Take the law with you. Anywhere.

LexisNexis® Electronic Books for Law Enforcement

Check criminal and traffic laws, research critical case notes, and study for promotion exams anywhere and in any way you want.

TABLET   SMARTPHONE   COMPUTER   BOOKS

After you download your new LexisNexis eBook you can access its content wherever, without the need to find Wi-Fi.

Covering over 40 states, LexisNexis print and eBook publications bring you:

- State Traffic and Criminal Laws
- Supreme Court Decisions
- Legal Guidelines
- Spanish Language Guides
- Case Notes
- Exam Prep Guides

SHOP
www.lexisnexis.com/lawenforcement

CALL
877.861.3389

FREE SAMPLE
lexisnexis.com/ebooks/le

WATCH VIDEO

 LexisNexis·

POLICE, CRIMES AND OFFENSES AND MOTOR VEHICLE LAWS OF VIRGINIA

2013 EDITION

VOLUME 1

Issued by
The Department of State Police

Reprinted from the Code of Virginia of 1950
and the 2013 Supplement

QUESTIONS ABOUT THIS PUBLICATION?

For CUSTOMER SERVICE ASSISTANCE concerning replacement pages, shipments, billing, reprint permission, or other matters,

> please call Customer Service Department at 800-833-9844
> email *customer.support@lexisnexis.com*
> or visit our interactive customer service website at *www.lexisnexis.com/printcdsc*

For EDITORIAL **content questions** concerning this publication,

> please email: *LEpublications@lexisnexis.com*

For **information on other LEXISNEXIS MATTHEW BENDER publications**,

> please call us at 877-461-8801
> or visit our online bookstore at *www.lexisnexis.com/bookstore*

ISBN: 978-0-7698-7290-2

Matthew Bender & Company, Inc.
Editorial Offices
701 E. Water Street
Charlottesville, VA 22902
800-446-3410
www.lexisnexis.com

Product Number 3551229

(Pub. 35453)

Table of Contents

VOLUME 1

VOLUME 2

Table of Comparable Sections

COMPARABLE SECTIONS OF TITLE 2.1

Former Section	Present Section
2.1-51.16	2.2-200
	2.2-221
2.1-51.17	2.2-200, 2.2-221, 2.2-222
2.1-51.17:01	2.2-223
2.1-51.18	2.2-221
2.1-51.18:3	2.2-222
2.1-116.01	2.2-1000
2.1-116.02	2.2-1000
2.1-116.03	2.2-1001
2.1-116.04	2.2-3000 B
2.1-116.05	2.2-3000 A, 2.2-3003
2.1-116.06	2.2-3004
2.1-116.07	2.2-3005
2.1-116.07:1	2.2-3006
2.1-116.08	2.2-3007
2.1-116.09	2.2-3001
2.1-116.012	2.2-3008
2.1-116.013	2.2-3002
2.1-116.1	9.1-500
2.1-116.2	9.1-501
2.1-116.3	9.1-503
2.1-116.4	9.1-502
2.1-116.5	9.1-504 A, B, C
2.1-116.6	9.1-505
2.1-116.7	9.1-504 D
2.1-116.8	9.1-506
2.1-116.9	9.1-507
2.1-121	2.2-507

Former Section	Present Section
2.1-124	2.2-511
2.1-133.5	9.1-400 A
2.1-133.6	9.1-400 B
2.1-133.7	9.1-402
2.1-133.7:1	9.1-401
2.1-133.8	9.1-403
2.1-133.9	9.1-404
2.1-133.10	9.1-405
2.1-133.11	9.1-406
2.1-340	2.2-3700 A
2.1-340.1	2.2-3700 B
2.1-341	2.2-3701
2.1-341.1	2.2-3702
2.1-341.2	2.2-3703
2.1-342	2.2-3704
2.1-342.01	2.2-3705
2.1-342.2	2.2-3706
2.1-343	2.2-3707
2.1-343.1	2.2-3708
2.1-343.1:1	2.2-3709
2.1-343.2	2.2-3710
2.1-344	2.2-3711
2.1-344.1	2.2-3712
2.1-346	2.2-3713
2.1-346.1	2.2-3714
2.1-346.2	30-178
2.1-346.3	30-179
2.1-346.4	30-180
2.1-346.5	30-181
2.1-457.2	2.2-1124
2.1-457.3	2.2-1125

Former Section	Present Section
2.1-639.1	2.2-3100
2.1-639.2	2.2-3101
2.1-639.3	2.2-3102
2.1-639.4	2.2-3103
2.1-639.4:1	2.2-3104
2.1-639.4:2	2.2-3104.1
2.1-639.5	2.2-3105
2.1-639.6	2.2-3106
2.1-639.7	2.2-3107
2.1-639.7:1	2.2-3108
2.1-639.8	2.2-3109
2.1-639.9	2.2-3110
2.1-639.10	2.2-3111
2.1-639.11	2.2-3112
2.1-639.12	2.2-3113
2.1-639.13	2.2-3114
2.1-639.14	2.2-3115
2.1-639.14:1	2.2-3116
2.1-639.15	2.2-3117
2.1-639.15:1	2.2-3118
2.1-639.16	2.2-3119
2.1-639.17	2.2-3120
2.1-639.18	2.2-3121
2.1-639.19	2.2-3122
2.1-639.20	2.2-3123
2.1-639.21	2.2-3124
2.1-639.22	2.2-3125
2.1-639.23	2.2-3126
2.1-639.24	2.2-3127

COMPARABLE SECTIONS OF TITLE 3.1

Former Section	Present Section
3.1-796.93:1	3.2-6540
3.1-796.104	3.2-6555
3.1-796.104:1	3.2-6556
3.1-796.105	3.2-6557
3.1-796.106	3.2-6558
3.1-796.106:1	3.2-6561
3.1-796.106:2	3.2-6559
3.1-796.107	3.2-6564
3.1-796.108	3.2-6565

Former Section	Present Section
3.1-796.109	Repealed
3.1-796.110	3.2-6560
3.1-796.111	3.2-6566
3.1-796.112	3.2-6567
3.1-796.113	3.2-6568
3.1-796.114	3.2-6563
3.1-796.115	3.2-6569
3.1-796.116	3.2-6552
3.1-796.117	Repealed

Former Section	Present Section
3.1-796.118	3.2-6553
3.1-796.119	3.2-6562
3.1-796.120	Deleted
3.1-796.121	3.2-6554
3.1-796.122	3.2-6570
3.1-796.123	Repealed
3.1-796.124	3.2-6571
3.1-796.125	3.2-6572
3.1-796.126	3.2-6573

COMPARABLE SECTIONS OF TITLE 6.1

Former Section	Present Section
6.1-225.62	6.2-1316

COMPARABLE SECTIONS OF TITLE 9

Former Section	Present Section
9-183.1	9.1-138
9-183.2	9.1-140
9-183.3	9.1-139
9-183.4	9.1-142
9-183.5	9.1-143
9-183.6	9.1-144
9-183.7	9.1-145

Former Section	Present Section
9-183.8	9.1-146
9-183.9	9.1-149
9-183.10	9.1-148
9-183.11	9.1-147
9-183.12	9.1-150
9-183.13	9.1-166
9-183.14	9.1-165

Former Section	Present Section
9-183.15	9.1-167
9-183.16	9.1-169
9-183.17	9.1-170
9-183.18	9.1-171
9-183.19	9.1-168 A, B, C
9-183.20	9.1-168 D
9-183.21	9.1-172

COMPARABLE SECTIONS OF TITLE 37.1

Former Section	Present Section
37.1-67.01	37.2-808
37.1-67.1	37.2-809
37.1-67.1	37.2-810
37.1-67.1	37.2-811
37.1-67.1	37.2-812
37.1-67.1	37.2-813
37.1-67.3	37.2-814

Former Section	Present Section
37.1-67.3	37.2-815
37.1-67.3	37.2-816
37.1-67.3	37.2-817
37.1-67.3	37.2-818
37.1-67.3	37.2-819
37.1-67.4	37.2-809, 37.2-820
37.1-67.5	37.2-802

Former Section	Present Section
37.1-67.5:01	37.2-802
37.1-67.6	37.2-821
37.1-75	37.2-833
37.1-76	37.2-834
37.1-77	37.2-835

COMPARABLE SECTIONS OF TITLE 63.1

Former Section	Present Section
63.1-112	63.2-513
63.1-124	63.2-522
63.1-124.1	63.2-523
63.1-171.3	46.2-932.1
63.1-248.1	63.2-1500
63.1-248.2	63.2-100
63.1-248.2	63.2-1501
63.1-248.2	63.2-1508
63.1-248.2:1	63.2-1504
63.1-248.3	63.2-1509
63.1-248.4	63.2-1510
64.1-248.4:1	63.2-1511

Former Section	Present Section
63.1-248.5	63.2-1512
63.1-248.5:1	63.2-1514
63.1-248.5:1.01	63.2-1513
63.1-248.6	63.2-1503
63.1-248.6:01	63.2-1505
63.1-248.6:02	63.2-1506
63.1-248.6:1	63.2-1526
63.1-248.6:2	63.2-1516
63.1-248.7	63.2-1502
63.1-248.7:1	63.2-1527
63.1-248.7:2	63.2-1726
63.1-248.8	63.2-1515

Former Section	Present Section
63.1-248.9	63.2-1517
63.1-248.10	63.2-1518
63.1-248.11	63.2-1519
63.1-248.13	63.2-1520
63.1-248.13:1	63.2-1521
63.1-248.13:2	63.2-1522
63.1-248.13:3	63.2-1523
63.1-248.14	63.2-1524
63.1-248.15	63.2-1525
63.1-248.16	63.2-1528
63.1-248.17	63.2-1507
63.1-248.19	63.2-1529

Motor Vehicle Laws and Related Statutes

This listing of motor vehicle laws and related statutes is reprinted as received by the publisher.

ACCIDENTS

46.2-371. Fail to report an accident to police (Injury/Fatal)
46.2-372. Fail to make a written report
46.2-707. Operate an uninsured motor vehicle (without having paid uninsured motorist fee to DMV)
46.2-894. Hit and Run (personal injury, death, attended property)
46.2-895. Hit and Run — passenger duties (must be at least 16 years old)
46.2-896. Hit and Run — unattended property
46.2-900. Penalties for Hit and Run (felony — personal injury, death; misdemeanor — property)
46.2-902. Fail to leave the scene of an accident
46.2-939. Authority to issue subpoenas

ALCOHOL RELATED

4.1-305. Possession of alcohol by a minor
4.1-308. Drinking in Public
4.1-309. Possession of alcohol on school property
4.1-310. Transportation of Alcohol
18.2-266. Driving Under the Influence of alcohol or other self-administered intoxicants
18.2-266.1. Persons under age 21 driving after illegally consuming alcohol
18.2-268.3. Unreasonable refusal to submit to blood or breath test
18.2-323.1. Drinking While Driving
18.2-388. Drunk in Public

BICYCLES, MOPEDS, ATV'S, AND MOTOR-DRIVEN CYCLES

46.2-800. Persons riding bicycles, mopeds or animals on highways subject to provision of chapter 8
46.2-911. Operation of motor-driven cycles on public highways prohibited
46.2-914. Operating a moped on the public highways while under 16 years of age
46.2-915.1. Illegal operation of an All-Terrain Vehicle on the highway
46.2-932. Unlawfully attaching to a motor vehicle

DRIVERS LICENSES

46.2-104. No driver's license in possession (this charge can be compiled with law)
46.2-300. No valid driver's license
46.2-301. Driving while suspended or revoked
46.2-328. No motorcycle license
46.2-335. Violation of Learner's Permit (must have licensed driver 21 or older in front seat)
46.2-346. Display, permit to display, possession of fictitious, altered, canceled, revoked or suspended driver's license
46.2-347. Use of forged, deceptive, or nongenuine driver's license to obtain alcoholic beverages
46.2-348. False statements in application for driver's license
46.2-349. Allowing an unlicensed person to drive
46.2-357. Drive while adjudicated an Habitual Offender
    First offense (if no endangerment to life, limb, or property) — misdemeanor (if driving, of itself, does endanger life, limb, or property) — Felony
    Second or subsequent offense — Felony
46.2-411.1. Driving after period of license suspension has expired
46.2-819.2. Driving from establishment where motor fuel offered for sale

COMMERCIAL DRIVER'S LICENSE (CDL)

Note: In order to enforce the Commercial Driver's License Act you must prove that the vehicle is or should be classified as a Commercial Motor Vehicle.
46.2-341.4. Definitions
46.2-341.6. Possession of more than one driver's license

Sections Affected by 2013 Legislation

NOTE: In addition to the sections below, users of this edition should be aware that additional section and case note annotations have been appropriately incorporated throughout this publication. The sections with new and/or revised annotations do *not* appear in this listing.

Code of Va. Section	Action	Chapter No.	Bill No.	Sec. No.
2.2-507	Amended	585	HB 2116	1
2.2-507	Amended	588	HB 2151	1
2.2-507	Amended	646	SB 1209	1
2.2-507	Amended	650	SB 1223	1
2.2-1202.1	Amended	572	HB 1845	1
2.2-1202.1	Amended	690	SB 1178	1
2.2-1202.1	Amended	717	HB 2114	1
2.2-1202.1	Amended	723	SB 1176	1
2.2-3014	Amended	572	HB 1845	1
2.2-3014	Amended	690	SB 1178	1
2.2-3101	Amended	475	SB 1119	1
2.2-3104	Amended	648	SB 1215	1
2.2-3104.01	Amended	583	HB 2079	1
2.2-3106	Amended	583	HB 2079	1
2.2-3109	Amended	583	HB 2079	1
2.2-3705.2	Amended	600	HB 2280	1
2.2-3705.3	Amended	571	HB 1844	1
2.2-3705.3	Amended	572	HB 1845	1
2.2-3705.3	Amended	690	SB 1178	1
2.2-3705.3	Amended	717	HB 2114	1
2.2-3705.3	Amended	723	SB 1176	1
2.2-3705.6	Amended	54	SB 1212	1
2.2-3705.6	Amended	482	SB 1350	1
2.2-3705.6, 2.2-3705.7	Amended	574	HB 1855	1
2.2-3705.7	Amended	199	HB 1639	1
2.2-3705.7	Amended	481	SB 1334	1
2.2-3705.7	Amended	554	HB 1524	1
2.2-3706	Amended	695	SB 1264	1
2.2-3708, 2.2-3708.1	Amended	694	SB 1263	1
2.2-3708.1	Amended	119	HB 2026	1
2.2-3711	Amended	571	HB 1844	1
2.2-3711	Amended	580	HB 2043	1
2.2-3711	Amended	695	SB 1264	1
3.2-6540	Amended	58	SB 828	1
3.2-6540	Amended	732	HB 1562	1
3.2-6540.1	Enacted	58	SB 828	1
3.2-6540.1	Enacted	732	HB 1562	1
3.2-6570	Amended	58	SB 828	1
3.2-6570	Amended	732	HB 1562	1
4.1-100	Amended	107	SB 1127	1
4.1-100	Amended	117	HB 1849	1
4.1-201	Amended	604	HB 2300	1
4.1-304	Amended	562	HB 1720	1
4.1-325	Amended	661	SB 1349	1
4.1-325.2	Amended	661	SB 1349	1
9.1-140	Amended	411	HB 1363	1
9.1-141	Amended	69	HB 1604	1
9.1-902	Amended	750	HB 1862	1
9.1-902	Amended	781	SB 1032	1
15.2-982	Enacted	246	HB 1521	1

Code of Va. Section	Action	Chapter No.	Bill No.	Sec. No.
15.2-1123	Amended	758	HB 2137	1
15.2-1705	Amended	307	HB 2121	1
15.2-1705	Amended	468	SB 1026	1
15.2-1707	Amended	307	HB 2121	1
15.2-1707	Amended	468	SB 1026	1
15.2-1713.1	Amended	695	SB 1264	1
15.2-1720	Amended	783	SB 1038	1
15.2-1724	Amended	428	HB 1826	1
15.2-1726	Amended	250	HB 1561	1
15.2-1726	Amended	472	SB 1047	1
15.2-1726	Amended	594	HB 2216	1
15.2-1726	Amended	775	SB 839	1
15.2-1752	Amended	66	HB 1569	1
15.2-1752	Amended	99	SB 1045	1
16.1-252, 16.1-253	Amended	130	HB 2117	1
16.1-253.2	Amended	761	HB 2269	1
16.1-253.2	Amended	774	SB 832	1
16.1-260	Amended	746	HB 1833	1
16.1-277.02	Amended	130	HB 2117	1
16.1-284.1	Amended	651	SB 1234	1
16.1-301	Amended	769	HB 2347	1
17.1-805	Amended	424	HB 1746	1
17.1-805	Amended	647	SB 1214	1
18.2-46.1	Amended	573	HB 1847	1
18.2-46.1	Amended	645	SB 1205	1
18.2-46.3:3	Amended	761	HB 2269	1
18.2-46.3:3	Amended	774	SB 832	1
18.2-48.1	Amended	707	HB 2065	1
18.2-48.1	Amended	782	SB 1033	1
18.2-57	Amended	698	HB 1927	1
18.2-57	Amended	707	HB 2065	1
18.2-57	Amended	711	SB 853	1
18.2-57	Amended	748	HB 1850	1
18.2-57	Amended	782	SB 1033	1
18.2-57.3	Amended	746	HB 1833	1
18.2-60.3	Amended	759	HB 2211	1
18.2-60.4	Amended	761	HB 2269	1
18.2-60.4	Amended	774	SB 832	1
18.2-60.5	Enacted	434	HB 1981	1
18.2-61	Amended	761	HB 2269	1
18.2-61	Amended	774	SB 832	1
18.2-64.2	Amended	602	HB 2294	1
18.2-67.1, 18.2-67.2	Amended	761	HB 2269	1
18.2-67.1, 18.2-67.2	Amended	774	SB 832	1
18.2-118	Amended	536	SB 1144	1
18.2-154	Amended	761	HB 2269	1
18.2-154	Amended	774	SB 832	1
18.2-174	Amended	410	HB 1358	1
18.2-174, 18.2-174.1	Amended	431	HB 1955	1
18.2-174	Amended	638	SB 1128	1
18.2-178.1	Enacted	419	HB 1682	1
18.2-178.1	Enacted	452	SB 706	1
18.2-186.3	Amended	420	HB 1684	1
18.2-186.3	Amended	466	SB 1010	1
18.2-213.1	Amended	482	SB 1350	1
18.2-213.2	Enacted	454	SB 811	1
18.2-246.13—18.2-246.15	Amended	625	SB 1019	1
18.2-248	Amended	426	HB 1806	1
18.2-248.02	Amended	743	HB 1816	1
18.2-248.1:1	Amended	295	HB 1941	1
18.2-248.1:1	Amended	785	SB 1083	1
18.2-270	Amended	415	HB 1559	1
18.2-270	Amended	655	SB 1272	1
18.2-271	Amended	415	HB 1559	1

Code of Va. Section	Action	Chapter No.	Bill No.	Sec. No.
18.2-271	Amended	655	SB 1272	1
18.2-287.01	Amended	746	HB 1833	1
18.2-307.1	Enacted	746	HB 1833	1
18.2-308	Amended	135	SB 703	1
18.2-308	Amended	559	HB 1679	1
18.2-308	Amended	659	SB 1335	1
18.2-308	Amended	746	HB 1833	1
18.2-308.01—18.2-308.015	Enacted	746	HB 1833	1
18.2-308.1	Amended	416	HB 1582	1
18.2-308.1:4	Amended	759	HB 2211	1
18.2-308.2:1	Amended	797	SB 1378	1
18.2-308.2:2	Amended	450	HB 2317	1
18.2-308.2:2	Amended	662	SB 1363	1
18.2-308.2:2	Amended	761	HB 2269	1
18.2-308.2:2	Amended	774	SB 832	1
18.2-308.2:2	Amended	797	SB 1378	1
18.2-311	Amended	746	HB 1833	1
18.2-334.2	Amended	36	SB 930	1
18.2-334.2	Amended	350	HB 2178	1
18.2-340.16	Amended	36	SB 930	1
18.2-340.16	Amended	350	HB 2178	1
18.2-340.19	Amended	36	SB 930	1
18.2-340.19	Amended	350	HB 2178	1
18.2-340.22	Amended	36	SB 930	1
18.2-340.22	Amended	350	HB 2178	1
18.2-340.28	Amended	36	SB 930	1
18.2-340.28	Amended	350	HB 2178	1
18.2-340.28:1	Enacted	36	SB 930	1
18.2-340.28:1	Enacted	350	HB 2178	1
18.2-340.33	Amended	36	SB 930	1
18.2-340.33	Amended	350	HB 2178	1
18.2-340.34:2	Enacted	36	SB 930	1
18.2-340.34:2	Enacted	350	HB 2178	1
18.2-345	Repealed	621	SB 969	1
18.2-346	Amended	417	HB 1606	1
18.2-346	Amended	467	SB 1015	1
18.2-370	Amended	423	HB 1745	1
18.2-370	Amended	470	SB 1031	1
18.2-374.1	Amended	761	HB 2269	1
18.2-374.1	Amended	774	SB 832	1
18.2-374.1:1	Amended	761	HB 2269	1
18.2-374.1:1	Amended	774	SB 832	1
18.2-374.3	Amended	423	HB 1745	1
18.2-374.3	Amended	470	SB 1031	1
18.2-431.1	Amended	707	HB 2065	1
18.2-431.1	Amended	782	SB 1033	1
18.2-459	Amended	615	SB 870	1
18.2-473.1—18.2-476	Amended	707	HB 2065	1
18.2-473.1—18.2-476	Amended	782	SB 1033	1
18.2-477.2	Amended	707	HB 2065	1
18.2-477.2	Amended	782	SB 1033	1
18.2-513	Amended	626	SB 1020	1
19.2-13	Amended	105	SB 1048	1
19.2-13	Amended	122	HB 2058	1
19.2-66	Amended	448	HB 2266	1
19.2-66	Amended	664	SB 1373	1
19.2-68	Amended	448	HB 2266	1
19.2-68	Amended	664	SB 1373	1
19.2-72	Amended	207	HB 1763	1
19.2-76	Amended	207	HB 1763	1
19.2-81	Amended	787	SB 1117	1
19.2-83.1	Amended	746	HB 1833	1
19.2-120.1	Amended	746	HB 1833	1
19.2-123	Amended	614	SB 847	1

Code of Va. Section	Action	Chapter No.	Bill No.	Sec. No.
19.2-124	Amended	408	HB 1311	1
19.2-124	Amended	474	SB 1118	1
19.2-132	Amended	408	HB 1311	1
19.2-132	Amended	474	SB 1118	1
19.2-188.1	Amended	60	HB 1376	1
19.2-215.1	Amended	83	HB 1870	1
19.2-215.1	Amended	314	HB 2248	1
19.2-215.1	Amended	459	SB 938	1
19.2-245.01	Amended	625	SB 1019	1
19.2-266.3	Enacted	154	SB 1135	1
19.2-305.1	Amended	273	HB 1705	1
19.2-324.1	Enacted	675	HB 2338	1
19.2-327.1	Amended	170	HB 1308	1
19.2-327.2, 19.2-327.3	Amended	170	HB 1308	1
19.2-327.3	Amended	180	HB 1432	1
19.2-327.5	Amended	170	HB 1308	1
19.2-327.5	Amended	180	HB 1432	1
19.2-327.10—19.2-327.13	Amended	170	HB 1308	1
19.2-327.11	Amended	180	HB 1432	1
19.2-327.13	Amended	180	HB 1432	1
19.2-368.15	Amended	273	HB 1705	1
19.2-386.21	Amended	627	SB 1022	1
19.2-386.27, 19.2-386.28	Amended	746	HB 1833	1
19.2-389	Amended	165	SB 1219	1
19.2-389	Amended	176	HB 1383	1
19.2-389	Amended	261	HB 1640	1
19.2-389	Amended	407	SB 1288	1
19.2-389	Amended	491	HB 1765	1
19.2-389	Amended	582	HB 2077	1
19.2-390	Amended	614	SB 847	1
22.1-177	Amended	778	SB 899	1
22.1-178	Amended	498	HB 2028	1
22.1-178	Amended	530	SB 986	1
27-14	Amended	356	HB 2301	1
27-14	Amended	616	SB 881	1
29.1-516	Amended	345	HB 1829	1
29.1-517	Amended	349	HB 2099	1
29.1-529	Amended	346	HB 1929	1
29.1-530	Amended	349	HB 2099	1
29.1-712—29.1-733.1	Repealed	787	SB 1117	2
29.1-733.2—29.1-733.29	Enacted	787	SB 1117	1
29.1-735.2	Amended	48	SB 1053	1
29.1-738	Amended	787	SB 1117	1
30-179	Amended	694	SB 1263	1
32.1-320	Amended	538	SB 1186	1
33.1-1	Amended	762	HB 2276	1
33.1-1	Amended	794	SB 1305	1
33.1-7	Amended	585	HB 2116	1
33.1-7	Amended	646	SB 1209	1
33.1-11, 33.1-12	Amended	585	HB 2116	1
33.1-11, 33.1-12	Amended	646	SB 1209	1
33.1-12	Amended	388	SB 1075	1
33.1-12	Amended	569	HB 1809	1
33.1-12	Amended	741	HB 1718	1
33.1-13.05	Enacted	585	HB 2116	1
33.1-13.05	Enacted	646	SB 1209	1
33.1-346	Amended	156	SB 1166	1
33.1-346.1	Repealed	156	SB 1166	2
33.1-348	Amended	127	HB 2105	1
33.1-351	Amended	127	HB 2105	1
33.1-370	Amended	585	HB 2116	1
33.1-370	Amended	646	SB 1209	1
33.1-371.1	Amended	737	HB 1633	1
33.1-373	Amended	457	SB 888	1

Code of Va. Section	Action	Chapter No.	Bill No.	Sec. No.
37.2-808	Amended	371	SB 920	1
37.2-809	Amended	87	HB 2091	1
37.2-809	Amended	321	SB 753	1
37.2-810	Amended	371	SB 920	1
37.2-817	Amended	179	HB 1423	1
40.1-54.3	Enacted	484	HB 1385	1
46.2-100	Amended	128	HB 2106	1
46.2-100	Amended	400	SB 1200	1
46.2-100	Amended	783	SB 1038	1
46.2-208	Amended	673	HB 2042	1
46.2-208	Amended	789	SB 1218	1
46.2-212.2	Enacted	673	HB 2042	1
46.2-212.2	Enacted	789	SB 1218	1
46.2-311	Amended	165	SB 1219	1
46.2-311	Amended	582	HB 2077	1
46.2-324.1	Amended	165	SB 1219	1
46.2-324.1	Amended	582	HB 2077	1
46.2-325	Amended	272	HB 1701	1
46.2-328	Amended	673	HB 2042	1
46.2-328	Amended	783	SB 1038	1
46.2-328	Amended	789	SB 1218	1
46.2-328.1	Amended	686	SB 1077	1
46.2-334.01	Amended	397	SB 1165	1
46.2-334.01	Amended	579	HB 2033	1
46.2-337	Amended	673	HB 2042	1
46.2-337	Amended	783	SB 1038	1
46.2-337	Amended	789	SB 1218	1
46.2-341.4	Amended	165	SB 1219	1
46.2-341.4	Amended	582	HB 2077	1
46.2-341.7—46.2-341.9	Amended	165	SB 1219	1
46.2-341.7—46.2-341.9	Amended	582	HB 2077	1
46.2-341.10	Amended	165	SB 1219	1
46.2-341.10	Amended	582	HB 2077	1
46.2-341.12	Amended	165	SB 1219	1
46.2-341.12	Amended	582	HB 2077	1
46.2-341.14	Amended	165	SB 1219	1
46.2-341.14	Amended	582	HB 2077	1
46.2-341.14:1—46.2-341.14:10	Enacted	165	SB 1219	1
46.2-341.14:1—46.2-341.14:10	Enacted	582	HB 2077	1
46.2-341.15, 46.2-341.16	Amended	165	SB 1219	1
46.2-341.15, 46.2-341.16	Amended	582	HB 2077	1
46.2-341.20	Amended	165	SB 1219	1
46.2-341.20	Amended	582	HB 2077	1
46.2-341.20:4, 46.2-341.20:5	Enacted	165	SB 1219	1
46.2-341.20:4, 46.2-341.20:5	Enacted	582	HB 2077	1
46.2-345.1	Enacted	673	HB 2042	1
46.2-348	Amended	165	SB 1219	1
46.2-348	Amended	312	HB 2243	1
46.2-348	Amended	477	SB 1284	1
46.2-348	Amended	582	HB 2077	1
46.2-380	Amended	80	HB 1830	1
46.2-380	Amended	104	SB 948	1
46.2-383	Amended	263	HB 1658	1
46.2-391	Amended	415	HB 1559	1
46.2-391	Amended	655	SB 1272	1
46.2-417	Amended	598	HB 2272	1
46.2-427	Amended	598	HB 2272	1
46.2-502	Amended	326	SB 770	1
46.2-600	Amended	244	HB 1475	1
46.2-600	Amended	367	SB 904	1
46.2-600	Amended	783	SB 1038	1
46.2-602.3	Amended	216	HB 1944	1
46.2-613	Amended	783	SB 1038	1
46.2-615	Amended	318	SB 715	1

Code of Va. Section	Action	Chapter No.	Bill No.	Sec. No.
46.2-626.1	Enacted	244	HB 1475	1
46.2-626.1	Enacted	367	SB 904	1
46.2-629	Amended	783	SB 1038	1
46.2-633.2	Enacted	318	SB 715	1
46.2-646	Amended	337	HB 1485	1
46.2-646.1	Enacted	673	HB 2042	1
46.2-646.1	Enacted	789	SB 1218	1
46.2-649	Amended	226	HB 2080	1
46.2-662	Amended	347	HB 1990	1
46.2-662	Amended	783	SB 1038	1
46.2-665, 46.2-666	Amended	776	SB 887	1
46.2-670	Amended	776	SB 887	1
46.2-674	Amended	777	SB 892	1
46.2-694	Amended	783	SB 1038	1
46.2-705	Amended	783	SB 1038	1
46.2-707	Amended	673	HB 2042	1
46.2-707	Amended	789	SB 1218	1
46.2-711	Amended	783	SB 1038	1
46.2-714, 46.2-715	Amended	783	SB 1038	1
46.2-720, 46.2-721	Amended	783	SB 1038	1
46.2-743	Amended	478	SB 1298	1
46.2-749.69:1	Amended	482	SB 1350	1
46.2-752	Amended	82	HB 1841	1
46.2-752.1	Amended	673	HB 2042	1
46.2-752.1	Amended	789	SB 1218	1
46.2-804, 46.2-805	Amended	128	HB 2106	1
46.2-804, 46.2-805	Amended	400	SB 1200	1
46.2-804	Amended	585	HB 2116	1
46.2-804	Amended	646	SB 1209	1
46.2-806	Amended	585	HB 2116	1
46.2-806	Amended	646	SB 1209	1
46.2-807	Amended	128	HB 2106	1
46.2-807	Amended	400	SB 1200	1
46.2-821, 46.2-822	Amended	128	HB 2106	1
46.2-821, 46.2-822	Amended	400	SB 1200	1
46.2-826	Amended	128	HB 2106	1
46.2-826	Amended	400	SB 1200	1
46.2-828.2	Enacted	312	HB 2243	1
46.2-828.2	Enacted	477	SB 1284	1
46.2-830	Amended	128	HB 2106	1
46.2-830	Amended	400	SB 1200	1
46.2-830	Amended	585	HB 2116	1
46.2-830	Amended	646	SB 1209	1
46.2-831—46.2-833	Amended	128	HB 2106	1
46.2-831—46.2-833	Amended	400	SB 1200	1
46.2-831	Amended	585	HB 2116	1
46.2-831	Amended	646	SB 1209	1
46.2-834—46.2-836	Amended	128	HB 2106	1
46.2-834—46.2-836	Amended	400	SB 1200	1
46.2-846	Amended	128	HB 2106	1
46.2-846	Amended	400	SB 1200	1
46.2-847	Amended	585	HB 2116	1
46.2-847	Amended	646	SB 1209	1
46.2-868	Amended	752	HB 1907	1
46.2-868	Amended	790	SB 1222	1
46.2-878	Amended	303	HB 2029	1
46.2-878.2	Amended	585	HB 2116	1
46.2-878.2	Amended	646	SB 1209	1
46.2-889	Amended	585	HB 2116	1
46.2-889	Amended	646	SB 1209	1
46.2-904, 46.2-905	Amended	783	SB 1038	1
46.2-907	Amended	783	SB 1038	1
46.2-908.1	Amended	783	SB 1038	1
46.2-908.3	Amended	783	SB 1038	1

Code of Va. Section	Action	Chapter No.	Bill No.	Sec. No.
46.2-914, 46.2-915	Amended	783	SB 1038	1
46.2-915.2	Amended	783	SB 1038	1
46.2-916.2	Amended	64	HB 1514	1
46.2-924	Amended	507	HB 2217	1
46.2-924	Amended	585	HB 2116	1
46.2-924	Amended	646	SB 1209	1
46.2-924	Amended	681	SB 959	1
46.2-1041	Amended	585	HB 2116	1
46.2-1041	Amended	646	SB 1209	1
46.2-1043.1	Enacted	430	HB 1886	1
46.2-1046	Amended	585	HB 2116	1
46.2-1046	Amended	646	SB 1209	1
46.2-1047	Amended	783	SB 1038	1
46.2-1076	Amended	165	SB 1219	1
46.2-1076	Amended	582	HB 2077	1
46.2-1078.1	Amended	752	HB 1907	1
46.2-1078.1	Amended	790	SB 1222	1
46.2-1104	Amended	118	HB 1985	1
46.2-1107—46.2-1109	Amended	585	HB 2116	1
46.2-1107—46.2-1109	Amended	646	SB 1209	1
46.2-1112	Amended	585	HB 2116	1
46.2-1112	Amended	646	SB 1209	1
46.2-1114	Amended	585	HB 2116	1
46.2-1114	Amended	646	SB 1209	1
46.2-1116, 46.2-1117	Amended	585	HB 2116	1
46.2-1116, 46.2-1117	Amended	646	SB 1209	1
46.2-1120	Amended	242	HB 1453	1
46.2-1120	Amended	385	SB 1050	1
46.2-1129.1	Amended	118	HB 1985	1
46.2-1139	Amended	118	HB 1985	1
46.2-1143	Amended	305	HB 2100	1
46.2-1143	Amended	618	SB 918	1
46.2-1148	Amended	118	HB 1985	1
46.2-1149	Amended	354	HB 2228	1
46.2-1178	Amended	634	SB 1102	1
46.2-1183.1	Enacted	673	HB 2042	1
46.2-1183.1	Enacted	789	SB 1218	1
46.2-1190	Amended	226	HB 2080	1
46.2-1190.2	Amended	111	HB 1476	1
46.2-1190.3	Amended	226	HB 2080	1
46.2-1190.5	Amended	226	HB 2080	1
46.2-1192	Amended	226	HB 2080	1
46.2-1203	Amended	241	HB 1395	1
46.2-1233.1	Amended	592	HB 2202	1
46.2-1241	Amended	137	SB 794	1
46.2-1516	Amended	247	HB 1539	1
46.2-1531	Amended	247	HB 1539	1
46.2-1571	Amended	260	HB 1632	1
46.2-1571	Amended	630	SB 1051	1
46.2-1916	Amended	247	HB 1539	1
46.2-1931	Amended	247	HB 1539	1
46.2-1992.14	Amended	247	HB 1539	1
46.2-1992.24	Amended	247	HB 1539	1
46.2-1993.14	Amended	247	HB 1539	1
46.2-1993.24	Amended	247	HB 1539	1
46.2-2001.1	Amended	165	SB 1219	1
46.2-2001.1	Amended	582	HB 2077	1
46.2-2001.3	Amended	165	SB 1219	1
46.2-2001.3	Amended	582	HB 2077	1
46.2-2005	Amended	165	SB 1219	1
46.2-2005	Amended	582	HB 2077	1
46.2-2011.9	Amended	165	SB 1219	1
46.2-2011.9	Amended	582	HB 2077	1
46.2-2011.11	Amended	165	SB 1219	1

Code of Va. Section	Action	Chapter No.	Bill No.	Sec. No.
46.2-2011.11	Amended	582	HB 2077	1
46.2-2011.23, 46.2-2011.24	Amended	165	SB 1219	1
46.2-2011.23, 46.2-2011.24	Amended	582	HB 2077	1
46.2-2099.19	Amended	165	SB 1219	1
46.2-2099.19	Amended	582	HB 2077	1
46.2-2108.4	Amended	165	SB 1219	1
46.2-2108.4	Amended	582	HB 2077	1
46.2-2122	Amended	165	SB 1219	1
46.2-2122	Amended	582	HB 2077	1
46.2-2132, 46.2-2133	Amended	165	SB 1219	1
46.2-2132, 46.2-2133	Amended	582	HB 2077	1
46.2-2176	Amended	165	SB 1219	1
46.2-2176	Amended	582	HB 2077	1
46.2-2900—46.2-2910	Enacted	312	HB 2243	1
46.2-2900—46.2-2910	Enacted	477	SB 1284	1
54.1-3401	Amended	412	HB 1422	1
54.1-3401	Amended	504	HB 2181	1
54.1-3401	Amended	544	SB 1285	1
54.1-3401	Amended	765	HB 2312	1
54.1-3408	Amended	114	HB 1759	1
54.1-3408	Amended	132	HB 2161	1
54.1-3408	Amended	183	HB 1444	1
54.1-3408	Amended	191	HB 1499	1
54.1-3408	Amended	252	HB 1564	1
54.1-3408	Amended	267	HB 1672	1
54.1-3408	Amended	328	SB 773	1
54.1-3408	Amended	336	HB 1468	1
54.1-3408	Amended	359	SB 807	1
54.1-3408	Amended	617	SB 893	1
54.1-3408.04	Enacted	412	HB 1422	1
54.1-3408.04	Enacted	544	SB 1285	1
54.1-3410.2	Amended	765	HB 2312	1
54.1-3434.1	Amended	412	HB 1422	1
54.1-3434.1	Amended	544	SB 1285	1
54.1-3434.1, 54.1-3434.2	Amended	765	HB 2312	1
54.1-3435.2	Amended	504	HB 2181	1
54.1-3446	Amended	295	HB 1941	1
54.1-3446	Amended	785	SB 1083	1
54.1-3450	Amended	233	HB 2136	1
54.1-3457	Amended	412	HB 1422	1
54.1-3457	Amended	544	SB 1285	1
54.1-4009, 54.1-4010	Amended	262	HB 1649	1
54.1-4101	Amended	262	HB 1649	1
58.1-2701	Amended	766	HB 2313	1
58.1-2701	Repealed	766	HB 2313	4
58.1-2706	Amended	766	HB 2313	1
58.1-3503	Amended	287	HB 1860	1
58.1-3503	Amended	652	SB 1236	1
58.1-3503	Amended	783	SB 1038	1
59.1-148.3	Amended	62	HB 1506	1
59.1-326	Amended	24	HB 2085	1
59.1-328	Amended	24	HB 2085	1
63.2-100	Amended	5	HB 1646	1
63.2-100	Amended	362	SB 863	1
63.2-100	Amended	564	HB 1743	1
63.2-1505	Amended	340	HB 1721	1
63.2-1505	Amended	506	HB 2193	1
63.2-1509	Amended	72	HB 1622	1
63.2-1509	Amended	331	SB 790	1
63.2-1726	Amended	96	SB 992	1
63.2-1726	Amended	181	HB 1439	1

Police, Crimes and Offenses and Motor Vehicles Laws of Virginia

VOLUME 1

TITLE 2.1.

ADMINISTRATION OF THE GOVERNMENT GENERALLY.

[Repealed.]

TITLE 2.2.

ADMINISTRATION OF GOVERNMENT.

SUBTITLE I.

ORGANIZATION OF STATE GOVERNMENT.

PART A.

OFFICE OF THE GOVERNOR.

CHAPTER 1.

GOVERNOR.

Article 1. General Provisions.

Section
2.2-100. Salaries of Governor and other officers; administrative assistants.

ARTICLE 1.

GENERAL PROVISIONS.

§ 2.2-100. Salaries of Governor and other officers; administrative assistants.

A. The Governor and all officers of the Commonwealth shall receive annually for their services such salaries as are fixed by law.

B. The Governor may employ the necessary administrative assistants, including a chief of staff, and fix their salaries within the limitation of funds appropriated for executive control of the Commonwealth. Any chief of staff appointed by the Governor shall be confirmed by a majority of the members in each house of the General Assembly.

C. The Governor may employ the staff required to perform necessary services in the operation of the Executive Mansion.

History.
Code 1950, §§ 2-34, 14-9 to 14-16, 14-18 to 14-26; 1962, c. 356; 1964, c. 386, § 14.1-12; 1966, cc. 55, 677, § 2.1-38; 1968, cc. 223, 562; 1970, cc. 262, 759; 1977, c. 672; 1984, cc. 104, 750, 779; 1998, c. 872; 2001, c. 844.

Cross references.
For constitutional provision as to compensation of Governor, see Va. Const., Art. V, § 4. For requirement that state agencies, boards, commissions, etc., submit environmental impact reports on major state projects, see § 10.1-1188.

Transition provisions.
In accordance with § 9-77.10 (now § 30-149), the Virginia Code Commission, in 1998, undertook a three-year recodification of Titles 2.1 and 9. Title 2.1 had last been recodified in 1966 and Title 9 had never been recodified. The Commission's draft of this revision, which was published as House Document 51 of the 2001 Session, was sent to the Governor and General Assembly in January, 2001. The revision, as amended by the General Assembly, became Acts 2001, c. 844, effective October 1, 2001.

Title 2.1 was rewritten primarily as new Title 2.2, with certain material now incorporated into Titles 6.1, 9.1, 17.1, 30, 37.1 and 51.1, and Title 9 was rewritten primarily as new Title 9.1, with certain material now incorporated into Titles 3.1, 2.2, and 30. In addition, the Virginia Public Procurement Act, §§ 11-35 to 11-80, was rewritten as § 2.2-4300 et seq., and §§ 53.1-180 to 53.1-185.3, the Comprehensive Community Corrections Act for Local-Responsible Offenders, was rewritten as § 9.1-173 to 9.1-183.

In addition to revision by Acts 2001, c. 844, Titles 2.1 and 9, § 11-35 et seq. and § 53.1-183 [see now § 9.1-178] were also amended by other acts passed at the 2001 Session. As required by § 9-77.11 (see new § 30-152), the Code Commission has incorporated the majority of these amendments into the new sections.

Where appropriate, the historical citations to former sections have been added to corresponding new sections.

The case notes appearing under new sections were decided under corresponding former sections or under prior law.

For tables of corresponding former and new sections, see the Table of Comparable Sections following the Table of Contents at the front of this volume.

Acts 2001, c. 844, cl. 2, provides: "That whenever any of the conditions, requirements, provisions or contents of any section or chapter of Title 2.1 or Title 9 or any other title of the Code of Virginia as such titles existed prior to October 1, 2001, are transferred in the same or modified form to a new section or chapter of Title 2.2 or Title 9.1 or any other title of the Code and whenever any such former section or chapter is given a new number in Title 2.2 or Title 9.1 or any other title, all references to any such former section or chapter of Title 2.1 or Title 9 or other title appearing in this Code shall be construed to apply to the new or renumbered section or chapter containing such conditions, requirements, provisions, contents or portions thereof."

Acts 2001, c. 844, cl. 3, provides: "That the regulations of any department or agency affected by the revision of Title 2.1, Title 9 or

1

such other titles in effect on the effective date of this act shall continue in effect to the extent that they are not in conflict with this act and shall be deemed to be regulations adopted under this act."

Acts 2001, c. 844, cl. 4, provides: "That this title revision of Title 2.1 as Title 2.2 and Title 9 as Title 9.1 and the repeal of Chapter 7 (§ 11-35 et seq.) of Title 11 shall not be construed to require the reappointment of any officer or any member of a board, council, committee or other appointed body referred to in Title 2.2 or Title 9.1 and each such officer and member shall continue to serve for the term for which appointed pursuant to the provisions of Title 2.1, Title 9, or Chapter 7 (§ 11-35 et seq.) of Title 11. The revision of Title 2.1 as Title 2.2 and Title 9 as Title 9.1 in this act shall not affect the classification or assignment of any state agency, institution, board, commission, council or other collegial body within the executive branch currently in effect pursuant to Title 2.1 or Title 9; such classifications and assignments within the executive branch which existed prior to the effective date of this act shall continue unless reclassified or reassigned by a later enactment of the General Assembly and signed by the Governor."

Acts 2001, c. 844, cl. 5, provides: "That this title revision of Title 2.1 as Title 2.2 or Title 9 as Title 9.1 shall not be construed to affect the term of office of any elected officeholder holding office on October 1, 2001."

Acts 2001, c. 844, cl. 6, provides: "That the provisions of § 30-152, formerly § 9-77.11, of the Code of Virginia shall apply to the codification of Title 2.2 and Title 9.1 so as to give effect to other laws enacted by the 2001 Session of the General Assembly notwithstanding the delay in the effective date of this act."

Acts 2001, c. 844, cl. 7, provides: "That the repeal of Title 2.1, Title 9, and Chapter 7 (§ 11-35 et seq.) of Title 11 effective as of October 1, 2001, shall not affect any act or offense done or committed, or any penalty incurred, or any right established, accrued or accruing on or before such date, or any proceeding, prosecution, suit or action pending on that day. Except as otherwise provided in this act, neither the repeal of Title 2.1, Title 9 or Chapter 7 (§ 11-35 et seq.) of Title 11 nor the enactment of Title 2.2 or the enactment of Title 9.1, shall apply to offenses committed prior to October 1, 2001, and prosecution for such offenses shall be governed by the prior law, which is continued in effect for that purpose. For the purpose of this enactment, an offense was committed prior to October 1, 2001, if any of essential elements of the offense occurred prior thereto."

Acts 2001, c. 844, cl. 8, provides: "That any notice given, recognizance taken, or process or writ issued before October 1, 2001, shall be valid although given, taken or to be returned to a day after such date, in like manner as if Title 2.2 and Title 9.1 had been effective before the same was given, taken or issued."

Acts 2001, c. 844, cl. 9, provides: "That if any clause, sentence, paragraph, subdivision, section or part of Title 2.2 and Title 9.1 shall be adjudged in any court of competent jurisdiction to be invalid, the judgment shall not affect, impair or invalidate the remainder thereof, but shall be confined in its operation to the clause, sentence, paragraph, subdivision, section or part thereof directly involved in the controversy in which the judgment shall have been rendered, and to this end the provisions of Title 2.2 and Title 9.1 are declared severable."

Acts 2001, c. 844, cl. 10, provides: "That any reference in the Code of Virginia or the Acts of Assembly to the Privacy Protection Act of 1976 shall be construed to mean the Government Data Collection and Dissemination Practices Act."

Law Review.

For survey of Virginia administrative law and utility regulation for the year 1978-1979, see 66 Va. L. Rev. 193 (1980). For an article, "Agency Adjudication, the Importance of Facts, and the Limitation of Labels," see 57 Wash. & Lee L. Rev. 351 (2000).

Michie's Jurisprudence.

For related discussion, see 2A M.J. Attorney General, § 3; 9A M.J. Governor, § 3; 11A M.J. Judges, § 26.

CASE NOTES

Editor's note.

The cases below were decided under former Title 2.1 or prior provisions.

The Virginia Department of Health is not a "corporate citizen" of the State, maintaining a separate identity from the State. Medicenters of Am., Inc. v. Virginia, 373 F. Supp. 305 (E.D. Va. 1974).

Rather, it is merely an "arm of the State," i.e., the State's alter ego. Medicenters of Am., Inc. v. Virginia, 373 F. Supp. 305 (E.D. Va. 1974).

And does not have certain powers apart from State. — The Virginia Department of Health has not the power to raise capital, engage in other financial and contractual relationships, or sue and be sued, in its own right, as an entity separate and distinct from the State. Medicenters of Am., Inc. v. Virginia, 373 F. Supp. 305 (E.D. Va. 1974).

Legislature cannot withhold from Attorney General the salary prescribed by law, nor can it delegate such power to the Auditor of Public Accounts (now Comptroller), and he may recover his salary by mandamus. Blair v. Marye, 80 Va. 485 (1885).

Attorney General's salary not subject to attachment, detention for debt, etc. — The salary of the Attorney General is of constitutional grant, and of public official right, and the doctrine of offset cannot be applied to it. It is not liable to attachment, garnishment, nor assignment in bankruptcy, and upon principles of public policy it has absolute immunity from detention for debt or counterclaims. Blair v. Marye, 80 Va. 485 (1885).

But the State may recover fees paid him by mistake. — The Commonwealth may recover from the Attorney General fees paid him by the Auditor of Public Accounts (now Comptroller) under the mistaken belief that he was entitled thereto as part of his compensation. Commonwealth v. Field, 84 Va. 26, 3 S.E. 882 (1887).

CHAPTER 2.

GOVERNOR'S SECRETARIES.

Article 1. General Provisions.

ARTICLE 1.

GENERAL PROVISIONS.

§ 2.2-200. Appointment of Governor's Secretaries; general powers; severance.

A. The Governor's Secretaries shall be appointed by the Governor, subject to confirmation by the General Assembly if in session when the appointment is made, and if not in session, then at its next succeeding session. Each Secretary shall hold office at the pleasure of the Governor for a term coincident with that of the Governor making the appointment or until a successor is appointed and qualified. Before entering upon the discharge of duties, each Secretary shall take an oath to faithfully execute the duties of the office.

B. Each Secretary shall be subject to direction and supervision by the Governor. Except as provided in

Article 5 (§ 2.2-208 et seq.) of this chapter, the agencies assigned to each Secretary shall:

1. Exercise their respective powers and duties in accordance with the general policy established by the Governor or by the Secretary acting on behalf of the Governor;

2. Provide such assistance to the Governor or the Secretary as may be required; and

3. Forward all reports to the Governor through the Secretary.

C. Unless the Governor expressly reserves such power to himself and except as provided in Article 5 (§ 2.2-208 et seq.) of this chapter, each Secretary may:

1. Resolve administrative, jurisdictional, operational, program, or policy conflicts between agencies or officials assigned;

2. Direct the formulation of a comprehensive program budget for the functional area identified in § 2.2-1508 encompassing the services of agencies assigned for consideration by the Governor;

3. Hold agency heads accountable for their administrative, fiscal and program actions in the conduct of the respective powers and duties of the agencies;

4. Direct the development of goals, objectives, policies and plans that are necessary to the effective and efficient operation of government;

5. Sign documents on behalf of the Governor that originate with agencies assigned to the Secretary; and

6. Employ such personnel and to contract for such consulting services as may be required to perform the powers and duties conferred upon the Secretary by law or executive order.

D. Severance benefits provided to any departing Secretary shall be publicly announced by the Governor prior to such departure.

E. As used in this chapter, "Governor's Secretaries" means the Secretary of Administration, the Secretary of Agriculture and Forestry, the Secretary of Commerce and Trade, the Secretary of Education, the Secretary of Finance, the Secretary of Health and Human Resources, the Secretary of Natural Resources, the Secretary of Public Safety, the Secretary of Technology, the Secretary of Transportation, and the Secretary of Veterans Affairs and Homeland Security.

History.
1972, c. 641, § 2.1-51.7; 1975, c. 390; 1976, cc. 729, 730, 732, 733, 734, 743, §§ 2.1-51.8:1, 2.1-51.13, 2.1-51.14, 2.1-51.16, 2.1-51.17, 2.1-51.26; 1984, c. 720, § 2.1-51.33; 1986, c. 492, § 2.1-51.39; 1998, c. 646; 1990, cc. 1, 317, §§ 2.1-51.41, 2.1-51.42; 1993, c. 699; 1996, cc. 500, 617; 1998, c. 793; 1999, cc. 412, 421, 433, §§ 2.1-51.44, 2.1-51.45; 2000, c. 937; 2001, c. 844; 2004, cc. 940, 963; 2006, c. 254; 2011, cc. 780, 858.

Editor's note.
The amendments to this section by Acts 2004, cc. 940 and 963 are effective no later than the beginning of the term of the Governor elected November 8, 2005. However, if funding for the position and expenses of the Secretary of Agriculture and Forestry is included in the 2004 Appropriation Act, the amendments shall become effective on the date set out in that act. The funding was provided in the 2004

appropriation act. See Acts 2004, Sp. Sess. 1, c. 4, Item 94.10. The provisions of Acts 2004, cc. 940 and 963, became effective July 1, 2004.

Acts 2004, cc. 940 and 963, cl. 2, provide: "That except as provided in the third enactment of this act, the provisions of this act shall become effective no later than the beginning of the term of the Governor elected November 8, 2005."

Acts 2004, cc. 940 and 963, cl. 3, provide: "That if funding for the position and expenses of the Secretary of Agriculture and Forestry created by this act is included in the 2004 Appropriation Act passed by the General Assembly, the provisions of this act shall become effective beginning on the date set out in the appropriation act."

The 2011 amendments.
The 2011 amendments by cc. 780 and 858, effective April 6, 2011, are identical and added "and the Secretary of Veterans Affairs and Homeland Security" in subsection E and made a related change.

OPINIONS OF THE ATTORNEY GENERAL

Role of Governor. — The Governor, having supervisory authority over the Secretary of Transportation under subsection B of § 2.2-200, may provide appropriate coordination and guidance as the Secretary of Transportation exercises his authority under subdivision 2 of § 56-573.1 to determine whether to give final approval before the responsible public entity signs a comprehensive agreement. See opinion of Attorney General to The Honorable Frank W. Wagner, Member, Senate of Virginia; The Honorable Barry D. Knight, Member, House of Delegates; The Honorable Jeffrey L. McWaters, Member, Senate of Virginia; The Honorable Christopher P. Stolle, M.D., Member, House of Delegates; The Honorable Ralph S. Northam, M.D., Member, Senate of Virginia, 12-078, 2012 Va. AG LEXIS 37 (10/3/2012).

ARTICLE 8.

SECRETARY OF PUBLIC SAFETY.

§ 2.2-221. Position established; agencies for which responsible.

The position of Secretary of Public Safety (the Secretary) is created. The Secretary shall be responsible to the Governor for the following agencies: Department of Alcoholic Beverage Control, Department of Corrections, Department of Juvenile Justice, Department of Criminal Justice Services, Department of Forensic Science, Virginia Parole Board, Department of Emergency Management, Department of Military Affairs, Department of State Police, Department of Fire Programs and the Commonwealth's Attorneys' Services Council. The Governor may, by executive order, assign any other state executive agency to the Secretary, or reassign any agency listed above to another Secretary.

History.
1976, c. 732, §§ 2.1-51.16, 2.1-51.18; 1978, cc. 455, 606, 607, 820; 1984, cc. 720, 779; 1985, cc. 447, 448; 1986, c. 60; 1988, cc. 67, 173, 888; 1989, c. 733; 1990, cc. 1, 317; 1992, c. 81; 1996, c. 503; 2001, c. 844; 2006, cc. 150, 326; 2011, cc. 780, 858; 2012, cc. 803, 835.

The 2011 amendments.
The 2011 amendments by cc. 780 and 858, effective April 6, 2011, are identical and deleted "Department of Veterans Services, Virginia Veterans Services Foundation" following "Department of Military Affairs."

The 2012 amendments.
The 2012 amendments by cc. 803 and 835, cl. 99, are identical, and deleted "Department of Correctional Education" following "Department of Juvenile Justice" in the second sentence.

§ 2.2-221.1. Secretary to coordinate system for offender transition and reentry services.

The Secretary of Public Safety shall establish an integrated system for coordinating the planning and provision of offender transitional and reentry services among and between state, local, and nonprofit agencies in order to prepare inmates for successful transition into their communities upon release from incarceration and for improving opportunities for treatment, employment, and housing while on subsequent probation, parole, or post-release supervision.

It is the intent of the General Assembly that funds used for the purposes of this section be leveraged to the fullest extent possible and that direct transitional and reentry employment and housing assistance for offenders be provided in the most cost effective means possible, including through agreements with local nonprofit pre- and post-release service organizations.

History.
2005, c. 153.

§ 2.2-222. Secretary to provide annual reports on juvenile offenders.

The Secretary shall provide annual reports to the Governor and the General Assembly on juvenile offender demographics by offense, age, committing court, previous court contacts of offenders, and, beginning in July 1998, recidivism rates of juveniles committed to agencies within the Secretariat. The annual report shall also include summaries of any juvenile program evaluations completed in the previous year on programs operated by the Departments of Juvenile Justice, Corrections or Criminal Justice Services and whose evaluation was directed by the General Assembly or the Secretary.

History.
1976, c. 732, § 2.1-51.17; 1984, c. 720; 1990, cc. 1, 317; 1996, c. 617; 2001, c. 844.

§ 2.2-223. Repealed by Acts 2012, cc. 164 and 456, cl. 2.

Editor's note.
Former § 2.2-223, pertaining to Interagency Drug Offender Screening and Assessment Committee, derived from Acts 1999, cc. 891, 913, § 2.1-51.18:3; 2001, c. 844; 2009, cc. 813, 840.

PART B.
[DEPARTMENT OF LAW].

CHAPTER 5.
DEPARTMENT OF LAW.

Article 1. General Provisions.

ARTICLE 1.
GENERAL PROVISIONS.

§ 2.2-507. Legal service in civil matters.

A. All legal service in civil matters for the Commonwealth, the Governor, and every state department, institution, division, commission, board, bureau, agency, entity, official, court, or judge, including the conduct of all civil litigation in which any of them are interested, shall be rendered and performed by the Attorney General, except as provided in this chapter and except for any litigation concerning a justice or judge initiated by the Judicial Inquiry and Review Commission. No regular counsel shall be employed for or by the Governor or any state department, institution, division, commission, board, bureau, agency, entity, or official. The Attorney General may represent personally or through one or more of his assistants any number of state departments, institutions, divisions, commissions, boards, bureaus, agencies, entities, officials, courts, or judges that are parties to the same transaction or that are parties in the same civil or administrative proceeding and may represent multiple interests within the same department, institution, division, commission, board, bureau, agency, or entity. The soil and water conservation district directors or districts may request legal advice from local, public, or private sources; however, upon request of the soil and water conservation district directors or districts, the Attorney General shall provide legal service in civil matters for such district directors or districts.

B. The Attorney General may represent personally or through one of his assistants any of the following persons who are made defendant in any civil action for damages arising out of any matter connected with their official duties:

1. Members, agents or employees of the Alcoholic Beverage Control Board;

2. Agents inspecting or investigators appointed by the State Corporation Commission;

3. Agents, investigators, or auditors employed by the Department of Taxation;

4. Members, agents or employees of the State Board of Behavioral Health and Developmental Services, the Department of Behavioral Health and Developmental Services, the State Board of Health, the State Department of Health, the Department of General Services, the State Board of Social Services, the Department of Social Services, the State Board of Corrections, the Department of Corrections, the State Board of Juvenile Justice, the Department of Juvenile Justice, the Virginia Parole Board, or the Department of Agriculture and Consumer Services;

5. Persons employed by the Commonwealth Transportation Board, the Department of Transportation, or the Department of Rail and Public Transportation;

6. Persons employed by the Commissioner of Motor Vehicles;

7. Persons appointed by the Commissioner of Marine Resources;

8. Police officers appointed by the Superintendent of State Police;

9. Conservation police officers appointed by the Department of Game and Inland Fisheries;

10. Hearing officers appointed to hear a teacher's grievance pursuant to § 22.1-311;

11. Staff members or volunteers participating in a court-appointed special advocate program pursuant to Article 5 (§ 9.1-151 et seq.) of Chapter 1 of Title 9.1;

12. Any emergency medical service agency that is a licensee of the Department of Health in any civil matter and any guardian ad litem appointed by a court in a civil matter brought against him for alleged errors or omissions in the discharge of his court-appointed duties;

13. Conservation officers of the Department of Conservation and Recreation; or

14. A person appointed by written order of a circuit court judge to run an existing corporation or company as the judge's representative, when that person is acting in execution of a lawful order of the court and the order specifically refers to this section and appoints such person to serve as an agent of the Commonwealth.

Upon request of the affected individual, the Attorney General may represent personally or through one of his assistants any basic or advanced emergency medical care attendant or technician possessing a valid certificate issued by authority of the State Board of Health in any civil matter in which a defense of immunity from liability is raised pursuant to § 8.01-225.

C. If, in the opinion of the Attorney General, it is impracticable or uneconomical for such legal service to be rendered by him or one of his assistants, he may employ special counsel for this purpose, whose compensation shall be fixed by the Attorney General. The compensation for such special counsel shall be paid out of the funds appropriated for the administration of the board, commission, division or department being represented or whose members, officers, inspectors, investigators, or other employees are being represented pursuant to this section. Notwithstanding any provision of this section to the contrary, the Supreme Court may employ its own counsel in any matter arising out of its official duties in which it, or any justice, is a party.

History.
Code 1950, § 2-87; 1958, c. 542; 1966, cc. 222, 677, § 2.1-121; 1974, cc. 44, 45, 432; 1975, c. 372; 1976, cc. 580, 726; 1978, c. 96; 1979, c. 450; 1980, c. 255; 1981, c. 427; 1982, c. 636; 1984, cc. 703, 742; 1987, c. 326; 1988, c. 435; 1989, c. 733; 1990, cc. 637, 752, 791; 2001, c. 844; 2005, c. 236; 2007, cc. 248, 595; 2008, c. 577; 2009, cc. 813, 840; 2012, c. 563; 2013, cc. 585, 588, 646, 650.

Editor's note.
Acts 2013, cc. 585 and 646, cl. 2 provides: "That the provisions of this act shall not be construed to invalidate any action taken or approval rendered by the Commonwealth Transportation Board prior to July 1, 2013, and that any and all actions taken and all approvals rendered by the Board prior to July 1, 2013, shall remain valid and in effect unless modified, superseded, or repealed by subsequent action of the Board."

The 2012 amendments.
The 2012 amendment by c. 563 added subdivision B 14 and made related changes.

The 2013 amendments.
The 2013 amendments by cc. 585 and 646 are identical, and added "the Department of Transportation, or the Department of Rail and Public Transportation" at the end of subdivision B 5.

The 2013 amendments by cc. 588 and 650 are identical, and in subdivision B 10, substituted "Hearing officers" for "Third impartial panel members" and "§ 22.1-311" for "§ 22.1-312."

Law Review.
For annual survey commentary, "Constitutional Crisis in the Commonwealth: Resolving the Conflict between Governors and Attorney General," see 41 U. Rich. L. Rev. 43 (2006). For annual survey of Virginia law, "Comment: Why Virginia's Challenges to the Patient Protection and Affordable Care Act Did Not Invoke Nullification," see 46 U. Rich. L. Rev. 917 (2012). For annual survey of Virginia law article, "Administrative Law," see 47 U. Rich. L. Rev. 7 (2012).

Michie's Jurisprudence.
For related discussion, see 2A M.J. Attorney General, § 2.

CASE NOTES

Editor's note.
Most of the cases below were decided under former Title 2.1 or prior provisions.

Assistance to hearing officer in case against medical provider. — The Attorney General complied with mandate to render all legal service in civil matters for the Commonwealth and all its agencies by assigning separate assistants to prosecute and to advise the hearing officer on procedure in case against doctor whose medical provider contract was terminated. Hladys v. Commonwealth, 235 Va. 145, 366 S.E.2d 98 (1988).

Doctor's right in a medical license revocation proceeding to a neutral decision maker was not improperly infringed when one assistant attorney general advised the board while another assistant attorney general prosecuted the case against the doctor. The doctor had not show the required bias or improper conduct and the General Assembly had directed the Attorney General to conduct legal services for every state board. Vuyyuru v. Va. Bd. of Med., 2008 Va. App. LEXIS 30 (Jan. 15, 2008).

Scope of inquiry. — While Supreme Court recognized that the Attorney General vigorously disputed the existence of any conflict of interests between her office and the Virginia Retirement System, it was not the province of the judicial branch of government to question the motives or judgment of the head of the executive branch; rather, inquiry for the Supreme Court was limited to whether the Governor exceeded the scope of authority vested in his office by his appointment of a "special counsel" and whether, in the exercise of that grant of power, the Governor's acts were arbitrary and capricious. Wilder v. Attorney Gen., 247 Va. 119, 439 S.E.2d 398 (1994).

Finding not binding on Supreme Court. — Where trial court's finding that the Governor appointed regular counsel was not merely a finding of fact, but a mixed question of law and fact, such finding was not binding on the Supreme Court. Wilder v. Attorney Gen., 247 Va. 119, 439 S.E.2d 398 (1994).

Arising from official duties. — Under subsection B of § 2.2-507, the Attorney General may represent members, agents, or employees of the Department of Corrections who are made defendant in any civil action for damages arising out of any matter connected with their official duties and, contrary to an inmate's contention, the statute does not require that an individual be a member, agent, or employee of the relevant department at the time the counterclaim is filed; all that is required is that the civil litigation for which damages are sought arise from the individual's official duties. Douglas v. McCarty, 2003 U.S. App. LEXIS 23585 (4th Cir. Nov. 19, 2003).

Exception to Attorney General's authority. — At a minimum, the Commonwealth's Attorney has standing to seek mandamus or prohibition in a matter involving an ongoing criminal prosecution. Moreau v. Fuller, 276 Va. 127, 661 S.E.2d 841, 2008 Va. LEXIS 68 (2008).

Attorney generals not proper parties in prison condition suit. — Where plaintiff failed to state what legal duties attorney generals owed him and how those duties were breached, all claims against them were properly dismissed in suit complaining of correctional facilities for morbidly obese inmate. Torcasio v. Murray, 862 F. Supp. 1482 (E.D. Va. 1994), aff'd in part, rev'd in part, 57 F.3d 1340 (4th Cir. 1995), cert. denied, 516 U.S. 1071, 116 S. Ct. 772, 133 L. Ed. 2d 724 (1996).

Legal services for Social Services Department mandatory. — This section provides that the Office of the Attorney General shall provide all legal services for the Department of Social Services in civil matters; the term "shall" is mandatory and reflects the General Assembly's intention that there be no discretion in complying with the statute, except as provided in the statute itself, an issue not raised on these facts. Brunty v. Smith, 22 Va. App. 191, 468 S.E.2d 161 (1996).

§ 2.2-507.1. Authority of Attorney General regarding charitable assets.

A. The assets of a charitable corporation incorporated in or doing any business in Virginia shall be deemed to be held in trust for the public for such purposes as are established by the governing documents of such charitable corporation, the gift or bequest made to such charitable corporation, or other applicable law. The Attorney General shall have the same authority to act on behalf of the public with respect to such assets as he has with respect to assets held by unincorporated charitable trusts and other charitable entities, including the authority to seek such judicial relief as may be necessary to protect the public interest in such assets.

B. Nothing contained in this section is intended to modify the standard of conduct applicable under existing law to the directors of charitable corporations incorporated in or doing any business in Virginia.

History.
2002, c. 792; 2004, c. 289.

Law Review.
For 2003/2004 survey of the law of wills, trusts and estates, see 39 U. Rich. L. Rev. 447 (2004).

Research references.
Harrison on Wills and Administration for Virginia and West Virginia (Matthew Bender). Chapter 17 Beneficiaries. § 17.25 Present Status. James P. Cox, III.

CASE NOTES

Suits filed prior to July 1, 2002. — Trial court had jurisdiction to decide a lawsuit that a fraternity filed against a foundation it created in 1966 seeking an order declaring that the foundation held title to property it owned in trust for the benefit of the fraternity, even though the Attorney General of Virginia was not a party to the lawsuit, because the suit was filed before July 1, 2002. Kappa Sigma Fraternity, Inc. v. Kappa Sigma Fraternity, 266 Va. 455, 587 S.E.2d 701, 2003 Va. LEXIS 105 (2003).

Applicability to a nonstock charitable corporation. — This section does not impose any duties upon a nonstock charitable corporation. Dodge v. Trs. of Randolph-Macon Woman's College, 276 Va. 10, 661 S.E.2d 805, 2008 Va. LEXIS 85 (2008).

Application of trust law. — This section does not require the application of trust law, rather than corporate law, to a college, which is a nonstock charitable corporation. Acceptance of that position would transform all charitable Virginia nonstock corporations into charitable trusts, and there was no language in § 2.2-507.1 that manifested any intent of the General Assembly to make such a drastic change in Virginia's established law. Dodge v. Trs. of Randolph-Macon Woman's College, 276 Va. 10, 661 S.E.2d 805, 2008 Va. LEXIS 85 (2008).

Authority of Attorney General to act. — Applying the plain meaning of the language the General Assembly chose to use when enacting § 2.2-507.1, the statute was quite narrow and simply conferred upon the Attorney General the authority to act on behalf of the public to protect the public's interest in assets held by charitable corporations. This statute was devoid of any language that imposed duties upon charitable corporations. Dodge v. Trs. of Randolph-Macon Woman's College, 276 Va. 10, 661 S.E.2d 805, 2008 Va. LEXIS 85 (2008).

Directors' duties and standards of conduct. — Under subsection B, directors of charitable nonstock corporations remained subject to existing statutory and common law related to those corporations. Subsection B of § 2.2-507.1, by its express and explicit language, negated the imposition of any additional duties upon directors of charitable corporations; rather, § 13.1-870, which was a part of the Virginia Nonstock Corporation Act, and the common law, governed the standards of conduct applicable to directors of nonstock charitable corporations. Dodge v. Trs. of Randolph-Macon Woman's College, 276 Va. 10, 661 S.E.2d 805, 2008 Va. LEXIS 85 (2008).

§ 2.2-511. Criminal cases.

A. Unless specifically requested by the Governor to do so, the Attorney General shall have no authority to institute or conduct criminal prosecutions in the circuit courts of the Commonwealth except in cases involving (i) violations of the Alcoholic Beverage Control Act (§ 4.1-100 et seq.), (ii) violation of laws relating to elections and the electoral process as provided in § 24.2-104, (iii) violation of laws relating to motor vehicles and their operation, (iv) the handling of funds by a state bureau, institution, commission or department, (v) the theft of state property, (vi) violation of the criminal laws involving child pornography and sexually explicit visual material involving children, (vii) the practice of law without being duly authorized or licensed or the illegal practice of law, (viii) violations of § 3.2-4212 or 58.1-1008.2, (ix) with the concurrence of the local attorney for the Commonwealth, violations of the Virginia Computer Crimes Act (§ 18.2-152.1 et seq.), (x) with the concurrence of the local attorney for the Commonwealth, violations of the Air Pollution Control Law (§ 10.1-1300 et seq.), the Virginia Waste Management Act (§ 10.1-1400 et seq.), and the State Water Control Law (§ 62.1-44.2 et seq.), (xi) with the concurrence of the local attorney for the Commonwealth, violations of Chapters 2 (§ 18.2-18 et seq.), 3 (§ 18.2-22 et seq.), and 10 (§ 18.2-434 et seq.) of Title 18.2, if such crimes relate to violations of law listed in clause (x) of this subsection, (xii) with the concurrence of the local attorney for the Commonwealth, criminal violations by Medicaid providers or their employees in the course of doing business, or violations of Chapter 13 (§ 18.2-512 et seq.) of Title 18.2, in which cases the Attorney General may leave the prosecution to the local attorney for the Commonwealth, or he may institute proceedings by information, presentment or indictment, as appropriate, and conduct the same, (xiii) with the concurrence of the local attorney for the Commonwealth, violations of Article 9 (§ 18.2-246.1 et seq.) of Chapter 6 of Title 18.2, (xiv) with the concurrence of the local attorney for the Commonwealth, assisting in the prosecution of violations of §§ 18.2-186.3 and 18.2-186.4, (xv) with the concurrence of the local attorney for the Commonwealth, assisting in the prosecution of violations of § 18.2-46.2, 18.2-46.3, or 18.2-46.5 when such violations are committed on the grounds of a state correctional facility, and (xvi) with the concurrence of the local attorney for the Commonwealth, assisting in the prosecution of violations of Article 10 (§ 18.2-246.6 et seq.) of Chapter 6 of Title 18.2.

In all other criminal cases in the circuit courts, except where the law provides otherwise, the authority of the Attorney General to appear or participate in the proceedings shall not attach unless and until a petition for appeal has been granted by the Court of Appeals or a writ of error has been granted by the Supreme Court. In all criminal cases before the Court of Appeals or the Supreme Court in which the Commonwealth is a party or is directly interested, the Attorney General shall appear and represent the Commonwealth. In any criminal case in which a petition for appeal has been granted by the Court of Appeals, the Attorney General shall continue to represent the Commonwealth in any further appeal of a case from the Court of Appeals to the Supreme Court.

B. The Attorney General shall, upon request of a person who was the victim of a crime and subject to such reasonable procedures as the Attorney General may require, ensure that such person is given notice of the filing, of the date, time and place and of the disposition of any appeal or habeas corpus proceeding involving the cases in which such person was a victim. For the purposes of this section, a victim is an individual who has suffered physical, psychological or economic harm as a direct result of the commission of a crime; a spouse, child, parent or legal guardian of a minor or incapacitated victim; or a spouse, child, parent or legal guardian of a victim of a homicide. Nothing in this subsection shall confer upon any person a right to appeal or modify any decision in a criminal, appellate or habeas corpus proceeding; abridge any right guaranteed by law; or create any cause of action for damages against the Commonwealth or any of its political subdivisions, the Attorney General or any of his employees or agents, any other officer, employee or agent of the Commonwealth or any of its political subdivisions, or any officer of the court.

History.
Code 1950, § 2-90; 1958, c. 235; 1966, c. 677, § 2.1-124; 1974, c. 490; 1975, c. 42; 1984, c. 703; 1993, c. 866; 1995, cc. 565, 839; 1997, c. 801; 1998, cc. 507, 510; 2000, c. 239; 2001, c. 844; 2002, cc. 588, 623; 2003, c. 103; 2004, cc. 450, 883, 996; 2007, c. 409; 2009, c. 847.

CASE NOTES

Proceedings conducted on motions to vacate orders releasing defendants from custody were civil in nature, and this section and Va. Const., Art. VI, § 1 and U.S. Const., Amend. 5 were inapplicable. Appeals from denial of such motions were properly before the Supreme Court. Virginia Dep't of Cors. v. Crowley, 227 Va. 254, 316 S.E.2d 439 (1984) (decided under former Title 2.1).

Attorney General represents state in criminal appeals. — Appellate court lacked jurisdiction over defendant's appeal of his driving under the influence conviction because defendant's notice of appeal listed the state as the prosecuting body when the city was prosecuting body, and defendant thus failed to join an indispensable party; the trial court's order, entered while the appeal was pending, purporting to show that the state was the prosecuting body, was improper because defendant's counsel failed to notify the Attorney General of the trial court's hearing. The Attorney General represented the state in all criminal appeals and had already participated on behalf of the state in the case. Roberson v. City of Va. Beach, 53 Va. App. 666, 674 S.E.2d 569, 2009 Va. App. LEXIS 153 (2009), aff'd, Roberson v. Commonwealth, 279 Va. 396, 689 S.E.2d 706, 2010 Va. LEXIS 38 (2010).

§ 2.2-515.2. Address confidentiality program established; victims of domestic violence; application; disclosure of records.

A. As used in this section:

"Address" means a residential street address, school address, or work address of a person as specified on the person's application to be a program participant.

"Applicant" means a person who is a victim of domestic violence or is a parent or guardian of a

minor child or incapacitated person who is the victim of domestic violence.

"Domestic violence" means an act as defined in § 38.2-508 and includes threat of such acts committed against an individual in a domestic situation, regardless of whether these acts or threats have been reported to law-enforcement officers. Such threat must be a threat of force which would place any person in reasonable apprehension of death or bodily injury.

"Domestic violence programs" means public and not-for-profit agencies the primary mission of which is to provide services to victims of sexual or domestic violence.

"Program participant" means a person certified by the Office of the Attorney General as eligible to participate in the Address Confidentiality Program.

B. The Statewide Facilitator for Victims of Domestic Violence shall establish a program to be known as the "Address Confidentiality Program" to protect victims of domestic violence by authorizing the use of designated addresses for such victims. An individual who is at least 18 years of age, a parent or guardian acting on behalf of a minor, a guardian acting on behalf of an incapacitated person, or an emancipated minor may apply in person, at domestic violence programs that provide services where the role of the services provider is (i) to assist the eligible person in determining whether the address confidentiality program should be part of such person's overall safety plan; (ii) to explain the address confidentiality program services and limitations; (iii) to explain the program participant's responsibilities; and (iv) to assist the person eligible for participation with the completion of application materials. The Office of the Attorney General shall approve an application if it is filed in the manner and on the form prescribed by the Attorney General and if the application contains the following:

1. A sworn statement by the applicant declaring to be true and correct under penalty of perjury that the applicant has good reason to believe that:

a. The applicant, or the minor or incapacitated individual on whose behalf the application is made, is a victim of domestic violence;

b. The applicant fears further violent acts from the applicant's assailant; and

c. The applicant is not on active parole or probation supervision requirements under federal, state, or local law.

2. A designation of the Office of the Attorney General as agent for the purpose of receiving mail on behalf of the applicant;

3. The applicant's actual address to which mail can be forwarded and a telephone number where the applicant can be called;

4. A listing of any minor children residing at the applicant's actual address, each minor child's date of birth, and each minor child's relationship to the applicant; and

5. The signature of the applicant and any person who assisted in the preparation of the application and the date.

C. Upon approval of a completed application, the Office of the Attorney General shall certify the applicant as a program participant. An applicant shall be certified for one year following the date of the approval, unless the certification is withdrawn or invalidated before that date. A program participant may apply to be recertified every year.

D. Upon receipt of first-class mail addressed to a program participant, the Attorney General or his designee shall forward the mail to the actual address of the program participant. The actual address of a program participant shall be available only to the Attorney General and to those employees involved in the operation of the Address Confidentiality Program and to law-enforcement officers. A program participant's actual address may be entered into the Virginia Criminal Information Network (VCIN) system so that it may be made known to law-enforcement officers accessing the VCIN system for law-enforcement purposes.

E. The Office of the Attorney General may cancel a program participant's certification if:

1. The program participant requests withdrawal from the program;

2. The program participant obtains a name change through an order of the court;

3. The program participant changes his residence address and does not provide seven days' notice to the Office of the Attorney General prior to the change of address;

4. The mail forwarded by the Office of the Attorney General to the address provided by the program participant is returned as undeliverable;

5. Any information contained in the application is false;

6. The program participant has been placed on parole or probation while a participant in the address confidentiality program; and

7. The applicant is required to register as a sex offender pursuant to Chapter 9 (§ 9.1-900 et seq.) of Title 9.1.

For purposes of the address confidentiality program, residents of temporary housing for 30 days or less are not eligible to enroll in the address confidentiality program until a permanent residential address is obtained.

The application form shall contain a statement notifying each applicant of the provisions of this subsection.

F. A program participant may request that any state or local agency use the address designated by the Office of the Attorney General as the program participant's address, except when the program participant is purchasing a firearm from a dealer in firearms. The agency shall accept the address designated by the Office of the Attorney General as a program participant's address, unless the agency has received a written exemption from the Office of the Attorney General demonstrating to the satisfaction of the Attorney General that:

1. The agency has a bona fide statutory basis for requiring the program participant to disclose to it the actual location of the program participant;

2. The disclosed confidential address of the program participant will be used only for that statutory purpose and will not be disclosed or made available in any way to any other person or agency; and

3. A state agency may request an exemption by providing in writing to the Office of the Attorney General identification of the statute or administrative rule that demonstrates the agency's bona fide requirement and authority for the use of the actual address of an individual. A request for a waiver from an agency may be for an individual program participant, a class of program participants, or all program participants. The denial of an agency's exemption request shall be in writing and include a statement of the specific reasons for the denial. Acceptance or denial of an agency's exemption request shall constitute final agency action.

Any state or local agency that discloses the program participant's confidential address provided by the Office of the Attorney General shall be immune from civil liability unless the agency acted with gross negligence or willful misconduct.

A program participant's actual address shall be disclosed pursuant to a court order.

G. Records submitted to or provided by the Office of the Attorney General in accordance with this section shall be exempt from disclosure under the Virginia Freedom of Information Act (§ 2.2-3700 et seq.) to the extent such records contain information identifying a past or current program participant, including such person's name, actual and designated address, telephone number, and any email address. However, access shall not be denied to the person who is the subject thereof, or the parent or legal guardian of a program participant in cases where the program participant is a minor child or an incapacitated person, except when the parent or legal guardian is named as the program participant's assailant.

H. Neither the Office of the Attorney General, its officers or employees, or others who have a responsibility to a program participant under this section shall have any liability nor shall any cause of action arise against them in their official or personal capacity from the failure of a program participant to receive any first class mail forwarded to him by the Office of the Attorney General pursuant to this section. Nor shall any such liability or cause of action arise from the failure of a program participant to timely receive any first class mail forwarded by the Office of the Attorney General pursuant to this section.

History.
2007, c. 599; 2008, c. 649; 2011, cc. 97, 172.

Editor's note.
Acts 2007, c. 599, cl. 2, as amended by Acts 2008, c. 649, cl. 2, made 2007 amendments to this section applicable only to certain localities (Counties of Albemarle, Arlington, Augusta, Dickenson, Fairfax, Henry, Lee, Rockbridge, Russell, Scott, Washington, and Wise as well as the Cities of Buena Vista, Charlottesville, Lexington, Martinsville, Norfolk, and Roanoke). Acts 2011, cc. 97 and 172, cl. 2 amended the clause to provide for statewide implementation.

Acts 2007, c. 599, cl. 2, as amended by Acts 2008, c. 649, cl. 2, and Acts 2011, cc. 97 and 172, cl. 2, provides: "That an evaluation of the statewide implementation of the program shall be prepared by the Office of the Attorney General and the results forwarded to the members of the Senate Committee on General Laws and the House Committee on General Laws by December 31, 2012."

Acts 2007, c. 599, cl. 3, as amended by Acts 2008, c. 649, cl. 2, which made continued implementation of this section contingent on an appropriation, was repealed by Acts 2011, cc. 97 and 172, cl. 3.

The 2011 amendments.
The 2011 amendments by cc. 97 and 172 are identical, and substituted "the date of the approval" for "the date of the institution of the program" in subsection C.

PART C.

STATE AGENCIES RELATED TO THE GENERAL OPERATION OF GOVERNMENT.

CHAPTER 10.

DEPARTMENT OF EMPLOYMENT DISPUTE RESOLUTION.

Section
2.2-1000, 2.2-1001. [Repealed.]

§§ 2.2-1000, 2.2-1001. Repealed by Acts 2012, cc. 803 and 835, cl. 9.

Cross references.
For current provisions related to employment dispute resolution, see § 2.2-1202.1.

Editor's note.
Acts 2012, cc. 803 and 835, enactment clauses 8 through 12, abolished the Department of Employment Dispute Resolution and transferred duties to the Department of Human Resource Management. For current provisions pertaining to employment dispute resolution, see § 2.2-1202.1.

Acts 2012, cc. 803 and 835, cl. 10 provides: "That as of July 1, 2012, the Department of Human Resource Management shall be deemed successor in interest to the Department of Employment Dispute Resolution to the extent the 8th enactment of this act transfers powers and duties. All right, title, and interest in and to any real or tangible personal property vested in the Department of Employment Dispute Resolution to the extent the 8th enactment of this act transfers powers and duties as of July 1, 2012, shall be transferred to and taken as standing in the name of the Department of Human Resource Management."

Acts 2012, cc. 803 and 835, cl. 11 provides: "That the Governor may transfer an appropriation or any portion thereof within a state agency established, abolished, or otherwise affected by the provisions of the 8th enactment of this act, or from one such agency to another, to support the changes in organization or responsibility resulting from or required by the provisions of the 8th enactment of this act."

Acts 2012, cc. 803 and 835, cl. 12 provides: "That all rules and regulations adopted by the Department of Employment Dispute Resolution that are in effect on July 1, 2012, and which pertain to the subject of the 8th enactment of this act shall remain in full force and effect until altered, amended, or rescinded by the Department of Human Resource Management."

Former § 2.2-1000, pertaining to creation of Department; appointment of Director; powers and duties, derived from 1995, cc. 770, 818, §§ 2.1-116.01, 2.1-116.02; 2000, cc. 947, 1006; 2001, c. 844. Former §

2.2-1001, pertaining to director's authority to administer Department; powers and duties, derived from 1995, cc. 16, 646, 770, 818, § 2.1-116.03; 1996, cc. 164, 869; 1998, c. 263; 2000, cc. 66, 657, 947, 1006; 2001, c. 844.

CHAPTER 11.

DEPARTMENT OF GENERAL SERVICES.

Article 3. Division Of Purchases And Supply.

ARTICLE 3.

DIVISION OF PURCHASES AND SUPPLY.

§ 2.2-1112. Standardization of materials, equipment and supplies.

A. So far as practicable, all materials, equipment and supplies, purchased by or for the officers, departments, agencies or institutions of the Commonwealth, shall be standardized by the Division, and no variation shall be allowed from any established standard without the written approval of the Division. The standard shall be determined upon the needs of all using agencies, so far as their needs are in common, and for groups of using agencies or single using agencies so far as their needs differ. When changes or alterations in equipment are necessary in order to permit the application of any standard, the changes and alterations shall be made as rapidly as possible.

B. The Division shall determine the proper equipment or electrical devices used to monitor the speed of any motor vehicle pursuant to § 46.2-882 and shall so advise the respective law-enforcement officials. Police chiefs and sheriffs shall ensure that all such equipment and devices meet or exceed the standards established by the Division. This subsection shall apply only to equipment and devices purchased on or after July 1, 1986.

C. The Division shall determine the proper equipment to be used to determine the decibel level of sound and shall so advise the respective law-enforcement officials. Police chiefs and sheriffs shall ensure that all such equipment and devices meet or exceed the standards established by the Division and shall maintain, inspect, calibrate, and test for accuracy all such equipment and devices on a schedule and in accordance with standards established by the Division.

History.
Code 1950, §§ 2-255, 2-256; 1958 c. 124; 1966, c. 677, §§ 2.1-279, 2.1-280; 1972, c. 494; 1977, c. 672, § 2.1-446; 1986, c. 530; 1991, c. 345; 2001, c. 844; 2010, c. 558.

The 2010 amendments.
The 2010 amendment by c. 558 inserted subsection A and B designations; substituted "subsection" for "provision" in subsection B; and added subsection C.

CASE NOTES

Editor's note.
The case below was decided under former Title 2.1 or prior provisions.

Presumptions. — Radar results of a machine that has been calibrated are entitled by statute to a presumption of correctness, and are admissible regardless of whether Commonwealth proves that the specific machine met or exceeded standards established by Division of Purchases and Supplies. White v. Commonwealth, No. 2991-98-3, 2000 Va. App. LEXIS 103 (Ct. of Appeals Feb. 15, 2000).

§ 2.2-1124. Disposition of surplus materials.

A. "Surplus materials" means personal property including, but not limited to, materials, supplies, equipment, and recyclable items, but shall not include property as defined in § 2.2-1147 that is determined to be surplus. Surplus materials shall not include finished products that a state hospital or training center operated by the Department of Behavioral Health and Developmental Services sells for the benefit of individuals receiving services in the state hospital or training center, provided that (i) most of the supplies, equipment, or products have been donated to the state hospital or training center; (ii) the individuals in the state hospital or training center have substantially altered the supplies, equipment, or products in the course of occupational or other therapy; and (iii) the substantial alterations have resulted in a finished product.

B. The Department shall establish procedures for the disposition of surplus materials from departments, divisions, institutions, and agencies of the Commonwealth. Such procedures shall:

1. Permit surplus materials to be transferred between or sold to departments, divisions, institutions, or agencies of the Commonwealth;

2. Permit surplus materials to be sold to Virginia charitable corporations granted tax-exempt status under § 501(c)(3) of the Internal Revenue Code and operating as clinics for the indigent and uninsured that are organized for the delivery of primary health care services (i) as federally qualified health centers designated by the Health Care Financing Administration or (ii) at a reduced or sliding fee scale or without charge;

3. Permit public sales or auctions, including online public auctions;

4. Permit surplus motor vehicles to be sold prior to public sale or auction to local social service departments for the purpose of resale at cost to TANF recipients;

5. Permit surplus materials to be sold to Virginia charitable corporations granted tax-exempt status under § 501(c)(3) of the Internal Revenue Code and operating as children's homes;

6. Permit donations to political subdivisions of the Commonwealth under the circumstances specified in this section;

7. Permit other methods of disposal when (a) the cost of the sale will exceed the potential revenue to be derived therefrom or (b) the surplus material is not suitable for sale;

8. Permit any dog especially trained for police work to be sold at an appropriate price to the handler who last was in control of the dog, which sale shall not be deemed a violation of the State and Local Government Conflict of Interests Act (§ 2.2-3100 et seq.);

9. Permit the transfer of surplus clothing to an appropriate department, division, institution, or agency of the Commonwealth for distribution to needy individuals by and through local social services boards;

10. Encourage the recycling of paper products, beverage containers, electronics, and used motor oil;

11. Require the proceeds from any sale or recycling of surplus materials be promptly deposited into the state treasury in accordance with § 2.2-1802 and report the deposit to the State Comptroller;

12. Permit donations of surplus computers and related equipment to public schools in the Commonwealth and Virginia charitable corporations granted tax-exempt status under § 501(c)(3) of the Internal Revenue Code and providing services to persons with disabilities, at-risk youths, or low-income families. For the purposes of this subdivision, "at-risk youths" means school-age children approved eligible to receive free or reduced price meals in the federally funded lunch program;

13. Permit surplus materials to be transferred or sold, prior to public sale or auction, to public television stations located in the state and other nonprofit organizations approved for the distribution of federal surplus materials;

14. Permit a public institution of higher education to dispose of its surplus materials at the location where the surplus materials are held and to retain any proceeds from such disposal, provided that the institution meets the conditions prescribed in subsection B of § 23-38.88 and § 23-38.112 (regardless of whether or not the institution has been granted any authority under Subchapter 3 (§ 23-38.91 et seq.) of Chapter 4.10 of Title 23); and

15. Require, to the extent practicable, the recycling and disposal of computers and other information technology assets. Additionally, for computers or information technology assets that may contain confidential state data or personal identifying information of citizens of the Commonwealth, the Department shall ensure all policies for the transfer or other disposition of computers or information technology assets are consistent with data and information security policies developed by the Virginia Information Technologies Agency.

C. The Department shall dispose of surplus materials pursuant to the procedures established in sub-section B or permit any department, division, institution, or agency of the Commonwealth to dispose of its surplus materials consistent with the procedures so established. No surplus materials shall be disposed of without prior consent of the head of the department, division, institution, or agency of the Commonwealth in possession of such surplus materials or the Governor.

D. Departments, divisions, institutions, or agencies of the Commonwealth or the Governor may donate surplus materials only under the following circumstances:

1. Emergencies declared in accordance with § 44-146.18:2 or 44-146.28;

2. As set forth in the budget bill as defined by § 2.2-1509, provided that (a) the budget bill contains a description of the surplus materials, the method by which the surplus materials shall be distributed, and the anticipated recipients, and (b) such information shall be provided by the Department to the Department of Planning and Budget in sufficient time for inclusion in the budget bill;

3. When the market value of the surplus materials, which shall be donated for a public purpose, is less than $500; however, the total market value of all surplus materials so donated by any department, division, institution, or agency shall not exceed 25 percent of the revenue generated by such department's, division's, institution's, or agency's sale of surplus materials in the fiscal year, except these limits shall not apply in the case of surplus computer equipment and related items donated to Virginia public schools; or

4. During a local emergency, upon written request of the head of a local government or a political subdivision in the Commonwealth to the head of a department, division, institution, or agency.

E. On or before October 1 of each year, the Department shall prepare, and file with the Secretary of the Commonwealth, a plan that describes the expected disposition of surplus materials in the upcoming fiscal year pursuant to subdivision B 6.

F. The Department may make available to any local public body of the Commonwealth the services or facilities authorized by this section; however, the furnishing of any such services shall not limit or impair any services normally rendered any department, division, institution or agency of the Commonwealth. All public bodies shall be authorized to use the services of the Department's Surplus Property Program under the guidelines established pursuant to this section and the surplus property policies and procedures of the Department. Proceeds from the sale of the surplus property shall be returned to the local body minus a service fee. The service fee charged by the Department shall be consistent with the fee charged by the Department to state public bodies.

History.
    1996, cc. 935, 978, § 2.1-457.2; 1999, cc. 159, 578, 629, 911; 2000, cc. 615, 636, 661; 2001, c. 844; 2004, c. 670; 2005, cc. 933, 945; 2006, cc. 468, 493; 2007, c. 701; 2009, c. 75; 2012, cc. 476, 507, 805, 836.

§ 2.2-1125. Proceeds from the sale or recycling of surplus materials.

A. The proceeds from the sale or recycling of surplus materials pursuant to § 2.2-1124 shall promptly be deposited into the state treasury and the deposit reported to the State Comptroller, along with a statement of total proceeds and the amount of the proceeds derived from the sale or recycling of surplus materials purchased in whole or in part from general fund appropriations.

B. At the end of each fiscal quarter, the State Comptroller shall (i) determine the total proceeds derived from the sale of surplus materials purchased in whole or in part from general fund appropriations and direct the State Treasurer to transfer fifty percent of the total of such proceeds to the Conservation Resources Fund and (ii) provide copies of the reports furnished to him pursuant to subsection A, or summaries thereof, to the Department of Planning and Budget.

C. Based on such reports, or summaries, the Department of Planning and Budget, pursuant to its authority in the appropriation act, may increase general fund appropriations to any department, division, institution, or agency of the Commonwealth by the amount of available proceeds derived from the sale or recycling of surplus materials pursuant to § 2.2-1124. The department, division, institution, or agency of the Commonwealth may use the additional appropriations to purchase materials, supplies, or equipment, or to defray the cost of disposing of surplus materials to the extent permitted pursuant to § 2.2-1124.

D. Departments, divisions, institutions, or agencies may retain the full net profits from the sale of recycled materials provided that a report is filed with the State Comptroller on or before October 1 of each year.

E. Departments, divisions, institutions, or agencies meeting management standards prescribed by the Governor may retain the net proceeds from the surplus materials sold pursuant to § 2.2-1124. Such retention shall be effective on July 1 following the determination that the department, division, institution, or agency meets the management standards.

History.
1996, cc. 935, 978, § 2.1-457.3; 2001, c. 844.

CHAPTER 12.

DEPARTMENT OF HUMAN RESOURCE MANAGEMENT.

Section
2.2-1202.1. Additional powers and duties of Director; employment dispute resolution.

§ 2.2-1202.1. Additional powers and duties of Director; employment dispute resolution.

The Director shall:
1. Establish a comprehensive program of employee relations management that includes alternative processes for resolving employment disputes;
2. Establish the grievance procedure and a statewide mediation program;
3. Adopt rules and set hearing officer fees for grievance hearings;
4. For employees who are covered by the grievance procedure, (i) provide forms necessary for the proper use of the grievance procedure; (ii) direct full compliance with the grievance procedure process; and (iii) investigate allegations of retaliation as the result of use of or participation in the grievance procedure or of reporting, in good faith, an allegation of fraud, waste, or abuse to the Fraud, Waste and Abuse Hotline and advise the agency head of the findings;
5. Render final decisions, containing the reasons for such decision, on all matters related to access to the grievance procedure, procedural compliance with the grievance procedure, and qualification for hearing;
6. Establish a process to select, on a rotating basis, hearing officers for grievance hearings from (i) the list maintained by the Executive Secretary of the Supreme Court or (ii) attorneys hired as classified employees by the Department through a competitive selection process; train and assign such hearing officers to conduct grievance hearings; evaluate the quality of their services to determine eligibility for continued selection; and, if deemed ineligible for continued selection, establish policies for removing such hearing officers from consideration for future selection;
7. Publish hearing officer decisions and Department rulings;
8. Establish a training program for human resources personnel on employee relations management and employment rights and responsibilities;
9. Implement a comprehensive training and instructional program for all supervisory personnel that includes the role of the grievance procedure in harmonious employee relations management. The training program shall also include methods for supervisors to instruct nonsupervisory personnel in the use of the grievance procedure. Use of the grievance procedure to resolve disputes shall be encouraged. In-house resources shall be developed to allow the Department and its personnel to conduct onsite

training of this nature for units and agencies of state government throughout Virginia. The Department shall assist agencies in establishing performance criteria for such supervisory personnel;

10. Provide information upon the request of any employee concerning personnel policies, regulations, and law applicable to the grievance procedure and counsel employees in the resolution of conflict in the workplace;

11. Establish and maintain a toll-free telephone number to facilitate access by employees to the services of the Department;

12. Collect information and statistical data regarding the use of the grievance procedure and the effectiveness of employee relations management in the various state agencies;

13. Make recommendations to the Governor and the General Assembly to improve the grievance procedure and employee relations management;

14. Conduct such training seminars and educational programs for the members and staff of agencies and public bodies and other interested persons on the use of dispute resolution proceedings as the Director determines appropriate;

15. Exercise such other powers and perform such other duties as may be requested by the Governor; and

16. Perform all acts and employ such personnel as may be required, necessary, or convenient to carry out the provisions of this section.

History.
1995, cc. 16, 646, 770, 818, § 2.1-116.03; 1996, cc. 164, 869; 1998, c. 263; 2000, cc. 66, 657, 947, 1006; 2001, c. 844, § 2.2-1001; 2012, cc. 56, 349, 803, 835; 2013, cc. 572, 690, 717, 723.

Cross references.
As to the effect of the Virginia Administrative Dispute Resolution Act, § 2.2-4115 et seq., on mediation programs administered by the Department of Employment Dispute Resolution, see § 2.2-4117. As to immunity from civil liability for mediators and mediation services established under this section, see § 8.01-581.23.

Editor's note.
Acts 2012, cc. 803 and 835, cl. 8 enacted this section. Acts 2012, cc. 803 and 835, enactment clauses 8 through 12, abolished the Department of Employment Dispute Resolution and transferred duties to the Department of Human Resource Management. The historical citations and annotations to former § 2.2-1001 have been added to this section.

Acts 2012, cc. 56 and 349 amended § 2.2-1001, from which this section is derived. Pursuant to § 30-152, the 2012 amendments by cc. 56 and 349 have been given effect in this section as set out above by deleting clause (iv) in subdivision 4, which read "(iv) rule on the qualification of a grievance or the question of access to the grievance procedure"; and inserting "access to the grievance procedure" and "and qualification for hearing" in subdivision 5.

Acts 2012, cc. 803 and 835, cl. 11 provides: "That the Governor may transfer an appropriation or any portion thereof within a state agency established, abolished, or otherwise affected by the provisions of the 8th enactment of this act, or from one such agency to another, to support the changes in organization or responsibility resulting from or required by the provisions of the 8th enactment of this act."

The 2013 amendments.
The 2013 amendments by cc. 572, 690, 717 and 723 are identical, and deleted "State Employee" preceding "Fraud, Waste and Abuse Hotline" in subdivision 4.

Research references.
Friend's Virginia Pleading and Practice (Matthew Bender). Chapter 34 Alternatives to Trial: Arbitration and Award and Dispute Resolution Proceedings. § 34.03 Dispute Resolution Proceedings. Charles E. Friend.

CASE NOTES

Editor's note.
Most of the cases below were decided under former Title 2.1 or prior provisions.

Authority of grievance panel to promote should be left to General Assembly. — The determination whether a grievance panel has the authority to promote clearly is best left to the wisdom of the General Assembly and the state officials charged with the administration of the grievance procedure. Therefore, the board was without authority to award a policeman, denied promotion, a retroactive promotion and compensation for back pay. Jones v. Carter, 234 Va. 621, 363 S.E.2d 921 (1988).

Legislative intent to preclude judicial review. — The "final authority" language in subdivision (7) of former § 2.1-114.5:6, which stated: 'To make and disseminate interpretations of the grievance procedure," supported and was consistent with a legislative intent shown throughout the act to preclude judicial review in certain areas. Murray v. Stokes, 237 Va. 653, 378 S.E.2d 834 (1989).

Judicial review of the interpretation of a personnel policy regarding employee compensation by the Director of the Department of Personnel and Training (now Department of Human Resource Management) is precluded under the Virginia Personnel Act, and therefore, the trial court had no jurisdiction to entertain a bill of complaint seeking review of the interpretation of Rule 8.3(d) of the Department's rules by the director of that department. Murray v. Stokes, 237 Va. 653, 378 S.E.2d 834 (1989).

Court lacked authority to treat petition as notice of grievance. — Where the trial court correctly determined that the employee's demotion upon reinstatement was an issue that had to be grieved separately and was not enforceable as part of the panel's reinstatement decision without exhausting the administrative grievance procedure, the trial court lacked authority to treat the petition filed pursuant to subsection F of former § 2.1-114.5:1 as filing notice of a grievance with an agency. Commonwealth, Dep't of Taxation v. Hogan, 11 Va. App. 306, 397 S.E.2d 902 (1990).

Reversal of hearing officer's decision in error. — Upon judicial review of a hearing officer's decision to amend a disciplinary notice against two penitentiary employees, the trial court erred by concluding that the hearing officer had no authority to amend the disciplinary notice and, therefore, dismissed the Group II disciplinary notice. Because the hearing officer's amendment of the disciplinary notice did not violate any statute, judicial precedent, or accepted legal principal, it was proper and should have been upheld. Commonwealth v. Doyle, 2005 Va. App. LEXIS 255 (July 5, 2005).

Agency decision not subject to review. — In a case involving Virginia's State Grievance Procedure, specifically §§ 2.2-3003, 2.2-3004, and 2.2-3006, the Department of Employment Dispute Resolution's decision was not subject to review by the circuit court because it involved an interpretation of agency procedures created pursuant to subdivision 2 of § 2.2-1001 rather than an issue of law; also, the delay by the Department of Human Resource Management (DHRM) in rendering its decision on the request for review did not nullify its ruling because subsection A of § 2.2-3006 contained no prohibitory or limiting language preventing the DHRM from ruling after the expiration of 60 days. Va. Dep't of Taxation v. Brailey, 2008 Va. App. LEXIS 19 (2008).

CIRCUIT COURT OPINIONS

Burden shifting proper. — Director of the Department of Employment Dispute Resolution had the authority under § 2.2-1001 to establish the grievance procedure, adopt rules for grievance hearings, and perform all acts as were necessary to carry out the provisions of the disciplining of a university employee, such that the use of the McDonnell Douglas burden-shifting analysis by a hearing officer regarding the employee's grievance over his termination, wherein the employee asserted racial discrimination, was not contrary to law. Old Dominion Univ. v. Birkmeyer, 73 Va. Cir. 341, 2007 Va. Cir. LEXIS 131 (Norfolk 2007).

PART E.

STATE OFFICERS AND EMPLOYEES.

CHAPTER 30.

STATE GRIEVANCE PROCEDURE.

§ 2.2-3000. Policy of the Commonwealth; responsibilities of state agencies under this chapter.

A. It shall be the policy of the Commonwealth, as an employer, to encourage the resolution of employee problems and complaints. To that end, employees shall be able to discuss freely, and without retaliation, their concerns with their immediate supervisors and management. To the extent that such concerns cannot be resolved informally, the grievance procedure shall afford an immediate and fair method for the resolution of employment disputes that may arise between state agencies and those employees who have access to the procedure under § 2.2-3001.

B. To fully achieve the objectives of this chapter and to create uniformity, each agency in the executive branch of state government shall:

1. Require supervisory personnel to be trained in the grievance procedure, personnel policies, and conflict resolution;

2. Familiarize employees with their grievance rights and promote the services of the Department of Human Resource Management;

3. Cooperate with investigations conducted pursuant to the authority granted by clause (iii) of subdivision 4 of § 2.2-1202.1;

4. Participate in the mediation program;

5. Evaluate supervisors on the effectiveness of employee relations management, including, but not limited to, their handling of grievances; and

6. Recognize the right of employees to fully participate in the grievance process without retaliation.

C. The Department of Human Resource Management shall monitor agencies' activities under this section.

History.
1995, cc. 770, 818, §§ 2.1-116.04, 2.1-116.05; 1996, cc. 164, 869; 1999, cc. 703, 726; 2000, cc. 947, 1006; 2001, c. 844; 2004, c. 674; 2012, cc. 803, 835.

Editor's note.
Acts 2012, cc. 803 and 835, cl. 11 provides: "That the Governor may transfer an appropriation or any portion thereof within a state agency established, abolished, or otherwise affected by the provisions of the 8th enactment of this act, or from one such agency to another, to support the changes in organization or responsibility resulting from or required by the provisions of the 8th enactment of this act."
Acts 2012, cc. 803 and 835, cl. 12 provides: "That all rules and regulations adopted by the Department of Employment Dispute Resolution that are in effect on July 1, 2012, and which pertain to the subject of the 8th enactment of this act shall remain in full force and effect until altered, amended, or rescinded by the Department of Human Resource Management."

The 2012 amendments.
The 2012 amendments by cc. 803 and 835, cl. 8, are identical, and in subdivision B 2 and in subsection C, substituted "Department of Human Resource Management" for "Department of Employment Dispute Resolution"; and updated the section reference in subdivision B 3.

CASE NOTES

Federal court jurisdiction. — Employee's action, which alleged disciplinary action by the employer was retaliation for engaging in protected communications, was dismissed because the Rooker-Feldman doctrine applied to Virginia's grievance procedure under § 2.2-3000 et seq. and dictated a conclusion that the court was without subject matter jurisdiction to entertain the employee's claims; the factual basis for the constitutional claims under 42 U.S.C.S. § 1983 did not differ, in any substantial part, from those essential facts presented in the state proceedings. Horner v. Dep't of Mental Health, 2003 U.S. Dist. LEXIS 10094 (W.D. Va. June 17, 2003).

State grievance process subject to *Rooker-Feldman* doctrine. — In an action by a former state employee against his former state employer and former supervisors, a magistrate correctly found that the court lacked subject matter jurisdiction over the employee's complaint based on the *Rooker-Feldman* doctrine because, although 28 U.S.C.S. § 1257 did not explicitly mention decisions by lower state courts or administrative agencies, the state grievance process under § 2.2-3000 et seq., which the employee had invoked, was an adjudicatory process subject to the *Rooker-Feldman* doctrine. Horner v. Dep't of Mental Health, 2003 U.S. Dist. LEXIS 26935 (W.D. Va. May 1, 2003).

Remedy by immediate supervisor precludes further review. — The language "Each level of management review shall have the authority to provide the employee with a remedy," meant that the decision of the employee's immediate supervisor that the employee should be reinstated, after the employee had committed offenses while working for the state employer that called for immediate dismissal, was not a mere recommendation, and precluded subsequent review by the state employer's higher-level management. Horner v. Dep't of Mental Health, Mental Retardation, & Substance Abuse Servs., 268 Va. 187, 597 S.E.2d 202, 2004 Va. LEXIS 83 (2004), reversing 40 Va. App. 338, 579 S.E.2d 372, 2003 Va. App. LEXIS 229 (2003), which held that the legislature did not intend that the low-level supervisor could make a final, conclusive determination on the grievance and thereby thwart review by more senior management. See also, 59 Va. Cir. 250 (2002).

CIRCUIT COURT OPINIONS

Local government employees are exempt. — Charlottesville Redevelopment and Housing Authority is not subject to the state grievance procedure. Although grievance-hearing decisions are grievable under the state grievance procedure, § 2.2-3002 and the Virginia Personnel Act, § 2.2-2905, expressly exempt local government employees. Crawley-Evans v. Charlottesville Redevelopment & Hous. Auth., 73 Va. Cir. 494, 2007 Va. Cir. LEXIS 209 (Charlottesville Aug. 7, 2007).

Discipline requiring grievance hearing. — State employment resolution department erred in determining that e-mail that an office director sent to petitioner was not disciplinary action that qualified for a hearing on petitioner's grievance regarding an altercation with a fellow employee over what material could be posted at work; the trial court determined that petitioner was entitled to a grievance hearing because the e-mail outlined a course of conduct that was to be followed and how future conduct regarding the issue would be handled, and, thus, qualified as a formal disciplinary action that entitled petitioner to a grievance hearing. Gillispie v. Va. Dep't of Envtl. Quality, 67 Va. Cir. 580, 2004 Va. Cir. LEXIS 356 (Richmond Dec. 16, 2004).

§ 2.2-3001. State employees.

A. Unless exempted by law, all nonprobationary state employees shall be covered by the grievance procedure established pursuant to this chapter and any regulations adopted pursuant thereto. Employees not covered by the grievance procedure may be covered by an alternative grievance procedure.

B. The Office of the Attorney General and every legislative, judicial, and independent agency that is not subject to the state grievance procedure shall establish and administer a grievance procedure.

History.
1995, cc. 770, 818, § 2.1-116.09; 1996, cc. 164, 869; 1997, c. 711; 1998, c. 245; 2000, cc. 947, 1006; 2001, c. 844.

CASE NOTES

Agency's alleged failure to comply with grievance procedures. — When an employee contesting the employee's termination asserted that the Department of Behavioral Health and Developmental Services did not follow procedures in the applicable grievance procedures manual, such alleged failure did not require reversal of the department's decision because: (1) under subsection A of § 2.2-3001, the Director of the Department of Employment Dispute Resolution policed compliance with grievance procedures; and (2) courts ensured an administrative decision was not "contradictory to law," under subsection B of § 2.2-3006, but the grievance procedures manual was not law. Burke v. Catawba Hosp., 59 Va. App. 828, 722 S.E.2d 684, 2012 Va. App. LEXIS 76 (2012).

§ 2.2-3002. Exemptions from chapter.

The provisions of this chapter shall not apply to:
1. Appointees of elected groups or individuals except as provided in subsection B of § 2.2-3001;
2. Agency heads or chief executive officers of government agencies and public institutions of higher education appointed by boards and commissions;
3. Law-enforcement officers as defined in § 9.1-500 whose grievances are subject to Chapter 5 (§ 9.1-500 et seq.) and who have elected to resolve such grievances under those provisions; and
4. Employees in positions designated in § 2.2-2905 as exempt from the Virginia Personnel Act (§ 2.2-2900 et seq.).

History.
1995, cc. 770, 818, § 2.1-116.013; 2001, c. 844.

§ 2.2-3003. Grievance procedure generally.

A. As part of the Commonwealth's program of employee relations management, the Department of Human Resource Management shall develop a grievance procedure that includes not more than three successively higher grievance resolution steps and a formal hearing as provided in this chapter. However, grievances involving dismissals due to formal discipline or unsatisfactory job performance shall proceed directly to a formal hearing, omitting the grievance resolution steps, the face-to-face meeting specified in subsection D, and the agency head qualification determination specified in subsection D of § 2.2-3004.

B. Prior to initiating a written grievance, the employee shall be encouraged to pursue an informal complaint with his immediate supervisor. The supervisor shall have authority to resolve the complaint if it involves actions within his control.

C. An employee may pursue a formal written grievance through the grievance resolution steps if the complaint has been presented to management within 30 calendar days of the employee's knowledge of the event that gave rise to the complaint. Employees' rights to pursue grievances shall not be used to harass or otherwise impede the efficient operations of government.

D. Except as provided in subsection A, upon receipt of a timely written complaint, management shall review the grievance and respond to the merits thereof. Each level of management review shall have the authority to provide the employee with a remedy, subject to the agency head's approval. At least one face-to-face meeting between the employee and management shall be required. The persons who may be present at this meeting are the employee, the appropriate manager, an individual selected by the employee, and an individual selected by the manager. Witnesses may be called by either party.

E. Absent just cause, all documents, as defined in the Rules of the Supreme Court of Virginia, relating to the actions grieved shall be made available, upon request from a party to the grievance, by the opposing party, in a timely fashion. Upon such request a party shall have a duty to search its records to ensure that all such relevant documents are provided. Documents pertaining to nonparties that are relevant to the grievance shall be produced in such a manner as to preserve the privacy of the individuals not personally involved in the grievance. A party shall not be required to create a document if the document does not exist.

F. All time limitations prescribed in the grievance procedure, including, but not limited to, submission of an initial complaint and employee appeal of management decisions, shall be reasonable, specific, and equally applicable to the agency and the employee. Expedited grievance procedures shall be established for terminations, demotions, suspensions, and lost wages or salaries.

G. Within five workdays of the receipt of a written notice of noncompliance, failure of the employee or the agency to comply with a substantial procedural requirement of the grievance procedure without just cause may result in a decision against the noncomplying party on any qualified issue. Written notice of noncompliance by the agency shall be made to the agency head. The Director of the Department of Human Resource Management shall render all decisions related to procedural compliance, and such decisions shall contain the reasons for such decision and shall be final.

H. Grievances qualified pursuant to § 2.2-3004 that have not been resolved through the grievance resolution steps shall advance to a hearing that shall be the final step in the grievance procedure.

History.
1995, cc. 770, 818, § 2.1-116.05; 1996, cc. 164, 869; 1999, cc. 703, 726; 2000, cc. 947, 1006; 2001, c. 844; 2003, c. 252; 2004, c. 674; 2012, cc. 56, 349, 803, 835.

The 2012 amendments.
The 2012 amendments by cc. 56 and 349 are identical, and added the second sentence of subsection A and the exception at the beginning of subsection D.
The 2012 amendments by cc. 803 and 835, cl. 8, are identical, and in subsections A and G, substituted "Department of Human Resource Management" for "Department of Employment Dispute Resolution."

CASE NOTES

Editor's note.
Many of the cases below were decided under former Title 2.1 or prior provisions.

Remedy by immediate supervisor precludes further review. — The language "Each level of management review shall have the authority to provide the employee with a remedy," meant that the decision of the employee's immediate supervisor that the employee should be reinstated, after the employee had committed offenses while working for the state employer that called for immediate dismissal, was not a mere recommendation, and precluded subsequent review by the state employer's higher-level management. Horner v. Dep't of Mental Health, Mental Retardation, & Substance Abuse Servs., 268 Va. 187, 597 S.E.2d 202, 2004 Va. LEXIS 83 (2004), reversing 40 Va. App. 338, 579 S.E.2d 372, 2003 Va. App. LEXIS 229 (2003), which held that the legislature did not intend that the low-level supervisor could make a final, conclusive determination on the grievance and thereby thwart review by more senior management. See also, 59 Va. Cir. 250 (2002).

Application of issue preclusion to hearing officer's findings of fact. — Issue preclusion applied to a former hospital employee's action that alleged retaliation in violation of the Rehabilitation Act, 29 U.S.C.S. § 794(a), and the First Amendment because the employee had previously litigated all of the issues presented in the instant case surrounding his termination in an impartial forum, the Virginia Department of Employment Dispute Resolution. There was no basis to find that the decisions of the hearing officer on the factual issues surrounding the discharge were contradictory to law or policy; thus, the hearing officer's findings that the employee was terminated for failing to follow a supervisor's instructions and failing to comply with written policy, not because of retaliation, were final and binding under Virginia law. Horner v. Dep't of Mental Health, 2004 U.S. Dist. LEXIS 29022 (W.D. Va. Apr. 26, 2004).

Court deference to administrative decision. — Where an agency failed to show that a hearing officer's decision contradicted any law, the circuit court's ruling, unduly limiting the officer's authority and overturning the officer's decision, was reversed to reinstate the officer's decision. Tatum v. Va. Dep't of Agric. &

Consumer Servs., 41 Va. App. 110, 582 S.E.2d 452, 2003 Va. App. LEXIS 356 (2003), reversing 59 Va. Cir. 262 (2002).

Virginia's layoff-rights scheme and rules on exemptions circumscribe property interest in continued employment. — Although a nonprobationary employee has a property interest in continued employment that is created by the state the scope of this interest, is circumscribed by Virginia's rules on exemptions from the classified employment scheme and from access to the grievance procedure and by Virginia's layoff-rights scheme. Mandel v. Allen, 889 F. Supp. 857 (E.D. Va. 1995), aff'd, 81 F.3d 478 (4th Cir. 1996).

No property interest when statute makes exercise of classification power non-grievable. — Where, as in the relevant Virginia statutes, the state statute vests the power to classify solely in management and then makes the exercise of that power non-grievable, there can be no property interest in the classification. Mandel v. Allen, 889 F. Supp. 857 (E.D. Va. 1995), aff'd, 81 F.3d 478 (4th Cir. 1996).

A nonprobationary employee does not serve at the will of the agency that employs him. Detweiler v. Virginia Dep't of Rehabilitative Servs., 705 F.2d 557 (4th Cir. 1983).

Nonprobationary employees of state have property interest in continued employment. — Former § 2.1-114.5:1's distinction between probationary employees and nonprobationary employees, its distinction between disciplinary discharges and discharges for reduction in work force, the specifications in the "Policy Standards of Conduct" for state employees concerning breaches of discipline for which an employee could be discharged, and the authority conferred on an impartial panel to reverse the agency's decision and to order reinstatement with back pay (pursuant to "The Rules for the Conduct of Panel Hearings"), established that a nonprobationary employee had a property interest in continued employment that was created by the State. Detweiler v. Virginia Dep't of Rehabilitative Servs., 705 F.2d 557 (4th Cir. 1983).

Probationary employee had no right to grievance procedures and no property interest in her job, and thus the protections of due process were not triggered by her firing. Assa'ad-Faltas v. Virginia, 738 F. Supp. 982 (E.D. Va. 1989), aff'd, 902 F.2d 1564 (4th Cir. 1990).

Former § 2.1-114.5:1 did not necessarily create a property interest in promotion, as promotions are not awarded as a matter of right or entitlement under Virginia law, but are based on merit and fitness. James v. Powell, 765 F. Supp. 314 (E.D. Va. 1991).

The protections in former § 2.1-114.5:1 were inapplicable to an at-will employee of the general district court who was not subject to the provisions of the Virginia Personnel Act. James v. Powell, 765 F. Supp. 314 (E.D. Va. 1991).

Virginia law required four basic elements in a post-termination grievance hearing. These requirements included: (1) Written notice of the termination with reasons therefor; (2) a hearing before an impartial three-member panel; (3) an opportunity to present, examine, and cross-examine witnesses; and (4) a panel discussion that adheres to "law and written policies." Leftwich v. Bevilacqua, 635 F. Supp. 238 (W.D. Va. 1986).

For discussion of the procedures required by the due process clause when an employee, who has established a property interest in continued employment, is discharged. Detweiler v. Virginia Dep't of Rehabilitative Servs., 705 F.2d 557 (4th Cir. 1983).

Retroactive application of 1985 amendment to former § 2.1-116. — A state official who simply enforces a presumptively valid state statute will rarely lose his immunity from suit. However, two defendants in instant case did not simply enforce a presumptively valid state statute. Rather, totally disregarding long-standing Virginia law prohibiting new legislation from being construed to eliminate pre-existing substantive rights, they attempted to apply the 1985 amendment to former § 2.1-116 retroactively to do precisely this. Moreover, they did this in the face of several holdings of this court that the act established a property interest in continued public employment, and a holding of the Virginia Supreme Court that the right to continued public employment is substantive and cannot be retroactively eliminated. Garraghty v. Virginia, Dep't of Cors., 52 F.3d 1274 (4th Cir. 1995).

Failure to apprise employee of rights. — Director of county board of public welfare (now local board of social services), charged with counseling employees on the rights and procedures available with regard to adverse personnel actions, was not denied due process where the board, after forcing her to resign, did not affirmatively apprise her of her grievance rights, due to director's actual knowledge of both their existence as well as the mechanics of the procedure, and the fact that she consulted with an attorney regarding this matter will within the time frame prescribed for filing a grievance. Crocker v. Fluvanna County Bd. of Pub. Welfare, 859 F.2d 14 (4th Cir. 1988).

Petition to implement panel action does not initiate or toll a grievance. — The filing of a petition in circuit court pursuant to subdivision F of former § 2.1-114.5:1, the purpose of which is to require a party to implement a grievance panel's decision, should not have been treated as the initiation of a grievance over a separate disciplinary action; the petition to implement a panel action did not serve to initiate a grievance or toll the limitation for doing so. Commonwealth, Dep't of Taxation v. Hogan, 11 Va. App. 306, 397 S.E.2d 902 (1990).

Where the trial court correctly determined that the employee's demotion upon reinstatement was an issue that had to be grieved separately and was not enforceable as part of the panel's reinstatement decision without exhausting the administrative grievance procedure, the trial court lacked authority to treat the petition filed pursuant to subdivision F of former § 2.1-114.5:1 as filing notice of a grievance with an agency. Commonwealth, Dep't of Taxation v. Hogan, 11 Va. App. 306, 397 S.E.2d 902 (1990).

Local committee at mental hospital not authorized to hear grievances. — The Local Human Rights Committee at the Western State Mental Hospital was created under proper Commonwealth regulations to investigate solely charges of patient abuse; it had no other authority. Any investigation of employee grievances is by state law differently provided for under a procedure laid out precisely under the law. For the Committee to have intruded into the area of employee grievances would have been an improper and illegal encroachment on the grievance procedure created by statute for investigating such complaints. Buschi v. Kirven, 775 F.2d 1240 (4th Cir. 1985).

Authority of grievance panel to promote should be left to General Assembly. — The determination whether a grievance panel has the authority to promote clearly is best left to the wisdom of the General Assembly and the state officials charged with the administration of the grievance procedure. Therefore, the board was without authority to award a policeman, denied promotion, a retroactive promotion and compensation for back pay. Jones v. Carter, 234 Va. 621, 363 S.E.2d 921 (1988).

Procedural due process where job abolition is cited as reason to terminate employee. — When the state chooses to terminate an employee for cause, it may not avoid the requirements of procedural due process by merely citing job abolition as a pretextual justification. It is the employee's burden, however, to present evidence that the job abolition was a pretext for action intended to target the individual rather than the abolished position. Only then can there be a claim for deprivation of procedural due process. Mandel v. Allen, 889 F. Supp. 857 (E.D. Va. 1995), aff'd, 81 F.3d 478 (4th Cir. 1996).

Plaintiff has burden to show state avoiding procedural due process. — To present sufficient evidence that the state in justifying elimination of positions is seeking to use administrative efficiency as a pretext for avoiding procedural due process is the plaintiff's burden. The burden is not onerous, nor does it necessarily require a "smoking gun" memorandum or the like. It may not be satisfied by conjecture or surmise. Mandel v. Allen, 889 F. Supp. 857 (E.D. Va. 1995), aff'd, 81 F.3d 478 (4th Cir. 1996).

Plaintiff has burden of showing that admission of evidence denied due process. — Even if evidence of prior similar acts by an employee was inadmissible in federal court, its admission in a grievance hearing does not violate due process unless notions of fundamental fairness were violated. Plaintiff has the burden of showing that the admission of the extraneous evidence denied him minimal due process. Leftwich v. Bevilacqua, 635 F. Supp. 238 (W.D. Va. 1986).

Preclusive effect of local administrative findings. — Findings of local administrative body are given preclusive effect in a federal Americans with Disabilities Act, 42 U.S.C. § 12101 et seq., suit, particularly where the body acted pursuant to a grievance procedure mandated by state law. Roberts v. County of Fairfax, 937 F. Supp. 541 (E.D. Va. 1996).

Grievance panel decision binding on sheriff. — Grievance panel decision against demoting police lieutenant for violation of

sheriff's orders was not recommendation but under former § 2.1-114.5:1 was binding, since if the sheriff was free to reject panel's decisions the grievance procedure mandated by the General Assembly would be rendered impotent. Angle v. Overton, 235 Va. 103, 365 S.E.2d 758 (1988).

Trial court decision final and nonappealable. — Decision of the trial court, which reversed city manager's decision that complaint was not "grievable," concluded that the complaint was grievable, and ordered a full hearing, was final and nonappealable. City of Danville v. Franklin, 234 Va. 275, 361 S.E.2d 634 (1987).

Jurisdiction on appeal. — The Court of Appeals does not have jurisdiction to review the judgment of a circuit court entered pursuant to subsection F of former § 2.1-114.5:1. Therefore, appeal should be transferred to the Supreme Court of Virginia. Virginia Dep't of Cors. v. Dillon, No. 1871-93-2 (Ct. of Appeals Nov. 15, 1994).

Where the grievance panel's decision was "final and binding", only its implementation could be granted or denied by the circuit court. Therefore, proceeding before the circuit court was not an appeal of the grievance panel's decision, thus, the Court of Appeals lacked jurisdiction and properly ordered the appeal transferred to the Supreme Court. Virginia Dep't of Taxation v. Daughtry, 19 Va. App. 135, 449 S.E.2d 57 (1994).

Agency decision not subject to review. — In a case involving Virginia's State Grievance Procedure, specifically §§ 2.2-3003, 2.2-3004, and 2.2-3006, the Department of Employment Dispute Resolution's decision was not subject to review by the circuit court because it involved an interpretation of agency procedures created pursuant to subdivision 2 of § 2.2-1001 rather than an issue of law; also, the delay by the Department of Human Resource Management (DHRM) in rendering its decision on the request for review did not nullify its ruling because subsection A of § 2.2-3006 contained no prohibitory or limiting language preventing the DHRM from ruling after the expiration of 60 days. Va. Dep't of Taxation v. Brailey, 2008 Va. App. LEXIS 19 (2008).

Dismissal of federal claim. — Due process claim which was in fact a mere pretext and simply a claim that the Virginia Employment Commission violated its own standards of conduct in handling plaintiff's grievance was a case of a Virginia resident suing Virginia employees, over an interpretation of Virginia law, and as such, would be dismissed from the district court for lack of jurisdiction. Davis v. Pak, 856 F.2d 648 (4th Cir. 1988).

City ordered to implement panel's decision. — Although a city employee does not have a vested right to remain in a personnel classification indefinitely, where the employee sought to be reinstated to his former position in accordance with the decision of the grievance panel, the court reversed the judgment of the trial court and remanded the case with directions that the trial court enter an order which required that the employee be reinstated to the position of golf course superintendent in accordance with the panel's decision. Zicca v. City of Hampton, 240 Va. 468, 397 S.E.2d 882 (1990).

Deputy sheriff served at the will of the sheriff under state law, and therefore had no property interest in his continued employment as deputy even though sheriff's department adopted regulations concerning dismissal and grievance procedures patterned on that outlined in former § 2.1-114.5:1. Jenkins v. Weatherholtz, 719 F. Supp. 468 (W.D. Va. 1989), aff'd, 909 F.2d 105 (4th Cir. 1990).

Adoption of handbook patterned after section did not compromise statutory authority. — Sheriff's adoption of employees handbook patterned after the procedures in this section could not compromise his statutory authority under former § 15.1-48 (see now § 15.2-1603) to remove deputies at his discretion. Jenkins v. Weatherholtz, 909 F.2d 105 (4th Cir. 1990).

District court erred to the extent that it held that defendants were not entitled to qualified immunity on plaintiff's claim that they had deprived him of a property right in the state grievance procedure without due process. Even if such a right is possible, there is nothing that suggests it is vested or substantive and so nothing to suggest that any property right to participation in the state grievance procedure survived the 1985 amendment to former § 2.1-116 (see now § 2.2-2905), let alone that this was clearly established. Garraghty v. Virginia, Dep't of Cors., 52 F.3d 1274 (4th Cir. 1995).

Threats to supervisor. — Where plaintiff made death threat to her supervisor, the department's transfer of plaintiff to another office and its requirement of a mental health evaluation before she resumed work were within management's prerogative under former section and consistent with its duty to provide a safe working environment for all employees. Virginia Dep't of Taxation v. Daughtry, 250 Va. 542, 463 S.E.2d 847 (1995).

Missing work and signing inaccurate reports. — The former section gave the department the right to transfer plaintiff to another job for which he was well-qualified at the same pay, where he had missed work although denied leave time and had signed grossly inaccurate sales reports for his department. Virginia Dep't of Taxation v. Daughtry, 250 Va. 542, 463 S.E.2d 847 (1995).

Applied in Doe v. Va. Bd. of Dentistry, 52 Va. App. 166, 662 S.E.2d 99, 2008 Va. App. LEXIS 411 (2008).

§ 2.2-3004. Grievances qualifying for a grievance hearing; grievance hearing generally.

A. A grievance qualifying for a hearing shall involve a complaint or dispute by an employee relating to the following adverse employment actions in which the employee is personally involved, including but not limited to (i) formal disciplinary actions, including suspensions, demotions, transfers and assignments, and dismissals resulting from formal discipline or unsatisfactory job performance; (ii) the application of all written personnel policies, procedures, rules and regulations where it can be shown that policy was misapplied or unfairly applied; (iii) discrimination on the basis of race, color, religion, political affiliation, age, disability, national origin or sex; (iv) arbitrary or capricious performance evaluations; (v) acts of retaliation as the result of the use of or participation in the grievance procedure or because the employee has complied with any law of the United States or of the Commonwealth, has reported any violation of such law to a governmental authority, has sought any change in law before the Congress of the United States or the General Assembly, or has reported an incidence of fraud, abuse, or gross mismanagement; and (vi) retaliation for exercising any right otherwise protected by law.

B. Management reserves the exclusive right to manage the affairs and operations of state government. Management shall exercise its powers with the highest degree of trust. In any employment matter that management precludes from proceeding to a grievance hearing, management's response, including any appropriate remedial actions, shall be prompt, complete, and fair.

C. Complaints relating solely to the following issues shall not proceed to a hearing: (i) establishment and revision of wages, salaries, position classifications, or general benefits; (ii) work activity accepted by the employee as a condition of employment or which may reasonably be expected to be a part of the job content; (iii) contents of ordinances, statutes or established personnel policies, procedures, and rules and regulations; (iv) methods, means, and personnel by which work activities are to be carried on; (v) termination, layoff, demotion, or suspension from duties because of lack of work, reduction in work force, or job abolition; (vi) hiring, promotion, transfer, assignment, and retention of employees within the agency; and (vii) relief of employees from duties of the agency in emergencies.

D. Except as provided in subsection A of § 2.2-3003, decisions regarding whether a grievance qualifies for a hearing shall be made in writing by the agency head or his designee within five workdays of the employee's request for a hearing. A copy of the decision shall be sent to the employee. The employee may appeal the denial of a hearing by the agency head to the Director of the Department of Human Resource Management (the Director). Upon receipt of an appeal, the agency shall transmit the entire grievance record to the Department of Human Resource Management within five workdays. The Director shall render a decision on whether the employee is entitled to a hearing upon the grievance record and other probative evidence.

E. The hearing pursuant to § 2.2-3005 shall be held in the locality in which the employee is employed or in any other locality agreed to by the employee, employer, and hearing officer. The employee and the agency may be represented by legal counsel or a lay advocate, the provisions of § 54.1-3904 notwithstanding. The employee and the agency may call witnesses to present testimony and be cross-examined.

History.
  1995, cc. 770, 818, § 2.1-116.06; 1996, cc. 164, 869; 2001, c. 844; 2012, cc. 56, 349, 803, 835.

The 2012 amendments.
  The 2012 amendments by cc. 56 and 349 are nearly identical, and added the exception at the beginning of subsection D, deleted former subsection E, redesignated former subsection F as E, and c. 56 made a minor stylistic change.
  The 2012 amendments by cc. 803 and 835, cl. 8, are identical, and in subsection D, twice substituted "Department of Human Resource Management" for "Department of Employment Dispute Resolution"; and made minor stylistic changes.

CASE NOTES

The judgment of the city court had no preclusive effect because, under Virginia law, subsequent actions are not barred by res judicata if the court in the first action did not have subject matter jurisdiction over the proceedings; the city court dismissed plaintiff's first action without reaching the merits because plaintiff had not exhausted his administrative remedies. Pignato v. Virginia Dep't of Envtl. Quality, 948 F. Supp. 532 (E.D. Va 1996) (decided under former Title 2.1).

Court deference to administrative decision. — Where an agency failed to show that a hearing officer's decision contradicted any law, the circuit court's ruling, unduly limiting the officer's authority and overturning the officer's decision, was reversed to reinstate the officer's decision. Tatum v. Va. Dep't of Agric. & Consumer Servs., 41 Va. App. 110, 582 S.E.2d 452, 2003 Va. App. LEXIS 356 (2003), reversing 59 Va. Cir. 262 (2002).

Letters not a "case decision." — Two letters, one written by an employee's attorney, and another written by the Department of Corrections, did not meet the definition of a "case decision," as defined in § 2.2-4001, as neither letter involved the application of law to the facts in an agency proceeding, the first amounted to merely a request for clarification of the Department's position concerning a grievance matter, and the Department's response to the same acknowledged that it had responded to the merits during the grievance process and that denial of a grievance hearing was affirmed; further, the letter written by the employee's attorney did not have the effect of filing a claim for retirement benefits. Garraghty v. Va. Ret. Sys., 45 Va. App. 1, 608 S.E.2d 477, 2005 Va. App. LEXIS 44 (2005).

Agency decision not subject to review. — In a case involving Virginia's State Grievance Procedure, specifically §§ 2.2-3003, 2.2-3004, and 2.2-3006, the Department of Employment Dispute Resolution's decision was not subject to review by the circuit court because it involved an interpretation of agency procedures created pursuant to subdivision 2 of § 2.2-1001 rather than an issue of law; also, the delay by the Department of Human Resource Management (DHRM) in rendering its decision on the request for review did not nullify its ruling because subsection A of § 2.2-3006 contained no prohibitory or limiting language preventing the DHRM from ruling after the expiration of 60 days. Va. Dep't of Taxation v. Brailey, 2008 Va. App. LEXIS 19 (2008).

Applied in Va. Dep't of State Police v. Barton, 39 Va. App. 439, 573 S.E.2d 319, 2002 Va. App. LEXIS 756 (2002); Ibrahim Martin-Bangura v. Commonwealth Dep't of Mental Health, 640 F. Supp. 2d 729, 2009 U.S. Dist. LEXIS 67800 (E.D. Va. 2009).

CIRCUIT COURT OPINIONS

Severity of discipline. — University was in its rights when it imposed a discipline upon a campus police officer following an auto accident that was more severe than the discipline it had imposed upon other police officers for similar conduct, but conduct that caused less damage; therefore, a hearing officer's decision in a grievance proceeding that the university could not impose a more severe discipline on the officer than what other officers had received for similar conduct was contradictory to law. Siewert v. Virginia Commonwealth Univ., 58 Va. Cir. 212, 2002 Va. Cir. LEXIS 143 (Richmond 2002).

Hearing officer misapplied subdivision C 6 of § 2.2-3005 in mitigating the termination of a grievant for patient abuse as mitigation was reserved by policy to a training center's management and subsection B of § 2.2-3004 reserved to the management of the center the right to manage the center's affairs and operations. Woodson v. Cent. Va. Training Ctr., 66 Va. Cir. 480, 2002 Va. Cir. LEXIS 457 (Amherst County 2002).

"Discipline" requiring a hearing. — State employment resolution department erred in determining that e-mail that an office director sent to petitioner, was not discipline that qualified for a hearing on petitioner's grievance regarding an altercation with a fellow employee over what material could be posted at work; the trial court determined that petitioner was entitled to a grievance hearing because the e-mail outlined a course of conduct that was to be followed and how future conduct regarding the issue would be handled, and, thus, qualified as a formal disciplinary action that entitled petitioner to a grievance hearing. Gillispie v. Va. Dep't of Envtl. Quality, 67 Va. Cir. 580, 2004 Va. Cir. LEXIS 356 (Richmond Dec. 16, 2004).

Failure to provide reasonable accommodation. — City's failure to provide a policeman with a "reasonable accommodation" given his medical condition was grievable under clause (ii) of subsection A of § 2.2-3004 where the duty to provide the policeman with sedentary employment in the light of his medical condition was a duty imposed on the city by its personnel rules and regulations. November v. City of Richmond, 66 Va. Cir. 326, 2005 Va. Cir. LEXIS 42 (Richmond Jan. 13, 2005).

Agency decision not subject to review. — Corrections employee was not entitled to a grievance hearing under subsection E of § 2.2-3004 because the record did not show that the employee's working conditions were intolerable; therefore, the employee voluntarily resigned from his position and no constructive discharge occurred. (Former subsection E repealed by 2011 amendments) Epperson v. Va. Dep't of Corr., 77 Va. Cir. 325, 2008 Va. Cir. LEXIS 257 (Sussex County 2008).

Employee not entitled to hearing. — Public employee was not entitled to a hearing on his employee grievance where memoranda cited behavior that supported a lower rating in the evaluation, a Lieutenant Colonel cited multiple infractions on the part of the employee, including errors in his case files and several days of not reporting to work, and there was credible evidence in the record to support Employment Dispute Resolution's decision that the employee's performance evaluation was based on his conduct. Kelly v. Dep't of State Police, 84 Va. Cir. 55, 2011 Va. Cir. LEXIS 188 (Fairfax County Dec. 12, 2011).

§ 2.2-3005. Hearing officers; duties.

A. Nothing in this chapter shall create, nor shall be construed to create, a property interest in selection or assignment to serve as a hearing officer for grievance hearings.

B. The Director of the Department of Human Resource Management shall assign a hearing officer to conduct the grievance hearing. All hearing officers shall be selected, on a rotating basis, (i) from the list of administrative hearing officers maintained by the Supreme Court of Virginia pursuant to § 2.2-4024 or (ii) from attorneys hired as classified employees by the Department through a competitive selection process. Hearing officer fees shall be reasonable, in accordance with compensation guidelines developed by the Department of Human Resource Management. In addition to the training requirements imposed by the Supreme Court, each hearing officer shall meet the criteria established by the Director pursuant to subdivision 6 of § 2.2-1202.1 and attend annually at least one day of training in employment law or state personnel policies and organizations. The training shall be conducted by the Department of Human Resource Management or an organization approved by the Virginia State Bar for continuing legal education.

C. Hearing officers shall have the following powers and duties:

1. Hold conferences for the settlement or simplification of issues;

2. Dispose of procedural requests;

3. Issue orders requiring testimony or the production of evidence;

4. Administer oaths and affirmations;

5. Receive probative evidence; exclude irrelevant, immaterial, insubstantial, privileged, or repetitive proofs, rebuttals, or cross-examinations; rule upon offers of proof; and oversee a verbatim recording of the evidence;

6. Receive and consider evidence in mitigation or aggravation of any offense charged by an agency in accordance with rules established by the Department of Human Resource Management pursuant to § 2.2-1202.1; and

7. Take other actions as necessary or specified in the grievance procedure.

History.
1995, cc. 770, 818, § 2.1-116.07; 1998, cc. 263, 438; 1999, c. 713; 2000, cc. 66, 657, 947, 1006; 2001, c. 844; 2004, c. 674; 2012, cc. 803, 835.

Cross references.
As to the jurisdiction of the Court of Appeals to hear appeals from any final decision of a circuit court on appeal from a grievance hearing decision issued pursuant to this section, see § 17.1-405.

The 2012 amendments.
The 2012 amendments by cc. 803 and 835, cl. 8, are identical, and throughout subsection B and in subdivision C 6, substituted "Department of Human Resource Management" for "Department of Employment Dispute Resolution"; and in the next-to-last sentence of subsection B and in subdivision C 6, updated the section reference.

Research references.
Friend's Virginia Pleading and Practice (Matthew Bender). Chapter 38 Appeals to the Court of Appeals of Virginia. § 38.04 Jurisdiction; Chapter 39A Interlocutory Appeals. § 39A.01 Interlocutory Appeal Statute. Charles E. Friend.

Michie's Jurisprudence.
For related discussion, see 15 M.J. Public Officers, § 46.

CASE NOTES

Locality procedure decisions. — Decision rendered under a locality procedure is not a decision issued pursuant to § 2.2-3005 or a final grievance hearing decision issued pursuant to subsection B of § 2.2-3007; thus, a city manager's decision refusing to abide by a personnel board decision that a police officer should be reinstated to his job could not be considered by a Virginia appellate court. Styles v. City of Colonial Heights, 43 Va. App. 588, 600 S.E.2d 174, 2004 Va. App. LEXIS 378 (2004).

Reversal of hearing officer's decision in error. — Upon judicial review of a hearing officer's decision to amend a disciplinary notice against two penitentiary employees, the trial court erred by concluding that the hearing officer had no authority to amend the disciplinary notice and, therefore, dismissed the Group II disciplinary notice. Because the hearing officer's amendment of the disciplinary notice did not violate any statute, judicial precedent, or accepted legal principal, it was proper and should have been upheld. Commonwealth v. Doyle, 2005 Va. App. LEXIS 255 (July 5, 2005).

Under the State Grievance Procedure, an appeal from a hearing officer's interpretation of policy went to the director of the Department of Human Resource Management, not the circuit court. The hearing officer's decision contained the findings of fact as to the material issues in the case, as required by subsection C of § 2.2-3005.1 and the circuit court was only to review the administrative record. Commonwealth v. Needham, 55 Va. App. 316, 685 S.E.2d 857, 2009 Va. App. LEXIS 538 (2009).

Hearing officer did not exceed his authority. — Hearing officer acted within the scope of the authority conferred when he held that a corrections officer's conduct, though apparently insufficient to sustain a conviction for assault, was enough to mandate termination for cause. Va. Dep't of Corr. v. Compton, 47 Va. App. 202, 623 S.E.2d 397, 2005 Va. App. LEXIS 517 (2005).

Jurisdiction of court of appeals. — When a party petitioned the circuit court pursuant to subsection D of § 2.2-3006, it did not seek a review of the hearing officer's decision on the merits, nor did it seek a modification of the hearing officer's decision; rather, those implementation proceedings recognized that the hearing officer's decision was final and binding, and the circuit court proceeding was analogous to a proceeding to domesticate and enforce a foreign judgment. The court found the analytical framework holding that enforcement proceedings were not appeals to trial courts over which the court of appeals had appellate jurisdiction convincing; accordingly the petition to the circuit court under subsection D of § 2.2-3006 was not an appeal of the grievance panel decision, and because the court of appeals lacked jurisdiction, the court of appeals ordered the appeal transferred to the Supreme Court of Virginia pursuant to § 8.01-677.1. Va. Dep't of Corr. v. Estep, 55 Va. App. 386, 685 S.E.2d 891, 2009 Va. App. LEXIS 549 (2009).

CIRCUIT COURT OPINIONS

Hearing officer exceeded his authority. — Hearing officer misapplied subdivision C 6 in mitigating the termination of a grievant for patient abuse as mitigation was reserved by policy to a training center's management and subsection B of § 2.2-3004 reserved to the management of the center the right to manage the center's affairs and operations. Woodson v. Cent. Va. Training Ctr., 66 Va. Cir. 480, 2002 Va. Cir. LEXIS 457 (Amherst County 2002).

§ 2.2-3005.1. Scope of hearing officer's decision; agency cooperation; cost of hearing; decision of hearing officer.

A. For those issues qualified for a hearing, the hearing officer may order appropriate remedies. Relief may include (i) reinstatement to the same position, or if the position is filled, to an equivalent position, (ii) back pay, (iii) full reinstatement of fringe benefits and seniority rights, (iv) mitigation or reduction of the agency disciplinary action, or (v) any combination of these remedies. In grievances challenging discharge, if the hearing officer finds that the employee has substantially prevailed on the merits of the grievance, the employee shall be entitled to recover reasonable attorney fees, unless special circumstances would make an award unjust. All awards of relief, including attorney fees, by a hearing officer must be in accordance with rules established by the Department of Human Resource Management.

B. The agency from which the grievance arises shall bear the costs for the hearing officer and other associated hearing expenses including the grievant's attorney fees that the hearing officer may award.

C. The decision of the hearing officer shall (i) be in writing, (ii) contain findings of fact as to the material issues in the case and the basis for those findings, including any award of reasonable attorney fees pursuant to this section, and (iii) be final and binding if consistent with law and policy.

D. The provisions of this section relating to the award of attorney fees shall not apply to any local government or agency thereof that is otherwise subject to the grievance procedure set forth in this chapter.

History.
2004, c. 674; 2011, c. 595; 2012, cc. 803, 835.

The 2011 amendments.
The 2011 amendment by c. 595 substituted "attorney fees" for "attorneys' fees" throughout the section; and in the second sentence in subsection A, inserted "to the same position, or if the position is filled, to an equivalent position" in clause (i).

The 2012 amendments.
The 2012 amendments by cc. 803 and 835, cl. 8, are identical, and substituted "Department of Human Resource Management" for "Department of Employment Dispute Resolution" in the last sentence of subsection A.

Research references.
Bryson on Virginia Civil Procedure (Matthew Bender). Chapter 14 Costs. § 14.01 Items included. W. Hamilton Bryson.

CASE NOTES

Appellant required to specify what law the decision contradicted. — State employee's appeal from a hearing officer's decision was properly dismissed because the employee failed to state how that decision was contradictory to law and what law was contradicted, as required by subsection C of § 2.2-3005.1. Issues relating to evidence, witness credibility, and findings of fact were beyond the scope of review of the trial court pursuant to subsection B of § 2.2-3006. Kone v. Va. Dep't of State Police, 2009 Va. App. LEXIS 517 (Nov. 24, 2009).

Application of issue preclusion to hearing officer's findings of fact. — Issue preclusion applied to a former hospital employee's action that alleged retaliation in violation of the Rehabilitation Act, 29 U.S.C.S. § 794(a), and the First Amendment because the employee had previously litigated all of the issues presented in the instant case surrounding his termination in an impartial forum, the Virginia Department of Employment Dispute Resolution. There was no basis to find that the decisions of the hearing officer on the factual issues surrounding the discharge were contradictory to law or policy; thus, the hearing officer's findings that the employee was terminated for failing to follow a supervisor's instructions and failing to comply with written policy, not because of retaliation, were final and binding under Virginia law. Horner v. Va. Dep't of Mental Health, 2004 U.S. Dist. LEXIS 29022 (W.D. Va. Apr. 26, 2004).

Circuit court's authority limited to implementing decision. — Under this section, the circuit court's authority with respect to a petition for enforcement of a hearing officer's decision is limited to the act of implementing or refusing to implement the hearing officer's ruling; the court lacks the authority to consider the grievance de novo, to modify the hearing officer's decision, to substitute the court's view of the facts for those of the hearing officer or to invoke its broad equitable powers to arrive at a decision that the court may think is fair. Commonwealth, Dep't of Envtl. Quality v. Wright, 256 Va. 236, 504 S.E.2d 862 (1998) (decided under former Title 2.1).

Where an agency failed to show that a hearing officer's decision contradicted any law, the circuit court's ruling, unduly limiting the officer's authority and overturning the officer's decision, was reversed to reinstate the officer's decision. Tatum v. Va. Dep't of Agric. & Consumer Servs., 41 Va. App. 110, 582 S.E.2d 452, 2003 Va. App. LEXIS 356 (2003), reversing 59 Va. Cir. 262 (2002).

Reversal of hearing officer's decision in error. — Upon judicial review of a hearing officer's decision to amend a disciplinary notice against two penitentiary employees, the trial court erred by concluding that the hearing officer had no authority to amend the disciplinary notice and, therefore, dismissed the Group II disciplinary notice. Because the hearing officer's amendment of the disciplinary notice did not violate any statute, judicial precedent, or accepted legal principal, it was proper and should have been upheld. Commonwealth v. Doyle, 2005 Va. App. LEXIS 255 (July 5, 2005).

Applied in Va. Dep't of Corr. v. Compton, 47 Va. App. 202, 623 S.E.2d 397, 2005 Va. App. LEXIS 517 (2005).

CIRCUIT COURT OPINIONS

Circuit court's authority limited to implementing decision. — Where an amendment to former § 2.1-116.07(1) (now § 2.2-3005) was substantive because it afforded a right of review that previously did not exist, the court lacked authority to implement a hearing officer's determination because it was not a "decision" subject to implementation under § 2.1-116.07(D); therefore, the matter had to be dismissed. Bala v. Dep't of Conservation & Rec., 57 Va. Cir. 132, 2001 Va. Cir. LEXIS 519 (Richmond 2001) (decided under former Title 2.1).

Attorney's fees. — University police officer who was terminated from an employment position and who was reinstated by a hearing officer was properly awarded substantial attorney's fees pursuant to § 2.2-3005.1, as the employee substantially prevailed on the merits of his grievance; arguments by the university regarding lack of timeliness were disregarded pursuant to authority under subdivision 5 of § 2.2-1001. Old Dominion Univ. v. Birkmeyer, 73 Va. Cir. 341, 2007 Va. Cir. LEXIS 131 (Norfolk 2007).

§ 2.2-3006. Review of hearing decisions; costs.

A. Upon the request of a party to a grievance hearing for an administrative review of the hearing decision, the Director of the Department of Human Resource Management shall determine, within 30 days of the conclusion of any other administrative reviews, whether the hearing decision is consistent with policy.

B. Within 30 days of a final decision, a party may appeal on the grounds that the determination is contradictory to law by filing a notice of appeal with the clerk of the circuit court in the jurisdiction in which the grievance arose. The agency shall request and receive prior approval of the Director before filing a notice of appeal. After a notice of appeal has been filed by either party, the agency shall then transmit a copy of the grievance record to the clerk of the court. The court, on motion of a party, shall issue a writ of certiorari requiring transmission of the record on or before a certain date. Within 30 days of receipt of the grievance record, the court, sitting without a jury, shall hear the appeal on the record. The court may affirm the decision or may reverse or modify the decision. The decision of the court shall be rendered no later than the fifteenth day from the date of the conclusion of the hearing. The circuit court hearing shall be at no cost to the Commonwealth or the grievant.

C. The hearing officer's final decision shall be effective from the latter of the date issued or the date of the conclusion of any administrative review and judicial appeal, and shall be implemented immediately thereafter, unless circumstances beyond the control of the agency delay such implementation.

D. Either party may petition the circuit court having jurisdiction in the locality in which the grievance arose for an order requiring implementation of the final decision of a hearing officer.

E. The court shall award reasonable attorneys' fees and costs to the employee if the employee substantially prevails on the merits of a case brought under subsection B or D.

History.
2000, cc. 947, 1006, § 2.1-116.07:1; 2001, cc. 393, 420, 844; 2003, c. 252; 2004, c. 229; 2012, cc. 56, 349.

Editor's note.
Acts 2001, cc. 393 and 420 amended § 2.1-116.07:1, from which this section is derived. Pursuant to § 30-152, Acts 2001, cc. 393 and 420 have been given effect in this section as set out above. The 2001 amendments by cc. 393 and 420 are identical, and deleted the former second sentence of subsection A, which read: "In grievances arising out of the Department of Mental Health, Mental Retardation and Substance Abuse Services that challenge allegations of patient abuse, the Director of the Department of Employment Dispute Resolution shall determine within sixty days of the decision whether the decision is consistent with law."

The 2012 amendments.
The 2012 amendments by cc. 56 and 349 are identical, and substituted "within 30 days of the conclusion of any other administrative reviews, whether" for "within 60 days of receipt of such request, whether" in subsection A, and deleted "or recommendation" following "final decision" in subsection D.

Law Review.
For annual survey article, "Labor and Employment Law," see 44 U. Rich. L. Rev. 513 (2009).

Research references.
Bryson on Virginia Civil Procedure (Matthew Bender). Chapter 14 Costs. § 14.01 Items included. W. Hamilton Bryson.

Michie's Jurisprudence.
For related discussion, see 15 M.J. Public Officers, § 46.

CASE NOTES

The decision must be contradictory to law. — State trooper failed to identify a specific statute, constitutional provision, regulation, or judicial decision that was violated by a hearing officer's suspension of the trooper for three days, and under § 2.2-3006 the trial court had no jurisdiction over the trooper's appeal of the hearing officer's decision. Va. Dep't of State Police v. Barton, 39 Va. App. 439, 573 S.E.2d 319, 2002 Va. App. LEXIS 756 (2002).

Where an agency failed to show that a hearing officer's decision contradicted any law, the circuit court's ruling, unduly limiting the officer's authority and overturning the officer's decision, was reversed to reinstate the officer's decision. Tatum v. Va. Dep't of Agric. & Consumer Servs., 41 Va. App. 110, 582 S.E.2d 452, 2003 Va. App. LEXIS 356 (2003), reversing 59 Va. Cir. 262 (2002).

When an employee contesting the employee's termination asserted that the Department of Behavioral Health and Developmental Services did not follow procedures in the applicable grievance procedures manual, such alleged failure did not require reversal of the department's decision because: (1) under subsection A of § 2.2-3001, the Director of the Department of Employment Dispute Resolution policed compliance with grievance procedures; and (2) courts ensured an administrative decision was not "contradictory to law," under subsection B of § 2.2-3006, but the grievance procedures manual was not law. Burke v. Catawba Hosp., 59 Va. App. 828, 722 S.E.2d 684, 2012 Va. App. LEXIS 76 (2012).

Findings of fact and evidence issues not subject to review. — State employee's appeal from a hearing officer's decision was properly dismissed because the employee failed to state how that decision was contradictory to law and what law was contradicted, as required by subsection C of § 2.2-3005.1. Issues relating to evidence, witness credibility, and findings of fact were beyond the scope of review of the trial court pursuant to subsection B of § 2.2-3006. Kone v. Va. Dep't of State Police, 2009 Va. App. LEXIS 517 (Nov. 24, 2009).

Several of a former employee's questions presented were not subject to judicial review in her appeal of a judgment affirming a hearing officer's finding that the Virginia Department of Veterans Services did not discriminate against her because the questions involved either factual determinations made by the hearing officer or policy determinations made by the the Director of the Department of Human Resource Management; Veterans Services' retaliatory motives in deciding to eliminate the employee's position and lay her off and the discriminatory nature of the layoff were factual questions, and whether Veterans Services misapplied the layoff policy involved a determination of whether the hearing officer's decision was consistent with policy and was not subject to judicial review. Earman v. Va. Dep't of Veterans Servs., 2010 Va. App. LEXIS 424 (Nov. 2, 2010).

Remand to the agency when the record is insufficient. — Circuit court's order remanding an employment matter to a hearing officer for a new hearing because a tape of the grievance proceedings had been lost, precluding its review of the hearing officer's decision, and was not a final order as required for jurisdiction pursuant to § 17.1-405; therefore, the court did not have jurisdiction of the employer's appeal. Va. Dep't of Corr. v. Hodges, 2011 Va. App. LEXIS 148 (May 3, 2011).

Interpretation of agency procedures not subject to review. — In a case involving Virginia's State Grievance Procedure, specifically §§ 2.2-3003, 2.2-3004, and 2.2-3006, the Department of Employment Dispute Resolution's decision was not subject to review by the circuit court because it involved an interpretation of agency procedures created pursuant to subdivision 2 of § 2.2-1001 rather than an issue of law; also, the delay by the Department of Human Resource Management (DHRM) in rendering its decision on the request for review did not nullify its ruling because subsection A of § 2.2-3006 contained no prohibitory or limiting language preventing the DHRM from ruling after the expiration of 60 days. Va. Dep't of Taxation v. Brailey, 2008 Va. App. LEXIS 19 (2008).

When an employee contesting a state agency's termination of the employee challenged the agency's interpretation of the agency's policy to be applicable to the employee, a trial court properly held the court had no jurisdiction to consider the employee's appeal of an administrative decision upholding the termination because (1) the issue presented involved an interpretation of agency policy; and (2) under subsection A of § 2.2-3006, such questions were properly presented to the director of the Department of Human Resource Management, rather than a court. Burke v. Catawba Hosp., 59 Va. App. 828, 722 S.E.2d 684, 2012 Va. App. LEXIS 76 (2012).

University employee afforded due process prior to termination. — University employee was afforded due process rights prior to her termination where: (1) she received notice of the reasons for the termination in two letters and a Group III Written Notice; (2) she was provided an opportunity to respond to the charges and did so in conjunction with the investigation conducted by the university's human resources department; and (3) she was afforded further opportunity to respond to the allegations through the grievance process of which she availed herself. Porter v. Dep't of Human Res. Mgmt., No. 3093-03-1, 2004 Va. App. LEXIS 225 (Ct. of Appeals May 18, 2004).

Probation officer afforded due process prior to termination. — Circuit court did not err in affirming a hearing officer's decision that despite the employer's failure to strictly comply with its own termination policy, that noncompliance was harmless error, as only the circuit court was authorized to rescind the employee's appointment as a probation officer serving that court; further, the action of the court could not have been challenged to the employer, even if the employee had been provided an opportunity to respond to the charges before her termination, as the employer could neither authorize nor rescind authorization for the employee to serve as a court-appointed probation officer under § 53.1-143. Barker v. Va. Dep't of Corr., No. 1003-05-02, 2005 Va. App. LEXIS 327 (Aug. 30, 2005).

Reversal of hearing officer's decision in error. — Upon judicial review of a hearing officer's decision to amend a disciplinary notice against two penitentiary employees, the trial court erred by concluding that the hearing officer had no authority to amend the disciplinary notice and, therefore, dismissed the Group II disciplinary notice. Because the hearing officer's amendment of the disciplinary notice did not violate any statute, judicial precedent, or accepted legal principal, it was proper and should have been upheld. Commonwealth v. Doyle, 2005 Va. App. LEXIS 255 (July 5, 2005).

Circuit court erred in reversing a hearing officer's decision sustaining disciplinary action against a state trooper for failing to follow a supervisor's instructions because the circuit court, in contravention of its standard of review under § 2.2-3006, improperly disregarded the hearing officer's factual finding that the trooper understood the supervisor's instructions. Va. Dep't of State Police v. Thompson, 2007 Va. App. LEXIS 476 (Dec. 27, 2007).

Court of appeals erred in affirming a circuit court's judgment reversing a hearing officer's decision to uphold a state employee's termination from his employment at a university because pursuant to subsection B of § 2.2-3006, the court of appeals and the circuit court lacked any basis for reviewing the officer's decision when the employee failed to identify any applicable law that the decision contradicted; because the officer specifically concluded that the employee had not engaged in "sexual harassment," there was no issue of "sexual harassment" before the circuit court, and the court of appeals erred in considering as persuasive authority federal court decisions interpreting "sexual harassment" under Title VII of the Civil Rights Act of 1964, 42 U.S.C.S. § 2000e et seq. when the employee's grievance did not involve a claim under Title VII but was an administrative proceeding conducted under the state grievance procedures provided in §§ 2.2-3000 through 2.2-3008. Va. Polytechnic Inst. v. Quesenberry, 277 Va. 420, 674 S.E.2d 854, 2009 Va. LEXIS 48 (2009).

Although a state employee threatened a co-worker outside the workplace, because the employee's behavior was an extension of a job-related incident where the employee cursed a crew leader, the circuit court exceeded its authority in subsection B of § 2.2-3006 by overruling a hearing officer's decision approving the employee's termination. Va. DOT v. Stevens, 53 Va. App. 654, 674 S.E.2d 563, 2009 Va. App. LEXIS 149 (2009).

Under the State Grievance Procedure, an appeal from a hearing officer's interpretation of policy went to the director of the Department of Human Resource Management, not the circuit court. The hearing officer's decision contained the findings of fact as to the material issues in the case as required by subsection C of § 2.2-3005.1 and the circuit court was only to review the administrative record. Commonwealth v. Needham, 55 Va. App. 316, 685 S.E.2d 857, 2009 Va. App. LEXIS 538 (2009).

Jurisdiction of court of appeals. — When a party petitioned the circuit court pursuant to subsection D of § 2.2-3006, it did not seek a review of the hearing officer's decision on the merits, nor did it seek a modification of the hearing officer's decision; rather, those implementation proceedings recognized that the hearing officer's decision was final and binding, and the circuit court proceeding was analogous to a proceeding to domesticate and enforce a foreign judgment. The court found the analytical framework holding that enforcement proceedings were not appeals to trial courts over which the court of appeals had appellate jurisdiction convincing; accordingly the petition to the circuit court under subsection D of § 2.2-3006 was not an appeal of the grievance panel decision, and because the court of appeals lacked jurisdiction, the court of appeals ordered the appeal transferred to the Supreme Court of Virginia pursuant to § 8.01-677.1. Va. Dep't of Corr. v. Estep, 55 Va. App. 386, 685 S.E.2d 891, 2009 Va. App. LEXIS 549 (2009).

Jurisdictional issue waived. — State employer waived the issue of whether the trial court had jurisdiction to hear the employee's grievance appeal from the hearing officer's denial of relief to the employee, based on the state employer's claim that the grievance appeal was not timely filed, as the state employer did not properly assign that alleged cross-error for review by the state supreme court. Horner v. Dep't of Mental Health, Mental Retardation, & Substance Abuse Servs., 268 Va. 187, 597 S.E.2d 202, 2004 Va. LEXIS 83 (2004).

Trial court did not err in affirming a hearing officer's finding that the Virginia Department of Veterans Services did not discriminate against a former employee because although the employee argued that the failure of the Department of Human Resource Management to issue a decision on Veterans Services' request for administrative review within the 60-day time limit required under subsection A of § 2.2-3006 constituted a procedural default on the part of Veterans Services, the employee offered no evidence that she was prejudiced as a result of the delay; rather, the employee made the conclusory argument that because the delayed decision favored Veterans Services, she was prejudiced by the delay, but there was no evidence that the employee would have prevailed but for the delay. Earman v. Va. Dep't of Veterans Servs., 2010 Va. App. LEXIS 424 (Nov. 2, 2010).

Delay in issuing decision. — Because subsection A of § 2.2-3006 contains no prohibitory or limiting language that prevents the Director of the Department of Human Resource Management from ruling after the expiration of 60 days, a delay would not constitute a procedural default on the part of Virginia Department of Veterans Services. Earman v. Va. Dep't of Veterans Servs., 2010 Va. App. LEXIS 424 (Nov. 2, 2010).

Procedures for making transcript part of record. — By sending the circuit court cassette tapes of an administrative hearing and a transcript of those tapes, both of which were part of the grievance record, the Virginia Department of Corrections (VDOC) complied with this section and, therefore, properly made the transcript part of the circuit court record. Once the transcript was part of the record, VDOC did not need to take any further steps to "file" the transcript for purposes of its appeal of the circuit court's decision. Va. Dep't of Corr. v. Compton, 47 Va. App. 202, 623 S.E.2d 397, 2005 Va. App. LEXIS 517 (2005).

Waiver of issue on appeal. — Virginia Department of Corrections failed to raise a question regarding whether no part of a hearing officer's decision was contradictory to law, by appealing the hearing officer's decision to a circuit court to challenge its legal correctness pursuant to subsection B of § 2.2-3006. Accordingly, the reviewing court deemed that argument waived and did not consider it. Va. Dep't of Corr. v. Estep, 281 Va. 660, 710 S.E.2d 95, 2011 Va. LEXIS 82 (2011).

Evidence supported trial court's findings. — Implementation of a hearing officer's order required restoration of a grievant, who was involuntarily demoted from the grievant's position with the Virginia Department of Corrections, to the grievant's original position with the Department of Corrections because the evidence supported the finding that the substitute position that the department provided to the grievant after the hearing officer's order was not a comparable substitute position. Va. Dep't of Corr. v. Estep, 281 Va. 660, 710 S.E.2d 95, 2011 Va. LEXIS 82 (2011).

Applied in Pound v. Dep't of Game & Inland Fisheries, 40 Va. App. 59, 577 S.E.2d 533, 2003 Va. App. LEXIS 119 (2003).

CIRCUIT COURT OPINIONS

Severity of discipline. — University was in its rights when it imposed a discipline upon a campus police officer following an auto accident that was more severe than the discipline it had imposed upon other police officers for similar conduct, but conduct that caused less damage; therefore, a hearing officer's decision in a grievance proceeding that the university could not impose a more severe discipline on the officer than what other officers had received for similar conduct was contradictory to law. Siewert v. Virginia Commonwealth Univ., 58 Va. Cir. 212, 2002 Va. Cir. LEXIS 143 (Richmond 2002).

The decision must be contradictory to law. — Hearing officer's decision that affirmed the state employer's decision to issue two separate "Group II" written violations and subsequently terminate the state employee based on those violations was affirmed as the only ground of appeal of the hearing officer's decision was that the decision was contradictory to law; since that ground was not apparent in the state employee's case, the hearing officer's decision was affirmed. Green v. Mary Washington College, 63 Va. Cir. 47, 2003 Va. Cir. LEXIS 196 (Fredericksburg 2003).

Because an employee failed to show that a decision by the Department of Employment Dispute Resolution terminating his employment, and the hearing officer's final decision upholding the same, were contradictory to law, the circuit court lacked jurisdiction to review the hearing officer's final decision. Thus, an appeal therefrom was dismissed. Shulz v. Univ. of Va., 73 Va. Cir. 482, 2007 Va. Cir. LEXIS 234 (Charlottesville Aug. 2, 2007).

Termination contradictory to law. — Virginia Department of Corrections erred in upholding an employee's termination for a positive marijuana result to a non-random oral swab drug test because the test was administered in violation of the Fourth Amendment since the time between the employee's initial test and the Department's "follow up" test was impermissibly long; because the second test was not random and was not administered pursuant to any individualized suspicion, but ordered arbitrarily to clear the agency for purposes of an audit, it failed any logical Fourth Amendment inquiry, and thus, the final agency decision to terminate the employee was contradictory to law pursuant to subsection B of § 2.2-3006 since it failed to account for the Fourth Amendment violation. Workman v. Va. Dep't of Corr., 82 Va. Cir. 160, 2011 Va. Cir. LEXIS 130 (Chesapeake Feb. 1, 2011).

Termination not contradictory to law. — Agency's termination of an employee was not contradictory to law, because the termination was supported by sufficient evidence showing, inter alia, that the employee was terminated for improper use of agency resources and equipment and causing agency expenses for things other than agency business. Jacobs v. Va. Empl. Comm'n, 69 Va. Cir. 66, 2005 Va. Cir. LEXIS 343 (Richmond 2005).

Scope of review. — Court had no authority to review decisions of a hearing officer that involved the sufficiency of the evidence pursuant to subsection B of § 2.2-3006, based on the plain wording therein and the explicit references to evidentiary support contained in §§ 8.01-680, 2.2-4027, and 60.2-625, with respect to the hearing officer's reversal of a university's termination of a university police officer and the hearing officer's award of attorney's fees to the officer. Old Dominion Univ. v. Birkmeyer, 73 Va. Cir. 341, 2007 Va. Cir. LEXIS 131 (Norfolk 2007).

Contents of notice of appeal. — University's appeal of a final decision of a hearing officer, which reversed its termination of a university police officer and awarded the officer substantial attorney's fees, was not subject to the officer's motion to dismiss, as the court's jurisdiction was granted by subsection B of § 2.2-3006 and accordingly, was not determined by a grievance procedure rule that required that a copy of the notice of appeal be served on the Employment Dispute Resolution Director at the university; there were no requirements imposed on the content of the notice of appeal. Old Dominion Univ. v. Birkmeyer, 73 Va. Cir. 341, 2007 Va. Cir. LEXIS 131 (Norfolk 2007).

§ 2.2-3007. Certain employees of the Departments of Corrections and Juvenile Justice.

A. Employees of the Departments of Corrections and Juvenile Justice who work in institutions or juvenile correctional centers or have client, inmate, or resident contact and who are terminated on the grounds of client, inmate, or resident abuse, criminal conviction, or as a result of being placed on probation under the provisions of § 18.2-251, may appeal their termination only through the grievance resolution steps.

B. If no resolution is reached by the conclusion of the last grievance step, the employee may advance the grievance to the circuit court of the jurisdiction in which the grievance occurred for a de novo hearing on the merits. In its discretion, the court may refer the matter to a commissioner in chancery to take such evidence as may be proper and to make a report to the court. Both the grievant and the respondent may call upon witnesses and be represented by legal counsel or other representatives before the court or the commissioner in chancery. Such representatives may examine, cross-examine, question and present evidence on behalf of the grievant or respondent before the court or commissioner in chancery without being in violation of the provisions of § 54.1-3904.

C. A termination shall be upheld unless shown to have been unwarranted by the facts or contrary to law or policy.

History.
1995, cc. 770, 818, § 2.1-116.08; 1996, cc. 755, 914; 2001, cc. 393, 420, 844.

Editor's note.
Acts 2001, cc. 393 and 420 amended § 2.1-116.08, from which this section is derived. Pursuant to § 30-152, Acts 2001, cc. 393 and 420 have been given effect in this section as set out above.

CASE NOTES

Locality procedure decisions. — Decision rendered under a locality procedure is not a decision issued pursuant to § 2.2-3005 or a final grievance hearing decision issued pursuant to subsection B of § 2.2-3007; thus, a city manager's decision refusing to abide by a personnel board decision that a police officer should be reinstated to his job could not be considered by a Virginia appellate court. Styles v. City of Colonial Heights, 43 Va. App. 588, 600 S.E.2d 174, 2004 Va. App. LEXIS 378 (2004).

§ 2.2-3008. Employees of local constitutional officers.

Constitutional officers shall not be required to provide a grievance procedure for their employees; however, such employees may be accepted in a local governing body's grievance procedure or personnel system if agreed to by the constitutional officer and the local governing body.

History.
1995, cc. 770, 818, § 2.1-116.012; 1996, cc. 164, 869; 2001, c. 844.

CHAPTER 30.1.

THE FRAUD AND ABUSE WHISTLE BLOWER PROTECTION ACT.

§ 2.2-3009. Policy.

It shall be the policy of the Commonwealth that employees of state government be freely able to report instances of wrongdoing or abuse committed by their employing agency, other state agencies, or independent contractors of state agencies.

History.
2009, c. 340.

Law Review.
For annual survey article, "Health Care Law," see 44 U. Rich. L. Rev. 473 (2009).

§ 2.2-3010. Definitions.

As used in this chapter:

"*Abuse*" means an employer's or employee's conduct or omissions that result in substantial misuse, destruction, waste, or loss of funds or resources belonging to or derived from federal, state, or local government sources.

"*Appropriate authority*" means a federal or state agency or organization having jurisdiction over criminal law enforcement, regulatory violations, professional conduct or ethics, or abuse; or a member, officer, agent, representative, or supervisory employee of the agency or organization. The term also includes the Office of the Attorney General, the Office of the State Inspector General, and the General Assembly and its committees having the power and duty to investigate criminal law enforcement, regulatory violations, professional conduct or ethics, or abuse.

"*Employee*" means any person who is regularly employed full time on either a salaried or wage basis, whose tenure is not restricted as to temporary or provisional appointment, in the service of and whose compensation is payable, no more often than biweekly, in whole or in part, by a state agency.

"*Employer*" means a person supervising one or more employees, including the employee filing a good faith report, a superior of that supervisor, or an agent of the state agency.

"*Good faith report*" means a report of conduct defined in this chapter as wrongdoing or abuse which is made without malice and which the person making the report has reasonable cause to believe is true.

"*Misconduct*" means conduct or behavior by an employee that is inconsistent with state or agency standards for which specific corrective or disciplinary action is warranted.

"*State agency*" means any agency, institution, board, bureau, commission, council, or instrumentality of state government in the executive branch listed in the appropriation act.

"Whistle blower" means an employee who witnesses or has evidence of wrongdoing or abuse and who makes or demonstrates by clear and convincing evidence that he is about to make a good faith report of, or testifies or is about to testify to, the wrongdoing or abuse to one of the employee's superiors, an agent of the employer, or an appropriate authority.

"Wrongdoing" means a violation, which is not of a merely technical or minimal nature, of a federal or state law or regulation or a formally adopted code of conduct or ethics of a professional organization designed to protect the interests of the public or employee.

History.
2009, c. 340; 2011, cc. 798, 871.

Editor's note.
Acts 2011, cc. 798 and 871, cl. 7 provides: "That the provisions of this act shall become effective on July 1, 2012, except that the provisions of the fifth enactment of this act shall become effective on July 1, 2011."

The 2011 amendments.
The 2011 amendments by cc. 798 and 871, effective July 1, 2012, are identical, and in the definition for "Appropriate authority," substituted "Office of the State Inspector General" for "Division of State Internal Audit of the Department of Accounts."

§ 2.2-3011. Discrimination and retaliatory actions against whistle blowers prohibited; good faith required.

A. No employer may discharge, threaten, or otherwise discriminate or retaliate against a whistle blower whether acting on his own or through a person acting on his behalf or under his direction.

B. No employer may discharge, threaten, or otherwise discriminate or retaliate against a whistle blower because the whistle blower is requested or subpoenaed by an appropriate authority to participate in an investigation, hearing, or inquiry by an appropriate authority or in a court action.

C. To be protected by the provisions of this chapter, an employee who discloses information about suspected wrongdoing or abuse shall do so in good faith and upon a reasonable belief that the information is accurate. Disclosures that are reckless or the employee knew or should have known were false, confidential by law, or malicious shall not be deemed good faith reports and shall not be protected.

D. Nothing in this chapter shall prohibit an employer from disciplining or discharging a whistle blower for his misconduct or any violation of criminal law.

History.
2009, c. 340.

§ 2.2-3012. Application of state grievance procedure; other remedies.

A. Any whistle blower covered by the state grievance procedure (§ 2.2-3000 et seq.) may initiate a grievance alleging retaliation and requesting relief through that procedure.

B. Any whistle blower disclosing information of wrongdoing or abuse under this chapter where the disclosure results in a savings of at least $10,000 may file a claim for reward under the Fraud and Abuse Whistle Blower Reward Fund established in § 2.2-3014.

C. Nothing in this chapter shall be construed to limit the remedies provided by the Virginia Fraud Against Taxpayers Act, Article 19.1 (§ 8.01-216.1 et seq.) of Chapter 3 of Title 8.01.

History.
2009, c. 340.

§ 2.2-3013. Notice to employees of whistle blower protection.

An employer shall post notices and use other appropriate means to notify employees and keep them informed of the protection and obligations set forth in the provisions of this chapter.

History.
2009, c. 340.

§ 2.2-3014. Fraud and Abuse Whistle Blower Reward Fund.

A. From such funds as may be authorized by the General Assembly, there is hereby created in the state treasury a special nonreverting fund to be known as the Fraud and Abuse Whistle Blower Reward Fund, hereafter referred to as "the Fund." The Fund shall be established on the books of the Comptroller and shall be administered by the State Inspector General. All moneys recovered by the State Inspector General as the result of whistle blower activity and alerts originating with the Office of the State Inspector General shall be deposited in the Fund. Interest earned on moneys in the Fund shall remain in the Fund and be credited to it. Except as provided in subsection B, any moneys remaining in the Fund, including interest thereon, at the end of each fiscal year shall not revert to the general fund but shall remain in the Fund. Moneys in the Fund shall be used solely to (i) provide monetary rewards to persons who have disclosed information of wrongdoing or abuse under the Fraud and Abuse Whistle Blower Protection Act (§ 2.2-3009 et seq.) and the disclosure results in a recovery of at least $5,000 or (ii) support the administration of the Fund, defray Fund advertising costs, or subsidize the operation of the Fraud, Waste and Abuse Hotline (previously known as the State Employee Fraud, Waste and Abuse Hotline).

B. By the end of each calendar quarter and upon authorization of the State Inspector General, 85 percent of all sums recovered shall be remitted to the institutions or agencies on whose behalf the recovery was secured by the State Inspector General unless otherwise directed by a court of law. Each such institution or agency on whose behalf the recovery was secured by the State Inspector General shall receive an amount equal to 85 percent of the actual amount recovered by the State Inspector General on its behalf.

C. The amount of the reward shall be up to 10 percent of the actual sums recovered by the Commonwealth as a result of the disclosure of the wrongdoing or abuse. Regardless of the sums recovered, at no time shall the amount of any reward, even if less than 10 percent, exceed the balance of the Fund. Reward disbursements from the Fund shall be made by the State Treasurer on warrants issued by the Comptroller upon written request signed by the State Inspector General. In the event that multiple whistle blowers contemporaneously report the same qualifying incident or occurrence of wrongdoing or abuse, the State Inspector General in his sole discretion may split the reward of up to 10 percent among the multiple whistle blowers. The decision of the State Inspector General regarding the allocation of the rewards shall be final and binding on all parties and shall not be appealable.

D. Five percent of all sums recovered shall be retained in the Fund to support the administration of the Fund, defray advertising costs, and subsidize the operation of the Fraud, Waste and Abuse Hotline. Expenditures for administrative costs for management of the Fund shall be managed as approved by the State Inspector General.

E. The Office of the State Inspector General shall promulgate regulations for the proper administration of the Fund including eligibility requirements and procedures for filing a claim. The Office of the State Inspector General shall submit an annual report to the General Assembly summarizing the activities of the Fund.

History.

2009, c. 340; 2011, cc. 798, 871; 2013, cc. 572, 690.

Editor's note.

Acts 2011, cc. 798 and 871, cl. 7 provides: "That the provisions of this act shall become effective on July 1, 2012, except that the provisions of the fifth enactment of this act shall become effective on July 1, 2011."

The 2011 amendments.

The 2011 amendments by cc. 798 and 871, effective July 1, 2012, are identical, and in subsection A, substituted "State Inspector General" for "Division of State Internal Audit of the Department of Accounts" at the end; and in subsection B, substituted "Office of the State Inspector General" for "Division of State Internal Audit of the Department of Accounts."

The 2013 amendments.

The 2013 amendments by cc. 572 and 690 are identical, and rewrote the section.

CHAPTER 31.

STATE AND LOCAL GOVERNMENT CONFLICT OF INTERESTS ACT.

ARTICLE 1.

GENERAL PROVISIONS.

§ 2.2-3100. Policy; application; construction.

The General Assembly, recognizing that our system of representative government is dependent in part upon (i) citizen legislative members representing fully the public in the legislative process and (ii) its citizens maintaining the highest trust in their public officers and employees, finds and declares that the citizens are entitled to be assured that the judgment of public officers and employees will be guided by a law that defines and prohibits inappropriate conflicts and requires disclosure of economic interests. To that end and for the purpose of establishing a single body of law applicable to all state and local government officers and employees on the subject of conflict of interests, the General Assembly enacts this State and Local Government Conflict of Interests Act so that the standards of conduct for such officers and employees may be uniform throughout the Commonwealth.

This chapter shall supersede all general and special acts and charter provisions which purport to deal with matters covered by this chapter except that the provisions of §§ 15.2-852, 15.2-2287, 15.2-2287.1, and 15.2-2289 and ordinances adopted pursuant thereto shall remain in force and effect. The provisions of this chapter shall be supplemented but not superseded by the provisions on ethics in public contracting in Article 6 (§ 2.2-4367 et seq.) of Chapter 43 of this title and ordinances adopted pursuant to § 2.2-3104.2 regulating receipt of gifts.

This chapter shall be liberally construed to accomplish its purpose.

History.
1987, Sp. Sess., c. 1, § 2.1-639.1; 1990, c. 672; 2001, c. 844; 2003, c. 694; 2008, c. 532.

Cross references.
As to the disposition of surplus materials by the Department of General Services, see § 2.2-1124.

Michie's Jurisprudence.
For related discussion, see 4A M.J. Commonwealth's and State's Attorney, § 7; 5A M.J. Counties, §§ 2, 19, 34; 13B M.J. Municipal Corporations, § 20; 15 M.J. Public Officers, §§ 2, 49; 16 M.J. Schools, §§ 7, 16, 19; 17 M.J. State, §§ 2, 4, 7, 11.

CASE NOTES

Editor's note.
Some of the cases below were decided under former Title 2.1 or prior provisions.

Applicability. — Since a majority of council members did not vote on the retailer's applications for rezoning and special use permits, the town council's vote, by less than a majority of council members, meant that a quorum had not voted on the applications, and, thus, the three council members vote to approve the applications was invalid; too, it did not matter that some of the missing council members had absented themselves pursuant to the State and Local Government Conflict of Interests Act (COIA), § 2.2-3100 et seq., since COIA did not apply the laws involving "Meetings of Governing Bodies" since those laws had nothing to do with conflicts of interests. Jakabcin v. Town of Front Royal, 271 Va. 660, 628 S.E.2d 319, 2006 Va. LEXIS 49 (2006).

Conflicts of interest are proscribed precisely because they may compromise or affect judgment of public servants at the expense of private citizens. If, at the time the transaction is pending, it is reasonably foreseeable that the public servant's personal interest could benefit or suffer from his participation in that transaction, the conflict and the danger it poses to the public interest arise at the moment the transaction occurs. West v. Jones, 228 Va. 409, 323 S.E.2d 96 (1984).

Public servant's interest may not exceed that as member of public at large. — A public servant whose interest is "involved" in a transaction may participate in that transaction only when his interest is one limited to that which he shares in common with other members of the public at large. West v. Jones, 228 Va. 409, 323 S.E.2d 96 (1984).

High school principal may not nominate or appoint school board members. — The former Comprehensive Conflict of Interests Act of 1984 prohibited school principal from participating in the nomination and appointment of members of the school board so long as he was employed by the board. West v. Jones, 228 Va. 409, 323 S.E.2d 96 (1984).

OPINIONS OF THE ATTORNEY GENERAL

Member of town council may serve on county school board, subject to certain restrictions. — Members of town councils generally are precluded from serving on appointed school boards by § 22.1-30, but § 22.1-30 applies only to appointed school boards; however, members of both town councils and school boards are subject to restrictions imposed by the State and Local Government Conflict of Interests Act. See opinion of Attorney General to Mr. William A. Bell, Jr., Secretary, Isle of Wight County Electoral Board, 11-070, 2011 Va. AG LEXIS 41 (9/30/11).

Although simultaneous service is not precluded, the potential interaction between the two bodies requires that any person so serving remain alert to any possible contractual and transactional conflicts that may arise. See opinion of Attorney General to Mr. William A. Bell, Jr., Secretary, Isle of Wight County Electoral Board, 11-070, 2011 Va. AG LEXIS 41 (9/30/11).

Breaks Interstate Park Commission or its members are not subject to application of the State and Local Government Conflict of Interests Act and the Virginia Public Procurement Act. See opinion of Attorney General to The Honorable Clarence E. "Bud" Phillips, Member, House of Delegates, 07-020 (6/20/07).

Employee of local school division cannot serve on the school board, while employed by the school board. See opinion of Attorney General to The Honorable Dave Nutter, Member, House of Delegates, 10-048, 2010 Va. AG LEXIS 63 (9/10/10).

Employee of the Department of Health may operate consulting business specializing in radon testing, as long as the employee does so during nonworking hours in a manner that does not conflict with his responsibilities to the Commonwealth, and the business does not conflict with any Department of Health policies governing outside employment. See opinion of Attorney General to The Honorable Dave Nutter, Member, House of Delegates, 10-048, 2010 Va. AG LEXIS 63 (9/10/10).

§ 2.2-3100.1. Copy of chapter; review by officers and employees.

Any person required to file a disclosure statement of personal interests pursuant to subsections A or B of § 2.2-3114, subsections A or B of § 2.2-3115 or

§ 2.2-3116 shall be furnished by the public body's administrator a copy of this chapter within two weeks following the person's election, reelection, employment, appointment or reappointment.

All officers and employees shall read and familiarize themselves with the provisions of this chapter.

History.
2004, cc. 134, 392.

§ 2.2-3101. Definitions.

As used in this chapter:

"Advisory agency" means any board, commission, committee or post which does not exercise any sovereign power or duty, but is appointed by a governmental agency or officer or is created by law for the purpose of making studies or recommendations, or advising or consulting with a governmental agency.

"Affiliated business entity relationship" means a relationship, other than a parent-subsidiary relationship, that exists when (i) one business entity has a controlling ownership interest in the other business entity, (ii) a controlling owner in one entity is also a controlling owner in the other entity, or (iii) there is shared management or control between the business entities. Factors that may be considered in determining the existence of an affiliated business entity relationship include that the same person or substantially the same person owns or manages the two entities, there are common or commingled funds or assets, the business entities share the use of the same offices or employees, or otherwise share activities, resources or personnel on a regular basis, or there is otherwise a close working relationship between the entities.

"Business" means a corporation, partnership, sole proprietorship, firm, enterprise, franchise, association, trust or foundation, or any other individual or entity carrying on a business or profession, whether or not for profit.

"Contract" means any agreement to which a governmental agency is a party, or any agreement on behalf of a governmental agency that involves the payment of money appropriated by the General Assembly or political subdivision, whether or not such agreement is executed in the name of the Commonwealth, or some political subdivision thereof. "Contract" includes a subcontract only when the contract of which it is a part is with the officer's or employee's own governmental agency.

"Dependent" means a son, daughter, father, mother, brother, sister or other person, whether or not related by blood or marriage, if such person receives from the officer or employee, or provides to the officer or employee, more than one-half of his financial support.

"Employee" means all persons employed by a governmental or advisory agency, unless otherwise limited by the context of its use.

"Financial institution" means any bank, trust company, savings institution, industrial loan association, consumer finance company, credit union, broker-dealer as defined in § 13.1-501, or investment company or advisor registered under the federal Investment Advisors Act or Investment Company Act of 1940.

"Gift" means any gratuity, favor, discount, entertainment, hospitality, loan, forbearance, or other item having monetary value. It includes services as well as gifts of transportation, local travel, lodgings and meals, whether provided in-kind, by purchase of a ticket, payment in advance or reimbursement after the expense has been incurred. "Gift" shall not include any offer of a ticket or other admission or pass unless the ticket, admission, or pass is used. "Gift" shall not include honorary degrees and presents from relatives. For the purpose of this definition, "relative" means the donee's spouse, child, uncle, aunt, niece, or nephew; a person to whom the donee is engaged to be married; the donee's or his spouse's parent, grandparent, grandchild, brother, or sister; or the donee's brother's or sister's spouse.

"Governmental agency" means each component part of the legislative, executive or judicial branches of state and local government, including each office, department, authority, post, commission, committee, and each institution or board created by law to exercise some regulatory or sovereign power or duty as distinguished from purely advisory powers or duties. Corporations organized or controlled by the Virginia Retirement System are "governmental agencies" for purposes of this chapter.

"Immediate family" means (i) a spouse and (ii) any other person residing in the same household as the officer or employee, who is a dependent of the officer or employee or of whom the officer or employee is a dependent.

"Officer" means any person appointed or elected to any governmental or advisory agency including local school boards, whether or not he receives compensation or other emolument of office. Unless the context requires otherwise, "officer" includes members of the judiciary.

"Parent-subsidiary relationship" means a relationship that exists when one corporation directly or indirectly owns shares possessing more than 50 percent of the voting power of another corporation.

"Personal interest" means a financial benefit or liability accruing to an officer or employee or to a member of his immediate family. Such interest shall exist by reason of (i) ownership in a business if the ownership interest exceeds three percent of the total equity of the business; (ii) annual income that exceeds, or may reasonably be anticipated to exceed, $10,000 from ownership in real or personal property or a business; (iii) salary, other compensation, fringe benefits, or benefits from the use of property, or any combination thereof, paid or provided by a business or governmental agency that exceeds, or may reasonably be anticipated to exceed, $10,000 annually; (iv) ownership of real or personal property if the interest exceeds $10,000 in value and excluding ownership in

a business, income, or salary, other compensation, fringe benefits or benefits from the use of property; (v) personal liability incurred or assumed on behalf of a business if the liability exceeds three percent of the asset value of the business; or (vi) an option for ownership of a business or real or personal property if the ownership interest will consist of (i) or (iv) above.

"Personal interest in a contract" means a personal interest that an officer or employee has in a contract with a governmental agency, whether due to his being a party to the contract or due to a personal interest in a business that is a party to the contract.

"Personal interest in a transaction" means a personal interest of an officer or employee in any matter considered by his agency. Such personal interest exists when an officer or employee or a member of his immediate family has a personal interest in property or a business or governmental agency, or represents or provides services to any individual or business and such property, business or represented or served individual or business (i) is the subject of the transaction or (ii) may realize a reasonably foreseeable direct or indirect benefit or detriment as a result of the action of the agency considering the transaction. Notwithstanding the above, such personal interest in a transaction shall not be deemed to exist where (a) an elected member of a local governing body serves without remuneration as a member of the board of trustees of a not-for-profit entity and such elected member or member of his immediate family has no personal interest related to the not-for-profit entity or (b) an officer, employee, or elected member of a local governing body is appointed by such local governing body to serve on a governmental agency, or an officer, employee, or elected member of a separate local governmental agency formed by a local governing body is appointed to serve on a governmental agency, and the personal interest in the transaction of the governmental agency is the result of the salary, other compensation, fringe benefits, or benefits provided by the local governing body or the separate governmental agency to the officer, employee, elected member, or member of his immediate family.

"State and local government officers and employees" shall not include members of the General Assembly.

"State filer" means those officers and employees required to file a disclosure statement of their personal interests pursuant to subsection A or B of § 2.2-3114.

"Transaction" means any matter considered by any governmental or advisory agency, whether in a committee, subcommittee, or other entity of that agency or before the agency itself, on which official action is taken or contemplated.

History.
1987, Sp. Sess., c. 1, § 2.1-639.2; 1988, c. 536; 1992, c. 865; 1993, c. 303; 1994, cc. 74, 724; 1995, c. 495; 1996, c. 77; 1997, c. 641; 2001, c. 844; 2003, c. 694; 2004, cc. 134, 392; 2012, cc. 345, 771; 2013, c. 475.

The 2012 amendments.
The 2012 amendments by cc. 345 and 771 are identical, and in the paragraph defining "Personal interest in a transaction," inserted the clause (a) designator and clause (b), and made a related change.

The 2013 amendments.
The 2013 amendment by c. 475, in the paragraph defining "Personal interest in a transaction," deleted "or" following "an officer" and "where an employee" preceding "or elected member," and inserted "or an officer, employee, or elected member of a separate local governmental agency formed by a local governing body is appointed to serve on a governmental agency" and "or the separate governmental agency" in clause (b).

OPINIONS OF THE ATTORNEY GENERAL

Chief Information Officer. — An individual may not serve simultaneously as the Secretary of Technology and the Chief Information Officer. See opinion of Attorney General to The Honorable Samuel A. Nixon, Jr., Member, House of Delegates, 09-053, 2009 Va. AG LEXIS 34 (8/14/09).

Member of town council may serve on county school board, subject to certain restrictions. — Members of town councils generally are precluded from serving on appointed school boards by § 22.1-30, but § 22.1-30 applies only to appointed school boards; however, members of both town councils and school boards are subject to restrictions imposed by the State and Local Government Conflict of Interests Act. See opinion of Attorney General to Mr. William A. Bell, Jr., Secretary, Isle of Wight County Electoral Board, 11-070, 2011 Va. AG LEXIS 41 (9/30/11).

Although simultaneous service is not precluded, the potential interaction between the two bodies requires that any person so serving remain alert to any possible contractual and transactional conflicts that may arise. See opinion of Attorney General to Mr. William A. Bell, Jr., Secretary, Isle of Wight County Electoral Board, 11-070, 2011 Va. AG LEXIS 41 (9/30/11).

Authority to enter into contracts. — The General Assembly has authorized the Virginia Information Technologies Agency, rather than the Information Technology Investment Board, to enter into or modify contracts for the purchase of information technology goods and services. See opinion of Attorney General to The Honorable Samuel A. Nixon, Jr., Member, House of Delegates, 09-053, 2009 Va. AG LEXIS 34 (8/14/09).

Employee of local school division cannot serve on the school board, while employed by the school board. See opinion of Attorney General to The Honorable Dave Nutter, Member, House of Delegates, 10-048, 2010 Va. AG LEXIS 63 (9/10/10).

Employee of the Department of Health may operate consulting business specializing in radon testing, as long as the employee does so during nonworking hours in a manner that does not conflict with his responsibilities to the Commonwealth, and the business does not conflict with any Department of Health policies governing outside employment. See opinion of Attorney General to The Honorable Dave Nutter, Member, House of Delegates, 10-048, 2010 Va. AG LEXIS 63 (9/10/10).

ARTICLE 2.

GENERALLY PROHIBITED AND UNLAWFUL CONDUCT.

§ 2.2-3102. Application.

This article applies to generally prohibited conduct that shall be unlawful and to state and local government officers and employees.

History.
1987, Sp. Sess., c. 1, § 2.1-639.3; 2001, c. 844.

§ 2.2-3103. Prohibited conduct.

No officer or employee of a state or local governmental or advisory agency shall:

1. Solicit or accept money or other thing of value for services performed within the scope of his official duties, except the compensation, expenses or other remuneration paid by the agency of which he is an officer or employee. This prohibition shall not apply to the acceptance of special benefits that may be authorized by law;

2. Offer or accept any money or other thing of value for or in consideration of obtaining employment, appointment, or promotion of any person with any governmental or advisory agency;

3. Offer or accept any money or other thing of value for or in consideration of the use of his public position to obtain a contract for any person or business with any governmental or advisory agency;

4. Use for his own economic benefit or that of another party confidential information that he has acquired by reason of his public position and which is not available to the public;

5. Accept any money, loan, gift, favor, service, or business or professional opportunity that reasonably tends to influence him in the performance of his official duties. This subdivision shall not apply to any political contribution actually used for political campaign or constituent service purposes and reported as required by Chapter 9.3 (§ 24.2-945 et seq.) of Title 24.2;

6. Accept any business or professional opportunity when he knows that there is a reasonable likelihood that the opportunity is being afforded him to influence him in the performance of his official duties;

7. Accept any honoraria for any appearance, speech, or article in which the officer or employee provides expertise or opinions related to the performance of his official duties. The term "honoraria" shall not include any payment for or reimbursement to such person for his actual travel, lodging, or subsistence expenses incurred in connection with such appearance, speech, or article or in the alternative a payment of money or anything of value not in excess of the per diem deduction allowable under § 162 of the Internal Revenue Code, as amended from time to time. The prohibition in this subdivision shall apply only to the Governor, Lieutenant Governor, Attorney General, Governor's Secretaries, and heads of departments of state government;

8. Accept a gift from a person who has interests that may be substantially affected by the performance of the officer's or employee's official duties under circumstances where the timing and nature of the gift would cause a reasonable person to question the officer's or employee's impartiality in the matter affecting the donor. Violations of this subdivision shall not be subject to criminal law penalties; or

9. Accept gifts from sources on a basis so frequent as to raise an appearance of the use of his public office for private gain. Violations of this subdivision shall not be subject to criminal law penalties.

History.
1987, Sp. Sess., c. 1, § 2.1-639.4; 1994, cc. 663, 815, 851; 2001, c. 844; 2006, cc. 787, 892.

OPINIONS OF THE ATTORNEY GENERAL

Health regulatory board members. — It is not a violation of the State and Local Government Conflict of Interests Act or the Virginia Public Procurement Act for a member of a health regulatory board to vote to authorize the board to contract with or join an organization in the business of administering licensure examinations, where the Department of Health Professions reimburses the board member for per diem and expenses as allowable under state law and travel regulations. See opinion of Attorney General to Mr. Robert A. Nebiker, Director, Department of Health Professions, 05-029 (6/21/05).

It would be a violation of the State and Local Government Conflict of Interests Act or the Virginia Public Procurement Act for a board member to vote to approve a contract or to join an organization where, at the time of the vote, there is an existing arrangement concerning prospective employment of such board member after departure from the board or the board member accepts the payment of monies in excess of allowable per diem payments and travel reimbursement allowances. See opinion of Attorney General to Mr. Robert A. Nebiker, Director, Department of Health Professions, 05-029 (6/21/05).

Member of town council may serve on county school board, subject to certain restrictions. — Members of town councils generally are precluded from serving on appointed school boards by § 22.1-30, but § 22.1-30 applies only to appointed school boards; however, members of both town councils and school boards are subject to restrictions imposed by the State and Local Government Conflict of Interests Act. See opinion of Attorney General to Mr. William A. Bell, Jr., Secretary, Isle of Wight County Electoral Board, 11-070, 2011 Va. AG LEXIS 41 (9/30/11).

Although simultaneous service is not precluded, the potential interaction between the two bodies requires that any person so serving remain alert to any possible contractual and transactional conflicts that may arise. See opinion of Attorney General to Mr. William A. Bell, Jr., Secretary, Isle of Wight County Electoral Board, 11-070, 2011 Va. AG LEXIS 41 (9/30/11).

Tax collection. — The Department may compensate a locality for actions taken by its treasurer to collect state taxes pursuant to subsection A of § 58.1-1803, provided the compensation is: (a) reasonable; (b) determined prior to the treasurer's undertaking of such actions; and (c) paid directly to the locality and not to the treasurer personally. See opinion of Attorney General to The Honorable Francis X. O'Leary, Arlington County Treasurer, 09-067, 2009 Va. AG LEXIS 47 (11/3/09).

Local treasurer collecting delinquent state taxes pursuant to an agreement with the Department of Taxation is not authorized to recover from the taxpayer a twenty-percent commission in addition to the delinquent state taxes collected on behalf of the Department. See opinion of Attorney General to The Honorable Francis X. O'Leary, Arlington County Treasurer, 09-067, 2009 Va. AG LEXIS 47 (11/3/09).

Employee of local school division cannot serve on the school board, while employed by the school board. See opinion of Attorney General to The Honorable Dave Nutter, Member, House of Delegates, 10-048, 2010 Va. AG LEXIS 63 (9/10/10).

Employee of the Department of Health may operate consulting business specializing in radon testing, as long as the employee does so during nonworking hours in a manner that does not conflict with his responsibilities to the Commonwealth, and the business does not conflict with any Department of Health policies governing outside employment. See opinion of Attorney General to The Honorable Dave Nutter, Member, House of Delegates, 10-048, 2010 Va. AG LEXIS 63 (9/10/10).

§ 2.2-3104. Prohibited conduct for certain officers and employees of state government.

For one year after the termination of public employment or service, no state officer or employee shall, before the agency of which he was an officer or employee, represent a client or act in a representative capacity on behalf of any person or group, for compensation, on matters related to legislation, executive orders, or regulations promulgated by the agency of which he was an officer or employee. This prohibition shall be in addition to the prohibitions contained in § 2.2-3103.

For the purposes of this section, "state officer or employee" shall mean (i) the Governor, Lieutenant Governor, Attorney General, and officers appointed by the Governor, whether confirmation by the General Assembly or by either house thereof is required or not, who are regularly employed on a full-time salaried basis; those officers and employees of executive branch agencies who report directly to the agency head; and those at the level immediately below those who report directly to the agency head and are at a payband 6 or higher and (ii) the officers and professional employees of the legislative branch designated by the joint rules committee of the General Assembly. For the purposes of this section, the General Assembly and the legislative branch agencies shall be deemed one agency.

Any person subject to the provisions of this section may apply to the Attorney General, as provided in § 2.2-3126, for an advisory opinion as to the application of the restriction imposed by this section on any post-public employment position or opportunity.

History.
1994, cc. 727, 776, § 2.1-639.4:1; 2001, c. 844; 2013, c. 648.

The 2013 amendments.
The 2013 amendment by c. 648 rewrote the first paragraph, which read: "In addition to the prohibitions contained in § 2.2-3103, no state officer or employee shall, during the one year after the termination of his public employment or service, represent a client or act in a representative capacity on behalf of any person or group, for compensation, on any matter before the agency of which he was an officer or employee" and deleted the former third paragraph, which read: "The prohibitions of this section shall apply only to persons engaged in activities that would require registration as a lobbyist under § 2.2-422."

§ 2.2-3104.01. Prohibited conduct; bids or proposals under the Virginia Public Procurement Act, Public-Private Transportation Act, and Public-Private Education Facilities and Infrastructure Act.

A. Neither the Governor, his political action committee, or the Governor's Secretaries, if the Secretary is responsible to the Governor for an executive branch agency with jurisdiction over the matters at issue, shall knowingly solicit or accept a contribution, gift, or other item with a value greater than $50 from any bidder, offeror, or private entity, or from an officer or director of such bidder, offeror, or private entity, who has submitted a bid or proposal to an executive branch agency that is directly responsible to the Governor pursuant to the Virginia Public Procurement Act (§ 2.2-4300 et seq.), the Public-Private Transportation Act of 1995 (§ 56-556 et seq.), or the Public-Private Education Facilities and Infrastructure Act of 2002 (§ 56-575.1 et seq.)(i) during the

period between the submission of the bid and the award of the public contract under the Virginia Public Procurement Act or (ii) following the submission of a proposal under the Public-Private Transportation Act of 1995 or the Public-Private Education Facilities and Infrastructure Act of 2002 until the execution of a comprehensive agreement thereunder.

B. **(Effective until July 1, 2014)** The provisions of this section shall apply only for public contracts, proposals, or comprehensive agreements where the stated or expected value of the contract is $5 million or more. The provisions of this section shall not apply to contracts awarded as the result of competitive sealed bidding as defined in § 2.2-4301.

B. **(Effective July 1, 2014)** The provisions of this section shall apply only for public contracts, proposals, or comprehensive agreements where the stated or expected value of the contract is $5 million or more. The provisions of this section shall not apply to contracts awarded as the result of competitive sealed bidding as set forth in § 2.2-4302.1.

C. Any person who knowingly violates this section shall be subject to a civil penalty of $500 or up to two times the amount of the contribution or gift, whichever is greater. The attorney for the Commonwealth shall initiate civil proceedings to enforce the civil penalties. Any civil penalties collected shall be payable to the State Treasurer for deposit to the general fund.

History.
2010, c. 732; 2011, c. 624; 2013, c. 583.

Subsection B set out twice. — The first version of subsection B above is effective until July 1, 2014. The second version of subsection B is effective July 1, 2014.

Editor's note.
Acts 2013, c. 583, cl. 2 provides: "That the provisions of the first enactment of this act shall become effective on July 1, 2014."

The 2011 amendments.
The 2011 amendment by c. 624, in subsection A, inserted "executive branch" and "to an executive branch agency that is directly responsible to the Governor"; and in subsection C, inserted "knowingly."

The 2013 amendments.
The 2013 amendment by c. 583, effective July 1, 2014, substituted "set forth in § 2.2-4302.1" for "defined in § 2.2-4301" at the end of subsection B.

§ 2.2-3104.02. Prohibited conduct for constitutional officers.

In addition to the prohibitions contained in § 2.2-3103, no constitutional officer shall, during the one year after the termination of his public service, act in a representative capacity on behalf of any person or group, for compensation, on any matter before the agency of which he was an officer.

The provisions of this section shall not apply to any attorney for the Commonwealth.

Any person subject to the provisions of this section may apply to the attorney for the Commonwealth for the jurisdiction where such person was elected as provided in § 2.2-3126, for an advisory opinion as to the application of the restriction imposed by this section on any post-public employment position or opportunity.

History.
2011, c. 591.

§ 2.2-3104.1. Exclusion of certain awards from scope of chapter.

The provisions of this chapter shall not be construed to prohibit or apply to the acceptance by (i) any employee of a local government, or (ii) a teacher or other employee of a local school board of an award or payment in honor of meritorious or exceptional services performed by the teacher or employee and made by an organization exempt from federal income taxation pursuant to the provisions of Section 501(c)(3) of the Internal Revenue Code.

History.
2001, c. 48, § 2.1-639.4:2; 2008, cc. 478, 497.

Editor's note.
Acts 2001, c. 48 enacted § 2.1-639.4:2, from which this section is derived. Pursuant to § 30-152, Acts 2001, c. 48 has been given effect in this section as set out above.

Law Review.
For annual survey article, "Election Law and Government," see 46 U. Rich. L. Rev. 119 (2011).

§ 2.2-3104.2. Ordinance regulating receipt of gifts.

The governing body of any county, city, or town may adopt an ordinance setting a monetary limit on the acceptance of any gift by the officers, appointees or employees of the county, city or town and requiring the disclosure by such officers, appointees or employees of the receipt of any gift.

History.
2003, c. 694.

ARTICLE 3.

PROHIBITED CONDUCT RELATING TO CONTRACTS.

§ 2.2-3105. Application.

This article proscribes certain conduct relating to contracts by state and local government officers and employees. The provisions of this article shall be supplemented but not superseded by the provisions on ethics in public contracting in Article 6 (§ 2.2-4367 et seq.) of Chapter 43 of this title.

History.
1987, Sp. Sess., c. 1, § 2.1-639.5; 2001, c. 844; 2003, c. 694.

§ 2.2-3106. Prohibited contracts by officers and employees of state government and Eastern Virginia Medical School.

A. No officer or employee of any governmental agency of state government or Eastern Virginia Medical School shall have a personal interest in a contract with the governmental agency of which he is an officer or employee, other than his own contract of employment.

B. **(Effective until July 1, 2014)** No officer or employee of any governmental agency of state government or Eastern Virginia Medical School shall have a personal interest in a contract with any other governmental agency of state government unless such contract is (i) awarded as a result of competitive sealed bidding or competitive negotiation as defined in § 2.2-4301 or (ii) is awarded after a finding, in writing, by the administrative head of the governmental agency that competitive bidding or negotiation is contrary to the best interest of the public.

B. **(Effective July 1, 2014)** No officer or employee of any governmental agency of state government or Eastern Virginia Medical School shall have a personal interest in a contract with any other governmental agency of state government unless such contract is (i) awarded as a result of competitive sealed bidding or competitive negotiation as set forth in § 2.2-4302.1 or 2.2-4302.2 or (ii) is awarded after a finding, in writing, by the administrative head of the governmental agency that competitive bidding or negotiation is contrary to the best interest of the public.

C. The provisions of this section shall not apply to:

1. An employee's personal interest in additional contracts of employment with his own governmental agency that accrue to him because of a member of his immediate family, provided the employee does not exercise any control over the employment or the employment activities of the member of his immediate family and the employee is not in a position to influence those activities;

2. The personal interest of an officer or employee of a state institution of higher education or the Eastern Virginia Medical School in additional contracts of employment with his own governmental agency that accrue to him because of a member of his immediate family, provided (i) the officer or employee and the immediate family member are engaged in teaching, research or administrative support positions at the educational institution or the Eastern Virginia Medical School, (ii) the governing board of the educational institution finds that it is in the best interests of the institution or the Eastern Virginia Medical School and the Commonwealth for such dual employment to exist, and (iii) after such finding, the governing board of the educational institution or the Eastern Virginia Medical School ensures that the officer or employee, or the immediate family member, does not have sole authority to supervise, evaluate or make personnel decisions regarding the other;

3. An officer's or employee's personal interest in a contract of employment with any other governmental agency of state government;

4. Contracts for the sale by a governmental agency or the Eastern Virginia Medical School of services or goods at uniform prices available to the general public;

5. An employee's personal interest in a contract between a public institution of higher education in Virginia or the Eastern Virginia Medical School and a publisher or wholesaler of textbooks or other educational materials for students, which accrues to him solely because he has authored or otherwise created such textbooks or materials;

6. An employee's personal interest in a contract with his or her employing public institution of higher education to acquire the collections or scholarly works owned by the employee, including manuscripts, musical scores, poetry, paintings, books or other materials, writings, or papers of an academic, research, or cultural value to the institution, provided the president of the institution approves the acquisition of such collections or scholarly works as being in the best interests of the institution's public mission of service, research, or education;

7. Subject to approval by the board of visitors, an employee's personal interest in a contract between the Eastern Virginia Medical School or a public institution of higher education in Virginia that operates a school of medicine or dentistry and a not-for-profit nonstock corporation that operates a clinical practice within such public institution of higher education or the Eastern Virginia Medical School and of which such employee is a member or employee;

8. Subject to approval by the relevant board of visitors, an employee's personal interest in a contract for research and development or commercialization of intellectual property between a public institution of higher education in Virginia or the Eastern Virginia Medical School and a business in which the employee has a personal interest, if (i) the employee's personal interest has been disclosed to and approved by such public institution of higher education or the Eastern Virginia Medical School prior to the time at which the contract is entered into; (ii) the employee promptly files a disclosure statement pursuant to § 2.2-3117 and thereafter files such statement annually on or before January 15; (iii) the institution has established a formal policy regarding such contracts, approved by the State Council of Higher Education or, in the case of the Eastern Virginia Medical School, a formal policy regarding such contracts in conformity with any applicable federal regulations that has been approved by its board of visitors; and (iv) no later than December 31 of each year, the institution or the Eastern Virginia Medical School files an annual report with the Secretary of the Commonwealth disclosing each open contract entered into subject to this provision, the names of the parties to each contract, the date each contract was executed and its term, the subject of each contractual arrangement,

the nature of the conflict of interest, the institution's or the Eastern Virginia Medical School's employee responsible for administering each contract, the details of the institution's or the Eastern Virginia Medical School's commitment or investment of resources or finances for each contract, and any other information requested by the Secretary of the Commonwealth; or

9. Subject to approval by the relevant board of visitors, an employee's personal interest in a contract between a public institution of higher education in Virginia or the Eastern Virginia Medical School and a business in which the employee has a personal interest, if (i) the personal interest has been disclosed to the institution or the Eastern Virginia Medical School prior to the time the contract is entered into; (ii) the employee files a disclosure statement pursuant to § 2.2-3117 and thereafter annually on or before January 15; (iii) the employee does not participate in the institution's or the Eastern Virginia Medical School's decision to contract; (iv) the president of the institution or the Eastern Virginia Medical School finds and certifies in writing that the contract is for goods and services needed for quality patient care, including related medical education or research, by the institution's medical center or the Eastern Virginia Medical School, its affiliated teaching hospitals and other organizations necessary for the fulfillment of its mission, including the acquisition of drugs, therapies and medical technologies; and (v) no later than December 31 of each year, the institution or the Eastern Virginia Medical School files an annual report with the Secretary of the Commonwealth disclosing each open contract entered subject to this provision, the names of the parties to each contract, the date each contract was executed and its term, the subject of each contractual arrangement, the nature of the conflict of interest, the institution's or the Eastern Virginia Medical School's employee responsible for administering each contract, the details of the institution's or the Eastern Virginia Medical School's commitment or investment of resources or finances for each contract, and any other information requested by the Secretary of the Commonwealth.

D. Notwithstanding the provisions of subdivisions C 8 and C 9, if the research and development or commercialization of intellectual property or the employee's personal interest in a contract with a business is subject to policies and regulations governing conflicts of interest promulgated by any agency of the United States government, including the adoption of policies requiring the disclosure and management of such conflicts of interests, the policies established by the Eastern Virginia Medical School pursuant to such federal requirements shall constitute compliance with subdivisions C 8 and C 9, upon notification by the Eastern Virginia Medical School to the Secretary of the Commonwealth by January 31 of each year of evidence of their compliance with such federal policies and regulations.

E. The board of visitors may delegate the authority granted under subdivision C 8 to the president of the institution. If the board elects to delegate such authority, the board shall include this delegation of authority in the formal policy required by clause (iii) of subdivision C 8. In those instances where the board has delegated such authority, on or before December 1 of each year, the president of the relevant institution shall file a report with the relevant board of visitors disclosing each open contract entered into subject to this provision, the names of the parties to each contract, the date each contract was executed and its term, the subject of each contractual arrangement, the nature of the conflict of interest, the institution's or the Eastern Virginia Medical School's employee responsible for administering each contract, the details of the institution's or the Eastern Virginia Medical School's commitment or investment of resources or finances for each contract, the details of how revenues are to be dispersed, and any other information requested by the board of visitors.

History.
1987, Sp. Sess., c. 1, § 2.1-639.6; 1989, c. 74; 1991, c. 470; 1993, c. 876; 1995, c. 403; 1998, c. 838; 2001, c. 844; 2002, cc. 87, 478; 2003, c. 646; 2006, c. 839; 2013, c. 583.

Subsection B set out twice. — The first version of subsection B above is effective until July 1, 2014. The second version of subsection B is effective July 1, 2014.

Editor's note.
Acts 2013, c. 583, cl. 2 provides: "That the provisions of the first enactment of this act shall become effective on July 1, 2014."

The 2013 amendments.
The 2013 amendment by c. 583, effective July 1, 2014, substituted "set forth in § 2.2-4302.1 or 2.2-4302.2" for "defined in § 2.2-4301" in clause (i) in subsection B.

OPINIONS OF THE ATTORNEY GENERAL

Member of town council may serve on county school board, subject to certain restrictions. — Members of town councils generally are precluded from serving on appointed school boards by § 22.1-30, but § 22.1-30 applies only to appointed school boards; however, members of both town councils and school boards are subject to restrictions imposed by the State and Local Government Conflict of Interests Act. See opinion of Attorney General to Mr. William A. Bell, Jr., Secretary, Isle of Wight County Electoral Board, 11-070, 2011 Va. AG LEXIS 41 (9/30/11).

Although simultaneous service is not precluded, the potential interaction between the two bodies requires that any person so serving remain alert to any possible contractual and transactional conflicts that may arise. See opinion of Attorney General to Mr. William A. Bell, Jr., Secretary, Isle of Wight County Electoral Board, 11-070, 2011 Va. AG LEXIS 41 (9/30/11).

Chief Information Officer. — An individual may not serve simultaneously as the Secretary of Technology and the Chief Information Officer. See opinion of Attorney General to The Honorable Samuel A. Nixon, Jr., Member, House of Delegates, 09-053, 2009 Va. AG LEXIS 34 (8/14/09).

Authority to enter into contracts. — The General Assembly has authorized the Virginia Information Technologies Agency, rather than the Information Technology Investment Board, to enter into or modify contracts for the purchase of information technology goods and services. See opinion of Attorney General to The Honorable Samuel A. Nixon, Jr., Member, House of Delegates, 09-053, 2009 Va. AG LEXIS 34 (8/14/09).

Employee of local school division cannot serve on the school board, while employed by the school board. See opinion of Attorney General to The Honorable Dave Nutter, Member, House of Delegates, 10-048, 2010 Va. AG LEXIS 63 (9/10/10).

Employee of the Department of Health may operate consulting business specializing in radon testing, as long as the employee does so during nonworking hours in a manner that does not conflict with his responsibilities to the Commonwealth, and the business does not conflict with any Department of Health policies governing outside employment. See opinion of Attorney General to The Honorable Dave Nutter, Member, House of Delegates, 10-048, 2010 Va. AG LEXIS 63 (9/10/10).

Conflict of interest. — No conflict of interest precludes members of local governing bodies who also serve on community action boards from voting in budgetary matters of the local government when such items may affect the community action program funding. See opinion of Attorney General to The Honorable Roslyn C. Tyler, Member, House of Delegates, 12-022, 2012 Va. AG LEXIS 14 (3/30/12).

§ 2.2-3107. Prohibited contracts by members of county boards of supervisors, city councils and town councils.

A. No person elected or appointed as a member of the governing body of a county, city or town shall have a personal interest in (i) any contract with his governing body, or (ii) any contract with any governmental agency that is a component part of his local government and which is subject to the ultimate control of the governing body of which he is a member, or (iii) any contract other than a contract of employment with any other governmental agency if such person's governing body appoints a majority of the members of the governing body of the second governmental agency.

B. The provisions of this section shall not apply to:

1. A member's personal interest in a contract of employment provided (i) the officer or employee was employed by the governmental agency prior to July 1, 1983, in accordance with the provisions of the former Conflict of Interests Act, Chapter 22 (§ 2.1-347 et seq.) of Title 2.1 as it existed on June 30, 1983, or (ii) the employment first began prior to the member becoming a member of the governing body;

2. Contracts for the sale by a governmental agency of services or goods at uniform prices available to the public; or

3. A contract awarded to a member of a governing body as a result of competitive sealed bidding where the governing body has established a need for the same or substantially similar goods through purchases prior to the election or appointment of the member to serve on the governing body. However, the member shall have no involvement in the preparation of the specifications for such contract, and the remaining members of the governing body, by written resolution, shall state that it is in the public interest for the member to bid on such contract.

History.
1987, Sp. Sess., c. 1, § 2.1-639.7; 2001, c. 844.

CASE NOTES

Editor's note.
The cases below were decided under former Title 2.1 or prior provisions.

Appointment of agency officers by agency employee not authorized by this section. — Former § 2.1-606 (see now this section) has two effects. It forbids a member of a local governing body to have a personal interest in certain contracts with a governmental agency if the majority of the officers of that agency are appointed by the local governing body. And, by way of exception, it permits a member of a local governing body to hold a job with such an agency. Nothing in the section authorizes such a person who works for such an agency to participate in the appointment of the officers of that agency. West v. Jones, 228 Va. 409, 323 S.E.2d 96 (1984).

No requirement that resolution be approved by unanimous vote. — Subdivision B 3 of this section does not state that the resolution must be approved by a unanimous vote of the remaining members of the governing body. It simply provides that only those members who do not have a personal interest in the contract may vote on the resolution. Harris v. Ingram, 240 Va. 46, 392 S.E.2d 816 (1990).

§ 2.2-3108. Prohibited contracts by members of school boards.

A. No person elected or appointed as a member of a local school board shall have a personal interest in (i) any contract with his school board or (ii) any contract with any governmental agency that is subject to the ultimate control of the school board of which he is a member.

B. The provisions of this section shall not apply to:

1. A member's personal interest in a contract of employment provided the employment first began prior to the member becoming a member of the school board;

2. Contracts for the sale by a governmental agency of services or goods at uniform prices available to the public; or

3. A contract awarded to a member of a school board as a result of competitive sealed bidding where the school board has established a need for the same or substantially similar goods through purchases prior to the election or appointment of the member to serve on the school board. However, the member shall have no involvement in the preparation of the specifications for such contract, and the remaining members of the school board, by written resolution, shall state that it is in the public interest for the member to bid on such contract.

History.
1996, c. 548, § 2.1-639.7:1; 2001, c. 844.

§ 2.2-3109. Prohibited contracts by other officers and employees of local governmental agencies.

A. No other officer or employee of any governmental agency of local government shall have a personal interest in a contract with the agency of which he is an officer or employee other than his own contract of employment.

B. **(Effective until July 1, 2014)** No officer or employee of any governmental agency of local government shall have a personal interest in a contract with any other governmental agency that is a component of the government of his county, city or town

unless such contract is (i) awarded as a result of competitive sealed bidding or competitive negotiation as defined in § 2.2-4301 or is awarded as a result of a procedure embodying competitive principles as authorized by subdivisions A 10 or A 11 of § 2.2-4343 or (ii) is awarded after a finding, in writing, by the administrative head of the governmental agency that competitive bidding or negotiation is contrary to the best interest of the public.

B. **(Effective July 1, 2014)** No officer or employee of any governmental agency of local government shall have a personal interest in a contract with any other governmental agency that is a component of the government of his county, city or town unless such contract is (i) awarded as a result of competitive sealed bidding or competitive negotiation as set forth in § 2.2-4302.1 or 2.2-4302.2 or is awarded as a result of a procedure embodying competitive principles as authorized by subdivisions A 10 or A 11 of § 2.2-4343 or (ii) is awarded after a finding, in writing, by the administrative head of the governmental agency that competitive bidding or negotiation is contrary to the best interest of the public.

C. The provisions of this section shall not apply to:

1. An employee's personal interest in additional contracts for goods or services, or contracts of employment with his own governmental agency that accrue to him because of a member of his immediate family, provided the employee does not exercise any control over (i) the employment or the employment activities of the member of his immediate family and (ii) the employee is not in a position to influence those activities or the award of the contract for goods or services;

2. An officer's or employee's personal interest in a contract of employment with any other governmental agency that is a component part of the government of his county, city or town;

3. Contracts for the sale by a governmental agency of services or goods at uniform prices available to the general public;

4. Members of local governing bodies who are subject to § 2.2-3107;

5. Members of local school boards who are subject to § 2.2-3108; or

6. Any ownership or financial interest of members of the governing body, administrators, and other personnel serving in a public charter school in renovating, lending, granting, or leasing public charter school facilities, as the case may be, provided such interest has been disclosed in the public charter school application as required by § 22.1-212.8.

History.
1987, Sp. Sess., c. 1, § 2.1-639.8; 1996, c. 548; 2001, c. 844; 2004, c. 530; 2009, c. 862; 2013, c. 583.

Subsection B set out twice. — The first version of subsection B above is effective until July 1, 2014. The second version of subsection B is effective July 1, 2014.

Editor's note.
Acts 2004, c. 530, added subdivision C 6 and in cl. 2 of that act, provided that subdivision C 6 would expire July 1, 2009. Acts 2004,

c. 530, cl. 2, as amended by Acts 2009, c. 441, cl. 2 provides: "That the provisions of this act amending and reenacting §§ 22.1-212.5, 22.1-212.6, 22.1-212.8, and 22.1-212.11 shall expire on July 1, 2009." Therefore, subdivision C 6 of § 2.2-3109 will not expire July 1, 2009.

Acts 2013, c. 583, cl. 2 provides: "That the provisions of the first enactment of this act shall become effective on July 1, 2014."

The 2013 amendments.

The 2013 amendment by c. 583, effective July 1, 2014, substituted "set forth in § 2.2-4302.1 or 2.2-4302.2" for "defined in § 2.2-4301" in clause (i) in subsection B.

Law Review.

For 2003/2004 survey of education law, see 39 U. Rich. L. Rev. 183 (2004).

§ 2.2-3110. Further exceptions.

A. The provisions of Article 3 (§ 2.2-3106 et seq.) of this chapter shall not apply to:

1. The sale, lease or exchange of real property between an officer or employee and a governmental agency, provided the officer or employee does not participate in any way as such officer or employee in such sale, lease or exchange, and this fact is set forth as a matter of public record by the governing body of the governmental agency or by the administrative head thereof;

2. The publication of official notices;

3. Contracts between the government or school board of a town or city with a population of less than 10,000 and an officer or employee of that town or city government or school board when the total of such contracts between the town or city government or school board and the officer or employee of that town or city government or school board or a business controlled by him does not exceed $10,000 per year or such amount exceeds $10,000 and is less than $25,000 but results from contracts arising from awards made on a sealed bid basis, and such officer or employee has made disclosure as provided for in § 2.2-3115;

4. An officer or employee whose sole personal interest in a contract with the governmental agency is by reason of income from the contracting firm or governmental agency in excess of $10,000 per year, provided the officer or employee or a member of his immediate family does not participate and has no authority to participate in the procurement or letting of such contract on behalf of the contracting firm and the officer or employee either does not have authority to participate in the procurement or letting of the contract on behalf of his governmental agency or he disqualifies himself as a matter of public record and does not participate on behalf of his governmental agency in negotiating the contract or in approving the contract;

5. When the governmental agency is a public institution of higher education, an officer or employee whose personal interest in a contract with the institution is by reason of an ownership in the contracting firm in excess of three percent of the contracting firm's equity or such ownership interest and income from the contracting firm is in excess of $10,000 per year, provided that (i) the officer or employee's ownership interest, or ownership and income interest, and that of any immediate family member in the contracting firm is disclosed in writing to the president of the institution, which writing certifies that the officer or employee has not and will not participate in the contract negotiations on behalf of the contracting firm or the institution, (ii) the president of the institution makes a written finding as a matter of public record that the contract is in the best interests of the institution, (iii) the officer or employee either does not have authority to participate in the procurement or letting of the contract on behalf of the institution or disqualifies himself as a matter of public record, and (iv) does not participate on behalf of the institution in negotiating the contract or approving the contract;

6. Except when the governmental agency is the Virginia Retirement System, contracts between an officer's or employee's governmental agency and a public service corporation, financial institution, or company furnishing public utilities in which the officer or employee has a personal interest, provided the officer or employee disqualifies himself as a matter of public record and does not participate on behalf of his governmental agency in negotiating the contract or in approving the contract;

7. Contracts for the purchase of goods or services when the contract does not exceed $500;

8. Grants or other payment under any program wherein uniform rates for, or the amounts paid to, all qualified applicants are established solely by the administering governmental agency; or

9. An officer or employee whose sole personal interest in a contract with his own governmental agency is by reason of his marriage to his spouse who is employed by the same agency, if the spouse was employed by such agency for five or more years prior to marrying such officer or employee.

B. Neither the provisions of this chapter nor, unless expressly provided otherwise, any amendments thereto shall apply to those employment contracts or renewals thereof or to any other contracts entered into prior to August 1, 1987, which were in compliance with either the former Virginia Conflict of Interests Act, Chapter 22 (§ 2.1-347 et seq.) or the former Comprehensive Conflict of Interests Act, Chapter 40 (§ 2.1-599 et seq.) of Title 2.1 at the time of their formation and thereafter. Those contracts shall continue to be governed by the provisions of the appropriate prior Act. Notwithstanding the provisions of subdivision (f) (4) of § 2.1-348 of Title 2.1 in effect prior to July 1, 1983, the employment by the same governmental agency of an officer or employee and spouse or any other relative residing in the same household shall not be deemed to create a material financial interest except when one of such persons is employed in a direct supervisory or administrative position, or both, with respect to such spouse or other relative residing in his household and the annual salary of such subordinate is $35,000 or more.

History.
1987, Sp. Sess., c. 1, § 2.1-639.9; 1990, c. 51; 1993, c. 303; 1994, cc. 450, 713; 1997, c. 641; 2001, c. 844; 2006, c. 839; 2010, cc. 301, 304.

The 2010 amendments.
The 2010 amendment by c. 301, in subdivision A 5, inserted "or such ownership interest and income from the contracting firm is in excess of $10,000 per year," substituted "interest, or ownership and income" for "or other equity," and made minor stylistic changes.
The 2010 amendment by c. 304 substituted "$35,000" for "$22,500" near the end of subsection B.

Michie's Jurisprudence.
For related discussion, see 5A M.J. Counties, § 36.

ARTICLE 4.

PROHIBITED CONDUCT RELATING TO TRANSACTIONS.

§ 2.2-3111. Application.

This article proscribes certain conduct by state and local government officers and employees having a personal interest in a transaction.

History.
1987, Sp. Sess., c. 1, § 2.1-639.10; 2001, c. 844.

§ 2.2-3112. Prohibited conduct concerning personal interest in a transaction; exceptions.

A. Each officer and employee of any state or local governmental or advisory agency who has a personal interest in a transaction:

1. Shall disqualify himself from participating in the transaction if (i) the transaction has application solely to property or a business or governmental agency in which he has a personal interest or a business that has a parent-subsidiary or affiliated business entity relationship with the business in which he has a personal interest or (ii) he is unable to participate pursuant to subdivision 2, 3 or 4. Any disqualification under the provisions of this subdivision shall be recorded in the public records of the officer's or employee's governmental or advisory agency. The officer or employee shall disclose his personal interest as required by subsection E of § 2.2-3114 or subsection F of § 2.2-3115 and shall not vote or in any manner act on behalf of his agency in the transaction. The officer or employee shall be prohibited from (i) attending any portion of a closed meeting authorized by the Virginia Freedom of Information Act (§ 2.2-3700 et seq.) when the matter in which he has a personal interest is discussed and (ii) discussing the matter in which he has a personal interest with other governmental officers or employees at any time;

2. May participate in the transaction if he is a member of a business, profession, occupation, or group of three or more persons the members of which are affected by the transaction, and he complies with the declaration requirements of subsection F of § 2.2-3114 or subsection H of § 2.2-3115;

3. May participate in the transaction when a party to the transaction is a client of his firm if he does not personally represent or provide services to such client and he complies with the declaration requirements of subsection G of § 2.2-3114 or subsection I of § 2.2-3115; or

4. May participate in the transaction if it affects the public generally, even though his personal interest, as a member of the public, may also be affected by that transaction.

B. Disqualification under the provisions of this section shall not prevent any employee having a personal interest in a transaction in which his agency is involved from representing himself or a member of his immediate family in such transaction provided he does not receive compensation for such representation and provided he complies with the disqualification and relevant disclosure requirements of this chapter.

C. Notwithstanding any other provision of law, if disqualifications of officers or employees in accordance with this section leave less than the number required by law to act, the remaining member or members shall constitute a quorum for the conduct of business and have authority to act for the agency by majority vote, unless a unanimous vote of all members is required by law, in which case authority to act shall require a unanimous vote of remaining members. Notwithstanding any provisions of this chapter to the contrary, members of a local governing body whose sole interest in any proposed sale, contract of sale, exchange, lease or conveyance is by virtue of their employment by a business involved in a proposed sale, contract of sale, exchange, lease or conveyance, and where such member's or members' vote is essential to a constitutional majority required pursuant to Article VII, Section 9 of the Constitution of Virginia and § 15.2-2100, such member or members of the local governing body may vote and participate in the deliberations of the governing body concerning whether to approve, enter into or execute such sale, contract of sale, exchange, lease or conveyance. Official action taken under circumstances that violate this section may be rescinded by the agency on such terms as the interests of the agency and innocent third parties require.

D. The provisions of subsection A shall not prevent an officer or employee from participating in a transaction merely because such officer or employee is a party in a legal proceeding of a civil nature concerning such transaction.

E. The provisions of subsection A shall not prevent an employee from participating in a transaction regarding textbooks or other educational material for students at state institutions of higher education, when those textbooks or materials have been authored or otherwise created by the employee.

History.
1987, Sp. Sess., c. 1, § 2.1-639.11; 2001, c. 844; 2003, c. 694; 2007, c. 613; 2012, c. 429.

The 2012 amendments.

The 2012 amendment by c. 429 substituted "required by subsection E of § 2.2-3114 E or subsection F of § 2.2-3115 E and shall" for "required by § 2.2-3114 E or 2.2-3115 E and shall" in the third sentence of subdivision A 1, substituted "requirements of subsection F of § 2.2-3114 F or subsection H of § 2.2-3115 G" for "requirements of § 2.2-3114 F or § 2.2-3115 G" in subdivision A 2, and substituted "requirements of subsection G of § 2.2-3114 G or subsection I of § 2.2-3115 H; or" for "requirements of § 2.2-3114 G or § 2.2-3115 H; or" in subdivision A 3.

CASE NOTES

Applicability. — Since a majority of council members did not vote on the retailer's applications for rezoning and special use permits, the town council's vote, by less than a majority of council members, meant that a quorum had not voted on the applications, and, thus, the three council members vote to approve the applications was invalid; too, it did not matter that some of the missing council members had absented themselves pursuant to the State and Local Government Conflict of Interests Act (COIA), § 2.2-3100 et seq., since COIA did not apply the laws involving "Meetings of Governing Bodies" since those laws had nothing to do with conflicts of interests. Jakabcin v. Town of Front Royal, 271 Va. 660, 628 S.E.2d 319, 2006 Va. LEXIS 49 (2006).

Public servant's interest may not exceed that as member of public at large. — A public servant whose interest is "involved" in a transaction may participate in that transaction only when his interest is one limited to that which he shares in common with other members of the public at large. West v. Jones, 228 Va. 409, 323 S.E.2d 96 (1984) (decided under prior law).

OPINIONS OF THE ATTORNEY GENERAL

Member of town council may serve on county school board, subject to certain restrictions. — Members of town councils generally are precluded from serving on appointed school boards by § 22.1-30, but § 22.1-30 applies only to appointed school boards; however, members of both town councils and school boards are subject to restrictions imposed by the State and Local Government Conflict of Interests Act. See opinion of Attorney General to Mr. William A. Bell, Jr., Secretary, Isle of Wight County Electoral Board, 11-070, 2011 Va. AG LEXIS 41 (9/30/11).

Although simultaneous service is not precluded, the potential interaction between the two bodies requires that any person so serving remain alert to any possible contractual and transactional conflicts that may arise. See opinion of Attorney General to Mr. William A. Bell, Jr., Secretary, Isle of Wight County Electoral Board, 11-070, 2011 Va. AG LEXIS 41 (9/30/11).

Conflict of interest. — No conflict of interest precludes members of local governing bodies who also serve on community action boards from voting in budgetary matters of the local government when such items may affect the community action program funding. See opinion of Attorney General to The Honorable Roslyn C. Tyler, Member, House of Delegates, 12-022, 2012 Va. AG LEXIS 14 (3/30/12).

Chief Information Officer. — An individual may not serve simultaneously as the Secretary of Technology and the Chief Information Officer. See opinion of Attorney General to The Honorable Samuel A. Nixon, Jr., Member, House of Delegates, 09-053, 2009 Va. AG LEXIS 34 (8/14/09).

Authority to enter into contracts. — The General Assembly has authorized the Virginia Information Technologies Agency, rather than the Information Technology Investment Board, to enter into or modify contracts for the purchase of information technology goods and services. See opinion of Attorney General to The Honorable Samuel A. Nixon, Jr., Member, House of Delegates, 09-053, 2009 Va. AG LEXIS 34 (8/14/09).

Employee of local school division cannot serve on the school board, while employed by the school board. See opinion of Attorney General to The Honorable Dave Nutter, Member, House of Delegates, 10-048, 2010 Va. AG LEXIS 63 (9/10/10).

Employee of the Department of Health may operate consulting business specializing in radon testing, as long as the employee does so during nonworking hours in a manner that does not conflict with his responsibilities to the Commonwealth, and the business does not conflict with any Department of Health policies governing outside employment. See opinion of Attorney General to The Honorable Dave Nutter, Member, House of Delegates, 10-048, 2010 Va. AG LEXIS 63 (9/10/10).

ARTICLE 5.

DISCLOSURE STATEMENTS REQUIRED TO BE FILED.

§ 2.2-3113. Application.

This article requires disclosure of certain personal and financial interests by state and local government officers and employees.

History.
1987, Sp. Sess., c. 1, § 2.1-639.12; 2001, c. 844.

§ 2.2-3114. Disclosure by state officers and employees.

A. The Governor, Lieutenant Governor, Attorney General, Justices of the Supreme Court, judges of the Court of Appeals, judges of any circuit court, judges and substitute judges of any district court, members of the State Corporation Commission, members of the Virginia Workers' Compensation Commission, members of the Commonwealth Transportation Board, members of the Board of Trustees of the Virginia Retirement System, and members of the State Lottery Board and other persons occupying such offices or positions of trust or employment in state government, including members of the governing bodies of authorities, as may be designated by the Governor or, in the case of officers or employees of the legislative branch, by the Joint Rules Committee of the General Assembly, shall file, as a condition to assuming office or employment, a disclosure statement of their personal interests and such other information as is specified on the form set forth in § 2.2-3117 and thereafter shall file such a statement annually on or before January 15. When the filing deadline falls on a Saturday, Sunday, or legal holiday, the disclosure statement shall be filed on the next day that is not a Saturday, Sunday, or legal holiday.

B. Nonsalaried citizen members of all policy and supervisory boards, commissions and councils in the executive branch of state government, other than the Commonwealth Transportation Board, members of the Board of Trustees of the Virginia Retirement System, and the State Lottery Board, shall file, as a condition to assuming office, a disclosure form of their personal interests and such other information as is specified on the form set forth in § 2.2-3118 and thereafter shall file such form annually on or before January 15. When the filing deadline falls on a Saturday, Sunday, or legal holiday, the disclosure statement shall be filed on the next day that is not a Saturday, Sunday, or legal holiday. Nonsalaried citizen members of other boards, commissions and councils, including advisory boards and authorities, may be required to file a disclosure form if so designated by the Governor, in which case the form shall be that set forth in § 2.2-3118.

C. The disclosure forms required by subsections A and B shall be provided by the Secretary of the Commonwealth to each officer and employee so designated, including officers appointed by legislative authorities, not later than November 30 of each year. Disclosure forms shall be filed and maintained as public records for five years in the Office of the Secretary of the Commonwealth.

D. Candidates for the offices of Governor, Lieutenant Governor or Attorney General shall file a disclosure statement of their personal interests as required by § 24.2-502.

E. Any officer or employee of state government who has a personal interest in any transaction before the governmental or advisory agency of which he is an officer or employee and who is disqualified from participating in that transaction pursuant to subdivision A 1 of § 2.2-3112, or otherwise elects to disqualify himself, shall forthwith make disclosure of the existence of his interest, including the full name and address of the business and the address or parcel number for the real estate if the interest involves a business or real estate, and his disclosure shall also be reflected in the public records of the agency for five years in the office of the administrative head of the officer's or employee's governmental agency or advisory agency or, if the agency has a clerk, in the clerk's office.

F. An officer or employee of state government who is required to declare his interest pursuant to subdivision A 2 of § 2.2-3112, shall declare his interest by stating (i) the transaction involved, (ii) the nature of the officer's or employee's personal interest affected by the transaction, (iii) that he is a member of a business, profession, occupation, or group the members of which are affected by the transaction, and (iv) that he is able to participate in the transaction fairly, objectively, and in the public interest. The officer or employee shall either make his declaration orally to be recorded in written minutes for his agency or file a signed written declaration with the clerk or administrative head of his governmental or advisory agency, as appropriate, who shall, in either case, retain and make available for public inspection such declaration for a period of five years from the date of recording or receipt. If reasonable time is not available to comply with the provisions of this subsection prior to participation in the transaction, the officer or employee shall prepare and file the required declaration by the end of the next business day.

G. An officer or employee of state government who is required to declare his interest pursuant to subdivision A 3 of § 2.2-3112, shall declare his interest by stating (i) the transaction involved, (ii) that a party to the transaction is a client of his firm, (iii) that he does not personally represent or provide services to the client, and (iv) that he is able to participate in the

transaction fairly, objectively, and in the public interest. The officer or employee shall either make his declaration orally to be recorded in written minutes for his agency or file a signed written declaration with the clerk or administrative head of his governmental or advisory agency, as appropriate, who shall, in either case, retain and make available for public inspection such declaration for a period of five years from the date of recording or receipt. If reasonable time is not available to comply with the provisions of this subsection prior to participation in the transaction, the officer or employee shall prepare and file the required declaration by the end of the next business day.

History.
1987, Sp. Sess., c. 1, § 2.1-639.13; 1988, cc. 767, 849; 1992, c. 710; 1993, c. 303; 1997, c. 641; 2001, cc. 217, 844; 2003, c. 694; 2005, c. 169; 2006, c. 779.

Editor's note.
Acts 2001, c. 217 amended § 2.1-639.13, from which this section is derived. Pursuant to § 30-152, Acts 2001, c. 217 has been given effect in this section as set out above. The 2001 amendment by c. 217 inserted "including members of the governing bodies of authorities" in subsection A; inserted "and authorities" in subsection B, in the last sentence; substituted "subdivision A 1 of § 2.2-3112" for "§ 2.2-3112 A 1" in subsection E; and substituted "subdivision A 2 of § 2.2-3112" for "§ 2.2-3112 A 2" in subsection F.

§ 2.2-3114.1. Filings of statements of economic interests by General Assembly members.

The filing of a current statement of economic interests by a General Assembly member, member-elect, or candidate for the General Assembly pursuant to §§ 30-110 and 30-111 of the General Assembly Conflict of Interests Act (§ 30-100 et seq.) shall suffice for the purposes of this chapter (§ 2.2-3100 et seq.). The Secretary of the Commonwealth may obtain from the Clerk of the House of Delegates or the Senate, as appropriate, a copy of the statement of a General Assembly member who is appointed to a position for which a statement is required pursuant to § 2.2-3114. No General Assembly member, member-elect, or candidate shall be required to file a separate statement of economic interests for the purposes of § 2.2-3114.

History.
2002, c. 36.

§ 2.2-3115. Disclosure by local government officers and employees.

A. The members of every governing body and school board of each county and city and of towns with populations in excess of 3,500 shall file, as a condition to assuming office or employment, a disclosure statement of their personal interests and other information as is specified on the form set forth in § 2.2-3117 and thereafter shall file such a statement annually on or before January 15.

The members of the governing body of any authority established in any county or city, or part or combination thereof, and having the power to issue bonds or expend funds in excess of $10,000 in any fiscal year, shall file, as a condition to assuming office, a disclosure statement of their personal interests and other information as is specified on the form set forth in § 2.2-3118 and thereafter shall file such a statement annually on or before January 15, unless the governing body of the jurisdiction that appoints the members requires that the members file the form set forth in § 2.2-3117.

Persons occupying such positions of trust appointed by governing bodies and persons occupying such positions of employment with governing bodies as may be designated to file by ordinance of the governing body shall file, as a condition to assuming office or employment, a disclosure statement of their personal interests and other information as is specified on the form set forth in § 2.2-3117 and thereafter shall file such a statement annually on or before January 15.

Persons occupying such positions of trust appointed by school boards and persons occupying such positions of employment with school boards as may be designated to file by an adopted policy of the school board shall file, as a condition to assuming office or employment, a disclosure statement of their personal interests and other information as is specified on the form set forth in § 2.2-3117 and thereafter shall file such a statement annually on or before January 15.

B. Nonsalaried citizen members of local boards, commissions and councils as may be designated by the governing body shall file, as a condition to assuming office, a disclosure form of their personal interests and such other information as is specified on the form set forth in § 2.2-3118 and thereafter shall file such form annually on or before January 15.

C. No person shall be mandated to file any disclosure not otherwise required by this article.

D. The disclosure forms required by subsections A and B shall be provided by the Secretary of the Commonwealth to the clerks of the governing bodies and school boards not later than November 30 of each year, and the clerks of the governing body and school board shall distribute the forms to designated individuals no later than December 10 of each year. Forms shall be filed and maintained as public records for five years in the office of the clerk of the respective governing body or school board. Forms filed by members of governing bodies of authorities shall be filed and maintained as public records for five years in the office of the clerk of the governing body of the county or city.

E. Candidates for membership in the governing body or school board of any county, city or town with a population of more than 3,500 persons shall file a disclosure statement of their personal interests as required by § 24.2-502.

F. Any officer or employee of local government who has a personal interest in any transaction before the governmental or advisory agency of which he is an officer or employee and who is disqualified from participating in that transaction pursuant to subdivision A 1 of § 2.2-3112 or otherwise elects to disqualify himself, shall forthwith make disclosure of the existence of his interest, including the full name and address of the business and the address or parcel number for the real estate if the interest involves a business or real estate, and his disclosure shall be reflected in the public records of the agency for five years in the office of the administrative head of the officer's or employee's governmental or advisory agency.

G. In addition to any disclosure required by subsections A and B, in each county and city and in towns with populations in excess of 3,500, members of planning commissions, boards of zoning appeals, real estate assessors, and all county, city and town managers or executive officers shall make annual disclosures of all their interests in real estate located in the county, city or town in which they are elected, appointed, or employed. Such disclosure shall include any business in which such persons own an interest, or from which income is received, if the primary purpose of the business is to own, develop or derive compensation through the sale, exchange or development of real estate in the county, city or town. Such disclosure shall be filed as a condition to assuming office or employment, and thereafter shall be filed annually with the clerk of the governing body of such county, city or town on or before January 15. Such disclosures shall be filed and maintained as public records for five years. Forms for the filing of such reports shall be prepared and distributed by the Secretary of the Commonwealth to the clerk of each governing body.

H. An officer or employee of local government who is required to declare his interest pursuant to subdivision A 2 of § 2.2-3112 shall declare his interest by stating (i) the transaction involved, (ii) the nature of the officer's or employee's personal interest affected by the transaction, (iii) that he is a member of a business, profession, occupation, or group the members of which are affected by the transaction, and (iv) that he is able to participate in the transaction fairly, objectively, and in the public interest. The officer or employee shall either make his declaration orally to be recorded in written minutes of his agency or file a signed written declaration with the clerk or administrative head of his governmental or advisory agency, as appropriate, who shall, in either case, retain and make available for public inspection such declaration for a period of five years from the date of recording or receipt. If reasonable time is not available to comply with the provisions of this subsection prior to participation in the transaction, the officer or employee shall prepare and file the required declaration by the end of the next business day. The officer or employee shall also orally disclose the existence of the interest during each meeting of the governmental or advisory agency at which the transaction is discussed and such disclosure shall be recorded in the minutes of the meeting.

I. An officer or employee of local government who is required to declare his interest pursuant to subdivision A 3 of § 2.2-3112, shall declare his interest by stating (i) the transaction involved, (ii) that a party to the transaction is a client of his firm, (iii) that he does not personally represent or provide services to the client, and (iv) that he is able to participate in the transaction fairly, objectively, and in the public interest. The officer or employee shall either make his declaration orally to be recorded in written minutes for his agency or file a signed written declaration with the clerk or administrative head of his governmental or advisory agency, as appropriate, who shall, in either case, retain and make available for public inspection such declaration for a period of five years from the date of recording or receipt. If reasonable time is not available to comply with the provisions of this subsection prior to participation in the transaction, the officer or employee shall prepare and file the required declaration by the end of the next business day.

History.
1987, Sp. Sess., c. 1, § 2.1-639.14; 1988, c. 849; 1995, c. 495; 1996, c. 526; 2000, c. 317; 2001, cc. 217, 844; 2003, c. 694; 2012, c. 429.

Editor's note.
Acts 2001, c. 217 amended § 2.1-639.14, from which this section is derived. Pursuant to § 30-152, Acts 2001, c. 217 has been given

effect in this section as set out above. The 2001 amendment by c. 217 added the second paragraph in subsection A; added the last sentence in subsection C; substituted "subdivision A 1 of § 2.2-3112" for "§ 2.2-3112 A 1" in subsection E; and substituted "subdivision A 2 of § 2.2-3112" for "§ 2.2-3112 A 2" in subsection G.

The 2012 amendments.
The 2012 amendment by c. 429 added subsection C and redesignated the following subsections accordingly.

§ 2.2-3116. Disclosure by certain constitutional officers.

For the purposes of this chapter, holders of the constitutional offices of treasurer, sheriff, attorney for the Commonwealth, clerk of the circuit court and commissioner of the revenue of each county and city, shall be deemed to be local officers and shall be required to file the Statement of Economic Interests set forth in § 2.2-3117. These officers shall file statements pursuant to § 2.2-3115 and candidates shall file statements as required by § 24.2-502.

History.
1988, c. 469, § 2.1-639.14:1; 2001, c. 844.

§ 2.2-3117. Disclosure form.

The disclosure form to be used for filings required by subsections A and D of § 2.2-3114 and subsections A and E of § 2.2-3115 shall be substantially as follows:

STATEMENT OF ECONOMIC INTERESTS.

Name ....
Office or position held or sought ....
Address ....
Names of members of immediate family ....

DEFINITIONS AND EXPLANATORY MATERIAL.

"Business" means a corporation, partnership, sole proprietorship, firm, enterprise, franchise, association, trust or foundation, or any other individual or entity carrying on a business or profession, whether or not for profit.

"Close financial association" means an association in which the person filing shares significant financial involvement with an individual and the filer would reasonably be expected to be aware of the individual's business activities and would have access to the necessary records either directly or through the individual. "Close financial association" does not mean an association based on (i) the receipt of retirement benefits or deferred compensation from a business by which the person filing this statement is no longer employed, or (ii) the receipt of compensation for work performed by the person filing as an independent contractor of a business that represents an entity before any state governmental agency when the person filing has had no communications with the state governmental agency.

"Contingent liability" means a liability that is not presently fixed or determined, but may become fixed or determined in the future with the occurrence of some certain event.

"Dependent" means any person, whether or not related by blood or marriage, who receives from the officer or employee, or provides to the officer or employee, more than one-half of his financial support.

"Gift" means any gratuity, favor, discount, entertainment, hospitality, loan, forbearance, or other item having monetary value. It includes services as well as gifts of transportation, local travel, lodgings and meals, whether provided in-kind, by purchase of a ticket, payment in advance or reimbursement after the expense has been incurred. "Gift" shall not include any offer of a ticket or other admission or pass unless the ticket, admission, or pass is used. "Gift" shall not include honorary degrees and presents from relatives. "Relative" means the donee's spouse, child, uncle, aunt, niece, or nephew; a person to whom the donee is engaged to be

married; the donee's or his spouse's parent, grandparent, grandchild, brother, or sister; or the donee's brother's or sister's spouse.

"Immediate family" means (i) a spouse and (ii) any other person residing in the same household as the officer or employee, who is a dependent of the officer or employee or of whom the officer or employee is a dependent.

TRUST. If you or your immediate family, separately or together, are the only beneficiaries of a trust, treat the trust's assets as if you own them directly. If you or your immediate family has a proportional interest in a trust, treat that proportion of the trust's assets as if you own them directly. For example, if you and your immediate family have a one-third interest in a trust, complete your Statement as if you own one-third of each of the trust's assets. If you or a member of your immediate family created a trust and can revoke it without the beneficiaries' consent, treat its assets as if you own them directly.

REPORT TO THE BEST OF INFORMATION AND BELIEF. Information required on this Statement must be provided on the basis of the best knowledge, information and belief of the individual filing the Statement as of the date of this report unless otherwise stated.

COMPLETE ITEMS 1 THROUGH 10. REFER TO SCHEDULES ONLY IF DIRECTED.

You may attach additional explanatory information.

1. Offices and Directorships.
   Are you or a member of your immediate family a paid officer or paid director of a business?
   EITHER check NO / / OR check YES / / and complete Schedule A.
2. Personal Liabilities.
   Do you or a member of your immediate family owe more than $10,000 to any one creditor including contingent liabilities? (Exclude debts to any government and loans secured by recorded liens on property at least equal in value to the loan.)
   EITHER check NO / / OR check YES / / and complete Schedule B.
3. Securities.
   Do you or a member of your immediate family, directly or indirectly, separately or together, own securities valued in excess of $10,000 invested in one business? Account for mutual funds, limited partnerships and trusts.
   EITHER check NO / / OR check YES / / and complete Schedule C.
4. Payments for Talks, Meetings, and Publications.
   During the past 12 months did you receive lodging, transportation, money, or anything else of value with a combined value exceeding $200 for a single talk, meeting, or published work in your capacity as an officer or employee of your agency?
   EITHER check NO / / OR check YES / / and complete Schedule D.
5. Gifts.
   During the past 12 months did a business, government, or individual other than a relative or personal friend (i) furnish you with any gift or entertainment at a single event, and the value received by you exceeded $50 in value or (ii) furnish you with gifts or entertainment in any combination and the value received by you exceeded $100 in total value; and for which you neither paid nor rendered services in exchange? Account for entertainment events only if the average value per person attending the event exceeded $50 in value. Account for all business entertainment (except if related to your private profession or occupation) even if unrelated to your official duties.
   EITHER check NO / / OR check YES / / and complete Schedule E.
6. Salary and Wages.
   List each employer that pays you or a member of your immediate family salary or wages in excess of $10,000 annually. (Exclude state or local government or advisory agencies.)
   If no reportable salary or wages, check here / /.
   ....
   ....
   ....
7. Business Interests.
   Do you or a member of your immediate family, separately or together, operate your own business, or own or control an interest in excess of $10,000 in a business?
   EITHER check NO / / OR check YES / / and complete Schedule F.
8. Payments for Representation and Other Services.
8A. Did you represent, excluding activity defined as lobbying in § 2.2-419, any businesses before any state governmental agencies, excluding courts or judges, for which you received total compensation during the past 12 months in excess of $1,000, excluding compensation for other services to such businesses and representation consisting solely of the filing of mandatory papers and subsequent representation

regarding the mandatory papers? (Officers and employees of local governmental and advisory agencies do NOT need to answer this question or complete Schedule G-1.)
EITHER check NO / / OR check YES / / and complete Schedule G-1.

8B. Subject to the same exceptions as in 8A, did persons with whom you have a close financial association (partners, associates or others) represent, excluding activity defined as lobbying in § 2.2-419, any businesses before any state governmental agency for which total compensation was received during the past 12 months in excess of $1,000? (Officers and employees of local governmental and advisory agencies do NOT need to answer this question or complete Schedule G-2.)
EITHER check NO / / OR check YES / / and complete Schedule G-2.

8C. Did you or persons with whom you have a close financial association furnish services to businesses operating in Virginia pursuant to an agreement between you and such businesses, or between persons with whom you have a close financial association and such businesses for which total compensation in excess of $1,000 was received during the past 12 months?
EITHER check NO / / OR check YES / / and complete Schedule G-3.

9. Real Estate.

9A. State Officers and Employees.
Do you or a member of your immediate family hold an interest, including a partnership interest, valued at $10,000 or more in real property (other than your principal residence) for which you have not already listed the full address on Schedule F? Account for real estate held in trust.
EITHER check NO / / OR check YES / / and complete Schedule H-1.

9B. Local Officers and Employees.
Do you or a member of your immediate family hold an interest, including a partnership interest, or option, easement, or land contract, valued at $10,000 or more in real property (other than your principal residence) for which you have not already listed the full address on Schedule F? Account for real estate held in trust.
EITHER check NO / / OR check YES / / and complete Schedule H-2.

10. Real Estate Contracts with Governmental Agencies.
Do you or a member of your immediate family hold an interest valued at more than $10,000 in real estate, including a corporate, partnership, or trust interest, option, easement, or land contract, which real estate is the subject of a contract, whether pending or completed within the past 12 months, with a governmental agency? If the real estate contract provides for the leasing of the property to a governmental agency, do you or a member of your immediate family hold an interest in the real estate valued at more than $1,000? Account for all such contracts whether or not your interest is reported in Schedule F, H-1, or H-2. This requirement to disclose an interest in a lease does not apply to an interest derived through an ownership interest in a business unless the ownership interest exceeds three percent of the total equity of the business.
EITHER check NO / / OR check YES / / and complete Schedule I.
Statements of Economic Interests are open for public inspection.

AFFIRMATION BY ALL FILERS.

I swear or affirm that the foregoing information is full, true and correct to the best of my knowledge.

Signature ....
(Return only if needed to complete Statement.)

SCHEDULES
to
STATEMENT OF ECONOMIC INTERESTS.

NAME ....

SCHEDULE A — OFFICES AND DIRECTORSHIPS.

Identify each business of which you or a member of your immediate family is a paid officer or paid director.

Name of Business	Address of Business	Position Held
_____	_____	_____
_____	_____	_____
_____	_____	_____

RETURN TO ITEM 2

SCHEDULE B — PERSONAL LIABILITIES.

Report personal liability by checking each category. Report only debts in excess of $10,000. Do not report debts to any government. Do not report loans secured by recorded liens on property at least equal in value to the loan.

Report contingent liabilities below and indicate which debts are contingent.

1. My personal debts are as follows:

Check appropriate categories	$10,001 to $50,000	Check one More than $50,000
Banks	_____	_____
Savings institutions	_____	_____
Other loan or finance companies	_____	_____
Insurance companies	_____	_____
Stock, commodity or other brokerage companies	_____	_____
Other businesses: (State principal business activity for each creditor.)		
_____	_____	_____
_____	_____	_____
Individual creditors: (State principal business or occupation of each creditor.)		
_____	_____	_____
_____	_____	_____

2. The personal debts of the members of my immediate family are as follows:

Check appropriate categories	$10,001 to $50,000	Check one More than $50,000
Banks	_____	_____
Savings institutions	_____	_____
Other loan or finance companies	_____	_____
Insurance companies	_____	_____
Stock, commodity or other brokerage companies	_____	_____
Other businesses: (State principal business activity for each creditor.)		
_____	_____	_____
_____	_____	_____
Individual creditors: (State principal business or		

occupation of each creditor.)

_____   _____   _____
_____   _____   _____
_____   _____   _____

RETURN TO ITEM 3

SCHEDULE C — SECURITIES.

"Securities" INCLUDES stocks, bonds, mutual funds, limited partnerships, and commodity futures contracts.

"Securities" EXCLUDES certificates of deposit, money market funds, annuity contracts, and insurance policies.

Identify each business or Virginia governmental entity in which you or a member of your immediate family, directly or indirectly, separately or together, own securities valued in excess of $10,000. Name each entity and type of security individually.

Do not list U.S. Bonds or other government securities not issued by the Commonwealth of Virginia or its authorities, agencies, or local governments. Do not list organizations that do not do business in this Commonwealth, but most major businesses conduct business in Virginia. Account for securities held in trust.

If no reportable securities, check here / / .

Name of Issuer	Type of Entity	Type of Security (stocks, bonds, mutual funds, etc.)	$10,001 to $50,000	Check one More than $50,000
_____	_____	_____	_____	_____
_____	_____	_____	_____	_____
_____	_____	_____	_____	_____

RETURN TO ITEM 4

SCHEDULE D — PAYMENTS FOR TALKS, MEETINGS, AND PUBLICATIONS.

List each source from which you received during the past 12 months lodging, transportation, money, or any other thing of value (excluding meals or drinks coincident with a meeting) with combined value exceeding $200 for your presentation of a single talk, participation in one meeting, or publication of a work in your capacity as an officer or employee of your agency.

List payments or reimbursements by an advisory or governmental agency only for meetings or travel outside the Commonwealth.

List a payment even if you donated it to charity.

Do not list information about a payment if you returned it within 60 days or if you received it from an employer already listed under Item 6 or from a source of income listed on Schedule F.

If no payment must be listed, check here / / .

Payer	Approximate Value	Circumstances	Type of payment (e.g. Honoraria, travel reimbursement, etc.)
_____	_____	_____	_____
_____	_____	_____	_____
_____	_____	_____	_____

RETURN TO ITEM 5

SCHEDULE E — GIFTS.

List each business, governmental entity, or individual that, during the past 12 months, (i) furnished you with any gift or entertainment at a single event and the value received by you exceeded $50 in value, or

(ii) furnished you with gifts or entertainment in any combination and the value received by you exceeded $100 in total value; and for which you neither paid nor rendered services in exchange. List each such gift or event. Do not list entertainment events unless the average value per person attending the event exceeded $50 in value. Do not list business entertainment related to your private profession or occupation. Do not list gifts or other things of value given by a relative or personal friend for reasons clearly unrelated to your public position. Do not list campaign contributions publicly reported as required by Chapter 9.3 (§ 24.2-945 et seq.) of Title 24.2 of the Code of Virginia.

Name of Business, Organization, or Individual	City or County and State	Gift or Event	Approximate Value
_____	_____	_____	_____
_____	_____	_____	_____
_____	_____	_____	_____
_____	_____	_____	_____

RETURN TO ITEM 6

SCHEDULE F — BUSINESS INTERESTS.

Complete this Schedule for each self-owned or family-owned business (including rental property, a farm, or consulting work), partnership, or corporation in which you or a member of your immediate family, separately or together, own an interest having a value in excess of $10,000.

If the enterprise is owned or operated under a trade, partnership, or corporate name, list that name; otherwise, merely explain the nature of the enterprise. If rental property is owned or operated under a trade, partnership, or corporate name, list the name only; otherwise, give the address of each property. Account for business interests held in trust.

Name of Business, Corporation, Partnership, Farm; Address of Rental Property	City or County and State	Nature of Enterprise (farming, law, rental property, etc.)	Gross Income		
			$50,000 or less	$50,001 to $250,000	More than $250,000
_____	_____	_____	_____	_____	_____
_____	_____	_____	_____	_____	_____
_____	_____	_____	_____	_____	_____

RETURN TO ITEM 8

SCHEDULE G-1 — PAYMENTS FOR REPRESENTATION BY YOU.

List the businesses you represented, excluding activity defined as lobbying in § 2.2-419, before any state governmental agency, excluding any court or judge, for which you received total compensation during the past 12 months in excess of $1,000, excluding compensation for other services to such businesses and representation consisting solely of the filing of mandatory papers and subsequent representation regarding the mandatory papers filed by you.

Identify each business, the nature of the representation and the amount received by dollar category from each such business. You may state the type, rather than name, of the business if you are required by law not to reveal the name of the business represented by you.

Only STATE officers and employees should complete this Schedule.

				Amount Received				
Name of Business	Type of Business	Purpose of Representation	Name of Agency	$1,001 to $10,000	$10,001 to $50,000	$50,001 to $100,000	$100,001 to $250,000	$250,001 and over
___	___	___	___	___	___	___	___	___
___	___	___	___	___	___	___	___	___
___	___	___	___	___	___	___	___	___
___	___	___	___	___	___	___	___	___

If you have received $250,001 or more from a single business within the reporting period, indicate the amount received, rounded to the nearest $10,000.

Amount Received:_____.

SCHEDULE G-2 — PAYMENTS FOR REPRESENTATION BY ASSOCIATES.

List the businesses that have been represented, excluding activity defined as lobbying in § 2.2-419, before any state governmental agency, excluding any court or judge, by persons who are your partners, associates or others with whom you have a close financial association and who received total compensation in excess of $1,000 for such representation during the past 12 months, excluding representation consisting solely of the filing of mandatory papers and subsequent representation regarding the mandatory papers filed by your partners, associates or others with whom you have a close financial association.

Identify such businesses by type and also name the state governmental agencies before which such person appeared on behalf of such businesses.

Only STATE officers and employees should complete this Schedule.

Type of business	Name of state governmental agency
___	___
___	___
___	___
___	___

SCHEDULE G-3 — PAYMENTS FOR SERVICES GENERALLY.

Indicate below types of businesses that operate in Virginia to which services were furnished by you or persons with whom you have a close financial association pursuant to an agreement between you and such businesses, or between persons with whom you have a close financial association and such businesses and for which total compensation in excess of $1,000 was received during the past 12 months. Identify opposite each category of businesses listed below (i) the type of business, (ii) the type of service rendered and (iii) the value by dollar category of the compensation received for all businesses falling within each category.

	Check if services were rendered	Type of service rendered	Value of Compensation				
			$1,001 to $10,000	$10,001 to $50,000	$50,001 to $100,000	$100,001 to $250,000	$250,001 and over
Electric utilities	___	___	___	___	___	___	___
Gas utilities	___	___	___	___	___	___	___
Telephone utilities	___	___	___	___	___	___	___
Water utilities	___	___	___	___	___	___	___
Cable television companies	___	___	___	___	___	___	___
Interstate transportation companies	___	___	___	___	___	___	___

	Check if services were rendered	Type of service rendered	Value of Compensation				
			$1,001 to $10,000	$10,001 to $50,000	$50,001 to $100,000	$100,001 to $250,000	$250,001 and over
Intrastate transportation companies	___	___	___	___	___	___	___
Oil or gas retail companies	___	___	___	___	___	___	___
Banks	___	___	___	___	___	___	___
Savings institutions	___	___	___	___	___	___	___
Loan or finance companies	___	___	___	___	___	___	___
Manufacturing companies (state type of product, e.g., textile, furniture, etc.)	___	___	___	___	___	___	___
Mining companies	___	___	___	___	___	___	___
Life insurance companies	___	___	___	___	___	___	___
Casualty insurance companies	___	___	___	___	___	___	___
Other insurance companies	___	___	___	___	___	___	___
Retail companies	___	___	___	___	___	___	___
Beer, wine or liquor companies or distributors	___	___	___	___	___	___	___
Trade associations	___	___	___	___	___	___	___
Professional associations	___	___	___	___	___	___	___
Associations of public employees or officials	___	___	___	___	___	___	___
Counties, cities or towns	___	___	___	___	___	___	___
Labor organizations	___	___	___	___	___	___	___
Other	___	___	___	___	___	___	___

RETURN TO ITEM 9

SCHEDULE H-1 — REAL ESTATE — STATE OFFICERS AND EMPLOYEES.

List real estate other than your principal residence in which you or a member of your immediate family holds an interest, including a partnership interest, option, easement, or land contract, valued at $10,000 or more. Each parcel shall be listed individually.

List each location (state, and county or city) where you own real estate.	Describe the type of real estate you own in each location (business, recreational, apartment, commercial, open land, etc.).	If the real estate is owned or recorded in a name other than your own, list that name.
___	___	___
___	___	___
___	___	___

SCHEDULE H-2 — REAL ESTATE — LOCAL OFFICERS AND EMPLOYEES.

List real estate other than your principal residence in which you or a member of your immediate family holds an interest, including a partnership interest or option, easement, or land contract, valued at $10,000 or more. Each parcel shall be listed individually. Also list the names of any co-owners of such property, if applicable.

List each location (state, and county or city) where you own real estate.	Describe the type of real estate you own in each location (business, recreational, apartment, commercial, open land, etc.).	If the real estate is owned or recorded in a name other than your own, list that name.	List the names of any co-owners, if applicable.
_____	_____	_____	_____
_____	_____	_____	_____
_____	_____	_____	_____
_____	_____	_____	_____

SCHEDULE I — REAL ESTATE CONTRACTS WITH GOVERNMENTAL AGENCIES.

List all contracts, whether pending or completed within the past 12 months, with a governmental agency for the sale or exchange of real estate in which you or a member of your immediate family holds an interest, including a corporate, partnership or trust interest, option, easement, or land contract, valued at $10,000 or more. List all contracts with a governmental agency for the lease of real estate in which you or a member of your immediate family holds such an interest valued at $1,000 or more. This requirement to disclose an interest in a lease does not apply to an interest derived through an ownership interest in a business unless the ownership interest exceeds three percent of the total equity of the business.
State officers and employees report contracts with state agencies.
Local officers and employees report contracts with local agencies.

List your real estate interest and the person or entity, including the type of entity, which is party to the contract. Describe any management role and the percentage ownership interest you or your immediate family member has in the real estate or entity.	List each governmental agency which is a party to the contract and indicate the county or city where the real estate is located.	State the annual income from the contract, and the amount, if any, of income you or any immediate family member derives annually from the contract.
_____	_____	_____
_____	_____	_____
_____	_____	_____
_____	_____	_____

History.
1987, Sp. Sess., c. 1, § 2.1-639.15; 1988, c. 849; 1994, cc. 724, 733, 777, 793; 1995, c. 763; 1996, c. 77; 1997, cc. 577, 844; 1998, c. 732; 2001, c. 844; 2006, cc. 310, 779, 787, 892; 2008, c. 239; 2010, c. 670; 2012, c. 429.

The 2010 amendments.
The 2010 amendment by c. 670 substituted "Each parcel shall be listed individually." for "You may list each parcel of real estate individually if you wish." in Schedule H-1 and Schedule H-2.

The 2012 amendments.
The 2012 amendment by c. 429 deleted the language following subdivision 10 which required acknowledgement of signature by notary public.

§ 2.2-3118. Disclosure form; certain citizen members.

A. The financial disclosure form to be used for filings required pursuant to subsection B of § 2.2-3114 and subsection B of § 2.2-3115 shall be signed by the filer either originally or by electronic signature as authorized by the Uniform Electronic Transactions Act (§ 59.1-479 et seq.). The financial disclosure form shall be substantially as follows:

DEFINITIONS AND EXPLANATORY MATERIAL.

"Business" means a corporation, partnership, sole proprietorship, firm, enterprise, franchise, association, trust or foundation, or any other individual or entity carrying on a business or profession, whether or not for profit.

"Close financial association" means an association in which the person filing shares significant financial involvement with an individual and the filer would reasonably be expected to be aware of the individual's business activities and would have access to the necessary records either directly or through the individual. "Close financial association" does not mean an association based on (i) the receipt of retirement benefits or deferred compensation from a business by which the person filing this statement is no longer employed, or (ii) the receipt of compensation for work performed by the person filing as an independent contractor of a business that represents an entity before any state governmental agency when the person filing has no communications with the state governmental agency.

"Contingent liability" means a liability that is not presently fixed or determined, but may become fixed or determined in the future with the occurrence of some certain event.

"Immediate family" means (i) a spouse and (ii) any other person residing in the same household as the filer, who is a dependent of the filer or of whom the filer is a dependent.

"Dependent" means any person, whether or not related by blood or marriage, who receives from the filer, or provides to the filer, more than one-half of his financial support.

"Personal interest" means, for the purposes of this form only, a personal and financial benefit or liability accruing to a filer or a member of his immediate family. Such interest shall exist by reason of (i) ownership in real or personal property, tangible or intangible; (ii) ownership in a business; (iii) income from a business; or (iv) personal liability on behalf of a business; however, unless the ownership interest in a business exceeds three percent of the total equity of the business, or the liability on behalf of a business exceeds three percent of the total assets of the business, or the annual income, and/or property or use of such property, from the business exceeds $10,000 or may reasonably be anticipated to exceed $10,000, such interest shall not constitute a "personal interest."

Name ....
Office or position held or to be held
....
Address ....

I. FINANCIAL INTERESTS

My personal interests and those of my immediate family are as follows:

Include all forms of personal interests held at the time of filing: real estate, stocks, bonds, equity interests in proprietorships and partnerships. You may exclude:

1. Deposits and interest bearing accounts in banks, savings institutions and other institutions accepting such deposits or accounts;

2. Interests in any business, other than a news medium, representing less than three percent of the total equity value of the business;

3. Liability on behalf of any business representing less than three percent of the total assets of such business; and

4. Income (other than from salary) less than $10,000 annually from any business. You need not state the value of any interest. You must state the name or principal business activity of each business in which you have a personal interest.

A. My personal interests are:
1. Residence, address, or, if no address, location ....
2. Other real estate, address, or, if no address, location ....
3. Name or principal business activity of each business in which stock, bond or equity interest is held . .

B. The personal interests of my immediate family are:
1. Real estate, address or, if no address, location ....
2. Name or principal business activity of each business in which stock, bond or equity interest is held . .

II. OFFICES, DIRECTORSHIPS AND SALARIED EMPLOYMENTS

The paid offices, paid directorships and salaried employments which I hold or which members of my immediate family hold and the businesses from which I or members of my immediate family receive retirement benefits are as follows:

(You need not state any dollar amounts.)

A. My paid offices, paid directorships and salaried employments are:

Position held	Name of business

B. The paid offices, paid directorships and salaried employments of members of my immediate family are:

Position held	Name of business

III. BUSINESSES TO WHICH SERVICES WERE FURNISHED

A. The businesses I have represented, excluding activity defined as lobbying in § 2.2-419, before any state governmental agency, excluding any court or judge, for which I have received total compensation in excess of $1,000 during the preceding year, excluding compensation for other services to such businesses and representation consisting solely of the filing of mandatory papers, are as follows:

Identify businesses by name and name the state governmental agencies before which you appeared on behalf of such businesses.

Name of business	Name of governmental agency

B. The businesses that, to my knowledge, have been represented, excluding activity defined as lobbying in § 2.2-419, before any state governmental agency, excluding any court or judge, by persons with whom I have a close financial association and who received total compensation in excess of $1,000 during the preceding year, excluding compensation for other services to such businesses and representation consisting solely of the filing of mandatory papers, are as follows:

Identify businesses by type and name the state governmental agencies before which such person appeared on behalf of such businesses.

Type of business	Name of state governmental agency

C. All other businesses listed below that operate in Virginia to which services were furnished pursuant to an agreement between you and such businesses and for which total compensation in excess of $1, 000 was received during the preceding year:

Check each category of business to which services were furnished.

Electric utilities	_____
Gas utilities	_____
Telephone utilities	_____
Water utilities	_____
Cable television companies	_____
Intrastate transportation companies	_____
Interstate transportation companies	_____
Oil or gas retail companies	_____

Banks _____
Savings institutions _____
Loan or finance companies _____
Manufacturing companies (state type of product, e.g., textile, furniture, etc.) _____
Mining companies _____
Life insurance companies _____
Casualty insurance companies _____
Other insurance companies _____
Retail companies _____
Beer, wine or liquor companies or distributors _____
Trade associations _____
Professional associations _____
Associations of public employees or officials _____
Counties, cities or towns _____
Labor organizations _____

IV. COMPENSATION FOR EXPENSES

The persons, associations, or other sources other than my governmental agency from which I or a member of my immediate family received remuneration in excess of $200 during the preceding year, in cash or otherwise, as honorariums or payment of expenses in connection with my attendance at any meeting or other function to which I was invited in my official capacity are as follows:

Name of source	Description of occasion	Amount of remuneration for each occasion
_____	_____	_____
_____	_____	_____

B. The provisions of Part III A and B of the disclosure form prescribed by this section shall not be applicable to officers and employees of local governmental and local advisory agencies.

C. Except for real estate located within the county, city or town in which the officer or employee serves or a county, city or town contiguous to the county, city or town in which the officer or employee serves, officers and employees of local governmental or advisory agencies shall not be required to disclose under Part I of the form any other interests in real estate.

History.
1988, c. 849, § 2.1-639.15:1; 1996, c. 77; 2001, c. 844; 2006, c. 779; 2011, cc. 123, 177.

The 2011 amendments.
The 2011 amendments by cc. 123 and 177 are identical, and in the introductory language in subsection A, inserted "signed by the filer either originally or by electronic signature as authorized by the Uniform Electronic Transactions Act (§ 59.1-479 et seq.)" and made a minor stylistic change.

§ 2.2-3118.1. Special provisions for individuals serving in or seeking multiple positions or offices; reappointees.

A. The filing of a single current statement of economic interests by a state officer or employee required to file the form prescribed in § 2.2-3117 shall suffice for the purposes of this chapter as filing for all state positions or offices held or sought by such individual during a single reporting period. The filing of a single current financial disclosure statement by a state officer or employee required to file the form prescribed in § 2.2-3118 shall suffice for the purposes of this chapter as filing for all state positions or offices held or sought by such individual and requiring the filing of the § 2.2-3118 form during a single reporting period.

B. Any individual who has met the requirement for annually filing a statement provided in § 2.2-3117 or 2.2-3118 shall not be required to file an additional statement upon such individual's reappointment to the same office or position for which he is required to file, provided such reappointment occurs within 12 months after the annual filing.

History.
2005, c. 397.

ARTICLE 6.

SCHOOL BOARDS AND EMPLOYEES OF SCHOOL BOARDS.

§ 2.2-3119. Additional provisions applicable to school boards and employees of school boards; exceptions.

A. Notwithstanding any other provision of this chapter, it shall be unlawful for the school board of any county or city or of any town constituting a separate school division to employ or pay any teacher or other school board employee from the public funds, federal, state or local, or for a division superintendent to recommend to the school board the employment of any teacher or other employee, if the teacher or other employee is the father, mother, brother, sister, spouse, son, daughter, son-in-law, daughter-in-law, sister-in-law or brother-in-law of the superintendent, or of any member of the school board.

This section shall apply to any person employed by any school board in the operation of the public free school system, adult education programs or any other program maintained and operated by a local county, city or town school board.

B. This section shall not be construed to prohibit the employment, promotion, or transfer within a school division of any person within a relationship described in subsection A when such person:

1. Has been employed pursuant to a written contract with a school board or employed as a substitute teacher or teacher's aide by a school board prior to the taking of office of any member of such board or division superintendent of schools; or

2. Has been employed pursuant to a written contract with a school board or employed as a substitute teacher or teacher's aide by a school board prior to the inception of such relationship; or

3. Was employed by a school board at any time prior to June 10, 1994, and had been employed at any time as a teacher or other employee of any Virginia school board prior to the taking of office of any member of such school board or division superintendent of schools.

C. A person employed as a substitute teacher may not be employed to any greater extent than he was employed by the school board in the last full school year prior to the taking of office of such board member or division superintendent or to the inception of such relationship. The exceptions in subdivisions B 1, B 2, and B 3 shall apply only if the prior employment has been in the same school divisions where the employee and the superintendent or school board member now seek to serve simultaneously.

D. If any member of the school board or any division superintendent knowingly violates these provisions, he shall be personally liable to refund to the local treasury any amounts paid in violation of this law, and the funds shall be recovered from the individual by action or suit in the name of the Commonwealth on the petition of the attorney for the Commonwealth. Recovered funds shall be paid into the local treasury for the use of the public schools.

E. The provisions of this section shall not apply to employment by a school district located in Planning Districts 3, 11, 12, and 13 of the father, mother, brother, sister, spouse, son, daughter, son-in-law, daughter-in-law, sister-in-law, or brother-in-law of any member of the school board provided (i) the member certifies that he had no involvement with the hiring decision and (ii) the superintendent certifies to the remaining members of the governing body in writing that the employment is based upon merit and fitness and the competitive rating of the qualifications of the individual and that no member of the board had any involvement with the hiring decision.

History.

1987, Sp. Sess., c. 1, § 2.1-639.16; 1994, c. 758; 1995, c. 186; 1997, c. 84; 2001, c. 844; 2010, cc. 676, 759; 2011, c. 517.

The 2010 amendments.

The 2010 amendments by cc. 676 and 759 are identical, and added subsection E, and made a minor stylistic change.

The 2011 amendments.

The 2011 amendment by c. 517 inserted "3" in subsection E.

CASE NOTES

Editor's note.
The case below was decided under former Title 2.1 or prior provisions.

Exemption not applicable. — Where the exemption applies to one who "has been employed" prior to a relative becoming a member of the school board, since the verb form used is the present perfect tense, which denotes an action beginning in the past and continuing to the present, and teacher's interpretation of the exemption, namely, employment at any time before the conflict arose, would require use of a verb form in the past perfect tense, that is, "had been employed," i.e., an event beginning and ending in the past, the exemption contained in this section was not applicable to teacher because she was not regularly employed by the board at the time her brother-in-law was appointed to the board. Williams v. Augusta County Sch. Bd., 248 Va. 124, 445 S.E.2d 118 (1994).

OPINIONS OF THE ATTORNEY GENERAL

Subsection E exception. — Subsection E of § 2.2-3119 can be harmonized with other statutes that require the school board to retain ultimate authority for hiring decisions. Subsection E does not require that the school board forfeit that authority; rather, it requires that the superintendent independently reaches a determination about the qualifications of an applicant who is married to or related to a school board member and to do so without any involvement of the school board in that hiring decision. Upon receiving the superintendent's recommendation, the non-conflicted school board members then can vote on the applicant. The requirements of subsection E are satisfied when a school board member recuses himself and certifies on the record that he had no involvement in the decision to hire his spouse or relative. Section 2.2-3126 authorizes a Commonwealth's Attorney or citizens to file suits for violations of the Conflicts Act, such a suit would be unsuccessful when the strictures of subsection E of § 2.2-3119 are followed because no violation of the Act would have occurred. See opinion of Attorney General to B. James Jefferson, Esquire, County Attorney, Franklin County, 11-039, 2011 Va. AG LEXIS 31 (5/27/11).

ARTICLE 7.

PENALTIES AND REMEDIES.

§ 2.2-3120. Knowing violation of chapter a misdemeanor.

Any person who knowingly violates any of the provisions of Articles 2 through 6 (§§ 2.2-3102 through 2.2-3119) of this chapter shall be guilty of a Class 1 misdemeanor, except that any member of a local governing body who knowingly violates subsection A of § 2.2-3112 or subsection D or F of § 2.2-3115 shall be guilty of a Class 3 misdemeanor. A knowing violation under this section is one in which the person engages in conduct, performs an act or refuses to perform an act when he knows that the conduct is prohibited or required by this chapter.

History.
1987, Sp. Sess., c. 1, § 2.1-639.17; 2001, c. 844; 2012, c. 429.

Cross references.
As to punishment for Class 1 and Class 3 misdemeanors, see § 18.2-11.

The 2012 amendments.
The 2012 amendment by c. 429 substituted "who knowingly violates subsection A of § 2.2-3112 or subsection D or F of § 2.2-3115 shall be guilty" for "who knowingly § 2.2-3112 A or § 2.2-3115 C or E shall be guilty" in the first sentence.

§ 2.2-3121. Advisory opinions.

A. A state officer or employee shall not be prosecuted for a knowing violation of this chapter if the alleged violation resulted from his good faith reliance on a written opinion of the Attorney General made in response to his written request for such opinion and the opinion was made after a full disclosure of the facts.

B. A local officer or employee shall not be prosecuted for a knowing violation of this chapter if the alleged violation resulted from his good faith reliance on a written opinion of the attorney for the Commonwealth made in response to his written request for such opinion and the opinion was made after a full disclosure of the facts. The written opinion shall be a public record and shall be released upon request.

C. If any officer or employee serving at the local level of government is charged with a knowing violation of this chapter, and the alleged violation resulted from his reliance upon a written opinion of his city, county or town attorney, made after a full disclosure of the facts, that such action was not in violation of this chapter, then the officer or employee shall have the right to introduce a copy of the opinion at his trial as evidence that he did not knowingly violate this chapter.

History.
1987, Sp. Sess., c. 1, § 2.1-639.18; 2001, c. 844; 2003, c. 694.

§ 2.2-3122. Knowing violation of chapter constitutes malfeasance in office or employment.

Any person who knowingly violates any of the provisions of this chapter shall be guilty of malfeasance in office or employment. Upon conviction thereof, the judge or jury trying the case, in addition to any other fine or penalty provided by law, may order the forfeiture of such office or employment.

History.
1987, Sp. Sess., c. 1, § 2.1-639.19; 2001, c. 844.

§ 2.2-3123. Invalidation of contract; recision of sales.

A. Any contract made in violation of § 2.2-3103 or §§ 2.2-3106 through 2.2-3109 may be declared void and may be rescinded by the governing body of the contracting or selling governmental agency within five years of the date of such contract. In cases in which the contract is invalidated, the contractor shall retain or receive only the reasonable value, with no increment for profit or commission, of the property or services furnished prior to the date of receiving notice that the contract has been voided. In cases of recision of a contract of sale, any refund or restitution shall be made to the contracting or selling governmental agency.

B. Any purchase by an officer or employee made in violation of § 2.2-3103 or §§ 2.2-3106 through 2.2-3109 may be rescinded by the governing body of the contracting or selling governmental agency within five years of the date of such purchase.

History.
1987, Sp. Sess., c. 1, § 2.1-639.20; 2001, c. 844.

Michie's Jurisprudence.
For related discussion, see 5A M.J. Counties, § 60.

§ 2.2-3124. Civil penalty from violation of this chapter.

In addition to any other fine or penalty provided by law, an officer or employee who knowingly violates any provision of §§ 2.2-3103 through 2.2-3112 shall be subject to a civil penalty in an amount equal to the amount of money or thing of value received as a result of such violation. If the thing of value received by the officer or employee in violation of §§ 2.2-3103 through 2.2-3112 increases in value between the time of the violation and the time of discovery of the violation, the greater value shall determine the amount of the civil penalty. Further, all money or other things of value received as a result of such violation shall be forfeited in accordance with the provisions of § 19.2-386.33.

History.

1987, Sp. Sess., c. 1, § 2.1-639.21; 1994, cc. 727, 776; 2001, c. 844; 2012, cc. 283, 756.

The 2012 amendments.

The 2012 amendments by cc. 283 and 756 are identical, and rewrote the section.

§ 2.2-3125. Limitation of actions.

The statute of limitations for the criminal prosecution of a person for violation of any provision of this chapter shall be one year from the time the Attorney General, if the violation is by a state officer or employee, or the attorney for the Commonwealth, if the violation is by a local officer or employee, has actual knowledge of the violation or five years from the date of the violation, whichever event occurs first. Any prosecution for malfeasance in office shall be governed by the statute of limitations provided by law.

History.

1987, Sp. Sess., c. 1, § 2.1-639.22; 2001, c. 844.

§ 2.2-3126. Enforcement.

A. The provisions of this chapter relating to an officer or employee serving at the state level of government shall be enforced by the Attorney General.

In addition to any other powers and duties prescribed by law, the Attorney General shall have the following powers and duties within the area for which he is responsible under this section:

1. He shall advise the agencies of state government and officers and employees serving at the state level of government on appropriate procedures for complying with the requirements of this chapter. He may review any disclosure statements, without notice to the affected person, for the purpose of determining satisfactory compliance, and shall investigate matters that come to his attention reflecting possible violations of the provisions of this chapter by officers and employees serving at the state level of government;

2. If he determines that there is a reasonable basis to conclude that any officer or employee serving at the state level of government has knowingly violated any provision of this chapter, he shall designate an attorney for the Commonwealth who shall have complete and independent discretion in the prosecution of such officer or employee;

3. He shall render advisory opinions to any state officer or employee who seeks advice as to whether the facts in a particular case would constitute a violation of the provisions of this chapter. He shall determine which opinions or portions thereof are of general interest to the public and may, from time to time, be published.

Irrespective of whether an opinion of the Attorney General has been requested and rendered, any person has the right to seek a declaratory judgment or other judicial relief as provided by law.

B. The provisions of this chapter relating to an officer or employee serving at the local level of government shall be enforced by the attorney for the Commonwealth within the political subdivision for which he is elected.

Each attorney for the Commonwealth shall be responsible for prosecuting violations by an officer or employee serving at the local level of government and, if the Attorney General designates such attorney for the Commonwealth, violations by an officer or employee serving at the state level of government. In the event the violation by an officer or employee serving at the local level of government involves more than one local jurisdiction, the Attorney General shall designate which of the attorneys for the Commonwealth of the involved local jurisdictions shall enforce the provisions of this chapter with regard to such violation.

Each attorney for the Commonwealth shall establish an appropriate written procedure for implementing the disclosure requirements of local officers and employees of his county, city or town, and for other political subdivisions, whose principal offices are located within the jurisdiction served by such attorney for the Commonwealth. The attorney for the Commonwealth shall provide a copy of this act to all local officers and employees in the jurisdiction served by such attorney who are required to file a disclosure statement pursuant to Article 5 (§ 2.2-3113 et seq.) of this chapter. Failure to receive a copy of the act shall not be a defense to such officers and employees if they are prosecuted for violations of the act.

Each attorney for the Commonwealth shall render advisory opinions as to whether the facts in a particular case would constitute a violation of the provisions of this chapter to the governing body and any local officer or employee in his jurisdiction and to political subdivisions other than a county, city or town, including regional political subdivisions whose principal offices are located within the jurisdiction served by such attorney for the Commonwealth. If the advisory opinion is written, then such written opinion shall be a public record and shall be released upon request. In case the opinion given by the attorney for the Commonwealth indicates that the facts would constitute a violation, the officer or employee affected thereby may request that the Attorney General review the opinion. A conflicting opinion by the Attorney General shall act to revoke the opinion of the attorney for the Commonwealth. The Attorney General shall determine which of his reviewing opinions or portions thereof are of general interest to the public and may, from time to time, be published.

Irrespective of whether an opinion of the attorney for the Commonwealth or the Attorney General has been requested and rendered, any person has the right to seek a declaratory judgment or other judicial relief as provided by law.

History.

1987, Sp. Sess., c. 1, § 2.1-639.23; 2001, c. 844; 2003, c. 694.

Michie's Jurisprudence.

For related discussion, see 4A M.J. Commonwealth's and State's Attorney, § 7.

CASE NOTES

Editor's note.

The case below was decided under former Title 2.1 or prior provisions.

The Commonwealth's attorneys have exclusive authority to enforce the provisions of this chapter as to violations by those serving at the local level of government. Commonwealth v. Holland, 211 Va. 530, 178 S.E.2d 506 (1971).

OPINIONS OF THE ATTORNEY GENERAL

Right to seek a judicial relief. — Subsection E of § 2.2-3119 creates an exception to the general rule that prohibits certain family members or spouses from working in a particular school division if their spouse or relative serves on the school board of that school division. Section 2.2-3126 authorizes a Commonwealth's Attorney or citizens to file suits for violations of the Conflicts Act, but such a suit would be unsuccessful when the strictures of subsection E of § 2.2-3119 are followed because no violation of the Act would have occurred. See opinion of Attorney General to B. James Jefferson, Esquire, County Attorney, Franklin County, 11-039, 2011 Va. AG LEXIS 31 (5/27/11).

§ 2.2-3127. Venue.

Any prosecution for a violation involving an officer serving at the state level of government shall be brought in the Circuit Court of the City of Richmond. Any prosecution for a violation involving an employee serving at the state level of government shall be within the jurisdiction in which the employee has his principal place of state employment.

Any proceeding provided in this chapter shall be brought in a court of competent jurisdiction within the county or city in which the violation occurs if the violation involves an officer or employee serving at the local level of government.

History.

1987, Sp. Sess., c. 1, § 2.1-639.24; 2001, c. 844.

ARTICLE 8.

ORIENTATION FOR STATE FILERS.

§ 2.2-3128. Semiannual orientation course.

Each state agency shall offer at least semiannually to each of its state filers an orientation course on this chapter, on ethics in public contracting pursuant to Article 6 (§ 2.2-4367 et seq.) of Chapter 43 of this title, if applicable to the filer, and on any other applicable regulations that govern the official conduct of state officers and employees.

History.

2004, cc. 134, 392.

Editor's note.

Acts 2004, cc. 134 and 392, cl. 2, provides: "On or before August 1, 2004, the Office of the Attorney General shall make available to all state agencies appropriate course content for the training requirements of § 2.2-3128 of the Code of Virginia. Such course content shall be updated periodically to conform with changes in applicable law. Completion of such course offered by the Office of the Attorney General by state filers shall satisfy the training requirements Article 8 (§ 2.2-3128 et seq.) of Chapter 31 of Title 2.2 of the Code of Virginia."

Acts 2004, cc. 134 and 392, cl. 3, provides: "The Virginia Information Technologies Agency shall provide any technical assistance required by the Office of the Attorney General in order to post all course content, including the ability to post course content as an interactive program, on the Internet."

§ 2.2-3129. Records of attendance.

Each state agency shall maintain records indicating the specific attendees, each attendee's job title, and dates of their attendance for each orientation course offered pursuant to § 2.2-3128 for a period of not less than five years after each course is given. These records shall be public records subject to inspection and copying consistent with § 2.2-3704.

History.

2004, cc. 134, 392.

§ 2.2-3130. Attendance requirements.

Except as set forth in § 2.2-3131, each state filer shall attend the orientation course required in § 2.2-3128, as follows:

1. For a state filer who holds a position with the agency on January 1, 2004, not later than December 31, 2004 and, thereafter, at least once during each consecutive period of two calendar years commencing on January 1, 2006.

2. For a person who becomes a state filer with the agency after January 1, 2004, within two months after he or she becomes a state filer and at least once during each consecutive period of two calendar years commencing on the first odd-numbered year thereafter.

History.

2004, cc. 134, 392.

§ 2.2-3131. Exemptions.

A. The requirements of § 2.2-3130 shall not apply to state filers with a state agency who have taken an equivalent ethics orientation course through another state agency within the time periods set forth in subdivision 1 or 2 of § 2.2-3130, as applicable.

B. State agencies may jointly conduct and state filers from more than one state agency may jointly attend an orientation course required by § 2.2-3128, as long as the course content is relevant to the official duties of the attending state filers.

C. Before conducting each orientation course required by § 2.2-3128, state agencies shall consult with the Attorney General regarding appropriate course content.

History.

2004, cc. 134, 392.

SUBTITLE II.

ADMINISTRATION OF STATE GOVERNMENT.

___

PART B.

TRANSACTION OF PUBLIC BUSINESS.

___

CHAPTER 37.

VIRGINIA FREEDOM OF INFORMATION ACT.

§ 2.2-3700. Short title; policy.

A. This chapter may be cited as "The Virginia Freedom of Information Act."

B. By enacting this chapter, the General Assembly ensures the people of the Commonwealth ready access to public records in the custody of a public body or its officers and employees, and free entry to meetings of public bodies wherein the business of the people is being conducted. The affairs of government are not intended to be conducted in an atmosphere of secrecy since at all times the public is to be the beneficiary of any action taken at any level of government. Unless a public body or its officers or employees specifically elect to exercise an exemption provided by this chapter or any other statute, every meeting shall be open to the public and all public records shall be available for inspection and copying upon request. All public records and meetings shall be presumed open, unless an exemption is properly invoked.

The provisions of this chapter shall be liberally construed to promote an increased awareness by all persons of governmental activities and afford every opportunity to citizens to witness the operations of government. Any exemption from public access to records or meetings shall be narrowly construed and no record shall be withheld or meeting closed to the public unless specifically made exempt pursuant to this chapter or other specific provision of law. This chapter shall not be construed to discourage the free discussion by government officials or employees of public matters with the citizens of the Commonwealth.

All public bodies and their officers and employees shall make reasonable efforts to reach an agreement with a requester concerning the production of the records requested.

Any ordinance adopted by a local governing body that conflicts with the provisions of this chapter shall be void.

History.
   1968, c. 479, § 2.1-340; 1976, c. 467, § 2.1-340.1; 1989, c. 358; 1990, c. 538; 1999, cc. 703, 726; 2001, c. 844; 2002, c. 393.

Cross references.
   As to the duty of the Secretary of the Commonwealth to report on gubernatorial appointments to certain committee chairmen and to the General Assembly, see § 2.2-406. As to the authority of agency directors to prohibit agency employees from discussing the functions and policies of the agency beyond the limitations of this act, see § 2.2-603. As to restrictions on the release of Department of Human Resource Management employee information, see § 2.2-1203. As to certain restrictions on the release of trade secrets submitted as part of a proposed workforce training program, see § 2.2-2673. As to the rights of data subjects to refuse to provide personal information, see § 2.2-3806. As to Protection of Social Security Numbers Act, see § 2.2-3815 et seq. As to the publication of the Virginia Register of Regulations, see § 2.2-4031. As to exemption of confidential information under the Virginia Administrative Dispute Resolution Act, § 2.2-4115 et seq., from the Virginia Freedom of Information Act, see § 2.2-4119. As to the availability of public records pertaining to procurement transactions, see § 2.2-4342. As to exemption of confidential records of and reports on adult persons under investigation by or placed on probation supervision

with a local community-based probation services agency, see § 9.1-177.1. As to exemption of confidential records of and reports on adult persons under investigation by or in the custody or supervision of a local pretrial service agency, see § 19.2-152.4:2. As to exemption from disclosure of trade secrets or proprietary information submitted to the Virginia Code Commission, see § 30-147. As to the powers and duties of the Virginia Freedom of Information Advisory Council, see § 30-179. As to restrictions on the release of information by the Disease Prevention and Control regarding the use of biological weapons, see § 32.1-39. As to confidentiality of certain information and records collected and maintained by the Office of the Chief Medical Examiner, see § 32.1-283.4. As to the confidentiality of certain records of the Office of the State Long-Term Care Ombudsman, see § 51.5-141. As to confidentiality of documents submitted to Advance Health Care Directive Registry, see § 54.1-2995.

Editor's note.

Acts 2002, c. 393, cl. 2, provides: "That it is the intent of the General Assembly to address the recent Virginia Supreme Court holding in the case styled Connell v. Kersey [262 Va. 154, 547 S.E.2d 228 (2001)], which held that attorneys for the Commonwealth are not 'public bodies' as defined in the Freedom of Information Act (§ 2.2-3700 et seq.), by clarifying that the Freedom of Information Act (FOIA) applies to constitutional officers and providing an exemption for attorneys for the Commonwealth."

Law Review.

For 2002 survey of Virginia technology law, see 37 U. Rich. L. Rev. 341 (2002). For article, "Some Assembly Required: The Application of State Open Meeting Laws to Email Correspondence," 12 Geo. Mason L. Rev. 719 (2004). For survey of the Virginia law on administrative law for the year 2007-2008, see 43 U. Rich. L. Rev. 73 (2008).

Research references.

Bryson on Virginia Civil Procedure (Matthew Bender). Chapter 9 Discovery. § 9.04 Privileges against discovery. W. Hamilton Bryson.

Friend's Virginia Pleading and Practice (Matthew Bender). Chapter 1 Courts. § 1.05 District Courts; Chapter 31 Proceedings in General District Courts. §§ 31.16 Trial, 31.21 Appeals; Chapter 39 Appeals to Circuit Courts. § 39.02 Appeals from District Courts to Circuit Courts in Civil Cases. Charles E. Friend.

Virginia Forms (Matthew Bender). No. 6-1205 Petition and Affidavit for Good Cause/For Injunction or Mandamus — Freedom of Information Act; No. 6-1206 Order Granting Petition for Injunction of Writ of Mandamus under Virginia Freedom of Information Act.

Michie's Jurisprudence.

For related discussion, see 5A M.J. Counties, § 2; 13B M.J. Municipal Corporations, § 22; 16 M.J. Right of Privacy, § 1; 21 M.J. Zoning and Planning, § 4.

CASE NOTES

Editor's note.

Some of the cases below were decided under former Title 2.1 or prior provisions.

Constitutionality. — Although the Virginia's Freedom of Information Act, § 2.2-3700 et seq., discriminates against noncitizens of Virginia, it does not discriminate against interstate commerce or out-of-state economic interests; the object of the Freedom of Information Act is to provide a mechanism for access and copying of public records to Virginia citizens to reflect that the affairs of government are not conducted in an atmosphere of secrecy, subsection B of § 2.2-3700. The Freedom of Information Act is wholly silent as to commerce or economic interests, both in and out of Virginia; therefore, the Freedom of Information Act does not facially, or in its effect, discriminate against interstate commerce or out-of-state economic interests. McBurney v. Young, 667 F.3d 454, 2012 U.S. App. LEXIS 1872 (4th Cir. 2012).

The policy expressly stated in this section is that this chapter shall be liberally construed to enable citizens to observe the operations of government and that the exemptions shall be narrowly construed in order that nothing which should be public may

be hidden from any person. City of Danville v. Laird, 223 Va. 271, 288 S.E.2d 429 (1982).

Purpose of this chapter is to remove any necessity for a reporter seeking access to a report or document in an agency's file to resort to subornation on the part of public employees, by providing him with a prompt and easy remedy to secure access to such document. If the agency refused access improperly, the reporter would have his remedy and would be awarded in addition attorney's fees and costs against the agency. There is accordingly no need for the reporter to engage in protracted pressure to induce a public employee to engage in subornation in violation of his duty under the regulations governing his employment. Jurgensen v. Fairfax County, 745 F.2d 868 (4th Cir. 1984).

There is no common-law right of the public or press to attend the meetings of governmental bodies. Roanoke City School Bd. v. Times-World Corp., 226 Va. 185, 307 S.E.2d 256 (1983).

An administrative request is a condition precedent to judicial remedies. — An administrative request for minutes or other records is a condition precedent to judicial remedies under the act. Hale v. Washington County School Bd., 241 Va. 76, 400 S.E.2d 175 (1991).

When prior request for records not required. — Where records exist, the legislative purpose was to require a request addressed to the public body, followed by a refusal, as a condition precedent to judicial proceedings for the production of those records. However, the act cannot be read to require either a request for records when the relief requested does not involve production of records, or a fruitless request for records which the requester knows to be nonexistent. Hale v. Washington County School Bd., 241 Va. 76, 400 S.E.2d 175 (1991).

Where school board superintendent alleged the nonexistence of any minutes of a closed meeting, the superintendent obviated any need to allege a prior request for, and denial of, those records. Hale v. Washington County School Bd., 241 Va. 76, 400 S.E.2d 175 (1991).

The purpose or motivation behind a request is irrelevant to a citizen's entitlement to requested information under the Freedom of Information Act. Associated Tax Serv., Inc. v. Fitzpatrick, 236 Va. 181, 372 S.E.2d 625 (1988).

Applicability. — Virginia Freedom of Information Act, § 2.2-3700 et seq., did not apply to the Virginia State Corporation Commission because the State Corporation Commission was governed by a separate and parallel structure of laws and was not a "public body" under the Virginia Freedom of Information Act; further, the Virginia Freedom of Information Act lacked a constitutional enforcement mechanism applicable to the State Corporation Commission. Christian v. State Corp. Comm'n, 282 Va. 392, 718 S.E.2d 767, 2011 Va. LEXIS 217 (2011).

Real estate assessment information. — City treasurer's reliance on the Privacy Protection Act (see now § 2.2-3900 et seq.) in denying a request for certain real estate tax information was totally misplaced, because the Act specifically excludes real estate assessment information. Associated Tax Serv., Inc. v. Fitzpatrick, 236 Va. 181, 372 S.E.2d 625 (1988).

Telephone conference call. — It was not the intent of the General Assembly that a telephone conference call between members of a public body be construed as a "meeting" of such members. Roanoke City School Bd. v. Times-World Corp., 226 Va. 185, 307 S.E.2d 256 (1983).

Mandamus erroneously denied. — Landowner, who alleged a violation of the rights and privileges afforded by the Virginia Freedom of Information Act, § 2.2-3700 et seq., and seeking relief by mandamus pursuant to § 2.2-3713, was not required to prove a lack of an adequate remedy at law, nor could his mandamus proceeding be barred on the ground that there might have been some other remedy at law available; moreover, because the circuit court did not reach the issue whether a sales brochure in connection with a highway construction project was subject to disclosure under the Act, the matter was remanded for further consideration of that issue and a determination as to whether the landowner was entitled to reasonable costs and attorneys' fees. Cartwright v. Commonwealth Transp. Comm'r, 270 Va. 58, 613 S.E.2d 449, 2005 Va. LEXIS 62 (2005).

Applied in Beck v. Shelton, 267 Va. 482, 593 S.E.2d 195, 2004 Va. LEXIS 40 (2004); White Dog Publ., Inc. v. Culpeper County Bd. of

Supervisors, 272 Va. 377, 634 S.E.2d 334, 2006 Va. LEXIS 81 (2006); Fenter v. Norfolk Airport Auth., 274 Va. 524, 649 S.E.2d 704, 2007 Va. LEXIS 102 (2007).

CIRCUIT COURT OPINIONS

Construction. — In order to discuss the performance of its city manager as it related to the rising crime in the city, the circuit court ordered the depositions transcribed be opened to allow public access, as the focus of the meeting was on the city's plans and programs to meet the soaring crime issue, and not on the city manager personally; thus, said discussion did not meet the requirements of subdivision A 1 of § 2.2-3711 to justify closure. Media Gen. Operations, Inc. v. City Council of Richmond, 64 Va. Cir. 406, 2004 Va. Cir. LEXIS 191 (Richmond 2004).

When recipient claims request is not for public record. — Following is the rule respecting the application of the Virginia Freedom of Information Act (FOIA), § 2.2-3700, to what are records that are not believed by the recipient of a request to be prepared or owned by, or in the possession of a public body or its officers, employees, or agents in the transaction of public business: first, the recipient should determine if the record is one arising out of the course of the public business of the recipient, that is, those matters over which the public governmental body or agent of the government has supervision, control, jurisdiction, or advisory power; second, if the record is determined by the recipient of the request to be a private rather than public record, he or she must make a response, denying production by reason of it being a private record within the five days required by statute unless an extension is afforded by the express provision of FOIA; third, the responding party claiming the record is not a public record should so state and in addition, describe the nature of the record not produced or disclosed in a manner that, without revealing the information or contents of the record itself, will enable the party making the request and the court to assess whether or not the record was prepared in the transaction of public business. Burton v. Mann, 74 Va. Cir. 471, 2008 Va. Cir. LEXIS 57 (Loudoun County 2008).

Redacted documents subject to disclosure. — Court redacted portions of certain documents sought from a town pursuant to the Freedom of Information Act, § 2.2-3700 et seq., because the nine letters were considered part business and part personal. Documents that were totally personal were not subject to disclosure and two of the documents fell within the Act. Town of Saltville v. Surrber, 83 Va. Cir. 161, 2011 Va. Cir. LEXIS 108 (Smyth County July 11, 2011).

Inmate's request for records. — Inmate was not denied rights and privileges conferred by the Virginia Freedom of Information Act (FOIA), § 2.2-3700 et seq., when his request for the release of certain police investigative reports was denied; the records sought were not subject to disclosure under express exemptions within FOIA. Chavez v. Manger, 62 Va. Cir. 146, 2003 Va. Cir. LEXIS 98 (Fairfax County 2003).

Proceedings before judicial inquiry and review commission. — Where a judge's request for an opinion regarding future conduct was not a proceeding or "papers filed" before the Virginia Judicial Inquiry and Review Commission, it was not confidential under § 17.1-913 and was subject to disclosure under the Virginia Freedom of Information Act, § 2.2-3700 et seq. Zaleski v. Judicial Inquiry & Review Comm'n, 64 Va. Cir. 495, 2004 Va. Cir. LEXIS 186 (Richmond 2004).

Burden of proof. — County school board had the burden of proving that it did not violate the Virginia Freedom of Information Act, § 2.2-3700 et seq., because while the board had to prove that its conduct was subject to an exemption, the citizen who file suit against it bore the burden of showing that the board's violations were intentional. Hill v. Fairfax County Sch. Bd., 83 Va. Cir. 172, 2011 Va. Cir. LEXIS 89 (Fairfax County July 13, 2011).

OPINIONS OF THE ATTORNEY GENERAL

Access to digital copies of court records. — The Virginia Freedom of Information Act and § 17.1-208 impose a duty on circuit court clerks to furnish copies of records requested by a citizen, without distinction between paper and digital formats, provided the records are not sealed by court order or otherwise exempt from disclosure by law. See opinion of Attorney General to The Honorable J. Jack Kennedy, Jr., Clerk, Circuit Court for Wise County and City of Norton, 02-095 (12/19/02).

Release of names of concealed handgun carry permittees. — The Department of State Police possesses the discretionary authority to release the names of concealed handgun carry permittees pursuant to a request under the The Virginia Freedom of Information Act. See opinion of Attorney General to The Honorable Dave Nutter, Member, House of Delegates, 07-027 (4/6/07).

§ 2.2-3701. Definitions.

As used in this chapter, unless the context requires a different meaning:

"Closed meeting" means a meeting from which the public is excluded.

"Electronic communication" means any audio or combined audio and visual communication method.

"Emergency" means an unforeseen circumstance rendering the notice required by this chapter impossible or impracticable and which circumstance requires immediate action.

"Meeting" or *"meetings"* means the meetings including work sessions, when sitting physically, or through telephonic or video equipment pursuant to § 2.2-3708 or 2.2-3708.1, as a body or entity, or as an informal assemblage of (i) as many as three members or (ii) a quorum, if less than three, of the constituent membership, wherever held, with or without minutes being taken, whether or not votes are cast, of any public body. The gathering of employees of a public body shall not be deemed a "meeting" subject to the provisions of this chapter.

"Open meeting" or *"public meeting"* means a meeting at which the public may be present.

"Public body" means any legislative body, authority, board, bureau, commission, district or agency of the Commonwealth or of any political subdivision of the Commonwealth, including cities, towns and counties, municipal councils, governing bodies of counties, school boards and planning commissions; boards of visitors of public institutions of higher education; and other organizations, corporations or agencies in the Commonwealth supported wholly or principally by public funds. It shall include (i) the Virginia Birth-Related Neurological Injury Compensation Program and its board of directors established pursuant to Chapter 50 (§ 38.2-5000 et seq.) of Title 38.2 and (ii) any committee, subcommittee, or other entity however designated, of the public body created to perform delegated functions of the public body or to advise the public body. It shall not exclude any such committee, subcommittee or entity because it has private sector or citizen members. Corporations organized by the Virginia Retirement System are "public bodies" for purposes of this chapter.

For the purposes of the provisions of this chapter applicable to access to public records, constitutional officers shall be considered public bodies and, except as otherwise expressly provided by law, shall have the same obligations to disclose public records as other custodians of public records.

"Public records" means all writings and recordings that consist of letters, words or numbers, or their equivalent, set down by handwriting, typewriting, printing, photostatting, photography, magnetic impulse, optical or magneto-optical form, mechanical or electronic recording or other form of data compilation, however stored, and regardless of physical form or characteristics, prepared or owned by, or in the possession of a public body or its officers, employees or agents in the transaction of public business. Records that are not prepared for or used in the transaction of public business are not public records.

"Regional public body" means a unit of government organized as provided by law within defined boundaries, as determined by the General Assembly, whose members are appointed by the participating local governing bodies, and such unit includes two or more counties or cities.

"Scholastic records" means those records containing information directly related to a student or an applicant for admission and maintained by a public body that is an educational agency or institution or by a person acting for such agency or institution.

History.
1968, c. 479, § 2.1-341; 1970, c. 456; 1974, c. 332; 1975, c. 307; 1977, c. 677; 1978, cc. 573, 826; 1979, cc. 369, 687; 1980, c. 754; 1984, c. 252; 1989, c. 358; 1990, c. 538; 1993, cc. 270, 720; 1994, cc. 845, 931; 1996, c. 609; 1997, c. 641; 1999, cc. 703, 726; 2001, c. 844; 2002, c. 393; 2003, c. 897; 2007, c. 945; 2008, cc. 233, 789; 2010, c. 706; 2011, c. 242.

Cross references.
As to Protection of Social Security Numbers Act, see § 2.2-3815 et seq. As to disclosure of a communication or information covered by attorney-client privilege or work product protection, see § 8.01-427.

Editor's note.
Acts 2002, c. 393, cl. 2, provides: "That it is the intent of the General Assembly to address the recent Virginia Supreme Court holding in the case styled Connell v. Kersey [262 Va. 154, 547 S.E.2d 228 (2001)], which held that attorneys for the Commonwealth are not 'public bodies' as defined in the Freedom of Information Act (§ 2.2-3700 et seq.), by clarifying that the Freedom of Information Act (FOIA) applies to constitutional officers and providing an exemption for attorneys for the Commonwealth."

The 2010 amendments.
The 2010 amendment by c. 706, effective April 13, 2010, inserted "or an applicant for admission" in the definition of "scholastic records."

The 2011 amendments.
The 2011 amendment by c. 242 added the last sentence in the definition for "Public records."

Law Review.
For survey of the Virginia law on administrative law for the year 2007-2008, see 43 U. Rich. L. Rev. 73 (2008). For essay, "Community Development Authorities," see 45 U. Rich. L. Rev. 81 (2010).

CASE NOTES

Information gathering session not a "meeting." — A "meeting," as defined by this section, did not include a conference where board of supervisors, without giving notice or keeping minutes, met with the Attorney General for the purpose of gathering information, where the board conducted no public business and did not exclude the public. Nageotte v. Board of Supvrs., 223 Va. 259, 288 S.E.2d 423 (1982) (decided under former Title 2.1).

Telephone conference call not a "meeting." — It was not the intent of the General Assembly that a telephone conference call between members of a public body be construed as a "meeting" of such members. Roanoke City School Bd. v. Times-World Corp., 226 Va. 185, 307 S.E.2d 256 (1983) (decided under former Title 2.1).

E-mail communications not "meeting." — Trial court did not err in finding that a school board had not conducted an improper closed meeting as the feature of simultaneity inherent in term "assemblage" in § 2.2-3701 was not established. E-mails that involved some sort of back-and-forth exchange were between only two members at a time, rather than the three required, and the messages did not generate group conversations or responses with multiple recipients. Hill v. Fairfax County Sch. Bd., 284 Va. 306, 727 S.E.2d 75, 2012 Va. LEXIS 136 (2012).

City council members-elect not "members" under FOIA. — Judgment was properly awarded to a mayor and city council members in plaintiff's action alleging that they e-mailed each other in a knowing, willful, and deliberate attempt to hold secret meetings, avoid public scrutiny, discuss city business, and decide city issues without the input of all of the council members and the public because the Virginia Freedom of Information Act did not apply to conduct of members-elect of the city council. Beck v. Shelton, 267 Va. 482, 593 S.E.2d 195, 2004 Va. LEXIS 40 (2004).

E-mail communications not "meeting." — Judgment was properly awarded to a mayor and city council members in an action alleging that they deliberately e-mailed each other in an attempt to hold secret meetings because e-mail communications did not constitute a "meeting" under the Virginia Freedom of Information Act. Beck v. Shelton, 267 Va. 482, 593 S.E.2d 195, 2004 Va. LEXIS 40 (2004).

Commonwealth's attorney. — A Commonwealth's attorney is not a "public body" within the meaning of the Virginia Freedom of Information Act (FOIA), and a request for information pursuant to § 2.1-342.2 [see now § 2.2-3706] is not subject to the procedures and time limits prescribed by § 2.1-342 [see now § 2.2-3704], which by its express terms relates only to requests made under the FOIA to "public bodies." Connell v. Kersey, 262 Va. 154, 547 S.E.2d 228, 2001 Va. LEXIS 67 (2001) (decided prior to the amendment by Acts 2002, c. 393.)

Distinction between "public bodies" and "public officials" under FOIA. — As used in the Virginia Freedom of Information Act (FOIA), the terms "authority" and "agency" clearly refer to entities to which responsibility to conduct the business of the people is delegated by legislative or executive action, whereas, by contrast, a Commonwealth's attorney derives his authority from the Constitution; while a Commonwealth's attorney, like a sheriff or other constitutional officer, is undoubtedly a public official, the FOIA distinguishes between "public officials" and "public bodies." Connell v. Kersey, 262 Va. 154, 547 S.E.2d 228, 2001 Va. LEXIS 67 (2001) (decided prior to the amendment by Acts 2002, c. 393.)

County's tape of calls to its 911 system is an official record where the system was created with public funds and created to provide for public safety. Tull v. Brown, 255 Va. 177, 494 S.E.2d 855 (1998) (decided under former Title 2.1).

Biological material not "public record." — Biological material recovered on swabs from the vagina of the victim did not meet the test of a "public record," and even if it did, the Virginia Freedom of Information Act (FOIA) allowed for inspection and copying, not testing. Globe Newspaper Co. v. Commonwealth, 264 Va. 622, 570 S.E.2d 809, 2002 Va. LEXIS 156 (2002).

CIRCUIT COURT OPINIONS

Redacted documents subject to disclosure. — Court redacted portions of certain documents sought from a town pursuant to the Freedom of Information Act, § 2.2-3700 et seq., because the nine letters were considered part business and part personal. Documents which were totally personal were not subject to disclosure and two of the documents fell within the Act. Town of Saltville v. Surrber, 83 Va. Cir. 161, 2011 Va. Cir. LEXIS 108 (Smyth County July 11, 2011).

E-mail communications not "meeting." — E-mails sent by county school board members in the days leading up to the vote to close an elementary school did not involve sufficient simultaneity to constitute a meeting under the Virginia Freedom of Information Act, § 2.2-3701, because the e-mails were used consecutively, rather than co-operatively, and the members never reached any sort of group consensus or discussed business as if they were sitting in a room, virtual or real, chatting with each other; individual attempts to ascertain other members' positions on the issue did not violate the Act's open meeting provisions because there was no evidence of a collective intent on behalf of any three members or the board as a whole to move toward a decision outside of the context of a public meeting. Hill v. Fairfax County Sch. Bd., 83 Va. Cir. 172, 2011 Va. Cir. LEXIS 89 (Fairfax County July 13, 2011).

Corporation not supported wholly by public funds. — Although the public broadcasting corporation had to be covered under the Freedom of Information Act, §§ 2.2-3700 through 2.2-3714, as a corporation that was supported wholly or principally by public funds; less than 25% of its funding came from government support and it did not perform a delegated governmental function. Wigand v. Wilkes, 65 Va. Cir. 437, 2004 Va. Cir. LEXIS 290 (Norfolk 2004).

Municipal liability pool is public body. — City's police officer, who was injured in a collision with an uninsured/underinsured motorist, could not recover under an insurance policy issued by a municipal liability pool where the pool was a § 2.2-3701 public body that had to keep minutes reflecting actions taken by resolution, and there was no resolution showing that the city elected UM/UIM insurance coverage. Johnson v. Va. Mun. Liab. Pool, 73 Va. Cir. 138, 2007 Va. Cir. LEXIS 231 (Richmond Mar. 23, 2007).

OPINIONS OF THE ATTORNEY GENERAL

An institutional review board of a public institution of higher learning in the Commonwealth engaged in human research projects is not a "public body" as defined by the statute as such a board is not an independent entity charged by law with the governance of, or responsibility for, some discrete public agency. See opinion of Attorney General to The Honorable Thomas C. Wright Jr., Member, House of Delegates, 01-101 (10/22/01).

Records generated by an institutional review board of a public institution of higher learning in the Commonwealth engaged in human research projects are not "public records" prepared or owned by, or in the possession of, a public body. See opinion of Attorney General to The Honorable Thomas C. Wright Jr., Member, House of Delegates, 01-101 (10/22/01).

Application to nonprofit organizations. — The fact that a nonprofit organization receives public funds from a locality does not result in the documents of the charitable organization being subject to the disclosure requirements of The Virginia Freedom of Information Act. See opinion of Attorney General to Mr. David W. Rowan, Town Attorney for the Town of Onancock, 01-094 (3/27/02).

A legislative caucus is not a "public body" as that term is defined in The Virginia Freedom of Information Act; therefore, the notice and open meeting requirements of the Act do not apply to such organizations. See opinion of Attorney General to The Honorable Clifton A. Woodrum, Member, House of Delegates, 03-063 (1/6/04).

An informal assemblage of three or more legislators at a meeting prearranged or called for the purpose of discussing expected votes on matters pending before the General Assembly constitutes a meeting under The Virginia Freedom of Information Act, requiring that such a meeting be open to the public. See opinion of Attorney General to The Honorable Clifton A. Woodrum, Member, House of Delegates, 03-063 (1/6/04).

§ 2.2-3702. Notice of chapter.

Any person elected, reelected, appointed or reappointed to any body not excepted from this chapter shall (i) be furnished by the public body's administrator or legal counsel with a copy of this chapter within two weeks following election, reelection, appointment or reappointment and (ii) read and become familiar with the provisions of this chapter.

History.

1976, c. 467, § 2.1-341.1; 1999, cc. 703, 726; 2001, c. 844; 2002, c. 393.

Editor's note.

Acts 2002, c. 393, cl. 2, provides: "That it is the intent of the General Assembly to address the recent Virginia Supreme Court holding in the case styled Connell v. Kersey [262 Va. 154, 547 S.E.2d 228 (2001)], which held that attorneys for the Commonwealth are not 'public bodies' as defined in the Freedom of Information Act (§ 2.2-3700 et seq.), by clarifying that the Freedom of Information Act (FOIA) applies to constitutional officers and providing an exemption for attorneys for the Commonwealth."

CASE NOTES

Applied in Beck v. Shelton, 267 Va. 482, 593 S.E.2d 195, 2004 Va. LEXIS 40 (2004).

§ 2.2-3703. Public bodies and records to which chapter inapplicable; voter registration and election records; access by persons incarcerated in a state, local, or federal correctional facility.

A. The provisions of this chapter shall not apply to:

1. The Virginia Parole Board, except that (i) information from the Virginia Parole Board providing the number of inmates considered by such Board for discretionary parole, the number of inmates granted or denied parole, and the number of parolees returned to the custody of the Department of Corrections solely as a result of a determination by such Board of a violation of parole shall be open to inspection and available for release, on a monthly basis, as provided by § 2.2-3704 and (ii) all records concerning the finances of the Virginia Parole Board shall be public records and subject to the provisions of this chapter. The information required by clause (i) shall be furnished by offense, sex, race, age of the inmate, and the locality in which the conviction was obtained, upon the request of the party seeking the information;

2. Petit juries and grand juries;

3. Family assessment and planning teams established pursuant to § 2.2-5207;

4. The Virginia State Crime Commission; and

5. The records required by law to be maintained by the clerks of the courts of record, as defined in § 1-212, and courts not of record, as defined in § 16.1-69.5. However, other records maintained by the clerks of such courts shall be public records and subject to the provisions of this chapter.

B. Public access to voter registration and election records shall be governed by the provisions of Title 24.2 and this chapter. The provisions of Title 24.2 shall be controlling in the event of any conflict.

C. No provision of this chapter or Chapter 21 (§ 30-178 et seq.) of Title 30 shall be construed to afford any rights to any person (i) incarcerated in a state, local or federal correctional facility, whether or not such facility is (a) located in the Commonwealth or (b) operated pursuant to the Corrections Private Management Act (§ 53.1-261 et seq.) or (ii) civilly committed pursuant to the Sexually Violent Predators Act (§ 37.2-900 et seq.). However, this subsection shall not be construed to prevent such persons from exercising their constitutionally protected rights, including, but not limited to, their right to call for evidence in their favor in a criminal prosecution.

History.
1999, cc. 703, 726, § 2.1-341.2; 2001, c. 844; 2003, cc. 989, 1018; 2004, cc. 398, 690; 2007, cc. 438, 548, 626.

CASE NOTES

Constitutionality. — The prisoner exclusion provision in subsection C is not subject to a facial overbreadth challenge because it does not carry the threat of prosecution for violating the statute and it does not restrict expressive speech but simply regulates access to information in the possession of Virginia state agencies. Fisher v. King, 232 F.3d 391, 2000 U.S. App. LEXIS 28962 (4th Cir. 2000) (decided under prior provisions).

The First Amendment did not provide a prisoner, as a member of the general public, a right of physical access to an audio tape that was played in open court in a criminal trial, admitted into evidence, and for which he possessed a complete verbatim transcript. Fisher v. King, 232 F.3d 391, 2000 U.S. App. LEXIS 28962 (4th Cir. 2000) (decided under prior provisions).

Prisoner exclusion provision of the Virginia Freedom of Information Act, subsection C of § 2.2-3703, was not facially unconstitutional as there were numerous rational reasons for it, such as preventing frivolous requests that would unduly burden state resources, and it was not unconstitutional as applied to an inmate, who sought records regarding his medical condition to determine if he had a viable claim against various state department of correction officials, because even if the inmate's request was not frivolous, he was not thereby denied equal protection, and the exclusion did not deny the inmate's access to the courts as it did not obstruct his ability to file suit challenging his medical treatment. Giarratano v. Johnson, 456 F. Supp. 2d 747, 2006 U.S. Dist. LEXIS 74882 (W.D. Va. 2006), aff'd, 521 F.3d 298, 2008 U.S. App. LEXIS 6144 (4th Cir. Va. 2008).

Prisoner exclusion from the Virginia Freedom of Information Act, subsection C of § 2.2-3703, did not violate equal protection, due process, or the right of access to the courts because an inmate's conclusory allegation that this provision was not rationally related to a legitimate state interest was insufficient to overcome the presumption of rationality of the law; while the inmate did not file frivolous complaints, his conclusory allegation also failed to show an as-applied equal protection violation; and denial of the inmate's information request under subsection C did not obstruct his capability to file suit. Giarratano v. Johnson, 521 F.3d 298, 2008 U.S. App. LEXIS 6144 (4th Cir. 2008).

Standing. — District court dismissed an action which a state inmate filed under 42 U.S.C.S. § 1983, alleging that Virginia officials violated his rights under the U.S. Constitution when they denied his request under the Virginia Freedom of Information Act for police reports and other information that pertained to his conviction on charges of abduction and spousal rape. The court found that the inmate did not have standing to challenge § 2.2-3703(C), the statute that allowed Commonwealth officials to deny requests for information they received from prisoners. Patterson v. Mundy, 2005 U.S. Dist. LEXIS 38216 (W.D. Va. Dec. 16, 2005).

CIRCUIT COURT OPINIONS

Inmate's request for records. — None of an inmate's constitutionally protected rights were denied as a result of a police official's exercise of an exemption pursuant to the Virginia Freedom of Information Act (FOIA) nor did the inmate point to any such

rights; in addition, the FOIA did not clearly establish any right on the part of the inmate to access the criminal investigative reports in the custody of the police department. Chavez v. Manger, 62 Va. Cir. 146, 2003 Va. Cir. LEXIS 98 (Fairfax County 2003).

OPINIONS OF THE ATTORNEY GENERAL

Patients in state mental institutions and individuals committed under the Civil Commitment of Sexually Violent Predators Act are not subject to application of the provision prohibiting use of the Virginia Freedom of Information Act by incarcerated individuals. See opinion of Attorney General to The Honorable H. Morgan Griffith, Member, House of Delegates, 06-063 (10/23/06).

§ 2.2-3704. Public records to be open to inspection; procedure for requesting records and responding to request; charges; transfer of records for storage, etc.

A. Except as otherwise specifically provided by law, all public records shall be open to inspection and copying by any citizens of the Commonwealth during the regular office hours of the custodian of such records. Access to such records shall not be denied to citizens of the Commonwealth, representatives of newspapers and magazines with circulation in the Commonwealth, and representatives of radio and television stations broadcasting in or into the Commonwealth. The custodian may require the requester to provide his name and legal address. The custodian of such records shall take all necessary precautions for their preservation and safekeeping.

B. A request for public records shall identify the requested records with reasonable specificity. The request need not make reference to this chapter in order to invoke the provisions of this chapter or to impose the time limits for response by a public body. Any public body that is subject to this chapter and that is the custodian of the requested records shall promptly, but in all cases within five working days of receiving a request, provide the requested records to the requester or make one of the following responses in writing:

1. The requested records are being entirely withheld because their release is prohibited by law or the custodian has exercised his discretion to withhold the records in accordance with this chapter. Such response shall identify with reasonable particularity the volume and subject matter of withheld records, and cite, as to each category of withheld records, the specific Code section that authorizes the withholding of the records.

2. The requested records are being provided in part and are being withheld in part because the release of part of the records is prohibited by law or the custodian has exercised his discretion to withhold a portion of the records in accordance with this chapter. Such response shall identify with reasonable particularity the subject matter of withheld portions, and cite, as to each category of withheld

records, the specific Code section that authorizes the withholding of the records. When a portion of a requested record is withheld, the public body may delete or excise only that portion of the record to which an exemption applies and shall release the remainder of the record.

3. The requested records could not be found or do not exist. However, if the public body that received the request knows that another public body has the requested records, the response shall include contact information for the other public body.

4. It is not practically possible to provide the requested records or to determine whether they are available within the five-work-day period. Such response shall specify the conditions that make a response impossible. If the response is made within five working days, the public body shall have an additional seven work days in which to provide one of the four preceding responses.

C. Any public body may petition the appropriate court for additional time to respond to a request for records when the request is for an extraordinary volume of records or requires an extraordinarily lengthy search, and a response by the public body within the time required by this chapter will prevent the public body from meeting its operational responsibilities. Before proceeding with the petition, however, the public body shall make reasonable efforts to reach an agreement with the requester concerning the production of the records requested.

D. Subject to the provisions of subsection G, no public body shall be required to create a new record if the record does not already exist. However, a public body may abstract or summarize information under such terms and conditions as agreed between the requester and the public body.

E. Failure to respond to a request for records shall be deemed a denial of the request and shall constitute a violation of this chapter.

F. A public body may make reasonable charges not to exceed its actual cost incurred in accessing, duplicating, supplying, or searching for the requested records. No public body shall impose any extraneous, intermediary or surplus fees or expenses to recoup the general costs associated with creating or maintaining records or transacting the general business of the public body. Any duplicating fee charged by a public body shall not exceed the actual cost of duplication. The public body may also make a reasonable charge for the cost incurred in supplying records produced from a geographic information system at the request of anyone other than the owner of the land that is the subject of the request. However, such charges shall not exceed the actual cost to the public body in supplying such records, except that the public body may charge, on a pro rata per acre basis, for the cost of creating topographical maps developed by the public body, for such maps or portions thereof, which encompass a contiguous area greater than 50 acres. All charges for the supplying of requested records shall be estimated in advance at the request of the citizen.

G. Public records maintained by a public body in an electronic data processing system, computer database, or any other structured collection of data shall be made available to a requester at a reasonable cost, not to exceed the actual cost in accordance with subsection F. When electronic or other databases are combined or contain exempt and nonexempt records, the public body may provide access to the exempt records if not otherwise prohibited by law, but shall provide access to the nonexempt records as provided by this chapter.

Public bodies shall produce nonexempt records maintained in an electronic database in any tangible medium identified by the requester, including, where the public body has the capability, the option of posting the records on a website or delivering the records through an electronic mail address provided by the requester, if that medium is used by the public body in the regular course of business. No public body shall be required to produce records from an electronic database in a format not regularly used by the public body. However, the public body shall make reasonable efforts to provide records in any format under such terms and conditions as agreed between the requester and public body, including the payment of reasonable costs. The excision of exempt fields of information from a database or the conversion of data from one available format to another shall not be deemed the creation, preparation or compilation of a new public record.

H. In any case where a public body determines in advance that charges for producing the requested records are likely to exceed $200, the public body may, before continuing to process the request, require the requester to agree to payment of a deposit not to exceed the amount of the advance determination. The deposit shall be credited toward the final cost of supplying the requested records. The period within which the public body shall respond under this section shall be tolled for the amount of time that elapses between notice of the advance determination and the response of the requester.

I. Before processing a request for records, a public body may require the requester to pay any amounts owed to the public body for previous requests for records that remain unpaid 30 days or more after billing.

J. In the event a public body has transferred possession of public records to any entity, including but not limited to any other public body, for storage, maintenance, or archiving, the public body initiating the transfer of such records shall remain the custodian of such records for purposes of responding to requests for public records made pursuant to this chapter and shall be responsible for retrieving and supplying such public records to the requester. In the event a public body has transferred public records for storage, maintenance, or archiving and such transferring public body is no longer in existence, any public body that is a successor to the transferring public body shall be deemed the custodian of such records. In the event no successor entity exists, the entity in possession of the public records shall be deemed the custodian of the records for purposes of compliance with this chapter, and shall retrieve and supply such records to the requester. Nothing in this subsection shall be construed to apply to records transferred to the Library of Virginia for permanent archiving pursuant to the duties imposed by the Virginia Public Records Act (§ 42.1-76 et seq.). In accordance with § 42.1-79, the Library of Virginia shall be the custodian of such permanently archived records and shall be responsible for responding to requests for such records made pursuant to this chapter.

History.
1968, c. 479, § 2.1-342; 1973, c. 461; 1974, c. 332; 1975, cc. 307, 312; 1976, cc. 640, 709; 1977, c. 677; 1978, c. 810; 1979, cc. 682, 684, 686, 689; 1980, cc. 678, 754; 1981, cc. 456, 464, 466, 589; 1982, cc. 225, 449, 452, 560, 635; 1983, cc. 372, 462, 607; 1984, cc. 85, 395, 433, 513, 532; 1985, cc. 81, 155, 502, 618; 1986, cc. 273, 291, 383, 469, 592; 1987, cc. 401, 491, 581; 1988, cc. 39, 151, 395, 411, 891, 902; 1989, cc. 56, 358, 478; 1990, cc. 217, 538, 721, 819, 968; 1991, cc. 213, 561; 1992, cc. 40, 150, 167, 200, 203, 207, 593, 612; 1993, cc. 205, 270, 296, 537, 552, 638, 750, 883; 1994, cc. 485, 532, 606, 839, 853, 918; 1995, cc. 299, 362, 499, 562, 638, 722, 812, 837; 1996, cc. 168, 469, 589, 599, 783, 786, 794, 855, 862, 902, 905, 1001, 1046; 1997, cc. 198, 295, 439, 567, 636, 641, 777, 782, 785, 838, 861; 1998, cc. 427, 891; 1999, cc. 438, 703, 726; 2001, c. 844; 2002, cc. 715, 830; 2003, cc. 275, 981, 1021; 2007, c. 439; 2009, c. 626; 2010, c. 627; 2011, c. 604.

Cross references.
As to the powers and duties of the Virginia Information Technologies Agency and Chief Information Officer, see §§ 2.2-2007 et seq. For provision that the Freedom of Information Act shall not apply to certified abstracts of votes or any other documents used by the State Board of Elections in ascertaining the results of an election until such results have been finally determined by the Board, see § 24.2-677. For provisions as to confidentiality of records of the Office of the State Long-Term Care Ombudsman, see § 51.5-141.

Editor's note.
For provisions of Acts 2003, cc. 981 and 1021, cls. 4 to 16, reflecting the intent of the General Assembly to provide for the consolidation of the procurement and operational functions of information technology for state agencies in a single agency, and related transitional and other provisions, see the Editor's note at § 2.2-2005.

The 2010 amendments.
The 2010 amendment by c. 627 added subsection J.

The 2011 amendments.
The 2011 amendment by c. 604 added the last two sentences in subsection J.

Law Review.
For survey of the Virginia law on administrative law for the year 2007-2008, see 43 U. Rich. L. Rev. 73 (2008). For article, "Litigation, Legislation, and Democracy in a Post-Newspaper America," see 68 Wash. & Lee L. Rev. 557 (2011).

Research references.
Bryson on Virginia Civil Procedure (Matthew Bender). Chapter 9 Discovery. § 9.08 Production of documents and things. W. Hamilton Bryson.
Virginia Forms (Matthew Bender). No. 9-1301 Freedom of Information Request.

CASE NOTES

Editor's note.
Most of the cases below were decided under former Title 2.1 or prior provisions.

Constitutionality. — Citizens-only provision of Virginia's Freedom of Information Act, § 2.2-3700 et seq., and specifically subsection A of § 2.2-3704, does not violate the Dormant Commerce Clause of U.S. Const., Art. I, § 8, cl. 3, because the Virginia Freedom of Information Act does not implicate principles of economic protectionism. While the law may have some incidental impact on out-of-state business, the goal is not to favor Virginia business over non-Virginia business. McBurney v. Cuccinelli, 2011 U.S. Dist. LEXIS 5926 (E.D. Va. Jan. 21, 2011).

State and local agencies in Virginia were entitled to deny certain requests for information from two individuals who were not Virginia citizens pursuant to subsection A of § 2.2-3704, a citizens-only provision of Virginia's Freedom of Information Act, because the provision did not burden a fundamental right within the meaning of the Privileges and Immunities Clause of U.S. Const., Art. IV, § 2, cl. 1, where the Virginia Freedom of Information Act did not interfere with the noncitizens' rights to pursue a common calling or to access the courts. The right to access information, the right to advocate for one's own interest, and the right to pursue economic interests were not fundamental rights. McBurney v. Cuccinelli, 2011 U.S. Dist. LEXIS 5926 (E.D. Va. Jan. 21, 2011).

No Commerce Clause violation. — Nothing in Virginia's Freedom of Information Act, § 2.2-3700 et seq., burdened the flow of interstate commerce — at most, it prevented individual one from using his chosen way of doing business, but it did not prevent him from engaging in business in the Commonwealth — the Freedom of Information Act simply did not fall within the type of provision to which the first tier test of analyzing dormant Commerce Clause claims applied. McBurney v. Young, 667 F.3d 454, 2012 U.S. App. LEXIS 1872 (4th Cir. 2012).

Virginia's Freedom of Information Act citizen's-only provision did not bar individual two from engaging in the political process, advocating his own interests, or advancing his political or legal arguments within the Commonwealth; therefore, individual two's argument that Freedom of Information Act impermissibly restricted his ability to advocate his own and others' interests was rejected. McBurney v. Young, 667 F.3d 454, 2012 U.S. App. LEXIS 1872 (4th Cir. 2012).

Nothing in the language of the Virginia's Freedom of Information Act, § 2.2-3700 et seq., prohibited individual one from pursuing his profession in Virginia, or regulated his ability as a noncitizen to enter or engage in business there. Any effect by the Virginia Freedom of Information Act was by happenstance; a circumstance never recognized by the U.S. Supreme Court in its Privileges and Immunities Clause case law. McBurney v. Young, 667 F.3d 454, 2012 U.S. App. LEXIS 1872 (4th Cir. 2012).

Policy of openness does not override need for confidentiality in every circumstance. — Although the General Assembly sought to ensure public access to governmental records and meetings, to avoid an "atmosphere of secrecy" in the conduct of government affairs, and to encourage resolution of disputes in these areas through agreement rather than litigation, the General Assembly does not consider the policy absolute, however, and currently has identified 44 instances in which certain information is exempt from mandatory disclosure; taken together, these exemptions reflect the General Assembly's determination that the policy of openness does not override the need for confidentiality in every circumstance, that the best interests of the Commonwealth may require that certain governmental records and activities not be subject to compelled disclosure. Taylor v. Worrell Enters., Inc., 242 Va. 219, 409 S.E.2d 136 (1991).

An administrative request is a condition precedent to judicial remedies. — An administrative request for minutes or other records is a condition precedent to judicial remedies under the act. Hale v. Washington County School Bd., 241 Va. 76, 400 S.E.2d 175 (1991).

When prior request for records not required. — Where records exist, the legislative purpose was to require a request addressed to the public body, followed by a refusal, as a condition precedent to judicial proceedings for the production of those records. However, the act cannot be read to require either a request for records when the relief requested does not involve production of records, or a fruitless request for records which the requester knows to be nonexistent. Hale v. Washington County School Bd., 241 Va. 76, 400 S.E.2d 175 (1991).

Where school board superintendent alleged the nonexistence of any minutes of a closed meeting, the superintendent obviated any need to allege a prior request for, and denial of, those records. Hale v. Washington County School Bd., 241 Va. 76, 400 S.E.2d 175 (1991).

The jury list is not an "official record" within the intent and meaning of the provisions of this chapter. Archer v. Mayes, 213 Va. 633, 194 S.E.2d 707 (1973).

Failure to cite Freedom of Information Act section. — Property owner was not entitled to the names of complainants redacted from documents disclosed to him pursuant to his Freedom of Information Act (FOIA) request to zoning administrator. The requester received all the information he was entitled to receive under FOIA and the administrator's failure to cite the FOIA section that established the exception did not deny any of the requester's rights and privileges under the Act. Lawrence v. Jenkins, 258 Va. 598, 521 S.E.2d 523 (1999).

Agency employee not authorized to remove and publish agency document. — This section gives no agency employee the right to remove a report or document from the files and records of the agency and to publish it. Jurgensen v. Fairfax County, 745 F.2d 868 (4th Cir. 1984).

Section does not authorize removal of documents in violation of departmental regulation. — This section relates only to the right to inspect and copy "during regular office hours" in the office of the "custodian" of "official records." It plainly did not clothe a police department employee with the right to remove files, reports or documents from the police department in knowing violation of his obligation as an employee under the regulations of the department. Jurgensen v. Fairfax County, 745 F.2d 868 (4th Cir. 1984).

Regulation granting certain officers exclusive authority to make reports public was not unreasonable. — A police department regulation which prescribed a formula for processing applications for the exercise of the right to inspect and copy reports by identifying the specific officers in the department with the exclusive authority to make a report public was not invalid for repugnancy to this chapter. There is nothing either illegal or unreasonable in such a regulation. Jurgensen v. Fairfax County, 745 F.2d 868 (4th Cir. 1984).

List of telephone calls by Governor does not need to be disclosed. — Itemized list of long distance telephone calls placed by the Governor's office does not need to be disclosed when requested pursuant to the Freedom of Information Act; a legislatively imposed disclosure requirement would constitute a violation of the separation of powers doctrine because disclosure of the information in question would unduly interfere with the chief executive officer's ability to perform his duties, and is not warranted by an overriding need to promote a policy of open government in this instance; therefore, the information at issue fell within exemption and was not subject to compelled disclosure under the act. Taylor v. Worrell Enters., Inc., 242 Va. 219, 409 S.E.2d 136 (1991).

High school election vote count does not need to be disclosed. — The Virginia Freedom of Information Act does not require the disclosure of the total number of votes received by each candidate in a public high school student election. Wall v. Fairfax County Sch. Bd., 252 Va. 156, 475 S.E.2d 803 (1996).

Failure to timely make statutorily required response. — City airport authority's response to appellant's request for information under the Freedom of Information Act (FOIA), § 2.2-3700 et seq., did not comply with the FOIA as it did not timely make one of the four statutorily required responses under § 2.2-3704 but merely stated that the matter had been referred to its legal counsel or to the transportation security administration; appellant was entitled to attorney's fees under § 2.2-3713(D) as the trial court's judgment was reversed on appeal. Fenter v. Norfolk Airport Auth., 274 Va. 524, 649 S.E.2d 704, 2007 Va. LEXIS 102 (2007).

Not applicable to State Corporation Commission. — Virginia Freedom of Information Act did not apply to the Virginia State Corporation Commission because the State Corporation Commission was governed by a separate and parallel structure of laws and was not a "public body" under the Virginia Freedom of Information Act; further, the Virginia Freedom of Information Act lacked a constitutional enforcement mechanism applicable to the State Corporation Commission. Christian v. State Corp. Comm'n, 282 Va. 392, 718 S.E.2d 767, 2011 Va. LEXIS 217 (2011).

CIRCUIT COURT OPINIONS

Failure to comply with document request. — Zoning administrator violated subsection B of § 2.2-3704 when the administrator did not timely respond to a document request. Ripol v. Westmoreland County Indus. Dev. Auth., 82 Va. Cir. 69, 2010 Va. Cir. LEXIS 203 (Westmoreland County Dec. 28, 2010).

Documents relating to volunteers. — County school board failed to comply in a timely manner with some of a citizen's document requests because five documents relating to volunteers, which were held not to fall under the exception to the Virginia Freedom of Information Act for personnel files, subdivision 1 of § 2.2-3705.1, should have been disclosed with the original documents, and the delay in the disclosure of documents that were produced voluntarily contravened the requirements of the Act, subsection B of § 2.2-3704; however, the violations were de minimis because the board was justified in withholding and redacting the numerous documents that qualified pursuant to exemptions under the Act, §§ 2.2-3705.1, 2.2-3705.4, and 2.2-3705.1. Hill v. Fairfax County Sch. Bd., 83 Va. Cir. 172, 2011 Va. Cir. LEXIS 89 (Fairfax County July 13, 2011).

Response improper. — Member of a county board of supervisors failed to make a proper response to a landowner's request for public records because his response, which was limited to the production of e-mails regarding the transaction of public business and withheld certain records deemed unrelated to the transaction of public business, was deficient; in the response, there had to be sufficient information to enable a court to make a meaningful review of the decision of the public official or body to whom the request has been made. Burton v. Mann, 74 Va. Cir. 471, 2008 Va. Cir. LEXIS 57 (Loudoun County 2008).

Records containing information exempt from disclosure do not have to be produced. — Language of the Virginia Freedom of Information Act, subdivision B 2 of § 2.2-3704, is unambiguous because it does not require that, in responding to a Freedom of Information Act request, all records containing information exempt from disclosure must, upon proper redaction, be produced; a court is thus bound by the plain meaning of the language of subdivision B 2 of § 2.2-3704. Virginian-Pilot Media Cos., L.L.C. v. City of Norfolk Sch. Bd., 81 Va. Cir. 450, 2010 Va. Cir. LEXIS 272 (Norfolk Dec. 28, 2010).

Redaction by public body. — Virginia Freedom of Information Act, § 2.2-3704, does not, in every instance, require a public body to redact an individual record subject to a Freedom of Information Act exclusion because its language is not sufficiently direct and clear to reach any such result; instead, this language requires only that, when a public body chooses in its discretion to engage in redaction, i.e., deletion or excision, it must limit itself to removal or obliteration of excludable information, and read in this way, the language of subdivision B 2 of § 2.2-3704 harmonizes with the language of subdivisions B 1, B 3 and B 4 of § 2.2-3704, which deal with legal prohibition from or hardship or impossibility of disclosure by a public body. Virginian-Pilot Media Cos., L.L.C. v. City of Norfolk Sch. Bd., 81 Va. Cir. 450, 2010 Va. Cir. LEXIS 272 (Norfolk Dec. 28, 2010).

Redaction not required. — School board was ordered to provide requested records to a media company, except for those records properly classified as scholastic records containing information concerning identifiable individuals, the Virginia Freedom of Information Act, subdivision 1 of § 2.2-3705.4, and personnel records containing information concerning identifiable individuals, because there was no specific requirement of "redaction" within the Virginia Freedom of Information Act with respect to minimum disclosure; the school board properly could exclude from production to the company any individual record properly considered in toto or in part a scholastic record or a personnel record, containing information concerning identifiable individuals, under subdivision 1 of §§ 2.2-3705.1 and 2.2-3705.4. Virginian-Pilot Media Cos., L.L.C. v. City of Norfolk Sch. Bd., 81 Va. Cir. 450, 2010 Va. Cir. LEXIS 272 (Norfolk Dec. 28, 2010).

Costs of redaction not reimbursable. — Labor costs, including travel and lodging expenses, related to redacting records to remove protected information, were not costs for which a department was allowed to charge for reimbursement under the Virginia Freedom of Information Act. Albright v. Woodfin, 68 Va. Cir. 115, 2005 Va. Cir. LEXIS 104 (Nelson County 2005).

Costs not reimbursed where fees not agreed upon. — Because the terms and conditions were not agreed between a city and a reporter prior to the city's preparation of a spreadsheet summary at the reporter's request, the costs requested by the city were not proper. Davis v. City of Chesapeake, 74 Va. Cir. 367, 2007 Va. Cir. LEXIS 299 (Chesapeake 2007).

Filing fees recoverable. — Landowner was entitled to recover her filing fees, which could be offset against the costs of conducting a search for a personal computer and the production of documents, because she was denied access to requested records in violation of the Virginia Freedom of Information Act; such a search was neither directed nor contemplated by a written order of a district court judge. Burton v. Mann, 74 Va. Cir. 471, 2008 Va. Cir. LEXIS 57 (Loudoun County 2008).

Statutory exemption not found. — Names of individual claimants were not protected by § 2.2-3803 under the Virginia Government Data Collection and Dissemination Practices Act, § 2.2-3800 et seq., where a reporter requested from a city information about claims against the city. Davis v. City of Chesapeake, 74 Va. Cir. 367, 2007 Va. Cir. LEXIS 299 (Chesapeake 2007).

OPINIONS OF THE ATTORNEY GENERAL

Records generated by an institutional review board of a public institution of higher learning in the Commonwealth engaged in human research projects are not required to be open for public inspection. See opinion of Attorney General to The Honorable Thomas C. Wright Jr., Member, House of Delegates, 01-101 (10/22/01).

Clerk of the circuit court is not required to produce records from an electronic database in a tangible medium that is not used in the regular course of business. See opinion of Attorney General to The Honorable Charles V. Mason, Clerk, Circuit Court of King George County, 03-101 (2/2/04).

Clerk's charge for reproduction of records from an electronic database must be reasonable and should not exceed the actual costs. See opinion of Attorney General to The Honorable Charles V. Mason, Clerk, Circuit Court of King George County, 03-101 (2/2/04).

A Clerk of Court may install recording systems into a Circuit Court, General District Court, and/or Juvenile and Domestic Relations Court and require such systems to be on at all times court is in session and, further, that the Clerk may charge a fee for access to such recordings provided that confidentiality is maintained for all proceedings as required by the Virginia Code or Court orders. See opinion of Attorney General to The Honorable Scott A. Surovell, Member, House of Delegates, 10-063, 2010 Va. AG LEXIS 40 (8/2/10).

§ 2.2-3704.1. Posting of notice of rights and responsibilities by state public bodies; assistance by the Freedom of Information Advisory Council.

A. All state public bodies created in the executive branch of state government and subject to the provisions of this chapter shall make available the following information to the public upon request and shall post such information on the Internet:

1. A plain English explanation of the rights of a requester under this chapter, the procedures to obtain public records from the public body, and the responsibilities of the public body in complying with this chapter. For purposes of this subdivision "plain English" means written in nontechnical, readily understandable language using words of common everyday usage and avoiding legal terms and phrases or other terms and words of art whose usage or special meaning primarily is limited to a particular field or profession;

2. Contact information for the person designated by the public body to (i) assist a requester in making a request for records or (ii) respond to requests for public records;

3. A general description, summary, list, or index of the types of public records maintained by such state public body;

4. A general description, summary, list, or index of any exemptions in law that permit or require such public records to be withheld from release; and

5. Any policy the public body has concerning the type of public records it routinely withholds from release as permitted by this chapter or other law.

B. The Freedom of Information Advisory Council, created pursuant to § 30-178, shall assist in the development and implementation of the provisions of subsection A, upon request.

History.
2004, c. 730; 2009, c. 626.

§ 2.2-3705. Repealed by Acts 2004, c. 690.

Cross references.
For present provisions as to exclusions to application of chapter, see §§ 2.2-3705.1 through 2.2-3705.8.

§ 2.2-3705.1. Exclusions to application of chapter; exclusions of general application to public bodies.

The following records are excluded from the provisions of this chapter but may be disclosed by the custodian in his discretion, except where such disclosure is prohibited by law:

1. Personnel records containing information concerning identifiable individuals, except that access shall not be denied to the person who is the subject thereof. Any person who is the subject of any personnel record and who is 18 years of age or older may waive, in writing, the protections afforded by this subdivision. If the protections are so waived, the public body shall open such records for inspection and copying.

2. Written advice of legal counsel to state, regional or local public bodies or the officers or employees of such public bodies, and any other records protected by the attorney-client privilege.

3. Legal memoranda and other work product compiled specifically for use in litigation or for use in an active administrative investigation concerning a matter that is properly the subject of a closed meeting under § 2.2-3711.

4. Any test or examination used, administered or prepared by any public body for purposes of evaluation of (i) any student or any student's performance, (ii) any employee or employment seeker's qualifications or aptitude for employment, retention, or promotion, or (iii) qualifications for any license or certificate issued by a public body.

As used in this subdivision, "test or examination" shall include (a) any scoring key for any such test or examination and (b) any other document that would jeopardize the security of the test or examination. Nothing contained in this subdivision shall prohibit the release of test scores or results as provided by law, or limit access to individual records as provided by law. However, the subject of such employment tests shall be entitled to review and inspect all records relative to his performance on such employment tests.

When, in the reasonable opinion of such public body, any such test or examination no longer has any potential for future use, and the security of future tests or examinations will not be jeopardized, the test or examination shall be made available to the public. However, minimum competency tests administered to public school children shall be made available to the public contemporaneously with statewide release of the scores of those taking such tests, but in no event shall such tests be made available to the public later than six months after the administration of such tests.

5. Records recorded in or compiled exclusively for use in closed meetings lawfully held pursuant to § 2.2-3711. However, no record that is otherwise open to inspection under this chapter shall be deemed exempt by virtue of the fact that it has been reviewed or discussed in a closed meeting.

6. Vendor proprietary information software that may be in the official records of a public body. For the purpose of this subdivision, "vendor proprietary software" means computer programs acquired from a vendor for purposes of processing data for agencies or political subdivisions of the Commonwealth.

7. Computer software developed by or for a state agency, state-supported institution of higher education or political subdivision of the Commonwealth.

8. Appraisals and cost estimates of real property subject to a proposed purchase, sale or lease, prior to the completion of such purchase, sale or lease.

9. Records concerning reserves established in specific claims administered by the Department of the Treasury through its Division of Risk Management as provided in Article 5 (§ 2.2-1832 et seq.) of Chapter 18 of this title, or by any county, city, or town; and investigative notes, correspondence and information furnished in confidence with respect to an investigation of a claim or a potential claim against a public body's insurance policy or self-insurance plan. However, nothing in this subdivision shall prohibit the disclosure of information taken from inactive reports upon expiration of the period of limitations for the filing of a civil suit.

10. Personal information, as defined in § 2.2-3801, including electronic mail addresses, furnished to a public body for the purpose of receiving electronic mail from the public body, provided that the electronic mail recipient has requested that the public body not disclose such information. However, access shall not be denied to the person who is the subject of the record.

11. Communications and materials required to be kept confidential pursuant to § 2.2-4119 of the Virginia Administrative Dispute Resolution Act (§ 2.2-4115 et seq.).

12. Records relating to the negotiation and award of a specific contract where competition or bargaining is involved and where the release of such records would adversely affect the bargaining position or negotiating strategy of the public body. Such records shall not be withheld after the public body has made a decision to award or not to award the contract. In the case of procurement transactions conducted pursuant to the Virginia Public Procurement Act (§ 2.2-4300 et seq.), the provisions of this subdivision shall not apply, and any release of records relating to such transactions shall be governed by the Virginia Public Procurement Act.

13. Those portions of records that contain account numbers or routing information for any credit card, debit card, or other account with a financial institution of any person or public body. However, access shall not be denied to the person who is the subject of the record. For the purposes of this subdivision, "financial institution" means any organization authorized to do business under state or federal laws relating to financial institutions, including, without limitation, banks and trust companies, savings banks, savings and loan companies or associations, and credit unions.

History.
1999, cc. 485, 518, 703, 726, 793, 849, 852, 867, 868, 881, § 2.1-342.01; 2000, cc. 66, 237, 382, 400, 430, 583, 589, 592, 594, 618, 632, 657, 720, 932, 933, 947, 1006, 1064; 2001, cc. 288, 518, 844, § 2.2-3705; 2002, cc. 87, 155, 242, 393, 478, 481, 499, 522, 571, 572, 633, 655, 715, 798, 830; 2003, cc. 274, 307, 327, 332, 358, 704, 801, 884, 891, 893, 897, 968; 2004, c. 690; 2010, c. 553.

The 2010 amendments.
The 2010 amendment by c. 553, effective April 11, 2010, added subdivision 13.

Research references.
Bryson on Virginia Civil Procedure (Matthew Bender). Chapter 9 Discovery. § 9.04 Privileges against discovery. W. Hamilton Bryson.

CASE NOTES

Documents to be made part of record on appeal. — Trial court erred in refusing to require a university to produce reports sought under the Freedom of Information Act so they could be made part of the record under Va. Sup. Ct. R. 5:10(a)(3), as the refusal prevented review by the appellate court of a professor's request for reports made by the university to an accrediting agency, and confidential personnel information under § 2.2-3705.1 could have been shielded by a protective order. Bland v. Va. State Univ., 272 Va. 198, 630 S.E.2d 525, 2006 Va. LEXIS 55 (2006).

Virginia Freedom of Information Act did not apply to State Corporation Commission. — Virginia Freedom of Information Act did not apply to the Virginia State Corporation Commission because the State Corporation Commission was governed by a separate and parallel structure of laws and was not a "public body" under the Virginia Freedom of Information Act; further, the Virginia Freedom of Information Act lacked a constitutional enforcement mechanism applicable to the State Corporation Commission. Christian v. State Corp. Comm'n, 282 Va. 392, 718 S.E.2d 767, 2011 Va. LEXIS 217 (2011).

Mandamus erroneously denied. — Landowner, who alleged a violation of the rights and privileges afforded by the Virginia Freedom of Information Act, § 2.2-3700 et seq., and seeking relief by mandamus pursuant to § 2.2-3713, was not required to prove a lack of an adequate remedy at law, nor could his mandamus proceeding be barred on the ground that there might have been some other remedy at law available; moreover, because the circuit court did not reach the issue whether a sales brochure in connection with a highway construction project was subject to disclosure under the Act, the matter was remanded for further consideration of that issue and a determination as to whether the landowner was entitled to reasonable costs and attorneys' fees. Cartwright v. Commonwealth Transp. Comm'r, 270 Va. 58, 613 S.E.2d 449, 2005 Va. LEXIS 62 (2005).

CIRCUIT COURT OPINIONS

Work product. — As "work product" has been applied to material compiled outside of the context of litigation, non-attorneys can create and compile such work product; when separated from its legal context, as is the case in the Virginia Freedom of Information Act, subdivision 3 of § 2.2-3705.1, "work product" means exactly that, the product, or materials and documents, of work. Virginian-Pilot Media Cos., L.L.C. v. City of Norfolk Sch. Bd., 81 Va. Cir. 450, 2010 Va. Cir. LEXIS 272 (Norfolk Dec. 28, 2010).

Personnel records. — "Personnel records" under the Virginia Freedom of Information Act, subdivision 1 of § 2.2-3705.1, are records of or pertaining to a specific, identifiable public school employee and touching directly upon that individual's performance, discipline, attendance, income, social security number, tax-related matters, personal background, circumstances and education, and other information bearing upon the individual's employment relationship with the public school and for which either the employee or the public school may have a reasonable expectation of confidentiality. Virginian-Pilot Media Cos., L.L.C. v. City of Norfolk Sch. Bd., 81 Va. Cir. 450, 2010 Va. Cir. LEXIS 272 (Norfolk Dec. 28, 2010). Police personnel records are, like all public personnel records, subject to the protections of subdivision 1 of § 2.2-3705.1; thus, a circuit court erred when it issued a mandamus order to a police department that required the department to produce information that was contained only in an officer's personnel record. Harmon v. Ewing, 285 Va. 335, 2013 Va. LEXIS 14 (Feb. 8, 2013).

Investigation no longer active. — Administrative investigation of a panel investigating testing irregularities at a school was no longer active, and as a result, the records the panel compiled were not longer subject to the exclusion of the Virginia Freedom of Information Act; the language of subdivision 3 of § 2.2-3705.1 appears clear and unambiguous on its face because the word "active" modifies only the term "administrative investigation," and not the term "litigation," which itself may be anticipated, or planned, active, or concluded. Virginian-Pilot Media Cos., L.L.C. v. City of Norfolk Sch. Bd., 81 Va. Cir. 450, 2010 Va. Cir. LEXIS 272 (Norfolk Dec. 28, 2010).

Investigation subject to closed meeting. — Panel investigating testing irregularities at a school investigated matters that were properly subject to a closed meeting under the Virginia Freedom of Information Act, § 2.2-3711, because the school board did, in fact, conduct a closed meeting on the panel's report, which derived from the panel's investigation, including the records; the panel's administrative investigation thus concerned matters that were "properly subject of a closed meeting under § 2.2-3711" pursuant to the Freedom of Information Act. Virginian-Pilot Media Cos., L.L.C. v. City of Norfolk Sch. Bd., 81 Va. Cir. 450, 2010 Va. Cir. LEXIS 272 (Norfolk Dec. 28, 2010).

Administrative investigation. — Work of a panel investigating testing irregularities at a school and its records constituted work product compiled specifically for use in an active administrative investigation concerning a matter properly subject to a closed meeting under the Virginia Freedom of Information Act, § 2.2-3711, because the work constituted an "administrative investigation" within the meaning of the Virginia Freedom of Information Act; as the investigation would have been "active" during the time that it occurred, the panel's work constituted an "active administrative investigation" under subdivision 3 of § 2.2-3705.1. Virginian-Pilot Media Cos., L.L.C. v. City of Norfolk Sch. Bd., 81 Va. Cir. 450, 2010 Va. Cir. LEXIS 272 (Norfolk Dec. 28, 2010).

Redaction not required. — School board was ordered to provide requested records to a media company, except for those records properly classified as scholastic records containing informa-

tion concerning identifiable individuals, the Virginia Freedom of Information Act, subdivision 1 of § 2.2-3705.4, and personnel records containing information concerning identifiable individuals, because there was no specific requirement of "redaction" within the Act with respect to minimum disclosure; the school board properly could exclude from production to the company any individual record properly considered in toto or in part a scholastic record or a personnel record, containing information concerning identifiable individuals, under subdivision 1 of §§ 2.2-3705.1 and 2.2-3705.4. Virginian-Pilot Media Cos., L.L.C. v. City of Norfolk Sch. Bd., 81 Va. Cir. 450, 2010 Va. Cir. LEXIS 272 (Norfolk Dec. 28, 2010).

Employment discrimination. — Because a county failed to prove that it advised the sources of information that information gathered would be treated confidentially, which was a necessary element in order to invoke the exception found in subdivision 3 of § 2.2-3705.3, a former employee was entitled to all information related to an employment discrimination complaint, investigation, and reprimand, pursuant to subdivision 1 of § 2.2-3705.1. McChrystal v. Fairfax County Bd. of Supervisors, 67 Va. Cir. 171, 2005 Va. Cir. LEXIS 26 (Fairfax County 2005).

Confidential information. — Even if a county could have shown that it advised the sources of information that information gathered would be treated confidentially, which was a necessary element in order to invoke the exception to the Virginia Freedom of Information Act found in § 2.2-3705.3, a former employee would have been entitled to all information in a report of a county's office of equity program but not the investigatory materials giving rise to it, pursuant to § 2.2-3705.1. McChrystal v. Fairfax County Bd. of Supervisors, 67 Va. Cir. 171, 2005 Va. Cir. LEXIS 26 (Fairfax County 2005).

Reporters' requests regarding claims against a city arising from sewer backups and overflows were not exempted from the Virginia Freedom of Information Act by subdivision 9 of § 2.2-3705.1 because the requested records were not correspondence furnished in confidence with respect to an investigation of a claim. Davis v. City of Chesapeake, 74 Va. Cir. 367, 2007 Va. Cir. LEXIS 299 (Chesapeake 2007).

Documents exempt. — County school board failed to comply in a timely manner with some of a citizen's document requests because five documents relating to volunteers, which were held not to fall under the exception to the Virginia Freedom of Information Act for personnel files, subdivision 1 of § 2.2-3705.1, should have been disclosed with the original documents, and the delay in the disclosure of documents that were produced voluntarily contravened the requirements of the Act, subsection B of § 2.2-3704; however, the violations were de minimis because the board was justified in withholding and redacting the numerous documents that qualified pursuant to exemptions under the Act, §§ 2.2-3705.1, 2.2-3705.4, and 2.2-3705.1. Hill v. Fairfax County Sch. Bd., 83 Va. Cir. 172, 2011 Va. Cir. LEXIS 89 (Fairfax County July 13, 2011).

Records not excluded from disclosure. — School board was ordered to provide requested records to a media company, except for those records properly classified as scholastic records containing information concerning identifiable individuals, the Virginia Freedom of Information Act, subdivision 1 of § 2.2-3705.4, and personnel records containing information concerning identifiable individuals, because the investigative notes, correspondence, and information assembled by a panel investigating testing irregularities at a school were not excluded from Freedom of Information Act disclosure as protected by the attorney-client privilege, subdivision 2 of § 2.2-3705.1; because of the nature of the two categories of Freedom of Information Act excludable records at issue, personnel and scholastic records, and their protected status under the Freedom of Information Act, such status was not affected by the outcome of any inquiry regarding whether the superintendent and/or the school board committed ultra vires acts in forming, charging, or otherwise permitting the panel to convene and act under their imprimatur. Virginian-Pilot Media Cos., L.L.C. v. City of Norfolk Sch. Bd., 81 Va. Cir. 450, 2010 Va. Cir. LEXIS 272 (Norfolk Dec. 28, 2010).

§ 2.2-3705.2. Exclusions to application of chapter; records relating to public safety.

The following records are excluded from the provisions of this chapter but may be disclosed by the custodian in his discretion, except where such disclosure is prohibited by law:

1. Confidential records, including victim identity, provided to or obtained by staff in a rape crisis center or a program for battered spouses.

2. Those portions of engineering and construction drawings and plans submitted for the sole purpose of complying with the Building Code in obtaining a building permit that would identify specific trade secrets or other information, the disclosure of which would be harmful to the competitive position of the owner or lessee. However, such information shall be exempt only until the building is completed. Information relating to the safety or environmental soundness of any building shall not be exempt from disclosure.

Those portions of engineering and construction drawings and plans that reveal critical structural components, security equipment and systems, ventilation systems, fire protection equipment, mandatory building emergency equipment or systems, elevators, electrical systems, telecommunications equipment and systems, and other utility equipment and systems submitted for the purpose of complying with the Uniform Statewide Building Code (§ 36-97 et seq.) or the Statewide Fire Prevention Code (§ 27-94 et seq.), the disclosure of which would jeopardize the safety or security of any public or private commercial office, multifamily residential or retail building or its occupants in the event of terrorism or other threat to public safety, to the extent that the owner or lessee of such property, equipment or system in writing (i) invokes the protections of this paragraph; (ii) identifies the drawings, plans, or other materials to be protected; and (iii) states the reasons why protection is necessary.

Nothing in this subdivision shall prevent the disclosure of information relating to any building in connection with an inquiry into the performance of that building after it has been subjected to fire, explosion, natural disaster or other catastrophic event.

3. Documentation or other information that describes the design, function, operation or access control features of any security system, whether manual or automated, which is used to control access to or use of any automated data processing or telecommunications system.

4. Plans and information to prevent or respond to terrorist activity, the disclosure of which would jeopardize the safety of any person, including (i) critical infrastructure sector or structural components; (ii) vulnerability assessments, operational, procedural, transportation, and tactical planning or training manuals, and staff meeting minutes or other records; and (iii) engineering or architectural records, or records containing information derived from such records, to the extent such records reveal the location or operation of security equipment and systems, elevators, ventilation, fire protection, emergency, electrical, telecommunications or utility equipment and systems of any public building, structure or information storage facility, or telecommunications or utility equipment or systems. The same categories of records of any governmental or nongovernmental person or entity submitted to a public body for the purpose of antiterrorism response planning may be withheld from disclosure if such person or entity in writing (a) invokes the protections of this subdivision, (b) identifies with specificity the records or portions thereof for which protection is sought, and (c) states with reasonable particularity why the protection of such records from public disclosure is necessary to meet the objective of antiterrorism planning or protection. Such statement shall be a public record and shall be disclosed upon request. Nothing in this subdivision shall be construed to prohibit the disclosure of records relating to the structural or environmental soundness of any building, nor shall it prevent the disclosure of information relating to any building in connection with an inquiry into the performance of that building after it has been subjected to fire, explosion, natural disaster or other catastrophic event.

5. Information that would disclose the security aspects of a system safety program plan adopted pursuant to 49 C.F.R. Part 659 by the Commonwealth's designated Rail Fixed Guideway Systems Safety Oversight agency; and information in the possession of such agency, the release of which would jeopardize the success of an ongoing investigation of a rail accident or other incident threatening railway safety.

6. Engineering and architectural drawings, operational, procedural, tactical planning or training manuals, or staff meeting minutes or other records, the disclosure of which would reveal surveillance techniques, personnel deployments, alarm or security systems or technologies, or operational and transportation plans or protocols, to the extent such disclosure would jeopardize the security of any governmental facility, building or structure or the safety of persons using such facility, building or structure.

7. Security plans and specific assessment components of school safety audits, as provided in § 22.1-279.8.

Nothing in this subdivision shall be construed to prohibit the disclosure of records relating to the effectiveness of security plans after (i) any school building or property has been subjected to fire, explosion, natural disaster or other catastrophic event, or (ii) any person on school property has suffered or been threatened with any personal injury.

8. [Expired.]

9. Records of the Commitment Review Committee concerning the mental health assessment of an individual subject to commitment as a sexually violent predator under Chapter 9 (§ 37.2-900 et

seq.) of Title 37.2; except that in no case shall records identifying the victims of a sexually violent predator be disclosed.

10. Subscriber data, which for the purposes of this subdivision, means the name, address, telephone number, and any other information identifying a subscriber of a telecommunications carrier, provided directly or indirectly by a telecommunications carrier to a public body that operates a 911 or E-911 emergency dispatch system or an emergency notification or reverse 911 system, if the data is in a form not made available by the telecommunications carrier to the public generally. Nothing in this subdivision shall prevent the release of subscriber data generated in connection with specific calls to a 911 emergency system, where the requester is seeking to obtain public records about the use of the system in response to a specific crime, emergency or other event as to which a citizen has initiated a 911 call.

11. Subscriber data, which for the purposes of this subdivision, means the name, address, telephone number, and any other information identifying a subscriber of a telecommunications carrier, collected by a local governing body in accordance with the Enhanced Public Safety Telephone Services Act (§ 56-484.12 et seq.), and other identifying information of a personal, medical, or financial nature provided to a local governing body in connection with a 911 or E-911 emergency dispatch system or an emergency notification or reverse 911 system, if such records are not otherwise publicly available. Nothing in this subdivision shall prevent the release of subscriber data generated in connection with specific calls to a 911 emergency system, where the requester is seeking to obtain public records about the use of the system in response to a specific crime, emergency or other event as to which a citizen has initiated a 911 call.

12. Records of the Virginia Military Advisory Council or any commission created by executive order for the purpose of studying and making recommendations regarding preventing closure or realignment of federal military and national security installations and facilities located in Virginia and relocation of such facilities to Virginia, or a local or regional military affairs organization appointed by a local governing body, to the extent such records (i) contain information relating to strategies under consideration or development by the Council or such commission or organizations to prevent the closure or realignment of federal military installations located in Virginia or the relocation of national security facilities located in Virginia, to limit the adverse economic effect of such realignment, closure, or relocation, or to seek additional tenant activity growth from the Department of Defense or federal government or (ii) disclose trade secrets, as defined in the Uniform Trade Secrets Act (§ 59.1-336 et seq.), provided to the Council or such commission or organizations in connection with their work. In order to invoke the trade secret protection provided by clause (ii), the submitting entity shall, in writing and at the time of submission (a) invoke this exclusion, (b) identify with specificity the information for which such protection is sought, and (c) state the reason why such protection is necessary. Nothing in this subdivision shall be construed to authorize the withholding of all or part of any record, other than a trade secret that has been specifically identified as required by this subdivision, after the Department of Defense or federal agency has issued a final, unappealable decision, or in the event of litigation, a court of competent jurisdiction has entered a final, unappealable order concerning the closure, realignment, or expansion of the military installation or tenant activities, or the relocation of the national security facility, for which records are sought.

13. Documentation or other information as determined by the State Comptroller that describes the design, function, operation, or implementation of internal controls over the Commonwealth's financial processes and systems, and the assessment of risks and vulnerabilities of those controls, including the annual assessment of internal controls mandated by the State Comptroller, the disclosure of which would jeopardize the security of the Commonwealth's financial assets. However, records relating to the investigation of and findings concerning the soundness of any fiscal process shall be disclosed in a form that does not compromise internal controls. Nothing in this subdivision shall be construed to prohibit the Auditor of Public Accounts or the Joint Legislative Audit and Review Commission from reporting internal control deficiencies discovered during the course of an audit.

14. Documentation or other information relating to the Statewide Agencies Radio System (STARS) or any other similar local or regional public safety communications system that (i) describes the design, function, programming, operation, or access control features of the overall system, components, structures, individual networks, and subsystems of the STARS or any other similar local or regional communications system or (ii) relates to radio frequencies assigned to or utilized by STARS or any other similar local or regional communications system, code plugs, circuit routing, addressing schemes, talk groups, fleet maps, encryption, programming maintained by or utilized by STARS or any other similar local or regional public safety communications system; those portions of engineering and construction drawings and plans that reveal critical structural components, interconnectivity, security equipment and systems, network monitoring, network operation center, master sites, ventilation systems, fire protection equipment, mandatory building emergency equipment, electrical systems, and other utility equipment and systems related to STARS or any other similar local or regional public safety communications system; and special event plans, operational plans, storm plans, or other pre-arranged programming, the disclosure of which would

reveal surveillance techniques, personnel deployments, alarm or security systems or technologies, or operational and transportation plans or protocols, to the extent such disclosure would jeopardize the security of any governmental facility, building, or structure or the safety of any person.

15. Records of a salaried or volunteer Fire/EMS company or Fire/EMS department, to the extent that the records disclose the telephone numbers for cellular telephones, pagers, or comparable portable communication devices provided to its personnel for use in the performance of their official duties.

16. Records of hospitals and nursing homes regulated by the Board of Health pursuant to Chapter 5 (§ 32.1-123 et seq.) of Title 32.1 provided to the Department of Health, to the extent such records reveal the disaster recovery plans or the evacuation plans for such facilities in the event of fire, explosion, natural disaster, or other catastrophic event. Nothing in this subdivision shall be construed to prohibit the disclosure of records relating to the effectiveness of executed evacuation plans after the occurrence of fire, explosion, natural disaster, or other catastrophic event.

History.
1999, cc. 485, 518, 703, 726, 793, 849, 852, 867, 868, 881, § 2.1-342.01; 2000, cc. 66, 237, 382, 400, 430, 583, 589, 592, 594, 618, 632, 657, 720, 932, 933, 947, 1006, 1064; 2001, cc. 288, 518, 844, § 2.2-3705; 2002, cc. 87, 155, 242, 393, 478, 481, 499, 522, 571, 572, 633, 655, 715, 798, 830; 2003, cc. 274, 307, 327, 332, 358, 704, 801, 884, 891, 893, 897, 968; 2004, cc. 398, 482, 690, 770; 2005, c. 410; 2008, c. 721; 2009, c. 418; 2010, c. 672; 2011, cc. 111, 536; 2012, cc. 617, 803, 835; 2013, c. 600.

Editor's note.
Acts 2004, c. 398 amended former § 2.2-3705, from which this section is derived. Pursuant to § 30-152, Acts 2004, c. 398 has been given effect in this section as set out above. The 2004 amendment by c. 398 added subdivision 9.

Acts 2004, c. 482 amended former § 2.2-3705, from which this section is derived. Pursuant to § 30-152, Acts 2004, c. 482 has been given effect in this section as set out above. The 2004 amendment by c. 482 inserted "or telecommunications or utility equipment or systems" following "structure or information storage facility" in clause (iii) of subdivision 4, and added subdivision 10.

Acts 2004, c. 770 amended former § 2.2-3705, from which this section is derived. Pursuant to § 30-152, Acts 2004, c. 770 has been given effect in this section as set out above. The 2004 amendment by c. 770, effective April 12, 2004, added subdivision 8.

Acts 2004, c. 770, which added subdivision 8, in cl. 2 provides: "That the provisions of this act shall expire on July 1, 2006."

The 2010 amendments.
The 2010 amendment by c. 672 added subdivision 14.

The 2011 amendments.
The 2011 amendments by cc. 111 and 536 are identical, and in subdivision 12, in the first sentence, inserted the language beginning "any commission created by executive order" and ending "and relocation of such facilities to Virginia," in clause 12 (i), inserted "commission or," "or the relocation of national security facilities located in Virginia," "or relocation," and "or federal government," and made a related change, and in clause 12 (ii), inserted "commission or," and in the last sentence, inserted "or federal agency" and "or the relocation of the national security facility."

The 2012 amendments.
The 2012 amendment by c. 617 added subdivision 15.
The 2012 amendments by cc. 803 and 835, cl. 51, are identical, and in the first sentence of subsection 12, deleted "the Virginia

National Defense Industrial Authority" following "Virginia Military Advisory Council" and inserted "or" preceding "any commission created," and twice deleted "the Authority" following "the Council."

The 2013 amendments.
The 2013 amendment by c. 600 added subdivision 16.

§ 2.2-3705.3. (Effective until January 1, 2014) Exclusions to application of chapter; records relating to administrative investigations.

The following records are excluded from the provisions of this chapter but may be disclosed by the custodian in his discretion, except where such disclosure is prohibited by law:

1. Confidential records of all investigations of applications for licenses and permits, and of all licensees and permittees, made by or submitted to the Alcoholic Beverage Control Board, the State Lottery Department, the Virginia Racing Commission, the Department of Agriculture and Consumer Services relating to investigations and applications pursuant to Article 1.1:1 (§ 18.2-340.15 et seq.) of Chapter 8 of Title 18.2, or the Private Security Services Unit of the Department of Criminal Justice Services.

2. Records of active investigations being conducted by the Department of Health Professions or by any health regulatory board in the Commonwealth.

3. Investigator notes, and other correspondence and information, furnished in confidence with respect to an active investigation of individual employment discrimination complaints made to the Department of Human Resource Management or to such personnel of any local public body, including local school boards as are responsible for conducting such investigations in confidence. However, nothing in this section shall prohibit the disclosure of information taken from inactive reports in a form that does not reveal the identity of charging parties, persons supplying the information or other individuals involved in the investigation.

4. Records of active investigations being conducted by the Department of Medical Assistance Services pursuant to Chapter 10 (§ 32.1-323 et seq.) of Title 32.1.

5. Investigative notes and other correspondence and information furnished in confidence with respect to an investigation or conciliation process involving an alleged unlawful discriminatory practice under the Virginia Human Rights Act (§ 2.2-3900 et seq.) or under any local ordinance adopted in accordance with the authority specified in § 2.2-524, or adopted pursuant to § 15.2-965, or adopted prior to July 1, 1987, in accordance with applicable law, relating to local human rights or human relations commissions. However, nothing in this section shall prohibit the distribution of information taken from inactive reports in a form that does not reveal the identity of the parties involved or other persons supplying information.

6. Records of studies and investigations by the State Lottery Department of (i) lottery agents, (ii) lottery vendors, (iii) lottery crimes under §§ 58.1-4014 through 58.1-4018, (iv) defects in the law or regulations that cause abuses in the administration and operation of the lottery and any evasions of such provisions, or (v) the use of the lottery as a subterfuge for organized crime and illegal gambling where such official records have not been publicly released, published or copyrighted. All studies and investigations referred to under clauses (iii), (iv), and (v) shall be open to inspection and copying upon completion of the study or investigation.

7. Investigative notes, correspondence and information furnished in confidence, and records otherwise exempted by this chapter or any Virginia statute, provided to or produced by or for (i) the Auditor of Public Accounts; (ii) the Joint Legislative Audit and Review Commission; (iii) an appropriate authority as defined in § 2.2-3010 with respect to an allegation of wrongdoing or abuse under the Fraud and Abuse Whistle Blower Protection Act (§ 2.2-3009 et seq.); (iv) the Office of the State Inspector General with respect to an investigation initiated through the Fraud, Waste and Abuse Hotline or an investigation initiated pursuant to Chapter 3.2 (§ 2.2-307 et seq.); (v) the committee or the auditor with respect to an investigation or audit conducted pursuant to § 15.2-825; or (vi) the auditors, appointed by the local governing body of any county, city or town or a school board, who by charter, ordinance, or statute have responsibility for conducting an investigation of any officer, department or program of such body. Records of completed investigations shall be disclosed in a form that does not reveal the identity of the complainants or persons supplying information to investigators. Unless disclosure is prohibited by this section, the records disclosed shall include, but not be limited to, the agency involved, the identity of the person who is the subject of the complaint, the nature of the complaint, and the actions taken to resolve the complaint. If an investigation does not lead to corrective action, the identity of the person who is the subject of the complaint may be released only with the consent of the subject person. Local governing bodies shall adopt guidelines to govern the disclosure required by this subdivision.

8. Records of the Virginia Office for Protection and Advocacy consisting of documentary evidence received or maintained by the Office or its agents in connection with specific complaints or investigations, and records of communications between employees and agents of the Office and its clients or prospective clients concerning specific complaints, investigations or cases. Upon the conclusion of an investigation of a complaint, this exclusion shall no longer apply, but the Office may not at any time release the identity of any complainant or person with mental illness, intellectual disability, developmental disabilities or other disability, unless (i) such

complainant or person or his legal representative consents in writing to such identification or (ii) such identification is required by court order.

9. Information furnished in confidence to the Department of Human Resource Management with respect to an investigation, consultation, or mediation under § 2.2-1202.1, and memoranda, correspondence and other records resulting from any such investigation, consultation or mediation. However, nothing in this section shall prohibit the distribution of information taken from inactive reports in a form that does not reveal the identity of the parties involved or other persons supplying information.

10. The names, addresses and telephone numbers of complainants furnished in confidence with respect to an investigation of individual zoning enforcement complaints or complaints relating to the Uniform Statewide Building Code (§ 36-97 et seq.) or the Statewide Fire Prevention Code (§ 27-94 et seq.) made to a local governing body.

11. Records of active investigations being conducted by the Department of Criminal Justice Services pursuant to Article 4 (§ 9.1-138 et seq.), Article 4.1 (§ 9.1-150.1 et seq.), Article 11 (§ 9.1-185 et seq.), and Article 12 (§ 9.1-186 et seq.) of Chapter 1 of Title 9.1.

12. Records furnished to or prepared by the Board of Education pursuant to subsection D of § 22.1-253.13:3 in connection with the review or investigation of any alleged breach in security, unauthorized alteration, or improper administration of tests by local school board employees responsible for the distribution or administration of the tests. However, this section shall not prohibit the disclosure of records to (i) a local school board or division superintendent for the purpose of permitting such board or superintendent to consider or to take personnel action with regard to an employee or (ii) any requester, after the conclusion of a review or investigation, in a form that (a) does not reveal the identity of any person making a complaint or supplying information to the Board on a confidential basis and (b) does not compromise the security of any test mandated by the Board.

13. Investigator notes, and other correspondence and information, furnished in confidence with respect to an active investigation conducted by or for the Board of Education related to the denial, suspension, or revocation of teacher licenses. However, this subdivision shall not prohibit the disclosure of records to a local school board or division superintendent for the purpose of permitting such board or superintendent to consider or to take personnel action with regard to an employee. Records of completed investigations shall be disclosed in a form that does not reveal the identity of any complainant or person supplying information to investigators. The records disclosed shall include information regarding the school or facility involved, the identity of the person who was the subject of the complaint, the

nature of the complaint, and the actions taken to resolve the complaint. If an investigation fails to support a complaint or does not lead to corrective action, the identity of the person who was the subject of the complaint may be released only with the consent of the subject person. No personally identifiable information in the records regarding a current or former student shall be released except as permitted by state or federal law.

14. Records, notes and information provided in confidence and related to an investigation by the Attorney General under Article 1 (§ 3.2-4200 et seq.) or Article 3 (§ 3.2-4204 et seq.) of Chapter 42 of Title 3.2, Article 10 (§ 18.2-246.6 et seq.) of Chapter 6 or Chapter 13 (§ 18.2-512 et seq.) of Title 18.2, or Article 1 (§ 58.1-1000) of Chapter 10 of Title 58.1. However, records related to an investigation that has been inactive for more than six months shall, upon request, be disclosed provided such disclosure is not otherwise prohibited by law and does not reveal the identity of charging parties, complainants, persons supplying information, witnesses or other individuals involved in the investigation.

History.
1999, cc. 485, 518, 703, 726, 793, 849, 852, 867, 868, 881, § 2.1-342.01; 2000, cc. 66, 237, 382, 400, 430, 583, 589, 592, 594, 618, 632, 657, 720, 932, 933, 947, 1006, 1064; 2001, cc. 288, 518, 844, § 2.2-3705; 2002, cc. 87, 155, 242, 393, 478, 481, 499, 522, 571, 572, 633, 655, 715, 798, 830; 2003, cc. 274, 307, 327, 332, 358, 704, 801, 884, 891, 893, 897, 968; 2004, cc. 605, 690, 766; 2005, c. 601; 2006, cc. 25, 95; 2008, cc. 387, 668, 689, 758; 2009, cc. 237, 326, 340; 2011, cc. 798, 871; 2012, cc. 476, 507, 803, 835; 2013, cc. 572, 690, 717, 723.

Section set out twice.
The section above is effective until January 1, 2014. For the version of this section effective January 1, 2014, see the following section, also numbered 2.2-3705.3.

Editor's note.
The reference in subdivision 5, was changed from "§ 2.2-254" to "§ 2.2-524" at the direction of the Virginia Code Commission.

Acts 2004, c. 605 amended former § 2.2-3705, from which this section is derived. Pursuant to § 30-152, Acts 2004, c. 605 has been given effect in this section as set out above. The 2004 amendment by c. 605, in subdivision 7, added clause (v) and added the last sentence.

Acts 2004, c. 766 amended former § 2.2-3705, from which this section is derived. Pursuant to § 30-152, Acts 2004, c. 766 has been given effect in this section as set out above. The 2004 amendment by c. 766 added "or the Private Security Services Unit of the Department of Criminal Justice Services" at the end of subdivision 1.

Acts 2011, cc. 798 and 871, cl. 7 provides: "That the provisions of this act shall become effective on July 1, 2012, except that the provisions of the fifth enactment of this act shall become effective on July 1, 2011."

Acts 2012, cc. 803 and 835, cl. 16 provides: "That the Governor may transfer an appropriation or any portion thereof within a state agency established, abolished, or otherwise affected by the provisions of the 13th enactment of this act, or from one such agency to another, to support the changes in organization or responsibility resulting from or required by the provisions of the 13th enactment of this act, provided that any such transfer shall be limited to salary and fringe benefits for any personnel transferred and reasonable administrative overhead and costs."

The 2011 amendments.
The 2011 amendments by cc. 798 and 871, effective July 1, 2012, are identical, and in the first sentence in subdivision 7, substituted

"the Office of the State Inspector General" for "Department of the State Internal Auditor," inserted "or an investigation initiated pursuant to Chapter 3.2 (§ 2.2-307 et seq.)" and made minor stylistic changes.

The 2012 amendments.
The 2012 amendments by cc. 476 and 507 are identical, and substituted "intellectual disability" for "mental retardation" in the second sentence of subdivision 8.

The 2012 amendments by cc. 803 and 835, cl. 8, are identical, and in subsection 9, substituted "Department of Human Resource Management" for "Department of Employment Dispute Resolution" and "§ 2.2-1202.1" for "Chapter 10 (§ 2.2-1000 et seq.) of this title." Clause 13 also amended this section by substituting "§ 2.2-252" for "§ 2.2-2638" in subsection 5; and by deleting "of this title" following "(§ 2.2-1000 et seq.)" in the first sentence of subsection 9.

The 2013 amendments.
The 2013 amendments by cc. 572, 690, 717 and 723 are identical, and deleted "State Employee" preceding "Fraud, Waste and Abuse Hotline" in clause (iv) in subdivision 7.

CIRCUIT COURT OPINIONS

Employment discrimination complaints. — Because a county failed to prove that it advised the sources of information that information gathered would be treated confidentially, which was a necessary element in order to invoke the exception found in § 2.2-3705.3, a former employee was entitled to all information related to an employment discrimination complaint, investigation, and reprimand, pursuant to § 2.2-3705.1. McChrystal v. Fairfax County Bd. of Supervisors, 67 Va. Cir. 171, 2005 Va. Cir. LEXIS 26 (Fairfax County 2005).

Investigatory materials. — Even if a county could have shown that it advised the sources of information that information gathered would be treated confidentially, which was a necessary element in order to invoke the exception to the Virginia Freedom of Information Act found in § 2.2-3705.3, a former employee would have been entitled to all information in a report of a county's office of equity program but not the investigatory materials giving rise to it, pursuant to § 2.2-3705.1. McChrystal v. Fairfax County Bd. of Supervisors, 67 Va. Cir. 171, 2005 Va. Cir. LEXIS 26 (Fairfax County 2005).

§ 2.2-3705.3. (Effective January 1, 2014) Exclusions to application of chapter; records relating to administrative investigations.

The following records are excluded from the provisions of this chapter but may be disclosed by the custodian in his discretion, except where such disclosure is prohibited by law:

1. Confidential records of all investigations of applications for licenses and permits, and of all licensees and permittees, made by or submitted to the Alcoholic Beverage Control Board, the State Lottery Department, the Virginia Racing Commission, the Department of Agriculture and Consumer Services relating to investigations and applications pursuant to Article 1.1:1 (§ 18.2-340.15 et seq.) of Chapter 8 of Title 18.2, or the Private Security Services Unit of the Department of Criminal Justice Services.

2. Records of active investigations being conducted by the Department of Health Professions or by any health regulatory board in the Commonwealth.

3. Investigator notes, and other correspondence and information, furnished in confidence with re-

spect to an active investigation of individual employment discrimination complaints made to the Department of Human Resource Management or to such personnel of any local public body, including local school boards as are responsible for conducting such investigations in confidence. However, nothing in this section shall prohibit the disclosure of information taken from inactive reports in a form that does not reveal the identity of charging parties, persons supplying the information or other individuals involved in the investigation.

4. Records of active investigations being conducted by the Department of Medical Assistance Services pursuant to Chapter 10 (§ 32.1-323 et seq.) of Title 32.1.

5. Investigative notes and other correspondence and information furnished in confidence with respect to an investigation or conciliation process involving an alleged unlawful discriminatory practice under the Virginia Human Rights Act (§ 2.2-3900 et seq.) or under any local ordinance adopted in accordance with the authority specified in § 2.2-524, or adopted pursuant to § 15.2-965, or adopted prior to July 1, 1987, in accordance with applicable law, relating to local human rights or human relations commissions. However, nothing in this section shall prohibit the distribution of information taken from inactive reports in a form that does not reveal the identity of the parties involved or other persons supplying information.

6. Records of studies and investigations by the State Lottery Department of (i) lottery agents, (ii) lottery vendors, (iii) lottery crimes under §§ 58.1-4014 through 58.1-4018, (iv) defects in the law or regulations that cause abuses in the administration and operation of the lottery and any evasions of such provisions, or (v) the use of the lottery as a subterfuge for organized crime and illegal gambling where such official records have not been publicly released, published or copyrighted. All studies and investigations referred to under clauses (iii), (iv), and (v) shall be open to inspection and copying upon completion of the study or investigation.

7. Investigative notes, correspondence and information furnished in confidence, and records otherwise exempted by this chapter or any Virginia statute, provided to or produced by or for (i) the Auditor of Public Accounts; (ii) the Joint Legislative Audit and Review Commission; (iii) an appropriate authority as defined in § 2.2-3010 with respect to an allegation of wrongdoing or abuse under the Fraud and Abuse Whistle Blower Protection Act (§ 2.2-3009 et seq.); (iv) the Office of the State Inspector General with respect to an investigation initiated through the Fraud, Waste and Abuse Hotline or an investigation initiated pursuant to Chapter 3.2 (§ 2.2-307 et seq.); (v) the committee or the auditor with respect to an investigation or audit conducted pursuant to § 15.2-825; or (vi) the auditors, appointed by the local governing body of any county, city or town or a school board, who by charter,

ordinance, or statute have responsibility for conducting an investigation of any officer, department or program of such body. Records of completed investigations shall be disclosed in a form that does not reveal the identity of the complainants or persons supplying information to investigators. Unless disclosure is prohibited by this section, the records disclosed shall include, but not be limited to, the agency involved, the identity of the person who is the subject of the complaint, the nature of the complaint, and the actions taken to resolve the complaint. If an investigation does not lead to corrective action, the identity of the person who is the subject of the complaint may be released only with the consent of the subject person. Local governing bodies shall adopt guidelines to govern the disclosure required by this subdivision.

8. Information furnished in confidence to the Department of Human Resource Management with respect to an investigation, consultation, or mediation under § 2.2-1202.1, and memoranda, correspondence and other records resulting from any such investigation, consultation or mediation. However, nothing in this section shall prohibit the distribution of information taken from inactive reports in a form that does not reveal the identity of the parties involved or other persons supplying information.

9. The names, addresses and telephone numbers of complainants furnished in confidence with respect to an investigation of individual zoning enforcement complaints or complaints relating to the Uniform Statewide Building Code (§ 36-97 et seq.) or the Statewide Fire Prevention Code (§ 27-94 et seq.) made to a local governing body.

10. Records of active investigations being conducted by the Department of Criminal Justice Services pursuant to Article 4 (§ 9.1-138 et seq.), Article 4.1 (§ 9.1-150.1 et seq.), Article 11 (§ 9.1-185 et seq.), and Article 12 (§ 9.1-186 et seq.) of Chapter 1 of Title 9.1.

11. Records furnished to or prepared by the Board of Education pursuant to subsection D of § 22.1-253.13:3 in connection with the review or investigation of any alleged breach in security, unauthorized alteration, or improper administration of tests by local school board employees responsible for the distribution or administration of the tests. However, this section shall not prohibit the disclosure of records to (i) a local school board or division superintendent for the purpose of permitting such board or superintendent to consider or to take personnel action with regard to an employee or (ii) any requester, after the conclusion of a review or investigation, in a form that (a) does not reveal the identity of any person making a complaint or supplying information to the Board on a confidential basis and (b) does not compromise the security of any test mandated by the Board.

12. Investigator notes, and other correspondence and information, furnished in confidence with re-

spect to an active investigation conducted by or for the Board of Education related to the denial, suspension, or revocation of teacher licenses. However, this subdivision shall not prohibit the disclosure of records to a local school board or division superintendent for the purpose of permitting such board or superintendent to consider or to take personnel action with regard to an employee. Records of completed investigations shall be disclosed in a form that does not reveal the identity of any complainant or person supplying information to investigators. The records disclosed shall include information regarding the school or facility involved, the identity of the person who was the subject of the complaint, the nature of the complaint, and the actions taken to resolve the complaint. If an investigation fails to support a complaint or does not lead to corrective action, the identity of the person who was the subject of the complaint may be released only with the consent of the subject person. No personally identifiable information in the records regarding a current or former student shall be released except as permitted by state or federal law.

13. Records, notes and information provided in confidence and related to an investigation by the Attorney General under Article 1 (§ 3.2-4200 et seq.) or Article 3 (§ 3.2-4204 et seq.) of Chapter 42 of Title 3.2, Article 10 (§ 18.2-246.6 et seq.) of Chapter 6 or Chapter 13 (§ 18.2-512 et seq.) of Title 18.2, or Article 1 (§ 58.1-1000) of Chapter 10 of Title 58.1. However, records related to an investigation that has been inactive for more than six months shall, upon request, be disclosed provided such disclosure is not otherwise prohibited by law and does not reveal the identity of charging parties, complainants, persons supplying information, witnesses or other individuals involved in the investigation.

History.
1999, cc. 485, 518, 703, 726, 793, 849, 852, 867, 868, 881, § 2.1-342.01; 2000, cc. 66, 237, 382, 400, 430, 583, 589, 592, 594, 618, 632, 657, 720, 932, 933, 947, 1006, 1064; 2001, cc. 288, 518, 844, § 2.2-3705; 2002, cc. 87, 155, 242, 393, 478, 481, 499, 522, 571, 572, 633, 655, 715, 798, 830; 2003, cc. 274, 307, 327, 332, 358, 704, 801, 884, 891, 893, 897, 968; 2004, cc. 605, 690, 766; 2005, c. 601; 2006, cc. 25, 95; 2008, cc. 387, 668, 689, 758; 2009, cc. 237, 326, 340; 2011, cc. 798, 871; 2012, cc. 476, 507, 803, 835; 2013, cc. 571, 572, 690, 717, 723.

Section set out twice.
The section above is effective January 1, 2014. For the version of this section effective until January 1, 2014, see the preceding section, also numbered 2.2-3705.3.

Editor's note.
Acts 2013, c. 571, cl. 3 provides: "That the provisions of this act amending §§ 2.2-2905, 2.2-3705.3, 37.2-304, and 37.2-709 of the Code of Virginia shall become effective January 1, 2014."

The 2013 amendments.
The 2013 amendment by c. 571, effective January 1, 2014, deleted former subdivision 8 pertaining to certain records of the Virginia Office for Protection and Advocacy and redesignated the remaining subdivisions accordingly.
The 2013 amendments by cc. 572, 690, 717 and 723 are identical, and deleted "State Employee" preceding "Fraud, Waste and Abuse Hotline" in clause (iv) in subdivision 7.

§ 2.2-3705.4. Exclusions to application of chapter; educational records and certain records of educational institutions.

The following records are excluded from the provisions of this chapter but may be disclosed by the custodian in his discretion, except where such disclosure is prohibited by law:

1. Scholastic records containing information concerning identifiable individuals, except that such access shall not be denied to the person who is the subject thereof, or the parent or legal guardian of the student. However, no student shall have access to (i) financial records of a parent or guardian or (ii) records of instructional, supervisory, and administrative personnel and educational personnel ancillary thereto, that are in the sole possession of the maker thereof and that are not accessible or revealed to any other person except a substitute.

The parent or legal guardian of a student may prohibit, by written request, the release of any individual information regarding that student until the student reaches the age of 18 years. For scholastic records of students under the age of 18 years, the right of access may be asserted only by his legal guardian or parent, including a noncustodial parent, unless such parent's parental rights have been terminated or a court of competent jurisdiction has restricted or denied such access. For scholastic records of students who are emancipated or attending a state-supported institution of higher education, the right of access may be asserted by the student.

Any person who is the subject of any scholastic record and who is 18 years of age or older may waive, in writing, the protections afforded by this subdivision. If the protections are so waived, the public body shall open such records for inspection and copying.

2. Confidential letters and statements of recommendation placed in the records of educational agencies or institutions respecting (i) admission to any educational agency or institution, (ii) an application for employment, or (iii) receipt of an honor or honorary recognition.

3. Records of the Brown v. Board of Education Scholarship Awards Committee relating to personally identifiable information, including scholarship applications, personal financial information, and confidential correspondence and letters of recommendation.

4. Data, records or information of a proprietary nature produced or collected by or for faculty or staff of public institutions of higher education, other than the institutions' financial or administrative records, in the conduct of or as a result of study or research on medical, scientific, technical or scholarly issues, whether sponsored by the institution alone or in conjunction with a governmental body or a private concern, where such data, records or information has not been publicly released, published, copyrighted or patented.

5. All records of the University of Virginia or the University of Virginia Medical Center or Eastern Virginia Medical School, as the case may be, that contain proprietary, business-related information pertaining to the operations of the University of Virginia Medical Center or Eastern Virginia Medical School, as the case may be, including business development or marketing strategies and activities with existing or future joint venturers, partners, or other parties with whom the University of Virginia Medical Center or Eastern Virginia Medical School, as the case may be, has formed, or forms, any arrangement for the delivery of health care, if disclosure of such information would be harmful to the competitive position of the Medical Center or Eastern Virginia Medical School, as the case may be.

6. Personal information, as defined in § 2.2-3801, provided to the Board of the Virginia College Savings Plan or its employees by or on behalf of individuals who have requested information about, applied for, or entered into prepaid tuition contracts or savings trust account agreements pursuant to Chapter 4.9 (§ 23-38.75 et seq.) of Title 23. Nothing in this subdivision shall be construed to prohibit disclosure or publication of information in a statistical or other form that does not identify individuals or provide personal information. Individuals shall be provided access to their own personal information.

7. Records maintained in connection with fundraising activities by or for a public institution of higher education to the extent that such records reveal (i) personal fundraising strategies relating to identifiable donors or prospective donors or (ii) wealth assessments; estate, financial, or tax planning information; health-related information; employment, familial, or marital status information; electronic mail addresses, facsimile or telephone numbers; birth dates or social security numbers of identifiable donors or prospective donors. Nothing in this subdivision, however, shall be construed to authorize the withholding of records relating to the amount, date, purpose, and terms of the pledge or donation, or the identity of the donor unless the donor has requested anonymity in connection with or as a condition of making a pledge or donation. The exclusion provided by this subdivision shall not apply to protect from disclosure (i) the identities of sponsors providing grants to or contracting with the institution for the performance of research services or other work or (ii) the terms and conditions of such grants or contracts.

8. Records of a threat assessment team established by a public institution of higher education pursuant to § 23-9.2:10 relating to the assessment or intervention with a specific individual. However, in the event an individual who has been under assessment commits an act, or is prosecuted for the commission of an act that has caused the death of, or caused serious bodily injury, including any felony sexual assault, to another person, the records of such threat assessment team concerning the individual under assessment shall be made available as provided by this chapter, with the exception of any criminal history records obtained pursuant to § 19.2-389 or 19.2-389.1, health records obtained pursuant to § 32.1-127.1:03, or scholastic records as defined in § 22.1-289. The public body providing such records shall remove information identifying any person who provided information to the threat assessment team under a promise of confidentiality.

History.
1999, cc. 485, 518, 703, 726, 793, 849, 852, 867, 868, 881, § 2.1-342.01; 2000, cc. 66, 237, 382, 400, 430, 583, 589, 592, 594, 618, 632, 657, 720, 932, 933, 947, 1006, 1064; 2001, cc. 288, 518, 844, § 2.2-3705; 2002, cc. 87, 155, 242, 393, 478, 481, 499, 522, 571, 572, 633, 655, 715, 798, 830; 2003, cc. 274, 307, 327, 332, 358, 704, 801, 884, 891, 893, 897, 968; 2004, c. 690; 2006, c. 518; 2008, cc. 561, 665; 2010, cc. 456, 524.

The 2010 amendments.
The 2010 amendments by cc. 456 and 524 are identical, and added subdivision 8.

CIRCUIT COURT OPINIONS

Documents relating to volunteers. — County school board failed to comply in a timely manner with some of a citizen's document requests because five documents relating to volunteers, which were held not to fall under the exception to the Virginia Freedom of Information Act for personnel files, subdivision 1 of § 2.2-3705.1, should have been disclosed with the original documents, and the delay in the disclosure of documents that were produced voluntarily contravened the requirements of the Act, subsection B of 2.2-3704; however, the violations were de minimis because the board was justified in withholding and redacting the numerous documents that qualified pursuant to exemptions under the Act, §§ 2.2-3705.1, 2.2-3705.4, and 2.2-3705.1. Hill v. Fairfax County Sch. Bd., 83 Va. Cir. 172, 2011 Va. Cir. LEXIS 89 (Fairfax County July 13, 2011).

Redaction not required. — School board was ordered to provide requested records to a media company, except for those records properly classified as scholastic records containing information concerning identifiable individuals, the Virginia Freedom of Information Act, subdivision 1 of § 2.2-3705.4, and personnel records containing information concerning identifiable individuals, because there was no specific requirement of "redaction" within the Freedom of Information Act with respect to minimum disclosure; the school board properly could exclude from production to the company any individual record properly considered in toto or in part a scholastic record or a personnel record, containing information concerning identifiable individuals, under subdivision 1 of §§ 2.2-3705.1 and 2.2-3705.4. Virginian-Pilot Media Cos., L.L.C. v. City of Norfolk Sch. Bd., 81 Va. Cir. 450, 2010 Va. Cir. LEXIS 272 (Norfolk Dec. 28, 2010).

§ 2.2-3705.5. Exclusions to application of chapter; health and social services records.

The following records are excluded from the provisions of this chapter but may be disclosed by the custodian in his discretion, except where such disclosure is prohibited by law:

1. Health records, except that such records may be personally reviewed by the individual who is the subject of such records, as provided in subsection F of § 32.1-127.1:03.

Where the person who is the subject of health records is confined in a state or local correctional facility, the administrator or chief medical officer of such facility may assert such confined person's right of access to the health records if the administrator or chief medical officer has reasonable cause to believe that such confined person has an infectious disease or other medical condition from which other persons so confined need to be protected. Health records shall only be reviewed and shall not be copied by such administrator or chief medical officer. The information in the health records of a person so confined shall continue to be confidential and shall not be disclosed by the administrator or chief medical officer of the facility to any person except the subject or except as provided by law.

Where the person who is the subject of health records is under the age of 18, his right of access may be asserted only by his guardian or his parent, including a noncustodial parent, unless such parent's parental rights have been terminated, a court of competent jurisdiction has restricted or denied such access, or a parent has been denied access to the health record in accordance with § 20-124.6. In instances where the person who is the subject thereof is an emancipated minor, a student in a public institution of higher education, or is a minor who has consented to his own treatment as authorized by § 16.1-338 or 54.1-2969, the right of access may be asserted by the subject person.

For the purposes of this chapter, statistical summaries of incidents and statistical data concerning abuse of individuals receiving services compiled by the Commissioner of Behavioral Health and Developmental Services shall be open to inspection and copying as provided in § 2.2-3704. No such summaries or data shall include any information that identifies specific individuals receiving services.

2. Applications for admission to examinations or for licensure and scoring records maintained by the Department of Health Professions or any board in that department on individual licensees or applicants. However, such material may be made available during normal working hours for copying, at the requester's expense, by the individual who is the subject thereof, in the offices of the Department of Health Professions or in the offices of any health regulatory board, whichever may possess the material.

3. Reports, documentary evidence and other information as specified in §§ 51.5-122, 51.5-141, and 63.2-104.

4. Investigative notes; proprietary information not published, copyrighted or patented; information obtained from employee personnel records; personally identifiable information regarding residents, clients or other recipients of services; other correspondence and information furnished in confidence to the Department of Social Services in connection with an active investigation of an applicant or licensee pursuant to Chapters 17 (§ 63.2-1700 et seq.) and 18 (§ 63.2-1800 et seq.) of Title 63.2; and records and information furnished to the Office of

the Attorney General in connection with an investigation or litigation pursuant to Article 19.1 (§ 8.01-216.1 et seq.) of Chapter 3 of Title 8.01 and Chapter 9 (§ 32.1-310 et seq.) of Title 32.1. However, nothing in this section shall prohibit disclosure of information from the records of completed investigations in a form that does not reveal the identity of complainants, persons supplying information, or other individuals involved in the investigation.

5. Information and records collected for the designation and verification of trauma centers and other specialty care centers within the Statewide Emergency Medical Services System and Services pursuant to Article 2.1 (§ 32.1-111.1 et seq.) of Chapter 4 of Title 32.1.

6. Reports and court documents relating to involuntary admission required to be kept confidential pursuant to § 37.2-818.

7. Data formerly required to be submitted to the Commissioner of Health relating to the establishment of new or the expansion of existing clinical health services, acquisition of major medical equipment, or certain projects requiring capital expenditures pursuant to former § 32.1-102.3:4.

8. Information required to be provided to the Department of Health Professions by certain licensees pursuant to § 54.1-2506.1.

9. Information and records acquired (i) during a review of any child death conducted by the State Child Fatality Review team established pursuant to § 32.1-283.1 or by a local or regional child fatality review team to the extent made confidential by § 32.1-283.2; (ii) during a review of any death conducted by a family violence fatality review team to the extent made confidential by § 32.1-283.3; or (iii) during a review of any adult death conducted by the Adult Fatality Review Team to the extent made confidential by § 32.1-283.5.

10. Patient level data collected by the Board of Health and not yet processed, verified, and released, pursuant to § 32.1-276.9, to the Board by the nonprofit organization with which the Commissioner of Health has contracted pursuant to § 32.1-276.4.

11. Records of the Health Practitioners' Monitoring Program Committee within the Department of Health Professions, to the extent such records may identify any practitioner who may be, or who is actually, impaired to the extent disclosure is prohibited by § 54.1-2517.

12. Records submitted as a grant application, or accompanying a grant application, to the Commonwealth Neurotrauma Initiative Advisory Board pursuant to Article 12 (§ 51.5-178 et seq.) of Chapter 14 of Title 51.5, to the extent such records contain (i) medical or mental health records, or other data identifying individual patients or (ii) proprietary business or research-related information produced or collected by the applicant in the conduct of or as a result of study or research on medical, rehabilitative, scientific, technical or scholarly issues, when such information has not been publicly released,

published, copyrighted or patented, if the disclosure of such information would be harmful to the competitive position of the applicant.

13. Any record copied, recorded or received by the Commissioner of Health in the course of an examination, investigation or review of a managed care health insurance plan licensee pursuant to §§ 32.1-137.4 and 32.1-137.5, including books, records, files, accounts, papers, documents, and any or all computer or other recordings.

14. Records, information and statistical registries required to be kept confidential pursuant to §§ 63.2-102 and 63.2-104.

15. All data, records, and reports relating to the prescribing and dispensing of covered substances to recipients and any abstracts from such data, records, and reports that are in the possession of the Prescription Monitoring Program pursuant to Chapter 25.2 (§ 54.1-2519 et seq.) of Title 54.1 and any material relating to the operation or security of the Program.

16. Records of the Virginia Birth-Related Neurological Injury Compensation Program required to be kept confidential pursuant to § 38.2-5002.2.

17. Records of the State Health Commissioner relating to the health of any person or persons subject to an order of quarantine or an order of isolation pursuant to Article 3.02 (§ 32.1-48.05 et seq.) of Chapter 2 of Title 32.1; this provision shall not, however, be construed to prohibit the disclosure of statistical summaries, abstracts or other information in aggregate form.

18. Records containing the names and addresses or other contact information of persons receiving transportation services from a state or local public body or its designee under Title II of the Americans with Disabilities Act, (42 U.S.C. § 12131 et seq.) or funded by Temporary Assistance for Needy Families (TANF) created under § 63.2-600.

History.
    1999, cc. 485, 518, 703, 726, 793, 849, 852, 867, 868, 881, § 2.1-342.01; 2000, cc. 66, 237, 382, 400, 430, 583, 589, 592, 594, 618, 632, 657, 720, 932, 933, 947, 1006, 1064; 2001, cc. 288, 518, 844, § 2.2-3705; 2002, cc. 87, 155, 242, 393, 478, 481, 499, 522, 571, 572, 633, 655, 715, 798, 830; 2003, cc. 274, 307, 327, 332, 358, 704, 801, 884, 891, 893, 897, 968; 2004, cc. 65, 666, 690, 773, 1014, 1021; 2005, cc. 181, 227, 716; 2008, c. 539; 2009, cc. 472, 813, 840; 2011, cc. 110, 175, 535; 2012, cc. 476, 479, 507, 803, 835.

Editor's note.
    Acts 2004, cc. 65 and 1014 amended former § 2.2-3705, from which this section is derived. Pursuant to § 30-152, Acts 2004, cc. 65 and 1014 have been given effect in this section as set out above. The 2004 amendments by cc. 65 and 1014 are identical, and rewrote the first paragraph of subdivision 1, which formerly read: "Medical and mental records, except that such records may be personally reviewed by the subject person or a physician of the subject person's choice. However, the subject person's mental records may not be personally reviewed by such person when the subject person's treating physician has made a part of such person's records a written statement that in his opinion a review of such records by the subject person would be injurious to the subject person's physical or mental health or well-being."
    Acts 2004, c. 666 amended former § 2.2-3705, from which this section is derived. Pursuant to § 30-152, Acts 2004, c. 666 has been

given effect in this section as set out above. The 2004 amendment by c. 666 added subdivision 18.
    Acts 2004, cc. 773 and 1021 amended former § 2.2-3705, from which this section is derived. Pursuant to § 30-152, Acts 2004, cc. 773 and 1021 have been given effect in this section as set out above. The 2004 amendments by cc. 773 and 1021, effective April 12, 2004 are identical, and added subdivision 17.
    Acts 2004, cc. 773 and 1021, cl. 2, provide: "That the Board of Health shall promulgate regulations to implement the provisions of this act to be effective within 280 days of its enactment."
    Acts 2002, c. 481, amended former § 2.2-3705 by adding subdivision 78, now subdivision 15 of this section. Amendments to former § 2.2-3705 by Acts 2002, c. 481, were limited to State Health Planning Region III and contingent on funding pursuant to Acts 2002, c. 481, cls. 4 and 5. Acts 2005, cc. 637 and 678, cl. 2, repealed the fourth and fifth enactment clauses of Acts 2002, c. 481.

The 2011 amendments.
    The 2011 amendments by cc. 110, 175, and 535 are identical, and added "and records and information furnished to the Office of the Attorney General in connection with an investigation pursuant to Chapter 9 (§ 32.1-310 et seq.) of Title 32.1" in the first sentence in subdivision 4 and made a related change.

The 2012 amendments.
    The 2012 amendments by cc. 476 and 507 are identical, and substituted "concerning abuse of individuals receiving services compiled" for "concerning patient abuse as may be compiled" and "shall include any information that identifies specific individuals receiving services" for "shall include any patient-identifying information" in the fourth paragraph of subdivision 1; and substituted "mental health records" for "mental records" in subdivision 12.
    The 2012 amendment by c. 479 substituted "or litigation pursuant to Article 19.1 (§ 8.01-216.1 et seq.) of Chapter 3 of Title 8.01 and Chapter 9 (§ 32.1-310 et seq.) of Title 32.1" for "pursuant to Chapter 9 (§ 32.1-310 et seq.) of Title 32.1" in the first sentence of subdivision 4.
    The 2012 amendment by cc. 803 and 835, cl. 59, are identical, and substituted "§§ 51.5-122, 51.5-141, and 63.2-104" for "§§ 2.2-706 and 63.2-104" in subsection 3; and substituted "Article 12 (§ 51.5-178 et seq.) of Chapter 14 of Title 51.5" for "Chapter 3.1 (§ 51.5-12.1 et seq.) of Title 51.5" in subsection 12.

§ 2.2-3705.6. Exclusions to application of chapter; proprietary records and trade secrets.

The following records are excluded from the provisions of this chapter but may be disclosed by the custodian in his discretion, except where such disclosure is prohibited by law:

1. Proprietary information gathered by or for the Virginia Port Authority as provided in § 62.1-132.4 or 62.1-134.1.

2. Financial statements not publicly available filed with applications for industrial development financings in accordance with Chapter 49 (§ 15.2-4900 et seq.) of Title 15.2.

3. Confidential proprietary records, voluntarily provided by private business pursuant to a promise of confidentiality from a public body, used by the public body for business, trade and tourism development or retention; and memoranda, working papers or other records related to businesses that are considering locating or expanding in Virginia, prepared by a public body, where competition or bargaining is involved and where, if such records are made public, the financial interest of the public body would be adversely affected.

4. Information that was filed as confidential under the Toxic Substances Information Act (§ 32.1-239 et seq.), as such Act existed prior to July 1, 1992.

5. Fisheries data that would permit identification of any person or vessel, except when required by court order as specified in § 28.2-204.

6. Confidential financial statements, balance sheets, trade secrets, and revenue and cost projections provided to the Department of Rail and Public Transportation, provided such information is exempt under the federal Freedom of Information Act or the federal Interstate Commerce Act or other laws administered by the Surface Transportation Board or the Federal Railroad Administration with respect to data provided in confidence to the Surface Transportation Board and the Federal Railroad Administration.

7. Confidential proprietary records related to inventory and sales, voluntarily provided by private energy suppliers to the Department of Mines, Minerals and Energy, used by that Department for energy contingency planning purposes or for developing consolidated statistical information on energy supplies.

8. Confidential proprietary information furnished to the Board of Medical Assistance Services or the Medicaid Prior Authorization Advisory Committee pursuant to Article 4 (§ 32.1-331.12 et seq.) of Chapter 10 of Title 32.1.

9. Proprietary, commercial or financial information, balance sheets, trade secrets, and revenue and cost projections provided by a private transportation business to the Virginia Department of Transportation and the Department of Rail and Public Transportation for the purpose of conducting transportation studies needed to obtain grants or other financial assistance under the Transportation Equity Act for the 21st Century (P.L. 105-178) for transportation projects, provided such information is exempt under the federal Freedom of Information Act or the federal Interstate Commerce Act or other laws administered by the Surface Transportation Board or the Federal Railroad Administration with respect to data provided in confidence to the Surface Transportation Board and the Federal Railroad Administration. However, the exemption provided by this subdivision shall not apply to any wholly owned subsidiary of a public body.

10. Confidential information designated as provided in subsection F of § 2.2-4342 as trade secrets or proprietary information by any person who has submitted to a public body an application for prequalification to bid on public construction projects in accordance with subsection B of § 2.2-4317.

11. a. Memoranda, staff evaluations, or other records prepared by the responsible public entity, its staff, outside advisors, or consultants exclusively for the evaluation and negotiation of proposals filed under the Public-Private Transportation Act of 1995 (§ 56-556 et seq.) or the Public Private Education Facilities and Infrastructure Act of 2002 (§ 56-575.1

et seq.), where (i) if such records were made public prior to or after the execution of an interim or a comprehensive agreement, § 56-573.1:1 or 56-575.17 notwithstanding, the financial interest or bargaining position of the public entity would be adversely affected, and (ii) the basis for the determination required in clause (i) is documented in writing by the responsible public entity; and

b. Records provided by a private entity to a responsible public entity, affected jurisdiction, or affected local jurisdiction pursuant to the provisions of the Public-Private Transportation Act of 1995 or the Public-Private Education Facilities and Infrastructure Act of 2002, to the extent that such records contain (i) trade secrets of the private entity as defined in the Uniform Trade Secrets Act (§ 59.1-336 et seq.); (ii) financial records of the private entity, including balance sheets and financial statements, that are not generally available to the public through regulatory disclosure or otherwise; or (iii) other information submitted by the private entity, where, if the records were made public prior to the execution of an interim agreement or a comprehensive agreement, the financial interest or bargaining position of the public or private entity would be adversely affected. In order for the records specified in clauses (i), (ii), and (iii) to be excluded from the provisions of this chapter, the private entity shall make a written request to the responsible public entity:

1. Invoking such exclusion upon submission of the data or other materials for which protection from disclosure is sought;

2. Identifying with specificity the data or other materials for which protection is sought; and

3. Stating the reasons why protection is necessary.

The responsible public entity shall determine whether the requested exclusion from disclosure is necessary to protect the trade secrets or financial records of the private entity. To protect other records submitted by the private entity from disclosure, the responsible public entity shall determine whether public disclosure prior to the execution of an interim agreement or a comprehensive agreement would adversely affect the financial interest or bargaining position of the public or private entity. The responsible public entity shall make a written determination of the nature and scope of the protection to be afforded by the responsible public entity under this subdivision. Once a written determination is made by the responsible public entity, the records afforded protection under this subdivision shall continue to be protected from disclosure when in the possession of any affected jurisdiction or affected local jurisdiction.

Except as specifically provided in subdivision 11 a, nothing in this subdivision shall be construed to authorize the withholding of (a) procurement records as required by § 56-573.1:1 or 56-575.17; (b) information concerning the terms and conditions of any interim or comprehensive agreement, service contract, lease, partnership, or any agreement of any kind entered into by the responsible public entity and the private entity; (c) information concerning the terms and conditions of any financing arrangement that involves the use of any public funds; or (d) information concerning the performance of any private entity developing or operating a qualifying transportation facility or a qualifying project.

For the purposes of this subdivision, the terms "affected jurisdiction," "affected local jurisdiction," "comprehensive agreement," "interim agreement," "qualifying project," "qualifying transportation facility," "responsible public entity," and "private entity" shall mean the same as those terms are defined in the Public-Private Transportation Act of 1995 or in the Public-Private Education Facilities and Infrastructure Act of 2002.

12. Confidential proprietary information or trade secrets, not publicly available, provided by a private person or entity to the Virginia Resources Authority or to a fund administered in connection with financial assistance rendered or to be rendered by the Virginia Resources Authority where, if such information were made public, the financial interest of the private person or entity would be adversely affected, and, after June 30, 1997, where such information was provided pursuant to a promise of confidentiality.

13. Trade secrets, as defined in the Uniform Trade Secrets Act (§ 59.1-336 et seq.), or confidential proprietary records that are not generally available to the public through regulatory disclosure or otherwise, provided by a (a) bidder or applicant for a franchise or (b) franchisee under Chapter 21 (§ 15.2-2100 et seq.) of Title 15.2 to the applicable franchising authority pursuant to a promise of confidentiality from the franchising authority, to the extent the records relate to the bidder's, applicant's, or franchisee's financial capacity or provision of new services, adoption of new technologies or implementation of improvements, where such new services, technologies or improvements have not been implemented by the franchisee on a nonexperimental scale in the franchise area, and where, if such records were made public, the competitive advantage or financial interests of the franchisee would be adversely affected.

In order for trade secrets or confidential proprietary information to be excluded from the provisions of this chapter, the bidder, applicant, or franchisee shall (i) invoke such exclusion upon submission of the data or other materials for which protection from disclosure is sought, (ii) identify the data or other materials for which protection is sought, and (iii) state the reason why protection is necessary.

No bidder, applicant, or franchisee may invoke the exclusion provided by this subdivision if the bidder, applicant, or franchisee is owned or controlled by a public body or if any representative of the applicable franchising authority serves on the management board or as an officer of the bidder, applicant, or franchisee.

14. Documents and other information of a proprietary nature furnished by a supplier of charitable gaming supplies to the Department of Agriculture and Consumer Services pursuant to subsection E of § 18.2-340.34.

15. Records and reports related to Virginia apple producer sales provided to the Virginia State Apple Board pursuant to § 3.2-1215.

16. Trade secrets, as defined in the Uniform Trade Secrets Act (§ 59.1-336 et seq.) of Title 59.1, submitted by CMRS providers as defined in § 56-484.12 to the Wireless Carrier E-911 Cost Recovery Subcommittee created pursuant to § 56-484.15, relating to the provision of wireless E-911 service.

17. Records submitted as a grant or loan application, or accompanying a grant or loan application, to the Innovation and Entrepreneurship Investment Authority pursuant to Article 3 (§ 2.2-2233.1 et seq.) of Chapter 22 of Title 2.2 or to the Commonwealth Health Research Board pursuant to Chapter 22 (§ 23-277 et seq.) of Title 23 to the extent such records contain proprietary business or research-related information produced or collected by the applicant in the conduct of or as a result of study or research on medical, rehabilitative, scientific, technical, technological, or scholarly issues, when such information has not been publicly released, published, copyrighted, or patented, if the disclosure of such information would be harmful to the competitive position of the applicant.

18. Confidential proprietary records and trade secrets developed and held by a local public body (i) providing telecommunication services pursuant to § 56-265.4:4 and (ii) providing cable television services pursuant to Article 1.1 (§ 15.2-2108.2 et seq.) of Chapter 21 of Title 15.2, to the extent that disclosure of such records would be harmful to the competitive position of the locality. In order for confidential proprietary information or trade secrets to be excluded from the provisions of this chapter, the locality in writing shall (a) invoke the protections of this subdivision, (b) identify with specificity the records or portions thereof for which protection is sought, and (c) state the reasons why protection is necessary.

19. Confidential proprietary records and trade secrets developed by or for a local authority created in accordance with the Virginia Wireless Service Authorities Act (§ 15.2-5431.1 et seq.) to provide qualifying communications services as authorized by Article 5.1 (§ 56-484.7:1 et seq.) of Chapter 15 of Title 56, where disclosure of such information would be harmful to the competitive position of the authority, except that records required to be maintained in accordance with § 15.2-2160 shall be released.

20. **(Effective until January 1, 2014)** Trade secrets as defined in the Uniform Trade Secrets Act (§ 59.1-336 et seq.) or financial records of a busi-

ness, including balance sheets and financial statements, that are not generally available to the public through regulatory disclosure or otherwise, provided to the Department of Minority Business Enterprise as part of an application for (i) certification as a small, women-owned, or minority-owned business in accordance with Chapter 14 (§ 2.2-1400 et seq.) of this title or (ii) a claim made by a disadvantaged business or an economically disadvantaged individual against the Capital Access Fund for Disadvantaged Businesses created pursuant to § 2.2-2311. In order for such trade secrets or financial records to be excluded from the provisions of this chapter, the business shall (a) invoke such exclusion upon submission of the data or other materials for which protection from disclosure is sought, (b) identify the data or other materials for which protection is sought, and (c) state the reasons why protection is necessary.

20. **(Effective January 1, 2014)** Trade secrets as defined in the Uniform Trade Secrets Act (§ 59.1-336 et seq.) or financial records of a business, including balance sheets and financial statements, that are not generally available to the public through regulatory disclosure or otherwise, provided to the Department of Small Business and Supplier Diversity as part of an application for (i) certification as a small, women-owned, or minority-owned business in accordance with Chapter 16.1 (§ 2.2-1603 et seq.) or (ii) a claim made by a disadvantaged business or an economically disadvantaged individual against the Capital Access Fund for Disadvantaged Businesses created pursuant to § 2.2-2311. In order for such trade secrets or financial records to be excluded from the provisions of this chapter, the business shall (a) invoke such exclusion upon submission of the data or other materials for which protection from disclosure is sought, (b) identify the data or other materials for which protection is sought, and (c) state the reasons why protection is necessary.

21. Documents and other information of a proprietary or confidential nature disclosed by a carrier to the State Health Commissioner pursuant to §§ 32.1-276.5:1 and 32.1-276.7:1.

22. Trade secrets, as defined in the Uniform Trade Secrets Act (§ 59.1-336 et seq.), including, but not limited to, financial records, including balance sheets and financial statements, that are not generally available to the public through regulatory disclosure or otherwise, and revenue and cost projections supplied by a private or nongovernmental entity to the State Inspector General for the purpose of an audit, special investigation, or any study requested by the Office of the State Inspector General in accordance with law.

In order for the records specified in this subdivision to be excluded from the provisions of this chapter, the private or nongovernmental entity shall make a written request to the State Inspector General:

1. Invoking such exclusion upon submission of the data or other materials for which protection from disclosure is sought;

2. Identifying with specificity the data or other materials for which protection is sought; and

3. Stating the reasons why protection is necessary.

The State Inspector General shall determine whether the requested exclusion from disclosure is necessary to protect the trade secrets or financial records of the private entity. The State Inspector General shall make a written determination of the nature and scope of the protection to be afforded by it under this subdivision.

23. Records submitted as a grant application, or accompanying a grant application, to the Virginia Tobacco Indemnification and Community Revitalization Commission to the extent such records contain (i) trade secrets as defined in the Uniform Trade Secrets Act (§ 59.1-336 et seq.), (ii) financial records of a grant applicant that is not a public body, including balance sheets and financial statements, that are not generally available to the public through regulatory disclosure or otherwise, or (iii) research-related information produced or collected by the applicant in the conduct of or as a result of study or research on medical, rehabilitative, scientific, technical, technological, or scholarly issues, when such information has not been publicly released, published, copyrighted, or patented, if the disclosure of such information would be harmful to the competitive position of the applicant; and memoranda, staff evaluations, or other records prepared by the Commission or its staff exclusively for the evaluation of grant applications. The exclusion provided by this subdivision shall apply to grants that are consistent with the powers of and in furtherance of the performance of the duties of the Commission pursuant to § 3.2-3103.

In order for the records specified in this subdivision to be excluded from the provisions of this chapter, the applicant shall make a written request to the Commission:

1. Invoking such exclusion upon submission of the data or other materials for which protection from disclosure is sought;

2. Identifying with specificity the data, records or other materials for which protection is sought; and

3. Stating the reasons why protection is necessary.

The Commission shall determine whether the requested exclusion from disclosure is necessary to protect the trade secrets, financial records or research-related information of the applicant. The Commission shall make a written determination of the nature and scope of the protection to be afforded by it under this subdivision.

24. a. Records of the Commercial Space Flight Authority relating to rate structures or charges for the use of projects of, the sale of products of, or services rendered by the Authority if public disclosure would adversely affect the financial interest or bargaining position of the Authority or a private entity providing records to the Authority; or

b. Records provided by a private entity to the Commercial Space Flight Authority, to the extent that such records contain (i) trade secrets of the private entity as defined in the Uniform Trade Secrets Act (§ 59.1-336 et seq.); (ii) financial records of the private entity, including balance sheets and financial statements, that are not generally available to the public through regulatory disclosure or otherwise; or (iii) other information submitted by the private entity, where, if the records were made public, the financial interest or bargaining position of the Authority or private entity would be adversely affected.

In order for the records specified in clauses (i), (ii), and (iii) of subdivision 24 b to be excluded from the provisions of this chapter, the private entity shall make a written request to the Authority:

1. Invoking such exclusion upon submission of the data or other materials for which protection from disclosure is sought;

2. Identifying with specificity the data or other materials for which protection is sought; and

3. Stating the reasons why protection is necessary.

The Authority shall determine whether the requested exclusion from disclosure is necessary to protect the trade secrets or financial records of the private entity. To protect other records submitted by the private entity from disclosure, the Authority shall determine whether public disclosure would adversely affect the financial interest or bargaining position of the Authority or private entity. The Authority shall make a written determination of the nature and scope of the protection to be afforded by it under this subdivision.

25. Documents and other information of a proprietary nature furnished by an agricultural landowner or operator to the Department of Conservation and Recreation, the Department of Environmental Quality, the Department of Agriculture and Consumer Services or any political subdivision, agency, or board of the Commonwealth pursuant to §§ 10.1-104.7, 10.1-104.8, and 10.1-104.9, other than when required as part of a state or federal regulatory enforcement action.

26. Trade secrets, as defined in the Uniform Trade Secrets Act (§ 59.1-336 et seq.), provided to the Department of Environmental Quality pursuant to the provisions of § 10.1-1458. In order for such trade secrets to be excluded from the provisions of this chapter, the submitting party shall (i) invoke this exclusion upon submission of the data or materials for which protection from disclosure is sought, (ii) identify the data or materials for which protection is sought, and (iii) state the reasons why protection is necessary.

27. Documents and other information of a proprietary nature furnished by a licensed public-use airport to the Department of Aviation for funding from programs administered by the Department of Aviation or the Virginia Aviation Board, where if the records were made public, the financial interest of the public-use airport would be adversely affected.

In order for the records specified in this subdivision to be excluded from the provisions of this chapter, the public-use airport shall make a written request to the Department of Aviation:

1. Invoking such exclusion upon submission of the data or other materials for which protection from disclosure is sought;

2. Identifying with specificity the data or other materials for which protection is sought; and

3. Stating the reasons why protection is necessary.

History.
1999, cc. 485, 518, 703, 726, 793, 849, 852, 867, 868, 881, § 2.1-342.01; 2000, cc. 66, 237, 382, 400, 430, 583, 589, 592, 594, 618, 632, 657, 720, 932, 933, 947, 1006, 1064; 2001, cc. 288, 518, 844, § 2.2-3705; 2002, cc. 87, 155, 242, 393, 478, 481, 499, 522, 571, 572, 633, 655, 715, 798, 830; 2003, cc. 274, 307, 327, 332, 358, 704, 801, 884, 891, 893, 897, 968; 2004, cc. 593, 690; 2005, cc. 258, 411; 2006, cc. 73, 76, 467, 831, 921, 936; 2006, Sp. Sess. I, c. 1; 2007, cc. 374, 693; 2008, cc. 71, 102, 266, 387, 633, 689, 736, 743; 2009, cc. 246, 311, 325, 765, 810, 869; 2010, cc. 310, 808; 2011, cc. 541, 781, 798, 871; 2012, cc. 693, 709; 2013, cc. 54, 482, 574.

Subdivision 20 set out twice. — The first version of subdivision 20 above is effective until January 1, 2014. The second version of subdivision 20 is effective January 1, 2014.

Editor's note.
Acts 2004, c. 593 amended former § 2.2-3705, from which this section is derived. Pursuant to § 30-152, Acts 2004, c. 593 has been given effect in this section as set out above. The 2004 amendment by c. 593 substituted "such entities" for "the Partnership" near the end in subdivision 3.

Acts 2006, c. 936, cl. 3, which amended subdivision 11, provides: "That the provisions of this act shall apply only to proposals for qualifying transportation facilities and qualifying projects filed on or after July 1, 2006."

Acts 2006, Sp. Sess. I, c. 1, which amended subdivision 11, in cl. 2 provides: "That the provisions of this act shall expire on July 1, 2007." The section is set out above without the amendments by Acts 2006, Sp. Sess. I, c. 1.

Acts 2011, cc. 798 and 871, cl. 7 provides: "That the provisions of this act shall become effective on July 1, 2012, except that the provisions of the fifth enactment of this act shall become effective on July 1, 2011."

Acts 2013, c. 482, cl. 7 provides: "That the provisions of this act shall become effective on January 1, 2014."

The 2010 amendments.
The 2010 amendments by cc. 310 and 808 are identical, and added subdivision 23.

The 2011 amendments.
The 2011 amendment by c. 541 added subdivision 24.
The 2011 amendment by c. 781 added subdivision 24 (now 25).
The 2011 amendments by cc. 798 and 871, effective July 1, 2012, are identical, and in subdivision 22, in the first and last paragraphs, substituted "State Inspector General" for "Inspector General of the Virginia Department of Transportation," in the first paragraph, substituted "Office of the State Inspector General" for "Inspector General's Office," in the second paragraph, substituted "State Inspector General" for "Department," and in the last paragraph, substituted "State Inspector General" for "Virginia Department of Transportation."

The 2012 amendments.
The 2012 amendments by cc. 693 and 709 are identical, and added "and 32.1-276.7:1" at the end of subdivision 21.

The 2013 amendments.
The 2013 amendment by c. 54 added subdivision 26.

The 2013 amendment by c. 482, effective January 1, 2014, in subdivision 20, substituted "Small Business and Supplier Diversity" for "Minority Business Enterprise" and "Chapter 16.1 (§ 2.2-1603 et seq.)" for "Chapter 14 (§ 2.2-1400 et seq.) of this title" in the first sentence.

The 2013 amendment by c. 574 added subdivision 26, which was subsequently renumbered as subdivision 27 at the direction of the Virginia Code Commission.

§ 2.2-3705.7. Exclusions to application of chapter; records of specific public bodies and certain other limited exemptions.

The following records are excluded from the provisions of this chapter but may be disclosed by the custodian in his discretion, except where such disclosure is prohibited by law:

1. State income, business, and estate tax returns, personal property tax returns, scholastic and confidential records held pursuant to § 58.1-3.

2. Working papers and correspondence of the Office of the Governor; Lieutenant Governor; the Attorney General; the members of the General Assembly, the Division of Legislative Services, or the Clerks of the House of Delegates and the Senate of Virginia; the mayor or chief executive officer of any political subdivision of the Commonwealth; or the president or other chief executive officer of any public institution of higher education in Virginia. However, no record, which is otherwise open to inspection under this chapter, shall be deemed exempt by virtue of the fact that it has been attached to or incorporated within any working paper or correspondence.

As used in this subdivision:

"Members of the General Assembly" means each member of the Senate of Virginia and the House of Delegates and their legislative aides when working on behalf of such member.

"Office of the Governor" means the Governor; his chief of staff, counsel, director of policy, Cabinet Secretaries, and the Assistant to the Governor for Intergovernmental Affairs; and those individuals to whom the Governor has delegated his authority pursuant to § 2.2-104.

"Working papers" means those records prepared by or for an above-named public official for his personal or deliberative use.

3. Library records that can be used to identify both (i) any library patron who has borrowed material from a library and (ii) the material such patron borrowed.

4. Contract cost estimates prepared for the confidential use of the Department of Transportation in awarding contracts for construction or the purchase of goods or services, and records and automated systems prepared for the Department's Bid Analysis and Monitoring Program.

5. Lists of registered owners of bonds issued by a political subdivision of the Commonwealth, whether the lists are maintained by the political subdivision itself or by a single fiduciary designated by the political subdivision.

6. Records and writings furnished by a member of the General Assembly to a meeting of a standing committee, special committee or subcommittee of his house established solely for the purpose of reviewing members' annual disclosure statements and supporting materials filed under § 30-110 or of formulating advisory opinions to members on standards of conduct, or both.

7. Customer account information of a public utility affiliated with a political subdivision of the Commonwealth, including the customer's name and service address, but excluding the amount of utility service provided and the amount of money paid for such utility service.

8. Personal information, as defined in § 2.2-3801, (i) filed with the Virginia Housing Development Authority concerning individuals who have applied for or received loans or other housing assistance or who have applied for occupancy of or have occupied housing financed, owned or otherwise assisted by the Virginia Housing Development Authority; (ii) concerning persons participating in or persons on the waiting list for federally funded rent-assistance programs; (iii) filed with any local redevelopment and housing authority created pursuant to § 36-4 concerning persons participating in or persons on the waiting list for housing assistance programs funded by local governments or by any such authority; or (iv) filed with any local redevelopment and housing authority created pursuant to § 36-4 or any other local government agency concerning persons who have applied for occupancy or who have occupied affordable dwelling units established pursuant to § 15.2-2304 or 15.2-2305. However, access to one's own information shall not be denied.

9. Records regarding the siting of hazardous waste facilities, except as provided in § 10.1-1441, if disclosure of them would have a detrimental effect upon the negotiating position of a governing body or on the establishment of the terms, conditions and provisions of the siting agreement.

10. Records containing information on the site specific location of rare, threatened, endangered or otherwise imperiled plant and animal species, natural communities, caves, and significant historic and archaeological sites if, in the opinion of the public body that has the responsibility for such information, disclosure of the information would jeopardize the continued existence or the integrity of the resource. This exemption shall not apply to requests from the owner of the land upon which the resource is located.

11. Records, memoranda, working papers, graphics, video or audio tapes, production models, data and information of a proprietary nature produced by or for or collected by or for the State Lottery Department relating to matters of a specific lottery game design, development, production, operation, ticket price, prize structure, manner of selecting the win-

ning ticket, manner of payment of prizes to holders of winning tickets, frequency of drawings or selections of winning tickets, odds of winning, advertising, or marketing, where such official records have not been publicly released, published, copyrighted or patented. Whether released, published or copyrighted, all game-related information shall be subject to public disclosure under this chapter upon the first day of sales for the specific lottery game to which it pertains.

12. Records of the Virginia Retirement System, acting pursuant to § 51.1-124.30, or of a local retirement system, acting pursuant to § 51.1-803, or of the Rector and Visitors of the University of Virginia, acting pursuant to § 23-76.1, or of the Virginia College Savings Plan, acting pursuant to § 23-38.77, relating to the acquisition, holding or disposition of a security or other ownership interest in an entity, where such security or ownership interest is not traded on a governmentally regulated securities exchange, to the extent that: (i) such records contain confidential analyses prepared for the Rector and Visitors of the University of Virginia, prepared by the retirement system or the Virginia College Savings Plan, or provided to the retirement system or the Virginia College Savings Plan under a promise of confidentiality, of the future value of such ownership interest or the future financial performance of the entity; and (ii) disclosure of such confidential analyses would have an adverse effect on the value of the investment to be acquired, held or disposed of by the retirement system, the Rector and Visitors of the University of Virginia, or the Virginia College Savings Plan. Nothing in this subdivision shall be construed to prevent the disclosure of records relating to the identity of any investment held, the amount invested, or the present value of such investment.

13. Names and addresses of subscribers to Virginia Wildlife magazine, published by the Department of Game and Inland Fisheries, provided the individual subscriber has requested in writing that the Department not release such information.

14. Financial, medical, rehabilitative and other personal information concerning applicants for or recipients of loan funds submitted to or maintained by the Assistive Technology Loan Fund Authority under Chapter 11 (§ 51.5-53 et seq.) of Title 51.5.

15. Records of the Virginia Commonwealth University Health System Authority pertaining to any of the following: an individual's qualifications for or continued membership on its medical or teaching staffs; proprietary information gathered by or in the possession of the Authority from third parties pursuant to a promise of confidentiality; contract cost estimates prepared for confidential use in awarding contracts for construction or the purchase of goods or services; data, records or information of a proprietary nature produced or collected by or for the Authority or members of its medical or teaching staffs; financial statements not publicly available that may be filed with the Authority from third parties; the identity, accounts or account status of any customer of the Authority; consulting or other reports paid for by the Authority to assist the Authority in connection with its strategic planning and goals; the determination of marketing and operational strategies where disclosure of such strategies would be harmful to the competitive position of the Authority; and data, records or information of a proprietary nature produced or collected by or for employees of the Authority, other than the Authority's financial or administrative records, in the conduct of or as a result of study or research on medical, scientific, technical or scholarly issues, whether sponsored by the Authority alone or in conjunction with a governmental body or a private concern, when such data, records or information have not been publicly released, published, copyrighted or patented.

16. Records of the Department of Environmental Quality, the State Water Control Board, State Air Pollution Control Board or the Virginia Waste Management Board relating to (i) active federal environmental enforcement actions that are considered confidential under federal law and (ii) enforcement strategies, including proposed sanctions for enforcement actions. Upon request, such records shall be disclosed after a proposed sanction resulting from the investigation has been proposed to the director of the agency. This subdivision shall not be construed to prohibit the disclosure of records related to inspection reports, notices of violation, and documents detailing the nature of any environmental contamination that may have occurred or similar documents.

17. As it pertains to any person, records related to the operation of toll facilities that identify an individual, vehicle, or travel itinerary including, but not limited to, vehicle identification data, vehicle enforcement system information; video or photographic images; Social Security or other identification numbers appearing on driver's licenses; credit card or bank account data; home addresses; phone numbers; or records of the date or time of toll facility use.

18. Records of the State Lottery Department pertaining to (i) the social security number, tax identification number, state sales tax number, home address and telephone number, personal and lottery banking account and transit numbers of a retailer, and financial information regarding the nonlottery operations of specific retail locations; and (ii) individual lottery winners, except that a winner's name, hometown, and amount won shall be disclosed.

19. Records of the Board for Branch Pilots relating to the chemical or drug testing of a person regulated by the Board, where such person has tested negative or has not been the subject of a disciplinary action by the Board for a positive test result.

20. Records, investigative notes, correspondence, and information pertaining to the planning, sched-

uling and performance of examinations of holder records pursuant to the Uniform Disposition of Unclaimed Property Act (§ 55-210.1 et seq.) prepared by or for the State Treasurer, his agents, employees or persons employed to perform an audit or examination of holder records.

21. Records of the Virginia Department of Emergency Management or a local governing body relating to citizen emergency response teams established pursuant to an ordinance of a local governing body, to the extent that such records reveal the name, address, including e-mail address, telephone or pager numbers, or operating schedule of an individual participant in the program.

22. Records of state or local park and recreation departments and local and regional park authorities to the extent such records contain information identifying a person under the age of 18 years. However, nothing in this subdivision shall operate to prohibit the disclosure of information defined as directory information under regulations implementing the Family Educational Rights and Privacy Act, 20 U.S.C. § 1232g, unless the public body has undertaken the parental notification and opt-out requirements provided by such regulations. Access shall not be denied to the parent, including a noncustodial parent, or guardian of such person, unless the parent's parental rights have been terminated or a court of competent jurisdiction has restricted or denied such access. For records of such persons who are emancipated, the right of access may be asserted by the subject thereof. Any parent or emancipated person who is the subject of the record may waive, in writing, the protections afforded by this subdivision. If the protections are so waived, the public body shall open such records for inspection and copying.

23. Records submitted for inclusion in the Statewide Alert Network administered by the Department of Emergency Management, to the extent that they reveal names, physical addresses, email addresses, computer or internet protocol information, telephone numbers, pager numbers, other wireless or portable communications device information, or operating schedules of individuals or agencies, where the release of such information would compromise the security of the Statewide Alert Network or individuals participating in the Statewide Alert Network.

24. Records of the Judicial Inquiry and Review Commission made confidential by § 17.1-913.

25. Records of the Virginia Retirement System acting pursuant to § 51.1-124.30, of a local retirement system acting pursuant to § 51.1-803 (hereinafter collectively referred to as the retirement system), or of the Virginia College Savings Plan, acting pursuant to § 23-38.77 relating to:

a. Internal deliberations of or decisions by the retirement system or the Virginia College Savings Plan on the pursuit of particular investment strategies, or the selection or termination of investment managers, prior to the execution of such investment

strategies or the selection or termination of such managers, to the extent that disclosure of such records would have an adverse impact on the financial interest of the retirement system or the Virginia College Savings Plan; and

b. Trade secrets, as defined in the Uniform Trade Secrets Act (§ 59.1-336 et seq.), provided by a private entity to the retirement system or the Virginia College Savings Plan, to the extent disclosure of such records would have an adverse impact on the financial interest of the retirement system or the Virginia College Savings Plan.

For the records specified in subdivision b to be excluded from the provisions of this chapter, the entity shall make a written request to the retirement system or the Virginia College Savings Plan:

(1) Invoking such exclusion prior to or upon submission of the data or other materials for which protection from disclosure is sought;

(2) Identifying with specificity the data or other materials for which protection is sought; and

(3) Stating the reasons why protection is necessary.

The retirement system or the Virginia College Savings Plan shall determine whether the requested exclusion from disclosure meets the requirements set forth in subdivision b.

Nothing in this subdivision shall be construed to authorize the withholding of the identity or amount of any investment held or the present value and performance of all asset classes and subclasses.

26. Records of the Department of Corrections made confidential by § 53.1-233.

27. Records maintained by the Department of the Treasury or participants in the Local Government Investment Pool (§ 2.2-4600 et seq.), to the extent such records relate to information required to be provided by such participants to the Department to establish accounts in accordance with § 2.2-4602.

28. Personal information, as defined in § 2.2-3801, contained in the Veterans Care Center Resident Trust Funds concerning residents or patients of the Department of Veterans Services Care Centers, except that access shall not be denied to the person who is the subject of the record.

29. Records maintained in connection with fundraising activities by the Veterans Services Foundation pursuant to § 2.2-2716 to the extent that such records reveal the address, electronic mail address, facsimile or telephone number, social security number or other identification number appearing on a driver's license, or credit card or bank account data of identifiable donors, except that access shall not be denied to the person who is the subject of the record. Nothing in this subdivision, however, shall be construed to authorize the withholding of records relating to the amount, date, purpose, and terms of the pledge or donation or the identity of the donor. The exclusion provided by this subdivision shall not apply to protect from disclosure (i) the identities of sponsors providing grants to

or contracting with the foundation for the performance of services or other work or (ii) the terms and conditions of such grants or contracts.

30. Names, physical addresses, telephone numbers, and email addresses contained in correspondence between an individual and a member of the governing body, school board, or other public body of the locality in which the individual is a resident, unless the correspondence relates to the transaction of public business. However, no record that is otherwise open to inspection under this chapter shall be deemed exempt by virtue of the fact that it has been attached to or incorporated within any such correspondence.

31. Records of the Commonwealth's Attorneys' Services Council, to the extent such records are prepared for and utilized by the Commonwealth's Attorneys' Services Council in the training of state prosecutors or law-enforcement personnel, where such records are not otherwise available to the public and the release of such records would reveal confidential strategies, methods or procedures to be employed in law-enforcement activities, or materials created for the investigation and prosecution of a criminal case.

32. Records provided to the Department of Aviation by other entities of the Commonwealth in connection with the operation of aircraft, where the records would not be subject to disclosure by the entity providing the records. The entity providing the records to the Department of Aviation shall identify the specific portion of the records to be protected and the applicable provision of this chapter that exempts the record or portions thereof from mandatory disclosure.

History.
1999, cc. 485, 518, 703, 726, 793, 849, 852, 867, 868, 881, § 2.1-342.01; 2000, cc. 66, 237, 382, 400, 430, 583, 589, 592, 594, 618, 632, 657, 720, 932, 933, 947, 1006, 1064; 2001, cc. 288, 518, 844, § 2.2-3705; 2002, cc. 87, 155, 242, 393, 478, 481, 499, 522, 571, 572, 633, 655, 715, 798, 830; 2003, cc. 274, 307, 327, 332, 358, 704, 801, 884, 891, 893, 897, 968; 2004, cc. 426, 690, 832; 2005, cc. 165, 508; 2007, cc. 406, 652, 660, 737, 739; 2008, cc. 16, 739; 2009, cc. 223, 827, 845; 2010, c. 300; 2011, cc. 827, 867; 2012, c. 726; 2013, cc. 199, 481, 554, 574.

Editor's note.
Acts 2004, c. 426 amended former § 2.2-3705, from which this section is derived. Pursuant to § 30-152, Acts 2004, c. 426 has been given effect in this section as set out above. The 2004 amendment by c. 426 added subdivision 21.
Acts 2004, c. 832 amended former § 2.2-3705, from which this section is derived. Pursuant to § 30-152, Acts 2004, c. 832 has been given effect in this section as set out above. The 2004 amendment by c. 832 added subdivision 22.
Acts 2005, c. 508, cl. 2, provides: "That the provisions of this act are declaratory of existing law."
Acts 2007, c. 660, which added subdivision 27, in cl. 2 provides: "That the provisions of this act shall expire on July 1, 2008." Subdivision 27 was subsequently deleted by Acts 2008, c. 16.

The 2010 amendments.
The 2010 amendment by c. 300 inserted "or the Clerks of the House of Delegates and the Senate of Virginia" in the first sentence of subdivision 2 and made a related change.

The 2011 amendments.
The 2011 amendments by cc. 827 and 867 are identical, and in subdivision 2, in the definition for "Office of the Governor," substi-

tuted "Assistant to the Governor for Intergovernmental Affairs" for "Director of the Virginia Liaison Office."

The 2012 amendments.
The 2012 amendment by c. 726 added subdivision 30.

The 2013 amendments.
The 2013 amendment by c. 199 added the definition of "Members of the General Assembly" in subdivision 2.
The 2013 amendment by c. 481 added subdivision 31.
The 2013 amendment by c. 554, in subdivision 22, deleted "where the parent or legal guardian of such person has requested in writing that such information not be disclosed" from the end of the first sentence and added the last two sentences.
The 2013 amendment by c. 574 added subdivision 31, which was subsequently renumbered as subdivision 32 at the direction of the Virginia Code Commission.

CIRCUIT COURT OPINIONS

E-mails received by superintendent of schools. — E-mails between county school board members are open to inspection, and the fact that the superintendent received or read a copy of these e-mails does not qualify them as part of his or her working papers or correspondence within the meaning of the Virginia Freedom of Information Act, § 2.2-3700 et seq., because such e-mails do not reflect the work of the superintendent, nor do they evidence communications intended only for the superintendent; therefore, those e-mails should be disclosed. Hill v. Fairfax County Sch. Bd., 83 Va. Cir. 172, 2011 Va. Cir. LEXIS 89 (Fairfax County July 13, 2011).

OPINIONS OF THE ATTORNEY GENERAL

Release of library records to parent of minor. — It is within the discretion of the records' custodian whether to release library records to the parent of a minor for the purpose of identifying and locating books checked out by the minor that are overdue. See opinion of Attorney General to The Honorable Robert G. Marshall, Member, House of Delegates, 02-002 (2/25/02) (decided under prior provisions).

Information provided to the Virginia Retirement System. — Confidential information provided to the Virginia Retirement System by limited partnerships in the private equity market may be exempt from disclosure under The Virginia Freedom of Information Act, provided such information meets the requirements of this section. See opinion of Attorney General to W. Forrest Matthews, Jr., Director, Virginia Retirement System, 02-149 (1/27/03) (decided under prior provisions).

Even though the Virginia Retirement System may deny public access to confidential information provided by limited partnerships, it is required to provide to a valid requester under the Act the identity of any private equity limited partnership in which it invests and the amount and present value of such investments. See opinion of Attorney General to W. Forrest Matthews, Jr., Director, Virginia Retirement System, 02-149 (1/27/03) (decided under prior provisions).

Information that is provided to the Virginia Retirement System by a private entity "relates to" the trade secrets of the entity. Such information is exempt from disclosure under The Virginia Freedom of Information Act provided the private entity meets the requirements of subdivision 25 of this section. See opinion of Attorney General to Mr. Robert P. Schultze, Director, Virginia Retirement System, 07-068 (9/4/07).

§ 2.2-3705.8. Limitation on record exclusions.

A. Neither any provision of this chapter nor any provision of Chapter 38 (§ 2.2-3800 et seq.) of this title shall be construed as denying public access to (i) contracts between a public body and its officers or employees, other than contracts settling public employment employment disputes held confidential as personnel records under § 2.2-3705.1; (ii) records of the position, job classification, official salary or rate of pay of, and records of the allowances or reimbursements for expenses paid to any officer, official or employee of a public body; or (iii) the compensation or benefits paid by any corporation organized by the Virginia Retirement System or its officers or employees.

The provisions of this subsection, however, shall not require public access to records of the official salaries or rates of pay of public employees whose annual rate of pay is $10,000 or less.

B. Nothing in this chapter shall be construed as denying public access to the nonexempt portions of a report of a consultant hired by or at the request of a local public body or the mayor or chief executive or administrative officer of such public body if (i) the contents of such report have been distributed or disclosed to members of the local public body or (ii) the local public body has scheduled any action on a matter that is the subject of the consultant's report.

History.

1999, cc. 485, 518, 703, 726, 793, 849, 852, 867, 868, 881, § 2.1-342.01; 2000, cc. 66, 237, 382, 400, 430, 583, 589, 592, 594, 618, 632, 657, 720, 932, 933, 947, 1006, 1064; 2001, cc. 288, 518, 844, § 2.2-3705; 2002, cc. 87, 155, 242, 393, 478, 481, 499, 522, 571, 572, 633, 655, 715, 798, 830; 2003, cc. 274, 307, 327, 332, 358, 704, 801, 884, 891, 893, 897, 968; 2004, c. 690.

§ 2.2-3706. Disclosure of criminal records; limitations.

A. All public bodies engaged in criminal law-enforcement activities shall provide requested records in accordance with this chapter as follows:

1. Records required to be released:

a. Criminal incident information relating to felony offenses, which shall include:

(1) A general description of the criminal activity reported;

(2) The date the alleged crime was committed;

(3) The general location where the alleged crime was committed;

(4) The identity of the investigating officer or other point of contact; and

(5) A general description of any injuries suffered or property damaged or stolen.

A verbal response as agreed to by the requester and the public body is sufficient to satisfy the requirements of subdivision a.

Where the release of criminal incident information, however, is likely to jeopardize an ongoing investigation or prosecution or the safety of an individual, cause a suspect to flee or evade detection, or result in the destruction of evidence, such information may be withheld until the above-referenced damage is no longer likely to occur from release of the information. Nothing in subdivision a shall be construed to authorize the withholding of those portions of such information that are not likely to cause the above-referenced damage;

b. Adult arrestee photographs taken during the initial intake following the arrest and as part of the routine booking procedure, except when necessary to avoid jeopardizing an investigation in felony cases until such time as the release of the photograph will no longer jeopardize the investigation; and

c. Information relative to the identity of any individual, other than a juvenile, who is arrested and charged, and the status of the charge or arrest;

2. Discretionary releases. The following records are excluded from the provisions of this chapter, but may be disclosed by the custodian, in his discretion, except where such disclosure is prohibited by law:

a. Criminal investigative files, defined as any documents and information, including complaints, court orders, memoranda, notes, diagrams, maps, photographs, correspondence, reports, witness statements, and evidence relating to a criminal investigation or prosecution, other than criminal incident information subject to release in accordance with subdivision 1 a;

b. Reports submitted in confidence to (i) state and local law-enforcement agencies, (ii) investigators authorized pursuant to Chapter 3.2 (§ 2.2-307 et seq.), and (iii) campus police departments of public institutions of higher education established pursuant to Chapter 17 (§ 23-232 et seq.) of Title 23;

c. Records of local law-enforcement agencies relating to neighborhood watch programs that include the names, addresses, and operating schedules of individual participants in the program that are provided to such agencies under a promise of anonymity;

d. All records of persons imprisoned in penal institutions in the Commonwealth provided such records relate to the imprisonment;

e. Records of law-enforcement agencies, to the extent that such records contain specific tactical plans, the disclosure of which would jeopardize the safety or security of law-enforcement personnel or the general public;

f. All records of adult persons under (i) investigation or supervision by a local pretrial services agency in accordance with Article 5 (§ 19.2-152.2 et seq.) of Chapter 9 of Title 19.2; (ii) investigation, probation supervision, or monitoring by a local community-based probation services agency in accordance with Article 9 (§ 9.1-173 et seq.) of Chapter 1 of Title 9.1; or (iii) investigation or supervision by state probation and parole services in accordance with Article 2 (§ 53.1-141 et seq.) of Chapter 4 of Title 53.1;

g. Records of a law-enforcement agency to the extent that they disclose the telephone numbers for cellular telephones, pagers, or comparable portable communication devices provided to its personnel for use in the performance of their official duties;

h. Those portions of any records containing information related to undercover operations or protective details that would reveal the staffing, logistics, or tactical plans of such undercover operations or protective details. Nothing in this subdivision shall operate to allow the withholding of information concerning the overall costs or expenses associated with undercover operations or protective details;

i. Records of (i) background investigations of applicants for law-enforcement agency employment, (ii) administrative investigations relating to allegations of wrongdoing by employees of a law-enforcement agency, and (iii) other administrative investigations conducted by law-enforcement agencies that are made confidential by law;

j. The identity of any victim, witness, or undercover officer, or investigative techniques or procedures. However, the identity of any victim or witness shall be withheld if disclosure is prohibited or restricted under § 19.2-11.2; and

k. Records of the Sex Offender and Crimes Against Minors Registry maintained by the Department of State Police pursuant to Chapter 9 (§ 9.1-900 et seq.) of Title 9.1, including information obtained from state, local, and regional officials, except to the extent that information is required to be posted on the Internet pursuant to § 9.1-913; and

3. Prohibited releases. The identity of any individual providing information about a crime or criminal activity under a promise of anonymity shall not be disclosed.

B. Noncriminal records. Records (i) required to be maintained by law-enforcement agencies pursuant to § 15.2-1722 or (ii) maintained by other public bodies engaged in criminal law-enforcement activities shall be subject to the provisions of this chapter except that those portions of noncriminal incident or other noncriminal investigative reports or materials that contain identifying information of a personal, medical, or financial nature may be withheld where the release of such information would jeopardize the safety or privacy of any person. Access to personnel records of persons employed by a law-enforcement agency shall be governed by the provisions of subdivision A 2 i of this section and subdivision 1 of § 2.2-3705.1, as applicable.

C. Records of any call for service or other communication to an emergency 911 system or communicated with any other equivalent reporting system shall be subject to the provisions of this chapter.

D. Conflict resolution. In the event of conflict between this section as it relates to requests made under this section and other provisions of law, this section shall control.

History.
1999, cc. 703, 726, § 2.1-342.2; 2000, c. 227; 2001, c. 844; 2002, cc. 393, 715, 769, 830; 2004, cc. 685, 735; 2006, cc. 857, 914; 2007, c. 133; 2010, c. 627; 2011, cc. 798, 871; 2013, c. 695.

Editor's note.
Acts 2002, c. 393, cl. 2, provides: "That it is the intent of the General Assembly to address the recent Virginia Supreme Court holding in the case styled Connell v. Kersey [262 Va. 154, 547 S.E.2d 228 (2001)], which held that attorneys for the Commonwealth are not 'public bodies' as defined in the Freedom of Information Act (§ 2.2-3700 et seq.), by clarifying that the Freedom of Information Act (FOIA) applies to constitutional officers and pro-

viding an exemption for attorneys for the Commonwealth."

Acts 2011, cc. 798 and 871, cl. 7 provides: "That the provisions of this act shall become effective on July 1, 2012, except that the provisions of the fifth enactment of this act shall become effective on July 1, 2011."

The 2010 amendments.
The 2010 amendment by c. 627, in subsection A, added the definition of "criminal investigative file"; rewrote subdivision F 1, which formerly read: "Complaints, memoranda, correspondence, case files or reports, witness statements, and evidence relating to a criminal investigation or prosecution, other than criminal incident information as defined in subsection A"; added subdivisions F 10 and F 11 and made related changes; and rewrote subsection G.

The 2011 amendments.
The 2011 amendments by cc. 798 and 871, effective July 1, 2012, are identical, and substituted "Chapter 3.2 (§ 2.2-307 et seq.)" for "§ 53.1-16 or § 66-3.1" in subdivision F 3.

The 2013 amendments.
The 2013 amendments by c. 695 rewrote the section.

Research references.
Virginia Forms (Matthew Bender). No. 9-1301 Freedom of Information Request.

CASE NOTES

Commonwealth's attorney not required to release actual records. — This section does not require a Commonwealth's attorney's office or other law enforcement official to release actual records relating to a criminal incident, but only to provide a summary of the information available from the specified records, subject to any mandatory or discretionary exemptions provided for in the statute. Connell v. Kersey, 262 Va. 154, 547 S.E.2d 228, 2001 Va. LEXIS 67 (2001) (decided under prior law).

Police personnel records. — Police personnel records are, like all public personnel records, subject to the protections of subdivision 1 of § 2.2-3705.1; thus, a circuit court erred when it issued a mandamus order to a police department that required the department to produce information that was contained only in an officer's personnel record. Harmon v. Ewing, 285 Va. 335, 2013 Va. LEXIS 14 (Feb. 8, 2013).

Production of information. — Contrary to a police department's position, it was required to provide both "information" and documents, and therefore, there was no error in an order from a circuit court that required the department to produce information relative to the identity of individuals who had been arrested by a particular police officer. Harmon v. Ewing, 285 Va. 335, 2013 Va. LEXIS 14 (Feb. 8, 2013).

Investigative files. — Arrests occurring merely on an officer's "information" or with him serving as a witness, for which the officer has not signed or been otherwise designated as the arresting officer, fall into the category of criminal investigative files and are exempt from freedom of information requests; thus, a circuit court erred when it directed a police department to produce records related to individuals arrested based on a specific officer's information or observations. Harmon v. Ewing, 285 Va. 335, 2013 Va. LEXIS 14 (Feb. 8, 2013).

CIRCUIT COURT OPINIONS

Undercover operations. — Certain portions of the records were properly redacted because they related to plans or resources dedicated to undercover operations, or contained credit card or account numbers, but other pages improperly redacted information concerning equipment and supplies which could have been used for many purposes, including general police work and surveillance. Albright v. Woodfin, 68 Va. Cir. 115, 2005 Va. Cir. LEXIS 104 (Nelson County 2005).

Decision not to prosecute. — Because a nine-page letter to the parents from the Commonwealth's attorney, detailing the decision not to prosecute a criminal case against the defendants, was far greater than what was required by the Virginia Freedom of

Information Act, subsection A of § 2.2-3706, a police lieutenant's motion to quash the parents' subpoena duces tecum in their wrongful death action was granted. Singh v. Agbemble, 77 Va. Cir. 242, 2008 Va. Cir. LEXIS 150 (Fairfax County 2008).

§ 2.2-3707. Meetings to be public; notice of meetings; recordings; minutes.

A. All meetings of public bodies shall be open, except as provided in §§ 2.2-3707.01 and 2.2-3711.

B. No meeting shall be conducted through telephonic, video, electronic or other communication means where the members are not physically assembled to discuss or transact public business, except as provided in § 2.2-3708, 2.2-3708.1 or as may be specifically provided in Title 54.1 for the summary suspension of professional licenses.

C. Every public body shall give notice of the date, time, and location of its meetings by placing the notice in a prominent public location at which notices are regularly posted and in the office of the clerk of the public body, or in the case of a public body that has no clerk, in the office of the chief administrator. All state public bodies subject to the provisions of this chapter shall also post notice of their meetings on their websites and on the electronic calendar maintained by the Virginia Information Technologies Agency commonly known as the Commonwealth Calendar. Publication of meeting notices by electronic means by other public bodies shall be encouraged. The notice shall be posted at least three working days prior to the meeting. Notices for meetings of state public bodies on which there is at least one member appointed by the Governor shall state whether or not public comment will be received at the meeting and, if so, the approximate point during the meeting when public comment will be received.

D. Notice, reasonable under the circumstance, of special or emergency meetings shall be given contemporaneously with the notice provided members of the public body conducting the meeting.

E. Any person may annually file a written request for notification with a public body. The request shall include the requester's name, address, zip code, daytime telephone number, electronic mail address, if available, and organization, if any. The public body receiving such request shall provide notice of all meetings directly to each such person. Without objection by the person, the public body may provide electronic notice of all meetings in response to such requests.

F. At least one copy of all agenda packets and, unless exempt, all materials furnished to members of a public body for a meeting shall be made available for public inspection at the same time such documents are furnished to the members of the public body.

G. Nothing in this chapter shall be construed to prohibit the gathering or attendance of two or more members of a public body (i) at any place or function where no part of the purpose of such gathering or attendance is the discussion or transaction of any public business, and such gathering or attendance was not called or prearranged with any purpose of discussing or transacting any business of the public body or (ii) at a public forum, candidate appearance, or debate, the purpose of which is to inform the electorate and not to transact public business or to hold discussions relating to the transaction of public business, even though the performance of the members individually or collectively in the conduct of public business may be a topic of discussion or debate at such public meeting. The notice provisions of this chapter shall not apply to informal meetings or gatherings of the members of the General Assembly.

H. Any person may photograph, film, record or otherwise reproduce any portion of a meeting required to be open. The public body conducting the meeting may adopt rules governing the placement and use of equipment necessary for broadcasting, photographing, filming or recording a meeting to prevent interference with the proceedings, but shall not prohibit or otherwise prevent any person from photographing, filming, recording, or otherwise reproducing any portion of a meeting required to be open. No public body shall conduct a meeting required to be open in any building or facility where such recording devices are prohibited.

I. Minutes shall be recorded at all open meetings. However, minutes shall not be required to be taken at deliberations of (i) standing and other committees of the General Assembly; (ii) legislative interim study commissions and committees, including the Virginia Code Commission; (iii) study committees or commissions appointed by the Governor; or (iv) study commissions or study committees, or any other committees or subcommittees appointed by the governing bodies or school boards of counties, cities and towns, except where the membership of any such commission, committee or subcommittee includes a majority of the governing body of the county, city or town or school board.

Minutes, including draft minutes, and all other records of open meetings, including audio or audio/visual records shall be deemed public records and subject to the provisions of this chapter.

Minutes shall be in writing and shall include (i) the date, time, and location of the meeting; (ii) the members of the public body recorded as present and absent; and (iii) a summary of the discussion on matters proposed, deliberated or decided, and a record of any votes taken. In addition, for electronic communication meetings conducted in accordance with § 2.2-3708, minutes of state public bodies shall include (a) the identity of the members of the public body at each remote location identified in the notice who participated in the meeting through electronic communications means, (b) the identity of the members of the public body who were physically assembled at the primary or central meeting location, and (c) the identity of the members of the public body who were not present at the locations identified in clauses (a) and (b), but who monitored such meeting through electronic communications means.

History.
1968, c. 479, § 2.1-343; 1973, c. 461; 1976, c. 467; 1977, c. 677; 1982, c. 333; 1989, c. 358; 1990, c. 538; 1993, c. 720; 1995, c. 562; 1999, cc. 696, 703, 726; 2000, c. 227; 2001, c. 844; 2004, cc. 730, 768; 2005, c. 352; 2007, c. 300; 2009, c. 628; 2010, c. 309.

Editor's note.
Acts 2004, c. 768, cl. 2, provides: "That technical assistance to the Joint Rules Committee for the implementation of the provisions of this act shall be provided by the Virginia Freedom of Information Advisory Council, upon request."
Acts 2009, c. 628, cl. 2, provides: "That the provisions of this act are declaratory of existing law."

The 2010 amendments.
The 2010 amendment by c. 309, in subsection H, inserted "but shall not prohibit or otherwise prevent any person from photographing, filming, recording, or otherwise reproducing any portion of a meeting required to be open" and added the last sentence.

Michie's Jurisprudence.
For related discussion, see 16 M.J. Right of Privacy, § 1.

CASE NOTES

Street gathering not "meeting." — Judgment was properly awarded to a mayor and city officials in an action alleging that a particular street gathering of citizens and city council members was a "meeting" under the Virginia Freedom of Information Act because the street gathering was a citizen-organized "informational forum;" no part of the purpose of the gathering or attendance was the discussion or transaction of any public business. Beck v. Shelton, 267 Va. 482, 593 S.E.2d 195, 2004 Va. LEXIS 40 (2004).

CIRCUIT COURT OPINIONS

Participation in meeting de minimus. — County school board member participated in a meeting without informing the public in violation of the open meeting provisions of the Virginia Freedom of Information Act, §§ 2.2-3707 and 2.2-3708, because her e-mail was an effort to communicate with the rest of the board, and there was no notice of her attendance; however, the member's participation in the meeting was de minimis and appeared to have no impact on the actions taken because the member did not vote or express her opinion about any substantive issue during the meeting. Hill v. Fairfax County Sch. Bd., 83 Va. Cir. 172, 2011 Va. Cir. LEXIS 89 (Fairfax County July 13, 2011).

OPINIONS OF THE ATTORNEY GENERAL

An institutional review board of a public institution of higher learning in the Commonwealth engaged in human research projects is not subject to the open meeting requirements set forth in the statute. See opinion of Attorney General to The Honorable Thomas C. Wright Jr., Member, House of Delegates, 01-101 (10/22/01).

A legislative caucus is not a "public body" as that term is defined in The Virginia Freedom of Information Act; therefore, the notice and open meeting requirements of the Act do not apply to such organizations. See opinion of Attorney General to The Honorable Clifton A. Woodrum, Member, House of Delegates, 03-063 (1/6/04).

An informal assemblage of three or more legislators at a meeting prearranged or called for the purpose of discussing expected votes on matters pending before the General Assembly constitutes a meeting under The Virginia Freedom of Information Act, requiring that such a meeting be open to the public. See opinion of Attorney General to The Honorable Clifton A. Woodrum, Member, House of Delegates, 03-063 (1/6/04).

Failure of a city council to give notice of meeting as required by subsection C of this section invalidates the appointment of a nominee to the school board. See opinions of Attorney General to The Honorable Roslyn C. Tyler, Member, House of Delegates 08-114 (1/6/09) and to H. Taylor Williams, IV, Esq., City Attorney for Franklin, 08-078 (1/6/09).

§ 2.2-3707.01. Meetings of the General Assembly.

A. Except as provided in subsection B, public access to any meeting of the General Assembly or a portion thereof shall be governed by rules established by the Joint Rules Committee and approved by a majority vote of each house at the next regular session of the General Assembly. At least 60 days before the adoption of such rules, the Joint Rules Committee shall (i) hold regional public hearings on such proposed rules and (ii) provide a copy of such proposed rules to the Virginia Freedom of Information Advisory Council.

B. Floor sessions of either house of the General Assembly; meetings, including work sessions, of any standing or interim study committee of the General Assembly; meetings, including work sessions, of any subcommittee of such standing or interim study committee; and joint committees of conference of the General Assembly; or a quorum of any such committees or subcommittees, shall be open and governed by this chapter.

C. Meetings of the respective political party caucuses of either house of the General Assembly, including meetings conducted by telephonic or other electronic communication means, without regard to (i) whether the General Assembly is in or out of regular or special session or (ii) whether such caucuses invite staff or guests to participate in their deliberations, shall not be deemed meetings for the purposes of this chapter.

D. No regular, special, or reconvened session of the General Assembly held pursuant to Article IV, Section 6 of the Constitution of Virginia shall be conducted using electronic communication means pursuant § 2.2-3708.

History.
2004, c. 768; 2005, c. 352.

Editor's note.
Acts 2004, c. 768, cl. 2, provides: "That technical assistance to the Joint Rules Committee for the implementation of the provisions of this act shall be provided by the Virginia Freedom of Information Advisory Council, upon request."

§ 2.2-3707.1. Posting of minutes for state boards and commissions.

All boards, commissions, councils, and other public bodies created in the executive branch of state government and subject to the provisions of this chapter shall post minutes of their meetings on such body's website, if any, and on the electronic calendar maintained by the Virginia Information Technologies Agency commonly known as the Commonwealth

Calendar. Draft minutes of meetings shall be posted as soon as possible but no later than ten working days after the conclusion of the meeting. Final approved meeting minutes shall be posted within three working days of final approval of the minutes.

History.
  2002, cc. 580, 618; 2006, cc. 474, 595; 2007, c. 300.

§ 2.2-3708. Electronic communication meetings; applicability; physical quorum required; exceptions; notice; report.

A. Except as expressly provided in subsection G of this section or § 2.2-3708.1, no local governing body, school board, or any authority, board, bureau, commission, district or agency of local government, any committee thereof, or any entity created by a local governing body, school board, or any local authority, board, or commission shall conduct a meeting wherein the public business is discussed or transacted through telephonic, video, electronic or other communication means where the members are not physically assembled. Nothing in this section shall be construed to prohibit the use of interactive audio or video means to expand public participation.

B. Except as provided in subsection G or H of this section or subsection D of § 2.2-3707.01, state public bodies may conduct any meeting wherein the public business is discussed or transacted through electronic communication means, provided (i) a quorum of the public body is physically assembled at one primary or central meeting location, (ii) notice of the meeting has been given in accordance with subsection C, and (iii) the remote locations, from which additional members of the public body participate through electronic communication means, are open to the public. All persons attending the meeting at any of the meeting locations shall be afforded the same opportunity to address the public body as persons attending the primary or central location.

If an authorized public body holds an electronic meeting pursuant to this section, it shall also hold at least one meeting annually where members in attendance at the meeting are physically assembled at one location and where no members participate by electronic communication means.

C. Notice of any meetings held pursuant to this section shall be provided at least three working days in advance of the date scheduled for the meeting. The notice shall include the date, time, place, and purpose for the meeting; shall identify the locations for the meeting; and shall include a telephone number that may be used at remote locations to notify the primary or central meeting location of any interruption in the telephonic or video broadcast of the meeting to the remote locations. Any interruption in the telephonic or video broadcast of the meeting shall result in the suspension of action at the meeting until repairs are made and public access restored.

D. Agenda packets and, unless exempt, all materials that will be distributed to members of the public body and that have been made available to the staff of the public body in sufficient time for duplication and forwarding to all locations where public access will be provided shall be made available to the public at the time of the meeting. Minutes of all meetings held by electronic communication means shall be recorded as required by § 2.2-3707. Votes taken during any meeting conducted through electronic communication means shall be recorded by name in roll-call fashion and included in the minutes.

E. Three working days' notice shall not be required for meetings authorized under this section held in accordance with subsection G or that are continued to address an emergency or to conclude the agenda of the meeting for which proper notice has been given, when the date, time, place, and purpose of the continued meeting are set during the meeting prior to adjournment. Public bodies conducting emergency meetings through electronic communication means shall comply with the provisions of subsection D requiring minutes of the meeting. The nature of the emergency shall be stated in the minutes.

F. Any authorized public body that meets by electronic communication means shall make a written report of the following to the Virginia Freedom of Information Advisory Council and the Joint Commission on Technology and Science by December 15 of each year:

1. The total number of electronic communication meetings held that year;

2. The dates and purposes of the meetings;

3. A copy of the agenda for the meeting;

4. The number of sites for each meeting;

5. The types of electronic communication means by which the meetings were held;

6. The number of participants, including members of the public, at each meeting location;

7. The identity of the members of the public body recorded as absent and those recorded as present at each meeting location;

8. A summary of any public comment received about the electronic communication meetings; and

9. A written summary of the public body's experience using electronic communication meetings, including its logistical and technical experience.

In addition, any authorized public body shall make available to the public at any meeting conducted in accordance with this section a public comment form prepared by the Virginia Freedom of Information Advisory Council in accordance with § 30-179.

G. Any public body may meet by electronic communication means without a quorum of the public body physically assembled at one location when the Governor has declared a state of emergency in accordance with § 44-146.17, provided (i) the catastrophic nature of the declared emergency makes it impracticable or unsafe to assemble a quorum in a single location and (ii) the purpose of the meeting is to address the emergency. The public body convening a meeting in accordance with this subsection shall (a) give public notice using the best available method given the nature of the emergency, which notice shall be given contemporaneously with the notice provided members of the public body conducting the meeting; (b) make arrangements for public access to such meeting; and (c) otherwise comply with the provisions of this section. The nature of the emergency, the fact that the meeting was held by electronic communication means, and the type of electronic communication means by which the meeting was held shall be stated in the minutes.

H. **(Expires July 1, 2014)** An advisory public body, defined as any state public body classified as advisory pursuant to § 2.2-2100 or any committee, subcommittee, or other entity, however designated, of a state public body created to advise the state public body, may meet by electronic communication means without a quorum of the advisory public body being physically assembled at one location, provided (i) the meeting is conducted utilizing a combined audio and visual communication method; (ii) a primary or central meeting location is established and identified in the notice in accordance with subsection C; (iii) the remote locations, from which additional members of the advisory public body participate through the combined audio and visual communication method, are open to the public and are identified in the notice in accordance with subsection C; (iv) all persons attending the meeting at any of the meeting locations shall be afforded the same opportunity to address the advisory public body as persons attending the primary or central location; and (v) all other provisions of this section are met. Any advisory public body holding electronic communication meetings in accordance with this subsection shall make an audiovisual recording of any such meeting, which recording shall be preserved by the advisory public body for a period of three years from the date of the meeting. The recording shall be available to the public for inspection and copying pursuant to § 2.2-3704. Any portion of the meeting that is closed to the public in accordance with this chapter may be recorded, but such recording is not required. Any audiovisual recording of any closed portion of the meeting shall not be subject to mandatory public disclosure.

History.
1984, c. 252, § 2.1-343.1; 1989, c. 358; 1991, c. 473; 1992, c. 153; 1993, c. 270; 1995, c. 278; 1996, c. 289; 1999, cc. 703, 726; 2001, c. 844; 2003, cc. 981, 1021; 2005, c. 352; 2007, cc. 512, 945; 2008, cc. 233, 789; 2013, c. 694.

Expiration date for subsection H. — Acts 2013, c. 694, cl. 2 provides: "That the provisions of subsection H of § 2.2-3708 of the Code of Virginia shall expire on July 1, 2014."

For provisions of Acts 2003, cc. 981 and 1021, cls. 4 to 16, reflecting the intent of the General Assembly to provide for the consolidation of the procurement and operational functions of information technology for state agencies in a single agency, and

related transitional and other provisions, see the Editor's note at § 2.2-2005.

The 2013 amendments.
The 2013 amendment by c. 694, in the first paragraph of subsection B, inserted "subsection G or H of this section or" near the beginning of the first sentence, and deleted the last sentence, which read: "State public bodies, however, may meet by electronic communication means without a quorum of the public body physically assembled at one location when (a) the Governor has declared a state of emergency in accordance with § 44-146.17, (b) the meeting is necessary to take action to address the emergency, and (c) the public body otherwise complies with the provisions of this section"; in subsection F, added subdivision 3 and renumbered the remaining subdivisions accordingly, and added the last paragraph; in subsection G, substituted "public body" for "local governing body, school board, or any authority, board, bureau, commission, district, or agency of local government" near the beginning of the first sentence, deleted "local" preceding "public body" twice in the second sentence, and in the third sentence, deleted "and" following emergency" and inserted "and the type of electronic communication means by which the meeting was held"; and added subsection H.

Law Review.
For survey of the Virginia law on administrative law for the year 2007-2008, see 43 U. Rich. L. Rev. 73 (2008).

Michie's Jurisprudence.
For related discussion, see 16 M.J. Right of Privacy, § 1.

CASE NOTES

Applied in Beck v. Shelton, 267 Va. 482, 593 S.E.2d 195, 2004 Va. LEXIS 40 (2004).

CIRCUIT COURT OPINIONS

Participation in meeting de minimus. — County school board member participated in a meeting without informing the public in violation of the open meeting provisions of the Virginia Freedom of Information Act, §§ 2.2-3707 and 2.2-3708, because her e-mail was an effort to communicate with the rest of the board, and there was no notice of her attendance; however, the member's participation in the meeting was de minimis and appeared to have no impact on the actions taken because the member did not vote or express her opinion about any substantive issue during the meeting. Hill v. Fairfax County Sch. Bd., 83 Va. Cir. 172, 2011 Va. Cir. LEXIS 89 (Fairfax County July 13, 2011).

§ 2.2-3708.1. Participation in meetings in event of emergency or personal matter; certain disabilities; distance from meeting location for certain public bodies.

A. A member of a public body may participate in a meeting governed by this chapter through electronic communication means from a remote location that is not open to the public only as follows and subject to the requirements of subsection B:

1. If, on or before the day of a meeting, a member of the public body holding the meeting notifies the chair of the public body that such member is unable to attend the meeting due to an emergency or personal matter and identifies with specificity the nature of the emergency or personal matter and the public body holding the meeting (a) approves such member's participation by a majority vote of the members present at a meeting and (b) records in its minutes the specific nature of the emergency or

personal matter and the remote location from which the member participated.

Such participation by the member shall be limited each calendar year to two meetings or 25 percent of the meetings of the public body, whichever is fewer;

2. If a member of a public body notifies the chair of the public body that such member is unable to attend a meeting due to a temporary or permanent disability or other medical condition that prevents the member's physical attendance and the public body records this fact and the remote location from which the member participated in its minutes; or

3. If, on the day of a meeting, a member of a regional public body notifies the chair of the public body that such member's principal residence is more than 60 miles from the meeting location identified in the required notice for such meeting and the public body holding the meeting (a) approves such member's participation by a majority vote of the members present and (b) records in its minutes the remote location from which the member participated.

B. Participation by a member of a public body as authorized under subsection A shall be only under the following conditions:

1. A quorum of the public body is physically assembled at the primary or central meeting location; and

2. The public body makes arrangements for the voice of the remote participant to be heard by all persons at the primary or central meeting location.

History.
2007, c. 945; 2013, cc. 119, 694.

The 2013 amendments.
The 2013 amendment by cc. 119 and 694, in the first paragraph of subdivision A 1, inserted "or before" near the beginning, inserted "or personal matter" three times, and inserted "at a meeting" near the end of clause (a).

§ 2.2-3709. Expired.

Editor's note.
Acts 1998, cc. 777 and 839, cl. 2, as amended by Acts 2000, c. 909, cl. 1, Acts 2002, c. 297, Acts 2003, c. 475, cl. 2, and Acts 2005, c. 17, cl. 1, provide: "That the provisions of this act shall expire on July 1, 2007. From July 1, 1998, to July 1, 2007, the Board of Visitors of the University of Virginia shall record the date and name of each board or committee meeting held pursuant to this chapter and, for each meeting, record the name of each board member who participates by video or telephone. The Board of Visitors also shall record any complaints about telephonic or video participation at meetings expressed by board members, members of the public, or members of the media. No later than January 1, 2007, the Board shall provide the Secretary of Education, the Virginia Freedom of Information Advisory Council, and the General Assembly a written report containing the information required to be recorded as well as a narrative summary of the positive and negative experiences of employing telephonic and video meetings."

§ 2.2-3710. Transaction of public business other than by votes at meetings prohibited.

A. Unless otherwise specifically provided by law, no vote of any kind of the membership, or any part

thereof, of any public body shall be taken to authorize the transaction of any public business, other than a vote taken at a meeting conducted in accordance with the provisions of this chapter. No public body shall vote by secret or written ballot, and unless expressly provided by this chapter, no public body shall vote by telephone or other electronic communication means.

B. Notwithstanding the foregoing, nothing contained herein shall be construed to prohibit (i) separately contacting the membership, or any part thereof, of any public body for the purpose of ascertaining a member's position with respect to the transaction of public business, whether such contact is done in person, by telephone or by electronic communication, provided the contact is done on a basis that does not constitute a meeting as defined in this chapter or (ii) the House of Delegates or the Senate of Virginia from adopting rules relating to the casting of votes by members of standing committees. Nothing in this subsection shall operate to exclude any public record from the provisions of this chapter.

History.
1987, c. 71, § 2.1-343.2; 1999, cc. 703, 726; 2000, c. 932; 2001, cc. 710, 844; 2002, c. 491.

Editor's note.
Acts 2001, c. 710 amended § 2.1-343.2, from which this section is derived. Pursuant to § 30-152, Acts 2001, c. 710 has been given effect in this section as set out above. The 2001 amendment by c. 710, in the second paragraph, inserted "whether such contact is done in person, by telephone or by electronic communication, provided the contact is done on a basis that does not constitute a meeting as defined in this chapter" at the end of the first sentence, and added the second sentence.

CASE NOTES

Applied in Beck v. Shelton, 267 Va. 482, 593 S.E.2d 195, 2004 Va. LEXIS 40 (2004).

CIRCUIT COURT OPINIONS

E-mail communications not "meeting." — E-mails sent by county school board members in the days leading up to the vote to close an elementary school did not involve sufficient simultaneity to constitute a meeting under the Virginia Freedom of Information Act, § 2.2-3701, because the e-mails were used consecutively, rather than co-operatively, and the members never reached any sort of group consensus or discussed business as if they were sitting in a room, virtual or real, chatting with each other; individual attempts to ascertain other members' positions on the issue did not violate the Act's open meeting provisions because there was no evidence of a collective intent on behalf of any three members or the board as a whole to move toward a decision outside of the context of a public meeting. Hill v. Fairfax County Sch. Bd., 83 Va. Cir. 172, 2011 Va. Cir. LEXIS 89 (Fairfax County July 13, 2011).

§ 2.2-3711. Closed meetings authorized for certain limited purposes.

A. Public bodies may hold closed meetings only for the following purposes:

1. Discussion, consideration, or interviews of prospective candidates for employment; assignment,

appointment, promotion, performance, demotion, salaries, disciplining, or resignation of specific public officers, appointees, or employees of any public body; and evaluation of performance of departments or schools of public institutions of higher education where such evaluation will necessarily involve discussion of the performance of specific individuals. Any teacher shall be permitted to be present during a closed meeting in which there is a discussion or consideration of a disciplinary matter that involves the teacher and some student and the student involved in the matter is present, provided the teacher makes a written request to be present to the presiding officer of the appropriate board.

2. Discussion or consideration of admission or disciplinary matters or any other matters that would involve the disclosure of information contained in a scholastic record concerning any student of any Virginia public institution of higher education or any state school system. However, any such student, legal counsel and, if the student is a minor, the student's parents or legal guardians shall be permitted to be present during the taking of testimony or presentation of evidence at a closed meeting, if such student, parents, or guardians so request in writing and such request is submitted to the presiding officer of the appropriate board.

3. Discussion or consideration of the acquisition of real property for a public purpose, or of the disposition of publicly held real property, where discussion in an open meeting would adversely affect the bargaining position or negotiating strategy of the public body.

4. The protection of the privacy of individuals in personal matters not related to public business.

5. Discussion concerning a prospective business or industry or the expansion of an existing business or industry where no previous announcement has been made of the business' or industry's interest in locating or expanding its facilities in the community.

6. Discussion or consideration of the investment of public funds where competition or bargaining is involved, where, if made public initially, the financial interest of the governmental unit would be adversely affected.

7. Consultation with legal counsel and briefings by staff members or consultants pertaining to actual or probable litigation, where such consultation or briefing in open meeting would adversely affect the negotiating or litigating posture of the public body; and consultation with legal counsel employed or retained by a public body regarding specific legal matters requiring the provision of legal advice by such counsel. For the purposes of this subdivision, "probable litigation" means litigation that has been specifically threatened or on which the public body or its legal counsel has a reasonable basis to believe will be commenced by or against a known party. Nothing in this subdivision shall be construed to permit the closure of a meeting merely because an attorney representing the public body is in attendance or is consulted on a matter.

8. In the case of boards of visitors of public institutions of higher education, discussion or consideration of matters relating to gifts, bequests and fund-raising activities, and grants and contracts for services or work to be performed by such institution. However, the terms and conditions of any such gifts, bequests, grants, and contracts made by a foreign government, a foreign legal entity, or a foreign person and accepted by a public institution of higher education in Virginia shall be subject to public disclosure upon written request to the appropriate board of visitors. For the purpose of this subdivision, (i) "foreign government" means any government other than the United States government or the government of a state or a political subdivision thereof; (ii) "foreign legal entity" means any legal entity created under the laws of the United States or of any state thereof if a majority of the ownership of the stock of such legal entity is owned by foreign governments or foreign persons or if a majority of the membership of any such entity is composed of foreign persons or foreign legal entities, or any legal entity created under the laws of a foreign government; and (iii) "foreign person" means any individual who is not a citizen or national of the United States or a trust territory or protectorate thereof.

9. In the case of the boards of trustees of the Virginia Museum of Fine Arts, the Virginia Museum of Natural History, the Jamestown-Yorktown Foundation, and The Science Museum of Virginia, discussion or consideration of matters relating to specific gifts, bequests, and grants.

10. Discussion or consideration of honorary degrees or special awards.

11. Discussion or consideration of tests, examinations, or other records excluded from this chapter pursuant to subdivision 4 of § 2.2-3705.1.

12. Discussion, consideration, or review by the appropriate House or Senate committees of possible disciplinary action against a member arising out of the possible inadequacy of the disclosure statement filed by the member, provided the member may request in writing that the committee meeting not be conducted in a closed meeting.

13. Discussion of strategy with respect to the negotiation of a hazardous waste siting agreement or to consider the terms, conditions, and provisions of a hazardous waste siting agreement if the governing body in open meeting finds that an open meeting will have an adverse effect upon the negotiating position of the governing body or the establishment of the terms, conditions and provisions of the siting agreement, or both. All discussions with the applicant or its representatives may be conducted in a closed meeting.

14. Discussion by the Governor and any economic advisory board reviewing forecasts of economic activity and estimating general and nongeneral fund revenues.

15. Discussion or consideration of medical and mental health records excluded from this chapter pursuant to subdivision 1 of § 2.2-3705.5.

16. Deliberations of the State Lottery Board in a licensing appeal action conducted pursuant to subsection D of § 58.1-4007 regarding the denial or revocation of a license of a lottery sales agent; and discussion, consideration or review of State Lottery Department matters related to proprietary lottery game information and studies or investigations exempted from disclosure under subdivision 6 of § 2.2-3705.3 and subdivision 11 of § 2.2-3705.7.

17. Those portions of meetings by local government crime commissions where the identity of, or information tending to identify, individuals providing information about crimes or criminal activities under a promise of anonymity is discussed or disclosed.

18. Those portions of meetings in which the Board of Corrections discusses or discloses the identity of, or information tending to identify, any prisoner who (i) provides information about crimes or criminal activities, (ii) renders assistance in preventing the escape of another prisoner or in the apprehension of an escaped prisoner, or (iii) voluntarily or at the instance of a prison official renders other extraordinary services, the disclosure of which is likely to jeopardize the prisoner's life or safety.

19. Discussion of plans to protect public safety as it relates to terrorist activity and briefings by staff members, legal counsel, or law-enforcement or emergency service officials concerning actions taken to respond to such activity or a related threat to public safety; or discussion of reports or plans related to the security of any governmental facility, building or structure, or the safety of persons using such facility, building or structure.

20. Discussion by the Board of the Virginia Retirement System, acting pursuant to § 51.1-124.30, or of any local retirement system, acting pursuant to § 51.1-803, or of the Rector and Visitors of the University of Virginia, acting pursuant to § 23-76.1, or by the Board of the Virginia College Savings Plan, acting pursuant to § 23-38.80, regarding the acquisition, holding or disposition of a security or other ownership interest in an entity, where such security or ownership interest is not traded on a governmentally regulated securities exchange, to the extent that such discussion (i) concerns confidential analyses prepared for the Rector and Visitors of the University of Virginia, prepared by the retirement system or by the Virginia College Savings Plan or provided to the retirement system or the Virginia College Savings Plan under a promise of confidentiality, of the future value of such ownership interest or the future financial performance of the entity, and (ii) would have an adverse effect on the value of the investment to be acquired, held or disposed of by the retirement system, the Rector and Visitors of the University of Virginia, or the Virginia College Savings Plan. Nothing in this subdivision shall be construed to prevent the disclosure of information relating to the identity of any investment held, the amount invested or the present value of such investment.

21. Those portions of meetings in which individual child death cases are discussed by the State Child Fatality Review team established pursuant to § 32.1-283.1, and those portions of meetings in which individual child death cases are discussed by a regional or local child fatality review team established pursuant to § 32.1-283.2, and those portions of meetings in which individual death cases are discussed by family violence fatality review teams established pursuant to § 32.1-283.3.

22. Those portions of meetings of the University of Virginia Board of Visitors or the Eastern Virginia Medical School Board of Visitors, as the case may be, and those portions of meetings of any persons to whom management responsibilities for the University of Virginia Medical Center or Eastern Virginia Medical School, as the case may be, have been delegated, in which there is discussed proprietary, business-related information pertaining to the operations of the University of Virginia Medical Center or Eastern Virginia Medical School, as the case may be, including business development or marketing strategies and activities with existing or future joint venturers, partners, or other parties with whom the University of Virginia Medical Center or Eastern Virginia Medical School, as the case may be, has formed, or forms, any arrangement for the delivery of health care, if disclosure of such information would adversely affect the competitive position of the Medical Center or Eastern Virginia Medical School, as the case may be.

23. In the case of the Virginia Commonwealth University Health System Authority, discussion or consideration of any of the following: the acquisition or disposition of real or personal property where disclosure would adversely affect the bargaining position or negotiating strategy of the Authority; operational plans that could affect the value of such property, real or personal, owned or desirable for ownership by the Authority; matters relating to gifts, bequests and fund-raising activities; grants and contracts for services or work to be performed by the Authority; marketing or operational strategies where disclosure of such strategies would adversely affect the competitive position of the Authority; members of its medical and teaching staffs and qualifications for appointments thereto; and qualifications or evaluations of other employees.

24. Those portions of the meetings of the Health Practitioners' Monitoring Program Committee within the Department of Health Professions to the extent such discussions identify any practitioner who may be, or who actually is, impaired pursuant to Chapter 25.1 (§ 54.1-2515 et seq.) of Title 54.1.

25. Meetings or portions of meetings of the Board of the Virginia College Savings Plan wherein personal information, as defined in § 2.2-3801, which has been provided to the Board or its employees by or on behalf of individuals who have requested information about, applied for, or entered into prepaid tuition contracts or savings trust account

agreements pursuant to Chapter 4.9 (§ 23-38.75 et seq.) of Title 23 is discussed.

26. Discussion or consideration, by the Wireless Carrier E-911 Cost Recovery Subcommittee created pursuant to § 56-484.15, of trade secrets, as defined in the Uniform Trade Secrets Act (§ 59.1-336 et seq.), submitted by CMRS providers as defined in § 56-484.12, related to the provision of wireless E-911 service.

27. Those portions of disciplinary proceedings by any regulatory board within the Department of Professional and Occupational Regulation, Department of Health Professions, or the Board of Accountancy conducted pursuant to § 2.2-4019 or 2.2-4020 during which the board deliberates to reach a decision or meetings of health regulatory boards or conference committees of such boards to consider settlement proposals in pending disciplinary actions or modifications to previously issued board orders as requested by either of the parties.

28. Discussion or consideration of records excluded from this chapter pursuant to subdivision 11 of § 2.2-3705.6 by a responsible public entity or an affected local jurisdiction, as those terms are defined in § 56-557, or any independent review panel appointed to review information and advise the responsible public entity concerning such records.

29. Discussion of the award of a public contract involving the expenditure of public funds, including interviews of bidders or offerors, and discussion of the terms or scope of such contract, where discussion in an open session would adversely affect the bargaining position or negotiating strategy of the public body.

30. Discussion or consideration of grant or loan application records excluded from this chapter pursuant to subdivision 17 of § 2.2-3705.6 by (i) the Commonwealth Health Research Board or (ii) the Innovation and Entrepreneurship Investment Authority or the Research and Technology Investment Advisory Committee appointed to advise the Innovation and Entrepreneurship Investment Authority.

31. Discussion or consideration by the Commitment Review Committee of records excluded from this chapter pursuant to subdivision 9 of § 2.2-3705.2 relating to individuals subject to commitment as sexually violent predators under Chapter 9 (§ 37.2-900 et seq.) of Title 37.2.

32. [Expired.]

33. Discussion or consideration of confidential proprietary records and trade secrets excluded from this chapter pursuant to subdivision 18 of § 2.2-3705.6.

34. Discussion or consideration by a local authority created in accordance with the Virginia Wireless Service Authorities Act (§ 15.2-5431.1 et seq.) of confidential proprietary records and trade secrets excluded from this chapter pursuant to subdivision 19 of § 2.2-3705.6.

35. Discussion or consideration by the State Board of Elections or local electoral boards of voting security matters made confidential pursuant to § 24.2-625.1.

36. Discussion or consideration by the Forensic Science Board or the Scientific Advisory Committee created pursuant to Article 2 (§ 9.1-1109 et seq.) of Chapter 11 of Title 9.1 of records excluded from this chapter pursuant to subdivision A 2 a of § 2.2-3706.

37. Discussion or consideration by the Brown v. Board of Education Scholarship Program Awards Committee of records or confidential matters excluded from this chapter pursuant to subdivision 3 of § 2.2-3705.4, and meetings of the Committee to deliberate concerning the annual maximum scholarship award, review and consider scholarship applications and requests for scholarship award renewal, and cancel, rescind, or recover scholarship awards.

38. Discussion or consideration by the Virginia Port Authority of records excluded from this chapter pursuant to subdivision 1 of § 2.2-3705.6.

39. Discussion or consideration by the Board of Trustees of the Virginia Retirement System acting pursuant to § 51.1-124.30, by the Investment Advisory Committee appointed pursuant to § 51.1-124.26, by any local retirement system, acting pursuant to § 51.1-803, by the Board of the Virginia College Savings Plan acting pursuant to § 23-38.80, or by the Virginia College Savings Plan's Investment Advisory Committee appointed pursuant to § 23-38.79:1 of records excluded from this chapter pursuant to subdivision 25 of § 2.2-3705.7.

40. Discussion or consideration of records excluded from this chapter pursuant to subdivision 3 of § 2.2-3705.6.

41. Discussion or consideration by the Board of Education of records relating to the denial, suspension, or revocation of teacher licenses excluded from this chapter pursuant to subdivision 12 of § 2.2-3705.3.

42. Those portions of meetings of the Virginia Military Advisory Council or any commission created by executive order for the purpose of studying and making recommendations regarding preventing closure or realignment of federal military and national security installations and facilities located in Virginia and relocation of such facilities to Virginia, or a local or regional military affairs organization appointed by a local governing body, during which there is discussion of records excluded from this chapter pursuant to subdivision 12 of § 2.2-3705.2.

43. Discussion or consideration by the Board of Trustees of the Veterans Services Foundation of records excluded from this chapter pursuant to subdivision 29 of § 2.2-3705.7.

44. Discussion or consideration by the Virginia Tobacco Indemnification and Community Revitalization Commission of records excluded from this chapter pursuant to subdivision 23 of § 2.2-3705.6.

45. Discussion or consideration by the board of directors of the Commercial Space Flight Authority of records excluded from this chapter pursuant to subdivision 24 of § 2.2-3705.6.

B. No resolution, ordinance, rule, contract, regulation or motion adopted, passed or agreed to in a closed meeting shall become effective unless the public body, following the meeting, reconvenes in open meeting and takes a vote of the membership on such resolution, ordinance, rule, contract, regulation, or motion that shall have its substance reasonably identified in the open meeting.

C. Public officers improperly selected due to the failure of the public body to comply with the other provisions of this section shall be de facto officers and, as such, their official actions are valid until they obtain notice of the legal defect in their election.

D. Nothing in this section shall be construed to prevent the holding of conferences between two or more public bodies, or their representatives, but these conferences shall be subject to the same procedures for holding closed meetings as are applicable to any other public body.

E. This section shall not be construed to (i) require the disclosure of any contract between the Department of Health Professions and an impaired practitioner entered into pursuant to Chapter 25.1 (§ 54.1-2515 et seq.) of Title 54.1 or (ii) require the board of directors of any authority created pursuant to the Industrial Development and Revenue Bond Act (§ 15.2-4900 et seq.), or any public body empowered to issue industrial revenue bonds by general or special law, to identify a business or industry to which subdivision A 5 applies. However, such business or industry shall be identified as a matter of public record at least 30 days prior to the actual date of the board's authorization of the sale or issuance of such bonds.

History.

1968, c. 479, § 2.1-344; 1970, c. 456; 1973, c. 461; 1974, c. 332; 1976, cc. 467, 709; 1979, cc. 369, 684; 1980, cc. 221, 475, 476, 754; 1981, cc. 35, 471; 1982, cc. 497, 516; 1984, cc. 473, 513; 1985, c. 277; 1988, c. 891; 1989, cc. 56, 358, 478; 1990, cc. 435, 538; 1991, c. 708; 1992, c. 444; 1993, cc. 270, 499; 1995, c. 499; 1996, cc. 855, 862, 902, 905, 1046; 1997, cc. 439, 641, 785, 861; 1999, cc. 485, 518, 703, 726, 849, 867, 868; 2000, cc. 382, 400, 720, 1064; 2001, cc. 231, 844; 2002, cc. 87, 393, 455, 478, 499, 655, 715, 830; 2003, cc. 274, 291, 332, 618, 703; 2004, cc. 398, 690, 770; 2005, cc. 258, 411, 568; 2006, cc. 430, 499, 518, 560; 2007, cc. 133, 374, 566, 739; 2008, cc. 626, 633, 668, 721, 743; 2009, cc. 223, 325, 472, 765, 810, 827, 845; 2010, cc. 310, 630, 808; 2011, cc. 89, 111, 147, 536, 541, 816, 874; 2012, cc. 476, 507, 803, 835; 2013, cc. 571, 580, 695.

Editor's note.

Acts 2001, c. 231 amended § 2.1-344, from which this section is derived. Pursuant to § 30-152, Acts 2001, c. 231 has been given effect in this section as set out above. The 2001 amendment by c. 231 inserted "or any other matters that would involve the disclosure of information contained in a scholastic record" in the first sentence in subdivision A 2.

Acts 2002, c. 393, cl. 2, provides: "That it is the intent of the General Assembly to address the recent Virginia Supreme Court holding in the case styled Connell v. Kersey [262 Va. 154, 547 S.E.2d 228 (2002)], which held that attorneys for the Commonwealth are not 'public bodies' as defined in the Freedom of Information Act (§ 2.2-3700 et seq.), by clarifying that the Freedom of Information Act (FOIA) applies to constitutional officers and providing an exemption for attorneys for the Commonwealth."

Acts 2003, c. 291, cl. 2, provides: "That the Board of Accountancy

shall promulgate regulations to implement the provisions of this act to be effective within 280 days of its enactment."

Acts 2004, c. 770, which added subdivision A 33 [now subdivision A 32], in cl. 2 provides: "That the provisions of this act shall expire on July 1, 2006."

The 2010 amendments.

The 2010 amendments by cc. 310 and 808 are identical, and added subdivision A 45.

The 2010 amendment by c. 630 substituted "Innovation and Entrepreneurship Investment" for "Innovative Technology" in subdivision A 30.

The 2011 amendments.

The 2011 amendments by cc. 89 and 147 are identical, and deleted former subdivision A 44, which read: "Discussion or consideration by the advisory committee for veterans care centers established by the Commissioner of the Virginia Department of Veterans Services pursuant to § 2.2-2004.1 of records excluded from this chapter pursuant to subdivision 28 of § 2.2-3705.7" and redesignated the remaining subdivisions accordingly.

The 2011 amendments by cc. 111 and 536 are identical, and inserted the language beginning "any commission created by executive order" and ending "and relocation of such facilities to Virginia" in subdivision A 42.

The 2011 amendment by c. 541 added subdivision A 46 (now A 45).

The 2011 amendments by cc. 816 and 874, effective April 6, 2011, are identical, and in subdivision A 30, substituted "or the Research and Technology Investment Advisory Committee" for "or a grant allocation committee" and deleted "on the grant applications" from the end.

The 2012 amendments.

The 2012 amendments by cc. 476 and 507 are identical, and inserted "health" in subdivision A 15.

The 2012 amendments by cc. 803 and 835, cl. 51, are identical, and at the beginning of subsection 42, deleted "the Virginia National Defense Industrial Authority" following "Virginia Military Council" and inserted "or" preceding "any commission created."

The 2013 amendments.

The 2013 amendment by c. 571 substituted "subdivision 12" for "subdivision 13" in subdivision A 41.

The 2013 amendment by c. 580 inserted "the Jamestown-Yorktown Foundation" in subdivision A 9.

The 2013 amendments by c. 695 substituted "subdivision A 2 a" for "subdivision F 1" near the end of subdivision A 36.

Law Review.

For survey of the Virginia law on administrative law for the year 2007-2008, see 43 U. Rich. L. Rev. 73 (2008).

Michie's Jurisprudence.

For related discussion, see 5A M.J. Counties, § 22; 13B M.J. Municipal Corporations, § 22.

CASE NOTES

Closed meeting to discuss previously awarded public contract improper. — Subdivision A 30 [now A 29] of § 2.2-3711 does not allow a public body to close a meeting in order to discuss the application or enforcement of the scope or terms of a previously awarded public contract. White Dog Publ., Inc. v. Culpeper County Bd. of Supervisors, 272 Va. 377, 634 S.E.2d 334, 2006 Va. LEXIS 81 (2006) (decided prior to 2007 amendments to subdivision A 29 of this section and subdivision 11 of § 2.2-3705.6).

CIRCUIT COURT OPINIONS

Requirements for holding closure. Where a city council previously voted to go into closed session in order to discuss the performance of its city manager as it related to the rising crime in the city, the circuit court ordered the depositions transcribed be opened to allow public access, as the focus of the meeting was on the city's plans and programs to meet the soaring crime issue, and not on the city manager personally; thus, said discussion did not meet the requirements for holding closed meetings. Media Gen. Operations, Inc. v. City Council of Richmond, 64 Va. Cir. 406, 2004 Va. Cir. LEXIS 191 (Richmond 2004).

Investigation subject to closed meeting. — Panel investigating testing irregularities at a school investigated matters that were properly subject to a closed meeting under the Virginia Freedom of Information Act, § 2.2-3711, because the school board did, in fact, conduct a closed meeting on the panel's report, which derived from the panel's investigation, including the records; the panel's administrative investigation thus concerned matters that were "properly subject to a closed meeting under § 2.2-3711." Virginian-Pilot Media Cos., L.L.C. v. City of Norfolk Sch. Bd., 81 Va. Cir. 450, 2010 Va. Cir. LEXIS 272 (Norfolk Dec. 28, 2010).

Discussion of zoning application improper in executive session — Written demurrer of defendants was overruled because the complaint set forth sufficient allegations that matters not lawfully exempted under the Freedom of Information Act were discussed at a county board of supervisors' executive session. While it is proper for a county board of supervisors to go into executive session for the purpose of consultation with legal counsel on specific legal matters requiring provision of legal advice under subdivision A 7 of § 2.2-3711, this does not authorize a general discussion of the merits of a zoning application or a decision to approve the application while in executive session. Robinson v. Brugiere, 72 Va. Cir. 109, 2006 Va. Cir. LEXIS 191 (Amherst County 2006).

Administrative investigation. — Work of a panel investigating testing irregularities at a school and its records constituted work product compiled specifically for use in an active administrative investigation concerning a matter properly subject to a closed meeting under the Virginia Freedom of Information Act, § 2.2-3711, because the work constituted an "administrative investigation" within the meaning of the Virginia Freedom of Information Act, subdivision 3 of § 2.2-3705.1; as the investigation would have been "active" during the time that it occurred, the panel's work constituted an "active administrative investigation" under subdivision 3 of § 2.2-3705.1. Virginian-Pilot Media Cos., L.L.C. v. City of Norfolk Sch. Bd., 81 Va. Cir. 450, 2010 Va. Cir. LEXIS 272 (Norfolk Dec. 28, 2010).

§ 2.2-3712. Closed meetings procedures; certification of proceedings.

A. No closed meeting shall be held unless the public body proposing to convene such meeting has taken an affirmative recorded vote in an open meeting approving a motion that (i) identifies the subject matter, (ii) states the purpose of the meeting and (iii) makes specific reference to the applicable exemption from open meeting requirements provided in § 2.2-3707 or subsection A of § 2.2-3711. The matters contained in such motion shall be set forth in detail in the minutes of the open meeting. A general reference to the provisions of this chapter, the authorized exemptions from open meeting requirements, or the subject matter of the closed meeting shall not be sufficient to satisfy the requirements for holding a closed meeting.

B. The notice provisions of this chapter shall not apply to closed meetings of any public body held solely for the purpose of interviewing candidates for the position of chief administrative officer. Prior to any such closed meeting for the purpose of interviewing candidates, the public body shall announce in an open meeting that such closed meeting shall be held at a disclosed or undisclosed location within 15 days thereafter.

C. The public body holding a closed meeting shall restrict its discussion during the closed meeting only to those matters specifically exempted from the provisions of this chapter and identified in the motion required by subsection A.

D. At the conclusion of any closed meeting, the public body holding such meeting shall immediately reconvene in an open meeting and shall take a roll call or other recorded vote to be included in the minutes of that body, certifying that to the best of each member's knowledge (i) only public business matters lawfully exempted from open meeting requirements under this chapter and (ii) only such public business matters as were identified in the motion by which the closed meeting was convened were heard, discussed or considered in the meeting by the public body. Any member of the public body who believes that there was a departure from the requirements of clauses (i) and (ii), shall so state prior to the vote, indicating the substance of the departure that, in his judgment, has taken place. The statement shall be recorded in the minutes of the public body.

E. Failure of the certification required by subsection D to receive the affirmative vote of a majority of the members of the public body present during a meeting shall not affect the validity or confidentiality of such meeting with respect to matters considered therein in compliance with the provisions of this chapter. The recorded vote and any statement made in connection therewith, shall upon proper authentication, constitute evidence in any proceeding brought to enforce the provisions of this chapter.

F. A public body may permit nonmembers to attend a closed meeting if such persons are deemed necessary or if their presence will reasonably aid the public body in its consideration of a topic that is a subject of the meeting.

G. A member of a public body shall be permitted to attend a closed meeting held by any committee or subcommittee of that public body, or a closed meeting of any entity, however designated, created to perform the delegated functions of or to advise that public body. Such member shall in all cases be permitted to observe the closed meeting of the committee, subcommittee or entity. In addition to the requirements of § 2.2-3707, the minutes of the committee or other entity shall include the identity of the member of the parent public body who attended the closed meeting.

H. Except as specifically authorized by law, in no event may any public body take action on matters discussed in any closed meeting, except at an open meeting for which notice was given as required by § 2.2-3707.

I. Minutes may be taken during closed meetings of a public body, but shall not be required. Such minutes shall not be subject to mandatory public disclosure.

History.
1989, c. 358, § 2.1-344.1; 1999, cc. 703, 726; 2001, c. 844; 2012, c. 428.

The 2012 amendments.

The 2012 amendment by c. 428 added subsection G and redesignated the following subsections accordingly.

CASE NOTES

Nonmember attendance. — Doctor involved in medical license revocation proceeding did not have the doctor's due process rights violated when the board allowed people who were not members of the state board of medicine to attend the board's closed session. The board, pursuant to subsection F of § 2.2-3712, was specifically authorized to permit nonmembers to attend a closed meeting if such persons were deemed necessary or if their presence would reasonably aid the public body in its consideration of a topic, and the doctor did not show prejudice from that decision. Vuyyuru v. Va. Bd. of Med., 2008 Va. App. LEXIS 30 (Jan. 15, 2008).

Closed meeting to discuss previously awarded public contract improper. — Subdivision A 30 [now A 29] of § 2.2-3711 does not allow a public body to close a meeting in order to discuss the application or enforcement of the scope or terms of a previously awarded public contract. White Dog Publ., Inc. v. Culpeper County Bd. of Supervisors, 272 Va. 377, 634 S.E.2d 334, 2006 Va. LEXIS 81 (2006).

Attorney's fees and costs. — As newspaper publishers "substantially prevailed" in their suit against a county board of supervisors for violating the Virginia Freedom of Information Act, § 2.2-3700 et seq., by holding a closed meeting, they were entitled to an award of attorney's fees and reasonable costs under subsection D of § 2.2-3713. The fact that the board's violation was not willful and knowing was not a "special circumstance" that would make such an award unjust. White Dog Publ., Inc. v. Culpeper County Bd. of Supervisors, 272 Va. 377, 634 S.E.2d 334, 2006 Va. LEXIS 81 (2006).

CIRCUIT COURT OPINIONS

Closed meeting improper. — County board of supervisors and industrial development authority violated subsection A of § 2.2-3712, a provision of the Freedom of Information Act, by convening a closed session to discuss a prospective business without explaining or justifying the purpose for the closed meeting in the minutes. Ripol v. Westmoreland County Indus. Dev. Auth., 82 Va. Cir. 69, 2010 Va. Cir. LEXIS 203 (Westmoreland County Dec. 28, 2010).

§ 2.2-3713. Proceedings for enforcement of chapter.

A. Any person, including the attorney for the Commonwealth acting in his official or individual capacity, denied the rights and privileges conferred by this chapter may proceed to enforce such rights and privileges by filing a petition for mandamus or injunction, supported by an affidavit showing good cause. Such petition may be brought in the name of the person notwithstanding that a request for public records was made by the person's attorney in his representative capacity. Venue for the petition shall be addressed as follows:

1. In a case involving a local public body, to the general district court or circuit court of the county or city from which the public body has been elected or appointed to serve and in which such rights and privileges were so denied;

2. In a case involving a regional public body, to the general district or circuit court of the county or city where the principal business office of such body is located; and

3. In a case involving a board, bureau, commission, authority, district, institution, or agency of the state government, including a public institution of higher education, or a standing or other committee of the General Assembly, to the general district court or the circuit court of the residence of the aggrieved party or of the City of Richmond.

B. In any action brought before a general district court, a corporate petitioner may appear through its officer, director or managing agent without the assistance of counsel, notwithstanding any provision of law or Rule of the Supreme Court of Virginia to the contrary.

C. Notwithstanding the provisions of § 8.01-644, the petition for mandamus or injunction shall be heard within seven days of the date when the same is made, provided the party against whom the petition is brought has received a copy of the petition at least three working days prior to filing. The hearing on any petition made outside of the regular terms of the circuit court of a locality that is included in a judicial circuit with another locality or localities shall be given precedence on the docket of such court over all cases that are not otherwise given precedence by law.

D. The petition shall allege with reasonable specificity the circumstances of the denial of the rights and privileges conferred by this chapter. A single instance of denial of the rights and privileges conferred by this chapter shall be sufficient to invoke the remedies granted herein. If the court finds the denial to be in violation of the provisions of this chapter, the petitioner shall be entitled to recover reasonable costs, including costs and reasonable fees for expert witnesses, and attorneys' fees from the public body if the petitioner substantially prevails on the merits of the case, unless special circumstances would make an award unjust. In making this determination, a court may consider, among other things, the reliance of a public body on an opinion of the Attorney General or a decision of a court that substantially supports the public body's position.

E. In any action to enforce the provisions of this chapter, the public body shall bear the burden of proof to establish an exemption by a preponderance of the evidence. Any failure by a public body to follow the procedures established by this chapter shall be presumed to be a violation of this chapter.

F. Failure by any person to request and receive notice of the time and place of meetings as provided in § 2.2-3707 shall not preclude any person from enforcing his rights and privileges conferred by this chapter.

History.

1968, c. 479, § 2.1-346; 1976, c. 709; 1978, c. 826; 1989, c. 358; 1990, c. 217; 1996, c. 578; 1999, cc. 703, 726; 2001, c. 844; 2007, c. 560; 2009, c. 634; 2010, c. 299; 2011, cc. 133, 783.

The 2010 amendments.

The 2010 amendment by c. 299 inserted the present next-to-last sentence in the introductory paragraph of subsection A; and inserted "including costs and reasonable fees for expert witnesses" following "reasonable costs" in the next-to-last sentence of subsection D.

The 2011 amendments.

The 2011 amendments by cc. 133 and 783 are nearly identical, and in subsection C, added the proviso at the end of the first sentence, and in the second sentence, substituted "The hearing on" for "However," "locality" for "county" and "locality or localities" for "county or counties, the hearing on the petition."

Law Review.

For article, "Civil Practice and Procedure," see 45 U. Rich. L. Rev. 183 (2010). For annual survey of Virginia law article, "Administrative Law," see 47 U. Rich. L. Rev. 7 (2012).

Research references.

Bryson on Virginia Civil Procedure (Matthew Bender). Chapter 14 Costs. § 14.01 Items included; Chapter 16 Miscellaneous Proceedings. § 16.02 Mandamus and prohibition. W. Hamilton Bryson.

Friend's Virginia Pleading and Practice (Matthew Bender). Chapter 1 Courts. § 1.04 Circuit Courts; Chapter 15 Sanctions. § 15.04 Sanctions in Connection with Petitions for Mandamus and Injunction; Chapter 31 Proceedings in General District Courts. §§ 31.03 Jurisdiction, 31.16 Trial; Chapter 33 Writs and Injunctions. § 33.01 Writs. Charles E. Friend.

Virginia Forms (Matthew Bender). No. 6-1201 Petition for Writ of Mandamus against Officer of a Corporation; No. 6-1205 Petition and Affidavit for Good Cause/For Injunction or Mandamus — Freedom of Information Act; No. 6-1206 Order Granting Petition for Injunction of Writ of Mandamus Under Virginia Freedom of Information Act; No. 9-1301 Freedom of Information Request.

CASE NOTES

Editor's note.

Some of the cases below were decided under former Title 2.1 or prior provisions.

This section is unconstitutional as applied to State Corporation Commission. — Where petitioner invoked jurisdiction of circuit court, and filed petition for writ of mandamus against State Corporation Commission (SCC), trial court correctly ruled that this section was not constitutional as applied to the SCC because of jurisdictional limitations of Va. Const., Art. IX, § 4. Framers of Va. Const., Art. IX, § 4, intended that Supreme Court have exclusive jurisdiction over all challenges to all actions of the SCC, both judgmental and ministerial, and issuance of writ of mandamus directing SCC to reverse its action in refusing petitioner's demand for access to official records was equivalent to entry of injunction restraining SCC in the performance of its official duties. Atlas Underwriters, Ltd. v. SCC, 237 Va. 45, 375 S.E.2d 733 (1989).

Actual controversy. — Production of documents did not resolve all of the issues raised in the appeal, namely, whether the requestor was entitled to recover fees and costs due to the insufficient original response; if the requestor were to prevail on the merits, then a determination of appropriate fees and costs under former § 2.2-3713 was needed; therefore, the finding that there was no actual controversy was rejected. Christian v. State Corp. Comm'n, 282 Va. 392, 718 S.E.2d 767, 2011 Va. LEXIS 217 (2011).

Extraordinary relief not to be casually or perfunctorily ordered. — Under this section, a single violation is sufficient to permit the grant of relief based on the inference that future violations will occur, but such an extraordinary and drastic remedy is not to be casually or perfunctorily ordered. Nageotte v. Board of Supvrs., 223 Va. 259, 288 S.E.2d 423 (1982).

The petition need not contain an allegation of "irreparable injury." WTAR Radio-TV Corp. v. City Council, 216 Va. 892, 223 S.E.2d 895 (1976).

Inference insufficient to justify sanction. — A previous course of conduct might raise an inference that such conduct would be repeated but a mere inference did not support an apprehension with reasonable probability such as would have justified imposition of a judicial sanction against a legislative body. WTAR Radio-TV Corp. v. City Council, 216 Va. 892, 223 S.E.2d 895 (1976).

When injunctive relief, etc., not justified. — The 1976 amendment to this section in effect permits a trial court to infer from a single violation that future violations will follow. However, where the court expresses the view that there will be no future violations, there is no justification for injunctive relief. Marsh v. Richmond Newspapers, Inc., 223 Va. 245, 288 S.E.2d 415 (1982).

Where violations occur under this chapter, but are not willful and knowing violations or violations that would invalidate board actions with which concerned citizens who brought suit were concerned, such violations do not justify injunctive relief or the award of attorneys' fees and costs. Nageotte v. Board of Supvrs., 223 Va. 259, 288 S.E.2d 423 (1982).

Injunctive relief discretionary and not granted unless violation willful, knowing, and substantial. — Although this section permits injunctive relief upon proof of a single violation of the act, based upon the inference that future violations will occur, such relief remains discretionary with the court and it will not be granted unless the court finds that the violation was willful, knowing, and substantial. Hale v. Washington County School Bd., 241 Va. 76, 400 S.E.2d 175 (1991).

Attorney's fees and costs awarded. — City airport authority's response to appellant's request for information under the Freedom of Information Act, § 2.2-3700 et seq., did not comply with the FOIA as it did not timely make one of the four statutorily required responses under § 2.2-3704 but merely stated that the matter had been referred to its legal counsel or to the transportation security administration; appellant was entitled to attorney's fees under subsection D of § 2.2-3713 as the trial court's judgment was reversed on appeal. Fenter v. Norfolk Airport Auth., 274 Va. 524, 649 S.E.2d 704, 2007 Va. LEXIS 102 (2007).

Attorney's fees and costs properly denied. — Trial court did not err in failing to award appellant attorneys' fees under subsection D of § 2.2-3713 as the purpose of appellant's mandamus petition was not to obtain the small number of documents that the trial court found should have been disclosed but was, rather, to overturn the result of the board's decision to close the school. Since she did not prevail on this issue, the request for attorneys' fees was properly denied. Hill v. Fairfax County Sch. Bd., 284 Va. 306, 727 S.E.2d 75, 2012 Va. LEXIS 136 (2012).

Attorney's fees and costs erroneously denied. — As newspaper publishers "substantially prevailed" in their suit against a county board of supervisors for violating the Virginia Freedom of Information Act, they were entitled to an award of attorney's fees and reasonable costs under subsection D of § 2.2-3713. The fact that the board's violation was not willful and knowing was not a "special circumstance" that would make such an award unjust. White Dog Publ., Inc. v. Culpeper County Bd. of Supervisors, 272 Va. 377, 634 S.E.2d 334, 2006 Va. LEXIS 81 (2006).

Mandamus erroneously denied. — Landowner, who alleged a violation of the rights and privileges afforded by the Virginia Freedom of Information Act, and seeking relief by mandamus pursuant to subsection A, was not required to prove a lack of an adequate remedy at law, nor could his mandamus proceeding be barred on the ground that there might have been some other remedy at law available; moreover, because the circuit court did not reach the issue whether a sales brochure in connection with a highway construction project was subject to disclosure under the Act, the matter was remanded for further consideration of that issue and a determination as to whether the landowner was entitled to reasonable costs and attorneys' fees. Cartwright v. Commonwealth Transp. Comm'r, 270 Va. 58, 613 S.E.2d 449, 2005 Va. LEXIS 62 (2005).

Newspaper publishers that sued a county board of supervisors for holding a closed meeting in violation of subsection A of § 2.2-3712 had been entitled to a writ of mandamus, as subdivision A 30 [now A 29] of § 2.2-3711 did not allow the board to close the meeting in order to discuss the application or enforcement of a previously awarded public contract. White Dog Publ., Inc. v. Culpeper County Bd. of Supervisors, 272 Va. 377, 634 S.E.2d 334, 2006 Va. LEXIS 81 (2006).

Applied in Harmon v. Ewing, 285 Va. 335, 2013 Va. LEXIS 14 (Feb. 8, 2013).

CIRCUIT COURT OPINIONS

Insufficient evidence to show knowing and willful intent to keep information from public. — Citizen was not entitled to an order requiring a county school board to hold a second meeting because evidence of the board's violations of the Virginia Freedom of Information Act, § 2.2-3700 et seq., was insufficient to show a knowing and willful intent to keep information from the citizen or from the public, nor could any such intent be inferred under the Act; the failures by the board were not substantial because the actions of the board or its members did not influence the outcome of the vote to close an elementary school or affect the public's ability to be informed of and participate in a decision that affected the community. Hill v. Fairfax County Sch. Bd., 83 Va. Cir. 172, 2011 Va. Cir. LEXIS 89 (Fairfax County July 13, 2011).

Records not excluded from disclosure. — School board was ordered to provide requested records to a media company because the investigative notes, correspondence, and information assembled by a panel investigating testing irregularities at a school were not excluded from Virginia Freedom of Information Act disclosure as protected by the attorney-client privilege. Virginian-Pilot Media Cos., L.L.C. v. City of Norfolk Sch. Bd., 81 Va. Cir. 450, 2010 Va. Cir. LEXIS 272 (Norfolk Dec. 28, 2010).

Burden of proof. — Burden is upon the public body to prove by a preponderance of the evidence that an exemption to the Virginia Freedom of Information Act exists. Davis v. City of Chesapeake, 74 Va. Cir. 367, 2007 Va. Cir. LEXIS 299 (Chesapeake 2007).

County school board had the burden of proving that it did not violate the Virginia Freedom of Information Act, § 2.2-3700 et seq., because while the board had to prove that its conduct was subject to an exemption, the citizen who filed suit against it bore the burden of showing that the board's violations were intentional. Hill v. Fairfax County Sch. Bd., 83 Va. Cir. 172, 2011 Va. Cir. LEXIS 89 (Fairfax County July 13, 2011).

Mandamus erroneously denied. — Landowner was entitled to recover her filing fees, which could be offset against the costs of conducting a search for a personal computer and the production of documents, because she was denied access to requested records in violation of the Virginia Freedom of Information Act; such a search was neither directed nor contemplated by a written order of a district court judge. Burton v. Mann, 74 Va. Cir. 471, 2008 Va. Cir. LEXIS 57 (Loudoun County 2008).

Costs and attorneys' fees. — Citizens were entitled to reasonable costs and attorneys' fees under subsection D of § 2.2-3713 where county officials violated §§ 2.2-3712 and 2.2-3704 of the Freedom of Information Act by convening a closed session without justification and by failing to timely respond to a document request. Ripol v. Westmoreland County Indus. Dev. Auth., 82 Va. Cir. 69, 2010 Va. Cir. LEXIS 203 (Westmoreland County Dec. 28, 2010).

It was unjust to order a county school board to pay a citizen's costs and fees because the citizen did not substantially prevail on the merits of her case against the board; the gravamen of the citizen's claim, that the board met secretly by e-mail and that the decision to close an elementary school had to be set aside, was rejected. Hill v. Fairfax County Sch. Bd., 83 Va. Cir. 172, 2011 Va. Cir. LEXIS 89 (Fairfax County July 13, 2011).

§ 2.2-3714. Violations and penalties.

In a proceeding commenced against any officer, employee, or member of a public body under § 2.2-3713 for a violation of § 2.2-3704, 2.2-3705.1 through 2.2-3705.8, 2.2-3706, 2.2-3707, 2.2-3708, 2.2-3708.1, 2.2-3710, 2.2-3711 or 2.2-3712, the court, if it finds that a violation was willfully and knowingly made, shall impose upon such officer, employee, or member in his individual capacity, whether a writ of mandamus or injunctive relief is awarded or not, a civil penalty of not less than $500 nor more than $2,000, which amount shall be paid into the State Literary Fund. For a second or subsequent violation, such civil penalty shall be not less than $2,000 nor more than $5,000.

History.
1976, c. 467, § 2.1-346.1; 1978, c. 826; 1984, c. 252; 1989, c. 358; 1996, c. 578; 1999, cc. 703, 726; 2001, c. 844; 2003, c. 319; 2004, c. 690; 2008, cc. 233, 789; 2011, c. 327.

The 2011 amendments.
The 2011 amendment by c. 327 substituted "any officer, employee, or member of a public body" for "members of public bodies," "such officer, employee, or member" for "such member," and "$500 nor more than $2,000" for "$250 nor more than $1,000," in the first sentence; and substituted "$2,000 nor more than $5,000" for "$1,000 nor more than $2,500" in the second sentence.

Research references.
Virginia Forms (Matthew Bender). No. 9-1301 Freedom of Information Request.

Michie's Jurisprudence.
For related discussion, see 5A M.J. Counties, § 22; 16 M.J. Schools, § 9.

CASE NOTES

Editor's note.
Some of the cases annotated below were decided under former Title 2.1 or prior provisions.

The evidentiary burden of a preponderance of the evidence is applicable to the proof of violations of this section. RF & P Corp. v. Little, 247 Va. 309, 440 S.E.2d 908 (1994).

The evidence was sufficient to support the trial court's finding that the chairman of the Virginia Retirement System Board willfully and knowingly violated Virginia Freedom of Information Act. RF & P Corp. v. Little, 247 Va. 309, 440 S.E.2d 908 (1994).

CIRCUIT COURT OPINIONS

Penalty not imposed when violation not knowingly or willfully made. — No civil penalty was imposed after it was determined that a chairman of a county board of supervisors violated the Virginia Freedom of Information Act by failing to adequately respond to a landowner's request for public records because the chairman's failure to timely respond to the request was not knowing or willful; the chairman's assistant acted promptly upon being informed of the failure to make a timely response, attempted to get an extension, and acted responsibly to fulfill his obligations under the provisions of a district court order. Burton v. Mann, 74 Va. Cir. 471, 2008 Va. Cir. LEXIS 57 (Loudoun County 2008).

TITLE 3.1.

AGRICULTURE, HORTICULTURE AND FOOD.

[Repealed.]

TITLE 3.2.

AGRICULTURE, ANIMAL CARE, AND FOOD.

SUBTITLE V.

DOMESTIC ANIMALS.

CHAPTER 65.

COMPREHENSIVE ANIMAL CARE.

Article 6. Authority of Local Governing Bodies.

ARTICLE 6.

AUTHORITY OF LOCAL GOVERNING BODIES.

§ 3.2-6540. Control of dangerous dogs; penalties.

A. As used in this section:

"Dangerous dog" means a canine or canine crossbreed that has bitten, attacked, or inflicted injury on a person or companion animal that is a dog or cat, or killed a companion animal that is a dog or cat. When a dog attacks or bites a companion animal that is a dog or cat, the attacking or biting dog shall not be deemed dangerous (i) if no serious physical injury as determined by a licensed veterinarian has occurred to the dog or cat as a result of the attack or bite; (ii) if both animals are owned by the same person; (iii) if such attack occurs on the property of the attacking or biting dog's owner or custodian; or (iv) for other good cause as determined by the court. No dog shall be found to be a dangerous dog as a result of biting, attacking, or inflicting injury on a dog or cat while engaged with an owner or custodian as part of lawful hunting or participating in an organized, lawful dog handling event. No dog that has bitten, attacked, or inflicted injury on a person shall be found to be a dangerous dog if the court determines, based on the totality of the evidence before it, that the dog is not dangerous or a threat to the community.

B. Any law-enforcement officer or animal control officer who has reason to believe that a canine or canine crossbreed within his jurisdiction is a dangerous dog shall apply to a magistrate serving the jurisdiction for the issuance of a summons requiring the owner or custodian, if known, to appear before a general district court at a specified time. The summons shall advise the owner of the nature of the proceeding and the matters at issue. If a law-enforcement officer successfully makes an application for the issuance of a summons, he shall contact the local animal control officer and inform him of the location of the dog and the relevant facts pertaining to his belief that the dog is dangerous. The animal control officer shall confine the animal until such time as evidence shall be heard and a verdict rendered. If the animal control officer determines that the owner or custodian can confine the animal in a manner that protects the public safety, he may permit the owner or custodian to confine the animal until such time as evidence shall be heard and a verdict rendered. The court, through its contempt powers, may compel the owner, custodian, or harborer of the animal to produce the animal. If, after hearing the evidence, the court finds that the animal is a dangerous dog, the court shall order the animal's owner to comply with the provisions of this section. The court, upon finding the animal to be a dangerous dog, may order the owner, custodian, or harborer thereof to pay restitution for actual damages to any person injured by the animal or whose companion animal was injured or killed by the animal. The court, in its discretion, may also order the owner to pay all reasonable expenses incurred in caring and providing for such dangerous dog from the time the animal is taken into custody until such time as the animal is disposed of or returned to the owner. The procedure for appeal and trial shall be the same as provided by law for misdemeanors. Trial by jury shall be as provided in Article 4 (§ 19.2-260 et seq.) of Chapter 15 of Title 19.2. The Commonwealth shall be required to prove its case beyond a reasonable doubt.

C. No canine or canine crossbreed shall be found to be a dangerous dog solely because it is a particular breed, nor is the ownership of a particular breed of canine or canine crossbreed prohibited. No animal shall be found to be a dangerous dog if the threat, injury, or damage was sustained by a person who was (i) committing, at the time, a crime upon the premises occupied by the animal's owner or custodian; (ii) committing, at the time, a willful trespass upon the premises occupied by the animal's owner or custodian; or (iii) provoking, tormenting, or physically abusing the animal, or can be shown to have repeatedly provoked, tormented, abused, or assaulted the animal at other times. No police dog that was engaged in the performance of its duties as such at the time of the acts complained of shall be found to be a dangerous dog. No animal that, at the time of the acts complained of, was responding to pain or injury, or was protecting itself, its kennel, its offspring, a person, or its owner's or custodian's property, shall be found to be a dangerous dog.

D. If the owner of an animal found to be a dangerous dog is a minor, the custodial parent or legal guardian shall be responsible for complying with all requirements of this section.

E. The owner of any animal found to be a dangerous dog shall, within 45 days of such finding, obtain a dangerous dog registration certificate from the local animal control officer or treasurer for a fee of $150, in addition to other fees that may be authorized by law. The local animal control officer or treasurer shall also provide the owner with a uniformly designed tag that identifies the animal as a dangerous dog. The owner shall affix the tag to the animal's collar and ensure that the animal wears the collar and tag at all times. By January 31 of each year, until such time as the dangerous dog is deceased, all certificates obtained pursuant to this subsection shall be updated and renewed for a fee of $85 and in the same manner as the initial certificate was obtained. The animal control officer shall post registration information on the Virginia Dangerous Dog Registry.

F. All dangerous dog registration certificates or renewals thereof required to be obtained under this section shall only be issued to persons 18 years of age or older who present satisfactory evidence (i) of the animal's current rabies vaccination, if applicable; (ii) that the animal has been neutered or spayed; and (iii) that the animal is and will be confined in a proper enclosure or is and will be confined inside the owner's residence or is and will be muzzled and confined in the owner's fenced-in yard until the proper enclosure is constructed. In addition, owners who apply for certificates or renewals thereof under this section shall not be issued a certificate or renewal thereof unless they present satisfactory evidence that (a) their residence is and will continue to be posted with clearly visible signs warning both minors and adults of the presence of a dangerous dog on the property and (b) the animal has been permanently identified by means of electronic implantation. All certificates or renewals thereof required to be obtained under this section shall only be issued to persons who present satisfactory evidence that the owner has liability insurance coverage, to the value of at least $100,000, that covers animal bites. The owner may obtain and maintain a bond in surety, in lieu of liability insurance, to the value of at least $100,000.

G. While on the property of its owner, an animal found to be a dangerous dog shall be confined indoors or in a securely enclosed and locked structure of sufficient height and design to prevent its escape or direct contact with or entry by minors, adults, or other animals. While so confined within the structure, the animal shall be provided for according to § 3.2-6503. When off its owner's property, an animal found to be a dangerous dog shall be kept on a leash and muzzled in such a manner as not to cause injury to the animal or interfere with the animal's vision or respiration, but so as to prevent it from biting a person or another animal.

H. The owner shall cause the local animal control officer to be promptly notified of (i) the names, addresses, and telephone numbers of all owners; (ii) all of the means necessary to locate the owner and the dog at any time; (iii) any complaints or incidents of attack by the dog upon any person or cat or dog; (iv) any claims made or lawsuits brought as a result of any attack; (v) chip identification information; (vi) proof of insurance or surety bond; and (vii) the death of the dog.

I. After an animal has been found to be a dangerous dog, the animal's owner shall immediately, upon learning of same, cause the local animal control authority to be notified if the animal (i) is loose or unconfined; (ii) bites a person or attacks another animal; or (iii) is sold, is given away, or dies. Any owner of a dangerous dog who relocates to a new address shall, within 10 days of relocating, provide written notice to the appropriate local animal control authority for the old address from which the animal has moved and the new address to which the animal has been moved.

J. Any owner or custodian of a canine or canine crossbreed or other animal is guilty of a:

1. Class 2 misdemeanor if the canine or canine crossbreed previously declared a dangerous dog pursuant to this section, when such declaration arose out of a separate and distinct incident, attacks and injures or kills a cat or dog that is a companion animal belonging to another person;

2. Class 1 misdemeanor if the canine or canine crossbreed previously declared a dangerous dog pursuant to this section, when such declaration arose out of a separate and distinct incident, bites a human being or attacks a human being causing bodily injury; or

3. Class 6 felony if any owner or custodian whose willful act or omission in the care, control, or containment of a canine, canine crossbreed, or other animal is so gross, wanton, and culpable as to show a reckless disregard for human life, and is the proximate cause of such dog or other animal attacking and causing serious bodily injury to any person.

The provisions of this subsection shall not apply to any animal that, at the time of the acts complained of, was responding to pain or injury, or was protecting itself, its kennel, its offspring, a person, or its owner's or custodian's property, or when the animal is a police dog that is engaged in the performance of its duties at the time of the attack.

K. The owner of any animal that has been found to be a dangerous dog who willfully fails to comply with the requirements of this section is guilty of a Class 1 misdemeanor.

Whenever an owner or custodian of an animal found to be a dangerous dog is charged with a violation of this section, the animal control officer shall confine the dangerous dog until such time as evidence shall be heard and a verdict rendered. The court, through its contempt powers, may compel the owner, custodian, or harborer of the animal to produce the animal.

Upon conviction, the court may (i) order the dangerous dog to be disposed of by a local governing body pursuant to § 3.2-6562 or (ii) grant the owner up to 45 days to comply with the requirements of this section, during which time the dangerous dog shall remain in the custody of the animal control officer until compliance has been verified. If the owner fails to achieve compliance within the time specified by the court, the court shall order the dangerous dog to be disposed of by a local governing body pursuant to § 3.2-6562. The court, in its discretion, may order the owner to pay all reasonable expenses incurred in caring and providing for such dangerous dog from the time the animal is taken into custody until such time that the animal is disposed of or returned to the owner.

L. All fees collected pursuant to this section, less the costs incurred by the animal control authority in producing and distributing the certificates and tags required by this section and fees due to the State Veterinarian for maintenance of the Virginia Dangerous Dog Registry, shall be paid into a special dedicated fund in the treasury of the locality for the purpose of paying the expenses of any training course required under § 3.2-6556.

M. The governing body of any locality may enact an ordinance parallel to this statute regulating dangerous dogs. No locality may impose a felony penalty for violation of such ordinances.

History.
1993, c. 977, § 3.1-796.93:1; 1994, c. 115; 1997, cc. 582, 892; 1998, c. 817; 2000, cc. 11, 727; 2003, cc. 785, 841; 2006, cc. 837, 864, 898; 2008, cc. 360, 551, 691, 860; 2009, c. 377; 2012, cc. 107, 236; 2013, cc. 58, 732.

Cross references.
As to recovery of damages when dog injures or kills other companion animals, see § 3.2-6586. As to punishment for Class 6 felonies, see § 18.2-10. As to punishment for Class 1 and 2 misdemeanors, see § 18.2-11.

Editor's note.
Acts 2008, c. 360 amended former § 3.1-796.93:1, from which this section is derived. Pursuant to § 30-152, the 2008 amendment by c. 360 has been given effect in this section as set out above, by inserting the last sentence in the definition of "Dangerous dog."

Acts 2008, cc. 551 and 691 amended former § 3.1-796.93:1, from which this section is derived. Pursuant to § 30-152, the 2008 amendments by cc. 551 and 691 have been given effect in this section as set out above, by substituting "magistrate serving the jurisdiction" for "magistrate of the jurisdiction" in the first sentence in subsection B.

The 2009 amendments.
The 2009 amendment by c. 377 inserted the ninth sentence in subsection B.

The 2012 amendments.
The 2012 amendments by cc. 107 and 236 are identical, and in subsection E, in the first sentence, substituted "45 days" for "10 days" and "$150" for "$50," in the next-to-last sentence, substituted "By January 31 of each year, until such time as the dangerous dog is deceased, all" for "All" and "shall be updated and renewed for a fee of $85" for "shall be renewed annually for the same fee" and substituted "post registration information on the Virginia Dangerous Dog Registry" for "provide a copy of the dangerous dog registration certificate and verification of compliance to the State Veterinarian" in the last sentence; deleted the first paragraph of subsection H, which formerly read: "The owner of any dog found to be dangerous shall register the animal with the Commonwealth of Virginia Dangerous Dog Registry, as established under § 3.2-6542, within 45 days of such a finding by any appropriate court" and deleted "also" following "owner shall" near the beginning of the second paragraph in subsection H; and inserted "and fees due to the State Veterinarian for maintenance of the Virginia Dangerous Dog Registry" in subsection L.

The 2013 amendments.
The 2013 amendments by cc. 58 and 732, in subsection A, deleted the paragraph defining "Vicious dog"; throughout the section, deleted "or vicious dog" following "dangerous dog" and "or vicious" following "dangerous"; deleted the former seventh sentence, which read: "If, after hearing the evidence, the court finds that the animal is a vicious dog, the court shall order the animal euthanized in accordance with the provisions of § 3.2-6562.", and inserted the present eighth sentence; in subsection F, deleted "a tattoo on the inside thigh or by" preceding "electronic implantation" near the end of clause (b); in subsection G, deleted the former second sentence, which read: "The structure shall be designed to provide the animal with shelter from the elements of nature."; in subsection H, deleted "tattoo or" at the beginning, and "or both" at the end, of clause (v); in subsection K, added the last two paragraphs; and made minor stylistic changes throughout. In addition, c. 58, in subsection F, changed the second occurrence of clause (i) and (ii) designators to (a) and (b). Also, c. 732 inserted the second sentence in subsection G.

Law Review.
For 2006 survey article, "Criminal Law and Procedure," see 41 U. Rich. L. Rev. 83 (2006). For annual survey article, "Animal Law," see 44 U. Rich. L. Rev. 185 (2009).

CIRCUIT COURT OPINIONS

Landlord's duty to passerby. — Pedestrian's case against a landlord arising from an attack by two dogs owned by the landlord's tenant was dismissed because the landlord had no duty to protect a passerby from the tenant's dogs; among other things, although the pedestrian alleged that the landlord should have known that the tenant's pit bulls were dangerous, subsection C of § 3.2-6540 was indicative of the policy of the Commonwealth of Virginia not to designate a particular breed as being dangerous. Walisser v. Harris, 81 Va. Cir. 14, 2010 Va. Cir. LEXIS 248 (Nelson County Feb. 26, 2010).

§ 3.2-6540.1. Vicious dogs; penalties.

A. As used in this section:

"*Serious injury*" means an injury having a reasonable potential to cause death or any injury other than a sprain or strain, including serious disfigurement, serious impairment of health, or serious impairment of bodily function and requiring significant medical attention.

"*Vicious dog*" means a canine or canine crossbreed that has (i) killed a person, (ii) inflicted serious injury to a person, or (iii) continued to exhibit the behavior that resulted in a previous finding by a court or, on or before July 1, 2006, by an animal control officer as authorized by ordinance that it is a dangerous dog, provided that its owner has been given notice of that finding.

B. Any law-enforcement officer or animal control officer who has reason to believe that a canine or canine crossbreed within his jurisdiction is a vicious dog shall apply to a magistrate serving the jurisdiction for the issuance of a summons requiring the owner or custodian, if known, to appear before a general district court at a specified time. The summons shall advise the owner of the nature of the proceeding and the matters at issue. If a law-enforcement officer successfully makes an application for the issuance of a summons, he shall contact the local animal control officer and inform him of the location of the dog and the relevant facts pertaining to his belief that the dog is vicious. The animal control officer shall confine the animal until such time as evidence shall be heard and a verdict rendered. The court, through its contempt powers, may compel the owner, custodian, or harborer of the animal to produce the animal. If, after hearing the evidence, the court finds that the animal is a vicious dog, the court shall order the animal euthanized in accordance with the provisions of § 3.2-6562. The court, upon finding the animal to be a vicious dog, may order the owner, custodian, or harborer thereof to pay restitution for actual damages to any person injured by the animal or to the estate of any person killed by the animal. The court, in its discretion, may also order the owner to pay all reasonable expenses incurred in caring and providing for such vicious dog from the time the animal is taken into custody until such time as the animal is disposed of. The procedure for appeal and trial shall be the same as provided by law for misdemeanors. Trial by jury shall be as provided in Article 4 (§ 19.2-260 et seq.) of Chapter 15 of Title 19.2. The Commonwealth shall be required to prove its case beyond a reasonable doubt.

C. No canine or canine crossbreed shall be found to be a vicious dog solely because it is a particular breed, nor is the ownership of a particular breed of canine or canine crossbreed prohibited. No animal shall be found to be a vicious dog if the threat, injury, or damage was sustained by a person who was (i) committing, at the time, a crime upon the premises occupied by the animal's owner or custodian; (ii) committing, at the time, a willful trespass upon the premises occupied by the animal's owner or custodian; or (iii) provoking, tormenting, or physically abusing the animal, or can be shown to have repeatedly provoked, tormented, abused, or assaulted the animal at other times. No police dog that was engaged in the performance of its duties as such at the time of the acts complained of shall be found to be a vicious dog. No animal that, at the time of the acts complained of, was responding to pain or injury

or was protecting itself, its kennel, its offspring, a person, or its owner's or custodian's property, shall be found to be a vicious dog.

D. Any owner or custodian of a canine or canine crossbreed or other animal whose willful act or omission in the care, control, or containment of a canine, canine crossbreed, or other animal is so gross, wanton, and culpable as to show a reckless disregard for human life and is the proximate cause of such dog or other animal attacking and causing serious injury to any person is guilty of a Class 6 felony. The provisions of this subsection shall not apply to any animal that, at the time of the acts complained of, was responding to pain or injury or was protecting itself, its kennel, its offspring, a person, or its owner's or custodian's property, or when the animal is a police dog that is engaged in the performance of its duties at the time of the attack.

E. The governing body of any locality may enact an ordinance parallel to this statute regulating vicious dogs. No locality may impose a felony penalty for violation of such ordinances.

History.
2013, cc. 58, 732.

§ 3.2-6552. Dogs killing, injuring or chasing livestock or poultry.

It shall be the duty of any animal control officer or other officer who may find a dog in the act of killing or injuring livestock or poultry to kill such dog forthwith whether such dog bears a tag or not. Any person finding a dog committing any of the depredations mentioned in this section shall have the right to kill such dog on sight as shall any owner of livestock or his agent finding a dog chasing livestock on land utilized by the livestock when the circumstances show that such chasing is harmful to the livestock. Any court shall have the power to order the animal control officer or other officer to kill any dog known to be a confirmed livestock or poultry killer, and any dog killing poultry for the third time shall be considered a confirmed poultry killer. The court, through its contempt powers, may compel the owner, custodian, or harborer of the dog to produce the dog.

Any animal control officer who has reason to believe that any dog is killing livestock or poultry shall be empowered to seize such dog solely for the purpose of examining such dog in order to determine whether it committed any of the depredations mentioned herein. Any animal control officer or other person who has reason to believe that any dog is killing livestock, or committing any of the depredations mentioned in this section, shall apply to a magistrate serving the locality wherein the dog may be, who shall issue a warrant requiring the owner or custodian, if known, to appear before a general district court at a time and place named therein, at which time evidence shall be heard. If it shall appear that the dog is a livestock killer, or has committed any of the depredations mentioned in this section, the district court shall order that the dog be: (i) killed immediately by the animal control officer or other officer designated by the court; or (ii) removed to another state that does not border on the Commonwealth and prohibited from returning to the Commonwealth. Any dog ordered removed from the Commonwealth that is later found in the Commonwealth shall be ordered by a court to be killed immediately.

History.
1984, c. 492, § 29-213.85; 1985, c. 385; 1987, c. 488, § 3.1-796.116; 1990, c. 222; 1993, c. 977; 1998, c. 817; 2008, cc. 551, 691, 860.

Editor's note.
Acts 2008, cc. 551 and 691 amended former § 3.1-796.116, from which this section is derived. Pursuant to § 30-152, the 2008 amendments by cc. 551 and 691 have been given effect in this section as set out above, by substituting "magistrate serving the locality" for "magistrate of the locality" in the second paragraph.

Michie's Jurisprudence.
For related discussion, see 1B M.J. Animals, § 9.

CASE NOTES

Editor's note.
The cases annotated below were decided under former § 29-213.85.

This section is intended to cover dogs killing or injuring poultry, and any person finding a dog killing fowls has the right to kill such dog on sight. Willeroy v. Commonwealth, 181 Va. 779, 27 S.E.2d 211 (1943).

When a dog, which had previously killed some of defendant's chickens, ran across defendant's lawn and charged against the chicken-wire fence surrounding his chicken yard, with every prospect of breaking it down, this was a depredation mentioned in this section, and defendant did not have to wait until the dog had bitten a chicken before killing it. Willeroy v. Commonwealth, 181 Va. 779, 27 S.E.2d 211 (1943).

Possession of sheep-killing dog not unlawful. — Neither this section nor any other section of the Code makes it unlawful to possess a sheep-killing dog. Laing v. Commonwealth, 203 Va. 682, 127 S.E.2d 142 (1962), cert. denied, 371 U.S. 962, 83 S. Ct. 542, 9 L. Ed. 2d 509 (1963).

The warrant prescribed by this section is a warrant requiring the owner or custodian of the dog to appear at the hearing of evidence as to whether the dog was guilty of the depredations mentioned in this section. Its purpose is to give notice to the owner or custodian of the time and place of the proceeding against the dog and an opportunity to be heard in its defense. Laing v. Commonwealth, 203 Va. 682, 127 S.E.2d 142 (1962), cert. denied, 371 U.S. 962, 83 S. Ct. 542, 9 L. Ed. 2d 509 (1963).

The purpose of the provision pertaining to the issuance of a warrant is for the court to determine if the dog is a killer of livestock, and the warrant is designed to require the owner or custodian, if known, to appear and make his defense in behalf of the dog, if he is so disposed. Laing v. Commonwealth, 205 Va. 511, 137 S.E.2d 896 (1964), cert. denied, 371 U.S. 962, 83 S. Ct. 542, 9 L. Ed. 2d 509 (1963).

Dog need not be in possession of warden when applying for warrant. — There is no language in this section which requires the dog to be in the physical possession or control of the game warden or other person when applying for a warrant requiring the owner of the dog to appear. Laing v. Commonwealth, 205 Va. 511, 137 S.E.2d 896 (1964), cert. denied, 371 U.S. 962, 83 S. Ct. 542, 9 L. Ed. 2d 509 (1963).

Nor in possession of court at time of hearing. — This section does not require that the court have the actual custody or posses-

sion of the dog at the time of the hearing. Laing v. Commonwealth, 205 Va. 511, 137 S.E.2d 896 (1964), cert. denied, 371 U.S. 962, 83 S. Ct. 542, 9 L. Ed. 2d 509 (1963).

§ 3.2-6553. Compensation for livestock and poultry killed by dogs.

Any person who has any livestock or poultry killed or injured by any dog not his own shall be entitled to receive as compensation the fair market value of such livestock or poultry not to exceed $400 per animal or $10 per fowl if: (i) the claimant has furnished evidence within 60 days of discovery of the quantity and value of the dead or injured livestock and the reasons the claimant believes that death or injury was caused by a dog; (ii) the animal control officer or other officer shall have been notified of the incident within 72 hours of its discovery; and (iii) the claimant first has exhausted his legal remedies against the owner, if known, of the dog doing the damage for which compensation under this section is sought. Exhaustion shall mean a judgment against the owner of the dog upon which an execution has been returned unsatisfied.

Local jurisdictions may by ordinance waive the requirements of (ii) or (iii) or both provided that the ordinance adopted requires that the animal control officer has conducted an investigation and that his investigation supports the claim. Upon payment under this section the local governing body shall be subrogated to the extent of compensation paid to the right of action to the owner of the livestock or poultry against the owner of the dog and may enforce the same in an appropriate action at law.

History.
1984, c. 492, § 29-213.87; 1986, c. 108; 1987, c. 488, § 3.1-796.118; 1992, c. 461; 1998, c. 817; 2008, c. 860.

CASE NOTES

Error for trial court to remand jury award to board of supervisors for satisfaction. — Where a breeder and trainer of horses filed a claim with the county board of supervisors to obtain compensation for two horses irreparably wounded by dogs of unknown origin and ownership, the board disallowed the claim, he appealed the board's decision, the appeal was tried in a de novo proceeding, and a jury awarded him an $18,000 verdict, he was entitled to a judgment against the county and the trial court erred in remanding the case to the board for satisfaction of the jury's verdict. Carlo v. County of Nottoway, 232 Va. 1, 348 S.E.2d 201 (1986) (decided under prior law).

§ 3.2-6554. Disposal of dead companion animals.

The owner of any companion animal shall forthwith cremate, bury, or sanitarily dispose of the animal upon its death. If, after notice, any owner fails to do so, the animal control officer or other officer shall bury or cremate the companion animal, and he may recover on behalf of the local jurisdiction from the owner his cost for this service.

History.
1984, c. 492, § 29-213.90; 1987, c. 488, § 3.1-796.121; 1993, c. 174; 1998, c. 817; 2008, c. 860.

ARTICLE 7.

ANIMAL CONTROL OFFICERS AND HUMANE INVESTIGATORS.

§ 3.2-6555. Position of animal control officer created.

The governing body of each county or city shall, or each town may, employ an officer to be known as the animal control officer who shall have the power to enforce this chapter, all ordinances enacted pursuant to this chapter and all laws for the protection of domestic animals. The governing body may also employ one or more deputy animal control officers to assist the animal control officer in the performance of his duties. Animal control officers and deputy animal control officers shall have knowledge of the animal control and protection laws of the Commonwealth that they are required to enforce. When in uniform or upon displaying a badge or other credentials of office, animal control officers and deputy animal control officers shall have the power to issue a summons or obtain a felony warrant as necessary, providing the execution of such warrant shall be carried out by any law-enforcement officer as defined in § 9.1-101, to any person found in the act of violating any such law or any ordinance enacted pursuant to such law of the locality where the animal control officer or deputy animal control officer is employed. Commercial dog breeding locations shall be subject to inspection by animal control at least twice annually and additionally upon receipt of a complaint or their own motion to ensure compliance with state animal care laws and regulations. The animal control officer and the deputy animal control officers shall be paid as the governing body of each locality shall prescribe.

Any locality where an animal control officer or deputy animal control officers have been employed may contract with one or more additional localities for enforcement of animal protection and control laws by the animal control officers or deputy animal control officers. Any such contract may provide that the locality employing the animal control officer or deputy animal control officers shall be reimbursed a portion of the salary and expenses of the animal control officer or deputy animal control officers.

Every locality employing an animal control officer shall submit to the State Veterinarian, on a form provided by him, information concerning the employment and training status of the animal control officers employed by the locality. The State Veterinarian may require that the locality notify him of any change in such information.

History.

1984, cc. 254, 492, § 29-213.73; 1987, c. 488, § 3.1-796.104; 1998, c. 817; 2003, c. 804; 2004, c. 181; 2008, cc. 852, 860.

Editor's note.

Acts 2008, c. 852 amended former § 3.1-796.104, from which this section is derived. Pursuant to § 30-152, the 2008 amendment by c.

852, effective January 1, 2009, has been given effect in this section as set out above, by inserting the next to last sentence in the first paragraph.

Acts 2008, c. 852, cl. 2, provides: "That the provisions of this act shall become effective on January 1, 2009."

Michie's Jurisprudence.

For related discussion, see 1B M.J. Animals, § 9.

§ 3.2-6556. Training of animal control officers.

A. Every locality employing animal control officers shall require that every animal control officer and deputy animal control officer completes the following training:

1. Within two years from the date of hire, a basic animal control course that has been approved by the State Veterinarian. The basic animal control course shall include training in recognizing suspected child abuse and neglect and information on how complaints may be filed and shall be approved and implemented; and

2. Every three years, additional training approved by the State Veterinarian, 15 hours of which shall be training in animal control and protection.

The State Veterinarian shall develop criteria to be used in approving training courses and shall provide an opportunity for public comment on proposed criteria before the final criteria are adopted.

Subdivision 1 shall not apply to animal control officers or deputy animal control officers hired before July 1, 1998. The State Veterinarian may grant exemptions from the requirements of subdivision 1 to animal control officers hired on or after July 1, 1998, based on the animal control officer's previous training.

The State Veterinarian shall work to ensure the availability of these training courses through regional criminal justice training academies or other entities as approved by him. Based on information provided by authorized training entities, the State Veterinarian shall maintain the training records for all animal control officers for the purpose of documenting and ensuring that they are in compliance with this subsection.

B. Upon cause shown by a locality, the State Veterinarian may grant additional time during which the training required by subsection A may be completed by an animal control officer for the locality.

C. Any animal control officer that fails to complete the training required by subsection A shall be removed from office, unless the State Veterinarian has granted additional time as provided in subsection B.

History.

1998, c. 817, § 3.1-796.104:1; 2002, c. 418; 2004, c. 181; 2008, c. 860.

§ 3.2-6557. Animal control officers and humane investigators; limitations; records; penalties.

A. No animal control officer, humane investigator, humane society or custodian of any pound or animal shelter shall: (i) obtain the release or transfer of an animal by the animal's owner to such animal control officer, humane investigator, humane society or custodian for personal gain; or (ii) give or sell or negotiate for the gift or sale to any individual, pet shop, dealer, or research facility of any animal that may come into his custody in the course of carrying out his official assignments. No animal control officer, humane investigator or custodian of any pound or animal shelter shall be granted a dealer's license. Violation of this subsection is a Class 1 misdemeanor. Nothing in this section shall preclude any animal control officer or humane investigator from lawfully impounding any animal pursuant to § 3.2-6569.

B. An animal control officer, law-enforcement officer, humane investigator or custodian of any pound or animal shelter, upon taking custody of any animal in the course of his official duties, or any representative of a humane society, upon obtaining custody of any animal on behalf of the society, shall immediately make a record of the matter. Such record shall include:

1. The date on which the animal was taken into custody;

2. The date of the making of the record;

3. A description of the animal including the animal's species, color, breed, sex, approximate age and approximate weight;

4. The reason for taking custody of the animal and the location where custody was taken;

5. The name and address of the animal's owner, if known;

6. Any license or rabies tag, tattoo, collar or other identification number carried by or appearing on the animal; and

7. The disposition of the animal.

Records required by this subsection shall be maintained for at least five years, and shall be available for public inspection upon request. A summary of such records shall be submitted annually to the State Veterinarian in a format prescribed by him.

C. Any animal control officer or custodian of any pound who violates any provision of this chapter that relates to the seizure, impoundment and custody of animals by an animal control officer may be subject to suspension or dismissal from his position.

D. Custodians and animal control officers engaged in the operation of a pound shall be required to have knowledge of the laws of the Commonwealth governing animals, including this chapter, as well as basic animal care.

History.
1984, c. 492, § 29-213.74; 1986, c. 315; 1987, c. 488, § 3.1-796.105; 1991, c. 65; 1993, c. 601; 1997, c. 286; 1998, c. 817; 2008, c. 860.

Cross references.
As to punishment for Class 1 misdemeanors, see § 18.2-11.

§ 3.2-6558. Humane investigators; qualifications; appointment; term.

A. A circuit court may reappoint any person as a humane investigator for any locality within its jurisdiction if the person:

1. Was appointed as a humane investigator prior to July 1, 2003; and

2. Has never been convicted of animal cruelty or neglect, any felony, or any crime of moral turpitude according to a criminal background check, which shall be performed by the attorney for the Commonwealth at the expense of the person seeking the appointment.

B. A circuit court may appoint a person to fill a vacancy in that jurisdiction created when a humane investigator who was appointed prior to July 1, 2003, is no longer willing or eligible to be a humane investigator, provided the person seeking appointment:

1. Has received a written recommendation from the administrative entity that oversees animal control in the locality where the humane investigator seeks appointment;

2. Has never been convicted of animal cruelty or neglect, any felony, or any crime of moral turpitude according to a criminal background check, which shall be performed by the attorney for the Commonwealth at the expense of the person seeking the appointment; and

3. Has completed a basic animal control course approved by the State Veterinarian pursuant to § 3.2-6556.

C. A person residing outside the Commonwealth may be appointed as a humane investigator only if he is employed by a humane society located within the locality where he is seeking appointment.

D. Reappointments of humane investigators shall be for terms of three years. Each humane investigator shall, during each term for which he is appointed, complete 15 hours of training in animal care and protection approved for animal control officers. If a humane investigator is appointed to a succeeding term before or within 30 days after his current term expires, a criminal background check shall not be required. If a humane investigator's term expires and he is not appointed to a succeeding term before or within 30 days after his current term expires, the humane investigator shall not be appointed to another term.

History.
1984, c. 492, § 29-213.75; 1987, c. 488, § 3.1-796.106; 1998, c. 817; 2003, c. 858; 2004, c. 181; 2008, c. 860.

§ 3.2-6559. Powers and duties of humane investigators.

A. Any humane investigator may, within the locality where he has been appointed, investigate violations of laws and ordinances regarding care and treatment of animals and disposal of dead animals.

B. Each humane investigator shall carry during the performance of his powers and duties under this chapter an identification card issued by the locality where the humane investigator is appointed. The identification card shall include the following information regarding the humane investigator:

1. His full name;

2. The locality where he has been appointed;

3. The name of the circuit court that appointed him;

4. The signature of the circuit court judge that appointed him;

5. A photograph of his face; and

6. The date of expiration of his appointment.

C. Each humane investigator shall record on a form approved by the administrative entity that oversees animal control every investigation he performs, maintain such record for five years, and make such record available upon request to any law-enforcement officer, animal control officer or State Veterinarian's representative. Each humane investigator shall file quarterly a report summarizing such records with the administrative agency that oversees animal control on an approved form. A humane investigator's appointment may be revoked as provided in § 3.2-6561 if he fails to file such report.

History.

1998, c. 817, § 3.1-796.106:2; 2003, c. 858; 2008, c. 860.

§ 3.2-6560. Expenses of humane investigators.

Neither the appointment of any humane investigator, nor the performance of any service or duty by him, shall require any locality or the Commonwealth to pay any cost or expense incurred by or on behalf of a humane investigator. Any locality may reimburse any humane investigator appointed for that locality for reasonable expenses incurred as the result of a specific request for services from the locality.

History.

1984, c. 492, § 29-213.79; 1986, c. 362; 1987, c. 488, § 3.1-796.110; 1998, c. 817; 2008, c. 860.

§ 3.2-6561. Revocation of appointment of humane investigators.

A. Upon a motion by the attorney for the Commonwealth, the circuit court that appointed a humane investigator may revoke his appointment if he is no longer able to perform the duties of a humane investigator; has been convicted of any felony, Class 1 misdemeanor, or a violation of any provision of this chapter or any other law regarding animals; or for good cause shown. The court shall notify the administrative entity that oversees animal control in the locality where the humane investigator was appointed of such revocation.

B. Any law-enforcement officer may investigate any allegation that a humane investigator has violated this chapter and report his findings and recommendations to the attorney for the Commonwealth.

History.

1998, c. 817, § 3.1-796.106:1; 1999, c. 376; 2003, c. 858; 2008, c. 860.

Cross references.

As to punishment for Class 1 misdemeanors, see § 18.2-11.

§ 3.2-6562. Capturing, confining, and euthanizing companion animals by animal control officers; approval of drugs used.

It shall be the duty of the animal control officer or any other officer to capture and confine any companion animal of unknown ownership found running at large on which the license fee has not been paid. Following the expiration of the holding period prescribed in § 3.2-6546, the animal control officer or other officer may deliver such companion animal to any person in his jurisdiction who will pay the required license fee on such companion animal. Prior to disposition by euthanasia or otherwise, all the provisions of § 3.2-6546 shall have been complied with. For all companion animals not otherwise disposed of as provided for in this chapter, it shall be the duty of the animal control officer or any other officer to euthanize such companion animals. Any person, animal control officer, or other officer euthanizing a companion animal under this chapter shall cremate, bury, or sanitarily dispose of the same.

All drugs and drug administering equipment used by animal control officers or other officers to capture companion animals pursuant to this chapter shall have been approved by the State Veterinarian.

History.

1984, c. 492, § 29-213.88; 1987, c. 488, § 3.1-796.119; 1991, c. 348; 1997, c. 159; 1998, c. 817; 2008, c. 860.

§ 3.2-6562.1. Rabies exposure; local authority and responsibility plan.

The local health director, in conjunction with the governing body of the locality, shall adopt a plan to control and respond to the risk of rabies exposure to persons and companion animals. Such plan shall set forth a procedure that promptly ensures the capture, confinement, isolation, or euthanasia of any animal that has exposed, or poses a risk of exposing, a person or companion animal to rabies. The plan shall identify the authority and responsibility of the local health department, law-enforcement officers, animal control officers, and any other persons with a duty to control or respond to a risk of rabies exposure. The plan shall provide for law-enforcement officers, animal control officers, and other persons to report to and be directed by the local health director for such purposes.

History.
2010, c. 834.

Editor's note.
Acts 2010, c. 834, cl. 2, provides: "That the Board of Health, in accordance with the Administrative Process Act (§ 2.2-4000 et seq. of the Code of Virginia), shall adopt regulations to implement the provisions of this act. Such regulations shall include a model plan that may be used by localities to comply with the requirements of § 3.2-6562.1 of this act. The model plan shall provide alternatives that reflect variations in local circumstances across the Commonwealth."

§ 3.2-6563. When animals to be euthanized; procedure.

Any humane investigator may lawfully cause to be euthanized any animal in his charge or found abandoned or not properly cared for when, in the judgment of the humane investigator and two reputable citizens called to view the same in his presence, and who shall give their written certificate, the animal appears to be injured, disabled or diseased, past recovery, or the injury, disease or disability is such that a reasonable owner would cause the animal to be euthanized.

Any humane investigator shall make every reasonable effort immediately to notify the owner of the animal that the humane investigator intends for the animal to be euthanized. The owner shall have a right to select one of the two reputable citizens called to view the animal and give written certificate of the animal's condition. In no event shall the determination as to disposition of the animal be delayed beyond 48 hours after such humane investigator first decides the animal should be euthanized. In the event that the two citizens called to give such certificate are unable to agree, they shall select a third reputable citizen and his decision shall be final.

History.
1984, c. 492, § 29-213.83; 1986, c. 362; 1987, c. 488, § 3.1-796.114; 1998, c. 817; 2008, c. 860.

OPINIONS OF THE ATTORNEY GENERAL

Dogs may not be euthanized based solely upon breed at publicly funded animal shelters or "pounds." See opinion of Attorney General to The Honorable Kenneth Cooper Alexander, Member, House of Delegates, 06-078 (10/30/06).

ARTICLE 8.

SEARCH, SEIZURE, IMPOUNDING, AND ENFORCEMENT.

§ 3.2-6564. Complaint of suspected violation; investigation.

A. Upon receiving a complaint of a suspected violation of this chapter, any ordinance enacted pursuant to this chapter or any law for the protection of domestic animals, any animal control officer, law-enforcement officer, or State Veterinarian's representative may, for the purpose of investigating the allegations of the complaint, enter upon, during business hours, any business premises, including any place where animals or animal records are housed or kept, of any dealer, pet shop, groomer, or boarding establishment. Upon receiving a complaint of a suspected violation of any law or ordinance regarding care or treatment of animals or disposal of dead animals, any humane investigator may, for the purpose of investigating the allegations of the complaint, enter upon, during business hours, any business premises, including any place where animals or animal records are housed or kept, of any dealer, pet shop, groomer, or boarding establishment.

Upon obtaining a warrant as provided for in § 3.2-6568, the law-enforcement officer, animal control officer, State Veterinarian's representative, or humane investigator may enter upon any other premises where the animal or animals described in the complaint are housed or kept. Attorneys for the Commonwealth and law-enforcement officials shall provide such assistance as may be required in the conduct of such investigations.

B. If the investigation discloses that a violation of § 3.2-6503 has occurred, the investigating official shall notify the owner or custodian of the complaint and of what action is necessary to comply with this chapter.

History.
1984, c. 492, § 29-213.76; 1987, c. 488, § 3.1-796.107; 1991, c. 451; 1993, c. 174; 1998, c. 817; 2008, c. 860.

§ 3.2-6565. Impoundment; expenses; lien; disposition of animal.

When an animal control officer, humane investigator, law-enforcement officer or State Veterinarian's representative finds that an apparent violation of this chapter has rendered an animal in such a condition as to constitute a direct and immediate threat to its life, safety or health that the owner or custodian has failed to remedy, such animal control officer, humane investigator, law-enforcement officer or State Veterinarian's representative may impound the animal pursuant to § 3.2-6569 in a facility that will provide the elements of good care as set forth in § 3.2-6503 and shall then proceed to take such steps as are required to dispose of the animal pursuant to § 3.2-6569.

History.
1984, c. 492, § 29-213.77; 1987, c. 488, § 3.1-796.108; 1994, c. 387; 1998, c. 817; 2008, c. 860.

CASE NOTES

Burden of proof. — Where appellant was found to have violated §§ 3.2-6569 and 3.2-6500 based on her inadequate care of her dog, the trial court's error in holding the Commonwealth to the preponderance of the evidence standard of proof, instead of proof beyond reasonable doubt as required by § 3.2-6569, was not harmless because there was little proof of a direct and immediate threat to the animal's life, safety, or health. Mosca v. Commonwealth, 2012 Va. App. LEXIS 379 (Nov. 27, 2012).

§ 3.2-6566. Preventing cruelty to animals; interference; penalty.

Each animal control officer, humane investigator or State Veterinarian's representative shall interfere to prevent the perpetration of any act of cruelty upon any animal in his presence. Any person who shall interfere with or obstruct or resist any humane investigator or State Veterinarian's representative in the discharge of his rights, powers, and duties as authorized and prescribed by law is guilty of a Class 4 misdemeanor.

History.
1984, c. 492, § 29-213.80; 1986, c. 362; 1987, c. 488, § 3.1-796.111; 1998, c. 817; 2008, c. 860; 2010, c. 240.

Cross references.
As to punishment for Class 4 misdemeanors, see § 18.2-11.

The 2010 amendments.
The 2010 amendment by c. 240 deleted "animal control officer" preceding "humane investigator or State Veterinarian's" in the last sentence.

OPINIONS OF THE ATTORNEY GENERAL

Acts of cruelty. — The question of whether there is an occurrence of an act of cruelty is a factual determination to be made by the animal control officer. See opinion of Attorney General to The Honorable Patricia S. Ticer, Member, Senate of Virginia, 08-068 (12/11/08).
Liability of officer. — An animal control officer is entitled to immunity for actions performed within the scope of his official duties, provided such actions were reasonable and in good faith. See opinion of Attorney General to The Honorable Patricia S. Ticer, Member, Senate of Virginia, 08-068 (12/11/08).

§ 3.2-6567. Enforcement authority.

All law-enforcement officers in the Commonwealth and State Veterinarian's representatives shall enforce the provisions of this chapter to the same extent other laws in the Commonwealth are enforced.

History.
1984, c. 492, § 29-213.81; 1987, c. 488, § 3.1-796.112; 1991, c. 121; 1998, c. 817; 2008, c. 860.

Law Review.
For annual survey article, "Animal Law," see 44 U. Rich. L. Rev. 185 (2009).

§ 3.2-6568. Power of search for violations of statutes against cruelty to animals.

When a sworn complaint is made to any proper authority by any animal control officer, humane investigator, law-enforcement officer or State Veterinarian's representative that the complainant believes and has reasonable cause to believe that the laws in relation to cruelty to animals have been, are being, or are about to be violated in any particular building or place, such authority, if satisfied that there is reasonable cause for such belief, shall issue a warrant authorizing any sheriff, deputy sheriff or police officer, to search the building or place.

History.
1984, c. 492, § 29-213.82; 1986, c. 362; 1987, c. 488, § 3.1-796.113; 1994, c. 168; 1998, c. 817; 2008, cc. 543, 707, 860.

Editor's note.
Acts 2008, cc. 543 and 707 amended former § 3.1-796.113, from which this section is derived. Pursuant to § 30-152, the 2008 amendments by cc. 543 and 707 have been given effect in this section as set out above, by deleting the last sentence, which read: "No search shall be made after sunset unless specially authorized by the authority upon satisfactory cause shown."
Acts 2008, cc. 543 and 707, cl. 3, provides: "That the provisions of this act may result in a net increase in periods of imprisonment or commitment. Pursuant to § 30-19.1:4, the estimated amount of the necessary appropriation cannot be determined for periods of imprisonment in state adult correctional facilities and cannot be determined for periods of commitment to the custody of the Department of Juvenile Justice."

§ 3.2-6569. Seizure and impoundment of animals; notice and hearing; disposition of animal; disposition of proceeds upon sale.

A. Any humane investigator, law-enforcement officer or animal control officer may lawfully seize and impound any animal that has been abandoned, has been cruelly treated, or is suffering from an apparent violation of this chapter that has rendered the animal in such a condition as to constitute a direct and immediate threat to its life, safety or health. The seizure or impoundment of an equine resulting from a violation of clause (iii) of subsection A or clause (ii) of subsection B of § 3.2-6570 may be undertaken only by the State Veterinarian or State Veterinarian's representative who has received training in the examination and detection of sore horses as required by 9 C.F.R. Part 11.7.

B. Before seizing or impounding any agricultural animal, the humane investigator, law-enforcement officer or animal control officer shall contact the State Veterinarian or State Veterinarian's representative, who shall recommend to the person the most appropriate action for effecting the seizure and impoundment. The humane investigator, law-enforcement officer or animal control officer shall notify the owner of the agricultural animal and the local attorney for the Commonwealth of the recommendation. The humane investigator, law-enforcement officer or animal control officer may impound the agricultural animal on the land where the agricultural animal is located if:

1. The owner or tenant of the land where the agricultural animal is located gives written permission;

2. A general district court so orders; or

3. The owner or tenant of the land where the agricultural animal is located cannot be immediately located, and it is in the best interest of the agricultural animal to be impounded on the land where it is located until the written permission of the owner or tenant of the land can be obtained.

If there is a direct and immediate threat to an agricultural animal, the humane investigator, law-enforcement officer or animal control officer may seize the animal, in which case the humane investigator, law-enforcement officer or animal control officer shall file within five business days on a form approved by the State Veterinarian a report on the condition of the animal at the time of the seizure, the location of impoundment, and any other information required by the State Veterinarian.

C. Upon seizing or impounding an animal, the humane investigator, law-enforcement officer or animal control officer shall petition the general district court in the city or county where the animal is seized for a hearing. The hearing shall be not more than 10 business days from the date of the seizure of the animal. The hearing shall be to determine whether the animal has been abandoned, has been cruelly treated, or has not been provided adequate care.

D. The humane investigator, law-enforcement officer, or animal control officer shall cause to be served upon the person with a right of property in the animal or the custodian of the animal notice of the hearing. If such person or the custodian is known and residing within the jurisdiction wherein the animal is seized, written notice shall be given at least five days prior to the hearing of the time and place of the hearing. If such person or the custodian is known but residing out of the jurisdiction where such animal is seized, written notice by any method or service of process as is provided by the Code of Virginia shall be given. If such person or the custodian is not known, the humane investigator, law-enforcement officer, or animal control officer shall cause to be published in a newspaper of general circulation in the jurisdiction wherein such animal is seized notice of the hearing at least one time prior to the hearing and shall further cause notice of the hearing to be posted at least five days prior to the hearing at the place provided for public notices at the city hall or courthouse wherein such hearing shall be held.

E. The procedure for appeal and trial shall be the same as provided by law for misdemeanors. Trial by jury shall be as provided in Article 4 (§ 19.2-260 et seq.) of Chapter 15 of Title 19.2. The Commonwealth shall be required to prove its case beyond a reasonable doubt.

F. The humane investigator, law-enforcement officer, or animal control officer shall provide for such animal until the court has concluded the hearing. Any locality may require the owner of any animal held pursuant to this subsection for more than thirty days to post a bond in surety with the locality for the amount of the cost of boarding the animal for a period of time set by ordinance, not to exceed nine months.

In any locality that has not adopted such an ordinance, a court may order the owner of an animal held pursuant to this subsection for more than 30 days to post a bond in surety with the locality for the amount of the cost of boarding the animal for a period of time not to exceed nine months. The bond shall not be forfeited if the owner is found to be not guilty of the violation.

If the court determines that the animal has been neither abandoned, cruelly treated, nor deprived of adequate care, the animal shall be returned to the owner. If the court determines that the animal has been (i) abandoned or cruelly treated, (ii) deprived of adequate care, as that term is defined in § 3.2-6500, or (iii) raised as a dog that has been, is, or is intended to be used in dogfighting in violation of § 3.2-6571, then the court shall order that the animal may be: (a) sold by a local governing body, if not a companion animal; (b) disposed of by a local governing body pursuant to subsection D of § 3.2-6546, whether such animal is a companion animal or an agricultural animal; or (c) delivered to the person with a right of property in the animal as provided in subsection G.

G. In no case shall the owner be allowed to purchase, adopt, or otherwise obtain the animal if the court determines that the animal has been abandoned, cruelly treated, or deprived of adequate care. The court shall direct that the animal be delivered to the person with a right of property in the animal, upon his request, if the court finds that the abandonment, cruel treatment, or deprivation of adequate care is not attributable to the actions or inactions of such person.

H. The court shall order the owner of any animal determined to have been abandoned, cruelly treated, or deprived of adequate care to pay all reasonable expenses incurred in caring and providing for such animal from the time the animal is seized until such time that the animal is disposed of in accordance with the provisions of this section, to the provider of such care.

I. The court may prohibit the possession or ownership of other companion animals by the owner of any companion animal found to have been abandoned, cruelly treated, or deprived of adequate care. In making a determination to prohibit the possession or ownership of companion animals, the court may take into consideration the owner's past record of convictions under this chapter or other laws prohibiting cruelty to animals or pertaining to the care or treatment of animals and the owner's mental and physical condition.

J. If the court finds that an agricultural animal has been abandoned or cruelly treated, the court may prohibit the possession or ownership of any other agricultural animal by the owner of the agricultural animal if the owner has exhibited a pattern of abandoning or cruelly treating agricultural animals as evidenced by previous convictions of violating § 3.2-6504 or 3.2-6570. In making a determination to prohibit the possession or ownership of agricultural animals, the court may take into consideration the owner's mental and physical condition.

K. Any person who is prohibited from owning or possessing animals pursuant to subsection I or J may petition the court to repeal the prohibition after two years have elapsed from the date of entry of the court's order. The court may, in its discretion, repeal the prohibition if the person can prove to the satisfaction of the court that the cause for the prohibition has ceased to exist.

L. When a sale occurs, the proceeds shall first be applied to the costs of the sale then next to the unreimbursed expenses for the care and provision of the animal, and the remaining proceeds, if any, shall be paid over to the owner of the animal. If the owner of the animal cannot be found, the proceeds remaining shall be paid into the Literary Fund.

M. Nothing in this section shall be construed to prohibit the humane destruction of a critically injured or ill animal for humane purposes by the impounding humane investigator, law-enforcement officer, animal control officer, or licensed veterinarian.

History.
1984, c. 492, § 29-213.84; 1986, c. 362; 1987, c. 488, § 3.1-796.115; 1990, c. 322; 1992, c. 123; 1993, c. 119; 1994, c. 387; 1998, c. 817; 1999, c. 113; 2002, c. 500; 2008, cc. 510, 860; 2011, cc. 754, 886.

Editor's note.
Acts 2008, c. 510 amended former § 3.1-796.115, from which this section is derived. Pursuant to § 30-152, the 2008 amendment by c. 510 has been given effect in this section as set out above. In subsection D, the second paragraph was added and, in the third paragraph, the clause (i) through (iii) designations and clause (iii) were inserted, "as that term is defined in § 3.2-6500" was inserted in clause (ii) and clause (a) to (d) designations were substituted for clause (i) to (iii) designations.

The 2011 amendments.
The 2011 amendments by cc. 754 and 886 are identical, and rewrote subsection A; added the first sentence and designator for subsection B; substituted "location of impoundment" for "disposition of the animal" near the end of the second paragraph of subdivision B 3; added subsection C designator and redesignated the remaining subsections accordingly; and rewrote the third paragraph of subsection F.

Law Review.
For annual survey article, "Animal Law," see 44 U. Rich. L. Rev. 185 (2009). For annual survey article, "Local Government Law," see 46 U. Rich. L. Rev. 175 (2011).

CASE NOTES

Appellate jurisdiction. — Former § 3.1-796.115 [now this section], the animal seizure statute, was not so punitive in effect as to transform the civil remedy into a criminal penalty; the Court of Appeals of Virginia had only limited jurisdiction in civil matters and statutory forfeiture procedures provided for appellate review only in the Supreme Court of Virginia. Settle v. Commonwealth, 55 Va. App. 212, 685 S.E.2d 182, 2009 Va. App. LEXIS 524 (2009).
Jurisdiction after nonsuit. — Circuit court erred when it exercised subject matter jurisdiction over a case alleging an unfit

pet owner pursuant to former § 3.1-796.115 that originated in general district court, was appealed to the circuit court and nonsuited there, was subsequently refiled in the general district court, dismissed, and then appealed to the circuit court. The county was required by subsection A of § 8.01-380 to refile its petition, following the nonsuit, in the circuit court. Although the circuit court did not have original or general jurisdiction over the § 3.1-796.115 petition pursuant to § 17.1-513, the circuit court did obtain appellate jurisdiction derivatively from the de novo appeal taken from the general district court. Davis v. County of Fairfax, 282 Va. 23, 710 S.E.2d 466, 2011 Va. LEXIS 125 (2011).
Exercise of police power. — An order prohibiting the defendant from owning or possessing companion animals was a valid exercise of the police power as authorized by the legislature in the statute. Green v. Commonwealth, No. 1724-97-3 (Ct. of Appeals Nov. 24, 1998) (decided under prior law).
Civil remedy. — Former § 3.1-796.115 [now this section] does not require a finding of scienter and the behavior at issue is clearly proscribed as a crime under a different statute, former § 3.1-796.122 [now § 3.2-6570]; further, although the owner of an animal found to be abandoned, abused, or neglected shall be required to pay for the animal's care, if the animal is sold, any proceeds from the sale remaining after expenses for the sale and care have been paid are to be returned to the animal's owner. Thus, the animal seizure statute is not so punitive in effect as to transform the civil remedy into a criminal penalty. Settle v. Commonwealth, 55 Va. App. 212, 685 S.E.2d 182, 2009 Va. App. LEXIS 524 (2009).
Former § 3.1-796.115 [now this section] does not define a crime or prescribe a penalty therefore the statute merely sets out the administrative process by which an animal warden or officer may seize an animal alleged to have been abused or neglected and provide for its care until the propriety of the seizure is resolved; the statute is civil in nature. Settle v. Commonwealth, 55 Va. App. 212, 685 S.E.2d 182, 2009 Va. App. LEXIS 524 (2009).
Due process. — Animal owner failed to state a due process claim against a county arising from seizure of the owner's animals, as the owner was given adequate process. The owner was notified of allegations of animal neglect in accordance with former § 3.1-796.115 (now § 3.2-6569); although the owner claimed that there was no avenue provided for return of the animals after a nonsuit was entered, the owner failed to file for a stay to prevent their adoption to other people. Root v. County of Fairfax, 2010 U.S. App. LEXIS 6381 (4th Cir. Mar. 26, 2010), cert. denied, 131 S. Ct. 655, 178 L. Ed. 2d 481, 2010 U.S. LEXIS 9412 (2010).
Burden of proof. — Where appellant was found to have violated §§ 3.2-6569 and 3.2-6500 based on her inadequate care of her dog, the trial court's error in holding the Commonwealth to the preponderance of the evidence standard of proof, instead of proof beyond reasonable doubt as required by § 3.2-6569, was not harmless because there was little proof of a direct and immediate threat to the animal's life, safety, or health. Mosca v. Commonwealth, 2012 Va. App. LEXIS 379 (Nov. 27, 2012).

ARTICLE 9.

CRUELTY TO ANIMALS.

Michie's Jurisprudence.
For related discussion, see 1B M.J. Animals, § 14.

§ 3.2-6570. Cruelty to animals; penalty.

A. Any person who: (i) overrides, overdrives, overloads, tortures, ill-treats, abandons, willfully inflicts inhumane injury or pain not connected with bona fide scientific or medical experimentation, or cruelly or unnecessarily beats, maims, mutilates, or kills any animal, whether belonging to himself or another; (ii) deprives any animal of necessary food, drink, shelter or emergency veterinary treatment; (iii) sores any equine for any purpose or administers drugs or medications to alter or mask such soring for the purpose of sale, show, or exhibition of any kind, unless such administration of drugs or medications is within the context of a veterinary client-patient relationship and solely for therapeutic purposes; (iv) willfully sets on foot, instigates, engages in, or in any way furthers any act of cruelty to any animal; (v) carries or causes to be carried by any vehicle, vessel or otherwise any animal in a cruel, brutal, or inhumane manner, so as to produce torture or unnecessary suffering; or (vi) causes any of the above things, or being the owner of such animal permits such acts to be done by another is guilty of a Class 1 misdemeanor.

In addition to the penalties provided in this subsection, the court may, in its discretion, require any person convicted of a violation of this subsection to attend an anger management or other appropriate treatment program or obtain psychiatric or psychological counseling. The court may impose the costs of such a program or counseling upon the person convicted.

B. Any person who: (i) tortures, willfully inflicts inhumane injury or pain not connected with bona fide scientific or medical experimentation, or cruelly and unnecessarily beats, maims, mutilates or kills any animal whether belonging to himself or another; (ii) sores any equine for any purpose or administers drugs or medications to alter or mask such soring for the purpose of sale, show, or exhibit of any kind, unless such administration of drugs or medications is under the supervision of a licensed veterinarian and solely for therapeutic purposes; (iii) maliciously deprives any companion animal of necessary food, drink, shelter or emergency veterinary treatment; (iv) instigates, engages in, or in any way furthers any act of cruelty to any animal set forth in clauses (i) through (iv); or (v) causes any of the actions described in clauses (i) through (iv), or being the owner of such animal permits such acts to be done by another; and has been within five years convicted of a violation of this subsection or subsection A, is guilty of a Class 6 felony if the current violation or any previous violation of this subsection or subsection A resulted in the death of an animal or the euthanasia of an animal based on the recommendation of a licensed veterinarian upon determination that such euthanasia was necessary due to the condition of the animal, and such condition was a direct result of a violation of this subsection or subsection A.

C. Nothing in this section shall be construed to prohibit the dehorning of cattle conducted in a reasonable and customary manner.

D. This section shall not prohibit authorized wildlife management activities or hunting, fishing or trapping as regulated under other titles of the Code of Virginia, including Title 29.1, or to farming activities as provided under this title or regulations adopted hereunder.

E. It is unlawful for any person to kill a domestic dog or cat for the purpose of obtaining the hide, fur or pelt of the dog or cat. A violation of this subsection is a Class 1 misdemeanor. A second or subsequent violation of this subsection is a Class 6 felony.

F. Any person who: (i) tortures, willfully inflicts inhumane injury or pain not connected with bona fide scientific or medical experimentation or cruelly and unnecessarily beats, maims or mutilates any dog or cat that is a companion animal whether belonging to him or another; and (ii) as a direct result causes the death of such dog or cat that is a companion animal, or the euthanasia of such animal on the recommendation of a licensed veterinarian upon determination that such euthanasia was necessary due to the condition of the animal, is guilty of a Class 6 felony. If a dog or cat is attacked on its owner's property by a dog so as to cause injury or death, the owner of the injured dog or cat may use all reasonable and necessary force against the dog at the time of the attack to protect his dog or cat. Such owner may be presumed to have taken necessary and appropriate action to defend his dog or cat and shall therefore be presumed not to have violated this subsection. The provisions of this subsection shall not overrule § 3.2-6540, 3.2-6540.1, or 3.2-6552.

G. Any person convicted of violating this section may be prohibited by the court from possession or ownership of companion animals.

History.
1984, c. 492, § 29-213.91; 1987, c. 488, § 3.1-796.122; 1992, c. 177; 1998, c. 817; 1999, cc. 209, 620, 645; 2002, cc. 351, 500, 583, 613; 2003, cc. 787, 788; 2004, c. 217; 2007, c. 743; 2008, c. 860; 2013, cc. 58, 732.

Cross references.
As to punishment for Class 6 felonies, see § 18.2-10. As to punishment for Class 1 misdemeanors, see § 18.2-11.

Editor's note.
Acts 2008, cc. 543 and 707 amended former § 3.1-796.122, from which this section is derived. The section was rewritten by Acts 2008, c. 860, making the changes by cc. 543 and 707 no longer applicable.

The 2013 amendments.
The 2013 amendments by cc. 58 and 732 are identical, and inserted "3.2-6540.1," near the end of subsection F.

Law Review.
For annual survey article, "Criminal Law and Procedure," see 46 U. Rich. L. Rev. 59 (2011).

CASE NOTES

Editor's note.
The cases annotated below were decided under prior law. The phrase "this section" refers to prior provisions.

Construction with other law. — Defendant's convictions in the circuit court for cruelty to animals in violation of this section after defendant had already been convicted in district court for failure to provide care for the same animals under § 3.1-796.68 [now § 3.2-6503], did not violate § 19.2-294 because the cruelty convictions occurred as part of the same prosecution as her convictions for failure to provide care, and § 19.2-294 did not apply to simultaneous prosecutions. Hillman v. Commonwealth, No. 1211-01-3, 2002 Va. App. LEXIS 195 (Ct. of Appeals Apr. 2, 2002).

Former § 3.1-796.115 [now this section] does not require a finding of scienter and the behavior at issue is clearly proscribed as a crime under a different statute, former § 3.1-796.122 [now § 3.2-6570]; further, although the owner of an animal found to be abandoned, abused, or neglected shall be required to pay for the animal's care, if the animal is sold, any proceeds from the sale remaining after expenses for the sale and care have been paid are to be returned to the animal's owner. Thus, the animal seizure statute is not so punitive in effect as to transform the civil remedy into a criminal penalty. Settle v. Commonwealth, 55 Va. App. 212, 685 S.E.2d 182, 2009 Va. App. LEXIS 524 (2009).

Failure to provide emergency veterinary treatment. — Evidence supported the trial court's conclusion that defendant committed cruelty to animals by failing to provide emergency veterinary treatment necessary for the dog; the trial court reasonably inferred that the dog's condition was so advanced that, in the three-week period during which the dog was missing, the worm eggs could not have entered the dog's system, matured into adult worms, and caused a near 20-percent weight loss. Buskey v. Commonwealth, No. 0919-02-1, 2003 Va. App. LEXIS 227 (Ct. of Appeals Apr. 15, 2003).

There was ample evidence to support a finding that defendant deprived her horse of necessary emergency veterinary treatment and therefore, to support defendant's conviction of misdemeanor animal cruelty under former § 3.1-796.122 [now § 3.2-6570], because the circuit court could readily have inferred from the expert testimony that the horse was becoming progressively weaker and emaciated over a period of weeks before she went down; the court could properly discard as incredible defendant's account that she was unaware that there was anything wrong with the horse until she found it down, removed the blanket and discovered that it had just wasted away; the court could have properly concluded from the evidence that it would have been apparent, over a considerable period of time, that the horse was in need of veterinary treatment to alleviate suffering and to prevent the progression of disease; and at the very least, the court could have properly concluded that the horse was in such a condition during a period of 30 to 48 hours before its death that emergency veterinary care was immediately necessary to alleviate suffering, during which time no such treatment was provided. Sullivan v. Commonwealth, 280 Va. 672, 701 S.E.2d 61, 2010 Va. LEXIS 266 (2010).

Felony conviction proper. — Trial court did not err in convicting defendant of a felony rather than a misdemeanor because the indictment was not ambiguous and it provided ample notice to defendant that defendant was being charged with violating the felony provision of this section. Ryan v. Commonwealth, — Va. App. —, — S.E.2d —, 2006 Va. App. LEXIS 335 (July 25, 2006).

Evidence sufficient for conviction. — Evidence was sufficient to support defendant's conviction of killing a companion animal because the record established that defendant lured a cat into a garage, closed the door, then released defendant's 50-pound pit bull into that confined space, directing it to "get the cat." When the cat tried to escape from the pit bull by jumping onto shelves and the car parked in the garage, defendant knocked the cat down with a broom. Ryan v. Commonwealth, — Va. App. —, — S.E.2d —, 2006 Va. App. LEXIS 335 (July 25, 2006).

County presented sufficient evidence to show that the pet owner provided inadequate care to 20 animals in violation of § 3.2-6570 such that the pet owner was unfit to own pets because the animal's health was directly and immediately threatened. A county officer testified about going to the pet owner's residence for the first time, smelling the odor of urine and feces before he got to the front door, and observing dogs and cats with injuries and skin conditions including open sores on some animals. Davis v. County of Fairfax, 2009 Va. App. LEXIS 346 (Aug. 4, 2009).

Defendant's conviction of animal cruelty in violation of former § 3.1-796.122 [now § 3.2-6570] was affirmed where: (1) the evidence in the record was that the horse was extremely thin, sick, dehydrated, and unable to move off of the ground; and (2) by the time a doctor finally arrived to administer veterinary care to the horse, defendant had known that the horse was down for more than 30 hours and still she had not put down the horse, nor had she summoned a veterinarian to try to save it. Sullivan v. Commonwealth, 2010 Va. App. LEXIS 22, aff'd, 280 Va. 672, 701 S.E.2d 61, 2010 Va. LEXIS 266 (2010).

In a prosecution for inadequate care by the owner of companion animals and dog at large, the evidence was sufficient to prove that defendant was the owner of the dogs in question because multiple witnesses who had interacted with defendant over the course of one year testified that defendant was the owner. Settle v. Commonwealth, 56 Va. App. 222, 692 S.E.2d 641, 2010 Va. App. LEXIS 243 (2010).

Self-defense instruction should have been given. — In an action charging defendant with felony cruelty to an animal resulting in death, the trial court erred in denying defendant's proffered self-defense jury instructions, because more than a scintilla of evidence supported such instructions including evidence that defendant believed the dog, who was barking, baring his teeth and appeared ready to attack, would have come onto defendant's deck and attacked him if he had not shot the dog. Smith v. Commonwealth, 2013 Va. App. LEXIS 29 (Jan. 29, 2013).

OPINIONS OF THE ATTORNEY GENERAL

Acts of cruelty. — The question of whether there is an occurrence of an act of cruelty is a factual determination to be made by the animal control officer. See opinion of Attorney General to The Honorable Patricia S. Ticer, Member, Senate of Virginia, 08-068 (12/11/08).

Liability of officer. — An animal control officer is entitled to immunity for actions performed within the scope of his official duties, provided such actions were reasonable and in good faith. See opinion of Attorney General to The Honorable Patricia S. Ticer, Member, Senate of Virginia, 08-068 (12/11/08).

§ 3.2-6570.1. Sale of animals after cruelty or neglect conviction; penalty.

Any person who has been convicted of a violation of any law concerning abuse, neglect, or cruelty to animals that sells, offers for sale, or trades any companion animal is guilty of a Class 1 misdemeanor. However, a person may dispose of animals under the provisions of a court order.

History.
2008, c. 852, § 3.1-796.122:1.

Cross references.
As to punishment for Class 1 misdemeanors, see § 18.2-11.

Editor's note.
Acts 2008, c. 852, enacted § 3.1-796.122:1. Pursuant to § 30-152, the section was given effect as set out above.

Acts 2008, c. 852, cl. 2, provides: "That the provisions of this act shall become effective on January 1, 2009."

§ 3.2-6571. Animal fighting; penalty.

A. No person shall knowingly:

1. Promote, prepare for, engage in, or be employed in, the fighting of animals for amusement, sport or gain;

2. Attend an exhibition of the fighting of animals;

3. Authorize or allow any person to undertake any act described in this section on any premises under his charge or control; or

4. Aid or abet any such acts.

Except as provided in subsection B, any person who violates any provision of this subsection is guilty of a Class 1 misdemeanor.

B. Any person who violates any provision of subsection A in combination with one or more of the following is guilty of a Class 6 felony:

1. When a dog is one of the animals;

2. When any device or substance intended to enhance an animal's ability to fight or to inflict

injury upon another animal is used, or possessed with intent to use it for such purpose;

3. When money or anything of value is wagered on the result of such fighting;

4. When money or anything of value is paid or received for the admission of a person to a place for animal fighting;

5. When any animal is possessed, owned, trained, transported, or sold with the intent that the animal engage in an exhibition of fighting with another animal; or

6. When he permits or causes a minor to (i) attend an exhibition of the fighting of any animals or (ii) undertake or be involved in any act described in this subsection.

C. 1. Any animal control officer, as defined in § 3.2-6500, shall confiscate any animal that he determines has been, is, or is intended to be used in animal fighting and any equipment used in training such animal or used in animal fighting.

2. Upon confiscation of an animal, the animal control officer shall petition the appropriate court for a hearing for a determination of whether the animal has been, is, or is intended to be used in animal fighting. The hearing shall be not more than 10 business days from the date of the confiscation of the animal. If the court finds that the animal has not been used, is not used and is not intended to be used in animal fighting, it shall order the animal released to its owner. However, if the court finds probable cause to believe that the animal has been, is, or is intended to be used in animal fighting, the court shall order the animal forfeited to the locality unless the owner posts bond in surety with the locality in an amount sufficient to compensate the locality for its cost of caring for the animal for a period of nine months. He shall post additional bond for each successive nine-month period until a final determination by the trial court on any criminal charges brought pursuant to subsections A or B.

3. Upon a final determination of guilt by the trial court on criminal charges brought pursuant to subsections A or B, the court shall order that the animal be forfeited to the locality. Upon a final determination of not guilty by the trial court on the underlying criminal charges, a confiscated animal shall be returned to its owner and any bond shall be refunded to him.

D. Any person convicted of violating any provision of subsection A or B shall be prohibited by the court from possession or ownership of companion animals or cocks.

E. In addition to fines and costs, the court shall order any person who is convicted of a violation of this section to pay all reasonable costs incurred in housing, caring for, or euthanizing any confiscated animal. If the court finds that the actual costs are reasonable, it may order payment of actual costs.

F. The provisions of this section shall not apply to any law-enforcement officer in the performance of his duties. This section shall not prohibit (i) authorized wildlife management activities or hunting, fishing, or trapping authorized under any title of the Code of Virginia or regulations promulgated thereto or (ii) farming activities authorized under Title 3.2 of the Code of Virginia or regulations promulgated thereto.

History.
1985, c. 408, § 29-213.92:1; 1987, c. 488, § 3.1-796.124; 1998, c. 817; 1999, c. 113; 2003, c. 857; 2008, cc. 543, 707, 860.

Cross references.
As to punishment for felonies and misdemeanors, see §§ 18.2-10, 18.2-11.

Editor's note.
Acts 2008, cc. 543 and 707, rewrote former § 3.1-796.124, from which this section is derived. Pursuant to § 30-152, the 2008 amendments by cc. 543 and 707 have been given effect in this section as set out above.

Acts 2008, cc. 543 and 707, cl. 3, provides: "That the provisions of this act may result in a net increase in periods of imprisonment or commitment. Pursuant to § 30-19.1:4, the estimated amount of the necessary appropriation cannot be determined for periods of imprisonment in state adult correctional facilities and cannot be determined for periods of commitment to the custody of the Department of Juvenile Justice."

Law Review.
For annual survey article, "Animal Law," see 44 U. Rich. L. Rev. 185 (2009).

CIRCUIT COURT OPINIONS

Evidence sufficient to support conviction. — In a case in which defendant was found guilty of dog fighting, in violation of former § 3.1-796.124 [now § 3.2-6571] and he filed a motion to set aside, he argued unsuccessfully that the evidence was insufficient to support the conviction. The Commonwealth was not required to prove that defendant engaged in organized dog fighting, but could prove in the alternative that he possessed, owned, trained, transported, or sold any dog with the intent that such dog engage in an exhibition of fighting with another dog; based upon the number of dogs that were there, the way they were restrained, the apparatus the dogs had on, the equipment that was found in the yard, the treadmill, the supplements, the medicine, and the literature that talked about how to train dogs to fight, which paralleled what was actually at the scene, the Commonwealth proved beyond a reasonable doubt that defendant was the person in charge and control of the premises when the alleged acts occurred. Commonwealth v. Taylor, 77 Va. Cir. 102, 2008 Va. Cir. LEXIS 228 (Chesapeake 2008).

Untimely challenge to indictment. — In a case in which defendant was convicted of violating former § 3.1-796.124 [now this section] and he filed a motion to set aside based on alleged deficiencies in the indictment, since he did not raise the issue of the validity of the indictment until 16 months after trial, defendant had waived his right to be more fully advised of the cause and nature of his accusation. Additionally, it was obvious that defendant, the Commonwealth, and the court all were fully aware of the cause and nature of the offense for which he was being tried and of which he was convicted. Commonwealth v. Taylor, 77 Va. Cir. 102, 2008 Va. Cir. LEXIS 228 (Chesapeake 2008).

§ 3.2-6572. Reserved.

Editor's note.
Acts 2008, cc. 543 and 707 repealed former § 3.1-796.125, from which this section is derived. Pursuant to § 30-152, this section has been set out as reserved at the direction of the Virginia Code Commission.

§ 3.2-6573. Shooting birds for amusement, and renting premises for such purposes; penalty.

Live pigeons or other birds or fowl shall not be kept or used for the purpose of a target, or to be shot at either for amusement or as a test of skill in marksmanship. It is a Class 4 misdemeanor to shoot at a bird kept or used as aforesaid, or to be a party to such shooting. Any person who lets any building, room, field or premises, or knowingly permits the use thereof for the purpose of such shooting is guilty of a Class 4 misdemeanor.

Nothing contained herein shall apply to the shooting of wild game.

History.

1984, c. 492, § 29-213.94; 1987, c. 488, § 3.1-796.126; 2008, c. 860.

Cross references.

As to punishment for Class 4 misdemeanors, see § 18.2-11.

TITLE 4.1.

ALCOHOLIC BEVERAGE CONTROL ACT.

CHAPTER 1.

DEFINITIONS AND GENERAL PROVISIONS.

Section
4.1-100. Definitions.

§ 4.1-100. Definitions.

As used in this title unless the context requires a different meaning:

"Alcohol" means the product known as ethyl or grain alcohol obtained by distillation of any fermented liquor, rectified either once or more often, whatever the origin, and shall include synthetic ethyl alcohol, but shall not include methyl alcohol and alcohol completely denatured in accordance with formulas approved by the government of the United States.

"Alcohol vaporizing device" means any device, machine, or process that mixes any alcoholic beverages with pure oxygen or other gas to produce a vaporized product for the purpose of consumption by inhalation.

"Alcoholic beverages" includes alcohol, spirits, wine, and beer, and any one or more of such varieties containing one-half of one percent or more of alcohol by volume, including mixed alcoholic beverages, and every liquid or solid, patented or not, containing alcohol, spirits, wine, or beer and capable of being consumed by a human being. Any liquid or solid containing more than one of the four varieties shall be considered as belonging to that variety which has the higher percentage of alcohol, however obtained, according to the order in which they are set forth in this definition; except that beer may be manufactured to include flavoring materials and other nonbeverage ingredients containing alcohol, as long as no more than 49 percent of the overall alcohol content of the finished product is derived from the addition of flavors and other nonbeverage ingredients containing alcohol for products with an alcohol content of no more than six percent by volume; or, in the case of products with an alcohol content of more than six percent by volume, as long as no more than one and one-half percent of the volume of the finished product consists of alcohol derived from added flavors and other nonbeverage ingredients containing alcohol.

"Barrel" means any container or vessel having a capacity of more than 43 ounces.

"Bed and breakfast establishment" means any establishment (i) having no more than 15 bedrooms; (ii) offering to the public, for compensation, transitory lodging or sleeping accommodations; and (iii) offering at least one meal per day, which may but need not be breakfast, to each person to whom overnight lodging is provided.

"Beer" means any alcoholic beverage obtained by the fermentation of an infusion or decoction of barley, malt, and hops or of any similar products in drinkable water and containing one-half of one percent or more of alcohol by volume.

"Board" means the Virginia Alcoholic Beverage Control Board.

"Bottle" means any vessel intended to contain liquids and having a capacity of not more than 43 ounces.

"Canal boat operator" means any nonprofit organization that operates tourism-oriented canal boats for recreational purposes on waterways declared nonnavigable by the United States Congress pursuant to 33 U.S.C. § 59ii.

"Club" means any private nonprofit corporation or association which is the owner, lessee, or occupant of an establishment operated solely for a national, social, patriotic, political, athletic, or other like purpose, but not for pecuniary gain, the advantages of which belong to all of the members. It also means the establishment so operated. A corporation or association shall not lose its status as a club because of the conduct of charitable gaming conducted pursuant to Article 1.1:1 (§ 18.2-340.15 et seq.) of Chapter 8 of Title 18.2 in which nonmembers participate frequently or in large numbers, provided that no alcoholic beverages are served or consumed in the room where such charitable gaming is being conducted while such gaming is being conducted and that no alcoholic beverages are made available upon the premises to any person who is neither a member nor a bona fide guest of a member.

Any such corporation or association which has been declared exempt from federal and state income taxes as one which is not organized and operated for pecuniary gain or profit shall be deemed a nonprofit corporation or association.

"*Container*" means any barrel, bottle, carton, keg, vessel or other receptacle used for holding alcoholic beverages.

"*Contract winemaking facility*" means the premises of a licensed winery or farm winery that obtains grapes, fruits, and other agricultural products from a person holding a farm winery license and crushes, processes, ferments, bottles, or provides any combination of such services pursuant to an agreement with the farm winery licensee. For all purposes of this title, wine produced by a contract winemaking facility for a farm winery shall be considered to be wine owned and produced by the farm winery that supplied the grapes, fruits, or other agricultural products used in the production of the wine. The contract winemaking facility shall have no right to sell the wine so produced but may charge the farm winery for its services.

"*Convenience grocery store*" means an establishment which (i) has an enclosed room in a permanent structure where stock is displayed and offered for sale and (ii) maintains an inventory of edible items intended for human consumption consisting of a variety of such items of the types normally sold in grocery stores.

"*Day spa*" means any commercial establishment that offers to the public both massage therapy, performed by persons certified in accordance with § 54.1-3029, and barbering or cosmetology services performed by persons licensed in accordance with Chapter 7 (§ 54.1-700 et seq.) of Title 54.1.

"*Designated area*" means a room or area approved by the Board for on-premises licensees.

"*Dining area*" means a public room or area in which meals are regularly served.

"*Establishment*" means any place where alcoholic beverages of one or more varieties are lawfully manufactured, sold, or used.

"*Farm winery*" means an establishment (i) located on a farm in the Commonwealth with a producing vineyard, orchard, or similar growing area and with facilities for fermenting and bottling wine on the premises where the owner or lessee manufactures wine that contains not more than 18 percent alcohol by volume or (ii) located in the Commonwealth with a producing vineyard, orchard, or similar growing area or agreements for purchasing grapes or other fruits from agricultural growers within the Commonwealth, and with facilities for fermenting and bottling wine on the premises where the owner or lessee manufactures wine that contains not more than 18 percent alcohol by volume. As used in this definition, the terms "owner" and "lessee" shall include a cooperative formed by an association of individuals for the purpose of manufacturing wine. In the event such cooperative is licensed as a farm winery, the term "farm" as used in this definition includes all of the land owned or leased by the

individual members of the cooperative as long as such land is located in the Commonwealth.

"*Gift shop*" means any bona fide retail store selling, predominantly, gifts, books, souvenirs, specialty items relating to history, original and handmade arts and products, collectibles, crafts, and floral arrangements, which is open to the public on a regular basis. Such shop shall be a permanent structure where stock is displayed and offered for sale and which has facilities to properly secure any stock of wine or beer. Such shop may be located (i) on the premises or grounds of a government registered national, state or local historic building or site or (ii) within the premises of a museum. The Board shall consider the purpose, characteristics, nature, and operation of the shop in determining whether it shall be considered a gift shop.

"*Gourmet brewing shop*" means an establishment which sells to persons to whom wine or beer may lawfully be sold, ingredients for making wine or brewing beer, including packaging, and rents to such persons facilities for manufacturing, fermenting and bottling such wine or beer.

"*Gourmet shop*" means an establishment provided with adequate inventory, shelving, and storage facilities, where, in consideration of payment, substantial amounts of domestic and imported wines and beers of various types and sizes and related products such as cheeses and gourmet foods are habitually furnished to persons.

"*Government store*" means a store established by the Board for the sale of alcoholic beverages.

"*Hotel*" means any duly licensed establishment, provided with special space and accommodation, where, in consideration of payment, food and lodging are habitually furnished to persons, and which has four or more bedrooms. It shall also mean the person who operates such hotel.

"*Interdicted person*" means a person to whom the sale of alcoholic beverages is prohibited by order pursuant to this title.

"*Internet wine retailer*" means a person who owns or operates an establishment with adequate inventory, shelving, and storage facilities, where, in consideration of payment, internet or telephone orders are taken and shipped directly to consumers and which establishment is not a retail store open to the public.

"*Intoxicated*" means a condition in which a person has drunk enough alcoholic beverages to observably affect his manner, disposition, speech, muscular movement, general appearance or behavior.

"*Licensed*" means the holding of a valid license issued by the Board.

"*Licensee*" means any person to whom a license has been granted by the Board.

"*Liquor*" means any of a class of highly flavored alcoholic beverages that do not exceed an alcohol content of 25 percent by volume.

"*Low alcohol beverage cooler*" means a drink containing one-half of one percent or more of alcohol by volume, but not more than seven and one-half percent alcohol by volume, and consisting of spirits mixed with nonalcoholic beverages or flavoring or coloring materials; it may also contain water, fruit juices, fruit adjuncts, sugar, carbon dioxide, preservatives or other similar products manufactured by fermenting fruit or fruit juices. Low alcohol beverage coolers shall be treated as wine for all purposes of this title; except that low alcohol beverage coolers shall not be sold in localities that have not approved the sale of mixed beverages pursuant to § 4.1-124. In addition, low alcohol beverage coolers shall not be sold for on-premises consumption other than by mixed beverage licensees.

"Meal-assembly kitchen" means any commercial establishment that offers its customers, for off-premises consumption, ingredients for the preparation of meals and entrees in professional kitchen facilities located at the establishment.

"Meals" means, for a mixed beverage license, an assortment of foods commonly ordered in bona fide, full-service restaurants as principal meals of the day. Such restaurants shall include establishments specializing in full course meals with a single substantial entree.

"Member of a club" means (i) a person who maintains his membership in the club by the payment of monthly, quarterly, or annual dues in the manner established by the rules and regulations thereof or (ii) a person who is a member of a bona fide auxiliary, local chapter, or squadron composed of direct lineal descendants of a bona fide member, whether alive or deceased, of a national or international organization to which an individual lodge holding a club license is an authorized member in the same locality. It shall also mean a lifetime member whose financial contribution is not less than 10 times the annual dues of resident members of the club, the full amount of such contribution being paid in advance in a lump sum.

"Mixed beverage" or *"mixed alcoholic beverage"* means a drink composed in whole or in part of spirits.

"Mixer" means any prepackaged ingredients containing beverages or flavoring or coloring materials, and which may also contain water, fruit juices, fruit adjuncts, sugar, carbon dioxide, or preservatives which are not commonly consumed unless combined with alcoholic beverages, whether or not such ingredients contain alcohol. Such specialty beverage product shall be manufactured or distributed by a Virginia corporation.

"Place or premises" means the real estate, together with any buildings or other improvements thereon, designated in the application for a license as the place at which the manufacture, bottling, distribution, use or sale of alcoholic beverages shall be performed, except that portion of any such building or other improvement actually and exclusively used as a private residence.

"Public place" means any place, building, or conveyance to which the public has, or is permitted to have, access, including restaurants, soda fountains, hotel dining areas, lobbies and corridors of hotels, and any park, place of public resort or amusement, highway, street, lane, or sidewalk adjoining any highway, street, or lane.

The term shall not include (i) hotel or restaurant dining areas or ballrooms while in use for private meetings or private parties limited in attendance to members and guests of a particular group, association or organization; (ii) restaurants licensed by the Board in office buildings or industrial or similar facilities while such restaurant is closed to the public and in use for private meetings or parties limited in attendance to employees and nonpaying guests of the owner or a lessee of all or part of such building or facility; (iii) offices, office buildings or industrial facilities while closed to the public and in use for private meetings or parties limited in attendance to employees and nonpaying guests of the owner or a lessee of all or part of such building or facility; or (iv) private recreational or chartered boats which are not licensed by the Board and on which alcoholic beverages are not sold.

"Residence" means any building or part of a building or structure where a person resides, but does not include any part of a building which is not actually and exclusively used as a private residence, nor any part of a hotel or club other than a private guest room thereof.

"Resort complex" means a facility (i) with a hotel owning year-round sports and recreational facilities located contiguously on the same property or (ii) owned by a nonstock, nonprofit, taxable corporation with voluntary membership which, as its primary function, makes available golf, ski and other recreational facilities both to its members and the general public. The hotel or corporation shall have a minimum of 140 private guest rooms or dwelling units contained on not less than 50 acres. The Board may consider the purpose, characteristics, and operation of the applicant establishment in determining whether it shall be considered as a resort complex. All other pertinent qualifications established by the Board for a hotel operation shall be observed by such licensee.

"Restaurant" means, for a beer, or wine and beer license or a limited mixed beverage restaurant license, any establishment provided with special space and accommodation, where, in consideration of payment, meals or other foods prepared on the premises are regularly sold.

"Restaurant" means, for a mixed beverage license other than a limited mixed beverage restaurant license, an established place of business (i) where meals with substantial entrees are regularly sold and (ii) which has adequate facilities and sufficient employees for cooking, preparing, and serving such meals for consumption at tables in dining areas on the premises, and includes establishments specializing in full course meals with a single substantial entree.

"Sale" and *"sell"* includes soliciting or receiving an order for; keeping, offering or exposing for sale; peddling, exchanging or bartering; or delivering otherwise than gratuitously, by any means, alcoholic beverages.

"Sangria" means a drink consisting of red or white wine mixed with some combination of sweeteners, fruit, fruit juice, soda, or soda water that may also be mixed with brandy, triple sec, or other similar spirits.

"Special agent" means an employee of the Department of Alcoholic Beverage Control whom the Board has designated as a law-enforcement officer pursuant to § 4.1-105.

"Special event" means an event sponsored by a duly organized nonprofit corporation or association and conducted for an athletic, charitable, civic, educational, political, or religious purpose.

"Spirits" means any beverage which contains alcohol obtained by distillation mixed with drinkable water and other substances, in solution, and includes, among other things, brandy, rum, whiskey, and gin, or any one or more of the last four named ingredients; but shall not include any such liquors completely denatured in accordance with formulas approved by the United States government.

"Wine" means any alcoholic beverage obtained by the fermentation of the natural sugar content of fruits or other agricultural products containing (i) sugar, including honey and milk, either with or without additional sugar; (ii) one-half of one percent or more of alcohol by volume; and (iii) no product of distillation. The term includes any wine to which wine spirits have been added, as provided in the Internal Revenue Code, to make products commonly known as "fortified wine" which do not exceed an alcohol content of 21 percent by volume.

"Wine cooler" means a drink containing one-half of one percent or more of alcohol by volume, and not more than three and two-tenths percent of alcohol by weight or four percent by volume consisting of wine mixed with nonalcoholic beverages or flavoring or coloring materials, and which may also contain water, fruit juices, fruit adjuncts, sugar, carbon dioxide, or preservatives and shall include other similar products manufactured by fermenting fruit or fruit juices. Wine coolers and similar fermented fruit juice beverages shall be treated as wine for all purposes except for taxation under § 4.1-236.

"With or without meals" means the selling and serving of alcoholic beverages by retail licensees for on-premises consumption whether or not accompanied by food so long as the total food-beverage ratio required by § 4.1-210, or the monthly food sale requirement established by Board regulation, is met by such retail licensee.

History.
　Code 1950, §§ 4-2, 4-99; 1952, c. 496; 1954, c. 682; 1962, c. 533; 1968, c. 7, § 4-98.1; 1970, cc. 302, 309; 1974, cc. 460, 497; 1975, c. 408; 1976, cc. 64, 702; 1977, c. 280; 1980, cc. 324, 490; 1983, c. 340; 1984, c. 200; 1985, cc. 448, 457; 1988, c. 261, § 4-127; 1990, cc. 707,

932; 1991, c. 426; 1993, cc. 190, 866, 910; 1995, cc. 497, 518, 661; 1996, cc. 558, 604; 1997, cc. 124, 425; 1999, cc. 93, 171, 481; 2000, cc. 786, 1037, 1052; 2005, c. 911; 2006, c. 714; 2007, cc. 101, 295, 454, 558; 2008, cc. 198, 513, 875; 2013, cc. 107, 117.

Cross references.
　As to the Attorney General's limited authority to institute and conduct criminal prosecutions in the circuit courts of the Commonwealth, see § 2.2-511.

Transition provisions.
　Senate Joint Resolution 13 of the 1992 General Assembly directed the Virginia Code Commission to undertake a revision of Title 4. In January of 1993, the Commission sent to the Governor and General Assembly its report containing the proposed revision of Title 4 which was published as Senate Document No. 26 of the 1993 Session. The Commission's draft of the revision of Title 4, as amended by the General Assembly, became c. 866 of the Acts of 1993 and was effective Oct. 1, 1993.
　Many of the cases cited in the notes under the various sections of this title were decided under corresponding provisions of Title 4 or prior law.
　Acts 1993, c. 866, cl. 2 provides: "That whenever any of the conditions, requirements, provisions or contents of any section or chapter of Title 4 or any other title of this Code as such titles existed prior to October 1, 1993, are transferred in the same or modified form to a new section or chapter of this title or any other title of this Code and whenever any such former section or chapter is given a new number in this or any other title, all references to any such former section or chapter of Title 4 or other title appearing in this Code shall be construed to apply to the new or renumbered section or chapter containing such conditions, requirements, provisions, or content or portions thereof."
　Acts 1993, c. 866, cl. 3 provides: "That the regulations of any department or agency affected by this title revision in effect on the effective date of this act [October 1, 1993] shall continue in effect to the extent that they are not in conflict with this act and shall be deemed to be regulations promulgated under this act."
　Acts 1993, c. 866, cl. 4 provides: "That this recodification of Title 4 as Title 4.1 shall not be construed to require the reappointment of any officer or any member of a board, council, committee or other appointed body referred to in Title 4.1, and each such officer and members shall continue to serve the term for which appointed pursuant to the provisions of Title 4."

Editor's note.
　Acts 1993, cc. 190 and 910 both amended former § 4-2, from which this section is derived. Pursuant to § 30-152 the 1993 amendments by cc. 190 and 910 have been given effect in this section as set out above. In accordance with c. 190, the paragraph defining "Resort complex" was added. In accordance with c. 910, "four or more bedrooms" was substituted for "ten or more bedrooms" in the first sentence of the paragraph defining "Hotel."

The 2013 amendments.
　The 2013 amendments by cc. 107 and 117 are identical, and added the paragraph defining "Contract winemaking facility."

Law Review.
　For comment on Virginia's dramshop immunity, see 10 G.M.U. L. Rev. 285 (1988). For article, "Wine Tasting Activities in Virginia: Is America's First Wine Producing State Destined to Wither on the Vine Due to Overregulation?," see 23 T.M. Cooley L. Rev. 221 (2006). For annual survey article, "Criminal Law and Procedure," see 44 U. Rich. L. Rev. 339 (2009).

Research references.
　James F. Mosher, Liquor Liability Law (Matthew Bender).

Michie's Jurisprudence.
　For related discussion, see 10B M.J. Intoxicating Liquors, §§ 2, 24; 17 M.J. Statutes, § 60.

CASE NOTES

I. Decisions Under Current Law.
II. Decisions Under Prior Law.

I. DECISIONS UNDER CURRENT LAW.

Probable cause to arrest for intoxication. — Police officer had probable cause to believe that defendant had consumed enough alcohol to visibly affect defendant's manner, disposition, speech, muscular movement, general appearance or behavior pursuant to § 4.1-100. The officer testified that as the officer spoke with defendant there was a very strong odor of alcohol coming from defendant's breath, defendant's speech was slurred, and defendant's eyes were very bloodshot. McGhee v. Commonwealth, 280 Va. 620, 701 S.E.2d 58, 2010 Va. LEXIS 260 (2010).

Evidence insufficient to infer intoxication. — Granting of a defendant's motion to suppress evidence in the form of a gun seized from his person and statements made to officers, where the officers lacked sufficient justification under the Fourth Amendment to perform a *Terry v. Ohio* stop, and to arrest and search defendant based on an uncorroborated anonymous tip, and where defendant admitted he had been drinking but was not intoxicated, was affirmed on appeal. United States v. Brown, 401 F.3d 588, 2005 U.S. App. LEXIS 4859 (4th Cir. 2005).

Evidence sufficient to prove intoxication. — Evidence was sufficient to prove beyond a reasonable doubt that defendant was intoxicated where he stopped his vehicle in the travel lane of a public road in the middle of the night and got out to clean it; staggered as he walked; had an odor of alcohol about him; slurred his speech; failed a sobriety test; and admitted earlier alcohol consumption. Leake v. Commonwealth, 27 Va. App. 101, 497 S.E.2d 522 (1998).

Where defendant's vehicle struck a barricade near a military base's gate, defendant's convictions for operating a motor vehicle on a military reservation while impaired by an intoxicant and operating a motor vehicle as an habitual offender while impaired by an intoxicant were upheld because substantial evidence supported the finding that defendant was intoxicated since it was clear that defendant's alcohol consumption so affected defendant's manner, disposition, speech, muscular movement, general appearance or behavior as to be apparent to observation. United States v. Scott, 188 Fed. Appx. 213, 2006 U.S. App. LEXIS 16899 (4th Cir. July 6, 2006).

Although the trial court erred in a DUI trial in allowing testimony that defendant was offered breath tests following a traffic stop, that evidence was harmless because there was overwhelming evidence that defendant drove while intoxicated; under § 4.1-100, "intoxicated" meant a condition in which a person had drunk enough alcoholic beverages to observably affect his manner, disposition, speech, muscular movement, general appearance, or behavior. The evidence at trial proved that defendant drove his car at a reckless speed and that, when stopped, he had an odor of alcohol about his breath, red and glassy eyes, and slurred speech, and performed poorly on field sobriety tests. Reid v. Commonwealth, 2009 Va. App. LEXIS 308 (July 14, 2009).

Scope of "place." — Defendants' search of plaintiff business owners' business did not violate the constitution, as the search was a proper exercise of the state and local governments' legitimate interest in investigating possible alcohol beverage control violations, and the business owners's private office was subject to inspection under 3 VAC 5-50-70 and § 4.1-100. Ruttenberg v. Jones, 283 Fed. Appx. 121, 2008 U.S. App. LEXIS 12907 (4th Cir. June 17, 2008).

Applied in Wyatt v. Commonwealth, 47 Va. App. 411, 624 S.E.2d 118, 2006 Va. App. LEXIS 5 (2006).

II. DECISIONS UNDER PRIOR LAW.

Editor's note.

The cases noted below were decided under former § 4-2, now repealed, which covered the same subject matter as this section.

The clear purpose of the Alcoholic Beverage Control Act is to permit the possession of spirits and alcoholic beverages legally acquired, and to prohibit and penalize possession when not so acquired. Miller v. Commonwealth, 172 Va. 639, 2 S.E.2d 343 (1939).

The purpose of the ABC Act is, among other things, to regulate and control the sale, possession, and use of alcoholic beverages. Harbour Enters., Inc. v. Ferro, 231 Va. 71, 340 S.E.2d 818 (1986).

Construction of act. — In order for the Supreme Court to construe properly the Alcoholic Beverage Control Act, it is necessary to consider under accepted principles the words used, their relation to the subject matter in which they are used, the purposes for which the act was intended, and such other sources, if any, as may throw light upon the intention of the legislature. Miller v. Commonwealth, 172 Va. 639, 2 S.E.2d 343 (1939).

The Alcoholic Beverage Control Act is severable, and the invalidity of subsection (a) of former § 4-51 did not affect the validity of the remaining portions of the act. Booth v. Commonwealth, 197 Va. 177, 88 S.E.2d 916 (1955).

The ABC Act mandates no statutory tort liability and creates no principal-agent relationships. Harbour Enters., Inc. v. Ferro, 231 Va. 71, 340 S.E.2d 818 (1986).

Former presumption as to possession wiped out. — The prima facie presumption that a person occupying or in control of premises is in possession of illegal liquor found thereon, which existed under former statutes, was wiped by the enactment of this act. Sutherland v. Commonwealth, 171 Va. 485, 198 S.E. 452 (1938); Charles v. Commonwealth, 184 Va. 63, 34 S.E.2d 136 (1945). See note to former § 4-75 [see now § 4.1-313].

Intoxication. — The definition of intoxication adopted by the General Assembly, if applied in all pertinent cases, tends to make the law consistent, uniform, certain, stable, and fair, a much desired goal. Gardner v. Commonwealth, 195 Va. 945, 81 S.E.2d 614 (1954).

In a prosecution for violation of § 18.2-266, instructions defining intoxication should be in the language of this section. Rodgers v. Commonwealth, 197 Va. 527, 90 S.E.2d 257 (1955).

For instruction containing definition of "intoxicated," see Oliphant v. Snyder, 206 Va. 932, 147 S.E.2d 122 (1966).

To be intoxicated the person must have drunk a sufficient amount of alcoholic beverages so as to affect him. Clemmer v. Commonwealth, 208 Va. 661, 159 S.E.2d 664 (1968).

The issue of intoxication is properly admitted when there are circumstances present other than the mere odor of alcohol on one's breath, such as evidence showing that the person's "manner, disposition, speech, muscular movement, general appearance or behavior" is affected. Hemming v. Hutchinson, 221 Va. 1143, 277 S.E.2d 230 (1981).

Odor of alcohol on one's breath. — The mere odor of alcohol on one's breath presents no question of intoxication for the determination of the jury. Hill v. Lee, 209 Va. 569, 166 S.E.2d 274 (1969).

But the odor of alcohol on a person's breath coupled with other circumstances, such as those indicated in the definition of "intoxicated", will be sufficient to support a finding of intoxication. Hill v. Lee, 209 Va. 569, 166 S.E.2d 274 (1969); United States v. Gholson, 319 F. Supp. 499 (E.D. Va. 1970).

The mere odor of alcohol on a person's breath is insufficient to prove intoxication. Hemming v. Hutchinson, 221 Va. 1143, 277 S.E.2d 230 (1981).

Court decisions establish the rule that the mere odor of alcohol on a person's breath is insufficient to establish either his intoxication, or his lack of control. But this rule does not apply, for example, where evidence shows that the consumption of alcohol has affected the person's "manner, disposition, speech, muscular movement, general appearance or behavior." These factors are listed in a statutory definition of intoxication contained in this section and applied in some of the decisions. Baker v. Taylor, 229 Va. 66, 326 S.E.2d 669 (1985).

Virginia adopts definition of "intoxicated" as the test for intoxication in civil cases. United States v. Gholson, 319 F. Supp. 499 (E.D. Va. 1970).

Definition of "intoxicated" provides test for intoxication of one arrested for drunken driving. — Even though former § 18.2-268 (now § 18.2-268.1 et seq.) provided a procedure for determining the alcoholic content of blood of one arrested for drunken driving, it is clear that this is not the only procedure for determining intoxication. In fact, this section provides for another test. United States v. Gholson, 319 F. Supp. 499 (E.D. Va. 1970).

Even where a blood sample was taken but was invalid because not sufficiently identified, the defendant could be retried for drunken driving under the definition set forth in this section. United States v. Gholson, 319 F. Supp. 499 (E.D. Va. 1970).

Definition of "intoxicated" adopted under federal Assimilative Crimes Act. — Since the blood test has been adopted as a definition of the crime of driving while intoxicated where the blood test is consented to and given, the definition of "intoxicated", which has been used by the courts of Virginia in defining intoxication where no blood test is given, should also be adopted under the Assimilative Crimes Act as a definition of the offense where there is no test. United States v. Gholson, 319 F. Supp. 499 (E.D. Va. 1970).

Blood test is more objective test of intoxication. — As compared with the statutory definitional test of intoxication set out in the definition of "intoxicated", the blood test is a new and more objective test and definition for an accused who consents to a blood analysis. United States v. Gholson, 319 F. Supp. 499 (E.D. Va. 1970).

Evidence sufficient to infer intoxication. — The consumption of four cans of beer within a 45-minute period, which ended three and one-half hours before automobile accident, is sufficient evidence to raise an inference of intoxication or impaired capacity, which the jury might draw or reject. Harrell v. Woodson, 233 Va. 117, 353 S.E.2d 770 (1987).

CHAPTER 2.

ADMINISTRATION OF LICENSES.

ARTICLE 1.

GENERAL PROVISIONS.

§ 4.1-200. Exemptions from licensure.

The licensure requirements of this chapter shall not apply to:

1. A person in charge of an institution regularly conducted as a hospital or sanatorium for the care of persons in ill health, or as a home devoted exclusively to the care of aged people, who administers or causes to be administered alcoholic beverages to any bona fide patient or inmate of the institution who is in need of the same, either by way of external application or otherwise for emergency medicinal purposes. Such person may charge for the alcoholic beverages so administered, and carry such stock as may be necessary for this purpose. No charge shall be made of any patient for the alcoholic beverages so administered to him where the same have been supplied to the institution by the Board free of charge.

2. The manufacture, sale and delivery or shipment by persons authorized under existing laws to engage in such business of any medicine containing sufficient medication to prevent it from being used as a beverage.

3. The manufacture, sale and delivery or shipment by persons authorized under existing laws to engage in such business of any medicinal preparations manufactured in accordance with formulas prescribed by the United States pharmacopoeia; national formulary, patent and proprietary preparations; and other bona fide medicinal and technical preparations; which contain no more alcohol than is necessary to extract the medicinal properties of the drugs contained in such preparations, and no more alcohol than is necessary to hold the medicinal agents in solution and to preserve the same, and which are manufactured and sold to be used exclusively as medicine and not as beverages.

4. The manufacture, sale and delivery or shipment of toilet, medicinal and antiseptic preparations and solutions not intended for internal human use nor to be sold as beverages.

5. The manufacture and sale of food products known as flavoring extracts which are manufactured and sold for cooking and culinary purposes only and not sold as beverages.

6. Any person who manufactures at his residence or at a gourmet brewing shop for domestic consumption at his residence, but not to be sold, dispensed or given away, except as hereinafter provided, wine or beer or both, in an amount not to exceed the limits permitted by federal law.

Any person who manufactures wine or beer in accordance with this subdivision may remove from his residence an amount not to exceed fifty liters of such wine or fifteen gallons of such beer on any one occasion for (i) personal or family use, provided such use does not violate the provisions of this title or Board regulations; (ii) giving to any person to whom wine or beer may be lawfully sold an amount not to exceed (a) one liter of wine per person per year or (b) seventy-two ounces of beer per person per year, provided such gift is for noncommercial purposes; or (iii) giving to any person to whom beer may lawfully be sold a sample of such wine or beer, not to exceed (a) one ounce of wine by volume or (b) two ounces of beer by volume for on-premises consumption at events organized for judging or exhibiting such wine or beer, including events held on the premises of a retail licensee. Nothing in this paragraph shall be construed to authorize the sale of such wine or beer.

The provision of this subdivision shall not apply to any person who resides on property on which a winery, farm winery, or brewery is located.

7. Any person who keeps and possesses lawfully acquired alcoholic beverages in his residence for his personal use or that of his family. However, such alcoholic beverages may be served or given to guests in such residence by such person, his family or servants when (i) such guests are 21 years of age or older or are accompanied by a parent, guardian, or spouse who is 21 years of age or older, (ii) the consumption or possession of such alcoholic beverages by family members or such guests occurs only in such residence where the alcoholic beverages are allowed to be served or given pursuant to this subdivision, and (iii) such service or gift is in no way a shift or device to evade the provisions of this title.

8. Any person who manufactures and sells cider to distillery licensees, or any person who manufactures wine from grapes grown by such person and sells it to winery licensees.

9. The sale of wine and beer in or through canteens or post exchanges on United States reservations when permitted by the proper authority of the United States.

10. The keeping and consumption of any lawfully acquired alcoholic beverages at a private meeting or private party limited in attendance to members and guests of a particular group, association or organization at a banquet or similar affair, or at a special event, if a banquet license has been granted. However, no banquet license shall be required for private meetings or private parties limited in attendance to the members of a common interest community as defined in § 54.1-2345 and their guests, provided (i) the alcoholic beverages shall not be sold or charged for in any way, (ii) the premises where the alcoholic beverages are consumed is limited to the common area regularly occupied and utilized for such private meetings or private parties, and (iii) such meetings or parties are not open to the public.

History.
Code 1950, §§ 4-50, 4-89, 4-90; 1954, c. 147; 1970, cc. 113, 541; 1972, cc. 75, 76, 741; 1973, c. 413; 1975, c. 408; 1976, c. 37; 1981, c. 410; 1984, c. 200; 1992, c. 349; 1993, c. 866; 1995, cc. 497, 518; 2001, c. 117; 2006, cc. 274, 740; 2010, c. 294; 2011, c. 8.

The 2010 amendments.
The 2010 amendment by c. 294 inserted clause (ii) in subdivision 7 and made related changes.

The 2011 amendments.
The 2011 amendment by c. 8 added the last sentence in subdivision 10.

§ 4.1-201. Conduct not prohibited by this title; limitation.

A. Nothing in this title or any Board regulation adopted pursuant thereto shall prohibit:

1. Any club licensed under this chapter from keeping for consumption by its members any alcoholic beverages lawfully acquired by such members, provided the alcoholic beverages are not sold, dispensed or given away in violation of this title.

2. Any person from having grain, fruit or fruit products and any other substance, when grown or lawfully produced by him, distilled by any distillery licensee, and selling the distilled alcoholic beverages to the Board or selling or shipping them to any person outside of the Commonwealth in accordance with Board regulations. However, no alcoholic beverages so distilled shall be withdrawn from the place where distilled except in accordance with Board regulations.

3. Any person licensed to manufacture and sell, or either, in the Commonwealth or elsewhere, alcoholic beverages other than wine or beer, from soliciting and taking orders from the Board for such alcoholic beverages.

4. The receipt by a person operating a licensed brewery of deliveries and shipments of beer in closed containers or the sale, delivery or shipment of such beer, in accordance with Board regulations to (i) persons licensed to sell beer at wholesale, (ii) persons licensed to sell beer at retail for the purpose of resale only as provided in subdivision B 4 of § 4.1-216, (iii) owners of boats registered under the laws of the United States sailing for ports of call of a foreign country or another state, and (iv) persons outside the Commonwealth for resale outside the Commonwealth.

5. The granting of any retail license to a brewery, distillery, or winery licensee, or to an applicant for such license, or to a lessee of such person, a wholly owned subsidiary of such person, or its lessee, provided the places of business or establishments for which the retail licenses are desired are located upon the premises occupied or to be occupied by such distillery, winery, or brewery, or upon property of such person contiguous to such premises, or in a development contiguous to such premises owned and operated by such person or a wholly owned subsidiary.

6. The receipt by a distillery licensee of deliveries and shipments of alcoholic beverages, other than wine and beer, in closed containers from other distilleries, or the sale, delivery or shipment of such alcoholic beverages, in accordance with Board regulations, to the Board and to persons outside the Commonwealth for resale outside the Commonwealth.

7. The receipt by a farm winery or winery licensee of deliveries and shipments of wine in closed containers from other wineries or farm wineries located inside or outside the Commonwealth, or the receipt by a winery licensee or farm winery licensee of deliveries and shipments of spirits distilled from fruit or fruit juices in closed containers from distilleries located inside or outside the Commonwealth to be used only for the fortification of wine produced by the licensee in accordance with Board regulations, or the sale, delivery or shipment of such wine, in accordance with Board regulations, to persons licensed to sell wine at wholesale for the purpose of resale, and to persons outside the Commonwealth for resale outside the Commonwealth.

8. The receipt by a fruit distillery licensee of deliveries and shipments of alcoholic beverages made from fruit or fruit juices in closed containers from other fruit distilleries owned by such licensee, or the sale, delivery or shipment of such alcoholic beverages, in accordance with Board regulations, to persons outside of the Commonwealth for resale outside of the Commonwealth.

9. Any farm winery or winery licensee from shipping or delivering its wine in closed containers to another farm winery or winery licensee for the purpose of additional bottling in accordance with Board regulations and the return of the wine so bottled to the manufacturing farm winery or winery licensee.

10. Any farm winery or winery licensee from selling and shipping or delivering its wine in closed containers to another farm winery or winery licensee, the wine so sold and shipped or delivered to be used by the receiving licensee in the manufacture of wine. Any wine received under this subsection shall be deemed an agricultural product produced in the Commonwealth for the purposes of § 4.1-219, to the extent it is produced from fresh fruits or agricultural products grown or produced in the Commonwealth. The selling licensee shall provide to the receiving licensee, and both shall maintain complete and accurate records of, the source of the fresh fruits or agricultural products used to produce the wine so transferred.

11. Any distiller licensed under this title from serving as an agent of the Board for the sale of alcoholic beverages, other than beer and wine, at a government store established by the Board on the licensed premises of the distiller in accordance with subsection D of § 4.1-119.

12. Any retail on-premises beer licensee, his agent or employee, from giving a sample of beer to persons to whom alcoholic beverages may be lawfully sold for on-premises consumption, or retail on-premises wine or beer licensee, his agent or employee, from giving a sample of wine or beer to persons to whom alcoholic beverages may be lawfully sold for on-premises consumption, or any mixed beverage licensee, his agent or employee, from giving a sample of wine, beer, or spirits to persons to whom alcoholic beverages may be lawfully sold for on-premises consumption. Samples of wine shall not exceed two ounces, samples of beer shall not exceed four ounces, and samples of spirits shall not exceed one-half ounce. No more than two product samples shall be given to any person per visit.

13. Any manufacturer, including any vendor authorized by any such manufacturer, whether or not licensed in the Commonwealth, from selling service items bearing alcoholic brand references to on-premises retail licensees or prohibit any such retail licensee from displaying the service items on the premises of his licensed establishment. Each such retail licensee purchasing such service items shall retain a copy of the evidence of his payment to the manufacturer or authorized vendor for a period of not less than two years from the date of each sale of the service items. As used in this subdivision, "service items" mean articles of tangible personal property normally used by the employees of on-premises retail licensees to serve alcoholic beverages to customers including, but not limited to, glasses, napkins, buckets, and coasters.

14. Any employee of an alcoholic beverage wholesaler or manufacturer, whether or not licensed in the Commonwealth, from distributing to retail licensees and their employees novelties and specialties, including wearing apparel, having a wholesale value of $10 or less and that bear alcoholic beverage

advertising. Such items may be distributed to retail licensees in quantities equal to the number of employees of the retail establishment present at the time the items are delivered. Thereafter, such employees may wear or display the items on the licensed premises.

15. Any retail on-premises wine or beer licensee, his agent or employee from offering for sale or selling for one price to any person to whom alcoholic beverages may be lawfully sold a flight of wines or beers consisting of samples of not more than five different wines or beers.

16. Any restaurant licensed under this chapter from permitting the consumption of lawfully acquired wine by bona fide customers on the premises in all areas and locations covered by the license. The licensee may charge a corkage fee to such customer for the wine so consumed; however, the licensee shall not charge any other fee to such customer.

B. No deliveries or shipments of alcoholic beverages to persons outside the Commonwealth for resale outside the Commonwealth shall be made into any state the laws of which prohibit the consignee from receiving or selling the same.

History.
    Code 1950, § 4-89; 1954, c. 147; 1970, cc. 113, 541; 1972, cc. 75, 76; 1973, c. 413; 1975, c. 408; 1981, c. 410; 1984, c. 200; 1992, c. 349; 1993, c. 866; 1995, cc. 253, 317; 1997, c. 386; 2000, c. 786; 2003, c. 630; 2004, c. 379; 2006, cc. 106, 826; 2007, c. 820; 2011, c. 559; 2012, c. 376; 2013, c. 604.

The 2011 amendments.
    The 2011 amendment by c. 559 added subdivision A 16.

The 2012 amendments.
    The 2012 amendment by c. 376 deleted "from other breweries owned by such person" following "in closed containers" in subdivision A 4.

The 2013 amendments.
    The 2013 amendment by c. 604 inserted "distillery" twice in subdivision A 5.

§ 4.1-201.1. Conduct not prohibited by this title; tastings conducted by manufacturers, wine or beer wholesalers, and authorized representatives.

A. Manufacturers of alcoholic beverages, whether or not licensed in the Commonwealth, and wine or beer wholesalers may conduct tastings of wine, beer, or spirits within hotels, restaurants, and clubs licensed for on-premises consumption provided:

1. The tastings are conducted only by (i) employees of such manufacturers or wholesalers or (ii) authorized representatives of such manufacturers or wholesalers, which authorized representatives have obtained a permit in accordance with subdivision A 15 of § 4.1-212;

2. Such employees or authorized representatives are present while the tastings are being conducted;

3. No category of alcoholic beverage products is offered to consumers unless the retail licensee on

whose premises the tasting is conducted is licensed to sell that category of alcoholic beverage product;

4. All alcoholic beverage products used in the tasting are served to the consumer by employees of the retail licensee;

5. The quantity of wine, beer, or spirits provided to any person during the tasting does not exceed 12 ounces of beer, five ounces of wine, or one and one-half ounces of spirits; however, for any spirits tastings, no single sample shall exceed one-half ounce per spirits product offered and no more than three spirits products may be offered to any patron; and

6. All alcoholic beverage products used in the tasting are purchased from the retail licensee on whose premises the tasting is conducted; except that no more than $100 may be expended by or on behalf of any such manufacturer or wholesaler at any retail licensed premises during any 24-hour period. For the purposes of this subdivision, the $100 limitation shall be exclusive of taxes and gratuities, which gratuities may not exceed 20 percent of the cost of the alcoholic beverages, including taxes, for the alcoholic beverages purchased for the tasting.

B. Manufacturers, wholesalers, and their authorized representatives shall keep complete records of each tasting authorized by this section for a period of not less than two years, which records shall include the date and place of each tasting conducted and the dollar amount expended by the manufacturer, wholesaler, or his agent or representative in the purchase of the alcoholic beverages used in the tasting.

C. Manufacturers and wholesalers shall be held liable for any violation of this section committed by their employees or authorized representative in connection with their employment or representation at any tasting event.

History.
2006, c. 826; 2007, cc. 452, 722.

ARTICLE 2.

LICENSES GRANTED BY BOARD; LIMITATIONS; REVOCATION AND SUSPENSION.

§ 4.1-212. Permits required in certain instances.

A. The Board may grant the following permits which shall authorize:

1. Wine and beer salesmen representing any out-of-state wholesaler engaged in the sale of wine and beer, or either, to sell or solicit the sale of wine or beer, or both in the Commonwealth.

2. Any person having any interest in the manufacture, distribution or sale of spirits or other alcoholic beverages to solicit any mixed beverage licensee, his agent, employee or any person connected with the licensee in any capacity in his licensed business to sell or offer for sale such spirits or alcoholic beverages.

3. Any person to keep upon his premises alcoholic beverages which he is not authorized by any license to sell and which shall be used for culinary purposes only.

4. Any person to transport lawfully purchased alcoholic beverages within, into or through the Commonwealth, except that no permit shall be required for any person shipping or transporting into the Commonwealth a reasonable quantity of alcoholic beverages when such person is relocating his place of residence to the Commonwealth in accordance with § 4.1-310.

5. Any person to keep, store or possess any still or distilling apparatus.

6. The release of alcoholic beverages not under United States custom bonds or internal revenue bonds stored in Board approved warehouses for delivery to the Board or to persons entitled to receive them within or outside of the Commonwealth.

7. The release of alcoholic beverages from United States customs bonded warehouses for delivery to the Board or to licensees and other persons enumerated in subsection B of § 4.1-131.

8. The release of alcoholic beverages from United States internal revenue bonded warehouses for delivery in accordance with subsection C of § 4.1-132.

9. A secured party or any trustee, curator, committee, conservator, receiver or other fiduciary appointed or qualified in any court proceeding, to continue to operate under the licenses previously issued to any deceased or other person licensed to sell alcoholic beverages for such period as the Board deems appropriate.

10. The one-time sale of lawfully acquired alcoholic beverages belonging to any person, or which may be a part of such person's estate, including a judicial sale, estate sale, sale to enforce a judgment lien or liquidation sale to satisfy indebtedness secured by a security interest in alcoholic beverages, by a sheriff, personal representative, receiver or other officer acting under authority of a court having jurisdiction in the Commonwealth, or by any secured party as defined in subdivision (a)(73) of § 8.9A-102 of the Virginia Uniform Commercial Code. Such sales shall be made only to persons who are licensed or hold a permit to sell alcoholic beverages in the Commonwealth or to persons outside the Commonwealth for resale outside the Commonwealth and upon such conditions or restrictions as the Board may prescribe.

11. Any person who purchases at a foreclosure, secured creditor's or judicial auction sale the premises or property of a person licensed by the Board and who has become lawfully entitled to the possession of the licensed premises to continue to operate the establishment to the same extent as a person holding such licenses for a period not to exceed 60 days or for such longer period as determined by the

Board. Such permit shall be temporary and shall confer the privileges of any licenses held by the previous owner to the extent determined by the Board. Such temporary permit may be issued in advance, conditioned on the above requirements.

12. The sale of wine and beer in kegs by any person licensed to sell wine or beer, or both, at retail for off-premises consumption.

13. The storage of lawfully acquired alcoholic beverages not under customs bond or internal revenue bond in warehouses located in the Commonwealth.

14. The storage of wine by a licensed winery or farm winery under internal revenue bond in warehouses located in the Commonwealth.

15. Any person to conduct tastings in accordance with § 4.1-201.1, provided that such person has filed an application for a permit in which the applicant represents (i) that he or she is under contract to conduct such tastings on behalf of the alcoholic beverage manufacturer or wholesaler named in the application; (ii) that such contract grants to the applicant the authority to act as the authorized representative of such manufacturer or wholesaler; and (iii) that such contract contains an acknowledgment that the manufacturer or wholesaler named in the application may be held liable for any violation of § 4.1-201.1 by its authorized representative. A permit issued pursuant to this subdivision shall be valid for at least one year, unless sooner suspended or revoked by the Board in accordance with § 4.1-229.

16. Any person who, through contract, lease, concession, license, management or similar agreement (hereinafter referred to as the contract), becomes lawfully entitled to the use and control of the premises of a person licensed by the Board to continue to operate the establishment to the same extent as a person holding such licenses, provided such person has made application to the Board for a license at the same premises. The permit shall (i) confer the privileges of any licenses held by the previous owner to the extent determined by the Board and (ii) be valid for a period of 120 days or for such longer period as may be necessary as determined by the Board pending the completion of the processing of the permittee's license application. No permit shall be issued without the written consent of the previous licensee. No permit shall be issued under the provisions of this subdivision if the previous licensee owes any state or local taxes, or has any pending charges for violation of this title or any Board regulation, unless the permittee agrees to assume the liability of the previous licensee for the taxes or any penalty for the pending charges. An application for a permit may be filed prior to the effective date of the contract, in which case the permit when issued shall become effective on the effective date of the contract. Upon the effective date of the permit, (a) the permittee shall be responsible for compliance with the provisions of this title and any Board

regulation and (b) the previous licensee shall not be held liable for any violation of this title or any Board regulation committed by, or any errors or omissions of, the permittee.

B. Nothing in subdivision 9, 10, or 11 shall authorize any brewery, winery or affiliate or a subsidiary thereof which has supplied financing to a wholesale licensee to manage and operate the wholesale licensee in the event of a default, except to the extent authorized by subdivision B 3 a of § 4.1-216.

History.
Code 1950, §§ 4-26, 4-59, 4-61.2, 4-72, 4-77, 4-86; 1950, p. 879; 1954, cc. 21, 351; 1962, c. 200, § 4-84.1; 1968, c. 7, § 4-98.16; 1972, cc. 138, 717; 1974, c. 460, § 4-72.1; 1975, c. 480; 1976, c. 696; 1978, c. 436; 1984, c. 53; 1986, c. 190; 1988, c. 786; 1990, cc. 442, 773; 1993, cc. 221, 866; 1994, cc. 825, 826; 1997, c. 801; 2003, c. 564; 2006, c. 826; 2008, c. 453; 2012, c. 155.

Editor's note.
Acts 1993, c. 221 amended former § 4-59, from which this section is derived. Pursuant to § 30-152, the 1993 amendment by c. 221 has been given effect in this section as set out above. In accordance with c. 221, "and upon such conditions or restrictions as the Board may prescribe" was added to the last sentence of subdivision 10 of this section.

Acts 2012, c. 155, cl. 3, provides: "That the provisions of this act shall become effective on July 1, 2013."

The 2012 amendments.
The 2012 amendment by c. 155, effective July 1, 2013, substituted "subdivision (a)(73)" for "subdivision (a)(72)" in subdivision A 10.

CHAPTER 3.

PROHIBITED PRACTICES; PENALTIES; PROCEDURAL MATTERS.

Article 1. Prohibited Practices Generally.

ARTICLE 1.

PROHIBITED PRACTICES GENERALLY.

Michie's Jurisprudence.

For related discussion, see 4C M.J. Constitutional Law, § 94; 10B M.J. Intoxicating Liquors, §§ 28, 33 - 36, 38, 41 - 44, 46, 48.

§ 4.1-300. Illegal manufacture and bottling; penalty.

A. Except as otherwise provided in §§ 4.1-200 and 4.1-201, no person shall manufacture alcoholic beverages in the Commonwealth without being licensed under this title to manufacture such alcoholic beverages. Nor shall any person, other than a brewery licensee or bottler's licensee, bottle beer for sale.

B. The presence of mash at an unlicensed distillery shall constitute manufacturing within the meaning of this section.

C. Any person convicted of a violation of this section shall be guilty of a Class 6 felony.

History.

Code 1950, § 4-57; 1954, c. 484; 1974, c. 460; 1993, c. 866.

Cross references.

As to punishment for Class 6 felonies, see § 18.2-10.

CASE NOTES

Editor's note.

The cases noted below were decided under former § 4-57, now repealed, which covered the same subject matter as this section.

Election to prosecute under former § 4-57 or former § 4-77. — Where accused was indicted for illegal manufacture of liquor in violation of former § 4-57 by the use of a still, and for illegal possession of the same still, in violation of former § 4-77 (see now §§ 4.1-212 and 4.1-314), the Commonwealth had the election to prosecute the greater offense, that is, the illegal manufacture, instead of the lesser offense of illegal possession, and when, upon appeal from convictions under both indictments, the Attorney General acquiesced in accused's view that the prosecution for illegal possession should be dismissed, this would be treated as such election. Wheeler v. Commonwealth, 192 Va. 665, 66 S.E.2d 605 (1951), overruled on other grounds, Watkins v. Commonwealth, 238 Va. 341, 385 S.E.2d 50 (1989).

Manufacture within the purview of the statute is a continuing process. It includes active efforts and means employed in producing or creating alcoholic beverages. Strange v. Commonwealth, 182 Va. 742, 30 S.E.2d 552 (1944).

Uncontradicted testimony regarding the presence of mash constituted illegal "manufacture" within the meaning of former § 4-57 (see now this section). Ruff v. Gathright, 373 F. Supp. 232 (W.D. Va. 1974).

For cases in which the accused was held to be present where a still was in operation within the meaning of a provision similar to subsection (b) of former § 4-57, see Johnson v. Commonwealth, 142 Va. 639, 128 S.E. 456 (1925); Langford v. Commonwealth, 154 Va. 879, 153 S.E. 821 (1930); Brown v. Commonwealth, 156 Va. 947, 157 S.E. 567 (1931); Ruff v. Gathright, 373 F. Supp. 232 (W.D. Va. 1974).

Confession by accused is a jury question. — In a prosecution for a violation of former § 4-57, it was held that the question as to whether a confession was made by accused was for the jury and was by their verdict resolved adversely to the accused. Upshur v. Commonwealth, 170 Va. 649, 197 S.E. 435 (1938).

As is the credibility of testimony of an accomplice. — In a prosecution for the unlawful manufacture of ardent spirits and possession of equipment for such manufacture under former § 4-57, the credibility of the testimony of an accomplice was a question for the jury. Upshur v. Commonwealth, 170 Va. 649, 197 S.E. 435 (1938).

Evidence held sufficient to sustain conviction of illegal manufacture. Strange v. Commonwealth, 182 Va. 742, 30 S.E.2d 552 (1944).

Evidence sustained conviction for an attempt to manufacture illegally alcoholic beverages. Anderson v. Commonwealth, 195 Va. 258, 77 S.E.2d 846 (1953).

Evidence held insufficient. — Evidence held insufficient to sustain conviction of aiding and abetting illegal manufacture. Strange v. Commonwealth, 182 Va. 742, 30 S.E.2d 552 (1944).

Evidence held insufficient to sustain conviction for illegal manufacture. Dotson v. Commonwealth, 171 Va. 514, 199 S.E. 471 (1938); Lyons v. Commonwealth, 204 Va. 375, 131 S.E.2d 407 (1963).

In prosecution for unlawfully and feloniously manufacturing alcoholic beverages without a license, the evidence was insufficient to support the defendant's conviction where the evidence did not establish beyond a reasonable doubt that the defendant was present at the distillery site. Moran v. Commonwealth, 4 Va. App. 310, 357 S.E.2d 551 (1987).

§ 4.1-301. Conspiracy to violate § 4.1-300; penalty.

If two or more persons conspire together to do any act which is in violation of § 4.1-300, and one or more of these persons does any act to effect the object of the conspiracy, each of the parties to such conspiracy shall be guilty of a Class 6 felony.

History.
1956, c. 70, § 4-57.1; 1993, c. 866.

Cross references.
As to punishment for Class 6 felonies, see § 18.2-10.

CASE NOTES

Editor's note.
The cases below were decided prior to Acts 2003, cc. 1029 and 1030, which enacted § 4.1-112.1 [see now §§ 4.1-209.1 and 4.1-212.1] and amended other sections of Title 4.1.

Constitutionality. — Virginia's ban on the direct shipment of wine to Virginia consumers from out-of-state entities, while Virginia not only permits, but encourages, direct shipment to consumers by in-state wineries and farm wineries, violates the dormant commerce clause and is unconstitutional. Bolick v. Roberts, 199 F. Supp. 2d 397, 2001 U.S. Dist. LEXIS 11118 (E.D. Va. 2001), modified and approved, Bolick v. Roberts, 199 F. Supp. 2d 397, 2002 U.S. Dist. LEXIS 6376 (E.D. Va. 2002), vacated and remanded sub nom. Bolick v. Danielson, 330 F.3d 274 (4th Cir. 2003), and partially rendered moot by 2003 legislation.

System whereby Virginia wineries, farm wineries, breweries, and off-premises licensees could directly ship beer and wine to Virginia and out-of-state consumers, where legal, but out-of-state vendors could neither obtain a Virginia license nor directly ship beer or wine to Virginia consumers, was the very definition of a facially discriminatory law; statutes were unconstitutional forms of discrimination in their in-state preferences for Virginia wine and beer. Bolick v. Roberts, 199 F. Supp. 2d 397, 2002 U.S. Dist. LEXIS 6376 (E.D. Va. 2002), vacated and remanded sub nom. Bolick v. Danielson, 330 F.3d 274 (4th Cir. 2003), and partially rendered moot by 2003 legislation.

§ 4.1-302. Illegal sale of alcoholic beverages in general; penalty.

If any person who is not licensed sells any alcoholic beverages except as permitted by this title, he shall be guilty of a Class 1 misdemeanor.

In the event of a second or subsequent conviction under this section, a jail sentence of no less than thirty days shall be imposed and in no case be suspended.

History.
Code 1950, § 4-58; 1952, c. 491; 1984, c. 603; 1993, c. 866.

Cross references.
As to punishment for Class 1 misdemeanors, see § 18.2-11.

CASE NOTES

Editor's note.
Most of the cases noted below were decided under former § 4-58, now repealed, which covered the same subject matter as this section.

The cases below were decided prior to Acts 2003, cc. 1029 and 1030, which enacted § 4.1-112.1 [see now §§ 4.1-209.1 and 4.1-212.1] and amended other sections of Title 4.1.

Constitutionality. — Virginia's ban on the direct shipment of wine to Virginia consumers from out-of-state entities, while Virginia not only permits, but encourages, direct shipment to consumers by in-state wineries and farm wineries, violates the dormant commerce clause and is unconstitutional. Bolick v. Roberts, 199 F. Supp. 2d 397, 2001 U.S. Dist. LEXIS 11118 (E.D. Va. 2001), modified and approved, Bolick v. Roberts, 199 F. Supp. 2d 397, 2002 U.S. Dist. LEXIS 6376 (E.D. Va. 2002), vacated and remanded sub nom. Bolick v. Danielson, 330 F.3d 274 (4th Cir. 2003), and partially rendered moot by 2003 legislation.

System whereby Virginia wineries, farm wineries, breweries, and off-premises licensees could directly ship beer and wine to Virginia and out-of-state consumers, where legal, but out-of-state vendors could neither obtain a Virginia license nor directly ship beer or wine to Virginia consumers, was the very definition of a facially discriminatory law; statutes were unconstitutional forms of discrimination in their in-state preferences for Virginia wine and beer. Bolick v. Roberts, 199 F. Supp. 2d 397, 2002 U.S. Dist. LEXIS 6376 (E.D. Va. 2002), vacated and remanded sub nom. Bolick v. Danielson, 330 F.3d 274 (4th Cir. 2003), and partially rendered moot by 2003 legislation.

The record on appeal did not support a theory of conspiracy to racially discriminate where the record consisted solely of a naked allegation of a percentage of black arrests under former § 4-58. Butler v. Cooper, 554 F.2d 645 (4th Cir. 1977).

Impeachment of witness. — In a prosecution under former § 4-58 the usual restrictive rules of evidence relating to the methods which may be used to impeach the truth and veracity of a witness were applicable to an undercover agent for the Alcoholic Beverage Control Commission (now Board) who was the primary witness against defendant. Clark v. Commonwealth, 202 Va. 787, 120 S.E.2d 270 (1961).

Hearsay evidence. — In prosecution under former § 4-58 admission of hearsay evidence was held to be reversible error. Boatright v. Commonwealth, 198 Va. 753, 96 S.E.2d 772 (1957).

Burden of proof. — In a prosecution under former § 4-58 there was no burden upon the Commonwealth to show that the defendant did not have a license. Baughan v. Commonwealth, 206 Va. 28, 141 S.E.2d 750 (1965).

Instructions. — See Boatright v. Commonwealth, 198 Va. 753, 96 S.E.2d 772 (1957).

In a prosecution under former § 4-58, since there was no evidence tending to show that investigators for the Alcoholic Beverage Control Commission (now Board), to whom defendant sold whiskey, conceived or planned to procure the illegal sales by one who would not otherwise have made them, there was no basis for giving defendant's requested instruction on entrapment. Swift v. Commonwealth, 199 Va. 420, 100 S.E.2d 9 (1957).

Sufficiency of evidence. — On the trial of a warrant charging the unlawful sale of alcoholic beverages the evidence was held sufficient to sustain the verdict of guilty. Simpson v. Commonwealth, 199 Va. 549, 100 S.E.2d 701 (1957).

Where the record contained testimony by the investigators of the Alcoholic Beverage Control Commission (now Board) to whom defendant had sold whiskey, that he was not properly licensed, there was no merit to his contention on appeal that the Commonwealth had failed to prove this fact. Swift v. Commonwealth, 199 Va. 420, 100 S.E.2d 9 (1957).

Evidence held sufficient to justify verdict of guilty in prosecution for illegal sale of intoxicating liquor. Nicholas v. Commonwealth, 186 Va. 979, 45 S.E.2d 302 (1947).

§ 4.1-302.1. Use of alcohol vaporizing devices prohibited; penalty.

A. No person shall purchase, offer for sale or use, sell or use any vaporized form of an alcoholic beverage produced by an alcohol vaporizing device.

B. Any person convicted of a violation of this section shall be guilty of a Class 1 misdemeanor.

History.
2006, c. 714.

Cross references.
As to punishment for Class 1 misdemeanors, see § 18.2-11.

§ 4.1-303. Purchase of alcoholic beverages from person not authorized to sell; penalty.

If any person buys alcoholic beverages from any person other than the Board, a government store or a person authorized under this title to sell alcoholic beverages, he shall be guilty of a Class 1 misdemeanor.

History.
Code 1950, § 4-71; 1968, c. 7; 1993, c. 866.

Cross references.
As to punishment for Class 1 misdemeanors, see § 18.2-11.

CASE NOTES

Editor's note.
One of the cases noted below was decided under former § 4-71, now repealed, which covered the same subject matter as this section.

The cases below were decided prior to Acts 2003, cc. 1029 and 1030, which enacted § 4.1-112.1 [see now §§ 4.1-209.1 and 4.1-212.1] and amended other sections of Title 4.1.

Constitutionality. — Virginia's ban on the direct shipment of wine to Virginia consumers from out-of-state entities, while Virginia not only permits, but encourages, direct shipment to consumers by in-state wineries and farm wineries, violates the dormant commerce clause and is unconstitutional. Bolick v. Roberts, 199 F. Supp. 2d 397, 2001 U.S. Dist. LEXIS 11118 (E.D. Va. 2001), modified and approved, Bolick v. Roberts, 199 F. Supp. 2d 397, 2002 U.S. Dist. LEXIS 6376 (E.D. Va. 2002), vacated and remanded sub nom. Bolick v. Danielson, 330 F.3d 274 (4th Cir. 2003), and partially rendered moot by 2003 legislation.

System whereby Virginia wineries, farm wineries, breweries, and off-premises licensees could directly ship beer and wine to Virginia and out-of-state consumers, where legal, but out-of-state vendors could neither obtain a Virginia license nor directly ship beer or wine to Virginia consumers, was the very definition of a facially discriminatory law; statutes were unconstitutional forms of discrimination in their in-state preferences for Virginia wine and beer. Bolick v. Roberts, 199 F. Supp. 2d 397, 2002 U.S. Dist. LEXIS 6376 (E.D. Va. 2002), vacated and remanded sub nom. Bolick v. Danielson, 330 F.3d 274 (4th Cir. 2003), and partially rendered moot by 2003 legislation.

Former § 4-71 was not applicable to officer of Board acting within scope of employment. — An officer of the Alcoholic Beverage Control Commission (now Board) who ascertains that a person is equipped to make illegal sales of whiskey and buys whiskey from that person is a "feigned accomplice," who, when he acts strictly within the scope of his employment, is not an accomplice in the sense that his uncorroborated testimony will not support a conviction, nor in the sense that his testimony should be condemned as unworthy of belief by the trial judge by an instruc-

tion that the jury must act upon it with caution. Guthrie v. Commonwealth, 171 Va. 461, 198 S.E. 481 (1938).

And testimony of such officer as to purchase was admissible. — In a prosecution under the former Alcoholic Beverage Control Act, the only evidence for the Commonwealth consisted in the testimony of an inspector of the Alcoholic Beverage Control Commission (now Board), who testified that he bought whiskey from accused and introduced a bottle of whiskey which he asserted he had purchased from accused. It was held that the evidence of the officer was admissible and, if believed by the jury, was sufficient to sustain a conviction. Guthrie v. Commonwealth, 171 Va. 461, 198 S.E. 481 (1938).

§ 4.1-304. Persons to whom alcoholic beverages may not be sold; proof of legal age; penalty.

A. No person shall, except pursuant to subdivisions 1 through 5 of § 4.1-200, sell any alcoholic beverages to any individual when at the time of such sale he knows or has reason to believe that the individual to whom the sale is made is (i) less than 21 years of age, (ii) interdicted, or (iii) intoxicated. Any person convicted of a violation of this subsection is guilty of a Class 1 misdemeanor.

B. Any person who sells, except pursuant to subdivisions 1 through 5 of § 4.1-200, any alcoholic beverage to an individual who is less than 21 years of age and at the time of the sale does not require the individual to present bona fide evidence of legal age indicating that the individual is 21 years of age or older is guilty of a violation of this subsection. Bona fide evidence of legal age is limited to any evidence that is or reasonably appears to be an unexpired driver's license issued by any state of the United States or the District of Columbia, military identification card, United States passport or foreign government visa, unexpired special identification card issued by the Department of Motor Vehicles, or any other valid government-issued identification card bearing the individual's photograph, signature, height, weight, and date of birth, or which bears a photograph that reasonably appears to match the appearance of the purchaser. A student identification card shall not constitute bona fide evidence of legal age for purposes of this subsection. Any person convicted of a violation of this subsection is guilty of a Class 3 misdemeanor. Notwithstanding the provisions of § 4.1-202, the Board shall not take administrative action against a licensee for the conduct of his employee who violates this subsection.

C. No person shall be convicted of both subsections A and B for the same sale.

History.
Code 1950, § 4-62; 1970, c. 686; 1974, c. 460; 1979, c. 537; 1981, c. 24; 1982, c. 66; 1983, c. 608; 1985, c. 559; 1990, c. 771; 1993, c. 866; 2013, c. 562.

Cross references.
As to punishment for Class 1 misdemeanors, see § 18.2-11.

The 2013 amendments.
The 2013 amendment by c. 562 added the subsection A designator, and in subsection A, substituted "individual" for "person" twice, added the last sentence and made a minor stylistic change; desig-

nated the former second paragraph as subsection B and rewrote it; and added subsection C.

Law Review.

For comment on Virginia's dramshop immunity, see 10 G.M.U. L. Rev. 285 (1988).

CASE NOTES

Editor's note.

Most of the cases noted below were decided under former § 4-62, now repealed, which covered the same subject matter as this section.

No constructive notice of order of interdiction. — The seller is not charged with constructive notice of the publication made under former § 4-51 (now § 4.1-333). He must have actual notice of the interdiction. Calamos v. Commonwealth, 184 Va. 397, 35 S.E.2d 397 (1945).

"Reason to believe" purchaser interdicted. — The failure of the seller before making the sale to inquire of the purchaser whether the latter had been interdicted is no indication that the seller had reason to believe that the purchaser was an interdicted person. Calamos v. Commonwealth, 184 Va. 397, 35 S.E.2d 397 (1945).

Circumstances were not sufficient to charge seller with "reason to believe" that the person to whom he sold had been interdicted. Calamos v. Commonwealth, 184 Va. 397, 35 S.E.2d 397 (1945).

Seller not guilty of contempt for violation of interdiction order. — A seller of intoxicants who had no actual knowledge or notice of an interdiction order entered against the purchaser cannot be held in contempt for violating such order. Calamos v. Commonwealth, 184 Va. 397, 35 S.E.2d 397 (1945).

As to meaning of "intoxicated," see Gardner v. Commonwealth, 195 Va. 945, 81 S.E.2d 614 (1954).

Duty to gauge level of intoxication of patrons. — As sellers, restaurant employees are charged with gauging the level of intoxication in their patrons; their failure to do so does not absolve the restaurant of the obligations of its license application. Sights & Brightwaters Investors, Ltd. v. Virginia Alcoholic Beverage Control Bd., No. 0378-98-1 (Ct. of Appeals Oct. 27, 1998).

Evidence sufficient to establish violation. — Employees of the restaurant had reason to believe that the patron was intoxicated, based on the patron's antagonistic and argumentative demeanor and the amount of alcohol consumed by him over the course of an evening. Sights & Brightwaters Investors, Ltd. v. Virginia Alcoholic Beverage Control Bd., No. 0378-98-1 (Ct. of Appeals Oct. 27, 1998).

Where a store relied to its detriment on subpoenas issued to witnesses (who failed to appear) by the Alcoholic Beverage Control Board and conceded that the Board had sufficient evidence to find an alcoholic beverage license violation, the store was not denied due process. 7-11, Inc. v. Va. Alcoholic Bev. Control Bd., No. 2740-02-4, 2003 Va. App. LEXIS 324 (Ct. of Appeals June 3, 2003).

At an administrative hearing at which a retailer was charged with selling alcohol to a minor, the evidence was sufficient to establish the retailer's violation of § 4.1-304 and 3 VAC 5-50-10 as the only identification card the minor had when he entered the retailer's store indicated he was 17, he gave the card to the retailer's employee, and the employee, after looking at it, sold the minor beer, and the clerk admitted looking at the card and miscalculating the minor's age due to blurred vision and anxiety about a long line of waiting customers. Mirabile Corp. v. Va. Alcoholic Bev. Control Bd., No. 2126-02-4, 2003 Va. App. LEXIS 493 (Ct. of Appeals Sept. 30, 2003).

Because a licensee stood in the shoes of its employee who served alcohol to an underage subject in violation of § 4.1-304 and 3 VAC 5-50-10, the licensee committed a violation cognizable under subdivision 1 c of § 4.1-225, which triggered the sanctions set forth therein. Commodore Assocs. v. Va. Alcoholic Bev. Control Bd., 2009 Va. App. LEXIS 68 (Feb. 10, 2009).

Customer's hearsay evidence that a patron appeared intoxicated while in a liquor store, and that the customer informed a cashier that the patron appeared intoxicated, but the cashier continued to ring up the patron's purchase was substantial evidence of a § 4.1-304 violation, particularly in light of a police officer's obser-vations of signs of intoxication after the patron's car accident. R K Enters. v. Va. Alcoholic Bev. Control Bd., 2009 Va. App. LEXIS 284 (June 23, 2009).

Attorney General not proper defendant for injunctive relief. — The mere fact that the Attorney General is clothed with enforcement power by former § 2.1-124 (see now § 2.2-511) does not warrant making him a defendant for purposes of injunctive relief against enforcement of former § 4-62, where the plaintiff did not assert any actual threatened enforcement by the Attorney General nor cite any history of prior enforcement of former § 4-62 by the Attorney General against himself or others. Fisher v. Coleman, 486 F. Supp. 311 (W.D. Va. 1979), aff'd, 639 F.2d 191 (4th Cir. 1981).

Former § 4-62 and the Virginia common law did not recognize dram shop liability on the part of a person who purveys an alcoholic beverage to someone else who then causes a tort to occur, specifically an automobile accident, while that person was intoxicated. Webb v. Blackie's House of Beef, Inc., 811 F.2d 840 (4th Cir. 1987).

In view of the fact that Virginia does not recognize dram shop liability, the federal government could not be found liable for negligence on such a legal principle arising out of an automobile accident caused by an intoxicated 19-year-old Army private who had done his drinking at taverns operated by the Army. Corrigan v. United States, 815 F.2d 954 (4th Cir.), cert. denied, 484 U.S. 926, 108 S. Ct. 290, 98 L. Ed. 2d 250 (1987).

Former § 4-62 did not create cause of action against seller by third party. — Former § 4-62 was a part of the Virginia Alcoholic Beverage Control Act, a self-contained statute with its own penalty provisions enacted solely with the legislative intent to regulate the sale and distribution of alcoholic beverages. It did not create a cause of action against the seller of alcoholic beverages by a third party for the negligent acts of a patron. Webb v. Regua Ltd. Partnership, 624 F. Supp. 471 (E.D. Va. 1985), aff'd sub nom. Webb v. Blackie's House of Beef, Inc., 811 F.2d 840 (4th Cir. 1987).

A person injured by an intoxicated customer of a seller of intoxicants is not a member of the class for whose benefit former § 4-62 was enacted. Thus, violation of former § 4-62 did not constitute negligence per se and does not furnish the basis for a civil action in damages. Williamson v. Old Brogue, Inc., 232 Va. 350, 350 S.E.2d 621 (1986).

A third party does not have a claim for relief against seller of intoxicating beverages for injuries sustained as a result of the intoxication of the vendor's patron, even if the patron is a minor. Byrd v. Gate Petro. Co., 845 F.2d 86 (4th Cir. 1988).

In Virginia there is no liability on seller of intoxicating liquor for negligence, resulting in personal injuries sustained by third parties, as a result of the negligence of the patron after leaving the seller's establishment. Webb v. Regua Ltd. Partnership, 624 F. Supp. 471 (E.D. Va. 1985), aff'd sub nom. Webb v. Blackie's House of Beef, Inc., 811 F.2d 840 (4th Cir. 1987).

§ 4.1-305. Purchasing or possessing alcoholic beverages unlawful in certain cases; venue; exceptions; penalty; forfeiture; deferred proceedings; treatment and education programs and services.

A. No person to whom an alcoholic beverage may not lawfully be sold under § 4.1-304 shall consume, purchase or possess, or attempt to consume, purchase or possess, any alcoholic beverage, except (i) pursuant to subdivisions 1 through 7 of § 4.1-200; (ii) where possession of the alcoholic beverages by a person less than 21 years of age is due to such person's making a delivery of alcoholic beverages in pursuance of his employment or an order of his parent; or (iii) by any state, federal, or local law-enforcement officer or his agent when possession of an alcoholic beverage is necessary in the performance of his duties. Such person may be prosecuted either in the county or city in which the alcohol was possessed or consumed, or in the county or city in which the person exhibits evidence of physical indicia of consumption of alcohol. It shall be an affirmative defense to a charge of a violation of this subsection if the defendant shows that such consumption or possession was pursuant to subdivision 7 of § 4.1-200.

B. No person under the age of 21 years shall use or attempt to use any (i) altered, fictitious, facsimile or simulated license to operate a motor vehicle, (ii) altered, fictitious, facsimile or simulated document, including, but not limited to a birth certificate or student identification card, or (iii) motor vehicle operator's license, birth certificate or student identification card of another person in order to establish a false identification or false age for himself to consume, purchase or attempt to consume or purchase an alcoholic beverage.

C. Any person found guilty of a violation of this section shall be guilty of a Class 1 misdemeanor; and upon conviction, (i) such person shall be ordered to pay a mandatory minimum fine of $500 or ordered to perform a mandatory minimum of 50 hours of community service as a condition of probation supervision and (ii) the license to operate a motor vehicle in the Commonwealth of any such person age 18 or older shall be suspended for a period of not less than six months and not more than one year; the license to operate a motor vehicle in the Commonwealth of any juvenile shall be handled in accordance with the provisions of § 16.1-278.9. The court, in its discretion and upon a demonstration of hardship, may authorize an adult convicted of a violation of this section the use of a restricted permit to operate a motor vehicle in accordance with the provisions of subsection E of § 18.2-271.1 or when referred to a local community-based probation services agency established pursuant to Article 9 (§ 9.1-173 et seq.) of Chapter 1 of Title 9.1. During the period of license suspension, the court may require an adult who is issued a restricted permit under the provisions of this subsection to be (a) monitored by an alcohol safety action program, or (b) supervised by a local community-based probation services agency established pursuant to Article 9 (§ 9.1-173 et seq.) of Chapter 1 of Title 9.1, if one has been established for the locality. The alcohol safety action program or local community-based probation services agency shall report to the court any violation of the terms of the restricted permit, the required alcohol safety action program monitoring or local community-based probation services and any condition related thereto or any failure to remain alcohol-free during the suspension period.

D. Any alcoholic beverage purchased or possessed in violation of this section shall be deemed contraband and forfeited to the Commonwealth in accordance with § 4.1-338.

E. Any retail licensee who in good faith promptly notifies the Board or any state or local law-enforcement agency of a violation or suspected violation of this section shall be accorded immunity from an administrative penalty for a violation of § 4.1-304.

F. When any adult who has not previously been convicted of underaged consumption, purchase or possession of alcoholic beverages in Virginia or any other state or the United States is before the court, the court may, upon entry of a plea of guilty or not guilty, if the facts found by the court would justify a finding of guilt of a violation of subsection A, without entering a judgment of guilt and with the consent of the accused, defer further proceedings and place him on probation subject to appropriate conditions. Such conditions may include the imposition of the license suspension and restricted license provisions in subsection C. However, in all such deferred proceedings, the court shall require the accused to enter a treatment or education program or both, if available, that in the opinion of the court best suits the needs of the accused. If the accused is placed on local community-based probation, the program or services shall be located in any of the judicial districts served by the local community-based probation services agency or in any judicial district ordered by the court when the placement is with an alcohol safety action program. The services shall be provided by (i) a program licensed by the Department of Behavioral Health and Developmental Services, (ii) certified by the Commission on VASAP, or (iii) by a program or services made available through a community-based probation services agency established pursuant to Article 9 (§ 9.1-173 et seq.) of Chapter 1 of Title 9.1, if one has been established for the locality. When an offender is ordered to a local community-based probation services rather than the alcohol safety action program, the local community-based probation services agency shall be responsible for providing for services or referring the offender to education or treatment services as a condition of probation.

Upon violation of a condition, the court may enter an adjudication of guilt and proceed as otherwise provided. Upon fulfillment of the conditions, the court shall discharge the person and dismiss the proceedings against him without an adjudication of guilt. A discharge and dismissal hereunder shall be treated as a conviction for the purpose of applying this section in any subsequent proceedings.

When any juvenile is found to have committed a violation of subsection A, the disposition of the case shall be handled according to the provisions of Article 9 (§ 16.1-278 et seq.) of Chapter 11 of Title 16.1.

History.
  Code 1950, § 4-62; 1970, c. 686; 1974, c. 460; 1979, c. 537; 1981, c. 24; 1982, c. 66; 1983, c. 608; 1985, c. 559; 1990, c. 771; 1993, c. 866; 1995, c. 374; 1996, cc. 626, 730; 2000, c. 325; 2002, c. 338; 2003, cc. 845, 849; 2004, cc. 322, 461; 2005, c. 895; 2006, c. 207; 2007, c. 133; 2009, cc. 248, 726, 813, 840; 2012, cc. 250, 260.

Cross references.
  As to punishment for Class 1 misdemeanors, see § 18.2-11. As to penalty for fraudulent use of a driver's license by a person under 18

in the case of beer, or under 21 in the case of other alcoholic beverages, in order to obtain alcoholic beverages, see § 46.2-347.

The 2009 amendments.

The 2009 amendment by c. 248 added the last sentence in subsection A; and redesignated former clauses (i) and (ii) designations as clauses (a) and (b) designations in the next-to-last sentence of subsection C.

The 2009 amendment by c. 726, in subsection C, inserted "the license to operate a motor vehicle in the Commonwealth of any juvenile shall be handled in accordance with the provisions of § 16.1-278.9" at the end of the first sentence; in the second sentence, substituted "an adult" for "any person" and deleted "subsection D of § 16.1-278.9 or" preceding "subsection E of"; and in the third sentence, substituted "an adult who is" for "a person"; in subsection F, substituted "adult" for "person" near the beginning; and added the last paragraph.

The 2009 amendments by cc. 813 and 840 are identical and substituted "Department of Behavioral Health and Developmental Services" for "Department of Mental Health, Mental Retardation and Substance Abuse Services" in clause (i) of subsection F.

The 2012 amendments.

The 2012 amendments by cc. 250 and 260 are identical, and inserted "or his agent" following "local law-enforcement officer" in clause (iii) of the first sentence in subsection A.

Law Review.

For article summarizing published Virginia criminal law decisions between July 1, 2002 and July 1, 2003, see 38 U. Rich. L. Rev. 87 (2003). For annual survey article on legal issues involving children, see 38 U. Rich. L. Rev. 161 (2003).

Research references.

Virginia Forms (Matthew Bender). No. 9-2801. Notice of Administrative Suspension of Driver's License/Driving Privilege. No. 9-2817. Driver's License Suspension Order (Underage Alcohol Violations). No. 9-2818. Driver's License Denial Order (Juvenile)/ Driver's License Suspension Order (Under Age Alcohol Violations).

CASE NOTES

Constitutionality. — The provisions of subsection B of former § 4-62 (see now subsection B of this section) did not threaten cruel and unusual punishment. Fisher v. Coleman, 639 F.2d 191 (4th Cir. 1981) (decided under former § 4-62).

Subsection B of former § 4-62 (see now subsection B of this section) did not make the status of alcoholism a criminal offense, but merely makes specific behavior, e.g. the purchase of alcoholic beverages by one who is interdicted, unlawful. This law in no way violates the Eighth Amendment when it is made applicable to an alcoholic. Fisher v. Coleman, 486 F. Supp. 311 (W.D. Va. 1979), aff'd, 639 F.2d 191 (4th Cir. 1981) (decided under former § 4-62).

Attorney General not proper defendant for injunctive relief. — The mere fact that the Attorney General is clothed with enforcement power by former § 2.1-124 (see now § 2.2-511) does not warrant making him a defendant for purposes of injunctive relief against enforcement of former § 4-62, where the plaintiff did not assert any actual threatened enforcement by the Attorney General nor cite any history of prior enforcement of former § 4-62 by the Attorney General against himself or others. Fisher v. Coleman, 486 F. Supp. 311 (W.D. Va. 1979), aff'd, 639 F.2d 191 (4th Cir. 1981) (decided under former § 4-62).

Possession: sufficient evidence. — Where the evidence proved that the defendant was under the age of 21, there was an odor of alcohol about his person, an Alcosensor test confirmed the presence of alcohol in his body system, and defendant told the investigating officer that he had consumed a beer earlier, this was sufficient to sustain a conviction for "possession" of an alcoholic beverage. Hale v. Commonwealth, 23 Va. App. 587, 478 S.E.2d 710 (1996).

Conviction as basis for enhancing federal sentence. — Sentence imposed on defendant could be enhanced under U.S. Sentencing Guidelines Manual § 4A1.1 based upon a prior conviction for being a minor in possession of alcohol; although the federal sentencing guidelines excluded consideration of several listed petty offenses, underage possession of alcohol was not "similar" to either

public intoxication or driving without a license, which were listed in the guidelines. United States v. Brown, 2005 U.S. App. LEXIS 436 (4th Cir. Jan. 11, 2005).

Sentence reasonable. — Where a jury found defendant guilty of possession of alcohol by a person under age twenty-one, in violation of 18 U.S.C.S. § 13, assimilating § 4.1-305, a sentence consisting of twelve months in prison, one year of supervised release, and a $500 fine was not unreasonable because the district court properly considered the 18 U.S.C.S. § 3353(a) factors, defendant was on probation at the time he committed the possession of alcohol offense, and an attendant assault charge stemmed from defendant's use of alcohol. United States v. Russell, 2007 U.S. App. LEXIS 11299 (4th Cir. May 14, 2007).

Motion to suppress properly denied. — Once an officer observed the seemingly underage individuals holding beer bottles and then fleeing from the police presence, he had probable cause to believe that a crime was being committed. Because the development of probable cause and the creation of the exigencies were virtually contemporaneous, the officer had no meaningful opportunity in which to obtain a search warrant for the property before exigent circumstances necessitated his further intrusion onto the premises; thus, the trial court did not err in concluding that the officer had both probable cause and exigent circumstances sufficient to justify his warrantless entry into defendant's backyard, the denial of his motion to suppress was affirmed, and his convictions for contributing to the delinquency of a minor were affirmed. Robinson v. Commonwealth, 47 Va. App. 533, 625 S.E.2d 651, 2006 Va. App. LEXIS 54 (2006).

CIRCUIT COURT OPINIONS

Evidence held sufficient. — A juvenile defendant's conviction under § 4.1-305 was supported by sufficient evidence; a state trooper's testimony that, at the time of defendant's apprehension, he detected the odor of alcohol on defendant's breath and that defendant admitted that he had previously consumed alcohol was credible, and when, as here, the commission of the crime had been fully confessed by the accused, only slight corroborative evidence was necessary to establish the corpus delicti. Commonwealth v. Villafana, 57 Va. Cir. 357, 2002 Va. Cir. LEXIS 216 (Norfolk 2002).

OPINIONS OF THE ATTORNEY GENERAL

A police officer may not arrest an underage person, without a warrant, for violating this section, unless the offense is committed in the presence of the officer within his territorial jurisdiction. See opinion of Attorney General to The Honorable Marsha L. Garst, Commonwealth's Attorney for the City of Harrisonburg and Rockingham County, 02-059 (7/24/02).

Despite the appearance of conflict between this section and § 16.1-278.9, the latter is the only statute applicable to juveniles: therefore, a juvenile court must dispose of charges of unlawful possession of alcohol by juveniles pursuant thereto. See opinion of Attorney General to The Honorable J. Dean Lewis, Judge, Fifteenth District Juvenile and Domestic Relations Court, 02-102 (10/29/02).

§ 4.1-306. Purchasing alcoholic beverages for one to whom they may not be sold; penalty; forfeiture.

A. Any person who purchases alcoholic beverages for another person, and at the time of such purchase knows or has reason to believe that the person for whom the alcoholic beverage was purchased was (i) interdicted, or (ii) intoxicated, is guilty of a Class 1 misdemeanor.

A1. Any person who purchases for, or otherwise gives, provides, or assists in the provision of alcoholic beverages to another person, when he knows or has reason to know that such person was less than

21 years of age, except (i) pursuant to subdivisions 1 through 7 of § 4.1-200; (ii) where possession of the alcoholic beverages by a person less than 21 years of age is due to such person's making a delivery of alcoholic beverages in pursuance of his employment or an order of his parent; or (iii) by any state, federal, or local law-enforcement officer when possession of an alcoholic beverage is necessary in the performance of his duties, is guilty of a Class 1 misdemeanor.

B. In addition to any other penalty authorized by law, any person found guilty of a violation of this section shall have his license to operate a motor vehicle suspended for a period of not more than one year. The court, in its discretion, may authorize any person convicted of a violation of this section the use of a restricted permit to operate a motor vehicle in accordance with the provisions of subsection D of § 16.1-278.9 or subsection E of § 18.2-271.1.

C. Any alcoholic beverages purchased in violation of this section shall be deemed contraband and forfeited to the Commonwealth in accordance with § 4.1-338.

History.
Code 1950, § 4-73; 1970, c. 686; 1993, c. 866; 2005, cc. 895, 898; 2006, c. 87; 2011, c. 31.

Cross references.
As to punishment for Class 1 misdemeanors, see § 18.2-11.

The 2011 amendments.
The 2011 amendment by c. 31 substituted "when he knows or has reason to know that such person was less than 21 years of age" for "knowing that such person was less than 21 years of age" in subsection A1.

§ 4.1-307. Persons by whom alcoholic beverages may not be sold or served for on-premises consumption; penalty.

No person shall permit anyone employed by him under the age of (i) eighteen years to sell, serve or dispense in any manner alcoholic beverages for on-premises consumption, except pursuant to subdivisions 1 through 5 of § 4.1-200 or (ii) twenty-one years to prepare or mix alcoholic beverages in the capacity of bartender.

Any person convicted of a violation of this section shall be guilty of a Class 1 misdemeanor.

History.
Code 1950, § 4-63; 1974, c. 460; 1982, c. 66; 1983, c. 608; 1993, c. 866.

Cross references.
As to punishment for Class 1 misdemeanors, see § 18.2-11.

§ 4.1-308. Drinking alcoholic beverages, or offering to another, in public place; penalty; exceptions.

A. If any person takes a drink of alcoholic beverages or offers a drink thereof to another, whether accepted or not, at or in any public place, he shall be guilty of a Class 4 misdemeanor.

B. This section shall not prevent any person from drinking alcoholic beverages or offering a drink thereof to another in any rooms or areas approved by the Board in a licensed establishment, provided such establishment or the person who operates the same is licensed to sell alcoholic beverages at retail for on-premises consumption and the alcoholic beverages drunk or offered were purchased therein.

C. This section shall not prevent any person from drinking alcoholic beverages or offering a drink thereof to another in any room or area approved by the Board at an event for which a banquet license or mixed beverage special events license has been granted. Nor shall this section prevent, upon authorization of the licensee, any person from drinking his own lawfully acquired alcoholic beverages or offering a drink thereof to another in approved areas and locations at events for which a coliseum or stadium license has been granted.

D. This section shall not prevent any person from drinking alcoholic beverages or offering a drink thereof to another on a chartered boat being used for the transportation of passengers for compensation which is not licensed by the Board and which does not sell alcoholic beverages.

History.
Code 1950, § 4-78; 1956, c. 23; 1972, c. 143; 1977, c. 439; 1979, c. 622; 1986, c. 113; 1988, c. 893; 1989, c. 42; 1990, c. 932; 1993, c. 866.

Cross references.
As to punishment for Class 4 misdemeanors, see § 18.2-11.

Michie's Jurisprudence.
For related discussion, see 6B M.J. Drunkenness, § 13.

§ 4.1-309. Drinking or possessing alcoholic beverages in or on public school grounds; penalty.

A. No person shall possess or drink any alcoholic beverage in or upon the grounds of any public elementary or secondary school during school hours or school or student activities.

B. In addition, no person shall drink and no organization shall serve any alcoholic beverage in or upon the grounds of any public elementary or secondary school after school hours or school or student activities, except for religious congregations using wine for sacramental purposes only.

C. Any person convicted of a violation of this section shall be guilty of a Class 2 misdemeanor.

D. This section shall not prohibit any person from possessing or drinking alcoholic beverages or any organization from serving alcoholic beverages in areas approved by the Board at a performing arts center owned by the City of Alexandria or the City of Portsmouth, provided the organization operating the performing arts center or its lessee has a license granted by the Board.

History.
1954, c. 651, § 4-78.1; 1982, c. 288; 1991, c. 710; 1993, c. 866; 1994, c. 844; 1997, cc. 784, 837; 2007, c. 813.

Cross references.

As to punishment for Class 2 misdemeanors, see § 18.2-11.

§ 4.1-309.1. Possessing or consuming alcoholic beverage while operating a school bus; penalty.

Any person who possesses or consumes an alcoholic beverage while operating a school bus and transporting children is guilty of a Class 1 misdemeanor. For purposes of this section, "school bus" shall have the same meaning as provided in § 46.2-100.

History.

2010, c. 169.

Cross references.

As to punishment for Class 1 misdemeanors, see § 18.2-11.

§ 4.1-310. Illegal importation, shipment and transportation of alcoholic beverages; penalty; exception.

A. No alcoholic beverages, other than wine or beer, shall be imported, shipped, transported or brought into the Commonwealth, other than to distillery licensees or winery licensees, unless consigned to the Board. However, the Board may permit such alcoholic beverages ordered by it from outside the Commonwealth for (i) persons, for industrial purposes, (ii) the manufacture of articles allowed to be manufactured under § 4.1-200, or (iii) hospitals, to be shipped or transported directly to such persons. On such orders or shipments of alcohol, the Board shall charge only a reasonable permit fee.

B. Except as otherwise provided in § 4.1-209.1 or 4.1-212.1, no wine shall be imported, shipped, transported or brought into the Commonwealth unless it is consigned to a wholesale wine licensee.

C. Except as otherwise provided in § 4.1-209.1 or 4.1-212.1, no beer shall be imported, shipped, transported or brought into the Commonwealth except to persons licensed to sell it.

D. Any person convicted of a violation of this section shall be guilty of a Class 1 misdemeanor.

E. The provisions of this chapter shall not prohibit (i) any person from bringing, in his personal possession, or through United States Customs in his accompanying baggage, into the Commonwealth not for resale, alcoholic beverages in an amount not to exceed one gallon or four liters if any part of the alcoholic beverages being transported is held in metric-sized containers, (ii) the shipment or transportation into the Commonwealth of a reasonable quantity of alcoholic beverages not for resale in the personal or household effects of a person relocating his place of residence to the Commonwealth, or (iii) the possession or storage of alcoholic beverages on passenger boats, dining cars, buffet cars and club cars, licensed under this title, or common carriers engaged in interstate or foreign commerce.

History.

Code 1950, § 4-84; 1970, c. 297; 1978, c. 436; 1983, c. 212; 1984, c. 200; 1993, c. 866; 1994, c. 826; 1995, cc. 253, 317; 2003, cc. 1029, 1030; 2007, cc. 99, 799.

Cross references.

As to punishment for Class 1 misdemeanors, see § 18.2-11.

CASE NOTES

Editor's note.

Some of the cases below were decided prior to Acts 2003, cc. 1029 and 1030, which enacted § 4.1-112.1 [see now §§ 4.1-209.1 and 4.1-212.1] and amended other sections of Title 4.1.

Constitutionality. — Virginia's ban on the direct shipment of wine to Virginia consumers from out-of-state entities, while Virginia not only permits, but encourages, direct shipment to consumers by in-state wineries and farm wineries, violates the dormant commerce clause and is unconstitutional. Bolick v. Roberts, 199 F. Supp. 2d 397, 2001 U.S. Dist. LEXIS 11118 (E.D. Va. 2001), modified and approved, Bolick v. Roberts, 199 F. Supp. 2d 397, 2002 U.S. Dist. LEXIS 6376 (E.D. Va. 2002), vacated and remanded sub nom. Bolick v. Danielson, 330 F.3d 274 (4th Cir. 2003), and partially rendered moot by 2003 legislation.

System whereby Virginia wineries, farm wineries, breweries, and off-premises licensees could directly ship beer and wine to Virginia and out-of-state consumers, where legal, but out-of-state vendors could neither obtain a Virginia license nor directly ship beer or wine to Virginia consumers, was the very definition of a facially discriminatory law; statutes were unconstitutional forms of discrimination in their in-state preferences for Virginia wine and beer. Bolick v. Roberts, 199 F. Supp. 2d 397, 2002 U.S. Dist. LEXIS 6376 (E.D. Va. 2002), vacated and remanded sub nom. Bolick v. Danielson, 330 F.3d 274 (4th Cir. 2003), and partially rendered moot by 2003 legislation.

Because the Twenty-first Amendment grants the states virtually complete control over whether to permit importation or sale of liquor and how to structure the liquor distribution system, and because the dormant Commerce Clause only prevents a state from enacting regulations that favor in-state producers and thus discriminates against interstate commerce, the Personal Import Exception to Virginia's Alcoholic Beverage Control Act, § 4.1-100 et seq., does not violate the Commerce Clause. Brooks v. Vassar, 462 F.3d 341, 2006 U.S. App. LEXIS 23144 (4th Cir. 2006), cert. denied, 550 U.S. 934, 127 S. Ct. 2251, 167 L. Ed. 2d 1090, 2007 U.S. LEXIS 5184 (U.S. 2007).

Personal Import Exception to Virginia's Alcoholic Beverage Control Act, § 4.1-100 et seq., is not economic protectionism but part of Virginia's import regulation, as it provides a de minimis exception to Virginia's import regulations, allowing consumers to import one gallon or four liters of wine for personal consumption (under no economic construct could such a provision be considered economic protectionism of local industry because it actually amounts to a disadvantage to local wineries whose wine may only be purchased through retailers); accordingly, the Personal Import Exception does not violate the dormant Commerce Clause. Brooks v. Vassar, 462 F.3d 341, 2006 U.S. App. LEXIS 23144 (4th Cir. 2006), cert. denied, 550 U.S. 934, 127 S. Ct. 2251, 167 L. Ed. 2d 1090, 2007 U.S. LEXIS 5184 (U.S. 2007).

Purpose of Alcoholic Beverage Control Act. — The provisions of the Virginia Alcoholic Beverage Control Act are designed to control the sale and distribution of alcoholic beverages within this State by channeling their importation into Virginia through the Alcoholic Beverage Control Commission (now Board). Milam v. Commonwealth, 200 Va. 68, 104 S.E.2d 60 (1958) (decided under former § 4-84).

Liquor is not exempt from seizure though imported in accordance with federal statute. — Assuming that liquor had been imported into Virginia in accordance with the federal statute, it did not follow that it was exempt from seizure and forfeiture under the laws of this State. Milam v. Commonwealth, 200 Va. 68, 104 S.E.2d 60 (1958) (decided under former § 4-84).

Or treated by United States customs officials as part of serviceman's baggage. — The fact that the United States customs officials may have treated liquor for tax purposes as a part of a serviceman's unaccompanied baggage is no reason why the state liquor control laws should be given a like interpretation. Milam v. Commonwealth, 200 Va. 68, 104 S.E.2d 60 (1958) (decided under former § 4-84).

"Baggage" defined. — "Baggage" is defined as "The trunks, valises, etc., which one carries on a journey." Milam v. Commonwealth, 200 Va. 68, 104 S.E.2d 60 (1958) (decided under former § 4-84).

"Possession" does not include constructive possession. — In order to be within the privilege of subsection (d) of former § 4-84 the traveler must bring the permitted quantity of alcoholic beverages "in his possession or in his baggage." The context does not support the interpretation that "possession," as here used, includes constructive possession, that is possession by a brokerage concern or its agent, a carrier. Milam v. Commonwealth, 200 Va. 68, 104 S.E.2d 60 (1958) (decided under former § 4-84).

The wording "bringing, in his possession," denotes personal custody by the traveler himself. Milam v. Commonwealth, 200 Va. 68, 104 S.E.2d 60 (1958) (decided under former § 4-84).

Liquor was imported in violation of former section and was subject to seizure and forfeiture under former § 4-55 (see now § 4.1-338), where it was imported pursuant to schemes by which United States naval personnel, who under naval regulations are not permitted to bring liquor into this country on naval vessels, placed orders with foreign brokers, either in foreign ports or in Norfolk before leaving for foreign ports, and the orders were sent by the brokers to distilleries in Canada, which consigned the liquor to warehouses in Norfolk where the purchasers could obtain it upon presentation of receipts. Milam v. Commonwealth, 200 Va. 68, 104 S.E.2d 60 (1958) (decided under former § 4-84).

§ 4.1-311. Limitations on transporting lawfully purchased alcoholic beverages; penalty.

A. The transportation of alcoholic beverages lawfully purchased in the Commonwealth in excess of the following limits is prohibited except in accordance with Board regulations:

1. Wine and beer, no limitation.

2. Alcoholic beverages other than wine and beer, three gallons, provided that not more than one gallon thereof shall be in containers holding less than one-fifth of a gallon. If any part of the alcoholic beverages being transported is held in metric-sized containers, the three-gallon limitation shall be construed to be 12 liters, and not more than 4 liters thereof shall be in containers smaller than 750 milliliters.

B. The transportation of alcoholic beverages lawfully purchased outside the Commonwealth, within, into or through the Commonwealth, in quantities in excess of one gallon or four liters if any part of the alcohol being transported is held in metric-sized containers, is prohibited except in accordance with Board regulations adopted pursuant to this section.

C. Any person transporting alcoholic beverages in violation of this section shall be guilty of a Class 1 misdemeanor.

History.
Code 1950, § 4-72; 1974, c. 460, § 4-72.1; 1975, c. 480; 1978, c. 436; 1993, c. 866.

Cross references.
As to punishment for Class 1 misdemeanors, see § 18.2-11.

Law Review.
For a note, "Alcohol Direct Shipment Laws, the Commerce Clause, and the Twenty-First Amendment," see 85 Va. L. Rev. 353 (1999).

CASE NOTES

Editor's note.
The cases noted below were decided under § 4-72, now repealed, which covered the same subject matter as this section.

Commerce power not invaded by regulations of Board. — The commerce power of Congress is not invaded by the regulations of the Alcoholic Beverage Control Commission (now Board), promulgated pursuant to former § 4-72, which provide that a vehicle transporting alcoholic beverages through the State must use the most direct route and carry a bill of lading showing the route it will travel, that the carrier must post a bond in the penal sum of $1,000 conditioned on lawful transportation, that the bill of lading must show the name of the true consignee, and that consignee must have a legal right to receive the beverages at the stated destination. Carter v. Virginia, 321 U.S. 131, 64 S. Ct. 464, 88 L. Ed. 605 (1944), aff'g Carter v. Commonwealth, 181 Va. 306, 24 S.E.2d 569 (1943), and Dickerson v. Commonwealth, 181 Va. 313, 24 S.E.2d 550 (1943), wherein it was stated that Williams v. Commonwealth, 169 Va. 857, 192 S.E. 795 (1937), and Surles v. Commonwealth, 172 Va. 573, 200 S.E. 636 (1939), which held certain provisions of this section unconstitutional as to interstate shipments, had, in effect, been overruled by later decisions of the United States Supreme Court. See Williams v. Commonwealth, 190 Va. 280, 56 S.E.2d 537 (1949).

Former § 4-72 is a criminal statute and must be strictly construed. Its breach by the accused must be shown beyond a reasonable doubt. Newman v. Commonwealth, 187 Va. 803, 48 S.E.2d 355 (1948).

Former § 4-72 nowhere prohibits the accumulation or storing of liquor lawfully acquired in a truck or vehicle. The prohibition is against "transportation." Newman v. Commonwealth, 187 Va. 803, 48 S.E.2d 355 (1948).

Evidence held insufficient to sustain a conviction under former § 4-72. Newman v. Commonwealth, 187 Va. 803, 48 S.E.2d 355 (1948).

§ 4.1-312. Limitation on carrying alcoholic beverages in motor vehicle transporting passengers for hire; penalty.

The transportation of alcoholic beverages in any motor vehicle which is being used, or is licensed, for the transportation of passengers for hire is prohibited, except when carried in the possession of a passenger who is being transported for compensation at the regular rate and fare charged other passengers.

Any person convicted of a violation of this section shall be guilty of a Class 1 misdemeanor.

History.
Code 1950, § 4-74; 1993, c. 866.

Cross references.
As to punishment for Class 1 misdemeanors, see § 18.2-11.

§ 4.1-313. Possessing, transporting, etc., alcoholic beverages illegally acquired; penalty.

A. No person, other than a common carrier, shall have, possess, keep, carry, ship or transport alcoholic beverages upon which the tax imposed by the laws of the United States has not been paid.

B. No person shall possess alcoholic beverages in amounts in excess of the limits provided in § 4.1-311 in containers not bearing evidence that they have been purchased from the Board or a person licensed to sell them, or other evidence that the tax due to the Commonwealth or the markup required by the Board has been paid, unless it can be proved that the alcoholic beverages were lawfully acquired by the possessor.

C. Any person convicted of a violation of this section shall be guilty of a Class 1 misdemeanor.

History.
Code 1950, § 4-75; 1954, c. 484; 1966, c. 408; 1974, c. 460; 1975, c. 481; 1976, c. 36; 1984, c. 603; 1993, c. 866.

Cross references.
As to punishment for Class 1 misdemeanors, see § 18.2-11. As to prior conviction of illegal sale of liquor as bar to prosecution for illegal possession, see note to § 19.2-294.

CASE NOTES

Editor's note.
The cases noted below were decided under former § 4-75, now repealed, which covered the same subject matter as this section.

Rules of law and evidence same as for other crimes. — Except so far as modified by statute the rules of law and evidence are the same in prosecutions for violation of statutes prohibiting the manufacture and possession of intoxicating liquor as in prosecutions for other crimes. Sutherland v. Commonwealth, 171 Va. 485, 198 S.E. 452 (1938).

The possession contemplated by this section is a guilty possession and the accused must have a connection with the ownership. Sutherland v. Commonwealth, 171 Va. 485, 198 S.E. 452 (1938); Fairfax v. Commonwealth, 177 Va. 824, 13 S.E.2d 315 (1941).

Both possession and want of stamps or seals must be proved. — Both the fact of possession and the further fact that the spirits have no legal stamps or seals thereon must be proved. Sutherland v. Commonwealth, 171 Va. 485, 198 S.E. 452 (1938); Saunders v. Commonwealth, 178 Va. 100, 16 S.E.2d 383 (1941), wherein the essential fact of possession was proven.

And possession cannot be presumed. — The fact of possession must be proved and is not presumed. Sutherland v. Commonwealth, 171 Va. 485, 198 S.E. 452 (1938).

The presence of liquor upon the premises of the owner or occupant is not sufficient, in the absence of statute, to overcome the presumption of innocence. Sutherland v. Commonwealth, 171 Va. 485, 198 S.E. 452 (1938); Pardue v. Commonwealth, 183 Va. 277, 32 S.E.2d 77 (1944).

The presence of the liquor in the home is undoubtedly a suspicious circumstance but of itself is not enough to justify a conviction. Sutherland v. Commonwealth, 171 Va. 485, 198 S.E. 452 (1938); Fairfax v. Commonwealth, 177 Va. 824, 13 S.E.2d 315 (1941).

The mere finding of liquor upon the premises occupied by accused and another created no presumption of law that accused was in the possession of it, either individually, or jointly with such other person. Powers v. Commonwealth, 182 Va. 669, 30 S.E.2d 22 (1944).

Wife's careless failure to keep all of her whiskey locked up was held insufficient to make husband guilty. Fairfax v. Commonwealth, 177 Va. 824, 13 S.E.2d 315 (1941); Saunders v. Commonwealth, 178 Va. 100, 16 S.E.2d 383 (1941).

Nor is the presence of a person in an automobile in which liquor is transported. — The mere presence of a person in an automobile in which intoxicating liquor is being illegally transported, with or without his knowledge, which is not shown to be owned by him or under his possession or control, single or joint, is not a crime, nor is it made by statute prima facie evidence of his transportation of or aiding or abetting the transportation of the intoxicating liquor in the automobile, nor is it alone sufficient to sustain a conviction of him upon a charge of illegally transporting intoxicating liquor. Worsham v. Commonwealth, 184 Va. 192, 34 S.E.2d 234 (1945).

Burden of showing that whiskey was being transported in interstate commerce. — In a prosecution for violating former § 4-75, the burden of showing that the whiskey is being transported in interstate commerce is upon the accused. Whitaker v. Commonwealth, 170 Va. 621, 195 S.E. 486 (1938).

Effect of storing and breaking original packages. — In a prosecution for violation of former § 4-75, cases of unstamped whiskey, two of which had been opened and bottles removed therefrom and distributed, were found in accused's automobile on his premises. Accused claimed that the whiskey was being transported in interstate commerce, and accused's nephew stated that the whiskey had been purchased by him in Kentucky for delivery in Florida and that accused had no knowledge that the whiskey was in the automobile. It was held that even if the shipment were interstate originally, the interstate character was changed by the storing of the liquor in accused's car and breaking the original packages. When the cases were broken and the bottles of whiskey removed and distributed, this destroyed the immunity, if it had ever been an interstate shipment. Whitaker v. Commonwealth, 170 Va. 621, 195 S.E. 486 (1938).

Sufficiency of evidence. — See Smith v. Commonwealth, 182 Va. 585, 30 S.E.2d 26 (1944); Pardue v. Commonwealth, 183 Va. 277, 32 S.E.2d 77 (1944); Worsham v. Commonwealth, 184 Va. 192, 34 S.E.2d 234 (1945); Sturgis v. Commonwealth, 197 Va. 264, 88 S.E.2d 919 (1955).

Remand of case. — Where the judgment of the trial court is reversed and the verdict of the jury set aside, and the Commonwealth has apparently fully developed its evidence, the case will be remanded to the trial court, with the direction to dismiss the accused from further prosecution under the charge in the warrant. Sutherland v. Commonwealth, 171 Va. 485, 198 S.E. 452 (1938).

§ 4.1-314. Keeping, possessing or storing still or distilling apparatus without a permit; penalty.

No person shall keep, store or have in his possession any still, or distilling apparatus, without a permit from the Board.

Any person convicted of a violation of this section shall be guilty of a Class 1 misdemeanor.

History.
Code 1950, § 4-77; 1993, c. 866.

Cross references.
As to punishment for Class 1 misdemeanors, see § 18.2-11.

CASE NOTES

Editor's note.
The cases noted below were decided under former § 4-77, now repealed, which covered the same subject matter as this section.

Use of still not necessary to support conviction. — The possession of a still constituted an offense under former § 4-77, regardless of whether or not it was used in the manufacturing of ardent spirits. So the refusal of an instruction to the effect that it must be so used was proper. Hawkins v. Commonwealth, 138 Va. 751, 120 S.E. 854 (1924).

Finding still within dwelling. — An instruction that distilling apparatus found within one's dwelling is presumed to be the property of the person occupying the premises, would be misleading and improper, except when relied upon in a prosecution against an occupant of the premises. Hudgins v. Commonwealth, 142 Va. 628, 128 S.E. 565 (1925).

Finding upon premises as possession. — Where stills, still sites, barrels of mash, and apparatuses used in the manufacturing of ardent spirits are found on the premises of the accused, together with some incriminating evidence, they are held sufficient to support a conviction of the accused of the possession of stills and appliances, etc. This is true even though there is evidence contradicting such possession. See Anthony v. Commonwealth, 142 Va. 577, 128 S.E. 633 (1925); Barrack v. Commonwealth, 142 Va. 596,

128 S.E. 638 (1925); Carr v. Commonwealth, 142 Va. 602, 128 S.E. 454 (1925); Hudgins v. Commonwealth, 142 Va. 628, 128 S.E. 565 (1925).

§ 4.1-315. Possession without license to sell alcoholic beverages upon premises of restaurant; exceptions; penalty.

A. No alcoholic beverages shall be kept or allowed to be kept upon any premises or upon the person of any proprietor or person employed upon the premises of a restaurant or other place where food or refreshments of any kind are furnished for compensation, except such alcoholic beverages as such person owning or operating such place of business is licensed to purchase and to sell at such place of business.

B. This section shall not apply to (i) any residence; (ii) alcoholic beverages in the possession of a passenger being transported for compensation as provided in subsection D of § 4.1-308; (iii) dining areas in restaurants licensed by the Board while such areas are in use for private meetings or parties limited in attendance to members and guests of a particular group, association or organization; (iv) licensed restaurants in office buildings, industrial or similar facilities while such restaurant is closed to the public and is in use for private meetings or parties limited in attendance to employees and nonpaying guests of the owner or a lessee of all or part of such building or facility; or (v) any dining areas or private rooms of residents in an assisted living facility as defined in § 63.2-100 and licensed in accordance with Article 1 (§ 63.2-1800 et seq.) of Chapter 18 of Title 63.2.

C. Any person convicted of a violation of this section shall be guilty of a Class 1 misdemeanor.

History.
Code 1950, p. 876, § 4-61; 1954, c. 512; 1958, c. 270; 1968, c. 7; 1972, c. 168; 1974, c. 497; 1990, c. 932; 1993, c. 866; 2010, c. 114.

Cross references.
As to punishment for Class 1 misdemeanors, see § 18.2-11.

The 2010 amendments.
The 2010 amendment by c. 114 added clause (v) of subsection B and made related changes.

§ 4.1-316. Keeping or drinking alcoholic beverages upon premises of club; penalty.

No person operating a club for profit or otherwise, either public or private, shall (i) keep or allow to be kept any alcoholic beverages, either by himself or any other person, upon the premises or (ii) permit the drinking of any alcoholic beverages upon the premises, unless he is licensed to sell alcoholic beverages.

Any person convicted of a violation of this section shall be guilty of a Class 1 misdemeanor.

History.
Code 1950, § 4-61.1; 1954, c. 147; 1993, c. 866.

Cross references.
As to punishment for Class 1 misdemeanors, see § 18.2-11.

§ 4.1-317. Maintaining common nuisances; penalties.

A. All houses, boathouses, buildings, club or fraternity or lodge rooms, boats, cars and places of every description where alcoholic beverages are manufactured, stored, sold, dispensed, given away or used contrary to law, by any scheme or device whatever, shall be deemed common nuisances.

No person shall maintain, aid, abet or knowingly associate with others in maintaining a common nuisance.

Any person convicted of a violation of this subsection shall be guilty of a Class 1 misdemeanor.

B. In addition, after due notice and opportunity to be heard on the part of any owner or lessor not involved in the original offense, by a proceeding analogous to that provided in §§ 4.1-339 through 4.1-348 and upon proof of guilty knowledge, judgment may be given that such house, building, boathouse, car or other place, or any room or part thereof, be closed. The court may, upon the owner or lessor giving bond in the penalty of not less than $500 and with security to be approved by the court, conditioned that the premises shall not be used for unlawful purposes, or in violation of the provisions of this chapter for a period of five years, turn the same over to its owner or lessor; or proceeding may be had in equity as provided in § 4.1-335.

C. In a proceeding under this section, judgment shall not be entered against the owner, lessor, or lienholder of the property unless it is proved he (i) knew of the unlawful use of the property and (ii) had the right, because of such unlawful use, to enter and repossess the property.

History.
Code 1950, p. 877, § 4-81; 1954, c. 484; 1993, c. 866.

Cross references.
As to punishment for Class 1 misdemeanors, see § 18.2-11. For general statutes relating to public or common nuisances, see §§ 48-1 through 48-6.

CASE NOTES

Editor's note.
The cases noted below were decided under former § 4-81, now repealed, which covered the same subject matter as this section.

Commonwealth must establish two distinct facts for conviction. — Before a conviction can be sustained under former § 4-81, it is necessary for the Commonwealth to establish two separate and distinct facts. First, that alcoholic beverages were habitually used upon the premises contrary to law, and, second, that the defendant maintained, aided, abetted, or knowingly was associated with another in such unlawful use. St. Clair v. Commonwealth, 174 Va. 480, 5 S.E.2d 512 (1939); Crowe v. Commonwealth, 193 Va. 752, 71 S.E.2d 77 (1952); Luttrell v. Commonwealth, 208 Va. 774, 160 S.E.2d 757 (1968).

Beyond a reasonable doubt. — The essential elements necessary to sustain a conviction under former § 4-81 must be established beyond a reasonable doubt. Crowe v. Commonwealth, 193 Va. 752, 71 S.E.2d 77 (1952).

A device for dispensing whiskey to persons who contribute a sufficient sum for juke box music is a subterfuge outlawed by former § 4-81. McCullough v. Commonwealth, 182 Va. 26, 27 S.E.2d 904 (1943).

Admissibility of evidence. — The evidence for the Commonwealth was that the home of accused was visited at various times by men and women, that some entered the home sober and left it drunk, others were intoxicated when they came and left in an intoxicated condition, and that some left carrying small packages. It was held that this class of evidence was admissible and was a circumstance to be considered, but it was only one of many circumstances to be considered by the jury in determining the guilt of accused. Woods v. Commonwealth, 171 Va. 543, 199 S.E. 465 (1938).

Evidence held sufficient. — While the evidence tending to establish the guilt of accused was circumstantial, considered as a whole it was sufficient to sustain a verdict of guilty. Woods v. Commonwealth, 171 Va. 543, 199 S.E. 465 (1938).

The evidence showed that the premises were so conducted that parties entering could first be surveyed by the inmates, a number of bottles of distilled spirits and beer were found on the premises, several of the people in the house were under the influence of liquor, and for some time prior to the search visitors to the house entered sober and came out in such an intoxicated condition that they were arrested for drunkenness. It was held that the evidence was conclusive that accused was the operator of what is commonly termed a "nip joint." Smith v. Commonwealth, 171 Va. 480, 198 S.E. 432 (1938).

In a prosecution for maintaining a common nuisance by dispensing alcoholic beverages in violation of former § 4-81, it was held that the evidence showed the guilt of accused. McCullough v. Commonwealth, 182 Va. 26, 27 S.E.2d 904 (1943).

Evidence held insufficient. — In a prosecution for maintaining a common nuisance as defined by former § 4-81, it was held that the evidence was not sufficient to establish beyond a reasonable doubt that alcoholic beverages were dispensed or otherwise used on the premises contrary to law. St. Clair v. Commonwealth, 174 Va. 480, 5 S.E.2d 512 (1939).

Evidence held insufficient to sustain a conviction for maintaining a common nuisance under former § 4-81. Dudley v. Commonwealth, 174 Va. 466, 5 S.E.2d 473 (1939); Crowe v. Commonwealth, 193 Va. 752, 71 S.E.2d 77 (1952).

In a prosecution under former § 4-81, evidence that the officers observed a number of persons visiting the home on one Sunday, and that some of them were drinking, tended to create a suspicion that the building may have been, in common parlance, a "nip joint," but this testimony alone was not sufficient to "produce the full assurance of moral certainty" that whiskey was illegally dispensed or used on the premises. St. Clair v. Commonwealth, 174 Va. 480, 5 S.E.2d 512 (1939).

In a prosecution for maintaining a common nuisance in violation of former § 4-81, police officers found in accused's home 12 pints of whiskey properly sealed and stamped, and three witnesses for the Commonwealth testified that they lived close to the accused but had never been in his home; that they had never seen any whiskey taken in or away from his home or sold there; that they had never heard any unusual noise or commotion there, but that more than the usual number of automobiles stopped in front of the accused's home and that people went in and out, some carrying packages. It was held that the evidence was insufficient to sustain a judgment of conviction. Campbell v. Commonwealth, 167 Va. 448, 187 S.E. 502 (1936).

Where the evidence showed a large number of people visiting defendants' home, including repeat visitors on the same day, the short length of the visits, the reputation of some visitors as drunks, and the presence of substantial quantities of whiskey in pint bottles of various brands on the premises, but no complaints of disturbance or disorder against defendants or the premises, and the evidence was not sufficient to show the whiskey was illegal, or disbursed, or used on the premises, the evidence was not sufficient for court or jury to declare the residence a common nuisance. Luttrell v. Commonwealth, 208 Va. 774, 160 S.E.2d 757 (1968).

§ 4.1-318. Violations by armed person; penalty.

No person shall unlawfully manufacture, transport or sell any alcoholic beverages, and at the time of the unlawful manufacturing, transporting, or selling or aiding or assisting in any manner in such act, shall carry on or about his person, or have on or in any vehicle which he may be using to aid him in any such purpose, or have in his possession, actual or constructive, at or within 100 yards of any place where any such alcoholic beverages are being unlawfully manufactured, transported or sold, any dangerous weapon as described in § 18.2-308.

Any person convicted of a violation of this section shall be guilty of a Class 6 felony.

History.
　Code 1950, § 4-83; 1993, c. 866.

Cross references.
　As to punishment for Class 6 felonies, see § 18.2-10.

CASE NOTES

Editor's note.
　Most of the cases noted below were decided under former § 4-83, now repealed, which covered the same subject matter as this section.

Former section was applicable to the officers of the law, and when they arm themselves and unlawfully transport ardent spirits, they are subject to the penalty. Hall v. Commonwealth, 143 Va. 554, 130 S.E. 416 (1925).

"Manufacture" as herein defined refers to the entire act, including the legislatively created definition of "manufacture" contained in former § 4-57 (d) (see now § 4.1-300). Ruff v. Gathright, 373 F. Supp. 232 (W.D. Va. 1974).

Actual manufacturing does not have to be established to prove a violation of former § 4-83. Ruff v. Gathright, 373 F. Supp. 232 (W.D. Va. 1974).

Possession of a firearm need not be exclusive, and if the weapon is in the immediate area and subject to dominion and control, there is constructive possession. Ruff v. Gathright, 373 F. Supp. 232 (W.D. Va. 1974).

Sufficiency of indictment. — An indictment which charges unlawful manufacture in one count and the possession of a dangerous weapon while so engaged in another, though loosely drawn, substantially follows the statute. If the second count had not referred to the first, it would probably have been held that it failed to follow the statute, making the gravamen the possession. Edens v. Commonwealth, 142 Va. 609, 128 S.E. 555 (1925).

Sufficiency of evidence. — Evidence was sufficient to support defendant's conviction of possessing a firearm while unlawfully selling alcoholic beverages. McLean v. Commonwealth, No. 1159-98-1 (Ct. of Appeals June 22, 1999).

§ 4.1-319. Disobeying subpoena; hindering conduct of hearing; penalty.

No person shall (i) fail or refuse to obey any subpoena issued by the Board, any Board member, or agent authorized by the Board to issue such subpoena or (ii) hinder the orderly conduct and decorum of any hearing held and conducted by the Board, any Board member, or agent authorized by the Board to hold and conduct such hearing.

Any person convicted of a violation of this section shall be guilty of a Class 1 misdemeanor.

History.
　Code 1950, § 4-70; 1993, c. 866.

Cross references.
　As to punishment for Class 1 misdemeanors, see § 18.2-11.

§ 4.1-320. Illegal advertising; penalty; exception.

A. Except in accordance with this title and Board regulations, no person shall advertise in or send any advertising matter into the Commonwealth about or concerning alcoholic beverages other than those which may legally be manufactured or sold without a license.

B. Manufacturers, wholesalers, and retailers may engage in the display of outdoor alcoholic beverage advertising on lawfully erected signs provided such display is done in accordance with § 4.1-112.2 and Board regulations.

C. Except as provided in subsection D, any person convicted of a violation of this section shall be guilty of a Class 1 misdemeanor.

D. For violations of § 4.1-112.2 relating to distance and zoning restrictions on outdoor advertising, the Board shall give the advertiser written notice to take corrective action to either bring the advertisement into compliance with this title and Board regulations or to remove such advertisement. If corrective action is not taken within 30 days, the advertiser shall be guilty of a Class 4 misdemeanor.

E. Neither this section nor any Board regulation shall prohibit (i) the awarding of watches of a wholesale value of less than $100 by a licensed distillery, winery or brewery, to participants in athletic contests; (ii) the exhibition or display of automobiles, boats, or aircraft regularly and normally used in racing or other competitive events and the sponsorship of an automobile, boat or aircraft racing team by a licensed distillery, winery or brewery and the display on the automobile, boat or aircraft and uniforms of the members of the racing team, the trademark or brand name of an alcoholic beverage manufactured by such distillery, winery or brewery; (iii) the sponsorship of a professional athletic event, including, but not limited to, golf, auto racing or tennis, by a licensed distillery, winery or brewery or the use of any trademark or brand name of any alcoholic beverage in connection with such sponsorship; (iv) the advertisement of beer by the display of such product's name on any airship, which advertising is paid for by the manufacturer of such product; (v) the advertisement of beer or any alcoholic beverage by the display of such product's name on any scale model, reproduction or replica of any motor vehicle, aircraft or watercraft offered for sale; (vi) the placement of billboard advertising within stadia, coliseums, or racetracks that are used primarily for professional or semiprofessional athletic or sporting events; or (vii) the sponsorship of an entertainment or cultural event.

History.
Code 1950, § 4-69; 1978, c. 630; 1979, c. 196; 1980, c. 407; 1993, c. 866; 1995, c. 222; 2009, c. 322; 2011, c. 728; 2012, cc. 760, 818.

Cross references.
As to punishment for Class 1 misdemeanors, see § 18.2-11.

Editor's note.
Acts 2011, c. 728, cl. 3, provides: "That the provisions of subsections B through E of § 4.1-320 of this act shall expire on January 1, 2013."Acts 2012, cc. 760 and 818, effective April 18, 2012, amended this section by deleting former subsections B through E. Therefore current subsections B through E will not expire.

Acts 2011, c. 728, cl. 4, provides: "That the expiration of certain provisions of § 4.1-320 in accordance with the third enactment of this act shall not invalidate any regulations adopted pursuant thereto by the Alcoholic Beverage Control Board."

Acts 2011, c. 728, cl. 5, provides: "That the provisions of this act or the application thereof to any person or circumstances that are held invalid shall not affect the validity of other provisions of this act or application of this act that can be given effect without the invalid provisions or applications."

The 2009 amendments.
The 2009 amendment by c. 322 added clause (vi) to the third paragraph and made a related change.

The 2011 amendments.
The 2011 amendment by c. 728, effective March 23, 2011, added subsections B through E and the subsection A, F, and G designators. See Editor's note for expiration for subsections B through E.

The 2012 amendments.
The 2012 amendments by cc. 760 and 818, effective April 18, 2012, are identical and inserted "this title and" in subsection A; deleted former subsection B, C, D, E, regarding signs and advertising; added new subsection B and substituted current subsection C for former F, which read: "Any person convicted of a violation of this section shall be guilty of a Class 1 misdemeanor."; added subsection D; and redesignated former subsection G as subsection E.

§ 4.1-321. Delivery of alcoholic beverages to prisoners in jail prohibited; penalty.

No person shall deliver, or cause to be delivered, to any prisoner in any local correctional facility, any alcoholic beverage.

Any person convicted of a violation of this section shall be guilty of a Class 1 misdemeanor.

History.
Code 1950, § 4-93; 1993, c. 866.

Cross references.
As to punishment for Class 1 misdemeanors, see § 18.2-11.

§ 4.1-322. Possession or consumption of alcoholic beverages by interdicted persons; penalty.

No person who has been interdicted pursuant to § 4.1-333 or § 4.1-334 shall possess any alcoholic beverages, except those acquired in accordance with subdivisions 1 through 5 of § 4.1-200, nor be drunk in public in violation of § 18.2-388.

Any interdicted person found to be in violation of this section shall be guilty of a Class 1 misdemeanor.

History.
Code 1950, § 4-52; 1954, c. 484; 1982, c. 66; 1993, c. 866; 1996, c. 717.

Cross references.
As to punishment for Class 1 misdemeanors, see § 18.2-11.

CASE NOTES

Constitutionality. — This section does not violate the Eighth Amendment by imposing criminal punishment for the status of being an alcoholic nor did it violate the Equal Protection Clause of the Fourteenth Amendment by treating homeless alcoholics disparately; further, because defendant failed to present evidence that he was homeless, he lacked standing to challenge the statute based on this classification. Jackson v. Commonwealth, 44 Va. App. 218, 604 S.E.2d 122, 2004 Va. App. LEXIS 514 (2004).

Sentence imposed was not disproportionate. — Given defendant's long history of arrests and continued failure to abide by the interdiction order, a 90-day jail sentence was not grossly disproportionate to the crime committed. Jackson v. Commonwealth, 44 Va. App. 218, 604 S.E.2d 122, 2004 Va. App. LEXIS 514 (2004).

CIRCUIT COURT OPINIONS

Constitutionality. — Because interdicted alcoholics were not a protected class, the Equal Protection Clause was not implicated; the charge under § 4.1-322 would not be dismissed since defendant was not facing criminal sanction for his mere status, but because he was drunk in public on a particular occasion. Commonwealth v. Reyes, 72 Va. Cir. 105, 2006 Va. Cir. LEXIS 279 (Alexandria 2006).

§ 4.1-323. Attempts; aiding or abetting; penalty.

No person shall attempt to do any of the things prohibited by this title or to aid or abet another in doing, or attempting to do, any of the things prohibited by this title.

On an indictment, information or warrant for the violation of this title, the jury or the court may find the defendant guilty of an attempt, or being an accessory, and the punishment shall be the same as if the defendant were solely guilty of such violation.

History.
Code 1950, § 4-87; 1993, c. 866.

CASE NOTES

Editor's note.
The cases noted below were decided under former § 4-87, now repealed, which covered the same subject matter as this section.

Effect of section as to attempts. — The effect of former § 4-87 is to write into each indictment charging unlawful manufacture of intoxicants the charge of an attempt, and the consummated crime and the attempt by statute stand upon exactly the same footing and the punishment in each instance is the same. Trent v. Commonwealth, 155 Va. 1128, 156 S.E. 567 (1931).

While the courts must exercise judgment and discretion in construing any doubtful provisions of the prohibition act, the terms of the statute leave no room to doubt that any willful attempt to violate the law in any substantial particular must be regarded as a crime, and punishable accordingly. In other words, whenever a conviction ought to be sustained if the offense had been consummated, a conviction for conduct which in law amounts to an attempt to commit the same offense should be sustained. Collins v. City of Radford, 134 Va. 518, 113 S.E. 735 (1922).

No evidence of attempt. — Accused drove up to still to get whiskey and was told that none was ready, but that he should wait. While he was waiting the still was raided. It was held that there was not evidence to convict the accused of an attempt to transport, the direct act toward its commission not having been committed. Andrews v. Commonwealth, 135 Va. 451, 115 S.E. 558 (1923). But see Collins v. City of Radford, 134 Va. 518, 113 S.E. 735 (1922).

Effect where principal guilty of prior offenses. — While it is true that the general rule is that an accessory is amenable to the same punishment as the principal, this general rule is not applicable to one aiding and abetting a principal who has been guilty of prior offenses. In derogation of the general rule this fixes the status of an aider or abettor and provides that the punishment shall be the same as if the defendant were solely guilty of such violation. Seay v. Commonwealth, 155 Va. 1087, 156 S.E. 574 (1931).

Accused held not principal or accessory. — Accused by taking two drinks from a bottle tendered him by a companion in an automobile did not become guilty of the offense of transporting the liquor as a principal in the second degree upon the principle that, being present, he aided and abetted the act. His conduct in drinking from the bottle may have indicated an approval of what they had done and were continuing to do, but it cannot be fairly said to have constituted him a participant in the transportation either as a principal or an accessory. Hitt v. Commonwealth, 131 Va. 752, 109 S.E. 597 (1921).

ARTICLE 2.

PROHIBITED PRACTICES BY LICENSEES.

Michie's Jurisprudence.
For related discussion, see 10B M.J. Intoxicating Liquors, §§ 35, 36.

§ 4.1-324. Illegal sale or keeping of alcoholic beverages by licensees; penalty.

A. No licensee or any agent or employee of such licensee shall:

1. Sell any alcoholic beverages of a kind other than that which such license or this title authorizes him to sell;

2. Sell beer to which wine, spirits or alcohol has been added, except that a mixed beverage licensee may combine wine or spirits, or both, with beer pursuant to a patron's order;

3. Sell wine to which spirits or alcohol, or both, have been added, otherwise than as required in the manufacture thereof under Board regulations, except that a mixed beverage licensee may (i) make sangria that contains brandy, triple sec, or other similar spirits and (ii) combine beer or spirits, or both, with wine pursuant to a patron's order;

4. Sell alcoholic beverages of a kind which such license or this title authorizes him to sell, but to any person other than to those to whom such license or this title authorizes him to sell;

5. Sell alcoholic beverages which such license or this title authorizes him to sell, but in any place or in any manner other than such license or this title authorizes him to sell;

6. Sell any alcoholic beverages when forbidden by this title;

7. Keep or allow to be kept, other than in his residence and for his personal use, any alcoholic beverages other than that which he is authorized to sell by such license or by this title;

8. Sell any beer to a retail licensee, except for cash, if the seller holds a brewery, bottler's or wholesale beer license;

9. Sell any beer on draft and fail to display to customers the brand of beer sold or misrepresent the brand of any beer sold;

10. Sell any wine for delivery within the Commonwealth to a retail licensee, except for cash, if the seller holds a wholesale wine or farm winery license;

11. Keep or allow to be kept or sell any vaporized form of an alcoholic beverage produced by an alcohol vaporizing device;

12. Keep any alcoholic beverage other than in the bottle or container in which it was purchased by him except: (i) for a frozen alcoholic beverage; and (ii) in the case of wine, in containers of a type approved by the Board pending automatic dispensing and sale of such wine; or

13. Establish any normal or customary pricing of its alcoholic beverages that is intended as a shift or device to evade any "happy hour" regulations adopted by the Board; however, a licensee may increase the volume of an alcoholic beverage sold to a customer if there is a commensurate increase in the normal or customary price charged for the same alcoholic beverage.

B. Any person convicted of a violation of this section shall be guilty of a Class 1 misdemeanor.

C. Neither this section nor any Board regulation shall prohibit an on-premises restaurant licensee from using alcoholic beverages that the licensee otherwise is authorized to purchase and possess for the purposes of preparing and selling for on-premises consumption food products with a final alcohol content of more than one-half of one percent by volume, as long as such food products are sold to and consumed by persons who are 21 years of age or older.

History.
Code 1950, § 4-60; 1970, c. 360; 1974, c. 460; 1984, c. 603; 1993, c. 866; 1998, c. 238; 2006, c. 714; 2008, cc. 513, 629, 875.

Cross references.
As to punishment for Class 1 misdemeanors, see § 18.2-11.

CASE NOTES

Editor's note.
The case noted below was decided under former § 4-60, now repealed, which covered the same subject matter as this section.

To allow a thing to be done is to acquiesce in or tolerate, and knowledge, express or implied, is essential. McDiarmid v. Commonwealth, 184 Va. 478, 35 S.E.2d 813 (1945).

Doctrine of respondeat superior not applicable. — Owner did not "allow" liquor found in club premises owned by him to be so kept in the club as to make him amenable to the doctrine of respondeat superior. McDiarmid v. Commonwealth, 184 Va. 478, 35 S.E.2d 813 (1945).

§ 4.1-325. Prohibited acts by mixed beverage licensees; penalty.

A. In addition to § 4.1-324, no mixed beverage licensee nor any agent or employee of such licensee shall:

1. Sell or serve any alcoholic beverage other than as authorized by law;

2. Sell any authorized alcoholic beverage to any person or at any place except as authorized by law;

3. Allow at the place described in his license the consumption of alcoholic beverages in violation of this title;

4. Keep at the place described in his license any alcoholic beverage other than that which he is licensed to sell;

5. Misrepresent the brand of any alcoholic beverage sold or offered for sale;

6. Keep any alcoholic beverage other than in the bottle or container in which it was purchased by him except (i) for a frozen alcoholic beverage, which may include alcoholic beverages in a frozen drink dispenser of a type approved by the Board; (ii) in the case of wine, in containers of a type approved by the Board pending automatic dispensing and sale of such wine; and (iii) as otherwise provided by Board regulation. Neither this subdivision nor any Board regulation shall prohibit any mixed beverage licensee from pre-mixing containers of sangria to be served and sold for consumption on the licensed premises;

7. Refill or partly refill any bottle or container of alcoholic beverage or dilute or otherwise tamper with the contents of any bottle or container of alcoholic beverage, except as provided by Board regulation adopted pursuant to § 4.1-111 B 11;

8. Sell or serve any brand of alcoholic beverage which is not the same as that ordered by the purchaser without first advising such purchaser of the difference;

9. Remove or obliterate any label, mark or stamp affixed to any container of alcoholic beverages offered for sale;

10. Deliver or sell the contents of any container if the label, mark or stamp has been removed or obliterated;

11. Allow any obscene conduct, language, literature, pictures, performance or materials on the licensed premises;

12. Allow any striptease act on the licensed premises;

13. Allow persons connected with the licensed business to appear nude or partially nude;

14. Consume or allow the consumption by an employee of any alcoholic beverages while on duty and in a position that is involved in the selling or serving of alcoholic beverages to customers.

The provisions of this subdivision shall not prohibit any retail licensee or his designated employee from (i) consuming product samples or sample servings of (a) beer or wine provided by a representative of a licensed beer or wine wholesaler or manufacturer or (b) a distilled spirit provided by a permittee of the Board who represents a distiller, if such samples are provided in accordance with Board regulations and the retail licensee or his designated employee does not violate the provisions of subdivision 1 f of § 4.1-225 or (ii) tasting an alcoholic beverage that has been or will be delivered to a customer for quality control purposes;

15. Deliver to a consumer an original bottle of an alcoholic beverage purchased under such license

whether the closure is broken or unbroken except in accordance with § 4.1-210.

The provisions of this subdivision shall not apply to the delivery of:

a. "Soju." For the purposes of this clause, "soju" means a traditional Korean alcoholic beverage distilled from rice, barley or sweet potatoes; or

b. Spirits, provided (i) the original container is no larger than 375 milliliters, (ii) the alcohol content is no greater than 15 percent by volume, and (iii) the contents of the container are carbonated and perishable;

16. Be intoxicated while on duty or employ an intoxicated person on the licensed premises;

17. Conceal any sale or consumption of any alcoholic beverages;

18. Fail or refuse to make samples of any alcoholic beverages available to the Board upon request or obstruct special agents of the Board in the discharge of their duties;

19. Store alcoholic beverages purchased under the license in any unauthorized place or remove any such alcoholic beverages from the premises;

20. Knowingly employ in the licensed business any person who has the general reputation as a prostitute, panderer, habitual law violator, person of ill repute, user or peddler of narcotics, or person who drinks to excess or engages in illegal gambling;

21. Keep on the licensed premises a slot machine or any prohibited gambling or gaming device, machine or apparatus;

22. Make any gift of an alcoholic beverage, other than as a gift made (i) to a personal friend, as a matter of normal social intercourse, so long as the gift is in no way a shift or device to evade the restriction set forth in this subdivision; (ii) to a person responsible for the planning, preparation or conduct on any conference, convention, trade show or event held or to be held on the premises of the licensee, when such gift is made in the course of usual and customary business entertainment and is in no way a shift or device to evade the restriction set forth in this subdivision; (iii) pursuant to subsection C of § 4.1-209; or (iv) pursuant to subdivision A 12 of § 4.1-201. Any gift permitted by this subdivision shall be subject to the taxes imposed by this title on sales of alcoholic beverages. The licensee shall keep complete and accurate records of gifts given in accordance with this subdivision; or

23. Establish any normal or customary pricing of its alcoholic beverages that is intended as a shift or device to evade any "happy hour" regulations adopted by the Board; however, a licensee may increase the volume of an alcoholic beverage sold to a customer if there is a commensurate increase in the normal or customary price charged for the same alcoholic beverage.

B. Any person convicted of a violation of this section shall be guilty of a Class 1 misdemeanor.

C. The provisions of subdivisions A 12 and A 13 shall not apply to persons operating theaters, con-cert halls, art centers, museums, or similar establishments that are devoted primarily to the arts or theatrical performances, when the performances that are presented are expressing matters of serious literary, artistic, scientific, or political value.

History.
1968, c. 7, § 4-98.10; 1970, c. 120; 1974, c. 548; 1975, c. 483; 1976, cc. 750, 768; 1978, c. 69; 1979, c. 227; 1982, c. 316; 1983, c. 608; 1993, c. 866; 2000, c. 780; 2002, c. 105; 2003, c. 856; 2004, c. 913; 2006, cc. 256, 826; 2008, cc. 513, 629, 794, 875; 2009, cc. 20, 509; 2010, c. 481; 2013, c. 661.

Cross references.
As to punishment for Class 1 misdemeanors, see § 18.2-11.

The 2009 amendments.
The 2009 amendments by cc. 20 and 509 are identical, and rewrote the second paragraph in subdivision A 15, inserting the A 15 a. designation and adding subdivision A 15 b.

The 2010 amendments.
The 2010 amendment by c. 481 inserted clause A 6 (iii) and made a related change; and inserted "except as provided by Board regulation adopted pursuant to § 4.1-111 B 11" at the end of subdivision A 7.

The 2013 amendments.
The 2013 amendments by c. 661 substituted "subdivision 1 f" for "subdivision 1 g" in clause (i) (b) of the second paragraph of subdivision A 14.

CASE NOTES

First Amendment analysis. — Virginia's alcohol licensing program, which allowed nightclubs employing erotic dancers to serve beer and wine but not mixed beverages, survived intermediate scrutiny, as the public interest served by the policy was substantial, the restriction on the clubs mild, and the burden on First Amendment values slight. Imaginary Images, Inc. v. Evans, 612 F.3d 736, 2010 U.S. App. LEXIS 14535 (4th Cir. July 15, 2010).

Offenses not crimes involving moral turpitude. — Indictments charging a defendant with keeping and selling unauthorized alcoholic beverages and with refilling and transferring alcoholic beverages in bottles other than those in which they were purchased, in violation of former § 4-98.10, did not describe crimes involving moral turpitude, so as to allow introduction of evidence of conviction for purposes of impeachment of credibility in a subsequent prosecution for perjury; although, under the circumstances of the case, the trial court's instruction to the jury allowing consideration of the evidence did not prejudice the defendant. Hackman v. Commonwealth, 220 Va. 710, 261 S.E.2d 555 (1980) (decided under former § 4-98.10).

§ 4.1-325.1. Falsifying application; penalty.

It shall be unlawful for any applicant for a banquet or special events license pursuant to § 4.1-209 or mixed beverage special events license pursuant to § 4.1-210 to knowingly make a false statement in order to secure a license or to alter, change, borrow, or lend or attempt to use, borrow, or lend a license. Any person violating this provision shall be guilty of a Class 3 misdemeanor.

History.
2002, c. 104.

Cross references.
As to punishment for Class 3 misdemeanors, see § 18.2-11.

§ 4.1-325.2. Prohibited acts by employees of wine or beer licensees; penalty.

A. In addition to the provisions of § 4.1-324, no retail wine or beer licensee or his agent or employee shall consume any alcoholic beverages while on duty and in a position that is involved in the selling or serving of alcoholic beverages to customers.

The provisions of this subsection shall not prohibit any retail licensee or his designated employee from (i) consuming product samples or sample servings of beer or wine provided by a representative of a licensed beer or wine wholesaler or manufacturer, if such samples are provided in accordance with Board regulations and the retail licensee or his designated employee does not violate the provisions of subdivision 1 f of § 4.1-225 or (ii) tasting an alcoholic beverage that has been or will be delivered to a customer for quality control purposes.

B. For the purposes of subsection A, a wine or beer wholesaler or farm winery licensee or its employees that participate in a wine or beer tasting sponsored by a retail wine or beer licensee shall not be deemed to be agents of the retail wine or beer licensee.

C. No retail wine or beer licensee, or his agent or employee shall make any gift of an alcoholic beverage, other than as a gift made (i) to a personal friend, as a matter of normal social intercourse, so long as the gift is in no way a shift or device to evade the restriction set forth in this subsection; (ii) to a person responsible for the planning, preparation or conduct on any conference, convention, trade show or event held or to be held on the premises of the licensee, when such gift is made in the course of usual and customary business entertainment and is in no way a shift or device to evade the restriction set forth in this subsection; (iii) pursuant to subsection C of § 4.1-209; or (iv) pursuant to subdivision A 12 of § 4.1-201. Any gift permitted by this subsection shall be subject to the taxes imposed by this title on sales of alcoholic beverages. The licensee shall keep complete and accurate records of gifts given in accordance with this subsection.

D. Any person convicted of a violation of this section shall be subject to a civil penalty in an amount not to exceed $500.

History.
2002, c. 105; 2003, c. 856; 2006, cc. 256, 826; 2013, c. 661.

The number of this section was assigned by the Virginia Code Commission, the number in the 2002 act having been 4.1-325.1.

The 2013 amendments.
The 2013 amendment by c. 661 substituted "subdivision 1 f" for "subdivision 1 g" in clause (i) of the second paragraph of subsection A.

§ 4.1-326. Sale of; purchase for resale; wine or beer from a person without a license; penalty.

No licensee, other than a common carrier operating in interstate or foreign commerce, licensed to sell wine or beer at retail shall purchase for resale or sell any wine or beer purchased from anyone other than a wholesale wine, farm winery, brewery, bottler's or wholesale beer licensee.

Any person convicted of a violation of this section shall be guilty of a Class 1 misdemeanor.

History.
Code 1950, §§ 4-64, 4-66; 1984, c. 200; 1988, c. 261; 1993, c. 866.

Cross references.
As to punishment for Class 1 misdemeanors, see § 18.2-11.

§ 4.1-327. Prohibiting transfer of wine or beer by licensees; penalty.

A. No retail licensee, except (i) a retail on-premises wine and beer licensee or (ii) a retail on-premises beer licensee, shall transfer any wine or beer from one licensed place of business to another licensed place of business whether such places of business are under the same ownership or not.

B. Any person convicted of a violation of this section shall be guilty of a Class 1 misdemeanor.

History.
1954, c. 338, § 4-34.1; 1993, c. 866.

Cross references.
As to punishment for Class 1 misdemeanors, see § 18.2-11.

§ 4.1-328. Prohibited trade practices; penalty.

A. No person subject to the jurisdiction of the Board shall violate, attempt to violate, solicit another person to violate or consent to any violation of § 4.1-216 or 4.1-216.1, or regulations adopted pursuant to subdivision B 3 of § 4.1-111.

B. Any person found by the Board to have committed a violation of this section shall be subject to a civil penalty as provided in § 4.1-227.

History.
1989, c. 528, § 4-79.1; 1992, c. 349; 1993, c. 866; 2007, c. 494.

Editor's note.
Acts 2007, c. 494, cl. 2, provides: "That the Alcoholic Beverage Control Board shall (i) include as part of its inspection of any retail licensee's records a review of evidence of procurement, including payment, required by this act to be maintained by that retail licensee involving the procurement of alcoholic beverage advertising materials and (ii) report annually to the House Committee on General Laws and the Senate Committee on Rehabilitation and Social Services the following information: (a) the results of any audits of retail records involving the procurement, including purchases, of alcoholic beverage advertising materials authorized by this act and (b) the extent to which the Board has achieved compliance with the provisions of this act."

§ 4.1-329. Illegal advertising materials; penalty.

No person subject to the jurisdiction of the Board shall induce, attempt to induce, or consent to, any manufacturer, as defined in § 4.1-216.1, or any wholesale licensee selling, renting, lending, buying for or giving to any person any advertising materials or decorations under circumstances prohibited by this title or Board regulations.

Any person found by the Board to have violated this section shall be subject to a civil penalty as provided in § 4.1-227.

History.
1981, c. 574, § 4-69.2; 1993, c. 866; 2007, c. 494.

Editor's note.
Acts 2007, c. 494, cl. 2, provides: "That the Alcoholic Beverage Control Board shall (i) include as part of its inspection of any retail licensee's records a review of evidence of procurement, including payment, required by this act to be maintained by that retail licensee involving the procurement of alcoholic beverage advertising materials and (ii) report annually to the House Committee on General Laws and the Senate Committee on Rehabilitation and Social Services the following information: (a) the results of any audits of retail records involving the procurement, including purchases, of alcoholic beverage advertising materials authorized by this act and (b) the extent to which the Board has achieved compliance with the provisions of this act."

§ 4.1-330. Solicitation by persons interested in manufacture, etc., of alcoholic beverages; penalty.

A. No person having any interest, direct or indirect, in the manufacture, distribution, or sale of spirits or other alcoholic beverages shall, without a permit granted by the Board and upon such conditions as the Board may prescribe, solicit either directly or indirectly (i) a mixed beverage licensee; (ii) any agent, servant, or employee of such licensee; or (iii) any person connected with the licensee in any capacity whatsoever in his licensed business, to sell or offer for sale the particular spirits or other alcoholic beverage in which such person may be so interested.

The Board, upon proof of any solicitation in violation of this subsection, may suspend or terminate the sale through government stores or its purchase of the brand of spirits or other alcoholic beverage which was the subject matter of the unlawful solicitation or promotion. In addition, the Board may suspend or terminate the sale through such stores or its purchase of all brands of spirits or other alcoholic beverages manufactured or distributed by either the employer or principal of such solicitor, the broker, or by the owner of the brand of spirits unlawfully solicited or promoted. The Board may impose a civil penalty not to exceed $250,000 in lieu of such suspension or termination of sales through government stores or purchases by the Board or portion thereof, or both.

Any person convicted of a violation of this subsection shall be guilty of a Class 1 misdemeanor.

B. No mixed beverage licensee or any agent, servant, or employee of such licensee, or any person connected with the licensee in any capacity whatsoever in his licensed business shall, either directly or indirectly, be a party to, consent to, solicit, or aid or abet another in a violation of subsection A.

The Board may suspend or revoke the license granted to such licensee, or may impose a civil penalty not to exceed $25,000 in lieu of such suspension or any portion thereof, or both.

Any person convicted of a violation of this subsection shall be guilty of a Class 1 misdemeanor.

History.
1968, c. 7, § 4-98.16; 1988, c. 786; 1990, c. 442; 1993, c. 866.

Cross references.
As to punishment for Class 1 misdemeanors, see § 18.2-11.

§ 4.1-331. Failure to pay tax or to deliver, keep and preserve records and accounts, or to allow examination and inspection; penalty.

No licensee shall fail or refuse to (i) pay any tax provided for in § 4.1-234 or § 4.1-236; (ii) deliver, keep and preserve such records, invoices and accounts as are required by § 4.1-204 or Board regulation; or (iii) allow such records, invoices and accounts or his place of business to be examined and inspected in accordance with § 4.1-204.

Any person convicted of a violation of this section shall be guilty of a Class 1 misdemeanor.

History.
Code 1950, § 4-65; 1988, c. 261, § 4-136; 1993, c. 866.

Cross references.
As to punishment for Class 1 misdemeanors, see § 18.2-11.

§ 4.1-332. Nonpayment of excise tax on beer and wine coolers; additional penalties.

A. No person shall sell beer or wine coolers to retailers or consumers without paying the excise tax imposed by § 4.1-236. No retailer shall purchase, receive, transport, store or sell any beer or wine coolers on which such retailer has reason to know such tax has not been paid and may not be paid.

Any person convicted of a violation of this subsection shall be guilty of a Class 1 misdemeanor.

B. In addition to subsection A, on each manufacturer, bottler or wholesaler who fails to make any return and pay the full amount of the tax required by § 4.1-236, there shall be imposed a civil penalty to be added to the tax in the amount of five percent of the proper tax due if the failure is for not more than thirty days, with an additional five percent for each additional thirty days, or fraction thereof, during which the failure continues. Such civil penalty shall not exceed twenty-five percent in the aggregate. In the case of a false or fraudulent return, where willful intent exists to defraud the Commonwealth of any excise tax due on beer and wine coolers, a civil penalty of fifty percent of the amount of the proper tax due shall be assessed. All penalties and interest shall be payable to the Board and if not so paid shall be collectible in the same manner as if they were a part of the tax imposed.

C. After reasonable notice to the manufacturer, bottler, wholesaler or retailer, the Board may suspend or revoke the license of the manufacturer, bottler, wholesaler or retailer who has failed to make any return or to pay the full amount of the excise tax.

History.
 1988, c. 261, §§ 4-139, 4-140; 1993, c. 866.

Cross references.
 As to punishment for Class 1 misdemeanors, see § 18.2-11.

ARTICLE 3.

PROCEDURAL MATTERS.

Michie's Jurisprudence.
 For related discussion, see 10B M.J. Intoxicating Liquors, §§ 28, 35, 38, 46, 48.

§ 4.1-333. Interdiction of intoxicated driver or habitual drunkard.

A. When after a hearing upon due notice it appears to the satisfaction of the circuit court of any county or city that any person, residing within such county or city, has been convicted of driving any automobile, truck, motorcycle, engine or train while intoxicated or has shown himself to be an habitual drunkard, the court may enter an order of interdiction prohibiting the sale of alcoholic beverages to such person until further ordered. The court entering any such order shall file a copy of the order with the Board.

B. The court entering any order of interdiction may alter, amend or cancel such order as it deems proper. A copy of any alteration, amendment or cancellation shall be filed with the Board.

History.
 Code 1950, § 4-51; 1956, c. 53; 1982, c. 66; 1993, c. 866.

CASE NOTES

Editor's note.
 Some of the cases noted below were decided under former § 4-51, now repealed, which covered the same subject matter as this section.

The term "habitual drunkard" clearly encompasses one who is admittedly in the continual habit of being intoxicated from alcohol. Fisher v. Coleman, 486 F. Supp. 311 (W.D. Va. 1979), aff'd, 639 F.2d 191 (4th Cir. 1981).

Plaintiff lacked standing to challenge the interdiction provisions of this section on vagueness and overbreadth grounds in light of his 59 convictions for public drunkenness over a period of slightly more than two years prior to his interdiction, which conduct fell clearly within the challenged language. Fisher v. Coleman, 639 F.2d 191 (4th Cir. 1981).

A person who had 59 convictions of public drunkenness during a period of slightly over two years and whose counselor at the local alcoholic treatment center described him as an incorrigible public drunkard was without standing to allege that the term "habitual drunkard," as used in this section governing interdiction of habitual drunkards, was void for vagueness, since claims of overbreadth and vagueness may not be brought by persons whose actions fall clearly within the terms of the statute in question. Fisher v. Coleman, 486 F. Supp. 311 (W.D. Va. 1979), aff'd, 639 F.2d 191 (4th Cir. 1981).

Application of section not unconstitutional. — Although

former § 4-51, governing interdiction of habitual drunkards, did not precisely define the term "habitual drunkard," it was not unconstitutionally vague as applied to a particular person, in light of that person's admitted alcoholism for 14 years and 59 convictions of public drunkenness in slightly more than two years, and his failure to make efforts to respond to court-ordered medical treatment, especially where he made no contention that had the statute's coverage been known to him, he would have acted differently. Fisher v. Coleman, 486 F. Supp. 311 (W.D. Va. 1979), aff'd, 639 F.2d 191 (4th Cir. 1981).

Section 4.1-322 did not violate the Eighth Amendment by imposing criminal punishment for the status of being an alcoholic nor did it violate the Equal Protection Clause of the Fourteenth Amendment by treating homeless alcoholics disparately; further, because defendant failed to present evidence that he was homeless, he lacked standing to challenge the statute based on this classification. Jackson v. Commonwealth, 44 Va. App. 218, 604 S.E.2d 122, 2004 Va. App. LEXIS 514 (2004).

Purpose of publication of order is to give actual notice. — There was nothing in either former § 4-51 or former § 4-62 (see now § 4.1-304) to indicate that the purpose of the publication of the order of interdiction is other than to give notice to one who might actually see it. There is no suggestion that all persons selling alcoholic beverages are to be charged with notice of such publication irrespective of whether they may have seen it. Calamos v. Commonwealth, 184 Va. 397, 35 S.E.2d 397 (1945).

§ 4.1-334. Interdiction for illegal manufacture, possession, transportation or sale of alcoholic beverages.

When any person has been found guilty of the illegal manufacture, possession, transportation, or sale of alcoholic beverages or maintaining a common nuisance as defined in § 4.1-317, the court may without further notice or additional hearing enter an order of interdiction prohibiting the sale of alcoholic beverages to such person for one year from the date of the entry of the order, and thereafter if further ordered.

History.
 Code 1950, § 4-52; 1954, c. 484; 1982, c. 66; 1993, c. 866.

CASE NOTES

Editor's note.
 The cases noted below were decided under former § 4-52, now repealed, which covered the same subject matter as this section.

Sale without knowledge of interdiction. — A seller should not be interdicted for selling alcoholic beverages to an interdicted person when he had no actual knowledge of or reason to believe the fact of the purchaser's interdiction. Calamos v. Commonwealth, 184 Va. 397, 35 S.E.2d 397 (1945).

Evidence of possession. — Evidence held insufficient to sustain conviction for unlawful possession under former § 4-52. Charles v. Commonwealth, 184 Va. 63, 34 S.E.2d 136 (1945).

§ 4.1-335. Enjoining nuisances.

A. In addition to the penalties imposed by § 4.1-317, the Board, its special agents, the attorney for the Commonwealth, or any citizen of the county, city, or town where a common nuisance as defined in § 4.1-317 exists may maintain a suit in equity in the name of the Commonwealth to enjoin the common nuisance.

B. The courts of equity shall have jurisdiction, and in every case where the bill charges, on the knowledge or belief of the complainant, and is sworn to by two reputable citizens, that alcoholic beverages are manufactured, stored, sold, dispensed, given away, or used in such house, building or other place described in § 4.1-317 contrary to the laws of the Commonwealth, an injunction shall be granted as soon as the bill is presented to the court. The injunction shall enjoin and restrain the owners, tenants, their agents, employees, servants, and any person connected with such house, building or other place, and all persons whomsoever from manufacturing, storing, selling, dispensing, giving away, or using alcoholic beverages on such premises. The injunction shall also restrain all persons from removing any alcoholic beverage then on such premises until the further order of the court. If the court is satisfied that the material allegations of the bill are true, although the premises complained of may not then be unlawfully used, it shall continue the injunction against such place for a period of time as the court deems proper. The injunction may be dissolved if a proper case is shown for dissolution.

History.
Code 1950, § 4-82; 1993, c. 866.

Research references.
Bryson on Virginia Civil Procedure (Matthew Bender). Chapter 5. Parties. § 5.02. Competency. W. Hamilton Bryson.

CASE NOTES

Editor's note.
The cases noted below were decided under former § 4-82, now repealed, which covered the same subject matter as this section.

Former § 4-82 was not in conflict with subdivision 3 of former § 4-89 (see now subdivision 7 of § 4.1-200). Nicholas v. Commonwealth, 186 Va. 315, 42 S.E.2d 306 (1947).

The injunction is intended to be preventive. — The injunction authorized by former § 4-82 was manifestly intended to be preventive rather than merely punitive. McCarron v. Commonwealth, 169 Va. 387, 193 S.E. 509 (1937).

The words "exists, or is kept or maintained," as used in former § 4-82 had a definite and clear meaning, and apply to an actual being, something, in fact, in existence, something continuing and not failing. McCarron v. Commonwealth, 169 Va. 387, 193 S.E. 509 (1937).

When nuisance abated before hearing. — The latter portion of former § 4-82, in providing for a continuation of the injunction, although the premises may not be unlawfully used at the time of the hearing of the matured case, was manifestly intended to cover those cases where nuisances exist at the time of the institution of the suit, but have been abated before such hearing. Under such circumstances, the provision allows the court to give consideration to the attitude of those who had formerly created or permitted a nuisance, but had abated it only after the institution of legal proceedings. McCarron v. Commonwealth, 169 Va. 387, 193 S.E. 509 (1937).

Plea of former jeopardy held no defense. — A plea of former jeopardy based on a conviction under former § 4-58 (see now § 4.1-302) for an illegal sale of alcoholic liquor stated no defense to a prosecution for violating, by the same sale, an injunction issued under former § 4-82 against selling alcoholic liquors on certain premises. Nicholas v. Commonwealth, 186 Va. 986, 45 S.E.2d 305 (1947).

§ 4.1-336. Contraband beverages and other articles subject to forfeiture.

All stills and distilling apparatus and materials for the manufacture of alcoholic beverages, all alcoholic beverages and materials used in their manufacture, all containers in which alcoholic beverages may be found, which are kept, stored, possessed, or in any manner used in violation of the provisions of this title, and any dangerous weapons as described in § 18.2-308, which may be used, or which may be found upon the person or in any vehicle which such person is using, to aid such person in the unlawful manufacture, transportation or sale of alcoholic beverages, or found in the possession of such person, or any horse, mule or other beast of burden, any wagon, automobile, truck or vehicle of any nature whatsoever which is found in the immediate vicinity of any place where alcoholic beverages are being unlawfully manufactured and which such animal or vehicle is being used to aid in the unlawful manufacture, shall be deemed contraband and shall be forfeited to the Commonwealth.

Proceedings for the confiscation of the above property shall be in accordance with § 4.1-338 for all such property except motor vehicles which proceedings shall be in accordance with Chapter 22.1 (§ 19.2-386.1 et seq.) of Title 19.2.

History.
Code 1950, § 4-53; 1954, c. 484; 1993, c. 866; 2012, cc. 283, 756.

The 2012 amendments.
The 2012 amendment by cc. 283 and 756 are identical, and substituted "Chapter 22.1 (§ 19.2-386.1 et seq.) of Title 19.2" for "§§ 4.1-339 through 4.1-348" at the end of the second paragraph and deleted the former third paragraph, which pertained to forfeiture and sale of dangerous weapons upon conviction.

Research references.
Bryson on Virginia Civil Procedure (Matthew Bender). Chapter 3. Active Jurisdiction. § 3.02. Types of Active Jurisdiction. W. Hamilton Bryson.

CASE NOTES

Editor's note.
The cases noted below were decided under former § 4-53, now repealed, which covered the same subject matter as this section.

Liquor being transported through Virginia for an unlawful purpose was contraband subject to immediate seizure under former § 4-53. Dickerson v. Commonwealth, 181 Va. 313, 24 S.E.2d 550 (1943), aff'd sub nom. Carter v. Virginia, 321 U.S. 131, 64 S. Ct. 464, 88 L. Ed. 605 (1944).

Effect of illegal seizure upon forfeiture. — The fact that ardent spirits and containers were seized by officers searching under an illegal warrant does not prevent them from being forfeited to the Commonwealth. Hall v. Commonwealth ex rel. Town of South Boston, 138 Va. 727, 121 S.E. 154 (1924).

§ 4.1-337. Search warrants.

A. If complaint on oath is made that alcoholic beverages are being manufactured, sold, kept, stored, or in any manner held, used or concealed in a particular house, or other place, in violation of law, the judge, magistrate, or other person having authority to issue criminal warrants, to whom such complaint is made, if satisfied that there is a probable cause for such belief, shall issue a warrant to search such house or other place for alcoholic beverages. Such warrants, except as herein otherwise provided, shall be issued, directed and executed in accordance with the laws of the Commonwealth pertaining to search warrants.

B. Warrants issued under this title for the search of any automobile, boat, conveyance or vehicle, whether of like kind or not, or for the search of any article of baggage, whether of like kind or not, for alcoholic beverages, may be executed in any part of the Commonwealth where they are overtaken and shall be made returnable before any judge within whose jurisdiction such automobile, boat, conveyance, vehicle, truck, or article of baggage, or any of them, was transported or attempted to be transported contrary to law.

History.
Code 1950, § 4-54; 1993, c. 866.

Cross references.
For prohibition of general warrants of search or seizure, see Va. Const., Art. I, § 10.

CASE NOTES

Sufficiency of evidence to justify issuance. — The evidence on which the issuance of a warrant is based does not have to be sufficient to establish the fact that the things sought are on the premises, but merely that the belief of the person making the affidavit is based on facts which permit a probable and reasonable cause for such belief. Zimmerman v. Town of Bedford, 134 Va. 787, 115 S.E. 362 (1922); Marshall v. Commonwealth, 140 Va. 541, 125 S.E. 329 (1924) (decided under former law).

§ 4.1-338. Confiscation proceedings; disposition of forfeited articles.

A. All proceedings for the confiscation of articles, except motor vehicles, declared contraband and forfeited to the Commonwealth under this chapter shall be as provided in this section.

B. Production of seized property. — Whenever any article declared contraband under the provisions of this title and required to be forfeited to the Commonwealth has been seized, with or without a warrant, by any officer charged with the enforcement of this title, he shall produce the contraband article and any person in whose possession it was found. In those cases where no person is found in possession of such articles the return shall so state and a copy of the warrant shall be posted on the door of the buildings or room where the articles were found, or if there is no door, then in any conspicuous place upon the premises.

In case of seizure of a still, doubler, worm, worm tub, mash tub, fermenting tub, or other distilling apparatus, for any offense involving their forfeiture, where it is impracticable to remove such distilling apparatus to a place of safe storage from the place where seized, the seizing officer may destroy such apparatus only as necessary to prevent use of all or any part thereof for the purpose of distilling. The destruction shall be in the presence of at least one credible witness, and such witness shall join the officer in a sworn report of the seizure and destruction, to be made to the Board. The report shall set forth the grounds of the claim of forfeiture, the reasons for seizure and destruction, an estimate of the fair cash value of the apparatus destroyed, and the materials remaining after such destruction. The report shall include a statement that, from facts within their own knowledge, the seizing officer and witness have no doubt whatever that the distilling apparatus was set up for use, or had been used in the unlawful distillation of spirits, and that it was impracticable to remove such apparatus to a place of safe storage.

In case of seizure of any quantity of mash, or of alcoholic beverages on which the tax imposed by the laws of the United States has not been paid, for any offense involving forfeiture of the same, the seizing officer may destroy them to prevent the use of all or any part thereof for the purpose of unlawful distillation of spirits or any other violation of this title. The destruction shall be in the presence of at least one credible witness, and such witness shall join the officer in a sworn report of the seizure and destruction, to be made to the Board. The report shall set forth the grounds of the claim of forfeiture, the reasons for seizure and destruction, and a statement that, from facts within their own knowledge, the seizing officer and witness have no doubt whatever that the mash was intended for use in the unlawful distillation of spirits, or that the alcoholic beverages were intended for use in violation of this title.

C. Hearing and determination. — Upon the return of the warrant as provided in this section, the court shall fix a time not less than ten days, unless waived by the accused in writing, and not more than thirty days thereafter, for the hearing on such return to determine whether or not the articles seized, or any part thereof, were used or in any manner kept, stored or possessed in violation of this title.

At such hearing if no claimant appears, the court shall declare the articles seized forfeited to the Commonwealth and, if such articles are not necessary as evidence in any pending prosecution, shall turn them over to the Board. Any person claiming an interest in any of the articles seized may appear at the hearing and file a written claim setting forth particularly the character and extent of his interest. The court shall certify the warrant and the articles seized along with any claim filed to the circuit court to hear and determine the validity of such claim.

If the evidence warrants, the court shall enter a judgment of forfeiture and order the articles seized to be turned over to the Board. Action under this section and the forfeiture of any articles hereunder shall not be a bar to any prosecution under any other provision of this title.

D. Disposition of forfeited beverages and other articles. — Any articles forfeited to the Commonwealth and turned over to the Board in accordance with this section shall be destroyed or sold by the Board as it deems proper. The net proceeds from such sales shall be paid into the Literary Fund. If the Board believes that any alcoholic beverages forfeited to the Commonwealth and turned over to the Board in accordance with this section cannot be sold and should not be destroyed, it may give such alcoholic beverages for medicinal purposes to any institution in the Commonwealth regularly conducted as a hospital, nursing home or sanatorium for the care of persons in ill health, or as a home devoted exclusively to the care of aged people, to supply the needs of such institution for alcoholic beverages for such purposes, provided that (i) the State Health Commissioner has issued a certificate stating that such institution has need for such alcoholic beverages and (ii) preference is accorded by the Board to institutions supported either in whole or in part by public funds. A record shall be made showing the amount issued in each case, to whom issued and the date when issued, and shall be kept in the offices of the State Health Commissioner and the Board. No charge shall be made to any patient for the alcoholic beverages supplied to him where they have been received from the Board pursuant to this section. Such alcoholic beverages shall be administered only upon approval of the patient's physician.

If the Board believes that any foodstuffs forfeited to the Commonwealth and turned over to the Board in accordance with this section are usable, should not be destroyed and cannot be sold or whose sale would be impractical, it may give such foodstuffs to any institution in the Commonwealth and shall prefer a gift to the local jail or other local correctional facility in the jurisdiction where seizure took place. A record shall be made showing the nature of the foodstuffs and amount given, to whom given and the date when given, and shall be kept in the offices of the Board.

History.
Code 1950, § 4-55; 1954, c. 484; 1958, c. 194; 1976, c. 37; 1993, c. 866; 1995, c. 196.

CASE NOTES

Editor's note.
The case noted below was decided under former § 4-55, now repealed, which covered the same subject matter as this section.

Section less stringent than state prohibition law. — Former § 4-55 and former § 4-56 were not quite so stringent as were similar provisions under the Layman Act (state prohibition law), Acts 1924, ch. 407. Cleek v. Commonwealth, 189 Va. 14, 52 S.E.2d 89 (1949).

§ 4.1-339. Search and seizure of conveyances or vehicles used in violation of law; arrests.

A. When any officer charged with the enforcement of the alcoholic beverage control laws of the Commonwealth has reason to believe that alcoholic beverages illegally acquired, or being illegally trans-

ported, are in any conveyance or vehicle of any kind, either on land or on water (except a conveyance or vehicle owned or operated by a railroad, express, sleeping or parlor car or steamboat company, other than barges, tugs or small craft), he shall obtain a search warrant and search such conveyance or vehicle. If illegally acquired alcoholic beverages or alcoholic beverages being illegally transported in amounts in excess of one quart or one liter if in a metric-sized container are found, the officer shall seize the alcoholic beverages, seize and take possession of such conveyance or vehicle, and deliver them to the chief law-enforcement officer of the locality in which such seizure was made, taking his receipt therefor in duplicate.

B. The officer making such seizure shall also arrest all persons found in charge of such conveyance or vehicle and shall forthwith report in writing such seizure and arrest to the attorney for the Commonwealth for the county or city in which seizure and arrest were made.

History.
Code 1950, § 4-56; 1954, c. 504; 1968, c. 763; 1971, Ex. Sess., c. 155; 1973, c. 16; 1978, cc. 434, 436; 1981, c. 365; 1983, c. 271; 1984, c. 52; 1993, c. 866.

Cross references.
For prohibition of general warrants of search or seizure, see Va. Const., Art. I, § 10. As to forfeiture of motor vehicles used in the commission of certain crimes, see § 19.2-386.16.

Law Review.
For comment on warrantless searches of automobiles in Virginia, see 12 U. Rich. L. Rev. 563 (1978).

CASE NOTES

Editor's note.
The cases noted below were decided under former § 4-56, now repealed, which covered the same subject matter as this section.

The burden of proof is upon the claimant. Forfeiture is the rule and release therefrom is the exception. Bandy v. Commonwealth, 185 Va. 1044, 41 S.E.2d 71 (1947); Universal C.I.T. Credit Corp. v. Commonwealth, 196 Va. 72, 82 S.E.2d 593 (1954).

Effect of price control regulations. — The right of a state to confiscate an automobile under former § 4-56 could not be successfully challenged on the ground that it would be in contravention of the United States price control regulations. Ives v. Commonwealth, 182 Va. 17, 27 S.E.2d 906 (1943).

Search warrant not always necessary for valid seizure and forfeiture of vehicle. — A search warrant is not, in all instances, a condition precedent to the valid seizure and forfeiture of a vehicle used for the illegal transportation of whiskey. One 1963 Chevrolet Pickup Truck v. Commonwealth, 208 Va. 506, 158 S.E.2d 755, cert. denied, 391 U.S. 964, 88 S. Ct. 2032, 20 L. Ed. 2d 877 (1968).

§§ 4.1-340 through 4.1-345. Repealed by Acts 2012, cc. 283 and 756, cl. 2.

Editor's note.
Former §§ 4.1-340 through 4.1-345, pertained to procedures involving forfeited property. For current procedures dealing with forfeiture see generally Chapters 22.1 (§ 19.2-386.1 et seq.) and Chapter 22.2 (§ 19.2-386.15 et seq.) of Title 19.2.
Former § 4.1-340 derived from Code 1950, § 4-56; Acts 1954, c. 504; 1968, c. 763; 1971, Ex. Sess., c. 155; 1973, c. 16; 1978, cc. 434,

436; 1981, c. 365; 1983, c. 271; 1984, c. 52; 1993, c. 866.

Former § 4.1-341 derived from Code 1950, § 4-56; Acts 1954, c. 504; 1968, c. 763; 1971, Ex. Sess., c. 155; 1973, c. 16; 1978, cc. 434, 436; 1981, c. 365; 1983, c. 271; 1984, c. 52; 1993, c. 866.

Former § 4.1-342 derived from Code 1950, § 4-56; Acts 1954, c. 504; 1968, c. 763; 1971, Ex. Sess., c. 155; 1973, c. 16; 1978, cc. 434, 436; 1981, c. 365; 1983, c. 271; 1984, c. 52; 1993, c. 866..

Former § 4.1-343 derived from Code 1950, § 4-56; Acts 1954, c. 504; 1968, c. 763; 1971, Ex. Sess., c. 155; 1973, c. 16; 1978, cc. 434, 436; 1981, c. 365; 1983, c. 271; 1984, c. 52; 1993, c. 866.

Former § 4.1-344 derived from Code 1950, § 4-56; Acts 1954, c. 504; 1968, c. 763; 1971, Ex. Sess., c. 155; 1973, c. 16; 1978, cc. 434, 436; 1981, c. 365; 1983, c. 271; 1984, c. 52; 1993, c. 866.

Former § 4.1-345 derived from Code 1950, § 4-56; Acts 1954, c. 504; 1968, c. 763; 1971, Ex. Sess., c. 155; 1973, c. 16; 1978, cc. 434, 436; 1981, c. 365; 1983, c. 271; 1984, c. 52; 1993, c. 866.

§ 4.1-346. Contraband beverages.

Alcoholic beverages seized pursuant to § 4.1-339 shall be deemed contraband as provided in § 4.1-336 and disposed of accordingly. Failure to maintain on a conveyance or vehicle a permit or other indicia of permission issued by the Board authorizing the transportation of alcoholic beverages within, into or through the Commonwealth when other Board regulations applicable to such transportation have been complied with shall not be cause for deeming such alcoholic beverages contraband.

History.
Code 1950, § 4-56; 1954, c. 504; 1968, c. 763; 1971, Ex. Sess., c. 155; 1973, c. 16; 1978, cc. 434, 436; 1981, c. 365; 1983, c. 271; 1984, c. 52; 1993, c. 866.

§ 4.1-347. Repealed by Acts 2012, cc. 283 and 756, cl. 2.

Editor's note.
Former § 4.1-347, pertaining to expenses incident to custody of seized property, derived from Code 1950, § 4-56; Acts 1954, c. 504; 1968, c. 763; 1971, Ex. Sess., c. 155; 1973, c. 16; 1978, cc. 434, 436; 1981, c. 365; 1983, c. 271; 1984, c. 52; 1993, c. 866.

§ 4.1-348. Beverages not licensed under this title.

The provisions of §§ 4.1-339 through 4.1-348 shall not apply to alcoholic beverages which may be manufactured and sold without any license under the provisions of this title.

History.
Code 1950, § 4-56; 1954, c. 504; 1968, c. 763; 1971, Ex. Sess., c. 155; 1973, c. 16; 1978, cc. 434, 436; 1981, c. 365; 1983, c. 271; 1984, c. 52; 1993, c. 866.

§ 4.1-349. Punishment for violations of title or regulations; bond.

A. Any person convicted of a misdemeanor under the provisions of this title without specification as to the class of offense or penalty, or convicted of violating any other provision thereof, or convicted of violating any Board regulation, shall be guilty of a Class 1 misdemeanor.

B. In addition to the penalties imposed by this title for violations, any court before whom any person is convicted of a violation of any provision of this title may require such defendant to execute bond, with approved security, in the penalty of not more than $1,000, with the condition that the defendant will not violate any of the provisions of this title for the term of one year. If any such bond is required and is not given, the defendant shall be committed to jail until it is given, or until he is discharged by the court, provided he shall not be confined for a period longer than six months. If any such bond required by a court is not given during the term of the court by which conviction is had, it may be given before any judge or before the clerk of such court.

C. The provisions of this title shall not prevent the Board from suspending, revoking or refusing to continue the license of any person convicted of a violation of any provision of this title.

D. No court shall hear such a case unless the respective attorney for the Commonwealth or his assistant has been notified that such a case is pending.

History.
Code 1950, § 4-92; 1984, c. 603; 1993, c. 866.

Cross references.
As to punishment for Class 1 misdemeanors, see § 18.2-11.

CASE NOTES

Editor's note.
The cases noted below were decided under former § 4-92, now repealed, which covered the same subject matter as this section.

The bond authorized by former § 4-92 is intended as a precautionary measure to prevent future violations of the law by a convicted person who is likely to be guilty of such violations. But where a man of good character has violated one of the provisions of the act, and there is no evidence indicating that he is likely again to do so, it is not proper to require him to execute a bond conditioned that he will not violate any of the provisions of the act for the term of one year. Snarr v. Commonwealth, 131 Va. 814, 109 S.E. 590 (1921).

And the imposition thereof is within discretion of trial judge. — The exercise of the authority given by former § 4-92 to impose a peace bond upon conviction of a violation of the Alcoholic Beverage Control Act, is left to the sound judicial discretion of the trial judge, and is only conditioned upon there being a conviction. Sutherland v. Commonwealth, 171 Va. 485, 198 S.E. 452 (1938).

When bond not required or vacated. — After an acquittal, or a final conclusion of the case favorable to the accused, no bond may be required. And a final judgment reversing the conviction vacates a peace bond required to be given under former § 4-92. Sutherland v. Commonwealth, 171 Va. 485, 198 S.E. 452 (1938).

§ 4.1-350. Witness not excused from testifying because of self-incrimination.

No person shall be excused from testifying for the Commonwealth as to any offense committed by another under this title by reason of his testimony tending to incriminate him. The testimony given by such person on behalf of the Commonwealth when called as a witness for the prosecution shall not be used against him and he shall not be prosecuted for the offense to which he testifies.

History.
Code 1950, § 4-94; 1993, c. 866.

§ 4.1-351. Previous convictions.

In any indictment, information or warrant charging any person with a violation of any provision of this title, it may be alleged and evidence may be introduced at the trial of such person to prove that such person has been previously convicted of a violation of this title.

History.
Code 1950, § 4-91; 1993, c. 866.

CASE NOTES

Editor's note.
The cases noted below were decided under former § 4-91, now repealed, which covered the same subject matter as this section.

The constitutionality of former § 4-91 has been considered and upheld. Simpson v. Commonwealth, 199 Va. 549, 100 S.E.2d 701 (1957).

The statute is a penal one, and must be construed strictly against the State and favorably to the liberty of the citizen. Campbell v. Commonwealth, 176 Va. 564, 11 S.E.2d 577 (1940).

But is not rendered ex post facto and invalid by the fact that under it convictions of offenses committed before its passage may be shown and considered by the jury in fixing the punishment for subsequent offenses. Surratt v. Commonwealth, 187 Va. 940, 48 S.E.2d 362 (1948).

Evidence of prior conviction is permitted in order to enhance the punishment of the accused should his guilt be established by independent testimony. Smith v. Commonwealth, 182 Va. 585, 30 S.E.2d 26 (1944); Wheeler v. Commonwealth, 192 Va. 665, 66 S.E.2d 605 (1951), overruled on other grounds, Watkins v. Commonwealth, 238 Va. 341, 385 S.E.2d 50 (1989); Crowe v. Commonwealth, 193 Va. 752, 71 S.E.2d 77 (1952); Simpson v. Commonwealth, 199 Va. 549, 100 S.E.2d 701 (1957).

Manner of introduction. — In a prosecution for unlawful possession of intoxicating liquors the Commonwealth inadvertently closed its evidence without proving alleged prior conviction of illegal transportation, and counsel for accused moved that the allegation be stricken. The trial court overruled the motion but indicated its readiness to instruct the jury that at that stage of the trial there was no evidence of such prior conviction. After accused had taken the stand and testified in chief, and had been cross-examined, he was asked, over the objection of his counsel, whether he had been previously convicted in the trial justice court of illegal transportation, and he admitted that he had. It was held that the ruling of the trial court was correct in allowing proof of the prior conviction. Smith v. Commonwealth, 182 Va. 585, 30 S.E.2d 26 (1944).

Evidence restricted to quantum of punishment. — In a prosecution for maintaining a nuisance in violation of former § 4-81 (see now § 4.1-317), accused objected to the introduction of evidence of prior convictions of similar offenses and contended that such evidence, if allowed at all, should be limited to the measure of punishment in the event of his conviction of the offense for which he was being tried. It was held that the evidence should be restricted to the quantum of punishment, since the terms of former section did not expressly make such evidence applicable to the case upon trial and it could not be said that its terms impliedly did so. Campbell v. Commonwealth, 176 Va. 564, 11 S.E.2d 577 (1940).

Instructions. — The trial court should instruct the jury to the effect that evidence of a prior conviction was to be considered only as to the quantum of punishment and was not to be considered as tending to prove the guilt of accused. However, the time of giving

instructions rests in the sound judicial discretion of the court, and, in the instant case, there was no abuse of the sound judicial discretion of the trial court in refusing to instruct the jury at the time the evidence was offered. Simpson v. Commonwealth, 199 Va. 549, 100 S.E.2d 701 (1957).

The refusal to instruct the jury "that the fact that the defendant has been heretofore convicted of similar or like offenses is not proof that he is guilty of the offense here charged and such fact should not be considered by the jury in reaching a conclusion as to his guilt or innocence on the present charge," was prejudicial error. Campbell v. Commonwealth, 176 Va. 564, 11 S.E.2d 577 (1940).

§ 4.1-352. Certificate of forensic scientist as evidence; requiring forensic scientist to appear.

The certificate of any forensic scientist employed by the Commonwealth on behalf of the Board or the Department of Forensic Science, when signed by him, shall be evidence in all prosecutions for violations of this title and all controversies in any judicial proceedings touching the mixture analyzed by him. On motion of the accused or any party in interest, the court may require the forensic scientist making the analysis to appear as a witness and be subject to cross-examination, provided such motion is made within a reasonable time prior to the day on which the case is set for trial.

History.
Code 1950, § 4-90; 1972, c. 741; 1981, c. 410; 1993, c. 866; 2003, c. 130; 2005, cc. 868, 881.

Law Review.
For comment on the admissibility of documentary evidence and the right to confrontation, see 12 Wm. & Mary L. Rev. 440 (1970).

Michie's Jurisprudence.
For related discussion, see 7B M.J. Evidence, § 86.

§ 4.1-353. Label on sealed container prima facie evidence of alcoholic content.

In any prosecution for violations of this title, where a sealed container is labeled as containing an alcoholic beverage as defined herein, such labeling shall be prima facie evidence of the alcoholic content of the container. Nothing shall preclude the introduction of other relevant evidence to establish the alcoholic content of a container, whether sealed or not.

History.
1962, c. 616, § 4-90.1; 1993, cc. 169, 866; 1997, c. 418.

Editor's note.
Acts 1993, c. 169 amended former § 4-90.1, from which this section is derived. Pursuant to § 30-152, the 1993 amendment by c. 169 has been given effect in this section as set out above. In accordance with c. 169, the phrase "where a sealed container" was substituted for "the alcoholic content as shown on the label of any sealed container," and the phrase "is labeled as containing an alcoholic beverage as defined herein, such labeling" was inserted.

§ 4.1-354. No recovery for alcoholic beverages illegally sold.

No action to recover the price of any alcoholic beverages sold in contravention of this title may be maintained.

History.

Code 1950, § 4-88; 1993, c. 866.

TITLE 5.1.

AVIATION.

CHAPTER 1.

AIRCRAFT, AIRMEN AND AIRPORTS GENERALLY.

Article 1. General Provisions.

ARTICLE 1.

GENERAL PROVISIONS.

Michie's Jurisprudence.

For related discussion, see 2B M.J. Aviation, §§ 1 - 3, 8.

§ 5.1-1. Definitions.

When used in this title, unless expressly stated otherwise:

"Aircraft" means any contrivance now known, or hereafter invented, used, or designed for navigation of or flight in the air, including a balloon or other contrivance designed for maneuvering in airspace at an altitude greater than 24 inches above ground or water level, except that any contrivance now or hereafter invented of fixed or flexible wing design, operating without the assistance of any motor, engine, or other mechanical propulsive device, which is designed to utilize the feet and legs of the operator or operators as the sole means of initiating and sustaining forward motion during the launch and of providing the point of contact with the ground upon

landing and commonly called a "hang glider" shall not be included within this definition.

"Aircraft based in this Commonwealth" means an aircraft that is either (i) domiciled in a county, city, or town in the Commonwealth or (ii) parked in a county, city, or town in the Commonwealth when not in flight for the period of time specified in § 5.1-5.

"Airman" means any individual, including the person in command and any pilot, mechanic, or member of the crew, who engages in the navigation of aircraft while under way within Virginia airspace; any individual who is directly in charge of the inspection, maintenance, overhauling, or repair of aircraft, aircraft engines, propellers, or accessories; and any individual who serves in the capacity of aircraft dispatcher.

"Air navigation facility" means any airport ground or air navigation facility, other than one owned and operated by the United States, used in, available for use in, or designed for use in aid of air navigation, including any structures, buildings, mechanisms, lights, beacons, markers, communicating systems, or other instrumentalities or devices, and any combination of any or all of such facilities, used or useful as an aid, or constituting any advantage or convenience, to the safe taking off, navigation, and landing of aircraft; in the safe and efficient operation or maintenance of an airport; in the safe, efficient and convenient handling or processing of aviation passengers, mail or cargo; or in the servicing or maintenance of aircraft or ground equipment.

"Airport" means any area of land or water which is used, or intended for public use, for the landing and takeoff of aircraft, and any appurtenant areas that are used, or intended for use, for airport buildings or other airport facilities or rights-of-way, easements and together with all airport buildings and facilities located thereon.

"Airport hazard" means any structure, object or natural growth, or use of land that obstructs the airspace required for the flight of aircraft in landing or taking off at an airport or is otherwise hazardous to such landing or taking off of aircraft.

"Airspace" means all that space above the land and waters within the boundary of the Commonwealth.

"Board" means the Virginia Aviation Board.

"Civil aircraft" means any aircraft other than a public aircraft.

"Commercial aircraft" means any civil aircraft used in flight activity for compensation or for hire.

"Contract carrier by aircraft" or *"contract carrier"* means any person not included under the definitions of "common carrier by aircraft" or "restricted common carrier by aircraft" as defined in § 5.1-89 who, under special and individual contracts or agreements, and whether directly or by a lease or any other arrangement, transports passengers or property by aircraft for compensation and in the transportation of passengers does not charge individual fares.

"Department" means the Department of Aviation.

"Drop zone" means any locality whether over land or water that is used, or intended for use, for the landing and recovery of sky divers or parachutists using a parachute or other contrivance designed for sport jumping.

"Landing area" or *"landing field"* means any locality, whether over land or water, including airports and intermediate landing fields, which is used or intended to be used for the landing and takeoff of aircraft and open to the public for such use, whether or not facilities are provided for the sheltering, servicing, or repair of aircraft or for receiving or discharging passengers or cargo.

"Person" means any individual, corporation, government, political subdivision of the Commonwealth, or governmental subdivision or agency, business trust, estate, trust, partnership, two or more of any of the foregoing having a joint or common interest, or any other legal or commercial entity.

"Public aircraft" means an aircraft used exclusively in the service of any state, or political subdivision thereof, or the federal government.

History.
Code 1950, § 5-1; 1966, c. 576; 1970, c. 717; 1975, c. 561; 1979, c. 272; 1980, c. 721; 1988, c. 588; 2011, c. 809.

Editor's note.
At its regular session of 1964 the General Assembly directed the Virginia Code Commission to revise certain titles of the Code, including Title 5, relating to aviation, and in July, 1965, the Commission sent to the Governor and General Assembly its report containing the proposed revision of Title 5, which was published as House Document 2 of the 1966 session. The Code Commission's draft of the revision, as amended by the General Assembly, became chapter 576 of the Acts of 1966. Effective July 1, 1966, it repealed Title 5 and enacted in lieu thereof a new Title 5.1.

Some of the cases cited in the notes under the various sections of this title were decided under corresponding provisions of Title 5.

Transition provisions.
Acts 1966, c. 576, clauses 3-6, provide as follows:

"3. All acts and parts of acts, all sections of the Code of Virginia, and all provisions of municipal charters inconsistent with the provisions of this act are, except as otherwise provided, repealed to the extent of such inconsistency.

"4. The repeal of Title 5 effective as of July 1, 1966, shall not affect any act or offense done or committed, or any penalty or forfeiture incurred, or any right established, accrued or accruing on or before such date, or any prosecution, suit or action pending on that date. Except as in this act otherwise provided, neither the repeal of Title 5 of the Code of Virginia nor the enactment of Title 5.1 shall apply to offenses committed prior to July 1, 1966, and prosecutions for such offenses shall be governed by the prior law, which is continued in effect for that purpose. For the purposes of this act, an offense was committed prior to July 1, 1966 if any of the essential elements of the offense occurred prior thereto.

"5. Whenever in Title 5.1 any of the conditions, requirements, provisions or contents of any section, article or chapter of Title 5, as such title existed prior to July 1, 1966, are transferred in the same or in modified form to a new section, article or chapter of Title 5.1, and whenever any such former section, article or chapter of Title 5 is given a new number in Title 5.1, all references to any such former section, article or chapter of Title 5 appearing elsewhere in the Code of Virginia than in Title 5.1 shall be construed to apply to the new or renumbered section, article or chapter containing such conditions, requirements, provisions or contents or portions thereof.

"6. It is the intention of the General Assembly that this act shall be liberally construed to effect the purposes set out herein, and if any clause, sentence, paragraph or section of this act shall ever be declared unconstitutional, it shall be deemed severable, and the remainder of this act shall continue in full force and effect."

Chapter 717 of the Acts of 1966 provides: "Whenever, during the regular session of the General Assembly of Virginia of nineteen hundred sixty-six there shall have been enacted any statute purporting to revise, rearrange, amend and recodify any title of the Code of Virginia, such statute shall be deemed to have been enacted prior in time to any other statute enacted at such session adding to, repealing or amending and reenacting any portion of such title; and every such other statute shall be deemed to have so added to, repealed or amended and reenacted, as the case may be, such title as so revised, rearranged, amended and recodified; provided, however, that effect shall be given to any such other, or subsequent, statute only to the extent of any apparent changes in the law as it existed prior to such session."

The 2011 amendments.
The 2011 amendment by c. 809 rewrote the section.

Law Review.
For survey of Virginia law on administrative law and utility regulation for the year 1978-1979, see 66 Va. L. Rev. 193 (1980). For an article, "Thou Canst Not Fly High With Borrowed Wings: Airline Finance and Bankruptcy Code Section 110," see 8 Geo. Mason L. Rev. 41 (1999).

CASE NOTES

Title applies to airports operated by government agencies. — The reenactment and amendment of Title 5 in 1966 as Title 5.1 emphasizes the intention of the General Assembly to make the general law apply to the operation of airports by governmental subdivisions or agencies as well as to other persons therein defined. Lillard v. Fairfax County Airport Auth., 208 Va. 8, 155 S.E.2d 338 (1967).

§ 5.1-1.1. Creation of Department of Aviation.

There is hereby created a Department of Aviation.

History.
1979, c. 272; 1984, c. 720.

§ 5.1-1.2. Appointment of Director; term; vacancies.

The Department shall be under the direction of a director, hereinafter referred to in this title as "Director," who shall be appointed by the Governor, subject to confirmation by the General Assembly if in session when such appointment is made, and, if not in session, then at its next succeeding session. He shall hold his office at the pleasure of the Governor for a term coincident with that of each Governor making the appointment or until his successor shall be appointed and qualified. Vacancies shall be filled for the unexpired term in the same manner as original appointments are made.

History.
1979, c. 272.

§ 5.1-1.3. Oath and bond of Director; salary.

The Director, before entering upon the discharge of his duties, shall take an oath that he will faithfully and impartially discharge and perform all the duties of his office and he shall give bond in such penalty as may be fixed by the Governor, conditioned upon the faithful discharge of his duties. The premium on such bond shall be paid out of the funds available for the maintenance and operation of his office. The Director shall receive such salary as may be appropriated for the purpose.

History.
1979, c. 272.

§ 5.1-1.4. Enforcement of laws, rules and regulations.

Except for the provisions of Chapter 9 (§ 5.1-89 et seq.) of this title, the Department shall have the authority to enforce any provision of this title and any rules and regulations promulgated by the Board in reference to aircraft, airfields, pilots and other similar subjects. Said rules and regulations, and enforcement actions taken in connection therewith, shall be in accordance with the substantive and procedural requirements of the Administrative Process Act, Chapter 40 (§ 2.2-4000 et seq.) of Title 2.2.

History.
1979, c. 272; 2002, c. 94.

Law Review.
For survey of Virginia administrative law and utility regulation for the year 1978-1979, see 66 Va. L. Rev. 193 (1980).

§ 5.1-1.5. General powers of Department.

The Department shall have the following general powers:

1. To employ such personnel as may be required to carry out the purposes of this chapter.

2. To make and enter into all contracts and agreements necessary or incidental to the performance of its duties and the execution of its powers under this chapter, including, but not limited to, contracts with the United States, other states, agencies and governmental subdivisions of the Commonwealth.

3. To accept grants from the United States government and agencies and instrumentalities thereof and any other source. To these ends, the Department shall have the power to comply with such conditions and execute such agreements as may be necessary, convenient or desirable.

4. To do all acts necessary or convenient to carry out the purposes of this chapter.

History.
1979, c. 272.

§ 5.1-1.6. Further powers and duties of Department; State Corporation Commission to administer Chapter 9.

A. The Department shall have the following powers and duties:

1. Administer the provisions of Chapters 1 (§ 5.1-1 et seq.), 3 (§ 5.1-31 et seq.), 5 (§ 5.1-51 et seq.) and 8.1 (§ 5.1-88.1 et seq.) of this title;

2. Plan for the development of a state aviation system;

3. Promote aviation in the Commonwealth in the interest of the public, including representing the interests of the Commonwealth before all tribunals, agencies or offices, federal, state and local, in any matter tending to affect any phase of Virginia aviation;

4. License aircraft, airports and landing areas; and

5. Provide assistance to cities, towns, counties and other governmental subdivisions for the planning, development, construction and operation of airports, landing fields and other aviation facilities.

B. The State Corporation Commission shall continue to administer Chapter 9 (§ 5.1-89 et seq.) of this title.

History.
1979, c. 272; 1991, c. 126; 1992, c. 108.

Law Review.
For survey of Virginia administrative law and utility regulation for the year 1978-1979, see 66 Va. L. Rev. 193 (1980).

§ 5.1-1.7. Suits to enjoin violations of title.

The Department may seek to enjoin any act in violation of any provision of this title, or of any rule or regulation promulgated under any provision of this title, by application for injunctive relief to the circuit court of the jurisdiction where the violation occurs, which shall give priority on its docket to suits brought by the Department.

History.
1979, c. 272.

§ 5.1-2. Repealed by Acts 1979, c. 272.

§ 5.1-2.1. Virginia Aviation Commission continued as Virginia Aviation Board; membership; terms; Chairman.

A. The Virginia Aviation Commission, a public body corporate and politic, is hereby continued within the Department of Aviation as a political subdivision of the Commonwealth and shall hereafter be known as the Virginia Aviation Board. The Board shall consist of eight members, selected so far as practicable from different geographic areas of the Commonwealth, appointed by the Governor, subject to confirmation by the General Assembly, to serve at the pleasure of the Governor. Members shall serve for four-year terms and no member shall serve for more than two full successive terms. Initial appointments to the Board shall be made as follows: one shall be for a term of one year, two shall be for terms of two years, two shall be for terms of three years, and two shall be for terms of four years each and thereafter all appointments shall be for terms of four years each. The Chairman of the Board shall be appointed by the Governor.

B. Whenever the Board shall acquire ownership or jurisdiction over an airport or airports previously operated by an agency of the United States, there may be a member appointed to the Board by the President of the United States. Such member shall have the powers and duties of other members of the Board only with respect to the airport or airports so acquired.

C. There may be a member of the Board from any county or city wherein the Board acquires or constructs an airport, to be elected by the governing body of the county or city and to serve at its pleasure. Such member shall have the powers and duties of other members of the Board only with respect to such airport. If the Board acquires an airport which was constructed by one political subdivision but is located in another, the political subdivision which constructed the airport, rather than the political subdivision in which it is located, shall be represented on the Board.

History.
1979, c. 272; 1980, c. 750; 1985, c. 448.

Law Review.
For survey of Virginia law on administrative law and utility regulation for the year 1978-1979, see 66 Va. L. Rev. 193 (1980).

§ 5.1-2.2. Powers and duties of Board.

The Board shall exercise the following powers and duties:

1. Provide a means of citizen access to the Department;

2. Provide a means of publicizing the policies and programs of the Department in order to educate the public and elicit public support for Department activities;

3. Monitor the policies and activities of the Department and have the right of access to departmental information;

4. Advise the Governor and the Director on matters relating to the Commonwealth's aviation policies and programs;

5. Promulgate such rules and regulations relating to airports, landing fields and other aviation facilities, aircraft, air traffic, construction and inspection of aircraft, qualifications and licensing of airmen, stunt flying, and such other kindred matters and things as may be proper and necessary to promote and develop safe aviation practices and operations; and

6. Develop on behalf of the Department recommendations for distribution of funds to localities by the State Corporation Commission for aviation development through the end of the 1978-80 biennium, after which time the Board shall be responsible for the allocation on behalf of the Department of all such funds as provided in this act, which funds shall be distributed by the Department in accordance with such allocation.

History.
1979, c. 272; 1980, c. 306; 1984, c. 720.

Editor's note.

The words "this act" in subdivision 6 of this section refer to Acts 1979, c. 272, which enacted §§ 5.1-1.1 through 5.1-1.7 and amended former §§ 2.1-1, 2.1-51.24 and numerous sections throughout this title.

§ 5.1-2.2:1. Further powers and duties of the Board.

The Board shall have all the powers necessary or convenient to carry out the purposes of this chapter including, but not limited to, the power:

1. To sue in its own name, to have a seal, and to have perpetual succession;

2. To execute such contracts and other instruments and take such other action as may be necessary or convenient to carry out the purposes of this chapter;

3. To plan, establish, develop, construct, enlarge, improve, maintain, equip, operate, regulate, and protect airports and air navigation facilities, within this Commonwealth and within any adjoining state, including the acquisition, construction, installation, equipment, maintenance, and operation at such airports of buildings and other facilities for the servicing of aircraft or for the comfort and accommodation of air travelers, and the purchase and sale of supplies, goods, and commodities as an incident to the operation of its airport properties. For such purposes the Board may, by purchase, gift, devise, lease, condemnation, or otherwise, acquire property, real or personal, or any interest therein, including easements in airport hazards or land outside the boundaries of an airport or airport site, as are necessary to permit the removal, elimination, obstruction marking or obstruction lighting of airport hazards or to prevent the establishment of airport hazards, or for the enlargement of an airport constructed or acquired under this subdivision 3; provided, however, such power of eminent domain shall not extend to the taking of any radio or television towers or installation in existence on June 27, 1958;

4. To acquire, by purchase, gift, devise, or lease, existing airports and air navigation facilities;

5. To establish or acquire and maintain airports in, over, and upon any public waters of this Commonwealth or any submerged lands under such public waters; and to construct and maintain terminal buildings, landing floats, causeways, roadways, and bridges for approaches to or connecting with any such airport, and landing floats and breakwaters for the protection thereof;

6. To construct, or permit the construction of, for sale or lease, on such terms and conditions as the Board may deem proper, industrial, commercial or recreational facilities and approaches thereto and appurtenances thereof, on any lands of the Board not acquired by eminent domain and not needed for operational use of an airport owned or operated by it; provided, that any such factory or manufacturing facility shall be so constructed as not to constitute an airport hazard. In the exercise of the powers conferred by this subdivision, the Board shall comply with any applicable zoning restrictions of the political subdivision in which any airport or facility is, or is proposed to be located.

History.
1980, c. 750.

OPINIONS OF THE ATTORNEY GENERAL

Aviation Board may borrow money and issue note for infrastructure projects. — If infrastructure projects fall within the context of constructing, enlarging, or improving an airport facility, the Aviation Board may enter into, execute, and deliver a loan agreement to borrow money and issue a note, subject to the receipt of appropriations or grants. See opinion of Attorney General to Mr. George P. Ramsey III, Chairman, Virginia Aviation Board, 01-032 (3/23/01).

§ 5.1-2.3. Meetings of Board; quorum.

The Board shall meet at least once every three months, and on the call of the Chairman, when in his opinion additional meetings are necessary. Four members of the Board shall constitute a quorum.

History.
1979, c. 272.

§ 5.1-2.4. Repealed by Acts 1980, c. 728.

Cross references.
As to compensation and expenses of boards, commissions and similar bodies, see § 2.2-2813.

§ 5.1-2.5. Eminent domain; right of entry.

The Board is hereby vested with the power of eminent domain and may exercise the same for the purposes set forth in subdivision 3 of § 5.1-2.2:1 in the manner set forth in Chapter 2 (§ 25.1-200 et seq.) of Title 25.1 and to the extent permitted to railroads by § 56-347; provided, however, such power of eminent domain shall not extend to the taking of any radio or television towers or installation in existence on June 27, 1958. If the owner, lessee or occupier of any property to be condemned or otherwise acquired shall refuse to remove his property therefrom or give up possession thereof, the Board may proceed to obtain possession in any manner provided by law. The authorized agents and employees may enter upon any lands, waters, and premises in the Commonwealth for the purpose of making surveys, soundings, drillings, and examinations as they may deem necessary or convenient for the purposes of this chapter, and such entry shall not be deemed a trespass, nor shall an entry for such purpose be deemed an entry under any condemnation proceedings that may be then pending. The Board shall make reimbursement for any actual damage resulting to such lands, waters, and premises as a result of such activities.

History.
1980, c. 750; 2003, c. 940.

Cross references.
As to application of this section, see § 5.1-2.24.

§ 5.1-2.6. Disposal of airport, air navigation facility or other property.

Except as may be limited by the terms and conditions of any grant, loan or agreement authorized by § 5.1-2.16 the Board may, by sale, lease, or otherwise, dispose of any airport, air navigation facility, or other property, or portion thereof or interest therein, acquired pursuant to this chapter. Such disposal by sale, lease, or otherwise, shall be in accordance with the laws of this Commonwealth governing the disposition of other public property, except that in the case of disposal to another authority, a municipality or an agency of the Commonwealth or federal government for use and operation as a public airport, the sale, lease, or other disposal may be effected in such manner and upon such terms as the commissioners of the Board may deem in the best interest of aviation.

History.
1980, c. 750.

§ 5.1-2.7. Revenue bonds generally.

The Board is hereby authorized to provide for the issuance, at one time or from time to time, of revenue bonds of the Board for the purpose of paying all or any part of the cost of any one or more airport projects or of any portion or portions thereof. The principal of and the interest on such bonds shall be payable solely from the funds provided in this chapter for such payment. Any bonds of the Board issued pursuant to this chapter shall not constitute a debt of the Commonwealth, or any political subdivision thereof other than the Board, and shall so state on their face. Neither the commissioners of the Board nor any person executing such bonds shall be liable personally thereon by reason of the issuance thereof. The bonds of each issue shall be dated, shall bear interest at such rate or rates as may be determined by the Board, shall mature at such time or times not exceeding forty years from their date or dates, as may be determined by the Board, and may be made redeemable before maturity, at the option of the Board, at such price or prices and under such terms and conditions as may be fixed by the Board prior to the issuance of the bonds. The Board shall determine the form and the manner of execution of the bonds, including any interest coupons to be attached thereto, and shall fix the denomination or denominations of the bonds and the place or places of payment of principal and interest, which may be at any bank or trust company within or without the Commonwealth. In case any officer whose signature or a facsimile of whose signature shall appear on any bonds or coupons shall cease to be such officer before the delivery of such bonds, such signature or such facsimile shall nevertheless be valid and sufficient for all purposes the same as if he had remained in office until such delivery. The bonds may be issued in coupon or in registered form or both, as the Board may determine, and provision may be made for the registration of any coupon bonds as to principal alone and also as to both principal and interest, for the reconversion into coupon bonds of any bonds registered as to both principal and interest, and for the interchange of registered and coupon bonds. The Board may sell such bonds in such manner, either at public or private sale, and for such price as it may determine will best effect the purposes of this chapter.

The proceeds of the bonds of each issue shall be used solely for the payment of the cost of the airport project or projects for which such bonds shall have been issued, and shall be disbursed in such manner and under such restrictions, if any, as the Board may provide in the resolution authorizing the issuance of such bonds or in the trust agreement hereinafter mentioned securing the same. If the proceeds of the bonds of any issue, by error of estimates or otherwise, shall be less than such cost, additional bonds may in like manner be issued to provide the amount of such deficit, and, unless otherwise provided in the resolution authorizing the issuance of such bonds or in the trust agreement securing the same, shall be deemed to be of the same issue and shall be entitled to payment from the same fund without preference or priority of the bonds first issued. If the proceeds of the bonds of any issue shall exceed such cost, the surplus shall be deposited to the credit of the sinking fund for such bonds, or may be applied to the payment of the cost of any additional airport project or projects.

Prior to the preparation of definitive bonds, the Board may, under like restrictions, issue interim receipts or temporary bonds with or without coupons, exchangeable for definitive bonds when such bonds shall have been executed and are available for delivery. The Board may also provide for the replacement of any bonds which shall become mutilated or shall be destroyed or lost. Bonds may be issued under the provisions of this chapter without obtaining the consent of any department, division, commission, board, bureau or agency of the Commonwealth, and without any other proceedings or the happening of any other conditions or things than those proceedings, conditions or things which are specifically required by this chapter.

History.
1980, c. 750; 1982, c. 563.

Cross references.
As to application of this section, see § 5.1-2.24.

§ 5.1-2.8. Trust agreement securing bonds.

In the discretion of the Board any bonds issued under the provisions of this chapter may be secured by a trust agreement by and between the Board and a corporate trustee, which may be any trust company or bank having the powers of a trust company within or without the Commonwealth. Such trust agreement or the resolution providing for the issuance of such bonds may pledge or assign the revenues to be received, but shall not convey or mortgage any airport project or any part thereof. Such trust agreement or resolution providing for the issuance of such bonds may contain such provisions for protecting and enforcing the rights and remedies of the bondholders as may be reasonable and proper and not in violation of law, including covenants setting forth the duties of the Board in relation to the acquisition of property and the acquisition, construction, establishment, improvement, extension, enlargement, equipment, maintenance, repair, operation, and insurance of the airport project or projects in connection with which such bonds shall have been authorized, the rates and fees to be charged, the custody, safeguarding, and application of all moneys, and conditions or limitations with respect to the issuance of additional bonds. It shall be lawful for any bank or trust company incorporated under the laws of the Commonwealth which may act as depositary of the proceeds of bonds or of revenues to furnish such indemnifying bonds or to pledge such securities as may be required by the Board. Any such trust agreement may set forth the rights and remedies of the bondholders and of the trustee, and may restrict the individual right of action by bondholders. In addition to the foregoing, any such trust agreement or resolution may contain such other provisions as the Board may deem reasonable and proper for the security of the bondholders. All expenses incurred in carrying out the provisions of such trust agreement or resolution may be treated as a part of the cost of the operation of the airport project or projects.

History.
1980, c. 750.

Cross references.
As to application of this section, see § 5.1-2.24.

§ 5.1-2.9. Rents, fees and charges for services or use of facilities; use and disposition of revenues.

The Board is hereby authorized to fix, revise, charge, and collect rates, fees, and other charges for the use of or for the services and facilities furnished by each airport project and the different parts thereof, and to contract with any person, partnership, association, or corporation desiring the use of any part thereof, and to fix the terms, conditions, rents and rates of charges for such use. Such rates, fees, and other charges shall be so fixed and adjusted that revenues of the Board, together with any other available funds, will be sufficient at all times to pay (i) the cost of maintaining, repairing and operating such airport project or projects, and (ii) the principal

of and the interest on such bonds as the same shall become due and payable, and to create reserves for such purposes. Such rates, fees and other charges shall not be subject to supervision or regulation by any other commission, board, bureau or agency of the Commonwealth. The revenues derived from the airport project or projects in connection with which the bonds shall have been issued, except such part thereof as may be necessary to pay such cost of maintenance, repair, and operation and to provide such reserves therefor as may be provided for in the resolution authorizing the issuance of such bonds or in the trust agreement securing the same, shall be set aside at such regular intervals as may be provided in such resolution or such trust agreement in a sinking fund which is hereby pledged to, and charged with, the payment of the principal of and the interest on such bonds as the same shall become due, and the redemption price or the purchase price of bonds retired by call or purchase as therein provided. Such pledge shall be valid and binding from the time when the pledge is made, the revenues or other moneys so pledged and thereafter received by the Board shall immediately be subject to the lien of such pledge without any physical delivery thereof or further act, and the lien of any such pledge shall be valid and binding as against all parties having claims of any kind against the Board, irrespective of whether such parties have notice thereof. Neither the resolution nor any trust agreement by which a pledge is created need be filed or recorded except in the records of the Board. The use and disposition of moneys to the credit of such sinking fund shall be subject to the provisions of the resolution authorizing the issuance of such bonds or of such trust agreement. Except as may otherwise be provided in such resolution or such trust agreement, such sinking fund shall be a fund for all such bonds without distinction or priority of one over another.

History.
1980, c. 750.

Cross references.
As to application of this section, see § 5.1-2.24.

§ 5.1-2.10. Moneys received deemed trust funds.

All moneys received pursuant to the authority of this chapter, whether as proceeds from the sale of bonds or as revenues, shall be deemed to be trust funds to be held and applied solely as provided in this chapter. The resolution authorizing the bonds of any issue or the trust agreement securing such bonds shall provide that any officer with whom, or any bank or trust company with which, such moneys shall be deposited shall act as trustee of such moneys and shall hold and apply the same for the purposes hereof, subject to such regulations as this chapter and such resolution or trust agreement may provide. In the case of revenues or the proceeds from the sale of revenue bonds, the trustee may invest and reinvest such funds in securities that are legal investments under the laws of the Commonwealth for funds held by fiduciaries pending their need for the construction of the projects. In the case of the proceeds of the sale of refunding bonds, the trustee may invest and reinvest such funds in direct obligations of, or obligations the principal of and the interest on which are guaranteed by, the United States of America. Such money and the interest, income and profits, if any, earned on such investment shall be available for the payment of all or any part of the principal, interest and redemption premium, if any, of the bonds being refunded. The proceeds of the sale of refunding bonds shall be so invested and applied as to ensure that the principal, interest and redemption premium, if any, on the bonds being refunded shall be paid in full on their respective maturity, redemption or interest payment dates. After the terms of the trust have been fully satisfied, any balance of such proceeds, interest, income and profits, if any, realized on the investments thereof may be returned to the Board for use by it in any lawful manner.

History.
1980, c. 750; 1982, c. 563.

Cross references.
As to application of this section, see § 5.1-2.24.

§ 5.1-2.11. Proceedings by bondholder or trustee to enforce rights.

Any holder of bonds issued under the provisions of this chapter or any of the coupons appertaining thereto, and the trustee under any trust agreement, except to the extent the rights herein given may be restricted by such trust agreement or the resolution authorizing the issuance of such bonds, may, either at law or in equity, by suit, action, mandamus, or other proceeding, protect and enforce any and all rights under the laws of the Commonwealth or granted hereunder or under such trust agreement or resolution, and may enforce and compel the performance of all duties required by this chapter or by such trust agreement or resolution to be performed by the Board or by any officer thereof, including the fixing, charging, and collecting of rates, fees and other charges.

History.
1980, c. 750.

Cross references.
As to application of this section, see § 5.1-2.24.

§ 5.1-2.12. Bonds made securities for investment and deposit.

Bonds issued by the Board under the provisions of this chapter are hereby made securities in which all public officers and public bodies of the Commonwealth and its political subdivisions, all insurance companies, trust companies, banking associations, investment companies, executors, administrators, trustees, and other fiduciaries may properly and legally invest funds, including capital in their control or belonging to them. Such bonds are hereby made securities which may properly and legally be deposited with and received by any state or municipal officer or any agency or political subdivision of the Commonwealth for any purpose for which the deposit of bonds or obligations of the Commonwealth is now or may hereafter be authorized by law.

History.
1980, c. 750.

Cross references.
As to application of this section, see § 5.1-2.24.

§ 5.1-2.13. Revenue refunding bonds; bonds for refunding and for cost of additional projects.

The Board is hereby authorized to provide for the issuance of revenue refunding bonds of the Board for the purpose of refunding any bonds then outstanding which shall have been issued under the provisions of this chapter, including the payment of any redemption premium thereon and any interest accrued or to accrue to the date of redemption of such bonds, and, if deemed advisable by the Board, for the additional purpose of constructing improvements, extensions, or enlargements of the airport project or projects in connection with which the bonds to be refunded shall have been issued. The Board is further authorized to provide by resolution for the issuance of its revenue bonds for the combined purpose of (i) refunding any bonds then outstanding which shall have been issued under the provisions of this chapter including the payment of any redemption premium thereon and any interest accrued or to accrue to the date of redemption of such bonds, and (ii) paying all or any part of the cost of any additional airport project or projects or of any portion or portions thereof. The issuance of such bonds, the maturities, and other details thereof, the rights of the holders thereof, and the rights, duties, and obligations of the Commonwealth in respect of the same shall be governed by the provisions of this chapter insofar as the same may be applicable.

History.
1980, c. 750.

Cross references.
As to application of this section, see § 5.1-2.24.

§ 5.1-2.14. Contracts, leases, and other arrangements.

A. In connection with the operation of an airport or air navigation facility owned or controlled by the Board, the Board may enter into contracts, leases, and other arrangements with any person or persons (i) granting the privilege of using or improving the airport or air navigation facility or any portion or facility thereof or space therein consistent with the purposes of this chapter; (ii) conferring the privileges of supplying goods, commodities, things, services, or facilities at the airport or air navigation facility; and (iii) making available services to be furnished by the Board or its agents at the airport or air navigation facility.

In each case the Board may establish the terms and conditions and fix the charges, rentals, or fee for the privilege or service, which shall be reasonable and uniform for the same class of privilege or service at each airport and shall be established with due regard to the property and improvements used and the expenses of operation to the Board; provided that in no case shall the public be deprived of its rightful, equal, and uniform use of the airport, air navigation facility, or portion of facility thereof.

B. Except as may be limited by the terms and conditions of any grant, loan, or agreement authorized by § 5.1-2.16, the Board may by contract, lease, or other arrangements, upon a consideration fixed by it, grant to any qualified person, for a term not to exceed thirty years, the privilege of operating, as agent of the Board or otherwise, any airport owned or controlled by the Board; provided that no person shall be granted any authority to operate an airport other than as a public airport or to enter into any contracts, leases, or other arrangements in connection with the operation of the airport which the Board might not have undertaken under subsection A of this section.

History.
1980, c. 750.

§ 5.1-2.15. Resolutions, rules and regulations, etc.

The Board is authorized to adopt, amend, and repeal such reasonable resolutions, rules, regulations, and orders as it shall deem necessary for the management, government, and use of any airport or air navigation facility owned by it or under its control. No rule, regulation, order, or standard prescribed by the Board shall be inconsistent with, or contrary to, any law of this Commonwealth or act of the Congress of the United States or any regulation promulgated or standard established pursuant thereto concerning such airport or the operation of aircraft. The Board shall keep on file at the principal office of the Board for public inspection a copy of all its rules and regulations.

History.
1980, c. 750.

§ 5.1-2.16. Grants or loans of public or private funds.

The Board is authorized to accept, receive, receipt for, disburse, and expend federal and state moneys and other moneys, public or private, made available by grant or loan or both, to accomplish, in whole or in part, any of the purposes of this chapter. All federal moneys accepted under this section shall be accepted and expended by the Board upon such terms and conditions as are prescribed by the United States and as are consistent with state law; and all state moneys accepted under this section shall be accepted and expended by the Board upon such terms and conditions as are prescribed by the Commonwealth.

In considering or evaluating the application for or award of any grant of moneys under this section, the Board shall take into account the capacities of all airports within the affected geographic region.

History.
1980, c. 750; 1998, c. 480.

OPINIONS OF THE ATTORNEY GENERAL

Aviation Board may borrow money and issue note for infrastructure projects. — If infrastructure projects fall within the context of constructing, enlarging, or improving an airport facility, the Aviation Board may enter into, execute, and deliver a loan agreement to borrow money and issue a note, subject to the receipt of appropriations or grants. See opinion of Attorney General to Mr. George P. Ramsey III, Chairman, Virginia Aviation Board, 01-032 (3/23/01).

§ 5.1-2.17. Exemptions from taxes or assessments; payments to county or city in lieu of taxes.

The exercise of the powers granted by this chapter will be in all respects for the benefit of the people of the Commonwealth, for the increase of their commerce and prosperity, and for the improvement of their health and living conditions, and as the operation and maintenance of airport projects by the Board will constitute the performance of essential governmental functions. The Board shall not be required to pay any taxes or assessments upon any airport project or any property acquired or used by the Board under the provisions of this chapter or upon the income therefrom, and any bonds issued under the provisions of this chapter, their transfer and the income therefrom, including any profit made on the sale thereof, shall at all times be free from taxation within the Commonwealth; provided that the exemption hereby granted shall not be construed to extend to persons conducting on the premises of an airport businesses for which local or state taxes would otherwise be required. When the bonds or other obligations of the Board issued in connection with the acquisition, construction or improvement of an airport or air navigation facility have been paid, or at an earlier date if the Board deems it financially feasible, the Board shall enter into negotiations with the governing body of the political subdivision in which such airport or facility is located and may agree with such governing body on sums to be paid to the county or city in lieu of taxes. In case of disagreement as to the value of the property, an appeal shall lie to the circuit court of the jurisdiction in which the airport or facility is located which court shall determine the value of such property and the ratio of assessed to true values of property in such political subdivision.

History.
1980, c. 750.

§ 5.1-2.18. Joint agency or authority; agreements authorized; terms.

The Board may, to the extent permitted by law, enter into agreements with agencies or authorities in this Commonwealth or from adjoining states or with an agency or authority of the United States for joint action pursuant to the provisions of this chapter. Each such agreement shall specify its duration, the proportionate interest which each participating authority or agency shall have in the property, facilities, and privileges of the joint undertaking; the apportionment of the costs of the undertaking among the participating authorities or agencies; the disposition of all property, facilities, and privileges jointly owned upon termination of such agreement or any renewal thereof; the payment or assumption of any indebtedness arising out of such joint operation which remains unpaid upon the disposal of all assets or upon the termination of the agreement or any renewal thereof; and such other provisions as may be necessary to insure efficient operation of the joint undertaking.

History.
1980, c. 750.

Editor's note.
As to the creation of the Virginia's Region 2000 Airport Authority Act, see Acts 2007, c. 812.

§ 5.1-2.19. Same; governing body; officers and agents; powers generally.

The agreement shall specify the composition of the governing body of the joint agency or authority created under § 5.1-2.18; provided, however, that the membership thereof from this Commonwealth shall be the same as the membership of the Board created by § 5.1-2.1. Each joint authority shall select officers for such terms as are fixed by the agreement and shall have the power to employ such agents and employees as it may require and as are reasonably necessary in carrying out the purposes of this chapter. Subject to the limitations and restrictions hereinafter set forth, such joint authority shall have the powers set forth in § 5.1-2.2:1.

History.
1980, c. 750.

§ 5.1-2.20. Same; eminent domain.

Eminent domain proceedings shall not be instituted by any joint authority except by majority vote

of each component agency or authority of such joint authority. If so instituted, any property or rights acquired thereunder shall be held by such agencies or authorities jointly, according to the terms of the agreement creating the joint authority.

History.
1980, c. 750.

Cross references.
As to application of this section, see § 5.1-2.24.

§ 5.1-2.21. Same; disposal of airport or facility.

The joint authority shall not dispose of any airport, airport navigational facility or real property under its jurisdiction except by majority vote of each component agency or authority; provided, however, that this restriction shall not be construed to apply to any disposition of property contemplated or permitted by § 5.1-2.2:1.

History.
1980, c. 750.

§ 5.1-2.22. Acquisition of airport previously operated by United States.

Whenever the Board shall acquire ownership and jurisdiction over any airport or airports previously operated by an agency of the United States, the Board is hereby authorized to enter into an agreement with such agency of the United States, as a condition of the acquisition of the airport, for the provision, necessary and appropriate use, maintenance, and operation, of such airport facilities as may be required by the United States or any specified agency or agencies thereof.

History.
1980, c. 750.

§ 5.1-2.23. Board as successor to Virginia Airports Authority.

The Board is the successor in interest to that political subdivision formerly known as the Virginia Airports Authority. As such, the Board stands in the place and stead of, and assumes all rights and duties formerly of, such Authority, including but not limited to all leases, contracts, grants-in-aid and all other agreements of whatsoever nature; holds title to all realty and personalty formerly held by such Authority; and may exercise all powers which might at any time past have been exercised by said Authority.

History.
1980, c. 750.

§ 5.1-2.24. Applicability of certain sections.

The provisions of §§ 5.1-2.5, 5.1-2.7, 5.1-2.8, 5.1-2.9, 5.1-2.10, 5.1-2.11, 5.1-2.12, 5.1-2.13, and 5.1-

2.20 of this chapter shall be applicable only to any airport owned by the Virginia Airports Authority or its successor agency on January 1, 1980.

History.
1980, c. 750.

§ 5.1-3. Repealed by Acts 1979, c. 272.

Cross references.
As to the Department of Aviation, see §§ 5.1-1.1 through 5.1-1.7. As to the Virginia Aviation Board, see §§ 5.1-2.1 through 5.1-2.3.

§ 5.1-4. Aircraft for use of Department; construction, etc., of aviation facilities by Department.

Within the limits of appropriations made for such purposes, the Department is authorized to purchase aircraft for the use of the Department, provided, however, that the Department shall not purchase any new or used executive aircraft unless specifically requested in the Governor's budget and approved by the General Assembly in the Appropriations Act, and to purchase land for and to construct, maintain and improve airports, landing fields and other aviation facilities within the Commonwealth for the promotion of aviation in the interest of the public; and neither the appropriations nor any part thereof may be transferred or used for any other purpose than is specified in this section.

History.
Code 1950, § 5-4; 1966, c. 576; 1970, c. 717; 1979, c. 272.

§ 5.1-5. Licensing of aircraft.

(a) Every resident of this Commonwealth owning a civil aircraft, every nonresident owning a civil aircraft based in this Commonwealth over sixty days during any twelve-month period and every owner of an aerial application aircraft operating within this Commonwealth or of a civil aircraft operated in this Commonwealth as a for-hire intrastate air carrier shall, before the same is operated in this Commonwealth, obtain from the Department an aircraft license for such aircraft.

(b) The Department shall provide for the issuance, expiration, suspension and revocation of licenses of aircraft in accordance with regulations promulgated by the Board. The Department shall furnish any necessary forms pursuant to the issuance of such licenses, and may assess a fee for such issuance not in excess of five dollars annually. The Department may in lieu of issuing aircraft licenses required by subsection (a) of this section, issue commercial aircraft licenses to air carriers and commercial dealers, and issue to noncommercial dealers noncommercial dealer fleet licenses, to cover all aircraft owned by such dealers and all aircraft for sale held by dealers on a consignment basis from an aircraft manufacturer. The Department may assess

a fee not in excess of $50 annually for any such noncommercial dealer fleet licenses issued and a fee not in excess of $100 annually for any such commercial fleet licenses issued. The fee for a commercial single aircraft license shall not be in excess of ten dollars annually.

History.
Code 1950, § 5-5; 1966, c. 576; 1970, c. 717; 1974, c. 431; 1979, c. 272; 1980, c. 721.

Law Review.
For survey of Virginia law on taxation for the year 1973-1974, see 60 Va. L. Rev. 1607 (1974). For survey of Virginia administrative law and utility regulation for the year 1978-1979, see 66 Va. L. Rev. 193 (1980).

CASE NOTES

Tax consequences for nonresident owners. — Section 58.1-1502 levies a tax on the use in the Commonwealth of any aircraft required to be licensed by the Department of Aviation pursuant to this section, which requires that every nonresident owning a civil aircraft based in Virginia over sixty days during any 12 month period shall obtain a license; thus plaintiff's aircraft was required to be licensed and was properly taxed accordingly. Charles E. Smith Mgt., Inc. v. Department of Taxation, 251 Va. 353, 467 S.E.2d 772 (1996).

§ 5.1-6. Repealed by Acts 1988, c. 45.

§ 5.1-7. Licensing of airports and landing areas.

Except as provided in § 5.1-7.2, every person, before operating an airport or landing area or adding or extending a runway, shall first secure from the Department a license. The application therefor shall be made on the form prescribed and furnished by the Department and shall be accompanied by a fee not exceeding $100.

Such license shall be issued for a period not to exceed seven years and shall be renewed every seven years. Before issuing such license, the Department shall require the holder of such license to furnish proof of financial responsibility prescribed in Chapter 8.2 (§ 5.1-88.7 et seq.).

It shall be unlawful for any person to operate any airport or landing area which is open to the general public for the landing or departure of any aircraft until a license therefor shall be issued by the Department.

Before issuing such license for the establishment of a new airport, the Department shall investigate the location of such airport or landing area with the relation to its proximity to and its runway orientation in relation to any other airport or landing area and shall provide for the safety of civil aircraft alighting thereon or departing therefrom. If the proposed airport or landing area shall be so situated as to endanger aircraft using the same or any other airport or landing area in close proximity, and if proper provisions have not been made in all other respects for the safety of aircraft alighting thereon or departing therefrom, the license shall not be granted. To be licensed, an airport required to be licensed under § 5.1-7.2 must meet this criterion and any applicable requirement provided for in regulation promulgated under this section, but no others.

The Board may, by regulation, adopt any other requirements for licensure that are related to the safety of civil aircraft using such airport or landing area. Any airport having a license issued prior to October 1, 1995, and not meeting one or more minimum standards as defined in Part III (24 VAC 5-20-120 et seq.) of the Virginia Aviation Regulations, shall be exempt from having to comply with those noncomplying standards for as long as the airport remains an active public-use facility unless those noncomplying standards are caused by natural growth. Should such airport cease to be open to the public for one year, and subsequently reopen, it shall be required to comply with all applicable minimum standards for licensure.

In addition to the above safety requirements, before a license is initially issued, the Department shall consider the reviews and comments of appropriate state agencies coordinated by the Department of Environmental Quality, and shall cause a public hearing to be held concerning the economic, social and environmental effects of the location or runway orientation of the airport or landing area if the facility is listed in the Virginia Air Transportation System Plan; however, such coordinated review by the Department of Environmental Quality shall not exceed 90 days after the Department has requested review by the Department of Environmental Quality. The public hearing required by this section shall be conducted by the Department of Environmental Quality in the jurisdiction in which the airport or landing area is located, after publication of notice of the hearing in a newspaper of general circulation in such jurisdiction at least 10 days in advance of such hearing.

Any license issued shall describe the number of runways, the length and orientation of each runway and/or, if appropriate, the landing area.

If a runway is to be extended or new runways are to be added, a revised license shall be applied for from the Department. If the airport or landing area is listed in the Virginia Air Transportation System Plan, the Department shall consider the reviews and comments of appropriate state agencies, coordinated by the Department of Environmental Quality, and shall cause a public hearing to be held concerning the economic, social and environmental effects of such changes to the license.

Whenever a public hearing is called for herein, if there has been a public hearing associated with the development of any environmental documents to comply with the receipt of federal funds, the Department and the Department of Environmental Quality may rely on such document or hearing in carrying out their respective duties set out in this section.

If an airport or landing area cannot meet the requirements for licensure that have been adopted by the Virginia Aviation Board, or having met those requirements cannot maintain compliance, the Department may issue conditional licenses to allow time for the airport or landing areas to take steps to meet those requirements or may revoke any license issued, if requirements for licensure are not met or cannot be met.

Any party aggrieved by the granting or refusal to grant any such license shall have a right of appeal to the circuit court of the jurisdiction where the airport or landing area is to be located, which appeal shall be filed in accordance with the Administrative Process Act (§ 2.2-4000 et seq.).

All airports or landing areas that hold licenses or permits shall be issued new licenses, without charge, on or before October 1, 1995, describing the number, length and orientation of the runway or runways or, if appropriate, the landing area, which shall be valid for up to seven years. The length of the new license term may be staggered so that all licenses will not become renewable at the same time. If any airport landing area does not meet the current requirements for licensure, a new license may be issued.

History.
Code 1950, § 5-7; 1966, c. 576; 1979, c. 272; 1980, c. 721; 1981, c. 326; 1991, c. 126; 1995, cc. 682, 690; 1996, cc. 148, 303; 2011, c. 75.

The 2011 amendments.
The 2011 amendment by c. 75 deleted "of this title" from the end of the second paragraph; in the first sentence in the fifth paragraph, inserted "(24 VAC 5-20-120 et seq.)," deleted "(VR 165-01-02:1)" following "Virginia Aviation Regulations," and added "unless those noncomplying standards are caused by natural growth"; made minor stylistic changes in the sixth paragraph; and updated the statutory reference in the next-to-last paragraph.

Law Review.
For article on state constitutions and the environment, see 58 Va. L. Rev. 193 (1972). For survey of Virginia administrative law and utility regulation for the year 1978-1979, see 66 Va. L. Rev. 193 (1980).

CASE NOTES

Editor's note.
The cases annotated below were decided under former § 5.1-8.

This section is a licensing statute, which makes it unlawful for any person, city, county or department of government to operate any airport without first obtaining a permit therefor from the Commission (now Board). Lillard v. Fairfax County Airport Auth., 208 Va. 8, 155 S.E.2d 338 (1967).

And should be applied meaningfully. — This section should be applied meaningfully. Whitman v. Waltrip, 210 Va. 40, 168 S.E.2d 109 (1969).

The University of Virginia is within the terms of this section requiring a permit to operate an airport engaged in commercial aviation. And the State Corporation Commission may issue it a permit although the main purpose of the University is the training of students in scientific aeronautics, and only an incidental portion of the transactions at the airport are commercial. Batcheller v. Commonwealth, 176 Va. 109, 10 S.E.2d 529 (1940).

Board must investigate safety conditions before issuing permit. — Before issuing a permit to operate an airport, the Commission (now Board) shall investigate and determine certain safety conditions with regard to the operation of the airport, its location, its proximity to other airports, and whether in the proposed use thereof "proper provisions have not been made in other respects for the safety of aircraft alighting thereon or departing therefrom." In the event of unfavorable findings, the permit shall be refused. Lillard v. Fairfax County Airport Auth., 208 Va. 8, 155 S.E.2d 338 (1967).

Duty of Board not altered by act creating county airport authority. — Chapter 642, Acts 1964, authorizing the establishment of the Fairfax County Airport Authority does not deprive the State Corporation Commission of the power and duty imposed on it by this section. Lillard v. Fairfax County Airport Auth., 208 Va. 8, 155 S.E.2d 338 (1967).

Matters not requiring denial of permit. — The noise incident to the operation of an airport engaged in commercial aviation, the mere apprehension of injury to homes in the vicinity from the falling of airplanes, the depreciation of the value of property in the community and the presence of nearby historic shrines were held not to require denial of a permit under this section. Batcheller v. Commonwealth, 176 Va. 109, 10 S.E.2d 529 (1940).

§ 5.1-7.1. Repealed by Acts 1980, c. 56.

§ 5.1-7.2. Registration of private landing areas not within five miles of commercial airport.

Any person owning an area for landing any aircraft, which area is not within five miles of a commercial airport and has been constructed by such person for his private use and which is not open to the general public, shall only be required to register, upon forms furnished by the Department, such landing area with the Department and with the Federal Aviation Administration.

History.
1981, c. 326.

§ 5.1-7.3. Duty of care and liability for damages of owners of private landing areas.

A. For the purposes of this section:
"Fee" means any payment or payments of money to a landowner for use of the premises or in order to engage in any activity described in subsections B and C, but does not include any action taken by another to improve the land or access to the land for the purposes set forth in subsections B and C or to remedy damage caused by such uses.

"Land" or "premises" means any privately owned area for landing any aircraft, that is not open to the general public, and that is registered with the Department and the Federal Aviation Administration pursuant to § 5.1-7.2.

"Landowner" means the legal title holder, lessee, occupant, or any other person in control of the land or premises.

B. A landowner shall not be liable for ordinary negligence related to conditions on his premises that proximately cause damage to property or injury to occupants of an aircraft or ultralight vehicle landing on or taking off from such premises, provided that no commercial operation is being conducted on or about the premises.

C. Any landowner who gives permission, express or implied, to another person to operate aircraft or ultralight vehicles of any type for the personal use of such person or for the use of an easement as set forth in subsection B does not thereby:

1. Impliedly or expressly represent that the premises are safe for such purposes;

2. Grant invitee status or its corresponding duty of care to the person to whom such permission has been granted; or

3. Assume responsibility for or incur liability for any intentional or negligent acts of such person or any other person, except as provided in subsection D.

D. Nothing contained in this section shall limit the liability of a landowner that may otherwise arise or exist by reason of his gross negligence or willful or malicious failure to guard or warn against a dangerous condition, use, structure, or activity. The provisions of this section shall not limit the liability of a landowner that may otherwise arise or exist when the landowner receives a fee for use of the premises or to engage in any activity described in subsection B or C. Nothing contained in this section shall relieve any landowner who sponsors or conducts any event or competition of the duty to exercise ordinary care in such events.

History.
2012, c. 302.

§ 5.1-8. Repealed by Acts 1995, cc. 682 and 690, effective October 1, 1995.

§ 5.1-9. Disposition of fees.

All fees or sums collected by the Department under the provisions of this chapter shall be paid into the special fund created by § 5.1-51.

History.
Code 1950, § 5-9; 1966, c. 576; 1979, c. 272.

§ 5.1-9.1. Certain privately owned airports declared to be works of public improvement; exemption from local taxation authorized.

(a) Any public use privately owned airport in this Commonwealth, or any improvements made thereto, which is open to the public at no charge and which has been licensed by the Department is hereby declared to be a work of internal improvement.

(b) The governing body of any city, town or county in this Commonwealth is authorized to exempt from local taxation, as an inducement to their location, the runways and taxiways of any privately owned, public use airport, which is available to the public at no charge and which has been licensed by the Department.

History.
Code 1950, § 5-9.1; 1966, c. 221; 1970, c. 717; 1979, c. 272; 1980, c. 721.

The number of this section was assigned by the Virginia Code Commission, the 1966 act having assigned no number.

§ 5.1-9.2. Contract carriers; permit and license required.

No person shall operate or engage in the business of a contract carrier by aircraft intrastate in the airspace of this Commonwealth unless such person has secured from the Department a permit authorizing him to conduct such operation or to engage in such business and has licensed under § 5.1-5 all aircraft used in this Commonwealth.

History.
Code 1950, § 5.1-103; 1970, c. 708; 1979, c. 357; 1980, c. 721.

§ 5.1-9.3. Same; application for permit; fee; action of Department.

Any person desiring a permit under this chapter shall file with the Department an application in the form prescribed by the Department with a fee of fifty dollars. Such application shall contain a promise of compliance by the applicant with the provisions of this title and with the lawful rules and regulations of the Department governing the operations of contract carriers by aircraft in the airspace of the Commonwealth. Such application may be filed with the Department by the applicant in person or transmitted by registered mail. Upon being satisfied that the provisions of this chapter and the lawful rules and regulations of the Department adopted pursuant hereto, which are prerequisite to the granting of a permit, have been complied with, the Department shall issue such permit to such applicant, subject to such terms, limitations and restrictions as the Department may deem proper, without further proceedings.

History.
Code 1950, § 5.1-104; 1970, c. 708; 1972, c. 232; 1980, c. 721.

§ 5.1-9.4. Repealed by Acts 1988, c. 45.

§ 5.1-9.5. Contract carriers; bonds, insurance or certificate of insurance required prior to issuance of license or permit; securities deposited in lieu thereof.

A. No license or permit shall be issued by the Department to any contract carrier by aircraft until and after such contract carrier has filed with the Department an insurance policy, a bond underwritten by an insurer, or certificate of insurance in lieu thereof, which certificate shall certify that such policy or bond covers the liability of such contract carrier in accordance with the provisions of this statute.

B. Such policy, bond or certificate of insurance shall be issued or underwritten only by an insurer approved or authorized to do business in Virginia, or by one who is eligible as a surplus lines insurer pursuant to Chapter 48 (§ 38.2-4800 et seq.) of Title 38.2, and shall be in amounts not less than the following minimum limits: liability for bodily injury to or death of any one person, passenger or other, aboard the aircraft; $75,000, liability for each occurrence in any one aircraft of at least an amount equal to the sum produced by multiplying $75,000 by seventy-five percent of the total number of passenger seats installed in the aircraft; and liability for loss or damage to cargo owned by others than the insured of at least $10,000 for each occurrence. However, the holder of a license or permit issued by the Department shall not be required to file any cargo insurance, bond, or bonds for cargo liability for the hauling of property transported under contract.

C. In no event shall the limits required herein for contract carriers be less than those prescribed for like carriers by the Civil Aeronautics Board or the Federal Aviation Administration or their successors.

D. In lieu of such policy, underwritten bond or certificate of insurance, a contract carrier may, with the consent of the Department, submit bonds, in an amount approved by the Department, of the United States of America, the Commonwealth of Virginia, or of any municipality of this Commonwealth as security for its bond. Such federal, state, or municipal bonds shall be deposited with the State Treasurer, and shall not be reduced in amount, pledged as security, or otherwise encumbered for any other purpose during the life of such license or permit, except with the prior written approval of the Department.

History.
1980, c. 721.

§ 5.1-9.6. Same; duration and custody of bonds, etc.

Insurance policies, bonds, certificates of insurance, or federal, state, or municipal bonds filed with the Department shall be kept in full force at all times. The policy, bond, or certificate of insurance shall remain in the custody of the Department six months after the insurance or bond has expired or has been canceled for any cause. If federal, state, or municipal bonds are deposited with the State Treasurer as security, such bonds shall remain so deposited until six months after the authority for use of equipment insured has expired or is cancelled for any cause, unless otherwise ordered by the Department.

History.
1980, c. 721.

§ 5.1-9.7. Same; condition of bond, etc.

The insurance bond, or other security, shall obligate the insurer or surety to pay any final judgment for damages sustained by the passengers, shippers, or consignees for injury to any passenger or passengers, or for loss or damage to property entrusted to such contract carrier when a cargo policy is required, and for any and all injuries to persons and loss of, or damage to, property resulting from the negligent operation of any aircraft.

History.
1980, c. 721.

§ 5.1-9.8. Same; effect of failure to give or maintain adequate security.

Failure of any contract carrier holding a license or permit issued by and under the authority of the Department to comply with any of the provisions of §§ 5.1-9.5 through 5.1-9.7 shall be a Class 1 misdemeanor and punishable as such.

History.
1980, c. 721.

Cross references.
As to punishment for Class 1 misdemeanors, see § 18.2-11.

§ 5.1-9.9. Same; duration of permits; suspension or revocation; penalty.

A. Contract carrier permits issued pursuant to this chapter shall be effective from the date of issuance and shall remain in effect only so long as the contract carrier's insurance, underwritten bond or certificate of insurance required by § 5.1-9.5 remains in full force and effect.

B. The Department may suspend or revoke such permit for violation of any of the aviation laws of this Commonwealth or of the United States of America, or for violation of any of the rules and regulations of the Virginia Aviation Board.

C. Willful misrepresentation of any material fact in obtaining a contract carrier permit shall be a Class 1 misdemeanor and punishable as such.

History.
1980, c. 721.

Cross references.
As to punishment for Class 1 misdemeanors, see § 18.2-11.

§ 5.1-10. Repealed by Acts 1979, c. 272.

§ 5.1-11. Government-owned aircraft.

This article shall not apply to public aircraft owned by the United States but shall apply to all other public aircraft.

History.
Code 1950, § 5-14; 1966, c. 576; 1980, c. 721.

§ 5.1-12. Federally certificated airlines and interstate service.

This article shall not apply to any aircraft operated by any air carrier operating under Federal Aviation Regulation Part 121 or Part 135 if operating with an exemption from Title IV of the Federal Aviation Act to provide scheduled passenger service.

History.
Code 1950, § 5-14; 1966, c. 576; 1980, c. 721; 1988, c. 45; 1991, c. 535.

ARTICLE 2.

ILLEGAL OPERATION, ETC.; PROCEDURE; PENALTIES.

§ 5.1-13. Operation of aircraft while under influence of intoxicating liquors or drugs; reckless operation.

Any person who shall operate any aircraft within the airspace over, above or upon the lands or waters of this Commonwealth, while under the influence of intoxicating liquor or of any narcotic or any habit-forming drugs shall be guilty of a felony and shall be confined in a state correctional facility not less than one nor more than five years, or, in the discretion of the court or jury trying the case, be confined in jail not exceeding twelve months and fined not exceeding $500, or both such fine and imprisonment.

Any person who shall operate any aircraft within the airspace over, above or upon the lands or waters of this Commonwealth carelessly or heedlessly in willful or wanton disregard of the rights or safety of others, or without due caution and circumspection and in a manner so as to endanger any person or property, shall be guilty of a misdemeanor.

History.
Code 1950, § 5-10.1; 1964, c. 416; 1966, c. 576.

CASE NOTES

As to meaning of "being intoxicated" or "under the influence of intoxicating liquor," see Gardner v. Commonwealth, 195 Va. 945, 81 S.E.2d 614 (1954).

A pilot has a right to assume that another pilot will obey air traffic regulations until he realizes, or in the exercise of ordinary care should have realized, that the other pilot is not going to do so. Mackey v. Miller, 221 Va. 715, 273 S.E.2d 550 (1981).

Violation of section was negligence per se. — Air Force pilot's violation of this section constituted negligence per se, where he flew his plane at such a low altitude that the turbulence from its wake caused a large limb from a tree to fall on and severely injure a timber cutter. Musick v. United States, 768 F. Supp. 183 (W.D. Va. 1991).

§ 5.1-14. Operation of unlicensed aircraft.

Any person who operates or causes to be operated any civil aircraft within the airspace over, above or upon the lands or waters of this Commonwealth, which aircraft has not been and is not at the time of such operation properly certificated under and in accordance with existing federal law and licensed under and in accordance with the existing laws of this Commonwealth and rules and regulations promulgated in pursuance thereof, shall be guilty of a misdemeanor.

History.
Code 1950, § 5-10.2; 1966, c. 576.

§ 5.1-15. Operation of aircraft by unlicensed persons.

Any person who operates any civil aircraft within the airspace over, above, or upon the lands or waters of this Commonwealth, without being, at the time of such operation, in possession of a valid airman's certificate for such operation, issued under and in accordance with existing federal law shall be deemed to be guilty of a Class 1 misdemeanor.

History.
Code 1950, § 5-10.3; 1966, c. 576; 1988, c. 45.

Cross references.
As to punishment for Class 1 misdemeanors, see § 18.2-11.

§ 5.1-16. Tampering with, etc., airplanes or markings of airports, landing fields or other aeronautical facilities.

It shall be unlawful for any person to tamper with, alter, destroy, remove, carry away, or cause to be carried away, an airplane or other flying device or instrumentality or any objects used for the marking of airports, landing fields, drop zones or other aeronautical facilities, or in any way change their position or location, except by and under the direction of the proper authorities charged with the maintenance and operation of such facilities. Any person violating any of the provisions of this section or who shall illegally have in his possession any objects or devices used for such markings, shall be guilty of a misdemeanor.

History.
Code 1950, § 5-10.4; 1966, c. 576.

Cross references.
As to breaking, injuring, defacing, destroying or preventing the operation of aircraft, see § 18.2-146.

§ 5.1-16.1. Misuse of licensed airports.

It shall be unlawful for any person or persons to use licensed airport runways, taxiways or ramp areas for other than aeronautical purposes without written approval of the controlling authority of such airport.

History.
1970, c. 717.

§ 5.1-17. Use of aircraft for hunting.

It shall be unlawful for any person to hunt, pursue or kill any wild waterfowl or other birds or animals by any means whatever during such time as such person is in flight in an aircraft in the airspace over the lands or waters of this Commonwealth. A violation of this section shall be deemed a misdemeanor.

History.
Code 1950, § 5-10.5; 1966, c. 576.

§§ 5.1-18, 5.1-19. Repealed by Acts 1988, c. 45.

§ 5.1-20. Pilot may restrain or arrest person interfering with operation of aircraft carrying passengers for hire.

The pilot of any aircraft carrying passengers for hire, or any person subject to his direction, may take such action as is reasonably necessary to restrain or arrest any person who interferes with, or threatens to interfere with, the operation of the aircraft in flight over the territory of this Commonwealth or to a destination within this Commonwealth.

History.
Code 1950, § 5-14.1; 1958, c. 561, § 1; 1966, c. 576.

§ 5.1-21. Powers of conservator of the peace conferred upon pilot.

The pilot of any aircraft carrying passengers for hire while actively engaged in the operation of such aircraft shall be a special policeman and have all the powers of a conservator of the peace in the enforcement of order on such aircraft and while in pursuit of persons for disorder upon such aircraft and until such persons as may be arrested by him shall have been placed in confinement or delivered to the custody of some other conservator of the peace or police officer.

History.
Code 1950, § 5-14.2; 1958, c. 561, § 2; 1966, c. 576.

§ 5.1-21.1. Powers of conservators of the peace conferred upon airport managers or designees.

The airport manager of any licensed Virginia airport or in his absence not more than two employees who are designated by him shall be special policemen and have all the powers of conservators of the peace in the enforcement of this title and its regulations as promulgated by the Board. Persons arrested by them shall be placed in confinement or delivered to the custody of some other conservator of the peace or police officer.

History.
1970, c. 717; 1979, c. 272; 1991, c. 339.

§ 5.1-22. Interference with operation of aircraft; penalties; venue.

Any person who interferes with or threatens to interfere with the operation of any aircraft, unless he is authorized by the Federal Aviation Administration or the armed forces of the United States, on or over the territory of the Commonwealth shall be guilty of a Class 1 misdemeanor. Where the act or acts of interference or threatened interference are of such a nature as to endanger the life of the aircraft's operator or the life of any other person, the person interfering or threatening to interfere shall be guilty of a Class 6 felony. Any person who knowingly and intentionally projects a point of light from a laser, laser gun sight, or any other device that simulates a laser at an aircraft is guilty of a Class 1 misdemeanor. Venue for the issuance of a warrant for the arrest and trial of any such person is hereby conferred upon any court having criminal jurisdiction in the political subdivision in the Commonwealth where the aircraft either took off prior to such offense, or where it lands or comes to rest subsequent to such offense, or in or over which the offense occurred.

History.
Code 1950, § 5-14.3; 1958, c. 561, § 3; 1966, c. 576; 1983, c. 560; 2012, c. 398.

Cross references.
As to punishment for Class 6 felonies, see § 18.2-10. As to punishment for Class 1 misdemeanors, see § 18.2-11.

The 2012 amendments.
The 2012 amendment by c. 398 inserted ", unless he is authorized by the Federal Aviation Administration or the armed forces of the United States," in the first sentence; inserted the third sentence; and substituted "the Commonwealth" for "this Commonwealth" twice.

Law Review.
For article surveying developments in criminal law and procedure in Virginia from July 2001 to September 2002, see 37 U. Rich. L. Rev. 45 (2002).

CASE NOTES

Intent. — Specific intent is not an element of § 5.1-22. Johnson v. Commonwealth, 37 Va. App. 634, 561 S.E.2d 1, 2002 Va. App. LEXIS 160 (2002).
Proof of misdemeanor. — Proof of a misdemeanor violation of § 5.1-22 does not require proof that the pilot or any other person was endangered, which is an element of the related felony. Johnson v. Commonwealth, 37 Va. App. 634, 561 S.E.2d 1, 2002 Va. App. LEXIS 160 (2002).

§ 5.1-23. Jurisdiction of local and State Police.

The local police authorities of any city, incorporated town or county shall have jurisdiction on the premises of any airport, drop zone or landing field operated hereunder, either individually or jointly and the State Police shall have jurisdiction to investigate any aircraft accident. In the exercise of such jurisdiction the State Police and officers of the department of law enforcement of any city or county with an optional form of government may enter with immunity and without a warrant upon private property for the purpose of conducting such investigations. This section shall not repeal the provisions of any city charter in conflict herewith.

History.
Code 1950, § 5-37; 1966, c. 576; 1968, c. 737; 1979, c. 394; 1980, c. 721.

§ 5.1-24. Penalties.

Any person violating any of the provisions of this chapter, or violating any of the rules or regulations promulgated pursuant thereto by the Board, except as otherwise specifically provided, shall be deemed guilty of a misdemeanor and upon conviction shall be punished by a fine of not more than $100 or imprisonment in jail not exceeding one month, or both, in the discretion of the judge or jury trying the case; provided, that any person (excepting any government, political subdivision of the Commonwealth, or governmental subdivision or agency) establishing or operating an airport without first obtaining a permit as provided in § 5.1-8 shall, upon conviction, be fined not less than $100 nor more than $500 for each offense, and each day that the airport is operated without such permit shall be construed as a separate offense.

History.
Code 1950, § 5-11; 1966, c. 576; 1979, c. 272.

§ 5.1-25. Operation of aircraft by nonresident.

A nonresident of this Commonwealth may operate aircraft engaged in operations other than for hire or reward in accordance with regulations promulgated by the Board, provided such nonresident and the aircraft to be so operated shall have been certified under federal law and shall have complied with the laws of the state in which such nonresident resides relative to aircraft and the operation thereof. A nonresident-owned aircraft engaged in intrastate operation for hire or reward must be licensed with the Department in accordance with this title and the Board's regulations.

History.
Code 1950, § 5-12; 1966, c. 576; 1970, c. 717; 1979, c. 272; 1988, c. 45.

ARTICLE 3.

STRUCTURES DANGEROUS TO AIRCRAFT.

§ 5.1-25.1. Permit required for erection of certain structures.

It shall be unlawful for any person to erect any structure, any part of which penetrates into or through any licensed airport's or United States government or military air facility's clear zone, approach zone, imaginary surface, obstruction clearance surface, obstruction clearance zone, or surface or zone as described in regulations of the Department of Aviation or the Federal Aviation Administration, without securing a permit for its erection from the Board. This section shall not apply to any structure to be erected in a county, city or town which has an ordinance regulating the height of such structures to prevent the penetration of zones and surfaces provided for in Federal Aviation Regulation Part 77 and Rule 19 of the Department of Aviation.

For the purpose of this section, *"structure"* shall mean any object, including a mobile object, constructed or erected by man, including but not limited to buildings, towers, cranes, smokestacks, earth formations, overhead transmission lines, flag poles, and ship masts.

History.
  1968, c. 744; 1979, c. 272; 1981, c. 326; 1989, cc. 202, 255; 1990, c. 384.

  The numbers of §§ 5.1-25.1 through 5.1-25.4 were assigned by the Virginia Code Commission, the 1968 act having assigned no numbers.

§ 5.1-25.2. Application for permit; notice and hearing.

Any person desiring to erect or cause to be erected any such structure shall make application to the Department for the issuance of a permit for such erection. Such application shall be forwarded immediately to the Board. The Department shall undertake an appropriate review of such application and submit its contents in writing to the Board as expeditiously as possible. The Board, after such notice to the public as it deems necessary, shall hold a public hearing not less than thirty days after the giving of such notice at which all interested parties shall be admitted to attend and state any objection which they may have to the erection of such structure.

History.
  1968, c. 744; 1979, c. 272.

§ 5.1-25.3. When permit issued or denied; conditions to issuance.

The Board, if it finds that the erection of such structure will not be dangerous to aircraft using the airways of this Commission, shall issue the permit requested; but if it shall find that the erection of such structure will create a hazard to aircraft using such airways, it shall refuse the issuance of such a permit. The Board may, as a condition to the issuance of any permit, require the installation and maintenance of warning lights and any other devices which may be reasonably required to reduce the hazard which might be presented by the erection of such structure.

History.
  1968, c. 744.

§ 5.1-25.4. Injunctions.

If any person commences the erection of a structure of the nature described in § 5.1-25.1 without securing the permit therein required, the Department shall have power to apply forthwith to the circuit court of the jurisdiction in which the structure is located or is to be located, for injunctive relief.

History.
  1968, c. 744; 1979, c. 272.

Law Review.
  For survey of Virginia administrative law and utility regulation for the year 1978-1979, see 66 Va. L. Rev. 193 (1980).

CHAPTER 2.1.

VIRGINIA AIRPORTS REVOLVING FUND.

§ 5.1-30.1. Definitions.

As used in this chapter, unless the context requires otherwise:

"Authority" means the Virginia Resources Authority created in Chapter 21 (§ 62.1-197 et seq.) of Title 62.1.

"Cost," as applied to any project financed under the provisions of this chapter, means the total of all costs incurred by the local government as reasonable and necessary for carrying out all works and undertakings necessary or incident to the accomplishment of any project. It includes, without limitation, all necessary developmental, planning and feasibility studies, surveys, plans and specifications; architectural, engineering, financial, legal or other special services; the cost of acquisition of land and any buildings and improvements thereon, including the discharge of any obligations of the sellers of such land, buildings or improvements; site preparation and development, including demolition or removal of existing structures; construction and reconstruction; labor; materials, machinery and equipment; the reasonable costs of financing incurred by the local government in the course of the development of the project; carrying charges incurred before placing the project in service; interest on funds borrowed to finance the project to a date subsequent to the estimated date the project is to be placed in service; necessary expenses incurred in connection with placing the project in service; the funding of accounts and reserves which the Authority may re-

quire; and the cost of other items which the Authority determines to be reasonable and necessary.

"*Fund*" means the Virginia Airports Revolving Fund created by this chapter.

"*Local government*" means any county, city, town, municipal corporation, authority, district, commission or political subdivision created by the General Assembly or pursuant to the Constitution or laws of the Commonwealth or any combination of any two or more of the foregoing.

"*Project*" means all or any part of an airport as defined in § 5.1-1 and may consist of or include any or all facilities related to the needs or convenience of passengers, shipping companies, and airlines, together with any or all buildings or other structures, improvements, additions, extensions, replacements, machinery or equipment, and any or all appurtenances, lands, rights in land, avigation rights, water rights, rights-of-way, franchises, furnishings, landscaping, utilities, approaches, roadways, or other facilities necessary or desirable in connection therewith or incidental thereto.

History.
1999, c. 897.

§ 5.1-30.2. Creation and management of Virginia Airports Revolving Fund.

There shall be set apart as a permanent and perpetual fund, to be known as the "Virginia Airports Revolving Fund," sums appropriated to the Fund by the General Assembly, all receipts by the Fund from loans made by it to local governments, all income from the investment of moneys held in the Fund, and any other sums designated for deposit to the Fund from any source public or private, including without limitation any federal grants, awards or other forms of assistance received by the Commonwealth that are eligible for deposit therein under federal law. The Authority shall administer and manage the Fund, and establish the interest rates and repayment terms of such loans as provided in this chapter, in accordance with a memorandum of agreement with the Board. The Board shall direct the distribution of loans from the Fund to particular local governments. Consistent with this chapter, the Board shall, after consultation with all interested parties, develop a guidance document governing project eligibility and project priority criteria. In order to carry out the administration and management of the Fund, the Authority, in consultation with the Board, is granted the power to employ officers, employees, agents, advisers and consultants, including, without limitation, attorneys, financial advisers, engineers and other technical advisers and public accountants and, the provisions of any other law to the contrary notwithstanding, to determine their duties and compensation without the approval of any other agency or instrumentality. The Authority may disburse from the Fund its reasonable costs and expenses incurred in the ad-

ministration and management of the Fund and a reasonable fee to be approved by the Board for its management services.

History.
1999, c. 897.

§ 5.1-30.3. Deposit of money; expenditures; investments.

All money belonging to the Fund shall be deposited in an account or accounts in banks or trust companies organized under the laws of the Commonwealth or in national banking associations located in Virginia or in savings institutions located in Virginia organized under the laws of the Commonwealth or the United States. The money in these accounts shall be paid by check signed by the Executive Director of the Authority or other officers or employees designated by the Board of Directors of the Authority. All deposits of money shall, if required by the Authority, be secured in a manner determined by the Authority to be prudent, and all banks, trust companies and savings institutions are authorized to give security for the deposits. Money in the Fund shall not be commingled with other money of the Authority. Money in the Fund not needed for immediate use or disbursement may be invested or reinvested by the Authority in obligations or securities which are considered lawful investments for public funds under the laws of the Commonwealth.

History.
1999, c. 897.

§ 5.1-30.4. Collection of money due Fund.

The Authority is empowered to collect, or to authorize others to collect on its behalf, amounts due to the Fund under any loan to a local government, including, if appropriate, taking the action required by § 15.2-2659 to obtain payment of any amounts in default. Proceedings to recover amounts due to the Fund may be instituted by the Authority in the name of the Fund in the appropriate circuit court.

History.
1999, c. 897.

§ 5.1-30.5. Loans to local governments.

Except as otherwise provided in this chapter, money in the Fund shall be used solely to make loans to local governments to finance or refinance the cost of any project. The local governments to which loans are to be made, the purposes of the loan, and the amount of each such loan, shall be designated in writing by the Board to the Authority following consultation with the Authority. No loan from the Fund shall exceed the total cost of the project to be financed or the outstanding principal amount of the indebtedness to be refinanced plus reasonable financing expenses.

Except as otherwise provided in this chapter, the Authority shall determine the interest rate and terms and conditions of any loan from the Fund, which may vary between local governments. Each loan shall be evidenced by appropriate bonds or notes of the local government payable to the Fund. The bonds or notes shall have been duly authorized by the local government and executed by its authorized legal representatives. The Authority is authorized to require in connection with any loan from the Fund such documents, instruments, certificates, legal opinions and other information as it may deem necessary or convenient. In addition to any other terms or conditions which the Authority may establish, the Authority may require, as a condition to making any loan from the Fund, that the local government receiving the loan covenant perform any of the following:

1. Establish and collect rents, rates, fees, and charges to produce revenue sufficient to pay all or a specified portion of (i) the costs of operation, maintenance, replacement, renewal, and repairs of the project; (ii) any outstanding indebtedness incurred for the purposes of the project, including the principal of, premium, if any, and interest on the loan from the Fund to the local government; and (iii) any amounts necessary to create and maintain any required reserve, including any rate stabilization fund deemed necessary or appropriate by the Authority to offset the need, in whole or in part, for future increases in rents, rates, fees, or charges.

2. Create and maintain a special fund or funds for the payment of the principal of, premium, if any, and interest on the loan from the Fund to the local government and any other amounts becoming due under any agreement entered into in connection with the loan, or for the operation, maintenance, repair, or replacement of the project or any portions thereof or other property of the local government, and deposit into any fund or funds amounts sufficient to make any payments on the loan as they become due and payable.

3. Create and maintain other special funds as required by the Authority.

4. Perform other acts otherwise permitted by applicable law to secure payment of the principal of, premium, if any, and interest on the loan from the Fund to the local government and to provide for the remedies of the Fund in the event of any default by the local government in the payment of the loan, including, without limitation, any of the following:

a. The procurement of insurance, guarantees, letters of credit and other forms of collateral, security, liquidity arrangements or credit supports for the loan from any source, public or private, and the payment therefor of premiums, fees, or other charges;

b. The combination of one or more projects, or the combination of one or more projects with one or more other undertakings, facilities, utilities, or systems, for the purpose of operations and financing, and the pledging of the revenues from such combined projects, undertakings, facilities, utilities, and systems to secure the loan from the Fund to the local government made in connection with such combination or any part or parts thereof;

c. The maintenance, replacement, renewal, and repair of the project; and

d. The procurement of casualty and liability insurance.

5. Obtain a review of the accounting and the internal controls from the Auditor of Public Accounts or his legally authorized representatives. The Authority may request additional reviews at any time during the term of the loan. In addition, anyone receiving a report in accordance with § 5.1-30.9 may request an additional review as set forth in this section.

All local governments borrowing money from the Fund are authorized to perform any acts, take any action, adopt any proceedings and make and carry out any contracts that are contemplated by this chapter. Such contracts need not be identical among all local governments, but may be structured as determined by the Authority according to the needs of the contracting local governments and the Fund.

Subject to the rights, if any, of the registered owners of any of the bonds of the Authority, the Authority may consent to and approve any modification in the terms of any loan to any local government.

History.
1999, c. 897.

§ 5.1-30.6. Pledge of loans to secure bonds of Authority.

The Authority is empowered at any time and from time to time to pledge, assign or transfer from the Fund to banks or trust companies designated by the Authority any or all of the assets of the Fund to be held in trust as security for the payment of the principal of, premium, if any, and interest on any or all of the bonds, as defined in § 62.1-199, issued to finance any project. The interests of the Fund in any assets so transferred shall be subordinate to the rights of the trustee under the pledge, assignment or transfer. To the extent funds are not available from other sources pledged for such purpose, any of the assets or payments of principal and interest received on the assets pledged, assigned or transferred or held in trust may be applied by the trustee thereof to the payment of the principal of, premium, if any, and interest on such bonds of the Authority secured thereby, and, if such payments are insufficient for such purpose, the trustee is empowered to sell any or all of such assets and apply the net proceeds from the sale to the payment of the principal of, premium, if any, and interest on such bonds of the Authority. Any assets of the Fund pledged, assigned or transferred in trust as set forth above and any payments of principal, interest or earnings received thereon shall remain part of the Fund but shall be subject to the pledge, assignment or transfer to secure the bonds of the Authority and shall be held by the trustee to which they are pledged, assigned or transferred until no longer required for such purpose by the terms of the pledge, assignment or transfer.

History.
1999, c. 897.

§ 5.1-30.7. Sale of loans.

The Authority is empowered at any time and from time to time to sell, upon such terms and conditions as the Authority shall deem appropriate, any loan, or interest therein, made pursuant to this chapter. The net proceeds of sale remaining after the payment of the costs and expenses of the sale shall be designated for deposit to, and become part of, the Fund.

History.
1999, c. 897.

§ 5.1-30.8. Powers of the Authority.

The Authority is authorized to do any act necessary or convenient to the exercise of the powers granted in this chapter or reasonably implied thereby.

History.
1999, c. 897.

§ 5.1-30.9. Report to the General Assembly and Governor.

The Board, in conjunction with the Authority, shall report annually on or before December 1 to the General Assembly and the Governor on all loans made from the Fund.

History.
1999, c. 897; 2005, c. 633.

§ 5.1-30.10. Liberal construction of chapter.

The provisions of this chapter shall be liberally construed to the end that its beneficial purposes may be effectuated. Insofar as the provisions of this chapter are inconsistent with the provisions of any other law, general, special or local, the provisions of this chapter shall be controlling.

History.
1999, c. 897.

CHAPTER 9.
AIR CARRIERS.

Article 1. In General.

ARTICLE 1.

IN GENERAL.

Michie's Jurisprudence.

For related discussion, see 2B M.J. Aviation, § 1; 3B M.J. Carriers, § 117; 15 M.J. Public Service and State Corporation Commissions, §§ 17, 21.

§ 5.1-89. Definitions.

Whenever used in this chapter unless expressly stated otherwise:

(a) The term *"person"* means any individual, firm, copartnership, corporation, company, association or joint-stock association, and includes any trustee, receiver, assignee, or personal representative thereof.

(b) The term *"aircraft"* means any contrivance, except a contrivance operating twenty-four inches or less above ground or water level, now known or hereafter invented, used, or designed for navigation of, or flight in, the airspace in the transportation of passengers, property or mail.

(c) The term *"common carrier by aircraft"* means any person who undertakes, whether directly or by a lease or any other arrangement, to transport passengers, property for the general public, or mail by aircrafts for compensation (wholly within the airspace of the Commonwealth), whether over regular or irregular routes, including such aircraft operations of carriers by rail, water or motor vehicle and of express or forwarding companies.

(d) The term *"restricted common carrier by aircraft"* means any person who undertakes, whether directly or by lease or other arrangement, to transport passengers or property of any restricted class or classes by aircraft for compensation whether over regular or irregular routes.

(e) [Repealed.]

(f) The term *"air carrier"* includes a common carrier by aircraft, a restricted common carrier by aircraft, and a contract carrier by aircraft.

(g) The term *"broker"* means any person not included in the term air carrier and not a bona fide employee or agent of any such carrier, who, as principal or agent, sells or offers for sale any transportation subject to this chapter, or negotiates for, or holds himself out by solicitation, advertisement, or otherwise as one who sells, provides, furnishes, contracts, or arranges for such transportation.

(h) The *"services"* and *"transportation"* to which this chapter applies include all aircraft operated by, for, or in the interest of, any air carrier irrespective of ownership or contract, express or implied, together with all facilities and property operated or controlled by any such carrier or carriers and used in the transportation of passengers, property or mail or in the performance of any service in connection therewith.

(i) The term *"certificate"* means a certificate of public convenience and necessity issued by the State Corporation Commission to common carriers by aircraft and restricted common carriers by aircraft under this chapter.

(j) [Repealed.]

(k) The term *"airport"* means a landing area used regularly by aircraft for receiving or discharging passengers or cargo, and open to the public for use.

(*l*) The term *"landing area"* means any locality, either of land or water, including airports and intermediate landing fields, which is used, or intended to be used, for the landing and takeoff of aircraft, whether or not facilities are provided for the shelter, servicing, or repair of aircraft, or for receiving or discharging passengers or cargo, and open to the public for such use.

(m) The term *"airspace"* means all airspace above the lands and waters within the boundary of this Commonwealth.

(n) For the purposes of this chapter, *"Commission"* means the State Corporation Commission.

History.

Code 1950, § 56-142; 1952, c. 597; 1970, c. 708; 1979, c. 272; 1980, c. 721.

§ 5.1-90. Exempted aircraft.

This chapter shall not be construed to cover or include aircraft used exclusively in transporting or handling United States mail, or aircraft while used exclusively in interstate commerce; provided, however, that any common carrier of passengers by airplane holding proper authority for and operating in interstate commerce on January 1, 1970, in the transportation of passengers between any licensed airport adjacent to or within three miles of the Virginia State Line on the one hand and any other licensed airport in Virginia on the other, shall, without further proceedings, be issued a certificate by the Commission authorizing such operations as a common carrier of passengers by aircraft in intrastate commerce if application is made to the Commission within 120 days after this section takes effect. Pending the determination of any such application, the continuance of such operation without a certificate shall be lawful.

History.
Code 1950, § 56-143; 1952, c. 597; 1970, c. 708.

§ 5.1-90.1. Incidental transportation of certain passengers and property by motor vehicle.

Nothing in this chapter or in Chapter 12 (§ 56-273 et seq.) of Title 56 shall be construed to prohibit the transportation of property or guards or other attendants of such property by motor vehicle when such transportation is incidental to transportation by aircraft, provided that such transportation shall not exceed twenty-five miles from airport to destination of such guards or other attendants or property.

History.
1972, c. 281.

Editor's note.
Chapter 12 of Title 56, referred to in this section, was repealed by Acts 1995, cc. 744 and 803, effective January 1, 1996.

§ 5.1-91. Air carriers to comply with chapter; subject to regulation by Commission.

No air carrier shall operate any aircraft for the transportation of passengers or property for compensation in the airspace of this Commonwealth except in accordance with the provisions of this chapter, and every such air carrier is hereby declared to be subject to control, supervision and regulation by the Commission.

History.
Code 1950, § 56-144; 1970, c. 708.

§ 5.1-92. Regulation by Commission; reports; prevention of discrimination.

The Commission shall supervise, regulate and control all air carriers, doing business in this Commonwealth, in all matters relating to the performance of their public duties and their charges therefor, and shall correct abuses therein by such air carriers; and to that end the Commission shall, from time to time, prescribe reasonable rules, regulations, forms and reports for such air carriers in furtherance of the administration and operation of this chapter; and the Commission shall have the right at all times to require from such air carriers special reports and statements under oath, concerning their business.

The Commission shall, from time to time, make and enforce such requirements, rules and regulations as may be necessary to prevent unjust and unreasonable discriminations by any air carrier in favor of, or against, any person, locality, community or connecting carrier in the matter of service, schedule, efficiency of transportation or otherwise, in connection with the public duties of such air carriers; and the Commission shall administer and enforce all provisions of this chapter, and prescribe reasonable rules, regulations and procedure looking to that end.

History.
Code 1950, § 56-145; 1970, c. 708.

§ 5.1-93. Regulation of brokers.

The Commission shall also regulate brokers and make and enforce reasonable requirements respecting their licenses, financial responsibility, accounts, records, reports, operations and practices.

History.
Code 1950, § 56-146; 1970, c. 708.

ARTICLE 2.

ISSUANCE OF CERTIFICATES OF CONVENIENCE AND RIGHTS THEREUNDER.

§ 5.1-94. Required certificate of public convenience and necessity.

No common carrier by aircraft or restricted common carrier by aircraft (not herein exempted) shall engage in intrastate operation in the airspace of this Commonwealth without first having obtained from the Commission a certificate of public convenience and necessity authorizing such operation.

History.
Code 1950, § 56-147; 1970, c. 708.

§ 5.1-95. Application for certificate; notices, etc.

The Commission shall prescribe the form of the application for a certificate of convenience and necessity, and such reasonable requirements as to notices, publication, proof of service and information as may in its judgment be necessary.

History.
Code 1950, § 56-148; 1970, c. 708.

§ 5.1-96. Fees in connection with certificates.

Every air carrier, upon filing with the Commission an application for a certificate, shall deposit with the Commission as a filing fee the sum of $100, and for the transfer of such certificate the sum of $100, and for the issuance of a duplicate certificate the sum of $5; provided, however, that an applicant for a certificate in lieu of an existing certificate, as provided by law, shall not be required to pay the fees prescribed in this section.

History.
Code 1950, § 56-149; 1970, c. 708.

§ 5.1-97. Hearing on application; action of Commission.

Upon the filing of an application for a certificate of public convenience and necessity, the Commission shall, within a reasonable time, fix a time and place of hearing on such application. If the Commission shall find that the proposed operation justified it, it shall issue a certificate to the applicant, subject to such terms, limitations and restrictions as the Commission may deem proper. If the Commission shall find the proposed operation not justified, the application shall be denied.

History.
Code 1950, § 56-150; 1970, c. 708.

§ 5.1-98. Factors to be considered by the Commission in granting certificates.

In granting certificates of public convenience and necessity pursuant to § 5.1-94, the Commission shall take into consideration, among other things, the business experience of the particular passenger air carrier in the field of air operations, the financial stability of the carrier, the insurance coverage of the carrier, the type of aircraft which the carrier would employ, proposed routes and minimum schedules to be established, whether the carrier could economically give adequate service to the communities involved, the need for the service, and any other factors which may affect the public interest.

History.
Code 1950, § 56-152; 1970, c. 708.

Law Review.
For article on state constitutions and the environment, see 58 Va. L. Rev. 193 (1972).

§ 5.1-99. Occasional deviations from authorized routes; emergency landings.

A common carrier by aircraft, or a restricted common carrier by aircraft, operating under a certificate issued by the Commission may occasionally deviate from the route over which it is authorized to operate under the certificate, under such general or special rules and regulations as the Commission may prescribe.

No air carrier shall be deemed to have violated any term, condition, or limitation of its certificate by landing or taking off during an emergency at a point not named in its certificate or by operating in an emergency, under regulations which may be prescribed by the Commission, between terminal and intermediate points other than those specified in its certificate.

History.
Code 1950, § 56-153; 1970, c. 708.

§ 5.1-100. Transportation of baggage, mail, etc., with passengers.

A certificate for the transportation of passengers may include, when so authorized by the Commission, authority to transport, in the same aircraft with passengers, the baggage of such passengers, newspapers, express parcels, or United States mail when the transportation thereof is authorized by the government of the United States of America; provided that the total weight of the aircraft and its contents shall not exceed that weight authorized by the "Operations Record" of the individual aircraft.

History.
Code 1950, § 56-154; 1970, c. 708.

§ 5.1-101. Chartered parties covered by common carriers.

Any common carrier by aircraft transporting passengers under a certificate issued by the Commission may operate to any place special or chartered parties, under such reasonable rules and regulations as the Commission may prescribe.

History.
Code 1950, § 56-155; 1970, c. 708.

§ 5.1-102. Schedule changes require Commission approval.

A common carrier by aircraft or a restricted common carrier by aircraft operation under a certificate issued by the Commission shall not make any change in schedules or service without having first received the approval of the Commission for such change in schedules or service.

History.
Code 1950, § 56-156; 1970, c. 708.

ARTICLE 3.

CONTRACT CARRIERS AND LIMITED FOR-HIRE SERVICE.

§§ 5.1-103 through 5.1-106. Repealed by Acts 1980, c. 721.

Cross references.
For present provisions as to contract carriers and limited for-hire service, see §§ 5.1-9.2 through 5.1-9.9.

ARTICLE 4.

TEMPORARY AUTHORITY.

§ 5.1-107. Issuance of temporary authority by Commission pending hearing on application for certificate.

To enable the provision of service for which there is an immediate and urgent need to a point or between points in Virginia, the Commission, may, pending its determination of an application for such permanent authority, in its discretion and without hearing or other proceeding, grant temporary authority for such service by common carrier by aircraft or restricted common carrier by aircraft, as the case may be. Such temporary authority shall be valid for such time as the Commission shall specify but not for more than an aggregate of 180 days, and shall create no presumption that corresponding permanent authority will be granted thereafter.

History.
1970, c. 708.

Michie's Jurisprudence.
For related discussion, see 8A M.J. Express Companies, § 2.

ARTICLE 5.

REGULATION OF BROKERS.

§ 5.1-108. When broker's license required.

No person shall for compensation sell or offer for sale transportation subject to this chapter or shall make any contract, agreement, or arrangement to provide, procure, furnish, or arrange for such transportation or shall hold himself or itself out by advertisement, solicitation, or otherwise as one who sells, provides, procures, contracts, or arranges for such transportation, unless such person holds a broker's license issued by the Commission to engage in such transactions; provided that the provisions of this section shall not apply to any carrier holding a certificate or permit under the provisions of this chapter or to any bona fide employee or agent of such carrier so far as concerns transportation to be furnished wholly by such carrier or jointly with other air carriers holding like certificates or permits, or with a common carrier by railroad, motor vehicle, express or water; nor shall they apply to any air carrier not engaged in intrastate operations or to any bona fide employee of such carrier.

History.
Code 1950, § 56-162; 1970, c. 708.

§ 5.1-109. Application for broker's license.

The Commission shall prescribe the form of application for a broker's license and such reasonable requirements and information as may in its judg-

ment be necessary, and may assess a fee of ten dollars for filing.

History.
Code 1950, § 56-163; 1970, c. 708.

§ 5.1-110. Hearing on such application and action thereon.

Upon the filing of an application for a broker's license the Commission may fix a time and place for the hearing of the application and require such notices, publication, or other service as may, in its judgment, be necessary. If the Commission finds the application proper and in the public interest it shall issue a license, subject to such terms, limitations and restrictions as the Commission may deem proper.

History.
Code 1950, § 56-164; 1970, c. 708.

§ 5.1-111. Authority over brokers; bond.

The Commission shall have the same authority over persons operating under and holding a brokerage license as it has over air carriers under this chapter and shall require a broker to furnish bond or other security approved by the Commission and sufficient for the protection of travelers or shippers by aircraft.

History.
Code 1950, § 56-165; 1970, c. 708.

§ 5.1-112. Broker's license not substitute for other certificates or permits required.

No person who holds a broker's license under this chapter shall engage in transportation subject to this chapter unless he holds a certificate or permit as provided in this chapter. In the execution of any contract, agreement, or arrangement to sell, provide, procure, furnish, or arrange for such transportation, it shall be unlawful for such person to employ any aircraft which is not the lawful holder of an effective certificate or permit issued as provided in this chapter.

History.
Code 1950, § 56-166; 1970, c. 708.

ARTICLE 6.

DURATION, REVOCATION, TRANSFER AND VALUE OF CERTIFICATES, ETC.; PENALTIES.

§ 5.1-113. Duration of certificates, etc.; suspension, revocation, or amendment; penalties.

Certificates, permits and licenses issued under the provisions of this chapter shall be effective from the dates specified therein and shall remain in effect until terminated as herein provided. The Commission may at any time, by its order duly entered after hearing held after notice to the holder of any such certificate, permit or license and an opportunity to such holder to be heard at which it shall be proved that such holder has willfully made any misrepresentation of a material fact in obtaining such certificate, permit or license, or has willfully violated or refused to observe the laws of this Commonwealth touching such certificate, permit or license, or any of the terms of his certificate, permit or license, or any of the Commission's proper orders, rules or regulations, impose a penalty not exceeding $1,000, which may be collected by the process of the Commission as provided by law; or the Commission may suspend, revoke, alter or amend any such certificate, permit or license for any of the causes set forth above. But no such certificate, permit or license shall be revoked, altered or amended (except upon application of the holder thereof) unless the holder thereof shall willfully fail to comply, within a reasonable time to be fixed by the Commission, with the lawful order of the Commission or with the lawful rule or regulation of the Commission, or with the term, condition or limitation of such certificate, permit or license, found by the Commission to have been violated by such holder.

Proceedings for the imposition of any penalty provided for in this section may be commenced upon the complaint of any person or upon the Commission's own initiative.

From any order of the Commission suspending, revoking, altering or amending any certificate, permit or license, the holder thereof shall have the right of appeal to the Supreme Court of Virginia, as a matter of right, as in other cases of appeals from the Commission.

History.
Code 1950, § 56-167; 1970, c. 708.

§ 5.1-114. Transfer or lease of certificate.

Any certificate issued under this chapter may be transferred or leased, subject to the approval of the Commission and under such reasonable rules and regulations as may be prescribed by the Commission. An application for such approval shall be made jointly by the transferor and transferee, or lessor and lessee.

No certificate shall be transferred, leased or otherwise disposed of when any consideration is paid or promised which exceeds the then value of the tangible property sold in connection with the transfer or lease of such certificate.

History.
Code 1950, § 56-168; 1970, c. 708.

§ 5.1-115. No value allowed for certificates.

No value shall be allowed for any purpose for any certificate issued under this chapter.

History.
Code 1950, § 56-169; 1970, c. 708.

ARTICLE 7.

BONDS OR INSURANCE.

§ 5.1-116. Bonds, insurance or certificate of insurance required prior to issuance of certificate or permit.

No certificate or permit shall be issued by the Commission to any air carrier until and after such air carrier shall have filed with, and the same has been approved by, the Commission, an insurance policy, bond or certificate of insurance in lieu thereof, certifying that such policy or bond covers the liability of such air carrier in accordance with the provisions of this article, issued by an insurance company or association or other insurer authorized to transact business in this Commonwealth, or bonds, to an amount approved by the Commission, of the Commonwealth of Virginia, of the United States of America, or of any municipality in this Commonwealth. Such state, federal, or municipal bonds shall be deposited with the State Treasurer, and such surety shall not be reduced during the life of such certificate or permit, except in accordance with an order of the Commission.

History.
Code 1950, § 56-170; 1970, c. 708; 1975, c. 211.

§ 5.1-117. Bonds or insurance to be kept in force.

Each holder of a certificate or permit issued by the Commission shall also keep in force at all times insurance or a bond underwritten by an insurer approved or authorized to do business in Virginia, or by one who is eligible as a surplus lines insurer in accordance with the provisions of Chapter 48 (§ 38.2-4800 et seq.) of Title 38.2 in amounts of not less than the following minimum limits: (a) liability for bodily injury to or death to any one person, passenger or other, aboard the aircraft, $75,000; and a limit for each occurrence in any one aircraft of at least an amount equal to the sum produced by multiplying $75,000 by seventy-five percent of the total number of passenger seats installed in the aircraft; and for the loss or damage to cargo owned by other than the insured, at least $10,000 for each occurrence; provided, however, that a holder of a permit issued by the Commission shall not be required to file any cargo insurance, bond or bonds for cargo liability for the hauling of property transported under contract. However, in no event shall the limits required herein for air common carriers be less than those prescribed for like carriers by the Civil Aeronautics Board or the Federal Aviation Administration.

History.
Code 1950, § 56-171; 1970, c. 708.

§ 5.1-118. Policies, bonds or certificates to be filed with Commission; securities deposited in lieu thereof.

Each holder of a certificate or permit issued by the Commission shall keep on file with the Commission an insurance policy, bond or certificate of insurance in lieu thereof, certifying that such policy or bond covers the liability of such air carrier in accordance with the provisions of this article, issued by an insurance company or association or other insurer authorized to transact business in this Commonwealth, and such insurance, bond or certificate of insurance filed with the Commission shall be kept in full force at all times. The policy, bond or certificate of insurance shall remain in the files of the Commission six months after the insurance or bond has expired or has been cancelled for any cause. If federal, state or municipal bonds are deposited with the State Treasurer in lieu thereof, such bonds shall remain so deposited until six months after the authority for use of equipment insured has expired or is cancelled for any cause, unless otherwise ordered by the Commission.

History.
Code 1950, § 56-172; 1970, c. 708; 1975, c. 211.

§ 5.1-119. Condition of bond, etc.

The insurance bond, or other security, shall obligate the insurer or surety to pay any final judgment for damages sustained by the passengers, shippers, or consignees for injury to any passenger or passengers, or for loss or damage to property entrusted to such air carrier when a cargo policy is required, and for any and all injuries to persons and loss of, or damage to, property resulting from the negligent operation of any aircraft.

History.
Code 1950, § 56-173; 1970, c. 708.

§ 5.1-120. Effect of failure to give security.

Failure of any holder of a certificate or permit issued by and under the authority of the Commission to comply with any of the requirements of §§ 5.1-116, 5.1-117 or 5.1-118 shall be cause without further proceedings for the revocation or suspension of the certificate or permit, and upon further proceedings for the imposition of a fine not exceeding $1,000.

History.
Code 1950, § 56-174; 1970, c. 708.

ARTICLE 8.

THROUGH ROUTES, SERVICE, RATES, ETC.

§ 5.1-121. Duties of carriers of passengers as to through routes, equipment, rates, regulations, etc.

Every common carrier or restricted common carrier of passengers by aircraft shall establish reasonable through routes with other such common carriers and provide safe and adequate service, equipment, and facilities for the transportation of passengers; shall establish, observe, and enforce just and reasonable individual and joint rates, fares and charges and just and reasonable regulations and practices relating thereto, and to the issuance, form, and substance of tickets, the carrying of personal, sample, and excess baggage, the facilities for transportation, and all other matters relating to or connected with the transportation of passengers; and in case of such joint rates, fares, and charges shall establish just, reasonable and equitable divisions thereof as between the carriers participating therein which shall not unduly prefer or prejudice any of such participating carriers.

History.
Code 1950, § 56-176; 1970, c. 708.

§ 5.1-122. Duties of carriers of property as to service, rates and regulations.

Every common carrier or restricted common carrier of property by aircraft shall provide safe and adequate service, equipment, and facilities for the transportation of property; and shall establish, observe, and enforce just and reasonable rates, charges, and classifications, and just and reasonable regulations and practices relating thereto and to the manner and method of presenting, marking, packing, and delivering property for transportation, the facilities for transportation, and all other matters relating to or connected with the transportation of property.

History.
Code 1950, § 56-177; 1970, c. 708.

§ 5.1-123. Through routes, joint rates, etc., not required may be established.

Common carriers or restricted common carriers of property by aircraft may establish reasonable routes and joint rates, charges, and classifications with other such carriers or with common carriers by railroad, motor vehicle, express and/or water; and common carriers or restricted common carriers of passengers by aircraft may establish reasonable through routes and joint rates, fares, or charges with common carriers by railroad, motor vehicle, and/or water. In case of such joint rates, fares or charges it shall be the duty of the carriers parties thereto to establish just and reasonable regulations and practices in connection therewith, and just, reasonable and equitable divisions thereof as between the carriers participating therein which shall not unduly prefer or prejudice any of such participating carriers.

History.
Code 1950, § 56-178; 1970, c. 708.

§ 5.1-124. Undue preference not permitted.

It shall be unlawful for any common carrier or restricted common carrier by aircraft to make, give, or cause any undue or unreasonable preference or advantage to any particular person, port, gateway, locality, or description of traffic in any respect whatsoever, or to subject any particular person, port, gateway, locality, or description of traffic to any unjust discrimination or any undue or unreasonable prejudice or disadvantage in any respect whatsoever; provided, however, that this section shall not be construed to apply to discriminations, prejudices or disadvantages to the traffic of any other carrier of whatever description.

History.
Code 1950, § 56-179; 1970, c. 708.

§ 5.1-125. Complaints; action of Commission thereon or on own initiative.

Any person, state board, organization, or body politic may make complaint in writing to the Commission that any rate, fare, charge, classification, rule, regulation, or practice of any common carrier or restricted common carrier by aircraft, in effect or proposed to be put into effect, is or will be in violation of §§ 5.1-121 to 5.1-124, or § 5.1-133. Whenever after hearing, upon complaint or in an investigation on its own initiative, the Commission shall be of the opinion that any individual or joint rate, fare, or charge, demanded, charged, or collected by any common carrier or restricted common carrier by aircraft or by any common or restricted common carrier by aircraft in conjunction with any common carrier by railroad, motor vehicle, express and/or water, or any classification, rule, regulation or practice whatsoever of such carrier affecting such rate, fare, or charge or the value of the service thereunder, is or will be unjust or unreasonable or unjustly discriminatory or unduly preferential or unduly prejudicial, it shall determine and prescribe

the lawful rate, fare, or charge or the maximum or minimum rate, fare, or charge thereafter to be observed, or the lawful classification, rule, regulation, or practice thereafter to be made effective.

History.
Code 1950, § 56-180; 1970, c. 708; 1971, Ex. Sess., c. 1.

§ 5.1-126. Establishment of through routes, etc., by Commission.

The Commission shall, whenever deemed by it to be necessary or desirable in the public interest, after hearing, upon complaint or upon its own initiative without a complaint, establish through routes, and joint rates, fares, charges, regulations, or practices, applicable to the transportation of passengers by common or restricted common carriers by aircraft, or the maximum or minimum to be charged, and the terms and conditions under which such through routes shall be operated.

History.
Code 1950, § 56-181; 1970, c. 708.

§ 5.1-127. Prescribing divisions of joint rates.

Whenever, after hearing, upon complaint or upon its own initiative, the Commission is of opinion that the divisions of joint rates, fares or charges, applicable to the transportation of passengers or property by common or restricted common carriers by aircraft or by such carriers in conjunction with common carriers by railroad, motor vehicle, express and/or water are or will be unjust, unreasonable, inequitable, or unduly preferential or prejudicial as between the carriers parties thereto (whether agreed upon by such carriers, or any of them, or otherwise established), the Commission shall by order prescribe the just, reasonable, and equitable divisions thereof to be received by the several carriers. In cases where the joint rate, fare, or charge was established pursuant to a finding or order of the Commission and the divisions thereof are found by it to have been unjust, unreasonable, or inequitable, or unduly preferential or prejudicial, the Commission may also by order determine what would have been the just, reasonable, and equitable divisions thereof to be received by the several carriers, and require adjustment to be made in accordance therewith. The order of the Commission may require the adjustment of divisions between the carriers, in accordance with the order, from the date of filing the complaint or entry of order of investigation or such other date subsequent as the Commission finds justified and, in the case of joint rates prescribed by the Commission, the order as to divisions may be made effective as a part of the original order.

History.
Code 1950, § 56-182; 1970, c. 708.

§ 5.1-128. New rate schedule; hearing; suspension; action thereon.

Whenever there shall be filed with the Commission any schedule stating a new individual or joint rate, fare, charge, or classification for the transportation of passengers or property by a common or restricted common carrier by aircraft, or by any such carrier in conjunction with a common carrier by railroad, motor vehicle, express and/or water, or any rule, regulation, or practice affecting such rate, fare, or charge, or the value of the service thereunder, the Commission, upon complaint of any interested party or upon its own initiative, if it so orders, without answer or other formal pleading by the interested carrier or carriers, but upon reasonable notice, may enter upon a hearing concerning the lawfulness of such rate, fare or charge, or such rule, regulations or practice.

Pending such hearing and the decision thereon the Commission, by filing with such schedule and delivering to the carrier or carriers affected thereby a statement in writing of its reasons for such suspension, may suspend the operation of such schedule and defer the use of such rate, fare, or charge, or such rule, regulation, or practice, for a period of 90 days and if the proceeding has not been concluded and a final order made within such period the Commission may, from time to time, extend the period of suspension by order, but not for a longer period in the aggregate than 180 days beyond the time when such rate, fare, charge, rule, regulation or practice would otherwise go into effect.

After such hearing, whether completed before or after the rate, fare, charge, classification, rule, regulation, or practice goes into effect, the Commission may make such order with reference thereto as would be proper in a proceeding instituted after it had become effective. If the proceeding has not been concluded and an order made within the period of suspension, the proposed change of rate, fare or charge, or classification, rule, regulation, or practice, shall go into effect at the end of such period.

History.
Code 1950, § 56-183; 1970, c. 708.

§ 5.1-129. Goodwill, certificate, etc., not element of value in rate making.

In any proceeding to determine the justness or reasonableness of any rate, fare, or charge of any common or restricted common carrier by aircraft there shall not be taken into consideration or allowed as evidence or elements of value of the property of such carrier either goodwill, earning power, or the certificate under which such carrier is operating; and in applying for and receiving a certificate under this chapter any such carrier shall be deemed to have agreed to the provisions of this section, on its own behalf and on behalf of all transferees or lessees of such certificate.

History.
Code 1950, § 56-184; 1970, c. 708.

§ 5.1-130. Criteria for establishment of rates.

In the exercise of its power to prescribe just and reasonable rates for the transportation of passengers or property by common or restricted common carriers by aircraft the Commission shall give due consideration, among other factors, to the inherent advantages of transportation by such carriers; to the effect of rates upon the movement of traffic by such carriers; to the need, in the public interest, of adequate and efficient transportation service by such carriers at the lowest cost consistent with the furnishing of such service; and to the need of such carriers for revenues sufficient to enable them, under honest, economical, and efficient management, to provide such service.

History.
Code 1950, § 56-185; 1970, c. 708.

§ 5.1-131. Other remedies not extinguished.

Nothing in the preceding nine sections (§§ 5.1-122 through 5.1-130) shall be held to extinguish any remedy or right of action not inconsistent therewith.

History.
Code 1950, § 56-186; 1970, c. 708.

§ 5.1-132. Tariffs showing rates, fares and charges, etc.

Every common carrier and restricted common carrier by aircraft shall file with the Commission, and print, and keep open to public inspection, tariffs showing all the rates, fares and charges for transportation, and all services in connection therewith, of passengers or property between points on its own route and between points on its own route and points on the route of any other such carrier, or on the route of any common carrier by railroad, motor vehicle, express and/or water, when a through route and joint rate shall have been established. Such rates, fares, and charges shall be stated in terms of lawful money of the United States. The tariffs required by this section shall be published, filed, and posted in such form and manner, and shall contain such information, as the Commission by regulations shall prescribe; and the Commission is authorized to reject any tariff filed with it which is not in consonance with this section and with such regulations. Any tariff so rejected by the Commission shall be void and its use shall be unlawful.

History.
Code 1950, § 56-187; 1970, c. 708.

§ 5.1-133. Unlawful to charge other than published tariff.

No common carrier or restricted common carrier by aircraft shall charge or demand or collect or receive a greater or less or different compensation for transportation or for any service in connection therewith between the points enumerated in such tariff than the rates, fares, and charges specified in the tariff in effect at the time; and no such carrier shall refund or remit in any manner or by any device, directly or indirectly, or through any agent or broker or otherwise, any portion of the rates, fares, or charges so specified, or extend to any person any privileges or facilities for transportation except such as specified in its tariffs.

History.
    Code 1950, § 56-188; 1970, c. 708.

§ 5.1-134. Changes in tariffs, etc.

No change shall be made in any rate, fare, charge, or classification, or any rule, regulation, or practice affecting such rate, fare, charge, or classification, or the value of the service thereunder, specified in any effective tariff of a common carrier or restricted common carrier by aircraft, except after thirty days' notice of the proposed change, filed and posted in accordance with § 5.1-132. Such notice shall plainly state the change proposed to be made and the time when such change will take effect. The Commission may, in its discretion and for good cause shown, allow such change upon notice less than that herein specified or modify the requirements of this section and § 5.1-132 with respect to posting and filing of tariffs either in particular instances or by general order applicable to special or peculiar circumstances or conditions.

History.
    Code 1950, § 56-189; 1970, c. 708.

§ 5.1-135. No transportation except when rates have been filed and published.

No common carrier or restricted common carrier by aircraft, unless otherwise provided by this chapter, shall engage in the transportation of passengers or property unless the rates, fares, and charges upon which the same are transported by such carrier have been filed and published in accordance with the provisions of this chapter.

History.
    Code 1950, § 56-190; 1970, c. 708.

§ 5.1-136. Free passes or reduced rates.

No air carrier subject to the provisions of this chapter shall, directly or indirectly, issue or give any free ticket, free pass or free transportation for passengers, but nothing in this section shall apply (1) to the carriage, storage or handling of property free or at reduced rates, when such rates have been authorized or prescribed by the Commission for the

United States, state or municipal governments, or for charitable purposes or to or from fairs and expositions for exhibition threat, or (2) to the free carriage of homeless and destitute persons and the necessary agents employed in such transportation, or (3) to mileage, excursion or commutation passenger tickets.

Nor shall anything in this section be construed to prohibit any air carrier from giving reduced rates or free passage to ministers of religion, or regular traveling secretaries of the Young Men's Christian Association or Young Women's Christian Association, whose duties require regular travel in supervising and directing Young Men's Christian or Young Women's Christian Association work, secretaries of duly organized religious work, or to indigent persons, or to inmates of the Confederate homes or State homes for disabled soldiers and sailors, or to disabled soldiers and sailors, including those about to enter, and those returning home after discharge; nor from giving free carriage to its own officers, employees, and members of their families, representatives of the press and members of the Department of State Police or to any other person or persons to whom the giving of such free carriage is not otherwise prohibited by the law; nor to prevent the principal officers of any air carrier from exchanging passes or tickets with other air carriers of any air, motor vehicle, steamship, or electric railway companies for their officers, employees and members of their families.

History.
    Code 1950, § 56-191; 1970, c. 708; 1971, Ex. Sess., c. 17.

§ 5.1-137. Payment of rates and charges before delivery of freight.

No common carrier or restricted common carrier by aircraft shall deliver or relinquish possession at destination of any freight transported by it until all tariff rates and charges thereon have been paid, except under such rules and regulations as the Commission may from time to time prescribe to govern the settlement of all such rates and charges, including rules and regulations for weekly or monthly settlement, and to prevent unjust discrimination or undue preference or prejudice; provided, that the provisions of this section shall not be construed to prohibit any such carrier from extending credit in connection with rates and charges on freight transported for the United States, for any department, bureau, or agency thereof, or for any state or territory or political subdivision thereof, or for the District of Columbia.

History.
    Code 1950, § 56-192; 1970, c. 708.

§ 5.1-138. Liability for additional charges.

When any common carrier by aircraft is instructed by a shipper or consignor to deliver property transported by such carrier to a consignee other than the shipper or consignor, such consignee shall not be legally liable for transportation charges in respect of the transportation of such property (beyond those billed against him at the time of delivery for which he is otherwise liable) which may be found to be due after the property has been delivered to him, if the consignee (a) is an agent only and had no beneficial title in the property, and (b) prior to delivery of the property has notified the delivering carrier in writing of the fact of such agency and absence of beneficial title, and, in the case of a shipment reconsigned or diverted to a point other than that specified in the original bill of lading, has also notified the delivering carrier in writing of the name and address of the beneficial owner of the property. In such cases the shipper or consignor, or, in the case of a shipment so reconsigned or diverted, the beneficial owner shall be liable for such additional charges, irrespective of any provisions to the contrary in the bill of lading or in the contract under which the shipment was made. If the consignee has given to the carrier erroneous information as to who is the beneficial owner, such consignee shall himself be liable for such additional charges, notwithstanding the foregoing provisions of this section. On shipments reconsigned or diverted by any agent who has furnished the carrier with a notice of agency and the proper name and address of the beneficial owner, and when such shipments are refused or abandoned at ultimate destination, the beneficial owner shall be liable for all legally applicable charges in connection therewith.

History.
Code 1950, § 56-193; 1970, c. 708.

§ 5.1-139. Commission may enter judgment for refunds due public and collect and distribute same.

If any air carrier or broker, upon the final decision of an appeal from the action of the Commission prescribing rates, charges, or classification of traffic, confirming or modifying the action of the Commission, shall fail to refund in the manner and within the time prescribed in the notice of the Commission all amounts which the appealing air carrier or broker may have collected pending the appeal, in excess of that authorized by such final decision, upon notice to such air carrier or broker by the Commission of such final decision, then the Commission, after thirty days' notice to any such air carrier or broker, may, unless the amount required by such order be paid to the clerk of the Commission, render and enter judgment in the name of the Commonwealth, for the use of the persons, firms and corporations entitled to the same, against any such air carrier or broker for the aggregate amount of such collections and for the costs, and may enforce the amount of such judgment and costs by process of execution, as hereinbefore provided as to the enforcement of the judgments of the Commission. The Commission shall, upon the collection of such judgment, forthwith distribute the amount thereof, through its clerk, among the parties entitled thereto, respectively, in such manner as it may by its rules or orders prescribe, and shall, upon the payment or collection of any such judgment enter the same satisfied upon its records, and have the same satisfied on the judgment lien docket of the court of any city or county where the same may have been docketed, and the satisfaction of any such judgment shall be a bar to any further action or recovery against any such air carrier or broker to the extent of such recovery.

History.
Code 1950, § 56-194; 1970, c. 708.

ARTICLE 9.

MISCELLANEOUS.

§ 5.1-140. Unlawful to disclose certain information.

It shall be unlawful for any air carrier or broker or any officer, receiver, trustee, lessee, agent, or employee of such carrier, broker, or person, or for any other person authorized by such carrier, broker, or person to receive information, knowingly to disclose to, or permit to be acquired by any person other than the shipper or consignee, without the consent of such shipper or consignee, any information concerning the nature, kind, quantity, destination, consignee, or routing of any property tendered or delivered to such air carrier or broker for such transportation, which information may be used to the detriment or prejudice of such shipper or consignee, or which may improperly disclose his business transactions to a competitor; and it shall also be unlawful for any person to solicit or receive knowingly any such information which may be so used.

Nothing in this chapter shall be construed to prevent the giving of such information in response to any legal process issued under the authority of any court, or to any officer or agent of the government of the United States or of any state, territory, or district thereof, in the exercise of his power, or to any officer or other duly authorized person seeking such information for the prosecution of persons charged with or suspected of crimes or to another carrier or broker, or its duly authorized agent, for the purpose of adjusting mutual traffic accounts in the ordinary course of business of such carriers or brokers.

History.
Code 1950, § 56-195; 1970, c. 708.

§ 5.1-141. Repealed by Acts 2001, c. 137.

§ 5.1-142. Reports, records, etc.

(a) The Commission is hereby authorized to require annual, periodic, or special reports from all air carriers except such as are exempted from the operation of the provisions of this chapter, to prescribe the manner and form in which such reports shall be made, and to require from such carriers specific answers to all questions upon which the Commission may deem information to be necessary. Such reports shall be under oath whenever the Commission so requires. The Commission may also require any air carrier to file with it a true copy of any contract, agreement, or arrangement between such carrier and any other carrier or person in relation to any traffic affected by the provisions of this chapter.

(b) The Commission may, in its discretion, prescribe the forms of any and all accounts, records, and memoranda to be kept by air carriers and the length of time such accounts, records and memoranda shall be preserved, including the accounts, records, and memoranda of the movement of traffic, as well as of the receipts and expenditures of money. The Commission or its employees shall at all times have access to all lands, buildings, and equipment of air carriers used in connection with their operation and also all accounts, records, and memoranda, including all documents, papers, and correspondence now existing, and kept, or required to be kept, by air carriers. The Commission and its employees shall have authority to inspect and examine any and all such lands, buildings, equipment, accounts, records, and memoranda, including all documents, papers, and correspondence now or hereafter existing and kept or required to be kept by such carriers. This provision shall apply to receivers of carriers and to operating trustees and, to the extent deemed necessary by the Commission, to persons having control, direct or indirect, over or affiliated with any air carrier.

(c) As used in this section the term "air carriers" includes brokers.

History.
  Code 1950, § 56-197; 1970, c. 708.

§ 5.1-143. Reports of accidents.

It shall be the duty of the manager, agent or other proper officer of every air carrier doing business or operating in this Commonwealth to make to the Commission such report or reports as may be required by it, under oath, of all accidents in this Commonwealth resulting in injury to persons, equipment, or property of any kind, under such rules and regulations as may be prescribed by the Commission.

History.
  Code 1950, § 56-198; 1970, c. 708.

§ 5.1-144. Certificate or permit holder not relieved of liability for negligence.

Nothing in this chapter shall relieve any holder of a certificate or permit by and under the authority of the Commission from any liability resulting from his negligence, whether or not he has complied with the requirements of this chapter.

History.
  Code 1950, § 56-199; 1970, c. 708.

§ 5.1-145. Enforcement under Department of State Police or Commission; concurrent jurisdiction for investigations of accidents.

The enforcement of any provision of this chapter requiring the use of police officers shall be under the Department of State Police or under the Commission; except the department of law enforcement of any city or county with an optional form of government shall have concurrent jurisdiction for the investigations of aircraft accidents occurring within such city or county.

History.
  Code 1950, § 56-200; 1964, c. 342; 1970, c. 708; 1979, c. 394; 1980, c. 721.

Law Review.
  For article on the evolution of the State Corporation Commission, see 14 Wm. & Mary L. Rev. 523 (1973).

§ 5.1-146. Violations and penalties.

(a) Any person knowingly and willfully violating any provision of this chapter, or any rule, regulation, requirement, or order thereunder for which a penalty is not otherwise herein provided, shall, after proper proceeding before the Commission, and upon conviction thereof, be fined not more than $100 for the first offense and not more than $500 for any subsequent offense. Each day of such violation shall constitute a separate offense.

(b) Any person, whether carrier, shipper, consignee, or broker, or any officer, employee, agent, or representative thereof, who shall knowingly offer, grant, or give, or solicit, accept, or receive any rebate, concession, or discrimination in violation of any provision of this chapter, or who, by means of any false statement or representation, or by the use of any false or fictitious bill, bill of lading, receipt, voucher, roll, account, claim, certificate, affidavit, deposition, lease, or bill of sale or by any other means or device, shall knowingly and willfully assist, suffer or permit any person, natural or artificial, to obtain transportation of passengers or property subject to this chapter for less than the applicable rate, fare, or charge, or who shall knowingly and willfully by any such means or otherwise fraudulently seek to evade or defeat regulation as in this chapter provided for air carriers or brokers, shall be deemed guilty of a misdemeanor and upon conviction thereof be fined not more than $500 for the first offense and not more than $2,000 for any subsequent offense.

(c) Any air carrier, or broker, or any officer, agent, employee, or representative thereof who shall willfully fail or refuse to make a report to the Commission as required by this chapter, or to keep accounts, records and memoranda in the form and manner approved or prescribed by the Commission, or shall knowingly and willfully falsify, destroy, mutilate, or alter any such report, account, record, or memorandum, or shall knowingly and willfully file any false report, account, record, or memorandum, shall, after proper proceeding before the Commission and upon conviction thereof, be subject for each offense to a fine of not less than $100 and not more than $5,000.

History.
Code 1950, § 56-201; 1970, c. 708.

§ 5.1-147. Disposition of fees or sums collected.

All fees or sums collected by the Commission under the provisions of this chapter shall be deposited with the State Treasurer, and shall be set aside by him for the use of the Commission for the administration and enforcement of this chapter.

History.
Code 1950, § 56-202; 1970, c. 708.

§ 5.1-148. Employees of Commission not to have interest in carriers.

No employee of the Commission appointed or employed in the administration of this chapter shall in any manner have any pecuniary interest in, own any securities of, or hold any position with any air carrier, motor carrier, railroad, steamboat or canal company.

History.
Code 1950, § 56-203; 1970, c. 708.

§ 5.1-149. No property rights in airspace conferred by chapter.

Nothing in this chapter shall confer any proprietary or property rights in the use of the airspace of this Commonwealth.

History.
Code 1950, § 56-204; 1970, c. 708.

§ 5.1-150. Licenses, taxes, etc., not affected.

Nothing in this chapter shall be construed to relieve any person from the payment of any licenses, fees, taxes or levies now or hereafter imposed by law.

History.
Code 1950, § 56-205; 1970, c. 708.

§ 5.1-151. Right to amend, revoke, etc., rights, certificates or franchises.

The right and power of the General Assembly to amend, alter, revoke or repeal any and all rights, certificates, or franchises granted pursuant to the provisions of this chapter is hereby reserved.

History.
Code 1950, § 56-206; 1970, c. 708.

CHAPTER 10.

METROPOLITAN WASHINGTON AIRPORTS AUTHORITY.

§ 5.1-152. Definitions.

For the purposes of this act, the following terms and phrases shall mean:

"Authority" shall mean the Metropolitan Washington Airports Authority created by this act and by similar enactment by the District of Columbia or, if the Authority shall be abolished, the board, body, or commission or agency succeeding to the principal functions thereof or upon whom the powers given by this act to the Authority shall be conferred by law;

"Authority Facilities" shall mean any or all airport facilities now existing or hereafter acquired or constructed or caused to be constructed by the Authority under this act, and together with any or all buildings, improvements, additions, extensions, replacements, appurtenances, lands, rights in land, water rights, air rights, franchises, machinery, equipment, furnishings, landscaping, easements, utilities, approaches, roadways and other facilities necessary or desirable in connection therewith or incidental thereto, including the existing Dulles Airport Access Road and its right-of-way, acquired or constructed by the Authority;

"Bonds" or *"revenue bonds"* shall mean bonds and notes or refunding bonds and notes or bond anticipation notes or other obligations of the Authority issued under the provisions of this act.

"Cost" shall mean, as applied to Authority Facilities, the cost of acquisition of all lands, structures, rights-of-way, franchises, easements and other property rights and interests, the cost of lease payments, the cost of construction, the cost of demolishing, removing or relocating any buildings or structures on lands acquired, including the cost of acquiring any lands to which such buildings or structures may be moved or relocated, the cost of any extensions,

enlargements, additions and improvements, the cost of all labor, materials, machinery and equipment, financing charges, interest on all bonds prior to and during construction and, if deemed advisable by the Authority, for a period not exceeding one year after completion of such construction, the cost of engineering, financial and legal services, plans, specifications, studies, surveys, estimates of cost and of revenues, other expenses necessary or incident to determining the feasibility or practicability of constructing the Authority Facilities, administrative expenses, provisions for working capital, reserves for interest and for extensions, enlargements, additions and improvements, the cost of bond issuance and other devices designed to enhance the creditworthiness of the bonds, and such other expenses as may be necessary or incidental to the construction of the Authority Facilities, the financing of such construction and the placing of the Authority Facilities in operation. Any obligation or expenses incurred by the Commonwealth or any agency thereof, with the approval of the Authority, for studies, surveys, borings, preparation of plans and specifications or other work or materials in connection with the construction of the Authority Facilities may be regarded as part of the cost of the Authority Facilities and may be reimbursed to the Commonwealth or such agency out of any funds available therefor or the proceeds of the revenue bonds issued for such Authority Facilities as hereinafter authorized.

History.
2001, c. 342.

Cross references.
For effective date of this chapter, see editor's note at § 5.1-178.

Editor's note.
Acts 2001, c. 342, cl. 2, provides: "That Chapter 598 of the Acts of Assembly of 1985, Chapter 665 of the Acts of Assembly of 1987, Chapter 180 and 610 of the Acts of Assembly of 1991, Chapter 402 of the Acts of Assembly of 1992, Chapters 647 and 661 of the Acts of Assembly of 1997, and Chapter 824 of the Acts of Assembly of 1998 are repealed."

Acts 2001, c. 342, cl. 3, provides: "That it is the intent of the General Assembly, through the passage of this act, to codify the provisions of Chapter 598 of the Acts of Assembly of 1985, Chapter 665 of the Acts of Assembly of 1987, Chapters 180 and 610 of the Acts of Assembly of 1991, Chapter 402 of the Acts of Assembly of 1992, Chapters 647 and 661 of the Acts of Assembly of 1997, and Chapter 824 of the Acts of Assembly of 1998, relating to the Metropolitan Washington Airports Authority, and the provisions of this act shall not be deemed to impair or otherwise affect any regulation promulgated, any contract entered into, any appointment made, or any other action lawfully taken under the provisions of the Acts of Assembly repealed by this act. Accordingly, the provisions of this act are declarative of existing law."

Acts 2003, c. 1012, cl. 1, provides:
"**§ 1. Limited waiver of sovereign immunity by Commonwealth of Virginia.**
"Notwithstanding any contrary provision of Chapter 10 (§ 5.1-152 et seq.) of Title 5.1 of the Code of Virginia, the Commonwealth of Virginia agrees to a limited waiver of its sovereign immunity, not to exceed $5 million, so as to indemnify the Metropolitan Washington Airports Authority against claims, damages, losses, and expenses arising out of, resulting from, or attributable to the Commonwealth's use of Authority property, in or near the Dulles Corridor, on which transportation facilities are constructed, to the extent required in any agreement between the Virginia Department of Transportation and the Authority. For purposes of this act and all provisions of law, "Dulles Corridor" means the transportation corridor with an eastern terminus of the East Falls Church Metrorail station and a western terminus of Route 772 in Loudoun County."

Acts 2013, c. 766, cl. 6 provides: "That $100 million of the increased revenues provided to the Highway Maintenance and Operating Fund pursuant to this act in fiscal years 2014, 2015, and 2016 shall be dedicated to Phase 2 of the Dulles Corridor Metrorail Extension Project, provided, however, that the Metropolitan Washington Airports Authority (MWAA) Board of Directors first address all recommendations cited in the Office of the Inspector General of the U.S. Department of Transportation's Report on MWAA Governance and the accountability officer appointed by the U.S. Secretary of Transportation determines that such recommendations have been addressed. Notwithstanding the foregoing provisions of this enactment, in the event that all conditions for dedication of funds are satisfied, the Commonwealth Transportation Board may provide funding from other available revenue sources to satisfy the requirements of this provision in order to maximize the use of increased revenues provided under this act."

CASE NOTES

Applied in Cont'l Airlines, Inc. v. United Airlines, Inc., 277 F.3d 499 (4th Cir. 2002); San Jose Constr. Group, Inc. v. Metro. Wash. Airports Auth., 415 F. Supp. 2d 643, 2006 U.S. Dist. LEXIS 5804 (E.D. Va. 2006).

CIRCUIT COURT OPINIONS

Authority facilities. — Because a road was part of the Dulles Airport Access Highway, it was recognized as part of the Airport Authority Facilities and an officer had the authority to make a warrantless arrest of the defendant because the road was part of Authority Facilities. Commonwealth v. Selby, 2002 Va. Cir. LEXIS 285 (Fairfax County Oct. 25, 2002).

OPINIONS OF THE ATTORNEY GENERAL

Whether a particular transportation facility constructed on the Metropolitan Washington Airports Authority property is in or near the Dulles Corridor is a factual determination to be resolved by the Commonwealth Transportation Board. See opinion of Attorney General to The Honorable Whittington W. Clement, Secretary of Transportation, 03-121 (2/17/04).

Authority. — Although the issue has not been conclusively resolved, under the only available precedent, the Governor was authorized to divest the Commonwealth of its interest in the Dulles Toll Road as part of the overall project to extend Metrorail. See opinion of Attorney General to The Honorable Robert G. Marshall, Member, Virginia House of Delegates, 11-004, 2012 Va. AG LEXIS 20 (5/25/12).

All the parties to the Compact governing Metropolitan Washington Airports Authority (MWAA) would not be required to approve the Authority's takeover of the Dulles Toll Road. Instead, the approval of MWAA's Board would be sufficient to confer upon MWAA the authority and responsibility to operate and maintain the Dulles Toll Road. See opinion of Attorney General to The Honorable Robert G. Marshall, Member, Virginia House of Delegates, 11-004, 2012 Va. AG LEXIS 20 (5/25/12).

§ 5.1-156. Powers and duties of the Authority.

A. For the purpose of acquiring, operating, maintaining, developing, promoting and protecting Ronald Reagan Washington National Airport and Washington Dulles International Airport together as primary airports for public purposes serving the metropolitan Washington area, the Authority shall have all necessary or convenient powers including, but not limited to, the power:

1. To adopt and amend bylaws for the regulation of its affairs and the conduct of its business;

2. To plan, establish, operate, develop, construct, enlarge, maintain, equip and protect the airports;

3. To adopt and amend regulations to carry out the powers granted by this section;

4. To adopt an official seal and alter the same at its pleasure;

5. To appoint one or more advisory committees;

6. To issue revenue bonds of the Authority for any of its purposes, payable solely from the fees and revenues pledged for their payment, and to refund its bonds, all as provided in this act;

7. To borrow money on a short-term basis and issue from time to time its notes therefor payable on such terms, conditions or provisions as it may deem advisable;

8. To fix, revise, charge, and collect rates, fees, rentals and other charges for the use of the airports;

9. To acquire, hold and dispose of real and personal property in the exercise of its powers and the performance of its duties under this act;

10. To employ, in its discretion, consulting engineers, attorneys, accountants, construction and financial experts, superintendents, managers, and such other employees and agents as may be necessary, and to fix their compensation and benefits. Employees of the Authority shall not participate in any strike or assert any right to strike against the Authority, and any employment agreement entered into by the Authority shall contain an explicit prohibition against strikes by the employee or employees covered by such agreement. The Authority shall comply with any act of Congress concerning former employees of the Federal Aviation Administration and Metropolitan Washington Airports;

11. To sue and be sued in its own name, plead and be impleaded;

12. To construct or permit the construction of commercial and other facilities consistent with the purposes of this act upon the airport property on terms established by the Authority;

13. To make and enter into all contracts and agreements necessary or desirable to the performance of its duties, the proper operation of the airports and the furnishing of services to the travelling public and airport users, including contracts for normal governmental services on a reimbursable basis with local political subdivisions where the Authority Facilities are situated and with the District of Columbia government; and any such contracts shall be exclusive or limited when it is necessary to further the public safety, improve the quality of service, avoid duplication of services, or conserve airport property and the airport environment;

14. To apply for, receive and accept such payments, appropriations, grants, gifts, loans, advances, and other funds, properties, and services as may be transferred or made available to it by the United States government or any other public or private entity or individual;

15. To make payments to reimburse the local political subdivisions where the Authority Facilities are situated for extraordinary law-enforcement costs incurred by such localities; and

16. To do all acts and things necessary or convenient to carry out the powers expressly granted in this act.

B. Pursuant to Section 6007 (b) of the Metropolitan Washington Airports Act of 1986, the Authority is established solely to operate and improve both metropolitan Washington airports as primary airports serving the metropolitan Washington area and shall be independent of the Commonwealth and its local political subdivisions, the District of Columbia and the federal government in the performance and exercise of the airport-related duties and powers enumerated in subdivisions 1 through 16 of subsection A of this section. Any conflict between the exercise of these enumerated powers by the Authority and the powers of any local political subdivision within which Authority Facilities are situated shall be resolved in favor of the Authority.

History.
2001, c. 342.

CASE NOTES

Applied in Washington-Dulles Transp., Ltd. v. Metropolitan Wash. Airports Auth., 263 F.3d 371, 2001 U.S. App. LEXIS 19298 (4th Cir. 2001); San Jose Constr. Group, Inc. v. Metro. Wash. Airports Auth., 415 F. Supp. 2d 643, 2006 U.S. Dist. LEXIS 5804 (E.D. Va. 2006).

CIRCUIT COURT OPINIONS

Illustrative cases. — Maintenance of airport runways was a proprietary function under Virginia law, and the Metropolitan Washington Airports Authority was not immune from suit by an airline which claimed that its plane was damaged when it hit debris that was on a runway. Alpine Air, Inc. v. Metro. Wash. Airports Auth., 62 Va. Cir. 215, 2003 Va. Cir. LEXIS 106 (Fairfax County 2003).

Sovereign immunity barred claims. — In an action filed by a group of residents against various state entities and an airport authority seeking both declaratory and injunctive relief, and alleging that the transfer of a toll road and toll revenue derived therefrom from the Commonwealth defendants to the airport authority was an unlawful delegation or assignment, and an unlawful transfer of state assets and the legislative ability to tax, demurrers and pleas in bar filed against said complaint were granted, and the case was dismissed, as the doctrine of sovereign immunity barred consideration of said claims. Gray v. Va. Secy. of Transp., 74 Va. Cir. 30, 2007 Va. Cir. LEXIS 150 (Richmond 2007).

OPINIONS OF THE ATTORNEY GENERAL

Procurement procedures. — State agency can negotiate to include in its grant agreement a provision that makes Metropolitan Washington Airports Authority's receipt of Virginia funds conditional upon Metropolitan Washington Airports Authority conducting the procurement in a manner that does not give a preference to offerors who will have a project labor agreement. Such a condition would be enforceable in accordance with general contract laws, but it could not be enforced through the special remedial provisions contained in subsection C of § 2.2-4321.2, because Metropolitan Washington Airports Authority is not subject to that statute. See opinion of Attorney General to The Honorable Mark D. Sickles, Member, House of Delegates, 12-025, 2012 Va. AG LEXIS 29 (7/6/2012).

§ 5.1-157. Authority rules and regulations; penalty.

A. The Authority shall have the power to adopt, amend, and repeal rules and regulations pertaining to use, maintenance and operation of its facilities and governing the conduct of persons and organizations using its facilities.

B. Unless the Authority shall by unanimous vote of all members present determine that an emergency exists, the Authority shall, prior to the adoption of any rule or regulation or alteration, amendment or modification thereof:

1. Make such rule, regulation, alteration, amendment, or modification in convenient form available for public inspection in the office of the Authority for at least ten days;

2. Publish a notice in a newspaper or newspapers of general circulation in the District of Columbia and in the local political subdivisions of the Commonwealth where the Authority Facilities are located declaring the Authority's intention to consider adopting such rule, regulation, alteration, amendment, or modification and informing the public that the Authority will hold a public hearing at which any person may appear and be heard for or against the adoption of such rule or regulation or such alteration, amendment, or modification, on a day and at a time to be specified in the notice, after the expiration of at least ten days from the day of the publication thereof; and

3. Hold the public hearing on the day and at the time specified in such notice or any adjournment thereof, and hear persons appearing for or against such rule, regulation, alteration, amendment or modification.

C. The Authority's rules and regulations shall be available for public inspection in the Authority's principal office.

D. The Authority's rules and regulations relating to:

(i) Air operations and motor vehicle traffic, including but not limited to, motor vehicle speed limits and the location of and payment for public parking;

(ii) Access to and use of Authority Facilities, including but not limited to, solicitation, handbilling, picketing and the conduct of commercial activities; and

(iii) Aircraft operation and maintenance; shall have the force and effect of law, as shall any other rule or regulation of the Authority which shall contain a determination by the Authority that it is necessary to accord the same force and effect of law in the public interest; provided, however, that with respect to motor vehicle traffic rules and regulations, the Authority shall obtain the approval of the traffic engineer or comparable official of the local political subdivision in which such rules or regulations are to be enforced.

E. The violation of any rule or regulation of the Authority establishing a noise limitation on aircraft that operate at the Authority Facilities shall subject the violator, in the discretion of the circuit court of any political subdivision where the facility is located, to a civil penalty not to exceed $5,000 for each violation. Such penalty shall be paid to the Authority. With the consent of the violator or the accused violator of a rule establishing aircraft noise limits, the Authority may provide, in an order issued against the violator or accused violator, for the payment of civil charges in specific sums not to exceed the limit that could be imposed by the court. Such civil charge when paid shall be in lieu of any civil penalty which could be imposed by the court. Any court proceeding shall be within the exclusive jurisdiction of the circuit court and shall be a civil proceeding at law brought by the Authority.

F. The violation of any Authority rule or regulation, having the force and effect of law, shall be a Class 1 misdemeanor unless otherwise specified by this chapter or unless a lesser penalty is set by the Authority in the rule or regulation. The rules of criminal procedure and evidence that apply throughout the Commonwealth shall apply to the adjudication of any case involving the violation of any Authority rule or regulation having the force and effect of law.

G. The courts of this Commonwealth shall take judicial notice of the Authority's regularly adopted rules and regulations. For the convenience of the courts which may regularly hear cases arising under the Authority's rules and regulations, the Authority may certify to the clerk of such court a copy of its rules and regulations. Any such certification, when signed by the chairman of the Metropolitan Washington Airports Authority, shall be accepted as evidence of the facts therein stated.

H. With respect to the violation of any statute of the Commonwealth, local ordinance or Authority rule or regulation having the force and effect of law occurring at the Authority Facilities:

1. The matter shall be within the jurisdiction of the state courts of the political subdivision where the violation occurred; violations occurring at Ronald Reagan Washington National Airport shall be within the jurisdiction of the courts for Arlington County;

2. The attorney for the Commonwealth shall have authority to prosecute those offenses in the name of the Commonwealth or local government as appropriate; and the county or city attorney, if otherwise authorized to prosecute offenses in the name of the county or city, shall have authority to prosecute those offenses in the name of the county or city; and

3. Sheriffs and clerks of the court shall provide those same services and exercise those same powers with respect to the Authority Facilities within their jurisdiction as for their political subdivisions.

History.
2001, c. 342.

Cross references.
As to punishment for Class 1 misdemeanor, see § 18.2-11.

§ 5.1-158. Police.

A. The Commonwealth hereby grants, accepts and agrees to concurrent police power authority over the Metropolitan Washington Airports as provided in Section 6009 (c) of the Metropolitan Washington Airports Act of 1986.

B. The Authority is authorized to establish and maintain a regular police force and to confer police powers to be exercised with respect to offenses occurring on the Authority Facilities upon its employees meeting the minimum requirements of the Department of Criminal Justice Services.

Such police officers shall have all powers vested in police officers under Chapter 17 of Title 15.2, Chapter 11 of Title 16.1, Title 18.2, Title 19.2, and Title 46.2 of the Code of Virginia as those titles may be amended from time to time and shall be responsible upon the Authority Facilities and within 300 yards of the Facilities for enforcing the laws of the Commonwealth, the Authority's rules and regulations and all other applicable ordinances, rules, and regulations.

Such police officers may issue summons to appear, or arrest on view or on information without warrant as permitted by law, and conduct before any judicial officer of competent jurisdiction any person violating, upon Authority Facilities, any rule or regulation of the Authority, any ordinance or regulation of any local political subdivision, or any other law of the Commonwealth.

C. The Department of State Police shall exercise the same powers upon Authority Facilities as elsewhere in the Commonwealth.

D. The Authority may enter into reciprocal or mutual aid agreements with the local political subdivisions in the National Capital Region as defined in § 2674(f)(2) of title 10 of the United States Code, those counties with a border abutting that area, and any municipalities therein; any agency of the Commonwealth, the District of Columbia, the State of Maryland; the federal government; or any combination of the foregoing for cooperation in the furnishing of services during a public service event, an emergency, or planned training, including law-enforcement, fire, rescue, emergency health, and medical services, transportation, communications, public works and engineering, mass care, and resource support. When responding to a request under such an agreement, Authority employees may go outside Authority facilities, and the Authority and its employees shall enjoy the same immunities from liability as localities and their employees do in responding under similar circumstances.

E. The police force of Arlington County shall have concurrent jurisdiction with the police force established herein at Ronald Reagan Washington National Airport. The Authority shall enter into an agreement with Arlington County regarding the exercise of police authority.

F. The sheriffs and police forces of Loudoun and Fairfax Counties shall continue to exercise concurrent jurisdiction with the police force established herein over the Authority Facilities situated within their respective counties.

History.
2001, c. 342; 2007, cc. 729, 742.

CASE NOTES

Sovereign immunity. — Metropolitan Washington Airports Authority was entitled to dismissal of plaintiff's claim for malicious prosecution because plaintiff's arrest by a Metropolitan Washington Airports Authority police officer clearly occurred in the performance of a governmental function. Mukuna v. Gibson, 2011 U.S. Dist. LEXIS 95408 (E.D. Va. Aug. 25, 2011).

§ 5.1-173. Jurisdiction of courts; liability for contracts and torts.

A. The courts of the Commonwealth of Virginia shall have original jurisdiction of all actions brought by or against the Authority, which courts shall in all cases apply the law of the Commonwealth of Virginia.

B. The Authority shall be liable for its contracts and for its torts and those of its members, officers, employees, and agents committed in the conduct of any proprietary function, in accordance with the law of the Commonwealth of Virginia but shall not be liable for any torts occurring in the performance of a governmental function. The exclusive remedy for such breach of contracts and torts for which the Authority shall be liable, as herein provided, shall be by suit against the Authority. Nothing in this act shall be construed as a waiver by the Commonwealth of Virginia or the District of Columbia or of their political subdivisions of any immunity from suit.

C. The Authority shall be responsible for all executory contracts entered into by the United States with respect to the former Metropolitan Washington Airports before the date of acquisition of those airports, except that the procedure for disputes resolution contained in any such contract shall continue to govern the performance of the contract unless otherwise agreed to by the parties to the contract.

D. The Authority shall not be responsible for any tort claims arising before the date of transfer.

History.
2001, c. 342.

Michie's Jurisprudence.
For related discussion, see 2B M.J. Aviation, § 8.

CASE NOTES

Sovereign immunity barred claims. — Pursuant to subsection B of § 5.1-173, the Metropolitan Washington Airports Authority was entitled to dismissal of plaintiff's claim for malicious prosecution because a police officer had probable cause to execute an arrest warrant after a complainant contacted the officer and told the officer that plaintiff had stolen the complainant's income tax refund. Mukuna v. Gibson, 2011 U.S. Dist. LEXIS 95408 (E.D. Va. Aug. 25, 2011).

Applied in Washington-Dulles Transp., Ltd. v. Metropolitan Wash. Airports Auth., 263 F.3d 371, 2001 U.S. App. LEXIS 19298 (4th Cir. 2001); San Jose Constr. Group, Inc. v. Metro. Wash. Airports Auth., 415 F. Supp. 2d 643, 2006 U.S. Dist. LEXIS 5804 (E.D. Va. 2006).

CIRCUIT COURT OPINIONS

Sovereign immunity barred claims. — In an action filed by a group of residents against various state entities and an airport authority seeking both declaratory and injunctive relief, and alleging that the transfer of a toll road and toll revenue derived therefrom from the Commonwealth defendants to the airport authority was an unlawful delegation or assignment, and an unlawful transfer of state assets and the legislative ability to tax, demurrers and pleas in bar filed against said complaint were granted, and the case was dismissed, as the doctrine of sovereign immunity barred consideration of said claims. Gray v. Va. Secy. of Transp., 74 Va. Cir. 30, 2007 Va. Cir. LEXIS 150 (Richmond 2007).

Illustrative cases. — Maintenance of airport runways was a proprietary function under Virginia law, and the Metropolitan Washington Airports Authority was not immune from suit by an airline which claimed that its plane was damaged when it hit debris that was on a runway. Alpine Air, Inc. v. Metro. Wash. Airports Auth., 62 Va. Cir. 215, 2003 Va. Cir. LEXIS 106 (Fairfax County 2003).

DECISIONS FROM COMPACT MEMBER STATES

Federal: In a case involving the Metropolitan Washington Airports Authority, the Court granted the motion to transfer venue to the Eastern District of Virginia where private interest factors did not outweigh public interest factors such as the Virginia Court's familiarity with Virginia law, relative congestion of court calendars and the local interest in deciding local controversies at home. Parkridge 6, LLC v. United States DOT, Civil Action No. 09-CV-01478(GK), 2009 U.S. Dist. LEXIS 104039 (D.D.C. November 9, 2009).

§ 5.1-178. Not set out.

History.
2001, c. 342.

Editor's note.
This section, pertaining to the effective date of Chapter 10, was enacted by Acts 2001, c. 342. Its provisions are deemed to have been accomplished by the following cited federal law: P.L. 99-591, Title VI; 100 Stat. 3341-376; 49 USC 49101 et seq. (October 28, 1986). In furtherance of the general policy of the Virginia Code Commission to include in the Code only provisions having general and permanent application, this section, which is limited in its purpose and scope, is not set out here, but attention is called to it by this reference.

The text of the act for this section read as follows: "This act shall only become effective upon the enactment into law by the Congress of the United States of legislation that authorizes and directs the sale, lease, or other disposition of the Metropolitan Washington Airports to the Authority; provided, however, the Governor may make appointments for initial Authority membership at such time

or times following the passage of this act as he may deem appropriate."

TITLE 6.1.

BANKING AND FINANCE.

[Repealed.]

TITLE 6.2.

FINANCIAL INSTITUTIONS AND SERVICES.

SUBTITLE II.

DEPOSITORY INSTITUTIONS AND TRUST ORGANIZATIONS.

CHAPTER 13.

CREDIT UNIONS.

Article 2. Supervision and Regulation.

Section
6.2-1316. Offenses; penalty.

ARTICLE 2.

SUPERVISION AND REGULATION.

§ 6.2-1316. Offenses; penalty.

Any officer, director, employee, receiver, or agent of a credit union who willfully does any of the following is guilty of a Class 6 felony:

1. With the intent to deceive, falsifies any book of account, report, statement, record, or other document of a credit union, whether by alteration, false entry, omission, or otherwise;

2. Signs, issues, publishes, or transmits to a government agency any book of account, report, statement, record, or other document that he knows to be false;

3. By means of deceit, obtains a signature to a writing that is a subject of forgery;

4. With intent to deceive, destroys any credit union book of account, report, statement, record, or other document; or

5. With the intent to defraud, shares or receives directly or indirectly any money, property, or benefits through any transaction of the credit union.

History.
  1985, c. 363, § 6.1-223.2; 1990, c. 373, § 6.1-225.62; 2010, c. 794.

Cross references.
  As to punishment for Class 6 felonies, see § 18.2-10.

TITLE 8.01.

CIVIL REMEDIES AND PROCEDURE.

CHAPTER 3.

ACTIONS.

Article 21. Miscellaneous Provisions.

ARTICLE 21.

MISCELLANEOUS PROVISIONS.

§ 8.01-226.9. Exemption from civil liability in connection with arrest or detention of person suspected of shoplifting.

A merchant, agent or employee of the merchant, who causes the arrest or detention of any person pursuant to the provisions of §§ 18.2-95, 18.2-96 or § 18.2-103, shall not be held civilly liable for unlawful detention, if such detention does not exceed one hour, slander, malicious prosecution, false imprisonment, false arrest, or assault and battery of the person so arrested or detained, whether such arrest or detention takes place on the premises of the merchant, or after close pursuit from such premises by such merchant, his agent or employee, provided that, in causing the arrest or detention of such person, the merchant, agent or employee of the merchant, had at the time of such arrest or detention probable cause to believe that the person had shoplifted or committed willful concealment of goods or merchandise. The activation of an electronic article surveillance device as a result of a person exiting the premises or an area within the premises of a merchant where an electronic article surveillance device is located shall constitute probable cause for the detention of such person by such merchant, his agent or employee, provided such person is detained only in a reasonable manner and only for such time as is necessary for an inquiry into the circumstances surrounding the activation of the device, and provided that clear and visible notice is posted at each exit and location within the premises where such a device is located indicating the presence of an antishoplifting or inventory control device. For purposes of this section, "electronic article

surveillance device" means an electronic device designed and operated for the purpose of detecting the removal from the premises, or a protected area within such premises, of specially marked or tagged merchandise.

History.
  Code 1950, § 18.1-127; 1960, c. 358; 1975, cc. 14, 15; 1976, c. 515; 1980, c. 149; 1985, c. 275, § 18.2-105; 2004, c. 462.

Michie's Jurisprudence.
  For related discussion, see 8B M.J. False Imprisonment, § 8.

CASE NOTES

Editor's note.
  Many of the cases annotated below were decided under former § 18.2-105.

Legislative intent. — The legislature, seeking remedies for the multi-billion dollar epidemic of shoplifting and recognizing that police officers cannot be omnipresent, intended to immunize a "merchant, agent or employee of the merchant" who, either on the store premises or after close pursuit off the premises, restrains and detains those he has "probable cause to believe" have "committed wilful concealment of goods or merchandise" against civil liability for certain torts committed in the course of such restraint and detention. F.B.C. Stores, Inc. v. Duncan, 214 Va. 246, 198 S.E.2d 595 (1973).

The scope of the exemption intended by the legislature was very broad. F.B.C. Stores, Inc. v. Duncan, 214 Va. 246, 198 S.E.2d 595 (1973).

The Supreme Court of Virginia would interpret the former version of this statute in a way giving expansive rather than restrictive scope to the probable cause defense, particularly where the expansive interpretation is that indicated by the plain language of the section. Brandau v. J.C. Penney Co., 646 F.2d 128 (4th Cir. 1981).

Under the former version of this section, the merchant's right to protect his property was enlarged but not infinitely; the litigable rights of the public were diminished but not extinguished. F.B.C. Stores, Inc. v. Duncan, 214 Va. 246, 198 S.E.2d 595 (1973).

This section does not provide a merchant with absolute immunity. — The balance between personal and property rights in the former version of this section is achieved by providing immunity from civil liability based on a wide range of torts, but not extending such immunity in circumstances in which the tort is committed in a willful, wanton or otherwise unreasonable or excessive manner. Merchants, their agents or employees are shielded from civil liability for actions reasonably necessary to protect the owners' property rights by detaining suspected shoplifters. But, individuals retain their "litigable rights." Jury v. Giant of Md., Inc., 254 Va. 235, 491 S.E.2d 718 (1997).

Qualified privilege. — The legal principles applicable to shoplifting, and to civil litigation arising from efforts to control this crime, do not include the concept of qualified privilege. Tweedy v. J.C. Penney Co., 216 Va. 596, 221 S.E.2d 152 (1976).

Unofficial restraint is within intendment of "causes the arrest." — Unofficial restraint or detention caused by the merchant or his agent is within the intendment of the phrase "causes the arrest." F.B.C. Stores, Inc. v. Duncan, 214 Va. 246, 198 S.E.2d 595 (1973).

Conduct and circumstances constituting an "unlawful detention" would also constitute the tort of false imprisonment. Since the legislature listed both false imprisonment and unlawful detention, the legislature considered detention to have particular significance in this context. F.B.C. Stores, Inc. v. Duncan, 214 Va. 246, 198 S.E.2d 595 (1973).

If formal arrest were the only predicate for the statutory exemption, the fact that a merchant or his agent had discovered a person's innocence and knew they had no probable cause for formal arrest would not necessarily dissuade them from attempting to so position themselves as to enable them, if faced with a civil suit, to assert the exemption or adduce testimony designed to prove probable cause for both the informal detention and the formal arrest. F.B.C. Stores, Inc. v. Duncan, 214 Va. 246, 198 S.E.2d 595 (1973).

Proof of intent to deprive not required. — The probable cause defense given merchants by this section requires with respect to all the civil claims enumerated in the section proof only that at the time of a claimant's unofficial detention the merchant had probable cause to believe that the claimant had willfully concealed merchandise, and does not require further proof that the merchant then or later had probable cause to believe that the suspect intended wrongfully to deprive the merchant of the merchandise. Brandau v. J.C. Penney Co., 646 F.2d 128 (4th Cir. 1981).

Test for probable cause. — In any trial whether probable cause is proven will depend upon whether the circumstances disclosed by the evidence were such as to justify an ordinarily prudent person in acting as defendants acted. F.B.C. Stores, Inc. v. Duncan, 214 Va. 246, 198 S.E.2d 595 (1973).

Later discovered facts suggesting innocence do not deprive the merchant of the defense provided under the former version of this statute if he nevertheless proceeds thereafter to cause an official arrest and criminal prosecution. Brandau v. J.C. Penney Co., 646 F.2d 128 (4th Cir. 1981).

Burden of proof. — The burden is on defendants to prove probable cause as an affirmative defense. Hence, the court erred in granting instruction tendered by defendants, which required plaintiff to prove lack of probable cause. Tweedy v. J.C. Penney Co., 216 Va. 596, 221 S.E.2d 152 (1976).

Question of fact. — Unless the evidence leaves no room for reasonable men to disagree, whether the circumstances were such as to justify an ordinarily prudent person in acting as defendants acted will be a question of fact properly within the province of the jury. F.B.C. Stores, Inc. v. Duncan, 214 Va. 246, 198 S.E.2d 595 (1973).

Probable cause found. — Store was immune from liability under § 8.01-226.9 in a customer's false imprisonment and malicious prosecution action, and therefore it was entitled to summary judgment, because it had probable cause to detain customer for committing petit larceny in violation of § 18.2-96 after she attempted to leave the store with a TV and VCR for which she had no receipt. At the time the store's employees detained the customer, they knew that: (1) she had received full credit on her mother's credit card for the returned merchandise; (2) she did not pay for the new television and VCR; (3) she had stood close to her friend while the friend shoplifted twice in the store; and (4) the customer attempted to leave the store with the TV and VCR without a receipt proving that she had paid for them. Jones v. Target Corp., 341 F. Supp. 2d 583, 2004 U.S. Dist. LEXIS 21425 (E.D. Va. 2004).

As plaintiff was not seeking punitive damages, she was not required to prove actual malice on the part of storekeeper as a prerequisite to recovery of compensatory damages for either insulting words or malicious prosecution. Tweedy v. J.C. Penney Co., 216 Va. 596, 221 S.E.2d 152 (1976).

Instruction. — The court erred in granting instruction tendered by defendants which directed the jury to find for defendants if they found that defendant acted "without personal animosity," i.e., actual malice, against plaintiff. Tweedy v. J.C. Penney Co., 216 Va. 596, 221 S.E.2d 152 (1976).

Store owner that detained a customer for shop lifting did so in a reasonable manner and for a reasonable length of time and was immune from civil claims for false imprisonment and malicious prosecution, and the harm to the customer was not outrageous; the store owner's motion for summary judgment was granted. Hall v. Wal-Mart Stores East, Inc., No. 1:03CV00056, 2003 U.S. Dist. LEXIS 21016 (W.D. Va. Nov. 21, 2003).

Conviction by a trial justice, though reversed on appeal, is conclusive evidence of probable cause, unless such conviction was procured by the defendant through fraud or by means of evidence which he knew to be false. Janney v. Arlan's Dep't Store, 247 F. Supp. 306 (W.D. Va. 1965).

§ 8.01-226.11. Civil immunity for operation of victim notification program.

The Virginia Sheriffs' Association and the Virginia Community Policing Institute, and the directors, managers, members, officers and employees of such entities shall be immune from civil liability for their acts or omissions relating to the establishment and operation of an automated victim notification system unless such act or omission was the result of gross negligence or willful misconduct.

History.
2006, c. 267.

Law Review.
For 2007 annual survey article, "Civil Practice and Procedure," see 42 U. Rich. L. Rev. 229 (2007).

CHAPTER 11.

JURIES.

Article 2. Jurors.

Section
8.01-341. Who are exempt from jury service.

ARTICLE 2.

JURORS.

§ 8.01-341. Who are exempt from jury service.

The following shall be exempt from serving on juries in civil and criminal cases:

1. The President and Vice President of the United States,

2. The Governor, Lieutenant Governor and Attorney General of the Commonwealth,

3. The members of both houses of Congress,

4. The members of the General Assembly, while in session or during a period when the member would be entitled to a legislative continuance as a matter of right under § 30-5,

5. Licensed practicing attorneys,

6. The judge of any court, members of the State Corporation Commission, members of the Virginia Workers' Compensation Commission, and magistrates,

7. Sheriffs, deputy sheriffs, state police, and police in counties, cities and towns,

8. The superintendent of the penitentiary and his assistants and the persons composing the guard,

9. Superintendents and jail officers, as defined in § 53.1-1, of regional jails.

History.
Code 1950, § 8-208.6; 1973, c. 439; 1977, cc. 458, 617; 1978, cc. 176, 340; 1980, c. 535; 1982, c. 315; 1987, c. 256; 1990, c. 758; 1993, c. 572; 1998, c. 83.

Editor's note.
Pursuant to § 30-152 and Acts 1977, c. 617, cl. 4, the Code Commission has given effect, in this section, to the amendment to former § 8-208.6, corresponding to this section, by Acts 1977, c. 458. The amendment deleted subdivisions 10 through 13, 18, 22, 23, 26 and 27. All of the classes exempted in the deleted subdivi-

sions are included as optional exemptions in § 8.01-341.1, also enacted by Acts 1977, c. 458.

Law Review.

For survey of Virginia constitutional law for the year 1972-1973, see 59 Va. L. Rev. 1445 (1973). For comment, "The Questionable Validity of the Automatic Exemption of Attorneys from Jury Service," see 14 U. Rich. L. Rev. 837 (1980). For article, "Improving the Jury System in Virginia: Jury Patriotism Legislation Is Needed," 11 Geo. Mason L. Rev. 657 (2003).

CASE NOTES

Disqualification and exemption provisions nondiscriminatory. — Virginia law has many disqualification and exemption provisions for selection to the jury list, none of which are discriminatory. Stephens v. Cox, 449 F.2d 657 (4th Cir. 1971) (decided under prior law).

Some of the Virginia disqualifications and exemptions, by an entirely impartial operation, may disqualify more African Americans than whites. Stephens v. Cox, 449 F.2d 657 (4th Cir. 1971) (decided under prior law).

OPINIONS OF THE ATTORNEY GENERAL

Licensed practicing attorney. — While subdivision 5 of § 8.01-341 provides an exemption from jury service for licensed practicing attorneys, it does not bar lawyers from serving on a jury when a lawyer is willing to waive the exemption. For the purpose of subdivision 5 of § 8.01-341, a "licensed practicing attorney" is a person licensed to practice law in any state or territory of the United States, including the District of Columbia, who is engaged in the active practice of law. See opinion of Attorney General to The Honorable Paul Ferguson, Clerk of the Circuit Court, Arlington County, 12-030, 2012 Va. AG LEXIS 16 (5/18/12).

TITLE 9.

COMMISSIONS, BOARDS AND INSTITUTIONS GENERALLY.

[Repealed.]

TITLE 9.1.

COMMONWEALTH PUBLIC SAFETY.

CHAPTER 1.

DEPARTMENT OF CRIMINAL JUSTICE SERVICES.

Article 1. General Provisions.

ARTICLE 1.

GENERAL PROVISIONS.

§ 9.1-100. Department of Criminal Justice Services.

A. There is created a Department of Criminal Justice Services (the "Department") that shall be headed by a Director appointed by the Governor, subject to confirmation by the General Assembly. The Director shall serve at the pleasure of the Governor.

B. The Director of the Department shall, under the direction and control of the Governor, exercise the powers and perform the duties conferred or imposed upon him by law and perform such other duties required by the Governor or the Criminal Justice Services Board.

History.

1981, c. 632, §§ 9-174, 9-175, 9-176; 1984, c. 720; 2001, c. 844.

Editor's note.

In accordance with § 9-77.10 (now § 30-149), the Virginia Code Commission, in 1998, undertook a three-year recodification of Titles 2.1 and 9. Title 2.1 had last been recodified in 1965 and Title 9 had never been recodified. The Commission's draft of this revision, which was published as House Document 51 of the 2001 Session, was sent to the Governor and General Assembly in January, 2001. The revision, as amended by the General Assembly, became Acts 2001, c. 844, effective October 1, 2001.

Title 2.1 was rewritten primarily as new Title 2.2, with certain material now incorporated into Titles 6.1, 9.1, 17.1, 30, 37.1 and 51.1, and Title 9 was rewritten primarily as new Title 9.1, with certain material now incorporated into Titles 3.1, 2.2, and 30. In addition, the Virginia Public Procurement Act, §§ 11-35 to 11-80, was rewritten as § 2.2-4300 et seq., and §§ 53.1-180 to 53.1-185.3, the Comprehensive Community Corrections Act for Local-Responsible Offenders, was rewritten as §§ 9.1-173 to 9.1-183.

Where appropriate, the historical citations to former sections have been added to corresponding new sections.

The case notes appearing under new sections were decided under corresponding former sections or under prior law.

For a table of corresponding former and new sections, see the Table of Comparable Sections following the Table of Contents at the front of this volume.

Acts 2001, c. 844, cl. 2, provides: "That whenever any of the conditions, requirements, provisions or contents of any section or chapter of Title 2.1 or Title 9 or any other title of the Code of Virginia as such titles existed prior to October 1, 2001, are transferred in the same or modified form to a new section or chapter of Title 2.2 or Title 9.1 or any other title of the Code and whenever any such former section or chapter is given a new number in Title 2.2 or Title 9.1 or any other title, all references to any such former section or chapter of Title 2.1 or Title 9 or other title appearing in this Code shall be construed to apply to the new or renumbered section or chapter containing such conditions, requirements, provisions, contents or portions thereof."

Acts 2001, c. 844, cl. 3, provides: "That the regulations of any department or agency affected by the revision of Title 2.1, Title 9 or such other titles in effect on the effective date of this act shall continue in effect to the extent that they are not in conflict with this act and shall be deemed to be regulations adopted under this act."

Acts 2001, c. 844, cl. 4, provides: "That this title revision of Title 2.1 as Title 2.2 and Title 9 as Title 9.1 and the repeal of Chapter 7 (§ 11-35 et seq.) of Title 11 shall not be construed to require the reappointment of any officer or any member of a board, council, committee or other appointed body referred to in Title 2.2 or Title 9.1 and each such officer and member shall continue to serve for the term for which appointed pursuant to the provisions of Title 2.1, Title 9, or Chapter 7 (§ 11-35 et seq.) of Title 11. The revision of Title 2.1 as Title 2.2 and Title 9 as Title 9.1 in this act shall not affect the classification or assignment of any state agency, institution, board, commission, council or other collegial body within the executive branch currently in effect pursuant to Title 2.1 or Title 9; such classifications and assignments within the executive branch which existed prior to the effective date of this act shall continue unless reclassified or reassigned by a later enactment of the General Assembly and signed by the Governor."

Acts 2001, c. 844, cl. 5, provides: "That this title revision of Title 2.1 as Title 2.2 or Title 9 as Title 9.1 shall not be construed to affect the term of office of any elected officeholder holding office on October 1, 2001."

Acts 2001, c. 844, cl. 6, provides: "That the provisions of § 30-152, formerly § 9-77.11, of the Code of Virginia shall apply to the codification of Title 2.2 and Title 9.1 so as to give effect to other laws enacted by the 2001 Session of the General Assembly notwithstanding the delay in the effective date of this act."

Acts 2001, c. 844, cl. 7, provides: "That the repeal of Title 2.1, Title 9, and Chapter 7 (§ 11-35 et seq.) of Title 11 effective as of October 1, 2001, shall not affect any act or offense done or committed, or any penalty incurred, or any right established, accrued or accruing on or before such date, or any proceeding, prosecution, suit or action pending on that day. Except as otherwise provided in this act, neither the repeal of Title 2.1, Title 9 or Chapter 7 (§ 11-35 et seq.) of Title 11 nor the enactment of Title 2.2 or the enactment of Title 9.1, shall apply to offenses committed prior to October 1, 2001, and prosecution for such offenses shall be governed by the prior law, which is continued in effect for that purpose. For the purpose of this enactment, an offense was committed prior to October 1, 2001, if any of essential elements of the offense occurred prior thereto."

Acts 2001, c. 844, cl. 8, provides: "That any notice given, recognizance taken, or process or writ issued before October 1, 2001, shall be valid although given, taken or to be returned to a day after such date, in like manner as if Title 2.2 and Title 9.1 had been effective before the same was given, taken or issued."

Acts 2001, c. 844, cl. 9, contains a severability clause.

Acts 2001, c. 844, cl. 14, provides: "That the provisions of this act shall become effective on October 1, 2001."

§ 9.1-101. Definitions.

As used in this chapter or in Chapter 23 (§ 19.2-387 et seq.) of Title 19.2, unless the context requires a different meaning:

"*Administration of criminal justice*" means performance of any activity directly involving the detection, apprehension, detention, pretrial release, posttrial release, prosecution, adjudication, correctional supervision, or rehabilitation of accused persons or criminal offenders or the collection, storage, and dissemination of criminal history record information.

"*Board*" means the Criminal Justice Services Board.

"*Conviction data*" means information in the custody of any criminal justice agency relating to a judgment of conviction, and the consequences arising therefrom, in any court.

"*Correctional status information*" means records and data concerning each condition of a convicted person's custodial status, including probation, confinement, work release, study release, escape, or termination of custody through expiration of sentence, parole, pardon, or court decision.

"*Criminal history record information*" means records and data collected by criminal justice agencies on adult individuals consisting of identifiable descriptions and notations of arrests, detentions, indictments, informations, or other formal charges, and any disposition arising therefrom. The term shall not include juvenile record information which is controlled by Chapter 11 (§ 16.1-226 et seq.) of Title 16.1, criminal justice intelligence information, criminal justice investigative information, or correctional status information.

"*Criminal justice agency*" means (i) a court or any other governmental agency or subunit thereof which as its principal function performs the administration of criminal justice and any other agency or subunit thereof which performs criminal justice activities, but only to the extent that it does so; (ii) for the purposes of Chapter 23 (§ 19.2-387 et seq.) of Title 19.2, any private corporation or agency which, within the context of its criminal justice activities, employs officers appointed under § 15.2-1737, or special conservators of the peace or special policemen appointed under Chapter 2 (§ 19.2-12 et seq.) of Title 19.2, provided that (a) such private corporation or agency requires its officers, special conservators or special policemen to meet compulsory training standards established by the Criminal Justice Services Board and submits reports of compliance with the training standards and (b) the private corporation or agency complies with the provisions of Article 3 (§ 9.1-126 et seq.), but only to the extent that the private corporation or agency so designated as a criminal justice agency performs criminal justice activities; and (iii) the Office of the Attorney

General, for all criminal justice activities otherwise permitted under clause (i) and for the purpose of performing duties required by the Civil Commitment of Sexually Violent Predators Act (§ 37.2-900 et seq.).

"Criminal justice agency" includes the Virginia State Crime Commission.

"Criminal justice agency" includes any program certified by the Commission on VASAP pursuant to § 18.2-271.2.

"*Criminal justice information system*" means a system including the equipment, facilities, procedures, agreements, and organizations thereof, for the collection, processing, preservation, or dissemination of criminal history record information. The operations of the system may be performed manually or by using electronic computers or other automated data processing equipment.

"*Department*" means the Department of Criminal Justice Services.

"*Dissemination*" means any transfer of information, whether orally, in writing, or by electronic means. The term shall not include access to the information by officers or employees of a criminal justice agency maintaining the information who have both a need and right to know the information.

"*Law-enforcement officer*" means any full-time or part-time employee of a police department or sheriff's office which is a part of or administered by the Commonwealth or any political subdivision thereof, and who is responsible for the prevention and detection of crime and the enforcement of the penal, traffic or highway laws of the Commonwealth, and shall include any (i) special agent of the Department of Alcoholic Beverage Control; (ii) police agent appointed under the provisions of § 56-353; (iii) officer of the Virginia Marine Police; (iv) conservation police officer who is a full-time sworn member of the enforcement division of the Department of Game and Inland Fisheries; (v) investigator who is a full-time sworn member of the security division of the State Lottery Department; (vi) conservation officer of the Department of Conservation and Recreation commissioned pursuant to § 10.1-115; (vii) full-time sworn member of the enforcement division of the Department of Motor Vehicles appointed pursuant to § 46.2-217; (viii) animal protection police officer employed under § 15.2-632; or (ix) campus police officer appointed under Chapter 17 (§ 23-232 et seq.) of Title 23. Part-time employees are those compensated officers who are not full-time employees as defined by the employing police department or sheriff's office.

"*School resource officer*" means a certified law-enforcement officer hired by the local law-enforcement agency to provide law-enforcement and security services to Virginia public elementary and secondary schools.

"*School security officer*" means an individual who is employed by the local school board for the singular purpose of maintaining order and discipline, preventing crime, investigating violations of school board policies, and detaining students violating the law or school board policies on school property or at school-sponsored events and who is responsible solely for ensuring the safety, security, and welfare of all students, faculty, staff, and visitors in the assigned school.

History.
1981, c. 632, § 9-169; 1982, c. 419; 1983, c. 357; 1984, c. 543; 1989, c. 233; 1991, c. 338; 1992, cc. 422, 569; 1993, cc. 533, 622, 866; 2000, c. 426; 2001, c. 844; 2002, cc. 789, 836, 868; 2003, cc. 744, 934, 937; 2004, c. 30; 2005, c. 914; 2007, c. 87; 2008, c. 460; 2010, c. 621; 2012, c. 776.

Cross references.
As to provisions establishing and developing crisis intervention teams, see Article 13 (§ 9.1-187) of Chapter 1 of Title 9.1. As to duty of law-enforcement officers to enforce certain provisions, see § 3.2-1010 pertaining to endangered plant and insect species; see § 3.2-6013 pertaining to execution of orders of the State Veterinarian. As to animal control officers, see §§ 3.2-6555 and 15.2-631. As to authority to serve capias or show cause order, see § 8.01-293. As to minimum qualifications of law-enforcement officers, see § 15.2-1705. As to special conservators of the peace, see § 9.1-150.1 et seq., § 19.2-13. As to availability of court ordered psychiatric reports of criminal defendants, see § 19.2-301. As to deeming of local social services department fraud prevention and investigation units to be criminal justice agencies as defined in § 9.1-101, see § 63.2-526.

Editor's note.
Acts 2012, c. 776, cl. 2, provides: "That the provisions of this act may result in a net increase in periods of imprisonment or commitment. Pursuant to § 30-19.1:4, the estimated amount of the necessary appropriation is $0 for periods of imprisonment in state adult correctional facilities and is $0 for periods of commitment to the custody of the Department of Juvenile Justice."

The 2012 amendments.
The 2012 amendment by c. 776, inserted clause (ix) under "Law-enforcement officer" and made related changes and updated references.

Michie's Jurisprudence.
For related discussion, see 11B M.J. Jury, § 17.

CASE NOTES

Editor's note.
The cases below were decided under former corresponding provisions.

Law-enforcement officer. — A police department employee responsible for monitoring the status of individuals subject to house arrest was not a "law enforcement officer" under this section; although the employee was expected to report observed violations to a law enforcement officer, she carried no badge, had only a civilian identification card, had no arrest authority and could not enforce the law. Jones v. Commonwealth, 32 Va. App. 30, 526 S.E.2d 281 (2000).

Commonwealth's Attorney constitutes criminal justice agency. — Because the administration of criminal justice, by definition, includes "the prosecution . . . of accused persons or criminal offenders," the Office of the Commonwealth's Attorney constitutes a "criminal justice agency" within the meaning of this section; thus, § 19.2-389 A 1 authorizes the Commonwealth's Attorney to review the criminal background records of prospective jurors. Salmon v. Commonwealth, 32 Va. App. 586, 529 S.E.2d 815, 2000 Va. App. LEXIS 428 (2000).

OPINIONS OF THE ATTORNEY GENERAL

A commissioner of accounts is not permitted access to criminal history records of delinquent fiduciaries through

the Virginia Criminal Information Network, unless such records are released pursuant to a circuit court order or rule. See opinion of Attorney General to The Honorable Thomas D. Horne, Judge, Twentieth Judicial Circuit, 00-011 (4/8/02).

State Police may provide mental health information to FBI to determine a person's eligibility to possess, purchase, or transfer a firearm. — The Department of State Police has the authority to provide certain mental health information maintained in the Central Criminal Records Exchange to the Federal Bureau of Investigation, so long as it is (i) kept confidential; and (ii) used only to determine a person's eligibility to possess, purchase or transfer a firearm. See opinion of Attorney General to Colonel W. Gerald Massengill, Superintendent, Department of State Police, 01-062 (4/4/02).

§ 9.1-101.1. Certified mail; subsequent mail or notices may be sent by regular mail.

Whenever in this chapter the Board or the Department is required to send any mail or notice by certified mail and such mail or notice is sent certified mail, return receipt requested, then any subsequent, identical mail or notice that is sent by the Board or the Department may be sent by regular mail.

History.
2011, c. 566.

ARTICLE 4.

PRIVATE SECURITY SERVICES BUSINESSES.

§ 9.1-138. Definitions.

In addition to the definitions set forth in § 9.1-101, as used in this article, unless the context requires a different meaning:

"*Alarm respondent*" means an individual who responds to the signal of an alarm for the purpose of detecting an intrusion of the home, business or property of the end user.

"*Armed*" means a private security registrant who carries or has immediate access to a firearm in the performance of his duties.

"*Armed security officer*" means a natural person employed to (i) safeguard and protect persons and property or (ii) deter theft, loss, or concealment of any tangible or intangible personal property on the premises he is contracted to protect, and who carries or has access to a firearm in the performance of his duties.

"*Armored car personnel*" means persons who transport or offer to transport under armed security from one place to another, money, negotiable instruments or other valuables in a specially equipped motor vehicle with a high degree of security and certainty of delivery.

"*Business advertising material*" means display advertisements in telephone directories, letterhead, business cards, local newspaper advertising and contracts.

"*Central station dispatcher*" means an individual who monitors burglar alarm signal devices, burglar alarms or any other electrical, mechanical or electronic device used (i) to prevent or detect burglary, theft, shoplifting, pilferage or similar losses; (ii) to prevent or detect intrusion; or (iii) primarily to summon aid for other emergencies.

"*Certification*" means the method of regulation indicating that qualified persons have met the minimum requirements as private security services training schools, private security services instructors, compliance agents, or certified detector canine handler examiners.

"*Compliance agent*" means an individual who owns or is employed by a licensed private security services business to ensure the compliance of the private security services business with this title.

"*Computer or digital forensic services*" means the use of highly specialized expertise for the recovery, authentication, and analysis of electronic data or computer usage.

"*Courier*" means any armed person who transports or offers to transport from one place to another documents or other papers, negotiable or nonnegotiable instruments, or other small items of value that require expeditious services.

"*Detector canine*" means any dog that detects drugs or explosives.

"*Detector canine handler*" means any individual who uses a detector canine in the performance of private security duties.

"*Detector canine handler examiner*" means any individual who examines the proficiency and reliability of detector canines and detector canine handlers in the detection of drugs or explosives.

"*Detector canine team*" means the detector canine handler and his detector canine performing private security duties.

"*Electronic security business*" means any person who engages in the business of or undertakes to (i) install, service, maintain, design or consult in the design of any electronic security equipment to an end user; (ii) respond to or cause a response to electronic security equipment for an end user; or (iii) have access to confidential information concerning the design, extent, status, password, contact list, or location of an end user's electronic security equipment.

"*Electronic security employee*" means an individual who is employed by an electronic security business in any capacity which may give him access to information concerning the design, extent, status, password, contact list, or location of an end user's electronic security equipment.

"*Electronic security equipment*" means (i) electronic or mechanical alarm signaling devices including burglar alarms or holdup alarms used to safeguard and protect persons and property; or (ii) cameras used to detect intrusions, concealment or theft, to safeguard and protect persons and property. This shall not include tags, labels, and other devices that are attached or affixed to items offered for sale, library books, and other protected articles as part of an electronic article surveillance and theft detection and deterrence system.

"Electronic security sales representative" means an individual who sells electronic security equipment on behalf of an electronic security business to the end user.

"Electronic security technician" means an individual who installs, services, maintains or repairs electronic security equipment.

"Electronic security technician's assistant" means an individual who works as a laborer under the supervision of the electronic security technician in the course of his normal duties, but who may not make connections to any electronic security equipment.

"Employed" means to be in an employer/employee relationship where the employee is providing work in exchange for compensation and the employer directly controls the employee's conduct and pays some taxes on behalf of the employee. The term "employed" shall not be construed to include independent contractors.

"End user" means any person who purchases or leases electronic security equipment for use in that person's home or business.

"Firearms training verification" means the verification of successful completion of either initial or retraining requirements for handgun or shotgun training, or both.

"General public" means individuals who have access to areas open to all and not restricted to any particular class of the community.

"Key cutting" means making duplicate keys from an existing key and includes no other locksmith services.

"License number" means the official number issued to a private security services business licensed by the Department.

"Locksmith" means any individual that performs locksmith services, or advertises or represents to the general public that the individual is a locksmith even if the specific term locksmith is substituted with any other term by which a reasonable person could construe that the individual possesses special skills relating to locks or locking devices, including use of the words lock technician, lockman, safe technician, safeman, boxman, unlocking technician, lock installer, lock opener, physical security technician or similar descriptions.

"Locksmith services" mean selling, servicing, rebuilding, repairing, rekeying, repinning, changing the combination to an electronic or mechanical locking device; programming either keys to a device or the device to accept electronic controlled keys; originating keys for locks or copying keys; adjusting or installing locks or deadbolts, mechanical or electronic locking devices, egress control devices, safes, and vaults; opening, defeating or bypassing locks or latching mechanisms in a manner other than intended by the manufacturer; with or without compensation for the general public or on property not his own nor under his own control or authority.

"Natural person" means an individual person.

"Personal protection specialist" means any individual who engages in the duties of providing close protection from bodily harm to any person.

"Private investigator" means any individual who engages in the business of, or accepts employment to make, investigations to obtain information on (i) crimes or civil wrongs; (ii) the location, disposition, or recovery of stolen property; (iii) the cause of accidents, fires, damages, or injuries to persons or to property; or (iv) evidence to be used before any court, board, officer, or investigative committee.

"Private security services business" means any person engaged in the business of providing, or who undertakes to provide, armored car personnel, security officers, personal protection specialists, private investigators, couriers, security canine handlers, security canine teams, detector canine handlers, detector canine teams, alarm respondents, locksmiths, central station dispatchers, electronic security employees, electronic security sales representatives or electronic security technicians and their assistants to another person under contract, express or implied.

"Private security services instructor" means any individual certified by the Department to provide mandated instruction in private security subjects for a certified private security services training school.

"Private security services registrant" means any qualified individual who has met the requirements under this article to perform the duties of alarm respondent, locksmith, armored car personnel, central station dispatcher, courier, electronic security sales representative, electronic security technician, electronic security technician's assistant, personal protection specialist, private investigator, security canine handler, detector canine handler, unarmed security officer or armed security officer.

"Private security services training school" means any person certified by the Department to provide instruction in private security subjects for the training of private security services business personnel in accordance with this article.

"Registration" means a method of regulation whereby certain personnel employed by a private security services business are required to register with the Department pursuant to this article.

"Registration category" means any one of the following categories: (i) unarmed security officer and armed security officer/courier, (ii) security canine handler, (iii) armored car personnel, (iv) private investigator, (v) personal protection specialist, (vi) alarm respondent, (vii) central station dispatcher, (viii) electronic security sales representative, (ix) electronic security technician, (x) electronic technician's assistant, (xi) detector canine handler, or (xii) locksmith.

"Security canine" means a dog that has attended, completed, and been certified as a security canine by a certified security canine handler instructor in accordance with approved Department procedures

and certification guidelines. "Security canines" shall not include detector dogs.

"*Security canine handler*" means any individual who utilizes his security canine in the performance of private security duties.

"*Security canine team*" means the security canine handler and his security canine performing private security duties.

"*Supervisor*" means any individual who directly or indirectly supervises registered or certified private security services business personnel.

"*Unarmed security officer*" means a natural person who performs the functions of observation, detection, reporting, or notification of appropriate authorities or designated agents regarding persons or property on the premises he is contracted to protect, and who does not carry or have access to a firearm in the performance of his duties.

History.
1976, c. 737, § 54-729.27; 1977, c. 376, § 54.1-1900; 1980, c. 425, cc. 57, 779; 1988, c. 765; 1992, c. 578, § 9-183.1; 1994, cc. 45, 335, 810; 1995, c. 79; 1996, c. 541; 1997, c. 80; 1998, cc. 122, 807; 1999, c. 33; 2001, cc. 821, 844; 2003, c. 124; 2004, c. 470; 2005, c. 365; 2008, c. 638; 2009, c. 375; 2011, c. 263.

Cross references.
As to exclusions under the Virginia Freedom of Information Act pertaining to records of active investigations being conducted by the Department of Criminal Justice Services pursuant to this article, see § 2.2-3705.3. As to exclusions for persons licensed under this Article as a private security services business from certain licensing requirements of § 54.1-1100 et seq., see § 54.1-1103.

Editor's note.
Acts 2001, c. 821 amended former § 9-183.1, from which this section is derived. Pursuant to § 30-152, Acts 2001, c. 821 has been given effect in this section as set out above. The 2001 amendment by c. 821 inserted paragraphs defining the terms "Employed," "General Public," and "Natural Person."

Acts 2008, c. 638, cl. 2, provides: "That the Criminal Justice Services Board shall adopt reasonable regulations in accordance with the Administrative Process Act (§ 2.2-4000 et seq.) to implement the provisions of this act."

Acts 2008, c. 638, cl. 3, provides: "That, in addition to the requirements of §§ 2.2-4007.01 and 2.2-4007.02, during the promulgation of regulations in accordance with the second enactment of this act, the Department of Criminal Justice Services shall meet with representatives of the various locksmith organizations and other interested parties to solicit input from such organizations and persons in the formation and development of regulations concerning (i) the appropriate educational and training requirements for locksmiths and (ii) the Department's investigation of complaints against its locksmith regulants, including the process by which anonymous complaints will be handled by the Department pursuant to the requirements of Article 3 (§ 2.2-4018 et seq.) of Chapter 40 of Title 2.2. For the purposes of clause (i), the educational and training requirements, to the extent practicable, shall not exceed such requirements for electronic security businesses."

Acts 2008, c. 638, cl. 4, provides: "That the Board of Criminal Justice Services shall promulgate regulations to implement the provisions of this act to be effective by July 1, 2008."

Acts 2008, c. 638, cl. 5, provides: "That the registration requirements of this act shall become effective on October 1, 2008. Applicants for licensing and registration for locksmiths may submit an application to the Department on or after July 1, 2008." At the direction of the Virginia Code Commission, amendments to subsection C of § 9.1-139 have been set out as effective October 1, 2008.

The 2011 amendments.
The 2011 amendment by c. 263 added the definition for "Computer or digital forensic services."

CASE NOTES

Applied in United States v. Day, 591 F.3d 679, 2010 U.S. App. LEXIS 429 (4th Cir. 2010).

OPINIONS OF THE ATTORNEY GENERAL

Licensing requirement. — When an employee installing wiring or equipment used to support electronic security equipment has access to "confidential information concerning the design, extent, status ... or location of an end user's electronic security equipment," the contractor or subcontractor employing this individual must obtain a license from the Department of Criminal Justice Services as required by § 9.1-138, et seq. See opinion of Attorney General to The Honorable William K. Barlow, Member, House of Delegates, 10-115, 2011 Va. AG LEXIS 13 (2/25/11).

No distinction is made between contractors and subcontractors under the statute, only whether the individual performing the work has access to confidential information concerning the "end user's electronic security equipment." See opinion of Attorney General to The Honorable William K. Barlow, Member, House of Delegates, 10-115, 2011 Va. AG LEXIS 13 (2/25/11).

A business that provides wiring and data services that might be used by others, such as licensed alarm companies, to support security equipment, would not necessarily trigger the licensing equipment. See opinion of Attorney General to The Honorable William K. Barlow, Member, House of Delegates, 10-115, 2011 Va. AG LEXIS 13 (2/25/11).

§ 9.1-139. Licensing, certification, and registration required; qualifications; temporary licenses.

A. No person shall engage in the private security services business or solicit private security business in the Commonwealth without having obtained a license from the Department. No person shall be issued a private security services business license until a compliance agent is designated in writing on forms provided by the Department. The compliance agent shall ensure the compliance of the private security services business with this article and shall meet the qualifications and perform the duties required by the regulations adopted by the Board. A compliance agent shall have either a minimum of (i) three years of managerial or supervisory experience in a private security services business; with a federal, state or local law-enforcement agency; or in a related field or (ii) five years of experience in a private security services business; with a federal, state or local law-enforcement agency; or in a related field.

B. No person shall act as private security services training school or solicit students for private security training in the Commonwealth without being certified by the Department. No person shall be issued a private security services training school certification until a school director is designated in writing on forms provided by the Department. The school director shall ensure the compliance of the school with the provisions of this article and shall meet the qualifications and perform the duties required by the regulations adopted by the Board.

C. No person shall be employed by a licensed private security services business in the Commonwealth as armored car personnel, courier, armed security officer, detector canine handler, unarmed security officer, security canine handler, private investigator, personal protection specialist, alarm respondent, locksmith, central station dispatcher, electronic security sales representative, electronic security technician's assistant, or electronic security technician without possessing a valid registration issued by the Department, except as provided in this article.

D. A temporary license may be issued in accordance with Board regulations for the purpose of awaiting the results of the state and national fingerprint search. However, no person shall be issued a temporary license until (i) he has designated a compliance agent who has complied with the compulsory minimum training standards established by the Board pursuant to subsection A of § 9.1-141 for compliance agents, (ii) each principal of the business has submitted his fingerprints for a National Criminal Records search and a Virginia Criminal History Records search, and (iii) he has met all other requirements of this article and Board regulations.

E. No person shall be employed by a licensed private security services business in the Commonwealth unless such person is certified or registered in accordance with this chapter.

F. A temporary registration may be issued in accordance with Board regulations for the purpose of awaiting the results of the state and national fingerprint search. However, no person shall be issued a temporary registration until he has (i) complied with, or been exempted from the compulsory minimum training standards established by the Board, pursuant to subsection A of § 9.1-141, for armored car personnel, couriers, armed security officers, detector canine handlers, unarmed security officers, security canine handlers, private investigators, personal protection specialists, alarm respondents, locksmith, central station dispatchers, electronic security sales representatives, electronic security technician's assistants, or electronic security technicians, (ii) submitted his fingerprints to be used for the conduct of a National Criminal Records search and a Virginia Criminal History Records search, and (iii) met all other requirements of this article and Board regulations.

G. A temporary certification as a private security instructor or private security training school may be issued in accordance with Board regulations for the purpose of awaiting the results of the state and national fingerprint search. However, no person shall be issued a temporary certification as a private security services instructor until he has (i) met the education, training and experience requirements established by the Board and (ii) submitted his fingerprints to be used for the conduct of a National Criminal Records search and a Virginia Criminal History Records search. No person shall be issued a temporary certification as a private security services training school until (a) he has designated a training director, (b) each principal of the training school has

submitted his fingerprints to be used for the conduct of a National Criminal Records search and a Virginia Criminal History Records search, and (c) he has met all other requirements of this article and Board regulations.

H. A licensed private security services business in the Commonwealth shall not employ as an unarmed security officer, electronic security technician's assistant, unarmed alarm respondent, central station dispatcher, electronic security sales representative, locksmith, or electronic security technician, any person who has not complied with, or been exempted from, the compulsory minimum training standards established by the Board, pursuant to subsection A of § 9.1-141, except that such person may be so employed for not more than 90 days while completing compulsory minimum training standards.

I. No person shall be employed as an electronic security employee, electronic security technician's assistant, unarmed alarm respondent, locksmith, central station dispatcher, electronic security sales representative, electronic security technician or supervisor until he has submitted his fingerprints to the Department to be used for the conduct of a National Criminal Records search and a Virginia Criminal History Records search. The provisions of this subsection shall not apply to an out-of-state central station dispatcher meeting the requirements of subdivision 19 of § 9.1-140.

J. The compliance agent of each licensed private security services business in the Commonwealth shall maintain documentary evidence that each private security registrant and certified employee employed by his private security services business has complied with, or been exempted from, the compulsory minimum training standards required by the Board. Before January 1, 2003, the compliance agent shall ensure that an investigation to determine suitability of each unarmed security officer employee has been conducted, except that any such unarmed security officer, upon initiating a request for such investigation under the provisions of subdivision A 11 of § 19.2-389, may be employed for up to 30 days pending completion of such investigation. After January 1, 2003, no person shall be employed as an unarmed security officer until he has submitted his fingerprints to the Department for the conduct of a National Criminal Records search and a Virginia Criminal History Records search. Any person who was employed as an unarmed security officer prior to January 1, 2003, shall submit his fingerprints to the Department in accordance with subsection B of § 9.1-145.

K. No person with a criminal conviction for a misdemeanor involving (i) moral turpitude, (ii) assault and battery, (iii) damage to real or personal property, (iv) controlled substances or imitation controlled substances as defined in Article 1 (§ 18.2-247 et seq.) of Chapter 7 of Title 18.2, (v) prohibited sexual behavior as described in Article 7 (§ 18.2-61 et seq.) of Chapter 4 of Title 18.2, or (vi) firearms, or any felony shall be (a) employed as a registered or certified employee by a private security services business or training school, or (b) issued a private security services registration, certification as an unarmed security officer, electronic security employee or technician's assistant, a private security services training school or instructor certification, compliance agent certification, or a private security services business license, except that, upon written request, the Director of the Department may waive such prohibition.

L. The Department may grant a temporary exemption from the requirement for licensure, certification, or registration for a period of not more than 30 days in a situation deemed an emergency by the Department.

M. All private security services businesses and private security services training schools in the Commonwealth shall include their license or certification number on all business advertising materials.

N. A licensed private security services business in the Commonwealth shall not employ as armored car personnel any person who has not complied with, or been exempted from, the compulsory minimum training standards established by the Board pursuant to subsection A of § 9.1-141, except such person may serve as a driver of an armored car for not more than 90 days while completing compulsory minimum training standards, provided such person does not possess or have access to a firearm while serving as a driver.

History.
1976, c. 737, § 54-729.29; 1977, c. 376, § 54.1-1902; 1978, cc. 28, 428; 1984, cc. 57, 779; 1988, cc. 48, 765; 1991, c. 589; 1992, c. 578, § 9-183.3; 1994, cc. 45, 47, 810; 1995, c. 79; 1996, c. 541; 1998, cc. 53, 122, 807; 2000, c. 26; 2001, cc. 821, 844; 2002, cc. 578, 597; 2003, c. 124; 2004, c. 470; 2008, c. 638.

Editor's note.
Acts 2001, c. 821 amended former § 9-183.3, from which this section is derived. Pursuant to § 30-152, Acts 2001, c. 821 has been given effect in this section as set out above. The 2001 amendment by c. 821, in subsection J, substituted "conviction for" for "record of," inserted "(i)" before "moral turpitude," inserted "(ii) assault and battery, (iii) damage to real or personal property, (iv) controlled substances or imitation controlled substances as defined in Article 1 (§ 18.2-247 et seq.) of Chapter 7 of Title 18.2, (v) prohibited sexual behavior as described in Article 7 (§ 18.2-61 et seq.) of Chapter 4 of Title 18.2, or (vi) firearms," following "moral turpitude" and substituted "(a)" and "(b)" for "(i)" and "(ii)."

Acts 2008, c. 638, cl. 2, provides: "That the Criminal Justice Services Board shall adopt reasonable regulations in accordance with the Administrative Process Act (§ 2.2-4000 et seq.) to implement the provisions of this act."

Acts 2008, c. 638, cl. 3, provides: "That, in addition to the requirements of §§ 2.2-4007.01 and 2.2-4007.02, during the promulgation of regulations in accordance with the second enactment of this act, the Department of Criminal Justice Services shall meet with representatives of the various locksmith organizations and other interested parties to solicit input from such organizations and persons in the formation and development of regulations concerning (i) the appropriate educational and training requirements for locksmiths and (ii) the Department's investigation of complaints against its locksmith regulants, including the process by which anonymous complaints will be handled by the Department pursuant to the requirements of Article 3 (§ 2.2-4018 et seq.) of Chapter 40 of Title 2.2. For the purposes of clause (i), the educational and

training requirements, to the extent practicable, shall not exceed such requirements for electronic security businesses."

Acts 2008, c. 638, cl. 4, provides: "That the Board of Criminal Justice Services shall promulgate regulations to implement the provisions of this act to be effective by July 1, 2008."

Acts 2008, c. 638, which inserted "locksmith" in subsections C, F, H and I, in cl. 5 provides: "That the registration requirements of this act shall become effective on October 1, 2008. Applicants for licensing and registration for locksmiths may submit an application to the Department on or after July 1, 2008." At the direction of the Virginia Code Commission, amendments by this act to subsection C of this section are effective October 1, 2008.

CASE NOTES

Applied in United States v. Day, 591 F.3d 679, 2010 U.S. App. LEXIS 429 (4th Cir. 2010).

CIRCUIT COURT OPINIONS

Unjust enrichment claim not viable where contract deemed void under statute. — Because a contract between a security services provider and a business was found to be illegal under subsection A of § 9.1-139, there was no basis to find an implied or quasi-contract; as a result, the business was granted summary judgment on the provider's unjust enrichment or quantum meruit claim, in which it sought retention of money it garnished from the business's bank account to pay for its security services. Urban Protective Servs. v. Great Latin Rests., L.L.C., 2007 Va. Cir. LEXIS 33 (Fairfax County Mar. 5, 2007).

OPINIONS OF THE ATTORNEY GENERAL

Licensing requirement. — When an employee installing wiring or equipment used to support electronic security equipment has access to "confidential information concerning the design, extent, status ... or location of an end user's electronic security equipment," the contractor or subcontractor employing this individual must obtain a license from the Department of Criminal Justice Services as required by § 9.1-138, et seq. See opinion of Attorney General to The Honorable William K. Barlow, Member, House of Delegates, 10-115, 2011 Va. AG LEXIS 13 (2/25/11).

No distinction is made between contractors and subcontractors under the statute, only whether the individual performing the work has access to confidential information concerning the "end user's electronic security equipment." See opinion of Attorney General to The Honorable William K. Barlow, Member, House of Delegates, 10-115, 2011 Va. AG LEXIS 13 (2/25/11).

A business that provides wiring and data services that might be used by others, such as licensed alarm companies, to support security equipment, would not necessarily trigger the licensing equipment. See opinion of Attorney General to The Honorable William K. Barlow, Member, House of Delegates, 10-115, 2011 Va. AG LEXIS 13 (2/25/11).

§ 9.1-140. Exceptions from article; training requirements for out-of-state central station dispatchers.

The provisions of this article shall not apply to:

1. An officer or employee of the United States, the Commonwealth, or a political subdivision of either, while the officer or employee is performing his official duties;

2. A person, except a private investigator as defined in § 9.1-138, engaged exclusively in the business of obtaining and furnishing information regarding an individual's financial rating or a person engaged in the business of a consumer reporting

agency as defined by the Federal Fair Credit Reporting Act;

3. An attorney or certified public accountant licensed to practice in Virginia or his employees;

4. The legal owner of personal property which has been sold under any security agreement while performing acts relating to the repossession of such property;

5. A person receiving compensation for private employment as a security officer, or receiving compensation under the terms of a contract, express or implied, as a security officer, who is also a law-enforcement officer as defined by § 9.1-101 and employed by the Commonwealth or any of its political subdivisions;

6. Any person appointed under § 46.2-2003 or 56-353 while engaged in the employment contemplated thereunder, unless they have successfully completed training mandated by the Department;

7. Persons who conduct investigations as a part of the services being provided as a claims adjuster, by a claims adjuster who maintains an ongoing claims adjusting business, and any natural person employed by the claims adjuster to conduct investigations for the claims adjuster as a part of the services being provided as a claims adjuster;

8. Any natural person otherwise required to be registered pursuant to § 9.1-139 who is employed by a business that is not a private security services business for the performance of his duties for his employer. Any such employee, however, who carries a firearm and is in direct contact with the general public in the performance of his duties shall possess a valid registration with the Department as required by this article;

9. Persons, sometimes known as "shoppers," employed to purchase goods or services solely for the purpose of determining or assessing the efficiency, loyalty, courtesy, or honesty of the employees of a business establishment;

10. Licensed or registered private investigators from other states entering Virginia during an investigation originating in their state of licensure or registration when the other state offers similar reciprocity to private investigators licensed and registered by the Commonwealth;

11. Unarmed regular employees of telephone public service companies where the regular duties of such employees consist of protecting the property of their employers and investigating the usage of telephone services and equipment furnished by their employers, their employers' affiliates, and other communications common carriers;

12. An end user;

13. A material supplier who renders advice concerning the use of products sold by an electronics security business and who does not provide installation, monitoring, repair or maintenance services for electronic security equipment;

14. Members of the security forces who are directly employed by electric public service companies;

15. Any professional engineer or architect licensed in accordance with Chapter 4 (§ 54.1-400 et seq.) of Title 54.1 to practice in the Commonwealth, or his employees;

16. Any person who only performs telemarketing or schedules appointments without access to information concerning the electronic security equipment purchased by an end user;

17. Any certified forensic scientist employed as an expert witness for the purpose of possibly testifying as an expert witness;

18. Members of the security forces who are directly employed by shipyards engaged in the construction, design, overhaul or repair of nuclear vessels for the United States Navy;

19. An out-of-state central station dispatcher employed by a private security services business licensed by the Department provided he (i) possesses and maintains a valid license, registration, or certification as a central station dispatcher issued by the regulatory authority of the state in which he performs the monitoring duties and (ii) has submitted his fingerprints to the regulatory authority for the conduct of a national criminal history records search;

20. Any person, or independent contractor or employee of any person, who (i) exclusively contracts directly with an agency of the federal government to conduct background investigations and (ii) possesses credentials issued by such agency authorizing such person, subcontractor or employee to conduct background investigations;

21. Any person whose occupation is limited to the technical reconstruction of the cause of accidents involving motor vehicles as defined in § 46.2-100, regardless of whether the information resulting from the investigation is to be used before a court, board, officer, or investigative committee, and who is not otherwise a private investigator as defined in § 9.1-138;

22. Retail merchants performing locksmith services, selling locks or engaged in key cutting activities conducted at the business location who do not represent themselves to the general public as locksmiths;

23. Law-enforcement, fire, rescue, emergency service personnel, or other persons performing locksmith services in an emergency situation without compensation and who do not represent themselves to the general public as locksmiths;

24. Motor vehicle dealers as defined in § 46.2-1500 performing locksmith services who do not represent themselves to the general public as locksmiths;

25. Taxicab and towing businesses performing locksmith services that do not represent themselves to the general public as locksmiths;

26. Contractors licensed under Chapter 11 (§ 54.1-1100 et seq.) of Title 54.1 performing locksmith services when acting within the scope of such license who do not represent themselves to the general public as locksmiths;

27. Any contractor as defined in § 54.1-1100 (i) who is exempt from the licensure requirements of Chapter 11 (§ 54.1-1100 et seq.) of Title 54.1, (ii) where the total value referred to in a single contract or project is less than $1,000, (iii) when the performance of locksmith services is ancillary to the work performed by such contractor, and (iv) who does not represent himself to the general public as a locksmith;

28. Any individual, employed by a retail merchant that also holds a private security services business license as a locksmith, where such individual's duties relating to such license are limited to key cutting and the key cutting is performed under the direct supervision of the licensee;

29. Any individual engaged in (i) computer or digital forensic services as defined in § 9.1-138 or in the acquisition, review, or analysis of digital or computer-based information, in order to obtain or furnish information for evidentiary purposes or to provide expert testimony before a court, or (ii) network or system vulnerability testing, including network scans and risk assessment and analysis of computers connected to a network; or

30. Employees and sales representatives of a retailer of electronic security equipment, provided such employees and sales representatives (i) sell electronic security equipment at a store location, online, or by telephone, but not at the end user's premises; (ii) are not electronic security technicians; and (iii) do not have access to end user confidential information regarding the end user's electronic security equipment.

History.
1976, c. 737, § 54-729.28; 1977, c. 376, § 54.1-1901; 1981, c. 538; 1983, c. 569; 1984, c. 375; 1988, c. 765; 1992, c. 578, § 9-183.2; 1994, cc. 45, 810; 1995, c. 79; 1996, cc. 541, 543, 576; 1997, cc. 80, 204; 2000, c. 26; 2001, cc. 388, 650, 821, 844; 2002, cc. 578, 597; 2003, c. 136; 2008, c. 638; 2009, c. 225; 2011, c. 263; 2013, c. 411.

Editor's note.
Acts 2001, cc. 388, 650 and 821 amended former § 9-183.2, from which this section is derived. Pursuant to § 30-152, Acts 2001, cc. 388, 650 and 821 have been given effect in this section as set out above.

Section 46.2-2003, referred to in subdivision 6, was repealed effective July 1, 2002, by Acts 2001, c. 596.

Acts 2008, c. 638, cl. 2, provides: "That the Criminal Justice Services Board shall adopt reasonable regulations in accordance with the Administrative Process Act (§ 2.2-4000 et seq.) to implement the provisions of this act."

Acts 2008, c. 638, cl. 3, provides: "That, in addition to the requirements of §§ 2.2-4007.01 and 2.2-4007.02, during the promulgation of regulations in accordance with the second enactment of this act, the Department of Criminal Justice Services shall meet with representatives of the various locksmith organizations and other interested parties to solicit input from such organizations and persons in the formation and development of regulations concerning (i) the appropriate educational and training requirements for locksmiths and (ii) the Department's investigation of complaints against its locksmith regulants, including the process by which anonymous complaints will be handled by the Department pursuant to the requirements of Article 3 (§ 2.2-4018 et seq.) of Chapter 40 of Title 2.2. For the purposes of clause (i), the educational and training requirements, to the extent practicable, shall not exceed such requirements for electronic security businesses."

Acts 2008, c. 638, cl. 4, provides: "That the Board of Criminal

Justice Services shall promulgate regulations to implement the provisions of this act to be effective by July 1, 2008."

Acts 2008, c. 638, cl. 5, provides: "That the registration requirements of this act shall become effective on October 1, 2008. Applicants for licensing and registration for locksmiths may submit an application to the Department on or after July 1, 2008."

The 2011 amendments.
The 2011 amendment by c. 263 added subdivision 29.

The 2013 amendments.
The 2013 amendment by c. 411 substituted "Law-enforcement" for "Law enforcement" in subdivision 23; added subdivision 30; made a minor stylistic change and made punctuation changes throughout the section.

OPINIONS OF THE ATTORNEY GENERAL

Licensing requirement. — When an employee installing wiring or equipment used to support electronic security equipment has access to "confidential information concerning the design, extent, status ... or location of an end user's electronic security equipment," the contractor or subcontractor employing this individual must obtain a license from the Department of Criminal Justice Services as required by § 9.1-138, et seq. See opinion of Attorney General to The Honorable William K. Barlow, Member, House of Delegates, 10-115, 2011 Va. AG LEXIS 13 (2/25/11).

§ 9.1-140.1. Registration; waiver of examination; locksmiths.

Notwithstanding any other provision of this article, unless an applicant is found by the Board to have engaged in any act that would constitute grounds for disciplinary action, the Board shall issue a registration, without examination, to any applicant who provides satisfactory proof to the Board of having been actively and continuously providing locksmith services immediately prior to July 1, 2008, for at least two years.

History.
2008, c. 638.

Editor's note.
Acts 2008, c. 638, cl. 2, provides: "That the Criminal Justice Services Board shall adopt reasonable regulations in accordance with the Administrative Process Act (§ 2.2-4000 et seq.) to implement the provisions of this act."

Acts 2008, c. 638, cl. 3, provides: "That, in addition to the requirements of §§ 2.2-4007.01 and 2.2-4007.02, during the promulgation of regulations in accordance with the second enactment of this act, the Department of Criminal Justice Services shall meet with representatives of the various locksmith organizations and other interested parties to solicit input from such organizations and persons in the formation and development of regulations concerning (i) the appropriate educational and training requirements for locksmiths and (ii) the Department's investigation of complaints against its locksmith regulants, including the process by which anonymous complaints will be handled by the Department pursuant to the requirements of Article 3 (§ 2.2-4018 et seq.) of Chapter 40 of Title 2.2. For the purposes of clause (i), the educational and training requirements, to the extent practicable, shall not exceed such requirements for electronic security businesses."

Acts 2008, c. 638, cl. 4, provides: "That the Board of Criminal Justice Services shall promulgate regulations to implement the provisions of this act to be effective by July 1, 2008."

Acts 2008, c. 638, cl. 5, provides: "That the registration requirements of this act shall become effective on October 1, 2008. Applicants for licensing and registration for locksmiths may submit an application to the Department on or after July 1, 2008." At the direction of the Virginia Code Commission, the amendment by Acts

2008, c. 638 to subsection C of § 9.1-139 was effective October 1, 2008.

§ 9.1-141. Powers of Board relating to private security services business.

A. The Board may adopt regulations in accordance with the Administrative Process Act (§ 2.2-4000 et seq.), establishing compulsory minimum, entry-level, in-service, and advanced training standards for persons employed by private security services businesses in classifications defined in § 9.1-138. The regulations may include provisions delegating to the Board's staff the right to inspect the facilities and programs of persons conducting training to ensure compliance with the law and Board regulations. In establishing compulsory training standards for each of the classifications defined in § 9.1-138, the Board shall be guided by the policy of this section to secure the public safety and welfare against incompetent or unqualified persons engaging in the activities regulated by this section and Article 4 (§ 9.1-138 et seq.) of this chapter. The regulations may provide for partial exemption from such compulsory, entry-level training for persons having previous employment as law-enforcement officers for a local, state or the federal government, to include units of the United States armed forces, or for persons employed in classifications defined in § 9.1-138. However, no such exemption shall be granted to persons having less than five continuous years of such employment, nor shall an exemption be provided for any person whose employment as a law-enforcement officer or whose employment as a private security services business employee was terminated because of his misconduct or incompetence. The regulations may include separate provisions for partial exemption from compulsory training for persons having previous training that meets or exceeds the minimum training standards and has been approved by the Department. No regulation adopted by the Board shall prevent any person employed by an electronic security business, other than an alarm respondent, or as a locksmith from carrying a firearm in the course of his duties when such person carries with him a valid concealed handgun permit issued in accordance with § 18.2-308.

B. The Board may enter into an agreement with other states for reciprocity or recognition of private security services businesses and their employees, duly licensed by such states. The agreements shall allow those businesses and their employees to provide and perform private security services within the Commonwealth to secure the public safety and welfare against incompetent, unqualified, unscrupulous, or unfit persons engaging in the activities of private security services businesses.

C. The Board may adopt regulations in accordance with the Administrative Process Act (§ 2.2-4000 et seq.) to secure the public safety and welfare against incompetent, unqualified, unscrupulous, or unfit persons engaging in the activities of private security services businesses that:

1. Establish the qualifications of applicants for registration, certification, or licensure under Article 4 (§ 9.1-138) of this chapter;

2. Examine, or cause to be examined, the qualifications of each applicant for registration, certification, or licensure, including when necessary the preparation, administration, and grading of examinations;

3. Certify qualified applicants for private security training schools and instructors or license qualified applicants as practitioners of private security services businesses;

4. Levy and collect fees for registration, certification, or licensure and renewal that are sufficient to cover all expenses for administration and operation of a program of registration, certification, and licensure for private security services businesses and training schools;

5. Are necessary to ensure continued competency, and to prevent deceptive or misleading practices by practitioners and effectively administer the regulatory system adopted by the Board;

6. Receive complaints concerning the conduct of any person whose activities are regulated by the Board, to conduct investigations, and to take appropriate disciplinary action if warranted; and

7. Revoke, suspend or fail to renew a registration, certification, or license for just cause as enumerated in Board regulations.

D. In adopting its regulations under subsections A and C, the Board shall seek the advice of the Private Security Services Advisory Board established pursuant to § 9.1-143.

History.
1981, c. 632, § 9-182; 1990, c. 354; 1992, c. 578; 1994, cc. 45, 335, 810; 1995, c. 79; 1998, cc. 122, 807; 2001, c. 844; 2009, c. 375; 2013, c. 69.

Cross references.
As to registration requirements for special conservators of the peace, see § 19.2-13.

The 2013 amendments.
The 2013 amendment by c. 69, in subsection A, substituted "armed forces" for "Armed Forces" in the fourth sentence and added the last sentence.

CASE NOTES

Applicability. — Virginia's licensing and registration requirements are inapplicable to private investigators working solely for the Federal Bureau of Investigation because the state regulations interfere with federal objectives. United States v. Commonwealth, 139 F.3d 984 (4th Cir. 1998) (decided under prior law).
Applied in United States v. Day, 591 F.3d 679, 2010 U.S. App. LEXIS 429 (4th Cir. 2010).

§ 9.1-142. Powers of Department relating to private security services businesses.

A. In addition to the powers otherwise conferred upon it by law, the Department may:

1. Charge each applicant for licensure, certification or registration a nonrefundable fee as established by the Board to cover the costs of the Department for processing an application for a registration, certification or license, and enforcement of these regulations, and other costs associated with the maintenance of this program of regulation.

2. Charge nonrefundable fees for private security services training as established by the Board for processing school certifications and enforcement of training standards.

3. Conduct investigations to determine the suitability of applicants for registration, licensure, or certification of compliance agents, training schools, and instructors. For purposes of this investigation, the Department shall have access to criminal history record information maintained by the Central Criminal Records Exchange of the Department of State Police and shall conduct a background investigation, to include a National Criminal Records search and a Virginia Criminal History Records search.

4. Issue subpoenas. The Director or a designated subordinate may make an ex parte application to the circuit court for the city or county wherein evidence sought is kept or wherein a licensee does business, for the issuance of a subpoena duces tecum in furtherance of the investigation of a sworn complaint within the jurisdiction of the Department or the Board to request production of any relevant records, documents and physical or other evidence of any person, partnership, association or corporation licensed or regulated by the Department pursuant to this article. The court may issue and compel compliance with such a subpoena upon a showing of reasonable cause. Upon determining that reasonable cause exists to believe that evidence may be destroyed or altered, the court may issue a subpoena duces tecum requiring the immediate production of evidence.

5. Recover costs of the investigation and adjudication of violations of this article or Board regulations. Such costs may be recovered from the respondent when a sanction is imposed to fine or place on probation, suspend, revoke, or deny the issuance of any license, certification, or registration. Such costs shall be in addition to any monetary penalty which may be imposed. All costs recovered shall be deposited into the state treasury to the credit of the Private Security Services Regulatory Fund.

6. Institute proceedings to enjoin any person from engaging in any lawful act enumerated in § 9.1-147. Such proceedings shall be brought in the name of the Commonwealth by the Department in circuit court of the city or county in which the unlawful act occurred or in which the defendant resides.

B. The Director, or agents appointed by him, shall be vested with the authority to administer oaths or affirmations for the purpose of receiving complaints and conducting investigations of violations of this article, or any Board regulation promulgated pursuant to authority given by this article. Information concerning alleged criminal violations shall be turned over to law-enforcement officers in appropriate jurisdictions. Agents shall be vested with authority to serve such paper or process issued by the Department or the Board under regulations approved by the Board.

History.
1976, c. 737, § 54-729.30; 1977, c. 376, § 54.1-1903; 1984, cc. 57, 779; 1985, c. 448; 1988, c. 765; 1991, c. 589; 1992, c. 578, § 9-183.4; 1994, c. 46; 1998, cc. 122, 807; 2001, c. 844.

§ 9.1-143. Private Security Services Advisory Board; membership.

The Private Security Services Advisory Board is established as an advisory board within the meaning of § 2.2-2100, in the executive branch of state government. The Private Security Services Advisory Board shall consist of 15 members as follows: two members shall be private investigators; two shall be representatives of electronic security businesses; two members shall be representatives of locksmith businesses; three shall be representatives of private security services businesses providing security officers, armed couriers, detector canine handlers, or security canine handlers; one shall be a representative of a private security services business providing armored car personnel; one shall be a representative of a private security services business involving personal protection specialists; one shall be a certified private security services instructor; one shall be a special conservator of the peace appointed pursuant to § 19.2-13; one shall be a licensed bail bondsman and one shall be a representative of law enforcement. The Private Security Services Advisory Board shall be appointed by the Criminal Justice Services Board and shall advise the Criminal Justice Services Board on all issues relating to regulation of private security services businesses.

History.
1976, c. 737, § 54-729.30; 1977, c. 376, § 54.1-1904; 1984, cc. 57, 779; 1985, c. 448; 1988, c. 765; 1992, c. 578, § 9-183.5; 1994, c. 810; 1997, c. 79; 2001, c. 844; 2003, c. 922; 2004, c. 460; 2008, c. 638; 2009, c. 375.

Editor's note.
Acts 2004, c. 460, cl. 5, provides: "That the provisions of this act, except for § 16.1-77, shall become effective on July 1, 2005."

Acts 2008, c. 638, cl. 2, provides: "That the Criminal Justice Services Board shall adopt reasonable regulations in accordance with the Administrative Process Act (§ 2.2-4000 et seq.) to implement the provisions of this act."

Acts 2008, c. 638, cl. 3, provides: "That, in addition to the requirements of §§ 2.2-4007.01 and 2.2-4007.02, during the promulgation of regulations in accordance with the second enactment of this act, the Department of Criminal Justice Services shall meet with representatives of the various locksmith organizations and other interested parties to solicit input from such organizations and persons in the formation and development of regulations concerning (i) the appropriate educational and training requirements for locksmiths and (ii) the Department's investigation of complaints against its locksmith regulants, including the process by which anonymous complaints will be handled by the Department pursuant to the requirements of Article 3 (§ 2.2-4018 et seq.) of Chapter

40 of Title 2.2. For the purposes of clause (i), the educational and training requirements, to the extent practicable, shall not exceed such requirements for electronic security businesses."

Acts 2008, c. 638, cl. 4, provides: "That the Board of Criminal Justice Services shall promulgate regulations to implement the provisions of this act to be effective by July 1, 2008."

Acts 2008, c. 638, cl. 5, provides: "That the registration requirements of this act shall become effective on October 1, 2008. Applicants for licensing and registration for locksmiths may submit an application to the Department on or after July 1, 2008." At the direction of the Virginia Code Commission, the amendment by Acts 2008, c. 638 to subsection C of § 9.1-139 was effective October 1, 2008.

§ 9.1-144. Bond or insurance required; actions against bond.

A. Every person licensed as a private security services business under subsection A of § 9.1-139 or certified as a private security services training school under subsection B of § 9.1-139 shall, at the time of receiving the license or certification and before the license or certification shall be operative, file with the Department (i) a cash bond or evidence that the licensee or certificate holder is covered by a surety bond, executed by a surety company authorized to do business in the Commonwealth, in a reasonable amount to be fixed by the Department, conditioned upon the faithful and honest conduct of his business or employment; or (ii) evidence of a policy of liability insurance in an amount and with coverage as fixed by the Department. The bond or liability insurance shall be maintained for so long as the licensee or certificate holder is licensed or certified by the Department.

B. If any person aggrieved by the misconduct of any person licensed or certified under subsection A or B of § 9.1-139 recovers judgment against the licensee or certificate holder, which judgment is unsatisfied in whole or in part, such person may bring an action in his own name on the bond of the licensee or certificate holder.

History.
1976, c. 737, § 54-729.31; 1988, c. 765, § 54.1-1905; 1992, c. 578, § 9-183.6; 1998, cc. 122, 807; 2001, c. 844.

§ 9.1-145. Fingerprints required; penalty.

A. Each applicant for initial registration, licensure or certification as a compliance agent, private security services training school or instructor or unarmed security officer under the provisions of this article and every person employed as an electronic security employee or electronic security technician's assistant shall submit his fingerprints to the Department on a form provided by the Department. The Department shall use the applicant's fingerprints and personal descriptive information for the conduct of a National Criminal Records search and a Virginia Criminal History Records search.

B. Each currently certified unarmed security officer applying for renewal between January 1, 2003, and December 31, 2004, shall submit his fingerprints to the Department on a form provided by the Department. The Department shall use the applicant's fingerprints and personal descriptive information for the conduct of a National Criminal Records search and a Virginia Criminal History Records search.

C. The Department may suspend the registration, license or certification of any applicant who is subsequently convicted of a misdemeanor involving (i) moral turpitude, (ii) assault and battery, (iii) damage to real or personal property, (iv) controlled substances or imitation controlled substances as defined in Article 1 (§ 18.2-247 et seq.) of Chapter 7 of Title 18.2, (v) prohibited sexual behavior as described in Article 7 (§ 18.2-61 et seq.) of Chapter 4 of Title 18.2, or (vi) firearms or any felony.

D. Any person willfully and intentionally making a false statement in the personal descriptive information required on the fingerprint card is guilty of a Class 5 felony.

History.
1976, c. 737, § 54-729.32; 1988, c. 765, § 54.1-1906; 1992, c. 578, § 9-183.7; 1994, c. 810; 1995, c. 79; 1998, cc. 122, 807; 2001, c. 844; 2002, cc. 578, 597.

Cross references.
As to punishment for Class 5 felonies, see § 18.2-10.

Editor's note.
Acts 2002, cc. 578 and 597, cl. 2, provide: "That the provisions of this act may result in a net increase in periods of imprisonment or commitment. Pursuant to § 30-19.1:4, the estimated amount of the necessary appropriation is $0 for periods of imprisonment in state adult correctional facilities and is $0 for periods of commitment to the custody of the Department of Juvenile Justice."

§ 9.1-146. Limitation on powers of registered armed security officers.

Compliance with the provisions of this article shall not itself authorize any person to carry a concealed weapon or exercise any powers of a conservator of the peace. A registered armed security officer of a private security services business while at a location which the business is contracted to protect shall have the power to effect an arrest for an offense occurring (i) in his presence on such premises or (ii) in the presence of a merchant, agent, or employee of the merchant the private security business has contracted to protect, if the merchant, agent, or employee had probable cause to believe that the person arrested had shoplifted or committed willful concealment of goods as contemplated by § 18.2-106. For the purposes of § 19.2-74, a registered armed security officer of a private security services business shall be considered an arresting officer.

History.
1976, c. 737, § 54-729.33; 1978, c. 560, § 54.1-1907; 1980, c. 425; 1988, cc. 48, 765; 1992, c. 578, § 9-183.8; 1994, c. 45; 2001, c. 844.

CASE NOTES

Registered security guard not "conservator of the peace." — In accordance with the express language in this section, a registered, armed security guard was not a "conservator of the peace" so as to be exempt from the prohibition on carrying weapons on school grounds for conservators of the peace. Frias v. Commonwealth, 34 Va. App. 193, 538 S.E.2d 374, 2000 Va. App. LEXIS 838 (2000) (decided under former Title 9).

Private security guards not agents of state. — Apartment complex's private security guards did not act as de facto police officers under the public function test when they restrained and questioned defendant after finding him with a gun in a parking lot because, under § 9.1-146, they had only the same power to arrest as private citizens did; thus, defendant's Fifth Amendment right to Miranda warnings was not violated. United States v. Day, 591 F.3d 679, 2010 U.S. App. LEXIS 429 (4th Cir. 2010).

Apartment complex's private security guards did not act as de facto police officers under the public function test when they questioned defendant after restraining him after finding him with a gun in a parking lot because, under § 9.1-146, they had only the same power to arrest as private citizens did; thus, defendant's Fourth Amendment right to protection against unreasonable search and seizure was not violated. United States v. Day, 591 F.3d 679, 2010 U.S. App. LEXIS 429 (4th Cir. 2010).

§ 9.1-147. Unlawful conduct generally; penalty.

A. It shall be unlawful for any person to:

1. Practice any trade or profession licensed, certified or registered under this article without obtaining the necessary license, certification or registration required by statute or regulation;

2. Materially misrepresent facts in an application for licensure, certification or registration;

3. Willfully refuse to furnish the Department information or records required or requested pursuant to statute or regulation; and

4. Violate any statute or regulation governing the practice of the private security services businesses or training schools regulated by this article.

B. Any person who is convicted of willful violation of subsection A shall be guilty of a Class 1 misdemeanor. Any person convicted of a third or subsequent offense under this section during a thirty-six-month period shall be guilty of a Class 6 felony.

History.
1992, c. 578, § 9-183.11; 1998, cc. 122, 807; 2001, c. 844.

Cross references.
As to punishment for Class 6 felonies, see § 18.2-10. As to punishment for Class 1 misdemeanors, see § 18.2-11.

§ 9.1-148. Unlawful procurement of a license; penalty.

A. It shall be unlawful for any person to:

1. Procure, or assist another to procure, through theft, fraud or other illegal means, a registration or license, by giving to, or receiving from, any person any information, oral, written or printed, during the administration of the examination, which is intended to, or will, assist any person taking the examination in passing the examination and obtaining the required registration or license;

2. Attempt to procure, through theft, fraud or other illegal means, any questions intended to be used by the Department conducting the examination, or the answers to the questions;

3. Promise or offer any valuable or other consideration to a person having access to the questions or answers as an inducement to procure for delivery to the promisor, or any other person, a copy of any questions or answers.

B. No person, other than a designee of the Department, shall procure or have in his possession prior to the beginning of an examination, without written authority of the Department, any question intended to be used by the Department, or receive or furnish to any person taking the examination, prior to or during the examination, any written or printed material purporting to be answers to, or aid in answering such questions;

C. If an examination is divided into separate parts, each of the parts shall be deemed an examination for the purposes of this section.

D. Any person convicted of a violation of subsections A or B shall be guilty of a Class 2 misdemeanor.

History.
1992, c. 578, § 9-183.10; 2001, c. 844.

Cross references.
As to punishment for Class 2 misdemeanors, see § 18.2-11.

§ 9.1-149. Unlicensed activity prohibited; penalty.

A. No person:

1. Required to possess a registration under subsection C of § 9.1-139 shall be employed by a private security services business, except as provided in this article, as armored car personnel, courier, armed security officer, security canine handler, personal protection specialist, private investigator, alarm respondent, central station dispatcher, electronic security sales representative or electronic security technician without possessing a valid registration.

2. Licensed or required to be licensed under subsection A of § 9.1-139 shall employ or otherwise utilize, except as provided in this article, as armored car personnel, courier, armed security officer, security canine handler, personal protection specialist, private investigator, alarm respondent, central station dispatcher, electronic security sales representative or electronic security technician, any person not possessing a valid registration.

3. Required to possess an instructor certification under subsection D of § 9.1-139 shall provide mandated instruction, except as provided in § 9.1-141 and Board regulations, without possessing a valid private security instructor certification.

4. Certified or required to be certified as a private security services training school under subsection B of § 9.1-139 shall employ or otherwise utilize, except as provided in § 9.1-141 and Board regulations, as a private security instructor, any person not possessing a valid instructor certification.

B. No compliance agent employed or otherwise utilized by a person licensed or required to be licensed under subsection A of § 9.1-139 shall:

1. Employ or otherwise utilize as an unarmed security officer, except as provided in this article, any individual for whom the compliance agent does not possess documentary evidence of compliance with, or exemption from, the compulsory minimum training standards established by the Board for unarmed security officers and before January 1, 2003, maintain documentary evidence that an investigation to determine suitability has been conducted.

2. Employ or otherwise utilize as an electronic security technician's assistant, except as provided in this article, any individual for whom the compliance agent does not possess documentary evidence of compliance with, or exemption from, the compulsory minimum training standards established by the Board for electronic security technician's assistants.

C. Any person convicted of a violation of subsections A or B shall be guilty of a Class 1 misdemeanor.

History.
1976, c. 737, § 54-729.34; 1980, c. 425, § 54.1-1908; 1988, cc. 48, 765; 1992, c. 578, § 9-183.9; 1994, cc. 45, 810; 1995, c. 79; 1998, cc. 122, 807; 2001, c. 844; 2002, cc. 578, 597.

Cross references.
As to punishment for Class 1 misdemeanors, see § 18.2-11.

§ 9.1-150. Monetary penalty.

Any person required to be licensed, certified or registered by the Board pursuant to this article who violates any statute or Board regulation who is not criminally prosecuted is subject to the monetary penalty provided in this section. If the Board determines that such person has violated any statute or Board regulation, the Board shall determine the amount of the monetary penalty for the violation, which shall not exceed $2,500 for each violation. The penalty may be sued for and recovered in the name of the Commonwealth. The monetary penalty shall be paid into the state treasury to the credit of the Literary Fund in accordance with § 19.2-353.

History.
1992, c. 578, § 9-183.12; 1994, c. 810; 1998, cc. 122, 807; 2001, c. 844; 2011, cc. 821, 854.

The 2011 amendments.
The 2011 amendments by cc. 821 and 854 are identical, and in the first sentence, inserted "required to be" and substituted "is subject to" for "shall be subject to," and in the second sentence, substituted "determines that such person has violated any statute or Board regulation" for "determines that a respondent is guilty of the violation complained of."

ARTICLE 4.1.
SPECIAL CONSERVATORS OF THE PEACE.

§ 9.1-150.1. Definitions.

In addition to the definitions set forth in § 9.1-101, as used in this article, unless the context requires a different meaning:

"Special conservator of the peace" means any individual appointed pursuant to § 19.2-13 on or after September 15, 2004.

History.
2003, c. 922.

Cross references.
As to exclusions under the Virginia Freedom of Information Act pertaining to records of active investigations being conducted by the Department of Criminal Justice Services pursuant to this article, see § 2.2-3705.3.

§ 9.1-150.2. Powers of Criminal Justice Services Board relating to special conservators of the peace appointed pursuant to § 19.2-13.

The Board may adopt regulations establishing compulsory minimum, entry-level, in-service, and advanced training standards for special conservators of the peace. The regulations may include provisions delegating to the Board's staff the right to inspect the facilities and programs of persons conducting training to ensure compliance with the law and its regulations. In establishing compulsory training standards for special conservators of the peace, the Board shall ensure the public safety and welfare against incompetent or unqualified persons engaging in the activities regulated by this section. The regulations may provide for exemption from training of persons having previous employment as law-enforcement officers for a state or the federal government. However, no such exemption shall be granted to persons having less than five continuous years of such employment, nor shall an exemption be provided for any person whose employment as a law-enforcement officer was terminated because of his misconduct or incompetence. The regulations may include provisions for partial exemption from such training for persons having previous training that meets or exceeds the minimum training standards and has been approved by the Department. The Board may also adopt regulations that (i) establish the qualifications of applicants for registration; (ii) cause to be examined the qualifications of each applicant for registration; (iii) provide for collection of fees for registration and renewal that are sufficient to cover all expenses for administration and operation of a program of registration; (iv) ensure continued competency and prevent deceptive or misleading practices by practitioners; (v) effectively administer the regulatory system promulgated by the Board; (vi) provide for receipt of complaints concerning the conduct of any person whose activities are regulated by the Board; (vii) provide for investigations, and appropriate disciplinary action if warranted; and (viii) allow the Board to revoke, suspend or refuse to renew a registration, certification, or license for just cause as enumerated in regulations of the Board. The Board shall not adopt compulsory, minimum, entry-level training standards in excess of 24 hours for unarmed special conservators of the peace or in excess of 40 hours for armed special conservators of the peace. In adopting its regulations, the Board shall seek the advice of the Private Security Services Advisory Board established pursuant to § 9.1-143.

History.
2003, c. 922.

§ 9.1-150.3. Powers of Department of Criminal Justice Services relating to special conservators of the peace appointed pursuant to § 19.2-13.

A. In addition to the powers otherwise conferred upon it by law, the Department may (i) charge each applicant for registration a nonrefundable fee as established by the Board to cover the costs of the Department for processing an application for registration, and enforcement of the regulations, and other costs associated with the maintenance of the program of regulation; (ii) charge nonrefundable fees for private security services training as established by the Board for processing school certifications and enforcement of training standards; and (iii) conduct investigations to determine the suitability of applicants for registration, including a drug and alcohol screening. For purposes of this investigation, the Department shall require the applicant to provide personal descriptive information to be forwarded, along with the applicant's fingerprints, to the Central Criminal Records Exchange for the purpose of conducting a Virginia criminal history records search. The Central Criminal Records Exchange shall forward the fingerprints and personal description to the Federal Bureau of Investigation for the purpose of obtaining a national criminal record check.

B. The Director or his designee may make an ex parte application to the circuit court for the city or county wherein evidence sought is kept or wherein a licensee does business for the issuance of a subpoena duces tecum in furtherance of the investigation of a sworn complaint within the jurisdiction of the Department or the Board to request production of any relevant records, documents and physical or other evidence of any person, partnership, association or corporation licensed or regulated by the Department pursuant to this article. The court may issue and compel compliance with such a subpoena upon a showing of reasonable cause. Upon determining that reasonable cause exists to believe that evidence may be destroyed or altered, the court may issue a subpoena duces tecum requiring the immediate production of evidence. Costs of the investigation and adjudication of violations of this article or Board regulations may be recovered. All costs recovered shall be deposited into the state treasury to the credit of the Conservators of the Peace Regulatory Fund. Such proceedings shall be brought in the name of the Commonwealth by the Department in the circuit court of the city or county in which the unlawful act occurred or in which the defendant resides. The Director, or agents appointed by him, shall have the authority to administer oaths or affirmations for the purpose of receiving complaints and conducting investigations of violations of this article, or any regulation promulgated hereunder and to serve process issued by the Department or the Board.

History.
2003, c. 922.

§ 9.1-150.4. Unlawful conduct; penalties.

A. It shall be unlawful for any person to (i) misrepresent facts in an application for registration; (ii) willfully refuse to furnish the Department information or records required or requested pursuant to statute or regulation; or (iii) violate any statute or regulation governing the practice of special conservators of the peace regulated by this article or § 19.2-13.

B. Any person registered by the Department pursuant to § 19.2-13 who the Department or the Board determines has violated any statute or Board regulation and who is not criminally prosecuted shall be subject to a monetary penalty not to exceed $2,500 for each violation. The penalty may be sued for and recovered in the name of the Commonwealth and shall be paid into the state treasury to the credit of the Literary Fund in accordance with § 19.2-353.

C. Any person who is convicted of a willful violation of the provisions of this article or § 19.2-13 is guilty of a Class 1 misdemeanor. Any person convicted of a third or subsequent offense under this article or § 19.2-13 during a 36-month period is guilty of a Class 6 felony.

History.
2003, c. 922.

Cross references.
As to penalty for Class 6 felonies, see § 18.2-10. As to penalty for Class 1 misdemeanors, see § 18.2-11.

ARTICLE 8.

LAW-ENFORCEMENT EXPENDITURES.

§ 9.1-165. Definitions.

As used in this article, unless the context requires a different meaning:

"*Adjusted crime index*" means the potential crime rate for a locality multiplied by the base year population of the locality as estimated by the Center for Public Service.

"*Average crime rate*" for a city or eligible county means the annual average number of violent and property index crimes per 100,000 persons, as reported by the Superintendent of State Police, for the base year and the fiscal year immediately preceding, and the fiscal year immediately following, the base year. If the data are not available for the fiscal year immediately following the base year, the average shall be based on the base year and the two immediately preceding fiscal years.

"Base year" means the most recent fiscal year for which comparable data are available for: (i) population estimates by the Center for Public Service or the United States Bureau of the Census, adjusted for annexation as determined by the Department, (ii) actual state expenditures for salaries and expenses of sheriffs as reported by the Compensation Board, (iii) number of persons eligible for Temporary Assistance to Needy Families as defined in § 63.2-100, (iv) number of persons in foster care, as defined in § 63.2-100, and (v) the number of persons receiving maintenance payments in a general relief program as defined in § 63.2-100.

"Distribution formula" means that linear equation derived biennially by the Department, using standard statistical procedures, which best predicts average crime rates in all cities and eligible counties in the Commonwealth on the basis of the following factors in their simplest form:

1. The total base year number of (i) persons enrolled in Temporary Assistance to Needy Families, (ii) persons in foster care, and (iii) persons receiving maintenance payments in a general relief program, per 100,000 base year population; and

2. The local population density, based on the base year population estimates of the Center for Public Service, adjusted for annexation as determined by the Department, and the land area in square miles of the city or eligible county as reported by the United States Census Bureau, adjusted for annexation as determined by the Department.

"Eligible county" means any county which operates a police department.

"Police department" means that organization established by ordinance by a local governing body that is responsible for the prevention and detection of crime, the apprehension of criminals, the safeguard of life and property, the preservation of peace and the enforcement of state and local laws, regulations, and ordinances. Such department shall have a chief of police, which in the case of counties may be the sheriff, and such officers, privates, and other personnel as may be provided for in the ordinance, one sworn member of which shall be a full-time employee. All law-enforcement officers serving as members of such police department, whether full-time or part-time, and whether permanently or temporarily employed, shall meet the minimum training standards established pursuant to §§ 9.1-102 and 9.1-114, unless such personnel are exempt from the minimum training standards as provided in §§ 9.1-113 and 9.1-116. Any police department established subsequent to July 1, 1981, shall also have, at a minimum, one officer on duty at all times for the purposes set forth above.

However, notwithstanding any contrary provision of this definition,

1. Any locality receiving funds under this article during the 1980-82 biennium shall be considered to have a valid police department eligible for funds as long as such police department continues in operation;

2. Any town receiving funds under this article during the 1986-1988 biennium shall be considered to have a valid police department eligible for funds even though police services for such town may thereafter be provided by the sheriff of the county in which the town is located by agreement made pursuant to § 15.2-1726. Eligibility for funds under this subdivision shall last as long as such agreement remains in effect. Police services for the town furnished by the sheriff shall be equal to or greater than the police services last furnished by the town's police department.

"Population served by police departments" means the total base year population of the Commonwealth less the population served by sheriffs only.

"Population served by sheriffs only" means the total base year population of those counties without a police department, less the latest available estimate from the United States Bureau of the Census of the total population of towns, or portions of towns, having police departments, located in such counties.

"Potential crime rate" means the number of crimes per 100,000 persons in the base year population for each city or eligible county, as derived from the distribution formula.

"State aid to localities with police" means that amount which bears the same relationship to the population served by police departments as state aid to sheriff-only localities bears to the population served by sheriffs only.

"State aid to sheriff-only localities" means the estimated total amount for salaries and expenses to be paid by the Commonwealth, pursuant to Article 3 (§ 15.2-1609 et seq.) of Chapter 16 of Title 15.2, to sheriffs' offices in those counties without a police department, based on the actual percentage of total state expenditures in the base year distributed to those counties without police departments.

History.

1979, c. 83, § 14.1-84.2; 1981, c. 485; 1982, c. 600; 1984, c. 779; 1985, c. 140; 1989, cc. 84, 292; 1998, c. 872, § 9-183.14; 2001, c. 844.

Cross references.

As to salaries and expense allowances to be paid by Commonwealth, see § 15.2-1609.7.

Editor's note.

Acts 2012, Sp. Sess. I, c. 3, as amended by Acts 2013, c. 806, effective for the biennium ending June 30, 2014, Item 395 A provides: "The funds appropriated in this Item shall be distributed to localities with qualifying police departments, as defined in §§ 9.1-165 through 9.1-172, Code of Virginia (HB 599), except that, in accordance with the requirements of § 15.2-1302, Code of Virginia, such funds shall also be distributed to a city without a qualifying police force that was created by the consolidation of a city and a county subsequent to July 1, 2011, pursuant to the provisions of § 15.2-3500 et seq. of the Code of Virginia. Notwithstanding the provisions of §§ 9.1-165 through 9.1-172, Code of Virginia, the total amount to be distributed to localities shall be $172,412,837 the first year and $172,412,837 the second year. The amount to be distributed to each locality in each year shall be equal to the amount distributed in FY 2012. The amount to be distributed to such a city created by consolidation shall equal the sum distributed to the city during the year prior to the effective date of the consolidation, net of any additional funds allocated by the Compensation Board to the sheriff of the consolidated city as a result of such consolidation, as adjusted in proportion to the increase or decrease in the total amount distributed to all localities during the applicable year."

§ 9.1-166. Local governments to receive state funds for law enforcement.

The Department of the Treasury shall disburse funds to cities, towns and counties, to aid in the law-enforcement expenditures of those local governments, pursuant to the terms of this article.

History.
  1979, c. 83, § 14.1-84.1; 1981, c. 485; 1998, c. 872, § 9-183.13; 2001, c. 844.

§ 9.1-167. Calculation of adjusted crime index; use.

By January 1 of each even-numbered year, the Department, using the relevant base year data, shall calculate the adjusted crime index for each city and each eligible county. Such calculation shall be used for the succeeding fiscal biennium adjusted for annexation as determined by the Department.

History.
  1979, c. 83, § 14.1-84.3; 1981, c. 485; 1989, c. 84; 1998, c. 872, § 9-183.15; 2001, c. 844.

§ 9.1-168. Eligibility for funds.

A. Any city, county, or town establishing a police department shall provide the Department written notice of its intent to seek state funds in accordance with the provisions of this article. Such city, county, or town shall become eligible to receive funds at the beginning of the next fiscal year which commences not sooner than twelve months after the filing of this notice.

B. No city, county, or town shall receive any funds in accordance with the terms of this article unless it notifies the Department prior to July 1 each year that its law-enforcement personnel, whether full-time or part-time and whether permanently or temporarily employed, have complied with the minimum training standards as provided in §§ 9.1-102 and 9.1-114, unless such personnel are exempt from the minimum training standards as provided in §§ 9.1-113 and 9.1-116 or that an effort will be made to have its law-enforcement personnel comply with such minimum training standards during the ensuing fiscal year. Any city, county, or town failing to make an effort to comply with the minimum training standards may be declared ineligible for funding in the succeeding fiscal year by the Department.

C. A change in the form of government from city to tier-city shall not preclude the successor tier-city which continues to provide a police department from eligibility for funds.

D. Any county consolidated under the provisions of Chapter 35 (§ 15.2-3500 et seq.) of Title 15.2 shall be eligible to receive financial assistance for law-enforcement expenditures subject to the provisions of this article. The consolidated county shall be eligible to receive, on behalf of the formerly incorporated towns that became shires, boroughs or special service tax districts within the consolidated county, law-enforcement assistance under the provisions of this article, provided that the consolidation agreement approved pursuant to Chapter 35 (§ 15.2-3500 et seq.) of Title 15.2 provides for the additional law-enforcement governmental services previously provided by the police department of such incorporated towns.

History.
  1981, c. 485, § 14.1-84.6:1; 1982, c. 600; 1983, c. 4, § 14.1-84.6:2; 1984, cc. 695, 779; 1998, c. 872, §§ 9-183.19, 9-183.20; 2001, c. 844.

§ 9.1-169. Total amount and method of distribution of funds to counties and cities.

A. The total amount of funds to be distributed as determined by the Department shall be equal to the amount of state aid to localities with police, as defined in § 9.1-165, minus (i) the salaries and expenses of sheriffs' offices in such cities and counties as estimated pursuant to Article 3 (§ 15.2-1609 et seq.) of Chapter 16 of Title 15.2 and (ii) five percent of the remainder, which shall be placed in a discretionary fund to be administered as specified in § 9.1-171. However, the percentage change in the total amount of funds to be distributed for any fiscal year from the preceding fiscal year shall be equal to the anticipated percentage change in total general fund revenue collections for the same time period as stated in the appropriation act.

B. Each city and eligible county shall receive a percentage of such total amount to be distributed equal to the percentage of the total adjusted crime index attributable to such city or county. Payments to the cities and eligible counties shall be made in equal quarterly installments by the State Treasurer on warrants issued by the Comptroller. Notwithstanding the foregoing provisions, the General Assembly, through the appropriation act, may appropriate specific dollar amounts to provide financial assistance to localities with police departments.

History.
  1979, c. 83, § 14.1-84.4; 1981, c. 485; 1986, c. 235; 1998, c. 872, § 9-183.16; 2001, c. 844.

§ 9.1-170. Distribution of funds to towns.

A. Towns located in eligible counties and which have police departments shall receive a percentage of the funds distributed to the county in accordance with § 9.1-169, such percentage to be equal to the ratio of the town's population as determined by the Department to the total population of the county.

B. Towns located in noneligible counties shall be assigned an adjusted crime index based on their population and the average of the three lowest predicted crime rates for cities. Such towns shall receive funds based on such adjusted crime index in the same manner as cities and eligible counties as provided in § 9.1-169.

History.
1979, c. 83, § 14.1-84.5; 1981, c. 485; 1998, c. 872, § 9-183.17; 2001, c. 844.

§ 9.1-171. Distribution of discretionary fund.

In the case of a city with a population of more than 200,000 receiving per capita aid for law enforcement in accordance with § 9.1-169 of less than sixty-five percent of the average per capita aid to law enforcement received by all other cities with a population of more than 200,000 under such provisions, exclusive of amounts payable by reason of this section, the discretionary fund established by § 9.1-169 shall first be used to pay such city an aggregate sum so as to make its per capita receipts for law enforcement under § 9.1-169 equal to sixty-five percent of the average per capita aid for law enforcement disbursed to all other cities with a population of more than 200,000. The remainder, if any, shall be distributed per capita among (i) cities with populations under 200,000, (ii) eligible counties, and (iii) towns having police departments.

History.
1979, c. 83, § 14.1-84.6; 1981, c. 485; 1998, c. 872, § 9-183.18; 2001, c. 844.

§ 9.1-172. Periodic determination of weights and constants.

Prior to the convening of the General Assembly in each even-numbered year, the Department shall determine whether the variables incorporated in the equation used in the distribution formula are statistically acceptable for such computation, and to determine whether any other variables would be better predictors of crime. If, as a result of this research, the Department determines that the variables used in the equation should be changed, it shall recommend to the General Assembly appropriate legislation to accomplish this change.

History.
1979, c. 83, § 14.1-84.7; 1981, c. 485; 1998, c. 872, § 9-183.21; 2001, c. 844.

CHAPTER 4.

LINE OF DUTY ACT.

§ 9.1-400. Title of chapter; definitions.

A. This chapter shall be known and designated as the Line of Duty Act.

B. As used in this chapter, unless the context requires a different meaning:

"Beneficiary" means the spouse of a deceased person and such persons as are entitled to take under the will of a deceased person if testate, or as his heirs at law if intestate.

"Deceased person" means any individual whose death occurs on or after April 8, 1972, as the direct or proximate result of the performance of his duty, including the presumptions under §§ 27-40.1, 27-40.2, 51.1-813, and 65.2-402, as a law-enforcement officer of the Commonwealth or any of its political subdivisions; a correctional officer as defined in § 53.1-1; a jail officer; a regional jail or jail farm superintendent; a sheriff, deputy sheriff, or city sergeant or deputy city sergeant of the City of Richmond; a police chaplain; a member of any fire company or department or rescue squad that has been recognized by an ordinance or a resolution of the governing body of any county, city or town of the Commonwealth as an integral part of the official safety program of such county, city or town; a member of any fire company providing fire protection services for facilities of the Virginia National Guard; a member of the Virginia National Guard or the Virginia Defense Force while such member is serving in the Virginia National Guard or the Virginia Defense Force on official state duty or federal duty under Title 32 of the United States Code; any special agent of the Virginia Alcoholic Beverage Control Board; any regular or special conservation police officer who receives compensation from a county, city or town or from the Commonwealth appointed pursuant to the provisions of § 29.1-200; any commissioned forest warden appointed under the provisions of § 10.1-1135; any member or employee of the Virginia Marine Resources Commission granted the power of arrest pursuant to § 28.2-900; any Department of Emergency Management hazardous materials officer; any other employee of the Department of Emergency Management who is performing official duties of the agency, when those duties are related to a major disaster or emergency, as defined in § 44-146.16, that has been or is later

declared to exist under the authority of the Governor in accordance with § 44-146.28; any employee of any county, city, or town performing official emergency management or emergency services duties in cooperation with the Department of Emergency Management, when those duties are related to a major disaster or emergency, as defined in § 44-146.16, that has been or is later declared to exist under the authority of the Governor in accordance with § 44-146.28 or a local emergency, as defined in § 44-146.16, declared by a local governing body; any nonfirefighter regional hazardous materials emergency response team member; any conservation officer of the Department of Conservation and Recreation commissioned pursuant to § 10.1-115; or any full-time sworn member of the enforcement division of the Department of Motor Vehicles appointed pursuant to § 46.2-217.

"Disabled person" means any individual who, as the direct or proximate result of the performance of his duty in any position listed in the definition of deceased person in this section, has become mentally or physically incapacitated so as to prevent the further performance of duty where such incapacity is likely to be permanent. The term shall also include any state employee included in the definition of a deceased person who was disabled on or after January 1, 1966.

"Line of duty" means any action the deceased or disabled person was obligated or authorized to perform by rule, regulation, condition of employment or service, or law.

History.
1995, cc. 112, 156, 597, §§ 2.1-133.5, 2.1-133.6; 1996, cc. 66, 174; 1998, c. 712; 2001, cc. 678, 844; 2003, cc. 37, 41, 1005; 2004, c. 30; 2005, cc. 907, 910; 2006, c. 824; 2007, c. 87; 2011, cc. 572, 586; 2012, cc. 374, 458, 573.

Editor's note.
Acts 2001, c. 678 amended former § 2.1-133.6, from which this section is derived. Pursuant to § 30-152, Acts 2001, c. 678 has been given effect in this section as set out above. The 2001 amendment by c. 678, in the paragraph defining "Deceased person," substituted "the Commonwealth" for "this Commonwealth" in two places, and inserted "a police chaplain in the City of Virginia Beach."

Acts 2005, cc. 907 and 910, cl. 2 provides: "That any person eligible for benefits solely by virtue of the provisions of § 9.1-400 of this act shall be entitled to such benefits only on a prospective basis upon approval of a claim pursuant to §§ 9.1-403 and 9.1-404 that is made on or after July 1, 2005."

Acts 2006, c. 824, cl. 2, provides: "That any person eligible for benefits solely by virtue of the provisions of § 9.1-400 of this act shall be entitled to such benefits only on a prospective basis upon approval of a claim pursuant to §§ 9.1-403 and 9.1-404 that is made on or after July 1, 2006."

The 2011 amendments.
The 2011 amendments by cc. 572 and 586 are identical, and twice deleted "State" preceding "Defense Force" in the definition for "Deceased person."

The 2012 amendments.
The 2012 amendments by cc. 374 and 573 are identical, and inserted "a member of any fire company providing fire protection services for facilities of the Virginia National Guard" preceding "a member of the Virginia National Guard" in the definition of "Deceased person" in subsection B.

The 2012 amendment by c. 458 added "or any full-time sworn member of the enforcement division of the Department of Motor Vehicles appointed pursuant to § 46.2-217" to the end in the definition of "Deceased person" and made a related change.

OPINIONS OF THE ATTORNEY GENERAL

Firefighters who are employees of the Commonwealth are not covered under the Line of Duty Act, § 9.1-400 et seq., unless they are members of a fire company or department or rescue squad that has been recognized by an ordinance or a resolution of the governing body of a Virginia county, city, or town as an integral part of the official safety program of such county, city, or town. See opinion of Attorney General to The Honorable Frank M. Ruff, Jr., Member, Senate of Virginia, 10-039, 2010 Va. AG LEXIS 42 (8/10/10).

§ 9.1-401. Continued health insurance coverage for disabled persons, their spouses and dependents, and for the surviving spouse and dependents of certain deceased law-enforcement officers, firefighters, etc.

A. The surviving spouse and any dependents of a deceased person shall be afforded continued health insurance coverage, the cost of which shall be paid in full out of the general fund of the state treasury.

B. If the disabled person's disability (i) occurred while in the line of duty as the direct or proximate result of the performance of his duty or (ii) was subject to the provisions of §§ 27-40.1, 27-40.2, 51.1-813 or § 65.2-402, and arose out of and in the course of his employment, the disabled person, his surviving spouse and any dependents shall be afforded continued health insurance coverage. The cost of such health insurance coverage shall be paid in full out of the general fund of the state treasury.

C. The continued health insurance coverage provided by this section shall be the same plan of benefits which the deceased or disabled person was entitled to on the last day of his active duty or comparable benefits established as a result of a replacement plan.

D. For any spouse, continued health insurance provided by this section shall terminate upon such spouse's death or coverage by alternate health insurance.

E. For dependents, continued health insurance provided by this section shall terminate upon such dependent's death, marriage, coverage by alternate health insurance or twenty-first birthday. Continued health care insurance shall be provided beyond the dependent's twenty-first birthday if the dependent is a full-time college student and shall continue until such time as the dependent ceases to be a full-time student or reaches his twenty-fifth birthday, whichever occurs first. Continued health care insurance shall also be provided beyond the dependent's twenty-first birthday if the dependent is mentally or physically disabled, and such coverage shall continue until three months following the cessation of the disability.

F. For any disabled person, continued health insurance provided by this section shall automatically terminate upon the disabled person's death, recovery or return to full duty in any position listed in the definition of deceased person in § 9.1-400.

History.
  1998, c. 712, § 2.1-133.7:1; 2000, c. 616; 2001, c. 844.

CASE NOTES

Award under § 9.1-402 reversed. — Because the evidence presented by a surviving spouse failed to prove the required subsection A of § 9.1-402 condition precedent that the decedent's performance of his law-enforcement duty was the direct or proximate cause of his death, and there was simply no nexus between a § 65.2-402 presumption of a statutory medical condition as a cause of death and whether the death was the proximate result of the performance of a duty, a $75,000 award to the spouse thereunder was reversed. But, she was entitled to $25,000 pursuant to subsection B of § 9.1-402, as well as an award of health insurance benefits. Commonwealth v. Barker, 275 Va. 529, 659 S.E.2d 502, 2008 Va. LEXIS 48 (2008).

OPINIONS OF THE ATTORNEY GENERAL

Payments through the state health benefits program. — Certain individuals entitled to health benefits under the Line of Duty Act may receive those benefits through the state health benefits program. See opinion of Attorney General to Ms. Sara Redding Wilson, Director, Department of Human Resource Management, 03-090 (12/18/03).

§ 9.1-401.1. Supplemental short-term disability benefit for state police officers.

A state police officer who is a participating employee, as defined in § 51.1-1100, and who incurs a work-related injury in the line of duty, shall receive supplemental short-term disability coverage, pursuant to § 51.1-1121, that provides income replacement for 100 percent of the officer's creditable compensation for the first six months and, pursuant to a certification by the Superintendent of State Police, based on a medical evaluation, that the officer is likely to return to service within another six months, up to one calendar year, that the officer is disabled, without regard to the officer's number of months of state service. Except as provided in this section with regard to the rate of income replacement and the duration of supplemental short-term disability coverage, such state police officers shall be eligible for work-related, supplemental short-term disability benefits upon the same terms and conditions that apply to other participating employees pursuant to Article 4 (§ 51.1-1119 et seq.) of Chapter 11 of Title 51.1. Upon the expiration of the one-calendar-year period, such state police officers shall be eligible for supplemental long-term disability benefits as provided in § 51.1-1123.

History.
  2010, c. 654.

§ 9.1-402. Payments to beneficiaries of certain deceased law-enforcement officers, firefighters, etc., and retirees.

A. The beneficiary of a deceased person whose death occurred on or before December 31, 2005, while in the line of duty as the direct or proximate result of the performance of his duty shall be entitled to receive the sum of $75,000, which shall be payable out of the general fund of the state treasury, in gratitude for and in recognition of his sacrifice on behalf of the people of the Commonwealth.

B. The beneficiary of a deceased person whose death occurred on or after January 1, 2006, while in the line of duty as the direct or proximate result of the performance of his duty shall be entitled to receive the sum of $100,000, which shall be payable out of the general fund of the state treasury, in gratitude for and in recognition of his sacrifice on behalf of the people of the Commonwealth.

C. Subject to the provisions of §§ 27-40.1, 27-40.2, 51.1-813, or § 65.2-402, if the deceased person's death (i) arose out of and in the course of his employment or (ii) was within five years from his date of retirement, his beneficiary shall be entitled to receive the sum of $25,000, which shall be payable out of the general fund of the state treasury.

History.
  1995, cc. 156, 597, § 2.1-133.7; 2000, c. 314; 2001, c. 844; 2006, c. 878.

CASE NOTES

Award reversed. — Because the evidence presented by a surviving spouse failed to prove the required subsection A of § 9.1-402 condition precedent that the decedent's performance of his law-enforcement duty was the direct or proximate cause of his death, and there was simply no nexus between a § 65.2-402 presumption of a statutory medical condition as a cause of death and whether the death was the proximate result of the performance of a duty, a $75,000 award to the spouse thereunder was reversed. But, she was entitled to $25,000 pursuant to subsection B of § 9.1-402, as well as an award of health insurance benefits. Commonwealth v. Barker, 275 Va. 529, 659 S.E.2d 502, 2008 Va. LEXIS 48 (2008).

§ 9.1-402.1. Payments for burial expenses.

It is the intent of the General Assembly that expeditious payments for burial expenses be made for persons whose death is determined to be a direct and proximate result of their performance in the line of duty as defined by the Line of Duty Act. The State Comptroller is hereby authorized to release, at the request of the family of a person who may be subject to the line of duty death benefits, payments to a funeral service provider for burial and transportation costs. These payments would be advanced from the death benefit that would be due to the beneficiary of the deceased person if it is determined that the person qualifies for line of duty coverage. Expenses advanced under this provision shall not exceed the coverage amounts outlined in § 65.2-512. In the event a determination is made that the death is not subject to the line of duty benefits, the Virginia Retirement System or other retirement fund to which the deceased is a member will deduct from benefit payments otherwise due to be paid to the beneficiaries of the deceased payments previously paid by the State Comptroller for burial and related transportation expenses and return such funds to the State Comptroller. The State Comptroller shall have the right to file a claim with the Virginia Workers' Compensation Commission against any employer to recover burial and related transportation expenses advanced under this provision.

History.
  2012, cc. 90, 576.

§ 9.1-403. Claim for payment; costs.

A. Every beneficiary, disabled person or his spouse, or dependent of a deceased or disabled person shall present his claim to the chief officer, or his designee, of the appropriate division or department that last employed the deceased or disabled person on forms to be provided by the State Comptroller's office.

B. In the case of a police department or a sheriff's office that is part of or administered by the Commonwealth or any political subdivision thereof, the chief officer, or his designee, of such department or office shall investigate and report upon the circumstances surrounding the deceased or disabled person and report his findings to the Comptroller within 10 business days after completion of the investigation. The Comptroller, the Attorney General, or any such chief officer, in his discretion, may submit a request to the Superintendent of the Department of State Police to perform the investigation pursuant to subsection C.

C. In all other cases, upon receipt of the claim the chief officer, or his designee, of the appropriate division or department shall submit a request to the Superintendent of the Department of the State Police, who shall investigate and report upon the circumstances surrounding the deceased or disabled person, calling upon the additional information and services of any other appropriate agents or agencies of the Commonwealth. The Superintendent, or his designee, shall report his findings to the Comptroller within 10 business days after completion of the investigation. The Department of State Police shall take action to conduct the investigation as expeditiously as possible. The Department shall be reimbursed for the cost of investigations conducted pursuant to this section from the appropriate employer that last employed the deceased or disabled employee.

D. Within 10 business days of being notified by an employee, or an employee's representative, that such employee is permanently and totally disabled due to a work-related injury suffered in the line of duty, the agency or department employing the disabled person shall provide him with information about the continued health insurance coverage provided under this act and the process for initiating a claim. The employer shall assist in filing a claim, unless such assistance is waived by the employee or the employee's representative.

History.
  1995, c. 156, § 2.1-133.8; 1998, c. 712; 2001, cc. 427, 844; 2007, c. 90; 2009, cc. 393, 580.

Editor's note.
  Acts 2001, c. 427 amended former § 2.1-133.8, from which this section is derived. Pursuant to § 30-152, Acts 2001, c. 427 has been given effect in this section as set out above. The 2001 amendment by c. 427, in the third sentence, substituted "Superintendent" for "chief officer," and substituted "ten business days after completion of the investigation" for "forty-five days of receipt of a claim," and added the last two sentences.

CASE NOTES

Applied in Commonwealth v. Barker, 275 Va. 529, 659 S.E.2d 502, 2008 Va. LEXIS 48 (2008).

§ 9.1-404. Order of Comptroller.

A. If it appears to the Comptroller that the requirements of either subsection A or B of § 9.1-402 have been satisfied, he shall issue his warrant in the appropriate amount for payment out of the general fund of the state treasury to the surviving spouse or to such persons and subject to such conditions as may be proper in his administrative discretion, and in the event there is no beneficiary, the Comptroller shall issue the payment to the estate of the deceased person. The Comptroller shall issue a decision, and payment, if appropriate, shall be made no later than forty-five days following receipt of the report required under § 9.1-403.

B. If it appears to the Comptroller that the requirements of either subsection A or B of § 9.1-401 have been satisfied, he shall issue his warrants in the appropriate amounts for payment from the general fund of the state treasury to ensure continued health care coverage for the persons designated under § 9.1-401. The Comptroller shall issue a decision, and payments, if appropriate, shall commence no later than forty-five days following receipt of the report required under § 9.1-403. The payments shall be retroactive to the first date that the disability existed.

History.
  1995, cc. 156, 597, § 2.1-133.9; 1998, c. 712; 2001, c. 844.

§ 9.1-405. Appeal from decision of Comptroller.

Any beneficiary, disabled person or his spouse or dependent of a deceased or disabled person aggrieved by the decision of the Comptroller shall present a petition to the court in which the will of the deceased person is probated or in which the personal representative of the deceased person is qualified or might qualify or in the jurisdiction in which the disabled person resides.

The Commonwealth shall be represented in such proceeding by the Attorney General or his designee. The court shall proceed as chancellor without a jury. If it appears to the court that the requirements of this chapter have been satisfied, the judge shall enter an order to that effect. The order shall also direct the Comptroller to issue his warrant in the appropriate amount for the payment out of the general fund of the state treasury to such persons and subject to such conditions as may be proper. If, in the case of a deceased person, there is no beneficiary, the judge shall direct such payment as is due under § 9.1-402 to the estate of the deceased person.

History.
1995, cc. 156, 597, § 2.1-133.10; 1998, c. 712; 2001, c. 844.

CASE NOTES

Applied in Commonwealth v. Barker, 275 Va. 529, 659 S.E.2d 502, 2008 Va. LEXIS 48 (2008).

§ 9.1-406. Appeals.

Appeals from judgments entered pursuant to this chapter shall be allowed as in civil actions generally.

History.
1995, c. 156, § 2.1-133.11; 2001, c. 844; 2005, c. 681.

§ 9.1-407. Training.

Any law-enforcement or public safety officer entitled to benefits under this Chapter shall receive training concerning the benefits available to himself or his beneficiary in case of disability or death in the line of duty. The Secretary of Public Safety shall develop training information to be distributed to agencies and localities with employees subject to this Chapter. The agency or locality shall be responsible for providing the training. Such training shall not count towards in-service training requirements for law-enforcement officers pursuant to § 9.1-102.

History.
2006, c. 535.

§ 9.1-408. Records of investigation confidential.

Evidence and documents obtained by or created by, and the report of investigation prepared by, the Department of State Police in carrying out the provisions of this chapter shall (i) be deemed confidential, (ii) be exempt from disclosure under the Freedom of Information Act (§ 2.2-3700 et seq.), and (iii) not be released in whole or in part by any person to any person except as provided in this chapter.

History.
2010, c. 568.

CHAPTER 5.

LAW-ENFORCEMENT OFFICERS PROCEDURAL GUARANTEE ACT.

§ 9.1-500. Definitions.

As used in this chapter, unless the context requires a different meaning:

"Agency" means the Department of State Police, the Division of Capitol Police, the Virginia Marine Resources Commission, the Virginia Port Authority, the Department of Game and Inland Fisheries, the Department of Alcoholic Beverage Control, the Department of Conservation and Recreation, or the Department of Motor Vehicles; or the political subdivision or the campus police department of any public institution of higher education of the Commonwealth employing the law-enforcement officer.

"Law-enforcement officer" means any person, other than a Chief of Police or the Superintendent of the Department of State Police, who, in his official capacity, is (i) authorized by law to make arrests and (ii) a nonprobationary officer of one of the following agencies:

a. The Department of State Police, the Division of Capitol Police, the Virginia Marine Resources Commission, the Virginia Port Authority, the Department of Game and Inland Fisheries, the Department of Alcoholic Beverage Control, the Department of Motor Vehicles, or the Department of Conservation and Recreation;

b. The police department, bureau or force of any political subdivision or the campus police department of any public institution of higher education of the Commonwealth where such department, bureau or force has ten or more law-enforcement officers; or

c. Any conservation police officer as defined in § 9.1-101.

For the purposes of this chapter, "law-enforcement officer" shall not include the sheriff's department of any city or county.

History.
1978, c. 19, § 2.1-116.1; 1979, c. 592; 1983, c. 357; 1995, c. 730; 2001, c. 844; 2007, cc. 87, 364.

Cross references.
As to exemptions from the provisions of the State Grievance Procedure, see § 2.2-3002. As to election of remedies for grievances by police officers, see § 15.2-723.

CASE NOTES

Editor's note.

The cases below were decided under former corresponding provisions.

Violation of guarantees does not necessarily compel finding of due process violation. — Police department's violation of the Law-Enforcement Officers' Procedural Guarantees does not necessarily compel a finding of a due process violation. Riccio v. County of Fairfax, 907 F.2d 1459 (4th Cir. 1990).

Statutory procedures exceed requirements of due process. — While this state law provides those to whom it applies with a property interest in employment, it also provides for more process than what the constitution would otherwise require and, for this reason, the specific procedures it establishes need not be complied with fully to satisfy federal due process. Mansoor v. County of Albemarle, 124 F. Supp. 2d 367, 2000 U.S. Dist. LEXIS 18612 (W.D. Va. 2000).

§ 9.1-501. Conduct of investigation.

The provisions of this section shall apply whenever an investigation by an agency focuses on matters which could lead to the dismissal, demotion, suspension or transfer for punitive reasons of a law-enforcement officer:

1. Any questioning of the officer shall take place at a reasonable time and place as designated by the investigating officer, preferably when the officer under investigation is on duty and at the office of the command of the investigating officer or at the office of the local precinct or police unit of the officer being investigated, unless matters being investigated are of such a nature that immediate action is required.

2. Prior to the officer being questioned, he shall be informed of (i) the name and rank of the investigating officer and of any individual to be present during the questioning and (ii) the nature of the investigation.

3. When a blood or urine specimen is taken from a law-enforcement officer for the purpose of determining whether the officer has used drugs or alcohol, the specimen shall be divided and placed into two separate containers. One specimen shall be tested while the other is held in a proper manner to preserve the specimen by the facility collecting or testing the specimen. Should the first specimen test positive, the law-enforcement officer shall have the right to require the second specimen be sent to a laboratory of his choice for independent testing in accordance generally with the procedures set forth in §§ 18.2-268.1 through 18.2-268.12. The officer shall notify the chief of his agency in writing of his request within 10 days of being notified of positive specimen results. The laboratory chosen by the officer shall be accredited or certified by one or more of the following bodies: the American Society of Crime Laboratory Directors/Laboratory Accreditation Board (ASCLD/LAB), the College of American Pathologists (CAP), the United States Department of Health and Human Services Substance Abuse and Mental Health Services Administration (SAMHSA), or the American Board of Forensic Toxicology (ABFT).

History.

1978, c. 19, § 2.1-116.2; 1992, c. 221; 1993, c. 229; 2001, c. 844; 2005, cc. 868, 881.

§ 9.1-502. Notice of charges; response; election to proceed under grievance procedure of local governing body.

A. Before any dismissal, demotion, suspension without pay or transfer for punitive reasons may be imposed, the following rights shall be afforded:

1. The law-enforcement officer shall be notified in writing of all charges, the basis therefor, and the action which may be taken;

2. The law-enforcement officer shall be given an opportunity, within a reasonable time limit after the date of the written notice provided for above, to respond orally and in writing to the charges. The time limit shall be determined by the agency, but in no event shall it be less than five calendar days unless agreed to by the law-enforcement officer;

3. In making his response, the law-enforcement officer may be assisted by counsel at his own expense; and

4. The law-enforcement officer shall be given written notification of his right to initiate a grievance under the grievance procedure established by the local governing body pursuant to §§ 15.2-1506 and 15.2-1507. A copy of the local governing body's grievance procedure shall be provided to the law-enforcement officer upon his request.

B. A law-enforcement officer may proceed under either the local governing body's grievance procedure or the law-enforcement officer's procedural guarantees, but not both.

History.

1978, c. 19, § 2.1-116.4; 1987, c. 461; 2001, c. 844.

CASE NOTES

Investigation after giving of notice did not deny due process. — Where plaintiff was given notice at the outset of the investigation, which could not in and of itself result in adverse action, and where a grievance procedure was provided for in the event the investigation would lead to collateral action such as dismissal, defendants could not be found to have violated due process in conducting the investigation. Morrell v. Stone, 638 F. Supp. 163 (W.D. Va. 1986) (decided under prior law).

Due process not denied where basis for dismissal existed and plaintiff voluntarily resigned. — Where plaintiff's threatened termination was made in good faith, as there was a for cause basis to substantiate his proposed dismissal, and where rather than resigning, plaintiff could have chosen to challenge through the grievance procedure made available to him under former § 2.1-116.5 (see now § 9.1-504) of the "Law-Enforcement Officers' Procedural Guarantees" any adverse disciplinary action taken against him by the defendants, and where plaintiff admitted that he talked with his attorney before making the decision to submit his resignation, plaintiff's resignation was voluntary as a matter of law, and having voluntarily resigned, plaintiff could not claim he was denied procedural protections that he waived. Morrell v. Stone, 638 F. Supp. 163 (W.D. Va. 1986) (decided under prior law).

CIRCUIT COURT OPINIONS

No notice of disciplinary sanction. — County manager's decision holding that a police officer's 80-hour suspension was non-grievable was reversed, where at the time the police officer submitted his resignation, he had not been informed that he was to receive a disciplinary sanction and the county's action of waiting until the eleventh hour to advise the officer of the sanction effectively deprived him of his right to participate in the grievance process. In re Williams, 62 Va. Cir. 383, 2003 Va. Cir. LEXIS 314 (Arlington County 2003).

§ 9.1-503. Personal assets of officers.

No law-enforcement officer shall be required or requested to disclose any item of his property, income, assets, source of income, debts, or personal or domestic expenditures, including those of any member of his family or household, unless (i) such information is necessary in investigating a possible conflict of interest with respect to the performance of his official duties(ii) such disclosure is required by law, or (iii) such information is related to an investigation. Nothing in this section shall preclude an agency from requiring the law-enforcement officer to disclose any place of off-duty employment and where he may be contacted.

History.
1978, c. 19, § 2.1-116.3; 2001, c. 844.

§ 9.1-504. Hearing; hearing panel recommendations.

A. Whenever a law-enforcement officer is dismissed, demoted, suspended or transferred for punitive reasons, he may, within a reasonable amount of time following such action, as set by the agency, request a hearing. If such request is timely made, a hearing shall be held within a reasonable amount of time set by the agency. However, the hearing shall not be set later than fourteen calendar days following the date of request unless a later date is agreed to by the law-enforcement officer. At the hearing, the law-enforcement officer and his agency shall be afforded the opportunity to present evidence, examine and cross-examine witnesses. The law-enforcement officer shall also be given the opportunity to be represented by counsel at the hearing unless the officer and agency are afforded, by regulation, the right to counsel in a subsequent de novo hearing.

B. The hearing shall be conducted by a panel consisting of one member from within the agency selected by the grievant, one member from within the agency of equal rank of the grievant but no more than two ranks above appointed by the agency head, and a third member from within the agency to be selected by the other two members. In the event that such two members cannot agree upon their selection, the chief judge of the judicial circuit wherein the duty station of the grievant lies shall choose such third member. The hearing panel may, and on the request of either the law-enforcement officer or his agency shall, issue subpoenas requiring the testimony of witnesses who have refused or failed to appear at the hearing. The hearing panel shall rule on the admissibility of the evidence. A record shall be made of the hearing.

C. At the option of the agency, it may, in lieu of complying with the provisions of § 9.1-502, give the law-enforcement officer a statement, in writing, of the charges, the basis therefor, the action which may be taken, and provide a hearing as provided for in this section prior to dismissing, demoting, suspending or transferring for punitive reasons the law-enforcement officer.

D. The recommendations of the hearing panel, and the reasons therefor, shall be in writing and transmitted promptly to the law-enforcement officer or his attorney and to the chief executive officer of the law-enforcement agency. Such recommendations shall be advisory only, but shall be accorded significant weight.

History.
1978, c. 19, §§ 2.1-116.5, 2.1-116.7; 1980, c. 191; 2001, c. 844.

CASE NOTES

Editor's note.
The cases below were decided under former corresponding provisions.

No automatic right to pretermination hearing. — Failure to afford police officers a hearing prior to discharge did not violate due process, because there is no automatic right to a pretermination hearing under subdivision 3 of former § 2.1-116.5 (see now subsection C of § 9.1-504). Kersey v. Shipley, 673 F.2d 730 (4th Cir.), cert. denied, 459 U.S. 836, 103 S. Ct. 80, 74 L. Ed. 2d 77 (1982).

Property interest in continued employment. — A law-enforcement officer's procedural guarantees as set out in this section provide the police officer with a property interest in his continued employment, and the due process clause of the Fourteenth Amendment becomes implicated if, as a factual matter, the officer is deprived of the benefits conferred by this chapter. Himmelbrand v. Harrison, 484 F. Supp. 803 (W.D. Va. 1980). But see Mandel v. Allen, 889 F. Supp. 857 (E.D. Va. 1995), aff'd, 81 F.3d 478 (4th Cir. 1996).

Investigation after giving of notice did not deny due process. — Where plaintiff was given notice at the outset of the investigation, which could not in and of itself result in adverse action, and where a grievance procedure was provided for in the event the investigation would lead to collateral action such as dismissal, defendants could not be found to have violated due process in conducting the investigation. Morrell v. Stone, 638 F. Supp. 163 (W.D. Va. 1986).

Due process not denied where basis for dismissal existed and plaintiff voluntarily resigned. — Where plaintiff's threatened termination was made in good faith, as there was a for cause basis to substantiate his proposed dismissal, and where rather than resigning, plaintiff could have chosen to challenge through the grievance procedure made available to him under this section of the "Law-Enforcement Officers' Procedural Guarantees" any adverse disciplinary action taken against him by the defendants, and where plaintiff admitted that he talked with his attorney before making the decision to submit his resignation, plaintiff's resignation was voluntary as a matter of law, and having voluntarily resigned, plaintiff could not claim he was denied procedural protections that he waived. Morrell v. Stone, 638 F. Supp. 163 (W.D. Va. 1986).

Immediate suspension. — Although former § 2.1-116.6 (see now § 9.1-505) does in certain specified circumstances permit "immediate suspension," even in such cases of "immediate suspension" the extensive post-termination procedures prescribed in this section must be complied with. Himmelbrand v. Harrison, 484 F. Supp. 803 (W.D. Va. 1980). But see Mandel v. Allen, 889 F. Supp. 857 (E.D. Va. 1995), aff'd, 81 F.3d 478 (4th Cir. 1996).

§ 9.1-505. Immediate suspension.

Nothing in this chapter shall prevent the immediate suspension without pay of any law-enforcement officer whose continued presence on the job is deemed to be a substantial and immediate threat to the welfare of his agency or the public, nor shall anything in this chapter prevent the suspension of a law-enforcement officer for refusing to obey a direct order issued in conformance with the agency's written and disseminated regulations. In such a case, the law-enforcement officer shall, upon request, be afforded the rights provided for under this chapter within a reasonable amount of time set by the agency.

History.
1978, c. 19, § 2.1-116.6; 2001, c. 844.

CASE NOTES

Editor's note.
The case below was decided under former corresponding provisions.

Immediate suspension. — Although this section does in certain specified circumstances permit "immediate suspension," even in such cases of "immediate suspension" the extensive post-termination procedures prescribed in former § 2.1-116.5 (see now § 9.1-504) must be complied with. Himmelbrand v. Harrison, 484 F. Supp. 803 (W.D. Va. 1980). But see Mandel v. Allen, 889 F. Supp. 857 (E.D. Va. 1995), aff'd, 81 F.3d 478 (4th Cir. 1996).

§ 9.1-506. Informal counseling not prohibited.

Nothing in this chapter shall be construed to prohibit the informal counseling of a law-enforcement officer by a supervisor in reference to a minor infraction of policy or procedure which does not result in disciplinary action being taken against the law-enforcement officer.

History.
1978, c. 19, § 2.1-116.8; 2001, c. 844.

§ 9.1-507. Chapter accords minimum rights.

The rights accorded law-enforcement officers in this chapter are minimum rights and all agencies shall adopt grievance procedures that are consistent with this chapter. However, an agency may provide for additional rights of law-enforcement officers in its grievance procedure.

History.
1978, c. 19, § 2.1-116.9; 2001, c. 844.

CHAPTER 9.

SEX OFFENDER AND CRIMES AGAINST MINORS REGISTRY ACT.

§ 9.1-900. Purpose of the Sex Offender and Crimes Against Minors Registry.

The purpose of the Sex Offender and Crimes Against Minors Registry (Registry) shall be to assist the efforts of law-enforcement agencies and others to protect their communities and families from repeat sex offenders and to protect children from becoming victims of criminal offenders by helping to prevent such individuals from being allowed to work directly with children.

History.
2003, c. 584.

Cross references.
As to effect of registration as sex offender on participation in the address confidentiality program for victims of domestic violence, see § 2.2-515.2. As to exclusions under the Virginia Freedom of Information Act for records of the Sex Offender and Crimes Against Minors Registry, see § 2.2-3706. As to personal information systems that are exempt from the Government Data Collection and Dissemination Practices Act, see § 2.2-3802. As to offense of providing false information or failing to provide registration information, see § 18.2-472.1.

Law Review.
For article, "Legal Issues Involving Children," see 35 U. Rich. L. Rev. 741 (2001). For comment, "Sex Offender Registration and Community Notification Laws: Will These Laws Survive?," see 37 U. Rich. L. Rev. 1245 (2003). For annual survey article on legal issues involving children, see 38 U. Rich. L. Rev. 161 (2003). For 2006 survey article, "Family and Juvenile Law," see 41 U. Rich. L. Rev. 151 (2006).

Research references.
Virginia Forms (Matthew Bender). No. 9-3117. Criminal Record Request.

CASE NOTES

Constitutionality. — Where defendant was convicted of rape and malicious wounding, and as part of defendant's sentence, defendant was requested to register with local law-enforcement officers as a sex offender pursuant to former § 19.2-298.1, and where former § 19.2-298.1 was enacted after the offenses occurred, the trial court did not violate defendant's federal and state constitutional rights against the imposition of an ex post facto law. Kitze v. Commonwealth, 23 Va. App. 213, 475 S.E.2d 830 (1996), cert. denied, 522 U.S. 817, 118 S. Ct. 66, 139 L. Ed. 2d 28 (1997) (decided under former § 19.2-298.1).

Inmate's challenge to the Virginia Sex Offender and Crimes Against Minors Registry Act (Sex Offender Act), § 9.1-900 et seq., was dismissed because the Sex Offender Act was civil in nature and did not violate the Ex Post Facto law and the protections against Double Jeopardy; the inmate's due process rights were not violated because the only issue that could be asserted at a hearing would be a challenge to the conviction, which was not contested, and the inmate did not have a protected liberty interest in precluding truthful information about his conviction being disseminated over the internet. Ballard v. Chief of FBI, 2004 U.S. Dist. LEXIS 1095 (W.D. Va. Jan. 20, 2004).

Purpose. — Sex offender registration requirement is not penal, and the General Assembly intended to facilitate law enforcement and protection of children. Kitze v. Commonwealth, 23 Va. App. 213, 475 S.E.2d 830 (1996), cert. denied, 522 U.S. 817, 118 S. Ct. 66, 139 L. Ed. 2d 28 (1997) (decided under former § 19.2-298.1).

Where plaintiff, having been reclassified as a sexually violent offender and thus being required to be on the sex offender registration list for life, sued defendant state police official alleging a procedural due process violation in connection with the reclassification and publicizing her status as a sexually violent offender on the registry without affording her a procedure through which to challenge that action, the claim failed because Conn. Dep't of Pub. Safety v. Doe precluded such a claim; while the mother sought to distinquist the Connecticut statute from the Virginia statute, arguing that § 9.1-900, unlike Connecticut's statute, made an offender's dangerousness a material part of the statute, the cases were not distinguishable on that ground because the United States Supreme Court had recognized that the Connecticut statute was likewise designed to protect its communities from sex offenders. Doe v. Va. Dep't of State Police, 2013 U.S. App. LEXIS 7403 (4th Cir. Apr. 12, 2013).

CIRCUIT COURT OPINIONS

Prosecutorial function and discretion. — Trial court lacked authority under the separate branches of government of Va. Const., Art. VII, § 4 to enjoin the Commonwealth's Attorney from prosecuting unnamed defendants for their failure to abide by the reporting requirements of the sex offender registry pursuant to § 9.1-900 et seq., as such a decision was within the prosecutor's executive function and sole discretion; the fact that there was a lawsuit pending as to whether they were required to report to the registry did not impede the prosecutor's decision. Doe v. Commonwealth, 74 Va. Cir. 75, 2007 Va. Cir. LEXIS 130 (Fairfax County 2007).

§ 9.1-901. Persons for whom registration required.

A. Every person convicted on or after July 1, 1994, including a juvenile tried and convicted in the circuit court pursuant to § 16.1-269.1, whether sentenced as an adult or juvenile, of an offense set forth in § 9.1-902 and every juvenile found delinquent of an offense for which registration is required under subsection G of § 9.1-902 shall register and reregister as required by this chapter. Every person serving a sentence of confinement on or after July 1, 1994, for a conviction of an offense set forth in § 9.1-902 shall register and reregister as required by this chapter. Every person under community supervision as defined by § 53.1-1 or any similar form of supervision under the laws of the United States or any political subdivision thereof, on or after July 1, 1994,

resulting from a conviction of an offense set forth in § 9.1-902 shall register and reregister as required by this chapter.

B. Every person found not guilty by reason of insanity on or after July 1, 2007, of an offense set forth in § 9.1-902 shall register and reregister as required by this chapter. Every person in the custody of the Commissioner of Behavioral Health and Developmental Services, or on conditional release on or after July 1, 2007, because of a finding of not guilty by reason of insanity of an offense set forth in § 9.1-902 shall register and reregister as required by this chapter.

C. Unless a specific effective date is otherwise provided, all provisions of the Sex Offender and Crimes Against Minors Registry Act shall apply retroactively. This subsection is declaratory of existing law.

History.
2003, c. 584; 2005, c. 586; 2007, cc. 718, 744; 2009, cc. 813, 840.

Law Review.
For survey of Virginia criminal law and procedure for the year 2004-2005, see 40 U. Rich. L. Rev. 197 (2005).

CASE NOTES

Constitutionality. — Inmate's challenge to the Virginia Sex Offender and Crimes Against Minors Registry Act (Sex Offender Act), § 9.1-900 et seq., was dismissed because the Sex Offender Act was civil in nature and did not violate the Ex Post Facto law and the protections against Double Jeopardy; the inmate's due process rights were not violated because the only issue that could be asserted at a hearing would be a challenge to the conviction, which was not contested, and the inmate did not have a protected liberty interest in precluding truthful information about his conviction being disseminated over the internet. Ballard v. Chief of FBI, 2004 U.S. Dist. LEXIS 1095 (W.D. Va. Jan. 20, 2004).

§ 9.1-902. Offenses requiring registration.

A. For purposes of this chapter:
"Offense for which registration is required" includes:

1. Any offense listed in subsection B;
2. Criminal homicide;
3. Murder;
4. A sexually violent offense;
5. Any offense similar to those listed in subdivisions 1 through 4 under the laws of any foreign country or any political subdivision thereof, the United States or any political subdivision thereof; and
6. Any offense for which registration in a sex offender and crimes against minors registry is required under the laws of the jurisdiction where the offender was convicted.

B. The offenses included under this subsection include any violation of, attempted violation of, or conspiracy to violate:

1. § 18.2-63; unless registration is required pursuant to subdivision E 1; § 18.2-64.1; former § 18.2-67.2:1; § 18.2-90 with the intent to commit rape;

former § 18.1-88 with the intent to commit rape; subsection B or C of § 18.2-374.1:1; former subsection D of § 18.2-374.1:1 as it was in effect from July 1, 1994, through June 30, 2007; former clause (iv) of subsection B of § 18.2-374.3 as it was in effect on June 30, 2007; or subsection B, C, or D of § 18.2-374.3; or a third or subsequent conviction of (i) § 18.2-67.4, (ii) § 18.2-67.4:2, (iii) subsection C of § 18.2-67.5, or (iv) § 18.2-386.1.

If the offense was committed on or after July 1, 2006, § 18.2-91 with the intent to commit any felony offense listed in this section; subsection A of § 18.2-374.1:1; or a felony under § 18.2-67.5:1.

2. Where the victim is a minor or is physically helpless or mentally incapacitated as defined in § 18.2-67.10, subsection A of § 18.2-47, clause (i) of § 18.2-48, § 18.2-67.4, subsection C of § 18.2-67.5, § 18.2-361, § 18.2-366, or a felony violation of former § 18.1-191.

3. § 18.2-370.6.

C. "Criminal homicide" means a homicide in conjunction with a violation of, attempted violation of, or conspiracy to violate clause (i) of § 18.2-371 or § 18.2-371.1, when the offenses arise out of the same incident.

D. "Murder" means a violation of, attempted violation of, or conspiracy to violate § 18.2-31 or § 18.2-32 where the victim is (i) under 15 years of age or (ii) where the victim is at least 15 years of age but under 18 years of age and the murder is related to an offense listed in this section or a violation of former § 18.1-21 where the victim is (a) under 15 years of age or (b) at least 15 years of age but under 18 years of age and the murder is related to an offense listed in this section.

E. "Sexually violent offense" means a violation of, attempted violation of, or conspiracy to violate:

1. Clause (ii) and (iii) of § 18.2-48, former § 18.1-38 with the intent to defile or, for the purpose of concubinage or prostitution, a felony violation of subdivision (2) or (3) of former § 18.1-39 that involves assisting or aiding in such an abduction, § 18.2-61, former § 18.1-44 when such act is accomplished against the complaining witness's will, by force, or through the use of the complaining witness's mental incapacity or physical helplessness, or if the victim is under 13 years of age, subsection A of § 18.2-63 where the perpetrator is more than five years older than the victim, § 18.2-67.1, § 18.2-67.2, § 18.2-67.3, former § 18.1-215 when the complaining witness is under 13 years of age, § 18.2-67.4 where the perpetrator is 18 years of age or older and the victim is under the age of six, subsections A and B of § 18.2-67.5, § 18.2-370, subdivision (1), (2), or (4) of former § 18.1-213, former § 18.1-214, or § 18.2-370.1 or § 18.2-374.1; or

2. § 18.2-63, § 18.2-64.1, former § 18.2-67.2:1, § 18.2-90 with the intent to commit rape or, where the victim is a minor or is physically helpless or mentally incapacitated as defined in § 18.2-67.10, subsection A of § 18.2-47, § 18.2-67.4, subsection C

of § 18.2-67.5, clause (i) of § 18.2-48, § 18.2-361, § 18.2-366, or subsection C of § 18.2-374.1:1. An offense listed under this subdivision shall be deemed a sexually violent offense only if the person has been convicted or adjudicated delinquent of any two or more such offenses, provided that person had been at liberty between such convictions or adjudications;

3. If the offense was committed on or after July 1, 2006, § 18.2-91 with the intent to commit any felony offense listed in this section. An offense listed under this subdivision shall be deemed a sexually violent offense only if the person has been convicted or adjudicated delinquent of any two or more such offenses, provided that the person had been at liberty between such convictions or adjudications; or

4. Chapter 117 (18 U.S.C. § 2421 et seq.) of Title 18 of the United States Code or sex trafficking (as described in § 1591 of Title 18, U.S.C.).

F. "Any offense listed in subsection B," "criminal homicide" as defined in this section, "murder" as defined in this section, and "sexually violent offense" as defined in this section includes (i) any similar offense under the laws of any foreign country or any political subdivision thereof, the United States or any political subdivision thereof or (ii) any offense for which registration in a sex offender and crimes against minors registry is required under the laws of the jurisdiction where the offender was convicted.

G. Juveniles adjudicated delinquent shall not be required to register; however, where the offender is a juvenile over the age of 13 at the time of the offense who is tried as a juvenile and is adjudicated delinquent on or after July 1, 2005, of any offense for which registration is required, the court may, in its discretion and upon motion of the attorney for the Commonwealth, find that the circumstances of the offense require offender registration. In making its determination, the court shall consider all of the following factors that are relevant to the case: (i) the degree to which the delinquent act was committed with the use of force, threat or intimidation, (ii) the age and maturity of the complaining witness, (iii) the age and maturity of the offender, (iv) the difference in the ages of the complaining witness and the offender, (v) the nature of the relationship between the complaining witness and the offender, (vi) the offender's prior criminal history, and (vii) any other aggravating or mitigating factors relevant to the case. The attorney for the Commonwealth may file such a motion at any time during which the offender is within the jurisdiction of the court for the offense that is the basis for such motion. Prior to any hearing on such motion, the court shall appoint a qualified and competent attorney-at-law to represent the offender unless an attorney has been retained and appears on behalf of the offender or counsel has already been appointed.

H. Prior to entering judgment of conviction of an offense for which registration is required if the victim of the offense was a minor, physically helpless, or mentally incapacitated, the court shall determine by a preponderance of the evidence whether the victim of the offense was a minor, physically helpless or mentally incapacitated, as defined in § 18.2-67.10, and shall also determine the age of the victim at the time of the offense if it determines the victim to be a minor. Upon such a determination the court shall advise the defendant of its determination and of the defendant's right to withdraw a plea of guilty or nolo contendere. If the defendant chooses to withdraw his plea of guilty or of nolo contendere, his case shall be heard by another judge, unless the parties agree otherwise.

History.
2003, cc. 584, 732; 2004, cc. 414, 444; 2005, cc. 586, 603, 631; 2006, cc. 857, 875, 914, 931; 2007, cc. 463, 718, 759, 823; 2008, cc. 592, 747, 772, 877; 2010, c. 858; 2012, c. 243; 2013, cc. 750, 781.

Cross references.
As to notice required by places of confinement upon intake of certain persons, see § 16.1-249.1. As to prohibiting entry onto school property by adults convicted of sexually violent offense, see § 18.2-370.5. As to offense of providing false information or failing to provide registration information, see § 18.2-472.1. As to obtaining records concerning electronic communication service or remote computing service, see § 19.2-70.3. As to required reports to the Central Criminal Records Exchange, see § 19.2-390. As to prohibition on adoption by violent sex offenders, see § 63.2-1205.1.

Editor's note.
Acts 2003, c. 732 amended § 19.2-298.1, which was repealed by Acts 2003, c. 584, cl. 2. At the direction of the Virginia Code Commission, effect has been given in this section, as set out above, to Acts 2003, c. 732. In accordance with c. 732, the amendment, in subdivision A 1, added clause designations (i) and (ii), deleted "or a third or subsequent conviction of" preceding "subsection C of § 18.2-67.5," and added clause (iii).

Acts 2013, cc. 750 and 781, cl. 2 provides: "That the provisions of this act may result in a net increase in periods of imprisonment or commitment. Pursuant to § 30-19.1:4, the estimated amount of the necessary appropriation cannot be determined for periods of imprisonment in state adult correctional facilities; therefore, Chapter 3 of the Acts of Assembly of 2012, Special Session I, requires the Virginia Criminal Sentencing Commission to assign a minimum fiscal impact of $50,000. Pursuant to § 30-19.1:4, the estimated amount of the necessary appropriation cannot be determined for periods of commitment to the custody of the Department of Juvenile Justice."

The 2012 amendments.
The 2012 amendment by c. 243 added the last two sentences in subsection G.

The 2013 amendments.
The 2013 amendments by cc. 750 and 781 are identical, and in subsection B, inserted "former § 18.1-88 with the intent to commit rape" in subdivision B 1; substituted "§ 18.2-361, § 18.2-366, or a felony violation of former § 18.1-191" for "§ 18.2-361, or 18.2-366" at the end of subdivision B 2; added "or a violation of former § 18.1-21 where the victim is (a) under 15 years of age or (b) at least 15 years of age but under 18 years of age and the murder is related to an offense listed in this section" at the end of subsection D; and in subdivision E 1, inserted references to former §§ 18.1-38, 18.1-39, 18.1-44, 18.1-215, 18.1-213 and 18.1-214.

Law Review.
For survey of Virginia criminal law and procedure for the year 2004-2005, see 40 U. Rich. L. Rev. 197 (2005). For 2006 survey article, "Criminal Law and Procedure," see 41 U. Rich. L. Rev. 83 (2006). For survey of Virginia law on criminal law and procedure for the year 2007-2008, see 43 U. Rich. L. Rev. 149 (2008).

Research references.
Virginia Forms (Matthew Bender). No. 9-2525. Order of Remand — Sex Offender and Crimes Against Minors Registry.

CASE NOTES

Constitutionality. — Where defendant was convicted of rape and malicious wounding, and as part of defendant's sentence, defendant was requested to register with local law-enforcement officers as a sex offender pursuant to this section, and where this section was enacted after the offenses occurred, the trial court did not violate his federal and state constitutional rights against the imposition of an ex post facto law. Kitze v. Commonwealth, 23 Va. App. 213, 475 S.E.2d 830 (1996), cert. denied, 522 U.S. 817, 118 S. Ct. 66, 139 L. Ed. 2d 28 (1997) (decided under former § 19.2-298.1).

Where plaintiff, having been reclassified as a sexually violent offender, sued defendant state police official alleging a procedural due process violation in connection with the reclassification and publicizing her status as a sexually violent offender on the sex offender registry without affording her a procedure through which to challenge that action, the claim failed because Conn. Dep't of Pub. Safety v. Doe precluded such a claim. Doe v. Va. Dep't of State Police, 2013 U.S. App. LEXIS 7403 (4th Cir. Apr. 12, 2013).

Purpose. — Sex offender registration requirement is not penal, and the General Assembly intended to facilitate law enforcement and protection of children. Kitze v. Commonwealth, 23 Va. App. 213, 475 S.E.2d 830 (1996), cert. denied, 522 U.S. 817, 118 S. Ct. 66, 139 L. Ed. 2d 28 (1997) (decided under former § 19.2-298.1).

Registration requirement proper. — Trial court did not err in requiring defendant to register as a sex offender based on defendant's conviction of computer solicitation for sex with a minor based on defendant's actions in using his computer to solicit sex from someone he thought was a 13-year-old girl, but who was, in fact, a police officer posing as a 13-year-old girl. Colbert v. Commonwealth, 47 Va. App. 390, 624 S.E.2d 108, 2006 Va. App. LEXIS 7 (2006).

When registration based on out-of-state conviction is required. — Plain language of § 9.1-902 requires registration as a sex offender if the statute under which a defendant was convicted in another state is "similar" to a Virginia statute that would require registration. Johnson v. Commonwealth, 53 Va. App. 608, 674 S.E.2d 541, 2009 Va. App. LEXIS 157 (2009).

Similar offenses. — Defendant was required to register as a sex offender based on North Carolina convictions, because any action that resulted in a conviction of second-degree rape under North Carolina law would necessarily result in a conviction of rape in Virginia, as the Virginia statute was broader and the statutes shared common essential elements. Johnson v. Commonwealth, 53 Va. App. 608, 674 S.E.2d 541, 2009 Va. App. LEXIS 157 (2009).

Subsection H directory, not mandatory. — As subsection H of § 9.1-902 contains no prohibitory or limiting language that prevents the trial court from convicting and sentencing a defendant without first determining that a victim was a minor and advising the defendant of his right to withdraw his plea of guilty, that provision is directory and procedural, rather than mandatory and jurisdictional; therefore, the claim cannot prevail in an appeal unless he can show some harm or prejudice caused by the failure to follow subsection H of § 9.1-902. Hamilton v. Commonwealth, 61 Va. App. 542, 738 S.E.2d 525, 2013 Va. App. LEXIS 82 (2013).

Withdrawal of plea. — Trial court's failure to apprise defendant of his substantive right to withdraw his guilty plea under subsection H of § 9.1-902 did not infringe or deny him that right, as he was aware of his right to withdraw his plea under subsection H but not did pursue it. Hamilton v. Commonwealth, 61 Va. App. 542, 738 S.E.2d 525, 2013 Va. App. LEXIS 82 (2013).

Assuming arguendo that subsection H of § 9.1-902 created a substantive right to withdraw a guilty plea, that the trial court failed to apprise defendant of this right in the precise manner detailed by subsection H of § 9.1-902 did not require reversal, as the court substantially complied with subsection H of § 9.1-902, and defendant was aware of his right to withdraw his plea. Hamilton v. Commonwealth, 61 Va. App. 542, 738 S.E.2d 525, 2013 Va. App. LEXIS 82 (2013).

CIRCUIT COURT OPINIONS

Registration requirement proper. — Pursuant to subdivision A 2 of § 9.1-902, plaintiff was required to register as a sex offender; the requirement did not violate any constitutional ex post facto prohibition, § 9.1-902 was not ambiguous, and a clear reading indicated that plaintiff was required to register. Corbett v. Commonwealth, 74 Va. Cir. 73, 2007 Va. Cir. LEXIS 282 (Chesapeake 2007).

Multiple contemporaneous convictions required registration. — Defendant was required to register as a sex offender pursuant to subdivision B 1 of § 9.1-902 after he was convicted of nine violations of § 18.2-386.1 because he had accumulated at least three convictions of § 18.2-386.1 and the contemporaneousness of his convictions was not a bar to enforcement of the registration requirement. Commonwealth v. Schneider, 78 Va. Cir. 320, 2009 Va. Cir. LEXIS 160 (Hanover County May 7, 2009).

§ 9.1-903. Registration procedures.

A. Every person convicted, including juveniles tried and convicted in the circuit courts pursuant to § 16.1-269.1, whether sentenced as an adult or juvenile, of an offense for which registration is required and every juvenile found delinquent of an offense for which registration is required under subsection G of § 9.1-902 shall be required upon conviction to register and reregister with the Department of State Police. The court shall order the person to provide to the local law-enforcement agency of the county or city where he physically resides all information required by the State Police for inclusion in the Registry. The court shall immediately remand the person to the custody of the local law-enforcement agency for the purpose of obtaining the person's fingerprints and photographs of a type and kind specified by the State Police for inclusion in the Registry. Upon conviction, the local law-enforcement agency shall forthwith forward to the State Police all the necessary registration information.

B. Every person required to register shall register in person within three days of his release from confinement in a state, local or juvenile correctional facility, in a state civil commitment program for sexually violent predators or, if a sentence of confinement is not imposed, within three days of suspension of the sentence or in the case of a juvenile of disposition. A person required to register shall register, and as part of the registration shall submit to be photographed, submit to have a sample of his blood, saliva, or tissue taken for DNA (deoxyribonucleic acid) analysis and submission to the DNA databank to determine identification characteristics specific to the person, provide electronic mail address information, any instant message, chat or other Internet communication name or identity information that the person uses or intends to use, submit to have his fingerprints and palm prints taken, provide information regarding his place of employment, and provide motor vehicle, watercraft and aircraft registration information for all motor vehicles, watercraft and aircraft owned by him. The local law-enforcement agency shall obtain from the person who presents himself for registration or reregistration one set of fingerprints, electronic mail address information, any instant message, chat or other Internet communication name or identity information that the person uses or intends to use, one set of palm prints, place of employment information, motor vehicle, watercraft and aircraft registration

information for all motor vehicles, watercraft and aircraft owned by the registrant, proof of residency and a photograph of a type and kind specified by the State Police for inclusion in the Registry and advise the person of his duties regarding reregistration. The local law-enforcement agency shall obtain from the person who presents himself for registration a sample of his blood, saliva or tissue taken for DNA (deoxyribonucleic acid) analysis to determine identification characteristics specific to the person. If a sample has been previously taken from the person, as indicated by the Local Inmate Data System (LIDS), no additional sample shall be taken. The local law-enforcement agency shall forthwith forward to the State Police all necessary registration information.

C. To establish proof of residence in Virginia, a person who has a permanent physical address shall present one photo-identification form issued by a governmental agency of the Commonwealth which contains the person's complete name, gender, date of birth and complete physical address. The local law-enforcement agency shall forthwith forward to the State Police a copy of the identification presented by the person required to register.

D. Any person required to register shall also reregister in person with the local law-enforcement agency following any change of name or any change of residence, whether within or without the Commonwealth. If his new residence is within the Commonwealth, the person shall register in person with the local law-enforcement agency where his new residence is located within three days following his change in residence. If the new residence is located outside of the Commonwealth, the person shall register in person with the local law-enforcement agency where he previously registered within 10 days prior to his change of residence. If a probation or parole officer becomes aware of a change of name or residence for any of his probationers or parolees required to register, the probation or parole officer shall notify the State Police forthwith of learning of the change. Whenever a person subject to registration changes residence to another state, the State Police shall notify the designated law-enforcement agency of that state.

E. Any person required to register shall reregister in person with the local law-enforcement agency where his residence is located within three days following any change of the place of employment, whether within or without the Commonwealth. If a probation or parole officer becomes aware of a change of the place of employment for any of his probationers or parolees required to register, the probation or parole officer shall notify the State Police forthwith upon learning of the change of the person's place of employment. Whenever a person subject to registration changes his place of employment to another state, the State Police shall notify the designated law-enforcement agency of that state.

F. Any person required to register shall reregister in person with the local law-enforcement agency where his residence is located within three days following any change of owned motor vehicle, watercraft and aircraft registration information, whether within or without the Commonwealth. If a probation or parole officer becomes aware of a change of owned motor vehicle, watercraft and aircraft registration information for any of his probationers or parolees required to register, the probation or parole officer shall notify the State Police forthwith upon learning of the change of the person's owned motor vehicle, watercraft and aircraft registration information. Whenever a person required to register changes his owned motor vehicle, watercraft and aircraft registration information to another state, the State Police shall notify the designated law-enforcement agency of that state.

G. Any person required to register shall reregister either in person or electronically with the local law-enforcement agency where his residence is located within 30 minutes following any change of the electronic mail address information, any instant message, chat or other Internet communication name or identity information that the person uses or intends to use, whether within or without the Commonwealth. If a probation or parole officer becomes aware of a change of the electronic mail address information, any instant message, chat or other Internet communication name or identity information for any of his probationers or parolees required to register, the probation or parole officer shall notify the State Police forthwith upon learning of the change.

H. The registration shall be maintained in the Registry and shall include the person's name, all aliases that he has used or under which he may have been known, the date and locality of the conviction for which registration is required, his fingerprints and a photograph of a type and kind specified by the State Police, his date of birth, social security number, current physical and mailing address and a description of the offense or offenses for which he was convicted. The registration shall also include the locality of the conviction and a description of the offense or offenses for previous convictions for the offenses set forth in § 9.1-902.

I. The local law-enforcement agency shall forthwith forward to the State Police all necessary registration or reregistration information received by it. Upon receipt of registration or reregistration information the State Police shall forthwith notify the chief law-enforcement officer of the locality listed as the person's address on the registration and reregistration.

J. If a person required to register does not have a legal residence, such person shall designate a location that can be located with reasonable specificity where he resides or habitually locates himself. For the purposes of this section, "residence" shall include such a designated location. If the person wishes to change such designated location, he shall do it pursuant to the terms of this section.

History.

2003, c. 584; 2004, c. 834; 2005, c. 586; 2006, cc. 857, 914; 2007, cc. 718, 759, 823; 2008, c. 220; 2010, c. 843.

Law Review.

For 2006 survey article, "Criminal Law and Procedure," see 41 U. Rich. L. Rev. 83 (2006). For 2007 annual survey article, "Criminal Law and Procedure," see 42 U. Rich. L. Rev. 311 (2007).

Research references.

Virginia Forms (Matthew Bender). No. 9-2525. Order of Remand — Sex Offender and Crimes Against Minors Registry.

CASE NOTES

Applicability. — Defendant argued that he was not required to register under the Sex Offender Registration and Notification Act (SORNA), Pub. L. 109-248, §§ 1-155, 120 Stat. 587, 590-611 (2006), because the Attorney General had not adopted the rule delegated in 42 U.S.C.S. § 16913(d) until after the dates alleged in the indictment — the court disagreed as the Attorney General's rule made no difference as to the instant case, as long as the government could prove that defendant was required to register or update his registration under the existing state law of his residence. Regardless of the applicability of SORNA to defendant as of the dates in question, the nature of his conviction required him, under a long-standing federal law, to register in his state of residence and any other state where he was employed, carried on a vocation, or was a student, 42 U.S.C.S. § 14071(b); furthermore, following his conviction, Virginia state law required him to register as a sex offender, which he did in 2001, and similarly, Tennessee law required him to register promptly once establishing residency there, Tenn. Code Ann. § 40-39-203. United States v. Hinen, 487 F. Supp. 2d 747, 2007 U.S. Dist. LEXIS 36003 (W.D. Va. 2007).

§ 9.1-904. Reregistration.

A. Every person required to register, other than a person convicted of a sexually violent offense or murder, shall reregister with the State Police on an annual basis from the date of the initial registration. Every person convicted of a sexually violent offense or murder shall reregister with the State Police every 90 days from the date of initial registration. Reregistration means that the person has notified the State Police, confirmed his current physical and mailing address and electronic mail address information, any instant message, chat or other Internet communication name or identity information that he uses or intends to use, and provided such other information, including identifying information, which the State Police may require. Upon registration and as may be necessary thereafter, the State Police shall provide the person with an address verification form to be used for reregistration. The form shall contain in bold print a statement indicating that failure to comply with the registration required is punishable as provided in § 18.2-472.1. Upon registration and as may be necessary thereafter, the person shall likewise be required to execute a consent form consistent with applicable law that authorizes a business or organization that offers electronic communications or remote computer services to provide to the Department of State Police any information pertaining to that person necessary to determine the veracity of his electronic identity information in the registry.

B. Any person convicted of a violation of § 18.2-472.1, other than a person convicted of a sexually violent offense or murder, shall reregister with the State Police every 180 days from the date of such conviction. Any person convicted of a violation of § 18.2-472.1, in which such person was included on the Registry for a conviction of a sexually violent offense or murder, shall reregister with the State Police every 30 days from the date of conviction. Reregistration means the person has notified the State Police, confirmed his current physical and mailing address and electronic mail address information, any instant message, chat or other Internet communication name or identity information that he uses or intends to use, and provided such other information, including identifying information, which the State Police may require. Upon registration and as may be necessary thereafter, the State Police shall provide the person with an address verification form to be used for reregistration. The form shall state the registration requirements and contain in bold print a statement indicating that failure to comply with the registration requirements is punishable as provided in § 18.2-472.1.

C. Every person required to register pursuant to this chapter shall submit to be photographed by a local law-enforcement agency every two years commencing with the date of initial registration. Photographs shall be in color, be taken with the registrant facing the camera, and clearly show the registrant's face and shoulders only. No person other than the registrant may appear in the photograph submitted. The photograph shall indicate the registrant's full name, date of birth and the date the photograph was taken. The local law-enforcement agency shall forthwith forward the photograph and the registration form to the State Police. Where practical, the local law-enforcement agency may electronically transfer a digital photograph containing the required information to the Sex Offender and Crimes Against Minors Registry within the State Police.

History.
2003, c. 584; 2006, cc. 857, 914; 2007, cc. 759, 823.

Law Review.
For 2006 survey article, "Criminal Law and Procedure," see 41 U. Rich. L. Rev. 83 (2006).

CASE NOTES

Failure to reregister. — Conviction for failure to reregister as a sex offender was suported by undisputed evidence that defendant was required to reregister by the date alleged, pursuant to subsection A of § 9.1-904, and that defendant failed to reregister until almost a month later. Harris v. Commonwealth, 53 Va. App. 494, 673 S.E.2d 483, 2009 Va. App. LEXIS 104 (2009).

§ 9.1-905. New residents and nonresident offenders; registration required.

A. All persons required to register shall register within three days of establishing a residence in the Commonwealth.

B. Nonresident offenders entering the Commonwealth for an extended visit, for employment, to carry on a vocation, or as a student attending school who are required to register in their state of residence or who would be required to register if a resident of the Commonwealth shall, within three days of entering the Commonwealth for an extended visit, accepting employment or enrolling in school in the Commonwealth, be required to register and reregister in person with the local law-enforcement agency.

C. To document employment or school attendance in Virginia a person shall present proof of enrollment as a student or suitable proof of temporary employment in the Commonwealth and one photo-identification form issued by a governmental agency of the person's state of residence which contains the person's complete name, gender, date of birth and complete address.

D. For purposes of this section:

"Employment" and *"carry on a vocation"* include employment that is full-time or part-time for a period of time exceeding 14 days or for an aggregate period of time exceeding 30 days during any calendar year, whether financially compensated, volunteered, or for the purpose of government or educational benefit.

"Extended visit" means a period of visitation for any purpose in the Commonwealth of 30 days or more.

"Student" means a person who is enrolled on a full-time or part-time basis, in any public or private educational institution, including any secondary school, trade or professional institution, or institution of higher education.

History.
2003, c. 584; 2005, c. 603; 2006, cc. 857, 914.

§ 9.1-906. Enrollment or employment at institution of higher learning; information required.

A. Persons required to register or reregister who are enrolled in or employed at institutions of higher learning shall, in addition to other registration requirements, indicate on their registration and reregistration form the name and location of the institution attended by or employing the registrant whether such institution is within or without the Commonwealth. In addition, persons required to register or reregister shall notify the local law-enforcement agency in person within three days of any change in their enrollment or employment status with an institution of higher learning. The local law-enforcement agency shall forthwith forward to the State Police all necessary registration or reregistration information received by it.

B. Upon receipt of a registration or reregistration indicating enrollment or employment with an institute of higher learning or notification of a change in status, the State Police shall notify the chief law-enforcement officer of the institution's law-enforcement agency or, if there is no institutional law-enforcement agency, the local law-enforcement agency serving that institution, of the registration, reregistration, or change in status. The law-enforcement agency receiving notification under this section shall make such information available upon request.

C. For purposes of this section:

"Employment" includes full- or part-time, temporary or permanent or contractual employment at an institution of higher learning either with or without compensation.

"Enrollment" includes both full- and part-time.

"Institution of higher learning" means any post-secondary school, trade or professional institution, or institution of higher education.

History.
2003, c. 584; 2006, cc. 857, 914.

§ 9.1-907. Procedures upon a failure to register or reregister.

A. Whenever it appears from the records of the State Police that a person has failed to comply with the duty to register or reregister, the State Police shall promptly investigate and, if there is probable cause to believe a violation has occurred, obtain a warrant or assist in obtaining an indictment charging a violation of § 18.2-472.1 in the jurisdiction in which the person last registered or reregistered or, if the person failed to comply with the duty to register, in the jurisdiction in which the person was last convicted of an offense for which registration or reregistration is required or if the person was convicted of an offense requiring registration outside the Commonwealth, in the jurisdiction in which the person resides. The State Police shall forward to the jurisdiction an affidavit signed by a custodian of the records that such person failed to comply with the duty to register or reregister. If such affidavit is admitted into evidence, it shall constitute prima facie evidence of the failure to comply with the duty to register or reregister in any trial or hearing for the violation of § 18.2-472.1, provided that in a trial or hearing other than a preliminary hearing, the requirements of subsection G of § 18.2-472.1 have been satisfied and the accused has not objected to the admission of the affidavit pursuant to subsection H of § 18.2-472.1. The State Police shall also promptly notify the local law-enforcement agency of

the jurisdiction of the person's last known residence as shown in the records of the State Police.

B. Nothing in this section shall prohibit a law-enforcement officer employed by a sheriff's office or police department of a locality from enforcing the provisions of this chapter, including obtaining a warrant, or assisting in obtaining an indictment for a violation of § 18.2-472.1. The local law-enforcement agency shall notify the State Police forthwith of such actions taken pursuant to this chapter or under the authority granted pursuant to this section.

C. The State Police shall physically verify or cause to be physically verified the registration information within 30 days of the initial registration and semiannually each year thereafter and within 30 days of a change of address of those persons who are not under the control of the Department of Corrections or Community Supervision as defined by § 53.1-1, who are required to register pursuant to this chapter. Whenever it appears that a person has provided false registration information, the State Police shall promptly investigate and, if there is probable cause to believe that a violation has occurred, obtain a warrant or assist in obtaining an indictment charging a violation of § 18.2-472.1 in the jurisdiction in which the person last registered or reregistered. The State Police shall forward to the jurisdiction an affidavit signed by a custodian of the records that such person failed to comply with the provisions of this chapter. If such affidavit is admitted into evidence, it shall constitute prima facie evidence of the failure to comply with the provisions of this chapter in any trial or hearing for the violation of § 18.2-472.1, provided that in a trial or hearing other than a preliminary hearing, the requirements of subsection G of § 18.2-472.1 have been satisfied and the accused has not objected to the admission of the affidavit pursuant to subsection H of § 18.2-472.1. The State Police shall also promptly notify the local law-enforcement agency of the jurisdiction of the person's last known residence as shown in the records of the State Police.

D. The Department of Corrections or Community Supervision as defined by § 53.1-1 shall physically verify the registration information within 30 days of the original registration and semiannually each year thereafter and within 30 days of a change of address of all persons who are under the control of the Department of Corrections or Community Supervision, and those who are under supervision pursuant to § 37.2-919, who are required to register pursuant to this chapter. The Department of Corrections or Community Supervision, upon request, shall provide the State Police the verification information, in an electronic format approved by the State Police, regarding persons under their control who are required to register pursuant to the chapter. Whenever it appears that a person has provided false registration information, the Department of Corrections or Community Supervision shall promptly notify the State Police, who shall investigate and, if there is probable cause to believe that a violation has occurred, obtain a warrant or assist in obtaining an indictment charging a violation of § 18.2-472.1 in the jurisdiction in which the person last registered or reregistered. The State Police shall forward to the jurisdiction an affidavit signed by a custodian of the records that such person failed to comply with the provisions of this chapter. If such affidavit is admitted into evidence, it shall constitute prima facie evidence of the failure to comply with the provisions of this chapter in any trial or hearing for the violation of § 18.2-472.1, provided that in a trial or hearing other than a preliminary hearing, the requirements of subsection G of § 18.2-472.1 have been satisfied and the accused has not objected to the admission of the affidavit pursuant to subsection H of § 18.2-472.1. The State Police shall also promptly notify the local law-enforcement agency of the jurisdiction of the person's last known residence as shown in the records of the State Police.

History.
2003, c. 584; 2005, c. 603; 2006, cc. 857, 914; 2007, c. 718; 2009, Sp. Sess. I, cc. 1, 4; 2010, c. 858.

Law Review.
For 2006 survey article, "Criminal Law and Procedure," see 41 U. Rich. L. Rev. 83 (2006).

Research references.
Virginia Forms (Matthew Bender). No. 9-2525. Order of Remand — Sex Offender and Crimes Against Minors Registry.

CIRCUIT COURT OPINIONS

Affidavit violated Confrontation Clause. — Affidavit filed pursuant to subsection D of § 18.2-472.1 in a failure to register case, which affidavit stated that state police records showed that no sex offender registration or re-registration form was filed for defendant, was accusatory, resembled "ex-parte examination," was a core testimonial statement, and thus violated the Confrontation Clause. Commonwealth v. Dickens, 72 Va. Cir. 533, 2007 Va. Cir. LEXIS 17 (Norfolk 2007).

§ 9.1-908. Duration of registration requirement.

Any person required to register or reregister shall be required to register until the duty to register and reregister is terminated by a court order as set forth in § 9.1-910, except that any person who has been convicted of (i) any sexually violent offense, (ii) murder or (iii) former § 18.2-67.2:1 shall have a continuing duty to reregister for life.

Any period of confinement in a federal, state or local correctional facility, hospital or any other institution or facility during the otherwise applicable period shall toll the registration period and the duty to reregister shall be extended. Persons confined in a federal, state, or local correctional facility shall not be required to reregister until released from custody. Persons civilly committed pursuant to Chapter 9 (§ 37.2-900 et seq.) of Title 37.2 shall not be required to reregister until released from custody.

History.
2003, c. 584; 2005, c. 631; 2006, cc. 857, 914; 2007, c. 718; 2008, c. 877; 2010, c. 858.

CASE NOTES

Adoption. — As § 9.1-908 did not operate to preclude a convicted sex offender who was required to register annually for ten years and who had not yet registered from adopting a child, and nothing in § 63.2-1205 automatically precluded adoption in such a case, a birth father's challenge to his child's adoption by withholding his consent was denied. Gray v. Bourne, 46 Va. App. 11, 614 S.E.2d 661, 2005 Va. App. LEXIS 237 (2005).

§ 9.1-909. Relief from registration or reregistration.

A. Upon expiration of three years from the date upon which the duty to register as a sexually violent offender or murderer is imposed, the person required to register may petition the court in which he was convicted or, if the conviction occurred outside of the Commonwealth, the circuit court in the jurisdiction where he currently resides, for relief from the requirement to reregister every 90 days. After five years from the date of his last conviction for a violation of § 18.2-472.1, a sexually violent offender or murderer may petition for relief from the requirement to reregister monthly. A person who is required to register may similarly petition the circuit court for relief from the requirement to reregister every 180 days after five years from the date of his last conviction for a violation of § 18.2-472.1. The court shall hold a hearing on the petition, on notice to the attorney for the Commonwealth, to determine whether the person suffers from a mental abnormality or a personality disorder that makes the person a menace to the health and safety of others or significantly impairs his ability to control his sexual behavior. Prior to the hearing the court shall order a comprehensive assessment of the applicant by a panel of three certified sex offender treatment providers as defined in § 54.1-3600. A report of the assessment shall be filed with the court prior to the hearing. The costs of the assessment shall be taxed as costs of the proceeding.

If, after consideration of the report and such other evidence as may be presented at the hearing, the court finds by clear and convincing evidence that the person does not suffer from a mental abnormality or a personality disorder that makes the person a menace to the health and safety of others or significantly impairs his ability to control his sexual behavior, the petition shall be granted and the duty to reregister more frequently than once a year shall be terminated. The court shall promptly notify the State Police upon entry of an order granting the petition. The person shall, however, be under a continuing duty to register annually for life. If the petition is denied, the duty to reregister with the same frequency as before shall continue. An appeal from the denial of a petition shall lie to the Supreme Court.

A petition for relief pursuant to this subsection may not be filed within three years from the date on which any previous petition for such relief was denied.

B. The duly appointed guardian of a person convicted of an offense requiring registration or reregistration as either a sex offender, sexually violent offender or murderer, who due to a physical condition is incapable of (i) reoffending and (ii) reregistering, may petition the court in which the person was convicted for relief from the requirement to reregister. The court shall hold a hearing on the petition, on notice to the attorney for the Commonwealth, to determine whether the person suffers from a physical condition that makes the person (i) no longer a menace to the health and safety of others and (ii) incapable of reregistering. Prior to the hearing the court shall order a comprehensive assessment of the applicant by at least two licensed physicians other than the person's primary care physician. A report of the assessment shall be filed with the court prior to the hearing. The costs of the assessment shall be taxed as costs of the proceeding.

If, after consideration of the report and such other evidence as may be presented at the hearing, the court finds by clear and convincing evidence that due to his physical condition the person (i) no longer poses a menace to the health and safety of others and (ii) is incapable of reregistering, the petition shall be granted and the duty to reregister shall be terminated. However, for a person whose duty to reregister was terminated under this subsection, the Department of State Police shall, annually for sex offenders and quarterly for persons convicted of sexually violent offenses and murder, verify and report to the attorney for the Commonwealth in the jurisdiction in which the person resides that the person continues to suffer from the physical condition that resulted in such termination.

The court shall promptly notify the State Police upon entry of an order granting the petition to terminate the duty to reregister.

If the petition is denied, the duty to reregister shall continue. An appeal from the denial of a petition shall be to the Virginia Supreme Court.

A petition for relief pursuant to this subsection may not be filed within three years from the date on which any previous petition for such relief was denied.

If, at any time, the person's physical condition changes so that he is capable of reoffending or reregistering, the attorney for the Commonwealth shall file a petition with the circuit court in the jurisdiction where the person resides and the court shall hold a hearing on the petition, with notice to the person and his guardian, to determine whether the person still suffers from a physical condition that makes the person (i) no longer a menace to the health and safety of others and (ii) incapable of reregistering. If the petition is granted, the duty to reregister shall commence from the date of the court's order. An appeal from the denial or granting of a petition shall be to the Virginia Supreme Court. Prior to the hearing the court shall order a comprehensive assessment of the applicant by at least two licensed physicians other than the person's primary care physician. A report of the assessment shall be filed with the court prior to the hearing. The costs of the assessment shall be taxed as costs of the proceeding.

History.
2003, c. 584; 2006, cc. 857, 914.

Law Review.
For 2006 survey article, "Criminal Law and Procedure," see 41 U. Rich. L. Rev. 83 (2006). For survey of Virginia law on criminal law and procedure for the year 2007-2008, see 43 U. Rich. L. Rev. 149 (2008).

CASE NOTES

Removal remedy. — After obtaining a judgment relieving appellant of quarterly reregistration requirements under former § 19.2-298.4 for sex offenders, appellant was not entitled to enjoin the reposting of his information on a sex offender internet registry after the 2006 amendment to § 9.1-909 as appellant did not have an accrued right under § 1-239 affected by the statute's retroactive application as the removal remedy under § 9.1-909 was self-executing and could be altered "at will" by the legislature. Morency v. Commonwealth, 274 Va. 569, 649 S.E.2d 682, 2007 Va. LEXIS 114 (2007), cert. denied, 128 S. Ct. 1717, 2008 U.S. LEXIS 2757, 170 L. Ed. 2d 524 (2008).

CIRCUIT COURT OPINIONS

No vested property right to be removed from registry. — Defendants who had previously reported to the sex offender registry and were thereafter excused from the 90-day reporting requirement pursuant to § 9.1-909 and a court order did not have a substantial and vested right under § 1-239 to be permanently removed from the State Police registry on the Internet based on the Police's removal of their names therefrom after the court order was issued, as the trial court's order did not require the State Police to remove their names from the registry; such removal was not a vested property right and accordingly, amendments to § 9.1-909 allowed the Police to re-record defendants' names on the Internet registry, and defendants' declaratory relief request under § 8.01-184 to be permanently removed from the registry failed. Doe v. Commonwealth, 74 Va. Cir. 75, 2007 Va. Cir. LEXIS 130 (Fairfax County 2007).

§ 9.1-910. Removal of name and information from Registry.

A. Any person required to register, other than a person who has been convicted of any (i) sexually violent offense, (ii) two or more offenses for which registration is required, (iii) a violation of former § 18.2-67.2:1, or (iv) murder, may petition the circuit court in which he was convicted or the circuit court in the jurisdiction where he then resides for removal of his name and all identifying information from the Registry. A petition may not be filed earlier than 15 years, or 25 years for violations of § 18.2-64.1, subsection C of § 18.2-374.1:1, or subsection C, D, or E of § 18.2-374.3, after the date of initial registration nor earlier than 15 years, or 25 years for violations of § 18.2-64.1, subsection C of § 18.2-

374.1:1, or subsection C, D, or E of § 18.2-374.3, from the date of his last conviction for (a) a violation of § 18.2-472.1 or (b) any felony. A petition may not be filed until all court ordered treatment, counseling, and restitution has been completed. The court shall obtain a copy of the petitioner's complete criminal history and registration and reregistration history from the Registry and then hold a hearing on the petition at which the applicant and any interested persons may present witnesses and other evidence. The Commonwealth shall be made a party to any action under this section. If, after such hearing, the court is satisfied that such person no longer poses a risk to public safety, the court shall grant the petition. In the event the petition is not granted, the person shall wait at least 24 months from the date of the denial to file a new petition for removal from the Registry.

B. The State Police shall remove from the Registry the name of any person and all identifying information upon receipt of an order granting a petition pursuant to subsection A.

History.
2003, c. 584; 2005, c. 631; 2006, cc. 857, 914; 2007, c. 718; 2008, c. 877.

CASE NOTES

Reclassification of status. — Where plaintiff, having been reclassified as a sexually violent offender and thus being required to be on the sex offender registration list for life, sued defendant state police official alleging a procedural due process violation in connection with the reclassification and publicizing her status as a sexually violent offender on the registry without affording her a procedure through which to challenge that action, the claim failed because Conn. Dep't of Pub. Safety v. Doe precluded such a claim. Doe v. Va. Dep't of State Police, 2013 U.S. App. LEXIS 7403 (4th Cir. Apr. 12, 2013).

§ 9.1-911. Registry maintenance.

The Registry shall include conviction data received from the courts, including the disposition records for juveniles tried and convicted in the circuit courts pursuant to § 16.1-269.1, on convictions for offenses for which registration is required and registrations and reregistrations received from persons required to do so. The Registry shall also include a separate indication that a person has been convicted of a sexually violent offense. The State Police shall forthwith transmit the appropriate information as required by the Federal Bureau of Investigation for inclusion in the National Sex Offender Registry.

History.
2003, c. 584.

§ 9.1-912. Registry access and dissemination; fees.

A. Except as provided in § 9.1-913 and subsection B or C of this section, Registry information shall be disseminated upon request made directly to the State Police or to the State Police through a local law-enforcement agency. Such information may be disclosed to any person requesting information on a specific individual in accordance with subsection B. The State Police shall make Registry information available, upon request, to criminal justice agencies including local law-enforcement agencies through the Virginia Criminal Information Network (VCIN). Registry information provided under this section shall be used for the purposes of the administration of criminal justice, for the screening of current or prospective employees or volunteers or otherwise for the protection of the public in general and children in particular. The Superintendent of State Police may by regulation establish a fee not to exceed $15 for responding to requests for information from the Registry. Any fees collected shall be deposited in a special account to be used to offset the costs of administering the Registry.

B. Information regarding a specific person shall be disseminated upon receipt of an official request form that may be submitted directly to the State Police or to the State Police through a local law-enforcement agency. The official request form shall include a statement of the reason for the request; the name and address of the person requesting the information; the name, address and, if known, the social security number of the person about whom information is sought; and such other information as the State Police may require to ensure reliable identification.

C. Registry information regarding all registered offender's electronic mail address information, any instant message, chat or other Internet communication name or identity information may be electronically transmitted by the Department of State Police to a business or organization that offers electronic communication or remote computing services for the purpose of prescreening users or for comparison with information held by the requesting business or organization. In order to obtain the information from the Department of State Police, the requesting business or organization that offers electronic communication or remote computing services shall agree to notify the Department of State Police forthwith when a comparison indicates that any such registered sex offender's electronic mail address information, any instant message, chat or other Internet communication name or identity information is being used on their system. The requesting business or organization shall also agree that the information will not be further disseminated.

History.
2003, c. 584; 2007, cc. 759, 823.

Research references.
Virginia Forms (Matthew Bender). No. 9-3117. Criminal Record Request.

CIRCUIT COURT OPINIONS

No ex post facto violation. — Based on the nonpunitive nature and purpose under subsection A of § 9.1-912 of the sex offender registry, § 9.1-900 et seq., the requirement that a defendant submit his current registry information to the Virginia State Police was not a violation of the U.S. or Virginia Constitutional prohibition against ex post facto laws under U.S. Const., Art. I, § 10, and Va. Const., Art. 1, § 9. Doe v. Commonwealth, 74 Va. Cir. 75, 2007 Va. Cir. LEXIS 130 (Fairfax County 2007).

§ 9.1-913. Public dissemination by means of the Internet.

The State Police shall develop and maintain a system for making certain Registry information on persons convicted of an offense for which registration is required publicly available by means of the Internet. The information to be made available shall include the offender's name; all aliases that he has used or under which he may have been known; the date and locality of the conviction and a brief description of the offense; his age, current address and photograph; and such other information as the State Police may from time to time determine is necessary to preserve public safety including but not limited to the fact that an individual is wanted for failing to register or reregister. The system shall be secure and not capable of being altered except by the State Police. The system shall be updated each business day with newly received registrations and reregistrations. The State Police shall remove all information that it knows to be inaccurate from the Internet system.

History.
2003, c. 584; 2005, c. 603; 2006, cc. 857, 914.

Cross references.
As to personal information systems that are exempt from the Government Data Collection and Dissemination Practices Act, see § 2.2-3802.

CASE NOTES

Constitutionality. — Inmate's challenge to the Virginia Sex Offender and Crimes Against Minors Registry Act (Sex Offender Act), § 9.1-900 et seq., was dismissed because the Sex Offender Act was civil in nature and did not violate the Ex Post Facto law and the protections against Double Jeopardy; the inmate's due process rights were not violated because the only issue that could be asserted at a hearing would be a challenge to the conviction, which was not contested, and the inmate did not have a protected liberty interest in precluding truthful information about his conviction being disseminated over the internet. Ballard v. Chief of FBI, 2004 U.S. Dist. LEXIS 1095 (W.D. Va. Jan. 20, 2004).

§ 9.1-914. Automatic notification of registration to certain entities; electronic notification to requesting persons.

Any school, day-care service and child-minding service, and any state-regulated or state-licensed child day center, child day program, children's residential facility, family day home, assisted living facility or foster home as defined in § 63.2-100, nursing home or certified nursing facility as defined in § 32.1-123, and any institution of higher education may request from the State Police and, upon compliance with the requirements therefor estab-

lished by the State Police, shall be eligible to receive from the State Police electronic notice of the registration or reregistration of any sex offender and if such entities do not have the capability of receiving such electronic notice, the entity may register with the State Police to receive written notification of sex offender registration or reregistration. Within three business days of receipt by the State Police of registration or reregistration, the State Police shall electronically or in writing notify an entity listed above that has requested such notification, has complied with the requirements established by the State Police and is located in the same or a contiguous zip code area as the address of the offender as shown on the registration.

The Virginia Council for Private Education shall annually provide the State Police, in an electronic format approved by the State Police, with the location of every private school in the Commonwealth that is accredited through one of the approved accrediting agencies of the Council, and an electronic mail address for each school if available, for purposes of receiving notice under this section.

Any person may request from the State Police and, upon compliance with the requirements therefor established by the State Police, shall be eligible to receive from the State Police electronic notice of the registration or reregistration of any sex offender. Within three business days of receipt by the State Police of registration or reregistration, the State Police shall electronically notify a person who has requested such notification, has complied with the requirements established by the State Police and is located in the same or a contiguous zip code area as the address of the offender as shown on the registration.

The State Police shall establish reasonable guidelines governing the automatic dissemination of Registry information, which may include the payment of a fee, whether a one-time fee or a regular assessment, to maintain the electronic access. The fee, if any, shall defray the costs of establishing and maintaining the electronic notification system and notice by mail.

For the purposes of this section:

"Child-minding service" means provision of temporary custodial care or supervisory services for the minor child of another;

"Day-care service" means provision of supplementary care and protection during a part of the day for the minor child of another; and

"School" means any public, religious or private educational institution, including any preschool, elementary school, secondary school, post-secondary school, trade or professional institution, or institution of higher education.

History.
2003, c. 584; 2005, c. 928; 2006, cc. 857, 914; 2007, cc. 119, 164.

Law Review.
For 2007 annual survey article, "Criminal Law and Procedure," see 42 U. Rich. L. Rev. 311 (2007).

§ 9.1-915. Regulations.

The Superintendent of State Police shall promulgate regulations and develop forms to implement and enforce this chapter; including the operation and maintenance of the Registry and the removal of records on persons who are deceased, whose convictions have been reversed or who have been pardoned, and those for whom an order of removal or relief from frequent registration has been entered. Such regulations and forms shall not be subject to the provisions of Article 2 (§ 2.2-4006 et seq.) of the Administrative Process Act.

History.
2003, c. 584.

§ 9.1-916. Requests for Registry data by Virginia Criminal Sentencing Commission; confidentiality.

Upon request of the Virginia Criminal Sentencing Commission, the Department of State Police shall provide the Commission with Registry data in an electronic format. The Commission may use the data for research, evaluative or statistical purposes only and shall ensure the confidentiality and security of the data.

History.
2003, c. 391.

The number of this section was assigned by the Virginia Code Commission, the section having been added as subsection E of § 19.2-390.1, by Acts 2003, c. 391.

§ 9.1-917. Limitation on liability.

No liability shall be imposed upon any law-enforcement official who disseminates information or fails to disseminate information in good faith compliance with the requirements of this chapter, but this provision shall not be construed to grant immunity for gross negligence or willful misconduct.

History.
2003, c. 584.

The number of this section was assigned by the Virginia Code Commission, the number in the 2003 act having been 9.1-916.

§ 9.1-918. Misuse of registry information; penalty.

Use of registry information for purposes not authorized by this chapter is prohibited, the unlawful use of the information contained in or derived from the Registry for purposes of intimidating or harassing another is prohibited, and a willful violation of this chapter is a Class 1 misdemeanor. For purposes of this section, absent other aggravating circumstances, the mere republication or reasonable distribution of material contained on or derived from the publicly available Internet sex offender database shall not be deemed intimidation or harassment.

History.
2003, c. 584; 2006, cc. 857, 914.

The number of this section was assigned by the Virginia Code Commission, the number in the 2003 act having been 9.1-917.

Cross references.
As to penalty for Class 1 misdemeanors, see § 18.2-11.

§ 9.1-919. Notice of penalty on forms and documents.

The Virginia Criminal Information Network and any form or document used by the Department of State Police to disseminate information from the Registry shall provide notice that any unauthorized use of the information with the intent to harass or intimidate another is a crime punishable as a Class 1 misdemeanor.

History.
2003, c. 391.

The number of this section was assigned by the Virginia Code Commission, the section having been added as subsection H of § 19.2-390.1, by Acts 2003, c. 391.

Cross references.
As to penalty for Class 1 misdemeanor, see § 18.2-11.

§ 9.1-920. Severability; liberal construction.

The provisions of this chapter are severable, and if any of its provisions shall be declared unconstitutional or invalid by any court of competent jurisdiction, the decision of such court shall not affect or impair any of the other provisions of this chapter. This chapter, being necessary for the welfare of the Commonwealth and its inhabitants, shall be liberally construed to effect the purposes hereof.

History.
2003, c. 584.

The number of this section was assigned by the Virginia Code Commission, the number in the 2003 act having been 9.1-918.

§ 9.1-921. Exemption of information systems from provisions related to the Virginia Information Technologies Agency.

The provisions of Chapter 20.1 (§ 2.2-2005 et seq.) of Title 2.2 shall not apply to the Sex Offender and Crimes Against Minors Registry pursuant to Chapter 9 (§ 9.1-900 et seq.) of Title 9.1, operated by the Department of State Police or to information technology as defined in § 2.2-2006 operated by the Department of Juvenile Justice, Department of Corrections or the Virginia Compensation Board that interact, furnish, update, contain or exchange information with the Sex Offender and Crimes Against Minors Registry.

History.
2006, cc. 857, 914.

§ 9.1-922. Use of Registry data by Statewide Automated Victim Notification (SAVIN) system; confidentiality.

Upon request of the Compensation Board, the Department of State Police shall provide the Statewide Automated Victim Notification (SAVIN) system with Registry data in an electronic format. The Board or its contractor may use the data for verification of registrant status and notification of victims and law enforcement regarding changes in status of persons on the Registry and shall ensure the confidentiality and security of the data.

History.
2008, cc. 76, 338.

Editor's note.
Acts 2008, c. 76, cl. 2, provides: "That an emergency exists and this act is in force from its passage [March 2, 2008]."
Acts 2008, c. 338, cl. 2, provides: "That an emergency exists and this act is in force from its passage [March 4, 2008]."

CHAPTER 13.

DOMESTIC AND SEXUAL ASSAULT POLICIES.

§ 9.1-1300. Domestic violence policies and procedures for law-enforcement agencies in the Commonwealth.

The Virginia Department of State Police and the police and sheriff's departments of every political subdivision in the Commonwealth shall establish an arrest policy and procedures for domestic violence and family abuse cases. Any local police or sheriff's department is authorized to adopt an arrest policy that prescribes additional requirements under this section. Any policies and procedures established under this section shall at a minimum provide guidance to law-enforcement officers on the following:

1. The department's arrest policy;
2. The standards for determining who is the predominant physical aggressor pursuant to § 19.2-81.3;
3. The standards for completion of a required incident report to be filed with the department including the existence of any special circumstances which would dictate a course of action other than arrest;
4. The department's policy on providing transportation to an allegedly abused person;
5. The legal and community resources available to allegedly abused persons in the department's jurisdiction;

6. The department's policy on domestic violence incidents involving law-enforcement officers; and
7. The department's policy on the handling of cases involving repeat offenders of family abuse or domestic violence.

History.
2008, cc. 600, 771.

§ 9.1-1301. Sexual assault policies for law-enforcement agencies in the Commonwealth.

The Virginia Department of State Police and the police and sheriff's departments of every political subdivision in the Commonwealth and every campus police department shall establish written policies and procedures regarding a law-enforcement officer's response to an alleged criminal sexual assault in violation of Article 7 (§ 18.2-61 et seq.) of Chapter 4 of Title 18.2. Such policies shall, at a minimum, provide guidance as to the department's policy on (i) training; (ii) compliance with §§ 19.2-9.1 and 19.2-165.1; (iii) transportation of alleged sexual assault victims; and (iv) the provision of information on legal and community resources available to alleged victims of sexual assault.

History.
2008, cc. 600, 771.

TITLE 10.1.

CONSERVATION.

SUBTITLE II.

ACTIVITIES ADMINISTERED BY OTHER ENTITIES.

CHAPTER 14.

VIRGINIA WASTE MANAGEMENT ACT.

Article 7. Transportation of Hazardous Materials.

ARTICLE 7.

TRANSPORTATION OF HAZARDOUS MATERIALS.

§ 10.1-1450. Waste Management Board to promulgate regulations regarding hazardous materials.

The Board shall promulgate regulations designating the manner and method by which hazardous materials shall be loaded, unloaded, packed, identi-fied, marked, placarded, stored and transported. Such regulations shall be no more restrictive than any applicable federal laws or regulations.

History.
  1986, c. 492, § 10-305; 1988, c. 891; 1992, c. 208; 1997, c. 260.

Cross references.
  For provisions relating to granting of variances for commercial drivers transporting hazardous wastes, see § 46.2-341.9:1. As to State Police authority to promulgate regulations pertaining to commercial motor vehicle safety, see § 52-8.4.

Michie's Jurisprudence.
  For related discussion, see 2B M.J. Aviation, § 1; 3B M.J. Carriers, § 96.

§ 10.1-1451. Enforcement of article and regulations.

The Department of State Police and all other law-enforcement officers of the Commonwealth who have satisfactorily completed the course in Hazardous Materials Compliance and Enforcement as prescribed by the U.S. Department of Transportation, Research and Special Programs Administration, Office of Hazardous Materials Transportation, in federal safety regulations and safety inspection procedures pertaining to the transportation of hazardous materials, shall enforce the provisions of this article, and any rule or regulation promulgated hereunder. Those law-enforcement officers certified to enforce the provisions of this article and any regulation promulgated hereunder, shall annually receive in-service training in current federal safety regulations and safety inspection procedures pertaining to the transportation of hazardous materials.

History.
  1986, c. 492, § 10-306; 1988, cc. 14, 891.

§ 10.1-1452. Article not to preclude exercise of certain regulatory powers.

The provisions of this article shall not preclude the exercise of the statutory and regulatory powers of any agency, department or political subdivision of the Commonwealth having statutory authority to regulate hazardous materials on specified highways or portions thereof.

History.
  1986, c. 492, § 10-307; 1988, c. 891.

§ 10.1-1453. Exceptions.

This article shall not apply to regular military or naval forces of the United States, the duly authorized militia of any state or territory thereof, police or fire departments, or sheriff's offices and regional jails of this Commonwealth, provided the same are acting within their official capacity and in the performance of their duties, or to the transportation of hazardous radioactive materials in accordance with § 44-146.30.

History.
  1986, c. 492, § 10-308; 1988, c. 891; 1995, c. 112.

§ 10.1-1454. Transportation under United States regulations.

Any person transporting hazardous materials in accordance with regulations promulgated under the laws of the United States, shall be deemed to have complied with the provisions of this article, except when such transportation is excluded from regulation under the laws or regulations of the United States.

History.
  1986, c. 492, § 10-309; 1988, c. 891.

Law Review.
  For 2003/2004 survey of environmental law, see 39 U. Rich. L. Rev. 203 (2004).

Michie's Jurisprudence.
  For related discussion, see 2B M.J. Aviation, § 1.

TITLE 15.2.

COUNTIES, CITIES AND TOWNS.

SUBTITLE II.

POWERS OF LOCAL GOVERNMENT.

CHAPTER 9.

GENERAL POWERS OF LOCAL GOVERNMENTS.

Article 1. Public Health and Safety; Nuisances.

ARTICLE 1.

PUBLIC HEALTH AND SAFETY; NUISANCES.

§ 15.2-922.1. Regulating or prohibiting the making of fires.

A. Any city or town may by ordinance regulate or prohibit the making of fires in streets, alleys, and other public places and regulate the making of fires on private property.

B. In addition to the authority provided under § 27-98, any county may by ordinance regulate or prohibit the making of fires in streets, alleys, and other public places and, when a declared emergency exists, pursuant to § 44-146.21, regulate the making of fires on private property.

History.
2007, c. 256.

ARTICLE 5.
ADDITIONAL POWERS.

§ 15.2-968.1. Use of photo-monitoring systems to enforce traffic light signals.

A. The governing body of any county, city, or town may provide by ordinance for the establishment of a traffic signal enforcement program imposing monetary liability on the operator of a motor vehicle for failure to comply with traffic light signals in such locality in accordance with the provisions of this section. Each such locality may install and operate traffic light signal photo-monitoring systems at no more than one intersection for every 10,000 residents within each county, city, or town at any one time, provided, however, that within planning District 8, each such locality may install and operate traffic light signal photo-monitoring systems at no more than 10 intersections, or at no more than one intersection for every 10,000 residents within each county, city, or town, whichever is greater, at any one time.

B. The operator of a vehicle shall be liable for a monetary penalty imposed pursuant to this section if such vehicle is found, as evidenced by information obtained from a traffic light signal violation monitoring system, to have failed to comply with a traffic light signal within such locality.

C. Proof of a violation of this section shall be evidenced by information obtained from a traffic light signal violation monitoring system authorized pursuant to this section. A certificate, sworn to or affirmed by a law-enforcement officer employed by a locality authorized to impose penalties pursuant to this section, or a facsimile thereof, based upon inspection of photographs, microphotographs, videotape, or other recorded images produced by a traffic light signal violation monitoring system, shall be prima facie evidence of the facts contained therein. Any photographs, microphotographs, videotape, or other recorded images evidencing such a violation shall be available for inspection in any proceeding to adjudicate the liability for such violation pursuant to an ordinance adopted pursuant to this section.

D. In the prosecution for a violation of any local ordinance adopted as provided in this section, prima facie evidence that the vehicle described in the summons issued pursuant to this section was oper-

ated in violation of such ordinance, together with proof that the defendant was at the time of such violation the owner, lessee, or renter of the vehicle, shall constitute in evidence a rebuttable presumption that such owner, lessee, or renter of the vehicle was the person who committed the violation. Such presumption shall be rebutted if the owner, lessee, or renter of the vehicle (i) files an affidavit by regular mail with the clerk of the general district court that he was not the operator of the vehicle at the time of the alleged violation or (ii) testifies in open court under oath that he was not the operator of the vehicle at the time of the alleged violation. Such presumption shall also be rebutted if a certified copy of a police report, showing that the vehicle had been reported to the police as stolen prior to the time of the alleged violation of this section, is presented, prior to the return date established on the summons issued pursuant to this section, to the court adjudicating the alleged violation.

E. For purposes of this section, "owner" means the registered owner of such vehicle on record with the Department of Motor Vehicles. For purposes of this section, "traffic light signal violation monitoring system" means a vehicle sensor installed to work in conjunction with a traffic light that automatically produces two or more photographs, two or more microphotographs, video, or other recorded images of each vehicle at the time it is used or operated in violation of § 46.2-833, 46.2-835, or 46.2-836. For each such vehicle, at least one recorded image shall be of the vehicle before it has illegally entered the intersection, and at least one recorded image shall be of the same vehicle after it has illegally entered that intersection.

F. Imposition of a penalty pursuant to this section shall not be deemed a conviction as an operator and shall not be made part of the operating record of the person upon whom such liability is imposed, nor shall it be used for insurance purposes in the provision of motor vehicle insurance coverage. No monetary penalty imposed under this section shall exceed $50, nor shall it include court costs.

G. A summons for a violation of this section may be executed pursuant to § 19.2-76.2. Notwithstanding the provisions of § 19.2-76, a summons for a violation of this section may be executed by mailing by first class mail a copy thereof to the owner, lessee, or renter of the vehicle. In the case of a vehicle owner, the copy shall be mailed to the address contained in the records of the Department of Motor Vehicles; in the case of a vehicle lessee or renter, the copy shall be mailed to the address contained in the records of the lessor or renter. Every such mailing shall include, in addition to the summons, a notice of (i) the summoned person's ability to rebut the presumption that he was the operator of the vehicle at the time of the alleged violation through the filing of an affidavit as provided in subsection D and (ii) instructions for filing such affidavit, including the address to which the affidavit is to be sent. If the summoned person fails to appear on the date of return set out in the summons mailed pursuant to this section, the summons shall be executed in the manner set out in § 19.2-76.3. No proceedings for contempt or arrest of a person summoned by mailing shall be instituted for failure to appear on the return date of the summons. Any summons executed for a violation of this section shall provide to the person summoned at least 30 business days from the mailing of the summons to inspect information collected by a traffic light signal violation monitoring system in connection with the violation.

H. Information collected by a traffic light signal violation monitoring system installed and operated pursuant to subsection A shall be limited exclusively to that information that is necessary for the enforcement of traffic light violations. On behalf of a locality, a private entity that operates a traffic light signal violation monitoring system may enter into an agreement with the Department of Motor Vehicles, in accordance with the provisions of subdivision B 21 of § 46.2-208, to obtain vehicle owner information regarding the registered owners of vehicles that fail to comply with a traffic light signal. Information provided to the operator of a traffic light signal violation monitoring system shall be protected in a database with security comparable to that of the Department of Motor Vehicles' system, and used only for enforcement against individuals who violate the provisions of this section. Notwithstanding any other provision of law, all photographs, microphotographs, electronic images, or other personal information collected by a traffic light signal violation monitoring system shall be used exclusively for enforcing traffic light violations and shall not (i) be open to the public; (ii) be sold or used for sales, solicitation, or marketing purposes; (iii) be disclosed to any other entity except as may be necessary for the enforcement of a traffic light violation or to a vehicle owner or operator as part of a challenge to the violation; or (iv) be used in a court in a pending action or proceeding unless the action or proceeding relates to a violation of § 46.2-833, 46.2-835, or 46.2-836 or requested upon order from a court of competent jurisdiction. Information collected under this section pertaining to a specific violation shall be purged and not retained later than 60 days after the collection of any civil penalties. If a locality does not execute a summons for a violation of this section within 10 business days, all information collected pertaining to that suspected violation shall be purged within two business days. Any locality operating a traffic light signal violation monitoring system shall annually certify compliance with this section and make all records pertaining to such system available for inspection and audit by the Commissioner of Highways or the Commissioner of the Department of Motor Vehicles or his designee. Any person who discloses personal information in violation of the provisions of this subsection shall be subject to a civil penalty of $1,000 per disclosure.

Any unauthorized use or disclosure of such personal information shall be grounds for termination of the agreement between the Department of Motor Vehicles and the private entity.

I. A private entity may enter into an agreement with a locality to be compensated for providing the traffic light signal violation monitoring system or equipment, and all related support services, to include consulting, operations and administration. However, only a law-enforcement officer employed by a locality may swear to or affirm the certificate required by subsection C. No locality shall enter into an agreement for compensation based on the number of violations or monetary penalties imposed.

J. When selecting potential intersections for a traffic light signal violation monitoring system, a locality shall consider factors such as (i) the accident rate for the intersection, (ii) the rate of red light violations occurring at the intersection (number of violations per number of vehicles), (iii) the difficulty experienced by law-enforcement officers in patrol cars or on foot in apprehending violators, and (iv) the ability of law-enforcement officers to apprehend violators safely within a reasonable distance from the violation. Localities may consider the risk to pedestrians as a factor, if applicable.

K. Before the implementation of a traffic light signal violation monitoring system at an intersection, the locality shall complete an engineering safety analysis that addresses signal timing and other location-specific safety features. The length of the yellow phase shall be established based on the recommended methodology of the Institute of Transportation Engineers. All traffic light signal violation monitoring systems shall provide a minimum 0.5-second grace period between the time the signal turns red and the time the first violation is recorded. If recommended by the engineering safety analysis, the locality shall make reasonable location-specific safety improvements, including signs and pavement markings.

L. Any locality that uses a traffic light signal violation monitoring system shall evaluate the system on a monthly basis to ensure all cameras and traffic signals are functioning properly. Evaluation results shall be made available to the public.

M. Any locality that uses a traffic light signal violation monitoring system to enforce traffic light signals shall place conspicuous signs within 500 feet of the intersection approach at which a traffic light signal violation monitoring system is used. There shall be a rebuttable presumption that such signs were in place at the time of the commission of the traffic light signal violation.

N. Prior to or coincident with the implementation or expansion of a traffic light signal violation monitoring system, a locality shall conduct a public awareness program, advising the public that the locality is implementing or expanding a traffic light signal violation monitoring system.

O. Notwithstanding any other provision of this section, if a vehicle depicted in images recorded by a traffic light signal photo-monitoring system is owned, leased, or rented by a county, city, or town, then the county, city, or town may access and use the recorded images and associated information for employee disciplinary purposes.

History.
2007, cc. 836, 903; 2010, c. 175; 2012, cc. 805, 836.

Editor's note.
Acts 2011, cc. 36 and 152, cl. 3 provides: "That the Virginia Code Commission shall carry out such editorial changes to the Code of Virginia as may be required to reflect the provisions of this act changing the title 'Commonwealth Transportation Commissioner' to 'Commissioner of Highways.'" "Commissioner of Highways" was substituted for "Commonwealth Transportation Commissioner" in this section.

The 2012 amendments.
The 2012 amendments by cc. 805 and 836 are identical, and deleted "A locality shall submit a list of intersections to the Virginia Department of Transportation for final approval." at the end of subsection J.

OPINIONS OF THE ATTORNEY GENERAL

Use of funds. — Since the funds collected by localities in enforcing their traffic light laws do not constitute "fines for offenses against the Commonwealth," the General Assembly constitutionally may permit localities to retain such funds. See opinion of Attorney General to The Honorable Joseph D. Morrissey, Member, House of Delegates, 11-034, 2011 Va. AG LEXIS 24 (4/15/11).

§ 15.2-971. Armories and markets; assistance to National Guard.

A. A locality may provide and operate armories and markets, or may contract with others for supplying such facilities.

B. Any locality may appropriate out of the general levy, except the school fund, and expend annually such sums of money as their judgment may warrant to aid and assist in the erection and maintenance of suitable armories for companies of the Virginia National Guard, or otherwise contribute towards the assistance and maintenance of such companies.

History.
Code 1950, §§ 15-77.44, 15-694; 1958, c. 328; 1962, c. 623, §§ 15.1-268, 15.1-880; 1970, c. 225; 1997, c. 587.

§ 15.2-974. Permits for display of fireworks; use and exhibitions.

The governing bodies of the several counties, cities and towns shall have the power to provide for the issuance of permits for the display of fireworks by fair associations, amusement parks, or by any organization or group of individuals, under the minimum terms and conditions set forth in the Virginia Statewide Fire Prevention Code (§ 27-94 et seq.) and any additional terms and conditions as may be prescribed by the locality. Any association, organization, or group that has been issued a permit may purchase and make use of fireworks under the terms and conditions of such permit.

History.
2002, c. 856.

§ 15.2-980. Civil penalties for violations of noise ordinances.

Any locality may, by ordinance, adopt a uniform schedule of civil penalties for violations of that locality's noise ordinance. This provision shall not apply to noise generated in connection with the business being performed on industrial property. Civil fines will not exceed $250 for the first offense and $500 for each subsequent offense. The provisions of this section shall not apply to railroads. No ordinance of any locality shall apply to sound emanating from any area permitted by the Virginia Department of Mines, Minerals and Energy or any division thereof.

History.
2010, cc. 501 788.

§ 15.2-981. Authority to sell dogs trained for police work.

A locality may sell any dog specially trained for police work to the handler who was last in control of such dog, at a price deemed by the locality to be appropriate. Such sale shall not be deemed a violation of the State and Local Government Conflict of Interests Act (§ 2.2-3100 et seq.).

History.
2010, c. 714.

The number of this section was assigned by the Virginia Code Commission, the number in the 2010 act having been § 15.2-980.

§ 15.2-982. Designation of tourism activity zones.

Any locality may designate one or more tourism activity zones as areas that may be used for special events, including parades, events requiring temporary street closures, and indoor and outdoor entertainment activities. The locality shall include any designated tourism activity zone as an amendment to the locality's zoning map.

History.
2013, c. 246.

CHAPTER 11.

POWERS OF CITIES AND TOWNS.

Article 1. Uniform Charter Powers.

ARTICLE 1.

UNIFORM CHARTER POWERS.

Michie's Jurisprudence.
For related discussion, see 13B M.J. Municipal Corporations, § 25.

§ 15.2-1119. Hospitals, sanatoria, homes, clinics, etc.

A municipal corporation may provide and operate, within or outside the municipal corporation, hospitals, sanatoria, homes, clinics, institutions and facilities for the care, treatment and maintenance of the sick, of children, the aged, destitute and indigent; may contract with others for supplying such services; and may charge and collect compensation for such care, treatment and maintenance.

History.
Code 1950, § 15-77.45; 1958, c. 328; 1962, c. 623, § 15.1-881; 1997, c. 587.

§ 15.2-1120. Detentive, correctional and penal institutions.

A municipal corporation may provide and operate, within or outside the municipal corporation, detentive, correctional and penal institutions; or may contract with others for supplying the services and facilities provided at such institutions.

History.
Code 1950, § 15-77.46; 1958, c. 328; 1962, c. 623, § 15.1-882; 1997, c. 587.

§ 15.2-1121. Cemeteries.

A municipal corporation may provide and operate, within or outside the municipal corporation, cemeteries; may contract for the perpetual care of lots and burial spaces therein; and may charge compensation for lots and burial spaces and services in connection with interments and the maintenance and operation of such cemeteries.

History.
Code 1950, § 15-77.47; 1958, c. 328; 1962, c. 623, § 15.1-883; 1997, c. 587.

§ 15.2-1122. Parking or storage of vehicles.

A municipal corporation may provide and operate places for, and limited to, the parking or storage of vehicles by the public, which shall include but shall not be limited to parking lots, garages, buildings and other land, structures, equipment and facilities; provide for their management and operation by an agency of the municipality; contract with others for the operation and management thereof upon such terms and conditions as shall be prescribed by the municipal corporation; and charge or authorize the charging of compensation for the parking or storage of vehicles.

History.
Code 1950, § 15-77.48; 1958, c. 328; 1962, c. 623, § 15.1-884; 1997, c. 587.

Law Review.
For discussion of some legal and financial considerations relating to parking facilities, see 46 Va. L. Rev. 595 (1960).

CIRCUIT COURT OPINIONS

Municipality may charge for parking vehicles. — City was statutorily-authorized to charge a fee for parking and the fact that it did so did not mean it waived its defense of governmental immunity to the injured party's claim for damages after she slipped and fell on snow and ice in the city paring lot, as providing off-street parking was a governmental function specifically authorized under Virginia law. Gambrell v. City of Norfolk, 60 Va. Cir. 328, 2002 Va. Cir. LEXIS 399 (Norfolk 2002).

§ 15.2-1123. Airports and facilities.

A. A municipal corporation may provide and operate within or outside the municipal corporation airports and lands, structures, equipment and facilities appurtenant thereto; provide for their management and operation by an agency of the municipality; contract with others for the operation and management thereof upon such terms and conditions as shall be prescribed by the municipal corporation; and charge or authorize the charging of compensation for the use of the airport or any of its appurtenances or facilities.

B. A municipal corporation located in Planning District 11 or a political subdivision located in Planning District 6 or 7 may apply any deicing agent containing urea for the purpose of deicing an airport that is classified by the Virginia Air Transportation System Plan as a Commercial Service airport or General Aviation Regional airport, provided the application does not exceed Virginia Pollutant Discharge Elimination System stormwater permit requirements.

History.
Code 1950, § 15-77.49; 1958, c. 328; 1962, c. 623, § 15.1-885; 1997, c. 587; 2013, c. 758.

The 2013 amendments.
The 2013 amendment by c. 758 added the subsection A designator and subsection B.

Michie's Jurisprudence.
For related discussion, see 2B M.J. Aviation, § 1.

§ 15.2-1124. Police jurisdiction over lands, buildings and structures; jurisdiction of offenses; appeals; jurisdiction in certain public buildings with magistrate's offices.

A. Lands, buildings or structures provided and operated by a municipality for any purpose defined in this article shall be under the police jurisdiction of the municipal corporation for the enforcement of its regulations respecting the use or occupancy thereof. All regular and special police officers of the municipal corporation shall have jurisdiction to make arrests on such land and in such buildings or structures for violations of such regulations. Such criminal case shall be prosecuted in the locality in which the offense was committed.

B. In any public building that is located in Henry County adjoining a municipal corporation and that contains a magistrate's office which serves the municipal corporation, the sheriff, any deputy sheriff, and any police officer of the municipal corporation shall have the same powers which such sheriff, deputy sheriff or police officer would have in the municipal corporation itself. The courts of the municipal corporation and the locality in which such public building is located shall have concurrent jurisdiction of any offense committed against or any escape from any such sheriff, deputy sheriff, or police officer in such public building, provided that the sheriff, deputy sheriff, or police officer was present in the public building while in the performance of his official duties. Such police powers and concurrent jurisdiction shall also apply during travel between the municipal corporation and the public building by such sheriff, deputy sheriffs, and police officers while in the performance of their official duties. For purposes of this subsection, a "public building" shall include the surrounding grounds of such building.

History.
Code 1950, § 15-77.51; 1958, c. 328; 1962, c. 623, § 15.1-887; 1997, cc. 587, 739; 2007, c. 813.

Editor's note.
Acts 2007, c. 813, cl. 2, provides: "That the provisions of this act shall not affect the powers of any locality with respect to any ordinance, resolution or bylaw validly adopted and not repealed or rescinded prior to July 1, 2007."

CASE NOTES

Authority given by section. — This section gives authority to police officers of the municipal corporation to make arrests on its land and facilities for any violation of regulations on use or occupancy thereof. Squire v. Commonwealth, 214 Va. 260, 199 S.E.2d 534 (1973), cert. denied, 417 U.S. 909, 94 S. Ct. 2606, 41 L. Ed. 2d 213 (1974) (decided under prior law).

CHAPTER 15.

LOCAL GOVERNMENT PERSONNEL, QUALIFICATION FOR OFFICE, BONDS, DUAL OFFICE HOLDING AND CERTAIN LOCAL GOVERNMENT OFFICERS.

Article 1. General Provisions for Certain Officers and Employees.

ARTICLE 1.

GENERAL PROVISIONS FOR CERTAIN OFFICERS AND EMPLOYEES.

§ 15.2-1511. Allowances to injured officials and employees and their dependents.

The governing body of any locality is authorized in its discretion to make allowances by appropriation of funds, payable in monthly or semimonthly installments, for the relief of any of its officials, employees, police officers, firefighters, sheriffs or deputy sheriffs, town sergeants and town deputy sergeants, or their dependents, who suffer injury or death as defined in Title 65.2, whether such injury was suffered or death occurs before or after June 29, 1948 (which date is the effective date of the section). The allowance shall not exceed the salary or wage being paid such official, employee, police officer, firefighter, sheriff or deputy sheriff, town sergeants and town deputy sergeants, at the time of such injury or death, and the payment of the allowance shall not extend beyond the period of disability resulting from such injury. In case death results from the injury, the allowance may be made for the dependents as defined in Title 65.2. In localities which have established retirement or pension systems for injured, retired or superannuated officials, employees, members of police or fire departments, sheriffs, deputy sheriffs, town sergeants and deputy sergeants, or for the dependents of those killed in line of duty, the agencies provided for the administration of such systems shall determine the existence of such injury or cause of death before any appropriation to pay such allowance is made and shall determine the extent of and period of disability resulting from such injury and the cause in case of death. All sums paid to any such official, employee, police officer, firefighter, sheriff or deputy sheriff, town sergeants and deputy sergeants, as compensation under Title 65.2 and all sums paid to the dependents of such official, employee, police officer, firefighter, sheriff or deputy sheriff, town sergeant and deputy sergeant, if he is killed, and all sums paid under any retirement or pension system shall be deducted from the allowance made under this section in such installments as the agency determines. If the agency determines that any official, employee, police officer, firefighter, sheriff or deputy sheriff, town sergeant and deputy sergeant, who suffered injury in the line of duty is engaged or is able to engage in a gainful occupation, then the allowance shall be reduced by the agency to an amount which, together with the amount earnable by him, equals the allowance. Should the earning capacity of the official, employee, police officer, firefighter, sheriff or deputy sheriff, town sergeant and deputy sergeant, be later changed, such allowance may be further modified, up or down, provided the new allowance shall not exceed the amount of the allowance originally made nor an amount which, when added to the amount earnable by him, exceeds such allowance.

The death of, or any condition or impairment of health of, any member of a local police department, or of a sheriff or deputy sheriff, caused by hypertension or heart disease resulting in total or partial disability shall be presumed to have been suffered in the line of duty unless the contrary be shown by competent evidence; provided that prior to making any claim based upon such presumption for retirement, sickness or other benefits on account of such death or total or partial disability, such member, sheriff, or deputy sheriff, shall have been found free from hypertension or heart disease, as the case may be, by a physical examination which shall include such appropriate laboratory and other diagnostic studies as such governing body shall prescribe and which shall have been conducted by physicians whose qualifications shall have been prescribed by such governing body. In the case of a claim for disability, that any such member, sheriff, or deputy sheriff, shall, if requested by such governing body or its authorized representative, submit himself to physical examination by any physician designated by such governing body, such examination to include such tests or studies as may reasonably be prescribed by the physician so designated. Such member, sheriff or deputy sheriff, or claimant shall have the right to have present at such examination, at his own expense, any qualified physician he may designate. In the case of a claim for death benefits, any person entitled to make a claim for such benefits, claiming that such person's death was suffered in the line of duty, shall submit the body of the deceased to a postmortem examination to be performed by the medical examiner for the county, city or town appointed under § 32.1-282.

History.
Code 1950, § 15-555; 1950, p. 315; 1954, c. 246; 1960, c. 487; 1962, c. 623, § 15.1-134; 1971, Ex. Sess., c. 155; 1973, c. 499; 1976, c. 769; 1977, c. 326; 1997, c. 587.

Cross references.
For other provisions as to power of police authorities to take fingerprints and photographs, see § 19.2-392.

§ 15.2-1511.01. Allowances to injured deputy sheriffs.

A. In addition to the allowances provided in § 15.2-1511, any deputy sheriff who suffers injury as defined in Title 65.2 and whose allowance as provided in § 15.2-1511 is less than 100 percent of his regular compensation shall be entitled to use any accrued vacation, compensatory, or sick leave to supplement the allowance so as to receive 100 percent of his regular compensation. In no case shall a deputy sheriff use such accrued leave so as to receive more than 100 percent of his regular compensation.

B. The governing body of a locality shall continue to pay the employer's share of the cost of health insurance to the same extent paid for other employees of the locality covered by the health insurance plan for a deputy sheriff who participates in the employer-provided health plan who suffers a compensable injury as defined under Title 65.2 so long as the deputy sheriff remains employed by the locality.

History.
2008, cc. 335, 766.

Cross references.
As to definition of "injury," see § 65.2-101.

CHAPTER 16.

LOCAL CONSTITUTIONAL OFFICERS, COURTHOUSES AND SUPPLIES.

ARTICLE 3.

SHERIFF.

§ 15.2-1613. Operation of sheriff's office.

Any county or city may appropriate funds for the operation of the sheriff's office.

In addition to those items listed in § 15.2-1615.1, counties and cities shall provide at their expense in accordance with standards set forth in § 15.2-1610 a reasonable number of uniforms and items of personal equipment required by the sheriff to carry out his official duties.

History.
1986, c. 139, § 15.1-137.3; 1990, c. 68; 1997, c. 587.

§ 15.2-1613.1. Processing fee may be imposed on certain individuals.

Any county or city may by ordinance authorize a processing fee not to exceed $25 on any individual admitted to a county, city, or regional jail following conviction. The fee shall be ordered as a part of court costs collected by the clerk, deposited into the account of the treasurer of the county or city and shall be used by the local sheriff's office to defray the costs of processing arrested persons into local or regional jails. If processing costs are incurred by a regional jail rather than a local sheriff's office, the fees collected pursuant to such ordinance may be used by the regional jail to defray the costs of processing arrested persons. Where costs are incurred by a sheriff's office and a regional jail the fees collected pursuant to such ordinance may be divided proportionately as determined by the local governing body or bodies, between the sheriff's office and the regional jail. Where costs are incurred by a police department for booking or fingerprinting services, the fees collected pursuant to such ordinance may be divided proportionately as determined by the local governing body or bodies, between the sheriff's office and the police department.

History.
2002, c. 840; 2003, c. 623; 2011, cc. 300, 664.

Cross references.
As to fees included in court costs, see § 17.1-275.5.

The 2011 amendments.
The 2011 amendments by cc. 300 and 664 are identical, and added the last sentence.

OPINIONS OF THE ATTORNEY GENERAL

Local sheriff's office. — Processing fee authorized by this section is reserved solely for use by the local sheriff's office. See opinion of Attorney General to Sharon E. Pandak, County Attorney for Prince William County, 02-118 (11/18/02).

To be assessed after conviction. — This section authorizes the fee to be assessed only when a person is admitted, or re-admitted, to jail after conviction. If a person is convicted, but is not admitted or readmitted to jail following conviction, the fee may not be assessed. See opinion of Attorney General to The Honorable Rex A. Davis, Clerk of the Circuit Court, 11-091, 2011 Va. AG LEXIS 57 (7/22/11).

ARTICLE 4.

ATTORNEY FOR THE COMMONWEALTH.

§ 15.2-1627.4. Coordination of multidisciplinary response to sexual assault.

The attorney for the Commonwealth in each political subdivision in the Commonwealth shall coordinate the establishment of a multidisciplinary response to criminal sexual assault as set forth in Article 7 (§ 18.2-61 et seq.) of Chapter 4 of Title 18.2, and hold a meeting, at least annually, to: (i) discuss implementation of protocols and policies for sexual assault response teams consistent with those established by the Department of Criminal Justice Services pursuant to subdivision 45 of § 9.1-102; and (ii) establish and review guidelines for the community's response, including the collection, preservation, and secure storage of evidence from Physical Evidence Recovery Kit examinations consistent with § 19.2-165.1. The following persons or their designees shall be invited to participate in the annual meeting: the attorney for the Commonwealth; the sheriff; the director of the local sexual assault crisis center providing services in the juris-

diction, if any; the chief of each police department and the chief of each campus police department of any institution of higher education in the jurisdiction, if any; a forensic nurse examiner or other health care provider who performs Physical Evidence Recovery Kit examinations in the jurisdiction, if any; and the director of the victim/witness program in the jurisdiction, if any.

History.
2009, c. 817; 2012, cc. 343, 625.

Editor's note.
Acts 2009, c. 817 was codified as this section at the direction of the Virginia Code Commission.

The 2012 amendments.
The 2012 amendments by cc. 343 and 625 are identical, and inserted "and the chief of each campus police department of any institution of higher education" near the middle of the second sentence.

CHAPTER 17.

POLICE AND PUBLIC ORDER.

Article 1. General Provisions.

ARTICLE 1.

GENERAL PROVISIONS.

§ 15.2-1700. Preservation of peace and good order.

Any locality may provide for the protection of its inhabitants and property and for the preservation of peace and good order therein.

History.
Code 1950, § 15-556; 1962, c. 623, § 15.1-137; 1997, c. 587.

Cross references.
As to powers and duties of governing body of sanitary district, see § 21-118.

Research references.
Police Civil Liability (Matthew Bender). Isidore Silver.

CASE NOTES

This section and former § 15.1-138 (see now §§ 15.2-1704, 15.2-1710) merely set out the general powers of a municipality to create a police force; the sections do not require a municipality to act, and therefore do not create any public rights; there is no public policy right of action for the enforcement of nonpublic rights, and thus the plaintiff officers stated no public policy claim. Childress v. City of Richmond, 907 F. Supp. 934 (E.D. Va. 1995), aff'd, 134 F.3d 1205 (4th Cir. 1998), cert. denied, 524 U.S. 927, 118 S. Ct. 2322, 141 L. Ed. 2d 696 (1998) (decided under prior law).

CIRCUIT COURT OPINIONS

Police officer responding to a call. — Sovereign immunity applies to a police officer involved in an automobile accident that occurs after the official call to which the officer was responding had been cancelled but before the officer was aware of the cancellation. Reid v. Hammer, 62 Va. Cir. 251, 2003 Va. Cir. LEXIS 284 (Richmond 2003).

§ 15.2-1701. Organization of police forces.

Any locality may, by ordinance, provide for the organization of its authorized police forces. Such forces shall include a chief of police, and such officers and other personnel as appropriate.

When a locality provides for a police department, the chief of police shall be the chief law-enforcement officer of that locality. However, in towns, the chief law-enforcement officer may be called the town sergeant.

History.
1979, c. 333, § 15.1-131.7; 1997, c. 587.

OPINIONS OF THE ATTORNEY GENERAL

Jurisdiction. — Jurisdiction encompasses any locality or political subdivision, so that if a town has organized its own police department, that department, rather than the surrounding county's sheriff's office or police department is the primary law-enforcement agency. If the town does not have its own police department, then the responsibility for the orders and accompanying transportation falls to the county police department if there is one, and to the sheriff's office if there is not. See opinion of Attorney General to Karen T. Mullins, Esquire, County Attorney, Wise County, 11-123, 2011 Va. AG LEXIS 44 (10/21/11).

Primary law-enforcement agency for purposes of execution of orders subjecting a person to emergency custody or temporary detention, or providing for the transportation of such persons. — In jurisdictions served by police departments, the police department rather than the sheriff is the "primary law-enforcement agency" to execute both emergency custody under § 37.2-808 and temporary detention orders under § 37.2-810 and to provide transportation pursuant to such orders. See opinion of Attorney General to Karen T. Mullins, Esquire, County Attorney, Wise County, 11-123, 2011 Va. AG LEXIS 44 (10/21/11).

Appointment of town sergeant. — A charter town is authorized to appoint a town sergeant and any other necessary officers to enforce the laws of the Commonwealth within the town and, pursuant to § 15.2-1726, is authorized to enter into a reciprocal agreement with another town for the provision of law-enforcement assistance. See opinion of Attorney General to Daniel M. Siegel, Esq., Town Attorney for Charlotte Court House, 08-076 (10/9/08).

Where a town charter specifically includes the office of "town sergeant, who shall be the conservator of the peace," the appointment of a town sergeant is authorized when the town council deems such appointment to be proper and necessary, and two charter towns may enter into a valid, reciprocal agreement to contract for the services of a town sergeant provided the town charters of both towns authorize the appointment of a town sergeant. See opinion of Attorney General to Jennifer LeLacheur Jones, Esq., Town Attorney for Drakes Branch, 08-071 (10/9/08).

§ 15.2-1702. Referendum required prior to establishment of county police force.

A. A county shall not establish a police force unless (i) such action is first approved by the voters of the county in accordance with the provisions of this section and (ii) the General Assembly enacts appropriate authorizing legislation.

B. The governing body of any county shall petition the court, by resolution, asking that a referendum be held on the question, "Shall a police force be established in the county and the sheriff's office be relieved of primary law-enforcement responsibilities?" The court, by order entered of record in accordance with Article 5 (§ 24.2-681 et seq.) of Chapter 6 of Title 24.2, shall require the regular election officials of the county to open the polls and take the sense of the voters on the question as herein provided.

The clerk of the circuit court for the county shall publish notice of the election in a newspaper of general circulation in the county once a week for three consecutive weeks prior to the election. The notice shall contain the ballot question and a statement of not more than 500 words on the proposed question. The explanation shall be presented in plain English, shall be limited to a neutral explanation, and shall not present arguments by either proponents or opponents of the proposal. The attorney for the county or city or, if there is no county or city attorney, the attorney for the Commonwealth shall prepare the explanation. "Plain English" means written in nontechnical, readily understandable language using words of common everyday usage and avoiding legal terms and phrases or other terms and words of art whose usage or special meaning primarily is limited to a particular field or profession.

C. The county may expend public funds to produce and distribute neutral information concerning the referendum; provided, however, public funds may not be used to promote a particular position on the question, either in the notice called for in subsection B, or in any other distribution of information to the public.

D. The regular election officers of the county shall open the polls on the date specified in such order and conduct the election in the manner provided by law. The election shall be by ballot which shall be prepared by the electoral board of the county and on which shall be printed the following:

"Shall a police force be established in the county and the sheriff's office be relieved of primary law-enforcement responsibilities?

☐ Yes
☐ No"

The ballots shall be counted, returns made and canvassed as in other elections, and the results certified by the electoral board to the court ordering the election. If a majority of the voters voting in the election vote "Yes," the court shall enter an order proclaiming the results of the election and a duly certified copy of such order shall be transmitted to the governing body of the county. The governing body shall proceed to establish a police force following the enactment of authorizing legislation by the General Assembly.

E. After a referendum has been conducted pursuant to this section, no subsequent referendum shall be conducted pursuant to this section in the same county for a period of four years from the date of the prior referendum.

History.
1983, c. 341, § 15.1-131.6:1; 1993, c. 630; 1997, c. 587; 2000, c. 298.

§ 15.2-1703. Referendum to abolish county police force.

The police force in any county which established the force subsequent to July 1, 1983, may be abolished and its responsibilities assumed by the sheriff's office after a referendum held pursuant to this section.

Either (i) the voters of the county by petition signed by not less than ten percent of the registered voters therein on the January 1 preceding the filing of the petition or (ii) the governing body of the county, by resolution, may petition the circuit court for the county that a referendum be held on the question, "Shall the county police force be abolished and its responsibilities assumed by the county sheriff's office?" The court, by order entered of record in accordance with Article 5 (§ 24.2-681 et seq.) of Chapter 6 of Title 24.2, shall require the regular election officials of the county at the next general election held in the county to open the polls and take the sense of the voters on the question as herein provided. The clerk of the circuit court for the county shall publish notice of the election in a newspaper of general circulation in the county once a week for three consecutive weeks prior to the election.

The ballot shall be printed as follows:

"Shall the county police force be abolished and its responsibilities assumed by the county sheriff's office?

☐ Yes
☐ No"

The election shall be held and the results certified as provided in § 24.2-684. If a majority of the voters voting in the election vote in favor of the question, the court shall enter an order proclaiming the results of the election, and a duly certified copy of such order shall be transmitted to the governing body of the county. The governing body shall proceed with the necessary action to abolish the police force and transfer its responsibilities to the sheriff's office, to become effective on July 1 following the referendum.

Once a referendum has been held pursuant to this section, no further referendum shall be held pursuant to this section within four years thereafter.

History.
1988, c. 660, § 15.1-131.6:2; 1997, c. 587.

§ 15.2-1704. Powers and duties of police force.

A. The police force of a locality is hereby invested with all the power and authority which formerly belonged to the office of constable at common law and is responsible for the prevention and detection of crime, the apprehension of criminals, the safeguard of life and property, the preservation of peace and the enforcement of state and local laws, regulations, and ordinances.

B. A police officer has no authority in civil matters, except (i) to execute and serve temporary detention and emergency custody orders and any other powers granted to law-enforcement officers in § 16.1-340, 16.1-340.1, 37.2-808, or 37.2-809, (ii) to serve an order of protection pursuant to §§ 16.1-253.1, 16.1-253.4, and 16.1-279.1, (iii) to execute all warrants or summons as may be placed in his hands by any magistrate serving the locality and to make due return thereof, and (iv) to deliver, serve, execute, and enforce orders of isolation and quarantine issued pursuant to §§ 32.1-48.09, 32.1-48.012, and 32.1-48.014 and to deliver, serve, execute, and enforce an emergency custody order issued pursuant to § 32.1-48.02. A town police officer, after receiving training under subdivision 8 of § 9.1-102, may, with the concurrence of the local sheriff, also serve civil papers, and make return thereof, only when the town is the plaintiff and the defendant can be found within the corporate limits of the town.

History.
Code 1950, § 15-557; 1960, c. 167; 1962, c. 623, § 15.1-138; 1982, c. 38; 1984, c. 661; 1992, cc. 729, 742; 1995, c. 844; 1997, c. 587; 1998, c. 425; 1999, c. 495; 2007, c. 724; 2008, cc. 551, 691; 2010, cc. 778, 825.

Law Review.
For article, "City of Canton v. Harris: Municipality Liability Under 42 U.S.C. Section 1983 for Inadequate Police Training," see 12 G.M.U. L. Rev. 757 (1990).

Michie's Jurisprudence.
For related discussion, see 2A M.J. Arrest, § 4; 15 M.J. Public Officers, § 45.

CASE NOTES

A police officer is an officer of the State and not a city officer. Burch v. Hardwicke, 71 Va. (30 Gratt.) 24, 32 Am. R. 640

(1878); Smith v. Bryan, 100 Va. 199, 40 S.E. 652 (1902); Sherry v. Lumpkin, 127 Va. 116, 102 S.E. 658 (1920); City of Alexandria v. McClary, 167 Va. 199, 188 S.E. 158 (1936) (decided under prior law).

This section and former § 15.1-137 (see now §§ 15.2-1704, 15.2-1710) merely set out the general powers of a municipality to create a police force; the sections do not require a municipality to act, and therefore do not create any public rights; there is no public policy right of action for the enforcement of nonpublic rights, and thus the plaintiff officers stated no public policy claim. Childress v. City of Richmond, 907 F. Supp. 934 (E.D. Va. 1995), aff'd, 134 F.3d 1205 (4th Cir. 1998), cert. denied, 524 U.S. 927, 118 S. Ct. 2322, 141 L. Ed. 2d 696 (1998) (decided under prior law).

Implied authority to issue barment notices. — Municipal police officers may be given the limited authority pursuant to a property owner's power of attorney to issue barment notices to unauthorized parties on the property as this authority furthers the objective of the police to prevent crime, to protect life and property and to preserve the peace, and is necessarily implied in the powers expressly granted by statute. Holland v. Commonwealth, 28 Va. App. 67, 502 S.E.2d 145 (1998) (decided under prior law).

The power of police to bar individuals from trespassing on premises pursuant to an ongoing request for assistance from the owner of the premises is necessarily implied in the powers expressly granted by statute. Collins v. Commonwealth, 30 Va. App. 443, 517 S.E.2d 277 (1999).

Policeman may act within city or one mile thereof. — The power of a policeman to make an arrest by virtue of his office is subject to well recognized territorial limits. He can act only within his city or within one mile of its corporate limits. City of Alexandria v. McClary, 167 Va. 199, 188 S.E. 158 (1936); Banks v. Bradley, 192 Va. 598, 66 S.E.2d 526 (1951) (decided under prior law).

OPINIONS OF THE ATTORNEY GENERAL

Police officers may not enforce fee limit imposed in lieu of towing trespassing vehicle. — Local police officers may not enforce the fee limit for which the owner of a trespassing vehicle is liable to a towing company, in lieu of towing the vehicle. See opinion of Attorney General to The Honorable Marsha L. Garst, Commonwealth's Attorney for the City of Harrisonburg and Rockingham County, 00-028 (11/31/00).

Duty to retrieve and return fugitive. — When a fugitive is held in another locality, it is the duty of the police department of the locality issuing the warrant to retrieve and return the fugitive to the court. See opinion of Attorney General to The Honorable H. S.Caudill, Sheriff for Tazewell County, 02-096 (12/20/02).

Virginia law-enforcement officers have authority to detain and arrest individuals who have committed violations of the laws of the United States and other states, and such authority extends to violations of federal criminal immigration law. It would not be advisable to enforce such violations outside of the scope of an agreement with federal authorities. See opinion of Attorney General to The Honorable Kenneth W. Stolle, Member, Senate of Virginia, and The Honorable David B. Albo, Member, House of Delegates, 07-086 (10/15/07).

Police officers may not distrain property. — Police officers do not have the civil authority to distrain property for payments owed to a city. See opinion of Attorney General to Ms. Barbara O. Carraway, City Treasurer for the City of Chesapeake, 10-040, 2010 Va. AG LEXIS 33 (7/8/10).

Law-enforcement officers may inquire into immigration status. — Virginia law-enforcement officers, including conservation officers, may inquire into the immigration status of persons stopped or arrested; however, persons tasked with enforcing zoning laws lack the authority to investigate criminal violations of the law, including criminal violations of the immigration laws of the United States. See opinion of Attorney General to The Honorable Robert G. Marshall, Member, Virginia House of Delegates, 10-047, 2010 Va. AG LEXIS 37 (7/30/10).

§ 15.2-1705. Minimum qualifications; waiver.

A. The chief of police and all police officers of any locality, all deputy sheriffs and jail officers in this

Commonwealth, and all law-enforcement officers as defined in § 9.1-101 who enter upon the duties of such office after July 1, 1994, are required to meet the following minimum qualifications for office. Such person shall (i) be a citizen of the United States, (ii) be required to undergo a background investigation including fingerprint-based criminal history records inquiries to both the Central Criminal Records Exchange and the Federal Bureau of Investigation, (iii) have a high school education or have passed the General Educational Development exam, (iv) possess a valid driver's license if required by the duties of office to operate a motor vehicle, (v) undergo a physical examination, subsequent to a conditional offer of employment, conducted under the supervision of a licensed physician, (vi) be at least eighteen years of age, (vii) not have been convicted of or pled guilty or no contest to a felony or any offense that would be a felony if committed in the Commonwealth, and (viii) not have produced a positive result on a pre-employment drug screening, if such screening is required by the hiring law-enforcement agency or jail, where the positive result cannot be explained to the law-enforcement agency or jail administrator's satisfaction. In addition, all such officers who enter upon the duties of such office on or after July 1, 2013, shall not have been convicted of or pled guilty or no contest to (a) any misdemeanor involving moral turpitude, including but not limited to petit larceny under § 18.2-96, or any offense involving moral turpitude that would be a misdemeanor if committed in the Commonwealth, (b) any misdemeanor sex offense in the Commonwealth, another state, or the United States, including but not limited to sexual battery under § 18.2-67.4 or consensual sexual intercourse with a minor 15 or older under clause (ii) of § 18.2-371, or (c) domestic assault under § 18.2-57.2 or any offense that would be domestic assault under the laws of another state or the United States.

B. Upon request of a sheriff or chief of police, or the director or chief executive of any agency or department employing law-enforcement officers as defined in § 9.1-101, or jail officers as defined in § 53.1-1, the Department of Criminal Justice Services is hereby authorized to waive the requirements for qualification as set out in subsection A of this section for good cause shown.

History.
1982, c. 442, § 15.1-131.8; 1988, c. 396; 1994, cc. 850, 905; 1995, c. 112; 1997, c. 587; 2013, cc. 307, 468.

Cross references.
As to appointment of special conservators of the peace, see § 19.2-13.

The 2013 amendments.
The 2013 amendments by cc. 307 and 468 are identical, and in subsection A, substituted "pled guilty" for "pleaded guilty" and "the Commonwealth" for "Virginia" in clause (vii), and added the last sentence.

§ 15.2-1706. Certification through training required for all law-enforcement officers; waiver of requirements.

A. All law-enforcement officers as defined in § 9.1-101 and all jail officers as defined in § 53.1-1 must be certified through the successful completion of training at an approved criminal justice training academy in order to remain eligible for appointment or employment. In order to obtain such certification, all entry level law-enforcement officers seeking certification on or after July 1, 2003, shall successfully complete statewide certification examinations developed and administered by the Department of Criminal Justice Services. The Department may delegate administration of the examinations to an approved criminal justice training academy and may revoke such delegation at its discretion. The appointee's or employee's hiring agency must provide the Department of Criminal Justice Services with verification that law-enforcement or jail officers first hired after July 1, 1994, have met the minimum standards set forth in § 15.2-1705.

B. The requirement for the successful completion of the law-enforcement certification examination may be waived by the Department of Criminal Justice Services based upon previous law-enforcement experience and training. To be eligible for such waiver, the individual must have applied for and been granted an exemption or partial exemption in accordance with § 9.1-116.

History.
1994, cc. 850, 905, § 15.1-131.8:1; 1995, c. 112; 1997, c. 587; 1999, c. 635; 2002, c. 345; 2004, c. 477.

Cross references.
As to the powers and duties of the Department of Criminal Justice Services and the Criminal Justice Services Board, see § 9.1-102. As to appointment of conservators of the peace, see § 19.2-12.

§ 15.2-1707. Decertification of law-enforcement officers.

A. The sheriff, chief of police, or agency administrator shall notify the Criminal Justice Services Board in writing when any certified law-enforcement or jail officer currently employed by his agency has (i) been convicted of or pled guilty or no contest to a felony or any offense that would be a felony if committed in the Commonwealth, (ii) been convicted of or pled guilty or no contest to a Class 1 misdemeanor involving moral turpitude or any offense that would be any misdemeanor involving moral turpitude, including but not limited to petit larceny under § 18.2-96, or any offense involving moral turpitude that would be a misdemeanor if committed in the Commonwealth, (iii) been convicted of or pled guilty or no contest to any misdemeanor sex offense in the Commonwealth, another state, or the United States, including but not limited to sexual battery under § 18.2-67.4 or consensual sexual intercourse with a minor 15 or older under clause (ii) of § 18.2-371, (iv) been convicted of or pled guilty or no contest to domestic assault under § 18.2-57.2 or any offense that would be domestic assault under the laws of another state or the United States, (v) failed to comply with or maintain compliance with mandated training requirements, or (vi) refused to submit to a drug screening or has produced a positive result on a drug screening reported to the employing agency, where the positive result cannot be explained to the agency administrator's satisfaction. Notification shall also be provided in writing for any employee who resigned or was terminated in advance of being convicted or found guilty of an offense that requires decertification or who resigned or was terminated in advance of a pending drug screening. The notification, where appropriate, shall be accompanied by a copy of the judgment of conviction. Upon receiving such notice from the sheriff, chief of police, or agency administrator, or from an attorney for the Commonwealth, the Criminal Justice Services Board shall decertify such law-enforcement or jail officer. Such officer shall not have the right to serve as a law-enforcement officer within the Commonwealth until his certification has been reinstated by the Board.

B. When a conviction has not become final, the Board may decline to decertify the officer until the conviction becomes final, after considering the likelihood of irreparable damage to the officer if such officer is decertified during the pendency of an ultimately successful appeal, the likelihood of injury or damage to the public if the officer is not decertified, and the seriousness of the offense.

C. The Department of Criminal Justice Services is hereby authorized to waive the requirements for decertification as set out in subsection A for good cause shown.

D. The Criminal Justice Services Board may initiate decertification proceedings against any former law-enforcement or jail officer whom the Board has found to have been convicted of an offense that requires decertification or who has failed to comply with or maintain compliance with mandated training requirements.

History.

1994, cc. 850, 905, § 15.1-131.8:2; 1995, c. 112; 1997, c. 587; 2013, cc. 307, 468.

Cross references.

As to the powers and duties of the Department of Criminal Justice Services and the Criminal Justice Services Board, see § 9.1-102.

The 2013 amendments.

The 2013 amendments by cc. 307 and 468 are identical, and added the subsection A and B designators to the former first and third paragraphs and rewrote the first paragraph which read: "Upon written notification from the sheriff, chief of police or agency administrator that any certified law-enforcement or jail officer has (i) been convicted of or pled guilty or no contest to a felony or any offense that would be a felony if committed in Virginia, (ii) failed to comply with or maintain compliance with mandated training requirements, or (iii) refused to submit to a drug screening or has produced a positive result on a drug screening reported to the employing agency, where the positive result cannot be explained to the agency administrator's satisfaction, which notification, where appropriate, shall be accompanied by a copy of the judgment of conviction, the Criminal Justice Services Board shall decertify such law-enforcement or jail officer. Such officer shall not have the right to serve as a law-enforcement officer within this Commonwealth until his certification has been reinstated by the Board"; deleted the former second paragraph which read: "The clerk of any court in which a conviction of a felony is made who has knowledge that a law-enforcement or jail officer has been convicted shall have a duty to report these findings promptly to the employing agency"; and added subsections C and D.

§ 15.2-1708. Notice of decertification.

A. Service of notice. The Board shall, within ten days of decertification, serve notice upon an affected officer, in person or by certified mail, and upon the law-enforcement or jail agency employing said officer, by certified mail, specifying the action taken and remedies available. The Board shall stay final action until the period for requesting a hearing expires.

B. Decertification hearing. Any law-enforcement or jail officer who has been decertified may, within thirty days of receipt of notice served by the Board, request, by certified mail, a hearing which shall be granted by the Board. Upon receipt of such request, the Board shall set a date, time, and place for the hearing within sixty days and serve notice by certified mail upon the affected officer. The Board, or a committee thereof, shall conduct such hearing. The affected officer may be represented by counsel. In the absence of a request for hearing, decertification shall, without further proceedings, become final thirty days after the initial notice.

C. Standard of review. The decertification of a law-enforcement or jail officer under § 15.2-1707 shall be sustained by the Board unless such law-enforcement or jail officer shows, by a preponderance of the evidence, good cause for his certification to be reinstated.

D. Final decision after request for hearing. The Board shall render a final decision within thirty days.

E. Notice of final action. The Board shall notify the officer and the law-enforcement or jail agency involved, by certified mail, of the final action regarding decertification.

F. Reinstatement after decertification. Any officer who is decertified may, after a period of not less than five years, petition the Board to be considered for reinstatement of certification.

History.

1994, cc. 850, 905, § 15.1-131.8:3; 1995, c. 112; 1997, c. 587.

§ 15.2-1709. Employer immunity from liability; disclosure of information regarding former deputy sheriffs and law-enforcement officers.

Any sheriff or chief of police, the director or chief executive of any agency or department employing deputy sheriffs or law-enforcement officers as defined § 9.1-101, or jail officers as defined in § 53.1-1, and the Director of the Department of Criminal Justice Services or his designee who discloses information about a former deputy sheriff's or law-enforcement officer's or jail officer's job performance to a prospective law-enforcement or jail employer of the former appointee or employee is presumed to be acting in good faith and, unless lack of good faith is shown by clear and convincing evidence, is immune from civil liability for such disclosure or its consequences. For purposes of this section, the presumption of good faith is rebutted upon a showing that the information disclosed by the former employer was knowingly false or deliberately misleading, was rendered with malicious purpose, or violated any civil right of the former employee or appointee.

History.
 1994, cc. 850, 905, § 15.1-131.8:4; 1995, c. 112; 1997, c. 587.

§ 15.2-1710. Fees and other compensation.

A police officer shall not receive any fee or other compensation out of the state treasury or the treasury of a locality for any service rendered under the provisions of this chapter other than the salary paid him by the locality and a fee as a witness in cases arising under the criminal laws of the Commonwealth. A police officer shall not receive any fee as a witness in any case arising under the ordinances of his locality, nor for attendance as a witness before any magistrate serving his locality. However, if it is necessary or expedient for him to travel beyond the limits of the locality in his capacity as a police officer, he shall be entitled to his actual expenses, as provided by law for other expenses in criminal cases.

Nothing in this section shall be construed as prohibiting a police officer of a locality from claiming and receiving any reward which may be offered for the arrest and detention of any offender against the criminal laws of this or any other state or nation.

History.
 Code 1950, § 15-557; 1960, c. 167; 1962, c. 623, § 15.1-138; 1982, c. 38; 1984, c. 661; 1992, cc. 729, 742; 1995, c. 844; 1997, c. 587; 2008, cc. 551, 691.

Cross references.
 As to right of sheriffs, sergeants, their deputies and other officers to receive rewards, see § 19.2-7.

Law Review.
 For comment, "Effect of Public Policy upon Reward Offers," see 20 Wash. & Lee L. Rev. 395 (1963).

Michie's Jurisprudence.
 For related discussion, see 15 M.J. Public Officers, § 45.

CASE NOTES

Right to receive rewards. — An exception to the general rule, that an officer cannot receive a reward for the discharge of a public duty with respect to the arrest and detention of a criminal, is made by this section in behalf of members of the police force of cities and towns. Buek v. Nance, 112 Va. 28, 70 S.E. 515 (1911) (decided under prior law).

Reward denied deputy sergeant. — A deputy sergeant of a city, who, as jailor, has custody of a prisoner, and obtains from him a confession which leads to the recovery and restoration of stolen property, is not a policeman within the meaning of this section and cannot recover a reward offered therefor. Buek v. Nance, 112 Va. 28, 70 S.E. 515 (1911) (decided under prior law).

§ 15.2-1711. Providing legal fees and expenses for law-enforcement officers; repayment to locality of two-thirds of amount by Compensation Board.

If any law-enforcement officer is investigated, arrested or indicted or otherwise prosecuted on any criminal charge arising out of any act committed in the discharge of his official duties, and no charges are brought, the charge is subsequently dismissed or upon trial he is found not guilty, the governing body of the locality wherein he is appointed may reimburse such officer for reasonable legal fees and expenses incurred by him in defense of such investigation or charge; such reimbursement shall be paid from the treasury of the locality.

When a governing body reimburses its sheriff or a law-enforcement officer in the sheriff's employment for reasonable legal fees and expenses as provided for in this section, then, upon certification of the reimbursement to the Chairman of the Compensation Board by the presiding officer of the governing body, the Compensation Board shall pay to the applicable locality two-thirds of the amount so certified.

History.
 1975, c. 31, § 15.1-131.6; 1979, c. 600; 1980, c. 106; 1985, c. 321; 1997, c. 587.

§ 15.2-1712. Employment of off-duty officers.

Notwithstanding the provisions of §§ 2.2-3100 through 2.2-3127, any locality may adopt an ordinance which permits law-enforcement officers and deputy sheriffs in such locality to engage in off-duty employment which may occasionally require the use of their police powers in the performance of such employment. Such ordinance may include reasonable rules to apply to such off-duty employment, or it may delegate the promulgation of such reasonable rules to the chief of the respective police departments or the sheriff of the county or city.

History.
 1978, c. 537, § 15.1-133.1; 1997, c. 587.

CASE NOTES

Plaintiff was not deprived of liberty interest with police regulation. — Police regulation, which placed limits on the outside employment of police officers by making such employment subject to the approval of the chief of police, under which plaintiff, a licensed private investigator, was denied permission to engage in outside employment as a private investigator performing domestic surveillance and background investigations, bore a rational connection to the promotion of safety of persons and property and was not arbitrary and irrational, and therefore, plaintiff suffered no deprivation of any assumed liberty interest thereby. Decker v. City of Hampton, 741 F. Supp. 1223 (E.D. Va. 1990) (decided under prior law).

CIRCUIT COURT OPINIONS

Sovereign immunity. — Police officer sued for negligence in directing traffic while off duty was entitled to sovereign immunity because regulating traffic was a governmental function, even when performed by an off-duty officer, which required the use discretion and judgment. Bailey v. Lewis, 2012 Va. Cir. LEXIS 92 (Portsmouth Oct. 5, 2012).

OPINIONS OF THE ATTORNEY GENERAL

Attorney General could not issue official advisory opinion on question requiring factual determination. — Whether law-enforcement officers employed pursuant to § 15.2-1712 are considered to be performing "law-enforcement activities" for purposes of workers' compensation and personal and property damage liability coverage under a local government risk management insurance program is a question requiring a factual determination rather than an interpretation of law; therefore, the Attorney General could not issue an official advisory opinion on the question. See opinion of Attorney General to The Honorable William C. Mims, Member, Senate of Virginia, 01-047 (12/27/01).

§ 15.2-1713. Localities authorized to offer and pay rewards in felony and misdemeanor cases.

When any felony or misdemeanor has been committed, or there has been any attempt to commit a felony in any locality, the governing body of the locality or its duly authorized agent may offer and pay a reward for the arrest and final conviction of the person or persons who committed the felony or misdemeanor or attempted to commit the felony. The reward may be paid out of the general fund of such locality.

History.
1983, c. 525, § 15.1-137.2; 1984, c. 661; 1997, c. 587.

Law Review.
For comment, "Effect of Public Policy upon Reward Offers," see 20 Wash. & Lee L. Rev. 395 (1963).

§ 15.2-1713.1. Local "Crime Stoppers" programs; confidentiality.

A. As used in this section, a "Crime Stoppers," "crime solvers," "crime line," or other similarly named organization is defined as a private, non-profit Virginia corporation governed by a civilian volunteer board of directors that is operated on a local or statewide level that (i) offers anonymity to persons providing information to the organization, (ii) accepts and expends donations for cash rewards to persons who report to the organization information about alleged criminal activity and that the organization forwards to the appropriate law-enforcement agency, and (iii) is established as a cooperative alliance between the news media, the community, and law-enforcement officials.

B. Evidence of a communication or any information contained therein between a person submitting

a report of an alleged criminal act to a "Crime Stoppers" organization and the person who accepted the report on behalf of the organization is not admissible in a court proceeding. Law-enforcement agencies receiving information concerning alleged criminal activity from a "Crime Stoppers" organization shall maintain confidentiality pursuant to subdivision A 3 of § 2.2-3706.

History.
2003, cc. 754, 760; 2013, c. 695.

Cross references.
As to dissemination of criminal history record information, see § 19.2-389.

The 2013 amendments.
The 2013 amendment by c. 695 substituted "subdivision A 3" for "subsection E" near the end of subsection B.

§ 15.2-1714. Establishing police lines, perimeters, or barricades.

Whenever fires, accidents, wrecks, explosions, crimes, riots or other emergency situations where life, limb or property may be endangered may cause persons to collect on the public streets, alleys, highways, parking lots or other public area, the chief law-enforcement officer of any locality or that officer's authorized representative who is responsible for the security of the scene may establish such areas, zones or perimeters by the placement of police lines or barricades as are reasonably necessary to (i) preserve the integrity of evidence at such scenes, (ii) notwithstanding the provisions of §§ 46.2-888 through 46.2-891, facilitate the movement of vehicular and pedestrian traffic into, out of and around the scene, (iii) permit firefighters, police officers and emergency services personnel to perform necessary operations unimpeded, and (iv) protect persons and property.

Any police line or barricade erected for these purposes shall be clearly identified by wording such as "Police Line — DO NOT CROSS" or other similar wording. If material or equipment is not available for identifying the prohibited area, then a verbal warning by identifiable law-enforcement officials positioned to indicate a location of a police line or barricade shall be given to any person or persons attempting to cross police lines or barricades without proper authorization.

Such scene may be secured no longer than is reasonably necessary to effect the above-described purposes. Nothing in this section shall limit or otherwise affect the authority of, or be construed to deny access to such scene by, any person charged by law with the responsibility of rendering assistance at or investigating any such fires, accidents, wrecks, explosions, crimes or riots.

Personnel from information services such as press, radio and television, when gathering news, shall be exempt from the provisions of this section except that it shall be unlawful for such persons to obstruct the police, firemen and rescue workers in the performance of their duties at such scene. Such personnel shall proceed at their own risk.

History.
1984, c. 533, § 15.1-140.1; 1990, c. 327; 1997, c. 587.

Cross references.
As to the penalty for crossing established police lines, perimeters or barricades, see § 18.2-414.2.

§ 15.2-1715. Authority to declare Intensified Drug Enforcement Jurisdictions; expenditure of funds.

Whenever, in the judgment of the Governor or his designee, a locality or multi-jurisdictional area is confronted with a drug trafficking problem of such a magnitude as to warrant additional resources to supplement the efforts of local officials responsible for the apprehension and prosecution of persons engaged in drug trafficking activities, he may declare such areas Intensified Drug Enforcement Jurisdictions. Upon such declaration, the Governor, or his designee, may make available funds from the Intensified Drug Enforcement Jurisdictions Fund provided for in § 9.1-105.

History.
1990, c. 971, § 15.1-131.12; 1997, c. 587.

Cross references.
As to powers and duties of a drug law enforcement and investigation division of State Police, see § 52-8.1:1.

§ 15.2-1716. Reimbursement of expenses incurred in responding to DUI and related incidents.

A. Any locality may provide by ordinance that a person convicted of violating any of the following provisions shall, at the time of sentencing or in a separate civil action, be liable to the locality or to any responding volunteer fire or rescue squad, or both, for restitution of reasonable expenses incurred by the locality for responding law enforcement, firefighting, rescue and emergency services, including those incurred by the sheriff's office of such locality, or by any volunteer fire or rescue squad, or by any combination of the foregoing, when providing an appropriate emergency response to any accident or incident related to such violation. The ordinance may further provide that a person convicted of violating any of the following provisions shall, at the time of sentencing or in a separate civil action, be liable to the locality or to any responding volunteer fire or rescue squad, or both, for restitution of reasonable expenses incurred by the locality when issuing any related arrest warrant or summons, including the expenses incurred by the sheriff's office of such locality, or by any volunteer fire or rescue squad, or by any combination of the foregoing:

1. The provisions of § 18.2-36.1, 18.2-51.4, 18.2-266, 18.2-266.1, 29.1-738, 29.1-738.02, or 46.2-341.24, or a similar ordinance, when such operation of a motor vehicle, engine, train or watercraft while so impaired is the proximate cause of the accident or incident;

2. The provisions of Article 7 (§ 46.2-852 et seq.) of Chapter 8 of Title 46.2 relating to reckless driving, when such reckless driving is the proximate cause of the accident or incident;

3. The provisions of Article 1 (§ 46.2-300 et seq.) of Chapter 3 of Title 46.2 relating to driving without a license or driving with a suspended or revoked license; and

4. The provisions of § 46.2-894 relating to improperly leaving the scene of an accident.

B. Personal liability under this section for reasonable expenses of an appropriate emergency response pursuant to subsection A shall not exceed $1,000 in the aggregate for a particular accident, arrest, or incident occurring in such locality. In determining the "reasonable expenses," a locality may bill a flat fee of $350 or a minute-by-minute accounting of the actual costs incurred. As used in this section, "appropriate emergency response" includes all costs of providing law-enforcement, firefighting, rescue, and emergency medical services. The court may order as restitution the reasonable expenses incurred by the locality for responding law enforcement, firefighting, rescue and emergency medical services. The provisions of this section shall not preempt or limit any remedy available to the Commonwealth, to the locality or to any volunteer rescue squad to recover the reasonable expenses of an emergency response to an accident or incident not involving impaired driving, operation of a vehicle or other conduct as set forth herein.

History.
1994, c. 617, § 15.1-132.1; 1995, cc. 683, 685, 830; 1997, cc. 587, 691; 2001, c. 505; 2003, c. 796; 2004, c. 273; 2005, cc. 148, 366; 2006, c. 679; 2009, c. 245; 2010, c. 343.

Cross references.
As to suspension for failure to satisfy motor vehicle accident judgment, see § 46.2-417.

Law Review.
For 2003/2004 survey of criminal law and procedure, see 39 U. Rich. L. Rev. 133 (2004).

OPINIONS OF THE ATTORNEY GENERAL

Reimbursement of expenses arising from DUI event. — County may not seek reimbursement pursuant to this section for expenses incurred by a law-enforcement officer performing routine duties that result in a DUI conviction. See opinion of Attorney General to Mr. J. Thompson Shrader, County Attorney for Amherst County, 04-054 (9/23/04) (but see later amendments to this section).

County may be compensated, in limited circumstances, for reasonable expenses incurred in providing an appropriate emergency response to an accident or incident related to the DUI conviction, even when fire, rescue, or extra law-enforcement personnel do not participate. See opinion of Attorney General to Mr. J. Thompson Shrader, County Attorney for Amherst County, 04-054 (9/23/04) (but see later amendments to this section).

Billing for emergency services. — Section 27-14 does not permit a locality to adopt an ordinance authorizing a volunteer fire department to assess and charge a fee to an individual's homeowners' or automobile insurance policy for responding to a fire emergency. See opinion of Attorney General to The Honorable Clarence E. "Bud" Phillips, Member, Virginia House of Delegates, 11-082, 2011 Va. AG LEXIS 55 (7/22/11).

Volunteer fire departments and rescue squads lack authority, either statutory or contractual, to bill home or automobile owners, or their insurance companies, for responding to a fire emergency. See opinion of Attorney General to The Honorable Clarence E. "Bud" Phillips, Member, Virginia House of Delegates, 11-052, 2011 Va. AG LEXIS 29 (5/13/11).

§ 15.2-1716.1. Reimbursement of expenses incurred in responding to terrorism hoax incident.

Any locality may provide by ordinance that any person who is convicted of a violation of subsection B or C of § 18.2-46.6, when his violation of such section is the proximate cause of any incident resulting in an appropriate emergency response, shall be liable at the time of sentencing or in a separate civil action to the locality or to any volunteer rescue squad, or both, which may provide such emergency response for the reasonable expense thereof, in an amount not to exceed $1,000 in the aggregate for a particular incident occurring in such locality. In determining the "reasonable expense," a locality may bill a flat fee of $250 or a minute-by-minute accounting of the actual costs incurred. As used in this section, "appropriate emergency response" includes all costs of providing law-enforcement, firefighting, rescue, and emergency medical services. The provisions of this section shall not preempt or limit any remedy available to the Commonwealth, to the locality or to any volunteer rescue squad to recover the reasonable expenses of an emergency response to an incident not involving a terroristic hoax as set forth herein.

History.
2002, cc. 588, 623; 2005, c. 479.

Cross references.
As to suspension for failure to satisfy motor vehicle accident judgment, see § 46.2-417.

§ 15.2-1716.2. Methamphetamine lab cleanup costs; localities may charge for reimbursement.

Any locality may provide by ordinance that any person who is convicted of an offense for manufacture of methamphetamine pursuant to § 18.2-248 or 18.2-248.03 shall be liable at the time of sentencing or in a separate civil action to the locality or to any other law-enforcement entity for the expense in cleaning up any methamphetamine lab related to the conviction. The amount charged shall not exceed the actual expenses associated with cleanup, removal, or repair of the affected property or the replacement cost of personal protective equipment used.

History.
2012, cc. 517, 616.

§ 15.2-1717. Preventing interference with pupils at schools.

Localities may adopt any reasonable ordinance necessary to prevent any improper interference with or annoyance of the pupils attending or boarding at any schools situated in such locality.

History.
Code 1950, § 15-558; 1962, c. 623, § 15.1-139; 1973, c. 401; 1984, c. 661; 1997, c. 587.

§ 15.2-1717.1. Designation of police to enforce trespass violations.

Any locality may by ordinance establish a procedure whereby the owner, lessee, custodian, or person lawfully in charge as those terms are used in § 18.2-119, of real property may designate the local law-enforcement agency as a "person lawfully in charge of the property" for the purpose of forbidding another to go or remain upon the lands, buildings or premises as specified in the designation. The ordinance shall require that any such designation be in writing and on file with the local law-enforcement agency.

History.
1999, c. 275; 2002, c. 328.

§ 15.2-1718. Receipt of missing child reports.

No police or sheriff's department shall establish or maintain any policy which requires the observance of any waiting period before accepting a missing child report as defined in § 52-32. Upon receipt of a missing child report by any police or sheriff's department, the department shall immediately, but in all cases within two hours of receiving the report, enter identifying and descriptive data about the child into the Virginia Criminal Information Network and the National Crime Information Center Systems, forward the report to the Missing Children Information Clearinghouse within the Department of State Police, notify all other law-enforcement agencies in the area, and initiate an investigation of the case.

History.
1985, c. 259, § 15.1-131.9; 1990, c. 239; 1997, c. 587; 2004, cc. 248, 443.

Michie's Jurisprudence.
For related discussion, see 9B M.J. Infants, § 81.

§ 15.2-1718.1. Receipt of missing senior adult reports.

A. No police or sheriff's department shall establish or maintain any policy which requires the observance of any waiting period before accepting a missing senior adult report. Upon receipt of a missing senior adult report by any police or sheriff's department, the department shall immediately, but in all cases within two hours of receiving the report, enter identifying and descriptive data about the senior adult into the Virginia Criminal Information Network and the National Crime Information Center Systems, forward the report to the Department of State Police, notify all other law-enforcement agencies in the area, and initiate an investigation of the case.

B. For purposes of this section:

"Missing senior adult report" means a report prepared in a format prescribed by the Superintendent of State Police for use by law-enforcement agencies to report missing senior adult information and photograph to the Department of State Police.

History.
2007, cc. 486, 723.

Law Review.
For 2007 annual survey article, "Health Care Law," see 42 U. Rich. L. Rev. 441 (2007).

§ 15.2-1719. Disposal of unclaimed property in possession of sheriff or police.

Any locality may provide by ordinance for (i) the public sale in accordance with the provisions of this section or (ii) the retention for use by the law-enforcement agency, of any unclaimed personal property which has been in the possession of its law-enforcement agencies and unclaimed for a period of more than 60 days, after payment of a reasonable storage fee to the sheriff or other agency storing such property. No storage fee shall be charged or accounted for if such property has been stored by and is to be retained by the sheriff's office or other law-enforcement agency. As used herein, "unclaimed personal property" shall be any personal property belonging to another which has been acquired by a law-enforcement officer pursuant to his duties, which is not needed in any criminal prosecution, which has not been claimed by its rightful owner and which the State Treasurer has indicated will be declined if remitted under the Uniform Disposition of Unclaimed Property Act (§ 55-210.1 et seq.). Unclaimed bicycles and mopeds may also be disposed of in accordance with § 15.2-1720. Unclaimed firearms may also be disposed of in accordance with § 15.2-1721.

Prior to the sale or retention for use by the law-enforcement agency of any unclaimed item, the chief of police, sheriff or their duly authorized agents shall make reasonable attempts to notify the rightful owner of the property, obtain from the attorney for the Commonwealth in writing a statement advising that the item is not needed in any criminal prosecution, and cause to be published in a newspaper of general circulation in the locality once a week for two successive weeks, notice that there will be a public display and sale of unclaimed personal property. Such property, including property selected for retention by the law-enforcement agency, shall be described generally in the notice, together with the date, time and place of the sale and shall be made available for public viewing at the sale. The chief of police, sheriff or their duly authorized agents shall pay from the proceeds of sale the costs of advertisement, removal, storage, investigation as to ownership and liens, and notice of sale. The balance of the funds shall be held by such officer for the owner and paid to the owner upon satisfactory proof of ownership. Any unclaimed item retained for use by the law-enforcement agency shall become the property of the locality served by the agency and shall be retained only if, in the opinion of the chief law-enforcement officer, there is a legitimate use for the property by the agency and that retention of the item is a more economical alternative than purchase of a similar or equivalent item.

If no claim has been made by the owner for the property or proceeds of such sale within 60 days of the sale, the remaining funds shall be deposited in the general fund of the locality and the retained property may be placed into use by the law-enforcement agency. Any such owner shall be entitled to apply to the locality within three years from the date of the sale and, if timely application is made therefor and satisfactory proof of ownership of the funds or property is made, the locality shall pay the remaining proceeds of the sale or return the property to the owner without interest or other charges or compensation. No claim shall be made nor any suit, action or proceeding be instituted for the recovery of such funds or property after three years from the date of the sale.

History.
1982, c. 163, § 15.1-133.01; 1994, c. 144; 1997, c. 587; 2010, c. 333.

§ 15.2-1720. Localities authorized to license bicycles, electric power-assisted bicycles, mopeds, and electric personal assistive mobility devices; disposition of unclaimed bicycles, electric power-assisted bicycles, mopeds, and electric personal assistive mobility devices.

Any locality may, by ordinance, (i) provide for the public sale or donation to a charitable organization of any bicycle, electric personal assistive mobility device, electric power-assisted bicycle, or moped that has been in the possession of the police or sheriff's department, unclaimed, for more than thirty days; (ii) require every resident owner of a bicycle, electric power-assisted bicycle, electric personal assistive mobility device, or moped to obtain a license therefor and a license plate, tag, or adhesive license decal of such design and material as the ordinance may prescribe, to be substantially attached to the bicycle, electric personal assistive mobility device, electric power-assisted bicycle, or moped; (iii) prescribe the license fee, the license application forms and the license form; and (iv) prescribe penalties for operating a bicycle, electric personal assistive mobility device, electric power-assisted bicycle, or moped on public roads or streets within the locality without an attached license plate, tag, or adhesive decal. The ordinance shall require the license plates, tags, or adhesive decals to be provided by and at the cost of the locality. Any locality may provide that the license plates, tags, or adhesive decals shall be valid for the life of the bicycles, electric personal assistive mobility devices, electric power-assisted bicycles, and mopeds to which they are attached or for such other period as it may prescribe and may prescribe such fee therefor as it may deem reasonable. When any town license is required as provided for herein, the license shall be in lieu of any license required by any county ordinance. Any bicycle, electric personal assistive mobility device, electric power-assisted bicycle, or moped found and delivered to the police or sheriff's department by a private person that thereafter remains unclaimed for thirty days after the final date of publication as required herein may be given to the finder; however, the location and description of the bicycle, electric personal assistive mobility device, electric power-assisted bicycle, or moped shall be published at least once a week for two successive weeks in a newspaper of general circulation within the locality. In addition, if there is a license, tag, or adhesive license decal affixed to the bicycle, electric personal assistive mobility device, or electric power-assisted bicycle, or moped, the record owner shall be notified directly.

History.
Code 1950, § 15-554; 1962, c. 623, § 15.1-133; 1968, c. 24; 1970, c. 285; 1975, c. 76; 1986, c. 52; 1994, c. 449; 1997, c. 587; 2001, c. 834; 2002, c. 254; 2013, c. 783.

The 2013 amendments.
The 2013 amendment by c. 783, in clause (ii) of the first sentence, inserted the first occurrence of "electric personal assistive mobility device," and substituted "tag, or adhesive license decal" for "tag, and, in the case of an electric personal assistive mobility device, an adhesive license decal."

§ 15.2-1721. Disposal of unclaimed firearms or other weapons in possession of sheriff or police.

Any locality may destroy unclaimed firearms and other weapons which have been in the possession of law-enforcement agencies for a period of more than sixty days. For the purposes of this section, "unclaimed firearms and other weapons" means any firearm or other weapon belonging to another which has been acquired by a law-enforcement officer pursuant to his duties, which is not needed in any criminal prosecution, which has not been claimed by its rightful owner and which the State Treasurer has indicated will be declined if remitted under the Uniform Disposition of Unclaimed Property Act (§ 55-210.1 et seq.).

At the discretion of the chief of police, sheriff, or their duly authorized agents, unclaimed firearms and other weapons may be destroyed by any means which renders the firearms and other weapons permanently inoperable. Prior to the destruction of such firearms and other weapons, the chief of police, sheriff, or their duly authorized agents shall comply with the notice provision contained in § 15.2-1719.

History.
1990, c. 324, § 15.1-133.01:1; 1997, c. 587.

§ 15.2-1722. Certain records to be kept by sheriffs and chiefs of police.

A. It shall be the duty of the sheriff or chief of police of every locality to insure, in addition to other records required by law, the maintenance of adequate personnel, arrest, investigative, reportable incidents, and noncriminal incidents records necessary for the efficient operation of a law-enforcement agency. Failure of a sheriff or a chief of police to maintain such records or failure to relinquish such records to his successor in office shall constitute a misdemeanor. Former sheriffs or chiefs of police shall be allowed access to such files for preparation of a defense in any suit or action arising from the performance of their official duties as sheriff or chief of police. The enforcement of this section shall be the duty of the attorney for the Commonwealth of the county or city wherein the violation occurs.

B. For purposes of this section, the following definitions shall apply:

"Arrest records" means a compilation of information, centrally maintained in law-enforcement custody, of any arrest or temporary detention of an individual, including the identity of the person arrested or detained, the nature of the arrest or detention, and the charge, if any.

"Investigative records" means the reports of any systematic inquiries or examinations into criminal or suspected criminal acts which have been committed, are being committed, or are about to be committed.

"Noncriminal incidents records" means compilations of noncriminal occurrences of general interest to law-enforcement agencies, such as missing persons, lost and found property, suicides and accidental deaths.

"Personnel records" means those records maintained on each and every individual employed by a law-enforcement agency which reflect personal data concerning the employee's age, length of service, amount of training, education, compensation level, and other pertinent personal information.

"Reportable incidents records" means a compilation of complaints received by a law-enforcement agency and action taken by the agency in response thereto.

History.
1975, c. 290, § 15.1-135.1; 1979, c. 686; 1981, c. 284; 1997, c. 587; 1999, cc. 703, 726.

Cross references.
As to limitations on the release of criminal incident information, see § 2.2-3706. As to dissemination of criminal history record

information, see § 19.2-389. As to reports to be made by local law-enforcement officers, etc., to Central Criminal Records Exchange, see § 19.2-390.

CASE NOTES

Release of transcript. — Sheriff's voluntary release of transcript of a 911 system call did not waive his right to deny access to the actual tape under the exemption in subdivision B 5 of this section. Tull v. Brown, 255 Va. 177, 494 S.E.2d 855 (1998) (decided under former § 15.1-135.1).

Tape of call to county's 911 system was exempt from disclosure under this section as "noncriminal incidents records"; the county's 911 system was operated by the county sheriff's office during the performance of its traditional law-enforcement responsibilities and therefore the tape was a law-enforcement record. Tull v. Brown, 255 Va. 177, 494 S.E.2d 855 (1998) (decided under former § 15.1-135.1).

CIRCUIT COURT OPINIONS

Statutory duty not delegable. — Sheriff's deputies had no right to bring a claim under *Bowman v. State Bank of Keysville*, 229 Va. 534, 331 S.E.2d 797 (1985), for wrongful termination against the sheriff based on either § 15.2-1722 or the Virginia Fraud Against Taxpayers Act, § 8.01-216.1 et seq.; however, they did state a *Bowman* claim based on their duty under § 19.2-201 to report wrongful conduct. Bowman v. Hunt, 2011 Va. Cir. LEXIS 116 (Franklin County Aug. 16, 2011).

§ 15.2-1723. Validation of certain police forces.

Any police force in existence on July 1, 1980, whose existence is authorized or was authorized by any provision of law, general or special, that was repealed by Chapter 333 of the Acts of Assembly of 1979 is hereby validated and shall continue. Any police force in existence on December 1, 1996, whose existence is authorized or was authorized by any provision of law, general or special, that is repealed by this act is hereby validated and shall continue.

History.
1979, c. 333, § 15.1-142.2; 1983, c. 576; 1997, c. 587.

ARTICLE 2.

INTERJURISDICTIONAL LAW-ENFORCEMENT AUTHORITY AND AGREEMENTS.

§ 15.2-1724. Police and other officers may be sent beyond territorial limits.

Whenever the necessity arises (i) for the enforcement of laws designed to control or prohibit the use or sale of controlled drugs as defined in § 54.1-3401 or laws contained in Article 3 (§ 18.2-47 et seq.) of Chapter 4 or Article 3 (§ 18.2-344 et seq.) of Chapter 8 of Title 18.2, (ii) in response to any law-enforcement emergency involving any immediate threat to life or public safety, (iii) during the execution of the provisions of Article 4 (§ 37.2-808 et seq.) of Chapter 8 of Title 37.2 or § 16.1-340 or 16.1-340.1 relating to orders for temporary detention or emergency custody for mental health evaluation or (iv) during any emergency resulting from the existence of a state of war, internal disorder, or fire, flood, epidemic or other public disaster, the police officers and other officers, agents and employees of any locality, the police officers of the Division of Capitol Police, and the police of any state-supported institution of higher learning appointed pursuant to § 23-233 may, together with all necessary equipment, lawfully go or be sent beyond the territorial limits of such locality, such agency, or such state-supported institution of higher learning to any point within or without the Commonwealth to assist in meeting such emergency or need, or while enroute to a part of the jurisdiction which is only accessible by roads outside the jurisdiction. However, the police of any state-supported institution of higher learning may be sent only to a locality within the Commonwealth, or locality outside the Commonwealth, whose boundaries are contiguous with the locality in which such institution is located. No member of a police force of any state-supported institution of higher learning shall be sent beyond the territorial limits of the locality in which such institution is located unless such member has met the requirements established by the Department of Criminal Justice Services as provided in clause (i) of subdivision 2 of § 9.1-102.

In such event the acts performed for such purpose by such police officers or other officers, agents or employees and the expenditures made for such purpose by such locality, such agency, or a state-supported institution of higher learning shall be deemed conclusively to be for a public and governmental purpose, and all of the immunities from liability enjoyed by a locality, agency, or a state-supported institution of higher learning when acting through its police officers or other officers, agents or employees for a public or governmental purpose within its territorial limits shall be enjoyed by it to the same extent when such locality, agency, or a state-supported institution of higher learning within the Commonwealth is so acting, under this section or under other lawful authority, beyond its territorial limits.

The police officers and other officers, agents and employees of any locality, agency, or a state-supported institution of higher learning when acting hereunder or under other lawful authority beyond the territorial limits of such locality, agency, or such state-supported institution of higher learning shall have all of the immunities from liability and exemptions from laws, ordinances and regulations and shall have all of the pension, relief, disability, workers' compensation and other benefits enjoyed by them while performing their respective duties within the territorial limits of such locality, agency, or such state-supported institution of higher learning.

History.
Code 1950, § 15-552; 1962, c. 623, § 15.1-131; 1968, c. 800; 1971, Ex. Sess., c. 238; 1976, c. 457; 1977, c. 79; 1979, c. 503; 1984, c. 779;

1992, c. 566; 1993, c. 860; 1995, c. 844; 1997, c. 587; 2008, c. 437; 2010, cc. 778, 825; 2013, c. 428.

Cross references.
As to powers, duties and functions of Capitol Police, see § 30-34.2:1.

The 2013 amendments.
The 2013 amendment by c. 428, in the first paragraph, inserted "Article 3 (§ 18.2-47 et seq.) of Chapter 4 or" in clause (i), and substituted "clause (i) of subdivision 2" for "subdivision 2 (i)" near the end.

Michie's Jurisprudence.
For related discussion, see 2A M.J. Arrest, § 7.

OPINIONS OF THE ATTORNEY GENERAL

Limitation on interjurisdictional law-enforcement authority. — The statute limits the interjurisdictional law-enforcement authority of a sheriff's office beyond the county to matters directly and incidentally related to the circumstances set forth in the statute; an officer properly engaged in one of the activities enumerated in the statute beyond the territorial limits of his locality is authorized to act in the same manner and is subject to the same limitations as would apply to a law-enforcement officer of the extraterritorial locality. See opinion of Attorney General to The Honorable Robert E. Maxey Jr., Sheriff for Campbell County, 00-078 (5/17/01).

Jurisdiction for purposes of execution of orders subjecting a person to emergency custody or temporary detention, or providing for the transportation of such persons. — Jurisdiction encompasses any locality or political subdivision, so that if a town has organized its own police department, that department, rather than the surrounding county's sheriff's office or police department is the primary law-enforcement agency. If the town does not have its own police department, then the responsibility for the orders and accompanying transportation falls to the county police department if there is one, and to the sheriff's office if there is not. See opinion of Attorney General to Karen T. Mullins, Esquire, County Attorney, Wise County, 11-123, 2011 Va. AG LEXIS 44 (10/21/11).

§ 15.2-1725. Extending police power of localities over lands lying beyond boundaries thereof; jurisdiction of courts.

Any locality owning and operating an airport, public hospital, sanitarium, nursing home, public water supply or watershed, public park, recreational area, sewage disposal plant or system, public landing, dock, wharf or canal, public school, public utility, public buildings and other public property located beyond the limits of the locality shall have and may exercise full police power over the property, and over persons using the property, and may, by ordinance, prescribe rules for the operation and use of the property and for the conduct of all persons using the property and may, further, provide penalties for the violation of such rules contained in an ordinance; such penalties, however, shall not exceed those provided by general law for misdemeanors. However, no ordinances in conflict with an ordinance of the jurisdiction wherein the property is located shall be enacted.

Any locality which maintains or operates in whole or in part any property enumerated in this section may lawfully send its law-enforcement officers to the property owned beyond the limits of the locality for the purpose of protecting the property, keeping order therein, or otherwise enforcing the laws of the Commonwealth and ordinances of the locality owning the property as such laws and ordinances may relate to the operation and use thereof. The law-enforcement officer shall have power to make an arrest for a violation of any law or ordinance relating to the operation and use of the property. The district court in the city or town where the offense occurs shall have jurisdiction of all cases arising therein, and the district court of the county where the offense occurs shall have jurisdiction of all cases arising therein.

It shall be the duty of the attorney for the Commonwealth for the locality wherein the offense occurs to prosecute all violators of the ordinances of the locality that pertain to the operation and use of the property enumerated in this section.

History.
Code 1950, § 15-560.1; 1952, c. 382; 1962, c. 623, § 15.1-142; 1979, c. 333; 1997, c. 587.

Michie's Jurisprudence.
For related discussion, see 2B M.J. Aviation, § 1.

§ 15.2-1725.1. Concurrent jurisdiction; limitations.

For the purposes of local public safety regulatory authority and enforcement, the territorial limits of the City of Virginia Beach shall extend from its coastal shorelines, the coastal shorelines of Camp Pendleton, the coastal shorelines of First Landing State Park, and the coastal shorelines of False Cape State Park in a perpendicular direction for three miles into the Atlantic Ocean and Chesapeake Bay waters. This territorial jurisdiction shall be concurrent with the jurisdiction of the Commonwealth. No ordinance enacted under this authority shall conflict with the laws or regulations promulgated by the Commonwealth or any of its agencies. This authority shall not extend to the regulatory authority held by the Virginia Marine Resources Commission as provided in § 28.2-101.

History.
2012, c. 809.

§ 15.2-1726. Agreements for consolidation of police departments or for cooperation in furnishing police services.

Any locality may, in its discretion, enter into a reciprocal agreement with any other locality, any agency of the federal government exercising police powers, the police of any state-supported institution of higher learning appointed pursuant to § 23-233, the Division of Capitol Police, any private police department certified by the Department of Criminal Justice Services, or any combination of the foregoing, for such periods and under such conditions as the contracting parties deem advisable, for cooperation in the furnishing of police services. Such agreements may include designation of mutually agreed-upon boundary lines between contiguous localities for purposes of organizing 911 dispatch and response and clarifying issues related to coverage under workers' compensation and risk management laws. Such localities also may enter into an agreement for the cooperation in the furnishing of police services with the Department of State Police. The governing body of any locality also may, in its discretion, enter into a reciprocal agreement with any other locality, or combination thereof, for the consolidation of police departments or divisions or departments thereof. Subject to the conditions of the agreement, all police officers, officers, agents and other employees of such consolidated or cooperating police departments shall have the same powers, rights, benefits, privileges and immunities in every jurisdiction subscribing to such agreement, including the authority to make arrests in every such jurisdiction subscribing to the agreement; however, no police officer of any locality shall have authority to enforce federal laws unless specifically empowered to do so by statute, and no federal law-enforcement officer shall have authority to enforce the laws of the Commonwealth unless specifically empowered to do so by statute.

The governing body of a county also may enter into a tripartite contract with the governing body of any town, one or more, in such county and the sheriff for such county for the purpose of having the sheriff furnish law-enforcement services in the town. The contract shall be structured as a service contract and may have such other terms and conditions as the contracting parties deem advisable. The sheriff and any deputy sheriff serving as a town law-enforcement officer shall have authority to enforce such town's ordinances. Likewise, subject to the conditions of the contract, the sheriff and deputy sheriffs while serving as a town's law-enforcement officers shall have the same powers, rights, benefits, privileges and immunities as those of regular town police officers. The sheriff under any such contract shall be the town's chief of police.

History.
1970, c. 271, § 15.1-131.3; 1978, c. 9; 1984, c. 622; 1989, c. 294; 1994, c. 268; 1997, c. 587; 2008, c. 437; 2013, cc. 250, 472, 594, 775.

Cross references.
As to law-enforcement expenditures, see § 9.1-165 et seq. As to powers, duties and functions of Capitol Police, see § 30-34.2:1.

The 2013 amendments.
The 2013 amendments by cc. 250 and 472 are identical, and in the first paragraph, inserted "the" following "police powers," and "§ 23-233," and substituted "any private police department certified by the Department of Criminal Justice Services, or" for "or with."
The 2013 amendments by cc. 594 and 775 are identical, and inserted the second sentence in the first paragraph.

CASE NOTES

Law-enforcement mutual aid agreements. — Defendant was properly convicted of assault and battery on a police officer under

subsection C of § 18.2-57 because while defendant claimed that the officer's public duties were limited to one mile outside the geographic borders of Virginia Beach under § 19.2-250, a law-enforcement mutual aid agreement permitted by § 15.2-1726 gave the officer authority to perform his public duties in Chesapeake based on the immediate threat to public safety presented by defendant's erratic driving. Rowe v. Commonwealth, 2008 Va. App. LEXIS 242 (May 20, 2008), aff'd, 277 Va. 495, 675 S.E.2d 161, 2009 Va. LEXIS 59 (2009).

Navy police officers. — Because Navy police officers were not employees of a Commonwealth or local law-enforcement agency, and because a reciprocal agreement under § 15.2-1726 did not incorporate itself into the assault and battery statute, the trial court erred as a matter of law in convicting defendant under subsection C of § 18.2-57. South v. Commonwealth, 47 Va. App. 247, 623 S.E.2d 419, 2005 Va. App. LEXIS 513 (2005); as to remanding the case for a new trial rather than remanding for new sentencing on the lesser included offense, see 2006 Va. LEXIS 56 (Va. 2006).

CIRCUIT COURT OPINIONS

Extra-jurisdictional arrest. — Although an agreement pursuant to §§ 15.2-1726 and 23-234 was invalid and defendant was arrested beyond a university police officer's jurisdictional limits, which made a certificate of breath analysis inadmissible, the rest of the evidence was admissible under the "good faith exception" to the Fourth Amendment's exclusionary rule. Commonwealth v. Borek, 68 Va. Cir. 323, 2005 Va. Cir. LEXIS 196 (Charlottesville Aug. 4, 2005).

OPINIONS OF THE ATTORNEY GENERAL

Agreement with the Department of Homeland Security to enforce selected immigration laws may be entered into pursuant to this section by a local law-enforcement agency. See opinion of Attorney General to The Honorable Thomas Davis Rust, Member, House of Delegates, 07-016 (5/10/07).

Virginia law-enforcement officers have authority to detain and arrest individuals who have committed violations of the laws of the United States and other states, and such authority extends to violations of federal criminal immigration law. It would not be advisable to enforce such violations outside of the scope of an agreement with federal authorities. See opinion of Attorney General to The Honorable Kenneth W. Stolle, Member, Senate of Virginia, and The Honorable David B. Albo, Member, House of Delegates, 07-086 (10/15/07).

Requirement for reciprocal agreement. — This section does not authorize a municipality that has a police charter and police force to enter into an agreement with another municipality that does not have such a charter or force. See opinion of Attorney General to The Honorable Thomas D. Jones, Sheriff, Charlotte County, 08-028 (7/28/08).

Appointment of town sergeant. — A charter town is authorized to appoint a town sergeant and any other necessary officers to enforce the laws of the Commonwealth within the town and, pursuant to § 15.2-1726, is authorized to enter into a reciprocal agreement with another town for the provision of law-enforcement assistance. See opinion of Attorney General to Daniel M. Siegel, Esq., Town Attorney for Charlotte Court House, 08-076 (10/9/08).

Where a town charter specifically includes the office of "a town sergeant, who shall be the conservator of the peace," the appointment of a town sergeant is authorized when the town council deems such appointment to be proper and necessary, and two charter towns may enter into a valid, reciprocal agreement to contract for the services of a town sergeant provided the town charters of both towns authorize the appointment of a town sergeant. See opinion of Attorney General to Jennifer LeLacheur Jones, Esq., Town Attorney for Drakes Branch, 08-071 (10/9/08).

§ 15.2-1727. Reciprocal agreements with localities outside the Commonwealth.

A locality or a state-supported or private institution of higher learning may, in its discretion, enter into reciprocal agreements for such periods as it deems advisable with any locality outside the Commonwealth, including the District of Columbia, in order to establish and carry into effect a plan to provide mutual aid through the furnishing of its police and other employees and agents, together with all necessary equipment, in the event of such need or emergency as provided herein. No state-supported or private institution of higher learning shall enter into such agreement unless the agreement provides that each of the parties to such agreement shall: (i) waive any and all claims against all the other parties thereto which may arise out of their activities outside their respective jurisdictions under such agreement and (ii) indemnify and save harmless the other parties to such agreement from all claims by third parties for property damage or personal injury which may arise out of the activities of the other parties to such agreement outside their respective jurisdictions under such agreement. Parties responding to a reciprocal agreement for mutual aid between localities shall be liable to third parties only to the extent permitted under and in accordance with the laws of the state of the party rendering aid.

The principal law-enforcement officer in any locality or of a state-supported or private institution of higher learning having a reciprocal agreement with a jurisdiction outside the Commonwealth for police mutual aid under the provisions hereof shall be responsible for directing the activities of all police officers and other officers and agents coming into his jurisdiction under the reciprocal agreement. While operating under the terms of the reciprocal agreement, the principal law-enforcement officer is empowered to authorize all police officers and other officers and agents from outside the Commonwealth to enforce the laws of the Commonwealth of Virginia to the same extent as if they were duly authorized law-enforcement officers of the locality or a state-supported or private institution of higher learning in Virginia.

The governing body of any locality or a state-supported or private institution of higher learning in the Commonwealth is authorized to procure or extend the necessary public liability insurance to cover claims arising out of mutual aid agreements executed with other localities outside the Commonwealth.

The police officers, and other officers, agents and employees of a locality or a state-supported or private institution of higher learning serving in a jurisdiction outside the Commonwealth under a reciprocal agreement entered into pursuant hereto are authorized to carry out the duties and functions provided for in the agreement under the command and supervision of the chief law-enforcement officer of the jurisdiction outside the Commonwealth.

In counties where no police department has been established and the sheriff is the chief law-enforcement officer, the sheriff may enter into mutual aid agreements and furnish and receive such assistance as provided by this section. Sheriffs and their deputies providing assistance pursuant to such a mutual aid agreement shall enjoy all of the authority, immunities and benefits as provided herein for police officers, including full police powers.

History.
Code 1950, § 15-552; 1962, c. 623, § 15.1-131; 1968, c. 800; 1971, Ex. Sess., c. 238; 1976, c. 457; 1977, c. 79; 1979, c. 503; 1984, c. 779; 1992, c. 566; 1993, c. 860; 1995, c. 844; 1997, cc. 587, 638, 668; 2004, c. 769; 2007, c. 724.

Cross references.
As to powers and duties of campus police departments, see § 23-234.

§ 15.2-1728. Mutual aid agreements between police departments and federal authorities.

In any case where exclusive jurisdiction over any property or territory has been granted by the Commonwealth to the United States government, or to a department or agency thereof, the governing body of any contiguous locality or the Division of Capitol Police may enter into a mutual aid agreement with the appropriate federal authorities to authorize police cooperation and assistance within such property or territory. Subject to the conditions of any such agreement, all police officers and agents of the contracting governing body or agency shall have the same powers, rights, benefits, privileges and immunities while acting in the performance of their duties on the property or territory under federal authority as are lawfully conferred upon them within their own jurisdictions.

History.
1987, c. 33, § 15.1-131.10; 1997, c. 587; 2008, c. 437.

Cross references.
As to powers, duties and functions of Capitol Police, see § 30-34.2:1.

§ 15.2-1729. Agreements for enforcement of state and county laws by federal officers on federal property.

A. The governing body of any county may enter into an agreement with the United States government or a department or agency thereof, under the terms of which agreement law-enforcement officers employed by such government, including but not limited to members of the United States Park Police, may enforce the laws of such county and the Commonwealth on federally owned properties within such county, and on the highways located therein and other public places abutting such properties. In the event such an agreement is entered into, all of the provisions of §§ 15.2-1724 and 15.2-1727 shall be applicable, mutatis mutandis.

B. The governing body of any county governed under the provisions of Chapter 8 (§ 15.2-800 et seq.) of Title 15.2 may enter into an agreement with the United States government or a department or agency thereof, under the terms of which agreement law-enforcement officers employed by such government, including but not limited to members of the United States Park Police, may enforce the laws of such county and the Commonwealth on federally owned properties within such county, and on the highways and other public places abutting such properties. In the event such an agreement is entered into, all of the provisions of §§ 15.2-1724 and 15.2-1727 shall be applicable, mutatis mutandis.

History.
  1972, c. 743, § 15.1-131.4; 1997, cc. 537, 587.

§ 15.2-1730. Calling upon law-enforcement officers of counties, cities or towns for assistance.

In case of an emergency declared by the chief law-enforcement officer of a locality, such officer may call upon the chief law-enforcement officer of towns within his county and the chief law-enforcement officer of an adjoining county or city, or towns in adjoining counties for assistance from him or his deputies or other police officers, without the necessity for deputizing such deputies or officers. Such deputies or officers shall have full police powers in such locality as are conferred upon them by law during the period of such emergency.

History.
  1974, c. 633, § 15.1-131.5; 1976, c. 206; 1997, c. 587.

§ 15.2-1730.1. Authority and immunity of sheriffs and deputies.

In counties where no police department has been established and the sheriff is the chief law-enforcement officer, the sheriff may enter into agreements with any other governmental entity providing law-enforcement services in the Commonwealth, and may furnish and receive interjurisdictional law-enforcement assistance for all law-enforcement purposes, including those described in this chapter, and for purposes of Chapter 3.2 (§ 44-146.13 et seq.) of Title 44. Sheriffs and their deputies, providing or receiving such assistance, shall have all the authority, benefits, immunity from liability and exemptions from laws, ordinances and regulations as officers acting within their own jurisdictions.

History.
  1999, c. 352.

Editor's note.
  Acts 1999, c. 352, cl. 2, provides: "That this act is declarative of existing law."

ARTICLE 3.

AUXILIARY POLICE FORCES IN LOCALITIES.

§ 15.2-1731. Establishment, etc., authorized; powers, authority and immunities generally.

A. Localities, for the further preservation of the public peace, safety, and good order of the community, may establish, equip, and maintain auxiliary police forces that have all the powers and authority and all the immunities of full-time law-enforcement officers, if all such forces have met the training requirements established by the Department of Criminal Justice Services under § 9.1-102.

B. Notwithstanding any other provision of this section, an auxiliary officer shall be exempted from any initial training requirement established under § 9.1-102 until a date one year subsequent to the approval by the Criminal Justice Services Board of compulsory minimum training standards for auxiliary police officers, except that (i) any such officer shall not be permitted to carry or use a firearm while serving as an auxiliary police officer unless such officer has met the firearms training requirements established in accordance with in-service training standards for law-enforcement officers as prescribed by the Criminal Justice Services Board, and (ii) any such officer shall have one year following the approval by the Board to comply with the compulsory minimum training standards.

History.
  1968, c. 157, § 15.1-159.2; 1987, c. 421; 1988, c. 864; 1997, c. 587; 2012, c. 827.

Cross references.
  As to emergency protective orders, see § 16.1-253.4. As to capital murder of police officer, see § 18.2-31. As to malicious bodily injury to law-enforcement officers, etc., see § 18.2-51.1. As to assault and battery of law-enforcement officers, etc., see § 18.2-57. As to arrest without warrant in cases of assault and battery against family or household member and stalking and for violations of protective orders, see § 19.2-81.3. As to authorization for emergency protective orders, see § 19.2-152.8. As to transportation of prisoners by auxiliary police forces, see § 53.1-31.1.

The 2012 amendments.
  The 2012 amendment by c. 827, effective April 18, 2012, rewrote the section.

§ 15.2-1732. Appropriations for equipment and maintenance.

Localities may make such appropriations as may be necessary to arm, equip, uniform and maintain such auxiliary police force.

History.
  1968, c. 157, § 15.1-159.3; 1997, c. 587.

CASE NOTES

Applied in Blankenship v. City of Portsmouth, 372 F. Supp. 2d 496, 2005 U.S. Dist. LEXIS 11124 (E.D. Va. 2005).

§ 15.2-1733. Appointment of auxiliary police officers; revocation of appointment; uniform; organization; rules and regulations.

The governing body of the locality may appoint or provide for the appointment as auxiliary police officers as many persons of good character as it deems necessary, not to exceed the number fixed by ordinance adopted by the governing body, and their appointment shall be revocable at any time by the governing body. The governing body may prescribe the uniform, organization, and such rules as it deems necessary for the operation of the auxiliary police force.

History.
1968, c. 157, § 15.1-159.4; 1997, c. 587.

Cross references.
As to capital murder of police officer, see § 18.2-31. As to malicious bodily injury to law-enforcement officers, etc., see § 18.2-51.1. As to assault and battery of law-enforcement officers, etc., see § 18.2-57.

§ 15.2-1734. Calling auxiliary police officers into service; police officers performing service to wear uniform; exception.

A. A locality may call into service or provide for calling into service such auxiliary police officers as may be deemed necessary (i) in time of public emergency, (ii) at such times as there are insufficient numbers of regular police officers to preserve the peace, safety and good order of the community, or (iii) at any time for the purpose of training such auxiliary police officers. At all times when performing such service, the members of the auxiliary police force shall wear the uniform prescribed by the governing body.

B. Members of any auxiliary police force who have been trained in accordance with the provisions of § 15.2-1731 may be called into service by the chief of police of any locality to aid and assist regular police officers in the performance of their duties.

C. When the duties of an auxiliary police officer are such that the wearing of the prescribed uniform would adversely limit the effectiveness of the auxiliary police officer's ability to perform his prescribed duties, then clothing appropriate for the duties to be performed may be required by the chief of police.

History.
1968, c. 157, § 15.1-159.5; 1987, c. 421; 1988, c. 190; 1997, c. 587.

§ 15.2-1735. Acting beyond limits of jurisdiction of locality.

The members of any such auxiliary police force shall not be required to act beyond the limits of the jurisdiction of any such locality except when called upon to protect any public property belonging to the locality which may be located beyond its boundaries, or as provided in § 15.2-1736.

History.
1968, c. 157, § 15.1-159.6; 1997, c. 587.

§ 15.2-1736. Mutual aid agreements among governing bodies of localities.

The governing bodies of localities, institutions of higher learning having a police force appointed pursuant to § 23-233, and institutions of higher education having a private police force, as well as sheriffs, and the Director of the Department of Conservation and Recreation with commissioned conservation officers, or any combination thereof may, by proper resolutions, enter in and become a party to contracts or mutual aid agreements for the use of their joint forces, both regular and auxiliary, their equipment and materials to maintain peace and good order. However, no such institution of higher learning shall enter into such agreement with another institution of higher education in a noncontiguous locality without the consent of all localities within which such institutions are located. Any police or other law-enforcement officer, regular or auxiliary, while performing his duty under any such contract or agreement, shall have the same authority in such locality as he has within the locality where he was appointed.

In counties where no police department has been established, the sheriff may, in his discretion, enter into mutual aid agreements as provided by this section.

History.
1968, c. 157, § 15.1-159.7; 1987, c. 421; 1994, c. 268; 1997, cc. 587, 604; 2002, cc. 684, 709, 876; 2005, c. 87; 2006, c. 286; 2009, cc. 461, 609; 2010, c. 523.

Cross references.
As to jurisdiction of conservation officers, see § 10.1-116.

ARTICLE 4.

SPECIAL POLICE OFFICERS IN LOCALITIES.

§ 15.2-1737. Circuit courts may appoint special police officers.

A. The circuit court for any locality may, upon the application of, and a showing of a necessity for the security of property or the peace by, the sheriff or chief of police, appoint special police officers for a locality within its jurisdiction. Effective July 1, 2002, no person employed by a local school board as a school security officer, as defined in § 9.1-101, shall be eligible for appointment as a special police officer for purposes of maintaining safety in a public school in the Commonwealth.

The special police officers shall be suitable and discreet persons and shall serve as such for such length of time as the court may designate, but not exceeding four years under any one appointment. Such person or persons so appointed shall be conservators of the peace under the supervision of the person or agency making application for the appointment, who shall likewise be civilly liable for any wrongful action or conduct committed by the appointee while within the scope of his employment.

B. The court shall, prior to appointment, order the applicant to conduct a background investigation, in accordance with clause A (ii) of § 15.2-1705 of each prospective appointee who is not a law-enforcement officer as defined in § 9.1-101.

C. All appointments made pursuant to this section shall become void on September 15, 2004, and any officers so appointed shall no longer be eligible to serve.

History.
Code 1950, § 15-562; 1962, cc. 234, 623, § 15.1-144; 1976, c. 199; 1996, c. 850; 1997, c. 587; 2002, cc. 836, 868; 2003, c. 922.

Cross references.
As to government clerk being appointed as special policeman pursuant to this section, see § 2.2-2801. For the State and Local Government Conflict of Interests Act, see § 2.2-3100 et seq. As to special conservators of the peace, see § 9.1-150.1 et seq., § 19.2-13. As to issuance of summons by special policemen and conservators of the peace, see § 19.2-74. As to arrest without warrant, see § 19.2-81. As to taxes and license fees imposed by counties, cities, and towns, see § 46.2-752.

Editor's note.
Acts 1996, c. 850, cl. 3, provides: "[t]hat the provisions of this statute do not apply to those special police officers regulated by the Nuclear Regulatory Commission or the Department of Defense."
Acts 1996, c. 850, cl. 4, provides: "[t]hat the provisions of this statute shall not apply to any persons appointed as special police officers or special conservators of the peace prior to July 1, 1996."

Michie's Jurisprudence.
For related discussion, see 2A M.J. Arrest, § 7; 14A M.J. Obstructing Justice, § 2.

CASE NOTES

Status of special police. — Special policemen, appointed under this section are peace officers — conservators of the peace — and there is no limitation upon their power to arrest persons charged with a felony, and found within their territorial jurisdiction, and, when actually in pursuit, to arrest persons outside of the counties for which they have been appointed, and hence they are within the protection of § 18.1-310 (see now § 18.2-460) relative to intimidating and impeding officers in the discharge of their duty. Williams v. Commonwealth, 142 Va. 667, 128 S.E. 572 (1925) (decided under prior law).

Authority to make police inspection. — Special police officers appointed under the section are conservators of the peace in their respective counties. The office of conservators of the peace is a very ancient one, and their common-law authority to make police inspection, without a search warrant, extends throughout the territory for which they are elected or appointed, as the case may be, in private as well as in public places, and upon private as well as public property, unless inhibited from entry for such purpose without a search warrant by some rule of the common law, or by Constitution, or by statute. McClannan v. Chaplain, 136 Va. 1, 116 S.E. 495 (1923) (decided under prior law).

In an action for trespass on the case against special police officers appointed under this section for entering upon plaintiff's farm in search of a still without a search warrant, the officers had the right under the law then in force, without a search warrant, and without the consent of the owner or tenant of the land (he offering no actual resistance or objection at the time thereto), to enter upon a part of the farm in question away from the dwelling house and curtilage, in the exercise of the duty of police inspection imposed upon them by the former law — i.e., to ascertain if an illegal still was where they had been informed it was hidden on the farm, away from the dwelling house and curtilage. McClannan v. Chaplain, 136 Va. 1, 116 S.E. 495 (1923) (decided under prior law).

Applied in United States v. Day, 591 F.3d 679, 2010 U.S. App. LEXIS 429 (4th Cir. 2010).

§ 15.2-1738. Application for appointment as special police officer; qualifications.

Before any person is appointed as a police officer under § 15.2-1737, the sheriff or chief of police shall make written application for such appointment to the circuit court. Such application shall state the necessity for the appointment and the prospective appointee's full name, age, place of residence, occupation and regular employer. A part-time deputy of the sheriff may be appointed as such police officer.

History.
Code 1950, § 15-563; 1956, Ex. Sess., c. 18; 1962, c. 623, § 15.1-145; 1971, Ex. Sess., c. 152; 1996, c. 850; 1997, c. 587; 1999, c. 278.

Editor's note.
Acts 1996, c. 850, cl. 3, provides: "[t]hat the provisions of this statute do not apply to those special police officers regulated by the Nuclear Regulatory Commission or the Department of Defense."
Acts 1996, c. 850, cl. 4, provides: "[t]hat the provisions of this statute shall not apply to any persons appointed as special police officers or special conservators of the peace prior to July 1, 1996."

§ 15.2-1739. Compensation of special police officer.

A locality, if deemed proper, except where the police officer is otherwise regularly employed and his duties as police officer are merely incidental to such private employment, may allow such compensation to the police officer appointed under the provisions of § 15.2-1737 as, together with any expenses incurred in executing his duties, shall be deemed right and proper by the governing body to be paid out of the local levy.

History.
Code 1950, § 15-564; 1962, c. 623, § 15.1-146; 1997, c. 587.

§ 15.2-1740. Certain special police officers not employees of Commonwealth or locality.

No police officer appointed under § 15.2-1737 who is otherwise regularly employed and whose duties as police officer are merely incidental to such private employment shall be deemed to be an employee of the Commonwealth or locality within the meaning of the Virginia Workers' Compensation Act (§ 65.2-100 et seq.).

History.
Code 1950, § 15-565; 1962, c. 623, § 15.1-147; 1997, c. 587.

§ 15.2-1741. Removal of special police officers; filling vacancies.

The court may, at any time, remove any or all of such police, and appoint others, and may fill any vacancy that may occur in such police force, or may add to the number previously appointed.

History.
Code 1950, § 15-567; 1962, c. 623, § 15.1-149; 1997, c. 587.

§ 15.2-1742. Removal from locality creates vacancy.

The removal from the locality in which he was appointed shall vacate the office of the person appointed, or the person may resign or decline appointment.

History.
Code 1950, § 15-568; 1962, c. 623, § 15.1-150; 1997, c. 587.

§ 15.2-1743. Bond of special police officers.

Before entering upon the duties of his office, any person initially appointed on or after July 1, 1996, shall give bond in the penalty of such sum as may be fixed by the court, with approved security before the circuit court clerk, with condition faithfully to discharge his official duties. No bond shall be required, however, if the person so appointed has successfully completed the minimum entry-level law-enforcement training requirements established by the Department of Criminal Justice Services under § 9.1-102 within three years of the date of initial appointment or has been employed as a law-enforcement officer as defined by § 9.1-101 within the preceding three years.

History.
Code 1950, § 15-569; 1962, c. 623, § 15.1-151; 1991, c. 260; 1996, c. 850; 1997, c. 587.

Editor's note.
Acts 1996, c. 850, cl. 3, provides: "[t]hat the provisions of this statute do not apply to those special police officers regulated by the Nuclear Regulatory Commission or the Department of Defense."
Acts 1996, c. 850, cl. 4, provides: "[t]hat the provisions of this statute shall not apply to any persons appointed as special police officers or special conservators of the peace prior to July 1, 1996."

§ 15.2-1744. Jurisdiction and authority of special police officers; evidence of their office.

The jurisdiction and authority of special police shall extend no further than the limits of the locality in which they are appointed, and a copy of the order of appointment made by the court, attested by the clerk of such court, shall in all cases be received as evidence of their official character. But the authority of special police shall extend throughout the Commonwealth when actually in pursuit of persons accused of crime and when acting under authority of a duly executed warrant for the arrest of persons accused of committing crime.

The jurisdiction and authority of special police upon order entered of record by the circuit court for the locality may be limited to a specific place or places in a locality; may limit or prohibit the carrying of weapons by special police; and shall prescribe the type of uniform, badge, insignia or identification to be worn or carried by special police to the extent that the uniform, badge, insignia or identification shall not resemble or be in facsimile of the uniform, badge, insignia or identification of the State Police or that of any sheriff, or member of a police department in the locality or an adjoining locality. Any special police officer initially appointed on or after July 1, 1996, whose order of appointment does not prohibit the carrying of weapons while within the scope of his employment as such may be required by the court to meet the minimum entry training requirements established by the Department of Criminal Justice Services under § 9.1-102 for law-enforcement officers within twelve months of his appointment. Such order may provide that special police shall, within the limits of their jurisdiction, have the same authority and responsibility as deputy sheriffs with regard to the service of civil and criminal process.

However, the jurisdiction and authority of special police, upon an order entered of record by the circuit court for an adjoining locality, may be extended into such adjoining locality or into such part thereof as the order may designate, provided that the special circumstances necessitating such extension of jurisdiction and authority are set forth in the order.

History.
Code 1950, § 15-570; 1954, c. 400; 1962, c. 623, § 15.1-152; 1964, c. 138; 1972, c. 218; 1976, c. 403; 1996, c. 850; 1997, c. 587.

Cross references.
As to appointment of special policemen by the circuit courts, see § 15.2-1737.

Editor's note.
Acts 1996, c. 850, cl. 3, provides: "[t]hat the provisions of this statute do not apply to those special police officers regulated by the Nuclear Regulatory Commission or the Department of Defense."
Acts 1996, c. 850, cl. 4, provides: "[t]hat the provisions of this statute shall not apply to any persons appointed as special police officers or special conservators of the peace prior to July 1, 1996."

Michie's Jurisprudence.
For related discussion, see 2A M.J. Arrest, § 7.

CIRCUIT COURT OPINIONS

Motion to suppress denied. — Although the evidence of field sobriety tests conducted on defendant by a university police officer who was outside the university police department's patrol area may have been gathered in violation of the "color of office" doctrine, the officer's actions were in reliance on the authority of former § 19.2-17, which the officer reasonably and in good faith believed to be the established law. Therefore, defendant's motion to suppress the evidence of the field sobriety tests was denied. Commonwealth v. Thompson, 69 Va. Cir. 283, 2005 Va. Cir. LEXIS 321 (Charlottesville 2005).

§ 15.2-1745. Duties and powers of special police officers.

Special police shall apprehend and carry before a judge or magistrate to be dealt with according to law, all persons whom they may be directed by the warrant of a judge or magistrate to apprehend, shall have the authority to make arrests and issue summonses in accordance with Chapter 7 (§ 19.2-71 et seq.) of Title 19.2; and may execute any search warrant issued under §§ 19.2-52 and 19.2-53. If property that is mentioned in these sections is found, the police shall proceed as officers acting under Chapter 5 (§ 19.2-52 et seq.) of Title 19.2.

History.
Code 1950, § 15-571; 1960, c. 371; 1962, c. 623, § 15.1-153; 1968, c. 639; 1996, c. 850; 1997, c. 587.

Cross references.
As to appointment of special policemen by the circuit courts, see § 15.2-1737.

Editor's note.
Acts 1996, c. 850, cl. 3, provides: "[t]hat the provisions of this statute do not apply to those special police officers regulated by the Nuclear Regulatory Commission or the Department of Defense."
Acts 1996, c. 850, cl. 4, provides: "[t]hat the provisions of this statute shall not apply to any persons appointed as special police officers or special conservators of the peace prior to July 1, 1996."

CASE NOTES

A policeman who does not use more force than is necessary to arrest a person who is engaged in riotous and disorderly conduct, and who resists the officer, is not guilty of an assault and battery. Mesmer v. Commonwealth, 67 Va. (26 Gratt.) 976 (1875) (decided under prior law).

§ 15.2-1746. Duty of district judge; may bind to good behavior, etc.

In all cases arising under § 15.2-1745, the district judge before whom the person so arrested is brought shall examine the case and dispose of it according to law. If he thinks the person so apprehended ought to enter into a recognizance to keep the peace and be of good behavior, he shall require him to do so, and in default thereof such person may be committed to jail.

History.
Code 1950, § 15-572; 1962, c. 623, § 15.1-154; 1997, c. 587.

Research references.
Virginia Forms (Matthew Bender). No. 9-201 Peace Bond.

Michie's Jurisprudence.
For related discussion, see 2A M.J. Arrest, § 7.

ARTICLE 5.

CRIMINAL JUSTICE TRAINING ACADEMIES.

§ 15.2-1747. Creation of academies.

A. The governing bodies of two or more localities or other political subdivisions or other public bodies hereinafter collectively referred to as "governmental units," may by ordinance or resolution enter into an agreement which creates a regional criminal justice academy under an appropriate name and title containing the words "criminal justice academy" or "criminal justice training academy" which shall be a public body politic and corporate. Any regional criminal justice training academy created under this article shall also be subject to the requirements of § 9.1-102.

B. The agreement shall set forth (i) the name of the academy, (ii) the governmental subdivision in which its principal office shall be situated, (iii) the effective date of the organization of the academy and the duration of the agreement, (iv) the composition of the board of directors of the academy which may include representation of each locality, political subdivision or governmental entity party to the agreement, the members of which shall be the governing body of the academy, (v) the method for selection and the terms of office of the board of directors, (vi) the voting rights of the directors which need not be equal, (vii) the procedure for amendment of the agreement, and (viii) such other matters as the governmental units creating the academy deem appropriate. Sheriffs and members of the governing bodies of the governmental units as well as other public officials or employees may be members of the board of directors.

C. Any governmental unit not a party to an original agreement creating an academy under this section or § 15.2-1300 may join the academy only by two-thirds vote of the board of directors of the academy. The governing body of the governmental unit seeking to join the academy shall request membership by resolution or ordinance. The board of directors shall provide for the addition of the joining governmental unit to the academy and the number, terms of office, and voting rights of members of the board of directors, if any, to be appointed by the joining governmental unit.

D. A governmental unit may withdraw from an academy created under this section or § 15.2-1300 only by two-thirds vote of the board of directors of the academy. The governing body of the governmental unit seeking to withdraw from the academy shall signify its desire by resolution or ordinance. The board of directors shall consider requests to withdraw in October 2001, and in October of every fifth year thereafter. No requests to withdraw shall be considered at any other time, unless agreed to unanimously. Any withdrawal approved by the board of directors shall be effective on June 30 of the following year. The board of directors shall provide for the conditions of withdrawal.

D1. The Division of Capitol Police may become a party to an agreement creating an academy or may join an existing academy. The Chief of the Capitol Police is authorized to enter into such agreement as necessary to join an academy. The chief or his designee may serve as a member of the board of directors of such academy, and in accordance with the bylaws of the academy, may serve as a member of the executive committee or other committee of the academy.

E. The chairman of the academy board shall serve as a member and as the chairman of an executive committee. The composition of the remaining membership of the executive committee, the term of office of its members and any alternate members, procedures for the conduct of its meetings, and any limitations upon the general authority of the executive committee shall be established in the bylaws of the academy. The bylaws shall also establish any other special standing committees, advisory, technical or otherwise, as the board of directors shall deem desirable for the transaction of its affairs.

History.
1993, c. 935, § 15.1-159.7:1; 1997, c. 587; 2000, c. 772; 2002, c. 350; 2010, c. 516.

§ 15.2-1748. Powers of the academies.

A. Upon organization of an academy, it shall be a public body corporate and politic, the purposes of which shall be to establish and conduct training for public law-enforcement and correctional officers, those being trained to be public law-enforcement and correctional officers and other personnel who assist or support such officers. The persons trained by an academy need not be employed by a locality which has joined in the agreement creating the academy.

B. Criminal justice training academies may:

1. Adopt and have a common seal and alter that seal at the pleasure of the board of directors;

2. Sue and be sued;

3. Adopt bylaws and make rules and regulations for the conduct of its business;

4. Make and enter into all contracts or agreements, as it may determine are necessary, incidental or convenient to the performance of its duties and to the execution of the powers granted under this article;

5. Apply for and accept, disburse and administer for itself or for a member governmental unit any loans or grants of money, materials or property from any private or charitable source, the United States of America, the Commonwealth, any agency or instrumentality thereof, or from any other source;

6. Employ engineers, attorneys, planners and such other professional experts or consultants, and general and clerical employees as may be deemed necessary and prescribe such experts, consultants, and employees' powers, duties, and compensation;

7. Perform any acts authorized under this article through or by means of its own officers, agents and employees, or by contracts with any person, firm or corporation;

8. Acquire, whether by purchase, exchange, gift, lease or otherwise, any interest in real or personal property, and improve, maintain, equip and furnish academy facilities;

9. Lease, sell, exchange, donate and convey any interest in any or all of its projects, property or facilities in furtherance of the purposes of the academy as set forth in this article;

10. Accept contributions, grants and other financial assistance from the United States of America and its agencies or instrumentalities thereof, the Commonwealth, any political subdivision, agency or public instrumentality thereof or from any other source, for or in aid of the construction, acquisition, ownership, maintenance or repair of the academy facilities, for the payment of principal of, or interest on, any bond of the academy, or other costs incident thereto, or make loans in furtherance of the purposes of this article of such money, contributions, grants, and other financial assistance, and comply with such conditions and to execute such agreements, trust indentures, and other legal instruments as may be necessary, convenient or desirable and agree to such terms and conditions as may be imposed;

11. Borrow money from any source for capital purposes or to cover current expenditures in any given year in anticipation of the collection of revenues;

12. Mortgage and pledge any or all of its projects, property or facilities or parts thereof and pledge the revenues therefrom or from any part thereof as security for the payment of principal and premium, if any, and interest on any bonds, notes or other evidences of indebtedness;

13. Create an executive committee which may exercise the powers and authority of the academy under this article pursuant to authority delegated to it by the board of directors;

14. Establish fees or other charges for the training services provided;

15. Exercise the powers granted in the agreement creating the academy; and

16. Execute any and all instruments and do and perform any and all acts necessary, convenient or desirable for its purposes or to carry out the powers expressly given in this article.

History.
1993, c. 935, § 15.1-159.7:2; 1997, c. 587.

§ 15.2-1749. Revenue bonds.

A. Each academy is hereby authorized, after a resolution adopted by a majority of its board of directors, to issue, at one time or from time to time, revenue bonds of the academy on a taxable or tax-exempt basis for the purpose of acquiring, purchasing, constructing, reconstructing, or improving training facilities and acquiring necessary land or equipment therefor, and to refund any bonds issued for such purposes. The bonds of each issue shall be dated, shall mature at such time or times not exceeding forty years from their issue date or dates and shall bear interest at such fixed or variable rate or rates as may be determined by the board of directors, and may be made redeemable before maturity at the option of the board of directors at such price or prices and under such terms and conditions as may be fixed by the authority prior to the issuance of the bonds. The board of directors shall determine the form of the bonds, including any interest coupons to be attached thereto, and the manner of execution of the bonds, and shall affix the denomination or denominations of the bonds and the place or places of payment of principal and interest, which may be at any bank or trust company within or outside the Commonwealth. In case any officer whose signature or a facsimile of whose signature appears on any bonds or coupons ceases to be such officer before the delivery of such bonds, such signature or facsimile shall nevertheless be valid and sufficient for all purposes the same as if he had remained in office until such delivery. Notwithstanding any of the other provisions of this article or any recitals in any bonds issued under the provisions of this article, all such bonds shall be deemed to be negotiable instruments under the laws of this Commonwealth. The bonds may be issued in coupon or registered form or both, as the board of directors may determine, and provision may be made for the registration of any coupon bonds as to principal alone and also as to both principal and interest, and for the reconversion into coupon bonds of any bonds registered as to both principal and interest. The board of directors may sell such bonds in such manner, either at public or private sale, and for such price as it may determine to be for the best interests of the academy.

B. The resolution providing for the issuance of revenue bonds, and any trust agreement securing such bonds, may also contain such limitations upon the issuance of additional revenue bonds as the board of directors may deem proper and such additional bonds as shall be issued under such restriction and limitations as may be prescribed by such resolution or trust agreement.

C. Bonds may be issued under the provisions of this article without obtaining the consent of any commission, board, bureau, or agency of the Commonwealth or of any political subdivision and without any other proceedings or conditions as are specifically required by this article.

D. Bonds issued under the provisions of this article shall not be deemed to constitute a debt of the Commonwealth or of any political subdivision thereof or a pledge of the faith and credit of the Commonwealth or of any political subdivision thereof. The bonds shall be payable solely from revenues or other property of the academy specifically pledged for such purpose.

E. "Bonds" or "revenue bonds" as used in this article shall embrace notes, bonds and other obligations authorized to be issued pursuant to this article.

History.
1993, c. 935, § 15.1-159.7:3; 1997, c. 587.

§ 15.2-1750. Governmental units authorized to appropriate or lend funds.

The governmental units which are parties of the agreement creating the academy or which arrange to have personnel trained at the academy are authorized to appropriate or lend funds; pay fees or charges for services; convey by sale, lease or gift real or personal property, or any interest therein; provide services to the academy; or enter into such other contracts with the academy as may be appropriate to carry out any other power granted to those localities or the academy.

History.
1993, c. 935, § 15.1-159.7:4; 1997, c. 587.

§ 15.2-1751. Exemption from taxation.

Any academy created under the provisions of this article shall not be required to pay taxes or assessments upon any project or upon any property acquired or used by it or upon the income therefrom and income derived from bonds shall be exempt at all times from every kind and nature of taxation by this Commonwealth or by any of its political subdivisions, municipal corporations, or public agencies of any kind.

History.
1993, c. 935, § 15.1-159.7:5; 1997, c. 587.

§ 15.2-1752. Governmental immunity.

Any academy created pursuant to this article shall be deemed to be a governmental entity exercising essential governmental powers. Any such academy; its directors, officers, and employees; and any person serving as a trainer at the academy who is certified by the Department of Criminal Justice Services or any person who is a criminal justice academy approved instructor shall be entitled to immunity in any civil action or proceeding for damages or injury to any person or property of any person to the same extent that counties and their officers and employees are immune. Members of the board of directors of the academy shall have the same immunity as members of county boards of supervisors.

History.
1993, c. 935, § 15.1-159.7:6; 1997, c. 587; 2013, cc. 66, 99.

The 2013 amendments.
The 2013 amendments by cc. 66 and 99 are identical, and divided the former first sentence into the first and second sentences by substituting "powers. Any such academy; its directors" for "powers, and any such academy and its directors" and inserted "and any person serving as a trainer at the academy who is certified by the Department of Criminal Justice Services or any person who is a criminal justice academy approved instructor" in the second sentence.

§ 15.2-1753. Liability of board members.

No member of the board of directors of an academy shall be personally liable for any indebtedness, obligation or other liability of an academy, barring willful misconduct.

History.
1993, c. 935, § 15.1-159.7:7; 1997, c. 587.

CHAPTER 18.

BUILDINGS, MONUMENTS AND LANDS GENERALLY.

Article 2. Parks, Recreation Facilities and Playgrounds.

Section
15.2-1808. Certain sports facilities.

ARTICLE 2.

PARKS, RECREATION FACILITIES AND PLAYGROUNDS.

§ 15.2-1808. Certain sports facilities.

A locality may provide and operate stadiums and arenas and the lands, structures, equipment and facilities appurtenant thereto; provide for their management and operation by an agency of the locality; contract with others for the operation and management thereof upon such terms and conditions as shall be prescribed by the locality; and charge or authorize the charging of compensation for the use of or admission to such stadiums and arenas and their appurtenances.

History.
Code 1950, § 15-77.50; 1958, c. 328; 1962, c. 623, § 15.1-886; 1997, c. 587.

CHAPTER 21.

FRANCHISES; SALE AND LEASE OF CERTAIN MUNICIPAL PUBLIC PROPERTY; PUBLIC UTILITIES.

Article 5. Water Supply Systems Generally.

Section
15.2-2143. Water supplies and facilities.

ARTICLE 5.

WATER SUPPLY SYSTEMS GENERALLY.

§ 15.2-2143. Water supplies and facilities.

Every locality may provide and operate within or outside its boundaries water supplies and water production, preparation, distribution and transmission systems, facilities and appurtenances for the purpose of furnishing water for the use of its inhabitants; or may contract with others for such purposes and services. Fees and charges for the services of such systems shall be fair and reasonable and payable as directed by the locality. Except in counties which are not otherwise authorized, a locality may require the connection of premises with facilities provided for furnishing water; charge and collect compensation for water thus furnished; and may provide penalties for the unauthorized use thereof.

No locality, after July 1, 1976, shall construct, provide or operate outside its boundaries any water supply system prior to obtaining the consent of the locality in which the system is to be located. No consent shall be required for the operation of any such water supply system in existence on July 1, 1976, in the process of construction or for which the site has been purchased, or for its orderly expansion.

In any case in which the approval by such locality's governing body is withheld, the party seeking such approval may petition for the convening of a special court, pursuant to §§ 15.2-2135 through 15.2-2141.

Notwithstanding any provision of law to the contrary, any town with a population between 11,000 and 14,000, with the concurrence of the affected county, which provides and operates outside its boundaries any such water supply system may provide water supplies to industrial and commercial users outside its boundaries and collect such compensation therefor as may be contracted for between the town and such user. Such town shall not thereby be obligated to provide water supplies to any other users outside its boundaries.

History.
Code 1950, § 15-77.39; 1958, c. 328; 1962, c. 623, § 15.1-875; 1975, c. 573; 1976, c. 69; 1997, c. 587; 1998, cc. 224, 328.

Michie's Jurisprudence.
For related discussion, see 20 M.J. Water Companies and Waterworks; § 6.

CASE NOTES

Municipal corporations are empowered to contract with others for water and sewer services. Marsh v. Gainesville-Haymarket San. Dist., 214 Va. 83, 197 S.E.2d 329 (1973) (decided under prior law).

Purpose sufficient for exercise of police power. — Although former § 15.1-873 designated other purposes which might justify the enactment of a mandatory connection ordinance pursuant to this section, the public health purpose alone was sufficient to constitute a valid exercise of the city's police power. McMahon v. City of Virginia Beach, 221 Va. 102, 267 S.E.2d 130, cert. denied, 449 U.S. 954, 101 S. Ct. 361, 66 L. Ed. 2d 219 (1980) (decided under prior law).

Ability to finance cost of water system is inherent in the ability to provide a water system. — In order to exercise the duty and authority to provide a water system, the corresponding ability to pay for the system must exist; the ability to finance the cost of providing this service is inherent in the authority to provide it, and the specific mechanism chosen by the city to finance the project need not be defined by statute. Tidewater Ass'n of

Homebuilders, Inc. v. City of Virginia Beach, 241 Va. 114, 400 S.E.2d 523 (1991) (decided under prior law).

A resolution requiring abutting property owners to connect with the public water system and to abandon the use of any privately owned well water was a valid exercise of police power as a public health measure, and did not constitute a taking of property without due process of law. McMahon v. City of Virginia Beach, 221 Va. 102, 267 S.E.2d 130, cert. denied, 449 U.S. 954, 101 S. Ct. 361, 66 L. Ed. 2d 219 (1980) (decided under prior law).

Fee imposed to pay costs of city's water supply project was not an impact fee where it was a proprietary fee and those who were paying the fee were receiving a present, particularized benefit. Tidewater Ass'n of Homebuilders, Inc. v. City of Virginia Beach, 241 Va. 114, 400 S.E.2d 523 (1991) (decided under prior law).

The provisions of Va. Const., Art. X, § 1 apply to taxation of property. — Fee imposed to pay costs of city's water supply project was not an impact fee assessed against property, since only those connecting to the city water system paid the fee; vacant lot owners did not; therefore, the fee was not a tax and was not prohibited by Va. Const., Art. X, § 1. Tidewater Ass'n of Homebuilders, Inc. v. City of Virginia Beach, 241 Va. 114, 400 S.E.2d 523 (1991) (decided under prior law).

Fair and reasonable rates. — Evidence supported water and sewer rates charged by a town to out-of-town customers because an expert's testimony that the water rate charged to out-of-town customers was fair and reasonable, and that the sewer rate charged to out-of-town customers was practicable, equitable, and uniform, supported by the expert's justifications for the expert's opinion, was sufficient to make the issue fairly debatable. Town of Leesburg v. Giordano, 280 Va. 597, 701 S.E.2d 783, 2010 Va. LEXIS 276 (2010).

Necessity of consent. — The legislature intended to impose the consent requirement of this section upon a Virginia municipality's construction, provision, or operation of those tangible parts of a water supply system that are to be built in another Virginia jurisdiction after July 1, 1976. Therefore, where reservoir in question was built before that date and the evidence indicated that the government's change in the allocation of a part of the storage capacity of the reservoir did not involve the city in its construction, provision, or operation, the city's contractual right to use water in the reservoir as a part of its water supply system did not require consent under this section. City of Va. Beach v. Board of Supvrs., 246 Va. 233, 435 S.E.2d 382 (1993) (decided under prior law).

Relationship to federal law. — Provision of water service in certain areas by appellee water authority was not preempted by four acts of Congress, as there was no clear and manifest purpose to supersede Virginia's traditional authority in the area of water utility regulation; the Act of March 3, 1859, ch. 84, 11 Stat. 435 (1859) and the Act of April 14, 1926, ch. 140, 44 Stat. 251 (1926) did not refer to or impact the city at all, the Act of June 26, 1947, ch. 149, § 1, Pub. L. No. 80-118, 61 Stat. 181 (1947), merely authorized the Secretary of War to permit the delivery of water to the city (the language was conspicuously and unequivocally permissive), and the core objective of Act of Aug. 6, 1996, § 306(d)(1), Pub. L. 104-182, 110 Stat. 1686 (1996), was to facilitate the federal government's departure from the water supply business. City of Falls Church v. Fairfax County Water Auth., 2008 U.S. App. LEXIS 7285 (4th Cir. Apr. 4, 2008).

Applied in Town of Leesburg v. Giordano, 276 Va. 318, 667 S.E.2d 552, 2008 Va. LEXIS 66 (2008).

CHAPTER 28.2.

VIRGINIA INDOOR CLEAN AIR ACT.

ARTICLE 1.

GENERAL PROVISIONS.

§ 15.2-2820. Definitions.

As used in this chapter, unless the context requires a different meaning:

"Bar or lounge area" means any establishment or portion of an establishment devoted to the sale and service of alcoholic beverages for consumption on the premises and where the sale or service of food or meals is incidental to the consumption of the alcoholic beverages.

"Educational facility" means any building used for instruction of enrolled students, including but not limited to any day-care center, nursery school, public or private school, college, university, medical school, law school, or career and technical education school.

"Health care facility" means any institution, place, building, or agency required to be licensed under Virginia law, including but not limited to any hospital, nursing facility or nursing home, boarding home, assisted living facility, supervised living facility, or ambulatory medical and surgical center.

"Private club" means an organization, whether incorporated or not, that (i) is the owner, lessee, or occupant of a building or portion thereof used exclusively for club purposes, including club or member sponsored events; (ii) is operated solely for recreational, fraternal, social, patriotic, political, benevolent, or athletic purposes, and only sells alcoholic beverages incidental to its operation; (iii) has established bylaws, a constitution, or both that govern its activities; and (iv) the affairs and management of which are conducted by a board of directors, executive committee, or similar body chosen by the members at an annual meeting.

"Private function" means any gathering of persons for the purpose of deliberation, education, instruction, entertainment, amusement, or dining that is not intended to be open to the public and for which membership or specific invitation is a prerequisite to entry.

"Private work place" means any office or work area that is not open to the public in the normal course of business except by individual invitation.

"*Proprietor*" means the owner or lessee of the public place, who ultimately controls the activities within the public place. The term "proprietor" includes corporations, associations, or partnerships as well as individuals.

"*Public conveyance*" or "*public vehicle*" means any air, land, or water vehicle used for the mass transportation of persons in intrastate travel for compensation, including but not limited to any airplane, train, bus, or boat that is not subject to federal smoking regulations.

"*Public place*" means any enclosed, indoor area used by the general public, including but not limited to any building owned or leased by the Commonwealth or any agency thereof or any locality, public conveyance or public vehicle, educational facility, hospital, nursing facility or nursing home, other health care facility, library, retail store of 15,000 square feet or more, auditorium, arena, theater, museum, concert hall, or other area used for a performance or an exhibit of the arts or sciences, or any meeting room.

"*Recreational facility*" means any enclosed, indoor area used by the general public and used as a stadium, arena, skating rink, video game facility, or senior citizen recreational facility.

"*Restaurant*" means any place where food is prepared for service to the public on or off the premises, or any place where food is served. Examples of such places include but are not limited to lunchrooms, short order places, cafeterias, coffee shops, cafes, taverns, delicatessens, dining accommodations of public or private clubs, kitchen facilities of hospitals and nursing homes, dining accommodations of public and private schools and colleges, and kitchen areas of local correctional facilities subject to standards adopted under § 53.1-68. "Restaurant" shall not include (i) places where packaged or canned foods are manufactured and then distributed to grocery stores or other similar food retailers for sale to the public, (ii) mobile points of service to the general public that are outdoors, or (iii) mobile points of service where such service and consumption occur in a private residence or in any location that is not a public place. "Restaurant" shall include any bar or lounge area that is part of such restaurant.

"*Smoke*" or "*smoking*" means the carrying or holding of any lighted pipe, cigar, or cigarette of any kind, or any other lighted smoking equipment, or the lighting, inhaling, or exhaling of smoke from a pipe, cigar, or cigarette of any kind.

"*Theater*" means any indoor facility or auditorium, open to the public, which is primarily used or designed for the purpose of exhibiting any motion picture, stage production, musical recital, dance, lecture, or other similar performance.

History.
2009, cc. 153, 154.

Cross references.
As to offense of smoking in proximity to a medical oxygen source in a health care facility, see § 18.2-511.1.

Editor's note.
Acts 2009, cc. 153 and 154, cl. 3 provides: "That the provisions of this act shall become effective on December 1, 2009."

CASE NOTES

Definition of "Restaurant." — Determination that a cafe was not exempt from compliance with the regulations of the Virginia Indoor Clean Air Act was proper because the cafe fit the definition of "restaurant" under subsection A of § 15.2-2825, and thus had to comply with the smoking ban, as it did not fall within one of the six expressly stated exemptions set forth in subdivisions A 1 through 6 of § 15.2-2825; contrary to the owner's argument, § 15.2-2825 did not conflict with § 15.2-2821. The owner did not substantially prevail on the merits of the case and the department's position was substantially justified, so it was inappropriate to award the owner attorneys' fees and costs under subsection A of § 2.2-4030. Kepa, Inc. v. Va. Dep't of Health, 2013 Va. App. LEXIS 113 (Apr. 9, 2013).

OPINIONS OF THE ATTORNEY GENERAL

Electronic cigarette. — Using an e-cigarette does not fall within the definition of "smoke" or "smoking" for purposes of § 15.2-2820. See opinion of Attorney General to The Honorable Christopher K. Peace, Member, House of Delegates, 10-029, 2010 Va. AG LEXIS 21 (4/27/10).

§ 15.2-2821. Applicability.

Nothing in this chapter shall be construed to:

1. Permit smoking where it is otherwise prohibited or restricted by other applicable provisions of law; or

2. Regulate smoking in retail tobacco stores, tobacco warehouses, or tobacco manufacturing facilities.

History.
2009, cc. 153, 154.

Editor's note.
Acts 2009, cc. 153 and 154, cl. 3 provides: "That the provisions of this act shall become effective on December 1, 2009."

CASE NOTES

Restaurant smoking ban upheld. — Determination that a cafe was not exempt from compliance with the regulations of the Virginia Indoor Clean Air Act was proper because the cafe fit the definition of "restaurant" under subsection A of § 15.2-2825, and thus had to comply with the smoking ban, as it did not fall within one of the six expressly stated exemptions set forth in subdivisions A 1 through 6 of § 15.2-2825; contrary to the owner's argument, § 15.2-2821 did not conflict with § 15.2-2821. The owner did not substantially prevail on the merits of the case and the department's position was substantially justified, so it was inappropriate to award the owner attorneys' fees and costs under subsection A of § 2.2-4030. Kepa, Inc. v. Va. Dep't of Health, 2013 Va. App. LEXIS 113 (Apr. 9, 2013).

§ 15.2-2822. Authority of law-enforcement officials.

Any law-enforcement officer may issue a summons regarding a violation of this chapter.

History.
2009, cc. 153, 154.

Editor's note.
Acts 2009, cc. 153 and 154, cl. 3 provides: "That the provisions of this act shall become effective on December 1, 2009."

§ 15.2-2823. Smoking in public buildings or facilities; exception.

A. The Commonwealth or any agency thereof and every locality shall provide reasonable no-smoking areas, considering the nature of the use and the size of the building, in any building owned or leased by the Commonwealth or any agency thereof or a locality.

B. The provisions of this chapter shall not apply to office, work, or other areas of the Department of Corrections that are not entered by the general public in the normal course of business or use of the premises.

History.
2009, cc. 153, 154.

Editor's note.
Acts 2009, cc. 153 and 154, cl. 3 provides: "That the provisions of this act shall become effective on December 1, 2009."

ARTICLE 2.

STATEWIDE REGULATION OF SMOKING.

§ 15.2-2824. Prohibitions on smoking generally; penalty for violation.

A. Smoking shall be prohibited in (i) elevators, regardless of capacity, except in any open material hoist elevator not intended for use by the general public; (ii) public school buses; (iii) the interior of any public elementary, intermediate, and secondary school; (iv) hospital emergency rooms; (v) local or district health departments; (vi) polling rooms; (vii) indoor service lines and cashier lines; (viii) public restrooms in any building owned or leased by the Commonwealth or any agency thereof; (ix) the interior of a child day center licensed pursuant to § 63.2-1701 that is not also used for residential purposes; however, this prohibition shall not apply to any area of a building not utilized by a child day center, unless otherwise prohibited by this chapter; and (x) public restrooms of health care facilities.

B. No person shall smoke in any area or place specified in subsection A and any person who continues to smoke in such area or place after having been asked to refrain from smoking shall be subject to a civil penalty of not more than $25.

C. Civil penalties assessed under this section shall be paid into the Virginia Health Care Fund established under § 32.1-366.

History.
2009, cc. 153, 154.

Editor's note.
Acts 2009, cc. 153 and 154, cl. 3 provides: "That the provisions of this act shall become effective on December 1, 2009."

OPINIONS OF THE ATTORNEY GENERAL

Electronic cigarette. — Using an e-cigarette does not fall within the definition of "smoke" or "smoking" for purposes of § 15.2-2820. See opinion of Attorney General to The Honorable Christopher K. Peace, Member, House of Delegates, 10-029, 2010 Va. AG LEXIS 21 (4/27/10).

§ 15.2-2825. Smoking in restaurants prohibited; exceptions; posting of signs; penalty for violation.

A. Effective December 1, 2009, smoking shall be prohibited and no person shall smoke in any restaurant in the Commonwealth or in any restroom within such restaurant, except that smoking may be permitted in:

1. Any place or operation that prepares or stores food for distribution to persons of the same business operation or of a related business operation for service to the public. Examples of such places or operations include the preparation or storage of food for catering services, pushcart operations, hotdog stands, and other mobile points of service;

2. Any outdoor area of a restaurant, with or without roof covering, at such times when such outdoor area is not enclosed in whole or in part by any screened walls, roll-up doors, windows or other seasonal or temporary enclosures;

3. Any restaurants located on the premises of any manufacturer of tobacco products;

4. Any portion of a restaurant that is used exclusively for private functions, provided such functions are limited to those portions of the restaurant that meet the requirements of subdivision 5;

5. Any portion of a restaurant that is constructed in such a manner that the area where smoking may be permitted is (i) structurally separated from the portion of the restaurant in which smoking is prohibited and to which ingress and egress is through a door and (ii) separately vented to prevent the recirculation of air from such area to the area of the restaurant where smoking is prohibited. At least one public entrance to the restaurant shall be into an area of the restaurant where smoking is prohibited. For the purposes of the preceding sentence, nothing shall be construed to require the creation of an additional public entrance in cases where the only public entrance to a restaurant in existence as of December 1, 2009, is through an outdoor area described in subdivision 2; and

6. Any private club.

B. For the purposes of this section:

"*Proprietor*" means the owner, lessee or other person who ultimately controls the activities within the restaurant. The term "proprietor" includes corporations, associations, or partnerships as well as individuals.

"*Structurally separated*" means a stud wall covered with drywall or other building material or other like barrier, which, when completed, extends from the floor to the ceiling, resulting in a physically separated room. Such wall or barrier may include portions that are glass or other gas-impervious building material.

C. No individual who is wait staff or bus staff in a restaurant shall be required by the proprietor to work in any area of the restaurant where smoking may be permitted without the consent of such individual. Nothing in this subsection shall be interpreted to create a cause of action against such proprietor.

D. The proprietor of any restaurant shall:

1. Post signs stating "No Smoking" or containing the international "No Smoking" symbol, consisting of a pictorial representation of a burning cigarette enclosed in a red circle with a bar across it, clearly and conspicuously in every restaurant where smoking is prohibited in accordance with this section; and

2. Remove all ashtrays and other smoking paraphernalia from any area in the restaurant where smoking is prohibited in accordance with this section.

E. Any proprietor of a restaurant who fails to comply with the requirements of this section shall be subject to the civil penalty of not more than $25.

F. No person shall smoke in any area of a restaurant in which smoking is prohibited as provided in this section. Any person who continues to smoke in such area after having been asked to refrain from smoking shall be subject to a civil penalty of not more than $25.

G. It shall be an affirmative defense to a complaint brought against a proprietor for a violation of this section that the proprietor or an employee of such proprietor:

1. Posted a "No Smoking" sign as required;

2. Removed all ashtrays and other smoking paraphernalia from all areas where smoking is prohibited;

3. Refused to seat or serve any individual who was smoking in a prohibited area; and

4. If the individual continued to smoke after an initial warning, asked the individual to leave the establishment.

H. Civil penalties assessed under this section shall be paid into the Virginia Health Care Fund established under § 32.1-366.

I. Any local health department or its designee shall, while inspecting a restaurant as otherwise required by law, inspect for compliance with this section.

History.
2009, cc. 153, 154.

Editor's note.
Acts 2009, cc. 153 and 154, cl. 3 provides: "That the provisions of this act shall become effective on December 1, 2009."

OPINIONS OF THE ATTORNEY GENERAL

Electronic cigarette. — Using an e-cigarette does not fall within the definition of "smoke" or "smoking" for purposes of § 15.2-2820. See opinion of Attorney General to The Honorable

Christopher K. Peace, Member, House of Delegates, 10-029, 2010 Va. AG LEXIS 21 (4/27/10).

§ 15.2-2826. Designation of "No-Smoking" areas; smoking prohibited in "No-Smoking" areas; penalty for violation.

A. The proprietor or other person in charge of (i) an educational facility, except any public elementary, intermediate, or secondary school; (ii) a health care facility; (iii) a retail establishment of 15,000 square feet or more serving the general public, including, but not limited to, department stores, grocery stores, drug stores, clothing stores, and shoe stores; and (iv) recreational facilities shall designate reasonable no-smoking areas, considering the nature of the use and the size of the building.

B. The proprietor or other person in charge of a space subject to the provisions of this section shall post signs conspicuous to public view stating "Smoking Permitted" or "No Smoking." Any person failing to post such signs shall be subject to a civil penalty of not more than $25.

C. No person shall smoke in a designated no-smoking area and any person who continues to smoke in such area after having been asked to refrain from smoking shall be subject to a civil penalty of not more than $25.

D. Civil penalties assessed under this section shall be paid into the Virginia Health Care Fund established under § 32.1-366.

History.
2009, cc. 153, 154.

Editor's note.
Acts 2009, cc. 153 and 154, cl. 3 provides: "That the provisions of this act shall become effective on December 1, 2009."

§ 15.2-2827. Responsibility of building proprietors and managers.

Except as provided in § 15.2-2825, proprietors or persons who manage or otherwise control any building, structure, space, place, or area governed by this chapter in which smoking is not otherwise prohibited may designate rooms or areas in which smoking is permitted as follows:

1. Designated smoking areas shall not encompass so much of the building, structure, space, place, or area open to the general public that reasonable no-smoking areas, considering the nature of the use and the size of the building, are not provided;

2. Designated smoking areas shall be separate to the extent reasonably practicable from those rooms or areas entered by the general public in the normal use of the particular business or institution; and

3. In designated smoking areas, ventilation systems and existing physical barriers shall be used when reasonably practicable to minimize the permeation of smoke into no-smoking areas. However, this chapter shall not be construed as requiring physical modifications or alterations to any structure.

History.
2009, cc. 153, 154.

Editor's note.
Acts 2009, cc. 153 and 154, cl. 3 provides: "That the provisions of this act shall become effective on December 1, 2009."

ARTICLE 3.

LOCAL REGULATION OF SMOKING.

§ 15.2-2828. Ordinances regulating smoking generally.

A. No ordinances enacted by a locality prior to January 1, 1990, shall be deemed invalid or unenforceable because of lack of consistency with the provisions of this chapter.

B. Except as provided in § 15.2-2829, no ordinances adopted after January 1, 1990, shall contain provisions or standards that exceed those established in this chapter.

C. However, any ordinance may provide that employers may regulate smoking in the private work place as they deem appropriate under the following circumstances: (i) if the designation of smoking and no-smoking areas is the subject of a written agreement between the employer and his employees, the provisions of the written agreement shall control such designation and (ii) a total ban on smoking in any work place shall only be enforced by the employer upon an affirmative vote of a majority of the affected employees voting, unless such ban is the subject of a contract of employment between the employer and the employees as a prior condition of employment. No ordinance adopted pursuant to this subsection shall affect no-smoking policies established by employers prior to the adoption of such ordinance.

History.
2009, cc. 153, 154.

Editor's note.
Acts 2009, cc. 153 and 154, cl. 3 provides: "That the provisions of this act shall become effective on December 1, 2009."

§ 15.2-2829. Mandatory provisions of ordinances.

If an ordinance is enacted by a locality in accordance with this chapter, it shall provide that it is unlawful for any person to smoke in any of the following places:

1. Common areas in an educational facility, including but not limited to, classrooms, hallways, auditoriums, and public meeting rooms;

2. School buses and public conveyances; and

3. Any of the places governed by § 15.2-2824 or 15.2-2825.

History.
2009, cc. 153, 154.

Editor's note.
Acts 2009, cc. 153 and 154, cl. 3 provides: "That the provisions of this act shall become effective on December 1, 2009."

§ 15.2-2830. Optional provisions of ordinances.

If an ordinance is enacted by a locality in accordance with this chapter, it may provide that management shall designate reasonable no-smoking areas, considering the nature of the use and the size of the building, in the following places:

1. Retail and service establishments of 15,000 square feet or more serving the general public, including, but not limited to, department stores, grocery stores, drug stores, clothing stores, and shoe stores;

2. Educational facilities, except as provided in § 15.2-2824;

3. Health care facilities;

4. Rooms in which a public meeting or hearing is being held;

5. Places of entertainment and cultural facilities, including but not limited to theaters, concert halls, gymnasiums, auditoriums, other enclosed arenas, art galleries, libraries, and museums;

6. Indoor facilities used for recreational purposes; or

7. Other public places.

History.
2009, cc. 153, 154.

Editor's note.
Acts 2009, cc. 153 and 154, cl. 3 provides: "That the provisions of this act shall become effective on December 1, 2009."

§ 15.2-2831. Other ordinances not authorized.

The provisions of §§ 15.2-2828, 15.2-2829, and 15.2-2830 shall not be construed to allow local regulation of smoking in:

1. Conference or meeting rooms and public or private assembly rooms while such rooms are being used for private functions;

2. Private work places;

3. Areas of enclosed shopping centers or malls that are external to the retail stores therein, are used by customers as a route of travel from one store to another, and consist primarily of walkways and seating arrangements; or

4. Lobby areas of hotels, motels, and other establishments open to the general public for overnight accommodation.

History.
2009, cc. 153, 154.

Editor's note.
Acts 2009, cc. 153 and 154, cl. 3 provides: "That the provisions of this act shall become effective on December 1, 2009."

§ 15.2-2832. Regulation of smoking; posting of signs.

Any person who owns, manages, or otherwise controls any building or area in which smoking is regulated by an ordinance shall post in an appropriate place, in a clear, conspicuous, and sufficient manner, "Smoking Permitted" signs, "No Smoking" signs, or "No-Smoking Section Available" signs.

History.
2009, cc. 153, 154.

Editor's note.
Acts 2009, cc. 153 and 154, cl. 3 provides: "That the provisions of this act shall become effective on December 1, 2009."

§ 15.2-2833. Enforcement of ordinances.

A. Any ordinance may provide a civil penalty of not more than $25 for violations of any provision of such ordinance.

B. Any ordinance may provide that no person shall smoke in a designated no-smoking area and any person who continues to smoke in such area after being asked to refrain from smoking may be subject to a civil penalty of not more than $25.

C. Any ordinance shall provide that any law-enforcement officer may issue a summons regarding a violation of the ordinance.

D. Any civil penalties assessed under this section shall be paid into the treasury of the locality where the offense occurred and shall be expended solely for public health purposes.

History.
2009, cc. 153, 154.

Editor's note.
Acts 2009, cc. 153 and 154, cl. 3 provides: "That the provisions of this act shall become effective on December 1, 2009."

TITLE 16.1.

COURTS NOT OF RECORD.

CHAPTER 4.1.

DISTRICT COURTS.

Article 5. Financing of the District System.

ARTICLE 5.

FINANCING OF THE DISTRICT SYSTEM.

§ 16.1-69.48:5. Fees for services of juvenile and domestic relations district court judges and clerks in certain civil cases.

Except as otherwise provided, upon the initial commencement of any case in the juvenile and domestic relations district court pursuant to subdi-

vision A 3 of § 16.1-241 when the custody or visitation of a child is a subject of controversy or requires determination, there shall be a filing fee of $25. However, only one $25 fee shall be required for all custody and visitation petitions simultaneously initiated by a single petitioner. Notwithstanding any other provision of law, there shall be no other fees or costs added to this fee as a condition of filing. No case to which this fee is applicable shall be set for hearing by the clerk until this fee has been paid except on account of poverty as provided in § 17.1-606. Fees shall be paid to the clerk in the jurisdiction in which the petition is filed.

This fee shall not be charged in any case brought by an agent of the Commonwealth or of a local government entity.

When service of process is had on the respondent named in a petition for which the filing fee established by this section has been paid, such petition may be reissued once by changing the return day of such process, for which service there shall be no charge; however, reissuance of such process shall be within three months after the original return day.

In the case of an appeal filed pursuant to § 16.1-296, the clerk shall collect any applicable fees for service of process of the notice of appeal in the circuit court from the appellant prior to transmitting the case to the clerk of the circuit court. For purposes of this section, service of process in the circuit court may include service on the appellee by the sheriff or private process server or certified or registered mail, and service on the attorney for the appellee by regular mail.

History.
2003, c. 906; 2004, cc. 366, 659, 727.

Law Review.
For 2003/2004 survey of family and juvenile law, see 39 U. Rich. L. Rev. 241 (2004).

Research references.
Virginia Forms (Matthew Bender). No. 5-208 Affidavit in Support of Application for Proceeding without Payment of Filing Fees. No. 5-275 Affidavit in Support of Application for Proceeding in Custody or Visitation Case Without Payment of Filing Fees.

CHAPTER 7.

JURISDICTION AND PROCEDURE IN CRIMINAL MATTERS.

Article 1. Jurisdiction in Criminal Matters.

ARTICLE 1.

JURISDICTION IN CRIMINAL MATTERS.

§ 16.1-123. Repealed by Acts 1984, c. 506.

§ 16.1-123.1. Criminal and traffic jurisdiction of general district courts.

1. Each general district court shall have, within the county, including the towns within such county, or city for which it is established, exclusive original jurisdiction for the trial of:

a. All offenses against the ordinances, laws and bylaws of such county, including the towns within such county, or city or of any service district within such county or city, except a city ordinance enacted pursuant to §§ 18.2-372 through 18.2-391.1. All offenses against the ordinances of a service district shall be prosecuted in the name of such service district;

b. All other misdemeanors and traffic infractions arising in such county, including the towns in such county, or city.

2. Each general district court which is established within a city shall also have:

a. Concurrent jurisdiction with the circuit court of such city for all violations of state revenue and election laws; and

b. Exclusive original jurisdiction, except as otherwise provided by general law or the city charter, within the area extending for one mile beyond the corporate limits thereof, for the trial of all offenses against the ordinances, laws and bylaws of the city.

3. If a city lying within a county has no general district court provided by city charter or under general law, then the general district court of the county within which such city lies shall have the same jurisdiction in such city as a general district court established for a city would have.

4. Each general district court shall have such other jurisdiction, exclusive or concurrent, as may be conferred on such court by general law or by provisions of the charter of the city for which the court was established.

5. Nothing herein shall affect the jurisdiction conferred on the juvenile and domestic relations district court by Chapter 11 (§ 16.1-226 et seq.) of this title.

History.
1984, c. 506.

Cross references.
For constitutional provisions, see Va. Const., Art. I, §§ 8, 11. For provision redesignating county courts as general district courts, see § 16.1-69.8. For right of appeal, see § 16.1-132. For right of jury trial, see § 16.1-136.

Law Review.
For article, "Trial by Jury and Speedy Justice," see 28 Wash. & Lee L. Rev. 309 (1971). For article, "Appeal De Novo in Virginia: An Examination of Its Present Utility," see 42 Wash. & Lee L. Rev. 1149 (1985). For article surveying developments in criminal law and procedure in Virginia from July 2001 to September 2002, see 37 U. Rich. L. Rev. 45 (2002).

Research references.
Friend's Virginia Pleading and Practice (Matthew Bender). Chapter 1 Courts. § 1.05 District Courts. Charles E. Friend.

Michie's Jurisprudence.
For related discussion, see 2B M.J. Automobiles, § 118; 5A M.J. Courts, §§ 43, 44.

CASE NOTES

Petty offenses not requiring jury trial. — Notwithstanding the broad language of the Virginia Constitution, there are many petty offenses against statutes or municipal ordinances which are triable without a jury, because they were so triable when the Constitution was adopted, and the right of trial by jury which is secured is the right as it existed at the time the Constitution was adopted. This was decided in Ex parte Marx, 86 Va. 40, 9 S.E. 475 (1889), and such is the settled law on the subject. Ragsdale v. City of Danville, 116 Va. 484, 82 S.E. 77 (1914).

Ordinance violations involving title to real estate. — See Martin v. City of Richmond, 108 Va. 765, 62 S.E. 800 (1980); City of Richmond v. Sutherland, 114 Va. 688, 77 S.E. 470 (1913).

Applied in Greenwalt v. Commonwealth, 224 Va. 498, 297 S.E.2d 709 (1982); Kelley v. Stamos, 285 Va. 68, 737 S.E.2d 218, 2013 Va. LEXIS 10 (2013).

§§ 16.1-124, 16.1-125. Repealed by Acts 1984, c. 506.

Cross references.
As to the criminal and traffic jurisdiction of general district courts, see now § 16.1-123.1.

§ 16.1-126. Certain courts of record may try misdemeanors; procedure.

Notwithstanding the provisions of this chapter, the circuit court of any county or city having criminal jurisdiction, shall have jurisdiction to try any person for any misdemeanor for which a presentment or indictment is brought in or for which an information is filed; or such court may certify the presentment, indictment or information for trial to the court not of record which would otherwise have jurisdiction of the offense; in which event the presentment, indictment or information shall be in lieu of any warrant, petition or other pleading which might otherwise be required by law.

History.
1956, c. 555.

Law Review.
For article, "Trial by Jury and Speedy Justice," see 28 Wash. & Lee L. Rev. 309 (1971).

§ 16.1-127. Courts may conduct preliminary examinations.

In addition to the power and authority conferred by this chapter on courts not of record having criminal jurisdiction, each such court shall have power to conduct preliminary examinations of persons charged with crime within its jurisdiction in the manner prescribed in Chapter 7 (§ 19.2-71 et seq.) of Title 19.2.

History.
1956, c. 555; 1960, c. 362.

CASE NOTES

County (now general district) courts have no jurisdiction over felonies. Kost v. Cox, 317 F. Supp. 884 (W.D. Va. 1970).
With the exception of conducting preliminary hearings. — See Kost v. Cox, 317 F. Supp. 884 (W.D. Va. 1970).
In Virginia, a preliminary hearing in an adult criminal case is merely a procedural requirement, not jurisdictionally significant. Nottingham v. Zahradnick, 573 F.2d 193 (4th Cir.), cert. denied, 439 U.S. 970, 99 S. Ct. 464, 58 L. Ed. 2d 430 (1978).
And may be preempted. — Determination by a grand jury of probable cause to indict preempts an adult defendant's right to a preliminary hearing. Nottingham v. Zahradnick, 573 F.2d 193 (4th Cir.), cert. denied, 439 U.S. 970, 99 S. Ct. 464, 58 L. Ed. 2d 430 (1978).

§ 16.1-128. Exception when jurisdiction in State Corporation Commission.

Nothing in this chapter shall be held to confer upon courts not of record any jurisdiction or power over offenses of which jurisdiction is specifically vested in the State Corporation Commission or in courts of record under the corporation laws of the Commonwealth.

History.
1956, c. 555.

ARTICLE 2.

PROCEDURE IN CRIMINAL CASES.

§ 16.1-129. Offenses tried on warrants, or as provided in Chapter 7 of Title 19.2.

Every offense of which a court not of record is given jurisdiction under this title may be tried upon a warrant; or the judge of such court may, in his discretion, make an examination into the offense and proceed according to the provisions of Chapter 7 (§ 19.2-71 et seq.) of Title 19.2. The word warrant as

used in this chapter shall be construed to include a summons or notice requiring a person to appear and answer a charge of having violated any statute, ordinance, or any regulation having the force and effect of law.

History.
1956, c. 555; 1960, c. 373.

Law Review.
For article, "Trial by Jury and Speedy Justice," see 28 Wash. & Lee L. Rev. 309 (1971).

Michie's Jurisprudence.
For related discussion, see 8B M.J. Forgery, §§ 9, 24; 12A M.J. Larceny, § 11.

CASE NOTES

No opportunity for vindictive deterrence of appeal. — The Virginia two-tier system of administering criminal justice does not present the opportunity for the vindictive deterrence of appeal condemned in North Carolina v. Pearce, 395 U.S. 711, 89 S. Ct. 2072, 23 L. Ed. 2d 656 (1969); McClung v. Weatherholtz, 351 F. Supp. 5 (W.D. Va. 1972).
Failure to appear on charging summons. — Traffic summons was a public record as it became the charging document on which a general district court tried an accused, under § 16.1-129, and if an accused willfully violated his written promise to appear in court, given when he signed the summons, he could be convicted for failure to appear under § 19.2-128, regardless of the disposition of, and in addition to, the charge upon which he was originally arrested, under subdivision A 3 of § 19.2-74, and, given this statutory scheme, each signed summons clearly could constitute a separate offense under § 18.2-168, regarding forgery of a public document. Hines v. Commonwealth, 39 Va. App. 752, 576 S.E.2d 781, 2003 Va. App. LEXIS 92 (2003).
On appeal, court properly granted motion to amend summons. — Where both an arrest warrant and a summons charged defendant with violating a city ordinance and § 18.2-266, each of which is a misdemeanor, and the defendant was convicted on the summons and appealed, and on appeal, the circuit court granted the Commonwealth's motion to amend the summons to delete the reference to the city ordinance, this action was proper, as the amendment did not change the nature or character of the offense charged. Hill v. Commonwealth, No. 1240-91-4 (Ct. of Appeals Feb. 2, 1993).
Applied in Bellinger v. Commonwealth, 23 Va. App. 471, 477 S.E.2d 779 (1996).

§ 16.1-129.1. Repealed by Acts 1990, c. 75.

§ 16.1-129.2. Procedure when warrant defective.

Upon the trial of a warrant, the court may, upon its own motion or upon the request either of the attorney for the prosecution or for the accused, amend the form of the warrant in any respect in which it appears to be defective. But when the warrant is so defective in form that it does not substantially appear from the same what is the offense with which the accused is charged, or even when it is not so seriously defective, the judge of the court having examined on oath the original complainant, if there be one, or if he sees good reason to believe that an offense has been committed, then without examination of witnesses, may issue under his own hand his warrant reciting the offense and requiring the defendant in the original warrant to be arrested and brought before him. Upon the arrest of the defendant on the new warrant and his production or appearance in court the trial shall proceed upon the new warrant. When there is an amendment of the original warrant the trial shall proceed on the amended warrant. But whether the warrant is amended or a new warrant is issued, the court before proceeding to trial on the same may grant a continuance to the prosecution or to the defendant upon such terms as to costs as may be proper under the circumstances of the case; provided, however, that if the warrant be amended or if a new warrant be issued after any evidence has been heard, the accused shall be entitled to a continuance as a matter of right.

When a warrant is amended or a new warrant is issued the costs already accrued shall be taxed against the defendant, if he is ultimately convicted, as a part of the costs arising under the new or amended warrant.

History.
1968, c. 495.

Cross references.
For provision on amendment of written pleadings, see Rule 8:8, Juvenile and Domestic Relations District Court Rules.

CASE NOTES

Judge's authority to amend warrant. — Assuming a trial judge never actually accepted a defendant's plea of guilty to a charge of driving under the influence, the judge retained the authority to amend the charging warrant and then find the defendant guilty of reckless driving. Kelley v. Stamos, 285 Va. 68, 737 S.E.2d 218, 2013 Va. LEXIS 10 (2013).

Amendment did not render warrant defective. — Arrest warrant issued was not defective as a result of having been amended sometime prior to a trial de novo in the lower appellate court, where the dates of the offense were amended, as the same particularity was not required in warrants of arrest as was required in formal indictments; pursuant to §§ 16.1-129.2 and 16.1-137, as long as the warrant was not so defective as to fail to notify the defendant of the nature and character of the offense charged, both district courts and circuit courts had the power to amend a warrant in any respect in which the warrant appeared to be defective, on the courts' own motion and without the consent of the parties. Raja v. Commonwealth, 40 Va. App. 710, 581 S.E.2d 237, 2003 Va. App. LEXIS 318 (2003).

Amendment did not render indictment defective. — Even though the trial court allowed the indictment to be amended, the indictment was not rendered defective by the amendment. The trial court merely allowed the indictment to be changed from reading that defendant robbed the store to defendant robbed the store clerk, but at all times, defendant was aware of the nature of the conduct forming the robbery charge against defendant. Thomas v. Commonwealth, 2006 Va. App. LEXIS 605 (Dec. 20, 2006).

CIRCUIT COURT OPINIONS

Amendment could not change nature and character of offense charged. — Amendment to a warrant could not change the nature and character of the offense originally charged; a trial court erred when, after hearing the evidence and without the agreement of the parties or the request of either, sua sponte, amended a DUI warrant to reckless driving and convicted defendant, since reckless driving was not a lesser included offense of DUI. Commonwealth v. Sumner, 66 Va. Cir. 266, 2004 Va. Cir. LEXIS 322 (Salem Dec. 3, 2004).

Dismissal of an appeal was required because, although defendant was tried on a charge of improper lane change, he was convicted of the charge of failure to give full time and attention to the operation of the vehicle, pursuant to Fairfax, Va., County Code § 82-4-24, and the district court had not amended the warrant, because an amendment could not change the nature and character of the offense originally charged. Commonwealth v. Dipietro, 79 Va. Cir. 55, 2009 Va. Cir. LEXIS 67 (Fairfax Apr. 22, 2009).

OPINIONS OF THE ATTORNEY GENERAL

Prosecutorial discretion. — While a prosecutor is permitted to move to amend a misdemeanor charge alleging a violation of a municipal ordinance to the equivalent misdemeanor charge alleging a violation of state law when such an arrest or summons was made by an officer of a local police department or a deputy for a local sheriff's department, any such an amendment is subject to judicial review and may be made only by an appropriate judicial officer. See opinion of Attorney General to The Honorable Richard K. Newman, Commonwealth Attorney for the City of Hopewell, 11-080, 2012 Va. AG LEXIS 8 (2/17/12).

§ 16.1-129.3. Repealed by Acts 1974, c. 481.

§ 16.1-130. Repealed by Acts 1983, c. 499.

Cross references.
For provision as to retention of records of criminal cases in the general district courts and juvenile and domestic relations district courts, see § 16.1-69.55.

§ 16.1-131. Subpoenas duces tecum and recognizances of witnesses; applicable provisions.

The provisions of § 16.1-90 with respect to recognizances for witnesses upon the continuation of any case, shall be applicable to proceedings of a criminal nature as well as to civil actions. The provisions of Rule 3A:12 of the Rules of the Supreme Court shall apply to the issuance of a subpoena duces tecum and punishment for failure to comply.

History.
1956, c. 555; 1986, c. 160.

§ 16.1-131.1. Procedure when constitutionality of a statute is challenged in a court not of record.

In any criminal or traffic case in a court not of record, if the court rules that a statute or local ordinance is unconstitutional, it shall upon motion of the Commonwealth, or the locality if a local ordinance is the subject of the ruling, stay the proceedings and issue a written statement of its findings of law and relevant facts, if any, in support of its ruling and shall transmit the case, together with all papers, documents, and evidence connected therewith, to the circuit court for a determination of constitutionality. Either party may file a brief with the circuit court. Either party may request oral argument before the circuit court. The circuit court shall give the issue priority on its docket. If the circuit court rules that the statute or local ordinance is unconstitutional, the Commonwealth or the locality may appeal such interlocutory order to the Court of Appeals and thereafter to the Supreme Court; however, if the circuit court rules that the statute or local ordinance is constitutional, the circuit court shall remand the case to the court not of record for trial consistent with the ruling of the circuit court.

History.

2006, cc. 571, 876; 2010, cc. 303, 609.

The 2010 amendments.

The 2010 amendments by cc. 303 and 609 are identical, and inserted "or the locality if a local ordinance is the subject of the ruling" following "Commonwealth" in the first sentence and "or the locality" following "Commonwealth" in the last sentence.

Law Review.

For 2006 survey article, "Criminal Law and Procedure," see 41 U. Rich. L. Rev. 83 (2006).

§ 16.1-132. Right of appeal.

Any person convicted in a district court of an offense not felonious shall have the right, at any time within ten days from such conviction, and whether or not such conviction was upon a plea of guilty, to appeal to the circuit court. There shall also be an appeal of right from any order or judgment of a district court forfeiting any recognizance or revoking any suspension of sentence.

History.

1956, c. 555.

Cross references.

For constitutional provision, see Va. Const., Art. I, § 8. For appeals in civil cases, see §§ 16.1-106 through 16.1-114.1.

Law Review.

For comment, "Right to Court-Appointed Counsel for Misdemeanants in Virginia," see 4 U. Rich. L. Rev. 306 (1970). For survey of Virginia law on criminal law and procedure for the year 1969-1970, see 56 Va. L. Rev. 1572 (1970). For survey of Virginia criminal law and procedure for the year 1970-1971, see 57 Va. L. Rev. 1438 (1971). For article, "Trial by Jury and Speedy Justice," see 28 Wash. & Lee L. Rev. 309 (1971). For survey of Virginia law on criminal law for the year 1971-1972, see 58 Va. L. Rev. 1206 (1972). For survey of Virginia law on criminal procedure for the year 1972-1973, see 59 Va. L. Rev. 1478 (1973). For note, "Limiting Judicial Incompetence: The Due Process Right to a Legally Learned Judge in State Minor Court Criminal Proceedings," see 61 Va. L. Rev. 1454 (1975). For article, "Appeal De Novo in Virginia: An Examination of Its Present Utility," see 42 Wash. & Lee L. Rev. 1149 (1985). For an article relating to all published Virginia criminal law decisions between July 1, 1997, and July 1, 1998, see 32 U. Rich. L. Rev. 1091 (1998).

Michie's Jurisprudence.

For related discussion, see 1B M.J. Appeal and Error, §§ 25, 85, 357, 376, 377, 380, 382; 4C M.J. Constitutional Law, §§ 128, 141; 5B M.J. Criminal Procedure, §§ 14, 77; 9A M.J. Habeas Corpus, § 15; 12A M.J. Larceny, § 33.

CASE NOTES

This section and § 16.1-136 were enacted pursuant to the Va. Const., Art. I, § 8, and provide the means of securing a trial by jury. Commonwealth v. Bass, 113 Va. 760, 74 S.E. 397 (1912), decided under former statute corresponding to this section.

No violation of Equal Protection Clause. — With respect to appellate procedure, the distinctions between felonies and misdemeanors either do not exist or, where they do, are based upon well-reasoned objectives which serve a legitimate state interest and protect the constitutional right of defendants convicted of crime and thus do not violate equal protection. Saunders v. Reynolds, 214 Va. 697, 204 S.E.2d 421 (1974).

The equal protection clause of the Fourteenth Amendment to the United States Constitution is not violated by the procedure in which a person convicted of a misdemeanor in a court not of record is given an automatic appeal to a higher court while a person originally convicted in a court of record has no such automatic right of appeal to a higher court. Saunders v. Reynolds, 214 Va. 697, 204 S.E.2d 421 (1974).

Construction with other laws. — Where the provisions of §§ 16.1-69.24 and 18.2-459 address the specific subject of appeals from summary contempt adjudications in the district courts, and the provisions of §§ 16.1-132 and 16.1-136 address the general subject of appeals from the district courts, to the extent that the more specific provisions of §§ 16.1-69.24 and § 18.2-459 are in conflict with the general provisions of §§ 16.1-132 and 16.1-136, the more specific statutes prevail. Gilman v. Commonwealth, 275 Va. 222, 657 S.E.2d 474, 2008 Va. LEXIS 23 (2008).

Because the provisions of § 16.1-69.24 and § 18.2-459 had to prevail over the more general provisions of §§ 16.1-132 and 16.1-136, a contemnor appealing an adjudication of summary contempt does not receive a trial de novo in the circuit court with attendant Sixth Amendment protections and, thus, does not have a Sixth Amendment right of confrontation in the circuit court. Gilman v. Commonwealth, 275 Va. 222, 657 S.E.2d 474, 2008 Va. LEXIS 23 (2008).

This section contains no unreasonable restrictions. Gaskill v. Commonwealth, 206 Va. 486, 144 S.E.2d 293 (1965).

Section does not limit appeals from other juvenile court orders or judgments. — Although this section mentions a right to an appeal only with respect to orders or judgments pertaining to convictions, filing for recognizance, or revoking suspension of sentences, this provision does not operate to limit the right of appeal from other juvenile court orders or judgments. Hairfield v. Commonwealth, 7 Va. App. 649, 376 S.E.2d 796 (1989).

Orders transferring juveniles are final, a contrary interpretation would contravene legislative intent, and such orders are immediately appealable to the circuit court and need not be preceded by a conviction under this section. Hairfield v. Commonwealth, 7 Va. App. 649, 376 S.E.2d 796 (1989).

This section insures an unrestricted right of appeal to the circuit court, where the accused can demand a jury. Lacey v. Palmer, 93 Va. 159, 24 S.E. 930 (1896), decided under former statute corresponding to this section.

Regardless of whether error was committed. — The intent of the former statutes relating to appeals from justices of the peace, and trial justices appointed under Chapter 2 of former Title 16, was to grant an appeal, in the nature of a new trial, as of right without inquiry as to whether the justice or trial justice has committed error or not. And considering the nature and procedure of these courts it seemed to be an undesirable practice to make appeals therefrom depend, in any case, upon the establishment by parol testimony that the justice had been guilty of judicial misconduct or had committed error. Dickerson v. Commonwealth, 162 Va. 787, 173 S.E. 543 (1934) (decided under former statute corresponding to this section).

The trial de novo procedure involves a fresh determination of guilt or innocence by the court of general jurisdiction, which is not the court that acted before and has no motive to deal more strictly with a de novo defendant than it would with any other. Griffith v. Kerkhoff, 345 F. Supp. 1160 (W.D. Va. 1972).

An appeal of a district court order revoking a suspended sentence must be heard de novo in the circuit court. Barnes v. City of Newport News, 9 Va. App. 466, 389 S.E.2d 481 (1990).

The effect of an appeal from the inferior court's decision is not only to deprive him of further jurisdiction but to annul his judgment of conviction. Malouf v. City of Roanoke, 177 Va. 846, 13 S.E.2d 319 (1941) (decided under former statute corresponding to this section).

An appeal under this section and § 16.1-136 is, in effect, a statutory grant of a new trial which annuls the judgment of the inferior court, and accordingly such judgment may not be introduced in evidence before the jury in the circuit court. Harbaugh v. Commonwealth, 209 Va. 695, 167 S.E.2d 329 (1969).

An appeal under this section is in effect a statutory grant of a new trial, which annuls the judgment of the inferior court as completely as if there had been no previous trial, and it is reversible error to mention such judgment of conviction in a trial of the case on appeal. Buck v. City of Danville, 213 Va. 387, 192 S.E.2d 758 (1972).

Whenever a defendant exercises his rights under § 16.1-132 and a conviction in general district court is appealed, the fact of that conviction is not admissible in the appeal or in a subsequent civil proceeding. Baker v. Elmendorf, 271 Va. 474, 628 S.E.2d 358, 2006 Va. LEXIS 39 (2006).

In a malicious prosecution suit, it was error to admit into evidence, under *Ricketts v. J.G. McCrory Co.,* 138 Va. 548 (1924), the fact of a previous conviction as conclusive evidence of probable cause; where the conviction was reversed on appeal, the de novo appeal annulled the judgment of the inferior tribunal completely as if there had been no previous trial and "wiped out" guilty pleas. Baker v. Elmendorf, 271 Va. 474, 628 S.E.2d 358, 2006 Va. LEXIS 39 (2006).

The right of appeal is not dependent upon the posting of a bond. — The right of an accused to appeal from the district court to the circuit court and obtain retrial of a misdemeanor charge pursuant to this section is not dependent upon his posting an appeal bond. Hill v. Middlesex County, 12 Va. App. 58, 402 S.E.2d 243 (1991).

No condition imposed except appeal be made within 10 days from conviction. — No condition is imposed upon the exercise of the statutory right to appeal in this section other than the requirement that the appeal be made within 10 days from conviction in the district court. Hill v. Middlesex County, 12 Va. App. 58, 402 S.E.2d 243 (1991).

The right to appeal is not waived by form of plea. — The words "and whether or not such conviction was upon a plea of guilty," make statutory the holding in Dickerson v. Commonwealth, 162 Va. 787, 173 S.E. 543 (1934), that a plea of guilty or not guilty does not operate to waive or bar the right of appeal given by that section. The case cited disapproves the contrary rule laid down in Cooper v. Town of Appalachia, 145 Va. 861, 134 S.E. 591 (1926).

Nor by motion to suspend jail sentence. — A motion to suspend a jail sentence made by or on behalf of the accused after he had been sentenced is not a waiver of, or a bar to, the right of the accused to appeal to the circuit court. Dickerson v. Commonwealth, 162 Va. 787, 173 S.E. 543 (1934) (decided under former statute corresponding to this section).

Accused, convicted by a trial justice and informed that if he paid his fine and costs he would not be granted an appeal, stated that he did not intend to appeal, paid the fine and costs, and was remanded to jail to begin the service of his sentence. Within the ten-day period in which an appeal is allowed by this section, his application to the trial justice for an appeal was denied. It was held that his right to appeal was not waived. Gravely v. Deeds, 185 Va. 662, 40 S.E.2d 175 (1946) (decided under former statute corresponding to this section).

And payment of fine and partial submission to judgment of trial justice do not constitute waiver of the right to appeal if proper steps are taken to perfect such an appeal within the period named in this section. Gravely v. Deeds, 185 Va. 662, 40 S.E.2d 175 (1946) decided under former statute corresponding to this section).

Assignment of errors not required. — An appeal of right is given by the statute to one convicted in the inferior court without assigning errors. Harrison v. Commonwealth, 81 Va. 491 (1886) (decided under former statute corresponding to this section).

Plea of guilty not to be considered on appeal. — The language of this section indicates that a plea of guilty in an inferior court should not be considered on appeal. Harbaugh v. Commonwealth, 209 Va. 695, 167 S.E.2d 329 (1969).

Since under the terms of this section an accused is given the right to a new trial whether or not such conviction was upon a plea of guilty in the inferior court, such plea of guilty was not admissible in evidence on the appeal to the court of record. Harbaugh v. Commonwealth, 209 Va. 695, 167 S.E.2d 329 (1969).

Double jeopardy is not violated where defendant is re-indicted on original offense after appeal de novo to the circuit court because the plea-based conviction is thereby vacated and

jeopardy continues until a final conviction is rendered. Peterson v. Commonwealth, 5 Va. App. 389, 363 S.E.2d 440 (1987).

When the defendant appealed her misdemeanor possession conviction to the circuit court, as she had a right to do under this section, her conviction was vacated; therefore, the defendant could be retried for the same or a greater offense without double jeopardy being violated. Peterson v. Commonwealth, 5 Va. App. 389, 363 S.E.2d 440 (1987).

Imposition of greater sentence on retrial. — Allowing a jury to impose a greater sentence on retrial without evidence of supervening misconduct does not place an unconstitutional condition on one's exercise of the right to a trial by jury. Manns v. Allman, 324 F. Supp. 1149 (W.D. Va. 1971), aff'd, 473 F.2d 909 (4th Cir. 1973).

When a jury in a de novo trial imposed a more severe sentence than was imposed in the lower court of record, there was no denial of either due process or equal protection. Manns v. Allman, 324 F. Supp. 1149 (W.D. Va. 1971), aff'd, 473 F.2d 909 (4th Cir. 1973).

When a greater sentence is imposed at a retrial by a jury, such a penalty will be valid in the absence of exceptional circumstances. Manns v. Allman, 324 F. Supp. 1149 (W.D. Va. 1971), aff'd, 473 F.2d 909 (4th Cir. 1973).

The imposition of a harsher sentence in the absence of any intervening misconduct at a de novo trial on appeal of the defendant's conviction of reckless driving does not violate the due process clause. Griffith v. Kerkhoff, 345 F. Supp. 1160 (W.D. Va. 1972).

No conviction of greater offense on appeal from conviction of lesser included offense. — One who was tried in a court not of record on a warrant charging him with driving under the influence of alcohol, and who was convicted of the lesser included offense of impaired driving, may not be tried and convicted of driving under the influence of intoxicants on an appeal of his conviction to the corporation (now circuit) court. Buck v. City of Danville, 213 Va. 387, 192 S.E.2d 758 (1972).

When a warrant charges an accused with an offense of several grades, and on his trial in a court not of record he is acquitted of the greater offense and convicted of the lesser included offense, on appeal from that conviction the defendant is not placed in the same position as to the offense of which he was acquitted as if no trial had been had. Buck v. City of Danville, 213 Va. 387, 192 S.E.2d 758 (1972).

Due process affords the appellant the right to a de novo hearing in the circuit court without having to risk an attempt by the Commonwealth to convict him of a more serious charge with a greater potential punishment for the same criminal incident. Allen v. Commonwealth, 36 Va. App. 334, 549 S.E.2d 652, 2001 Va. App. LEXIS 447 (2001).

Commonwealth's indictment and conviction of the appellant for a felony offense upon his invocation of this section was constitutionally impermissible as a violation of due process; appellant could only be tried in the circuit court for the original misdemeanor, and the indictment for the felony offense should have been dismissed. Allen v. Commonwealth, 36 Va. App. 334, 549 S.E.2d 652, 2001 Va. App. LEXIS 447 (2001).

Reopening of case by district court where appeal withdrawn. — Where an appeal had been perfected to the circuit court, and where appellant withdrew his appeal, until a de novo hearing on the merits had commenced, the district court could "for good cause shown" reopen and reconsider its judgment within sixty days from the final judgment. Zamani v. Commonwealth, 26 Va. App. 59, 492 S.E.2d 854 (1997), aff'd, 256 Va. 391, 507 S.E.2d 608 (1998).

Evidence of statements or admissions. — There is nothing in the language of this section or § 16.1-136 which excludes evidence of statements or admissions made by an accused while testifying in the inferior court. Harbaugh v. Commonwealth, 209 Va. 695, 167 S.E.2d 329 (1969).

Evidence of guilty plea that was followed by appeal to circuit court was properly excluded in later civil trial. — In a civil suit by plaintiff buyer against defendant individual to recover damages for personal injuries arising from an altercation, the trial court did not err in excluding evidence that the individual had pleaded guilty to a misdemeanor charge in relation to the altercation, as the individual had appealed the conviction to the circuit court under § 16.1-132, which effectively "wiped out" the guilty plea, making evidence of the plea inadmissible. Santen v. Tuthill, 265 Va. 492, 578 S.E.2d 788, 2003 Va. LEXIS 48 (2003).

Timeliness of appeal. — In a case in which a circuit court quashed defendant's appeal of a revocation of suspension of his sentence for contributing to the delinquency of a minor based on an excessive number of unexcused school absences of one of his four minor children, from the juvenile and domestic relations district court (juvenile court) because it was untimely, the circuit court incorrectly determined that the December 17, 2008, order was a final order by the juvenile court and that his appeal within ten days after entry of the February 11, 2009, order was untimely. Not until the juvenile court heard additional evidence on February 11, 2009, regarding compliance with the conditions of suspension did it make a final, appealable determination regarding whether to impose the previously suspended 30-day sentence or to re-suspend some or all of that time, and defendant's appeal was filed on the same day. Smith v. Commonwealth, 2009 Va. App. LEXIS 557 (Dec. 15, 2009).

Applied in Robinson v. Commonwealth, 206 Va. 766, 146 S.E.2d 197 (1966); Hogan v. Lukhard, 351 F. Supp. 1112 (E.D. Va. 1972); White v. Commonwealth, 214 Va. 559, 203 S.E.2d 443 (1974); Preston v. Commonwealth, 14 Va. App. 731, 419 S.E.2d 288 (1992).

CIRCUIT COURT OPINIONS

Jurisdiction. — When defendant failed to file a notice of a appeal of his driving under the influence conviction within 10 days, he was not entitled to a trial de novo as the appellate court lacked jurisdiction. Commonwealth v. Copto-Lavalle, 58 Va. Cir. 148, 2002 Va. Cir. LEXIS 29 (Fairfax County 2002).

§ 16.1-133. Withdrawal of appeal.

Notwithstanding the provisions of § 16.1-135, any person convicted in a general district court, a juvenile and domestic relations district court, or a court of limited jurisdiction of an offense not felonious may, at any time before the appeal is heard, withdraw an appeal which has been noted, pay the fine and costs to such court, and serve any sentence which has been imposed.

A person withdrawing an appeal shall give written notice of withdrawal to the court and counsel for the prosecution prior to the hearing date of the appeal. If the appeal is withdrawn more than ten days after conviction, the circuit court shall forthwith enter an order affirming the judgment of the lower court and the clerk shall tax the costs as provided by statute. Fines and costs shall be collected by the circuit court, and all papers shall be retained in the circuit court clerk's office.

Where the withdrawal is within ten days after conviction, no additional costs shall be charged, and the judgment of the lower court shall be imposed without further action of the circuit court.

History.
1956, c. 555; 1973, c. 18; 1974, c. 228; 1979, c. 536; 1982, c. 366; 1983, c. 105; 1990, c. 25.

Editor's note.
Acts 1993, c. 929, cl. 3, as amended by Acts 1994, c. 564, cl. 1, and Acts 1996, c. 616, cl. 3, provides that the amendment to this section by Acts 1993, c. 929, cl. 1, shall become effective June 1, 1998, "only if state funds are provided by the General Assembly sufficient to provide adequate resources, including all local costs, for the court to carry out the purposes of this act and to fulfill its mission to serve children and families of the Commonwealth." The funding was not provided.

Law Review.
For survey of Virginia law on criminal procedure for the year 1972-1973, see 59 Va. L. Rev. 1478 (1973). For 2003/2004 survey of criminal law and procedure, see 39 U. Rich. L. Rev. 133 (2004).

Michie's Jurisprudence.
For related discussion, see 1B M.J. Appeal and Error, §§ 232, 381.

CASE NOTES

Construction with § 16.1-133.1. — The General Assembly intended to make fully available to a person convicted of a misdemeanor both the right to seek review by a de novo appeal and the right, within the specified period, to petition to reopen the case in the district court; this section and § 16.1-133.1 must be construed in a manner that affords a convicted person the full opportunity to employ both post-trial procedures to the extent the exercise of one does not conflict with the exercise of the other. Commonwealth v. Zamani, 256 Va. 391, 507 S.E.2d 608 (1998).

Termination of district court's jurisdiction following appeal to circuit court. — Where a case is brought in the circuit court on appeal from the district court, a de novo hearing on the merits must commence before the district court's jurisdiction to reopen the case is terminated; accordingly, where a defendant had noted his appeal to the circuit court and, at the only hearing in that court, the defendant had waived his right to a jury trial and the case was continued, such incidents did not rise to the dignity of a de novo hearing on the merits, the district court retained jurisdiction to reopen its judgment and the defendant could withdraw his appeal to the circuit court. Commonwealth v. Zamani, 256 Va. 391, 507 S.E.2d 608 (1998).

Validity of district court's jurisdiction following appeal to circuit court. — Where defendant withdrew an appeal of a district court judgment, pursuant to § 16.1-133, more than 10 days after the date of the judgment, and a de novo hearing was not held, the judgment was stayed, but remained valid; a circuit court's appellate order did not annul or abrogate the district court judgment. Commonwealth v. Diaz, 266 Va. 260, 585 S.E.2d 552, 2003 Va. LEXIS 90 (2003).

Reopening of case by district court. — Where an appeal had been perfected to the circuit court, and where appellant withdrew his appeal, until a de novo hearing on the merits had commenced, the district court could "for good cause shown" reopen and reconsider its judgment within sixty days from the final judgment. Zamani v. Commonwealth, 26 Va. App. 59, 492 S.E.2d 854 (1997), aff'd, 256 Va. 391, 507 S.E.2d 608 (1998).

Applied in Turner v. Commonwealth, 49 Va. App. 381, 641 S.E.2d 771, 2007 Va. App. LEXIS 78 (2007).

CIRCUIT COURT OPINIONS

Responsibility for costs. — Defendant's appeal of a district court conviction for unreasonably failing to permit his blood or breath to be tested when charged with driving while intoxicated was a criminal matter to which the same procedures applied as appeals from misdemeanor convictions, and defendant was therefore responsible for the jury expense incurred in the circuit court when defendant withdrew his appeal on the day of trial when a jury had been assembled and resolved his case via plea bargain; to avoid the charge, defendant would have had to have withdrawn his jury demand at least 10 days prior to trial. Commonwealth v. Franklin, 54 Va. Cir. 214, 2000 Va. Cir. LEXIS 579 (Northampton County 2000).

§ 16.1-133.1. Reopening case after conviction.

Within sixty days from the date of conviction of any person in a general district court or juvenile and domestic relations district court for an offense not felonious, the case may be reopened upon the application of such person and for good cause shown. Such application shall be heard by the judge who presided at the trial in which the conviction was had, but if he be not in office, or be absent from the county or city or is otherwise unavailable to hear the application, it may be heard by his successor or by any other judge or substitute judge of such court. If the case is reopened after the case documents have been filed with the circuit court, the clerk of the circuit court shall return the case documents to the district court in which the case was originally tried.

History.
1973, c. 440; 1975, c. 298; 1983, c. 21.

Editor's note.
Acts 1993, c. 930, cl. 3, as amended by Acts 1994, c. 564, cl. 2, and Acts 1996, c. 616, cl. 4, provides that the amendment to this section by Acts 1993, c. 930, cl. 1, shall become effective June 1, 1998, "if state funds are provided, including all local costs, to carry out the purposes of this bill by the General Assembly." The funding was not provided.

CASE NOTES

Construction with § 16.1-133. — The General Assembly intended to make fully available to a person convicted of a misdemeanor both the right to seek review by a de novo appeal and the right, within the period specified in this section, to petition to reopen the case in the district court; this section and § 16.1-133 must be construed in a manner that affords a convicted person the full opportunity to employ both post-trial procedures to the extent the exercise of one does not conflict with the exercise of the other. Commonwealth v. Zamani, 256 Va. 391, 507 S.E.2d 608 (1998).

Termination of district court's jurisdiction following appeal to circuit court. — Where a case is brought in the circuit court on appeal from the district court, a de novo hearing on the merits must commence before the district court's jurisdiction to reopen the case is terminated; accordingly, where a defendant had noted his appeal to the circuit court and, at the only hearing in that court, the defendant had waived his right to a jury trial and the case was continued, such incidents did not rise to the dignity of a de novo hearing on the merits, the district court retained jurisdiction to reopen its judgment and the defendant could withdraw his appeal to the circuit court. Commonwealth v. Zamani, 256 Va. 391, 507 S.E.2d 608 (1998).

Juvenile court lost jurisdiction since no timely appeal filed. — Because a mother did not comply with subsection A of § 16.1-296 and § 16.1-133.1 by appealing a dispositional order within 10 days of its entry or applying to reopen the case within 60 days, pursuant to Va. Sup. Ct. R. 1:1, the juvenile court lost jurisdiction of a charge and the court's dismissal of that charge had no force; therefore, since the juvenile court had authority under subdivision A 13 c of § 16.1-278.8 to maintain custody of the child with the social services department, the circuit court properly denied the mother's motion to dismiss proceedings and return custody of her son. Lee v. Frederick County Dep't of Soc. Servs., 2008 Va. App. LEXIS 370 (Aug. 5, 2008).

Reopening of case where appeal withdrawn. — Where an appeal had been perfected to the circuit court, and where appellant withdrew his appeal, until a de novo hearing on the merits had commenced, the district court could "for good cause shown" reopen and reconsider its judgment within sixty days from the final judgment. Zamani v. Commonwealth, 26 Va. App. 59, 492 S.E.2d 854 (1997), aff'd, 256 Va. 391, 507 S.E.2d 608 (1998).

Finding of contempt based on valid conviction. — Trial court's finding that defendant was in contempt of court was based on a valid conviction; as the district court did not dismiss defendant's conviction within 21 days of the conviction order, the district court no longer had jurisdiction and could not dismiss defendant's conviction. Wilson v. Commonwealth, No. 1959-01-4, 2002 Va. App. LEXIS 465 (Ct. of Appeals Aug. 13, 2002).

§ 16.1-134. Appeal by Commonwealth in revenue cases.

In any case involving the violation of a law relating to the state revenue tried in a court not of record

under this title, the Commonwealth shall also have the right at any time within ten days from final judgment to appeal to the circuit court.

History.
1956, c. 555.

Michie's Jurisprudence.
For related discussion, see 1B M.J. Appeal and Error, §§ 47, 376.

§ 16.1-135. Bail and recognizance; papers filed with circuit court.

A person who has been convicted of an offense in a district court and who has noted an appeal, either at the time judgment is rendered or subsequent to its entry, shall be given credit for any bond that he may have posted in the court from which he appeals and shall be treated in accordance with the provisions of Article 1 (§ 19.2-119 et seq.) of Chapter 9 of Title 19.2. Any new bond which may be required for the release of such person pending the appeal shall be given before the judge or the clerk of the district court and treated in accordance with Article 1 of Chapter 9 of Title 19.2; however, if the judge or clerk is not available to take the bond, the bond may be given before a magistrate serving the jurisdiction. Whenever an appeal is taken and the ten-day period prescribed by § 16.1-133 has expired the papers shall be promptly filed with the clerk of the circuit court.

History.
1956, c. 555; 1981, c. 159; 1999, cc. 829, 846; 2008, cc. 551, 691.

Michie's Jurisprudence.
For related discussion, see 1B M.J. Appeal and Error, §§ 376, 378; 5B M.J. Criminal Procedure, § 14.

CASE NOTES

Authority of justice after judgment of conviction. — The only prerogative that can be lawfully exercised, after judgment of conviction has been pronounced, by a justice of the peace (now district court judge) is to admit the accused to bail, if applied for immediately, or grant bail if subsequently applied for within ten days, or carry into execution the judgment. Seay v. Commonwealth, 155 Va. 1087, 156 S.E. 574 (1931) (decided under former statute corresponding to this section).

He cannot grant a new trial or hold judgment in abeyance. — There is no statutory provision for a new trial to be had before a justice of the peace (now district court judge) in a criminal case, nor is there any warrant of law authorizing him to hold in abeyance the judgment of conviction. Seay v. Commonwealth, 155 Va. 1087, 156 S.E. 574 (1931) (decided under former statute corresponding to this section).

It is his mandatory duty to forthwith return and file all papers with the clerk of the court having appellate jurisdiction of the case. Seay v. Commonwealth, 155 Va. 1087, 156 S.E. 574 (1931), cited in Omohundro v. Palmer, 158 Va. 693, 164 S.E. 541 (1932) (decided under former statute corresponding to this section).

When such filing has been done by the justice his jurisdiction is at an end and any further act committed in connection with the judgment is ultra vires and void. Seay v. Commonwealth, 155 Va. 1087, 156 S.E. 574 (1931) (decided under former statute corresponding to this section).

A police justice (now district court judge) loses all jurisdiction over a case when he notes the appeal, admits the accused to bail and delivers the papers to the clerk of the hustings court. Malouf v.

City of Roanoke, 177 Va. 846, 13 S.E.2d 319 (1941) (decided under former statute corresponding to this section).

The right of appeal is not dependent upon the posting of a bond. — The right of an accused to appeal from the district court to the circuit court and obtain retrial of a misdemeanor charge pursuant to § 16.1-132 is not dependent upon his posting an appeal bond. Hill v. Middlesex County, 12 Va. App. 58, 402 S.E.2d 243 (1991).

This section authorizes the requirement of bail and describes the manner of taking and handling bail bonds. It does not require the accused to secure his release on bail, nor does it impose a bonding condition upon his exercise of his right to trial de novo. Hill v. Middlesex County, 12 Va. App. 58, 402 S.E.2d 243 (1991).

No condition imposed except appeal be made within 10 days from conviction. — No condition is imposed upon the exercise of the statutory right to appeal in § 16.1-132 other than the requirement that the appeal be made within 10 days from conviction in the district court. Hill v. Middlesex County, 12 Va. App. 58, 402 S.E.2d 243 (1991).

§ 16.1-136. How appeal tried.

Any appeal taken under the provisions of this chapter shall be heard de novo in the appellate court and shall be tried without formal pleadings in writing; and, except in the case of an appeal from any order or judgment of a court not of record forfeiting any recognizance or revoking any suspension of sentence, the accused shall be entitled to trial by a jury in the same manner as if he had been indicted for the offense in the circuit court.

History.
1956, c. 555.

Cross references.
As to procedure on appeal in civil cases, see §§ 16.1-106, 16.1-113 and 16.1-114.1. See §§ 16.1-132, 16.1-137, and notes.

Law Review.
For survey of Virginia law on criminal law and procedure for the year 1969-1970, see 56 Va. L. Rev. 1572 (1970). For survey of Virginia criminal law and procedure for the year 1970-1971, see 57 Va. L. Rev. 1438 (1971). For article, "Trial by Jury and Speedy Justice," see 28 Wash. & Lee L. Rev. 309 (1971). For survey of Virginia law on criminal law for the year 1971-1972, see 58 Va. L. Rev. 1206 (1972). For survey of Virginia law on criminal procedure for the year 1972-1973, see 59 Va. L. Rev. 1478 (1973). For survey of Virginia practice and pleading for the year 1975-1976, see 62 Va. L. Rev. 1460 (1976). For article, "Appeal De Novo in Virginia: An Examination of Its Present Utility," see 42 Wash. & Lee L. Rev. 1149 (1985).

Research references.
Friend's Virginia Pleading and Practice (Matthew Bender). Chapter 39 Appeals to Circuit Courts. § 39.09 Appeals to Circuit Courts from Juvenile Courts. Charles E. Friend.

Michie's Jurisprudence.
For related discussion, see 1B M.J. Appeal and Error, §§ 379, 380, 382; 2B M.J. Automobiles, § 118; 2B M.J. Autrefois, Acquit and Convict, § 11; 4C M.J. Constitutional Law, §§ 128, 141; 5B M.J. Criminal Procedure, § 77; 9A M.J. Habeas Corpus, § 15; 19 M.J. Warrants, § 6.

CASE NOTES

I. In General.
II. Trial de novo.
III. Appeals from Juvenile and Domestic Relations District Courts.

I. IN GENERAL.

Constitutionality of distinctions between felonies and misdemeanors with respect to appeals. — With respect to appellate procedure, the distinctions between felonies and misdemeanors either do not exist or, where they do, are based upon well-reasoned objectives which serve a legitimate state interest and protect the constitutional rights of defendants convicted of crime and thus do not violate equal protection. Saunders v. Reynolds, 214 Va. 697, 204 S.E.2d 421 (1974).

Construction with other laws. — Where the provisions of §§ 16.1-69.24 and 18.2-459 address the specific subject of appeals from summary contempt adjudications in the district courts, and the provisions of §§ 16.1-132 and 16.1-136 address the general subject of appeals from the district courts, to the extent that the more specific provisions of §§ 16.1-69.24 and § 18.2-459 are in conflict with the general provisions of §§ 16.1-132 and 16.1-136, the more specific statutes prevail. Gilman v. Commonwealth, 275 Va. 222, 657 S.E.2d 474, 2008 Va. LEXIS 23 (2008).

Because the provisions of § 16.1-69.24 and § 18.2-459 had to prevail over the more general provisions of §§ 16.1-132 and 16.1-136, a contemnor appealing an adjudication of summary contempt does not receive a trial de novo in the circuit court with attendant Sixth Amendment protections and, thus, does not have a Sixth Amendment right of confrontation in that summary contempt adjudication in the circuit court. Gilman v. Commonwealth, 275 Va. 222, 657 S.E.2d 474, 2008 Va. LEXIS 23 (2008).

Double jeopardy does not attach. — Assertion that the trial on the new warrant under this section was barred by the double jeopardy clause was without merit. An appeal de novo from a general district court to a circuit court annuls the former judgment as completely as if no trial had ever occurred. To allow a defendant to appeal a conviction in the general district court de novo and then plead double jeopardy in the circuit court would grant every criminal defendant who appealed an automatic pass to freedom. Ledbetter v. Commonwealth, 18 Va. App. 805, 447 S.E.2d 250 (1994).

Trial by jury. — This section and § 16.1-132 were enacted pursuant to Va. Const., Art. I, § 8, and provide the means of securing a trial by jury. Commonwealth v. Bass, 113 Va. 760, 74 S.E. 397 (1912) (decided under former statutes corresponding to this section and § 16.1-132).

Improper denial of de novo appeal. — Circuit court committed clear error in denying a mother her right to a de novo appeal of an order awarding a father custody of the parties' child because the circuit court considered the transcript of the juvenile and domestic relations district court hearing on the matter and pronounced that its ruling would be the same unless the mother presented different evidence; the circuit court improperly shifted the burden of production and persuasion from the father to the mother by requiring the mother to present new or different evidence and imposed an award of attorney's fees as a punitive measure to punish the mother for pursuing her right to a trial de novo. Alexander v. Flowers, 51 Va. App. 404, 658 S.E.2d 355, 2008 Va. App. LEXIS 139 (2008).

No opportunity for vindictive deterrence of appeal. — The Virginia two-tier system of administering criminal justice does not present the opportunity for the vindictive deterrence of appeal condemned in North Carolina v. Pearce, 395 U.S. 711, 89 S. Ct. 2072, 23 L. Ed. 2d 656 (1969). McClung v. Weatherholtz, 351 F. Supp. 5 (W.D. Va. 1972).

Applied in Eames v. Town of Rocky Mount, 217 Va. 16, 225 S.E.2d 197 (1976); Fairfax County Dep't of Family Servs. v. Nordel, 29 Va. App. 400, 512 S.E.2d 830 (1999).

II. TRIAL DE NOVO.

The court is given a free hand in conducting the trial on appeal, under this section and § 16.1-137, in such a way as to guarantee every substantial right, on the one hand, and, on the other, to cut off frivolous and formal objections. Collins v. City of Radford, 134 Va. 518, 113 S.E. 735 (1922) (decided under former statute corresponding to this section).

The de novo trial is a two-edged sword. Just as a defendant is protected against having anything that happened in the lower court used against him in the de novo trial, he may not seek to incur any of the benefits. The fact that the prosecution may have agreed to a lesser penalty below is irrelevant in the de novo trial. McClung v. Weatherholtz, 351 F. Supp. 5 (W.D. Va. 1972).

Which is to be heard de novo. — Under the provisions of this section appeals from convictions by mayors, police justices, justices of the peace and trial justices appointed under Chapter 2 of former

Title 16 (now district court judges), are to be tried de novo. Postal Telegraph-Cable Co. v. City of Charlottesville, 126 Va. 800, 101 S.E. 357 (1919); Ossa v. Town of Appalachia, 137 Va. 795, 119 S.E. 51 (1923); Seay v. Commonwealth, 155 Va. 1087, 156 S.E. 574 (1931); Peak v. Commonwealth, 171 Va. 535, 199 S.E. 473 (1938); Gravely v. Deeds, 185 Va. 662, 40 S.E.2d 175 (1946). The above cases were decided under former statute corresponding to this section; Laing v. Commonwealth, 203 Va. 682, 127 S.E.2d 142 (1962), cert. denied, Gamble v. Gamble, 14 Va. App. 558, 421 S.E.2d 635 (1992).

In Virginia, on appeal from convictions of misdemeanors in courts not of record to courts of record, the defendant is entitled to a trial de novo under this section. Griffin v. Wilkerson, 335 F. Supp. 1272 (W.D. Va. 1972).

And without formal pleadings. — This section dispenses with formal pleadings in writing on the trial where an appeal has been taken from the judgment of a justice convicting one of an offense. Harding v. Commonwealth, 105 Va. 858, 52 S.E. 832 (1906); Harley v. Commonwealth, 131 Va. 664, 108 S.E. 648 (1921); Collins v. City of Radford, 134 Va. 518, 113 S.E. 735 (1922); Ossa v. Town of Appalachia, 137 Va. 795, 119 S.E. 51 (1923); McWilliams v. Commonwealth, 165 Va. 725, 181 S.E. 391 (1935); Peak v. Commonwealth, 171 Va. 535, 199 S.E. 473 (1938). The above cases were decided under former statute corresponding to this section.

This section does not deprive an accused of the right or relieve him of the duty to file informal or special pleas, if he intends to rely on them. Royals v. City of Hampton, 201 Va. 552, 111 S.E.2d 795 (1960).

A trial de novo in the circuit court grants to a litigant every advantage which would have been his had the case been tried originally in such court. Walker v. Department of Pub. Welfare, 223 Va. 557, 290 S.E.2d 887 (1982).

Consideration of evidence. — A trial court is required to consider any relevant evidence developed prior to the hearing date that may impact on the child's best interests. Parish v. Spaulding, 20 Va. App. 130, 455 S.E.2d 728 (1995).

The appeal is in effect a statutory grant of a new trial to the accused to be had before the appellate court. Dickerson v. Commonwealth, 162 Va. 787, 173 S.E. 543 (1934); Gravely v. Deeds, 185 Va. 662, 40 S.E.2d 175 (1946); Baylor v. Commonwealth, 190 Va. 116, 56 S.E.2d 77 (1949). These cases were decided under former statute corresponding to this section.

The intent of this section and § 16.1-137 is to afford the accused, by giving him a new trial before the court on appeal, the opportunity to have every advantage which would have been his had he been tried originally in such court. Dickerson v. Commonwealth, 162 Va. 787, 173 S.E. 543 (1934) (decided under former corresponding statutes).

The appeal is in effect a statutory grant of a new trial to the accused, to be had before a court of record having original criminal jurisdiction. Gaskill v. Commonwealth, 206 Va. 486, 144 S.E.2d 293 (1965).

The intent of this section and § 16.1-137, is to grant a new trial to the accused, with the opportunity to have every advantage which he would have had had he been tried originally in a circuit court, and to give such court a free hand in conducting such new trial in such a way as to guarantee to the accused every substantial right on the one hand, and, on the other hand, to cut frivolous and purely formal objections. Royals v. City of Hampton, 201 Va. 552, 111 S.E.2d 795 (1960).

It annuls the judgment of the trial justice, and it is reversible error to permit such judgment to be introduced in evidence before the jury on the trial of the case on appeal. Malouf v. City of Roanoke, 177 Va. 846, 13 S.E.2d 319 (1941); Gravely v. Deeds, 185 Va. 662, 40 S.E.2d 175 (1946); Baylor v. Commonwealth, 190 Va. 116, 56 S.E.2d 77 (1949). These cases were decided under former statute corresponding to this section.

The appeal annuls the judgment of the inferior tribunal as completely as if there had been no previous trial. Gaskill v. Commonwealth, 206 Va. 486, 144 S.E.2d 293 (1965); Walker v. Department of Pub. Welfare, 223 Va. 557, 290 S.E.2d 887 (1982).

The appeal not only annuls the judgment of the inferior court, but it is reversible error to permit such judgment to be introduced in evidence before the jury on a trial of the case on appeal. Gaskill v. Commonwealth, 206 Va. 486, 144 S.E.2d 293 (1965).

An appeal under this section and § 16.1-132 is, in effect, a statutory grant of a new trial which annuls the judgment of the inferior court, and accordingly such judgment may not be introduced in evidence before the jury in the circuit court. Harbaugh v. Commonwealth, 209 Va. 695, 167 S.E.2d 329 (1969).

The statutory grant of a new trial under this section annuls the judgment of the inferior court. Griffin v. Wilkerson, 335 F. Supp. 1272 (W.D. Va. 1972).

This section annuls the judgment of the court not of record as completely as if there had been no previous trial. The amount of punishment awarded in the previous trial may not be imparted to the jury. The judgment appealed from is completely annulled, and is not thereafter available for any purpose. Griffin v. Wilkerson, 335 F. Supp. 1272 (W.D. Va. 1972).

Where a hearing is de novo, an appeal to the circuit court from a juvenile court under this section annuls the judgment of the juvenile court as completely as if there had been no previous trial. Cox v. Cox, 16 Va. App. 146, 428 S.E.2d 515 (1993).

Also a former plea of guilty. — The appeal in effect annuls or wipes out a former plea of guilty entered before the trial justice. The purpose of this section is to give the accused a new trial in the circuit court, unhampered and unprejudiced by such plea. Baylor v. Commonwealth, 190 Va. 116, 56 S.E.2d 77 (1949) (decided under former § 16-10, corresponding to this section).

And a plea of guilty by accused before the trial justice is not admissible in the circuit court as "a confession." Baylor v. Commonwealth, 190 Va. 116, 56 S.E.2d 77 (1949) (decided under former § 16-10, corresponding to this section).

A plea of guilty in the court not of record may not be considered in the appeal. Griffin v. Wilkerson, 335 F. Supp. 1272 (W.D. Va. 1972).

And the trial on appeal is not a review of the proceedings before the justice. Malouf v. City of Roanoke, 177 Va. 846, 13 S.E.2d 319 (1941) (decided under former statute corresponding to this section).

Where the court made no factual findings, offered no independent basis for its decision and rendered no independent final judgment based on the facts, the trial court has acted inconsistently with its duty to render a new and inherently independent judgment upon the evidence presented to it. In re Fener, No. 0588-03-1, 2003 Va. App. LEXIS 596 (Ct. of Appeals Nov. 18, 2003).

The statute contemplates that the accused shall plead anew in the circuit court, for unless he does so he could not be tried by a jury in the same manner as if he had been indicted for the offense in said court. Baylor v. Commonwealth, 190 Va. 116, 56 S.E.2d 77 (1949) (decided under former § 16-10, corresponding to this section).

The judgment of the inferior court may not be introduced in evidence before the jury in the court of record. Griffin v. Wilkerson, 335 F. Supp. 1272 (W.D. Va. 1972).

And record of such court may not be used as reason for increased punishment. — In a de novo trial in Virginia, it is improper for the sentencing judge in the court of record to consider the record in the inferior court so that he can state his reasons for giving increased punishment. The jury verdict of a finding of guilt and fixing punishment, of course, states no reasons. The judge, after a verdict, merely imposes the sentence fixed by the jury. Griffin v. Wilkerson, 335 F. Supp. 1272 (W.D. Va. 1972).

Imposition of greater sentence on retrial. — Allowing a jury to impose a greater sentence on retrial without evidence of supervening misconduct does not place an unconstitutional condition on one's exercise of the right to a trial by jury. Manns v. Allman, 324 F. Supp. 1149 (W.D. Va. 1971), aff'd, 473 F.2d 909 (4th Cir. 1973).

When a jury in a de novo trial imposed a more severe sentence than was imposed in the lower court of record, there was no denial of either due process or equal protection. Manns v. Allman, 324 F. Supp. 1149 (W.D. Va. 1971), aff'd, 473 F.2d 909 (4th Cir. 1973).

When a greater sentence is imposed at a retrial by a jury, such a penalty will be valid in the absence of exceptional circumstances. Manns v. Allman, 324 F. Supp. 1149 (W.D. Va. 1971), aff'd, 473 F.2d 909 (4th Cir. 1973).

The fact that a state's law provides for a de novo trial on appeal does not prevent the prohibition of a longer sentence after appeal. Griffin v. Wilkerson, 335 F. Supp. 1272 (W.D. Va. 1972).

The question on appeal is whether the accused is guilty of the offense charged and for which he has been tried. In determining this issue the judgment of the trial justice is disregarded. Malouf v. City of Roanoke, 177 Va. 846, 13 S.E.2d 319 (1941); Gravely v.

Deeds, 185 Va. 662, 40 S.E.2d 175 (1946); Baylor v. Commonwealth, 190 Va. 116, 56 S.E.2d 77 (1949). These cases were decided under former statute corresponding to this section. See also, Royals v. City of Hampton, 201 Va. 552, 111 S.E.2d 795 (1960).

The question on the appeal is not whether the county court (now general district court) was in error, but whether the defendant is guilty or not guilty. And that matter is determined by an entirely new trial. McClung v. Weatherholtz, 351 F. Supp. 5 (W.D. Va. 1972).

And not whether the judgment of the justice is correct. — The question on appeal from a justice's decision is not whether his judgment is correct, and in determining the guilt or innocence of the accused the judgment is disregarded. Malouf v. City of Roanoke, 177 Va. 846, 13 S.E.2d 319 (1941); Gravely v. Deeds, 185 Va. 662, 40 S.E.2d 175 (1946). These cases were decided under former statute corresponding to this section.

It is improper to inform the jury of the punishment given accused by the trial justice, since this section provides that the appeal must be tried de novo. Green v. Commonwealth, 170 Va. 619, 195 S.E. 520 (1938) (decided under former statute corresponding to this section).

It was improper for the prosecutor in argument to refer to the punishment requested in the lower court, but since there was no reference to the punishment actually imposed, the impropriety was not grounds for reversal, particularly since the jury was appropriately instructed. Mawyer v. Commonwealth, 203 Va. 898, 128 S.E.2d 433 (1962).

Arguments in general district court not binding. — The Commonwealth, on appeal from a conviction in general district court, is no more bound by the assertions of the prosecutor in the first trial than is the defendant bound by his counsel's actions therein. Ledbetter v. Commonwealth, 18 Va. App. 805, 447 S.E.2d 250 (1994).

Amendment of judgment changing acquittal to conviction. — Courts cannot alter the language of the judgment of a police justice (now district court judge) so as to change an acquittal to a conviction, in order to secure a trial de novo. Peak v. Commonwealth, 171 Va. 535, 199 S.E. 473 (1938) (decided under former statute corresponding to this section).

Evidence of statements or admissions. — There is nothing in the language of this section or § 16.1-132 which excludes evidence of statements or admissions made by an accused while testifying in the inferior court. Harbaugh v. Commonwealth, 209 Va. 695, 167 S.E.2d 329 (1969).

No conviction of greater offense on appeal from conviction of lesser included offense. — One who was tried in a court not of record on a warrant charging him with driving under the influence of alcohol, and who was convicted of the lesser included offense of impaired driving, may not be tried and convicted of driving under the influence of intoxicants on an appeal of his conviction to the corporation (now circuit) court. Buck v. City of Danville, 213 Va. 387, 192 S.E.2d 758 (1972).

When a warrant charges an accused with an offense of several grades, and on his trial in a court not of record he is acquitted of the greater offense and convicted of the lesser included offense, on appeal from that conviction the defendant is not placed in the same position as to the offense of which he was acquitted as if no trial had been had. Buck v. City of Danville, 213 Va. 387, 192 S.E.2d 758 (1972).

Although a circuit court had discretion under § 16.1-137 to amend a defective warrant, defendant's double jeopardy rights were violated when the circuit court, in an appeal de novo under § 16.1-136, improperly amended the warrant to charge driving under the influence (DUI) second offense under § 18.2-266 after defendant had been acquitted of that charge by a district court, which had then convicted defendant of a lesser offense of DUI first offense. Turner v. Commonwealth, 49 Va. App. 381, 641 S.E.2d 771, 2007 Va. App. LEXIS 78 (2007).

An appeal of a district court order revoking a suspended sentence must be heard de novo in the circuit court. Barnes v. City of Newport News, 9 Va. App. 466, 389 S.E.2d 481 (1990).

An appeal of a district court order suspending driver's license. — Because the appeal of a conviction from a general district court to circuit court results in a trial de novo, perfecting the appeal in the district court renders the judgment a nullity under § 16.1-136; if the judgment in the district court is void, there is no conviction and therefore no suspension of the license. The

license is returned to the accused simply because the court has no authority to retain physical custody of it; the language of § 46.2-398 requiring the return of the license upon effecting an appeal would be unnecessary if this statute did not apply to appeals from the circuit court. Corbin v. Commonwealth, 44 Va. App. 196, 604 S.E.2d 111, 2004 Va. App. LEXIS 516 (2004).

Validity of district court's jurisdiction following appeal to circuit court. — Where defendant withdrew an appeal of a district court judgment more than 10 days after the date of the judgment, and a de novo hearing was not held, the judgment was stayed but remained valid; a circuit court's appellate order did not annul or abrogate the district court judgment. Commonwealth v. Diaz, 266 Va. 260, 585 S.E.2d 552, 2003 Va. LEXIS 90 (2003), reversing 38 VA. App. 713, 568 S.E.2d 401 (2002).

III. APPEALS FROM JUVENILE AND DOMESTIC RELATIONS DISTRICT COURTS.

Transfer decision appeal. — The circuit court that hears an appeal of a juvenile court's transfer decision de novo pursuant to this section must, in the absence of any provision specifying a different procedure, follow the mandatory provisions that govern juvenile court transfer proceedings. Hairfield v. Commonwealth, 7 Va. App. 649, 376 S.E.2d 796 (1989).

Review of juvenile court record in making determination on transfer issue. — The critical requirement is that the circuit court make an independent determination on the issue of transfer but it is permissible for the circuit court to review the transcripts and written records from the juvenile court. Grogg v. Commonwealth, 6 Va. App. 598, 371 S.E.2d 549 (1988).

Section only vehicle for appeal from juvenile court. — Although this chapter relates to "Jurisdiction and Procedure in Criminal Matters," this section remains the only vehicle for appeal from the juvenile court to the circuit court, having been reenacted as a part of the Juvenile and Domestic Relations District Court Law of 1977. Walker v. Department of Pub. Welfare, 223 Va. 557, 290 S.E.2d 887 (1982).

Distinction between appeal and divestiture of further jurisdiction in juvenile court. — Under the statutory scheme this distinction between an appeal under this section and a divestiture of further jurisdiction in the juvenile court by operation of subsection A of § 16.1-244 is intentional and consistent with and conducive to the best interests of children who are the subjects of custody disputes between their natural parents, the protection of parental rights, and, less significantly, with the notion of judicial economy. Peple v. Peple, 5 Va. App. 414, 364 S.E.2d 232 (1988).

In an appeal to the circuit court, the "advantage" granted to the noncustodial parent is simply the avoidance of the additional burden of proof imposed by the change in circumstance test; in the de novo appeal, the issue is simply what is in the best interests of the child. Accordingly, the procedural distinction between an appeal under this section and a divestiture of further jurisdiction in the juvenile court by operation of subsection A of § 16.1-244 is significant and perhaps controlling in most cases. Peple v. Peple, 5 Va. App. 414, 364 S.E.2d 232 (1988).

The procedural distinction between an appeal under this section and a divestiture of further jurisdiction in the juvenile court by operation of subsection A of § 16.1-244 relating to divorce proceedings is significant. An order adjudicating an appeal from the juvenile court to the circuit court is not entitled to the procedural convenience of transfer provided by § 20-79. Rather, such order, together with related issues embraced by the appeal, rests within the exclusive jurisdiction of the circuit court pending disposition by that court. Calfee v. Calfee, 29 Va. App. 88, 509 S.E.2d 552 (1999).

De novo review precludes issues concerning notice provided by JDR court. — Because the custody case was heard de novo in the trial court, the decision of the juvenile and domestic relations district court (JDR court) was annulled under § 16.1-136. Any issues concerning the notice provided by the JDR court were moot. Harris v. Burd, 2006 Va. App. LEXIS 393 (Aug. 22, 2006).

Impartial de novo standard of review not denied. — Trial court did not deny a mother an impartial de novo standard of review on appeal from an order of a juvenile and domestic relations district court because although the trial court reviewed the JDR court's opinion in issuing its pendente lite order, the trial court stated that it reached its own conclusions; from the trial court's letter opinion, and the fact that the pendente lite hearing lasted for two days, it was apparent that the mother was allowed to put on evidence, and in addition, the final hearing took place over two days, with one day devoted to custody issues. Huston v. Huston, 2010 Va. App. LEXIS 407 (Oct. 19, 2010).

Circuit court retained jurisdiction of juvenile proceeding following disposition of appeal. — Where the circuit court acquired jurisdiction over an appeal de novo of a juvenile proceeding, the circuit court retained jurisdiction to hear a parole revocation proceeding concerning the juvenile upon her release from the department of juvenile justice. Austin v. Commonwealth, 42 Va. App. 33, 590 S.E.2d 68, 2003 Va. App. LEXIS 676 (2003), aff'd, 268 Va. 439, 604 S.E.2d 430 (2004).

Admission of orders terminating parental rights. — Record belied a parent's assertion that the trial court did not afford the parent a trial de novo and shifted the burden of going forward with evidence to the parent as a result of its admission of orders terminating the parent's residual parental rights. To the contrary, the record showed that the trial court admitted the orders, but limited their use to show the procedural history of the case, not the substantive history. Chappell v. Alexandria Dep't of Human Servs., 2008 Va. App. LEXIS 267 (June 3, 2008).

Burden of proof. — A de novo hearing means a trial anew, with the burden of proof remaining upon the party with whom it rested in the juvenile court. Box v. Talley, 1 Va. App. 289, 338 S.E.2d 349 (1986).

Burden on appeal of termination order on social services department. — On appeal to circuit court brought by parents under this section from orders of the juvenile and domestic relations district court terminating their residual parental rights pursuant to § 16.1-283, the circuit court erred in placing the burden of proof on the parents rather than the department, as should have occurred in a trial de novo. Walker v. Department of Pub. Welfare, 223 Va. 557, 290 S.E.2d 887 (1982).

Civil contempt of court did not alter nature of relief. — Where judgment was for arrearages in child support payments established by the terms of a previously-entered property settlement agreement, and where husband filed his notice of appeal with the circuit court but posted no appeal bond, upon the expiration of 30 days, the circuit court was without jurisdiction to entertain the appeal; the fact that husband also was found in civil contempt of court, and a sanction was imposed, did not alter the fundamental nature of the relief sought by wife; the case was treated as a civil proceeding in the juvenile and domestic relations court and the appeal to the circuit court was, therefore, civil in nature. Scheer v. Isaacs, 10 Va. App. 338, 392 S.E.2d 201 (1990).

Absence of reference to appeal bond does not abrogate § 16.1-107 provisions. — The provisions of this section and following sections indeed make no provision for an appeal bond; however, the absence of any reference to an appeal bond in this section in no way abrogates the mandatory provisions of § 16.1-107, which requires a bond in an appeal of a civil case. Scheer v. Isaacs, 10 Va. App. 338, 392 S.E.2d 201 (1990).

Award of attorney's fees. — Circuit court erred in awarding a father attorney's fees in his child custody action because it denied the mother a de novo review on appeal and used the attorney's fees award as a punitive measure to punish the mother for pursuing her right to a trial de novo; the circuit court's action imposed upon the mother the burden of proving that the juvenile and domestic relations court judge had decided the parties' custody dispute wrongly and/or had weighed the evidence incorrectly, and the circuit court abdicated its responsibility to independently weigh the evidence, make its own credibility determinations, and decide in the exercise of its sound discretion in which parent custody would be vested so as to serve the best interest of the child. Alexander v. Flowers, 51 Va. App. 404, 658 S.E.2d 355, 2008 Va. App. LEXIS 139 (2008).

CIRCUIT COURT OPINIONS

Jurisdiction. — When defendant failed to file a notice of a appeal of his driving under the influence conviction within 10 days, he was not entitled to a trial de novo as the appellate court lacked jurisdiction. Commonwealth v. Copto-Lavalle, 58 Va. Cir. 148, 2002 Va. Cir. LEXIS 29 (Fairfax County 2002).

Nonsuit. — Nonsuit in de novo appeal from child support

proceedings could be taken by the Division of Child Support Enforcement under subsection D of § 8.01-380 because although the appeal was heard de novo without formal pleadings under § 16.1-136, the father was not relieved of the duty to file an actual counterclaim. Div. of Child Support Enforcement ex rel. Abediyi v. Ferguson, 77 Va. Cir. 341, 2008 Va. Cir. LEXIS 163 (Roanoke 2008).

§ 16.1-137. Procedure on appeal when warrant defective.

Upon the trial of the warrant on appeal the court may, upon its own motion or upon the request either of the attorney for the prosecution or for the accused, amend the form of the warrant in any respect in which it appears to be defective. But when the warrant is so defective in form that it does not substantially appear from the same what is the offense with which the accused is charged, or even when it is not so seriously defective, the judge of the court having examined on oath the original complainant, if there be one, or if he sees good reason to believe that an offense has been committed, then without examination of witnesses, may issue under his own hand his warrant reciting the offense and requiring the defendant in the original warrant to be arrested and brought before him. Upon the arrest of the defendant on the new warrant and his production or appearance in court the trial shall proceed upon the new warrant. When there is an amendment of the original warrant the trial shall proceed on the amended warrant. But whether the warrant is amended or a new warrant is issued, the court before proceeding to trial on the same may grant a continuance to the prosecution or to the defendant upon such terms as to costs as may be proper under the circumstances of the case; provided, however, that if the warrant be amended or if a new warrant be issued after any evidence has been heard, the accused shall be entitled to a continuance as a matter of right.

When a warrant is amended or a new warrant is issued the costs already accrued shall be taxed against the defendant, if he is ultimately convicted, as a part of the costs arising under the new or amended warrant.

History.
1956, c. 555; 1958, c. 399.

Michie's Jurisprudence.
For related discussion, see 1B M.J. Appeal and Error, §§ 376, 380; 19 M.J. Warrants, §§ 2, 6.

CASE NOTES

Legislative intent. — This section was intended to provide broad powers and abundant opportunity to amend a defective warrant where justice so requires. Watkins v. Commonwealth, No. 0975-96-3 (Ct. of Appeals May 6, 1997).

Formal pleadings are dispensed with. — Formal pleadings are dispensed with on the trial of an appeal from the judgment of a justice of the peace (now district court judge) convicting one of an offense. Harding v. Commonwealth, 105 Va. 858, 52 S.E. 832 (1906) (decided under former statute corresponding to this section). See § 16.1-136.

And a warrant does not require technical precision. — A

warrant need not have the particularity or technical precision of pleading required in an indictment. Harding v. Commonwealth, 105 Va. 858, 52 S.E. 832 (1906). See Harley v. Commonwealth, 131 Va. 664, 108 S.E. 648 (1921). These cases were decided under former statute corresponding to this section.

But it must recite the offense charged. — While a warrant is not required to describe the offense with that particularity demanded of indictments, it must recite the offense charged. Commonwealth v. Doss, 159 Va. 968, 167 S.E. 371 (1933); Smith v. Commonwealth, 160 Va. 943, 169 S.E. 550 (1933). Both cases were decided under former statute corresponding to this section.

It was error for the trial court to convict the defendant of a violation of a state statute upon a warrant which, at the time of conviction, charged a violation of a county ordinance. Robinson v. Commonwealth, 206 Va. 766, 146 S.E.2d 197 (1966).

With sufficient clarity. — Where an appeal has been taken from the judgment of a justice of the peace (now district court judge) convicting one of an offense, the charge of the offense must be sufficiently clear and specific to inform the accused of the precise offense with which he is charged. Harding v. Commonwealth, 105 Va. 858, 52 S.E. 832 (1906) (decided under former statute corresponding to this section).

A warrant charging the accused with the violation of § 36 of Michie's Virginia Code of 1930, by hunting during the closed season, was held fatally defective as legal notice to the accused of the offense with which he was charged. Smith v. Commonwealth, 160 Va. 943, 169 S.E. 550 (1933) (decided under former statute corresponding to this section).

The court is given a free hand in conducting the trial on appeal, under this section and § 16.1-136, in such way as to guarantee every substantial right, on the one hand, and, on the other, to cut off frivolous and formal objections. Collins v. City of Radford, 134 Va. 518, 113 S.E. 735 (1922) (decided under former statutes corresponding to this section and § 16.1-136).

It may amend warrants or issue new ones. — Under this section, on appeals from convictions before a mayor, justice of the peace or police justice (now district court judges), the appellate court has full power to amend the warrants in any particular, or to issue new warrants in lieu thereof. Postal Telegraph-Cable Co. v. City of Charlottesville, 126 Va. 800, 101 S.E. 357 (1919); Ossa v. Town of Appalachia, 137 Va. 795, 119 S.E. 51 (1923); Commonwealth v. Doss, 159 Va. 968, 167 S.E. 371 (1933); Smith v. Commonwealth, 160 Va. 943, 169 S.E. 550 (1933). These cases were decided under former statute corresponding to this section.

Under this section abundant opportunity is afforded to correct a warrant. Harley v. Commonwealth, 131 Va. 664, 108 S.E. 648 (1921) (decided under former statute corresponding to this section).

Under this section there is ample power to correct formal objection to a warrant. Flint v. Commonwealth, 114 Va. 820, 76 S.E. 308 (1912) (decided under former statute corresponding to this section).

Where the original warrant was sufficient to inform the accused of the charge against him, the court did not err in permitting amendments thereto instead of issuing a new warrant. McWilliams v. Commonwealth, 165 Va. 725, 181 S.E. 391 (1935) (decided under former statute corresponding to this section).

Because a warrant provided defendant with notice of the nature and character of the offense with which defendant was charged, and because §§ 16.1-137 and 19.2-226 authorized the trial court to amend the warrant to delete reference to a city code, which was mere surplusage, the trial court properly denied defendant's motion to dismiss, and found defendant guilty of a second offense of driving under the influence under § 18.2-266. Dennis v. Commonwealth, 2008 Va. App. LEXIS 530 (Dec. 9, 2008).

The court may change a warrant to cover another offense. — Under the broad powers conferred by this section, the court of its own motion may direct the attorney for the Commonwealth to change a warrant from an attempt to commit larceny of oats to an attempt to obtain money by false pretenses. Robinson v. Commonwealth, 111 Va. 844, 69 S.E. 518 (1910), distinguished in, Eddy v. Commonwealth, 119 Va. 873, 89 S.E. 899 (1916). These cases were decided under former statute corresponding to this section.

Where the real subject of prosecution was the violation of a local law against catching fish with nets, and the warrant charged defendant with a violation of the fish laws of the State, the defect could have been corrected by amendment under this section. Burks

v. Commonwealth, 126 Va. 763, 101 S.E. 230 (1919) (decided under former statute corresponding to this section).

And it may be duty bound to do so. — When it was brought to the attention of the trial court by accused that the appeal warrant charged him with an offense against the State, whereas he had been tried before the police justice for an offense against a city ordinance, it became the duty of the trial court, under this section, to amend the warrant so as to conform it to the facts so brought to its attention. Malouf v. City of Roanoke, 177 Va. 846, 13 S.E.2d 319 (1941) (decided under former statute corresponding to this section).

Instead of remanding case to trial justice. — See Read v. Commonwealth, 65 Va. (24 Gratt.) 618 (1873); Malouf v. City of Roanoke, 177 Va. 846, 13 S.E.2d 319 (1941). Both cases were decided under former statute corresponding to this section.

The court was bound to take the warrant as it read when the evidence was concluded and the defendant's motion to strike was made. Robinson v. Commonwealth, 206 Va. 766, 146 S.E.2d 197 (1966).

Substitution of warrant pending appeal may be error. — Where a prisoner convicted by a police justice of the violation of a city ordinance against houses of ill fame appeals to the corporation court, neither the attorney for the Commonwealth nor the police justice can, pending the appeal, change the warrant so as to charge an offense under former § 18.1-196 (now § 18.2-347). There having been no conviction of any offense under the statute, the provisions of this section as to amendments and changes of the warrant have no application, and until such conviction, the corporation court has no jurisdiction, with or without the consent of the accused, to hear and determine a charge of misdemeanor under former § 18.1-196 (now § 18.2-347). Eddy v. Commonwealth, 119 Va. 873, 89 S.E. 899 (1916). Both cases were decided under former statute corresponding to this section.

The court may try a case on a new warrant. — Under the broad terms of this section if there is any substantial reason to suppose that the accused does not know from the warrant what he is charged with, the court may discard the original warrant and proceed to trial on a new warrant for the offense. Collins v. City of Radford, 134 Va. 518, 113 S.E. 735 (1922) (decided under former statute corresponding to this section).

Or on a warrant issued before commission of offense. — In a prosecution for the unlawful sale of ardent spirits, it was held that the defendant was not prejudiced by the fact that the warrant was issued, though not served, before the sale for which he was tried, since, under the broad powers given by this section, the court could have issued a warrant in the exact words of the warrant on which the defendant was tried. Robinson v. Commonwealth, 118 Va. 785, 87 S.E. 553 (1916) (decided under former statute corresponding to this section).

The circuit court is the proper forum to try cases when it issues a new warrant. Ledbetter v. Commonwealth, 18 Va. App. 805, 447 S.E.2d 250 (1994).

Failure to allege venue not ground for reversal. — Where the accused could have been tried without a warrant in the first instance under former § 16.1-129.1, and as abundant opportunity is afforded under this section to correct the warrant where one has been issued, and as in either event the appeal is to be tried "without formal pleadings in writing" (§ 16.1-136), the Supreme Court ought not to reverse the judgment of the trial court simply because the warrant failed to allege the venue of the offense. Harley v. Commonwealth, 131 Va. 664, 108 S.E. 648 (1921) (decided under former statutes corresponding to this section, former § 16.1-129.1 and § 16.1-136).

Where no objection to the warrant is made in the trial court, and no motion is made to correct it under the comprehensive provisions of this section, the Supreme Court will not reverse the judgment of the trial court for formal imperfections of the warrant unless the ends of justice require it. Harley v. Commonwealth, 131 Va. 664, 108 S.E. 648 (1921) (decided under former statute corresponding to this section).

Where no objection was made in the trial court to the sufficiency of a warrant in a prosecution for disorderly conduct, and no demurrer thereto was interposed, defendant cannot object for the first time in the Supreme Court that the warrant did not specify the acts of disorderly conduct complained of. Harley v. Commonwealth, 131 Va. 664, 108 S.E. 648 (1921) (decided under former statute corresponding to this section).

On appeal from the judgment of a civil and police justice (now district court judge) to the corporation court (now circuit court) in a criminal case, a general motion to quash the warrant on appeal, which points out no specific objections, cannot under the terms of this section and § 16.1-136, avail after verdict as against any defect in form unless it appears from the record of the trial that the accused was or could have been prejudiced thereby. Collins v. City of Radford, 134 Va. 518, 113 S.E. 735 (1922) (decided under former statutes corresponding to this section and § 16.1-136).

Amendment of warrant and conviction constituted double jeopardy. — Although a circuit court had discretion under § 16.1-137 to amend a defective warrant, defendant's double jeopardy rights were violated when the circuit court, in an appeal de novo under § 16.1-136, improperly amended the warrant to charge driving under the influence (DUI) second offense under § 18.2-266 after defendant had been acquitted of that charge by a district court, which had then convicted defendant of a lesser offense of DUI first offense. Turner v. Commonwealth, 49 Va. App. 381, 641 S.E.2d 771, 2007 Va. App. LEXIS 78 (2007).

On appeal, court properly granted motion to amend summons. — Where both an arrest warrant and a summons charged defendant with violating a city ordinance and § 18.2-266, each of which is a misdemeanor, and the defendant was convicted on the summons and appealed, and on appeal, the circuit court granted the Commonwealth's motion to amend the summons to delete the reference to the city ordinance, this action was proper, as the amendment did not change the nature or character of the offense charged. Hill v. Commonwealth, No. 1240-91-4 (Ct. of Appeals Feb. 2, 1993).

Defective warrant held not prejudicial. — For a case where a defective warrant was held not to be prejudicial, see Laing v. Commonwealth, 203 Va. 682, 127 S.E.2d 142 (1962), cert. denied, 371 U.S. 962, 83 S. Ct. 542, 9 L. Ed. 2d 509 (1963).

Amendment did not render warrant defective. — Arrest warrant issued was not defective as a result of having been amended sometime prior to a trial de novo in the lower appellate court, where the dates of the offense were amended, as the same particularity was not required in warrants of arrest as was required in formal indictments; pursuant to §§ 16.1-129.2 and 16.1-137, as long as the warrant was not so defective as to fail to notify the defendant of the nature and character of the offense charged, both district courts and circuit courts had the power to amend a warrant in any respect in which the warrant appeared to be defective, on the courts' own motion and without the consent of the parties. Raja v. Commonwealth, 40 Va. App. 710, 581 S.E.2d 237, 2003 Va. App. LEXIS 318 (2003).

Even though the trial court allowed the indictment to be amended, the indictment was not rendered defective by the amendment. The trial court merely allowed the indictment to be changed from reading that defendant robbed the store to defendant robbed the store clerk, but at all times, defendant was aware of the nature of the conduct forming the robbery charge against defendant. Thomas v. Commonwealth, 2006 Va. App. LEXIS 605 (Dec. 20, 2006).

§ 16.1-138. Repealed by Acts 1983, c. 499.

Cross references.

As to retention and disposition of district court records, see § 16.1-69.53 et seq.

CHAPTER 11.

JUVENILE AND DOMESTIC RELATIONS DISTRICT COURTS.

Article 1. General Provisions.

ARTICLE 1.

GENERAL PROVISIONS.

Michie's Jurisprudence.
　For related discussion, see 5B M.J. Criminal Procedure, § 72; 9B M.J. Infants, §§ 13, 15, 81, 82, 84, 86.

§ 16.1-226. Short title.

The short title of the statutes embraced in this chapter is "Juvenile and Domestic Relations District Court Law."

History.
　Code 1950, § 16.1-139; 1956, c. 555; 1972, c. 708; 1973, c. 546; 1977, c. 559.

Cross references.
　As to constitutional authority to establish and regulate jurisdiction of inferior courts, see Va. Const., Art. IV, § 14. As to the definitions used in the chapter regarding the Department of Criminal Justice Services, see § 9.1-101. As to duty of the Commissioner of Social Services to encourage and direct training of personnel of local boards and departments engaged in administering programs within the purview of § 16.1-226 et seq., see § 63.2-204. As to initiation by the Commissioner of Social Services of collection procedures upon an administrative support order, pursuant to § 16.1-226 et seq., see § 63.2-1916.

Editor's note.
　Acts 1993, c. 929, cl. 3, as amended by Acts 1994, c. 564, cl. 1, and Acts 1996, c. 616, cl. 3, provides that the amendment to this section by Acts 1993, c. 929, cl. 1, shall become effective June 1, 1998, "only if state funds are provided by the General Assembly sufficient to provide adequate resources, including all local costs, for the court to carry out the purposes of this act and to fulfill its mission to serve children and families of the Commonwealth." The funding was not provided.
　Many of the cases cited in the notes under the various sections of

this chapter were decided under corresponding provisions of former Chapter 8 of this title.

Law Review.

For article on the problem of the juvenile, see 18 Wash. & Lee L. Rev. 187 (1961). For comment, "Right to Counsel in Virginia Juvenile Proceedings," see 3 U. Rich. L. Rev. 316 (1969). For note, "Publicity in the Juvenile Court," see 3 U. Rich. L. Rev. 348 (1969). For note entitled, "The Dilemma of the 'Uniquely Juvenile' Offender," see 14 Wm. & Mary L. Rev. 386 (1972). For survey of Virginia law on domestic relations for the year 1976-1977, see 63 Va. L. Rev. 1418 (1977). For article, "The Revision of Virginia's Juvenile Court Law," see 13 U. Rich. L. Rev. 847 (1979). For article, "The Rights of Adolescents," see 23 Wm. & Mary L. Rev. 363 (1982). For a book review, "Random Violence and the Transformation of the Juvenile Justice Debate," see 86 Va. L. Rev. 1095 (2000). For annual survey article on legal issues involving children, see 38 U. Rich. L. Rev. 161 (2003). For 2003/2004 survey of family and juvenile law, see 39 U. Rich. L. Rev. 241 (2004).

CASE NOTES

The jurisdiction, practice, and procedure of the juvenile and domestic relations district courts are entirely statutory, and are set forth in this chapter. Walker v. Department of Pub. Welfare, 223 Va. 557, 290 S.E.2d 887 (1982).

Strict compliance with substantive statutes required. — Taken as a whole, the Virginia cases compel strict compliance with the requirements of the juvenile statutes that are not merely procedural. Hailey v. Dorsey, 580 F.2d 112 (4th Cir. 1978), cert. denied, 440 U.S. 937, 99 S. Ct. 1282, 59 L. Ed. 2d 495 (1979).

But failure to comply with any statute may not be jurisdictional defect. — Virginia cases do not indicate that the failure to comply with any juvenile statute is a jurisdictional defect and establish no per se rule to that effect. Hailey v. Dorsey, 580 F.2d 112 (4th Cir. 1978), cert. denied, 440 U.S. 937, 99 S. Ct. 1282, 59 L. Ed. 2d 495 (1979).

OPINIONS OF THE ATTORNEY GENERAL

Cases arising within boundaries of United States Naval Weapons Station. — Virginia courts have jurisdiction to issue and enforce orders pursuant to Chapter 11 of Title 16.1 and Title 63.2 for child-protective services cases arising within the boundaries of the United States Naval Weapons Station. See opinion of Attorney General to Mr. James E. Barnett, County Attorney for York County, 03-034 (3/3/04).

A local department of social services is obligated to provide child welfare services within the Naval Weapons Station, including removal and protective orders, and to apply current abuse and neglect statutes. See opinion of Attorney General to Mr. James E. Barnett, County Attorney for York County, 03-034 (3/3/04).

Local courts may order social workers to enter the Naval Weapons Station to perform home studies and conduct investigations regarding allegations of abuse, neglect, or delinquency. See opinion of Attorney General to Mr. James E. Barnett, County Attorney for York County, 03-034 (3/3/04).

Release of information to local commissioner of revenue. — This section does not prohibit a landlord or managing agent of an apartment complex from releasing to the local commissioner of the revenue a tenant list and vehicle information. See opinion of Attorney General to The Honorable Geraldine M. Whiting, Commissioner of the Revenue for Arlington County, 03-022 (10/8/03).

§ 16.1-227. Purpose and intent.

This law shall be construed liberally and as remedial in character, and the powers hereby conferred are intended to be general to effect the beneficial purposes herein set forth. It is the intention of this law that in all proceedings the welfare of the child and the family, the safety of the community and the protection of the rights of victims are the paramount concerns of the Commonwealth and to the end that these purposes may be attained, the judge shall possess all necessary and incidental powers and authority, whether legal or equitable in their nature.

This law shall be interpreted and construed so as to effectuate the following purposes:

1. To divert from or within the juvenile justice system, to the extent possible, consistent with the protection of the public safety, those children who can be cared for or treated through alternative programs;

2. To provide judicial procedures through which the provisions of this law are executed and enforced and in which the parties are assured a fair hearing and their constitutional and other rights are recognized and enforced;

3. To separate a child from such child's parents, guardian, legal custodian or other person standing in loco parentis only when the child's welfare is endangered or it is in the interest of public safety and then only after consideration of alternatives to out-of-home placement which afford effective protection to the child, his family, and the community; and

4. To protect the community against those acts of its citizens, both juveniles and adults, which are harmful to others and to reduce the incidence of delinquent behavior and to hold offenders accountable for their behavior.

History.

Code 1950, § 16.1-140; 1956, c. 555; 1977, c. 559; 1990, c. 554; 1991, c. 392; 1996, cc. 755, 914.

Law Review.

For survey of Virginia domestic relations law for the year 1977-1978, see 64 Va. L. Rev. 1439 (1978). For comment on termination of parental rights, see 15 U. Rich. L. Rev. 213 (1980). For survey of Virginia law on criminal procedure for the year 1978-1979, see 66 Va. L. Rev. 261 (1980).

CASE NOTES

The primary function of the juvenile courts properly considered is not conviction or punishment for crime; but crime prevention and juvenile rehabilitation. Kiracofe v. Commonwealth, 198 Va. 833, 97 S.E.2d 14 (1957).

Strict compliance with substantive statutes required. — Taken as a whole, the Virginia cases compel strict compliance with the requirements of the juvenile statutes that are not merely procedural. Hailey v. Dorsey, 580 F.2d 112 (4th Cir. 1978), cert. denied, 440 U.S. 937, 99 S. Ct. 1282, 59 L. Ed. 2d 495 (1979).

But failure to comply with any statute may not be jurisdictional defect. — Virginia cases do not indicate that the failure to comply with any juvenile statute is a jurisdictional defect and establish no per se rule to that effect. Hailey v. Dorsey, 580 F.2d 112 (4th Cir. 1978), cert. denied, 440 U.S. 937, 99 S. Ct. 1282, 59 L. Ed. 2d 495 (1979).

Impeachment with prior juvenile adjudications. — A prosecutor may not impeach the defendant with evidence of prior juvenile adjudications, and the attempt to so cross-examine defendant was not harmless error. Lavinder v. Commonwealth, 395 S.E.2d 211 (1990).

Authority to issue interlocutory order. — Trial court properly affirmed juvenile and domestic relations court's order which held the juvenile in contempt for failing to attend school, as § 16.1-227 provided the court with authority to issue the interlocutory order. B.P. v. Commonwealth, 38 Va. App. 735, 568 S.E.2d 412, 2002 Va. App. LEXIS 498 (2002).

Best interests of child. — Mother and father's apparent stipulation to the correctness of the juvenile and domestic relations court's adjudicatory order making a nonspecific finding that their child was abused was not binding on the trial court to the extent that agreement conflicted with the trial court's duty to determine what disposition would serve the best interest of the child. Thus, the trial court needed to hear evidence and make findings about who was inflicting the abuse, and what type of abuse was being inflicted, since § 16.1-227 expressed the intent of the legislature that the welfare of the child and the family were the paramount concerns of the Commonwealth. Anonymous B v. Anonymous C, 51 Va. App. 657, 660 S.E.2d 307, 2008 Va. App. LEXIS 201 (2008).

Trial court did not err in denying a mother's request for a nonsuit under § 8.01-380 because the evidence supported a finding that it was in the best interests of her child for the trial court to transfer the right to advocate for the protective order to the father and the guardian ad litem, and since the mother was a respondent to the preliminary protective order, her right to nonsuit the case against her was subordinate to the welfare of the child; in cases where allegations of child sexual abuse have been presented to the trial court and a preliminary protective order has been issued pursuant to those allegations, an alleged abuser's "right" to nonsuit must be subordinate to the welfare of the child, and the right to advocate a protective order on behalf of the child can be transferred to a party of interest. Anonymous C v. Anonymous B, No. 2232-09-2, 2011 Va. App. LEXIS 14 (Ct. of Appeals Jan. 11, 2011).

Applied in Ballard v. Commonwealth, 228 Va. 213, 321 S.E.2d 284 (1984); Kaywood v. Halifax County Dep't of Social Servs., 10 Va. App. 535, 394 S.E.2d 492 (1990); Tross v. Commonwealth, 21 Va. App. 362, 464 S.E.2d 523 (1995).

CIRCUIT COURT OPINIONS

Equitable powers of juvenile court. — Juvenile court erred in concluding that it did not have jurisdiction over the petition the city social services agency filed that alleged the minor child was a child in need of services and that continued placement in the home would be contrary to the minor child's welfare; evidence showing that the mother had previously abused the minor child's brother was sufficient to invoke the juvenile court's equitable jurisdiction even though the evidence did not show that the minor child had been abused, as the juvenile court was authorized to prevent the minor child's placement with a known abuser and did not have to wait for the minor child herself to be abused. Norfolk Dep't of Soc. Servs. v. Petermore, 63 Va. Cir. 315, 2003 Va. Cir. LEXIS 351 (Norfolk 2003).

§ 16.1-228. Definitions.

When used in this chapter, unless the context otherwise requires:

"Abused or neglected child" means any child:

1. Whose parents or other person responsible for his care creates or inflicts, threatens to create or inflict, or allows to be created or inflicted upon such child a physical or mental injury by other than accidental means, or creates a substantial risk of death, disfigurement or impairment of bodily or mental functions, including, but not limited to, a child who is with his parent or other person responsible for his care either (i) during the manufacture or attempted manufacture of a Schedule I or II controlled substance, or (ii) during the unlawful sale of such substance by that child's parents or other person responsible for his care, where such manufacture, or attempted manufacture or unlawful sale would constitute a felony violation of § 18.2-248;

2. Whose parents or other person responsible for his care neglects or refuses to provide care necessary for his health; however, no child who in good faith is under treatment solely by spiritual means through prayer in accordance with the tenets and practices of a recognized church or religious denomination shall for that reason alone be considered to be an abused or neglected child;

3. Whose parents or other person responsible for his care abandons such child;

4. Whose parents or other person responsible for his care commits or allows to be committed any sexual act upon a child in violation of the law;

5. Who is without parental care or guardianship caused by the unreasonable absence or the mental or physical incapacity of the child's parent, guardian, legal custodian, or other person standing in loco parentis; or

6. Whose parents or other person responsible for his care creates a substantial risk of physical or mental injury by knowingly leaving the child alone in the same dwelling, including an apartment as defined in § 55-79.2, with a person to whom the child is not related by blood or marriage and who the parent or other person responsible for his care knows has been convicted of an offense against a minor for which registration is required as a violent sexual offender pursuant to § 9.1-902.

If a civil proceeding under this chapter is based solely on the parent having left the child at a hospital or rescue squad, it shall be an affirmative defense that such parent safely delivered the child to a hospital that provides 24-hour emergency services or to an attended rescue squad that employs emergency medical technicians, within 14 days of the child's birth. For purposes of terminating parental rights pursuant to § 16.1-283 and placement for adoption, the court may find such a child is a neglected child upon the ground of abandonment.

"Adoptive home" means the place of residence of any natural person in which a child resides as a member of the household and in which he has been placed for the purposes of adoption or in which he has been legally adopted by another member of the household.

"Adult" means a person 18 years of age or older.

"Ancillary crime" or *"ancillary charge"* means any delinquent act committed by a juvenile as a part of the same act or transaction as, or which constitutes a part of a common scheme or plan with, a delinquent act which would be a felony if committed by an adult.

"Boot camp" means a short term secure or nonsecure juvenile residential facility with highly structured components including, but not limited to, military style drill and ceremony, physical labor, education and rigid discipline, and no less than six months of intensive aftercare.

"Child," "juvenile," or *"minor"* means a person less than 18 years of age.

"Child in need of services" means (i) a child whose behavior, conduct or condition presents or results in a serious threat to the well-being and physical safety

of the child or (ii) a child under the age of 14 whose behavior, conduct or condition presents or results in a serious threat to the well-being and physical safety of another person; however, no child who in good faith is under treatment solely by spiritual means through prayer in accordance with the tenets and practices of a recognized church or religious denomination shall for that reason alone be considered to be a child in need of services, nor shall any child who habitually remains away from or habitually deserts or abandons his family as a result of what the court or the local child protective services unit determines to be incidents of physical, emotional or sexual abuse in the home be considered a child in need of services for that reason alone.

However, to find that a child falls within these provisions, (i) the conduct complained of must present a clear and substantial danger to the child's life or health or to the life or health of another person, (ii) the child or his family is in need of treatment, rehabilitation or services not presently being received, and (iii) the intervention of the court is essential to provide the treatment, rehabilitation or services needed by the child or his family.

"Child in need of supervision" means:

1. A child who, while subject to compulsory school attendance, is habitually and without justification absent from school, and (i) the child has been offered an adequate opportunity to receive the benefit of any and all educational services and programs that are required to be provided by law and which meet the child's particular educational needs, (ii) the school system from which the child is absent or other appropriate agency has made a reasonable effort to effect the child's regular attendance without success, and (iii) the school system has provided documentation that it has complied with the provisions of § 22.1-258; or

2. A child who, without reasonable cause and without the consent of his parent, lawful custodian or placement authority, remains away from or deserts or abandons his family or lawful custodian on more than one occasion or escapes or remains away without proper authority from a residential care facility in which he has been placed by the court, and (i) such conduct presents a clear and substantial danger to the child's life or health, (ii) the child or his family is in need of treatment, rehabilitation or services not presently being received, and (iii) the intervention of the court is essential to provide the treatment, rehabilitation or services needed by the child or his family.

"Child welfare agency" means a child-placing agency, child-caring institution or independent foster home as defined in § 63.2-100.

"The court" or the *"juvenile court"* or the *"juvenile and domestic relations court"* means the juvenile and domestic relations district court of each county or city.

"Delinquent act" means (i) an act designated a crime under the law of this Commonwealth, or an ordinance of any city, county, town or service district, or under federal law, (ii) a violation of § 18.2-308.7, or (iii) a violation of a court order as provided for in § 16.1-292, but shall not include an act other than a violation of § 18.2-308.7, which is otherwise lawful, but is designated a crime only if committed by a child. For purposes of §§ 16.1-241 and 16.1-278.9, the term shall include a refusal to take a blood or breath test in violation of § 18.2-268.2 or a similar ordinance of any county, city or town.

"Delinquent child" means a child who has committed a delinquent act or an adult who has committed a delinquent act prior to his 18th birthday, except where the jurisdiction of the juvenile court has been terminated under the provisions of § 16.1-269.6.

"Department" means the Department of Juvenile Justice and *"Director"* means the administrative head in charge thereof or such of his assistants and subordinates as are designated by him to discharge the duties imposed upon him under this law.

"Family abuse" means any act involving violence, force, or threat that results in bodily injury or places one in reasonable apprehension of death, sexual assault, or bodily injury and that is committed by a person against such person's family or household member. Such act includes, but is not limited to, any forceful detention, stalking, criminal sexual assault in violation of Article 7 (§ 18.2-61 et seq.) of Chapter 4 of Title 18.2, or any criminal offense that results in bodily injury or places one in reasonable apprehension of death, sexual assault, or bodily injury.

"Family or household member" means (i) the person's spouse, whether or not he or she resides in the same home with the person, (ii) the person's former spouse, whether or not he or she resides in the same home with the person, (iii) the person's parents, stepparents, children, stepchildren, brothers, sisters, half-brothers, half-sisters, grandparents and grandchildren, regardless of whether such persons reside in the same home with the person, (iv) the person's mother-in-law, father-in-law, sons-in-law, daughters-in-law, brothers-in-law and sisters-in-law who reside in the same home with the person, (v) any individual who has a child in common with the person, whether or not the person and that individual have been married or have resided together at any time, or (vi) any individual who cohabits or who, within the previous 12 months, cohabited with the person, and any children of either of them then residing in the same home with the person.

"Foster care services" means the provision of a full range of casework, treatment and community services for a planned period of time to a child who is abused or neglected as defined in § 63.2-100 or in need of services as defined in this section and his family when the child (i) has been identified as needing services to prevent or eliminate the need for foster care placement, (ii) has been placed through an agreement between the local board of social services or a public agency designated by the community policy and management team and the par-

ents or guardians where legal custody remains with the parents or guardians, (iii) has been committed or entrusted to a local board of social services or child welfare agency, or (iv) has been placed under the supervisory responsibility of the local board pursuant to § 16.1-293.

"Independent living arrangement" means placement of a child at least 16 years of age who is in the custody of a local board or licensed child-placing agency and has been placed by the local board or licensed child-placing agency in a living arrangement in which he does not have daily substitute parental supervision.

"Independent living services" means services and activities provided to a child in foster care 14 years of age or older and who has been committed or entrusted to a local board of social services, child welfare agency, or private child-placing agency. "Independent living services" may also mean services and activities provided to a person who was in foster care on his 18th birthday and has not yet reached the age of 21 years. Such services shall include counseling, education, housing, employment, and money management skills development and access to essential documents and other appropriate services to help children or persons prepare for self-sufficiency.

"Intake officer" means a juvenile probation officer appointed as such pursuant to the authority of this chapter.

"Jail" or *"other facility designed for the detention of adults"* means a local or regional correctional facility as defined in § 53.1-1, except those facilities utilized on a temporary basis as a court holding cell for a child incident to a court hearing or as a temporary lock-up room or ward incident to the transfer of a child to a juvenile facility.

"The judge" means the judge or the substitute judge of the juvenile and domestic relations district court of each county or city.

"This law" or *"the law"* means the Juvenile and Domestic Relations District Court Law embraced in this chapter.

"Legal custody" means (i) a legal status created by court order which vests in a custodian the right to have physical custody of the child, to determine and redetermine where and with whom he shall live, the right and duty to protect, train and discipline him and to provide him with food, shelter, education and ordinary medical care, all subject to any residual parental rights and responsibilities or (ii) the legal status created by court order of joint custody as defined in § 20-107.2.

"Permanent foster care placement" means the place of residence in which a child resides and in which he has been placed pursuant to the provisions of §§ 63.2-900 and 63.2-908 with the expectation and agreement between the placing agency and the place of permanent foster care that the child shall remain in the placement until he reaches the age of majority unless modified by court order or unless removed pursuant to § 16.1-251 or 63.2-1517. A permanent foster care placement may be a place of residence of any natural person or persons deemed appropriate to meet a child's needs on a long-term basis.

"Residual parental rights and responsibilities" means all rights and responsibilities remaining with the parent after the transfer of legal custody or guardianship of the person, including but not limited to the right of visitation, consent to adoption, the right to determine religious affiliation and the responsibility for support.

"Secure facility" or *"detention home"* means a local, regional or state public or private locked residential facility that has construction fixtures designed to prevent escape and to restrict the movement and activities of children held in lawful custody.

"Shelter care" means the temporary care of children in physically unrestricting facilities.

"State Board" means the State Board of Juvenile Justice.

"Status offender" means a child who commits an act prohibited by law which would not be criminal if committed by an adult.

"Status offense" means an act prohibited by law which would not be an offense if committed by an adult.

"Violent juvenile felony" means any of the delinquent acts enumerated in subsection B or C of § 16.1-269.1 when committed by a juvenile 14 years of age or older.

History.
Code 1950, § 16.1-141; 1956, c. 555; 1972, c. 708; 1973, c. 546; 1974, cc. 44, 45; 1977, c. 559; 1978, c. 605; 1979, c. 15; 1981, c. 491; 1984, c. 631; 1985, c. 260; 1986, cc. 281, 308; 1987, c. 632; 1988, c. 794; 1990, cc. 704, 769, 842; 1991, c. 534; 1992, cc. 742, 830, 886; 1993, cc. 435, 467, 494; 1994, cc. 859, 865, 949; 1996, cc. 755, 914; 1999, cc. 453, 665, 697, 721; 2002, cc. 810, 818; 2003, cc. 538, 547, 835; 2004, cc. 245, 753; 2006, c. 868; 2008, cc. 475, 483; 2011, cc. 445, 480.

Cross references.
As to the availability of confidential medical and mental health records of children maintained by the Department of Juvenile Justice, see § 16.1-300. For the definition in this section applying to the Juvenile and Domestic Relations District Court rules, see Rule 8:2, in Volume 11. As to foster care services for a child who is abused or neglected as defined in § 63.2-100 or in need of services as defined in § 16.1-228, see § 63.2-905. As to parental or agency consent for adoption, and exceptions to consent requirement, see § 63.2-1202.

Editor's note.
Acts 1993, c. 929, cl. 3, as amended by Acts 1994, c. 564, cl. 1, and Acts 1996, c. 616, cl. 3, provides that the amendment to this section by Acts 1993, c. 929, cl. 1, shall become effective June 1, 1998, "only if state funds are provided by the General Assembly sufficient to provide adequate resources, including all local costs, for the court to carry out the purposes of this act and to fulfill its mission to serve children and families of the Commonwealth." The funding was not provided.

Acts 2011, cc. 445 and 480, cl. 2 provides: "That the provisions of this act may result in a net increase in periods of imprisonment or commitment. Pursuant to § 30-19.1:4, the estimated amount of the necessary appropriation is $93,767 for periods of imprisonment in state adult correctional facilities and cannot be determined for periods of commitment to the custody of the Department of Juvenile Justice."

The 2011 amendments.

The 2011 amendments by cc. 445 and 480 are identical, and in the definition for "Family abuse," in the first sentence, deleted "including, but not limited to, any forceful detention" following "threat," inserted "death, sexual assault, or" and made minor stylistic changes, and added the last sentence.

Law Review.

For note, "The Constitutionality of Excluding Young People From Jury Service," see 29 Wash. & Lee L. Rev. 131 (1972). For comment on termination of parental rights, see 15 U. Rich. L. Rev. 213 (1980). For survey of Virginia law on criminal procedure for the year 1978-1979, see 66 Va. L. Rev. 261 (1980). For overview of Virginia Supreme Court decisions on domestic relations, see 15 U. Rich. L. Rev. 321 (1981). For 1987 survey of Virginia law as to children, see 21 U. Rich. L. Rev. 789 (1987). For survey on evidence in Virginia for 1989, see 23 U. Rich. L. Rev. 647 (1989). For survey on legal issues involving children in Virginia for 1989, see 23 U. Rich. L. Rev. 705 (1989). For a review of Virginia legal issues involving children, see 33 U. Rich. L. Rev. 1001 (1999). For article, "Gender Bias Task Force: Comments on Family Law Issues," see 58 Wash. & Lee L. Rev. 1089 (2001). For article, "Family Law," see 35 U. Rich. L. Rev. 651 (2001). For article surveying developments in criminal law and procedure in Virginia from July 2001 to September 2002, see 37 U. Rich. L. Rev. 45 (2002). For article surveying developments in family law in Virginia, see 37 U. Rich. L. Rev. 155 (2002). For 2006 survey article, "Criminal Law and Procedure," see 41 U. Rich. L. Rev. 83 (2006). For 2006 survey article, "Family and Juvenile Law," see 41 U. Rich. L. Rev. 151 (2006). For article, "Marriage Mimicry: The Law of Domestic Violence," see 47 Wm. & Mary L. Rev. 1841 (2006).

Research references.

Virginia Forms (Matthew Bender). No. 5-153 Adjudicatory Order for Abuse or Neglect Cases.

CASE NOTES

Guardianship, legal custody distinguished. — The distinction between "legal custody" and "guardianship" is a reflection of the extent of the power over, and the responsibility to, the child involved in each. Thus, in the Commonwealth, legal custody is the right to have physical charge of the child and generally direct the day-to-day activities of the child's life. Guardianship of the person and estate of a child, by contrast, is a broader power to have the custody of the ward and the right to take possession of the ward's estate, real and personal, and out of the proceeds of such estate provide for the ward's maintenance and education. Additionally, the legal custodian, while being required to provide for the child, is not fiduciary or guarantor of the child. Rather, it is the guardian of the person and estate who carries the burden of managing the ward's estate and making good the lawful debts of his ward. In re O'Neil, 18 Va. App. 674, 446 S.E.2d 475 (1994).

Legal custodian not required to pay support for child in physical custody of another. — Under the definition of "legal custody" in this section, a divorced grandmother and grandfather who had been granted joint legal custody of their granddaughter had the duty to provide her "with food, shelter, education and ordinary medical care," but no more; the grandfather was required to provide these necessities for the child during the periods of the year that she stayed with him, but he was not similarly responsible for her needs while she was staying with her grandmother. Russell v. Russell, 35 Va. App. 360, 545 S.E.2d 548, 2001 Va. App. LEXIS 224 (2001).

Code contemplates intervention where severe injury likely if child returned to parent. — The Code contemplates intervention in circumstances, which are without realistic probability of improvement of conditions, by allowing for the emergency removal of children before placement into an environment where the child would be subjected to an imminent threat to life or health to the extent that severe or irreversible injury would be likely to result if the child were returned to or left in the custody of his parent. Jenkins v. Winchester Dep't of Social Servs., 12 Va. App. 1178, 409 S.E.2d 16 (1991).

Definition of abuse or neglected child does not require proof of actual harm. — The statutory definitions of an abused or neglected child do not require proof of actual harm or impairment having been experienced by the child. The term "substantial risk" speaks in futuro. Jenkins v. Winchester Dep't of Social Servs., 12 Va. App. 1178, 409 S.E.2d 16 (1991).

Evidence was sufficient to show that the mother's child was neglected, as it showed that the mother violated a protective order that directed her to keep the child away from the mother's suspected abusive boyfriend and no showing had to be made that the child had been actually harmed, as the evidence showed that the child was at a substantial risk of future harm from him becuase the mother would not keep the child away from him although he was already suspected of having abused the child once. S.V.R. v. Hampton Dep't of Soc. Servs., No. 0073-04-1, 2004 Va. App. LEXIS 450 (Ct. of Appeals Sept. 21, 2004).

No evidence of active abuse but court found "passive" abuse. — Where appellant contended that because there was no visible evidence of active abuse and trial court found "passive" abuse, that the requirements of this section were unmet, this position was without merit. The fact that the child suffered no injury while her parent was under the influence of self-induced drugs was not a mitigating circumstance. The evidence clearly supported the trial court's finding of neglect. Deskin v. Clarke County Dep't of Social Servs., No. 0623-97-4 (Ct. of Appeals Nov. 25, 1997).

Ties between parent and child severed forever when parental rights terminated. — When a court orders termination of parental rights, the ties between the parent and child are severed forever and the parent becomes "a legal stranger to the child." Cage v. Harrisonburg Dep't of Social Servs., 13 Va. App. 246, 410 S.E.2d 405 (1991).

Juvenile court abuse and neglect action in relation to termination of parental rights action. — Circuit court properly terminated a mother's parental rights pursuant to subsection C of § 16.1-283; in an appeal de novo from a juvenile court, an agency was not limited to the evidence and arguments presented in an earlier abuse and neglect action in the juvenile court pursuant to this section § 16.1-228, and thus the agency was not limited to seeking termination pursuant to subsection B of § 16.1-283. Nguyen v. Fairfax County Dep't of Family Servs., No. 0938-04-4, 2004 Va. App. LEXIS 465 (Ct. of Appeals Sept. 28, 2004).

In a case in which the Petersburg Department of Social Services (DSS) filed petitions alleging that two children were abused and/or neglected within the meaning of § 16.1-228, and the father appealed the § 16.1-283 termination of his parental rights arguing that the trial court erred in terminating his parental rights where he was exercising his Fifth Amendment right to remain silent due to pending criminal charges related to the present proceedings, even if the trial court erroneously based its decisions to terminate the father's parental rights in part on the allegations of father's sexual abuse and his decision to assert his Fifth Amendment rights, any such error was harmless because sufficient evidence not related to the sexual abuse allegations or the criminal charges supported the trial court's decisions. In addition to the father's failure to participate in a psychosexual evaluation, he had not provided the DSS with verification of employment or housing, he had not participated in parenting classes, he had not paid child support or visited the children, and he had tested positive for drug use in the recent past. White v. Petersburg Dep't of Soc. Servs., 2009 Va. App. LEXIS 481 (Oct. 27, 2009).

"Family or household member." — In a prosecution for domestic assault in violation of § 18.2-57.2, evidence that defendant considered the victim's child to be his daughter was sufficient to prove the victim was his "family or household member" as defined in § 16.1-228 and incorporated in § 18.2-57.2. As he made no timely request for court-ordered DNA testing, he could not challenge the sufficiency of the evidence on this issue on appeal. Graves v. Commonwealth, 2007 Va. App. LEXIS 63 (Feb. 20, 2007).

History of family abuse. — Award of primary physical custody of the children to the father was proper, in part because the mother's argument that the circuit court abused its discretion in disregarding the history of family abuse that she endured throughout the marriage was without merit. All facts pertaining to the allegation of family abuse were before the circuit court, and it appeared from the record that the court did consider them; the court simply gave greater weight to the testimony of father and that finding was not plainly wrong or without evidence to support it.

Gudino v. Gudino, 2011 Va. App. LEXIS 327 (Nov. 1, 2011).

Reasonable fear of bodily injury. — Threats which placed defendant's wife in reasonable apprehension of death or bodily injury were part of Virginia's definition of domestic abuse under § 16.1-228, and 18 U.S.C.S. § 922(g)(8)(B) reached those restrained from engaging in other conduct that would place an intimate partner in reasonable fear of bodily injury to the partner, and the absence of findings in the protective order of prior violence or prior bodily injury inflicted on the wife did not suffice to vitiate defendant's § 922(g)(8) conviction on Second Amendment grounds. United States v. Mahin, 668 F.3d 119, 2012 U.S. App. LEXIS 2083 (4th Cir. 2012).

Definition of "child." — Evidence was sufficient to convict defendant of possession of a firearm after having been convicted of a felony under § 18.2-308.2, as an undated juvenile adjudication order stating that a "child" was found guilty of breaking and entering and larceny and was committed to the Virginia Department of Juvenile Justice (DJJ) was adequate proof that defendant, while a juvenile, committed two acts that would have been felonies if committed by an adult. Under § 16.1-228, "child" meant a person less than 18 years of age; and under § 16.1-278.7, only a juvenile 11 years or older could be committed to DJJ. Perez v. Commonwealth, 274 Va. 724, 652 S.E.2d 95, 2007 Va. LEXIS 129 (2007).

Definition of "delinquent." — By unsuccessfully soliciting oral sex from a minor, defendant willfully encouraged her to engage in a criminal act in violation of § 18.2-29. As his solicitation was clearly designed to encourage her to commit that act, which would have rendered her delinquent under this section, the evidence established that he contributed to the delinquency of a minor in violation of § 18.2-371. MacDonald v. Commonwealth, 2007 Va. App. LEXIS 7 (Jan. 9, 2007).

Trial court had subject matter jurisdiction under § 17.1-513 over defendant's trial, even though under subsection A of § 16.1-241, the juvenile and domestic relations district courts had exclusive original jurisdiction over all cases involving a juvenile who was alleged to be delinquent, defined under this section as one under 18 years old, as defendant gave defendant's birthdate as December 13, 1986, and the indictment stated that the offense occurred on December 16, 2006. Hall v. Commonwealth, 2009 Va. App. LEXIS 73 (Feb. 17, 2009).

Definition of "adoptive parents." — Phrase "adoptive parents" in subsection K of § 16.1-241 must be interpreted to describe, as set forth in this section, the residence of any natural person in which the child resides as a member of the household and in which he has been placed for the purposes of adoption. Segura v. Fairfax County Dep't of Family Servs., 2008 Va. App. LEXIS 93 (Feb. 26, 2008).

Insurer may condition coverage on obtaining guardianship. — Because the statutory definition of legal custody in this Commonwealth includes the power to direct medical care, legal guardianship of the person was not a necessary legal status for grandparents who had such custody to obtain to direct such care for their granddaughter. However, the status of legal custodian does not require a non-governmental entity such as their insurance carrier to recognize their financial responsibility for her medical care. Therefore, their insurance carrier could decline to recognize the child as an insured person until they obtained the status of legal guardians of the person in order to comply with their contract. In re O'Neil, 18 Va. App. 674, 446 S.E.2d 475 (1994).

Civil rights claims. — In a family's suit against numerous state, county, and private defendants for separating the daughter from the mother and stepfather based upon allegations of sexual abuse, certain substantive due process, procedural due process, and unlawful seizure claims survived dismissal, but the emergency removal of the daughter was authorized by Virginia law. Gedrich v. Fairfax County Dep't of Family Servs., 282 F. Supp. 2d 439, 2003 U.S. Dist. LEXIS 16312 (E.D. Va. 2003).

Right to bear arms. — While the Second Amendment did not historically protect individuals subject to domestic protective orders, as defendant had committed an act of family violence under § 16.1-253.1, and as the deprivation of defendant's right to bear arms was only temporary, defendant's prosecution under 18 U.S.C.S. § 922(g)(8) was not unconstitutional. United States v. Elkins, 2011 U.S. Dist. LEXIS 47105 (W.D. Va. May 2, 2011).

Circuit court has subject matter jurisdiction to determine parentage in domestic assault cases. — Florida circuit court does not err in exercising subject matter jurisdiction to determine parentage for purposes of adjudicating a defendant's guilt on charges of felony domestic assault, whether or not other proceedings involving a determination of parentage are then pending in the juvenile and domestic relations district court. Graves v. Commonwealth, 2007 Va. App. LEXIS 63 (Feb. 20, 2007).

Sufficient evidence of neglected child. — There was sufficient credible evidence for the trial court to find that the infant was a neglected child as defined in this section where while in mother's care, the infant's weight dropped to a dangerously low level, risking permanent damage to her physical development; instructions and assistance by case workers had little effect in alleviating mother's problems; and mother's own testimony demonstrated that she remained confused about her child's nutritional needs. Barr v. Winchester Dep't of Social Servs., No. 1144-93-4 (Ct. of Appeals May 31, 1994).

Evidence that the mother was not an appropriate caretaker because she had a history of serious emotional disturbance characterized by aggressive and emotional outbursts, poor impulse control, poor judgment, and poor problem-solving skills that interfered with her ability to provide a safe and secure environment was sufficient to support a finding of neglect and/or abuse. Wilson v. Fairfax County Dep't of Family Servs., No. 2606-02-4, 2003 Va. App. LEXIS 405 (Ct. of Appeals July 15, 2003).

Evidence showed that father's action in taking his children to a bank where he and the mother uttered a forgery, which caused the police to take the father and mother away to jail, caused the father to be unreasonably absent and the children to be without parental care; accordingly, the trial court's finding that the children were neglected, for the purposes of the city welfare agency's request for an emergency order of removal of the children, was not clearly erroneous and was affirmed. Lewis v. Fredericksburg Dep't of Soc. Servs., No. 2832-02-2, 2003 Va. App. LEXIS 432 (Ct. of Appeals Aug. 12, 2003).

Where the evidence showed that a child's mother was a heroin abuser, was unable to stop using heroin, was occasionally incarcerated, was often discovered having left her son unattended, and was unable to remedy her heroin addiction or provide her son with a stable environment, and where her son had been in foster care for 29.5 months, was returned to her mother's care, and was soon after removed from her care because the mother was using heroin within a week, the Department of Family Services proved by clear and convincing evidence that statutory grounds for termination of the mother's parental rights existed and that the child's best interests would be served through adoption. Foster v. Fairfax County Dep't of Family Servs., No. 0026-04-4, 2004 Va. App. LEXIS 346 (Ct. of Appeals July 20, 2004).

Court properly terminated a father's parental rights because the father admitted that he smoked marijuana after the department removed the children the second time, and an expert noted that the father suffered from alcohol dependence, a history of polysubstance abuse, along with a narcissistic personality disorder with antisocial traits. Farrell v. Warren County Dep't of Soc. Servs., 59 Va. App. 375, 719 S.E.2d 329, 2012 Va. App. LEXIS 1 (2012).

Evidence was sufficient to terminate a mother's parental rights on the basis that the children were abused or neglected because the mother's continued drug use created an unsafe environment, and the mother's failure to adequately address one child's medical needs created an unsafe environment for all the children because a doctor expressed concerns regarding the child's weight and malnourishment. Farrell v. Warren County Dep't of Soc. Servs., 59 Va. App. 342, 719 S.E.2d 313, 2012 Va. App. LEXIS 4 (2012).

Sufficient evidence of abuse and neglect. — Record contained credible evidence that the mother inflicted physical and mental abuse on her child, as she refused to allow him to attend a public school, requiring him instead to stay at home and essentially home-school himself, provided the child with no social activities, and failed to provide a safe, comfortable environment in which the child could thrive mentally or physically; accordingly, the trial court's finding of abuse and neglect was not plainly wrong or without evidence to support it, pursuant to subdivisions 1 and 2 of § 16.1-228. Parker v. Lynchburg Div. of Soc. Servs., No. 0301-03-3, 2003 Va. App. LEXIS 450 (Ct. of Appeals Aug. 26, 2003).

Evidence was sufficient to support the trial court's finding that the father's two-year-old daughter was abused or neglected, as proof of actual harm or impairment was not required because the statutory term "substantial risk" spoke in futuro; accordingly, the father's admission that he was in violation of the conditions of his probation and parole, that he was a fugitive, and that he knew a warrant would be issued for his arrest yet he exposed the two-year-old daughter to the potential for harm during his arrest was sufficient to support the trial court's finding. Seibert v. Alexandria Div. of Soc. Servs., 2005 Va. App. LEXIS 163 (Apr. 26, 2005).

Appellant's residual parental rights to her daughter were properly terminated pursuant to subdivision C 2 of § 16.1-283, as the evidence established that the child was abused and neglected as defined in § 16.1-228, because appellant was not prepared to care for the child at home, and because of her mental retardation and mental health issues, appellant did not understand how to feed an infant or the frequency of feedings, and the evidence established that appellant did not have the cognitive ability to care for the child, and that further time would not remedy appellant's cognitive functioning. Sylvia v. Hampton Dep't of Soc. Servs., 2007 Va. App. LEXIS 109 (Mar. 20, 2007).

Because a doctor's education, experience, knowledge, and skill regarding child abuse qualified the doctor as an expert, and because the parents did not preserve their arguments under Va. Sup. Ct. R. 5A:18 and 5A:20(c) that the doctor relied on hearsay and that their child was injured while in their care, the child was properly found to be abused and neglected under § 16.1-228. Hersey v. New Kent Dep't of Soc. Servs., 2007 Va. App. LEXIS 321 (Aug. 28, 2007).

Finding that the children, a boy and a girl, were abused or neglected under § 16.1-228, was supported by evidence that the mother allowed the father to commit sexual acts upon the girl by continuing to leave the girl in father's care after the girl reported the sexual abuse to the mother, the father created physical injury by throwing objects at the boy, and the boy was a child whose parent committed a sexual act upon a child. Kelly v. Hopewell Dep't of Soc. Servs., 2009 Va. App. LEXIS 206 (May 5, 2009).

Sufficient evidence of child in need of services. — Clear and convincing evidence supported the trial court's finding that sixteen-year-old was a "child in need of services" under this section where she was taken by appellant to her home where she spent the night with appellant's son without her parents' permission and was involved in sexual activity and appellant was involved in preplanning this event, took the child from her home, lied both to her parents and the police about her departure and the circumstances surrounding her overnight stay. The court was justified in concluding that her family needed assistance and services to regain control over their daughter and to remove appellant's detrimental influence. Watkins v. Commonwealth, No. 0975-96-3 (Ct. of Appeals May 6, 1997).

Child in need of services. — Child was not in need of services under this section where child's situation quickly improved without the necessity of court intervention once the child was removed from the defendant's control. DeAmicis v. Commonwealth, 29 Va. App. 751, 514 S.E.2d 788 (1999).

The trial judge is required to consider any history of family abuse as defined in this section when determining custody of minor children. Davenport v. Davenport, No. 1517-93-2 (Ct. of Appeals Jan. 31, 1995).

Circuit court had jurisdiction where defendant failed to prove he was under 18 when offenses were committed. — Although there was conflicting evidence as to defendant's age, credible evidence supported trial court's conclusion that defendant failed to meet his burden of proving he was less than 18 years of age on date offenses were committed, and therefore trial court did not err in denying defendant's motion to set aside his conviction for lack of subject matter jurisdiction. Winston v. Commonwealth, 26 Va. App. 746, 497 S.E.2d 141 (1998).

Applied in Grigg v. Commonwealth, 224 Va. 356, 297 S.E.2d 799 (1982); Deahl v. Winchester Dep't of Social Servs., 224 Va. 664, 299 S.E.2d 863 (1983); Kauffman v. Commonwealth, 8 Va. App. 400, 382 S.E.2d 279 (1989); Stanley v. Fairfax County Dep't of Social Servs., 10 Va. App. 596, 395 S.E.2d 199 (1990); Pfoltzer v. County of Fairfax, 775 F. Supp. 874 (E.D. Va. 1991); Kluis v. Commonwealth, 14 Va. App. 720, 418 S.E.2d 908 (1992); Goodwin v. Commonwealth, 23 Va. App. 475, 477 S.E.2d 781 (1996); DeAmicis v. Commonwealth, 31 Va. App. 437, 524 S.E.2d 151 (2000); Virginia Farm Bureau Mut. Ins. Co. v. Gile, 259 Va. 164, 524 S.E.2d 642 (2000); Justus v. Commonwealth, 274 Va. 143, 645 S.E.2d 284, 2007 Va. LEXIS 74 (2007).

CIRCUIT COURT OPINIONS

Truancy. — Though a Child in Need of Supervision order may have been defective and thus voidable because of improperly documented compliance with § 22.1-258, because no motion to reconsider was made within 21 days and no appeal to the circuit court was lodged within 10 days, the order could not be collaterally attacked in a contempt proceeding. Commonwealth v. May, 62 Va. Cir. 360, 2003 Va. Cir. LEXIS 275 (Rockingham County 2003).

Sufficient evidence of abuse or neglect. — Although parents claimed they did not cause their 11-month-old daughter's injuries and did not allow someone else to cause her injuries, a doctor's testimony that the child displayed symptoms of shaken baby syndrome was sufficient for the court to find that the child was abused or neglected, within the meaning of § 16.1-228, and the court found that the child was abused or neglected and that her two-year-old brother was a child at risk of being abused or neglected because of the injuries his sister sustained. In re McBride, 60 Va. Cir. 261, 2002 Va. Cir. LEXIS 391 (Richmond 2002).

Insufficient evidence of abuse or neglect. — County department of social services' (DSS) neglect/abuse petition was dismissed as when the petition was filed, the child was in a residential program and had not been subjected to physical assaults by his father for a significant period of time; the child had been adjudicated a child in need of services and DSS did not show that the child was now being abused or neglected. Madison County Dep't of Soc. Servs. v. Aylor, 2006 Va. Cir. LEXIS 149 (Madison County Aug. 14, 2006).

Finding that a father's daughter was abused and neglected under § 16.1-228 was not supported by the evidence; instead, pursuant to § 20-124.2, the court gave regard to the primacy of the parent-child relationship. While the father used poor judgment in taking the daughter out of school, in not taking her to two court-ordered visits with her counselor, and in moving her out of state, this did not show that the father had refused to provide care necessary for the daughter's health. In re Baxter, 73 Va. Cir. 520, 2007 Va. Cir. LEXIS 133 (Henrico County 2007).

OPINIONS OF THE ATTORNEY GENERAL

Petition by emancipated minors for protective orders. — Emancipated minor may file petitions for protective orders under applicable statutes. See opinion of Attorney General to The Honorable Charniele L. Herring, Member, House of Delegates, 10-116, 2011 Va. AG LEXIS 2 (01/21/11).

§ 16.1-229. This chapter controlling in event of conflict.

Whenever any specific provision of this chapter differs from or is in conflict with any provision or requirement of any other chapters of this title relating to the same or a similar subject, then such specific provision shall be controlling with respect to such subject or requirement.

History.
Code 1950, § 16.1-142; 1956, c. 555; 1977, c. 559.

ARTICLE 2.

ORGANIZATION AND PERSONNEL.

§ 16.1-232. Attorney for the Commonwealth to prosecute certain cases and represent Commonwealth on appeal.

The attorney for the Commonwealth shall prosecute felony charges before the juvenile court, unless relieved of such responsibility by order of the court. In his discretion, the attorney for the Commonwealth may prosecute misdemeanor charges before such court.

The attorney for the Commonwealth shall represent the Commonwealth in all cases appealed from the juvenile and domestic relations district court to the circuit court.

History.
Code 1950, § 16.1-155; 1956, c. 555; 1977, c. 559; 1980, c. 530; 1991, c. 262.

Editor's note.
Acts 1993, c. 930, cl. 3, as amended by Acts 1994, c. 564, cl. 2, and Acts 1996, c. 616, cl. 4, provides that the amendment to this section by Acts 1993, c. 930, cl. 1, shall become effective June 1, 1998, "if state funds are provided, including all local costs, to carry out the purposes of this bill by the General Assembly." The funding was not provided.

Michie's Jurisprudence.
For related discussion, see 4A M.J. Commonwealth's and State's Attorney, § 4.

CASE NOTES

Purpose. — This section, in effect, gives the Commonwealth's attorney some discretion in prosecuting certain criminal cases in the juvenile and domestic relations courts and requires him to prosecute all cases appealed to the circuit court. But the statute does not confer authority to represent parties in civil cases in which the Commonwealth is not a party in interest. Walthall v. Commonwealth, 3 Va. App. 674, 353 S.E.2d 169 (1987).

Duty to prosecute foreign support orders. — The Commonwealth's attorney has a duty to prosecute foreign support orders that are properly before a Virginia court pursuant to the Revised Uniform Reciprocal Enforcement of Support Act (§§ 20-88.12 to 20-88.31) [see now the Uniform Interstate Family Support Act (§ 20-88.32 et. seq.)] Walthall v. Commonwealth, 3 Va. App. 674, 353 S.E.2d 169 (1987).

The word "case," as used in the second paragraph of this section, refers to the cases described in the paragraph immediately preceding it. The first paragraph provides that the Commonwealth shall prosecute felony charges before the juvenile court and may prosecute misdemeanor charges before that court, but shall be required to do so only when the court so directs. Walthall v. Commonwealth, 3 Va. App. 674, 353 S.E.2d 169 (1987).

The second paragraph of this section, which states that the Commonwealth shall represent the state in all cases appealed from the juvenile and domestic relations district court to the circuit court, refers only to cases in which the Commonwealth is a party or, at least, has an interest. Walthall v. Commonwealth, 3 Va. App. 674, 353 S.E.2d 169 (1987).

Real party in interest has right to own counsel. — In civil matters appealed to the circuit court, the Commonwealth may have a theoretical interest in seeing that the best interests of children are provided for in both custody disputes and support proceedings. However, the real party in interest has a right to his or her own counsel. Certainly the legislature never intended that under these circumstances the Commonwealth's attorney be allowed to control litigation in a purely civil case. Walthall v. Commonwealth, 3 Va. App. 674, 353 S.E.2d 169 (1987).

§ 16.1-236.1. Court services unit directors.

A. State-operated court services units. A court services unit director shall be designated for each state-operated court services unit. The judge or judges of the juvenile and domestic relations district court shall, from a list of eligible persons submitted by the Director appoint one court services unit director for the state-operated court services unit serving that district court. The list of eligible persons shall be developed in accordance with state personnel laws and regulations, and Department policies and procedures.

If any list of eligible persons submitted by the Director is unsatisfactory to the judge or judges, the judge or judges may request the Director to submit a new list containing the names of additional eligible persons. Upon such request by the judge or judges, the Director shall develop and submit a new list of eligible persons in accordance with state personnel laws and regulations, and Department policies and procedures.

The transfer, demotion, or separation of a court services unit director, appointed pursuant to this subsection shall be under the authority of the Director and shall be only for good cause shown, after consulting with the judge or judges of that juvenile and domestic relations district court, and in accordance with the Virginia Personnel Act (§ 2.2-2900 et seq.).

B. Locally operated court services units. A court services unit director shall be designated for each locally operated court services unit. The judge or judges of the juvenile and domestic relations district court shall, from a list of eligible persons submitted by the governing body or bodies of the district, appoint one court services unit director for the locally operated court services unit serving that district court. The list of eligible persons shall be in accordance with locally established qualifications that are consistent with state personnel laws and regulations, and Department policies and procedures.

If any list of eligible persons submitted by the governing body or bodies of the district is unsatisfactory to the judge or judges, the judge or judges may request the governing body or bodies to submit a new list containing the names of additional eligible persons. Upon such request by the judge or judges, the governing body or bodies shall develop and submit a new list of eligible persons in accordance with locally established qualifications that are consistent with state personnel laws and regulations, and Department policies and procedures.

The transfer, demotion, or separation of a court services unit director appointed pursuant to this subsection shall be under the authority of the local governing body or bodies and shall be only for good cause shown after consulting with the judge or judges of that juvenile and domestic relations district court and in accordance with the Virginia Personnel Act (§ 2.2-2900 et seq.).

History.
2003, c. 648.

OPINIONS OF THE ATTORNEY GENERAL

"List of eligible persons," for state-operated court services unit directors consists of those individuals submitted by the

Director of the Department of Juvenile Justice pursuant to state personnel laws and regulations and Department policies and procedures. Such list is the only list from which judges may appoint a director. Should the list be unsatisfactory to judges, they may request new lists. See opinion of Attorney General to Mr. Barry R. Green, Director, Department of Juvenile Justice, 05-068 (10/19/05).

ARTICLE 3.
JURISDICTION AND VENUE.

§ 16.1-241. Jurisdiction; consent for abortion.

The judges of the juvenile and domestic relations district court elected or appointed under this law shall be conservators of the peace within the corporate limits of the cities and the boundaries of the counties for which they are respectively chosen and within one mile beyond the limits of such cities and counties. Except as hereinafter provided, each juvenile and domestic relations district court shall have, within the limits of the territory for which it is created, exclusive original jurisdiction, and within one mile beyond the limits of said city or county, concurrent jurisdiction with the juvenile court or courts of the adjoining city or county, over all cases, matters and proceedings involving:

A. The custody, visitation, support, control or disposition of a child:

1. Who is alleged to be abused, neglected, in need of services, in need of supervision, a status offender, or delinquent except where the jurisdiction of the juvenile court has been terminated or divested;

2. Who is abandoned by his parent or other custodian or who by reason of the absence or physical or mental incapacity of his parents is without parental care and guardianship;

2a. Who is at risk of being abused or neglected by a parent or custodian who has been adjudicated as having abused or neglected another child in the care of the parent or custodian;

3. Whose custody, visitation or support is a subject of controversy or requires determination. In such cases jurisdiction shall be concurrent with and not exclusive of courts having equity jurisdiction, except as provided in § 16.1-244;

4. Who is the subject of an entrustment agreement entered into pursuant to § 63.2-903 or 63.2-1817 or whose parent or parents for good cause desire to be relieved of his care and custody;

5. Where the termination of residual parental rights and responsibilities is sought. In such cases jurisdiction shall be concurrent with and not exclusive of courts having equity jurisdiction, as provided in § 16.1-244; and

6. Who is charged with a traffic infraction as defined in § 46.2-100.

In any case in which the juvenile is alleged to have committed a violent juvenile felony enumerated in subsection B of § 16.1-269.1, and for any charges ancillary thereto, the jurisdiction of the juvenile court shall be limited to conducting a preliminary hearing to determine if there is probable cause to believe that the juvenile committed the act alleged and that the juvenile was 14 years of age or older at the time of the commission of the alleged offense, and any matters related thereto. In any case in which the juvenile is alleged to have committed a violent juvenile felony enumerated in subsection C of § 16.1-269.1, and for all charges ancillary thereto, if the attorney for the Commonwealth has given notice as provided in subsection C of § 16.1-269.1, the jurisdiction of the juvenile court shall be limited to conducting a preliminary hearing to determine if there is probable cause to believe that the juvenile committed the act alleged and that the juvenile was 14 years of age or older at the time of the commission of the alleged offense, and any matters related thereto. A determination by the juvenile court following a preliminary hearing pursuant to subsection B or C of § 16.1-269.1 to certify a charge to the grand jury shall divest the juvenile court of jurisdiction over the charge and any ancillary charge. In any case in which a transfer hearing is held pursuant to subsection A of § 16.1-269.1, if the juvenile court determines to transfer the case, jurisdiction of the juvenile court over the case shall be divested as provided in § 16.1-269.6.

In all other cases involving delinquent acts, and in cases in which an ancillary charge remains after a violent juvenile felony charge has been dismissed or a violent juvenile felony has been reduced to a lesser offense not constituting a violent juvenile felony, the jurisdiction of the juvenile court shall not be divested unless there is a transfer pursuant to subsection A of § 16.1-269.1.

The authority of the juvenile court to adjudicate matters involving the custody, visitation, support, control or disposition of a child shall not be limited to the consideration of petitions filed by a mother, father or legal guardian but shall include petitions filed at any time by any party with a legitimate interest therein. A party with a legitimate interest shall be broadly construed and shall include, but not be limited to, grandparents, stepparents, former stepparents, blood relatives and family members. A party with a legitimate interest shall not include any person (i) whose parental rights have been terminated by court order, either voluntarily or involuntarily, (ii) whose interest in the child derives from or through a person whose parental rights have been terminated by court order, either voluntarily or involuntarily, including, but not limited to, grandparents, stepparents, former stepparents, blood relatives and family members, if the child subsequently has been legally adopted, except where a final order of adoption is entered pursuant to § 63.2-1241, or (iii) who has been convicted of a violation of subsection A of § 18.2-61, § 18.2-63, subsection B of § 18.2-366, or an equivalent offense of another state, the United States, or any foreign jurisdiction, when the child who is the subject of the petition was conceived as a result of such violation. The authority of the juvenile court to consider a petition involving the custody of a child shall not be proscribed or limited where the child has previously been awarded to the custody of a local board of social services.

B. The admission of minors for inpatient treatment in a mental health facility in accordance with the provisions of Article 16 (§ 16.1-335 et seq.) and the involuntary admission of a person with mental illness or judicial certification of eligibility for admission to a training center for persons with intellectual disability in accordance with the provisions of Chapter 8 (§ 37.2-800 et seq.) of Title 37.2. Jurisdiction of the involuntary admission and certification of adults shall be concurrent with the general district court.

C. Except as provided in subsections D and H, judicial consent to such activities as may require parental consent may be given for a child who has been separated from his parents, guardian, legal custodian or other person standing in loco parentis and is in the custody of the court when such consent is required by law.

D. Judicial consent for emergency surgical or medical treatment for a child who is neither married nor has ever been married, when the consent of his parent, guardian, legal custodian or other person standing in loco parentis is unobtainable because such parent, guardian, legal custodian or other person standing in loco parentis (i) is not a resident of the Commonwealth, (ii) has his whereabouts unknown, (iii) cannot be consulted with promptness, reasonable under the circumstances, or (iv) fails to give such consent or provide such treatment when requested by the judge to do so.

E. Any person charged with deserting, abandoning or failing to provide support for any person in violation of law.

F. Any parent, guardian, legal custodian or other person standing in loco parentis of a child:

1. Who has been abused or neglected;

2. Who is the subject of an entrustment agreement entered into pursuant to § 63.2-903 or 63.2-1817 or is otherwise before the court pursuant to subdivision A 4; or

3. Who has been adjudicated in need of services, in need of supervision, or delinquent, if the court finds that such person has by overt act or omission induced, caused, encouraged or contributed to the conduct of the child complained of in the petition.

G. Petitions filed by or on behalf of a child or such child's parent, guardian, legal custodian or other person standing in loco parentis for the purpose of obtaining treatment, rehabilitation or other services that are required by law to be provided for that child or such child's parent, guardian, legal custodian or other person standing in loco parentis. Jurisdiction in such cases shall be concurrent with and not exclusive of that of courts having equity jurisdiction as provided in § 16.1-244.

H. Judicial consent to apply for a work permit for a child when such child is separated from his parents, legal guardian or other person standing in loco parentis.

I. The prosecution and punishment of persons charged with ill-treatment, abuse, abandonment or neglect of children or with any violation of law that causes or tends to cause a child to come within the purview of this law, or with any other offense against the person of a child. In prosecution for felonies over which the court has jurisdiction, jurisdiction shall be limited to determining whether or not there is probable cause.

J. All offenses in which one family or household member is charged with an offense in which another family or household member is the victim and all offenses under § 18.2-49.1.

In prosecution for felonies over which the court has jurisdiction, jurisdiction shall be limited to determining whether or not there is probable cause. Any objection based on jurisdiction under this subsection shall be made before a jury is impaneled and sworn in a jury trial or, in a nonjury trial, before the earlier of when the court begins to hear or receive evidence or the first witness is sworn, or it shall be conclusively waived for all purposes. Any such objection shall not affect or be grounds for challenging directly or collaterally the jurisdiction of the court in which the case is tried.

K. Petitions filed by a natural parent, whose parental rights to a child have been voluntarily relinquished pursuant to a court proceeding, to seek a reversal of the court order terminating such parental rights. No such petition shall be accepted, however, after the child has been placed in the home of adoptive parents.

L. Any person who seeks spousal support after having separated from his spouse. A decision under this subdivision shall not be res judicata in any subsequent action for spousal support in a circuit court. A circuit court shall have concurrent original jurisdiction in all causes of action under this subdivision.

M. Petitions filed for the purpose of obtaining an order of protection pursuant to § 16.1-253.1, 16.1-253.4, or 16.1-279.1, and all petitions filed for the purpose of obtaining an order of protection pursuant to § 19.2-152.8, 19.2-152.9, or 19.2-152.10 if either the alleged victim or the respondent is a juvenile.

N. Any person who escapes or remains away without proper authority from a residential care facility in which he had been placed by the court or as a result of his commitment to the Virginia Department of Juvenile Justice.

O. Petitions for emancipation of a minor pursuant to Article 15 (§ 16.1-331 et seq.).

P. Petitions for enforcement of administrative support orders entered pursuant to Chapter 19 (§ 63.2-1900 et seq.) of Title 63.2, or by another state in the same manner as if the orders were entered by a juvenile and domestic relations district court upon the filing of a certified copy of such order in the juvenile and domestic relations district court.

Q. Petitions for a determination of parentage pursuant to Chapter 3.1 (§ 20-49.1 et seq.) of Title

20. A circuit court shall have concurrent original jurisdiction to the extent provided for in § 20-49.2.

R. [Repealed.]

S. Petitions filed by school boards against parents pursuant to §§ 16.1-241.2 and 22.1-279.3.

T. Petitions to enforce any request for information or subpoena that is not complied with or to review any refusal to issue a subpoena in an administrative appeal regarding child abuse and neglect pursuant to § 63.2-1526.

U. Petitions filed in connection with parental placement adoption consent hearings pursuant to § 63.2-1233. Such proceedings shall be advanced on the docket so as to be heard by the court within 10 days of filing of the petition, or as soon thereafter as practicable so as to provide the earliest possible disposition.

V. Petitions filed for the purpose of obtaining the court's assistance with the execution of consent to an adoption when the consent to an adoption is executed pursuant to the laws of another state and the laws of that state provide for the execution of consent to an adoption in the court of the Commonwealth.

W. Petitions filed by a juvenile seeking judicial authorization for a physician to perform an abortion if a minor elects not to seek consent of an authorized person.

After a hearing, a judge shall issue an order authorizing a physician to perform an abortion, without the consent of any authorized person, if he finds that (i) the minor is mature enough and well enough informed to make her abortion decision, in consultation with her physician, independent of the wishes of any authorized person, or (ii) the minor is not mature enough or well enough informed to make such decision, but the desired abortion would be in her best interest.

If the judge authorizes an abortion based on the best interests of the minor, such order shall expressly state that such authorization is subject to the physician or his agent giving notice of intent to perform the abortion; however, no such notice shall be required if the judge finds that such notice would not be in the best interest of the minor. In determining whether notice is in the best interest of the minor, the judge shall consider the totality of the circumstances; however, he shall find that notice is not in the best interest of the minor if he finds that (i) one or more authorized persons with whom the minor regularly and customarily resides is abusive or neglectful, and (ii) every other authorized person, if any, is either abusive or neglectful or has refused to accept responsibility as parent, legal guardian, custodian or person standing in loco parentis.

The minor may participate in the court proceedings on her own behalf, and the court may appoint a guardian ad litem for the minor. The court shall advise the minor that she has a right to counsel and shall, upon her request, appoint counsel for her.

Notwithstanding any other provision of law, the provisions of this subsection shall govern proceedings relating to consent for a minor's abortion. Court proceedings under this subsection and records of such proceedings shall be confidential. Such proceedings shall be given precedence over other pending matters so that the court may reach a decision promptly and without delay in order to serve the best interests of the minor. Court proceedings under this subsection shall be heard and decided as soon as practicable but in no event later than four days after the petition is filed.

An expedited confidential appeal to the circuit court shall be available to any minor for whom the court denies an order authorizing an abortion without consent or without notice. Any such appeal shall be heard and decided no later than five days after the appeal is filed. The time periods required by this subsection shall be subject to subsection B of § 1-210. An order authorizing an abortion without consent or without notice shall not be subject to appeal.

No filing fees shall be required of the minor at trial or upon appeal.

If either the original court or the circuit court fails to act within the time periods required by this subsection, the court before which the proceeding is pending shall immediately authorize a physician to perform the abortion without consent of or notice to an authorized person.

Nothing contained in this subsection shall be construed to authorize a physician to perform an abortion on a minor in circumstances or in a manner that would be unlawful if performed on an adult woman.

A physician shall not knowingly perform an abortion upon an unemancipated minor unless consent has been obtained or the minor delivers to the physician a court order entered pursuant to this section and the physician or his agent provides such notice as such order may require. However, neither consent nor judicial authorization nor notice shall be required if the minor declares that she is abused or neglected and the attending physician has reason to suspect that the minor may be an abused or neglected child as defined in § 63.2-100 and reports the suspected abuse or neglect in accordance with § 63.2-1509; or if there is a medical emergency, in which case the attending physician shall certify the facts justifying the exception in the minor's medical record.

For purposes of this subsection:

"*Authorization*" means the minor has delivered to the physician a notarized, written statement signed by an authorized person that the authorized person knows of the minor's intent to have an abortion and consents to such abortion being performed on the minor.

"*Authorized person*" means (i) a parent or duly appointed legal guardian or custodian of the minor or (ii) a person standing in loco parentis, including, but not limited to, a grandparent or adult sibling with whom the minor regularly and customarily resides and who has care and control of the minor.

Any person who knows he is not an authorized person and who knowingly and willfully signs an authorization statement consenting to an abortion for a minor is guilty of a Class 3 misdemeanor.

"*Consent*" means that (i) the physician has given notice of intent to perform the abortion and has received authorization from an authorized person, or (ii) at least one authorized person is present with the minor seeking the abortion and provides written authorization to the physician, which shall be witnessed by the physician or an agent thereof. In either case, the written authorization shall be incorporated into the minor's medical record and maintained as a part thereof.

"*Medical emergency*" means any condition which, on the basis of the physician's good faith clinical judgment, so complicates the medical condition of the pregnant minor as to necessitate the immediate abortion of her pregnancy to avert her death or for which a delay will create a serious risk of substantial and irreversible impairment of a major bodily function.

"*Notice of intent to perform the abortion*" means that (i) the physician or his agent has given actual notice of his intention to perform such abortion to an authorized person, either in person or by telephone, at least 24 hours previous to the performance of the abortion; or (ii) the physician or his agent, after a reasonable effort to notify an authorized person, has mailed notice to an authorized person by certified mail, addressed to such person at his usual place of abode, with return receipt requested, at least 72 hours prior to the performance of the abortion.

"*Perform an abortion*" means to interrupt or terminate a pregnancy by any surgical or nonsurgical procedure or to induce a miscarriage as provided in § 18.2-72, 18.2-73, or 18.2-74.

"*Unemancipated minor*" means a minor who has not been emancipated by (i) entry into a valid marriage, even though the marriage may have been terminated by dissolution; (ii) active duty with any of the Armed Forces of the United States; (iii) willingly living separate and apart from his or her parents or guardian, with the consent or acquiescence of the parents or guardian; or (iv) entry of an order of emancipation pursuant to Article 15 (§ 16.1-331 et seq.).

X. Petitions filed pursuant to Article 17 (§ 16.1-349 et seq.) relating to standby guardians for minor children.

The ages specified in this law refer to the age of the child at the time of the acts complained of in the petition.

Notwithstanding any other provision of law, no fees shall be charged by a sheriff for the service of any process in a proceeding pursuant to subdivision A 3, except as provided in subdivision A 6 of § 17.1-272, or subsection B, D, M, or R.

Notwithstanding the provisions of § 18.2-71, any physician who performs an abortion in violation of subsection W shall be guilty of a Class 3 misdemeanor.

History.

Code 1950, § 16.1-158; 1956, c. 555; 1960, c. 388; 1968, c. 225; 1970, cc. 232, 600; 1973, c. 440; 1976, cc. 42, 324; 1977, cc. 525, 559; 1978, c. 648; 1979, cc. 597, 605, 628; 1980, cc. 527, 529; 1981, cc. 454, 475, 488, 491, 501, 502, 510; 1982, c. 46; 1983, c. 280; 1984, cc. 631, 645, 651, 665, 669; 1985, c. 270; 1986, cc. 59, 506; 1987, c. 632; 1988, cc. 797, 906; 1989, cc. 368, 733; 1990, cc. 704, 975; 1991, cc. 511, 715; 1992, cc. 585, 742; 1994, cc. 575, 719, 813, 859, 949; 1995, cc. 7, 665, 772, 826, 852; 1996, cc. 755, 914; 1997, cc. 690, 708; 1998, c. 829; 1999, cc. 697, 721, 1028; 2000, c. 830; 2003, cc. 229, 960, 962; 2004, c. 588; 2005, cc. 716, 839, 890; 2007, cc. 284, 370; 2008, cc. 164, 201; 2010, c. 402; 2012, cc. 424, 476, 507, 637.

Cross references.

As to punishment for Class 3 misdemeanors, see § 18.2-11. As to notice of right to counsel, see § 16.1-266. As to the one year deadline for claims of error or defect, see § 16.1-272.1. As to visitation of child placed in foster care, see § 63.2-912. As to testimony of child by use of two-way closed circuit television in civil proceedings involving alleged abuse or neglect of a child, see § 63.2-1521. As to admission of out-of-court statements made by certain children in civil proceedings involving alleged abuse or neglect of a child, see § 63.2-1522. As to use of videotaped statements of certain children who are complaining witnesses in in civil proceedings involving alleged abuse or neglect of a child, see § 63.2-1523.

Editor's note.

Acts 1993, c. 929, cl. 3, as amended by Acts 1994, c. 564, cl. 1, and Acts 1996, c. 616, cl. 3, provides that the amendment to this section by Acts 1993, c. 929, cl. 1, shall become effective June 1, 1998, "only if state funds are provided by the General Assembly sufficient to provide adequate resources, including all local costs, for the court to carry out the purposes of this act and to fulfill its mission to serve children and families of the Commonwealth." The funding was not provided.

Acts 2003, cc. 960 and 962, cl. 2, provide: "That if the amendments made by this act to § 16.1-241 are ever temporarily or permanently restrained or enjoined by judicial order, the provisions of § 16.1-241 shall be enforced as though the amendments were not enacted; however, if such temporary or permanent restraining order or injunction is ever stayed or dissolved, or otherwise ceases to have effect, § 16.1-241, as amended by this act, shall have full force and effect."

The 2010 amendments.

The 2010 amendment by c. 402 deleted former subsection X, which read: "Petitions filed pursuant to § 18.2-370.5 for an order allowing the petitioner to enter and be present on school or child day center property. In such cases jurisdiction shall be concurrent with and not exclusive of circuit courts."

The 2012 amendments.

The 2012 amendment by c. 424 added subsection V and redesignated former subsection V as W; substituted "subsection W" for "subsection V" in the last paragraph, and made related and minor stylistic changes throughout the section.

The 2012 amendments by cc. 476 and 507 are identical, and substituted "persons with intellectual disability in accordance with the provisions of Chapter 8 (§ 37.2-800 et seq.) of Title 37.2" for "persons with mental retardation in accordance with the provisions of Chapters 1 (§ 37.2-100 et seq.) and 8 (§ 37.2-800 et seq.) of Title 37.2" at the end of the first sentence of subsection B; and made minor stylistic changes throughout the section.

The 2012 amendment by c. 637 added ", 16.1-253.4, or 16.1-279.1, and all petitions filed for the purpose of obtaining an order of protection pursuant to § 19.2-152.8, 19.2-152.9, or 19.2-152.10 if either the alleged victim or the respondent is a juvenile" at the end of subsection M; repealed former subsection R, whch read: "Petitions for the purpose of obtaining an emergency protective order pursuant to § 16.1-253.4."; and made a minor stylistic change.

Law Review.

For survey on legal issues involving children in Virginia for 1989, see 23 U. Rich. L. Rev. 705 (1989). For 1994 survey of Virginia domestic relations law, see 28 U. Rich. L. Rev. 981 (1994). For 1995 survey of criminal law and procedure, see 29 U. Rich. L. Rev. 951 (1995). For an article relating to recent changes of formidable importance in major areas of domestic relations, both nationally and in Virginia, see 32 U. Rich. L. Rev. 1165 (1998). For an article, "Legal Issues Involving Children," see 32 U. Rich. L. Rev. 1345 (1998). For an article, "Blood Ties: A Rationale for Child Visitation by Legal Strangers," see 55 Wash. & Lee L. Rev. 351 (1998). For annual survey article on legal issues involving children, see 38 U. Rich. L. Rev. 161 (2003).

Research references.

Friend's Virginia Pleading .and Practice (Matthew Bender). Chapter 32 Juvenile and Domestic Relations Courts, etc. § 32.02 Proceedings in Juvenile and Domestic Relations Courts. Charles E. Friend

Virginia Forms (Matthew Bender). No. 6-739 Petition Requesting Authorization for Medical Treatment of Juvenile. No. 6-743 Petition by Juvenile for Judicial Authorization of Abortion Without Notice to Authorized Person. No. 6-746 Order in Proceeding for Judicial Authorization of Abortion in Juvenile and Domestic Relations District Court. No. 6-747 Notice of Appeal — Judicial Authorization of Abortion. No. 6-749 Order in Proceeding for Judicial Authorization of Abortion.

Michie's Jurisprudence.

For related discussion, see 1A M.J. Abortion, § 1; 4A M.J. Commonwealth's and State's Attorney, § 4; 6A M.J. Divorce and Alimony, § 69; 9B M.J. Infants, §§ 13, 82, 84; 10A M.J. Insane and Other Incompetent Persons, § 4; 11B M.J. Jurisdiction, § 21; 14A M.J. Parent and Child, §§ 1, 4.

CASE NOTES

Constitutionality of parental notice provision. — The Parental Notice Act, as legislation that respects the fundamental interests of responsible parents in the rearing and in the educational, moral and religious development of their children, without unduly burdening the fundamental abortion right, is facially constitutional under the Fourth Amendment. Planned Parenthood of the Blue Ridge v. Camblos, 155 F.3d 352 (4th Cir. 1998).

The unmistakable implication in this section and the guidelines given by the supreme court to its lower courts is that, whenever possible, bypass petitions should be resolved within the four-day statutory period required for holding hearings and no more is required to sustain the statute against a facial challenge to its constitutionality. Planned Parenthood of the Blue Ridge v. Camblos, 155 F.3d 352 (4th Cir. 1998).

The imposing confidentiality protections provided for in this and other statutes and promulgated by the supreme court in the form of instructions to the judges and clerks who will handle cases under the parental notification law, would be adequate to sustain a statute requiring parental consent and they are clearly adequate to sustain this statute requiring only notice. Planned Parenthood of the Blue Ridge v. Camblos, 155 F.3d 352 (4th Cir. 1998).

Provided that a parental notice statute, such as this one, does not condition the minor's access to abortion upon notice to abusive or neglectful parents, absent parents who have not assumed their parental responsibilities or parents with similar relationships with their daughters, nothing more is required in order to withstand a facial challenge to its constitutionality. Planned Parenthood of the Blue Ridge v. Camblos, 155 F.3d 352 (4th Cir. 1998).

Power of circuit court. — A circuit court possesses the inherent power to punish juveniles for criminal contempt for disobedience to its orders, decrees, and processes. Wilson v. Commonwealth, 23 Va. App. 318, 477 S.E.2d 7 (1996).

The juvenile code does not require a circuit court seeking to punish a juvenile for contempt of a court's subpoena power to refer the legal or factual issues to a separate juvenile and domestic relations court. Wilson v. Commonwealth, 23 Va. App. 318, 477 S.E.2d 7 (1996).

Jurisdiction. — This section grants the juvenile court exclusive original jurisdiction over all cases, matters and proceedings concerning a juvenile who is alleged to have been delinquent. Moore v. Commonwealth, 259 Va. 405, 527 S.E.2d 415 (2000), rev'd on other grounds, Pope v. Commonwealth, 37 Va. App. 451, 559 S.E.2d 388 (2002).

The jurisdiction of a juvenile and domestic relations district court is remarkably broad and includes concurrent jurisdiction with the circuit courts over the custody, visitation and support of a child whose custody, visitation or support is a subject of controversy or requires determination. Croteau v. Croteau, 246 Bankr. 254, 2000 Bankr. LEXIS 302 (Bankr. E.D. Va. 2000).

Subdivision A 1 of § 16.1-241, by its plain language, does not predicate subject matter jurisdiction on the residence of the child but grants exclusive jurisdiction to juvenile and domestic relations district courts over all cases, matters and proceedings involving the custody of a child who was alleged to be abused or neglected. Wilson v. Fairfax County Dep't of Family Servs., No. 2606-02-4, 2003 Va. App. LEXIS 405 (Ct. of Appeals July 15, 2003).

Circuit court properly declined jurisdiction over appellant mother's subsection K § 16.1-241 petition to reverse a prior adjudication terminating her parental rights because the phrase "adoptive parents" had to be interpreted to describe, as set forth in § 16.1-228, the residence of any natural person in which the child resided as a member of the household and in which he had been placed for the purposes of adoption; thus, the circuit court lacked jurisdiction over the petition because the child had been placed in the home of adoptive parents, even though a final order of adoption had not been entered. Segura v. Fairfax County Dep't of Family Servs., 2008 Va. App. LEXIS 93 (Feb. 26, 2008).

Because the circuit court did not have jurisdiction under subdivision A 3 of § 16.1-241 and § 20-124.3 to determine visitation for a person who was 18 years old, the appellant's motion was moot; therefore, the circuit court properly dismissed the matter. Crossman v. Harrisonburg Rockingham Soc. Servs. Dist., 2008 Va. App. LEXIS 369 (Aug. 5, 2008).

Trial court had subject matter jurisdiction under § 17.1-513 over defendant's trial, even though under subsection A of this section, the juvenile and domestic relations district courts had exclusive original jurisdiction over all cases involving a juvenile who was alleged to be delinquent, defined under § 16.1-228 as one under 18 years old, as defendant gave defendant's birthdate as December 13, 1986, and the indictment stated that the offense occurred on December 16, 2006. Hall v. Commonwealth, 2009 Va. App. LEXIS 73 (Feb. 17, 2009).

Juvenile and domestic relations district court had subject matter jurisdiction under subdivision A 3 of § 16.1-241 to enter an order granting joint custody of a child to the mother and an adoptee because the custody of the child was the subject of controversy and/or required determination, and the rights of the biological father were also at issue; subdivision A 3 of § 16.1-241 does not restrict a juvenile and domestic relations district court's jurisdiction only to matters in which a disagreement exists between parents or other interested parties. Morgan v. Kifus, 2011 Va. App. LEXIS 126 (Apr. 12, 2011).

Waiver of jurisdiction. — Nothing in either this section or § 16.1-244 permits the juvenile court to "waive" its jurisdiction and allow a party to bring an original action in the circuit court without meeting the statutory requirements. Willis v. Gamez, 20 Va. App. 75, 455 S.E.2d 274 (1995).

When the legislature enacted subsection (J), it created an exception to the general rule that lack of subject-matter jurisdiction cannot be waived. Burke v. Commonwealth, 29 Va. App. 183, 510 S.E.2d 743 (1999).

Defendant waived his objection to the juvenile court's exercise of jurisdiction over his preliminary hearing by not raising such objection before trial in the circuit court. Burke v. Commonwealth, 29 Va. App. 183, 510 S.E.2d 743 (1999).

Defendant waived jurisdictional objection to his preliminary hearing, where he failed to raise his objection before trial in circuit court. Waller v. Commonwealth, No. 0657-98-2 (Ct. of Appeals June 8, 1999).

Award of custody to non-parents. — Because there was sufficient evidence to show that child's father was unfit, there was a compelling state interest for the court to award custody to non-parents; the father, therefore, was not deprived of substantive due process and this section was not unconstitutional. Switzer v. Smith, Nos. 0779-00-3, 1159-00-3, 2001 Va. App. LEXIS 454 (Ct. of Appeals July 31, 2001).

Court of appeals erred when the court upheld a circuit court's decision awarding custody of a child who had been adjudicated as abused and neglected and removed the child from the child's parents, pursuant to §§ 16.1-251 and 16.1-252, giving custody to the child's grandparents, based on the court's conclusion that language in subsection A of § 16.1-241 and subsection B of § 16.1-278.15 subordinated Virginia statutes on foster care to Virginia's general custody statutes. The only interpretation of Titles 16.1 and 20 that gave effect to both statutory schemes and the intent of the Virginia General Assembly was that a trial court had to make the specific factual findings required by the foster care statutes in a custody case involving a child who was subject to a foster care plan. Lynchburg Div. of Soc. Servs. v. Cook, 276 Va. 465, 666 S.E.2d 361, 2008 Va. LEXIS 97 (2008).

Custody order did not violate Marriage Affirmation Amendment. — Custody order granting joint custody of a child to the mother and an adoptee was not void as violative of the Virginia Marriage Amendment, Va. Const., Art. I, § 15-A, or the Marriage Affirmation Act, § 20-45.3, because the custody order was premised on the adoptee's status as a party with a legitimate interest under subsection A of § 16.1-241 and stated that the adoptee was a fit and proper person to care for the minor child; there was no language in the custody order recognizing a legal relationship between the mother and adoptee or indicating the juvenile and domestic relations district court's decision to award joint custody to the adoptee was based on the relationship between the mother, adoptee, and father, rather than the relationship between the adoptee and child. Morgan v. Kifus, 2011 Va. App. LEXIS 126 (Apr. 12, 2011).

Court had jurisdiction and authority to order mother's alcohol evaluation. — While defendant argued that the evidence was insufficient to prove that she was a contributing factor to her daughter's need for supervision as required under this section, the evidence was sufficient to support the trial court's finding that she contributed to the need for supervision and, therefore, the juvenile court had jurisdiction to order the alcohol evaluation. Hanson v. Commonwealth, No. 2899-95-3 (Ct. of Appeals Apr. 1, 1997).

Circuit court retained jurisdiction over a juvenile's parole revocation proceeding. — Where the circuit court acquired jurisdiction over an appeal of a juvenile proceeding originally heard by the juvenile court, the circuit court retained jurisdiction to hear a parole revocation proceeding concerning the juvenile upon her release from the department of juvenile justice. Austin v. Commonwealth, 42 Va. App. 33, 590 S.E.2d 68, 2003 Va. App. LEXIS 676 (2003), aff'd, 268 Va. 439, 604 S.E.2d 430 (2004).

Commonwealth not "victim" in all criminal cases. — Although it is true that the Commonwealth is the plaintiff party in any criminal case in the Virginia courts, one cannot infer from that fact that the Commonwealth is the victim in all criminal cases for purposes of applying this section. By the Commonwealth's rationale, no family or household member could ever be the victim of a crime committed by a family member, because the Commonwealth would be the victim. That analysis effectively would render subdivision J meaningless. Pope v. Commonwealth, 19 Va. App. 130, 449 S.E.2d 269 (1994).

The term "party with a legitimate interest" means not only a party possessed of legal rights with respect to the child, but also any party having a cognizable and reasonable interest in maintaining a close relationship with the child. Thrift v. Baldwin, 23 Va. App. 18, 473 S.E.2d 715 (1996).

Person with a legitimate interest. — Great great stepaunt of a nine-year-old child was a family member under subsection A of § 16.1-241; because the statutory phrase "person with a legitimate interest" was to be broadly construed to accommodate the best interest of the child, the trial court erred in ruling the great great stepaunt was not a person with a legitimate interest. Joseph v. Portsmouth Dep't of Soc. Servs., 2006 Va. App. LEXIS 264 (June 13, 2006).

"Adoptive parents." — Phrase "adoptive parents" in subsection K must be interpreted to describe, as set forth in § 16.1-228, the residence of any natural person in which the child resides as a member of the household and in which he has been placed for the purposes of adoption. Segura v. Fairfax County Dep't of Family Servs., 2008 Va. App. LEXIS 93 (Feb. 26, 2008).

Court did not have authority to order visitation by man determined not to be father. — Subdivision A of this section does not confer upon the juvenile and domestic relations district courts, or upon the circuit courts on appeal, authority and jurisdiction to order visitation with a child by one, not married to the mother, previously thought to be the father but later determined not to be. Kogon v. Ulerick, 12 Va. App. 595, 405 S.E.2d 441 (1991).

Although the adoption of the children by the defendants

extinguished the plaintiffs' grandparental and sibling relationship, the blood relationship continued, and this section particularly confers standing to all plaintiffs to seek visitation. Thrift v. Baldwin, 23 Va. App. 18, 473 S.E.2d 715 (1996).

Forgery conviction vacated for lack of jurisdiction. — Because defendant's brother was the victim of forgery committed by defendant, the juvenile and domestic relations district court had exclusive, original jurisdiction to determine whether there was probable cause. Therefore, since defendant was never brought before a juvenile and domestic relations district court for the purpose of determining probable cause, or for any purpose, but rather was brought before the general district court which acted in the absence of jurisdiction and thus had no power to certify the case to the circuit court, the forgery conviction should be vacated. Pope v. Commonwealth, 19 Va. App. 130, 449 S.E.2d 269 (1994).

Jurisdiction properly exercised. — The defendant burglarized the house of the widow of his father. He was brought before general district court for a preliminary hearing, indicted, and tried in the circuit court. The fact that the defendant was the illegitimate son of the victim's deceased husband was stipulated. The defendant contended that he was a stepchild of the victim and should have been tried under this section. Without a former marriage no stepchild is possible and the defendant fell under neither the technical definition of a stepchild nor in the statutory intent to protect and preserve family harmony. Consequently, the general district court was the proper forum for the defendant's criminal prosecution to begin. Bell v. Commonwealth, No. 0799-95-1 (Ct. of Appeals June 11, 1996).

Trial court did not err when it denied a mother's motion to dismiss the Virginia Beach Department of Social Services' action to terminate the mother's parental rights pursuant to § 16.1-283 based upon a petition filed in Norfolk because, even if a Virginia Beach juvenile and domestic relations court lacked jurisdiction to issue an emergency removal order pursuant to which the child was removed from the mother, the mother lost her parental rights through a petition that originated out of Norfolk, which was the proper venue under § 16.1-243 and had jurisdiction under this section. Paris v. City of Va. Beach Dep't of Soc. Servs., No. 2009-04-1, 2005 Va. App. LEXIS 30 (Ct. of Appeals Jan. 25, 2005).

Because trial court had subject matter jurisdiction under § 16.1-241 in earlier proceeding, any defects in order awarding mother custody rendered it voidable, not void. Department waived issue of whether the mother was a "party with a legitimate interest" to seek custody by failing to timely appeal the trial court's earlier order. Hudson v. Franklin County Dep't of Soc. Servs., 2007 Va. App. LEXIS 53 (Feb. 13, 2007).

Circuit court did not err in denying parents' motions to dismiss petitions filed by a county department of family services pursuant to subdivision A 1 of § 16.1-241 alleging that their children were abused and neglected because the circuit court had the power to exercise its subject matter jurisdiction since subsection B of § 16.1-251 was procedural and directory, rather than mandatory and jurisdictional, and the parents failed to show that they suffered any prejudice as a result of the juvenile and domestic relations district court's alleged failure to comply with subsection B of § 16.1-251; the department's action invoked the subject matter jurisdiction of the district court, upon appeal to the circuit court, the circuit court's jurisdiction was derivative of that of the district court, and therefore, if the district court had subject matter jurisdiction, so too did the circuit court upon appeal from the district court order. Marrison v. Fairfax County Dep't of Family Servs., 59 Va. App. 61, 717 S.E.2d 146, 2011 Va. App. LEXIS 336 (2011).

Exclusive, original jurisdiction. — This section provides that each juvenile and domestic relations district court has exclusive, original jurisdiction over proceedings involving delinquent children, unless the case is transferred to the circuit court. Tross v. Commonwealth, 21 Va. App. 362, 464 S.E.2d 523 (1995).

The juvenile and domestic relations district courts have exclusive, original jurisdiction over criminal offenses alleged to have been committed by a juvenile. Burfoot v. Commonwealth, 23 Va. App. 38, 473 S.E.2d 724 (1996).

Circuit court had jurisdiction where defendant failed to prove he was under 18 when offenses were committed. — Although there was conflicting evidence as to defendant's age, credible evidence supported trial court's conclusion that defendant failed to meet his burden of proving he was less than 18 years of age on date offenses were committed, and therefore trial court did not err in denying defendant's motion to set aside his conviction for lack of subject matter jurisdiction. Winston v. Commonwealth, 26 Va. App. 746, 497 S.E.2d 141 (1998).

The circuit court, sitting as chancery court in divorce case, lacked jurisdiction to terminate father's parental rights and, with that termination, father's child support obligation. Church v. Church, 24 Va. App. 502, 483 S.E.2d 498 (1997).

Jurisdiction based on entrustment agreement. — By the plain language of this statutory provision, a valid and effective entrustment agreement which meets the requirements set forth in former § 63.1-56 (see now § 63.2-900) must be executed before the court may adjudicate a petition for the termination of parental rights. Fredericksburg Dep't of Social Servs. v. Brown, 33 Va. App. 313, 533 S.E.2d 12, 2000 Va. App. LEXIS 634 (2000).

Validity of entrustment agreements jurisdictional and not subject to waiver. — Parents did not waive their challenge to the validity of entrustment agreements signed by their children's aunt when the termination issue was tried de novo in the circuit court because the question of whether requirements of this section were met, and particularly whether the children were the subjects of a valid entrustment agreement, was jurisdictional in nature; because the exercise of subject matter jurisdiction could not be waived by the parties, the validity of the entrustment agreements was properly before the circuit court even assuming the parents had entered an agreed order in the juvenile and domestic relations court approving the execution of the challenged agreements. Fredericksburg Dep't of Social Servs. v. Brown, 33 Va. App. 313, 533 S.E.2d 12, 2000 Va. App. LEXIS 634 (2000).

Jurisdiction of circuit court coincident with juvenile and domestic relations court. — Because the jurisdiction of the circuit court to hear and decide the issues raised in a petition to terminate parental rights is wholly derivative of that of the juvenile and domestic relations court, its power to adjudicate such a petition is coincident with that of the lower court. Fredericksburg Dep't of Social Servs. v. Brown, 33 Va. App. 313, 533 S.E.2d 12, 2000 Va. App. LEXIS 634 (2000).

Authority to issue interlocutory order. — Trial court properly affirmed juvenile and domestic relations court's order which held the juvenile in contempt for failing to attend school, as § 16.1-241 A. provided the court with authority to issue the interlocutory order. B.P. v. Commonwealth, 38 Va. App. 735, 568 S.E.2d 412, 2002 Va. App. LEXIS 498 (2002).

Probable cause finding divested juvenile court of jurisdiction. — Defendant juvenile, tried as an adult on a charge of malicious wounding and convicted of the lesser included offense of unlawful wounding, could not have the case transferred back to the juvenile court, as once the juvenile court made a probable cause finding, the juvenile court had no further jurisdiction; under subdivision A 6 of § 16.1-241, the jurisdiction of the juvenile court was limited to conducting a preliminary hearing to determine if there is probable cause to believe that the juvenile committed the act alleged and that the juvenile was fourteen years of age or older at the time of the commission of the alleged offense, and any matters related thereto. Hughes v. Commonwealth, 39 Va. App. 448, 573 S.E.2d 324, 2002 Va. App. LEXIS 765 (2002).

Applied in Ward v. Commonwealth, Dep't of Social Servs., 13 Va. App. 144, 408 S.E.2d 921 (1991); Fauquier County Dep't of Social Servs. v. Robinson, 20 Va. App. 142, 455 S.E.2d 734 (1995); Catron v. Morrison, 186 Bankr. 197 (Bankr. E.D. Va. 1995); Calfee v. Calfee, 29 Va. App. 88, 509 S.E.2d 552 (1999); Fairfax County Dep't of Family Servs. v. Nordel, 29 Va. App. 400, 512 S.E.2d 830 (1999).

CIRCUIT COURT OPINIONS

"Person with legitimate interest." — Since petitioner was a child's foster parent for the first eighteen months of the child's life, cared for the child continuously during that period, held the same place in the emotional life of the foster child, and fulfilled the same socializing functions as a natural family, she qualified as a "persona with a legitimate interest" and had standing to pursue her petition for custody of the child. Welch v. Wise County Dep't of Soc. Servs., 84 Va. Cir. 245, 2012 Va. Cir. LEXIS 27 (Wise County Jan. 27, 2012).

While petitioner's name did not appear on the foster care agreement that placed a child in petitioner's home and was not the child's foster parent, petitioner was an approved foster care household member, she performed parental duties, and she contributed to the maintenance and well-being of the child; therefore, she qualified as a "persona with a legitimate interest" and had standing to pursue her petition for custody of the child. Welch v. Wise County Dep't of Soc. Servs., 84 Va. Cir. 245, 2012 Va. Cir. LEXIS 27 (Wise County Jan. 27, 2012).

Finding that a child is at risk of being abused or neglected. — Although parents claimed they did not cause their 11-month-old daughter's injuries and did not allow someone else to cause her injuries, a doctor's testimony that the child displayed symptoms of shaken baby syndrome was sufficient for the court to find that the child was abused or neglected, within the meaning of § 16.1-228, and the court found that the child was abused or neglected and that her two-year-old brother was a child at risk of being abused or neglected because of the injuries his sister sustained. In re McBride, 60 Va. Cir. 261, 2002 Va. Cir. LEXIS 391 (Richmond 2002).

Jurisdiction over child in need of services petition. — Juvenile court erred in concluding that it did not have jurisdiction over the petition the city social services agency filed that alleged the minor child was a child in need of services and that continued placement in the home would be contrary to the minor child's welfare; evidence showing that the mother had previously abused the minor child's brother was sufficient to invoke the juvenile court's equitable jurisdiction even though the evidence did not show that the minor child had been abused, as the juvenile court was authorized to prevent the minor child's placement with a known abuser and did not have to wait for the minor child herself to be abused. Norfolk Dep't of Soc. Servs. v. Petermore, 63 Va. Cir. 315, 2003 Va. Cir. LEXIS 351 (Norfolk 2003).

Jurisdiction. — Motion filed by a mother and father to dismiss foster parents' adoption petition was granted because the case did not involve a parental placement within the meaning of §§ 63.2-1230 through 63.2-1240 when the custody order did not mention any placement for the purpose of foster care or adoption, and neither birth parent placed the child with the foster parents for adoption; jurisdiction could not rest on subdivision A 5 of § 16.1-241 because there was no pleading filed to request termination of parental rights, the juvenile court's order did not refer to a termination proceeding, and a separate proceeding was not instituted as required by subsection A of § 16.1-283. In re Terry, 78 Va. Cir. 25, 2008 Va. Cir. LEXIS 272 (Henrico County 2008).

Power of circuit court. — In a case in which a consent decree was entered in the juvenile and domestic relations district court in which a husband was ordered to pay spousal support through November 30, 2008, at which time the spousal support would terminate, and the husband later filed for divorce, the res judicata language of subsection L of § 16.1-241 did not apply to the consent decree entered by the juvenile and domestic relations district court. Since the consent decree was reduced to writing in a court order and signed by or on behalf of the husband and the wife, it constituted a binding stipulation or contract as contemplated by subsection C of § 20-109, and, since it was filed before the entry of a final decree, the circuit court was prevented from entering a spousal support order contrary to the terms of the parties' agreement. Paul v. Paul, 77 Va. Cir. 124, 2008 Va. Cir. LEXIS 250 (Salem 2008).

OPINIONS OF THE ATTORNEY GENERAL

Juvenile court has jurisdiction over adult charged with driving in reckless manner which places juvenile in danger. — The juvenile court, and not the general district court, has jurisdiction to try a case involving an adult charged with driving in a reckless manner which places the person of a juvenile in danger. See opinion of Attorney General to The Honorable Michael J. Valentine, Judge, Juvenile and Domestic Relations District Court, 01-021 (9/28/01).

Consent for medical treatment of minor by substitute judge. — Without a specific appointment, a substitute judge is not a sitting judge, and therefore should not be called upon by a hospital seeking judicial consent for medical treatment of a minor. See opinion of Attorney General to The Honorable Charles E. Poston, Judge, Fourth Judicial Circuit, 01-112 (2/28/02).

§ 16.1-241.1. Repealed by Acts 2002, c. 305.

§ 16.1-241.2. Proceedings against certain parents.

A. Upon the failure of a parent to comply with the provisions of § 22.1-279.3, the school board may, by petition to the juvenile and domestic relations court, proceed against such parent for willful and unreasonable refusal to participate in efforts to improve the student's behavior as follows:

1. If the court finds that the parent has willfully and unreasonably failed to meet, pursuant to a request of the principal as set forth in subsection D of § 22.1-279.3, to review the school board's standards of student conduct and the parent's responsibility to assist the school in disciplining the student, maintaining order, or ensuring the child's school attendance, and to discuss improvement of the child's behavior, school attendance, or educational progress, it may order the parent to so meet; or

2. If the court finds that the parent has willfully and unreasonably failed to accompany a suspended student to meet with school officials pursuant to subsection F of § 22.1-279.3, or upon the student receiving a second suspension or being expelled, it may order (i) the student or his parent to participate in such programs or such treatment as the court deems appropriate to improve the student's behavior, including, but not limited to, extended day programs and summer school or other education programs and counseling, or (ii) the student or his parent to be subject to such conditions and limitations as the court deems appropriate for the supervision, care, and rehabilitation of the student or his parent; in addition, the court may order the parent to pay a civil penalty not to exceed $500.

The court may use its contempt power to enforce any order entered under this section.

B. The civil penalties established pursuant to this section shall be enforceable in the juvenile and domestic relations court or its successor in interest in which the student's school is located and shall be paid into a fund maintained by the appropriate local governing body to support programs or treatments designed to improve the behavior and school attendance of students as described in subdivision 2 of subsection G of § 22.1-279.3. Upon the failure to pay any civil penalties imposed by this section and § 22.1-279.3, the attorney for the appropriate county, city, or town shall enforce the collection of such civil penalties.

C. For the purposes of this section and § 22.1-279.3, *"parent"* or *"parents"* means any parent, guardian, legal custodian, or other person having control or charge of a child.

History.
1994, c. 813; 1995, c. 852; 1996, c. 771; 2004, c. 573.

Law Review.
For 2003/2004 survey of family and juvenile law, see 39 U. Rich. L. Rev. 241 (2004).

Research references.
Virginia Forms (Matthew Bender). No. 5-142 Petition and Order for Parental Participation.

§ 16.1-241.3. Newborn children; substance abuse.

Upon the filing of a petition alleging that an investigation has been commenced in response to a report of suspected abuse or neglect of the child based upon a factor specified in subsection B of § 63.2-1509, the court may enter any order authorized pursuant to this chapter which the court deems necessary to protect the health and welfare of the child pending final disposition of the investigation pursuant to Chapter 15 (§ 63.2-1500 et seq.) of Title 63.2 or other proceedings brought pursuant to this chapter. Such orders may include, but shall not be limited to, an emergency removal order pursuant to § 16.1-251, a preliminary protective order pursuant to § 16.1-253 or an order authorized pursuant to subdivisions A 1 through 4 of § 16.1-278.2. The fact that an order was entered pursuant to this section shall not be admissible as evidence in any criminal, civil or administrative proceeding other than a proceeding to enforce the order.

The order shall be effective for a limited duration not to exceed the period of time necessary to conclude the investigation and any proceedings initiated pursuant to Chapter 15 (§ 63.2-1500 et seq.) of Title 63.2, but shall be a final order subject to appeal.

History.
1998, cc. 704, 716; 2002, c. 860; 2012, cc. 504, 640.

Cross references.
As to filing of a petition pursuant to § 16.1-241.3 by a local social services department upon a report or complaint based upon one of the factors in § 63.2-1509 B, see § 63.2-1505 B 1 and § 63.2-1506 B 1.

The 2012 amendments.
The 2012 amendments by cc. 504 and 640 are identical, and in the first paragraph, deleted "within twenty-one days of a child's birth" following "filing of a petition" in the first sentence and substituted "subdivisions A 1 through 4 of § 16.1-278.2" for "subdivisions 1 through 4 of subsection A of § 16.1-278.2" at the end of the next-to-last sentence.

§ 16.1-242. Retention of jurisdiction.

When jurisdiction has been obtained by the court in the case of any child, such jurisdiction may be retained by the court until such person becomes twenty-one years of age, except when the person is in the custody of the Department or when jurisdiction is divested under the provisions of § 16.1-244. In any event, when such person reaches the age of twenty-one and a prosecution has not been commenced against him, he shall be proceeded against as an adult, even if he was a juvenile when the offense was committed.

History.
Code 1950, § 16.1-159; 1956, c. 555; 1977, c. 559; 1978, c. 740; 1992, c. 509.

Editor's note.

Acts 1993, c. 929, cl. 3, as amended by Acts 1994, c. 564, cl. 1, and Acts 1996, c. 616, cl. 3, provides that the amendment to this section by Acts 1993, c. 929, cl. 1, shall become effective June 1, 1998, "only if state funds are provided by the General Assembly sufficient to provide adequate resources, including all local costs, for the court to carry out the purposes of this act and to fulfill its mission to serve children and families of the Commonwealth." The funding was not provided.

Law Review.

For discussion of retrial of infant as adult, see 4 U. Rich. L. Rev. 142 (1969). For comment, "The Uniform Child Custody Jurisdiction Act in Virginia," see 14 U. Rich. L. Rev. 435 (1979). For article, "Legal Issues Involving Children," see 26 U. Rich. L. Rev. 797 (1992).

Research references.

Bryson on Virginia Civil Procedure (Matthew Bender). Chapter 2 Potential Jurisdiction. § 2.03 Courts. W. Hamilton Bryson.

CASE NOTES

Prosecution as adult after loss of jurisdiction. — A defendant who is charged with the commission of a crime when a juvenile and is not validly tried therefor before he reaches 21 years of age, is no longer within the jurisdiction of the juvenile court but may be proceeded against as an adult. Pruitt v. Guerry, 210 Va. 268, 170 S.E.2d 1 (1969).

Statutes governing insanity defense not applicable in juvenile proceedings. — If the statutory scheme governing the disposition of persons acquitted by reason of insanity were available to a juvenile, that scheme's indeterminate period of commitment for inpatient hospitalization could run afoul of the limited duration of the juvenile and domestic relations district courts' jurisdiction pursuant to this section; therefore, the statutory provisions relating to the insanity defense are inapplicable in juvenile proceedings. Commonwealth v. Chatman, 260 Va. 562, 538 S.E.2d 304, 2000 Va. LEXIS 131 (2000).

OPINIONS OF THE ATTORNEY GENERAL

Probation revocation proceedings. — A juvenile court retains jurisdiction over a probationer although he has reached the age of twenty-one prior to a probation revocation proceeding. See opinion of Attorney General to Honorable Harvey L. Bryant, Commonwealth's Attorney for the City of Virginia Beach, 05-037 (6/20/05).

§ 16.1-242.1. Retention of jurisdiction; appeals involving children in foster care.

Upon appeal to the circuit court of any case involving a child placed in foster care and in any appeal to the Court of Appeals or Supreme Court of Virginia, the juvenile court shall retain jurisdiction to continue to hear petitions filed pursuant to §§ 16.1-282 and 16.1-282.1. Orders of the juvenile court in such cases shall continue to be reviewed and enforced by the juvenile court until the circuit court, Court of Appeals or Supreme Court rules otherwise.

History.

1998, c. 550.

§ 16.1-243. Venue.

A. Original venue:

1. Cases involving children, other than support or where protective order issued: Proceedings with respect to children under this law, except support proceedings as provided in subdivision 2 or family abuse proceedings as provided in subdivision 3, shall:

a. Delinquency: If delinquency is alleged, be commenced in the city or county where the acts constituting the alleged delinquency occurred or they may, with the written consent of the child and the attorney for the Commonwealth for both jurisdictions, be commenced in the city or county where the child resides;

b. Custody or visitation: In cases involving custody or visitation, be commenced in the court of the city or county which, in order of priority, (i) is the home of the child at the time of the filing of the petition, or had been the home of the child within six months before the filing of the petition and the child is absent from the city or county because of his removal or retention by a person claiming his custody or for other reasons, and a parent or person acting as a parent continues to live in the city or county, (ii) has significant connection with the child and in which there is substantial evidence concerning the child's present or future care, protection, training and personal relationships, (iii) is where the child is physically present and the child has been abandoned or it is necessary in an emergency to protect the child because he has been subjected to or threatened with mistreatment or abuse or is otherwise neglected or dependent or (iv) it is in the best interest of the child for the court to assume jurisdiction as no other city or county is an appropriate venue under the preceding provisions of this subdivision;

c. Adoption: In parental placement adoption consent hearings pursuant to §§ 16.1-241, 63.2-1233, and 63.2-1237, be commenced in any city or county, provided, however, that diligent efforts shall first be made to commence such hearings (i) in the city or county where the child to be adopted was born, (ii) in the city or county where the birth parent(s) reside, or (iii) in the city or county where the prospective adoptive parent(s) reside. In cases in which a hearing is commenced in a city or county other than one described in clauses (i) through (iii), the petitioner shall certify in writing to the court that diligent efforts to commence a hearing in such city or county have been made but have proven ineffective; and

d. All other cases: In all other proceedings, be commenced in the city or county where the child resides or in the city or county where the child is present when the proceedings are commenced.

2. Support: Proceedings that involve child or spousal support or child and spousal support, exclusive of proceedings arising under Chapter 5 (§ 20-61 et seq.) of Title 20, shall be commenced in the city or county where either party resides or in the city or county where the respondent is present when the proceeding commences.

3. Family abuse: Proceedings in which an order of protection is sought as a result of family abuse shall

be commenced where (i) either party has his or her principal residence (ii) the abuse occurred or (iii) a protective order was issued if at the time the proceeding is commenced the order is in effect to protect the petitioner or a family or household member of the petitioner.

B. Transfer of venue:

1. Generally: Except in custody, visitation and support cases, if the child resides in a city or county of the Commonwealth and the proceeding is commenced in a court of another city or county, that court may at any time, on its own motion or a motion of a party for good cause shown, transfer the proceeding to the city or county of the child's residence for such further action or proceedings as the court receiving the transfer may deem proper. However, such transfer may occur only after adjudication in delinquency proceedings.

2. Custody and visitation: In custody and visitation cases, if venue lies in one of several cities or counties, the court in which the motion for transfer is made shall determine which such city or county is the most appropriate venue unless the parties mutually agree to the selection of venue. In the consideration of the motion, the best interests of the child shall determine the most appropriate forum.

3. Support: In support proceedings, exclusive of proceedings arising under Chapter 5 of Title 20, if the respondent resides in a city or county in the Commonwealth and the proceeding is commenced in a court of another city or county, that court may, at any time on its own motion or a motion of a party for good cause shown or by agreement of the parties, transfer the proceeding to the city or county of the respondent's residence for such further action or proceedings as the court receiving the transfer may deem proper. For the purposes of determining venue of cases involving support, the respondent's residence shall include any city or county in which the respondent has resided within the last six months prior to the commencement of the proceeding or in which the respondent is residing at the time that the motion for transfer of venue is made. If venue is transferable to one of several cities or counties, the court in which the motion for transfer is made shall determine which such city or county is the most appropriate venue unless the parties mutually agree to the selection of such venue.

When the support proceeding is a companion case to a child custody or visitation proceeding, the provisions governing venue in the proceeding involving the child's custody or visitation shall govern.

4. Subsequent transfers: Any court receiving a transferred proceeding as provided in this section may in its discretion transfer such proceeding to a court in an appropriate venue for good cause shown based either upon changes in circumstances or mistakes of fact or upon agreement of the parties. In any transfer of venue in cases involving children, the best interests of the child shall be considered in deciding if and to which court a transfer of venue would be appropriate.

5. Enforcement of orders for support, maintenance and custody: Any juvenile and domestic relations district court to which a suit is transferred for enforcement of orders pertaining to support, maintenance, care or custody pursuant to § 20-79 (c) may transfer the case as provided in this section.

C. Records: Originals of all legal and social records pertaining to the case shall accompany the transfer of venue. Records imaged from the original documents shall be considered original documents for purposes of the transfer of venue. The transferor court may, in its discretion, retain copies as it deems appropriate.

History.

Code 1950, § 16.1-160; 1956, c. 555; 1977, c. 559; 1985, c. 367; 1987, cc. 598, 608, 620; 1989, c. 545; 1995, cc. 772, 826; 1996, c. 866; 2000, c. 830; 2010, cc. 717, 760; 2012, c. 424.

Editor's note.

Acts 1993, c. 929, cl. 3, as amended by Acts 1994, c. 564, cl. 1, and Acts 1996, c. 616, cl. 3, provides that the amendment to this section by Acts 1993, c. 929, cl. 1, shall become effective June 1, 1998, "only if state funds are provided by the General Assembly sufficient to provide adequate resources, including all local costs, for the court to carry out the purposes of this act and to fulfill its mission to serve children and families of the Commonwealth." The funding was not provided.

The 2010 amendments.

The 2010 amendments by cc. 717 and 760 are identical, and in subsection C, inserted the second sentence and deleted "such" preceding "copies" in the last sentence.

The 2012 amendments.

The 2012 amendment by c. 424 rewrote subdivision A 1 c, which formerly read "Adoption: In parental placement adoption consent hearings pursuant to §§ 16.1-241, 63.2-1233 and 63.2-1237, be commenced (i) in the city or county where the child to be adopted was born, (ii) in the city or county where the birth parent(s) reside, or (iii) in the city or county where the prospective adoptive parent(s) reside" and made minor stylistic changes.

Law Review.

For 1987 survey of Virginia law as to children, see 21 U. Rich. L. Rev. 789 (1987). For survey on domestic relations in Virginia for 1989, see 23 U. Rich. L. Rev. 561 (1989).

Research references.

Bryson on Virginia Civil Procedure (Matthew Bender). Chapter 4 Venue. § 4.03 Venue in miscellaneous cases. W. Hamilton Bryson.

Michie's Jurisprudence.

For related discussion, see 14A M.J. Parent and Child, § 4.

CASE NOTES

Propriety of action where child was removed pursuant to emergency removal ordered by court lacking jurisdiction. — Trial court did not err when it denied a mother's motion to dismiss the Virginia Beach Department of Social Services' action to terminate the mother's parental rights pursuant to § 16.1-283 based upon a petition filed in Norfolk because, even if a Virginia Beach juvenile and domestic relations court lacked jurisdiction to issue an emergency removal order pursuant to which the child was removed from the mother, the mother lost her parental rights through a petition that originated out of Norfolk, which was the proper venue under this section and had jurisdiction under § 16.1-241. Paris v. City of Va. Beach Dep't of Soc. Servs., No. 2009-04-1, 2005 Va. App. LEXIS 30 (Ct. of Appeals Jan. 25, 2005).

OPINIONS OF THE ATTORNEY GENERAL

Proper venue for a juvenile detention hearing is the place where the proceeding has been commenced. See opinion of Attorney General to The Honorable Michael W. Lee, Commonwealth's Attorney for City of Colonial Heights, 05-002 (3/29/05).

§ 16.1-244. Concurrent jurisdiction; exceptions.

A. Nothing contained in this law shall deprive any other court of the concurrent jurisdiction to determine the custody of children upon a writ of habeas corpus under the law, or to determine the custody, guardianship, visitation or support of children when such custody, guardianship, visitation or support is incidental to the determination of causes pending in such courts, nor deprive a circuit court of jurisdiction to determine spousal support in a suit for separate maintenance. However, when a suit for divorce has been filed in a circuit court, in which the custody, guardianship, visitation or support of children of the parties or spousal support is raised by the pleadings and a hearing, including a pendente lite hearing, is set by the circuit court on any such issue for a date certain or on a motions docket to be heard within 21 days of the filing, the juvenile and domestic relations district courts shall be divested of the right to enter any further decrees or orders to determine custody, guardianship, visitation or support when raised for such hearing and such matters shall be determined by the circuit court unless both parties agreed to a referral to the juvenile court. Nothing in this section shall deprive a circuit court of the authority to refer any such case to a commissioner for a hearing or shall deprive the juvenile and domestic relations district courts of the jurisdiction to enforce its valid orders prior to the entry of a conflicting order of any circuit court for any period during which the order was in effect or to temporarily place a child in the custody of any person when that child has been adjudicated abused, neglected, in need of services or delinquent subsequent to the order of any circuit court.

B. Jurisdiction of cases involving violations of federal law by a child shall be concurrent and shall be assumed only if waived by the federal court or the United States attorney.

History.

Code 1950, § 16.1-161; 1956, c. 555; 1977, c. 559; 1978, c. 740; 1984, cc. 657, 669; 1985, c. 183; 1987, c. 36; 1989, c. 509; 1990, c. 600; 2000, c. 781; 2003, c. 129.

Editor's note.

Acts 1993, c. 929, cl. 3, as amended by Acts 1994, c. 564, cl. 1, and Acts 1996, c. 616, cl. 3, provides that the amendment to this section by Acts 1993, c. 929, cl. 1, shall become effective June 1, 1998, "only if state funds are provided by the General Assembly sufficient to provide adequate resources, including all local costs, for the court to carry out the purposes of this act and to fulfill its mission to serve children and families of the Commonwealth." The funding was not provided.

Law Review.

For survey of Virginia law on domestic relations for the year 1969-1970, see 56 Va. L. Rev. 1411 (1970). For comment, "The

Uniform Child Custody Jurisdiction Act in Virginia," see 14 U. Rich. L. Rev. 435 (1979). For survey on domestic relations in Virginia for 1989, see 23 U. Rich. L. Rev. 561 (1989). For survey on legal issues involving children in Virginia for 1989, see 23 U. Rich. L. Rev. 705 (1989). For annual survey article on legal issues involving children, see 38 U. Rich. L. Rev. 161 (2003).

Research references.

Bryson on Virginia Civil Procedure (Matthew Bender). Chapter 2 Potential Jurisdiction. § 2.03 Courts. W. Hamilton Bryson.

Michie's Jurisprudence.

For related discussion, see 6A M.J. Divorce and Alimony, § 69; 9A M.J. Habeas Corpus, § 16.

CASE NOTES

Generally, under statutory scheme, juvenile courts have exclusive original jurisdiction in custody cases unless and until circuit courts assume jurisdiction. The circuit courts may assume jurisdiction either by an appeal from the juvenile courts or by the direct filing of an appropriate proceeding in the circuit courts. The procedural standard to be applied in the circuit courts is dictated by the manner in which those courts assume jurisdiction. Peple v. Peple, 5 Va. App. 414, 364 S.E.2d 232 (1988).

Waiver of jurisdiction. — Nothing in either § 16.1-241 or this section permits the juvenile court to "waive" its jurisdiction and allow a party to bring an original action in the circuit court without meeting the statutory requirements. Willis v. Gamez, 20 Va. App. 75, 455 S.E.2d 274 (1995).

Mere filing of divorce suit by husband prior to participating in subsequent juvenile court proceeding did not sufficiently "challenge" juvenile court order to relieve him of meeting the extra burden of proof imposed by the "change in circumstances test." Peple v. Peple, 5 Va. App. 414, 364 S.E.2d 232 (1988).

Courts of equity not divested of all power to determine custody of children. — It is evident, as indicated by the language of this section, that it was not the purpose of the legislature to divest courts of equity of all power to determine the custody of children. Under this section a court of record has concurrent jurisdiction to determine the custody of children: (1) upon a writ of habeas corpus; and (2) in a suit in equity when custody is incidental to the determination of the cause. Poole v. Poole, 210 Va. 442, 171 S.E.2d 685 (1970).

Jurisdiction of circuit court over custody petition. — Although a circuit court had acquired jurisdiction solely by virtue of an appealed visitation petition, custody was incidental to visitation under the circumstances and the circuit court had subject matter jurisdiction to transfer custody. Cintron v. Long, No. 2169-99-2, 2000 Va. App. LEXIS 487 (Ct. of Appeals July 5, 2000).

Authority of circuit court to reinstate case on docket. — Circuit court had authority to reinstate the case on its docket and to entertain the parties' motions to enforce visitation rights and to modify child support after having transferred "all matters ... pertaining to child support, visitation rights [and] custody of the minor children" to the juvenile and domestic relations district court pursuant to § 20-79(c). Although a final divorce decree had been entered, when the case was reinstated on the docket of the circuit court, the case was "pending" for consideration of those matters over which the circuit court had continuing jurisdiction. Crabtree v. Crabtree, 17 Va. App. 81, 435 S.E.2d 883 (1993).

A "transfer" of "any other matters pertaining to support and maintenance ... and custody" to the juvenile and domestic relations district court pursuant to § 20-79(c) conveys concurrent jurisdiction on the juvenile and domestic relations district court to hear those matters, but the transfer does not divest the circuit court of its continuing jurisdiction to consider those issues, should it exercise its discretion to do so. Accordingly, the circuit court had the authority to reinstate the case on its docket and to consider the motions to modify child support and visitation. Crabtree v. Crabtree, 17 Va. App. 81, 435 S.E.2d 883 (1993).

Distinction between appeal and divestiture of jurisdiction. — Under the statutory scheme this distinction between an appeal under § 16.1-136 and a divestiture of further jurisdiction in the juvenile court by operation of subsection A is intentional and consistent with and conducive to the best interests of children who are the subjects of custody disputes between their natural parents, the protection of parental rights, and, less significantly, with the notion of judicial economy. Peple v. Peple, 5 Va. App. 414, 364 S.E.2d 232 (1988).

In an appeal to the circuit court, the "advantage" granted to the noncustodial parent is simply the avoidance of the additional burden of proof imposed by the change in circumstance test; in the de novo appeal, the issue is simply what is in the best interests of the child. Accordingly, the procedural distinction between an appeal under § 16.1-136 and a divestiture of further jurisdiction in the juvenile court by operation of this section is significant and perhaps controlling in most cases. Peple v. Peple, 5 Va. App. 414, 364 S.E.2d 232 (1988).

The procedural distinction between an appeal under § 16.1-136 and a divestiture of further jurisdiction in the juvenile court by operation of this section relating to divorce proceedings is significant. An order adjudicating an appeal from the juvenile court to the circuit court is not entitled to the procedural convenience of transfer provided by § 20-79. Rather, such order, together with related issues embraced by the appeal, rests within the exclusive jurisdiction of the circuit court pending disposition by that court. Calfee v. Calfee, 29 Va. App. 88, 509 S.E.2d 552 (1999).

Divestiture of jurisdiction in juvenile court simply provides for orderly transfer of concurrent jurisdiction to the sole jurisdiction of the superior circuit court. Peple v. Peple, 5 Va. App. 414, 364 S.E.2d 232 (1988).

Unlike an appeal, divestiture provisions of subsection A do not annul judgment of juvenile court as if no previous hearing occurred. Rather the judgment of the juvenile court remains in full force and effect until modified by the circuit court to which jurisdiction has been transferred. In modifying the prior order, the procedural standard to be applied is the "change in circumstances" test which affords the benefit of stability to the child. It further ensures an orderly administration of the judicial process in both levels of courts with concurrent jurisdiction in these cases in which natural parents regrettably too often find themselves. Peple v. Peple, 5 Va. App. 414, 364 S.E.2d 232 (1988).

Hearing not scheduled as required; divestiture not successful. — Although husband fully utilized the concurrent jurisdiction initially available to him in both the trial and juvenile and domestic courts, simultaneously filing a bill of complaint for divorce in the trial court seeking, inter alia, child custody and support, and a petition pursuing identical relief in the juvenile and domestic court, the record did not reveal that a hearing on the matters of custody or support was thereafter scheduled in the trial court for a date certain to be heard within 21 days of filing, as required by subsection A. Thus, the institution of the divorce proceedings, together with the related prayers, did not divest the juvenile and domestic court from shared jurisdiction. Rose v. Bartlett, No. 2776-99-3, 2000 Va. App. LEXIS 438 (Ct. of Appeals June 13, 2000).

Jurisdiction as to custody and support of children of parties to divorce suit. — Section 20-108 and other related sections give courts of equity ample authority to deal with matters of custody and support of children if one or both of the parties to the divorce suit should die. Morris v. Henry, 193 Va. 631, 70 S.E.2d 417 (1952); Judd. v. Van Horn, 195 Va. 988, 81 S.E.2d 432 (1954).

Writ of prohibition against juvenile and domestic relations court held properly denied. — Court properly denied petition for writ of prohibition sought by father to prevent further action by the juvenile and domestic relations district court on the ground that it lacked subject matter jurisdiction by virtue of the Parental Kidnapping Prevention Act and the Uniform Child Custody Jurisdiction Act. The juvenile and domestic relations district courts of Virginia have general jurisdiction over all proceedings involving the custody, visitation, support, control or disposition of a child, except as otherwise provided in this section. In re Johnston, 3 Va. App. 492, 350 S.E.2d 681 (1986).

Limited jurisdiction of district court after filing for divorce where spousal support in issue. — When a suit for divorce has been filed and spousal support is at issue, the district court is divested of jurisdiction to enter any further decrees or order relating to spousal support except to enforce its orders entered prior to an order of the circuit court. Martin v. Bales, 7 Va. App. 141, 371 S.E.2d 823 (1988).

Applied in Fauquier County Dep't of Soc. Servs. v. Ridgeway, 59 Va. App. 185, 717 S.E.2d 811, 2011 Va. App. LEXIS 381 (2011).

CIRCUIT COURT OPINIONS

Effect of 21-day rule. — The 21-day rule of § 16.1-244 divests the juvenile and domestic relations court of jurisdiction even though the circuit court has entered no orders on the issue involved as long as a hearing is set within 21 days of the filing of the divorce case. Forand v. Mutchler, 59 Va. Cir. 68, 2002 Va. Cir. LEXIS 109 (Loudoun County 2002).

No exception for concurrent jurisdiction present. — Juvenile and domestic relations (J&DR) court was without authority to enter a protective order as between two divorcing parties because a circuit court had previously acquired jurisdiction and entered an order addressing support, custody, and visitation and none of the exceptions allowing an exercise of concurrent jurisdiction by the J&DR court applied. Wyrick v. Wyrick, 61 Va. Cir. 74, 2003 Va. Cir. LEXIS 9 (Roanoke County 2003).

Circuit court's child support award retroactive to juvenile court's petition. — Based upon the jurisdictional provisions of § 16.1-244, which indicated that upon a wife's filing of a divorce action, which included a request for child support, the juvenile and domestic relations district court no longer had authority over a previously filed child support petition, the circuit court awarded child support retroactively to the date of the commencement of the initial request for support in the domestic relations court, which was in compliance with the dictates of subsection B of § 20-108.1. Nagpaul v. Nagpaul, 2003 Va. Cir. LEXIS 178 (Fairfax County Aug. 7, 2003).

Jurisdiction not divested. — This section did not preclude the juvenile court from enforcing a support order because the circuit court orders relied on by the mother did not include any support provision that applied during the time period covered by the juvenile court support order, rather they dealt with custody. Federico v. DCSE, 70 Va. Cir. 260, 2006 Va. Cir. LEXIS 23 (Madison County 2006).

§ 16.1-245. Transfer from other courts.

If, during the pendency of a proceeding in any other court, it is ascertained for the first time that exclusive jurisdiction lies within the juvenile and domestic relations district court, such court shall forthwith transfer the case, together with all papers, documents and evidence connected therewith, to the juvenile and domestic relations district court of the city or county having jurisdiction. The court making the transfer shall determine who is to have custody of the child pending action by the juvenile and domestic relations district court pursuant to § 16.1-247. If, during the pendency of a proceeding in the juvenile and domestic relations district court, it is ascertained for the first time that exclusive jurisdiction lies in the general district or circuit court, the juvenile and domestic relations district court shall likewise transfer the case to the appropriate court.

History.
Code 1950, § 16.1-175; 1956, c. 555; 1977, c. 559; 1992, c. 496.

Editor's note.
Acts 1993, c. 930, cl. 3, as amended by Acts 1994, c. 564, cl. 2, and Acts 1996, c. 616, cl. 4, provides that the amendment to this section by Acts 1993, c. 930, cl. 1, shall become effective June 1, 1998, "if state funds are provided, including all local costs, to carry out the purposes of this bill by the General Assembly." The funding was not provided.

Law Review.
For survey of Virginia law on criminal law and procedure for the year 1969-1970, see 56 Va. L. Rev. 1572 (1970).

Michie's Jurisprudence.
For related discussion, see 9A M.J. Habeas Corpus, § 8; 9B M.J. Infants, §§ 13, 84.

CIRCUIT COURT OPINIONS

Transferee court lacked subject matter jurisdiction. — Circuit Court for the City of Norfolk did not have subject matter jurisdiction to consider the parties' motions to amend a husband's child and spousal support obligations upon a transfer from the Norfolk Juvenile and Domestic Relations District Court since: (1) the circuit court did not have concurrent jurisdiction to amend the support orders; (2) § 16.1-245 allowed the district court to transfer a case to the circuit court if the circuit court had exclusive jurisdiction, but the circuit court did not have exclusive jurisdiction; (3) the circuit court only had appellate jurisdiction over a Juvenile and Domestic Relations District Court order under subsections A and J of § 16.1-296; (4) there was no authority to transfer a case from a lower court to a circuit court pendente lite; and (5) the Virginia Constitution and the statutes enacted pursuant to it were the sources of the circuit court's subject matter jurisdiction. Cunningham v. Cunningham, 2013 Va. Cir. LEXIS 10 (Norfolk Jan. 24, 2013).

§ 16.1-245.1. Medical evidence admissible in juvenile and domestic relations district court.

In any civil case heard in a juvenile and domestic relations district court involving allegations of child abuse or neglect or family abuse, any party may present evidence, by a report from the treating or examining health care provider as defined in § 8.01-581.1 or the records of a hospital, medical facility or laboratory at which the treatment, examination or laboratory analysis was performed, or both, as to the extent, nature, and treatment of any physical condition or injury suffered by a person and the examination of the person or the result of the laboratory analysis.

A medical report shall be admitted if the party intending to present such evidence at trial or hearing gives the opposing party or parties a copy of the evidence and written notice of intention to present it at least ten days, or in the case of a preliminary removal hearing under § 16.1-252 or § 16.1-253.1 at least twenty-four hours, prior to the trial or hearing and if attached to such evidence is a sworn statement of the treating or examining health care provider or laboratory analyst who made the report that (i) the information contained therein is true, accurate, and fully describes the nature and extent of the physical condition or injury and (ii) the patient named therein was the person treated or examined by such health care provider; or, in the case of a laboratory analysis, that the information contained therein is true and accurate.

A hospital or other medical facility record shall be admitted if attached to it is a sworn statement of the custodian thereof that the same is a true and accurate copy of the record of such hospital or other medical facility. If thereafter a party summons the health care provider or custodian making such statement to testify in proper person or by deposition taken de bene esse, the court shall determine which party shall pay the fees and costs for such appearance or depositions, or may apportion the same among the parties in such proportion as the ends of justice may require. If such health care provider or custodian is not subject to subpoena for cross-examination in court or by a deposition de bene esse, then the court shall allow a reasonable opportunity for the party seeking the subpoena for such health care provider or custodian to obtain his testimony as the ends of justice may require.

History.
1990, c. 560; 1996, c. 866; 2000, c. 163.

Editor's note.
Acts 1993, c. 930, cl. 3, as amended by Acts 1994, c. 564, cl. 2, and Acts 1996, c. 616, cl. 4, provides that the amendment to this section by Acts 1993, c. 930, cl. 1, shall become effective June 1, 1998, "if state funds are provided, including all local costs, to carry out the purposes of this bill by the General Assembly." The funding was not provided.

CASE NOTES

Introduction into evidence of psychological evaluation. — In a proceeding to terminate parental rights, the court properly allowed the introduction into evidence of the mother's psychological evaluation as the report was previously made a part of the file in the juvenile court and the juvenile court documents were admitted in evidence. Padilla v. Norfolk Division of Social Services, No. 1388-98-1 (Ct. of Appeals Jan. 26, 1999).

ARTICLE 4.

IMMEDIATE CUSTODY, ARREST, DETENTION AND SHELTER CARE.

§ 16.1-246. When and how child may be taken into immediate custody.

No child may be taken into immediate custody except:

A. With a detention order issued by the judge, the intake officer or the clerk, when authorized by the judge, of the juvenile and domestic relations district court in accordance with the provisions of this law or with a warrant issued by a magistrate; or

B. When a child is alleged to be in need of services or supervision and (i) there is a clear and substantial danger to the child's life or health or (ii) the assumption of custody is necessary to ensure the child's appearance before the court; or

C. When, in the presence of the officer who makes the arrest, a child has committed an act designated a crime under the law of this Commonwealth, or an ordinance of any city, county, town or service district, or under federal law and the officer believes that such is necessary for the protection of the public interest; or

C1. When a child has committed a misdemeanor offense involving (i) shoplifting in violation of § 18.2-103, (ii) assault and battery or (iii) carrying a weapon on school property in violation of § 18.2-308.1 and, although the offense was not committed in the presence of the officer who makes the arrest, the arrest is based on probable cause on reasonable complaint of a person who observed the alleged offense; or

D. When there is probable cause to believe that a child has committed an offense which if committed by an adult would be a felony; or

E. When a law-enforcement officer has probable cause to believe that a person committed to the Department of Juvenile Justice as a child has run away or that a child has escaped from a jail or detention home; or

F. When a law-enforcement officer has probable cause to believe a child has run away from a residential, child-caring facility or home in which he had been placed by the court, the local department of social services or a licensed child welfare agency; or

G. When a law-enforcement officer has probable cause to believe that a child (i) has run away from home or (ii) is without adult supervision at such hours of the night and under such circumstances that the law-enforcement officer reasonably concludes that there is a clear and substantial danger to the child's welfare; or

H. When a child is believed to be in need of inpatient treatment for mental illness as provided in § 16.1-340.

History.
Code 1950, § 16.1-194; 1956, c. 555; 1958, c. 344; 1974, cc. 585, 671; 1977, c. 559; 1978, cc. 643, 740; 1979, c. 701; 1981, c. 487; 1982, c. 683; 1985, c. 540; 1990, cc. 635, 642, 743, 744, 975; 2002, c. 747.

Cross references.
As to bail for juveniles taken into custody pursuant to this section, see § 19.2-119 et seq. As to recognizances for juveniles taken into custody pursuant to this section, see § 19.2-135 et seq. As to local boards of social services accepting temporary custody of persons under 18 years of age taken into custody pursuant to § 16.1-246 B or § 63.2-1517, see § 63.2-900.

Editor's note.
Acts 1993, c. 930, cl. 3, as amended by Acts 1994, c. 564, cl. 2, and Acts 1996, c. 616, cl. 4, provides that the amendment to this section by Acts 1993, c. 930, cl. 1, shall become effective June 1, 1998, "if state funds are provided, including all local costs, to carry out the purposes of this bill by the General Assembly." The funding was not provided.

Law Review.
For comment, "Right to Counsel in Virginia Juvenile Proceedings," see 3 U. Rich. L. Rev. 316 (1969). For note, "Publicity in the Juvenile Court," see 3 U. Rich. L. Rev. 348 (1969). For survey of Virginia law on domestic relations for the year 1974-1975, see 61 Va. L. Rev. 1732 (1975). For survey of Virginia criminal procedure for the year 1977-1978, see 64 Va. L. Rev. 1419 (1978). For article, "The Revision of Virginia's Juvenile Court Law," see 13 U. Rich. L. Rev. 847 (1979). For comment, "The Uniform Child Custody Jurisdiction Act in Virginia," see 14 U. Rich. L. Rev. 435 (1979). For survey of Virginia law on criminal procedure for the year 1978-1979, see 66 Va. L. Rev. 261 (1980). For annual survey article on legal issues involving children, see 38 U. Rich. L. Rev. 161 (2003). For 2003/2004 survey of family and juvenile law, see 39 U. Rich. L. Rev. 241 (2004).

Michie's Jurisprudence.
For related discussion, see 19 M.J. Warrants, § 2.

CASE NOTES

Failure to conform strictly with this section and the sections following pertaining to arrest and detention did not deprive the

Commonwealth of the right to prosecute where no constitutional violations were involved. Durrette v. Commonwealth, 201 Va. 735, 113 S.E.2d 842 (1960).

It is not an unconstitutional denial of equal protection for children taken into protective custody under former § 63.1-248.9 [see now § 63.2-1517] in order to protect them from imminent harm to be afforded different procedural protections than children taken into custody under this section on suspicion of criminal or other misconduct. Jordan v. Jackson, 15 F.3d 333 (4th Cir. 1994).

OPINIONS OF THE ATTORNEY GENERAL

Out-of-state runaway children can be detained within Commonwealth. — Amendment to statute was not necessary to authorize law-enforcement officers of the Commonwealth to detain nonresident runaway children as subsection G already authorized law-enforcement officers to take into custody out-of-state runaway children who were within the Commonwealth. See opinion of Attorney General to The Honorable William C. Mims, Member, Senate of Virginia, 00-096 (11/29/00).

§ 16.1-247. Duties of person taking child into custody.

A. A person taking a child into custody pursuant to the provisions of subsection A of § 16.1-246, during such hours as the court is open, shall, with all practicable speed, and in accordance with the provisions of this law and the orders of court pursuant thereto, bring the child to the judge or intake officer of the court and the judge, intake officer or arresting officer shall, in the most expeditious manner practicable, give notice of the action taken, together with a statement of the reasons for taking the child into custody, orally or in writing to the child's parent, guardian, legal custodian or other person standing in loco parentis.

B. A person taking a child into custody pursuant to the provisions of subsection B, C, or D of § 16.1-246, during such hours as the court is open, shall, with all practicable speed, and in accordance with the provisions of this law and the orders of court pursuant thereto:

1. Release the child to such child's parents, guardian, custodian or other suitable person able and willing to provide supervision and care for such child and issue oral counsel and warning as may be appropriate; or

2. Release the child to such child's parents, guardian, legal custodian or other person standing in loco parentis upon their promise to bring the child before the court when requested; or

3. If not released, bring the child to the judge or intake officer of the court and, in the most expeditious manner practicable, give notice of the action taken, together with a statement of the reasons for taking the child into custody, in writing to the judge or intake officer, and the judge, intake officer or arresting officer shall give notice of the action taken orally or in writing to the child's parent, guardian, legal custodian or other person standing in loco parentis. Nothing herein shall prevent the child from being held for the purpose of administering a blood or breath test to determine the alcoholic con-

tent of his blood where the child has been taken into custody pursuant to § 18.2-266.

C. A person taking a child into custody pursuant to the provisions of subsections E and F of § 16.1-246, during such hours as the court is open, shall, with all practicable speed and in accordance with the provisions of this law and the orders of court pursuant thereto:

1. Release the child to the institution, facility or home from which he ran away or escaped; or

2. If not released, bring the child to the judge or intake officer of the court and, in the most expeditious manner practicable, give notice of the action taken, together with a statement of the reasons for taking the child into custody, in writing to the judge or intake officer, and the judge, intake officer or arresting officer shall give notice of the action taken orally or in writing to the institution, facility or home in which the child had been placed and orally or in writing to the child's parent, guardian, legal custodian or other person standing in loco parentis.

D. A person taking a child into custody pursuant to the provisions of subsection A of § 16.1-246, during such hours as the court is not open, shall with all practicable speed and in accordance with the provisions of this law and the orders of court pursuant thereto:

1. Release the child taken into custody pursuant to a warrant on bail or recognizance pursuant to Chapter 9 (§ 19.2-119 et seq.) of Title 19.2; or

2. Place the child in a detention home or in shelter care; or

3. Place the child in a jail subject to the provisions of § 16.1-249.

E. A person taking a child into custody pursuant to the provisions of subsection B, C, or D of § 16.1-246 during such hours as the court is not open, shall:

1. Release the child pursuant to the provisions of subdivision B 1 or B 2 of this section; or

2. Release the child on bail or recognizance pursuant to Chapter 9 (§ 19.2-119 et seq.) of Title 19.2; or

3. Place the child taken into custody pursuant to subsection B of § 16.1-246 in shelter care after the issuance of a detention order pursuant to § 16.1-255; or

4. Place the child taken into custody pursuant to subsection C or D of § 16.1-246 in shelter care or in a detention home after the issuance of a warrant by a magistrate; or

5. Place the child in a jail subject to the provisions of § 16.1-249 after the issuance of a warrant by a magistrate or after the issuance of a detention order pursuant to § 16.1-255; or

6. In addition to any other provisions of this subsection, detain the child for a reasonably necessary period of time in order to administer a breath or blood test to determine the alcohol content of his blood, if such child was taken into custody pursuant to § 18.2-266.

F. A person taking a child into custody pursuant to the provisions of subsection E of § 16.1-246, during such hours as the court is not open, shall:

1. Release the child to the institution or facility from which he ran away or escaped; or

2. Detain the child in a detention home or in a jail subject to the provisions of § 16.1-249 after the issuance of a warrant by a magistrate or after the issuance of a detention order pursuant to § 16.1-255.

G. A person taking a child into custody pursuant to the provisions of subsection F of § 16.1-246, during such hours as the court is not open, shall:

1. Release the child to the facility or home from which he ran away; or

2. Detain the child in shelter care after the issuance of a detention order pursuant to § 16.1-255 or after the issuance of a warrant by a magistrate.

H. If a parent, guardian or other custodian fails, when requested, to bring the child before the court as provided in subdivisions B 2 and E 1, the court may issue a detention order directing that the child be taken into custody and be brought before the court.

I. A law-enforcement officer taking a child into custody pursuant to the provisions of subsection G of § 16.1-246 shall notify the intake officer of the juvenile court of the action taken. The intake officer shall determine if the child's conduct or situation is within the jurisdiction of the court and if a petition should be filed on behalf of the child. If the intake officer determines that a petition should not be filed, the law-enforcement officer shall as soon as practicable:

1. Return the child to his home;

2. Release the child to such child's parents, guardian, legal custodian or other person standing in loco parentis;

3. Place the child in shelter care for a period not longer than 24 hours after the issuance of a detention order pursuant to § 16.1-255; or

4. Release the child.

During the period of detention authorized by this subsection no child shall be confined in any detention home, jail or other facility for the detention of adults.

J. If a child is taken into custody pursuant to the provisions of subsection B, F, or G of § 16.1-246 by a law-enforcement officer during such hours as the court is not in session and the child is not released or transferred to a facility or institution in accordance with subsection E, G, or I of this section, the child shall be held in custody only so long as is reasonably necessary to complete identification, investigation and processing. The child shall be held under visual supervision in a nonlocked, multipurpose area which is not designated for residential use. The child shall not be handcuffed or otherwise secured to a stationary object.

K. When an adult is taken into custody pursuant to a warrant or detention order alleging a delinquent act committed when he was a juvenile, he may be released on bail or recognizance pursuant to Chapter 9 (§ 19.2-119 et seq.) of Title 19.2.

History.

Code 1950, § 16.1-197; 1956, c. 550; 1958, c. 344; 1973, c. 440; 1974, c. 584; 1975, c. 248; 1977, c. 559; 1978, c. 643; 1979, c. 701; 1984, c. 567; 1992, cc. 728, 830; 2004, cc. 415, 439; 2012, c. 253.

Editor's note.

Acts 1993, c. 930, cl. 3, as amended by Acts 1994, c. 564, cl. 2, and Acts 1996, c. 616, cl. 4, provides that the amendment to this section by Acts 1993, c. 930, cl. 1, shall become effective June 1, 1998, "if state funds are provided, including all local costs, to carry out the purposes of this bill by the General Assembly." The funding was not provided.

The 2012 amendments.

The 2012 amendment by c. 253 inserted "(§ 19.2-119 et seq.)" following "Chapter 9" in subdivision E 2; deleted "hereof" following "subdivisions B 2 and E 1" in subsection H; and added subsection K.

Law Review.

For survey of Virginia criminal procedure for the year 1977-1978, see 64 Va. L. Rev. 1419 (1978).

Research references.

Virginia Forms (Matthew Bender). No. 5-154 Shelter Care Order.

CASE NOTES

This section is not intended to safeguard a juvenile's Fifth and Sixth Amendment rights. Roberts v. Commonwealth, 18 Va. App. 554, 445 S.E.2d 709 (1994).

No constitutional violation. — The Equal Protection Clause is not violated by the absence from former § 63.1-248.9 [see now § 63.2-1517], and the presence in subdivision E 3 of this section of a requirement of administrative intake officer review prior to continued detention; the difference in procedures is neither irrational or capricious. Jordan v. Jackson, 15 F.3d 333 (4th Cir. 1994).

Confession by 17-year-old, after being arrested and taken to the police station and interrogated, was voluntary, as the absence of a parent did not necessarily invalidate a waiver of a juvenile's Fifth Amendment rights, but instead constituted a circumstance and factor to be considered in the totality of the circumstances; § 16.1-247 was procedural, and any failure of the police to adhere to the provisions of § 16.1-247 did not result in a per se violation of Fifth Amendment rights. Cary v. Commonwealth, 40 Va. App. 480, 579 S.E.2d 691, 2003 Va. App. LEXIS 284 (2003).

CIRCUIT COURT OPINIONS

This section is not intended to safeguard a juvenile's Fifth and Sixth Amendment rights. — Section 16.1-247, requiring that a juvenile in custody be brought before a judge or intake officer in the most expeditious manner practicable was not intended to safeguard a juvenile's Fifth and Sixth Amendment rights, as the statute set forth a procedural requirement, and violation of the requirement reached a constitutional dimension only if it resulted in defendant's loss of exculpatory evidence. Commonwealth v. Malvo, 63 Va. Cir. 22, 2003 Va. Cir. LEXIS 188 (Fairfax County 2003).

"With all practicable speed." — When a juvenile defendant released from federal custody to state custody was taken before a judicial officer within 24 hours of being received into state custody, he was taken before the judicial officer "with all practicable speed," as required by § 16.1-247, particularly when the chief juvenile court judge was advised of and reviewed his circumstances and the conditions of his detention in the interim. Commonwealth v. Malvo, 63 Va. Cir. 22, 2003 Va. Cir. LEXIS 188 (Fairfax County 2003).

§ 16.1-248. Repealed by Acts 1985, c. 260.

Cross references.

For present provisions as to criteria for detention or shelter care, see § 16.1-248.1.

§ 16.1-248.1. Criteria for detention or shelter care.

A. A juvenile taken into custody whose case is considered by a judge, intake officer or magistrate pursuant to § 16.1-247 shall immediately be released, upon the ascertainment of the necessary facts, to the care, custody and control of such juvenile's parent, guardian, custodian or other suitable person able and willing to provide supervision and care for such juvenile, either on bail or recognizance pursuant to Chapter 9 (§ 19.2-119 et seq.) of Title 19.2 or under such conditions as may be imposed or otherwise. However, at any time prior to an order of final disposition, a juvenile may be detained in a secure facility, pursuant to a detention order or warrant, only upon a finding by the judge, intake officer, or magistrate, that there is probable cause to believe that the juvenile committed the act alleged, and that at least one of the following conditions is met:

1. The juvenile is alleged to have (a) violated the terms of his probation or parole when the charge for which he was placed on probation or parole would have been a felony or Class 1 misdemeanor if committed by an adult; (b) committed an act that would be a felony or Class 1 misdemeanor if committed by an adult; or (c) violated any of the provisions of § 18.2-308.7, and there is clear and convincing evidence that:

a. Considering the seriousness of the current offense or offenses and other pending charges, the seriousness of prior adjudicated offenses, the legal status of the juvenile and any aggravating and mitigating circumstances, the liberty of the juvenile, constitutes a clear and substantial threat to the person or property of others;

b. The liberty of the juvenile would present a clear and substantial threat of serious harm to such juvenile's life or health; or

c. The juvenile has threatened to abscond from the court's jurisdiction during the pendency of the instant proceedings or has a record of willful failure to appear at a court hearing within the immediately preceding 12 months.

2. The juvenile has absconded from a detention home or facility where he has been directed to remain by the lawful order of a judge or intake officer.

3. The juvenile is a fugitive from a jurisdiction outside the Commonwealth and subject to a verified petition or warrant, in which case such juvenile may be detained for a period not to exceed that provided for in § 16.1-323 while arrangements are made to return the juvenile to the lawful custody of a parent, guardian or other authority in another state.

4. The juvenile has failed to appear in court after having been duly served with a summons in any case in which it is alleged that the juvenile has committed a delinquent act or that the child is in need of services or is in need of supervision; however, a child alleged to be in need of services or in

need of supervision may be detained for good cause pursuant to this subsection only until the next day upon which the court sits within the county or city in which the charge against the child is pending, and under no circumstances longer than 72 hours from the time he was taken into custody. If the 72-hour period expires on a Saturday, Sunday, legal holiday or day on which the court is lawfully closed, the 72 hours shall be extended to the next day that is not a Saturday, Sunday, legal holiday or day on which the court is lawfully closed.

5. The juvenile failed to adhere to the conditions imposed upon him by the court, intake officer or magistrate following his release upon a Class 1 misdemeanor charge or a felony charge.

When a juvenile is placed in secure detention, the detention order shall state the offense for which the juvenile is being detained, and, to the extent practicable, other pending and previous charges.

B. Any juvenile not meeting the criteria for placement in a secure facility shall be released to a parent, guardian or other person willing and able to provide supervision and care under such conditions as the judge, intake officer or magistrate may impose. However, a juvenile may be placed in shelter care if:

1. The juvenile is eligible for placement in a secure facility;

2. The juvenile has failed to adhere to the directions of the court, intake officer or magistrate while on conditional release;

3. The juvenile's parent, guardian or other person able to provide supervision cannot be reached within a reasonable time;

4. The juvenile does not consent to return home;

5. Neither the juvenile's parent or guardian nor any other person able to provide proper supervision can arrive to assume custody within a reasonable time; or

6. The juvenile's parent or guardian refuses to permit the juvenile to return home and no relative or other person willing and able to provide proper supervision and care can be located within a reasonable time.

C. When a juvenile is detained in a secure facility, the juvenile's probation officer may review such placement for the purpose of seeking a less restrictive alternative to confinement in that secure facility.

D. The criteria for continuing the juvenile in detention or shelter care as set forth in this section shall govern the decisions of all persons involved in determining whether the continued detention or shelter care is warranted pending court disposition. Such criteria shall be supported by clear and convincing evidence in support of the decision not to release the juvenile.

E. Nothing in this section shall be construed to deprive the court of its power to punish a juvenile summarily for contempt for acts set forth in § 18.2-456, other than acts of disobedience of the court's dispositional order which are committed outside the presence of the court.

F. A detention order may be issued pursuant to subdivision 2 of subsection A by the committing court or by the court in the jurisdiction from which the juvenile fled or where he was taken into custody.

G. The court is authorized to detain a juvenile based upon the criteria set forth in subsection A at any time after a delinquency petition has been filed, both prior to adjudication and after adjudication pending final disposition subject to the time limitations set forth in § 16.1-277.1.

H. If the intake officer or magistrate releases the juvenile, either on bail or recognizance or under such conditions as may be imposed, no motion to revoke bail, or change such conditions may be made unless (i) the juvenile has violated a term or condition of his release, or is convicted of or taken into custody for an additional offense, or (ii) the attorney for the Commonwealth presents evidence that incorrect or incomplete information regarding the factors in subsection A was relied upon by the intake officer or magistrate establishing the initial terms of release. If the juvenile court releases the juvenile, either on bail or recognizance or under such conditions as may be imposed, over the objection of the attorney for the Commonwealth, the attorney for the Commonwealth may appeal such decision to the circuit court. The order of the juvenile court releasing the juvenile shall remain in effect until the circuit court, Court of Appeals or Supreme Court rules otherwise.

History.
1977, c. 559; 1979, c. 701; 1985, c. 260; 1986, c. 517; 1987, c. 632; 1989, c. 725; 1990, c. 257; 1996, cc. 755, 914; 2000, c. 836; 2001, c. 837; 2002, cc. 55, 359; 2003, cc. 104, 851; 2004, c. 374; 2005, c. 647; 2010, c. 683; 2011, c. 644.

Cross references.
As to punishment for Class 1 misdemeanors, see § 18.2-11. As to medical records of juvenile in secure facility, see § 16.1-248.3.

The 2010 amendments.
The 2010 amendment by c. 683 added clause (c) in subdivision A 1 and made a related change.

The 2011 amendments.
The 2011 amendment by c. 644 added the subdivision A 5 designation and the first paragraph therein.

Law Review.
For 1985 survey of Virginia law affecting children, see 19 U. Rich. L. Rev. p. 753 (1985). For survey on legal issues involving children in Virginia for 1989, see 23 U. Rich. L. Rev. 705 (1989). For 2000 survey of Virginia criminal law and procedure, see 34 U. Rich. L. Rev. 749 (2000). For 2000 survey of Virginia law regarding children, see 34 U. Rich. L. Rev. 939 (2000). For article, "Legal Issues Involving Children," see 35 U. Rich. L. Rev. 741 (2001).

Research references.
Virginia Forms (Matthew Bender). No. 5-154 Shelter Care Order.

CASE NOTES

Officer's accommodation of juvenile's request to use toilet facilities did not change juvenile's custodial status. Moss v. Commonwealth, 30 Va. App. 219, 516 S.E.2d 246 (1999).

Detention of juvenile not already in custody. — Juvenile court judge has no statutory authority to temporarily detain a juvenile after an adjudication hearing where the juvenile is determined delinquent but pending the disposition hearing, when the juvenile was not originally taken into custody and detained pursuant to subsection A of this section. See opinion of Attorney General to The Honorable J. Dean Lewis, Judge, Fifteenth District Juvenile and Domestic Relations Court, 02-047 (8/7/02).

§ 16.1-248.2. Mental health screening and assessment for certain juveniles.

Whenever a juvenile is placed in a secure facility pursuant to § 16.1-248.1, the staff of the facility shall gather such information from the juvenile and the probation officer as is reasonably available and deemed necessary by the facility staff. As part of the intake procedures at each such facility, the staff shall ascertain the juvenile's need for a mental health assessment. If it is determined that the juvenile needs such an assessment, the assessment shall take place within twenty-four hours of such determination. The community services board serving the jurisdiction where the facility is located shall be responsible for conducting the assessments and shall be compensated from funds appropriated to the Department of Juvenile Justice for this purpose. The Department of Juvenile Justice shall develop criteria and a compensation plan for such assessments.

History.
1996, cc. 755, 914; 1998, c. 434.

Law Review.
For an article, "Legal Issues Involving Children," see 32 U. Rich. L. Rev. 1345 (1998).

§ 16.1-248.3. Medical records of juveniles in secure facility.

Whenever a juvenile is placed in a secure facility or a shelter care facility pursuant to § 16.1-248.1, the director of the facility or his designee shall be entitled to obtain medical records concerning the juvenile from a provider. Prior to using the authority granted by this section to obtain such records, the director of the facility or his designee shall make a reasonable attempt to obtain consent for the release of the records from the juvenile's parent or legal guardian or, in instances where the juvenile may consent pursuant to § 54.1-2969, from the juvenile. The director of the facility or his designee may proceed to obtain the records from the provider if such consent is refused or is not readily obtainable and the records are necessary (i) for the provision of health care to the juvenile, (ii) to protect the health and safety of the juvenile or other residents or staff of the facility or (iii) to maintain the security and safety of the facility.

The director or his designee shall document in writing the reason that the records were requested and that a reasonable attempt was made to obtain consent for the release of records and that consent was refused or not readily obtainable.

No person to whom disclosure of records was made pursuant to this section shall redisclose or otherwise reveal the records, beyond the purpose for which such disclosure was made, without first obtaining specific consent to redisclose from the juvenile's parent or legal guardian or, in instances where the juvenile may consent pursuant to § 54.1-2969, from the juvenile.

Substance abuse records subject to federal regulations, Confidentiality of Alcohol and Drug Abuse Patient Records, 42 C.F.R. Part 2, shall not be subject to the provisions of this section. The disclosure of results of a test for human immunodeficiency virus shall not be permitted except as provided in § 32.1-36.1.

The definitions of "provider" and "records" in § 32.1-127.1:03 shall apply to this section.

History.
2003, c. 983.

Law Review.
For annual survey article discussing the state of health care law in Virginia, see 38 U. Rich. L. Rev. 137(2003).

§ 16.1-249. Places of confinement for juveniles.

A. If it is ordered that a juvenile remain in detention or shelter care pursuant to § 16.1-248.1, such juvenile may be detained, pending a court hearing, in the following places:

1. An approved foster home or a home otherwise authorized by law to provide such care;

2. A facility operated by a licensed child welfare agency;

3. If a juvenile is alleged to be delinquent, in a detention home or group home approved by the Department;

4. Any other suitable place designated by the court and approved by the Department;

5. To the extent permitted by federal law, a separate juvenile detention facility located upon the site of an adult regional jail facility established by any county, city or any combination thereof constructed after 1994, approved by the Department of Juvenile Justice and certified by the Board of Juvenile Justice for the holding and detention of juveniles.

B. No juvenile shall be detained or confined in any jail or other facility for the detention of adult offenders or persons charged with crime except as provided in subsection D, E, F or G of this section.

C. The official in charge of a jail or other facility for the detention of adult offenders or persons charged with crime shall inform the court immediately when a juvenile who is or appears to be under the age of 18 years is received at the facility, and shall deliver him to the court upon request, or transfer him to a detention facility designated by the court.

D. When a case is transferred to the circuit court in accordance with the provisions of subsection A of § 16.1-269.1 and an order is entered by the circuit court in accordance with § 16.1-269.6, or in accordance with the provisions of § 16.1-270 where the juvenile has waived the jurisdiction of the district court, or when the district court has certified a charge to the grand jury pursuant to subsection B or C of § 16.1-269.1, the juvenile, if in confinement, shall be placed in a juvenile secure facility, unless the court determines that the juvenile is a threat to the security or safety of the other juveniles detained or the staff of the facility, in which case the court may transfer the juvenile to a jail or other facility for the detention of adults and need no longer be entirely separate and removed from adults.

E. If, in the judgment of the custodian, a juvenile has demonstrated that he is a threat to the security or safety of the other juveniles detained or the staff of the home or facility, the judge shall determine whether such juvenile should be transferred to another juvenile facility or, if the child is 14 years of age or older, a jail or other facility for the detention of adults; provided, that (i) the detention is in a room or ward entirely separate and removed from adults, (ii) adequate supervision is provided, and (iii) the facility is approved by the State Board of Corrections for detention of juveniles.

F. If, in the judgment of the custodian, it has been demonstrated that the presence of a juvenile in a facility creates a threat to the security or safety of the other juveniles detained or the staff of the home or facility, the custodian may transfer the juvenile to another juvenile facility, or, if the child is 14 years of age or older, a jail or other facility for the detention of adults pursuant to the limitations of clauses (i), (ii) and (iii) of subsection E for a period not to exceed six hours prior to a court hearing and an additional six hours after the court hearing unless a longer period is ordered pursuant to subsection E.

G. If a juvenile 14 years of age or older is charged with an offense which, if committed by an adult, would be a felony or Class 1 misdemeanor, and the judge or intake officer determines that secure detention is needed for the safety of the juvenile or the community, such juvenile may be detained for a period not to exceed six hours prior to a court hearing and six hours after the court hearing in a temporary lock-up room or ward for juveniles while arrangements are completed to transfer the juvenile to a juvenile facility. Such room or ward may be located in a building which also contains a jail or other facility for the detention of adults, provided (i) such room or ward is totally separate and removed from adults or juveniles transferred to the circuit court pursuant to Article 7 (§ 16.1-269.1 et seq.) of this chapter, (ii) constant supervision is provided, and (iii) the facility is approved by the State Board of Corrections for the detention of juveniles. The State Board of Corrections is authorized and directed to prescribe minimum standards for temporary lock-up rooms and wards based on the requirements set out in this subsection.

G1. Any juvenile who has been ordered detained in a secure detention facility pursuant to § 16.1-248.1 may be held incident to a court hearing (i) in a court holding cell for a period not to exceed six hours provided the juvenile is entirely separate and removed from detained adults or (ii) in a nonsecure area provided constant supervision is provided.

H. If a judge, intake officer or magistrate orders the predispositional detention of persons 18 years of age or older, such detention shall be in an adult facility; however, if the predispositional detention is ordered for a violation of the terms and conditions of release from a juvenile correctional center, the judge, intake officer or magistrate may order such detention be in a juvenile facility.

I. The Departments of Corrections, Juvenile Justice and Criminal Justice Services shall assist the localities or combinations thereof in implementing this section and ensuring compliance herewith.

History.
1977, c. 559; 1979, c. 655; 1983, c. 336; 1985, c. 260; 1988, c. 886; 1989, c. 557; 1993, c. 435; 1994, cc. 859, 904, 949; 1995, cc. 746, 748, 798, 802; 1996, cc. 755, 914; 1998, cc. 576, 830; 2002, c. 558; 2004, cc. 415, 439; 2010, c. 739.

Cross references.
As to punishment for Class 1, 2 or 3 felonies, see § 18.2-10. As to punishment for Class 1 misdemeanors, see § 18.2-11.

The 2010 amendments.
The 2010 amendment by c. 739 substituted "shall be placed in a juvenile secure facility, unless the court determines that the juvenile is a threat to the security or safety of the other juveniles detained or the staff of the facility, in which case the court may transfer the juvenile" for "may be transferred" in subsection D.

Law Review.
For 1985 survey of Virginia law affecting children, see 19 U. Rich. L. Rev. p. 753 (1985). For survey on legal issues involving children in Virginia for 1989, see 23 U. Rich. L. Rev. 705 (1989). For an article, "Legal Issues Involving Children," see 32 U. Rich. L. Rev. 1345 (1998).

Research references.
Virginia Forms (Matthew Bender). No. 5-154 Shelter Care Order.

CASE NOTES

If the decision to waive juvenile jurisdiction were not immediately appealable, those legislative protections afforded children under the juvenile justice system once lost, would be irretrievable. Hairfield v. Commonwealth, 7 Va. App. 649, 376 S.E.2d 796 (1989).

OPINIONS OF THE ATTORNEY GENERAL

Housing in adult jail facility pending transfer. — A juvenile who has been convicted as an adult may be housed in an adult jail facility pending transfer to the Department of Juvenile Justice. See opinion of Attorney General to Mr. Robert J. McCabe, Sheriff for the City of Norfolk, 05-012 (3/29/05).

§ 16.1-249.1. Places of confinement to give notice of intake of certain persons.

A. At the time of receipt of any person, for whom registration with the Sex Offender and Crimes

Against Minors Registry is required pursuant to Chapter 9 (§ 9.1-900 et seq.) of Title 9.1 into a secure facility, the secure facility shall obtain from that person all necessary registration information, including fingerprints and photographs of a type and kind approved by the Department of State Police. A person required to register shall register and submit to be photographed as part of the registration. The facility shall forthwith forward the registration information to the Department of State Police on the date of the receipt of the prisoner.

B. Whenever a person required to register has failed to comply with the provisions of subsection A, the facility shall promptly investigate or request the State Police promptly investigate and, if there is probable cause to believe a violation has occurred, obtain a warrant, or assist in obtaining an indictment charging a violation of § 18.2-472.1 in the jurisdiction in which the person was received. The facility shall notify the State Police forthwith of such actions taken pursuant to this section.

History.
2006, cc. 857, 914.

§ 16.1-250. Procedure for detention hearing.

A. When a child has been taken into immediate custody and not released as provided in § 16.1-247 or § 16.1-248.1, such child shall appear before a judge on the next day on which the court sits within the county or city wherein the charge against the child is pending. In the event the court does not sit within the county or city on the following day, such child shall appear before a judge within a reasonable time, not to exceed 72 hours, after he has been taken into custody. If the 72-hour period expires on a Saturday, Sunday or other legal holiday, the 72 hours shall be extended to the next day which is not a Saturday, Sunday or legal holiday. In the event the court does not sit on the following day within the county or city wherein the charge against the child is pending, the court may conduct the hearing in another county or city, but only if two-way electronic video and audio communication is available in the courthouse of the county or city wherein the charge is pending.

B. The appearance of the child, the attorney for the Commonwealth, the attorney for the child and the parent, guardian, legal custodian or other person standing in loco parentis may be by (i) personal appearance before the judge or (ii) use of two-way electronic video and audio communication. If two-way electronic video and audio communication is used, a judge may exercise all powers conferred by law and all communications and proceedings shall be conducted in the same manner as if the appearance were in person, and any documents filed may be transmitted by electronically transmitted facsimile process. The facsimile may be served or executed by the officer or person to whom sent, and returned in the same manner, and with the same force, effect, authority, and liability as an original document. All signatures thereon shall be treated as original signatures. Any two-way electronic video and audio communication system used for an appearance shall meet the standards as set forth in subsection B of § 19.2-3.1.

C. Notice of the detention hearing or any rehearing, either oral or written, stating the time, place and purpose of the hearing shall be given to the parent, guardian, legal custodian or other person standing in loco parentis if he can be found, to the child's attorney, to the child if 12 years of age or older and to the attorney for the Commonwealth.

D. During the detention hearing, the parties shall be informed of the child's right to remain silent with respect to any allegation of delinquency and of the contents of the petition. The attorney for the child and the attorney for the Commonwealth shall be given the opportunity to be heard.

E. If the judge finds that there is not probable cause to believe that the child committed the delinquent act alleged, the court shall order his release. If the judge finds that there is probable cause to believe that the child committed the delinquent act alleged but that the full-time detention of a child who is alleged to be delinquent is not required, the court shall order his release, and in so doing, the court may impose one or more of the following conditions singly or in combination:

1. Place the child in the custody of a parent, guardian, legal custodian or other person standing in loco parentis under their supervision, or under the supervision of an organization or individual agreeing to supervise him;

2. Place restrictions on the child's travel, association or place of abode during the period of his release;

3. Impose any other condition deemed reasonably necessary and consistent with the criteria for detaining children specified in § 16.1-248.1; or

4. Release the child on bail or recognizance in accordance with the provisions of Chapter 9 (§ 19.2-119 et seq.) of Title 19.2.

F. An order releasing a child on any of the conditions specified in this section may, at any time, be amended to impose additional or different conditions of release or to return the child who is alleged to be delinquent to custody for failure to conform to the conditions previously imposed.

G. All relevant and material evidence helpful in determining probable cause under this section or the need for detention may be admitted by the court even though not competent in a hearing on the petition.

H. If the child is not released and a parent, guardian, legal custodian or other person standing in loco parentis is not notified and does not appear or does not waive appearance at the hearing, upon the written request of such person stating that such person is willing and available to supervise the child upon release from detention and to return the child to court for all scheduled proceedings on the pending charges, the court shall rehear the matter on the next day on which the court sits within the county or city wherein the charge against the child is pending. If the court does not sit within the county or city on the following day, such hearing shall be held before a judge within a reasonable time, not to exceed 72 hours, after the request.

I. In considering probable cause under this section, if the court deems it necessary to summon witnesses to assist in such determination then the hearing may be continued and the child remain in detention, but in no event longer than three consecutive days, exclusive of Saturdays, Sundays, and legal holidays.

History.

1977, c. 559; 1979, c. 338; 1985, c. 260; 1986, c. 542; 1988, c. 220; 1989, c. 549; 1992, c. 508; 1995, c. 451; 2004, c. 437; 2006, c. 89.

Law Review.

For survey of Virginia law on criminal procedure for the year 1978-1979, see 66 Va. L. Rev. 261 (1980). For 1985 survey of Virginia law affecting children, see 19 U. Rich. L. Rev. p. 753 (1985). For survey on legal issues involving children in Virginia for 1989, see 23 U. Rich. L. Rev. 705 (1989). For 2006 survey article, "Family and Juvenile Law," see 41 U. Rich. L. Rev. 151 (2006).

OPINIONS OF THE ATTORNEY GENERAL

Venue for juvenile detention hearing. — The proper venue for a juvenile detention hearing is the place where the proceeding has been commenced. See opinion of Attorney General to Mr. Michael W. Lee, Commonwealth's Attorney for the City of Colonial Heights, 05-002 (3/29/05).

§ 16.1-250.1. Repealed by Acts 2004, c. 437, cl. 2, effective July 1, 2005.

§ 16.1-251. Emergency removal order.

A. A child may be taken into immediate custody and placed in shelter care pursuant to an emergency removal order in cases in which the child is alleged to have been abused or neglected. Such order may be issued ex parte by the court upon a petition supported by an affidavit or by sworn testimony in person before the judge or intake officer which establishes that:

1. The child would be subjected to an imminent threat to life or health to the extent that severe or irremediable injury would be likely to result if the child were returned to or left in the custody of his parents, guardian, legal custodian or other person standing in loco parentis pending a final hearing on the petition.

2. Reasonable efforts have been made to prevent removal of the child from his home and there are no alternatives less drastic than removal of the child from his home which could reasonably protect the child's life or health pending a final hearing on the petition. The alternatives less drastic than removal may include but not be limited to the provision of medical, educational, psychiatric, psychological,

homemaking or other similar services to the child or family or the issuance of a preliminary protective order pursuant to § 16.1-253.

If the petitioner fails to obtain an emergency removal order within four hours of taking custody of the child, the affidavit or sworn testimony before the judge or intake officer shall state the reasons therefor.

When a child is removed from his home and there is no reasonable opportunity to provide preventive services, reasonable efforts to prevent removal shall be deemed to have been made.

B. Whenever a child is taken into immediate custody pursuant to an emergency removal order, a hearing shall be held in accordance with § 16.1-252 as soon as practicable, but in no event later than five business days after the removal of the child.

C. In the emergency removal order the court shall give consideration to temporary placement of the child with a relative or other interested individual, including grandparents, under the supervision of the local department of social services, until such time as the hearing in accordance with § 16.1-252 is held.

D. The local department of social services having "legal custody" of a child as defined in § 16.1-228 (i) shall not be required to comply with the requirements of this section in order to redetermine where and with whom the child shall live, notwithstanding that the child had been placed with a natural parent.

History.

1977, c. 559; 1984, c. 499; 1985, c. 584; 1986, c. 308; 1990, c. 769; 2000, c. 385; 2003, c. 508.

Cross references.

As to foster care plans, placement of child, permissible plan goals, and court review of foster children, see § 63.2-906. As to permanent foster care placements, see § 63.2-908. As to testimony of child by use of two-way closed circuit television in civil proceedings involving alleged abuse or neglect of a child, see § 63.2-1521. As to admission of out-of-court statements made by certain children in civil proceedings involving alleged abuse or neglect of a child, see § 63.2-1522. As to use of videotaped statements of certain children who are complaining witnesses in in civil proceedings involving alleged abuse or neglect of a child, see § 63.2-1523.

Law Review.

For comment, "The Uniform Child Custody Jurisdiction Act in Virginia," see 14 U. Rich. L. Rev. 435 (1979). For article, "Family Law," see 35 U. Rich. L. Rev. 651 (2001).

Research references.

Virginia Forms (Matthew Bender). No. 5-152 Emergency Removal Order.

CASE NOTES

Statute is procedural and directory. — Because subsection B of § 16.1-251 does not expressly prohibit the juvenile and domestic relations district court from conducting a preliminary removal hearing beyond the five-business-day period, is not prohibitive or limiting, and does not contain any manifestation of a contrary intent, subsection B of § 16.1-251 is procedural and directory, rather than mandatory and jurisdictional; although subsection B does provide that the hearing shall be held "in no event" later than five business days after the removal of the child, this phrase does not suggest an intent that the statute be deemed mandatory and jurisdictional because subsection B of § 16.1-251 contains no explicit penalty for failure to comply with the five-day requirement nor explicitly renders a hearing held beyond the five-day period invalid. Marrison v. Fairfax County Dep't of Family Servs., 59 Va. App. 61, 717 S.E.2d 146, 2011 Va. App. LEXIS 336 (2011).

Jurisdiction. — Circuit court did not err in denying parents' motions to dismiss petitions filed by a county department of family services pursuant to subdivision A 1 of § 16.1-241 alleging that their children were abused and neglected because the circuit court had the power to exercise its subject matter jurisdiction since subsection B of § 16.1-251 was procedural and directory, rather than mandatory and jurisdictional, and the parents failed to show that they suffered any prejudice as a result of the juvenile and domestic relations district court's alleged failure to comply with subsection B of § 16.1-251; under subdivision A 1 of § 16.1-241, the department's action invoked the subject matter jurisdiction of the district court, upon appeal to the circuit court, the circuit court's jurisdiction was derivative of that of the district court, and therefore, if the district court had subject matter jurisdiction, so too did the circuit court upon appeal from the district court order. Marrison v. Fairfax County Dep't of Family Servs., 59 Va. App. 61, 717 S.E.2d 146, 2011 Va. App. LEXIS 336 (2011).

Code contemplates intervention where severe injury likely if child returned to parent. — The Code contemplates intervention in circumstances, which are without realistic probability of improvement of conditions, by allowing for the emergency removal of children before placement into an environment where the child would be subjected to an imminent threat to life or health to the extent that severe or irreversible injury would be likely to result if the child were returned to or left in the custody of his parent. Jenkins v. Winchester Dep't of Social Servs., 12 Va. App. 1178, 409 S.E.2d 16 (1991).

Relation to custody statutes. — Court of appeals erred when the court upheld a circuit court's decision awarding custody of a child who had been adjudicated as abused and neglected and removed the child from the child's parents, pursuant to §§ 16.1-251 and 16.1-252, giving custody to the child's grandparents, based on the court's conclusion that language in subsection A of § 16.1-241 and subsection B of § 16.1-278.15 subordinated Virginia statutes on foster care to Virginia's general custody statutes. The only interpretation of Titles 16.1 and 20 that gave effect to both statutory schemes and the intent of the Virginia General Assembly was that a trial court had to make the specific factual findings required by the foster care statutes in a custody case involving a child who was subject to a foster care plan. Lynchburg Div. of Soc. Servs. v. Cook, 276 Va. 465, 666 S.E.2d 361, 2008 Va. LEXIS 97 (2008).

Parents given specific written notice of subsequent hearing. — Under this section, §§ 16.1-252 and 16.1-253 the parents shall be given specific notice in writing of a subsequent hearing on the merits by a petition stating the factual circumstances which allegedly necessitated removal of the children. Rader v. Montgomery County Dep't of Social Servs., 5 Va. App. 523, 365 S.E.2d 234 (1988).

Evidence of neglect supported emergency order of removal. — Evidence showed that father's action in taking his children to a bank where he and the mother uttered a forgery, which caused the police to take the father and mother away to jail, caused the father to be unreasonably absent and the children to be without parental care; accordingly, the trial court's finding that the children were neglected, for the purposes of the city welfare agency's request for an emergency order of removal of the children, was not clearly erroneous and was affirmed. Lewis v. Fredericksburg Dep't of Soc. Servs., No. 2832-02-2, 2003 Va. App. LEXIS 432 (Ct. of Appeals Aug. 12, 2003).

Applied in Robinette v. Keene, 2 Va. App. 578, 347 S.E.2d 156 (1986).

§ 16.1-252. (Effective until July 1, 2014) Preliminary removal order; hearing.

A. A preliminary removal order in cases in which a child is alleged to have been abused or neglected may be issued by the court after a hearing wherein the court finds that reasonable efforts have been made to prevent removal of the child from his home. The hearing shall be in the nature of a preliminary hearing rather than a final determination of custody.

B. Prior to the removal hearing, notice of the hearing shall be given at least twenty-four hours in advance of the hearing to the guardian ad litem for the child, to the parents, guardian, legal custodian or other person standing in loco parentis of the child and to the child if he or she is twelve years of age or older. If notice to the parents, guardian, legal custodian or other person standing in loco parentis cannot be given despite diligent efforts to do so, the hearing shall be held nonetheless, and the parents, guardian, legal custodian or other person standing in loco parentis shall be afforded a later hearing on their motion regarding a continuation of the summary removal order. The notice provided herein shall include (i) the time, date and place for the hearing; (ii) a specific statement of the factual circumstances which allegedly necessitate removal of the child; and (iii) notice that child support will be considered if a determination is made that the child must be removed from the home.

C. All parties to the hearing shall be informed of their right to counsel pursuant to § 16.1-266.

D. At the removal hearing the child and his parent, guardian, legal custodian or other person standing in loco parentis shall have the right to confront and cross-examine all adverse witnesses and evidence and to present evidence on their own behalf. If the child was fourteen years of age or under on the date of the alleged offense and is sixteen or under at the time of the hearing, the child's attorney or guardian ad litem, or if the child has been committed to the custody of the Department of Social Services, the local department of social services, may apply for an order from the court that the child's testimony be taken in a room outside the courtroom and be televised by two-way closed-circuit television. The provisions of § 63.2-1521 shall apply, mutatis mutandis, to the use of two-way closed-circuit television except that the person seeking the order shall apply for the order at least forty-eight hours before the hearing, unless the court for good cause shown allows the application to be made at a later time.

E. In order for a preliminary order to issue or for an existing order to be continued, the petitioning party or agency must prove:

1. The child would be subjected to an imminent threat to life or health to the extent that severe or irremediable injury would be likely to result if the child were returned to or left in the custody of his parents, guardian, legal custodian or other person standing in loco parentis pending a final hearing on the petition; and

2. Reasonable efforts have been made to prevent removal of the child from his home and there are no alternatives less drastic than removal of the child from his home which could reasonably and ad-

equately protect the child's life or health pending a final hearing on the petition. The alternatives less drastic than removal may include but not be limited to the provision of medical, educational, psychiatric, psychological, homemaking or other similar services to the child or family or the issuance of a preliminary protective order pursuant to § 16.1-253.

When a child is removed from his home and there is no reasonable opportunity to provide preventive services, reasonable efforts to prevent removal shall be deemed to have been made.

F. If the court determines that pursuant to subsection E hereof the removal of the child is proper, the court shall:

1. Order that the child be placed in the temporary care and custody of a suitable person, subject to the provisions of subsection F1 of this section and under the supervision of the local department of social services, with consideration being given to placement in the temporary care and custody of a relative or other interested individual, including grandparents, until such time as the court enters an order of disposition pursuant to § 16.1-278.2, or, if such placement is not available, in the care and custody of a suitable agency;

2. Order that reasonable visitation be allowed between the child and his parents, guardian, legal custodian or other person standing in loco parentis, and between the child and his siblings, if such visitation would not endanger the child's life or health; and

3. Order that the parent or other legally obligated person pay child support pursuant to § 16.1-290.

In addition, the court may enter a preliminary protective order pursuant to § 16.1-253 imposing requirements and conditions as specified in that section which the court deems appropriate for protection of the welfare of the child.

F1. Prior to the entry of an order pursuant to subsection F of this section transferring temporary custody of the child to a relative or other interested individual, including grandparents, the court shall consider whether the relative or other interested individual is one who (i) is willing and qualified to receive and care for the child; (ii) is willing to have a positive, continuous relationship with the child; and (iii) is willing and has the ability to protect the child from abuse and neglect. The court's order transferring temporary custody to a relative or other interested individual should provide for compliance with any preliminary protective order entered on behalf of the child in accordance with the provisions of § 16.1-253; initiation and completion of the investigation as directed by the court and court review of the child's placement required in accordance with the provisions of § 16.1-278.2; and, as appropriate, ongoing provision of social services to the child and the temporary custodian.

G. At the conclusion of the preliminary removal order hearing, the court shall determine whether the allegations of abuse or neglect have been proven by a preponderance of the evidence. Any finding of abuse or neglect shall be stated in the court order. However, if, before such a finding is made, a person responsible for the care and custody of the child, the child's guardian ad litem or the local department of social services objects to a finding being made at the hearing, the court shall schedule an adjudicatory hearing to be held within thirty days of the date of the initial preliminary removal hearing. The adjudicatory hearing shall be held to determine whether the allegations of abuse and neglect have been proven by a preponderance of the evidence. Parties who are present at the preliminary removal order hearing shall be given notice of the date set for the adjudicatory hearing and parties who are not present shall be summoned as provided in § 16.1-263. The hearing shall be held and an order may be entered, although a party to the preliminary removal order hearing fails to appear and is not represented by counsel, provided personal or substituted service was made on the person, or the court determines that such person cannot be found, after reasonable effort, or in the case of a person who is without the Commonwealth, the person cannot be found or his post office address cannot be ascertained after reasonable effort.

The preliminary removal order and any preliminary protective order issued shall remain in full force and effect pending the adjudicatory hearing.

H. If the preliminary removal order includes a finding of abuse or neglect and the child is removed from his home or a preliminary protective order is issued, a dispositional hearing shall be held pursuant to § 16.1-278.2. The dispositional hearing shall be scheduled at the time of the preliminary removal order hearing and shall be held within seventy-five days of the preliminary removal order hearing. If an adjudicatory hearing is requested pursuant to subsection G, the dispositional hearing shall nonetheless be scheduled at the initial preliminary removal order hearing. All parties present at the preliminary removal order hearing shall be given notice of the date scheduled for the dispositional hearing; parties who are not present shall be summoned to appear as provided in § 16.1-263.

I. The local department of social services having "legal custody" of a child as defined in § 16.1-228 (i) shall not be required to comply with the requirements of this section in order to redetermine where and with whom the child shall live, notwithstanding that the child had been placed with a natural parent.

J. Violation of any order issued pursuant to this section shall constitute contempt of court.

History.

1977, c. 559; 1984, c. 499; 1985, c. 584; 1986, c. 308; 1990, c. 769; 1994, c. 42; 1995, c. 817; 1997, c. 790; 1999, c. 668; 2000, c. 385; 2008, c. 397.

Section set out twice.

The section above is effective until July 1, 2014. For the version of this section effective July 1, 2014, see the following section, also numbered 16.1-252.

Cross references.

As to foster care plans, placement of child, permissible plan goals, and court review of foster children, see § 63.2-906. As to testimony of child by use of two-way closed circuit television in civil proceedings involving alleged abuse or neglect of a child, see § 63.2-1521. As to admission of out-of-court statements made by certain children in civil proceedings involving alleged abuse or neglect of a child, see § 63.2-1522. As to use of videotaped statements of certain children who are complaining witnesses in in civil proceedings involving alleged abuse or neglect of a child, see § 63.2-1523.

Research references.

Virginia Forms (Matthew Bender). No. 5-151 Preliminary Removal Order. No. 5-153 Adjudicatory Order for Abuse or Neglect Cases. No. 5-154 Shelter Care Order.

CASE NOTES

Relation to custody statutes. — Court of appeals erred when the court upheld a circuit court's decision awarding custody of a child who had been adjudicated as abused and neglected and removed the child from the child's parents, pursuant to §§ 16.1-251 and 16.1-252, giving custody to the child's grandparents, based on the court's conclusion that language in subsection A of § 16.1-241 and subsection B of § 16.1-278.15 subordinated Virginia statutes on foster care to Virginia's general custody statutes. The only interpretation of Titles 16.1 and 20 that gave effect to both statutory schemes and the intent of the Virginia General Assembly was that a trial court had to make the specific factual findings required by the foster care statutes in a custody case involving a child who was subject to a foster care plan. Lynchburg Div. of Soc. Servs. v. Cook, 276 Va. 465, 666 S.E.2d 361, 2008 Va. LEXIS 97 (2008).

Parents given specific written notice of subsequent hearing. — Under this section, §§ 16.1-251 and 16.1-253 the parents shall be given specific notice in writing of a subsequent hearing on the merits by a petition stating the factual circumstances which allegedly necessitated removal of the children. Rader v. Montgomery County Dep't of Social Servs., 5 Va. App. 523, 365 S.E.2d 234 (1988).

Immunity of social workers. — State social workers are absolutely immune from liability resulting from their decision to file a removal petition. Vosburg v. Department of Social Servs., 884 F.2d 133 (4th Cir. 1989).

Appealability of juvenile court order. — Because the plain language of §§ 16.1-278.2 D, 16.1-252, and 16.1-296 A provided that a preliminary removal order was not a dispositional order and was not a final order, the trial court did not err in finding that it lacked jurisdiction to entertain a department of social services' appeal of a juvenile court's order. Richmond Dep't of Soc. Servs. v. Petersburg Dep't of Soc. Servs., 2006 Va. App. LEXIS 263 (June 13, 2006).

CIRCUIT COURT OPINIONS

Sufficient evidence of abuse or neglect. — Although parents claimed they did not cause their 11-month-old daughter's injuries and did not allow someone else to cause her injuries, a doctor's testimony that the child displayed symptoms of shaken baby syndrome was sufficient for the court to find that the child was abused or neglected, within the meaning of § 16.1-228, and the court found that the child was abused or neglected and that her two-year-old brother was a child at risk of being abused or neglected because of the injuries his sister sustained. In re McBride, 60 Va. Cir. 261, 2002 Va. Cir. LEXIS 391 (Richmond 2002).

§ 16.1-252. (Effective July 1, 2014) Preliminary removal order; hearing.

A. A preliminary removal order in cases in which a child is alleged to have been abused or neglected may be issued by the court after a hearing wherein the court finds that reasonable efforts have been made to prevent removal of the child from his home. The hearing shall be in the nature of a preliminary hearing rather than a final determination of custody.

B. Prior to the removal hearing, notice of the hearing shall be given at least 24 hours in advance of the hearing to the guardian ad litem for the child, to the parents, guardian, legal custodian or other person standing in loco parentis of the child and to the child if he or she is 12 years of age or older. If notice to the parents, guardian, legal custodian or other person standing in loco parentis cannot be given despite diligent efforts to do so, the hearing shall be held nonetheless, and the parents, guardian, legal custodian or other person standing in loco parentis shall be afforded a later hearing on their motion regarding a continuation of the summary removal order. The notice provided herein shall include (i) the time, date and place for the hearing; (ii) a specific statement of the factual circumstances which allegedly necessitate removal of the child; and (iii) notice that child support will be considered if a determination is made that the child must be removed from the home.

C. All parties to the hearing shall be informed of their right to counsel pursuant to § 16.1-266.

D. At the removal hearing the child and his parent, guardian, legal custodian or other person standing in loco parentis shall have the right to confront and cross-examine all adverse witnesses and evidence and to present evidence on their own behalf. If the child was 14 years of age or under on the date of the alleged offense and is 16 or under at the time of the hearing, the child's attorney or guardian ad litem, or if the child has been committed to the custody of the Department of Social Services, the local department of social services, may apply for an order from the court that the child's testimony be taken in a room outside the courtroom and be televised by two-way closed-circuit television. The provisions of § 63.2-1521 shall apply, mutatis mutandis, to the use of two-way closed-circuit television except that the person seeking the order shall apply for the order at least 48 hours before the hearing, unless the court for good cause shown allows the application to be made at a later time.

E. In order for a preliminary order to issue or for an existing order to be continued, the petitioning party or agency must prove:

1. The child would be subjected to an imminent threat to life or health to the extent that severe or irremediable injury would be likely to result if the child were returned to or left in the custody of his parents, guardian, legal custodian or other person standing in loco parentis pending a final hearing on the petition; and

2. Reasonable efforts have been made to prevent removal of the child from his home and there are no alternatives less drastic than removal of the child from his home which could reasonably and adequately protect the child's life or health pending a

final hearing on the petition. The alternatives less drastic than removal may include but not be limited to the provision of medical, educational, psychiatric, psychological, homemaking or other similar services to the child or family or the issuance of a preliminary protective order pursuant to § 16.1-253.

When a child is removed from his home and there is no reasonable opportunity to provide preventive services, reasonable efforts to prevent removal shall be deemed to have been made.

F. If the court determines that pursuant to subsection E hereof the removal of the child is proper, the court shall:

1. Order that the child be placed in the temporary care and custody of a suitable person, subject to the provisions of subsection F1 of this section and under the supervision of the local department of social services, with consideration being given to placement in the temporary care and custody of a relative or other interested individual, including grandparents, until such time as the court enters an order of disposition pursuant to § 16.1-278.2, or, if such placement is not available, in the care and custody of a suitable agency;

2. Order that reasonable visitation be allowed between the child and his parents, guardian, legal custodian or other person standing in loco parentis, and between the child and his siblings, if such visitation would not endanger the child's life or health; and

3. Order that the parent or other legally obligated person pay child support pursuant to § 16.1-290.

In addition, the court may enter a preliminary protective order pursuant to § 16.1-253 imposing requirements and conditions as specified in that section which the court deems appropriate for protection of the welfare of the child.

F1. Prior to the entry of an order pursuant to subsection F of this section transferring temporary custody of the child to a relative or other interested individual, including grandparents, the court shall consider whether the relative or other interested individual is one who (i) is willing and qualified to receive and care for the child; (ii) is willing to have a positive, continuous relationship with the child; and (iii) is willing and has the ability to protect the child from abuse and neglect. The court's order transferring temporary custody to a relative or other interested individual should provide for compliance with any preliminary protective order entered on behalf of the child in accordance with the provisions of § 16.1-253; initiation and completion of the investigation as directed by the court and court review of the child's placement required in accordance with the provisions of § 16.1-278.2; and, as appropriate, ongoing provision of social services to the child and the temporary custodian.

G. At the conclusion of the preliminary removal order hearing, the court shall determine whether the allegations of abuse or neglect have been proven by a preponderance of the evidence. Any finding of abuse or neglect shall be stated in the court order. However, if, before such a finding is made, a person responsible for the care and custody of the child, the child's guardian ad litem or the local department of social services objects to a finding being made at the hearing, the court shall schedule an adjudicatory hearing to be held within 30 days of the date of the initial preliminary removal hearing. The adjudicatory hearing shall be held to determine whether the allegations of abuse and neglect have been proven by a preponderance of the evidence. Parties who are present at the preliminary removal order hearing shall be given notice of the date set for the adjudicatory hearing and parties who are not present shall be summoned as provided in § 16.1-263. The hearing shall be held and an order may be entered, although a party to the preliminary removal order hearing fails to appear and is not represented by counsel, provided personal or substituted service was made on the person, or the court determines that such person cannot be found, after reasonable effort, or in the case of a person who is without the Commonwealth, the person cannot be found or his post office address cannot be ascertained after reasonable effort.

The preliminary removal order and any preliminary protective order issued shall remain in full force and effect pending the adjudicatory hearing.

H. If the preliminary removal order includes a finding of abuse or neglect and the child is removed from his home or a preliminary protective order is issued, a dispositional hearing shall be held pursuant to § 16.1-278.2. The dispositional hearing shall be scheduled at the time of the preliminary removal order hearing and shall be held within 60 days of the preliminary removal order hearing. If an adjudicatory hearing is requested pursuant to subsection G, the dispositional hearing shall nonetheless be scheduled at the initial preliminary removal order hearing. All parties present at the preliminary removal order hearing shall be given notice of the date scheduled for the dispositional hearing; parties who are not present shall be summoned to appear as provided in § 16.1-263.

I. The local department of social services having "legal custody" of a child as defined in § 16.1-228 (i) shall not be required to comply with the requirements of this section in order to redetermine where and with whom the child shall live, notwithstanding that the child had been placed with a natural parent.

J. Violation of any order issued pursuant to this section shall constitute contempt of court.

History.
1977, c. 559; 1984, c. 499; 1985, c. 584; 1986, c. 308; 1990, c. 769; 1994, c. 42; 1995, c. 817; 1997, c. 790; 1999, c. 668; 2000, c. 385; 2008, c. 397; 2013, c. 130.

Section set out twice.
The section above is effective July 1, 2014. For this section as in effect until July 1, 2014, see the preceding section, also numbered 16.1-252.

Editor's note.

Acts 2013, c. 130, cl. 2 provides: "That the provisions of this act shall become effective on July 1, 2014."

The 2013 amendments.

The 2013 amendment by c. 130, effective July 1, 2014, substituted "60 days" for "seventy-five days" in the second sentence of subsection H, and made numeric stylistic changes throughout the section.

§ 16.1-253. Preliminary protective order.

A. Upon the motion of any person or upon the court's own motion, the court may issue a preliminary protective order, after a hearing, if necessary to protect a child's life, health, safety or normal development pending the final determination of any matter before the court. The order may require a child's parents, guardian, legal custodian, other person standing in loco parentis or other family or household member of the child to observe reasonable conditions of behavior for a specified length of time. These conditions shall include any one or more of the following:

1. To abstain from offensive conduct against the child, a family or household member of the child or any person to whom custody of the child is awarded;

2. To cooperate in the provision of reasonable services or programs designed to protect the child's life, health or normal development;

3. To allow persons named by the court to come into the child's home at reasonable times designated by the court to visit the child or inspect the fitness of the home and to determine the physical or emotional health of the child;

4. To allow visitation with the child by persons entitled thereto, as determined by the court;

5. To refrain from acts of commission or omission which tend to endanger the child's life, health or normal development; or

6. To refrain from such contact with the child or family or household members of the child, as the court may deem appropriate, including removal of such person from the residence of the child. However, prior to the issuance by the court of an order removing such person from the residence of the child, the petitioner must prove by a preponderance of the evidence that such person's probable future conduct would constitute a danger to the life or health of such child, and that there are no less drastic alternatives which could reasonably and adequately protect the child's life or health pending a final determination on the petition.

B. A preliminary protective order may be issued ex parte upon motion of any person or the court's own motion in any matter before the court, or upon petition. The motion or petition shall be supported by an affidavit or by sworn testimony in person before the judge or intake officer which establishes that the child would be subjected to an imminent threat to life or health to the extent that delay for the provision of an adversary hearing would be likely to result in serious or irremediable injury to the child's life or health. If an ex parte order is issued without an affidavit being presented, the court, in its order, shall state the basis upon which the order was entered, including a summary of the allegations made and the court's findings. Following the issuance of an ex parte order the court shall provide an adversary hearing to the affected parties within the shortest practicable time not to exceed five business days after the issuance of the order.

C. Prior to the hearing required by this section, notice of the hearing shall be given at least 24 hours in advance of the hearing to the guardian ad litem for the child, to the parents, guardian, legal custodian, or other person standing in loco parentis of the child, to any other family or household member of the child to whom the protective order may be directed and to the child if he or she is 12 years of age or older. The notice provided herein shall include (i) the time, date and place for the hearing and (ii) a specific statement of the factual circumstances which allegedly necessitate the issuance of a preliminary protective order.

D. All parties to the hearing shall be informed of their right to counsel pursuant to § 16.1-266.

E. At the hearing the child, his or her parents, guardian, legal custodian or other person standing in loco parentis and any other family or household member of the child to whom notice was given shall have the right to confront and cross-examine all adverse witnesses and evidence and to present evidence on their own behalf.

F. If a petition alleging abuse or neglect of a child has been filed, at the hearing pursuant to this section the court shall determine whether the allegations of abuse or neglect have been proven by a preponderance of the evidence. Any finding of abuse or neglect shall be stated in the court order. However, if, before such a finding is made, a person responsible for the care and custody of the child, the child's guardian ad litem or the local department of social services objects to a finding being made at the hearing, the court shall schedule an adjudicatory hearing to be held within 30 days of the date of the initial preliminary protective order hearing. The adjudicatory hearing shall be held to determine whether the allegations of abuse and neglect have been proven by a preponderance of the evidence. Parties who are present at the hearing shall be given notice of the date set for the adjudicatory hearing and parties who are not present shall be summoned as provided in § 16.1-263. The adjudicatory hearing shall be held and an order may be entered, although a party to the hearing fails to appear and is not represented by counsel, provided personal or substituted service was made on the person, or the court determines that such person cannot be found, after reasonable effort, or in the case of a person who is without the Commonwealth, the person cannot be found or his post office address cannot be ascertained after reasonable effort.

Any preliminary protective order issued shall remain in full force and effect pending the adjudicatory hearing.

G. **(Effective until July 1, 2014)** If at the preliminary protective order hearing held pursuant to this section the court makes a finding of abuse or neglect and a preliminary protective order is issued, a dispositional hearing shall be held pursuant to § 16.1-278.2. The court shall forthwith, but in all cases no later than the end of the business day on which the order was issued, enter and transfer electronically to the Virginia Criminal Information Network the respondent's identifying information and the name, date of birth, sex, and race of each protected person provided to the court. A copy of the preliminary protective order containing any such identifying information shall be forwarded forthwith to the primary law-enforcement agency responsible for service and entry of protective orders. Upon receipt of the order by the primary law-enforcement agency, the agency shall forthwith verify and enter any modification as necessary to the identifying information and other appropriate information required by the Department of State Police into the Virginia Criminal Information Network established and maintained by the Department of State Police pursuant to Chapter 2 (§ 52-12 et seq.) of Title 52 and the order shall be served forthwith on the allegedly abusing person in person as provided in § 16.1-264 and due return made to the court. However, if the order is issued by the circuit court, the clerk of the circuit court shall forthwith forward an attested copy of the order containing the respondent's identifying information and the name, date of birth, sex, and race of each protected person provided to the court to the primary law-enforcement agency providing service and entry of protective orders and upon receipt of the order, the primary law-enforcement agency shall enter the name of the person subject to the order and other appropriate information required by the Department of State Police into the Virginia Criminal Information Network established and maintained by the Department pursuant to Chapter 2 (§ 52-12 et seq.) of Title 52 and the order shall be served forthwith upon the allegedly abusing person in person as provided in § 16.1-264. Upon service, the agency making service shall enter the date and time of service and other appropriate information required by the Department of State Police into the Virginia Criminal Information Network and make due return to the court. The preliminary order shall specify a date for the dispositional hearing. The dispositional hearing shall be scheduled at the time of the hearing pursuant to this section, and shall be held within 75 days of this hearing. If an adjudicatory hearing is requested pursuant to subsection F, the dispositional hearing shall nonetheless be scheduled at the hearing pursuant to this section. All parties present at the hearing shall be given notice of the date and time scheduled for the dispositional hearing; parties who are not present shall be summoned to appear as provided in § 16.1-263.

G. **(Effective July 1, 2014)** If at the preliminary protective order hearing held pursuant to this sec-

tion the court makes a finding of abuse or neglect and a preliminary protective order is issued, a dispositional hearing shall be held pursuant to § 16.1-278.2. The court shall forthwith, but in all cases no later than the end of the business day on which the order was issued, enter and transfer electronically to the Virginia Criminal Information Network the respondent's identifying information and the name, date of birth, sex, and race of each protected person provided to the court. A copy of the preliminary protective order containing any such identifying information shall be forwarded forthwith to the primary law-enforcement agency responsible for service and entry of protective orders. Upon receipt of the order by the primary law-enforcement agency, the agency shall forthwith verify and enter any modification as necessary to the identifying information and other appropriate information required by the Department of State Police into the Virginia Criminal Information Network established and maintained by the Department of State Police pursuant to Chapter 2 (§ 52-12 et seq.) of Title 52 and the order shall be served forthwith on the allegedly abusing person in person as provided in § 16.1-264 and due return made to the court. However, if the order is issued by the circuit court, the clerk of the circuit court shall forthwith forward an attested copy of the order containing the respondent's identifying information and the name, date of birth, sex, and race of each protected person provided to the court to the primary law-enforcement agency providing service and entry of protective orders and upon receipt of the order, the primary law-enforcement agency shall enter the name of the person subject to the order and other appropriate information required by the Department of State Police into the Virginia Criminal Information Network established and maintained by the Department pursuant to Chapter 2 (§ 52-12 et seq.) of Title 52 and the order shall be served forthwith upon the allegedly abusing person in person as provided in § 16.1-264. Upon service, the agency making service shall enter the date and time of service and other appropriate information required by the Department of State Police into the Virginia Criminal Information Network and make due return to the court. The preliminary order shall specify a date for the dispositional hearing. The dispositional hearing shall be scheduled at the time of the hearing pursuant to this section, and shall be held within 60 days of this hearing. If an adjudicatory hearing is requested pursuant to subsection F, the dispositional hearing shall nonetheless be scheduled at the hearing pursuant to this section. All parties present at the hearing shall be given notice of the date and time scheduled for the dispositional hearing; parties who are not present shall be summoned to appear as provided in § 16.1-263.

H. Nothing in this section enables the court to remove a child from the custody of his or her parents, guardian, legal custodian or other person standing in loco parentis, except as provided in § 16.1-278.2, and no order hereunder shall be entered against a person over whom the court does not have jurisdiction.

I. Neither a law-enforcement agency, the attorney for the Commonwealth, a court nor the clerk's office, nor any employee of them, may disclose, except among themselves, the residential address, telephone number, or place of employment of the person protected by the order or that of the family of such person, except to the extent that disclosure is (i) required by law or the Rules of the Supreme Court, (ii) necessary for law-enforcement purposes, or (iii) permitted by the court for good cause.

J. Violation of any order issued pursuant to this section shall constitute contempt of court.

K. The court shall forthwith, but in all cases no later than the end of the business day on which the order was issued, enter and transfer electronically to the Virginia Criminal Information Network the respondent's identifying information and the name, date of birth, sex, and race of each protected person provided to the court. A copy of the preliminary protective order containing any such identifying information shall be forwarded forthwith to the primary law-enforcement agency responsible for service and entry of protective orders. Upon receipt of the order by the primary law-enforcement agency, the agency shall forthwith verify and enter any modification as necessary to the identifying information and other appropriate information required by the Department of State Police into the Virginia Criminal Information Network established and maintained by the Department pursuant to Chapter 2 (§ 52-12 et seq.) of Title 52 and the order shall be served forthwith on the allegedly abusing person in person as provided in § 16.1-264 and due return made to the court. However, if the order is issued by the circuit court, the clerk of the circuit court shall forthwith forward an attested copy of the order containing the respondent's identifying information and the name, date of birth, sex, and race of each protected person provided to the court to the primary law-enforcement agency providing service and entry of protective orders and upon receipt of the order, the primary law-enforcement agency shall enter the name of the person subject to the order and other appropriate information required by the Department of State Police into the Virginia Criminal Information Network established and maintained by the Department pursuant to Chapter 2 (§ 52-12 et seq.) of Title 52 and the order shall be served forthwith on the allegedly abusing person in person as provided in § 16.1-264. Upon service, the agency making service shall enter the date and time of service and other appropriate information required by the Department of State Police into the Virginia Criminal Information Network and make due return to the court. The preliminary order shall specify a date for the full hearing.

Upon receipt of the return of service or other proof of service pursuant to subsection C of § 16.1-264,

the clerk shall forthwith forward an attested copy of the preliminary protective order to the primary law-enforcement agency and the agency shall forthwith verify and enter any modification as necessary into the Virginia Criminal Information Network as described above. If the order is later dissolved or modified, a copy of the dissolution or modification order shall also be attested, forwarded forthwith to the primary law-enforcement agency responsible for service and entry of protective orders, and upon receipt of the order by the primary law-enforcement agency, the agency shall forthwith verify and enter any modification as necessary to the identifying information and other appropriate information required by the Department of State Police into the Virginia Criminal Information Network as described above and the order shall be served forthwith and due return made to the court.

L. No fee shall be charged for filing or serving any petition or order pursuant to this section.

History.
  1977, c. 559; 1985, c. 595; 1986, c. 308; 1987, c. 497; 1996, c. 866; 1997, c. 790; 1998, c. 550; 2002, cc. 508, 810, 818; 2008, cc. 73, 246; 2009, c. 732; 2013, c. 130.

  Subsection G set out twice. — The first version of subsection G above is effective until July 1, 2014. The second version of subsection G is effective July 1, 2014.

Cross references.
  As to testimony of child by use of two-way closed circuit television in civil proceedings involving alleged abuse or neglect of a child, see § 63.2-1521. As to admission of out-of-court statements made by certain children in civil proceedings involving alleged abuse or neglect of a child, see § 63.2-1522. As to use of videotaped statements of certain children who are complaining witnesses in in civil proceedings involving alleged abuse or neglect of a child, see § 63.2-1523.

Editor's note.
  Acts 2013, c. 130, cl. 2 provides: "That the provisions of this act shall become effective on July 1, 2014."

The 2009 amendments.
  The 2009 amendment by c. 732, in subsection G, in the second sentence, inserted "electronically to the Virginia Criminal Information Network the respondent's" and "and the name, date of birth, sex, and race of each protected person," and deleted "electronically to the Virginia Criminal Information Network" from the end, in the third sentence, deleted "and an addendum" preceding "containing any such," in the fourth sentence, deleted "and addendum" preceding "by the primary," in the fifth sentence, deleted "and an addendum" following "copy of the order" and "receipt of the order" inserted "the respondent's" and "and the name, date of birth, sex, and race of each protected person provided to the court"; in subsection K, in the first sentence, inserted "electronically to the Virginia Criminal Information Network the respondent's" and "and the name, date of birth, sex, and race of each protected person," and deleted "electronically to the Virginia Criminal Information Network" from the end, in the second sentence, deleted "and an addendum" following "protective order," in the third sentence, deleted "and addendum" following "receipt of the order," in the fourth sentence, deleted "and an addendum" following "copy of the order," inserted "the respondent's" and "and the name, date of birth, sex, and race of each protected person provided to the court" and deleted "and addendum" following "receipt of the order"; and deleted subsection M, which read: "If any identifying information in the addendum is determined to be incorrect by the entering agency, the agency shall enter the corrected information into the Virginia Criminal Information Network."

The 2013 amendments.

The 2013 amendment by c. 130, effective July 1, 2014, substituted "60 days" for "75 days" in the eighth sentence of subsection G.

Research references.

Virginia Forms (Matthew Bender). No. 5-149 Preliminary Child Protective Order. No. 5-153 Adjudicatory Order for Abuse or Neglect Cases.

CASE NOTES

Parents given specific written notice of subsequent hearing. — Under this section, §§ 16.1-251 and 16.1-252 the parents shall be given specific notice in writing of a subsequent hearing on the merits by a petition stating the factual circumstances which allegedly necessitated removal of the children. Rader v. Montgomery County Dep't of Social Servs., 5 Va. App. 523, 365 S.E.2d 234 (1988).

Writ of prohibition against juvenile and domestic relations court held properly denied. — Court properly denied petition for writ of prohibition sought by father to prevent further action by the juvenile and domestic relations district court on the ground that it lacked subject matter jurisdiction by virtue of the Parental Kidnapping Prevention Act and the Uniform Child Custody Jurisdiction Act. The juvenile and domestic relations district courts of Virginia have general jurisdiction over all proceedings involving the custody, visitation, support, control or disposition of a child, except as otherwise provided in § 16.1-244. In re Johnston, 3 Va. App. 492, 350 S.E.2d 681 (1986).

Court has authority to seek a preliminary protective order. — Under most circumstances, an action under § 16.1-253 does not involve the infringement of a right personal to the movant because it involves the protection of a third party: the child; the fact that the trial court has authority to seek a preliminary protective order sua sponte indicates that no personal right of the movant is involved. Anonymous C v. Anonymous B, No. 2232-09-2, 2011 Va. App. LEXIS 14 (Ct. of Appeals Jan. 11, 2011).

Protective order appropriately entered. — Father's argument that the trial court erred in issuing a protective order, based on his neglect and abuse of his child, for a period of five years in contravention of subdivision A 3 of § 16.1-278.2 was without merit because that code section only limited the duration of a protective order excluding from the home parents or other adults living in the same dwelling with the abused child, and at the time the order was entered, the father was no longer living in the same home as the child; further, the five-year limitation on visitation was clearly within the trial court's discretion as appropriate to protect the child's life, health, and normal development, pursuant to § 16.1-253. Altice v. Roanoke County Dep't of Soc. Servs., 45 Va. App. 400, 611 S.E.2d 628, 2005 Va. App. LEXIS 154 (2005).

Further proceedings required to enter proper protective order. — Despite mother and father's apparent stipulation to the judicial and domestic relations court's nonspecific finding of abuse, the trial court was required to hear evidence and make findings on the issues of which parent or parents committed abuse inflicted on child and what type of abuse was involved. Only then could the trial court enter a § 16.1-253 protective order designed to meet the best interests of the child while also taking into consideration the rights of her mother and father. Anonymous B v. Anonymous C, 51 Va. App. 657, 660 S.E.2d 307, 2008 Va. App. LEXIS 201 (2008).

Nonsuit. — Trial court did not err in denying a mother's request for a nonsuit under § 8.01-380 because the evidence supported a finding that it was in the best interests of her child for the trial court to transfer the right to advocate for the protective order to the father and the guardian ad litem, and since the mother was a respondent to the preliminary protective order, her right to nonsuit the case against her was subordinate to the welfare of the child; in cases where allegations of child sexual abuse have been presented to the trial court and a preliminary protective order has been issued pursuant to those allegations, an alleged abuser's "right" to nonsuit must be subordinate to the welfare of the child, and the parties to an action under § 16.1-253 are not in the same positions as plaintiffs and defendants in a traditional action. Anonymous C v. Anonymous B, No. 2232-09-2, 2011 Va. App. LEXIS 14 (Ct. of Appeals Jan. 11, 2011).

OPINIONS OF THE ATTORNEY GENERAL

"Offensive conduct." — "Offensive conduct" includes the acts of harassing, stalking, threatening, or placing a person in reasonable fear of bodily injury. See opinion of Attorney General to Colonel W.S. (Steve) Flaherty, Superintendent, Department of State Police, 09-048, 2009 Va. AG LEXIS 39 (8/27/09).

§ 16.1-253.1. Preliminary protective orders in cases of family abuse; confidentiality.

A. Upon the filing of a petition alleging that the petitioner is or has been, within a reasonable period of time, subjected to family abuse, the court may issue a preliminary protective order against an allegedly abusing person in order to protect the health and safety of the petitioner or any family or household member of the petitioner. The order may be issued in an ex parte proceeding upon good cause shown when the petition is supported by an affidavit or sworn testimony before the judge or intake officer. Immediate and present danger of family abuse or evidence sufficient to establish probable cause that family abuse has recently occurred shall constitute good cause. Evidence that the petitioner has been subjected to family abuse within a reasonable time and evidence of immediate and present danger of family abuse may be established by a showing that (i) the allegedly abusing person is incarcerated and is to be released from incarceration within 30 days following the petition or has been released from incarceration within 30 days prior to the petition, (ii) the crime for which the allegedly abusing person was convicted and incarcerated involved family abuse against the petitioner, and (iii) the allegedly abusing person has made threatening contact with the petitioner while he was incarcerated, exhibiting a renewed threat to the petitioner of family abuse.

A preliminary protective order may include any one or more of the following conditions to be imposed on the allegedly abusing person:

1. Prohibiting acts of family abuse or criminal offenses that result in injury to person or property.

2. Prohibiting such contacts by the respondent with the petitioner or family or household members of the petitioner as the court deems necessary for the health or safety of such persons.

3. Granting the petitioner possession of the premises occupied by the parties to the exclusion of the allegedly abusing person; however, no such grant of possession shall affect title to any real or personal property.

4. Enjoining the respondent from terminating any necessary utility service to a premises that the petitioner has been granted possession of pursuant to subdivision 3 or, where appropriate, ordering the respondent to restore utility services to such premises.

5. Granting the petitioner temporary possession or use of a motor vehicle owned by the petitioner alone or jointly owned by the parties to the exclusion

of the allegedly abusing person; however, no such grant of possession or use shall affect title to the vehicle.

6. Requiring that the allegedly abusing person provide suitable alternative housing for the petitioner and any other family or household member and, where appropriate, requiring the respondent to pay deposits to connect or restore necessary utility services in the alternative housing provided.

7. Any other relief necessary for the protection of the petitioner and family or household members of the petitioner.

B. The court shall forthwith, but in all cases no later than the end of the business day on which the order was issued, enter and transfer electronically to the Virginia Criminal Information Network the respondent's identifying information and the name, date of birth, sex, and race of each protected person provided to the court. A copy of a preliminary protective order containing any such identifying information shall be forwarded forthwith to the primary law-enforcement agency responsible for service and entry of protective orders. Upon receipt of the order by the primary law-enforcement agency, the agency shall forthwith verify and enter any modification as necessary to the identifying information and other appropriate information required by the Department of State Police into the Virginia Criminal Information Network established and maintained by the Department pursuant to Chapter 2 (§ 52-12 et seq.) of Title 52 and the order shall be served forthwith on the allegedly abusing person in person as provided in § 16.1-264 and due return made to the court. However, if the order is issued by the circuit court, the clerk of the circuit court shall forthwith forward an attested copy of the order containing the respondent's identifying information and the name, date of birth, sex, and race of each protected person provided to the court to the primary law-enforcement agency providing service and entry of protective orders and upon receipt of the order, the primary law-enforcement agency shall enter the name of the person subject to the order and other appropriate information required by the Department of State Police into the Virginia Criminal Information Network established and maintained by the Department pursuant to Chapter 2 (§ 52-12 et seq.) of Title 52 and the order shall be served forthwith on the allegedly abusing person in person as provided in § 16.1-264. Upon service, the agency making service shall enter the date and time of service and other appropriate information required by the Department of State Police into the Virginia Criminal Information Network and make due return to the court. The preliminary order shall specify a date for the full hearing. The hearing shall be held within 15 days of the issuance of the preliminary order. If the respondent fails to appear at this hearing because the respondent was not personally served, or if personally served was incarcerated and not transported to the hearing, the court may extend the protective order for a period not to exceed six months. The extended protective order shall be served forthwith on the respondent. However, upon motion of the respondent and for good cause shown, the court may continue the hearing. The preliminary order shall remain in effect until the hearing. Upon request after the order is issued, the clerk shall provide the petitioner with a copy of the order and information regarding the date and time of service. The order shall further specify that either party may at any time file a motion with the court requesting a hearing to dissolve or modify the order. The hearing on the motion shall be given precedence on the docket of the court.

Upon receipt of the return of service or other proof of service pursuant to subsection C of § 16.1-264, the clerk shall forthwith forward an attested copy of the preliminary protective order to the primary law-enforcement agency, and the agency shall forthwith verify and enter any modification as necessary into the Virginia Criminal Information Network as described above. If the order is later dissolved or modified, a copy of the dissolution or modification order shall also be attested, forwarded forthwith to the primary law-enforcement agency responsible for service and entry of protective orders, and upon receipt of the order by the primary law-enforcement agency, the agency shall forthwith verify and enter any modification as necessary to the identifying information and other appropriate information required by the Department of State Police into the Virginia Criminal Information Network as described above and the order shall be served forthwith and due return made to the court.

C. The preliminary order is effective upon personal service on the allegedly abusing person. Except as otherwise provided in § 16.1-253.2, a violation of the order shall constitute contempt of court.

D. At a full hearing on the petition, the court may issue a protective order pursuant to § 16.1-279.1 if the court finds that the petitioner has proven the allegation of family abuse by a preponderance of the evidence.

E. Neither a law-enforcement agency, the attorney for the Commonwealth, a court nor the clerk's office, nor any employee of them, may disclose, except among themselves, the residential address, telephone number, or place of employment of the person protected by the order or that of the family of such person, except to the extent that disclosure is (i) required by law or the Rules of the Supreme Court, (ii) necessary for law-enforcement purposes, or (iii) permitted by the court for good cause.

F. As used in this section, "copy" includes a facsimile copy.

G. No fee shall be charged for filing or serving any petition or order pursuant to this section.

History.
1984, c. 631; 1987, c. 497; 1988, c. 165; 1992, c. 886; 1994, c. 907; 1996, c. 866; 1997, c. 603; 1998, c. 684; 2000, cc. 34, 654; 2001, c.

101; 2002, cc. 508, 810, 818; 2006, c. 308; 2007, c. 205; 2008, cc. 73, 246; 2009, cc. 343, 732; 2011, cc. 445, 480.

Editor's note.

Acts 2011, cc. 445 and 480, cl. 2 provides: "That the provisions of this act may result in a net increase in periods of imprisonment or commitment. Pursuant to § 30-19.1:4, the estimated amount of the necessary appropriation is $93,767 for periods of imprisonment in state adult correctional facilities and cannot be determined for periods of commitment to the custody of the Department of Juvenile Justice."

The 2009 amendments.

The 2009 amendment by c. 343, in subsection A, in the first paragraph, added the last sentence; in subsection B, in the first paragraph, in the seventh sentence, inserted "or if personally served was incarcerated and not transported to the hearing."

The 2009 amendment by c. 732, in subsection B, in the first sentence, inserted "electronically to the Virginia Criminal Information Network the respondent's" and "and the name, date of birth, sex, and race of each protected person," and deleted "electronically to the Virginia Criminal Information Network" from the end, in the second sentence, deleted "and an addendum" preceding "containing any such," in the third sentence, deleted "and addendum" preceding "by the primary," in the fourth sentence, deleted "and an addendum" following "copy of the order," inserted "the respondent's" and "and the name, date of birth, sex, and race of each protected person provided to the court" and deleted "and addendum" following "receipt of the order"; and deleted subsection H, which read: "If any identifying information in the addendum is determined to be incorrect by the entering agency, the agency shall enter the corrected information into the Virginia Criminal Information Network."

The 2011 amendments.

The 2011 amendments by cc. 445 and 480 are identical, and in subdivision A 1, added "or criminal offenses that result in injury to person or property"; rewrote subdivision A 2, which read: "Prohibiting such other contacts between the parties as the court deems appropriate"; and deleted subdivision A 3, which read: "Prohibiting such other contacts with the allegedly abused family or household member as the court deems necessary to protect the safety of such persons," redesignated the remaining subdivisions accordingly and made a related reference change.

Law Review.

For an article, "Domestic Relations," see 31 U. Rich. L. Rev. 1069 (1997). For 2000 survey of Virginia law regarding children, see 34 U. Rich. L. Rev. 939 (2000). For 2006 survey article, "Family and Juvenile Law," see 41 U. Rich. L. Rev. 151 (2006).

Research references.

Virginia Forms (Matthew Bender). No. 5-157 Preliminary Protective Order — Family Abuse.

OPINIONS OF THE ATTORNEY GENERAL

Petition by unemancipated minors for protective orders. — A minor may seek an emergency protective order in certain situations, but a minor who has not been emancipated, however mature that individual may be, can seek a protective order only through a next friend. See opinion of Attorney General to The Honorable Charniele L. Herring, Member, House of Delegates, 10-116, 2011 Va. AG LEXIS 2 (01/21/11).

Petition by emancipated minors for protective orders. — Emancipated minor may file petitions for protective orders under applicable statutes. See opinion of Attorney General to The Honorable Charniele L. Herring, Member, House of Delegates, 10-116, 2011 Va. AG LEXIS 2 (01/21/11).

§ 16.1-253.2. Violation of provisions of protective orders; penalty.

In addition to any other penalty provided by law, any person who violates any provision of a protective

order issued pursuant to § 16.1-253, 16.1-253.1, 16.1-253.4, 16.1-278.14, or 16.1-279.1 or subsection B of § 20-103, when such violation involves a provision of the protective order that prohibits such person from (i) going or remaining upon land, buildings, or premises; (ii) further acts of family abuse; or (iii) committing a criminal offense, or which prohibits contacts by the respondent with the allegedly abused person or family or household members of the allegedly abused person as the court deems appropriate, is guilty of a Class 1 misdemeanor. The punishment for any person convicted of a second offense of violating a protective order, when the offense is committed within five years of the prior conviction and when either the instant or prior offense was based on an act or threat of violence, shall include a mandatory minimum term of confinement of 60 days. Any person convicted of a third or subsequent offense of violating a protective order, when the offense is committed within 20 years of the first conviction and when either the instant or one of the prior offenses was based on an act or threat of violence is guilty of a Class 6 felony and the punishment shall include a mandatory minimum term of confinement of six months. The mandatory minimum terms of confinement prescribed for violations of this section shall be served consecutively with any other sentence.

If the respondent commits an assault and battery upon any party protected by the protective order, resulting in serious bodily injury to the party, he is guilty of a Class 6 felony. Any person who violates such a protective order by furtively entering the home of any protected party while the party is present, or by entering and remaining in the home of the protected party until the party arrives, is guilty of a Class 6 felony, in addition to any other penalty provided by law.

Upon conviction of any offense hereunder for which a mandatory minimum term of confinement is not specified, the person shall be sentenced to a term of confinement and in no case shall the entire term imposed be suspended. Upon conviction, the court shall, in addition to the sentence imposed, enter a protective order pursuant to § 16.1-279.1 for a specified period not exceeding two years from the date of conviction.

History.

1987, c. 700; 1988, c. 501; 1991, cc. 534, 715; 1992, c. 886; 1996, c. 866; 2003, c. 219; 2004, cc. 972, 980; 2007, cc. 745, 923; 2012, c. 637; 2013, cc. 761, 774.

Cross references.

As to punishment for Class 6 felonies, see § 18.2-10. As to punishment for Class 1 misdemeanors, see § 18.2-11.

Editor's note.

Acts 2013, cc. 761 and 774, cl. 2 provides: "That the provisions of this act may result in a net increase in periods of imprisonment or commitment. Pursuant to § 30-19.1:4, the estimated amount of the necessary appropriation cannot be determined for periods of imprisonment in state adult correctional facilities; therefore, Chapter 3 of the Acts of Assembly of 2012, Special Session I, requires the Virginia Criminal Sentencing Commission to assign a minimum fiscal impact of $50,000. Pursuant to § 30-19.1:4, the estimated amount of the necessary appropriation cannot be determined for periods of commitment to the custody of the Department of Juvenile Justice."

The 2012 amendments.

The 2012 amendment by c. 637 rewrote the first sentence of the first paragraph.

The 2013 amendments.

The 2013 amendments by cc. 761 and 774 are identical, and added the last sentence of the first paragraph.

Law Review.

For 2007 annual survey article, "Criminal Law and Procedure," see 42 U. Rich. L. Rev. 311 (2007). For annual survey article, "Criminal Law and Procedure," see 44 U. Rich. L. Rev. 339 (2009).

CASE NOTES

"Serious bodily injury." — Definition of "serious bodily injury" in subsection E of § 16.1-283 is inapplicable to a case under § 16.1-253.2. By its terms, it applies only to § 16.1-283. Nolen v. Commonwealth, 53 Va. App. 593, 673 S.E.2d 920, 2009 Va. App. LEXIS 138 (2009).

"Serious bodily injury" under § 16.1-253.2 is one that can fairly and reasonably be deemed not trifling, grave, giving rise to apprehension, giving rise to considerable care, and attended with danger. The victim's injuries satisfied this definition when she was bruised and lacerated, bore marks on her body, bled, missed several days of work, and suffered pain, requiring medication for an extended period of time. Nolen v. Commonwealth, 53 Va. App. 593, 673 S.E.2d 920, 2009 Va. App. LEXIS 138 (2009).

Specifications of "serious injury" in § 18.2-371.1 do not limit the court's consideration of the term "serious bodily injury" in a case under § 16.1-253.2. They relate to a specific legislative concern, the protection of children in custodial relationships; furthermore, the statute expressly provides that the term "serious injury" is not limited to the enumerated specifications. Nolen v. Commonwealth, 53 Va. App. 593, 673 S.E.2d 920, 2009 Va. App. LEXIS 138 (2009).

Conviction for violating protective order reversed. — Because insufficient evidence showed that defendant had notice of the terms of a protective order entered against her, and the victim never testified that a judge verbally ordered defendant to have no further contact with him, defendant's conviction for disobeying the terms of said order, in violation of § 16.1-279.1, was reversed and the warrant was dismissed. Hsiu Tsai v. Commonwealth, 51 Va. App. 649, 659 S.E.2d 594, 2008 Va. App. LEXIS 187 (2008).

§ 16.1-253.3. Repealed by Acts 1992, c. 886.

§ 16.1-253.4. Emergency protective orders authorized in certain cases; penalty.

A. Any judge of a circuit court, general district court, juvenile and domestic relations district court or magistrate may issue a written or oral ex parte emergency protective order pursuant to this section in order to protect the health or safety of any person.

B. When a law-enforcement officer or an allegedly abused person asserts under oath to a judge or magistrate, and on that assertion or other evidence the judge or magistrate (i) finds that a warrant for a violation of § 18.2-57.2 has been issued or issues a warrant for violation of § 18.2-57.2 and finds that there is probable danger of further acts of family abuse against a family or household member by the respondent or (ii) finds that reasonable grounds exist to believe that the respondent has committed family abuse and there is probable danger of a

further such offense against a family or household member by the respondent, the judge or magistrate shall issue an ex parte emergency protective order, except if the respondent is a minor, an emergency protective order shall not be required, imposing one or more of the following conditions on the respondent:

1. Prohibiting acts of family abuse or criminal offenses that result in injury to person or property;

2. Prohibiting such contacts by the respondent with the allegedly abused person or family or household members of the allegedly abused person as the judge or magistrate deems necessary to protect the safety of such persons; and

3. Granting the family or household member possession of the premises occupied by the parties to the exclusion of the respondent; however, no such grant of possession shall affect title to any real or personal property.

When the judge or magistrate considers the issuance of an emergency protective order pursuant to clause (i), he shall presume that there is probable danger of further acts of family abuse against a family or household member by the respondent unless the presumption is rebutted by the allegedly abused person.

C. An emergency protective order issued pursuant to this section shall expire at 11:59 p.m. on the third day following issuance. If the expiration occurs on a day that the court is not in session, the emergency protective order shall be extended until 11:59 p.m. on the next day that the juvenile and domestic relations district court is in session. When issuing an emergency protective order under this section, the judge or magistrate shall provide the protected person or the law-enforcement officer seeking the emergency protective order with the form for use in filing petitions pursuant to § 16.1-253.1 and written information regarding protective orders that shall include the telephone numbers of domestic violence agencies and legal referral sources on a form prepared by the Supreme Court. If these forms are provided to a law-enforcement officer, the officer may provide these forms to the protected person when giving the emergency protective order to the protected person. The respondent may at any time file a motion with the court requesting a hearing to dissolve or modify the order issued hereunder. The hearing on the motion shall be given precedence on the docket of the court.

D. A law-enforcement officer may request an emergency protective order pursuant to this section and, if the person in need of protection is physically or mentally incapable of filing a petition pursuant to § 16.1-253.1 or 16.1-279.1, may request the extension of an emergency protective order for an additional period of time not to exceed three days after expiration of the original order. The request for an emergency protective order or extension of an order may be made orally, in person or by electronic means, and the judge of a circuit court, general district court, or juvenile and domestic relations district court or a magistrate may issue an oral emergency protective order. An oral emergency protective order issued pursuant to this section shall be reduced to writing, by the law-enforcement officer requesting the order or the magistrate on a preprinted form approved and provided by the Supreme Court of Virginia. The completed form shall include a statement of the grounds for the order asserted by the officer or the allegedly abused person.

E. The court or magistrate shall forthwith, but in all cases no later than the end of the business day on which the order was issued, enter and transfer electronically to the Virginia Criminal Information Network the respondent's identifying information and the name, date of birth, sex, and race of each protected person provided to the court or magistrate. A copy of an emergency protective order issued pursuant to this section containing any such identifying information shall be forwarded forthwith to the primary law-enforcement agency responsible for service and entry of protective orders. Upon receipt of the order by the primary law-enforcement agency, the agency shall forthwith verify and enter any modification as necessary to the identifying information and other appropriate information required by the Department of State Police into the Virginia Criminal Information Network established and maintained by the Department pursuant to Chapter 2 (§ 52-12 et seq.) of Title 52 and the order shall be served forthwith upon the respondent and due return made to the court. However, if the order is issued by the circuit court, the clerk of the circuit court shall forthwith forward an attested copy of the order containing the respondent's identifying information and the name, date of birth, sex, and race of each protected person provided to the court to the primary law-enforcement agency providing service and entry of protective orders and upon receipt of the order, the primary law-enforcement agency shall enter the name of the person subject to the order and other appropriate information required by the Department of State Police into the Virginia Criminal Network established and maintained by the Department pursuant to Chapter 2 (§ 52-12 et seq.) of Title 52 and the order shall be served forthwith on the respondent. Upon service, the agency making service shall enter the date and time of service and other appropriate information required by the Department of State Police into the Virginia Criminal Information Network and make due return to the court. One copy of the order shall be given to the allegedly abused person when it is issued, and one copy shall be filed with the written report required by subsection D of § 19.2-81.3. The judge or magistrate who issues an oral order pursuant to an electronic request by a law-enforcement officer shall verify the written order to determine whether the officer who reduced it to writing accurately transcribed the contents of the oral order. The original copy shall be filed with the clerk of the juvenile and

domestic relations district court within five business days of the issuance of the order. If the order is later dissolved or modified, a copy of the dissolution or modification order shall also be attested, forwarded forthwith to the primary law-enforcement agency responsible for service and entry of protective orders, and upon receipt of the order by the primary law-enforcement agency, the agency shall forthwith verify and enter any modification as necessary to the identifying information and other appropriate information required by the Department of State Police into the Virginia Criminal Information Network as described above and the order shall be served forthwith and due return made to the court. Upon request, the clerk shall provide the allegedly abused person with information regarding the date and time of service.

F. The availability of an emergency protective order shall not be affected by the fact that the family or household member left the premises to avoid the danger of family abuse by the respondent.

G. The issuance of an emergency protective order shall not be considered evidence of any wrongdoing by the respondent.

H. As used in this section, a "law-enforcement officer" means any (i) full-time or part-time employee of a police department or sheriff's office which is part of or administered by the Commonwealth or any political subdivision thereof and who is responsible for the prevention and detection of crime and the enforcement of the penal, traffic, or highway laws of the Commonwealth and (ii) member of an auxiliary police force established pursuant to § 15.2-1731. Part-time employees are compensated officers who are not full-time employees as defined by the employing police department or sheriff's office.

I. Neither a law-enforcement agency, the attorney for the Commonwealth, a court nor the clerk's office, nor any employee of them, may disclose, except among themselves, the residential address, telephone number, or place of employment of the person protected by the order or that of the family of such person, except to the extent that disclosure is (i) required by law or the Rules of the Supreme Court, (ii) necessary for law-enforcement purposes, or (iii) permitted by the court for good cause.

J. As used in this section, "copy" includes a facsimile copy.

K. No fee shall be charged for filing or serving any petition or order pursuant to this section.

History.
1991, c. 715; 1992, c. 742; 1994, c. 907; 1996, c. 866; 1997, c. 603; 1998, cc. 677, 684; 1999, c. 807; 2001, c. 474; 2002, cc. 508, 706, 810, 818; 2007, cc. 396, 661; 2008, cc. 73, 246; 2009, c. 732; 2011, cc. 445, 480; 2012, cc. 637, 827.

Editor's note.
Acts 1993, c. 930, cl. 3, as amended by Acts 1994, c. 564, cl. 2, and Acts 1996, c. 616, cl. 4, provides that the amendment to this section by Acts 1993, c. 930, cl. 1, shall become effective June 1, 1998, "if state funds are provided, including all local costs, to carry out the

purposes of this bill by the General Assembly." The funding was not provided.

Acts 2011, cc. 445 and 480, cl. 2 provides: "That the provisions of this act may result in a net increase in periods of imprisonment or commitment. Pursuant to § 30-19.1:4, the estimated amount of the necessary appropriation is $93,767 for periods of imprisonment in state adult correctional facilities and cannot be determined for periods of commitment to the custody of the Department of Juvenile Justice."

The 2009 amendments.

The 2009 amendment by c. 732, in subsection C, in the first sentence, substituted "11:59 p.m. on" for "the end of," in the second sentence, substituted "on a day" for "at a time" and "11:59 p.m. on" for "the end of" and deleted "business" preceding "day that the"; in subsection E, in the first sentence, inserted "electronically to the Virginia Criminal Information Network the respondent's" and "and the name, date of birth, sex, and race of each protected person," and deleted "electronically to the Virginia Criminal Information Network" from the end, in the second sentence, deleted "and an addendum" preceding "containing any such," in the third sentence, deleted 'and addendum" preceding "by the primary," in the fourth sentence, deleted "and an addendum" following "copy of the order," inserted "the respondent's" and "and the name, date of birth, sex, and race of each protected person provided to the court" and deleted "and addendum" following "receipt of the order"; and deleted subsection L, which read: "If any identifying information in the addendum is determined to be incorrect by the entering agency, the agency shall enter the corrected information into the Virginia Criminal Information Network."

The 2011 amendments.

The 2011 amendments by cc. 445 and 480 are identical, and added "or criminal offenses that result in injury to person or property" in subdivision B 1; deleted "of this subsection" following "clause (i)" in the last paragraph in subsection B; made a minor stylistic change in subsection D; and corrected the subsection reference near the middle in subsection E.

The 2012 amendments.

The 2012 amendment by c. 637 inserted "the allegedly abused person or" and substituted "of the allegedly abused person" for "of the respondent" in subdivision B 2.

The 2012 amendment by c. 827, effective April 18, 2012, deleted "subsection B of" preceding "§ 15.2-1731" at the end of H (ii).

Law Review.

For an article relating to recent changes of formidable importance in major areas of domestic relations, both nationally and in Virginia, see 32 U. Rich. L. Rev. 1165 (1998).

Research references.

Friend's Virginia Pleading and Practice (Matthew Bender). Chapter 1 Courts. § 1.05 District Courts. Charles E. Friend.

Virginia Forms (Matthew Bender). No. 5-158 Emergency Protective Order — Family Abuse.

Michie's Jurisprudence.

For related discussion, see 2A M.J. Assault and Battery, § 5; 3B M.J. Civil Rights, § 2; 9B M.J. Husband and Wife, § 87.

CASE NOTES

Police officer brandishing firearm at wife. — In the context of procedural due process protections, it was perfectly reasonable for an investigating officer to have obtained an emergency protective order from the magistrate judge who issued an arrest warrant for another police officer where the officer was charged with brandishing a firearm at his wife during a heated argument. Myers v. Shaver, 245 F. Supp. 2d 805, 2003 U.S. Dist. LEXIS 2547 (W.D. Va. 2003).

OPINIONS OF THE ATTORNEY GENERAL

Petition for protective orders by law enforcement on behalf of minors. — Law-enforcement officers may file petitions for emergency protective orders on behalf of minors who are victims of family abuse, stalking, sexual assault or other acts of criminal violence. See opinion of Attorney General to The Honorable Charniele L. Herring, Member, House of Delegates, 10-116, 2011 Va. AG LEXIS 2 (01/21/11).

Petition by unemancipated minors for protective orders. — A minor may seek an emergency protective order in certain situations, but a minor who has not been emancipated, however mature that individual may be, can seek a protective order only through a next friend. See opinion of Attorney General to The Honorable Charniele L. Herring, Member, House of Delegates, 10-116, 2011 Va. AG LEXIS 2 (01/21/11).

Petition by emancipated minors for protective orders. — Emancipated minor may file petitions for protective orders under applicable statutes. See opinion of Attorney General to The Honorable Charniele L. Herring, Member, House of Delegates, 10-116, 2011 Va. AG LEXIS 2 (01/21/11).

§ 16.1-254. Responsibility for and limitation on transportation of children.

A. The detention home having custody or responsibility for supervision of a child pursuant to §§ 16.1-246, 16.1-247, 16.1-248.1, 16.1-249, and 16.1-250 shall be responsible for transportation of the child to all local medical appointments, dental appointments, psychological and psychiatric evaluations. Transportation of youth to special placements pursuant to § 16.1-286 shall be the responsibility of the court service unit.

B. However, the chief judge of the juvenile and domestic relations district court, on the basis of guidelines approved by the Board, shall designate the appropriate agencies in each county, city and town, other than the Department of State Police, to be responsible for (i) the transportation of violent and disruptive children and (ii) the transportation of children to destinations other than those set forth in subsection A of this section, pursuant to §§ 16.1-246, 16.1-247, 16.1-248.1, 16.1-249, and 16.1-250, and as otherwise ordered by the judge.

No child shall be transported with adults suspected of or charged with criminal acts.

History.

Code 1950, § 16.1-196; 1956, c. 555; 1958, c. 344; 1971, Ex. Sess., c. 109; 1973, c. 440; 1974, c. 358; 1977, c. 559; 1979, c. 202; 1990, cc. 629, 673.

Editor's note.

Acts 1993, c. 930, cl. 3, as amended by Acts 1994, c. 564, cl. 2, and Acts 1996, c. 616, cl. 4, provides that the amendment to this section by Acts 1993, c. 930, cl. 1, shall become effective June 1, 1998, "if state funds are provided, including all local costs, to carry out the purposes of this bill by the General Assembly." The funding was not provided.

§ 16.1-255. Limitation on issuance of detention orders for juveniles; appearance by juvenile.

No detention order shall be issued for any juvenile except when authorized by the judge or intake officer of a juvenile court or by a magistrate as provided in § 16.1-256.

In matters involving the issuance of detention orders each state or local court service unit shall ensure the capability of a prompt response by an intake officer who is either on duty or on call.

A child may appear before an intake officer either (i) by personal appearance before the intake officer or (ii) by the use of two-way electronic video and audio communication. All communications and proceedings shall be conducted in the same manner and the intake officer shall have the same powers as if the appearance were in person. Any documents filed may be transmitted by facsimile and the facsimile and any signatures thereon shall serve, for all purposes, as an original document. Any two-way electronic video and audio communication system used shall comply with the provisions of subsection B of § 19.2-3.1.

History.
1977, c. 559; 1985, c. 260; 1996, cc. 755, 914; 1997, c. 862; 2002, c. 700.

Cross references.
As to the provision of court services and replacement intake officers, see § 16.1-235.1.

Editor's note.
Acts 1993, c. 930, cl. 3, as amended by Acts 1994, c. 564, cl. 2 and Acts 1996, c. 616, cl. 4, provides that the amendment to this section by Acts 1993, c. 930, cl. 1, shall become effective June 1, 1998, "if state funds are provided, including all local costs, to carry out the purposes of this bill by the General Assembly." The funding was not provided.

Law Review.
For 1985 survey of Virginia law affecting children, see 19 U. Rich. L. Rev. p. 753 (1985). For an article, "Legal Issues Involving Children," see 32 U. Rich. L. Rev. 1345 (1998).

§ 16.1-256. Limitations as to issuance of warrants for juveniles; detention orders.

No warrant of arrest shall be issued for any juvenile by a magistrate, except as follows:

1. As provided in § 16.1-260 on appeal from a decision of an intake officer; or

2. Upon a finding of probable cause to believe that the child is in need of services or is a delinquent, when (i) the court is not open and (ii) the judge and the intake officer of the juvenile and domestic relations district court are not reasonably available. For purposes of this section, the phrase "not reasonably available" means that neither the judge nor the intake officer of the juvenile and domestic relations district court could be reached after the appearance by the juvenile before a magistrate or that neither could arrive within one hour after he was contacted.

When a magistrate is authorized to issue a warrant pursuant to subdivision 2, he may also issue a detention order, if the criteria for detention set forth in § 16.1-248.1 have been satisfied.

Warrants issued pursuant to this section shall be delivered forthwith to the juvenile court.

History.
Code 1950, § 16.1-195; 1956, c. 555; 1958, c. 344; 1973, c. 440; 1977, c. 559; 1979, c. 701; 1980, c. 234; 1981, c. 184; 1983, c. 349; 1986, c. 295; 1996, cc. 755, 914.

Editor's note.
Acts 1993, c. 930, cl. 3, as amended by Acts 1994, c. 564, cl. 2, and Acts 1996, c. 616, cl. 4, provides that the amendment to this section by Acts 1993, c. 930, cl. 1, shall become effective June 1, 1998, "if state funds are provided, including all local costs, to carry out the purposes of this bill by the General Assembly." The funding was not provided.

Law Review.
For survey of Virginia law on criminal procedure for the year 1978-1979, see 66 Va. L. Rev. 261 (1980). For 1985 survey of Virginia law affecting children, see 19 U. Rich. L. Rev. p. 753 (1985).

Research references.
Virginia Forms (Matthew Bender). No. 5-154 Shelter Care Order.

§ 16.1-257. Interference with or obstruction of officer; concealment or removal of child.

No person shall interfere with or obstruct any officer, juvenile probation officer or other officer or employee of the court in the discharge of his duties under this law, nor remove or conceal or cause to be removed or concealed any child in order that he or she may not be brought before the court, nor interfere with or remove or attempt to remove any child who is in the custody of the court or of an officer or who has been lawfully committed under this law. Any person willfully violating any provision of this section is guilty of a Class 1 misdemeanor.

History.
Code 1950, § 16.1-191; 1956, c. 555; 1977, c. 559.

Cross references.
As to punishment for Class 1 misdemeanors, see § 18.2-11.

ARTICLE 5.

INTAKE, PETITION AND NOTICE.

§ 16.1-259. Procedure in cases of adults.

A. In cases where an adult is charged with violations of the criminal law pursuant to subsection I or J of § 16.1-241, the procedure and disposition applicable in the trial of such cases in general district court shall be applicable to trial in juvenile court. The provisions of this law shall govern in all other cases involving adults.

B. Proceedings in cases of adults may be instituted on petition by any interested party, or on a warrant issued as provided by law, or upon the court's own motion.

History.
Code 1950, § 16.1-186; 1956, c. 555; 1977, c. 559; 1986, c. 95.

Cross references.
For provision on amendment of written pleadings, see Rule 8:8, Juvenile and Domestic Relations District Court Rules.

Editor's note.
In subsection A, "subsection I or J" was substituted for "subdivisions I or J" at the direction of the Virginia Code Commission.
Acts 1993, c. 930, cl. 3, as amended by Acts 1994, c. 564, cl. 2, and Acts 1996, c. 616, cl. 4, provides that the amendment to this section by Acts 1993, c. 930, cl. 1, shall become effective June 1, 1998, "if

state funds are provided, including all local costs, to carry out the purposes of this bill by the General Assembly." The funding was not provided.

Law Review.

For article, "The Revision of Virginia's Juvenile Court Law," see 13 U. Rich. L. Rev. 847 (1979). For annual survey article on legal issues involving children, see 38 U. Rich. L. Rev. 161 (2003). For 2003/2004 survey of family and juvenile law, see 39 U. Rich. L. Rev. 241 (2004).

CASE NOTES

Applied in Burke v. Commonwealth, 29 Va. App. 183, 510 S.E.2d 743 (1999).

§ 16.1-260. Intake; petition; investigation.

A. All matters alleged to be within the jurisdiction of the court shall be commenced by the filing of a petition, except as provided in subsection H and in § 16.1-259. The form and content of the petition shall be as provided in § 16.1-262. No individual shall be required to obtain support services from the Department of Social Services prior to filing a petition seeking support for a child. Complaints, requests and the processing of petitions to initiate a case shall be the responsibility of the intake officer. However, (i) the attorney for the Commonwealth of the city or county may file a petition on his own motion with the clerk, (ii) designated nonattorney employees of the Department of Social Services may complete, sign and file petitions and motions relating to the establishment, modification, or enforcement of support on forms approved by the Supreme Court of Virginia with the clerk, and (iii) any attorney may file petitions on behalf of his client with the clerk except petitions alleging that the subject of the petition is a child alleged to be in need of services, in need of supervision or delinquent. Complaints alleging abuse or neglect of a child shall be referred initially to the local department of social services in accordance with the provisions of Chapter 15 (§ 63.2-1500 et seq.) of Title 63.2. Motions and other subsequent pleadings in a case shall be filed directly with the clerk. The intake officer or clerk with whom the petition or motion is filed shall inquire whether the petitioner is receiving child support services or public assistance. No individual who is receiving support services or public assistance shall be denied the right to file a petition or motion to establish, modify or enforce an order for support of a child. If the petitioner is seeking or receiving child support services or public assistance, the clerk, upon issuance of process, shall forward a copy of the petition or motion, together with notice of the court date, to the Division of Child Support Enforcement.

B. The appearance of a child before an intake officer may be by (i) personal appearance before the intake officer or (ii) use of two-way electronic video and audio communication. If two-way electronic video and audio communication is used, an intake officer may exercise all powers conferred by law. All communications and proceedings shall be conducted in the same manner as if the appearance were in person, and any documents filed may be transmitted by facsimile process. The facsimile may be served or executed by the officer or person to whom sent, and returned in the same manner, and with the same force, effect, authority, and liability as an original document. All signatures thereon shall be treated as original signatures. Any two-way electronic video and audio communication system used for an appearance shall meet the standards as set forth in subsection B of § 19.2-3.1.

When the court service unit of any court receives a complaint alleging facts which may be sufficient to invoke the jurisdiction of the court pursuant to § 16.1-241, the unit, through an intake officer, may proceed informally to make such adjustment as is practicable without the filing of a petition or may authorize a petition to be filed by any complainant having sufficient knowledge of the matter to establish probable cause for the issuance of the petition.

An intake officer may proceed informally on a complaint alleging a child is in need of services, in need of supervision or delinquent only if the juvenile (i) is not alleged to have committed a violent juvenile felony or (ii) has not previously been proceeded against informally or adjudicated delinquent for an offense that would be a felony if committed by an adult. A petition alleging that a juvenile committed a violent juvenile felony shall be filed with the court. A petition alleging that a juvenile is delinquent for an offense that would be a felony if committed by an adult shall be filed with the court if the juvenile had previously been proceeded against informally by intake or had been adjudicated delinquent for an offense that would be a felony if committed by an adult.

If a juvenile is alleged to be a truant pursuant to a complaint filed in accordance with § 22.1-258 and the attendance officer has provided documentation to the intake officer that the relevant school division has complied with the provisions of § 22.1-258, then the intake officer shall file a petition with the court. The intake officer may defer filing the complaint for 90 days and proceed informally by developing a truancy plan. The intake officer may proceed informally only if the juvenile has not previously been proceeded against informally or adjudicated in need of supervision for failure to comply with compulsory school attendance as provided in § 22.1-254. The juvenile and his parent or parents, guardian or other person standing in loco parentis must agree, in writing, for the development of a truancy plan. The truancy plan may include requirements that the juvenile and his parent or parents, guardian or other person standing in loco parentis participate in such programs, cooperate in such treatment or be subject to such conditions and limitations as necessary to ensure the juvenile's compliance with compulsory school attendance as provided in § 22.1-254. The intake officer may refer the juvenile to the appropriate public agency for the purpose of developing a truancy plan using an interagency interdisciplinary team approach. The team may include qualified personnel who are reasonably available from the appropriate department of social services, community services board, local school division, court service unit and other appropriate and available public and private agencies and may be the family assessment and planning team established pursuant to § 2.2-5207. If at the end of the 90-day period the juvenile has not successfully completed the truancy plan or the truancy program, then the intake officer shall file the petition.

Whenever informal action is taken as provided in this subsection on a complaint alleging that a child is in need of services, in need of supervision or delinquent, the intake officer shall (i) develop a plan for the juvenile, which may include restitution and the performance of community service, based upon community resources and the circumstances which resulted in the complaint, (ii) create an official record of the action taken by the intake officer and file such record in the juvenile's case file, and (iii) advise the juvenile and the juvenile's parent, guardian or other person standing in loco parentis and the complainant that any subsequent complaint alleging that the child is in need of supervision or delinquent based upon facts which may be sufficient to invoke the jurisdiction of the court pursuant to § 16.1-241 will result in the filing of a petition with the court.

C. The intake officer shall accept and file a petition in which it is alleged that (i) the custody, visitation or support of a child is the subject of controversy or requires determination, (ii) a person has deserted, abandoned or failed to provide support for any person in violation of law, (iii) a child or such child's parent, guardian, legal custodian or other person standing in loco parentis is entitled to treatment, rehabilitation or other services which are required by law, (iv) family abuse has occurred and a protective order is being sought pursuant to § 16.1-253.1, 16.1-253.4, or 16.1-279.1, or (v) an act of violence, force, or threat has occurred, a protective order is being sought pursuant to § 19.2-152.8, 19.2-152.9, or 19.2-152.10, and either the alleged victim or the respondent is a juvenile. If any such complainant does not file a petition, the intake officer may file it. In cases in which a child is alleged to be abused, neglected, in need of services, in need of supervision or delinquent, if the intake officer believes that probable cause does not exist, or that the authorization of a petition will not be in the best interest of the family or juvenile or that the matter may be effectively dealt with by some agency other than the court, he may refuse to authorize the filing of a petition. The intake officer shall provide to a person seeking a protective order pursuant to § 16.1-253.1, 16.1-253.4, or 16.1-279.1 a written explanation of the conditions, procedures and time limits applicable to the issuance of protective orders pursuant to § 16.1-253.1, 16.1-253.4, or 16.1-279.1.

If the person is seeking a protective order pursuant to § 19.2-152.8, 19.2-152.9, or 19.2-152.10, the intake officer shall provide a written explanation of the conditions, procedures, and time limits applicable to the issuance of protective orders pursuant to § 19.2-152.8, 19.2-152.9, or 19.2-152.10.

D. Prior to the filing of any petition alleging that a child is in need of supervision, the matter shall be reviewed by an intake officer who shall determine whether the petitioner and the child alleged to be in need of supervision have utilized or attempted to utilize treatment and services available in the community and have exhausted all appropriate nonjudicial remedies which are available to them. When the intake officer determines that the parties have not attempted to utilize available treatment or services or have not exhausted all appropriate nonjudicial remedies which are available, he shall refer the petitioner and the child alleged to be in need of supervision to the appropriate agency, treatment facility or individual to receive treatment or services, and a petition shall not be filed. Only after the intake officer determines that the parties have made a reasonable effort to utilize available community treatment or services may he permit the petition to be filed.

E. If the intake officer refuses to authorize a petition relating to an offense that if committed by an adult would be punishable as a Class 1 misdemeanor or as a felony, the complainant shall be notified in writing at that time of the complainant's right to apply to a magistrate for a warrant. If a magistrate determines that probable cause exists, he shall issue a warrant returnable to the juvenile and domestic relations district court. The warrant shall be delivered forthwith to the juvenile court, and the intake officer shall accept and file a petition founded upon the warrant. If the court is closed and the magistrate finds that the criteria for detention or shelter care set forth in § 16.1-248.1 have been satisfied, the juvenile may be detained pursuant to the warrant issued in accordance with this subsection. If the intake officer refuses to authorize a petition relating to a child in need of services or in need of supervision, a status offense, or a misdemeanor other than Class 1, his decision is final.

Upon delivery to the juvenile court of a warrant issued pursuant to subdivision 2 of § 16.1-256, the intake officer shall accept and file a petition founded upon the warrant.

F. The intake officer shall notify the attorney for the Commonwealth of the filing of any petition which alleges facts of an offense which would be a felony if committed by an adult.

G. Notwithstanding the provisions of Article 12 (§ 16.1-299 et seq.), the intake officer shall file a report with the division superintendent of the school division in which any student who is the subject of a petition alleging that such student who is a juvenile has committed an act, wherever committed, which would be a crime if committed by an adult, or that such student who is an adult has committed a crime and is alleged to be within the jurisdiction of the court. The report shall notify the division superintendent of the filing of the petition and the nature of the offense, if the violation involves:

1. A firearm offense pursuant to Article 4 (§ 18.2-279 et seq.), 5 (§ 18.2-288 et seq.), 6 (§ 18.2-299 et seq.), 6.1 (§ 18.2-307.1 et seq.), or 7 (§ 18.2-308.1 et seq.) of Chapter 7 of Title 18.2;

2. Homicide, pursuant to Article 1 (§ 18.2-30 et seq.) of Chapter 4 of Title 18.2;

3. Felonious assault and bodily wounding, pursuant to Article 4 (§ 18.2-51 et seq.) of Chapter 4 of Title 18.2;

4. Criminal sexual assault, pursuant to Article 7 (§ 18.2-61 et seq.) of Chapter 4 of Title 18.2;

5. Manufacture, sale, gift, distribution or possession of Schedule I or II controlled substances, pursuant to Article 1 (§ 18.2-247 et seq.) of Chapter 7 of Title 18.2;

6. Manufacture, sale or distribution of marijuana or synthetic cannabinoids pursuant to Article 1 (§ 18.2-247 et seq.) of Chapter 7 of Title 18.2;

7. Arson and related crimes, pursuant to Article 1 (§ 18.2-77 et seq.) of Chapter 5 of Title 18.2;

8. Burglary and related offenses, pursuant to §§ 18.2-89 through 18.2-93;

9. Robbery pursuant to § 18.2-58;

10. Prohibited criminal street gang activity pursuant to § 18.2-46.2;

11. Recruitment of other juveniles for a criminal street gang activity pursuant to § 18.2-46.3; or

12. An act of violence by a mob pursuant to § 18.2-42.1.

The failure to provide information regarding the school in which the student who is the subject of the petition may be enrolled shall not be grounds for refusing to file a petition.

The information provided to a division superintendent pursuant to this section may be disclosed only as provided in § 16.1-305.2.

H. The filing of a petition shall not be necessary:

1. In the case of violations of the traffic laws, including offenses involving bicycles, hitchhiking and other pedestrian offenses, game and fish laws or a violation of the ordinance of any city regulating surfing or any ordinance establishing curfew violations, animal control violations or littering violations. In such cases the court may proceed on a summons issued by the officer investigating the violation in the same manner as provided by law for adults. Additionally, an officer investigating a motor vehicle accident may, at the scene of the accident or at any other location where a juvenile who is involved in such an accident may be located, proceed on a summons in lieu of filing a petition.

2. In the case of seeking consent to apply for the issuance of a work permit pursuant to subsection H of § 16.1-241.

3. In the case of a misdemeanor violation of § 18.2-250.1, 18.2-266, 18.2-266.1, or 29.1-738, or

the commission of any other alcohol-related offense, provided the juvenile is released to the custody of a parent or legal guardian pending the initial court date. The officer releasing a juvenile to the custody of a parent or legal guardian shall issue a summons to the juvenile and shall also issue a summons requiring the parent or legal guardian to appear before the court with the juvenile. Disposition of the charge shall be in the manner provided in § 16.1-278.8, 16.1-278.8:01, or 16.1-278.9. If the juvenile so charged with a violation of § 18.2-51.4, 18.2-266, 18.2-266.1, 18.2-272, or 29.1-738 refuses to provide a sample of blood or breath or samples of both blood and breath for chemical analysis pursuant to §§ 18.2-268.1 through 18.2-268.12 or 29.1-738.2, the provisions of these sections shall be followed except that the magistrate shall authorize execution of the warrant as a summons. The summons shall be served on a parent or legal guardian and the juvenile, and a copy of the summons shall be forwarded to the court in which the violation is to be tried. When a violation of § 18.2-250.1 is charged by summons, the juvenile shall be entitled to have the charge referred to intake for consideration of informal proceedings pursuant to subsection B, provided such right is exercised by written notification to the clerk not later than 10 days prior to trial. At the time such summons alleging a violation of § 18.2-250.1 is served, the officer shall also serve upon the juvenile written notice of the right to have the charge referred to intake on a form approved by the Supreme Court and make return of such service to the court. If the officer fails to make such service or return, the court shall dismiss the summons without prejudice.

4. In the case of offenses which, if committed by an adult, would be punishable as a Class 3 or Class 4 misdemeanor. In such cases the court may direct that an intake officer proceed as provided in § 16.1-237 on a summons issued by the officer investigating the violation in the same manner as provided by law for adults provided that notice of the summons to appear is mailed by the investigating officer within five days of the issuance of the summons to a parent or legal guardian of the juvenile.

I. Failure to comply with the procedures set forth in this section shall not divest the juvenile court of the jurisdiction granted it in § 16.1-241.

History.
Code 1950, § 16.1-164; 1956, c. 555; 1972, cc. 672, 835; 1973, c. 440; 1977, c. 559; 1979, c. 701; 1982, c. 91; 1983, c. 349; 1985, c. 488; 1986, c. 381; 1987, cc. 203, 632; 1988, cc. 792, 803; 1990, c. 742; 1991, cc. 496, 511, 534; 1992, cc. 502, 527, 542; 1993, c. 981; 1995, cc. 347, 429; 1996, cc. 755, 914; 1997, c. 862; 1999, cc. 54, 526, 952; 2002, c. 747; 2003, c. 587; 2004, cc. 105, 255, 309, 416, 517, 558; 2006, c. 677; 2008, cc. 136, 845; 2009, cc. 385, 726; 2010, c. 742; 2011, cc. 384, 410, 825; 2012, c. 637; 2013, c. 746.

Cross references.
As to the provision of court services and replacement intake officers, see § 16.1-235.1. As to punishment for Class 3 and Class 4 misdemeanors, see § 18.2-11.

Editor's note.
Acts 1993, c. 929, cl. 3, as amended by Acts 1994, c. 564, cl. 1, and Acts 1996, c. 616, cl. 3, provides that the amendment to this section

by Acts 1993, c. 929, cl. 1, shall become effective June 1, 1998, "only if state funds are provided by the General Assembly sufficient to provide adequate resources, including all local costs, for the court to carry out the purposes of this act and to fulfill its mission to serve children and families of the Commonwealth." The funding was not provided.

Acts 2008, cc. 136 and 845, cl. 2, provides: "That the provisions of this act amending subsection A of § 16.1-260 and the provisions of this act amending § 54.1-3900 are declarative of existing law."

Acts 2011, cc. 384 and 410, cl. 3 provides: "That the provisions of this act may result in a net increase in periods of imprisonment or commitment. Pursuant to § 30-19.1:4, the estimated amount of the necessary appropriation cannot be determined for periods of imprisonment in state adult correctional facilities; therefore, Chapter 874 of the Acts of Assembly of 2010 requires the Virginia Criminal Sentencing Commission to assign a minimum fiscal impact of $50,000. Pursuant to § 30-19.1:4, the estimated amount of the necessary appropriation cannot be determined for periods of commitment to the custody of the Department of Juvenile Justice."

Acts 2013, c. 746, cl. 2 provides: "That the provisions of this act are declaratory of existing law."

The 2009 amendments.

The 2009 amendment by c. 385, in subsection G, deleted former subdivision G 10, which read: "Prohibited street gang participation pursuant to § 18.2-46.2" and redesignated former subdivisions G 11 through G 13 as subdivisions G 10 and G 12; and substituted "An act of violence by a mob pursuant to § 18.2-42.1" for "Recruitment of juveniles for criminal street gang pursuant to § 18.2-46.3" in subdivision G 12.

The 2009 amendment by c. 726 added "for an offense that would be a felony if committed by an adult" at the end of the third paragraph of subsection B.

The 2010 amendments.

The 2010 amendment by c. 742 inserted "or that such student who is an adult has committed a crime and is alleged to be within the jurisdiction of the court" in the first sentence of subsection G; and substituted "student" for "juvenile" in the next-to-last paragraph of subsection G.

The 2011 amendments.

The 2011 amendments by cc. 384 and 410, effective March 23, 2011, are identical, and inserted "or synthetic cannabinoids" in subdivision G 6.

The 2011 amendment by c. 825, in subdivision H 3, in the first sentence, inserted "misdemeanor," "18.2-250.1," and "18.2-266.1," in the third sentence, inserted "16.1-278.8:01," and added the last two sentences.

The 2012 amendments.

The 2012 amendment by c. 637, in subsection C, inserted clause (v) of the first sentence and added the last sentence, and made related and minor stylistic changes.

The 2013 amendments.

The 2013 amendment by c. 746 substituted "6 (§ 18.2-299 et seq.), 6.1 (§ 18.2-307.1 et seq.), or 7 (§ 18.2-308.1 et seq.)" for "6 (§ 18.2-299 et seq.), or 7 (§ 18.2-308 et seq.)" in subdivision G 1.

Law Review.

For comment, "Jury Trials for Juvenile Delinquents in Virginia," see 28 Wash. & Lee L. Rev. 135 (1971). For survey on legal issues involving children in Virginia for 1989, see 23 U. Rich. L. Rev. 705 (1989). For article, "Legal Issues Involving Children," see 26 U. Rich. L. Rev. 797 (1992). For an article, "Legal Issues Involving Children," see 32 U. Rich. L. Rev. 1345 (1998). For 2006 survey article, "Family and Juvenile Law," see 41 U. Rich. L. Rev. 151 (2006). For annual survey, "A Look Back and Forward: Legislative and Regulatory Highlights for 2008 and 2009 and a Discussion of Juvenile Transfer," see 44 U. Rich. L. Rev. 53 (2009). For annual survey article, "Civil Practice and Procedure," see 44 U. Rich. L. Rev. 269 (2009).

Michie's Jurisprudence.

For related discussion, see 9B M.J. Infants, § 84; 14A M.J. Parent and Child, § 1.

CASE NOTES

This section, in pertinent part, requires filing of petition to invoke jurisdiction of juvenile court and subsection F of this section does not waive the requirement of the filing of a petition but, rather, addresses the duties of the intake officer and the actions taken in regard to the petition. Rader v. Montgomery County Dep't of Social Servs., 5 Va. App. 523, 365 S.E.2d 234 (1988).

Separation of powers. — Because juvenile intake officers exercise only a limited judicial function, and the juvenile and domestic relations district court retains actual control over the juveniles, the intake officer's authority to issue criminal petitions does not violate the separation of powers guaranteed by the Virginia Constitution. Roach v. Commonwealth, 251 Va. 324, 468 S.E.2d 98, cert. denied, 519 U.S. 951, 117 S. Ct. 365, 136 L. Ed. 2d 256 (1996), overruled in part on other grounds by Morrisette v. Warden of the Sussex I State Prison, 270 Va. 188, 613 S.E.2d 551 (2005).

Procedural defects do not divest juvenile court of jurisdiction. — Juvenile and domestic relations district court acted on a petition of the guardian ad litem, and therefore exercised jurisdiction over residential placement proceedings notwithstanding any latent procedural defect. Comprehensive Servs. Act Office v. J.M., No. 1620-98-2 (Ct. of Appeals Aug. 3, 1999).

Applied in Tross v. Commonwealth, 21 Va. App. 362, 464 S.E.2d 523 (1995); Burke v. Commonwealth, 29 Va. App. 183, 510 S.E.2d 743 (1999).

CIRCUIT COURT OPINIONS

Right to counsel. — There is no Virginia case deciding whether a petition obtained pursuant to § 16.1-260 charging a juvenile with a delinquent act is the equivalent of an indictment for the purposes of determining whether the Sixth Amendment right to counsel has attached. Commonwealth v. Malvo, 63 Va. Cir. 22, 2003 Va. Cir. LEXIS 188 (Fairfax County 2003).

OPINIONS OF THE ATTORNEY GENERAL

Petition by unemancipated minors for protective orders. — A minor may seek an emergency protective order in certain situations, but a minor who has not been emancipated, however mature that individual may be, can seek a protective order only through a next friend. See opinion of Attorney General to The Honorable Charniele L. Herring, Member, House of Delegates, 10-116, 2011 Va. AG LEXIS 2 (01/21/11).

Petition by emancipated minors for protective orders. — Emancipated minor may file petitions for protective orders under applicable statutes. See opinion of Attorney General to The Honorable Charniele L. Herring, Member, House of Delegates, 10-116, 2011 Va. AG LEXIS 2 (01/21/11).

§ 16.1-261. Statements made at intake or mental health screening and assessment.

Statements made by a child to the intake officer or probation officer during the intake process or during a mental health screening or assessment conducted pursuant to § 16.1-248.2 and prior to a hearing on the merits of the petition filed against the child, shall not be admissible at any stage of the proceedings.

History.

1977, c. 559; 1996, cc. 755, 914.

Law Review.

For 1991 survey on legal issues involving children, see 25 U. Rich. L. Rev. 773 (1991).

§ 16.1-262. Form and content of petition.

The petition shall contain the facts below indicated:

"Commonwealth of Virginia, In re ...." a
(name of child)
child under eighteen years of age.

"In the Juvenile and Domestic Relations District Court of the county (or city) of ...."

1. Statement of name, age, date of birth, if known, and residence of the child.

2. Statement of names and residence of his parents, guardian, legal custodian or other person standing in loco parentis and spouse, if any.

3. Statement of names and residence of the nearest known relatives if no parent or guardian can be found.

4. Statement of the specific facts which allegedly bring the child within the purview of this law. If the petition alleges a delinquent act, it shall make reference to the applicable sections of the Code which designate the act a crime.

5. Statement as to whether the child is in custody, and if so, the place of detention or shelter care, and the time the child was taken into custody, and the time the child was placed in detention or shelter care.

If any of the facts herein required to be stated are not known by the petitioner, the petition shall so state. The petition shall be verified, except that petitions filed under § 63.2-1237 may be signed by the petitioner's counsel, and may be upon information.

In accordance with § 16.1-69.32, the Supreme Court may formulate rules for the form and content of petitions in the juvenile court concerning matters related to the custody, visitation or support of a child and the protection, support or maintenance of an adult where the provisions of this section are not appropriate.

History.
Code 1950, § 16.1-165; 1956, c. 555; 1977, c. 559; 1979, c. 615; 1984, c. 631; 1995, cc. 772, 826; 2000, c. 830.

Editor's note.
Acts 1993, c. 929, cl. 3, as amended by Acts 1994, c. 564, cl. 1, and Acts 1996, cl. 3, provides that the amendment to this section by Acts 1993, c. 929, cl. 1, shall become effective June 1, 1998, "only if state funds are provided by the General Assembly sufficient to provide adequate resources, including all local costs, for the court to carry out the purposes of this act and to fulfill its mission to serve children and families of the Commonwealth." The funding was not provided.

§ 16.1-263. Summonses.

A. After a petition has been filed, the court shall direct the issuance of summonses, one directed to the juvenile, if the juvenile is twelve or more years of age, and another to at least one parent, guardian, legal custodian or other person standing in loco parentis, and such other persons as appear to the court to be proper or necessary parties to the proceedings. The summons shall require them to appear personally before the court at the time fixed to answer or testify as to the allegations of the petition. Where the custodian is summoned and such person is not a parent of the juvenile in question, a parent shall also be served with a summons. The court may direct that other proper or necessary parties to the proceedings be notified of the pendency of the case, the charge and the time and place for the hearing.

Any such summons shall be deemed a mandate of the court, and willful failure to obey its requirements shall subject any person guilty thereof to liability for punishment for contempt. Upon the failure of any person to appear as ordered in the summons, the court shall immediately issue an order for such person to show cause why he should not be held in contempt.

B. The summons shall advise the parties of their right to counsel as provided in § 16.1-266. A copy of the petition shall accompany each summons for the initial proceedings. The summons shall include notice that in the event that the juvenile is committed to the Department or to a secure local facility, at least one parent or other person legally obligated to care for and support the juvenile may be required to pay a reasonable sum for support and treatment of the juvenile pursuant to § 16.1-290. Notice of subsequent proceedings shall be provided to all parties in interest. In all cases where a party is represented by counsel and counsel has been provided with a copy of the petition and due notice as to time, date and place of the hearing, such action shall be deemed due notice to such party, unless such counsel has notified the court that he no longer represents such party.

C. The judge may endorse upon the summons an order directing a parent or parents, guardian or other custodian having the custody or control of the juvenile to bring the juvenile to the hearing.

D. A party, other than the juvenile, may waive service of summons by written stipulation or by voluntary appearance at the hearing.

E. No such summons or notification shall be required if the judge shall certify on the record that (i) the identity of a parent or guardian is not reasonably ascertainable or (ii) in cases in which it is alleged that a juvenile has committed a delinquent act, crime, status offense or traffic infraction or is in need of services or supervision, the location, or in the case of a parent or guardian located outside of the Commonwealth the location or mailing address, of a parent or guardian is not reasonably ascertainable. An affidavit of the mother that the identity of the father is not reasonably ascertainable shall be sufficient evidence of this fact, provided there is no other evidence before the court which would refute such an affidavit. In cases referred to in clause (ii), an affidavit of a law-enforcement officer or juvenile probation officer that the location of a parent or guardian is not reasonably ascertainable shall be sufficient evidence of this fact, provided that there is no other evidence before the court which would refute the affidavit.

History.
Code 1950, §§ 16.1-166, 16.1-172; 1956, c. 555; 1974, c. 620; 1975, c. 128; 1977, c. 559; 1978, cc. 613, 740; 1996, cc. 755, 914; 1997, c. 441; 1999, c. 952; 2004, c. 573.

Editor's note.
Acts 1993, c. 929, cl. 3, as amended by Acts 1994, c. 564, cl. 1, and Acts 1996, c. 616, cl. 3, provides that the amendment to this section by Acts 1993, c. 929, cl. 1, shall become effective June 1, 1998, "only if state funds are provided by the General Assembly sufficient to provide adequate resources, including all local costs, for the court to carry out the purposes of this act and to fulfill its mission to serve children and families of the Commonwealth." The funding was not provided.

Law Review.
For an article, "Legal Issues Involving Children," see 32 U. Rich. L. Rev. 1345 (1998). For 2000 survey of Virginia law regarding children, see 34 U. Rich. L. Rev. 939 (2000). For 2000 survey of Virginia criminal law and procedure, see 34 U. Rich. L. Rev. 749 (2000). For article, "Legal Issues Involving Children," see 35 U. Rich. L. Rev. 741 (2001).

Michie's Jurisprudence.
For related discussion, see 9B M.J. Infants, §§ 82, 84, 85; 14A M.J. Parent and Child, § 19.

CASE NOTES

Claim that § 16.1-263 was unconstitutionally vague was without sufficient substance to warrant the convening of a three-judge court. McGhee v. Moyer, 60 F.R.D. 578 (W.D. Va. 1973).

Proceedings jurisdictional. — The proceedings in the juvenile court are jurisdictional rather than procedural. Evans v. Cox, 327 F. Supp. 1057 (E.D. Va. 1971).

This section establishes procedures only for the juvenile court and has no application once the case has been certified to the court of record. Ferguson v. Slayton, 340 F. Supp. 276 (W.D. Va. 1972).

And such procedures are mandatory. — The statutes relating to the procedure applicable to proceedings for cases tried in a juvenile court are mandatory and must be followed. Evans v. Cox, 327 F. Supp. 1057 (E.D. Va. 1971).

Failure of the juvenile court to comply with the statutory provisions of procedure will render the certification to a court of record void. Evans v. Cox, 327 F. Supp. 1057 (E.D. Va. 1971); Ferguson v. Slayton, 340 F. Supp. 276 (W.D. Va. 1972).

Identity of parent and guardian was required to be addressed on record. — Where the mother's testimony failed to suggest even a clue as to the father's identity, his whereabouts, or that a reasonable inquiry or search would successfully identify and locate him, the identity of the father was "not reasonably ascertainable." Unknown Father of Baby Girl Janet v. Division of Social Servs., 15 Va. App. 110, 422 S.E.2d 407 (1992).

Juvenile court's failure to properly issue summons made transfer of jurisdiction ineffectual. — Where juvenile court had address of defendant's mother but issued a summons to a different jurisdiction and later issued another summons at a time which made mother's timely arrival at transfer hearing impossible, transfer of jurisdiction over defendant from juvenile to circuit court was ineffectual and subsequent convictions were void. Williams v. Commonwealth, 26 Va. App. 776, 497 S.E.2d 156 (1998).

Father held not entitled to notice where divested of parental rights. — Defendant's biological father was not his parent within the meaning of subsection A of this section as it read at the time of transfer proceedings and was not entitled to notice under this section, because an earlier final adoption order divested the defendant's biological parents of all legal rights with respect to him. Thomas v. Garraghty, 258 Va. 530, 522 S.E.2d 865 (1999).

Failure to serve father required reversal of conviction. —

Without either a certification on the record that the identity of a juvenile's father was not reasonably ascertainable or proof of service of a summons on the father by publication, the provisions of this section requiring service of process on the parents of a juvenile have not been met and noncompliance with these requirements necessitated reversal of the juvenile's conviction. Baker v. Commonwealth, 28 Va. App. 306, 504 S.E.2d 394 (1998), aff'd, 258 Va. 1, 516 S.E.2d 219 (1999) (superseded by statute as stated in Smith v. Commonwealth, 38 Va. App. 840, 568 S.E.2d 462 (2002)) See note below .

Service of summons to both parents not required. — Trial court had subject matter jurisdiction over juvenile even though father was not notified of criminal proceedings, pursuant to subsection E of § 16.1-263, which allowed the trial court to rely upon an affidavit of the mother that the identity of the father was not reasonably ascertainable, and did not require that both parents be served with a summons. Smith v. Commonwealth, 38 Va. App. 840, 568 S.E.2d 462, 2002 Va. App. LEXIS 526 (2002).

Verbal notice to grandmother of illegitimate son of deceased mother and unknown father. — See Cradle v. Peyton, 208 Va. 243, 156 S.E.2d 874 (1967), cert. denied, 392 U.S. 945, 88 S. Ct. 2296, 20 L. Ed. 2d 1407 (1968).

Waiver of parental notice. — Subsection D of this section, as it read at the time, referred only to the initial summons to be served on parties in interest and did not prescribe a method of notice for subsequent proceedings. Roach v. Director, Dep't of Cors., 258 Va. 537, 522 S.E.2d 869 (1999).

Under subsection E of § 16.1-269.1, any objection based on an alleged failure to give notice to a juvenile's parent of a preliminary hearing, as required by this section, is waived if such objection is not made before an indictment is returned in circuit court if the offense was committed on or after July 1, 1996. Carter v. Commonwealth, 31 Va. App. 393, 523 S.E.2d 544 (2000).

Any defect in the manner of notice to juvenile defendant's father was cured by the father's appearances at the hearings, denoted in the court records, and the absence of any objection at the hearing to the adequacy of that notice. Howerton v. Commonwealth, 36 Va. App. 205, 548 S.E.2d 914, 2001 Va. App. LEXIS 425 (2001).

Actual notice to parent of hearing satisfies statutory requirements. — Where a defendant's mother had actual notice of the hearing in circuit court in which the defendant challenged the transfer of his case to such court, this notice satisfied any statutory notice requirements of subsection B of this section. Shackleford v. Commonwealth, 262 Va. 196, 547 S.E.2d 899, 2001 Va. LEXIS 78 (2001).

Effect of actual notice. — Where a parent has actual notice of a transfer hearing, any departure from the statutory requirement of written notice is a procedural, rather than a jurisdictional, defect that may be cured or waived by the appearance of the parties and a failure to object to the adequacy of the notice. Roach v. Director, Dep't of Cors., 258 Va. 537, 522 S.E.2d 869 (1999).

Notice of subsequent proceedings. — Failure to notify juvenile's mother of his appeal from transfer hearing did not constitute error, where she received notice of original proceedings, she had opportunity, following juvenile's appeal, to appear and be involved in subsequent proceedings, including de novo hearings in circuit court. Shackleford v. Commonwealth, No. 2883-98-3 (Ct. of Appeals Mar. 28, 2000).

Certification proceedings. — Juvenile defendant had no right to have a parent notified of the pendency of certification proceedings in juvenile court. Angel v. Commonwealth, 2009 Va. App. LEXIS 125 (Mar. 24, 2009).

Custody inured to mother where court order relieved agency of custody. — Where the defendant's mother had been deprived of his custody in 1960, but a department of public welfare (now department of social services), which had obtained custody from the mother in 1960, had been relieved of his custody by court order in 1967, and no other person or agency was granted custody over the defendant, custody inured to the mother, and at the hearing four months after the order, the defendant's mother was a proper person under this section. Muse v. Slayton, 333 F. Supp. 1007 (W.D. Va. 1971).

Failure to serve biological parents cured by indictment in circuit court. — Juvenile's indictment in circuit court cured alleged defects in service of summonses. Souksengmany v. Commonwealth, No. 1641-99-4 (Ct. of Appeals Apr. 4, 2000) (decided under prior version of § 16.1-263).

Any error from Commonwealth's failure to notify juvenile's biological parents of juvenile court proceedings was cured when grand jury returned indictments on offenses certified to it by juvenile court. Gilbert v. Commonwealth, No. 1515-99-1 (Ct. of Appeals Mar. 28, 2000) (decided under prior version of § 16.1-263).

Indictment by grand jury cures any defect or error, except one regarding defendant's age, which occurred in juvenile and domestic relations district court proceeding, including Commonwealth's failure to comply with statutory notice requirements. Nelson v. Commonwealth, No. 0283-99-1 (Ct. of Appeals Apr. 4, 2000) (decided under prior version of § 16.1-263).

Because juvenile failed to raise jurisdictional issue of lack of notice to his father before indictments were returned in circuit court, failure to comply with parental notification provisions did not deprive circuit court of jurisdiction. Shackleford v. Commonwealth, No. 2883-98-3 (Ct. of Appeals Mar. 28, 2000) (decided under prior version of § 16.1-263).

Applied in Spain v. Commonwealth, 35 Va. App. 431, 545 S.E.2d 583, 2001 Va. App. LEXIS 242 (2001).

CIRCUIT COURT OPINIONS

The primary purpose behind the requirements of notice to a child's parents in the initiation of proceedings involving a juvenile is to protect the juvenile from the critically important decision of trying the juvenile as an adult. Commonwealth v. Carter, 54 Va. Cir. 230, 2000 Va. Cir. LEXIS 583 (Norfolk 2000).

Notice requirements must be met. — The notice requirements of subsection E, requiring notice of juvenile proceedings to a child's parent, are jurisdictional rather than procedural and, more specifically, bear directly on whether a court has subject matter jurisdiction to hear a particular case, and failure to strictly adhere to the notice procedures results in the denial of a juvenile defendant's substantial right and constitutional guarantee of due process. Commonwealth v. Carter, 54 Va. Cir. 230, 2000 Va. Cir. LEXIS 583 (Norfolk 2000).

Where father of defendant, a juvenile, was not notified of the juvenile or transfer proceedings that were initiated against defendant as required by former § 16.1-263, the juvenile court never acquired jurisdiction over the case and the subsequent transfer to the circuit court for trial as an adult was void, as were the convictions rendered in the circuit court against defendant. Sampson v. Commonwealth, 56 Va. Cir. 287, 2001 Va. Cir. LEXIS 460 (Norfolk 2001).

And are not waivable. — The failure of a juvenile court to comply with statutory requirements of procedure, such as the notice requirements of this section, renders a certification to another court void, and any subsequent conviction in that court also void, and, since the notice requirement is considered to be jurisdictional, and particularly subject matter jurisdiction, it is not waivable despite the existence of waiver provisions. Commonwealth v. Carter, 54 Va. Cir. 230, 2000 Va. Cir. LEXIS 583 (Norfolk 2000).

Notice not required. — Notice to juvenile's father of the initiation of juvenile proceedings was not required where the father had had no involvement in the juvenile's life since birth and the mother, who was notified, had been awarded full custody of the juvenile. Commonwealth v. Carter, 54 Va. Cir. 230, 2000 Va. Cir. LEXIS 583 (Norfolk 2000).

Waiver of parental notice. — A juvenile's motion to vacate his convictions was denied. Because both the juvenile's parents appeared at an initial appearance and a certification hearing, an alleged failure by the State to properly notify both parents as required by §§ 16.1-263 and 16.1-264 was waived pursuant to § 16.1-263 D. Commonwealth v. Haskins, 56 Va. Cir. 373, 2001 Va. Cir. LEXIS 474 (Norfolk 2001).

§ 16.1-264. Service of summons; proof of service; penalty.

A. If a party designated in subsection A of § 16.1-263 to be served with a summons can be found within the Commonwealth, the summons shall be served upon him in person or by substituted service as prescribed in subdivision 2 of § 8.01-296.

If a party designated to be served in § 16.1-263 is without the Commonwealth but can be found or his address is known, or can with reasonable diligence be ascertained, service of summons may be made either by delivering a copy thereof to him personally or by mailing a copy thereof to him by certified mail return receipt requested.

If after reasonable effort a party other than the person who is the subject of the petition cannot be found or his post-office address cannot be ascertained, whether he is within or without the Commonwealth, the court may order service of the summons upon him by publication in accordance with the provisions of §§ 8.01-316 and 8.01-317.

A1. Any person who is subject to an emergency protective order issued pursuant to § 16.1-253.4 or 19.2-152.8 shall have been personally served with the protective order if a law-enforcement officer, as defined in § 9.1-101, personally provides to such person a notification of the issuance of the order, which shall be on a form approved by the Executive Secretary of the Supreme Court of Virginia, provided that all of the information and individual requirements of the order are included on the form. The officer making service shall enter or cause to be entered the date and time of service and other appropriate information required by the Department of State Police into the Virginia Criminal Information Network and make due return to the court.

B. Service of summons may be made under the direction of the court by sheriffs, their deputies and police officers in counties and cities or by any other suitable person designated by the court. However, in any case in which custody or visitation of a minor child or children is at issue and a summons is issued for the attendance and testimony of a teacher or other school personnel who is not a party to the proceeding, if such summons is served on school property, it shall be served only by a sheriff or his deputy.

C. Proof of service may be made by the affidavit of the person other than an officer designated in subsection B hereof who delivers a copy of the summons to the person summoned, but if served by a state, county or municipal officer his return shall be sufficient without oath.

D. The summons shall be considered a mandate of the court and willful failure to obey its requirements shall subject any person guilty thereof to liability for punishment as for contempt.

History.
Code 1950, §§ 16.1-167 to 16.1-170; 1956, c. 555; 1977, c. 559; 1984, c. 594; 1987, c. 632; 1991, c. 62; 2004, c. 588; 2011, c. 482.

Cross references.
As to the Court-Appointed Special Advocate Program and notice of hearings and proceedings, see § 9.1-155.

Editor's note.
Acts 1993, c. 929, cl. 3, as amended by Acts 1994, c. 564, cl. 1, and Acts 1996, c. 616, cl. 3, provides that the amendment to this section

by Acts 1993, c. 929, cl. 1, shall become effective June 1, 1998, "only if state funds are provided by the General Assembly sufficient to provide adequate resources, including all local costs, for the court to carry out the purposes of this act and to fulfill its mission to serve children and families of the Commonwealth." The funding was not provided.

The 2011 amendments.
The 2011 amendment by c. 482 made a minor stylistic change in the first paragraph in subsection A; and added subsection A1.

Research references.
Bryson on Virginia Civil Procedure (Matthew Bender). Chapter 3 Active Jurisdiction. § 3.01 Process. W. Hamilton Bryson.

Michie's Jurisprudence.
For related discussion, see 9B M.J. Infants, § 85.

CASE NOTES

Section 8.01-288 is not applicable to the service of a summons under this section, which provides for service in juvenile cases, since it excepts process commencing actions wherein service of process is specifically prescribed by statute. Garrity v. Virginia Dep't of Social Servs. ex rel. Sinift, 11 Va. App. 39, 396 S.E.2d 150 (1990).

Since there is no provision in this section for substituted service by "posting" a summons on the front door of the person's abode, the summons in a child support case was not properly served on the defendant because a copy was not sent to him by certified mail as required by this section. Service would be invalid even if it was shown that a copy of the summons was posted on the front door of his residence and a copy of the pleading was mailed to him less than 10 days prior to entry of the default judgment. Garrity v. Virginia Dep't of Social Servs. ex rel. Sinift, 11 Va. App. 39, 396 S.E.2d 150 (1990).

Waiver of objection based on failure to notify parent. — The legislature has provided in subsection E of § 16.1-269.1 that, as to offenses committed on or after July 1, 1996, once an indictment has been returned in the circuit court, any failure to comply with the parental notification provisions of § 16.1-263 and this section does not deprive the court of subject matter jurisdiction. Carter v. Commonwealth, 31 Va. App. 393, 523 S.E.2d 544 (2000).

Applied in Spain v. Commonwealth, 35 Va. App. 431, 545 S.E.2d 583, 2001 Va. App. LEXIS 242 (2001).

CIRCUIT COURT OPINIONS

Waiver of parental notice. — A juvenile's motion to vacate his convictions was denied. Because both the juvenile's parents appeared at an initial appearance and a certification hearing, an alleged failure by the State to properly notify both parents as required by §§ 16.1-263 and 16.1-264 was waived pursuant to subsection D of § 16.1-263. Commonwealth v. Haskins, 56 Va. Cir. 373, 2001 Va. Cir. LEXIS 474 (Norfolk 2001).

Posted witness subpoena not a substitute for service of process. — Because a posted witness subpoena was not a substitute for service of process in a juvenile court procedure pursuant to subsection A of § 16.1-264, and a summons was returned "not found," a father did not have adequate actual notice of a child support hearing. Hankins v. Hankins, 60 Va. Cir. 449, 2003 Va. Cir. LEXIS 2 (Spotsylvania County 2003).

§ 16.1-265. Subpoena; attorney-issued subpoena.

Upon application of a party and pursuant to the rules of the Supreme Court of Virginia for the issuance of subpoenas, the clerk of the court shall issue, and the court on its own motion may issue, subpoenas requiring attendance and testimony of witnesses and production of records, documents or other tangible objects at any hearing.

Subpoenas duces tecum for medical records shall be subject to the provisions of §§ 8.01-413 and 32.1-127.1:03 except that no separate fee shall be imposed. A subpoena may also be issued in a civil proceeding by an attorney-at-law who is an active member of the Virginia State Bar at the time of issuance, as an officer of the court. Any such subpoena shall be on a form approved by the Committee on District Courts, signed by the attorney as if a pleading and shall include the attorney's address. A copy, together with the attorney's certificate of service pursuant to Rule 1:12, shall be mailed or delivered to the clerk's office of the court in which the case is pending on the day of issuance by the attorney. The law governing subpoenas issued by a clerk shall apply mutatis mutandis, except that attorneys may not issue subpoenas in those cases in which they may not issue a summons as provided in § 8.01-407. When an attorney-at-law transmits one or more subpoenas or subpoenas duces tecum to a sheriff to be served in his jurisdiction, the provisions in § 8.01-407 regarding such transmittals shall apply. A sheriff shall not be required to serve an attorney-issued subpoena that is not issued at least five business days prior to the date production of evidence is required.

If the time for compliance with a subpoena issued by an attorney is less than 14 days after service of the subpoena, the person to whom it is directed may serve upon the party issuing the subpoena a written objection setting forth any grounds therefor. If objection is made, the party on whose behalf the subpoena was issued and served shall not be entitled to compliance, except pursuant to an order of the court, but may, upon notice to the person to whom the subpoena was directed, move for an order to compel compliance. Upon such timely motion, the court may quash, modify or sustain the subpoena.

History.
1977, c. 559; 2000, c. 813; 2004, c. 335.

Editor's note.
Acts 2001, cc. 514 and 551, repealed Acts 2000, c. 813, cl. 2, which had provided: "That the provisions of this act shall expire on July 1, 2001, unless reenacted by the 2001 General Assembly. Any subpoena or subpoena duces tecum issued by an attorney in compliance with this act shall remain valid notwithstanding the expiration of this act."

Law Review.
For 2003/2004 survey of civil practice and procedure, see 39 U. Rich. L. Rev. 87 (2004).

Research references.
Friend's Virginia Pleading and Practice (Matthew Bender). Chapter 17 Subpoenas and Witnesses. § 17.05 Subpoena Duces Tecum. Charles E. Friend.
Virginia Forms (Matthew Bender). No. 2-1401 Subpoena for Witness in District Court. No. 2-1402 Subpoena for Witness (Civil)

— Attorney Issued. No. 2-1403 Checklist for Attorney-Issued Subpoena.

ARTICLE 6.

APPOINTMENT OF COUNSEL.

§ 16.1-266. Appointment of counsel and guardian ad litem.

A. Prior to the hearing by the court of any case involving a child who is alleged to be abused or neglected or who is the subject of an entrustment agreement or a petition seeking termination of residual parental rights or who is otherwise before the court pursuant to subdivision A 4 of § 16.1-241 or § 63.2-1230, the court shall appoint a discreet and competent attorney-at-law as guardian ad litem to represent the child pursuant to § 16.1-266.1.

B. Prior to the detention hearing held pursuant to § 16.1-250, the court shall appoint a qualified and competent attorney-at-law to represent the child unless an attorney has been retained and appears on behalf of the child. For the purposes of appointment of counsel for the detention hearing held pursuant to § 16.1-250 only, a child's indigence shall be presumed. Nothing in this subsection shall prohibit a judge from releasing a child from detention prior to appointment of counsel.

C. Subsequent to the detention hearing, if any, and prior to the adjudicatory or transfer hearing by the court of any case involving a child who is alleged to be in need of services, in need of supervision or delinquent, such child and his parent, guardian, legal custodian or other person standing in loco parentis shall be informed by a judge, clerk or probation officer of the child's right to counsel and of the liability of the parent, guardian, legal custodian or other person standing in loco parentis for the costs of such legal services pursuant to § 16.1-267 and be given an opportunity to:

1. Obtain and employ counsel of the child's own choice; or

2. Request that the court appoint counsel, provided that before counsel is appointed or the court continues any appointment previously made pursuant to subsection B, the court shall determine that the child is indigent within the contemplation of the law pursuant to guidelines set forth in § 19.2-159 by requiring the child's parent, guardian, legal custodian or other person standing in loco parentis to complete a statement of indigence substantially in the form provided by § 19.2-159 and a financial statement, and upon determination of indigence the court shall appoint an attorney from the list maintained by the Indigent Defense Commission pursuant to § 19.2-163.01 to represent the child; or

3. Waive the right to representation by an attorney, if the court finds the child and the parent, guardian, legal custodian or other person standing in loco parentis of the child consent, in writing, and such waiver is consistent with the interests of the child. Such written waiver shall be in accordance with law and shall be filed with the court records of the case. A child who is alleged to have committed an offense that would be a felony if committed by an adult, may waive such right only after he consults with an attorney and the court determines that his waiver is free and voluntary. The waiver shall be in writing, signed by both the child and the child's attorney and shall be filed with the court records of the case.

D. A judge, clerk or probation officer shall inform the parent or guardian of his right to counsel prior to the adjudicatory hearing of a petition in which a child is alleged to be abused or neglected or at risk of abuse or neglect as provided in subdivision A 2a of § 16.1-241 and prior to a hearing at which a parent could be subjected to the loss of residual parental rights. In addition, prior to the hearing by the court of any case involving any other adult charged with abuse or neglect of a child, this adult shall be informed of his right to counsel. This adult and the parent or guardian shall be given an opportunity to:

1. Obtain and employ counsel of the parent's, guardian's or other adult's own choice; or

2. If the court determines that the parent, guardian or other adult is indigent within the contemplation of the law pursuant to the guidelines set forth in § 19.2-159, a statement substantially in the form provided by § 19.2-159 and a financial statement shall be executed by such parent, guardian or other adult and the court shall appoint an attorney-at-law to represent him; or

3. Waive the right to representation by an attorney in accordance with the provisions of § 19.2-160.

If the identity or location of a parent or guardian is not reasonably ascertainable or a parent or guardian fails to appear, the court shall consider appointing an attorney-at-law to represent the interests of the absent parent or guardian, and the hearing may be held.

Prior to a hearing at which a child is the subject of an initial foster care plan filed pursuant to § 16.1-281, a foster care review hearing pursuant to § 16.1-282 and a permanency planning hearing pursuant to § 16.1-282.1, the court shall consider appointing counsel to represent the child's parent or guardian.

E. In those cases described in subsections A, B, C and D, which in the discretion of the court require counsel or a guardian ad litem to represent the child or children or the parent or guardian or other adult party in addition to the representation provided in those subsections, a discreet and competent attorney-at-law may be appointed by the court as counsel or a guardian ad litem.

F. In all other cases which in the discretion of the court require counsel or a guardian ad litem, or both, to represent the child or children or the parent or guardian, discreet and competent attorneys-at-law may be appointed by the court. However, in cases where the custody of a child or children is the subject of controversy or requires determination and each of the parents or other persons claiming a right to custody is represented by counsel, the court shall not appoint counsel or a guardian ad litem to represent the interests of the child or children unless the court finds, at any stage in the proceedings in a specific case, that the interests of the child or children are not otherwise adequately represented.

G.　Any state or local agency, department, authority or institution and any school, hospital, physician or other health or mental health care provider shall permit a guardian ad litem or counsel for the child appointed pursuant to this section to inspect and copy, without the consent of the child or his parents, any records relating to the child whom the guardian or counsel represents upon presentation by him of a copy of the court order appointing him or a court order specifically allowing him such access. Upon request therefor by the guardian ad litem or counsel for the child made at least 72 hours in advance, a mental health care provider shall make himself available to conduct a review and interpretation of the child's treatment records which are specifically related to the investigation. Such a request may be made in lieu of or in addition to inspection and copying of the records.

History.

Code 1950, §§ 16.1-173, 63.1-248.12; 1956, c. 555; 1966, c. 709; 1968, c. 581; 1970, c. 87; 1973, c. 440; 1974, c. 513; 1975, cc. 341, 465, 559; 1977, c. 559; 1980, c. 572; 1982, c. 451; 1984, c. 709; 1985, c. 260; 1987, c. 632; 1994, c. 36; 1997, c. 790; 2002, c. 687; 2003, c. 98; 2004, cc. 66, 437, 884, 921, 1014; 2005, c. 427.

Editor's note.

Acts 1993, c. 929, cl. 3, as amended by Acts 1994, c. 564, cl. 1, and Acts 1996, c. 616, cl. 3, provides that the amendment to this section by Acts 1993, c. 929, cl. 1, shall become effective June 1, 1998, "only if state funds are provided by the General Assembly sufficient to provide adequate resources, including all local costs, for the court to carry out the purposes of this act and to fulfill its mission to serve children and families of the Commonwealth." The funding was not provided.

Acts 2004, c. 437, cl. 3, provides: "That the Office of the Executive Secretary of the Supreme Court, in conjunction with the Commonwealth's Attorneys' Service Council, the Public Defender Commission and the Department of Juvenile Justice, shall develop written guidelines and procedures for implementing subsections B and C of § 16.1-266 as amended by this act. The Executive Secretary shall submit a report of its findings and recommendations concerning the implementation of subsections B and C of § 16.1-266 to the Chairmen of the Senate Courts of Justice and House Courts of Justice Committees by December 1, 2004."

Acts 2005, c. 427, cl. 2, provides: "That to facilitate implementation of the requirements of Chapter 437 of the 2004 Acts of Assembly, the Office of the Executive Secretary, Supreme Court of Virginia is authorized to issue payments out of the Criminal Fund for the appointment of two attorneys, appointed consecutively, when such payment is authorized by the appointing court and such consecutive appointments are necessary to provide the juvenile with representation at the detention hearing as required by subsection B of § 16.1-266, and representation subsequently, by separate counsel, pursuant to subsection C of § 16.1-266. Such dual, consecutive representation shall be deemed to satisfy the standard for relieving and replacing counsel for cause when continuing representation of the juvenile beyond the detention hearing through all stages of the proceeding would be unreasonably burdensome to the detention hearing attorney due to lack of proximity to the subsequent proceeding."

Law Review.

For survey of Virginia law on criminal procedure for the year 1972-1973, see 59 Va. L. Rev. 1478 (1973). For article, "The Revision of Virginia's Juvenile Court Law," see 13 U. Rich. L. Rev. 847 (1979). For comment on termination of parental rights, see 15 U. Rich. L. Rev. 213 (1980). For 1985 survey of Virginia law affecting children, see 19 U. Rich. L. Rev. p. 753 (1985). For survey on legal issues involving children in Virginia for 1989, see 23 U. Rich. L. Rev. 705 (1989). For an article, "Legal Issues Involving Children," see 32 U. Rich. L. Rev. 1345 (1998). For annual survey article on legal issues involving children, see 38 U. Rich. L. Rev. 161 (2003).

Research references.

Bryson on Virginia Civil Procedure (Matthew Bender). Chapter 5 Parties. § 5.02 Competency. W. Hamilton Bryson.

Soler, Bell, Jameson, Representing the Child Client (Matthew Bender).

Virginia Forms (Matthew Bender). No. 5-141 Order for Appointment of Guardian ad Litem.

Michie's Jurisprudence.

For related discussion, see 4C M.J. Constitutional Law, § 42; 5B M.J. Criminal Procedure, § 24; 9B M.J. Infants, § 84.

CASE NOTES

Legislative intent. — The General Assembly did not intend to require a circuit court to appoint a guardian ad litem whenever the court issues a subpoena to compel a juvenile's testimony or where the circuit court initiates criminal contempt proceedings against the juvenile where juvenile is represented by counsel. Wilson v. Commonwealth, 23 Va. App. 318, 477 S.E.2d 7 (1996).

Purpose. — This section is a prophylactic device designed to ensure that before a child and his parent or legal guardian waives assistance of counsel, the child understands the consequences of waiver and waiver is in the best interest of the child. Grogg v. Commonwealth, 6 Va. App. 598, 371 S.E.2d 549 (1988).

Applicability. — Trial court did not err in allowing the guardian ad litem to remain on the child custody case even after the mother appealed the decision of the juvenile and domestic relations district court awarding primary custody to the father to the trial court. The mother could not use subsection F of § 16.1-266, which the mother cited, as a sword to remove the guardian ad litem. Lewis v. Hyman, 2008 Va. App. LEXIS 281 (June 10, 2008).

Counsel not required where loss of parental rights not sought. — A trial court erred in finding that counsel for the parents was required at the time of a hearing in which entrustment agreements were signed by the children's aunt and approved by the juvenile and domestic relations court, because no petition for termination of parental rights was either filed or pending at that time and, therefore, neither parent could be subjected to the loss of residual rights and responsibilities at the time of that hearing. Fredericksburg Dep't of Social Servs. v. Brown, 33 Va. App. 313, 533 S.E.2d 12, 2000 Va. App. LEXIS 634 (2000).

Guardian ad litem fee not subject to fee limitations set forth in § 16.1-267. — The Attorney General of Virginia has opined that the fee of a guardian ad litem appointed to represent a minor child pursuant to subsection D [now subsection E] is not subject to the maximum fee limitations for court-appointed counsel set forth in § 16.1-267. Op. Va. Att'y Gen. 177 (Dec. 2, 1980); Op. Va. Att'y Gen. 153 (Oct. 27, 1986); see Patterson v. Old Dominion Trust Co., 156 Va. 763, 775, 159 S.E. 168, 172 (1931). Kaplan v. Kaplan, No. 0987-92-1 (Ct. of Appeals Sept. 14, 1993).

Inquiry as to financial ability to pay fees applies only to appointments pursuant to subsection A or B. — That statutory mandate, to inquire as to financial ability to pay guardian ad litem fees as required by § 16.1-267 A applies only to a guardian ad litem appointed pursuant to subsection A or B of this section. Where, the guardian ad litem was appointed pursuant to subsection D [now subsection E] of this section; wife's claim is without merit. Kaplan v. Kaplan, No. 0987-92-1 (Ct. of Appeals Sept. 14, 1993).

Reimbursement by parents of guardian ad litem fee. — Trial court did not abuse its discretion in ordering a mother to pay one-half of a guardian ad litem's fee, where the evidence presented demonstrated that the guardian was appointed to protect the interests of the children and favorably addressed an issue related to the mother's successful treatment for depression. Leake v. Leake, No. 3268-03-4, 2004 Va. App. LEXIS 491 (Ct. of Appeals Oct. 12, 2004).

Substantive rights and interests of child. — This section recognizes that the substantive rights and interests of the child are often separate and distinct from those of the other parties to the litigation, and that these rights and interests are best protected by an independent party. Stanley v. Fairfax County Dep't of Social Servs., 10 Va. App. 596, 395 S.E.2d 199 (1990), aff'd, Stanley v. Fairfax, 242 Va. 60, 405 S.E.2d 621 (1991).

The preliminary hearing is a "critical stage" of the criminal process at which an accused is as much entitled to assistance of counsel as at the actual trial. Evans v. Cox, 327 F. Supp. 1057 (E.D. Va. 1971).

The proceedings in the juvenile court are jurisdictional rather than procedural. Evans v. Cox, 327 F. Supp. 1057 (E.D. Va. 1971).

These jurisdictional procedures apply to juvenile court hearings. Evans v. Cox, 327 F. Supp. 1057 (E.D. Va. 1971).

And not to proceedings in a court of record. — See Evans v. Cox, 327 F. Supp. 1057 (E.D. Va. 1971).

And such procedures are mandatory. — The statutes relating to the procedure applicable to proceedings for cases tried in a juvenile court are mandatory and must be followed. Evans v. Cox, 327 F. Supp. 1057 (E.D. Va. 1971).

Failure of the juvenile court to comply with the statutory provisions of procedure will render the certification to a court of record void. Evans v. Cox, 327 F. Supp. 1057 (E.D. Va. 1971); Ferguson v. Slayton, 340 F. Supp. 276 (W.D. Va. 1972).

Failure of the juvenile court to appoint a guardian ad litem to represent the interest of a juvenile offender is violative of this section and is jurisdictional and not procedural, and renders void the subsequent proceedings in the court of record. Jones v. Commonwealth, 213 Va. 425, 192 S.E.2d 775 (1972).

Counsel at transfer stage. — A juvenile is entitled to the assistance of counsel in having a court of proper jurisdiction determine, upon proper facts, whether he should be tried and sentenced as a juvenile. Cradle v. Cox, 327 F. Supp. 1169 (E.D. Va. 1971).

Counsel appointed over parent's objection. — A judge of the juvenile and domestic relations district court has jurisdiction to appoint counsel to represent a minor charged with assault and battery over the objections of one parent where the child's age and the parents' animosity towards each other and inability to agree on an attorney to represent their son lead the court to determine that such an appointment is in the child's best interests. Oxenham v. J.S.M., 256 Va. 180, 501 S.E.2d 765 (1998).

Continuing authority to appoint guardian ad litem. — Trial court retained jurisdiction over child custody matters sufficient to empower it to order the continued appointment of a guardian ad litem until the children reached majority. Ferguson v. Grubb, 39 Va. App. 549, 574 S.E.2d 769, 2003 Va. App. LEXIS 5 (2003).

Appointment of guardian ad litem resulting in conflict of interest. — Trial court abused its discretion under §§ 16.1-266 and 8.01-9 in appointing counsel who was hired by a parent to act as the child's guardian ad litem in a parentage action as a conflict of interest was created. Breit v. Mason, 59 Va. App. 322, 718 S.E.2d 482, 2011 Va. App. LEXIS 414 (2011).

Guardian ad litem of unknown father has standing to appeal entrustment agreement. — In proceedings involving custody of the child of an unwed minor, the guardian ad litem for the unknown father had standing to appeal the entrustment agreement decision by the juvenile and domestic relations district court. Norfolk Div. of Social Servs. v. Unknown Father, 2 Va. App. 420, 345 S.E.2d 533 (1986).

Re-appointment of guardian ad litem. — Trial court did not err in involving and re-appointing a guardian ad litem after a mother filed a motion to enforce and modify custody order because the mother and father could not represent the best interests of the children when they were at odds with each other; the father admitted that he did not like the mother and did not communicate with her, and the father used the children as messengers. Sandhir v. Ahuja-Sandhir, 2009 Va. App. LEXIS 265 (June 16, 2009).

Application to ensuring court proceedings. — This section applies to waiver of counsel at a detention hearing, and the waiver of counsel contemplated under the statute applies to ensuing court proceedings and prosecution without assistance of counsel. Grogg v. Commonwealth, 6 Va. App. 598, 371 S.E.2d 549 (1988).

Paramount concern of Commonwealth is child's best interest. — The strong public policy of this Commonwealth posits that the paramount concern where children are concerned is their best interests and this public policy would be thwarted if a child were bound by a paternity determination in which the child's independent rights and interests were not adequately protected. Commonwealth ex rel. Gray v. Johnson, 7 Va. App. 614, 376 S.E.2d 787 (1989).

Power to file petition seeking termination of residual parental rights. — No specific statutory provision either grants or denies the guardian ad litem the power to file a petition seeking the termination of residual parental rights, but such action is implicit in the general charge of authority given the guardian ad litem in § 8.01-9 to represent faithfully the interests of the individual under disability for whom he or she is appointed. Stanley v. Fairfax County Dep't of Social Servs., 10 Va. App. 596, 395 S.E.2d 199 (1990), aff'd, Stanley v. Fairfax, 242 Va. 60, 405 S.E.2d 621 (1991).

A guardian ad litem has standing to file a petition for termination of residual parental rights. Stanley v. Fairfax, 242 Va. 60, 405 S.E.2d 621 (1991).

Failure to timely file notice of appeal naming guardian ad litem required dismissal. — Mother's appeal of the termination of her parental rights was dismissed due to her failure to timely name the children's guardian ad litem, an indispensable party under this section, as an appellee in either the notice of appeal or the accompanying certificate of service; the failure to name the guardian ad litem as an appellee meant that the appeal was not perfected under Rule 5A:16, and the appellate court never acquired jurisdiction over the guardian ad litem. Watkins v. Fairfax County Dep't of Family Servs., 42 Va. App. 760, 595 S.E.2d 19, 2004 Va. App. LEXIS 164 (2004).

Guardian ad litem not required. — Because case was properly characterized as one "where custody of a child or children is the subject of controversy," rather than one involving "a child who is alleged to be abused or neglected," trial court was not required to appoint a guardian ad litem for the child. Santoro v. Owens, No. 1801-99-1 (Ct. of Appeals Feb. 8, 2000).

When a grandmother appealed the denial of her petition for visitation with her granddaughter, and her incarcerated son joined in her appeal, §§ 8.01-9 and 16.1-266 D [now § 16.1-266 E] did not require the appointment of a guardian ad litem for the son because he was not "a party defendant" to the appeal, and the case did not involve an entrustment agreement, a custody dispute, a termination of the father's parental rights, or any of the actions described in § 16.1-266. Harris v. Boxler, No. 0604-03-3, 2003 Va. App. LEXIS 461 (Ct. of Appeals Sept. 2, 2003).

Guardian ad litem who was appointed to represent the interests of a minor child in a suit filed by the child's grandfather, seeking visitation rights, was not an indispensable party to the action, and the appellate court held that it did not lack jurisdiction to hear the child's mother's appeal from the circuit court's judgment granting the child's grandparents visitation rights because the mother did not serve the guardian ad litem with notice that she was appealing. Yopp v. Hodges, 43 Va. App. 427, 598 S.E.2d 760, 2004 Va. App. LEXIS 310 (2004).

Guardian ad litem issue waived on appeal. — Award of primary physical custody of the children to the father was proper, in part because the mother was not permitted to complain on appeal of error in the circuit court where she herself failed to follow through with her motion to exclude the guardian ad litem and where she failed to properly notify the court of the statutory requirements for the appointment. The issue was waived. Gudino v. Gudino, 2011 Va. App. LEXIS 327 (Nov. 1, 2011).

OPINIONS OF THE ATTORNEY GENERAL

No authority to appoint guardian ad litem in addition to legal counsel. — A juvenile and domestic relations district court does not have authority to appoint a guardian ad litem for a juvenile defendant, in addition to the appointment of legal counsel, to represent the child. See opinion of Attorney General to The Honorable W. Edward Meeks III, Commonwealth's Attorney for Amherst County, 00-106 (12/14/01).

Applicability of section. — Subsection D of this section is not applicable to proceedings within the purview of subsections A — C;

further, a judge may appoint a guardian ad litem or counsel pursuant to subsection D, but not both. See opinion of Attorney General to The Honorable Robert N. Baldwin, Executive Secretary of the Supreme Court of Virginia, 02-046 (7/16/02).

Reimbursement by parents of guardian ad litem fee. — The court may order reimbursement by the parents when the appointment of a guardian ad litem for the child is required in abuse or neglect cases. See opinion of Attorney General to The Honorable J. Dean Lewis, Judge, Fifteenth District Juvenile and Domestic Relations Court, 02-058 (7/16/02).

§ 16.1-266.1. Standards for attorneys appointed as guardians ad litem; list of qualified attorneys.

A. On or before January 1, 1995, the Judicial Council of Virginia, in conjunction with the Virginia State Bar and the Virginia Bar Association, shall adopt standards for attorneys appointed as guardians ad litem pursuant to § 16.1-266. The standards shall, in so far as practicable, take into consideration the following criteria: (i) license or permission to practice law in Virginia, (ii) current training in the roles, responsibilities and duties of guardian ad litem representation, (iii) familiarity with the court system and general background in juvenile law, and (iv) demonstrated proficiency in this area of the law.

B. The Judicial Council shall maintain a list of attorneys admitted to practice law in Virginia who are qualified to serve as guardians ad litem based upon the standards and shall make the names available to the courts. If no attorney who is on the list is reasonably available, a judge in his discretion, may appoint any discreet and competent attorney who is admitted to practice law in Virginia.

History.
1994, c. 36; 1995, c. 273.

Research references.
Virginia Forms (Matthew Bender). No. 5-141 Order for Appointment of Guardian ad Litem.

CASE NOTES

Guardian ad litem's use of staff was proper. — Nothing prevented a guardian ad litem from using staff members to carry out his or her duties. Ferguson v. Grubb, 39 Va. App. 549, 574 S.E.2d 769, 2003 Va. App. LEXIS 5 (2003).

§ 16.1-266.2. Appointment of pro bono counsel by judges of the First and Second Judicial District in certain cases.

The judges of the juvenile and domestic relations district court of the First and Second Judicial District are authorized to appoint pro bono counsel for alleged victims in family abuse cases in which the court is authorized to issue a preliminary protective order under § 16.1-253.1, or an emergency protective order under § 16.1-253.4. Such counsel shall have no prosecutorial authority except as granted in writing by the attorney for the Commonwealth for the jurisdiction in which the representation is to occur.

Any attorney appointed under the provisions of this section shall be a volunteer and serve without compensation and shall be subject to any rules adopted by the court and approved by the Virginia Supreme Court providing for the establishment and conduct of a project providing pro bono services to victims of family abuse.

History.
1995, c. 806.

Editor's note.
Acts 1995, c. 806, cl. 2, which provided for the expiration of § 16.1-266.2 on July 1, 1997, was repealed by Acts 1997, c. 151, cl. 1. Therefore, this section remains in effect.

Law Review.
For an article, "Legal Issues Involving Children," see 32 U. Rich. L. Rev. 1345 (1998).

§ 16.1-267. Compensation of appointed counsel.

A. When the court appoints counsel to represent a child pursuant to subsection A of § 16.1-266 and, after an investigation by the court services unit, finds that the parents are financially able to pay for the attorney and refuse to do so, the court shall assess costs against the parents for such legal services in the maximum amount of that awarded the attorney by the court under the circumstances of the case, considering such factors as the ability of the parents to pay and the nature and extent of the counsel's duties in the case. Such amount shall not exceed the maximum amount specified in subdivision 1 of § 19.2-163 if the action is in district court.

When the court appoints counsel to represent a child pursuant to subsection B or C of § 16.1-266 and, after an investigation by the court services unit, finds that the parents are financially able to pay for the attorney in whole or in part and refuse to do so, the court shall assess costs in whole or in part against the parents for such legal services in the amount awarded the attorney by the court. Such amount shall not exceed $100 if the action is in circuit court or the maximum amount specified in subdivision 1 of § 19.2-163 if the action is in district court. In determining the financial ability of the parents to pay for an attorney to represent the child, the court shall utilize the financial statement required by § 19.2-159.

In all other cases, except as provided in § 16.1-343, counsel appointed to represent a child shall be compensated for his services pursuant to § 19.2-163.

B. When the court appoints counsel to represent a parent, guardian or other adult pursuant to § 16.1-266, such counsel shall be compensated for his services pursuant to § 19.2-163.

History.
Code 1950, § 16.1-173; 1956, c. 555; 1966, c. 709; 1968, c. 581; 1970, c. 87; 1973, c. 440; 1974, c. 513; 1975, cc. 465, 559; 1977, c. 559; 1981, c. 213; 1984, c. 709; 1986, c. 425; 1993, c. 344; 2004, cc. 342, 437.

Law Review.

For 2003/2004 survey of family and juvenile law, see 39 U. Rich. L. Rev. 241 (2004).

Research references.

Virginia Forms (Matthew Bender). No. 5-141 Order for Appointment of Guardian ad Litem. No. 5-236 Assessment of Costs/Payment Order.

CASE NOTES

Court erred in assessing transcript costs against Commonwealth. — The trial court erred in assessing to the Commonwealth the costs related to preparation of the trial transcript since subsection B expressly assures compensation only for appointed counsel's "services" not "expenses." Kerns v. Winchester Dep't of Social Servs., No. 2211-91-4 (Ct. of Appeals Sept. 15, 1992).

Inquiry as to financial ability to pay fees applies only to appointments pursuant to § 16.1-266 A and B [now § 16.1-266 A and C]. — That statutory mandate, to inquire as to financial ability to pay guardian ad litem fees as required by subsection A of this section, applies only to a guardian ad litem appointed pursuant to § 16.1-266 A or B [now § 16.1-266 A and C]. Where, the guardian ad litem was appointed pursuant to § 16.1-266 D [now § 16.1-266 E]; wife's claim is without merit. Kaplan v. Kaplan, No. 0987-92-1 (Ct. of Appeals Sept. 14, 1993).

Guardian ad litem fee not subject to fee limitation. — The Attorney General of Virginia has opined that the fee of a guardian ad litem appointed to represent a minor child pursuant to § 16.1-266 D [now § 16.1-266 E] is not subject to the maximum fee limitations for court-appointed counsel set forth in this section. Op. Va. Att'y Gen. 177 (Dec. 2, 1980); Op. Va. Att'y Gen. 153 (Oct. 27, 1986); see Patterson v. Old Dominion Trust Co., 156 Va. 763, 775, 159 S.E. 168, 172 (1931). Kaplan v. Kaplan, No. 0987-92-1 (Ct. of Appeals Sept. 14, 1993).

Guardian ad litem fees can be divided between parties. — Trial court did not err in dividing a guardian ad litem's fees equally between a mother and a father because nothing in Virginia jurisprudence indicated that allocating guardian ad litem costs equally amongst the parties was error. Anonymous C v. Anonymous B, No. 2232-09-2, 2011 Va. App. LEXIS 14 (Ct. of Appeals Jan. 11, 2011).

§ 16.1-268. Order of appointment.

The order of appointment of counsel pursuant to § 16.1-266 shall be filed with and become a part of the record of such proceeding. The attorney so appointed shall represent the child or parent, guardian or other adult at any such hearing and at all other stages of the proceeding unless relieved or replaced in the manner provided by law.

History.

1977, c. 559.

Michie's Jurisprudence.

For related discussion, see 4C M.J. Constitutional Law, § 142; 5B M.J. Criminal Procedure, § 24.

CASE NOTES

Representation of child. — Trial court was authorized to allow the guardian ad litem to remain on the child custody case despite the mother seeking to remove the guardian ad litem after appealing an adverse decision from the juvenile and domestic relations district court to the trial court. This section authorized a properly appointed guardian ad litem to remain on such a case, and the mother did not show that the guardian ad litem was not properly appointed. Lewis v. Hyman, 2008 Va. App. LEXIS 281 (June 10, 2008).

Applied in Norfolk Div. of Social Servs. v. Unknown Father, 2 Va. App. 420, 345 S.E.2d 533 (1986).

ARTICLE 7.

TRANSFER AND WAIVER.

§ 16.1-269.1. Trial in circuit court; preliminary hearing; direct indictment; remand.

A. Except as provided in subsections B and C, if a juvenile 14 years of age or older at the time of an alleged offense is charged with an offense which would be a felony if committed by an adult, the court shall, on motion of the attorney for the Commonwealth and prior to a hearing on the merits, hold a transfer hearing and may retain jurisdiction or transfer such juvenile for proper criminal proceedings to the appropriate circuit court having criminal jurisdiction of such offenses if committed by an adult. Any transfer to the appropriate circuit court shall be subject to the following conditions:

1. Notice as prescribed in §§ 16.1-263 and 16.1-264 shall be given to the juvenile and his parent, guardian, legal custodian or other person standing in loco parentis; or attorney;

2. The juvenile court finds that probable cause exists to believe that the juvenile committed the delinquent act as alleged or a lesser included delinquent act which would be a felony if committed by an adult;

3. The juvenile is competent to stand trial. The juvenile is presumed to be competent and the burden is on the party alleging the juvenile is not competent to rebut the presumption by a preponderance of the evidence; and

4. The court finds by a preponderance of the evidence that the juvenile is not a proper person to remain within the jurisdiction of the juvenile court. In determining whether a juvenile is a proper person to remain within the jurisdiction of the juvenile court, the court shall consider, but not be limited to, the following factors:

a. The juvenile's age;

b. The seriousness and number of alleged offenses, including (i) whether the alleged offense was committed in an aggressive, violent, premeditated, or willful manner; (ii) whether the alleged offense was against persons or property, with greater weight being given to offenses against persons, especially if death or bodily injury resulted; (iii) whether the maximum punishment for such an offense is greater than 20 years confinement if committed by an adult; (iv) whether the alleged offense involved the use of a firearm or other dangerous weapon by brandishing, threatening, displaying or otherwise employing such weapon; and (v) the nature of the juvenile's participation in the alleged offense;

c. Whether the juvenile can be retained in the juvenile justice system long enough for effective treatment and rehabilitation;

d. The appropriateness and availability of the services and dispositional alternatives in both the criminal justice and juvenile justice systems for dealing with the juvenile's problems;

e. The record and previous history of the juvenile in this or other jurisdictions, including (i) the number and nature of previous contacts with juvenile or circuit courts, (ii) the number and nature of prior periods of probation, (iii) the number and nature of prior commitments to juvenile correctional centers, (iv) the number and nature of previous residential and community-based treatments, (v) whether previous adjudications and commitments were for delinquent acts that involved the infliction of serious bodily injury, and (vi) whether the alleged offense is part of a repetitive pattern of similar adjudicated offenses;

f. Whether the juvenile has previously absconded from the legal custody of a juvenile correctional entity in this or any other jurisdiction;

g. The extent, if any, of the juvenile's degree of intellectual disability or mental illness;

h. The juvenile's school record and education;

i. The juvenile's mental and emotional maturity; and

j. The juvenile's physical condition and physical maturity.

No transfer decision shall be precluded or reversed on the grounds that the court failed to consider any of the factors specified in subdivision 4.

B. The juvenile court shall conduct a preliminary hearing whenever a juvenile 14 years of age or older is charged with murder in violation of § 18.2-31, 18.2-32 or 18.2-40, or aggravated malicious wounding in violation of § 18.2-51.2.

C. The juvenile court shall conduct a preliminary hearing whenever a juvenile 14 years of age or older is charged with murder in violation of § 18.2-33; felonious injury by mob in violation of § 18.2-41; abduction in violation of § 18.2-48; malicious wounding in violation of § 18.2-51; malicious wounding of a law-enforcement officer in violation of § 18.2-51.1; felonious poisoning in violation of § 18.2-54.1; adulteration of products in violation of § 18.2-54.2; robbery in violation of § 18.2-58 or carjacking in violation of § 18.2-58.1; rape in violation of § 18.2-61; forcible sodomy in violation of § 18.2-67.1; object sexual penetration in violation of § 18.2-67.2; manufacturing, selling, giving, distributing, or possessing with intent to manufacture, sell, give, or distribute a controlled substance or an imitation controlled substance in violation of § 18.2-248 if the juvenile has been previously adjudicated delinquent on two or more occasions of violating § 18.2-248 provided the adjudications occurred after the juvenile was at least 14 years of age; manufacturing, selling, giving, distributing, or possessing with intent to manufacture, sell, give, or distribute methamphetamine in violation of § 18.2-248.03 if the juvenile has been previously adjudicated delinquent on two or more occasions of violating § 18.2-248.03 provided the adjudications occurred after the juvenile was at least 14 years of age; or felonious manufacturing, selling, giving, distributing, or possessing with intent to manufacture, sell, give, or distribute anabolic steroids in violation of § 18.2-248.5 if the juvenile has been previously adjudicated delinquent on two or more occasions of violating § 18.2-248.5 provided the adjudications occurred after the juvenile was at least 14 years of age, provided the attorney for the Commonwealth gives written notice of his intent to proceed pursuant to this subsection. The notice shall be filed with the court and mailed or delivered to counsel for the juvenile or, if the juvenile is not then represented by counsel, to the juvenile and a parent, guardian or other person standing in loco parentis with respect to the juvenile at least seven days prior to the preliminary hearing. If the attorney for the Commonwealth elects not to give such notice, or if he elects to withdraw the notice prior to certification of the charge to the grand jury, he may proceed as provided in subsection A.

D. Upon a finding of probable cause pursuant to a preliminary hearing under subsection B or C, the juvenile court shall certify the charge, and all ancillary charges, to the grand jury. Such certification shall divest the juvenile court of jurisdiction as to the charge and any ancillary charges. Nothing in this subsection shall divest the juvenile court of jurisdiction over any matters unrelated to such charge and ancillary charges which may otherwise be properly within the jurisdiction of the juvenile court.

If the court does not find probable cause to believe that the juvenile has committed the violent juvenile felony as charged in the petition or warrant or if the petition or warrant is terminated by dismissal in the juvenile court, the attorney for the Commonwealth may seek a direct indictment in the circuit court. If the petition or warrant is terminated by nolle prosequi in the juvenile court, the attorney for the Commonwealth may seek an indictment only after a preliminary hearing in juvenile court.

If the court finds that the juvenile was not 14 years of age or older at the time of the alleged commission of the offense or that the conditions specified in subdivision A 1, 2, or 3 have not been met, the case shall proceed as otherwise provided for by law.

E. An indictment in the circuit court cures any error or defect in any proceeding held in the juvenile court except with respect to the juvenile's age. If an indictment is terminated by nolle prosequi, the Commonwealth may reinstate the proceeding by seeking a subsequent indictment.

History.

1994, cc. 859, 949; 1996, cc. 755, 914; 1997, c. 862; 2012, cc. 476, 507, 772.

Cross references.

As to the one year deadline for claims of error or defect, see § 16.1-272.1. As to Sex Offenders and Crimes Against Minors Registry, see § 9.1-900 et seq.

Editor's note.

Acts 1993, c. 929, cl. 3, as amended by Acts 1994, c. 564, cl. 1, and Acts 1996, c. 616, cl. 3, provides that the contingent enactment of this section by Acts 1994, cc. 859 and 949, cl. 2, shall become effective June 1, 1998, "only if state funds are provided by the General Assembly sufficient to provide adequate resources for the court to carry out the purposes of this act and to fulfill its mission to serve children and families of the Commonwealth." The funding was not provided.

Acts 2012, c. 772, cl. 2, provides: "That the provisions of this act may result in a net increase in periods of imprisonment or commitment. Pursuant to § 30-19.1:4, the estimated amount of the necessary appropriation cannot be determined for periods of imprisonment in state adult correctional facilities; therefore, Chapter 890 of the Acts of Assembly of 2011 requires the Virginia Criminal Sentencing Commission to assign a minimum fiscal impact of $50,000. Pursuant to § 30-19.1:4, the estimated amount of the necessary appropriation cannot be determined for periods of commitment to the custody of the Department of Juvenile Justice."

The 2012 amendments.

The 2012 amendments by cc. 476 and 507 are identical, and substituted "intellectual disability or mental illness" for "mental retardation or mental illness" in subdivision A 4 g; and made minor stylistic changes throughout the section.

The 2012 amendment by c. 772 inserted the language following "§ 18.2-67.2" and preceding "providing the attorney" in subsection C, and made minor stylistic changes throughout.

Law Review.

For article, "Legal Issues Involving Children," see 28 U. Rich. L. Rev. 1075 (1994). For note, "Novak v. Commonwealth: Are Virginia Courts Providing Special Protection to Virginia's Juvenile Defendants?", see 30 U. Rich. L. Rev. 935 (1996). For an article relating to all published Virginia criminal law decisions between July 1, 1997, and July 1, 1998, see 32 U. Rich. L. Rev. 1091 (1998). For an article, "Legal Issues Involving Children," see 32 U. Rich. L. Rev. 1345 (1998). For a review of Virginia legal issues involving children, see 33 U. Rich. L. Rev. 1001 (1999). For 2000 survey of Virginia law regarding children, see 34 U. Rich. L. Rev. 939 (2000). For article, "Legal Issues Involving Children," see 35 U. Rich. L. Rev. 741 (2001). For article summarizing published Virginia criminal law decisions between July 1, 2002 and July 1, 2003, see 38 U. Rich. L. Rev. 87 (2003). For annual survey article on legal issues involving children, see 38 U. Rich. L. Rev. 161 (2003). For survey of Virginia criminal law and procedure for the year 2004-2005, see 40 U. Rich. L. Rev. 197 (2005). For note, "Let the Jury Do the Waive: How Apprendi v. New Jersey Applies to Juvenile Transfer Proceedings," see 48 Wm. & Mary L. Rev. 723 (2006). For annual survey, "A Look Back and Forward: Legislative and Regulatory Highlights for 2008 and 2009 and a Discussion of Juvenile Transfer," see 44 U. Rich. L. Rev. 53 (2009).

Michie's Jurisprudence.

For related discussion, see 9B M.J. Infants, §§ 13, 19, 82.

CASE NOTES

I. General Consideration.
II. Constitutional Consideration.
III. Nature and Requirements of Proceedings Generally.
IV. Study and Report.
V. Practice and Procedure.

I. GENERAL CONSIDERATION.

Editor's note.

Most of the cases below were decided under former § 16.1-269.

Effect of section. — In effect, if not intent, this section and § 16.1-241 provide a chance for different, less rigorous treatment for certain persons whose immaturity at the time of the offense works not only to make special rehabilitation efforts more fitting but also decreases the moral blame attached to the act, and the punishment flowing from it. James v. Cox, 323 F. Supp. 15 (E.D. Va. 1971).

Effect of 1990 amendment. — A de novo hearing is required under subsection E of this section on the issue of transfer and the 1990 amendment to this section did not do away with the de novo hearing requirement, but merely prohibited the circuit court from redetermining the juvenile court's finding of probable cause. Broadnax v. Commonwealth, 16 Va. App. 36, 427 S.E.2d 741 (1993).

A juvenile is entitled to the protection of the juvenile system and the Commonwealth can only try the juvenile as an adult if the requirements for juvenile transfer proceedings under this section have been strictly followed; for without such an approach, there may be grounds for concern that the child receives the worst of both worlds: that he gets neither the protections accorded to adults nor the solicitous care and regenerative treatment postulated for children. In re Baskins, 16 Va. App. 241, 430 S.E.2d 555 (1993), but see Jamborsky v. Baskins, 247 Va. 506, 442 S.E.2d 636 (1994).

Interests of child and the public protected. — The authority of the juvenile court either to retain jurisdiction or to transfer jurisdiction in serious cases protects the interests of both the child and the public. Grogg v. Commonwealth, 6 Va. App. 598, 371 S.E.2d 549 (1988).

Indictment in circuit court cures failure to notify biological father. — The failure to notify a defendant's biological father of the initiation of juvenile proceedings was a defect but, under this section, that defect was cured when the grand jury returned indictments against the defendant on the offenses certified to it by the juvenile court and this section permitted the circuit court to exercise its subject matter jurisdiction and to try the defendant on the offenses set forth in the indictments. Moore v. Commonwealth, 259 Va. 405, 527 S.E.2d 415 (2000), rev'd on other grounds, Pope v. Commonwealth, 37 Va. App. 451, 559 S.E.2d 388 (2002).

Unless competency of juvenile is challenged, explicit finding of competency is not required. Panameno v. Commonwealth, 255 Va. 473, 498 S.E.2d 920 (1998).

The availability of appropriate services in the juvenile system does not render it improper to try a juvenile as an adult; such availability of services is only one of several relevant factors. Brown v. Commonwealth, No. 2858-97-2 (Ct. of Appeals Mar. 30, 1999).

The trial court properly authorized trial of a juvenile as an adult where: (1) several months prior to his 18th birthday, the juvenile was charged with six counts of distributing cocaine to his half-brother, who was a police informant; (2) over the preceding years, the juvenile had been found guilty of several crimes, including assault and battery; (3) at the time of the hearing, the juvenile was charged with an unrelated offense of brandishing a firearm; and (4) he had also been jailed because he failed to complete a community service requirement mandated by a court order. Brown v. Commonwealth, No. 2858-97-2 (Ct. of Appeals Mar. 30, 1999).

The transfer hearing, with or without evidence, is a vital and integral procedural step in the process of the juvenile court system. As such it is designed to achieve fairness both to the public and to the juvenile. Brown v. Cox, 481 F.2d 622 (4th Cir. 1973), cert. denied, 414 U.S. 1136, 94 S. Ct. 881, 38 L. Ed. 2d 761 (1976).

Review of juvenile court record in making determination on transfer issue. — The critical requirement is that the circuit court make an independent determination on the issue of transfer but it is permissible for the circuit court to review the transcripts and written records from the juvenile court. Grogg v. Commonwealth, 6 Va. App. 598, 371 S.E.2d 549 (1988).

Cameras in courtroom. — Once a juvenile is transferred to the circuit court pursuant to this section, he is thereafter prosecuted as an adult. In such circumstances, a decision to permit cameras in the courtroom rests with the sound discretion of the trial court, and absent a showing of prejudice of constitutional dimensions, the mere presence of cameras does not result in an unfair trial. Novak v. Commonwealth, 20 Va. App. 373, 457 S.E.2d 402 (1995).

Section prohibits trial of juvenile under fifteen as adult. — This section prohibits the indictment and trial of a child under the age of fifteen on a charge of murder and felonious assault. Lee v. Jones, 212 Va. 792, 188 S.E.2d 102 (1972).

No authority to proceed against appellant as adult. — Where circuit court failed to conduct the required hearing to juvenile defendant, the Commonwealth lacked the authority to proceed against appellant as an adult and, accordingly, appellant's conviction for possession of cocaine with intent to distribute must be vacated and case to be remanded to the circuit court to provide the required hearing before determining whether the Commonwealth should be authorized to seek an indictment. Broadnax v. Commonwealth, No. 1458-91-2 (Ct. of Appeals Sept. 9, 1993).

Emancipation alone is not a sufficient reason to transfer a felony charge from a juvenile and domestic relations district court to a circuit court for trial. Kluis v. Commonwealth, 14 Va. App. 720, 418 S.E.2d 908 (1992).

Waiver based solely on seriousness of offense contemplated. — The attitude that a waiver of a juvenile court's jurisdiction over a child may be premised solely on the basis of the seriousness of the offense is reflected in this section. Pollard v. Riddle, 482 F. Supp. 260 (E.D. Va. 1979).

Right to different judge at adjudicatory hearing. — It would strain reason to hold that a juvenile is not afforded the right to a different circuit judge at an adjudicatory hearing following appeal of the transfer to circuit court, when the juvenile has that right pursuant to specific language in subsection D for the identical proceeding in juvenile court, and in subsection E for the identical proceeding in circuit court incident to the Commonwealth's appeal; therefore, the circuit court erred in failing to follow the procedure in this section for transfer hearings by denying defendant his right to a different judge at the adjudicatory hearing. Hairfield v. Commonwealth, 7 Va. App. 649, 376 S.E.2d 796 (1989).

Sentencing. — When defendant appeared before a circuit court for sentencing on criminal charges under § 16.1-269.1, the jury was correctly allowed to sentence defendant because he was not a juvenile in that he had been previously convicted as an adult on an unrelated charge and given an adult sentence. Section 16.1-272 did not apply to youthful offenders who fell within the scope of § 16.1-271, while § 16.1-271 applied to any juvenile who was tried and convicted in a circuit court as an adult. Saunders v. Commonwealth, 281 Va. 448, 706 S.E.2d 350, 2011 Va. LEXIS 45 (2011).

Applied in Tross v. Commonwealth, 21 Va. App. 362, 464 S.E.2d 523 (1995); Burke v. Commonwealth, 29 Va. App. 183, 510 S.E.2d 743 (1999); Bramblett v. Commonwealth, 257 Va. 263, 513 S.E.2d 400 (1999); Roach v. Angelone, 176 F.3d 210 (4th Cir. 1999); Woodfork v. Commonwealth, 31 Va. App. 154, 521 S.E.2d 781 (1999); Brown v. Commonwealth, 279 Va. 210, 688 S.E.2d 185, 2010 Va. LEXIS 9 (2010).

II. CONSTITUTIONAL CONSIDERATION.

All constitutional rights of adult need not be available to juvenile. — The United States Supreme Court has never held that all rights constitutionally assured to an adult accused of crime also are to be enforced or made available to the juvenile in his delinquency proceeding. Brown v. Cox, 481 F.2d 622 (4th Cir. 1973), cert. denied, 414 U.S. 1136, 94 S. Ct. 881, 38 L. Ed. 2d 761 (1976).

Test. — The United States Supreme Court has enunciated the test for ascertaining to what extent constitutional requirements are to be "superimposed" on the juvenile process. That test is a two-fold one, namely, whether the application of the right is necessary to the achievement of "fundamental fairness" and whether it will disrupt the juvenile court system. Brown v. Cox, 481 F.2d 622 (4th Cir. 1973), cert. denied, 414 U.S. 1136, 94 S. Ct. 881, 38 L. Ed. 2d 761 (1976).

Due process. — The juvenile hearing need not conform with all of the requirements of a criminal trial or even of the usual administrative hearing, but it must measure up to the essentials of due process and fair treatment. Cradle v. Cox, 327 F. Supp. 1169 (E.D. Va. 1971).

Juvenile waiver of jurisdiction hearings requires basic elements of procedural due process, including a hearing, effective assistance of counsel and a statement of reasons. The procedures under this section generally provide appropriate constitutional safeguards. Wansley v. Miller, 353 F. Supp. 42 (E.D. Va.), rev'd on other grounds, 487 F.2d 90 (4th Cir. 1973).

A juvenile is entitled to the assistance of counsel in having a court of proper jurisdiction determine, upon proper facts, whether he should be tried and sentenced as a juvenile. Cradle v. Cox, 327 F. Supp. 1169 (E.D. Va. 1971).

Juvenile charged with first degree murder was barred from claiming a deprivation of due process for not being allowed a preliminary hearing before being transferred for prosecution as an adult because this section did not mandate a preliminary hearing prior to a dismissal of the charges in juvenile court. Lampkins v. Commonwealth, 44 Va. App. 709, 607 S.E.2d 722, 2005 Va. App. LEXIS 22 (2005).

There was no reversible error in denying defendant's appeal of the order of the juvenile court certifying the charges against defendant to the grand jury pursuant to subsection B of § 16.1-269.1, because, while defendant's parents were not provided with notification of the advisement hearing or the transfer hearing, there was no violation of defendant's constitutional due process rights because no such rights exist with regard to non-adjudicatory hearings. Angel v. Commonwealth, 281 Va. 248, 704 S.E.2d 386, 2011 Va. LEXIS 26 (2011), cert. denied, 2011 U.S. LEXIS 7091, 132 S. Ct. 344, 181 L. Ed. 2d 216 (U.S. 2011).

Violation of speedy trial statute. — When the district court certified and transferred defendant for trial as an adult in the circuit court, the district court necessarily found the requisite probable cause contemplated by the speedy trial statute. Because the transfer order directed that defendant be "remanded to jail," the prescribed five month limitation of § 19.2-243 commenced on October 4, 1995. It was immaterial that such custody coincided with detention of defendant incidental to an unrelated commitment. Irrespective of the trial court's order to quash, the initial indictments of defendant were a nullity, obtained without the benefit of the enabling order required by subsection B of § 16.1-269.6, and the court simply remedied of record an error or oversight in the proceedings, without disturbing the legal efficacy of the pending transfer order or effecting a nolle prosequi. Accordingly, defendant was held continuously from the finding of probable cause in the district court on October 4, 1995, until trial on July 11, 1996, in violation of Section 19.2-243, and the court had to reverse and dismiss the convictions. Price v. Commonwealth, 25 Va. App. 655, 492 S.E.2d 447 (1997), aff'd, 256 Va. 373, 506 S.E.2d 317 (1998).

Speedy trial rights attach upon determination by juvenile court that probable cause exists to believe that the juvenile committed the delinquent act as alleged. Jackson v. Commonwealth, 255 Va. 625, 499 S.E.2d 538 (1998), cert. denied, 525 U.S. 1067, 119 S. Ct. 796, 142 L. Ed. 2d 658 (1999).

Transfer hearing. — Juvenile court's certification to the grand jury of the murder charge filed against defendant, a 14-year-old, did not violate defendant's constitutional rights even though defendant was not granted a transfer hearing as no constitutional right existed to a transfer hearing and the juvenile court had made the required statutory findings that defendant was 14 years old or older and probable cause existed to believe defendant committed the murder at issue. Rodriguez v. Commonwealth, 40 Va. App. 144, 578 S.E.2d 78, 2003 Va. App. LEXIS 153 (2003).

Capital murder. — A 16-year-old person who is convicted of capital murder may be subjected to capital punishment. Jackson v. Commonwealth, 255 Va. 625, 499 S.E.2d 538 (1998), cert. denied, 525 U.S. 1067, 119 S. Ct. 796, 142 L. Ed. 2d 658 (1999).

III. NATURE AND REQUIREMENTS OF PROCEEDINGS GENERALLY.

Scope of hearing. — A hearing held under the Juvenile and Domestic Relations (District) Court Law is not as limited in its scope as a preliminary hearing under the criminal procedures applicable to an adult. The juvenile court judge is expressly empowered with the discretion of either retaining jurisdiction of the child charged with the commission of a felony or certifying the child for criminal proceedings in a proper court of record. Peyton v. French, 207 Va. 73, 147 S.E.2d 739 (1966).

Distinction between transfer and adjudicatory proceedings. — Distinction should be made for double jeopardy purposes between the transfer or certification proceeding and an adjudicatory or dispositional proceeding. A confinement order "imposes a sentence of confinement" and will constitute jeopardy. On the other hand, a certification order transfers the case to another court for original determination whether the accused child shall be confined. In such order, the court makes no finding of innocence or guilt, only a finding that the juvenile should stand trial on the merits in another court. Brown v. Cox, 481 F.2d 622 (4th Cir. 1973), cert. denied, 414 U.S. 1136, 94 S. Ct. 881, 38 L. Ed. 2d 761 (1976).

Minimum requirements needed when transfer is made to circuit court. — Circuit court is not required to conduct a de novo hearing in transfer or removal proceedings from juvenile court to the circuit court, nonetheless certain minimum requirements must be met, however there must be a hearing that gives meaningful review; the juvenile must be given notice of the hearing and afforded an opportunity to appear with counsel and argue his position. Russell v. Commonwealth, 16 Va. App. 660, 432 S.E.2d 12 (1993).

Hearing does not constitute jeopardy. — To hold that the transfer hearing constituted jeopardy, and to apply to it the rules applicable to the criminal trial on the merits of an adult, would effectively undermine the juvenile court system. There is no warrant for any such conclusion. Brown v. Cox, 481 F.2d 622 (4th Cir. 1973), cert. denied, 414 U.S. 1136, 94 S. Ct. 881, 38 L. Ed. 2d 761 (1976).

The problem of double jeopardy has been eliminated from this section. Lewis v. Howard, 374 F. Supp. 446 (W.D. Va.), aff'd, 504 F.2d 426 (4th Cir. 1974), cert. denied, 421 U.S. 999, 95 S. Ct, 2396, 44 L. Ed. 2d 666 (1975).

The proceedings in the juvenile court are jurisdictional rather than procedural. Evans v. Cox, 327 F. Supp. 1057 (E.D. Va. 1971).

Effect of significant defect in transfer proceeding. — If there be a significant defect in the transfer proceeding, the circuit court never gains jurisdiction over the juvenile and therefore has no authority to impose a sentence on the offender. Hailey v. Dorsey, 580 F.2d 112 (4th Cir. 1978), cert. denied, 440 U.S. 937, 99 S. Ct. 1282, 59 L. Ed. 495 (1979).

Failure of the juvenile court to comply with the statutory provisions of procedure will render the certification to a court of record void. Evans v. Cox, 327 F. Supp. 1057 (E.D. Va. 1971).

The Virginia Supreme Court has consistently insisted upon strict compliance with the statutes governing transfer for adult trial. A failure to conduct an investigation before discretion is exercised, a failure to provide a hearing in a juvenile court, and a failure to notify a child's parents of a juvenile court certification hearing or to appoint a guardian ad litem, all render a decision to try a defendant as an adult invalid and ineffective to oust the original jurisdiction of the juvenile and domestic relations court. James v. Cox, 323 F. Supp. 15 (E.D. Va. 1971).

A preliminary hearing in a juvenile court is jurisdictional and not procedural, and before a circuit court can acquire jurisdiction to try petitioner there must be a compliance with the provisions of the Juvenile and Domestic Relations [District] Court Law. Peyton v. French, 207 Va. 73, 147 S.E.2d 739 (1966).

Limited jurisdiction of juvenile court. — This section limits the juvenile court to conducting a preliminary hearing and certifying the charge to the grand jury; once the juvenile court finds probable cause and certifies the charge, it loses jurisdiction. Williams v. Commonwealth, 33 Va. App. 725, 536 S.E.2d 916, 2000 Va. App. LEXIS 734 (2000).

Defendant juvenile, tried as an adult on a charge of malicious wounding and convicted of the lesser included offense of unlawful wounding, could not have the case transferred back to the juvenile court, as once the juvenile court made a probable cause finding, the juvenile court had no further jurisdiction; subsection C of § 16.1-269.1 defined the class of "violent felonies" that mandated certification to the circuit court upon a finding of probable cause and limited the role of the juvenile court in those cases. Hughes v. Commonwealth, 39 Va. App. 448, 573 S.E.2d 324, 2002 Va. App. LEXIS 765 (2002).

Findings required by the transfer statute are jurisdictional and, because neither the juvenile court nor the circuit court made such findings, the circuit court was without jurisdiction to try defendant as an adult. Matthews v. Commonwealth, 216 Va. 358, 218 S.E.2d 538 (1975).

To make a transfer, the transferring judge must have conducted a transfer hearing, and he must have made the findings in subdivision A 3. Absent such findings, the circuit court never gains jurisdiction over the minor to try him as an adult. United States v. Blevins, 802 F.2d 768 (4th Cir. 1986).

Transfer order void where findings not made. — Where at the conclusion of a hearing held pursuant to this section, the juvenile court judge transferred defendant to the circuit court for trial as an adult, but the transfer order failed to indicate that the juvenile court judge made the findings required by subdivisions (A) (3) (b), (c) and (d) as the appropriate boxes on the form order were not checked, the juvenile court order transferring defendant to the circuit court for trial as an adult was void since the findings required by this section are jurisdictional and if these findings are

not made, the transfer order of the juvenile court is void and the circuit court is without jurisdiction to try the juvenile as an adult. Hairfield v. Commonwealth, 7 Va. App. 649, 376 S.E.2d 796 (1989).

If the juvenile and domestic relations district court fails to hold a transfer hearing or to make the required findings, then the circuit court proceedings against a juvenile are void for lack of jurisdiction to try him or her as an adult. Burfoot v. Commonwealth, 23 Va. App. 38, 473 S.E.2d 724 (1996).

Incomplete form transfer order rendered trial court without jurisdiction. — Where juvenile district court made some, but not all, of the required findings by checking some, but not all, of the boxes provided on a form transfer order used by the juvenile and domestic relations district court, the trial court had no jurisdiction to try the defendant as an adult on charges of first degree murder and use of a firearm while committing a felony. Harrell v. Commonwealth, No. 1308-91-1 (Ct. of Appeals Dec. 15, 1992).

Provisions mandatory. — The statutes relating to the procedure applicable to proceedings for cases tried in a juvenile court are mandatory and must be followed. Evans v. Cox, 327 F. Supp. 1057 (E.D. Va. 1971).

Where court referred to "violent felony," it was not addressing sentencing requirements — Where appellant correctly pointed out that neither of his offenses of conviction, attempted armed robbery and use of a firearm in the commission of a felony, was enumerated as a "violent juvenile felony" under this section, the court's reference to "violent felony" did not ineluctably lead to the conclusion that it was referring to the "violent juvenile felony" provision of this section when it stated its findings. Indeed, the record, taken as a whole, supported the conclusion that the court had before it and gave consideration to all the relevant factors under the juvenile sentencing provisions in determining whether appellant was more properly sentenced under the criminal law applicable to adults or that governing the disposition of juveniles, and that, in announcing its finding, it was not particularly addressing the requirements for sentencing under this section. Pressley v. Commonwealth, No. 3019-96-4 (Ct. of Appeals Jan. 13, 1998).

Waiver of objection based on failure to notify parent. — The legislature has provided in subsection E of this section that, as to offenses committed on or after July 1, 1996, once an indictment has been returned in the circuit court, any failure to comply with the parental notification provisions of § 16.1-263 and this section does not deprive the court of subject matter jurisdiction. Carter v. Commonwealth, 31 Va. App. 393, 523 S.E.2d 544 (2000).

Because the defendant failed to raise the jurisdictional issue of lack of notice to his father when he was certified for trial as an adult in another county before the indictments were returned in the circuit court in the instant case, failure to comply with the parental notification provisions of the statutes did not deprive the circuit court of jurisdiction in the instant case. Monteon v. Commonwealth, No. 2038-99-3, 2000 Va. App. LEXIS 316 (Ct. of Appeals May 2, 2000).

IV. STUDY AND REPORT.

Report as jurisdictional prerequisite. — The Supreme Court has held that the statute requiring that the juvenile court's investigation report be transmitted to the court of record laid down a jurisdictional prerequisite. James v. Cox, 323 F. Supp. 15 (E.D. Va. 1971).

The investigation required by this section is a prerequisite to the exercise of judicial discretion, informed and aided by the data compiled. James v. Cox, 323 F. Supp. 15 (E.D. Va. 1971).

The purpose of the investigation is to enable the court to reach a proper decision as to whether or not to transfer the defendant for trial to the juvenile court. Tilton v. Commonwealth, 196 Va. 774, 85 S.E.2d 368 (1955) (decided under former § 16-172.42, corresponding to this section).

The juvenile court can rely on information previously supplied to itself in a subsequent case involving the same defendant. Muse v. Slayton, 333 F. Supp. 1007 (W.D. Va. 1971).

No requirement court must consider juvenile's prior treatment or rehabilitation. — Where judge, basing his decision on defendant's age and nature of offenses, transferred him to be tried in circuit court as adult pursuant to this section, finding of nonamenability did not require that juvenile must fail to respond to previously offered treatment or rehabilitation since plain language of former § 16.1-269 (A) (3) (b) authorizes juvenile court judge in determining nonamenability to look to either nature of offense or other factors set forth in statutes; use of word "or" in former § 16.1-269 (A) (3) (b) allows finding of nonamenability based solely on nature of offense. Hutcherson v. Commonwealth, 7 Va. App. 534, 375 S.E.2d 403 (1989).

Determination of nonamenability based solely on face of charge is only permissible when offense is one of those enumerated in statute. Hutcherson v. Commonwealth, 7 Va. App. 534, 375 S.E.2d 403 (1989).

Finding of nonamenability held proper. — Finding of nonamenability was permissible under statute and transfer was proper where defendant and two other boys were accused of luring 81-year-old man from his apartment, where they assaulted him and one held him there against his will while other two burglarized his apartment. Hutcherson v. Commonwealth, 7 Va. App. 534, 375 S.E.2d 403 (1989).

V. PRACTICE AND PROCEDURE.

If the decision to waive juvenile jurisdiction were not immediately appealable, those legislative protections afforded children under the juvenile justice system once lost, would be irretrievable. Hairfield v. Commonwealth, 7 Va. App. 649, 376 S.E.2d 796 (1989).

The defendant's failure to object to the circuit court's exercise of jurisdiction before arraignment cannot constitute a waiver of jurisdiction. Burfoot v. Commonwealth, 23 Va. App. 38, 473 S.E.2d 724 (1996).

Orders transferring juveniles are final, a contrary interpretation would contravene legislative intent, and such orders are immediately appealable to the circuit court and need not be preceded by a conviction under § 16.1-132. Hairfield v. Commonwealth, 7 Va. App. 649, 376 S.E.2d 796 (1989).

Defendant properly transferred under subsection B. — The defendant was transferred under subsection B. Under that subsection, the court is not required to consider the factors under subsection A 4 if the offender is 14 or older and charged with an unclassified felony violation of Chapter 4 or Title 18.2 punishable by life imprisonment. The defendant was 17 at the time of the offense and charged with first-degree murder, an offense punishable by life imprisonment. She could thus be transferred upon a finding of probable cause without considering other factors. Dara v. Commonwealth, No. 2795-95-1 (Ct. of Appeals Feb. 11, 1997).

Commonwealth may seek direct indictment in circuit court under subsection D. Even if juvenile court found evidence insufficient to establish probable cause to believe defendant committed aggravated malicious wounding and intended to certify only lesser offense of malicious wounding to grand jury, Commonwealth was free to proceed by direct indictment for the original offense, notwithstanding the order of the juvenile court certifying lesser offense. Nelson v. Commonwealth, No. 0283-99-1 (Ct. of Appeals Apr. 4, 2000).

No requirement in subsection E that removal order be predicated on findings in subsection A. — The language of subsection E of this section is plain, and unambiguous, in its omission of any requirement that a removal order be predicated on the findings set forth in subsection A of this section. Green v. Commonwealth, No. 0524-89-4 (Ct. of Appeals Nov. 6, 1990) (decided under former §§ 16.1-269 A and 16.1-269 E).

Compliance with time period held directory and procedural. — This section contains no prohibitory or limiting language that prevents the circuit court from entering its order beyond the expiration date of the 21-day period; absent such limiting language, the provision at issue, compliance with the 21-day time period, is directory and procedural, rather than mandatory and jurisdictional. Jamborsky v. Baskins, 247 Va. 506, 442 S.E.2d 636 (1994) (decided under former § 16.1-269 E).

The circuit court which hears an appeal of a juvenile court's transfer decision de novo pursuant to § 16.1-136 must, in the absence of any provision specifying a different procedure, follow the mandatory provisions that govern juvenile court transfer proceedings. Hairfield v. Commonwealth, 7 Va. App. 649, 376 S.E.2d 796 (1989).

Failure to give written notice of transfer hearing as required by former § 16.1-176 (a) (3) held procedural defect cured or waived by appearance and failure to object. See Turner v. Commonwealth, 216 Va. 666, 222 S.E.2d 517 (1976).

Failure to give notice to parent cured by indictment. — The provisions of subsection E apply to offenses committed on or after July 1, 1996, and clearly cured any deficiency in notice to a defendant's mother arising from charges certified as the result of a juvenile court proceeding. Nelson v. Commonwealth, No. 0283-99-1, 2000 Va. App. LEXIS 245 (Ct. of Appeals Apr. 4, 2000).

Because the defendant failed to raise the jurisdictional issue of lack of notice to his father before indictments were returned in the circuit court, failure to comply with the parental notification provisions of the code did not deprive the circuit court of jurisdiction. Shackleford v. Commonwealth, 32 Va. App. 307, 528 S.E.2d 123, 2000 Va. App. LEXIS 233 (2000), aff'd, 262 Va. 196, 547 S.E.2d 899 (2001).

Any error from Commonwealth's failure to notify juvenile's biological parents of juvenile court proceedings was cured when grand jury returned indictments on offenses certified to it by juvenile court. Gilbert v. Commonwealth, No. 1515-99-1 (Ct. of Appeals Mar. 28, 2000).

Although a defendant timely raised his objection to the jurisdiction of the circuit court before his arraignment, the alleged defect based on the failure to comply with the parental notice requirements was cured by the indictment; in other words, the indictment cured the defect raised in the defendant's objection before he made the objection. Shackleford v. Commonwealth, 262 Va. 196, 547 S.E.2d 899, 2001 Va. LEXIS 78 (2001).

Lack of parental notice of transfer appeal cured by indictment. — The rule established by subsection E that an indictment cures any error or defect in any proceeding held in the juvenile court applies to the lack of notice to a defendant's parent of a hearing to be held in circuit court appealing the transfer of the case; while subsection E speaks in terms of curing defects in the proceedings in the juvenile court, an appeal from a transfer decision is the final step in the transfer process, and the legislature intended for an indictment to cure any defects in that entire process. Shackleford v. Commonwealth, 262 Va. 196, 547 S.E.2d 899, 2001 Va. LEXIS 78 (2001).

Error cured by indictment in circuit court. — Indictment by grand jury cures any defect or error, except one regarding defendant's age, which occurred in juvenile and domestic relations district court proceeding, including Commonwealth's failure to comply with statutory notice requirements. Nelson v. Commonwealth, No. 0283-99-1 (Ct. of Appeals Apr. 4, 2000).

Because juvenile failed to raise jurisdictional issue of lack of notice to his father before indictments were returned in circuit court, failure to comply with parental notification provisions did not deprive circuit court of jurisdiction. Shackleford v. Commonwealth, No. 2883-98-3 (Ct. of Appeals Mar. 28, 2000).

Juvenile's indictment in circuit court cured alleged defects in service of summonses. Souksengmany v. Commonwealth, No. 1641-99-4 (Ct. of Appeals Apr. 4, 2000).

Juvenile's indictment in circuit court cured any defect that may have occurred in his transfer proceedings in juvenile and domestic relations district court. Ballard v. Commonwealth, No. 0075-99-1 (Ct. of Appeals Mar. 21, 2000).

Although defendant juvenile timely raised her objection to the jurisdiction of the circuit court, once the grand jury returned an indictment, the alleged defects in the transfer proceedings from the juvenile court to the circuit court were cured by the indictment; also, because any procedural errors in the appeal were cured by the indictment, the circuit court was not in any manner divested of its jurisdiction to try defendant on the charges set forth in the indictment. Thus, the circuit court did not err in exercising jurisdiction over the felony charges against defendant. Overdorff v. Commonwealth, 45 Va. App. 222, 609 S.E.2d 626, 2005 Va. App. LEXIS 81 (2005).

Confession of juvenile prior to certification and transfer. — If a juvenile has been fully advised of his constitutional rights, and it is apparent from the totality of the circumstances that a criminal prosecution might follow, his confession, if freely and voluntarily made, is admissible in a criminal trial in a circuit court notwithstanding the confession was made prior to certification and transfer of the juvenile case by the juvenile and domestic relations district court. Harris v. Commonwealth, 217 Va. 715, 232 S.E.2d 751 (1977).

None of juvenile defendant's substantive rights was infringed as a result of the three-day delay in the circuit court's assumption of jurisdiction over his felony charges; in fact, at oral argument in this appeal, his counsel acknowledged that the 21-day requirement is procedural in that it does not convey a substantive right, and that the defendant did not suffer even minor prejudice because of the delay. Jamborsky v. Baskins, 247 Va. 506, 442 S.E.2d 636 (1994) (decided under former § 16.1-269 E).

Any error made by the juvenile court in failing to make findings as to the defendant's mental retardation was cured by the return of indictments in the trial court. Scott v. Commonwealth, 31 Va. App. 461, 524 S.E.2d 162 (2000).

Failure to enter timely order corrected by nunc pro tunc order. — Where the nonentry of a timely order certifying a juvenile for trial as an adult under subsection E of this section was caused by the prosecutor's failure to follow directions, and that mistake was compounded by the failure of defense counsel to return the order either to the court or the prosecutor, a nunc pro tunc order correcting the error was proper. Harris v. Commonwealth, 222 Va. 205, 279 S.E.2d 395 (1981).

Imposition of juvenile treatment requires full results of juvenile hearing. — Since, under this section, the reports of the juvenile court are certified to the court of record in the event of transfer, and the latter court may impose juvenile treatment rather than adult sentence under § 16.1-272, for consideration of that alternative the court of record needs the full results of a proper juvenile hearing. James v. Cox, 323 F. Supp. 15 (E.D. Va. 1971).

A writ of prohibition will lie where necessary to prevent a court of record from exercising jurisdiction to try indictments returned against a juvenile in violation of this section. Lee v. Jones, 212 Va. 792, 188 S.E.2d 102 (1972).

Defects in juvenile court cured by indictment. — Under the plain language of this statute, an indictment by a grand jury cures any defect or error, except one regarding a juvenile's age, which has occurred in any juvenile court proceeding. Ballard v. Commonwealth, No. 0075-99-1, 2000 Va. App. LEXIS 201 (Ct. of Appeals Mar. 21, 2000).

Assuming that, in addition to notifying a juvenile's legal custodian, the Commonwealth was required to notify both of the juvenile's biological parents of the commencement of proceedings, any failure to do so was cured when the grand jury returned indictments on the charges against him. Gilbert v. Commonwealth, No. 1515-99-1, 2000 Va. App. LEXIS 231 (Ct. of Appeals Mar. 28, 2000).

Each case considered on own facts in determining remedy. — While ordinarily a reconstructed transfer hearing is the appropriate remedy where a prior transfer order of the juvenile court has been invalidated on procedural due process grounds and the juvenile court has lost jurisdiction of the defendant by reason of his age, each case must be considered on its own facts, and, if some other remedy or determination will not result in fundamental unfairness to the petitioner and is more appropriate under the facts of the case and will contribute to a more expeditious resolution of the issue, that procedure should be adopted. Brown v. Cox, 481 F.2d 622 (4th Cir. 1973), cert. denied, 414 U.S. 1136, 94 S. Ct. 881, 38 L. Ed. 2d 761 (1976).

Certification of lesser offense not bar to indictment for greater offense. — Even if it was assumed that the juvenile court found the evidence insufficient to establish probable cause to believe a defendant committed a more serious offense and intended to certify a lesser offense to the grand jury, the Commonwealth was free to proceed by direct indictment for the original offense, notwithstanding such order. Nelson v. Commonwealth, No. 0283-99-1, 2000 Va. App. LEXIS 245 (Ct. of Appeals Apr. 4, 2000).

Evidence of date of receipt of case was properly a part of the record. — Testimony of deputy clerk of the circuit court as to date of receipt of case from juvenile court did not impeach the accuracy of the record but, rather, established a fact not evident on the face of the record therefore the date of the receipt of the juvenile court case by the circuit court was properly a part of the record in the proceedings to determine whether request to have juvenile be prosecuted as an adult was timely. In re Baskins, 16 Va. App. 241, 430 S.E.2d 555 (1993).

Discretion of trial court. — Whether, in addition to examining all papers, reports and orders of the juvenile court in transfer of case from juvenile court to circuit court, circuit court hears additional evidence is a matter addressed to the sound discretion of the trial court and will not be disturbed by Court of Appeals unless there has been an abuse of discretion. Russell v. Commonwealth, 16 Va. App. 660, 432 S.E.2d 12 (1993).

Transfer review. — When defendant sought de novo review in the circuit court of the order of the juvenile court transferring his prosecution for arson and related offenses to the circuit court, the record showed the circuit court properly conducted such a review by holding a hearing and taking substantial evidence on the issue, before finding defendant was not a proper person to remain within the jurisdiction of the juvenile court. Schwartz v. Commonwealth, 41 Va. App. 61, 581 S.E.2d 891, 2003 Va. App. LEXIS 339 (2003), aff'd, 267 Va. 751, 594 S.E.2d 925 (2004).

CIRCUIT COURT OPINIONS

Request for transfer denied. — Commonwealth's request for transfer under subsection A of § 16.1-269.1 was denied as defendant, a juvenile, was considered at low risk for re-offense, had been compliant with the rules of supervision, actively participated in treatment, had no prior criminal history, performed well in school, and was engaged in extracurricular activities. Commonwealth v. T. D. S., 74 Va. Cir. 455, 2008 Va. Cir. LEXIS 63 (Loudoun County 2008).

OPINIONS OF THE ATTORNEY GENERAL

Appeal of transfer order. — The circuit court is not required to enter an enabling order where the transfer decision of the juvenile court has not been appealed. Furthermore, a Commonwealth's attorney may seek an indictment after the period for an appeal has expired, provided no appeal has been noted. See opinion of Attorney General to The Honorable V. Thomas Forehand, Jr., Chief Judge, First Judicial Circuit of Virginia, 09-031, 2009 Va. AG LEXIS 31 (6/26/09).

§ 16.1-269.2. Admissibility of statement; investigation and report; bail.

A. Statements made by the juvenile at the transfer hearing provided for under § 16.1-269.1 shall not be admissible against him over objection in any criminal proceedings following the transfer, except for purposes of impeachment.

B. Prior to a transfer hearing pursuant to subsection A of § 16.1-269.1, a study and report to the court, in writing, relevant to the factors set out in subdivision A 4 of § 16.1-269.1, as well as an assessment of any affiliation with a criminal street gang as defined in § 18.2-46.1, shall be made by the probation services or other qualified agency designated by the court. Upon motion of the attorney for the Commonwealth for a transfer hearing pursuant to subsection A of § 16.1-269.1, the attorney for the Commonwealth shall provide notice to the designated probation services or other qualified agency of the need for a transfer report. Counsel for the juvenile and the attorney for the Commonwealth shall have full access to the study and report and any other report or data concerning the juvenile which are available to the court. The court shall not consider the report until a finding has been made concerning probable cause. If the court so orders, the study and report may be expanded to include matters provided for in § 16.1-273, whereupon it may also serve as the report required by this subsection, but on the condition that it will not be submitted to the judge who will preside at any subsequent hearings except as provided for by law.

C. After the completion of the hearing, whether or not the juvenile court decides to retain jurisdiction over the juvenile or transfer such juvenile for criminal proceedings in the circuit court, the juvenile court shall set bail for the juvenile in accordance with Chapter 9 (§ 19.2-119 et seq.) of Title 19.2, if bail has not already been set.

History.
1994, cc. 859, 949; 1999, c. 350; 2005, cc. 590, 843.

Editor's note.
Acts 1993, c. 929, cl. 3, as amended by Acts 1994, c. 564, cl. 1, and Acts 1996, c. 616, cl. 3, provides that the contingent enactment of this section by Acts 1994, cc. 859 and 949, cl. 2, shall become effective June 1, 1998, "only if state funds are provided by the General Assembly sufficient to provide adequate resources for the court to carry out the purposes of this act and to fulfill its mission to serve children and families of the Commonwealth." The funding was not provided.

§ 16.1-269.3. Retention by juvenile court; appeal.

If a case is not transferred following a transfer hearing or is not certified following a probable cause hearing, the judge who conducted the hearing shall not, over the objection of any interested party, preside at the adjudicatory hearing on the petition, but rather it shall be presided over by another judge of that court. If the attorney for the Commonwealth deems it to be in the public interest, and the juvenile is fourteen years of age or older he may, within ten days after the juvenile court's final decision to retain the case in accordance with subsection A of § 16.1-269.1, file a notice of appeal of the decision to the appropriate circuit court. A copy of such notice shall be furnished at the same time to the counsel for the juvenile.

History.
1994, cc. 859, 949; 1996, cc. 755, 914.

Editor's note.
Acts 1993, c. 929, cl. 3, as amended by Acts 1994, c. 564, cl. 1, and Acts 1996, c. 616, cl. 3, provides that the contingent enactment of this section by Acts 1994, cc. 859 and 949, cl. 2, shall become effective June 1, 1998, "only if state funds are provided by the General Assembly sufficient to provide adequate resources for the court to carry out the purposes of this act and to fulfill its mission to serve children and families of the Commonwealth." The funding was not provided.

§ 16.1-269.4. Transfer to circuit court; appeal by juvenile.

If the juvenile court transfers the case pursuant to subsection A of § 16.1-269.1, the juvenile may, within ten days after the juvenile court's final decision, file a notice of appeal of the decision to the appropriate circuit court. A copy of the notice shall be furnished at the same time to the attorney for the Commonwealth.

History.
1994, cc. 859, 949; 1996, cc. 755, 914.

Editor's note.
Acts 1993, c. 929, cl. 3, as amended by Acts 1994, c. 564, cl. 1, and Acts 1996, c. 616, cl. 3, provides that the contingent enactment of this section by Acts 1994, cc. 859 and 949, cl. 2, shall become effective June 1, 1998, "only if state funds are provided by the General Assembly sufficient to provide adequate resources for the court to carry out the purposes of this act and to fulfill its mission to serve children and families of the Commonwealth." The funding was not provided.

§ 16.1-269.5. Placement of juvenile.

The juvenile court may order placement of the transferred juvenile in either a local correctional facility as approved by the State Board of Corrections pursuant to the limitations of subsections D and E of § 16.1-249 or a juvenile detention facility.

History.
1994, cc. 859, 949; 1995, cc. 746, 798, 802; 2010, c. 739.

Editor's note.
Acts 1993, c. 929, cl. 3, as amended by Acts 1994, c. 564, cl. 1, and Acts 1996, c. 616, cl. 3, provides that the contingent enactment of this section by Acts 1994, cc. 859 and 949, cl. 2, shall become effective June 1, 1998, "only if state funds are provided by the General Assembly sufficient to provide adequate resources for the court to carry out the purposes of this act and to fulfill its mission to serve children and families of the Commonwealth." The funding was not provided.

The 2010 amendments.
The 2010 amendment by c. 739 substituted "subsections D and E" for "subsection E."

§ 16.1-269.6. Circuit court hearing; jury; termination of juvenile court jurisdiction; objections and appeals.

A. Within seven days after receipt of notice of an appeal from the transfer decision pursuant to subsection A of § 16.1-269.1, by either the attorney for the Commonwealth or the juvenile, or if an appeal to such a decision to transfer is not noted, upon expiration of the time in which to note such an appeal, the clerk of the court shall forward to the circuit court all papers connected with the case, including any report required by subsection B of § 16.1-269.2, as well as a written court order setting forth the reasons for the juvenile court's decision. Within seven days after receipt of notice of an appeal, the clerk shall forward copies of the order to the attorney for the Commonwealth and other counsel of record.

B. The circuit court, when practicable, shall, within 45 days after receipt of the case from the juvenile court pursuant to subsection A of § 16.1-269.1, (i) if either the juvenile or the attorney for the Commonwealth has appealed the transfer decision, examine all such papers, reports and orders and conduct a hearing to take further evidence on the issue of transfer, to determine if there has been substantial compliance with subsection A of § 16.1-269.1, but without redetermining whether the juvenile court had sufficient evidence to find probable cause; and (ii) enter an order either remanding the case to the juvenile court or advising the attorney for the Commonwealth that he may seek an indictment. A juvenile held continuously in secure detention shall be released from confinement if there is no hearing on the merits of his case within 45 days of the filing of the appeal. The circuit court may extend the time limitations for a reasonable period of time based upon good cause shown, provided the basis for such extension is recorded in writing and filed among the papers of the proceedings. However, in cases where a charge has been certified by the juvenile court to the grand jury pursuant to subsection B or C of § 16.1-269.1, the attorney for the Commonwealth may seek an indictment upon such charge and any ancillary charge without obtaining an order of the circuit court advising him that he may do so.

C. The circuit court order advising the attorney for the Commonwealth that he may seek an indictment shall divest the juvenile court of its jurisdiction over the case as well as the juvenile court's jurisdiction over any other allegations of delinquency arising from the same act, transaction or scheme giving rise to the charge for which the juvenile has been transferred. In addition, upon conviction of the juvenile following transfer or certification and trial as an adult, the circuit court shall issue an order terminating the juvenile court's jurisdiction over that juvenile with respect to any future criminal acts alleged to have been committed by such juvenile and with respect to any pending allegations of delinquency which have not been disposed of by the juvenile court at the time of the criminal conviction. However, such an order terminating the juvenile court's jurisdiction shall not apply to any allegations of criminal conduct that would properly be within the jurisdiction of the juvenile and domestic relations district court if the defendant were an adult. Upon receipt of the order terminating the juvenile court's jurisdiction over the juvenile, the clerk of the juvenile court shall forward any pending petitions of delinquency for proceedings in the appropriate general district court.

D. The judge of the circuit court who reviewed the case after receipt from the juvenile court shall not, over the objection of any interested party, preside over the trial of such charge or charges.

E. Any objection to the jurisdiction of the circuit court pursuant to this article shall be waived if not made before arraignment.

F. The time period beginning with the filing of a notice of appeal pursuant to § 16.1-269.3 or § 16.1-269.4 and ending with the order of the circuit court disposing of the appeal shall not be included as applying to the provisions of § 19.2-243.

History.
1994, cc. 859, 949; 1996, cc. 755, 914; 1997, c. 862; 2003, c. 144; 2004, c. 468; 2010, c. 739.

Cross references.
As to the one year deadline for claims of error or defect, see § 16.1-272.1.

Editor's note.
Acts 1993, c. 929, cl. 3, as amended by Acts 1994, c. 564, cl. 1 and Acts 1996, c. 616, cl. 3, provides that the contingent enactment of this section by Acts 1994, cc. 859 and 949, cl. 2, shall become effective June 1, 1998, "only if state funds are provided by the General Assembly sufficient to provide adequate resources for the court to carry out the purposes of this act and to fulfill its mission to serve children and families of the Commonwealth." The funding was not provided.

The 2010 amendments.
The 2010 amendment by c. 739 deleted the former fourth sentence of subsection B, which read: "Upon advising the attorney for the Commonwealth that he may seek an indictment, the circuit court may issue an order transferring the juvenile from the juvenile detention facility to an appropriate local correctional facility where the juvenile need no longer be entirely separate and removed from adults, unless, upon motion of counsel, good cause is shown for placement of the juvenile pursuant to the limitations of subdivision E (i), (ii), and (iii) of § 16.1-249."

Law Review.
For 2003/2004 survey of family and juvenile law, see 39 U. Rich. L. Rev. 241 (2004). For survey of Virginia criminal law and procedure for the year 2004-2005, see 40 U. Rich. L. Rev. 197 (2005). For note, "Let the Jury Do the Waive: How Apprendi v. New Jersey Applies to Juvenile Transfer Proceedings," see 48 Wm. & Mary L. Rev. 723 (2006).

CASE NOTES

The terms of subsection E establish a deadline before which any objections to the jurisdiction of the circuit court based on defects in the transfer process must be raised; the deadline for making such objections is the date of arraignment, and if objections are not raised before that date, the objections are waived. Shackleford v. Commonwealth, 262 Va. 196, 547 S.E.2d 899, 2001 Va. LEXIS 78 (2001).

Defects in transfer to Circuit Court cured. — Although defendant juvenile timely raised her objection to the jurisdiction of the circuit court, once the grand jury returned an indictment, the alleged defects in the transfer proceedings from the juvenile court to the circuit court were cured by the indictment; also, because any procedural errors in the appeal were cured by the indictment, the circuit court was not in any manner divested of its jurisdiction to try defendant on the charges set forth in the indictment. Thus, the circuit court did not err in exercising jurisdiction over the felony charges against defendant. Overdorff v. Commonwealth, 45 Va. App. 222, 609 S.E.2d 626, 2005 Va. App. LEXIS 81 (2005).

Return to juvenile court no longer required. — The nolle prosequi in the instant case did not have the same effect as it would have if decided under the old statute. Under the new statute, the circuit court retains jurisdiction and the Commonwealth may, as it did, seek new indictments without having to return to the juvenile court. Dara v. Commonwealth, No. 2795-95-1 (Ct. of Appeals Feb. 11, 1997).

Violation of speedy trial statute. — When the district court certified and transferred defendant for trial as an adult in the circuit court, the district court necessarily found the requisite probable cause contemplated by the speedy trial statute. Because the transfer order directed that defendant be "remanded to jail," the prescribed five month limitation of Section 19.2-243 commenced on October 4, 1995. It was immaterial that such custody coincided with detention of defendant incidental to an unrelated commitment. Irrespective of the trial court's order to quash, the initial indictments of defendant were a nullity, obtained without the benefit of the enabling order required by subsection B, and the court simply remedied of record an error or oversight in the proceedings, without disturbing the legal efficacy of the pending transfer order or effecting a nolle prosequi. Accordingly, defendant was held continuously in custody from the finding of probable cause in the district court on October 4, 1995, until trial on July 11, 1996, in violation of § 19.2-243, and the court had to reverse and dismiss the convictions. Price v. Commonwealth, 25 Va. App. 655, 492 S.E.2d 447 (1997), aff'd, 256 Va. 373, 506 S.E.2d 317 (1998).

Waiver of defect. — The plain language of this section clearly manifests legislative intent that any defect in the transfer proceedings conducted in the juvenile court as provided in this article is waived unless the juvenile raises an objection based on a defect in the juvenile court transfer hearing prior to arraignment in the circuit court. It is beyond question that the legislature has the authority to provide for a waiver of a defect in the transfer proceeding in this manner. Moore v. Commonwealth, 259 Va. 405, 527 S.E.2d 415 (2000), rev'd on other grounds, Pope v. Commonwealth, 37 Va. App. 451, 559 S.E.2d 388 (2002).

Review by circuit court. — The statute presently in effect does not require review if the transfer decision is not appealed; however, prior to the 1996 amendments, the statute clearly provided review, even if neither party filed an appeal to the juvenile court's transfer order. Jackson v. Commonwealth, 255 Va. 625, 499 S.E.2d 538 (1998), cert. denied, 525 U.S. 1067, 119 S. Ct. 796, 142 L. Ed. 2d 658 (1999).

Applied in Willis v. Commonwealth, 37 Va. App. 224, 556 S.E.2d 60, 2001 Va. App. LEXIS 689 (2001).

OPINIONS OF THE ATTORNEY GENERAL

Appeal of transfer order. — The circuit court is not required to enter an enabling order where the transfer decision of the juvenile court has not been appealed. Furthermore, a Commonwealth's attorney may seek an indictment after the period for an appeal has expired, provided no appeal has been noted. See opinion of Attorney General to The Honorable V. Thomas Forehand, Jr., Chief Judge, First Judicial Circuit of Virginia, 09-031, 2009 Va. AG LEXIS 31 (6/26/09).

§ 16.1-270. Waiver of jurisdiction of juvenile court in certain cases.

At any time prior to commencement of the adjudicatory hearing, a juvenile fourteen years of age or older charged with an offense which if committed by an adult could be punishable by confinement in a state correctional facility, with the written consent of his counsel, may elect in writing to waive the jurisdiction of the juvenile court and have his case transferred to the appropriate circuit court, in which event his case shall thereafter be dealt with in the same manner as if he had been transferred pursuant to this article.

History.
Code 1950, § 16.1-176.2; 1973, c. 440; 1977, c. 559; 1994, cc. 859, 949.

Editor's note.
Acts 1993, c. 930, cl. 3, as amended by Acts 1994, c. 564, cl. 2, and Acts 1996, c. 616, cl. 4, provides that the amendment to this section by Acts 1993, c. 930, cl. 1, shall become effective June 1, 1998, "if state funds are provided, including all local costs, to carry out the purposes of this bill by the General Assembly." The funding was not provided.

Michie's Jurisprudence.
For related discussion, see 9B M.J. Infants, § 13.

CASE NOTES

Waiver ineffective where juvenile and domestic court without jurisdiction. — Although this section provides that a juvenile, with the written consent of his counsel, may elect in writing to waive the jurisdiction of the juvenile and domestic court and have his case transferred to the appropriate circuit court, such waiver provision relates to transfer and does not dispense with the statutory parental notice necessary to confer subject matter jurisdiction upon the juvenile and domestic court at the inception of the proceedings; manifestly, a waiver permitted by this section is

predicated upon the existence of authority in the juvenile and domestic court to act, and cannot cure an antecedent and fatal defect in the underlying jurisdiction. Spain v. Commonwealth, 35 Va. App. 431, 545 S.E.2d 583, 2001 Va. App. LEXIS 242 (2001).

Equal protection not denied. — Defendant juvenile was not denied his equal protection rights under U.S. Const., amend. XIV, § 1 because he had no right in juvenile court to assert an insanity defense to attempting to poison his mother's tea with intent to kill or injure her in violation of § 18.2-54.1 as defendant suffered no disparate treatment as he had the same ability as an adult to assert an insanity defense under § 19.2-168 in the trial court, but he did not exercise his right under § 16.1-270 to be tried as adult and to assert the insanity defense available to him under the adult system. D.L.G. v. Commonwealth, 60 Va. App. 77, 724 S.E.2d 208, 2012 Va. App. LEXIS 123 (2012).

§ 16.1-271. Subsequent offenses by juvenile.

Conviction of a juvenile as an adult pursuant to the provisions of this chapter shall preclude the juvenile court from taking jurisdiction of such juvenile for subsequent offenses committed by that juvenile.

Any juvenile who is tried and convicted in a circuit court as an adult under the provisions of this article shall be considered and treated as an adult in any criminal proceeding resulting from any alleged future criminal acts and any pending allegations of delinquency which have not been disposed of by the juvenile court at the time of the criminal conviction.

All procedures and dispositions applicable to adults charged with such a criminal offense shall apply in such cases, including, but not limited to, arrest; probable cause determination by a magistrate or grand jury; the use of a warrant, summons, or capias instead of a petition to initiate the case; adult bail; preliminary hearing and right to counsel provisions; trial in a court having jurisdiction over adults; and trial and sentencing as an adult. The provisions of this article regarding a transfer hearing shall not be applicable to such juveniles.

History.
1977, c. 559; 1989, c. 675; 1990, c. 668; 1994, cc. 859, 949; 2007, c. 221.

Editor's note.
At the direction of the Virginia Code Commission, "from taking" has been substituted for "for taking" in the first sentence to correct an error in the 2007 act.
Acts 1993, c. 930, cl. 3, as amended by Acts 1994, c. 564, cl. 2, and Acts 1996, c. 616, cl. 4, provides that the amendment to this section by Acts 1993, c. 930, cl. 1, shall become effective June 1, 1998, "if state funds are provided, including all local costs, to carry out the purposes of this bill by the General Assembly." The funding was not provided.

Law Review.
For survey on legal issues involving children in Virginia for 1989, see 23 U. Rich. L. Rev. 705 (1989). For an article, "Criminal Law and Procedure," see 31 U. Rich. L. Rev. 1015 (1997). For 2000 survey of Virginia law regarding children, see 34 U. Rich. L. Rev. 939 (2000). For 2003/2004 survey of criminal law and procedure, see 39 U. Rich. L. Rev. 133 (2004). For 2003/2004 survey of family and juvenile law, see 39 U. Rich. L. Rev. 241 (2004). For 2007 annual survey article, "Criminal Law and Procedure," see 42 U. Rich. L. Rev. 311 (2007). For annual survey article, "Criminal Law and Procedure," see 46 U. Rich. L. Rev. 59 (2011).

Michie's Jurisprudence.
For related discussion, see 9B M.J. Infants, § 84; 17 M.J. Statutes, § 47.

CASE NOTES

Effect of 1994 amendment. — Prior to 1994, the treatment of a juvenile as an adult specifically did not prohibit the juvenile court from exercising jurisdiction on subsequent charges. However, the 1994 amendment intentionally altered that procedure and now precludes the juvenile court from exercising jurisdiction over a juvenile once the juvenile has been tried or treated as an adult on an earlier charge. Broadnax v. Commonwealth, 24 Va. App. 808, 485 S.E.2d 666 (1997).

Conviction in circuit court divests juvenile court of jurisdiction. — A juvenile who has been convicted as an adult in circuit court under the provisions of this article is not entitled to a transfer hearing in juvenile court for any pending unrelated allegations of delinquency which have not been disposed of by the juvenile court at the time of the criminal conviction. A prior conviction in the circuit court for unrelated offenses precludes the juvenile court from thereafter exercising jurisdiction regardless of the defendant's age at the time of the institution of the proceedings. Asby v. Commonwealth, 34 Va. App. 217, 539 S.E.2d 742, 2001 Va. App. LEXIS 4 (2001).

Although defendant was only 17 years old, jury sentencing was proper in his adult trial because pursuant to this section, § 16.1-272 did not apply where defendant had previously been tried and convicted as an adult on an unrelated charge. Saunders v. Commonwealth, 56 Va. App. 139, 692 S.E.2d 252, 2010 Va. App. LEXIS 169 (2010), aff'd, 281 Va. 448, 706 S.E.2d 350, 2011 Va. LEXIS 45 (2011).

Probable cause finding divested juvenile court of jurisdiction for future offenses. — Defendant juvenile, tried as an adult on a charge of malicious wounding and convicted of the lesser included offense of unlawful wounding, could not have the case transferred back to the juvenile court, as once the juvenile court made a probable cause finding, the juvenile court had no further jurisdiction; the juvenile court was also precluded from taking jurisdiction subsequent offenses committed by that juvenile, pursuant to § 16.1-271. Hughes v. Commonwealth, 39 Va. App. 448, 573 S.E.2d 324, 2002 Va. App. LEXIS 765 (2002).

Prior conviction as adult renders transfer procedures inapplicable. — A defendant's argument that original indictments were void because the circuit court failed to review the transfer record from the juvenile court as required by statute before the indictments were obtained was without merit because the defendant previously had been tried and convicted as an adult in another circuit court for rape and such prior conviction as an adult eliminated the requirement that the circuit court review the transfer proceedings. Johnson v. Commonwealth, 259 Va. 654, 529 S.E.2d 769, 2000 Va. LEXIS 60, cert. denied, 531 U.S. 981, 121 S. Ct. 432, 148 L. Ed. 2d 439 (2000).

Juvenile procedures inapplicable to subsequent offense. — Where the defendant had previously been tried and convicted of a rape which occurred several days before the rape and capital murder with which he was presently charged, the later rape and capital murder constituted "alleged future criminal acts" for purposes of this section and rendered inapplicable the procedures for transferring a case so that a juvenile may be charged as an adult and for giving notice to the juvenile's parents. Johnson v. Commonwealth, 259 Va. 654, 529 S.E.2d 769, 2000 Va. LEXIS 60, cert. denied, 531 U.S. 981, 121 S. Ct. 432, 148 L. Ed. 2d 439 (2000).

Failure to challenge certification in other proceeding. — Because the defendant failed to raise the jurisdictional issue of lack of notice to his father when he was certified for trial as an adult in another county before the indictments were returned in the circuit court in the instant case, failure to comply with the parental notification provisions of the statutes did not deprive the circuit court of jurisdiction in the instant case. Monteon v. Commonwealth, No. 2038-99-3, 2000 Va. App. LEXIS 316 (Ct. of Appeals May 2, 2000).

Sentencing by a jury. — The fact that a defendant was convicted as an adult of crimes committed when he was a juvenile after he had previously been convicted of another crime as an adult did not mean he was entitled to be sentenced by a jury. The offenses for which he was to be sentenced occurred before the offense of which he had previously been convicted as an adult and were not, therefore, "future criminal acts," nor were they the subject of delinquency allegations pending in the juvenile court at the time of

his first conviction as an adult. Ingram v. Commonwealth, No. 1791-01-1, 2002 Va. App. LEXIS 593 (Ct. of Appeals Oct. 8, 2002).

Jury sentencing was proper in a minor defendant's adult trial because § 16.1-271 permitted all adult sentencing procedures and dispositions, including jury sentencing. Saunders v. Commonwealth, 56 Va. App. 139, 692 S.E.2d 252, 2010 Va. App. LEXIS 169 (2010), aff'd, 281 Va. 448, 706 S.E.2d 350, 2011 Va. LEXIS 45 (2011).

When defendant appeared before a circuit court for sentencing on criminal charges under § 16.1-269.1, the jury was correctly allowed to sentence defendant because he was not a juvenile in that he had been previously convicted as an adult on an unrelated charge and given an adult sentence. Section 16.1-272 did not apply to youthful offenders who fell within the scope of § 16.1-271, while § 16.1-271 applied to any juvenile who was tried and convicted in a circuit court as an adult. Saunders v. Commonwealth, 281 Va. 448, 706 S.E.2d 350, 2011 Va. LEXIS 45 (2011).

Trial as an adult proper where previous charges ended by nolle prosequi. — Defendant was properly tried as an adult under § 16.1-271 on attempted murder, use of a firearm in the commission of attempted murder, robbery, and use of a firearm in the commission of robbery charges, where he had been certified as adult under subsection C of § 16.1-269.1 on previous charges of robbery and aggravated malicious wounding; although the previous charges terminated by nolle prosequi, defendant was treated as an adult during the pendency of the prior proceedings, which status continued pursuant to § 16.1-271. Cook v. Commonwealth, No. 1968-02-2, 2003 Va. App. LEXIS 375 (Ct. of Appeals July 1, 2003), aff'd, 268 Va. 111, 597 S.E.2d 84 (2004) But see the 2007 amendment to this section which substituted "Conviction of a juvenile" for "The trial or treatment of a juvenile." .

Applied in Willis v. Commonwealth, 37 Va. App. 224, 556 S.E.2d 60, 2001 Va. App. LEXIS 689 (2001).

CIRCUIT COURT OPINIONS

Juvenile court retained jurisdiction to enforce previous order. — Despite the fact that defendant had already been tried and convicted on unrelated charges as an adult in the circuit court, the juvenile court retained jurisdiction to enforce its previous order sentencing him to jail time, and the juvenile proceedings subsequent to his conviction were simply an exercise of the court's inherent authority to enforce its orders. Commonwealth v. Stewart, 71 Va. Cir. 313, 2006 Va. Cir. LEXIS 224 (Page County 2006).

§ 16.1-272. Power of circuit court over juvenile offender.

A. In any case in which a juvenile is indicted, the offense for which he is indicted and all ancillary charges shall be tried in the same manner as provided for in the trial of adults, except as otherwise provided with regard to sentencing. Upon a finding of guilty of any charge, the court shall fix the sentence without the intervention of a jury.

1. If a juvenile is convicted of a violent juvenile felony, for that offense and for all ancillary crimes the court may order that (i) the juvenile serve a portion of the sentence as a serious juvenile offender under § 16.1-285.1 and the remainder of such sentence in the same manner as provided for adults; (ii) the juvenile serve the entire sentence in the same manner as provided for adults; or (iii) the portion of the sentence to be served in the same manner as provided for adults be suspended conditioned upon successful completion of such terms and conditions as may be imposed in a juvenile court upon disposition of a delinquency case including, but not limited to, commitment under subdivision A 14 of § 16.1-278.8 or § 16.1-285.1.

2. If the juvenile is convicted of any other felony, the court may sentence or commit the juvenile offender in accordance with the criminal laws of this Commonwealth or may in its discretion deal with the juvenile in the manner prescribed in this chapter for the hearing and disposition of cases in the juvenile court, including, but not limited to, commitment under § 16.1-285.1 or may in its discretion impose an adult sentence and suspend the sentence conditioned upon successful completion of such terms and conditions as may be imposed in a juvenile court upon disposition of a delinquency case.

3. If the juvenile is not convicted of a felony but is convicted of a misdemeanor, the court shall deal with the juvenile in the manner prescribed by law for the disposition of a delinquency case in the juvenile court.

B. If the circuit court decides to deal with the juvenile in the same manner as a case in the juvenile court and places the juvenile on probation, the juvenile may be supervised by a juvenile probation officer.

C. Whether the court sentences and commits the juvenile as a juvenile under this chapter or under the criminal law, in cases where the juvenile is convicted of a felony in violation of § 18.2-61, 18.2-63, 18.2-64.1, 18.2-67.1, 18.2-67.2, 18.2-67.3, 18.2-67.5, 18.2-370 or 18.2-370.1 or, where the victim is a minor or is physically helpless or mentally incapacitated as defined in § 18.2-67.10, subsection B of § 18.2-361 or subsection B of § 18.2-366, the clerk shall make the report required by § 19.2-390 to the Sex Offender and Crimes Against Minors Registry established pursuant to Chapter 9 (§ 9.1-900 et seq.) of Title 9.1.

D. A juvenile sentenced pursuant to clause (i) of subdivision A 1 shall be eligible to earn sentence credits in the manner prescribed by § 53.1-202.2 for the portion of the sentence served as a serious juvenile offender under § 16.1-285.1.

E. If the court sentences the juvenile as a juvenile under this chapter, the clerk shall provide a copy of the court's final order or judgment to the court service unit in the same locality as the juvenile court to which the case had been transferred.

History.
Code 1950, § 16.1-177; 1956, c. 555; 1977, c. 559; 1994, c. 362; 1996, cc. 755, 914; 2000, c. 793; 2002, c. 511; 2003, c. 584; 2005, c. 590; 2007, c. 460; 2008, c. 517.

Editor's note.
Acts 1993, c. 930, cl. 3, as amended by Acts 1994, c. 564, cl. 2, and Acts 1996, c. 616, cl. 4, provides that the amendment to this section by Acts 1993, c. 930, cl. 1, shall become effective June 1, 1998, "if state funds are provided, including all local costs, to carry out the purposes of this bill by the General Assembly." The funding was not provided.

Law Review.
For a review of Virginia legal issues involving children, see 33 U. Rich. L. Rev. 1001 (1999). For 2000 survey of Virginia law regarding children, see 34 U. Rich. L. Rev. 939 (2000). For annual survey article, "Criminal Law and Procedure," see 46 U. Rich. L. Rev. 59 (2011).

Michie's Jurisprudence.
For related discussion, see 5B M.J. Criminal Procedure, § 72; 6B M.J. Drugs and Druggists, § 5; 9B M.J. Infants, § 13.

CASE NOTES

Construction with § 18.2-53.1. — The terms of § 18.2-53.1, providing for a mandatory, unsuspended sentence for persons convicted of use of a firearm in the commission of certain felonies "notwithstanding any other provision of law," require a trial court to impose the mandatory, unsuspended sentence on a juvenile convicted of one of the enumerated felonies despite the provisions of this section. Green v. Commonwealth, 28 Va. App. 567, 507 S.E.2d 627 (1998).

Notwithstanding the 2004 amendment to § 18.2-53.1, *Green v. Commonwealth*, 28 Va. App. 567, 507 S.E.2d 627 (1998), remains valid and precludes the courts from applying clause (iii) of subdivision A 1 of § 16.1-272 to suspend any part of a mandatory minimum sentence imposed under § 18.2-53.1. Bullock v. Commonwealth, 48 Va. App. 359, 631 S.E.2d 334, 2006 Va. App. LEXIS 296 (2006).

Juvenile defendant who was charged as an adult and pled guilty to five counts of use of a firearm in the commission of a felony, in violation of § 18.2-53.1, should have been sentenced to the mandatory minimum rather than sentenced to juvenile dispositions under § 16.1-272 because the statutes were in conflict, and § 18.2-53.1 was the more specific statute. Brown v. Commonwealth, 279 Va. 210, 688 S.E.2d 185, 2010 Va. LEXIS 9 (2010).

Use of firearm in commission of felony. — Even after the 2004 statutory amendments, the mandatory sentencing provisions of § 18.2-53.1 control over the juvenile sentencing options contained in subdivision A 1 of § 16.1-272 that allow suspension of an adult sentence. Commonwealth v. Brown, 2008 Va. App. LEXIS 517 (2008), aff'd in part and rev'd in part, 279 Va. 210, 688 S.E.2d 185, 2010 Va. LEXIS 9 (2010).

Convictions for using a firearm in the commission of robbery were clearly "ancillary crimes" requiring sentencing under subdivision A 1 of § 16.1-272 rather than subdivision A 2 of § 16.1-272, and the mandatory sentencing provisions of § 18.2-53.1 controlled over the juvenile sentencing options in subdivision A 1 of § 16.1-272. Thus, defendants had to receive the mandatory minimum sentences. Commonwealth v. Brown, 2008 Va. App. LEXIS 517 (2008), aff'd in part and rev'd in part, 279 Va. 210, 688 S.E.2d 185, 2010 Va. LEXIS 9 (2010).

This statute places solely upon the trial judge the obligation to sentence the juvenile offender in accordance with the criminal laws or in the manner prescribed for juvenile court cases. Stephens v. Commonwealth, No. 1690-93-1 (Ct. of Appeals March 28, 1995).

The word "or" in subdivision A 2 does not reflect a legislative intent to prohibit a judge from sentencing a juvenile both as an adult and as a juvenile "serious offender" pursuant to § 16.1-285.1. Jackson v. Commonwealth, 29 Va. App. 418, 512 S.E.2d 838 (1999).

Fixing of sentence by judge does not deprive juveniles of equal protection. — Juveniles are not deprived of equal protection by the Virginia procedure in criminal cases, whereby an adult tried by jury has his sentence fixed by the jury under § 19.2-295, while a juvenile transferred to circuit court and tried by jury has his sentence fixed by the judge under this section. Ballard v. Commonwealth, 228 Va. 213, 321 S.E.2d 284 (1984), cert. denied, 470 U.S. 1085, 105 S. Ct. 1848, 85 L. Ed. 2d 146 (1985).

Rational basis exists for different sentencing procedure for juveniles. — A rational basis does exist for the classification under which sentences of adults are fixed by juries but sentences of juveniles transferred to the circuit court are fixed by the judge. While, for the purpose of determining guilt or innocence, a transferred juvenile is treated as an adult, and although he may be subject to adult penalties in the sentencing phase of his case, this section permits a circuit court to treat him in all respects as a juvenile, with the full panoply of beneficent alternatives available in juvenile court, including the use of a juvenile probation officer. Ballard v. Commonwealth, 228 Va. 213, 321 S.E.2d 284 (1984), cert. denied, 470 U.S. 1085, 105 S. Ct. 1848, 85 L. Ed. 2d 146 (1985).

Purpose of having judge rather than jury set sentence. —

In enacting this section, the General Assembly obviously opted for judge-sentencing for transferred juveniles because it perceived the inability of juries to adequately comprehend the differences in the sentencing of a juvenile defendant as an adult, and the treatment of that same child within the framework of the juvenile court laws. Ballard v. Commonwealth, 228 Va. 213, 321 S.E.2d 284 (1984), cert. denied, 470 U.S. 1085, 105 S. Ct. 1848, 85 L. Ed. 2d 146 (1985).

When child dealt with as adult. — This section recognizes that cases arise of such serious character as to require that the child be dealt with as an adult under the general criminal laws. Durrette v. Commonwealth, 201 Va. 735, 113 S.E.2d 842 (1960).

Defendant who was convicted as an adult of crimes committed when he was a juvenile had to be sentenced by the court, without the intervention of a jury, because he was not convicted of capital murder. Ingram v. Commonwealth, No. 1791-01-1, 2002 Va. App. LEXIS 593 (Ct. of Appeals Oct. 8, 2002).

Although defendant was only 17 years old, jury sentencing was proper in his adult trial because pursuant to § 16.1-271, § 16.1-272 did not apply where defendant had previously been tried and convicted as an adult on an unrelated charge. Saunders v. Commonwealth, 56 Va. App. 139, 692 S.E.2d 252, 2010 Va. App. LEXIS 169 (2010), aff'd, 281 Va. 448, 706 S.E.2d 350, 2011 Va. LEXIS 45 (2011).

Probable cause finding divested juvenile court of jurisdiction. — Defendant juvenile, tried as an adult on a charge of malicious wounding and convicted of the lesser included offense of unlawful wounding, could not have the case transferred back to the juvenile court, as once the juvenile court made a probable cause finding, the juvenile court had no further jurisdiction; the trial court had express authority to impose sentence on defendant, under subsection A of § 16.1-272, as there was a felony conviction, even though the felony was not a violent juvenile felony, because the case was transferred to the circuit court following a probable cause determination. Hughes v. Commonwealth, 39 Va. App. 448, 573 S.E.2d 324, 2002 Va. App. LEXIS 765 (2002).

Sentencing by jury in capital murder case. — A juvenile who is convicted by a jury of capital murder should be sentenced by the jury pursuant to §§ 19.2-264.3 and 19.2-264.4. Thomas v. Commonwealth, 244 Va. 1, 419 S.E.2d 606, cert. denied, 506 U.S. 958, 113 S. Ct. 421, 121 L. Ed. 2d 343 (1992).

Sentencing by jury. — When defendant appeared before a circuit court for sentencing on criminal charges under § 16.1-269.1, the jury was correctly allowed to sentence defendant because he was not a juvenile in that he had been previously convicted as an adult on an unrelated charge and given an adult sentence. Section 16.1-272 did not apply to youthful offenders who fell within the scope of § 16.1-271, while § 16.1-271 applied to any juvenile who was tried and convicted in a circuit court as an adult. Saunders v. Commonwealth, 281 Va. 448, 706 S.E.2d 350, 2011 Va. LEXIS 45 (2011).

Discretion of court. — The discretion lodged in the court of record is a sound judicial discretion, to be exercised not arbitrarily or willfully, but based upon knowledge of facts upon which the discretion might properly operate. Tilton v. Commonwealth, 196 Va. 774, 85 S.E.2d 368 (1955).

Where a juvenile was properly certified to a court of record in connection with offenses committed when he was sixteen and thereafter was tried as an adult when he was seventeen, there was no merit in the contention that the trial court erred in not trying him as a juvenile. It was not shown that there was abuse of the discretion given the court of record by this section. Holt v. City of Richmond, 204 Va. 364, 131 S.E.2d 394 (1963), cert. denied, 376 U.S. 917, 84 S. Ct. 672, 11 L. Ed. 2d 613 (1964).

Defendant, a juvenile who was certified to be tried as adult, was properly sentenced to an adult facility because, his assertions to the contrary notwithstanding, the trial court was aware of its authority to allow him to serve part of his sentence in a juvenile facility; it simply elected not to do so. Bullock v. Commonwealth, 48 Va. App. 359, 631 S.E.2d 334, 2006 Va. App. LEXIS 296 (2006).

Accommodation defense. — In a prosecution for distribution of cocaine, the trial court did not err by not allowing the jury to consider the juvenile's accommodation defense during the guilt phase of the trial; this defense was only relevant to sentencing, and the trial court, not the jury, determined sentence in a juvenile case. Foster v. Commonwealth, 38 Va. App. 549, 567 S.E.2d 547, 2002 Va. App. LEXIS 447 (2002).

Defendant who was convicted as an adult of crimes committed when he was a juvenile had to be sentenced by the court, without the intervention of a jury, because he was not convicted of capital murder. Ingram v. Commonwealth, No. 1791-01-1, 2002 Va. App. LEXIS 593 (Ct. of Appeals Oct. 8, 2002).

Court had authority to order combination of sentences which imposed a juvenile commitment and an adult prison sentence. Jackson v. Commonwealth, 29 Va. App. 418, 512 S.E.2d 838 (1999).

Imposition of juvenile treatment requires full results of juvenile hearing. — Since, under former § 16.1-269, the reports of the juvenile court are certified to the court of record in the event of transfer, and the latter court may impose juvenile treatment rather than adult sentence under this section, for consideration of that alternative the court of record needs the full results of a proper juvenile hearing. James v. Cox, 323 F. Supp. 15 (E.D. Va. 1971).

Question whether sentence is constitutionally excessive. — The question of whether the imposition of an aggregate sentence of 80 years upon a 17-year-old defendant following his pleas of guilty to three charges of robbery was constitutionally excessive should be initially litigated in the courts of Virginia. Saunders v. Cox, 470 F.2d 734 (4th Cir. 1972), cert. denied, 412 U.S. 951, 93 S. Ct. 3018, 37 L. Ed. 2d 1004 (1973).

Applied in Thomas v. Taylor, 170 F.3d 466 (4th. Cir. 1999).

OPINIONS OF THE ATTORNEY GENERAL

Juvenile who has been convicted as an adult may be housed in an adult jail facility pending transfer to the Department of Juvenile Justice. See opinion of Attorney General to The Honorable Robert J. McCabe, Sheriff for City of Norfolk, 05-012 (3/29/05).

§ 16.1-272.1. Claim of error to be raised within one year.

In addition to any other curative provisions, waivers, procedural defaults, or requirements for timely objection, including but not limited to those in subsection J of § 16.1-241, subsection E of § 16.1-269.1 and subsection E of § 16.1-269.6, any claim of error or defect under this chapter, jurisdictional or otherwise, that is not raised within one year from the date of final judgment of the circuit court or one year from the effective date of this act, whichever is later, shall not constitute a ground for relief in any judicial proceeding.

History.
2000, c. 418.

Editor's note.
Acts 1993, c. 929, cl. 3, as amended by Acts 1994, c. 564, cl. 1, and Acts 1996, c. 616, cl. 3, provides that the enactment of §§ 16.1-272.1 and 16.1-272.2 by Acts 1993, c. 929, cl. 1, shall become effective June 1, 1998, "only if state funds are provided by the General Assembly sufficient to provide adequate resources, including all local costs, for the court to carry out the purposes of this act and to fulfill its mission to serve children and families of the Commonwealth." The funding was not provided.

CASE NOTES

Section did not intend to abrogate Va. Sup. Ct. R. 1:1. — As to appellant's motions to vacate his conviction for sexual battery filed ten months after entry of the conviction order, the language of § 16.1-272.1 was not susceptible to an interpretation that suggested it was intended to abrogate Va. Sup. Ct. R. 1:1 and other procedural requirements that had to be satisfied before asserting a claim of error, as appellant claimed. Locklear v. Commonwealth, 46 Va. App. 488, 618 S.E.2d 361, 2005 Va. App. LEXIS 361 (2005).

CIRCUIT COURT OPINIONS

Failure to timely file. — Because a circuit court had jurisdiction over defendant after defendant was certified as an adult for trial, because defendant's motion to vacate was untimely, and because defendant did not raise a Fourth Amendment challenge prior to filing the motion, pursuant to § 16.1-272.1, defendant's arguments were waived. Commonwealth v. Douglas, 72 Va. Cir. 385, 2007 Va. Cir. LEXIS 3 (Fairfax County 2007).

ARTICLE 8.

ADJUDICATION.

§ 16.1-273. Court may require investigation of social history and preparation of victim impact statement.

A. When a juvenile and domestic relations district court or circuit court has adjudicated any case involving a child subject to the jurisdiction of the court hereunder, except for a traffic violation, a violation of the game and fish law or a violation of any city ordinance regulating surfing or establishing curfew violations, the court before final disposition thereof may require an investigation, which (i) shall include a drug screening and (ii) may, and for the purposes of § 16.1-278.7 shall, include the physical, mental and social conditions, including an assessment of any affiliation with a criminal street gang as defined in § 18.2-46.1, and personality of the child and the facts and circumstances surrounding the violation of law. However, in the case of a juvenile adjudicated delinquent on the basis of an act committed on or after January 1, 2000, which would be a felony if committed by an adult, or a violation under Article 1 (§ 18.2-247 et seq.) or Article 1.1 (§ 18.2-265.1 et seq.) of Chapter 7 of Title 18.2 and such offense would be punishable as a Class 1 or Class 2 misdemeanor if committed by an adult, the court shall order the juvenile to undergo a drug screening. If the drug screening indicates that the juvenile has a substance abuse or dependence problem, an assessment shall be completed by a certified substance abuse counselor as defined in § 54.1-3500 employed by the Department of Juvenile Justice or by a locally operated court services unit or by an individual employed by or currently under contract to such agencies and who is specifically trained to conduct such assessments under the supervision of such counselor.

B. The court also shall, on motion of the attorney for the Commonwealth with the consent of the victim, or may in its discretion, require the preparation of a victim impact statement in accordance with the provisions of § 19.2-299.1 if the court determines that the victim may have suffered significant physical, psychological or economic injury as a result of the violation of law.

History.

Code 1950, § 16.1-164; 1956, c. 555; 1972, cc. 672, 835; 1973, c. 440; 1977, cc. 559, 627; 1993, c. 603; 1998, cc. 783, 840; 1999, cc. 350, 891, 913; 2000, cc. 1020, 1041; 2005, c. 843; 2007, c. 510.

Cross references.

For disposition of court-ordered studies and reports, see Rule 8:5, Juvenile and Domestic Relations District Court Rules.

Editor's note.

Acts 1993, c. 930, cl. 3, as amended by Acts 1994, c. 564, cl. 2, and Acts 1996, c. 616, cl. 4, provides that the amendment to this section by Acts 1993, c. 930, cl. 1, shall become effective June 1, 1998, "if state funds are provided, including all local costs, to carry out the purposes of this bill by the General Assembly." The funding was not provided.

Acts 2012, Sp. Sess. I, c. 3, as amended by Acts 2013, c. 806, effective for the biennium ending June 30, 2014, Item 407 provides: "Notwithstanding the provisions of § 16.1-273 of the Code of Virginia, the Department of Juvenile Justice, including locally-operated court services units, shall not be required to provide drug screening and assessment services in conjunction with investigations ordered by the courts."

Law Review.

For article, "The Revision of Virginia's Juvenile Court Law," see 13 U. Rich. L. Rev. 847 (1979).

§ 16.1-274. Time for filing of reports; copies furnished to attorneys; amended reports; fees.

A. Whenever any court directs an investigation pursuant to subdivision A of § 16.1-237 or § 16.1-273 or 9.1-153, or an evaluation pursuant to § 16.1-278.5, the probation officer, court-appointed special advocate, or other agency conducting such investigation shall file such report with the clerk of the court directing the investigation. The clerk shall furnish a copy of such report to all attorneys representing parties in the matter before the court no later than 72 hours, and in cases of child custody, 15 days, prior to the time set by the court for hearing the matter. If such probation officer or other agency discovers additional information or a change in circumstance after the filing of the report, an amended report shall be filed forthwith and a copy sent to each person who received a copy of the original report. Whenever such a report is not filed or an amended report is filed, the court shall grant such continuance of the proceedings as justice requires. All attorneys receiving such report or amended report shall return such to the clerk upon the conclusion of the hearing and shall not make copies of such report or amended report or any portion thereof. However, the chief judge of each juvenile and domestic relations district court may provide for an alternative means of copying and distributing reports or amended reports filed pursuant to § 9.1-153.

B. Notwithstanding the provisions of §§ 16.1-69.48:2 and 17.1-275, when the court directs the appropriate local department of social services to conduct supervised visitation or directs the appropriate local department of social services or court services unit to conduct an investigation pursuant to § 16.1-273 or to provide mediation services in matters involving a child's custody, visitation, or support, the court shall assess a fee against the petitioner, the respondent, or both, in accordance with fee schedules established by the appropriate local board of social services when the service is provided by a local department of social services or by a court services unit. The fee schedules shall include (i) standards for determining the paying party's or parties' ability to pay and (ii) a scale of fees based on the paying party's or parties' income and family size and the actual cost of the services provided. The fee charged shall not exceed the actual cost of the service. The fee shall be assessed as a cost of the case and shall be paid as prescribed by the court to the local department of social services, locally operated court services unit or Department of Juvenile Justice, whichever performed the service, unless payment is waived. The method and medium for payment for such services shall be determined by the local department of social services, Department of Juvenile Justice, or the locally operated court services unit that provided the services.

C. When a local department of social services or any court services unit is requested by another local department or court services unit in the Commonwealth or by a similar department or entity in another state to conduct an investigation involving a child's custody, visitation or support pursuant to § 16.1-273 or, in the case of a request from another state pursuant to a provision corresponding to § 16.1-273, or to provide mediation services, or for a local department of social services to provide supervised visitation, the local department or the court services unit performing the service may require payment of fees prior to conducting the investigation or providing mediation services or supervised visitation.

History.
Code 1950, § 16.1-208.1; 1972, c. 111; 1975, c. 286; 1977, c. 559; 1983, c. 174; 1987, c. 5; 1989, c. 725; 1990, c. 752; 1991, cc. 534, 618; 1992, c. 554; 1993, c. 975; 2001, c. 364; 2006, c. 675; 2012, cc. 164, 456.

Cross references.
For disposition of court-ordered studies and reports, see Rule 8:5, Juvenile and Domestic Relations District Court Rules. As to the Court-Appointed Special Advocate Program and volunteer court-appointed special advocates, see § 9.1-153. As to fee assessed in adoption proceedings, see § 17.1-275. For provision authorizing local boards to establish regulations and fee schedules and receive fees for services that a court directs a local department to perform pursuant to § 16.1-274, see § 63.2-314. As to fees assessed for adoption services, see § 63.2-1248.

The 2012 amendments.
The 2012 amendments by cc. 164 and 456 are identical, and substituted "pursuant to subdivision A of § 16.1-237 or § 16.1-273 or 9.1-153, or" for "pursuant to subsection A of § 16.1-237, § 16.1-273, or § 9.1-153, or" in the first sentence of subsection A; substituted "social services or by a court services unit" for "social services and by the State Board of Juvenile Justice when the service is provided by a court services unit" at the end of the first sentence of subsection B; and made a stylistic change.

Law Review.
For article, "Legal Issues Involving Children," see 35 U. Rich. L. Rev. 741 (2001).

Research references.
Virginia Forms (Matthew Bender). No. 5-236 Assessment of Costs/Payment Order.

CASE NOTES

Preparation and filing of reports. — Statutory law permitted court-appointed special advocate to submit to the court a written report of the advocate's investigation into what was best for the child's welfare in a proceeding to terminate parental rights and directed the advocate to file that report with the clerk of the court directing the investigation, and, thus, the trial court did not err in admitting that report into evidence; accordingly, the father's objection that the report violated the hearsay rule had to be rejected. Holley v. Amherst County Dep't of Soc. Servs., No. 3397-02-3, 2003 Va. App. LEXIS 330 (Ct. of Appeals June 10, 2003).

§ 16.1-274.1. Admission of evidence of juvenile's age.

In any proceeding in a district court or circuit court where a juvenile is alleged to have committed a delinquent act, the Commonwealth shall be permitted to introduce evidence establishing the age of the juvenile at any time prior to adjudication of the case.

History.
1994, c. 913; 1996, cc. 755, 914.

§ 16.1-276.1. Repealed by Acts 2002, c. 305.

§ 16.1-276.2. Transportation orders in certain proceedings.

In any proceeding (i) pursuant to subdivisions 2, 4 or 5 of subsection A of § 16.1-241, (ii) pursuant to subsections K or U of § 16.1-241, (iii) involving a child who is alleged to be abused or neglected, or (iv) involving a child who is before the court pursuant to §§ 16.1-281, 16.1-282 or § 16.1-282.1, if the judge finds that the presence at a hearing of a prisoner in a state, local or regional correctional institution is essential to the just adjudication and disposition of the proceeding, the judge may issue an order to the Director of the Department of Corrections or the administrator of the state, local or regional correctional institution to deliver such witness to the sheriff of the jurisdiction of the court issuing the order. Such orders shall be executed in accordance with § 8.01-410. Any such orders shall issue only upon consideration of the importance of the personal appearance of the person.

The party seeking the testimony of such prisoner shall advance a sum sufficient to defray the expenses and compensation of the officers, which the court shall tax as costs. When the party seeking the attendance of the prisoner is an agency of the Commonwealth or when the attendance is sought on motion of the court, no sum shall be advanced to defray the expenses or compensation of the correctional officers and sheriff nor shall any such sum be taxed as costs.

History.
2001, c. 513.

Law Review.
For article, "Legal Issues Involving Children," see 35 U. Rich. L. Rev. 741 (2001).

§ 16.1-276.3. Use of telephonic communication systems or electronic video and audio communication systems to conduct hearing.

Notwithstanding any other provision of law, in any civil proceeding under this chapter in which a party or witness is incarcerated or when otherwise authorized by the court, the court may, in its discretion, conduct any hearing using a telephonic communication system or an electronic audio and video communication system to provide for the appearance of any parties and witnesses. Any electronic audio and video communication system used to conduct such a hearing shall meet the standards set forth in subsection B of § 19.2-3.1.

History.
2001, c. 513.

Law Review.
For article, "Legal Issues Involving Children," see 35 U. Rich. L. Rev. 741 (2001).

§ 16.1-277.01. Approval of entrustment agreement.

A. In any case in which a child has been entrusted pursuant to § 63.2-903 or 63.2-1817 to the local board of social services or to a child welfare agency, a petition for approval of the entrustment agreement by the board or agency:

1. Shall be filed within a reasonable period of time, no later than 89 days after the execution of an entrustment agreement for less than 90 days, if the child is not returned to the caretaker from whom he was entrusted within that period;

2. Shall be filed within a reasonable period of time, not to exceed 30 days after the execution of an entrustment agreement for 90 days or longer or for an unspecified period of time, if such entrustment agreement does not provide for the termination of all parental rights and responsibilities with respect to the child; and

3. May be filed in the case of a permanent entrustment agreement which provides for the termination of all parental rights and responsibilities with respect to the child.

The board or agency shall file a foster care plan pursuant to § 16.1-281 to be heard with any petition for approval of an entrustment agreement.

B. Upon the filing of a petition for approval of an entrustment agreement pursuant to subsection A of § 16.1-241, the court shall appoint a guardian ad litem to represent the child in accordance with the provisions of § 16.1-266, and shall schedule the matter for a hearing to be held as follows: within 45 days of the filing of a petition pursuant to subdivision A 1, A 2 or A 3, except where an order of publication has been ordered by the court, in which case the hearing shall be held within 75 days of the filing of the petition. The court shall provide notice of the hearing and a copy of the petition to the

following, each of whom shall be a party entitled to participate in the proceeding:

1. The local board of social services or child welfare agency;

2. The child, if he is 12 years of age or older;

3. The guardian ad litem for the child; and

4. The child's parents, guardian, legal custodian or other person standing in loco parentis to the child. No such notification shall be required, however, if the judge certifies on the record that the identity of the parent or guardian is not reasonably ascertainable. A birth father shall be given notice of the proceedings if he is an acknowledged father pursuant to § 20-49.1, adjudicated pursuant to § 20-49.8, or presumed pursuant to § 63.2-1202, or has registered with the Putative Father Registry pursuant to Article 7 (§ 63.2-1249 et seq.). An affidavit of the mother that the identity of the father is not reasonably ascertainable shall be sufficient evidence of this fact, provided there is no other evidence before the court which would refute such an affidavit. Failure to register with the Putative Father Registry pursuant to Article 7 (§ 63.2-1249 et seq.) of Chapter 12 of Title 63.2 shall be evidence that the identity of the father is not reasonably ascertainable. The hearing shall be held and an order may be entered, although a parent, guardian, legal custodian or person standing in loco parentis fails to appear and is not represented by counsel, provided personal or substituted service was made on the person, or the court determines that such person cannot be found, after reasonable effort, or in the case of a person who is without the Commonwealth, the person cannot be found or his post office address cannot be ascertained after reasonable effort. However, when a petition seeks approval of a permanent entrustment agreement which provides for the termination of all parental rights and responsibilities with respect to the child, a summons shall be served upon the parent or parents and the other parties specified in § 16.1-263. The summons or notice of hearing shall clearly state the consequences of a termination of residual parental rights. Service shall be made pursuant to § 16.1-264. The remaining parent's parental rights may be terminated even though that parent has not entered into an entrustment agreement if the court finds, based upon clear and convincing evidence, that it is in the best interest of the child and that (i) the identity of the parent is not reasonably ascertainable; (ii) the identity and whereabouts of the parent are known or reasonably ascertainable, and the parent is personally served with notice of the termination proceeding pursuant to § 8.01-296 or 8.01-320; (iii) the whereabouts of the parent are not reasonably ascertainable and the parent is given notice of the termination proceedings by certified or registered mail to the last known address and such parent fails to object to the proceedings within 15 days of the mailing of such notice; or (iv) the whereabouts of the parent are not reasonably ascertainable and the parent is given

notice of the termination proceedings through an order of publication pursuant to §§ 8.01-316 and 8.01-317, and such parent fails to object to the proceedings.

C. At the hearing held pursuant to this section, the court shall hear evidence on the petition filed and shall review the foster care plan for the child filed by the local board or child welfare agency in accordance with § 16.1-281.

D. At the conclusion of the hearing, the court shall make a finding, based upon a preponderance of the evidence, whether approval of the entrustment agreement is in the best interest of the child. However, if the petition seeks approval of a permanent entrustment agreement which provides for the termination of all parental rights and responsibilities with respect to the child, the court shall make a finding, based upon clear and convincing evidence, whether termination of parental rights is in the best interest of the child. If the court makes either of these findings, the court may make any of the orders of disposition permitted in a case involving an abused or neglected child pursuant to § 16.1-278.2. Any such order transferring legal custody of the child shall be made in accordance with the provisions of subdivision A 5 of § 16.1-278.2 and shall be subject to the provisions of subsection D1. This order shall include, but need not be limited to, the following findings: (i) that there is no less drastic alternative to granting the requested relief; and (ii) that reasonable efforts have been made to prevent removal and that continued placement in the home would be contrary to the welfare of the child, if the order transfers legal custody of the child to a local board of social services. At any time subsequent to the transfer of legal custody of the child pursuant to this section, a birth parent or parents of the child and the pre-adoptive parent or parents may enter into a written post-adoption contact and communication agreement in accordance with the provisions of § 16.1-283.1 and Article 1.1 (§ 63.2-1220.2 et seq.) of Chapter 12 of Title 63.2. The court shall not require a written post-adoption contact and communication agreement as a precondition to entry of an order in any case involving the child.

The effect of the court's order approving a permanent entrustment agreement is to terminate an entrusting parent's residual parental rights. Any order terminating parental rights shall be accompanied by an order (i) continuing or granting custody to a local board of social services or to a licensed child-placing agency or (ii) granting custody or guardianship to a relative or other interested individual. Such an order continuing or granting custody to a local board of social services or to a licensed child-placing agency shall indicate whether that board or agency shall have the authority to place the child for adoption and consent thereto. A final order terminating parental rights pursuant to this section renders the approved entrustment agreement irrevocable. Such order may be appealed in accordance with the provisions of § 16.1-296.

D1. Any order transferring custody of the child to a relative or other interested individual pursuant to subsection D shall be entered only upon a finding, based upon a preponderance of the evidence, that the relative or other interested individual is one who (i) after an investigation as directed by the court, is found by the court to be willing and qualified to receive and care for the child; (ii) is willing to have a positive, continuous relationship with the child; (iii) is committed to providing a permanent, suitable home for the child; and (iv) is willing and has the ability to protect the child from abuse and neglect; and the order shall so state. The court's order transferring custody to a relative or other interested individual should further provide for, as appropriate, any terms and conditions which would promote the child's interest and welfare; ongoing provision of social services to the child and the child's custodian; and court review of the child's placement.

E. The local board or licensed child-placing agency to which authority is given to place the child for adoption and consent thereto after an order terminating parental rights is entered pursuant to this section shall file a written Adoption Progress Report with the juvenile court on the progress being made to place the child in an adoptive home. The report shall be filed with the court every six months from the date of the final order terminating parental rights until a final order of adoption is entered on behalf of the child in the circuit court. At the conclusion of the hearing at which termination of parental rights is ordered and authority is given to the local board or licensed child-placing agency to place the child for adoption, the juvenile court shall schedule a date by which the board or agency shall file the first Adoption Progress Report required by this section. A copy of the Adoption Progress Report shall be sent by the court to the guardian ad litem for the child. The court may schedule a hearing on the report with or without the request of a party.

History.
  1999, c. 889; 2000, c. 385; 2006, c. 825; 2009, cc. 98, 260; 2010, c. 331.

Editor's note.
  Acts 2006, c. 825, cl. 3, provides: "That the provisions of this act that establish the Putative Father Registry shall not become effective unless an appropriation of general funds effectuating the purposes of this act is included in the general appropriation act passed by the 2006 Session of the General Assembly, which becomes law." The funding was provided in the 2006 appropriation act. See Acts 2006, Sp. Sess. I, c. 3.

The 2009 amendments.
  The 2009 amendments by cc. 98 and 260 are identical, and added the last two sentences in the first paragraph of subsection D.

The 2010 amendments.
  The 2010 amendment by c. 331 substituted "§ 16.1-283.1 and Article 1.1 (§ 63.2-1220.2 et seq.) of Chapter 12 of Title 63.2" for "§§ 16.1-283.1 and 63.2-1228.1" in the first paragraph of subsection D and made minor stylistic changes.

CASE NOTES

Termination pursuant to entrustment agreement. — Termination of the mother's parental rights pursuant to an entrustment agreement was proper, where the evidence showed that it was in the best interests of the child; the mother had inadequate coping skills and limited cognitive abilities, leading to impulsivity and poor decision-making, and despite an evaluator's recommendation, the mother stopped her individual therapy sessions and stopped taking her psychotropic medications. Ferrell v. Alexandria Dep't of Cmty. & Human Servs., 2012 Va. App. LEXIS 215 (July 3, 2012).

§ 16.1-277.02. Petition for relief of care and custody.

A. Requests for petitions for relief of the care and custody of a child shall be referred initially to the local department of social services for investigation and the provision of services, if appropriate, in accordance with the provisions of § 63.2-319 or Chapter 15 (§ 63.2-1500 et seq.) of Title 63.2. Upon the filing of a petition for relief of a child's care and custody pursuant to subdivision A 4 of § 16.1-241, the court shall appoint a guardian ad litem to represent the child in accordance with the provisions of § 16.1-266, and shall schedule the matter for a hearing on the petition. Such hearing on the petition may include partial or final disposition of the matter. The court shall provide notice of the hearing and a copy of the petition to the following, each of whom shall be a party entitled to participate in the proceeding:

1. The child, if he is 12 years of age or older;

2. The guardian ad litem for the child;

3. The child's parents, custodian or other person standing in loco parentis to the child. No such notification shall be required, however, if the judge certifies on the record that the identity of the parent is not reasonably ascertainable. An affidavit of the mother that the identity of the father is not reasonably ascertainable shall be sufficient evidence of this fact, provided there is no other evidence before the court which would refute such an affidavit. The hearing on the petition shall be held pursuant to this section although a parent fails to appear and is not represented by counsel, provided personal or substituted service was made on the parent, or the court determines that such person cannot be found, after reasonable effort, or in the case of a person who is without the Commonwealth, the person cannot be found or his post office address cannot be ascertained after reasonable effort. However, in the case of a hearing to grant a petition for permanent relief of custody and terminate a parent's residual parental rights, notice to the parent whose rights may be affected shall be provided in accordance with the provisions of §§ 16.1-263 and 16.1-264; and

4. The local board of social services. Upon receiving notice of the hearing pursuant to this section, the local board of social services shall investigate the matter and provide services, as appropriate, in accordance with the provisions of § 63.2-319 or Chapter 15 (§ 63.2-1500 et seq.) of Title 63.2.

B. At the hearing, the local board of services, the child, the child's parents, guardian, legal custodian or other person standing in loco parentis and any other family or household member of the child to whom notice was given shall have the right to confront and cross-examine all adverse witnesses and evidence and to present evidence on their own behalf.

C. **(Effective until July 1, 2014)** At the conclusion of the hearing on the petition, the court shall make a finding, based upon a preponderance of the evidence, whether there is good cause shown for the petitioner's desire to be relieved of the child's care and custody, unless the petition seeks permanent relief of custody and termination of parental rights. If the petition seeks permanent relief of custody and termination of parental rights, the court shall make a finding, based upon clear and convincing evidence, whether termination of parental rights is in the best interest of the child. If the court makes either of these findings, the court may enter:

1. A preliminary protective order pursuant to § 16.1-253;

2. An order that requires the local board of social services to provide services to the family as required by law;

3. An order that is consistent with any of the dispositional alternatives pursuant to § 16.1-278.3; or

4. Any combination of these orders.

Any such order transferring legal custody of the child shall be made in accordance with the provisions of subdivision A 5 of § 16.1-278.2 and shall be subject to the provisions of subsection C1. This order shall include, but need not be limited to, the following findings: (i) that there is no less drastic alternative to granting the requested relief; and (ii) that reasonable efforts have been made to prevent removal and that continued placement in the home would be contrary to the welfare of the child, if the order transfers legal custody of the child to a local board of social services. Any order terminating residual parental rights shall be accompanied by an order continuing or granting custody to a local board of social services, to a licensed child-placing agency or the granting of custody or guardianship to a relative or other interested individual. Such an order continuing or granting custody to a local board of social services or to a licensed child-placing agency shall indicate whether that board or agency shall have the authority to place the child for adoption and consent thereto. At any time subsequent to the transfer of legal custody of the child pursuant to this section, a birth parent or parents of the child and the pre-adoptive parent or parents may enter into a written post-adoption contact and communication agreement in accordance with the provisions of § 16.1-283.1 and Article 1.1 (§ 63.2-1220.2 et seq.) of Chapter 12 of Title 63.2. The court shall not require a written post-adoption contact and communication agreement as a precondition to entry of an order in any case involving the child.

The court shall schedule a subsequent hearing within 75 days of the hearing held pursuant to this section: (i) to enter a final order of disposition pursuant to § 16.1-278.3 or (ii) if the child is placed in foster care, for review of the foster care plan filed pursuant to § 16.1-281. If a party is required to be present at the subsequent hearing, and (i) is present at the hearing on the petition, the party shall be given notice of the date set for the subsequent hearing; (ii) if not present, shall be summoned as provided in § 16.1-263.

C. **(Effective July 1, 2014)** At the conclusion of the hearing on the petition, the court shall make a finding, based upon a preponderance of the evidence, whether there is good cause shown for the petitioner's desire to be relieved of the child's care and custody, unless the petition seeks permanent relief of custody and termination of parental rights. If the petition seeks permanent relief of custody and termination of parental rights, the court shall make a finding, based upon clear and convincing evidence, whether termination of parental rights is in the best interest of the child. If the court makes either of these findings, the court may enter:

1. A preliminary protective order pursuant to § 16.1-253;

2. An order that requires the local board of social services to provide services to the family as required by law;

3. An order that is consistent with any of the dispositional alternatives pursuant to § 16.1-278.3; or

4. Any combination of these orders.

Any such order transferring legal custody of the child shall be made in accordance with the provisions of subdivision A 5 of § 16.1-278.2 and shall be subject to the provisions of subsection C1. This order shall include, but need not be limited to, the following findings: (i) that there is no less drastic alternative to granting the requested relief; and (ii) that reasonable efforts have been made to prevent removal and that continued placement in the home would be contrary to the welfare of the child, if the order transfers legal custody of the child to a local board of social services. Any order terminating residual parental rights shall be accompanied by an order continuing or granting custody to a local board of social services, to a licensed child-placing agency or the granting of custody or guardianship to a relative or other interested individual. Such an order continuing or granting custody to a local board of social services or to a licensed child-placing agency shall indicate whether that board or agency shall have the authority to place the child for adoption and consent thereto. At any time subsequent to the transfer of legal custody of the child pursuant to this section, a birth parent or parents of the child and the pre-adoptive parent or parents may enter into a written post-adoption contact and communication agreement in accordance with the provisions of § 16.1-283.1 and Article 1.1 (§ 63.2-1220.2 et seq.) of Chapter 12 of Title 63.2. The court shall not require a written post-adoption contact and communication agreement as a precondition to entry of an order in any case involving the child.

The court shall schedule a subsequent hearing within 60 days of the hearing held pursuant to this section: (a) to enter a final order of disposition pursuant to § 16.1-278.3 or (b) if the child is placed in foster care, for review of the foster care plan filed pursuant to § 16.1-281. If a party is required to be present at the subsequent hearing, and (1) is present at the hearing on the petition, the party shall be given notice of the date set for the subsequent hearing; (2) if not present, shall be summoned as provided in § 16.1-263.

C1. Any order transferring temporary custody of the child to a relative or other interested individual pursuant to subsection C shall be entered only upon a finding, based upon a preponderance of the evidence, that the relative or other interested individual is one who (i) is found by the court to be willing and qualified to receive and care for the child; (ii) is willing to have a positive, continuous relationship with the child; and (iii) is willing and has the ability to protect the child from abuse and neglect. The court's order transferring temporary custody to a relative or other interested individual should further provide for compliance with any preliminary protective order entered on behalf of the child in accordance with the provisions of § 16.1-253; and, as appropriate, ongoing provision of social services to the child and the child's custodian; and court review of the child's placement with the relative or other individual. Any final order transferring custody of the child to a relative or other interested individual pursuant to this section shall, in addition, be entered only after an investigation as directed by the court and upon a finding, stated in the court's order, that the relative or other interested individual is one who satisfies clauses (i), (ii), and (iii) and is committed to providing a permanent, suitable home for the child.

D. The local board or licensed child-placing agency to which authority is given to place the child for adoption and consent thereto after an order terminating parental rights is entered pursuant to this section shall file a written Adoption Progress Report with the juvenile court on the progress being made to place the child in an adoptive home. The report shall be filed with the court every six months from the date of the final order terminating parental rights until a final order of adoption is entered on behalf of the child in the circuit court. At the conclusion of the hearing at which termination of parental rights is ordered and authority is given to the local board or licensed child-placing agency to place the child for adoption, the juvenile court shall schedule a date by which the board or agency shall file the first Adoption Progress Report required by this section. A copy of the Adoption Progress Report shall be sent by the court to the guardian ad litem for the child. The court may schedule a hearing on the report with or without the request of a party.

History.
  1999, c. 889; 2000, c. 385; 2009, cc. 98, 260; 2010, c. 331; 2013, c. 130.

Subsection C set out twice. — The first version of subsection C above is effective until July 1, 2014. The second version of subsection C is effective July 1, 2014.

Cross references.

As to foster care plans, placement of child, permissible plan goals, and court review of foster children, see § 63.2-906.

The 2009 amendments.

The 2009 amendments by cc. 98 and 260 are identical, and added the last two sentences in the next-to-last paragraph of subsection C.

The 2010 amendments.

The 2010 amendment by c. 331 substituted "§ 16.1-283.1 and Article 1.1 (§ 63.2-1220.2 et seq.) of Chapter 12 of Title 63.2" for "§§ 16.1-283.1 and 63.2-1228.1" in the next-to-last sentence of the second full paragraph of subsection C and made minor stylistic changes.

The 2013 amendments.

The 2013 amendment by c. 130, effective July 1, 2014, in the last paragraph of subsection C, subsituted "60 days" for "75 days" and changed the clause (i) and (ii) designators to (a) and (b) in the first sentence, and changed the clause (i) and (ii) designators to (1) and (2) in the second sentence.

Research references.

Virginia Forms (Matthew Bender). No. 5-150 Child Protective Order.

CASE NOTES

Statute provided no basis for father's petition to terminate his parental obligations. — Because a father was not the children's custodial parent, he provided no actual care and custody from which he could have been relieved, and, thus, § 16.1-278.3 provided him no basis for seeking termination of his parental rights and obligations; furthermore, subsection D of § 16.1-278.3 authorized consideration of the status and rights of a remaining parent only following the granting of a petition properly filed under § 16.1-277.02. No such petition was filed or granted, and a trial court properly dismissed the father's petition. Cartwright v. Cartwright, 49 Va. App. 25, 635 S.E.2d 691, 2006 Va. App. LEXIS 473 (2006).

§ 16.1-277.1. Time limitation.

A. When a child is held continuously in secure detention, he shall be released from confinement if there is no adjudicatory or transfer hearing conducted by the court for the matters upon which he was detained within twenty-one days from the date he was first detained.

B. If a child is not held in secure detention or is released from same after having been confined, an adjudicatory or transfer hearing on the matters charged in the petition or petitions issued against him shall be conducted within 120 days from the date the petition or petitions are filed.

C. When a child is held in secure detention after the completion of his adjudicatory hearing or is detained when the juvenile court has retained jurisdiction as a result of a transfer hearing, he shall be released from such detention if the disposition hearing is not completed within thirty days from the date of the adjudicatory or transfer hearing.

D. The time limitations provided for in this section shall be tolled during any period in which (i) the whereabouts of the child are unknown, (ii) the child has escaped from custody, or (iii) the child has failed to appear pursuant to a court order. The limitations also may be extended by the court for a reasonable period of time based upon good cause shown, provided that the basis for such extension is recorded in writing and filed among the papers of the proceedings. For the purposes of this section, good cause includes, but is not limited to, extension of limitations necessary to obtain the presence of a witness to testify regarding the results of scientific analyses or examinations.

History.

1985, c. 260; 1988, c. 220; 1999, c. 58; 2009, Sp. Sess. I, cc. 1, 4.

Editor's note.

Acts 1993, c. 930, cl. 3, as amended by Acts 1994, c. 564, cl. 2, and Acts 1996, c. 616, cl. 4, provides that the amendment to this section by Acts 1993, c. 930, cl. 1, shall become effective June 1, 1998, "if state funds are provided, including all local costs, to carry out the purposes of this bill by the General Assembly." The funding was not provided.

The 2009 amendments.

The 2009 amendments by Sp. Sess. I, c. 1, effective August 21, 2009, and Sp. Sess. I, c. 4, effective September 15, 2009, are identical, and added the last sentence of subsection D.

Law Review.

For 1985 survey of Virginia law affecting children, see 19 U. Rich. L. Rev. p. 753 (1985). For annual survey article, "Criminal Law and Procedure," see 44 U. Rich. L. Rev. 339 (2009).

CASE NOTES

Section only applicable to juvenile detention. — This section applies when the juvenile court has authority to adjudicate the matter or decide whether to transfer it for trial under adult procedures; where a defendant has been transferred to jail after his first preliminary hearing and is no longer held in juvenile detention, this section does not apply. Williams v. Commonwealth, 33 Va. App. 725, 536 S.E.2d 916, 2000 Va. App. LEXIS 734 (2000).

Construction with other law. — Circuit court properly determined that the termination of a father's parental rights on grounds that he was unfit as a parent was in the best interest of the child, and that the child should be placed for adoption, as sufficient evidence was presented of the father's inability to provide for the welfare of his child due to his incarceration and status as a convicted felon, his lack of employment and a stable home, his past drug abuse, and a history of violence toward women. Wheless v. Commonwealth Catholic Charities, 2007 Va. App. LEXIS 401 (Nov. 6, 2007).

Dismissal not required for failure to hold hearing within 120-day period. — Failure of the juvenile and domestic relations court to timely hold an adjudicatory or transfer hearing did not require dismissal of the charges against defendant, because subsection B of § 16.1-277.1 merely directed the mode of proceeding and did not expressly prohibit a hearing after 120 days. Harris v. Commonwealth, 52 Va. App. 735, 667 S.E.2d 809, 2008 Va. App. LEXIS 479 (2008).

ARTICLE 9.

DISPOSITION.

§ 16.1-278.1. Definitions.

As used in this article, unless the context clearly indicates otherwise:

"Parent" includes parent, guardian, legal custodian, or other person standing in loco parentis.

"Public service project" means any governmental or quasi-governmental agency project or any project of a nonprofit corporation or association operated exclusively for charitable or community purposes.

History.
1991, c. 534.

§ 16.1-278.8. Delinquent juveniles.

A. If a juvenile is found to be delinquent, except where such finding involves a refusal to take a blood or breath test in violation of § 18.2-268.2 or a similar ordinance, the juvenile court or the circuit court may make any of the following orders of disposition for his supervision, care and rehabilitation:

1. Enter an order pursuant to the provisions of § 16.1-278;

2. Permit the juvenile to remain with his parent, subject to such conditions and limitations as the court may order with respect to the juvenile and his parent;

3. Order the parent of a juvenile living with him to participate in such programs, cooperate in such treatment or be subject to such conditions and limitations as the court may order and as are designed for the rehabilitation of the juvenile and his parent;

4. Defer disposition for a specific period of time established by the court with due regard for the gravity of the offense and the juvenile's history, after which time the charge may be dismissed by the judge if the juvenile exhibits good behavior during the period for which disposition is deferred;

4a. Defer disposition and place the juvenile in the temporary custody of the Department to attend a boot camp established pursuant to § 66-13 provided bed space is available for confinement and the juvenile (i) has been found delinquent for an offense that would be a Class 1 misdemeanor or felony if committed by an adult, (ii) has not previously been and is not currently being adjudicated delinquent or found guilty of a violent juvenile felony, (iii) has not previously attended a boot camp, (iv) has not previously been committed to and received by the Department, and (v) has had an assessment completed by the Department or its contractor concerning the appropriateness of the candidate for a boot camp. Upon the juvenile's withdrawal, removal or refusal to comply with the terms and conditions of participation in the program, he shall be brought before the court for a hearing at which the court may impose any other disposition as authorized by this section which could have been imposed at the time the juvenile was placed in the custody of the Department;

5. Without entering a judgment of guilty and with the consent of the juvenile and his attorney, defer disposition of the delinquency charge for a specific period of time established by the court with due regard for the gravity of the offense and the juve-

nile's history, and place the juvenile on probation under such conditions and limitations as the court may prescribe. Upon fulfillment of the terms and conditions, the court shall discharge the juvenile and dismiss the proceedings against him. Discharge and dismissal under these provisions shall be without adjudication of guilt;

6. Order the parent of a juvenile with whom the juvenile does not reside to participate in such programs, cooperate in such treatment or be subject to such conditions and limitations as the court may order and as are designed for the rehabilitation of the juvenile where the court determines this participation to be in the best interest of the juvenile and other parties concerned and where the court determines it reasonable to expect the parent to be able to comply with such order;

7. Place the juvenile on probation under such conditions and limitations as the court may prescribe;

7a. Place the juvenile on probation and order treatment for the abuse or dependence on alcohol or drugs in a program licensed by the Department of Behavioral Health and Developmental Services for the treatment of juveniles for substance abuse provided that (i) the juvenile has received a substance abuse screening and assessment pursuant to § 16.1-273 and that such assessment reasonably indicates that the commission of the offense was motivated by, or closely related to, the habitual use of alcohol or drugs and indicates that the juvenile is in need of treatment for this condition; (ii) the juvenile has not previously been and is not currently being adjudicated for a violent juvenile felony; and (iii) such facility is available. Upon the juvenile's withdrawal, removal, or refusal to comply with the conditions of participation in the program, he shall be brought before the court for a hearing at which the court may impose any other disposition authorized by this section. The court shall review such placements at 30-day intervals;

8. Impose a fine not to exceed $500 upon such juvenile;

9. Suspend the motor vehicle and driver's license of such juvenile or impose a curfew on the juvenile as to the hours during which he may operate a motor vehicle. Any juvenile whose driver's license is suspended may be referred for an assessment and subsequent referral to appropriate services, upon such terms and conditions as the court may order. The court, in its discretion and upon a demonstration of hardship, may authorize the use of a restricted permit to operate a motor vehicle by any juvenile who enters such program for any of the purposes set forth in subsection E of § 18.2-271.1 or for travel to and from school. The restricted permit shall be issued in accordance with the provisions of such subsection. However, only an abstract of the court order that identifies the juvenile and the conditions under which the restricted license is to be issued shall be sent to the Department of Motor Vehicles.

If a curfew is imposed, the juvenile shall surrender his driver's license, which shall be held in the physical custody of the court during any period of curfew restriction. The court shall send an abstract of any order issued under the provisions of this section to the Department of Motor Vehicles, which shall preserve a record thereof. Notwithstanding the provisions of Article 12 (§ 16.1-299 et seq.) of this chapter or the provisions of Title 46.2, this record shall be available only to all law-enforcement officers, attorneys for the Commonwealth and courts. A copy of the court order, upon which shall be noted all curfew restrictions, shall be provided to the juvenile and shall contain such information regarding the juvenile as is reasonably necessary to identify him. The juvenile may operate a motor vehicle under the court order in accordance with its terms.

Any juvenile who operates a motor vehicle in violation of any restrictions imposed pursuant to this section shall be guilty of a violation of § 46.2-301.

The Department of Motor Vehicles shall refuse to issue a driver's license to any juvenile denied a driver's license until such time as is stipulated in the court order or until notification by the court of withdrawal of the order imposing the curfew;

10. Require the juvenile to make restitution or reparation to the aggrieved party or parties for actual damages or loss caused by the offense for which the juvenile was found to be delinquent;

11. Require the juvenile to participate in a public service project under such conditions as the court prescribes;

12. In case of traffic violations, impose only those penalties that are authorized to be imposed on adults for such violations. However, for those violations punishable by confinement if committed by an adult, confinement shall be imposed only as authorized by this title;

13. Transfer legal custody to any of the following:

a. A relative or other individual who, after study, is found by the court to be qualified to receive and care for the juvenile;

b. A child welfare agency, private organization or facility that is licensed or otherwise authorized by law to receive and provide care for such juvenile. The court shall not transfer legal custody of a delinquent juvenile to an agency, organization or facility outside of the Commonwealth without the approval of the Director; or

c. The local board of social services of the county or city in which the court has jurisdiction or, at the discretion of the court, to the local board of the county or city in which the juvenile has residence if other than the county or city in which the court has jurisdiction. The board shall accept the juvenile for care and custody, provided that it has been given reasonable notice of the pendency of the case and an opportunity to be heard. However, in an emergency in the county or city in which the court has jurisdiction, such local board may be required to temporarily accept a juvenile for a period not to exceed 14 days without prior notice or an opportunity to be heard if the judge entering the placement order describes the emergency and the need for such temporary placement in the order. Nothing in this subdivision shall prohibit the commitment of a juvenile to any local board of social services in the Commonwealth when such local board consents to the commitment. The board to which the juvenile is committed shall have the final authority to determine the appropriate placement for the juvenile. Any order authorizing removal from the home and transferring legal custody of a juvenile to a local board of social services as provided in this subdivision shall be entered only upon a finding by the court that reasonable efforts have been made to prevent removal and that continued placement in the home would be contrary to the welfare of the juvenile, and the order shall so state;

14. Commit the juvenile to the Department of Juvenile Justice, but only if he is 11 years of age or older and the current offense is (i) an offense that would be a felony if committed by an adult, (ii) an offense that would be a Class 1 misdemeanor if committed by an adult and the juvenile has previously been found to be delinquent based on an offense that would be a felony if committed by an adult, or (iii) an offense that would be a Class 1 misdemeanor if committed by an adult and the juvenile has previously been adjudicated delinquent of three or more offenses that would be a Class 1 misdemeanor if committed by an adult, and each such offense was not a part of a common act, transaction or scheme;

15. Impose the penalty authorized by § 16.1-284;

16. Impose the penalty authorized by § 16.1-284.1;

17. Impose the penalty authorized by § 16.1-285.1;

18. Impose the penalty authorized by § 16.1-278.9; or

19. Require the juvenile to participate in a gang-activity prevention program including, but not limited to, programs funded under the Virginia Juvenile Community Crime Control Act pursuant to § 16.1-309.7, if available, when a juvenile has been found delinquent of any of the following violations: § 18.2-51, 18.2-51.1, 18.2-52, 18.2-53, 18.2-55, 18.2-56, 18.2-57, 18.2-57.2, 18.2-121, 18.2-127, 18.2-128, 18.2-137, 18.2-138, 18.2-146, or 18.2-147, or any violation of a local ordinance adopted pursuant to § 15.2-1812.2.

B. If the court finds a juvenile delinquent of any of the following offenses, the court shall require the juvenile to make at least partial restitution or reparation for any property damage, for loss caused by the offense, or for actual medical expenses incurred by the victim as a result of the offense: § 18.2-51, 18.2-51.1, 18.2-52, 18.2-53, 18.2-55, 18.2-56, 18.2-57, 18.2-57.2, 18.2-121, 18.2-127, 18.2-128, 18.2-137, 18.2-138, 18.2-146, or 18.2-147; or for any violation of a local ordinance adopted pursuant to § 15.2-1812.2. The court shall further require the juvenile to participate in a community service project under such conditions as the court prescribes.

History.

1991, c. 534; 1992, c. 830; 1994, cc. 859, 949; 1996, cc. 755, 914; 1997, c. 318; 1999, cc. 350, 622; 2000, cc. 954, 978, 981, 988, 1020, 1041; 2004, cc. 325, 462; 2005, c. 810; 2009, cc. 813, 840.

Cross references.

As to foster care plans, placement of child, permissible plan goals, and court review of foster children, see § 63.2-906.

Editor's note.

Acts 1993, c. 930, cl. 3, as amended by Acts 1994, c. 564, cl. 2, and Acts 1996, c. 616, cl. 4, provides that the amendment to this section by Acts 1993, c. 930, cl. 1, shall become effective June 1, 1998, "if state funds are provided, including all local costs, to carry out the purposes of this bill by the General Assembly." The funding was not provided.

Acts 2000, c. 978, cl. 2, as amended by Acts 2002, c. 648, cl. 1, provides: "That the Department of Juvenile Justice shall establish a uniform risk assessment instrument for use when making a detention decision pursuant to § 16.1-248.1 and when making recommendations to the court at a detention hearing pursuant to § 16.1-250. The uniform risk assessment instrument and related procedure shall be implemented by each court service unit and distributed to each juvenile court judge no later than October 1, 2002."

The 2009 amendments.

The 2009 amendments by cc. 813 and 840 are identical, and substituted "Department of Behavioral Health and Developmental Services" for "Department of Mental Health, Mental Retardation and Substance Abuse Services" in subdivision A 7a.

Law Review.

For 2000 survey of Virginia law regarding children, see 34 U. Rich. L. Rev. 939 (2000). For annual survey article on legal issues involving children, see 38 U. Rich. L. Rev. 161 (2003). For survey of Virginia criminal law and procedure for the year 2004-2005, see 40 U. Rich. L. Rev. 197 (2005).

Research references.

Virginia Forms (Matthew Bender). No. 5-150 Child Protective Order.

Michie's Jurisprudence.

For related discussion, see 9B M.J. Infants, § 19.

CASE NOTES

Commitment for probation violation. — Because defendant juvenile did not provide a transcript or refer to it in the appellate brief, as required by Va. Sup. Ct. R. 5A:8(b) and 5A:20(c), the appellate court was unable to consider whether the proper underlying offense was present to commit defendant to the Department of Juvenile Justice. Williams v. Commonwealth, 2005 Va. App. LEXIS 378 (Oct. 4, 2005).

Commitment to Department of Juvenile Justice. — Trial court did not err in finding, upon determining that the juvenile violated the juvenile's probation, that the juvenile should be committed to the Department of Juvenile Justice for an indeterminate period; although the juvenile argued that the "original disposition" and "current offense" for such a disposition had to be a felony or Class 1 misdemeanor and the juvenile's case merely involved a probation violation, the underlying offense on which the juvenile received probation was a felony robbery, and, thus, commitment to the Department of Juvenile Justice was permissible because it could have been made in originally deciding the juvenile's punishment even though the juvenile's proceeding was indeed a probation revocation proceeding. Kerns v. Commonwealth, 2007 Va. App. LEXIS 175 (May 1, 2007).

Trial court had authority pursuant to §§ 16.1-278.8 and 16.1-291

to impose a suspended Department of Juvenile Justice commitment upon defendant juvenile's violation of the conditions of his probation because defendant's underlying offense, larceny of animals, was a form of grand larceny, and it remained a felony each time defendant came before the trial court on a probation violation; the term, "original disposition" in subsection B of § 16.1-291 plainly refers to the dispositional proceeding for the larceny of animals offense held under subsection A of § 16.1-278.8, in which the original conditions of probation were imposed. Rivas v. Commonwealth, 51 Va. App. 507, 659 S.E.2d 524, 2008 Va. App. LEXIS 173 (2008).

Commitment for probation violation improper. — Because the plain language of subdivision A 14 of this section bars the commitment of a juvenile absent a delinquency finding on either a felony or a second Class 1 misdemeanor, a probation violation is insufficient to commit a juvenile to the Department of Juvenile Justice. Salvatierra v. City of Falls Church, 35 Va. App. 453, 546 S.E.2d 214, 2001 Va. App. LEXIS 265 (2001).

Juvenile court could maintain custody of child. — Because a mother did not comply with subsection A of § 16.1-296 and § 16.1-133.1 by appealing a dispositional order within 10 days of its entry or applying to reopen the case within 60 days, pursuant to Va. Sup. Ct. R. 1:1, the juvenile court lost jurisdiction of a charge and its dismissal of that charge had no force; therefore, since the juvenile court had authority under clause c of subdivision A 13 of § 16.1-278.8 to maintain custody of the child with the social services department, the circuit court properly denied the mother's motion to dismiss proceedings and return custody of her son. Lee v. Frederick County Dep't of Soc. Servs., 2008 Va. App. LEXIS 370 (Aug. 5, 2008).

Effect of adjudication of guilt. — Sufficient evidence of a prior adjudication of delinquency supported defendant's conviction of possession of a firearm after having been adjudicated delinquent of an act which would be a felony if committed by an adult under § 18.2-308.2 where; (1) an adjudication order was admitted that described an adjudicatory hearing based on a § 18.2-308.2 A felony charge and stated that defendant pled guilty and that the juvenile court accepted the plea; (2) the adjudication order tended to prove that defendant had been previously adjudicated delinquent; and (3) although the disposition order was not admitted, there was no evidence that defendant's conviction changed after the adjudication hearing, and the juvenile court could not have dismissed the prior charge under subdivision A 5 of § 16.1-278.8 because an adjudication of guilt had been made. Perry v. Commonwealth, 61 Va. App. 502, 737 S.E.2d 922, 2013 Va. App. LEXIS 66 (2013).

OPINIONS OF THE ATTORNEY GENERAL

Fingerprinting of juvenile. — A juvenile who has been issued a summons but is not taken into custody may not be fingerprinted. See opinion of Attorney General to The Honorable Edward DeJ. Berry, Judge, Juvenile and Domestic Relations District Court, 01-093 (6/19/01).

This statute does not require the issuance of a subpoena to a local department of social services, because the department, as a non-party, is not required to attend any proceeding. However, should a court want the local department to be present for such proceedings, then a subpoena or other court order can be issued to compel the local department to appear. See opinion of Attorney General to The Honorable Gayl Branum Carr, Juvenile and Domestic Relations District Court, 19th Judicial District, 12-027, 2012 Va. AG LEXIS 19 (5/25/12).

§ 16.1-278.8:01. Juveniles found delinquent of first drug offense; screening; assessment; drug tests; costs and fees; education or treatment programs.

Whenever any juvenile who has not previously been found delinquent of any offense under Article 1 (§ 18.2-247 et seq.) of Chapter 7 of Title 18.2 or under any statute of the United States or of any state relating to narcotic drugs, marijuana, synthetic cannabinoids, or stimulant, depressant or hallucinogenic drugs, or has not previously had a proceeding against him for a violation of such an offense dismissed as provided in § 18.2-251, is found delinquent of any offense concerning the use, in any manner, of drugs, controlled substances, narcotics, marijuana, synthetic cannabinoids, noxious chemical substances and like substances, the juvenile court or the circuit court shall require such juvenile to undergo a substance abuse screening pursuant to § 16.1-273 and to submit to such periodic substance abuse testing, to include alcohol testing, as may be directed by the court. Such testing shall be conducted by a court services unit of the Department of Juvenile Justice, or by a locally operated court services unit or by personnel of any program or agency approved by the Department. The cost of such testing ordered by the court shall be paid by the Commonwealth from funds appropriated to the Department for this purpose. The court shall also order the juvenile to undergo such treatment or education program for substance abuse, if available, as the court deems appropriate based upon consideration of the substance abuse assessment. The treatment or education shall be provided by a program licensed by the Department of Behavioral Health and Developmental Services or by a similar program available through a facility or program operated by or under contract to the Department of Juvenile Justice or a locally operated court services unit or a program funded through the Virginia Juvenile Community Crime Control Act (§ 16.1-309.2 et seq.).

History.
2000, cc. 1020, 1041; 2009, cc. 813, 840; 2011, cc. 384, 410.

Editor's note.
Acts 2011, cc. 384 and 410, cl. 3 provides: "That the provisions of this act may result in a net increase in periods of imprisonment or commitment. Pursuant to § 30-19.1:4, the estimated amount of the necessary appropriation cannot be determined for periods of imprisonment in state adult correctional facilities; therefore, Chapter 874 of the Acts of Assembly of 2010 requires the Virginia Criminal Sentencing Commission to assign a minimum fiscal impact of $50,000. Pursuant to § 30-19.1:4, the estimated amount of the necessary appropriation cannot be determined for periods of commitment to the custody of the Department of Juvenile Justice."

The 2009 amendments.
The 2009 amendments by cc. 813 and 840 are identical, and substituted "Department of Behavioral Health and Developmental Services" for "Department of Mental Health, Mental Retardation and Substance Abuse Services" in the last sentence.

The 2011 amendments.
The 2011 amendments by cc. 384 and 410, effective March 23, 2011, are identical, and twice inserted "synthetic cannabinoids" in the first sentence.

Law Review.
For 2000 survey of Virginia law regarding children, see 34 U. Rich. L. Rev. 939 (2000).

§ 16.1-278.9. Delinquent children; loss of driving privileges for alcohol, firearm, and drug offenses; truancy.

A. If a court has found facts which would justify a finding that a child at least 13 years of age at the time of the offense is delinquent and such finding involves (i) a violation of § 18.2-266 or of a similar ordinance of any county, city or town, (ii) a refusal to take a blood or breath test in violation of § 18.2-268.2, (iii) a felony violation of § 18.2-248, 18.2-248.1 or 18.2-250, (iv) a misdemeanor violation of § 18.2-248, 18.2-248.1, or 18.2-250 or a violation of § 18.2-250.1, (v) the unlawful purchase, possession or consumption of alcohol in violation of § 4.1-305 or the unlawful drinking or possession of alcoholic beverages in or on public school grounds in violation of § 4.1-309, (vi) public intoxication in violation of § 18.2-388 or a similar ordinance of a county, city or town, (vii) the unlawful use or possession of a handgun or possession of a "streetsweeper" as defined below, or (viii) a violation of § 18.2-83, the court shall order, in addition to any other penalty that it may impose as provided by law for the offense, that the child be denied a driver's license. In addition to any other penalty authorized by this section, if the offense involves a violation designated under clause (i) and the child was transporting a person 17 years of age or younger, the court shall impose the additional fine and order community service as provided in § 18.2-270. If the offense involves a violation designated under clause (i), (ii), (iii) or (viii), the denial of a driver's license shall be for a period of one year or until the juvenile reaches the age of 17, whichever is longer, for a first such offense or for a period of one year or until the juvenile reaches the age of 18, whichever is longer, for a second or subsequent such offense. If the offense involves a violation designated under clause (iv), (v) or (vi) the denial of driving privileges shall be for a period of six months unless the offense is committed by a child under the age of 16 years and three months, in which case the child's ability to apply for a driver's license shall be delayed for a period of six months following the date he reaches the age of 16 and three months. If the offense involves a first violation designated under clause (v) or (vi), the court shall impose the license sanction and may enter a judgment of guilt or, without entering a judgment of guilt, may defer disposition of the delinquency charge until such time as the court disposes of the case pursuant to subsection F of this section. If the offense involves a violation designated under clause (iii) or (iv), the court shall impose the license sanction and shall dispose of the delinquency charge pursuant to the provisions of this chapter or § 18.2-251. If the offense involves a violation designated under clause (vii), the denial of driving privileges shall be for a period of not less than 30 days, except when the offense involves possession of a concealed handgun or a striker 12, commonly called a "streetsweeper," or any semiautomatic folding stock shotgun of like kind with a spring tension drum magazine capable of holding 12 shotgun shells, in which case the denial of driving privileges shall be for a period of two years unless the offense is committed by a child under the age of

16 years and three months, in which event the child's ability to apply for a driver's license shall be delayed for a period of two years following the date he reaches the age of 16 and three months.

A1. If a court finds that a child at least 13 years of age has failed to comply with school attendance and meeting requirements as provided in § 22.1-258, the court shall order the denial of the child's driving privileges for a period of not less than 30 days. If such failure to comply involves a child under the age of 16 years and three months, the child's ability to apply for a driver's license shall be delayed for a period of not less than 30 days following the date he reaches the age of 16 and three months.

If the court finds a second or subsequent such offense, it may order the denial of a driver's license for a period of one year or until the juvenile reaches the age of 18, whichever is longer, or delay the child's ability to apply for a driver's license for a period of one year following the date he reaches the age of 16 and three months, as may be appropriate.

B. Any child who has a driver's license at the time of the offense or at the time of the court's finding as provided in subsection A1 shall be ordered to surrender his driver's license, which shall be held in the physical custody of the court during any period of license denial.

C. The court shall report any order issued under this section to the Department of Motor Vehicles, which shall preserve a record thereof. The report and the record shall include a statement as to whether the child was represented by or waived counsel or whether the order was issued pursuant to subsection A1 of this section. Notwithstanding the provisions of Article 12 (§ 16.1-299 et seq.) of this chapter or the provisions of Title 46.2, this record shall be available only to all law-enforcement officers, attorneys for the Commonwealth and courts. No other record of the proceeding shall be forwarded to the Department of Motor Vehicles unless the proceeding results in an adjudication of guilt pursuant to subsection F.

The Department of Motor Vehicles shall refuse to issue a driver's license to any child denied a driver's license until such time as is stipulated in the court order or until notification by the court of withdrawal of the order of denial under subsection E.

D. If the finding as to the child involves a violation designated under clause (i), (ii), (iii) or (vi) of subsection A, the child may be referred to a certified alcohol safety action program in accordance with § 18.2-271.1 upon such terms and conditions as the court may set forth. If the finding as to such child involves a violation designated under clause (iii), (iv), (v), (vii) or (viii) of subsection A, such child may be referred to appropriate rehabilitative or educational services upon such terms and conditions as the court may set forth.

The court, in its discretion and upon a demonstration of hardship, may authorize the use of a restricted permit to operate a motor vehicle by any child who has a driver's license at the time of the offense or at the time of the court's finding as provided in subsection A1 for any of the purposes set forth in subsection E of § 18.2-271.1 or for travel to and from school, except that no restricted license shall be issued for travel to and from home and school when school-provided transportation is available and no restricted license shall be issued if the finding as to such child involves a violation designated under clause (iii) or (iv) of subsection A, or if it involves a second or subsequent violation of any offense designated in subsection A or a second finding by the court of failure to comply with school attendance and meeting requirements as provided in subsection A1. The issuance of the restricted permit shall be set forth within the court order, a copy of which shall be provided to the child, and shall specifically enumerate the restrictions imposed and contain such information regarding the child as is reasonably necessary to identify him. The child may operate a motor vehicle under the court order in accordance with its terms. Any child who operates a motor vehicle in violation of any restrictions imposed pursuant to this section shall be guilty of a violation of § 46.2-301.

E. Upon petition made at least 90 days after issuance of the order, the court may review and withdraw any order of denial of a driver's license if for a first such offense or finding as provided in subsection A1. For a second or subsequent such offense or finding, the order may not be reviewed and withdrawn until one year after its issuance.

F. If the finding as to such child involves a first violation designated under clause (vii) of subsection A, upon fulfillment of the terms and conditions prescribed by the court and after the child's driver's license has been restored, the court shall or, in the event the violation resulted in the injury or death of any person or if the finding involves a violation designated under clause (i), (ii), (v), or (vi) of subsection A, may discharge the child and dismiss the proceedings against him. Discharge and dismissal under these provisions shall be without an adjudication of guilt but a record of the proceeding shall be retained for the purpose of applying this section in subsequent proceedings. Failure of the child to fulfill such terms and conditions shall result in an adjudication of guilt. If the finding as to such child involves a violation designated under clause (iii) or (iv) of subsection A, the charge shall not be dismissed pursuant to this subsection but shall be disposed of pursuant to the provisions of this chapter or § 18.2-251. If the finding as to such child involves a second violation under clause (v), (vi) or (vii) of subsection A, the charge shall not be dismissed pursuant to this subsection but shall be disposed of under § 16.1-278.8.

History.
1991, cc. 534, 696; 1992, cc. 701, 736, 830; 1993, cc. 482, 866, 972; 1994, c. 338; 2000, c. 835; 2001, cc. 248, 266; 2002, cc. 519, 755; 2003, c. 118; 2005, c. 895; 2007, c. 731; 2010, cc. 522, 569, 570.

The 2010 amendments.

The 2010 amendment by c. 522 inserted "no restricted license shall be issued for travel to and from home and school when school-provided transportation is available and" in the second paragraph of subsection D.

The 2010 amendment by c. 569 substituted "and may enter a judgment of guilt or, without entering a judgment of guilt, may" for "without entering a judgment of guilt and shall," in the fifth sentence of subsection A; and in subsection F, substituted "clause (vii)" for "clause (v), (vi) or (vii)" and "clause (i), (ii), (v), or (vi)" for "clause (i) or (ii)."

The 2010 amendment by c. 570, in subsection A, inserted "first" in the fifth sentence; and in subsection F, inserted "first" in the first sentence and inserted the last sentence.

Law Review.

For a book review, "Random Violence and the Transformation of the Juvenile Justice Debate," see 86 Va. L. Rev. 1095 (2000). For 2000 survey of Virginia law regarding children, see 34 U. Rich. L. Rev. 939 (2000). For article, "Legal Issues Involving Children," see 35 U. Rich. L. Rev. 741 (2001). For article summarizing published Virginia criminal law decisions between July 1, 2002 and July 1, 2003, see 38 U. Rich. L. Rev. 87 (2003).

Michie's Jurisprudence.

For related discussion, see 2B M.J. Automobiles, § 118.

OPINIONS OF THE ATTORNEY GENERAL

Despite the appearance of conflict between § 4.1-305 and this section, this section is the only statute applicable to juveniles: therefore, a juvenile court must dispose of charges of unlawful possession of alcohol by juveniles pursuant thereto. See opinion of Attorney General to The Honorable J. Dean Lewis, Judge, Fifteenth District Juvenile and Domestic Relations Court, 02-102 (10/29/02).

§ 16.1-278.10. Traffic infractions.

In cases involving a child who is charged with a traffic infraction, the court may impose only those penalties which are authorized to be imposed on adults for such infractions.

History.

1991, c. 534.

Cross references.

As to restrictions on licenses issued to persons less than 19 years old, see § 46.2-334.01.

CIRCUIT COURT OPINIONS

License suspension. — Court-imposed penalties for traffic infractions were penal in nature and served to deter and punish drivers who violated the rules of the road, while an administrative license suspension by the Commissioner was primarily remedial in nature and was a reflection of the legislature's concern for young drivers and the public safety. Thus, the juvenile's petition to have the court review the suspension of her operator's license was denied because there was no conflict between the permitted punishment that could be imposed by the court and the administrative action of the Commissioner. Commonwealth v. Dimuzio, 58 Va. Cir. 63, 2001 Va. Cir. LEXIS 391 (Loudoun County 2001).

Administrative suspension of juvenile's license did not conflict with juvenile court's action. — Where a juvenile motorist committed a traffic infraction, the decision of the juvenile and domestic relations court, in accordance with § 16.1-278.10, not to suspend the juvenile's operator's license did not conflict with the decision of the Commissioner of the Department of Motor Vehicles to suspend the juvenile's license pursuant to a separate legislative mandate, and was not manifestly unjust, as court-imposed penalties for traffic infractions were penal in nature and served to deter

and punish drivers who violated the rules of the road, where, the administrative license suspension in issue was mainly remedial and reflected concern for young drivers and the public safety. Commonwealth v. Dimuzio, 58 Va. Cir. 63, 2001 Va. Cir. LEXIS 391 (Louisa County 2001).

§ 16.1-278.14. Criminal jurisdiction; protective orders; family offenses.

In cases involving the violation of any law, regulation or ordinance for the education, protection or care of children or involving offenses committed by one family or household member against another, the juvenile court or the circuit court may impose a penalty prescribed by applicable sections of the Code and may impose conditions and limitations upon the defendant to protect the health or safety of family or household members, including, but not limited to, a protective order as provided in § 16.1-279.1, treatment and counseling for the defendant and payment by the defendant for crisis shelter care for the complaining family or household member.

History.

1991, c. 534; 1992, c. 742; 1996, c. 866.

Editor's note.

Acts 1993, c. 930, cl. 3, as amended by Acts 1994, c. 564, cl. 2, and Acts 1996, c. 616, cl. 4, provides that the amendment to this section by Acts 1993, c. 930, cl. 1, shall become effective June 1, 1998, "if state funds are provided, including all local costs, to carry out the purposes of this bill by the General Assembly." The funding was not provided.

CASE NOTES

Order authorized. — Where the evidence showed that husband grabbed, pushed, and elbowed his former wife during a verbal argument relating to visitation schedule, evidence was sufficient to show that husband committed an act of abuse against a family member, and the trial court was authorized to issue a protective order. Lord v. Lord, No. 0049-02-4, 2002 Va. App. LEXIS 362 (Ct. of Appeals June 25, 2002).

Petition denied. — Denial of a wife's petition for a protective order against her husband was not error under circumstances in which the parties presented different versions of the extent and content of the argument which led to the petition, and the trial court heard testimony from both parties and announced it found the wife's testimony less than credible; the trial court disbelieved the wife's version of the events and repeatedly admonished the wife during the hearing for interrupting the court with her outbursts and erratic behavior. Blake v. Blake, 2007 Va. App. LEXIS 306 (Aug. 14, 2007).

The section did not preclude the trial judge from sentencing defendant in the criminal matter after another judge had issued a protective order based on the same act of assault and battery. Goodwin v. Commonwealth, 23 Va. App. 475, 477 S.E.2d 781 (1996).

§ 16.1-284. When adult sentenced for juvenile offense.

When the juvenile court sentences an adult who has committed, before attaining the age of eighteen, an offense which would be a crime if committed by an adult, the court may impose the penalties which are authorized to be imposed on adults for such violations, not to exceed the punishment for a Class

1 misdemeanor for a single offense or multiple offenses.

History.
Code 1950, § 16.1-177.1; 1956, c. 555; 1973, c. 440; 1977, c. 559; 1978, c. 142; 1980, c. 235; 1983, c. 336; 1985, c. 260; 1996, cc. 755, 914.

Cross references.
For exception to confidentiality of proceedings in cases where a child is sentenced as an adult in accordance with this section, see § 16.1-309.1. As to punishment for Class 1 misdemeanors, see § 18.2-11.

Law Review.
For survey of Virginia statutory changes in substantive criminal law for the year 1970-1971, see 57 Va. L. Rev. 1467 (1971). For article discussing double jeopardy and waiver of jurisdiction to criminal courts in juvenile proceedings, see 14 Wm. & Mary L. Rev. 266 (1972). For 1985 survey of Virginia law affecting children, see 19 U. Rich. L. Rev. p. 753 (1985).

Michie's Jurisprudence.
For related discussion, see 9B M.J. Infants, §§ 13, 84.

CASE NOTES

Editor's note.
The cases cited below were decided under former § 16.1-177.1.

A juvenile is not immune from incarceration in jail. Rather, alternative and less harsh measures are preferred for the juvenile offender, but when the best interests of the child demand such confinement, that is available as an alternate discipline. Hailey v. Dorsey, 580 F.2d 112 (4th Cir. 1978), cert. denied, 440 U.S. 937, 99 S. Ct. 1282, 59 L. Ed. 2d 495 (1979).

The jail sentence is merely an additional remedial alternative applied, if at all, to incorrigibles who have committed an offense which would be a felony or misdemeanor if they were adult. Hailey v. Dorsey, 580 F.2d 112 (4th Cir. 1978), cert. denied, 440 U.S. 937, 99 S. Ct. 1282, 59 L. Ed. 2d 495 (1979).

When jail sentence may not be imposed. — Because the power of the court under this section to impose a jail sentence is limited in application to offenses committed by a juvenile which would have been either misdemeanors or felonies had they been committed by an adult, a juvenile who has been accorded juvenile delinquent status for any other reason may not be sentenced to jail. Hailey v. Dorsey, 580 F.2d 112 (4th Cir. 1978), cert. denied, 440 U.S. 937, 99 S. Ct. 1282, 59 L. Ed. 2d 495 (1979).

Finding of incorrigibility is procedural. — The statutory requirement of a finding of incorrigibility is a procedural prerequisite to the exercise of the court's general remedial powers which are granted elsewhere in the statute, and not a prerequisite to the jurisdiction of the court. Hailey v. Dorsey, 580 F.2d 112 (4th Cir. 1978), cert. denied, 440 U.S. 937, 99 S. Ct. 1282, 59 L. Ed. 2d 495 (1979).

Effect of failure to record such finding formally. — Since the failure of a circuit court to formally record a finding of incorrigibility is a State procedural error in sentencing and not a prerequisite to the jurisdiction of the court, such failure is not a ground for federal habeas corpus relief. Hailey v. Dorsey, 580 F.2d 112 (4th Cir. 1978), cert. denied, 440 U.S. 937, 99 S. Ct. 1282, 59 L. Ed. 2d 495 (1979).

The finding of incorrigibility must be supported by evidence obtained by an investigation. Norwood v. City of Richmond, 203 Va. 886, 128 S.E.2d 425 (1962).

§ 16.1-284.1. Placement in secure local facility.

A. If a juvenile 14 years of age or older is found to have committed an offense which if committed by an adult would be punishable by confinement in a state or local correctional facility as defined in § 53.1-1, and the court determines (i) that the juvenile has not previously been and is not currently adjudicated delinquent of a violent juvenile felony or found guilty of a violent juvenile felony, (ii) that the juvenile has not been released from the custody of the Department within the previous 18 months, (iii) that the interests of the juvenile and the community require that the juvenile be placed under legal restraint or discipline, and (iv) that other placements authorized by this title will not serve the best interests of the juvenile, then the court may order the juvenile confined in a detention home or other secure facility for juveniles for a period not to exceed six months from the date the order is entered, for a single offense or multiple offenses.

The period of confinement ordered may exceed 30 calendar days if the juvenile has had an assessment completed by the secure facility to which he is ordered concerning the appropriateness of the placement.

B. If the period of confinement in a detention home or other secure facility for juveniles is to exceed 30 calendar days, and the juvenile is eligible for commitment pursuant to subdivision A 14 of § 16.1-278.8, then the court shall order the juvenile committed to the Department, but suspend such commitment. In suspending the commitment to the Department as provided for in this subsection, the court shall specify conditions for the juvenile's satisfactory completion of one or more community or facility based treatment programs as may be appropriate for the juvenile's rehabilitation.

C. During any period of confinement which exceeds 30 calendar days ordered pursuant to this section, the court shall conduct a mandatory review hearing at least once during each 30 days and at such other times upon the request of the juvenile's probation officer, for good cause shown. If it appears at such hearing that the purpose of the order of confinement has been achieved, the juvenile shall be released on probation for such period and under such conditions as the court may specify and remain subject to the order suspending commitment to the State Department of Juvenile Justice. If the juvenile's commitment to the Department has been suspended as provided in subsection B of this section, and if the court determines at the first or any subsequent review hearing that the juvenile is consistently failing to comply with the conditions specified by the court or the policies and program requirements of the facility, then the court shall order that the juvenile be committed to the State Department of Juvenile Justice. If the court determines at the first or any subsequent review hearing that the juvenile is not actively involved in any community facility based treatment program through no fault of his own, then the court shall order that the juvenile be released under such conditions as the court may specify subject to the suspended commitment.

C1. The appearance of the juvenile before the court for a hearing pursuant to subsection C may be by (i) personal appearance before the judge or (ii) use of two-way electronic video and audio communication. If two-way electronic video and audio communication is used, a judge may exercise all powers conferred by law and all communications and proceedings shall be conducted in the same manner as if the appearance were in person, and any documents filed may be transmitted by facsimile process. A facsimile may be served or executed by the officer or person to whom sent, and returned in the same manner, and with the same force, effect, authority, and liability as an original document. All signatures thereon shall be treated as original signatures. Any two-way electronic video and audio communication system used for an appearance shall meet the standards as set forth in subsection B of § 19.2-3.1.

D. A juvenile may only be ordered confined pursuant to this section to a facility in compliance with standards established by the State Board for such placements. Standards for these facilities shall require juveniles placed pursuant to this section for a period which exceeds 30 calendar days be provided separate services for their rehabilitation, consistent with the intent of this section.

E. The Department of Juvenile Justice shall assist the localities or combinations thereof in implementing this section consistent with the statewide plan required by § 16.1-309.4 and pursuant to standards promulgated by the State Board, in order to ensure the availability and reasonable access of each court to the facilities the use of which is authorized by this section.

History.
1985, c. 260; 1989, c. 733; 1995, cc. 696, 699; 1996, cc. 755, 914; 2000, c. 978; 2001, c. 140; 2012, c. 94; 2013, c. 651.

Editor's note.
Acts 2000, c. 978, cl. 2, as amended by Acts 2002, c. 648, cl. 1, provides: "That the Department of Juvenile Justice shall establish a uniform risk assessment instrument for use when making a detention decision pursuant to § 16.1-248.1 and when making recommendations to the court at a detention hearing pursuant to § 16.1-250. The uniform risk assessment instrument and related procedure shall be implemented by each court service unit and distributed to each juvenile court judge no later than October 1, 2002."

The 2012 amendments.
The 2012 amendment by c. 94 added subsection C1; and made minor stylistic changes throughout the section.

The 2013 amendments.
The 2013 amendment by c. 651, in the first sentence of subsection B, inserted "and the juvenile is eligible for commitment pursuant to subdivision A 14 of § 16.1-278.8" and deleted "if he is eligible pursuant to subdivision A 14 of § 16.1-278.8" following "Department."

Law Review.
For article, "Legal Issues Involving Children," see 35 U. Rich. L. Rev. 741 (2001).

§ 16.1-285. Duration of commitments.

Except as provided in § 16.1-285.1, all commitments under this chapter shall be for an indeterminate period having regard to the welfare of the juvenile and interests of the public, but no juvenile committed hereunder shall be held or detained longer than thirty-six continuous months or after such juvenile has attained the age of twenty-one years. However, the thirty-six month limitation shall not apply in cases of commitment for an act of murder or manslaughter. The Department shall have the authority to discharge any juvenile or person from its custody, including releasing a juvenile or person to parole supervision, in accordance with policies and procedures established by the State Board and with other provisions of law. Parole supervision programs shall be operated through the court services units established pursuant to § 16.1-233. A juvenile or person who violates the conditions of his parole granted pursuant to this section may be proceeded against for a revocation or modification of parole status pursuant to § 16.1-291.

History.
Code 1950, § 16.1-180; 1956, c. 555; 1977, c. 559; 1985, cc. 260, 388; 1996, cc. 755, 914; 2000, cc. 954, 981, 988; 2001, c. 853.

Law Review.
For survey of Virginia law on criminal procedure for the year 1973-1974, see 60 Va. L. Rev. 1505 (1974). For 1985 survey of Virginia law affecting children, see 19 U. Rich. L. Rev. p. 753 (1985). For article, "Legal Issues Involving Children," see 35 U. Rich. L. Rev. 741 (2001).

CASE NOTES

Immunity of officials who determined length of confinement. — Department officials who determined the length of juvenile's indeterminate confinement under former § 16.1-180 were entitled to quasi-judicial immunity and could not be sued for personal injuries suffered by victim assaulted by juvenile after his release. Harlow v. Clatterbuck, 230 Va. 490, 339 S.E.2d 181 (1986).

§ 16.1-285.1. Commitment of serious offenders.

A. In the case of a juvenile fourteen years of age or older who has been found guilty of an offense which would be a felony if committed by an adult, and either (i) the juvenile is on parole for an offense which would be a felony if committed by an adult, (ii) the juvenile was committed to the state for an offense which would be a felony if committed by an adult within the immediately preceding twelve months, (iii) the felony offense is punishable by a term of confinement of greater than twenty years if the felony was committed by an adult, or (iv) the juvenile has been previously adjudicated delinquent for an offense which if committed by an adult would be a felony punishable by a term of confinement of twenty years or more, and the circuit court, or the juvenile or family court, as the case may be, finds that commitment under this section is necessary to meet the rehabilitative needs of the juvenile and would serve the best interests of the community, then the court may order the juvenile committed to the Department of Juvenile Justice for placement in a juvenile correctional center for the period of time prescribed pursuant to this section.

Alternatively, in order to determine if a juvenile, transferred from a juvenile and domestic relations district court to a circuit court pursuant to § 16.1-269.1, appropriately qualifies for commitment pursuant to this section, notwithstanding the inapplicability of the qualification criteria set forth in clauses (i) through (iv), the circuit court may consider the commitment criteria set forth in subdivisions 1, 2, and 3 of subsection B as well as other components of the juvenile's life history and, if upon such consideration in the opinion of the court the needs of the juvenile and the interests of the community would clearly best be served by commitment hereunder, may so commit the juvenile.

B. Prior to committing any juvenile pursuant to this section, the court shall consider:

1. The juvenile's age;

2. The seriousness and number of the present offenses, including (i) whether the offense was committed in an aggressive, violent, premeditated, or willful manner; (ii) whether the offense was against persons or property, with greater weight being given to offenses against persons, especially if death or injury resulted; (iii) whether the offense involved the use of a firearm or other dangerous weapon by brandishing, displaying, threatening with or otherwise employing such weapon; and (iv) the nature of the juvenile's participation in the alleged offense;

3. The record and previous history of the juvenile in this or any other jurisdiction, including (i) the number and nature of previous contacts with courts, (ii) the number and nature of prior periods of probation, (iii) the number and nature of prior commitments to juvenile correctional centers, (iv) the number and nature of previous residential and community-based treatments, (v) whether previous adjudications and commitments were for delinquent acts that involved the infliction of serious bodily injury, and (vi) whether the offense is part of a repetitive pattern of similar adjudicated offenses; and

4. The Department's estimated length of stay.

Such commitment order must be supported by a determination that the interests of the juvenile and community require that the juvenile be placed under legal restraint or discipline and that the juvenile is not a proper person to receive treatment or rehabilitation through other juvenile programs or facilities.

C. In ordering commitment pursuant to this section, the court shall specify a period of commitment not to exceed seven years or the juvenile's twenty-first birthday, whichever shall occur first. The court may also order a period of determinate or indeterminate parole supervision to follow the commitment but the total period of commitment and parole supervision shall not exceed seven years or the juvenile's twenty-first birthday, whichever occurs first.

D. Upon receipt of a juvenile committed under the provisions of this section, the Department shall evaluate the juvenile for the purpose of considering placement of the juvenile in an appropriate juvenile correctional center for the time prescribed by the committing court. Such a placement decision shall be made based on the availability of treatment programs at the facility; the level of security at the facility; the offense for which the juvenile has been committed; and the welfare, age and gender of the juvenile.

E. The court which commits the juvenile to the Department under this section shall have continuing jurisdiction over the juvenile throughout his commitment. The continuing jurisdiction of the court shall not prevent the Department from removing the juvenile from a juvenile correctional center without prior court approval for the sole purposes of routine or emergency medical treatment, routine educational services, or family emergencies.

F. Any juvenile committed under the provisions of this section shall not be released at a time earlier than that specified by the court in its dispositional order except as provided for in § 16.1-285.2. The Department may petition the committing court for a hearing as provided for in § 16.1-285.2 for an earlier release of the juvenile when good cause exists for an earlier release. In addition, the Department shall petition the committing court for a determination as to the continued commitment of each juvenile sentenced under this section at least sixty days prior to the second anniversary of the juvenile's date of commitment and sixty days prior to each annual anniversary thereafter.

History.
1985, c. 260; 1989, c. 717; 1992, c. 484; 1994, cc. 859, 949; 1996, cc. 755, 914; 2001, c. 563.

Law Review.
For 1985 survey of Virginia law affecting children, see 19 U. Rich. L. Rev. p. 753 (1985). For survey on legal issues involving children in Virginia for 1989, see 23 U. Rich. L. Rev. 705 (1989). For article, "Legal Issues Involving Children," see 28 U. Rich. L. Rev. 1075 (1994). For article, "Legal Issues Involving Children," see 35 U. Rich. L. Rev. 741 (2001).

Michie's Jurisprudence.
For related discussion, see 9B M.J. Infants, §§ 81, 86.

CASE NOTES

Court had authority to order combination of sentences which imposed a juvenile commitment and an adult prison sentence. The word "or" in subdivision A 2 of § 16.1-272 does not reflect a legislative intent to prohibit a judge from sentencing a juvenile both as an adult and as a juvenile "serious offender" under this section. Jackson v. Commonwealth, 29 Va. App. 418, 512 S.E.2d 838 (1999).

Commitment upheld on appeal. — Commitment and sentence of a juvenile as a serious offender was upheld on appeal based on his conviction of felony hit and run, reckless driving, and assault and battery because the trial court properly considered the juvenile's age and the aggressive, violent, and willful manner of the incident, along with the extensive injuries suffered by the victim, which resulted from the juvenile purposely hitting a park game warden with his ATV when the game warden was trying to stop the juvenile. Mattox v. Commonwealth, 46 Va. App. 577, 620 S.E.2d 550, 2005 Va. App. LEXIS 390 (2005).

§ 16.1-285.2. Release and review hearing for serious offender.

A. Upon receipt of a petition of the Department of Juvenile Justice for a hearing concerning a juvenile committed under § 16.1-285.1, the court shall schedule a hearing within thirty days and shall appoint counsel for the juvenile pursuant to § 16.1-266. The court shall provide a copy of the petition, the progress report required by this section, and notice of the time and place of the hearing to (i) the juvenile, (ii) the juvenile's parent, legal guardian, or person standing in loco parentis, (iii) the juvenile's guardian ad litem, if any, (iv) the juvenile's legal counsel, and (v) the attorney for the Commonwealth who prosecuted the juvenile during the delinquency proceeding. The attorney for the Commonwealth shall provide notice of the time and place of the hearing by first-class mail to the last known address of any victim of the offense for which the juvenile was committed if such victim has submitted a written request for notification to the attorney for the Commonwealth.

B. The petition shall be filed in the committing court and shall be accompanied by a progress report from the Department. This report shall describe (i) the facility and living arrangement provided for the juvenile by the Department, (ii) the services and treatment programs afforded the juvenile, (iii) the juvenile's progress toward treatment goals and objectives, which shall include a summary of his educational progress, (iv) the juvenile's potential for danger to either himself or the community, and (v) a comprehensive aftercare plan for the juvenile.

B1. The appearance of the juvenile before the court may be by (i) personal appearance before the judge, or (ii) use of two-way electronic video and audio communication. If two-way electronic video and audio communication is used, a judge may exercise all powers conferred by law and all communications and proceedings shall be conducted in the same manner as if the appearance were in person, and any documents filed may be transmitted by facsimile process. A facsimile may be served or executed by the officer or person to whom sent, and returned in the same manner, and with the same force, effect, authority, and liability as an original document. All signatures thereon shall be treated as original signatures. Any two-way electronic video and audio communication system used for an appearance shall meet the standards as set forth in subsection B of § 19.2-3.1.

C. At the hearing the court shall consider the progress report. The court may also consider additional evidence from (i) probation officers, the juvenile correctional center, treatment professionals, and the court service unit; (ii) the juvenile, his legal counsel, parent, guardian or family member; or (iii) other sources the court deems relevant. The hearing and all records relating thereto shall be governed by the confidentiality provisions of Article 12 (§ 16.1-299 et seq.) of this chapter.

D. At the conclusion of the hearing, the court shall order (i) continued commitment of the juvenile to the Department for completion of the original determinate period of commitment or such lesser time as the court may order or (ii) release of the juvenile under such terms and conditions as the court may prescribe. In making a determination under this section, the court shall consider (i) the experiences and character of the juvenile before and after commitment, (ii) the nature of the offenses that the juvenile was found to have committed, (iii) the manner in which the offenses were committed, (iv) the protection of the community, (v) the recommendations of the Department, and (vi) any other factors the court deems relevant. The order of the court shall be final and not subject to appeal.

E. In the case of a juvenile convicted as an adult and committed as a serious offender under subdivision A 1 of § 16.1-272, at the conclusion of the review hearing, the circuit court shall order (i) the juvenile to begin serving any adult sentence in whole or in part that may include any remaining part of the original determinate period of commitment, or (ii) the suspension of the unserved portion of the adult sentence in whole or in part based upon the juvenile's successful completion of the commitment as a serious offender, or (iii) the continued commitment of the juvenile to the Department for completion of the original determinate period of commitment or such lesser time as the court may order, or (iv) the release of the juvenile under such terms and conditions as the court may prescribe.

History.
1994, cc. 859, 949; 1995, c. 536; 1996, cc. 755, 914; 2002, c. 511.

CASE NOTES

Jurisdiction. — Defendant's §§ 16.1-289 and 16.1-285.2 challenges were not jurisdictional as they pertained to specific proceedings that were part of particular, individual cases before the court, and governed the trial court's authority to exercise its subject matter jurisdiction, not the subject of cases that could be heard and ruled upon by trial courts; subject matter jurisdiction was conferred by statute according to the subject of the case rather than according to a particular proceeding that might be one part of the case. Edmonds v. Commonwealth, No. 1577-11-4, 2013 Va. App. LEXIS 71 (Mar. 5, 2013).

Progress report. — Defendant waived his non-jurisdictional challenges to the absence of the progress report required under subsections B and C of § 16.1-285.2 as he did not object at either the initial or the continued hearing; the ends of justice exception to Va. Sup. Ct. R. 5A:18 did not apply as the untimely filing of the progress report was corrected by presenting the progress report at the hearing and continuing the hearing to consider the report. Edmonds v. Commonwealth, No. 1577-11-4, 2013 Va. App. LEXIS 71 (Mar. 5, 2013).

Time constraints. — Defendant waived his non-jurisdictional challenges to the continuance of the initial hearing that put his hearing outside of the § 16.1-285.2 time constraints and the ruling that was made outside of the time constraints as he did not object at either the initial or the continued hearing; the ends of justice exception to Va. Sup. Ct. R. 5A:18 did not apply as: (1) the order revoking defendant's suspended sentence was voidable, not void as the trial court had jurisdiction; (2) the trial court scheduled and initiated a hearing on May 4, 2011, during which it granted a continuance and scheduled a date for the review hearing; and (3) both of these actions took place 28 days after the April 6, 2011, petition, and were within the § 16.1-285.2 time period for scheduling and holding the initial hearing, and scheduling the continued hearing. Edmonds v. Commonwealth, No. 1577-11-4, 2013 Va. App. LEXIS 71 (Mar. 5, 2013).

OPINIONS OF THE ATTORNEY GENERAL

Computerized system to notify crime victims could not be used for inmates who were juveniles when crimes were committed. — Because the statutes relating to rights of victims involved in juvenile matters contained in Chapter 11 of Title 16.1 control over the general statutes relating to rights of victims as set forth in the Crime Victim and Witness Rights Act, a computerized system by which registered crime victims would be updated with information regarding future court dates, transfers, and releases of active inmates incarcerated in the city jail could not be used to provide information to victims in cases where the inmate was a juvenile when the crime was committed. See opinion of Attorney General to The Honorable Robert J. McCabe, Sheriff for the City of Norfolk, 01-058 (12/17/01).

§ 16.1-289. Review of order of commitment.

The juvenile court or the circuit court, as the case may be, of its own motion may reopen any case and may modify or revoke its order. The juvenile court or the circuit court shall before modifying or revoking such order grant a hearing after notice in writing to the complainant, if any, and to the person or agency having custody of the child; provided, however, that this section shall not apply in the case of a child committed to the Department after sixty days from the date of the order of commitment.

History.
Code 1950, § 16.1-183; 1956, c. 555; 1977, c. 559.

Editor's note.
Acts 1993, c. 929, cl. 3, as amended by Acts 1994, c. 564, cl. 1, and Acts 1996, c. 616, cl. 3, provides that the amendment to this section by Acts 1993, c. 929, cl. 1, shall become effective June 1, 1998, "only if state funds are provided by the General Assembly sufficient to provide adequate resources, including all local costs, for the court to carry out the purposes of this act and to fulfill its mission to serve children and families of the Commonwealth." The funding was not provided.

Michie's Jurisprudence.
For related discussion, see 9B M.J. Infants, § 86.

CASE NOTES

A commitment review is not a reexamination of the underlying order of delinquency or commitment but it permits the trial court to evaluate the utility of continuing commitment in the light of post-commitment developments and circumstances. Richardson v. Commonwealth, 28 Va. App. 389, 504 S.E.2d 884 (1998).

Sixty-day limitation. — Trial court properly concluded that it did not have the authority to review the juvenile's commitment order where it had entered an order committing the juvenile to the state juvenile justice department, it had continued that commitment order at a second hearing, and at the third hearing it was pointed out to the trial court that the trial court could not again review the commitment order because more than 60 days had passed since entry of the initial commitment order, which contravened the express language of § 16.1-289 regarding review of commitment orders. Washington v. Commonwealth, 2007 Va. App. LEXIS 278 (July 24, 2007).

Defendant's §§ 16.1-289 and 16.1-285.2 challenges were not jurisdictional as they pertained to specific proceedings that were

part of particular, individual cases before the court, and governed the trial court's authority to exercise its subject matter jurisdiction, not the subject of cases that could be heard and ruled upon by trial courts; subject matter jurisdiction was conferred by statute according to the subject of the case rather than according to a particular proceeding that might be one part of the case. Edmonds v. Commonwealth, No. 1577-11-4, 2013 Va. App. LEXIS 71 (Mar. 5, 2013).

ARTICLE 10.

PROBATION AND PAROLE.

§ 16.1-291. Revocation or modification of probation, protective supervision or parole; proceedings; disposition.

A. A juvenile or person who violates an order of the juvenile court entered into pursuant to §§ 16.1-278.2 through 16.1-278.10, who violates the conditions of his probation granted pursuant to § 16.1-278.5 or § 16.1-278.8, or who violates the conditions of his parole granted pursuant to §§ 16.1-285, 16.1-285.1 or § 16.1-293, may be proceeded against for a revocation or modification of such order or parole status. A proceeding to revoke or modify probation, protective supervision or parole shall be commenced by the filing of a petition. Except as otherwise provided, such petitions shall be screened, reviewed and prepared in the same manner and shall contain the same information as provided in §§ 16.1-260 and 16.1-262. The petition shall recite the date that the juvenile or person was placed on probation, under protective supervision or on parole and shall state the time and manner in which notice of the terms of probation, protective supervision or parole were given.

B. If a juvenile or person is found to have violated a prior order of the court or the terms of probation or parole, the court may, in accordance with the provisions of §§ 16.1-278.2 through 16.1-278.10, upon a revocation or modification hearing, modify or extend the terms of the order of probation or parole, including termination of probation or parole. However, notwithstanding the contempt power of the court as provided in § 16.1-292, the court shall be limited in the actions it may take to those that the court may have taken at the time of the court's original disposition pursuant to §§ 16.1-278.2 through 16.1-278.10, except as hereinafter provided.

C. In the event that a child in need of supervision is found to have willfully and materially violated an order of the court or the terms of his probation granted pursuant to § 16.1-278.5, in addition to or in lieu of the dispositions specified in that section, the court may enter any of the following orders of disposition:

1. Suspend the child's driver's license upon terms and conditions which may include the issuance of a restricted license for those purposes set forth in subsection E of § 18.2-271.1; or

2. Order any such child fourteen years of age or older to be (i) placed in a foster home, group home or other nonsecure residential facility, or, (ii) if the

court finds that such placement is not likely to meet the child's needs, that all other treatment options in the community have been exhausted, and that secure placement is necessary in order to meet the child's service needs, detained in a secure facility for a period of time not to exceed ten consecutive days for violation of any order of the court or violation of probation arising out of the same petition. The court shall state in its order for detention the basis for all findings required by this section. When any child is detained in a secure facility pursuant to this section, the court shall direct the agency evaluating the child pursuant to § 16.1-278.5 to reconvene the interdisciplinary team participating in such evaluation, develop further treatment plans as may be appropriate and submit its report to the court of its determination as to further treatment efforts either during or following the period the child is in secure detention. A child may only be detained pursuant to this section in a detention home or other secure facility in compliance with standards established by the State Board. Any order issued pursuant to this subsection is a final order and is appealable as provided by law.

D. Nothing in this section shall be construed to reclassify a child in need of supervision as a delinquent.

E. If a person adjudicated delinquent and found to have violated an order of the court or the terms of his probation or parole was a juvenile at the time of the original offense and is eighteen years of age or older when the court enters disposition for violation of the order of the court or the terms of his probation or parole, the dispositional alternative specified in § 16.1-284 shall be available to the court.

History.
Code 1950, § 16.1-188; 1956, c. 555; 1977, c. 559; 1991, c. 534; 1992, c. 90; 2001, c. 853.

Editor's note.
Acts 1993, c. 930, cl. 3, as amended by Acts 1994, c. 564, cl. 2, and Acts 1996, c. 616, cl. 4, provides that the amendment to this section by Acts 1993, c. 930, cl. 1, shall become effective June 1, 1998, "if state funds are provided, including all local costs, to carry out the purposes of this bill by the General Assembly." The funding was not provided.

Law Review.
For article, "The Revision of Virginia's Juvenile Court Law," see 13 U. Rich. L. Rev. 847 (1979). For article, "Legal Issues Involving Children," see 35 U. Rich. L. Rev. 741 (2001). For annual survey article on legal issues involving children, see 38 U. Rich. L. Rev. 161 (2003).

Michie's Jurisprudence.
For related discussion, see 9B M.J. Infants, § 84.

CASE NOTES

Circuit court retained jurisdiction over juvenile parole revocation proceeding. — Where the circuit court acquired jurisdiction over an appeal de novo of a juvenile proceeding, the circuit court retained jurisdiction to hear a parole revocation proceeding concerning the juvenile upon her release from the department of juvenile justice. Austin v. Commonwealth, 42 Va.

App. 33, 590 S.E.2d 68, 2003 Va. App. LEXIS 676 (2003), aff'd, 268 Va. 439, 604 S.E.2d 430 (2004).

Petition to revoke parole need not be filed in juvenile court. — Subsection A describes the process necessary to initiate a revocation proceeding. It does not require the petition to be filed only in the juvenile court. Austin v. Commonwealth, 42 Va. App. 33, 590 S.E.2d 68, 2003 Va. App. LEXIS 676 (2003), aff'd, 268 Va. 439, 604 S.E.2d 430 (2004).

Meaning of "original proceedings." — The "original proceedings" referred to in the former last sentence of subsection A, which prior to its deletion by the General Assembly in 2001 provided that proceedings to revoke or modify probation, protective supervision or parole should be governed by the procedures, safeguards, rights and duties applicable to the original proceedings, were not the original adjudicatory proceedings in the prosecution, but the original dispositional proceedings. Commonwealth v. Pannell, 263 Va. 497, 561 S.E.2d 724, 2002 Va. LEXIS 53 (2002).

The General Assembly's elimination of the sentence at issue as part of the 2001 amendments to § 16.1-291 does not require a finding that the General Assembly's action was undertaken to alter the meaning of the phrase "original proceedings." Commonwealth v. Pannell, 263 Va. 497, 561 S.E.2d 724, 2002 Va. LEXIS 53 (2002).

Commitment to Department of Juvenile Justice. — Trial court did not err in finding, upon determining that the juvenile violated the juvenile's probation, that the juvenile should be committed to the Department of Juvenile Justice for an indeterminate period; although the juvenile argued that the "original disposition" and "current offense" for such a disposition had to be a felony or Class 1 misdemeanor and the juvenile's case merely involved a probation violation, the underlying offense on which the juvenile received probation was a felony robbery, and, thus, commitment to the Department of Juvenile Justice was permissible because it could have been made in originally deciding the juvenile's punishment even though the juvenile's proceeding was indeed a probation revocation proceeding. Kerns v. Commonwealth, 2007 Va. App. LEXIS 175 (May 1, 2007).

Trial court had authority pursuant to §§ 16.1-278.8 and 16.1-291 to impose a suspended Department of Juvenile Justice commitment upon defendant juvenile's violation of the conditions of his probation because defendant's underlying offense, larceny of animals, was a form of grand larceny, and it remained a felony each time defendant came before the trial court on a probation violation; the term, "original disposition" in subsection B of § 16.1-291 plainly refers to the dispositional proceeding for the larceny of animals offense held under subsection A of § 16.1-278.8, in which the original conditions of probation were imposed. Rivas v. Commonwealth, 51 Va. App. 507, 659 S.E.2d 524, 2008 Va. App. LEXIS 173 (2008).

Standard in juvenile probation revocation proceedings. — There is no constitutional requirement that a court apply a reasonable doubt standard or exclude hearsay evidence in an adult probation revocation proceeding, nor are such standards required in juvenile proceedings. Commonwealth v. Pannell, 263 Va. 497, 561 S.E.2d 724, 2002 Va. LEXIS 53 (2002).

OPINIONS OF THE ATTORNEY GENERAL

Probation revocation proceedings. — A juvenile court retains jurisdiction over a probationer although he has reached the age of twenty-one prior to a probation revocation proceeding. See opinion of Attorney General to Honorable Harvey L. Bryant, Commonwealth's Attorney for the City of Virginia Beach, 05-037 (6/20/05).

§ 16.1-292. Violation of court order by any person.

A. Any person violating an order of the juvenile court entered pursuant to §§ 16.1-278.2 through 16.1-278.19, including a parent subject to an order issued pursuant to subdivision 3 of § 16.1-278.8, may be proceeded against (i) by an order requiring the person to show cause why the order of the court entered pursuant to §§ 16.1-278.2 through 16.1-278.19 has not been complied with, (ii) for contempt of court pursuant to § 16.1-69.24 or as otherwise provided in this section, or (iii) by both. Except as otherwise expressly provided herein, nothing in this chapter shall deprive the court of its power to punish summarily for contempt for such acts as set forth in § 18.2-456, or to punish for contempt after notice and an opportunity for a hearing on the contempt except that confinement in the case of a juvenile shall be in a secure facility for juveniles rather than in jail and shall not exceed a period of ten days for each offense. However, if the person violating the order was a juvenile at the time of the original act and is eighteen years of age or older when the court enters a disposition for violation of the order, the judge may order confinement in jail.

B. Upon conviction of any party for contempt of court in failing or refusing to comply with an order of a juvenile court for spousal support or child support under § 16.1-278.15, the court may commit and sentence such party to confinement in a jail, workhouse, city farm or work squad as provided in §§ 20-61 and 20-62, for a fixed or indeterminate period or until the further order of the court. In no event, however, shall such sentence be imposed for a period of more than twelve months. The sum or sums as provided for in § 20-63 shall be paid as therein set forth, to be used for the support and maintenance of the spouse or the child or children for whose benefit such order or decree provided.

C. Notwithstanding the contempt power of the court, the court shall be limited in the actions it may take with respect to a child violating the terms and conditions of an order to those which the court could have taken at the time of the court's original disposition pursuant to §§ 16.1-278.2 through 16.1-278.10, except as hereinafter provided. However, this limitation shall not be construed to deprive the court of its power to (i) punish a child summarily for contempt for acts set forth in § 18.2-456 or (ii) punish a child for contempt for violation of a dispositional order in a delinquency proceeding after notice and an opportunity for a hearing regarding such contempt, including acts of disobedience of the court's dispositional order which are committed outside the presence of the court.

D. In the event a child in need of services is found to have willfully and materially violated for a second or subsequent time the order of the court pursuant to § 16.1-278.4, the dispositional alternatives specified in subdivision 9 of § 16.1-278.8 shall be available to the court.

E. In the event a child in need of supervision is found to have willfully and materially violated an order of the court pursuant to § 16.1-278.5, the court may enter any of the following orders of disposition:

1. Suspend the child's motor vehicle driver's license;

2. Order any such child fourteen years of age or older to be (i) placed in a foster home, group home or other nonsecure residential facility, or, (ii) if the court finds that such placement is not likely to meet the child's needs, that all other treatment options in the community have been exhausted, and that secure placement is necessary in order to meet the child's service needs, detained in a secure facility for a period of time not to exceed ten consecutive days for violation of any order of the court arising out of the same petition. The court shall state in its order for detention the basis for all findings required by this section. When any child is detained in a secure facility pursuant to this section, the court shall direct the agency evaluating the child pursuant to § 16.1-278.5 to reconvene the interdisciplinary team participating in such evaluation as promptly as possible to review its evaluation, develop further treatment plans as may be appropriate and submit its report to the court for its determination as to further treatment efforts either during or following the period the child is in secure detention. A juvenile may only be detained pursuant to this section in a detention home or other secure facility in compliance with standards established by the State Board. Any order issued pursuant to this subsection is a final order and is appealable to the circuit court as provided by law.

F. Nothing in this section shall be construed to reclassify a child in need of services or in need of supervision as a delinquent.

History.
1977, c. 559; 1983, c. 501; 1985, cc. 1, 260; 1987, c. 632; 1988, c. 771; 1989, c. 725; 1990, c. 110; 1991, c. 534; 1993, c. 632; 1994, c. 21; 2000, c. 978.

Cross references.
As to escapes from residential care facilities, see § 18.2-477.1.

Editor's note.
Acts 1993, c. 929, cl. 3, as amended by Acts 1994, c. 564, cl. 1, and Acts 1996, c. 616, cl. 3, provides that the amendment to this section by Acts 1993, c. 929, cl. 1, shall become effective June 1, 1998, "only if state funds are provided by the General Assembly sufficient to provide adequate resources, including all local costs, for the court to carry out the purposes of this act and to fulfill its mission to serve children and families of the Commonwealth." The funding was not provided.

Acts 2000, c. 978, cl. 2, as amended by Acts 2002, c. 648, cl. 1, provides: "That the Department of Juvenile Justice shall establish a uniform risk assessment instrument for use when making a detention decision pursuant to § 16.1-248.1 and when making recommendations to the court at a detention hearing pursuant to § 16.1-250. The uniform risk assessment instrument and related procedure shall be implemented by each court service unit and distributed to each juvenile court judge no later than October 1, 2002."

Law Review.
For 1985 survey of Virginia law affecting children, see 19 U. Rich. L. Rev. p. 753 (1985). For survey on legal issues involving children in Virginia for 1989, see 23 U. Rich. L. Rev. 705 (1989). For an article, "Legal Issues Involving Children," see 32 U. Rich. L. Rev. 1345 (1998).

CASE NOTES

Authority to punish for contempt of order to attend school. — Where an order to attend school had been violated, subsection A of § 16.1-292 authorized the juvenile and domestic relations court and the trial court to punish for contempt; thus, as the record clearly supported the trial court's finding that the juvenile violated the school attendance order, subsection A of § 16.1-292 provided for the penalty adjudicated. B.P. v. Commonwealth, 38 Va. App. 735, 568 S.E.2d 412, 2002 Va. App. LEXIS 498 (2002).

The circuit court lacked authority to sentence juvenile to jail, where the proceeding was one in which the juvenile had not been certified as an adult. Wilson v. Commonwealth, 23 Va. App. 318, 477 S.E.2d 7 (1996).

"Jail." — For case construing the word "jail" in circuit court's order to mean "the appropriate location for juvenile confinement," see Wilson v. Commonwealth, 23 Va. App. 318, 477 S.E.2d 7 (1996).

Placement in a residential facility and requiring the parents to pay for the placement was proper. — Trial court's order placing a juvenile in a non-secure residential facility and requiring the parents to pay for the placement did not violate subsection E of § 16.1-292. The circuit judge found that the juvenile was "doing well and making progress," and the judge's interlocutory order was consistent with the primary purpose of the juvenile system in Virginia, which was corrective in nature rather than penal. Aylor v. Madison County Dep't of Soc. Servs., 2006 Va. App. LEXIS 496 (Oct. 31, 2006).

CIRCUIT COURT OPINIONS

Multiple confinement orders proper. — Under either § 18.2-456 or subsection E of § 16.1-292, there can be multiple confinement orders for violations of orders to attend school, issued under the same Child In Need of Supervision petition. Commonwealth v. May, 62 Va. Cir. 360, 2003 Va. Cir. LEXIS 275 (Rockingham County 2003).

Punishment for contempt. — Under this section, detention may be ordered for contempt of a court order to go to school (with no need to show the futility of less restrictive remedies), but the failure to go to school without a court order can only be punished by detention if the procedural and substantive safeguards of subsection E of § 16.1-292 are observed. Commonwealth v. May, 62 Va. Cir. 360, 2003 Va. Cir. LEXIS 275 (Rockingham County 2003).

Virginia juvenile and domestic relations district court was authorized to punish by contempt a student's failure to obey its order to go to school, and the student could be sentenced to 10 consecutive days for each violation of such orders. Commonwealth v. May, 62 Va. Cir. 360, 2003 Va. Cir. LEXIS 275 (Rockingham County 2003).

§ 16.1-295. Transfer of supervision from one county or city to another, or to another state.

If any person on probation to or under the supervision of any juvenile probation officer or other officer of the court removes his residence or place of abode from the county or city in which he was so placed on probation or under supervision to another county or city in the Commonwealth, the court in the city or county from which he removed his residence or place of abode may then arrange the transfer of the supervision to the city or county to which he moves his place of residence or abode, or such transfer may be ordered by the transferring court.

The Director of the Department of Juvenile Justice may make provision for the transfer of a juvenile placed on probation in this Commonwealth to another state to be there placed on probation under the terms of Article 4 (§ 53.1-166 et seq.) of Chapter 4 of Title 53.1.

The costs of returning juveniles on probation or parole to their places of residence, whether within or outside of this Commonwealth, shall be paid in accordance with regulations established by the State Board from funds appropriated in the general appropriation act for criminal costs.

History.
Code 1950, § 16.1-212; 1956, c. 555; 1972, c. 708; 1973, c. 546; 1974, cc. 44, 45; 1977, c. 559; 1989, c. 733.

ARTICLE 11.

APPEAL.

§ 16.1-296. Jurisdiction of appeals; procedure.

A. From any final order or judgment of the juvenile court affecting the rights or interests of any person coming within its jurisdiction, an appeal may be taken to the circuit court within 10 days from the entry of a final judgment, order or conviction and shall be heard de novo. However, in a case arising under the Uniform Interstate Family Support Act (§ 20-88.32 et seq.), a party may take an appeal pursuant to this section within 30 days from entry of a final order or judgment. Protective orders issued pursuant to § 16.1-279.1 in cases of family abuse and orders entered pursuant to § 16.1-278.2 are final orders from which an appeal may be taken.

B. Upon receipt of notice of such appeal the juvenile court shall forthwith transmit to the attorney for the Commonwealth a report incorporating the results of any investigation conducted pursuant to § 16.1-273, which shall be confidential in nature and made available only to the court and the attorney for the defendant (i) after the guilt or innocence of the accused has been determined or (ii) after the court has made its findings on the issues subject to appeal. After final determination of the case, the report and all copies thereof shall be forthwith returned to such juvenile court.

C. Where an appeal is taken by a child on a finding that he or she is delinquent and on a disposition pursuant to § 16.1-278.8, trial by jury on the issue of guilt or innocence of the alleged delinquent act may be had on motion of the child, the attorney for the Commonwealth or the circuit court judge. If the alleged delinquent act is one which, if committed by an adult, would constitute a felony, the child shall be entitled to a jury of 12 persons. In all other cases, the jury shall consist of seven persons. If the jury in such a trial finds the child guilty, disposition shall be by the judge pursuant to the provisions of § 16.1-278.8 after taking into consideration the report of any investigation made pursuant to § 16.1-237 or 16.1-273.

C1. In any hearing held upon an appeal taken by a child on a finding that he is delinquent and on a disposition pursuant to § 16.1-278.8, the provisions of § 16.1-302 shall apply mutatis mutandis, except in the case of trial by jury which shall be open. If proceedings in the circuit court are closed pursuant to this subsection, any records or portions thereof relating to such closed proceedings shall remain confidential.

C2. Where an appeal is taken by a juvenile on a finding that he is delinquent and on a disposition pursuant to § 16.1-278.8 and the juvenile is in a secure facility pending the appeal, the circuit court, when practicable, shall hold a hearing on the merits of the case within 45 days of the filing of the appeal. Upon receipt of the notice of appeal from the juvenile court, the circuit court shall provide a copy of the order and a copy of the notice of appeal to the attorney for the Commonwealth within seven days after receipt of notice of an appeal. The time limitations shall be tolled during any period in which the juvenile has escaped from custody. A juvenile held continuously in secure detention shall be released from confinement if there is no hearing on the merits of his case within 45 days of the filing of the appeal. The circuit court may extend the time limitations for a reasonable period of time based upon good cause shown, provided the basis for such extension is recorded in writing and filed among the papers of the proceedings.

D. When an appeal is taken in a case involving termination of parental rights brought under § 16.1-283, the circuit court shall hold a hearing on the merits of the case within 90 days of the perfecting of the appeal. An appeal of the case to the Court of Appeals shall take precedence on the docket of the Court.

E. Where an appeal is taken by an adult on a finding of guilty of an offense within the jurisdiction of the juvenile and domestic relations district court, the appeal shall be dealt with in all respects as is an appeal from a general district court pursuant to §§ 16.1-132 through 16.1-137; however, where an appeal is taken by any person on a charge of non-support, the procedure shall be as is provided for appeals in prosecutions under Chapter 5 (§ 20-61 et seq.) of Title 20.

F. In all other cases on appeal, proceedings in the circuit court shall be heard without a jury; however, hearing of an issue by an advisory jury may be allowed, in the discretion of the judge, upon the motion of any party. An appeal from an order of protection issued pursuant to § 16.1-279.1 shall be given precedence on the docket of the court over other civil appeals taken to the circuit court from the district courts, but shall otherwise be docketed and processed as other civil cases.

G. Costs, taxes and fees on appealed cases shall be assessed only in those cases in which a trial fee could have been assessed in the juvenile and domestic relations court and shall be collected in the circuit court, except that the appeal to circuit court of any case in which a fee either was or could have been assessed pursuant to § 16.1-69.48:5 shall also be in accordance with § 16.1-296.2.

H. No appeal bond shall be required of a party appealing from an order of a juvenile and domestic relations district court except for that portion of any order or judgment establishing a support arrearage or suspending payment of support during pendency of an appeal. In cases involving support, no appeal shall be allowed until the party applying for the same or someone for him gives bond, in an amount and with sufficient surety approved by the judge or by his clerk if there is one, to abide by such judgment as may be rendered on appeal if the appeal is perfected or, if not perfected, then to satisfy the judgment of the court in which it was rendered. Upon appeal from a conviction for failure to support or from a finding of civil or criminal contempt involving a failure to support, the juvenile and domestic relations district court may require the party applying for the appeal or someone for him to give bond, with or without surety, to insure his appearance and may also require bond in an amount and with sufficient surety to secure the payment of prospective support accruing during the pendency of the appeal. An appeal will not be perfected unless such appeal bond as may be required is filed within 30 days from the entry of the final judgment or order. However, no appeal bond shall be required of the Commonwealth or when an appeal is proper to protect the estate of a decedent, an infant, a convict or an insane person, or the interest of a county, city or town.

If bond is furnished by or on behalf of any party against whom judgment has been rendered for money, the bond shall be conditioned for the performance and satisfaction of such judgment or order as may be entered against the party on appeal, and for the payment of all damages which may be awarded against him in the appellate court. If the appeal is by a party against whom there is no recovery, the bond shall be conditioned for the payment of any damages as may be awarded against him on the appeal. The provisions of § 16.1-109 shall apply to bonds required pursuant to this subsection.

This subsection shall not apply to release on bail pursuant to other subsections of this section or § 16.1-298.

I. In all cases on appeal, the circuit court in the disposition of such cases shall have all the powers and authority granted by the chapter to the juvenile and domestic relations district court. Unless otherwise specifically provided by this Code, the circuit court judge shall have the authority to appoint counsel for the parties and compensate such counsel in accordance with the provisions of Article 6 (§ 16.1-266 et seq.) of this chapter.

J. In any case which has been referred or transferred from a circuit court to a juvenile court and an appeal is taken from an order or judgment of the juvenile court, the appeal shall be taken to the circuit court in the same locality as the juvenile court to which the case had been referred or transferred.

History.
Code 1950, § 16.1-214; 1956, c. 555; 1966, c. 237; 1977, c. 559; 1978, c. 445; 1981, c. 109; 1982, c. 465; 1983, c. 88; 1984, c. 631;

1986, cc. 143, 465; 1989, c. 473; 1991, c. 534; 1993, c. 970; 1994, c. 673; 1995, c. 517; 1996, c. 866; 1997, cc. 654, 664, 790, 862; 1998, c. 550; 2004, cc. 468, 659, 727; 2005, c. 681; 2007, c. 464; 2009, c. 729.

Editor's note.

Acts 1993, c. 929, cl. 3, as amended by Acts 1994, c. 564, cl. 1, and Acts 1996, c. 616, cl. 3, provides that the amendment to this section by Acts 1993, c. 929, cl. 1, shall become effective June 1, 1998, "only if state funds are provided by the General Assembly sufficient to provide adequate resources, including all local costs, for the court to carry out the purposes of this act and to fulfill its mission to serve children and families of the Commonwealth." The funding was not provided.

Acts 1993, c. 970, cl. 2, as amended by Acts 1994, c. 564, cl. 3 and Acts 1996, c. 616, cl. 5, provides that the amendment to this section by Acts 1993, c. 970, cl. 1, "shall expire on May 31, 1998; provided, however, that the provisions of this act shall apply on and after June 1, 1998, only to any final order which disposes of a proceeding in a support case, when such proceeding was commenced in a juvenile and domestic relations district court prior to June 1, 1998, and when such case is appealed to the circuit court, regardless of whether such proceeding was commenced by a petition, motion or other pleading."

Acts 1994, c. 673, cl. 3, provides that the provisions of § 16.1-296 as amended by this act shall expire on the effective date of Chapter 929 of the 1993 Acts of Assembly. Chapter 929 never became effective.

Acts 1995, c. 517, cl. 2, provides: "That the provisions of this act shall expire on July 1, 1996, if funds are provided pursuant to the provisions of the third enactment of Chapter 930 of the Acts of Assembly of 1993 as amended by the second enactment of Chapter 564 of the Acts of Assembly of 1994." The funding was never provided.

Acts 2009, c. 729, cl. 2, provides: "That the provisions of this act are declarative of existing law."

The 2009 amendments.

The 2009 amendment by c. 729, in subsection A, in the first sentence, inserted "to the circuit court" and "and shall be heard de novo."

Law Review.

For comment, "Jury Trials for Juvenile Delinquents in Virginia," see 28 Wash. & Lee L. Rev. 135 (1971). For note, "Review of Improper Juvenile Transfer Hearings," see 60 Va. L. Rev. 818 (1974). For article, "The Revision of Virginia's Juvenile Court Law," see 13 U. Rich. L. Rev. 847 (1979). For survey on domestic relations in Virginia for 1989, see 23 U. Rich. L. Rev. 561 (1989). For survey on legal issues involving children in Virginia for 1989, see 23 U. Rich. L. Rev. 705 (1989). For 1994 survey of Virginia domestic relations law, see 28 U. Rich. L. Rev. 981 (1994). For 2003/2004 survey of family and juvenile law, see 39 U. Rich. L. Rev. 241 (2004). For 2006 survey article, "Family and Juvenile Law," see 41 U. Rich. L. Rev. 151 (2006). For annual survey, "A Look Back and Forward: Legislative and Regulatory Highlights for 2008 and 2009 and a Discussion of Juvenile Transfer," see 44 U. Rich. L. Rev. 53 (2009).

Research references.

Bryson on Virginia Civil Procedure (Matthew Bender). Chapter 2 Potential Jurisdiction. § 2.03 Courts. W. Hamilton Bryson.

Friend's Virginia Pleading and Practice (Matthew Bender). Chapter 1 Courts. § 1.05 District Courts. Charles E. Friend.

Virginia Forms (Matthew Bender). No. 5-231 Notice of Appeal — Support Proceeding. No. 5-232 Civil Appeal Bond.

Michie's Jurisprudence.

For related discussion, see 9B M.J. Infants, § 87.

CASE NOTES

The cross-reference in the first sentence of this section relates to § 16.1-136. Walker v. Department of Pub. Welfare, 223 Va. 557, 290 S.E.2d 887 (1982).

Application of standards to appeals from district courts to circuit courts. — Where appellants contended that the application of standards to appeals from district courts to circuit courts, which are different that those standards applied to appeals from

circuit courts to the court of appeals or to the Supreme Court, violated due process, this contention was without merit. In light of the opportunity to have the matter heard de novo in the circuit court, the appellants did not demonstrate that they were denied due process by the statutory requirement that they await entry of the district court's final order before seeking an appeal. Green v. Morgan, No. 1281-97-4 (Ct. of Appeals Jan. 20, 1998).

Evidentiary hearing required. — Comprehensive Services Act Office was entitled to an evidentiary hearing on order of juvenile and domestic relations district court directing it to provide residential placement for child found to be in need of supervision. Comprehensive Servs. Act Office v. J.M., No. 1620-98-2 (Ct. of Appeals Aug. 3, 1999).

Documentary evidence during termination of parental rights proceeding. — Trial court did not improperly consider documentary evidence in during a hearing regarding the termination of a father's parental rights to his child because a circuit court order terminating the father's parental rights to the child's sibling was properly considered as a basis for termination pursuant to subsection C of § 16.1-283; all documentary evidence was made part of the record by operation of the law because under § 16.1-296, an appeal from a juvenile and domestic relations district court to a circuit court necessarily transferred the entire record to the circuit court for retrial as though the case had been originally brought there. Ridgley v. Fairfax County Dep't of Family Servs., 2010 Va. App. LEXIS 465 (Nov. 30, 2010).

Commitment review order final and appealable. — The language of this section makes plain that the appellate jurisdiction in the circuit court encompasses "any final order" without qualification or limitation; an order determining whether to modify, revoke or continue a juvenile's commitment following a review hearing is final and appealable because it concludes that issue and leaves nothing to be done by the court. Richardson v. Commonwealth, 28 Va. App. 389, 504 S.E.2d 884 (1998).

This section makes no distinction between consent orders and nonconsent orders. It also does not qualify or limit the word "any." Cox v. Cox, 16 Va. App. 146, 428 S.E.2d 515 (1993).

Section 16.1-136 is only vehicle for appeal from juvenile court to circuit court. — Although Chapter 7 of Title 16.1 relates to "Jurisdiction and Procedure in Criminal Matters," § 16.1-136 remains the only vehicle for appeal from the juvenile court to the circuit court, having been reenacted as a part of the Juvenile and Domestic Relations District Court Law of 1977. Walker v. Department of Pub. Welfare, 223 Va. 557, 290 S.E.2d 887 (1982).

Nonsuit order not a final appealable order. — In a custody and visitation matter, a juvenile court's order of nonsuit was not a final appealable order under § 16.1-296 because the effect of the nonsuit was to put an end to the pending action without precluding another for the same cause of action. Sharman v. Gillepsie, 2010 Va. App. LEXIS 47 (Feb. 9, 2010).

Appeal from a juvenile court sanction order. — Upon review of a sanctions order entered against an attorney for misconduct in the juvenile court, the circuit court erred by failing to conduct a de novo review. In re Fener, No. 0588-03-1, 2003 Va. App. LEXIS 596 (Ct. of Appeals Nov. 18, 2003).

Applicability to appeal following incarceration for failing to pay child support. — Denial of a parent's appeal of the denial of a bond motion for an appeal of an order incarcerating the parent for failure to pay child support was summarily affirmed as a parent did not post an appeal bond and there was no indigency exception to subsection H of § 16.1-296; section 16.1-107 concerned appeals of the general district court, rather than the juvenile courts, and § 8.01-676.1 did not apply to appeals of the juvenile courts. Shadwell v. Commonwealth, 2008 Va. App. LEXIS 444 (Sept. 30, 2008).

Appealability of juvenile court order. — Because the plain language of §§ 16.1-278.2 D, 16.1-252, and 16.129-6 A provided that a preliminary removal order was not a dispositional order and was not a final order, the trial court did not err in finding that it lacked jurisdiction to entertain a department of social services' appeal of a juvenile court's order. Richmond Dep't of Soc. Servs. v. Petersburg Dep't of Soc. Servs., 2006 Va. App. LEXIS 263 (June 13, 2006).

Father could not leave Virginia with a child involved in an international custody dispute during appellee mother's appeal and refuse to recognize the continuing jurisdiction of Virginia's courts as to do so would defeat the mother's § 16.1-296 rights. Sasson v. Shenhar, 276 Va. 611, 667 S.E.2d 555, 2008 Va. LEXIS 124 (2008).

Circuit court did not err in dismissing a mother's appeals of a juvenile and domestic relations district court's adjudicatory orders that her children were abused and neglected because the juvenile and domestic relations district court's dispositional orders, the final orders, were not entered until July 16, 2010, but the mother never appealed those orders, and the filing of the dispositional order appeal forms on June 1, 2010, was premature since there were no final orders from which the mother could appeal at that time; pursuant to subsection A of § 16.1-296, only final orders of the district court could be appealed to the circuit court, and adjudicatory orders entered by a district court in child abuse and neglect cases are not final orders for purposes of appeal because they are not entered pursuant to § 16.1-278.2 as required by the General Assembly. Chavis v. Hopewell Dep't of Soc. Servs., 2011 Va. App. LEXIS 118 (Apr. 5, 2011).

Final judgment. — Order at issue was a final order under subsection D of § 16.1-278.2 and subsection A of § 16.1-296 because it was captioned "dispositional order," transferred custody of a child to the department of social services, made the finding required by subdivision A 5 c. of § 16.1-278.2, established specific terms for visitation, authorized placement with the mother, and was entered after an adjudicatory order. Blevins v. Prince William County Dep't of Soc. Servs., 61 Va. App. 94, 733 S.E.2d 674, 2012 Va. App. LEXIS 347 (2012).

Circuit court retained jurisdiction over juvenile parole revocation proceeding. — Where the circuit court acquired jurisdiction over an appeal de novo of a juvenile proceeding, the circuit court retained jurisdiction to hear a parole revocation proceeding concerning the juvenile upon her release from the department of juvenile justice. Austin v. Commonwealth, 42 Va. App. 33, 590 S.E.2d 68, 2003 Va. App. LEXIS 676 (2003), aff'd, 268 Va. 439, 604 S.E.2d 430 (2004).

Subsection H of this section places the burden on the party applying for the appeal to ask for and to have the district court set the bond and approve the surety. Thus, in the instant case, just because the district court failed to require bond, the circuit court could not obtain jurisdiction of the appeal. Commonwealth, Va. Dep't of Social Servs. ex rel. May v. Walker, 253 Va. 319, 485 S.E.2d 134 (1997).

Failure to post the appeal bond deprived the trial court of jurisdiction as subsection H of § 16.1-296 placed the burden on the father as the party applying for the appeal to ask for and to have the district court set the bond and approve the surety; thus, the argument that the district court had set the bond at zero failed. Espinoza v. Espinoza, No. 0536-03-4, 2003 Va. App. LEXIS 426 (Ct. of Appeals Aug. 5, 2003).

Appeal from juvenile court without posting of bond. — Where a father was required to file an appeal bond by subsection H of § 16.1-296, but failed to do so, the circuit court lacked jurisdiction to hear his appeal of the registration of certain out-of-state child support orders. Jones v. Dep't of Soc. Servs. ex rel. Dye, No. 2376-03-3, 2004 Va. App. LEXIS 251 (Ct. of Appeals June 1, 2004).

Trial court properly dismissed a husband's appeal from an order of the juvenile court finding him in contempt and establishing an arrearage amount of $50,000, due to his failure to post the entire appeal bond, as the husband could not choose to bifurcate his appeal by appealing the show cause and other portions of the order but not that part establishing a support arrearage. Hall v. Hall, No. 0432-04-2, 2004 Va. App. LEXIS 485 (Ct. of Appeals Oct. 12, 2004).

Trial court properly dismissed a father's appeal of a juvenile court order which modified his child support obligation and assessed an arrearage; a court clerk's act of setting an appeal bond at "0" did not excuse the father of the requirement to post an appeal bond under subsection H of this section and § 16.1-109 did not allow for a cure where there was a total failure to comply with the bond requirement, and thus the failure to post the bond divested the trial court of jurisdiction. Sharma v. Sharma, 46 Va. App. 584, 620 S.E.2d 553, 2005 Va. App. LEXIS 389 (2005).

Bond not required of convict. — Under plain meaning of section, father's status as a convict and a person under a legal disability exempted him from the requirement to post an appeal bond in child support case. Frazier v. Commonwealth, Dep't of Social Servs. ex rel. Sandridge, 27 Va. App. 131, 497 S.E.2d 879 (1998).

Appeal bond timely filed. — On the husband's appeal from the parties' final decree of divorce, the record showed that the wife filed the appeal bond within 30 days of the entry of the written order, as required by subsection H of § 16.1-296. Thus, the appeal bond was timely filed. Leake v. Taylor, 2010 Va. App. LEXIS 126 (Mar. 30, 2010).

Appellate proceedings under this section are a trial de novo. Hailey v. Dorsey, 580 F.2d 112 (4th Cir. 1978), cert. denied, 440 U.S. 937, 99 S. Ct. 1282, 59 L. Ed. 2d 495 (1979).

The award of a greater punishment on trial de novo under this section is not constitutionally impermissible under the holding in Colten v. Kentucky, 407 U.S. 104, 92 S. Ct. 1953, 32 L. Ed. 2d 584 (1972); Hailey v. Dorsey, 580 F.2d 112 (4th Cir. 1978), cert. denied, 440 U.S. 937, 99 S. Ct. 1282, 59 L. Ed. 2d 495 (1979).

Effect of de novo appeal. — On appeal under § 16.1-296, the circuit court did not err in declining to reverse a juvenile court's grant of a nonsuit in a termination of parental rights case. Because the de novo appeal vacated the juvenile court's proceedings, the grant of the nonsuit had already been vacated; the circuit court's only authority at that point was to conduct a new trial. Berger v. Harris, 2012 Va. App. LEXIS 172 (May 22, 2012).

The requirement that the investigation report be made and forwarded to the court of record is mandatory and unless complied with, the appeal cannot be heard. Norwood v. City of Richmond, 203 Va. 886, 128 S.E.2d 425 (1962).

Void court orders. — Where the order of the juvenile and domestic relations court was void the order of the circuit court on appeal therefrom was likewise void. Lowe v. Grasty, 203 Va. 168, 122 S.E.2d 867 (1961).

Conformance with equity practice. — In the appeal to the circuit court from the juvenile court's finding of no child abuse, the circuit court acts as a court of equity and, therefore, is required to conform to equity practice. Donald v. Fairfax County Dep't of Human Dev., 20 Va. App. 155, 455 S.E.2d 740 (1995), rev'd on other grounds, 251 Va. 227, 467 S.E.2d 803 (1996).

Denial of advisory jury held not abuse of discretion. — Where the record did not reflect that the factual issues to be decided were necessarily more appropriate for a jury than for the judge, the trial judge did not abuse his discretion in denying the request for an advisory jury. Edwards v. County of Arlington, 5 Va. App. 294, 361 S.E.2d 644 (1987).

Unauthorized early closing of clerk's office on last day of period to file appeal bond grievously interfered with appellant's right to appeal under this section. Furthermore, neither this section, nor § 16.1-114.1 which applies only to an irregularity in the proceedings, provides an adequate postdeprivation remedy for the loss of the right to appeal. Hutchins v. Carrillo, 27 Va. App. 595, 500 S.E.2d 277 (1998).

Appeal by board of public welfare (now board of social services). — See Board of Pub. Welfare v. Blackburn, 214 Va. 425, 201 S.E.2d 777 (1974).

Mother, although not the named guardian, could appeal. — Since, under the statute, an appeal may be taken "from any final order or judgment of the juvenile court affecting the rights or interests of any person coming within its jurisdiction," a mother could properly appeal, even though the child's grandparents had been named as guardians. Evans v. Division of Child Support Enforcement, No. 1290-95-1 (Ct. of Appeals Feb. 6, 1996).

Appeal from experimental family courts. — The statutes that created the experimental family courts did not set forth an alternative scheme for appeals from the juvenile and domestic relations courts following the expiration of their status as family courts. Rhoades v. Rhoades, 16 Va. App. 757, 433 S.E.2d 487 (1993).

The statutes providing for appeals from that [experimental family] court confer no substantive rights; they are procedural in nature. The procedures are applied to cases depending upon the designation of the court at the time of the appeal. Rhoades v. Rhoades, 16 Va. App. 757, 433 S.E.2d 487 (1993).

It is the designation of the court at the time the final order is entered that determines where this appeal will lie. Rhoades v. Rhoades, 16 Va. App. 757, 433 S.E.2d 487 (1993).

Effect of failure to hold hearing within 90 days. — In absence of any showing of harm, failure to hold hearing within 90 days did not require reversal of termination orders. Cook v. Petersburg Dep't of Social Servs., No. 1385-99-2 (Ct. of Appeals Mar. 7,

2000) (decided prior to 2004 amendment requiring that hearing shall be held within 45 days).

Time limit for hearing. — Because a hearing date was already past the 90-day statutory requirement in subsection D of § 16.1-296, and because a mother had ample time to obtain counsel to prepare her case, the trial court did not abuse its discretion by denying the mother's motions for a continuance. Black v. Charlottesville Dep't of Soc. Servs., 2012 Va. App. LEXIS 63 (Mar. 6, 2012).

Juvenile court lost jurisdiction since no timely appeal filed. — Because a mother did not comply with subsection A of § 16.1-296 and § 16.1-133.1 by appealing a dispositional order within 10 days of its entry or applying to reopen the case within 60 days, pursuant to Va. Sup. Ct. R. 1:1, the juvenile court lost jurisdiction of a charge and the court's dismissal of that charge had no force; therefore, since the juvenile court had authority under clause c of subdivision A 13 of § 16.1-278.8 to maintain custody of the child with the social services department, the circuit court properly denied the mother's motion to dismiss proceedings and return custody of her son. Lee v. Frederick County Dep't of Soc. Servs., 2008 Va. App. LEXIS 370 (Aug. 5, 2008).

Impermissible collateral attack. — Mother's claim that the Interstate Compact on the Placement of Children, § 63.2-1000 et seq., was unconstitutional was an impermissible collateral attack on the juvenile court's foster care review orders, from which the mother did not timely appeal. Hogue v. Alexandria Dep't of Soc. Servs., No. 3063-03-4, 2004 Va. App. LEXIS 466 (Ct. of Appeals Oct. 5, 2004).

Bond only required for portion of order establishing support arrearage. — Subsection H. specifying that a bond shall be required for an appeal of a judgment establishing support arrearages implicitly recognizes that an order that sets arrearages may have a component that does not establish a support arrearage and, in such a case, an appeal bond is required only for that portion of the order establishing a support arrearage. Mahoney v. Mahoney, 32 Va. App. 139, 526 S.E.2d 780 (2000).

Appeal bond was not required when an appealed child support order did not establish arrearage; since the order which increased child support obligation made no mention of any child support arrearage that existed as of the date of the order, and did not establish an arrearage, an appeal bond was not needed. Nero v. Williams, 2007 Va. App. LEXIS 10 (Jan. 16, 2007).

Appeal from contempt order allowed without posting of bond. — A finding of contempt is not an order establishing a support arrearage; thus this section permitted the defendant to appeal from the juvenile court's contempt order without the necessity of posting a bond. Avery v. Commonwealth, Dep't of Social Servs. ex rel. Clark, 22 Va. App. 698, 472 S.E.2d 675 (1996).

Bond not required for appeal challenging jurisdiction. — A husband's appeal challenging the jurisdiction of the juvenile court to enter any order was not an appeal of a portion of an order or judgment establishing a support arrearage and, under subsection H, the husband was not required to post a bond to pursue such an appeal. Mahoney v. Mahoney, 32 Va. App. 139, 526 S.E.2d 780 (2000).

Dismissal of appeal from contempt order based on inability to post appeal bond. — The dismissal of a father's appeal from an order finding him in civil contempt for failure to pay past-due child support and interest and sentencing him to six months in jail, based on his failure, due to inability, to post an appeal bond, did not violate his right to a trial and to due process in violation of the Sixth and Fourteenth Amendments to the United States Constitution, since the contempt proceeding was civil in nature. Scales, Jr. v. Commonwealth, No. 2295-97-3 (Ct. of Appeals May 19, 1998).

Bond amount found abuse of discretion. — The juvenile and domestic relations court abused its discretion when setting bond at $500 for an appeal of a judgment of arrearage of $18,975. Smiley v. Erickson, 29 Va. App. 426, 512 S.E.2d 842 (1999).

Attorney's fees award authorized. — Trial court was authorized to award costs and attorney's fees to the mother in a case brought by a father seeking to terminate his parental obligations. Cartwright v. Cartwright, 49 Va. App. 25, 635 S.E.2d 691, 2006 Va. App. LEXIS 473 (2006).

Contempt jurisdiction present. — The appeal of the motion to amend child support placed in issue the question of child support and invoked the jurisdiction of the circuit court. Therefore, the

circuit court had jurisdiction to initiate contempt proceedings against appellant for failure to obey the juvenile and domestic relations district court order. Grizzle v. Commonwealth, No. 1014-93-3 (Ct. of Appeals Dec. 20, 1994).

Timeliness of appeal. — In a case in which a circuit court quashed defendant's appeal of a revocation of suspension of his sentence for contributing to the delinquency of a minor in violation of § 18.2-371, based on an excessive number of unexcused school absences of one of his four minor children, from the juvenile and domestic relations district court (juvenile court) because it was untimely, the circuit court incorrectly determined that the December 17, 2008, order was a final order by the juvenile court and that his appeal within ten days after entry of the February 11, 2009, order was untimely. Not until the juvenile court heard additional evidence on February 11, 2009, regarding compliance with the conditions of suspension did it make a final, appealable determination regarding whether to impose the previously suspended 30-day sentence or to re-suspend some or all of that time, and defendant's appeal was filed on the same day. Smith v. Commonwealth, 2009 Va. App. LEXIS 557 (Dec. 15, 2009).

Because a father argued, for the first time on appeal, that his guardian ad litem was ineffective for failing to inform him of an appeal deadline in subsection A of § 16.1-296, and did not dispute the fact that his appeal was late, pursuant to Va. Sup. Ct. R. 5A:18, the father's arguments on appeal would not be considered and his appeal was properly dismissed. Thinnes v. Thinnes, 2012 Va. App. LEXIS 146 (May 8, 2012).

Appeal dismissed. — Where a juvenile expressly waived his right to appeal to the circuit court under subsection A of § 16.1-296 when he entered into his written plea agreement and did not claim the prosecutor, the district court, or anyone else coerced him into making the agreement, the circuit court properly dismissed his appeal. Congdon v. Commonwealth, 57 Va. App. 692, 705 S.E.2d 526, 2011 Va. App. LEXIS 53 (2011).

Although a mother had indicated her intention to appeal an order terminating her parental rights, a trial court properly dismissed the appeal because the mother failed to file her written notice of appeal within the 10-day time period for doing so. Burch v. City of Alexandria, 2013 Va. App. LEXIS 30 (Jan. 29, 2013).

Applied in Leisge v. Leisge, 223 Va. 688, 292 S.E.2d 352 (1982); Jones v. Robinson, 229 Va. 276, 329 S.E.2d 794 (1985); Box v. Talley, 1 Va. App. 289, 338 S.E.2d 349 (1986); Calfee v. Calfee, 29 Va. App. 88, 509 S.E.2d 552 (1999); Alexander v. Flowers, 51 Va. App. 404, 658 S.E.2d 355, 2008 Va. App. LEXIS 139 (2008).

CIRCUIT COURT OPINIONS

Appeal from juvenile court without posting of bond. — Though no appeal bonds were set by the juvenile court, the appeals could proceed and the dismissal of consolidated appeals because of the failure to post appeal bonds was not required. Commonwealth v. Neal, 58 Va. Cir. 205, 2002 Va. Cir. LEXIS 142 (Richmond 2002).

Circuit Court for the City of Norfolk did not have subject matter jurisdiction to consider the parties' motions to amend a husband's child and spousal support obligations upon a transfer from the Norfolk Juvenile and Domestic Relations District Court since: (1) the circuit court did not have concurrent jurisdiction to amend the support orders; (2) § 16.1-245 allowed the district court to transfer a case to the circuit court if the circuit court had exclusive jurisdiction, but the circuit court did not have exclusive jurisdiction; (3) the circuit court only had appellate jurisdiction over a Juvenile and Domestic Relations District Court under subsections A and J of § 16.1-296; (4) there was no authority to transfer a case from a lower court to a circuit court pendente lite; and (5) the Virginia Constitution and the statutes enacted pursuant to it were the sources of the circuit court's subject matter jurisdiction. Cunningham v. Cunningham, 2013 Va. Cir. LEXIS 10 (Norfolk Jan. 24, 2013).

Burden on party applying for appeal to ask for bond. — Subsection H of § 16.1-296 places the burden on the party applying for the appeal to ask for and to have the district court set the bond and approve the surety; it is fundamental that the appealing party has the burden of perfecting his appeal. Commonwealth v. Neal, 58 Va. Cir. 205, 2002 Va. Cir. LEXIS 142 (Richmond 2002).

Appeal from contempt order allowed without posting of

bond. — Failure of a father to post appeal bonds when appealing orders holding him in contempt for failure to pay child support was not fatal because the father was not appealing the amount of the arrearages. Commonwealth v. Neal, 58 Va. Cir. 205, 2002 Va. Cir. LEXIS 142 (Richmond 2002).

Jury trial inappropriate. — Father did not have a right to a jury trial of his appeal from his civil contempt conviction and sentence for failure to pay child support as the appeal was in the posture of a show cause for civil contempt and was governed by subsection F of § 16.1-296, which provided for equity procedures when the evidence was heard ore tenus; a jury trial was granted in equity practice only for a plea in equity and an issue out of chancery, neither of which was appropriate. McGann v. Royer, 66 Va. Cir. 483, 2003 Va. Cir. LEXIS 365 (Amherst County 2003).

OPINIONS OF THE ATTORNEY GENERAL

Appeal bond must be posted to perfect an appeal of a civil contempt. — Subsection H requires the posting of an appeal bond to perfect an appeal of a civil contempt finding within thirty days of the court order, if arrearages are set forth in the order finding the payor in contempt. See opinion of Attorney General to The Honorable J. Dean Lewis, Judge, Fifteenth District Juvenile and Domestic Relations Court, 01-108 (4/11/02).

§ 16.1-297. Final judgment; copy filed with juvenile court; proceeding may be remanded to juvenile court.

Upon the rendition of final judgment upon an appeal from the juvenile and domestic relations district court, the circuit court shall cause a copy of its judgment to be filed with the juvenile court within twenty-one days of entry of its order, which shall thereupon become the judgment of the juvenile court. In the event such circuit court does not dismiss the proceedings or discharge such child or adult, the circuit court may remand the child or adult to the jurisdiction of the juvenile court for its supervision and care, under the terms of its order or judgment, and thereafter such child or adult shall be and remain under the jurisdiction of the juvenile court in the same manner as if such court had rendered the judgment in the first instance.

History.
Code 1950, § 16.1-215; 1956, c. 555; 1977, c. 559; 1996, c. 828.

Editor's note.
Acts 1993, c. 929, cl. 3, as amended by Acts 1994, c. 564, cl. 1, and Acts 1996, c. 616, cl. 3, provides that the amendment to this section by Acts 1993, c. 929, cl. 1, shall become effective June 1, 1998, "only if state funds are provided by the General Assembly sufficient to provide adequate resources, including all local costs, for the court to carry out the purposes of this act and to fulfill its mission to serve children and families of the Commonwealth." The funding was not provided.

Law Review.
For 2003/2004 survey of criminal law and procedure, see 39 U. Rich. L. Rev. 133 (2004).

Michie's Jurisprudence.
For related discussion, see 9B M.J. Infants, §§ 84, 87.

CASE NOTES

Filing requirement gives juvenile court information concerning disposition of appeal. — Statutory filing requirement of § 16.1-297 permits the juvenile court to have information not only as to the disposition of the appeal, but also to have important information necessary to guide its actions should the juvenile be the subject of other proceedings within the jurisdiction of the juvenile court. Austin v. Commonwealth, 42 Va. App. 33, 590 S.E.2d 68, 2003 Va. App. LEXIS 676 (2003), aff'd, 268 Va. 439, 604 S.E.2d 430 (2004).

Circuit court retains jurisdiction in the absence of a remand. — This section directs the circuit court to file a copy of its final judgment with the juvenile court in a delinquency appeal case. However, the language of the statute providing the circuit court with discretion to remand, demonstrates that the failure to do so does not result in the loss of jurisdiction by the circuit court. Austin v. Commonwealth, 42 Va. App. 33, 590 S.E.2d 68, 2003 Va. App. LEXIS 676 (2003), aff'd, 268 Va. 439, 604 S.E.2d 430 (2004).

Trial court's final judgment. — Trial court did not render a final judgment in defendant's marijuana possession case because it did not sentence defendant, and, thus, no final judgment existed for the appellate court to review and the trial court prematurely transferred the case to the juvenile court after finding defendant guilty. Brown v. Commonwealth, No. 1596-02-1, 2003 Va. App. LEXIS 141 (Ct. of Appeals Mar. 18, 2003).

Applied in Calfee v. Calfee, 29 Va. App. 88, 509 S.E.2d 552 (1999).

CIRCUIT COURT OPINIONS

Court lacked authority to transfer. — Circuit Court for the City of Norfolk could not transfer a case to the Norfolk Juvenile and Domestic Relations District Court or the Circuit Court of the City of Chesapeake after finding that the circuit court did not have subject matter jurisdiction since: (1) § 16.1-297 allowed the circuit court to remand a case to the district court upon the rendition of final judgment upon an appeal, but the parties' motions to amend child and spousal support were not before the circuit court on appeal and the the circuit court's order was not a final judgment; (2) § 20-79(c) did not apply as the circuit court was not making an order regarding support; and (3) § 20-88.49 had been construed as a venue statute. Cunningham v. Cunningham, 2013 Va. Cir. LEXIS 10 (Norfolk Jan. 24, 2013).

ARTICLE 12.

CONFIDENTIALITY AND EXPUNGEMENT.

§ 16.1-299. Fingerprints and photographs of juveniles.

A. All duly constituted police authorities having the power of arrest shall take fingerprints and photographs of any juvenile who is taken into custody and charged with a delinquent act an arrest for which, if committed by an adult, is required to be reported to the Central Criminal Records Exchange pursuant to subsection A of § 19.2-390. Whenever fingerprints are taken, they shall be maintained separately from adult records and a copy shall be filed with the juvenile court on forms provided by the Central Criminal Records Exchange.

B. If a juvenile of any age (i) is convicted of a felony, (ii) is adjudicated delinquent of an offense that would be a felony if committed by an adult, (iii) has a case involving an offense, which would be a felony if committed by an adult, that is dismissed pursuant to the deferred disposition provisions of § 16.1-278.8, or (iv) is convicted or adjudicated delinquent of any other offense for which a report to the Central Criminal Records Exchange is required by subsection C of § 19.2-390 if the offense were committed by an adult, copies of his fingerprints and a report of the disposition shall be forwarded to the Central Criminal Records Exchange and to the jurisdiction making the arrest by the clerk of the court which heard the case.

C. If a petition or warrant is not filed against a juvenile whose fingerprints or photographs have been taken in connection with an alleged violation of law, the fingerprint card, all copies of the fingerprints and all photographs shall be destroyed 60 days after fingerprints were taken. If a juvenile charged with a delinquent act other than a violent juvenile felony or a crime ancillary thereto is found not guilty, or in any other case resulting in a disposition for which fingerprints are not required to be forwarded to the Central Criminal Records Exchange, the court shall order that the fingerprint card, all copies of the fingerprints and all photographs be destroyed within six months of the date of disposition of the case.

History.
1977, c. 559; 1978, c. 383; 1979, c. 267; 1982, c. 514; 1985, c. 211; 1986, c. 264; 1993, cc. 468, 926; 1994, cc. 859, 949; 1996, cc. 755, 914; 1997, c. 657; 2000, c. 431; 2004, c. 464; 2008, c. 636.

Cross references.
As to reports to school authorities of certain acts, notwithstanding the provisions of this article, see § 22.1-279.3:1.

Editor's note.
Acts 1993, c. 930, cl. 3, as amended by Acts 1994, c. 564, cl. 2, and Acts 1996, c. 616, c. 4, provides that the amendment to this section by Acts 1993, c. 930, cl. 1, shall become effective June 1, 1998, "if state funds are provided, including all local costs, to carry out the purposes of this bill by the General Assembly." The funding was not provided.

Law Review.
For article, "The Revision of Virginia's Juvenile Court Law," see 13 U. Rich. L. Rev. 847 (1979). For survey of Virginia law on criminal procedure for the year 1978-1979, see 66 Va. L. Rev. 261 (1980). For an article, "Legal Issues Involving Children," see 32 U. Rich. L. Rev. 1345 (1998). For 2003/2004 survey of family and juvenile law, see 39 U. Rich. L. Rev. 241 (2004).

CASE NOTES

Use of defendant's juvenile record in capital sentencing. — Virginia law does not prohibit the use of a defendant's juvenile record in capital sentencing. Peterson v. Murray, 904 F.2d 882 (4th Cir.), cert. denied, 498 U.S. 992, 111 S. Ct. 537, 112 L. Ed. 2d 547 (1990).

§ 16.1-299.1. Sample required for DNA analysis upon conviction or adjudication of felony.

A juvenile convicted of a felony or adjudicated delinquent on the basis of an act which would be a felony if committed by an adult shall have a sample of his blood, saliva or tissue taken for DNA analysis provided the juvenile was 14 years of age or older at the time of the commission of the offense.

The provisions of Article 1.1 (§ 19.2-310.2 et seq.) of Chapter 18 of Title 19.2 shall apply to all persons

and all DNA samples taken as required by this section, mutatis mutandis.

The Department of Juvenile Justice shall verify that a DNA sample required to be taken has been received by the Department of Forensic Science. In any case where a DNA sample has not been received, the Department of Juvenile Justice shall notify the court and the court shall require the person to submit a sample for DNA analysis.

History.
1996, cc. 755, 914; 1998, c. 280; 2003, cc. 150, 607; 2007, c. 528.

§ 16.1-299.2. Repealed by Acts 2005, c. 843, cl. 2.

§ 16.1-300. Confidentiality of Department records.

A. The social, medical, psychiatric and psychological reports and records of children who are or have been (i) before the court, (ii) under supervision, or (iii) receiving services from a court service unit or who are committed to the Department of Juvenile Justice shall be confidential and shall be open for inspection only to the following:

1. The judge, prosecuting attorney, probation officers and professional staff assigned to serve a court having the child currently before it in any proceeding;

2. Any public agency, child welfare agency, private organization, facility or person who is treating or providing services to the child pursuant to a contract with the Department or pursuant to the Virginia Juvenile Community Crime Control Act as set out in Article 12.1 (§ 16.1-309.2 et seq.);

3. The child's parent, guardian, legal custodian or other person standing in loco parentis and the child's attorney;

4. Any person who has reached the age of majority and requests access to his own records or reports;

5. Any state agency providing funds to the Department of Juvenile Justice and required by the federal government to monitor or audit the effectiveness of programs for the benefit of juveniles which are financed in whole or in part by federal funds;

6. Any other person, agency or institution, including any law-enforcement agency, school administration, or probation office by order of the court, having a legitimate interest in the case, the juvenile, or in the work of the court;

7. Any person, agency, or institution, in any state, having a legitimate interest (i) when release of the confidential information is for the provision of treatment or rehabilitation services for the juvenile who is the subject of the information, (ii) when the requesting party has custody or is providing supervision for a juvenile and the release of the confidential information is in the interest of maintaining security in a secure facility, as defined by § 16.1-228 if the facility is located in Virginia, or as similarly defined by the law of the state in which such facility

is located if it is not located in Virginia, or (iii) when release of the confidential information is for consideration of admission to any group home, residential facility, or postdispositional facility, and copies of the records in the custody of such home or facility shall be destroyed if the child is not admitted to the home or facility;

8. Any attorney for the Commonwealth, any pretrial services officer, local community-based probation officer and adult probation and parole officer for the purpose of preparing pretrial investigation, including risk assessment instruments, presentence reports, including those provided in § 19.2-299, discretionary sentencing guidelines worksheets, including related risk assessment instruments, as directed by the court pursuant to subsection C of § 19.2-298.01 or any court-ordered post-sentence investigation report;

9. Any person, agency, organization or institution outside the Department that, at the Department's request, is conducting research or evaluation on the work of the Department or any of its divisions; or any state criminal justice agency that is conducting research, provided that the agency agrees that all information received shall be kept confidential, or released or published only in aggregate form;

10. With the exception of medical, psychiatric, and psychological records and reports, any full-time or part-time employee of the Department of State Police or of a police department or sheriff's office that is a part of or administrated by the Commonwealth or any political subdivision thereof, and who is responsible for the enforcement of the penal, traffic, or motor vehicle laws of the Commonwealth, is entitled to any information related to a criminal street gang including that a person is a member of a criminal street gang as defined in § 18.2-46.1. Information shall be provided by the Department to law enforcement without their request to aid in initiating an investigation or assist in an ongoing investigation of a criminal street gang as defined in § 18.2-46.1. The Department shall not release the identifying information of a juvenile not affiliated with or involved in a criminal street gang unless that information relates to a specific criminal act. No person who obtains information pursuant to this subdivision shall divulge such information except in connection with a criminal investigation regarding a criminal street gang as defined in § 18.2-46.1 that is authorized by the Attorney General or by the attorney for the Commonwealth or in connection with a prosecution or proceeding in court;

11. The Commonwealth's Attorneys' Services Council and any attorney for the Commonwealth, as permitted under subsection B of § 66-3.2;

12. Any state or local correctional facility as defined in § 53.1-1 when such facility has custody of or is providing supervision for a person convicted as an adult who is the subject of the reports and records. The reports and records shall remain confidential and shall be open for inspection only in accordance with this section; and

13. The Office of the Attorney General, for all criminal justice activities otherwise permitted and for purposes of performing duties required by Chapter 9 (§ 37.2-900 et seq.) of Title 37.2.

A designated individual treating or responsible for the treatment of a person may inspect such reports and records as are kept by the Department on such person or receive copies thereof, when the person who is the subject of the reports and records or his parent, guardian, legal custodian or other person standing in loco parentis if the person is under the age of 18, provides written authorization to the Department prior to the release of such reports and records for inspection or copying to the designated individual.

B. The Department may withhold from inspection by a child's parent, guardian, legal custodian or other person standing in loco parentis that portion of the records referred to in subsection A hereof, when the staff of the Department determines, in its discretion, that disclosure of such information would be detrimental to the child or to a third party, provided that the juvenile and domestic relations district court (i) having jurisdiction over the facility where the child is currently placed or (ii) that last had jurisdiction over the child if such child is no longer in the custody or under the supervision of the Department shall concur in such determination.

If any person authorized under subsection A to inspect Department records requests to inspect the reports and records and if the Department withholds from inspection any portion of such record or report pursuant to the preceding provisions, the Department shall (i) inform the individual making the request of the action taken to withhold any information and the reasons for such action; (ii) provide such individual with as much information as is deemed appropriate under the circumstances; and (iii) notify the individual in writing at the time of the request of his right to request judicial review of the Department's decision. The circuit court (a) having jurisdiction over the facility where the child is currently placed or (b) that had jurisdiction over the original proceeding or over an appeal of the juvenile and domestic relations district court final order of disposition concerning the child if such child is no longer in the custody or under the supervision of the Department shall have jurisdiction over petitions filed for review of the Department's decision to withhold reports or records as provided herein.

History.

1977, c. 559; 1978, cc. 738, 740; 1981, c. 487; 1988, c. 541; 1989, c. 733; 1994, c. 19; 2000, c. 212; 2002, c. 735; 2003, cc. 108, 143; 2006, cc. 431, 500; 2007, c. 511; 2009, c. 740; 2010, cc. 367, 472; 2011, cc. 99, 169; 2012, cc. 262, 421.

Editor's note.

Acts 1993, c. 929, cl. 3, as amended by Acts 1994, c. 564, cl. 1, and Acts 1996, c. 616, cl. 3, provides that the amendment to this section by Acts 1993, c. 929, cl. 1, shall become effective June 1, 1998, "only if state funds are provided by the General Assembly sufficient to provide adequate resources, including all local costs, for the court to carry out the purposes of this act and to fulfill its mission to serve children and families of the Commonwealth." The funding was not provided.

Acts 2006, cc. 431 and 500, in cl. 2 provide: "That the information forwarded by the Department of Corrections and the Department of Juvenile Justice to the Commonwealth's Attorneys' Services Council shall be in a form mutually agreeable to all parties."

Acts 2009, c. 740, cl. 2, provides: "That the provisions of this act may result in a net increase in periods of imprisonment or commitment. Pursuant to § 30-19.1:4, the estimated amount of the necessary appropriation cannot be determined for periods of imprisonment in state adult correctional facilities and is $0 for periods of commitment to the custody of the Department of Juvenile Justice."

The 2009 amendments.
The 2009 amendment by c. 740 added subdivision A 12 and made a related change.

The 2010 amendments.
The 2010 amendments by cc. 367 and 472 are identical, and in subdivision A 10, substituted "is entitled to any information related to a criminal street gang including" for "for purposes of a criminal investigation of an allegation of criminal gang activity involving a predicate criminal act as defined in § 18.2-46.1 or information" in the first sentence, and inserted the second and third sentences.

The 2011 amendments.
The 2011 amendments by cc. 99 and 169 are identical, and deleted "of Chapter 11 of this title" from the end of subdivision A 2; and in subdivision A 7, inserted "in any state," "if the facility is located in Virginia, or as similarly defined by law of the state in which such facility is located if it is not located in Virginia," and the last occurrence of "when release of the confidential information is" and made a minor stylistic change.

The 2012 amendments.
The 2012 amendments by cc. 262 and 421 are identical, and added subdivision A 12, redesignated former subdivision 12 as 13, and made related changes.

Law Review.
For article, "Legal Issues Involving Children," see 35 U. Rich. L. Rev. 741 (2001). For annual survey article on legal issues involving children, see 38 U. Rich. L. Rev. 161 (2003). For 2006 survey article, "Family and Juvenile Law," see 41 U. Rich. L. Rev. 151 (2006).

CASE NOTES

Impeachment with evidence of prior juvenile adjudications. — A prosecutor may not impeach the defendant with evidence of prior juvenile adjudications, and the attempt to so cross-examine defendant was not harmless error. Lavinder v. Commonwealth, 395 S.E.2d 211 (1990).

§ 16.1-301. Confidentiality of juvenile law-enforcement records; disclosures to school principal.

A. The court shall require all law-enforcement agencies to take special precautions to ensure that law-enforcement records concerning a juvenile are protected against disclosure to any unauthorized person. The police departments of the cities of the Commonwealth, and the police departments or sheriffs of the counties, as the case may be, shall keep separate records as to violations of law other than violations of motor vehicle laws committed by juveniles. Such records with respect to such juvenile shall not be open to public inspection nor their contents disclosed to the public unless a juvenile 14 years of age or older is charged with a violent juvenile felony as specified in subsections B and C of § 16.1-269.1.

B. Notwithstanding any other provision of law, the chief of police or sheriff of a jurisdiction or his designee may disclose, for the protection of the juvenile, his fellow students and school personnel, to the school principal that a juvenile is a suspect in or has been charged with (i) a violent juvenile felony, as specified in subsections B and C of § 16.1-269.1; (ii) a violation of any of the provisions of Article 1 (§ 18.2-77 et seq.) of Chapter 5 of Title 18.2; or (iii) a violation of law involving any weapon as described in subsection A of § 18.2-308. If a chief of police, sheriff or a designee has disclosed to a school principal pursuant to this section that a juvenile is a suspect in or has been charged with a crime listed above, upon a court disposition of a proceeding regarding such crime in which a juvenile is adjudicated delinquent, convicted, found not guilty or the charges are reduced, the chief of police, sheriff or a designee shall, within 15 days of the expiration of the appeal period, if there is no notice of appeal, provide notice of the disposition ordered by the court to the school principal to whom disclosure was made. If the court defers disposition or if charges are withdrawn, dismissed or nolle prosequi, the chief of police, sheriff or a designee shall, within 15 days of such action provide notice of such action to the school principal to whom disclosure was made. If charges are withdrawn in intake or handled informally without a court disposition or if charges are not filed within 90 days of the initial disclosure, the chief of police, sheriff or a designee shall so notify the school principal to whom disclosure was made. In addition to any other disclosure that is permitted by this subsection, the principal in his discretion may provide such information to a threat assessment team established by the local school division. No member of a threat assessment team shall (a) disclose any juvenile record information obtained pursuant to this section or (b) use such information for any purpose other than evaluating threats to students and school personnel. For the purposes of this subsection, "principal" also refers to the chief administrator of any private primary or secondary school.

C. Inspection of law-enforcement records concerning juveniles shall be permitted only by the following:

1. A court having the juvenile currently before it in any proceeding;

2. The officers of public and nongovernmental institutions or agencies to which the juvenile is currently committed, and those responsible for his supervision after release;

3. Any other person, agency, or institution, by order of the court, having a legitimate interest in the case or in the work of the law-enforcement agency;

4. Law-enforcement officers of other jurisdictions, by order of the court, when necessary for the discharge of their current official duties;

5. The probation and other professional staff of a court in which the juvenile is subsequently convicted

of a criminal offense for the purpose of a presentence report or other dispositional proceedings, or by officials of penal institutions and other penal facilities to which he is committed, or by a parole board in considering his parole or discharge or in exercising supervision over him;

6. The juvenile, parent, guardian or other custodian and counsel for the juvenile by order of the court; and

7. As provided in §§ 19.2-389.1 and 19.2-390.

D. The police departments of the cities and towns and the police departments or sheriffs of the counties may release, upon request to one another and to state and federal law-enforcement agencies, and to law-enforcement agencies in other states, current information on juvenile arrests. The information exchanged shall be used by the receiving agency for current investigation purposes only and shall not result in the creation of new files or records on individual juveniles on the part of the receiving agency.

E. Upon request, the police departments of the cities and towns and the police departments or sheriffs of the counties may release current information on juvenile arrests or juvenile victims to the Virginia Workers' Compensation Commission solely for purposes of determining whether to make an award to the victim of a crime, and such information shall not be disseminated or used by the Commission for any other purpose than provided in § 19.2-368.3.

F. Nothing in this section shall prohibit the exchange of other criminal investigative or intelligence information among law-enforcement agencies.

History.
Code 1950, § 16.1-163; 1956, c. 555; 1977, cc. 559, 618; 1978, c. 740; 1981, c. 175; 1993, cc. 468, 926; 1994, cc. 859, 949; 1995, c. 752; 1996, cc. 755, 914; 1997, c. 430; 2000, c. 211; 2001, c. 770; 2003, c. 119; 2005, c. 683; 2009, c. 286; 2013, c. 769.

The 2009 amendments.
The 2009 amendment by c. 286 inserted "and to law-enforcement agencies in other states" in subsection D.

The 2013 amendments.
The 2013 amendment by c. 769 added the fifth through seventh sentences of subsection B.

Law Review.
For an article, "Legal Issues Involving Children," see 32 U. Rich. L. Rev. 1345 (1998). For article, "Legal Issues Involving Children," see 35 U. Rich. L. Rev. 741 (2001). For annual survey, "A Look Back and Forward: Legislative and Regulatory Highlights for 2008 and 2009 and a Discussion of Juvenile Transfer," see 44 U. Rich. L. Rev. 53 (2009).

Michie's Jurisprudence.
For related discussion, see 5B M.J. Criminal Procedure, § 59.

CASE NOTES

If the decision to waive juvenile jurisdiction were not immediately appealable, those legislative protections afforded children under the juvenile justice system once lost, would be irretrievable. Hairfield v. Commonwealth, 7 Va. App. 649, 376 S.E.2d 796 (1989).

Impeachment with evidence of prior juvenile adjudications. — A prosecutor may not impeach the defendant with evidence of prior juvenile adjudications, and the attempt to so cross-examine defendant was not harmless error. Lavinder v. Commonwealth, 395 S.E.2d 211 (1990).

§ 16.1-302. Dockets, indices and order books; when hearings and records private; right to public hearing; presence of juvenile in court.

A. Every juvenile court shall keep a separate docket of cases arising under this law.

B. Every circuit court shall keep a separate docket, index, and, for entry of its orders, a separate order book or file for cases on appeal from the juvenile court except: (i) cases involving support pursuant to § 20-61 or subdivisions A 3, F or L of § 16.1-241; (ii) cases involving criminal offenses committed by adults which are commenced on a warrant or a summons as described in Title 19.2; and (iii) cases involving civil commitments of adults pursuant to Title 37.2. Such cases shall be docketed on the appropriate docket and the orders in such cases shall be entered in the appropriate order book as used with similar cases commenced in circuit court.

C. The general public shall be excluded from all juvenile court hearings and only such persons admitted as the judge shall deem proper. However, proceedings in cases involving an adult charged with a crime and hearings held on a petition or warrant alleging that a juvenile fourteen years of age or older committed an offense which would be a felony if committed by an adult shall be open. Subject to the provisions of subsection D for good cause shown, the court may, sua sponte or on motion of the accused or the attorney for the Commonwealth close the proceedings. If the proceedings are closed, the court shall state in writing its reasons and the statement shall be made a part of the public record.

D. In any hearing held for the purpose of adjudicating an alleged violation of any criminal law, or law defining a traffic infraction, the juvenile or adult so charged shall have a right to be present and shall have the right to a public hearing unless expressly waived by such person. The chief judge may provide by rule that any juvenile licensed to operate a motor vehicle who has been charged with a traffic infraction may waive court appearance and admit to the infraction or infractions charged if he or she and a parent, legal guardian, or person standing in loco parentis to the juvenile appear in person at the court or before a magistrate or sign and either mail or deliver to the court or magistrate a written form of appearance, plea and waiver, provided that the written form contains the notarized signature of the parent, legal guardian, or person standing in loco parentis to the juvenile. An emancipated juvenile charged with a traffic infraction shall have the opportunity to waive court appearance and admit to the infraction or infractions if he or she appears in person at the court or before a magistrate or signs and either mails or delivers to the court or magistrate a written form of appearance, plea, and waiver, provided that the written plea form containing the signature of the emancipated juvenile is accompanied by a notarized sworn statement which details the facts supporting the claim of emancipated status. Whenever the sole purpose of a proceeding is to determine the custody of a child of tender years, the presence of such juvenile in court may be waived by the judge at any stage thereof.

History.
Code 1950, § 16.1-162; 1956, c. 555; 1958, c. 353; 1971, Ex. Sess., c. 228; 1975, c. 334; 1977, cc. 559, 585; 1978, c. 605; 1979, c. 393; 1983, c. 293; 1996, cc. 755, 914.

Editor's note.
Acts 1993, c. 929, cl. 3, as amended by Acts 1994, c. 564, cl. 1, and Acts 1996, c. 616, cl. 3, provides that the amendment to this section by Acts 1993, c. 929, cl. 1, shall become effective June 1, 1998, "only if state funds are provided by the General Assembly sufficient to provide adequate resources, including all local costs, for the court to carry out the purposes of this act and to fulfill its mission to serve children and families of the Commonwealth." The funding was not provided.

Law Review.
For survey of Virginia statutory changes in substantive criminal law for the year 1970-1971, see 57 Va. L. Rev. 1467 (1971).

Research references.
Virginia Forms (Matthew Bender). No. 5-292 Confidential Materials — Juvenile Case Appeal/Transfer Transmittal.

Michie's Jurisprudence.
For related discussion, see 5B M.J. Criminal Procedure, § 59.

CASE NOTES

Mandamus not available to challenge closure order. — Writs of mandamus had been improperly issued to reporters and newspapers granting them access to certain criminal proceedings where the proper procedure would have been for the petitioners to have filed motions to intervene and objections to the courts' closure orders and, if such had been rejected, to appeal those orders. Hertz v. Times-World Corp., 259 Va. 599, 528 S.E.2d 458, 2000 Va. LEXIS 81 (2000).

§ 16.1-302.1. Right of victim or representative to attend certain proceedings; notice of hearings.

During proceedings involving petitions or warrants alleging that a juvenile is delinquent, including proceedings on appeal, a victim may remain in the courtroom and shall not be excluded unless the court determines in its discretion, that the presence of the victim would impair the conduct of a fair trial. In any such case involving a minor victim, the court may permit an adult chosen by the minor victim to be present in the courtroom during the proceedings in addition to or in lieu of the minor's parent or guardian.

The attorney for the Commonwealth shall give prior notice of any such proceedings and changes in the scheduling thereof to any known victim and to any known adult chosen in accordance with this section by a minor victim at the address or telephone number, or both, provided in writing by such persons.

History.
1996, cc. 755, 914; 2000, c. 339.

Law Review.
For 2000 survey of Virginia law regarding children, see 34 U. Rich. L. Rev. 939 (2000).

§ 16.1-305. Confidentiality of court records.

A. Social, medical and psychiatric or psychological records, including reports or preliminary inquiries, predisposition studies and supervision records, of neglected and abused children, children in need of services, children in need of supervision and delinquent children shall be filed with the other papers in the juvenile's case file. All juvenile case files shall be filed separately from adult files and records of the court and shall be open for inspection only to the following:

1. The judge, probation officers and professional staff assigned to serve the juvenile and domestic relations district courts;

2. Representatives of a public or private agency or department providing supervision or having legal custody of the child or furnishing evaluation or treatment of the child ordered or requested by the court;

3. The attorney for any party, including the attorney for the Commonwealth;

4. Any other person, agency or institution, by order of the court, having a legitimate interest in the case or in the work of the court. However, for the purposes of an investigation conducted by a local community-based probation services agency, preparation of a pretrial investigation report, or of a presentence or postsentence report upon a finding of guilty in a circuit court or for the preparation of a background report for the Parole Board, adult probation and parole officers, including United States Probation and Pretrial Services Officers, any officer of a local pretrial services agency established or operated pursuant to Article 5 (§ 19.2-152.2 et seq.) of Chapter 9 of Title 19.2, and any officer of a local community-based probation services agency established or operated pursuant to the Comprehensive Community Corrections Act for Local-Responsible Offenders (§ 9.1-173 et seq.) shall have access to an accused's or inmate's records in juvenile court without a court order and for the purpose of preparing the discretionary sentencing guidelines worksheets and related risk assessment instruments as directed by the court pursuant to subsection C of § 19.2-298.01, the attorney for the Commonwealth and any pretrial services or probation officer shall have access to the defendant's records in juvenile court without a court order;

5. Any attorney for the Commonwealth and any local pretrial services or community-based probation officer or state adult probation or parole officer shall

have direct access to the defendant's juvenile court delinquency records maintained in an electronic format by the court for the strictly limited purposes of preparing a pretrial investigation report, including any related risk assessment instrument, any presentence report, any discretionary sentencing guidelines worksheets, including related risk assessment instruments, any post-sentence investigation report or preparing for any transfer or sentencing hearing.

A copy of the court order of disposition in a delinquency case shall be provided to a probation officer or attorney for the Commonwealth, when requested for the purpose of calculating sentencing guidelines. The copies shall remain confidential, but reports may be prepared using the information contained therein as provided in §§ 19.2-298.01 and 19.2-299.

6. The Office of the Attorney General, for all criminal justice activities otherwise permitted and for purposes of performing duties required by Chapter 9 (§ 37.2-900 et seq.) of Title 37.2.

A1. Any person, agency, or institution that may inspect juvenile case files pursuant to subdivisions A 1 through A 4 shall be authorized to have copies made of such records, subject to any restrictions, conditions, or prohibitions that the court may impose.

B. All or any part of the records enumerated in subsection A, or information secured from such records, which is presented to the judge in court or otherwise in a proceeding under this law shall also be made available to the parties to the proceedings and their attorneys.

B1. If a juvenile 14 years of age or older at the time of the offense is adjudicated delinquent on the basis of an act which would be a felony if committed by an adult, all court records regarding that adjudication and any subsequent adjudication of delinquency, other than those records specified in subsection A, shall be open to the public. However, if a hearing was closed, the judge may order that certain records or portions thereof remain confidential to the extent necessary to protect any juvenile victim or juvenile witness.

C. All other juvenile records, including the docket, petitions, motions and other papers filed with a case, transcripts of testimony, findings, verdicts, orders and decrees shall be open to inspection only by those persons and agencies designated in subsections A and B of this section. However, a licensed bail bondsman shall be entitled to know the status of a bond he has posted or provided surety on for a juvenile under § 16.1-258. This shall not authorize a bail bondsman to have access to or inspect any other portion of his principal's juvenile court records.

D. Attested copies of papers filed in connection with an adjudication of guilty for an offense for which the clerk is required by § 46.2-383 to furnish an abstract to the Department of Motor Vehicles, which shows the charge, finding, disposition, name of the attorney for the juvenile, or waiver of attorney shall be furnished to an attorney for the Commonwealth upon certification by the prosecuting attorney that such papers are needed as evidence in a pending criminal, traffic, or habitual offender proceeding and that such papers will be only used for such evidentiary purpose.

D1. Attested copies of papers filed in connection with an adjudication of guilt for a delinquent act that would be a felony if committed by an adult, which show the charge, finding, disposition, name of the attorney for the juvenile, or waiver of attorney by the juvenile, shall be furnished to an attorney for the Commonwealth upon his certification that such papers are needed as evidence in a pending criminal prosecution for a violation of § 18.2-308.2 and that such papers will be only used for such evidentiary purpose.

E. Upon request, a copy of the court order of disposition in a delinquency case shall be provided to the Virginia Workers' Compensation Commission solely for purposes of determining whether to make an award to the victim of a crime, and such information shall not be disseminated or used by the Commission for any other purpose including but not limited to actions pursuant to § 19.2-368.15.

F. Staff of the court services unit or the attorney for the Commonwealth shall provide notice of the disposition in a case involving a juvenile who is committed to state care after being adjudicated for a criminal sexual assault as specified in Article 7 (§ 18.2-61 et seq.) of Chapter 4 of Title 18.2 to the victim or a parent of a minor victim, upon request. Additionally, if the victim or parent submits a written request, the Department of Juvenile Justice shall provide advance notice of such juvenile offender's anticipated date of release from commitment.

G. Any record in a juvenile case file which is open for inspection by the professional staff of the Department of Juvenile Justice pursuant to subsection A and is maintained in an electronic format by the court, may be transmitted electronically to the Department of Juvenile Justice. Any record so transmitted shall be subject to the provisions of § 16.1-300.

History.

Code 1950, § 16.1-162; 1956, c. 555; 1958, c. 353; 1971, Ex. Sess., c. 228; 1975, c. 334; 1977, c. 559; 1979, c. 605; 1983, c. 389; 1984, c. 34; 1988, c. 541; 1989, c. 182; 1990, c. 258; 1992, c. 547; 1994, c. 603; 1995, c. 430; 1996, cc. 755, 870, 914; 1998, cc. 278, 521; 2002, cc. 701, 735, 741; 2003, c. 143; 2004, c. 446; 2007, c. 133; 2009, cc. 138, 308, 740.

Editor's note.

Acts 1993, c. 929, cl. 3, as amended by Acts 1994, c. 564, cl. 1, and Acts 1996, c. 616, cl. 3, provides that the amendment to this section by Acts 1993, c. 929, cl. 1, shall become effective June 1, 1998, "only if state funds are provided by the General Assembly sufficient to provide adequate resources, including all local costs, for the court to carry out the purposes of this act and to fulfill its mission to serve children and families of the Commonwealth." The funding was not provided.

Acts 2009, c. 740, cl. 2, provides: "That the provisions of this act may result in a net increase in periods of imprisonment or commitment. Pursuant to § 30-19.1:4, the estimated amount of the necessary appropriation cannot be determined for periods of imprisonment in state adult correctional facilities and is $0 for periods of commitment to the custody of the Department of Juvenile Justice."

The 2009 amendments.

The 2009 amendments by cc. 138 and 308 are identical, and added subsection A1.

The 2009 amendment by c. 740 added subdivision A 6.

Law Review.

For survey on legal issues involving children in Virginia for 1989, see 23 U. Rich. L. Rev. 705 (1989). For an article, "Legal Issues Involving Children," see 32 U. Rich. L. Rev. 1345 (1998). For annual survey, "A Look Back and Forward: Legislative and Regulatory Highlights for 2008 and 2009 and a Discussion of Juvenile Transfer," see 44 U. Rich. L. Rev. 53 (2009).

Michie's Jurisprudence.

For related discussion, see 16 M.J. Right of Privacy, § 1.

CASE NOTES

Impeachment with evidence of prior juvenile adjudications. — A prosecutor may not impeach the defendant with evidence of prior juvenile adjudications, and the attempt to so cross-examine defendant was not harmless error. Lavinder v. Commonwealth, 395 S.E.2d 211 (1990).

Defendant was not entitled to examine the juvenile records of an adverse witness where he was given a list of juvenile adjudications, and defendant did not assert the witness' prior juvenile adjudications involved defendant. Scott v. Commonwealth, 7 Va. App. 252, 372 S.E.2d 771 (1988), cert. denied, 490 U.S. 1095, 109 S. Ct. 2441, 104 L. Ed. 2d 997 (1989).

Use of juvenile record in capital sentencing. — Virginia law does not prohibit the use of a defendant's juvenile record in capital sentencing. Peterson v. Murray, 904 F.2d 882 (4th Cir.), cert. denied, 498 U.S. 992, 111 S. Ct. 537, 112 L. Ed. 2d 547 (1990).

Applied in Fulcher v. Commonwealth, 226 Va. 96, 306 S.E.2d 874 (1983).

OPINIONS OF THE ATTORNEY GENERAL

Access to court files of cases must be given to self-represented individuals by juvenile and domestic relations district courts. However, juvenile courts are not required to provide such self-represented litigants with notice regarding their rights of access. See opinion of Attorney General to The Honorable Onzlee Ware, Member, House of Delegates, 06-107 (2/20/07).

Where records are designated as "open for inspection" to certain individuals, such individuals are not authorized to copy the records. See opinion of Attorney General to The Honorable Robert B. Wilson, V, Chief Judge, Eighth Judicial Circuit Juvenile & Domestic Relations District Court, 08-041 (6/16/08).

§ 16.1-306. Expungement of court records.

A. Notwithstanding the provisions of § 16.1-69.55, the clerk of the juvenile and domestic relations district court shall, on January 2 of each year or on a date designated by the court, destroy its files, papers and records, including electronic records, connected with any proceeding concerning a juvenile in such court, if such juvenile has attained the age of 19 years and five years have elapsed since the date of the last hearing in any case of the juvenile which is subject to this section. However, if the juvenile was found guilty of an offense for which the clerk is required by § 46.2-383 to furnish an abstract to the Department of Motor Vehicles, the records shall be destroyed when the juvenile has attained the age of 29. If the juvenile was found guilty of a delinquent act which would be a felony if committed by an adult, the records shall be retained.

B. In all files in which the court records concerning a juvenile contain a finding of guilty of a delinquent act which would be a felony if committed by an adult or an offense for which the clerk is required by § 46.2-383 to furnish an abstract to the Department of Motor Vehicles together with findings of not innocent of other acts, all of the records of such juvenile subject to this section shall be retained and available for inspection as provided in § 16.1-305.

C. A person who has been the subject of a delinquency or traffic proceeding and (i) has been found innocent thereof or (ii) such proceeding was otherwise dismissed, may file a motion requesting the destruction of all records pertaining to the charge of such an act of delinquency. Notice of such motion shall be given to the attorney for the Commonwealth. Unless good cause is shown why such records should not be destroyed, the court shall grant the motion, and shall send copies of the order to all officers or agencies that are repositories of such records, and all such officers and agencies shall comply with the order.

D. Each person shall be notified of his rights under subsections A and C of this section at the time of his dispositional hearing.

E. Upon destruction of the records of a proceeding as provided in subsections A, B, and C, the violation of law shall be treated as if it never occurred. All index references shall be deleted and the court and law-enforcement officers and agencies shall reply and the person may reply to any inquiry that no record exists with respect to such person.

F. All docket sheets shall be destroyed in the sixth year after the last hearing date recorded on the docket sheet.

History.

Code 1950, § 16.1-193; 1956, c. 555; 1977, c. 559; 1979, cc. 736, 737; 1989, c. 183; 1990, c. 258; 1993, cc. 468, 589, 926; 1994, cc. 859, 949; 1996, c. 463; 2008, c. 519.

Editor's note.

Acts 1993, c. 929, cl. 3, as amended by Acts 1994, c. 564, cl. 1, and Acts 1996, c. 616, cl. 3, provides that the amendment to this section, and enactment of § 16.1-306.1, by Acts 1993, c. 929, cl. 1, shall become effective June 1, 1998, "only if state funds are provided by the General Assembly sufficient to provide adequate resources, including all local costs, for the court to carry out the purposes of this act and to fulfill its mission to serve children and families of the Commonwealth." The funding was not provided.

Law Review.

For survey of Virginia law on criminal procedure for the year 1978-1979, see 66 Va. L. Rev. 261 (1980). For survey on legal issues involving children in Virginia for 1989, see 23 U. Rich. L. Rev. 705 (1989). For an article, "Legal Issues Involving Children," see 32 U. Rich. L. Rev. 1345 (1998).

CASE NOTES

Impeachment with evidence of prior juvenile adjudications. — A prosecutor may not impeach the defendant with evidence of prior juvenile adjudications, and the attempt to so cross-examine defendant was not harmless error. Lavinder v. Commonwealth, 395 S.E.2d 211 (1990).

Admissibility of juvenile records in sexually violent predator proceedings. — Circuit court erred when it excluded juvenile records in a sexually violent predator proceeding under the Sexually Violent Predators Act (SVPA), § 37.2-900 et seq., because the 1996 amendment to § 16.1-306, providing retention of juvenile records for certain offenses, came into effect before the inmate's 29th birthday, the date on which the right to record destruction would otherwise have vested. Thus, the inmate did not have a due process right under the Fourteenth Amendment to the U.S. Constitution to have his juvenile records destroyed and considered inadmissible in the SVPA proceedings. Commonwealth v. Garrett, 276 Va. 590, 667 S.E.2d 739, 2008 Va. LEXIS 116 (2008).

§ 16.1-307. Circuit court records regarding juveniles.

In proceedings against a juvenile in the circuit court in which the circuit court deals with the child in the same manner as a case in the juvenile court, the clerk of the court shall preserve all records connected with the proceedings in files separate from other files and records of the court as provided in § 16.1-302. Except as provided in §§ 19.2-389.1 and 19.2-390, such records shall be open for inspection only in accordance with the provisions of § 16.1-305 and shall be subject to expungement provisions of § 16.1-306. In proceedings in which a juvenile, fourteen years of age or older at the time of the offense, was adjudicated delinquent in juvenile court on the basis of an act which would be a felony if committed by an adult, or was found guilty of a felony in the circuit court, any court records, other than those specified in subsection A of § 16.1-305, regarding that adjudication or conviction and any subsequent adjudication of delinquency or conviction of a crime, shall be available and shall be treated in the same manner as adult criminal records.

History.
1977, c. 559; 1990, c. 258; 1993, cc. 468, 926; 1996, cc. 755, 914.

Editor's note.
Acts 1993, c. 930, cl. 3, as amended by Acts 1994, c. 564, cl. 2, and Acts 1996, c. 616, cl. 4, provides that the amendment to this section by Acts 1993, c. 930, cl. 1, shall become effective June 1, 1998, "if state funds are provided, including all local costs, to carry out the purposes of this bill by the General Assembly." The funding was not provided.

§ 16.1-308. Effect of adjudication on status of child.

Except as otherwise provided by law for a juvenile found guilty of a felony in circuit court whose case is disposed of in the same manner as an adult criminal case, a finding of guilty on a petition charging delinquency under the provisions of this law shall not operate to impose any of the civil disabilities ordinarily imposed by conviction for a crime, nor shall any such finding operate to disqualify the child for employment by any state or local governmental agency.

Nothing in this section shall prohibit the State Police or a police department or sheriff's office that is a part of or administered by the Commonwealth or any political subdivision thereof from denying employment to a person who had been adjudicated delinquent where such denial is based on the nature and gravity of the offense, the time since adjudication, the time since completion of any sentence, and the nature of the job sought.

History.
Code 1950, § 16.1-179; 1956, c. 555; 1977, c. 559; 1996, cc. 755, 914; 2011, c. 622.

The 2011 amendments.
The 2011 amendment by c. 622 added the last paragraph.

Law Review.
For comment, "Jury Trials for Juvenile Delinquents in Virginia," see 28 Wash. & Lee L. Rev. 135 (1971).

Michie's Jurisprudence.
For related discussion, see 5B M.J. Criminal Procedure, § 59; 9B M.J. Infants, § 19; 17 M.J. Statutes, § 40; 20 M.J. Weapons, §§ 7.2, 13.

CASE NOTES

Policy of section. — Statutes of this character originated in a policy not to permit the same uses to be made of records of juvenile courts as are frequently made of criminal records of courts of general jurisdiction, for the reason that juvenile proceedings are corrective in nature rather than penal. The child is looked upon not as a bad man, who should be punished, but as an erring child who needs help. Kiracofe v. Commonwealth, 198 Va. 833, 97 S.E.2d 14 (1957).

Predicate conviction for 18 U.S.C.S. § 922(g)(1). — Dismissal of indictments for possession of a firearm after having been convicted of a crime punishable by more than one year of imprisonment in violation of 18 U.S.C.S. § 922(g)(1) was affirmed, where the predicate convictions were juvenile adjudications in Virginia state court; a juvenile adjudication was not a conviction under Virginia law, so such an adjudication could not serve as the underlying conviction. United States v. Walters, 359 F.3d 340, 2004 U.S. App. LEXIS 3021 (4th Cir. 2004).

Conviction for purposes of 18 U.S.C.S. § 922(g)(1). — The clearest general statement of Virginia law on whether an adjudication of juvenile delinquency qualifies as a "conviction" for purposes of 18 U.S.C.S. § 922(g)(1) is § 16.1-308. United States v. Walters, 359 F.3d 340, 2004 U.S. App. LEXIS 3021 (4th Cir. 2004).

Impeachment with evidence of prior juvenile adjudications. — A prosecutor may not impeach the defendant with evidence of prior juvenile adjudications, and the attempt to so cross-examine defendant was not harmless error. Lavinder v. Commonwealth, 395 S.E.2d 211 (1990).

Interaction with § 18.2-308.2. — Regarding defendant's unlawful possession of a firearm, any ambiguity over juvenile protections between this section and § 18.2-308.2, which applies to adult felons and juveniles of a certain age convicted of acts that would be felonies for adults, must be resolved in favor of section 18.2-308.2, which is the more specific statute and prevails over the general statute concerning collateral disabilities for convicted juveniles. Griffin v. Commonwealth, 33 Va. App. 413, 533 S.E.2d 653, 2000 Va. App. LEXIS 649 (2000).

Juvenile conviction under Virginia law was not a criminal conviction for purposes of defining "prohibited person" under 18 U.S.C.S. § 922 and U.S. Sentencing Guidelines Manual § 2K2.1(a)(6); the fact that defendant was considered a "prohibited person" under § 18.2-308.2 A was irrelevant for purposes of a federal firearms conviction. United States v. Bugg, 248 F. Supp. 2d 507, 2003 U.S. Dist. LEXIS 3215 (E.D. Va. 2003).

Questioning witness as to adjudication as delinquent not permitted. — In view of the provisions of the juvenile statutes no error was committed in refusing to allow defendant's counsel to ask a witness for the prosecution whether he had ever been adjudged a juvenile delinquent in a proceeding in a juvenile court involving a felonious offense or larceny, the purpose of the question being to affect the credibility of the witness. Questions which refer to the disposition of the child in a juvenile court are not permitted. Kiracofe v. Commonwealth, 198 Va. 833, 97 S.E.2d 14 (1957). But, see McCain v. Commonwealth, 5 Va. App. 81, 360 S.E.2d 854 (1987).

Cross examination as to juvenile record where witness found "guilty" by juvenile court. — Once it was established that defendant had the right to cross-examine co-defendant by referring to his juvenile record, the right included an effective cross examination and not one limited so as to convey to the jury that "within the purview of the juvenile court law" was something other than a finding of guilty. The trial court erred in limiting the cross-examination of co-defendant, the Commonwealth's chief witness, to questions which did not include "not innocent" or "guilty" because the phrase "within the purview of the juvenile court law" did not effectively convey to the jury that co-defendant had, in fact, been found "guilty" by the juvenile court. McCain v. Commonwealth, 5 Va. App. 81, 360 S.E.2d 854 (1987).

Applied in United States v. Davis, 234 F. Supp. 2d 601, 2002 U.S. Dist. LEXIS 24781 (E.D. Va. 2002); Conkling v. Commonwealth, 45 Va. App. 518, 612 S.E.2d 235, 2005 Va. App. LEXIS 173 (2005).

§ 16.1-309. Penalty.

A. Except as provided in §§ 16.1-299, 16.1-300, 16.1-301, 16.1-305 and 16.1-307, any person who (i) files a petition, (ii) receives a petition or has access to court records in an official capacity, (iii) participates in the investigation of allegations which form the basis of a petition, (iv) is interviewed concerning such allegations and whose information is derived solely from such interview or (v) is present during any court proceeding, who discloses or makes use of or knowingly permits the use of identifying information not otherwise available to the public concerning a juvenile who is suspected of being or is the subject of a proceeding within the jurisdiction of the juvenile court pursuant to subdivisions 1 through 5 of subsection A of § 16.1-241 or who is in the custody of the State Department of Juvenile Justice, which information is directly or indirectly derived from the records or files of a law-enforcement agency, court or the Department of Juvenile Justice or acquired in the course of official duties, shall be guilty of a Class 3 misdemeanor.

B. The provisions of this section shall not apply to any law-enforcement officer or school employee who discloses to school personnel identifying information concerning a juvenile who is suspected of committing or has committed a delinquent act that has met applicable criteria of § 16.1-260 and is committed or alleged to have been committed on school property during a school-sponsored activity or on the way to or from such activity, if the disclosure is made solely for the purpose of enabling school personnel to take appropriate disciplinary action within the school setting against the juvenile. Further, the provisions of this section shall not apply to school personnel who disclose information obtained pursuant to §§ 16.1-305.1 and 22.1-288.2, if the disclosure is made in compliance with those sections.

History.
1977, c. 559; 1978, c. 626; 1979, c. 481; 1989, cc. 520, 733; 1993, cc. 645, 889; 1994, cc. 835, 913; 1996, cc. 755, 914; 2003, c. 119.

Cross references.
As to punishment for Class 3 misdemeanors, see § 18.2-11.

Editor's note.
Acts 1993, c. 930, cl. 3, as amended by Acts 1994, c. 564, cl. 2, and Acts 1996, c. 616, cl. 4, provides that the amendment to this section by Acts 1993, c. 930, cl. 1, shall become effective June 1, 1998, "if state funds are provided, including all local costs, to carry out the purposes of this bill by the General Assembly." The funding was not provided.

Law Review.
For survey on legal issues involving children in Virginia for 1989, see 23 U. Rich. L. Rev. 705 (1989). For an article, "Legal Issues Involving Children," see 32 U. Rich. L. Rev. 1345 (1998). For annual survey article on legal issues involving children, see 38 U. Rich. L. Rev. 161 (2003).

CASE NOTES

Impeachment with evidence of prior juvenile adjudications. — A prosecutor may not impeach the defendant with evidence of prior juvenile adjudications, and the attempt to so cross-examine defendant was not harmless error. Lavinder v. Commonwealth, 395 S.E.2d 211 (1990).

§ 16.1-309.1. Exception as to confidentiality.

A. Notwithstanding any other provision of this article, where consideration of public interest requires, the judge shall make available to the public the name and address of a juvenile and the nature of the offense for which a juvenile has been adjudicated delinquent (i) for an act which would be a Class 1, 2, or 3 felony, forcible rape, robbery or burglary or a related offense as set out in Article 2 (§ 18.2-89 et seq.) of Chapter 5 of Title 18.2 if committed by an adult or (ii) in any case where a juvenile is sentenced as an adult in circuit court.

B. 1. a. At any time prior to disposition, if a juvenile charged with a delinquent act which would constitute a felony if committed by an adult, or held in custody by a law-enforcement officer, or held in a secure facility pursuant to such charge becomes a fugitive from justice, the attorney for the Commonwealth or, upon notice to the Commonwealth's attorney, the Department of Juvenile Justice or a locally operated court services unit, may, with notice to the juvenile's attorney of record, petition the court having jurisdiction of the offense to authorize public release of the juvenile's name, age, physical description and photograph, the charge for which he is sought or for which he was adjudicated and any other information which may expedite his apprehension. Upon a showing that the juvenile is a fugitive and for good cause, the court shall order release of this information to the public. If a juvenile charged with a delinquent act that would constitute a felony if committed by an adult, or held in custody by a law-enforcement officer, or held in a secure facility pursuant to such charge becomes a fugitive from justice at a time when the court is not in session, the Commonwealth's attorney, the Department of Juvenile Justice, or a locally operated court services unit may, with notice to the juvenile's attorney of record, authorize the public release of the juvenile's name, age, physical description and photograph, the charge for which he is sought, and any other information which may expedite his apprehension.

b. At any time prior to disposition, if a juvenile charged with a delinquent act which would constitute a misdemeanor if committed by an adult, or held in custody by a law-enforcement officer, or held in a secure facility pursuant to such charge becomes a fugitive from justice, the attorney for the Commonwealth may, with notice to the juvenile's attorney of record, petition the court having jurisdiction of the offense to authorize public release of the juvenile's name, age, physical description and photograph, the charge for which he is sought or for which he was adjudicated and any other information which may expedite his apprehension. Upon a showing that the juvenile is a fugitive and for good cause, the court shall order release of this information to the public. If a juvenile charged with a delinquent act that would constitute a misdemeanor if committed by an adult, or held in custody by a law-enforcement officer, or held in a secure facility pursuant to such charge becomes a fugitive from justice at a time when the court is not in session, the attorney for the Commonwealth may, with notice to the juvenile's attorney of record, authorize the public release of the juvenile's name, age, physical description and photograph, the charge for which he is sought, and any other information which may expedite his apprehension.

2. After final disposition, if a juvenile (i) found to have committed a delinquent act becomes a fugitive from justice or (ii) who has been committed to the Department of Juvenile Justice pursuant to subdivision 14 of § 16.1-278.8 or 16.1-285.1 becomes a fugitive from justice by escaping from a facility operated by or under contract with the Department or from the custody of any employee of such facility, the Department may release to the public the juvenile's name, age, physical description and photograph, the charge for which he is sought or for which he was committed, and any other information which may expedite his apprehension. The Department shall promptly notify the attorney for the Commonwealth of the jurisdiction in which the juvenile was tried whenever information is released pursuant to this subdivision. If a juvenile specified in clause (i) being held after disposition in a secure facility not operated by or under contract with the Department becomes a fugitive by such escape, the attorney for the Commonwealth of the locality in which the facility is located may release the information as provided in this subdivision.

C. Whenever a juvenile 14 years of age or older is charged with a delinquent act that would be a criminal violation of Article 2 (§ 18.2-38 et seq.) of Chapter 4 of Title 18.2, a felony involving a weapon, a felony violation of Article 1 (§ 18.2-247 et seq.) of Chapter 7 of Title 18.2, or an "act of violence" as defined in subsection A of § 19.2-297.1 if committed by an adult, the judge may, where consideration of

the public interest requires, make the juvenile's name and address available to the public.

D. Upon the request of a victim of a delinquent act which would be a felony if committed by an adult, the court may order that such victim be informed of the charge or charges brought, the findings of the court, and the disposition of the case. For purposes of this section, "victim" shall be defined as in § 19.2-11.01.

E. Upon request, the judge or clerk may disclose if an order of emancipation of a juvenile pursuant to § 16.1-333 has been entered, provided (i) the order is not being appealed, (ii) the order has not been terminated, or (iii) there has not been a judicial determination that the order is void ab initio.

F. Notwithstanding any other provision of law, a copy of any court order that imposes a curfew or other restriction on a juvenile may be provided to the chief law-enforcement officer of the county or city wherein the juvenile resides. The chief law-enforcement officer shall only disclose information contained in the court order to other law-enforcement officers in the conduct of official duties.

G. Notwithstanding any other provision of law, where consideration of public safety requires, the Department and locally operated court service unit shall release information relating to a juvenile's criminal street gang involvement, if any, and the criminal street gang-related activity and membership of others, as criminal street gang is defined in § 18.2-46.1, obtained from an investigation or supervision of a juvenile and shall include the identity or identifying information of the juvenile; however, the Department and local court service unit shall not release the identifying information of a juvenile not affiliated with or involved in a criminal street gang unless that information relates to a specific criminal act. Such information shall be released to any State Police, local police department, sheriff's office, or law-enforcement task force that is a part of or administered by the Commonwealth or any political subdivision thereof, and that is responsible for the prevention and detection of crime and the enforcement of the penal, traffic, or highway laws of the Commonwealth. The exchange of information shall be for the purpose of an investigation into criminal street gang activity.

H. Notwithstanding any other provision of Article 12 (§ 16.1-299 et seq.), an intake officer shall report to the Bureau of Immigration and Customs Enforcement of the United States Department of Homeland Security a juvenile who has been detained in a secure facility based on an allegation that the juvenile committed a violent juvenile felony and who the intake officer has probable cause to believe is in the United States illegally.

History.
1979, c. 94; 1981, c. 307; 1986, c. 506; 1988, c. 749; 1993, c. 297; 1994, cc. 499, 542; 1995, cc. 558, 687, 804; 1997, cc. 434, 452; 1999, c. 710; 2000, cc. 563, 603; 2005, c. 364; 2006, cc. 259, 309, 682; 2008, c. 798; 2010, cc. 367, 472, 526.

Cross references.

As to punishment for Class 1, 2 and 3 felonies, see § 18.2-10.

The 2010 amendments.

The 2010 amendments by cc. 367 and 472 are identical, and rewrote subsection G, which formerly read: "Notwithstanding any other provision of law, where consideration of public safety requires, the Department or locally operated court service unit may release any information relating to gang involvement or the gang-related activity of others, obtained from an investigation or supervision of a juvenile identified as affiliated with a criminal street gang, as defined in § 18.2-46.1. Such information may be released to any State Police, local police department or sheriff's office, that is a part of or administered by the Commonwealth or any political subdivision thereof, and that is responsible for the prevention and detection of crime and the enforcement of the penal, traffic, or highway laws of the Commonwealth. The exchange of information shall be for the purpose of an investigation into criminal street gang activity."

The 2010 amendment by c. 526 in subsection B, inserted the a. designation and added subdivision B 1 b.; in subdivision B 1 a., twice substituted "constitute a felony" for "be forcible rape, robbery, burglary or a related offense as set out in Article 2 (§ 18.2-289 et seq.) of Chapter 5 of Title 18.2 or a Class 1, 2, or 3 felony"; and inserted "with notice to the juvenile's attorney of record" in the last sentence; in subdivision B 2, deleted "which would be forcible rape, robbery, burglary or a related offense as set out in Article 2 (§ 18.2-89 et seq.) of Chapter 5 of Title 18.2, or a Class 1, 2, or 3 felony if committed by an adult" following "a delinquent act" in the first sentence.

Law Review.

For 2006 survey article, "Family and Juvenile Law," see 41 U. Rich. L. Rev. 151 (2006). For annual survey, "A Look Back and Forward: Legislative and Regulatory Highlights for 2008 and 2009 and a Discussion of Juvenile Transfer," see 44 U. Rich. L. Rev. 53 (2009).

OPINIONS OF THE ATTORNEY GENERAL

Computerized system to notify crime victims could not be used for inmates who were juveniles when crimes were committed. — Because the statutes relating to rights of victims involved in juvenile matters contained in Chapter 11 of Title 16.1 control over the general statutes relating to rights of victims as set forth in the Crime Victim and Witness Rights Act, a computerized system by which registered crime victims would be updated with information regarding future court dates, transfers, and releases of active inmates incarcerated in the city jail could not be used to provide information to victims in cases where the inmate was a juvenile when the crime was committed. See opinion of Attorney General to The Honorable Robert J. McCabe, Sheriff for the City of Norfolk, 01-058 (12/17/01).

ARTICLE 13.

FACILITIES FOR DETENTION AND OTHER RESIDENTIAL CARE.

§§ 16.1-310 through 16.1-314. Repealed by Acts 1995, cc. 698 and 840.

Editor's note.

Acts 1995, cc. 698 and 840, cls. 3 provide: "That this act shall become effective January 1, 1996, if state funds are provided to carry out the purposes of this act during the 1995 Session of the General Assembly." These funds were provided pursuant to Acts 1995, c. 853, item 578.

ARTICLE 16.

PSYCHIATRIC TREATMENT OF MINORS ACT.

§ 16.1-339.1. Minors in detention homes or shelter care facilities.

If a minor admitted to a mental health facility pursuant to this article was in a detention home or a shelter care facility at the time of his admission, the director of the detention home or shelter care facility or his designee shall provide, if available, the charges against the minor that are the basis of the detention and the names and addresses of the minor's parents and the juvenile and domestic relations district court ordering the minor's placement in detention or shelter care to the mental health facility and to the juvenile and domestic relations district court for the jurisdiction in which the mental health facility is located if different from the court ordering the minor's placement in detention or shelter care.

History.

2009, cc. 455, 555.

ARTICLE 18.

JUVENILE COMPETENCY.

§ 16.1-356. Raising question of competency to stand trial; evaluation and determination of competency.

A. If, at any time after the attorney for the juvenile has been retained or appointed pursuant to a delinquency proceeding and before the end of trial, the court finds, sua sponte or upon hearing evidence or representations of counsel for the juvenile or the attorney for the Commonwealth, that there is probable cause to believe that the juvenile lacks substantial capacity to understand the proceedings against him or to assist his attorney in his own defense, the court shall order that a competency evaluation be performed by at least one psychiatrist, clinical psychologist, licensed professional counselor, licensed clinical social worker, or licensed marriage and family therapist, who is qualified by training and experience in the forensic evaluation of juveniles.

The Commissioner of Behavioral Health and Developmental Services shall approve the training and qualifications for individuals authorized to conduct juvenile competency evaluations and provide restoration services to juveniles pursuant to this article. The Commissioner shall also provide all juvenile courts with a list of guidelines for the court to use in the determination of qualifying individuals as experts in matters relating to juvenile competency and restoration.

B. The evaluation shall be performed on an outpatient basis at a community services board or behavioral health authority, juvenile detention home or juvenile justice facility unless the court specifically finds that (i) the results of the outpatient competency evaluation indicate that hospitalization of the juvenile for evaluation of competency is necessary or (ii) the juvenile is currently hospitalized in a psychiatric hospital. If one of these findings is made, the court, under authority of this subsection, may order the juvenile sent to a hospital designated by the Commissioner of Behavioral Health and Developmental Services as appropriate for the evaluation of juveniles against whom a delinquency petition has been filed.

C. The court shall require the attorney for the Commonwealth to provide to the evaluators appointed under subsection A any information relevant to the evaluation, including, but not limited to (i) a copy of the warrant or petition, (ii) the names and addresses of the attorney for the Commonwealth, the attorney for the juvenile, and the judge ordering the evaluation; and (iii) information about the alleged offense. The court shall require the attorney for the juvenile to provide to the evaluator only the psychiatric records and other information that is deemed relevant to the evaluation of competency. The moving party shall provide the evaluator a summary of the reasons for the evaluation request. All information required by this subsection shall be provided to the evaluator within 96 hours of the issuance of the court order requiring the evaluation and when applicable, shall be submitted prior to admission to the facility providing the inpatient evaluation. If the 96-hour period expires on a Saturday, Sunday or other legal holiday, the 96 hours shall be extended to the next day which is not a Saturday, Sunday or legal holiday.

D. If the juvenile is hospitalized under the provisions of subsection B, the juvenile shall be hospitalized for such time as the director of the hospital deems necessary to perform an adequate evaluation of the juvenile's competency, but not to exceed 10 days from the date of admission to the hospital. All evaluations shall be completed and the report filed with the court within 14 days of receipt by the evaluator of all information required under subsection C.

E. Upon completion of the evaluation, the evaluator shall promptly and in no event exceeding 14 days after receipt of all required information submit the report in writing to the court and the attorneys of record concerning (i) the juvenile's capacity to understand the proceedings against him; (ii) his ability to assist his attorney; and (iii) his need for services in the event he is found incompetent, including a description of the suggested necessary services and least restrictive setting to assist the juvenile in restoration to competency. No statements of the juvenile relating to the alleged offense shall be included in the report.

F. After receiving the report described in subsection E, the court shall promptly determine whether the juvenile is competent to stand trial for adjudication or disposition. A hearing on the juvenile's competency is not required unless one is requested by the attorney for the Commonwealth or the attorney for the juvenile or when required under § 16.1-357 B. If a hearing is held, the party alleging that the juvenile is incompetent shall bear the burden of proving by a preponderance of the evidence the juvenile's incompetency. The juvenile shall have the right to notice of the hearing and the right to personally participate in and introduce evidence at the hearing.

If the juvenile is otherwise able to understand the charges against him and assist in his defense, a finding of incompetency shall not be made based solely on any or all of the following: (i) the juvenile's age or developmental factors, (ii) the juvenile's claim to be unable to remember the time period surrounding the alleged offense, or (iii) the fact that the juvenile is under the influence of medication.

History.
  1999, cc. 958, 997; 2000, c. 337; 2005, c. 110; 2009, cc. 813, 840.

The 2009 amendments.
  The 2009 amendments by cc. 813 and 840 are identical, and substituted "Behavioral Health and Developmental Services" for "Mental Health, Mental Retardation and Substance Abuse Services" in the second paragraph of subsection A and in subsection B.

Law Review.
  For a review of Virginia legal issues involving children, see 33 U. Rich. L. Rev. 1001 (1999). For 2000 survey of Virginia law regarding children, see 34 U. Rich. L. Rev. 939 (2000).

CASE NOTES

  Licensed professional counselor qualified to testify as to post-traumatic stress disorder. — Appellate court's judgment that affirmed defendant's convictions for sex offenses was affirmed; the trial court did not err, and the appellate court did not err in affirming, the decision that permitted the licensed professional counselor to testify about the alleged victim's post-traumatic stress disorder, as Virginia law authorized licensed professional counselors to diagnose that disorder and the record showed that the licensed professional counselor possessed the requisite skill, knowledge, and experience to testify about it. Fitzgerald v. Commonwealth, 273 Va. 596, 643 S.E.2d 162, 2007 Va. LEXIS 63 (2007).

§ 16.1-357. Disposition when juvenile found incompetent.

A. Upon finding pursuant to subsection F of § 16.1-356 that the juvenile is incompetent, the court shall order that the juvenile receive services to restore his competency in either a nonsecure community setting or a secure facility as defined in § 16.1-228. A copy of the order shall be forwarded to the Commissioner of Behavioral Health and Developmental Services, who shall arrange for the provision of restoration services in a manner consistent with the order. Any report submitted pursuant to subsection E of § 16.1-356 shall be made available to the agent providing restoration.

B. If the court finds the juvenile incompetent but restorable to competency in the foreseeable future, it shall order restoration services for up to three months. At the end of three months from the date restoration is ordered under subsection A of this section, if the juvenile remains incompetent in the opinion of the agent providing restoration, the agent shall so notify the court and make recommendations concerning disposition of the juvenile. The court shall hold a hearing according to the procedures specified in subsection F of § 16.1-356 and, if it finds the juvenile unrestorably incompetent, shall order one of the dispositions pursuant to § 16.1-358. If the court finds the juvenile incompetent but restorable to competency, it may order continued restoration services for additional three-month periods, provided a hearing pursuant to subsection F of § 16.1-356 is held at the completion of each such period and the juvenile continues to be incompetent but restorable to competency in the foreseeable future.

C. If, at any time after the juvenile is ordered to undergo services under subsection A of this section, the agent providing restoration believes the juvenile's competency is restored, the agent shall immediately send a report to the court as prescribed in subsection E of § 16.1-356. The court shall make a ruling on the juvenile's competency according to the procedures specified in subsection F of § 16.1-356.

History.
1999, cc. 958, 997; 2009, cc. 813, 840.

The 2009 amendments.
The 2009 amendments by cc. 813 and 840 are identical, and substituted "Behavioral Health and Developmental Services" for "Mental Health, Mental Retardation and Substance Abuse Services" in the second sentence of subsection A.

§ 16.1-358. Disposition of the unrestorably incompetent juvenile.

If, at any time after the juvenile is ordered to undergo services pursuant to subsection A of § 16.1-357, the agent providing restoration concludes that the juvenile is likely to remain incompetent for the foreseeable future, he shall send a report to the court so stating. The report shall also indicate whether, in the agent's opinion, the juvenile should be (i) committed pursuant to Article 16 (§ 16.1-335 et seq.) of this chapter or, if the juvenile has reached the age of eighteen years at the time of the competency determination, pursuant to Article 5 (§ 37.2-814 et seq.) of Chapter 8 of Title 37.2, (ii) certified pursuant to § 37.2-806, (iii) provided other services by the court, or (iv) released. Upon receipt of the report, the court shall make a competency determination according to the procedures specified in subsection F of § 16.1-356. If the court finds that the juvenile is incompetent and is likely to remain so for the foreseeable future, it shall order that the juvenile (i) be committed pursuant to Article 16 (§ 16.1-

335 et seq.) of this chapter or, if the juvenile has reached the age of eighteen years at the time of the competency determination, pursuant to Article 5 (§ 37.2-814 et seq.) of Chapter 8 of Title 37.2, (ii) be certified pursuant to § 37.2-806, (iii) have a child in need of services petition filed on his behalf pursuant to § 16.1-260 D, or (iv) be released. If the court finds the juvenile incompetent but restorable to competency in the foreseeable future, it may order restoration services continued until three months have elapsed from the date of the provision of restoration ordered under subsection A of § 16.1-357.

If not dismissed without prejudice at an earlier time, charges against an unrestorably incompetent juvenile shall be dismissed in compliance with the time frames as follows: in the case of a charge which would be a misdemeanor, one year from the date of the juvenile's arrest for such charge; and in the case of a charge which would be a felony, three years from the date of the juvenile's arrest for such charges.

History.
1999, cc. 958, 997; 2000, c. 216.

Editor's note.
At the direction of the Virginia Code Commission, "Article 5 (§ 37.2-814 et seq.) of Chapter 8 of Title 37.2" was substituted for "§ 37.1-67.01 or § 37.1-67.1" twice in the first paragraph.

§ 16.1-359. Litigating certain issues when the juvenile is incompetent.

A finding of incompetency does not preclude the adjudication, at any time before trial, of a motion objecting to the sufficiency of the petition, nor does it preclude the adjudication of similar legal objections which, in the court's opinion, may be undertaken without the personal participation of the juvenile.

History.
1999, cc. 958, 997.

§ 16.1-360. Disclosure by juvenile during evaluation or restoration; use at guilt phase of trial adjudication or disposition hearing.

No statement or disclosure by the juvenile concerning the alleged offense made during a competency evaluation ordered pursuant to § 16.1-356, or services ordered pursuant to § 16.1-357 may be used against the juvenile at the adjudication or disposition hearings as evidence or as a basis for such evidence.

History.
1999, cc. 958, 997.

§ 16.1-361. Compensation of experts.

Each psychiatrist, clinical psychologist, licensed clinical social worker, licensed professional counselor, licensed marriage and family therapist, or other expert appointed by the court to render professional service pursuant to § 16.1-356, shall receive a reasonable fee for such service. With the exception of services provided by state hospitals or training centers, the fee shall be determined in each instance by the court that appointed the expert, in accordance with guidelines established by the Supreme Court after consultation with the Department of Behavioral Health and Developmental Services. If any such expert is required to appear as a witness in any hearing held pursuant to § 16.1-356, he shall receive mileage and a fee of $100 for each day during which he is required to serve. An itemized account of expenses, duly sworn to, must be presented to the court, and when allowed shall be certified to the Supreme Court for payment out of the state treasury, and be charged against the appropriations made to pay criminal charges. Allowance for the fee and for the per diem authorized shall also be made by order of the court, duly certified to the Supreme Court for payment out of the appropriation to pay criminal charges.

History.
1999, cc. 958, 997; 2000, c. 337; 2005, c. 110; 2009, cc. 813, 840; 2012, cc. 476, 507.

The 2009 amendments.
The 2009 amendments by cc. 813 and 840 are identical, and substituted "Behavioral Health and Developmental Services" for "Mental Health, Mental Retardation and Substance Abuse Services" at the end of the second sentence.

The 2012 amendments.
The 2012 amendments by cc. 476 and 507 are identical, and substituted "state hospitals or training centers" for "state mental health or mental retardation facilities" in the second sentence.

TITLE 17.

COURTS OF RECORD.

[Repealed.]

TITLE 17.1.

COURTS OF RECORD.

CHAPTER 3.

SUPREME COURT.

Article 1. Composition, Jurisdiction, etc.

ARTICLE 1.

COMPOSITION, JURISDICTION, ETC.

§ 17.1-313. Review of death sentence.

A. A sentence of death, upon the judgment thereon becoming final in the circuit court, shall be reviewed on the record by the Supreme Court.

B. The proceeding in the circuit court shall be transcribed as expeditiously as practicable, and the transcript filed forthwith upon transcription with the clerk of the circuit court, who shall, within ten days after receipt of the transcript, compile the record as provided in Rule 5:14 and transmit it to the Supreme Court.

C. In addition to consideration of any errors in the trial enumerated by appeal, the court shall consider and determine:

1. Whether the sentence of death was imposed under the influence of passion, prejudice or any other arbitrary factor; and

2. Whether the sentence of death is excessive or disproportionate to the penalty imposed in similar cases, considering both the crime and the defendant.

D. In addition to the review and correction of errors in the trial of the case, with respect to review of the sentence of death, the court may:

1. Affirm the sentence of death;

2. Commute the sentence of death to imprisonment for life; or

3. Remand to the trial court for a new sentencing proceeding.

E. The Supreme Court may accumulate the records of all capital felony cases tried within such period of time as the court may determine. The court shall consider such records as are available as a guide in determining whether the sentence imposed in the case under review is excessive. Such records as are accumulated shall be made available to the circuit courts.

F. Sentence review shall be in addition to appeals, if taken, and review and appeal may be consolidated. The defendant and the Commonwealth shall have the right to submit briefs within time limits imposed by the court, either by rule or order, and to present oral argument.

G. The Supreme Court shall, in setting its docket, give priority to the review of cases in which the sentence of death has been imposed over other cases pending in the Court. In setting its docket, the Court shall also give priority to the consideration and disposition of petitions for writs of habeas corpus filed by prisoners held under sentence of death.

History.
1977, c. 492, §§ 17-110.1, 17-110.2; 1983, c. 519; 1995, c. 503; 1998, c. 872.

Cross references.
As to the trial of capital cases, see § 19.2-264.2 et seq. For a special rule applicable to cases in which sentence of death has been imposed, see Supreme Court Rule 5:22.

Law Review.
For survey of Virginia criminal procedure for the year 1976-1977, see 63 Va. L. Rev. 1408 (1977). For article, "Psychiatry and the Death Penalty: Emerging Problems in Virginia," see 66 Va. L. Rev. 167 (1980). For survey of Virginia law on criminal procedure for the year 1978-1979, see 66 Va. L. Rev. 261 (1980). For note, "Criminal Procedure and Criminal Law: Virginia Supreme Court Decisions During the 70's," see 15 U. Rich. L. Rev. 585 (1981). For article, "Virginia's Capital Murder Sentencing Proceeding: A Defense Perspective," see 18 U. Rich. L. Rev. 341 (1984). For case note, "Atkins

v. Virginia: Nothing Left of the Independent Legislative Power to Punish and Define Crime," 11 Geo. Mason L. Rev. 805 (2003).

Michie's Jurisprudence.
For related discussion, see 5B M.J. Criminal Procedure, § 80; 9B M.J. Homicide, § 132.1.

CASE NOTES

I. General Consideration.
II. Review for Influence of Passion, Prejudice, etc.
III. Review for Excessive or Disproportionate Sentence.

I. GENERAL CONSIDERATION.

Editor's note.
Many of the cases cited below were decided under prior law.

Constitutionality. — Virginia's capital sentencing procedure statutes are not facially invalid on grounds that the death penalty is cruel and unusual punishment under the Eighth and Fourteenth Amendments. Mason v. Commonwealth, 219 Va. 1091, 254 S.E.2d 116, cert. denied, 444 U.S. 919, 100 S. Ct. 239, 62 L. Ed. 2d 176 (1979).

The statutes which limit review of a death penalty case to the Supreme Court do not violate equal protection rights, as it is rational for the General Assembly, given the gravity of cases involving a sentence to death, to provide death-penalty defendants as automatic, plenary review in the Commonwealth's highest court. Payne v. Commonwealth, 233 Va. 460, 357 S.E.2d 500, cert. denied, 484 U.S. 933, 108 S. Ct. 308, 98 L. Ed. 2d 267 (1987).

Where the Virginia Supreme Court, in considering the proportionality review, decided that this case was the worst on record, question of whether scope of proportionality review was constitutionally invalid was not decided. Clozza v. Murray, 913 F.2d 1092 (4th Cir. 1990), cert. denied, 499 U.S. 913, 111 S. Ct. 1123, 113 L. Ed. 2d 231 (1991).

Given that proportionality review is not constitutionally required, it cannot be argued that Virginia's scheme is unconstitutional simply because the relevant comparison has been limited to death cases. Turner v. Williams, 812 F. Supp. 1400 (E.D. Va. 1993), aff'd, 35 F.3d 872 (4th Cir. 1994), cert. denied, 514 U.S. 1017, 115 S. Ct. 1359, 131 L. Ed. 2d 216 (1995), overruled on other grounds, O'Dell v. Netherland, 95 F.3d 1214 (4th Cir. 1996).

Although the Virginia capital sentencing statute requires a proportionality review, the federal Constitution does not; therefore, defendant's claims that the review was inadequate did not provide sufficient constitutional grounds to warrant a writ of habeas corpus. Buchanan v. Angelone, 103 F.3d 344 (4th Cir. 1996), aff'd, 522 U.S. 269, 118 S. Ct. 757, 139 L. Ed. 2d 702 (1998).

Proportionality review not constitutionally required. — Proportionality review by an appellate court has been deemed important in insuring that the sentence was not imposed in an arbitrary or capricious manner. However comparative proportionality review of a death sentence with penalties imposed in similar cases is not constitutionally required. Briley v. Bass, 584 F. Supp. 807 (E.D. Va.), aff'd, 742 F.2d 155 (4th Cir.), cert. denied, 469 U.S. 893, 105 S. Ct. 270, 83 L. Ed. 2d 206 (1984).

Supreme Court did not violate due process by not reviewing all capital murder cases. — In reviewing the proportionality of a death penalty sentence, the Virginia Supreme Court did not violate due process by not reviewing all capital murder cases but giving particular emphasis to the cases which were most like the defendant's in that the death sentences were based on the probability that the defendants would be continuing threats to society. Peterson v. Murray, 904 F.2d 882 (4th Cir.), cert. denied, 498 U.S. 992, 111 S. Ct. 537, 112 L. Ed. 2d 547 (1990).

Due process does not require maintenance of complete records. — Nothing in this statute suggests that the maintenance of complete records is requisite to the preservation of a defendant's right to a proportionality review or prescribes the method by which an appellate court conducts a proportionality review of a death sentence; rather, so long as the methods employed assure that the death sentence is not disproportionate to the penalty generally imposed for comparable crimes, due process will be satisfied and

the defendant's constitutional rights protected. Bailey v. Commonwealth, 259 Va. 723, 529 S.E.2d 570, 2000 Va. LEXIS 59, cert. denied, 531 U.S. 995, 121 S. Ct. 488, 148 L. Ed. 2d 460 (2000).

Mandatory review limited to certain issues. — Although this section requires that the Supreme Court review every case in which a sentence of death has been entered, mandatory review in the Supreme Court is limited to certain issues. The Court is required to review only whether the sentence of death was imposed under the influence of passion, prejudice or any other arbitrary factor and whether the sentence of death is excessive or disproportionate to the penalty imposed in similar cases, considering both the crime and the defendant. The contemporaneous objection rule applies to other issues and the Court has applied it in capital cases. Briley v. Bass, 584 F. Supp. 807 (E.D. Va.), aff'd, 742 F.2d 155 (4th Cir.), cert. denied, 469 U.S. 893, 105 S. Ct. 270, 83 L. Ed. 2d 206 (1984).

State supreme court was required to determine whether the death sentence imposed on defendant was excessive or disproportionate to the penalty imposed in similar cases, considering both the defendant and the crime, and upon doing so, was satisfied that defendant's acts of hiring two murderers to kill her husband and stepson as they laying sleeping in their home, for the money she would receive, meant her crimes were so heinous compared to other, similar crimes that the death sentence imposed was warranted. Lewis v. Commonwealth, 267 Va. 302, 593 S.E.2d 220, 2004 Va. LEXIS 47, cert. denied, 543 U.S. 904, 125 S. Ct. 201, 160 L. Ed. 2d 177 (2004).

Mandatory review of death sentence required. — Mandatory review by the supreme court was required in case where defendant entered a plea of guilty to capital murder and was sentenced to death, even though he instructed his counsel not to pursue an appeal. Zirkle v. Commonwealth, 262 Va. 631, 553 S.E.2d 520, 2001 Va. LEXIS 125 (2001).

When defendant waived his right to appeal his death sentence, the Virginia Supreme Court was still required, under subsections A and C of § 17.1-313 to review the sentence, as the purpose of the review process was to assure the fair and proper application of the death penalty statutes in Virginia and to instill public confidence in the administration of justice. Hudson v. Commonwealth, 267 Va. 29, 590 S.E.2d 362, 2004 Va. LEXIS 5 (2004).

Cumulation of records in death penalty cases. — This statute uses discretionary language permitting the court to determine the period of time within which the records of all capital felony cases will be accumulated for purposes of a proportionality review of a death sentence. Bailey v. Commonwealth, 259 Va. 723, 529 S.E.2d 570, 2000 Va. LEXIS 59, cert. denied, 531 U.S. 995, 121 S. Ct. 488, 148 L. Ed. 2d 460 (2000).

Circuit court not required to request records for proportionality review. — Although the Supreme Court has previously supplied its records of capital murder cases to a circuit court upon request, nothing in the statute requires the circuit court to make such a request, the matter being one committed to the trial court's discretion. Bailey v. Commonwealth, 259 Va. 723, 529 S.E.2d 570, 2000 Va. LEXIS 59, cert. denied, 531 U.S. 995, 121 S. Ct. 488, 148 L. Ed. 2d 460 (2000).

Error in failure of trial court to consider probation report held cured. — Although original sentencing order was entered in error for failure of the trial court to consider the probation report required by § 19.2-264.5, where the trial judge recognized the omission, vacated the order, directed the probation officer to prepare a report, authorized a private psychiatric examination, and afforded defendant a second opportunity to show good cause why the death penalty should not be imposed, the error was cured, and absent anything to support defendant's claim that the final sentencing order was the product of passion or prejudice, such assignment of error was to be rejected. Edmonds v. Commonwealth, 229 Va. 303, 329 S.E.2d 807, cert. denied, 474 U.S. 975, 106 S. Ct. 339, 88 L. Ed. 2d 324 (1985).

Reviewing court conducts proportionality review. — State supreme court dismissed the petition for habeas corpus filed by petitioner in petitioner's capital murder case; although petitioner claimed that petitioner's trial counsel provided ineffective assistance for not requesting that the trial court conduct a proportionality review of the jury's imposition of the death penalty, § 17.1-313 imposed the requirement of conducting such review on the reviewing courts and not on a trial court. Jackson v. Warden of the Sussex

I State Prison, 2005 Va. LEXIS 107 (June 16, 2005).

The Supreme Court's review of a petitioner's sentence was not constitutionally inadequate where the evidence demonstrated that the court had a clear awareness of the mitigating factors and stated that it had reviewed the records of all its capital murder cases and found no disproportion, particularly when the number of people the petitioner was found to have killed was taken into account. Goins v. Angelone, 52 F. Supp. 2d 638 (E.D. Va. 1999), appeal dismissed, 226 F.3d 312 (4th Cir. 2000).

Elimination of juror for bias in favor of death penalty permitted. — The process of selection of an impartial jury permits elimination for cause of those veniremen who are biased in favor of the death penalty under all circumstances as well as those who are biased against its imposition under all circumstances. Patterson v. Commonwealth, 222 Va. 653, 283 S.E.2d 212 (1981).

And failure to question jury invalidates sentence. — In a prosecution for robbery and capital murder, the refusal by the trial judge to ask the jury whether, if the jury should happen to convict the defendant of capital murder, each juror would be able to consider voting for a sentence less than death, or to ask an equivalent question, was prejudicial error invalidating the sentence to death. Patterson v. Commonwealth, 222 Va. 653, 283 S.E.2d 212 (1981).

Applied in Bramblett v. Commonwealth, 257 Va. 263, 513 S.E.2d 400 (1999); Hedrick v. Commonwealth, 257 Va. 328, 513 S.E.2d 634; Cherrix v. Commonwealth, 257 Va. 292, 513 S.E.2d 642; Walker v. Commonwealth, 258 Va. 54, 515 S.E.2d 565 (1999); Johnson v. Commonwealth, 259 Va. 654, 529 S.E.2d 769, 2000 Va. LEXIS 60; Akers v. Commonwealth, 260 Va. 358, 535 S.E.2d 674, 2000 Va. LEXIS 118 (2000); Lenz v. Commonwealth, 261 Va. 451, 544 S.E.2d 299, 2001 Va. LEXIS 58 (2001); Schmitt v. Commonwealth, 262 Va. 127, 547 S.E.2d 186, 2001 Va. LEXIS 85 (2001); Morrisette v. Commonwealth, 264 Va. 386, 569 S.E.2d 47, 2002 Va. LEXIS 100 (2002); Atkins v. Commonwealth, 260 Va. 73, 581 S.E.2d 514, 2003 Va. LEXIS 71 (2003); Elliott v. Warden of the Sussex I State Prison, 274 Va. 598, 652 S.E.2d 465, 2007 Va. LEXIS 137 (2007); Prieto v. Commonwealth, 278 Va. 366, 682 S.E.2d 910, 2009 Va. LEXIS 94 (2009).

II. REVIEW FOR INFLUENCE OF PASSION, PREJUDICE, ETC.

Court's consideration of constitutional claims during subdivision C 1 review. — In conducting its mandatory review of the death sentence pursuant to subdivision C 1, the Supreme Court of Virginia ascertains only whether the imposition of the death penalty was influenced by improper considerations; the provision simply does not require the court to examine the record for constitutional errors not specified on appeal. Mu'Min v. Pruett, 125 F.3d 192 (4th Cir. 1997).

Where defendant claimed that in performing its statutory duty the Supreme Court of Virginia necessarily determined that his conviction and sentence were free of fundamental constitutional error because such errors would constitute arbitrary factors requiring the invalidation of his death sentence, and where defendant concluded that because the Supreme Court of Virginia considered the merits of his constitutional claims the Fourth Circuit Court of Appeals could do likewise, the fact that the Supreme Court of Virginia applied the procedural default rule set forth in Slayton v. Parrigan, 215 Va. 27, 205 S.E. 2d 680 (1974) mandated the conclusion that the court did not implicitly consider the merits of defendant's constitutional claims during the course of its mandatory review. Mu'Min v. Pruett, 125 F.3d 192 (4th Cir. 1997).

Mandatory review after appeal withdrawn. — Mandatory review of a death sentence, where defendant withdrew his appeal, required the review of possible trial errors for their potential impact on the decision to impose the death penalty; the mandatory review process, mandated by § 17.1-313 C 1, would be meaningless without the recognition that the erroneous admission of some evidence or some other error might have resulted in a prejudicial verdict. Emmett v. Commonwealth, 264 Va. 364, 569 S.E.2d 39, 2002 Va. LEXIS 102 (2002), cert. denied, 538 U.S. 929, 123 S. Ct. 1586, 155 L. Ed. 2d 324 (2003).

The fact that a capital murder case is well publicized does not prove that a sentence of death is improperly imposed. Beaver v. Commonwealth, 232 Va. 521, 352 S.E.2d 342, cert. denied, 483 U.S. 1033, 107 S. Ct. 3277, 97 L. Ed. 2d 781 (1987).

Jury request for explanation of "the terms of life imprisonment" and "eligibility for parole" tended to show that the jury's deliberations were dispassionate, unprejudiced, and guided by earnest consideration of every factor relevant to the portentous decision they were required to make. DeLong v. Commonwealth, 234 Va. 357, 362 S.E.2d 669 (1987), cert. denied, 485 U.S. 929, 108 S. Ct. 1100, 99 L. Ed. 2d 263 (1988); Mu'Min v. Commonwealth, 239 Va. 433, 389 S.E.2d 886 (1990), aff'd, 500 U.S. 415, 111 S. Ct. 1899, 114 L. Ed. 2d 493, rehearing denied, 501 U.S. 1269, 112 S. Ct. 13, 115 L. Ed. 2d 1097 (1991).

Prosecutorial misconduct claims were unfounded in black defendant's conviction by all-white jury, since there was nothing to suggest that the jury's sentence was imposed under the influence of passion or prejudice. Satcher v. Netherland, 944 F. Supp. 1222 (E.D. Va. 1996), aff'd in part and rev'd in part on other grounds sub nom. Satcher v. Pruett, 126 F.3d 561 (4th Cir.), cert. denied, 522 U.S. 1010, 118 S. Ct. 595, 139 L. Ed. 2d 431 (1997).

Statements about failure to support children. — Where defendant asserted that trial court statements, particularly statement about the number and nonsupport of his children, showed "high emotion," passion or prejudice, and reflected consideration of the type of arbitrary factors upon which the trial court could not properly impose the death penalty, the supreme court's review of the judge's statements showed that they were made in the context of reciting factors in defendant's background, including his age, his children, and the various parts of his criminal record therefore, the trial court did not impose the death sentence based on passion, prejudice, or any other arbitrary factor. Dubois v. Commonwealth, 246 Va. 260, 435 S.E.2d 636 (1993), cert. denied, 511 U.S. 1012, 114 S. Ct. 1389, 128 L. Ed. 2d 63 (1994).

Photographs of victim's decomposed body. — Death sentence was not infected by impermissible passion and prejudice resulting from photographs of victim's decomposed body that were admitted into evidence; the admission of photographs is a matter resting within the sound discretion of the trial court and will not be disturbed unless a clear abuse of discretion is shown. Stockton v. Commonwealth, 241 Va. 192, 402 S.E.2d 196, cert. denied, 502 U.S. 280, 112 S. Ct. 280, 116 L. Ed. 2d 231 (1991).

Sentence not imposed under the influence of passion, prejudice or other arbitrary factor. — The defendant's death sentence was not the result of passion, prejudice or other arbitrary factor where the defendant had killed two people and injured three others when he opened fire with a high-powered rifle on employees entering the CIA; the death sentence was not imposed because the defendant had a political motive, but because he had murdered two innocent men and maimed three others in an extremely brutal and premeditated manner. Kasi v. Commonwealth, 256 Va. 407, 508 S.E.2d 57 (1998), cert. denied, 527 U.S. 1038, 119 S. Ct. 2399, 144 L. Ed. 2d 798 (1999) overruled in part on other grounds by Jay v. Commonwealth, 275 Va. 510, 659 S.E.2d 311, 2008 Va. LEXIS 53 (2008).

While the killing of one's own child is undeniably among the most abhorrent crimes for a jury to contemplate when considering an appropriate sentence, especially when that crime occurs in conjunction with the equally abhorrent crime of the killing of one's wife, the mere fact that a crime is abhorrent does not raise a presumption that the jury will be unable to set aside its natural emotions and fairly consider all the evidence; thus, where the record did not disclose that the jury failed to give fair consideration to all the evidence both in favor and in mitigation of the death sentences and the there was nothing in the record which suggested that the jury, or the trial court in reviewing the verdicts, imposed the death sentences under the influence of passion, prejudice, or other arbitrary factors, there was no grounds to set aside the sentences imposed by the jury. Bailey v. Commonwealth, 259 Va. 723, 529 S.E.2d 570, 2000 Va. LEXIS 59, cert. denied, 531 U.S. 995, 121 S. Ct. 488, 148 L. Ed. 2d 460 (2000).

With regard to defendant's convictions on two capital murder counts and the imposition of two death sentences against him, the Supreme Court of Virginia, in conducting its mandatory review under subsection C of § 17.1-313, determined that the jury was not influenced by passion, prejudice, or any other arbitrary factor in sentencing defendant to death and that in looking at similar cases in which, after a finding of both aggravating factors of future dangerousness and vileness, a death sentence was imposed, his capital sentences were neither excessive nor disproportionate to sentences imposed in capital murder cases for comparable crimes. Prieto v. Commonwealth, 283 Va. 149, 721 S.E.2d 484, 2012 Va. LEXIS 20 (2012).

Defendant's death sentences, imposed upon his pleas of guilty to two charges of capital murder, were not imposed under influence of passion, prejudice, or any other arbitrary factor, in violation of subdivision C 1 of § 17.1-313 as the trial court was meticulous in ensuring that defendant was competent, and the record made clear that defendant consistently had advice from stand-by counsel throughout the proceedings. The trial court took great pains to explain to defendant the procedure, the law, and his rights; defendant was permitted to change his plea in the first case several times; and the trial court granted each of defendant's requests for a continuance, appointed every expert he requested, and granted all accommodations within its power to grant. Gleason v. Commonwealth, 284 Va. 166, 726 S.E.2d 351, 2012 Va. LEXIS 135 (2012).

III. REVIEW FOR EXCESSIVE OR DISPROPORTIONATE SENTENCE.

In determining in a given case whether a sentence of death is excessive or disproportionate, the Supreme Court inquires whether juries in this jurisdiction generally approve the supreme penalty for comparable or similar crimes. Townes v. Commonwealth, 234 Va. 307, 362 S.E.2d 650 (1987), cert. denied, 485 U.S. 971, 108 S. Ct. 1249, 99 L. Ed. 2d 447 (1988); Smith v. Commonwealth, 239 Va. 243, 389 S.E.2d 871 (1990).

The test of proportionality is whether juries in this jurisdiction generally approve the supreme penalty for comparable or similar crimes. Yeatts v. Commonwealth, 242 Va. 121, 410 S.E.2d 254 (1991), cert. denied, 503 U.S. 946, 112 S. Ct. 1500, 117 L. Ed. 2d 639 (1992).

Death sentence was affirmed because the Supreme Court of Virginia completed a review of the record and found no basis to conclude that the jury or trial court were influenced by passion, prejudice, or other arbitrary factor in sentencing defendant to death. Further, the court found that defendant's sentence of death was not excessive or disproportionate to the sentences imposed by other sentencing bodies in the Commonwealth of Virginia in comparable cases with comparable defendants. Juniper v. Commonwealth, 271 Va. 362, 626 S.E.2d 383, 2006 Va. LEXIS 29 (2006).

What cases compared in disproportionality review. — The legislature did not limit the disproportionality review to cases chosen selectively. The Supreme Court's comparison extends to the records in all the capital cases presented to the Court, including those in which the trial court imposed a penalty of imprisonment for life. Because the Court is directed by subdivision C 2 to compare "similar" cases, it gives special attention to those in which the underlying felony, the penalty predicate, and the facts and circumstances surrounding the commission of the crime are fairly comparable. Boggs v. Commonwealth, 229 Va. 501, 331 S.E.2d 407 (1985), cert. denied, 475 U.S. 1031, 106 S. Ct. 1240, 89 L. Ed. 2d 347 (1986), 495 U.S. 940, 110 S. Ct. 2193, 109 L. Ed. 2d 521 (1990).

In a proportionality review, the court inquires whether "juries in this jurisdiction generally approve the supreme penalty for comparable or similar crimes." Turner v. Commonwealth, 234 Va. 543, 364 S.E.2d 483 (1988).

In determining whether a sentence of death is excessive or disproportionate, the Supreme Court inquires if juries in this jurisdiction generally approve the supreme penalty for comparable or similar crimes. Pruett v. Commonwealth, 232 Va. 266, 351 S.E.2d 1 (1986), cert. denied, 482 U.S. 931, 107 S. Ct. 3220, 96 L. Ed. 2d 706 (1987).

Test in consideration of similar cases. — The Supreme Court cannot fairly determine whether a death sentence is excessive or disproportionate by comparing it with sentences imposed upon convictions for lesser included offenses, reached perhaps by compromise verdicts, even where there may be similarities in the evidence. The test is not whether a jury may have declined to recommend the death penalty in a particular case but whether generally juries in this jurisdiction impose the death sentence for conduct similar to that of the defendant. Stamper v. Commonwealth, 220 Va. 260, 257 S.E.2d 808 (1979), cert. denied, 445 U.S. 972, 100 S. Ct. 1666, 64 L. Ed. 2d 249 (1980).

If juries generally in Virginia impose the death sentence for conduct similar to that of the defendant, then the sentence is not excessive or disproportionate. Peterson v. Commonwealth, 225 Va.

289, 302 S.E.2d 520, cert. denied, 464 U.S. 865, 104 S. Ct. 202, 78 L. Ed. 2d 176 (1983).

Defendant's death sentence was not excessive or disproportionate to penalties generally imposed by other sentencing bodies in the Commonwealth for comparable crimes; such sentencing bodies generally impose death for a capital murder in which a defendant is also convicted of murdering another person or persons. Goins v. Commonwealth, 251 Va. 442, 470 S.E.2d 114, cert. denied, 519 U.S. 887, 117 S. Ct. 222, 136 L. Ed. 2d 154 (1996); Kasi v. Commonwealth, 256 Va. 407, 508 S.E.2d 57 (1998), cert. denied, 527 U.S. 1038, 119 S. Ct. 2399, 144 L. Ed. 2d 798 (1999).

Based upon the appellate court's review and a consideration of both the defendant and the crime he committed, the court was satisfied that, while there were exceptions, other sentencing bodies in the state generally imposed the death sentence for comparable or similar offenses. Accordingly, the appellate court concluded that the defendant's sentence of death was neither excessive nor disproportionate. Williams v. Commonwealth, 252 Va. 3, 472 S.E.2d 50 (1996), cert. denied, 519 U.S. 998, 117 S. Ct. 493, 136 L. Ed. 2d 386 (1996).

Proportionality review does not require that a given capital murder case equal in horror the worst possible scenario yet encountered. Reid v. Commonwealth, 256 Va. 561, 506 S.E.2d 787 (1998), cert. denied, 528 U.S. 833, 120 S. Ct. 91, 145 L. Ed. 2d 77 (1999).

Limitation on consideration of similar cases. — In determining whether a death penalty sentence is excessive or disproportionate to the penalty imposed in similar cases, considering both the crime and the defendant, the Supreme Court's consideration of similar cases should be limited generally to cases arising in Virginia under revised death penalty statutes. Coppola v. Commonwealth, 220 Va. 243, 257 S.E.2d 797 (1979), cert. denied, 444 U.S. 1103, 100 S. Ct. 1069, 62 L. Ed. 2d 788 (1980).

Where basis of imposition of death sentence is "dangerousness," the Supreme Court gives particular emphasis to those cases where the death penalty was based upon the same predicate. Townes v. Commonwealth, 234 Va. 307, 362 S.E.2d 650 (1987), cert. denied, 485 U.S. 971, 108 S. Ct. 1249, 99 L. Ed. 2d 447 (1988).

Future dangerousness established. — Evidence which showed that defendant raped three women, killing the first, was sufficient to establish the future dangerousness of defendant. Beavers v. Commonwealth, 245 Va. 268, 427 S.E.2d 411, cert. denied, 510 U.S. 859, 114 S. Ct. 171, 126 L. Ed. 2d 130 (1993).

Where basis of imposition of death sentence is "vileness," the reviewing court gives particular attention to those cases in which the death penalty was based upon the same predicate. Yet no concept of proportionality requires that each new capital murder case equal in horror the worst possible scenario yet encountered, else the death penalty may not be imposed. Turner v. Commonwealth, 234 Va. 543, 364 S.E.2d 483 (1988).

Ample evidence of vileness and future dangerousness. — Where defendant was the sole participant in prior murders and arson and suggested the robbery, rapes, and the execution-type killings of victims in the instant case, and the arson of their house, evidence amply justified the jury's finding of vileness and future dangerousness. Williams v. Commonwealth, 248 Va. 528, 450 S.E.2d 365 (1994), cert. denied, 515 U.S. 1161, 115 S. Ct. 2616, 132 L. Ed. 2d 858 (1995).

Where a defendant killed a robbery victim in front of her husband with multiple gunshots and left them both to die, merely to rob them, the Virginia Supreme Court found that the evidence established both the "vileness" and "future dangerousness" aggravators, and that the death sentence was proportional to sentences imposed in similar cases. Green v. Commonwealth, 266 Va. 81, 580 S.E.2d 834, 2003 Va. LEXIS 55 (2003), cert. denied, 540 U.S. 1194, 124 S. Ct. 1448, 158 L. Ed. 2d 107 (2004).

Death penalty for one codefendant despite life sentence for other. — A codefendant is not necessarily entitled to commutation of a death sentence because an equally culpable confederate, on substantially the same evidence, has been sentenced to life imprisonment. Coppola v. Commonwealth, 220 Va. 243, 257 S.E.2d 797 (1979), cert. denied, 444 U.S. 1103, 100 S. Ct. 1069, 62 L. Ed. 2d 788 (1980).

A death sentence against one defendant will be upheld when a sentence of life imprisonment, or less, has been imposed upon a codefendant, provided the death sentence is in accord with the general statewide standard. Coppola v. Commonwealth, 220 Va.

243, 257 S.E.2d 797 (1979), cert. denied, 444 U.S. 1103, 100 S. Ct. 1069, 62 L. Ed. 2d 788 (1980).

Effect of accomplice's punishment. — Defendant's punishment of death sentence for capital murder was not excessive or disproportionate although his accomplices did not receive a sentence of death. Murphy v. Commonwealth, 246 Va. 136, 431 S.E.2d 48, cert. denied, 510 U.S. 928, 114 S. Ct. 336, 126 L. Ed. 2d 281 (1993).

Death penalty for murder of police officer held not disproportionate. See DeLong v. Commonwealth, 234 Va. 357, 362 S.E.2d 669 (1987), cert. denied, 485 U.S. 929, 108 S. Ct. 1100, 99 L. Ed. 2d 263 (1988).

Defendant's sentence of death was neither excessive nor disproportionate. — Defendant's sentence of death for capital murder for hire was neither excessive nor disproportionate when compared to sentences generally imposed by sentencing bodies in this jurisdiction for crimes of a similar nature. Murphy v. Commonwealth, 246 Va. 136, 431 S.E.2d 48, cert. denied, 510 U.S. 928, 114 S. Ct. 336, 126 L. Ed. 2d 281 (1993).

The defendant's death sentence was not excessive or disproportionate where the defendant had killed the victim and another person and had injured three other people when he opened fire with a high-powered rifle into vehicles stopped at a red light and where the jury had based the death sentence on the vileness factor; the death sentence is generally imposed when, as in this case, the defendant is also convicted of killing another person. Kasi v. Commonwealth, 256 Va. 407, 508 S.E.2d 57 (1998), cert. denied, 527 U.S. 1038, 119 S. Ct. 2399, 144 L. Ed. 2d 798 (1999) overruled in part on other grounds by Jay v. Commonwealth, 275 Va. 510, 659 S.E.2d 311, 2008 Va. LEXIS 53 (2008).

The death sentence was not excessive or disproportionate where the evidence established that, several months before killing his wife and son, the defendant began to make elaborate efforts to divert suspicion away from himself, that the defendant obtained the murder weapon several weeks in advance of the killings, that the defendant shot his wife three times in the head while she was sleeping and that his son's wounds resulted from an execution-style shooting. Bailey v. Commonwealth, 259 Va. 723, 529 S.E.2d 570, 2000 Va. LEXIS 59, cert. denied, 531 U.S. 995, 121 S. Ct. 488, 148 L. Ed. 2d 460 (2000).

Death sentence was not excessive or disproportionate to penalties imposed by other sentencing bodies in the Commonwealth for comparable or similar crimes, where the evidence showed that after robbing victim, the defendant repeatedly cut the front and rear of the victim's neck in a "sawing motion" with a pocket knife, while victim was concious and begging the defendant to stop attacking him, and that victim sustained a minimum of ten separate knife wounds to the neck, which were of a type usually associated with an attempted decapitation. Yarbrough v. Commonwealth, 262 Va. 388, 551 S.E.2d 306, 2001 Va. LEXIS 112 (2001), cert. denied, 535 U.S. 1060, 122 S. Ct. 1925, 152 L. Ed. 2d 832 (2002).

Where defendant, a prison inmate, was sentenced to death for participating in the fatal stabbing of another inmate, the death sentence was neither excessive nor disproportionate. Remington v. Commonwealth, 262 Va. 333, 551 S.E.2d 620, 2001 Va. LEXIS 107 (2001), cert. denied, 535 U.S. 1062, 122 S. Ct. 1928, 152 L. Ed. 2d 834 (2002).

Defendant's sentence of death was neither excessive nor disproportionate, and was not imposed under the influence of passion, prejudice or other arbitrary factor, where evidence showed that he violated a protective order, went to his estranged girlfriend's home, stabbed to death her daughter from a previous relationship, removed his biological daughter with the woman from the home, and then stabbed his daughter to death. Zirkle v. Commonwealth, 262 Va. 631, 553 S.E.2d 520, 2001 Va. LEXIS 125 (2001).

State supreme court found that the death penalty was not an excessive or disproportionate punishment for defendant who was convicted of killing a 79 year old woman who was stabbed five times in the neck and face, anally sodomized with her cane, and had the cane driven into her mouth. Jackson v. Commonwealth, 266 Va. 423, 587 S.E.2d 532, 2003 Va. LEXIS 101 (2003), cert. denied, 543 U.S. 842, 125 S. Ct. 281, 160 L. Ed. 2d 68 (2004).

In its review under subsection C of § 17.1-313, the court held that defendant's sentence of death was not imposed under the influence of passion, prejudice, or other arbitrary factors, and, after comparing the case with "similar cases" by focusing on instances where a victim was murdered during the commission of robbery or rape and the death penalty was imposed based upon the future dangerousness aggravating factor, it also determined that the sentence was not excessive or disproportionate to the penalty imposed in Virginia for capital murders comparable to defendant's murder of the victim. Jackson v. Commonwealth, 267 Va. 178, 590 S.E.2d 520, 2004 Va. LEXIS 8 (2004), cert. denied, 543 U.S. 891, 125 S. Ct. 168, 160 L. Ed. 2d 155 (2004).

Defendant's death sentence was neither excessive nor disproportionate to sentences imposed in similar capital murder cases; among other things, the prosecutor's statement that defendant could pick up a phone and order another murder did not directly suggest a connection between the jurors and defendant's future criminal activity. Teleguz v. Commonwealth, 273 Va. 458, 643 S.E.2d 708, 2007 Va. LEXIS 64 (2007), cert. denied, Teleguz v. Virginia, 522 U.S. 1191, 2008 U.S. LEXIS 1412, 128 S.Ct. 1228 (2008).

Death sentences imposed upon defendant for two murder convictions under subdivision 12 of § 18.2-31, were not influenced by passion, prejudice, or any other arbitrary factor, and were not excessive or disproportionate to the sentences of death imposed by other sentencing bodies in comparable cases with comparable defendants. Gray v. Commonwealth, 274 Va. 290, 645 S.E.2d 448, 2007 Va. LEXIS 94 (2007), cert. denied, 128 S. Ct. 1111, 2008 U.S. LEXIS 1072, 169 L. Ed. 2d 826 (U.S. 2008).

In accordance with subsection E of § 17.1-313, the appellate court reviewed similar cases in which a life sentence was imposed, and based on that review, determined that defendant's sentence was not excessive or disproportionate to sentences imposed in capital murder cases for comparable crimes. Morva v. Commonwealth, 278 Va. 329, 683 S.E.2d 553, 2009 Va. LEXIS 84 (2009), cert. denied, 131 S. Ct. 97, 178 L. Ed. 2d 61, 2010 U.S. LEXIS 5806 (U.S. 2010).

Defendant's death sentences, imposed upon his pleas of guilty to two charges of capital murder, were not excessive or disproportionate. The murders were both clearly premeditated and accomplished by means of ligature strangulation, a very deliberate and personal method of killing; they both involved taunting or torture indicative of a particularly high level of cruelty; and defendant was very clear that he had "no remorse for it, zero." Gleason v. Commonwealth, 284 Va. 166, 726 S.E.2d 351, 2012 Va. LEXIS 135 (2012).

Sentence held not excessive. — Insofar as it is possible to quantify "vileness" and "dangerousness" and to correlate the culpability of one criminal act resulting in death with that of another, sentence imposed upon defendant held not excessive or disproportionate to the penalty imposed in similar cases, considering both the crime and the defendant. Edmonds v. Commonwealth, 229 Va. 303, 329 S.E.2d 807, cert. denied, 474 U.S. 975, 106 S. Ct. 339, 88 L. Ed. 2d 324 (1985).

Where the defendant, implementing a carefully conceived plan, locked his victim in a small area, doused the area with a fluid that was more volatile than gasoline, and set the victim afire, this conduct revealed depravity of mind and fully warranted imposition of the death penalty. Payne v. Commonwealth, 233 Va. 460, 357 S.E.2d 500, cert. denied, 484 U.S. 933, 108 S. Ct. 308, 98 L. Ed. 2d 267 (1987).

Where defendant pled guilty to capital murder in commission of robbery, where defendant had expressed remorse and where defendant asserted that he had not intended to commit murder at onset of robbery and that multiple wounds were not involved in murder, death sentence was not excessive or disproportionate. Stout v. Commonwealth, 237 Va. 126, 376 S.E.2d 288, cert. denied, 492 U.S. 925, 109 S. Ct. 3263, 106 L. Ed. 2d 609 (1989).

The sentence of death imposed upon defendant was neither excessive nor disproportionate to the penalties imposed in similar cases where there were multiple victims and the deaths did not occur instantaneously as each victim suffered a great deal of pain in the interval before death. Each of the three victims suffered multiple fractures and penetrations of skull as a result of having been hit repeatedly with a crowbar. Davidson v. Commonwealth, 244 Va. 129, 419 S.E.2d 656, cert. denied, 506 U.S. 959, 113 S. Ct. 423, 121 L. Ed. 2d 345 (1992).

The sentence of death was not excessive or disproportionate to sentences generally imposed in the commonwealth for capital murders comparable to that committed by the defendant where the defendant had inflicted 21 stab wounds on a 63-year-old quadriplegic while in the course of committing a robbery. Overton v. Commonwealth, 260 Va. 599, 539 S.E.2d 421, 2000 Va. LEXIS 140 (2000), cert. dismissed, 532 U.S. 968, 121 S. Ct. 1651, 149 L. Ed. 2d 464 (2001).

The death sentence was neither excessive nor disproportionate to penalties imposed by other sentencing bodies in the commonwealth for comparable crimes, considering both the crime and the defendant, where the record showed that the defendant planned to commit the offense of robbery and murdered the victim for the sole reason of eliminating any witness to the robbery, the multiple stab wounds inflicted on the victim reflected an escalation of the violent and dangerous criminal activity detailed in the defendant's prior criminal record, which included numerous felony convictions, including a conviction for attempted robbery and multiple convictions on burglary charges, and the defendant had committed several of these prior crimes while on supervised probation or parole, which was further evidence of his continuing failure to refrain from serious criminal conduct. Lovitt v. Commonwealth, 260 Va. 497, 537 S.E.2d 866, 2000 Va. LEXIS 149 (2000), cert. denied, 534 U.S. 815, 122 S. Ct. 41, 151 L. Ed. 2d 14 (2001).

A defendant's death sentence was not excessive when considered in the light of other cases in which a person was murdered during the commission of rape and/or forcible sodomy, and the death penalty was imposed upon both the future dangerousness and vileness predicates. The defendant had broken into and entered the home of his elderly mother-in-law, raped and sodomized her and killed her by breaking her ribs in 24 places and rupturing her heart. The defendant also had a lengthy criminal record and had repeatedly raped a former girlfriend. Burns v. Commonwealth, 261 Va. 307, 541 S.E.2d 872, 2001 Va. LEXIS 29 (2001), cert. denied, 534 U.S. 1043, 122 S. Ct. 621, 151 L. Ed. 2d 542 (2001) and overruled in part on other grounds by Jay v. Commonwealth, 275 Va. 510, 659 S.E.2d 311, 2008 Va. LEXIS 53 (2008).

Murder for hire was shown to have been particularly heinous in defendant's case; therefore, the jury's decision that a death sentence was called for was neither provoked by passion or prejudice nor was it disproportionate to sentences generally imposed in Virginia. Wolfe v. Commonwealth, 265 Va. 193, 576 S.E.2d 471, 2003 Va. LEXIS 32, cert. denied, 540 U.S. 1019, 124 S. Ct. 566, 157 L. Ed. 2d 434 (2003).

Death sentence was neither excessive nor disproportionate when compared to similar cases despite defendant's claim that the trial court failed to adequately consider his history of mental health problems and failure to receive adequate treatment when in state custody as a juvenile since, inter alia, the expert called by defendant did not testify that defendant lacked the ability to appreciate the criminality of his conduct or that his condition significantly impairs his ability to conform his conduct to the requirements of the law. Powell v. Commonwealth, 267 Va. 107, 590 S.E.2d 537, 2004 Va. LEXIS 6, cert. denied, — U.S. —, 125 S. Ct. 86, 160 L. Ed. 2d 157 (2004).

Death sentence was neither excessive nor disproportionate where the record showed, inter alia, that defendant committed five rapes within a period of seven months, that he stabbed one of the victims, and that he inflicted multiple stab wounds on the victim in the instant case indicating the vileness of the murder and representing the culmination of a pattern of escalating violence. Johnson v. Commonwealth, 267 Va. 53, 591 S.E.2d 47, 2004 Va. LEXIS 7 (2004), vacated and remanded, 125 S.Ct. 1589, 161 L.Ed.2d 270, 2005 U.S. LEXIS 2208, for further consideration in light of Roper v. Simmons, 544 U.S. 551, 161 L.Ed.2d 1, 125 S.Ct. 1183 (2005).

Defendant's sentence was not found to have been imposed under the influence of passion, prejudice, or any other arbitrary factor, nor was it excessive or disproportionate to the penalty imposed in similar cases, considering both the crime and the defendant; although defendant had a long career as a soldier and a non-commissioned officer in the U.S. Army, there was also evidence that he had an illicit relationship although he was married for 23 years, that he squandered hundreds of thousands of dollars on the relationship, which was with a prostitute, and that he brutally murdered two innocent people with no remorse. Elliott v. Commonwealth, 267 Va. 396, 593 S.E.2d 270, 2004 Va. LEXIS 44 (2004), cert. denied, 543 U.S. 1081, 125 S. Ct. 875, 160 L. Ed. 2d 825 (2005) and overruled in part on other grounds by Jay v. Commonwealth, 275 Va. 510, 659 S.E.2d 311, 2008 Va. LEXIS 53 (2008).

Death penalty was not an excessive or a disproportionate penalty in defendant's capital murder case, with evidence of ten murders and six malicious woundings; similarly, the evidence presented on the terrorism count independently supported the imposition of the death penalty. Defendant's crimes could not be compared to any other case in the Commonwealth, and the evidence of vileness and future dangerousness in support of the jury's verdict justified its sanction of death. Muhammad v. Commonwealth, 269 Va. 451, 611 S.E.2d 537, 2005 Va. LEXIS 39 (2005), cert. denied, 547 U.S. 1136, 126 S. Ct. 2035, 164 L. Ed. 2d 794 (2006), and overruled in part on other grounds by Jay v. Commonwealth, 275 Va. 510, 659 S.E.2d 311, 2008 Va. LEXIS 53 (2008).

CHAPTER 8.

VIRGINIA CRIMINAL SENTENCING COMMISSION.

Section
17.1-805. Adoption of initial discretionary sentencing guideline midpoints.

§ 17.1-805. Adoption of initial discretionary sentencing guideline midpoints.

A. The Commission shall adopt an initial set of discretionary felony sentencing guidelines which shall become effective on January 1, 1995. The initial recommended sentencing range for each felony offense shall be determined first, by computing the actual time-served distribution for similarly situated offenders, in terms of their conviction offense and prior criminal history, released from incarceration during the base period of calendar years 1988 through 1992, increased by 13.4 percent, and second, by eliminating from this range the upper and lower quartiles. The midpoint of each initial recommended sentencing range shall be the median time served for the middle two quartiles and subject to the following additional enhancements:

1. The midpoint of the initial recommended sentencing range for first degree murder, second degree murder, rape in violation of § 18.2-61, forcible sodomy, object sexual penetration, and aggravated sexual battery, shall be further increased by (i) 125 percent in cases in which the defendant has no previous conviction of a violent felony offense; (ii) 300 percent in cases in which the defendant has previously been convicted of a violent felony offense punishable by a maximum punishment of less than 40 years; or (iii) 500 percent in cases in which the defendant has previously been convicted of a violent felony offense punishable by a maximum punishment of 40 years or more, except that the recommended sentence for a defendant convicted of first degree murder who has previously been convicted of a violent felony offense punishable by a maximum term of imprisonment of 40 years or more shall be imprisonment for life;

2. The midpoint of the initial recommended sentencing range for voluntary manslaughter, robbery, aggravated malicious wounding, malicious wounding, and any burglary of a dwelling house or statu-

tory burglary of a dwelling house or any burglary committed while armed with a deadly weapon or any statutory burglary committed while armed with a deadly weapon shall be further increased by (i) 100 percent in cases in which the defendant has no previous conviction of a violent felony offense, (ii) 300 percent in cases in which the defendant has previously been convicted of a violent felony offense punishable by a maximum term of imprisonment of less than 40 years, or (iii) 500 percent in cases in which the defendant has previously been convicted of a violent felony offense punishable by a maximum term of imprisonment of 40 years or more;

3. The midpoint of the initial recommended sentencing range for manufacturing, selling, giving or distributing, or possessing with the intent to manufacture, sell, give or distribute a Schedule I or II controlled substance shall be increased by (i) 200 percent in cases in which the defendant has previously been convicted of a violent felony offense punishable by a maximum punishment of less than 40 years or (ii) 400 percent in cases in which the defendant has previously been convicted of a violent felony offense punishable by a maximum term of imprisonment of 40 years or more; and

4. The midpoint of the initial recommended sentencing range for felony offenses not specified in subdivision 1, 2, or 3 shall be increased by 100 percent in cases in which the defendant has previously been convicted of a violent felony offense punishable by a maximum punishment of less than 40 years, and by 300 percent in cases in which the defendant has previously been convicted of a violent felony offense punishable by a maximum term of imprisonment of 40 years or more.

B. For purposes of this chapter, previous convictions shall include prior adult convictions and juvenile convictions and adjudications of delinquency based on an offense which would have been at the time of conviction a felony if committed by an adult under the laws of any state, the District of Columbia, the United States or its territories.

C. For purposes of this chapter, violent felony offenses shall include any felony violation of § 16.1-253.2; solicitation to commit murder under § 18.2-29; any violation of § 18.2-31, 18.2-32, 18.2-32.1, 18.2-32.2, 18.2-33, or 18.2-35; any violation of subsection B of § 18.2-36.1; any violation of § 18.2-40 or 18.2-41; any violation of clause (c)(i) or (ii) of subsection B of § 18.2-46.3; any violation of § 18.2-46.5, 18.2-46.6, or 18.2-46.7; any Class 5 felony violation of § 18.2-47; any felony violation of § 18.2-48, 18.2-48.1, or 18.2-49; any violation of § 18.2-51, 18.2-51.1, 18.2-51.2, 18.2-51.3, 18.2-51.4, 18.2-51.6, 18.2-52, 18.2-52.1, 18.2-53, 18.2-53.1, 18.2-54.1, 18.2-54.2, or 18.2-55; any violation of subsection B of § 18.2-57; any felony violation of § 18.2-57.2; any violation of § 18.2-58 or 18.2-58.1; any felony violation of § 18.2-60.1, 18.2-60.3, or 18.2-60.4; any violation of § 18.2-61, 18.2-64.1, 18.2-67.1, 18.2-67.2, former § 18.2-67.2:1, 18.2-67.3, 18.2-67.5, or 18.2-

67.5:1 involving a third conviction of either sexual battery in violation of § 18.2-67.4 or attempted sexual battery in violation of subsection C of § 18.2-67.5; any Class 4 felony violation of § 18.2-63; any violation of subsection A of § 18.2-67.4:1; any violation of subsection A of § 18.2-77; any Class 3 felony violation of § 18.2-79; any Class 3 felony violation of § 18.2-80; any violation of § 18.2-85, 18.2-89, 18.2-90, 18.2-91, 18.2-92, or 18.2-93; any felony violation of § 18.2-152.7; any Class 4 felony violation of § 18.2-153; any Class 4 felony violation of § 18.2-154; any Class 4 felony violation of § 18.2-155; any felony violation of § 18.2-162; any violation of § 18.2-279 involving an occupied dwelling; any felony violation of subsection A or B of § 18.2-280; any violation of § 18.2-281; any felony violation of subsection A of § 18.2-282; any felony violation of § 18.2-282.1; any violation of § 18.2-286.1, 18.2-287.2, 18.2-289, or 18.2-290; any violation of subsection A of § 18.2-300; any felony violation of subsection C of § 18.2-308.1 or 18.2-308.2; any violation of § 18.2-308.2:1 or subsection M or N of § 18.2-308.2:2; any violation of § 18.2-308.3 or 18.2-312; any violation of subdivision (2) or (3) of § 18.2-355; any violation of former § 18.2-358; any violation of subsection B of § 18.2-361; any violation of subsection B of § 18.2-366; any violation of § 18.2-368, 18.2-370, or 18.2-370.1; any violation of subsection A of § 18.2-371.1; any felony violation of § 18.2-369 resulting in serious bodily injury or disease; any violation of § 18.2-374.1; any felony violation of § 18.2-374.1:1; any violation of § 18.2-374.3 or 18.2-374.4; any second or subsequent offense under §§ 18.2-379 and 18.2-381; any felony violation of § 18.2-405 or 18.2-406; any violation of § 18.2-408, 18.2-413, 18.2-414, 18.2-423, 18.2-423.01, 18.2-423.1, 18.2-423.2, or 18.2-433.2; any felony violation of § 18.2-460, 18.2-474.1, or 18.2-477.1; any violation of § 18.2-477, 18.2-478, 18.2-480, 18.2-481, or 18.2-485; any violation of § 37.2-917; any violation of § 52-48; any violation of § 53.1-203; or any conspiracy or attempt to commit any offense specified in this subsection, and any substantially similar offense under the laws of any state, the District of Columbia, the United States or its territories.

History.

1994, 2nd Sp. Sess., cc. 1, 2, § 17-237; 1995, c. 482; 1998, cc. 277, 872; 1999, c. 349; 2004, cc. 459, 866; 2005, c. 631; 2011, c. 282; 2013, cc. 424, 647.

Cross references.

As to presumption of no bail for illegal aliens charged with certain crimes, see § 19.2-120.1.

Editor's note.

Acts 2011, c. 282, cl. 2, provides: "That the provisions of this act may result in a net increase in periods of imprisonment or commitment. Pursuant to § 30-19.1:4, the estimated amount of the necessary appropriation is $0 for periods of imprisonment in state adult correctional facilities and cannot be determined for periods of commitment to the custody of the Department of Juvenile Justice."

Acts 2013, cc. 424 and 647, cl. 2 provides: "That the provisions of this act may result in a net increase in periods of imprisonment or commitment. Pursuant to § 30-19.1:4, the estimated amount of the necessary appropriation cannot be determined for periods of imprisonment in state adult correctional facilities; therefore, Chapter 3 of the Acts of Assembly of 2012, Special Session I, requires the Virginia Criminal Sentencing Commission to assign a minimum fiscal impact of $50,000. Pursuant to § 30-19.1:4, the estimated amount of the necessary appropriation cannot be determined for periods of commitment to the custody of the Department of Juvenile Justice."

The 2011 amendments.

The 2011 amendment by c. 282 substituted "any felony violation of subsection C of § 18.2-308.1 or 18.2-308.2" for "any felony violation of §§ 18.2-308.1 and 18.2-308.2" in subsection C.

The 2013 amendments.

The 2013 amendments by cc. 424 and 647 are nearly identical, and rewrote subsection C.

Michie's Jurisprudence.

For related discussion, see 19 M.J. Warrants, § 6; 20 M.J. Weapons, § 4.1.

CASE NOTES

Prior conviction was not a violent felony. — Because of his prior conviction in the military for housebreaking the defendant was guilty of possession of a firearm by a convicted felon; however, the trial court improperly sentenced the defendant because the crime was not a violent felony. Turner v. Commonwealth, 38 Va. App. 851, 568 S.E.2d 468, 2002 Va. App. LEXIS 525 (2002).

Prior conviction was a violent felony. — Defendant's sentence to a mandatory five-year term under § 18.2-308.2 for possession of a firearm by a convicted felon, was affirmed as he had been convicted of possessing a firearm after conviction of a felony in violation of § 18.2-308.2 when he was 14, which would have been classified as a violent felony under subsections B and C of § 17.1-805, if he had been tried as an adult; defendant's argument that his juvenile conviction could not serve as the necessary predicate act for § 18.2-308.2 because he was not convicted under an indictment was rejected, and § 19.2-217, relied upon by defendant, was inapplicable. Parks v. Commonwealth, No. 2780-02-1, 2003 Va. App. LEXIS 385 (Ct. of Appeals July 8, 2003).

Evidence was sufficient to establish that defendant possessed a firearm, and since defendant did not dispute that he was previously convicted of a violent felony, the supreme court further held that the jury verdict convicting defendant of possession of a firearm by a convicted felon under subsection A of § 18.2-308.2 was not plainly wrong. When police arrived at defendant's residence, defendant was alone in the bedroom in which the firearm was found, and the bedroom contained defendant's clothes and personal effects. Rawls v. Commonwealth, 272 Va. 334, 634 S.E.2d 697, 2006 Va. LEXIS 77 (2006).

Jury was required to fix defendant's sentence for possession of a firearm by a convicted felon in violation of subsection A of § 18.2-308.2 to a mandatory sentence of five years of imprisonment as: (1) defendant possessed a handgun found in a pillowcase located at defendant's feet in a car in which defendant was a passenger; and (2) defendant had been previously convicted of possession of a firearm by a felon, which was classified as a violent felony under § 17.1-805. Lee v. Commonwealth, 2008 Va. App. LEXIS 324 (July 15, 2008).

Juvenile and domestic relations district court records received under § 8.01-389 showed that defendant committed a prior violent felony as the petition alleged a violation of § 18.2-91, which was a violent felony under § 17.1-805, and the Record of Proceedings stated that defendant was convicted and referenced the only pending case. Preston v. Commonwealth, 2009 Va. App. LEXIS 603 (Nov. 12, 2009).

Violent felony not sufficiently proven. — As the Commonwealth failed to prove that appellant juvenile was previously adjudicated delinquent of an act that would have been a violent felony under subsection C of § 17.1-805 if committed by an adult, his conviction for possession of a firearm, in violation of subsection A of § 18.2-308.2, could not stand; the Commonwealth's attempt to prove a prior breaking and entering conviction, in violation of § 18.2-91, was insufficient where the nature of the delinquent act

for which the juvenile was adjudicated was unclear by the document in support of that conviction. Preston v. Commonwealth, 281 Va. 52, 704 S.E.2d 127, 2011 Va. LEXIS 23 (2011).

Applied in Jackson v. Commonwealth, No. 0388-99-2, 2000 Va. App. LEXIS 398 (Ct. of Appeals May 23, 2000); Conkling v. Commonwealth, 45 Va. App. 518, 612 S.E.2d 235, 2005 Va. App. LEXIS 173 (2005).

TITLE 18.2.

CRIMES AND OFFENSES GENERALLY.

CHAPTER 1.

IN GENERAL.

Article 1. Transition Provisions.

Article 2. Construction and Definitions.

Article 3. Classification of Criminal Offenses and Punishment Therefor.

ARTICLE 1.

TRANSITION PROVISIONS.

§ 18.2-1. Repealing clause.

All acts and parts of acts, all sections of this Code, and all provisions of municipal charters, inconsistent with the provisions of this title, are, except as herein otherwise provided, repealed to the extent of such inconsistency.

History.
1975, cc. 14, 15.

Editor's note.
At its special session of 1971 the General Assembly directed the Code Commission to make a thorough study of the criminal laws of the State and make recommendations for the review and recodification of all statutes of the State relating to crime and criminal procedure. In November of 1973 the Commission sent to the Governor and General Assembly its report containing a proposed revision of Title 18.1, which was published as House Document 10 of the 1974 Session. This report contains revisor's notes and other explanatory matter, which, while valuable, are too lengthy for inclusion here. The proposed revision of Title 18.1 was not adopted by the 1974 General Assembly, but was carried over to the 1975 Session, when it was adopted, with modifications, as Chapters 14 and 15 of the Acts of 1975, the two acts being substantially identical. Effective Oct. 1, 1975, the 1975 acts repeal Title 18.1 of the Code and enact in lieu thereof a new Title 18.2. In addition to its revision by Chapters 14 and 15, former Title 18.1 was also amended by certain other acts passed at the 1975 Session. As required by § 30-152, the Code Commission has incorporated the majority of these amendments into new Title 18.2.

Many of the cases cited in the notes under the various sections of this title were decided under corresponding provisions of former Title 18.1 or prior law.

Law Review.
For survey of the Virginia criminal law for the year 1961-1962, see 48 Va. L. Rev. 1342 (1962). For case note on the burden of proof as to perpetrators of crimes, see 19 Wash. & Lee L. Rev. 262 (1962). For survey of Virginia criminal law for the year 1963-1964, see 50 Va. L. Rev. 1287 (1964); for the year 1964-1965, see 51 Va. L. Rev. 1409 (1965); for survey of Virginia criminal law and procedure for the year 1967-1968, see 54 Va. L. Rev. 1579 (1968); for the year 1968-1969, see 55 Va. L. Rev. 1581 (1969). For survey of Virginia law on evidence for the year 1967-1968, see 54 Va. L. Rev. 1611 (1968).

Research references.
Stanley S. Arkin, Business Crime: Criminal Liability of the Business Community (Matthew Bender)

§ 18.2-2. Effect of repeal of Title 18.1 and enactment of this title.

The repeal of Title 18.1, effective as of October 1, 1975, shall not affect any act or offense done or committed, or any penalty or forfeiture incurred, or any right established, accrued or accruing on or before such date, or any prosecution, suit or action pending on that day. Except as herein otherwise provided, neither the repeal of Title 18.1 nor the enactment of this title shall apply to offenses committed prior to October 1, 1975, and prosecutions for such offenses shall be governed by the prior law, which is continued in effect for that purpose. For the purposes of this section, an offense was committed prior to October 1, 1975, if any of the essential elements of the offense occurred prior thereto.

History.
1975, cc. 14, 15.

§ 18.2-3. Certain notices, recognizances and processes validated.

Any notice given, recognizance taken, or process or writ issued before October 1, 1975, shall be valid although given, taken or to be returned to a day after such date, in like manner as if this title had been effective before the same was given, taken or issued.

History.
1975, cc. 14, 15.

§ 18.2-4. References to former sections, articles and chapters of Title 18.1 and others.

Whenever in this title any of the conditions, requirements, provisions or contents of any section, article or chapter of Title 18.1 or any other title of this Code as such titles existed prior to October 1, 1975, are transferred in the same or in modified form to a new section, article or chapter of this title or any other title of this Code and whenever any such former section, article or chapter is given a new number in this or any other title, all references to any such former section, article or chapter of Title 18.1 or such other title appearing elsewhere in this Code than in this title shall be construed to apply to the new or renumbered section, article or chapter containing such conditions, requirements, provisions or contents or portions thereof.

History.
1975, cc. 14, 15.

ARTICLE 2.

CONSTRUCTION AND DEFINITIONS.

§ 18.2-5. Repealed by Acts 2005, c. 839, cl. 10, effective October 1, 2005.

§ 18.2-6. Meaning of certain terms.

As used in this title:

The word *"court,"* unless otherwise clearly indicated by the context in which it appears, shall mean and include any court vested with appropriate jurisdiction under the Constitution and laws of this Commonwealth.

The word *"judge,"* unless otherwise clearly indicated by the context in which it appears, shall mean and include any judge, associate judge or substitute judge, or police justice, of any court.

The words *"motor vehicle," "semitrailer," "trailer"* and *"vehicle"* shall have the respective meanings assigned to them by § 46.2-100.

History.

Code 1950, § 18.1-5; 1960, c. 358; 1975, cc. 14, 15.

§ 18.2-7. Criminal act not to merge civil remedy.

The commission of a crime shall not stay or merge any civil remedy.

History.

Code 1950, § 18.1-7; 1960, c. 358; 1975, cc. 14, 15.

Michie's Jurisprudence.

For related discussion, see 5B M.J. Criminal Procedure, § 11.

ARTICLE 3.

CLASSIFICATION OF CRIMINAL OFFENSES AND PUNISHMENT THEREFOR.

§ 18.2-8. Felonies, misdemeanors and traffic infractions defined.

Offenses are either felonies or misdemeanors. Such offenses as are punishable with death or confinement in a state correctional facility are felonies; all other offenses are misdemeanors. Traffic infractions are violations of public order as defined in § 46.2-100 and not deemed to be criminal in nature.

History.

Code 1950, § 18.1-6; 1960, c. 358; 1975, cc. 14, 15; 1977, c. 585.

Law Review.

For comment, "Right to Court-Appointed Counsel for Misdemeanants in Virginia," see 4 U. Rich. L. Rev. 306 (1970). For article, "Trial by Jury and Speedy Justice," see 28 Wash. & Lee L. Rev. 309 (1971). For comment on rights of the convicted felon on parole, see 13 U. Rich. L. Rev. 367 (1979). For article, "Appeal De Novo in Virginia: An Examination of Its Present Utility," see 42 Wash. & Lee L. Rev. 1149 (1985). For article, "Preclusion of Evidence of Criminal Conviction in Civil Action Arising from the Same Incident," see 10 G.M.U. L. Rev. 107 (1988).

Research references.

Cipes, Bernstein, and Hall, Criminal Defense Techniques (Matthew Bender).

Criminal Law Advocacy Reporter (Matthew Bender).

Erickson, Neighbors, and George, United States Supreme Court Cases and Comments: Criminal Law and Procedure (Matthew Bender).

Kadish, Brofman, Criminal Law Advocacy (Matthew Bender).

McCloskey and Schoenberg, Criminal Law Deskbook (Matthew Bender)

Rudstein, Erlinder, and Thomas, Criminal Constitutional Law (Matthew Bender).

Michie's Jurisprudence.

For related discussion, see 2A M.J. Assault and Battery, § 10; 5B M.J. Criminal Procedure, § 3; 21A M.J. Words and Phrases.

CASE NOTES

The same act cannot at the same time constitute a felony and a misdemeanor. They cannot coexist as the result of one and the same transaction. The crime must be one or the other, not both, or either. Benton v. Commonwealth, 89 Va. 570, 16 S.E. 725 (1893).

And the grade of the offense is fixed by the punishment provided by statute. Bell v. Commonwealth, 167 Va. 526, 189 S.E. 441 (1937).

For the legislature never intended to leave the grade of any offense to the discretion of a jury. Benton v. Commonwealth, 89 Va. 570, 16 S.E. 725 (1893).

A felony is such an offense as may be (not must be) punished by death or confinement in the penitentiary (now state correctional facility). Canada v. Commonwealth, 63 Va. (22 Gratt.) 899 (1872); Benton v. Commonwealth, 89 Va. 570, 16 S.E. 725 (1893); Forbes v. Commonwealth, 90 Va. 550, 19 S.E. 164 (1894); Benton v. Commonwealth, 91 Va. 782, 21 S.E. 495 (1895); Fletcher v. Commonwealth, 163 Va. 1007, 175 S.E. 895 (1934).

Notwithstanding lesser jury verdict. — Where the punishment prescribed may be death or confinement in the penitentiary (now state correctional facility), it is a felony notwithstanding that the jury actually imposes a less penalty, by virtue of a discretion allowed them. Quillin v. Commonwealth, 105 Va. 874, 54 S.E. 333 (1906). See Fletcher v. Commonwealth, 163 Va. 1007, 175 S.E. 895 (1934).

Whatever is not a felony is a misdemeanor. Commonwealth v. Callaghan, 4 Va. (2 Va. Cas.) 460 (1825).

All offenses which cannot be punished with death or confinement in the penitentiary (now state correctional facility) are misdemeanors. Trimble v. Commonwealth, 4 Va. (2 Va. Cas.) 143 (1818); Benton v. Commonwealth, 89 Va. 570, 16 S.E. 725 (1893); Forbes v. Commonwealth, 90 Va. 550, 19 S.E. 164 (1894); Benton v. Commonwealth, 91 Va. 782, 21 S.E. 495 (1895).

There is no distinction between "capital cases" and "felonies" as exists in some other jurisdictions or as existed at common law. This section classifies offenses as either felonies or misdemeanors. Such offenses as are punishable with death or confinement in the penitentiary (now state correctional facility) are felonies; all other offenses are misdemeanors. Roach v. Commonwealth, 157 Va. 954, 162 S.E. 50 (1932).

The committing magistrate does not by his warrant fix the grade of the offense for which the accused is tried. Hawley v. Commonwealth, 75 Va. 847 (1880).

In case of doubt, court will construe crime as misdemeanor. — This section defines felonies to be "such offenses as are punishable with death or confinement in the penitentiary (now state correctional facility), all other offenses are misdemeanors." There is nothing in the statute which prohibits imprisonment in jail for a longer period than one year. Where a crime may be construed either a misdemeanor or a felony, the court will construe it a misdemeanor, thus applying the well-recognized principle that a penal statute must be construed strictly in favor of the accused. Young v. Commonwealth, 155 Va. 1152, 156 S.E. 565 (1931).

Forgery. — This section makes clear that whether forgery is a felony or is a misdemeanor is determined by the sentence lawfully possible under former § 18.1-96 (now § 18.2-172) and does not depend upon the sentence actually imposed or the nature of the offense. United States v. Johnson, 497 F.2d 548 (4th Cir. 1974).

Applied in Turner v. Commonwealth, 38 Va. App. 851, 568 S.E.2d 468, 2002 Va. App. LEXIS 525 (2002).

OPINIONS OF THE ATTORNEY GENERAL

Trial court may not order a person convicted of felony to serve any confinement in jail on weekends or nonconsecutive days. — The plain language of § 53.1-131.1, limits the court's authority to convictions for misdemeanors, traffic offenses and violations of Chapter 5 (§ 20-61 et seq.) Title 20. See opinion of Attorney General to The Honorable Harvey L. Bryant, Commonwealth's Attorney, City of Virginia Beach, 12-062, 2012 Va. AG LEXIS 30 (7/20/2012).

§ 18.2-9. Classification of criminal offenses.

(1) Felonies are classified, for the purposes of punishment and sentencing, into six classes:
  (a) Class 1 felony
  (b) Class 2 felony
  (c) Class 3 felony
  (d) Class 4 felony
  (e) Class 5 felony
  (f) Class 6 felony.

(2) Misdemeanors are classified, for the purposes of punishment and sentencing, into four classes:
  (a) Class 1 misdemeanor
  (b) Class 2 misdemeanor
  (c) Class 3 misdemeanor
  (d) Class 4 misdemeanor.

History.
1975, cc. 14, 15.

Law Review.
For survey of Virginia law on criminal law for the year 1974-1975, see 61 Va. L. Rev. 1697 (1975). For comment on sentencing in criminal cases, see 13 U. Rich. L. Rev. 899 (1979).

Michie's Jurisprudence.
For related discussion, see 5B M.J. Criminal Procedure, § 3.

CASE NOTES

Applied in Turner v. Commonwealth, 38 Va. App. 851, 568 S.E.2d 468, 2002 Va. App. LEXIS 525 (2002).

§ 18.2-10. Punishment for conviction of felony; penalty.

The authorized punishments for conviction of a felony are:
(a) For Class 1 felonies, death, if the person so convicted was 18 years of age or older at the time of the offense and is not determined to be mentally retarded pursuant to § 19.2-264.3:1.1, or imprisonment for life and, subject to subdivision (g), a fine of not more than $100,000. If the person was under 18 years of age at the time of the offense or is determined to be mentally retarded pursuant to § 19.2-264.3:1.1, the punishment shall be imprisonment for life and, subject to subdivision (g), a fine of not more than $100,000.
(b) For Class 2 felonies, imprisonment for life or for any term not less than 20 years and, subject to subdivision (g), a fine of not more than $100,000.
(c) For Class 3 felonies, a term of imprisonment of not less than five years nor more than 20 years and, subject to subdivision (g), a fine of not more than $100,000.
(d) For Class 4 felonies, a term of imprisonment of not less than two years nor more than 10 years and, subject to subdivision (g), a fine of not more than $100,000.
(e) For Class 5 felonies, a term of imprisonment of not less than one year nor more than 10 years, or in the discretion of the jury or the court trying the case without a jury, confinement in jail for not more than 12 months and a fine of not more than $2,500, either or both.
(f) For Class 6 felonies, a term of imprisonment of not less than one year nor more than five years, or in the discretion of the jury or the court trying the case without a jury, confinement in jail for not more than 12 months and a fine of not more than $2,500, either or both.
(g) Except as specifically authorized in subdivision (e) or (f), or in Class 1 felonies for which a sentence of death is imposed, the court shall impose either a sentence of imprisonment together with a fine, or imprisonment only. However, if the defendant is not a natural person, the court shall impose only a fine.

For any felony offense committed (i) on or after January 1, 1995, the court may, and (ii) on or after July 1, 2000, shall, except in cases in which the court orders a suspended term of confinement of at least six months, impose an additional term of not less than six months nor more than three years, which shall be suspended conditioned upon successful completion of a period of post-release supervision pursuant to § 19.2-295.2 and compliance with such other terms as the sentencing court may require. However, such additional term may only be imposed when the sentence includes an active term of incarceration in a correctional facility.

For a felony offense prohibiting proximity to children as described in subsection A of § 18.2-370.2, the sentencing court is authorized to impose the punishment set forth in that section in addition to any other penalty provided by law.

History.
1975, cc. 14, 15; 1977, c. 492; 1990, c. 788; 1991, c. 7; 1994, 2nd Sp. Sess., cc. 1, 2; 1995, c. 427; 2000, cc. 361, 767, 770; 2003, cc. 1031, 1040; 2006, cc. 36, 733; 2008, c. 579.

Cross references.
As to the trial of capital cases, see § 19.2-264.2 et seq.

Editor's note.
Acts 1975, cc. 14 and 15, cl. 4 provides: "All acts of the General Assembly of Virginia in its Session of nineteen hundred seventy-five, which provide for punishment by class instead of a specific penalty shall be deemed to be incorporated by reference to §§ 18.2-10 and 18.2-11 of this act, which will become effective Oct. one, nineteen hundred seventy-five."

Acts 2008, c. 579, cl. 2 provides: "That the provisions of this act may result in a net increase in periods of imprisonment or commitment. Pursuant to § 30-19.1:4, the estimated amount of the necessary appropriation is cannot be determined for periods of imprisonment in state adult correctional facilities and $0 for periods of commitment to the custody of the Department of Juvenile Justice."

The 2008 amendments.
The 2008 amendment by c. 579 deleted "subsection B of" preceding "that section in" near the middle of the last paragraph.

Law Review.
For comment on the constitutional parameters for capital punishment, see 11 U. Rich. L. Rev. 101 (1976). For survey of Virginia criminal law for the year 1975-1976, see 62 Va. L. Rev. 1400 (1976). For survey of Virginia criminal procedure for the year 1976-1977, see 63 Va. L. Rev. 1408 (1977). For survey of Virginia criminal law

for the year 1978-1979, see 66 Va. L. Rev. 241 (1980). For article discussing the legislative history of sexual assault law reform in Virginia, see 68 Va. L. Rev. 459 (1982). For note, "Predicate Offenses for First Degree Felony Murder in Virginia," see 57 Wash. & Lee L. Rev. 561 (2000). For 2000 survey of Virginia criminal law and procedure, see 34 U. Rich. L. Rev. 749 (2000). For 2006 survey article, "Family and Juvenile Law," see 41 U. Rich. L. Rev. 151 (2006).

Michie's Jurisprudence.

For related discussion, see 3A M.J. Burglary and Housebreaking, § 21; 4A M.J. Conspiracy, § 4.1; 5B M.J. Criminal Procedure, §§ 3, 80; 8B M.J. Forgery, § 25; 9B M.J. Homicide, §§ 37, 133, 135, 136; 12A M.J. Lotteries, § 4; 12B M.J. Mayhem, §§ 2, 11; 15 M.J. Rape, §§ 3, 27.

CASE NOTES

Constitutionality of death penalty statutes. — The death penalty statute, set out in Article 4.1 of Chapter 15 of Title 19.2, is not facially unconstitutional under the Eighth and Fourteenth Amendments. Smith v. Commonwealth, 219 Va. 455, 248 S.E.2d 135 (1978), cert. denied, 441 U.S. 967, 99 S. Ct. 2419, 60 L. Ed. 2d 1074 (1979), aff'd, 477 U.S. 527, 106 S. Ct. 2661, 91 L. Ed. 2d 434 (1986).

Construction. — Fine provisions of subsection C of § 18.2-270 and subdivision (f) of § 18.2-10 directly conflict with each other. Because the provisions cannot be harmonized, the more specific statute, subsection C of § 18.2-270, prevails. Neria v. Commonwealth, — Va. App. —, — S.E.2d —, 2009 Va. App. LEXIS 136 (Mar. 24, 2009).

The effect of a commutation was to substitute a sentence of life imprisonment for the death penalty, a substitution the Governor was empowered to make without the defendant's consent. Lewis v. Commonwealth, 218 Va. 31, 235 S.E.2d 320 (1977).

And substituted penalty is only sentence considered on appeal. — After commutation of a sentence of death, the penalty substituted therefor is the only sentence to be considered on appeal. In such circumstances, the defendant's status is to be viewed as though the substituted sentence, and not the allegedly invalid death penalty, had been imposed originally. Lewis v. Commonwealth, 218 Va. 31, 235 S.E.2d 320 (1977).

Thus, constitutionality of death penalty is rendered moot. — Where a life term is substituted validly by commutation for a viable sentence of death, the conclusion is inescapable that the question of the constitutionality of the death penalty has been rendered moot. Lewis v. Commonwealth, 218 Va. 31, 235 S.E.2d 320 (1977).

Death penalty availability. — State supreme court granted the petition for writ of mandamus filed by the Commonwealth Attorney, as the trial court did not have the discretion to prohibit the Commonwealth Attorney from seeking the death penalty; the Commonwealth Attorney was entitled to seek that penalty pursuant to statutory law and the trial court erred by exercising an executive function in determining that the Commonwealth Attorney was prohibited from seeking it in defendant's case where defendant was charged with capital murder pursuant to § 18.2-31. In re Horan, 271 Va. 258, 634 S.E.2d 675, 2006 Va. LEXIS 23 (2006).

Capital murder verdict form must allow for life sentence and fine. — Subsection (g) and § 19.2-264.4 are in conflict; this section, the statute that prescribes the punishment for capital murder, is the more specific of the two and, accordingly, it must prevail; thus, at a minimum, a jury must receive a verdict form that, in addition to addressing the imposition of a sentence of death and the imposition of a sentence of life imprisonment, also allows the jury to impose a sentence of life imprisonment and a fine of up to $ 100,000. Powell v. Commonwealth, 261 Va. 512, 552 S.E.2d 344, 2001 Va. LEXIS 86 (2001).

Imposition of post-release terms of suspended incarceration and supervision. — The imposition of post-release terms of suspended incarceration and supervision under this section and § 19.2-295.2 does not violate a due process right of a defendant to be sentenced by a jury. Boyd v. Commonwealth, 28 Va. App. 537, 507 S.E.2d 107 (1998).

Purpose of the enactment of § 18.2-10 was to provide the authority, following the abolition of parole in Virginia, to allow for

a period of at least six months' supervision, and thus, the trial court erred in imposing an additional term of post-release supervision on defendant after defendant's probation was revoked since statutory authority existed at time of sentencing to impose post-release supervision. Lamb v. Commonwealth, 40 Va. App. 52, 577 S.E.2d 530, 2003 Va. App. LEXIS 120 (2003).

Trial court did not err in imposing an additional sentence of three years supervision on to defendant's life sentence after defendant pled guilty to first-degree murder in exchange for the life sentence; although the plea agreement was a contract, contract law included the law in force on the date the contract was formed, which included the suspended sentence and post-release supervision provisions of subdivision (g) of § 18.2-10 and § 19.2-295.2. Wright v. Commonwealth, 49 Va. App. 58, 636 S.E.2d 489, 2006 Va. App. LEXIS 503 (2006).

Defendant entered into a plea agreement with the Commonwealth pursuant to Va. Sup. Ct. R. 3A:8(c)(1)(C); as contract principles applied to plea agreements, and the law in effect when the contract was made became part of the contract, the trial court, after accepting the plea agreement, properly imposed terms of suspended incarceration and post-release supervision under § 18.2-10(g) and subsection A of § 19.2-295.2, even though such terms were not mentioned in the plea agreement. Wright v. Commonwealth, 275 Va. 77, 655 S.E.2d 7, 2008 Va. LEXIS 12 (2008).

Imposition of term of post-release supervision. — As defendant's sentence, which included three years of imprisonment fixed by the jury and a three-year term of post-release supervision imposed by the trial court under § 19.2-295.2, was within the 10-year range set by the legislature for voluntary manslaughter, it was not illegal. Alston v. Commonwealth, 49 Va. App. 115, 637 S.E.2d 344, 2006 Va. App. LEXIS 544 (2006).

No error in denying concurrent sentence. — Given that the record on appeal adequately demonstrated that the sentencing judge correctly understood his discretion and sentenced defendant within the lawful scope of that discretion, the Court of Appeals of Virginia declined to apply the ends of justice exception to Va. Sup. Ct. R. 5A:18. As a result, no error resulted in the denial of defendant's request for a concurrent sentence. Scalf v. Commonwealth, 2008 Va. App. LEXIS 230 (May 13, 2008).

Former provisions of § 53-291 not automatically invalidated. — The former provisions of § 53-291, including a mandatory death penalty provision subsequently incorporated into this section, were not automatically invalidated and the defendant's death sentence for the killing of a prison guard was not immediately voided, by the decisions in *Woodson v. North Carolina*, 428 U.S. 280, 96 S. Ct. 2978, 49 L. Ed. 2d 944 (1976), and *Roberts v. Louisiana*, 428 U.S. 325, 96 S. Ct. 3001, 49 L. Ed. 2d 974 (1976), which invalidated mandatory death penalty statutes in North Carolina and Louisiana. Lewis v. Commonwealth, 218 Va. 31, 235 S.E.2d 320 (1977).

The former provisions of § 53-291, including a mandatory death penalty provision subsequently incorporated into this section, and any sentence imposed thereunder stand, at least presumptively, valid and enforceable despite the similarity between the provision and the mandatory death penalty statutes struck down in *Woodson v. North Carolina*, 428 U.S. 280, 96 S. Ct. 2978, 49 L. Ed. 2d 944 (1976), and *Roberts v. Louisiana*, 428 U.S. 325, 96 S. Ct. 3001, 49 L. Ed. 2d 974 (1976), unless and until directly struck down in light of these opinions by the Virginia Supreme Court in an appropriate future case. Lewis v. Commonwealth, 218 Va. 31, 235 S.E.2d 320 (1977).

Convicted felon must take affirmative action to restore rights. — A convicted felon in Virginia retains the civil disabilities resulting from his conviction until he himself takes affirmative action to have his civil rights restored. Almond v. United States, 854 F. Supp. 439 (W.D. Va. 1994).

Excessive sentence. — Where defendant's abduction sentence exceeded the maximum, it had to be reduced. Barron v. Commonwealth, No. 1798-02-3, 2003 Va. App. LEXIS 358 (Ct. of Appeals June 24, 2003).

Defendant's sentence on his conviction for possession of marijuana with intent to distribute was excessive and, thus, the sentence for that offense had to be corrected on remand of defendant's case to the trial court; a 15-year sentence was imposed for that offense, but since it was a Class 5 felony, the maximum punishment that could be imposed was 10 years. Lathram v.

Commonwealth, — Va. App. —, — S.E.2d —, 2006 Va. App. LEXIS 168 (May 2, 2006).

When defendant was sentenced to 15 years for attempted murder, not attempted capital murder, resentencing was required, as first- or second-degree attempted murder was a Class 4 felony and the lawful term of confinement for such a felony was two to ten years. Baldwin v. Commonwealth, 2006 Va. App. LEXIS 236 (May 30, 2006), rev'd, on other grounds, 274 Va. 276, 645 S.E.2d 433 (2007).

Defendant's sentence to twenty years in prison, with fifteen years suspended, for unlawful wounding was excessive because the crime was a class 6 felony for which the maximum sentence was five years in prison under § 18.2-10. Ferguson v. Commonwealth, 51 Va. App. 427, 658 S.E.2d 692, 2008 Va. App. LEXIS 367 (2008).

Trial court erred by sentencing defendant to ten years' incarceration for each of defendant's two convictions of unlawful wounding, in violation of § 18.2-51, because § 18.2-10(f) authorized the imposition of a maximum five years' incarceration for unlawful wounding, a Class 6 felony. Furthermore, because the appellate court could only speculate as to the sentence which the trial court might have imposed on remand for each conviction of unlawful wounding, using the correct statutory sentencing range, each case had to be remanded to the trial court for resentencing. Gordon v. Commonwealth, No. 0940-12-2, 61 Va. App. 682, 739 S.E.2d 276, 2013 Va. App. LEXIS 102 (Apr. 2, 2013).

Sentence within range set by legislature. — Trial court did not abuse its discretion in imposing a 43-year sentence against defendant, as said sentence was within the ranges set by the legislature and well below the total statutory maximum for the various felony offenses for which he was convicted. Clark v. Commonwealth, — Va. App. —, — S.E.2d —, 2008 Va. App. LEXIS 234 (May 13, 2008).

Defendant's involuntary manslaughter sentence was appropriate because it was a Class 5 felony under § 18.2-36, punishable by imprisonment for 1 to 10 years under subsection (e) of § 18.2-10, and defendant was sentenced to 10 years imprisonment, which fell within the statutory range set by the legislature. Thus, no abuse of discretion occurred with regard to his sentence. Scott v. Commonwealth, 58 Va. App. 35, 707 S.E.2d 17, 2011 Va. App. LEXIS 104 (2011).

Defendant's sentence of death was neither excessive nor disproportionate. Defendant's sentence of death for capital murder for hire was neither excessive nor disproportionate when compared to sentences generally imposed by sentencing bodies in this jurisdiction for crimes of a similar nature. Murphy v. Commonwealth, 246 Va. 136, 431 S.E.2d 48, cert. denied, 510 U.S. 928, 114 S. Ct. 336, 126 L. Ed. 2d 281 (1993).

Revocation of suspended sentence. — There was a miscarriage of justice for Va. Sup. Ct. R. 5A:18 purposes in the revocation of defendant's 1999 sentences as the maximum sentence for the 1999 convictions was five years and 30 days under §§ 18.2-308.2, 18.2-10, and 18.2-250.1, and the revocation of defendant's 1999 suspended sentences occurred two years after the maximum period for which defendant might originally have been sentenced to imprisonment under subsection A of § 19.2-306. Keen v. Commonwealth, 2010 Va. App. LEXIS 268 (July 6, 2010).

Order revoking defendant's suspended sentences for three distributing marijuana convictions was proper as defendant failed to object and did not show a miscarriage of justice under Va. Sup. Ct. R. 5A:18 since the trial court had jurisdiction to revoke defendant's suspended sentences under subsection A of § 19.2-306 since such revocation was allowed during the maximum period for which defendant might originally have been sentenced to imprisonment, or 30 years, under § 18.2-10. Keen v. Commonwealth, 2010 Va. App. LEXIS 268 (July 6, 2010).

Mental retardation. — Punishment is death for Class 1 felonies, if the person convicted was 16 [now 18] years of age or older at the time of the offense and is not determined to be mentally retarded, but the finding of mental retardation does not increase the penalty for the crime beyond the statutory maximum — death, rather, a defendant facing the death penalty may avoid that penalty if defendant successfully raises and proves by a preponderance of the evidence that defendant is mentally retarded (§ 19.2-264.3:1.2 E and § 19.2-264.3:1.1 C); the state does not have a corollary duty to prove that a defendant is not retarded in order to be entitled to the death penalty, and accordingly, an increase in a defendant's sentence is not predicated on the outcome of the mental retardation determination, only a decrease. Walker v. True, 399 F.3d 315, 2005 U.S. App. LEXIS 2775 (4th Cir. 2005).

Verdict form must include option of life imprisonment and fine. — In 1991, the General Assembly amended this section to include the additional option of imposing a fine of not more than $ 100,000 in addition to a sentence of life imprisonment in a capital case but failed to amend § 19.2-264.4 D to reflect this change in the range of sentences available for capital murder, and the two statutes have since remained in conflict; since this section is more specific than § 19.2-264.4 D, which sets forth the terms of the verdict forms that are to be provided to the jury, it must prevail, and thus, at a minimum, a jury in a capital case must receive a verdict form that, in addition to addressing the imposition of a sentence of death and the imposition of a sentence of life imprisonment, also allows the jury to impose a sentence of life imprisonment and a fine of up to $100,000. Accordingly, in a capital murder trial, the trial court must give the jury verdict forms providing expressly for the imposition of a sentence of imprisonment for life and a fine of not more than $100,000 when the jury finds that one or both of the aggravating factors have been proven beyond a reasonable doubt. Powell v. Commonwealth, 261 Va. 512, 552 S.E.2d 344, 2001 Va. LEXIS 86 (2001).

Sentence which the trial court imposed on defendant who was convicted of statutory rape was within the range prescribed by §§ 18.2-10 and 18.2-63, and the trial court did not abuse its discretion by considering defendant's risk factors and imposing an active sentence that exceeded the length of the active sentence recommended by the sentencing guidelines. Brooks v. Commonwealth, No. 2540-02-3, 2004 Va. App. LEXIS 29 (Ct. of Appeals Jan. 28, 2004).

Sentence was proper. — Sentence for taking indecent liberties with a minor was affirmed where, before passing sentence, the trial court emphasized the seriousness of the offense committed, addressed two of the arguments made by the defense in mitigation of the offense, explained that it did not feel either of those claims undermined the seriousness of the criminal acts committed against the victim, and gave reasons for exceeding the sentencing guidelines: "gravity of the offense" and "failure to truly accept responsibility"; contrary to defendant's contention, the record did not reflect that the trial court refused to consider any of the mitigating facts or circumstances presented on his behalf. The sentence imposed by the trial court was within the range set by the legislature. Harmon v. Commonwealth, 2012 Va. App. LEXIS 107 (Apr. 10, 2012).

Attempted malicious wounding is class 3 felony. — Facts showed that (1) defendant drove his truck down a 100-foot driveway at a high rate of speed; (2) the victim testified he believed that defendant was going to hit him, and he had to jump between two parked cars to escape being struck; (3) defendant admitted threatening the victim, drinking alcohol before the incident, and confirmed that he and the victim had prior confrontations; (4) the victim's father also heard defendant's threats and saw skid marks in the gravel driveway; (5) a police officer investigating the incident also observed fresh skid marks and testified defendant appeared to have been drinking; and (6) a motor vehicle, wrongfully used, could be a weapon as deadly as a gun or a knife. Thus, the trial court's determination that defendant attempted to run over the victim and cause him serious bodily injury was not plainly wrong or without evidence to support it; therefore, the evidence was sufficient to convict defendant of attempted malicious wounding. Sprouse v. Commonwealth, — Va. App. —, — S.E.2d —, 2006 Va. App. LEXIS 45 (Feb. 7, 2006).

Applied in Patterson v. Commonwealth, 222 Va. 653, 283 S.E.2d 212 (1981); Smith v. Commonwealth, 222 Va. 700, 284 S.E.2d 590 (1981); Brown v. Commonwealth, 226 Va. 56, 307 S.E.2d 239 (1983); Evans v. Commonwealth, 228 Va. 468, 323 S.E.2d 114 (1984); Dargan v. Commonwealth, 27 Va. App. 495, 500 S.E.2d 228 (1998); Turner v. Commonwealth, 38 Va. App. 851, 568 S.E.2d 468, 2002 Va. App. LEXIS 525 (2002); McBride v. Commonwealth, 44 Va. App. 526, 605 S.E.2d 773, 2004 Va. App. LEXIS 597 (2004); Conkling v. Commonwealth, 45 Va. App. 518, 612 S.E.2d 235, 2005 Va. App. LEXIS 173 (2005).

CIRCUIT COURT OPINIONS

Trial court has broad discretion. — In non-jury trials, a presiding judge has broad discretion in sentencing and, as long as the sentence does not exceed the statutory authority, he may impose whatever sentence he deems appropriate. Commonwealth v. Boone, 73 Va. Cir. 277, 2007 Va. Cir. LEXIS 232 (Portsmouth Apr. 26, 2007).

§ 18.2-11. Punishment for conviction of misdemeanor.

The authorized punishments for conviction of a misdemeanor are:

(a) For Class 1 misdemeanors, confinement in jail for not more than twelve months and a fine of not more than $2,500, either or both.

(b) For Class 2 misdemeanors, confinement in jail for not more than six months and a fine of not more than $1,000, either or both.

(c) For Class 3 misdemeanors, a fine of not more than $500.

(d) For Class 4 misdemeanors, a fine of not more than $250.

For a misdemeanor offense prohibiting proximity to children as described in subsection A of § 18.2-370.2, the sentencing court is authorized to impose the punishment set forth in subsection B of that section in addition to any other penalty provided by law.

History.
1975, cc. 14, 15; 1990, c. 788; 2000, c. 770.

Cross references.
As to mandatory purchases from the Department for the Blind and Vision Impaired, see § 2.2-1117.

Editor's note.
Acts 1975, cc. 14 and 15, cl. 4 provides: "All acts of the General Assembly of Virginia in its Session of nineteen hundred seventy-five, which provide for punishment by class instead of a specific penalty shall be deemed to be incorporated by reference to §§ 18.2-10 and 18.2-11 of this act, which will become effective Oct. one, nineteen hundred seventy-five."

Law Review.
For survey of Virginia criminal law for the year 1974-1975, see 61 Va. L. Rev. 1697 (1975); for the year 1975-1976, see 62 Va. L. Rev. 1400 (1976). For survey of Virginia criminal law for the year 1978-1979, see 66 Va. L. Rev. 241 (1980). For article on injuries to business under the Virginia Conspiracy Act, see 38 Wash. & Lee L. Rev. 377 (1981). For article on the Virginia Conspiracy Statute, see 38 Wash. & Lee L. Rev. 1147 (1981). For note, "Criminal Procedure and Criminal Law: Virginia Supreme Court Decisions During the 70's," see 15 U. Rich. L. Rev. 585 (1981). For article, "Appeal De Novo in Virginia: An Examination of Its Present Utility," see 42 Wash. & Lee. L. Rev. 1149 (1985). For article, "What's Current in Asbestos Regulations," see 23 U. Rich. L. Rev. 375 (1989). For survey on environmental law in Virginia for 1989, see 23 U. Rich. L. Rev. 625 (1989). For note, "Predicate Offenses for First Degree Felony Murder in Virginia," see 57 Wash. & Lee L. Rev. 561 (2000).

Michie's Jurisprudence.
For related discussion, see 5B M.J. Criminal Procedure, §§ 79, 91; 9A M.J. Gaming and Gaming Contracts, § 4; 12A M.J. Lotteries, § 4; 15 M.J. Rape, § 3.

CASE NOTES

Punishment for violation of an ordinance may not exceed penalties prescribed by general law for like offenses. — Virginia Beach ordinance, which punished destruction of property by fine of up to $2,500 and up to 12 months in jail, manifested a conflict with state law because the penalty that attached exceeded the penalty under the state code destruction of property statute, § 18.2-137, a violation of which was punishable only by a fine not exceeding $500. Strout v. City of Va. Beach, 43 Va. App. 99, 596 S.E.2d 529, 2004 Va. App. LEXIS 240 (2004).

Excessive sentence for Class 2 misdemeanor. — A trial court's sentence of a term of incarceration of 12 months, suspended upon certain terms and conditions, for a Class 2 misdemeanor clearly exceeded the time limitation set forth in subdivision (b). Olgers v. Commonwealth, No. 0856-99-2, 2000 Va. App. LEXIS 342 (Ct. of Appeals May 9, 2000).

Trial court erred in imposing sentence of 30 days in jail, where appellant was convicted for obstruction of justice in violation of § 18.2-460 A, a Class 4 misdemeanor. The punishment for a Class 4 misdemeanor is a fine of not more than $250. Nesbit v. Commonwealth, 15 Va. App. 391, 424 S.E.2d 239 (1992).

Applied in Freedlander v. Edens Broadcasting, Inc., 734 F. Supp. 221 (E.D. Va. 1990); United States v. Montigue, 357 F. Supp. 2d 939, 2005 U.S. Dist. LEXIS 2450 (E.D. Va. 2005); Smith v. Commonwealth, 59 Va. App. 710, 722 S.E.2d 310, 2012 Va. App. LEXIS 56 (2012).

§ 18.2-12. Same; where no punishment or maximum punishment prescribed.

A misdemeanor for which no punishment or no maximum punishment is prescribed by statute shall be punishable as a Class 1 misdemeanor.

History.
Code 1950, § 18.1-9; 1960, c. 358; 1975, cc. 14, 15.

Law Review.
For discussion of jury sentencing, see 53 Va. L. Rev. 968 (1967). For comment, "Right to Court-Appointed Counsel for Misdemeanants in Virginia," see 4 U. Rich. L. Rev. 306 (1970). For article, "Trial by Jury and Speedy Justice," see 28 Wash. & Lee L. Rev. 309 (1971). For article discussing the requirement of counsel in misdemeanor cases and its implementation in Virginia, see 30 Wash. & Lee L. Rev. 431 (1973). For survey of Virginia criminal procedure for the year 1972-1973, see 59 Va. L. Rev. 1478 (1973). For survey of Virginia criminal law for the year 1974-1975, see 61 Va. L. Rev. 1697 (1975).

Michie's Jurisprudence.
For related discussion, see 1A M.J. Adultery, Fornication and Lewdness, §§ 8, 15; 2A M.J. Assault and Battery, § 17; 5B M.J. Criminal Procedure, §§ 4, 79.

CASE NOTES

This section should be construed strictly. Waller v. Commonwealth, 192 Va. 83, 63 S.E.2d 713 (1951).

It cannot be extended by implication or construction so as to impose a jail sentence for conviction of simple adultery. Waller v. Commonwealth, 192 Va. 83, 63 S.E.2d 713 (1951).

Power to impose sentences in all misdemeanor and felony cases resides in the jury. Witcher v. Peyton, 382 F.2d 707 (4th Cir. 1967).

§ 18.2-12.1. Mandatory minimum punishment; definition.

"Mandatory minimum" wherever it appears in this Code means, for purposes of imposing punishment upon a person convicted of a crime, that the court shall impose the entire term of confinement, the full amount of the fine and the complete requirement of community service prescribed by law. The court shall not suspend in full or in part any punishment described as mandatory minimum punishment.

History.
2004, c. 461.

Law Review.
For 2003/2004 survey of criminal law and procedure, see 39 U. Rich. L. Rev. 133 (2004).

CASE NOTES

Use of weapon in commission of crime. — Read in conjunction with this section, § 18.2-53.1 expressly requires the court to impose the entire term of confinement and provides that the court shall not suspend the sentence in full or in part. Thus, a trial court may not set the mandatory minimum sentences imposed for multiple convictions under § 18.2-53.1 to run concurrently with each other. Bullock v. Commonwealth, 48 Va. App. 359, 631 S.E.2d 334, 2006 Va. App. LEXIS 296 (2006).

Neither § 18.2-12.1 nor § 18.2-53.1, the use or display of a firearm while commiting a felony, prohibit a trial court from running multiple sentences imposed for convictions of § 18.2-53.1 concurrently with each other. To the extent that the holding in *Bullock v. Commonwealth,* 631 S.E.2d 334 (2006), is inconsistent, it is overruled. Brown v. Commonwealth, 284 Va. 538, 733 S.E.2d 638, 2012 Va. LEXIS 190 (2012).

Concurrent sentences proper. — Subdivision C1 of § 18.2-374.1 does not prohibit mandatory minimum sentences imposed under that section from running concurrently as: (1) § 18.2-12.1, defining mandatory minimum, does not require that mandatory minimum sentences run consecutively; (2) § 19.2-308 provides that when any person is convicted of two or more offenses, and sentenced to confinement, such sentences shall not run concurrently, unless expressly ordered by the court; and (3) if subdivision C1 of § 18.2-374.1 were interpreted to require the mandatory minimum sentences to run consecutively, it would render superfluous the words the Virginia general assembly used in at least 11 other criminal statutes explicitly requiring that mandatory minimum sentences run consecutively. Commonwealth v. Jefferson, 60 Va. App. 749, 732 S.E.2d 728, 2012 Va. App. LEXIS 323 (2012).

Trial court did not abuse its discretion in ordering defendant's six § 18.2-374.1 sentences to run concurrently with each other as: (1) § 18.2-12.1, defining mandatory minimum, did not require that mandatory minimum sentences run consecutively; (2) § 19.2-308 provided that when any person was convicted of two or more offenses, and sentenced to confinement, such sentences were not to run concurrently, unless expressly ordered by the court; and (3) if subdivision C1 of § 18.2-374.1 were interpreted to require the mandatory minimum sentences to run consecutively, it would render superfluous the words the Virginia general assembly used in at least 11 other criminal statutes explicitly requiring that mandatory minimum sentences run consecutively. Commonwealth v. Jefferson, 60 Va. App. 749, 732 S.E.2d 728, 2012 Va. App. LEXIS 323 (2012).

Applied in Brown v. Commonwealth, 279 Va. 210, 688 S.E.2d 185, 2010 Va. LEXIS 9 (2010).

§ 18.2-13. Same; by reference.

Where a statute in this Code prescribes punishment by stating that the offense is a misdemeanor, or that it is punishable as provided for in § 18.2-12, the offense shall be deemed to be a Class 1 misdemeanor.

History.
1975, cc. 14, 15.

Michie's Jurisprudence.
For related discussion, see 5B M.J. Criminal Procedure, §§ 3, 91.

§ 18.2-14. How unclassified offenses punished.

Offenses defined in Title 18.2 and in other titles in the Code, for which punishment is prescribed without specification as to the class of the offense, shall be punished according to the punishment prescribed in the section or sections thus defining the offense.

History.
1975, cc. 14, 15.

Law Review.
For annual survey of Virginia law article, "Criminal Law and Procedure," see 47 U. Rich. L. Rev. 143 (2012).

CASE NOTES

Applied in Hines v. Commonwealth, 59 Va. App. 567, 721 S.E.2d 792, 2012 Va. App. LEXIS 45 (2012).

§ 18.2-15. Place of punishment.

Imprisonment for conviction of a felony shall be by confinement in a state correctional facility, unless in Class 5 and Class 6 felonies the jury or court trying the case without a jury fixes the punishment at confinement in jail. Imprisonment for conviction of a misdemeanor shall be by confinement in jail.

History.
1975, cc. 14, 15.

§ 18.2-16. How common-law offenses punished.

A common-law offense, for which punishment is prescribed by statute, shall be punished only in the mode so prescribed.

History.
Code 1950, § 18.1-8; 1960, c. 358; 1975, cc. 14, 15.

Michie's Jurisprudence.
For related discussion, see 5B M.J. Criminal Procedure, § 79.

§ 18.2-17. When capital punishment inflicted.

No crime shall be punished with death unless it be authorized by statute.

History.
Code 1950, § 18.1-10; 1960, c. 358; 1975, cc. 14, 15.

Michie's Jurisprudence.
For related discussion, see 5B M.J. Criminal Procedure, § 80.

CHAPTER 2.

PRINCIPALS AND ACCESSORIES.

§ 18.2-18. How principals in second degree and accessories before the fact punished.

In the case of every felony, every principal in the second degree and every accessory before the fact may be indicted, tried, convicted and punished in all respects as if a principal in the first degree; provided, however, that except in the case of a killing for hire under the provisions of subdivision 2 of § 18.2-31 or a killing pursuant to the direction or order of one who is engaged in a continuing criminal enterprise under the provisions of subdivision 10 of § 18.2-31 or a killing pursuant to the direction or order of one who is engaged in the commission of or attempted commission of an act of terrorism under the provisions of subdivision 13 of § 18.2-31, an accessory before the fact or principal in the second degree to a capital murder shall be indicted, tried, convicted and punished as though the offense were murder in the first degree.

History.

Code 1950, § 18.1-11; 1960, c. 358; 1975, cc. 14, 15; 1977, c. 478; 1997, c. 313; 2002, cc. 588, 623.

Cross references.

As to the Attorney General's limited authority to institute and conduct criminal prosecutions in the circuit courts of the Commonwealth, see § 2.2-511.

Law Review.

For survey of Virginia criminal law for the year 1975-1976 see 62 Va. L. Rev. 1400 (1976). For note, "Toward a Level Playing Field: Challenges to Accomplice Testimony in the Wake of United States v. Singleton," see 57 Wash. & Lee L. Rev. 515 (2000).

Michie's Jurisprudence.

For related discussion, see 1A M.J. Accomplices and Accessories, §§ 2, 5, 8, 9, 12; 2B M.J. Autrefois, Acquit and Convict, § 3; 5A M.J. Counterfeiting, § 8; 5B M.J. Criminal Procedure, § 11; 9B M.J. Homicide, § 26; 9B M.J. Indictments, Informations and Presentments, § 20.

CASE NOTES

I. General Consideration.
II. Who Are Principals and Accessories.
   A. Principal in First Degree.
   B. Principal in Second Degree.
   C. Accessory Before the Fact.
   D. Capital Murder.
III. Prosecution.
   A. Indictment.
   B. Evidence.
   C. Other Matters.

I. GENERAL CONSIDERATION.

Criminal responsibility. — Unless it is otherwise stated, if a statute makes an act criminal, it imposes on all persons who are present purposely giving aid and comfort to the actual wrongdoer criminal responsibility equal to that of the wrongdoer. Spradlin v. Commonwealth, 195 Va. 523, 79 S.E.2d 443 (1954).

If there is concert of action with the resulting crime one of its incidental probable consequences, then whether such crime was originally contemplated or not, all who participate in any way in bringing it about are equally answerable and bound by the acts of every other person connected with the consummation of such resulting crime. The question of whether the offense is the natural and probable result of the intended wrongful act is usually for the jury. Spradlin v. Commonwealth, 195 Va. 523, 79 S.E.2d 443 (1954).

A principal in the second degree is liable for the same punishment as the person who commits the crime. Blankenship v. Commonwealth, No. 1112-99-3, 2000 Va. App. LEXIS 293 (Ct. of Appeals Apr. 25, 2000).

This section makes no exception for those who plan a crime, do not involve themselves with the details of its execution, and are not present for its consummation; this section and the cases direct that an accessory before the fact is accountable in all respects as the principal who carries out the intended crime, as well as any of its natural, probable, and incidental crimes. Charlton v. Commonwealth, 32 Va. App. 47, 526 S.E.2d 289 (2000).

The court treats concert of action as a species of accomplice liability, carrying with it the principle that the punishment imposed on each accomplice may be the same. Davis v. Commonwealth, 36 Va. App. 291, 549 S.E.2d 631, 2001 Va. App. LEXIS 445 (2001).

If there is concert of action with the resulting crime one of its incidental probable consequences, then whether such crime was originally contemplated or not, all who participate in any way in bringing it about are equally answerable and bound by the acts of every other person connected with the consummation of such resulting crime. Davis v. Commonwealth, 36 Va. App. 291, 549 S.E.2d 631, 2001 Va. App. LEXIS 445 (2001).

Concert of action instruction required. — In a second degree murder prosecution, the trial court was required to give a concert of action instruction where co-defendants were part of a group of people who kicked and stomped the victim while he was on the ground. Davis v. Commonwealth, 36 Va. App. 291, 549 S.E.2d 631, 2001 Va. App. LEXIS 445 (2001).

Accomplice may be punished despite silence of statute creating an offense. — Where the statute creating an offense fails to provide for the guilt of an accomplice, the omission is not generally considered to indicate an intent to exclude such parties from criminal responsibility. Adkins v. Commonwealth, 175 Va. 590, 9 S.E.2d 349 (1940).

Lack of intent no defense. — Each co-actor is responsible for the acts of the others and may not interpose his personal lack of intent as a defense. Charlton v. Commonwealth, 32 Va. App. 47, 526 S.E.2d 289 (2000).

Commonwealth not required to elect between theories. — Because an accessory before the fact and a principal in the second degree may be tried in all respects as a principal in the first degree, the Commonwealth is not required to elect between those two theories, and depending on the evidence, a defendant can be convicted under either theory. Buchanan v. Commonwealth, No. 0960-88-3 (Ct. of Appeals May 8, 1990).

Applied in Simpson v. Commonwealth, 221 Va. 109, 267 S.E.2d 134 (1980); Riddick v. Commonwealth, 226 Va. 244, 308 S.E.2d 117 (1983); Sutton v. Commonwealth, 228 Va. 654, 324 S.E.2d 665 (1985); Pancoast v. Commonwealth, 2 Va. App. 28, 340 S.E.2d 833 (1986); Rogers v. Commonwealth, 242 Va. 307, 410 S.E.2d 621 (1991); Jones v. Commonwealth, 15 Va. App. 384, 424 S.E.2d 563 (1992); Barlow v. Commonwealth, 26 Va. App. 421, 494 S.E.2d 901 (1998); Hansford v. Angelone, 244 F. Supp. 2d 606, 2002 U.S. Dist. LEXIS 26217 (E.D. Va. 2002); Johnson v. Commonwealth, 53 Va. App. 608, 674 S.E.2d 541, 2009 Va. App. LEXIS 157 (2009).

II. WHO ARE PRINCIPALS AND ACCESSORIES.

A. Principal in First Degree.

Principals in the first degree are those who are actors, actual perpetrators of the crime; those who are the immediate perpetrators of the act. Horton v. Commonwealth, 99 Va. 848, 38 S.E. 184 (1901).

A principal in the first degree is the actual perpetrator of the crime. Jones v. Commonwealth, 208 Va. 370, 157 S.E.2d 907 (1967).

One who effects a criminal act through an innocent or unwitting agent is a principal in the first degree, even if the person accused was not present at the time and place of the offense. Bailey v. Commonwealth, 229 Va. 258, 329 S.E.2d 37 (1985).

Defendant held principal in first degree despite absence of proof defendant was actual perpetrator. — Evidence was held sufficient to prove defendant, on trial for charges of attempted capital murder by arson, was a principal in the first degree, despite absence of proof that defendant was the perpetrator who lit the fire, rather than his accomplice. Hancock v. Commonwealth, 12 Va. App. 774, 407 S.E.2d 301 (1991).

Instigation of larceny. — Where accused was the instigator and moving spirit in bringing about the larceny, procured his associates to commit the crime, and with intent to steal the property, before the event instigated and directed the acts done by his associates in the commission of the crime, and also assisted them in taking and carrying away the goods, he is guilty of actual larceny and subject to punishment as a principal in the first degree. Stapleton v. Commonwealth, 140 Va. 475, 124 S.E. 237 (1924).

Driving the getaway car in destruction of property/mailbox case. — Defendant was properly convicted of misdemeanor destruction of property, under § 18.2-137, as a principal in the first degree, for driving a getaway car in which those who actually damaged a victim's mailbox tried to escape, because: (1) § 18.2-18, concerning felony principals and accessories before the fact, did not abrogate the common-law rule that, in misdemeanors, all participants were principals; and (2) defendant admitted participating in this criminal episode. Wade v. Commonwealth, 56 Va. App. 689, 696 S.E.2d 258, 2010 Va. App. LEXIS 321 (2010).

B. Principal in Second Degree.

To prove that one is a principal in the second degree, the Commonwealth must prove: (1) the accused's presence at the crime's commission; and (2) committing an overt act such as inciting, encouraging, advising, or assisting in the commission of the crime; or (3) sharing in the perpetrator's criminal intent. Buchanan v. Commonwealth, No. 0960-88-3 (Ct. of Appeals May 8, 1990).

To convict a principal in the second degree as one in the first degree, the Commonwealth must prove the defendant was present at the scene and shared the criminal intent of the parties who actually committed the crime or was guilty of some act in furtherance thereof. Allard v. Commonwealth, 24 Va. App. 57, 480 S.E.2d 139 (1997).

To show an accused guilty of a crime as a principal in the second degree, the Commonwealth must show that the accused was present, aiding and abetting, and intended his or her words, gestures, signals, or actions to in some way encourage, advise, urge or in some way help the person committing the crime to commit it. Porter v. Commonwealth, No. 0637-00-1, 2001 Va. App. LEXIS 176 (Ct. of Appeals Apr. 3, 2001); Painter v. Commonwealth, No. 1953-00-2, 2001 Va. App. LEXIS 190 (Ct. of Appeals Apr. 10, 2001).

Commonwealth did not need to prove that defendant actually committed the burglary and grand larceny with which he was charged as, pursuant to § 18.2-18, a principal in the second degree was equally guilty as a principal in the first degree. The Commonwealth was only required to prove that defendant was present and that he, in some way, procured, encouraged, countenanced, or approved commission of the crime. Wilkins v. Commonwealth, 2008 Va. App. LEXIS 483 (Oct. 28, 2008).

A principal in the second degree is one not the perpetrator, but present, aiding and abetting the act done, or keeping watch or guard at some convenient distance. Brown v. Commonwealth, 130 Va. 733, 107 S.E. 809 (1921); Spradlin v. Commonwealth, 195 Va. 523, 79 S.E.2d 443 (1954); Ward v. Commonwealth, 205 Va. 564, 138 S.E.2d 293 (1964). See Grant v. Commonwealth, 216 Va. 166, 217 S.E.2d 806 (1975); Powell v. Commonwealth, No. 0549-89-2 (Ct. of Appeals Aug. 28, 1990).

A principal in the second degree, or an aider or abettor as he is sometimes termed, is one who is present, actually or constructively, assisting the perpetrator in the commission of the crime. In order to make a person a principal in the second degree actual participation in the commission of the crime is not necessary. The test is whether or not he was encouraging, inciting, or in some manner offering aid in the commission of the crime. If he was present lending countenance, or otherwise aiding while another did the act, he is an aider and abettor or principal in the second degree. Jones v. Commonwealth, 208 Va. 370, 157 S.E.2d 907 (1967).

Principals in the second degree are those who did not with their own hands commit the act, but were present, aiding and abetting it. It is not necessary in order to make a person principal in the second degree that he be actually present when the crime was committed, or that he should have actually participated in the commission of the crime. The test as to whether or not he is a principal in the second

degree is, was he encouraging, inciting, or in some manner offering aid or consent to the crime. All persons present lending countenance or otherwise aiding, while another does the act, are principals in the second degree. Horton v. Commonwealth, 99 Va. 848, 38 S.E. 184 (1901).

A principal in the second degree is one who is not only present at a crime's commission, but one who also commits some overt act, such as inciting, encouraging, advising, or assisting in the commission of the crime or shares the perpetrator's criminal intent. Moehring v. Commonwealth, 223 Va. 564, 290 S.E.2d 891 (1982).

A principal in the second degree is a person who is present, aiding and abetting, by helping some way in the commission of the crime. Presence or consent alone is not sufficient to constitute aiding and abetting. It must be shown that the defendant intended his words, gestures, signals or actions to in some way encourage, advise, or urge, or in some way help the person committing the crime to commit it. A principal in the second degree is equally accountable and is subject to the same punishment as the actual perpetrator. Ramsey v. Commonwealth, 2 Va. App. 265, 343 S.E.2d 465 (1986).

A person who is present at the commission of a crime, inciting, encouraging, advising or assisting in the act done, is deemed to be an aider and abettor, and is liable as principal. Taylor v. Commonwealth, 260 Va. 683, 537 S.E.2d 592, 2000 Va. LEXIS 126 (2000).

Or if not present, within easy call. — If P. and L., at the house of the accused, by the use of false pretenses, obtained from F. the sum of $570, the accused is not guilty of the offense, unless he was present, aiding and abetting therein, or suffered or permitted the said P. and L. to use said house, with knowledge that they intended to use the same for the employing of such pretenses. But if the accused was within easy call with intent to aid or assist them in their purpose, or in escaping, or in getting rid of or misleading the person from whom such money was obtained, that is a presence, aiding and abetting, and the accused is as guilty as if he were personally present. Dull v. Commonwealth, 66 Va. (25 Gratt.) 965 (1875).

But mere presence is insufficient. — It is well settled law that mere presence is not sufficient to render one guilty of aiding and abetting the commission of crime. There must be something done or said by him showing his consent to the felonious purpose and contributing to its execution. Reynolds v. Commonwealth, 74 Va. (33 Gratt.) 834 (1880); Kemp v. Commonwealth, 80 Va. 443 (1885). See Wren v. Commonwealth, 67 Va. (26 Gratt.) 952 (1875); Horton v. Commonwealth, 99 Va. 848, 38 S.E. 184 (1901); Brown v. Commonwealth, 130 Va. 733, 107 S.E. 809 (1921); Spradlin v. Commonwealth, 195 Va. 523, 79 S.E.2d 443 (1954).

Mere presence of a party when a crime is committed is not sufficient to constitute one an aider and abettor in the commission of a crime. Jones v. Commonwealth, 208 Va. 370, 157 S.E.2d 907 (1967).

Mere presence is not sufficient to establish that one is a principal in the second degree, an aider and abettor to the commission of a crime. The prosecution must prove that the accused did or said something showing his consent to the felonious purpose and his contribution to its execution. Hall v. Commonwealth, 225 Va. 533, 303 S.E.2d 903 (1983); Augustine v. Commonwealth, 226 Va. 120, 306 S.E.2d 886 (1983).

Unless assembled to commit a wrongful act. — All those who assemble themselves together with an intent to commit a wrongful act, the execution whereof makes probable, in the nature of things, a crime not specifically designed, but incidental to that which was the object of the confederacy, are responsible for such incidental crime. Brown v. Commonwealth, 130 Va. 733, 107 S.E. 809 (1921).

Mere presence during the commission of a crime and subsequent flight do not constitute sufficient evidence to convict a person as a principal in the second degree. Moehring v. Commonwealth, 223 Va. 564, 290 S.E.2d 891 (1982).

Criminal intent must be present. — To constitute an aider or abettor it is essential that the aider and abettor share the criminal intent of the principal, and if a reasonable doubt exists as to the intention of a party, in interfering in a fight between two other persons, he cannot be found guilty as an aider and abettor. Horton v. Commonwealth, 99 Va. 848, 38 S.E. 184 (1901).

To prove defendant was an aider and abettor, the evidence must show that the defendant was not only present but that the defendant procured, encouraged, countenanced, or approved commission of the crime. In other words, defendant must share the criminal intent of the party who actually committed the crime or be guilty of some overt act in furtherance thereof. Hall v. Commonwealth, 225 Va. 533, 303 S.E.2d 903 (1983); Augustine v. Commonwealth, 226 Va. 120, 306 S.E.2d 886 (1983).

Aiders or abettors must either share the perpetrator's criminal intent or commit an overt act in furtherance of the crime, thereby making the offense "more likely" to occur. Whether an accused aided and abetted in the commission of an offense is a question of fact to be determined from the circumstances of each case. Lyne v. Commonwealth, No. 2428-94-2 (Ct. of Appeals Mar. 26, 1996).

Section 18.2-18 cannot be interpreted to mean that any overt act that is advantageous to the principal's criminal plan is sufficient; to be guilty as a principal in the second degree the defendant must also share in the principal's criminal intent. McMorris v. Commonwealth, 276 Va. 500, 666 S.E.2d 348, 2008 Va. LEXIS 91 (2008).

And presence, plus encouragement, will suffice. — An aider and abettor is one who is present, actually or constructively, and participates in the crime of the principal; but any encouragement or act of assistance is a participation in the crime. Horton v. Commonwealth, 99 Va. 848, 38 S.E. 184 (1901); Spradlin v. Commonwealth, 195 Va. 523, 79 S.E.2d 443 (1954).

If a person is present at the commission of a crime inciting, encouraging, advising or assisting in the act done, he is deemed to be an aider and abettor, and is liable as principal. Snyder v. Commonwealth, 202 Va. 1009, 121 S.E.2d 452 (1961); Tasker v. Commonwealth, 202 Va. 1019, 121 S.E.2d 459 (1961).

Whether a person does in fact aid or abet another in the commission of a crime is a question that may be determined by circumstances as well as by direct evidence. — See Tuck v. Commonwealth, No. 3376-02-3, 2003 Va. App. LEXIS 623 (Ct. of Appeals Dec. 9, 2003).

Incapacity to commit the offense is no defense. — The mere fact of incapacity to commit an offense as a principal in the first degree does not prevent one who aids and abets the principal offender from being held criminally liable as a principal in the second degree. Adkins v. Commonwealth, 175 Va. 590, 9 S.E.2d 349 (1940).

A principal in the second degree is held as culpable as one in the first degree. Briley v. Commonwealth, 221 Va. 563, 273 S.E.2d 57 (1980).

It is well established that a "principal in the first degree is the actual perpetrator of the crime." A principal in the second degree is a person present at the scene of the offense, either actively or constructively, aiding or abetting its commission through "words, gestures, signals or actions to in some way encourage advise, . . . urge, or . . . help" the primary actor. A principal in the second degree "may be indicted, tried, convicted and punished in all respects as if a principal in the first degree." Lyne v. Commonwealth, No. 2428-94-2 (Ct. of Appeals Mar. 26, 1996).

In the case of a felony, every principal in the second degree may be indicted, tried, convicted, and punished as if a principal in the first degree. Allard v. Commonwealth, 24 Va. App. 57, 480 S.E.2d 139 (1997).

Evidence was sufficient to establish that defendant was principal in the second degree to malicious wounding where the defendant and others acted in concert in attacking the victim and one of the defendant's coperpetrators struck the victim in the head with a glass bottle, knocking him unconscious. Simmons v. Commonwealth, No. 1624-97-3 (Ct. of Appeals July 14, 1998).

Evidence was sufficient to establish that defendant was principal in the second degree in both the manufacture and distribution of cocaine where: (1) the defendant accompanied her coperpetrator on trips to purchase cocaine; (2) she provided him with the use of her apartment to cook cocaine, was present when he cooked powder cocaine into crack cocaine, and directly assisted him with cooking the cocaine; (3) she knowingly allowed him to use her apartment as a distribution center for cocaine; (4) she was present in her apartment when he transferred cocaine to others to pass along to customers and was also present when he sold cocaine directly to customers in her apartment; and (5) she was unemployed, and he paid the rent and damages fees for her apartment. Timbers v. Commonwealth, No. 2249-97-2 (Ct. of Appeals August 18, 1998).

Evidence was sufficient to establish that defendant was principal in the second degree where defendant admitted knowing the plan to steal items from victim's home, he was present and watched while the others took the items, thereby approving of the principals'

actions and sharing in their criminal intent, and he was aware of the location of some of the stolen items after the theft. Cooke v. Commonwealth, No. 1603-99-1, 2000 Va. App. LEXIS 410 (Ct. of Appeals May 30, 2000).

Appellate court affirmed defendant's conviction for robbery as a principal in the second degree because the evidence was sufficient to prove defendant aided and abetted in the commission of a robbery, as defendant knew the perpetrators were going to commit a robbery, he waited for them in the get-away vehicle to facilitate their escape, during the escape he tried to hide the clothing they wore during the robbery by placing it in the glove compartment or at his feet, and a reasonable person could conclude that defendant shared the intent to commit a robbery. Bradner v. Commonwealth, No. 2640-00-3, 2001 Va. App. LEXIS 572 (Ct. of Appeals Oct. 23, 2001).

Defendant's presence at the scene, coupled with the fact that he remained at the scene, fled with the actual perpetrators and shared in the fruits of the crime, was sufficient to prove his guilt of the charged offenses as a principal in the second degree. Toney v. Commonwealth, No. 1024-01-2, 2002 Va. App. LEXIS 254 (Ct. of Appeals Apr. 30, 2002).

Actual presence at the scene of the commission of a crime was not required to convict an accused as a principal in the second degree, and defendant, in the instant case, was constructively present at the crime's commission and was aiding and abetting by helping in the commission of the crime, under § 18.2-18. Paige v. Commonwealth, No. 1444-02-4, 2003 Va. App. LEXIS 492 (Ct. of Appeals Sept. 30, 2003).

There was ample evidence from which a jury could have reasonably found that defendant was a principal in the second degree in violation of § 18.2-35 because by the defendant's words, gestures, and actions, viewed in the light most favorable to the Commonwealth, defendant explicitly demonstrated that the defendant shared a friend's criminal intent to kill the victim; immediately prior to the killing, defendant specifically commanded the friend to shoot the victim and did nothing to dissuade the friend. McKinney v. Commonwealth, 2008 Va. App. LEXIS 344 (July 8, 2008).

There was sufficient evidence to support defendant's conviction as a principal in the second degree of abduction and felony murder, in violation of §§ 18.2-48 and 18.2-32, where he and others lured the victim to a co-defendant's home with the purpose of robbing the victim of drugs and money, they restrained the victim while attempting to determine the whereabouts of the drugs, walked him out to the trunk of his car, drove him away, and fatally shot him; although there was blood in the house, the fact that the victim was "walked" outside to his car and that he "squirmed like a worm" when he was shot supported the finding that he was not killed in the house and accordingly, that defendant participated in abducting defendant while he was still alive. Brooks v. Commonwealth, No. 1629-03-2, 2004 Va. App. LEXIS 284 (Ct. of Appeals June 15, 2004).

Trial court did not err in finding that the evidence proved beyond a reasonable doubt that defendant acted as a principal in the second degree to use of a firearm in the commission of a robbery as the evidence showed that defendant aided in the commission of and shared the main actor's intent to rob a clothing retail store during normal business hours, where he was likely to encounter both store employees and customers. The evidence showed that defendant transported the main actor to and from the immediate area where he committed the robbery and abduction; that defendant remained in her SUV at a nearby apartment complex, where neither she nor the main actor lived, when the main actor departed the vehicle to commit the robbery; that she tried to assist him in eluding police, and that she tried to provide him with an alibi when questioned about the offenses, and that she gave false and contradictory statements to officers when questioned about her part in the robbery. Wade v. Commonwealth, 2012 Va. App. LEXIS 161 (May 15, 2012).

Sufficient evidence supported defendant's § 18.2-53.1 conviction as the victim observed that the accomplice had a semi-automatic gun, felt the cold, hard barrel of the gun that defendant placed against his neck, and saw the tip of that gun; further, defendant was guilty as a principal in the second degree of possessing the firearm used by his accomplice. Gibbs v. Commonwealth, No. 1726-11-1, 2012 Va. App. LEXIS 324 (Oct. 16, 2012).

Evidence was insufficient. — Assuming the driver of the truck in which defendant had been riding stole a handgun, since there was neither proof that defendant failed to oppose the theft, nor proof of other circumstances upon which to find he acted as a principal in the second degree, his conviction of grand larceny on an aiding and abetting theory was not supported by sufficient evidence. Myers v. Commonwealth, 43 Va. App. 113, 596 S.E.2d 536, 2004 Va. App. LEXIS 238 (2004).

Defendant was not a principal in the second degree pursuant to § 18.2-18 because the defendant could not have procured, encouraged, countenanced, approved or knowingly committed an overt act in furtherance of a robbery without the knowledge that the crime was occurring. McMorris v. Commonwealth, 276 Va. 500, 666 S.E.2d 348, 2008 Va. LEXIS 91 (2008).

Invited error. — Trial court did not err in finding defendant guilty of petit larceny, a misdemeanor under § 18.2-96, when she was indicted as a principal in the second degree to third offense petit larceny, a felony under §§ 18.2-104 and 18.2-18, where defendant requested the trial court to treat her actions as misdemeanor petit larceny, and she was subject to the misdemeanor finding that her counsel requested, as she was precluded from raising the same on appeal under the invited error doctrine; additionally, misdemeanor petit larceny was a lesser-included offense of a violation of § 18.2-104. Brumfield v. Commonwealth, No. 0794-04-3, 2004 Va. App. LEXIS 625 (Ct. of Appeals Dec. 21, 2004).

Evidence sufficient to support conviction. — Defendant's convictions for first-degree murder and use of a firearm in the commission of a felony were appropriate because the jury was entitled to disbelieve defendant's assertion that she did not know that her boyfriend had a weapon when they entered the victim's home. Further, there was sufficient evidence of concert of action because defendant and her boyfriend arrived at the home of defendant's father knowing that they were forbidden to be there; they gained entrance through the back door; they were intent upon forcing her father to surrender the welfare checks; and when defendant's father refused, they pursued him up the stairs where he was shot and brutally beaten. Thomas v. Commonwealth, 279 Va. 131, 688 S.E.2d 220, 2010 Va. LEXIS 11, cert. denied, 131 S. Ct. 143, 178 L. Ed. 2d 8, 2010 U.S. LEXIS 6109 (U.S. 2010).

C. Accessory Before the Fact.

Elements of crime. — In order for a person to be an accessory before the fact, the Commonwealth is required to prove: (1) commission of the crime by the principal, and (2) prior to the crime's commission, the accessory was in someway concerned as a contriver, instigator or advisor. Buchanan v. Commonwealth, No. 0960-88-3 (Ct. of Appeals May 8, 1990).

An accessory before the fact is one who, being absent at the time the crime is committed, procures, counsels, or commands another to commit a crime. Absence is necessary to make one an accessory. See Rasnick v. Commonwealth, 4 Va. (2 Va. Cas.) 356 (1823).

To be guilty of accessory before the fact, the accused must either know or have reason to know of the principal's criminal intention and must intend to encourage, incite or aid the principal's commission of the crime. Charlton v. Commonwealth, 32 Va. App. 47, 526 S.E.2d 289 (2000).

In the trial of an accessory before the fact the Commonwealth must establish the following elements beyond a reasonable doubt: the commission of the crime by the principal, the accessory's absence at the commission of the offense and that before the commission of the crime, the accessory was in some way concerned therein as a contriver, instigator or advisor. McGhee v. Commonwealth, 221 Va. 422, 270 S.E.2d 729 (1980).

Although conviction of a principal in the first degree is not a condition precedent to conviction of an accessory, before the accessory to a crime can be convicted as such, it must be shown that the crime has been committed by the principal. Dusenbery v. Commonwealth, 220 Va. 770, 263 S.E.2d 392 (1980).

Procedure. — Trial court did not err in submitting a murder charge to the jury based on the theory that defendant was "an accessory before the fact or co-conspirator" in the commission of the charged murder; the Commonwealth is entitled to an accessory-before-the-fact instruction on a felony indictment even when the defendant is not charged in the indictment with being an accessory before the fact to the felony. Schwartz v. Commonwealth, 45 Va. App. 407, 611 S.E.2d 631, 2005 Va. App. LEXIS 156 (2005).

D. Capital Murder.

Only immediate perpetrator may be convicted of capital murder. — Except in the case of murder for hire, only the immediate perpetrator of a homicide, the one who fired the fatal shot, and not an accessory before the fact or a principal in the second degree, may be convicted of capital murder under the provisions of § 18.2-31, as qualified by this section. Coppola v. Commonwealth, 220 Va. 243, 257 S.E.2d 797 (1979), cert. denied, 444 U.S. 1103, 100 S. Ct. 1069, 62 L. Ed. 2d 788 (1980).

It is essential in a prosecution for capital murder, except in the case of murder for hire, that the heretofore unnecessary distinction be drawn between principals in the first and second degree, assuring that only the person who is the immediate perpetrator may be a principal in the first degree and thus liable to conviction for capital murder. Johnson v. Commonwealth, 220 Va. 146, 255 S.E.2d 525 (1979), cert. denied, 454 U.S. 920, 102 S. Ct. 422, 70 L. Ed. 2d 231 (1981).

When the offense constituting the charge of capital murder is the willful, deliberate and premeditated killing of a person in the commission of robbery while armed with a deadly weapon, only the actual perpetrator of the crime may be convicted of capital murder. Johnson v. Commonwealth, 220 Va. 146, 255 S.E.2d 525 (1979), cert. denied, 454 U.S. 920, 102 S. Ct. 422, 70 L. Ed. 2d 231 (1981).

This section does not permit a principal in the second degree to be convicted of capital murder. Cortner v. Commonwealth, 222 Va. 557, 281 S.E.2d 908 (1981).

Except in the case of murder for hire, "only the actual perpetrator of the crime may be convicted of capital murder." Thus, neither an accessory before the fact nor a principal in the second degree may be so convicted. Cheng v. Commonwealth, 240 Va. 26, 393 S.E.2d 599 (1990).

And instruction to contrary is reversible error. — Harmful, reversible error occurred in a capital murder prosecution when the trial court instructed the jury in such a manner that the jury could have believed that it could convict the defendant of capital murder though it was unable to determine who fired the fatal shots, or if it determined that the defendant's brother fired the fatal shots; the error was compounded when the Commonwealth was permitted to argue to the jury that it could convict the defendant regardless of who pulled the trigger. Johnson v. Commonwealth, 220 Va. 146, 255 S.E.2d 525 (1979), cert. denied, 454 U.S. 920, 102 S. Ct. 422, 70 L. Ed. 2d 231 (1981).

Construction with § 18.2-31. — Defendant gave a direction or order sufficient to satisfy the requirements of § 18.2-18 such that even if he were a criminal actor ordinarily demonstrating culpability as a principal in the second degree, he was nonetheless guilty of capital murder under subdivision 13 of § 18.2-31 and § 18.2-18; the record showed defendant directed and ordered his companion in the entire criminal enterprise, defendant had the military background in shooting and snipering skills, and it was defendant who provided the weapons. Muhammad v. Commonwealth, 269 Va. 451, 611 S.E.2d 537, 2005 Va. LEXIS 39 (2005), cert. denied, 547 U.S. 1136, 126 S. Ct. 2035, 164 L. Ed. 2d 794 (2006), and overruled in part on other grounds by Jay v. Commonwealth, 275 Va. 510, 659 S.E.2d 311, 2008 Va. LEXIS 53 (2008).

Failure to establish presence of another perpetrator. — In a capital case, defendant unsuccessfully argued that the evidence was insufficient to convict him as an immediate perpetrator or triggerman, which was required under § 18.2-18 for his conviction as a principal in the first degree, making him eligible for the death penalty. There was no conclusive evidence of the presence of another perpetrator, and the evidence was overwhelming that defendant was the sole perpetrator of the murders. Prieto v. Commonwealth, 278 Va. 366, 682 S.E.2d 910, 2009 Va. LEXIS 94 (2009), cert. denied, 177 L. Ed. 2d 332, 2010 U.S. LEXIS 4926 (U.S. 2010).

III. PROSECUTION.

A. Indictment.

Indictment against accessory need not aver conviction of principal. — It is not necessary that the indictment against the accessory should aver the conviction of the principal, for they may be jointly indicted. Commonwealth v. Williamson, 4 Va. (2 Va. Cas.) 211 (1820).

Refusal to furnish bill of particulars. — The defendant was deprived of no substantial right by the trial court's refusal to require the Commonwealth to furnish a bill of particulars stating whether defendant was being tried as a principal in the first degree or second degree, particularly where the motion for bill of particulars was not made until the time of trial. Tasker v. Commonwealth, 202 Va. 1019, 121 S.E.2d 459 (1961).

Amendment to indictment by adding "or an accessory before the fact." — Where the indictment returned by the grand jury charged that appellant did, as a principal in the second degree, deliberately, and with premeditation kill victim during a killing for hire, in violation of this section and § 18.2-31 and where prior to the trial, the Commonwealth requested and received the trial court's permission to amend the indictment by adding the words "or an accessory before the fact" between "second degree," and "unlawfully," trial court did not err in failing to grant defendant's motion for a bill of particulars, and by permitting the Commonwealth to amend the indictment over his objection; the indictment sufficiently informed defendant of the charge upon which he was to be tried and moreover, under the indictment he could be convicted either as a principal in the first or second degree or as an accessory before the fact. Harris v. Commonwealth, 8 Va. App. 424, 382 S.E.2d 292 (1989).

The Commonwealth was not required to elect whether it would prosecute the defendant on a charge of aiding and abetting or being a principal in the first degree since the indictment contained but one single count and charged only one homicide. Ward v. Commonwealth, 205 Va. 564, 138 S.E.2d 293 (1964).

B. Evidence.

Aiding and abetting may be shown by circumstantial evidence. — Whether a person does in fact aid or abet another in the commission of a crime is a question which may be determined by circumstances as well as by direct evidence. Brown v. Commonwealth, 130 Va. 733, 107 S.E. 809 (1921); Spradlin v. Commonwealth, 195 Va. 523, 79 S.E.2d 443 (1954).

Circumstantial evidence was sufficient to support conclusion that defendant was an aider and abetter in a purse snatching and was the driver of the "getaway" car. Powell v. Commonwealth, No. 0549-89-2 (Ct. of Appeals Aug. 28, 1990).

Where defendant robbed the victim after the victim was distracted by another person with a gun, the evidence was sufficient to prove that defendant acted in concert with the other person in using a firearm to commit a felony. Nelson v. Commonwealth, No. 1868-02-2, 2003 Va. App. LEXIS 363 (Ct. of Appeals June 24, 2003).

Evidence was sufficient to support defendant's conviction for attempting to obtain money by false pretenses and uttering a forged check drawn on the account of her employer in violation of §§ 18.2-178 and 18.2-172 because the only reasonable hypothesis flowing from the direct and circumstantial evidence was that defendant shared in an accomplice's intent to utter a forged check and to attempt to obtain money by false pretenses; defendant, who worked across the hall from the victim and had access to her office, admitted to the victim that she had possessed the check at issue, defendant accompanied the accomplice to a check cashing business and admitted knowing that the accomplice was there to cash a check, and defendant, the only one of the three people at the business that day who had a direct tie to the employer, remained in the car during the transaction, fabricated a reason to enter the business after police arrived and entered, and attempted to flee the scene alone after learning that the accomplice had been handcuffed. Bell v. Commonwealth, 2010 Va. App. LEXIS 461 (Nov. 30, 2010).

Conviction as accessory before the fact by totality of evidence. — While no single piece of evidence, standing alone, tied the defendant directly to the killing, the totality of the evidence supported the jury's finding that the defendant was an accessory before the fact of first degree murder. Cirios v. Commonwealth, 7 Va. App. 292, 373 S.E.2d 164 (1988).

Jury does not have to accept defendant's testimony. — Although defendant's testimony could have absolved himself of any complicity in the robbery/murder, circumstances leading up to and after the crimes were such that the jury could reasonably have concluded that defendant participated in the robbery and aided and abetted in the murder; jury did not have to accept defendant's statement. Pugliese v. Commonwealth, 16 Va. App. 82, 428 S.E.2d 16 (1993).

Abduction by prisoners. — Evidence was sufficient to establish that the defendant was a principal in the second degree to abduction by prisoners where, inter alia, he came twice to a breezeway with other inmates more directly involved in the incident, remained present while the inmates subdued two correctional officers, stood within three feet of one officer as he lay restrained on the ground, and assisted in dealing with another officer. Wicker v. Commonwealth, No. 2607-97-2 (Ct. of Appeals Dec. 22, 1998).

Driving the getaway car. — Evidence was sufficient to sustain a burglary conviction where defendant drove the other participants to the crime scene, waited for their return from a safe distance across the street in the dark, and then provided the transportation for their flight from the scene of the crime by driving the getaway car. Defendant admitted on cross-examination to knowing before the burglary that "something bad was going to happen at the burglary scene." Thomas v. Commonwealth, — Va. App. —, — S.E.2d —, 2006 Va. App. LEXIS 73 (Feb. 28, 2006).

Videotape properly admitted. — For a case upholding admission of partially unintelligible videotape of drug transaction in conviction of defendant as principal in second degree, see Brooks v. Commonwealth, 15 Va. App. 407, 424 S.E.2d 566 (1992).

Evidence held sufficient. — In a prosecution for malicious wounding, the evidence was sufficient to show that defendant's actions caused the victim's wounds as the evidence showed that defendant, at a minimum, acted as a principal, within the meaning of § 18.2-18, in the malicious wounding of the victim, in that the evidence showed that defendant was present during the malicious wounding of the victim and performed an overt act of assistance by striking the initial blow against the victim. Johnson v. Commonwealth, 58 Va. App. 303, 709 S.E.2d 175, 2011 Va. App. LEXIS 185 (2011).

C. Other Matters.

Verdict should determine degree of accessory. — A verdict which finds a person indicted as being an accessory to a murder guilty thereof, but does not determine whether he is guilty as accessory to the murder in the first or second degree, is erroneous, and ought to be set aside, and a venire facias de novo awarded. Commonwealth v. Williamson, 4 Va. (2 Va. Cas.) 211 (1820).

To convict accessory, commission of offense by principal must be shown. — In order to convict an accessory, although it is not necessary now to show that the principal felon has been convicted, it is necessary to show that the substantive offense, to which he is charged as having been accessory, has been committed by the principal felon. Hatchett v. Commonwealth, 75 Va. 925 (1882); Snyder v. Commonwealth, 202 Va. 1009, 121 S.E.2d 452 (1961).

Before an accessory to a crime can be convicted as such, it must be shown that the crime has been committed by the principal, but it is not necessary that the principal should be convicted of the basic offense. Taylor v. Commonwealth, 260 Va. 683, 537 S.E.2d 592, 2000 Va. LEXIS 126 (2000).

Although the commonwealth must prove a principal in the first degree committed the underlying offense, conviction of the principal in the first degree is not a condition precedent to convicting the accessory. Blankenship v. Commonwealth, No. 1112-99-3, 2000 Va. App. LEXIS 293 (Ct. of Appeals Apr. 25, 2000).

New trial required for accessory where principal acquitted. — M. is prosecuted for subornation of perjury, found guilty, and judgment rendered against him. At the same term of the court, but after the conviction of M., G. is tried for the perjury, and is acquitted. M. then moves the court for a new trial. G. having been acquitted of the perjury, M. should have a new trial, for if G. was not guilty of the perjury, M. could not be guilty of subornation. Maybush v. Commonwealth, 70 Va. (29 Gratt.) 857 (1878).

New trial for accessory not required where principal acquitted. — Where the evidence was sufficient to support a finding that the defendant's brother committed the charged offenses as a principal in the first degree and that the defendant actively aided and abetted his brother's commission of the offenses, the fact that the jury acquitted the defendant's brother did not render the defendant's conviction improper. Blankenship v. Commonwealth, No. 1112-99-3, 2000 Va. App. LEXIS 293 (Ct. of Appeals Apr. 25, 2000).

Aiding and abetting robbery incurs same punishment as being actual robber. — Upon a plea of guilty to aiding and abetting in the robbery, the court is authorized to impose the same punishment upon the defendant as if he were the actual robber. Hern v. Cox, 212 Va. 644, 186 S.E.2d 85 (1972).

CIRCUIT COURT OPINIONS

Lookout during petit larceny guilty of petit larceny. — Defendant, who served as a lookout while another person broke into cars and stole electronic components, was guilty of petit larceny. Commonwealth v. Howlett, 61 Va. Cir. 509, 2003 Va. Cir. LEXIS 136 (Norfolk 2003).

§ 18.2-19. How accessories after the fact punished; certain exceptions.

In the case of every felony, every accessory after the fact shall be guilty of a Class 1 misdemeanor; provided, however, no person in the relation of husband or wife, parent or grandparent, child or grandchild, brother or sister, by consanguinity or affinity, or servant to the offender, who, after the commission of a felony, shall aid or assist a principal felon or accessory before the fact to avoid or escape from prosecution or punishment, shall be deemed an accessory after the fact.

History.
Code 1950, §§ 18.1-11, 18.1-12; 1960, c. 358; 1975, cc. 14, 15.

Law Review.
For note, "The Attorney-Client Privilege," see 19 U. Rich. L. Rev. 559 (1985).

Michie's Jurisprudence.
For related discussion, see 1A M.J. Accomplices and Accessories, § 5; 9B M.J. Husband and Wife, § 87.

CASE NOTES

Common-law definition. — This charge constitutes what the law denominates an accessory after the fact. The common law definitely and distinctly defines who is such an offender. He is a person who, knowing a felony to have been committed by another, receives, relieves, comforts or assists the felon. Wren v. Commonwealth, 67 Va. (26 Gratt.) 952 (1875).

To constitute one an accessory after the fact, three things are requisite: (1) the felony must be completed; (2) he must know that the felon is guilty; and (3) he must receive, relieve, comfort or assist him. It is necessary that the accessory have notice, direct or implied, at the time he assists or comforts the felon, that he has committed a felony. Wren v. Commonwealth, 67 Va. (26 Gratt.) 952 (1875).

Kind of help unimportant. — The true test whether one is accessory after the fact, is to consider whether what he did was done by way of personal help to his principal, with the view of enabling his principal to elude punishment, the kind of help rendered appearing to be unimportant. Wren v. Commonwealth, 67 Va. (26 Gratt.) 952 (1875). See Buck v. Commonwealth, 116 Va. 1031, 83 S.E. 390 (1914).

Detective who allows prisoner to escape not an accessory. — A detective who allows a prisoner to go away without being arrested, and who knows that such criminal has committed a felony, is not an accessory after the fact. Wren v. Commonwealth, 67 Va. (26 Gratt.) 952 (1875).

Whether accessory after the fact had knowledge of commission of felony is a jury question. Wren v. Commonwealth, 67 Va. (26 Gratt.) 952 (1875).

Particular evidence necessary to show notice of felony to accessory. — And although it seemed at one time to be doubted whether an implied notice of the felony would not in some cases suffice, as where a man received a felon in the same county in which

he has been attainted, which was supposed to have been a matter of notoriety, it seems to be the better opinion that some more particular evidence is requisite to raise the presumption of knowledge. Wren v. Commonwealth, 67 Va. (26 Gratt.) 952 (1875).

Evidence sufficient. — Evidence, including 911 tape recording giving a narrative report of a larceny in progress, and that defendant was seen with another individual pushing a large bin containing stole machinery to sell at for scrap, was sufficient to convict defendant of grand larceny in violation of § 18.2-19. However, conviction was reversed because 911 recording was improperly admitted. Wilder v. Commonwealth, 55 Va. App. 579, 687 S.E.2d 542, 2010 Va. App. LEXIS 24 (2010).

§ 18.2-20. Reserved.

§ 18.2-21. When and where accessories tried; how indicted.

An accessory, either before or after the fact, may, whether the principal felon be convicted or not, or be amenable to justice or not, be indicted, tried, convicted and punished in the county or corporation in which he became accessory, or in which the principal felon might be indicted. Any such accessory before the fact may be indicted either with such principal or separately.

History.
Code 1950, § 18.1-13; 1960, c. 358; 1975, cc. 14, 15.

Michie's Jurisprudence.
For related discussion, see 1A M.J. Accomplices and Accessories, §§ 2, 8, 9, 10.

CASE NOTES

It must be shown that a crime has been committed by the principal before the accessory to the crime can be convicted as such. However, it is not necessary that the principal should be convicted of the basic offense. Snyder v. Commonwealth, 202 Va. 1009, 121 S.E.2d 452 (1961); Sult v. Commonwealth, 221 Va. 915, 275 S.E.2d 608 (1981).

Although conviction of a principal in the first degree is not a condition precedent to conviction of an accessory, before the accessory to a crime can be convicted as such, it must be shown that the crime has been committed by the principal. Dusenbery v. Commonwealth, 220 Va. 770, 263 S.E.2d 392 (1980).

CHAPTER 3.

INCHOATE OFFENSES.

ARTICLE 1.
CONSPIRACIES.

Michie's Jurisprudence.
For related discussion, see 4A M.J. Conspiracy, §§ 2, 4, 7, 8, 9, 10; 7B M.J. Evidence, § 284.

§ 18.2-22. Conspiracy to commit felony.

(a) If any person shall conspire, confederate or combine with another, either within or without this Commonwealth, to commit a felony within this Commonwealth, or if he shall so conspire, confederate or combine with another within this Commonwealth to commit a felony either within or without this Commonwealth, he shall be guilty of a felony which shall be punishable as follows:

(1) Every person who so conspires to commit an offense which is punishable by death shall be guilty of a Class 3 felony;

(2) Every person who so conspires to commit an offense which is a noncapital felony shall be guilty of a Class 5 felony; and

(3) Every person who so conspires to commit an offense the maximum punishment for which is confinement in a state correctional facility for a period of less than five years shall be confined in a state correctional facility for a period of one year, or, in the discretion of the jury or the court trying the case without a jury, may be confined in jail not exceeding twelve months and fined not exceeding $500, either or both.

(b) However, in no event shall the punishment for a conspiracy to commit an offense exceed the maximum punishment for the commission of the offense itself.

(c) Jurisdiction for the trial of any person accused of a conspiracy under this section shall be in the county or city wherein any part of such conspiracy is planned or in the county or city wherein any act is done toward the consummation of such plan or conspiracy.

(d) The penalty provisions of this section shall not apply to any person who conspires to commit any offense defined in Chapter 34 of Title 54.1 or of Article 1 (§ 18.2-247 et seq.), Chapter 7 of this title. The penalty for any such violation shall be as provided in § 18.2-256.

History.
Code 1950, § 18.1-15.3; 1972, c. 484; 1973, c. 399; 1975, cc. 14, 15; 1983, c. 19.

Cross references.
As to the Attorney General's limited authority to institute or conduct criminal prosecutions for violations of this chapter, see § 2.2-511.

Law Review.
For article on the law of inchoate crimes, see 59 Va. L. Rev. 1235 (1973).

Research references.
Paul Marcus, Prosecution and Defense of Criminal Conspiracy Cases (Matthew Bender).

CASE NOTES

This section must be strictly construed against the Commonwealth. Cartwright v. Commonwealth, 223 Va. 368, 288 S.E.2d 491 (1982).

Definition. — Conspiracy is an agreement between two or more persons by some concerted action to commit an offense. Falden v. Commonwealth, 167 Va. 542, 189 S.E. 326 (1937); Cartwright v. Commonwealth, 223 Va. 368, 288 S.E.2d 491 (1982).

In Virginia, the crime of conspiracy is complete when the parties agree to commit an offense. Gray v. Commonwealth, 260 Va. 675, 537 S.E.2d 862, 2000 Va. LEXIS 141 (2000).

A conspiracy is committed when the agreement to commit the offense is complete and no overt act in furtherance of the underlying crime is necessary. Stevens v. Commonwealth, 14 Va. App. 238, 415 S.E.2d 881 (1992).

Commonwealth must prove an agreement was made. — In order to prove a conspiracy to distribute heroin, the Commonwealth is required to prove an agreement between defendant and another person to do so; if the Commonwealth fails to produce such evidence, defendant's false testimony alone cannot support his conviction. Cosby v. Commonwealth, — Va. App. —, — S.E.2d —, 2005 Va. App. LEXIS 161 (Apr. 26, 2005).

Shared intent may not be inferred from mere proximity. — In a prosecution for conspiracy to distribute heroin, the fact finder may not infer the shared intent necessary to an agreement from mere proximity and eyeshot. Cosby v. Commonwealth, — Va. App. —, — S.E.2d —, 2005 Va. App. LEXIS 161 (Apr. 26, 2005).

Intent to cooperate in a joint venture. — In a prosecution for conspiracy to distribute heroin, the fact finder may not infer an intent to cooperate in a joint venture from the mere possession of partial proceeds from a sale. Cosby v. Commonwealth, — Va. App. —, — S.E.2d —, 2005 Va. App. LEXIS 161 (Apr. 26, 2005).

Two reasons have been given for making conspiracy illegal: one is to punish the special dangers inherent in group criminal activity, and the second is to permit preventive steps against those who show a disposition to commit crime. Cartwright v. Commonwealth, 223 Va. 368, 288 S.E.2d 491 (1982).

A single agreement can form the basis for multiple violations of this section. Cartwright v. Commonwealth, 223 Va. 368, 288 S.E.2d 491 (1982).

Prosecution for conspiracy to commit robbery barred where previous acquittal of underlying robbery. — Defendant's prosecution for conspiracy to commit robbery was barred under principles of double jeopardy where defendant had previously been acquitted of the underlying robbery. Ginanni v. Commonwealth, 13 Va. App. 1, 408 S.E.2d 767 (1991).

Conspiring with police officer and officer's informant. — An accused may not be convicted under this section for conspiring to distribute cocaine with a police officer and the officer's confidential informant. Fortune v. Commonwealth, 12 Va. App. 643, 406 S.E.2d 47 (1991).

Case fell within "third party" exception to Wharton's Rule. — Case involving prosecution for conspiracy to distribute heroin fell within the recognized "third party" exception to Wharton's Rule, where the number of conspirators exceeded the essential participants in the contemplated crime. Brown v. Commonwealth, 10 Va. App. 73, 390 S.E.2d 386 (1990).

For case discussing the application of "Wharton's Rule" in forgery and conspiracy to commit a felony case, see Ramsey v. Commonwealth, 2 Va. App. 265, 343 S.E.2d 465 (1986).

Applicability of Wharton's Rule. — Wharton's Rule did not operate to bar defendant's conviction and punishment under § 18.2-22 for conspiracy to commit murder; defendant's reliance on the fact that she was convicted of murder under a theory of accomplice liability was misplaced, as the focus was on the underlying criminal act of the particular substantive offense rather than on the accomplice aspect of the offense, and application of Wharton's Rule would be in direct contravention of legislative intent to the contrary. Schwartz v. Commonwealth, 45 Va. App. 407, 611 S.E.2d 631, 2005 Va. App. LEXIS 156 (2005).

Indictment sufficient even though it did not identify the object felony as murder. — Because count two of her indictment fully informed defendant that she was charged with conspiring to commit a felony and because conspiracy to commit a felony was the only crime set forth in § 18.2-22, count two was sufficient to advise defendant of the cause and nature of the accusation lodged against her, as required by the United States and Virginia Constitutions, even though it did not identify the object felony as murder. Schwartz v. Commonwealth, 45 Va. App. 407, 611 S.E.2d 631, 2005 Va. App. LEXIS 156 (2005).

Plea agreement. — Although defendant was originally indicted for robbery in violation of § 18.2-58, and defendant pled guilty to an amended indictment for conspiracy to commit robbery, § 18.2-22, the Commonwealth was free to seek a new indictment for robbery when defendant failed to comply with a condition of the plea agreement that defendant would cooperate fully in the prosecution of a codefendant. Williams v. Commonwealth, 2010 Va. App. LEXIS 382 (Sept. 28, 2010).

Conspiracy alone and not murder itself enough to establish jurisdiction in Virginia. — Even if the defendant could not have been charged by Virginia with a murder that took place in the Philippines, both the defendant and his assassin, because they conspired to kill the intended victim in Virginia, would have committed the Virginia crime of conspiracy to commit capital murder. United States v. Morin, 80 F.3d 124 (4th Cir. 1996).

Venue may be proper in more than one place. — Because conspiracy is a continuing offense, venue may be proper in more than one place. Brown v. Commonwealth, 10 Va. App. 73, 390 S.E.2d 386 (1990).

Where "strong presumption," venue proper for conspiracy. — Where the evidence was sufficient to give rise to a "strong presumption" that the robbery and abduction were committed in Arlington County, it followed, therefore, that, pursuant to this section, Arlington County was a proper venue for the trial of the conspiracy indictment. Cheng v. Commonwealth, 240 Va. 26, 393 S.E.2d 599 (1990).

Venue held proper in county where marijuana stored for defendant. — Defendant's directing of alleged co-conspirator to retrieve the marijuana at another alleged co-conspirator's house in Henrico County, which was then stored with the other marijuana held for defendant, was an act in furtherance of the conspiracy, and, accordingly, venue was proper in the Circuit Court for Henrico County. Barber v. Commonwealth, 5 Va. App. 172, 360 S.E.2d 888 (1987).

Evidentiary factors. — Proof of an explicit agreement is not required and oftentimes the prosecution must rely only on circumstantial evidence to establish the conspiracy. Stevens v. Commonwealth, 14 Va. App. 238, 415 S.E.2d 881 (1992).

Circumstantial proof. — The crime of conspiracy may be proved by circumstantial evidence; indeed, because of the very nature of the offense, it often may be established only by indirect and circumstantial evidence. Gray v. Commonwealth, 260 Va. 675, 537 S.E.2d 862, 2000 Va. LEXIS 141 (2000).

Declaration of co-conspirator admissible. — When the evidence establishes a prima facie case of conspiracy, that is, that two or more persons have entered into an agreement to commit a crime, any declaration of a conspirator during such conspiracy, and in furtherance thereof, is admissible, in a prosecution for the target crime, as substantive evidence against any co-conspirator on trial. Such evidence is admitted on the theory that the declarant is the agent of the other conspirator. Berger v. Commonwealth, 217 Va. 332, 228 S.E.2d 559 (1976).

But not certain declarations after end of conspiracy. — Incriminating, inculpatory, extrajudicial declarations of a co-conspirator made in the absence of or without the knowledge of the accused, after the conspiracy has come to an end through withdrawal or arrest of the participants, or termination of the plan in success or failure, are inadmissible in evidence in a criminal trial to prove the guilt of one other than the declarant. Berger v. Commonwealth, 217 Va. 332, 228 S.E.2d 559 (1976).

Evidence held sufficient. — Evidence of conspiracy to commit murder held sufficient where the defendant agreed with estranged wife of the intended victim to have her husband killed so that she could receive a financial windfall and, as part of the agreement, the defendant made a firearm silencer that he contemplated the wife would use to accomplish the homicide. Gray v. Commonwealth, 260 Va. 675, 537 S.E.2d 862, 2000 Va. LEXIS 141 (2000).

Evidence was sufficient to sustain defendant's conspiracy conviction where the evidence proved that defendant and a co-conspirator acted in tandem to distribute drugs; each played a role in the distribution process — defendant received the money and the co-conspirator retrieved the drugs from the area near the tree. After the transactions, the two remained together near a parked vehicle. Banks v. Commonwealth, — Va. App. —, — S.E.2d —, 2006 Va. App. LEXIS 60 (Feb. 14, 2006).

Defendant's use of the victim's cell phone shortly after it was stolen and the undisputed DNA evidence establishing that DNA recovered from the victim matched defendant's DNA profile provided sufficient evidence to prove that defendant was the criminal agent who committed the crimes of forcible sodomy, abduction, robbery, and conspiracy to commit robbery. Hayden v. Commonwealth, — Va. App. —, — S.E.2d —, 2006 Va. App. LEXIS 275 (June 27, 2006).

Defendant's conviction of conspiracy to commit a felony was affirmed; defendant's brandishing of a weapon only moments after a statement by defendant's brother ("We're going to shoot their ass") would allow a rational fact finder to reasonably conclude that defendant agreed with the statement, planned to shoot the victim, but at the last minute changed defendant's mind. Berry v. Commonwealth, — Va. App. —, — S.E.2d —, 2007 Va. App. LEXIS 77 (Mar. 6, 2007).

Homeowner's presence in the residence, thereby disrupting defendant's plan to commit burglary and grand larceny, did not relieve defendant of criminal liability for conspiracy to commit burglary and grand larceny there, as the conspiracy was complete when defendant formed the agreement with a companion to unlawfully enter and take property from the targeted residences. Seis v. Commonwealth, 2007 Va. App. LEXIS 432 (Nov. 27, 2007).

There was ample support in the record for the trial court's determination that defendant conspired to rob the sporting goods store, notwithstanding defendant's failure to carry out a robbery. Defendant and the co-conspirator agreed to rob the store and had discussed how to accomplish the robbery on several occasions; the co-conspirator's testimony was sufficient proof of an explicit agreement to carry out a taking of the store's property. Anderson v. Commonwealth, 52 Va. App. 501, 664 S.E.2d 514, 2008 Va. App. LEXIS 377 (2008), aff'd, 683 S.E.2d 536, 2009 Va. LEXIS 86 (Va. 2009).

Sufficient evidence supported defendant's conspiracy conviction under § 18.2-22 as defendant conspired with two accomplices to commit a felony as they discussed an affront by a victim the day of a burglary, defendant told an officer that defendant went to the apartment at an accomplice's direction, and their actions were indicative of a pre-designed plan as an accomplice told one of the victim's roommates that if anything happened, it had nothing to do with the roommate. Jones v. Commonwealth, — Va. App. —, — S.E.2d —, 2009 Va. App. LEXIS 44 (Feb. 3, 2009), aff'd, 279 Va. 295, 687 S.E.2d 738 (2010).

Evidence, including that there was an agreement to go to the victim's apartment for purposes stemming from an argument with the victim, was sufficient to establish a conspiracy under § 18.2-22. Jones v. Commonwealth, 279 Va. 295, 687 S.E.2d 738, 2010 Va. LEXIS 4 (2010).

Conviction for conspiracy to maim by mob was supported by a finding that a reasonable fact finder could have inferred from the circumstances and overt actions of the parties that the mob did not form spontaneously, but was the result of a collective, agreed upon effort to punish anyone involved in the earlier flight inside the club. Johnson v. Commonwealth, 58 Va. App. 625, 712 S.E.2d 751, 2011 Va. App. LEXIS 259 (2011).

Evidence was sufficient to support defendant's conviction for conspiracy to commit robbery, as defendant was present and hung around the rea and shared the proceeds of the robbery. Defendant knew his role was to wait with the getaway driver in the vehicle to pick up the principals, and he played that role. Whitley v. Commonwealth, 2013 Va. App. LEXIS 63 (Feb. 26, 2013).

There was sufficient evidence supporting a conviction for conspiracy to commit robbery. After the victim opened his wallet, defendant and the others surrounded him, announced their intention to rob him, then without speaking to each other took coordinated positions around him to prevent his escape; and defendant's acting as if he had a weapon contributed to the robbery. Lewis v. Commonwealth, 2012 Va. App. LEXIS 381 (Nov. 27, 2012).

Evidence sufficient to support conviction for conspiracy to commit robbery. — Where the evidence showed that defendant said that defendant planned to rob the victim and put defendant's plan into action with an intent to rob the victim, and that, from that starting premise, a co-conspirator agreed to participate in defendant's plan, defendant's conviction for conspiracy to commit robbery in violation of §§ 18.2-58 and 18.2-22 was supported by sufficient evidence. James v. Commonwealth, 53 Va. App. 671, 674 S.E.2d 571, 2009 Va. App. LEXIS 155 (2009).

Evidence was sufficient to support defendant's conviction for conspiracy to commit robbery, as there was sufficient proof of an agreement to commit robbery between defendant and a woman; there was a reasonable inference that defendant and the woman had a prearranged plan to take the television from the victim. Searcy v. Commonwealth, 2012 Va. App. LEXIS 383 (Nov. 27, 2012).

Evidence insufficient. — Because the Commonwealth conceded that the evidence of an intent to defraud was insufficient to sustain defendant's conviction of obtaining goods by false pretenses in violation of § 43-13, there had to be a concession that the evidence was insufficient to prove the conviction of conspiracy to commit a felony in violation of § 18.2-22; both required the intent to defraud, and the conspiracy alleged and tried was a conspiracy to violate § 18.2-178, and not a conspiracy to violate § 43-13. Hinote v. Commonwealth, No. 2570-10-2, 2011 Va. App. LEXIS 362 (Ct. of Appeals Nov. 22, 2011).

Evidence did not exclude the reasonable hypothesis of innocence that defendant was merely aiding and abetting the commission of the murder of the victim as the trial court expressly found that no agreement existed prior to when defendant, the other individual, and a third person arrived at the apartment complex where the victim was socializing, thereby negating any inference that defendant and the other individual entered into a conspiracy to kill the victim. Because the evidence did not establish beyond a reasonable doubt that defendant and the other individual entered into an agreement to kill the victim, the evidence was insufficient as a matter of law to support his conviction for conspiracy to commit murder. Nichols v. Commonwealth, 2012 Va. App. LEXIS 416 (Dec. 18, 2012).

Although the evidence supported a finding that the parties agreed to entered the subject house in order to commit a larceny, the conspiracy conviction could not be upheld, because the evidence did not establish that they agreed to enter the house at night. Derrick v. Commonwealth, 2013 Va. App. LEXIS 101 (Apr. 2, 2013).

Withdrawal from conspiracy not a defense. — In Virginia, unlike some other jurisdictions, withdrawal is not a defense to conspiracy; the crime of conspiracy is complete when the parties agree to commit an offense and no action subsequent to the formation of the agreement can exonerate the conspirator of that crime. Gray v. Commonwealth, 260 Va. 675, 537 S.E.2d 862, 2000 Va. LEXIS 141 (2000).

Conviction for both statutory burglary and conspiracy. — One who has been convicted of statutory burglary may be convicted of conspiracy to commit statutory burglary and grand larceny. The conspiracy is not merged into the consummated statutory burglary. Bell v. Commonwealth, 220 Va. 87, 255 S.E.2d 498 (1979).

Applied in Stewart v. Commonwealth, 225 Va. 473, 303 S.E.2d 877 (1983); Henry v. Commonwealth, 2 Va. App. 194, 342 S.E.2d 655 (1986); Graves v. Commonwealth, 234 Va. 578, 363 S.E.2d 705 (1988); Johnson v. Commonwealth, 8 Va. App. 34, 377 S.E.2d 636 (1989); Jay v. Commonwealth, 275 Va. 510, 659 S.E.2d 311, 2008 Va. LEXIS 53 (2008).

§ 18.2-23. Conspiring to trespass or commit larceny.

A. If any person shall conspire, confederate or combine with another or others in the Commonwealth to go upon or remain upon the lands, buildings or premises of another, or any part, portion or area thereof, having knowledge that any of them have been forbidden, either orally or in writing, to do so by the owner, lessee, custodian or other person lawfully in charge thereof, or having knowledge that any of them have been forbidden to do so by a sign or signs posted on such lands, buildings, premises or part, portion or area thereof at a place or places where it or they may reasonably be seen, he shall be deemed guilty of a Class 3 misdemeanor.

B. If any person shall conspire, confederate or combine with another or others in the Commonwealth to commit larceny or counsel, assist, aid or abet another in the performance of a larceny, where the aggregate value of the goods or merchandise involved is more than $200, he is guilty of a felony punishable by confinement in a state correctional facility for not less than one year nor more than 20 years. The willful concealment of goods or merchandise of any store or other mercantile establishment, while still on the premises thereof, shall be prima facie evidence of an intent to convert and defraud the owner thereof out of the value of the goods or merchandise. A violation of this subsection constitutes a separate and distinct felony.

C. Jurisdiction for the trial of any person charged under this section shall be in the county or city wherein any part of such conspiracy is planned, or in the county or city wherein any act is done toward the consummation of such plan or conspiracy.

History.
Code 1950, § 18.1-15.1; 1960, cc. 99, 358; 1975, cc. 14, 15; 2003, c. 831.

Michie's Jurisprudence.
For related discussion, see 4A M.J. Conspiracy, §§ 2, 8.

CASE NOTES

Applied in Swisher v. Commonwealth, 256 Va. 471, 506 S.E.2d 763 (1998).

Evidence sufficient to support conviction. — Evidence supported a finding that defendant and two accomplices had agreed to commit grand larceny in violation of subsection B of § 18.2-23 and § 18.2-95 because testimony revealed that they were in a store, together, for one-and-a-half hours, taking merchandise and thereafter concealing the merchandise, and the trial court could properly infer that defendant and the accomplices, prior to entering the store, agreed upon a course of action that would provide the means to conceal the merchandise to be stolen from the store; because the evidence proved conspiracy, and the aggregate value of the merchandise concealed by defendant and the accomplices exceeded $200, the trial court did not err in convicting defendant of grand larceny. Brown v. Commonwealth, 2010 Va. App. LEXIS 299 (July 27, 2010).

§ 18.2-23.1. Completed substantive offense bars conviction for conspiracy.

Notwithstanding any other provision of this article or of § 18.2-256, in any case where a defendant has been tried and convicted of an act he has also conspired to commit, such defendant shall be subject to conviction only for the completed substantive offense and not thereafter be convicted for the underlying conspiracy.

History.
1985, c. 376.

Law Review.
For 1991 survey on criminal law and procedure, see 25 U. Rich. L. Rev. 731 (1991).

Michie's Jurisprudence.

For related discussion, see 4A M.J. Conspiracy, § 4; 6B M.J. Drugs and Druggists, § 5.

CASE NOTES

Presumption of prospective application. — There are no words in this section which can be construed as legislative intent to override the presumption that new laws are to be prospective in their operation. Shilling v. Commonwealth, 4 Va. App. 500, 359 S.E.2d 311 (1987).

Even if this section applied retroactively, there was sufficient evidence to convict the defendant of distribution and conspiracy to distribute a controlled substance, where the indictments were tried simultaneously and the evidence concerning all three indictments was heard by the jury at the same time, no objection was raised that the trial court failed to instruct the jury that evidence relating to the distribution charges should not have been considered in arriving at its verdict on the conspiracy charge, and if the defendant had made that request of the trial judge and it was granted, the conspiracy conviction could have been supported by the evidence of the defendant's actions for which no substantive offense charges were brought. Shilling v. Commonwealth, 4 Va. App. 500, 359 S.E.2d 311 (1987).

Application of section to offenses prior to effective date. — Since the effect of this section is to mitigate punishment by barring conviction for the underlying conspiracy if a defendant has been convicted of the completed substantive offense, the Commonwealth's consent was necessary for application of this section to a defendant's trial on offenses that occurred prior to the effective date of this section. Naito v. Commonwealth, No. 1421-86-4 (Ct. of Appeals Nov. 22, 1988).

This section is a substantive penal provision which must be further construed with § 1-16. Naito v. Commonwealth, No. 1421-86-4 (Ct. of Appeals Nov. 22, 1988).

This section does not prescribe a mode of trial conduct, and the fact that it may be asserted in the course of trial proceedings does not make it a procedural provision. Naito v. Commonwealth, No. 1421-86-4 (Ct. of Appeals Nov. 22, 1988).

The word "thereafter," as used in this section, means "at a subsequent trial," and does not mean just any moment of time subsequent to conviction of the substantive offense. Boyd v. Commonwealth, 236 Va. 346, 374 S.E.2d 301 (1988).

Conspiracy convictions not barred where based on separate acts from substantive conviction. — A conviction for distribution of narcotics did not bar a subsequent prosecution of the same defendant for conspiracies to distribute narcotics on dates different from that of the distribution conviction; the distribution conviction was not a bar to the conspiracy convictions, as the conspiracy convictions did not involve the particular acts upon which the substantive conviction was based. However, as there was one overall, ongoing conspiracy encompassing various transactions, the second conspiracy prosecution was barred under principles of double jeopardy. Bowman v. Commonwealth, 11 Va. App. 259, 397 S.E.2d 886 (1990).

Conviction of substantive offense and conspiracy in same trial not prohibited. — This section bars conviction for conspiracy in a subsequent trial after an earlier conviction for the substantive offense; this section does not prohibit, however, conviction of both the completed substantive offense and the underlying conspiracy, provided the convictions occur in a single trial, regardless of the order in which the trial court announced the convictions. Boyd v. Commonwealth, 236 Va. 346, 374 S.E.2d 301 (1988).

Applied in Stevens v. Commonwealth, 14 Va. App. 238, 415 S.E.2d 881 (1992).

§ 18.2-24. Reserved.

ARTICLE 2.
ATTEMPTS.

§ 18.2-25. Attempts to commit capital offenses; how punished.

If any person attempts to commit an offense which is punishable with death, he shall be guilty of a Class 2 felony.

History.

Code 1950, § 18.1-16; 1960, c. 358; 1975, cc. 14, 15; 1985, c. 280.

Cross references.

As to shooting in attempt to commit a felony, see § 18.2-53. As to attempt to commit rape, see note to § 18.2-61. As to indictment for felony and conviction of attempt, see § 19.2-286.

Law Review.

For note, "Capital Punishment in Virginia," see 58 Va. L. Rev. 97 (1972). For article on the law of inchoate crimes, see 59 Va. L. Rev. 1235 (1973). For survey of Virginia criminal law for the year 1973-1974, see 60 Va. L. Rev. 1499 (1974).

Michie's Jurisprudence.

For related discussion, see 2A M.J. Attempts and Solicitations, §§ 3, 6; 5B M.J. Criminal Procedure, §§ 11, 79; 9B M.J. Homicide, § 37; 15 M.J. Rape, § 10.

CASE NOTES

  I. General Consideration.
 II. Elements Of Attempt.
III. Prosecution.
    A. Indictment.
    B. Evidence.
    C. Verdict.

I. GENERAL CONSIDERATION.

Legislative intent as to phrase "an offense which is punishable with death." — The General Assembly intended the phrase "an offense which is punishable with death" to incorporate by reference the substantive offenses to which the highest penalty for attempt would attach. Evans v. Commonwealth, 214 Va. 694, 204 S.E.2d 413 (1974).

Attempt penalty not dependent on existence of death penalty. — There was no legislative intent to make the attempt penalty dependent upon the existence or nonexistence of the death penalty attached to the substantive offenses incorporated by reference. Evans v. Commonwealth, 214 Va. 694, 204 S.E.2d 413 (1974).

An attempt is an offense of a lower grade than the consummated felony. The intention to commit a felony, and the doing of some act towards its commission without actually committing it, is an attempt and is, from its very nature, an offense of a lower grade than the consummated felony. Cates v. Commonwealth, 111 Va. 837, 69 S.E. 520 (1910).

This article supersedes the common law. — This article, providing for punishment for attempts to commit crime, supersedes the common law. But it does not change the common law as to the grade of the offense, so far as murder is concerned, except as to murder in the first degree. Lee v. Commonwealth, 144 Va. 594, 131 S.E. 212 (1926).

But does not change the common-law definition of attempt. Merritt v. Commonwealth, 164 Va. 653, 180 S.E. 395 (1935).

For this article does not undertake to state what shall constitute an attempt to commit a crime. Merritt v. Commonwealth, 164 Va. 653, 180 S.E. 395 (1935).

Double jeopardy considerations. — Section 19.2-294 is not a bar to prosecution for attempted murder after a conviction of obstructing justice; while obstructing justice may be a statutory offense, attempted murder is a common-law offense. Martin v. Commonwealth, 242 Va. 1, 406 S.E.2d 15, cert. denied, 502 U.S. 945, 112 S. Ct. 388, 116 L. Ed. 2d 339 (1991).

Where defendant was first convicted of, inter alia, obstruction of justice by threats or force (a misdemeanor) and later convicted of attempted murder (a felony), the "same conduct" rule enunciated in Grady v. Corbin, 495 U.S. 508, 110 S. Ct. 2084, 109 L.Ed. 2d 548 (1990), did not apply to bar prosecution of the charge of attempted murder on principles of double jeopardy. Martin v. Commonwealth, 242 Va. 1, 406 S.E.2d 15, cert. denied, 502 U.S. 945, 112 S. Ct. 388, 116 L. Ed. 2d 339 (1991).

Multiple punishments for the crimes of attempted murder and malicious wounding do not violate the double jeopardy clause when the convictions are obtained in a single trial. Creamer v. Commonwealth, No. 1298-91-3 (Ct. of Appeals Dec. 15, 1992).

Defendant's conviction in city for the rape that occurred there did not bar proof of that rape as a predicate offense in his prosecution in neighboring county for attempted capital murder. Curtis v. Commonwealth, 13 Va. App. 622, 414 S.E.2d 421 (1992).

Double jeopardy not a bar. — Defendant's double jeopardy rights were not violated in a case where defendant pled guilty to solicitation to commit murder in violation of § 18.2-29 and a jury then convicted defendant in a trial of attempted capital murder for hire in violation of subdivision 2 of § 18.2-31 and § 18.2-25. Double jeopardy did not apply because: (1) defendant's offenses were considered in a single proceeding and, thus, there were not successive prosecutions for the same offense; and (2) solicitation to commit murder and attempted capital murder for hire were not the same offenses and, thus, defendant could be convicted and punished for both offenses since solicitation for murder required that a defendant solicit another person whereas attempted capital murder for hire did not require such proof. Ostrander v. Commonwealth, 51 Va. App. 386, 658 S.E.2d 346, 2008 Va. App. LEXIS 126 (2008).

II. ELEMENTS OF ATTEMPT.

Common law. — While the punishments for attempts to commit felonies are fixed by statute, what constitutes an attempt must be ascertained from the common law. Johnson v. Commonwealth, 209 Va. 291, 163 S.E.2d 570 (1968).

An attempt consists of intent plus a direct act. — An attempt to commit a crime consists of: (1) the intent; (2) a direct, ineffectual act towards its commission; and that act must reach far enough towards the accomplishment of the desired result to amount to the commencement of the consummation. Hicks v. Commonwealth, 86 Va. 223, 9 S.E. 1024 (1889); Barrett v. Commonwealth, 210 Va. 153, 169 S.E.2d 449 (1969); Sizemore v. Commonwealth, 218 Va. 980, 243 S.E.2d 212 (1978).

An attempt in criminal law is an unfinished crime and is composed of two elements, the intent to commit the crime and the doing of some direct act toward its consummation, but falling short of the accomplishment of the ultimate design. Martin v. Commonwealth, 195 Va. 1107, 81 S.E.2d 574 (1954); Johnson v. Commonwealth, 209 Va. 291, 163 S.E.2d 570 (1968).

Intent necessary. — A person cannot be guilty of an attempt to commit murder unless he has a specific intent to kill. Merritt v. Commonwealth, 164 Va. 653, 180 S.E. 395 (1935).

The necessary intent is the intent in fact, as distinguished from an intent in law. Epps v. Commonwealth, 216 Va. 150, 216 S.E.2d 64 (1975); Nobles v. Commonwealth, 218 Va. 548, 238 S.E.2d 808 (1977).

Under this article "attempt" embraces the full meaning of "intent," and may be, and frequently is, shown by circumstances. It is a state of mind which may be proved by a person's conduct or by his statements. Barrett v. Commonwealth, 210 Va. 153, 169

S.E.2d 449 (1969); Nobles v. Commonwealth, 218 Va. 548, 238 S.E.2d 808 (1977).

Intent in fact is the purpose formed in a person's mind which may be shown by his conduct. Epps v. Commonwealth, 216 Va. 150, 216 S.E.2d 64 (1975).

State of mind is the subject of any inquiry concerning whether an intent to kill exists in an attempted murder case. Nobles v. Commonwealth, 218 Va. 548, 238 S.E.2d 808 (1977).

Presumption of intention. — A person is presumed to intend the immediate, direct, and necessary consequences of his voluntary act. Nobles v. Commonwealth, 218 Va. 548, 238 S.E.2d 808 (1977).

Whether the required intent exists is generally a question for the trier of fact. Nobles v. Commonwealth, 218 Va. 548, 238 S.E.2d 808 (1977).

Preparation and attempt distinguished. — Preparation consists in devising or arranging the means or measures necessary for the commission of the offense and the attempt is a direct movement towards the commission after the preparations are made. Martin v. Commonwealth, 195 Va. 1107, 81 S.E.2d 574 (1954).

The act must amount to the commencement of the consummation. — The act must reach far enough towards the accomplishment of the desired result to amount to the commencement of the consummation. Thacker v. Commonwealth, 134 Va. 767, 114 S.E. 504 (1922). See Dixon v. Commonwealth, 162 Va. 798, 173 S.E. 521 (1934). See also Merritt v. Commonwealth, 164 Va. 653, 180 S.E. 395 (1935), holding that where the intent appears as a part of the act alleged it need not be expressly stated.

But need not be last proximate act prior to the consummation. — The overt act, composing one of the two essential elements of an attempt, need not be the last proximate act prior to the consummation of the felony attempted to be perpetrated. Uhl v. Commonwealth, 47 Va. (6 Gratt.) 706 (1849); Glover v. Commonwealth, 86 Va. 382, 10 S.E. 420 (1889).

An attempt need not be the last proximate act towards the consummation of the crime in contemplation, but is sufficient if it be an act apparently adopted to produce the result intended; mere preparation is not sufficient. Martin v. Commonwealth, 195 Va. 1107, 81 S.E.2d 574 (1954).

Sufficient evidence to show attempted capital murder for hire. — Defendant asked two people to kill his wife, formulated diagrams of his wife's house, explained when she would be at home, and paid two thousand dollars to the hit man. The evidence was sufficient to convict defendant of attempted capital murder for hire, in violation of §§ 18.2-25 and 18.2-31, and solicitation of capital murder for hire in violation of §§ 18.2-29 and 18.2-31; the Commonwealth did not err by failing to elect between the charges, because the solicitation and attempt were both parts of a common scheme or plan. Ashford v. Commonwealth, 47 Va. App. 676, 626 S.E.2d 464, 2006 Va. App. LEXIS 70 (2006).

III. PROSECUTION.

A. Indictment.

The Supreme Court has been liberal in sustaining indictments charging an attempt to commit a crime under this section. Merritt v. Commonwealth, 164 Va. 653, 180 S.E. 395 (1935).

The allegations of an indictment must be read as a whole. Fields v. Commonwealth, 129 Va. 774, 106 S.E. 333 (1921).

Indictments must allege act that constitutes an attempt. — It is an elementary rule of criminal pleading that an indictment for an attempt to commit an offense must allege some act done by the defendant of such a nature as to constitute an attempt, in a legal sense, to commit the contemplated offense, otherwise the indictment will not be sufficient. Commonwealth v. Clark, 47 Va. (6 Gratt.) 675 (1849). See Hicks v. Commonwealth, 86 Va. 223, 9 S.E. 1024 (1889); Cunningham v. Commonwealth, 88 Va. 37, 13 S.E. 309 (1891).

But need not allege intent. — Where the statute under which the indictment is found expressly makes the "intent" descriptive of the offense, the prevailing rule is that the indictment must expressly allege the "intent," but this is not true of this section on attempts to commit crime. Broaddus v. Commonwealth, 126 Va. 733, 101 S.E. 321 (1919).

If it is an attempt to do an act in its nature evil. — An indictment under this section charged that accused made an assault upon a woman and he feloniously did attempt to ravish and carnally know, against her will and by force. The indictment thus followed the statute in the use of the word "attempt," without further expansion. It charged, however, an assault, and that the "attempt" was "to ravish and carnally know" the prosecutrix "against her will and by force." This was an act in its nature evil, and an act, therefore, "prima facie evil also in intent; so this intent need not be alleged," since the statute under which the indictment was found has not made the intent "affirmatively or descriptively an element of the offense." Broaddus v. Commonwealth, 126 Va. 733, 101 S.E. 321 (1919).

But intent must be alleged if it would not be inferred. — The indictment should charge the intent as well as the overt act unless the specific intent to commit the crime charged might be inferred, either from the nature of the act alleged or from the use of the word "attempt" in the indictment, as "attempt" embraces the full meaning of "intent"; the only distinction between an "intent" and an "attempt" is that the former implies purpose only, while the latter implies both purpose and the effort to carry that purpose into effect. Merritt v. Commonwealth, 164 Va. 653, 180 S.E. 395 (1935).

An indictment charging an attempt to commit a crime should charge both the intent and the overt act; but it has been held that where the intent appeared as a part of the act alleged, it need not be expressly stated. Johnson v. Commonwealth, 209 Va. 291, 163 S.E.2d 570 (1968).

Indictment need not specify degree of attempted murder. — The indictment is not invalid because it failed to specify that the murder alleged to have been attempted was murder in the first degree. Fields v. Commonwealth, 129 Va. 774, 106 S.E. 333 (1921).

Indictment held good. — An indictment under this section alleged that accused "did feloniously attempt to commit the crime of murder by then and there" with a loaded pistol, which pistol accused feloniously, willfully, and of malice aforethought did discharge and shoot off at and towards one David Tabb, the accused being close enough to said Tabb to be within carrying distance of the pistol. It was held that the indictment sufficiently charged the overt acts done towards the commission of the offense. The indictment followed the statute in its use of the word "attempt," and both charged the assault and descended into the particulars of that charge. Fields v. Commonwealth, 129 Va. 774, 106 S.E. 333 (1921).

B. Evidence.

To sustain a conviction of attempted murder, the evidence must establish both a specific intent to kill the victim and an overt but ineffectual act committed in furtherance of this criminal purpose. Nobles v. Commonwealth, 218 Va. 548, 238 S.E.2d 808 (1977); Howard v. Commonwealth, 221 Va. 904, 275 S.E.2d 602 (1981).

Evidence showing preparation only. — The evidence in this case shows only a procurement of the poison and an ineffectual solicitation of a third party to put it in the drink of the intended victim, which acts constitute not an attempt, but only a preparation. Goin v. Absher, 189 Va. 372, 53 S.E.2d 50 (1949).

Evidence not brought before Supreme Court. — Where accused was convicted of an attempt to commit murder in the first degree and the evidence introduced at the trial was not brought before the Supreme Court, that court must presume that it was sufficient to establish that the attempted murder was murder in the first degree. Fields v. Commonwealth, 129 Va. 774, 106 S.E. 333 (1921).

Sufficient evidence. — Where the defendant pointed a loaded rifle at a state trooper and threatened to kill him, the evidence was sufficient to support a conviction for attempted murder, even though the defendant did not pull or attempt to pull the trigger. Sizemore v. Commonwealth, 218 Va. 980, 243 S.E.2d 212 (1978).

Evidence was sufficient to support defendant's attempted robbery conviction, in violation of §§ 18.2-58 and 18.2-25, when the victims testified that defendant said he would "take your stuff, " did not appear to be joking, and, when they ran from him, lifted his shirt and displayed a firearm, as this showed defendant intended to take, with intent to steal, the personal property of another, from his person or in his presence, against his will, by violence or intimidation, and engaged in a direct, ineffectual, act towards its commission. Jones v. Commonwealth, No. 1730-03-1, 2004 Va. App. LEXIS 300 (Ct. of Appeals June 29, 2004).

Court did not make an error of law in ruling that the evidence had been sufficient to support a habeas petitioner's conviction for attempted murder; the inmate's driving a truck, armed with a deadly weapon, from Florida to within one-half mile of the intended victim's workplace in Virginia was the overt act that supported his conviction. Littlefield v. Hinkle, — F. Supp. 2d —, 2005 U.S. Dist. LEXIS 31344 (W.D. Va. Nov. 22, 2005).

Because defendant swerved a car toward a police officer rather than driving straight ahead to escape, the evidence was sufficient to prove premeditation and the specific intent to kill; consequently, defendant was properly convicted of violating § 18.2-25. Coles v. Commonwealth, 270 Va. 585, 621 S.E.2d 109, 2005 Va. LEXIS 88 (2005).

Sufficient evidence supported defendant's conviction under § 18.2-25 and subdivision 6 of § 18.2-31 of attempted capital murder of a police officer because the specific intent required for the crime could be inferred by defendant veering the defendant's automobile from the defendant's path of travel directly towards a second police officer, resulting in defendant striking the second officer at about 40 to 50 mph, knocking the second officer to the ground, and running over the officer's foot. Piggott v. Commonwealth, — Va. App. —, — S.E.2d —, 2008 Va. App. LEXIS 432 (Sept. 23, 2008).

Evidence that defendant did not brake or attempt to avoid the collision and collided head-on with the officer while still accelerating, supported the finding that defendant had the specific intent to kill the officer and thus, was sufficient to convict defendant of attempted capital murder. McMillan v. Commonwealth, 2009 Va. App. LEXIS 118 (Mar. 17, 2009).

C. Verdict.

Need not show degree of murder attempted. — In a prosecution for an attempt to commit murder, the jury found the accused guilty as charged in the indictment and fixed her punishment at two years confinement in the penitentiary (now state correctional facility). It was held that the verdict was not invalid because it did not expressly appear therefrom that the jury found the accused guilty of the attempt to commit murder in the first degree. Fields v. Commonwealth, 129 Va. 774, 106 S.E. 333 (1921).

Improper conviction where offense not lesser included one. — Defendant was improperly convicted of assault on a law-enforcement officer where that crime was not a lesser-included offense of attempted capital murder of an officer. Edwards v. Commonwealth, 40 Va. App. 529, 580 S.E.2d 450, 2003 Va. App. LEXIS 298 (2003).

§ 18.2-26. Attempts to commit noncapital felonies; how punished.

Every person who attempts to commit an offense which is a noncapital felony shall be punished as follows:

(1) If the felony attempted is punishable by a maximum punishment of life imprisonment or a term of years in excess of twenty years, an attempt thereat shall be punishable as a Class 4 felony.

(2) If the felony attempted is punishable by a maximum punishment of twenty years' imprisonment, an attempt thereat shall be punishable as a Class 5 felony.

(3) If the felony attempted is punishable by a maximum punishment of less than twenty years' imprisonment, an attempt thereat shall be punishable as a Class 6 felony.

History.
Code 1950, §§ 18.1-17, 18.1-18; 1960, c. 358; 1975, cc. 14, 15; 1994, c. 639.

Law Review.
For survey of Virginia criminal law for the year 1973-1974, see 60 Va. L. Rev. 1499 (1974). For survey of Virginia criminal law for the year 1974-1975, see 61 Va. L. Rev. 1697 (1975). For article discuss-

ing the legislative history of sexual assault law reform in Virginia, see 68 Va. L. Rev. 459 (1982). For article, "Modal Retributivism: A Theory of Sanctions for Attempts and Other Criminal Wrongs," see 45 U. Rich. L. Rev. 647 (2011).

Michie's Jurisprudence.

For related discussion, see 9B M.J. Homicide, § 37; 15 M.J. Rape, § 27.

CASE NOTES

Double jeopardy considerations. — Multiple punishments for the crimes of attempted murder and malicious wounding do not violate the double jeopardy clause when the convictions are obtained in a single trial. Creamer v. Commonwealth, No. 1298-91-3 (Ct. of Appeals Dec. 15, 1992).

Proof of attempted murder does not require proof of an actual injury, and therefore aggravated malicious wounding and attempted murder each contain an element not contained by the other, and neither crime is a lesser-included offense of the other for double jeopardy purposes. Dennis v. Commonwealth, No. 1285-98-1 (Ct. of Appeals Oct. 19, 1999).

The word "punishable," as here used, means the maximum punishment which may be imposed. Slusher v. Commonwealth, 196 Va. 440, 83 S.E.2d 719 (1954).

No retroactive assignment of punishment. — Although the amendments to this section subsequent to defendant's misconduct included attempts at § 18.2-32 offenses, the revised statute may not retroactively assign punishment to prior acts. Cook v. Commonwealth, 20 Va. App. 510, 458 S.E.2d 317 (1995).

No error in indictment amendment which substituted § 18.2-257 for this section. — Where prior to trial, the trial court granted the Commonwealth's motion to amend the second count of indictment, thereby changing the attempt statute on which the Commonwealth was relying from this section, the general attempt statute, to § 18.2-257, which covers attempts to violate the Drug Control Act, the trial court did not err in granting the Commonwealth's motion to amend the indictment against defendant. The amendment did not change the nature or character of the offense charged; it merely substituted reference to § 18.2-257, the specific provision covering attempts to commit drug offenses, for this section, the general provision covering attempts to commit general, non-capital felonies. Robinson v. Commonwealth, No. 1840-90-1 (Ct. of Appeals July 21, 1992).

Conviction for conduct not constituting crime. — This section, at the time of defendant's offense, did not provide a punishment for an attempted felony which was punishable by confinement for a maximum of 40 years. Thus, although defendant's conduct may have been proscribed by § 18.2-32, it was an offense without a penalty. Therefore, defendant was convicted for conduct which constituted no crime at the time of the offense. Accordingly, the judgment of the trial court was reversed. Cook v. Commonwealth, 20 Va. App. 510, 458 S.E.2d 317 (1995).

Instructions which permitted the jury to find defendant guilty of attempted murder in either first or second degree, and set forth the punishment for either offense, were not confusing and prejudicial on the ground that in Virginia there are no "specific offenses for varying degrees of attempted murder." Even though there are no specific statutory provisions which establish the degrees of attempted murder, the statutes set forth the punishment for attempts to commit noncapital offenses. Martin v. Commonwealth, 217 Va. 847, 234 S.E.2d 62 (1977).

The defendant's statement that he was going to shoot the victim and take his money was sufficient to prove beyond a reasonable doubt that he intended to rob the victim. Furthermore, the defendant committed numerous overt acts in furtherance of the robbery by placing his hand in his pocket in a manner that caused the victim to believe that he had a gun, following the victim into the store and stating that he did not "want anybody to get hurt," and attempting to enter the taxi after leaving the store. Accordingly, the evidence was sufficient to sustain the defendant's conviction for attempted robbery. Chrisman v. Commonwealth, No. 1724-95-3 (Ct. of Appeals April 30, 1996).

Attempted robbery. — Evidence was sufficient to show that defendant committed an overt act for purposes of attempted robbery under §§ 18.2-26 and 18.2-58 where: (1) defendant and his

co-defendant talked about robbing a bank the day before; (2) defendant drove to a remote location in town; (3) the two pulled bandanas over their faces outside the bank; (4) defendant carried a knapsack with his hand inside, and the two men walked toward the entrance to the bank; and (5) when they made eye contact with the witness, they pulled down the masks, but continued walking toward the entrance to the bank, where they paused at the entrance, but at the last minute, aborted their plan and walked away. Williams v. Commonwealth, No. 0641-03-1, 2004 Va. App. LEXIS 154 (Ct. of Appeals Apr. 6, 2004).

In an attempted robbery prosecution, where defendant and his companions intended to rob "some people" in a house, demanded money from the persons they found in the house, and shot and killed a man who later entered, the evidence had been insufficient to convict defendant of attempting to rob this man, as the evidence showed he never formed an intent to rob him, and that he and companions took no action toward realizing the ultimate purpose of robbing him. Lewis v. Commonwealth, 43 Va. App. 126, 596 S.E.2d 542, 2004 Va. App. LEXIS 252 (2004).

Evidence defendant admitted that, the day after defendant and another planned the attack on the victim, the two of them met in the evening at a gas station near the scene of the attack, pursuant to their plan, and then proceeded to their hiding place behind the bushes next to the government building, where they waited for 30 minutes for the victim to appear, was sufficient to support defendant's attempted robbery and aggravated malicious wounding convictions. Goode v. Commonwealth, 52 Va. App. 380, 663 S.E.2d 532, 2008 Va. App. LEXIS 331 (2008).

Evidence was insufficient to convict defendant of attempted robbery of a particular person in violation of § 18.2-26 because defendant placed a gun to the victim's neck and told the victim to keep ringing the bell for entry to his place of employment, which showed an intent to gain access to the building, but it did not show an intent to deprive the victim of his property. DeSilva v. Commonwealth, 2009 Va. App. LEXIS 482 (Oct. 27, 2009).

Evidence was sufficient to support defendant's conviction for attempted robbery where an accomplice testified that the accomplice approached the passenger side of a vehicle to buy drugs, defendant pulled out a gun by the driver's side of the vehicle, the accomplice ran, but heard the sound of gunshots, and the accomplice's testimony was corroborated by the presence of the accomplice's fingerprints on the passenger side of the vehicle. Moreover, after the shooting defendant hid out at a friend's house and then fled the state, the gun was found in the friend's backyard, and other crimes evidence tended to prove that defendant stole the gun in another robbery. Rayford v. Commonwealth, 2007 Va. App. LEXIS 506 (Aug. 9, 2007).

Attempted grand larceny. — In a case in which defendant appealed his convictions for uttering a forged check in violation of § 18.2-172 and attempted grand larceny in violation of §§ 18.2-95 and 18.2-26, he argued unsuccessfully that the evidence was insufficient to support his convictions. Because he possessed the forged check, the circumstantial evidence allowed for the inference that defendant had the requisite intent to fraudulently induce the bank to give him the money and not return it, and his possession of the forged check, in conjunction with the other circumstantial evidence, allowed the inference that defendant knew the check was forged; therefore, the evidence was sufficient to support his convictions for uttering and attempted grand larceny. Coles v. Commonwealth, 2009 Va. App. LEXIS 484 (Oct. 27, 2009).

Attempted murder. — Evidence was insufficient to prove that defendant acted with specific intent to kill bank employee when he drove his vehicle through bank's automatic teller machine lane. Willson v. Commonwealth, No. 2004-98-2 (Ct. of Appeals Sept. 21, 1999).

Evidence was sufficient to support defendant's attempted murder conviction, as it showed that defendant entered the victim's house armed with a knife, that defendant threatened to kill her, and that defendant tried unsuccessfully to kill her. Singleton v. Commonwealth, No. 1432-02-1, 2003 Va. App. LEXIS 185 (Ct. of Appeals Apr. 1, 2003).

Evidence that defendant turned the car into traffic in order to flee while the officer was standing toward the rear of the vehicle and slightly behind the driver's side door was insufficient to show that defendant possessed the requisite specific intent to kill the officer; there was no evidence that defendant aimed the vehicle directly at the officer or otherwise had any intent to inflict bodily harm on the officer, much less that defendant had formed the intent to murder the officer. The facts better supported the conclusion that defendant was attempting to escape. Baldwin v. Commonwealth, 274 Va. 276, 645 S.E.2d 433, 2007 Va. LEXIS 76 (2007).

Evidence was sufficient to prove attempted murder and use of a firearm while attempting to commit murder, violations of §§ 18.2-26, 18.2-32, and 18.2-154, where defendant pointed a gun at the victim's car, firing four or five times. Thus, defendant must have intended the immediate, direct, and necessary consequences of his voluntary act. Stullenberg v. Commonwealth, 2010 Va. App. LEXIS 179 (May 4, 2010).

Trial court's finding that defendant was guilty of the attempted murder of his wife in violation of §§ 18.2-32 and 18.2-26 and use of a firearm in the commission of that offense was not plainly wrong or without evidence to support it because defendant shoved, punched, and choked his wife in the presence of their three minor children and his father and obtained a shotgun and went to the front door of the house looking for his wife; the trial court found that the evidence proved that defendant was aiming the shotgun generally around with his finger on the trigger. Herring v. Commonwealth, 2013 Va. App. LEXIS 123 (Apr. 16, 2013).

Attempted malicious wounding. — Sufficient evidence supported defendant's convictions for attempted malicious wounding in violation of §§ 18.2-26 and 18.2-51 and felony hit-and-run, in violation of § 46.2-894, where the evidence presented at trial showed that, while trying to help her sister escape from a store where the sister had been stopped for shoplifting, defendant hit two store employees with her car, dragging one of them for several feet, and then fled the scene of the accident without stopping and giving the information required by § 46.2-894. Brooks v. Commonwealth, No. 0898-01-2, 2002 Va. App. LEXIS 311 (Ct. of Appeals May 14, 2002).

Facts showed that: (1) defendant drove his truck down a 100-foot driveway at a high rate of speed; (2) the victim testified he believed that defendant was going to hit him, and he had to jump between two parked cars to escape being struck; (3) defendant admitted threatening the victim, drinking alcohol before the incident, and confirmed that he and the victim had prior confrontations; (4) the victim's father also heard defendant's threats and saw skid marks in the gravel driveway; (5) a police officer investigating the incident also observed fresh skid marks and testified defendant appeared to have been drinking; and (6) a motor vehicle, wrongfully used, could be a weapon as deadly as a gun or a knife. Thus, the trial court's determination that defendant attempted to run over the victim and cause him serious bodily injury was not plainly wrong or without evidence to support it; therefore, the evidence was sufficient to convict defendant of attempted malicious wounding. Sprouse v. Commonwealth, — Va. App. —, — S.E.2d —, 2006 Va. App. LEXIS 45 (Feb. 7, 2006).

Evidence was insufficient to support a conviction for attempted malicious wounding, although the circumstances were suspicious, because the evidence failed to establish an overt act necessary to prove an attempted malicious wounding where the scenario was interrupted when the victim made contact with defendant, and the evidence also failed to exclude the reasonable hypotheses that defendant acted with the intent to do no more than scare the victim. Small v. Commonwealth, 2009 Va. App. LEXIS 556 (Dec. 15, 2009).

Conviction for attempted malicious wounding under §§ 18.2-26 and 18.2-51, was supported by evidence that defendant entered the victim's apartment and attempted to take money from the victim by intimidating him at gunpoint, and defendant and the victim struggled; defendant's exclusive possession of defendant's gun during the entire time the incident was occurring supported a finding that the gunshot was deliberate, not accidental, and the trial court was entitled to infer that defendant intended the natural and probable consequences of pointing a gun at someone during a robbery, that the circumstances might result in the gun firing. Reid v. Commonwealth, 2010 Va. App. LEXIS 334 (Aug. 17, 2010).

Attempted malicious wounding of police officer. — Commonwealth sufficiently proved that defendant acted with the intent to maim, disfigure, disable or kill, as required by § 18.2-51.1, through his actions of attempting to elude a police officer and accelerating his van into the direct path of the police officer without making an effort to veer or avoid hitting said officer; moreover, the evidence raised the sole inference that defendant intended to

escape even if in so doing he had to drive his accelerating vehicle into the officer who stood before him. Holley v. Commonwealth, 44 Va. App. 228, 604 S.E.2d 127, 2004 Va. App. LEXIS 515 (2004).

Use of a firearm in commission of a felony. — Commonwealth presented sufficient evidence to sustain two convictions of using a firearm in commission of both a charge of attempted murder and a charge of malicious wounding, based on the victim's testimony, and the inferences drawn therefrom, in which the jury could reasonably conclude that: (1) defendant had a firearm in her possession when she hit the victim with the hammer; (2) when defendant shot the victim, and before she hit the victim with a hammer, nothing in the record indicated that she put the gun down before she hit him with the hammer; and, (3) by having the firearm in her possession, defendant displayed the firearm in a threatening manner during the hammer attack; furthermore, although the record did not indicate that defendant presented the pistol in a threatening manner, the jury could properly conclude that her mere possession of the pistol during the hammer attack, coupled with the fact she had already used the pistol, could create a legitimate fear of further use and constituted display of a firearm in a threatening manner. Coleman v. Commonwealth, — Va. App. —, — S.E.2d —, 2005 Va. App. LEXIS 379 (Oct. 4, 2005).

Upon defendant's sufficiency challenge, because the Commonwealth had the burden to prove beyond a reasonable doubt that defendant committed the crime of attempted robbery and it failed to do so, as one would have to resort to speculation and conjecture in order to find that he was attempting to rob as opposed to attempting to obtain money by false pretenses, an attempted robbery conviction could not stand; moreover, given reversal of the attempted robbery conviction, defendant's conviction for attempted use of a firearm during the commission of attempted robbery also had to be reversed. Jay v. Commonwealth, 275 Va. 510, 659 S.E.2d 311, 2008 Va. LEXIS 53 (2008).

Attempted abduction. — Because defendant, a North Carolina bail bondsman, did not have authority pursuant to §§ 9.1-185.18 and 9.1-186.13, to seize a fugitive or the victim, and the Commonwealth showed that defendant intended to abduct the fugitive, there was no legal justification for his actions and defendant's convictions for attempted abduction, a violation of §§ 18.2-26 and 18.2-47, and use of a firearm in the commission of an attempted abduction, a violation of § 18.2-53.1, were proper. Collins v. Commonwealth, 57 Va. App. 355, 702 S.E.2d 267, 2010 Va. App. LEXIS 480 (2010), aff'd, 283 Va. 263, 720 S.E.2d 530, 2012 Va. LEXIS 17 (2012).

Sufficient evidence supported defendant's conviction for attempted abduction because his use of foul language, his pointing of a deadly weapon at the deputy chief of police, his allowance of an employee to confront the deputy chief with mace and a handgun, and his use of physical force in pulling the deputy chief toward the truck all proved beyond a reasonable doubt that, without legal justification or excuse, defendant seized another person with the intent to deprive such other person of his personal liberty. As a bail bondsman licensed in another state, he was not justified in apprehending a fugitive bailee and his abandonment (when he realized he had the wrong person) came after the attempt was complete. Collins v. Commonwealth, 283 Va. 263, 720 S.E.2d 530, 2012 Va. LEXIS 17 (2012).

Attempt to distribute marijuana. — Where evidence showed: (1) discussions were held on three separate occasions between defendant/seller and juvenile/purchaser regarding when and how much marijuana could be obtained; (2) parties met at a prearranged location for transfer of marijuana; (3) defendant/seller had some marijuana on hand; (4) but a misunderstanding regarding the amount of drugs to be sold prevented consummation of the sale, evidence was sufficient to prove that defendant intended and attempted to distribute marijuana to juvenile for further distribution. Wescoat v. Commonwealth, No. 1256-98-2 (Ct. of Appeals Feb. 15, 2000).

Attempted statutory burglary. — Evidence was sufficient to convict defendant of attempted statutory burglary because the evidence was sufficient to prove that defendant attempted to break into his sister's house with the intent to steal money or items from her house at a time when he needed "a fix" for his drug addiction because: (1) defendant knew his sister was not at home because no one responded to his "banging" on the door; (2) defendant pulled off the screens on some windows, but was unable to open the windows;

(3) defendant then beat on the lock on the back door with a shovel; (4) a neighbor informed defendant that his sister was not at home and defendant walked to the front of the house where the neighbor heard more loud noise but did not investigate further; and (5) defendant's sister testified that she had not given defendant permission to enter her house and that he later told her that he did try and break into her house. Perkins v. Commonwealth, No. 1025-03-1, 2004 Va. App. LEXIS 419 (Ct. of Appeals Sept. 7, 2004).

In a prosecution for attempted burglary with the intent to commit larceny, assault and battery, or a felony other than rape, robbery or arson in violation of §§ 18.2-91 and 18.2-26, there was sufficient evidence that defendant had the specific intent to commit larceny when he broke a window in an attempt to enter a garage. His codefendant's knowledge that the victim stored property there was imputed to defendant. Bourne v. Commonwealth, 2012 Va. App. LEXIS 171 (May 22, 2012).

In a prosecution for attempted burglary with the intent to commit larceny, assault and battery, or a felony other than rape, robbery or arson in violation of §§ 18.2-91 and 18.2-26, the evidence was sufficient to support the theory that defendant broke the victim's window in an attempt to enter his garage. The fact finder could conclude that the victim heard the noise of a breaking glass and metallic window frame, which had been intact earlier, and that the fleeing defendant and codefendant had broken the window and frame in an attempt to gain entry to the garage. Bourne v. Commonwealth, 2012 Va. App. LEXIS 171 (May 22, 2012).

Attempted escape from a correctional facility. — Defendant's attempted escape from a correctional facility conviction was upheld, as his combined acts of leaving his assigned residential unit and culminating in climbing one of the last three remaining fences within a correctional facility's secured perimeter, amounted to more than mere preparation and were performed in furtherance of the exclusive purpose of escaping the facility, supporting an attempted escape charge; moreover, defendant's statement, when confronted by an official that he was going to see his daughter, showed his specific intent to escape the facility and that he had committed said series of acts aimed at the consummation of that escape. Harvey v. Commonwealth, No. 0712-05-2, 2006 Va. App. LEXIS 256 (Ct of Appeals June 6, 2006).

Because defendant and another inmate specifically focused their combined efforts on reaching and attempting to drive away in a truck, which was crucial to the success of their attempted escape, the evidence was sufficient to find that there was an agreement between them to attempt an escape, in violation of § 53.1-203; the fact that there was no evidence of an actual conversation between defendant and the other inmate was not dispositive. Charity v. Commonwealth, 49 Va. App. 581, 643 S.E.2d 503, 2007 Va. App. LEXIS 173 (2007).

Section inapplicable to attempt to commit act of sodomy for money. — The General Assembly, by its amendment of § 18.2-346 to include within its proscription an act of sodomy for money, precluded prosecution of an attempt to commit such act under the general statutory scheme under which attempts to commit felonies are prosecuted. McFadden v. Commonwealth, 3 Va. App. 226, 348 S.E.2d 847 (1986).

Validity of indictment for attempted sodomy. — Where defendant was convicted of taking indecent liberties with a child, an indictment charging defendant with attempted sodomy was not invalid for failure to allege an overt, ineffectual act to commit sodomy since the present statutes contain no language which provides specified punishment for a person "who attempts to commit an offense, and in such attempt does any act toward its commission," as was provided in Section 3888 of the 1887 Code. Howard v. Commonwealth, 221 Va. 904, 275 S.E.2d 602 (1981).

Attempt to take indecent liberties with child. — Where evidence showed that defendant knew that he was chatting with a 13-year-old girl, who was actually a detective, in an internet chat room, based on the so-called victim's statement telling him her age and that she was in the seventh grade, lived at home, and had little, if any, sexual experience, and that defendant turned on his webcam and exposed himself to the victim, such was sufficient to support his convictions of attempting to take indecent liberties with a child under the age of 14, in violation of §§ 18.2-370 and 18.2-26. Deecheandia v. Commonwealth, No. 1885-03-2, 2004 Va. App. LEXIS 266 (Ct. of Appeals June 8, 2004).

Attempted rape. — Evidence was sufficient to support a con-

viction of attempted rape, § 18.2-61, because a reasonable fact finder could have found that by asking the victim for "a favor," forcing her to the ground from behind, and attempting to remove her pants, defendant was preparing to have nonconsensual sexual intercourse with the victim; because the Commonwealth proved that defendant had the requisite intent, only a slight act in furtherance of the crime was required. Moreover, because, after the victim threw money behind her head, defendant did not get off of her, but instead he remained on top of her, and continued to force her to the ground, a reasonable fact finder could have found these actions to have been overt acts in furtherance of the commission of a rape. Futrell v. Commonwealth, — Va. App. —, — S.E.2d —, 2007 Va. App. LEXIS 83 (Mar. 13, 2007).

Defendant's convictions for abduction with intent to defile, in violation of § 18.2-48, and attempted rape, in violation of §§ 18.2-26 and 18.2-61 were proper because the trial court did not err in finding the facts sufficient to show the abduction or detention was separate and apart from, rather than incidental to, the attempted rape. The evidence showed the detention by deception posed an additional danger to the victim, was accomplished before the attempted rape, and was not intrinsic to or inherent in the separate offense. Smith v. Commonwealth, 56 Va. App. 711, 697 S.E.2d 14, 2010 Va. App. LEXIS 336 (2010).

Defendant's convictions for abduction with intent to defile, in violation of § 18.2-48, and attempted rape, in violation of §§ 18.2-26 and 18.2-61, were proper because the jury heard the victim's conflicting accounts and in its role as factfinder, it alone was entitled to judge credibility given the discrepancy and assign her testimony what weight it deemed appropriate. Moreover, the officer's testimony and the victim's own actions corroborated the remainder of the victim's account of the incident; the victim immediately notified her mother and a friend about the incident. Smith v. Commonwealth, 56 Va. App. 711, 697 S.E.2d 14, 2010 Va. App. LEXIS 336 (2010).

Applied in United States v. Teplin, 775 F.2d 1261 (4th Cir. 1985); Wolfe v. Commonwealth, 42 Va. App. 776, 595 S.E.2d 27, 2004 Va. App. LEXIS 168 (2004).

CIRCUIT COURT OPINIONS

Attempt to possess cocaine. — Because the question of whether or not defendant attempted to possess cocaine could only be determined from all of the evidence presented at a trial, defendant's pretrial motion to dismiss was denied. Commonwealth v. Sheely, 68 Va. Cir. 245, 2005 Va. Cir. LEXIS 252 (Salem July 8, 2005).

§ 18.2-27. Attempts to commit misdemeanors; how punished.

Every person who attempts to commit an offense which is a misdemeanor shall be punishable by the same punishment prescribed for the offense the commission of which was the object of the attempt.

History.
Code 1950, § 18.1-19; 1960, c. 358; 1972, c. 52; 1975, cc. 14, 15.

CASE NOTES

Evidence sufficient. — Evidence was sufficient for the trial court to rationally find defendant guilty of attempting to photograph a victim in violation of § 18.2-386.1 because as defendant was charged with and convicted of attempting to photograph the victim in violation of §§ 18.2-27 and 18.2-386.1, not the completed crime; therefore, it was not necessary for the Commonwealth to prove that defendant, in fact, accomplished "directly" photographing the victim in the proscribed manner under the statute or that defendant actually photographed anything. Wilson v. Commonwealth, 53 Va. App. 599, 673 S.E.2d 923, 2009 Va. App. LEXIS 137 (2009).

§ 18.2-28. Maximum punishment for attempts.

Any provision in this article notwithstanding, in no event shall the punishment for an attempt to commit an offense exceed the maximum punishment had the offense been committed.

History.
Code 1950, § 18.1-20; 1960, c. 358; 1975, cc. 14, 15.

Law Review.
For article on the law of inchoate crimes, see 59 Va. L. Rev. 1235 (1973).

Michie's Jurisprudence.
For related discussion, see 2A M.J. Attempts and Solicitations, § 6; 5B M.J. Criminal Procedure, §§ 11, 79.

§ 18.2-29. Criminal solicitation; penalty.

Any person who commands, entreats, or otherwise attempts to persuade another person to commit a felony other than murder, shall be guilty of a Class 6 felony. Any person age eighteen or older who commands, entreats, or otherwise attempts to persuade another person under age eighteen to commit a felony other than murder, shall be guilty of a Class 5 felony. Any person who commands, entreats, or otherwise attempts to persuade another person to commit a murder is guilty of a felony punishable by confinement in a state correctional facility for a term not less than five years or more than forty years.

History.
1975, cc. 14, 15; 1994, cc. 364, 440; 2002, cc. 615, 635.

Law Review.
For survey of Virginia criminal law for the year 1974-1975, see 61 Va. L. Rev. 1697 (1975). For article surveying developments in criminal law and procedure in Virginia from July 2001 to September 2002, see 37 U. Rich. L. Rev. 45 (2002).

Michie's Jurisprudence.
For related discussion, see 2A M.J. Attempts and Solicitations, §§ 3, 6, 7, 9; 15 M.J. Rape, § 10.

CASE NOTES

This section is designed as a deterrent to a person who, by any means, attempts to persuade another to commit a felony. Huffman v. Commonwealth, 222 Va. 823, 284 S.E.2d 837 (1981).

Section is not unconstitutionally vague. Fletcher v. Commonwealth, No. 0405-85 (Ct. of Appeals Oct. 10, 1986).

Section gives notice that solicitation is felony. — A person of ordinary intelligence is given notice by this section that solicitation to commit any felony is a crime. Persons of ordinary intelligence need not speculate or guess as to the nature of the conduct proscribed by this section. They are properly notified that soliciting another to commit a felony is a crime accorded a specific punishment and encompasses the solicitation of all acts which are defined as felonies. Fletcher v. Commonwealth, No. 0405-85 (Ct. of Appeals Oct. 10, 1986).

Section does not unconstitutionally abridge First Amendment right of free speech. The constitutionally guaranteed right of free speech does not extend to statements constituting solicitation to commit a felony in violation of this section. Fletcher v. Commonwealth, No. 0405-85 (Ct. of Appeals Oct. 10, 1986).

Defendant's argument that § 18.2-29, along with § 18.2-361, is unconstitutional because it deters constitutionally protected conduct, in defendant's case, requesting an act of oral sodomy from an undercover police officer in a public place, had to be rejected, as such speech did not request a legal act, but instead requested an illegal act. Singson v. Commonwealth, 46 Va. App. 724, 621 S.E.2d 682, 2005 Va. App. LEXIS 452 (2005).

Prosecution under statute with more severe penalty held not denial of equal protection. — Defendant's right of equal protection under the Fourteenth Amendment was not denied by being prosecuted under the state statute, on grounds that the penalty for the state crime of solicitation to commit a felony is greater than the federal penalty applicable to the National Park Service nuisance regulation, where he made no assertion or showing that he was invidiously singled out for prosecution under the state solicitation statute. The fact that a federal statute exists, proscribing the same conduct but providing a lesser penalty range than a state statute, does not create an equal protection deprivation where one is prosecuted under the statute allowing a greater penalty. Fletcher v. Commonwealth, No. 0405-85 (Ct. of Appeals Oct. 10, 1986).

Prosecution under this section and § 18.2-361 for a crime committed on federal land does not violate the Fourteenth Amendment right of equal protection even though similar conduct is proscribed by federal law and is punishable by lesser penalties. Fletcher v. Commonwealth, No. 0405-85 (Ct. of Appeals Oct. 10, 1986).

Statutory scheme did not violate Equal Protection Clause. — The fact that solicitation to commit prostitution, § 18.2-346, is a misdemeanor and is, therefore, considered a less serious crime than solicitation to commit a felony, which includes solicitation to commit sodomy, does not create an impermissible classification between groups of people similarly situated. Therefore, the court rejected the defendant's claim that the statutory scheme violated the Equal Protection Clause. Branche v. Commonwealth, 25 Va. App. 480, 489 S.E.2d 692 (1997).

No discrimination of one gender where absence of attempts to apprehend other gender. — The police do not intentionally discriminate against one gender by the absence of attempts to detect and apprehend offenders of the other gender, when no evidence is presented that offenders of the other gender are engaged in similar criminal behavior; the defendant offered no evidence that similarly situated females could have been prosecuted but were not. Branche v. Commonwealth, 25 Va. App. 480, 489 S.E.2d 692 (1997).

Double jeopardy not a bar. — Defendant's double jeopardy rights were not violated in a case where defendant pled guilty to solicitation to commit murder in violation of § 18.2-29 and a jury then convicted defendant in a trial of attempted capital murder for hire in violation of subdivision 2 of § 18.2-31 and § 18.2-25. Double jeopardy did not apply because: (1) defendant's offenses were considered in a single proceeding and, thus, there were not successive prosecutions for the same offense; and (2) solicitation to commit murder and attempted capital murder for hire were not the same offenses and, thus, defendant could be convicted and punished for both offenses since solicitation for murder required that a defendant solicit another person whereas attempted capital murder for hire did not require such proof. Ostrander v. Commonwealth, 51 Va. App. 386, 658 S.E.2d 346, 2008 Va. App. LEXIS 126 (2008).

Section does not conflict with federal regulation. — The regulatory provision of this section and former 36 C.F.R. § 50.26(d), pertaining to nuisances and solicitation for immoral purposes on areas under the jurisdiction of the National Park Service, are not in actual conflict, even though they contain disparate penalty provisions. In fact, such differing penalty provisions exist routinely, and their coexistence has withstood constitutional scrutiny. Fletcher v. Commonwealth, No. 0405-85 (Ct. of Appeals Oct. 10, 1986).

Gist of offense is incitement. — It is immaterial whether the solicitation is of any effect and whether the crime solicited is in fact committed; the gist of the offense is incitement. Branche v. Commonwealth, 25 Va. App. 480, 489 S.E.2d 692 (1997).

Criminal solicitation involves the attempt of the accused to incite another to commit a criminal offense; it is immaterial whether the solicitation has any effect and whether the crime solicited is in fact committed. Scott v. Commonwealth, No. 2132-00-1, 2001 Va. App. LEXIS 173 (Ct. of Appeals Apr. 3, 2001).

Criminal solicitation involves the attempt of the accused to incite another to commit a criminal offense; it is immaterial whether the solicitation is of any effect and whether the crime solicited is in fact committed as the gist of the offense is incitement.

Jeffers v. Commonwealth, No. 1350-00-1, 2001 Va. App. LEXIS 111 (Ct. of Appeals Mar. 6, 2001).

For crime of solicitation to be completed, it is not necessary that the intended conduct approach the moment of an attempt. Therefore, the offense of solicitation was completed once defendant attempted to persuade the plainclothes investigator to commit oral sodomy. Fletcher v. Commonwealth, No. 0405-85 (Ct. of Appeals Oct. 10, 1986).

Entreaty to perform criminal act exceeded mere statement of desire. — A defendant's words and actions were more than an expression of his desire for oral sex and the trial court could have properly concluded that the defendant expressed both a desire and entreaty to induce the victim to allow him to sodomize her where, after his initial suggestion had been rebuffed, he asked, "Are you sure?" and then, in a demanding tone of voice, ordered her to get in his car; the defendant's entire course of conduct underscored his desire for the victim to act upon his entreaty. Jeffers v. Commonwealth, No. 1350-00-1, 2001 Va. App. LEXIS 111 (Ct. of Appeals Mar. 6, 2001).

Solicitation may comprise a course of conduct, intended to induce another to act, that continues over an extended period. Jeffers v. Commonwealth, No. 1350-00-1, 2001 Va. App. LEXIS 111 (Ct. of Appeals Mar. 6, 2001).

Entrapment was no defense in a prosecution for solicitation to commit murder where the intended crime originated in the evil mind of the defendant and police were brought in merely as a means of permitting the original defendant an opportunity to carry out her criminal plan. Huffman v. Commonwealth, 222 Va. 823, 284 S.E.2d 837 (1981).

Failure to prove defendant spoke with intent to induce act. — Where defendant's statements were no more than the expression of his own desire and did not constitute a command, entreaty or attempt to persuade either student to engage in oral sodomy, and where several minutes after first encounter defendant stated "I'll get you, I'll find you," the trial court was plainly wrong in concluding that the Commonwealth had sustained its burden of proving that defendant spoke to either student with the intent "to induce" either of them to act. Ford v. Commonwealth, 10 Va. App. 224, 391 S.E.2d 603 (1990).

Failure to name victim. — The fact that the defendant did not name or specify the identity of her intended victim when she solicited another to commit murder was no defense in a prosecution under this section. Huffman v. Commonwealth, 222 Va. 823, 284 S.E.2d 837 (1981).

Solicitation of capital murder for hire. — Defendant asked two people to kill his wife, formulated diagrams of his wife's house, explained when she would be at home, and paid two thousand dollars to the hit man. The evidence was sufficient to convict defendant of attempted capital murder for hire, in violation of §§ 18.2-25 and 18.2-31, and solicitation of capital murder for hire, in violation of §§ 18.2-29 and 18.2-31; the Commonwealth did not err by failing to elect between the charges, because the solicitation and attempt were both parts of a common scheme or plan. Ashford v. Commonwealth, 47 Va. App. 676, 626 S.E.2d 464, 2006 Va. App. LEXIS 70 (2006).

Solicitation to become an accessory before the fact to murder. — Evidence proved that defendant entreated his friend to procure an untraceable gun to be used to kill his ex-wife, and therefore Commonwealth properly characterized wrongful act that defendant solicited as being an accessory before the fact to murder. Santora v. Commonwealth, No. 2962-98-4 (Ct. of Appeals Feb. 22, 2000).

Evidence of telephone calls from person soliciting murder held admissible. — The trial court's decision to admit evidence of telephone calls from a person soliciting the murder of another solely upon the Commonwealth's assurance that it would provide sufficient evidence to create a jury issue as to the identity of the caller was not an abuse of discretion, in view of the long-standing rule in Virginia that the order of proof is within the sound discretion of the trial court, and where there was sufficient circumstantial evidence to create a jury issue. Armes v. Commonwealth, 3 Va. App. 189, 349 S.E.2d 150 (1986).

There is no crime in Virginia of entreat to commit fornication. The word "entreat" is found in this section — Criminal Solicitation. A key element of solicitation is that the substantive crime solicited be a felony; fornication is a misdemeanor.

Weatherford v. Commonwealth, No. 1489-90-1 (Ct. of Appeals, March 3, 1992).

Solicitation of oral sex from minor. — By unsuccessfully soliciting oral sex from a minor, defendant willfully encouraged her to engage in a criminal act. As his solicitation was clearly designed to encourage her to commit that act, which would have rendered her delinquent under § 16.1-228, the evidence established that he contributed to the delinquency of a minor in violation of § 18.2-371. MacDonald v. Commonwealth, 2007 Va. App. LEXIS 7 (Jan. 9, 2007).

Evidence sufficient to convict. — Although defendant's conviction of solicitation to commit a felony was reversed because improper impeachment evidence was admitted, the evidence that she asked another person to commit an arson against a dwelling house was sufficient to support her conviction, and thus the Commonwealth could retry her if it was so inclined. Goodson v. Commonwealth, — Va. App. —, — S.E.2d —, 2006 Va. App. LEXIS 515 (Nov. 14, 2006).

Defendant's conviction for solicitation to commit a felony was proper; based on the content of a letter, the trial court could have concluded beyond a reasonable doubt that defendant, a convicted murderer, planned to ask defendant's accomplices to kill the witnesses against defendant. Rodriguez v. Commonwealth, 2012 Va. App. LEXIS 229 (July 10, 2012).

CHAPTER 4.

CRIMES AGAINST THE PERSON.

Article 1. Homicide.

Article 2. Crimes by Mobs.

Article 2.1. Crimes by Gangs.

Section
18.2-75.   Conscience clause.
18.2-76.   Informed written consent required; civil penalty.
18.2-76.1.   Encouraging or promoting abortion.
18.2-76.2.   [Not set out.]

ARTICLE 1.

HOMICIDE.

§ 18.2-30. Murder and manslaughter declared felonies.

Any person who commits capital murder, murder of the first degree, murder of the second degree, voluntary manslaughter, or involuntary manslaughter, shall be guilty of a felony.

History.
1975, cc. 14, 15.

Cross references.
As to presumption of no bail for illegal aliens charged with certain crimes, see § 19.2-120.1. For definition of "barrier crime" as including a conviction of murder or manslaughter as set out in § 18.2-30 et seq., or an equivalent offense in another state, and prohibition against assisted living facilities, adult day care centers or child welfare agencies hiring for certain compensated employment persons who have committed such an offense, see §§ 63.2-1719, 63.2-1720. As to report to children's residential facility for which a background check is being performed on whether the applicant has ever been convicted of or is the subject of pending charges for various crimes, including murder or manslaughter as set out in § 18.2-30 et seq., or an equivalent offense in another state, see § 63.2-1726.

CASE NOTES

Evidence of telephone calls from person soliciting murder held admissible. — The trial court's decision to admit evidence of telephone calls from a person soliciting the murder of another solely upon the Commonwealth's assurance that it would provide sufficient evidence to create a jury issue as to the identity of the caller was not an abuse of discretion, in view of the long-standing rule in Virginia that the order of proof is within the sound discretion of the trial court, and where there was sufficient circumstantial evidence to create a jury issue. Armes v. Commonwealth, 3 Va. App. 189, 349 S.E.2d 150 (1986).

Jury instruction on justifiable homicide refused. — Defendant, convicted of multiple charges that included a conviction as a principal in the first degree for second-degree murder, in violation of §§ 18.2-30 and 18.2-32, was not entitled to an instruction on theory of justifiable homicide, as defendant was not totally free from fault, where defendant admitted that approaching defendant's adversary and threatening him; in addition, defendant was not entitled to a voluntary manslaughter instruction, as the evidence did not support defendant's argument that defendant shot in the heat of passion and without reflection, where defendant's statement to the police reflected deliberation and intent, rather than the heat of passion, and there was a reasonable opportunity to cool. Martin v. Commonwealth, No. 0470-02-1, 2003 Va. App. LEXIS 205 (Ct. of Appeals Apr. 8, 2003).

Jury instruction on self-defense with and without fault was proper. — Defendant was properly convicted of voluntary manslaughter where an instruction on self-defense with fault and without fault was properly given; evidence existed that defendant may have initiated the confrontation that led to the victim being shot and he may have armed himself with a gun prior to engaging in the confrontation. Workman v. Commonwealth, — Va. App. —, — S.E.2d —, 2005 Va. App. LEXIS 303 (Aug. 2, 2005), rev'd, remanded, 272 Va. 633, 636 S.E.2d 368 (2006).

Applied in Jenkins v. Commonwealth, 220 Va. 104, 255 S.E.2d 504 (1979).

§ 18.2-31. Capital murder defined; punishment.

The following offenses shall constitute capital murder, punishable as a Class 1 felony:

1. The willful, deliberate, and premeditated killing of any person in the commission of abduction, as defined in § 18.2-48, when such abduction was committed with the intent to extort money or a pecuniary benefit or with the intent to defile the victim of such abduction;

2. The willful, deliberate, and premeditated killing of any person by another for hire;

3. The willful, deliberate, and premeditated killing of any person by a prisoner confined in a state or local correctional facility as defined in § 53.1-1, or while in the custody of an employee thereof;

4. The willful, deliberate, and premeditated killing of any person in the commission of robbery or attempted robbery;

5. The willful, deliberate, and premeditated killing of any person in the commission of, or subsequent to, rape or attempted rape, forcible sodomy or attempted forcible sodomy or object sexual penetration;

6. The willful, deliberate, and premeditated killing of a law-enforcement officer as defined in § 9.1-101, a fire marshal appointed pursuant to § 27-30 or a deputy or an assistant fire marshal appointed pursuant to § 27-36, when such fire marshal or deputy or assistant fire marshal has police powers as set forth in §§ 27-34.2 and 27-34.2:1, an auxiliary police officer appointed or provided for pursuant to §§ 15.2-1731 and 15.2-1733, an auxiliary deputy sheriff appointed pursuant to § 15.2-1603, or any law-enforcement officer of another state or the United States having the power to arrest for a felony under the laws of such state or the United States, when such killing is for the purpose of interfering with the performance of his official duties;

7. The willful, deliberate, and premeditated killing of more than one person as a part of the same act or transaction;

8. The willful, deliberate, and premeditated killing of more than one person within a three-year period;

9. The willful, deliberate, and premeditated killing of any person in the commission of or attempted commission of a violation of § 18.2-248, involving a Schedule I or II controlled substance, when such killing is for the purpose of furthering the commission or attempted commission of such violation;

10. The willful, deliberate, and premeditated killing of any person by another pursuant to the direction or order of one who is engaged in a continuing criminal enterprise as defined in subsection I of § 18.2-248;

11. The willful, deliberate, and premeditated killing of a pregnant woman by one who knows that the

woman is pregnant and has the intent to cause the involuntary termination of the woman's pregnancy without a live birth;

12. The willful, deliberate, and premeditated killing of a person under the age of fourteen by a person age twenty-one or older;

13. The willful, deliberate, and premeditated killing of any person by another in the commission of or attempted commission of an act of terrorism as defined in § 18.2-46.4;

14. The willful, deliberate, and premeditated killing of a justice of the Supreme Court, a judge of the Court of Appeals, a judge of a circuit court or district court, a retired judge sitting by designation or under temporary recall, or a substitute judge appointed under § 16.1-69.9:1 when the killing is for the purpose of interfering with his official duties as a judge; and

15. The willful, deliberate, and premeditated killing of any witness in a criminal case after a subpoena has been issued for such witness by the court, the clerk, or an attorney, when the killing is for the purpose of interfering with the person's duties in such case.

If any one or more subsections, sentences, or parts of this section shall be judged unconstitutional or invalid, such adjudication shall not affect, impair, or invalidate the remaining provisions thereof but shall be confined in its operation to the specific provisions so held unconstitutional or invalid.

History.
Code 1950, §§ 18.1-21, 53-291; 1960, c. 358; 1962, c. 42; 1966, c. 300; 1970, c. 648; 1973, c. 403; 1975, cc. 14, 15; 1976, c. 503; 1977, c. 478; 1979, c. 582; 1980, c. 221; 1981, c. 607; 1982, c. 636; 1983, c. 175; 1985, c. 550; 1989, c. 527; 1990, c. 746; 1991, c. 232; 1995, c. 340; 1996, cc. 876, 959; 1997, cc. 235, 313, 514, 709; 1998, c. 887; 2002, cc. 588, 623; 2007, cc. 844, 845, 846; 2010, cc. 399, 428, 475.

Editor's note.
Acts 2010, cc. 399, 428, and 475, in cl. 2 provide: "That the provisions of this act may result in a net increase in periods of imprisonment or commitment. Pursuant to § 30-19.1:4, the estimated amount of the necessary appropriation is $0 for periods of imprisonment in state adult correctional facilities and is $0 for periods of commitment to the custody of the Department of Juvenile Justice."

The 2010 amendments.
The 2010 amendment by c. 399 inserted "a fire marshal appointed pursuant to § 27-30 or a deputy or an assistant fire marshal appointed pursuant to § 27-36, when such fire marshal or deputy or assistant fire marshal has police powers as set forth in §§ 27-34.2 and 27-34.2:1" in subdivision 6.
The 2010 amendments by cc. 428 and 475 are identical, and inserted "an auxiliary police officer appointed or provided for pursuant to §§ 15.2-1731 and 15.2-1733, an auxiliary deputy sheriff appointed pursuant to § 15.2-1603" in subdivision 6.

Law Review.
For survey of Virginia criminal law for the year 1974-1975, see 61 Va. L. Rev. 1697 (1975). For comment on the constitutional parameters for capital punishment, see 11 U. Rich. L. Rev. 101 (1976). For survey of Virginia criminal procedure for the year 1975-1976, see 62 Va. L. Rev. 1412 (1976). For survey of Virginia criminal law for the year 1976-1977, see 63 Va. L. Rev. 1396 (1977). For article, "Psychiatry and the Death Penalty: Emerging Problems in Virginia," see 66 Va. L. Rev. 167 (1980). For comment discussing

possible effects on Virginia's death penalty of recent United States Supreme Court decisions, see 15 U. Rich. L. Rev. 951 (1981). For note on premeditation, see 40 Wash. & Lee L. Rev. 341 (1983). For comment on Virginia's death penalty, see 17 U. Rich. L. Rev. 603 (1983). For article, "Virginia's Capital Murder Sentencing Proceeding: A Defense Perspective," see 18 U. Rich. L. Rev. 341 (1984). For comment on multiple murder, multiple punishment and double jeopardy in Virginia, see 9 G.M.U. L. Rev. 107 (1986). For an article relating to all published Virginia criminal law decisions between July 1, 1997, and July 1, 1998, see 32 U. Rich. L. Rev. 1091 (1998). For note, "Fetal Homicide: Woman or Fetus as Victim? A Survey of Current State Approaches and Recommendations for Future State Application," see 41 Wm. & Mary L. Rev. 1845 (2000). For note, "Predicate Offenses for First Degree Felony Murder in Virginia," see 57 Wash. & Lee L. Rev. 561 (2000). For article, "Criminal Law and Procedure," see 35 U. Rich. L. Rev. 537 (2001). For article, "Virginia's Capital Jurors," 44 Wm. & Mary L. Rev. 2063 (2003). For survey of Virginia criminal law and procedure for the year 2004-2005, see 40 U. Rich. L. Rev. 197 (2005). For 2007 annual survey article, "Criminal Law and Procedure," see 42 U. Rich. L. Rev. 311 (2007).

Michie's Jurisprudence.
For related discussion, see 1A M.J. Accomplices and Accessories, § 11; 2B M.J. Automobiles, § 122; 5B M.J. Criminal Procedure, §§ 70, 80, 87; 9B M.J. Homicide, §§ 10, 17, 20, 26, 54, 101, 132.1.

CASE NOTES

I. In General.
II. Elements.
III. Underlying Felony.
  A. Robbery.
  B. Rape.
  C. Others.
IV. Trial.
  A. In General.
  B. Evidentiary Matters.

I. IN GENERAL.

Constitutionality. — Virginia's capital murder statutes are not unconstitutional. Clark v. Commonwealth, 220 Va. 201, 257 S.E.2d 784 (1979), cert. denied, 444 U.S. 1049, 100 S. Ct. 741, 62 L. Ed. 2d 736 (1980); Pope v. Commonwealth, 234 Va. 114, 360 S.E.2d 352 (1987), cert. denied, 485 U.S. 1015, 108 S. Ct. 1489, 99 L. Ed. 2d 716 (1988).

Section is constitutional under U.S. Const., Amends. V and XIV, and Va. Const., Art. I, § 2. Fitzgerald v. Commonwealth, 223 Va. 615, 292 S.E.2d 798 (1982), cert. denied, 459 U.S. 1228, 103 S. Ct. 1235, 75 L. Ed. 2d 469, rehearing denied, 460 U.S. 1105, 103 S. Ct. 1809, 76 L. Ed. 2d 371 (1983).

The capital murder statutes are not unconstitutional. Edmonds v. Commonwealth, 229 Va. 303, 329 S.E.2d 807, cert. denied, 474 U.S. 975, 106 S. Ct. 339, 88 L. Ed. 2d 324 (1985).

The Virginia Capital Murder Statute is constitutional. Poyner v. Commonwealth, 229 Va. 401, 329 S.E.2d 815, cert. denied, 474 U.S. 865, 106 S. Ct. 189, 88 L. Ed. 2d 158 (1985), 474 U.S. 888, 106 S. Ct. 208, 88 L. Ed. 2d 178 (1985), 506 U.S. 958, 113 S. Ct. 419, 121 L. Ed. 2d 342 (1992).

The death sentence is not unconstitutional on grounds that it is cruel and unusual. Beaver v. Commonwealth, 232 Va. 521, 352 S.E.2d 342, cert. denied, 483 U.S. 1033, 107 S. Ct. 3277, 97 L. Ed. 2d 781 (1987).

Where the evidence showed that two murders were committed at the same location, about the same time, and under the same circumstances, defendant, given his conduct, reasonably should have been on notice that this section applied to his actions when it defined capital murder as killing "more than one person as a part of the same act or transaction." Thus, this section satisfied the constitutional requirement of definiteness and complied with the standard forbidding arbitrary and erratic law enforcement. Woodfin v. Commonwealth, 236 Va. 89, 372 S.E.2d 377 (1988), cert. denied, 490 U.S. 1009, 109 S. Ct. 1649, 104 L. Ed. 2d 163 (1989).

Virginia terrorism statutes, subdivision 13 of § 18.2-31 and

§ 18.2-46.4 were not unconstitutionally overbroad and vague, as claimed by defendant; nothing in the words of the statutes evinced an intent to limit their application to criminal actors with political motives, and the statutes provided notice sufficient for ordinary people to understand what conduct they prohibited, and did not authorize and/or encourage arbitrary and discriminatory enforcement. Muhammad v. Commonwealth, 269 Va. 451, 611 S.E.2d 537, 2005 Va. LEXIS 39 (2005), cert. denied, 547 U.S. 1136, 126 S. Ct. 2035, 164 L. Ed. 2d 794 (2006), and overruled in part on other grounds by Jay v. Commonwealth, 275 Va. 510, 659 S.E.2d 311, 2008 Va. LEXIS 53 (2008).

Terrorism statutes, subdivision 13 of § 18.2-31 and § 18.2-46.4, were not unconstitutionally overbroad and vague; by referencing established criminal offenses as acts of violence subject to the statutory scheme, the legislature included offenses with previously defined elements and mens rea requirements. Muhammad v. Commonwealth, 269 Va. 451, 619 S.E.2d 16, 2005 Va. LEXIS 85 (2005), cert. denied, — U.S. —, 126 S. Ct. 2035, 164 L. Ed. 2d 794 (2006) and overruled in part on other grounds by Jay v. Commonwealth, 275 Va. 510, 659 S.E.2d 311, 2008 Va. LEXIS 53 (2008).

Subdivision 12 of § 18.2-31 was not unconstitutional because it exposed some murders to the death penalty because there was a rational basis for imposition of the death penalty on persons over the age of 21 who murdered a child, that such persons should have sufficient maturity and judgment to be held responsible for conduct that might be excusable in a younger person; rational basis, not strict scrutiny, was proper standard of review for such a claim. Gray v. Commonwealth, 274 Va. 290, 645 S.E.2d 448, 2007 Va. LEXIS 94 (2007), cert. denied, 128 S. Ct. 1111, 2008 U.S. LEXIS 1072, 169 L. Ed. 2d 826 (U.S. 2008).

Joinder of capital murder with predicate murder. — In adopting subdivision 8 of § 18.2-31, making the murder of more than one person within three years a capital offense, the Virginia General Assembly implicitly modified Va. Sup. Ct. Rule 3A:6(b), concerning the joinder of offenses for trial, to the extent that the meaning of the words "connected crimes," i.e. "so intimately connected and blended with the main facts adduced in evidence, that they cannot be departed from with propriety," no longer applied, since, to establish the required connection for a joint trial of offenses under the statute, it is only necessary to show that the capital murder and the predicate murder(s) occurred within three years. Commonwealth v. Smith, 263 Va. 13, 557 S.E.2d 223, 2002 Va. LEXIS 8 (2002).

A prisoner is not entitled to use habeas corpus to circumvent the trial and appellate processes for an inquiry into an alleged non-jurisdictional defect of a judgment of conviction. Strickler v. Murray, 249 Va. 120, 452 S.E.2d 648, cert. denied, 516 U.S. 850, 116 S. Ct. 146, 133 L. Ed. 2d 92 (1995).

For case adhering to prior rulings upholding constitutionality of this section, classifying capital offenses, and of §§ 19.2-264.2 to 19.2-264.4, outlining sentencing procedures in capital cases, see Frye v. Commonwealth, 231 Va. 370, 345 S.E.2d 267 (1986).

Section enacted to conform to decision in Furman v. Georgia. — This section, defining capital murder, was first enacted by the General Assembly in 1975 as part of a statutory scheme enacted to eliminate the unbridled choice between the death penalty and a lesser sentence prohibited by Furman v. Georgia, 408 U.S. 238, 92 S. Ct. 2726, 33 L. Ed. 2d 346 (1972); Fitzgerald v. Commonwealth, 223 Va. 615, 292 S.E.2d 798 (1982), cert. denied, 459 U.S. 1228, 103 S. Ct. 1235, 75 L. Ed. 2d 469, reh'g denied, 460 U.S. 1105, 103 S. Ct. 1809, 76 L. Ed. 2d 371 (1983).

For brief history of first-degree murder statutes and death sanction, see Fitzgerald v. Commonwealth, 223 Va. 615, 292 S.E.2d 798 (1982), cert. denied, 459 U.S. 1228, 103 S. Ct. 1235, 75 L. Ed. 2d 469, rehearing denied, 460 U.S. 1105, 103 S. Ct. 1809, 76 L. Ed. 2d 371 (1983).

Purpose of murder statutes is gradation. Fitzgerald v. Commonwealth, 223 Va. 615, 292 S.E.2d 798 (1982), cert. denied, 459 U.S. 1228, 103 S. Ct. 1235, 75 L. Ed. 2d 469, rehearing denied, 460 U.S. 1105, 103 S. Ct. 1809, 76 L. Ed. 2d 371 (1983).

General Assembly grades murder in order to assign punishment consistent with prevailing societal and legal views of what is appropriate and procedurally fair. Fitzgerald v. Commonwealth, 223 Va. 615, 292 S.E.2d 798 (1982), cert. denied, 459 U.S. 1228, 103 S. Ct. 1235, 75 L. Ed. 2d 469, rehearing denied, 460 U.S.

1105, 103 S. Ct. 1809, 76 L. Ed. 2d 371 (1983).

Capital murder statute is not overbroad in failing to distinguish capital from felony murder. Briley v. Bass, 584 F. Supp. 807 (E.D. Va.), aff'd, 742 F.2d 155 (4th Cir.), cert. denied, 469 U.S. 893, 105 S. Ct. 270, 83 L. Ed. 2d 206 (1984).

No intent to eliminate punishment for other offenses included in murder statutes. — The overriding purpose of the murder statutes being gradation, there was no legislative intent to eliminate punishment for other offenses which were included in the murder statutes solely for the purpose of categorizing the murder. Fitzgerald v. Commonwealth, 223 Va. 615, 292 S.E.2d 798 (1982), cert. denied, 459 U.S. 1228, 103 S. Ct. 1235, 75 L. Ed. 2d 469, rehearing denied, 460 U.S. 1105, 103 S. Ct. 1809, 76 L. Ed. 2d 371 (1983).

The legislature did not intend any elimination of underlying sentencing authority for rape and robbery when it modified the murder statutes in 1975, or on any prior occasion. Fitzgerald v. Commonwealth, 223 Va. 615, 292 S.E.2d 798 (1982), cert. denied, 459 U.S. 1228, 103 S. Ct. 1235, 75 L. Ed. 2d 469, rehearing denied, 460 U.S. 1105, 103 S. Ct. 1809, 76 L. Ed. 2d 371 (1983).

Commonwealth Attorney may seek death penalty. — State Supreme Court granted the petition for writ of mandamus filed by the Commonwealth Attorney, as the trial court did not have the discretion to prohibit the Commonwealth Attorney from seeking the death penalty; the Commonwealth Attorney was entitled to seek that penalty pursuant to statutory law and the trial court erred by exercising an executive function in determining that the Commonwealth Attorney was prohibited from seeking it in defendant's case where defendant was charged with capital murder pursuant to § 18.2-31. In re Horan, 271 Va. 258, 634 S.E.2d 675, 2006 Va. LEXIS 23 (2006).

Applied in Briley v. Commonwealth, 221 Va. 532, 273 S.E.2d 48 (1980); Patterson v. Commonwealth, 222 Va. 653, 283 S.E.2d 212 (1981); Whitley v. Commonwealth, 223 Va. 66, 286 S.E.2d 162 (1982); Coleman v. Commonwealth, 226 Va. 31, 307 S.E.2d 864 (1983); Wall Distribs., Inc. v. City of Newport News, 228 Va. 358, 323 S.E.2d 75 (1984); Evans v. Commonwealth, 228 Va. 468, 323 S.E.2d 114 (1984); Jones v. Commonwealth, 228 Va. 427, 323 S.E.2d 554 (1984); Bradshaw v. Commonwealth, 228 Va. 484, 323 S.E.2d 567 (1984); Washington v. Commonwealth, 228 Va. 535, 323 S.E.2d 577 (1984); Briley v. Bass, 750 F.2d 1238 (4th Cir. 1984); Clanton v. Blair, 619 F. Supp. 1491 (E.D. Va. 1985); Gray v. Commonwealth, 233 Va. 313, 356 S.E.2d 157 (1987); Harris v. Commonwealth, 8 Va. App. 424, 382 S.E.2d 292 (1989); Mu'Min v. Commonwealth, 239 Va. 433, 389 S.E.2d 886 (1990); Cheng v. Commonwealth, 240 Va. 26, 393 S.E.2d 599 (1990); George v. Commonwealth, 242 Va. 264, 411 S.E.2d 12 (1991); Stamper v. Muncie, 944 F.2d 170 (4th Cir. 1991); George v. Angelone, 901 F. Supp. 1070 (E.D. Va. 1995); Roach v. Angelone, 176 F.3d 210 (4th Cir. 1999); Williams v. Commonwealth, 30 Va. App. 378, 517 S.E.2d 246 (1999); Abraham v. Commonwealth, 32 Va. App. 22, 526 S.E.2d 277 (2000); Barnabei v. Angelone, 214 F.3d 463, 2000 U.S. App. LEXIS 12183 (4th Cir.); Powell v. Commonwealth, 261 Va. 512, 552 S.E.2d 344, 2001 Va. LEXIS 86 (2001); Edwards v. Commonwealth, 41 Va. App. 752, 589 S.E.2d 444, 2003 Va. App. LEXIS 637 (2003).

II. ELEMENTS.

Generally, only immediate perpetrator may be convicted. — Except in the case of murder for hire, only the immediate perpetrator of a homicide, the one who fired the fatal shot, and not an accessory before the fact or a principal in the second degree, may be convicted of capital murder under the provisions of this section, as qualified by § 18.2-18. Coppola v. Commonwealth, 220 Va. 243, 257 S.E.2d 797 (1979), cert. denied, 444 U.S. 1103, 100 S. Ct. 1069, 62 L. Ed. 2d 788 (1980).

In a prosecution for willful, deliberate and premeditated killing of any person in the commission of robbery while armed with a deadly weapon, only the triggerman can be a principal in the first degree to capital murder. Harrison v. Commonwealth, 220 Va. 188, 257 S.E.2d 777 (1979).

When the offense constituting the charge of capital murder is the willful, deliberate and premeditated killing of a person in the commission of robbery while armed with a deadly weapon, only the actual perpetrator of the crime may be convicted of capital murder. Johnson v. Commonwealth, 220 Va. 146, 255 S.E.2d 525 (1979), cert. denied, 454 U.S. 920, 102 S. Ct. 422, 70 L. Ed. 2d 231 (1981).

A defendant who was found not to be the "triggerman" in the willful, deliberate and premeditated killing of a person in the commission of robbery while armed with a deadly weapon, could not be convicted of capital murder under this section, but could be convicted of first-degree murder punishable as a Class 2 felony. Harrison v. Commonwealth, 220 Va. 188, 257 S.E.2d 777 (1979).

Under the "triggerman" rule, only the actual perpetrator of a crime delineated in this section may be convicted of capital murder and subjected to the penalty of execution, except in the case of murder for hire. Frye v. Commonwealth, 231 Va. 370, 345 S.E.2d 267 (1986).

And instruction to contrary is reversible error. — Harmful, reversible error occurred in a capital murder prosecution when the trial court instructed the jury in such a manner that the jury could have believed that it could convict the defendant of capital murder though it was unable to determine who fired the fatal shots or if it determined that the defendant's brother fired the fatal shots; the error was compounded when the Commonwealth was permitted to argue to the jury that it could convict the defendant regardless of who pulled the trigger. Johnson v. Commonwealth, 220 Va. 146, 255 S.E.2d 525 (1979), cert. denied, 454 U.S. 920, 102 S. Ct. 422, 70 L. Ed. 2d 231 (1981).

Triggerman instruction not required. — The trial court was not required to instruct the jury on the Commonwealth's burden to prove beyond a reasonable doubt that defendant was the triggerman or principal in the first degree, where defendant's defense was that he was not at the scene of the murder, while the Commonwealth's evidence was that defendant and co-defendant acted jointly to murder the victim. Hash v. Commonwealth, No. 1290-01-4, 2002 Va. App. LEXIS 541 (Ct. of Appeals Sept. 3, 2002).

Defendant need not be triggerman in both murders under subdivision 8. — Subdivision 8 requires proof only that the defendant was the triggerman in the principal murder charged and that he was at least an accomplice in the murder of an additional person or persons within a three-year period; the Commonwealth is not required to prove that the defendant was the triggerman in both murders. Burlile v. Commonwealth, 32 Va. App. 796, 531 S.E.2d 26, 2000 Va. App. LEXIS 532 (2000), aff'd, 261 Va. 501, 544 S.E.2d 360 (2001).

One who is present, aiding and abetting actual murder, but who does not actually fire fatal shot, is a principal in the second degree and may be convicted of no greater offense than first-degree murder. Frye v. Commonwealth, 231 Va. 370, 345 S.E.2d 267 (1986).

When joint participant is "immediate perpetrator." — Where two or more persons take a direct part in inflicting fatal injuries, each joint participant is an "immediate perpetrator" for the purposes of the capital murder statutes. Strickler v. Commonwealth, 241 Va. 482, 404 S.E.2d 227, cert. denied, 502 U.S. 944, 112 S. Ct. 386, 116 L. Ed. 2d 337 (1991).

Defendant, a prison inmate, was properly convicted of capital murder for participating in the fatal stabbing of another prison inmate; the evidence established that defendant jointly participated in the stabbing and that all the victim's stab wounds contributed to the victim's death. Remington v. Commonwealth, 262 Va. 333, 551 S.E.2d 620, 2001 Va. LEXIS 107 (2001), cert. denied, 535 U.S. 1062, 122 S. Ct. 1928, 152 L. Ed. 2d 834 (2002).

Proof was sufficient to establish beyond a reasonable doubt that defendant acted as a principal in the first degree, as an immediate perpetrator, in the death of a victim in a shooting; the "sniper theory" advanced by the Commonwealth was supported through expert testimony, the ample evidence of such a methodology, and prior decisions. As an immediate perpetrator of the death of the victim in a murder that qualified as an act of violence under § 19.2-297.1, defendant was a principal in the first degree in the willful, deliberate, and premeditated killing of a person in the commission of an act of terrorism. Muhammad v. Commonwealth, 269 Va. 451, 611 S.E.2d 537, 2005 Va. LEXIS 39 (2005), cert. denied, 547 U.S. 1136, 126 S. Ct. 2035, 164 L. Ed. 2d 794 (2006), and overruled in part on other grounds by Jay v. Commonwealth, 275 Va. 510, 659 S.E.2d 311, 2008 Va. LEXIS 53 (2008).

Evidence was sufficient to convict defendant of capital murder for the willful, deliberate, and premeditated killing of the victim in the commission of an act of terrorism as defined in § 18.2-46.4. Defendant was a principal in the first degree and was a criminal actor in the second degree who gave an order or direction to the shooter, who

was firing from inside the trunk of the car defendant was driving, to kill the victim. Muhammad v. Commonwealth, 269 Va. 451, 619 S.E.2d 16, 2005 Va. LEXIS 85 (2005), cert. denied, — U.S. —, 126 S. Ct. 2035, 164 L. Ed. 2d 794 (2006) and overruled in part on other grounds by Jay v. Commonwealth, 275 Va. 510, 659 S.E.2d 311, 2008 Va. LEXIS 53 (2008).

Jury instructions given by the trial court accurately conveyed the applicable law, without confusion to the jury, by requiring that defendant be a principal in the first degree for the jury to convict for capital murder. The evidence supported the Commonwealth's theory of a shooter and a spotter and the direction by the spotter to shoot at the opportune time. Muhammad v. Commonwealth, 269 Va. 451, 619 S.E.2d 16, 2005 Va. LEXIS 85 (2005), cert. denied, — U.S. —, 126 S. Ct. 2035, 164 L. Ed. 2d 794 (2006) and overruled in part on other grounds by Jay v. Commonwealth, 275 Va. 510, 659 S.E.2d 311, 2008 Va. LEXIS 53 (2008).

Instructions, premised on theory that killing was accomplished by sole perpetrator, correctly refused. — Where the weight and dimensions of the 69-pound bloodstained rock, which was introduced in evidence as an exhibit, made it apparent that a single person could not have lifted it and dropped or thrown it while simultaneously holding victim down, and where the bloodstains on coperpetrator's jacket as well as on defendant's clothing further tended to corroborate the Commonwealth's theory that two men had been in the immediate presence of the victim's body when the fatal blows were struck and, hence, had jointly participated in the killing, trial court correctly refused defendant's tendered instructions which were premised upon the theory that the killing was accomplished by a sole perpetrator. Strickler v. Commonwealth, 241 Va. 482, 404 S.E.2d 227, cert. denied, 502 U.S. 944, 112 S. Ct. 386, 116 L. Ed. 2d 337 (1991).

Defendant held principal in first degree despite absence of proof defendant was perpetrator. — Evidence was held sufficient to prove defendant, on trial for charges of attempted capital murder by arson, was a principal in the first degree, despite absence of proof that defendant was the perpetrator who lit the fire, rather than his accomplice. Hancock v. Commonwealth, 12 Va. App. 774, 407 S.E.2d 301 (1991).

Sufficient evidence to convict defendant of attempted capital murder for hire. — Defendant asked two people to kill his wife, formulated diagrams of his wife's house, explained when she would be at home, and paid two thousand dollars to the hit man. The evidence was sufficient to convict defendant of attempted capital murder for hire, in violation of §§ 18.2-25 and 18.2-31, and solicitation of capital murder for hire, in violation of §§ 18.2-29 and 18.2-31; the Commonwealth did not err by failing to elect between the charges, because the solicitation and attempt were both parts of a common scheme or plan. Ashford v. Commonwealth, 47 Va. App. 676, 626 S.E.2d 464, 2006 Va. App. LEXIS 70 (2006).

Sufficient evidence of attempted capital murder of officer. — Sufficient evidence supported defendant's conviction under §§ 18.2-25 and 18.2-31(6) of attempted capital murder of a police officer because the specific intent required for the crime could be inferred by defendant veering the defendant's automobile from the defendant's path of travel directly toward a second police officer, resulting in defendant striking the second officer at about 40 to 50 mph, knocking the second officer to the ground, and running over the officer's foot. Piggott v. Commonwealth, — Va. App. —, — S.E.2d —, 2008 Va. App. LEXIS 432 (Sept. 23, 2008).

Malice is element of murder but not manslaughter. — Malice, a requisite element for murder of any kind, is unnecessary in manslaughter cases and is the touchstone by which murder and manslaughter cases are distinguished. Essex v. Commonwealth, 228 Va. 273, 322 S.E.2d 216 (1984).

Neither premeditation nor an intent to kill is an element of felony murder; only malice is required. Goodson v. Commonwealth, 22 Va. App. 61, 467 S.E.2d 848 (1996).

Willfulness, deliberation, and premeditation are jury questions. — The question whether a defendant is guilty of a willful, deliberate, and premeditated killing of the victim is usually a question for the jury to determine from all the facts and circumstances. Clozza v. Commonwealth, 228 Va. 124, 321 S.E.2d 273 (1984), cert. denied, 469 U.S. 1230, 105 S. Ct. 1233, 84 L. Ed. 2d 370 (1985).

Factors considered as to willfulness, deliberation, and premeditation. — In deciding the question of whether the killing was willful, deliberate, and premeditated, the jury properly may consider the brutality of the attack, whether more than one blow was struck, the disparity in size and strength between the accused and the victim, the concealment of the victim's body, and the defendant's efforts to avoid detection. Clozza v. Commonwealth, 228 Va. 124, 321 S.E.2d 273 (1984), cert. denied, 469 U.S. 1230, 105 S. Ct. 1233, 84 L. Ed. 2d 370 (1985).

Where witness testified that defendant in a robbery-murder prosecution had had problems with the victim before and that defendant had a motive to kill the victim, witness's testimony was crucial in the Commonwealth's proof that the killing was "willful, deliberate, and premeditated." Ortega v. Commonwealth, No. 0713-94-2 (Ct. of Appeals Jan. 30, 1996).

A capital murder instruction that did not refer to specific intent and required proof only that the attempted killing was "willful, deliberate and premeditated" was insufficient; the inclusion of language in a later instruction defining "willful, deliberate and premeditated" as "a specific intent to kill" was likewise insufficient to compensate for the absence of intent language from the earlier instruction. Herbert v. Commonwealth, No. 0888-00-4, 2001 Va. App. LEXIS 184 (Ct. of Appeals Apr. 10, 2001).

Intention to kill need not exist for any specified length of time prior to the actual killing. Clozza v. Commonwealth, 228 Va. 124, 321 S.E.2d 273 (1984), cert. denied, 469 U.S. 1230, 105 S. Ct. 1233, 84 L. Ed. 2d 370 (1985).

Evidence showed that defendant committed the underlying offense of robbery while armed with a deadly weapon where, although when the robbery began defendant was unarmed, he rendered victim helpless by physical force, then took from his person what items of value could be found, and subsequently, after the beating and stabbing of the victim with knife removed from his car, defendant and his accomplices fled the scene in the car they had earlier commandeered, as only at this point was the taking of the car consummated and the robbery completed, so that defendant was clearly armed with the knife during the commission of a portion of the robbery. Correll v. Commonwealth, 232 Va. 454, 352 S.E.2d 352, cert. denied, 482 U.S. 931, 107 S. Ct. 3219, 96 L. Ed. 2d 705 (1987).

Whether killing was accidental or intentional and premeditated is a question of fact and, absent eyewitness testimony or a voluntary confession, that question necessarily turns upon the import of circumstantial evidence. Edmonds v. Commonwealth, 229 Va. 303, 329 S.E.2d 807, cert. denied, 474 U.S. 975, 106 S. Ct. 339, 88 L. Ed. 2d 324 (1985).

To establish premeditation, the intention to kill need only exist for a moment. Peterson v. Commonwealth, 225 Va. 289, 302 S.E.2d 520, cert. denied, 464 U.S. 865, 104 S. Ct. 202, 78 L. Ed. 2d 176 (1983).

A design to kill may be formed only a moment before the fatal act is committed, provided the accused had time to think and did intend to kill. Clozza v. Commonwealth, 228 Va. 124, 321 S.E.2d 273 (1984), cert. denied, 469 U.S. 1230, 105 S. Ct. 1233, 84 L. Ed. 2d 370 (1985); Barnes v. Commonwealth, 234 Va. 130, 360 S.E.2d 196 (1987), cert. denied, 484 U.S. 1036, 108 S. Ct. 763, 98 L. Ed. 2d 779 (1988), cert. denied, 499 U.S. 913, 111 S. Ct. 1123, 113 L. Ed. 2d 231 (1991).

The question of premeditation is usually one for determination by the trier of fact from all the facts and circumstances of the case. Barnes v. Commonwealth, 234 Va. 130, 360 S.E.2d 196 (1987), cert. denied, 484 U.S. 1036, 108 S. Ct. 763, 98 L. Ed. 2d 779 (1988).

Double jeopardy not a bar. — Defendant's double jeopardy rights were not violated in a case where defendant pled guilty to solicitation to commit murder in violation of § 18.2-29 and a jury then convicted defendant in a trial of attempted capital murder for hire in violation of subdivision 2 of § 18.2-31 and § 18.2-25. Double jeopardy did not apply because: (1) defendant's offenses were considered in a single proceeding and, thus, there were not successive prosecutions for the same offense; and (2) solicitation to commit murder and attempted capital murder for hire were not the same offenses and, thus, defendant could be convicted and punished for both offenses since solicitation for murder required that a defendant solicit another person whereas attempted capital murder for hire did not require such proof. Ostrander v. Commonwealth, 51 Va. App. 386, 658 S.E.2d 346, 2008 Va. App. LEXIS 126 (2008).

III. UNDERLYING FELONY.

A. Robbery.

This section does not require proof that a defendant charged with murder during the commission of a robbery or a rape was a principal in the first degree to the crimes of robbery or rape. It is only necessary that the Commonwealth prove that the defendant was the triggerman in the murder and an accomplice in the robbery or rape to convict him of capital murder. Briley v. Commonwealth, 221 Va. 563, 273 S.E.2d 57 (1980).

When robbery involved, all elements to convict of first-degree murder must be established. — To convict of capital murder under subsection (d) (now subdivision 4) of this section, the Commonwealth must establish all the elements necessary to convict of first-degree murder, i.e., that the killing was willful, deliberate and premeditated and, in addition, all the elements necessary to convict of an armed robbery. Johnson v. Commonwealth, 221 Va. 736, 273 S.E.2d 784, cert. denied, 454 U.S. 920, 102 S. Ct. 422, 70 L. Ed. 2d 231 (1981).

Murder in an attempted robbery violates § 18.2-32, but not this section, the capital-murder statute. Ball v. Commonwealth, 221 Va. 754, 273 S.E.2d 790 (1981).

Murder in the commission of a robbery is a killing which takes place before, during, or after the robbery and is so closely related thereto in time, place, and causal connection as to make the killing part of the same criminal enterprise as the robbery; under Virginia law, the robbery must have been one of the motivating factors for the killing. George v. Angelone, 100 F.3d 353 (4th Cir. 1996), cert. denied, 519 U.S. 1103, 117 S. Ct. 854, 136 L. Ed. 2d 829 (1997).

To support a capital murder conviction under subdivision 4, the Commonwealth is not required to prove the robbery was a motivating factor for the homicide that was committed; rather, it is sufficient if the killing and robbery were interdependent objects of a common criminal design. Winckler v. Commonwealth, 32 Va. App. 836, 531 S.E.2d 45, 2000 Va. App. LEXIS 526 (2000).

Subsections (d) and (e) (now subdivisions 4 and 5) expand the definition of capital murder to include the "willful, deliberate and premeditated killing" of any person "in the commission of, or subsequent to, rape," and "in the commission of robbery while armed with a deadly weapon." Fitzgerald v. Commonwealth, 223 Va. 615, 292 S.E.2d 798 (1982), cert. denied, 459 U.S. 1228, 103 S. Ct. 1235, 75 L. Ed. 2d 469, rehearing denied, 460 U.S. 1105, 103 S. Ct. 1809, 76 L. Ed. 2d 371 (1983).

Evidence showed that defendant committed the underlying offense of robbery while armed with a deadly weapon where, although when the robbery began defendant was unarmed, he rendered victim helpless by physical force, then took from his person what items of value could be found, and subsequently, after the beating and stabbing of the victim with knife removed from his car, defendant and his accomplices fled the scene in the car they had earlier commandeered, as only at this point was the taking of the car consummated and the robbery completed, so that defendant was clearly armed with the knife during the commission of a portion of the robbery. Correll v. Commonwealth, 232 Va. 454, 352 S.E.2d 352, cert. denied, 482 U.S. 931, 107 S. Ct. 3219, 96 L. Ed. 2d 705 (1987).

"During the commission of." — For case where evidence was held sufficient to establish a murder during the commission of a robbery, see Bunch v. Thompson, 949 F.2d 1354 (4th Cir. 1991), cert. denied, 505 U.S. 1230, 112 S. Ct. 3056, 120 L. Ed. 2d 922 (1992).

In Virginia, conviction of capital murder during the commission of a robbery was sufficient by itself to support defendant's death sentence, pursuant to § 18.2-31(4). Hedrick v. True, 2004 U.S. Dist. LEXIS 4600 (W.D. Va. Mar. 23, 2004), aff'd, 443 F.3d 342 (4th Cir. 2006).

Sufficient nexus between predicate offenses and murders. — A sufficient nexus was present between the defendant's murder of three victims and the related offenses of robbery and rape where, although the defendant may not have entered the house where the crimes occurred with the specific intent to kill all three victims and to rob all three and rape one of them, and while the victims perhaps may not have died simultaneously with the commission of a robbery or rape, they were in fact raped and robbed as part of the same criminal enterprise which surrounded the murders. Beck

v. Angelone, 113 F. Supp. 2d 941, 2000 U.S. Dist. LEXIS 14194 (E.D. Va. 2000).

Both robbery and deliberate, premeditated killing required under subsection (d) (now subdivision 4). — Subsection (d) (now subdivision 4) of this section limits capital murder; murder committed in the course of a robbery, standing alone, is not capital murder; nor is murder committed with deliberation and premeditation standing alone capital murder. Rather, capital murder is an appropriate finding only while both an ongoing robbery with a deadly weapon and a premeditated murder are present simultaneously, only where the defendant while engaged in the robbery with the use of a deadly weapon has killed willfully, with premeditation, and with deliberation. Briley v. Bass, 584 F. Supp. 807 (E.D. Va.), aff'd, 742 F.2d 155 (4th Cir.), cert. denied, 469 U.S. 893, 105 S. Ct. 270, 83 L. Ed. 2d 206 (1984).

Robbery need not be the sole motive to sustain a charge of capital murder during the commission of a robbery. To prove a defendant guilty, the prosecution must show that the murder and the robbery were interdependent objects of a common criminal design. Savino v. Murray, 82 F.3d 593 (4th Cir.), cert. denied, 518 U.S. 1036, 117 S. Ct. 1, 135 L. Ed. 2d 1098 (1996); Winckler v. Commonwealth, 32 Va. App. 836, 531 S.E.2d 45, 2000 Va. App. LEXIS 526 (2000).

Where killing and taking of property are so closely related in time, place, and causal connection as to make them parts of the same criminal enterprise, the predicates for capital murder under subsection (d) (now subdivision 4) are established. Further, these relationships need not necessarily be jury questions. They may, in a proper case, be determined as a matter of law. Pope v. Commonwealth, 234 Va. 114, 360 S.E.2d 352 (1987).

The fact that stealing occurs after a killing does not prove that the decision to steal was an afterthought and that the two crimes were unrelated so as to preclude a conviction for capital murder. Beck v. Angelone, 113 F. Supp. 2d 941, 2000 U.S. Dist. LEXIS 14194 (E.D. Va. 2000).

Possession of property as proof of single criminal enterprise. — The defendant's possession of some fruit of the robbery may show conclusively that the violence against the victim and the trespass to his property were so closely related in time, place and causal connection as to make the killing, as a matter of law, a part of the same criminal enterprise as the robbery. Winckler v. Commonwealth, 32 Va. App. 836, 531 S.E.2d 45, 2000 Va. App. LEXIS 526 (2000).

Distinction between crimes in subsection (d) (now subdivision 4) of this section and § 18.2-32 is plain: To be found guilty of capital murder, a defendant must be proved, beyond a reasonable doubt, not only to have killed during the commission of a robbery, but to have killed willfully, deliberately, and with premeditation and while armed with a deadly weapon. The defendant found guilty of first degree murder is the defendant who killed during the course of a robbery, but did not kill with willfulness, deliberation, and premeditation. Briley v. Bass, 584 F. Supp. 807 (E.D. Va.), aff'd, 742 F.2d 155 (4th Cir.), cert. denied, 469 U.S. 893, 105 S. Ct. 270, 83 L. Ed. 2d 206 (1984).

Capital murder in commission of robbery without being principal in first degree. — Under this section, a defendant may be convicted of capital murder in the commission of a robbery without being a principal in the first degree to the crime of robbery. The Commonwealth need only prove that the defendant actually committed the murder and was an accomplice in the robbery. Watkins v. Commonwealth, 229 Va. 469, 331 S.E.2d 422 (1985), cert. denied, 475 U.S. 1099, 106 S. Ct. 1503, 89 L. Ed. 2d 903 (1986).

Corpus delicti held adequately established both as to robbery and cause of death. — Williams v. Commonwealth, 234 Va. 168, 360 S.E.2d 361 (1987), cert. denied, 484 U.S. 1020, 108 S. Ct. 733, 98 L. Ed. 2d 681 (1988). See.

For case dealing with the mandatory death penalty for the killing by an inmate of an employee or other person in a penal institution under a provision contained in provisions of former § 53-291 and subsequently incorporated into § 18.2-10, see notes under § 18.2-10.

B. Rape.

Sequence of rape and murder not dispositive. — A defendant was properly convicted of capital murder under subdivision 5 where the sequence of events were sufficient to establish that the rape of the victim and the murder of the victim were interconnected as part of the same criminal enterprise; it was not necessary for the Commonwealth to show that the rape occurred before the murder. Beck v. Angelone, 113 F. Supp. 2d 941, 2000 U.S. Dist. LEXIS 14194 (E.D. Va. 2000).

Defense of consent not advanced by not guilty plea. — In a prosecution for capital murder following rape, the defense of consent is not advanced solely by a plea of not guilty. That plea could be grounded upon the defendant's belief that the Commonwealth is unable to prove identification, opportunity, or the physical elements of carnal knowledge. The defense of consent can be "advanced" only by evidence adduced by one of the parties. Whether the evidence is sufficient for that purpose necessarily is a question of law. Smith v. Commonwealth, 219 Va. 455, 248 S.E.2d 135 (1978), cert. denied, 441 U.S. 967, 99 S. Ct. 2419, 60 L. Ed. 2d 1074 (1979), aff'd, 477 U.S. 527, 106 S. Ct. 2661, 91 L. Ed. 2d 434 (1986).

Proof of unchaste character of victim in murder following rape case. — Rape is an essential element of the crime of capital murder charged under this section. Thus, where consent is advanced as a defense, the previous unchaste character of the victim may be shown by proof of general reputation. Smith v. Commonwealth, 219 Va. 455, 248 S.E.2d 135 (1978), cert. denied, 441 U.S. 967, 99 S. Ct. 2419, 60 L. Ed. 2d 1074 (1979), aff'd, 477 U.S. 527, 106 S. Ct. 2661, 91 L. Ed. 2d 434 (1986).

Testimony of victim's daughter. — In a prosecution for capital murder following rape, the admission of testimony of the victim's daughter which supplemented a testimonial narrative of the sequence of events preceding and following the commission of the crime was not improper. Smith v. Commonwealth, 219 Va. 455, 248 S.E.2d 135 (1978), cert. denied, 441 U.S. 967, 99 S. Ct. 2419, 60 L. Ed. 2d 1074 (1979), aff'd, 477 U.S. 527, 106 S. Ct. 2661, 91 L. Ed. 2d 434 (1986).

Evidence sufficient for finding murder following rape. — See Keil v. Commonwealth, 222 Va. 99, 278 S.E.2d 826 (1981).

Introduction of evidence of three other similar crimes upheld. — In trial in which defendant was convicted of capital murder and rape, introduction of evidence of three other similar crimes would be upheld in view of the similarities between the offenses, particularly the indications of a common modus operandi and the scientific evidence that the defendant was the common criminal agent. Spencer v. Commonwealth, 240 Va. 78, 393 S.E.2d 609, cert. denied, 498 U.S. 908, 111 S. Ct. 281, 112 L. Ed. 2d 235 (1990).

Double Jeopardy Clause did not bar second trial. — After petitioner's conviction for the capital murder of a murder victim during or subsequent to the rape of the murder victim's sister was reversed, a state court did not unreasonably apply federal law in concluding that the Double Jeopardy Clause of the Fifth Amendment did not bar petitioner's second trial for capital murder during the commission of rape or attempted rape of the murder victim because under Virginia law, a defendant could be prosecuted for multiple violations of § 18.2-31 where there was a single murder victim but different gradation crime victims. Powell v. Kelly, 562 F.3d 656, 2009 U.S. App. LEXIS 7867 (4th Cir. 2009), cert. denied, 2010 U.S. LEXIS 1011 (U.S. 2010).

C. Others.

General Assembly's classification of murder for hire as a capital offense does not deny the accused either due process or equal protection of the law. Stockton v. Commonwealth, 227 Va. 124, 314 S.E.2d 371, cert. denied, 469 U.S. 873, 105 S. Ct. 229, 83 L. Ed. 2d 158 (1984).

Section 18.2-33 and its companion, § 18.2-32, codify the common-law doctrine of felony-murder, a doctrine developed to elevate to murder a homicide committed during the course of a felony by imputing malice to the killing. King v. Commonwealth, 6 Va. App. 351, 368 S.E.2d 704 (1988).

The word "purpose" in subsection (f) (now subdivision 6) of this section equates with intent, rather than motive. Martin v. Commonwealth, 221 Va. 436, 271 S.E.2d 123 (1980).

By its clear terms, this section makes purpose a key factor in any prosecution thereunder; the death penalty may be imposed only where the Commonwealth proves beyond a reasonable doubt that the killing of a law-enforcement officer is accompanied by the purpose of interfering with the performance of his official duties and is not unconstitutionally vague. Martin v. Commonwealth, 221 Va. 436, 271 S.E.2d 123 (1980).

The "purpose of interfering" language of subsection (f) (now subdivision 6) of this section does not change the established rule of law that motive is not an essential element of murder, although proof of motive may tend to establish intent in cases of circumstantial evidence. Martin v. Commonwealth, 221 Va. 436, 271 S.E.2d 123 (1980).

A person of ordinary intelligence would also conclude that the term "to defile" is interchangeable with the phrase intent to "sexually molest." Swisher v. Commonwealth, 256 Va. 471, 506 S.E.2d 763 (1998), cert. denied, 528 U.S. 812, 120 S. Ct. 46, 145 L. Ed. 2d 41 (1999).

The Commonwealth must prove that the accused was a convict at the time of the homicide in order to convict him of the murder of a guard under this section. Brown v. Commonwealth, 132 Va. 606, 111 S.E. 112 (1922).

Although victim killed elsewhere, hiring of killer in Virginia sufficient. — It was without consequence that the defendant intended for the killing to take place in the Philippines, because the hiring of the killer took place in Virginia and that was sufficient to violate this section. United States v. Morin, 80 F.3d 124 (4th Cir. 1996).

Defendant need not be principal in first degree in each murder. — Subdivision 8 of this section does not require proof that a defendant charged with capital murder in the premeditated killing of more than one person within a three-year period was a principal in the first degree in each murder referenced in the indictment; the jury need be instructed only that they must find the defendant was a principal in the first degree, or triggerman, in the principal murder charged, and that he was at least an accomplice in the murder of one or more persons other than the victim within a three-year period. Burlile v. Commonwealth, 261 Va. 501, 544 S.E.2d 360, 2001 Va. LEXIS 56 (2001).

What constitutes "armed with a deadly weapon." — A person is criminally armed with a deadly weapon from the moment he seizes a weapon with intent to use it for a criminal purpose. Quintana v. Commonwealth, 224 Va. 127, 295 S.E.2d 643 (1982), cert. denied, 460 U.S. 1029, 103 S. Ct. 1280, 75 L. Ed. 2d 501, rehearing denied, 461 U.S. 940, 103 S. Ct. 2113, 77 L. Ed. 2d 316 (1983).

Evidence insufficient that defendant intended to murder officers. — Where from the Commonwealth's evidence, it was just as likely, if not more likely, that defendant attempted to avoid police apprehension by driving toward their cars, indifferent to the consequences in risking a collision, because he believed that he could crash through any vehicle in his way or that the police would move out of his way, which they did, because the Commonwealth presented no direct evidence that defendant in running the road blocks intended to murder the police officers and because its circumstantial evidence did not exclude a reasonable hypothesis of innocence, defendant's convictions for attempted murder under this section were reversed. Haywood v. Commonwealth, 20 Va. App. 562, 458 S.E.2d 606 (1995).

Sufficient evidence of attempt to kill officer. — Evidence of intent to kill a police officer in violation of subdivision 6 held sufficient where the officer testified that after the defendant's companion, who was being pursued by the officer, entered the vehicle that was waiting for him in the back of the alley, the defendant revved the engine and drove toward toward the officer and the officer saw the tires of the vehicle turn completely in his direction and away from the alley exit; and where the defendant's assertion that he only struck the officer with his vehicle while attempting to escape was belied by the evidence that the defendant could have driven from the scene without steering toward the officer or without hitting the retaining wall. Salaam v. Commonwealth, No. 1694-99-2, 2000 Va. App. LEXIS 609 (Ct. of Appeals Aug. 22, 2000).

Because defendant swerved a car toward a police officer rather than driving straight ahead to escape, the evidence was sufficient to prove premeditation and the specific intent to kill; consequently, defendant was properly convicted of violating subdivision 6 of § 18.2-31 and § 18.2-25. Coles v. Commonwealth, 270 Va. 585, 621 S.E.2d 109, 2005 Va. LEXIS 88 (2005).

Evidence that defendant operated vehicle that tried to run down police officer. — Although the incident occurred very quickly while the vehicle sped past the officer, brushing up against his leg, and while the officer was firing three rounds into the vehicle, the officer's identification of the defendant was not inherently incredible; the officer had an unobstructed view of the defendant as he drove past him in the vehicle, the officer positively identified the defendant as the driver and testified that only two people were in the vehicle, neither that officer nor another officer saw a third person occupying the vehicle or flee from the vehicle after it crashed, as the defendant claimed, and the defendant was irrefutably an occupant of the vehicle. Salaam v. Commonwealth, No. 1694-99-2, 2000 Va. App. LEXIS 609 (Ct. of Appeals Aug. 22, 2000).

Sufficient evidence of abduction for pecuniary benefit. — Where transporting of murder victim from robbery scene was a detention separate and apart from, and not merely incidental to, the robbery, and was greater than the restraint intrinsic in a robbery, and further, the evidence clearly supported a finding that the abduction was committed to protect the fruits of the robbery and to escape an arrest, the evidence supported the charge of an abduction with the intent to extort a pecuniary benefit. Cardwell v. Commonwealth, 248 Va. 501, 450 S.E.2d 146 (1994), cert. denied, 514 U.S. 1097, 115 S. Ct. 1826, 131 L. Ed. 2d 747 (1995).

Single indictment under subsection (g) (now subdivision 7) will support only one conviction and sentence. — When a defendant is charged under only one indictment for capital murder in violation of subsection (g) (now subdivision 7), he cannot be sentenced to two life sentences on that one indictment. Whether the indictment charges one offense or two, the result is the same. If only one offense is charged, the indictment can support only one conviction and sentence; but even if two offenses are charged, because they are contained in a single count, only one conviction and one sentence are permissible. Morris v. Commonwealth, 228 Va. 206, 321 S.E.2d 633 (1984).

Single trial for two murders if committed within three years not contradicted by federal law. — Certificate of appealability was granted under 28 U.S.C.S. § 2253 on the habeas petitioner's claim that the Sixth Amendment right to effective assistance of counsel was violated when counsel did not challenge a single trial for two murders under subdivision 8 of § 18.2-31, but on the merits the district court's dismissal of that claim was affirmed because the Supreme Court of Virginia had held that two murder counts could be joined under subdivision 8 of § 18.2-31 despite any prejudice if the murders occurred within three years and the United States Supreme Court had never addressed the issue; thus, there was no clearly established federal law for the state court to contradict. Walker v. True, — F.3d —, 2003 U.S. App. LEXIS 8557 (4th Cir. May 6, 2003).

Where four people were killed, it was theoretically possible that the defendant could have been convicted of two capital murders since it takes the killing of at least two people as part of the same act or transaction to constitute one capital murder under this section. Buchanan v. Commonwealth, 238 Va. 389, 384 S.E.2d 757 (1989), cert. denied, 493 U.S. 1063, 110 S. Ct. 880, 107 L. Ed. 2d 963 (1990).

The theoretical limitation on the number of possible capital murder convictions that can be supported by four murders does not control the way in which the Commonwealth can frame indictments, since the Commonwealth is free to indict an individual for as many separate crimes as the Commonwealth, in good faith, thinks it can prove and the Commonwealth is free to charge the commission of a single offense in several different ways in order to meet the contingencies of proof. Buchanan v. Commonwealth, 238 Va. 389, 384 S.E.2d 757 (1989), cert. denied, 493 U.S. 1063, 110 S. Ct. 880, 107 L. Ed. 2d 963 (1990).

If all four individuals were killed in one act or transaction, defendant could only be convicted of one capital murder but if two individuals were killed as part of one act or transaction and the two others were killed as part of a second, different act or transaction, then defendant could be convicted of two capital murders. Buchanan v. Commonwealth, 238 Va. 389, 384 S.E.2d 757 (1989), cert. denied, 493 U.S. 1063, 110 S. Ct. 880, 107 L. Ed. 2d 963 (1990).

Burden of proof as to killing of law-enforcement officer. — The burden the statute imposes upon the Commonwealth is the burden of proving that the killing of a law-enforcement officer is accompanied by the purpose of interfering with the performance of his official duties. The crucial inquiry contemplated by the statute is not whether the officer was in fact engaged at the time he was killed in performing a law-enforcement duty but, rather, whether the killer acted with the purpose of interfering with what he perceived to be an officer's performance of a law-enforcement duty. DeLong v. Commonwealth, 234 Va. 357, 362 S.E.2d 669 (1987), cert. denied, 485 U.S. 929, 108 S. Ct. 1100, 99 L. Ed. 2d 263 (1988).

In a habeas corpus proceeding, evidence was sufficient to establish beyond a reasonable doubt that petitioner killed a police officer for the purpose of interfering with the performance of his official duties, an essential element of capital murder. DeLong v. Thompson, 790 F. Supp. 594 (E.D. Va. 1991), aff'd, 985 F.2d 553 (4th Cir. 1993).

Killing and theft held objects of common criminal design. — Where the jury properly could have found that the theft occurred during or sometime after the first shot was fired but before the victim was submerged in the water where he drowned, and, even if the wallet was taken from the truck after the victim expired, the homicide was a capital offense because the evidence supported the conclusion that the killing and the theft were interdependent objects of a common criminal design. Wise v. Commonwealth, 230 Va. 322, 337 S.E.2d 715 (1985), cert. denied, 475 U.S. 1112, 106 S. Ct. 1524, 89 L. Ed. 2d 921 (1986), cert. denied, 508 U.S. 964, 113 S. Ct. 2940, 124 L. Ed. 2d 689 (1993).

IV. TRIAL.

A. In General.

Defendant implicitly acknowledged fair notice that indictment charged him with capital murder at the pretrial hearings when he moved to quash the indictment, assigning only challenges to the facial constitutionality of the capital statutes. Boggs v. Commonwealth, 229 Va. 501, 331 S.E.2d 407 (1985), cert. denied, 475 U.S. 1031, 106 S. Ct. 1240, 89 L. Ed. 2d 347 (1986).

Indictment for capital murder following arrest and hearing for noncapital murder. — Where the defendant was originally detained on a noncapital charge of first-degree murder, was granted a preliminary hearing on that charge, and was certified to the grand jury, and where the Commonwealth's attorney then obtained indictments for both capital murder and first-degree murder and proceeded to trial on the capital but not the noncapital offense, the procedure employed in obtaining the indictment was not manipulative, and it did not work a denial of any statutory right to which the defendant was entitled, since the defendant was not arrested on the charge of capital murder, but was indicted on that charge directly by the grand jury. Waye v. Commonwealth, 219 Va. 683, 251 S.E.2d 202, cert. denied, 442 U.S. 924, 99 S. Ct. 2850, 61 L. Ed. 2d 292 (1979).

No additional peremptory strikes. — There is no basis in Virginia law for additional peremptory strikes in a capital murder trial. Buchanan v. Commonwealth, 238 Va. 389, 384 S.E.2d 757 (1989), cert. denied, 493 U.S. 1063, 110 S. Ct. 880, 107 L. Ed. 2d 963 (1990).

Instruction on "force and violence" in murder following rape case. — In a prosecution for capital murder following rape, an instruction to the jury that the Commonwealth was required to prove that the act of intercourse was accomplished "by force and violence" was not improper. Smith v. Commonwealth, 219 Va. 455, 248 S.E.2d 135 (1978), cert. denied, 441 U.S. 967, 99 S. Ct. 2419, 60 L. Ed. 2d 1074 (1979), aff'd, 477 U.S. 527, 106 S. Ct. 2661, 91 L. Ed. 2d 434 (1986).

Defendant held not entitled to first-degree murder instruction. — Where the sole issue presented by the evidence was whether it was defendant or his codefendant who killed state trooper, and defendant was either guilty or innocent of the capital offense, he was not entitled to an instruction on first-degree murder. Frye v. Commonwealth, 231 Va. 370, 345 S.E.2d 267 (1986).

Instructions on intent proper. — As the jury was instructed that defendant's act had to have been "willful, deliberate, and premeditated," that willful, deliberate and premeditated meant a specific intent to kill, and that an attempted crime required a specific intent to commit the completed crime, the trial court instructed the jury exactly as subdivision 6 of § 18.2-31 directed. Jordan v. Commonwealth, 50 Va. App. 322, 649 S.E.2d 709, 2007 Va. App. LEXIS 327 (2007).

Accused is not entitled to instructions on lesser included

offenses solely because the case is one of murder. A second-degree murder instruction is appropriate only where there is evidence to support it. Bunch v. Commonwealth, 225 Va. 423, 304 S.E.2d 271, cert. denied, 464 U.S. 977, 104 S. Ct. 414, 78 L. Ed. 2d 352 (1983), 505 U.S. 1230, 112 S. Ct. 3056, 120 L. Ed. 2d 922 (1992).

It is well established that a defendant accused of capital or first degree murder is not entitled to an instruction on second degree murder based on the legal presumption that all homicides are second degree murder. Williams v. Commonwealth, No. 2584-96-1 (Ct. of Appeals Feb. 10, 1998).

Entitlement to lesser included offense instructions. — To be entitled to a lesser included offense instruction of first degree murder, petitioner, convicted of capital murder, had to provide some evidence that the killing was not done with willfulness, deliberation, and premeditation. Given the absence of any evidence to support petitioner's accidental shooting theory, petitioner could not show entitlement to an instruction on that theory. Orbe v. True, 233 F. Supp. 2d 749, 2002 U.S. Dist. LEXIS 22958 (E.D. Va. 2002).

Conviction under this section and § 18.2-53.1 not double jeopardy. — Conviction for the use of a firearm in the commission of a felony, § 18.2-53.1, as well as murder in the commission of a robbery while armed with a deadly weapon, does not violate the double jeopardy clause of the United States Constitution. Turner v. Commonwealth, 221 Va. 513, 273 S.E.2d 36 (1980), cert. denied, 451 U.S. 1011, 101 S. Ct. 2347, 68 L. Ed. 2d 863 (1981).

Defendant's sentence of death was neither excessive nor disproportionate. — Defendant's sentence of death for capital murder for hire was neither excessive nor disproportionate when compared to sentences generally imposed by sentencing bodies in this jurisdiction for crimes of a similar nature. Murphy v. Commonwealth, 246 Va. 136, 431 S.E.2d 48, cert. denied, 510 U.S. 928, 114 S. Ct. 336, 126 L. Ed. 2d 281 (1993).

Defendant's punishment of death for capital murder based on a finding of vileness was not disproportionate to similar offenses. Yarbrough v. Commonwealth, 262 Va. 388, 551 S.E.2d 306, 2001 Va. LEXIS 112 (2001), cert. denied, 535 U.S. 1060, 122 S. Ct. 1925, 152 L. Ed. 2d 832 (2002).

Multiple punishments not double jeopardy. — The convictions and imposition of multiple punishments for capital murder, robbery and use of a firearm in the commission of a felony did not violate appellant's rights under the double jeopardy clause of the Fifth Amendment. Since those convictions and punishments did not violate the double jeopardy clause, his counsel was not ineffective for failing to raise the issue. Peterson v. Bass, 2 Va. App. 314, 343 S.E.2d 475 (1986).

Defendant's guilty plea to first-degree murder with regard to death of one victim did not bar, on double jeopardy grounds, capital murder prosecution with regard to death of second victim. Same conduct is used to support more than one conviction in a single proceeding. Defendant can be prosecuted in single proceeding for both murder charges involving victims. Thomas v. Commonwealth, 244 Va. 1, 419 S.E.2d 606, cert. denied, 506 U.S. 958, 113 S. Ct. 421, 121 L. Ed. 2d 343 (1992).

Where the killing of one victim constituted two capital offenses, the imposition of multiple death sentences did not violate the constitutional guarantee of protection against multiple punishments for the same offense. Payne v. Commonwealth, 257 Va. 216, 509 S.E.2d 293 (1999).

Petitioner's application for a writ of habeas corpus was dismissed because he failed to satisfy the "performance" and "prejudice" prong of the two-part test enunciated in Strickland; there was no double jeopardy violation because the elements of capital murder while in custody, subdivision 3 of § 18.2-31, capital murder of a law-enforcement officer, subdivision 6 of § 18.2-31, and capital murder of more than one person within a three-year period, subdivision 8 of § 18.2-31 were different and each carried its own separate penalty. Morva v. Warden of the Sussex I State Prison, 2013 Va. LEXIS 43 (Apr. 12, 2013).

Defendant placed in double jeopardy. — Since the defendant had previously been tried for a rape in Richmond, the use of that rape as an element in an attempted capital murder charge in Chesterfield county violated the defendant's right against double jeopardy. Curtis v. Commonwealth, 12 Va. App. 527, 405 S.E.2d 230 (1991).

Commonwealth is free to indict a defendant under subdivision 8 of § 18.2-31 for the murder of more than one person within a three-year period when each of the constituent murders occurred as part of the same act or transaction, and also indict the defendant for capital murder under subdivision 7 of § 18.2-31 for the same murders; however, if the Commonwealth obtains convictions on both indictments it may not seek to have separate punishments imposed for each offense, but rather it must elect which indictment it will proceed upon in the penalty-determination phase of the trial. Andrews v. Commonwealth, 280 Va. 231, 699 S.E.2d 237, 2010 Va. LEXIS 239 (2010), cert. denied, 131 S. Ct. 2999, 2011 U.S. LEXIS 4469, 180 L. Ed. 2d 827 (U.S. 2011).

Imposition of two death sentences upon defendant for convictions under subdivisions 7 and 8 of § 18.2-31 violated the double jeopardy prohibition against multiple punishments for the same offense, as the Commonwealth was free to indict a defendant under subdivisions 7 and 8 for the same murders, when each of the constituent murders occurred as part of the same act or transaction, but if the Commonwealth obtained convictions on both indictments it could not seek to have separate punishments imposed for each offense, but rather it had to elect which indictment it would proceed upon in the penalty-determination phase. Andrews v. Commonwealth, 280 Va. 231, 699 S.E.2d 237, 2010 Va. LEXIS 239 (2010), cert. denied, 131 S. Ct. 2999, 2011 U.S. LEXIS 4469, 180 L. Ed. 2d 827 (U.S. 2011).

Habeas petitioner was granted a writ as to sentences imposed under subdivisions 7 and 8 of § 18.2-31 because the petitioner satisfied the performance and prejudice prongs of the Strickland test by showing ineffective assistance of counsel because counsel failed to protect petitioner's rights to be free from double jeopardy where petitioner was tried and punished for separate counts of capital murder of more than one person as part of the same transaction under subdivision 7 and capital murder of more than one person within a three-year period under subdivision 8, even though the crimes arose from the same criminal act and one punishment was for a crime that was a lesser included offense of the other. There was a reasonable probability that, but for counsel's failure to raise this issue at trial, the Commonwealth would have been permitted to proceed to sentencing on only one of the two indictments. Gray v. Warden of the Sussex I State Prison, 281 Va. 303, 707 S.E.2d 275, 2011 Va. LEXIS 62 (2011), cert. denied, 2011 U.S. LEXIS 7334, 132 S. Ct. 403, 181 L. Ed. 2d 263 (U.S. 2011).

A remark made by the prosecutor during argument in the penalty phase that "if he is not a candidate for being a possible threat in the future, I don't know what would be" was not an improper expression of personal opinion by counsel, but rather was a statement, based on the evidence, that the defendant would constitute a future danger to society in view of his prior history. Payne v. Commonwealth, 233 Va. 460, 357 S.E.2d 500, cert. denied, 484 U.S. 933, 108 S. Ct. 308, 98 L. Ed. 2d 267 (1987).

Where the trial court sustained defendant's objection to the prosecutor's use of the words, "I believe," and, upon defendant's motion for a mistrial, instructed the jury that "I believe" has no place in the attorney's argument, this prompt action by the court cured any possible error that may have occurred. Payne v. Commonwealth, 233 Va. 460, 357 S.E.2d 500, cert. denied, 484 U.S. 933, 108 S. Ct. 308, 98 L. Ed. 2d 267 (1987).

B. Evidentiary Matters.

Expert opinion as to effect of drugs or alcohol. — In capital murder case, the jury was entitled to have the benefit of expert opinion as to the cumulative effect of LSD, tranxene, and alcohol, in answer to a hypothetical question based upon evidence in the record. Fitzgerald v. Commonwealth, 223 Va. 615, 292 S.E.2d 798 (1982), cert. denied, 459 U.S. 1228, 103 S. Ct. 1235, 75 L. Ed. 2d 469, rehearing denied, 460 U.S. 1105, 103 S. Ct. 1809, 76 L. Ed. 2d 371 (1983).

Conflicting DNA test results involving defendant only indicated a disagreement among scientific experts and were not sufficient to establish a miscarriage of justice to allow for federal habeas corpus review of defendant's procedurally defaulted federal constitutional claims in absence of showing of cause and prejudice for default, where defendant was convicted in state court of various crimes, including capital murder, and sentenced to death. Satcher v. Netherland, 944 F. Supp. 1222 (E.D. Va. 1996), aff'd in part and rev'd in part on other grounds sub nom. Satcher v. Pruett, 126 F.3d 561 (4th Cir.), cert. denied, 522 U.S. 1010, 118 S. Ct. 595, 139 L. Ed. 2d 431 (1997).

Mere intoxication from drugs or alcohol is not sufficient to negate premeditation. Fitzgerald v. Commonwealth, 223 Va. 615, 292 S.E.2d 798 (1982), cert. denied, 459 U.S. 1228, 103 S. Ct. 1235, 75 L. Ed. 2d 469, rehearing denied, 460 U.S. 1105, 103 S. Ct. 1809, 76 L. Ed. 2d 371 (1983).

But one so greatly intoxicated as to be unable to deliberate and premeditate cannot be convicted of a class of murder that requires proof of a willful, deliberate, and premeditated killing. Fitzgerald v. Commonwealth, 223 Va. 615, 292 S.E.2d 798 (1982), cert. denied, 459 U.S. 1228, 103 S. Ct. 1235, 75 L. Ed. 2d 469, rehearing denied, 460 U.S. 1105, 103 S. Ct. 1809, 76 L. Ed. 2d 371 (1983).

The defendant may negate the specific intent requisite for capital or first-degree murder by showing that he was so greatly intoxicated as to be incapable of deliberation or premeditation, but voluntary intoxication is no defense to the lesser degrees of homicide, or to any other crime. Particularly, his state of intoxication, however great, will not repel an inference of malice, implied by the circumstances surrounding his conduct. Essex v. Commonwealth, 228 Va. 273, 322 S.E.2d 216 (1984).

Evidence of premeditation held sufficient. — First degree murder conviction was affirmed as the evidence was sufficient to prove defendant's attack on his six-week-old baby was premeditated, based on the *Epperly* factors: (1) the brutality of the attack, (2) the disparity in size between defendant and the victim, (3) his efforts to conceal his guilt, (4) his lack of remorse, and (5) the period of time between the two blows he struck. Knight v. Commonwealth, 41 Va. App. 617, 587 S.E.2d 736, 2003 Va. App. LEXIS 550 (2003).

Evidence held sufficient to support judge's finding that killing was willful, deliberate, and premeditated. — Evidence held to support the conclusion that killing and theft were interdependent objects of a common criminal design, and conviction of capital murder in the commission of robbery would be affirmed. Edmonds v. Commonwealth, 229 Va. 303, 329 S.E.2d 807, cert. denied, 474 U.S. 975, 106 S. Ct. 339, 88 L. Ed. 2d 324 (1985).

The fact that defendant had money in hand before he shot victim did not mean that he could escape a charge and conviction of capital murder; robbery is a continuing offense. Poyner v. Commonwealth, 229 Va. 401, 329 S.E.2d 815, cert. denied, 474 U.S. 865, 106 S. Ct. 189, 88 L. Ed. 2d 158 (1985), 474 U.S. 888, 106 S. Ct. 208, 88 L. Ed. 2d 178 (1985), 506 U.S. 958, 113 S. Ct. 419, 121 L. Ed. 2d 342 (1992).

Evidence of the brutality of the attack, including the number and nature of the knife wounds inflicted, was sufficient to support the jury's finding that killing was willful, deliberate and premeditated. Boyce v. Commonwealth, No. 1820-91-1 (Ct. of Appeals Feb. 2, 1993).

Jury was entitled to ignore the self-serving statement made by defendant to a defense witness, after the fact, that the person hired to rob the victim had messed things up and killed the victim instead; therefore, defendant was properly convicted of capital murder instead of felony murder. Wolfe v. Commonwealth, 265 Va. 193, 576 S.E.2d 471, 2003 Va. LEXIS 32, cert. denied, 540 U.S. 1019, 124 S. Ct. 566, 157 L. Ed. 2d 434 (2003).

Evidence that defendant shot a store owner without warning and, after his accomplice exited the store with stolen cash, fired two more shots at the victim and did not leave the store until his gun was empty clearly established premeditation; thus, the circuit court did not err in refusing to strike the Commonwealth's evidence regarding capital murder. Green v. Commonwealth, 266 Va. 81, 580 S.E.2d 834, 2003 Va. LEXIS 55 (2003), cert. denied, 540 U.S. 1194, 124 S. Ct. 1448, 158 L. Ed. 2d 107 (2004).

When proof of premeditation is the subject of a sufficiency challenge, evidence showing that the premeditation was only slight or momentary is sufficient to sustain the conviction because premeditation is an intent to kill that needs to exist only for a moment, and the question of premeditation is generally a factual issue; thus, the court declined to reverse a jury's finding of premeditation where, despite defendant's self-serving testimony that he did not smother the victim with a pillow and told another to stop doing so, the jury could have concluded, based on defendant's confession, that he placed a pillow over the victim's face and held it there for four to six minutes even though she would have become unconscious within 15 to 30 seconds because that evidence was sufficient to show that defendant had a willful, premeditated, and deliberate intent to kill the victim. Jackson v. Commonwealth, 267 Va. 178,

590 S.E.2d 520, 2004 Va. LEXIS 8 (2004), cert. denied, 543 U.S. 891, 125 S. Ct. 168, 160 L. Ed. 2d 155 (2004).

Admissibility of photographs. — In prosecution for capital murder following rape, photographs depicting contusions about the victim's back, and multiple stab wounds in her body were relevant and material and were no more inflammatory than the medical testimony detailing the results of the autopsy. Such photographs would be properly admitted. Smith v. Commonwealth, 219 Va. 455, 248 S.E.2d 135 (1978), cert. denied, 441 U.S. 967, 99 S. Ct. 2419, 60 L. Ed. 2d 1074 (1979), aff'd, 477 U.S. 527, 106 S. Ct. 2661, 91 L. Ed. 2d 434 (1986).

The admission in evidence of photographs of a murder victim's body is within the discretion of the trial court. Peterson v. Commonwealth, 225 Va. 289, 302 S.E.2d 520, cert. denied, 464 U.S. 865, 104 S. Ct. 202, 78 L. Ed. 2d 176 (1983).

It is not an abuse of discretion for the court to admit a photograph showing the location of the entry wound, since this might tend to support an inference that the killer did not shoot wildly in panic but drew his weapon and took aim before firing. Peterson v. Commonwealth, 225 Va. 289, 302 S.E.2d 520, cert. denied, 464 U.S. 865, 104 S. Ct. 202, 78 L. Ed. 2d 176 (1983).

If photographs are relevant and material to establish premeditation and malice and to show the degree of atrociousness of the crime, their admission does not constitute an abuse of discretion. Stockton v. Commonwealth, 227 Va. 124, 314 S.E.2d 371, cert. denied, 469 U.S. 873, 105 S. Ct. 229, 83 L. Ed. 2d 158 (1984).

In prosecution for capital murder of a fellow inmate, the trial court did not err by the admitting of three color photographs of the victim taken after death showing front and rear views of the victim's unclothed body and depicting the severe burns he received, where the photos tended to show motive, intent, method, premeditation, malice, and the degree of atrociousness of the crime. Payne v. Commonwealth, 233 Va. 460, 357 S.E.2d 500, cert. denied, 484 U.S. 933, 108 S. Ct. 308, 98 L. Ed. 2d 267 (1987).

Evidence of homosexual defilement. — Introduction during the guilt phase of evidence regarding the homosexual defilement of the victim did not create an impermissible risk that defendant's conviction and sentence were the product of passion, prejudice, and arbitrary factors. George v. Angelone, 100 F.3d 353 (4th Cir. 1996), cert. denied, 519 U.S. 1103, 117 S. Ct. 854, 136 L. Ed. 2d 829 (1997).

Where no insanity defense is interposed, the defendant's mental condition is only relevant insofar as it might be probative of a fact in issue; i.e., premeditation at the time of the killing. LeVasseur v. Commonwealth, 225 Va. 564, 304 S.E.2d 644 (1983), cert. denied, 464 U.S. 1063, 104 S. Ct. 744, 79 L. Ed. 2d 202 (1984).

Resistance of victims not a defense. — As a matter of law, one who, armed with a deadly weapon, approaches others intending to rob them will not be heard to assert that he was provoked by the resistance of his victims to his criminal enterprise. Barnes v. Commonwealth, 234 Va. 130, 360 S.E.2d 196 (1987), cert. denied, 484 U.S. 1036, 108 S. Ct. 763, 98 L. Ed. 2d 779 (1988).

Testimony by expert witness about pain suffered by victim. — The severity of the burning which caused the death of the victim was relevant to the questions of malice and premeditation, and testimony by the medical examiner about pain suffered by the victim as the result of the burns was properly admitted. Payne v. Commonwealth, 233 Va. 460, 357 S.E.2d 500, cert. denied, 484 U.S. 933, 108 S. Ct. 308, 98 L. Ed. 2d 267 (1987).

Testimony of fellow inmate. — In prosecution for capital murder by a fellow inmate, the trial court did not err by admitting testimony from a fellow inmate that the defendant wished to be a member of a motorcycle group, which apparently had an active local chapter within the correctional facility, where one motive for the murder was the defendant's desire to be feared as a killer in order to join the local chapter of the group. Payne v. Commonwealth, 233 Va. 460, 357 S.E.2d 500, cert. denied, 484 U.S. 933, 108 S. Ct. 308, 98 L. Ed. 2d 267 (1987).

Murder victim's affidavit not admissible. — Admission at trial of a murder victim's affidavit in support of her request for a protective order against defendant, her husband, violated the Confrontation Clause of the Sixth Amendment to the U.S. Constitution, and the error was not harmless because in it she swore he had threatened and raped her; therefore, his convictions for rape under § 18.2-61, abduction with the intent to defile under § 18.2-48, use of a firearm during the commission of an abduction, and capital murder, which was predicated on the former three offenses,

were unconstitutional as well as based on insufficient evidence. Crawford v. Commonwealth, 53 Va. App. 138, 670 S.E.2d 15, 2008 Va. App. LEXIS 554 (2008).

In a capital murder case, the trial court's admission of the victim's affidavit, which had been attached to her request for a protective order and stated that defendant, her husband, had previously threatened and raped her, in order to prove that defendant later raped and murdered his estranged wife, violated the Confrontation Clause; however, the affidavit's admission was harmless as to defendant's conviction for grand larceny because it did not affect the jury's determination of guilt as to defendant's theft of the victim's car. Crawford v. Commonwealth, 53 Va. App. 138, 670 S.E.2d 15, 2008 Va. App. LEXIS 554 (2008).

Evidence of second murder held admissible to show effort to conceal first murder. — As a general rule, evidence that the accused committed other crimes similar to the offense charged is inadmissible to prove the particular crime charged. But where the only reasonable inference which can be drawn from the testimony was that the victim of a second murder knew the defendant killed the victim of the first murder, and the defendant, believing the victim of a second murder was telling others about the murder, killed him to silence him. Clearly, the two offenses were interrelated, and the testimony showed both the defendant's guilty knowledge of the first murder and his desire to conceal his guilt. The conduct of an accused following the crime is often relevant, particularly when its purpose is to conceal his guilt. The testimony was so relevant and probative to the truth-finding process that its probative value greatly outweighed any prejudicial effect. Stockton v. Commonwealth, 227 Va. 124, 314 S.E.2d 371, cert. denied, 469 U.S. 873, 105 S. Ct. 229, 83 L. Ed. 2d 158 (1984).

Commonwealth did not have the burden of excluding the hypothesis that defendant might have given the gun to the other man, who then shot the victims. Nothing in the evidence suggested that defendant may have given the gun to the other man in the interval between the time one victim closed his eyes and he and the other victim were shot. Instead, defendant's ownership of the gun, his retention of the gun even when sleeping, victim's testimony, and defendant's direction to friend to "get rid of the bag" containing the gun, taken together, amply justified the conclusion that defendant was the person who shot the victims. Graham v. Commonwealth, 250 Va. 79, 459 S.E.2d 97, cert. denied, 516 U.S. 997, 116 S. Ct. 535, 133 L. Ed. 2d 440 (1995).

Robbery predicate for capital murder was established. — Where defendant and cohort were in the process of stealing money when they were interrupted by victim, where defendant left the room where he had found the money, chased victim, shot him, returned to the room, and retrieved the money, and where defendant and cohort then left the premises, the robbery and killing of the victim were interdependent objects of a common criminal design, and therefore, the robbery predicate for capital murder was established. Quesinberry v. Commonwealth, 241 Va. 364, 402 S.E.2d 218, cert. denied, 502 U.S. 834, 112 S. Ct. 113, 116 L. Ed. 2d 82 (1991), and overruled in part on other grounds by Jay v. Commonwealth, 275 Va. 510, 659 S.E.2d 311, 2008 Va. LEXIS 53 (2008).

This section does not require proof that a defendant charged with capital murder during the commission of a robbery or a rape was a principal in the first degree to the crimes of robbery or rape; it is only necessary that the Commonwealth prove that the defendant was the triggerman in the murder and an accomplice in the robbery or rape to convict him of capital murder. Graham v. Commonwealth, 250 Va. 487, 464 S.E.2d 128 (1995).

Where defendant took victim's motorcycle and helmet, hid them apart from his body, and marked their location on a map, the evidence was sufficient to permit a reasonable trier of fact to conclude beyond a reasonable doubt that defendant robbed victim of his motorcycle and helmet or that the robbery was a motivating factor for the murder. George v. Angelone, 100 F.3d 353 (4th Cir. 1996), cert. denied, 519 U.S. 1103, 117 S. Ct. 854, 136 L. Ed. 2d 829 (1997).

The evidence was sufficient to establish that the killing of the victim immediately after she was robbed was so closely related in time, place and causal connection as to the make the killing, as a matter of law, a part of the same criminal enterprise where defendant, acting in concert with others, beat the victim in one location and then transported her in the trunk of a car to another location where they robbed her and, immediately thereafter, further beat and cut her, inflicting fatal injuries. Tibbs v. Commonwealth, 31 Va. App. 687, 525 S.E.2d 579 (2000).

Evidence of intent sufficient. — Where the evidence was undisputed that the defendant deliberately shot the victim twice in the chest with a high-powered assault rifle and the defendant stated in his confession that he planned and carried out the attack with premeditation and without provocation and that he deliberately aimed his weapon at the victim's chest, it was established as a matter of law that the murder was intentional. Kasi v. Commonwealth, 256 Va. 407, 508 S.E.2d 57 (1998), cert. denied, 527 U.S. 1038, 119 S. Ct. 2399, 144 L. Ed. 2d 798 (1999) overruled in part on other grounds by Jay v. Commonwealth, 275 Va. 510, 659 S.E.2d 311, 2008 Va. LEXIS 53 (2008).

Evidence held sufficient for conviction. — Where the main witness for the prosecution explained the details of the plan, in which he participated, to kill the victim, he related the specifics of the defendant's motive for the murder, he was an eyewitness to the defendant's acts of throwing the liquid into the victim's cell and igniting the fluid with matches, prison employees corroborated the witness' account of the incident, and the jurors were instructed fully on the manner in which they were to judge the testimony and credibility of convicted felons, there was no inherently incredible testimony by the Commonwealth's witnesses, and there was abundant evidence to support the conviction. Payne v. Commonwealth, 233 Va. 460, 357 S.E.2d 500, cert. denied, 484 U.S. 933, 108 S. Ct. 308, 98 L. Ed. 2d 267 (1987).

Defendant's sentence to death for having committed several crimes, including the murder of two people, one of which was a willful, deliberate, and premeditated killing of more than one person as part of the same act in violation of subdivision 7 of § 18.2-31, was not found to have been imposed under the influence of passion, prejudice, or any other arbitrary factor pursuant to subdivision C 1 of § 17.1-313, nor was it excessive or disproportionate to the penalty imposed in similar cases, considering both the crime and the defendant, pursuant to subdivision C 2 of § 17.1-313; although defendant had a long career as a soldier and a non-commissioned officer in the U.S. Army, there was also evidence that he had an illicit relationship although he was married for 23 years, that he squandered hundreds of thousands of dollars on the relationship, which was with a prostitute, and that he brutally murdered two innocent people with no remorse. Elliott v. Commonwealth, 267 Va. 396, 593 S.E.2d 270, 2004 Va. LEXIS 44 (2004), cert. denied, 543 U.S. 1081, 125 S. Ct. 875, 160 L. Ed. 2d 825 (2005) and overruled in part on other grounds by Jay v. Commonwealth, 275 Va. 510, 659 S.E.2d 311, 2008 Va. LEXIS 53 (2008).

Testimony that defendant was involved in a stormy relationship with one of the four victims, one witness gave defendant a ride to the victim's apartment, defendant began arguing with the victim and remained behind when the witness left, defendant called a friend from the victim's apartment and told him that he had killed them, a neighbor went to the victim's apartment and saw defendant was in the apartment with a gun and the bodies of the victim, the victim's two children, and the victim's brother were in the apartment, and an inmate testified that defendant had confessed to him during defendant's detention that he had killed the victims; evidence that the victim was both stabbed and shot, and that defendant's DNA and fingerprint matched that found on a knife in the victim's apartment was sufficient to support defendant's conviction for capital murder. Juniper v. Commonwealth, 271 Va. 362, 626 S.E.2d 383, 2006 Va. LEXIS 29 (2006).

Trial court did not err in denying defendant's motion to strike evidence on the count for capital murder in the commission of abduction with the intent to defile, as the beating the victim 47 times with a blunt object was not a manner of effectuating a capital murder in the commission of a rape or attempted rape and thus, the evidence was sufficient to establish capital murder in the commission of abduction with the intent to defile separately and apart from, and not merely incidental to, capital murder in the commission of a rape or attempted rape. Lawlor v. Commonwealth, 285 Va. 187, 738 S.E.2d 847, 2013 Va. LEXIS 13 (2013).

No reversal where record failed to show actual prejudice. — Defendant's four capital murder convictions, and conviction for use of a firearm in the commission of murder, were not reversed, despite his contention that he was deprived of a fair trial when the trial court allowed spectators in the courtroom to wear badges displaying photographs of the victims, where the court took active steps to ensure that the jurors were not negatively influenced by the spectators, including segregating the jurors from persons in the hallways and elevators, and by excluding the victim's family members, many of whom were wearing the badges, from the front row of the gallery, and there were always some people seated in the front row between the spectators wearing the badges and the jury. Cooper v. Commonwealth, No. 0819-03-4, 2004 Va. App. LEXIS 403 (Ct. of Appeals Aug. 24, 2004).

Retrial. — After defendant's capital murder conviction was reversed because an appellate court found insufficient evidence to support his convictions for the predicate offenses of rape, abduction with intent to defile, and use of a firearm in the commission of abduction, double jeopardy principles required the court to remand for retrial on a lesser-included offense of no greater than first-degree murder. Crawford v. Commonwealth, 53 Va. App. 138, 670 S.E.2d 15, 2008 Va. App. LEXIS 554 (2008).

Ineffective assistance of counsel not shown. — State Supreme Court dismissed the petition for writ of habeas corpus that petitioner filed as to petitioner's claim in petitioner's capital murder case that the indictments, jury instructions, and verdict forms were inadequate because they did not specify which other person petitioner had killed during a three-year period or which act of terrorism petitioner had committed; petitioner's claim in that regard did not satisfy either the performance or prejudice prong of the two-part *Strickland* test since under subdivision 8 of § 18.2-31, there was no requirement that the relevant documents specify which other killing was being included within the three-year period and the indictment, under § 18.2-46.4, did not have to specify the petitioner's intent under that statute's two subsections. Muhammad v. Warden of the Sussex I State Prison, 274 Va. 3, 646 S.E.2d 182, 2007 Va. LEXIS 97 (2007), cert. denied, 128 S. Ct. 1889, 2008 U.S. LEXIS 3275 (U.S. 2008).

Admissibility of other crimes evidence. — Circuit court did not abuse its discretion by admitting evidence of defendant's prior felony conviction during the Commonwealth's case-in-chief for the limited purpose of proving defendant's motivation for shooting a police officer and to prove an essential element of the offense charged under subdivision 6 of § 18.2-31; i.e., the murder was to interfere with the performance of the police officer's duties. Porter v. Commonwealth, 276 Va. 203, 661 S.E.2d 415, 2008 Va. LEXIS 78 (2008), cert. denied, 129 S. Ct. 1999, 173 L. Ed. 2d 1097, 2009 U.S. LEXIS 3047 (U.S. 2009).

§ 18.2-32. First and second degree murder defined; punishment.

Murder, other than capital murder, by poison, lying in wait, imprisonment, starving, or by any willful, deliberate, and premeditated killing, or in the commission of, or attempt to commit, arson, rape, forcible sodomy, inanimate or animate object sexual penetration, robbery, burglary or abduction, except as provided in § 18.2-31, is murder of the first degree, punishable as a Class 2 felony.

All murder other than capital murder and murder in the first degree is murder of the second degree and is punishable by confinement in a state correctional facility for not less than five nor more than forty years.

History.
Code 1950, § 18.1-21; 1960, c. 358; 1962, c. 42; 1975, cc. 14, 15; 1976, c. 503; 1977, cc. 478, 492; 1981, c. 397; 1993, cc. 463, 490; 1998, c. 281.

Cross references.
As to death caused by injury, etc., to railroad equipment, see § 18.2-155. As to the trial of capital cases, see § 19.2-264.2 et seq. As to fixing degree of murder in verdict, see § 19.2-288.

Law Review.
For article on the corpus delicti of murder, see 48 Va. L. Rev. 173 (1962). For discussion of proof of malice under this section, see 7

Wm. & Mary L. Rev. 399 (1966). For note, "Capital Punishment in Virginia," see 58 Va. L. Rev. 97 (1972). For article on the law of homicide, see 59 Va. L. Rev. 1270 (1973). For survey of Virginia criminal law for the year 1973-1974, see 60 Va. L. Rev. 1499 (1974); for the year 1974-1975, see 61 Va. L. Rev. 1697 (1975). For comments, "Has the Burger Court Dealt a Death Blow to the Presumption of Malice in Virginia?" see 10 U. Rich. L. Rev. 687 (1976). For survey of Virginia law on evidence for the year 1975-1976, see 62 Va. L. Rev. 1442 (1976). For survey of Virginia criminal law for the year 1976-1977, see 63 Va. L. Rev. 1396 (1977). For survey of Virginia criminal procedure for the year 1976-1977, see 63 Va. L. Rev. 1408 (1977). For the year 1977-1978, see 64 Va. L. Rev. 1407 (1978). For note, "Criminal Procedure and Criminal Law: Virginia Supreme Court decisions During the 70's," see 15 U. Rich. L. Rev. 585 (1981). For article discussing the legislative history of sexual assault law reform in Virginia, see 68 Va. L. Rev. 459 (1982). For note on premeditation, see 40 Wash. & Lee L. Rev. 341 (1983). For note comparing states' recognition of reduced degrees of felony murder, see 40 Wash. & Lee L. Rev. 1601 (1983). For comment on admissibility of expert testimony on the battered woman syndrome in Virginia, see 10 G.M.U. L. Rev. 171 (1988). For an article relating to all published Virginia criminal law decisions between July 1, 1997, and July 1, 1998, see 32 U. Rich. L. Rev. 1091 (1998). For note, "Predicate Offenses for First Degree Felony Murder in Virginia," see 57 Wash. & Lee L. Rev. 561 (2000). For article, "Interrogation Stories," see 95 Va. L. Rev. 1599 (2009). For article, "Medical Malpractice Law," see 45 U. Rich. L. Rev. 319 (2010). For article, "Modal Retributivism: A Theory of Sanctions for Attempts and Other Criminal Wrongs," see 45 U. Rich. L. Rev. 647 (2011).

Michie's Jurisprudence.

For related discussion, see 5B M.J. Criminal Procedure, § 70; 9B M.J. Homicide, §§ 17, 20, 133, 134; 14B M.J. Poisons and Poisoning, § 1; 21A M.J. Words and Phrases.

CASE NOTES

I. What Constitutes Murder.
  A. Definitions and Illustrations.
  B. Elements.
    1. Malice.
    2. Other Elements.
II. Degree of Murder.
  A. First and Second Degree Distinguished.
  B. Murder in the First Degree.
  C. Murder in the Second Degree.
III. Trial.
  A. Indictment.
  B. Defenses.
    1. Self-Defense.
    2. Drunkenness and Insanity.
    3. Other Defenses.
  C. Evidence.
    1. Presumptions and Burden of Proof.
      a. Degree of Offense.
      b. Other Matters.
    2. Admissibility.
    3. Weight and Sufficiency.
  D. Instructions.
  E. Verdict.

I. WHAT CONSTITUTES MURDER.

A. Definitions and Illustrations.

This section distinguishes the degrees of murder, but it does not define murder itself. Biddle v. Commonwealth, 206 Va. 14, 141 S.E.2d 710 (1965).

Distinction between crimes in § 18.2-31(d) (now § 18.2-31 4) and this section is plain: To be found guilty of capital murder, a defendant must be proved, beyond a reasonable doubt, not only to have killed during the commission of a robbery, but to have killed willfully, deliberately, and with premeditation and while armed with a deadly weapon. The defendant found guilty of first degree murder is the defendant who killed during the course of a robbery,

but did not kill with willfulness, deliberation, and premeditation. Briley v. Bass, 584 F. Supp. 807 (E.D. Va.), aff'd, 742 F.2d 155 (4th Cir.), cert. denied, 469 U.S. 893, 105 S. Ct. 270, 83 L. Ed. 2d 206 (1984).

Murder is the unlawful killing of another with malice. Robertson v. Commonwealth, 1 Va. Dec. 851, 20 S.E. 362 (1894).

Whoever kills a human being with malice aforethought is guilty of murder. Stapleton v. Commonwealth, 123 Va. 825, 96 S.E. 801 (1918).

Murder is where a man of sound sense unlawfully kills another with malice aforethought, either express or implied. Harrison v. Commonwealth, 79 Va. 374 (1884).

Murder is defined as the unlawful killing of another with malice aforethought. Jackson v. Virginia, 443 U.S. 307, 99 S. Ct. 2781, 61 L. Ed. 2d 560 (1979).

And it is murder even though deceased might have recovered but for improper treatment. — If the prisoner willfully inflicted upon the deceased a dangerous wound, one that was calculated to endanger and destroy life, and death ensued therefrom within a year and a day, the prisoner is nonetheless responsible for the result although it may appear that the deceased might have recovered but for the aggravation of the wound by unskillful or improper treatment. Clark v. Commonwealth, 90 Va. 360, 18 S.E. 441 (1893).

But it is not murder when wound quickens progress of fatal disease. — Where in a cause of homicide it appeared that a wound or beating was inflicted on the deceased which was not mortal and the deceased, while laboring under the effect of the violence, became sick of a disease not caused by such violence, from which disease death ensued within a year and a day, the party charged with the homicide was not criminally responsible for the death, although it also appeared that the symptoms of the disease were aggravated, and the fatal progress quickened, by the enfeebled or irritated condition of the deceased, caused by the violence. Livingston v. Commonwealth, 55 Va. (14 Gratt.) 592 (1857).

Doctrine of transferred intent. — Under the doctrine of transferred intent, if an accused shoots at another intending to kill him, and a third person is killed because of the act, that same intent follows the bullet and is transferred to the killing of the third person, even if such death was accidental or unintentional. Riddick v. Commonwealth, 226 Va. 244, 308 S.E.2d 117 (1983).

When "intent" required. — To commit murder one need not intend to take a life; but to be guilty of an attempt to murder he must so intend. It is not sufficient that his act, had it been fatal, would have been murder. Goodson v. Commonwealth, 22 Va. App. 61, 467 S.E.2d 848 (1996).

To sustain a conviction for attempted murder, the evidence must establish a specific intent to kill the victim, as well as an overt but ineffectual act committed in furtherance of this criminal purpose. Parrott v. Commonwealth, No. 1014-99-2, 2001 Va. App. LEXIS 253 (Ct. of Appeals May 15, 2001).

Felony-murder defined. — Murder, for purposes of felony-murder under this section, is common-law murder coupled with the contemporaneous commission or attempted commission of one of the listed felonies. Wooden v. Commonwealth, 222 Va. 758, 284 S.E.2d 811 (1981).

Although felony-murder is a statutory offense, it includes the elements of common-law murder. Wooden v. Commonwealth, 222 Va. 758, 284 S.E.2d 811 (1981).

Purpose of felony-murder doctrine of this section was to deter inherently dangerous felonies by holding the felons responsible for the consequences of the felony, whether intended or not. While the range of felonies which may be a predicate for the felony-murder conviction has changed, the function of the doctrine is still to elevate to murder a homicide resulting from a felony by imputing malice. King v. Commonwealth, 6 Va. App. 351, 368 S.E.2d 704 (1988).

Section 18.2-33 and its companion, this section, codify common-law doctrine of felony-murder, a doctrine developed to elevate to murder a homicide committed during the course of a felony by imputing malice to the killing. King v. Commonwealth, 6 Va. App. 351, 368 S.E.2d 704 (1988).

Defendant is responsible even if victim killed by one acting in concert with him. — If defendant was the slayer, his intent to kill the intended victim was transferred to the slaying of the actual victim and his conviction is valid. If, however, the one acting in concert with defendant fired the fatal shot, defendant's conviction is still valid, as the two were acting in concert. The one acting in concert with defendant intended to kill the intended victim, and that intent was transferred to the slaying of the actual victim. Due to concert of action, defendant is deemed to have shared his intent. Thus, even if the one acting in concert with defendant killed the victim, defendant was responsible for his acts as a principal in the second degree. Riddick v. Commonwealth, 226 Va. 244, 308 S.E.2d 117 (1983).

Ample evidence existed from which the jury reasonably could have concluded that defendant, at a minimum, was guilty of murder as a principal in the second degree because although the evidence did not show with certainty which of the gunmen fired the fatal bullet, the evidence showed that several persons, including defendant, fired guns toward a crowd of people; because the victim died as a result of the gunfire, defendant aided and abetted the other shooters by joining in the gunfire, and, by so doing, acted at least as a principal in the second degree to the murder of the victim. Cooper v. Commonwealth, 2010 Va. App. LEXIS 403 (Oct. 19, 2010).

Exposure or neglect of infant resulting in death. — If the exposure or neglect of an infant or other dependent person, resulting in death, is an act of mere carelessness wherein the danger to life does not clearly appear, the homicide is only manslaughter; whereas if the exposure or neglect is of a dangerous kind, it is murder. Biddle v. Commonwealth, 206 Va. 14, 141 S.E.2d 710 (1965).

If from an infant of tender years the person under obligation to provide for it willfully withholds needful food or any other needful thing, though not with intent to kill, and by reason thereof the child dies, he commits murder. Biddle v. Commonwealth, 206 Va. 14, 141 S.E.2d 710 (1965).

If death is the direct consequence of the malicious omission of the performance of a duty, such as of a mother to feed her child, this is a case of murder; but if the omission is not willful, and arose out of neglect only, it is manslaughter. Biddle v. Commonwealth, 206 Va. 14, 141 S.E.2d 710 (1965).

Convictions for murder and lynching by mob upheld. — Defendant was not entitled to reversal of convictions for both felony murder and lynching by mob, because both the felony murder statute, § 18.2-32, and the lynching-by-mob statute, § 18.2-40, included at least one element the other did not, and the appellate court presumed that the General Assembly did not intend either statute to displace the other. Gaddie v. Commonwealth, 2010 Va. App. LEXIS 247 (June 22, 2010).

Former § 19.1-249 (now § 19.2-285) and this section are in pari materia and should be read together. Puckett v. Commonwealth, 182 Va. 237, 28 S.E.2d 619 (1944).

Applied in Pender v. Angelone, 257 Va. 501, 514 S.E.2d 756 (1999); Orndorff v. Commonwealth, 271 Va. 486, 628 S.E.2d 344, 2006 Va. LEXIS 43 (2006); Osman v. Osman, 285 Va. 384, 737 S.E.2d 876, 2013 Va. LEXIS 26 (Feb. 28, 2013).

B. Elements.

1. Malice.

The test of murder is malice. Every malicious killing is murder either in the first or second degree — the former if deliberate and premeditated, and the latter if not. Furthermore, there is a prima facie presumption of malice arising from the mere fact of a homicide, but there is no presumption therefrom of deliberation and premeditation. That is merely another way of stating the familiar rule of law that every homicide is prima facie murder in the second degree, and that the burden is on the accused to reduce, and on the Commonwealth to elevate, the grade of the offense. Painter v. Commonwealth, 210 Va. 360, 171 S.E.2d 166 (1969); Perkins v. Commonwealth, 215 Va. 69, 205 S.E.2d 385 (1974); Wooden v. Commonwealth, 222 Va. 758, 284 S.E.2d 811 (1981).

Malice aforethought is the grand criterion which distinguishes murder from other killings. M'Whirt's Case, 44 Va. (3 Gratt.) 594 (1846); Wooden v. Commonwealth, 222 Va. 758, 284 S.E.2d 811 (1981).

Every unlawful homicide must be either murder or manslaughter, and whether it be the one or the other depends alone upon whether the party who perpetrated the act did it with malice or not — malice either expressed or implied. Read v. Commonwealth, 63 Va. (22 Gratt.) 924 (1872); Moxley v. Commonwealth, 195 Va. 151, 77 S.E.2d 389 (1953).

Malice is element of murder but not manslaughter. — Malice, a requisite element for murder of any kind, is unnecessary in manslaughter cases and is the touchstone by which murder and manslaughter cases are distinguished. Essex v. Commonwealth, 228 Va. 273, 322 S.E.2d 216 (1984).

Malice, an essential element of all grades of murder, distinguishes murder from manslaughter. Parrott v. Commonwealth, No. 1014-99-2, 2001 Va. App. LEXIS 253 (Ct. of Appeals May 15, 2001).

Without malice there cannot be murder. Coleman v. Commonwealth, 184 Va. 197, 35 S.E.2d 96 (1945).

Malice, express or implied, is an essential element in murder of either the first or second degree. Richardson v. Commonwealth, 128 Va. 691, 104 S.E. 788 (1920); Mercer v. Commonwealth, 150 Va. 588, 142 S.E. 369 (1928).

Malicious intent is an element of both first-degree murder and second-degree murder. What elevates the lesser crime to the greater grade and invokes the heavier penalty is the element of premeditation. Baker v. Commonwealth, 218 Va. 193, 237 S.E.2d 88 (1977).

Malice is an element of felony-murder. Wooden v. Commonwealth, 222 Va. 758, 284 S.E.2d 811 (1981).

Malice inheres in the doing of a wrongful act intentionally or without just cause or excuse, or as a result of ill will. Thus, where a person maliciously engages in criminal activity, such as robbery, and homicide of the victim results, the malice inherent in the robbery provides the malice prerequisite to a finding that the homicide was murder. All of the criminal participants in the initial felony may be found guilty of the felony-murder of the victim so long as the homicide was within the res gestae of the initial felony. Wooden v. Commonwealth, 222 Va. 758, 284 S.E.2d 811 (1981).

Malice, in a legal sense, means any wrongful act done willfully or purposely. Sun Life Assurance Co. v. Bailey, 101 Va. 443, 44 S.E. 692 (1903).

Malice is a subjective condition of mind, discoverable only by words and conduct, and the significance of the words and conduct of an accused person, wherever there can be doubt about such significance, addresses itself peculiarly to the consideration of the jury. Painter v. Commonwealth, 210 Va. 360, 171 S.E.2d 166 (1969); Perkins v. Commonwealth, 215 Va. 69, 205 S.E.2d 385 (1974).

And is presumed from the act of killing. — Malice is presumed from the act of killing, unaccompanied with circumstances of extenuation, and the burden of disproving the malice is thrown upon the accused. Hill v. Commonwealth, 43 Va. (2 Gratt.) 594 (1845); Johnston's Case, 46 Va. (5 Gratt.) 660 (1848); Dejarnette v. Commonwealth, 75 Va. 867 (1881); Lewis v. Commonwealth, 78 Va. 732 (1884); Honesty v. Commonwealth, 81 Va. 283 (1886); Coleman v. Commonwealth, 184 Va. 197, 35 S.E.2d 96 (1945); Essex v. Commonwealth, 228 Va. 273, 322 S.E.2d 216 (1984).

On a charge of murder, malice is presumed from the fact of killing, and when the Commonwealth has proven the commission of a homicide and has pointed out the accused as the criminal agent, then it may rest its case, and, unless the accused shows circumstances of justification, excuse, or palliation, a verdict of murder in the second degree will be warranted. Adams v. Commonwealth, 163 Va. 1053, 178 S.E. 29 (1935).

Or from the deliberate use of a deadly weapon. Commonwealth v. Jones, 28 Va. (1 Leigh) 598 (1829); Hill v. Commonwealth, 43 Va. (2 Gratt.) 594 (1845); Johnston's Case, 46 Va. (5 Gratt.) 660 (1848); Murphy v. Commonwealth, 64 Va. (23 Gratt.) 960 (1873); Wright v. Commonwealth, 74 Va. (33 Gratt.) 880 (1880); Wright v. Commonwealth, 75 Va. 914 (1882); Stapleton v. Commonwealth, 123 Va. 825, 96 S.E. 801 (1918); Henry v. Commonwealth, 195 Va. 281, 77 S.E.2d 863 (1953).

The use of a deadly weapon, standing alone, is not sufficient to prove the specific intent required to establish attempted murder. Goodson v. Commonwealth, 22 Va. App. 61, 467 S.E.2d 848 (1996).

Malice may be evident in post-shooting conduct. — The finder of fact may consider the defendant's conduct and words at the time of the shooting and thereafter, including evidence of flight, to determine whether the shooting was accompanied by malice. Betancourt v. Commonwealth, No. 0142-93-2 (Ct. of Appeals Sept. 13, 1994).

Malice may be either express or implied by conduct. Essex v. Commonwealth, 228 Va. 273, 322 S.E.2d 216 (1984).

Express malice is evidenced when one person kills another with a sedate, deliberate mind and formed design. Essex v. Commonwealth, 228 Va. 273, 322 S.E.2d 216 (1984).

Implied malice exists when any purposeful, cruel act is committed by one individual against another without any, or without great provocation. Essex v. Commonwealth, 228 Va. 273, 322 S.E.2d 216 (1984).

Malice cannot be implied from negligent killing. — If a killing results from negligence, however gross or culpable, and the killing is contrary to the defendant's intention, malice cannot be implied. In order to elevate the crime to second-degree murder, the defendant must be shown to have willfully or purposefully, rather than negligently, embarked upon a course of wrongful conduct likely to cause death or great bodily harm. Essex v. Commonwealth, 228 Va. 273, 322 S.E.2d 216 (1984).

Generally, implied malice is equivalent to "constructive malice"; that is, malice as such does not exist but the law regards the circumstances of the act as so harmful that the law punishes the act as though malice did in fact exist. Pugh v. Commonwealth, 223 Va. 663, 292 S.E.2d 339 (1982).

Defendant's conduct rather than degree of intoxication is relied upon to establish malice. — The defendant's degree of intoxication, however great, neither enhances nor impairs the set of facts relied upon to establish implied malice. In making the determination whether malice exists, the fact finder must be guided by the quality of the defendant's conduct, its likelihood of causing death or great bodily harm, and whether it was volitional or inadvertent; not by the defendant's blood-alcohol level. Essex v. Commonwealth, 228 Va. 273, 322 S.E.2d 216 (1984).

Malicious purpose to do deceased a serious personal injury is sufficient. — If the prisoner, in the execution of a malicious purpose to do the deceased a serious personal injury or hurt by wounding and beating him, killed him, the offense is murder. Dock v. Commonwealth, 62 Va. (21 Gratt.) 909 (1872). See Honesty v. Commonwealth, 81 Va. 283 (1886); M'Whirt's Case, 44 Va. (3 Gratt.) 594 (1846); Johnston's Case, 46 Va. (5 Gratt.) 660 (1848).

Malice and passion distinguished. — "Malice aforethought" implies a mind under the sway of reason, whereas "passion," while it does not imply a dethronement of reason, yet is the furor brevis which renders a man deaf to the voice of reason so that, although the act done was intentional of death, it was not the result of malignity of heart, but imputable to human infirmity. Passion and malice are, therefore, inconsistent motive powers and, hence, an act which proceeds from the one cannot also proceed from the other. Brown v. Commonwealth, 86 Va. 466, 10 S.E. 745 (1890).

Malice and heat of passion are mutually exclusive; malice excludes passion, and passion presupposes the absence of malice. In other words, malice and passion cannot coexist. Jenkins v. Commonwealth, 244 Va. 445, 423 S.E.2d 360 (1992), cert. denied, 507 U.S. 1036, 113 S. Ct. 1862, 123 L. Ed. 2d 483 (1993), overruled in part on other grounds by Jay v. Commonwealth, 275 Va. 510, 659 S.E.2d 311, 2008 Va. LEXIS 53 (2008).

Whether a defendant acted with malice is generally a question to be decided by the trier of fact. Pugh v. Commonwealth, 223 Va. 663, 292 S.E.2d 339 (1982); Essex v. Commonwealth, 228 Va. 273, 322 S.E.2d 216 (1984).

Implied malice in death of three year old. — Implied malice was shown beyond a reasonable doubt and was fairly deducible where victim, a three year old child, had been forcefully fed a stomach full of pepper, was starving and had been beaten; this was sufficient evidence to find the mother-defendant guilty of murder in the second degree. Pugh v. Commonwealth, 223 Va. 663, 292 S.E.2d 339 (1982).

Malice intrinsic in commission of predicate felony provides element needed to find murder. — While this section contemplates a killing with malice, the malice intrinsic in the commission of one of the predicate felonies provides the malice prerequisite to a finding that the homicide was murder. The same imputation of malice is implicit in § 18.2-33 which contemplates an accidental killing; the commission of any felonious act during the prosecution of which a death occurs supplies the malice which raises the incidental homicide to the level of second-degree murder. Heacock v. Commonwealth, 228 Va. 397, 323 S.E.2d 90 (1984).

Participant not guilty of felony-murder of co-felon killed by victim. — Under this section, a criminal participant in a felony may not be convicted of the felony-murder of a co-felon killed by the victim of the initial felony as this would require the elimination of proof of malice as a prerequisite to conviction under this section. Wooden v. Commonwealth, 222 Va. 758, 284 S.E.2d 811 (1981).

Sufficient evidence of malice. — The evidence was sufficient to support a finding of malice where appellant's wife died as a result of a gunshot wound to the chest inflicted at close range; appellant admitted that the gun went off in his hands; a neighbor testified that she heard a gunshot and then heard a woman moan and say, "I can't believe you did that to me"; and appellant then immediately fled the scene without administering aid, disposed of the weapon, and failed to report the incident when stopped by the police a short time later. Betancourt v. Commonwealth, No. 0142-93-2 (Ct. of Appeals Sept. 13, 1994).

Proof of malice was established by testimony that defendant and victim had argued, that defendant had angrily refused to allow victim to leave, and that victim suffered two deep stab wounds. Bowler v. Commonwealth, No. 0404-99-4 (Ct. of Appeals Mar. 21, 2000).

There were no mitigating circumstances that would have stripped defendant's conduct in submerging her newborn baby in the bathtub of its inherent malice, as it was not a provoked killing, nor was defendant acting in self-defense, but rather admitted that she knew her actions could result in the death of her baby, but deliberately engaged in those actions because she was worried that people would be ashamed of her. Aldridge v. Commonwealth, 44 Va. App. 618, 606 S.E.2d 539, 2004 Va. App. LEXIS 631 (2004).

2. Other Elements.

Proof of corpus delicti. — In homicide cases, the corpus delicti must consist of proof (1) of the victim's death, and (2) that it resulted from the criminal act or agency of another. Epperly v. Commonwealth, 224 Va. 214, 294 S.E.2d 882 (1982).

The corpus delicti may be proven by circumstantial evidence. Epperly v. Commonwealth, 224 Va. 214, 294 S.E.2d 882 (1982).

Premeditated murder, one of the forms of first degree murder defined by statute, contemplates: (1) a killing; (2) a reasoning process antecedent to the act of killing, resulting in the formation of a specific intent to kill; and (3) the performance of that act with malicious intent. Rhodes v. Commonwealth, 238 Va. 480, 384 S.E.2d 95 (1989).

Deliberation and premeditation. — While the absence of self defense is not an element of murder, deliberation and premeditation undoubtedly are elements of first-degree murder which the state must prove beyond a reasonable doubt. Baker v. Muncy, 619 F.2d 327 (4th Cir. 1980).

Premeditation and deliberation, which the Commonwealth must prove beyond a reasonable doubt to obtain a first-degree murder conviction, require the adoption of a specific intent to kill, which is something more than malice. Epperly v. Commonwealth, 224 Va. 214, 294 S.E.2d 882 (1982).

Premeditation and deliberation are jury questions. — The question whether premeditation and deliberation exist, so as to elevate a homicide to first-degree murder, is in the province of the jury. In deciding it, the jury may properly consider the brutality of the attack, and whether more than one blow was struck, the disparity in size and strength between the defendant and the victim, the concealment of the victim's body, and the defendant's lack of remorse and efforts to avoid detection. Epperly v. Commonwealth, 224 Va. 214, 294 S.E.2d 882 (1982).

Premeditation shown by circumstantial evidence. — Supreme Court will affirm a conviction of premeditated murder, even though based upon wholly circumstantial evidence, whenever the reasonable import of such evidence, considered as a whole, is sufficient to show beyond a reasonable doubt that the accused was the criminal agent and that he acted with a premeditated intent to kill. Rhodes v. Commonwealth, 238 Va. 480, 384 S.E.2d 95 (1989).

Defendant's actions following her baby's death provided ample circumstantial evidence of her specific intent to kill; specifically, defendant concealed the infant's body so effectively that it was not discovered until almost three months had elapsed, in her effort to avoid detection she cleaned the hotel bathroom and disposed of soiled towels and bathmats in an outside dumpster, and she informed nurses at a hospital that she had given her child up for adoption rather than telling them that she had given birth to a stillborn baby. Aldridge v. Commonwealth, 44 Va. App. 618, 606 S.E.2d 539, 2004 Va. App. LEXIS 631 (2004).

Premeditation inferred from wound. — Evidence of a mortal wound inflicted by a deadly weapon with little or no provocation creates an inference from which the trier of fact may conclude that the killer acted with premeditation. McNair v. Commonwealth, No. 0062-00-1, 2000 Va. App. LEXIS 784 (Ct. of Appeals Dec. 5, 2000).

Analysis of intent. — The intention to kill need not exist for any specified length of time prior to the actual killing; the design to kill may be formed only a moment before the fatal act is committed provided the accused had time to think and did intend to kill. In deciding the question, the jury may consider, among other things, the brutality of the attack and whether more than one shot was fired. Weeks v. Commonwealth, 248 Va. 460, 450 S.E.2d 379 (1994), cert. denied, 516 U.S. 829, 116 S. Ct. 100, 133 L. Ed. 2d 55 (1995).

To constitute murder, the killing must be predetermined, yet the design to kill need not have existed for any particular length of time and may be formed at the moment of committing the act. Commonwealth v. Brown, 90 Va. 671, 19 S.E. 447 (1894).

Unless committed by specific means enumerated in this section. — Murder committed by any of the specific means enumerated in the statute is murder in the first degree, whether there was any actual intent to kill or not. Howell v. Commonwealth, 67 Va. (26 Gratt.) 995 (1875). See Burgess v. Commonwealth, 4 Va. (2 Va. Cas.) 483 (1826); Whiteford v. Commonwealth, 27 Va. (6 Rand.) 721 (1828); Commonwealth v. Jones, 28 Va. (1 Leigh) 598 (1829).

Killing must be done on purpose and not by accident or without design. Epperly v. Commonwealth, 224 Va. 214, 294 S.E.2d 882 (1982).

Defendant's state of mind determines intent. — The exact state of the defendant's mind at the time of the killing is the crucial factor in determining intent. Epperly v. Commonwealth, 224 Va. 214, 294 S.E.2d 882 (1982).

The test of the criminal intent in the use of a deadly weapon is to be found, not in the manner in which or the purpose for which the previous possession of the weapon was acquired, but in its deliberate use for a deadly purpose. Adams v. Commonwealth, 163 Va. 1053, 178 S.E. 29 (1935).

Motive is not an essential element of the crime of murder. Ward v. Commonwealth, 205 Va. 564, 138 S.E.2d 293 (1964).

Motive has never been a requisite element of the crime of murder in Virginia. Cantrell v. Commonwealth, 229 Va. 387, 329 S.E.2d 22 (1985).

Motive relevant to intent. — While motive is not an essential element of the crime of murder, motive is usually an element relevant to establish intent when a conviction is based primarily on circumstantial evidence. Smith v. Commonwealth, 220 Va. 696, 261 S.E.2d 550 (1980).

Defendant's admission that a motive existed was a circumstance which the jury had a right to consider in determining if the murder of which he was accused was a willful, deliberate and premeditated act, one prompted by a cause or reason or by an inducement which moved the will and induced the action by the defendant. Smith v. Commonwealth, 220 Va. 696, 261 S.E.2d 550 (1980).

While motive is not an essential element of the crime, it is relevant and often most persuasive upon the question of the actor's intent. Epperly v. Commonwealth, 224 Va. 214, 294 S.E.2d 882 (1982).

Striking with a walking stick held not to warrant presumption of intent to kill. McDaniel v. Commonwealth, 77 Va. 281 (1883).

Premeditation was not shown. — Where accused was an adult and the victim an infant, and the deceased suffered grievous injuries caused by a number of blows struck on several occasions, evidence was insufficient to show defendant acted with premeditated intent to kill since defendant did not conceal evidence or avoid the risk of detection and blame, but to the contrary, she initiated a call for medical help for a child who had suffered respiratory problems from birth. Rhodes v. Commonwealth, 238 Va. 480, 384 S.E.2d 95 (1989).

Premeditation amply proved. — On probation, riding in a stolen vehicle, and possessing a weapon that the evidence showed had been used in a previous North Carolina murder, defendant shot the state trooper at virtually point blank range at least six times to avoid arrest. Several of the bullet wounds, according to the evi-

dence, probably were the result of ricochet, indicating that the trooper may have been fired upon while lying on the pavement. These and other factors surrounding the killing amply proved premeditation. Weeks v. Commonwealth, 248 Va. 460, 450 S.E.2d 379 (1994), cert. denied, 516 U.S. 829, 116 S. Ct. 100, 133 L. Ed. 2d 55 (1995).

Circuit court did not err in denying defendant's motion to strike a first-degree murder charge because a reasonable jury could have found that defendant underwent the necessary premeditation to commit first-degree murder; the attack was quite brutal, defendant attacked a pregnant woman, and he failed to demonstrate remorse. Riddick v. Commonwealth, — Va. App. —, — S.E.2d —, 2008 Va. App. LEXIS 237 (May 13, 2008).

Neither premeditation nor an intent to kill is an element of felony-murder under this section. Wooden v. Commonwealth, 222 Va. 758, 284 S.E.2d 811 (1981).

For a murder conviction, it is not necessary that the wounds, injuries or trauma be the direct cause of death. — It is sufficient if the initial wound, injury or trauma causes death indirectly through a chain of natural causes such as a defendant's beating death of a fellow inmate, which caused the fellow inmate to have a heart attack as well as suffer a brain injury from striking his head on the steel frame of a bunk bed. Wyche v. Commonwealth, No. 3113-02-1, 2004 Va. App. LEXIS 163 (Ct. of Appeals Apr. 6, 2004).

Felony-murder. — Defendant's conviction on a felony-murder theory was affirmed where the record established all the requisite elements that he confessed to a burglary as a principal in the first degree and the victim was murdered during commission of the offense, even though a codefendant's conviction had been reversed based on improperly admitted evidence. Smith v. Commonwealth, No. 2752-00-1, 2002 Va. App. LEXIS 124 (Ct. of Appeals Feb. 26, 2002).

Insufficient evidence of causation. — Commonwealth failed to present evidence that death resulted from the criminal act or agency of another — a necessary element for successful prosecution for commission of homicide in the state — where Commonwealth failed to show by medical examiner's testimony whether the aspiration simply occurred after or was caused by the gunshot wound. Jenkins v. Commonwealth, No. 1093-96-1 (Ct. of Appeals June 3, 1997).

Evidence was insufficient as a matter of law to convict defendant under this section where the victim died of a cocaine overdose; taken in the light most favorable to the Commonwealth, the evidence did not exclude the hypothesis that the victim died as a result of an accidental or deliberate self-inflicted overdose. Betancourt v. Commonwealth, 26 Va. App. 363, 494 S.E.2d 873 (1998).

II. DEGREE OF MURDER.

A. First and Second Degree Distinguished.

Degree depends upon the intent. — Whether a homicide is murder in the first or second degree depends upon the intent of the prisoner at the time of the killing. Williams v. Commonwealth, 128 Va. 698, 104 S.E. 853 (1920).

And whether the killing was willful, deliberate and premeditated. — The difference between murder in the first and murder in the second degree turns upon whether the homicide was wilful, deliberate and premeditated or not. Williams v. Commonwealth, 128 Va. 698, 104 S.E. 853 (1920).

Every malicious homicide is murder. If in addition, the killing be wilful, deliberate and premeditated it is murder in the first degree. Sims v. Commonwealth, 134 Va. 736, 115 S.E. 382 (1922).

Premeditation, or specific intent to kill, distinguishes murder in the first from murder in the second degree. Jackson v. Virginia, 443 U.S. 307, 99 S. Ct. 2781, 61 L. Ed. 2d 560.

To premeditate means to adopt a specific intent to kill, and that is what distinguishes first and second-degree murder. Smith v. Commonwealth, 220 Va. 696, 261 S.E.2d 550 (1980).

Evidence was sufficient to show that defendant acted with malice in starving her infant son; however, there was no evidence of premeditation as her plan to blame the child's death on an inherited disorder was made after the child's death. Thus, defendant's conviction for first-degree murder was reversed and the case was remanded for retrial for an offense no greater than second-degree murder. Welch v. Commonwealth, — Va. App. —, — S.E.2d —, 2005 Va. App. LEXIS 264 (July 12, 2005).

Will and purpose to kill determines grade of offense. — It is the will and purpose to kill, not necessarily the interval of time, which determines the grade of the offense. Epperly v. Commonwealth, 224 Va. 214, 294 S.E.2d 882 (1982).

In Virginia, every homicide is presumed to be second degree murder. To elevate murder to first degree the Commonwealth must prove additional aggravating factors. Willis v. Commonwealth, 10 Va. App. 430, 393 S.E.2d 405 (1990).

Question for jury. — The question of whether a particular homicide is murder in the first or second degree is one of fact for the jury. Williamson v. Commonwealth, 180 Va. 277, 23 S.E.2d 240 (1942); Plymale v. Commonwealth, 195 Va. 582, 79 S.E.2d 610 (1954); Smith v. Commonwealth, 220 Va. 696, 261 S.E.2d 550 (1980).

The determination of the grade or degree of homicide is a question for the jury. Painter v. Commonwealth, 210 Va. 360, 171 S.E.2d 166 (1969); Perkins v. Commonwealth, 215 Va. 69, 205 S.E.2d 385 (1974).

Determination of the degree is ordinarily a question for the jury. Hodges v. Commonwealth, 213 Va. 316, 191 S.E.2d 794 (1972).

B. Murder in the First Degree.

There must be a premeditated design to kill. — As to willful, deliberate and premeditated killings, other than those enumerated in the statute, proof must be adduced to satisfy the mind that the death of the party slain was the ultimate result which the concurring will, deliberation and premeditation of the attempt sought. King v. Commonwealth, 4 Va. (2 Va. Cas.) 78 (1817); Whiteford v. Commonwealth, 27 Va. (6 Rand.) 721 (1828); Commonwealth v. Jones, 28 Va. (1 Leigh) 598 (1829); McDaniel v. Commonwealth, 77 Va. 281 (1883); Wells v. Commonwealth, 190 Va. 619, 57 S.E.2d 898 (1950).

A willful, deliberate and premeditated killing is murder in the first degree. It must be a predetermined killing upon consideration, and not a sudden killing done in the momentary excitement and impulse of a passion which was engendered by adequate provocation. Bailey v. Commonwealth, 191 Va. 510, 62 S.E.2d 28 (1950).

Only a homicide proved to be committed willfully, deliberately, and with premeditation constitutes first-degree murder. Cooper v. Mitchell, 647 F.2d 437 (4th Cir.), cert. denied, 454 U.S. 849, 102 S. Ct. 171, 70 L. Ed. 2d 139 (1981).

Without provocation recently received. — The premeditated design to kill need not have existed any particular length of time, but if the design at the time of killing was then formed, and the killing was done without provocation then or recently received, it is murder in the first degree. Whiteford v. Commonwealth, 27 Va. (6 Rand.) 721 (1828). See Commonwealth v. Jones, 28 Va. (1 Leigh) 598 (1829); Howell v. Commonwealth, 67 Va. (26 Gratt.) 995 (1875); Mitchell v. Commonwealth, 74 Va. (33 Gratt.) 872 (1880). See also Wright v. Commonwealth, 75 Va. 914 (1882); McDaniel v. Commonwealth, 77 Va. 281 (1883); Price v. Commonwealth, 77 Va. 393 (1883); Williams v. Commonwealth, 128 Va. 698, 104 S.E. 853 (1920); Thompson v. Commonwealth, 131 Va. 847, 109 S.E. 447 (1921); Bailey v. Commonwealth, 191 Va. 510, 62 S.E.2d 28 (1950).

Intent to kill must come into existence at some time before killing; it need not exist for any particular length of time. Smith v. Commonwealth, 220 Va. 696, 261 S.E.2d 550 (1980); Epperly v. Commonwealth, 224 Va. 214, 294 S.E.2d 882 (1982).

A measurable period of time for pondering need not have elapsed in order for a killing to be rendered first-degree murder. The intention to kill may have come into being only at the time of the killing and the act still be first-degree murder. It is the will and purpose to kill and not the interval of time which fixes the grade of the offense. Bailey v. Commonwealth, 191 Va. 510, 62 S.E.2d 28 (1950); Hairston v. Commonwealth, 217 Va. 429, 230 S.E.2d 626 (1976).

It is not the interval of time, but the will and purpose to kill which fixes the grade of the offense. Fuller v. Commonwealth, 201 Va. 724, 113 S.E.2d 667 (1960); Akers v. Commonwealth, 216 Va. 40, 216 S.E.2d 28 (1975).

To constitute willful, deliberate and premeditated murder, it is not necessary that the intent to kill exist for any particular length of time prior to the killing. The intent to kill may spring into existence for the first time at the time of the killing or at any time

previously. Akers v. Commonwealth, 216 Va. 40, 216 S.E.2d 28 (1975); Hairston v. Commonwealth, 217 Va. 429, 230 S.E.2d 626 (1976); Beck v. Commonwealth, 2 Va. App. 170, 342 S.E.2d 642 (1986).

In first-degree murder, the intent to kill must come into existence at some time before the killing; it need not exist for any particular length of time. Smith v. Commonwealth, 220 Va. 696, 261 S.E.2d 550 (1980).

Premeditation need not exist for any particular length of time; an intent to kill may be formed at the moment of the commission of the unlawful act. Jackson v. Virginia, 443 U.S. 307, 99 S. Ct. 2781, 61 L. Ed. 2d 560 (1979).

It is the will and purpose to kill, not necessarily the interval of time, which determine the grade of homicide. Smith v. Commonwealth, 220 Va. 696, 261 S.E.2d 550 (1980).

To constitute a willful, deliberate and premeditated homicide, the intention to kill need not exist for any specified length of time prior to the actual killing. Giarratano v. Commonwealth, 220 Va. 1064, 266 S.E.2d 94 (1980).

A design to kill may be formed only a moment before the fatal act is committed provided the accused had time to think and did intend to kill. Giarratano v. Commonwealth, 220 Va. 1064, 266 S.E.2d 94 (1980); Epperly v. Commonwealth, 224 Va. 214, 294 S.E.2d 882 (1982).

In finding first-degree murder, the fact finder need not have found that defendant harbored the intent to kill for any particular time prior to its enactment. The intent to kill may arise prior to or at the time of the murder. Beck v. Commonwealth, 2 Va. App. 170, 342 S.E.2d 642 (1986).

To establish premeditation, the intent to kill need only exist for a moment. McNair v. Commonwealth, No. 0062-00-1, 2000 Va. App. LEXIS 784 (Ct. of Appeals Dec. 5, 2000).

Anger does not necessarily preclude premeditation. Bailey v. Commonwealth, 193 Va. 814, 71 S.E.2d 368 (1952).

A killing in anger without provocation or upon very slight provocation may still be murder in the first degree. Bailey v. Commonwealth, 193 Va. 814, 71 S.E.2d 368 (1952).

The intent to kill need not be directed against any specific person. — If it be an intent to kill any person who may attempt a certain thing, and one is killed because he attempted that thing, the intent is the same as if it were directed against that specific person. Williams v. Commonwealth, 128 Va. 698, 104 S.E. 853 (1920).

Murder by enumerated means is murder in first degree. — Murder by poison, lying in wait, imprisonment, starving or any willful, deliberate, and premeditated killing, or in the commission of, or attempt to commit arson, rape, robbery, or burglary, is murder in the first degree. Commonwealth v. Jones, 28 Va. (1 Leigh) 598 (1829); Harrison v. Commonwealth, 79 Va. 374 (1884); Stapleton v. Commonwealth, 123 Va. 825, 96 S.E. 801 (1918).

Murder by enumerated means. — As to murder by poison, see Commonwealth v. Jones, 28 Va. (1 Leigh) 598 (1829); Hatchett v. Commonwealth, 76 Va. 1026 (1882); Hicks v. Commonwealth, 86 Va. 223, 3 S.E. 1024 (1889). As to murder by lying in wait, see Commonwealth v. Jones, 28 Va. (1 Leigh) 598 (1829). As to murder by imprisonment, confinement or starvation, see Commonwealth v. Jones, 28 Va. (1 Leigh) 598 (1829).

In a case in which defendant had been convicted of first-degree murder and the Commonwealth moved for a rehearing, asking that the court reconsider its holding that the evidence did not prove premeditation, the Commonwealth was correct that § 18.2-32 did not require proof of premeditation for first-degree murder by starvation. Murder by starvation was one of the enumerated crimes. Welch v. Commonwealth, 2005 Va. App. LEXIS 540 (Oct. 18, 2005).

Whether there was intent to kill or not. — Murder committed by any of the specific means enumerated in the statute is murder in the first degree, whether there was any actual intent to kill or not. Howell v. Commonwealth, 67 Va. (26 Gratt.) 995 (1875).

Imprisonment may be with a view to reducing the victim to the necessity of yielding to some proposed conditions, as well as a punishment for the failure of prompt obedience, without any certain and final determination to destroy life. Gilreath v. Robinson, 544 F. Supp. 569 (E.D. Va. 1982), aff'd, 705 F.2d 109 (4th Cir. 1983), decided under former § 18.1-21.

In cases of imprisonment, as with poisoning and the other enumerated actions, the underlying legislative intent was to hold the perpetrator guilty of first-degree murder without further proof that the death was the ultimate result, which the will, deliberation, and premeditation of the party accused sought. Gilreath v. Robinson, 544 F. Supp. 569 (E.D. Va. 1982), aff'd, 705 F.2d 109 (4th Cir. 1983), decided under former § 18.1-21.

Homicide committed in course of robbery. — Where the intention of the defendants changed from the commission of larceny to robbery to accomplish their original purpose by overcoming a property owner's interference with the taking, and homicide was committed in the course thereof, then the homicide may be first-degree murder. Durham v. Commonwealth, 214 Va. 166, 198 S.E.2d 603 (1973).

Murder in an attempted robbery violates this section, but not § 18.2-31, the capital-murder statute. Ball v. Commonwealth, 221 Va. 754, 273 S.E.2d 790 (1981).

Even if unintentional. — Even an unintentional killing during a robbery or an attempted robbery violates this section and is punishable as murder of the first degree. Ball v. Commonwealth, 221 Va. 754, 273 S.E.2d 790 (1981).

Conviction of both murder and robbery. — The clear conclusion of the trial court, sitting without a jury, that defendant was a principal in the second degree to a willful, deliberate and premeditated killing provided an independent statutory basis for his first-degree murder conviction, apart from any association with or relation to the crime of robbery out of which course of action the killing arose, and defendant could be convicted of both murder and robbery. Simpson v. Commonwealth, 221 Va. 109, 267 S.E.2d 134 (1980).

When felony-murder statute applies. — The felony-murder statute applies where the killing is so closely related to the felony in time, place, and causal connection as to make it a part of the same criminal enterprise. Haskell v. Commonwealth, 218 Va. 1033, 243 S.E.2d 477 (1978).

Question of fact. — Whether a homicide committed during escape from a felony comes within the felony-murder statute usually will present an issue of fact to be determined from the evidence. Haskell v. Commonwealth, 218 Va. 1033, 243 S.E.2d 477 (1978).

Defendant's activities prior to breaking and entering and subsequent thereto provided sufficient evidence of his intent to kill at the time of entry, where he had threatened to kill the victim the previous week, in a statement given to the police he stated: "I remember taking the glass out to get in because I wanted to see my kids for the last time," he took with him to the victim's apartment a screwdriver and a carpenter's knife, upon entry, he obtained a larger knife from the kitchen, he confessed to the killing, physical evidence demonstrated 18 knife wounds, including seven fatal wounds inflicted both in the chest and back, blood was splattered over the entire apartment, upstairs and down, the upstairs phone was unplugged and blood stained, and blood was splattered in the area of the phone downstairs. Patterson v. Commonwealth, No. 0819-85 (Ct. of Appeals July 30, 1986).

The trial court properly considered, as evidence of premeditation, the manner of death as well as the circumstances surrounding the death. The fact that the decedent died from manual strangulation and suffocation, which in themselves required some prolonged physical effort by appellant, coupled with the same facts which identified defendant as the criminal agent, were relevant to the determination whether defendant acted willfully, deliberately and with premeditation. Beck v. Commonwealth, 2 Va. App. 170, 342 S.E.2d 642 (1986).

Evidence supported first degree murder instruction. — Where trial judge give instructions on first and second degree murder, there was evidence to support a first degree murder instruction; the jury could have found that the shots were fired by appellant in a fearful response to the victim reaching under the counter; from this, the jury could have found that the killing was not willful, deliberate and premeditated; under these circumstances, the court properly instructed the jury as to the crime of felony murder, and felony murder under these circumstances is murder in the first degree. Moats v. Commonwealth, 12 Va. App. 349, 404 S.E.2d 244 (1991).

C. Murder in the Second Degree.

Homicide is presumed to be murder in second degree. McDaniel v. Commonwealth, 77 Va. 281 (1883); Bradshaw v. Com-

monwealth, 174 Va. 391, 4 S.E.2d 752 (1939); Hodge v. Commonwealth, 217 Va. 338, 228 S.E.2d 692 (1976).

Every homicide is prima facie a case of murder in the second degree. And it is incumbent upon the Commonwealth where the offense was not committed by any of the specific means enumerated in the statute in order to elevate it to murder in the first degree, to prove by evidence, either direct or circumstantial, beyond rational doubt, that the killing was "willful, deliberate and premeditated." And on the other hand, the burden is upon the accused, if he would reduce the offense below murder in the second degree, to show the absence of malice and the other mitigating circumstances necessary for that purpose. Painter v. Commonwealth, 210 Va. 360, 171 S.E.2d 166 (1969).

Every unlawful homicide is presumed to be murder in the second degree, and an instruction to that effect is usually necessary in a homicide case. But it is not always necessary. Painter v. Commonwealth, 210 Va. 360, 171 S.E.2d 166 (1969).

Every homicide is presumed to be murder in the second degree, the burden resting on the accused to reduce it and on the Commonwealth to elevate it to murder in the first degree. Hodges v. Commonwealth, 213 Va. 316, 191 S.E.2d 794 (1972); Evans v. Commonwealth, 215 Va. 609, 212 S.E.2d 268 (1975).

In Virginia, every unlawful homicide is "presumed" to be murder in the second degree. The so-called "presumption," however, amounts to no more than an "inference" which the trier of fact is permitted, but is not required, to draw from proven facts. The constitutional guarantee of due process is protected if the evidence necessary to invoke the presumption or inference is sufficient for a rational juror to find the presumed or inferred fact beyond a reasonable doubt. Bell v. Commonwealth, 2 Va. App. 48, 341 S.E.2d 654 (1986).

The intention to kill is not essential. — In all cases of slight and insufficient provocation, if it may be reasonably inferred from the weapon made use of, or the manner of using it, or from any other circumstance that the party intended merely to do some great bodily harm, such homicide will be murder in the second degree in like manner as if no provocation had been given, but not a case of murder in the first degree. McDaniel v. Commonwealth, 77 Va. 281 (1883).

Second degree murder does not require a willful, deliberate and premeditated act; it is defined simply as a malicious killing. Maddox v. Commonwealth, No. 1129-99-4, 2000 Va. App. LEXIS 575 (Ct. of Appeals Aug. 1, 2000).

Conviction of second-degree murder for beating death of child. — See Evans v. Commonwealth, 215 Va. 609, 212 S.E.2d 268 (1975).

Principles governing second-degree murder conviction based upon use of an automobile are the same as those which apply to any other kind of second-degree murder: The victim must be shown to have died as a result of the defendant's conduct, and the defendant's conduct must be shown to be malicious. In the absence of express malice, this element may only be implied from conduct likely to cause death or great bodily harm, willfully or purposefully undertaken. Essex v. Commonwealth, 228 Va. 273, 322 S.E.2d 216 (1984).

Evidence supported second degree murder. — Viewed in the light most favorable to the Commonwealth, where the evidence proved the defendant struck the back of the victim's head five times with an object, causing impressed skull fractures, the brutal and vicious nature of the killing was evidence from which the trial judge could infer malice; the evidence supported second-degree murder. Tratzinski v. Commonwealth, No. 0419-02-2, 2003 Va. App. LEXIS 158 (Ct. of Appeals Mar. 25, 2003).

Evidence was sufficient to support defendant's conviction for second-degree murder, despite her claim that she could not be found guilty of any crime greater than voluntary manslaughter, as it showed that she was an active and joint participant in the beating death of the victim; indeed, the evidence showed that she struck defendant on the back of the head with a metal folding chair before he was beaten to death, that she told an inquiring neighbor that what was going on was none of his business, that she cleaned blood off of her two "co-actors" after the beating, and that she lied to police when they investigated the death. Whitehead v. Commonwealth, — Va. App. —, — S.E.2d —, 2006 Va. App. LEXIS 89 (Mar. 14, 2006).

Direct eyewitness testimony of two witnesses identifying defendant as the gunman was not inherently incredible as a matter of law and was, thus, sufficient to support defendant's convictions for second-degree murder, in violation of § 18.2-32, and use of a firearm in the commission of murder, in violation of § 18.2-53.1. The witnesses' testimony was corroborated by other testimony and the physical evidence, including shell casings recovered from the scene of the murder. Jones v. Commonwealth, 2007 Va. App. LEXIS 265 (July 17, 2007).

Evidence, while primarily circumstantial, supported the fact finder's determination that defendant was a principal in the second degree to the crimes of murder, malicious wounding, and use of a firearm during the commission of a felony because the fact finder could conclude that after having left a convenience store and returning to his father's car, defendant followed the victims back into the store and confronted one of them with the accusation that he touched or hit the father's car, and defendant's repeated questioning and interaction drew the victims towards the car, exposing them to the father's gunfire; the evidence further supported the jury's finding that defendant's conduct was knowingly in furtherance of the commission of the father's crime because rather than expressing surprise, fleeing, or intervening when the shots were fired, defendant stood by observing his father shoot the victims. Stagg v. Commonwealth, 2010 Va. App. LEXIS 416 (Oct. 26, 2010).

Evidence supported attempted second degree murder. — Evidence was sufficient to support defendant's conviction for the attempted second-degree murder of a victim, and under the doctrine of transferred intent, this same evidence supported defendant's conviction for the attempted second-degree murder of a witness's daughter. The testimony of the witness, coupled with tire marks left in the grass by defendant's vehicle, supported a finding that defendant struck the victim and the witness's daughter when they were at a location in the grass more than six feet from the edge of a roadway. Patrick v. Commonwealth, 2008 Va. App. LEXIS 231 (May 13, 2008).

III. TRIAL.

A. Indictment.

An indictment in the common-law form for murder is good and will support a conviction for murder in the first or second degree, or manslaughter. Livingston v. Commonwealth, 55 Va. (14 Gratt.) 592 (1857); cited in Bull v. Commonwealth, 55 Va. (14 Gratt.) 613 (1857); Cluverius v. Commonwealth, 81 Va. 787 (1886); Kibler v. Commonwealth, 94 Va. 804, 26 S.E. 858 (1897). See, in accord, Commonwealth v. Miller, 3 Va. (1 Va. Cas.) 310 (1812); Wicks v. Commonwealth, 4 Va. (2 Va. Cas.) 387 (1824); Thompson v. Commonwealth, 61 Va. (20 Gratt.) 724 (1870). See also Thurman v. Commonwealth, 107 Va. 912, 60 S.E. 99 (1908).

Where the indictment was sufficient to convict on first as well as second-degree murder, the petitioner's plea of guilty was a plea of guilty to first-degree murder. Davis v. Slayton, 353 F. Supp. 571 (W.D. Va. 1973).

Manner of killing. — Under an indictment for murder in the form prescribed by § 19.2-221 or Rule 3A:7, Form 5, the Commonwealth may prove a killing in any manner or in different manners. Thus, the Commonwealth was not required to elect whether it was proceeding against the defendant on the theory that the killing was willful, deliberate and premeditated or under the felony-murder doctrine that the killing occurred in the commission of an abduction. Akers v. Commonwealth, 216 Va. 40, 216 S.E.2d 28 (1975).

Must charge that killing was done with "malice aforethought." — In an indictment for murder, it is indispensable that the killing and murder should be charged to be done with "malice aforethought." And if the assault and stabbing be charged to have been done with "malice aforethought" and the conclusion substitutes for those words the word "maliciously," the indictment is not sufficient. Commonwealth v. Gibson, 4 Va. (2 Va. Cas.) 70 (1817).

But it may omit words "deliberately" and "premeditate." — In an indictment for murder, the omission of the word "deliberately," will not be fatal on general demurrer. Bull v. Commonwealth, 55 Va. (14 Gratt.) 613 (1857). Nor omission of the word "premeditate." Weatherman v. Commonwealth, 1 Va. Dec. 819, 19 S.E. 778 (1894). See Livingston v. Commonwealth, 55 Va. (14 Gratt.) 592 (1857).

The deletion from an indictment of the words "willfully, deliberately and premeditatedly," and the inclusion of the phrase "during the commission of robbery while armed with a deadly weapon" did not constitute a binding prosecutorial commitment to prove first-degree murder under this section solely through the mechanism of proving a robbery. Simpson v. Commonwealth, 221 Va. 109, 267 S.E.2d 134 (1980).

Defects as to time are not fatal. — The decisions holding that the defect in the indictment as to the elements of time is fatal were prior to § 19.2-231 as it now reads. Prior to this time there could be no amendment after the indictment was returned by the grand jury. Section 19.2-231 changed this rule. Woods v. Commonwealth, 140 Va. 491, 124 S.E. 468 (1924).

And it is not error to set out dates in figures. Lazier v. Commonwealth, 51 Va. (10 Gratt.) 708 (1853).

Or to designate the name of murdered person by initials. — An indictment concluding "against the peace and dignity of the Commonwealth of Virginia," and designating the murdered person by the initials of his name, though not signed by the Commonwealth's attorney is sufficient. Brown v. Commonwealth, 86 Va. 466, 10 S.E. 745 (1890).

It is not necessary to set out the length, breadth or depth of the wound. Lazier v. Commonwealth, 51 Va. (10 Gratt.) 708 (1853).

Nor is it necessary to specify the kind of missile used. — An averment that the killing was done with a loaded shotgun would have been sufficient without specifying the kind of missiles employed. Green v. Commonwealth, 122 Va. 862, 94 S.E. 940 (1918).

Or that accused knew the killing substance was a deadly poison. — In an indictment for murder by poison, it is not necessary to charge that the accused knew the substance alleged to have been used in producing death was a deadly poison. Thornton v. Commonwealth, 65 Va. (24 Gratt.) 657 (1874).

Amendment properly denied. — In prosecution for first-degree murder it was held proper under the evidence for the court to deny motion to amend indictment to charge only manslaughter. Bailey v. Commonwealth, 193 Va. 814, 71 S.E.2d 368 (1952).

Prosecution's switch of theories on retrial does not violate due process. — The prosecution's switch on retrial of petitioner for murder from a theory of premeditated murder in petitioner's original trial to a theory of felony murder in petitioner's retrial did not violate petitioner's due process rights, as petitioner's indictment gave him adequate notice that he might be tried for felony murder, and the evidence at petitioner's first trial was substantially the same as that at his retrial. Moore v. Garraghty, 739 F. Supp. 285 (E.D. Va. 1990), aff'd, 932 F.2d 963 (4th Cir. 1991).

B. Defenses.

1. Self-Defense.

Self-defense is an affirmative defense and the state may cast upon the accused the burden of proving self-defense. Baker v. Muncy, 619 F.2d 327 (4th Cir. 1980).

Defense must be necessary to protect against grievous bodily harm. — To make out a case of self-defense in a case of homicide, the accused must show to the jury that the defense was necessary to protect his own life, or to protect himself against grievous bodily harm. Vaiden v. Commonwealth, 53 Va. (12 Gratt.) 717 (1855); Clark v. Commonwealth, 90 Va. 360, 18 S.E. 440 (1893). See Brown v. Commonwealth, 86 Va. 466, 10 S.E. 745 (1890).

And the necessity must not arise out of accused's misconduct. — With regard to the necessity that will justify the slaying of another in self-defense, the accused must not have wrongfully occasioned the necessity, for a man shall not in any case justify the killing of another by a pretense of necessity, unless he were without fault in bringing that necessity upon himself. Vaiden v. Commonwealth, 53 Va. (12 Gratt.) 717 (1855); Bristow v. Commonwealth, 56 Va. (15 Gratt.) 634 (1859); Lewis v. Commonwealth, 78 Va. 732 (1884); Honesty v. Commonwealth, 81 Va. 283 (1886); Gaines v. Commonwealth, 88 Va. 682, 14 S.E. 375 (1892); Clark v. Commonwealth, 90 Va. 360, 18 S.E. 440 (1893); Gray v. Commonwealth, 92 Va. 772, 22 S.E. 858 (1895); Jackson v. Commonwealth, 98 Va. 845, 36 S.E. 487 (1900); McCoy v. Commonwealth, 125 Va. 771, 99 S.E. 644 (1919); Bausell v. Commonwealth, 165 Va. 669, 181 S.E. 453 (1935). See Looney v. Commonwealth, 115 Va. 921, 78 S.E. 625 (1913).

Homicide in self-defense may be either justifiable or excusable. If it is either, it entitles the prisoner to an acquittal. But if the difficulty is brought about by the accused and he finds that it is necessary to kill his assailant in order to save his own life, such killing is not in the eye of the law excusable. Sims v. Commonwealth, 134 Va. 736, 115 S.E. 382 (1922).

Accused must retreat as far as he safely can before killing. — When a man is assaulted in the course of a sudden brawl or quarrel, he may in some cases protect himself by slaying the person who assaults him, and excuse himself on the ground of self-defense. Before a party thus assaulted, however, can kill his adversary, he must have retreated as far as he safely could to avoid the assault, until his further going back was prevented by some impediment, or as far as the fierceness of the assault permitted. He must show to the jury that the defense was necessary to protect his own life, or to protect himself against grievous bodily harm. Vaiden v. Commonwealth, 53 Va. (12 Gratt.) 717 (1855).

Justified self-defense applies if the defendant was without fault in bringing on the altercation. Epps v. Commonwealth, No. 2921-02-3, 2003 Va. App. LEXIS 641 (Ct. of Appeals Dec. 16, 2003).

Failure to retreat. — Defendant's conviction for first-degree murder was proper because defendant's own testimony revealed that he did not retreat as far as possible; additionally, when the victim, without a weapon and wounded by a shotgun, was on the ground after a blow from defendant, defendant was not acting out of a reasonably apparent necessity to preserve his own life. Accordingly, the trial court did not err when it denied defendant's motion to strike on the basis of excusable homicide in self-defense. Avent v. Commonwealth, 279 Va. 175, 688 S.E.2d 244, 2010 Va. LEXIS 10 (2010).

To reduce the offense to killing in self-defense the accused must prove two things, to wit: (1) that before the mortal blow was given he declined further combat, and retreated as far as he could with safety; and (2) that he killed the deceased through the necessity of preserving his life or to save himself from great bodily harm. Vaiden v. Commonwealth, 53 Va. (12 Gratt.) 717 (1855); Dock v. Commonwealth, 62 Va. (21 Gratt.) 909 (1872); Clark v. Commonwealth, 90 Va. 360, 18 S.E. 440 (1894).

Distinction between accident and self-defense. — The defense that a killing was accidental presents a different issue from a claim that a killing was done in self-defense; in making a claim of self-defense a defendant implicitly admits the killing was intentional and assumes the burden of introducing evidence of justification or excuse that raises a reasonable doubt in the minds of jurors. Bowler v. Commonwealth, No. 0404-99-4, 2000 Va. App. LEXIS 207 (Ct. of Appeals Mar. 21, 2000).

Death may result accidentally from action taken in self-defense and, under such circumstances, defenses of accident and self-defense are not mutually exclusive and instructions on both defenses should be given upon request. Bowler v. Commonwealth, No. 0404-99-4, 2000 Va. App. LEXIS 207 (Ct. of Appeals Mar. 21, 2000).

Unless assaulted while in the discharge of a lawful act. — A person assaulted while in discharge of a lawful act, and reasonably apprehending that his assailant will do him bodily harm, has the right to repel the assault by all force he deems necessary and is not compelled to retreat from his assailant, but may in turn become the assailant, inflicting bodily wounds until his person is out of danger. Jackson v. Commonwealth, 96 Va. 107, 30 S.E. 452 (1898); McCoy v. Commonwealth, 125 Va. 771, 99 S.E. 644 (1919).

There must be an overt act by deceased to warrant a killing. — There must be some act by the deceased meaning present peril, or something in the attending circumstances indicative of a present purpose to make the apprehended attack. The act so done, or circumstances thus existing, must be of such a character as to afford a reasonable ground for believing there is a design to commit a felony, or to do some serious bodily harm, and imminent danger of carrying such design into immediate execution. Then the killing will be justifiable, though there was in fact no such design by the deceased. Stoneman v. Commonwealth, 66 Va. (25 Gratt.) 887 (1874).

For fear alone that a man intends to commit murder will not suffice. — The bare fear that a man intends to commit murder or other atrocious felony, however well grounded, unaccompanied by any overt act indicative of any such intention will not warrant killing the party by way of prevention. There must be some overt act indicative of imminent danger at the time. Stoneman v. Commonwealth, 66 Va. (25 Gratt.) 887 (1874).

Whether the defendant shot in self-defense depends on whether he reasonably believed that it was necessary to shoot as he did in order to save his own life or avoid serious bodily harm. Fear alone would not excuse the killing. There must have been some overt act by the deceased indicative of imminent danger at the time. Boone v. Commonwealth, 195 Va. 708, 80 S.E.2d 412 (1954).

An overt act of sufficient imminence. — In a first degree murder prosecution, where the victim had a history of assaulting defendant, and had allegedly assaulted her and refused to leave her residence, his allegedly advancing towards her after threatening her was an overt act of sufficient imminence on his part that would warrant her to use deadly force in self-defense. Thus, the trial court erred in denying her proffered self-defense instruction. Commonwealth v. Cary, 271 Va. 87, 623 S.E.2d 906, 2006 Va. LEXIS 22 (2006).

A person reasonably apprehending attack has a right to arm himself for his necessary self-defense. Stapleton v. Commonwealth, 123 Va. 825, 96 S.E. 801 (1918).

As to distinction between killing in self-defense proper and accidental or unintentional killing while in the exercise of self-defense, see Braxton v. Commonwealth, 195 Va. 275, 77 S.E.2d 840 (1953).

As to admissibility of evidence of decedent's prior character, see notes under analysis line III, C, 2.

As to issue of remoteness of evidence showing decedent's prior character, see note under analysis line III, C, 3.

The trier of fact determines the weight of evidence in support of a claim of self-defense. Gardner v. Commonwealth, 3 Va. App. 418, 350 S.E.2d 229 (1986).

2. Drunkenness and Insanity.

Effect of intoxication on ability to commit first degree murder. — When a man has become so greatly intoxicated as not to be able to deliberate and premeditate, he cannot commit murder of the first degree, or that class of murder under the statute denominated a willful, deliberate and premeditated killing. But so long as he retains the faculty of willing, deliberating and premeditating, though drunk, he is capable of committing murder in the first degree; and if a drunk man is guilty of a willful, deliberate and premeditated killing, he is guilty of murder in the first degree. Hatcher v. Commonwealth, 218 Va. 811, 241 S.E.2d 756 (1978).

A person who voluntarily has become so intoxicated as to be unable to deliberate and premeditate cannot commit any class of murder that is defined as a willful, deliberate and premeditated killing. Giarratano v. Commonwealth, 220 Va. 1064, 266 S.E.2d 94 (1980).

Mere intoxication from drugs or alcohol will not suffice to negate premeditation. Giarratano v. Commonwealth, 220 Va. 1064, 266 S.E.2d 94 (1980).

Voluntary drunkenness will not reduce offense to manslaughter. — "Voluntary immediate drunkenness is not admissible to disprove malice, or to reduce the offense to manslaughter. But where, by reason of it, there is wanting that deliberation and premeditation which are necessary to elevate the offense to murder in the first degree, it is properly ranked as murder in the second degree, as the courts have repeatedly decided." Willis v. Commonwealth, 73 Va. (32 Gratt.) 929 (1879). See also Honesty v. Commonwealth, 81 Va. 283 (1886).

Mere intoxication will not negate premeditation. However, when a person voluntarily becomes so intoxicated that he is incapable of deliberation or premeditation, he cannot commit a class of murder that requires proof of a deliberate and premeditated killing. Wright v. Commonwealth, 234 Va. 627, 363 S.E.2d 711 (1988).

While a person who has become so intoxicated as to be unable to deliberate and premeditate cannot commit any class of murder that is defined as a willful, deliberate, and premeditated killing, mere intoxication from drugs or alcohol will not suffice to negate premeditation. Jenkins v. Commonwealth, 244 Va. 445, 423 S.E.2d 360 (1992), cert. denied, 507 U.S. 1036, 113 S. Ct. 1862, 123 L. Ed. 2d 483 (1993), overruled in part on other grounds by Jay v. Commonwealth, 275 Va. 510, 659 S.E.2d 311, 2008 Va. LEXIS 53 (2008).

But is admissible to show the murder was not premeditated. — "Drunkenness is only entitled to weight when and so far as it tends to show that the offender did not act in a frame of mind to act with that determination and premeditation which is necessary to constitute murder in the first degree. Great caution is required in applying this doctrine because there are few cases of premeditated violent homicide in which the defendant does not nerve himself to the encounter by liquor." Willis v. Commonwealth, 73 Va. (32 Gratt.) 929 (1879). See Baccigalupo v. Commonwealth, 74 Va. (33 Gratt.) 807 (1880); Honesty v. Commonwealth, 81 Va. 283 (1886).

Voluntary drunkenness (as distinguished from permanent insanity produced by drink) affords no excuse for crime, save only that where premeditation is a material question the intoxication of the accused may be considered by the jury. As between murder in the first degree and murder in the second degree, voluntary drunkenness may be a legitimate subject of inquiry; but, as between murder in the second degree and manslaughter, it is never material and cannot be considered. Gills v. Commonwealth, 141 Va. 445, 126 S.E. 51 (1925).

Voluntary intoxication is material to the element of premeditation and may be found to have negated it. Jackson v. Virginia, 443 U.S. 307, 99 S. Ct. 2781, 61 L. Ed. 2d 560 (1979).

The defendant may negate the specific intent requisite for capital or first-degree murder by showing that he was so greatly intoxicated as to be incapable of deliberation or premeditation, but voluntary intoxication is no defense to the lesser degrees of homicide, or to any other crime. Particularly, his state of intoxication, however great, will not repel an inference of malice, implied by the circumstances surrounding his conduct. Essex v. Commonwealth, 228 Va. 273, 322 S.E.2d 216 (1984).

When partial insanity is no defense. — In every case, although the accused may be laboring under partial insanity, if he still understands the nature and character of his act, and its consequences, and has a knowledge that it is wrong and criminal, and a mental power sufficient to apply that knowledge to his own case, and to know that if he does the act he will do wrong and receive punishment, and possesses withal a will sufficient to restrain the impulse that may arise from a diseased mind, such partial insanity is not sufficient to exempt him from responsibility to the law for his crime. Dejarnette v. Commonwealth, 75 Va. 867 (1881).

The doctrine of irresistible impulse is applicable only where the defendant knows that the act is wrong but is driven by an irresistible impulse to commit it. Thompson v. Commonwealth, 193 Va. 704, 70 S.E.2d 284 (1952).

The irresistible impulse doctrine is applicable only to that class of cases where the accused is able to understand the nature and consequences of his act and knows it is wrong, but his mind has become so impaired by disease that he is totally deprived of the mental power to control or restrain his act. Thompson v. Commonwealth, 193 Va. 704, 70 S.E.2d 284 (1952); McLane v. Commonwealth, 202 Va. 197, 116 S.E.2d 274 (1960); Christian v. Commonwealth, 202 Va. 311, 117 S.E.2d 72 (1960).

In prosecution for homicide although instruction to the effect that the only degree of insanity the law recognizes as an excuse for a crime is that determined by the "right and wrong test" was inaccurate, the failure to include in such instruction the doctrine of irresistible impulse did not constitute reversible error as applied to the evidence in the case. Thompson v. Commonwealth, 193 Va. 704, 70 S.E.2d 284 (1952).

The defense of irresistible impulse is applicable only where the accused's mind has become so impaired by disease that he is totally deprived of the mental power to control or restrain his act. Godley v. Commonwealth, 2 Va. App. 249, 343 S.E.2d 368 (1986).

How sanity to be determined. — Defendant in murder prosecution was, under the evidence, entitled to have the question of his sanity determined by a fair and impartial jury, uninfluenced or affected by any testimony except that produced in open court. Thompson v. Commonwealth, 193 Va. 704, 70 S.E.2d 284 (1952).

Burden on accused to show he was rendered incapable of doing premeditated act by drunkenness. — The onus rests on accused to prove, if he relies on intoxication as a defense, that when he committed the offense his condition, from intoxication was such as to render him incapable of doing a willful, deliberate and premeditated act. And so of insanity. Both must be proved as independent facts. Honesty v. Commonwealth, 81 Va. 283 (1886).

Burden on accused to show insanity. — If the accused relies on the defense of insanity, the burden is on him to prove to the satisfaction of the jury that he was insane at the time. Reasonable

doubt as to his insanity is not enough to excuse him. Thompson v. Commonwealth, 193 Va. 704, 70 S.E.2d 284 (1952).

The accused has the burden of proving that he was insane when the offense was committed. Bloodgood v. Commonwealth, 212 Va. 253, 183 S.E.2d 737 (1971).

When the corpus delicti has been established and proof adduced that the accused committed the act it is not sufficient for the accused to raise a reasonable doubt as to his sanity; he must go one step further and prove to the satisfaction of the jury that he was insane at the time of the commission of the act. Jones v. Commonwealth, 202 Va. 236, 117 S.E.2d 67 (1960); Christian v. Commonwealth, 202 Va. 311, 117 S.E.2d 72 (1960).

The Commonwealth having established the corpus delicti and that the act was committed by the defendant, had made out its case, and the burden rested upon the accused to prove to the satisfaction of the jury that at the time of the commission of the act he was insane. This burden rests upon the accused by reason of the presumption of law that every person of the age of discretion is of sound mind. Lucas v. Commonwealth, 201 Va. 599, 112 S.E.2d 915 (1960).

Effect of expert testimony. — Although the Commonwealth produced no expert testimony, the jurors were not bound to accept the testimony of defendant's expert to the effect that defendant committed the crime under an "irresistible impulse." The evidence of an expert witness should be given the same consideration as is given that of any other witness, considering his opportunity for knowledge of the subject, his appearance, conduct, and demeanor on the stand. McLane v. Commonwealth, 202 Va. 197, 116 S.E.2d 274 (1960).

Opinion of lay witness. — It was improper, though not reversible error, to admit the opinion of a lay witness as to whether defendant acted "like he was out of his mind." Jones v. Commonwealth, 202 Va. 236, 117 S.E.2d 67 (1960).

Issue of sanity held for the jury even though medical witnesses were unable to state an opinion as to whether or not defendant was insane at the time of the crime. Lucas v. Commonwealth, 201 Va. 599, 112 S.E.2d 915 (1960).

Instruction on partial insanity upheld. — An instruction is not misleading or confusing which plainly tells the jury that although the defendant may be laboring under partial insanity, if he still understands the nature and character of his act and its consequences, and has knowledge that it is wrong and criminal and has mental power sufficient to apply that knowledge to his own case, and has knowledge sufficient to know that if he does the act he will do wrong and receive punishment, and possesses a will sufficient to restrain the impulse that may arise from a diseased mind, that such partial insanity is not sufficient to exempt him from responsibility to the law for his crime. Jones v. Commonwealth, 202 Va. 236, 117 S.E.2d 67 (1960).

Intoxication held not so great to render defendant incapable of premeditated murder. — Where defendant was at his mother's home before the murder and had the ability to talk with her and determine that he wanted to visit his children, who were living with the victim, although at an inappropriate hour; he had the mental capacity to determine that he would need a screwdriver and a carpenter's knife to get into the victim's apartment; he was able to walk to her residence four or five blocks away and then use the tools he brought with him to break and enter the door; he decided that he might need a butcher knife and found his way to the kitchen to obtain it; he went to the victim's bedroom and discussed with her the visitation of the children; and after the killing he was able to go to the telephone, dial the police, and report that he had killed the victim, the defendant's level of intoxication from alcohol and drug use was not so great as to render him incapable of committing a deliberate and premeditated murder. Patterson v. Commonwealth, No. 0819-85 (Ct. of Appeals July 30, 1986).

Voluntary intoxication defense rejected. — Defendant's conviction for first-degree murder was proper because, by his own testimony, it was clear that on the day in question he comprehended what was occurring; he recalled the chain of events and he articulated reasons for his reaction to the developing situation in a way that supported a finding that he was capable of deliberation despite his consumption of intoxicants. Accordingly, the trial court did not err when it denied defendant's motion to strike the charge of first-degree murder on the grounds that he was voluntarily intoxicated. Avent v. Commonwealth, 279 Va. 175, 688 S.E.2d 244, 2010 Va. LEXIS 10 (2010).

3. Other Defenses.

A homicide committed to prevent a felony is justifiable. Cooke v. Commonwealth, 114 Va. 882, 77 S.E. 608 (1913).

Duress. — A person subject to duress may justifiably violate the literal language of the criminal law in order to avoid a harm of greater magnitude. Sam v. Commonwealth, 13 Va. App. 312, 411 S.E.2d 832 (1991).

To support a defense of duress, a defendant must demonstrate that his criminal conduct was the product of an unlawful threat that caused him reasonably to believe that performing the criminal conduct was his only reasonable opportunity to avoid imminent death or serious bodily harm, either to himself or to another. Sam v. Commonwealth, 13 Va. App. 312, 411 S.E.2d 832 (1991).

A defendant may not rely on the defense of duress if he has a reasonable opportunity both to refuse to do the criminal act and also to avoid the threatened harm. Sam v. Commonwealth, 13 Va. App. 312, 411 S.E.2d 832 (1991).

Defense of duress requires showing of imminent harm. — The more appropriate approach to the defense of duress is to require a showing of "imminent" harm rather than the stricter and more limiting "immediate" harm. Sam v. Commonwealth, 13 Va. App. 312, 411 S.E.2d 832 (1991).

"Threats of future harm" denotes threats of harm that might occur at some uncertain time that is distant and separate from the period of duress or coercion; therefore, the temporal proximity of the threat and the threatened harm is the true issue, and the proper distinction between imminent and immediate harm is how far in the future is the harm to occur from the time the threat is made. Sam v. Commonwealth, 13 Va. App. 312, 411 S.E.2d 832 (1991).

Vague threats of future harm, however alarming, will not suffice to excuse criminal conduct. Sam v. Commonwealth, 13 Va. App. 312, 411 S.E.2d 832 (1991).

Duress is available in cases involving threats against family members. — The defense of duress is applicable to cases involving threats of harm against a defendant's family members. Sam v. Commonwealth, 13 Va. App. 312, 411 S.E.2d 832 (1991).

The defense of duress may be available to a defendant who has committed a criminal act because of threats made against members of the defendant's family. Sam v. Commonwealth, 13 Va. App. 312, 411 S.E.2d 832 (1991).

When balanced against a lesser evil, a greater evil, whether committed against the defendant or a member of the defendant's family, is still less desirable for reasons of social policy. Sam v. Commonwealth, 13 Va. App. 312, 411 S.E.2d 832 (1991).

One may kill to protect his family. — On the trial of S. for the murder of E., if S. shot E. under a reasonable apprehension that his own life or that of some member of his family was in imminent danger, or under a reasonable apprehension that the deceased intended to burn the dwelling house of his mother, or commit some other known felony, and that there was imminent danger of such design being carried into execution, he is justified in so doing, though such danger was unreal. Stoneman v. Commonwealth, 66 Va. (25 Gratt.) 887 (1874). See Green v. Commonwealth, 122 Va. 862, 94 S.E. 940 (1918).

Killing to resist entry of dwelling. — The owner may resist the entry of his dwelling but he has no right to kill, unless it be rendered necessary to prevent loss of life or great bodily harm. If he kills where there is not a reasonable ground of apprehension of imminent danger to his person or property, it is manslaughter, and if done with malice, express or implied, it is then murder. Bausell v. Commonwealth, 165 Va. 669, 181 S.E. 453 (1935). But see Stoneman v. Commonwealth, 66 Va. (25 Gratt.) 887 (1874); Parrish v. Commonwealth, 81 Va. 1 (1884).

A mere trespass upon land is insufficient provocation. — For a mere trespass upon land, the owner has no right to assault the trespasser with a deadly weapon, the result of which may be to kill him or do him great bodily harm. Montgomery v. Commonwealth, 98 Va. 840, 36 S.E. 371 (1900).

Provocation not proved. — Defendant's conviction for first-degree murder was proper because the victim's alleged statements regarding his disapproval of African Americans was so removed in time that it was irrelevant to the issue of reasonable provocation.

Avent v. Commonwealth, 279 Va. 175, 688 S.E.2d 244, 2010 Va. LEXIS 10 (2010).

And words, however grievous, will not justify an assault. McCoy v. Commonwealth, 125 Va. 771, 99 S.E. 644 (1919). See Sims v. Commonwealth, 134 Va. 736, 115 S.E. 382 (1922).

In a prosecution for homicide, where the deceased, who was intoxicated, applied a vile epithet to the accused and others to which the accused took exception and invited the deceased outside to fight, and in the fight the accused stabbed the deceased eight times and killed him, the deceased not being armed, it was held that vile as the epithet was that deceased employed, it afforded no legal excuse to the accused to assault him and was not in law such a provocation as justified the killing. Adams v. Commonwealth, 163 Va. 1053, 178 S.E. 29 (1935).

Self-induced unconsciousness goes only to the grade of the offense and not to the existence of a complete defense. Greenfield v. Commonwealth, 214 Va. 710, 204 S.E.2d 414 (1974).

Where not self-induced, unconsciousness is a complete defense to a criminal homicide. Greenfield v. Commonwealth, 214 Va. 710, 204 S.E.2d 414 (1974).

Evidence contradicting assertion of accident. — The jury was presented with evidence contradicting defendant's assertion that his gun discharged accidentally as he was raising the weapon from his leg holster, where the autopsy report showed that the bullet traveled at a slightly downward angle through the victim's chest. From this fact, the jury was entitled to infer that defendant was not truthful about the manner in which the shooting occurred. Gardner v. Commonwealth, 3 Va. App. 418, 350 S.E.2d 229 (1986).

Conviction for conduct not constituting crime. — Section 18.2-26, at the time of defendant's offense, did not provide a punishment for an attempted felony which was punishable by confinement for a maximum of 40 years. Thus, although defendant's conduct may have been proscribed by this section, it was an offense without a penalty. Therefore, defendant was convicted for conduct which constituted no crime at the time of the offense. Accordingly, the judgment of the trial court was reversed. Cook v. Commonwealth, 20 Va. App. 510, 458 S.E.2d 317 (1995).

No retroactive assignment of punishment. — Although the amendments to § 18.2-26 subsequent to defendant's misconduct included attempts at offenses under this section, the revised statute may not retroactively assign punishment to prior acts. Cook v. Commonwealth, 20 Va. App. 510, 458 S.E.2d 317 (1995).

C. Evidence.

1. Presumptions and Burden of Proof.

a. Degree of Offense.

Nothing in Mullaney v. Wilbur, 421 U.S. 684, 95 S. Ct. 1881, 44 L. Ed. 2d 508 (1975) casts any shadow upon the constitutionality of this section. Warlitner v. Commonwealth, 217 Va. 348, 228 S.E.2d 698 (1976), cert. denied, 430 U.S. 957, 97 S. Ct. 1604, 51 L. Ed. 2d 807 (1977).

This section does not mention, much less establish, any presumptions or burdens. Warlitner v. Commonwealth, 217 Va. 348, 228 S.E.2d 698 (1976), cert. denied, 430 U.S. 957, 97 S. Ct. 1604, 51 L. Ed. 2d 807 (1977).

Ultimate burden of proof on prosecution. — Neither the due process clause nor Mullaney v. Wilbur, 421 U.S. 684, 95 S. Ct. 1881, 44 L. Ed. 2d 508 (1975) prohibits the use of presumptions or inferences as procedural devices to shift to the accused the burden of producing some evidence contesting the otherwise presumed or inferred fact. These devices, however, must satisfy certain due process requirements, and the ultimate burden of proof beyond a reasonable doubt must remain upon the prosecution. Hodge v. Commonwealth, 217 Va. 338, 228 S.E.2d 692 (1976).

The presumption of innocence to which an accused is entitled follows him throughout the trial. This presumption is sufficient to require his acquittal on the charge brought against him unless the Commonwealth proves beyond a reasonable doubt every material element of that charge. The burden of proof is always upon the Commonwealth, and this burden never shifts. Hodge v. Commonwealth, 217 Va. 338, 228 S.E.2d 692 (1976).

The presumption is that every killing is murder in the second degree. Hill v. Commonwealth, 43 Va. (2 Gratt.) 594 (1845); Watson v. Commonwealth, 85 Va. 867, 9 S.E. 418 (1889);

Vance v. Commonwealth, 1 Va. Dec. 830, 19 S.E. 785 (1894); Williams v. Commonwealth, 128 Va. 698, 104 S.E. 853 (1920); Blankenship v. Commonwealth, 193 Va. 587, 70 S.E.2d 335 (1952).

And burden is on state to raise offense to murder in the first degree. — The presumption arising from the homicide being that the killing is murder in the second degree, if the state would make it murder in the first degree, the burden is upon the state to establish the elements of the crime. Hill v. Commonwealth, 43 Va. (2 Gratt.) 594 (1845); Willis v. Commonwealth, 73 Va. (32 Gratt.) 929 (1879); McDaniel v. Commonwealth, 77 Va. 281 (1883); Watson v. Commonwealth, 85 Va. 867, 9 S.E. 418 (1889); Tilley v. Commonwealth, 89 Va. 136, 15 S.E. 526 (1892); Smith v. Commonwealth, 192 Va. 186, 64 S.E.2d 761 (1951); Blankenship v. Commonwealth, 193 Va. 587, 70 S.E.2d 335 (1952); Henry v. Commonwealth, 195 Va. 281, 77 S.E.2d 863 (1953).

In establishing first-degree murder the Commonwealth has the burden of showing both premeditation and malice. Brown v. Commonwealth, 212 Va. 515, 184 S.E.2d 786 (1971).

By showing malice aforethought and intent to kill. — Under this section, in order to elevate the crime of murder to murder in the first degree, the burden is upon the Commonwealth to show not only that the killing was done with malice aforethought, but also that the homicide was committed with the intent to kill, not merely to do great bodily harm. Williams v. Commonwealth, 128 Va. 698, 104 S.E. 853 (1920).

Second-degree murder presumption is no more than inference. — The Virginia presumption of second-degree murder arising from the commission of an unlawful homicide amounts, in practical effect, to no more than an inference which the trier of fact is permitted, but is not required, to draw from proven facts. Warlitner v. Commonwealth, 217 Va. 348, 228 S.E.2d 698 (1976), cert. denied, 430 U.S. 957, 97 S. Ct. 1604, 51 L. Ed. 2d 807 (1977).

The presumption of second-degree murder employed in Virginia is the type of procedural, evidentiary device permitted by Mullaney v. Wilbur, 421 U.S. 684, 95 S. Ct. 1881, 44 L. Ed. 2d 508 (1975). Neither the presumption nor the resulting burden imposed upon the accused has the effect of shifting from the prosecution the ultimate burden of persuasion upon the critical issue of malice or its corollary, the absence of heat of passion. Hodge v. Commonwealth, 217 Va. 338, 228 S.E.2d 692 (1976).

The Virginia presumption that an unlawful homicide is murder of the second degree differs substantially, both in nature and effect, from the Maine presumption struck down in Mullaney v. Wilbur, 421 U.S. 684, 95 S. Ct. 1881, 44 L. Ed. 2d 508 (1975). Unlike the Maine presumption, the Virginia presumption is not conclusive. Unlike the Maine presumption, the Virginia presumption does not cast upon the accused the burden of proving by a fair preponderance of the evidence that he acted in the heat of passion in order to put that critical fact in issue and to require the Commonwealth to negate passion beyond a reasonable doubt. The Virginia burden is satisfied when the accused produces some credible evidence that he acted in the heat of passion. But even if he produces no evidence, he may rely upon the Commonwealth's evidence to secure a manslaughter instruction and an acquittal on the charge of murder, if that evidence indicates he acted in the heat of passion. In practical effect, therefore, the Virginia presumption amounts to no more than an inference which the trier of fact is permitted, but is not required, to draw from proven facts. Hodge v. Commonwealth, 217 Va. 338, 228 S.E.2d 692 (1976).

This section merely prescribes what shall constitute murder of the first degree and then declares that all other murders shall be of the second degree. Warlitner v. Commonwealth, 217 Va. 348, 228 S.E.2d 698 (1976), cert. denied, 430 U.S. 957, 97 S. Ct. 1604, 51 L. Ed. 2d 807 (1977).

When the Commonwealth makes a prima facie showing that malice exists, it thereby establishes prima facie that heat of passion is absent. Hodge v. Commonwealth, 217 Va. 338, 228 S.E.2d 692 (1976).

The Virginia presumption or inference of malice arising from the commission of an unlawful homicide is clothed with due process safeguards. Hodge v. Commonwealth, 217 Va. 338, 228 S.E.2d 692 (1976).

Evidence must prove inference beyond reasonable doubt. — Virginia law comports with the rule that the evidence necessary to invoke the presumption or inference must be sufficient for a rational juror to find the presumed or inferred fact beyond a

reasonable doubt. Hodge v. Commonwealth, 217 Va. 338, 228 S.E.2d 692 (1976).

The burden of going forward with the evidence may, from time to time during the course of trial, shift from one side to the other as the exigencies of the situation may require. For example, the burden of production may first shift to the accused to neutralize, by evidence raising a reasonable doubt, a prima facie showing by the Commonwealth of guilt and then to the Commonwealth to overcome the showing made by the accused. But the ultimate burden of persuasion remains upon the Commonwealth, and if, upon the evidence as a whole, both for the Commonwealth and the accused, there remains a reasonable doubt of the guilt of the accused, he must be acquitted or convicted only of a lesser included charge established by the evidence. Hodge v. Commonwealth, 217 Va. 338, 228 S.E.2d 692 (1976).

Burden of persuasion as to malice cannot be shifted to accused. — There is no violation of the rule of Mullaney v. Wilbur, 421 U.S. 684, 95 S. Ct. 1881, 44 L. Ed. 2d 508 (1975) that the burden of persuasion may not be shifted to the accused upon the critical issue of malice. Virginia has long recognized that malice and heat of passion cannot coexist. Proof of malice excludes the presence of passion, and proof of passion presupposes the absence of malice. Hodge v. Commonwealth, 217 Va. 338, 228 S.E.2d 692 (1976).

The Commonwealth is not entitled to the presumption of malice in the absence of evidence showing that defendant's use of the pistol was deliberate, that is, not accidental. Lawhorne v. Commonwealth, 213 Va. 608, 194 S.E.2d 747 (1973).

Similarly, burden is on accused to reduce offense to manslaughter. — And if the accused would reduce the crime to manslaughter, the burden of proof is on him to overcome the presumption of murder arising from the killing. Hill v. Commonwealth, 43 Va. (2 Gratt.) 594 (1845); Willis v. Commonwealth, 73 Va. (32 Gratt.) 929 (1879); Watson v. Commonwealth, 85 Va. 867, 9 S.E. 418 (1889); Tilley v. Commonwealth, 89 Va. 136, 15 S.E. 526 (1892); Vance v. Commonwealth, 1 Va. Dec. 830, 19 S.E. 785 (1894); Smith v. Commonwealth, 192 Va. 186, 64 S.E.2d 761 (1951); Blankenship v. Commonwealth, 193 Va. 587, 70 S.E.2d 335 (1952); Henry v. Commonwealth, 195 Va. 281, 77 S.E.2d 863 (1953).

By showing justification or excuse. — Every homicide is prima facie murder in the second degree, and the burden is upon the defendant to establish to the satisfaction of the jury any justification or excuse relied upon by him. Bryan v. Commonwealth, 131 Va. 709, 109 S.E. 477 (1921); Blankenship v. Commonwealth, 193 Va. 587, 70 S.E.2d 335 (1952).

When the Commonwealth has proved the commission of a homicide, and has pointed out the accused as a criminal agent, then it may rest its case, and unless the accused shows circumstances of justification, alleviation or excuse, a verdict of murder in the second degree will be warranted. Braxton v. Commonwealth, 195 Va. 275, 77 S.E.2d 840 (1953); Boone v. Commonwealth, 195 Va. 708, 80 S.E.2d 412 (1954).

All homicide is, in presumption of law, malicious, and of course amounts to murder, unless justified, excused or alleviated. It is incumbent upon the prisoner to make out to the satisfaction of the court and jury the circumstances of justification, excuse and alleviation. M'Whirt's Case, 44 Va. (3 Gratt.) 594 (1846).

Once the Commonwealth proves an unlawful homicide and establishes the accused as the criminal agent, the presumption of second-degree murder arises and he has the burden of showing circumstances of justification, excuse or alleviation. Hodge v. Commonwealth, 217 Va. 338, 228 S.E.2d 692 (1976).

Which raises a reasonable doubt that offense was murder. — In order to reduce a homicide from murder in the second degree to manslaughter or excusable homicide, the burden is upon the accused to introduce evidence sufficient to raise a reasonable doubt in the minds of the jury as to whether the offense is murder in the second degree. Sims v. Commonwealth, 134 Va. 736, 115 S.E. 328 (1922).

In a given situation, the accused, without producing evidence, may be entitled to an instruction on manslaughter, or even to a verdict on that lesser charge, if it can reasonably be inferred from the Commonwealth's evidence that he acted in the heat of passion. Where the Commonwealth's evidence does not permit such an inference, however, the burden of production shifts to the accused. But when he produces some credible evidence that he acted in the heat of passion, he is entitled to an instruction on manslaughter and also, if the evidence as a whole raises a reasonable doubt that he acted maliciously, to a verdict on the lesser charge of homicide. Hodge v. Commonwealth, 217 Va. 338, 228 S.E.2d 692 (1976).

Guilty plea held involuntary. — Where the defendant's guilty plea to a short form indictment of murder was based upon the advice of counsel who mistakenly understood that the Commonwealth would have the burden of raising the degree of the offense to first-degree murder through a showing of evidence of premeditation, when in fact the Virginia Supreme Court has determined that a guilty plea is always to the highest degree of the offense charged in the indictment and that the statutory short form of indictment for murder includes murder in the first degree, the plea could not be viewed as voluntary, intelligent or made with an awareness of the likely consequences. Harlow v. Murray, 443 F. Supp. 1327 (W.D. Va.), aff'd, 588 F.2d 1348 (4th Cir. 1978).

b. Other Matters.

Fact of death must be shown by direct proof or strongest presumptive evidence. — The corpus delicti consists of two fundamental facts: first, the death, and second, the existence of the criminal agency as the cause thereof. The former must be shown either by direct proof, or by presumptive evidence of the strongest kind, which is clearly satisfactory to the jury, and convinces them beyond a reasonable doubt. Smith v. Commonwealth, 62 Va. (21 Gratt.) 809 (1871); Dean v. Commonwealth, 73 Va. (32 Gratt.) 912 (1879); Hatchett v. Commonwealth, 76 Va. 1026 (1882); Russell v. Commonwealth, 78 Va. 400 (1884); Sutton v. Commonwealth, 85 Va. 128, 7 S.E. 323 (1888).

A man must be taken to intend that which he does, or which is the natural and necessary consequence of his act. Hill v. Commonwealth, 43 Va. (2 Gratt.) 594 (1845); Murphy v. Commonwealth, 64 Va. (23 Gratt.) 960 (1873); McDaniel v. Commonwealth, 77 Va. 281 (1883); Price v. Commonwealth, 77 Va. 393 (1883). See Lewis v. Commonwealth, 78 Va. 732 (1884).

The burden of showing that a killing is accidental is upon the accused. Lawhorne v. Commonwealth, 213 Va. 608, 194 S.E.2d 747 (1973).

Restrictions on cross-examination. — Second-degree murder conviction would be reversed, and case would be remanded for new trial, where trial judge erred in limiting counsel's cross-examination of adverse witnesses about pending charges and their dispositions for purposes of showing bias and motive to testify, where from proffered evidence the jury could have inferred that both had agreements for leniency with the State. Fogg v. Commonwealth, No. 3062-00-2, 2002 Va. App. LEXIS 323 (Ct. of Appeals May 28, 2002).

Appellate review standard. — Defendant's convictions for second-degree murder of defendant's wife and for the use of a firearm in the commission of the murder were reinstated, after having been reversed on initial appeal, by the lower appellate court, which found that there was evidence to support defendant's hypothesis of innocence, and that there was some evidence that defendant's wife may have fatally fired the gun; the issue upon appellate review was not whether there was some evidence to support defendant's hypotheses, the issue was whether a reasonable jury, upon consideration of all the evidence, could have rejected defendant's theories in defendant's defense and found defendant guilty of murder beyond a reasonable doubt, which the jury could have done in the instant case. Commonwealth v. Hudson, 265 Va. 505, 578 S.E.2d 781, 2003 Va. LEXIS 49 (2003), cert. denied, 540 U.S. 972, 124 S. Ct. 444, 157 L. Ed. 2d 322 (2003).

2. Admissibility.

Proof violating defendant's right against self-incrimination. — Proof in a murder trial of the defendant's identity primarily through the testimony of a state-employed psychiatrist hired to determine competency to stand trial that the defendant had admitted the crime, was in violation of the defendant's constitutional right against self-incrimination. Gibson v. Zahradnick, 581 F.2d 75 (4th Cir.), cert. denied, 439 U.S. 996, 99 S. Ct. 597, 58 L. Ed. 2d 669 (1978).

False information leading to confession not error to admit. — Trial court did not err in denying motion to suppress defendant's confession where he gave an inculpatory statement only after police created and showed him falsified fingerprint and DNA reports implicating him in the crime. Arthur v. Commonwealth, 24 Va. App. 102, 480 S.E.2d 749 (1997).

Previous quarrels and ill feelings between accused and deceased are admissible. Poindexter v. Commonwealth, 74 Va. (33 Gratt.) 766 (1880); Hardy v. Commonwealth, 110 Va. 910, 67 S.E. 522 (1910).

Also, threats by deceased communicated to accused. — Threats by deceased communicated to the prisoner, directly or indirectly, or through others are admissible to show the motive of the killing. Lewis v. Commonwealth, 78 Va. 732 (1884). See Hardy v. Commonwealth, 110 Va. 910, 67 S.E. 522 (1910); Stapleton v. Commonwealth, 123 Va. 825, 96 S.E. 801 (1918).

Antecedent threats of accused. — On a trial for homicide, antecedent threats are competent evidence both on a question of deliberation and premeditation. Lewis v. Commonwealth, 78 Va. 732 (1884); Honesty v. Commonwealth, 81 Va. 283 (1886); Snodgrass v. Commonwealth, 89 Va. 679, 17 S.E. 238 (1893); Nicholas v. Commonwealth, 91 Va. 741, 21 S.E. 364 (1895). See Muscoe v. Commonwealth, 87 Va. 460, 12 S.E. 790 (1891); Hardy v. Commonwealth, 110 Va. 910, 67 S.E. 522 (1910).

Including impersonal threats. — See Snodgrass v. Commonwealth, 89 Va. 679, 17 S.E. 238 (1893); Hardy v. Commonwealth, 110 Va. 910, 67 S.E. 522 (1910).

Evidence of discussion of murder and how to get away with it. — Trial court did not err in allowing prosecution to present evidence that several months prior to the killing, defendant had engaged in a discussion with two classmates centered on how to murder someone and get away with it. Because the circumstances of the shooting generally conformed to the suggestions that arose from the conversation, and because evidence of the discussion went to establish premeditation, the trial court did not abuse its discretion in admitting evidence of that discussion, despite its potential for prejudicial impact. Miller v. Commonwealth, 15 Va. App. 301, 422 S.E.2d 795 (1992), aff'd, 246 Va. 336, 437 S.E.2d 411 (1993).

Evidence of use of stolen weapon. — Trial court did not err in admitting evidence that, eight to nine months prior to the offense, defendant committed an uncharged theft of the weapon used to shoot victim. At issue was whether defendant planned the killing. Use of a stolen weapon in the commission of a killing could make the tracing of the bullets to the perpetrator more difficult. The fact that defendant used a stolen weapon, not whether he stole it, was relevant at trial to the critical question of premeditation. Miller v. Commonwealth, 15 Va. App. 301, 422 S.E.2d 795 (1992), aff'd, 246 Va. 336, 437 S.E.2d 411 (1993).

And the subsequent possession by accused of shells fitting gun used. Litton v. Commonwealth, 101 Va. 833, 44 S.E. 923 (1903).

Attempt to purchase untraceable weapon. — The fact that defendant sought to obtain a deadly weapon that could not be traced to her was relevant to prove that she attempted to obtain the means to inflict death or serious bodily harm to another at a time when she had a reason or motive for wanting to do so. The fact that she was present at the time of victim's death and had given false and conflicting accounts of what occurred tended to enhance the relevance of the evidence. Therefore, trial court did not abuse its discretion by admitting testimony that defendant attempted to purchase an untraceable, concealable handgun within 10 months of victim's murder. Monroe v. Commonwealth, No. 2604-92-2 (Ct. of Appeals May 2, 1995).

Evidence of assault on other members of family. — Where defendant went to deceased's home, talked with deceased at front door, shot and killed him, it was not error to admit evidence that defendant then went into the home and assaulted other members of the family. The actions were continuous and interwoven and necessary to show jury the circumstances surrounding the killing, and tended to show motive and that the killing was willful and deliberate. Williams v. Commonwealth, 208 Va. 724, 160 S.E.2d 781 (1968).

Evidence that defendant killed other members of same family. — In a prosecution for murder of one member of a family, evidence that defendant killed other members of the same family was properly admitted to show motive. Rees v. Commonwealth, 203 Va. 850, 127 S.E.2d 406 (1962), cert. denied, 372 U.S. 964, 83 S. Ct. 1088, 10 L. Ed. 2d 128 (1963).

Evidence of good character and peaceable nature of deceased. — It is true that the Commonwealth may not ordinarily, in its case-in-chief, offer evidence of the good character and peaceable nature of the deceased. However, where the Commonwealth has the burden of proving by circumstantial evidence that the victim was dead as a result of the criminal act of another, the evidence must be such as to foreclose every reasonable hypothesis of innocence, including suicide, natural death, accidental death, justifiable or excusable homicide, or continuing life in absentia. Epperly v. Commonwealth, 224 Va. 214, 294 S.E.2d 882 (1982).

Evidence of infidelity or disharmony in prosecution for murder of spouse. — In a prosecution for the murder of one's spouse the Commonwealth generally may introduce evidence of marital infidelity and may offer relevant evidence to show marital disharmony or to rebut evidence of marital bliss. Brown v. Commonwealth, 3 Va. App. 182, 348 S.E.2d 849 (1986).

Evidence of fight between husband and wife 18 months prior to her murder was properly admitted for the purpose of showing the relations between the parties, their state of feeling and course of conduct towards each other, and as reflecting light upon the motive and intent with which the act was done. Cox v. Commonwealth, No. 2177-93-2 (Ct. of Appeals May 9, 1995).

Evidence of previous unchaste character of accused's wife. — Evidence of the previous unchaste character of the wife, and that accused had knowledge of this reputation, is admissible when accused claimed to have acted in hot blood after a confession of his wife of her illicit relations with deceased. Bryan v. Commonwealth, 131 Va. 709, 109 S.E. 477 (1921).

Proof of truth of confession of unchastity by accused's wife inadmissible. — The trial court did not err in refusing to permit accused to introduce proof of the truth of his wife's confession. Bryan v. Commonwealth, 131 Va. 709, 109 S.E. 477 (1921).

Testimony that victim suffered from battered child syndrome admissible. — Where doctor was qualified as an expert based on both his professional training and professional experiences with physically abused children, the trial court did not abuse its discretion in admitting his testimony as to whether the deceased infant had suffered from a pattern of intentional physical abuse referred to as battered child syndrome. Price v. Commonwealth, 18 Va. App. 760, 446 S.E.2d 642 (1994).

Evidence of defendant's prior attacks on the victim improperly admitted. — In a case where deliberation and premeditation were the only issues, it was reversible error to permit the prosecutor on cross-examination of defendant to question him as to a prior beating and to elicit the information that defendant had been convicted of a felony. This evidence served only to prejudice the accused in the minds of the jury. Williams v. Commonwealth, 203 Va. 837, 127 S.E.2d 423 (1962).

Photographic evidence. — In defendant's trial for first-degree murder, a violation of § 18.2-32, and use of a firearm in the commission of murder, a violation of § 18.2-53.1, the trial court did not abuse its discretion when it admitted into evidence six photographs of defendant's bedroom, which served as an independent silent witness corroborating a witness's testimony that defendant handled a firearm. Although the photographs supported the prosecution's case, the photographs also supported defendant's testimony regarding intoxication. Therefore, the photographs were relevant evidence and were not prejudicial. Szenasy v. Commonwealth, 2010 Va. App. LEXIS 412 (Oct. 26, 2010).

Photographs of the victim were relevant and admissible to show the degree of atrociousness of the crime, or the malice with which it was committed, even though the defense was based only on insanity and did not question that defendant committed the act. Timmons v. Commonwealth, 204 Va. 205, 129 S.E.2d 697 (1963).

Admission of photographs of the victim's body, which accurately represent the true condition of the victim and the handiwork of the killer, and are relevant and material to establish premeditation and malice and to show the degree of atrociousness of the crime, does not constitute an abuse of discretion by the trial court. Brown v. Commonwealth, 212 Va. 515, 184 S.E.2d 786 (1971).

Evidence of decedent's prior character is admissible on self-defense issue. — Where an accused adduces evidence that he acted in self-defense, evidence of specific acts is admissible to show the character of the decedent for turbulence and violence, even if the accused is unaware of such character. Barnes v. Commonwealth, 214 Va. 24, 197 S.E.2d 189 (1973).

Where there is evidence that the victim was intoxicated at the time of the shooting, evidence of his character or reputation for turbulence when in such condition is admissible on the issue of self-defense. Barnes v. Commonwealth, 214 Va. 24, 197 S.E.2d 189 (1973).

The test of admissibility on self-defense is whether the evidence of prior character is so distant in time as to be void of real probative value in showing present character. Barnes v. Commonwealth, 214 Va. 24, 197 S.E.2d 189 (1973).

Incriminating statement that defendant was at scene of crime. — Appellate court's reversal of the trial court's denial of defendant's motion to suppress an incriminating statement made during police questioning was upheld on appeal, because defendant's third reference to an attorney during the police questioning was an unequivocal request for the presence of counsel and police questioning should have ceased, therefore, the trial court erred by refusing to grant defendant's motion to suppress the statement. Commonwealth v. Hilliard, 270 Va. 42, 613 S.E.2d 579, 2005 Va. LEXIS 64 (2005).

Interrogation conducted appropriately. — Defendant's convictions for first-degree murder and the use of a firearm in the commission of a felony were proper because the record in the case, which included defendant's own testimony, indicated that his will was not overborne during questioning and that his capacity for self-determination was not impaired. Defendant was apprised of his Miranda rights by the interrogating officer; he was given food and an opportunity to sleep; and he described himself as calm and comfortable throughout the questioning. Avent v. Commonwealth, 279 Va. 175, 688 S.E.2d 244, 2010 Va. LEXIS 10 (2010).

Hypnotic evidence, whether in the form of the murder defendant testifying in court under hypnosis or through another's revelation of what the murder defendant said while under a hypnotic trance, is not admissible. Greenfield v. Commonwealth, 214 Va. 710, 204 S.E.2d 414 (1974).

Expert testimony. — Trial court did not abuse its discretion in allowing the Commonwealth's forensic expert to opine that the physical facts were inconsistent with defendant's differing versions of how his wife's fatal injury occurred, as these evidentiary facts were useful to the jury in deciding whether the death was accidental, self-inflicted, or a homicide, and whether any of the versions defendant gave to the police were credible; moreover, not only was it important for the Commonwealth's expert witnesses to explain the impact of the physical and forensic evidence to the jury to aid it in evaluating defendant's differing versions to the police of how his wife died, the significance of these evidentiary factors was beyond the scope of knowledge of the average juror. Smallwood v. Commonwealth, — Va. App. —, — S.E.2d —, 2005 Va. App. LEXIS 196 (May 17, 2005).

In a prosecution for second-degree murder under § 18.2-32, the trial court did not err in allowing medical examiner's opinion testimony as to cause of victim's death as record showed that her opinions were supported by her own observations and examinations of victim's body. Observations obtained during autopsy overcame any suggestion that examiner relied in part on hospital records not admitted into evidence. Jones v. Commonwealth, 54 Va. App. 219, 677 S.E.2d 61, 2009 Va. App. LEXIS 238 (2009).

Second expert's testimony properly excluded. — In a prosecution for first-degree murder, because the trial court specifically found that defendant's personality could be understood by men of ordinary intelligence, and testimony from defendant's first expert on this issue sufficiently placed that issue before the jury, it properly excluded testimony from defendant's second expert on the same. Moreover, given defendant's limited proffer, and the second expert's admitted lack of specialized expertise in the area the first expert testified about, no error resulted. Downs v. Commonwealth, — Va. App. —, — S.E.2d —, 2008 Va. App. LEXIS 222 (May 6, 2008).

Admission of evidence held not a federal question. — The admission of evidence to show robbery when the accused is indicted for murder in the common form, and thus raising the offense to murder in the first degree, under this section, is not a federal question. In re Robertson, 156 U.S. 183, 15 S. Ct. 324, 39 L. Ed. 389 (1895).

Evidence properly admitted. — It was not an abuse of discretion to allow the jury to consider the evidence of defendant's attempted escape as evidence of his consciousness of guilt as to the attempted murder charge; defendant clearly was aware, at the time, that the police had information connecting him to that crime and that he would likely be prosecuted for it, although he was not yet charged with that offense when he attempted to escape from jail. Leonard v. Commonwealth, 39 Va. App. 134, 571 S.E.2d 306, 2002 Va. App. LEXIS 657 (2002), cert. denied, 540 U.S. 989, 124 S. Ct. 479, 157 L. Ed. 2d 384 (2003).

During defendant's trial on charges of murder and using a firearm in the commission of a murder, the trial court properly admitted an affidavit defendant's ex-wife submitted when she sought a restraining order and allowed the prosecutor to use that affidavit in an attempt to impeach defendant's expert after the expert testified that defendant suffered from a major depressive disorder and post-traumatic stress disorder, that these disorders were present when defendant shot his ex-wife. Araya v. Commonwealth, No. 0044-02-4, 2002 Va. App. LEXIS 754 (Ct. of Appeals Dec. 17, 2002).

Trial court did not err in allowing defendant's former girlfriend to read portions of her affidavit to the jury on the basis of the past recollection recorded hearsay exception as there was no abuse of discretion in the trial court's determination that the vouching foundation requirement to the present recollection recorded doctrine was met. Further, defendant's Sixth Amendment right to confront witnesses was met because defendant had an opportunity to confront the witness and test the recollection of the witness. Abney v. Commonwealth, 51 Va. App. 337, 657 S.E.2d 796, 2008 Va. App. LEXIS 103 (2008).

Where defendant was convicted of second-degree murder, items seized at defendant's residence pursuant to a search warrant were properly admitted because: (1) the totality of the circumstances could be considered when deciding the question of good faith; and (2) the Leon good-faith exception to the exclusionary rule applied since the warrant stated that the residence was located on the same street as the shooting and the criminal complaint listed defendant's address, which was the same address as the residence. Adams v. Commonwealth, 275 Va. 260, 657 S.E.2d 87, 2008 Va. LEXIS 40 (2008).

Defendant's convictions for murder in violation of § 18.2-32, use of a firearm in the commission of a felony in violation of § 18.2-53.1, and grand larceny in violation of § 18.2-95 were appropriate because the trial court did not err in admitting evidence of prior crimes to establish defendant's identity since he disputed his identity as the perpetrator of the instant offenses. Additionally, given the substantial evidence of prior bad acts, evidence of a damaged fence did not substantially influence the jury; its admission was therefore harmless. McMillian v. Commonwealth, 2011 Va. App. LEXIS 74 (Mar. 1, 2011).

In a murder prosecution, because defendant did not possess the firearm that police later recovered near the area where he was seized, nor was he seen discarding it, the trial court did not err in denying his motion to suppress the firearm. Osorio v. Commonwealth, 2010 Va. App. LEXIS 508 (Oct. 28, 2010).

Evidence inadmissible. — In a murder prosecution in which defendant claimed self-defense, evidence that the victim was seen panhandling was properly excluded because panhandling was not an act of violence. Osorio v. Commonwealth, 2010 Va. App. LEXIS 508 (Oct. 28, 2010).

Harmless error in admission of evidence. — Any error in the admission at trial of an autopsy report prepared by a then deceased medical examiner and a medical examiner's testimony based on the report was harmless beyond a reasonable doubt because any error did not affect the verdict. Similarly, any error in admitting DNA evidence was harmless beyond a reasonable doubt as it did not affect the verdict. Abney v. Commonwealth, 51 Va. App. 337, 657 S.E.2d 796, 2008 Va. App. LEXIS 103 (2008).

Admission of hearsay held harmless. — Based on the overwhelming evidence of defendant's guilt, including testimony from an expert, a police detective, and defendant himself, the latter of which demonstrated a motive and intent to kill, the trial court's admission of alleged hearsay testimony under the "state of mind" exception to the hearsay rule was harmless error. West v. Commonwealth, 2008 Va. App. LEXIS 193 (Apr. 22, 2008).

Alleged error harmless given proof of specific intent to kill. — When defendant claimed that he was guilty only of second-degree murder, not first-degree murder, any violation of § 8.01-381 by not allowing the jury to replay defendant's videotaped confession while deliberating was harmless error under

§ 8.01-678. The facts that defendant entered his wife's room and retrieved a loaded gun from a closet, fired twice at her at point-blank range, buried her in a makeshift grave, lied about her whereabouts, and admitted that he killed her because he did not want to take any more verbal harassment from her were irrefutable proof of his specific intent to kill; replaying the videotape would have added little to the deliberative process, given the Commonwealth's stipulation of its narrative content, the jury's previous viewing of it, the jury's in-court review of an agreed transcript, and the nearly identical evidence presented from an investigator. Kirby v. Commonwealth, 50 Va. App. 691, 653 S.E.2d 600, 2007 Va. App. LEXIS 442 (2007).

3. Weight and Sufficiency.

The corpus delicti may be established by circumstantial as well as direct evidence, and it takes only slight evidence to establish the corpus delicti where the commission of the crime has been fully confessed by the accused. Lucas v. Commonwealth, 201 Va. 599, 112 S.E.2d 915 (1960).

Circumstantial evidence standard. — The malicious infliction of injury can be shown through circumstantial evidence, but the Commonwealth is required to exclude hypotheses of innocence that flow from the evidence. Maddox v. Commonwealth, No. 1129-99-4, 2000 Va. App. LEXIS 575 (Ct. of Appeals Aug. 1, 2000).

Evidence sufficient to prove cause of death. — Where medical testimony was to the effect that the victim died one month after being shot by defendant as a result of peritonitis caused by the bullet wounds, such testimony was sufficient to carry the question of causation to the jury. Jones v. Commonwealth, 202 Va. 236, 117 S.E.2d 67 (1960).

Consideration of sufficiency confined to evidence bearing upon the sole defense. — Where the plea of self-defense was the sole defense relied on by the accused to justify the shooting on the trial of a prosecution for homicide, a consideration of the sufficiency of the evidence to support the verdict and judgment must be confined to a consideration of the evidence as bearing upon that defense. Pendleton v. Commonwealth, 131 Va. 676, 109 S.E. 201 (1921).

Evidence sufficient to warrant jury finding deceased shot while fleeing. — See Pendleton v. Commonwealth, 131 Va. 676, 109 S.E. 201 (1921).

Criminal agency of defendant sufficiently proved. — Where evidence showed that during the course of an altercation defendant struck deceased on the head with a deadly weapon (a pair of wire cutters) and that the sole cause of death was a brain hemorrhage resulting from a fracture of the skull, these facts sufficiently proved the criminal agency of defendant. Henry v. Commonwealth, 195 Va. 281, 77 S.E.2d 863 (1953).

Evidence sufficient to prove malice. — In the instant case, accused, upon the confession of his wife of illicit relations with deceased, immediately got his pistol, walked to deceased's office about one hundred and twenty-five yards, stopping at a drug store for an instant to inquire about deceased, and at once opened fire upon deceased. It was held that even if the evidence had disclosed no circumstance to discredit accused's claim that he acted solely under the propulsion of hot blood and frenzy, engendered by his wife's confession, it is not at all certain that the trial court would not have improperly invaded the province of the jury if it had set aside the verdict of guilty of murder in the second degree on the ground that the evidence was insufficient to show that the killing was malicious. Bryan v. Commonwealth, 131 Va. 709, 109 S.E. 477 (1921); Burgess v. Commonwealth, 4 Va. (2 Va. Cas.) 483 (1825). See Bristow v. Commonwealth, 65 Va. (15 Gratt.) 634 (1859).

Evidence sufficiently showed malice aforethought to support defendant's second-degree murder conviction where: (1) defendant, who had given birth in her bedroom and wished to keep her pregnancy a secret from her mother, left her newborn infant son outside near some trash cans wrapped in some sweat pants before going herself to the hospital; and (2) the medical evidence showed that the infant's later death despite medical attention was the result of blunt force head injuries and abandonment. Smith v. Commonwealth, No. 2284-01-1, 2002 Va. App. LEXIS 668 (Ct. of Appeals Nov. 5, 2002).

Defendant's convictions for first-degree murder and the use of a firearm in the commission of a felony were proper because he admitted to purposefully using a sawed-off shotgun both to shoot and bludgeon the victim; therefore, there was sufficient evidence from which the jury could have inferred malice, and the charges of first- and second-degree murder were properly before the jury. Accordingly, the trial court did not err when it denied defendant's motion to strike those charges; for the same reasons, the trial court did not err when it failed to strike the charge of use of a firearm in the commission of a felony. Avent v. Commonwealth, 279 Va. 175, 688 S.E.2d 244, 2010 Va. LEXIS 10 (2010).

Evidence insufficient to prove malice. — The evidence was insufficient, as a matter of law, to support a finding that the defendant killed the victim maliciously where, although the defendant admitted striking the victim in the face after their truck became stuck in a flood and began to fill with water, the blow itself did not cause the death of the victim and there was no evidence that it caused her to drown. Maddox v. Commonwealth, No. 1129-99-4, 2000 Va. App. LEXIS 575 (Ct. of Appeals Aug. 1, 2000).

Evidence sufficient to show intent. — Evidence that defendant intended to kill the victim held sufficient where the defendant, who was a stranger to the victim, shouted a racial epithet at the victim, got out of the car with a loaded gun and chased the victim, made no demand of the victim to turn over personal property nor call for him to halt, and where the defendant fired from twenty-five feet behind the victim, who was about to enter the safety of his apartment building. King v. Commonwealth, No. 2834-98-2, 2000 Va. App. LEXIS 555 (Ct. of Appeals July 25, 2000).

Evidence was sufficient to support defendant's attempted murder and use of a firearm in the commission of attempted murder charges where defendant's intent to kill the victim was shown by defendant's actions in climbing on the top of the victim's truck, and repeatedly firing his weapon toward the victim, who was on the ground trying to shield himself with the truck. Cook v. Commonwealth, No. 1968-02-2, 2003 Va. App. LEXIS 375 (Ct. of Appeals July 1, 2003), aff'd, 268 Va. 111, 597 S.E.2d 84 (2004).

Evidence was sufficient to prove attempted murder and use of a firearm while attempting to commit murder, violations of §§ 18.2-26, 18.2-32, and 18.2-154, where defendant pointed a gun at the victim's car, firing four or five times. Thus, defendant must have intended the immediate, direct, and necessary consequences of his voluntary act. Stullenberg v. Commonwealth, 2010 Va. App. LEXIS 179 (May 4, 2010).

Evidence insufficient to show intent required for attempted murder. — Evidence that defendant turned the car into traffic in order to flee while the officer was standing toward the rear of the vehicle and slightly behind the driver's side door was insufficient to show that defendant possessed the requisite specific intent to kill the officer; there was no evidence that defendant aimed the vehicle directly at the officer or otherwise had any intent to inflict bodily harm on the officer, much less that defendant had formed the intent to murder the officer. The facts better supported the conclusion that defendant was attempting to escape. Baldwin v. Commonwealth, 274 Va. 276, 645 S.E.2d 433, 2007 Va. LEXIS 76 (2007).

Evidence sufficient to prove attempted murder. — Trial court's finding that defendant was guilty of the attempted murder of his wife in violation of §§ 18.2-32 and 18.2-26 and use of a firearm in the commission of that offense was not plainly wrong or without evidence to support it because defendant shoved, punched, and choked his wife in the presence of their three minor children and his father and obtained a shotgun and went to the front door of the house looking for his wife; the trial court found that the evidence proved that defendant was aiming the shotgun generally around with his finger on the trigger. Herring v. Commonwealth, 2013 Va. App. LEXIS 123 (Apr. 16, 2013).

Evidence warranted a verdict of murder in the first degree. See Bennett v. Commonwealth, 35 Va. (8 Leigh) 745 (1837); Howell v. Commonwealth, 67 Va. (26 Gratt.) 995 (1875); Mitchell v. Commonwealth, 74 Va. (33 Gratt.) 845 (1880); Wright v. Commonwealth, 74 Va. (33 Gratt.) 880 (1880); Wright v. Commonwealth, 75 Va. 914 (1882); Harrison v. Commonwealth, 79 Va. 374 (1884); Barbour v. Commonwealth, 80 Va. 287 (1885); Thompson v. Commonwealth, 193 Va. 704, 70 S.E.2d 284 (1952); Bailey v. Commonwealth, 193 Va. 814, 71 S.E.2d 368, cert. denied, 344 U.S. 886, 73 S. Ct. 186, 97 L. Ed. 686 (1952); Fuller v. Commonwealth, 201 Va. 724, 113 S.E.2d 667 (1960); Williams v. Commonwealth, 214 Va. 338, 200 S.E.2d 579 (1973); Hairston v. Commonwealth, 217 Va. 429, 230 S.E.2d 626 (1976); O'Brien v. Commonwealth, 4 Va. App. 261, 356 S.E.2d 449 (1987); Cantrell v. Commonwealth, 7 Va. App. 269, 373 S.E.2d 328 (1988); Etheridge v. Commonwealth, No. 1487-97-1 (Ct. of Appeals June 9, 1998); Dickens v. Radford-Willis S. Ry., 121 Va. 353, 93 S.E. 625 (1917); Simon v. Commonwealth, No. 0294-03-3, 2003 Va. App. LEXIS 689 (Ct. of Appeals Dec. 23, 2003).

Defendant's conviction of first-degree murder in violation of § 18.2-32 was affirmed, because the trial court did not allow the Commonwealth to impeach its own witness as prohibited by § 8.01-403, but rather properly allowed the Commonwealth to refresh the memory of the witness after the witness stated that she was unable to recall certain statements she had made to police investigators, and defendant failed to include either the tape played to refresh the witness's memory or the contents of the tape in the record on appeal as required by Va. Sup. Ct. R. 5A:25, so the appellate court had no basis for determining whether the trial court committed error in permitting the tape to be played in the presence of the jury. Brockenbrough v. Commonwealth, No. 3023-01-2, 2003 Va. App. LEXIS 243 (Ct. of Appeals Apr. 22, 2003).

The evidence is sufficient to support the conviction for first-degree murder. The jury reasonably could have inferred, from the unbroken chain of necessary circumstances, established to its satisfaction, that defendant had a motive to kill the victim; that he was placed within several hundred yards of the victim shortly before and shortly after the time of the crime; that he had the means to commit the crime, in that he owned a camper and had access to a shotgun; that his conduct before and after the crime was consistent with guilt and inconsistent with innocence; and that all of these factors concur in pointing him out as the perpetrator of the crime. Inge v. Commonwealth, 217 Va. 360, 228 S.E.2d 563 (1976), cert. denied, 474 U.S. 833, 106 S. Ct. 104, 88 L. Ed. 2d 85 (1985).

Any error in admitting defendant's confession was harmless beyond a reasonable doubt, where Commonwealth's other evidence overwhelmingly proved that he committed a willful, deliberate and premeditated act, and his wife's fresh defensive injuries belied his theory that her death was an accident. Xayapheth v. Commonwealth, No. 0524-99-3 (Ct. of Appeals Mar. 14, 2000).

Court confirmed convictions for first-degree murder and use of a firearm in the commission of the murder where blood spatter analysis was proper expert testimony for which a sufficient evidentiary foundation was established. Smith v. Commonwealth, 265 Va. 250, 576 S.E.2d 465, 2003 Va. LEXIS 36 (2003).

Evidence was sufficient to support defendant's conviction of first-degree murder as a principal in the second degree where: (1) defendant was a lookout for his accomplice, assisted in the abduction, and countenanced the murder as a retaliation against a drug dealer, erroneously believed to be related to the victim, (2) he drove his accomplice and the victim to a secluded area and allowed his accomplice to exit the vehicle with the victim, (3) he provided the murder weapon, and (4) he drove the accomplice home from the spot where the victim was later found dead. Hood v. Commonwealth, No. 2469-02-2, 2004 Va. App. LEXIS 82 (Ct. of Appeals Feb. 17, 2004), aff'd, — Va. —, 608 S.E.2d 913 (2005).

Evidence was sufficient to conclude that defendant willfully, deliberately, and with premeditation, killed the victim, who came to collect a drug debt, where defendant brutally beat the victim with a metal pipe, sealed a plastic bag over his head, wrapped him in a carpet, and concealed him in a bedroom, and then admitted to the murder to several witnesses. Hurt v. Commonwealth, — Va. App. —, — S.E.2d —, 2008 Va. App. LEXIS 127 (Mar. 18, 2008).

Because a letter found in defendant's jail cell was properly admitted as relevant to whether he was faking symptoms of insanity, and any error in excluding defendant's statement or in granting the jury instruction was harmless, his first-degree murder conviction, in violation of § 18.2-32 was upheld on appeal. Pahno v. Commonwealth, 2008 Va. App. LEXIS 199 (Apr. 22, 2008).

Fact that defendant apparently found and loaded a pistol, defendant fired all five rounds and still continued pulling the trigger, and defendant initially packed a bag for flight were circumstances that the jury properly considered in concluding that defendant acted with malice and supported defendant's convictions for first-degree murder and the use of a firearm in committing the murder. Cayton v. Commonwealth, — Va. App. —, — S.E.2d —, 2008 Va. App. LEXIS 393 (Aug. 12, 2008).

Defendant's conviction for first-degree murder, in violation of § 18.2-32, was sufficiently supported by evidence showing that the victim rejected defendant's request to have sex, that defendant convinced the victim, who was described as a little bit slow mentally, to let him walk her to her sister's home, that the victim never arrived at her intended destination, that defendant pretended to be a deaf juvenile and used false names in order to gain transportation out of Virginia, that the victim's body was found in a wooded area, and that the victim's clothes contained semen from defendant. Jordan v. Commonwealth, 2008 Va. App. LEXIS 417 (Sept. 9, 2008).

Defendant's convictions for first-degree murder and use of a firearm in the commission of a felony in violation of §§ 18.2-32 and 18.2-53.1 were appropriate because the jury was entitled to disbelieve defendant's assertion that she did not know that her boyfriend had a weapon when they entered the victim's home. Further, there was sufficient evidence of concert of action because defendant and her boyfriend arrived at the home of defendant's father knowing that they were forbidden to be there; they gained entrance through the back door; they were intent upon forcing her father to surrender the welfare checks; and when defendant's father refused, they pursued him up the stairs where he was shot and brutally beaten. Thomas v. Commonwealth, 279 Va. 131, 688 S.E.2d 220, 2010 Va. LEXIS 11, cert. denied, 131 S. Ct. 143, 178 L. Ed. 2d 8, 2010 U.S. LEXIS 6109 (U.S. 2010).

Evidence was sufficient to support defendant's convictions on three counts of first-degree murder where defendant hid out at a friend's house and then fled the state, the murder weapon was found in the friend's backyard, other crimes evidence tended to prove that defendant stole the murder weapon in a robbery, and an accomplice's testimony identifying defendant as the shooter was corroborated by fingerprint evidence. Rayford v. Commonwealth, 2007 Va. App. LEXIS 506 (Aug. 9, 2007).

Evidence was sufficient beyond a reasonable doubt to support defendant's convictions for first-degree murder, a violation of § 18.2-32, and use of a firearm in the commission of murder, a violation of § 18.2-53.1, where the trial court's rejection of defendant's heat of passion argument was not plainly wrong or without evidentiary support because the victim's words alone, no matter how insulting, were not sufficient to constitute heat of passion and defendant's mere intoxication did not suffice to negate premeditation. Szenasy v. Commonwealth, 2010 Va. App. LEXIS 412 (Oct. 26, 2010).

Evidence was sufficient to support defendant's conviction for first-degree murder because the jury could have concluded that defendant acted as a principal in the first degree and that he was the person whose shot struck and killed the victim; the victim was killed by a medium caliber bullet, several witnesses testified that defendant was firing a pistol and firing it in the victim's direction, and defendant admitted that he had access to a 9 mm gun on the night of the shooting. Cooper v. Commonwealth, 2010 Va. App. LEXIS 403 (Oct. 19, 2010).

Evidence was sufficient to support defendant's convictions where, taken in the light most favorable to the Commonwealth, it established that defendant shot and killed the victim; the jury was free to disbelieve defendant's testimony that defendant was not at scene when the victim was shot and to believe the testimony of other witnesses that defendant was there and shot and killed the victim. Mayfield v. Commonwealth, 59 Va. App. 839, 722 S.E.2d 689, 2012 Va. App. LEXIS 88 (2012).

Defendant was properly convicted of first-degree murder, as evidence that he deliberately shot and killed an unarmed man at close range, immediately left the scene, tried to avoid questioning by police, and initially admitted that the victim was unarmed, was sufficient to establish that he acted with premeditation and malice. Osorio v. Commonwealth, 2010 Va. App. LEXIS 508 (Oct. 28, 2010).

Ample evidence supported a finding that defendant committed the offenses of first-degree murder and use of a firearm in the commission of a felony as the testimony of an eyewitness, who was at the scene at the time of the offenses, proved that defendant shot and killed two unarmed men without provocation, in that the eyewitness testified that defendant obtained a rifle, that he had a brief verbal exchange with the first victim before he shot the first victim twice, that defendant then turned the gun toward the second victim and shot him twice in the back, that the eyewitness did not have a gun, and that the eyewitness did not see any weapons in the possession of the two victims. Additionally, the evidence showed that defendant moved the two bodies to a location behind his garage

and fled from police. Daugherty v. Commonwealth, 2012 Va. App. LEXIS 136 (May 1, 2012).

Conviction for first-degree murder, based on robbery as the underlying felony, was supported by sufficient evidence, where the record contained ample evidence demonstrating that defendant took marijuana from a victim's car on the day of the shooting, including testimony that the victim weighed out one ounce of marijuana in the car but police recovered less than two-tenths of an ounce and defendant admitted he took a pill bottle containing marijuana. Person v. Commonwealth, 2012 Va. App. LEXIS 187 (June 5, 2012).

Evidence insufficient to prove first-degree murder. — See Wells v. Commonwealth, 190 Va. 619, 57 S.E.2d 898 (1950).

Defendant's conviction for first-degree murder was reversed because, at its best, the inculpatory evidence showed only that defendant knew that the triggerman killed the victim and that, two months after the killing, defendant and another decided to "roll up" or leave the area. No reasonable interpretation of defendant's statement that defendant knew the triggerman implied that defendant, even if present at the scene of the murder, aided and abetted the triggerman in committing the murder. Jones v. Virginia, — Va. App. —, — S.E.2d —, 2007 Va. App. LEXIS 430 (Nov. 27, 2007).

Evidence warranted a verdict of murder in the second degree. — See Slaughter v. Commonwealth, 38 Va. (11 Leigh) 681 (1841); M'Whirt's Case, 44 Va. (3 Gratt.) 594 (1846); Lewis v. Commonwealth, 81 Va. 416 (1886); Boone v. Commonwealth, 195 Va. 708, 80 S.E.2d 412 (1954).

Evidence was sufficient to sustain defendant's conviction for murdering her newborn baby where: (1) the baby's lungs were filled with air indicating that the baby had been alive; (2) the jury could infer that defendant caused the death, as she denied giving birth, and was the only one who knew that the baby was in her closet; and (3) malice could be inferred from defendant's denial of the birth, testimony of a friend that defendant told her that she wanted to cremate the body, and testimony that defendant faced eviction for having another baby. Corrales v. Commonwealth, No. 2797-01-2, 2002 Va. App. LEXIS 687 (Ct. of Appeals Nov. 19, 2002).

Evidence was sufficient to support defendant's second-degree murder conviction where: (1) the position of the victim's body was inconsistent with defendant's explanation that she had committed suicide; (2) defendant gave inconsistent factual accounts to the EMTs, law-enforcement officers, friends, and the jury; (3) despite defendant's claims that his relationship with the victim had no problems or difficulties, the victim moved out four months earlier, bought a new home, removed defendant as beneficiary on her life insurance policy, and started dating other men; (4) the victim's friends described her as happy and upbeat following her separation from defendant; and (5) defendant testified that immediately prior to the victim's death, he and the victim engaged in an emotional discussion over the victim's admitted relationships with other men that hurt defendant's feelings and emotionally upset him. Sluder v. Commonwealth, No. 2531-02-3, 2003 Va. App. LEXIS 605 (Ct. of Appeals Nov. 25, 2003).

Evidence was sufficient to support defendant's conviction for murder, as it showed that the three-year-old boy who died after being placed in defendant's care was healthy when he was initially placed in defendant's care, that he had severe and extensive injuries when he was taken to a hospital after being in defendant's care, that defendant did not have a plausible explanation for how the boy sustained the injuries, and that the boy's medical care providers opined that the injuries had been caused by blunt force trauma caused by an external force. Covington v. Coleman, No. 2450-02-2, 2003 Va. App. LEXIS 606 (Ct. of Appeals Nov. 25, 2003).

Evidence was sufficient to support defendant's conviction for second-degree murder as a fellow inmate's testimony that defendant had confessed to him was not inherently incredible and was corroborated by other evidence where: (1) the inmate was not directed to extract defendant's confession, and had nothing to gain by fabricating the confession; (2) defendant's stepson observed a clean ashtray, which fit with the inmate's testimony that the weapon was an ashtray and that defendant wiped it clean; (3) defendant was wearing different clothing the next day, which fit with the inmate's testimony that he returned to the house later to clean up; (4) defendant asked the arresting officer whether he was only being arrested for being drunk in public, which implied that he thought that the police might have cause to arrest him for something else; and (5) the victim's autopsy and a bloodstain pattern expert supported a conclusion that the victim died from a blow to the head. Lester v. Commonwealth, No. 1719-03-3, 2004 Va. App. LEXIS 198 (Ct. of Appeals Apr. 27, 2004).

Evidence supported defendant's conviction for second-degree murder as: (1) defendant arrived at a witness's home with blood on her T-shirt and arm; (2) defendant's statement to the witness that the police were looking for her, that she had cut her boyfriend because he called her a bitch, and that she had left him on the floor, bleeding, was not speculative; (3) defendant wielded a deadly weapon to kill the victim and malice could be inferred from the deliberate use of a deadly weapon; and (4) defendant's hypothesis that the victim stabbed himself was properly rejected as the medical examiner had never seen such a self-inflicted wound. Oliver v. Commonwealth, — Va. App. —, — S.E.2d —, 2006 Va. App. LEXIS 297 (July 5, 2006).

Because defendant admitted to being at the victim's residence, because glitter similar to that worn by defendant was found on the victim, because defendant's driver testified that defendant was taken to the victim's residence and left an hour later with the victim's property, and because the victim's property was later discovered in defendant's home and purse, defendant was properly found to have assisted her husband in the victim's death and shared the requisite criminal intent; accordingly, the evidence was sufficient to convict defendant of second-degree murder and robbery under §§ 18.2-32 and 18.2-58. McLean v. Commonwealth, — Va. App. —, — S.E.2d —, 2008 Va. App. LEXIS 449 (Oct. 7, 2008).

Defendant's challenge to the sufficiency of the evidence to support convictions for second-degree murder, use of a firearm in the commission of murder, malicious wounding, and use of a firearm in the commission of malicious wounding lacked merit, because the testimony of defendant's grandfather, identifying defendant as the person who shot the pistol that wounded the grandfather and killed another victim, was not inherently incredible as a matter of law; any challenge based on the grandfather's admission that the grandfather had been drinking and doing drugs before the killing did not render the testimony inherently incredible. Carrington v. Commonwealth, 2009 Va. App. LEXIS 152 (Mar. 31, 2009).

Trial court did not err in denying defendant's motion to strike the charge of murder to voluntary manslaughter because the evidence supported a rational trier of fact's conclusion that defendant committed second-degree murder by maliciously suffocating the victim, who died as a result of the suffocation; defendant's conduct showed that she willfully undertook an act that would likely cause death or great bodily harm without reasonable provocation. Durand v. Commonwealth, 2009 Va. App. LEXIS 419 (Sept. 22, 2009).

Evidence that defendant purchased a handgun five weeks before using it to kill the victim, defendant fired twice at point blank range hitting the victim in the side and the back, and the handgun had to be manually squeezed was sufficient to support defendant's conviction for second-degree murder. Tizon v. Commonwealth, 60 Va. App. 1, 723 S.E.2d 260, 2012 Va. App. LEXIS 105 (2012).

Stress-induced heart attack. — Evidence that 86-year-old victim who was beaten and robbed had a preexisting heart disease which contributed to her death, but that she died of a stress-induced heart attack, and that the robbery of a woman in her condition was sufficient stress to trigger such a heart attack, was more than sufficient to support a finding that the trauma of the robbery caused her death and to support a verdict of felony murder. Spain v. Commonwealth, 7 Va. App. 385, 373 S.E.2d 728 (1988).

Evidence sufficient to find defendant present at scene of crimes. — Defendant's fingerprint, impressed in blood on a moveable object (a flashlight), found at the scene of the crimes was sufficient in light of attendant circumstances to find that the defendant was at the scene at the time the crimes were committed in a prosecution for murder and breaking and entering with intent to commit murder. Turner v. Commonwealth, 218 Va. 141, 235 S.E.2d 357 (1977).

Evidence sufficient to prove victim was alive during abduction. — There was sufficient evidence to support defendant's conviction as a principal in the second degree, § 18.2-18, of abduction and felony murder, in violation of §§ 18.2-48 and 18.2-32, where he and others lured the victim to a co-defendant's home with the purpose of robbing the victim of drugs and money, they restrained the victim while attempting to determine the where-

abouts of the drugs, walked him out to the trunk of his car, drove him away, and fatally shot him; although there was blood in the house, the fact that the victim was "walked" outside to his car and that he "squirmed like a worm" when he was shot supported the finding that he was not killed in the house and accordingly, that defendant participated in abducting defendant while he was still alive. Brooks v. Commonwealth, No. 1629-03-2, 2004 Va. App. LEXIS 284 (Ct. of Appeals June 15, 2004).

Sufficiency of provocation is question of fact. — Whether provocation, shown by credible evidence, is sufficient to engender the furor brevis necessary to rebut the presumption of malice arising from a homicide is a question of fact. McClung v. Commonwealth, 215 Va. 654, 212 S.E.2d 290 (1975).

Sufficiency of evidence showing premeditation is a jury question. — The law presumes malice from the fact of the killing, but it does not presume that the act was willful, deliberate, and premeditated. The sufficiency of the evidence on the one hand to establish the willful, deliberate and premeditated character of the act, or, on the other, to rebut the presumption of malice, is generally a question which lies peculiarly within the province of the jury. Bryan v. Commonwealth, 131 Va. 709, 109 S.E. 477 (1921).

The sufficiency of the evidence on one hand to establish the willful, deliberate and premeditated character of the act, or, on the other, to rebut the presumption of malice, is generally a question which lies peculiarly within the province of the jury. Painter v. Commonwealth, 210 Va. 360, 171 S.E.2d 166 (1969).

Evidence sufficient to support finding of premeditation. — See Martinez v. Commonwealth, 42 Va. App. 9, 590 S.E.2d 57, 2003 Va. App. LEXIS 678 (2003).

Defendant's convictions for first-degree murder and the use of a firearm in the commission of a felony were proper because the record revealed a brutal attack where, after the victim was shot, more than one blow was struck, and defendant attempted to conceal the crime and avoid detection; defendant expressed no remorse for the killing. Accordingly, there was ample evidence to support the jury's finding of premeditated killing in the first degree and the trial court did not err when it denied defendant's motion to set aside the verdict on the grounds that there was insufficient evidence to support a finding of premeditation. Avent v. Commonwealth, 279 Va. 175, 688 S.E.2d 244, 2010 Va. LEXIS 10 (2010).

Jury decides if killing induced by previous grudge or immediate provocation. — Where there has been a previous grudge and also an immediate provocation, it is for the jury to determine whether the shooting was induced by the previous grudge or the immediate provocation, and it is not for an appellate court to reverse their judgment, when the judge who tried the case declines to set aside. Read v. Commonwealth, 63 Va. (22 Gratt.) 924 (1872).

Trial court's determination of issue as a matter of law held proper. — Where defendant was on trial for murder of police officer during an attempted arrest, the evidence justified the trial court in determining as a matter of law that the attempted arrest was legal, although without a warrant. Fuller v. Commonwealth, 201 Va. 724, 113 S.E.2d 667 (1960).

Circumstantial evidence justifying verdict. — The evidence, which is circumstantial only, justifies the verdict of murder in the first degree. Russell v. Commonwealth, 78 Va. 400 (1884). As to sufficiency of circumstantial evidence, see also Dean v. Commonwealth, 73 Va. (32 Gratt.) 912 (1879); Holmes v. Cooper, 872 F. Supp. 298 (W.D. Va. 1995); Bullion v. Gadaleto, 872 F. Supp. 303 (W.D. Va. 1995); Vannoy v. Cooper, 872 F. Supp. 1485 (E.D. Va. 1995).

Circumstantial evidence held sufficient to uphold verdict of first-degree murder. Rees v. Commonwealth, 203 Va. 850, 127 S.E.2d 406 (1962), cert. denied, 372 U.S. 964, 83 S. Ct. 1088, 10 L. Ed. 2d 128 (1963).

Circumstantial evidence was sufficient to prove that the defendant was the person who committed the murder at issue where: (1) the victim's companion identified the defendant as the person she saw approach their car on three occasions attempting to sell cocaine to the victim; (2) in close proximity to her, the defendant and the victim discussed the quantity of cocaine the victim was trying to buy; (3) the defendant had the victim exit the car and led him to an apartment breezeway; (4) within seconds, the companion heard a gunshot and saw the victim run toward the car holding his chest; and (5) when he arrived at the car, he stated that he "shot me."

Fentress v. Commonwealth, No. 2056-97-2 (Ct. of Appeals Sept. 15, 1998).

Whether evidence of decedent's prior character is remote concerns weight, etc. — Once a nexus for relevancy of prior conduct or character of decedent has been established in a defendant's self-defense contentions, the issue of remoteness concerns the weight of the evidence and the credibility of the witnesses, both of which are within the province of the jury. Barnes v. Commonwealth, 214 Va. 24, 197 S.E.2d 189 (1973).

D. Instructions.

The jury should be instructed as to the degrees of homicide and the punishment therefor provided by statute. Bradshaw v. Commonwealth, 174 Va. 391, 4 S.E.2d 752 (1939); Henry v. Commonwealth, 195 Va. 281, 77 S.E.2d 863 (1953).

Instruction on second-degree murder not given unless warranted by evidence. — An instruction on murder in the second degree should not be given unless it was warranted by the evidence before the jury. Wright v. Commonwealth, 213 Va. 352, 192 S.E.2d 748 (1972).

The trial court did not err in refusing the instruction on murder in the second degree where the jury could have properly returned only one of two verdicts: guilty of murder in the first degree, or not guilty. Wright v. Commonwealth, 213 Va. 352, 192 S.E.2d 748 (1972).

The presumption of second-degree murder yields to facts. No instruction should be given unless it is supported by evidence, and such evidence must be more than a scintilla. LeVasseur v. Commonwealth, 225 Va. 564, 304 S.E.2d 644 (1983), cert. denied, 464 U.S. 1063, 104 S. Ct. 744, 79 L. Ed. 2d 202 (1984).

The trial court properly refuses an instruction on second-degree murder where the evidence would support only findings of first-degree murder or not guilty. This is so notwithstanding the presumption that every homicide is second-degree murder. LeVasseur v. Commonwealth, 225 Va. 564, 304 S.E.2d 644 (1983), cert. denied, 464 U.S. 1063, 104 S. Ct. 744, 79 L. Ed. 2d 202 (1984).

The fact that a killer and his victim argue prior to the murder does not, of itself, mandate that a second degree murder instruction be given. Casey v. Commonwealth, No. 1326-94-3 (Ct. of Appeals July 25, 1995).

It is well established that a defendant accused of capital or first degree murder is not entitled to an instruction on second degree murder based on the legal presumption that all homicides are second degree murder. Williams v. Commonwealth, No. 2584-96-1 (Ct. of Appeals Feb. 10, 1998).

Instructions as to malice, deliberation, and premeditation held valid. — See Honesty v. Commonwealth, 81 Va. 283 (1886); Bryan v. Commonwealth, 131 Va. 709, 109 S.E. 477 (1921); Thompson v. Commonwealth, 131 Va. 847, 109 S.E. 447 (1921); Sims v. Commonwealth, 134 Va. 736, 115 S.E. 382 (1922); Adams v. Commonwealth, 163 Va. 1053, 178 S.E. 29 (1935); Hodges v. Commonwealth, 213 Va. 316, 191 S.E.2d 794 (1972).

Instruction in a prosecution for first-degree murder that "to constitute a willful, deliberate and premeditated killing" it is only necessary that the intention to kill come into existence at the time of the killing is not error when thrust of instructions is to define time frame of malicious intent to kill and additional instruction clearly differentiates between malicious intent and premeditation. The preferable practice, however, is to omit the words "and premeditated." Baker v. Commonwealth, 218 Va. 193, 237 S.E.2d 88 (1977).

An instruction to the effect that to constitute a willful, deliberate and premeditated killing, it is not necessary that the intention to kill should exist for any length of time prior to the actual killing; it is only necessary that such intention should have come into existence for the first time at the time of such killing or at any time previously, although misleading, was not so erroneous as to require habeas corpus relief, though the words "and premeditation" should be omitted in the future. Baker v. Muncy, 619 F.2d 327 (4th Cir. 1980).

Instruction as to concert of action. — Because the jury instructions on concert of action fully and fairly covered the principle of law, and because defendant acted with an accomplice pursuant to a scheme that involved robbing the victim with a gun, defendant was accountable for the victim's death; consequently, defendant was properly convicted of first-degree murder and use of

a firearm during the commission of a felony. Baker v. Commonwealth, 2010 Va. App. LEXIS 507 (Mar. 31, 2010).

Instructions properly refused. — See Dejarnette v. Commonwealth, 75 Va. 867 (1881); Smith v. Commonwealth, 192 Va. 186, 64 S.E.2d 761 (1951).

In a prosecution of accused, as a principal in the second degree, for murder in the commission of a robbery, the trial judge committed no error in refusing to grant an instruction that would have told the jury that every unlawful homicide is presumed to be murder in the second degree and that, in order to elevate an unlawful homicide to murder in the first degree, the Commonwealth has the burden of proving the elements of first-degree murder, or in refusing instructions that defined and set forth the permissible punishment for murder in the second degree, since, under the evidence, the jury could have properly returned only one of two verdicts, guilty of first-degree murder or not guilty. Wooden v. Commonwealth, 208 Va. 629, 159 S.E.2d 623 (1968).

Where defendant's only defense at trial was that he was not the killer, defendant was not entitled to an instruction on first degree murder or on the grade of the offense of homicide. Bennett v. Commonwealth, 236 Va. 448, 374 S.E.2d 303 (1988), cert. denied, 490 U.S. 1028, 109 S. Ct. 1765, 104 L. Ed. 2d 200 (1989).

Where evidence fell short of establishing provocation, anger, passion, or any other fact that might serve to convince a jury that defendant acted without premeditation, the trial court did not err in refusing to instruct the jury on second degree murder. Casey v. Commonwealth, No. 1326-94-3 (Ct. of Appeals July 25, 1995).

The trial court did not err in refusing to instruct the jury on self-defense where the defendant asserted that, after he and the victim had begun to argue, she attacked him with a knife, they fought over the knife and, in the struggle, they fell down the stairs and the victim was fatally wounded when she fell on the knife; the defendant never claimed that he had stabbed the victim in self-defense and the only instruction warranted by his account was for an accidental death, which instruction was given by the court. Bowler v. Commonwealth, No. 0404-99-4, 2000 Va. App. LEXIS 207 (Ct. of Appeals Mar. 21, 2000).

Request for a jury instruction on self-defense in defendant's trial for murder, under § 18.2-32, was properly refused where defendant was not engaged in a lawful activity when he shot the gun, killing the victim; defendant had instigated two separate confrontations at the time of the killing. Coleman v. Commonwealth, No. 1654-01-2, 2002 Va. App. LEXIS 734 (Ct. of Appeals Dec. 10, 2002).

Defendant, convicted of multiple charges that included a conviction as a principal in the first degree for second-degree murder, in violation of §§ 18.2-30 and 18.2-32, was not entitled to an instruction on theory of justifiable homicide, as defendant was not totally free from fault, as defendant admitted that approaching defendant's adversary and threatening him; in addition, defendant was not entitled to a voluntary manslaughter instruction, as the evidence did not support defendant's argument that defendant shot in the heat of passion and without reflection, where defendant's statement to the police reflected deliberation and intent, rather than the heat of passion, and there was a reasonable opportunity to cool. Martin v. Commonwealth, No. 0470-02-1, 2003 Va. App. LEXIS 205 (Ct. of Appeals Apr. 8, 2003).

Trial court's denial of defendant's requested jury instruction to support his defense of heat of passion and absence of malice was proper where he was convicted of being a principal to a murder due to his friend having shot at a carload of individuals that defendant and his friend were engaged in a dispute with, which caused the death of an innocent passerby when the bullet went astray; the court indicated that defendant's intent was irrelevant because he did not have the gun, and his friend's actions clearly evidenced no indication of provocation that would have justified giving the instruction. Williams v. Commonwealth, No. 0552-02-1, 2003 Va. App. LEXIS 206 (Ct. of Appeals Apr. 8, 2003).

Where defendant preserved the argument for a voluntary manslaughter instruction and the Commonwealth did not argue at trial that the evidence did not support the instruction, the trial court erred in excluding the instruction; therefore, defendant's conviction for second-degree murder and use of a firearm during the commission of a felony, violations of §§ 18.2-32 and 18.2-53.1, had to be reversed. Fox v. Commonwealth, No. 1717-02-1, 2003 Va. App. LEXIS 362 (Ct. of Appeals June 24, 2003).

Defendant's request for a jury instruction on justifiable self-defense was properly denied as both defendant and the victim were responsible for the altercation that resulted in the shooting. Epps v. Commonwealth, No. 2921-02-3, 2003 Va. App. LEXIS 641 (Ct. of Appeals Dec. 16, 2003).

In trial for second-degree murder, the trial court did not err in refusing to instruct on voluntary manslaughter, because defendant presented no evidence that defendant acted in the heat of passion; no evidence suggested that the victim provoked defendant or that defendant acted in rage or fear, and even if defendant did act in rage or fear initially, the time necessary to get gun and return was sufficient for defendant's passion to cool. Monroe v. Commonwealth, — Va. App. —, — S.E.2d —, 2009 Va. App. LEXIS 111 (Mar. 17, 2009).

Defendant's convictions for first-degree murder and the use of a firearm in the commission of a felony were proper because, under either account of the events given by defendant, either his trial testimony or his statements made to investigators, he forfeited his right to a self-defense jury instruction because he was not without fault in bringing on the difficulty that resulted in the victim's death, and he was not in reasonable fear of death or great bodily harm when he killed the victim. Accordingly, the trial court did not err when it refused defendant's proffered jury instruction on justifiable homicide. Avent v. Commonwealth, 279 Va. 175, 688 S.E.2d 244, 2010 Va. LEXIS 10 (2010).

Trial court did not abuse its discretion by refusing to give defendant's proposed jury instruction defining concert of action because defendant did not meet his burden of showing that the proposed language was a correct statement of the law, applicable to the facts of the case on trial, and expressed in appropriate language; the trial court gave an instruction on concert of action that adequately stated the law and addressed the issues raised in the case related to that legal principle. Cooper v. Commonwealth, 2010 Va. App. LEXIS 403 (Oct. 19, 2010).

Defendant's conviction for first-degree murder was appropriate because any error in refusing to give his requested justifiable self-defense jury instruction was harmless since the trial court instructed the jury on the elements of first-degree murder, second-degree murder, and voluntary manslaughter, as well as excusable self-defense. By convicting defendant of first-degree murder, the jury found that defendant acted with premeditation, and willfully, maliciously, and deliberately killed his father. Lancaster v. Commonwealth, 2011 Va. App. LEXIS 29 (Feb. 1, 2011).

Defendant's convictions for first-degree murder and use of a firearm in the commission of a felony were proper because the jury did not err in refusing to award an instruction on voluntary manslaughter. The jury rejected the instruction on second-degree murder and convicted defendant of first-degree murder; it followed that the jury would never have reached a voluntary manslaughter verdict. Cortez-Hernandez v. Commonwealth, 58 Va. App. 66, 706 S.E.2d 893, 2011 Va. App. LEXIS 114 (2011).

In a murder prosecution in which defendant claimed self-defense, as the evidence showed that he did not arm himself after being threatened or assaulted, but shot the victim during their only confrontation, he was not entitled to a "right to arm" instruction. Osorio v. Commonwealth, 2010 Va. App. LEXIS 508 (Oct. 28, 2010).

Instruction on unsupported hypothesis properly refused. — It is proper for the trial court to refuse defendant's request to instruct the jury on a hypothesis of the case which finds no support in the evidence. Fuller v. Commonwealth, 201 Va. 724, 113 S.E.2d 667 (1960).

Variance not created by instruction. — Jury instruction on transferred intent did not create a fatal variance between the indictment of first-degree murder and the evidence, where the instruction accurately reflected the evidence adduced at trial, that defendant intended to shoot a person other than the victim, and did not broaden the charge defendant faced. Coleman v. Commonwealth, No. 1654-01-2, 2002 Va. App. LEXIS 734 (Ct. of Appeals Dec. 10, 2002).

Failure to give elements of robbery in felony murder instruction. — While failure of court on trial for felony murder to instruct the jury as to the elements of robbery or attempted robbery in giving felony murder instruction was error, it was not so prejudicial as to warrant federal habeas relief. Moore v. Garraghty, 739 F. Supp. 285 (E.D. Va. 1990), aff'd, 932 F.2d 963 (4th Cir. 1991).

Improper felony murder instruction. — Although a felony homicide instruction under § 18.2-33 incorrectly included the of-

fense of attempted robbery, which was an enumerated offense for first-degree felony murder under § 18.2-32, defendant could not show that a miscarriage of justice had occurred in order to invoke the ends of justice exception to Va. Sup. Ct. R. 5A:18 as defendant benefitted from the error in the jury instruction. Chalk v. Commonwealth, — Va. App. —, — S.E.2d —, 2009 Va. App. LEXIS 36 (Feb. 3, 2009).

Instruction as to lapse of cooling time after provocation. — An instruction to the effect that if accused, in heat of passion caused by insult to his wife, and before lapse of time enough for his passion to cool, killed deceased, it was murder in the second degree, but that it was murder in the first degree if such time had elapsed, and then he went with deadly weapon to kill, and did kill him with malice aforethought, was proper. Watson v. Commonwealth, 87 Va. 608, 13 S.E. 22 (1891). See M'Whirt's Case, 44 Va. (3 Gratt.) 594 (1846).

Instruction presenting defendant's theory of accidental killing as defense. — Where the evidence warrants, an accused is entitled to an instruction presenting his theory of accidental killing as a defense. Martin v. Commonwealth, 218 Va. 4, 235 S.E.2d 304 (1977).

Where the undisputed physical evidence renders an accident impossible, the trial court does not err in refusing to instruct on accidental shooting. Epps v. Commonwealth, No. 2921-02-3, 2003 Va. App. LEXIS 641 (Ct. of Appeals Dec. 16, 2003).

Accidental killing instruction denied. — In trial for second-degree murder, the trial court did not err in refusing to instruct on accidental killing, because the evidence did not support defendant's claim that a ricochet bullet hit the victim accidentally and the instructions given fully denied the elements of murder and the meaning of the terms. Monroe v. Commonwealth, — Va. App. —, — S.E.2d —, 2009 Va. App. LEXIS 111 (Mar. 17, 2009).

To justify an instruction on voluntary drunkenness, the evidence must show more than the mere drinking of alcohol. Hatcher v. Commonwealth, 218 Va. 811, 241 S.E.2d 756 (1978).

Instruction which read: "Voluntary intoxication is a defense to first degree murder. If you find that the defendant was so greatly intoxicated by the voluntary use of alcohol that he was incapable of forming the specific intent necessary to deliberate and premeditate, which are elements of the crime of first degree murder, you may not find him guilty of any offense greater than second degree murder," read as a whole, contained a clear, accurate statement of the law, although deletion of the first sentence of the instruction perhaps would have been an improvement. Wright v. Commonwealth, 234 Va. 627, 363 S.E.2d 711 (1988).

Instruction as to burden of proof. — It was error for the trial court to refuse an instruction to the jury that the burden was on the Commonwealth to prove a killing was not accidental and that the jury should acquit the defendant if it entertained a reasonable doubt whether the death was accidental or intentional where the evidence warranted such an instruction. Martin v. Commonwealth, 218 Va. 4, 235 S.E.2d 304 (1977).

The instruction "The Court instructs the jury that every person is presumed to have intended the natural and probable consequences of his voluntary acts" is error, since a reasonable jury could view the presumption either as conclusive or as shifting the burden of persuasion to the defendant. Stokes v. Warden, Powhatan Correctional Center, 226 Va. 111, 306 S.E.2d 882 (1983).

For case involving an analysis of specific jury instructions vis-à-vis the due process standards of Mullaney v. Wilbur, 421 U.S. 684, 95 S. Ct. 1881, 44 L. Ed. 2d 508 (1975), see Hodge v. Commonwealth, 217 Va. 338, 228 S.E.2d 692 (1976); Warlitner v. Commonwealth, 217 Va. 348, 228 S.E.2d 698 (1976), cert. denied, 430 U.S. 957, 97 S. Ct. 1604, 51 L. Ed. 2d 807 (1977).

Requiring defendant to show extenuating circumstances unconstitutional. — An instruction which tells the jury that the delivery of a mortal wound with a deadly weapon and without sufficient provocation throws upon the slayer the necessity of showing extenuating circumstances to overcome the presumption of willful, deliberate and premeditated killing and which directs that the presumption may be overcome by proof of extenuating circumstances sufficient to create a reasonable doubt, is an unconstitutional shifting to the defendant of the burden of persuasion as to an essential element of the crime. Baker v. Muncy, 619 F.2d 327 (4th Cir. 1980).

Proper instruction on self-defense. — An instruction that the law of self-defense is the law of necessity, and necessity relied on to justify the killing must not arise out of the prisoner's own conduct, and that if the prisoner assaulted the deceased, and thereby brought about the necessity of killing him, then the prisoner could not justify the killing by a plead of necessity unless he were without fault in bringing that necessity on himself, was proper. Jackson v. Commonwealth, 98 Va. 845, 36 S.E. 487 (1900).

Instruction on self-defense properly refused when no evidence to support it. — In a trial for homicide it is not error to refuse an instruction on self-defense, where there is no evidence to support it, it not appearing that accused was threatened with any danger. Jones v. Commonwealth, 135 Va. 545, 115 S.E. 572 (1923).

Failure to instruct on self-defense, right to arm, voluntary manslaughter, and heat of passion, constituted reversible error, where the court's exclusion of the victim's prior threats and violence toward defendant, evidence which rebutted the Commonwealth's anticipated argument as to premeditation, and evidence which would have created a jury issue on whether a significant cooling off period was presented, failed to allow the fact finder to conclude that the murder was anything but premeditated. Cary v. Commonwealth, No. 2031-03-1, 2004 Va. App. LEXIS 623 (Ct. of Appeals Dec. 21, 2004), aff'd, — Va. —, 623 S.E.2d 906 (2006).

Instruction on apprehension of danger. — See Byrd v. Commonwealth, 89 Va. 536, 16 S.E. 727 (1893); McCoy v. Commonwealth, 125 Va. 771, 99 S.E. 644 (1919).

Instructions on duty to retreat. — See Stoneham v. Commonwealth, 86 Va. 523, 10 S.E. 238 (1889); McCoy v. Commonwealth, 125 Va. 771, 99 S.E. 644 (1919).

Instruction that lack of motive affords presumption of innocence held valid. — Where there is no evidence of motive, it is prejudicial error to refuse to instruct the jury "that the absence of all evidence of an inducing cause or motive to commit the crime, when the fact is in reasonable doubt as to who committed it, affords a strong presumption of innocence." Vaughan v. Commonwealth, 85 Va. 671, 8 S.E. 584 (1889). See also Sutton v. Commonwealth, 85 Va. 128, 7 S.E. 323 (1888).

Instructions as to reasonable doubt. — See Horton v. Commonwealth, 99 Va. 848, 38 S.E. 184 (1901).

Instructions on unique method of committing crime. — Trial judge erred by referring in jury instructions to the "unique nature of the method of committing the crime," where no evidence of modus operandi was proffered at trial. Fogg v. Commonwealth, No. 3062-00-2, 2002 Va. App. LEXIS 323 (Ct. of Appeals May 28, 2002).

Instructions as to res gestae. — It was proper to instruct the jury that a killing could take place before, during, or after the arson if the killing was so closely related to the arson in time, place, and causal connection as to make it a part of the same criminal enterprise. It was unnecessary to give a more elaborate restatement with regard to res gestae; there was nothing in the brevity or clarity of the instruction to suggest that the jury could find defendant guilty without any showing of causal connection between the killing and the arson or attempted arson. Kennemore v. Commonwealth, 50 Va. App. 703, 653 S.E.2d 606, 2007 Va. App. LEXIS 439 (2007).

Instructions as to lesser offenses. — In murder prosecution where facts were sufficient to establish the killing of the deceased by the defendant and defendant was convicted of involuntary manslaughter the court did not err in instructing the jury as to voluntary manslaughter, involuntary manslaughter, or assault and battery, because there was no evidence which tended to prove the commission of any of these lesser offenses. Blankenship v. Commonwealth, 193 Va. 587, 70 S.E.2d 335 (1952).

Denial of defendant's request for a voluntary manslaughter instruction was proper, because the overwhelming evidence demonstrated that defendant committed a malicious killing; with a sedate, deliberate mind, and formed design, he placed a barbell on his daughter's neck and suffocated her and then took a larger barbell and pummeled his wife's head with it and used it to suffocate her. Kenston v. Commonwealth, No. 2487-11-4, 2013 Va. App. LEXIS 35 (Jan. 29, 2013).

Curative instructions. — In a first degree murder case, the prosecutor's comment, in rebuttal to defense counsel's closing argument, that defendant did not obtain the house or any money after her husband's murder because she was in jail 10 days after his death, was not so prejudicial as to require a mistrial, especially in light of the trial court's cautionary instruction and the prosecutor's corrective statement. Blanton v. Commonwealth, 280 Va. 447, 699 S.E.2d 279, 2010 Va. LEXIS 237 (2010).

Preservation for review. — Where defendant did not preserve for appeal the issues regarding admission and exclusion of testimony and did not show "good cause" or that review was necessary to attain the "ends of justice," the issues could not be raised on direct appeal of defendant's conviction for first-degree murder and for use of a firearm in the commission of the murder. Nguyen v. Commonwealth, No. 0432-02-4, 2003 Va. App. LEXIS 155 (Ct. of Appeals March 25, 2003).

In a first-degree murder prosecution, defendant's proffer of a correct instruction on self-defense was sufficient to preserve for appeal the question of whether the trial court erred in refusing that instruction. It was not necessary for her to expressly articulate each element necessary to her defense, because the trial court heard the evidence and could evaluate its application to the proffered instruction. Commonwealth v. Cary, 271 Va. 87, 623 S.E.2d 906, 2006 Va. LEXIS 22 (2006).

Defendant did not preserve for review the claim that the trial court's response to the jury's question caused the jury instruction to incorrectly state the law because defendant did not make a contemporaneous objection at the time the trial court informed defendant how the trial court would respond to the question. However, in defendant's murder case, the jury instruction did correctly state the law because defendant could be found not guilty of murder under § 18.2-32 yet be convicted of use of a firearm in attempting to commit murder under § 18.2-53.1. Ludwig v. Commonwealth, 52 Va. App. 1, 660 S.E.2d 679, 2008 Va. App. LEXIS 227 (2008).

***Batson* motion correctly denied.** — Defendant's convictions for first-degree murder and the use of a firearm in the commission of a felony were proper because the trial court was not clearly erroneous in denying defendant's *Batson* motion. The Commonwealth offered facially valid race-neutral reasons for the exercise of its strikes and defendant failed to offer any evidence or argument that the proffered rationale behind the strikes challenged were pretextual. Avent v. Commonwealth, 279 Va. 175, 688 S.E.2d 244, 2010 Va. LEXIS 10 (2010).

E. Verdict.

A jury's determination of guilt and punishment in a single trial does not impair the right of an accused to an impartial jury in contravention of the Sixth Amendment to the Constitution of the United States. Bloodgood v. Commonwealth, 212 Va. 253, 183 S.E.2d 737 (1971).

A unitary trial at which the jury determines guilt and punishment in a single trial does not impair the right of the accused to an impartial trial in contravention of the Sixth Amendment to the Constitution of the United States. Brown v. Commonwealth, 212 Va. 515, 184 S.E.2d 786 (1971).

From a constitutional standpoint, it is not impermissible for a state to consider that the compassionate purposes of jury sentencing in capital cases are better served by having the issues of guilt and punishment determined in a single trial than by focusing the jury's attention solely on punishment after the issue of guilt has been determined. Bloodgood v. Commonwealth, 212 Va. 253, 183 S.E.2d 737 (1971).

Defendant entitled to new sentencing hearing. — Circuit court erred by reducing defendant's second degree murder conviction to a sentence of twenty years imprisonment because defendant was entitled to a new sentencing hearing when his original twenty-five year sentence exceeded the maximum range of punishment set forth in § 18.2-32; a sentence imposed in violation of a prescribed statutory range of punishment is void ab initio because the character of the judgment was not such as the circuit court had the power to render, and, thus, a criminal defendant in that situation is entitled to a new sentencing hearing. Rawls v. Commonwealth, 278 Va. 213, 683 S.E.2d 544, 2009 Va. LEXIS 82 (2009).

Double jeopardy was not violated when defendant was convicted of both felony murder and the underlying felony in a single trial, since the purpose of the reference to felonies in the murder statutes is gradation and not prohibition of punishment for the underlying felonies. Spain v. Commonwealth, 7 Va. App. 385, 373 S.E.2d 728 (1988).

Double jeopardy not violated by convictions for aggravated malicious wounding and attempted murder. — Proof of attempted murder does not require proof of an actual injury, and therefore aggravated malicious wounding and attempted murder each contain an element not contained by the other, and neither crime is a lesser-included offense of the other for double jeopardy purposes. Dennis v. Commonwealth, No. 1285-98-1 (Ct. of Appeals Oct. 19, 1999).

Double jeopardy not violated by convictions for aggravated malicious wounding and second-degree murder. — Two offenses required elements of proof that the other did not since the aggravated malicious wounding statute, § 18.2-51.2, prohibited certain methods of violence resulting in severe and permanent injury, and the murder statute, § 18.2-32, punished the taking of life without regard to the method. Aggravated malicious wounding required proof of a specific intent, whereas second-degree murder required no specific intent, and with different elements of proof, aggravated malicious wounding was not a lesser-included offense of second-degree murder, malicious wounding was not a lesser-included offense of attempted murder and the legislature intended multiple punishments; therefore, the offenses, having separate and distinct elements, allowed for prosecution under both statutes, the legislature authorized separate punishments for those acts, and the defendant's convictions for both aggravated malicious wounding and second-degree murder did not violate the Fifth Amendment prohibition against double jeopardy. Bomber v. Commonwealth, 2013 Va. App. LEXIS 75 (Mar. 5, 2013).

Jury verdict finding accused guilty of a lesser degree of homicide will not be disturbed even though the evidence adduced tends to prove murder in the first degree and none other. Blankenship v. Commonwealth, 193 Va. 587, 70 S.E.2d 335 (1952).

On an indictment for murder, a verdict of manslaughter will not be set aside at the instance of the accused because the evidence shows "murder by lying in wait" which the statute declares to be murder of first degree. The statutes of this state allow juries a certain degree of latitude and discretion in applying the law to the facts, and in fixing the degree of guilt of one convicted of crime. Burton v. Commonwealth, 108 Va. 892, 62 S.E. 376 (1908).

Verdict set aside where jury examined photographs not admitted. — The trial court erred in refusing to sustain defendant's motion to set aside the verdicts of guilty of first-degree murder and use of a firearm in the commission of murder made upon the ground that numerous photographs of the crime scene, not admitted in evidence, were examined and considered by the jurors during deliberations, since the information supplied by some of the photographs tended to incriminate the accused and affected the grade of the offense. Brittle v. Commonwealth, 222 Va. 518, 281 S.E.2d 889 (1981).

CIRCUIT COURT OPINIONS

Admissibility of evidence. — Trial court denied defendant's motion in limine to exclude evidence that defendant had an altercation with another person whiled defendant was incarcerated for premeditated murder and use of a firearm while committing a murder, and that altercation led to a charge and conviction for assault and battery; that evidence, plus evidence that defendant made incriminating statements regarding his crimes were relevant and probative, and were not unduly prejudicial. Commonwealth v. Wallace, 70 Va. Cir. 341, 2006 Va. Cir. LEXIS 32 (Portsmouth 2006).

§ 18.2-32.1. Murder of a pregnant woman; penalty.

The willful and deliberate killing of a pregnant woman without premeditation by one who knows that the woman is pregnant and has the intent to cause the involuntary termination of the woman's pregnancy without a live birth shall be punished by a term of imprisonment of not less than ten years nor more than forty years.

History.
1997, c. 709.

Law Review.
For note, "Fetal Homicide: Woman or Fetus as Victim? A Survey of Current State Approaches and Recommendations for Future State Application," see 41 Wm. & Mary L. Rev. 1845 (2000).

§ 18.2-32.2. Killing a fetus; penalty.

A. Any person who unlawfully, willfully, deliberately, maliciously and with premeditation kills the fetus of another is guilty of a Class 2 felony.

B. Any person who unlawfully, willfully, deliberately and maliciously kills the fetus of another is guilty of a felony punishable by confinement in a state correctional facility for not less than five nor more than 40 years.

History.
2004, cc. 1023, 1026.

Law Review.
For 2003/2004 survey of criminal law and procedure, see 39 U. Rich. L. Rev. 133 (2004). For 2003/2004 survey of family and juvenile law, see 39 U. Rich. L. Rev. 241 (2004).

§ 18.2-32.3. Human infant; independent and separate existence.

For the purposes of this article, the fact that the umbilical cord has not been cut or that the placenta remains attached shall not be considered in determining whether a human infant has achieved an independent and separate existence.

History.
2010, cc. 810, 851.

Editor's note.
Acts 2010, cc. 810 and 851, cl. 2, provides: "That the provisions of this act may result in a net increase in periods of imprisonment or commitment. Pursuant to § 30-19.1:4, the estimated amount of the necessary appropriation cannot be determined for periods of imprisonment in state adult correctional facilities; therefore, Chapter 781 of the Acts of Assembly of 2009 requires the Virginia Criminal Sentencing Commission to assign a minimum fiscal impact of $50,000. Pursuant to § 30-19.1:4, the estimated amount of the necessary appropriation is $0 for periods of commitment to the custody of the Department of Juvenile Justice."
Acts 2010, cc. 810 and 851, cl. 3 provides: "That an emergency exists and this act is in force from its passage [April 21, 2010]."

§ 18.2-33. Felony homicide defined; punishment.

The killing of one accidentally, contrary to the intention of the parties, while in the prosecution of some felonious act other than those specified in §§ 18.2-31 and 18.2-32, is murder of the second degree and is punishable by confinement in a state correctional facility for not less than five years nor more than forty years.

History.
1975, cc. 14, 15; 1999, c. 282.

Law Review.
For survey of Virginia criminal law for the year 1974-1975, see 61 Va. L. Rev. 1697 (1975); for the year 1977-1978, see 64 Va. L. Rev. 1407 (1978). For note comparing states' recognition of reduced degrees of felony murder, see 40 Wash. & Lee L. Rev. 1601 (1983).

For an article relating to all published Virginia criminal law decisions between July 1, 1997, and July 1, 1998, see 32 U. Rich. L. Rev. 1091 (1998).

Michie's Jurisprudence.

For related discussion, see 2B M.J. Automobiles, § 122; 9B M.J. Homicide, § 22.

CASE NOTES

Purpose. — The purpose of the doctrine of this section was to deter inherently dangerous felonies by holding the felons responsible for the consequences of the felony, whether intended or not. While the range of felonies which may be a predicate for the felony-murder conviction has changed, the function of the doctrine is still to elevate to murder a homicide resulting from a felony by imputing malice. King v. Commonwealth, 6 Va. App. 351, 368 S.E.2d 704 (1988).

Applicability. — This section applies where the initial felony and the accidental killing are parts of one continuous transaction and are closely related in point of time, place and causal connection. Griffin v. Commonwealth, 33 Va. App. 413, 533 S.E.2d 653, 2000 Va. App. LEXIS 649 (2000).

Under the res gestae rule, which has been adopted in Virginia and represents the prevailing view among other jurisdictions, the felony-murder statute applies where the killing is so closely related to the felony in time, place and causal connection as to make it a part of the same criminal enterprise. Commonwealth v. Montague, 260 Va. 697, 536 S.E.2d 910, 2000 Va. LEXIS 139 (2000).

In the prosecution of some felonious act. — The phrase "in the prosecution" requires proof that the killing resulted from an act which was an integral part of the felony or an act in direct furtherance of or necessitated by the felony; where the evidence fails to support a finding that the killing occurred "in the prosecution of" or "in the furtherance of" the underlying felony, there is no basis to find that the accidental death was part or a result of the criminal enterprise. Griffin v. Commonwealth, 33 Va. App. 413, 533 S.E.2d 653, 2000 Va. App. LEXIS 649 (2000).

Elements of offense. — The required elements of the res gestae rule, i.e., time, place, and causal connection, are stated in the conjunctive and, therefore, all three elements must be established for the felony-murder statute to apply. Commonwealth v. Montague, 260 Va. 697, 536 S.E.2d 910, 2000 Va. LEXIS 139 (2000).

The conduct proscribed by this statute involves the substantial risk to human life common to all other forms of malicious homicide: intent to kill, intent to inflict grievous bodily harm, or extreme recklessness demonstrating total indifference to human life. Cotton v. Commonwealth, 35 Va. App. 511, 546 S.E.2d 241, 2001 Va. App. LEXIS 277 (2001).

Causation. — One of the most significant factors in defining the scope of the felony-murder involves the causation required between the felony and the death. King v. Commonwealth, 6 Va. App. 351, 368 S.E.2d 704 (1988).

Causal connection is not the criterion by which culpability for felony murder is determined; for felony murder to exist, the killer must act with malice, which is imputed to him by his commission of the underlying felony. Barrett v. Commonwealth, 32 Va. App. 693, 530 S.E.2d 437, 2000 Va. App. LEXIS 480 (2000).

Existence of causal connection determines whether felony murder committed. — In determining whether a felony murder has been committed, the critical factor is the existence of a causal connection between the felony and the accidental killing. Davis v. Commonwealth, 12 Va. App. 408, 404 S.E.2d 377 (1991).

This section and § 18.2-32 codify common-law doctrine of felony-murder. The doctrine was developed to elevate to murder a homicide committed during the course of a felony by imputing malice to the killing. King v. Commonwealth, 6 Va. App. 351, 368 S.E.2d 704 (1988).

Imputation of malice. — While § 18.2-32 contemplates a killing with malice, the malice intrinsic in the commission of one of the predicate felonies provides the malice prerequisite to a finding that the homicide was murder. The same imputation of malice is implicit in this section which contemplates an accidental killing; the commission of any felonious act during the prosecution of which a death occurs supplies the malice which raises the incidental homicide to the level of second-degree murder. Heacock v. Common-

wealth, 228 Va. 397, 323 S.E.2d 90 (1984).

The court adopted the Pennsylvania Supreme Court's analysis in Commonwealth v. Redline, 391 Pa. 486, 137 A.2d 472 (1958) that the felony-murder rule provides for imputing malice to an accidental killing; it does not impute the act of killing. Therefore, if the accidental death, in the absence of imputed malice, would not have been a criminal homicide, then the statute does not elevate it to second-degree murder and impute culpability for the death to a co-felon. King v. Commonwealth, 6 Va. App. 351, 368 S.E.2d 704 (1988).

The second degree felony-murder statute in Virginia contemplates a killing with malice. The commission of any felonious act supplies the malice which raises the incidental homicide to the level of second-degree murder. It does not follow, however, that any death of any person which occurs during the period in which a felony is being committed will subject the felon to criminal liability under the felony-murder rule. King v. Commonwealth, 6 Va. App. 351, 368 S.E.2d 704 (1988).

Where a person engages in felonious activity and homicide results, the malice inherent in the original felony provides the malice necessary to a finding that the homicide was murder. Hickman v. Commonwealth, 11 Va. App. 369, 398 S.E.2d 698 (1990), aff'd, 242 Va. 263, 410 S.E.2d 88 (1991).

This section provides that an accidental killing accompanied by some felonious act, other than those specified in §§ 18.2-31 and 18.2-32, will support a second degree murder conviction; in such case, malice is imputed and raises an accidental homicide to the level of second degree murder. Pavlick v. Commonwealth, 25 Va. App. 538, 489 S.E.2d 720 (1997).

Trial court did not err by imputing malice to defendant's drunk driving since: (1) § 18.2-33 encompassed all felonious acts not expressly excluded and included defendant's felonious driving while intoxicated; (2) driving while intoxicated or recklessly was a felony considered to be inherently dangerous and by implication presented a substantial risk to life; and (3) the increased risk of death or serious harm occasioned by the commission of defendant's felony DWI demonstrated his lack of concern for human life and justified imputing malice. Montano v. Commonwealth, 61 Va. App. 610, 739 S.E.2d 241, 2013 Va. App. LEXIS 91 (Mar. 26, 2013).

This section does not create a presumption that shifts the burden of proof to the defendant; the Commonwealth must prove beyond a reasonable doubt a felony that involved substantial risk to life. Cotton v. Commonwealth, 35 Va. App. 511, 546 S.E.2d 241, 2001 Va. App. LEXIS 277 (2001).

Homicide within res gestae of initial felony. — It is clear when the homicide is within the res gestae of the initial felony and emanates therefrom, it is committed in the perpetration of that felony. King v. Commonwealth, 6 Va. App. 351, 368 S.E.2d 704 (1988).

To convict a defendant of felony homicide, there must be a connection between the felony and the death, and the connection must be found within the res gestae doctrine: the death must be related by time, place and causal connection to the commission of the felony. Cotton v. Commonwealth, 35 Va. App. 511, 546 S.E.2d 241, 2001 Va. App. LEXIS 277 (2001).

Felony child abuse as predicate offense. — Felony child abuse requires proof that the assailant is a person responsible for the care of a child, and since that requirement of a special relationship is not an element of murder, felony child abuse is not a lesser-included offense of murder; hence, the doctrine of merger does not preclude use of felony child abuse as the predicate offense required to establish felony homicide. Cotton v. Commonwealth, 35 Va. App. 511, 546 S.E.2d 241, 2001 Va. App. LEXIS 277 (2001).

All criminal participants in the initial felony may be found guilty of the felony-murder so long as the homicide was within the res gestae of the initial felony. Hickman v. Commonwealth, 11 Va. App. 369, 398 S.E.2d 698 (1990), aff'd, 242 Va. 263, 410 S.E.2d 88 (1991).

Felons not absolutely liable for accidental death of another during commission of felony. — To misconstrue the statute to encompass every accidental death occurring during the commission of a felony, regardless of whether it causally relates to or results from the commission of the felony, is to make felons absolutely liable for the accidental death of another even though such death is fortuitous and the product of causes wholly unrelated to the commission of the felony. King v. Commonwealth, 6 Va. App. 351, 368 S.E.2d 704 (1988).

Requirement of section not satisfied by extending common-law fiction of larceny. — The requirement of this section that the accidental killing occur while the defendant is in the prosecution of a felonious act is not satisfied by extending the common-law fiction of larceny as a continuing offense. Doane v. Commonwealth, 218 Va. 500, 237 S.E.2d 797 (1977).

There was neither a showing of causal relationship nor a showing of nexus between a larceny which was complete with the defendant's asportation of a car in Richmond, and the accidental killing of a person in a collision the following day. Doane v. Commonwealth, 218 Va. 500, 237 S.E.2d 797 (1977).

The accidental death of child riding his bicycle who was hit when car driven by defendant jumped a curb while defendant was fleeing from a police traffic checkpoint was not related in time to defendant's larceny of the car approximately 12 hours earlier and defendant was not prosecuting the felonious act of larceny at the time of the accident. Hence, the evidence was insufficient to support defendant's conviction for felony murder. Montague v. Commonwealth, 31 Va. App. 187, 522 S.E.2d 379 (1999), aff'd, 260 Va. 697, 536 S.E.2d 910 (2000).

Where death results from ingestion of a controlled substance. — classified in law as dangerous to human life, the homicide constitutes murder of the second degree within the intendment of this section if that substance had been distributed to the decedent in violation of the felony statutes of the Commonwealth. Heacock v. Commonwealth, 228 Va. 397, 323 S.E.2d 90 (1984).

One who assists another in the illegal possession and consumption of a lethal dose of a controlled substance may be convicted of murder under the felony-murder doctrine. Hickman v. Commonwealth, 11 Va. App. 369, 398 S.E.2d 698 (1990), aff'd, 242 Va. 263, 410 S.E.2d 88 (1991).

Evidence was insufficient to sustain defendant's felony-murder conviction under § 18.2-33 where: (1) the underlying offense was the sale of ecstasy in violation of § 18.2-248; (2) the place element for felony-murder was missing because defendant sold the ecstasy to the victim in a store parking lot, and the drug transaction was completed; (3) the victim ingested the ecstasy over two hours after the drug buy, after she went to dinner, stopped at a gas station for cigarettes, and went to a friend's apartment; and (4) the place element for felony-murder was missing because the underlying felony took place in the store parking lot, and the victim did not ingest the ecstasy until she was at the apartment. Woodard v. Commonwealth, 61 Va. App. 567, 739 S.E.2d 220, 2013 Va. App. LEXIS 96 (Mar. 26, 2013).

Killing during police chase held not felony-murder. — A grand larceny and a homicide were not parts of the same criminal enterprise where the theft of a motor vehicle occurred at least 11 hours before the defendant struck and killed the victim with the vehicle while attempting to evade the police; the accidental killing of the victim was not related in time to the larceny and the larceny and the homicide transpired in different parts of the city. Commonwealth v. Montague, 260 Va. 697, 536 S.E.2d 910, 2000 Va. LEXIS 139 (2000).

Instructions when death occurs while defendant is allegedly attempting to elude police. — Trial court erred by instructing the jury that it could find defendant guilty of violating § 46.2-817 B if it found that defendant "willfully or wantonly" disregarded a police officer's signal to stop, instead of instructing the jury that it had to find defendant "willfully and wantonly" disregarded the signal, and although defendant did not object to the trial court's instruction, the error was not harmless, as it affected defendant's convictions for eluding police and second degree murder. Bazemore v. Commonwealth, No. 0103-02-1, 2003 Va. App. LEXIS 291 (Ct. of Appeals May 13, 2003).

Held not felony-murder. — A death which results not from actions of the felons nor from acts directly calculated to further the felony or necessitated by the felony, but from circumstances coincident to the felony, is not a death for which a felony-murder conviction will obtain. King v. Commonwealth, 6 Va. App. 351, 368 S.E.2d 704 (1988).

Where defendant and co-felon were in the airplane to further the felony of possession of marijuana with the intent to distribute and were flying over the mountains while committing the felony, the time and the place of the death were closely connected with the felony. However, no causal connection existed between the felony of

drug distribution and the killing by a plane crash. Thus, no basis existed to find that the accidental death was part or a result of the criminal enterprise. Had the plane been flying low or recklessly to avoid detection, for example, the crash would have been a consequence or action which was directly intended to further the felony and a different result might have been obtained. King v. Commonwealth, 6 Va. App. 351, 368 S.E.2d 704 (1988).

The evidence was insufficient to support a conviction of a mother under this section where the mother's daughter had drowned her infant brother after the mother had fallen asleep, leaving the children unattended; the daughter was not involved in the underlying felony of the mother's child abuse or neglect, her conduct involved no effort on her part to further that felony, she acted independently and her conduct could not be attributed to the mother. Although the mother's commission of the underlying felony would impute malice to her in the commission of any act in furtherance of that felony, the daughter's conduct did not constitute a killing attributable to the mother, which, clothed with the imputation of malice, constituted felony murder. Barrett v. Commonwealth, 32 Va. App. 693, 530 S.E.2d 437, 2000 Va. App. LEXIS 480 (2000).

Where defendant returned to his apartment after work, saw a gun which he and victim/friend had previously purchased lying on victim's bed, picked up the gun and began dancing to music, and the gun discharged and a bullet hit victim in the chest from a distance of three feet or less, the evidence was insufficient to establish that the accidental killing of victim occurred in furtherance of the charge of possession of a firearm by a convicted felon, and the killing could not be considered within the res gestae of the underlying felony. Griffin v. Commonwealth, 33 Va. App. 413, 533 S.E.2d 653, 2000 Va. App. LEXIS 649 (2000).

Sufficient evidence of causation. — Commonwealth proved an unbroken chain of events leading from appellant's sale of the heroin to victim's death where evidence established that: (1) Appellant sold the heroin to buyer at 9:00 p.m.; (2) Appellant knew buyer was going to resell the heroin to victim and warned her of the strength of the drugs; (3) 30 to 45 minutes later, buyer sold the heroin to victim; (4) Victim remained in her kitchen with the bag of heroin and cotton, which is used for injecting heroin; and (5) Victim fell asleep on her sofa and died. Hillman v. Commonwealth, No. 2194-93-4 (Ct. of Appeals May 16, 1995).

Evidence was sufficient to convict defendant of second-degree felony murder based on the victim's death after consuming methadone purchased from defendant because the causal connection between the victim's ingestion of methadone and his death was not broken by the victim's ingestion of a prescription drug. Carrowiano v. Commonwealth, 2009 Va. App. LEXIS 548 (Dec. 8, 2009).

Double jeopardy. — Because a jury determined that defendant engaged in a felony hit-and-run when she fatally struck the pedestrian and that she was driving while intoxicated and in a manner so gross, wanton, and culpable as to show a reckless disregard for human life in violation of subsection B of § 18.2-36.1 when she struck and killed the pedestrian, while the separate criminal offenses each resulted in the death of a single victim, the convictions and punishments imposed did not violate the constitutional prohibition against double jeopardy. Payne v. Commonwealth, 52 Va. App. 120, 661 S.E.2d 513, 2008 Va. App. LEXIS 265 (2008).

Conviction for both felony murder and aggravated involuntary manslaughter was proper, because subsection C of § 18.2-36.1 supported and proved that the legislature intended multiple punishments and the two convictions required proof of different elements and thus, did not violate the prohibition against double jeopardy. To convict defendant under the felony homicide statute, the Commonwealth had to prove that defendant committed the killing in the commission of a felonious act; however, the Commonwealth was not required to prove any level of intoxication or recklessness, as it was under aggravated involuntary manslaughter statute. Payne v. Commonwealth of Virginia, 277 Va. 531, 674 S.E.2d 835, 2009 Va. LEXIS 49 (2009).

Homicide was felony murder within purview of section. — Where case involved an habitual offender who accidentally killed a person while driving in a reckless manner in order to avoid being caught committing his felonious act of driving after being declared an habitual offender, the act of driving recklessly was directly calculated to further the felonious act of driving after having been declared an habitual offender, and therefore, the homicide caused by defendant's reckless driving was within the res gestae of his felony and emanated from it; the homicide was committed in the perpetration of defendant's felony and was subject to the felony-murder doctrine. Davis v. Commonwealth, 12 Va. App. 408, 404 S.E.2d 377 (1991).

Improper instruction. — Instruction in dispute did not properly admonish the jury that second degree felony-murder must be a part of the res gestae of the predicate felony. Instead, it required only that the Commonwealth prove that defendant "had committed" the underlying felony, distribution of cocaine, at some previous time, perhaps transactionally distinct from the death, and, therefore, erroneously stated the law. Accordingly, the judgment of the trial court was reversed with respect to the murder conviction. Talbert v. Commonwealth, 17 Va. App. 239, 436 S.E.2d 286 (1993).

Jury instruction properly stated that for a firearm conviction, the jury had to find the defendant committed murder and his proffered instruction did not permit inconsistent verdicts; the court did not err refusing the defendant's instruction or motion to set aside. Gaines v. Commonwealth, 39 Va. App. 562, 574 S.E.2d 775, 2003 Va. App. LEXIS 75 (2003).

Although a felony homicide instruction under § 18.2-33 incorrectly included the offense of attempted robbery, which was an enumerated offense for first-degree felony murder under § 18.2-32, defendant could not show that a miscarriage of justice had occurred in order to invoke the ends of justice exception to Va. Sup. Ct. R. 5A:18 as defendant benefitted from the error in the jury instruction. Chalk v. Commonwealth, — Va. App. —, — S.E.2d —, 2009 Va. App. LEXIS 36 (Feb. 3, 2009).

Evidence sufficient. — Evidence that defendant poured the methadone into a cup that the child used to take medicine to test the accuracy of her purchase and left the cup on the counter while she went to discuss it with someone else, giving the victim access to the methadone and an incentive to drink it was sufficient to support defendant's conviction for second-degree felony murder under § 18.2-33. Hylton v. Commonwealth, 60 Va. App. 50, 723 S.E.2d 628, 2012 Va. App. LEXIS 111 (2012).

Elements of res gestae were proved and supported the application of the felony-murder rule under § 18.2-33 to a victim's death after a drunk driving car accident where: (1) the expert testimony made clear that the car accident occurred because defendant was highly intoxicated while he was driving; (2) defendant's vision, motor skills, and reaction time were all adversely affected by his intoxication; (3) the underlying felony driving while intoxicated caused the collision and resulted in an accidental death; and (4) defendant's intoxicated operation of his vehicle was inextricably linked and integral to the victim's death. Montano v. Commonwealth, 61 Va. App. 610, 739 S.E.2d 241, 2013 Va. App. LEXIS 91 (Mar. 26, 2013).

Applied in Ball v. Commonwealth, 221 Va. 754, 273 S.E.2d 790 (1981); Essex v. Commonwealth, 228 Va. 273, 322 S.E.2d 216 (1984); Hickman v. Commonwealth, 242 Va. 263, 410 S.E.2d 88 (1991).

CIRCUIT COURT OPINIONS

Not felony murder. — Felony homicide resulting from felony child neglect indictment under § 18.2-33 was dismissed as the victim died from Sudden Infant Death Syndrome (SIDS), and under § 32.1-285.1, a death caused by SIDS resulted from an unexplained cause; the Commonwealth could not prove that defendant's or her employees' acts or omissions caused the victim's death, even if defendant's or her employees' acts or omissions exposed the victim to SIDS risk factors. Commonwealth v. Futrell, 83 Va. Cir. 389, 2012 Va. Cir. LEXIS 48 (Norfolk Jan. 3, 2012).

§ 18.2-34. Reserved.

§ 18.2-35. How voluntary manslaughter punished.

Voluntary manslaughter is punishable as a Class 5 felony.

History.
Code 1950, § 18.1-24; 1960, c. 358; 1972, cc. 14, 15.

Law Review.
For survey of Virginia criminal law for the year 1974-1975, see 61 Va. L. Rev. 1697 (1975). For comments, "Has the Burger Court Dealt a Death Blow to the Presumption of Malice in Virginia?" see 10 U. Rich. L. Rev. 687 (1976). For comment on admissibility of expert testimony on the battered woman syndrome in Virginia, see 10 G.M.U. L. Rev. 171 (1988).

Michie's Jurisprudence.
For related discussion, see 9B M.J. Homicide, § 135.

CASE NOTES

Malice is element of murder but not manslaughter. — Malice, a requisite element for murder of any kind, is unnecessary in manslaughter cases and is the touchstone by which murder and manslaughter cases are distinguished. Essex v. Commonwealth, 228 Va. 273, 322 S.E.2d 216 (1984).

Manslaughter is the unlawful killing of another, without malice, either express or implied. Commonwealth v. Mitchell, 3 Va. (1 Va. Cas.) 116 (1796); King v. Commonwealth, 4 Va. (2 Va. Cas.) 78 (1817); M'Whirt's Case, 44 Va. (3 Gratt.) 594 (1846); Byrd v. Commonwealth, 89 Va. 536, 16 S.E. 727 (1893); Clark v. Commonwealth, 90 Va. 360, 18 S.E. 440 (1893).

And is distinguished from murder by the absence of malice, either express or implied, which is the essence of murder. Commonwealth v. Mitchell, 3 Va. (1 Va. Cas.) 116 (1796); King v. Commonwealth, 4 Va. (2 Va. Cas.) 78 (1817); M'Whirt's Case, 44 Va. (3 Gratt.) 594 (1846); Briggs v. Commonwealth, 82 Va. 554 (1886). See Read v. Commonwealth, 63 Va. (22 Gratt.) 924 (1872); Moxley v. Commonwealth, 195 Va. 151, 77 S.E.2d 389 (1953).

Such as when death blow struck in heat of combat. — Where defendant and deceased were actually engaged in combat, during the heat of which defendant dealt the blow which caused the death of deceased, such killing is manslaughter only. King v. Commonwealth, 4 Va. (2 Va. Cas.) 78 (1817). See Watson v. Commonwealth, 87 Va. 608, 13 S.E. 22 (1891); Horton v. Commonwealth, 99 Va. 848, 38 S.E. 184 (1901).

There can be a principal in the second degree to the offense of manslaughter. Campbell v. Commonwealth, 130 Va. 741, 107 S.E. 812 (1921). See § 18.2-18.

There was ample evidence from which a jury could have reasonably found that defendant was a principal in the second degree in violation of § 18.2-35 because by the defendant's words, gestures, and actions, viewed in the light most favorable to the Commonwealth, defendant explicitly demonstrated that the defendant shared a friend's criminal intent to kill the victim; immediately prior to the killing, defendant specifically commanded the friend to shoot the victim and did nothing to dissuade the friend. McKinney v. Commonwealth, 2008 Va. App. LEXIS 344 (July 8, 2008).

Voluntary manslaughter defined. — Voluntary manslaughter is the unlawful killing of another without malice actual or implied, upon a sudden heat, on reasonable provocation, or in mutual combat. King v. Commonwealth, 4 Va. (2 Va. Cas.) 78 (1817).

Mutual combat supporting voluntary manslaughter conviction absent where although defendant arguably brought about the difficulty that eventually led to the shootout by taking the victims' cocaine, he attempted several times to prevent the violence that ultimately ensued. The mutual voluntariness necessary for such combat was not present. Smith v. Commonwealth, 17 Va. App. 68, 435 S.E.2d 414 (1993).

Provocation and passion must concur. Read v. Commonwealth, 63 Va. (22 Gratt.) 924 (1872).

And continue till instant of mortal stroke. — The suspension of reason arising from sudden passion must continue from the time provocation is received to the very instant of the mortal stroke given, for if from any circumstances whatever it appears that the party reflected, deliberated, or cooled any time before the fatal stroke was given, or if in legal presumption there was time or opportunity for cooling, the killing will amount to murder. M'Whirt's Case, 44 Va. (3 Gratt.) 594 (1846). See Dock v. Commonwealth, 62 Va. (21 Gratt.) 909 (1872); Byrd v. Commonwealth, 89

Va. 536, 16 S.E. 727 (1893); Campbell v. Commonwealth, 130 Va. 741, 107 S.E. 812 (1921).

Nature of provocation determines if killing is from sudden heat of passion. — The test of whether killing is from the sudden heat of passion is found in the nature and degree of the provocation and the manner in which it is resented. Richardson v. Commonwealth, 128 Va. 691, 104 S.E. 788 (1920). See Read v. Commonwealth, 63 Va. (22 Gratt.) 924 (1872).

And words alone are not sufficient. — Words alone, however insulting or contemptuous, are never a sufficient provocation to have the effect of reducing a homicide to manslaughter, at least where a deadly weapon is used, so tender is the law of human life and so much opposed is it to the use of such a weapon. Read v. Commonwealth, 63 Va. (22 Gratt.) 924 (1872).

Successful assertion of self-defense. — Although defendant may have provoked the initial confrontation with the two victims by taking their cocaine, he attempted to withdraw from the conflict several times, and he shot them only when it became necessary to do so in order to save his life or prevent serious bodily injury to him. The danger was real and immediate, and he had no other course available to him. He literally was looking down the barrel of a loaded gun with another assailant standing nearby armed with a cocked pistol. Therefore, defendant was entitled to an acquittal, as a matter of law, on a finding of excusable homicide in self-defense. Smith v. Commonwealth, 17 Va. App. 68, 435 S.E.2d 414 (1993).

It is no defense that defendant did not intend to kill. — While neither of defendants in a prosecution for murder may have premeditated the death of deceased, yet where they went with a joint unlawful purpose of attacking deceased, and deceased was killed in a pistol duel developing out of such attack, the death of deceased was not an improbable consequence of the fight which defendants clearly contemplated, and which the jury, upon ample testimony, evidently believed they precipitated. This being true, it matters not that neither of the defendants intended to kill deceased, and a verdict of voluntary manslaughter is warranted. Campbell v. Commonwealth, 130 Va. 741, 107 S.E. 812 (1921).

Evidence sufficient for voluntary manslaughter. — Since the jury could have concluded that the defendant lied during the defendant's testimony when the defendant stated that the victim initially attacked the defendant with the knife that the defendant used to stab the victim, and the victim, who either never had a knife, or had lost the knife, was stabbed four times, the evidence was sufficient to convict the defendant of voluntary manslaughter under § 18.2-35. Caison v. Commonwealth, 52 Va. App. 423, 663 S.E.2d 553, 2008 Va. App. LEXIS 361 (2008).

Jury instruction to the effect that the accused had the burden of proving self-defense to the extent of raising in the minds of the jury a reasonable doubt as to whether or not he acted in the lawful exercise of such right was constitutional. Frazier v. Weatherholtz, 572 F.2d 994 (4th Cir.), cert. denied, 439 U.S. 876, 99 S. Ct. 215, 58 L. Ed. 2d 191 (1978).

Trial court properly refused to instruct the jury on justified self-defense and defense of others, because there was no evidence to support such instructions; although defendant and his wife testified that the victim was yelling and screaming cruel obscenities in the face of defendant's wife, such behavior did not constitute an overt act indicative of imminent danger entitling defendant to the proffered defense theories. Garrard v. Commonwealth, 2010 Va. App. LEXIS 376 (Sept. 21, 2010).

Applied in Blythe v. Commonwealth, 222 Va. 722, 284 S.E.2d 796 (1981).

§ 18.2-36. How involuntary manslaughter punished.

Involuntary manslaughter is punishable as a Class 5 felony.

History.
Code 1950, § 18.1-25; 1960, c. 358; 1975, cc. 14, 15; 1982, c. 301.

Law Review.
For comment on 1982 amendments to Virginia's driving while intoxicated laws, see 17 U. Rich. L. Rev. 189 (1982). For comment on admissibility of expert testimony on the battered woman syndrome

in Virginia, see 10 G.M.U. L. Rev. 171 (1988). For survey on evidence in Virginia for 1989, see 23 U. Rich. L. Rev. 647 (1989).

Research references.
Campbell, Fisher, and Mansfield, Defense of Speeding, Reckless Driving & Vehicular Homicide (Matthew Bender).

Michie's Jurisprudence.
For related discussion, see 9B M.J. Homicide, § 136.

CASE NOTES

I. In General.
II. Involuntary Manslaughter in Operation of a Motor Vehicle.

I. IN GENERAL.

Involuntary manslaughter is the killing of one accidentally contrary to the intention of the parties, in the prosecution of some unlawful, but not felonious act; or in the improper performance of a lawful act. Commonwealth v. Jones, 28 Va. (1 Leigh) 598 (1829); Souther v. Commonwealth, 48 Va. (7 Gratt.) 673 (1851). See also M'Whirt's Case, 44 Va. (3 Gratt.) 594 (1846); Byrd v. Commonwealth, 89 Va. 536, 16 S.E. 727 (1893); Fadely v. Commonwealth, 208 Va. 198, 156 S.E.2d 773 (1967); Lewis v. Commonwealth, 211 Va. 684, 179 S.E.2d 506 (1971); Gooden v. Commonwealth, 226 Va. 565, 311 S.E.2d 780 (1984).

Criminal negligence is element of offense. — Criminal negligence is the basis for involuntary manslaughter and has been defined as acting consciously in disregard of another person's rights or acting with reckless indifference to the consequences, with the defendant aware, from his knowledge of existing circumstances and conditions, that his conduct probably would cause injury to another. Gray v. Commonwealth, No. 2017-99-3, 2000 Va. App. LEXIS 548 (Ct. of Appeals July 25, 2000).

Criminal negligence is acting consciously in disregard of another person's rights or acting with reckless indifference to the consequences, with the defendant aware, from his knowledge of existing circumstances and conditions, that his conduct probably would cause injury to another. Craig v. Commonwealth, 34 Va. App. 155, 538 S.E.2d 355, 2000 Va. App. LEXIS 837 (2000).

Knowledge is element of offense. — To be guilty of involuntary manslaughter, a defendant must have had prior knowledge of specific conditions that would likely cause injury to others. Gray v. Commonwealth, No. 2017-99-3, 2000 Va. App. LEXIS 548 (Ct. of Appeals July 25, 2000).

Intentional, willful and wanton violation of safety statutes, resulting in death, will justify conviction of involuntary manslaughter. King v. Commonwealth, 217 Va. 601, 231 S.E.2d 312 (1977).

To convict defendant of involuntary manslaughter the Commonwealth was required to prove that defendant committed acts of commission or omission of a wanton or wilful nature, showing a reckless or indifferent disregard of the rights of others, under circumstances reasonably calculated to produce injury, or which make it not improbable that injury will be occasioned, and the offender knows, or is charged with the knowledge of, the probable result of his acts. Gallimore v. Commonwealth, 246 Va. 441, 436 S.E.2d 421 (1993).

To support an involuntary manslaughter conviction, the Commonwealth must prove a homicide was not improbable under all of the facts existing at the time and that the knowledge of such facts should have had an influence on the conduct of the offender. Craig v. Commonwealth, 34 Va. App. 155, 538 S.E.2d 355, 2000 Va. App. LEXIS 837 (2000).

Evidence that defendant left the child in the van and casually instructed other children to get all the children out of the van and into the house without ensuring that his instructions were obeyed, and that, over a period of more than seven hours, defendant assumed but never ascertained that the child was asleep in the house was sufficient to show defendant's total and utter disregard for her well-being, safety, and life and thus, to support convictions for involuntary manslaughter and felony child neglect. Kelly v. Commonwealth, 42 Va. App. 347, 592 S.E.2d 353, 2004 Va. App. LEXIS 47 (2004).

"Objective awareness" test. — Whether a defendant knows of the dangerous risk she or he causes is measured by an "objective awareness" test — whether the defendant knew or should have known of the risk her or his conduct created. Gallimore v. Commonwealth, 15 Va. App. 288, 422 S.E.2d 613 (1992), aff'd, 246 Va. 441, 436 S.E.2d 421 (1993).

Criminal negligence, as the basis for involuntary manslaughter, is judged under an objective standard and, therefore, may be found to exist where the offender either knew or should have known the probable results of his acts. Craig v. Commonwealth, 34 Va. App. 155, 538 S.E.2d 355, 2000 Va. App. LEXIS 837 (2000).

Construction with other law. — While the statutory requirements of former § 18.2-268 [now see § 18.2-268.1 et seq.] are to be strictly applied, they apply only to DUI prosecutions under § 18.2-266, and not to an involuntary manslaughter prosecution under this section. Taylor v. Commonwealth, No. 1977-94-4 (Ct. of Appeals July 18, 1995).

The "improper" performance of a lawful act, to constitute involuntary manslaughter, must amount to an unlawful commission of such lawful act, not merely a negligent performance. The negligence must be criminal negligence. Gooden v. Commonwealth, 226 Va. 565, 311 S.E.2d 780 (1984).

The accidental killing must be the proximate result of a lawful act performed in a manner so gross, wanton, and culpable as to show a reckless disregard of human life. Gooden v. Commonwealth, 226 Va. 565, 311 S.E.2d 780 (1984).

The improper performance of a lawful act proximately causing an accidental killing is insufficient to support a conviction for involuntary manslaughter unless that improper performance constitutes criminal negligence. King v. Commonwealth, 217 Va. 601, 231 S.E.2d 312 (1977).

Showing necessary where charge predicated on improper performance of lawful act. — When the Commonwealth predicates the charge upon an improper performance of a lawful act, it must show that the performance was so improper as to constitute negligence so gross and culpable as to indicate a callous disregard of human life. But the negligence need not be so gross as to raise the presumption of malice. Beck v. Commonwealth, 216 Va. 1, 216 S.E.2d 8 (1975).

Where intentional violation of statute involves inherently dangerous act which is the proximate cause of the resulting homicide, the killing is involuntary manslaughter. Bailey v. Commonwealth, 5 Va. App. 331, 362 S.E.2d 750 (1987).

Malice is element of murder but not manslaughter. — Malice, a requisite element for murder of any kind, is unnecessary in manslaughter cases and is the touchstone by which murder and manslaughter cases are distinguished. Essex v. Commonwealth, 228 Va. 273, 322 S.E.2d 216 (1984).

Reckless conduct must amount to unlawful conduct in order to sustain a charge of involuntary manslaughter; it is immaterial whether the unlawful act was unlawful in its inception — that is, an inherently unlawful act, such as discharging a deadly weapon into a crowded street — or became unlawful after it was begun, such as lawfully operating a vehicle in a public street but so accelerating its speed that it may cause death or serious bodily harm to persons in that street. Gooden v. Commonwealth, 226 Va. 565, 311 S.E.2d 780 (1984).

Ordinary negligence is insufficient to convict of involuntary manslaughter. — The degree of negligence must be more than ordinary negligence in order for negligent violation of a safety statute to justify conviction of involuntary manslaughter. King v. Commonwealth, 217 Va. 601, 231 S.E.2d 312 (1977).

In the operation of motor vehicles violation of a safety statute amounting to mere negligence proximately causing an accidental death is not sufficient to support a conviction of involuntary manslaughter. King v. Commonwealth, 217 Va. 601, 231 S.E.2d 312 (1977).

Where evidence in a criminal prosecution showed at most only an inadvertent failure by the defendant to turn on her white headlights rather than her amber running or parking lights, this act of omission was no more than ordinary negligence, an insufficient predicate for a conviction of involuntary manslaughter. King v. Commonwealth, 217 Va. 601, 231 S.E.2d 312 (1977).

When the proximate cause of a death is simply ordinary negligence, i.e., the failure to exercise reasonable care, the negligent party cannot be convicted of involuntary manslaughter. To consti-

tute criminal negligence essential to a conviction of involuntary manslaughter, an accused's conduct must be of such reckless, wanton or flagrant nature as to indicate a callous disregard for human life and of the probable consequences of the act. Davis v. Commonwealth, 230 Va. 201, 335 S.E.2d 375 (1985).

A higher degree of negligence in the operation of a motor vehicle is required to establish criminal liability for involuntary manslaughter than to establish liability in a civil action for ordinary or even gross negligence. This higher degree of negligence has come to be known as "criminal negligence." Keech v. Commonwealth, 9 Va. App. 272, 386 S.E.2d 813 (1989).

In determining the degree of negligence sufficient to support a conviction of vehicular involuntary manslaughter, the accused's conscious awareness of the risk of injury created by his conduct is necessarily a significant factor. Obviously, when the driver proceeds in the face of a known risk, the degree of the negligence is increased, and may turn that which would have been ordinary negligence into gross, willful or wanton negligence. Keech v. Commonwealth, 9 Va. App. 272, 386 S.E.2d 813 (1989).

Effect of contributory negligence of victim. — Contributory negligence has no place in a case of involuntary manslaughter. If the criminal negligence of the accused is found to be the cause of the death, he is criminally responsible, whether the decedent's failure to use due care contributed to the injury or not. Only if the conduct of the deceased amounts to an independent, intervening act alone causing the fatal injury can the accused be exonerated from liability for his or her criminal negligence. In such case, the conduct of the accused becomes a remote cause. Hubbard v. Commonwealth, 243 Va. 1, 413 S.E.2d 875 (1992).

Reasonably foreseeable intervening acts do not break the chain of causal connection between the original act of negligence and subsequent injury. For defendant's negligence to have been a remote cause of victim's death, action of person who shot victim must have been an independent, intervening act alone causing the death. Gallimore v. Commonwealth, 15 Va. App. 288, 422 S.E.2d 613 (1992), aff'd, 246 Va. 441, 436 S.E.2d 421 (1993).

It was not necessary that defendant foresaw the specific manner in which injury and death occurred. It was sufficient that she reasonably could have foreseen that risk of death or serious harm might result from her actions. Gallimore v. Commonwealth, 15 Va. App. 288, 422 S.E.2d 613 (1992), aff'd, 246 Va. 441, 436 S.E.2d 421 (1993).

Accidental killing of person at whom loaded gun was pointed. — Where defendant intentionally pointed a loaded gun at the victim who was no more than five to ten feet away and the killing, while accidental, was a foreseeable result of defendant's conduct, his conduct was so gross, wanton and culpable as to show a reckless disregard for human life constituting involuntary manslaughter. Alternatively, his conduct was an unlawful act committed with criminal negligence constituting involuntary manslaughter. Bailey v. Commonwealth, 5 Va. App. 331, 362 S.E.2d 750 (1987).

Violation not a crime of violence under 18 U.S.C.S. § 16(b). — Violation of § 18.2-36 is not a crime of violence under 18 U.S.C.S. § 16(b); although the crime of violating § 18.2-36 intrinsically involves a substantial risk that the defendant's actions will cause physical harm, it does not intrinsically involve a substantial risk that force will be applied "as a means to an end." Bejarano-Urrutia v. Gonzales, 413 F.3d 444, 2005 U.S. App. LEXIS 13318 (4th Cir. 2005).

Removability of alien. — Where the court found that involuntary manslaughter was not a crime of violence, the immigrant's finding of removability under 8 U.S.C.S. § 1227 was erroneous because the immigrant had not been convicted of an aggravated felony. Bejarano-Urrutia v. Gonzales, 413 F.3d 444, 2005 U.S. App. LEXIS 13318 (4th Cir. 2005).

Duty to avoid danger by revealing truth. — Where defendant knew that a dangerous condition had been created by her deceit, and knew or should have known that the situation she created had escalated and was fraught with imminent danger that someone might be killed or seriously injured, yet she took no steps to defuse the danger that she knowingly and purposefully set in motion, and where she knew or should have known that she could avoid the danger by revealing the truth, she had a duty to act to avoid the danger. Gallimore v. Commonwealth, 15 Va. App. 288, 422 S.E.2d 613 (1992), aff'd, 246 Va. 441, 436 S.E.2d 421 (1993).

For case upholding conviction of daughter for involun-

tary manslaughter of mother by starvation and freezing, see Davis v. Commonwealth, 230 Va. 201, 335 S.E.2d 375 (1985).

Hunting accident. — Fact that defendant, alerted by a noise which he supposed to be a squirrel jumping from a tree but which could well have been something else, fired at an unidentified target which he perceived only to be "a flash of movement," supported a finding that he fired blindly and wildly and in utter disregard of the safety of others, and was sufficient to support defendant's conviction of involuntary manslaughter. Cable v. Commonwealth, 12 Va. App. 565, 405 S.E.2d 444 (1991), aff'd. 243 Va. 236, 415 S.E.2d 218 (1992).

Admissibility of perception expert testimony in hunting shooting. — Testimony by sensation and perception expert would have explained to the jury how the camouflage contributed to the possibility of misperception. Some jurors might not appreciate how the victim, being camouflaged and using a turkey call, and defendant, expecting a turkey, could combine to cause defendant reasonably to believe he saw a turkey. The jury might have wondered how defendant could have made such a mistake unless he was grossly, wantonly, and wilfully negligent. The expert testimony could have provided the jury with an explanation that the jury could have found to be a reasonable hypothesis of innocence. Therefore, the testimony would have assisted the jury in resolving an essential issue and should not have been rejected on the grounds that it would not assist the jury or was a matter of common knowledge. Farley v. Commonwealth, 20 Va. App. 495, 458 S.E.2d 310 (1995).

Criminal negligence in training and supervision of dogs. — Evidence supported defendant's involuntary manslaughter conviction under § 18.2-36 as the jury could find that the cumulative effect of defendant's acts, including lack of adequate training and supervision of defendant's dogs culminating in their repeated history of actual harm and threatening behavior to animals and humans, followed by defendant's indifferent attitude to their actions caused a victim's death, and constituted criminal negligence. Large v. Commonwealth, 2007 Va. App. LEXIS 399 (Oct. 30, 2007).

Supplying legal substance in lethal doses constituted involuntary manslaughter. — Evidence that defendant provided a lawful drug to a victim that he packaged in quantities that he knew were potentially lethal, knowing that the victim intended to ingest them in order to "trip," was sufficient evidence of defendant's criminal negligence to support his conviction of involuntary manslaughter. Coyle v. Commonwealth, 50 Va. App. 656, 653 S.E.2d 291, 2007 Va. App. LEXIS 422 (2007).

Defendant was charged with involuntary manslaughter for supplying a legal, but dangerous, drug to a person who died from an overdose. Although the victim's voluntary act of ingesting the drug was a contributing cause of his death, his voluntary act did not interrupt the natural and probable consequence of defendant's criminally negligent act of purposefully distributing the drug for ingestion in large dosages to the victim so that he could experience a "trip." Coyle v. Commonwealth, 50 Va. App. 656, 653 S.E.2d 291, 2007 Va. App. LEXIS 422 (2007).

Evidence sufficient to convict. — Where defendant, knowing that victim was intoxicated, nearly blind, and in an agitated state of mind, orchestrated a scenario whose finale was bound to include harmful consequences to victim, either in the form of his arrest or his injury or death, having aroused victim's wrath and led him to expect a violent confrontation, and then made two anonymous telephone calls to the police in which he falsely reported that victim had threatened to "shoot up" the neighborhood and to shoot anything that moved, defendant could properly be convicted of involuntary manslaughter for victim's death, which occurred when victim opened fire upon the police and the officers returned fire. Bailey v. Commonwealth, 229 Va. 258, 329 S.E.2d 37 (1985).

Evidence that defendant assaulted the victim and left him lying injured on unlit exit ramp and that it was the assault that left the victim lying in the road to be subsequently hit by an oncoming car was sufficient to sustain his conviction for involuntary manslaughter. Banks v. Commonwealth, 41 Va. App. 539, 586 S.E.2d 876, 2003 Va. App. LEXIS 495 (2003).

Evidence supported defendant's involuntary manslaughter conviction under § 18.2-36 as: (1) a victim's daughter identified dogs one and two as two of dogs involved in the fatal attack on the victim; (2) defendant admitted that defendant owned dog one; and (3) five witnesses identified dog two as belonging to defendant. Large v. Commonwealth, 2007 Va. App. LEXIS 399 (Oct. 30, 2007).

In a prosecution for involuntary manslaughter, where experts testified that the victim had elevated levels of a drug in his bodily fluids and tissues, and that he died from the toxicity of that drug, which defendant had supplied him, the jury's finding that the victim died from an overdose of the drug was not plainly wrong or without evidence to support it. Coyle v. Commonwealth, 50 Va. App. 656, 653 S.E.2d 291, 2007 Va. App. LEXIS 422 (2007).

Defendant's conduct in placing cardboard and a thirty-three and one-quarter pound, collapsed dog crate atop a toddler's crib to prevent the toddler from standing up in the crib and failing to visually check on the toddler for about three hours was wanton and willful, supporting defendant's conviction for involuntary manslaughter. Noakes v. Commonwealth, 280 Va. 338, 699 S.E.2d 284, 2010 Va. LEXIS 240 (2010).

Convictions of involuntary manslaughter, § 18.2-36, and felony child neglect, § 18.2-371.1 B were supported by sufficient evidence under circumstances in which defendant, a daycare van driver, left a child in the van for a full day, and the child died of heat exposure; defendant failed to look for the child after unloading the other children from the van, despite having personally strapped the child into his car seat, did not use the van logbook designed to prevent this kind of tragedy, took the child's diaper bag inside the daycare without confirming that the child was also safely inside, failed to use the logbook inside the daycare, and then drove home, completely oblivious to the child sitting behind him. After returning home, defendant did not check to make sure the van was empty, silenced his phone, making it impossible for anyone to reach him when questions later arose concerning the child's delivery, and then slept all day leading to the reasonable inference that lack of sleep compromised his alertness that morning. Whitfield v. Commonwealth, 57 Va. App. 396, 702 S.E.2d 590, 2010 Va. App. LEXIS 502 (2010).

Sentence appropriate within statutory range. — Defendant's involuntary manslaughter sentence was appropriate because it was a Class 5 felony under § 18.2-36, punishable by imprisonment for 1 to 10 years under subdivision (e) of § 18.2-10, and defendant was sentenced to 10 years imprisonment, which fell within the statutory range set by the legislature. Thus, no abuse of discretion occurred with regard to his sentence. Scott v. Commonwealth, 58 Va. App. 35, 707 S.E.2d 17, 2011 Va. App. LEXIS 104 (2011).

II. INVOLUNTARY MANSLAUGHTER IN OPERATION OF A MOTOR VEHICLE.

Involuntary manslaughter in operation of motor vehicle defined. — Involuntary manslaughter arising from the operation of a motor vehicle should be predicated solely upon criminal negligence proximately causing death. Accordingly, involuntary manslaughter in the operation of a motor vehicle is defined as the accidental killing which, although unintended, is the proximate result of negligence so gross, wanton and culpable as to show a reckless disregard of human life. King v. Commonwealth, 217 Va. 601, 231 S.E.2d 312 (1977).

In order for driving an automobile at an excessive speed to constitute the basis for a manslaughter conviction the act must be so flagrant, culpable, and wanton as to show utter disregard of the safety of others under circumstances likely to cause injury. Shrader v. Commonwealth, 2 Va. App. 287, 343 S.E.2d 375 (1986).

In a prosecution for involuntary manslaughter, the manner of operation and speed of the appellant's automobile was material to the issue of whether his conduct was willful or wanton or showed a total disregard of the safety and well-being of others. Shrader v. Commonwealth, 2 Va. App. 287, 343 S.E.2d 375 (1986).

In a prosecution for involuntary manslaughter, evidence which tends to prove the rate of speed at which the automobile was driven, if competent, is relevant. Shrader v. Commonwealth, 2 Va. App. 287, 343 S.E.2d 375 (1986).

Degree of intoxication is a circumstance relevant to a determination of the question whether, in light of all other circumstances, the act of driving an automobile was such an improper performance of a lawful act as to constitute negligence so gross and culpable as to indicate a callous disregard of human life. Beck v. Commonwealth, 216 Va. 1, 216 S.E.2d 8 (1975).

Defendant's negligence not remote cause of double homicide where evidence established beyond reasonable doubt that the defendant's vehicle was proceeding at an exorbitant rate of speed, running out of control, and swerving from one lane to the other up to the very point in time and place that the fatal collision occurred. At best, failure of driver of victims' car to steer to the right would have been only a contributing cause of the collision, not rising to the level of an independent, intervening act which could be classified as alone causing the fatal injuries and thus exonerating the defendant. Hubbard v. Commonwealth, 243 Va. 1, 413 S.E.2d 875 (1992).

Concurring causes of death. — Where, in a prosecution under this section, the negligence of the defendant and another person, in operating their vehicles around a curve at speeds of 80 to 100 miles per hour, occurred contemporaneously and continued in operation up to the very point in time and place that the defendant's vehicle went out of control and resulted in death of a pedestrian, the negligence of the other person was not an intervening but a concurring cause. Delawder v. Commonwealth, 214 Va. 55, 196 S.E.2d 913 (1973).

Reckless driving and involuntary manslaughter are two separate and distinct offenses, although arising out of the same occurrence. The lesser offense is not included within the other. Delawder v. Commonwealth, 214 Va. 55, 196 S.E.2d 913 (1973).

Distinction between reckless driving and involuntary manslaughter. — What distinguishes a speeding violation from the misdemeanor of reckless driving, and the misdemeanor from the felony of involuntary manslaughter, is the likelihood of injury to other users of the highways. And the degree of the hazard posed by a speeding automobile depends upon the circumstances in each case. Mayo v. Commonwealth, 218 Va. 644, 238 S.E.2d 831 (1977).

Evidence that defendant, after drinking enough beer to affect his behavior, knowingly drove an overcrowded, defective vehicle and attempted to negotiate a curve at a speed in excess of the posted speed limit during unfavorable weather conditions was a sufficient basis for the jury to conclude that defendant's negligence was so gross, wanton, and culpable as to show a reckless disregard of human life. Jetton v. Commonwealth, 2 Va. App. 557, 347 S.E.2d 141 (1986).

Prosecution not barred by prior acquittal of driving under influence. — The doctrine of collateral estoppel may not bar the prosecution for involuntary manslaughter of a person previously acquitted of driving under the influence of intoxicants, since the issue of intoxication is not necessarily dispositive of the crime of involuntary manslaughter. Simon v. Commonwealth, 220 Va. 412, 258 S.E.2d 567 (1979).

But evidence of intoxication barred under collateral estoppel. — Although the defendant could be tried for involuntary manslaughter, even though he previously had been acquitted of driving under the influence of intoxicants, based upon failure of the Commonwealth to prove legal intoxication, the Commonwealth should have been barred, under the doctrine of collateral estoppel, from introducing in the manslaughter trial evidence to show that the defendant was intoxicated while operating the motor vehicle. Simon v. Commonwealth, 220 Va. 412, 258 S.E.2d 567 (1979).

Though consumption of alcohol could be shown. — If the Commonwealth elected to try a defendant previously acquitted of driving under the influence for involuntary manslaughter, the Commonwealth would not be estopped from introducing evidence to show that the defendant consumed alcohol shortly before the accident in question, since the quantity of alcohol consumed by an automobile driver, even though not enough to cause legal intoxication, may be sufficient to impair his capacity to perceive the dangers with the clarity, make decisions with the prudence, and operate the vehicle with the skill and caution required by law. If such evidence is introduced in a subsequent trial, the jury should be instructed that such conduct is a circumstance to be considered in considering whether the defendant was guilty of negligence so gross, wanton and culpable as to show a reckless disregard of human life; and in addition, that the defendant was not legally intoxicated within the definition contained in former § 4-2 [now § 4.1-100]. Simon v. Commonwealth, 220 Va. 412, 258 S.E.2d 567 (1979).

But blood tests not admissible to prove consumption of alcohol. — Where the prosecution would be estopped from introducing evidence of intoxication in a prosecution for involuntary manslaughter following acquittal of the defendant in a prosecution for driving under the influence of intoxicants on the basis of the failure of the Commonwealth to prove legal intoxication, the Commonwealth could not introduce into evidence the results of

defendant's blood test, to prove that the defendant had been drinking before the accident in question, even though not estopped from proving that fact, since the prejudicial effect of the evidence would outweigh its probative value. If, however, the defendant presented evidence that he was not drinking before the accident, evidence of the test results would be competent on rebuttal, because its probative value would then outweigh its prejudicial effect. Simon v. Commonwealth, 220 Va. 412, 258 S.E.2d 567 (1979).

Admissibility of blood test. — In an involuntary manslaughter prosecution, the degree of the driver's intoxication or impairment from alcohol ingestion is relevant to a determination of the driver's negligence, whether ordinary, gross, or wanton so as to demonstrate a reckless disregard of human life. For blood test results to be admissible to prove the degree of impairment or intoxication, the evidence must prove the reliability of the procedures used, that is, that the procedures utilized are likely to produce a reliable result. The burden is on the Commonwealth, as the proponent of the evidence, to prove that the procedures used yielded a reliable result. Taylor v. Commonwealth, No. 1977-94-4 (Ct. of Appeals July 18, 1995).

Where nurse testified that, except when drawing blood for DUI prosecutions, the traditional and customary procedure for cleansing and sterilizing the puncture area was with an isopropyl alcohol solution and that before drawing the blood, she dried the area with a sterile gauze pad; while no direct evidence was offered that the procedure could not affect the test results, from nurse's testimony, the fact finder could infer that because the area was dry, no isopropyl alcohol remained to contaminate the area or the blood sample and, therefore, that the test results were accurate and reliable. Accordingly, the Commonwealth met its burden of proving the reliability of the testing procedure. Taylor v. Commonwealth, No. 1977-94-4 (Ct. of Appeals July 18, 1995).

Conviction for involuntary manslaughter in the operation of a motor vehicle upheld. — An involuntary manslaughter conviction was upheld where a pedestrian on a bridge, who could be clearly seen for 400 feet, was killed by a drinking driver operating a car with defective brakes. Lewis v. Commonwealth, 211 Va. 684, 179 S.E.2d 506 (1971).

Evidence that the driver, with an unobstructed view for 1,000 feet, "zigzagged" across the road and collided with another vehicle on the wrong side of the highway was held sufficient to convict him of involuntary manslaughter. Lewis v. Commonwealth, 211 Va. 684, 179 S.E.2d 506 (1971).

Where defendant was travelling at a high rate of speed while following a vehicle so closely that he was unable to stop when the other driver hit his brakes, while his intellectual and motor functions were substantially impaired by alcohol, the record clearly supported his conviction under this section for involuntary manslaughter. Stover v. Commonwealth, 31 Va. App. 225, 522 S.E.2d 397 (1999).

Evidence of defendant's reckless and violent driving, directed toward known location of a pedestrian, supported trial court's finding that defendant's conduct constituted negligence so gross, wanton and culpable as to show a reckless disregard of human life. Hancock v. Commonwealth, No. 0182-99-1 (Ct. of Appeals Jan. 27, 2000).

The evidence was sufficient to support defendant's conviction where the defendant crashed into the rear end of a vehicle that was stopped behind a school bus that was unloading children and the evidence established that the defendant, who was driving a large wrecker truck, had been driving erratically for a number of miles prior to the accident, that the defendant was distracted by repeatedly checking his clipboard while he was driving, that the defendant failed to observe the signs warning of a school bus stop ahead, that the defendant failed to observe the school bus from a reasonable distance and that, when he finally did see the bus, he maintained a 55 mile per hour speed until slamming on the brakes just prior to the collision. Gray v. Commonwealth, No. 2017-99-3, 2000 Va. App. LEXIS 548 (Ct. of Appeals July 25, 2000).

Sufficient evidence supported defendant's convictions of involuntary manslaughter stemming from a drag race where the other driver ran into a tree, killing him and his passenger. Defendant's conduct of racing at speeds over 100 miles per hour during rush hour on a busy road near a residential area after he had been drinking was criminal negligence, and as defendant set the course of events in motion and did nothing to prevent the risk, the other driver's negligence was not an intervening act that alone caused the accident. O'Connell v. Commonwealth, 48 Va. App. 719, 634 S.E.2d 379, 2006 Va. App. LEXIS 415 (2006).

Evidence supported defendant's conviction for involuntary manslaughter in the operation of a motor vehicle as: (1) defendant was on notice that the road conditions ahead required a modification of his speed, but he continued to travel at 75 to 80 miles per hour both before and after he crested a hill, and he failed to slow as he approached the merging traffic that was traveling at 5 to 7 miles per hour; (2) defendant was in a fully-loaded tractor-trailer; (3) his failure to heed the warning signs and to slow down and drive at a safe speed and his unusual maneuver in merging caused him to crush the victim's vehicle; and (4) he showed a disregard for others and a reckless indifference to the consequences, which he knew or should have known would cause injury to another. Kreider v. Commonwealth, — Va. App. —, — S.E.2d —, 2006 Va. App. LEXIS 486 (Oct. 31, 2006).

Where defendant made a wrong turn onto the highway, and traveled the next seven or eight miles, with westbound traffic visible to him at various points, with other motorists traveling both east and west warning him by blowing horns and flashing lights, with reversed traffic signs and several wrong way and one way signs visible to him, prior to hitting an oncoming automobile killing three people, he should have known that he was traveling in the wrong lane, and therefore, should have known of the risk his conduct created; his conduct of continuing to drive against oncoming traffic once armed with this knowledge, which was chargeable to him, was a callous act of indifference to the safety of others and constituted conduct so gross, wanton and culpable as to show a reckless disregard of human life. The degree of his negligence, as determined by the great risk of injury together with the knowledge he had or should have had of that risk, was sufficient to support the convictions of involuntary manslaughter. Keech v. Commonwealth, 9 Va. App. 272, 386 S.E.2d 813 (1989).

Evidence sufficient to convict. — Defendant's conviction of involuntary manslaughter was proper. The trial court did not err in its finding that defendant acted in a criminally negligent manner, with a wanton and culpable disregard of human life, when defendant fired at a target defendant did not fully identify and thought incorrectly to be a turkey. Vance v. Commonwealth, — Va. App. —, — S.E.2d —, 2008 Va. App. LEXIS 508 (Nov. 18, 2008).

Evidence insufficient to convict. — In a prosecution for involuntary manslaughter, where the evidence showed that the defendant drove down the center of a narrow, unlighted, unmarked, rural, secondary road in the early morning hours at a time when he was unlikely to encounter other traffic or pedestrians, and that he was driving at a speed well within the posted speed limit, and there was no evidence of drinking or of recklessness in the operation of his truck, the evidence, at most, showed ordinary negligence and not such gross, wanton, and culpable negligence as to show a reckless disregard of human life necessary to sustain a conviction of involuntary manslaughter. Jenkins v. Commonwealth, 220 Va. 104, 255 S.E.2d 504 (1979).

The defendant's conduct did not rise to the level of willful or wanton negligence, evidencing a reckless disregard for human life, and, therefore, did not support a conviction for involuntary manslaughter where the most that could be said against him was that he failed to maintain a proper lookout. Sullivan, Jr. v. Commonwealth, No. 1038-98-3 (Ct. of Appeals Apr. 6, 1999).

§ 18.2-36.1. Certain conduct punishable as involuntary manslaughter.

A. Any person who, as a result of driving under the influence in violation of clause (ii), (iii), or (iv) of § 18.2-266 or any local ordinance substantially similar thereto unintentionally causes the death of another person, shall be guilty of involuntary manslaughter.

B. If, in addition, the conduct of the defendant was so gross, wanton and culpable as to show a reckless disregard for human life, he shall be guilty of aggravated involuntary manslaughter, a felony

punishable by a term of imprisonment of not less than one nor more than 20 years, one year of which shall be a mandatory minimum term of imprisonment.

C. The provisions of this section shall not preclude prosecution under any other homicide statute. This section shall not preclude any other revocation or suspension required by law. The driver's license of any person convicted under this section shall be revoked pursuant to subsection B of § 46.2-391.

History.
  1989, cc. 554, 574; 1992, c. 862; 1994, cc. 635, 682; 1999, cc. 945, 987; 2000, cc. 956, 982; 2004, c. 461.

Cross references.
  As to admissibility of written results of blood alcohol tests conducted in the regular course of providing emergency medical treatment, see § 19.2-187.02.

Law Review.
  For note, "Fetal Homicide: Woman or Fetus as Victim? A Survey of Current State Approaches and Recommendations for Future State Application," see 41 Wm. & Mary L. Rev. 1845 (2000). For article surveying developments in criminal law and procedure in Virginia from July 2001 to September 2002, see 37 U. Rich. L. Rev. 45 (2002).

Michie's Jurisprudence.
  For related discussion, see 2B M.J. Automobiles, § 118; 2B M.J. Autrefois, Acquit and Convict, § 18.

Research references.
  Campbell, Fisher, and Mansfield, Defense of Speeding, Reckless Driving & Vehicular Homicide (Matthew Bender).

CASE NOTES

Elements of offense under this action. — A conviction under this section requires proof both that the accused violated § 18.2-266 (ii), (iii), or (iv) and that such misconduct caused the death of another, elements not necessary to common-law involuntary manslaughter. Subsection C of this section expressly provides that the provisions of the section shall not preclude prosecution under any other homicide statute. Stover v. Commonwealth, 31 Va. App. 225, 522 S.E.2d 397 (1999), upholding defendant's conviction under this section for voluntary manslaughter.

Under § 18.2-36.1, the Commonwealth cannot rely on the presumption in § 18.2-266 (i) that a defendant with a .08 blood alcohol concentration is driving under the influence to convict that defendant, but instead must prove that he was under the influence as proscribed in § 18.2-266 (ii), (iii), or (iv). Dalo v. Commonwealth, 37 Va. App. 156, 554 S.E.2d 705, 2001 Va. App. LEXIS 637 (2001), aff'd, 264 Va. 431, 570 S.E.2d 840 (2002).

Necessity for causal connection. — The phrase "as a result of driving under the influence ... causes the death" requires proof of a causal connection between the driver's intoxication and the death of another person. Pollard v. Commonwealth, 20 Va. App. 94, 455 S.E.2d 283 (1995).

Because there was evidence from which jury might have found that defendant turned on a green arrow, issue of causal connection between defendant's intoxication and accident was a significant issue that jury had to resolve, and thus trial court erred in refusing to give jury instruction which fully explained requirements of causal connection. Hall v. Commonwealth, No. 1280-98-4 (Ct. of Appeals Sept. 28, 1999).

Intervening causation not shown. — In an aggravated involuntary manslaughter conviction, where the first vehicle struck a backhoe in a construction zone, and where defendant's vehicle, which was closely following the first vehicle, struck the first vehicle, and where the combined force of the two impacts caused the backhoe to strike and kill a worker, who was aiding the backhoe operator, the first driver's negligence and any acts of the backhoe operator and other construction site workers were not independent intervening acts, excusing defendant's negligence. Dupree v. Commonwealth, 2010 Va. App. LEXIS 170 (May 4, 2010).

Sufficient evidence of causation. — In an aggravated involuntary manslaughter conviction, the evidence was sufficient to establish a causal connection between defendant's intoxication and the victim's death because defendant's failure to keep a proper lookout was exacerbated by the extent of her intoxication since an unimpaired driver would have seen the backhoe in the lane of traffic and braked or swerved to avoid it. Nininger v. Commonwealth, 2010 Va. App. LEXIS 174 (May 4, 2010).

Multiple convictions for same act upheld. — The Virginia legislature intended to permit the imposition of multiple punishments for involuntary manslaughter while driving under the influence, under this section, and driving under the influence, under § 18.2-266 (ii), (iii) or (iv) upon convictions obtained in a single trial. Goodman v. Commonwealth, 37 Va. App. 374, 558 S.E.2d 555, 2002 Va. App. LEXIS 45 (2002).

Section 19.2-294 does not bar multiple convictions arising out of the same act if they are prosecuted simultaneously. Thus, where warrants for involuntary manslaughter and driving while under the influence of alcohol were issued at the same time, although the charges were heard at different times in different courts, because the charges were initiated simultaneously, the proceedings were concurrent, not successive, and thus, both convictions were permitted under § 19.2-294. Doss v. Commonwealth, No. 2003-93-3, 1995 Va. App. LEXIS 425 (May 9, 1995).

Defendant, who was convicted of driving under the influence under § 18.2-266 (ii), (iii), or (iv), could also be convicted of involuntary manslaughter under § 18.2-36.1, providing that one who caused a death while driving under the influence was guilty of involuntary manslaughter, without violating double jeopardy. Dalo v. Commonwealth, 37 Va. App. 156, 554 S.E.2d 705, 2001 Va. App. LEXIS 637 (2001), aff'd, 264 Va. 431, 570 S.E.2d 840 (2002).

Conviction for both felony murder and aggravated involuntary manslaughter was proper, because subsection C of § 18.2-36.1 supported and proved that the legislature intended multiple punishments and the two convictions required proof of different elements and thus, did not violate the prohibition against double jeopardy. To convict defendant under the felony homicide statute, the Commonwealth had to prove that defendant committed the killing in the commission of a felonious act; however, the Commonwealth was not required to prove any level of intoxication or recklessness, as it was under aggravated involuntary manslaughter statute. Payne v. Commonwealth of Virginia, 277 Va. 531, 674 S.E.2d 835, 2009 Va. LEXIS 49 (2009).

Double jeopardy. — Because a jury determined that defendant engaged in a felony hit-and-run when she fatally struck the pedestrian and that she was driving while intoxicated and in a manner so gross, wanton, and culpable as to show a reckless disregard for human life in violation of subsection B of § 18.2-36.1 when she struck and killed the pedestrian, while the separate criminal offenses each resulted in the death of a single victim, the convictions and punishments imposed did not violate the constitutional prohibition against double jeopardy. Payne v. Commonwealth, 52 Va. App. 120, 661 S.E.2d 513, 2008 Va. App. LEXIS 265 (2008).

Convictions for aggravated involuntary manslaughter and common-law involuntary manslaughter. — Defendant was entitled to habeas corpus relief for defendant's conviction for common-law involuntary manslaughter as defense counsel provided ineffective assistance of counsel by failing to raise a double jeopardy challenge to defendant's conviction of both common-law involuntary manslaughter and aggravated involuntary manslaughter under § 18.2-36.1 as common-law involuntary manslaughter did not require proof of a fact different from those required for a conviction of aggravated involuntary manslaughter, and defendant received multiple punishments for the same offense; defendant was prejudiced as the additional manslaughter conviction resulted in defendant being convicted of two felonies with two distinct punishments imposed, instead of one felony conviction with one punishment, even though the sentences were imposed concurrently. West v. Dir. of the Dep't of Corr., 273 Va. 56, 639 S.E.2d 190, 2007 Va. LEXIS 17 (2007).

Contributory negligence irrelevant. — The fact that the decedent had a blood alcohol concentration of .13 did not exonerate the defendant from liability, as contributory negligence has no place in a case of involuntary manslaughter; only if the conduct of the decedent amounted to an independent, intervening act alone causing the fatal injury could the accused be exonerated from liability for his criminal negligence. Hall v. Commonwealth, 32 Va. App. 616, 529 S.E.2d 829, 2000 Va. App. LEXIS 466 (2000).

Proof of aggravated involuntary manslaughter. — Such acts of egregious misconduct as driving on the wrong side of the road and driving without headlights after dark combined with prolonged and excessive consumption of alcohol clearly aggregate to gross, wanton, and culpable behavior reflecting a reckless disregard for human life. Cottee v. Commonwealth, 31 Va. App. 398, 524 S.E.2d 132 (2000).

Results of preliminary breath test inadmissible. — By express wording of statute, a prosecution for violation of this section was necessarily a "prosecution under § 18.2-266," and thus subsection E of § 18.2-267 applied to bar results of preliminary breath test in prosecution under this section. Hall v. Commonwealth, No. 1280-98-4 (Ct. of Appeals Sept. 28, 1999).

Proof required in alcohol related vehicular homicide. — In a prosecution for involuntary manslaughter, the Commonwealth must prove an "accidental killing which, although unintended, is the proximate result of negligence so gross wanton, and culpable as to show a reckless disregard for human life." However, in a prosecution under this section as in this case, the Commonwealth is obligated to prove the accused drove "under the influence in violation of subdivision (ii), (iii), or (iv) of § 18.2-266," thus, reversal was required. Castillo v. Commonwealth, 21 Va. App. 482, 465 S.E.2d 146 (1995).

Blood alcohol tests properly admitted. — In a prosecution for aggravated involuntary manslaughter, the trial court did not commit reversible error in allowing into evidence the results of a blood alcohol content test performed on a blood sample taken from a defendant in violation of his Fourth, Fifth, and Fourteenth Amendment rights, as: (1) a test conducted by hospital personnel had been independently performed and the written report thereof was admissible under subsection A of § 19.2-187.02; (2) defendant consented to a second blood test administered by a deputy sheriff under the implied consent law; (3) evidence of defendant's intoxication was overwhelming despite testing over three times the legal limit; and (4) it was unreasonable to believe that the jury would have rejected the hospital-administered test and accepted, instead, the implied consent law test. Stevens v. Commonwealth, 272 Va. 481, 634 S.E.2d 305, 2006 Va. LEXIS 87 (2006), cert. denied, 549 U.S. 1350, 127 S. Ct. 2053, 167 L. Ed. 2d 784, 2007 U.S. LEXIS 4119 (U.S. 2007).

Trial court did not err in denying defendant's motion to exclude from evidence a blood alcohol content certificate showing his state of intoxication because defendant introduced substantially similar evidence during his case in chief, thereby waiving his objection and rendering harmless any alleged error; defendant's evidence, a 0.14 percent blood alcohol content certificate of analysis, dealt with the same subject as, and was sufficiently similar to, the Commonwealth's 0.16 percent blood alcohol content certificate, and both established blood alcohol content levels in excess of 0.08 percent, thereby triggering the inference of § 18.2-269 that defendant was under the influence of alcohol intoxicants at the time of the alleged offense. Isaac v. Commonwealth, 58 Va. App. 255, 708 S.E.2d 435, 2011 Va. App. LEXIS 164 (2011).

Expert testimony. — Trial court did not err in allowing blood alcohol test results into evidence, where exigent circumstances justified warrantless arrest and search of defendant, and Commonwealth relied on expert opinion to explain significance of defendant's blood alcohol level and did not rely on statutory presumption contained in § 18.2-269. Felts v. Commonwealth, No. 1997-98-3 (Ct. of Appeals Oct. 5, 1999).

Prosecution for aggravated involuntary manslaughter was not foreclosed. — Despite defendant's contention that the Commonwealth failed to comply with the procedural requirements of a DUI charge, where given defendant's admission to being intoxicated and his statements asking what he had hit, even without a blood test, the jury properly convicted defendant on all other evidence showing he was intoxicated. Stevens v. Commonwealth, 44 Va. App. 122, 603 S.E.2d 642, 2004 Va. App. LEXIS 496 (2004).

Defendant's aggravated involuntary manslaughter conviction

was upheld on appeal, as the trial court did not err by: (1) failing to foreclose prosecution of the aggravated involuntary manslaughter charge on the ground that the Commonwealth did not comply with the procedural requirements of a driving under the influence charge; (2) failing to exclude a hospital toxicology report based on insufficient proof of reliability; (3) failing to instruct the jury on criminal negligence; and (4) finding the evidence sufficient to prove he was guilty of aggravated involuntary manslaughter, as (a) evidence of defendant's intoxication was overwhelming without the need for blood test results, given defendant's admissions and eyewitness testimony about strong odor of alcohol on his person; (b) the State's failure to substantially comply with the procedural requirements for testing blood and breath samples under the implied consent law did not apply to a prosecution under § 18.2-36.1 or 18.2-266; (c) trial court did not abuse its discretion in refusing to admit one instruction on grounds that it might have confused the jury, and two other instructions, as redundant; and (d) along with defendant's intoxication, the combination of defendant's act of ignoring traffic signals and running a red light and the lack of skid marks showing no evidence of him braking or attempting to slow down, provided sufficient evidence to establish his gross, wanton, and culpable conduct. Stevens v. Commonwealth, 46 Va. App. 234, 616 S.E.2d 754, 2005 Va. App. LEXIS 407 (2005), aff'd, — Va. —, 634 S.E.2d 305 (2006).

Even if the State's failure to comply with the implied consent law procedural requirements did not forbid a prosecution for aggravated manslaughter, blood test results were not required for a conviction under either § 18.2-266 or 18.2-36.1. Stevens v. Commonwealth, 46 Va. App. 234, 616 S.E.2d 754, 2005 Va. App. LEXIS 407 (2005), aff'd, — Va. —, 634 S.E.2d 305 (2006).

Evidence was sufficient to support defendant's involuntary manslaughter conviction by unintentionally causing death as the result of driving an automobile while under the influence of alcohol where the defendant sped down a curvy, mountain road at night, that he proceeded into a right-hand curve in his lane of travel, then swerved right onto the shoulder of his lane and left across the median and struck the victim's car, and although he claimed that he saw headlights in his lane, other eyewitnesses refuted his testimony and expert testimony showed that he was under the influence of alcohol. Tipton v. Commonwealth, 18 Va. App. 370, 444 S.E.2d 1 (1994).

Evidence was sufficient to show that the death of the defendant's passenger in a single car accident was caused by the defendant's extreme intoxication, notwithstanding his assertion that he drove off the road because a "big black truck" drove toward him from the opposite direction and forced him off the road, where: (1) the defendant admitted that he drove off the road, causing the accident; (2) tire marks at the scene were inconsistent with his claim that he swerved to avoid a truck; and (3) the defendant was in a dangerously intoxicated state. Faltz v. Commonwealth, No. 0650-97-1 (Ct. of Appeals 1998).

Evidence, viewed in the light most favorable to the Commonwealth, was sufficient to show that defendant was under the influence of alcohol at the time he crashed his vehicle into the back end of a pickup truck and caused the death of its driver; the trial court had several certificates of analysis indicating defendant was driving with a blood-alcohol level of over .08 grams, which permitted the trial court to presume that defendant was under the influence of alcohol intoxicants at the time of the alleged offense, and other evidence in the form of eyewitness testimony also supported that conviction. West v. Commonwealth, 43 Va. App. 327, 597 S.E.2d 274, 2004 Va. App. LEXIS 276 (2004).

Defendant's gross, wanton, and culpable conduct in killing the victim while driving well beyond the legal limit, running a red light, and failing to apply his brakes before the collision amply supported his aggravated voluntary manslaughter conviction. Stevens v. Commonwealth, 272 Va. 481, 634 S.E.2d 305, 2006 Va. LEXIS 87 (2006), cert. denied, 549 U.S. 1350, 127 S. Ct. 2053, 167 L. Ed. 2d 784, 2007 U.S. LEXIS 4119 (U.S. 2007).

Evidence that defendant disregarded warning signs and speed limits, causing defendant to loose control of defendant's vehicle supported the conclusion that defendant showed a reckless disregard for human life constituting criminal negligence sufficient to support defendant's conviction for involuntary manslaughter.

Gochez v. Commonwealth, — Va. App. —, — S.E.2d —, 2008 Va. App. LEXIS 450 (Oct. 7, 2008).

Defendant's conviction for involuntary manslaughter in violation of subsection A of § 18.2-36.1 after the victim was thrown off defendant's motorcycle was proper. The trial court could conclude that defendant's intoxication caused the accident and the victim's subsequent death; it was reasonable to infer defendant's reaction time was impaired. Rodriguez v. Commonwealth, — Va. App. —, — S.E.2d —, 2009 Va. App. LEXIS 43 (Feb. 3, 2009).

Aggravated involuntary manslaughter shown. — The evidence was sufficient to establish the defendant's gross, wanton and culpable driving behavior where the defendant's blood alcohol level was .22 and where witnesses testified that the defendant was "cutting the corner" while attempting to make a left turn across oncoming traffic, which had a green light, at the time the decedent struck the side of the defendant's vehicle. Hall v. Commonwealth, 32 Va. App. 616, 529 S.E.2d 829, 2000 Va. App. LEXIS 466 (2000).

Evidence that defendant drank almost 22 ounces of beer before he got into his vehicle and that he was driving at least 25 miles per hour over the posted speed limit on the highway before his vehicle slammed into a pick-up truck and caused the death of the driver inside was sufficient to show that his conduct was so gross, wanton, and culpable as to show defendant's reckless disregard for human life, and supported his conviction for aggravated involuntary manslaughter. West v. Commonwealth, 43 Va. App. 327, 597 S.E.2d 274, 2004 Va. App. LEXIS 276 (2004).

Knowing that he: (a) was beneath the legal drinking age, (b) had consumed six or seven alcoholic beverages in under three hours, and (c) was buzzed, defendant's act of choosing to get behind the wheel of his automobile and drive home after dark on a clear, dry night on a straight, well-paved and clearly marked two-lane road, was sufficient to show his reckless disregard for human life; further, the evidence sufficiently showed that defendant failed to maintain proper control of his vehicle, drove so that it was entirely in the lane of oncoming traffic, and hence, failed to see a car approaching from the opposite direction until it was too late to avoid impact, so as to support a finding of criminal negligence. Wyatt v. Commonwealth, 47 Va. App. 411, 624 S.E.2d 118, 2006 Va. App. LEXIS 5 (2006).

Evidence that defendant, who had been drinking alcohol at a birthday party, was driving under the influence and sending text messages on a dark, rainy night, and failed to take evasive action to avoid the victim was sufficient to support a conviction for vehicular aggravated involuntary manslaughter. Davis v. Commonwealth, 57 Va. App. 446, 703 S.E.2d 259, 2011 Va. App. LEXIS 3 (2011).

Reckless disregard for human life shown. — Evidence was sufficient to show that defendant acted with a reckless disregard for human life under subsection B of § 18.2-36.1 because defendant was highly intoxicated at the time of the vehicular collision, which led to the victim's death; he was following another vehicle, which was driven by a drinking companion, too closely; and defendant was talking on his cellular telephone at the time of the collision. Dupree v. Commonwealth, 2010 Va. App. LEXIS 170 (May 4, 2010).

Sufficient evidence of reckless disregard for human life. — In an aggravated involuntary manslaughter conviction, the evidence was sufficient to establish that defendant acted with a reckless disregard for human life under subsection B of § 18.2-36.1 because she failed to keep a proper lookout and was so intoxicated that she did not see the backhoe in her lane of traffic and thus, did not attempt to stop or swerve to avoid it; in addition, defendant was so intoxicated that she did not realize the seriousness of the accident and expressed concern for damages to her car, rather than for the injured victim. Nininger v. Commonwealth, 2010 Va. App. LEXIS 174 (May 4, 2010).

Proximate cause jury instruction improper. — A trial court properly rejected an instruction regarding proximate cause which stated that the causal connection required was a cause "which in the natural and continuous sequence, unbroken by any efficient intervening cause, produces the injury without which the result would not have occurred," in that such instruction was based on the civil instruction for proximate cause and the injection of inapplicable principles of civil negligence into a criminal trial would have created confusion and would have been misleading. Hall v. Commonwealth, 32 Va. App. 616, 529 S.E.2d 829, 2000 Va. App. LEXIS 466 (2000).

§ 18.2-36.2. Involuntary manslaughter; operating a watercraft while under the influence; penalties.

A. Any person who, as a result of operating a watercraft or motorboat in violation of clause (ii), (iii), or (iv) of subsection B of § 29.1-738 or a similar local ordinance, unintentionally causes the death of another person, is guilty of involuntary manslaughter.

B. If, in addition, the conduct of the defendant was so gross, wanton, and culpable as to show a reckless disregard for human life, he shall be guilty of aggravated involuntary manslaughter, a felony punishable by a term of imprisonment of not less than one nor more than 20 years, one year of which shall be a mandatory minimum term of imprisonment.

C. The provisions of this section shall not preclude prosecution under any other homicide statute. The court shall order any person convicted under this section not to operate a watercraft or motorboat that is underway upon the waters of the Commonwealth. After five years have passed from the date of the conviction, the convicted person may petition the court that entered the conviction for the right to operate a watercraft or motorboat upon the waters of the Commonwealth. Upon consideration of such petition, the court may restore the right to operate a watercraft or motorboat subject to such terms and conditions as the court deems appropriate, including the successful completion of a water safety alcohol rehabilitation program described in § 29.1-738.5.

History.
2005, c. 376.

§ 18.2-37. How and where homicide prosecuted and punished if death occur without the Commonwealth.

If any person be stricken or poisoned in this Commonwealth, and die by reason thereof out of this Commonwealth, the offender shall be as guilty, and shall be prosecuted and punished, as if the death had occurred in the county or corporation in which the stroke or poison was given or administered.

History.
Code 1950, § 18.1-26; 1960, c. 358; 1975, cc. 14, 15.

Michie's Jurisprudence.
For related discussion, see 9B M.J. Homicide, § 50; 14B M.J. Poisons and Poisoning, § 1; 19 M.J. Venue, § 14.

CASE NOTES

Effect of section. — The effect of this section and § 19.2-246 is merely to give the courts of the counties or corporations in which the accused and the deceased may have been, respectively, at the time of the commission of the offense, concurrent jurisdiction, so that the offender may be prosecuted and punished in either county where the offense is not wholly committed within one county. Covington v. Commonwealth, 136 Va. 665, 116 S.E. 462 (1923).

Section changed former rule. — This section changed the rule established by Commonwealth v. Linton, 4 Va. (2 Va. Cas.) 205 (1820), in which it was held that if one be stricken within the state, but die of the wound in another state, the offender may be indicted and tried within the state for wounding with intent to maim, disable, etc., but not for murder, and constituted the act of giving a mortal wound in this state which results in death out of the state a statutory offense of murder punishable in this state. By necessary implication from its terms, the statute provided that the venue of such offense should be in the county or corporation in which the stroke was given. Covington v. Commonwealth, 136 Va. 665, 116 S.E. 462 (1923).

ARTICLE 2.
CRIMES BY MOBS.

Michie's Jurisprudence.
For related discussion, see 13A M.J. Mobs, Riots and Lynchings, §§ 1, 4.

§ 18.2-38. "Mob" defined.

Any collection of people, assembled for the purpose and with the intention of committing an assault or a battery upon any person or an act of violence as defined in § 19.2-297.1, without authority of law, shall be deemed a *"mob."*

History.
Code 1950, § 18.1-27; 1960, c. 358; 1975, cc. 14, 15; 1999, c. 623.

Law Review.
For 2006 survey article, "Criminal Law and Procedure," see 41 U. Rich. L. Rev. 83 (2006).

CASE NOTES

Meaning of "assemble." — For a group of persons lawfully gathered for whatever purpose to "assemble" as a mob within the intendment of this section, they need only to collectively band together with the common purpose and intention of committing an assault and battery upon a person. Harrell v. Commonwealth, 11 Va. App. 1, 396 S.E.2d 680 (1990).

Assembled as a mob. — The evidence which proves that a group assembled as a mob may consist solely of proof that characterizes the purpose, circumstances or the setting of the group's initial assemblage. Harrell v. Commonwealth, 11 Va. App. 1, 396 S.E.2d 680 (1990).

Proof of what transpired after the original assemblage, when considered in relation to the purpose for which the persons were present, may establish that persons gathered for a lawful purpose "assembled" as a mob. Harrell v. Commonwealth, 11 Va. App. 1, 396 S.E.2d 680 (1990).

Trial court erred in admitting the grand jury testimony of two codefendants to show that defendant assembled as part of a mob in order to show that he was guilty of lynching, but the error was harmless beyond a reasonable doubt in light of considerable other evidence showing that defendant was part of the mob that attacked a rival gang at a hotel and was responsible for stabbing to death anther person during the attack. Corado v. Commonwealth, 47 Va. App. 315, 623 S.E.2d 452, 2005 Va. App. LEXIS 528 (2005).

A mob need not have a common motivation or underlying reason for the assault, they need only to collectively band together with the common purpose and intention of committing an assault and battery upon a person. Jones v. Commonwealth, No. 2922-99-1, 2000 Va. App. LEXIS 844 (Ct. of Appeals Dec. 28, 2000).

But specific intent must be shown. — Statutory definition of a mob requires that the act of assembling be done for a specific purpose and with a specific intent — to commit an assault or a battery without lawful authority. Hughes v. Commonwealth, 43 Va. App. 391, 598 S.E.2d 743, 2004 Va. App. LEXIS 308 (2004).

What transforms group into mob. — Whether a group of individuals lawfully assembled has been transformed into a "mob" depends upon the circumstances; no particular words or express agreements are required to effect a change in a group's purpose or intentions. Events or emotionally charged circumstances suddenly may focus individuals toward a common goal or purpose without an express or stated call to join forces. Harrell v. Commonwealth, 11 Va. App. 1, 396 S.E.2d 680 (1990).

It is possible that individuals who are lawfully assembled may become members of a "mob" without great deliberation and for them to become part of a group that is moved or controlled by those impulsive and irrational forces that perpetuate mob violence. Hughes v. Commonwealth, 43 Va. App. 391, 598 S.E.2d 743, 2004 Va. App. LEXIS 308 (2004).

Purpose of assembling. — The definition of a mob in this section requires that the act of assembling be done for a specific purpose and with a specific intent — to commit an assault or a battery without lawful authority. Sheikh v. Commonwealth, 32 Va. App. 9, 526 S.E.2d 271 (2000).

Every person in mob criminally culpable. — Once a group assembled comprises a mob, if the assault or battery which is committed is a simple assault or battery, then under § 18.2-57, every person composing the mob becomes criminally culpable even though the member may not have actively encouraged, aided, or countenanced the act. Harrell v. Commonwealth, 11 Va. App. 1, 396 S.E.2d 680 (1990).

If a defendant was part of a mob which attacked a victim, then the defendant is criminally culpable for all the acts of the mob even though he may not have actively encouraged, aided or countenanced the act; criminal accountability flows from being a member of the mob, regardless of whether the member aids and abets in the assault and battery. Jones v. Commonwealth, No. 2922-99-1, 2000 Va. App. LEXIS 844 (Ct. of Appeals Dec. 28, 2000).

Indictment using word "mob" without elaboration is sufficient. — Defendant was charged with being one of a "mob" and in that capacity with feloniously assaulting another. The "lynch law" (this section) defines a mob. Therefore, an elaboration in the indictment of these statutory provisions defining a mob is not necessary, as they are too plain for argument and could not possibly have been misunderstood. Hagood v. Commonwealth, 157 Va. 918, 162 S.E. 10 (1932).

Statement of member of mob at time of assault admissible. — Objection was made to the admissibility in evidence of statements made by a member of the mob at the time of the assault to the effect that the person assaulted had run his wife away from home and put her in an institution. It was held that all that was then done and said was part of the res gestae and competent. Hagood v. Commonwealth, 157 Va. 918, 162 S.E. 10 (1932).

Evidence sufficient. — Evidence was sufficient to support defendant's conviction for maiming by mob as it showed that the group of men emerged from the McDonald's en masse, followed the victim and his friend, surrounding them, and then beat the victim and struck and chased his friend. The evidence also suggested that the group acted in concert to attack the victim following one of the group member's stated intent to hit the victim or his friend. Johnson v. Commonwealth, 58 Va. App. 303, 709 S.E.2d 175, 2011 Va. App. LEXIS 185 (2011).

Evidence insufficient. — The evidence was insufficient to sustain a conviction under § 18.2-41 because the Commonwealth failed to prove that when the defendant committed the battery, he was a member of a mob assembled with a purpose and intention of committing an assault and battery under this section where the uncontradicted evidence established that the group assembled to attend a neighborhood party, after which many congregated in a boisterous gathering in the street nearby, lingering there for over two hours after the party ended and before the confrontation with the victim. Harrell v. Commonwealth, 11 Va. App. 1, 396 S.E.2d 680 (1990).

The circumstantial evidence necessary to prove that a group assembled with a common purpose and intent to commit an assault and battery does not have to be completely independent of proving the original purpose for which the group assembled and how they behaved thereafter. Harrell v. Commonwealth, 11 Va. App. 1, 396 S.E.2d 680 (1990).

Although a brawl ensued after the patrons of the bowling alley watched appellant argue with man and another person punched man, no evidence proved that appellant joined in any mob that could have formed. Although the evidence would have been sufficient to prove individual assaultive conduct, it was insufficient to prove beyond a reasonable doubt that appellant acted as part of a mob. Iverson v. Commonwealth, No. 1825-93-1 (Ct. of Appeals June 20, 1995).

Although a brawl ensued after the patrons of the bowling alley watched appellant's friend argue with man and appellant punched man, no evidence proved that appellant joined in any mob that could have formed. At best, the Commonwealth proved that appellant hit man and threw more than one chair. Although the evidence would have been sufficient to prove individual assaultive conduct, it was insufficient to prove beyond a reasonable doubt that appellant acted as part of a mob. Simmons v. Commonwealth, No. 1805-93-1 (Ct. of Appeals June 20, 1995).

Where testimony proved that appellant was seen moving to the area where fight was, and although appellant admitted that he threw a chair, the evidence proved that after the fight began many people threw chairs, including people who the Commonwealth conceded were not part of the mob, thus, the fact that appellant threw chairs did not prove beyond a reasonable doubt that he was acting as part of a mob. Wynn v. Commonwealth, No. 1804-93-1 (Ct. of Appeals June 20, 1995).

Evidence failed to prove that group of which defendant was alleged to be a member assembled for specific purpose of maliciously wounding and assaulting victims named in indictment. Forrester v. Commonwealth, No. 0701-98-2 (Ct. of Appeals June 22, 1999).

Applied in Hamilton v. Commonwealth, 279 Va. 94, 688 S.E.2d 168, 2010 Va. LEXIS 6 (2010).

CIRCUIT COURT OPINIONS

What transforms group into mob. — Even if defendant were originally at an apartment complex to fight a shooting culprit one-on-one, evidence that, once everyone arrived at the apartment, they agreed to move across the street to "handle it" indicated that the group, at that time, fell within the definition of a mob as contemplated by § 18.2-38 as the group had transformed into a collection of people who had the intention of committing an assault or battery upon any person or an act of violence. Moreover, the evidence showed that, during the altercation, the victim and the shooting culprit became focused on the common goal of fighting defendant; thus, defendant's motion to strike under Va. Sup. Ct. R. 3A:15 was denied. Commonwealth v. Puryear, 2009 Va. Cir. LEXIS 18 (Fairfax County Feb. 3, 2009).

§ 18.2-39. "Lynching" defined.

Any act of violence by a mob upon the body of any person, which shall result in the death of such person, shall constitute a *"lynching."*

History.
Code 1950, § 18.1-28; 1960, c. 358; 1975, cc. 14, 15.

Law Review.
For 2006 survey article, "Criminal Law and Procedure," see 41 U. Rich. L. Rev. 83 (2006).

CASE NOTES

Attack on "any" person. — Trial court did not err in the jury instructions it gave in regard to the lynching charge against defendant; the victim of the attack did not have to be the initial, specific target of the mob and since the jury instructions correctly stated the law in that regard, the jury was not improperly instructed. Corado v. Commonwealth, 47 Va. App. 315, 623 S.E.2d 452, 2005 Va. App. LEXIS 528 (2005).

§ 18.2-40. Lynching deemed murder.

Every lynching shall be deemed murder. Any and every person composing a mob and any and every accessory thereto, by which any person is lynched, shall be guilty of murder, and upon conviction, shall be punished as provided in Article 1 (§ 18.2-30 et seq.) of this chapter.

History.
Code 1950, § 18.1-29; 1960, c. 358; 1975, cc. 14, 15.

CASE NOTES

Convictions for felony murder and lynching by mob upheld. — Defendant was not entitled to reversal of convictions for both felony murder and lynching by mob, because both the felony murder statute, § 18.2-32, and the lynching-by-mob statute, § 18.2-40, included at least one element the other did not, and the appellate court presumed that the General Assembly did not intend either statute to displace the other. Gaddie v. Commonwealth, 2010 Va. App. LEXIS 247 (June 22, 2010).

§ 18.2-41. Shooting, stabbing, etc., with intent to maim, kill, etc., by mob.

Any and every person composing a mob which shall maliciously or unlawfully shoot, stab, cut or wound any person, or by any means cause him bodily injury with intent to maim, disable, disfigure or kill him, shall be guilty of a Class 3 felony.

History.
Code 1950, § 18.1-30; 1960, c. 358; 1975, cc. 14, 15.

Cross references.
For definition of "barrier crime" as including a conviction of malicious wounding by mob as set out in § 18.2-41, or an equivalent offense in another state, and prohibition against assisted living facilities, adult day care centers or child welfare agencies hiring certain compensated employment persons who have committed such an offense, see §§ 63.2-1719, 63.2-1720.

Law Review.
For survey of Virginia criminal law for the year 1974-1975, see 61 Va. L. Rev. 1697 (1975).

Michie's Jurisprudence.
For related discussion, see 10A M.J. Instructions, § 20; 12B M.J. Mayhem, § 2.

CASE NOTES

Meaning of "assemble." — For a group of persons lawfully gathered for whatever purpose to "assemble" as a mob within the intendment of § 18.2-38, they need only to collectively band together with the common purpose and intention of committing an assault and battery upon a person. Harrell v. Commonwealth, 11 Va. App. 1, 396 S.E.2d 680 (1990).

Assembled as a mob. — The evidence which proves that a group assembled as a mob may consist solely of proof that characterizes the purpose, circumstances or the setting of the group's initial assemblage. Harrell v. Commonwealth, 11 Va. App. 1, 396 S.E.2d 680 (1990).

Proof of what transpired after the original assemblage, when considered in relation to the purpose for which the persons were present, may establish that persons gathered for a lawful purpose "assembled" as a mob. Harrell v. Commonwealth, 11 Va. App. 1, 396 S.E.2d 680 (1990).

What transforms group into mob. — Whether a group of individuals lawfully assembled has been transformed into a "mob" depends upon the circumstances; no particular words or express agreements are required to effect a change in a group's purpose or intentions. Events or emotionally charged circumstances suddenly may focus individuals toward a common goal or purpose without an express or stated call to join forces. Harrell v. Commonwealth, 11 Va. App. 1, 396 S.E.2d 680 (1990).

Every person in mob criminally culpable. — Once a group assembled comprises a mob, if the assault or battery which is committed is a simple assault or battery, then under § 18.2-57, every person composing the mob becomes criminally culpable even though the member may not have actively encouraged, aided, or countenanced the act. Harrell v. Commonwealth, 11 Va. App. 1, 396 S.E.2d 680 (1990).

Double jeopardy. — Defendant's convictions for malicious wounding and maiming by mob did not violate principles of double jeopardy as malicious wounding contained an additional element not found in maiming by mob, namely that the defendant acted with malice. Thus, it followed that one who was guilty of maiming by mob was not necessarily guilty of malicious wounding. Johnson v. Commonwealth, 58 Va. App. 303, 709 S.E.2d 175, 2011 Va. App. LEXIS 185 (2011).

Lesser-included offense. — Assault and battery by a mob, in violation of § 18.2-42, is a lesser-included offense of malicious wounding by a mob, because the only difference between the two offenses is the requisite intent, and one cannot have the malicious intent required for the latter offense without also having an intent to do bodily harm, required for the former offense, making the former crime a lesser-included offense of the latter. Leal v. Commonwealth, 37 Va. App. 525, 559 S.E.2d 874, 2002 Va. App. LEXIS 108 (2002), rev'd on grounds that the jury instruction was not supported by "more than a scintilla of evidence," 265 Va. 142, 574 S.Ed.2d 285 (2003).

Evidence insufficient. — The evidence was insufficient to sustain a conviction under this section because the Commonwealth failed to prove that when the defendant committed the battery, he was a member of a mob assembled with a purpose and intention of committing an assault and battery under § 18.2-38 where the uncontradicted evidence established that the group assembled to attend a neighborhood party, after which many congregated in a boisterous gathering in the street nearby, lingering there for over two hours after the party ended and before the confrontation with the victim. Harrell v. Commonwealth, 11 Va. App. 1, 396 S.E.2d 680 (1990).

The circumstantial evidence necessary to prove that a group assembled with a common purpose and intent to commit an assault and battery does not have to be completely independent of proving the original purpose for which the group assembled and how they behaved thereafter. Harrell v. Commonwealth, 11 Va. App. 1, 396 S.E.2d 680 (1990).

Although a brawl ensued after the patrons of the bowling alley watched appellant argue with man and another person punched man, no evidence proved that appellant joined in any mob that could have formed. Although the evidence would have been sufficient to prove individual assaultive conduct, it was insufficient to prove beyond a reasonable doubt that appellant acted as part of a mob. Iverson v. Commonwealth, No. 1825-93-1 (Ct. of Appeals June 20, 1995).

Although a brawl ensued after the patrons of the bowling alley watched appellant's friend argue with man and appellant punched man, no evidence proved that appellant joined in any mob that could have formed. At best, the Commonwealth proved that appellant hit man and threw more than one chair. Although the evidence would have been sufficient to prove individual assaultive conduct, it was insufficient to prove beyond a reasonable doubt that appellant acted as part of a mob. Simmons v. Commonwealth, No. 1805-93-1 (Ct. of Appeals June 20, 1995).

Where testimony proved that appellant was seen moving to the area where fight was, and although appellant admitted that he threw a chair, the evidence proved that after the fight began many people threw chairs, including people who the Commonwealth conceded were not part of the mob, thus, the fact that appellant threw chairs did not prove beyond a reasonable doubt that he was acting as part of a mob. Wynn v. Commonwealth, No. 1804-93-1 (Ct. of Appeals June 20, 1995).

Evidence sufficient. — The evidence was sufficient to establish beyond a reasonable doubt that a defendant was a member of a mob for purposes of this section where the defendant met with a group of fellow gang members in order to assault another individual, the defendant admitted that they made a plan to seek out the intended victim and to physically assault him and the defendant knew that one of the members of the gang had a rifle and had made repeated statements regarding his intent to kill the person they were seeking. Sheikh v. Commonwealth, 32 Va. App. 9, 526 S.E.2d 271 (2000).

Defendant's convictions for malicious wounding while part of a mob under § 18.2-41, and aggravated malicious wounding under § 18.2-51.2 were appropriate because defendant was not permitted to complain on appeal of the trial court's refusal to suppress the very evidence that he elicited on his own behalf. Defendant himself elicited the testimony about his statements to the Security Threat Unit that he was a gang member. Boone v. Commonwealth, 2010 Va. App. LEXIS 37 (Feb. 2, 2010).

Evidence was sufficient to support defendant's conviction for maiming by mob as it showed that the group of men emerged from the McDonald's en masse, followed the victim and his friend, surrounding them, and then beat the victim and struck and chased his friend. The evidence also suggested that the group acted in concert to attack the victim following one of the group member's stated intent to hit the victim or his friend. Johnson v. Commonwealth, 58 Va. App. 303, 709 S.E.2d 175, 2011 Va. App. LEXIS 185 (2011).

Conviction for maiming by mob under § 18.2-41, was supported by evidence that a mob formed at a club with the specific intent of committing violence and beat the victim for five minutes, leaving the victim with two fractured vertebrae; the duration of the beating and the gravity of the victim's injuries showed that the mob, which included defendant, intended to seriously injure and maim the victim. Johnson v. Commonwealth, 58 Va. App. 625, 712 S.E.2d 751, 2011 Va. App. LEXIS 259 (2011).

Jury instructions. — In a prosecution for maiming by mob and causing bodily injury in violation of § 18.2-41, the trial court properly refused a jury instruction requested by defendant which would have permitted the jury to find defendant guilty of assault or battery by mob, under § 18.2-42; the evidence warranted a conviction of the crime charged, and there was not more than a scintilla of independent evidence to show that defendant was entitled to an instruction on the lesser offense. Commonwealth v. Leal, 265 Va. 142, 574 S.E.2d 285, 2003 Va. LEXIS 8 (2003).

§ 18.2-42. Assault or battery by mob.

Any and every person composing a mob which shall commit a simple assault or battery shall be guilty of a Class 1 misdemeanor.

History.
Code 1950, § 18.1-31; 1960, c. 358; 1975, cc. 14, 15.

Michie's Jurisprudence.
For related discussion, see 10A M.J. Instructions, § 20; 12B M.J. Mayhem, § 2.

CASE NOTES

Lesser-included offense. — Assault and battery by a mob is a lesser-included offense of malicious wounding by a mob, in violation of § 18.2-41, because the only difference between the two offenses is the requisite intent, and one cannot have the malicious intent required for the latter offense without also having an intent to do bodily harm, required for the former offense, making the former crime a lesser-included offense of the latter. Leal v. Commonwealth, 37 Va. App. 525, 559 S.E.2d 874, 2002 Va. App. LEXIS 108 (2002), rev'd on grounds that the jury instruction was not supported by "more than a scintilla of evidence," 265 Va. 142, 574 S.Ed.2d 285 (2003).

In a prosecution for maiming by mob and causing bodily injury in violation of § 18.2-41, the trial court properly refused a jury instruction requested by defendant which would have permitted the jury to find defendant guilty of assault or battery by mob, under § 18.2-42; the evidence warranted a conviction of the crime charged, and there was not more than a scintilla of independent evidence to show that defendant was entitled to an instruction on the lesser offense. Commonwealth v. Leal, 265 Va. 142, 574 S.E.2d 285, 2003 Va. LEXIS 8 (2003).

Evidence properly admitted as hearsay exception. — Where a witness testified that a third party relayed defendant's license plate number to the witness, the evidence of the license plate number was properly admitted as a present sense impression; as a result, defendant's conviction of misdemeanor assault by mob was proper. Brooke v. Commonwealth, No. 0006-03-4, 2004 Va. App. LEXIS 104 (Ct. of Appeals Mar. 9, 2004).

Evidence sufficient. — There was sufficient evidence supporting the jury's decision that defendant participated in the assault and battery of three victims in violation of § 18.2-42, as a witness who knew defendant saw defendant "doing something" to one victim's back while the victim was on the ground unconscious, and according to the witness, defendant was not trying to help the victim. While the victim was unconscious, the victim's back was twice burned with a cigarette. Hamilton v. Commonwealth, 2008 Va. App. LEXIS 487 (Nov. 4, 2008), aff'd, 279 Va. 94, 688 S.E.2d 168 (2010).

Evidence was sufficient to support defendant's conviction for misdemeanor assault while part of a mob, where the victim testified that defendant was one of the men who surrounded the victim, who converged on the victim, and who prevented the victim from escaping. Abdullah v. Commonwealth, 53 Va. App. 750, 675 S.E.2d 215, 2009 Va. App. LEXIS 169 (2009).

Sufficient evidence supported convictions for participating in a criminal street gang and three counts of assault and battery by a mob, where defendant was dressed in red, the gang color, he was seen with gang members at the scene, and the gang used hand-signs and a war cry before the attacks Hamilton v. Commonwealth, 279 Va. 94, 688 S.E.2d 168, 2010 Va. LEXIS 6 (2010).

Evidence insufficient. — Although a brawl ensued after the patrons of the bowling alley watched appellant's friend argue with man and appellant punched man, no evidence proved that appellant joined in any mob that could have formed. At best, the Commonwealth proved that appellant hit man and threw more than one chair. Although the evidence would have been sufficient to prove individual assaultive conduct, it was insufficient to prove beyond a reasonable doubt that appellant acted as part of a mob. Simmons v. Commonwealth, No. 1805-93-1 (Ct. of Appeals June 20, 1995).

Where testimony proved that appellant was seen moving to the area where fight was, and although appellant admitted that he threw a chair, the evidence proved that after the fight began many people threw chairs, including people who the Commonwealth conceded were not part of the mob, thus, the fact that appellant threw chairs did not prove beyond a reasonable doubt that he was acting as part of a mob. Wynn v. Commonwealth, No. 1804-93-1 (Ct. of Appeals June 20, 1995).

§ 18.2-42.1. Acts of violence by mob.

Any and every person composing a mob which commits an act of violence as defined in § 19.2-297.1 shall be guilty of that act of violence and, upon conviction, shall be punished as provided in the section of this title which makes that act of violence unlawful.

History.
1999, c. 623.

CASE NOTES

Liability of members. — Defendant's convictions under § 18.2-53.1 were reversed and dismissed because even though defendant was a member of a mob, § 18.2-42.1 did not render him criminally responsible for using a firearm in the commission of lynching and using a firearm in the commission of malicious wounding by mob simply by being a member of such mob. Paiz v. Commonwealth, 54 Va. App. 688, 682 S.E.2d 71, 2009 Va. App. LEXIS 380 (2009).

§ 18.2-43. Apprehension and prosecution of participants in lynching.

The attorney for the Commonwealth of any county or city in which a lynching may occur shall promptly and diligently endeavor to ascertain the identity of the persons who in any way participated therein, or who composed the mob which perpetrated the same, and have them apprehended, and shall promptly proceed with the prosecution of any and all persons so found; and to the end that such offenders may not escape proper punishment, such attorney for the Commonwealth may be assisted in all such endeavors and prosecutions by the Attorney General, or other prosecutors designated by the Governor for the purpose; and the Governor may have full authority to spend such sums as he may deem necessary for the purpose of seeking out the identity, and apprehending the members of such mob.

History.
Code 1950, § 18.1-32; 1960, c. 358; 1975, cc. 14, 15.

§ 18.2-44. Civil liability for lynching.

No provisions of this article shall be construed to relieve any member of a mob from civil liability to the personal representative of the victim of a lynching.

History.
Code 1950, § 18.1-33; 1960, c. 358; 1975, cc. 14, 15.

§ 18.2-45. Persons suffering death from mob attempting to lynch another person.

Every person suffering death from a mob attempting to lynch another person shall come within the provisions of this article, and his personal representative shall be entitled to relief in the same manner and to the same extent as if he were the originally intended victim of such mob.

History.
Code 1950, § 18.1-34; 1960, c. 358; 1975, cc. 14, 15.

§ 18.2-46. Venue.

Venue for all actions and prosecutions under any of the provisions of this article shall be in the county or city wherein a lynching or other violation of any of the provisions of this article may have occurred, or of the county or city from which the person lynched or assaulted may have been taken as aforesaid.

History.
Code 1950, § 18.1-35; 1960, c. 358; 1975, cc. 14, 15; 2004, c. 144.

ARTICLE 2.1.

CRIMES BY GANGS.

§ 18.2-46.1. Definitions.

As used in this article unless the context requires otherwise or it is otherwise provided:

"*Act of violence*" means those felony offenses described in subsection A of § 19.2-297.1.

"*Criminal street gang*" means any ongoing organization, association, or group of three or more persons, whether formal or informal, (i) which has as one of its primary objectives or activities the commission of one or more criminal activities; (ii) which has an identifiable name or identifying sign or symbol; and (iii) whose members individually or collectively have engaged in the commission of, attempt to commit, conspiracy to commit, or solicitation of two or more predicate criminal acts, at least one of which is an act of violence, provided such acts were not part of a common act or transaction.

"*Predicate criminal act*" means (i) an act of violence; (ii) any violation of § 18.2-31, 18.2-42, 18.2-46.3, 18.2-51, 18.2-51.1, 18.2-51.2, 18.2-51.3, 18.2-51.6, 18.2-52, 18.2-52.1, 18.2-53, 18.2-53.1, 18.2-55, 18.2-56.1, 18.2-57, 18.2-57.2, 18.2-59, 18.2-83, 18.2-89, 18.2-90, 18.2-95, 18.2-108.1, 18.2-121, 18.2-127, 18.2-128, 18.2-137, 18.2-138, 18.2-146, 18.2-147, 18.2-248.01, 18.2-248.03, 18.2-255, 18.2-255.2, 18.2-279, 18.2-282.1, 18.2-286.1, 18.2-287.4, 18.2-289, 18.2-300, 18.2-308.1, 18.2-308.2, 18.2-308.2:01, 18.2-308.4, 18.2-355, 18.2-356, or 18.2-357; (iii) a felony violation of § 18.2-60.3 or 18.2-248.1:1; (iv) a felony violation of § 18.2-248 or of 18.2-248.1 or a conspiracy to commit a felony violation of § 18.2-248 or 18.2-248.1; (v) any violation of a local ordinance adopted pursuant to § 15.2-1812.2; or (vi) any substantially similar offense under the laws of another state or territory of the United States, the District of Columbia, or the United States.

History.
2000, c. 332; 2004, cc. 396, 435, 462, 867; 2005, cc. 764, 813; 2006, cc. 262, 319, 844, 895; 2007, c. 499; 2012, c. 364; 2013, cc. 573, 645.

Editor's note.
At the direction of the Virginia Code Commission, "subsection H, H1 or H2" was substituted for "subsection H, H 1 or H 2."
Acts 2012, c. 364, cl. 2, provides: "That the provisions of this act may result in a net increase in periods of imprisonment or commitment. Pursuant to § 30-19.1:4, the estimated amount of the necessary appropriation is $3,358 for periods of imprisonment in state adult correctional facilities and is $0 for periods of commitment to the custody of the Department of Juvenile Justice."
Acts 2013, cc. 573 and 645, cl. 2 provides: "That the provisions of this act may result in a net increase in periods of imprisonment or commitment. Pursuant to § 30-19.1:4, the estimated amount of the necessary appropriation is at least $574,916 for periods of imprisonment in state adult correctional facilities and cannot be determined for periods of commitment to the custody of the Department of Juvenile Justice."
Acts 2013, cc. 573 and 645, cl. 3 provides: "That the provisions of this act shall not become effective unless an appropriation of general funds effectuating the purposes of this act is included in a general appropriation act passed by the 2013 Session of the General Assembly, which becomes law."
Acts 2013, cc. 573 and 645, cl. 4 provides: "That the General Assembly determines that the requirements of the third enactment of this act have been met."

The 2012 amendments.
The 2012 amendment by c. 364 substituted "18.2-308.1, 18.2-355, 18.2-356, or 18.2-357;" for "18.2-308.1, or 18.2-356;" in the paragraph defining "Predicate criminal act."

The 2013 amendments.

The 2013 amendments by cc. 573 and 645 are identical, and rewrote the paragraph defining "Predicate criminal act."

Law Review.

For 2003/2004 survey of criminal law and procedure, see 39 U. Rich. L. Rev. 133 (2004). For 2006 survey article, "Criminal Law and Procedure," see 41 U. Rich. L. Rev. 83 (2006). For 2007 annual survey article, "Criminal Law and Procedure," see 42 U. Rich. L. Rev. 311 (2007). For annual survey article, "Criminal Law and Procedure," see 46 U. Rich. L. Rev. 59 (2011).

CASE NOTES

"Criminal street gang." — Because defendant prison officials had established a zero tolerance policy for inappropriate or criminal behavior committed by groups of inmates meeting § 18.2-46.1's definition of a criminal street gang, and plaintiff inmate did not challenge such a designation as to his "religious" materials as Security Threat Group materials, and he retained other avenues of religious exercise, and the ban of the materials promoted the goal of a zero tolerance of gang affiliation to reduce dangers to other inmates and staff, the ban withstood First Amendment and Religious Land Use and Institutionalized Persons Act, 42 U.S.C.S. §§ 2000cc to 2000cc-5, challenges. Holley v. Johnson, 2010 U.S. Dist. LEXIS 65356 (W.D. Va. June 30, 2010).

Because the two people whose convictions the Commonwealth relied on as predicate criminal acts to establish the existence of a criminal street gang were not members of defendant's subset gang, the crimes committed by those two people did not qualify as predicate criminal acts under clause (iii) of the definition of "criminal street gang." Taybron v. Commonwealth, 57 Va. App. 470, 703 S.E.2d 270, 2011 Va. App. LEXIS 1 (2011).

Evidence was insufficient to convict defendant of participation in a criminal street gang because the Commonwealth proved only one predicate crime committed by a gang member and thus failed to prove that the gang was a "criminal street gang" under § 18.2-46.1, an essential element of the offense. Rushing v. Commonwealth, 284 Va. 270, 726 S.E.2d 333, 2012 Va. LEXIS 133 (2012).

"Criminal gang activity." — Trial court did not err in admitting evidence of the prior convictions of two codefendants; based on defendant's involvement in an attack at a hotel on a rival gang, he was charged with "criminal street gang participation" and to prove the requisite street gang activity, the Commonwealth had to prove predicate criminal acts by "two or more persons" who were members of the same gang, thus allowing for admission of the prior conviction evidence. Corado v. Commonwealth, 47 Va. App. 315, 623 S.E.2d 452, 2005 Va. App. LEXIS 528 (2005).

Where there was ample evidence of criminal activities, including at least one violent act, from which a trial court could have inferred that the requisite predicate acts to establish a criminal street gang occurred prior to defendant recruiting a juvenile to join a gang, the evidence proved that a criminal street gang existed prior to and independent of defendant's recruitment of the juvenile and was sufficient to support defendant's conviction for recruitment of a juvenile for membership in a criminal street gang, in violation of § 18.2-46.3. Phillips v. Commonwealth, 56 Va. App. 526, 694 S.E.2d 805, 2010 Va. App. LEXIS 271 (2010).

Expert testimony on gang culture. — In a case in which defendant appealed his conviction for violating §§ 18.2-51, 18.2-53.1, and 18.2-286.1, he unsuccessfully argued that the trial court erred in permitting an expert witness to testify about gang practices and terminology, including his involvement with a gang. The trial court reasonably concluded that the probative value of the expert's testimony outweighed any prejudicial effect; the evidence was relevant to prove the identity of the shooter, and the testimony about his gang affiliation was probative as to defendant's identity. Wyche v. Commonwealth, 2012 Va. App. LEXIS 227 (July 10, 2012).

Evidence of criminal street gang. — Expert testimony indicating that the Latin Kings gang members engaged in criminal enterprises, have adopted black and gold as their identifying colors, wore the symbols of the "sacred crown" and colored beads as part of their clothing attire, and used identifiable hand signals to identify themselves was sufficient to prove that the Latin Kings were a criminal street gang as defined in § 18.2-46.1. Salcedo v. Common-

wealth, 58 Va. App. 525, 712 S.E.2d 8, 2011 Va. App. LEXIS 239 (2011).

Evidence, in the form of testimony by a police detective, a stipulation of facts, and a sentencing order, of prior criminal acts committed by two purported gang members was admissible because the evidence was relevant and was admitted to prove the existence of a criminal street gang, pursuant to § 18.2-46.1. Newton v. Commonwealth, 2011 Va. App. LEXIS 212 (June 28, 2011).

Officer's expert opinion that a convicted felon was a gang member because he was seen at an unspecified time wearing beads the officer considered to be gang insignia had an insufficient factual basis, because 1) wearing gang insignia did not logically entail gang membership; and 2) the officer's observation of the beads was not related in time to the purported member's commission of the crime for which he was convicted. Rushing v. Commonwealth, 284 Va. 270, 726 S.E.2d 333, 2012 Va. LEXIS 133 (2012).

Applied in Hamilton v. Commonwealth, 279 Va. 94, 688 S.E.2d 168, 2010 Va. LEXIS 6 (2010).

§ 18.2-46.2. Prohibited criminal street gang participation; penalty.

A. Any person who actively participates in or is a member of a criminal street gang and who knowingly and willfully participates in any predicate criminal act committed for the benefit of, at the direction of, or in association with any criminal street gang shall be guilty of a Class 5 felony. However, if such participant in or member of a criminal street gang is age eighteen years or older and knows or has reason to know that such criminal street gang also includes a juvenile member or participant, he shall be guilty of a Class 4 felony.

B. Violation of this section shall constitute a separate and distinct offense. If the acts or activities violating this section also violate another provision of law, a prosecution under this section shall not prohibit or bar any prosecution or proceeding under such other provision or the imposition of any penalties provided for thereby.

History.

2000, c. 332.

Law Review.

For annual survey article, "Criminal Law and Procedure," see 46 U. Rich. L. Rev. 59 (2011). For annual survey of Virginia law article, "Criminal Law and Procedure," see 47 U. Rich. L. Rev. 143 (2012).

CASE NOTES

Predicate act need not be gang related. — This section does not require that the predicate criminal act be gang related. Johnson v. Commonwealth, 58 Va. App. 625, 712 S.E.2d 751, 2011 Va. App. LEXIS 259 (2011).

Evidence that robbery committed in association with gang. — Evidence that defendant, a high-ranking gang member told another to commit the robbery, and that defendant was seen wearing the gangs trademark colors and beads, while the robbery was committed by an individual wearing gang colors, supporting an inference that the robbery was committed for the benefit of or in association with the gang. Salcedo v. Commonwealth, 58 Va. App. 525, 712 S.E.2d 8, 2011 Va. App. LEXIS 239 (2011).

Evidence sufficient. — There was sufficient evidence supporting the jury's decision that defendant participated in a criminal street gang in violation of § 18.2-46.2. During cross-examination defendant reluctantly admitted defendant might have been wearing a baseball hat, and an expert in gang activity testified that such a hat was frequently worn by members of a gang. Hamilton v.

Commonwealth, 2008 Va. App. LEXIS 487 (Nov. 4, 2008), aff'd, 279 Va. 94, 688 S.E.2d 168 (2010).

Sufficient evidence supported convictions for participating in a criminal street gang and three counts of assault and battery by a mob, where defendant was dressed in red, the gang color, he was seen with gang members at the scene, and the gang used hand-signs and a war cry before the attacks Hamilton v. Commonwealth, 279 Va. 94, 688 S.E.2d 168, 2010 Va. LEXIS 6 (2010).

Conviction for participating in criminal street gang under subsection A of § 18.2-46.2 was supported by evidence that defendant wore a bandanna in gang colors during a home invasion, and defendant planned and executed the crime with another, who wore a telltale bandanna during the crime and had evidence of the crime in his home and of the hand sign and other gang symbols. Rushing v. Commonwealth, 58 Va. App. 594, 712 S.E.2d 41, 2011 Va. App. LEXIS 247 (2011).

Evidence defendant was present when a high-ranking gang member told the person who robbed to store to do so, and defendant was seen wearing gang colors and beads associated with the gang, both of which were shown when the gang members wanted other to know they were part of the gang and supported an inference the robbery was committed for the benefit of the gang, was sufficient to support a conviction for participating in a criminal act for the benefit of a prohibited street gang. Lebron v. Commonwealth, 58 Va. App. 540, 712 S.E.2d 15, 2011 Va. App. LEXIS 238 (2011).

Defendant's conviction for criminal street gang participation under § 18.2-46.2 was appropriate because he associated himself with gang members in order to attack innocent individuals; he was present at a party where gang members discussed going on gang missions; and defendant then participated in those attacks. Morris v. Commonwealth, 58 Va. App. 744, 716 S.E.2d 139, 2011 Va. App. LEXIS 316 (2011).

Evidence insufficient. — Evidence was insufficient to support defendant's conviction for felony participation in criminal activity for the benefit of a criminal street gang that includes a juvenile, pursuant to § 18.2-46.2, because the conclusion that the juvenile was a member of the gang during the recruitment process was not supported by the evidence where the testimony indicated that the juvenile was not a member of the gang until after he participated in a "beating in." Logically, the recruitment activity performed by defendant ceased at the time the juvenile became an actual member of the gang. Phillips v. Commonwealth, 56 Va. App. 526, 694 S.E.2d 805, 2010 Va. App. LEXIS 271 (2010).

Evidence was not sufficient to sustain defendant's conviction for willfully participating in a criminal act for the benefit of criminal street gang of which he was a member, in violation of § 18.2-46.2, because the two people whose convictions the Commonwealth relied on as predicate criminal acts to establish existence of a criminal street gang were not members of defendant's subset gang. Taybron v. Commonwealth, 57 Va. App. 470, 703 S.E.2d 270, 2011 Va. App. LEXIS 1 (2011).

Evidence was insufficient to convict defendant of participation in a criminal street gang, because the Commonwealth proved only one predicate crime committed by a gang member and thus failed to prove that the gang was a "criminal street gang" under § 18.2-46.1, an essential element of the offense. Rushing v. Commonwealth, 284 Va. 270, 726 S.E.2d 333, 2012 Va. LEXIS 133 (2012).

Sentence within the range set by legislature is proper. — Trial court did not abuse its discretion in imposing a 43-year sentence against defendant, as said sentence was within the ranges set by the legislature and well below the total statutory maximum for the various felony offenses for which he was convicted. Clark v. Commonwealth, — Va. App. —, — S.E.2d —, 2008 Va. App. LEXIS 234 (May 13, 2008).

Applied in Saunders v. Commonwealth, 281 Va. 448, 706 S.E.2d 350, 2011 Va. LEXIS 45 (2011).

CIRCUIT COURT OPINIONS

Severance of charges. — Where the charges of assault and battery and assault and battery by mob were inextricably entwined with a felony gang charge, defendant's motion to sever had to be denied. Commonwealth v. Mendez, 60 Va. Cir. 242, 2002 Va. Cir. LEXIS 303 (Alexandria 2002).

§ 18.2-46.3. Recruitment of persons for criminal street gang; penalty.

A. Any person who solicits, invites, recruits, encourages or otherwise causes or attempts to cause another to actively participate in or become a member of what he knows to be a criminal street gang is guilty of a Class 1 misdemeanor. Any person age 18 years or older who solicits, invites, recruits, encourages or otherwise causes or attempts to cause a juvenile to actively participate in or become a member of what he knows to be a criminal street gang is guilty of a Class 6 felony.

B. Any person who, in order to encourage an individual (a) to join a criminal street gang, (b) to remain as a participant in or a member of a criminal street gang, or (c) to submit to a demand made by a criminal street gang to commit a felony violation of this title, (i) uses force against the individual or a member of his family or household or (ii) threatens force against the individual or a member of his family or household, which threat would place any person in reasonable apprehension of death or bodily injury, is guilty of a Class 6 felony. The definition of "family or household member" set forth in § 16.1-228 applies to this section.

History.
2000, c. 332; 2004, cc. 396, 435.

Law Review.
For 2003/2004 survey of family and juvenile law, see 39 U. Rich. L. Rev. 241 (2004).

CASE NOTES

Evidence sufficient. — Where there was ample evidence of criminal activities, including at least one violent act, from which a trial court could have inferred that the requisite predicate acts to establish a criminal street gang occurred prior to defendant recruiting a juvenile to join a gang, the evidence proved that a criminal street gang existed prior to and independent of defendant's recruitment of the juvenile and was sufficient to support defendant's conviction for recruitment of a juvenile for membership in a criminal street gang. Phillips v. Commonwealth, 56 Va. App. 526, 694 S.E.2d 805, 2010 Va. App. LEXIS 271 (2010).

§ 18.2-46.3:1. Third or subsequent conviction of criminal street gang crimes.

Upon a felony conviction of § 18.2-46.2 or § 18.2-46.3, where it is alleged in the warrant, information or indictment on which a person is convicted that (i) such person has been previously convicted twice under any combination of § 18.2-46.2 or § 18.2-46.3, within 10 years of the third or subsequent offense, and (ii) each such offense occurred on different dates, such person is guilty of a Class 3 felony.

History.
2004, cc. 396, 435, 847.

§ 18.2-46.3:2. Forfeiture.

All property, both personal and real, of any kind or character used in substantial connection with, intended for use in the course of, derived from, traceable to, or realized through, including any profit or interest derived from, any conduct in violation of any provision of this article is subject to civil forfeiture to the Commonwealth. Further, all property, both personal and real, of any kind or character used or intended to be used in substantial connection with, during the course of, derived from, traceable to, or realized through, including any profit or interest derived from, criminal street gang member recruitment as prohibited under § 18.2-46.3 is subject to civil forfeiture to the Commonwealth. The forfeiture proceeding shall utilize the provisions of Chapter 22.1 (§ 19.2-386.1 et seq.) of Title 19.2 and the procedures specified therein shall apply, mutatis mutandis, to all forfeitures under this article. The application of one civil remedy under the article does not preclude the application of any other remedy, civil or criminal, under this article or any other provision of the Code.

History.
2004, cc. 396, 435.

§ 18.2-46.3:3. Enhanced punishment for gang activity taking place in a gang-free zone; penalties.

Any person who violates § 18.2-46.2 (i) upon the property, including buildings and grounds, of any public or private elementary, secondary, or postsecondary school, or any public or private two-year or four-year institution of higher education; (ii) upon public property or any property open to public use within 1,000 feet of such school property; (iii) on any school bus as defined in § 46.2-100; or (iv) upon the property, including buildings and grounds, of any publicly owned or operated community center or any publicly owned or operated recreation center is guilty of a felony punishable as specified in § 18.2-46.2, and shall be sentenced to a mandatory minimum term of imprisonment of two years to be served consecutively with any other sentence. A person who violates subsection A of § 18.2-46.3 upon any property listed in this section is guilty of a Class 6 felony, except that any person 18 years of age or older who violates subsection A of § 18.2-46.3 upon any property listed in this section, when such offense is committed against a juvenile, is guilty of a Class 5 felony. Any person who violates subsection B of § 18.2-46.3 upon any property listed in this section is guilty of a Class 5 felony. It is a violation of this section if the person violated § 18.2-46.2 or 18.2-46.3 on the property described in clauses (i) through (iii) regardless of where the person intended to commit such violation.

History.
2005, cc. 764, 813; 2010, c. 364; 2013, cc. 761, 774.

Editor's note.
Acts 2010, c. 364, cl. 2, provides: "That the provisions of this act may result in a net increase in periods of imprisonment or commit-

ment. Pursuant to § 30-19.1:4, the estimated amount of the necessary appropriation cannot be determined for periods of imprisonment in state adult correctional facilities; therefore, Chapter 781 of the Acts of Assembly of 2009 requires the Virginia Criminal Sentencing Commission to assign a minimum fiscal impact of $50,000. Pursuant to § 30-19.1:4, the estimated amount of the necessary appropriation cannot be determined for periods of commitment to the custody of the Department of Juvenile Justice."

Acts 2013, cc. 761 and 774, cl. 2 provides: "That the provisions of this act may result in a net increase in periods of imprisonment or commitment. Pursuant to § 30-19.1:4, the estimated amount of the necessary appropriation cannot be determined for periods of imprisonment in state adult correctional facilities; therefore, Chapter 3 of the Acts of Assembly of 2012, Special Session I, requires the Virginia Criminal Sentencing Commission to assign a minimum fiscal impact of $50,000. Pursuant to § 30-19.1:4, the estimated amount of the necessary appropriation cannot be determined for periods of commitment to the custody of the Department of Juvenile Justice."

The 2010 amendments.
The 2010 amendment by c. 364 inserted "or (iv) upon the property, including buildings and grounds, of any publicly owned or operated community center or any publicly owned or operated recreation center" and made a related change.

The 2013 amendments.
The 2013 amendments by cc. 761 and 774 are identical, and added "to be served consecutively with any other sentence" at the end of the first sentence.

ARTICLE 2.2.

TERRORISM OFFENSES.

§ 18.2-46.4. Definitions.

As used in this article unless the context requires otherwise or it is otherwise provided:

"Act of terrorism" means an act of violence as defined in clause (i) of subdivision A of § 19.2-297.1 committed with the intent to (i) intimidate the civilian population at large; or (ii) influence the conduct or activities of the government of the United States, a state or locality through intimidation.

"Base offense" means an act of violence as defined in clause (i) of subdivision A of § 19.2-297.1 committed with the intent required to commit an act of terrorism.

"Weapon of terrorism" means any device or material that is designed, intended or used to cause death, bodily injury or serious bodily harm, through the release, dissemination, or impact of (i) poisonous chemicals; (ii) an infectious biological substance; or (iii) release of radiation or radioactivity.

History.
2002, cc. 588, 623.

Cross references.
As to inclusion of killing in the commission or attempted commission of an act of terrorism in the definition of capital murder, see § 18.2-31.

Law Review.
For survey of Virginia criminal law and procedure for the year 2004-2005, see 40 U. Rich. L. Rev. 197 (2005).

CASE NOTES

Constitutionality. — Terrorism statutes, subdivision 13 of § 18.2-31 and § 18.2-46.4, were not unconstitutionally overbroad and vague; by referencing established criminal offenses as acts of violence subject to the statutory scheme, the legislature included offenses with previously defined elements and mens rea requirements. Muhammad v. Commonwealth, 269 Va. 451, 619 S.E.2d 16, 2005 Va. LEXIS 85 (2005), cert. denied, — U.S. —, 126 S. Ct. 2035, 164 L. Ed. 2d 794 (2006) and overruled in part on other grounds by Jay v. Commonwealth, 275 Va. 510, 659 S.E.2d 311, 2008 Va. LEXIS 53 (2008).

Not limited to actors with political motives. — Virginia terrorism statutes, subdivision 13 of § 18.2-31 and § 18.2-46.4 were not unconstitutionally overbroad and vague, as claimed by defendant; nothing in the words of the statutes evinced an intent to limit their application to criminal actors with political motives, and the statutes provided notice sufficient for ordinary people to understand what conduct they prohibited, and did not authorize and/or encourage arbitrary and discriminatory enforcement. Muhammad v. Commonwealth, 269 Va. 451, 611 S.E.2d 537, 2005 Va. LEXIS 39 (2005), cert. denied, 547 U.S. 1136, 126 S. Ct. 2035, 164 L. Ed. 2d 794 (2006), and overruled in part on other grounds by Jay v. Commonwealth, 275 Va. 510, 659 S.E.2d 311, 2008 Va. LEXIS 53 (2008).

Evidence sufficient in sniper case. — Evidence was sufficient to convict defendant of capital murder pursuant to subdivision 13 of § 18.2-31 for the willful, deliberate, and premeditated killing of the victim in the commission of an act of terrorism. Defendant was a principal in the first degree and was a criminal actor in the second degree who gave an order or direction to the shooter, who was firing from inside the trunk of the car defendant was driving, to kill the victim. Muhammad v. Commonwealth, 269 Va. 451, 619 S.E.2d 16, 2005 Va. LEXIS 85 (2005), cert. denied, — U.S. —, 126 S. Ct. 2035, 164 L. Ed. 2d 794 (2006) and overruled in part on other grounds by Jay v. Commonwealth, 275 Va. 510, 659 S.E.2d 311, 2008 Va. LEXIS 53 (2008).

Ineffective assistance of counsel not shown. — State supreme court dismissed the petition for writ of habeas corpus that petitioner filed as to petitioner's claim in petitioner's capital murder case that the indictments, jury instructions, and verdict forms were inadequate because they did not specify which other person petitioner had killed during a three-year period or which act of terrorism petitioner had committed; petitioner's claim in that regard did not satisfy either the performance or prejudice prong of the two-part *Strickland* test since under subdivision 8 of § 18.2-31, there was no requirement that the relevant documents specify which other killing was being included within the three-year period and the indictment, under § 18.2-46.4, did not have to specify the petitioner's intent under that statute's two subsections. Muhammad v. Warden of the Sussex I State Prison, 274 Va. 3, 646 S.E.2d 182, 2007 Va. LEXIS 97 (2007), cert. denied, 128 S. Ct. 1889, 2008 U.S. LEXIS 3275 (U.S. 2008).

§ 18.2-46.5. Committing, conspiring and aiding and abetting acts of terrorism prohibited; penalty.

A. Any person who commits or conspires to commit, or aids and abets the commission of an act of terrorism, as defined in § 18.2-46.4, is guilty of a Class 2 felony if the base offense of such act of terrorism may be punished by life imprisonment, or a term of imprisonment of not less than twenty years.

B. Any person who commits, conspires to commit, or aids and abets the commission of an act of terrorism, as defined in § 18.2-46.4, is guilty of a Class 3 felony if the maximum penalty for the base offense of such act of terrorism is a term of imprisonment or incarceration in jail of less than twenty years.

C. Any person who solicits, invites, recruits, encourages, or otherwise causes or attempts to cause another to participate in an act or acts of terrorism, as defined in § 18.2-46.4, is guilty of a Class 4 felony.

History.
2002, cc. 588, 623; 2007, c. 409.

§ 18.2-46.6. Possession, manufacture, distribution, etc. of weapon of terrorism or hoax device prohibited; penalty.

A. Any person who, with the intent to commit an act of terrorism, possesses, uses, sells, gives, distributes or manufactures (i) a weapon of terrorism or (ii) a "fire bomb," "explosive material," or "device," as those terms are defined in § 18.2-85, is guilty of a Class 2 felony.

B. Any person who, with the intent to commit an act of terrorism, possesses, uses, sells, gives, distributes or manufactures any device or material that by its design, construction, content or characteristics appears to be or appears to contain a (i) weapon of terrorism or (ii) a "fire bomb," "explosive material," or "device," as those terms are defined in § 18.2-85, but that is an imitation of any such weapon of terrorism, "fire bomb," "explosive material," or "device" is guilty of a Class 3 felony.

C. Any person who, with the intent to (i) intimidate the civilian population, (ii) influence the conduct or activities of the government of the United States, a state or locality through intimidation, (iii) compel the emergency evacuation of any place of assembly, building or other structure or any means of mass transportation, or (iv) place any person in reasonable apprehension of bodily harm, uses, sells, gives, distributes or manufactures any device or material that by its design, construction, content or characteristics appears to be or appears to contain a weapon of terrorism, but that is an imitation of any such weapon of terrorism is guilty of a Class 6 felony.

History.
2002, cc. 588, 623.

Cross references.
As to civil action and reimbursement of expenses incurred in responding to terrorism hoax incident, see § 15.2-1716.1.

§ 18.2-46.7. Act of bioterrorism against agricultural crops or animals; penalty.

Any person who maliciously destroys or devastates agricultural crops or agricultural animals having a value of $2,500 or more through the use of an infectious biological substance with the intent to (i) intimidate the civilian population or (ii) influence the conduct or activities of the government of the United States, a state or locality through intimidation, is guilty of a Class 3 felony.

For the purposes of this section *"agricultural animal"* means all livestock and poultry as defined in § 3.2-5900 and *"agricultural crop"* means cultivated plants or produce, including grain, silage, forages, oilseeds, vegetables, fruits, nursery stock or turf grass.

History.
2002, cc. 588, 623.

Editor's note.
At the direction of the Virginia Code Commission, Title 3.2 references were substituted for Title 3.1 references to conform to the title revision by Acts 2008, c. 860.

§ 18.2-46.8. Venue.

Venue for any violation of this article may be had in the county or city where such crime is alleged to have occurred or where any act in furtherance of an act prohibited by this article was committed.

History.
2002, cc. 588, 623.

§ 18.2-46.9. Repealed by Acts 2004, c. 995.

Cross references.
For current provisions concerning seizure of property used in connection with or derived from terrorism, see § 19.2-386.15.

§ 18.2-46.10. Violation of sections within article separate and distinct offenses.

A violation of any section in this article shall constitute a separate and distinct offense. If the acts or activities violating any section within this article also violate another provision of law, a prosecution under any section in this article shall not prohibit or bar any prosecution or proceeding under such other provision or the imposition of any penalties provided for thereby.

History.
2002, cc. 588, 623.

Cross references.
As to seizure of property used in connection with or derived from terrorism, see §§ 19.2-386.15, 57-59.

ARTICLE 3.

KIDNAPPING AND RELATED OFFENSES.

Michie's Jurisprudence.
For related discussion, see 1A M.J. Abduction and Kidnapping, §§ 1, 3; 14A M.J. Parent and Child, § 4.

§ 18.2-47. Abduction and kidnapping defined; punishment.

A. Any person who, by force, intimidation or deception, and without legal justification or excuse, seizes, takes, transports, detains or secretes another person with the intent to deprive such other person of his personal liberty or to withhold or conceal him from any person, authority or institution lawfully entitled to his charge, shall be deemed guilty of "abduction."

B. Any person who, by force, intimidation or deception, and without legal justification or excuse, seizes, takes, transports, detains or secretes another person with the intent to subject him to forced labor or services shall be deemed guilty of "abduction." For purposes of this subsection, the term "intimidation" shall include destroying, concealing, confiscating, withholding, or threatening to withhold a passport, immigration document, or other governmental identification or threatening to report another as being illegally present in the United States.

C. The provisions of this section shall not apply to any law-enforcement officer in the performance of his duty. The terms "abduction" and "kidnapping" shall be synonymous in this Code. Abduction for which no punishment is otherwise prescribed shall be punished as a Class 5 felony.

D. If an offense under subsection A is committed by the parent of the person abducted and punishable as contempt of court in any proceeding then pending, the offense shall be a Class 1 misdemeanor in addition to being punishable as contempt of court. However, such offense, if committed by the parent of the person abducted and punishable as contempt of court in any proceeding then pending and the person abducted is removed from the Commonwealth by the abducting parent, shall be a Class 6 felony in addition to being punishable as contempt of court.

History.
Code 1950, §§ 18.1-36, 18.1-37; 1960, c. 358; 1975, cc. 14, 15; 1979, c. 663; 1980, c. 506; 1997, c. 747; 2009, c. 662.

Cross references.
For provision making it unlawful to work or volunteer on school grounds following convictions of certain sex offenses, see § 18.2-370.4. As to Sex Offenders and Crimes Against Minors Registry, see § 9.1-900 et seq. For definition of "barrier crime" as including a conviction of abduction as set out in subsection A of § 18.2-47, or an equivalent offense in another state, and prohibition against assisted living facilities, adult day care centers or child welfare agencies hiring for certain compensated employment persons who have committed such an offense, see §§ 63.2-1719, 63.2-1720.

Editor's note.
Acts 2009, c. 662, cl. 2, provides: "That the provisions of this act may result in a net increase in periods of imprisonment or commitment. Pursuant to § 30-19.1:4, the estimated amount of the necessary appropriation cannot be determined for periods of imprisonment in state adult correctional facilities and cannot be determined for periods of commitment to the custody of the Department of Juvenile Justice."

The 2009 amendments.
The 2009 amendment by c. 662 inserted subsection designations; in subsection A, substituted "secretes another person" for "secretes the person of another" and transferred the end of the subsection to new subsection C; added subsection B; and in subsection D, substituted "an offense under subsection A" for "such offense."

Law Review.
For survey of Virginia law on evidence for the year 1969-1970, see 56 Va. L. Rev. 1325 (1970). For survey of Virginia criminal law for the year 1978-1979, see 66 Va. L. Rev. 241 (1980). For survey on legal issues involving children in Virginia for 1989, see 23 U. Rich. L. Rev. 705 (1989). For note, "Predicate Offenses for First Degree Felony Murder in Virginia," see 57 Wash. & Lee L. Rev. 561 (2000). For 2007 annual survey article, "Criminal Law and Procedure," see 42 U. Rich. L. Rev. 311 (2007).

CASE NOTES

This section supersedes the common law. Scott v. Commonwealth, 228 Va. 519, 323 S.E.2d 572 (1984).

This section is not unconstitutionally vague because it does not inform an individual whether they can be held in contempt in a court of the Commonwealth or that of a sister state. Bennett v. Commonwealth, 8 Va. App. 228, 380 S.E.2d 17 (1989).

Each prohibited act independently sufficient to support conviction. — Because this section casts its several prohibited acts in the disjunctive, each is independently sufficient to support a conviction. Accordingly, the physical detention of a person, with the intent to deprive him of his personal liberty, by force, intimidation or deception, without any asportation of the victim from one place to another, is sufficient. Scott v. Commonwealth, 228 Va. 519, 323 S.E.2d 572 (1984).

The abduction statute casts its several prohibited acts in the disjunctive, [and therefore,] each is independently sufficient to support a conviction. Cheng v. Commonwealth, 240 Va. 26, 393 S.E.2d 599 (1990).

Robbery, burglary, grand larceny and abduction, are each treated separately and are governed by a separate statutory provision. Austin v. Peyton, 279 F. Supp. 227 (W.D. Va. 1968).

Included in offense defined in § 18.2-48. — The offense defined in this section is an offense lesser-included in the offense defined in § 18.2-48. Hawks v. Commonwealth, 228 Va. 244, 321 S.E.2d 650 (1984).

Detention of trespasser not legally justified. — The defendant did not have legal justification to confront and detain victims who trespassed onto his property, since the common law has long recognized the right of a landowner to order a trespasser to leave his property, and, should the trespasser refuse, to employ proper force to expel him, but does not allow the landowner to seize or detain a trespasser; thus, the evidence was sufficient to prove that the defendant abducted the victims and used a firearm in the commission of the abductions where the defendant and his brother jumped out of the woods, brandished rifles at the victims, and commanded that they "freeze," and then coerced them into going to the defendant's house by falsely telling them that the police had been called. Hitchcock v. Commonwealth, No. 1387-97-4 (Ct. of Appeals April 21, 1998).

Specific intent. — The distinguishing feature between the offenses of abduction "with the intent to deprive such other person of his personal liberty" and abduction "with intent to defile" is the specific intent entertained by the accused. McKinley v. Commonwealth, 217 Va. 1, 225 S.E.2d 352 (1976) (decided under former §§ 18.1-36 and 18.1-38).

Physical detention of a person, with intent to deprive him of his personal liberty, by force, intimidation, or deception, without any asportation of the victim from one place to another, is sufficient to support a conviction of abduction. Simms v. Commonwealth, 2 Va. App. 614, 346 S.E.2d 734 (1986).

Momentary deprivation of liberty furthering sexual advances. — Where defendant put his arms around prosecutrix and held her tightly this was done in furtherance of his sexual advances and not with the intent to deprive her of her personal liberty, although such a deprivation did occur momentarily; thus, the evidence was not sufficient to sustain his conviction of abduction. Johnson v. Commonwealth, 221 Va. 872, 275 S.E.2d 592 (1981).

When defendant grabbed the victim around the waist and thrust his pelvic area into her buttocks for about five seconds, the requisite specific intent to deprive the victim of her personal liberty, sufficient to sustain a charge of abduction under this section, was not present. Hartnett v. Commonwealth, No. 1507-00-2, 2001 Va. App. LEXIS 346 (Ct. of Appeals June 19, 2001).

Because the evidence was insufficient to prove that defendant intended to deprive a victim of the victim's personal liberty, defendant's conviction for abduction, in violation of subsection A of § 18.2-47, was improper; defendant's intent was to deceive the victim into positioning herself in such a way that defendant could gain sexual gratification, and although the victim was briefly detained by defendant's ruse, defendant's actions were made in pursuit of sexual gratification and not with the intent to deprive the victim of personal liberty. Burton v. Commonwealth, 281 Va. 622, 708 S.E.2d 892, 2011 Va. LEXIS 97 (2011).

For detention falling under the definition of abduction as set out in this section, see Joyce v. Commonwealth, 210 Va. 272, 170 S.E.2d 9 (1969).

The type of detention set forth in the abduction statute is defined as detention separate and apart from, and not merely incidental to, the restraint employed in the commission of the other crime. Coram v. Commonwealth, 3 Va. App. 623, 352 S.E.2d 532 (1987).

Claim of right to property no defense. — There is no authority in Virginia for a defense of bona fide claim of right that would allow the abduction of an individual in order to recover property. Jackson v. Commonwealth, No. 2994-99-2, 2001 Va. App. LEXIS 249 (Ct. of Appeals May 8, 2001).

The defense of legal excuse is personal to the parent and is not available to an accomplice of the parent. Taylor v. Commonwealth, 31 Va. App. 54, 521 S.E.2d 293 (1999), aff'd, 260 Va. 683, 537 S.E.2d 592 (2000).

Abduction of biological child from mother's custody. — Where the father of an illegitimate child had only a biological relationship, and none other, with his child, the father had no legal justification for taking the child from the mother's custody by intimidation and deception, and proof that he had done so was sufficient to establish that the father had committed the crime of abduction; his fiance, who was present at the commission of the crime and incited, encouraged and assisted the father in committing the crime, was liable as an accomplice. Taylor v. Commonwealth, 260 Va. 683, 537 S.E.2d 592, 2000 Va. LEXIS 126 (2000).

A custodial parent may be prosecuted for the felony murder of his or her child, using abduction as the underlying felony as set forth in this section. Diehl v. Commonwealth, 9 Va. App. 191, 385 S.E.2d 228 (1989).

Parent could be charged with felony instead of misdemeanor. — Where custodial parent was convicted of abduction of his child, parent could be convicted of a felony instead of a misdemeanor; the misdemeanor provision was inapplicable since there was no "proceeding then pending" at the time of the offense. Diehl v. Commonwealth, 9 Va. App. 191, 385 S.E.2d 228 (1989).

Photograph of victim was relevant. — Where a primary defense at trial was that the parents were merely disciplining a child for his misconduct, there was no abuse of discretion in admitting photograph of victim's buttocks disclosing extent of injury inflicted on him; the picture was relevant to the issue of whether the punishment inflicted exceeded the bounds of moderation so as to subject defendant to criminal liability. Diehl v. Commonwealth, 9 Va. App. 191, 385 S.E.2d 228 (1989).

One accused of abduction by detention and another crime involving restraint of victim, both growing out of a continuing course of conduct, is subject upon conviction to separate penalties for separate offenses only when the detention committed in the act of abduction is separate and apart from, and not merely incidental to, the restraint employed in the commission of the other crime. Brown v. Commonwealth, 230 Va. 310, 337 S.E.2d 711 (1985).

A defendant may be convicted and receive separate punishments for abduction and another crime involving restraint, both growing out of a continuing course of conduct, when the detention committed in the act of abduction is separate and apart from, and not merely incidental to, the restraint employed in the commission of the other crime. Redmond v. Commonwealth, No. 1726-00-1, 2001 Va. App. LEXIS 308 (Ct. of Appeals June 5, 2001).

Restraint was not brief prelude to victim's murder. — Defendant's restraint of a victim was not simply a brief prelude to her murder that could not be separately criminalized as an abduction, because it occurred before defendant sealed off the victim's airways with a plastic bag where he physically held the victim down while his wife obtained the tape he requested and he then taped the victim so she could not escape while he went to retrieve the plastic bag. Pryor v. Commonwealth, 48 Va. App. 1, 628 S.E.2d 47, 2006 Va. App. LEXIS 131 (2006).

Abduction preceding a murder may lead to separate convictions for each. Pryor v. Commonwealth, 48 Va. App. 1, 628 S.E.2d 47, 2006 Va. App. LEXIS 131 (2006).

Restraint intrinsic in rape, robbery, etc., not separate offense. — Detention is a discrete species of abduction. However, in the enactment of the abduction statute the General Assembly did not intend to make the kind of restraint which is an intrinsic element of crimes such as rape, robbery, and assault a criminal act, punishable as a separate offense. Brown v. Commonwealth, 230 Va. 310, 337 S.E.2d 711 (1985).

A defendant may be convicted of abduction in addition to robbery if the victim's detention is separate and apart from, and not merely incidental to, the restraint employed in the commission of robbery.

To constitute an abduction, separate and apart from a robbery, the victim's detention must be greater than the restraint that is intrinsic in a robbery. Herbin v. Commonwealth, No. 0223-00-3, 2001 Va. App. LEXIS 40 (Ct. of Appeals Jan. 30, 2001).

A defendant was improperly convicted of abduction under this section where the evidence failed to prove that the acts which gave rise to the attempted robbery were separate and apart from the attempted abduction charged in the indictment. The attack and struggles were continuous and not shown to be motivated by an intent to deprive the victim of his personal liberty except as an incident of the attempt to rob him. Burgess v. Commonwealth, No. 0275-00-1, 2000 Va. App. LEXIS 828 (Ct. of Appeals Dec. 19, 2000).

For case holding that abduction and rape were different offenses and that the several penalties imposed did not offend the double jeopardy guarantee against multiple punishments, see Brown v. Commonwealth, 230 Va. 310, 337 S.E.2d 711 (1985).

Abduction and attempted rape as separate crimes. — It could not be said as a matter of law that the evidence was insufficient to support a conviction for abduction with intent to defile, where when defendant grabbed the victim, he transported her from a location that was lighted and visible to one out of sight of potential passersby or others, as defendant's asportation of the victim substantially increased the risk of harm to the victim by decreasing the possibility of detecting his criminal activity, and as, moreover, asportation to decrease the possibility of detection is not an act inherent in or necessary to the restraint required in the commission of attempted rape. Thus, the jury could reasonably infer that the abduction was separate and apart from, and not merely incidental to, the crime of attempted rape. Accordingly, multiple punishments for defendant's abduction and attempted rape of victim did not offend the double jeopardy guarantee. Coram v. Commonwealth, 3 Va. App. 623, 352 S.E.2d 532 (1987).

Abduction not incidental to sexual assault. — Trial court properly denied defendant's motion to strike the abduction charge, because defendant's detention of the victim was not incidental to the sexual assault; defendant's act of covering the victim's mouth did nothing to further the sexual assault itself, but made it more difficult for the victim to call for help and, consequently, more difficult for the public to detect the crime. Mitchell v. Commonwealth, 2010 Va. App. LEXIS 342 (Aug. 17, 2010).

Evidence supported defendant's conviction for abduction with the intent to defile, in violation of §§ 18.2-47, 18.2-48, and 18.2-67.5:3, because defendant lured the victim to a house and proceeded to force himself onto the victim once the victim manifested the victim's discomfort with defendant's advances and attempted to leave. Defendant's conduct and statements to the victim supported the conclusion that the abduction that preceded the rape was effected with the intent to defile. Shepperson v. Commonwealth, 2012 Va. App. LEXIS 329 (Oct. 16, 2012).

Evidence of rape admissible to show intent to deprive of personal liberty. — Although intent to defile was not charged, evidence of rape was not irrelevant to the charge that the defendant intended to deprive his victim of personal liberty, since restraint imposed upon a rape victim was a deprivation of personal liberty. Such evidence was relevant to show that the abduction was committed with intent to deprive his victim of personal liberty. Hawks v. Commonwealth, 228 Va. 244, 321 S.E.2d 650 (1984).

Where trial court allowed charges of attempted rape and abduction to go to the jury, defendant was not placed in double jeopardy. Johnson v. Commonwealth, 221 Va. 872, 275 S.E.2d 592 (1981).

Defendant's conviction for assault did not bar, under double jeopardy, his subsequent conviction for abduction since the offense of assault and that of abduction each required proof of a fact that the other did not. Johnson v. Commonwealth, 13 Va. App. 515, 412 S.E.2d 731 (1992).

The fact that the same evidence, in whole or in part, was used in both trials does not give rise to a double jeopardy objection. Johnson v. Commonwealth, 13 Va. App. 515, 412 S.E.2d 731 (1992).

The conduct used to support the second prosecution was not the same conduct as that used to support the first conviction; evidence of separate, discrete conduct by the defendant supported each offense. Johnson v. Commonwealth, 13 Va. App. 515, 412 S.E.2d 731 (1992).

The assault required proof of an attempt or offer to do bodily harm through an unlawful show of force and violence; the abduc-

tion required proof of an asportation or detention by force, intimidation or deception. Johnson v. Commonwealth, 13 Va. App. 515, 412 S.E.2d 731 (1992).

Assault, therefore, required proof of force while abduction, although it may have been accomplished by force, did not require proof of force because it may also have been accomplished through intimidation or deception; abduction, on the other hand, required proof of asportation or detention while assault did not. Johnson v. Commonwealth, 13 Va. App. 515, 412 S.E.2d 731 (1992).

A defendant's prosecution for abduction was not barred by his previous prosecution for assault, because the abduction prosecution was based on different conduct; the trial court, as the trier of fact, could have reasonably concluded from the evidence that the defendant abducted, as well as assaulted, the victim, that the commission of the abduction was complete when the defendant shut the door to the victim's office and put his foot against it to keep the victim from leaving the room, and that this initial act of detention was not inherent in the later acts of assault in that, only after that initial, separate act of detention did the defendant's actions, including his hitting the victim's hand off the doorknob and wrapping his arms around the victim, constitute acts of assault involving incidental acts of restraint. Jackson v. Commonwealth, No. 2994-99-2, 2001 Va. App. LEXIS 249 (Ct. of Appeals May 8, 2001).

Abduction was incidental to robbery. — Because: (1) the duration of the detention and the distance of asportation were slight; (2) the detention and asportation of the first robbery victim occurred during the commission of the separate offense of robbery, but, they were not acts separate and apart from the robbery itself; (3) the detention and asportation of that same victim was inherent in the robbery; (4) the detention and asportation did not pose a danger to that victim independent of and significantly greater than that posed by the robbery itself; and (5) the evidence did not support an inference that defendant detained and moved the victim in order to avoid the detection of the robbery. Hoyt v. Commonwealth, 44 Va. App. 489, 605 S.E.2d 755, 2004 Va. App. LEXIS 599 (2004).

Attempted abduction by out-of-state bail bondsman. — Sufficient evidence supported defendant's conviction for attempted abduction because his use of foul language, his pointing of a deadly weapon at the deputy chief of police, his allowance of an employee to confront the deputy chief with mace and a handgun, and his use of physical force in pulling the deputy chief toward the truck all proved beyond a reasonable doubt that, without legal justification or excuse, defendant seized another person with the intent to deprive such other person of his personal liberty. As a bail bondsman licensed in another state, he was not justified in apprehending a fugitive bailee and his abandonment (when he realized he had the wrong person) came after the attempt was complete. Collins v. Commonwealth, 283 Va. 263, 720 S.E.2d 530, 2012 Va. LEXIS 17 (2012).

Motion to withdraw guilty plea. — In a case in which defendant pled guilty to violating §§ 18.2-90, 18.2-47, 18.2-67.1 and 18.2-53.1, he argued unsuccessfully that the circuit court abused its discretion in denying his motion to withdraw his guilty pleas prior to sentencing; defendant failed to show a good faith basis for seeking to withdraw his guilty pleas. He was clearly aware of the potential range of punishments available to the court at the time he pled guilty; as such, the fact that the sentencing guidelines recommended a higher sentence than he had hoped did not constitute a good faith basis for rescinding his pleas. Mack v. Commonwealth, 2009 Va. App. LEXIS 417 (Sept. 22, 2009).

Defendant's conviction for assault. — Detaining the boyfriend and later ordering the victim back to her room were separate and apart from the attempted robbery as they were not inherent in or necessary to complete the attempted robbery; the evidence showed the defendant committed two acts of abduction under § 18.2-47. Bell v. Commonwealth, No. 0318-02-1, 2003 Va. App. LEXIS 373 (Ct. of Appeals July 1, 2003).

Defendant may not be convicted of both abduction and attempted robbery unless the detention committed in the act of abduction is separate and apart from, and not merely incidental to, the restraint employed in the commission of the attempted robbery. Bell v. Commonwealth, No. 0318-02-1, 2003 Va. App. LEXIS 373 (Ct. of Appeals July 1, 2003).

Abduction conviction required reversal under the incidental detention doctrine, because the entire encounter lasted no more than three minutes; the assault and the detention were simultaneous, there was no difference in the time or place of the assault and the time or place of the resulting restraint on the victim's personal liberty; everything defendant did that contributed to the deprivation of the victim's liberty, pointing the gun at the victim as he walked toward him, perfectly fit a definition of common-law assault; and there was no evidence that the restraint of the victim's liberty inherent in the assault posed any physical danger to the victim apart from the danger created by the assault itself. Seddiq v. Commonwealth, 2010 Va. App. LEXIS 238 (June 15, 2010).

Conviction as accessory or principal in second degree to abduction. — The evidence was sufficient to prove that the defendant was either an accessory before the fact or a principal in the second degree to the victim's abduction where the Commonwealth proved that, after the victim accused the defendant of stealing cocaine, the defendant hit the victim and knocked him to the ground, and the defendant then instructed four men to beat the victim, tie him up, "get rid of him." Smith v. Commonwealth, 3 Va. App. 65, 531 S.E.2d 608, 2000 Va. App. LEXIS 577 (2000).

Indictment sufficient. — The indictment which, although not drawn in the precise language of the statute, did charge the defendant with having feloniously seized and abducted his victim by force and intimidation and without legal justification or excuse in violation of former § 18.1-36 was sufficient to sustain a conviction of abduction "with the intent to deprive such other person of his personal liberty." McKinley v. Commonwealth, 217 Va. 1, 225 S.E.2d 352 (1976) (decided under former § 18.1-36).

The Commonwealth by specifying in the indictment that the abduction was accomplished "by threat, force or intimidation" sufficiently notified the defendant of the nature of the charge against him and to require it to further describe the nature of the force used would have required disclosure of the evidence upon which it planned to rely to prove this element. Sims v. Commonwealth, 28 Va. App. 611, 507 S.E.2d 648 (1998).

Evidence sufficient to show victim did not voluntarily accompany defendant. — In trial for simple abduction in connection with murder, where victim lived in apartments within sight of another apartment complex where defendant talked about abducting and killing a college girl the previous year, and victim was last seen at the hotel lounge where she and several friends had gone for an after-dinner drink and victim did not have a car and was depending on her friends to drive her back to her apartment, some two miles from hotel, victim disappeared less than eight hours before she was scheduled to leave for trip, she had arranged her affairs in order and reconfirmed her plans for the trip shortly before her disappearance, and when she telephoned friend who was to accompany her on trip only a few hours before her disappearance, she stressed her desire to get an early start on the following morning, evidence was sufficient to justify jury's conclusion that the victim would not voluntarily have travelled to county where her body was found or otherwise accompanied defendant willingly. Lafon v. Commonwealth, 17 Va. App. 411, 438 S.E.2d 279 (1993).

Use of force or intimidation. — The only reasonable hypothesis flowing from the evidence was that the victims entered the bathroom and remained there for over two hours based on the defendant's intimidation and threat to use force if they did not cooperate where, immediately upon entering the victims' apartment, the defendant locked the door's deadbolt, then, a few minutes later, ripped the telephone out of the wall to prevent one of the victims from calling for help, pulled out a gun while standing only three or four feet away from the victims and, while displaying the weapon, said he "didn't want to hurt [them]," "made [them] go in the bathroom," and told them to stay there without making any noise until he said they could come out. Griffin v. Commonwealth, No. 0949-99-2, 2000 Va. App. LEXIS 264 (Ct. of Appeals Apr. 11, 2000).

Evidence held sufficient. — Evidence was sufficient to sustain the abduction and felony murder charges where defendant shackled an unclothed child to the floor of a bus for several weeks, where during that time the child was required to drink his own urine, eat his own feces and where child was subjected to body and head blows which caused his death. Diehl v. Commonwealth, 9 Va. App. 191, 385 S.E.2d 228 (1989).

Because mother was not entitled to custody of the children, and the father could and did entrust the care of the children to their grandparents, and mother broke into grandparents' home and took the children, the evidence was sufficient to sustain the jury's finding that the children were taken from one "lawfully entitled to their charge." Bennett v. Commonwealth, 8 Va. App. 228, 380 S.E.2d 17 (1989).

Where transporting of murder victim from robbery scene was a detention separate and apart from, and not merely incidental to, the robbery and was greater than the restraint intrinsic in a robbery, and further, the evidence clearly supported a finding that the abduction was committed to protect the fruits of the robbery and to escape an arrest, the evidence supported the charge of an abduction with the intent to extort a pecuniary benefit. Cardwell v. Commonwealth, 248 Va. 501, 450 S.E.2d 146 (1994), cert. denied, 514 U.S. 1097, 115 S. Ct. 1826, 131 L. Ed. 2d 747 (1995).

Defendant's initial act of forcing the victims upstairs at knifepoint satisfies the elements of this crime. Wilson v. Commonwealth, 249 Va. 95, 452 S.E.2d 669, cert. denied, 516 U.S. 841, 116 S. Ct. 127, 133 L. Ed. 2d 76 (1995).

Making victims get out of their car and onto ground during robbery and attempted robbery constituted the separate crime of abduction. Taylor v. Commonwealth, No. 0995-94-1 (Ct. of Appeals May 23, 1995).

The detention of the victim in this case was separate and apart from the robbery charge, and was sufficient to support a charge and conviction for abduction. Coward v. Commonwealth, No. 2631-94-2 (Ct. of Appeals April 2, 1996).

The evidence was sufficient for the trial judge to find beyond a reasonable doubt both that the defendant detained a boy and that he did so with the intent to deprive the boy of his personal liberty while the defendant's son, at the defendant's direction, assaulted the boy where several witnesses testified that the defendant restrained the boy on the ground while his son kicked the boy and one of the witnesses heard the defendant tell his son to kick the boy and testified that the defendant's son kicked the boy's head for approximately a minute while the defendant held the boy. Barfield v. Commonwealth, No. 1050-00-1, 2001 Va. App. LEXIS 75 (Ct. of Appeals Feb. 20, 2001).

Where defendant grabbed a 10-year-old girl by her wrists, victim told defendant to let her go, and defendant did not let go of her until she kicked him, abduction was upheld under this section. Moreno v. Commonwealth, No. 2237-98-4, 2000 Va. App. LEXIS 396 (Ct. of Appeals May 23, 2000).

When, in the course of a robbery of a restaurant cash register, defendant ordered a victim to move approximately 15 feet to lie down next to another victim, defendant was properly convicted of abduction because the victim's movement was not necessary to accomplish the robbery, and the victim's asportation and detention were not merely incidental to the restraint employed in the commission of the robbery. Ortega v. Commonwealth, No. 3394-01-1, 2003 Va. App. LEXIS 132 (Ct. of Appeals Mar. 11, 2003).

Because the evidence was sufficient to convict petitioner of abduction (the first abduction was accomplished through asportation by deception, and the second abduction occurred when the victim's body was carried out of the house, through the backyard to the fence, and dumped over the fence; in both acts of abduction petitioner acted, as a minimum, as a principal in the second degree), there was not a reasonable probability, under the Strickland prejudice prong, that there would have been a different outcome if petitioner's trial counsel had moved, at the close of evidence, to strike the evidence on the abduction charge. Jerman v. Dir., Dep't of Corr., 267 Va. 432, 593 S.E.2d 255, 2004 Va. LEXIS 43 (2004).

Evidence that, after blocking the victim's path of escape, defendant personally detained the victim at gunpoint and forcibly moved him from the back of the tow truck into the truck cab by picking him up by his belt showed that defendant physically detained the victim, with the intent to deprive him of his personal liberty, using force and intimidation, thereby supporting a conviction for abduction. Walker v. Commonwealth, 47 Va. App. 114, 622 S.E.2d 282, 2005 Va. App. LEXIS 482 (2005).

Trial court's denial of defendant's motion to strike a jury instruction on abduction was proper where the evidence was sufficient to support a finding that he committed that crime by gaining control of the victim's vehicle, even if only for a short time, and driving in a direction other than where the victim wanted to go, and by his intent to deprive her of her personal liberty; defendant had flagged down a local mail carrier, gotten a ride to his allegedly dead car, and then he pulled a knife on the carrier, jumped into her vehicle, and engaged in a struggle with her while stabbing her. Ford v. Commonwealth, — Va. App. —, —, S.E.2d —, 2006 Va. App. LEXIS 100 (Mar. 21, 2006).

Defendant's use of the victim's cell phone shortly after it was stolen and the undisputed DNA evidence establishing that DNA recovered from the victim matched defendant's DNA profile provided sufficient evidence to prove that defendant was the criminal agent who committed the crimes of forcible sodomy, abduction, robbery, and conspiracy to commit robbery. Hayden v. Commonwealth, — Va. App. —, — S.E.2d —, 2006 Va. App. LEXIS 275 (June 27, 2006).

Evidence that defendant, armed with a handgun that he pointed against the victim's chest, lifted the victim in the air, moved the victim seven or eight feet, and "stuffed" the victim into the tow truck the victim was using to repossess defendant's vehicle, as the victim screamed and begged defendant to cease was sufficient to show that defendant deprived the victim of his liberty by using the handgun to prevent the victim from leaving during the detention and support defendant's conviction for abduction. Walker v. Commonwealth, 272 Va. 511, 636 S.E.2d 476, 2006 Va. LEXIS 96 (2006).

Evidence that the victim reported the incident to the victim's husband as soon as the victim returned to their hotel room, reported it to the police after the victim discovered evidence identifying the assailant, and located several landmarks the victim had seen while defendant held the victim captive was sufficient to support convictions for carjacking, abduction, and robbery; based on defendant's display of a gun and defendant's bizarre behavior, the victim reasonably feared defendant would kill the victim, explaining the victim's failure to make a more determined attempt to escape. Corbin v. Commonwealth, — Va. App. —, — S.E.2d —, 2007 Va. App. LEXIS 359 (Oct. 2, 2007).

Conviction for abduction under § 18.2-47, was supported by evidence that the infant was taken from the infant's father in order to facilitate the attempted robbery of the father; § 18.2-47 did not require that the force, intimidation, or deceit be directed at the infant or that the infant be aware of such conduct and resist it. Clanton v. Commonwealth, 53 Va. App. 561, 673 S.E.2d 904, 2009 Va. App. LEXIS 202 (2009).

Because defendant, a North Carolina bail bondsman, did not have authority pursuant to §§ 9.1-185.18 and 9.1-186.13, to seize a fugitive or the victim, and the Commonwealth showed that defendant intended to abduct the fugitive, there was no legal justification for his actions and defendant's convictions for attempted abduction, a violation of §§ 18.2-26 and 18.2-47, and use of a firearm in the commission of an attempted abduction, a violation of § 18.2-53.1, were proper. Collins v. Commonwealth, 57 Va. App. 355, 702 S.E.2d 267, 2010 Va. App. LEXIS 480 (2010), aff'd, 283 Va. 263, 720 S.E.2d 530, 2012 Va. LEXIS 17 (2012).

Evidence was sufficient to prove beyond a reasonable doubt that defendant was guilty of abduction because defendant both detained and asported the victim, defendant's wife, using force and without legal excuse. As the victim tried to leave the bedroom, defendant grabbed the victim and threw her on the bed. Defendant restrained the victim on the bed for several minutes despite the victim's repeated entreaties that defendant release the victim. Bradbury v. Commonwealth, 2010 Va. App. LEXIS 421 (Nov. 2, 2010).

Defendant's convictions for robbery, abduction, and malicious wounding were proper because the fact that he was not wearing a white coat did not negate a detective's reasonable suspicion that defendant was somehow involved in criminal activity. The trial court accepted the explanation that defendant had abandoned his coat as he fled. Diaz v. Commonwealth, 2010 Va. App. LEXIS 417 (Oct. 26, 2010).

Evidence was sufficient to support the trial court's finding that defendant abducted a victim, as defendant's attempt to remove the victim from a register kiosk in the front of a convenience store was legally sufficient to constitute a detention, and thus an abduction. Ellis v. Commonwealth, 2012 Va. App. LEXIS 92 (Mar. 27, 2012).

Trial court did not err in finding that the evidence proved beyond a reasonable doubt that defendant acted as a principal in the second degree to use of a firearm in the commission of a robbery and abduction as the evidence showed that defendant aided in the commission of and shared the main actor's intent to rob a clothing retail store during normal business hours, where he was likely to encounter both store employees and customers. The evidence showed that defendant transported the main actor to and from the immediate area where he committed the robbery and abduction; that defendant remained in her SUV at a nearby apartment complex, where neither she nor the main actor lived, when the main actor departed the vehicle to commit the robbery; that she tried to assist him in eluding police, and that she tried to provide him with an alibi when questioned about the offenses, and that she gave false and contradictory statements to officers when questioned about her part in the robbery. Wade v. Commonwealth, 2012 Va. App. LEXIS 161 (May 15, 2012).

Although no witness was able to identify defendant by facial recognition, as the robber was wearing a mask during the robbery, there was sufficient evidence to convict defendant of abduction during a robbery where the surveillance camera photographs showed the robber wearing a dark, hooded jacket or sweatshirt of some type, with a tag or label on the lower left front side, as well as distinctively marked gloves, the store owner testified that defendant's height was about the same as the height of the robber and the robber was African-American, as was defendant, a police officer later encountered defendant wearing a dark jacket, zipped up, with a knit cap on his head and the hood of his jacket pulled over his head, with a tag or label on the lower left front side, and the officer discovered a pair of gloves and a handgun lying on the ground in a haphazard fashion, as if someone had quickly or carelessly tossed them there, defendant's DNA profile was consistent with that found on the gloves, and the gloves had the same color and distinctive markings as the gloves worn by the robber. Spence v. Commonwealth, 60 Va. App. 355, 727 S.E.2d 786, 2012 Va. App. LEXIS 221 (2012).

Conviction for abduction under § 18.2-47 was supported by the fact that nearly all of the elements of abduction occurred entirely before the assault and battery began and that defendant could have committed assault and battery without first detaining the victim in the bathroom but instead, defendant blocked only exit while he questioned the victim. Breland v. Commonwealth, 2012 Va. App. LEXIS 307 (Oct. 2, 2012).

Sufficient evidence supported defendant's conviction for abduction under subsection A of § 18.2-47 where: (1) the victim testified that she was scared because she did not know what was going to happen and did not know when defendant's rage was going to return; (2) it could be inferred that defendant, by force or intimidation, intended to and did prevent the victim from leaving the home against her will when he took off her clothes, refused to seek help after rendering her helpless, insisted on holding her, and disabled or hid the telephones; and (3) the abduction conduct occurred after the malicious wounding, was separate from the malicious wounding and was not merely incidental to it. Chatman v. Commonwealth, No. 0858-11-2, 61 Va. App. 618, 739 S.E.2d 245, 2013 Va. App. LEXIS 98 (Mar. 26, 2013).

Failure to preserve legal justification argument for appeal. — Defendant failed to preserve for appeal his argument that his alleged abduction of a victim in violation of § 18.2-47 was legally justified since he was acting in self-defense because he did not make that argument to the trial court, but instead, his counsel argued just the opposite to the trial court in summation, that defendant used no force against the victim; the court of appeals would not consider defendant's justification/self-defense argument under the ends of justice exception to Rule 5A:18 because defendant failed to establish any grave injustice or denial of essential rights implicated by his convictions. Stone v. Commonwealth, 2010 Va. App. LEXIS 414 (Oct. 26, 2010).

Double jeopardy. — Because the two statutes require proof of additional facts, and they therefore constitute two distinct offenses, the double jeopardy clause was not offended by defendant's convictions under this section and § 40.1-103. Long v. Commonwealth, No. 0399-95-1, 1995 Va. App. LEXIS 874 (Ct. of Appeals Dec. 5, 1995).

Where the acts constituting abduction and carjacking were separate and distinct, double jeopardy did not attach; however, where defendant's abduction sentence exceeded the maximum, it had to be reduced. Barron v. Commonwealth, No. 1798-02-3, 2003 Va. App. LEXIS 358 (Ct. of Appeals June 24, 2003).

Jury instructions. — Under the instruction given in petitioner's case, the evidence proved abduction by deception before the assault and abduction by force after the assault. Neither involved the restraint or force inherent in the act of murdering the victim, and that restraint was the subject of the instruction proposed by petitioner. Jerman v. Dir., Dep't of Corr., 267 Va. 432, 593 S.E.2d 255, 2004 Va. LEXIS 43 (2004).

Defendant's request that the trial court instruct the jury that if the detention of the victim was incidental to an assault, defendant could not be guilty of abduction, was properly denied as defendant followed the victim after she fled from the car and grabbed her, which was not incidental to the malicious wounding charge based on the restraint defendant used at the time he bit off the victim's finger, before she fled. Lewis v. Commonwealth, No. 1770-03-2, 2004 Va. App. LEXIS 296 (Ct. of Appeals June 29, 2004).

Where a defendant is charged with both abduction and another crime, such as rape or assault, arising out of the same criminal episode, as the requirement that the restraint involved in the abduction be separate and apart from the restraint involved in the other offense is not an element of the crime of abduction, the jury does not have to be instructed on this matter. Anderson v. Commonwealth, — Va. App. —, — S.E.2d —, 2006 Va. App. LEXIS 555 (Dec. 12, 2006).

As a trial court found as matter of law that the evidence was sufficient for the jury to consider both the crime of abduction and of assault and battery, it was not obliged to instruct the jury about the test for determining whether the abduction was merely incidental to the assault and battery. Anderson v. Commonwealth. — Va. App. —, — S.E.2d —, 2006 Va. App. LEXIS 555 (Dec. 12, 2006).

Since *Blakely* applies to increases of the penalty for a crime beyond the prescribed maximum, not the penalty for a course of conduct, a trial judge's refusal to instruct the jury on the possible merger of charges of abduction and assault and battery did not violate defendant's Sixth Amendment right to a jury trial. Anderson v. Commonwealth, — Va. App. —, — S.E.2d —, 2006 Va. App. LEXIS 555 (Dec. 12, 2006).

Trial court properly refused to give defendant's requested instructions on the merger of charges of abduction and assault and battery, as the question whether the abduction was incidental to the assault and battery was a question of law, and the trial court determined that the evidence was sufficient to go to the jury on both charges. Mawyer v. Commonwealth, — Va. App. —, — S.E.2d —, 2006 Va. App. LEXIS 554 (Dec. 12, 2006).

Relationship with federal sentencing. — Fact that defendant was ultimately convicted of only misdemeanors had no bearing on the district court's finding of a Grade A violation; defendant was charged under Virginia law with abduction and malicious wounding, both felonies punishable by a year or more in prison. These crimes met the requirements of U.S. Sentencing Guidelines Manual § 7B1.1(a)(1)(A), Pol'y Statement, in that they were state crimes of violence punishable by more than one year's imprisonment; thus, they constituted Grade A violations. United States v. Washington, 2009 U.S. App. LEXIS 14801 (4th Cir. July 2, 2009).

Applied in Pearson v. Commonwealth, 221 Va. 936, 275 S.E.2d 893 (1981); Crawford v. Commonwealth, 281 Va. 84, 704 S.E.2d 107, 2011 Va. LEXIS 20 (2011).

CIRCUIT COURT OPINIONS

Evidence held insufficient. — Evidence that defendant stood in front of a door and temporarily prevented a woman from leaving her house by using that door did not prove that defendant seized, took, transported, detained, or secreted the woman by force, threat, intimidation, or deception, and was not sufficient to prove abduction, in violation of § 18.2-47. Commonwealth v. Harrington, — Va. Cir. —, 2002 Va. Cir. LEXIS 268 (Newport News June 11, 2002).

§ 18.2-48. Abduction with intent to extort money or for immoral purpose.

Abduction (i) of any person with the intent to extort money or pecuniary benefit, (ii) of any person with intent to defile such person, (iii) of any child under sixteen years of age for the purpose of concubinage or prostitution, (iv) of any person for the purpose of prostitution, or (v) of any minor for the purpose of manufacturing child pornography shall be punishable as a Class 2 felony. If the sentence

imposed for a violation of (ii), (iii), (iv), or (v) includes a term of confinement less than life imprisonment, the judge shall impose, in addition to any active sentence, a suspended sentence of no less than 40 years. This suspended sentence shall be suspended for the remainder of the defendant's life subject to revocation by the court.

History.
Code 1950, § 18.1-38; 1960, c. 358; 1966, c. 214; 1975, cc. 14, 15; 1993, c. 317; 1997, c. 747; 2006, cc. 853, 914; 2011, c. 785.

Cross references.
For provision making it unlawful to work or volunteer on school grounds following convictions of certain sex offenses, see § 18.2-370.4. As to Sex Offenders and Crimes Against Minors Registry, see § 9.1-900 et seq. For definition of "barrier crime" as including a conviction of abduction for immoral purposes as set out in § 18.2-48, or an equivalent offense in another state, and prohibition against assisted living facilities, adult day care centers or child welfare agencies hiring for certain compensated employment persons who have committed such an offense, see §§ 63.2-1719, 63.2-1720. As to report to children's residential facility for which a background check is being performed on whether the applicant has ever been convicted of or is the subject of pending charges for various crimes, including abduction for immoral purposes as set out in § 18.2-48, or an equivalent offense in another state, see § 63.2-1726. For provision making it unlawful for any person to operate a family day home if he, or if he knows that any other person who resides in the home, has been convicted of a felony in violation of this section, see § 63.2-1727.

Editor's note.
Acts 2011, c. 785, cl. 2, provides: "That the provisions of this act may result in a net increase in periods of imprisonment or commitment. Pursuant to § 30-19.1:4, the estimated amount of the necessary appropriation cannot be determined for periods of imprisonment in state adult correctional facilities; therefore, Chapter 874 of the Acts of Assembly of 2010 requires the Virginia Criminal Sentencing Commission to assign a minimum fiscal impact of $50,000. Pursuant to § 30-19.1:4, the estimated amount of the necessary appropriation cannot be determined for periods of commitment to the custody of the Department of Juvenile Justice."

The 2011 amendments.
The 2011 amendment by c. 785, in the first sentence, added "of any person" in (i), added (iv) and (v) and inserted "punishable as" near the end; and in the second sentence, substituted "(ii), (iii), (iv), or (v)" for "(ii) or (iii)."

Law Review.
For survey of Virginia criminal law for the year 1974-1975, see 61 Va. L. Rev. 1697 (1975). For note, "Predicate Offenses for First Degree Felony Murder in Virginia," see 57 Wash. & Lee L. Rev. 561 (2000). For 2006 survey article, "Criminal Law and Procedure," see 41 U. Rich. L. Rev. 83 (2006).

Michie's Jurisprudence.
For related discussion, see 5B M.J. Criminal Procedure, § 80; 9B M.J. Homicide, § 17; 21A M.J. Words and Phrases.

CASE NOTES

The clear purpose of this section is to punish more severely those who abduct with the intent to effectuate the taking of money or its equivalent. Newson v. Commonwealth, No. 1498-90-1 (Ct. of Appeals July 30, 1991).

Offense under § 18.2-47 included in offense under this section. — The offense defined in § 18.2-47 is an offense lesser-included in the offense defined in this section. Hawks v. Commonwealth, 228 Va. 244, 321 S.E.2d 650 (1984).

Specific intent. — The distinguishing feature between the offenses of abduction "with the intent to deprive such other person of his personal liberty" and abduction "with intent to defile" is the specific intent entertained by the accused. McKinley v. Commonwealth, 217 Va. 1, 225 S.E.2d 352 (1976) (decided under former §§ 18.1-36 and 18.1-38).

Pecuniary benefit. — The term "pecuniary benefit" means not only money, but everything that can be valued in money. Griffin v. Commonwealth, No. 0949-99-2, 2000 Va. App. LEXIS 264 (Ct. of Appeals Apr. 11, 2000).

Although the evidence supported multiple hypotheses regarding the defendant's intent at the time of the abduction, all involved the intent to obtain a pecuniary benefit — by intending to steal something the defendant found while looking through closets and cabinets in the victims' apartment, by taking the car operated by a key he duplicated or by duplicating a key to the bank where one of the victims worked in order to rob or facilitate a subsequent bank robbery; in light of this evidence and the absence of any evidence of a prior relationship between the defendant and the victims or any other motive for their abduction, the trier of fact was entitled to conclude that the defendant did not act merely to deprive the victims of their personal liberty. Griffin v. Commonwealth, No. 0949-99-2, 2000 Va. App. LEXIS 264 (Ct. of Appeals Apr. 11, 2000).

The statutory element is the intent to extort money or obtain a pecuniary benefit; it is not necessary that the criminal actually succeed in realizing his or her desired gain. Barnes v. Commonwealth, 234 Va. 130, 360 S.E.2d 196 (1987), cert. denied, 484 U.S. 1036, 108 S. Ct. 763, 98 L. Ed. 2d 779 (1988).

Physical detention of a person, with intent to deprive him of his personal liberty, by force, intimidation, or deception, without any asportation of the victim from one place to another, is sufficient to support a conviction of abduction. Simms v. Commonwealth, 2 Va. App. 614, 346 S.E.2d 734 (1986).

Either one of two intents is criminal; the "intent to extort money, or pecuniary benefit." There may be an intent to extort money, or the offender may otherwise intend to benefit himself pecuniarily; either is sufficient. Krummert v. Commonwealth, 186 Va. 581, 43 S.E.2d 831 (1947).

Use of hostage to escape robbery scene. — Where defendants, by using a hostage as a shield and by threatening to "blow him away," safely left the scene of a robbery with stolen money and drugs, they acted with intent to extort or acquire pecuniary benefit for themselves. Cortner v. Commonwealth, 222 Va. 557, 281 S.E.2d 908 (1981).

Abduction as means of committing robbery. — Abducting a person as a means of gaining access to the scene or otherwise facilitating the commission of an intended robbery violates the statute. Barnes v. Commonwealth, 234 Va. 130, 360 S.E.2d 196 (1987), cert. denied, 484 U.S. 1036, 108 S. Ct. 763, 98 L. Ed. 2d 779 (1988).

In a case involving defendant's conviction for abduction with the intent to extort money and using a firearm in the commission of a felony, because the victims' detention was no greater than that necessary to carry out two armed robberies of restaurants, the detentions were incidental to, rather than separate and apart from, the underlying robberies. Neither of the victims was forced to move a significant distance, walking instead from one area of the restaurant to another, and neither of the victims was detained for a significant length of time. Wiggins v. Commonwealth, 47 Va. App. 173, 622 S.E.2d 774, 2005 Va. App. LEXIS 507 (2005).

A conviction for abduction in connection with a robbery requires proof of a detention greater than the restraint that is intrinsic in a robbery. Abraham v. Commonwealth, 32 Va. App. 22, 526 S.E.2d 277 (2000).

Abduction not incidental to other crimes. — Defendant's conviction for abduction was not incidental to animate object sexual penetration, § 18.2-67.2, and taking indecent liberties with a minor, § 18.2-370, and was a separate offense, as the victim testified that he grabbed her as she tried to leave the room and tricked her into leaving the bathroom and into entering his bedroom; neither of these acts was inherent in the commission of object sexual penetration or taking indecent liberties with a minor. Dade v. Commonwealth, No. 2042-02-1, 2003 Va. App. LEXIS 368 (Ct. of Appeals June 24, 2003).

Defendant's claim that he did not abduct a victim because the detention was incidental to the restraint employed in a rape was not preserved for appeal; the victim testified that defendant grabbed her wrists and pulled her to a bedroom, and those actions were not inherent to the commission of rape or forcible sodomy,

defendant failed to establish than an element of the offense did not occur. Payne v. Commonwealth, No. 0678-03-1, 2004 Va. App. LEXIS 135 (Ct. of Appeals Mar. 30, 2004).

In a case involving defendant's conviction for abduction with the intent to extort money and using a firearm in the commission of a felony, the degree of restraint used in an abduction during a robbery of a restaurant was greater than, rather than incidental to, the restraint inherent in the underlying robbery. During this incident the victim was forced to walk a total of thirty-one feet, and by giving additional directions defendant exercised a great degree of control over the victim and her exact movements. Wiggins v. Commonwealth, 47 Va. App. 173, 622 S.E.2d 774, 2005 Va. App. LEXIS 507 (2005).

Multiple victims. — Trial court did not err in denying defendant's motions to strike the charge of abduction for pecuniary benefit of one victim, under § 18.2-48, because the abduction was not merely incidental to the robbery, under § 18.2-58, as the victim of the abduction and the victim of the robbery were two separate persons. El-Shabazz v. Commonwealth, 2012 Va. App. LEXIS 99 (Apr. 3, 2012).

Terms "sexually molest" and "defile" are interchangeable within the meaning of this section. Fitzgerald v. Commonwealth, 223 Va. 615, 292 S.E.2d 798 (1982), cert. denied, 459 U.S. 1228, 103 S. Ct. 1235, 75 L. Ed. 2d 469 (1983), rehearing denied, 460 U.S. 1105, 103 S. Ct. 1809, 76 L. Ed. 2d 371 (1983).

Attempted rape and abduction with intent to defile compared. — Attempted rape includes the intent to engage in sexual intercourse with a female victim, whereas abduction with intent to defile requires an intent to sexually molest a victim of any sex. Simms v. Commonwealth, 2 Va. App. 614, 346 S.E.2d 734 (1986).

The elements of the offense of abduction with intent to defile are separate and distinct from the elements of attempted rape. Simms v. Commonwealth, 2 Va. App. 614, 346 S.E.2d 734 (1986).

Abduction and attempted rape as separate crimes. — It could not be said as a matter of law that the evidence was insufficient to support a conviction for abduction with intent to defile, where when defendant grabbed the victim, he transported her from a location that was lighted and visible to one out of sight of potential passersby or others, as defendant's asportation of the victim substantially increased the risk of harm to the victim by decreasing the possibility of detecting his criminal activity, and as, moreover, asportation to decrease the possibility of detection is not an act inherent in or necessary to the restraint required in the commission of attempted rape. Thus, the jury could reasonably infer that the abduction was separate and apart from, and not merely incidental to the crime of attempted rape. Accordingly, multiple punishments for defendant's abduction and attempted rape of victim did not offend the double jeopardy guarantee. Coram v. Commonwealth, 3 Va. App. 623, 352 S.E.2d 532 (1987).

Evidence sufficient to prove abduction was separate and distinct from restraint inherent in rape. — Evidence was sufficient to prove as a matter of law that defendant's abduction, detention of the victim was separate and distinct from the restraint inherent in the commission of the crimes of rape and forcible sodomy; accordingly, defendant's conviction for abduction with intent to defile was affirmed. Defendant clearly restricted the victim's liberty, with the intent to defile the victim, by the use of force far in excess of that inherent in the commission of rape and sodomy where defendant twice choked the victim to the point of unconsciousness; those acts substantially increased the risk of harm to the victim. Fields v. Commonwealth, 48 Va. App. 393, 632 S.E.2d 8, 2006 Va. App. LEXIS 312 (2006).

Conviction for abduction with the intent to defile was supported by sufficient evidence to prove defendant's asportation and detention of the victim within her home. The abduction-detention and abduction-asportation of the victim were factually distinct from the restraint inherent in the perpetration of the rape as defendant forced the victim to walk with him through her house twice, he threw her on the bed and slice her arm and finger with a knife, and then he sexually assaulted her. Morales v. Commonwealth, 2010 Va. App. LEXIS 452 (Nov. 16, 2010).

Trial court record showed defendant was arraigned. — Court affirmed defendant's conviction for abduction because, in spite of defendant's argument to the contrary, the trial court's jury trial order clearly stated that defendant was arraigned and entered a plea of not guilty on the abduction charge and defendant failed to rebut the presumptive verity of the jury trial order. Lewis v. Commonwealth, — Va. App. —, — S.E.2d —, 2006 Va. App. LEXIS 485 (Oct. 31, 2006).

No error in denying motion to withdraw guilty plea. — Trial court did not err in refusing defendant's motion to withdraw his guilty plea to abduction with intent to defile because defendant failed to establish a good faith basis for seeking to withdraw his plea and to proffer evidence of a reasonable basis for contesting guilt, and defendant knew, prior to entering his plea, exactly what his sentence was going to be and that it would run concurrent to his sentence in an earlier case; the defense proffer failed to mention anything about defendant touching the victim's clothing over her vagina, an act which defendant admitted to during police questioning. Williams v. Commonwealth, 59 Va. App. 238, 717 S.E.2d 837, 2011 Va. App. LEXIS 392 (2011).

Evidence admitted in violation of Confrontation Clause. — Admission at trial of a murder victim's affidavit in support of her request for a protective order against defendant, her husband, violated the Confrontation Clause of the Sixth Amendment to the U.S. Constitution, and the error was not harmless because in it she swore he had threatened and raped her; therefore, his convictions for rape under § 18.2-61, abduction with the intent to defile under § 18.2-48, use of a firearm during the commission of an abduction, and capital murder, which was predicated on the former three offenses, were unconstitutional as well as based on insufficient evidence. Crawford v. Commonwealth, 53 Va. App. 138, 670 S.E.2d 15, 2008 Va. App. LEXIS 554 (2008).

Admission of an abuse affidavit into evidence, although violative of defendant's U.S. Const., Amend. VI right to confrontation, was harmless beyond a reasonable doubt for convictions for capital murder, abduction with intent to defile, rape, grand larceny, and two counts of use of a firearm, where the evidence was sufficient to support the convictions absent the affidavit. Crawford v. Commonwealth, 281 Va. 84, 704 S.E.2d 107, 2011 Va. LEXIS 20 (2011).

Testimony from caller ID device not inadmissible hearsay. — In trial of simple abduction, testimony regarding what was displayed on caller ID device did not constitute inadmissible hearsay because the caller ID display was based on computer generated information and not simply the repetition of prior recorded human input or observation. Tatum v. Commonwealth, 17 Va. App. 585, 440 S.E.2d 133 (1994).

Evidence sufficient to sustain conviction. — The evidence showed that the accused took deceased with him under such circumstances as amounted to fraud and coercion on his part, and for the purpose of pecuniary benefit, and the same was, therefore, sufficient to sustain a conviction under the statute. Kent v. Commonwealth, 165 Va. 840, 183 S.E. 177 (1936).

Trial court reasonably concluded from the evidence that defendant's beating of the victim, his demand for more money, the victim's fear of another beating, and defendant's taking the victim to his residence to obtain more money proved beyond a reasonable doubt that defendant abducted the victim with the intent to extort pecuniary benefit. Robinson v. Commonwealth, No. 1169-03-1, 2004 Va. App. LEXIS 317 (Ct. of Appeals July 6, 2004).

Because defendant and two others moved the victims' children to another room after spraying all the victims with pepper spray, the evidence was sufficient to find that the children were abducted in violation of subdivision 1 of § 18.2-48 to facilitate a robbery or to minimize their interference with the robbery and the getaway. Gonzalez-Tenas v. Commonwealth, — Va. App. —, — S.E.2d —, 2005 Va. App. LEXIS 430 (Nov. 1, 2005).

Evidence, when viewed in the light most favorable to the Commonwealth, supported the jury's verdicts that defendant was guilty of abduction to extort money for pecuniary benefit in violation of § 18.2-48 and use of a firearm during the commission of a felony in violation of § 18.2-53.1 because the jury, as it was entitled to do, ostensibly disregarded some of the testimony from the Commonwealth's witnesses; defendant pointed a handgun at the victim and demanded money, the victim's boyfriend gave defendant money after an initial attempt to obtain money from the victim's brother failed, over the course of the next two hours, defendant accompanied the victim to numerous locations in an attempt to obtain more money, and numerous witnesses testified on behalf of the Commonwealth confirming the victim's allegations. Brown v. Commonwealth, 2009 Va. App. LEXIS 575 (Dec. 22, 2009).

Defendant's convictions for abduction with intent to defile, in

violation of § 18.2-48, and attempted rape, in violation of §§ 18.2-26 and 18.2-61, were proper because the trial court did not err in finding the facts sufficient to show the abduction or detention was separate and apart from, rather than incidental to, the attempted rape. The evidence showed the detention by deception posed an additional danger to the victim, was accomplished before the attempted rape, and was not intrinsic to or inherent in the separate offense. Smith v. Commonwealth, 56 Va. App. 711, 697 S.E.2d 14, 2010 Va. App. LEXIS 336 (2010).

Defendant's convictions for abduction with intent to defile, in violation of § 18.2-48, and attempted rape, were proper because the jury heard the victim's conflicting accounts and in its role as factfinder, it alone was entitled to judge credibility given the discrepancy and assign her testimony what weight it deemed appropriate. Moreover, the officer's testimony and the victim's own actions corroborated the remainder of the victim's account of the incident; the victim immediately notified her mother and a friend about the incident. Smith v. Commonwealth, 56 Va. App. 711, 697 S.E.2d 14, 2010 Va. App. LEXIS 336 (2010).

Evidence was sufficient to sustain defendant's conviction for abduction with intent to defile, in violation of § 18.2-48, where the victim, defendant's wife, had previously obtained a protective order, the victim failed to report to work despite telling a supervisor what time she would report, the victim had plans for a hair appointment and a date with another man on the day that she disappeared, the driver's side window of the victim's car was broken, and the victim was found dead in a motel room, her body positioned in a particularly gruesome and suggestive manner. Crawford v. Commonwealth, 281 Va. 84, 704 S.E.2d 107, 2011 Va. LEXIS 20 (2011).

Commonwealth's evidence was competent, not inherently incredible, and sufficient to prove beyond a reasonable doubt attempted rape and abduction with intent to defile, because jury believed the victim's version of what happened and the Commonwealth's evidence and rejected defendant's version of those events, and the jury was permitted to consider defendant's prior felony convictions in assessing his credibility; the victim testified that defendant held her down, partially removed her pants, exposed his penis, pulled out a knife, and repeatedly threatened to kill the victim. Gay v. Commonwealth, 2011 Va. App. LEXIS 134 (Apr. 19, 2011).

Evidence was sufficient to support defendant's conviction for abduction with intent to defile because defendant physically detained the victim by force when he handcuffed her, and his subsequent actions and his statements were sufficient to show his intent to sexually molest the victim. Dillingham v. Commonwealth, 2011 Va. App. LEXIS 184 (2011).

Evidence was sufficient to support the trial court's finding that defendant abducted a victim within the meaning of § 18.2-48, as defendant's attempt to remove the victim from a register kiosk in the front of a convenience store was legally sufficient to constitute a detention, and thus an abduction. Ellis v. Commonwealth, 2012 Va. App. LEXIS 92 (Mar. 27, 2012).

Evidence sufficient to support conviction as principal in the second degree. — There was sufficient evidence to support defendant's conviction as a principal in the second degree, pursuant to § 18.2-18, of abduction and felony murder, in violation of §§ 18.2-48 and 18.2-32, where he and others lured the victim to a co-defendant's home with the purpose of robbing the victim of drugs and money, they restrained the victim while attempting to determine the whereabouts of the drugs, walked him out to the trunk of his car, drove him away, and fatally shot him; although there was blood in the house, the fact that the victim was "walked" outside to his car and that he "squirmed like a worm" when he was shot supported the finding that he was not killed in the house and accordingly, that defendant participated in abducting defendant while he was still alive. Brooks v. Commonwealth, No. 1629-03-2, 2004 Va. App. LEXIS 284 (Ct. of Appeals June 15, 2004).

Sufficient evidence of sexual motive. — Evidence in the instant case proved that appellant had a sexual motive the evening of the child's disappearance as opposed to any other motive. He spent much of his time at the Christmas party standing alone staring at women, including the child's mother. When he talked to male at the party, he talked about sexual infidelity and pointed out women who sexually attracted him and he also asked two women to leave the party with him. From all of this, the jury could believe that appellant was sexually focused up until he abducted the child. Hughes v. Commonwealth, 18 Va. App. 510, 446 S.E.2d 451 (1994).

Evidence sufficient to show intent to defile. — The fact that appellant abducted a five-year-old female child who was a stranger to him and who has never been heard from since, when no other purpose reasonably flows from the evidence, supports the inference that his abduction was with the intent to defile the child. When the circumstances surrounding the abduction are considered, appellant's inexplicable guilt-implying behavior and comments to the police, and his general attitude after the abduction, the jury's finding that he abducted the child with the intent to defile her is amply supported by credible evidence. Hughes v. Commonwealth, 18 Va. App. 510, 446 S.E.2d 451 (1994).

A defendant's intent to abduct and defile a 14-year-old girl could fairly be inferred from the evidence that he had just abducted, raped, and sodomized that girl's companion at the time he told the companion to call the other girl to the door of his house and, when the other girl approached the door, the defendant attempted to seize the other girl by the strap of her bib shorts and pull her inside; such circumstantial evidence sufficed to show intent and the defendant's act of grabbing the girl's shoulder strap also constituted a direct, ineffectual act toward the completion of the crime of abduction, an act that failed only because the strap broke and the girl was able to flee. Brown v. Commonwealth, 33 Va. App. 296, 533 S.E.2d 4, 2000 Va. App. LEXIS 626 (2000).

Circumstantial evidence was sufficient to show defendant abducted a victim with the intent to defile the victim, as surveillance footage plainly demonstrated defendant's active attempt to remove the victim from a convenience store register kiosk, and given defendant's prior statement that defendant wanted to "mess around" with the victim in the back room, the reasonable inference from defendant's acts was that defendant was attempting to take the victim to a more secluded area of the convenience store so that defendant might carry out defendant's lascivious desire by force. Ellis v. Commonwealth, 2012 Va. App. LEXIS 92 (Mar. 27, 2012).

Evidence supported defendant's conviction for abduction with intent to defile, in violation of §§ 18.2-47, 18.2-48, and 18.2-67.5:3, because defendant lured the victim to a house and proceeded to force himself onto the victim once the victim manifested the victim's discomfort with defendant's advances and attempted to leave. Defendant's conduct and statements to the victim supported the conclusion that the abduction that preceded the rape was effected with the intent to defile. Shepperson v. Commonwealth, 2012 Va. App. LEXIS 329 (Oct. 16, 2012).

Evidence of attempted escape. — It was not an abuse of discretion to permit the admission of evidence of defendant's attempted escape to show consciousness of guilt as to the rape and abduction with intent to defile charges, even though he was also incarcerated at the time of the attempted escape on two other charges. Leonard v. Commonwealth, 39 Va. App. 134, 571 S.E.2d 306, 2002 Va. App. LEXIS 657 (2002), cert. denied, 540 U.S. 989, 124 S. Ct. 479, 157 L. Ed. 2d 384 (2003).

Instruction as to attempted rape. — Even if the proof adduced at defendant's trial for abduction with intent to defile was sufficient to show that a rape was attempted, defendant was not entitled to an instruction on the offense of attempted rape, with which he was not specifically charged, as it was not a necessarily included lesser offense of the crime with which he was charged. Simms v. Commonwealth, 2 Va. App. 614, 346 S.E.2d 734 (1986).

Sentence appropriate. — Defendant's sentences after he pled guilty to rape, in violation of § 18.2-61, and two counts of abduction with intent to defile, in violation of § 18.2-48, were appropriate because the circuit court did not base his three life sentences on a prior molestation investigation, but on his history as a "career criminal" and on defendant's lack of remorse. Therefore, even if the testimony regarding a prior molestation investigation was inadmissible, such error was harmless. Pagan v. Commonwealth, 2011 Va. App. LEXIS 7 (Jan. 11, 2011).

On petition for writ of actual innocence. — Defendant's petition for a writ of actual innocence based on newly-discovered, non-biological evidence was denied, although the codefendant's confession that he acted alone in killing the victim was credible, because the recantation did not provide the court with clear and convincing evidence that no rational fact finder could have found that defendant used deception to abduct the victim with the intent to have sexual intercourse with her against her will. Turner v. Commonwealth, 56 Va. App. 391, 694 S.E.2d 251, 2010 Va. App. LEXIS 263 (2010).

Applied in Johnson v. Commonwealth, 221 Va. 872, 275 S.E.2d 592 (1981); Jennings v. Commonwealth, 20 Va. App. 9, 454 S.E.2d 752 (1995).

§ 18.2-48.1. Abduction by prisoners or committed persons; penalty.

Any person confined in a state, local, or community correctional facility or committed to the Department of Juvenile Justice in any juvenile correctional center, or in the custody of an employee thereof, or who has escaped from any such facility or from any person in charge of such prisoner or committed person, who abducts or takes any person hostage is guilty of a Class 3 felony.

History.
1985, c. 526; 1986, c. 414; 2013, cc. 707, 782.

Editor's note.
Acts 2013, c. 707, cl. 2 provides: "That the provisions of this act may result in a net increase in periods of imprisonment or commitment. Pursuant to § 30-19.1:4, the estimated amount of the necessary appropriation cannot be determined for periods of imprisonment in state adult correctional facilities; therefore, Chapter 3 of the Acts of Assembly of 2012, Special Session I, requires the Virginia Criminal Sentencing Commission to assign a minimum fiscal impact of $50,000. Pursuant to § 30-19.1:4, the estimated amount of the necessary appropriation cannot be determined for periods of commitment to the custody of the Department of Juvenile Justice."

Acts 2013, c. 782, cl. 2 provides: "Pursuant to § 30-19.1:4, the estimated amount of the necessary appropriation is at least $299,513 for periods of imprisonment in state adult correctional facilities and cannot be determined for periods of commitment to the custody of the Department of Juvenile Justice."

The 2013 amendments.
The 2013 amendments by cc. 707 and 782 are identical, and rewrote the section.

CASE NOTES

Evidence was sufficient to establish that the defendant was a principal in the second degree to abduction by prisoners where, inter alia, he came twice to a breezeway with other inmates more directly involved in the incident, remained present while the inmates subdued two correctional officers, stood within three feet of one officer as he lay restrained on the ground, and assisted in dealing with another officer. Wicker v. Commonwealth, No. 2607-97-2 (Ct. of Appeals Dec. 22, 1998).

Evidence was sufficient to establish that two nurses were abducted where they were forced to lie on the floor in a hallway, taken to a classroom, and ordered to remain in the room under the watch of several inmates for the duration of the night. Wicker v. Commonwealth, No. 2607-97-2 (Ct. of Appeals Dec. 22, 1998).

Jury instructions. — As a trial court found as matter of law that the evidence was sufficient for the jury to consider both the crime of abduction by a prisoner and the crime of assault and battery, it was not obliged to instruct the jury about the test for determining whether the abduction was merely incidental to the assault and battery. Anderson v. Commonwealth, — Va. App. —, — S.E.2d —, 2006 Va. App. LEXIS 555 (Dec. 12, 2006).

Where a defendant is charged with both abduction and another crime, such as rape or assault, arising out of the same criminal episode, as the requirement that the restraint involved in the abduction be separate and apart from the restraint involved in the other offense is not an element of the crime of abduction, the jury does not have to be instructed on this matter. Anderson v. Commonwealth, — Va. App. —, — S.E.2d —, 2006 Va. App. LEXIS 555 (Dec. 12, 2006).

Since *Blakely* applies to increases of the penalty for a crime beyond the prescribed maximum, not the penalty for a course of conduct, a trial judge's refusal to instruct the jury on the possible merger of charges of abduction and assault and battery did not violate defendant's Sixth Amendment right to a jury trial. Anderson v. Commonwealth, — Va. App. —, — S.E.2d —, 2006 Va. App. LEXIS 555 (Dec. 12, 2006).

§ 18.2-49. Threatening, attempting or assisting in such abduction.

Any person who (1) threatens, or attempts, to abduct any other person with intent to extort money, or pecuniary benefit, or (2) assists or aids in the abduction of, or threatens to abduct, any person with the intent to defile such person, or (3) assists or aids in the abduction of, or threatens to abduct, any female under sixteen years of age for the purpose of concubinage or prostitution, shall be guilty of a Class 5 felony.

History.
Code 1950, § 18.1-39; 1960, c. 358; 1966, c. 214; 1975, cc. 14, 15.

§ 18.2-49.1. Violation of court order regarding custody and visitation; penalty.

A. Any person who knowingly, wrongfully and intentionally withholds a child from either of a child's parents or other legal guardian in a clear and significant violation of a court order respecting the custody or visitation of such child, provided such child is withheld outside of the Commonwealth, is guilty of a Class 6 felony.

B. Any person who knowingly, wrongfully and intentionally engages in conduct that constitutes a clear and significant violation of a court order respecting the custody or visitation of a child is guilty of a Class 3 misdemeanor upon conviction of a first offense. Any person who commits a second violation of this section within 12 months of a first conviction is guilty of a Class 2 misdemeanor, and any person who commits a third violation occurring within 24 months of the first conviction is guilty of a Class 1 misdemeanor.

History.
1987, c. 704; 1989, c. 486; 1994, c. 575; 2002, cc. 576, 596; 2003, c. 261.

Law Review.
For survey on legal issues involving children in Virginia for 1989, see 23 U. Rich. L. Rev. 705 (1989). For 1994 survey of Virginia domestic relations law, see 28 U. Rich. L. Rev. 981 (1994). For note, "Predicate Offenses for First Degree Felony Murder in Virginia," see 57 Wash. & Lee L. Rev. 561 (2000). For article surveying developments in family law in Virginia, see 37 U. Rich. L. Rev. 155 (2002).

CASE NOTES

Editor's note.
The cases below were decided prior to 2003 amendments substituting "either of a child's parents or other legal guardians" for "the child's custodial parent."

The act that elevates this offense from a misdemeanor to a felony occurs only when the child is "withheld" from a custodial parent outside of the Commonwealth. Foster-Zahid

v. Commonwealth, 23 Va. App. 430, 477 S.E.2d 759 (1996).

Proper venue found. — Where the evidence established that the father was a resident of Fairfax County at the time of the abduction by out-of-state mother and that the child was to be returned to Fairfax County pursuant to a valid and enforceable custody order, the harm contemplated by this section was clearly established as occurring in this locus for venue purposes. Foster-Zahid v. Commonwealth, 23 Va. App. 430, 477 S.E.2d 759 (1996).

Defendant's failure to relinquish custody of her minor child to the father in Virginia Beach constituted an offense committed within that circuit under § 19.2-244. Accordingly, venue was proper in that jurisdiction as that was the jurisdiction to which the defendant was ordered to relinquish temporary custody and from which the defendant withheld custody. Dunn v. Commonwealth, No. 1689-02-1, 2003 Va. App. LEXIS 219 (Ct. of Appeals Apr. 15, 2003).

Mother was the custodial parent only for the time of her visitation. — Despite the fact that the defendant was the custodial parent at the time the defendant left the Commonwealth with her minor child, the defendant was the custodial parent or rightful custodian only for that period of visitation until the defendant was to return the child to the father. Accordingly, the defendant was properly charged and convicted of custodial interference under § 18.2-49.1 A. Dunn v. Commonwealth, No. 1689-02-1, 2003 Va. App. LEXIS 219 (Ct. of Appeals Apr. 15, 2003).

CIRCUIT COURT OPINIONS

Constitutionality. — Subsection A of § 18.2-49.1, criminalizing parental abduction, is unconstitutionally vague, as "clear and significant" terminology is not defined with sufficient particularity, and individuals are left to speculate as to the meaning of the statute; in addition, the statute fails to establish minimal guidelines for law enforcement. Commonwealth v. Dumont, 58 Va. Cir. 475, 2002 Va. Cir. LEXIS 164 (Chesterfield County 2002).

§ 18.2-50. Disclosure of information and assistance to law-enforcement officers required.

Whenever it is brought to the attention of the members of the immediate family of any person that such person has been abducted, or that threats or attempts have been made to abduct any such person, such members shall make immediate report thereof to the police or other law-enforcement officers of the county, city or town where such person resides, and shall render all such possible assistance to such officers in the capture and conviction of the person or persons guilty of the alleged offense. Any person violating any of the provisions of this section shall be guilty of a Class 2 misdemeanor.

History.
Code 1950, § 18.1-40; 1960, c. 358; 1975, cc. 14, 15.

§ 18.2-50.1. Repealed by Acts 1992, c. 479.

Cross references.
For present provisions as to emergency control of telephone service in hostage or barricaded person situation, see § 18.2-50.2.

§ 18.2-50.2. Emergency control of telephone service in hostage or barricaded person situation.

A. The Superintendent of the State Police or the chief law-enforcement officer or sheriff of any county, city or town may designate one or more law-enforcement officers with appropriate technical training or expertise as a hostage and barricade communications specialist.

B. Each telephone company providing service to Virginia residents shall designate a department or one or more individuals to provide liaison with law-enforcement agencies for the purposes of this section and shall designate telephone numbers, not exceeding two, at which such law-enforcement liaison department or individual can be contacted.

C. The supervising law-enforcement officer, who has jurisdiction in any situation in which there is probable cause to believe that the criminal enterprise of hostage holding is occurring or that a person has barricaded himself within a structure and poses an immediate threat to the life, safety or property of himself or others, may order a telephone company, or a hostage and barricade communications specialist to interrupt, reroute, divert, or otherwise control any telephone communications service involved in the hostage or barricade situation for the purpose of preventing telephone communication by a hostage holder or barricaded person with any person other than a law-enforcement officer or a person authorized by the officer.

D. A hostage and barricade communication specialist shall be ordered to act under subsection C only if the telephone company providing service in the area has been contacted and requested to act under subsection C or an attempt to contact has been made, using the telephone company's designated liaison telephone numbers and:

1. The officer's attempt to contact after ten rings for each call is unsuccessful;

2. The telephone company declines to respond to the officer's request because of a threat of personal injury to its employees; or

3. The telephone company indicates when contacted that it will be unable to respond appropriately to the officer's request within a reasonable time from the receipt of the request.

E. The supervising law-enforcement officer may give an order under subsection C only after that supervising law-enforcement officer has given or attempted to give written notification or oral notification of the hostage or barricade situation to the telephone company providing service to the area in which it is occurring. If an order is given on the basis of an oral notice, the oral notice shall be followed by a written confirmation of that notice within forty-eight hours of the order.

F. Good faith reliance on an order by a supervising law-enforcement officer who has the real or apparent authority to issue an order under this section shall constitute a complete defense to any action against a telephone company or a telephone company employee that rises out of attempts by the telephone company or the employees of the telephone company to comply with such an order.

History.
1992, c. 479.

Michie's Jurisprudence.
For related discussion, see 1A M.J. Abduction and Kidnapping, § 1; 18 M.J. Telegraph and Telephone Companies, § 2.

ARTICLE 4.

ASSAULTS AND BODILY WOUNDINGS.

Michie's Jurisprudence.
For related discussion, see 5B M.J. Criminal Procedure, § 95; 9B M.J. Husband and Wife, § 87; 12B M.J. Mayhem, §§ 2, 3, 4, 5, 8, 10, 11; 13A M.J. Mobs, Riots and Lynchings, § 4.

§ 18.2-51. Shooting, stabbing, etc., with intent to maim, kill, etc.

If any person maliciously shoot, stab, cut, or wound any person or by any means cause him bodily injury, with the intent to maim, disfigure, disable, or kill, he shall, except where it is otherwise provided, be guilty of a Class 3 felony. If such act be done unlawfully but not maliciously, with the intent aforesaid, the offender shall be guilty of a Class 6 felony.

History.
Code 1950, § 18.1-65; 1960, c. 358; 1975, cc. 14, 15.

Cross references.
As to certain employees of the Departments of Corrections and Juvenile Justice and the grievance resolution steps, see § 2.2-3007. For definition of "barrier crime" as including a conviction of assault and bodily woundings as set out in § 18.2-51 et seq., or an equivalent offense in another state, and prohibition against assisted living facilities, adult day care centers or child welfare agencies hiring for certain compensated employment persons who have committed such an offense, see §§ 63.2-1719, 63.2-1720. As to report to children's residential facility for which a background check is being performed on whether the applicant has ever been convicted of or is the subject of pending charges for various crimes, including assault and bodily woundings as set out in § 18.2-51 et seq., or an equivalent offense in another state, see § 63.2-1726.

Law Review.
For survey of Virginia criminal law for the year 1974-1975, see 61 Va. L. Rev. 1697 (1975). For comment on spouse abuse in Virginia, see 17 U. Rich. L. Rev. 633 (1983). For article, "Preclusion of Evidence of Criminal Conviction in Civil Action Arising from the Same Incident," see 10 G.M.U. L. Rev. 107 (1988). For annual survey of Virginia law article, "Criminal Law and Procedure," see 47 U. Rich. L. Rev. 143 (2012).

CASE NOTES

I. General Consideration.
II. Nature and Elements of Offenses.
    A. In General.
    B. Intent.
III. Prosecution.
    A. Indictment.
    B. Defenses.
    C. Evidence.
    D. Instructions.
    E. Verdict, Sentence and Punishment.

I. GENERAL CONSIDERATION.

This section is commonly referred to as the maiming statute. Fletcher v. Commonwealth, 209 Va. 636, 166 S.E.2d 269 (1969).

Purpose of act. — The true purpose and meaning of the

maiming act was doubtless conceived to be to define and punish as felonies those acts which had theretofore been considered misdemeanors only in those cases where it also appeared that there was the felonious intent to maim, disfigure, disable, or kill. Harris v. Commonwealth, 150 Va. 580, 142 S.E. 354 (1928); Bryant v. Commonwealth, 189 Va. 310, 53 S.E.2d 54 (1949).

An assault is not punishable under this section. Jones v. Commonwealth, 184 Va. 679, 36 S.E.2d 571 (1946).

"Unlawful maiming," "unlawful wounding," "unlawful shooting" and "unlawful stabbing" standing alone are not crimes embraced under this section. Banner v. Commonwealth, 204 Va. 640, 133 S.E.2d 305 (1964).

Aggravated malicious wounding distinguished. — Unlike the crime of aggravated malicious wounding under § 18.2-51.2, which requires proof that the victim suffered a permanent and significant physical impairment as a result of the wound inflicted by the defendant, the crime of malicious wounding under § 18.2-51, does not require that the wound inflicted by the defendant be permanent or significant; the crime of malicious wounding lacks the severity and permanence elements required for the offense of aggravated malicious wounding, and merely requires that the defendant intended to inflict a permanent wound. An Trong Tran v. Commonwealth, No. 2565-02-4, 2004 Va. App. LEXIS 195 (Ct. of Appeals Apr. 27, 2004).

Compared to assault with a dangerous weapon under federal law. — Defendants sought dismissal of counts under 18 U.S.C.S. §§ 1959 and 924(c), of the indictment on the ground that the elements of Virginia's malicious or unlawful wounding statute, § 18.2-51, and brandishing statute, § 18.2-282, the state laws that the charged assaults allegedly violated, did not match — element-by-element — with the elements of assault with a dangerous weapon under federal law, but, the elements of malicious or unlawful wounding under Virginia law were adequately similar to those of assault with a dangerous weapon and aggravated assault as generically defined, the indictment charging assault with a dangerous weapon was sufficient, and the motion to dismiss was denied. United States v. Cuong Gia Le, 316 F. Supp. 2d 355, 2004 U.S. Dist. LEXIS 7786 (E.D. Va. 2004).

Double jeopardy considerations. — Multiple punishments for the crimes of attempted murder and malicious wounding do not violate the double jeopardy clause when the convictions are obtained in a single trial. Creamer v. Commonwealth, No. 1298-91-3 (Ct. of Appeals Dec. 15, 1992).

Crimes of attempted murder and malicious wounding had different elements, and therefore defendant's convictions of both did not violate double jeopardy. Coleman v. Commonwealth, No. 2871-97-2, 1999 Va. App. LEXIS 445 (July 20, 1999).

Defendant's convictions for malicious wounding and maiming by mob did not violate principles of double jeopardy as malicious wounding contained an additional element not found in maiming by mob, namely that the defendant acted with malice. Thus, it followed that one who was guilty of maiming by mob was not necessarily guilty of malicious wounding. Johnson v. Commonwealth, 58 Va. App. 303, 709 S.E.2d 175, 2011 Va. App. LEXIS 185 (2011).

Lesser included offense. — The shooting of another unlawfully but without malicious intent to maim, disfigure, disable, or kill, is a lesser included offense of malicious shooting and is also a felony. Jones v. Blankenship, 458 F. Supp. 521 (W.D. Va. 1978), rev'd on other grounds, 602 F.2d 650 (4th Cir. 1979).

Assault and battery and unlawful wounding are lesser included offenses of malicious wounding. Brown v. Commonwealth, 222 Va. 111, 279 S.E.2d 142 (1981).

Unlawful wounding is a lesser included offense of malicious wounding; the element of malice constitutes the distinction between malicious and unlawful wounding. Miller v. Commonwealth, 5 Va. App. 22, 359 S.E.2d 841 (1987).

Malicious wounding is not a lesser included offense of robbery. Walker v. Commonwealth, 14 Va. App. 203, 415 S.E.2d 446 (1992).

Assault and battery is a lesser-included offense of malicious wounding. Vaughn v. Commonwealth, 34 Va. App. 263, 540 S.E.2d 516, 2001 Va. App. LEXIS 48 (2001), rev'd on other grounds, 263 Va. 31, 557 S.E.2d 220 (2002).

The intent to maim, disfigure, disable or kill is not necessarily included in the definition of murder or manslaughter and, therefore, malicious wounding is not a lesser-included offense embraced within the crime of murder or manslaughter. Hampton v. Commonwealth, 34 Va. App. 412, 542 S.E.2d 41, 2001 Va. App. LEXIS 86 (2001).

Applied in Barrett v. Commonwealth, 231 Va. 102, 341 S.E.2d 190 (1986); Akers v. Commonwealth, 31 Va. App. 521, 525 S.E.2d 13 (2000); Cottee v. Commonwealth, 31 Va. App. 546, 525 S.E.2d 25 (2000); Jaccard v. Commonwealth, 268 Va. 56, 597 S.E.2d 30, 2004 Va. LEXIS 87 (2004).

II. NATURE AND ELEMENTS OF OFFENSES.

A. In General.

Attempted malicious wounding. — An attempt to commit the crime of malicious wounding consists of: (1) the specific intent to maim, disfigure, disable or kill and (2) an ineffectual act done towards the crime's completion. Moody v. Commonwealth, 28 Va. App. 702, 508 S.E.2d 354 (1998).

In order to convict an accused of attempted malicious wounding, the Commonwealth must prove that the accused: (1) intended to maliciously shoot, stab, cut or wound any person or by any means cause bodily injury with the intent to maim, disfigure, disable or kill; and (2) committed a direct but ineffectual act toward this purpose. Smith v. Commonwealth, No. 3001-99-1, 2001 Va. App. LEXIS 120 (Ct. of Appeals Mar. 13, 2001); Knox v. Commonwealth, No. 0533-00-1, 2001 Va. App. LEXIS 226 (Ct. of Appeals May 1, 2001).

Evidence was insufficient to support a conviction for attempted malicious wounding, although the circumstances were suspicious, because the evidence failed to establish an overt act necessary to prove an attempted malicious wounding where the scenario was interrupted when the victim made contact with defendant, and the evidence also failed to exclude the reasonable hypotheses that defendant acted with the intent to do no more than scare the victim. Small v. Commonwealth, 2009 Va. App. LEXIS 556 (Dec. 15, 2009).

Malice inheres in the intentional doing of a wrongful act without legal justification or excuse, or as the result of ill will. Fletcher v. Commonwealth, 209 Va. 636, 166 S.E.2d 269 (1969).

Malice inheres in the doing of a wrongful act intentionally, or without just cause or excuse, or as a result of ill will. Robertson v. Commonwealth, 31 Va. App. 814, 525 S.E.2d 640 (2000).

Malice is evidenced either when the accused acted with a sedate, deliberate mind and formed design or committed a purposeful and cruel act without any or without great provocation. Robertson v. Commonwealth, 31 Va. App. 814, 525 S.E.2d 640 (2000).

Malice may be directly evidenced by words or inferred form the acts and conduct which necessarily result in injury. Robertson v. Commonwealth, 31 Va. App. 814, 525 S.E.2d 640 (2000).

The words "shoot," "stab," "cut" or "wound" are analogous for the purpose employed in this section. Lane v. Commonwealth, 190 Va. 58, 55 S.E.2d 450 (1949).

Causing bodily injury is a distinct offense. — To "shoot, stab, cut or wound," under this section comprise distinct offenses, and to cause bodily injury is likewise a distinct offense. Johnson v. Commonwealth, 184 Va. 409, 35 S.E.2d 594 (1945).

And the fist and knee of defendant are "means" within the language of the statute, viz., "by any means." Dawkins v. Commonwealth, 186 Va. 55, 41 S.E.2d 500 (1947).

"Bodily injury" is caused where one is struck on the face and head and kicked so that as a result of the beating blood ran from his ears, nose and mouth and he suffered a small cut inside of his mouth. Bryant v. Commonwealth, 189 Va. 310, 53 S.E.2d 54 (1949).

Under this section a "wound" is a breach of the skin, or of the skin and flesh, produced by external violence. Without such parting of the skin there can be no wounding. Johnson v. Commonwealth, 184 Va. 409, 35 S.E.2d 594 (1945).

Under the maiming act it is necessary, in order to constitute a wounding and support a conviction for such wounding, that the skin be broken or cut. Harris v. Commonwealth, 150 Va. 580, 142 S.E. 354 (1928).

Thus, two broken ribs do not constitute a wounding as contemplated by this section. Johnson v. Commonwealth, 184 Va. 409, 35 S.E.2d 594 (1945).

Test to determine if guilty of malicious shooting. — Whether a prisoner on trial is guilty of malicious shooting with intent to kill, depends upon the question, whether if he had killed the person at whom he shot, instead of only wounding him with intent to kill him, the offense would have been murder. Commonwealth v. Chapple, 3 Va. (1 Va. Cas.) 184 (1811); Read v. Commonwealth, 63 Va. (22 Gratt.) 924 (1872); Price v. Commonwealth, 77 Va. 393 (1883); Harris v. Commonwealth, 134 Va. 688, 114 S.E. 597 (1922); Gills v. Commonwealth, 141 Va. 445, 126 S.E. 51 (1925).

Malice and heat of passion mutually exclusive. — Malice and heat of passion are mutually exclusive; malice excludes passion and passion presupposes the absence of malice. Robertson v. Commonwealth, 31 Va. App. 814, 525 S.E.2d 640 (2000).

Malicious wounding in intent to maim, disfigure, disable, or kill by shaking baby. — Defendant was properly convicted of malicious wounding for shaking his six-week-old baby to the point of causing the baby severe and permanent brain damage because, in part, evidence of defendant's mental retardation was irrelevant absent an insanity defense and further, the evidence permitted a finding beyond a reasonable doubt that defendant intended to maim, disfigure, disable, or kill the baby given the baby's permanent brain damage suffered under the sole care of defendant, who initially blamed the injury on a toy, but later admitted shaking the baby. Funk v. Commonwealth, No. 1821-02-4, 2003 Va. App. LEXIS 383 (Ct. of Appeals July 8, 2003).

Use of a pit bull terrier. — Because this section specifies "any means," the Commonwealth was not constrained to prove that the method defendant used to cause bodily harm was inherently dangerous, and the defendant's use of a pit bull terrier to inflict the injury by releasing the dog to "sic him, kill" met the requirements of this section since, by its explicit terms, this section does not contain a limitation upon the means employed. Long v. Commonwealth, 8 Va. App. 194, 379 S.E.2d 473 (1989).

Evidence held sufficient. — Evidence was sufficient to support defendant's malicious wounding conviction under § 18.2-51 where: (1) defendant struck the victim with a shiny object, causing a wound that required stitches; (2) the statute proscribed the infliction of bodily injury by any means, and the nature of the intent with which the result was accomplished, and not the nature of the means, determined whether the act was malicious; (3) defendant's argument that he inflicted the blows on the victim as a response to being pushed by the victim was rejected, as the victim, a landowner, lawfully attempted to escort defendant, a trespasser, from the victim's property after asking defendant to leave; and (4) the victim's lawful act did not justify defendant's violent response. Carnes v. Commonwealth, No. 2016-02-1, 2003 Va. App. LEXIS 371 (Ct. of Appeals July 1, 2003).

B. Intent.

Intent is a necessary element in the crime of shooting and wounding; intent must be proved either directly, or from facts from which an intentional shooting could be inferred. Where the evidence fails to show such intent a conviction is not warranted. Hay v. Commonwealth, 139 Va. 578, 123 S.E. 333 (1924).

In accordance with the use of the disjunctive "or" in the portion of this section requiring that a defendant act with the intent to maim, disfigure, disable or kill, a malicious wounding charge does not require proof of the specific intent to kill. Coleman v. Commonwealth, 261 Va. 196, 539 S.E.2d 732, 2001 Va. LEXIS 12 (2001).

Intent in fact. — The necessary intent constituting one element in an attempt to commit murder is the intent in fact, as distinguished from an intent in law. Hargrave v. Commonwealth, 214 Va. 436, 201 S.E.2d 597 (1974).

Intent may be inferred. — The fact finder may infer that a person intends the immediate, direct and necessary consequences of his voluntary act. Moody v. Commonwealth, 28 Va. App. 702, 508 S.E.2d 354 (1998).

Trial court's judgment following a bench trial that found defendant guilty of eight counts of attempted malicious wounding and eight counts of felonious use of a firearm was not plainly wrong or without evidence to support it and, thus, was affirmed; an inference that defendant tried to maim eight police officers providing security at a nightclub could be drawn by defendant's conduct in firing a fusillade of gunfire in their direction. Coleman v. Commonwealth, — Va. App. —, — S.E.2d —, 2006 Va. App. LEXIS 502 (Nov. 7, 2006).

Intent not derived from means of injury and may be shown by circumstances. Hargrave v. Commonwealth, 214 Va. 436, 201 S.E.2d 597 (1974).

Intent in fact is a state of mind which may be shown by a person's conduct or by his statements. Hargrave v. Commonwealth, 214 Va. 436, 201 S.E.2d 597 (1974).

Intent is the purpose formed in a person's mind. It may be shown by the circumstances surrounding the offense, including the person's conduct and his statements. Lindsey v. Commonwealth, No. 0137-89-2 (Ct. of Appeals Oct. 9, 1990).

Intent is the purpose formed in a person's mind which may, and often must, be inferred from the facts and circumstances in a particular case, and the state of mind of an alleged offender may be shown by his acts and conduct. Waller v. Commonwealth, No. 1696-89-3 (Ct. of Appeals Nov. 20, 1990).

Under the maiming statute proof of specific intent to maim, disfigure, disable or kill is necessary. Such intent may be proved by circumstantial evidence, but cannot be presumed from an act which does not naturally indicate it. Banovitch v. Commonwealth, 196 Va. 210, 83 S.E.2d 369 (1954).

The defendant can be convicted of unlawful wounding with the intent to maim, disfigure, disable or kill when there is no direct evidence of a subjective intent to inflict bodily harm to the injured person. Such intent may be inferred when the defendant intentionally commits an act from which he or she reasonably could have anticipated that the injury would result. Waller v. Commonwealth, No. 1696-89-3 (Ct. of Appeals Nov. 20, 1990).

The requisite state of mind for malicious wounding derives not from the means employed to inflict the bodily injury, but from the intent with which the injury is inflicted. Fleshman v. Commonwealth, No. 1495-96-3 (Ct. of Appeals May 13, 1997).

The presumption is that the natural and necessary consequences of the act were intended. Murphy v. Commonwealth, 64 Va. (23 Gratt.) 960 (1873); Price v. Commonwealth, 77 Va. 393 (1883).

And wounding with a deadly weapon imputes malicious intent. — Where one wounds another with a deadly weapon, the law, in the absence of evidence to the contrary, imputes the malicious intent. Gills v. Commonwealth, 141 Va. 445, 126 S.E. 51 (1925).

In a prosecution for malicious shooting, where it was shown that the shooting was unlawful and without reasonable provocation, and the evidence failed to disclose any circumstances of palliation, the jury were compelled to find, as a matter of fact, that the shooting was done with malice. Harris v. Commonwealth, 134 Va. 688, 114 S.E. 597 (1922).

But intent to disfigure cannot be presumed from a blow with the fist. — Men are presumed to intend the natural and probable consequences of their acts, and a permanent disfigurement would be the natural and probable consequences of a violent blow in the face with sharp instrument like a knife or steel knuckles. But it cannot be presumed from a blow with the fist that the striker intended to permanently disfigure his adversary. Lee v. Commonwealth, 135 Va. 572, 115 S.E. 671 (1923). But see Dawkins v. Commonwealth, 186 Va. 55, 41 S.E.2d 500 (1947).

Nor may an intent to maim be presumed from a blow with a bare fist under ordinary circumstances. Fletcher v. Commonwealth, 209 Va. 636, 166 S.E.2d 269 (1969).

Intent to kill may be presumed. — But an assault with a bare fist may be attended with such circumstances of violence and brutality that an intent to kill may be presumed. Fletcher v. Commonwealth, 209 Va. 636, 166 S.E.2d 269 (1969).

Intent may be inferred from assault with bare fists. — The intent to maim, disfigure, disable or kill a person may be inferred from an assault with bare fists if it is attended with circumstances of such violence and brutality that the fact finder can reasonably conclude that the assailant intended one of those results. Bland v. Commonwealth, No. 1733-91-4 (Ct. of Appeals March 16, 1993).

Although blows inflicted with bare fists do not ordinarily imply intent to kill, disable, disfigure or maim, such blows, if applied with sufficient violence or brutality, may allow trier of fact to infer that defendant possessed the requisite intent. Coleman v. Commonwealth, No. 2008-98-2 (Ct. of Appeals Dec. 14, 1999).

Though defendant struck the victim only once with his bare fist, the evidence was sufficient to convict him of malicious wounding, as he struck the victim with such force as to seriously injure him, and defendant's threats and boasts about his strength indicated his awareness of the harm he could inflict, which demonstrated his intent to permanently harm the victim. Burkeen v. Commonwealth, 2012 Va. App. LEXIS 384 (Nov. 27, 2012).

Intent inferred from repeated blows applied to vital parts. — The intent to maim, disfigure, disable, or kill a person can be inferred from repeated blows applied to vital and delicate parts of the body of a defenseless, unresisting person on the ground. Bland v. Commonwealth, No. 1733-91-4 (Ct. of Appeals March 16, 1993).

Doctrine of transferred intent had no application to attempted malicious wounding. — The Commonwealth conceded that the doctrine of transferred intent had no application to the charge of attempted malicious wounding, the crime at issue in this appeal. N. was not injured when appellant shot A. Because in this case appellant did not escape criminal liability, neither the express terms of the doctrine nor its underlying policy dictated that it apply. Thus, the Commonwealth was required to prove that the appellant specifically intended to wound N. Crawley v. Commonwealth, 25 Va. App. 768, 492 S.E.2d 503 (1997).

Doctrine of transferred intent applicable. — Doctrine of transferred intent was properly applied in finding defendant guilty of the malicious wounding of defendant's daughter because the daughter's injury was reasonably related to the criminal act defendant directed at the wife and defendant had the requisite intent to maim the wife when defendant cut the daughter. Blow v. Commonwealth, 52 Va. App. 533, 665 S.E.2d 254, 2008 Va. App. LEXIS 400 (2008).

"Disfigure" in this section means a permanent and not merely a temporary and inconsequential disfigurement. Lee v. Commonwealth, 135 Va. 572, 115 S.E. 671 (1923).

When comparative weakness of victim and strength of aggressor considered. — In determining the probable consequences of an aggressor's actions and his or her intent to achieve those consequences, the comparative weakness of the victim and the strength of the aggressor may be considered. Campbell v. Commonwealth, 12 Va. App. 476, 405 S.E.2d 1 (1991).

Facts sufficient to show intent. — One may be convicted of unlawful wounding with intent to maim, disfigure, disable or kill another, when there is no direct evidence of a subjective intent to inflict bodily harm to the injured person, where, while only two feet from the victim, he fires a bullet onto the cement drive where it reasonably could be anticipated that the bullet would be deflected, and in fact it deflected into the victim's foot causing serious injury. David v. Commonwealth, 2 Va. App. 1, 340 S.E.2d 576 (1986).

Evidence showed beyond a reasonable doubt that defendant acted with malice and intended to maim or disable victim, an 81 year old man, where the defendant intentionally grabbed and threw to the ground the victim during the course of a robbery, and given the victim's age and the nature of the attack upon him, a disability such as a broken ankle was a natural and probable consequence of the defendant's act. Davis v. Commonwealth, No. 0302-92-1 (Ct. of Appeals Sept. 7, 1993).

Evidence that the defendant threw a brick at the victim as he attempted to close garage door, breaking a toe, lacerating his shin to the bone, and causing a large welt, supported a finding that he maliciously intended to maim, disfigure, or disable the victim. Williams v. Commonwealth, No. 0540-94-1 (Ct. of Appeals March 21, 1995).

Trial court was not plainly wrong in finding defendant acted with the requisite intent to maim or kill his wife when he pinned her to the wall and choked her into unconsciousness. The trial court is entitled to infer defendant's intent from the facts and circumstances, and it appropriately concluded beyond a reasonable doubt that these were acts from which appellant reasonably should have anticipated that disabling injury or death might result to his wife. Graber v. Commonwealth, No. 0688-94-2 (Ct. of Appeals Oct. 3, 1995).

Where without provocation, assailant grabbed pizza delivery woman in a choke hold; forcing her into submission, he repeatedly punched her in the neck, exhibiting a callous and violent disregard for a vulnerable part of her body; in responding to her pleas for mercy, he spoke coarsely and without concern; this attendant brutality continued even after the robbery was accomplished; and as a result, she suffered permanent disability, these facts and circumstances support the fact finder's inference that he intended the natural and probable consequences of the beating he administered to the delivery woman. Fleshman v. Commonwealth, No. 1495-96-3 (Ct. of Appeals May 13, 1997).

The Commonwealth presented sufficient evidence of intent to sustain the defendant's conviction for attempted malicious wounding where the defendant, while attempting to leave a parking lot in a stolen vehicle, saw a pedestrian blocking his only avenue of escape and deliberately chose to accelerate the car toward the pedestrian, never decelerating, braking or swerving to avoid him, even when the pedestrian was only five to ten feet away from being struck. Moody v. Commonwealth, 28 Va. App. 702, 508 S.E.2d 354 (1998).

Where defendant's blow to the victim's head was sufficient to break the cup, inflict a cut to the head, and require stitches to close, then the finder of fact could reasonably infer that the defendant employed the plastic cup to enhance the blow he intended to strike and that he intended the cup to break and become a cutting weapon; thus, the evidence was sufficient to support the finding that the defendant maliciously struck the victim with the intent to maim, disfigure, disable, or kill him under this section. Summers v. Commonwealth, No. 1797-99-3, 2000 Va. App. LEXIS 451 (Ct. of Appeals June 20, 2000).

The evidence was sufficient for the fact finder to conclude that the defendant acted with the malicious intent to maim, disfigure or disable the victim in light of the defendant's threatening words, his invitation for the victim "to go outside," his return to join a fight between a third party and the victim, the force of the defendant's initial blow and the severity of the resulting injury and the fact that the defendant continued to beat the victim when he was on the floor and had to be pulled away. Clark v. Commonwealth, No. 2226-99-2, 2000 Va. App. LEXIS 728 (Ct. of Appeals Nov. 14, 2000).

The fact finder could reasonably have found that, in striking the victim in the face with a bottle, the defendant acted with malice where the evidence showed that the defendant unlawfully entered the victim's residence and proceeded to the victim's bedroom where he assaulted another person, accused the victim of infidelity and, while standing a short distance in front of the victim, threw a bottle towards her head. Robertson v. Commonwealth, 31 Va. App. 814, 525 S.E.2d 640 (2000).

Severity and number of blows demonstrated defendant's intent to maim, disfigure, disable or kill his victim. Roebuck v. Commonwealth, No. 1060-99-1 (Ct. of Appeals Jan. 27, 2000).

Facts sufficient to show intent to maim, disfigure, disable, or kill. Jenkins v. Commonwealth, No. 0967-01-4, 2002 Va. App. LEXIS 660 (Ct. of Appeals Nov. 5, 2002).

Where the Commonwealth proceeded against defendant as a principal in the second degree, and each participant became accountable for the incidental crimes committed by the other participants, the trial court properly imputed malice to the defendant, due to a co-defendant's actions in throwing an elderly lady against a wall, as the use of such force could have foreseen an injury, and the evidence of the nature of the attack permitted said finding. Ward v. Commonwealth, No. 0306-02-1, 2003 Va. App. LEXIS 226 (Ct. of Appeals Apr. 15, 2003).

Defendant's use of a shiny object, whether his ring or another object, supported an inference of intent for purposes of malicious wounding, in violation of § 18.2-51, as disfigurement would be the natural and probable consequence of a violent blow in the face with the weapon. Carnes v. Commonwealth, No. 2016-02-1, 2003 Va. App. LEXIS 371 (Ct. of Appeals July 1, 2003).

Where defendant lunged toward a co-employee while swinging a dry wall knife near his throat area, the evidence was sufficient to establish a basis from which the trial court could infer defendant's conduct demonstrated his intent to wound the co-employee and that his conduct went beyond mere preparation to carry out his intention; the mere fact that defendant stopped short of cutting the other employee did not negate the significance of the evidence of his intent, nor his conduct in furtherance of the crime. Peck v. Commonwealth, No. 1972-02-1, 2003 Va. App. LEXIS 581 (Ct. of Appeals Nov. 12, 2003).

Trial court erred in failing to instruct the jury that in order to convict defendant of malicious wounding, he had to have intended to permanently maim, disfigure, disable, or kill the victim; however, the error was harmless based on defendant's use of a metal knife and fork to stab the victim in the face very close to the eye, with sufficient force to cut and pierce the victim's skin and cause the wound to bleed, causing three holes and one cut on the right side of the victim's face, as the jury could only have inferred that a permanent disfigurement was the natural and probable consequence of defendant's actions. An Trong Tran v. Commonwealth,

No. 2565-02-4, 2004 Va. App. LEXIS 195 (Ct. of Appeals Apr. 27, 2004).

Evidence was sufficient to prove that defendant acted with malice when defendant, who suspected that defendant's paramour was seeing the victim, entered the victim's trailer home in the middle of the night, physically assaulted the victim while the victim was sleeping in bed with defendant's paramour, and injured the victim. Furthermore, defendant's own testimony, that defendant realized that defendant did not have to be there, undermined defendant's claim that heat of passion motivated the final blow, when defendant left the victim's home and then reentered the home, which knocked the victim to the floor of the trailer. King v. Commonwealth, 2011 Va. App. LEXIS 349 (Nov. 15, 2011).

Trial court did not err in finding the evidence sufficient to support defendant's conviction for attempted malicious shooting of a victim and use of a firearm in the commission of the attempted shooting, as circumstantial evidence regarding defendant's state of mind at the time of the shooting did not indicate that another victim was defendant's only intended target, as claimed by defendant. Cuffee v. Commonwealth, 61 Va. App. 353, 735 S.E.2d 693, 2013 Va. App. LEXIS 7 (2013).

Facts insufficient to show intent to disfigure. — See Banovitch v. Commonwealth, 196 Va. 210, 83 S.E.2d 369 (1954).

Defendant's conviction for malicious wounding in violation of § 18.2-51 was reversed because it was unsupported by the evidence. Although the trial court found that defendant's striking the victim, causing him to lose an eye, was malicious, it also found that defendant did not have the intent to maim or disfigure the victim. Williams v. Commonwealth, 2011 Va. App. LEXIS 151 (May 3, 2011).

Facts insufficient to show malicious intent. — Court reasonably disbelieved the defendant's claim he used a hip-toss, body slamming the victim, to calm victims and found the defendant guilty of unlawful wounding but the court noted that the final sentencing order entered by the trial court erroneously reflected that the defendant was found guilty of malicious wounding and this required remand. Townes v. Commonwealth, No. 0577-02-2, 2003 Va. App. LEXIS 184 (Ct. of Appeals Apr. 1, 2003).

Evidence was insufficient to support defendant's conviction for unlawful wounding under § 18.2-51 as there was no showing that defendant had intent to maim, disable, or kill the victim when he delivered a single punch to the victim's face, in that, although the evidence supported a finding that the attack was unprovoked by the victim, there was no evidence of any significant injury caused by defendant's single blow to the victim, there was no evidence showing that defendant repeatedly bragged about it or vowed to do the same thing again, and there was no evidence linking any particular injury to defendant's initial blow. Without any special evidence of the nature, force, and results of the single blow delivered by defendant, the court could not say that the isolated punch rose above the level of a blow that would be delivered in a typical fistfight. Worrell v. Commonwealth, 2010 Va. App. LEXIS 497 (Dec. 21, 2010).

No estoppel as to proof of intent. — A verdict in a prior trial which found defendant guilty of involuntary manslaughter did not necessarily mean that defendant's wounding of another victim in the same shooting for which he was prosecuted in a subsequent trial was without malicious intent so as to preclude conviction under this section on grounds of collateral estoppel embodied in the Fifth Amendment. Jones v. Commonwealth, 217 Va. 231, 228 S.E.2d 127 (1976); Jones v. Blankenship, 602 F.2d 650 (4th Cir. 1979).

III. PROSECUTION.

A. Indictment.

Indictments for statutory offenses should be couched in the language of the statute. It is not requisite to charge in an indictment for a violation of this section any more than is necessary to accurately and adequately charge the felony. Dean v. Commonwealth, 189 Va. 426, 53 S.E.2d 141 (1949).

And should charge intents conjunctively. — Although the statute against unlawful shooting, etc., affixes a penalty when the act is done with intent to maim, disfigure, disable or kill, in the disjunctive, yet the indictment should charge the intents conjunctively. Angel v. Commonwealth, 4 Va. (2 Va. Cas.) 231 (1820).

Failure to allege malice. — Where the indictment charged that

the defendant "did unlawfully and feloniously stab, cut, or cause bodily injury to [the victim] with the intent to maim, disfigure, disable or kill" and contained no allegation that the act was committed maliciously, the indictment charged the defendant with unlawful wounding, rather than malicious wounding, and the defendant could not be convicted of or sentenced for malicious wounding. Terrell v. Commonwealth, No. 1669-99-2, 2000 Va. App. LEXIS 266 (Ct. of Appeals Apr. 11, 2000).

Failure to allege specific intent fatal. — An indictment failing to allege the specific intent to wound, disfigure, disable and kill, as required by this section, is insufficient. Williamson v. Commonwealth, 165 Va. 750, 181 S.E. 351 (1935); Tompkins v. Commonwealth, 177 Va. 858, 13 S.E.2d 409 (1941).

And is not cured by statute of jeofails. — An indictment not in compliance with this section in that it failed to charge that the cutting was done with the intent to maim, disable or kill is not cured by § 19.2-227. Tompkins v. Commonwealth, 177 Va. 858, 13 S.E.2d 409 (1941).

Where an indictment charged that one feloniously did strike, cut, and stab another, with intent to kill, etc., although the words strike and cut were not in the statute, the indictment was not quashed. Derieux v. Commonwealth, 4 Va. (2 Va. Cas.) 379 (1823).

Unnecessary to state weapon used. — In an indictment for malicious assault with intent to kill it is unnecessary to state the weapon with which the assault was made. Jackson v. Commonwealth, 96 Va. 107, 30 S.E. 452 (1898).

Indictment for malicious shooting ought to charge that it was done feloniously. Trimble v. Commonwealth, 4 Va. (2 Va. Cas.) 143 (1818).

Section 19.2-294 does not prohibit prosecution in a single trial for violation of this section and § 18.2-51.2. Powell v. Commonwealth, No. 0554-89-1 (Ct. of Appeals Oct. 6, 1992).

Variance between record of examining court and indictment. — The record of the examining court showed that the prisoner was charged with a felonious stabbing with intent to kill. The indictment contained four counts, of which the first charged a malicious stabbing, with intent to kill; the second, a malicious stabbing, with intent to maim, disfigure, and disable; the third and fourth, an unlawful stabbing, with the same intents, respectively. It was held that this variance between the record of the examining court, and the indictment is no ground for quashing the latter. Derieux v. Commonwealth, 4 Va. (2 Va. Cas.) 379 (1823).

Indictment; prosecutorial vindictiveness not found. — Defendant failed to offer objective evidence that his indictment for malicious wounding under § 18.2-51 was obtained as a result of prosecutorial vindictiveness, even though it was obtained after defendant received a continuance of his trial for robbery; the Commonwealth stated that the malicious wounding indictment was not originally sought due to an oversight, and the indictment was sought from the next available grand jury. Muhammad v. Commonwealth, No. 1300-01-2, 2002 Va. App. LEXIS 731 (Ct. of Appeals Dec. 10, 2002).

Indictments held sufficient. — An indictment charging that prisoner, "at the county and within the jurisdiction of the court, feloniously and maliciously did stab one P.T. with intention to maim, etc., and kill him," will not be quashed, upon objection that it does not allege any assault, striking or wounding, nor that P.T. was within the county or jurisdiction, nor that the intent was felonious or malicious. Commonwealth v. Woodson, 36 Va. (9 Leigh) 669 (1839).

Indictment charging that accused made an assault with a stone, and did feloniously, maliciously and unlawfully beat, wound, illtreat and cause bodily injury, etc., sufficiently conforms to this section. Jones v. Commonwealth, 87 Va. 63, 12 S.E. 226 (1890).

B. Defenses.

Self-defense. — A person assaulted while in the discharge of a lawful act, and reasonably apprehending that his assailant will do him bodily harm, has the right to repel the assault by all the force he deems necessary, and is not compelled to retreat from his assailant, but may, in turn, become the assailant, inflicting bodily wounds until his person is out of danger. Jackson v. Commonwealth, 96 Va. 107, 30 S.E. 452 (1898). See Stoneman v. Commonwealth, 66 Va. (25 Gratt.) 887 (1874); Brown v. Commonwealth, 86

Va. 466, 10 S.E. 745 (1890); Montgomery v. Commonwealth, 99 Va. 833, 37 S.E. 841 (1901).

An instruction which failed to point out that self-defense is not available to the aggressor was properly refused. Banner v. Commonwealth, 204 Va. 640, 133 S.E.2d 305 (1963).

Where an accused responds to a threat of harm from another and the amount of force the accused uses is reasonable in relation to the harm threatened, the accused may be acquitted based on self-defense. Thornton v. Commonwealth, No. 2579-99-1, 2000 Va. App. LEXIS 794 (Ct. of Appeals Dec. 5, 2000).

If a wounding remains unlawful but results from the heat of passion, such as rage or fear, rather than malice, it constitutes unlawful wounding rather than malicious wounding. Thornton v. Commonwealth, No. 2579-99-1, 2000 Va. App. LEXIS 794 (Ct. of Appeals Dec. 5, 2000).

Because defendant's daughter testified that defendant neither initiated nor provoked a fight with the victim, the trial court erred in denying defendant's proffered instruction on self-defense without fault; consequently, defendant was entitled to a new trial for malicious wounding. Sanders v. Commonwealth, — Va. App. —, — S.E.2d —, 2005 Va. App. LEXIS 386 (Oct. 4, 2005).

Defense of others. — In order to justifiably defend another, the defendant must reasonably believe that the person being defended was free from fault; whether the defended person was, in fact, free from fault is legally irrelevant to the defense. Foster v. Commonwealth, 13 Va. App. 380, 412 S.E.2d 198 (1991).

The law pertaining to defense of others is that one may avail himself or herself of the defense only where he or she reasonably believes, based on the attendant circumstances, that the person defended is without fault in provoking the fray. Foster v. Commonwealth, 13 Va. App. 380, 412 S.E.2d 198 (1991).

No duty to retreat. — If a defendant is completely without fault in precipitating a violent confrontation, he is under no duty to retreat but, rather, is free to stand his ground and repel the attack by force. Swain v. Commonwealth, No. 2430-99-1, 2000 Va. App. LEXIS 701 (Ct. of Appeals Oct. 31, 2000).

An illegal arrest of itself does not give the person being arrested the right to shoot or take the officer's life. Banner v. Commonwealth, 204 Va. 640, 133 S.E.2d 305 (1963).

Protection of property. — A man may rightfully use as much force as is necessary for the protection of his person or property, provided he does not endanger human life or do great bodily harm. But for a mere trespass upon land the owner has no right to assault the trespasser with a deadly weapon, the result of which may be to kill or do him great bodily harm. Montgomery v. Commonwealth, 98 Va. 840, 36 S.E. 371 (1900); Montgomery v. Commonwealth, 99 Va. 833, 37 S.E. 841 (1901).

Insanity. — Trial court did not abuse its discretion by precluding defendant from presenting evidence to the jury in support of a settled insanity defense because defendant conceded his insanity was not permanent. Morgan v. Commonwealth, 50 Va. App. 120, 646 S.E.2d 899, 2007 Va. App. LEXIS 251 (2007).

Acquittal of shooting one no defense to charge of shooting another. — If a person be indicted for shooting S.W. and acquitted thereof, and then indicted for shooting J.W. her plea of autrefois acquit will not be supported, although the same act of shooting is charged in each indictment; for, the jury who tried the first indictment might have acquitted the prisoner on several grounds, which would not affect the second trial, as that the shot did not strike and wound S.W. or that she did not shoot S.W. with intent to maim, disfigure, disable or kill the said S.W. Vaughan v. Commonwealth, 4 Va. (2 Va. Cas.) 273 (1821).

Conviction is acquittal of lesser offenses. — Where, in a prosecution for unlawfully, maliciously, and feloniously wounding one with intent to maim, disfigure, disable and kill him, accused was convicted of the highest offense charged, this conviction was equivalent to an acquittal of all lesser ones necessarily included therein, the latter being merged in the former. Lee v. Commonwealth, 135 Va. 572, 115 S.E. 671 (1923).

C. Evidence.

Commonwealth's burden to prove malice and intent. — To support a conviction for malicious wounding under this section, the Commonwealth must prove that the defendant inflicted the victim's injuries maliciously and with the intent to maim, disfigure, disable

or kill. Robertson v. Commonwealth, 31 Va. App. 814, 525 S.E.2d 640 (2000).

Opportunity insufficient to prove criminal agency. — In a prosecution for causing bodily injury to a child, while the defendant's opportunity to injure her daughter and certain other circumstances in the case raised inferences which created a suspicion of guilt or even a probability of guilt, the evidence was insufficient to exclude a reasonable hypothesis that someone other than the defendant was the criminal agent; thus circumstantial evidence alone was not sufficient enough to prove criminal agency. Christian v. Commonwealth, 221 Va. 1078, 277 S.E.2d 205 (1981).

To prove the crime of attempted murder two essential elements must be established. The specific intent to kill the victim must be shown and this must be coupled with evidence of some overt but ineffectual act in furtherance of this purpose. Hargrave v. Commonwealth, 214 Va. 436, 201 S.E.2d 597 (1974).

Conviction can rest upon the uncorroborated testimony of the prosecuting witness. Robinson v. Commonwealth, 186 Va. 992, 45 S.E.2d 162 (1947).

Weight of evidence is question for jury. — In the instant case accused was convicted of malicious cutting with intent to kill. The evidence for the Commonwealth was sufficient to sustain the conviction, and while several witnesses for the defense contradicted some of the testimony for the Commonwealth, and testified that accused bore a good reputation, the credibility of the witnesses and the weight of the evidence were questions for the jury, and the Supreme Court could not say that the judgment was plainly wrong or without evidence to support it. Jones v. Commonwealth, 135 Va. 545, 115 S.E. 572 (1923).

Proof establishing wounding and bodily injury. — Proof established both a wounding within the purview of the ancient definition and a bodily injury, within the broadened meaning of this section. Shackelford v. Commonwealth, 183 Va. 423, 32 S.E.2d 682 (1945).

Evidence that the defendant, acting in concert with two accomplices, stomped repeatedly on the victim's arm was sufficient to show he caused bodily injury to the victim. Hall v. Commonwealth, No. 1375-99-3, 2000 Va. App. LEXIS 703 (Ct. of Appeals Oct. 31, 2000).

And specific intent. — Evidence of express malice, plus the unprovoked and brutal attack by the accused, a strong man, upon a defenseless woman in her own home in the early hours of the morning, is clearly sufficient to establish the specific intent defined in this section. Shackelford v. Commonwealth, 183 Va. 423, 32 S.E.2d 682 (1945).

Malice and the specific intent to maim, etc., may be evidenced by words or inferred from acts and conduct under the rule that a person is presumed to have intended the natural and probable consequences of his voluntary act. Fletcher v. Commonwealth, 209 Va. 636, 166 S.E.2d 269 (1969).

Lack of direct evidence of subjective intent does not preclude conviction. — One may be convicted of unlawful wounding with intent to maim, disfigure, disable or kill another when there is no direct evidence of a subjective intent to inflict bodily harm to the injured person. David v. Commonwealth, 2 Va. App. 1, 340 S.E.2d 576 (1986).

The use of a deadly weapon, standing alone, is not sufficient to prove the specific intent required to establish attempted murder. Hargrave v. Commonwealth, 214 Va. 436, 201 S.E.2d 597 (1974).

A verdict of unlawful wounding is sustained by evidence that the accused struck the prosecuting witness on his face and head and kicked him so that blood ran from his ears, nose and mouth and he suffered a small cut inside the mouth. Bryant v. Commonwealth, 189 Va. 310, 53 S.E.2d 54 (1949).

Confidential communication need not be disclosed. Murphy v. Commonwealth, 64 Va. (23 Gratt.) 960 (1873).

Expert testimony on gang culture. — Trial court did not abuse its discretion in admitting expert testimony on gang culture in defendant's criminal trial for malicious wounding and use of a firearm during the commission of a felony; the Commonwealth provided a sufficient foundation for the admission of the testimony, the testimony was relevant in that it established a motive for the shooting, and the evidence was not outweighed by prejudice. Hubbard v. Commonwealth, 2006 Va. App. LEXIS 72 (Feb. 28, 2006).

In a case in which defendant appealed his conviction for violating §§ 18.2-51, 18.2-53.1, and 18.2-286.1, he unsuccessfully argued that the trial court erred in permitting an expert witness to testify about gang practices and terminology, including his involvement with a gang. The trial court reasonably concluded that the probative value of the expert's testimony outweighed any prejudicial effect; the evidence was relevant to prove the identity of the shooter, and the testimony about his gang affiliation was probative as to defendant's identity. Wyche v. Commonwealth, 2012 Va. App. LEXIS 227 (July 10, 2012).

Evidence held irrelevant. — See Jackson v. Commonwealth, 96 Va. 107, 30 S.E. 452 (1898).

Introduction of prior convictions during guilt phase improper. — Trial judge erred in admitting defendant's two prior robbery convictions during the guilt phase of the trial because the felony convictions, which had to be proved to invoke § 19.2-297.1, were not elements of the malicious wounding offense; § 19.2-297.1 unambiguously related to the punishment to be imposed upon conviction. Washington v. Commonwealth, 44 Va. App. 157, 604 S.E.2d 92, 2004 Va. App. LEXIS 503 (2004).

Where evidence shows beyond reasonable doubt that two defendants participated in the commission of an assault, it is immaterial whether they actually inflicted the specific injuries received by the victims. Allison v. Commonwealth, No. 0295-85 (Ct. of Appeals Mar. 19, 1986).

There was evidence to support the defendant's theory of unlawful wounding, where the evidence indicated that the fight was provoked by the victim and the shooting occurred several minutes thereafter, there was evidence that prior to the shooting the defendant was upset and was shouting for someone to give him a gun, after he obtained the gun several people tried unsuccessfully to restrain him, and the defendant fired two shots, one of which missed the victim; a jury could find from the evidence that the defendant did not act maliciously, but acted upon a reasonable provocation, in the heat of passion. Miller v. Commonwealth, 5 Va. App. 22, 359 S.E.2d 841 (1987).

Evidence that parent or stepparent has caused his or her child bodily injury, has done so maliciously, and with an intent to cause permanent injury, even if he fails in this intention, is sufficient to support a conviction of malicious wounding. Campbell v. Commonwealth, 12 Va. App. 476, 405 S.E.2d 1 (1991).

Evidence of malice sufficient. — The evidence was sufficient to prove that the defendant acted with malice and not in the heat of passion where the evidence showed that the defendant entered the victim's residence in the early morning hours after he was informed that he was not welcome, that the entry was both unlawful and planned and that, after entering, the defendant attacked a third person and the victim and accused the victim of infidelity. Robertson v. Commonwealth, 31 Va. App. 814, 525 S.E.2d 640 (2000).

Given that the Commonwealth presented sufficient evidence that defendant burglarized an apartment with the requisite specific intent and malice to disfigure, maim, disable, or kill at least three of the victims, without provocation, his convictions based upon said actions were upheld on appeal. Slayton v. Commonwealth, — Va. App. —, — S.E.2d —, 2007 Va. App. LEXIS 180 (May 1, 2007).

Where defendant drove his girlfriend's car at speeds of 77 to 107 miles per hour, 42 to 72 miles per hour over the posted speed limit of 35 miles per hour while driving in a populated area, and he moved out of the through lane of traffic and into the left turn lane, and drove his car into another vehicle causing the two vehicles to hit a third vehicle, there was sufficient evidence to convict him of malicious wounding in violation of § 18.2-51 as there was sufficient evidence from which a rational fact finder could infer that defendant's actions constituted implied malice. Knight v. Commonwealth, 61 Va. App. 148, 733 S.E.2d 701, 2012 Va. App. LEXIS 363 (2012).

Evidence held sufficient. — Evidence was sufficient to support conviction for malicious wounding with intent to maim, disfigure, disable, or kill of defendant where without provocation, defendant repeatedly struck victim on the side of his head, opening a wound that required several stitches to close, and after administering several of these blows, the defendant attempted to reach into one of the victim's pockets as if to take his wallet, and when the defendant was unsuccessful in his attempt to procure whatever he was seeking, he again struck the victim "real hard in the head two or three or four more times," stopping only upon the appearance of a security guard. Williams v. Commonwealth, No. 0844-92-1 (Ct. of Appeals Aug. 17, 1993).

Evidence was sufficient to show intent, notwithstanding the defendant's assertion that he acted in self-defense, where the victim testified that the defendant stabbed her after he wrestled a knife from her, the defendant stabbed the victim seven times, including twice in the back, and one wound was inflicted with sufficient force that it punctured the victim's lung. Murray v. Commonwealth, No. 1995-97-2 (Ct. of Appeals July 14, 1998).

Evidence held sufficient to sustain verdict. See Pyliaris v. Commonwealth, No. 2193-97-2 (Ct. of Appeals Sept. 15, 1998); Jenkins v. Commonwealth, No. 0967-01-4, 2002 Va. App. LEXIS 660 (Ct. of Appeals Nov. 5, 2002); Muhammad v. Commonwealth, No. 1300-01-2, 2002 Va. App. LEXIS 731 (Ct. of Appeals Dec. 10, 2002).

The Commonwealth presented sufficient evidence of intent to sustain the defendant's conviction for attempted malicious wounding where the defendant, while attempting to leave a parking lot in a stolen vehicle, saw a pedestrian blocking his only avenue of escape and deliberately chose to accelerate the car toward the pedestrian, never decelerating, braking or swerving to avoid him, even when the pedestrian was only five to ten feet away from being struck. Moody v. Commonwealth, 28 Va. App. 702, 508 S.E.2d 354 (1998).

Evidence was sufficient to support a conviction where testimony of an uninterested witness established: (1) that a violent argument erupted between the defendant and the victim; (2) that the defendant armed herself with a knife; and (3) that the defendant stabbed the victim. Hall v. Commonwealth, No. 0642-98-4 (Ct. of Appeals Apr. 13, 1999).

Sufficient evidence supported defendant's convictions for attempted malicious wounding in violation of §§ 18.2-26 and 18.2-51, and felony hit-and-run, in violation of § 46.2-894, where the evidence presented at trial showed that, while trying to help her sister escape from a store where the sister had been stopped for shoplifting, defendant hit two store employees with her car, dragging one of them for several feet, and then fled the scene of the accident without stopping and giving the information required by § 46.2-894. Brooks v. Commonwealth, No. 0898-01-2, 2002 Va. App. LEXIS 311 (Ct. of Appeals May 14, 2002).

Sufficient evidence supported defendant's conviction for unlawful wounding; the contextual circumstances coupled with defendant's notable age, size, and weight advantages over his victim supported the trial court's judgment. Parrish v. Commonwealth, No. 1688-02-3, 2003 Va. App. LEXIS 505 (Ct. of Appeals Oct. 7, 2003).

Commonwealth's evidence regarding a fight in a nightclub parking lot, although circumstantial, was competent, was not inherently incredible, and was sufficient to prove beyond a reasonable doubt that the defendant was guilty of maiming the person with whom she was fighting. Harris v. Commonwealth, No. 2083-02-1, 2003 Va. App. LEXIS 631 (Ct. of Appeals Dec. 9, 2003).

Sufficient evidence was presented to prove malicious wounding where defendant: (1) maliciously and intentionally struck the victim in the face without provocation with the intent to inflict serious injury; (2) prepared for the assault by wrapping a belt around his hand and knuckles, converting his bare fist into a more effective weapon; (3) ensured that the buckle would strike his victim and inflict serious injury; and (4) caused a four to five inch cut which, although healed, left a visible scar; moreover, because the court could find that defendant lied when he testified that the victim was the aggressor, it could infer that he was lying to conceal his guilt and the true nature of the intention with which he struck her. Branch v. Commonwealth, No. 1283-03-1, 2004 Va. App. LEXIS 153 (Ct. of Appeals Apr. 6, 2004).

Evidence supported defendant's conviction for malicious wounding where: (1) the victim testified that while he was incarcerated, he was assaulted by a group of inmates, including defendant; (2) another inmate overheard the group talking about the planned assault and then heard an attack; (3) photographs showed the victim's injuries; and (4) the medical testimony confirmed that the victim suffered hearing and vision injuries from the beating. Stump v. Commonwealth, No. 1112-03-3, 2004 Va. App. LEXIS 471 (Ct. of Appeals Oct. 5, 2004).

Defendant's unlawful wounding conviction was upheld, as the trial court properly disallowed evidence of prior specific acts of violence allegedly committed by the victim and sustained an objection to evidence of the victim's long-term alcohol use, given defendant's failure to: (1) proffer any evidence which would have supported his self-defense defense; (2) lay a proper foundation to support said defense; and (3) preserve for appeal the trial court's failure to rule on whether any expert testimony was necessary on the issue of the victim's long-term alcohol abuse, and whether there was a nexus between the same and her violent behavior, especially where the trial court specifically ruled that the long-term pattern of alcohol use was irrelevant. Witterman v. Commonwealth, — Va. App. —, — S.E.2d —, 2005 Va. App. LEXIS 281 (July 19, 2005).

Commonwealth presented sufficient evidence to sustain two convictions of using a firearm in commission of both a charge of attempted murder and a charge of malicious wounding, based on the victim's testimony, and the inferences drawn therefrom, in which the jury could reasonably conclude that: (1) defendant had a firearm in her possession when she hit the victim with the hammer; (2) when defendant shot the victim, and before she hit the victim with a hammer, nothing in the record indicated that she put the gun down before she hit him with the hammer; and (3) by having the firearm in her possession, defendant displayed the firearm in a threatening manner during the hammer attack; furthermore, although the record did not indicate that defendant presented the pistol in a threatening manner, the jury could properly conclude that her mere possession of the pistol during the hammer attack, coupled with the fact she had already used the pistol, could create a legitimate fear of further use and constituted display of a firearm in a threatening manner. Coleman v. Commonwealth, — Va. App. —, — S.E.2d —, 2005 Va. App. LEXIS 379 (Oct. 4, 2005).

Facts showed that: (1) defendant drove his truck down a 100-foot driveway at a high rate of speed; (2) the victim testified he believed that defendant was going to hit him, and he had to jump between two parked cars to escape being struck; (3) defendant admitted threatening the victim, drinking alcohol before the incident, and confirmed that he and the victim had prior confrontations; (4) the victim's father also heard defendant's threats and saw skid marks in the gravel driveway; (5) a police officer investigating the incident also observed fresh skid marks and testified defendant appeared to have been drinking; and (6) a motor vehicle, wrongfully used, could be a weapon as deadly as a gun or a knife. Thus, the trial court's determination that defendant attempted to run over the victim and cause him serious bodily injury was not plainly wrong or without evidence to support it; therefore, the evidence was sufficient to convict defendant of attempted malicious wounding. Sprouse v. Commonwealth, — Va. App. —, — S.E.2d —, 2006 Va. App. LEXIS 45 (Feb. 7, 2006).

Evidence was sufficient to prove that defendant had the intent to maim, disfigure, disable, or kill his wife in a case where he was charged with unlawful wounding following an altercation with her in which he punched her in the nose so hard that he broke her nose in two places; the evidence showed that defendant was a much bigger person than his wife and that she needed surgery to correct the damage. Thornburgh v. Commonwealth, — Va. App. —, — S.E.2d —, 2006 Va. App. LEXIS 90 (Mar. 14, 2006).

Defendant's malicious wounding, aggravated malicious wounding, and use of a firearm in the commission of a felony convictions were upheld on appeal, as sufficient evidence linked him to a shooting while driving a jeep loaned to him and his cohorts in exchange for drugs, and based on the same, the trial judge could reject defendant's hypothesis that another group of men gained possession of the jeep and committed the crimes alleged. Powell v. Commonwealth, — Va. App. —, — S.E.2d —, 2006 Va. App. LEXIS 537 (Nov. 28, 2006).

Commonwealth's evidence was sufficient to convict defendant of malicious wounding, where the evidence showed that defendant pushed the victim onto the floor, hit the victim's head facedown on the floor, and continued to push the victim's face into the floor for several minutes. Paris Antwan Barnes v. Commonwealth, — Va. App. —, — S.E.2d —, 2006 Va. App. LEXIS 525 (Nov. 21, 2006).

Evidence that defendant beat the oldest child with defendant's hand, kicked the oldest child with defendant's feet, and struck the oldest child repeatedly with a cable cord using sufficient force to inflict welts, bruising, and scabs was sufficient to support a conviction for malicious wounding. Ferguson v. Commonwealth, 50 Va. App. 351, 649 S.E.2d 724, 2007 Va. App. LEXIS 338 (2007).

Evidence was sufficient to support defendant's conviction for the malicious wounding of a victim and a witness's daughter. The testimony of the witness, coupled with tire marks left in the grass by defendant's vehicle, supported a finding that defndant struck the victim and the witness's daughter when they were at a location in the grass more than six feet from the edge of a roadway. Patrick v. Commonwealth, 2008 Va. App. LEXIS 231 (May 13, 2008).

Defendant's challenge to the sufficiency of the evidence to support convictions for second-degree murder, use of a firearm in the commission of murder, malicious wounding, and use of a firearm in the commission of malicious wounding lacked merit, because the testimony of defendant's grandfather, identifying defendant as the person who shot the pistol that wounded the grandfather and killed another victim, was not inherently incredible as a matter of law; any challenge based on the grandfather's admission that the grandfather had been drinking and doing drugs before the shooting did not render the testimony inherently incredible. Carrington v. Commonwealth, 2009 Va. App. LEXIS 152 (Mar. 31, 2009).

Evidence that the victim suffered multiple stab wounds to the abdomen, lower back, and fingers, that the victim said defendant stabbed the victim, and that the knives used to stab the victim were found where victim said defendant put them was sufficient to support defendant's conviction for malicious wounding. Salahmand v. Commonwealth, 2009 Va. App. LEXIS 324 (July 21, 2009).

Evidence was sufficient to support defendant's convictions for robbery, shooting within an occupied dwelling, using a firearm in the commission of a felony, armed burglary, and malicious wounding, because ample evidence supported a finding that defendant was a perpetrator in a home invasion: three of the victims identified defendant at trial, and a co-defendant testified that defendant said he intended to rob the home, that he entered the home wearing a bullet-proof vest and armed with a handgun, and that he later told the co-defendant that he had struck one of the victim's in the head. Trial court did not abuse discretion in ruling on misidentification of accomplices by witnesses. Streater v. Commonwealth, 2009 Va. App. LEXIS 504 (Nov. 10, 2009).

Evidence was sufficient to convict defendant of unlawful wounding because the natural and probable consequence of defendant's high speed chase and bumping of another vehicle was causing an accident, which resulted in injury to the occupants of the other vehicle. Kelley v. Commonwealth, 2010 Va. App. LEXIS 11 (Jan. 12, 2010).

Conviction for attempted malicious wounding under §§ 18.2-26 and 18.2-51, was supported by evidence that defendant entered the victim's apartment and attempted to take money from the victim by intimidating him at gunpoint, and defendant and the victim struggled; defendant's exclusive possession of defendant's gun during the entire time the incident was occurring supported a finding that the gunshot was deliberate, not accidental, and the trial court was entitled to infer that defendant intended the natural and probable consequences of pointing a gun at someone during a robbery, that the circumstances might result in the gun firing. Reid v. Commonwealth, 2010 Va. App. LEXIS 334 (Aug. 17, 2010).

Defendant's convictions for robbery, abduction, and malicious wounding, were proper because the fact that he was not wearing a white coat did not negate a detective's reasonable suspicion that defendant was somehow involved in criminal activity. The trial court accepted the explanation that defendant had abandoned his coat as he fled. Diaz v. Commonwealth, 2010 Va. App. LEXIS 417 (Oct. 26, 2010).

In a prosecution for malicious wounding, the evidence was sufficient to show that defendant's actions caused the victim's wounds as the evidence showed that defendant, at a minimum, acted as a principal, within the meaning of § 18.2-18, in the malicious wounding of the victim, in that the evidence showed that defendant was present during the malicious wounding of the victim and performed an overt act of assistance by striking the initial blow against the victim. Johnson v. Commonwealth, 58 Va. App. 303, 709 S.E.2d 175, 2011 Va. App. LEXIS 185 (2011).

Evidence was sufficient to establish that the victim was wounded in a manner sufficient to satisfy the requirements of § 18.2-51, in that the evidence showed that, following the attack, there was a very large pool of blood beside the victim's head, with blood coming out of his nose, mouth, and eye. These breaks or cuts in the skin were sufficient to show that the victim suffered a qualified wound under § 18.2-51. Johnson v. Commonwealth, 58 Va. App. 303, 709 S.E.2d 175, 2011 Va. App. LEXIS 185 (2011).

Evidence that defendant's beating of the victim lasted for a sustained period, involving 25 to 30 blows; that the beating caused the victim intense shooting pain, temporarily leaving the victim barely able to move; and that months later the victim was still partially incapacitated and continued to need medical treatment for nerve damage and chronic radiating pain, supported a conviction for maliciously causing bodily injury. English v. Commonwealth, 58 Va. App. 711, 715 S.E.2d 391, 2011 Va. App. LEXIS 298 (2011).

Evidence was sufficient to support defendant's malicious wounding conviction, where the trier of fact was free to conclude that defendant did not act in the heat of passion, as defendant left the room to get a pistol before the fight began, and that there was no provocation that reasonably produced such fear or anger in defendant as would have caused defendant to act on impulse without conscious reflection. Cook v. Commonwealth, 2011 Va. App. LEXIS 409 (Dec. 20, 2011).

Where the trial court expressly found that the "pocket discharge" that wounded the unintended victim was negligent or accidental and defendant had the intent to maim, disfigure or kill codefendant's intended victim when defendant began the process of withdrawing the gun from his pocket, the action causing the shooting, the evidence supported a finding that defendant had the intent to maim, disfigure, disable, or kill the victim. Moore v. Commonwealth, 2012 Va. App. LEXIS 218 (July 3, 2012).

Evidence held insufficient to sustain verdict. — Evidence raised no more than a suspicion of the defendant's guilt and, therefore, was insufficient to support his conviction where: (1) after drinking with a friend for much of a day, the victim had an altercation with the defendant, during which the defendant hit the victim in the back and stomach; (2) the victim passed out shortly thereafter and, when he awoke, he was in a hospital being treated for stab wounds; (3) the victim testified that he did not perceive being stabbed and that the defendant struck him with his fists, but that some stab wounds were in places he recalled being hit by the defendant; (4) there was no evidence of the time of the altercation with the defendant, the length of time he was passed out, or the time he was taken to the hospital; and (5) the defendant stated that he knew that the victim had been stabbed, but that he did not inflict the wounds. Smith v. Commonwealth, No. 2130-97-2 (Ct. of Appeals Mar. 2, 1999).

Evidence presented by the Commonwealth that the defendant and a gunman entered a home, demanded the contents of a safe and tied the victim up, and that a table was broken and that the victim received scratches on her body presumably from the glass was insufficient to support the defendant's conviction; the evidence did not show that the defendant broke the glass table, that the glass caused the victim's injuries, or that the defendant intended to injure someone by breaking the table. Anderson v. Commonwealth, No. 0235-99-1, 2000 Va. App. LEXIS 539 (Ct. of Appeals July 25, 2000).

Evidence that established nothing more than that defendant was one of four passengers in a vehicle from which shots were fired wounding the victim in another car was not sufficient to support conviction of defendant for malicious wounding; suspicion that defendant was the shooter, no matter how strong, could not support the conviction. Hudgins v. Commonwealth, No. 0960-00-2, 2001 Va. App. LEXIS 526 (Ct. of Appeals Sept. 25, 2001).

There was insufficient evidence to support the defendant's conviction for malicious wounding where the stabbing victim testified that the defendant attacked him with his fists, and the record at trial contained no evidence of the length of time the victim lay unconscious on the sidewalk or what transpired in the interval of time preceding his arrival at the hospital. The evidence of record supported two hypotheses: (1) that the period of unconsciousness resulted from a fist attack that developed into a knife attack by the defendant or (2) that the victim's unconsciousness resulted from his state of intoxication which inspired an unidentified pedestrian present at the scene (or one arriving later) to use a knife to terrorize the victim in order to achieve some ulterior motive and, consequently, the Commonwealth failed to prove the guilt of the accused to the exclusion of every reasonable hypothesis consistent with his innocence. Commonwealth v. Smith, 259 Va. 780, 529 S.E.2d 78, 2000 Va. LEXIS 76 (2000).

Firing weapon into floor of upstairs apartment. — Evidence was sufficient to support the trial court's finding that defendant possessed the specific intent required to convict him of malicious wounding. After eruption of an argument between himself and

women he had just had intercourse with and requested that she leave before his girlfriend returned home, he intentionally twice fired a powerful weapon into the floor of his upstairs apartment at three o'clock in the morning, almost severing the leg of the sleeping resident above. Such conduct was inherently dangerous and imposed grave risk to anyone in the vicinity, thus, the fact finder was entitled to infer from this that defendant intended the direct and probable consequences of his act. Shimhue v. Commonwealth, No. 1736-97-2 (Ct. of Appeals June 30, 1998).

D. Instructions.

Jury should be charged as to offenses of which accused may be convicted. — Generally, on an indictment for malicious wounding under this section, the accused may be convicted of either malicious wounding, unlawful wounding, or simple assault and battery, and the jury are so charged by the clerk under the authority of the court, stating the punishment annexed to each. The pleadings are made up before this charge is given, and if the charge is not correct, objection to it should then be made. Honacker v. Commonwealth, 136 Va. 752, 118 S.E. 85 (1923).

A jury should be instructed that this section contemplates that a cutting or wounding may either be a malicious or unlawful wounding. Shifflett v. Commonwealth, 221 Va. 191, 269 S.E.2d 353 (1980).

And intent must be to disfigure permanently. — On a prosecution for maiming under this section, where it was an open question whether the wound was caused by the blow of accused's fist or by a blow with a sharp instrument, it was error for the court to refuse to instruct the jury that the accused could not be convicted of the felony charged unless they believed he intended to kill, or maim, or disfigure permanently, the prosecutor, and to give the same instruction with the word "permanently" stricken out. Lee v. Commonwealth, 135 Va. 572, 115 S.E. 671 (1923).

Instruction not based on evidence refused. — In a prosecution under this section, defendant objected that in declining to give instructions asked by him on provocation, self-defense, and his intoxication at the time of the shooting, the court refused to present to the jury the law covering accused's theory of the case. It was held, that, as the record failed to disclose any evidence upon which the instructions would have been based, their refusal was not error. Harris v. Commonwealth, 134 Va. 688, 114 S.E.2d 597 (1922).

Defendant's request that the trial court instruct the jury that if the detention of the victim was incidental to an assault, defendant could not be guilty of abduction, was properly denied as defendant followed the victim after she fled from the car and grabbed her, which was not incidental to the malicious wounding charge based on the restraint defendant used at the time he bit off the victim's finger, before she fled. Lewis v. Commonwealth, No. 1770-03-2, 2004 Va. App. LEXIS 296 (Ct. of Appeals June 29, 2004).

Instruction when defendant not charged with malicious cutting. — Where defendants were indicted upon the charge of having "unlawfully and feloniously" cut and wounded another, but the indictments contained no charge of "malicious" cutting, the court erred in permitting the clerk to read the jury this section without explaining to them that they were not to regard that portion of it which related to the punishment for maliciously doing the acts therein described, and in refusing an instruction requested by counsel for defendants that under the indictment defendants could not be found guilty of maliciously cutting or stabbing. Hummer v. Commonwealth, 122 Va. 826, 94 S.E. 157 (1917).

Instruction on the lesser offense of unlawful wounding. — Where a defendant produces evidence that he acted in the heat of passion, he is entitled to an instruction on the lesser offense of unlawful wounding. If the evidence as a whole raises a reasonable doubt that he acted maliciously, he is entitled to a verdict on the lesser charge. Miller v. Commonwealth, 5 Va. App. 22, 359 S.E.2d 841 (1987).

Failure to give a jury instruction on unlawful wounding, as a lesser-included offense of malicious wounding required reversal, because there was more than a scintilla of evidence to support the theory that defendant pulled a gun only after the victim first shot him. Person v. Commonwealth, 2012 Va. App. LEXIS 187 (June 5, 2012).

Instruction on lesser offenses of assault and battery. — Defendant, convicted of malicious wounding in violation of § 18.2-51, was not entitled to a jury instruction on the lesser-included offenses of assault and battery, as the evidence showed he had the specific intent to maim, disfigure, disable, or kill the victim, which would violate the malicious wounding statute, and the evidence did not show that defendant only had the intent to cause bodily harm to the victim. Commonwealth v. Vaughn, 263 Va. 31, 557 S.E.2d 220, 2002 Va. LEXIS 7 (2002).

Although defendant claimed he intended merely to rob the victim, he shoved her into a brick wall, threatened to kill her by slitting her throat, pushed his gloves into her eyes to the point the victim thought she would lose her eyes, participated in brutally beating and kicking the victim, and smashed her head into the brick wall and doorway; the victim suffered injuries to her face, hands, wrists, arms, ribs, legs, and ankles as a result of the attack. The gravity of the victim's uncontroverted physical injuries inflicted by defendant, his brutal conduct in attacking her, and his verbal threats to kill her belied any finding that he did not maliciously intend to maim, disfigure, disable, or kill the victim; thus, there was no scintilla of evidence that he did not intend to maim, disfigure, disable, or kill her, and the trial court did not err in denying the jury instruction on the lesser-included offense of assault and battery. Thomas v. Commonwealth, — Va. App. —, — S.E.2d —, 2006 Va. App. LEXIS 37 (Jan. 31, 2006).

Jury to be given complete definition of malice. — In order to properly distinguish malicious wounding from unlawful wounding, the jury must be given a complete definition of malice; thus, when the trial court instructed the jury that it could ignore the concepts of heat of passion and control of reason, its definition of malice was rendered incomplete. Mason v. Commonwealth, 7 Va. App. 339, 373 S.E.2d 603 (1988).

Instruction on self-defense. — In a prosecution for malicious wounding, the trial court erred by refusing defendant's request to charge the jury on self-defense and the burden of proving self-defense, as the defense evidence supported defendant's theory that the victim advanced on defendant, kicked and swung at her, and defendant reacted by striking the victim. Brooks v. Commonwealth, 2012 Va. App. LEXIS 397 (Dec. 11, 2012).

Self-defense without fault. — In a case in which defendant was convicted of malicious wounding and use of a firearm in the commission of malicious wounding, because the evidence failed to support an instruction on self-defense without fault, defendant was not entitled to such an instruction, as a matter of law, and the trial court properly refused defendant's proffered instruction on self-defense without fault. Robinson v. Commonwealth, — Va. App. —, — S.E.2d —, 2006 Va. App. LEXIS 474 (Oct. 24, 2006).

It was error not to give assault and battery instruction where from defendant's testimony, the jury reasonably could have concluded that defendant acted only with the intent to do victim bodily harm, albeit with malice; jury should have received, in addition to the malicious wounding instruction given, an instruction giving them the opportunity to assess the evidence as it related to assault and battery, an offense that may be accompanied by malice, but does not require intent to maim, disfigure or kill. Boone v. Commonwealth, 14 Va. App. 130, 415 S.E.2d 250 (1992).

A trial court erred in failing to instruct the jury on both malicious wounding and the lesser included offense of assault and battery where the jury could have concluded that the defendant lacked the specific intent to maim, disfigure, disable or kill and acted only with the intent to do bodily harm to the victim, whether with or without malice; credible evidence was before the jury that, if believed, supported an instruction on assault and battery and it was immaterial that the jury might have rejected the lesser-included offense. Maye v. Commonwealth, No. 2311-98-2, 2000 Va. App. LEXIS 629 (Ct. of Appeals Aug. 29, 2000).

Instruction on insanity defense. — Because the instruction given by the trial court was an accurate statement of law regarding the burden of proof, the trial court did not err in refusing defendant's proffered instructions. Moreover, Virginia's allocation to defendant of both the burden of production and the burden of persuasion with respect to the affirmative defense of insanity was constitutionally permissible. Morgan v. Commonwealth, 50 Va. App. 120, 646 S.E.2d 899, 2007 Va. App. LEXIS 251 (2007).

Instruction on heat of passion defense. — In a prosecution on a charge of malicious wounding, the trial court erred in refusing to instruct the jury concerning heat of passion as a rational jury could have concluded that the attack by the victim and his friend on defendant from the front and the back in the form of a choke hold

and the friend's perceived attempted theft together constituted a reasonable provocation. This testimony provided more than a scintilla of evidence that provocation caused fear for defendant's own safety and the safety of his girlfriend. Parisi v. Commonwealth, — Va. App. —, — S.E.2d —, 2009 Va. App. LEXIS 130 (Mar. 24, 2009).

In a prosecution for malicious wounding, although the jury instructions properly defined malice, defendant was nevertheless entitled to have "heat of passion" defined in support of her theory of defense, as there was evidence to support that defense. Brooks v. Commonwealth, 2012 Va. App. LEXIS 397 (Dec. 11, 2012).

E. Verdict, Sentence and Punishment.

Accused may be convicted of any offense substantially charged. — Under an indictment with only one count, for malicious shooting, stabbing or cutting, with the intent to kill, the accused may be convicted of the offense charged, or of unlawfully doing such acts, or indeed, of any other offense — felony or misdemeanor — which is substantially charged in the indictment. Canada v. Commonwealth, 63 Va. (22 Gratt.) 899 (1872); Stuart v. Commonwealth, 69 Va. (28 Gratt.) 950 (1877); Montgomery v. Commonwealth, 98 Va. 840, 36 S.E. 371 (1900). See § 18.2-54.

Under an indictment charging that accused "in and upon one Dorothy Crutchfield feloniously did make an assault and her, the said Dorothy Crutchfield then and there unlawfully, feloniously and maliciously did stab, cut and wound with intent then and there, the said Dorothy Crutchfield, to maim, disfigure, disable and kill," accused could have been convicted: (1) of a malicious wounding with intent to maim, disfigure, disable and kill; (2) of unlawful wounding with the same intent; or (3) of simple assault and battery. Crutchfield v. Commonwealth, 187 Va. 291, 46 S.E.2d 340 (1948). See Williams v. Commonwealth, 153 Va. 987, 151 S.E. 151 (1930); Smyth v. Gay, 197 Va. 800, 91 S.E.2d 425 (1956).

Under an indictment charging felonious and malicious maiming with intent to maim, disfigure, disable or kill, the jury, if warranted by the evidence, may find the accused guilty of: (1) malicious wounding with the intent to maim, disfigure, disable or kill; or (2) unlawful wounding with the same intent; or (3) simple assault and battery. Spradlin v. Commonwealth, 195 Va. 523, 79 S.E.2d 443 (1954); Banner v. Commonwealth, 204 Va. 640, 133 S.E.2d 305 (1963).

Imposition of improper sentence. — Trial court erred by sentencing defendant to ten years' incarceration for each of defendant's two convictions of unlawful wounding, in violation of § 18.2-51, because § 18.2-10(f) authorized the imposition of a maximum five years' incarceration for unlawful wounding, a Class 6 felony. Furthermore, because the appellate court could only speculate as to the sentence that the trial court might have imposed on remand for each conviction of unlawful wounding, using the correct statutory sentencing range, each case had to be remanded to the trial court for resentencing. Gordon v. Commonwealth, No. 0940-12-2, 61 Va. App. 682, 739 S.E.2d 276, 2013 Va. App. LEXIS 102 (Apr. 2, 2013).

Sufficient finding of intent. — J. was indicted for the malicious stabbing, etc., of W., with intent to maim, etc., and the jury found J. "guilty of unlawful cutting, as charged in the within indictment," etc. The language, "as charged in the within indictment," has reference both to the cutting and the intent, and is sufficient finding of the intent with which the unlawful act was done, to meet the requirement of the statute. Jones v. Commonwealth, 72 Va. (31 Gratt.) 830 (1878).

Verdict need not specify degree of crime charged. — This section does not require either that the verdict of a jury or the finding of a court specify the degree of the crime charged. Smyth v. Gay, 197 Va. 800, 91 S.E.2d 425 (1956).

Nor inform defendant of what offense he was convicted. — In the instant case accused was indicted for unlawfully, maliciously, and feloniously wounding one B. with intent to maim, disfigure, disable and kill him. The jury found the accused guilty as charged in the indictment and fixed his punishment at two years in the penitentiary (now state correctional facility). It was claimed for accused that the trial court should have set aside the verdict, because, as the punishment fixed therein could have been lawfully imposed for either unlawful or malicious maiming, it failed to inform the defendant of the offense for which he was convicted. It was held that there was no merit in this contention. The statute did not require the jury to specify the degree or grade of the crime, and, the verdict being general, the presumption is that they found the defendant guilty of the highest degree charged in the indictment and to which the punishment prescribed was applicable. Lee v. Commonwealth, 135 Va. 572, 115 S.E. 671 (1923).

Conviction not invalid because verdict form lacked recitation of intent. — Where appellant asserted that the unlawful wounding verdict form was invalid because it failed to specify that he wounded victim with an intent to maim, disfigure, disable, or kill, the verdict form included the phrase "on the issue joined." Additionally, the instructions defining unlawful wounding included the requisite intent. Appellant's conviction for unlawful wounding was therefore not invalid merely because the verdict form lacked recitation of the requisite intent. McKenley v. Commonwealth, No. 1910-96-3 (Ct. of Appeals Oct. 28, 1997).

Verdict of "unlawful maiming" is acquittal of malicious wounding. — A verdict of "unlawful maiming," although fatally defective, necessarily manifested an acquittal of malicious wounding, and therefore defendant could not upon a new trial be convicted of malicious wounding with intent to maim, but might be convicted of unlawful wounding with the requisite intent or of the lesser and included offense of assault and battery. Banner v. Commonwealth, 204 Va. 640, 133 S.E.2d 305 (1963).

Verdicts of unlawful wounding and unlawful use of firearm in malicious wounding not inconsistent. — Defendant did not have to be charged with malicious wounding to be convicted of the unlawful use of a firearm in commission of malicious wounding. Guilty verdicts on both unlawful wounding and unlawful use of a firearm in commission of malicious wounding charges were not inconsistent because the evidence supported both verdicts. Reese v. Commonwealth, No. 1279-03-4, 2004 Va. App. LEXIS 316 (Ct. of Appeals July 6, 2004).

Verdict read in connection with indictment. — On an indictment for maliciously shooting with intent to kill, etc., one S., the jury returned their verdict: "We, the jury, find the prisoner guilty of unlawful shooting with intent to kill, as charged in the indictment, and fix the term of imprisonment, at three years in the penitentiary (now state correctional facility)." The verdict is to be read in connection with the indictment, and therefore sufficiently indicates the person shot. Price v. Commonwealth, 77 Va. 393 (1883). See Hoback v. Commonwealth, 69 Va. (28 Gratt.) 922 (1877); Hairston v. Commonwealth, 97 Va. 754, 32 S.E. 797 (1899). But see Randall v. Commonwealth, 65 Va. (24 Gratt.) 644 (1874), overruled on another point, Jolly v. Commonwealth, 136 Va. 756, 118 S.E. 109 (1923).

Verdicts held valid. — Verdicts in which the jury found the defendant guilty of malicious wounding and unlawful wounding were valid since the requisite intent, while not stated specifically in the verdicts, was necessarily implied. Jackson v. Commonwealth, 218 Va. 490, 237 S.E.2d 791 (1977).

Defendant was not improperly convicted of malicious wounding when an indictment charged defendant with the crime of unlawful wounding, under § 18.2-51, because even though the trial court used the words "malicious wounding" when pronouncing guilt at the close of a bench trial, the trial court's written order convicted defendant as charged. However, defendant's sentence to twenty years in prison, with fifteen years suspended, for unlawful wounding was excessive because the crime was a class 6 felony for which the maximum sentence was five years in prison under § 18.2-10. Ferguson v. Commonwealth, 51 Va. App. 427, 658 S.E.2d 692, 2008 Va. App. LEXIS 367 (2008).

Verdicts held insufficient. — A prisoner was tried upon an indictment containing two counts. The first charged that he unlawfully, feloniously, willfully, voluntarily, maliciously, etc., stabbed a person with intent to maim, disfigure and kill said person. The second count charged that the person unlawfully, feloniously, voluntarily and with purpose stabbed the said person with intent to maim, disable, disfigure and kill said person. The jury returned a verdict finding "the person not guilty under the first count of the indictment but guilty of unlawful stabbing." It was held that the verdict is insufficient and will not authorize a judgment, but the court should direct a new trial. Marshall v. Commonwealth, 46 Va. (5 Gratt.) 663 (1848).

A judgment of conviction cannot be sustained, where it was not possible under the verdict of the jury to determine the crime of which the jury intended to find the accused guilty, as so much of the verdict as found accused guilty of "unjustful assault" might be fairly construed as finding him guilty of unlawful assault; that is, simple assault and battery; but the concluding clause of the verdict in which the punishment was fixed at two years in the penitentiary (now state correctional facility) contradicts this finding of simple assault. The punishment as for a felony is inconsistent with the finding that accused was guilty of a misdemeanor. Williams v. Commonwealth, 153 Va. 987, 151 S.E. 151 (1930).

A verdict which merely found the defendant guilty of "unlawful wounding" and failed to name the person wounded, to recite that the wounding was done "with intent to maim," etc., or to state that it was committed "as charged in the indictment," was fatally defective. Lane v. Commonwealth, 190 Va. 58, 55 S.E.2d 450 (1949).

A verdict finding defendant guilty of "unlawful maiming" was fatally defective in that it failed to recite the requisite intent or to state "as charged in the indictment." Banner v. Commonwealth, 204 Va. 640, 133 S.E.2d 305 (1963).

A jury verdict stating "We, the jury, find the accused guilty of unlawful wounding and fix his punishment at 12 months in jail — $500 fine," is void, except insofar as it served to acquit the defendant of malicious wounding, for failure to recite that the wounding was done with the necessary intent or as charged in the indictment. Bacci v. Commonwealth, 213 Va. 236, 191 S.E.2d 182 (1972).

Verdict of guilty of assault and battery properly accepted by trial court. — Defendant, indicted and tried for violation of the maiming act, was found guilty of assault and battery. Since the evidence was sufficiently conflicting to create a reasonable difference of opinion, the verdict was properly accepted by the trial court. Harper v. Commonwealth, 196 Va. 723, 85 S.E.2d 249 (1955).

Verdict of guilty of assault and battery improper. — In a prosecution for attempted murder where the jury concluded that the evidence was not sufficient to show an intent by the defendant to murder the wounded victim or that the defendant's act was committed maliciously, and where the jury did find that the defendant committed an unlawful wounding of the victim and convicted him accordingly, this conviction barred the defendant's further conviction of all other offenses of a higher grade and of any lesser included offense encompassed by a malicious wounding indictment, and it therefore was improper for the jury to have returned a verdict finding the defendant guilty of assault and battery under the indictment charging attempted murder. Brown v. Commonwealth, 222 Va. 111, 279 S.E.2d 142 (1981).

Sentence excessive after plea of guilty to misdemeanor accepted. — In a prosecution under this section, accused was allowed to plead guilty to unlawful assault, and was sentenced to three years in the penitentiary (now state correctional facility). It was held that, by reason of the acceptance of the plea of guilty, accused could have been found guilty of no greater offense than simple assault, a misdemeanor, and that the sentence imposed was in excess of that prescribed for a misdemeanor, and as to the excess was invalid. Crutchfield v. Commonwealth, 187 Va. 291, 46 S.E.2d 340 (1948).

Relationship with federal sentencing. — Fact that defendant was ultimately convicted of only misdemeanors had no bearing on the district court's finding of a Grade A violation; defendant was charged under Virginia law with abduction and malicious wounding, both felonies punishable by a year or more in prison. These crimes met the requirements of U.S. Sentencing Guidelines Manual § 7B1.1(a)(1)(A), Pol'y Statement, in that they were state crimes of violence punishable by more than one year's imprisonment; thus, they constituted Grade A violations. United States v. Washington, 2009 U.S. App. LEXIS 14801 (4th Cir. July 2, 2009).

CIRCUIT COURT OPINIONS

Speedy trial considerations. — Defendant's motion to dismiss an alleged violation of § 18.2-51 on speedy trial grounds was denied, as: (1) he was more responsible than the Commonwealth for the delay in bringing him to trial, due to his deportation; and (2) he failed to advise the Commonwealth of his whereabouts after illegally entering the country and returning to Virginia. Commonwealth v. Manzanares, 2008 Va. Cir. LEXIS 34 (Fairfax County Mar. 26, 2008).

Facts insufficient to show malice. — Evidence did not establish that defendant acted with malice when he kicked a victim who was on top of defendant's uncle and struggling with defendant's uncle on the floor of a bedroom, and the trial court reduced a charge of malicious wounding to the lesser included offense of unlawful wounding. Commonwealth v. Harrington, — Va. Cir. —, 2002 Va. Cir. LEXIS 268 (Newport News June 11, 2002).

§ 18.2-51.1. Malicious bodily injury to law-enforcement officers, firefighters, search and rescue personnel, or emergency medical service providers; penalty; lesser-included offense.

If any person maliciously causes bodily injury to another by any means including the means set out in § 18.2-52, with intent to maim, disfigure, disable or kill, and knowing or having reason to know that such other person is a law-enforcement officer, as defined hereinafter, firefighter, as defined in § 65.2-102, search and rescue personnel as defined hereinafter, or emergency medical services personnel, as defined in § 32.1-111.1 engaged in the performance of his public duties as a law-enforcement officer, firefighter, search and rescue personnel, or emergency medical services personnel, such person shall be guilty of a felony punishable by imprisonment for a period of not less than five years nor more than 30 years and, subject to subdivision (g) of § 18.2-10, a fine of not more than $100,000. Upon conviction, the sentence of such person shall include a mandatory minimum term of imprisonment of two years.

If any person unlawfully, but not maliciously, with the intent aforesaid, causes bodily injury to another by any means, knowing or having reason to know such other person is a law-enforcement officer, firefighter, as defined in § 65.2-102, search and rescue personnel, or emergency medical services personnel, engaged in the performance of his public duties as a law-enforcement officer, firefighter, search and rescue personnel, or emergency medical services personnel, he shall be guilty of a Class 6 felony, and upon conviction, the sentence of such person shall include a mandatory minimum term of imprisonment of one year.

Nothing in this section shall be construed to affect the right of any person charged with a violation of this section from asserting and presenting evidence in support of any defenses to the charge that may be available under common law.

As used in this section, "law-enforcement officer" means any full-time or part-time employee of a police department or sheriff's office that is part of or administered by the Commonwealth or any political subdivision thereof, who is responsible for the prevention or detection of crime and the enforcement of the penal, traffic or highway laws of this Commonwealth; any conservation officer of the Department of Conservation and Recreation commissioned pursuant to § 10.1-115; any conservation police officer appointed pursuant to § 29.1-200 and auxiliary police officers appointed or provided for pursuant to §§ 15.2-1731 and 15.2-1733 and auxiliary deputy sheriffs appointed pursuant to § 15.2-1603.

As used in this section, "search and rescue personnel" means any employee or member of a search and rescue organization that is authorized by a resolution or ordinance duly adopted by the governing body of any county, city or town of the Commonwealth or any member of a search and rescue organization operating under a memorandum of understanding with the Virginia Department of Emergency Management.

The provisions of § 18.2-51 shall be deemed to provide a lesser-included offense hereof.

History.
1983, c. 578; 1985, c. 444; 1994, cc. 205, 427; 1997, cc. 8, 120; 2002, cc. 588, 623; 2004, cc. 461, 841; 2007, c. 87; 2010, c. 344.

Cross references.
As to pointing a laser at law-enforcement officers, see § 18.2-57.01. As to disarming a law-enforcement officer, see § 18.2-57.02.

Editor's note.
Acts 2010, c. 344, cl. 2, provides: "That the provisions of this act may result in a net increase in periods of imprisonment or commitment. Pursuant to § 30-19.1:4, the estimated amount of the necessary appropriation is $0 for periods of imprisonment in state adult correctional facilities and cannot be determined for periods of commitment to the custody of the Department of Juvenile Justice."

The 2010 amendments.
The 2010 amendment by c. 344 inserted "or any member of a search and rescue organization operating under a memorandum of understanding with the Virginia Department of Emergency Management" at the end of the next-to-last paragraph.

Michie's Jurisprudence.
For related discussion, see 9B M.J. Homicide, § 17.

CASE NOTES

Officer acting in private capacity. — Although officer encountered defendant while acting in a private capacity, he was fully empowered by his public office to pursue an investigation, detain defendant if necessary, and arrest if justified; he was, therefore, "engaged in the performance of his public duties as a law-enforcement officer" when attacked and unlawfully wounded by defendant. Key v. Commonwealth, 21 Va. App. 311, 464 S.E.2d 171 (1995).

Intent may be inferred from assault with bare fists. — Ordinarily, an assault with fists does not reflect an intent to maim, disfigure, disable or kill, but it may be accompanied with sufficient violence and brutality that such intent may be presumed. Clark v. Commonwealth, No. 0445-92-1 (Ct. of Appeals Dec. 14, 1993).

Effect of indictment amendment. — Adding the words "with the intent to maime [sic], disfigure, disable or kill," was a permissible, although unnecessary, amendment to indictment in the instant case. The amendment neither changed the nature or character of the offense charged, nor resulted in prejudice or surprise to appellant. Appellant was sufficiently informed of the felony offense with which he was charged and could fairly prepare his defense. Trusty v. Commonwealth, No. 0278-93-1 (Ct. of Appeals Dec. 20, 1994).

Indictment adequately informing defendant. — Clearly, an element of unlawfully and feloniously causing malicious bodily injury to a law-enforcement officer is the intent to maim, disfigure, disable or kill. Supported by the reference to this section, which includes the language "with intent to maim, disfigure, disable or kill," indictment adequately informed appellant of the nature and character of the offense charged. Trusty v. Commonwealth, No. 0278-93-1 (Ct. of Appeals Dec. 20, 1994).

Sufficient evidence of malice. — Finding of malice by the trial court was well supported by the circumstances attending the attack and the resulting injury, where after continued struggle with officer after arrest for assault and battery, defendant bit officer's arm. Defendant "reached out and clamped on to [his] arm and just bit as hard as he could," the officer said, noting that he "could see the muscles in [defendant's] jaw just clamping down," and "he had to pull it out because [defendant] wasn't letting it go." Cooper v. Commonwealth, No. 0553-94-1 (Ct. of Appeals May 30, 1995).

Intent to maim or act maliciously shown where defendant repeatedly rammed a police vehicle while traveling at 80 miles per hour while weaving in and out of traffic. Luck v. Commonwealth, 32 Va. App. 827, 531 S.E.2d 41, 2000 Va. App. LEXIS 530 (2000).

Evidence sufficient to support conviction. — The evidence was sufficient to support a finding that the defendant maliciously attempted to injure a state trooper in furtherance of his criminal purpose where the defendant, in an attempt to evade apprehension, ignored emergency lights and sirens of two law-enforcement vehicles, together with an officer's entreaties to stop, fled along interstate highways at excessive speed, dangerously operated his truck and, in a continuing effort to escape capture, twice collided with the police vehicle operated by the trooper, intentionally driving forward on both occasions. Simmons v. Commonwealth, No. 1202-99-3, 2000 Va. App. LEXIS 563 (Ct. of Appeals Aug. 1, 2000).

Evidence was sufficient to support defendant's conviction for assaulting a police officer, as the trial court found defendant's testimony to be unworthy of belief and the conviction was supported by the testimony of an officer, which the trial court was entitled to believe. McCray v. Commonwealth, — Va. App. —, — S.E.2d —, 2008 Va. App. LEXIS 38 (Jan. 22, 2008).

Evidence that defendant deliberately crashed into a trooper's car to avoid being stopped, after leading officers on a dangerous, high-speed, 28-mile long car chase supported the finding that defendant intended to wound officer. Blow v. Commonwealth, 52 Va. App. 533, 665 S.E.2d 254, 2008 Va. App. LEXIS 400 (2008).

Intent demonstrated. — When a police officer intervened during an altercation, he was wearing a "raid shirt" which was emblazoned with large "POLICE" letters. He also testified that when he entered the foray, he announced that he was a police officer. The record also contained evidence that he had a clear view of defendant's face and made eye contact with him prior to his throwing a cinder block, which came within three feet of striking the police officer, it also indicates that defendant apologized to the police officer for throwing the cinder block. Accordingly, the conviction was affirmed. Gill v. Commonwealth, No. 0334-96-3 (Ct. of Appeals Feb. 25, 1997).

Where defendant followed police officer into the bedroom, attempted to stab him with a knife and missed, and struck a third person who was injured, the trial court, as fact finder, could reasonably conclude that defendant acted with the intent to maim, disfigure, disable or kill the officer. Starkes v. Commonwealth, No. 1458-96-2 (Ct. of Appeals Apr. 1, 1997).

Commonwealth sufficiently proved that defendant acted with the intent to maim, disfigure, disable or kill, as required by § 18.2-51.1, through his actions of attempting to elude a police officer and accelerating his van into the direct path of a police officer without making an effort to veer or avoid hitting said officer; moreover, the evidence raised the sole inference that defendant intended to escape even if in so doing he had to drive his accelerating vehicle into the officer who stood before him. Holley v. Commonwealth, 44 Va. App. 228, 604 S.E.2d 127, 2004 Va. App. LEXIS 515 (2004).

Evidence that defendant repeatedly rammed defendant's pickup truck in a trooper's cruiser demonstrated defendant's intent to maim, disfigure, disable, or kill the trooper, and supported defendant's conviction for attempted malicious wounding under § 18.2-51.1. Swanson v. Commonwealth, 2008 Va. App. LEXIS 406 (Aug. 26, 2008).

Evidence of bodily injury. — Two troopers suffered bodily injury when the defendant repeatedly rammed his vehicle into the vehicle the officers were occupying, causing soft-tissue injuries that required medical treatment and caused pain and stiffness; this section does not require that an officer suffer broken bones or bruises or that the injuries be observable or determinable by objective means. Luck v. Commonwealth, 32 Va. App. 827, 531 S.E.2d 41, 2000 Va. App. LEXIS 530 (2000).

Applied in Lowery v. Stovall, 92 F.3d 219 (4th Cir. 1996).

§ 18.2-51.2. Aggravated malicious wounding; penalty.

A. If any person maliciously shoots, stabs, cuts or wounds any other person, or by any means causes bodily injury, with the intent to maim, disfigure, disable or kill, he shall be guilty of a Class 2 felony if the victim is thereby severely injured and is caused to suffer permanent and significant physical impairment.

B. If any person maliciously shoots, stabs, cuts or wounds any other woman who is pregnant, or by any other means causes bodily injury, with the intent to maim, disfigure, disable or kill the pregnant woman or to cause the involuntary termination of her pregnancy, he shall be guilty of a Class 2 felony if the victim is thereby severely injured and is caused to suffer permanent and significant physical impairment.

C. For purposes of this section, the involuntary termination of a woman's pregnancy shall be deemed a severe injury and a permanent and significant physical impairment.

History.
1986, c. 460; 1991, c. 670; 1997, c. 709.

Cross references.
For provision making it unlawful to work or volunteer on school grounds following convictions of certain sex offenses, see § 18.2-370.4.

Law Review.
For note, "Fetal Homicide: Woman or Fetus as Victim? A Survey of Current State Approaches and Recommendations for Future State Application," see 41 Wm. & Mary L. Rev. 1845 (2000).

CASE NOTES

Constitutionality. — Because defendant had no standing to make a broad and general facial statutory challenge, and he agreed that victim's injuries qualified as both "significant" and "permanent" injuries, the trial court properly denied defendant's motion to dismiss the aggravated malicious wounding conviction based solely upon his facial constitutional challenge. Cottee v. Commonwealth, 31 Va. App. 546, 525 S.E.2d 25 (2000).

Right to counsel not violated. — Defendant's aggravated malicious wounding and use of a firearm in the commission of a felony convictions were not subject to reversal on appeal, as the trial court did not violate his right to counsel by erroneously disqualifying his retained trial counsel prior to trial, and appointing substitute counsel to defend him, based on an existing conflict of interest due to counsel's representation of a Commonwealth's witness. Johnson v. Commonwealth, 50 Va. App. 600, 652 S.E.2d 156, 2007 Va. App. LEXIS 406 (2007).

Non-vocational quality of life. — In determining the extent of disability, courts must apply both a functional and humane approach, taking into consideration not only the injured person's permanent unemployability, but also his non-vocational quality of life. Branch v. Commonwealth, 14 Va. App. 836, 419 S.E.2d 422 (1992).

Totally disabled. — The term "totally ... disabled" does not mean a state of absolute helplessness, but means the "inability to do substantially all of the material acts necessary to the prosecution of any occupation for remuneration or profit in substantially the customary and usual manner in which such occupation is prosecuted." Branch v. Commonwealth, 14 Va. App. 836, 419 S.E.2d 422 (1992).

Victim is "totally ... disabled" because he is unable to use his legs, has no bowel and bladder control, and has only limited use of his hands and arms. As a result of his paralysis, his ability to continue his former employment, his chances of pursuing other employment, and his quality of life are substantially diminished. His condition is the type intended by the General Assembly to be covered by this section. Branch v. Commonwealth, 14 Va. App. 836, 419 S.E.2d 422 (1992).

Malicious wounding distinguished. — Unlike the crime of aggravated malicious wounding under § 18.2-51.2, which requires proof that the victim suffered a permanent and significant physical impairment as a result of the wound inflicted by the defendant, the crime of malicious wounding under § 18.2-51, does not require that the wound inflicted by the defendant be permanent or significant. An Trong Tran v. Commonwealth, No. 2565-02-4, 2004 Va. App. LEXIS 195 (Ct. of Appeals Apr. 27, 2004).

Section 19.2-294 does not prohibit prosecution in a single trial for violation of § 18.2-51 and this section. Powell v. Commonwealth, No. 0554-89-1 (Ct. of Appeals Oct. 6, 1992).

Double jeopardy considerations. — Multiple punishments for the crimes of attempted murder and malicious wounding do not violate the double jeopardy clause when the convictions are obtained in a single trial. Creamer v. Commonwealth, No. 1298-91-3 (Ct. of Appeals Dec. 15, 1992).

Proof of attempted murder does not require proof of an actual injury, and therefore aggravated malicious wounding and attempted murder each contain an element not contained by the other, and neither crime is a lesser-included offense of the other for double jeopardy purposes. Dennis v. Commonwealth, No. 1285-98-1 (Ct. of Appeals Oct. 19, 1999).

Two offenses required elements of proof that the other did not since the aggravated malicious wounding statute, § 18.2-51.2, prohibited certain methods of violence resulting in severe and permanent injury, and the murder statute, § 18.2-32, punished the taking of life without regard to the method. Aggravated malicious wounding required proof of a specific intent, whereas second-degree murder required no specific intent, and with different elements of proof, aggravated malicious wounding was not a lesser-included offense of second-degree murder, malicious wounding was not a lesser-included offense of attempted murder and the legislature intended multiple punishments; therefore, the offenses, having separate and distinct elements, allowed for prosecution under both statutes, the legislature authorized separate punishments for those acts, and the defendant's convictions for both aggravated malicious wounding and second-degree murder did not violate the Fifth Amendment prohibition against double jeopardy. Bomber v. Commonwealth, 2013 Va. App. LEXIS 75 (Mar. 5, 2013).

Court rejected defendant's contention that he was punished twice for the same offense as the Virginia General Assembly intended to impose multiple punishments when enacting § 18.2-53. Moreover, the statutes each contained an element that the other did not: aggravated malicious wounding required malice, an intent to maim, and resulting permanent physical injury, while unlawful stabbing required a wounding during the commission of an underlying felony. Franklin v. Commonwealth, 2012 Va. App. LEXIS 356 (Nov. 6, 2012).

Intent to wound does not preclude intent to steal. — The mere fact that appellant had the intent to commit malicious wounding did not exclude the hypothesis that he also formed the intent to steal victim's property. Saunders v. Commonwealth, 18 Va. App. 825, 447 S.E.2d 526 (1994).

Sufficiency of indictment. — Pursuant to § 19.2-220 and Va. Sup. Ct. R. 3A:6(a), the citation to § 18.2-51.2 in the indictment incorporated by reference the complete definition of aggravated malicious wounding and supplemented the charging language of the indictment; therefore, the statutory citation, coupled with the facts alleged, was sufficient to set forth all relevant elements of the aggravated malicious wounding offense. Robinson v. Commonwealth, No. 1623-02-2, 2003 Va. App. LEXIS 327 (Ct. of Appeals June 3, 2003).

Jury instructions. — The words "maim" and "disable" do not have a distinct legal meaning, and trial court did not err by instructing jury that they should apply ordinary meanings of those words. Morgan v. Commonwealth, No. 1590-98-3 (Ct. of Appeals Oct. 5, 1999).

In a prosecution for aggravated malicious wounding, evidence that defendant directed racial epithets against the victim was properly admitted, as it was relevant to prove defendants' malice, and the trial court did not abuse its discretion in ruling that the probative value of this evidence outweighed its prejudicial effect. Landeck v. Commonwealth, 59 Va. App. 744, 722 S.E.2d 643, 2012 Va. App. LEXIS 72 (2012).

In a prosecution for aggravated malicious wounding, the trial court's heat of passion instruction was proper, as the jury could

have inferred from the evidence that there was a reasonable opportunity for defendants' passions to cool before they attacked the victim. Landeck v. Commonwealth, 59 Va. App. 744, 722 S.E.2d 643, 2012 Va. App. LEXIS 72 (2012).

Jury instructions on self-defense. — Trial court did not abuse its discretion by giving the jury a curative instruction that stated that self-defense was not an issue in defendant's trial for aggravated malicious wounding and use of a firearm in the commission of that offense since the victim was a transsexual prostitute whose true gender defendant claimed to have learned only moments before the shooting during what began as a consensual sexual encounter, and defendant said he became fearful and pulled his firearm when the prostitute suggested that they continue the sexual encounter despite the fact that the prostitute, like defendant, was male; defendant came perilously close to a claim that the act of shooting the victim was excusable as it was done in self-defense, and claimed that the fear he experienced negated a finding of malice, without supporting a heat-of-passion defense. Rollison v. Commonwealth, — Va. App. —, — S.E.2d —, 2007 Va. App. LEXIS 61 (Feb. 20, 2007).

Trial court did not abuse its discretion by giving the jury a curative instruction that stated that self-defense was not an issue in defendant's trial for aggravated malicious wounding and use of a firearm in the commission of that offense after defendant made defendant's closing argument and before the Commonwealth delivered its rebuttal argument; defendant did not object to the Commonwealth's right to argue in rebuttal that self-defense was not an issue, and the instruction was worded in a neutral fashion that did not mention defendant's argument. Rollison v. Commonwealth, — Va. App. —, — S.E.2d —, 2007 Va. App. LEXIS 61 (Feb. 20, 2007).

Jury instruction defining physical impairment. — Where appellant stabbed a victim and was convicted of aggravated malicious wounding, a jury instruction defining physical impairment was proper because: (1) the jury instruction was a correct statement of the law; and (2) sufficient evidence supported the trial court granting the instruction since the victim received a permanent and significant injury due to leg numbness and a limp, which were not likely to improve. Toler v. Commonwealth, 2008 Va. App. LEXIS 277 (June 10, 2008).

Lesser-included offense instruction rejected. — The crime of malicious wounding lacks the severity of injury and permanence of impairment elements required for the offense of aggravated malicious wounding; an instruction on the lesser offense is properly refused where there is not a scintilla of evidence in the record to support a finding that the injury was not severe or that it did not result in a significant and permanent impairment and the jury's ability to reject the commonwealth's evidence may not be treated as a substitute for the evidentiary support required to grant a defendant's request for an instruction on the lesser-included offense of malicious wounding. Commonwealth v. Donkor, 256 Va. 443, 507 S.E.2d 75 (1998).

Evidence sufficient. — Evidence that defendant threatened victim, coupled with defendant's use of a gun to get revenge, proved defendant's intent to "maim, disfigure, disable or kill" victim. As a result of the shooting, victim was paralyzed. The evidence thus proved beyond a reasonable doubt the elements of the crime of malicious wounding. Nicholas v. Commonwealth, 15 Va. App. 188, 422 S.E.2d 790 (1992).

Under the statute, the trial court reasonably could have found from the number of wounds, the need for stitches for some of them, and the resulting scars still visible after five months, that victim's injuries constituted "permanent and significant physical impairment." Newton v. Commonwealth, 21 Va. App. 86, 462 S.E.2d 117 (1995).

Despite conflicting testimony as to circumstances of fight, evidence of severe, brutal beating received by victim was sufficient to support defendant's conviction of unlawful wounding. Morgan v. Commonwealth, No. 1590-98-3 (Ct. of Appeals Oct. 5, 1999).

Commonwealth produced sufficient evidence to prove defendant's aggravated malicious wounding of the victim beyond a reasonable doubt where, viewed in the light most favorable to the Commonwealth, the evidence showed that defendant beat the victim with the intent to maim, disfigure, disable or kill him, as well as with malice, given the brutal nature of the attack, which supported the jury's finding of malice and intent, and defendant's actions in covering up the crime also indicated that he acted with specific intent and malice. U-Thasoonthorn v. Commonwealth, No. 1879-01-4, 2002 Va. App. LEXIS 607 (Ct. of Appeals Oct. 8, 2002).

Evidence was sufficient to support defendant's conviction for aggravated malicious wounding for defendant's attack with a hammer on the victim outside a bar after the victim confronted a codefendant about breaking into cars at the bar, as evidence that the victim still had facial scarring and numbness in his face more than two years after the attack was sufficient to show that the victim had sustained the severe, permanent, and significant injuries required to support an aggravated malicious wounding conviction. Swick v. Commonwealth, No. 1282-02-4, 2003 Va. App. LEXIS 360 (Ct. of Appeals June 24, 2003).

Trial court did not err in entering a judgment of conviction against defendant on a charge of aggravated malicious wounding, as the evidence was sufficient to show that defendant was acting with malice when he shot another man; defendant, knowing the man was at defendant's residence, armed himself with a gun, followed and shot the other man as he attempted to leave the property, and fled, and the jury was entitled to reject defendant's claim that the shooting was an accident and conclude defendant acted with malice. Hood v. Commonwealth, No. 2419-02-2, 2004 Va. App. LEXIS 33 (Ct. of Appeals Jan. 28, 2004).

Defendant's malicious wounding, aggravated malicious wounding, and use of a firearm in the commission of a felony convictions were upheld on appeal, as sufficient evidence linked him to a shooting while driving a jeep loaned to him and his cohorts in exchange for drugs, and based on the same, the trial judge could reject defendant's hypothesis another group of men gained possession of the Jeep and committed the crimes alleged. Powell v. Commonwealth, — Va. App. —, — S.E.2d —, 2006 Va. App. LEXIS 537 (Nov. 28, 2006).

Given that the Commonwealth presented sufficient evidence that defendant burglarized an apartment with the requisite specific intent and malice to disfigure, maim, disable, or kill at least three of the victims, without provocation, his convictions based upon said actions were upheld on appeal. Slayton v. Commonwealth, — Va. App. —, — S.E.2d —, 2007 Va. App. LEXIS 180 (May 1, 2007).

Where appellant stabbed a victim, sufficient evidence supported the conviction for aggravated malicious wounding because the jury could reasonably conclude that the victim had a permanent and significant physical impairment as a result of the stabbing based on the victim's need for stitches, the resulting scar, a limp, leg numbness, and random abdominal spasms. Toler v. Commonwealth, 2008 Va. App. LEXIS 277 (June 10, 2008).

Evidence defendant admitted that, the day after defendant and another planned the attack on the victim, the two of them met in the evening at a gas station near the scene of the attack, pursuant to their plan, and then proceeded to their hiding place behind the bushes next to the government building, where they waited for 30 minutes for the victim to appear, was sufficient to support defendant's attempted robbery and aggravated malicious wounding convictions. Goode v. Commonwealth, 52 Va. App. 380, 663 S.E.2d 532, 2008 Va. App. LEXIS 331 (2008).

There was sufficient evidence to support convictions of aggravated malicious wounding and use of a firearm in the commission of aggravated malicious wounding. Ample credible evidence, including the victim's identification of defendant, placed him in close proximity to the crime scene both immediately before and after the shooting; a rational finder of fact could determine that, notwithstanding another person's fingerprint on the firearm, defendant was present at the crime scene and fired the weapon, even though his prints were not on the weapon. Barnes v. Commonwealth, 2008 Va. App. LEXIS 533 (Dec. 9, 2008), aff'd, 279 Va. 22, 688 S.E.2d 210, 2010 Va. LEXIS 17 (Va. Jan. 15, 2010).

There was sufficient evidence to support the convictions for unlawful, felonious and malicious shooting of the victim and for the unlawful and felonious use and display of a firearm while committing an aggravated malicious wounding where: (1) the victim and numerous witnesses identified defendant as the armed assailant who shot the victim with a 9mm pistol discovered at defendants' house; (2) a doctor testified that the bullet that entered the victim's body damaged the lining of his left hip joint, thereby causing traumatic arthritis; and (3) traumatic arthritis could result in chronic pain and a limitation of the range of motion of that joint.

Barnes v. Commonwealth, 279 Va. 22, 688 S.E.2d 210, 2010 Va. LEXIS 17 (2010).

Defendant's convictions for malicious wounding while part of a mob under § 18.2-41, and aggravated malicious wounding under § 18.2-51.2 were appropriate because defendant was not permitted to complain on appeal of the trial court's refusal to suppress the very evidence that he elicited on his own behalf. Defendant himself elicited the testimony about his statements to the Security Threat Unit that he was a gang member. Boone v. Commonwealth, 2010 Va. App. LEXIS 37 (Feb. 2, 2010).

Evidence was sufficient to convict defendants of aggravated malicious wounding, as the jury could have found that they harbored a malicious intent as evidenced by their actions calculated to instigate a fight with the victim. Landeck v. Commonwealth, 59 Va. App. 744, 722 S.E.2d 643, 2012 Va. App. LEXIS 72 (2012).

Injuries sustained constituted "permanent and significant physical impairment." Cottee v. Commonwealth, 31 Va. App. 546, 525 S.E.2d 25 (2000).

The evidence was sufficient to show that the victim had suffered a "permanent and significant physical impairment" as a result of being shot by the defendant where the victim had a scar running from his chest to his navel that was still clearly visible at trial, three months after the surgery required by the shooting, the bullet, which was lodged against the victim's spinal cord, had not been removed and might never be removed, due to the location of the bullet, doctors had forbade the victim to lift any weight heavier than five pounds, thereby limiting his ability to find work and to live normally, the position of the bullet threatened the victim with the possibility of paralysis and the victim testified that he was in constant pain. Terry v. Commonwealth, No. 0716-99-2, 2000 Va. App. LEXIS 355 (Ct. of Appeals May 9, 2000).

Trial court did not err by failing to reduce the aggravated malicious wounding under § 18.2-51.2 to simple malicious wounding under § 18.2-51 because considering the victim's testimony and physical evidence, the jury could reasonably conclude that the victim had a permanent and significant physical impairment as a result of the shooting; defendant shot the victim in her left shoulder, she had two entrance wounds and one exit wound, the bullet lodged next to the victim's spine had to be removed during surgery; the victim had scars, and the victim testified that two years after the shooting she still had not regained full use of her left arm and hand. Martinez v. Commonwealth, 42 Va. App. 9, 590 S.E.2d 57, 2003 Va. App. LEXIS 678 (2003).

When defendant was convicted of aggravated malicious wounding and use of a firearm in the commission of aggravated malicious wounding, the evidence was sufficient to show that the victim was permanently and significantly impaired. A treating physician testified that his injury resulted in traumatic arthritis and abdominal scarring and that he faced the potential of a bowel obstruction. Barnes v. Commonwealth, 2008 Va. App. LEXIS 533 (Dec. 9, 2008), aff'd, 279 Va. 22, 688 S.E.2d 210, 2010 Va. LEXIS 17 (Va. Jan. 15, 2010).

New evidence that a victim's sense of smell had returned did not entitle defendant to a new aggravated malicious wounding trial under Va. Sup. Ct. R. 3A:15 because the evidence did not definitively prove that the results would have been different where metal plates in the victim's face showed that she was permanently and significantly injured. Lamm v. Commonwealth, 55 Va. App. 637, 688 S.E.2d 295, 2010 Va. App. LEXIS 48 (2010).

Evidence was sufficient to convict defendant of aggravated malicious wounding because evidence that the victim was hospitalized for 11 days after defendant stabbed him, had a prolonged recovery, was scarred, and had to use a machine to treat his lung supported the jury's finding that his physical impairment was permanent and significant. Van Kersey v. Commonwealth, 2012 Va. App. LEXIS 225 (July 10, 2012).

Sentence within the range set by legislature is proper. — Trial court did not abuse its discretion in imposing a 43-year sentence against defendant, as said sentence was within the ranges set by the legislature and well below the total statutory maximum for the various felony offenses for which he was convicted. Clark v. Commonwealth, — Va. App. —, — S.E.2d —, 2008 Va. App. LEXIS 234 (May 13, 2008).

Applied in Saunders v. Commonwealth, 281 Va. 448, 706 S.E.2d 350, 2011 Va. LEXIS 45 (2011).

§ 18.2-51.3. Prohibition against reckless endangerment of others by throwing objects from places higher than one story; penalty.

A. It shall be unlawful for any person, with the intent to cause injury to another, to intentionally throw from a balcony, roof top, or other place more than one story above ground level any object capable of causing any such injury.

B. A violation of this section shall be punishable as a Class 6 felony.

History.
1990, c. 761.

CASE NOTES

Applied in Newton v. Commonwealth, 21 Va. App. 86, 462 S.E.2d 117 (1995).

§ 18.2-51.4. Maiming, etc., of another resulting from driving while intoxicated.

A. Any person who, as a result of driving while intoxicated in violation of § 18.2-266 or any local ordinance substantially similar thereto in a manner so gross, wanton and culpable as to show a reckless disregard for human life, unintentionally causes the serious bodily injury of another person resulting in permanent and significant physical impairment shall be guilty of a Class 6 felony. The driver's license of any person convicted under this section shall be revoked pursuant to subsection B of § 46.2-391.

B. The provisions of Article 2 (§ 18.2-266 et seq.) of Chapter 7 of Title 18.2 shall apply, mutatis mutandis, upon arrest for a violation of this section.

History.
1997, c. 691; 1999, cc. 945, 987; 2000, cc. 956, 982.

Cross references.
For authorization for locality to provide by ordinance for reimbursement of certain expenses incurred in responding to DUI and other traffic incidents related to violation of §§ 18.2-51.4, 18.2-266, 29.1-738, 46.2-300 et seq., 46.2-852 et seq., and 46.2-894, see § 15.2-1716. As to admissibility of written results of blood alcohol tests conducted in the regular course of providing emergency medical treatment, see § 19.2-187.02.

Law Review.
For note, "Fetal Homicide: Woman or Fetus as Victim? A Survey of Current State Approaches and Recommendations for Future State Application," see 41 Wm. & Mary L. Rev. 1845 (2000). For article summarizing published Virginia criminal law decisions between July 1, 2002 and July 1, 2003, see 38 U. Rich. L. Rev. 87 (2003). For annual survey article, "Criminal Law and Procedure," see 44 U. Rich. L. Rev. 339 (2009).

Michie's Jurisprudence.
For related discussion, see 2B M.J. Automobiles, § 118.

CASE NOTES

Common-law criminal negligence. — While no Virginia appellate court has issued a decision interpreting § 18.2-51.4, the common law definition of criminal negligence, as stated in the statute, is well settled; conduct is culpable or criminal when accompanied by acts of commission or omission of a wanton or willful nature, showing a reckless or indifferent disregard of the rights of others, under circumstances reasonably calculated to produce injury, or which make it not improbable that injury will be occasioned, and the offender knows, or is charged with the knowledge of, the probable result of the offender's acts. Wright v. Commonwealth, 39 Va. App. 698, 576 S.E.2d 242, 2003 Va. App. LEXIS 60 (2003).

Blood test results not required. — Even if the State's failure to comply with the implied consent law procedural requirements did not forbid a prosecution for aggravated manslaughter, blood test results were not required for a conviction under either § 18.2-266 or 18.2-36.1. Stevens v. Commonwealth, 46 Va. App. 234, 616 S.E.2d 754, 2005 Va. App. LEXIS 407 (2005), aff'd, — Va. —, 634 S.E.2d 305 (2006).

Under the influence of drugs. — Reading §§ 18.2-51.4 and 18.2-266(iii) together, their plain meaning is that a person violates § 18.2-51.4 when he or she recklessly causes serious bodily injury to another person resulting in permanent and significant physical impairment to that person while operating a vehicle under the influence of any narcotic drug that impairs the driver's ability to operate a motor vehicle in violation of § 18.2-266(iii). Ratliff v. Commonwealth, 53 Va. App. 443, 672 S.E.2d 913, 2009 Va. App. LEXIS 83 (2009).

Defendant was properly convicted of recklessly causing serious and permanent bodily injury to another person while driving under the influence of narcotic drugs, as she admitted having controlled substances in her system, and § 18.2-51.4 did not apply only to those who operated a vehicle under the influence of alcohol. Ratliff v. Commonwealth, 53 Va. App. 443, 672 S.E.2d 913, 2009 Va. App. LEXIS 83 (2009).

Evidence sufficient to establish gross, wanton and culpable manner. — Evidence was sufficient to establish that defendant drove in manner so gross, wanton and culpable as to show reckless disregard for human life where defendant drove the car in a manner too fast for defendant to control it properly, and where defendant's intellectual and motor functions were impaired by the voluntary consumption of drugs and alcohol; defendant was properly convicted of maiming. Wright v. Commonwealth, 39 Va. App. 698, 576 S.E.2d 242, 2003 Va. App. LEXIS 60 (2003).

Sufficient evidence supporting conviction. — Sufficient evidence supported defendant's conviction for maiming another as a result of driving while intoxicated because defendant drove into the victim, other vehicles, and a tree without braking after he voluntarily ingested an overdose of sleeping pills and while he was in an intoxicated state. Riley v. Commonwealth, — Va. App. —, — S.E.2d —, 2008 Va. App. LEXIS 159 (Apr. 8, 2008), aff'd, 277 Va. 467, 675 S.E.2d 168, 2009 Va. LEXIS 50 (2009).

Evidence was sufficient to convict defendant of maiming another person as a result of driving while intoxicated. Defendant voluntarily ingested an overdose of sleeping medication in conjunction with other medications, and in an intoxicated state drove a vehicle and struck the victim and two other vehicles before hitting a tree, all without any apparent braking. Riley v. Commonwealth, 277 Va. 467, 675 S.E.2d 168, 2009 Va. LEXIS 50 (2009).

Applied in Stevens v. Commonwealth, 44 Va. App. 122, 603 S.E.2d 642, 2004 Va. App. LEXIS 496 (2004); Bristol v. Commonwealth, 272 Va. 568, 636 S.E.2d 460, 2006 Va. LEXIS 115 (2006).

§ 18.2-51.5. Maiming, etc., of another resulting from operating a watercraft while intoxicated; penalty.

A. Any person who, as a result of operating a watercraft or motorboat in violation of subsection B of § 29.1-738 or a similar local ordinance in a manner so gross, wanton, and culpable as to show reckless disregard for human life, unintentionally causes the serious bodily injury of another person resulting in permanent and significant physical impairment is guilty of a Class 6 felony. The court shall order any person convicted under this section not to operate a watercraft or motorboat that is underway upon the waters of the Commonwealth. After two years have passed from the date of the conviction, the convicted person may petition the court that entered the conviction for the right to operate a watercraft or motorboat upon the waters of the Commonwealth. Upon consideration of such petition, the court may restore the right to operate a watercraft or motorboat subject to such terms and conditions as the court deems appropriate, including the successful completion of a water safety alcohol rehabilitation program described in § 29.1-738.5.

B. The provisions of Article 3 (§ 29.1-734 et seq.) of Chapter 7 of Title 29.1 shall apply, mutatis mutandis, upon arrest for a violation of this section.

History.
2007, cc. 379, 679.

§ 18.2-51.6. Strangulation of another; penalty.

Any person who, without consent, impedes the blood circulation or respiration of another person by knowingly, intentionally, and unlawfully applying pressure to the neck of such person resulting in the wounding or bodily injury of such person is guilty of strangulation, a Class 6 felony.

History.
2012, cc. 577, 602.

Editor's note.
Acts 2012, cc. 577 and 602, cl. 2 provides: "That the provisions of this act may result in a net increase in periods of imprisonment or commitment. Pursuant to § 30-19.1:4, the estimated amount of the necessary appropriation cannot be determined for periods of imprisonment in state adult correctional facilities; therefore, Chapter 890 of the Acts of Assembly of 2011 requires the Virginia Criminal Sentencing Commission to assign a minimum fiscal impact of $50,000. Pursuant to § 30-19.1:4, the estimated amount of the necessary appropriation cannot be determined for periods of commitment to the custody of the Department of Juvenile Justice."

§ 18.2-52. Malicious bodily injury by means of any caustic substance or agent or use of any explosive or fire.

If any person maliciously causes any other person bodily injury by means of any acid, lye or other caustic substance or agent or use of any explosive or fire, he shall be guilty of a felony and shall be punished by confinement in a state correctional facility for a period of not less than five years nor more than thirty years. If such act is done unlawfully but not maliciously, the offender shall be guilty of a Class 6 felony.

History.
Code 1950, § 18.1-67; 1960, c. 358; 1975, cc. 14, 15, 604; 1995, c. 439.

Editor's note.
The above section is § 18.2-52 as enacted by Acts 1975, c. 604. Pursuant to § 30-152, it has been substituted for § 18.2-52 as enacted by Acts 1975, cc. 14 and 15.

Law Review.
For survey of Virginia criminal law for the year 1974-1975, see 61 Va. L. Rev. 1697 (1975).

CASE NOTES

Caustic substance. — Spray that smelled like pepper, caused victim's eyes and skin to burn, temporarily blinded her, and required medical attention was a caustic substance, even though the substance was not recovered, tested, or introduced into evidence. Floyd v. Commonwealth, 31 Va. App. 193, 522 S.E.2d 382 (1999).

Pepper spray. — Defendant's conviction for being part of a mob that maliciously caused bodily injury by means of a caustic substance was affirmed, as the pepper spray used during his gang's attack on a rival gang at a hotel was a caustic substance within the meaning of the term "caustic substance or agent." Corado v. Commonwealth, 47 Va. App. 315, 623 S.E.2d 452, 2005 Va. App. LEXIS 528 (2005).

Sufficient evidence. — Commonwealth proved beyond a reasonable doubt that the pepper spray used during the attack against a rival gang was a caustic substance, as testimony established that the pepper spray caused burning and significant irritation. Corado v. Commonwealth, 47 Va. App. 315, 623 S.E.2d 452, 2005 Va. App. LEXIS 528 (2005).

§ 18.2-52.1. Possession of infectious biological substances or radiological agents; penalties.

A. Any person who possesses, with the intent thereby to injure another, an infectious biological substance or radiological agent is guilty of a Class 5 felony.

B. Any person who (i) destroys or damages, or attempts to destroy or damage, any facility, equipment or material involved in the sale, manufacturing, storage or distribution of an infectious biological substance or radiological agent, with the intent to injure another by releasing the substance, or (ii) manufactures, sells, gives, distributes or uses an infectious biological substance or radiological agent with the intent to injure another is guilty of a Class 4 felony.

C. Any person who maliciously and intentionally causes any other person bodily injury by means of an infectious biological substance or radiological agent is guilty of a felony and shall be punished by confinement in a state correctional facility for a period of not less than five years nor more than 30 years.

An *"infectious biological substance"* includes any bacteria, viruses, fungi, protozoa, or rickettsiae capable of causing death or serious bodily injury. This definition shall not include HIV as defined in § 18.2-67.4:1, syphilis or hepatitis B.

A *"radiological agent"* includes any substance able to release radiation at levels that are capable of causing death or serious bodily injury.

History.
1996, c. 769; 2002, cc. 588, 623, 816; 2004, c. 833.

Law Review.
For article surveying developments in criminal law and procedure in Virginia from July 2001 to September 2002, see 37 U. Rich. L. Rev. 45 (2002).

§ 18.2-53. Shooting, etc., in committing or attempting a felony.

If any person, in the commission of, or attempt to commit, felony, unlawfully shoot, stab, cut or wound another person he shall be guilty of a Class 6 felony.

History.
Code 1950, § 18.1-68; 1960, c. 358; 1975, cc. 14, 15.

Michie's Jurisprudence.
For related discussion, see 20 M.J. Weapons, § 9.

CASE NOTES

The purpose of this section is to deter the use of specific forms of violence and thus lessen the risk of bodily harm to the potential victims of felonious crime. To effectuate this purpose, the General Assembly employed the only appropriate means available, viz., the imposition of punishment for the use of such violence in addition to the penalty prescribed for the primary felony. Blythe v. Commonwealth, 222 Va. 722, 284 S.E.2d 796 (1981).

Legislative intent regarding multiple punishments. — Defendant's punishment for two counts of malicious wounding resulting from the stabbing of two victims and for two counts of stabbing/cutting the same victims during the commission of a felony does not offend the double jeopardy clause because the General Assembly intended to impose multiple punishments when enacting this section. Hall v. Commonwealth, 14 Va. App. 892, 421 S.E.2d 455 (1992).

Court rejected defendant's contention that he was punished twice for the same offense as the Virginia General Assembly intended to impose multiple punishments when enacting § 18.2-53. Moreover, the statutes each contained an element that the other did not: aggravated malicious wounding required malice, an intent to maim, and resulting permanent physical injury, while unlawful stabbing required a wounding during the commission of an underlying felony. Franklin v. Commonwealth, 2012 Va. App. LEXIS 356 (Nov. 6, 2012).

The legislative intent to authorize cumulative punishment is clear in this section, despite the absence of an express statement to that effect. Blythe v. Commonwealth, 222 Va. 722, 284 S.E.2d 796 (1981).

Section 19.2-294 does not prohibit defendant's prosecution in a single trial for aggravated malicious wounding and use of a firearm in the commission of the aggravated malicious wounding. Powell v. Commonwealth, No. 0554-89-1 (Ct. of Appeals Oct. 6, 1992).

Intent to wound does not preclude intent to steal. — The mere fact that appellant had the intent to commit malicious wounding did not exclude the hypothesis that he also formed the intent to steal victim's property. Saunders v. Commonwealth, 18 Va. App. 825, 447 S.E.2d 526 (1994).

§ 18.2-53.1. Use or display of firearm in committing felony.

It shall be unlawful for any person to use or attempt to use any pistol, shotgun, rifle, or other firearm or display such weapon in a threatening manner while committing or attempting to commit murder, rape, forcible sodomy, inanimate or animate object sexual penetration as defined in § 18.2-67.2, robbery, carjacking, burglary, malicious wounding as defined in § 18.2-51, malicious bodily injury to a law-enforcement officer as defined in § 18.2-51.1, aggravated malicious wounding as defined in § 18.2-51.2, malicious wounding by mob as defined in § 18.2-41 or abduction. Violation of this section shall constitute a separate and distinct felony and any person found guilty thereof shall be sentenced to a mandatory minimum term of imprisonment of three years for a first conviction, and to a mandatory minimum term of five years for a second or subsequent conviction under the provisions of this section. Such punishment shall be separate and apart from, and shall be made to run consecutively with, any punishment received for the commission of the primary felony.

History.
1975, cc. 624, 628; 1976, c. 371; 1980, c. 333; 1982, c. 654; 1991, c. 506; 1992, cc. 191, 726; 1993, cc. 549, 835; 1994, c. 950; 2004, c. 461.

Law Review.
For survey of Virginia criminal law for the year 1978-1979, see 66 Va. L. Rev. 241 (1980). For 1995 survey of criminal law and procedures, see 29 U. Rich. L. Rev. 951 (1995). For survey of Virginia criminal law and procedure for the year 2004-2005, see 40 U. Rich. L. Rev. 197 (2005). For annual survey article, "Criminal Law and Procedure," see 44 U. Rich. L. Rev. 339 (2009). For article, "Construction Law," see 45 U. Rich. L. Rev. 227 (2010). For annual survey article, "Criminal Law and Procedure," see 46 U. Rich. L. Rev. 59 (2011). For annual survey of Virginia law article, "Criminal Law and Procedure," see 47 U. Rich. L. Rev. 143 (2012).

Michie's Jurisprudence.
For related discussion, see 1A M.J. Abduction and Kidnapping, § 1; 2B M.J. Autrefois, Acquit and Convict, §§ 16, 18, 20; 5B M.J. Criminal Procedure, §§ 4, 86, 87; 16 M.J. Robbery, §§ 3, 4; 20 M.J. Weapons, § 4.

CASE NOTES

I. In General.
II. Elements of Offense.
  A. Underlying Offenses.
  B. Use of a Firearm.
III. Evidentiary Matters.
IV. Punishment.

I. IN GENERAL.

Effect of 1976 amendment. — As a result of the 1976 amendment to this section, the use of a firearm "while committing a felony" no longer is sufficient to constitute a violation of the section. Now, a violation occurs only when a firearm is used with respect to the felonies specified in this section. Bundy v. Commonwealth, 220 Va. 485, 259 S.E.2d 826 (1979).

Legislative intent. — General Assembly clearly indicated its intent to impose multiple punishments for capital murder and use of a firearm in the commission of a felony pursuant to this section. Wolfe v. Commonwealth, 6 Va. App. 640, 371 S.E.2d 314 (1988).

The General Assembly, in adopting this section, intended to discourage the use of a firearm at any time during the course of the specified criminal endeavors. Creasy v. Commonwealth, 9 Va. App. 470, 389 S.E.2d 316 (1990).

The purpose of § 18.2-53.1 is not only to deter violent criminal conduct, but also to discourage criminal conduct that produces fear of physical harm to a victim from an instrument that gives the appearance of having a firing capability. Wubneh v. Commonwealth, 51 Va. App. 224, 656 S.E.2d 418, 2008 Va. App. LEXIS 56 (2008), overruled in part by Startin v. Commonwealth, 56 Va. App. 26, 690 S.E.2d 310, 2010 Va. App. LEXIS 115 (2010).

The purpose of this section is to deter violent criminal conduct rather than to reform the most dangerous class of criminals. Ansell v. Commonwealth, 219 Va. 759, 250 S.E.2d 760 (1979).

The purpose of this section is to deter violent criminal conduct. Creasy v. Commonwealth, 9 Va. App. 470, 389 S.E.2d 316 (1990).

The purpose of this section, keyed to serious crimes and prescribing inflexible penalties, is to deter violent criminal conduct. Holloman v. Commonwealth, 221 Va. 196, 269 S.E.2d 356 (1980).

This section not only is aimed at preventing actual physical injury or death but also is designed to discourage criminal conduct that produces fear of physical harm. Holloman v. Commonwealth, 221 Va. 196, 269 S.E.2d 356 (1980).

The purpose of this section is to deter violent crimes, not to reform or rehabilitate criminals. It expressly prohibits a court from either suspending the sentence or placing a defendant on probation. The statute provides that the sentence "shall not be suspended," and this language means that the court can neither delay imposition of the sentence nor stay its execution. In re Commonwealth, 229 Va. 159, 326 S.E.2d 695 (1985).

The mandatory sentence in this section aims to deter violent criminal conduct by imposing a mandatory penalty. The purpose of [this statute], keyed to serious crimes and prescribing inflexible penalties, is to deter violent criminal conduct. By replacing a wide range of discretionary penalties with inflexible penalties, the General Assembly intended to deter violent criminal conduct rather than to reform the most dangerous class of criminals. LaFleur v. Commonwealth, 6 Va. App. 190, 366 S.E.2d 712 (1988).

The purpose of this section would be eroded by committing an offender under § 19.2-311 in lieu of sentencing him under this section. This would substitute a discretionary penalty for an inflexible one. The General Assembly has directed a contrary policy which courts must follow. LaFleur v. Commonwealth, 6 Va. App. 190, 366 S.E.2d 712 (1988).

Construction. — This section is penal in nature and therefore must be strictly construed and any ambiguity or reasonable doubt as to its meaning must be resolved in defendant's favor. Ansell v. Commonwealth, 219 Va. 759, 250 S.E.2d 760 (1979); Holloman v. Commonwealth, 221 Va. 196, 269 S.E.2d 356 (1980).

Construction with § 16.1-272. — The terms of this section are not limited by other incongruous laws including subdivision A 1 of § 16.1-272, which provides for the conditional suspension of sentence for juveniles convicted of violent felonies; this section requires a trial court to impose a three-year, unsuspended sentence on a juvenile convicted of use of a firearm in the commission of one of the enumerated felonies despite the provisions of § 16.1-272. Green v. Commonwealth, 28 Va. App. 567, 507 S.E.2d 627 (1998).

Preservation for review. — Where defendant did not preserve for appeal the issues regarding admission and exclusion of testimony and did not show "good cause" or that review was necessary to attain the "ends of justice," the issues could not be raised on direct appeal of defendant's conviction for first-degree murder and for use of a firearm in the commission of the murder. Nguyen v. Commonwealth, No. 0432-02-4, 2003 Va. App. LEXIS 155 (Ct. of Appeals March 25, 2003).

Where defendant did not preserve an insufficiency claim and the record did not "affirmatively prove" that defendant did not commit the offenses of robbery, use of a firearm in the robbery, and wearing a mask in public, in violation of §§ 18.2-58, 18.2-53.1, and 18.2-422, the Va. Sup. Ct. R. 5A:18 "ends of justice" exception did not apply because no manifest injustice occurred. Young v. Commonwealth, No. 0363-03-1, 2003 Va. App. LEXIS 588 (Ct. of Appeals Nov. 12, 2003).

Because § 18.2-91 did not require the use or display of a firearm during a burglary, and because defendant's challenge to the sufficiency of the evidence under § 18.2-53.1 for use of a firearm in the commission of a breaking and entering was waived, the ends of justice exception in Va. Sup. Ct. R. 5A:18 did not apply. Blackwell v. Commonwealth, 2012 Va. App. LEXIS 9 (Jan. 17, 2012).

Defendant waived the right to appellate review of the issue of the sufficiency of the evidence to support defendant's conviction under § 18.2-53.1 because defendant's appellate brief was utterly devoid of any case law or legal argument — as required by Va. Sup. Ct. R. 5A:20(e) — with which to judge the correctness or viability of defendant's position on the issue. Mitchell v. Commonwealth, 60 Va. App. 349, 727 S.E.2d 783, 2012 Va. App. LEXIS 219 (2012).

In a case in which defendant appealed his conviction for violating §§ 18.2-51, 18.2-53.1, and 18.2-286.1, he argued that evidence of other crimes was inadmissible. The appellate court lacked jurisdiction to consider his argument as it was not presented in the assignment of error on his brief, as required by Va. Sup. Ct. R. 5A:12(c)(1), and was not included as part of the assignment of error on which the appeal was granted at the petition stage. Wyche v. Commonwealth, 2012 Va. App. LEXIS 227 (July 10, 2012).

Self-defense without fault. — In a case in which defendant was convicted of malicious wounding and use of a firearm in the commission of malicious wounding, because the evidence failed to support an instruction on self-defense without fault, defendant was not entitled to such an instruction, as a matter of law, and the trial court properly refused defendant's proffered instruction on self-defense without fault. Robinson v. Commonwealth, — Va. App. —, — S.E.2d —, 2006 Va. App. LEXIS 474 (Oct. 24, 2006).

Batson motion correctly denied. — Defendant's convictions for first-degree murder and the use of a firearm in the commission of a felony were proper because the trial court was not clearly erroneous in denying defendant's Batson motion. The Commonwealth offered facially valid race-neutral reasons for the exercise of its strikes and defendant failed to offer any evidence or argument that the proffered rationale behind the strikes challenged were pretextual. Avent v. Commonwealth, 279 Va. 175, 688 S.E.2d 244, 2010 Va. LEXIS 10 (2010).

Proper jury instruction. — Jury instruction properly stated that for a firearm conviction, the jury had to find the defendant committed murder and his proffered instruction did not permit inconsistent verdicts; the court did not err refusing the defendant's instruction or motion to set aside. Gaines v. Commonwealth, 39 Va. App. 562, 574 S.E.2d 75, 2003 Va. App. LEXIS 75 (2003).

Where defendant preserved the argument for a voluntary manslaughter instruction and the Commonwealth did not argue at trial that the evidence did not support the instruction, the trial court erred in excluding the instruction; therefore, defendant's conviction for second-degree murder and use of a firearm during the commission of a felony, violations of §§ 18.2-32 and 18.2-53.1, had to be reversed. Fox v. Commonwealth, No. 1717-02-1, 2003 Va. App. LEXIS 362 (Ct. of Appeals June 24, 2003).

Timing of jury instruction. — Trial court did not abuse its discretion by giving the jury a curative instruction that stated that self-defense was not an issue in defendant's trial for aggravated malicious wounding and use of a firearm in the commission of that offense after defendant made defendant's closing argument and before the Commonwealth delivered its rebuttal argument; defendant did not object to the Commonwealth's right to argue in rebuttal that self-defense was not an issue, and the instruction was worded in a neutral fashion that did not mention defendant's argument. Rollison v. Commonwealth, — Va. App. —, — S.E.2d —, 2007 Va. App. LEXIS 61 (Feb. 20, 2007).

Jury instructions. — Trial court did not abuse its discretion by giving the jury a curative instruction that stated that self-defense was not an issue in defendant's trial for aggravated malicious wounding and use of a firearm in the commission of that offense since the victim was a transsexual prostitute whose true gender defendant claimed to have learned only moments before the shooting during what began as a consensual sexual encounter, and defendant said he became fearful and pulled his firearm when the prostitute suggested that they continue the sexual encounter despite the fact that the prostitute, like defendant, was male; defendant came perilously close to a claim that the act of shooting the victim was excusable as it was done in self-defense, and claimed that the fear he experienced negated a finding of malice, without supporting a heat-of-passion defense. Rollison v. Commonwealth, — Va. App. —, — S.E.2d —, 2007 Va. App. LEXIS 61 (Feb. 20, 2007).

Defendant did not preserve for review the claim that the trial court's response to the jury's question caused the jury instruction to incorrectly state the law because defendant did not make a contemporaneous objection at the time the trial court informed defendant how the trial court would respond to the question. However, in defendant's murder case, the jury instruction did correctly state the law because defendant could be found not guilty of murder under § 18.2-32 yet be convicted of use of a firearm in attempting to commit murder under § 18.2-53.1. Ludwig v. Commonwealth, 52 Va. App. 1, 660 S.E.2d 679, 2008 Va. App. LEXIS 227 (2008).

Defendant's convictions for first-degree murder and use of a firearm in the commission of a felony were proper because the jury did not err in refusing to award an instruction on voluntary manslaughter. The jury rejected the instruction on second-degree murder and convicted defendant of first-degree murder; it followed that the jury would never have reached a voluntary manslaughter verdict. Cortez-Hernandez v. Commonwealth, 58 Va. App. 66, 706 S.E.2d 893, 2011 Va. App. LEXIS 114 (2011).

Defense of justification not proved. — Defendant's convictions for first-degree murder and the use of a firearm in the commission of a felony were proper because, under either account of the events given by defendant, either his trial testimony or his statements made to investigators, he forfeited his right to a self-defense jury instruction since he was not without fault in bringing on the difficulty that resulted in the victim's death; he was not in reasonable fear of death or great bodily harm when he killed the victim. Accordingly, the trial court did not err when it refused defendant's proffered jury instruction on justifiable homicide. Avent v. Commonwealth, 279 Va. 175, 688 S.E.2d 244, 2010 Va. LEXIS 10 (2010).

Evidence sufficient. — It is possible to brandish a firearm during a violation of § 18.2-53.1 because brandishing often does occur when one uses or displays a firearm in the commission of a felony; nevertheless, the prosecution is not required to prove a criminal defendant actually brandished his or her firearm in order to obtain a conviction under § 18.2-53.1 because § 18.2-53.1 is written in the disjunctive, prohibiting either the actual use of a firearm, or the display of a firearm in a threatening manner, and thus, the Commonwealth can obtain a conviction under § 18.2-53.1 if it proves the defendant "used or attempted to use" his or her firearm, even in the absence of evidence that the defendant brandished it, but the prosecution is not required to prove the defendant displayed his or her firearm in a threatening manner to obtain a conviction for brandishing a firearm under § 18.2-282. Nasser Nasser Ghalambor Dezfuli v. Commonwealth, 58 Va. App. 1, 707 S.E.2d 1, 2011 Va. App. LEXIS 105 (2011).

Word "threaten" means to utter threats against, promise punishment, reprisal, or other distress to, whereas the word "induce" means to move and lead, to bring in, or to bring on or bring about: effect, cause; thus, in cases involving the threatening display of a firearm under § 18.2-53.1, the defendant must display his or her firearm to promise punishment, reprisal or other distress to the victim, whereas in cases involving brandishing under § 18.2-282, the defendant must merely brandish or display a firearm in such a manner as to reasonably bring about or cause fear in the mind of the victim, and while the concepts are concededly similar, they are not the same. Nasser Nasser Ghalambor Dezfuli v. Commonwealth, 58 Va. App. 1, 707 S.E.2d 1, 2011 Va. App. LEXIS 105 (2011).

Brandishing not a lesser-included offense of use of a firearm in commission of felony. — Trial court erred in convicting defendant of brandishing a firearm in violation of § 18.2-282 as a lesser-included offense of use of a firearm in the commission of a felony, § 18.2-53.1, because brandishing under § 18.2-282 was not a lesser-included offense of use of a firearm in the commission of a felony under § 18.2-53.1; the Commonwealth can obtain a conviction for use of a firearm during the commission of a felony without proof that the defendant brandished the firearm, and a conviction for brandishing without also proving use of the firearm in the commission of a felony, and although the evidence presented to prove the former offense may, overlap with the evidence used to prove the latter, the Commonwealth must submit proof of completely different elements for a finding of guilt as to each separate offense, and thus, these offenses are different for purposes of Blockburger. Nasser Nasser Ghalambor Dezfuli v. Commonwealth, 58 Va. App. 1, 707 S.E.2d 1, 2011 Va. App. LEXIS 105 (2011).

Because it is possible to commit a violation of § 18.2-53.1 without brandishing a firearm, and because one can brandish a firearm without also committing a violation of § 18.2-53.1, the act of brandishing is not a lesser-included offense of use of a firearm in the commission of a felony; viewed in the abstract, these code sections each require proof of a fact that the other does not because the offense of using a firearm in the commission of a felony requires proof that the defendant either used or attempted to use a firearm or that he or she displayed a firearm in a threatening manner during the commission or attempt to commit one of the felonies enumerated in the statute, and thus, in such cases, the Commonwealth must prove that the defendant used or threateningly displayed the firearm expressly to assist him or her in attempting or completing a specified underlying criminal act, but, in a prosecution for the act of brandishing, the Commonwealth must merely prove that the defendant pointed, held or brandished a firearm in a manner that reasonably induced fear in the mind of some nearby person. Nasser Nasser Ghalambor Dezfuli v. Commonwealth, 58 Va. App. 1, 707 S.E.2d 1, 2011 Va. App. LEXIS 105 (2011).

Applied in Brown v. Commonwealth, 222 Va. 111, 279 S.E.2d 142 (1981); Blythe v. Commonwealth, 222 Va. 722, 284 S.E.2d 796

(1981); Bradshaw v. Commonwealth, 228 Va. 484, 323 S.E.2d 567 (1984); Barrett v. Commonwealth, 231 Va. 102, 341 S.E.2d 190 (1986); Hill v. Commonwealth, 2 Va. App. 683, 347 S.E.2d 913 (1986); Colclasure v. Commonwealth, 10 Va. App. 200, 390 S.E.2d 790 (1990); Akers v. Commonwealth, 31 Va. App. 521, 525 S.E.2d 13 (2000); Wolfe v. Commonwealth, 265 Va. 193, 576 S.E.2d 471, 2003 Va. LEXIS 32; Hoyt v. Commonwealth, 44 Va. App. 489, 605 S.E.2d 755, 2004 Va. App. LEXIS 599 (2004); Orndorff v. Commonwealth, 271 Va. 486, 628 S.E.2d 344, 2006 Va. LEXIS 43 (2006); Morgan v. Commonwealth, 50 Va. App. 120, 646 S.E.2d 899, 2007 Va. App. LEXIS 251 (2007); Saunders v. Commonwealth, 281 Va. 448, 706 S.E.2d 350, 2011 Va. LEXIS 45 (2011); Ellis v. Commonwealth, 281 Va. 499, 706 S.E.2d 849, 2011 Va. LEXIS 46 (2011).

II. ELEMENTS OF OFFENSE.

A. Underlying Offenses.

Violation of this section occurs only when the firearm is used with respect to specified felonies of murder, rape, robbery, burglary, malicious wounding or abduction. Wolfe v. Commonwealth, 6 Va. App. 640, 371 S.E.2d 314 (1988).

The common-law crime of robbery and the crime defined in this section are separate and distinct offenses for double jeopardy purposes. Jones v. Commonwealth, 218 Va. 18, 235 S.E.2d 313 (1977).

And have different elements as matter of law. — The crime of robbery and the crime of using a firearm in committing robbery have different elements as a matter of law, although they may have common elements as a matter of fact, since the "gist" of robbery is the taking and carrying away of the personal property of another, not necessarily by the use of a firearm, whereas the "gist" of this section is the use of a firearm in situations where it is likely that weapons may be used to injure victims of robbery or bystanders. Jones v. Commonwealth, 218 Va. 18, 235 S.E.2d 313 (1977).

To convict a defendant on a charge of using or displaying a weapon in the commission of a felony under this section, requires proof of a different element and evidence additional to that required for the offense of robbery. The use of a firearm is not one of the essential elements of the underlying felony. Jones v. Commonwealth, 218 Va. 18, 235 S.E.2d 313 (1977).

Elements Commonwealth must show. — To support a conviction of use of a firearm in the commission of a felony, the Commonwealth must prove that the accused actually had a firearm in his possession and that he used or attempted to use the firearm or displayed the firearm in a threatening manner while committing or attempting to commit robbery or one of the other specified felonies. Yarborough v. Commonwealth, 247 Va. 215, 441 S.E.2d 342 (1994).

To sustain a conviction for attempted capital murder, the evidence must establish "both a specific intent to kill the victim and an overt but ineffectual act committed in furtherance of the criminal purpose." Davis v. Commonwealth, No. 1244-95-3 (Ct. of Appeals Mar. 25, 1997).

Guilty of compound offense though not guilty of underlying offense. — A judgment may be entered on a guilty verdict of the compound offense of using a firearm in the commission of a robbery, even though, in the same trial, the jury finds the defendant not guilty of the underlying robbery. Reed v. Commonwealth, 239 Va. 594, 391 S.E.2d 75 (1990).

Use of predicate offense. — Where trial court acquitted defendant of the murder charge used as the predicate offense in the first indictment to support the use of a firearm charge, trial court did not err when it used the murder charge in the second indictment as the predicate offense to support the firearm charge. Strohecker v. Commonwealth, 23 Va. App. 242, 475 S.E.2d 844 (1996).

Reversal of predicate felony required reversal of firearm charge. — Upon defendant's sufficiency challenge, because the Commonwealth had the burden to prove beyond a reasonable doubt that defendant committed the crime of attempted robbery and it failed to do so, as one would have to resort to speculation and conjecture in order to find that he was attempting to rob as opposed to attempting to obtain money by false pretenses, an attempted robbery conviction could not stand; moreover, given reversal of the attempted robbery conviction, defendant's conviction for attempted use of a firearm during the commission of attempted robbery also had to be reversed. Jay v. Commonwealth, 275 Va. 510, 659 S.E.2d 311, 2008 Va. LEXIS 53 (2008).

Evidence was insufficient to convict defendant of use of a firearm during the attempted commission of a robbery because the evidence was insufficient to conviction of attempted robbery of a particular person because defendant placed a gun to the victim's neck and told the victim to keep ringing the bell for entry to his place of employment, which showed an intent to gain access to the building, but it did not show an intent to deprive the victim of his property. DeSilva v. Commonwealth, 2009 Va. App. LEXIS 482 (Oct. 27, 2009).

Because the trial court acquitted defendant of a robbery charge after a jury's verdict finding him guilty, defendant's conviction for use of a firearm in the commission of robbery in violation of § 18.2-53.1 was required to be reversed and dismissed on appeal pursuant to the ends of justice requirement, although defendant failed to raise this argument in the trial court. Martin v. Commonwealth, 2009 Va. App. LEXIS 511 (Nov. 17, 2009).

Conviction under this section not barred by determination defendant only guilty of unlawful wounding. — Defendant's conviction for use of a firearm in the commission of malicious wounding was not barred by the jury's determination that he was guilty of unlawful wounding only; a defendant may not attack his conviction on one count simply because it is inconsistent with the jury's acquittal on another count. Whitehurst v. Commonwealth, No. 0178-91-1 (Ct. of Appeals Mar. 31, 1992).

Conviction of use of firearm in commission of unlawful wounding. — The Code of Virginia contains no statute by which a defendant may be convicted of use of a firearm in the commission of unlawful wounding. A violation of this section occurs only when a firearm is used with respect to the statutorily specified felonies. Johnson v. Commonwealth, 20 Va. App. 547, 458 S.E.2d 599 (1995).

Convictions under this section and unlawful wounding section not inconsistent. — Defendant did not have to be charged with malicious wounding to be convicted of the unlawful use of a firearm in commission of malicious wounding; guilty verdicts on both were not inconsistent because the evidence supported both verdicts. Reese v. Commonwealth, No. 1279-03-4, 2004 Va. App. LEXIS 316 (Ct. of Appeals July 6, 2004).

Statute applies until underlying crime is completed in fact. — This section is not limited in application to the period of time from the commencement of the underlying crime until the point in time when the acts of the defendant make successful prosecution possible. The statute applies to the conduct of the accused until the underlying crime is completed in fact. Creasy v. Commonwealth, 9 Va. App. 470, 389 S.E.2d 316 (1990).

One-to-one relationship between underlying felonies and firearms convictions is not required. It is the identity of offenses which is dispositive, and, if a single act results in injury to two or more persons, a corresponding number of distinct offenses may result. Morris v. Commonwealth, 228 Va. 206, 321 S.E.2d 633 (1984).

Murder by "malicious shooting" does not preclude conviction under this section. — Murder under § 18.2-154 accomplished by a "malicious shooting" does not preclude a conviction under this section for use of a firearm in the commission of murder. Willis v. Commonwealth, 10 Va. App. 430, 393 S.E.2d 405 (1990).

Conviction under this section and § 18.2-31 not double jeopardy. — Conviction for the use of a firearm in the commission of a felony under this section as well as murder in the commission of a robbery while armed with a deadly weapon under § 18.2-31 (d) (now § 18.2-31 4) does not violate the double jeopardy clause of the United States Constitution. Turner v. Commonwealth, 221 Va. 513, 273 S.E.2d 36 (1980), cert. denied, 451 U.S. 1011, 101 S. Ct. 2347, 68 L. Ed. 2d 863 (1981).

Not necessary to separately indict and prosecute the underlying felony for conviction under this section. — Where an indictment is returned for an alleged violation of this section, the underlying felony must be proved beyond a reasonable doubt, and to obtain a conviction for violation of this section it is not necessary to separately indict and prosecute the underlying felony. Davis v. Commonwealth, 4 Va. App. 27, 353 S.E.2d 905 (1987).

Common-law burglary as underlying offense. — Defendant could be convicted of use of a firearm in the commission of burglary based on common-law burglary, as § 18.2-53.1 does not distinguish between common-law and statutory burglary. Rashad v. Commonwealth, 50 Va. App. 528, 651 S.E.2d 407, 2007 Va. App. LEXIS 395 (2007).

Member of mob. — Defendant's convictions under § 18.2-53.1 were reversed and dismissed because even though defendant was a member of a mob, § 18.2-42.1 did not render him criminally responsible for using a firearm in the commission of lynching and using a firearm in the commission of malicious wounding by mob simply by being a member of such mob. Paiz v. Commonwealth, 54 Va. App. 688, 682 S.E.2d 71, 2009 Va. App. LEXIS 380 (2009).

B. Use of a Firearm.

In deciding whether a firearm was used or displayed in a threatening manner under this section, the evidence is examined from the victim's point of view. Ballentine v. Commonwealth, No. 1457-89-3 (Ct. of Appeals May 7, 1991).

It is irrelevant that defendant did not in fact have a firearm if his victim rationally believed he had one. Cross v. Commonwealth, No. 1559-92-4 (Ct. of Appeals Feb. 22, 1994).

Firearm need not be used as firearm. — Application of § 18.2-53.1 is not restricted to instances where a firearm is used to expel a projective force; once an object satisfies the definition of a firearm, any use of that firearm that is intended to cause physical injury is a violation of § 18.2-53.1. Rose v. Commonwealth, 53 Va. App. 505, 673 S.E.2d 489, 2009 Va. App. LEXIS 106 (2009).

Need to show firearm was in fact present. — If an object is used to inflict fear or intimidation to accomplish its purpose of rape or robbery, the fear or intimidation may be proved by showing that the victim had reason to believe the object was a firearm although, in fact, it was not a firearm. However, that defendant may not be convicted for the use of a firearm under this section unless the evidence discloses beyond a reasonable doubt that the object used to cause the victim to reasonably believe it was a firearm was, in fact, a firearm. Sprouse v. Commonwealth, No. 1696-93-2 (Ct. of Appeals Jan. 24, 1995).

It was error for trial court to give instruction that relieved Commonwealth of burden of proving beyond a reasonable doubt that object used was in fact a firearm. Castillo v. Commonwealth, No. 0090-99-4 (Ct. of Appeals Feb. 22, 2000).

Instrument giving appearance of firearm. — Evidence was sufficient to convict defendant of using a firearm in violation of this section upon proof that defendant employed an instrument which gave the appearance of having a firing capability, whether or not the object actually had the capacity to propel a bullet by the force of gunpowder. Holloman v. Commonwealth, 221 Va. 196, 269 S.E.2d 356 (1980).

An instrument which gave the appearance of having a firing capability was sufficient to support a conviction under this section, whether or not the object actually had the capacity to propel a bullet by the force of gunpowder. Vanzant v. Commonwealth, No. 0713-95-1 (Ct. of Appeals April 9, 1996).

The evidence was sufficient to convict the defendant under this section even though the pistol and grenade were fake, where he brandished the pistol, a weapon whose use was specifically proscribed by this section, to threaten and intimate the persons in the bank where the robbery was committed, and the defendant conceded the evidence adduced at trial was sufficient to convict him of robbery. Cox v. Commonwealth, 218 Va. 689, 240 S.E.2d 524 (1978).

A BB gun appearing to be a .45 caliber pistol was a "firearm" within the meaning of this section. Vanzant v. Commonwealth, No. 0713-95-1 (Ct. of Appeals April 9, 1996).

The evidence was sufficient to prove that the BB pistol used by appellant while robbing the victim was a "firearm" under this section. Thomas v. Commonwealth, 25 Va. App. 681, 492 S.E.2d 460 (1997).

Rusted, inoperable revolver used in robberies constituted a firearm within the meaning of this section. Miller v. Commonwealth, 23 Va. App. 208, 475 S.E.2d 828 (1996).

Even though it was inoperable, the display of a replica of a handgun during two robberies supported a conviction of use of a firearm during the commission of a felony under § 18.2-53 because it looked like a firearm, it had not lost its identity as a firearm, and it had the capacity to operate as if to fire. Startin v. Commonwealth, 54 Va. App. 778, 682 S.E.2d 115, 2009 Va. App. LEXIS 394 (2009).

Evidence was sufficient to convict defendant of using a firearm in the commission of a felony in violation of § 18.2-53.1 because defendant employed a replica of a handgun during robberies which gave the appearance of having a firing capability, whether or not the object actually had the capacity to propel a bullet by the force of gunpowder, and was capable of evoking fear of physical harm. Startin v. Commonwealth, 281 Va. 374, 706 S.E.2d 873, 2011 Va. LEXIS 57 (2011).

Victim's perception of firearm not relevant. — In an action charging defendant with use of a firearm while in the commission of robbery, the victim's perception was not relevant because the victim sustained actual physical injury when struck with the weapon; the victim's perception is only relevant in those instances when a perpetrator is displaying a weapon in a threatening manner. Rose v. Commonwealth, 53 Va. App. 505, 673 S.E.2d 489, 2009 Va. App. LEXIS 106 (2009).

Actual possession of firearm required. — A victim's perception that an accused is armed, without more, is insufficient to support a conviction under this section which requires actual possession of a firearm as a necessary element of the offense. Wilkins v. Commonwealth, No. 2606-98-2, 2000 Va. App. LEXIS 619 (Ct. of Appeals Aug. 22, 2000).

Proof of "actual" possession of a firearm under this section may be established by circumstantial evidence, direct evidence, or both. Byers v. Commonwealth, 23 Va. App. 146, 474 S.E.2d 852 (1996).

Circumstantial evidence, such as an assailant's statement that he possesses a firearm, can be sufficient evidence to prove beyond a reasonable doubt that an accused indeed possessed a firearm. Williams v. Commonwealth, No. 0326-00-1, 2001 Va. App. LEXIS 147 (Ct. of Appeals Mar. 20, 2001).

By defendant's own statements. — Proof of "actual" possession of a firearm under this section may be established by defendant's own statements that he had a gun and that he threatened to hurt the victims if they didn't follow his instruction; despite the fact that police never found a gun, the jury was entitled to resolve the conflicts in the evidence against defendant, and in doing so, concluded that defendant had a gun. Powell v. Commonwealth, 268 Va. 233, 602 S.E.2d 119, 2004 Va. LEXIS 120 (2004).

Acting in concert with accomplice. — Where defendant never actually possessed the gun used in robberies, but he acted in concert with an accomplice who did display the weapon, defendant effectively "used" the revolver and was thereby subject to the terms of this section. Cortner v. Commonwealth, 222 Va. 557, 281 S.E.2d 908 (1981).

Although defendant did not personally possess weapon used in robbery of cab driver, by acting in concert with others to commit robbery, defendant was criminally accountable for use of weapon in commission of a felony. Broggin v. Commonwealth, No. 0131-98-3 (Ct. of Appeals Oct. 5, 1999).

Commonwealth was not required to prove that defendant, as opposed to a co-defendant, was in actual possession of firearm during robbery. Wallace v. Commonwealth, No. 2331-98-1 (Ct. of Appeals Nov. 9, 1999).

Where defendant robbed the victim after the victim was distracted by another person with a gun, the evidence was sufficient to prove that defendant acted in concert with the other person in using a firearm to commit a felony. Nelson v. Commonwealth, No. 1868-02-2, 2003 Va. App. LEXIS 363 (Ct. of Appeals June 24, 2003).

Evidence sufficient to find principal in the second degree. — Defendant's conviction for using a firearm in the commission of a felony in violation of § 18.2-53.1 as a principal in the second degree was supported by sufficient evidence as: (1) in accordance with a prior association, when defendant took a gun to a job interview and gave a principal the gun, defendant intended that the principal use it to obtain the victim's keys and drive away in the victim's vehicle; (2) defendant's theory that defendant was an innocent bystander was rejected; (3) defendant admitted that defendant knew the principal intended to carjack the victim and that defendant observed the crimes; (4) defendant did not discourage the principal or attempt to reclaim defendant's gun; and (5) defendant returned to the scene, retrieved the keys based on knowledge defendant obtained from the principal, and stole the car. Kirksey-Waugh v. Commonwealth, — Va. App. —, — S.E.2d —, 2008 Va. App. LEXIS 290 (June 17, 2008).

Jury instruction's definition of firearm. — Where defendant failed to object to jury instruction's definition of firearm and the definition that included a BB gun was correct under § 18.2-53.1, the issue was procedurally defaulted on appeal and no miscarriage

of justice warranted application of "ends of justice" exception to Va. Sup Ct. R. 5A:18. Wubneh v. Commonwealth, 51 Va. App. 224, 656 S.E.2d 418, 2008 Va. App. LEXIS 56 (2008), overruled in part by Startin v. Commonwealth, 56 Va. App. 26, 690 S.E.2d 310, 2010 Va. App. LEXIS 115 (2010).

Reasonable inference of actual possession. — Where evidence established that: (1) appellant twice told victim "this is a stickup"; (2) appellant threatened to "butt" victim in the head if victim turned around; (3) victim felt a metal object which he thought was a gun against the back of his neck; and (4) appellant took part in a similar robbery a week before in which a firearm was used, in light of this evidence, the trial court, as trier of fact, could reasonably have inferred that appellant "actually" possessed a firearm while robbing victim. Byers v. Commonwealth, 23 Va. App. 146, 474 S.E.2d 852 (1996).

Evidence was sufficient to establish that the defendant used a firearm in the commission of abduction, notwithstanding that the victim did not see a weapon, where the victim believed that the object that the defendant placed at her back was a weapon and, when the victim pleaded that the defendant not shoot her, the defendant did not respond that she did not have a gun and merely told the victim that she would not shoot. Washington v. Commonwealth, No. 0568-98-1 (Ct. of Appeals Apr. 6, 1999).

The evidence was sufficient to support a defendant's conviction under this section where the defendant handed a note to a hotel desk clerk on which he had written "have gun, will shoot, large bills"; although the defendant later claimed that he was unarmed and the clerk testified that she had seen no evidence of a firearm, the trier of fact could have concluded from the contents of the note that the defendant was armed at the time of the crime. Wilkins v. Commonwealth, No. 2606-98-2, 2000 Va. App. LEXIS 619 (Ct. of Appeals Aug. 22, 2000).

Credible evidence supported defendant's convictions for robbery, abduction, and use of a firearm as, during the hold-up, his statements, his assertive conduct, and the circumstances surrounding them were an "implied assertion" that he had a firearm. Powell v. Commonwealth, No. 1490-02-1, 2003 Va. App. LEXIS 427 (Ct. of Appeals Aug. 5, 2003), aff'd, 268 Va. 233, 602 S.E.2d 119 (2004).

Evidence was sufficient to convict defendant of using a firearm in the commission of a felony in violation of § 18.2-53.1, as the victim testified that the firearms used to rob him matched those recovered from the car in which defendant was found riding 15 minutes after the crime, and an officer testified that defendant had been sitting in the car next to where one of the guns was recovered. Berry v. Commonwealth, 2012 Va. App. LEXIS 385 (Nov. 27, 2012).

III. EVIDENTIARY MATTERS.

Evidence properly admitted. — Trial court did not abuse its discretion in allowing the Commonwealth's forensic expert to opine that the physical facts were inconsistent with defendant's differing versions of how his wife's fatal injury occurred, as these evidentiary facts were useful to the jury in deciding whether the death was accidental, self-inflicted, or a homicide, and whether any of the versions defendant gave to the police were credible; moreover, not only was it important for the Commonwealth's expert witnesses to explain the impact of the physical and forensic evidence to the jury to aid it in evaluating defendant's differing versions to the police of how his wife died, the significance of these evidentiary factors was beyond the scope of knowledge of the average juror. Smallwood v. Commonwealth, — Va. App. —, — S.E.2d —, 2005 Va. App. LEXIS 196 (May 17, 2005).

In a prosecution for robbery and the use of a firearm during the commission of robbery, the trial court did not err in admitting testimony by the police regarding other crimes committed by his accomplices that had no relevance to the crimes for which he was being tried, as he failed to restate his objection to the same when the first of two officers testified about those crimes, and also failed to object when the second officer testified about much of the same evidence; thus, in permitting the admission of said evidence, he waived any complaint on appeal regarding the same. Boggs v. Commonwealth, — Va. App. —, — S.E.2d —, 2006 Va. App. LEXIS 66 (Feb. 21, 2006).

Defendant's convictions for first-degree murder and the use of a firearm in the commission of a felony were proper because the record in the case, which included defendant's own testimony, indicated that his will was not overborne during questioning and that his capacity for self-determination was not impaired. Defendant was apprised of his Miranda rights by the interrogating officer; he was given food and an opportunity to sleep; and he described himself as calm and comfortable throughout the questioning. Avent v. Commonwealth, 279 Va. 175, 688 S.E.2d 244, 2010 Va. LEXIS 10 (2010).

Defendant's convictions for murder in violation of § 18.2-32, use of a firearm in the commission of a felony in violation of § 18.2-53.1, and grand larceny in violation of § 18.2-95 were appropriate because the trial court did not err in admitting evidence of prior crimes to establish defendant's identity since he disputed his identity as the perpetrator of the instant offenses. Additionally, given the substantial evidence of prior bad acts, evidence of a damaged fence did not substantially influence the jury; its admission was therefore harmless. McMillian v. Commonwealth, 2011 Va. App. LEXIS 74 (Mar. 1, 2011).

Admission of hearsay held harmless error. — Based on the overwhelming evidence of defendant's guilt, including testimony from an expert, a police detective, and defendant himself, the latter of which demonstrated a motive and intent to kill, the trial court's admission of alleged hearsay testimony under the "state of mind" exception to the hearsay rule was harmless error. West v. Commonwealth, 2008 Va. App. LEXIS 193 (Apr. 22, 2008).

Admission of an abuse affidavit into evidence, although violative of defendant's U.S. Const., Amend. VI right to confrontation, was harmless beyond a reasonable doubt for convictions for capital murder, abduction with intent to defile, rape, grand larceny, and two counts of use of a firearm, where the evidence was sufficient to support the convictions absent the affidavit. Crawford v. Commonwealth, 281 Va. 84, 704 S.E.2d 107, 2011 Va. LEXIS 20 (2011).

Gang culture evidence admitted. — Trial court did not abuse its discretion in admitting expert testimony on gang culture in defendant's criminal trial for malicious wounding and use of a firearm during the commission of a felony; the Commonwealth provided a sufficient foundation for the admission of the testimony, the testimony was relevant in that it established a motive for the shooting, and the evidence was not outweighed by prejudice. Hubbard v. Commonwealth, 2006 Va. App. LEXIS 72 (Feb. 28, 2006).

In a case in which defendant appealed his conviction for violating §§ 18.2-51, 18.2-53.1, and 18.2-286.1, he unsuccessfully argued that the trial court erred in permitting an expert witness to testify about gang practices and terminology, including his involvement with a gang. The trial court reasonably concluded that the probative value of the expert's testimony outweighed any prejudicial effect; the evidence was relevant to prove the identity of the shooter, and the testimony about his gang affiliation was probative as to defendant's identity. Wyche v. Commonwealth, 2012 Va. App. LEXIS 227 (July 10, 2012).

Photographs admitted into evidence. — In defendant's trial for first-degree murder, a violation of § 18.2-32, and use of a firearm in the commission of murder, a violation of § 18.2-53.1, the trial court did not abuse its discretion when it admitted into evidence six photographs of defendant's bedroom, which served as an independent silent witness corroborating a witness's testimony that defendant handled a firearm. Although the photographs supported the prosecution's case, the photographs also supported defendant's testimony regarding intoxication. Therefore, the photographs were relevant evidence and were not prejudicial. Szenasy v. Commonwealth, 2010 Va. App. LEXIS 412 (Oct. 26, 2010).

Expert improperly qualified. — In a prosecution for the use of a deadly weapon with the intent to commit larceny and the use of a firearm in the commission of a robbery, the trial court erred in qualifying a detective as an expert in firearms, as the BB gun defendant used was clearly not a "firearm." However, the error was harmless as the detective had the requisite knowledge to be classified as an expert on BB guns, and his improper classification could have only had a slight effect on the jury, if any. Justiss v. Commonwealth, 61 Va. App. 261, 734 S.E.2d 699, 2012 Va. App. LEXIS 404 (2012).

Evidence sufficient where victim believed defendant was armed. — Where victim said that he saw defendant with his hands in his pocket, that defendant approached him and stuck something in his stomach which he did not see, but that "it felt hard like a pistol, the end of a pistol," and that he assumed it was a pistol, and it was clear from the evidence that he responded to the orders and

directions of the robber with that belief, the evidence was sufficient to prove defendant guilty under this section beyond a reasonable doubt. Cromite v. Commonwealth, 3 Va. App. 64, 348 S.E.2d 38 (1986).

Where defendant pushed an object into the victim's back and told him he would "shoot" if the victim did not cooperate, then, while defendant did not explicitly state that he had a gun, the clear inference to be drawn from his threat to "shoot," is that he did have a gun. McBride v. Commonwealth, 22 Va. App. 730, 473 S.E.2d 85 (1996), aff'd on reh'g en banc, 24 Va. App. 603, 484 S.E.2d 165 (1997).

Commonwealth presented competent and credible evidence sufficient to prove beyond a reasonable doubt that defendant possessed and used a firearm during a robbery, § 18.2-53.1. The victim testified that the object felt like and appeared to be a real firearm, and the only evidence that the weapon was a BB gun came from defendant's accomplice, whose testimony the fact finder rejected. Wubneh v. Commonwealth, — Va. App. —, — S.E.2d —, 2008 Va. App. LEXIS 6 (Jan. 8, 2008).

Defendant's conviction for use of a firearm in the commission of a robbery was appropriate because the evidence was sufficient; defendant stated that he had a gun and the victim believed that he had one. Defendant had told the victim that he had a gun, to quit looking at him, and to get back in her car; the victim testified that she never saw a gun but that defendant pointed his finger under his sweatshirt like he had a gun, and she believed that he had a gun based on his words and actions. Courtney v. Commonwealth, 2010 Va. App. LEXIS 111 (Mar. 23, 2010), aff'd, 281 Va. 363, 706 S.E.2d 344, 2011 Va. LEXIS 51 (2011).

Identification evidence. — Defendant's convictions for robbery and the felonious use of a firearm were appropriate because the evidence was sufficient where the victims identified defendant as the robber; both victims had ample opportunity to observe defendant; the victims were certain that they had identified defendant correctly; and the victims' identification testimony was corroborated by others who had observed defendant at the crime scenes. Griffin v. Commonwealth, 2007 Va. App. LEXIS 504 (Nov. 7, 2007).

Identification evidence supported defendant's conviction of use of a firearm in the commission of a felony (attempted malicious shooting), as the victims' identification of defendant was sufficient to prove defendant's identity as the shooter; one victim reliably identified defendant as the person with whom the victim argued on the night of the subject shooting and another victim testified unequivocally that the same person who argued with the first victim was the shooter. Cuffee v. Commonwealth, 61 Va. App. 353, 735 S.E.2d 693, 2013 Va. App. LEXIS 7 (2013).

Evidence held sufficient. — Evidence supported conviction of robbery and use of a firearm in commission of robbery where there was positive identification testimony by witness and two other employees, who were in close proximity to defendant during robbery, who testified that the defendant was the armed robber who entered store alone, threatened them, and left with money, and where defendant was also identified by his accomplice as person who entered store and committed crime. Lewis v. Commonwealth, 7 Va. App. 596, 376 S.E.2d 295 (1989), aff'd en banc, 8 Va. App. 574, 383 S.E.2d 736 (1989).

Where the defendant gave a bank teller a note stating that he had a gun and pointed to his pocket, and saying he did not want to hurt anyone, this evidence was sufficient to prove beyond a reasonable doubt that the defendant actually possessed a firearm and used it in a threatening manner, even though he was acquitted in the same bench trial of entering the bank with a deadly weapon. Elmore v. Commonwealth, 22 Va. App. 424, 470 S.E.2d 588 (Va. App. 1996).

In this case, defendant aimed his loaded gun at police officer while he was in the car and attempted to aim at him again after he partially emerged from the car. Even though defendant did not verbally threaten the officer, the trial court could have reasonably concluded that his actions amounted to the commencement of the consummation of his murder of this officer. Davis v. Commonwealth, No. 1244-95-3 (Ct. of Appeals Mar. 25, 1997).

Evidence was sufficient to support the defendant's conviction of using a firearm in the commission of robbery where he aided and abetted another, who used a gun during a robbery, as, by such conduct, the defendant effectively "used" the firearm used by his coperpetrator. Turner v. Commonwealth, No. 2117-97-1 (Ct. of Appeals Oct. 6, 1998).

The evidence was sufficient to support a defendant's conviction under this section where a participant in a robbery identified the defendant and described his involvement in the crime. Kingsberry v. Commonwealth, No. 0142-99-1, 2000 Va. App. LEXIS 622 (Ct. of Appeals Aug. 22, 2000).

A defendant's statements and his menacing actions provided sufficient evidence from which the trial judge could conclude beyond a reasonable doubt that the defendant was guilty of using a firearm in the commission of two robberies where the evidence proved that the defendant threatened to "shoot" a store owner while gesturing and pointing at him with what appeared to the owner to be a heavy object and that the defendant told a bank teller that he would "blow her head off" and kept his hand tucked under his belt buckle during the course of robbing the bank. Williams v. Commonwealth, No. 0326-00-1, 2001 Va. App. LEXIS 147 (Ct. of Appeals Mar. 20, 2001).

Evidence was sufficient to support defendant's conviction of possession of a firearm, as defendant entered the victim's store with defendant's hand behind defendant's back, and threatened to shoot the victim; although the victim did not know whether defendant had a gun, defendant's threat was sufficient to cause the victim to relinquish all the money in the cash register. Artis v. Commonwealth, No. 3259-01-1, 2002 Va. App. LEXIS 749 (Ct. of Appeals Dec. 17, 2002).

Evidence was sufficient to support defendant's attempted murder and use of a firearm in the commission of attempted murder charges where defendant's intent to kill the victim was shown by defendant's actions in climbing on the top of the victim's truck, and repeatedly firing his weapon toward the victim, who was on the ground trying to shield himself with the truck. Cook v. Commonwealth, No. 1968-02-2, 2003 Va. App. LEXIS 375 (Ct. of Appeals July 1, 2003), aff'd, 268 Va. 111, 597 S.E.2d 84 (2004).

Evidence was sufficient to support defendant's illegal use of a firearm in the commission of a second-degree murder conviction where: (1) the position of the victim's body was inconsistent with defendant's explanation that she had committed suicide; (2) defendant gave inconsistent factual accounts to the EMTs, law enforcement officers, friends, and the jury; (3) despite defendant's claims that his relationship with the victim had no problems or difficulties, the victim moved out four months earlier, bought a new home, removed defendant as beneficiary on her life insurance policy, and started dating other men; (4) the victim's friends described her as happy and upbeat following her separation from defendant; and (5) defendant testified that immediately prior to the victim's death, he and the victim engaged in an emotional discussion over the victim's admitted relationships with other men that hurt defendant's feelings and emotionally upset him. Sluder v. Commonwealth, No. 2531-02-3, 2003 Va. App. LEXIS 605 (Ct. of Appeals Nov. 25, 2003).

Evidence was sufficient to support defendant's conviction where the Commonwealth proved that defendant raped a woman and held a gun the entire time as well as put the gun under his chin and told the victim he was going to blow his head off if she did not have intercourse with him. Breeden v. Commonwealth, 43 Va. App. 169, 596 S.E.2d 563, 2004 Va. App. LEXIS 257 (2004).

Trial court's judgment following a bench trial that found defendant guilty of eight counts of attempted malicious wounding and eight counts of felonious use of a firearm was not plainly wrong or without evidence to support it and, thus, was affirmed; an inference that defendant tried to maim eight police officers providing security at a nightclub could be drawn by defendant's conduct in firing a fusillade of gunfire in their direction. Coleman v. Commonwealth, — Va. App. —, — S.E.2d —, 2006 Va. App. LEXIS 502 (Nov. 7, 2006).

Defendant's malicious wounding, aggravated malicious wounding, and use of a firearm in the commission of a felony convictions were upheld on appeal, as sufficient evidence linked him to a shooting while driving a Jeep loaned to him and his cohorts in exchange for drugs, and based on the same, the trial judge could reject defendant's hypothesis that another group of men gained possession of the Jeep and committed the crimes alleged. Powell v. Commonwealth, — Va. App. —, — S.E.2d —, 2006 Va. App. LEXIS 537 (Nov. 28, 2006).

Testimony offered by two victims was not inherently incredible, and the trial court did not err in finding the evidence sufficient to support defendant's convictions for robbery, § 18.2-58, and using a firearm in the commission of a felony, § 18.2-53.1. Both victims described defendant as having played an active role in the robbery, and nothing in the record rendered their testimony inherently incredible. Winckler v. Commonwealth, — Va. App. —, — S.E.2d —, 2007 Va. App. LEXIS 73 (Mar. 6, 2007).

Direct eyewitness testimony of two witnesses identifying defendant as the gunman was not inherently incredible as a matter of law and was, thus, sufficient to support defendant's convictions for second-degree murder, in violation of § 18.2-32, and use of a firearm in the commission of murder, in violation of § 18.2-53.1. The witnesses' testimony was corroborated by other testimony and the physical evidence, including shell casings recovered from the scene of the murder. Jones v. Commonwealth, 2007 Va. App. LEXIS 265 (July 17, 2007).

Fact that defendant apparently found and loaded a pistol, defendant fired all five rounds and still continued pulling the trigger, and defendant initially packed a bag for flight were circumstances that the jury properly considered in concluding that the defendant acted with malice and supported defendant's convictions for first-degree murder and the use of a firearm in committing the murder. Cayton v. Commonwealth, — Va. App. —, — S.E.2d —, 2008 Va. App. LEXIS 393 (Aug. 12, 2008).

Defendant's challenge to the sufficiency of the evidence to support conviction for use of a firearm in the commission of murder and use of a firearm in the commission of malicious wounding lacked merit, because the testimony of defendant's grandfather, identifying defendant as the person who shot the pistol that wounded the grandfather and killed another victim, was not inherently incredible as a matter of law; any challenge based on the grandfather's admission that the grandfather had been drinking and doing drugs before the shooting did not render the testimony inherently incredible. Carrington v. Commonwealth, 2009 Va. App. LEXIS 152 (Mar. 31, 2009).

Fact that the infant was unaware of defendant's use of the gun did not invalidate defendant's conviction for use of a firearm in the commission of abduction. Clanton v. Commonwealth, 53 Va. App. 561, 673 S.E.2d 904, 2009 Va. App. LEXIS 202 (2009).

Evidence was sufficient to support a jury's verdict convicting defendant of robbery, use of a firearm in the commission of a felony, § 18.2-53.1, and wearing a mask in public, § 18.2-422, under circumstances in which defendant did not contest the victim's testimony that a robbery occurred, defendant and another individual were identified when the victim's purse was found in a creek near the other individual's residence and the other individual's fingerprint was found on the victim's credit card still inside the purse, when the other individual was arrested, defendant was with him, and, in a subsequent videotaped confession, defendant told a detective that he was the robber and gave numerous specific details about the offense, his subsequent flight from the scene, and the disposal of the purse in the creek; defendant admitted wearing a mask and using a BB gun to commit the offense. Defendant's actions did not support his claim that he confessed to prevent the other individual from being held responsible for the robbery. Sears v. Commonwealth, 2009 Va. App. LEXIS 319 (July 14, 2009).

There was sufficient evidence to support the convictions for unlawful, felonious and malicious shooting of the victim and for the unlawful and felonious use and display of a firearm while committing an aggravated malicious wounding where: (1) the victim and numerous witnesses identified defendant as the armed assailant who shot the victim with a 9mm pistol discovered at defendants' house; (2) a doctor testified that the bullet that entered the victim's body damaged the lining of his left hip joint, thereby causing traumatic arthritis; and (3) traumatic arthritis could result in chronic pain and a limitation of the range of motion of that joint. Barnes v. Commonwealth, 279 Va. 22, 688 S.E.2d 210, 2010 Va. LEXIS 17 (2010).

Defendant's convictions for first-degree murder and the use of a firearm in the commission of a felony were proper because he admitted to purposefully using a sawed-off shotgun both to shoot and bludgeon the victim; therefore, there was sufficient evidence from which the jury could have inferred malice, and the charges of first- and second-degree murder were properly before the jury. Accordingly, the trial court did not err when it denied defendant's motion to strike those charges; for the same reasons, the trial court did not err when it failed to strike the charge of use of a firearm in the commission of a felony. Avent v. Commonwealth, 279 Va. 175,

688 S.E.2d 244, 2010 Va. LEXIS 10 (2010).

Evidence was sufficient to support defendant's convictions for robbery, shooting within an occupied dwelling, using a firearm in the commission of a felony, armed burglary, and malicious wounding, because ample evidence supported a finding that defendant was a perpetrator in a home invasion: three of the victims identified defendant at trial, and a co-defendant testified that defendant said he intended to rob the home, that he entered the home wearing a bullet-proof vest and armed with a handgun, and that he later told the co-defendant that he had struck one of the victim's in the head. Trial court did not abuse discretion in ruling on misidentification of accomplices by witnesses. Streater v. Commonwealth, 2009 Va. App. LEXIS 504 (Nov. 10, 2009).

Evidence, when viewed in the light most favorable to the Commonwealth, supported the jury's verdicts that defendant was guilty of abduction to extort money for pecuniary benefit in violation of § 18.2-48 and use of a firearm during the commission of a felony in violation of § 18.2-53.1 because the jury, as it was entitled to do, ostensibly disregarded some of the testimony from the Commonwealth's witnesses; defendant pointed a handgun at the victim and demanded money, the victim's boyfriend gave defendant money after an initial attempt to obtain money from the victim's brother failed, over the course of the next two hours, defendant accompanied the victim to numerous locations in an attempt to obtain more money, and numerous witnesses testified on behalf of the Commonwealth confirming the victim's allegations. Brown v. Commonwealth, 2009 Va. App. LEXIS 575 (Dec. 22, 2009).

Evidence was sufficient to prove attempted murder and use of a firearm while attempting to commit murder, violations of §§ 18.2-26, 18.2-32, and 18.2-154, where defendant pointed a gun at the victim's car, firing four or five times. Thus, defendant must have intended the immediate, direct, and necessary consequences of his voluntary act. Stullenberg v. Commonwealth, 2010 Va. App. LEXIS 179 (May 4, 2010).

Evidence was sufficient to support defendant's convictions on four counts of using a firearm in the commission of a felony where after the fatal shooting of three people defendant hid out at a friend's house and then fled the state, the murder weapon was found in the friend's backyard, other crimes evidence tended to prove that defendant stole the murder weapon in a robbery, and an accomplice's testimony identifying defendant as the shooter was corroborated by fingerprint evidence. Rayford v. Commonwealth, 2007 Va. App. LEXIS 506 (Aug. 9, 2007).

Appellant's convictions for two counts of robbery, one count of statutory burglary, and three counts of use of a firearm in the commission of the felonies were affirmed because it was reasonable for the fact finder to conclude the intruder knew the victims' habits and DNA evidence indicated at some point in time, appellant had touched the BB gun. Swinson v. Commonwealth, 2010 Va. App. LEXIS 311 (Aug. 3, 2010).

Evidence was sufficient to sustain defendant's convictions for use of a firearm in the commission of a murder and use of a firearm in the commission of an abduction, violations of § 18.2-53.1, where defendant purchased a gun just prior to the victim's disappearance and death, and defendant admitted to shooting the victim, although defendant claimed that the shooting was accidental. Crawford v. Commonwealth, 281 Va. 84, 704 S.E.2d 107, 2011 Va. LEXIS 20 (2011).

Because defendant, a North Carolina bail bondsman, did not have authority pursuant to §§ 9.1-185.18 and 9.1-186.13, to seize a fugitive or the victim, and the Commonwealth showed that defendant intended to abduct the fugitive, there was no legal justification for his actions and defendant's convictions for attempted abduction, a violation of §§ 18.2-26 and 18.2-47, and use of a firearm in the commission of an attempted abduction, a violation of § 18.2-53.1, were proper. Collins v. Commonwealth, 57 Va. App. 355, 702 S.E.2d 267, 2010 Va. App. LEXIS 480 (2010), aff'd, 283 Va. 263, 720 S.E.2d 530, 2012 Va. LEXIS 17 (2012).

Defendant's conviction for use or display of a firearm in the commission of a felony was appropriate because his statements, combined with is opportunity to discard an actual firearm, were sufficient to find him guilty under § 18.2-53.1. Because there was evidence to support defendant's conviction, the supreme court was not permitted to substitute its own judgment. Courtney v. Commonwealth, 281 Va. 363, 706 S.E.2d 344, 2011 Va. LEXIS 51 (2011).

Evidence defendant repeatedly entered the store robbed wearing gang colors, a witness observed guns in the van used to get to and from the store, defendant drove van used to and from the store, and defendant was present when the person who robbed the store came running out with the register drawer and defendant drove the van away supported defendant's convictions for robbery and use of a firearm during the robbery. Lebron v. Commonwealth, 58 Va. App. 540, 712 S.E.2d 15, 2011 Va. App. LEXIS 238 (2011).

There was sufficient evidence to prove defendant was guilty of use of a firearm in the commission of a robbery, including testimony that defendant repeatedly entered the store that day of the robbery; told another he needed to "man up," meaning he needed to commit the robbery; and was in the get away van, which had been seen with firearms in it earlier that day, when the individual committing the robbery came running out with the register drawer. Salcedo v. Commonwealth, 58 Va. App. 525, 712 S.E.2d 8, 2011 Va. App. LEXIS 239 (2011).

Where the object defendant used had the appearance of being capable of firing a projective by explosion, the evidence was sufficient evidence to support defendant's conviction for use of a firearm in the commission of a felony. Cook v. Commonwealth, 2011 Va. App. LEXIS 409 (Dec. 20, 2011).

Evidence was sufficient to support defendant's convictions for two counts of use of a firearm in the commission of robbery and burglary under § 18.2-53.1, where defendant clearly displayed the weapon in a threatening manner when he demanded money, threatened to kill the pharmacy technician, and lifted his shirt to reveal a weapon. Towler v. Commonwealth, 59 Va. App. 284, 718 S.E.2d 463, 2011 Va. App. LEXIS 402 (2011).

Evidence was sufficient to support defendant's convictions where, taken in the light most favorable to the Commonwealth, it established that defendant shot and killed the victim; the jury was free to disbelieve defendant's testimony that defendant was not at scene when the victim was shot and to believe the testimony of other witnesses that defendant was there and shot and killed the victim. Mayfield v. Commonwealth, 59 Va. App. 839, 722 S.E.2d 689, 2012 Va. App. LEXIS 88 (2012).

Trial court did not err in finding that the evidence proved beyond a reasonable doubt that defendant acted as a principal in the second degree to use of a firearm in the commission of a robbery as the evidence showed that defendant aided in the commission of and shared the main actor's intent to rob a clothing retail store during normal business hours, where he was likely to encounter both store employees and customers. The evidence showed that defendant transported the main actor to and from the immediate area where he committed the robbery and abduction; that defendant remained in her SUV at a nearby apartment complex, where neither she nor the main actor lived, when the main actor departed the vehicle to commit the robbery; that she tried to assist him in eluding police, and that she tried to provide him with an alibi when questioned about the offenses, and that she gave false and contradictory statements to officers when questioned about her part in the robbery. Wade v. Commonwealth, 2012 Va. App. LEXIS 161 (May 15, 2012).

Ample evidence supported a finding that defendant committed the offenses of first-degree murder and use of a firearm in the commission of a felony as the testimony of an eyewitness, who was at the scene at the time of the offenses, proved that defendant shot and killed two unarmed men without provocation, in that the eyewitness testified that defendant obtained a rifle, that he had a brief verbal exchange with the first victim before he shot the first victim twice, that defendant then turned the gun toward the second victim and shot him twice in the back, that the eyewitness did not have a gun, and that the eyewitness did not see any weapons in the possession of the two victims. Additionally, the evidence showed that defendant moved the two bodies to a location behind his garage and fled from police. Daugherty v. Commonwealth, 2012 Va. App. LEXIS 136 (May 1, 2012).

Conviction for use of a firearm in the commission of a robbery was supported by sufficient evidence, where the record contained ample evidence demonstrating that defendant took marijuana from a victim's car on the day of the shooting, including testimony that the victim weighed out one ounce of marijuana in the car but police recovered less than two-tenths of an ounce and defendant admitted he took a pill bottle containing marijuana. Person v. Commonwealth, 2012 Va. App. LEXIS 187 (June 5, 2012).

Sufficient evidence supported defendant's conviction as the victim observed that the accomplice had a semi-automatic gun, felt the cold, hard barrel of the gun that defendant placed against his neck, and saw the tip of that gun; further, defendant was guilty as a principal in the second degree of possessing the firearm used by his accomplice. Gibbs v. Commonwealth, No. 1726-11-1, 2012 Va. App. LEXIS 324 (Oct. 16, 2012).

Evidence was sufficient to support defendant's conviction for using a firearm in the commission of burglary under § 18.2-53.1 because the way defendant used a gun after entering the victims home supported the jury's finding that he used it during the entry for the same purpose: in order to be ready to subdue the victim as necessary. Smith v. Commonwealth, 61 Va. App. 690, 739 S.E.2d 280, 2013 Va. App. LEXIS 104 (Apr. 2, 2013).

Evidence sufficient to prove use of firearm. — Evidence was sufficient to support defendant's conviction for use of a firearm in the commission of a felony, in violation of § 18.2-53.1, when the victims testified that defendant, while threatening to rob them, lifted his shirt and displayed a firearm, and the fact that only one victim saw the firearm did not require a different result, nor did the facts that a firearm was not found on defendant's person and his house was not searched for a weapon. Jones v. Commonwealth, No. 1730-03-1, 2004 Va. App. LEXIS 300 (Ct. of Appeals June 29, 2004).

Commonwealth presented sufficient evidence to sustain two convictions of using a firearm in commission of both a charge of attempted murder and a charge of malicious wounding, based on the victim's testimony, and the inferences drawn therefrom, in which the jury could reasonably conclude that: (1) defendant had a firearm in her possession when she hit the victim with the hammer; (2) when defendant shot the victim, and before she hit the victim with a hammer, nothing in the record indicated that she put the gun down before she hit him with the hammer; and (3) by having the firearm in her possession, defendant displayed the firearm in a threatening manner during the hammer attack; furthermore, although the record did not indicate that defendant presented the pistol in a threatening manner, the jury could properly conclude that her mere possession of the pistol during the hammer attack, coupled with the fact she had already used the pistol, could create a legitimate fear of further use and constituted display of a firearm in a threatening manner. Coleman v. Commonwealth, — Va. App. —, — S.E.2d —, 2005 Va. App. LEXIS 379 (Oct. 4, 2005).

Circumstantial evidence was sufficient to prove that defendant possessed a firearm and used it in a threatening way in the commission of a robbery of a convenience store; defendant kept his concealed hand beneath his clothing during the robbery, he nodded his head up and down in a gesture of yes when asked by the clerk if he had a gun, and defendant gestured with his concealed hand by "jiggling" it. Kendrick v. Commonwealth, — Va. App. —, — S.E.2d —, 2006 Va. App. LEXIS 39 (Jan. 31, 2006).

Conviction for use of a firearm while in the commission of robbery was supported by evidence that defendant used the gun to inflict physical harm in order to accomplish the robbery when the victim was struck with the weapon. Rose v. Commonwealth, 53 Va. App. 505, 673 S.E.2d 489, 2009 Va. App. LEXIS 106 (2009).

Reversal of defendant's conviction for use of a firearm in an attempted robbery was not required because the victim, who was deaf, did not see any gestures indicating the presence of a gun and could not hear any verbal threats regarding a gun. Section 18.2-53.1 was not restricted to situations in which the victim was aware of or able to comprehend the use of a firearm; the trial court could find that in making threats to use the gun and keeping his hand cocked under his clothing as though he was holding a gun, defendant used a firearm or attempted to use a firearm. Corprew v. Commonwealth, — Va. App. —, — S.E.2d —, 2009 Va. App. LEXIS 145 (Mar. 24, 2009).

There was sufficient evidence of a firearm to support defendant's convictions for use of a firearm in an attempted robbery and use of a firearm in a robbery. The trial court had concluded that defendant had a gun based on defendant's assertions that he had a gun and the motions he made toward his clothing. Corprew v. Commonwealth, — Va. App. —, — S.E.2d —, 2009 Va. App. LEXIS 145 (Mar. 24, 2009).

There was sufficient evidence to support convictions of aggravated malicious wounding and use of a firearm in the commission of aggravated malicious wounding. Ample credible evidence, including the victim's identification of defendant, placed him in close proximity to the crime scene both immediately before and after the shooting; a rational finder of fact could determine that, notwithstanding another person's fingerprint on the firearm, defendant was present at the crime scene and fired the weapon, even though his prints were not on the weapon. Barnes v. Commonwealth, 2008 Va. App. LEXIS 533 (Dec. 9, 2008), aff'd, 279 Va. 22, 688 S.E.2d 210, 2010 Va. LEXIS 17 (Va. Jan. 15, 2010).

Where no weapon was fired. — Evidence was sufficient to support conviction for use of a firearm during a burglary despite the fact that no weapon was fired until after defendant gained entry because § 18.2-53.1 applied until the underlying crime was complete. Tucker v. Commonwealth, — Va. App. —, — S.E.2d —, 2006 Va. App. LEXIS 526 (Nov. 21, 2006).

Sufficient evidence to show acting in concert. — Evidence that defendant, in concert with the gunman, intentionally attempted to seize control of the vehicle by trying to enter the vehicle while the gunman pointed a firearm at the driver was sufficient to support defendant's convictions for attempted carjacking, in violation of § 18.2-58.1, and use of a firearm in the commission of a felony, in violation of § 18.2-53.1. Walker v. Commonwealth, 2007 Va. App. LEXIS 214 (May 22, 2007).

Where no weapon was found. — There was sufficient evidence to convict defendant of the use of a firearm in the commission of a felony, even thought a firearm was never found, because the victim testified that he saw defendant holding a gun and the trial judge, as finder of fact, was entitled to accept this testimony. McCray v. Commonwealth, — Va. App. —, — S.E.2d —, 2008 Va. App. LEXIS 38 (Jan. 22, 2008).

Evidence held insufficient. — Defendant's conviction for use of a firearm during the commission of a felony was reversed because, at its best, the inculpatory evidence showed only that defendant knew that the triggerman killed the victim and that, two months after the killing, defendant and another decided to "roll up" or leave the area. No reasonable interpretation of defendant's statement that defendant knew the triggerman implied that defendant, even if present at the scene of the murder, aided and abetted the triggerman in committing the murder. Jones v. Virginia, — Va. App. —, — S.E.2d —, 2007 Va. App. LEXIS 430 (Nov. 27, 2007).

In a case in which the Commonwealth appealed the Court of Appeals of Virginia's reversal of defendant's convictions for violating §§ 18.2-58 and 18.2-53.1, the evidence was insufficient to support the circuit court's factual findings, to establish that a store department lead was intimidated, or to support the circuit court's judgment convicting defendant of robbery and use of a firearm in the commission of robbery. In the end, about all that the Commonwealth was left with was the robber's eye contact with the department lead and the latter's testimony that he stopped because there was a weapon involved and that gave him some concern. Commonwealth v. Anderson, 278 Va. 419, 683 S.E.2d 536, 2009 Va. LEXIS 86 (2009).

Evidence was insufficient to support a conviction of use or display of a firearm during the commission of the burglary, in violation of § 18.2-53.1, because the elements of statutory burglary were complete before defendant used or displayed a firearm. Rowland v. Commonwealth, 281 Va. 396, 707 S.E.2d 331, 2011 Va. LEXIS 60 (2011).

Where defendant's accomplice shot an occupant of a home after they broke in, the evidence was insufficient to convict defendant of the use of a firearm in commission of burglary, as the Commonwealth was required to prove that the firearm was used before entry was fully accomplished. Rushing v. Commonwealth, 284 Va. 270, 726 S.E.2d 333, 2012 Va. LEXIS 133 (2012).

Although no witness was able to identify defendant by facial recognition, as the robber was wearing a mask during the robbery, there was sufficient evidence to convict defendant of displaying a firearm during a robbery where the surveillance camera photographs showed the robber wearing a dark, hooded jacket or sweatshirt of some type, with a tag or label on the lower left front side, as well as distinctively marked gloves, the store owner testified that defendant's height was about the same as the height of the robber and the robber was African-American, as was defendant, a police officer later encountered defendant wearing a dark jacket, zipped up, with a knit cap on his head and the hood of his jacket pulled over his head, with a tag or label on the lower left front side, and the officer discovered a pair of gloves and a handgun lying on the ground in a haphazard fashion, as if someone had quickly or carelessly tossed them there, defendant's DNA profile was consistent with that found on the gloves, and the gloves had the same color and distinctive markings as the gloves worn by the robber. Spence v. Commonwealth, 60 Va. App. 355, 727 S.E.2d 786, 2012 Va. App. LEXIS 221 (2012).

Sufficient evidence to support conviction as principal in the second degree. — Defendant's convictions, as a principal in second degree, of robbery, § 18.2-58, and use of a firearm in the commission of a felony, § 18.2-53.1, were proper because, as the "getaway" driver, defendant contributed to the execution of the robbery and his actions belied his claim that he was merely a bystander who knew nothing of the perpetrator's intent to rob; defendant spent the afternoon with the perpetrator, held the perpetrator's gun, drove the perpetrator to the parking lot where the victim was standing, and stopped the car "directly" in front of the victim. Defendant remained in the car in the driver's seat and watched the perpetrator get out of the car while carrying a gun, and it was reasonable to conclude that defendant knew what the perpetrator intended to do and assisted him by driving him directly in front of victim and waiting in the driver's seat until the perpetrator returned. Hayes v. Commonwealth, — Va. App. —, — S.E.2d —, 2009 Va. App. LEXIS 132 (Mar. 24, 2009).

Evidence sufficient to support conviction. — Defendant's convictions for first-degree murder and use of a firearm in the commission of a felony in violation of §§ 18.2-32 and 18.2-53.1 were appropriate because the jury was entitled to disbelieve defendant's assertion that she did not know that her boyfriend had a weapon when they entered the victim's home. Further, there was sufficient evidence of concert of action because defendant and her boyfriend arrived at the home of defendant's father knowing that they were forbidden to be there; they gained entrance through the back door; they were intent upon forcing her father to surrender the welfare checks; and when defendant's father refused, they pursued him up the stairs where he was shot and brutally beaten. Thomas v. Commonwealth, 279 Va. 131, 688 S.E.2d 220, 2010 Va. LEXIS 11, cert. denied, 131 S. Ct. 143, 178 L. Ed. 2d 8, 2010 U.S. LEXIS 6109 (U.S. 2010).

IV. PUNISHMENT.

Section aimed at punishment not reform. — This section is not a general recidivist statute, but a "specific recidivist" statute; this section imposes additional punishment for a subsequent conviction for the same offense; such statutes are aimed at punishment of specific behavior, not reform. Stubblefield v. Commonwealth, 10 Va. App. 343, 392 S.E.2d 197 (1990).

Where the offense for the predicate conviction was committed after the charged offense, this section was intended to impose additional punishment for a subsequent conviction for the same offense. Miller v. Commonwealth, 22 Va. App. 497, 471 S.E.2d 780 (1996).

This statute is recidivist in nature because it is aimed at punishment of specific behavior, not reform. Batts v. Commonwealth, 30 Va. App. 1, 515 S.E.2d 307 (1999).

No double jeopardy when multiple convictions and punishments obtained in same trial. — Even where a single act is the subject of multiple punishments, there is no double jeopardy violation when multiple convictions and punishments are obtained in a single trial if the General Assembly has clearly indicated its intent to impose multiple punishments. The statute's language plainly expresses the legislature's intent to impose an enhanced punishment on an accused when he uses a firearm in the commission of a felony. This intent and its deterrence policy is the same whether the felonies are committed against several victims, or as in this case, one person. Ballentine v. Commonwealth, No. 1457-89-3 (Ct. of Appeals May 7, 1991).

Convictions under this section and § 18.2-93 not double jeopardy. — In order to prove the offense pursuant to this section, the commonwealth must establish that the defendant used or displayed a gun in the commission of a robbery and the location of the robbery is irrelevant whereas, under § 18.2-93, the commonwealth must show that the defendant entered a bank while armed with a deadly weapon but evidence of use or display of the weapon is not an element of the crime and, therefore, convicting a defendant for use of a firearm in the commission of a robbery and for entry into a banking house while armed with a deadly weapon does not violate the double jeopardy clause. Collins v. Commonwealth,

No. 0253-00-1, 2001 Va. App. LEXIS 90 (Ct. of Appeals Feb. 27, 2001).

Concurrent sentences for multiple convictions. — Neither § 18.2-53.1 nor the mandatory minimum sentencing statute, § 18.2-12.1, prohibit a trial court from running multiple sentences imposed for convictions of § 18.2-53.1 concurrently with each other. To the extent that the holding in *Bullock v. Commonwealth*, 631 S.E.2d 334 (2006), is inconsistent, it is overruled. Brown v. Commonwealth, 284 Va. 538, 733 S.E.2d 638, 2012 Va. LEXIS 190 (2012).

Motion to withdraw guilty plea. — In a case in which defendant pled guilty to violating §§ 18.2-90, 18.2-47, 18.2-67.1 and 18.2-53.1, he argued unsuccessfully that the circuit court abused its discretion in denying his motion to withdraw his guilty pleas prior to sentencing; defendant failed to show a good faith basis for seeking to withdraw his guilty pleas. He was clearly aware of the potential range of punishments available to the court at the time he pled guilty; as such, the fact that the sentencing guidelines recommended a higher sentence than he had hoped did not constitute a good faith basis for rescinding his pleas. Mack v. Commonwealth, 2009 Va. App. LEXIS 417 (Sept. 22, 2009).

Applicability of enhanced punishment provisions. — The enhanced punishment provision of this section applied to three separate offenses committed on the same day and tried together. Ansell v. Commonwealth, 219 Va. 759, 250 S.E.2d 760 (1979).

The enhanced punishment provided by this statute is not geared to whether an accused has committed one or more acts, but rather, it is geared to the number of actual convictions suffered by an accused; thus, where several convictions result from the same act, each conviction is separate and distinct from the other. Flythe v. Commonwealth, 221 Va. 832, 275 S.E.2d 582 (1981).

Final sentencing order predicate to instruction on enhanced punishment. — A final sentencing order with respect to the prior prosecution is a necessary predicate to an instruction on the enhanced punishment provisions for a second or subsequent conviction; a jury's verdict in the prior prosecution is not a final conviction without the entry of the sentencing order and, therefore, cannot be used to establish the predicate first offense. Batts v. Commonwealth, 30 Va. App. 1, 515 S.E.2d 307 (1999).

Number of actual convictions and not how many acts committed. — The statute is geared to the number of actual convictions suffered by an accused and not how many acts the accused has committed. Ballentine v. Commonwealth, No. 1457-89-3 (Ct. of Appeals May 7, 1991).

Identity of offense and not act is dispositive. — Where defendant argued that each of the two criminal events, although comprised of several felonies, was continuous in nature, involving only a single victim and a single "criminal intent," and he, therefore, reasoned that punishment for successive and distinct firearm offenses arising from each component felony amounted to multiple punishments for the same offense, the court of appeals found no merit in defendant's argument. This section addresses itself not to the act or the incident, but to the offenses committed with a firearm. It is the identity of the offense and not of the act which is dispositive. Brown v. Commonwealth, No. 3084-96-1 (Ct. of Appeals Nov. 18, 1997).

Subsequent conviction defined. — Any conviction that follows a first conviction is a subsequent conviction within the purview of this section. Flythe v. Commonwealth, 221 Va. 832, 275 S.E.2d 582 (1981).

Conviction for use of firearm in killing of second victim as part of same act constituted second conviction. — Where the defendant was convicted under § 18.2-31 (g) (now § 18.2-31 7) for killing two persons as part of the same act or transaction and the evidence showed he shot both his victims, he committed a corresponding number of distinct firearms offenses in the commission of those killings. Accordingly, his conviction of the use of a firearm in the murder of the second victim constituted a second or subsequent conviction under this section. Morris v. Commonwealth, 228 Va. 206, 321 S.E.2d 633 (1984).

Multiple firearms convictions for commission of more than one felony against victim. — It is possible to commit more than one of the felonies listed in this section against one victim and to incur multiple firearm convictions as a result thereof. Goad v. Commonwealth, No. 0137-86-3 (Ct. of Appeals July 13, 1987).

No requirement of prior notice to defendant. — Even

though the Commonwealth failed to inform defendant that he was being charged as a second offender, defendant was validly convicted of use of firearm as a second offense; Ansell v. Commonwealth, 219 Va. 759, 250 S.E.2d 760 (1979), makes clear that this section has no requirement of prior notice to the defendant. Stubblefield v. Commonwealth, 10 Va. App. 343, 392 S.E.2d 197 (1990).

An indictment alleging an offense need not notify a defendant that he is being charged as a second or subsequent offender, because the essential purpose of the statute, deterrence through punishment, is achieved despite the lack of such a recitation. Thus, when defendant was charged with violating § 18.2-53.1 and had previously been convicted under the statute, it was not necessary for the indictment to notify him that he was being tried as a second or subsequent offender. Hillard v. Commonwealth, — Va. App. —, — S.E.2d —, 2006 Va. App. LEXIS 234 (Apr. 18, 2006).

Use of firearm in commission of abduction. — Where the defendant was convicted of robbery, the use of a firearm in the commission of robbery, and three counts of abduction, all arising out of the same robbery, the three counts of use of a firearm in the commission of abduction were clearly second or subsequent convictions. Scaggs v. Commonwealth, 5 Va. App. 1, 359 S.E.2d 830 (1987).

Indictment not required to charge second or subsequent offense. — Virginia law clearly provides that § 18.2-53.1 does not require the Commonwealth to charge in an indictment, for using a firearm in the commission of an enumerated felony, that the particular crime is a second or subsequent offense before the offender may be sentenced to the enhanced mandatory minimum penalty. Totten v. Commonwealth, — Va. App. —, — S.E.2d —, 2006 Va. App. LEXIS 178 (May 9, 2006).

Proof of prior conviction. — When a defendant is charged with violating § 18.2-53.1 and has previously been convicted under the statute, the Commonwealth need not prove a defendant's prior use of a firearm conviction during the guilt phase of trial; rather, the Commonwealth is permitted to introduce evidence at sentencing to prove that conviction. Accordingly, when the Commonwealth offered no evidence of the prior conviction during the guilt phase, but offered a certified copy of an order to prove the conviction at sentencing, there was no error. Hillard v. Commonwealth, — Va. App. —, — S.E.2d —, 2006 Va. App. LEXIS 234 (Apr. 18, 2006).

Existence of more than one conviction, not sequence of offenses, is what gives rise to enhanced punishment. — It is the existence of more than one conviction under the statute, not the sequence of offenses, which gives rise to the enhanced punishment. To the extent that the indictment alleges "the second or subsequent time while committing Armed Robbery," the allegation is surplusage. The purpose of an indictment is to inform the defendant of the charge against him, and any variance between the indictment and proof is not fatal where there is not prejudice to the defendant in preparing for his trial. The indictment fulfilled its function, and defendant suffered no prejudice. Goad v. Commonwealth, No. 0137-86-3 (Ct. of Appeals July 13, 1987).

The order in which the crimes are committed, the order in which the verdicts are returned, or the order in which the acts are alleged in the indictment are all irrelevant to second or subsequent convictions for firearm offenses. Goad v. Commonwealth, No. 0137-86-3 (Ct. of Appeals July 13, 1987).

This section addresses itself not to the act or incident, but to the offenses committed with a firearm and the convictions that result therefrom; where several convictions result from the same act, each conviction is separate and distinct from the other. Scaggs v. Commonwealth, 5 Va. App. 1, 359 S.E.2d 830 (1987).

Here, the defendant had been previously convicted in another county of violating this section at the time of sentencing for the charged offense. Therefore, the charged offense was a second or subsequent conviction and the trial court did not err by sentencing the defendant as a recidivist. Miller v. Commonwealth, 22 Va. App. 497, 471 S.E.2d 780 (1996).

Judges divested of discretion respecting punishment. — Because this statute's purpose is "to deter violent criminal conduct," it provides an "inflexible" penalty. Clearly, therefore, by prescribing a mandatory sentence, the General Assembly has divested trial judges of all discretion respecting punishment. In re Commonwealth, 229 Va. 159, 326 S.E.2d 695 (1985).

Notwithstanding the 2004 amendment to § 18.2-53.1, Green v. Commonwealth, 28 Va. App. 567, 507 S.E.2d 627 (1998), remains

valid and precludes the courts from applying § 16.1-272 to suspend any part of a mandatory minimum sentence imposed. Bullock v. Commonwealth, 48 Va. App. 359, 631 S.E.2d 334, 2006 Va. App. LEXIS 296 (2006).

Read in conjunction with § 18.2-12.1, this section expressly requires the court to impose the entire term of confinement and provides that the court shall not suspend the sentence in full or in part. Thus, a trial court may not set the mandatory minimum sentences imposed for multiple convictions under § 18.2-53.1 to run concurrently with each other. Bullock v. Commonwealth, 48 Va. App. 359, 631 S.E.2d 334, 2006 Va. App. LEXIS 296 (2006).

Sentencing of juvenile. — Even after the 2004 statutory amendments, the mandatory sentencing provisions of § 18.2-53.1 control over the juvenile sentencing options contained in subdivision A 1 of § 16.1-272 that allow suspension of an adult sentence. Commonwealth v. Brown, 2008 Va. App. LEXIS 517 (2008), aff'd in part and rev'd in part, 279 Va. 210, 688 S.E.2d 185, 2010 Va. LEXIS 9 (2010).

Convictions for using a firearm in the commission of robbery were clearly "ancillary crimes" requiring sentencing under subdivision A 1 of § 16.1-272 rather than subdivision A 2 of § 16.1-272, and the mandatory sentencing provisions of § 18.2-53.1 controlled over the juvenile sentencing options in § 16.1-272. Thus, defendants had to receive the mandatory minimum sentences. Commonwealth v. Brown, 2008 Va. App. LEXIS 517 (2008), aff'd in part and rev'd in part, 279 Va. 210, 688 S.E.2d 185, 2010 Va. LEXIS 9 (2010).

Juvenile defendant who was charged as an adult and pled guilty to five counts of use of a firearm in the commission of a felony, in violation of § 18.2-53.1, should have been sentenced to the mandatory minimum rather than sentenced to juvenile dispositions under § 16.1-272 because the statutes were in conflict, and § 18.2-53.1 was the more specific statute. Brown v. Commonwealth, 279 Va. 210, 688 S.E.2d 185, 2010 Va. LEXIS 9 (2010).

Multiple punishments did not violate double jeopardy clause. — The convictions and imposition of multiple punishments for capital murder, robbery and use of a firearm in the commission of a felony did not violate appellant's rights under the double jeopardy clause of the Fifth Amendment. Since those convictions and punishments did not violate the double jeopardy clause, his counsel was not ineffective for failing to raise the issue. Peterson v. Bass, 2 Va. App. 314, 343 S.E.2d 475 (1986).

Where defendant was indicted and convicted for the offense of capital murder and the separate offense of robbery during the commission of which he used a firearm, the prosecution and convictions for dual violations of this section were proper. Walton v. Commonwealth, No. 0900-85 (Ct. of Appeals Dec. 11, 1986).

Conviction in jury trial held proper where defendant found guilty of voluntary manslaughter. — Neither principles of double jeopardy or collateral estoppel were applicable in a single criminal jury trial, where defendant was found guilty of voluntary manslaughter but not murder, and did not bar his conviction for use of a firearm in the commission of murder. Wolfe v. Commonwealth, 6 Va. App. 640, 371 S.E.2d 314 (1988).

Inconsistent with verdict of guilty of involuntary manslaughter. — A finding that a defendant is guilty beyond a reasonable doubt of murder is a necessary element of the firearm offense, as charged under this section, and a finding by a jury that the defendant is guilty of the lesser offense of involuntary manslaughter is inconsistent with a guilty verdict under this section; the use of a firearm during the commission of involuntary manslaughter is not a criminal offense under this section. Gray v. Commonwealth, 28 Va. App. 227, 503 S.E.2d 252 (1998).

All defendants held responsible for shooting by one of them in course of robbery. — Where defendant was one of four men, acting in concert, who decided to rob the victim; they followed him, surrounded him, and accosted him; it then appeared to at least one of them that shooting the victim would be expedient for their common purpose, and that the shooting was done as an incident of that common purpose, each co-actor was criminally responsible for the shooting, even those who did not intend it or anticipate that it would occur. Because they shared the common intent to rob, they shared the common intent to commit all of the elements of robbery, an incidental probable consequence of which was the use of a weapon, including a firearm if one should be at hand. In such circumstances, each co-actor is responsible for the acts of the others, and may not interpose his personal lack of intent as a defense. Carter v. Commonwealth, 232 Va. 122, 348 S.E.2d 265 (1986).

Mandatory term of imprisonment. — Upon a conviction under § 18.2-53.1, the use of a firearm statute, a trial court may sentence a defendant only to a mandatory term of imprisonment of three years for the first conviction or a mandatory term of imprisonment of five years for a second or subsequent conviction. Hines v. Commonwealth, 59 Va. App. 567, 721 S.E.2d 792, 2012 Va. App. LEXIS 45 (2012).

Commitment under § 19.2-311 contrary to mandatory provisions of this section. — The sentencing alternatives under § 19.2-311 differ from those required by this section. Thus, a commitment under § 19.2-311 is contrary to the mandatory provision of this section. LaFleur v. Commonwealth, 6 Va. App. 190, 366 S.E.2d 712 (1988).

Court confirmed convictions for first-degree murder and use of a firearm in the commission of the murder where blood spatter analysis was proper expert testimony for which a sufficient evidentiary foundation was established. Smith v. Commonwealth, 265 Va. 250, 576 S.E.2d 465, 2003 Va. LEXIS 36 (2003).

Sentence to indeterminate commitment held improper. — The mandatory sentence required upon a conviction for the use of a firearm during the commission of a felony prevents a trial court from sentencing a person to an indeterminate commitment to the Department of Corrections. LaFleur v. Commonwealth, 6 Va. App. 190, 366 S.E.2d 712 (1988).

Sentence not improper. — Trial court had subject matter jurisdiction and did not err in sentencing defendant after defendant pled guilty to two counts of robbery and one count of using a firearm while committing a robbery; Apprendi did not apply because defendant's sentences for those offenses was within the statutory ranges set by the legislature. Barnes v. Commonwealth, — Va. App. —, — S.E.2d —, 2006 Va. App. LEXIS 506 (Nov. 7, 2006).

Trial court did not abuse its discretion in imposing a 43-year sentence against defendant, as said sentence was within the ranges set by the legislature and well below the total statutory maximum for the various felony offenses for which he was convicted. Clark v. Commonwealth, — Va. App. —, — S.E.2d —, 2008 Va. App. LEXIS 234 (May 13, 2008).

Sentence improper. — Judgment was reversed and the case was remanded for a new sentencing hearing on defendant's robbery, conspiracy, and wearing a mask in public convictions as the ends of justice exception in Va. Sup. Ct. R. 5A:18 applied because defendant was sentenced to a maximum total sentence of 33 years' in violation of § 19.2-295, when the jury imposed a maximum total sentence of 15 years of imprisonment. Gibbs v. Commonwealth, No. 1726-11-1, 2012 Va. App. LEXIS 324 (Oct. 16, 2012).

Trial court followed the clear mandate of subdivision C1 of § 18.2-374.1 in convicting defendant of six counts of production of child pornography, first offense, for taking six sexually explicit photographs within a two-minute window and sentenced defendant to six minimum terms to be served concurrently with each other as *Bullock v. Commonwealth*, 631 S.E.2d 334 (Va. App. 2006), was not a predicate for the application of stare decisis here as *Bullock's* holding was limited to the imposition of multiple mandatory minimum sentences under § 18.2-53.1, and § 18.2-53.1 specified that the punishment for violating the statute was to be separate and apart from, and was to be made to run consecutively with, any punishment received for the primary felony. Commonwealth v. Jefferson, 60 Va. App. 749, 732 S.E.2d 728, 2012 Va. App. LEXIS 323 (2012).

CIRCUIT COURT OPINIONS

Admissibility of evidence. — Trial court denied defendant's motion in limine to exclude evidence that defendant had an altercation with another person while defendant was incarcerated for premeditated murder and use of a firearm while committing a murder, and that altercation led to a charge and conviction for assault and battery; that evidence, plus evidence that defendant made incriminating statements regarding his crimes were relevant and probative, and were not unduly prejudicial. Commonwealth v. Wallace, 70 Va. Cir. 341, 2006 Va. Cir. LEXIS 32 (Portsmouth 2006).

Evidence insufficient. — Court vacated the finding of guilt on two counts of using a firearm in the commission of robbery where

neither the defendant nor his accomplice had ever uttered to their victims that either actually had a firearm, each victim was left to infer that the object he or she saw during the course of the robbery was an operational firearm, and while the "gun" in question was never found, the Commonwealth was unable to rebut the testimony of its own witness, the defendant's accomplice, that he and the defendant had in fact stolen a toy pistol and covered it with black tape to give it an authentic appearance. Commonwealth v. Ruiz, 64 Va. Cir. 431, 2004 Va. Cir. LEXIS 177 (Norfolk 2004).

§ 18.2-54. Conviction of lesser offenses under certain indictments.

On any indictment for maliciously shooting, stabbing, cutting or wounding a person or by any means causing him bodily injury, with intent to maim, disfigure, disable or kill him, or of causing bodily injury by means of any acid, lye or other caustic substance or agent, the jury or the court trying the case without a jury may find the accused not guilty of the offense charged but guilty of unlawfully doing such act with the intent aforesaid, or of assault and battery if the evidence warrants.

History.
Code 1950, § 19.1-251; 1960, c. 366; 1975, cc. 14, 15.

Michie's Jurisprudence.
For related discussion, see 9B M.J. Homicide, § 119.

CASE NOTES

On charge of malicious cutting, accused may be convicted of unlawful cutting. — On an indictment for malicious cutting and wounding with intent to maim, disfigure and kill, the defendant may be convicted of unlawful cutting and wounding with like intent, or of assault and battery, if the evidence warrants. Canada v. Commonwealth, 63 Va. (22 Gratt.) 899 (1872); Hoback v. Commonwealth, 69 Va. (28 Gratt.) 922 (1877); Stuart v. Commonwealth, 69 Va. (28 Gratt.) 950 (1877); Montgomery v. Commonwealth, 98 Va. 840, 36 S.E. 371 (1900).

Unlawful wounding is a lessor offense included under malicious wounding. Hewitt v. Commonwealth, 213 Va. 605, 194 S.E.2d 893 (1973).

But may not be convicted of malicious cutting under indictment for unlawful cutting. Hummer v. Commonwealth, 122 Va. 826, 94 S.E. 157 (1917).

It was error not to give assault and battery instruction where from defendant's testimony, the jury reasonably could have concluded that defendant acted only with the intent to do victim bodily harm, albeit with malice; jury should have received, in addition to the malicious wounding instruction given, an instruction giving them the opportunity to assess the evidence as it related to assault and battery, an offense that may be accompanied by malice, but does not require intent to maim, disfigure or kill. Boone v. Commonwealth, 14 Va. App. 130, 415 S.E.2d 250 (1992).

Applied in Jackson v. Commonwealth, 218 Va. 490, 237 S.E.2d 791 (1977).

§ 18.2-54.1. Attempts to poison.

If any person administers or attempts to administer any poison or destructive substance in food, drink, prescription or over-the-counter medicine, or otherwise, or poisons any spring, well, waterworks as defined in § 32.1-167, or reservoir of water with intent to kill or injure another person, he shall be guilty of a Class 3 felony.

History.

Code 1950, § 18.1-64; 1960, c. 358; 1975, cc. 14, 15; 1983, c. 129; 2006, c. 300.

Cross references.

As to adulteration of food, drink, drugs, cosmetics, etc., see § 18.2-54.2. As to alleging intent in indictment, see § 19.2-225.

Michie's Jurisprudence.

For related discussion, see 9B M.J. Homicide, § 37; 14B M.J. Poisons and Poisoning, §§ 1, 2.

CASE NOTES

Delivery of poison does not constitute an attempt to administer. — The mere delivery of poison by one person to another does not constitute an attempt to administer poison within the meaning of the statute because it is not such an act as is likely, in the natural course of events, to bring about the result desired. Hicks v. Commonwealth, 86 Va. 223, 9 S.E. 1024 (1889).

Indictment demurrable that alleges preparatory acts only. — An indictment, under this section, for an attempt to administer poison, that does not allege such acts as, in a legal sense, constitute an attempt to commit the offense charged, but only such as show preparation, is demurrable. Hicks v. Commonwealth, 86 Va. 223, 9 S.E. 1024 (1889).

Insanity defense of juvenile. — Defendant juvenile was not denied his equal protection rights under U.S. Const., amend. XIV, § 1 because he had no right in juvenile court to assert an insanity defense to attempting to poison his mother's tea with intent to kill or injure her in violation of § 18.2-54.1 as defendant suffered no disparate treatment as he had the same ability as an adult to assert an insanity defense under § 19.2-168 in the trial court, but he did not exercise his right under § 16.1-270 to be tried as adult and to assert the insanity defense available to him under the adult system. D.L.G. v. Commonwealth, 60 Va. App. 77, 724 S.E.2d 208, 2012 Va. App. LEXIS 123 (2012).

§ 18.2-54.2. Adulteration of food, drink, drugs, cosmetics, etc.; penalty.

Any person who adulterates or causes to be adulterated any food, drink, prescription or over-the-counter medicine, cosmetic or other substance with the intent to kill or injure any individual who ingests, inhales or uses such substance shall be guilty of a Class 3 felony.

History.

1983, c. 129.

Cross references.

As to administering or attempting to administer poisons, etc., in food, drink or medicine and poisoning of springs, wells or reservoirs, see § 18.2-54.1.

§ 18.2-55. Bodily injuries caused by prisoners, state juvenile probationers and state and local adult probationers or adult parolees.

A. It shall be unlawful for a person confined in a state, local or regional correctional facility as defined in § 53.1-1; in a secure facility or detention home as defined in § 16.1-228 or in any facility designed for the secure detention of juveniles; or while in the custody of an employee thereof to knowingly and willfully inflict bodily injury on:

1. An employee thereof, or

2. Any other person lawfully admitted to such facility, except another prisoner or person held in legal custody, or

3. Any person who is supervising or working with prisoners or persons held in legal custody, or

4. Any such employee or other person while such prisoner or person held in legal custody is committing any act in violation of § 53.1-203.

B. It shall be unlawful for an accused, probationer or parolee under the supervision of, or being investigated by, (i) a probation or parole officer whose powers and duties are defined in § 16.1-237 or § 53.1-145, (ii) a local pretrial services officer associated with an agency established pursuant to Article 5 (§ 19.2-152.2) of Chapter 9 of Title 19.2, or (iii) a local community-based probation officer associated with an agency established pursuant to Article 9 (§ 9.1-173 et seq.) of Chapter 1 of Title 9.1, to knowingly and willfully inflict bodily injury on such officer while he is in the performance of his duty, knowing or having reason to know that the officer is engaged in the performance of his duty.

Any person violating any provision of this section is guilty of a Class 5 felony.

History.

1975, cc. 14, 15; 1977, c. 553; 1982, c. 636; 1985, c. 508; 1996, c. 527; 1999, cc. 618, 658; 2001, cc. 818, 848; 2007, c. 133.

Law Review.

For article, "Legal Issues Involving Children," see 35 U. Rich. L. Rev. 741 (2001).

CASE NOTES

The specific intent to "knowingly and willfully inflict bodily injury" is an essential element of proof of a violation of this section. Seegars v. Commonwealth, 18 Va. App. 641, 445 S.E.2d 720 (1994).

"Bodily injury." — The burning of the eyes of a correctional officer which lasted for ten to fifteen minutes, requiring medical treatment, caused by prisoner who threw urine at the officer constituted "bodily injury" under the provisions of this section. Karnes v. Commonwealth, No. 0982-88-2 (Ct. of Appeals Dec. 19, 1989).

Instruction on lesser included offense required. — The jury could have found that while the defendant might not have had the specific intent to "knowingly and willfully inflict bodily injury" under this section, he was nonetheless guilty of the lesser included offense of misdemeanor assault and battery, and the jury should have been instructed on the lesser included offense. Kelly v. Commonwealth, No. 0495-96-4 (Ct. of Appeals Feb. 4, 1997).

Administrative punishment not bar to prosecution. — The Department of Correction's administrative hearing was not a judicial proceeding or prosecution and the administrative punishment for striking and injuring a corrections officer imposed by prison officials did not render the subsequent judicial proceeding under this section violative of the prohibition against double jeopardy. Wild v. Commonwealth, 18 Va. App. 716, 446 S.E.2d 626 (1994).

Applied in Williams v. Commonwealth, 21 Va. App. 616, 466 S.E.2d 754 (1996).

§ 18.2-55.1. Hazing of youth gang members unlawful; criminal liability.

It shall be unlawful to cause bodily injury by hazing (i) any member of a criminal street gang as defined in § 18.2-46.1, or (ii) a person seeking to become a member of a youth gang or criminal street gang. Any person found guilty of hazing is guilty of a Class 1 misdemeanor.

For the purposes of this section, *"hazing"* means to recklessly or intentionally endanger the health or safety of a person or to inflict bodily injury on a person in connection with or for the purpose of initiation, admission into or affiliation with or as a condition for continued membership in a youth gang or criminal street gang regardless of whether the person so endangered or injured participated voluntarily in the relevant activity.

History.
2004, c. 850; 2005, c. 843.

§ 18.2-56. Hazing unlawful; civil and criminal liability; duty of school, etc., officials.

It shall be unlawful to haze so as to cause bodily injury, any student at any school, college, or university.

Any person found guilty thereof shall be guilty of a Class 1 misdemeanor.

Any person receiving bodily injury by hazing shall have a right to sue, civilly, the person or persons guilty thereof, whether adults or infants.

The president or other presiding official of any school, college or university receiving appropriations from the state treasury shall, upon satisfactory proof of the guilt of any student hazing another student, sanction and discipline such student in accordance with the institution's policies and procedures. The institution's policies and procedures shall provide for expulsions or other appropriate discipline based on the facts and circumstances of each case. The president or other presiding official of any school, college or university receiving appropriations from the state treasury shall report hazing which causes bodily injury to the attorney for the Commonwealth of the county or city in which such school, college or university is, who shall take such action as he deems appropriate.

For the purposes of this section, *"hazing"* means to recklessly or intentionally endanger the health or safety of a student or students or to inflict bodily injury on a student or students in connection with or for the purpose of initiation, admission into or affiliation with or as a condition for continued membership in a club, organization, association, fraternity, sorority, or student body regardless of whether the student or students so endangered or injured participated voluntarily in the relevant activity.

History.
Code 1950, § 18.1-71; 1960, c. 358; 1975, cc. 14, 15; 2003, cc. 62, 67.

Law Review.
For annual survey article on legal issues involving children, see 38 U. Rich. L. Rev. 161 (2003).

§ 18.2-56.1. Reckless handling of firearms; reckless handling while hunting.

A. It shall be unlawful for any person to handle recklessly any firearm so as to endanger the life, limb or property of any person. Any person violating this section shall be guilty of a Class 1 misdemeanor.

B. If this section is violated while the person is engaged in hunting, trapping or pursuing game, the trial judge may, in addition to the penalty imposed by the jury or the court trying the case without a jury, revoke such person's hunting or trapping license and privileges to hunt or trap while possessing a firearm for a period of one to five years.

C. Upon a revocation pursuant to subsection B hereof, the clerk of the court in which the case is tried pursuant to this section shall forthwith send to the Department of Game and Inland Fisheries (i) such person's revoked hunting or trapping license or notice that such person's privilege to hunt or trap while in possession of a firearm has been revoked and (ii) a notice of the length of revocation imposed. The Department shall keep a list which shall be furnished upon request to any law-enforcement officer, the attorney for the Commonwealth or court in this Commonwealth, and such list shall contain the names and addresses of all persons whose license or privilege to hunt or trap while in possession of a firearm has been revoked and the court which took such action.

D. If any person whose license to hunt and trap, or whose privilege to hunt and trap while in possession of a firearm, has been revoked pursuant to this section, thereafter hunts or traps while in possession of a firearm, he shall be guilty of a Class 1 misdemeanor, and, in addition to any penalty imposed by the jury or the court trying the case without a jury, the trial judge may revoke such person's hunting or trapping license and privileges to hunt or trap while in possession of a firearm for a period of one year to life. The clerk of the court shall notify the Department of Game and Inland Fisheries as is provided in subsection C herein.

History.
1977, c. 194; 1985, c. 182; 1991, c. 384; 2010, c. 183; 2011, c. 684.

The 2010 amendments.
The 2010 amendment by c. 183, in subsection B, substituted "and privileges" for "or privilege"; and in subsection D, substituted "and privileges" for "or privilege," made related changes, and substituted "of one to five years" for "not to exceed five years."

The 2011 amendments.
The 2011 amendment by c. 684 substituted "for a period of one to five years" for "for a period of one year to life" in subsection B; and substituted "possession of a firearm for a period of one year to life" for "possession of a firearm for an additional period of one to five years" in the first sentence in subsection D.

Law Review.
For article reviewing recent developments and changes in legislation, case law, and Virginia Supreme Court Rules affecting civil litigation, "Civil Practice and Procedure," see 40 U. Rich. L. Rev. 95 (2005).

Michie's Jurisprudence.
For related discussion, see 9A M.J. Game and Game Laws, § 5; 20 M.J. Weapons, § 9.

CASE NOTES

Subsection A is not limited to activity of hunters; subsection B provides for additional penalties in cases where firearms are handled recklessly during hunting activities. Bailey v. Commonwealth, 5 Va. App. 331, 362 S.E.2d 750 (1987).

Where intentional violation of statute involves inherently dangerous act which is the proximate cause of the resulting homicide, the killing is involuntary manslaughter. Bailey v. Commonwealth, 5 Va. App. 331, 362 S.E.2d 750 (1987).

Violation resulting in death not necessarily involuntary manslaughter. — Every statutory violation of reckless handling of a firearm resulting in death does not constitute involuntary manslaughter. Darnell v. Commonwealth, 6 Va. App. 485, 370 S.E.2d 717 (1988).

Reckless handling of firearms may or may not equate to criminal negligence. — The recklessness involved in reckless handling of a firearm may or may not equate with the "recklessness" involved in criminal negligence, and the fact that a jury determines that a defendant violated the statute prohibiting the "reckless" handling of a firearm does not necessarily imply that they have also determined that he or she did so with a callous disregard for human life. Darnell v. Commonwealth, 6 Va. App. 485, 370 S.E.2d 717 (1988).

The meaning of "reckless" varies significantly depending on who uses it and in what circumstances, and the reckless handling of a firearm may not be limited to a handling so gross, wanton or culpable as to show a reckless disregard of human life. Luck v. Commonwealth, 30 Va. App. 36, 515 S.E.2d 325 (1999).

Negligence per se. — Where a hunter was sued for shooting appellant during a hunt, and as a result of that shooting had pled guilty to reckless handling of a firearm, the trial court erred in refusing to instruct the jury on negligence per se. Schlimmer v. Poverty Hunt Club, 268 Va. 74, 597 S.E.2d 43, 2004 Va. LEXIS 85 (2004).

Reckless handling. — Evidence was sufficient to show that defendant recklessly handled a firearm and in doing so endangered the spouse as the spouse's testimony showed that defendant, while angry and intoxicated, obtained the spouse's gun and fired two shots into the bedroom floor while the spouse was sitting in the nearby living room since the evidence showed the ammunition had a tendency to deflect and the spouse could have been harmed; also, defendant later apologized for having scared the spouse. Kirby v. Commonwealth, 264 Va. 440, 570 S.E.2d 832, 2002 Va. LEXIS 164 (2002).

Section 18.2-371.1 punished willful omissions, which require an awareness that defendant's conduct would cause or permit serious injury; where the evidence against defendant did not establish that he knew danger ensued from only ordering his son to put a gun away rather than taking it from him, and failed to establish defendant's knowledge and consciousness that an injury will result from the act done, his child abuse and reckless handling of a firearm convictions were reversed. Mangano v. Commonwealth, 44 Va. App. 210, 604 S.E.2d 118, 2004 Va. App. LEXIS 511 (2004).

Pointing of loaded gun at another. — Defendant's acts of intentionally removing the loaded gun from his pocket and holding it down in the direction of the victim who was lying on the ground no more than five to ten feet away constituted reckless handling of a firearm. Furthermore, under these circumstances it was clearly foreseeable that another could be seriously injured or killed if the gun was discharged. Consequently, defendant's violation of subsection A proximately caused the homicide. Bailey v. Commonwealth, 5 Va. App. 331, 362 S.E.2d 750 (1987).

Probable cause to arrest. — Court was unable to conclude that there was probable cause to arrest for reckless use of a firearm, under § 18.2-56.1, because the complaint indicated that the arrestee did not match the description of the individual identified by a neighbor, the arrestee lived approximately 300 yards from the neighbor's house, the arrestee had obviously just used his gun to shoot a rodent in his backyard, and his gun remained pointed toward the ground the entire time. Botkin v. Fisher, 2009 U.S. Dist. LEXIS 24554 (W.D. Va. Mar. 25, 2009).

Admissibility of perception expert testimony in hunting shooting. — Testimony by sensation and perception expert would have explained to the jury how the camouflage contributed to the possibility of misperception. Some jurors might not appreciate how the victim, being camouflaged and using a turkey call, and defendant, expecting a turkey, could combine to cause defendant reasonably to believe he saw a turkey. The jury might have wondered how defendant could have made such a mistake unless he was grossly, wantonly, and wilfully negligent. The expert testimony could have provided the jury with an explanation that the jury could have found to be a reasonable hypothesis of innocence. Therefore, the testimony would have assisted the jury in resolving an essential issue and should not have been rejected on the grounds that it would not assist the jury or was a matter of common knowledge. Farley v. Commonwealth, 20 Va. App. 495, 458 S.E.2d 310 (1995).

§ 18.2-56.2. Allowing access to firearms by children; penalty.

A. It shall be unlawful for any person to recklessly leave a loaded, unsecured firearm in such a manner as to endanger the life or limb of any child under the age of fourteen. Any person violating the provisions of this subsection shall be guilty of a Class 3 misdemeanor.

B. It shall be unlawful for any person knowingly to authorize a child under the age of twelve to use a firearm except when the child is under the supervision of an adult. Any person violating this subsection shall be guilty of a Class 1 misdemeanor. For purposes of this subsection, *"adult"* shall mean a parent, guardian, person standing in loco parentis to the child or a person twenty-one years or over who has the permission of the parent, guardian, or person standing in loco parentis to supervise the child in the use of a firearm.

History.
1991, c. 537; 1994, c. 832.

Michie's Jurisprudence.
For related discussion, see 20 M.J. Weapons, § 2.

CASE NOTES

Evidence insufficient to sustain conviction. — Section § 18.2-371.1 punished willful omissions, which require an awareness that defendant's conduct would cause or permit serious injury; where the evidence against defendant did not establish that he knew danger ensued from only ordering his son to put a gun away rather than taking it from him, and failed to establish defendant's knowledge and consciousness that an injury will result from the act done, his child abuse and reckless handling of a firearm convictions were reversed. Mangano v. Commonwealth, 44 Va. App. 210, 604 S.E.2d 118, 2004 Va. App. LEXIS 511 (2004).

§ 18.2-57. Assault and battery.

A. Any person who commits a simple assault or assault and battery is guilty of a Class 1 misdemeanor, and if the person intentionally selects the person against whom a simple assault is committed because of his race, religious conviction, color or national origin, the penalty upon conviction shall include a term of confinement of at least six months, 30 days of which shall be a mandatory minimum term of confinement.

B. However, if a person intentionally selects the person against whom an assault and battery resulting in bodily injury is committed because of his race, religious conviction, color or national origin, the person is guilty of a Class 6 felony, and the penalty upon conviction shall include a term of confinement of at least six months, 30 days of which shall be a mandatory minimum term of confinement.

C. In addition, if any person commits an assault or an assault and battery against another knowing or having reason to know that such other person is a judge, a magistrate, a law-enforcement officer as defined in subsection F, a correctional officer as defined in § 53.1-1, a person directly involved in the care, treatment, or supervision of inmates in the custody of the Department of Corrections or an employee of a local or regional correctional facility directly involved in the care, treatment, or supervision of inmates in the custody of the facility, a person directly involved in the care, treatment, or supervision of persons in the custody of or under the supervision of the Department of Juvenile Justice, an employee or other individual who provides control, care, or treatment of sexually violent predators committed to the custody of the Department of Behavioral Health and Developmental Services, a firefighter as defined in § 65.2-102, or a volunteer firefighter or any emergency medical services personnel member who is employed by or is a volunteer of an emergency medical services agency or as a member of a bona fide volunteer fire department or volunteer emergency medical services agency, regardless of whether a resolution has been adopted by the governing body of a political subdivision recognizing such firefighters or emergency medical services personnel as employees, engaged in the performance of his public duties, such person is guilty of a Class 6 felony, and, upon conviction, the sentence of such person shall include a mandatory minimum term of confinement of six months.

Nothing in this subsection shall be construed to affect the right of any person charged with a violation of this section from asserting and presenting evidence in support of any defenses to the charge that may be available under common law.

D. In addition, if any person commits a battery against another knowing or having reason to know that such other person is a full-time or part-time teacher, principal, assistant principal, or guidance counselor of any public or private elementary or secondary school and is engaged in the performance of his duties as such, he is guilty of a Class 1 misdemeanor and the sentence of such person upon conviction shall include a sentence of 15 days in jail, two days of which shall be a mandatory minimum term of confinement. However, if the offense is committed by use of a firearm or other weapon prohibited on school property pursuant to § 18.2-308.1, the person shall serve a mandatory minimum sentence of confinement of six months.

E. In addition, any person who commits a battery against another knowing or having reason to know that such individual is a health care provider as defined in § 8.01-581.1 who is engaged in the per-

formance of his duties as an emergency health care provider in an emergency room of a hospital or clinic or on the premises of any other facility rendering emergency medical care is guilty of a Class 1 misdemeanor. The sentence of such person, upon conviction, shall include a term of confinement of 15 days in jail, two days of which shall be a mandatory minimum term of confinement.

F. As used in this section:

"Judge" means any justice or judge of a court of record of the Commonwealth including a judge designated under § 17.1-105, a judge under temporary recall under § 17.1-106, or a judge pro tempore under § 17.1-109, any member of the State Corporation Commission, or of the Virginia Workers' Compensation Commission, and any judge of a district court of the Commonwealth or any substitute judge of such district court.

"Law-enforcement officer" means any full-time or part-time employee of a police department or sheriff's office that is part of or administered by the Commonwealth or any political subdivision thereof who is responsible for the prevention or detection of crime and the enforcement of the penal, traffic or highway laws of the Commonwealth, any conservation officer of the Department of Conservation and Recreation commissioned pursuant to § 10.1-115, any special agent of the Department of Alcoholic Beverage Control, conservation police officers appointed pursuant to § 29.1-200, and full-time sworn members of the enforcement division of the Department of Motor Vehicles appointed pursuant to § 46.2-217, and such officer also includes jail officers in local and regional correctional facilities, all deputy sheriffs, whether assigned to law-enforcement duties, court services or local jail responsibilities, auxiliary police officers appointed or provided for pursuant to §§ 15.2-1731 and 15.2-1733, auxiliary deputy sheriffs appointed pursuant to § 15.2-1603, police officers of the Metropolitan Washington Airports Authority pursuant to § 5.1-158, and fire marshals appointed pursuant to § 27-30 when such fire marshals have police powers as set out in §§ 27-34.2 and 27-34.2:1.

"School security officer" means an individual who is employed by the local school board for the purpose of maintaining order and discipline, preventing crime, investigating violations of school board policies and detaining persons violating the law or school board policies on school property, a school bus or at a school-sponsored activity and who is responsible solely for ensuring the safety, security and welfare of all students, faculty and staff in the assigned school.

G. "Simple assault" or "assault and battery" shall not be construed to include the use of, by any teacher, teacher aide, principal, assistant principal, guidance counselor, school security officer, school bus driver or school bus aide, while acting in the course and scope of his official capacity, any of the following: (i) incidental, minor or reasonable physical contact or other actions designed to maintain order and control; (ii) reasonable and necessary force to quell a disturbance or remove a student from the scene of a disturbance that threatens physical injury to persons or damage to property; (iii) reasonable and necessary force to prevent a student from inflicting physical harm on himself; (iv) reasonable and necessary force for self-defense or the defense of others; or (v) reasonable and necessary force to obtain possession of weapons or other dangerous objects or controlled substances or associated paraphernalia that are upon the person of the student or within his control.

In determining whether a person was acting within the exceptions provided in this subsection, due deference shall be given to reasonable judgments that were made by a teacher, teacher aide, principal, assistant principal, guidance counselor, school security officer, school bus driver, or school bus aide at the time of the event.

History.

1975, cc. 14, 15; 1994, c. 658; 1997, c. 833; 1999, cc. 771, 1036; 2000, cc. 288, 682; 2001, c. 129; 2002, c. 817; 2004, cc. 420, 461; 2006, cc. 270, 709, 829; 2008, c. 460; 2009, c. 257; 2011, cc. 230, 233, 374; 2013, cc. 698, 707, 711, 748, 782.

Cross references.

As to disarming a law-enforcement or correctional officer and penalty involved, see § 18.2-57.02. As to approval as an adoptive parent by a child-placing agency of an applicant who has been convicted of not more than one misdemeanor as set out in § 18.2-57 not involving abuse, neglect or moral turpitude, provided 10 years have elapsed, see § 63.2-1721 E. As to grant of waiver from disqualification to a family day home for an adult living in the home for a misdemeanor offense under § 18.2-57 or § 18.2-57.2 under certain circumstances, see § 63.2-1723.

Editor's note.

Acts 2008, c. 460, cl. 2, provides: "That the provisions of this act may result in a net increase in periods of imprisonment or commitment. Pursuant to § 30-19.1:4, the estimated amount of the necessary appropriation is $12,475 for periods of imprisonment in state adult correctional facilities and $0 for periods of commitment to the custody of the Department of Juvenile Justice."

Acts 2009, c. 257, cl. 2 provides: "That the provisions of this act may result in a net increase in periods of imprisonment or commitment. Pursuant to § 30-19.1:4, the estimated amount of the necessary appropriation is $13,810 for periods of imprisonment in state adult correctional facilities and is $0 for periods of commitment to the custody of the Department of Juvenile Justice."

Acts 2011, c. 230, cl. 2, provides: "That the provisions of this act may result in a net increase in periods of imprisonment or commitment. Pursuant to § 30-19.1:4, the estimated amount of the necessary appropriation is $32,029 for periods of imprisonment in state adult correctional facilities and is $0 for periods of commitment to the custody of the Department of Juvenile Justice."

Acts 2011, c. 374, cl. 2, provides: "That the provisions of this act may result in a net increase in periods of imprisonment or commitment. Pursuant to § 30-19.1:4, the estimated amount of the necessary appropriation is $12,818 for periods of imprisonment in state adult correctional facilities and cannot be determined for periods of commitment to the custody of the Department of Juvenile Justice."

Acts 2013, cc. 698 and 707, cl. 2 provides: "That the provisions of this act may result in a net increase in periods of imprisonment or commitment. Pursuant to § 30-19.1:4, the estimated amount of the necessary appropriation cannot be determined for periods of imprisonment in state adult correctional facilities; therefore, Chapter 3 of the Acts of Assembly of 2012, Special Session I, requires the Virginia Criminal Sentencing Commission to assign a minimum fiscal impact of $50,000. Pursuant to § 30-19.1:4, the estimated

amount of the necessary appropriation cannot be determined for periods of commitment to the custody of the Department of Juvenile Justice."

Acts 2013, c. 698, cl. 3 provides: "That the provisions of this act shall not become effective unless an appropriation of general funds effectuating the purposes of this act is included in a general appropriation act passed by the 2013 Session of the General Assembly, which becomes law."

Acts 2013, c. 698, cl. 4 provides: "That the General Assembly determines that the requirements of the third enactment of this act have been met."

Acts 2013, c. 711, cl. 2 provides: "That the provisions of this act may result in a net increase in periods of imprisonment or commitment. Pursuant to § 30-19.1:4, the estimated amount of the necessary appropriation is $7,680 for periods of imprisonment in state adult correctional facilities and cannot be determined for periods of commitment to the custody of the Department of Juvenile Justice."

Acts 2013, c. 748, cl. 2 provides: "That the provisions of this act may result in a net increase in periods of imprisonment or commitment. Pursuant to § 30-19.1:4, the estimated amount of the necessary appropriation cannot be determined for periods of imprisonment in state adult correctional facilities; therefore, Chapter 3 of the Acts of Assembly of 2012, Special Session I, requires the Virginia Criminal Sentencing Commission to assign a minimum fiscal impact of $50,000. Pursuant to § 30-19.1:4, the estimated amount of the necessary appropriation is $0 for periods of commitment to the custody of the Department of Juvenile Justice."

Acts 2013, c. 748, cl. 3 provides: "That the provisions of this act shall not become effective unless an appropriation of general funds effectuating the purposes of this act is included in a general appropriation act passed by the 2013 Session of the General Assembly, which becomes law."

Acts 2013, c. 748, cl. 4 provides: "That the General Assembly determines that the requirements of the third enactment of this act have been met."

Acts 2013, c. 782, cl. 2 provides: "Pursuant to § 30-19.1:4, the estimated amount of the necessary appropriation is at least $299,513 for periods of imprisonment in state adult correctional facilities and cannot be determined for periods of commitment to the custody of the Department of Juvenile Justice."

The 2008 amendments.

The 2008 amendment by c. 460, in subsection E, in the definition of "Law-enforcement officer," deleted "and" following "of this Commonwealth," and "§ 10.1-115," and inserted "and full-time sworn members of the enforcement division of the Department of Motor Vehicles appointed pursuant to § 46.2-217."

The 2009 amendments.

The 2009 amendment by c. 257 added "and police officers of the Metropolitan Washington Airports Authority pursuant to § 5.1-158" to the end of the second paragraph of subsection E and made a related change.

The 2011 amendments.

The 2011 amendment by c. 230 inserted "any special agent of the Department of Alcoholic Beverage Control" in the definition for "Law-enforcement officer" in subsection F.

The 2011 amendment by c. 233 added subsection E and redesignated the remaining subsections accordingly.

The 2011 amendment by c. 374, in subsection F, inserted "and fire marshals appointed pursuant to § 27-30 when such fire marshals have police powers as set out in §§ 27-34.2 and 27-34.2:1" at the end of the definition of "law-enforcement officer," and made stylistic changes.

The 2013 amendments.

The 2013 amendment by c. 698, in subsection C, substituted "any emergency medical services personnel member who is employed by or is a volunteer of an emergency medical services agency or as a" for "lifesaving or rescue squad member who is a," "emergency medical services agency" for "rescue or emergency medical squad" and "emergency medical services personnel" for "members."

The 2013 amendment by 707, in subsection C, substituted "in subsection F" for "hereinafter" following "defined," deleted "employed by the Department of Corrections" preceding "directly involved," inserted "of Corrections" preceding "a firefighter"; and made stylistic changes throughout.

The 2013 amendments by c. 711 inserted "a magistrate" in the first paragraph of subsection C.

The 2013 amendment by c. 748 inserted "or an employee of a local or regional correctional facility directly involved in the care, treatment, or supervision of inmates in the custody of the facility" near the middle of the first paragraph of subsection C.

The 2013 amendment by c. 782 substituted "is guilty" for "shall be guilty" throughout the section; and in the first paragraph of subsection C, substituted "as defined in subsection F, a" for "as defined hereinafter, a," deleted "employed by the Department of Corrections" following "§ 53.1-1, a person," and inserted "of Corrections, a person directly involved in the care, treatment, or supervision of persons in the custody of or under the supervision of the Department of Juvenile Justice, an employee or other individual who provides control, care, or treatment of sexually violent predators committed to the custody of the Department of Behavioral Health and Developmental Services."

Law Review.

For survey of Virginia criminal law for the year 1974-1975, see 61 Va. L. Rev. 1697 (1975). For article discussing the legislative history of sexual assault law reform in Virginia, see 68 Va. L. Rev. 459 (1982). For comment on spouse abuse in Virginia, see 17 U. Rich. L. Rev. 633 (1983). For note, "The Battered Woman Syndrome and Self-Defense: A Legal and Empirical Dissent," see 72 Va. L. Rev. 619 (1986). For survey on evidence in Virginia for 1989, see 23 U. Rich. L. Rev. 647 (1989). For article summarizing published Virginia criminal law decisions between July 1, 2002 and July 1, 2003, see 38 U. Rich. L. Rev. 87 (2003). For 2006 survey article, "Criminal Law and Procedure," see 41 U. Rich. L. Rev. 83 (2006). For 2006 survey article, "Family and Juvenile Law," see 41 U. Rich. L. Rev. 151 (2006). For article summarizing Virginia labor and employment law cases from 2007, see 43 U. Rich. L. Rev. 211 (2008). For annual survey article, "Criminal Law and Procedure," see 46 U. Rich. L. Rev. 59 (2011).

Michie's Jurisprudence.

For related discussion, see 2A M.J. Assault and Battery, §§ 5, 17; 5B M.J. Criminal Procedure, § 78; 13A M.J. Mobs, Riots and Lynchings, § 4.

CASE NOTES

Assault defined. — An assault is an attempt or offer, with force and violence, to do some bodily hurt to another by means calculated to produce the end if carried into execution, as by leveling a gun at another within a distance from which, supposing it to be loaded, the contents might injure, or any similar act accompanied with circumstances denoting an intention coupled with a present ability of using actual violence against the person of another. Stith v. Commonwealth, No. 1210-00-2, 2001 Va. App. LEXIS 245 (Ct. of Appeals May 8, 2001).

Assault as predicate offense. — Defendant's offense in the 1989 assault case met the elements under 18 U.S.C.S. § 921(a)(33)(A) as interpreted by the U.S. Supreme Court in Hayes; she was convicted of a misdemeanor offense under § 18.2-57, involving the element of force against her husband. Accordingly, that state conviction qualified as a predicate offense under 18 U.S.C.S. § 922(g)(9), making defendant's possession of the firearm unlawful; in turn, her false statement on the firearms form met the materiality element required for a conviction under § 922(a)(6). United States v. Holbrook, 613 F. Supp. 2d 745, 2009 U.S. Dist. LEXIS 39737 (W.D. Va. 2009).

Victim's knowledge or fear of threat not required. — One may commit an assault even though the victim is not aware of or frightened by any acts directed at him, provided the perpetrator has the specific intent to commit a battery and commits an overt act in furtherance of that intent. Stith v. Commonwealth, No. 1210-00-2, 2001 Va. App. LEXIS 245 (Ct. of Appeals May 8, 2001).

Common-law battery compared with sexual battery. — The legislature imposed a greater burden on the Commonwealth to prove sexual battery than to prove common-law battery, the latter requiring only a showing of nonconsensual touching. To prove the crime of sexual battery, the Commonwealth has to establish beyond a reasonable doubt that the accused touched the intimate parts of

the complaining witness, or that the complaining witness was forced to touch the intimate parts of the accused, with the intent to sexually molest, arouse or gratify any person. The acts must have been against the will of the complaining witness. Doss v. Commonwealth, No. 0019-85 (Ct. of Appeals July 30, 1986).

From the language of the statutes, the legislature intended some force other than merely that force required to accomplish the unlawful touching to be included within the statutorily defined criminal acts of either sexual battery or aggravated sexual battery. Where the complaining witness is at least 13 years old, unless some force is used to overcome the will of the complaining witness, the unlawful touching constitutes common-law assault and battery. Johnson v. Commonwealth, 5 Va. App. 529, 365 S.E.2d 237 (1988).

No authority to defer or dismiss charge. — Trial court did not have the inherent authority to either defer a finding of guilt, defer sentencing, or dismiss defendant's charge of feloniously assaulting a police officer, in violation of subsection C of § 18.2-57, where there was no statutory authorization for deferral or dismissal of the charge. Hernandez v. Commonwealth, 55 Va. App. 190, 684 S.E.2d 845, 2009 Va. App. LEXIS 509 (2009), rev'd, remanded, 2011 Va. LEXIS 11 (Va. 2011).

Justified shooting not assault and battery. — Police officer, who shot running handcuffed arrestee believed to be armed, was justified, therefore, arrestee's assault and battery claim against the officer was patently without merit. McLenagan v. Karnes, 27 F.3d 1002 (4th Cir.), cert. denied, 513 U.S. 1018, 115 S. Ct. 581, 130 L. Ed. 2d 496 (1994).

Must prove officer performing public duties. — The prosecution must prove a law-enforcement officer was performing his public duties to sustain a felony conviction under this section. Oulds v. Commonwealth, 260 Va. 210, 532 S.E.2d 33 (2000).

Self-defense argument prohibited. — Defendant's conviction for assault and battery of a law-enforcement officer in violation of subsection C of § 18.2-57 was appropriate because the trial court did not err in refusing to accept defendant's self-defense argument. Whether the police had probable cause to arrest defendant for disorderly conduct was immaterial because police did have probable cause to arrest him for public intoxication; thus, the police officers were acting properly when they arrested defendant and he had no legal justification for head-butting a law-enforcement officer who was carrying out his lawful duties. Davis v. Commonwealth, 2010 Va. App. LEXIS 209 (May 18, 2010).

Performance of public duties shown. — The evidence was sufficient to establish that the police officer assaulted by the defendant was engaged in his public duties where the off-duty officer was working as a security guard when he attempted to arrest the defendant for trespassing after the defendant had been warned to stay off of the premises. Oulds v. Commonwealth, 260 Va. 210, 532 S.E.2d 33 (2000).

Defendant was properly convicted of assault and battery on a police officer under subsection C of § 18.2-57 because while defendant claimed that the officer's public duties were limited to one mile outside the geographic borders of Virginia Beach under § 19.2-250, a law-enforcement mutual aid agreement permitted by § 15.2-1726 gave the officer authority to perform his public duties in Chesapeake based on the immediate threat to public safety presented by defendant's erratic driving. Rowe v. Commonwealth, 2008 Va. App. LEXIS 242 (May 20, 2008), aff'd, 277 Va. 495, 675 S.E.2d 161, 2009 Va. LEXIS 59 (2009).

Failure to challenge victims' status as firefighters. — Defendant failed to preserve her contention that the evidence was insufficient to support her convictions for felonies rather than misdemeanors when she failed to challenge the victims' statutory status as "firefighters." McClung v. Commonwealth, No. 0641-01-2, 2002 Va. App. LEXIS 391 (Ct. of Appeals July 16, 2002).

Federal law-enforcement officers. — Because Navy police officers were not employees of a Commonwealth or local law-enforcement agency, and because a reciprocal agreement under § 15.2-1726 did not incorporate itself into the assault and battery statute, the trial court erred as a matter of law in convicting defendant under subsection C of § 18.2-57. South v. Commonwealth, 47 Va. App. 247, 623 S.E.2d 419, 2005 Va. App. LEXIS 513 (2005) as to remanding the case for a new trial rather than remanding for new sentencing on the lesser included offense, see 2006 Va. LEXIS 56 (Va. 2006); .

Campus police officer of private university. — Campus

police officer at a private university is not a "law-enforcement officer" as defined by the language of subsection E of § 18.2-57. Guinyard v. Commonwealth, — Va. App. —, — S.E.2d —, 2007 Va. App. LEXIS 287 (July 31, 2007).

Metro Transit Police. — Officer of the Metro Transit Police meets the definition of a law-enforcement officer described in subsection E of § 18.2-57. Fox v. Commonwealth, 2009 Va. App. LEXIS 574 (Dec. 22, 2009).

Purely verbal threat insufficient. — A purely verbal threat with no appearance of an overt physical act does not constitute an assault. Therefore, where defendant only stated to officer from his jail cell that he was going to kill him before the new year and defendant did not make any physical movements while officer was in his presence at that time, defendant could not properly be found guilty of assault. Taylor v. Commonwealth, No. 0665-96-3 (Ct. of Appeals Apr. 22, 1997).

Racial epithets sufficient evidence of racial motivation. — Evidence was sufficient to sustain defendant's convictions of felonious and unlawful assault and battery on two victims selected because of their race in violation of subsection B of § 18.2-57 where defendant used racial epithets to initiate a conversation with the victims, and continued to use them during his unprovoked assault of them; defendant's use of racial epithets constituted sufficient evidence of the speaker's racial motivation in committing the crime, and the sentence was properly enhanced. Carfagno v. Commonwealth, 39 Va. App. 718, 576 S.E.2d 765, 2003 Va. App. LEXIS 77 (2003).

Specific intent to strike officer not required. — A person violates this section if he commits an assault or an assault and battery against another person, knowing or having reason to know that the other person is a law-enforcement officer engaged in the performance of his public duties; the statute does not require proof that the defendant intentionally selected the officer as a target. O'Connell v. Commonwealth, No. 0286-00-4, 2001 Va. App. LEXIS 42 (Ct. of Appeals Jan. 30, 2001).

Assault and battery as part of mob. — Once a group assembled comprises a mob, if the assault or battery which is committed is a simple assault or battery, then under this section, every person composing the mob becomes criminally culpable even though the member may not have actively encouraged, aided, or countenanced the act. Harrell v. Commonwealth, 11 Va. App. 1, 396 S.E.2d 680 (1990).

Assaulting a police officer. — To sustain a conviction under subsection C of this section, the Commonwealth must prove that the defendant assaulted an individual that he knew or had reason to know was a police officer engaged in the performance of his duties. Wright v. Commonwealth, No. 1019-99-1, 2000 Va. App. LEXIS 263 (Ct. of Appeals Apr. 11, 2000).

Based on defendant's actions and statements while drunk at county fair, trial court did not err in finding that he intended to strike police officer as officer assisted him into his friend's car. Stallings v. Commonwealth, No. 0609-99-3 (Ct. of Appeals Mar. 21, 2000).

Defendant's conviction was reinstated where he used force to resist an illegal detention, and was consequently indicted and convicted for assault and battery of a law-enforcement officer, in violation of subsection C of § 18.2-57. Commonwealth v. Hill, 264 Va. 541, 570 S.E.2d 805, 2002 Va. LEXIS 170 (2002).

Trial court's finding that defendant intended to spit on the officer, thereby committing an assault and battery, was not plainly wrong or without supporting evidence and had to be upheld on appeal. English v. Commonwealth, No. 0675-02-3, 2002 Va. App. LEXIS 789 (Ct. of Appeals Dec. 31, 2002).

Although defendant moved to strike the evidence, he failed to specifically assert any grounds upon which the alleged evidence was insufficient to prove that he was guilty of assaulting a police officer in violation of subdivision C of § 18.2-57; therefore, defendant was precluded from raising that issue, with regard to the particular element of intent, for the first time on appeal, and finding no "good cause" supporting defendant's failure to raise the specific issue, nor justification to apply the ends of justice exception in Va. Sup. Ct. R. 5A:18, the trial court's judgment convicting him of assaulting a police officer was affirmed. Bowman v. Commonwealth, No. 2169-02-1, 2003 Va. App. LEXIS 379 (Ct. of Appeals July 1, 2003).

Where defendant aimed and gunned a speeding vehicle at a police officer, the facts clearly established a malicious attempt, with force and violence, to harm the officer by means calculated to produce that end if carried into execution, in violation of subsection C of § 18.2-57. Zimmerman v. Commonwealth, 266 Va. 384, 585 S.E.2d 538, 2003 Va. LEXIS 89 (2003).

Although defendant did not possess a gun and had no actual ability to harm a police officer, defendant's conduct in pointing a finger at the officer and saying "pow," reasonably and unequivocally denoted an intention and the present ability to harm the officer; defendant's actions, therefore, constituted an assault. Carter v. Commonwealth, 41 Va. App. 448, 585 S.E.2d 848, 2003 Va. App. LEXIS 472 (2003).

Evidence that defendant who was a passenger in a vehicle that was stopped by a police officer moved his right hand from a position where it was hidden, extended his index finger and thumb, pointed his finger at the officer, and said "Pow" was sufficient to sustain defendant's conviction for assaulting a police officer. Carter v. Commonwealth, 42 Va. App. 681, 594 S.E.2d 284, 2004 Va. App. LEXIS 215 (2004), aff'd, — Va. —, 606 S.E.2d 839 (2005).

In an assault and battery case in which defendant urinated on a law-enforcement officer, sufficient evidence supported defendant's conviction. The fact finder could infer that defendant had enough control over his faculties and movements to avoid urinating directly onto the officer, if he in fact could not avoid the urge to urinate, and the jury could reasonably reject defendant's claim that he accidentally urinated directly on the officer while attempting to urinate on the side door of the jail transport van. Determan v. Commonwealth, — Va. App. —, — S.E.2d —, 2007 Va. App. LEXIS 308 (Aug. 21, 2007).

Defendant was properly convicted of assault upon a law-enforcement officer under subsection C of § 18.2-57 as defendant was not entitled to claim self-defense since defendant expressly disclaimed that defendant committed any violence when defendant pointed a butter knife at a police officer responding to a breaking and entering call; there was no evidentiary basis to support counsel's closing argument raising self-defense. Terry v. Commonwealth, — Va. App. —, — S.E.2d —, 2008 Va. App. LEXIS 386 (Aug. 12, 2008).

Evidence, including that defendant behaved belligerently in the presence of a magistrate and that the contact between defendant and the police officer occurred as the officer was attempting to escort defendant from the magistrate's office, was sufficient to find defendant committed assault and battery on an individual he knew was a law enforcement officer in violation of § 18.2-57. Holloway v. Commonwealth, 55 Va. App. 609, 687 S.E.2d 557, 2010 Va. App. LEXIS 32 (2010).

Insurance action for death following assault on officer. — In a civil action in which an insurer denied coverage under an accidental death policy because the insured's death arose out of the insured's commission of the felony of assaulting a police officer, the denial of coverage was improper since there was no basis to conclude that the insured knew or had reason to know that the persons in his house were police officers; only a few seconds passed between the insured being awakened, pointing his rifle, and being shot, and there was no evidence that the officers identified themselves or that the room was sufficiently lit to permit a visual identification. Cox v. Reliance Std. Life Ins. Co., — F.3d —, 2002 U.S. App. LEXIS 16216 (4th Cir. Aug. 13, 2002).

Where the circumstantial evidence established that defendant was carrying a weapon and had the ability to harm a police officer, the trial court could reasonably infer that defendant made an "attempt" to assault the officer in violation of subsection C of § 18.2-57, and the evidence was sufficient to support the conviction. Agee v. Commonwealth, 40 Va. App. 123, 578 S.E.2d 68, 2003 Va. App. LEXIS 151 (2003).

Persons engaged in performance of public duties. — Police officer who was off-duty and in full uniform, working as a private security guard, was "engaged in the performance of his public duties" when he was assaulted by defendant during course of defendant's arrest for trespassing. Oulds v. Commonwealth, No. 2062-98-3 (Ct. of Appeals Sept. 28, 1999).

When defendant knew a police officer, greeting him by his nickname, and assaulted the officer during an arrest, there was sufficient evidence to show that defendant knew the police officer was engaged in the performance of his public duty. Davis v. Commonwealth, 44 Va. App. 562, 605 S.E.2d 790, 2004 Va. App. LEXIS 618 (2004).

Defendant's conviction for assault did not bar, under double jeopardy, his subsequent conviction for abduction since the offense of assault and that of abduction each required proof of a fact that the other did not. Johnson v. Commonwealth, 13 Va. App. 515, 412 S.E.2d 731 (1992).

The fact that the same evidence, in whole or in part, was used in both trials does not give rise to a double jeopardy objection. Johnson v. Commonwealth, 13 Va. App. 515, 412 S.E.2d 731 (1992).

The conduct used to support the second prosecution was not the same conduct as that used to support the first conviction; evidence of separate, discrete conduct by the defendant supported each offense. Johnson v. Commonwealth, 13 Va. App. 515, 412 S.E.2d 731 (1992).

The assault required proof of an attempt or offer to do bodily harm through an unlawful show of force and violence; the abduction required proof of an asportation or detention by force, intimidation or deception. Johnson v. Commonwealth, 13 Va. App. 515, 412 S.E.2d 731 (1992).

Assault, therefore, required proof of force while abduction, although it may have been accomplished by force, did not require proof of force because it may also have been accomplished through intimidation or deception; abduction, on the other hand, required proof of asportation or detention while assault did not. Johnson v. Commonwealth, 13 Va. App. 515, 412 S.E.2d 731 (1992).

No double jeopardy violation. — Because defendant's commission of an assault and the brandishing of a firearm were two distinct and separate acts, separated in time and space, and each conviction was sustained by different evidence, his double jeopardy rights were not violated. Jackson v. Commonwealth, — Va. App. —, — S.E.2d —, 2008 Va. App. LEXIS 251 (May 27, 2008).

Force in resisting illegal arrest. — In case in which the Court of Appeals held that defendant could use reasonable force to resist an illegal detention and search, the Virginia Supreme Court reversed, holding in part that allowing resistance to a brief "pat down" search for weapons would only increase the danger and violence involved in those detentions. Commonwealth v. Hill, 264 Va. 541, 570 S.E.2d 805, 2002 Va. LEXIS 170 (2002).

Defendant's conviction was reinstated where he used force to resist an illegal detention, and was consequently indicted and convicted for assault and battery of a law-enforcement officer, in violation of subsection C of § 18.2-57. Commonwealth v. Hill, 264 Va. 541, 570 S.E.2d 805, 2002 Va. LEXIS 170 (2002).

Resistance to unlawful arrest or detention not shown. — Where the evidence was sufficient to convict defendant of felony assault on a police officer under § 18.2-57 because she approached the officer as she tried to issue a summons to another person, and defendant swatted the officer, and then, when he tried to arrest her, she dug her fingernails into his hand, causing cuts and scrapes, defendant's conduct was not justified on the basis of resisting an unlawful arrest or detention. Bennett v. Commonwealth, 2010 Va. App. LEXIS 12 (Jan. 12, 2010).

To sustain a conviction for assault, the evidence need only prove an attempt or offer, with force and violence, to do some bodily hurt to another. Adams v. Commonwealth, 33 Va. App. 463, 534 S.E.2d 347 (2000).

Slight injury sufficient. — When the injury is actually inflicted, a battery has been committed regardless of how small the injury might be. Adams v. Commonwealth, 33 Va. App. 463, 534 S.E.2d 347 (2000).

Touching by intangible substance. — For purposes of determining whether a battery has occurred, contact by an intangible substance such as light must be considered in terms of its effect on the victim; there need be no actual injury for a touching to have occurred but the evidence must prove that the substance made objectively offensive or forcible contact with the victim's person resulting in some manifestation of a physical consequence or corporeal hurt. Adams v. Commonwealth, 33 Va. App. 463, 534 S.E.2d 347 (2000).

A defendant was properly convicted of assault and battery on a police officer where the evidence established that the defendant hit the officer in the eye with a laser light, the officer felt a stinging sensation in his eye as a "red dot" hit him and the defendant admitted he did not get along with the officer and that he had been waving the laser in the area where the officer was standing; the defendant, by aiming the laser at the officer, effected a contact that caused bodily harm to the officer. Adams v. Commonwealth, 33 Va. App. 463, 534 S.E.2d 347 (2000).

Evidence properly admitted. — Fact that defendant threatened a deputy verbally 90 minutes after defendant's arrest and was still angry and combative at that time was probative of defendant's intent when defendant struck the deputy and took the deputy's weapon, and was more probative of defendant's intent than prejudicial; the evidence was properly admitted as defendant was being tried for assaulting the deputy and taking defendant's weapon under subsection C of § 18.2-57. Bufford v. Commonwealth, 2009 Va. App. LEXIS 335 (July 28, 2009).

Evidence held sufficient. — The evidence was sufficient to support the conviction of a teacher for assault and battery where the teacher had touched a female student on the nape of the neck on two occasions while making statements that the student understood to relate to sex. Perkins v. Commonwealth, 31 Va. App. 326, 523 S.E.2d 512 (2000).

Where burglar came within 12 to 18 inches of victim's face and, in a menacing and threatening manner, pointed his finger at victim within an inch of her face and threatened to kill her, he committed an "overt act" sufficient to constitute assault. Monteiro v. Commonwealth, No. 1842-98-1 (Ct. of Appeals Jan. 4, 2000).

Evidence that defendant resisted officers who were trying to put her in shackles, inter alia, by kicking her feet, and that she kicked an officer in the face was sufficient to sustain her conviction for felonious assault and battery of a law-enforcement officer. Morrison v. Commonwealth, No. 2645-00-2, 2002 Va. App. LEXIS 244 (Ct. of Appeals Apr. 23, 2002).

Evidence, which included expert testimony by two physicians, showed that defendant was the only adult present with the baby several hours prior to the appearance of her symptoms of limpness and unresponsiveness, and that the injuries were inflicted by defendant in rudeness or anger, with force and violence, and with reckless disregard for the baby's well-being. Given the totality of the evidence, the appellate court found that the jury was entitled to reject defendant's explanations of innocence and to conclude that the evidence was sufficient to establish she inflicted the baby's injuries with the requisite state of mind. Morton v. Commonwealth, No. 2677-02-2, 2004 Va. App. LEXIS 40 (Ct. of Appeals Jan. 28, 2004).

Defendant's conviction for assault was affirmed where, during a confrontation with a police officer, defendant raised her hand and threw a cup at the officer. Davis v. Commonwealth, No. 2638-03-2, 2004 Va. App. LEXIS 489 (Ct. of Appeals Oct. 12, 2004).

Where defendant, was in a car at night in an area of frequent drug activity, quickly raised previously concealed hand toward the police officer as if holding a gun, causing the officer to back away from defendant's vehicle, defendant was properly convicted of assault; present ability to inflict harm is not required for an assault conviction, as a well-founded fear or apprehension of harm, combined with an intent to instill that fear, is sufficient to support a conviction for common-law assault. Carter v. Commonwealth, 269 Va. 44, 606 S.E.2d 839, 2005 Va. LEXIS 5 (2005).

Evidence that defendant spit on an officer; kicked the dashboard, cursed, and screamed after his arrest; and threatened to kill both responding officers and their families, was sufficient to support an assault and battery on a law-enforcement officer conviction, as said circumstances abundantly supported a finding that defendant's acts were committed in a rude, insolent, or angry manner. Gilbert v. Commonwealth, 45 Va. App. 67, 608 S.E.2d 509, 2005 Va. App. LEXIS 60 (2005).

Evidence was sufficient to support defendant's assault and battery conviction where, during an argument with his wife, defendant grabbed a knife, advanced toward her, and when she fell, reached out, knife in hand, and cut the hand she raised defensively; defendant made no claim of accident in the emergency call or in his initial conversations with the police, which suggested that defendant's accident claim was a later contrivance. Walker v. Commonwealth, — Va. App. —, — S.E.2d —, 2005 Va. App. LEXIS 433 (Nov. 1, 2005).

In a prosecution for assault and battery of a firefighter, as the victim's uniform identified her as a firefighter, and defendant had reason to know she was a member of an emergency rescue team because he was strapped to a stretcher with an oxygen mask on his face, the evidence was sufficient to convict him of the charges.

Solorzano v. Commonwealth, — Va. App. —, — S.E.2d —, 2008 Va. App. LEXIS 39 (Jan. 22, 2008).

Because defendant's initial arrest for being drunk in public under § 18.2-388 was supported by probable cause, defendant had no right to resist; consequently, defendant was properly convicted of assault and battery of a police officer under § 18.2-57 when defendant later fled and then struggled with and injured a police officer. Brower v. Commonwealth, — Va. App. —, — S.E.2d —, 2008 Va. App. LEXIS 83 (Feb. 19, 2008).

Defendant's assault conviction was supported by the evidence as the totality of the evidence supported a finding that defendant assaulted the victim under the assimilated tort definition of assault by engaging in an overt act intended to place the victim in fear or apprehension of bodily harm and creating such reasonable fear or apprehension in the victim. Defendant blocked the victim's only path of escape by blocking the victim's bus with her car; she threatened the victim with her arms across her chest and her lips pursed; she stood outside the bus cursing at the victim until the principal came up, thereby blocking the victim's only reasonable means of escaping on foot; and she repeated this same conduct later the same afternoon. Clark v. Commonwealth, 54 Va. App. 120, 676 S.E.2d 332, 2009 Va. App. LEXIS 225 (2009), aff'd, 279 VA. 636, 691 S.E.2d 786, 2010 Va. LEXIS 58 (2010).

In a case in which defendant appealed his conviction for violating subsection C of § 18.2-57, he argued unsuccessfully that the evidence was insufficient to support his conviction for assault and battery of a law-enforcement officer. The evidence showed that defendant pushed a police officer and struck him in the chest with an elbow while defendant was trying to prevent the police officers from taking him into custody on outstanding arrest warrants; that was sufficient to establish that defendant acted with the intent to inflict physical harm on the officer in order to impede the officers' ability to subdue him. Montague v. Commonwealth, 278 Va. 532, 684 S.E.2d 583, 2009 Va. LEXIS 113 (2009), cert. denied, 130 S. Ct. 1537, 176 L. Ed. 2d 133, 2010 U.S. LEXIS 1456 (U.S. 2010).

Sufficient evidence supported an assault conviction where defendant threatened to harm a school bus driver and then, later the same day, approached and threatened the driver a second time because, viewing defendant's words and actions in the context of her first threat, defendant's approach to the door of the bus a second time was an act sufficient to create a reasonable fear or apprehension of bodily harm on the part of the driver. Clark v. Commonwealth, 279 Va. 636, 691 S.E.2d 786, 2010 Va. LEXIS 58 (2010).

Evidence was sufficient to convict defendant of assault and battery because after yelling at the victim, a postal service employee, to deliver her mail sooner, defendant grabbed the victim by the shoulder as she was walking away, and pulled her back so that they were standing face-to-face, while pulling the victim's hair and twisting her head and body. Parish v. Commonwealth, 56 Va. App. 324, 693 S.E.2d 315, 2010 Va. App. LEXIS 225 (2010).

Evidence that defendant engaged police in a 13-mile pursuit, during which time defendant was speeding and swerved from lane to lane to avoid the troopers, hit a cruiser but still drove erratically, and swerved and hit back of another cruiser, causing the trooper to hit a jersey wall was sufficient to support defendant's conviction for assault and battery of law-enforcement officer under subsection C of § 18.2-54. Bell v. Commonwealth, 2012 Va. App. LEXIS 114 (Apr. 10, 2012).

Insufficient evidence of assault. — The evidence was insufficient, as a matter of law, to prove that defendant assaulted two police officers in the course of a confrontation in which the defendant insisted that the officers leave his house, where both officers testified that the defendant was not armed and made no threatening gestures with his hands and, although the defendant stood within inches of the officers, he made no overt act or attempt to physically harm either officer during the time the officers remained in his home after being asked to leave. Bennett v. Commonwealth, 35 Va. App. 442, 546 S.E.2d 209, 2001 Va. App. LEXIS 262 (2001).

Sufficient evidence for assault and battery of law-enforcement officer. — Sufficient evidence supported defendant's conviction for assault and battery of a law-enforcement officer, under subsection C of § 18.2-57, because circumstantial evidence showed defendant's intent, as the evidence showed defendant purposely resisted officers who were attempting to arrest defendant and that defendant struck an officer as a natural consequence of defendant's voluntary actions. Montague v. Commonwealth, — Va. App. —, —

S.E.2d —, 2009 Va. App. LEXIS 15 (Jan. 20, 2009).

With regard to defendant's conviction for assault and battery of a law-enforcement officer, there was sufficient evidence to sustain the conviction based on the testimony of another officer who witnessed defendant smirk and wink after he initiated the handshake with the officer who was the victim and then, along with the victim officer, observed what appeared to be blood on the victim officer's palm. The fact finder properly inferred that defendant must have been aware of the incision on his hand and that he should likewise have been aware of the copious blood flow, especially since its substantial wetness was transferred at some point prior to the handshake from defendant's left hand to his right hand and, while defendant testified to the contrary, the fact finder was permitted to reject his testimony and conclude that defendant was aware that the handshake he initiated would convey his blood to the victim officer. Harman v. Commonwealth, 2009 Va. App. LEXIS 74 (Feb. 17, 2009).

Evidence that the officer was acting pursuant to a Mutual Aid Agreement signed by the officer's town and the town where the encounter took place gave the officer authority to enforce the laws and to perform the other duties of a law-enforcement officer in instances where an apparent, immediate threat to public safety precluded the option of deferring action to the local law-enforcement agency and was sufficient to support the finding that the officer was engaged in his public duties when defendant assaulted the officer. Rowe v. Commonwealth, 277 Va. 495, 675 S.E.2d 161, 2009 Va. LEXIS 59 (2009).

Although defendant argued that his conviction should be reversed because the trial court erred in refusing to instruct the jury on the statutory definition of law-enforcement officer and as a matter of law the victim was not a law-enforcement officer within the meaning of subsection E of § 18.2-57, the jury was instructed that proof that the victim was a police officer engaged in the performance of his public duties was essential for conviction, thus the refusal to give the instruction requested by defendant did not permit the jury to convict defendant without proof of an element of the offense. The Metro Transit Police were a police department administered by the Commonwealth pursuant to the Washington Metropolitan Area Transit Authority Compact. Fox v. Commonwealth, 2009 Va. App. LEXIS 574 (Dec. 22, 2009).

Defendant's conviction for assault and battery of a law-enforcement officer under subsection C of § 18.2-57 was appropriate because the evidence was sufficient. Defendant was intent upon preventing the officer from discharging her duties; he squeezed the officer's hand after she grabbed the bags; and he then rushed at the officer to destabilize her before he grabbed the box containing the contraband. Jimenez-Calcano v. Commonwealth, 2010 Va. App. LEXIS 135 (Apr. 6, 2010).

Conviction for assault and battery of a law-enforcement officer in the performance of his duties, in violation of subsection C of § 18.2-57, was appropriate because defendant was not under arrest, and the police officer did not exceed the scope of a limited detention by placing handcuffs on defendant's wrists, thereby precluding defendant from using force to resist the officer's limited detention. The officer decided to detain defendant for further investigation, and because of defendant's agitated state, the officer wanted to place defendant in the handcuffs for the safety of everybody who was at the scene. Cooper v. Commonwealth, 2011 Va. App. LEXIS 341 (Nov. 8, 2011).

Conviction as lesser-included offense of attempted capital murder. — Defendant could not challenge defendant's conviction for assault and battery of a law-enforcement officer, as a lesser included offense of attempted capital murder of a law-enforcement officer, where defendant advanced the assault charge as a more lenient alternative and maintaining that it was a lesser-included offense. Rowe v. Commonwealth, 277 Va. 495, 675 S.E.2d 161, 2009 Va. LEXIS 59 (2009).

Preliminary hearing. — Defendant's conviction for assaulting a police officer in violation of subsection C of § 18.2-57 had to stand, as defendant was not denied the right to a preliminary hearing on that charge after the district court terminated the charge by entering a nolle prosequi officer and the Commonwealth then obtained a direct indictment for the same offense and proved its case in the trial court. Since the case had been terminated in the district court once the nolle prosequi order was entered, defendant was not under actual arrest for that charge as required by the preliminary hearing statute, § 19.2-218, and not holding the preliminary hearing was a statutory, not constitutional, matter, which meant that defendant's due process rights under Va. Const., Art. I, § 11 were not violated because a preliminary hearing was not held. Wright v. Commonwealth, 52 Va. App. 690, 667 S.E.2d 787, 2008 Va. App. LEXIS 509 (2008).

Jury instructions. — Trial court properly refused to give defendant's requested instructions on the merger of charges of abduction and assault and battery, as the question whether the abduction was incidental to the assault and battery was a question of law, and the trial court determined that the evidence was sufficient to go to the jury on both charges. Mawyer v. Commonwealth, — Va. App. —, — S.E.2d —, 2006 Va. App. LEXIS 554 (Dec. 12, 2006).

Defendant was not entitled to a self-defense instruction because there was no evidence that the victim committed an overt act indicating immediate injury to justify or excuse the assault, and as there was no evidence that defendant was threatened with an immediate injury, a duress instruction was not warranted. Taylor v. Commonwealth, 2010 Va. App. LEXIS 114 (Mar. 23, 2010).

Exclusionary rule. — With regard to defendant's conviction for assault and battery of a law-enforcement officer and his contention on appeal that the trial court erred by ordering him to submit to a blood test since the officer alleged that defendant transferred blood onto him via a handshake, the court held that the exclusionary rule did not apply, therefore, the trial court did not err by denying defendant's motion to suppress the blood evidence. Application of the exclusionary rule was not the proper remedy since the defendant made no allegation of police misconduct relevant to the appeal. Harman v. Commonwealth, 2009 Va. App. LEXIS 74 (Feb. 17, 2009).

Suppression motion properly denied. — Defendant's suppression motion was properly denied, and the Fourth Amendment was not violated, where: (1) a police officer had a reasonable, articulable suspicion that defendant was the man who was wanted on the capias as defendant's physical characteristics and clothing matched the description provided by dispatch, and defendant was near the address provided by dispatch in the backseat of a taxi matching the description provided by dispatch; (2) the officer was justified in detaining defendant further as he gave obviously false identifying information; and (3) when defendant struck the officer, he had probable cause for the arrest, which led to the search incident to a lawful arrest in which the drugs were discovered. Jackson v. Commonwealth, No. 0628-02-3, 2003 Va. App. LEXIS 340 (Ct. of Appeals June 17, 2003).

Because defendant's post-entry assaults on police officers were outside the scope of the exclusionary rule, and because police officers had probable cause under § 19.2-81 to make a warrantless arrest for public intoxication, the Fourth Amendment was irrelevant; since defendant had no right to resist the arrest, defendant's motion to suppress was properly denied and defendant was properly convicted of assault and battery on a police officer and obstruction of justice. Messier v. Commonwealth, 2007 Va. App. LEXIS 201 (May 15, 2007).

In a case in which defendant had been convicted of violating §§ 18.2-250, 18.2-308.2, 18.2-308.4, and subsection C of § 18.2-57, he argued unsuccessfully that the Court of Appeals of Virginia erroneously upheld the circuit court's denial of his motion to suppress the evidence because his encounter with the police officers was not consensual, and the officers lacked any reasonable suspicion to believe that he was engaged in criminal activity. During the encounter, which lasted only two or three minutes, the police checked the "ban list" but did not engage in any show of force or use language indicating that defendant was required to remain at that location, the police did not tell him that he was required to stay, and defendant did not make any attempt to leave; instead, defendant remained in the area, standing about five feet away from the officers while his companion moved to sit on some nearby steps. Montague v. Commonwealth, 278 Va. 532, 684 S.E.2d 583, 2009 Va. LEXIS 113 (2009), cert. denied, 130 S. Ct. 1537, 176 L. Ed. 2d 133, 2010 U.S. LEXIS 1456 (U.S. 2010).

Improper admission of evidence not harmless. — In a rape and assault and battery prosecution, the incriminating statements defendant made after he unambiguously invoked his right to counsel were admitted over his objections. As it could not be said that his statements that he choked and knocked the alleged victim

down before having consensual sex with her did not contribute to his convictions or to the severity of his sentence, the error in admitting the statements was not harmless. Zektaw v. Commonwealth, 278 Va. 127, 677 S.E.2d 49, 2009 Va. LEXIS 76 (2009).

Applied in Edwards v. Commonwealth, 41 Va. App. 752, 589 S.E.2d 444, 2003 Va. App. LEXIS 637 (2003); Jones v. West, 46 Va. App. 309, 616 S.E.2d 790, 2005 Va. App. LEXIS 307 (2005).

CIRCUIT COURT OPINIONS

Mandatory minimum sentence for assaulting police officer precludes electronic incarceration. — Defendant was convicted of assaulting a police officer in violation of § 18.2-57, which carried a mandatory minimum term of six months; probation could not be imposed during this period. Therefore, she was not eligible for electronic incarceration under § 53.1-131.2. Commonwealth v. Wright, 72 Va. Cir. 215, 2006 Va. Cir. LEXIS 220 (Fairfax County 2006).

Metro Transit police officer. — Metro Transit police officer with whom defendant allegedly engaged in an altercation was a law-enforcement officer within the definition set forth in subsection E of § 18.2-57. Commonwealth v. Fox, 78 Va. Cir. 40, 2008 Va. Cir. LEXIS 177 (Fairfax County 2008).

OPINIONS OF THE ATTORNEY GENERAL

Rejection of plea agreement after amendment of arrest warrant. — A Juvenile and Domestic Relations District Court judge may reject a plea agreement when an arrest warrant is amended from assault and battery against a family or household member under § 18.2-57.2 to "simple" assault under this section. See opinion of Attorney General to The Honorable Michael J. Valentine, Judge, Juvenile and Domestic Relations District Court, Nineteenth Judicial District, 06-061 (3/22/07).

Enhanced punishment provisions. — Except for employees of the Department of Corrections involved in the care of inmates, and volunteers and members of a bona fide rescue squad who are engaged in the performance of their duties, medical personnel who provide care to inmates are not covered by the enhanced punishment provisions of § 18.2-57. See opinion of Attorney General to The Honorable Ralph S. Northam, Member, Senate of Virginia, 10-090, 2010 Va. AG LEXIS 58 (9/24/10).

§ 18.2-57.01. Pointing laser at law-enforcement officer unlawful; penalty.

If any person, knowing or having reason to know another person is a law-enforcement officer as defined in § 18.2-57, a probation or parole officer appointed pursuant to § 53.1-143, a correctional officer as defined in § 53.1-1, or a person employed by the Department of Corrections directly involved in the care, treatment or supervision of inmates in the custody of the Department engaged in the performance of his public duties as such, intentionally projects at such other person a beam or a point of light from a laser, a laser gun sight, or any device that simulates a laser, shall be guilty of a Class 2 misdemeanor.

History.
2000, c. 350.

§ 18.2-57.02. Disarming a law-enforcement or correctional officer; penalty.

Any person who knows or has reason to know a person is a law-enforcement officer as defined in

§ 18.2-57, a correctional officer as defined in § 53.1-1, or a person employed by the Department of Corrections directly involved in the care, treatment or supervision of inmates in the custody of the Department, who is engaged in the performance of his duties as such and, with the intent to impede or prevent any such person from performing his official duties, knowingly and without the person's permission removes a chemical irritant weapon or impact weapon from the possession of the officer or deprives the officer of the use of the weapon is guilty of a Class 1 misdemeanor. However, if the weapon removed or deprived in violation of this section is the officer's firearm or stun weapon as defined in § 18.2-308.1, he shall be guilty of a Class 6 felony. A violation of this section shall constitute a separate and distinct offense.

History.
2001, c. 2; 2007, c. 519.

CASE NOTES

Evidence properly admitted. — Fact that defendant threatened a deputy verbally 90 minutes after defendant's arrest and was still angry and combative at that time was probative of defendant's intent when defendant struck the deputy and took the deputy's weapon, and was more probative of defendant's intent than prejudicial; the evidence was properly admitted as defendant was being tried for assaulting the deputy and taking defendant's weapon under § 18.2-57.02. Bufford v. Commonwealth, 2009 Va. App. LEXIS 335 (July 28, 2009).

Evidence supported intent finding. — Evidence supported the finding that when defendant disarmed a deputy, defendant acted with the intent to impede or prevent the deputy from performing the deputy's official duties under § 18.2-57.02; that defendant might also have acted with the intent to avoid the pain or disability associated with being stunned did not negate a finding of an intent to disarm the deputy. Bufford v. Commonwealth, 2009 Va. App. LEXIS 335 (July 28, 2009).

§ 18.2-57.1. Repealed by Acts 1997, c. 833.

Editor's note.
This section was amended by Acts 1997, cc. 8 and 120. At the direction of the Code Commission, the repeal by Acts 1997, c. 833, was implemented. For comparable current provisions, see § 18.2-57, which was amended by Acts 1997, c. 833.

§ 18.2-57.2. Assault and battery against a family or household member; penalty.

A. Any person who commits an assault and battery against a family or household member is guilty of a Class 1 misdemeanor.

B. Upon a conviction for assault and battery against a family or household member, where it is alleged in the warrant, petition, information, or indictment on which a person is convicted, that such person has been previously convicted of two offenses against a family or household member of (i) assault and battery against a family or household member in violation of this section, (ii) malicious wounding in violation of § 18.2-51, (iii) aggravated malicious wounding in violation of § 18.2-51.2, (iv) malicious

bodily injury by means of a substance in violation of § 18.2-52, or (v) an offense under the law of any other jurisdiction which has the same elements of any of the above offenses, in any combination, all of which occurred within a period of 20 years, and each of which occurred on a different date, such person is guilty of a Class 6 felony.

C. Whenever a warrant for a violation of this section is issued, the magistrate shall issue an emergency protective order as authorized by § 16.1-253.4, except if the defendant is a minor, an emergency protective order shall not be required.

D. The definition of "family or household member" in § 16.1-228 applies to this section.

History.
1991, c. 238; 1992, cc. 526, 886; 1996, c. 866; 1997, c. 603; 1999, cc. 697, 721, 807; 2004, cc. 448, 738; 2009, c. 726.

Cross references.
As to presumption of no bail for illegal aliens charged with certain crimes, see § 19.2-120.1. As to grant of waiver from disqualification to a family day home for an adult living in the home for a misdemeanor offense under § 18.2-57 or § 18.2-57.2 under certain circumstances, see § 63.2-1723.

The 2009 amendments.
The 2009 amendment by c. 726 inserted "petition" near the beginning of subsection B.

Law Review.
For article, "Marriage Mimicry: The Law of Domestic Violence," see 47 Wm. & Mary L. Rev. 1841 (2006). For note, "Estop in the Name of Love: A Case for Constructive Marriage in Virginia," see 49 Wm. & Mary L. Rev. 973 (2007).

Michie's Jurisprudence.
For related discussion, see 9B M.J. Husband and Wife, § 87.

CASE NOTES

Household member. — Evidence was sufficient to support a conviction of assault and battery against a household member under subsection B of § 18.2-57.2 where defendant and the victim were in a long-term romantic relationship and where they lived together in a motel room when defendant assaulted the victim. Harris v. Commonwealth, No. 2818-01-4 CHIEF, 2002 Va. App. LEXIS 622 (Ct. of Appeals Oct. 15, 2002).

Circuit court has subject matter jurisdiction to determine parentage. — Florida circuit court does not err in exercising subject matter jurisdiction to determine parentage for purposes of adjudicating a defendant's guilt on charges of felony domestic assault, whether or not other proceedings involving a determination of parentage are then pending in the juvenile and domestic relations district court. Graves v. Commonwealth, 2007 Va. App. LEXIS 63 (Feb. 20, 2007).

Self-defense claim. — Defendant's conviction for third-offense assault and battery of a family or household member in violation of § 18.2-57.2 would stand because the evidence failed to show that he acted in self-defense; the evidence did not show that defendant struck his wife in self-defense after she struck him, but, rather, that defendant struck her in an act of retaliation after she struck him. Washington v. Commonwealth, — Va. App. —, — S.E.2d —, 2006 Va. App. LEXIS 517 (Nov. 14, 2006).

Self-defense claim fails where force is unreasonable in relation to threat. — Appellant's conviction for assault and battery was affirmed; the trial court found that when appellant struck appellant's roommate, the roommate was unarmed, and his claim of self-defense failed. There was sufficient evidence to support the trial court's finding that the amount of force used by appellant was unreasonable in relation to the threat presented. Davis v.

Commonwealth, — Va. App. —, — S.E.2d —, 2007 Va. App. LEXIS 5 (Jan. 9, 2007).

Relationship to federal law. — Phrase physical force meant violent force — that is, force capable of causing physical pain or injury to another person — and it was clear that physical force, so defined, was not an element of assault and battery under the well-established law of Virginia; therefore, defendant's conviction under § 18.2-57.2 was not, on its face, a misdemeanor crime of domestic violence under 18 U.S.C.S. § 922(g)(9) because the Virginia statute was not an offense that had, as an element, the use or attempted use of physical force. Applying the modified categorical approach, the record was devoid of any qualifying documentation to show defendant's conviction under § 18.2-57.2 was otherwise a misdemeanor crime of domestic violence under 18 U.S.C.S. § 922(g)(9). United States v. White, 606 F.3d 144, 2010 U.S. App. LEXIS 11026 (4th Cir. 2010).

Evidence that victim is "family or household member." — In a prosecution for domestic assault in violation of § 18.2-57.2, evidence that defendant considered the victim's child to be his daughter was sufficient to prove the victim was his "family or household member" as defined in § 16.1-228 and incorporated in § 18.2-57.2. As he made no timely request for court-ordered DNA testing, he could not challenge the sufficiency of the evidence on this issue on appeal. Graves v. Commonwealth, 2007 Va. App. LEXIS 63 (Feb. 20, 2007).

Jury instruction defining "cohabitation" denied. — Jury instruction defining "cohabitation" was properly denied where it incorrectly stated the applicable law and failing to inform the jury that it had to employ a totality of the circumstances analysis, and would have misled the jury that it could only consider the specific factors listed in the instruction. Cowell v. Commonwealth, No. 3198-03-1, 2005 Va. App. LEXIS 42 (Ct. of Appeals Feb. 1, 2005).

Sufficiency of evidence. — The evidence was sufficient to support the defendant's conviction where the victim, his estranged girlfriend, testified that the defendant followed her out of her trailer, pursued her until he caught her, picked her up and carried her away from where she was standing, while she pounded on him and yelled at him to let her down; although the victim suffered from memory loss, paranoia, and bi-polar disorder due to an earlier car crash, her testimony to the assault events did not seem inherently incredible and the trial court had been entitled to weigh these facts in determining the victim's credibility. Whitby v. Commonwealth, No. 1343-99-1, 2000 Va. App. LEXIS 551 (Ct. of Appeals July 25, 2000).

The evidence was sufficient to support defendant's assault conviction where defendant, after consuming alcohol and admittedly "frustrated" by his children's behavior, smacked his son on the face with a closed hand. Guzman v. Commonwealth, No. 2329-01-2, 2002 Va. App. LEXIS 361 (Ct. of Appeals June 25, 2002).

Certified copies of two domestic assault conviction orders entered by another circuit court which bore defendant's name, birth date, and social security number were sufficient to raise an inference that defendant was the person named in those orders, and the trial court which tried defendant on a charge of felony domestic assault did not err by overruling defendant's objections to the orders or by finding that defendant was the person named in the orders. Holmes v. Commonwealth, 41 Va. App. 690, 589 S.E.2d 11, 2003 Va. App. LEXIS 609 (2003).

Despite the absence of specific evidence that defendant threatened the victim, or evidence of his specific intent to harm her, upon his admission that he began to throw things at her in anger and that his action of doing so showed a reckless disregard for her safety, his assault and battery of a household member conviction was upheld. Trent v. Commonwealth, No. 1844-03-2, 2004 Va. App. LEXIS 263 (Ct. of Appeals June 8, 2004).

Victim's testimony that defendant grabbed her by her throat and pushed her down on a bed and that, on a second occasion, he snatched her up out of her bed and punched her in the nose, was sufficient to prove beyond a reasonable doubt that defendant assaulted and battered the victim in violation of § 18.2-57.2. Graves v. Commonwealth, 2007 Va. App. LEXIS 63 (Feb. 20, 2007).

Conviction of felony domestic assault and battery was not supported by sufficient evidence because the warrant at issue, which alleged that defendant assaulted a family or household member "on or about 06/11/2004 to 06/13/2004," failed to indicate any finding of guilt and thus, was insufficient to prove a prior conviction on any date; nonetheless, the lesser-included misdemeanor was proven beyond a reasonable doubt. Sensabaugh v. Commonwealth, — Va. App. —, — S.E.2d —, 2007 Va. App. LEXIS 199 (May 15, 2007).

Commonwealth's evidence was competent, not inherently incredible, and sufficient to prove beyond a reasonable doubt two counts of domestic assault and battery. The testimony of officers, the victim's written report, defendant's statements, and the physical evidence of the victim's injuries constituted sufficient evidence to permit a finding that defendant committed one of the counts. Cabrera-Sanchez v. Commonwealth, — Va. App. —, — S.E.2d —, 2008 Va. App. LEXIS 71 (Feb. 12, 2008).

When the relevant evidence showed that defendant threw a beer can at his girlfriend, with whom he had a relationship for over ten years, which hit her on the shoulder, such was sufficient to support defendant's conviction for assault and battery of a family member, in violation of § 18.2-57.2. Gray v. Commonwealth, — Va. App. —, — S.E.2d —, 2008 Va. App. LEXIS 224 (May 6, 2008).

Evidence was sufficient to convict defendant of assault on his domestic partner because the trial court was entitled to credit her testimony that, after they struggled over possession of her cell phone, defendant dragged her by her hair and upper body to the front door of their residence and threw her out. Pitt v. Commonwealth, 2009 Va. App. LEXIS 470 (Oct. 20, 2009).

Although the victim denied being hit by defendant, the testimony of a police officer, the victim's demeanor, defendant's statements, and the physical evidence of the victim's injury constituted sufficient circumstantial evidence to permit a finding that defendant committed domestic assault and battery on the victim in violation of § 18.2-57.2. Watkins v. Commonwealth, 2012 Va. App. LEXIS 147 (May 8, 2012).

Lesser offense. — Where the Commonwealth proved that defendant committed the felony charged, assault and battery on a family or household member, third offense, the trial court, sitting without a jury, had the power to convict defendant of something less but defendant had no right to have it do so. Kirby v. Commonwealth, No. 1788-01-3, 2002 Va. App. LEXIS 592 (Ct. of Appeals Oct. 8, 2002).

Applied in St. Clair v. Town of Rocky Mount, — F. Supp. 2d —, 2005 U.S. Dist. LEXIS 1376 (W.D. Va. Feb. 1, 2005); Epps v. Commonwealth, 59 Va. App. 71, 717 S.E.2d 151, 2011 Va. App. LEXIS 351 (2011).

OPINIONS OF THE ATTORNEY GENERAL

No authority to grant general continuance. — Courts do not have the authority to grant a "general continuance" as an alternative to § 18.2-57.3 for cases involving an adult charged with a first offense of assault and battery against a family or household member under this section. See opinion of Attorney General to the Honorable Michael J. Valentine, Judge, Juvenile and Domestic Relations District Court, 05-013 (3/31/05).

Rejection of plea agreement after amendment of arrest warrant. — A Juvenile and Domestic Relations District Court judge may reject a plea agreement when an arrest warrant is amended from assault and battery against a family or household member under this section to "simple" assault under § 18.2-57. See opinion of Attorney General to The Honorable Michael J. Valentine, Judge, Juvenile and Domestic Relations District Court, Nineteenth Judicial District, 06-061 (3/22/07).

§ 18.2-57.3. Persons charged with first offense of assault and battery against a family or household member may be placed on local community-based probation; conditions; education and treatment programs; costs and fees; violations; discharge.

A. When a person is charged with a violation of § 18.2-57.2, the court may defer the proceedings against such person, without a finding of guilt, and place him on probation under the terms of this section.

B. For a person to be eligible for such deferral, the court shall find that (i) the person was an adult at the time of the commission of the offense, (ii) the person has not previously been convicted of any offense under this article or under any statute of the United States or of any state or any ordinance of any local government relating to assault and battery against a family or household member, (iii) the person has not previously had a proceeding against him for violation of such an offense dismissed as provided in this section, (iv) the person pleads guilty to, or enters a plea of not guilty or nolo contendere and the court finds the evidence is sufficient to find the person guilty of, a violation of § 18.2-57.2, and (v) the person consents to such deferral.

C. The court may (i) where a local community-based probation services agency established pursuant to Article 9 (§ 9.1-173 et seq.) of Chapter 1 of Title 9.1 is available, order that the eligible person be placed with such agency and require, as a condition of local community-based probation, the person to successfully complete all treatment, education programs or services, or any combination thereof indicated by an assessment or evaluation obtained by the local community-based probation services agency if such assessment, treatment or education services are available; or (ii) require successful completion of treatment, education programs or services, or any combination thereof, such as, in the opinion of the court, may be best suited to the needs of the person.

D. The court shall require the person entering such education or treatment program or services under the provisions of this section to pay all or part of the costs of the program or services, including the costs of any assessment, evaluation, testing, education and treatment, based upon the person's ability to pay. Such programs or services shall offer a sliding-scale fee structure or other mechanism to assist participants who are unable to pay the full costs of the required programs or services.

The court shall order the person to be of good behavior for a total period of not less than two years following the deferral of proceedings, including the period of supervised probation, if available.

The court shall, unless done at arrest, order the person to report to the original arresting law-enforcement agency to submit to fingerprinting.

E. Upon fulfillment of the terms and conditions specified in the court order, the court shall discharge the person and dismiss the proceedings against him. Discharge and dismissal under this section shall be without adjudication of guilt and is a conviction only for the purposes of applying this section in subsequent proceedings. No charges dismissed pursuant to this section shall be eligible for expungement under § 19.2-392.2.

F. Upon violation of a term or condition of supervised probation or of the period of good behavior, the court may enter an adjudication of guilt and proceed as otherwise provided by law.

G. Notwithstanding any other provision of this section, whenever a court places a person on probation upon terms and conditions pursuant to this section, such action shall be treated as a conviction for purposes of Article 6.1 (§ 18.2-307.1 et seq.) of Chapter 7.

History.
1999, c. 963; 2000, c. 1040; 2003, cc. 33, 38; 2004, c. 377; 2007, c. 133; 2009, cc. 313, 347; 2013, c. 746.

Editor's note.
Acts 2004, cc. 972 and 980, cl. 6, provide: "That the Office of the Executive Secretary of the Supreme Court shall determine appropriate standards for the approval of education and treatment programs for persons accused of assault and battery against a family or household member pursuant to § 18.2-57.3 and arrange for such programs to be approved by an appropriate entity."
Acts 2013, c. 746, cl. 2 provides: "That the provisions of this act are declaratory of existing law."

The 2009 amendments.
The 2009 amendment by cc. 313 and 347 are identical, and rewrote this section.

The 2013 amendments.
The 2013 amendment by c. 746 substituted "for purposes of Article 6.1 (§ 18.2-307.1 et seq.) of Chapter 7" for "for purposes of § 18.2-308" at the end of subsection G.

CASE NOTES

Applied in Epps v. Commonwealth, 59 Va. App. 71, 717 S.E.2d 151, 2011 Va. App. LEXIS 351 (2011).

OPINIONS OF THE ATTORNEY GENERAL

Deferred finding of guilt relating to first-offense assault and battery under this section is not a "conviction" in the legal sense of the word, but such a deferred finding is considered a "conviction" for purposes of applying this section in subsequent proceedings and for purposes of § 18.2-308 during a defendant's term of probation; also, the person's "conviction" terminates once the person completes probation and the deferred finding proceedings against him are dismissed, except for purposes of applying this section in any future proceeding under the section. See opinion of Attorney General to The Honorable Gary A. Mills, Judge, Seventh Judicial District, 04-066 (9/27/04).

No authority to grant general continuance. — Courts do not have the authority to grant a "general continuance" as an alternative to this section for cases involving an adult charged with a first offense of assault and battery against a family or household member under § 18.2-57.2. See opinion of Attorney General to the Honorable Michael J. Valentine, Judge, Juvenile and Domestic Relations District Court, 05-013 (3/31/05).

§ 18.2-57.4. Reporting findings of assault and battery to military family advocacy representatives.

If any active duty member of the United States Armed Forces is found guilty of a violation of § 18.2-57.2 or § 18.2-57.3, the court shall report the conviction to family advocacy representatives of the United States Armed Forces.

History.
2004, c. 681.

ARTICLE 5.

ROBBERY.

§ 18.2-58. How punished.

If any person commit robbery by partial strangulation, or suffocation, or by striking or beating, or by other violence to the person, or by assault or otherwise putting a person in fear of serious bodily harm, or by the threat or presenting of firearms, or other deadly weapon or instrumentality whatsoever, he shall be guilty of a felony and shall be punished by confinement in a state correctional facility for life or any term not less than five years.

History.
Code 1950, § 18.1-91; 1960, c. 358; 1966, c. 361; 1975, cc. 14, 15, 605; 1978, c. 608.

Cross references.
For definition of "barrier crime" as including a conviction of robbery as set out in § 18.2-58, or an equivalent offense in another state, and prohibition against assisted living facilities, adult day care centers or child welfare agencies hiring for certain compensated employment persons who have committed such an offense, see §§ 63.2-1719, 63.2-1720. As to report to children's residential facility for which a background check is being performed on whether the applicant has ever been convicted of or is the subject of pending charges for various crimes, including robbery as set out in § 18.2-58, or an equivalent offense in another state, see § 63.2-1726.

Editor's note.
The above section is § 18.2-58 as enacted by Acts 1975, c. 605. Pursuant to § 30-152, it has been substituted for § 18.2-58 as enacted by Acts 1975, cc. 14 and 15.

Law Review.
For survey of Virginia criminal law and procedure for the year 1969-1970, see 56 Va. L. Rev. 1572 (1970). For survey of Virginia criminal law and procedure for the year 1970-1971, see 57 Va. L. Rev. 1438 (1971). For article on justification as a defense to crime, see 59 Va. L. Rev. 1326 (1973). For survey of Virginia criminal law for the year 1974-1975, see 61 Va. L. Rev. 1697 (1975). For note, "Predicate Offenses for First Degree Felony Murder in Virginia," see 57 Wash. & Lee L. Rev. 561 (2000).

Michie's Jurisprudence.
For related discussion, see 16 M.J. Robbery, §§ 2, 9.

CASE NOTES

I. General Consideration.
II. Elements of Common-Law Robbery.
III. Illustrative Cases.

I. GENERAL CONSIDERATION.

This section fixes the punishment for, but does not define, the crime of robbery; consequently, the Supreme Court looks to the common law for its definition. Pierce v. Commonwealth, 205 Va. 528, 138 S.E.2d 28 (1964); Pettus v. Peyton, 207 Va. 906, 153 S.E.2d 278 (1967); Durham v. Commonwealth, 214 Va. 166, 198 S.E.2d 603 (1973).

The crime of robbery in Virginia is not defined by statute. This section fixes the punishments for robbery, but the definition of the crime is found in the common law. Johnson v. Commonwealth, 209 Va. 291, 163 S.E.2d 570 (1968).

Robbery is a common-law crime in Virginia, although its punishment is prescribed by this section. Pritchard v. Commonwealth, 225 Va. 559, 303 S.E.2d 911 (1983).

Although the punishment for robbery is fixed by statute, the offense is not statutorily defined, and the court must look to the common law for its definition. Robbery at common law is defined as the taking, with intent to steal, of the personal property of another, from his person or in his presence, against his will, by violence or intimidation. George v. Commonwealth, 242 Va. 264, 411 S.E.2d 12 (1991), cert. denied, 503 U.S. 973, 112 S. Ct. 1591, 118 L. Ed. 2d 308 (1992).

When a statute prescribes a maximum imprisonment penalty and the sentence does not exceed that maximum, the sentence will not be overturned as being an abuse of discretion. West v. Commonwealth, No. 1146-91-1 (Ct. of Appeals Jan. 19, 1993).

"Unit of prosecution" for double jeopardy purposes. — Because the essential character of both this section and common-law robbery is violence against a person for the purpose of theft, the appropriate "unit of prosecution" for double jeopardy purposes is determined by the number of persons from whose possession property is taken separately by force or intimidation. Jordan v. Commonwealth, 2 Va. App. 590, 347 S.E.2d 152 (1986).

Convictions under this section and § 18.2-93 not double jeopardy. — Convictions for both robbery and entry of a banking house with the intent to commit larceny while armed with a deadly weapon did not violate the double jeopardy clause. Hill v. Commonwealth, 2 Va. App. 683, 347 S.E.2d 913 (1986).

Multiple punishments did not violate double jeopardy clause. — The convictions and imposition of multiple punishments for capital murder, robbery and use of a firearm in the commission of a felony did not violate appellant's rights under the double jeopardy clause of the Fifth Amendment. Since those convictions and punishments did not violate the double jeopardy clause, his counsel was not ineffective for failing to raise the issue. Peterson v. Bass, 2 Va. App. 314, 343 S.E.2d 475 (1986).

Armed robbery trial not barred by first degree murder conviction. — See Harrison v. Commonwealth, 220 Va. 188, 257 S.E.2d 777 (1979).

Conviction for both robbery and carjacking allowed. — The Commonwealth is clearly permitted to try and convict an offender of both robbery and carjacking where the evidence supports convictions for those crimes. Brown v. Commonwealth, 37 Va. App. 507, 559 S.E.2d 415, 2002 Va. App. LEXIS 88 (2002).

Robbery is not an incidental, probable consequence of an assault. — Robbery pursuant to § 18.2-58 is not an incidental, probable consequence of an assault; robbery requires a completely different type of wrongdoing: stealing. McMorris v. Commonwealth, 276 Va. 500, 666 S.E.2d 348, 2008 Va. LEXIS 91 (2008).

Double jeopardy. — Court of Appeals erred in reversing defendant's conviction of grand larceny of a person, in violation of § 18.2-95, due to defendant's earlier acquittal of robbery, charged pursuant to this section, as proof of violence or intimidation was required in a robbery prosecution, but not for grand larceny from the person, and proof of the value of the property stolen was required in a prosecution for grand larceny from the person, but not for robbery; hence, double jeopardy did not bar prosecution on the grand larceny charge upon a robbery acquittal. Commonwealth v. Hudgins, 269 Va. 602, 611 S.E.2d 362, 2005 Va. LEXIS 37 (2005), reversing 43 Va. App. 219, 597 S.E.2d 221 (2004); overruling Jones v. Commonwealth, 218 Va. 757, 240 S.E.2d 658 (1978).

Where defendant pled guilty to conspiracy to commit robbery, § 18.2-22, defendant's subsequent indictment for robbery, in violation of § 18.2-58, did not violate double jeopardy because each statute required proof of an element that the other did not. Williams v. Commonwealth, 2010 Va. App. LEXIS 382 (Sept. 28, 2010).

Where defendant pled guilty to an amended indictment for conspiracy to commit robbery, § 18.2-22, and the amendment occurred because defendant entered the plea, defendant's subsequent indictment for robbery did not violate double jeopardy. Williams v. Commonwealth, 2010 Va. App. LEXIS 382 (Sept. 28, 2010).

Plea agreement. — Although defendant was originally indicted for robbery in violation of § 18.2-58, and defendant pled guilty to an amended indictment for conspiracy to commit robbery, § 18.2-22, the Commonwealth was free to seek a new indictment for robbery when defendant failed to comply with a condition of the plea agreement that defendant would cooperate fully in the prosecution of a codefendant. Williams v. Commonwealth, 2010 Va. App. LEXIS 382 (Sept. 28, 2010).

Common-law indictment is good. — A "robbery" under this section differs in no respect from a robbery purely at the common law; hence, if an indictment would be good as a common-law indictment, it is good also under this section. Houston v. Commonwealth, 87 Va. 257, 12 S.E. 385 (1890). See Brookman v. Commonwealth, 151 Va. 522, 145 S.E. 358 (1928).

Robbery and crime defined in § 18.2-53.1 are separate offenses. — The common-law crime of robbery and the crime defined in § 18.2-53.1 (use or display of a firearm in committing certain felonies) are separate and distinct offenses for double jeopardy purposes. Jones v. Commonwealth, 218 Va. 18, 235 S.E.2d 313 (1977).

And have different elements as matter of law. — The crime of robbery and the crime of using a firearm in committing robbery have different elements as a matter of law, although they may have common elements as a matter of fact, since the "gist" of robbery is the taking and carrying away of the personal property of another, not necessarily by the use of a firearm, whereas the "gist" of § 18.2-53.1 is the use of a firearm in situations where it is likely that weapons may be used to injure victims of robbery or bystanders. Jones v. Commonwealth, 218 Va. 18, 235 S.E.2d 313 (1977).

The crime of robbery as defined at common law involves a forceful taking "by violence or intimidation" but such force need not be by means of the use or threat of presenting a firearm. Robbery may be committed in many ways, such as by partial strangulation or suffocation, or by striking or beating with the fist or other less dangerous devices. Jones v. Commonwealth, 218 Va. 18, 235 S.E.2d 313 (1977).

To convict a defendant on a charge of using or displaying a weapon in the commission of a felony under § 18.2-53.1, requires proof of a different element and evidence additional to that required for the offense of robbery. The use of a firearm is not one of the essential elements of the underlying felony. Jones v. Commonwealth, 218 Va. 18, 235 S.E.2d 313 (1977).

Jury instructions accurately stated the law. — Trial court's taking instruction accurately stated the law regarding the taking element of the robbery given that the robbery victim asported the money from a safe under the command of defendant. Furthermore, it was not error for the trial court to have refused an instruction on circumstantial evidence regarding the taking of the money because the Commonwealth of Virginia did not rely on circumstantial evidence, but, instead, relied on the direct evidence that the robbery victim asported the money under the command of defendant. El-Shabazz v. Commonwealth, 2012 Va. App. LEXIS 99 (Apr. 3, 2012).

Sentence. — The import of § 19.2-295 is that the jury, upon determining a petitioner's guilt of robbery, has to set the sentence between the statutory limits for robbery as set forth in this section. Roman v. Parrish, 328 F. Supp. 882 (E.D. Va. 1971).

Trial court had subject matter jurisdiction and did not err in sentencing defendant after defendant pled guilty to two counts of robbery and one count of using a firearm while committing a robbery; Apprendi did not apply because defendant's sentences for those offenses was within the statutory ranges set by the legislature. Barnes v. Commonwealth, — Va. App. —, — S.E.2d —, 2006 Va. App. LEXIS 506 (Nov. 7, 2006).

No error in denying concurrent sentence. — Given that the record on appeal adequately demonstrated that the sentencing judge correctly understood his discretion and sentenced defendant within the lawful scope of that discretion, the Court of Appeals of Virginia declined to apply the ends of justice exception to Va. Sup. Ct. R. 5A:18. As a result, no error resulted in the denial of defendant's request for a concurrent sentence. Scalf v. Commonwealth, 2008 Va. App. LEXIS 230 (May 13, 2008).

Applied in Goode v. Commonwealth, 217 Va. 863, 234 S.E.2d 239 (1977); Clay v. Commonwealth, 30 Va. App. 254, 516 S.E.2d 684 (1999); Hoyt v. Commonwealth, 44 Va. App. 489, 605 S.E.2d 755, 2004 Va. App. LEXIS 599 (2004); Goode v. Commonwealth, 52 Va. App. 380, 663 S.E.2d 532, 2008 Va. App. LEXIS 331 (2008); Rowland v. Commonwealth, 281 Va. 396, 707 S.E.2d 331, 2011 Va. LEXIS 60 (2011); Newton v. Commonwealth, 2011 Va. App. LEXIS 212 (June 28, 2011).

II. ELEMENTS OF COMMON-LAW ROBBERY.

This section is silent on the elements of robbery and merely provides how the crime, when committed under given circum-

stances, shall be punished. Falden v. Commonwealth, 167 Va. 542, 189 S.E. 326 (1937).

While fixing the punishment by this section, Virginia has never codified the elements of common-law robbery. Cox v. Commonwealth, 218 Va. 689, 240 S.E.2d 524 (1978).

It does not change the common-law essentials of the crime. At common-law robbery is defined as the taking, with intent to deprive the owner permanently, of personal property, from his person or in his presence, against his will, by violence or intimidation. Ayres v. Commonwealth, 157 Va. 897, 161 S.E. 888 (1932); Smyth v. White, 195 Va. 169, 77 S.E.2d 454 (1953).

Robbery, at common law, as defined by text writers, is the felonious and forcible taking from the person of another of goods or money to any value, by violence or putting in fear. Houston v. Commonwealth, 87 Va. 257, 12 S.E. 385 (1890); Falden v. Commonwealth, 167 Va. 542, 189 S.E. 326 (1937).

Robbery at common law is defined as the taking, with intent to steal, of the personal property of another, from his person or in his presence, against his will, by violence or intimidation. Mason v. Commonwealth, 200 Va. 253, 105 S.E.2d 149 (1958); Whitley v. Cunningham, 205 Va. 251, 135 S.E.2d 823 (1964); Pierce v. Commonwealth, 205 Va. 528, 138 S.E.2d 28 (1964); Pettus v. Peyton, 207 Va. 906, 153 S.E.2d 278 (1967); Johnson v. Commonwealth, 209 Va. 291, 163 S.E.2d 570 (1968); Mitchell v. Commonwealth, 213 Va. 149, 191 S.E.2d 261 (1972); Durham v. Commonwealth, 214 Va. 166, 198 S.E.2d 603 (1973); Hunt v. Haga, 368 F. Supp. 527 (W.D. Va. 1973); Johnson v. Commonwealth, 215 Va. 495, 211 S.E.2d 71 (1975); Jones v. Commonwealth, 218 Va. 18, 235 S.E.2d 313 (1977); Bunch v. Commonwealth, 225 Va. 423, 304 S.E.2d 271, cert. denied, 464 U.S. 977, 104 S. Ct. 414, 78 L. Ed. 2d 352 (1983), 505 U.S. 1230, 112 S. Ct. 3056, 120 L. Ed. 2d 922 (1992).

Robbery is a common-law crime in this State, and while this section regulates the punishment, it does not attempt to define robbery, but leaves the crime as it was defined at common law. Houston v. Commonwealth, 87 Va. 257, 12 S.E. 385 (1890); Brookman v. Commonwealth, 151 Va. 522, 145 S.E. 358 (1928); Maxwell v. Commonwealth, 165 Va. 860, 183 S.E. 452 (1936); Jones v. Commonwealth, 172 Va. 615, 1 S.E.2d 300 (1939); Haughey v. Smyth, 187 Va. 320, 46 S.E.2d 419 (1948).

Robbery in Virginia is common-law robbery. Dove v. Peyton, 343 F.2d 210 (4th Cir. 1965); Johnson v. Commonwealth, 215 Va. 495, 211 S.E.2d 71 (1975).

All common-law elements must exist. — To constitute the crime of robbery in Virginia, all of the elements essential at common law must exist. Fleming v. Commonwealth, 170 Va. 636, 196 S.E. 696 (1938).

No statute in Virginia defines robbery, and to constitute robbery all of the elements essential at common law must exist. Mason v. Commonwealth, 200 Va. 253, 105 S.E.2d 149 (1958).

All elements of the common-law offense must be proved beyond a reasonable doubt in order to establish that a robbery has occurred. Mitchell v. Commonwealth, 213 Va. 149, 191 S.E.2d 261 (1972).

Robbery is an offense against the person. Whitley v. Cunningham, 205 Va. 251, 135 S.E.2d 823 (1964); Johnson v. Commonwealth, 215 Va. 495, 211 S.E.2d 71 (1975); Pritchard v. Commonwealth, 225 Va. 559, 303 S.E.2d 911 (1983).

Violence must be directed at person of victim. — The element of violence is related to the violence or intimidation directed at the person of the victim not violence used on the object taken. In the absence of evidence of physical contact or a struggle with the victim, there is no violence used in the taking of a purse. Henderson v. Commonwealth, No. 3017-99-1, 2000 Va. App. LEXIS 809 (Ct. of Appeals Dec. 12, 2000).

The distinctive elements of robbery are: (1) the use of violence, or the threat thereof, against the victim; and (2) the theft of property from his person or in his presence. Briley v. Commonwealth, 221 Va. 532, 273 S.E.2d 48 (1980), cert. denied, 451 U.S. 1031, 101 S. Ct. 3022, 69 L. Ed. 2d 400 (1981).

The principal elements of robbery, a crime against the person of the victim, are the taking, the intent to steal, and the violence (or intimidation). Definitionally, there is a temporal correlation among these elements. The violence must occur before or at the time of the taking. The intent to steal and the taking must coexist. And the offense is not robbery unless the animus furandi (intent to steal) was conceived before or at the time the violence was committed. Branch v. Commonwealth, 225 Va. 91, 300 S.E.2d 758 (1983).

Elements of robbery are the taking, with intent to steal, of the personal property of another, from his person or in his presence, against his will, by violence or intimidation. Pritchard v. Commonwealth, 225 Va. 559, 303 S.E.2d 911 (1983).

The essential element of violence must precede or be concomitant with the taking of property from the person or presence of the owner. Bunch v. Commonwealth, 225 Va. 423, 304 S.E.2d 271, cert. denied, 464 U.S. 977, 104 S. Ct. 414, 78 L. Ed. 2d 352 (1983), 505 U.S. 1230, 112 S. Ct. 3056, 120 L. Ed. 2d 922 (1992).

In order to sustain a robbery conviction, the commonwealth has the burden of proving beyond a reasonable doubt the elements of robbery, which include a taking, with intent to steal, of the personal property of another, from his person or in his presence, against his will, by violence or intimidation which precedes or is concomitant with the taking. Henderson v. Commonwealth, No. 3017-99-1, 2000 Va. App. LEXIS 809 (Ct. of Appeals Dec. 12, 2000).

A conviction for robbery requires proof beyond a reasonable doubt that the defendant took property from the victim by force, threats or violence and that the intent to steal co-existed with the act of force. Abraham v. Commonwealth, 32 Va. App. 22, 526 S.E.2d 277 (2000).

Robbery is larceny from the person, or in his presence, by violence or intimidation. Comer v. Commonwealth, 211 Va. 246, 176 S.E.2d 432 (1970).

Restraint in attempted robbery may not be abduction. — Defendant may not be convicted of both abduction and attempted robbery unless the detention committed in the act of abduction is separate and apart from, and not merely incidental to, the restraint employed in the commission of the attempted robbery. Bell v. Commonwealth, No. 0318-02-1, 2003 Va. App. LEXIS 373 (Ct. of Appeals July 1, 2003).

A store empty of persons cannot be robbed. Crawford v. Commonwealth, 217 Va. 595, 231 S.E.2d 309 (1977).

Robbery must be accomplished by violence or putting in fear. — Under the authorities the taking in common-law robbery must be accomplished by violence to the person who theretofore had the property in his possession (on his person or in his presence), or must be accomplished by putting such person in fear of immediate injury to his person. Mason v. Commonwealth, 200 Va. 253, 105 S.E.2d 149 (1958).

Where the owner of personal property, or another having custody or constructive possession of the same, interposes himself to prevent a thief from taking the property and the force and violence used to overcome the opposition to the taking is concurrent or concomitant with the taking, the thief's action constitutes robbery. Durham v. Commonwealth, 214 Va. 166, 198 S.E.2d 603 (1973).

In the commission of robbery, the property must be taken by force and violence, not necessarily from the owner, but from any person in possession thereof whose right of possession is superior to that of the robber. Johnson v. Commonwealth, 215 Va. 495, 211 S.E.2d 71 (1975).

Violence or force requires a physical touching or violation of the victim's person; the touching or violation necessary to prove the offense may be indirect but cannot result merely from the force associated with the taking. Henderson v. Commonwealth, No. 3017-99-1, 2000 Va. App. LEXIS 809 (Ct. of Appeals Dec. 12, 2000).

In a case in which the Commonwealth appealed the Court of Appeals of Virginia's reversal of defendant's convictions for violating §§ 18.2-58 and 18.2-53.1, the evidence was insufficient to support the circuit court's factual findings, to establish that a store department lead was intimidated, or to support the circuit court's judgment convicting defendant of robbery and use of a firearm in the commission of robbery. In the end, about all that the Commonwealth was left with was the robber's eye contact with the department lead and the latter's testimony that he stopped because there was a weapon involved and that gave him some concern. Commonwealth v. Anderson, 278 Va. 419, 683 S.E.2d 536, 2009 Va. LEXIS 86 (2009).

Which must precede or be concomitant with taking. — The violence of putting in fear, to constitute the essential element in robbery, must precede, or be concomitant with, the taking of the property from the person or presence of the owner. No violence, no excitation of fear, resorted to merely for the purpose of retaining a possession already acquired, or to effect escape, will, in point of time, supply the element of force or intimidation, an essential

ingredient of the offense. Mason v. Commonwealth, 200 Va. 253, 105 S.E.2d 149 (1958).

The violence, in order to constitute an essential element of robbery, must precede or be concomitant with the appropriation of the property from the person or presence of the owner. Patterson v. Commonwealth, 222 Va. 653, 283 S.E.2d 212 (1981).

Defendant is properly found guilty of robbery and use of a firearm in the commission of a robbery where, after the proprietor of a service station fills his tank with gasoline at his request, defendant intimidates the proprietor with a firearm. Use of the firearm subdues the proprietor's ability to resist and enables defendant to convert his custody of the gasoline into possession by carrying the goods away in violation of the condition of prompt payment, with the intent to steal. The use of force thus precedes the conversion and enables defendant to obtain possession. Pritchard v. Commonwealth, 225 Va. 559, 303 S.E.2d 911 (1983).

To establish a robbery, the act of violence or intimidation employed must precede or be concomitant with the taking; if the violence or intimidation preceded or was concomitant with the taking, the offense of robbery is established, but if the taking was accomplished before the violence toward or intimidation of the victim, then it was not robbery. Gary v. Commonwealth, No. 1099-00-3, 2001 Va. App. LEXIS 202 (Ct. of Appeals Apr. 17, 2001).

The evidence was sufficient to establish a robbery where the defendant had taken a wallet from the victim's purse but had not yet left the premises when he was discovered by the victim and another person, at which time he pulled out a gun; it was logical and reasonable to infer that the defendant's intention changed from the commission of larceny to robbery when, in order to accomplish his original purpose, he used force to overcome the interference with his asportation of the property. Gary v. Commonwealth, No. 1099-00-3, 2001 Va. App. LEXIS 202 (Ct. of Appeals Apr. 17, 2001).

The violence used does not need to be great or cause any actual harm to the victim; tapping the victim on the shoulder and jerking her around is sufficient violence to support a robbery conviction even though the victim isn't knocked down. Henderson v. Commonwealth, No. 3017-99-1, 2000 Va. App. LEXIS 809 (Ct. of Appeals Dec. 12, 2000).

But violence for purposes of retaining possession does not suffice. — No violence or excitation of fear, resorted to merely for the purpose of retaining a possession already acquired, or to effect escape, will, in point of time, supply the element of force or intimidation, an essential element of robbery. Gary v. Commonwealth, No. 1099-00-3, 2001 Va. App. LEXIS 202 (Ct. of Appeals Apr. 17, 2001).

Timing. — For theft by violence or intimidation to constitute robbery, the intent to steal must exist at the time of the violence or intimidation. Shepperson v. Commonwealth, 19 Va. App. 586, 454 S.E.2d 5 (1995).

Such acts concurrent with larceny may indicate intent to commit robbery. — Where the putting in fear and violence of the owner were concurrent or concomitant with the larceny or attempt to commit larceny, those acts may indicate an intent to commit, or an attempt to commit, robbery. Durham v. Commonwealth, 214 Va. 166, 198 S.E.2d 603 (1973).

The fear of bodily harm must result from the words or conduct of the accused, rather than the temperamental timidity of the victim. Harris v. Commonwealth, 3 Va. App. 519, 351 S.E.2d 356 (1986).

But threats of violence are not indispensable. — Threats of violence or bodily harm are not an indispensable ingredient of intimidation. It is only necessary that the victim actually be put in fear of bodily harm by the willful conduct or words of the accused. Harris v. Commonwealth, 3 Va. App. 519, 351 S.E.2d 356 (1986).

Victim's fear is not judged by objective standard. — There is no requirement in Virginia that the "fear" induced by the defendant's intimidating words or conduct be judged by an objective standard of reasonableness. Harris v. Commonwealth, 3 Va. App. 519, 351 S.E.2d 356 (1986).

Robbery continues while violence and trespass continues. — Where the violence against the victim and the trespass to his property combine in a continuing, unbroken sequence of events, the robbery itself continues as well for the same period of time. Briley v. Commonwealth, 221 Va. 532, 273 S.E.2d 48 (1980), cert. denied, 451 U.S. 1031, 101 S. Ct. 2022, 69 L. Ed. 2d 400 (1981).

Theft of property is a trespass upon the rights of the

owner therein for as long as he is deprived of the use thereof; he retains legal possession of the goods stolen even when they are in the actual possession of the thief. Briley v. Commonwealth, 221 Va. 532, 273 S.E.2d 48 (1980), cert. denied, 451 U.S. 1031, 101 S. Ct. 3022, 69 L. Ed. 2d 400 (1981).

But robbery includes the offense of larceny. Dove v. Peyton, 343 F.2d 210 (4th Cir. 1965).

Larceny, robbery distinguished. — If appellant killed victim intending to steal his property, the theft was robbery. If appellant killed victim only for a purpose unrelated to theft, and as an after thought decided to steal his property, the theft was larceny. Shepperson v. Commonwealth, 19 Va. App. 586, 454 S.E.2d 5 (1995).

Where the victim was violently flung around as defendant forcefully pulled the victim's purse from the victim's hands and arm, the conduct was sufficiently violent to support a burglary conviction rather than a larceny conviction. Taylor v. Commonwealth, No.0735-02-1, 2003 Va. App. LEXIS 117 (Ct. of Appeals Mar. 4, 2003).

Malicious wounding is not a lesser included offense of robbery. Walker v. Commonwealth, 14 Va. App. 203, 415 S.E.2d 446 (1992).

Brandishing not a lesser included offense. — Given that robbery did not require the use of a firearm, and brandishing did not require the taking of property, but required pointing or brandishing a firearm, it was clear that robbery could be committed without brandishing and brandishing could be committed without the taking of property. Morris v. Commonwealth, 45 Va. App. 181, 609 S.E.2d 92, 2005 Va. App. LEXIS 79 (2005).

The accused may be found guilty of larceny under an indictment for robbery. Dove v. Peyton, 343 F.2d 210 (4th Cir. 1965).

And is liable to conviction as a criminal receiver. — The accused in an indictment for robbery is apprised of his liability to conviction as a criminal receiver. Dove v. Peyton, 343 F.2d 210 (4th Cir. 1965).

The robber must have a fraudulent intent, and must intend to deprive the owner permanently of his property. Pierce v. Commonwealth, 205 Va. 528, 138 S.E.2d 28 (1964).

The felonious intent to steal, or the animus furandi, is as necessary to constitute robbery as it is to constitute larceny. Pierce v. Commonwealth, 205 Va. 528, 138 S.E.2d 28 (1964).

Proof of intent to steal is necessary to a conviction of robbery. It is definitely an element of the crime. Pierce v. Commonwealth, 205 Va. 528, 138 S.E.2d 28 (1964).

Where defendant possessed no intent to steal at the moment the shooting occurred, the evidence was insufficient as a matter of law to support his conviction of robbery. Branch v. Commonwealth, 225 Va. 91, 300 S.E.2d 758 (1983).

"Intent to steal." — An intent to steal is an intent to feloniously deprive the owner permanently of his property. But "feloniously" in this connection simply means with criminal intent. Pierce v. Commonwealth, 205 Va. 528, 138 S.E.2d 28 (1964).

Where defendant said, "Give me your wallet," victim thereupon handed his wallet to defendant, stating he had no money, and defendant looked in the wallet and, seeing that there was no money in it, threw it on the ground as he backed away, the court correctly refused the attempted robbery instruction. Through the use of force, defendant demanded and received the victim's wallet with the intent to deprive the victim permanently of his money. Brown v. Commonwealth, No. 1341-94-2 (Ct. of Appeals Nov. 21, 1995).

No evidence supported attempted robbery instruction because the record indisputably showed that defendant completed the crime. Through the use of force, defendant demanded and received victim's wallet with the intent to deprive him permanently of his money. His direct acts did not fall short of the accomplishment of the ultimate design. The fact that the wallet contained no money and was thereafter abandoned did not nullify defendant's intent to deprive victim of his money when he demanded and received the wallet. Brown v. Commonwealth, 24 Va. App. 292, 482 S.E.2d 75 (1997).

Animus furandi is generally translated as "an intent to steal." Pierce v. Commonwealth, 205 Va. 528, 138 S.E.2d 28 (1964).

An intent to commit robbery does not have to exist for any particular length of time. It may occur momentarily. Durham v. Commonwealth, 214 Va. 166, 198 S.E.2d 603 (1973).

A custodian, holding the property of another upon condition of prompt payment in cash, has committed no larceny until he carries the goods away in violation of the condition, with requisite intent. If, before carrying the goods away, he uses violence or intimidation to avoid payment, that violence or intimidation precedes the taking. Custody is converted into possession by the exercise of force, and the offense is robbery. Pritchard v. Commonwealth, 225 Va. 559, 303 S.E.2d 911 (1983).

Whether such an intent did exist is to be determined from the particular facts and circumstances of the acts committed. Durham v. Commonwealth, 214 Va. 166, 198 S.E.2d 603 (1973).

The jury may infer the felonious intent from the immediate asportation and conversion of the property, in the absence of satisfactory countervailing evidence by the prisoner. The whole question is one peculiarly for their consideration, to be determined upon all the facts and circumstances. Pierce v. Commonwealth, 205 Va. 528, 138 S.E.2d 28 (1964).

The degree of asportation necessary to constitute a taking under the common-law definition of robbery need be only slight. Durham v. Commonwealth, 214 Va. 166, 198 S.E.2d 603 (1973).

A "taking" in a robbery requires dominion or absolute control of the property and the absolute dominion must exist at some time, though it be only momentary. Brown v. Commonwealth, No. 2559-99-1, 2000 Va. App. LEXIS 810 (Ct. of Appeals Dec. 12, 2000).

Requirement of asportation for defendant's robbery conviction was satisfied by the undisputed evidence that the robbery victim put the money from the safe in a bag at defendant's command at gunpoint. El-Shabazz v. Commonwealth, 2012 Va. App. LEXIS 99 (Apr. 3, 2012).

Possession. — The very fact that property is taken from a person by the use of firearms, violence or threatened violence is, within and of itself, sufficient to show that the person from whom it was taken was in possession thereof. Johnson v. Commonwealth, 215 Va. 495, 211 S.E.2d 71 (1975).

Defendant cannot avoid a robbery conviction by developing a modus operandi of committing the crime by implicitly threatening or intimidating his victim while at the same time making explicit statements that, taken out of the context, belie his true intent. Braxton v. Commonwealth, 13 Va. App. 585, 414 S.E.2d 410 (1992).

Taking under claim of right is not robbery. — To take property under a bona fide claim of right, as under a claim of ownership, or in a bona fide attempt to enforce payment of a debt, is not robbery, though the taking be accompanied by violence or putting in fear. Pierce v. Commonwealth, 205 Va. 528, 138 S.E.2d 28 (1964).

There can be no larceny of the property taken if it, in fact, is the property of the taker, or if he, in good faith, believes it is his, for there is lacking the criminal intent which is an essential element of larceny. Pierce v. Commonwealth, 205 Va. 528, 138 S.E.2d 28 (1964).

Unless claim of right is a mere pretext. — If the claim of right is a mere pretext covering the intent to steal, the taking by violence is robbery. Pierce v. Commonwealth, 205 Va. 528, 138 S.E.2d 28 (1964).

No need to prove ultimate ownership of property taken. — Because robbery is a crime against the person, the prosecution need not prove the ultimate ownership of the property taken but need only prove that the possessory rights of the victim were superior to those of the thief. As such, it is not "legally essential" to allege or identify the ultimate owner of the property taken. Hairston v. Commonwealth, 2 Va. App. 211, 343 S.E.2d 355 (1986).

It is not necessary that there be distinct proof of specific value. A description is sufficient to show some value. Pierce v. Commonwealth, 205 Va. 528, 138 S.E.2d 28 (1964).

III. ILLUSTRATIVE CASES.

Evidence showing elements of crime. — In a prosecution for robbery, the evidence showed that the accused struck a boy 16 years old and took from him a gun and mining lamp, and some frogs that the boy had caught; that he made the boy get into a car and drove off with him; and that the accused refused to halt when commanded to do so by officers of the law, but drove rapidly away and was caught only after a chase. The accused assigned as error the refusal of the trial court to set aside the verdict because the same was contrary to the law and the evidence and without evidence to support it. It was held that the evidence met every element of the crime of common-law robbery. Fleming v. Commonwealth, 170 Va. 636, 196 S.E. 696 (1938).

Under the robbery statute the state's evidence must prove a defendant used violence or intimidation against a victim, as a necessary element to support a conviction. Winn v. Commonwealth, 21 Va. App. 179, 462 S.E.2d 911 (1995).

Indictment should set out form of violence employed. — A demurrer was sustained to an indictment for robbery, which only alleged that the accused made "an assault and in bodily fear feloniously did put and violently did take and steal," but did not set out the form of violence, whether it was by strangulation, or suffocation, of striking, or beating, etc., the court holding that it was necessary to state specifically the form of violence by which the robbery was committed. Commonwealth v. Stollings, 11 Va. L. Reg. 148 (1905).

Evidence of violence sufficient. — The evidence was sufficient to establish beyond a reasonable doubt the violence requisite to a robbery conviction where the defendant ran toward the victim, lowered his right shoulder and swung it forward in a football-blocking-type motion and appeared to prepare to strike the victim before the contact occurred and where, after being hit, the victim fell to the ground as the defendant ran away with her purse; the violence was directed at the victim and did not result merely from the force associated with the taking. Henderson v. Commonwealth, No. 3017-99-1, 2000 Va. App. LEXIS 809 (Ct. of Appeals Dec. 12, 2000).

Evidence of asportation sufficient. — The requisite asportation occurred when a defendant concealed merchandise inside his coat and that asportation continued through his struggle with the store manager. The evidence established that the defendant exercised absolute control over the merchandise as he walked away and during the struggle and the fact that the defendant was prevented from leaving the store did not mean that there had been no taking. Brown v. Commonwealth, No. 2559-99-1, 2000 Va. App. LEXIS 810 (Ct. of Appeals Dec. 12, 2000).

Identification evidence. — Defendant's convictions for robbery and the felonious use of a firearm were appropriate because the evidence was sufficient where the victims identified defendant as the robber; both victims had ample opportunity to observe defendant; the victims were certain that they had identified defendant correctly; and the victims' identification testimony was corroborated by others who had observed defendant at the crime scenes. Griffin v. Commonwealth, 2007 Va. App. LEXIS 504 (Nov. 7, 2007).

Prosecution for conspiracy to commit robbery barred where previous acquittal of underlying robbery. — Defendant's prosecution for conspiracy to commit robbery was barred under principles of double jeopardy where defendant had previously been acquitted of the underlying robbery. Ginanni v. Commonwealth, 13 Va. App. 1, 408 S.E.2d 767 (1991).

Robbery conviction properly used as predicate under federal act. — Because robbery in Virginia has as an element the use or threatened use of force, defendant's robbery convictions were properly used as predicates under the federal Armed Career Criminal Act. United States v. Presley, 52 F.3d 64 (4th Cir.), cert. denied, 516 U.S. 891, 116 S. Ct. 237, 133 L. Ed. 2d 165 (1995).

Offenses not substantially similar for purposes of § 19.2-297.1. — Defendant's robbery, third or subsequent offense, conviction under § 18.2-58 and 19.2-297.1 was reversed as defendant's two prior robbery offenses in Maryland were not substantially similar for purposes of § 19.2-297.1 since in Virginia, there was a requirement that the intent to steal had to have existed before or at the time the force or violence was used; Maryland law, by contrast, did not require that the intent to steal precede or co-exist with the violence, and permitted a conviction for robbery even if the intent to steal was formed only after the force or violence, as an afterthought, as long as it occurred as part of the same general events and coexisted with the later taking. Dean v. Commonwealth, 61 Va. App. 209, 734 S.E.2d 673, 2012 Va. App. LEXIS 394 (2012).

Use of a pistol with a blocked barrel and which fired only blank cartridges was sufficient to sustain a charge of robbery with firearms. Johnson v. Commonwealth, 209 Va. 291, 163 S.E.2d 570 (1968).

Separate sentences for robbery of employer's money from several employees not double jeopardy. — Where defendant pointed a gun at a restaurant employee and demanded that he turn over money in a cash register and he also threatened another employee and demanded that he turn over money from his pockets, although the money yielded by the two employees was the property of their employer, both employees were subjected to the threat of violence by the presenting of firearms as money was taken from each of them. Therefore, defendant committed the two robberies of which he was convicted; thus, the trial court's imposition of separate sentences for the robbery of each of the two employees did not punish defendant twice for the "same offense." Jordan v. Commonwealth, 2 Va. App. 590, 347 S.E.2d 152 (1986).

Conduct arguably constituted two criminal offenses. — Court of appeals declined to invoke the "ends of justice" exception to Va. Sup. Ct. R. 5A:18 to consider defendant's argument that he could not lawfully be convicted of both robbery and grand larceny from the person since they arose from a single act because defendant could not affirmatively prove that an element of the offense did not occur since it was unclear from the record whether the evidence adduced at trial established two distinct criminal acts or one, and defendant's conduct arguably constituted two criminal offenses; arguably, the instant defendant removed money from a register's drawer since the crime of grand larceny from the person was complete, but when the cashier realized what defendant was doing, she tried to stop him, and because defendant was able to pry the money out of the cashier's grasp and flee the store, the second taking constituted a robbery as it was accomplished through force, violence or intimidation. Ali v. Commonwealth, 2009 Va. App. LEXIS 500 (Nov. 10, 2009), aff'd in part, rev'd in part, 280 Va. 665, 701 S.E.2d 64 (2010).

When an indictment charged that the defendant robbed a corporation the offense of robbery was sufficiently stated in the original indictment and amendment was unnecessary, though desirable, since it in effect charged that he committed robbery by putting the agents of the corporation in fear and taking its money from their personal protection and in their presence. Crawford v. Commonwealth, 217 Va. 595, 231 S.E.2d 309 (1977).

Although indictment which charged that defendant "robbed Pizza Hut" came uncomfortably close to alleging that a store was robbed, a charge which the Virginia Supreme Court implied might be defective, because the indictment named the entity and because § 1-13.19 [see now § 1-230] broadly defines "person," the offense of robbery was sufficiently stated. Waters v. Commonwealth, 29 Va. App. 133, 510 S.E.2d 262 (1999).

Indictment held sufficient. — See Smyth v. White, 195 Va. 169, 77 S.E.2d 454 (1953); Pettus v. Peyton, 207 Va. 906, 153 S.E.2d 278 (1967).

Where no objection to the form of the indictment was made in the trial court, and any evidence in the record that defendant or his counsel were under any misapprehension as to the fact that defendant had been indicted for robbery, an indictment charging "robbery" with no mention of force is not faulty. Hunt v. Haga, 368 F. Supp. 527 (W.D. Va. 1973).

Use of victim's bank card. — Where defendant and abduction victim drove to money machine and in victim's presence using her bank card, he was able to get 50 dollars and victim testified that she permitted him to get the money because she thought he would physically hurt her, there was sufficient evidence to support robbery conviction. When one takes cash from the presence of a person whose right to possession is superior to that of the thief, the robbery is complete. Clay v. Commonwealth, 13 Va. App. 617, 414 S.E.2d 432 (1992).

Conviction of both robbery and murder. — The clear conclusion of the trial court, sitting without a jury, that defendant was a principal in the second degree to a willful, deliberate and premeditated killing provided an independent statutory basis for his first-degree murder conviction, apart from any association with or relation to the crime of robbery out of which course of action the killing arose, and defendant could be convicted of both murder and robbery. Simpson v. Commonwealth, 221 Va. 109, 267 S.E.2d 134 (1980).

Because defendant admitted to being at the victim's residence, because glitter similar to that worn by defendant was found on the victim, because defendant's driver testified that defendant was taken to the victim's residence and left an hour later with the victim's property, and because the victim's property was later discovered in defendant's home and purse, defendant was properly found to have assisted her husband in the victim's death and shared the requisite criminal intent; accordingly, the evidence was sufficient to convict defendant of second-degree murder and robbery under §§ 18.2-32 and 18.2-58. McLean v. Commonwealth, — Va. App. —, — S.E.2d —, 2008 Va. App. LEXIS 449 (Oct. 7, 2008).

Conviction of both robbery and abduction. — Making victims get out of their car and onto ground during robbery and attempted robbery constituted the separate crime of abduction. Taylor v. Commonwealth, No. 0995-94-1 (Ct. of Appeals May 23, 1995).

Evidence of death of defendant's accomplice properly admitted. — Where defendant was charged with committing a home invasion robbery and a carjacking with the aid of an accomplice, the trial court did not abuse its discretion in admitting evidence of the killing of his accomplice in another robbery attempt shortly thereafter, as this evidence was highly probative of defendant's identity as one of the perpetrators of the charged offenses, which he challenged throughout his trial. Layug v. Commonwealth, — Va. App. —, — S.E.2d —, 2007 Va. App. LEXIS 369 (Oct. 2, 2007).

Evidence held sufficient to support conviction for armed robbery. Lewis v. Commonwealth, 193 Va. 612, 70 S.E.2d 293 (1952).

Testimony offered by two victims was not inherently incredible, and the trial court did not err in finding the evidence sufficient to support defendant's convictions for robbery, § 18.2-58, and using a firearm in the commission of a felony, § 18.2-53.1. Both victims described defendant as having played an active role in the robbery, and nothing in the record rendered their testimony inherently incredible. Winckler v. Commonwealth, — Va. App. —, — S.E.2d —, 2007 Va. App. LEXIS 73 (Mar. 6, 2007).

Evidence sufficient to support a conviction of attempted robbery. — See Johnson v. Commonwealth, 209 Va. 291, 163 S.E.2d 570 (1968).

Evidence supported conviction for attempted robbery where defendant told bank teller he wanted to make a withdrawal, he failed to respond in an appropriate manner after she queried him to determine if he sought to make an ordinary lawful withdrawal, thus, making it obvious to teller that he did not desire to make a lawful transaction, he advised her that she did not understand, apparently referring to some other manner by which he wished to make his withdrawal, his repeated assurance to her that he would not hurt her implied that he had the capability to do so, and he held his hand in his pocket, conduct that frightened teller and further caused her to believe she was about to be robbed. In light of all of the circumstances, a reasonable person in her position would have reacted as she did and would have believed that defendant intended for her to believe she was in danger if she did not turn over money to him. Braxton v. Commonwealth, 13 Va. App. 585, 414 S.E.2d 410 (1992).

The defendant's statement that he was going to shoot the victim and take his money was sufficient to prove beyond a reasonable doubt that he intended to rob the victim. Furthermore, the defendant committed numerous overt acts in furtherance of the robbery by placing his hand in his pocket in a manner that caused the victim to believe that he had a gun, following the victim into the store and stating that he did not "want anybody to get hurt," and attempting to enter the taxi after leaving the store. Accordingly, the evidence was sufficient to sustain the defendant's conviction for attempted robbery. Chrisman v. Commonwealth, No. 1724-95-3 (Ct. of Appeals April 30, 1996).

Evidence was sufficient to support defendant's attempted robbery conviction, in violation of §§ 18.2-58 and 18.2-25, when the victims testified that defendant said he would "take your stuff," did not appear to be joking, and, when they ran from him, lifted his shirt and displayed a firearm, as this showed defendant intended to take, with intent to steal, the personal property of another, from his person or in his presence, against his will, by violence or intimidation, and engaged in a direct, ineffectual, act towards its commission. Jones v. Commonwealth, No. 1730-03-1, 2004 Va. App. LEXIS 300 (Ct. of Appeals June 29, 2004).

Victim's testimony that defendant pointed a gun at the victim and told the victim to give defendant what the victim had in the victim's pocket provided sufficient evidence to support defendant's conviction for attempted robbery. Totten v. Commonwealth, — Va. App. —, — S.E.2d —, 2006 Va. App. LEXIS 178 (May 9, 2006).

Fact that defendant told an on-duty undercover officer that defendant would take the officer's money and defendant's brisk walk back toward the officer supported defendant's conviction for attempted robbery under § 18.5-57. Jordan v. Commonwealth, — Va. App. —, — S.E.2d —, 2007 Va. App. LEXIS 259 (June 26, 2007).

In a case in which the only issue before the appellate court was whether there was sufficient evidence to support defendant's conviction for attempted robbery, while he testified that he played no role in the robbery, the jury disbelieved his testimony. Thus, the evidence viewed in the light most favorable to the Commonwealth proved that defendant intended to steal personal property from the victim, against his will, by force, violence, or intimidation and committed a direct, but ineffectual, act to accomplish the crime. Drew v. Commonwealth, 2009 Va. App. LEXIS 415 (Sept. 22, 2009).

Sufficient evidence of robbery. — The taking of the money and the taking of the cab, under the circumstances shown by the evidence in the instant case, constituted two distinct offenses, i.e., a robbery of money and an "unauthorized use" of an automobile. Comer v. Commonwealth, 211 Va. 246, 176 S.E.2d 432 (1970).

Under circumstances in which the trier of fact could reasonably infer that the money was actually taken and that defendant was at least an aider and abettor to the taking, defendant could be convicted of robbery. Hunt v. Haga, 368 F. Supp. 527 (W.D. Va. 1973).

Evidence supported robbery conviction where defendant threatened sheriff deputy's life while brandishing an object which appeared to be a weapon, and as a result, the deputy was fearful and surrendered the vehicle to defendant who then escaped with both the automobile and the deputy's pistol, apparently taken by defendant while the deputy was in extremity. Jones v. Commonwealth, 13 Va. App. 566, 414 S.E.2d 193 (1992).

Evidence supported robbery conviction where after defendant got possession of the purse in the hotel room, he fled from the room, chased by the victim, and defendant pushed victim six to eight feet against the hood of her automobile after the purse fell to the ground in the parking lot and defendant then got away with the purse. Broady v. Commonwealth, 16 Va. App. 281, 429 S.E.2d 468 (1993).

In view of the testimony that the victim was on the ground, that he "just felt the guy on me," observer's testimony that the defendant was "over top of" the victim, and that his cousin "tackled" the defendant in order to get him "from on top of" the victim, the evidence was sufficient for the fact finder to infer that observer and his cousin subdued the defendant and held him until the officers arrived because the defendant was robbing the victim. Branch v. Commonwealth, No. 1408-96-1 (Ct. of Appeals July 8, 1997).

The evidence was sufficient to support the defendant's conviction where the victim, his estranged girlfriend, testified that when she would not go with the defendant, he snatched her purse and fled; although the victim suffered from memory loss, paranoia, and bi-polar disorder due to an earlier car crash, her testimony to the relevant events did not seem inherently incredible. Whitby v. Commonwealth, No. 1343-99-1, 2000 Va. App. LEXIS 551 (Ct. of Appeals July 25, 2000).

The evidence was sufficient to support the defendant's conviction for robbery where one of the other participants in the crime identified the defendant and a third party as the men who were with him. Kingsberry v. Commonwealth, No. 0142-99-1, 2000 Va. App. LEXIS 622 (Ct. of Appeals Aug. 22, 2000).

The evidence was sufficient to support the defendant's conviction for robbery of motel where he had been staying, where it was established that the defendant had obtained access to the office where the cash box was kept under false pretenses, that he had savagely beaten the elderly manager who had the keys to the cash box into unconsciousness, that when the police arrived and the manager regained consciousness, the money and the defendant were gone, and that the defendant had obtained a ride to North Carolina immediately following the incident but had taken no luggage or personal possessions with him. Watson v. Commonwealth, No. 0494-00-1, 2001 Va. App. LEXIS 219 (Ct. of Appeals Apr. 24, 2001).

Testimony from the victim that identified defendant and provided that defendant threatened the victim with a knife, demanded money from him, and stabbed him in the back was sufficient to support the convictions for robbery. Muhammad v. Commonwealth, No. 1300-01-2, 2002 Va. App. LEXIS 731 (Ct. of Appeals Dec. 10, 2002).

Where defendant did not preserve an insufficiency claim and the record did not "affirmatively prove" that defendant did not commit the offenses of robbery, use of a firearm in the robbery, and wearing a mask in public, in violation of §§ 18.2-58, 18.2-53.1, and 18.2-422, the Va. Sup. Ct. R. 5A:18 "ends of justice" exception did not apply because no manifest injustice occurred. Young v. Commonwealth, No. 0363-03-1, 2003 Va. App. LEXIS 588 (Ct. of Appeals Nov. 12, 2003).

Evidence sufficient to support two convictions of robbery against two separate victims, where each victim had constructive possession of the property taken in their presence, and defendant subjected each victim to intimidation in taking the same; in other words, the stolen property did not have to be taken separately from each victim. Barksdale v. Commonwealth, No. 3028-03-2, 2005 Va. App. LEXIS 132 (Ct. of Appeals Mar. 29, 2005).

Evidence was sufficient to support defendant's robbery conviction, as it was reasonable for the trial court to have found defendant was referring to the victim's cell phone during a conversation with an investigator and defendant's mother confirmed that it was defendant calling the mother from the victim's cell phone number; in addition, the conviction was not solely based on defendant's possession of the victim's cell phone, but was also based on the victim's description of the assailant. Harris v. Commonwealth, — Va. App. —, — S.E.2d —, 2007 Va. App. LEXIS 121 (Mar. 27, 2007).

Where a pizza delivery man was robbed of money, his cell phone, and a pizza at the house where he went to deliver the pizza, evidence that: (1) an officer recovered the phone from defendant's person; (2) pizza boxes found in the house had defendant's fingerprints on them; and (3) defendant confessed, was sufficient to convict him of robbery. McCray v. Commonwealth, — Va. App. —, — S.E.2d —, 2008 Va. App. LEXIS 38 (Jan. 22, 2008).

Considering the totality of the circumstances, including the victim's observation of defendant before the robbery for thirty minutes from twenty feet away, the victim's observation of defendant during the robbery for five to eight minutes, and defendant's return to the scene to demand the victim's cell phone, together with the victim's description of defendant to officers within minutes of the robbery, the evidence was sufficient to prove defendant committed the robbery, in violation of § 18.2-58. Shelton v. Commonwealth, 2008 Va. App. LEXIS 28 (Jan. 15, 2008).

Since all three robbery victims, who each were able to get a good look at the robber, picked defendant out of the same photo lineup, the evidence was sufficient to convict the defendant, even without considering the defendant's incriminating statements. Taylor v. Commonwealth, 52 Va. App. 388, 663 S.E.2d 536, 2008 Va. App. LEXIS 330 (2008).

Evidence was sufficient to support defendant's convictions for robbery, shooting within an occupied dwelling, using a firearm in the commission of a felony, armed burglary, and malicious wounding, because ample evidence supported a finding that defendant was a perpetrator in a home invasion: three of the victims identified defendant at trial, and a co-defendant testified that defendant said he intended to rob the home, that he entered the home wearing a bullet-proof vest and armed with a handgun, and that he later told the co-defendant that he had struck one of the victim's in the head. Trial court did not abuse discretion in ruling on misidentification of accomplices by witnesses. Streater v. Commonwealth, 2009 Va. App. LEXIS 504 (Nov. 10, 2009).

Defendant's robbery conviction in violation of § 18.2-58 was appropriate because the evidence was sufficient. The victim testified that, upon walking outside of an apartment complex, he was hit in the face and knocked down; he further testified that every time he got up, he was knocked down again and that everything was taken out of his pocket, which included a cell phone, keys, and money. Young v. Commonwealth, 2010 Va. App. LEXIS 164 (Apr. 27, 2010).

Appellant's convictions for two counts of robbery, one count of statutory burglary, and three counts of use of a firearm in the commission of the felonies were affirmed because it was reasonable for the fact finder to conclude the intruder knew the victims' habits and DNA evidence indicated at some point in time, appellant had touched the BB gun. Swinson v. Commonwealth, 2010 Va. App. LEXIS 311 (Aug. 3, 2010).

Evidence defendant repeatedly entered the store robbed wearing gang colors, a witness observed guns in the van used to get to and from the store, defendant drove van used to and from the store, and defendant was present when the person who robbed the store came

running out with the register drawer and defendant drove the van away supported defendant's convictions for robbery and use of a firearm during the robbery. Lebron v. Commonwealth, 58 Va. App. 540, 712 S.E.2d 15, 2011 Va. App. LEXIS 238 (2011).

There was sufficient evidence to support defendant's conviction for robbery, including testimony that defendant repeatedly entered the store that day of the robbery; told another he needed to "man up," meaning he needed to commit the robbery; and was in the get away van when the individual committing the robbery came running out with the register drawer. Salcedo v. Commonwealth, 58 Va. App. 525, 712 S.E.2d 8, 2011 Va. App. LEXIS 239 (2011).

Conviction for robbery under § 18.2-58 was supported by defendant's statements, including "damn right I'm going to take it. I'm going to take it all," and defendant's continued use of violence after the victim offered his property to defendant, indicating an intent to permanently deprive the victim of the property through the ongoing use of violence. Carlstrom v. Commonwealth, 2011 Va. App. LEXIS 335 (Nov. 8, 2011).

In a prosecution on a charge of robbery, the items taken from the victim's purse located in another room of the trailer where the victim was held were close enough to the victim and sufficiently under her control that, had she not been subjected to violence and intimidation by the intruders, she could have tried to prevent the taking of her personal items. Because the victim was in the residence during the acts of violence and the taking of the property, her property was taken from her presence. Oliver v. Commonwealth, 2012 Va. App. LEXIS 71 (Mar. 13, 2012).

Conviction for robbery was supported by sufficient evidence, where the record contained ample evidence demonstrating that defendant took marijuana from a victim's car on the day of the shooting, including testimony that the victim weighed out one ounce of marijuana in the car but police recovered less than two-tenths of an ounce and defendant admitted he took a pill bottle containing marijuana. Person v. Commonwealth, 2012 Va. App. LEXIS 187 (June 5, 2012).

Although no witness was able to identify defendant by facial recognition, as the robber was wearing a mask during the robbery, there was sufficient evidence to convict defendant of robbery where the surveillance camera photographs showed the robber wearing a dark, hooded jacket or sweatshirt of some type, with a tag or label on the lower left front side, as well as distinctively marked gloves, the store owner testified that defendant's height was about the same as the height of the robber and the robber was African-American, as was defendant, a police officer later encountered defendant wearing a dark jacket, zipped up, with a knit cap on his head and the hood of his jacket pulled over his head, with a tag or label on the lower left front side, and the officer discovered a pair of gloves and a handgun lying on the ground in a haphazard fashion, as if someone had quickly or carelessly tossed them there, defendant's DNA profile was consistent with that found on the gloves, and the gloves had the same color and distinctive markings as the gloves worn by the robber. Spence v. Commonwealth, 60 Va. App. 355, 727 S.E.2d 786, 2012 Va. App. LEXIS 221 (2012).

Evidence was sufficient to convict defendant of robbery in violation of § 18.2-58, because 15 minutes after the crime, he was found 17 blocks away from the crime scene, in a sedan matching the victim's description of the car that had passed him just before the robbery, and guns that matched the victim's decription of those used by the robbers were found in or on the ground near the car. Berry v. Commonwealth, 2012 Va. App. LEXIS 385 (Nov. 27, 2012).

Evidence held insufficient. — The Commonwealth's circumstantial evidence did not exclude the hypothesis that defendant may have handled the bottle for an innocent purpose before the robbery. At best, the Commonwealth's case only proved that defendant once handled the bottle. The print evidence did not show when defendant handled the bottle or that he handled it at the scene of the crime. Moreover, defendant's prints were found on the handle and body of the half-gallon bottle, a location not inconsistent with someone holding the bottle to pour from it. Other than the fingerprints on the bottle, there was no evidence of other circumstances tending to reasonably exclude the hypothesis that the print was impressed at a time other than that of the crime. Accordingly, under the circumstances of this case, the evidence was insufficient to support the conviction. Granger v. Commonwealth, 20 Va. App. 576, 459 S.E.2d 106 (1995).

Upon defendant's sufficiency challenge, because the Commonwealth had the burden to prove beyond a reasonable doubt that defendant committed the crime of attempted robbery and it failed to do so, as one would have to resort to speculation and conjecture in order to find that he was attempting to rob as opposed to attempting to obtain money by false pretenses, an attempted robbery conviction could not stand; moreover, given reversal of the attempted robbery conviction, defendant's conviction for attempted use of a firearm during the commission of attempted robbery also had to be reversed. Jay v. Commonwealth, 275 Va. 510, 659 S.E.2d 311, 2008 Va. LEXIS 53 (2008).

Evidence was insufficient to support defendant's robbery conviction, where the robbery arose during the attack on the victim, the attack was not initiated with the purpose of robbing the victim, and no evidence was presented linking defendant, any even any other man involved in the assault, with the taking of the victim's laptop. Abdullah v. Commonwealth, 53 Va. App. 750, 675 S.E.2d 215, 2009 Va. App. LEXIS 169 (2009).

Evidence was insufficient to convict defendant of attempted robbery of a particular person in violation of § 18.2-58 because defendant placed a gun to the victim's neck and told the victim to keep ringing the bell for entry to his place of employment, which showed an intent to gain access to the building, but it did not show an intent to deprive the victim of his property. DeSilva v. Commonwealth, 2009 Va. App. LEXIS 482 (Oct. 27, 2009).

Sufficient evidence to support conviction. — There was sufficient evidence to support the conviction for robbery in violation of § 18.2-58 because appellant's larceny became a robbery when the victim and another individual confronted appellant, demanded return of the cell phone, and appellant reached into his waistband and pulled out a "flat, black object." Williams v. Commonwealth, 278 Va. 633, 685 S.E.2d 178, 2009 Va. LEXIS 109 (2009).

Evidence was sufficient to convict defendant as an accomplice to a robbery because, knowing that his friend needed money to support his girlfriend, he discussed a robbery with the friend, drove the friend to obtain a gun, approved an intended victim, and drove the friend from the robbery scene. Battin v. Commonwealth, 2010 Va. App. LEXIS 116 (Mar. 30, 2010).

Defendant's convictions for robbery, abduction, and malicious wounding, were proper because the fact that he was not wearing a white coat did not negate a detective's reasonable suspicion that defendant was somehow involved in criminal activity. The trial court accepted the explanation that defendant had abandoned his coat as he fled. Diaz v. Commonwealth, 2010 Va. App. LEXIS 417 (Oct. 26, 2010).

Trial court did not err in finding that the evidence proved beyond a reasonable doubt that defendant acted as a principal in the second degree to use of a firearm in the commission of a robbery as the evidence showed that defendant aided in the commission of and shared the main actor's intent to rob a clothing retail store during normal business hours, where he was likely to encounter both store employees and customers. The evidence showed that defendant transported the main actor to and from the immediate area where he committed the robbery and abduction; that defendant remained in her SUV at a nearby apartment complex, where neither she nor the main actor lived, when the main actor departed the vehicle to commit the robbery; that she tried to assist him in eluding police, and that she tried to provide him with an alibi when questioned about the offenses, and that she gave false and contradictory statements to officers when questioned about her part in the robbery. Wade v. Commonwealth, 2012 Va. App. LEXIS 161 (May 15, 2012).

Evidence was sufficient to convict defendant of robbery, because from evidence that intruders entered an apartment for the purpose of committing robbery and departed with a bag full of items of value, the jury could reasonably have concluded that the "something" an intruder removed from a victim's pocket possessed some inherent value. Jackson v. Commonwealth, 2012 Va. App. LEXIS 224 (July 10, 2012).

Defendant's confession and the corroborating DNA evidence was sufficient to support defendant's convictions for murder, rape, statutory burglary, and robbery. Farmer v. Commonwealth, 61 Va. App. 402, 737 S.E.2d 32, 2013 Va. App. LEXIS 34 (2013).

Evidence supported conviction of robbery and use of a firearm in commission of robbery where there was positive identification testimony by witness and two other employees, who were in close proximity to defendant during robbery, who testified that the defendant was the armed robber who entered store alone, threatened them, and left with money, and where defendant was also identified by his accomplice as person who entered store and committed crime. Lewis v. Commonwealth, 7 Va. App. 596, 376 S.E.2d 295 (1989).

Evidence sufficient to support two counts of robbery. — Appropriate unit of prosecution was determined by the number of persons from whose possession property was taken separately by force or intimidation. Because the clerk and the supervisor were both custodians of the hotel's money, and therefore, had joint constructive possession of the money in the cash register, the evidence was clear that, although the supervisor did not actually turn over the money to defendant, by pointing his gun at her, defendant insured that the supervisor would make no effort to stop him from taking the property that was in her constructive possession; therefore, because defendant intimidated each employee and obtained the money through the agency of that intimidation, the evidence was sufficient to prove that he committed two counts of robbery in violation of § 18.2-58. Crichlow v. Commonwealth, 2009 Va. App. LEXIS 564 (Dec. 15, 2009).

Evidence of taking by violence or intimidation. — Where, viewed in the light most favorable to the Commonwealth, the evidence disclosed that appellant "stalked" victim for a considerable period before taking the van, lingered near her while she loaded her groceries, entered her vehicle, and twice ordered her to get inside the van, and victim testified that she feared bodily harm, even death before the appellant "gunned" the van's motor and drove away, the totality of appellant's words and willful conduct were sufficient to support a rational finder of fact's conclusion that appellant robbed victim of personal property from her presence and possession, against her will, by intimidation. Jackson v. Commonwealth, 19 Va. App. 557, 453 S.E.2d 567 (1995).

The evidence supports a finding that the taking was effected through the use of violence or intimidation. From the evidence of the beating of the handcuffed victim, and the use of pliers to remove the gold crown from Bonner's mouth, the fact finder could have found beyond a reasonable doubt that the beating and the theft of the crown were "interdependent objects of a common criminal design" to obtain something of monetary value from the victim. Thus, the violence and intimidation, through both the beating and the forceful extraction of the gold crown, preceded or was concomitant with the taking. Therefore, the evidence was sufficient to prove beyond a reasonable doubt that the defendant committed the robbery. Perry v. Commonwealth, No. 0237-95-2 (Ct. of Appeals July 9, 1996).

Required element of violence was sufficiently close in time and effect to be concomitant with defendant's taking, where defendant struck victim within two or three seconds after her purse was removed from her shoulder and while she was trying to resist the taking. Stanley v. Commonwealth, No. 1902-98-2 (Ct. of Appeals Dec. 28, 1999).

Evidence was sufficient to support defendant's robbery conviction in a case where he attacked the victim from behind in a wooded area, and raped and sodomized before taking money from her; although defendant claimed that nothing he did intimidated the victim into giving defendant money, the violence he engaged in immediately preceding the demand for money, the rape and sodomy, was sufficient to convert mere thievery into robbery. Anderson v. Commonwealth, 48 Va. App. 704, 634 S.E.2d 372, 2006 Va. App. LEXIS 414 (2006), aff'd, 274 Va. 469, 650 S.E.2d 702, 2007 Va. LEXIS 115 (Va. 2007).

Evidence was sufficient to support defendant's conviction for robbery, as the Commonwealth introduced evidence showing that defendant entered the store where the store clerk was working and demanded money in a forceful manner. The trial court was entitled to conclude that the store clerk was put in fear of incurring serious bodily harm based on the store clerk's testimony that defendant held a screwdriver in defendant's hand and that the store clerk was frightened as a result. Thomas v. Commonwealth, 2006 Va. App. LEXIS 605 (Dec. 20, 2006).

Insufficient evidence of violence or intimidation. — Defendant's conviction for robbery was unfounded because no violence or intimidation was directed at the alleged victim to accomplish the taking. The alleged victim's subjective fear induced by a co-conspirator's actions did not facilitate the taking, but merely resulted from the taking; no force or intimidation was directed at the alleged victim's person. Anderson v. Commonwealth, 52 Va. App. 501, 664 S.E.2d 514, 2008 Va. App. LEXIS 377 (2008), aff'd, 683 S.E.2d 536, 2009 Va. LEXIS 86 (Va. 2009).

Sufficient evidence of a taking. — The fact that the appellant did not specify money or drugs when demanding the victim empty his pockets does nothing to alter the fact that defendant exercised dominion and control over the money when at the defendant's command the victim retrieved the money and dropped it. When the victim took the money from his pocket and dropped it, he no longer exercised control over the money and merely acted on the defendant's behalf. Accordingly, the defendant constructively possessed the money as soon as the victim complied with the defendant's order. Therefore, the evidence was sufficient to sustain the trial court's finding that a taking occurred and that the defendant had the intent to deprive the victim of his property. Spencer v. Commonwealth, No. 2074-95-3 (Ct. of Appeals Nov. 26, 1996).

Where a victim was detained in a bedroom while her property was stolen from the living room, as she was in the residence during the acts of violence and the taking of her property, the trial court properly found that her property was taken from her presence; therefore, the evidence was sufficient to convict defendant of robbery in violation of § 18.2-58. Price v. Commonwealth, 59 Va. App. 764, 722 S.E.2d 653, 2012 Va. App. LEXIS 68 (2012).

Sufficient evidence to support conviction as principal in the second degree to robbery. — Appellate court affirmed defendant's conviction for robbery as a principal in the second degree because the evidence was sufficient to prove that defendant aided and abetted in the commission of a robbery, as defendant knew the perpetrators were going to commit a robbery, he waited for them in the get-away vehicle to facilitate their escape, during the escape he tried to hide the clothing they wore during the robbery by placing it in the glove compartment or at his feet, and a reasonable person could conclude that defendant shared the intent to commit a robbery. Bradner v. Commonwealth, No. 2640-00-3, 2001 Va. App. LEXIS 572 (Ct. of Appeals Oct. 23, 2001).

Evidence showing that the principal used intimidation to accomplish the taking and that defendant knew what the principal was going to do and acted as the driver of the car was sufficient to support defendant's conviction for robbery as a principal in the second degree. Young v. Commonwealth, — Va. App. —, — S.E.2d —, 2009 Va. App. LEXIS 98 (Mar. 10, 2009).

Defendant's convictions, as a principal in second degree, of robbery, § 18.2-58, and use of a firearm in the commission of a felony, § 18.2-53.1, were proper because, as the "getaway" driver, defendant contributed to the execution of the robbery, and his actions belied his claim that he was merely a bystander who knew nothing of the perpetrator's intent to rob; defendant spent the afternoon with the perpetrator, held the perpetrator's gun, drove the perpetrator to the parking lot where the victim was standing, and stopped the car "directly" in front of the victim. Defendant remained in the car in the driver's seat and watched the perpetrator get out of the car while carrying a gun, and it was reasonable to conclude that defendant knew what the perpetrator intended to do and assisted him by driving him directly in front of victim and waiting in the driver's seat until the perpetrator returned. Hayes v. Commonwealth, — Va. App. —, — S.E.2d —, 2009 Va. App. LEXIS 132 (Mar. 24, 2009).

Defendant was properly convicted of robbery as a principal in the second degree, because defendant, although not the driver, was part of the getaway team. Defendant was present during the planning, he remained with the getaway driver, he reentered the car when he saw the principals fleeing the scene, and he was given the same amount of money as the lookout, permitting an inference that he performed an act of similar value to the accomplishment of the overall crime. Whitley v. Commonwealth, 2013 Va. App. LEXIS 63 (Feb. 26, 2013).

Evidence insufficient to support principal in the second degree conviction. — Defendant's conviction for robbery as a principal in the second degree pursuant to § 18.2-58 was improper because the circumstantial evidence presented by the Commonwealth was insufficient to prove that defendant knowingly committed an overt act in furtherance of robbery, shared in the criminal intent of the principal, or that the robbery was a natural and probable consequence of wrongful assaults. McMorris v. Commonwealth, 276 Va. 500, 666 S.E.2d 348, 2008 Va. LEXIS 91 (2008).

Proof of overt act for attempted robbery. — Evidence was sufficient to show that defendant committed an overt act for purposes of attempted robbery where: (1) defendant and his co-defendant talked about robbing a bank the day before; (2) defendant drove to a remote location in town; (3) the two pulled bandanas over their faces outside the bank; (4) defendant carried a knapsack with his hand inside, and the two men walked toward the entrance to the bank; and (5) when they made eye contact with the witness, they pulled down the masks, but continued walking toward the entrance to the bank, where they paused at the entrance, but at the last minute, aborted their plan and walked away. Williams v. Commonwealth, No. 0641-03-1, 2004 Va. App. LEXIS 154 (Ct. of Appeals Apr. 6, 2004).

In an attempted robbery prosecution, where defendant and his companions intended to rob "some people" in a house, demanded money from the persons they found in the house, and shot a killed a man who later entered, the evidence had been insufficient to convict defendant of attempting to rob this man, as the evidence showed he never formed an intent to rob him, and that he and companions took no action toward realizing the ultimate purpose of robbing him. Lewis v. Commonwealth, 43 Va. App. 126, 596 S.E.2d 542, 2004 Va. App. LEXIS 252 (2004).

Evidence sufficient to support conviction for conspiracy to commit robbery. — Where the evidence showed that defendant said that defendant planned to rob the victim and put defendant's plan into action with an intent to rob the victim, and that, from that starting premise, a co-conspirator agreed to participate in defendant's plan, defendant's conviction for conspiracy to commit robbery in violation of §§ 18.2-58 and 18.2-22 was supported by sufficient evidence. James v. Commonwealth, 53 Va. App. 671, 674 S.E.2d 571, 2009 Va. App. LEXIS 155 (2009).

Evidence was sufficient to support defendant's conviction for conspiracy to commit robbery, as there was sufficient proof of an agreement to commit robbery between defendant and a woman; there was a reasonable inference that defendant and the woman had a prearranged plan to take the television from the victim. Searcy v. Commonwealth, 2012 Va. App. LEXIS 383 (Nov. 27, 2012).

No error in limiting cross-examination of co-conspirator witness. — In an armed robbery trial under § 18.2-58, defendant's cross-examination of a co-conspirator witness regarding prior plea agreements that the witness had reached in other unrelated cases was properly denied because "bare bones" proffer was inadequate to determine that the line of questioning was relevant to bias or credibility and other evidence was overwhelming. Williams v. Commonwealth, — Va. App. —, — S.E.2d —, 2007 Va. App. LEXIS 74 (Mar. 6, 2007).

No error in admitting other crimes evidence against defendant. — In a prosecution for robbery and the use of a firearm during the commission of robbery, the trial court did not err in admitting testimony by the police regarding other crimes committed by his accomplices that had no relevance to the crimes for which he was being tried, as he failed to restate his objection to the same when the first of two officers testified about those crimes, and also failed to object when the second officer testified about much of the same evidence; thus, in permitting the admission of said evidence, he waived any complaint on appeal regarding the same. Boggs v. Commonwealth, — Va. App. —, — S.E.2d —, 2006 Va. App. LEXIS 66 (Feb. 21, 2006).

Mistrial and new trial unwarranted. — Because the record on appeal sufficiently showed that the trial judge thoroughly admonished a challenged witness, who was also defendant's former girlfriend, and determined that her alleged inflammatory testimony did not prejudice defendant, both a mistrial and a new trial were unwarranted. Moreover, because the jury necessarily determined that the Commonwealth's evidence proved the robbery charged, and were worthy of belief, that determination was upheld. White v. Commonwealth, — Va. App. —, — S.E.2d —, 2005 Va. App. LEXIS 538 (Sept. 15, 2005).

"Ends of justice" exception applicable. — Evidence clearly and affirmatively showed that an element of one of the crimes of which defendant was convicted did not occur. Accordingly, there was error in the judgment appealed from and application of the ends of justice exception was necessary to avoid a grave injustice. Ali v. Commonwealth, 280 Va. 665, 701 S.E.2d 64, 2010 Va. LEXIS 273 (2010).

§ 18.2-58.1. Carjacking; penalty.

A. Any person who commits carjacking, as herein defined, shall be guilty of a felony punishable by imprisonment for life or a term not less than fifteen years.

B. As used in this section, *"carjacking"* means the intentional seizure or seizure of control of a motor vehicle of another with intent to permanently or temporarily deprive another in possession or control of the vehicle of that possession or control by means of partial strangulation, or suffocation, or by striking or beating, or by other violence to the person, or by assault or otherwise putting a person in fear of serious bodily harm, or by the threat or presenting of firearms, or other deadly weapon or instrumentality whatsoever. *"Motor vehicle"* shall have the same meaning as set forth in § 46.2-100.

C. The provisions of this section shall not preclude the applicability of any other provision of the criminal law of the Commonwealth which may apply to any course of conduct which violates this section.

History.
   1993, c. 500.

Cross references.
   For definition of "barrier crime" as including a conviction of carjacking as set out in § 18.2-58.1, or an equivalent offense in another state, and prohibition against assisted living facilities, adult day care centers or child welfare agencies hiring for certain compensated employment persons who have committed such an offense, see §§ 63.2-1719, 63.2-1720.

Law Review.
   For article surveying developments in criminal law and procedure in Virginia from July 2001 to September 2002, see 37 U. Rich. L. Rev. 45 (2002).

Michie's Jurisprudence.
   For related discussion, see 12A M.J. Larceny, § 2.

CASE NOTES

When the defendant took possession of the victim's keys, he took "possession and control" of her vehicle. Bell v. Commonwealth, 21 Va. App. 693, 467 S.E.2d 289 (1996).

Violence or intimidation required. — Carjacking must be viewed as a crime against the person as well as against the person's property; thus, the requisite violence or intimidation must precede or be concomitant with the taking. Bell v. Commonwealth, 21 Va. App. 693, 467 S.E.2d 289 (1996).

The carjacking statute does not cover every case where a defendant takes a victim's keys and then deprives the victim of her vehicle; rather the Commonwealth must prove an act of violence against the victim that precedes or is concomitant with the taking of the vehicle from the possession or control of the victim. Bell v. Commonwealth, 21 Va. App. 693, 467 S.E.2d 289 (1996).

The carjacking provision is confined by the same limitations which apply to robbery and, therefore, the requisite violence or intimidation must precede or be concomitant with the taking. Abraham v. Commonwealth, 32 Va. App. 22, 526 S.E.2d 277 (2000).

Elements of crime. — To prove that an accused violated the provisions of this section, the Commonwealth must prove beyond a reasonable doubt that the carjacker took possession or control of the vehicle; it is not sufficient to prove that the accused merely attempted to seize the vehicle or seize control of the vehicle. Keyser v. Commonwealth, 22 Va. App. 747, 473 S.E.2d 93 (1996).

Proof of intent. — Evidence that defendant and the gunman attempted to seize control and possession of the vehicle was sufficient to show intent to take the vehicle, as defendant's attempt

to enter the vehicle from the rear door was inconsistent with an attempt to accost the driver, as claimed by defendant. Walker v. Commonwealth, 2007 Va. App. LEXIS 214 (May 22, 2007).

Possessory interest not necessary. — This section does not require any ownership or possessory interest on the part of the victim; the evidence was sufficient to support defendant's conviction because it proved that the victim was in control of the vehicle at the time of the offense. Walker v. Commonwealth, 2007 Va. App. LEXIS 214 (May 22, 2007).

Assault and battery not lesser-included offense. — Carjacking is defined as a particularized form of robbery and, because assault and battery is not a lesser-included offense of robbery, neither is it a lesser-included offense of carjacking. Sanchez v. Commonwealth, 32 Va. App. 238, 527 S.E.2d 461, 2000 Va. App. LEXIS 282 (2000).

Larceny not lesser included offense. — Larceny could not be a lesser-included offense of carjacking as larceny requires the intent to permanently deprive, but the lesser intent to temporarily deprive is sufficient to prove carjacking; carjacking does not always require proof of the specific intent to permanently deprive another of property because § 18.2-58.1 employs the disjunctive "or." Chambers v. Commonwealth, No. 0805-01-4, 2002 Va. App. LEXIS 452 (Ct. of Appeals Aug. 6, 2002).

Evidence of death of defendant's accomplice properly admitted. — Where defendant was charged with committing a home invasion robbery and a carjacking with the aid of an accomplice, the trial court did not abuse its discretion in admitting evidence of the killing of his accomplice in another robbery attempt shortly thereafter, as this evidence was highly probative of defendant's identity as one of the perpetrators of the charged offenses, which he challenged throughout his trial. Layug v. Commonwealth, — Va. App. —, — S.E.2d —, 2007 Va. App. LEXIS 369 (Oct. 2, 2007).

Prior acts evidence admissible. — Prior domestic dispute between defendant and the victim had a logical and natural connection to the events at carjacking and the facts that established their nexus were probative of the existence or non-existence of the elements of carjacking set forth in § 18.2-58.1. Smallwood v. Commonwealth, — Va. App. —, — S.E.2d —, 2008 Va. App. LEXIS 211 (Apr. 29, 2008).

Evidence of prior carjackings admitted. — Admission of evidence of 10 to 20 prior carjackings by defendant and a principal in defendant's trial for carjacking under § 18.2-58.1 was not an abuse of discretion as: (1) the evidence was relevant to intent; (2) the prior offenses involved defendant and the principal operating as a team using a similar weapon to perpetrate carjackings; (3) acting in accord with their prior association, defendant brought a gun to a job interview, gave the gun to the principal, accompanied the principal, and observed the crimes without attempting to prevent them; and (4) the probative value of the prior carjackings outweighed any prejudice. Kirksey-Waugh v. Commonwealth, — Va. App. —, — S.E.2d —, 2008 Va. App. LEXIS 290 (June 17, 2008).

Evidence sufficient to sustain conviction. — Evidence that defendant entered car while passenger was waiting for owner to return, held a knife to passenger's throat, and took passenger's purse and owner's car was sufficient to sustain defendant's conviction for carjacking and robbery. Brown v. Commonwealth, 37 Va. App. 507, 559 S.E.2d 415, 2002 Va. App. LEXIS 88 (2002).

Where defendant admitted at trial that he met with the victim at the same location indicated by the victim, defendant corroborated the victim's testimony that the two were together sometime that evening, and the detective partially corroborated the victim's description of the attack, the evidence was sufficient to sustain defendant's conviction for carjacking. Mitchell v. Commonwealth, No. 3325-02-1, 2004 Va. App. LEXIS 44 (Ct. of Appeals Feb. 3, 2004).

Evidence that the victim retained possession of her vehicle when defendant entered it in her presence and that, in an unbroken sequence of events, she was forced by defendant, through violence and intimidation, to give up possession was sufficient to support a carjacking conviction. Spencer v. Commonwealth, 42 Va. App. 443, 592 S.E.2d 400, 2004 Va. App. LEXIS 56 (2004).

Evidence that defendant, in concert with the gunman, intentionally attempted to seize control of the vehicle by trying to enter the vehicle while the gunman pointed a firearm at the driver was sufficient to support defendant's convictions for attempted carjacking, in violation of § 18.2-58.1, and use of a firearm in the commission of a felony, in violation of § 18.2-53.1. Walker v. Commonwealth, 2007 Va. App. LEXIS 214 (May 22, 2007).

Evidence that the victim reported the incident to the victim's husband as soon as the victim returned to their hotel room, reported it to the police after the victim discovered evidence identifying the assailant, and located several landmarks the victim had seen while defendant held the victim captive was sufficient to support convictions for carjacking, abduction, and robbery; based on defendant's display of a gun and defendant's bizarre behavior, the victim reasonably feared defendant would kill the victim, explaining the victim's failure to make a more determined attempt to escape. Corbin v. Commonwealth, — Va. App. —, — S.E.2d —, 2007 Va. App. LEXIS 359 (Oct. 2, 2007).

Evidence supported defendant's conviction for carjacking as the evidence showed that defendant demanded the car keys from the victim, that the car was no longer in the parking lot ten minutes after the victim handed over the keys to defendant, that the police found the car three hours after its disappearance within a mile from the scene of the robbery, and that defendant and his accomplice were the only people with the means to move the car. This evidence was sufficient to infer that defendant and his accomplice took possession or control of the car. Parham v. Commonwealth, — Va. App. —, — S.E.2d —, 2009 Va. App. LEXIS 58 (Feb. 10, 2009).

Evidence that defendant approached the victim at night, on a partially lit street, with a mask covering lower half of defendant's face, demanded the victim's possession, and made persistent requests for the victim's car keys was sufficient to support a finding that the victim surrendered the victim's vehicle because the victim was intimidated and to support defendant's conviction for carjacking under § 18.2-58.1. Pressley v. Commonwealth, 54 Va. App. 380, 679 S.E.2d 551, 2009 Va. App. LEXIS 341 (2009).

Evidence sufficient to find principal in the second degree. — Defendant's conviction for carjacking in violation of § 18.2-58.1 as a principal in the second degree was supported by sufficient evidence as: (1) in accordance with a prior association, when defendant took a gun to a job interview and gave a principal the gun, defendant intended that the principal use it to obtain the victim's keys and drive away in the victim's vehicle; (2) defendant's theory that defendant was an innocent bystander was rejected; (3) defendant admitted that defendant knew the principal intended to carjack the victim and that defendant observed the crimes; (4) defendant did not discourage the principal or attempt to reclaim defendant's gun; and (5) defendant returned to the scene, retrieved the keys based on knowledge defendant obtained from the principal, and stole the car. Kirksey-Waugh v. Commonwealth, — Va. App. —, — S.E.2d —, 2008 Va. App. LEXIS 290 (June 17, 2008).

ARTICLE 6.

EXTORTION AND OTHER THREATS.

§ 18.2-59. Extortion of money, property or pecuniary benefit.

Any person who (i) threatens injury to the character, person, or property of another person, (ii) accuses him of any offense, (iii) threatens to report him as being illegally present in the United States, or (iv) knowingly destroys, conceals, removes, confiscates, withholds or threatens to withhold, or possesses any actual or purported passport or other immigration document, or any other actual or purported government identification document, of another person, and thereby extorts money, property, or pecuniary benefit or any note, bond, or other evidence of debt from him or any other person, is guilty of a Class 5 felony.

For the purposes of this section, injury to property includes the sale, distribution, or release of identifying information defined in clauses (iii) through (xii) of subsection C of § 18.2-186.3, but does not

include the distribution or release of such information by a person who does so with the intent to obtain money, property or a pecuniary benefit to which he reasonably believes he is lawfully entitled.

History.
Code 1950, § 18.1-184; 1960, c. 358; 1975, cc. 14, 15; 2006, c. 313; 2007, cc. 453, 547; 2010, c. 298.

Cross references.
For definition of "barrier crime" as including a conviction of extortion by threat as set out in § 18.2-59, or an equivalent offense in another state, and prohibition against assisted living facilities, adult day care centers or child welfare agencies hiring for certain compensated employment persons who have committed such an offense, see §§ 63.2-1719, 63.2-1720. As to report to children's residential facility for which a background check is being performed on whether the applicant has ever been convicted of or is the subject of pending charges for various crimes, including extortion by threat as set out in § 18.2-59, or an equivalent offense in another state, see § 63.2-1726.

Editor's note.
Acts 2010, c. 298, cl. 2, provides: "That the provisions of this act may result in a net increase in periods of imprisonment or commitment. Pursuant to § 30-19.1:4, the estimated amount of the necessary appropriation is $0 for periods of imprisonment in state adult correctional facilities and is $0 for periods of commitment to the custody of the Department of Juvenile Justice."

The 2010 amendments.
The 2010 amendment by c. 298 added the last paragraph.

Law Review.
For article on justification as a defense to crime, see 59 Va. L. Rev. 1326 (1973). For article on model abusive debt collection statute for Virginia, see 15 Wm. & Mary L. Rev. 567 (1974). For article, "Labor and Employment Law," see 35 U. Rich. L. Rev. 725 (2001). For 2007 annual survey article, "Criminal Law and Procedure," see 42 U. Rich. L. Rev. 311 (2007).

Michie's Jurisprudence.
For related discussion, see 4A M.J. Conspiracy, § 4.1; 8A M.J. Extortion, § 1.

CASE NOTES

Constitutionality. — This section is not vague and is facially constitutional; the words "threat," "character," and "pecuniary benefit" are all ordinary, everyday words whose meanings are plain to a person of normal intelligence and education; furthermore, the trial court defined "pecuniary benefit" in a jury instruction as "benefits that can be valued in money," and this definition was accepted by the defendant without objection; finally the concept and proscription of extortion have long existed in the law of this Commonwealth. Stein v. Commonwealth, 12 Va. App. 65, 402 S.E.2d 238 (1991).

This section is constitutional in that it is not overbroad and does not impinge upon the First Amendment right to free speech. Stein v. Commonwealth, 12 Va. App. 65, 402 S.E.2d 238 (1991).

The threat to do a legal act is not per se protected speech. Morrissey v. Commonwealth, 16 Va. App. 172, 428 S.E.2d 503 (1993).

Guilt or innocence of victim of extortion is irrelevant. — Questions propounded by the counsel of the accused concerning the guilt or innocence of the victim of the extortion, were irrelevant, immaterial and properly excluded. Whether persons upon whom extortion is practiced are vicious or virtuous they are equally entitled to the protection of the law. Mitchell v. Commonwealth, 75 Va. 856 (1880).

Claim of right is not considered a defense to extortion under Virginia law. United States v. Teplin, 775 F.2d 1261 (4th Cir. 1985).

Claim of right no defense to extortion. — Appellant's alleged claim of right to the money he sought to obtain by extortion from the victim provided no defense. Strohecker v. Commonwealth, 23 Va. App. 242, 475 S.E.2d 844 (1996).

The absence of any "claim of right" defense demonstrates that, under the Virginia extortion statute, the lawfulness of the demanded object is irrelevant; therefore, an extortionate means is sufficient to establish liability under § 18.2-59. Smithfield Foods, Inc. v. United Food & Commer. Workers Int'l Union, 585 F. Supp. 2d 789, 2008 U.S. Dist. LEXIS 81889 (E.D. Va. 2008).

Public disclosure or even proposed public disclosure is not extortion unless coupled with an effort to obtain money or other value from the victim. Wood v. Commonwealth, 8 Va. App. 560, 382 S.E.2d 306 (1989).

Constructive breaking. — Where entry is gained by threats, fraud or conspiracy, a constructive breaking is deemed to have occurred; thus, breaking may be actual or constructive. Broady v. Commonwealth, 16 Va. App. 281, 429 S.E.2d 468 (1993).

Money demanded to remain silent about invalid revocation of prenuptial agreement. — Defendant had no claim of right to the money he demanded, where he was clearly demanding "hush money" to remain silent about the alleged invalidity of a revocation agreement nullifying a prenuptial agreement between defendant's former legal client and her husband. The revocation agreement allowed the wife to claim her statutory share of her husband's estate. United States v. Teplin, 775 F.2d 1261 (4th Cir. 1985).

Commonwealth did not need to prove that accusation underlying threat was false. — Where defendant had accused victim of raping her and where the Commonwealth elected to charge defendant with threatening to injure victim's character, it was not necessary for the Commonwealth to prove that an accusation underlying the threat was false, even though the threatened injury was to the character of a person and did not constitute an accusation of an offense. Wood v. Commonwealth, 8 Va. App. 560, 382 S.E.2d 306 (1989).

Extortion held alleged. — Where it was alleged that: (a) defendants entered into a contract with plaintiff, knowing at the time that they did not intend to perform and knowing also that plaintiff would rely on their contract to expose itself to economic risk; (b) plaintiff in reliance on the contract with defendant entered into a commercial arrangement with another; and (c) defendants exacted moneys, property and pecuniary benefits on the threat of causing plaintiff the economic harm which would stem from non-performance of its other commercial arrangement, extortion was alleged. Battlefield Bldrs., Inc. v. Swango, 743 F.2d 1060 (4th Cir. 1984).

Evidence sufficient. — Trial court did not err in finding defendant guilty, following a bench trial, of computer fraud, computer trespass, embezzlement, and attempted extortion, as the evidence showed that defendant transferred computer files from his computer at work to a third-party server before he was terminated from his position as human resource director, that he used the removed material to threaten the company in an attempt to forgive a loan it had made to him, and that the company established the value of the material removed as required to support convictions on those offenses. DiMaio v. Commonwealth, 46 Va. App. 755, 621 S.E.2d 696, 2005 Va. App. LEXIS 456 (2005).

§ 18.2-60. Threats of death or bodily injury to a person or member of his family; threats to commit serious bodily harm to persons on school property; penalty.

A. 1. Any person who knowingly communicates, in a writing, including an electronically transmitted communication producing a visual or electronic message, a threat to kill or do bodily injury to a person, regarding that person or any member of his family, and the threat places such person in reasonable apprehension of death or bodily injury to himself or his family member, is guilty of a Class 6 felony. However, any person who violates this subsection with the intent to commit an act of terrorism as defined in § 18.2-46.4 is guilty of a Class 5 felony.

2. Any person who communicates a threat, in a writing, including an electronically transmitted communication producing a visual or electronic message, to kill or do bodily harm, (i) on the grounds or premises of any elementary, middle or secondary school property, (ii) at any elementary, middle or secondary school-sponsored event or (iii) on a school bus to any person or persons, regardless of whether the person who is the object of the threat actually receives the threat, and the threat would place the person who is the object of the threat in reasonable apprehension of death or bodily harm, is guilty of a Class 6 felony.

B. Any person who orally makes a threat to any employee of any elementary, middle or secondary school, while on a school bus, on school property or at a school-sponsored activity, to kill or to do bodily injury to such person, is guilty of a Class 1 misdemeanor.

A prosecution pursuant to this section may be either in the county, city or town in which the communication was made or received.

History.
Code 1950, § 18.1-257; 1960, c. 358; 1973, c. 118; 1975, cc. 14, 15; 1994, c. 265; 1998, cc. 687, 788; 2001, cc. 644, 653; 2002, cc. 588, 623.

Cross references.
As to threats of violence to judge, etc., as contempt, see § 18.2-456. As to obstructing justice by threats, see § 18.2-460.

Law Review.
For article on model abusive debt collection statute for Virginia, see 15 Wm. & Mary L. Rev. 567 (1974). For article, "Criminal Law and Procedure," see 35 U. Rich. L. Rev. 537 (2001). For article, "Legal Issues Involving Children," see 35 U. Rich. L. Rev. 741 (2001). For article summarizing published Virginia criminal law decisions between July 1, 2002 and July 1, 2003, see 38 U. Rich. L. Rev. 87 (2003). For annual survey article, "Criminal Law and Procedure," see 46 U. Rich. L. Rev. 59 (2011).

CASE NOTES

What constitutes threats. — Defendant's posts on his MySpace profile constituted threats under subdivision A 1 of § 18.2-60 as the graphic and violent imagery used in the messages specifically referred to the victim and her family, referring to the victim by using her maiden name, referencing specific incidents involving the victim, and identifying details that were unique to the acrimonious history between defendant and the victim. Defendant frequently stated in his messages that he "just had to stab" the victim and "slit her neck into a fountain drink." Holcomb v. Commonwealth, 58 Va. App. 339, 709 S.E.2d 711, 2011 Va. App. LEXIS 190 (2011).

In determining whether a statement is threatening and places the recipient in reasonable apprehension of death or bodily injury under subdivision A 1 of § 18.2-60, proof of the effect of the alleged threat upon the addressee is highly relevant. Holcomb v. Commonwealth, 58 Va. App. 339, 709 S.E.2d 711, 2011 Va. App. LEXIS 190 (2011).

Electronic communications. — Defendant's posts on his MySpace profile were electronic communications capable of constituting threats in violation of § 18.2-60. Posting a message on a MySpace profile was an electronic communication because it produced a visual message that could be viewed by anyone who had access to that page. Holcomb v. Commonwealth, 58 Va. App. 339, 709 S.E.2d 711, 2011 Va. App. LEXIS 190 (2011).

Reasonable apprehension of death or injury. — Defendant's threats on his MySpace profile placed the victim in fear of death or bodily injury as the evidence showed that the victim, in response to reading the posts, moved into her parents' home to take advantage of their security system and cameras and that she was scared that she was going to be killed or maimed and that her daughter was going to be kidnapped. Holcomb v. Commonwealth, 58 Va. App. 339, 709 S.E.2d 711, 2011 Va. App. LEXIS 190 (2011).

Malice not element of offense. — In a prosecution under this section, a trial court is not required to instruct the jury on malice, as malice is not an element of the offense. Saunders v. Commonwealth, 31 Va. App. 321, 523 S.E.2d 509 (2000).

Threatening letter. — Evidence showed a defendant prisoner sent a threatening letter when he put it in the institutional mail. Keyes v. Commonwealth, 39 Va. App. 294, 572 S.E.2d 512, 2002 Va. App. LEXIS 698 (2002).

Letter from defendant to girlfriend threatening to kill her stepfather. — Letter from defendant to 15-year-old girl he had been dating, which contained a threat to kill her stepfather, who, along with the girl's mother, had been trying to "break up" the relationship between the girl and defendant, was held to violate this section. Flint v. Commonwealth, No. 0588-85 (Ct. of Appeals Oct. 30, 1986).

Search and seizure. — District court properly denied defendant's motion to suppress evidence in his trial for possession of an unregistered machine gun and an unregistered silencer in violation of 26 U.S.C.S. §§ 5861(d) and 5871 because the seizure of the gun and silencer was justified under the plain-view exception to the warrant requirement under U.S. Const., Amend. IV; a valid warrant had been issued to search for evidence and instrumentalities of criminal activity under § 18.2-60, evidence such as disks and thumbnail drives could easily have been stored in the lockbox with the gun and silencer, and the incriminating character of the gun and silencer became immediately apparent during the course of a legitimate safety inspection. United States v. Williams, 592 F.3d 511, 2010 U.S. App. LEXIS 1327 (4th Cir. 2010), cert. denied, 131 S. Ct. 595, 178 L. Ed. 2d 434, 2010 U.S. LEXIS 8864 (U.S. 2010).

§ 18.2-60.1. Threatening the Governor or his immediate family.

Any person who shall knowingly and willfully send, deliver or convey, or cause to be sent, delivered or conveyed, to the Governor or his immediate family any threat to take the life of or inflict bodily harm upon the Governor or his immediate family, whether such threat be oral or written, shall be guilty of a Class 6 felony.

History.
1982, c. 568.

§ 18.2-60.2. Members of the Governor's immediate family.

As used in § 18.2-60.1, the immediate family of the Governor shall include any parent, sibling, child, grandchild, spouse, parent of a spouse, and spouse of a sibling, child or grandchild who resides in the same household as the Governor.

History.
1982, c. 568.

§ 18.2-60.3. Stalking; penalty.

A. Any person, except a law-enforcement officer, as defined in § 9.1-101, and acting in the performance of his official duties, and a registered private investigator, as defined in § 9.1-138, who is regulated in accordance with § 9.1-139 and acting in the course of his legitimate business, who on more than one occasion engages in conduct directed at another person with the intent to place, or when he knows or reasonably should know that the conduct places that other person in reasonable fear of death, criminal sexual assault, or bodily injury to that other person or to that other person's family or household member is guilty of a Class 1 misdemeanor.

B. Any person who is convicted of a second offense of subsection A occurring within five years of a prior conviction of such an offense when the person was also convicted within the five-year period prior to the instant offense of a violation of (i) § 18.2-51, 18.2-51.2, 18.2-51.6, 18.2-52, or 18.2-57 and the victim of that crime was the same person who is the victim of the stalking activity in the instant conviction, (ii) § 18.2-57.2, or (iii) a protective order, is guilty of a Class 6 felony.

C. Any person convicted of a third or subsequent conviction of subsection A occurring within five years of a conviction for an offense under this section or for a similar offense under the law of any other jurisdiction is guilty of a Class 6 felony.

D. A person may be convicted under this section irrespective of the jurisdiction or jurisdictions within the Commonwealth wherein the conduct described in subsection A occurred, if the person engaged in that conduct on at least one occasion in the jurisdiction where the person is tried. Evidence of any such conduct that occurred outside the Commonwealth may be admissible, if relevant, in any prosecution under this section provided that the prosecution is based upon conduct occurring within the Commonwealth.

E. Upon finding a person guilty under this section, the court shall, in addition to the sentence imposed, issue an order prohibiting contact between the defendant and the victim or the victim's family or household member.

F. The Department of Corrections, sheriff or regional jail director shall give notice prior to the release from a state correctional facility or a local or regional jail of any person incarcerated upon conviction of a violation of this section, to any victim of the offense who, in writing, requests notice, or to any person designated in writing by the victim. The notice shall be given at least 15 days prior to release of a person sentenced to a term of incarceration of more than 30 days or, if the person was sentenced to a term of incarceration of at least 48 hours but no more than 30 days, 24 hours prior to release. If the person escapes, notice shall be given as soon as practicable following the escape. The victim shall keep the Department of Corrections, sheriff or regional jail director informed of the current mailing address and telephone number of the person named in the writing submitted to receive notice.

All information relating to any person who receives or may receive notice under this subsection shall remain confidential and shall not be made available to the person convicted of violating this section.

For purposes of this subsection, "release" includes a release of the offender from a state correctional facility or a local or regional jail (i) upon completion of his term of incarceration or (ii) on probation or parole.

No civil liability shall attach to the Department of Corrections nor to any sheriff or regional jail director or their deputies or employees for a failure to comply with the requirements of this subsection.

G. For purposes of this section:

"*Family or household member*" has the same meaning as provided in § 16.1-228.

History.

1992, c. 888; 1994, cc. 360, 521, 739; 1995, c. 824; 1996, cc. 540, 866; 1998, c. 570; 2001, c. 197; 2002, c. 377; 2013, c. 759.

Cross references.

For definition of "barrier crime" as including a conviction of felony stalking as set out in § 18.2-60.3, or an equivalent offense in another state, and prohibition against assisted living facilities, adult day care centers or child welfare agencies hiring for certain compensated employment persons who have committed such an offense, see §§ 63.2-1719, 63.2-1720.

Editor's note.

Acts 2013, c. 759, cl. 2 provides: "That the provisions of this act may result in a net increase in periods of imprisonment or commitment. Pursuant to § 30-19.1:4, the estimated amount of the necessary appropriation is at least $23,197 for periods of imprisonment in state adult correctional facilities and cannot be determined for periods of commitment to the custody of the Department of Juvenile Justice."

The 2013 amendments.

The 2013 amendment by c. 759 added present subsection B and redesignated the following subsections accordingly; in subsection C, substituted "Any person convicted of a third" for "A third," inserted "of subsection A" and substituted "is guilty of a Class 6 felony" for "shall be a Class 6 felony"; and made minor stylistic changes.

Law Review.

For note, "'Stalk Talk': A First Look at Anti-Stalking Legislation," see 50 Wash. & Lee L. Rev. 1303 (1993). For article, "Criminal Law and Procedure," see 31 U. Rich. L. Rev. 1015 (1997). For article, "Criminal Law and Procedure," see 35 U. Rich. L. Rev. 537 (2001). For article, "Gender Bias Task Force: Comments on Substantive Law Issues," see 58 Wash. & Lee L. Rev. 1095 (2001).

CASE NOTES

Constitutionality. — For a case upholding the constitutionality of this section as it read prior to the 1994 amendments, see Woolfolk v. Commonwealth, 18 Va. App. 840, 447 S.E.2d 530 (1994).

This section is not unconstitutionally vague either on its face or as applied to defendant. Both the "reasonable fear" element and the requirement of specific intent make this section sufficiently clear to inform both citizens and law-enforcement officers of what acts constitute stalking. Parker v. Commonwealth, 24 Va. App. 681, 485 S.E.2d 150 (1997), cert. denied, 523 U.S. 1071, 118 S. Ct. 1510, 140 L. Ed. 2d 665 (1998).

This section is not unconstitutionally overbroad on the ground that it chills protected speech. The purpose is legitimate: to protect innocent citizens from intentional or knowingly threatening conduct that subjects them to a reasonable fear of harm. And it is not directed primarily at speech nor does it overreach to prevent contact, speech or otherwise between quarreling lovers. The statute permits all communications between individuals that are conducted in a time, place and manner that do not intentionally or knowingly cause the receiver of the message reasonably to fear for his or her physical safety. Parker v. Commonwealth, 24 Va. App. 681, 485 S.E.2d 150 (1997), cert. denied, 523 U.S. 1071, 118 S. Ct. 1510, 140 L. Ed. 2d 665 (1998).

Evidence proved that appellant stalked his ex-wife where from mid-summer 1992 until his arrest in September 1992, he persistently followed her, he watched her in her home at all hours of the day and night, and even began to follow her boyfriend, who lived 40 miles away; threatened to shoot his ex-wife and her boyfriend; followed this threat by driving through the boyfriend's apartment complex and repeatedly driving by his ex-wife's residence; and ex-wife testified that appellant's threat, combined with his persistent course of conduct, "terrified" her and that she believed that appellant wanted to shoot or kill her. Woolfolk v. Commonwealth, 18 Va. App. 840, 447 S.E.2d 530 (1994).

Reasonableness of victim's fear. — Upon rehearing en banc it was determined that where a prior stalking conviction provided only a historical context in which defendant's subsequent conduct was adjudged, neither double jeopardy nor res judicata applied; the evidence abundantly supported the reasonableness of the victim's fear. Burwell v. Commonwealth, No. 1777-99-2, 2001 Va. App. LEXIS 711 (Ct. of Appeals Apr. 17, 2001).

Proof of accused's intent or knowledge. — To convict a defendant of stalking under this section, the Commonwealth must prove beyond a reasonable doubt that, on at least two occasions, the defendant either intended to cause the victim fear of the enumerated harms or knew his conduct would cause the victim such fear; the knowledge of the accused may be inferred from the surrounding facts and circumstances and, in drawing inferences from all the circumstances, the fact finder may discount defendant's explanation for his acts. Gilbert v. Commonwealth, No. 0418-00-2, 2001 Va. App. LEXIS 273 (Ct. of Appeals May 22, 2001).

Where Commonwealth fails to prove specific intent to cause fear, proof that the defendant actually knew that his conduct would place the victim in fear of the enumerated harms is a necessary element of the offense. Bowen v. Commonwealth, 27 Va. App. 377, 499 S.E.2d 20 (1998).

Evidence of prior conduct. — Trial court did not err by instructing the jury that the facts and circumstances relating to a prior charge could be considered as evidence of a common scheme or plan in the prosecution of the defendant for stalking in violation of § 18.2-60.3 and violating a protective order in violation of § 18.2-60.4 because defendant's 2007 prior conduct tended to prove that he knew or should have reasonably known that his 2008 conduct would reasonably cause the victim to fear bodily harm, and the jury instructions properly informed the jury for what specific purposes the victim's testimony could be considered; the 2007 events, as described by the victim at trial, were pertinent to the jury's determination regarding whether or not defendant had motive and intent when he violated the protective order in 2008 and went to the victim's home, followed her in various vehicles, and called her repeatedly at work, and defendant's pursuit of the victim in his car in 2008 was comparable to his pursuits in 2007. Jordan v. Commonwealth, 2011 Va. App. LEXIS 139 (Apr. 26, 2011).

Sufficient evidence of accused's intent or knowledge. — In a prosecution for stalking, where the evidence showed that defendant had continued his unwelcome advances toward the victim after she had told him that she was not interested and after the parties' employer had terminated defendant for sexual harassment, that the victim had moved out of state to avoid defendant, that the victim had communicated her fear of defendant to police, and that she had posted warning posters inside her apartment building with defendant's picture on it identifying defendant as a stalker, there was credible evidence to support the trial court's conclusion beyond a reasonable doubt that the victim had reasonable cause to fear that defendant would harm her and that he knew or should have known that his conduct caused her to have that fear. Schoenberger v. Commonwealth, No. 0156-04-4, 2005 Va. App. LEXIS 15 (Ct. of Appeals Jan. 11, 2005).

Sufficient evidence. — Where defendant engaged in frenzied sprees of phone calls that he knew would cause the victim to worry for her safety upon his pending release from jail; he was aware of his past abusive relationship with victim and that he had previously been convicted for placing her in reasonable fear of bodily harm; he knew his release from jail was in two months; and he continued his barrage of calls after he knew they were unwelcome, evidence was sufficient of a violation of this section. Parker v.

Commonwealth, 24 Va. App. 681, 485 S.E.2d 150 (1997), cert. denied, 523 U.S. 1071, 118 S. Ct. 1510, 140 L. Ed. 2d 665 (1998).

Evidence was sufficient to support convictions of stalking where the defendant repeatedly threw sexually explicit materials toward three minors and repeatedly drove by two minors and engaged in conversations that would reasonably frighten young girls. Hartman v. Commonwealth, No. 0569-98-3 (Ct. of Appeals Mar. 30, 1999).

The evidence was sufficient to support the defendant's conviction for stalking where the victim testified that she did not know the defendant very well when he began making daily telephone calls to her, that the initial calls were friendly but in later conversations the defendant began interjecting sexual comments and asserting his desire to have sex with her, that the defendant scared her when he said he would rape her if he saw her wearing a certain bathing suit, that the defendant made repeated and unwanted calls to her workplace, that the defendant continued calling her after having been told by the victim's boyfriend to stop because the victim was afraid of him, and that the defendant threatened victim over the telephone when she refused to help him raise bail money. Gilbert v. Commonwealth, No. 0418-00-2, 2001 Va. App. LEXIS 273 (Ct. of Appeals May 22, 2001).

Evidence was sufficient to sustain defendant's conviction for stalking as a rational fact finder could reasonably conclude that defendant, a complete stranger to the victim, engaged in conduct directed at the victim on more than one occasion that he reasonably should have known would place the victim in reasonable fear of death, criminal sexual assault, or bodily injury, in that defendant followed the victim for a year, driving up and down her neighborhood every evening for a month. Defendant's conduct persisted despite the fact that the victim moved to two different unpublished addresses, changed her telephone number, protected the number as unlisted, and rejected defendant's advances by stating that she was married. Frazier v. Commonwealth, — Va. App. —, — S.E.2d —, 2007 Va. App. LEXIS 285 (July 31, 2007).

Sufficiency of the evidence argument not preserved. — Where defendant appealed his conviction for stalking, claiming that the evidence was insufficient to support the conviction, the appellate court did not consider the argument on the merits because it was barred by Va. Sup. Ct. Rule 5A:18, as the issue was not properly preserved for review; although defendant had made two motions to strike against the Commonwealth's evidence, those motions were not supported with any specificity as to the grounds of the objections and accordingly, the trial court did not have an opportunity to consider the issue of sufficiency of the evidence. Hurley v. Commonwealth, No. 1332-03-3, 2004 Va. App. LEXIS 255 (Ct. of Appeals June 1, 2004).

Evidence sufficiently proved appropriateness of venue. — Ordinarily, a criminal case has to be prosecuted in the county or city in which the offense was committed, under § 19.2-244; despite the special venue provision of former § 18.2-60.3.A, there was no error in the refusal to grant defendant's motion to strike a stalking charge based upon an allegation of improper venue, as the evidence gave rise to a strong presumption that at least one of the stalking events occurred within the jurisdiction of the court where defendant was tried. Raja v. Commonwealth, 40 Va. App. 710, 581 S.E.2d 237, 2003 Va. App. LEXIS 318 (2003).

§ 18.2-60.4. Violation of protective orders; penalty.

Any person who violates any provision of a protective order issued pursuant to § 19.2-152.8, 19.2-152.9, or 19.2-152.10 is guilty of a Class 1 misdemeanor. Conviction hereunder shall bar a finding of contempt for the same act. The punishment for any person convicted of a second offense of violating a protective order, when the offense is committed within five years of the prior conviction and when either the instant or prior offense was based on an act or threat of violence, shall include a mandatory minimum term of confinement of 60 days. Any person convicted of a third or subsequent offense of violating a protective order, when the offense is

committed within 20 years of the first conviction and when either the instant or one of the prior offenses was based on an act or threat of violence, is guilty of a Class 6 felony and the punishment shall include a mandatory minimum term of confinement of six months. The mandatory minimum terms of confinement prescribed for violations of this section shall be served consecutively with any other sentence.

If the respondent commits an assault and battery upon any party protected by the protective order resulting in serious bodily injury to the party, he is guilty of a Class 6 felony. Any person who violates such a protective order by furtively entering the home of any protected party while the party is present, or by entering and remaining in the home of the protected party until the party arrives, is guilty of a Class 6 felony, in addition to any other penalty provided by law.

Upon conviction of any offense hereunder for which a mandatory minimum term of confinement is not specified, the person shall be sentenced to a term of confinement and in no case shall the entire term imposed be suspended.

Upon conviction, the court shall, in addition to the sentence imposed, enter a protective order pursuant to § 19.2-152.10 for a specified period not exceeding two years from the date of conviction.

History.
1998, c. 569; 2003, c. 219; 2011, cc. 445, 480; 2013, cc. 761, 774.

Editor's note.
Acts 2011, cc. 445 and 480, cl. 2 provides: "That the provisions of this act may result in a net increase in periods of imprisonment or commitment. Pursuant to § 30-19.1:4, the estimated amount of the necessary appropriation is $93,767 for periods of imprisonment in state adult correctional facilities and cannot be determined for periods of commitment to the custody of the Department of Juvenile Justice."

Acts 2013, cc. 761 and 774, cl. 2 provides: "That the provisions of this act may result in a net increase in periods of imprisonment or commitment. Pursuant to § 30-19.1:4, the estimated amount of the necessary appropriation cannot be determined for periods of imprisonment in state adult correctional facilities; therefore, Chapter 3 of the Acts of Assembly of 2012, Special Session I, requires the Virginia Criminal Sentencing Commission to assign a minimum fiscal impact of $50,000. Pursuant to § 30-19.1:4, the estimated amount of the necessary appropriation cannot be determined for periods of commitment to the custody of the Department of Juvenile Justice."

The 2011 amendments.
The 2011 amendments by cc. 445 and 480 are nearly identical, and in the first paragraph, added the last sentence and made a stylistic change; added the second and third paragraphs.

The 2013 amendments.
The 2013 amendments by cc. 761 and 774 are identical, and added the last sentence of the first paragraph.

CASE NOTES

Evidence of prior conduct. — Trial court did not err by instructing the jury that the facts and circumstances relating to a prior charge could be considered as evidence of a common scheme or plan in the prosecution of the defendant for stalking in violation of § 18.2-60.3 and violating a protective order in violation of § 18.2-60.4 because defendant's 2007 prior conduct tended to prove that he knew or should have known that his 2008 conduct would reasonably cause the victim to fear bodily harm, and the jury instructions properly informed the jury for what specific purposes the victim's testimony could be considered; the 2007 events, as described by the victim at trial, were pertinent to the jury's determination regarding whether or not defendant had motive and intent when he violated the protective order in 2008 and went to the victim's home, followed her in various vehicles, and called her repeatedly at work, and defendant's pursuit of the victim in his car in 2008 was comparable to his pursuits in 2007. Jordan v. Commonwealth, 2011 Va. App. LEXIS 139 (Apr. 26, 2011).

§ 18.2-60.5. Unauthorized use of electronic tracking device; penalty.

A. Any person who installs or places an electronic tracking device through intentionally deceptive means and without consent, or causes an electronic tracking device to be installed or placed through intentionally deceptive means and without consent, and uses such device to track the location of any person is guilty of a Class 3 misdemeanor.

B. The provisions of this section shall not apply to the installation, placement, or use of an electronic tracking device by:

1. A law-enforcement officer, judicial officer, probation or parole officer, or employee of the Department of Corrections when any such person is engaged in the lawful performance of official duties and in accordance with other state or federal law;

2. The parent or legal guardian of a minor when tracking (i) the minor or (ii) any person authorized by the parent or legal guardian as a caretaker of the minor at any time when the minor is under the person's sole care;

3. A legally authorized representative of an incapacitated adult, as defined in § 18.2-369;

4. The owner of fleet vehicles, when tracking such vehicles;

5. An electronic communications provider to the extent that such installation, placement, or use is disclosed in the provider's terms of use, privacy policy, or similar document made available to the customer; or

6. A registered private investigator, as defined in § 9.1-138, who is regulated in accordance with § 9.1-139 and is acting in the normal course of his business and with the consent of the owner of the property upon which the electronic tracking device is installed and placed. However, such exception shall not apply if the private investigator is working on behalf of a client who is subject to a protective order under § 16.1-253, 16.1-253.1, 16.1-253.4, 16.1-279.1, 19.2-152.8, 19.2-152.9, 19.2-152.10, or subsection B of § 20-103, or if the private investigator knows or should reasonably know that the client seeks the private investigator's services to aid in the commission of a crime.

C. For the purposes of this section:

"Electronic tracking device" means an electronic or mechanical device that permits a person to remotely determine or track the position and movement of another person.

"Fleet vehicle" means (i) one or more motor vehicles owned by a single entity and operated by employees or agents of the entity for business or government purposes, (ii) motor vehicles held for lease or rental to the general public, or (iii) motor vehicles held for sale by motor vehicle dealers.

History.
2013, c. 434.

ARTICLE 7.

CRIMINAL SEXUAL ASSAULT.

§ 18.2-61. Rape.

A. If any person has sexual intercourse with a complaining witness, whether or not his or her spouse, or causes a complaining witness, whether or not his or her spouse, to engage in sexual intercourse with any other person and such act is accomplished (i) against the complaining witness's will, by force, threat or intimidation of or against the complaining witness or another person; or (ii) through the use of the complaining witness's mental incapacity or physical helplessness; or (iii) with a child under age 13 as the victim, he or she shall be guilty of rape.

B. A violation of this section shall be punishable, in the discretion of the court or jury, by confinement in a state correctional facility for life or for any term not less than five years; and in addition:

1. For a violation of clause (iii) of subsection A where the offender is more than three years older than the victim, if done in the commission of, or as part of the same course of conduct as, or as part of a common scheme or plan as a violation of (i) subsection A of § 18.2-47 or § 18.2-48, (ii) § 18.2-89, 18.2-90, or 18.2-91, or (iii) § 18.2-51.2, the punishment shall include a mandatory minimum term of confinement of 25 years; or

2. For a violation of clause (iii) of subsection A where it is alleged in the indictment that the offender was 18 years of age or older at the time of the offense, the punishment shall include a mandatory minimum term of confinement for life.

The mandatory minimum terms of confinement prescribed for violations of this section shall be served consecutively with any other sentence. If the term of confinement imposed for any violation of clause (iii) of subsection A, where the offender is more than three years older than the victim, is for a term less than life imprisonment, the judge shall impose, in addition to any active sentence, a suspended sentence of no less than 40 years. This suspended sentence shall be suspended for the remainder of the defendant's life, subject to revocation by the court.

There shall be a rebuttable presumption that a juvenile over the age of 10 but less than 12, does not possess the physical capacity to commit a violation of this section. In any case deemed appropriate by the court, all or part of any sentence imposed for a violation under this section against a spouse may be suspended upon the defendant's completion of counseling or therapy, if not already provided, in the manner prescribed under § 19.2-218.1 if, after consideration of the views of the complaining witness and such other evidence as may be relevant, the court finds such action will promote maintenance of the family unit and will be in the best interest of the complaining witness.

C. Upon a finding of guilt under this section, when a spouse is the complaining witness in any case tried by the court without a jury, the court, without entering a judgment of guilt, upon motion of the defendant who has not previously had a proceeding against him for violation of this section dismissed pursuant to this subsection and with the consent of the complaining witness and the attorney for the Commonwealth, may defer further proceedings and place the defendant on probation pending completion of counseling or therapy, if not already provided, in the manner prescribed under § 19.2-218.1. If the defendant fails to so complete such counseling or therapy, the court may make final disposition of the case and proceed as otherwise provided. If such counseling is completed as prescribed under § 19.2-218.1, the court may discharge the defendant and dismiss the proceedings against him if, after consideration of the views of the complaining witness and such other evidence as may be relevant, the court finds such action will promote maintenance of the family unit and be in the best interest of the complaining witness.

History.
Code 1950, § 18.1-44; 1960, c. 358; 1972, c. 394; 1975, cc. 14, 15, 606; 1981, c. 397; 1982, c. 506; 1986, c. 516; 1994, cc. 339, 772, 794; 1997, c. 330; 1999, c. 367; 2002, cc. 810, 818; 2005, c. 631; 2006, cc. 853, 914; 2012, cc. 575, 605; 2013, cc. 761, 774.

Cross references.
As to punishment for attempted rape, see §§ 18.2-26 and 18.2-67.5. As to admissibility of evidence regarding the prosecutrix' chastity or prior sexual conduct, see § 18.2-67.7. For provision making it unlawful to work or volunteer on school grounds following convictions of certain sex offenses, see § 18.2-370.4. As to arrest policies and procedures in domestic violence and family abuse cases, see Chapter 13 (§ 9.1-1300 et seq.) of Title 9.1. For provision that consent to adoption shall not be required of the birth father when the father has been convicted of a violation of § 18.2-61 A, § 18.2-63, or § 18.2-366 B, see § 63.2-1202 F. As to validity of an entrustment agreement for termination of parental rights, despite lack of birth father's signature, when the father has been convicted of a violation of § 18.2-61 A, § 18.2-63, or § 18.2-366 B, and the child in question was conceived as a result of such violation, see § 63.2-903 C and § 63.2-1222. As to Sex Offenders and Crimes Against Minors Registry, see § 9.1-900 et seq. For definition of "barrier crime" as including a conviction of sexual assault as set out in § 18.2-61 et seq., or an equivalent offense in another state, and prohibition against assisted living facilities, adult day care centers or child welfare agencies hiring for certain compensated employment persons who have committed such an offense, see §§ 63.2-1719, 63.2-1720. As to report to children's residential facility for which a background check is being performed on whether the applicant has ever been convicted of or is the subject of pending charges for various crimes, including sexual assault as set out in § 18.2-61 et seq., or an equivalent offense in another state, see § 63.2-1726. For provision making it unlawful for any person to operate a family day home if he, or if he knows that any other person who resides in the home, has been convicted of a felony in violation of this section, see § 63.2-1727.

Editor's note.
This article was enacted by Acts 1975, c. 606. Pursuant to § 30-152, it has been substituted for §§ 18.2-61 through 18.2-67 as enacted by Acts 1975, cc. 14 and 15.

Acts 2012, cc. 575 and 605, cl. 2 provides: "That the provisions of this act may result in a net increase in periods of imprisonment or commitment. Pursuant to § 30-19.1:4, the estimated amount of the necessary appropriation cannot be determined for periods of imprisonment in state adult correctional facilities; therefore, Chapter 890 of the Acts of Assembly of 2011 requires the Virginia Criminal Sentencing Commission to assign a minimum fiscal impact of $50,000. Pursuant to § 30-19.1:4, the estimated amount of the necessary appropriation is $0 for periods of commitment to the custody of the Department of Juvenile Justice."

Acts 2013, cc. 761 and 774, cl. 2 provides: "That the provisions of this act may result in a net increase in periods of imprisonment or commitment. Pursuant to § 30-19.1:4, the estimated amount of the necessary appropriation cannot be determined for periods of imprisonment in state adult correctional facilities; therefore, Chapter 3 of the Acts of Assembly of 2012, Special Session I, requires the Virginia Criminal Sentencing Commission to assign a minimum fiscal impact of $50,000. Pursuant to § 30-19.1:4, the estimated amount of the necessary appropriation cannot be determined for periods of commitment to the custody of the Department of Juvenile Justice."

The 2012 amendments.
The 2012 amendments by cc. 575 and 605 are identical, and rewrote subsection B.

The 2013 amendments.
The 2013 amendments by cc. 761 and 774 are identical, and added the first sentence of the paragraph following subdivision B 2.

Law Review.
For note, "Recent Statutory Developments in the Definition of Forcible Rape," see 61 Va. L. Rev. 1500 (1975). For survey of Virginia criminal law for the year 1974-1975, see 61 Va. L. Rev. 1697 (1975). For article discussing constitutional problems with "rape shield" laws, see 18 Wm. & Mary L. Rev. 1 (1976). For survey of Virginia law on evidence for the year 1975-1976, see 62 Va. L. Rev. 1442 (1976). For article discussing the legislative history of sexual assault law reform in Virginia, see 68 Va. L. Rev. 459 (1982). For comment on spouse abuse in Virginia, see 17 U. Rich. L. Rev. 633 (1983). For note, "Checking the Allure of Increased Conviction Rates: The Admissibility of Expert Testimony on Rape Trauma Syndrome in Criminal Proceedings," see 70 Va. L. Rev. 1657 (1984). For comment, "Sexism and the Common Law: Spousal Rape in Virginia," see 8 Geo. Mason U.L. Rev. 369 (1986). For an article, "Sex and Guilt," see 84 Va. L. Rev. 1 (1998). For note, "Predicate Offenses for First Degree Felony Murder in Virginia," see 57 Wash. & Lee L. Rev. 561 (2000). For article surveying developments in criminal law and procedure in Virginia from July 2001 to September 2002, see 37 U. Rich. L. Rev. 45 (2002). For article surveying developments in family law in Virginia, see 37 U. Rich. L. Rev. 155 (2002). For survey of Virginia criminal law and procedure for the year 2004-2005, see 40 U. Rich. L. Rev. 197 (2005). For 2006 survey article, "Criminal Law and Procedure," see 41 U. Rich. L. Rev. 83 (2006). For 2006 survey article, "Family and Juvenile Law," see 41 U. Rich. L. Rev. 151 (2006). For 2007 annual survey article, "Criminal Law and Procedure," see 42 U. Rich. L. Rev. 311 (2007).

Research references.
Anthony Morosco, The Prosecution and Defense of Sex Crimes (Matthew Bender).

Michie's Jurisprudence.
For related discussion, see 2B M.J. Autrefois, Acquit and Convict, § 16; 15 M.J. Rape, §§ 1-6, 9, 17-19, 21, 23, 27.

CASE NOTES

I. General Consideration.

I. GENERAL CONSIDERATION.

Editor's note.

Attention is directed to the fact that many of the cases in the following annotations were decided under this article as it read before the extensive amendments in Acts 1981, c. 397.

Rape may be committed as well on a woman unchaste, or a common prostitute, as on any other woman. In matter of evidence, however, want of chastity may, within recognized limits, be shown as rendering it more probable that she consented. Christian v. Commonwealth, 64 Va. (23 Gratt.) 954 (1873); Bailey v. Commonwealth, 82 Va. 107 (1886); Fry v. Commonwealth, 82 Va. 334 (1886). But see § 18.2-67.7.

History of section. — See Hart v. Commonwealth, 131 Va. 726, 109 S.E. 582 (1921).

For case holding that abduction and rape were different offenses and that the several penalties imposed did not offend the double jeopardy guarantee against multiple punishments, see Brown v. Commonwealth, 230 Va. 310, 337 S.E.2d 711 (1985).

Court erred in failing to strike a juror where she would have required a defendant to prove sexual consent from a rape victim and this burden on the defendant was impermissible and the problem of the juror's "feeling" on consent was unaddressed. Bradbury v. Commonwealth, 40 Va. App. 176, 578 S.E.2d 93, 2003 Va. App. LEXIS 146 (2003).

Consensual intercourse with mentally retarded/impaired persons. — Statutes like this section must not be interpreted and applied in a manner that creates an unintended rule that would prohibit all mentally impaired or retarded persons from engaging in consensual sexual intercourse without having their partners commit a felony. Adkins v. Commonwealth, 20 Va. App. 332, 457 S.E.2d 382 (1995).

When a mentally impaired or mentally retarded person has sufficient cognitive and intellectual capacity to comprehend or appreciate that he or she is engaging in intimate or personal sexual behavior which later may have some effect or residual impact upon the person, upon the person's partner, or upon others, then the person does not have a "mental incapacity" within the meaning of the statute. Adkins v. Commonwealth, 20 Va. App. 332, 457 S.E.2d 382 (1995).

If a person is mentally incapacitated but, nevertheless, has the capacity to understand the nature and consequences of the sexual act, which understanding includes the capacity to make a volitional choice to engage or not engage in such act, then that person's sexual partner has not violated the rape statute merely because a mentally impaired person has made an unwise decision or has chosen to be sexually active. Adkins v. Commonwealth, 20 Va. App. 332, 457 S.E.2d 382 (1995).

Failure to order bill of particulars when Commonwealth amended indictment not abuse of discretion. — Trial judge did not abuse his discretion by failing to order a bill of particulars when the Commonwealth amended one of the three rape indictments to allege a new offense date. The indictment was sufficient to apprise the appellant of the nature and character of the offense, as he had already entered his plea prior to his bill of particulars request. In a statutory rape case, when the age of the victim is not in dispute, time is not of the essence of such an offense, and the Commonwealth is not required to specify the exact date. Yeager v. Commonwealth, 16 Va. App. 761, 433 S.E.2d 248 (1993).

Two-year reporting delay not inherently incredible. — Although two years passed before victim — who was 12 years of age at time of the offense — reported the crime to police, she had related the incident to two friends immediately after it occurred, and one testified at trial, corroborating victim's evidence. Under the circumstances, her failure to immediately report the rape did not render her testimony inherently incredible as a matter of law. The jury was entitled to attribute such significance as it deemed appropriate to this delay. West v. Commonwealth, No. 1766-93-2 (Ct. of Appeals Feb. 7, 1995).

No error in failing to strike juror. — In a case in which defendant appealed his conviction for rape, in violation of § 18.2-61, he argued unsuccessfully on appeal that the trial court erred in denying his motion to strike two prospective jurors, who indicated they were friends with police officers, based on their statements during voir dire. In light of the *O'Dell* decision, the two prospective jurors were not impermissibly biased in favor of police testimony, bias could not be presumed from the entirety of their statements during voir dire, and defendant had made claim during jury selection that any credibility determinations involving a police officer's testimony would be put to the jury. Weeks v. Commonwealth, 2009 Va. App. LEXIS 368 (Aug. 18, 2009).

Lesser-included offense. — Under this section, aggravated sexual battery is not a lesser-included offense of rape. Fisher v. Commonwealth, No. 0278-00-4 CHIEF, 2001 Va. App. LEXIS 342 (Ct. of Appeals June 19, 2001).

The offense of carnally knowing a child under 14 years of age without the use of force is not a lesser-included offense of rape, and the Commonwealth did not violate defendant's right against double jeopardy under the federal or state Constitutions by seeking an indictment for carnally knowing a child after a rape charge against defendant was dismissed. Ragsdale v. Commonwealth, 38 Va. App. 421, 565 S.E.2d 331, 2002 Va. App. LEXIS 366 (2002).

Applied in Woodward v. Commonwealth, 12 Va. App. 118, 402 S.E.2d 244 (1991); Clifton v. Commonwealth, 22 Va. App. 178, 468 S.E.2d 155 (1996); Crawford v. Commonwealth, 23 Va. App. 661, 479 S.E.2d 84 (1996); Terry v. Cross, 112 F. Supp. 2d 543, 2000 U.S. Dist. LEXIS 13315 (E.D. Va. 2000); Richardson v. Commonwealth, 42 Va. App. 236, 590 S.E.2d 618, 2004 Va. App. LEXIS 8 (2004); McBride v. Commonwealth, 44 Va. App. 526, 605 S.E.2d 773, 2004 Va. App. LEXIS 597 (2004); Johnson v. Commonwealth, 53 Va. App. 608, 674 S.E.2d 541, 2009 Va. App. LEXIS 157 (2009).

II. ELEMENTS OF OFFENSE.

A. Penetration.

Penetration is an essential element of the crime of rape, and without it there can be no rape. Bailey v. Commonwealth, 82 Va. 107 (1886).

The essential element of penetration must be proved beyond a reasonable doubt. McCall v. Commonwealth, 192 Va. 422, 65 S.E.2d 540 (1951).

Under an indictment charging statutory rape of a child, as well as one charging the common-law offense of rape of an adult woman, the prosecution must prove that there has been an actual penetration to some extent of the male sexual organ into the female sexual organ. McCall v. Commonwealth, 192 Va. 422, 65 S.E.2d 540 (1951); Strawderman v. Commonwealth, 200 Va. 855, 108 S.E.2d 376 (1959).

If penetration did not occur, under Virginia law, the substantive crime would not have been committed. Coles v. Peyton, 389 F.2d 224 (4th Cir.), cert. denied, 393 U.S. 849, 89 S. Ct. 80, 21 L. Ed. 2d 120 (1968).

Rape contemplates and requires penetration as an essential element of the crime. Black v. Peyton, 292 F. Supp. 45 (W.D. Va. 1968).

Because the terms "intimate relations," "sexual relations," "intimate," and "regular sex," employed by the police during an interview with defendant were not precise, and might or might not include penetration, the evidence was insufficient to prove penetration, which was an essential element of rape. Motameni v. Commonwealth, — Va. App. —, — S.E.2d —, 2005 Va. App. LEXIS 441 (Nov. 1, 2005).

But emission is not. — It seems, however, that penetration alone, without emission, constitutes the crime of rape. Commonwealth v. Thomas, 3 Va. (1 Va. Cas.) 307 (1812).

Virginia law does not require proof of emission as an element of the crime of rape, although it recognizes negative proof of emission as a strong circumstance indicating lack of penetration. Coles v. Peyton, 389 F.2d 224 (4th Cir.), cert. denied, 393 U.S. 849, 89 S. Ct. 80, 21 L. Ed. 2d 120 (1968).

The fact that the man's penis was placed on, not in, the woman's sexual organ was insufficient to establish the element of penetration. Moore v. Commonwealth, 254 Va. 184, 491 S.E.2d 739 (1997).

Slight penetration sufficient. — Penetration by a penis of a vagina is an essential element of the crime of rape; proof of penetration, however slight the entry may be, is sufficient. Johnson v. Commonwealth, 259 Va. 654, 529 S.E.2d 769, 2000 Va. LEXIS 60, cert. denied, 531 U.S. 981, 121 S. Ct. 432, 148 L. Ed. 2d 439 (2000).

Penetration can be established by circumstantial, as well as direct, evidence. Kehinde v. Commonwealth, 1 Va. App. 342, 338 S.E.2d 356 (1986).

Commonwealth need only exclude reasonable hypotheses of innocence that flow from the evidence. Patrick v. Commonwealth, 27 Va. App. 655, 500 S.E.2d 839 (1998).

Testimonies of victim and doctor sufficient to prove penetration. — Although 12-year-old victim never testified directly that defendant achieved penetration, her testimony, in conjunction with the testimony of doctor was sufficient to prove the element of penetration. Morrison v. Commonwealth, 10 Va. App. 300, 391 S.E.2d 612 (1990).

Use of doll in order to aid 11-year-old victim in explaining her testimony, was entirely appropriate and there was no abuse of discretion in the trial court's ruling allowing it. Kehinde v. Commonwealth, 1 Va. App. 342, 338 S.E.2d 356 (1986).

Testimony of 11-year-old victim sufficient if penetration can be reasonably inferred. — Where an 11-year-old girl was attempting to describe, with difficulty, where the defendant had put his penis "in" her, since it could not be expected that children would know enough to use the word "vagina," nor was such specificity required, it was enough if the trier of fact could reasonably infer from the evidence adduced where the penetration took place. Kehinde v. Commonwealth, 1 Va. App. 342, 338 S.E.2d 356 (1986).

Victim's testimony sufficient to prove penetration. — Victim's use of the term "into" connoted penetration, particularly when viewed with her testimony that defendant undressed her, got on top of her, and wore a condom when they had sex, and thus, was sufficient to show the essential element of penile-vaginal penetration necessary to support defendant's conviction for rape. Robinson v. Commonwealth, No. 0301-04-2, 2005 Va. App. LEXIS 63 (Ct. of Appeals Feb. 15, 2005).

Separate acts of penetration. — Defendant was guilty of three separate counts of rape when as he raped victim the first time, he had the knife at her throat; the second rape occurred after he had taken the victim down the hall to the bathroom, returned, told her to get on the bed and turn over; the third rape occurred after the act of sodomy and after he had told her to sleep. Clearly, the evidence supported three separate acts of penetration. Carter v. Commonwealth, 16 Va. App. 118, 428 S.E.2d 34 (1993).

B. Force.

The legislative intent in the 1981 amendment was to include a prohibition against sexual intercourse with a woman against her will by threat or intimidation, which expanded the parameters of rape. Sutton v. Commonwealth, 228 Va. 654, 324 S.E.2d 665 (1985).

Under this section prior to its 1981 amendment, it was necessary to prove sexual intercourse against the victim's will by force. Under the amended statute it is sufficient to prove sexual intercourse against the victim's will by force, threat or intimidation. Sutton v. Commonwealth, 228 Va. 654, 324 S.E.2d 665 (1985).

Meaning of "threat" and "intimidation." — There is a difference between threat and intimidation. As used in this section, threat means expression of an intention to do bodily harm. Intimidation may occur without threats. Intimidation, as used in this section, means putting a victim in fear of bodily harm by exercising such domination and control of her as to overcome her mind and overbear her will. Intimidation may be caused by the imposition of psychological pressure on one who, under the circumstances, is vulnerable and susceptible to such pressure. Sutton v. Commonwealth, 228 Va. 654, 324 S.E.2d 665 (1985).

There is no standard of reasonableness expressly pro-

vided by this section. Moreover, the cases from other jurisdictions do not universally hold that in rape cases the fear induced by the defendant's intimidating actions must be judged by an objective standard of reasonableness. Sutton v. Commonwealth, 228 Va. 654, 324 S.E.2d 665 (1985).

Where the evidence shows that an atmosphere of fear was developed and maintained by the defendant to intimidate a 15-year-old physically handicapped girl and that her fear of bodily harm was reasonable, such evidence is sufficient to affirm defendant's conviction of rape. Sutton v. Commonwealth, 228 Va. 654, 324 S.E.2d 665 (1985); Mings v. Commonwealth, 85 Va. 638, 8 S.E. 474 (1889); Bradley v. Commonwealth, 196 Va. 1126, 86 S.E.2d 828 (1955); Satterwhite v. Commonwealth, 201 Va. 478, 111 S.E.2d 820 (1960); Barnett v. Commonwealth, 216 Va. 200, 217 S.E.2d 828 (1975); Schrum v. Commonwealth, 219 Va. 204, 246 S.E.2d 893 (1978); Snyder v. Commonwealth, 220 Va. 792, 263 S.E.2d 55 (1980).

A carnal connection with no consent may provide sufficient force. — Whenever there is a carnal connection and no consent in fact, fraudulently obtained, or otherwise, there is evidently, in the wrongful act itself, all the force which the law demands as an element of the crime. Bailey v. Commonwealth, 82 Va. 107 (1886).

Commonwealth not required to prove force when victim is under thirteen. — Because a complaining witness was under the age of thirteen at the time of alleged sexual abuse by petitioner, the Commonwealth was not required to prove force, threat, or intimidation under §§ 18.2-61 and 18.2-67.1. Cairns v. Johnson, — F.3d —, 2008 U.S. App. LEXIS 4128 (4th Cir. Feb. 26, 2008), cert. denied, 129 S. Ct. 581, 2008 U.S. LEXIS 8293, 172 L. Ed. 2d 439 (U.S. 2008).

Evidence of intimidation sufficient. — Defendant's statement that he was angry and displayed a knife when he ordered his 14-year-old stepdaughter to disrobe and that he threatened her supported the trial court's conclusion that he used intimidation to facilitate sexual intercourse with the victim. Campbell v. Commonwealth, — Va. App. —, — S.E.2d —, 2006 Va. App. LEXIS 571 (Dec. 19, 2006).

Finding that petitioner accomplished forcible sodomy and rape by intimidation within the meaning of §§ 18.2-61 and 18.2-67.1 was supported by evidence showing that the complaining witness, petitioner's stepdaughter, did not want to engage in sexual activity with petitioner, that the stepdaughter did not resist because petitioner was more powerful than she was, that the stepdaughter was afraid of petitioner when he was angry, that the stepdaughter's mother participated in the abuse, and that petitioner had physically abused his wife and one of his sons in the stepdaughter's presence. Cairns v. Johnson, — F.3d —, 2008 U.S. App. LEXIS 4128 (4th Cir. Feb. 26, 2008), cert. denied, 129 S. Ct. 581, 2008 U.S. LEXIS 8293, 172 L. Ed. 2d 439 (U.S. 2008).

As to jury questions on issue of force, see Carpenter v. Commonwealth, 193 Va. 851, 71 S.E.2d 377 (1952); Schrum v. Commonwealth, 219 Va. 204, 246 S.E.2d 893 (1978).

Use of force shown. — Evidence that defendant pushed the victim down a hall toward a bedroom where he raped her was sufficient proof of the use of force. Sabol v. Commonwealth, 37 Va. App. 9, 553 S.E.2d 533, 2001 Va. App. LEXIS 567 (2001).

Use of force not shown. — Evidence that defendant threatened to withhold victim's privilege to use the family car and to withhold money from her, if she did not have sex with him, was not sufficient evidence of force, threat or intimidation to support a rape conviction, since the victim was not in fear of bodily harm. Sabol v. Commonwealth, 37 Va. App. 9, 553 S.E.2d 533, 2001 Va. App. LEXIS 567 (2001).

C. Consent.

In general. — It is essential in order to constitute the crime of rape that the accused should have had connection with the prosecutrix against her will and consent. Bailey v. Commonwealth, 82 Va. 107 (1886); Brown v. Commonwealth, 82 Va. 653 (1886).

Viewing the evidence in the light most favorable to the Commonwealth, it did not prove its contention that the victim was so drunk that she could not give her consent to the acts committed by appellant. Howard v. Commonwealth, 21 Va. App. 473, 465 S.E.2d 142 (1995).

Purpose. — The legislative purpose of clause (ii) of subsection A of this section is to protect persons who are mentally impaired or retarded from being sexually exploited due to their mental incapacity. Adkins v. Commonwealth, 20 Va. App. 332, 457 S.E.2d 382 (1995).

Legislative intent. — Manifestly, the legislature did not intend to include as part of the protected class of people under clause (ii) of subsection A of this section those whose mental impairment or handicap may prevent them from comprehending the more complex aspects of the nature or consequences of sexual intercourse, but who, nevertheless, have the mental capacity to have a basic understanding of the elementary and rudimentary nature and consequences of sexual intercourse. Adkins v. Commonwealth, 20 Va. App. 332, 457 S.E.2d 382 (1995).

Employee's proposed amendment (amending her complaint to allege that her discharge followed from her refusal to commit fornication, lewd and lascivious behavior and sexual assault under Virginia law) would have been futile because the Virginia Supreme Court had struck down § 18.2-344 as unconstitutional, the hug the employee complained of did not even begin to approach the sort of "open and gross lewdness" § 18.2-345 prohibited, and it was legally impossible to consent to sexual assault. Balas v. Huntington Ingalls Indus., 711 F.3d 401, 2013 U.S. App. LEXIS 5199 (4th Cir. Mar. 15, 2013).

Virginia law interposes consent as an absolute bar to a prosecution for rape when the alleged victim is over the age of consent. Coles v. Peyton, 389 F.2d 224 (4th Cir. 1968), cert. denied, 393 U.S. 849, 89 S. Ct. 80, 21 L. Ed. 2d 120 (1968).

Previous want of chastity is relevant and probative evidence of consent. Coles v. Peyton, 389 F.2d 224 (4th Cir. 1968), cert. denied, 393 U.S. 849, 89 S. Ct. 80, 21 L. Ed. 2d 120 (1968). But see § 18.2-67.7.

A consent induced by fear of bodily harm or personal violence is no consent; and though a man lay no hands on a woman, yet if by an array of physical force he so overpowers her mind that she dares not resist, he is guilty of rape by having the unlawful intercourse. Bailey v. Commonwealth, 82 Va. 107 (1886).

Likewise, submission through fear to sexual intercourse is not consent. Even under the pre-1981 definition of rape, where the intercourse was induced through fear of a person whom the victim was accustomed to obey, such as a person standing in loco parentis. Sutton v. Commonwealth, 228 Va. 654, 324 S.E.2d 665 (1985).

Mental incapacity. — Term "mental incapacity" as used in §§ 18.2-67.10 and 18.2-61 may extend to a transitory circumstance such as intoxication if the nature and degree of the intoxication has gone beyond the stage of merely reduced inhibition and has reached a point where the victim does not understand "the nature and consequences of the sexual act." Molina v. Commonwealth, 272 Va. 666, 636 S.E.2d 470, 2006 Va. LEXIS 106 (2006).

Evidence was sufficient to show the complaining witness' mental incapacity and defendant's knowledge thereof, where the complainant's IQ was well below the cutoff point and she, while 18 years old, functioned on the level of an eight year old. Desper v. Commonwealth, 2011 Va. App. LEXIS 343 (Nov. 8, 2011).

Not all persons who are mentally retarded or handicapped need the special protection of clause (ii) of subsection A of this section. The range of intellectual functioning among the mentally impaired and mentally retarded varies widely. The statute was not designed to unfairly punish the sexual partners of those mentally impaired or mentally retarded persons who have a basic understanding of the act and consequences of sexual intercourse and are capable of making volitional choice to engage or not engage in such conduct. Adkins v. Commonwealth, 20 Va. App. 332, 457 S.E.2d 382 (1995).

Corroboration of defense of consent. — In a prosecution for rape and sodomy, where the defense was that prosecutrix consented to the sexual acts, it was error for the court not to permit corroborative testimony suggesting that prosecutrix's conduct was sexually solicitous, not merely affectionate. Massey v. Commonwealth, 230 Va. 436, 337 S.E.2d 754 (1985).

Evidence that act was not consensual held sufficient. — Although defendant claimed he engaged with victim in consensual sexual intercourse, victim testified that when these events were occurring, she said she didn't want to, she said she didn't want to get pregnant, and she said she wanted to go home; evidence, believed by the jury, was sufficient to prove beyond a reasonable doubt that the sexual intercourse was committed against her will and without her consent. Inge v. Commonwealth, No. 1628-98-2, 2000 Va. App. LEXIS 457 (Ct. of Appeals June 20, 2000).

Prosecutrix in second trial could not testify as to lack of consent in first trial. — The court's ruling in the first trial of defendant for rape that the testimony of the prosecutrix in the second trial of defendant for rape was proper to prove a lack of consent by the prosecutrix in the first trial was reversible error. The fact that prosecutrix in the second trial had been attacked nine days after the offenses under indictment had no bearing as to whether prosecutrix in the first trial consented to the intercourse. It merely showed that defendant had a propensity to commit this type of crime. This is precisely what the prosecution is not allowed to show in a criminal case. Foster v. Commonwealth, 5 Va. App. 316, 362 S.E.2d 745 (1987).

III. ATTEMPT TO COMMIT RAPE.

Attempted rape consists of the intent to engage in sexual intercourse, and some direct, yet ineffectual, act towards its consummation. Siquina v. Commonwealth, 28 Va. App. 694, 508 S.E.2d 350 (1998).

Double jeopardy. — Sexual battery and attempted rape were separate and distinct offenses under facts in case at bar, and thus defendant could not have been twice convicted for the same offense in violation of double jeopardy. Haynes v. Commonwealth, No. 1778-98-3 (Ct. of Appeals Oct. 5, 1999).

This section and § 18.2-26, relating to attempts, are in pari materia and must be considered together, and compared with each other in the construction of their various material provisions. Buzzard v. Commonwealth, 134 Va. 641, 114 S.E. 664 (1922).

Upon an indictment for rape, the accused may be found guilty of an attempt to commit a rape. Givens v. Commonwealth, 70 Va. (29 Gratt.) 830 (1878); Lawrence v. Commonwealth, 71 Va. (30 Gratt.) 845 (1878) overruled on another point in Jones v. Commonwealth, 87 Va. 65, 12 S.E. 226 (1890); Mings v. Commonwealth, 85 Va. 638, 8 S.E. 474 (1889); Glover v. Commonwealth, 86 Va. 382, 10 S.E. 420 (1889); Cates v. Commonwealth, 111 Va. 837, 69 S.E. 520 (1910). See § 19.2-286.

The intent to commit rape is an essential element of the crime of an attempt to commit rape. Glover v. Commonwealth, 86 Va. 382, 10 S.E. 420 (1889); Broaddus v. Commonwealth, 126 Va. 733, 101 S.E. 321 (1919). See Lufty v. Commonwealth, 126 Va. 707, 100 S.E. 829 (1919).

Inference of specific intent. — The evidence need not show that the defendant touched the victim's sexual organs or removed the victim's clothing to reasonably infer the specific intent to rape. Siquina v. Commonwealth, 28 Va. App. 694, 508 S.E.2d 350 (1998).

Sufficiency of evidence of intent. — Where the purpose of the accused to have intercourse with the prosecutrix appeared from his own testimony, and his employment of force to accomplish that purpose was sworn to by the prosecutrix, and by her brother, in corroboration of her testimony, there was sufficient evidence before the jury to support their verdict in finding the existence of a felonious intent on the part of the accused. Broaddus v. Commonwealth, 126 Va. 733, 101 S.E. 321 (1919).

The evidence that the defendant forcibly took a young child into a vacant bathroom, covering her mouth so that she could not call for her mother, and that while removing his erect penis from his pants he directed the child to bend over in a position that would facilitate his rape, was sufficient to prove that the defendant took direct, yet ineffectual, steps towards the commission of rape. Siquina v. Commonwealth, 28 Va. App. 694, 508 S.E.2d 350 (1998).

Proof of mere persuasion or solicitation on the part of the accused is insufficient to support the charge. Mings v. Commonwealth, 85 Va. 638, 8 S.E. 474 (1889); Hairston v. Commonwealth, 97 Va. 754, 32 S.E. 797 (1899). See Commonwealth v. Fields, 31 Va. (4 Leigh) 648 (1832); Woodson v. Commonwealth, 107 Va. 895, 59 S.E. 1097 (1908); Broaddus v. Commonwealth, 126 Va. 733, 101 S.E. 321 (1919).

An element is the doing of some act towards the commission of the crime. Christian v. Commonwealth, 64 Va. (23 Gratt.) 954 (1873); Glover v. Commonwealth, 86 Va. 382, 10 S.E. 420 (1889); Cunningham v. Commonwealth, 88 Va. 37, 13 S.E. 309 (1891). See Commonwealth v. Clark, 47 Va. (6 Gratt.) 675 (1849).

The elements of the offense of abduction with intent to defile are separate and distinct from the elements of attempted rape. Simms

v. Commonwealth, 2 Va. App. 614, 346 S.E.2d 734 (1986).

Instruction as to attempted rape in trial for abduction with intent to defile. — Even if the proof adduced at defendant's trial for abduction with intent to defile was sufficient to show that a rape was attempted, defendant was not entitled to an instruction on the offense of attempted rape, with which he was not specifically charged, as it was not a necessarily included lesser offense of the crime with which he was charged. Simms v. Commonwealth, 2 Va. App. 614, 346 S.E.2d 734 (1986).

Error in admitting evidence of attempted rape. — The trial court in defendant's rape trial erred in admitting evidence of an attempted rape for which he was not being tried, since entering a women's public restroom and displaying a knife to a victim is not so unusual as to serve as a signature, and the similarities of the two crimes were not sufficient to establish a common perpetrator. White v. Commonwealth, 9 Va. App. 366, 388 S.E.2d 645 (1990), overruled on other grounds, Lavinder v. Commonwealth, 12 Va. App. 1003, 407 S.E.2d 910 (1991).

Evidence sufficient to support attempted rape conviction. — Evidence was sufficient to support a conviction of attempted rape, § 18.2-61, because a reasonable fact finder could have found that by asking the victim for "a favor," forcing her to the ground from behind, and attempting to remove her pants, defendant was preparing to have nonconsensual sexual intercourse with the victim; because the Commonwealth proved that defendant had the requisite intent, only a slight act in furtherance of the crime was required. Moreover, because, after the victim threw money behind her head, defendant did not get off of her, but instead he remained on top of her, and continued to force her to the ground, a reasonable fact finder could have found these actions to have been overt acts in furtherance of the commission of a rape. Futrell v. Commonwealth, — Va. App. —, — S.E.2d —, 2007 Va. App. LEXIS 83 (Mar. 13, 2007).

IV. EVIDENCE.

A. Complaints and Outcries.

An out-of-court complaint alone does not constitute sufficient evidence of rape. McManus v. Commonwealth, 16 Va. App. 475, 429 S.E.2d 475 (1993).

Fact that prosecutrix made complaint is admissible. — In prosecutions for rape the fact that the person injured made complaint recently after the commission of the offense is admissible, and the absence of such complaint would be suspicious. The proof of such offenses depends in a great measure upon the testimony of a single witness, and therefore every test should be applied to her integrity for the safety of the accused. Brogy v. Commonwealth, 51 Va. (10 Gratt.) 722 (1853).

The only exception to the general rule excluding, as hearsay evidence, the statements or declarations of parties which constitute complaints is the exception in cases of rape. Such a victim must at once make complaint, or she will be suspected of consent. But even in such cases the evidence is confined to the complaint, and no detailed statement of the transaction is permitted to go in evidence. Haynes v. Commonwealth, 69 Va. (28 Gratt.) 942 (1877).

Under a rule unique to rape cases, evidence of an out-of-court complaint by an alleged rape victim is admissible, not as independent evidence of the offense, but as corroboration of the victim's testimony. Cartera v. Commonwealth, 219 Va. 516, 248 S.E.2d 784 (1978).

But particulars of complaint are not. — Though it is competent to prove the fact of a recent complaint by the female for the purpose of sustaining her credit, it is not competent to prove the particulars of her complaint. Brogy v. Commonwealth, 51 Va. (10 Gratt.) 722 (1853).

Only the fact that the complaint was made is admissible, neither the details of the alleged offense nor a description of the alleged assailant, as reported by the victim, may be admitted. Cartera v. Commonwealth, 219 Va. 516, 248 S.E.2d 784 (1978).

The failure to report an alleged rape by force and violence for an unreasonable period after the incident occurred casts suspicion and doubt on the truthfulness of the story of a prosecutrix unless there is a credible explanation given for such a delay. Willis v. Commonwealth, 218 Va. 560, 238 S.E.2d 811 (1977).

The testimony concerning rape victim's mental disability bears directly upon the issue of her resistance and the amount of

force necessary to overcome her will. Jerry v. Commonwealth, No. 0075-86-2 (Ct. of Appeals Feb. 13, 1990).

Weight of failure to make outcry or complaint a jury question. — The failure to make outcry in prosecutions for rape, or attempt to commit rape, is a fact tending to disprove the good faith of the charge, but raises no presumption of law that the prosecutrix has sworn falsely; it is a circumstance to be weighed by the jury. Delay in making complaint is treated likewise. Broaddus v. Commonwealth, 126 Va. 733, 101 S.E. 321 (1919).

Appearance of female admissible to show force and resistance. — The state and appearance of the female, any marks of violence, and the condition of her dress shortly after the occurrence, are admissible to show force and resistance. Brogy v. Commonwealth, 51 Va. (10 Gratt.) 722 (1853); Bailey v. Commonwealth, 82 Va. 107 (1886). See Boxley v. Commonwealth, 65 Va. (24 Gratt.) 649 (1874).

Victim's failure to testify not bar. — A rape victim's complaint corroborates more than his or her testimony; it also corroborates the occurrence of the rape itself, no reason justifies limiting the rule to corroboration of a victim's testimony and therefore the rule allowing admission of rape victim's out-of-court complaint is applicable to corroborate other independent evidence of the offense. McManus v. Commonwealth, 16 Va. App. 475, 429 S.E.2d 475 (1993).

Magazine properly admitted. — Pornographic magazine which contained sexually explicit photographs and articles depicting male and female genitalia and persons engaged in heterosexual and homosexual sex, which defendant possessed in back pocket at the time of the attempted rape was relevant to prove his state of mind and motive. The trial court specifically instructed the jury that the magazine was admissible only to show the defendant's state of mind at the time and that they were free to accept or reject its probative value on this issue. Therefore, the trial court did not abuse its discretion in admitting the pornographic magazine for this purpose. Washington v. Commonwealth, No. 1730-94-2 (Ct. of Appeals Nov. 7, 1995).

B. Weight and Sufficiency.

Circumstantial evidence will uphold verdict. — A verdict of guilty of rape ought not to be set aside by the appellate court because it depends on circumstantial evidence, especially where the court which tried the cause did not think proper to disturb it. Commonwealth v. Bennet, 4 Va. (2 Va. Cas.) 235 (1820).

The necessary element of sexual intercourse may be proven by circumstantial as well as by direct evidence. McCall v. Commonwealth, 192 Va. 422, 65 S.E.2d 540 (1951).

As will the uncorroborated testimony of prosecutrix. — In prosecutions for rape the accused may be legally convicted on the sole and uncorroborated testimony of the prosecutrix and this is true even though the prosecutrix be a child of tender years. The weight to be given to her testimony is a question exclusively for the jury. Givens v. Commonwealth, 70 Va. (29 Gratt.) 830 (1878); Bailey v. Commonwealth, 82 Va. 107 (1886). See Smith v. Commonwealth, 85 Va. 924, 9 S.E. 148 (1889); Glover v. Commonwealth, 86 Va. 382, 10 S.E. 420 (1889); Lear v. Commonwealth, 195 Va. 187, 77 S.E.2d 424 (1953); Robinson v. Commonwealth, 197 Va. 754, 91 S.E.2d 396 (1956).

If the evidence of the Commonwealth is credible and from it the guilt of the accused is believed by the jury beyond a reasonable doubt, it is sufficient to sustain a conviction of rape, and this is true even though the evidence consists only of the uncorroborated testimony of the prosecutrix. But if the evidence is inherently incredible or so contrary to human experience or to usual human behavior as to render it unworthy of belief, it is not sufficient to warrant a verdict of guilty beyond a reasonable doubt. Bradley v. Commonwealth, 196 Va. 1126, 86 S.E.2d 828 (1955).

Corroboration of the prosecutrix in a rape case is not essential and her testimony alone is sufficient to sustain a conviction if it is credible and the guilt of the accused is believed by the jury beyond a reasonable doubt. Fogg v. Commonwealth, 208 Va. 541, 159 S.E.2d 616 (1968).

In a rape case, it is not necessary for the testimony of the prosecutrix to be corroborated, and her testimony alone is sufficient to sustain a conviction. Barnett v. Commonwealth, 216 Va. 200, 217 S.E.2d 828 (1975).

A conviction of rape may be sustained on the uncorroborated

testimony of a prosecutrix if her evidence is credible, and the guilt of the accused is believed by the jury beyond a reasonable doubt. Willis v. Commonwealth, 218 Va. 560, 238 S.E.2d 811 (1977).

A conviction of rape may be sustained solely upon the testimony of the prosecutrix. Snyder v. Commonwealth, 220 Va. 792, 263 S.E.2d 55 (1980).

Unless incredible. — While the uncorroborated testimony of the prosecutrix, when credible, is sufficient to support a conviction, the Supreme Court has consistently refused to approve a conviction where such testimony is contrary to human experience and is inherently incredible. Barker v. Commonwealth, 198 Va. 500, 95 S.E.2d 135 (1956).

The conviction of a man 70 years of age of the crime of rape on the uncorroborated evidence of the woman, who made no complaint until after the birth of a child, and whose evidence otherwise bears the impress of falsehood on its face, cannot be sustained, although the plaintiff in error stands in the Supreme Court as a demurrant to the evidence. The court cannot be expected to believe the incredible. Harvey v. Commonwealth, 103 Va. 850, 49 S.E. 481 (1905).

It is not sufficient to warrant a verdict of guilty beyond a reasonable doubt if the evidence is inherently incredible, or so contrary to human experience or to usual human behavior as to render it unworthy of belief. Willis v. Commonwealth, 218 Va. 560, 238 S.E.2d 811 (1977); Snyder v. Commonwealth, 220 Va. 792, 263 S.E.2d 55 (1980).

Burden of proof. — In a prosecution for rape the burden is on the Commonwealth to prove the identity of the accused beyond a reasonable doubt. Fogg v. Commonwealth, 208 Va. 541, 159 S.E.2d 616 (1968).

While it is true that the burden was on the Commonwealth to prove the identity of the accused beyond a reasonable doubt, the related evidence, which the trial court sitting as a jury accepted, was sufficient to meet this requirement and warrant a finding that the defendant was identified beyond a reasonable doubt as one of the persons who assaulted and raped the prosecutrix. Such finding is conclusive on appeal. Brickhouse v. Commonwealth, 208 Va. 533, 159 S.E.2d 611 (1968).

A person may passively or suggestively take advantage of a mentally retarded or incapacitated individual; however, the fact that a victim may have diminished mental capacity does not relieve the Commonwealth of its burden of proving that the "mental incapacity" is that defined by subdivision 3 of § 18.2-67.10. Adkins v. Commonwealth, 20 Va. App. 332, 457 S.E.2d 382 (1995).

Seven of eight convictions against defendant for rape of a child less than 13-years-old in violation of § 18.2-61 could not stand because the Commonwealth did not meet its burden of proving beyond a reasonable doubt those offenses. The victim's testimony regarding the seven convictions that the sexual activity the victim had with defendant after a move to a new home was either "oral or intercourse sex" left the jury to speculate about whether the required rape element of sexual intercourse had occurred. Slate v. Commonwealth, — Va. App. —, — S.E.2d —, 2008 Va. App. LEXIS 113 (Mar. 11, 2008).

The fact finder cannot infer from proof of general mental incapacity or retardation or an IQ range or mental age that a victim is prevented or unable to understand the nature and consequences of a sexual act, unless the evidence proves that the victim lacks the ability to comprehend or appreciate either the distinguishing characteristics or physical qualities of the sexual act or the future natural behavioral or societal results or effects which may flow from the sexual act. Adkins v. Commonwealth, 20 Va. App. 332, 457 S.E.2d 382 (1995).

Evidence was sufficient to support finding that defendant was the criminal agent. — Where record contained evidence that appellant applied force, an element of rape, to victim when he abducted her; that the victim had been sexually assaulted; that both the victim and appellant had Type B blood (found only in 12 percent of the population) and both were Type B secretors; that Type B blood was found on appellant's shorts, inside the fly area and on his underpants; and that a foreign hair consistent with that of appellant was found in the victim's pubic hair, there was no other evidence in this record from which it reasonably could be inferred that a person other than appellant was the criminal agent. Vanegas v. Commonwealth, 17 Va. App. 451, 438 S.E.2d 289 (1993).

The evidence was sufficient to support the jury's finding

that the act of intercourse was against victim's will and resulted from force, threat, or intimidation where the medical examiner found red, fresh bruises on victim's body, two inside the left wrist, one on the right forearm, and one on the upper right arm and her wrists and ankles had been tightly bound with electrical cords, her mouth was snugly gagged, and she was 56 years old and weighed only 125 pounds. Hoke v. Commonwealth, 237 Va. 303, 377 S.E.2d 595, cert. denied, 491 U.S. 910, 109 S. Ct. 3201, 105 L. Ed. 2d 709 (1989).

Lighting in room was sufficient for victim to identify defendant. — Jury was entitled to conclude from rape victim's testimony that the lighting in the room was sufficient for the victim to identify the defendant. Maynard v. Commonwealth, 11 Va. App. 437, 399 S.E.2d 635 (1990).

It is not sufficient that facts and circumstances proven be consistent with defendant's guilt. To sustain a conviction they must be inconsistent with every reasonable hypothesis of his innocence. McCall v. Commonwealth, 192 Va. 422, 65 S.E.2d 540 (1951); Strawderman v. Commonwealth, 200 Va. 855, 108 S.E.2d 376 (1959).

The evidence was sufficient to establish penetration where the victim testified that, when she and the defendant fell to the floor, the defendant was on top of her, that he pulled her pants and underwear down to her knees and did the same to his pants and underwear, that she felt a sharp pain inside of her vagina area when the defendant's head was on the top of her stomach, his waist was between her knees and his hands were on the floor lying flat beside her hips and that the pain continued for five minutes as the defendant's bottom half was making an up and down movement. In addition, there was testimony by a sexual assault nurse examiner that the victim had recent injuries, including lacerations in the vagina. Velazquez v. Commonwealth, 35 Va. App. 189, 543 S.E.2d 631, 2001 Va. App. LEXIS 157 (2001), aff'd in part and rev'd in part, 263 Va. 95, 557 S.E.2d 213 (2002).

Evidence of penetration was sufficient to support defendant's rape conviction, where, in addition to defendant's admission to having sexual intercourse with the complainant, the complainant provided testimony to corroborate defendant's confession, stating that she and defendant had sex three times and testifying that defendant put "his thing," which she said was between his legs, in hers. Desper v. Commonwealth, 2011 Va. App. LEXIS 343 (Nov. 8, 2011).

Evidence was sufficient to support finding that defendant used force, threat, or intimidation. — Evidence was sufficient to prove defendant used "force, threat, or intimidation" against the stepdaughter for the purposes of conviction under the forcible rape statute as it showed defendant accomplished the intercourse which occurred when the stepdaughter was 13 years old through fear and intimidation; the evidence showed defendant had beaten both the stepdaughter's mother and the stepdaughter prior to the time he had intercourse with the stepdaughter, that he had also committed other acts of physical abuse on the stepdaughter prior to that time, and, even though the acts of intercourse were against her will, she was fearful of not submitting to them. Rankin v. Commonwealth, No. 3065-00-3, 2002 Va. App. LEXIS 224 (Ct. of Appeals Apr. 9, 2002).

Evidence was sufficient to support the conviction. — There was sufficient evidence to find that defendant was guilty of rape, forcible sodomy, and indecent liberties with a child for acts upon defendant's wife's four-year-old cousin because the evidence supported the victim's account of the events and defendant did have an opportunity to commit the acts on at least two occasions; the victim gave her foster mother a substantially similar account when she initially made her complaint, the victim's testimony was consistent with a drawing she did at the psychologist's instruction, and the medical evidence showed that the victim was a sexually abused child as her hymen was consistent with a painful penetrating injury. Johnson v. Commonwealth, 40 Va. App. 605, 580 S.E.2d 486, 2003 Va. App. LEXIS 303 (2003).

Evidence was sufficient to support defendant's conviction for rape, where the Commonwealth proved the use of force, threat, or intimidation by providing evidence from the complaining witness that defendant broke into her home and waited for her, held a gun to her the entire time, as well as repeatedly pushed, kicked, and hit her. Breeden v. Commonwealth, 43 Va. App. 169, 596 S.E.2d 563, 2004 Va. App. LEXIS 257 (2004).

Evidence was sufficient to support defendant's conviction for rape, as the trial court was under no obligation to believe the rape victim's testimony that she lied about being raped because she was angry and jealous, especially since other competent evidence that was not inherently incredible was sufficient to prove defendant was guilty of rape. Mejia-Martinez v. Commonwealth, 2006 Va. App. LEXIS 80 (Mar. 7, 2006).

In a prosecution for rape of a child under age 13, the child's detailed account of two acts of sexual intercourse was sufficient to convict, despite minor inconsistencies in her testimony, her history of mental illness, and the lack of corroborating physical evidence. Nobrega v. Commonwealth, 271 Va. 508, 628 S.E.2d 922, 2006 Va. LEXIS 48 (2006).

Where defendant admitted to having sexual intercourse with his 14-year-old stepdaughter after displaying a knife, his flight from the state provided the basis for a reasonable inference that he committed the rape to which he confessed. Campbell v. Commonwealth, — Va. App. —, — S.E.2d —, 2006 Va. App. LEXIS 571 (Dec. 19, 2006).

Evidence was sufficient to support defendant's conviction on one count of rape of a child under the age of 13, as the evidence showed that defendant penetrated the victim when the victim was 12 years old by sticking the tip of defendant's penis in the victim's vagina; that evidence supported the finding of the legal definition of penetration as being penetration by the penis of the vagina however slight and the evidence was sufficient despite the fact that the victim testified on cross-examination that defendant did not penetrate the victim until the victim was 13 years old, as that testimony was pursuant to the lay definition of penetration where complete penetration or putting the penis all of the way in the vagina was involved. Perez-Amaya v. Commonwealth, — Va. App. —, — S.E.2d —, 2006 Va. App. LEXIS 569 (Dec. 19, 2006).

Because a child victim testified that defendant put his "thingy" "up in" "where she peed out of," which was located at her "bottom," and "started to hump her," the evidence was sufficient to convict defendant of aggravated sexual battery, animate object sexual penetration, and statutory rape under §§ 18.2-67.3, 18.2-67.2, and 18.2-61. Tinsley v. Commonwealth, 2007 Va. App. LEXIS 207 (May 15, 2007).

Defendant's challenge to the sufficiency of the evidence supporting defendant's rape conviction failed because the victim's delay in reporting the rape by the victim's stepfather was explained by the victim's testimony that the victim was afraid of defendant, shocked, embarrassed, and feared destroying the victim's relationship with the victim's mother. Smart v. Commonwealth, — Va. App. —, — S.E.2d —, 2007 Va. App. LEXIS 319 (Aug. 28, 2007).

Defendant's rape conviction under § 18.2-61 was not against the weight of the evidence as the discrepancies in the victim's account presented by a mother's and a school official's statements, and the victim's claim that the victim fell asleep following the rape and later accepted a ride from defendant and defendant's friend without telling the friend of the rape, did not render the victim's account inherently incredible as the mother could not have been home at the time of the incident, and the school attendance records could have been inaccurate; the victim's delay in reporting the rape did not make the victim's testimony incredible. Elam v. Commonwealth, — Va. App. —, — S.E.2d —, 2007 Va. App. LEXIS 436 (Dec. 11, 2007).

Evidence admitted at defendant's bench trial sufficiently supported defendant's convictions for the rape and forcible sodomy of defendant's teenage stepdaughter. That evidence showed that defendant forcibly required defendant's teenage stepdaughter to submit to defendant's sexual advances on three occasions, that the victim credibly testified to those events, and that defendant's explanations of recorded, incriminating statements defendant made to the victim's mother, defendant's wife, were lacking in credibility. Carpenter v. Commonwealth, 51 Va. App. 84, 654 S.E.2d 345, 2007 Va. App. LEXIS 463 (2007).

Because the victim's testimony and the documentary evidence established that defendant had sexual intercourse with a child under the age of 13, in violation of subsection A of § 18.2-61, and that the offense occurred on a date within the time period set forth in the indictment, the evidence was sufficient to sustain defendant's conviction. Booth v. Commonwealth, 2009 Va. App. LEXIS 198 (Apr. 28, 2009).

Victim's identification along with a wide range of circumstantial evidence, including the fact that defendant was acting strangely the day after the incident and had changed defendant's appearance, that clothing matching what the victim said the attacker wore was found in defendant's home, and that duct tape like that used on the victim was found in defendant's home were sufficient to support defendant's convictions for rape, robbery, statutory burglary, malicious wounding, and unlawful wounding in the commission of a felony. Parker v. Commonwealth, 2009 Va. App. LEXIS 235 (May 19, 2009).

There was sufficient evidence to convict appellant of rape where: (1) the victim testified that she woke up with sharp pains between her legs; (2) the sexual assault nurse examiner observed small hemorrhagic spots, abrasions, and skin breaking on the victim's genitalia, which she testified was consistent with trauma; (3) a rational trier of fact could find beyond a reasonable doubt that the degree of the victim's intoxication reached a point where she did not understand the nature or consequences of the sexual act; and (4) appellant knew of the victim's condition because he was at the party, and he was one of the people who walked her home from the party. Roberts v. Commonwealth, 2010 Va. App. LEXIS 13 (Jan. 12, 2010).

Defendant's convictions for abduction with intent to defile, in violation of § 18.2-48, and attempted rape, in violation of §§ 18.2-26 and 18.2-61, were proper because the trial court did not err in finding the facts sufficient to show the abduction or detention was separate and apart from, rather than incidental to, the attempted rape. The evidence showed the detention by deception posed an additional danger to the victim, was accomplished before the attempted rape, and was not intrinsic to or inherent in the separate offense. Smith v. Commonwealth, 56 Va. App. 711, 697 S.E.2d 14, 2010 Va. App. LEXIS 336 (2010).

Defendant's convictions for abduction with intent to defile, in violation of § 18.2-48, and attempted rape, in violation of §§ 18.2-26 and 18.2-61, were proper because the jury heard the victim's conflicting accounts and in its role as factfinder, it alone was entitled to judge credibility given the discrepancy and assign her testimony what weight it deemed appropriate. Moreover, the officer's testimony and the victim's own actions corroborated the remainder of the victim's account of the incident; the victim immediately notified her mother and a friend about the incident. Smith v. Commonwealth, 56 Va. App. 711, 697 S.E.2d 14, 2010 Va. App. LEXIS 336 (2010).

Evidence was sufficient to sustain defendant's conviction for rape, in violation of § 18.2-61, where the victim, defendant's wife, was found dead in a motel room, her body positioned in a particularly gruesome and suggestive manner, and defendant's semen was found inside the victim's vagina, and sperm was found in or around the victim's mouth and anus. Crawford v. Commonwealth, 281 Va. 84, 704 S.E.2d 107, 2011 Va. LEXIS 20 (2011).

Commonwealth's evidence was competent, not inherently incredible, and sufficient to prove beyond a reasonable doubt attempted rape and abduction with intent to defile, because jury believed the victim's version of what happened and the Commonwealth's evidence and rejected defendant's version of those events, and the jury was permitted to consider defendant's prior felony convictions in assessing his credibility; the victim testified that defendant held her down, partially removed her pants, exposed his penis, pulled out a knife, and repeatedly threatened to kill the victim. Gay v. Commonwealth, 2011 Va. App. LEXIS 134 (Apr. 19, 2011).

Defendant's convictions for forcible sodomy and rape were supported by sufficient evidence as the victim's testimony showed that defendant handcuffed her, placed her face-down over a desk, pushed her down so that she could not stand up, vaginally penetrated her without her consent, and forced her to perform fellatio on him without her consent. Because defendant penetrated the victim both vaginally and orally without her consent and through the use of force, despite her resistance, the evidence was sufficient to show that defendant committed rape and forcible sodomy. Dillingham v. Commonwealth, 2011 Va. App. LEXIS 184 (2011).

Testimony of the victim, which the fact finder accepted and which was corroborated by (1) the victim's statements in the immediate aftermath of the crimes to the victim's parent and the police; (2) the DNA evidence; and (3) defendant's initial denial that defendant even knew the victim, a denial that the trial court could reasonably have concluded was a lie offered to conceal defendant's guilt, when combined with defendant's later acknowledgement that defendant had consensual sexual intercourse with the victim, fully justified the trial court's conclusion that the prosecution sufficiently established defendant's guilt of the crimes of rape, object sexual penetration, and sodomy. Shepperson v. Commonwealth, 2012 Va. App. LEXIS 329 (Oct. 16, 2012).

Defendant's confession and the corroborating DNA evidence was sufficient to support defendant's convictions for murder, rape, statutory burglary, and robbery. Farmer v. Commonwealth, 61 Va. App. 402, 737 S.E.2d 32, 2013 Va. App. LEXIS 34 (2013).

Intent to rape not proven. — Where a trier of fact could find an intent to rape only by resorting to surmise and speculation, and neither a spoken word of defendant nor any other action on his part justifies the inference that he harbored the intent to rape, so far as the evidence shows, the defendant's intent might just as well have been to commit larceny or any of a number of offenses other than rape. Patterson v. Commonwealth, 215 Va. 698, 213 S.E.2d 752 (1975).

The proof must go beyond the mere showing of injury to the genital organs of the female and an opportunity on the part of the accused to have committed the offense. McCall v. Commonwealth, 192 Va. 422, 65 S.E.2d 540 (1951); Strawderman v. Commonwealth, 200 Va. 855, 108 S.E.2d 376 (1959).

Statement by doctor that injury to child was caused by a male sexual organ is not sufficient to prove the act of sexual intercourse beyond a reasonable doubt. Strawderman v. Commonwealth, 200 Va. 855, 108 S.E.2d 376 (1959).

Evidence of child rape sufficient. — Evidence was sufficient to support defendant's convictions for forcible sodomy, in violation of subsection A of § 18.2-67.1, rape, in violation of § 18.2-61, and producing sexually explicit material, in violation of § 18.2-374.1, where evidence showed that a victim and defendant engaged in oral sex while the victim's mother was at work, during a strip poker game in which the victim ran out of clothes and had to do favors for defendant, which included putting defendant's penis in the victim's mouth and defendant putting defendant's penis in the victim's vagina; in addition, there was testimony that a victim made videos at defendant's direction and that these were termed a type of punishment, and the videos detailed various instances of sexual abuse, at least one of which was seen by the victims' 13-year-old brother. Cairns v. Commonwealth, 40 Va. App. 271, 579 S.E.2d 340, 2003 Va. App. LEXIS 221 (2003).

Identification of accused by prosecutrix held insufficient. Boxley v. Commonwealth, 65 Va. (24 Gratt.) 649 (1874).

The female having declined to give a description of the person who committed the outrage when upon oath, it is not competent to prove the description given by her when not upon oath. Brogy v. Commonwealth, 51 Va. (10 Gratt.) 722 (1853).

Evidence held sufficient to support rape conviction. — Where a rape victim testified that defendant raped her at knifepoint, coerced her at gunpoint to sign an agreement promising not to reveal what had occurred, and officers searching defendant's house found both the knife and the agreement written in his handwriting, and the victim appeared distraught and made a prompt complaint after the incident, the evidence supported defendant's conviction of rape. Dowdy v. Commonwealth, No. 2509-02-3, 2003 Va. App. LEXIS 705 (Ct. of Appeals Dec. 30, 2003).

Reversal required where evidence erroneously admitted. — Admission of similar crimes evidence was not harmless error in defendant's trial for rape and sodomy as: (1) the required intent was established upon proof that the accused knowingly and intentionally committed the acts constituting the elements of rape; (2) the required lack of consent for rape involved the victim's mental state, not the defendant's; (3) the fact that one woman was raped had no tendency to prove that another woman did not consent; and (4) the testimony of two escorts that defendant had attacked them in a manner similar to that described by the victim was highly prejudicial and encouraged the inference that defendant committed the charged crimes as he had committed similar crimes in the past. Gonzales v. Commonwealth, No. 1351-03-4, 2004 Va. App. LEXIS 337 (Ct. of Appeals July 13, 2004).

C. Other Matters.

Age of prosecutrix a jury question. — Buzzard v. Commonwealth, 134 Va. 641, 114 S.E. 664 (1922).

Question of force or consent one for jury. — Where a rape case presents a typical situation where the prosecutrix maintains that she was forced by the accused to have intercourse with him and he insists that the act occurred with her consent, the case is subject to the general rule that whether the act was forcible or consensual was a question for the jury to decide. Snyder v. Commonwealth, 220 Va. 792, 263 S.E.2d 55 (1980).

Affidavits requesting dismissal of prosecution are not after-discovered evidence. — Affidavits made after the trial merely requesting that the prosecution be dismissed have no bearing on the case as after-discovered evidence. Salyer v. Commonwealth, 163 Va. 1027, 175 S.E. 757 (1934).

Error to admit murder victim's affidavit in support of a request for protective order. — Admission at trial of a murder victim's affidavit in support of her request for a protective order against defendant, her husband, violated the Confrontation Clause of the Sixth Amendment to the U.S. Constitution, and the error was not harmless because in it she swore he had threatened and raped her; therefore, his convictions for rape under § 18.2-61, abduction with the intent to defile under § 18.2-48, use of a firearm during the commission of an abduction, and capital murder, which was predicated on the former three offenses, were unconstitutional as well as based on insufficient evidence. Crawford v. Commonwealth, 53 Va. App. 138, 670 S.E.2d 15, 2008 Va. App. LEXIS 554 (2008).

Subpoena of victim's psychiatric records denied where request based on speculation. — Subpoena duces tecum sought by defendant, on trial for rape and forcible sodomy, directing the victim, to produce records "of any psychiatrist or psychologist which she has visited for treatment and/or other services within the last five (5) years," was properly denied where defendant hoped that victim's psychiatric records would show that she had fantasies of being raped, thereby creating the inference that she consented to the sexual activity to punish her husband for arguing with her, but where defendants' theory of consent was based on nothing more than surmise and speculation. Farish v. Commonwealth, 2 Va. App. 627, 346 S.E.2d 736 (1986).

No right to have psychiatric exam of child victim. — Trial court judge lacked authority to order a medical examination of the complaining witness and, therefore, did not err by denying defendant's motion for a psychiatric examination of the child victim, namely his daughter, though, as a matter of law, the trial court judge erred by denying the motion for incorrect reasons. Nobrega v. Commonwealth, — Va. App. —, — S.E.2d —, 2005 Va. App. LEXIS 189 (May 10, 2005), aff'd, 271 Va. 508, 628 S.E.2d 922 (2006).

Psychiatric or psychological evaluation of complaining witness not authorized. — In a prosecution for rape of a child under age 13, the trial court properly denied defendant's motion for a psychiatric or psychological evaluation of the complaining witness, as no Virginia statute or rule authorized the trial court to do so, even though the witness had a history of mental illness and her testimony was uncorroborated. Nobrega v. Commonwealth, 271 Va. 508, 628 S.E.2d 922, 2006 Va. LEXIS 48 (2006).

Error in permitting testimony regarding previous rape. — It was reversible error for the court to allow the victim of a previous rape perpetrated by the defendant to testify regarding that crime where there was no confusion or issue regarding the defendant's state of mind at the time of the events at issue and the only question was whether the defendant or the victim told the truth about the events. Baker v. Commonwealth, No. 2875-97-1 (Ct. of Appeals Mar. 9, 1999).

Error in admitting paternity test result. — The trial court erred in admitting the HLA paternity test result where the record showed that the sample tested as the victim's daughter was taken from a male child and the evidence proved that the victim's aunt gave birth to appellant's son shortly after the victim gave birth to a daughter. The admissibility of the test result turned on the identity of the child tested and this discrepancy in the testing documentation eliminated the reliability of the connection between the appellant and the matters in issue, therefore, further inquiry as to the identity of the child tested was required before the paternity test could be deemed admissible. Townsend v. Commonwealth, No. 0212-93-2 (Ct. of Appeals June 7, 1994).

Testimony as to prior offense which was characteristic of numerous other offenses was not admissible. — Testimony of prosecutrix that on a previous occasion defendant approached her with a small handgun and forced her into her apartment where he raped and robbed her characterized numerous offenses by other perpetrators. Accordingly, its probative value was minimal, especially in light of the extreme prejudice that resulted from such a detailed account of a prior rape and robbery. Such testimony also was inadmissible to prove defendant's intent to commit rape and robbery. If evidence of another crime is offered ostensibly to prove intent, it is still not admissible if the actual issue is identity or commission of the act itself. Foster v. Commonwealth, 5 Va. App. 316, 362 S.E.2d 745 (1987).

Evidence of acquittal in prior similar case. — Court's exclusion of the Maryland trial and acquittal verdict in similar case involving appellant and victim was not an abuse of discretion. The blanket acquittal in the Maryland trial failed to prove that the victim "lied" or made a "false accusation." Rather, a general verdict of acquittal can be read only for the proposition that the prosecution failed to prove each of the required elements beyond a reasonable doubt. Wooden v. Commonwealth, No. 2173-93-4 (Ct. of Appeals May 2, 1995).

Evidence of defendant's relationship with victim allowed. — State was allowed to introduce evidence of defendant's relationship with the victim, his niece, such explained the victim's presence at defendant's house and her conduct towards him throughout the evening on the night of the crime, and her willingness to accompany him to a remote area at night; further, it bore on the issues of fear or intimidation, and lack of consent and defendant was not entitled to have the evidence sanitized so as to deny the jury knowledge of all but the immediate crime for which he was on trial. Chinn v. Commonwealth, No. 2547-03-2, 2004 Va. App. LEXIS 469 (Ct. of Appeals Oct. 5, 2004).

Capability of consent. — Evidence clearly showed the 28-year-old victim, who had a performance IQ of 57, and was not able to live outside her family home, was not capable of giving consent to defendant, who offered to take her to work, but instead drove her to his home and had sex with her. Sene v. Commonwealth, 2009 Va. App. LEXIS 333 (July 28, 2009).

Insufficient evidence of non-spousal relationship with victim. — Where defendant was charged for violating this section, evidence that defendant was not a resident in the victim's house, that he dated the victim's sister, that defendant had a different last name than the victim, and that the victim was a virgin, did not suffice to prove beyond a reasonable doubt that he was not the victim's spouse. Smith v. Commonwealth, No. 1902-93-1 (Ct. of Appeals March 28, 1995).

Evidence of attempted escape. — It was not an abuse of discretion to permit the admission of evidence of defendant's attempted escape to show consciousness of guilt as to the rape and abduction with intent to defile charges, even though he was also incarcerated at the time of the attempted escape on two other charges. Leonard v. Commonwealth, 39 Va. App. 134, 571 S.E.2d 306, 2002 Va. App. LEXIS 657 (2002), cert. denied, 540 U.S. 989, 124 S. Ct. 479, 157 L. Ed. 2d 384 (2003).

Inculpatory statements admitted in violation of defendant's right to counsel. — Defendant's Sixth Amendment right to counsel was violated and a trial court erred by permitting the Commonwealth to use inculpatory statements made by defendant in its case-in-chief where the statements, made by defendant while in custody in the hospital being treated for asthma, were made without defendant voluntarily waiving his right to counsel. The Commonwealth failed to meet its burden of showing that defendant waived his right to counsel since the questioning police officer obtained the statements at the hospital through deception and duplicity by acting as a friend toward defendant, while wearing a recorder, and defendant was never aware that the purpose of the casual conversation was to gather evidence for use against him at trial. Bellamy v. Commonwealth, — Va. App. —, — S.E.2d —, 2005 Va. App. LEXIS 259 (July 5, 2005).

During police interrogation, defendant said, "I'd really like to talk to a lawyer because this—oh my God, oh, my Jesus, why?" Under an objective test, this statement was a clear and unambiguous invocation of defendant's right to counsel under Miranda; therefore, his subsequent inculpatory statements were improperly admitted in his rape trial. Zektaw v. Commonwealth, 278 Va. 127, 677 S.E.2d 49, 2009 Va. LEXIS 76 (2009).

Recanted allegations. — In a case where the victim testified regarding two incidents of sexual assault by defendant, her brother, but later recanted her allegations, the evidence was sufficient to sustain defendant's conviction, because the appellate court found nothing in the record to suggest it should overtake the fact finder's role, and recantations by the victim and her other brother were explored at trial and would not have produced a different result because DNA evidence corroborated the sexual assault and polygraph tests indicated the victim's recantations and defendant's denial of the allegations were false. Linkous v. Commonwealth, No. 2725-02-3, 2003 Va. App. LEXIS 644 (Ct. of Appeals Dec. 16, 2003).

Reputation for untruthfulness. — In a rape case, defendant claimed that the trial court erred in preventing the victim's aunt from testifying as to the victim's reputation for untruthfulness; as his proffer did not address the question whether the aunt ever discussed the victim's reputation with members of the community or which community might have been involved, the proffer was insufficient to allow the appellate court to determine whether the testimony was admissible and whether defendant was prejudiced by its exclusion. Newsome v. Commonwealth, 2012 Va. App. LEXIS 386 (Nov. 27, 2012).

Improper admission of evidence held harmless. — In a rape prosecution under § 18.2-61, the trial court's admission as a business record of a nurse's report stating that the victim's genitalia appeared abnormal, if error, was harmless because the DNA evidence provided overwhelming proof of sexual contact between defendant and the victim. Campbell v. Commonwealth, — Va. App. —, — S.E.2d —, 2006 Va. App. LEXIS 571 (Dec. 19, 2006).

Admission of an abuse affidavit into evidence, although violative of defendant's U.S. Const., Amend. VI right to confrontation, was harmless beyond a reasonable doubt for convictions for capital murder, abduction with intent to defile, rape, grand larceny, and two counts of use of a firearm, where the evidence was sufficient to support the convictions absent the affidavit. Crawford v. Commonwealth, 281 Va. 84, 704 S.E.2d 107, 2011 Va. LEXIS 20 (2011).

Improper admission of evidence not harmless. — In a rape and assault and battery prosecution, the incriminating statements defendant made after he unambiguously invoked his right to counsel were admitted over his objections. As it could not be said that his statements that he choked and knocked the alleged victim down before having consensual sex with her did not contribute to his convictions or to the severity of his sentence, the error in admitting the statements is not harmless. Zektaw v. Commonwealth, 278 Va. 127, 677 S.E.2d 49, 2009 Va. LEXIS 76 (2009).

V. INDICTMENT.

In general. — Where an indictment for rape is in the usual form and in the words of the statute defining the offense, or is, in substance, sufficiently specific to put the prisoner fairly upon trial for the offense therein charged, such an indictment will generally be held sufficient. Smith v. Commonwealth, 85 Va. 924, 9 S.E. 148 (1889); Mitchell v. Commonwealth, 89 Va. 826, 17 S.E. 480 (1893).

Word "female" held not necessary. — An indictment for rape did not charge that it was committed on a female, but the name given is a woman's name, and the indictment uses the pronouns "she" and "her," in speaking of the person upon whom the rape was committed. Though it would have been better to use the word female, as it is the word used in the statute, yet the language used sufficiently shows that rape was committed on a female, and therefore is good. Taylor v. Commonwealth, 61 Va. (20 Gratt.) 825 (1871). See Commonwealth v. Bennet, 4 Va. (2 Va. Cas.) 235 (1820).

Whether names idem sonans a jury question. — Where the indictment charged that rape was committed upon Ellen Frances Davis and the true name was Helen Frances Davids, the question whether the names were idem sonans was for the jury and not for the court. Taylor v. Commonwealth, 61 Va. (20 Gratt.) 825 (1871).

Offense must be described as in indictment for rape. — In an indictment for an attempt to commit a rape under the statute, it is sufficient to charge the attempt in the terms of the statute, but the offense must be described with the same legal precision and certainty and in the terms in which it is necessary to describe it in an indictment for a rape. Christian v. Commonwealth, 64 Va. (23 Gratt.) 954 (1873).

And must allege overt acts. — Christian v. Commonwealth, 64 Va. (23 Gratt.) 954 (1873); Cunningham v. Commonwealth, 88 Va. 37, 13 S.E. 309 (1891).

Variance as to time of offense not basis for reversal. — Generally, time is not a material ingredient of the offense of rape, and it need not be proven precisely as alleged. Accordingly, the variance between the date on which the bill of particulars alleged the rape occurred and the date which the evidence ultimately established as the day the crime occurred was not of itself a basis for reversal of defendant's conviction. Evans v. Commonwealth, No. 0503-85 (Ct. of Appeals Oct. 10, 1986).

Defendant could be convicted of raping his daughter on October 17 when the Commonwealth, in its bill of particulars, alleged that the rape occurred on October 19, since whether the rape was shown to have occurred on the 17th or 19th, the elements of the crime, for which the Commonwealth had the burden of proof, would remain the same. The indictment charging defendant with the rape, and to which he personally entered a plea of not guilty, alleged the commission of the rape "on or about" the 17th of October. The evidence presented at trial varied from the bill of particulars only as to the date on which the crime occurred and not as to the nature of the offense. This was, therefore, no basis upon which defendant could argue that he was, as a result of a discrepancy between the bill and indictment or between the bill and the facts as shown at trial, subjected to the possibility of being tried for a crime for which he was not indicted. Evans v. Commonwealth, No. 0503-85 (Ct. of Appeals Oct. 10, 1986).

Amendment of indictment proper. — Pursuant to § 19.2-231, the trial court properly allowed the prosecution, after trial began, to amend an indictment charging rape (§ 18.2-61) to object sexual penetration (§ 18.2-67.2), because the amendment did not change the nature or character of the underlying conduct, penetrating victim's vagina against her will by force, only the object used to accomplish the penetration. Jackson v. Commonwealth, 2012 Va. App. LEXIS 224 (July 10, 2012).

VI. INSTRUCTIONS.

In general. — The courts should not be unmindful of that just observation by Lord Hale that rape "is an accusation easily made, hard to be proved, and still harder to be defended by one ever so innocent." The court, however, will refuse to put this language in the form of an independent instruction to the jury, because it is rather a statement of the conclusion of the judicial mind from experience in the trial of this class of offenses than an enunciation of a principle of law. Crump v. Commonwealth, 98 Va. 833, 23 S.E. 760 (1895). See Bailey v. Commonwealth, 82 Va. 107 (1886).

Force and resistance. — On a trial for rape prisoner asked for an instruction "that such force is essential to the crime as may be adequate to overcome the resistance of the woman, taking into consideration the relative strength of the parties and other circumstances"; and the court giving it adds: "such as making outcries and giving alarm." It was held that the instruction was proper. Mings v. Commonwealth, 85 Va. 638, 8 S.E. 474 (1889).

Consent. — Where consent was crucial to appellant's defense and the instructions granted by the court did not sufficiently inform the jury that if the act of intercourse was consensual there could not be a conviction, the conviction was reversed and remanded. Bryant v. Commonwealth, 216 Va. 390, 219 S.E.2d 669 (1975).

There was sufficient evidence of consent by the prosecutrix to justify an instruction specifically directed to such defense. Bryant v. Commonwealth, 216 Va. 390, 219 S.E.2d 669 (1975).

Mental incapacity. — Jury was properly instructed that defendant could be found guilty of rape in violation of subsection A of § 18.2-61 if it found he had intercourse with the victim by using her mental incapacity. The evidence showed the victim had lost consciousness after a blow to the head, and blacked-out due to aggravation of her bipolar condition by alcohol and drug abuse; as used in subdivision 3 of § 18.2-67.10, the term "mental incapacity" could extend to a transitory circumstance such as voluntary intoxication. Molina v. Commonwealth, 272 Va. 666, 636 S.E.2d 470, 2006 Va. LEXIS 106 (2006).

Instruction going beyond charge in indictment. — In a prosecution for attempted rape an instruction to the jury that if they found the accused guilty they should do so under this section and former § 18.1-16 (now § 18.2-26) was held to be error since it might have tended to confuse and mislead the jury. The instruction went beyond the charge in the indictment and was also in conflict with the other instruction. Richards v. Commonwealth, 161 Va. 1073, 171 S.E. 525 (1933).

Inference permitted. — Trial court did not err in instructing the jury that it could infer that defendant's unauthorized presence in a building of another was with the intent to commit rape, absent evidence to the contrary, because the inference referred to in the subject instruction was justified by the rape itself; given the surrounding facts and circumstances and the context of other instructions given, the subject instruction recited a "proper principal of law." Velasquez v. Commonwealth, 2007 Va. App. LEXIS 313 (Aug. 21, 2007), aff'd, 661 S.E.2d 454, 2008 Va. LEXIS 67 (Va. 2008).

Inference not permitted. — While an instruction telling the jury that an intent to rape could be inferred from defendant's unauthorized presence in the victim's home was incorrect, as rape was a general intent crime and it was not the function of the court to suggest to the jury what conclusion it should draw from the facts in evidence, granting the instruction was harmless because of the overwhelming evidence of defendant's guilt where the victim identified defendant as her rapist, there was DNA evidence, and defendant confessed. Velasquez v. Commonwealth, 276 Va. 326, 661 S.E.2d 454, 2008 Va. LEXIS 67 (2008), cert. denied, 129 S. Ct. 580, 2008 U.S. LEXIS 8260, 172 L. Ed. 2d 438 (U.S. 2008).

Instructions that combine alternatives. — In a prosecution for rape, the trial court did not err in granting an instruction merely because it combined two alternatives upon which to convict defendant, as: (1) the theory under each alternative was stated in the disjunctive; (2) the jury was not misled by the instruction; and (3) the evidence was clearly sufficient to support an instruction on mental incapacity at the time of the alleged rape based on the victim's intoxication; moreover, based on the same, any error in giving the instruction was harmless. Molina v. Commonwealth, 47 Va. App. 338, 624 S.E.2d 83, 2006 Va. App. LEXIS 6 (2006).

An instruction that accused may be found guilty of a lesser offense than attempted rape should be given. Richards v. Commonwealth, 161 Va. 1073, 171 S.E. 525 (1933).

Jury instruction on defendant fleeing was improper. — Circuit court erred by instructing a jury on defendant's purported flight from an alleged victim's apartment because the record was devoid of more than a scintilla of evidence that defendant left the apartment as defendant sought to avoid detection, apprehension, arrest, or criminal prosecution. Turman v. Commonwealth, 276 Va. 558, 667 S.E.2d 767, 2008 Va. LEXIS 123 (2008).

VII. VERDICT.

The verdict in a criminal case is always to be read in connection with the indictment, and if, upon reading them together, the meaning of the verdict is certain, that is sufficient. The verdict need not give the name of the prisoner, nor of the person assaulted. Hairston v. Commonwealth, 97 Va. 754, 32 S.E. 797 (1899).

Verdict of jury rendered after their discharge invalid. — Where the court told the jury after a verdict of guilty of rape that they were discharged, and the jurors thereupon returned to the jury room accompanied by the sheriff to claim attendance fees, but were thereafter recalled by the court upon discovery that the jury had made a mistake fixing the penalty under this section, and again retired and returned another verdict, such other verdict would not support a conviction, having been rendered after discharge. Melton v. Commonwealth, 132 Va. 703, 111 S.E. 291 (1922).

Motion to set aside verdict because prosecutrix did not understand oath. — Where prosecutrix, twelve years old, has been critically examined as to her understanding the motive of an oath by the trial court to its satisfaction, and the jury instructed that they were the judges of her credibility, motion to set aside a verdict of guilty, on the ground that she could not understand the same, will not be sustained. Smith v. Commonwealth, 85 Va. 924, 9 S.E. 148 (1889).

New trial ordered. — Where appellant's conviction was based altogether on the testimonial accusation of victim and proposed new witness stood in a special, advisory and protective relationship to the victim, his proffered testimony, describing her failure to make outcry or complaint at the time of the alleged rape and sodomy and her statement to him exonerating the appellant, would have weighed heavily in the assessment of her credibility and the appellant's. Therefore, trial court erred in denying the appellant's motion for a new trial on the ground of after-discovered evidence. Gatling v. Commonwealth, 14 Va. App. 60, 414 S.E.2d 862 (1992).

VIII. PUNISHMENT.

Punishment does not vary according to race. — The degrees of punishment determined by different juries for the crime of rape vary. This variation does not depend upon the race of the accused, but upon the circumstances, aggravation, and enormity of the crime proven in each case. The law applies to all alike, regardless of race or creed. Hampton v. Commonwealth, 190 Va. 531, 58 S.E.2d 288 (1950).

Probation revocation. — Trial court did not err in determining that a convicted rapist violated the terms of probation when defendant refused to admit guilt during the course of court-ordered sex-offender treatment, although defendant's conviction was entered upon an Alford plea and defendant was not advised at the time of the plea that such refusal could have resulted in probation revocation. Carroll v. Commonwealth, 280 Va. 641, 701 S.E.2d 414, 2010 Va. LEXIS 277 (2010).

Sentence appropriate. — Defendant's sentences after he pled guilty to rape, in violation of § 18.2-61, and two counts of abduction with intent to defile, in violation of § 18.2-48, were appropriate because the circuit court did not base his three life sentences on a prior molestation investigation, but on his history as a "career criminal" and on defendant's lack of remorse. Therefore, even if the testimony regarding a prior molestation investigation was inadmissible, such error was harmless. Pagan v. Commonwealth, 2011 Va. App. LEXIS 7 (Jan. 11, 2011).

IX. MARITAL RAPE.

Editor's note.

Note that many cases annotated below were decided prior to amendments in 1986 and 2005.

Spouses living together. — Neither the rape statute nor the marital sexual assault statute prohibits sexual intercourse accomplished against the will of a spouse by "intimidation" where at the time of the act the spouses are living together. Morse v. Commonwealth, 17 Va. App. 627, 440 S.E.2d 145 (1994).

When husband guilty of raping wife. — A wife can unilaterally revoke her implied consent to marital sex where she has made manifest her intent to terminate the marital relationship by living separate and apart from her husband; refraining from voluntary sexual intercourse with her husband; and, in light of all the circumstances, conducting herself in a manner that establishes a de facto end to the marriage. And, once the implied consent is revoked, even though the parties have not yet obtained a divorce, the husband can be found guilty of raping his wife, if the evidence against him establishes a violation of this section. Weishaupt v. Commonwealth, 227 Va. 389, 315 S.E.2d 847 (1984), decided prior to 1986 amendment.

Common-law rule that wife cannot revoke implied consent is rejected. — So much of the English common-law rule regarding a husband's marital exemption from a charge of raping his wife and the implied consent to marital intercourse as provides that a wife cannot unilaterally revoke her implied consent to marital intercourse is rejected. Weishaupt v. Commonwealth, 227 Va. 389, 315 S.E.2d 847 (1984), decided prior to 1986 amendment.

Revocation of consent must be demonstrated by manifest intent to terminate marriage. — In order to sustain a conviction of marital rape, the prosecution, in addition to establishing a violation of this section, must prove beyond a reasonable doubt that the wife unilaterally had revoked her implied consent to marital intercourse. The wife's revocation of consent must be demonstrated by a manifest intent to terminate the marital relationship. The facts necessary to show this intention to terminate must reveal that the wife: has lived separate and apart from the husband; has refrained from voluntary sexual intercourse with her husband; and, in light of all the circumstances, has conducted herself in a manner that establishes a de facto end to the marriage. Kizer v. Commonwealth, 228 Va. 256, 321 S.E.2d 291 (1984), decided prior to 1986 amendment.

Spouse's express intent to terminate the marriage not required. — Virginia General Assembly refused to require proof of a spouse's express intent to end the relationship in order to sustain convictions for marital rape and marital sexual assault. Thus, the Commonwealth was not required to show that the victim communicated to defendant an express and unequivocal desire to terminate her marriage; accordingly, his convictions for marital rape and attempted marital sexual assault were affirmed. Walker v. Commonwealth, — Va. App. —, — S.E.2d —, 2005 Va. App. LEXIS 425 (Oct. 25, 2005).

Wife's subjective intent not manifest due to vacillating conduct. — In a prosecution for marital rape, where the wife subjectively considered the marriage fractured beyond repair when the parties separated, but this subjective intent was not manifested objectively to the husband, in view of the wife's vacillating conduct, so that he perceived that the marriage actually was ended, the evidence was insufficient to sustain a conviction. Kizer v. Commonwealth, 228 Va. 256, 321 S.E.2d 291 (1984), decided prior to 1986 amendment.

Separate and apart. — From the language of the marital rape statute, former subsection B of § 18.2-61, it is clear that the legislature did not intend for separate and apart to include the requirement that the parties refrain from any cohabitation, or that the period of separation be without interruption, which was one of the requirements for divorce under subsection A of § 20-91. Had the legislature intended such an interpretation, it would have included such language in the marital rape statute. Walker v. Commonwealth, — Va. App. —, — S.E.2d —, 2005 Va. App. LEXIS 425 (Oct. 25, 2005) (decided prior to 2005 amendment deleting former subsection B).

Evidence clearly established that defendant and the victim, his wife, lived separate and apart because (1) he had a home in Virginia Beach and she lived in Chesapeake; (2) he did not have a key to her apartment; (3) he did not contribute financially to her household; (4) she did not pay any of the bills at his house; (5) she testified they were separated; and (6) defendant's counsel conceded that defendant and the victim were not living together. Walker v. Commonwealth, — Va. App. —, — S.E.2d —, 2005 Va. App. LEXIS 425 (Oct. 25, 2005) (decided prior to 2005 amendment deleting former subsection B).

Evidence of conduct prior to marital rape properly admitted. — There was no abuse of discretion in the trial court's admission of evidence of defendant's beating and forcible taking of the victim to a remote area prior to committing marital rape, as the evidence tended to prove that defendant used a present threat of force, and the prior bad acts were also important in establishing defendant's state of mind toward the victim; defendant was not entitled to have the evidence "sanitized," so as to deny the jury knowledge of all but the immediate crime for which defendant was on trial. Beale v. Commonwealth, No. 1252-02-1, 2003 Va. App. LEXIS 251 (Ct. of Appeals Apr. 29, 2003).

Reliability of expert testimony. — Where a sexual assault nurse examiner's scientific methodology did not depend upon the reliability of the procedures for the results to be sound or valid, the trial court did not have to make a reliability finding before admitting the testimony; as a result, defendant's conviction for rape and forcible sodomy was affirmed. Beale v. Commonwealth, No. 1808-03-2, 2004 Va. App. LEXIS 180 (Ct. of Appeals Apr. 20, 2004).

§ 18.2-62. Testing of certain persons for human immunodeficiency virus or hepatitis B or C viruses.

A. As soon as practicable following arrest, the attorney for the Commonwealth may request, after consultation with any complaining witness, that any person charged with (i) any crime involving sexual assault pursuant to this article, (ii) any offenses against children as prohibited by §§ 18.2-361, 18.2-366, 18.2-370, and 18.2-370.1, or (iii) any assault and battery in which the complaining witness was exposed to body fluids of the person arrested, be requested to submit to testing for infection with human immunodeficiency virus or hepatitis B or C viruses. The person so charged shall be counseled about the meaning of the test, about acquired immunodeficiency syndrome or hepatitis B or C viruses, and about the transmission and prevention of infection with human immunodeficiency virus or hepatitis B or C viruses.

If the person so charged refuses to submit to the test or the competency of the person to consent to the test is at issue, the court with jurisdiction of the case shall hold a hearing to determine whether there is probable cause that the individual has committed the crime with which he is charged. If the court finds probable cause, the court shall order the accused to undergo testing for infection with human immunodeficiency virus or hepatitis B or C viruses. The court may enter such an order in the absence of the defendant if the defendant is represented at the hearing by counsel or a guardian ad litem. The court's finding shall be without prejudice to either the Commonwealth or the person charged and shall not be evidence in any proceeding, civil or criminal.

B. At any point following indictment, arrest by warrant, or service of a petition in the case of a juvenile, of any crime involving sexual assault pursuant to this article or any offenses against children as prohibited by §§ 18.2-361, 18.2-366, 18.2-370, and 18.2-370.1, the attorney for the Commonwealth may request, or after consultation with a complaining witness and, upon the request of the complaining witness shall request, and the court shall order the defendant to submit to testing for infection with human immunodeficiency virus or hepatitis B or C viruses within 48 hours, and follow-up testing as may be medically appropriate. Any test conducted following indictment, arrest by warrant, or service of a petition shall be in addition to such tests as may have been conducted following arrest pursuant to subsection A.

C. Confirmatory tests shall be conducted before any test result shall be determined to be positive. The results of the tests for infection with human immunodeficiency virus or hepatitis B or C viruses shall be confidential as provided in § 32.1-36.1; however, the Department of Health shall also disclose the results to any victim and offer appropriate counseling as provided by subsection B of § 32.1-37.2. The Department shall conduct surveillance and investigation in accordance with § 32.1-39.

The results of such tests shall not be admissible as evidence in any criminal proceeding.

The cost of such tests shall be paid by the Commonwealth and taxed as part of the cost of such criminal proceedings.

History.
1990, c. 957; 1992, cc. 500, 587; 1993, c. 512; 2001, c. 862; 2005, c. 661; 2008, c. 756.

The 2008 amendments.
The 2008 amendment by c. 756 substituted "complaining witness" for "victim" twice in the first sentence in subsection A; and in subsection B, substituted "At any point following indictment, arrest by warrant, or service of a petition" for "Upon conviction, or adjudication as delinquent" at the beginning and substituted "the Commonwealth may request, or after consultation with a complaining witness and, upon the request of the complaining witness shall request, and the court shall order the defendant to submit to testing for infection with human immunodeficiency virus or hepatitis B or C viruses within 48 hours, and follow-up testing as may be medically appropriate" for "the Commonwealth may, after consul-

tation with any victim and, upon the request of any victim shall, request and the court shall order the defendant to submit to testing for infection with human immunodeficiency virus or hepatitis B or C viruses" in the first sentence and substituted "following indictment, arrest by warrant, or service of a petition shall" for "following conviction shall" in the second sentence.

Michie's Jurisprudence.
For related discussion, see 9A M.J. Health and Sanitation, § 1; 9B M.J. Infants, § 89.

§ 18.2-63. Carnal knowledge of child between thirteen and fifteen years of age.

A. If any person carnally knows, without the use of force, a child thirteen years of age or older but under fifteen years of age, such person shall be guilty of a Class 4 felony.

B. If any person carnally knows, without the use of force, a child thirteen years of age or older but under fifteen years of age who consents to sexual intercourse and the accused is a minor and such consenting child is three years or more the accused's junior, the accused shall be guilty of a Class 6 felony. If such consenting child is less than three years the accused's junior, the accused shall be guilty of a Class 4 misdemeanor.

In calculating whether such child is three years or more a junior of the accused minor, the actual dates of birth of the child and the accused, respectively, shall be used.

C. For the purposes of this section, (i) a child under the age of thirteen years shall not be considered a consenting child and (ii) "carnal knowledge" includes the acts of sexual intercourse, cunnilingus, fellatio, anilingus, anal intercourse, and animate and inanimate object sexual penetration.

History.
Code 1950, § 18.1-44; 1960, c. 358; 1972, c. 394; 1975, cc. 14, 15, 606; 1981, c. 397; 1993, c. 852; 2007, c. 718.

Cross references.
As to Sex Offenders and Crimes Against Minors Registry, see § 9.1-900 et seq. As to validity of an entrustment agreement for termination of parental rights, despite lack of birth father's signature, when the father has been convicted of a violation of § 18.2-61 A, § 18.2-63, or § 18.2-366 B, and the child in question was conceived as a result of such violation, see § 63.2-903 C and § 63.2-1222. For provision that consent to adoption shall not be required of the birth father when the father has been convicted of a violation of § 18.2-61 A, § 18.2-63, or § 18.2-366 B, see § 63.2-1202 F.

Law Review.
For survey of Virginia criminal law for the year 1974-1975, see 61 Va. L. Rev. 1697 (1975). For article discussing constitutional problems with "rape shield" laws, see 18 Wm. & Mary L. Rev. 1 (1976). For 2006 survey article, "Family and Juvenile Law," see 41 U. Rich. L. Rev. 151 (2006).

CASE NOTES

Not a lesser-included offense of rape. — The offense of carnally knowing a child under 14 years of age without the use of force is not a lesser-included offense of rape, and the Commonwealth did not violate defendant's right against double jeopardy under the federal or state Constitutions by seeking an indictment for carnally knowing a child after a rape charge against defendant was dismissed. Ragsdale v. Commonwealth, 38 Va. App. 421, 565 S.E.2d 331, 2002 Va. App. LEXIS 366 (2002).

Constructive force is present when consent given by one under age of consent. — A female under the age of consent cannot legally consent to the act, and constructive force is present, even though she does in fact consent. Buzzard v. Commonwealth, 134 Va. 641, 114 S.E. 664 (1922).

When force essential element. — In prosecution under this section verdict finding defendant guilty of having carnal knowledge of prosecutrix without force was properly amended to show that prosecutrix was under the age of 16 (now 15) where evidence unquestionably showed that she was under 16. The original verdict was ambiguous according to the definition of rape under this section, because if the female be 16 (now 15) or more force must be used but if she be under that age force is not an essential ingredient. Carpenter v. Commonwealth, 193 Va. 851, 71 S.E.2d 377 (1952).

Knowledge of victim's age not essential to constitute attempt to commit statutory rape. Rainey v. Commonwealth, 169 Va. 892, 193 S.E. 501 (1937).

Failure to allege exact age of prosecutrix. — In a prosecution for statutory rape where the indictment alleged that the prosecutrix was under the age of 15, it was held that the defendant was not in any way prejudiced by the failure to allege the exact age of the prosecutrix. Stump v. Commonwealth, 137 Va. 804, 119 S.E. 72 (1923).

When consent immaterial, evidence of subsequent intercourse is admissible. — The authorities are in conflict upon the general question as to whether, in a prosecution for statutory rape, evidence may be admitted of intercourse between the accused and the prosecutrix subsequent to the act upon which the prosecution is based. The better doctrine is that where the consent of the prosecutrix is immaterial, such evidence is admissible as tending to show the disposition of the defendant with respect to the particular act charged. Stump v. Commonwealth, 137 Va. 804, 119 S.E. 72 (1923).

And consent of infant is no defense to attempt charge. — Since a 14-year-old girl's consent would have been no defense to a charge of statutory rape if the sexual act had taken place, it was no defense to an attempt to commit the crime of statutory rape. Rainey v. Commonwealth, 169 Va. 892, 193 S.E. 501 (1937).

Failure to make outcry held not to make prosecutrix's testimony incredible. — In a prosecution under this section the accused having been indicted for statutory rape and the testimony having conclusively shown that the prosecutrix was 14 years of age and that intercourse had been had with her, she having given birth to a child, the fact that she failed to make any outcry was not sufficient to warrant the Supreme Court in holding that her testimony was so incredible that it could not be believed. Salyer v. Commonwealth, 163 Va. 1027, 175 S.E. 757 (1934).

As a general rule, time is not a material ingredient of the offense of rape, and it need not be proved precisely as alleged, it being sufficient in prosecutions for the offense on females under the age of consent to prove the commission of the offense on any day when the female was still under the statutory age. Lear v. Commonwealth, 195 Va. 187, 77 S.E.2d 424 (1953).

Chastity of a female is not made an ingredient of the offense of statutory rape. Carpenter v. Commonwealth, 193 Va. 851, 71 S.E.2d 377 (1952).

Evidence of prior sexual act admissible. — Evidence of prior sexual act with child rape victim was admissible and relevant for the limited purposes of showing defendant's inclination to commit the acts with which defendant was charged and as tending to corroborate the testimony of the alleged victim. Mangum v. Commonwealth, No. 0761-02-2, 2003 Va. App. LEXIS 43 (Ct. of Appeals Feb. 4, 2003).

Defendant's age established. — Even if defendant's appearance did not establish that defendant was well over 18 at the time of a § 18.2-63 incident, defendant's appearance, combined with defendant's statements that defendant had graduated from high school, that defendant was celebrating a birthday, and that defendant was one of the people over 21 who had been drinking established that defendant was over 18 at the time of the incident. Hall v. Commonwealth, 2009 Va. App. LEXIS 73 (Feb. 17, 2009).

Evidence held sufficient. — Where evidence showed that defendant's mouth came in contact with the minor's penis, trial

court's conclusion that the defendant had carnal knowledge of the minor by the mouth in violation of this section was not plainly wrong. Shull v. Commonwealth, 16 Va. App. 667, 431 S.E.2d 924 (1993).

Testimony by the victim that she was 14 years old and that she had sexual relations with defendant over 20 times and testimony of the victims' mother that she suspected that defendant and the victim were having sexual relations, and that defendant confirmed that her suspicions were true, provided sufficient evidence to support defendant's conviction for having carnal knowledge of child between 13 and 15, in violation of § 18.2-63. Welch v. Commonwealth, — Va. App. —, — S.E.2d —, 2005 Va. App. LEXIS 253 (June 28, 2005).

Defendant asserted that, in granting his motion to strike on the ground that the Commonwealth's evidence was insufficient to prove the charge of animate object sexual penetration under § 18.2-67.2, the trial court effectively acquitted him of that charge and dismissed the indictment, but the trial court concluded that, although the Commonwealth's evidence was insufficient to prove the element of force, threat, intimidation, or physical helplessness, the evidence was sufficient, as a matter of law, to sustain a conviction for carnal knowledge under this section; thus, the trial court's granting of the motion to strike did not constitute a judgment of acquittal under Va. Sup. Ct. R. 3A:15. Therefore, the trial court's ruling on the motion to strike did not preclude the Commonwealth from proceeding on the amended charge of carnal knowledge; accordingly, his conviction was affirmed. Sandoval v. Commonwealth, 2006 Va. App. LEXIS 51 (Feb. 7, 2006).

Because defendant pleaded guilty to the offense of unlawful carnal knowledge, defendant supplied all of the evidence necessary to support a conviction; accordingly, the trial court did not err in finding defendant guilty of violating § 18.2-63. Armstrong v. Commonwealth, — Va. App. —, — S.E.2d —, 2006 Va. App. LEXIS 593 (Dec. 28, 2006).

Victim testified at trial that defendant put defendant's tongue on the victim's vagina on monthly occasions after the victim moved with her family and defendant to a new home. Thus, the evidence sufficiently proved that defendant committed the six offenses at issue of carnal knowledge of a child between the ages of 13 and 15 in violation of § 18.2-63. Slate v. Commonwealth, — Va. App. —, — S.E.2d —, 2008 Va. App. LEXIS 113 (Mar. 11, 2008).

Denial of motion to suppress was affirmed because the trial court's factual determination that the officers did not deliberately use improper tactics or coercion was not plainly wrong or without the evidence to support it. Defendant told the officer that he understood the warnings, which he conceded were accurate and complete, and then confessed to having sexual intercourse with the 13-year-old victim in violation of § 18.2-63. Crosby v. Commonwealth, 2009 Va. App. LEXIS 514 (Nov. 17, 2009).

Evidence not sufficient. — Defendant's conviction of carnal knowledge of a child in violation of § 18.2-63 was reversed and the indictment was dismissed, as testimony of a 14-year-old girl that she had "sexual relations" with defendant was too vague to prove carnal knowledge under the terms of the statute. Welch v. Commonwealth, 271 Va. 558, 628 S.E.2d 340, 2006 Va. LEXIS 50 (2006).

Evidence sustained conviction under this section for carnal knowledge, without force, of 15-year-old female. Carpenter v. Commonwealth, 193 Va. 851, 71 S.E.2d 377 (1952).

Evidence held sufficient for multiple convictions. — Because the statutory elements of carnal knowledge of a child were satisfied with each successive act of sexual intercourse, the trial court properly found that each penetration constituted a separate act of sexual intercourse during the four hours defendant was present, permitting a separate punishment for each act of sexual intercourse under § 18.2-63. Evans v. Commonwealth, — Va. App. —, — S.E.2d —, 2008 Va. App. LEXIS 25 (Jan. 15, 2008).

Severance of indictments. — Because: (1) evidence of defendant's separate misdemeanor offenses, in violation of § 18.2-371, with two separate victims was not necessary to prove any relevant element of the felony offenses charged involving a third victim or necessary to prove defendant's motive, intent or knowledge, and in a separate trial involving only the felony offenses; and (2) evidence of defendant's sexual offenses involving the two misdemeanor victims would do little more than show that defendant was a bad man likely to commit that sort of crime, the trial court abused its discretion by not granting defendant's motion to sever the felony indictments from the misdemeanor indictments for separate trials; however, said error was harmless due to the overwhelming evidence of defendant's guilt. Smith v. Commonwealth, No. 1004-04-1, 2005 Va. App. LEXIS 140 (Ct. of Appeals Apr. 5, 2005).

Jury instructions. — Trial judge did not commit reversible error by omitting an element of the offense in instructing the jury, specifically admitting the phrase "without the use of force," as defendant was barred from presenting this issue on appeal by the invited error doctrine, as he, by tendering the jury instructions to the trial judge, could not take advantage of his own wrong on appeal; but, the matter was remanded for the sole purpose of correcting a clerical error in one of the conviction orders. McBride v. Commonwealth, 44 Va. App. 526, 605 S.E.2d 773, 2004 Va. App. LEXIS 597 (2004).

Sentence. — Sentence which the trial court imposed on defendant who was convicted of statutory rape was within the range prescribed by §§ 18.2-10 and 18.2-63, and the trial court did not abuse its discretion by considering defendant's risk factors and imposing an active sentence that exceeded the length of the active sentence recommended by the sentencing guidelines. Brooks v. Commonwealth, No. 2540-02-3, 2004 Va. App. LEXIS 29 (Ct. of Appeals Jan. 28, 2004).

Sentence enhancement under the federal Armed Career Criminal Act improper. — Conviction under Virginia's carnal knowledge offense was not associated with a likelihood of future violent, aggressive, and purposeful armed career criminal behavior and thus, defendant's Virginia's carnal knowledge offense under § 18.2-63 was not sufficiently similar to the enumerated crimes in kind or in degree of risk to constitute a violent felony under the Armed Career Criminal Act, 18 U.S.C.S. § 924(e)(2)(B). Therefore, defendant's sentence as an armed career criminal subject to a sentence enhancement based in part on a 1986 statutory rape conviction was vacated, and the case was remanded for resentencing. United States v. Thornton, 554 F.3d 443, 2009 U.S. App. LEXIS 1988 (4th Cir. 2009).

Applied in McDonald v. Commonwealth, 48 Va. App. 325, 630 S.E.2d 754, 2006 Va. App. LEXIS 259 (2006).

CIRCUIT COURT OPINIONS

No double jeopardy violation. — Trial court denied defendant's motion to dismiss, as the county juvenile court's dismissal of the contributing to the delinquency of a minor charge filed against him, which was done without explanation, did not mean that the county juvenile court found that he did not have sexual intercourse with the 14-year-old victim; as a result, defendant was not entitled to have the felony charge filed against him of carnal knowledge dismissed, as the prosecution of him on that charge did not violate double jeopardy principals since he was not being tried in the trial court on the same charge as the county juvenile court dismissed. Commonwealth v. Hopkinson, 67 Va. Cir. 520, 2004 Va. Cir. LEXIS 362 (Loudoun County July 19, 2004).

OPINIONS OF THE ATTORNEY GENERAL

Duty to report sexual relationship of students. — A teacher or school administrator who suspects that an 18 year old student is having a sexual relationship with a 13 or 14 year old student in violation of this section has a duty to report the matter to the local department of social services in accordance with former §§ 63.1-248.2 and 63.1-248.3 [see now §§ 63.2-1508 and 63.2-1509]; similarly, a teacher or school administrator who suspects that two students, who are minors and whose age difference falls within the purview of this section, are engaging in sexual conduct in violation of this section has a duty to report his or her knowledge of such activity in accordance with former §§ 63.1-248.2 and 63.1-248.3 [see now §§ 63.2-1508 and 63.2-1509]. See opinion of Attorney General to The Honorable Raymond C. Robertson, Commonwealth's Attorney for the City of Staunton, 00-111 (12/27/01).

§ 18.2-63.1. Death of victim.

When the death of the victim occurs in connection with an offense under this article, it shall be imma-

terial in the prosecution thereof whether the alleged offense occurred before or after the death of the victim.

History.
1978, c. 803; 1981, c. 397.

CASE NOTES

Applied in Coleman v. Commonwealth, 226 Va. 31, 307 S.E.2d 864 (1983).

§ 18.2-64. Repealed by Acts 1981, c. 397.

§ 18.2-64.1. Carnal knowledge of certain minors.

If any person providing services, paid or unpaid, to juveniles under the purview of the Juvenile and Domestic Relations District Court Law, or to juveniles who have been committed to the custody of the State Department of Juvenile Justice, carnally knows, without the use of force, any minor fifteen years of age or older, when such minor is confined or detained in jail, is detained in any facility mentioned in § 16.1-249, or has been committed to the custody of the Department of Juvenile Justice pursuant to § 16.1-278.8, knowing or having good reason to believe that (i) such minor is in such confinement or detention status, (ii) such minor is a ward of the Department of Juvenile Justice, or (iii) such minor is on probation, furlough, or leave from or has escaped or absconded from such confinement, detention, or custody, he shall be guilty of a Class 6 felony.

For the purposes of this section, "carnal knowledge" includes the acts of sexual intercourse, cunnilingus, fellatio, anallingus, anal intercourse, and animate and inanimate object sexual penetration.

History.
1977, c. 304; 1981, c. 397; 1989, c. 733; 1991, c. 534; 1993, c. 852.

Cross references.
As to Sex Offenders and Crimes Against Minors Registry, see § 9.1-900 et seq. For provision making it unlawful for any person to operate a family day home if he, or if he knows that any other person who resides in the home, has been convicted of a felony in violation of this section, see § 63.2-1727.

Editor's note.
Acts 1993, c. 930, cl. 3, as amended by Acts 1994, c. 564, cl. 2, and Acts 1996, c. 616, cl. 4, provided that the amendment to this section by Acts 1993, c. 930, cl. 1, would become effective June 1, 1998, "if state funds are provided, including all local costs, to carry out the purposes of this bill by the General Assembly." The funding was not provided.

§ 18.2-64.2. Carnal knowledge of an inmate, parolee, probationer, detainee, or pretrial or posttrial offender; penalty.

An accused is guilty of carnal knowledge of an inmate, parolee, probationer, detainee, or pretrial defendant or posttrial offender if he is an employee or contractual employee of, or a volunteer with, a state or local correctional facility or regional jail, the Department of Corrections, the Department of Juvenile Justice, a secure facility or detention home, as defined in § 16.1-228, a state or local court services unit, as defined in § 16.1-235, a local community-based probation services agency or a pretrial services agency; is in a position of authority over the inmate, probationer, parolee, detainee, or a pretrial defendant or posttrial offender; knows that the inmate, probationer, parolee, detainee, or pretrial defendant or posttrial offender is under the jurisdiction of the state or local correctional facility, a regional jail, the Department of Corrections, the Department of Juvenile Justice, a secure facility or detention home, as defined in § 16.1-228, a state or local court services unit, as defined in § 16.1-235, a local community-based probation services agency, or a pretrial services agency; and carnally knows, without the use of force, threat or intimidation (i) an inmate who has been committed to jail or convicted and sentenced to confinement in a state or local correctional facility or regional jail or (ii) a probationer, parolee, detainee, or a pretrial defendant or posttrial offender under the jurisdiction of the Department of Corrections, the Department of Juvenile Justice, a secure facility or detention home, as defined in § 16.1-228, a state or local court services unit, as defined in § 16.1-235, a local community-based probation services agency, a pretrial services agency, a local or regional jail for the purposes of imprisonment, a work program or any other parole/probationary or pretrial services program or agency. Such offense is a Class 6 felony.

An accused is guilty of carnal knowledge of a pretrial defendant or posttrial offender if he (a) is an owner or employee of the bail bond company that posted the pretrial defendant's or posttrial offender's bond, (b) has the authority to revoke the pretrial defendant's or posttrial offender's bond, and (c) carnally knows, without use of force, threat, or intimidation, a pretrial defendant or posttrial offender. Such offense is a Class 1 misdemeanor.

For the purposes of this section, "carnal knowledge" includes the acts of sexual intercourse, cunnilingus, fellatio, anallingus, anal intercourse and animate or inanimate object sexual penetration.

History.
1999, c. 294; 2000, c. 1040; 2001, c. 385; 2007, c. 133; 2013, c. 602.

The 2013 amendments.
The 2013 amendment by c. 602, in the first sentence of the first paragraph, substituted "An accused is" for "An accused shall be" and "if he" for "if he or she"; and inserted the second paragraph.

Law Review.
For article, "Legal Issues Involving Children," see 35 U. Rich. L. Rev. 741 (2001).

CASE NOTES

Sufficient evidence. — Male correctional facility officer's conviction for carnal knowledge of a female inmate was based upon sufficient evidence, including the inmate's statement, a nurse's report and testimony after her physical examination which found the inmate's vaginal laceration was not self-induced, and defendant's voluntary post-Miranda confession. Martin v. Commonwealth, — Va. App. —, — S.E.2d —, 2005 Va. App. LEXIS 395 (Oct. 11, 2005).

Although there were some inconsistencies in the inmate's testimony, her testimony alone constituted sufficient evidence to convict a defendant of carnal knowledge of an inmate. Martin v. Commonwealth, — Va. App. —, — S.E.2d —, 2005 Va. App. LEXIS 395 (Oct. 11, 2005).

Applied in Ward v. Commonwealth, 2011 Va. App. LEXIS 81 (Mar. 8, 2011).

§ 18.2-65. Repealed by Acts 1981, c. 397.

§ 18.2-66. Repealed by Acts 2008, cc. 174 and 206, cl. 2.

§ 18.2-67. Depositions of complaining witnesses in cases of criminal sexual assault and attempted criminal sexual assault.

Before or during the trial for an offense or attempted offense under this article, the judge of the court in which the case is pending, with the consent of the accused first obtained in open court, by an order of record, may direct that the deposition of the complaining witness be taken at a time and place designated in the order, and the judge may adjourn the taking thereof to such other time and places as he may deem necessary. Such deposition shall be taken before a judge of a circuit court in the county or city in which the offense was committed or the trial is had, and the judge shall rule upon all questions of evidence, and otherwise control the taking of the same as though it were taken in open court. At the taking of such deposition the attorney for the Commonwealth, as well as the accused and his attorneys, shall be present and they shall have the same rights in regard to the examination of such witness as if he or she were testifying in open court. No other person shall be present unless expressly permitted by the judge. Such deposition shall be read to the jury at the time such witness might have testified if such deposition had not been taken, and shall be considered by them, and shall have the same force and effect as though such testimony had been given orally in court. The judge may, in like manner, direct other depositions of the complaining witness, in rebuttal or otherwise, which shall be taken and read in the manner and under the conditions herein prescribed as to the first deposition. The cost of taking such depositions shall be paid by the Commonwealth.

History.
Code 1950, § 18.1-47; 1960, c. 358; 1975, cc. 14, 15, 606; 1981, c. 397.

Law Review.
For article discussing constitutional problems with "rape shield" laws, see 18 Wm. & Mary L. Rev. 1 (1976). For note, "Checking the Allure of Increased Conviction Rates: The Admissibility of Expert

Testimony on Rape Trauma Syndrome in Criminal Proceedings," see 70 Va. L. Rev. 1657 (1984). For 2006 survey article, "Criminal Law and Procedure," see 41 U. Rich. L. Rev. 83 (2006).

Michie's Jurisprudence.

For related discussion, see 4A M.J. Continuances, § 7; 5B M.J. Criminal Procedure, § 23.

CASE NOTES

Only statute authorizing depositions in criminal prosecution. — With the exception of this section there is no statute in Virginia which authorizes depositions to be taken or used in a criminal prosecution. Setliff v. Commonwealth, 162 Va. 805, 173 S.E. 517 (1934).

Convening of court, without order of record, in home of bedridden prosecutrix, and the hearing of her testimony and that of a third party and the defendant, could not be considered a harmless substitute for the process permitted by this section. Lewis v. Peyton, 352 F.2d 791 (4th Cir. 1965).

Attempted aggravated sexual battery. — General assembly passed a law, § 18.2-67.5, stating the punishment for attempted sexual assault offenses, including attempted aggravated sexual battery, and passed § 18.2-67, permitting the deposition of a "complaining witness" in cases of sexual assault and attempted sexual assault, and, if it had intended to exclude attempt crimes from § 18.2-67.3, it would not have passed a law permitting a deposition of a "complaining witness" in attempted aggravated sexual battery and would not have passed a law stating the punishment for attempted aggravated sexual battery, so there was no evidence the general assembly intended to abrogate common-law attempt when it passed § 18.2-67.3, and the crime of attempted aggravated sexual battery existed in Virginia. Moody v. Commonwealth, No. 1395-02-2, 2003 Va. App. LEXIS 696 (Ct. of Appeals Dec. 30, 2003).

§ 18.2-67.01. Not in effect.

Editor's note.

This section, which was enacted by Acts 1987, c. 448, was to become effective only if reenacted by the 1988 Session of the General Assembly. This section was not reenacted at the 1988 Session and therefore did not become effective.

§ 18.2-67.1. Forcible sodomy.

A. An accused shall be guilty of forcible sodomy if he or she engages in cunnilingus, fellatio, anilingus, or anal intercourse with a complaining witness whether or not his or her spouse, or causes a complaining witness, whether or not his or her spouse, to engage in such acts with any other person, and

1. The complaining witness is less than 13 years of age; or

2. The act is accomplished against the will of the complaining witness, by force, threat or intimidation of or against the complaining witness or another person, or through the use of the complaining witness's mental incapacity or physical helplessness.

B. Forcible sodomy is a felony punishable by confinement in a state correctional facility for life or for any term not less than five years; and in addition:

1. For a violation of subdivision A 1, where the offender is more than three years older than the victim, if done in the commission of, or as part of the same course of conduct as, or as part of a common scheme or plan as a violation of (i) subsection A of § 18.2-47 or § 18.2-48, (ii) § 18.2-89, 18.2-90, or 18.2-91, or (iii) § 18.2-51.2, the punishment shall include a mandatory minimum term of confinement of 25 years; or

2. For a violation of subdivision A 1 where it is alleged in the indictment that the offender was 18 years of age or older at the time of the offense, the punishment shall include a mandatory minimum term of confinement for life.

The mandatory minimum terms of confinement prescribed for violations of this section shall be served consecutively with any other sentence. If the term of confinement imposed for any violation of subdivision A 1, where the offender is more than three years older than the victim, is for a term less than life imprisonment, the judge shall impose, in addition to any active sentence, a suspended sentence of no less than 40 years. This suspended sentence shall be suspended for the remainder of the defendant's life, subject to revocation by the court.

In any case deemed appropriate by the court, all or part of any sentence imposed for a violation under this section against a spouse may be suspended upon the defendant's completion of counseling or therapy, if not already provided, in the manner prescribed under § 19.2-218.1 if, after consideration of the views of the complaining witness and such other evidence as may be relevant, the court finds such action will promote maintenance of the family unit and will be in the best interest of the complaining witness.

C. Upon a finding of guilt under this section, when a spouse is the complaining witness in any case tried by the court without a jury, the court, without entering a judgment of guilt, upon motion of the defendant who has not previously had a proceeding against him for violation of this section dismissed pursuant to this subsection and with the consent of the complaining witness and the attorney for the Commonwealth, may defer further proceedings and place the defendant on probation pending completion of counseling or therapy, if not already provided, in the manner prescribed under § 19.2-218.1. If the defendant fails to so complete such counseling or therapy, the court may make final disposition of the case and proceed as otherwise provided. If such counseling is completed as prescribed under § 19.2-218.1, the court may discharge the defendant and dismiss the proceedings against him if, after consideration of the views of the complaining witness and such other evidence as may be relevant, the court finds such action will promote maintenance of the family unit and be in the best interest of the complaining witness.

History.

1981, c. 397; 1986, c. 516; 1994, cc. 772, 794; 1999, c. 367; 2005, c. 631; 2006, cc. 853, 914; 2012, cc. 575, 605; 2013, cc. 761, 774.

Cross references.

For provision making it unlawful to work or volunteer on school grounds following convictions of certain sex offenses, see § 18.2-

370.4. As to Sex Offenders and Crimes Against Minors Registry, see § 9.1-900 et seq. For provision making it unlawful for any person to operate a family day home if he, or if he knows that any other person who resides in the home, has been convicted of a felony in violation of this section, see § 63.2-1727.

Editor's note.

Acts 2012, cc. 575 and 605, cl. 2 provides: "That the provisions of this act may result in a net increase in periods of imprisonment or commitment. Pursuant to § 30-19.1:4, the estimated amount of the necessary appropriation cannot be determined for periods of imprisonment in state adult correctional facilities; therefore, Chapter 890 of the Acts of Assembly of 2011 requires the Virginia Criminal Sentencing Commission to assign a minimum fiscal impact of $50,000. Pursuant to § 30-19.1:4, the estimated amount of the necessary appropriation is $0 for periods of commitment to the custody of the Department of Juvenile Justice."

Acts 2013, cc. 761 and 774, cl. 2 provides: "That the provisions of this act may result in a net increase in periods of imprisonment or commitment. Pursuant to § 30-19.1:4, the estimated amount of the necessary appropriation cannot be determined for periods of imprisonment in state adult correctional facilities; therefore, Chapter 3 of the Acts of Assembly of 2012, Special Session I, requires the Virginia Criminal Sentencing Commission to assign a minimum fiscal impact of $50,000. Pursuant to § 30-19.1:4, the estimated amount of the necessary appropriation cannot be determined for periods of commitment to the custody of the Department of Juvenile Justice."

The 2012 amendments.

The 2012 amendments by cc. 575 and 605 are identical, and rewrote subsection B.

The 2013 amendments.

The 2013 amendments by cc. 761 and 774 are identical, and added the first sentence of the paragraph following subdivision B 2.

Law Review.

For article discussing the legislative history of sexual assault law reform in Virginia, see 68 Va. L. Rev. 459 (1982). For note, "Predicate Offenses for First Degree Felony Murder in Virginia," see 57 Wash. & Lee L. Rev. 561 (2000). For 2006 survey article, "Family and Juvenile Law," see 41 U. Rich. L. Rev. 151 (2006).

Michie's Jurisprudence.

For related discussion, see 16 M.J. Sodomy, § 1.

CASE NOTES

Definition. — Forcible sodomy is, inter alia, the act of cunnilingus accomplished against the will of the complaining witness and by force, threat or intimidation. An attempt is an unfinished crime, composed of the intent to commit the crime and the doing of some direct act toward its consummation, but falling short of the accomplishment of the ultimate design. Jones v. Commonwealth, No. 0033-96-2 (Ct. of Appeals Feb. 25, 1997).

Commonwealth not required to prove force when victim is under thirteen. — Because a complaining witness was under the age of thirteen at the time of alleged sexual abuse by petitioner, the Commonwealth was not required to prove force, threat, or intimidation under §§ 18.2-61 and 18.2-67.1. Cairns v. Johnson, — F.3d —, 2008 U.S. App. LEXIS 4128 (4th Cir. Feb. 26, 2008), cert. denied, 129 S. Ct. 581, 2008 U.S. LEXIS 8293, 172 L. Ed. 2d 439 (U.S. 2008).

Proof of intimidation. — In order to prove that defendant intimidated victim into submitting to a sex act, evidence must show that defendant caused his victim to fear some bodily harm if he or she failed to comply, or that, under the circumstances, defendant imposed such a degree of psychological or emotional pressure on a vulnerable and susceptible victim as to cause that person to submit. Stoudt v. Commonwealth, No. 2386-98-4 (Ct. of Appeals Feb. 15, 2000).

Evidence was sufficient to support defendant's conviction for forcible sodomy, under subsection A of § 18.2-67.1, as intimidation could be caused by the imposition of psychological pressure on one who, under the circumstances, was vulnerable and susceptible to such pressure; proof that the victim feared some type of bodily

harm other than the harm inherent in the sexual assault was not required, and instead, matters such as the victim's age, the relative size of defendant and the victim, and the familial relationship between defendant and the victim, were relevant matters to be considered with other testimony when determining whether the victim was put in fear of bodily harm. Cairns v. Commonwealth, 40 Va. App. 271, 579 S.E.2d 340, 2003 Va. App. LEXIS 221 (2003).

Defendant was not entitled to reversal of his conviction for forcible sodomy under § 18.2-67.1 because there was sufficient evidence that he used his position of authority to coerce the victim into engaging in sexual acts against his will; defendant assumed a parental role in victim's upbringing, required the victim to perform sexual acts as a means of punishment, and isolated the victim from his friends and family. Bell v. Commonwealth, — Va. App. —, — S.E.2d —, 2007 Va. App. LEXIS 456 (Dec. 18, 2007).

Finding that petitioner accomplished forcible sodomy and rape by intimidation within the meaning of §§ 18.2-61 and 18.2-67.1 was supported by evidence showing that the complaining witness, petitioner's stepdaughter, did not want to engage in sexual activity with petitioner, that the stepdaughter did not resist because petitioner was more powerful than she was, that the stepdaughter was afraid of petitioner when he was angry, that the stepdaughter's mother participated in the abuse, and that petitioner had physically abused his wife and one of his sons in the stepdaughter's presence. Cairns v. Johnson, — F.3d —, 2008 U.S. App. LEXIS 4128 (4th Cir. Feb. 26, 2008), cert. denied, 129 S. Ct. 581, 2008 U.S. LEXIS 8293, 172 L. Ed. 2d 439 (U.S. 2008).

Defendant's position of trust and victim's vulnerable condition. — Evidence was sufficient to establish that defendant used his position of trust and the victim's vulnerable condition to commit forcible sodomy where: (1) although the victim was able to communicate and a conviction could not be based on physical helplessness under § 18.2-67.10(4), his Parkinson's disease severely limited his abilities; (2) defendant, while bathing the victim, took the victim's penis in his hand and washed him up and down, which made the victim uncomfortable; (3) defendant put the victim's penis in defendant's mouth for 15-20 seconds before the victim was able to move away from defendant; (4) defendant's claim that the victim's "body language" led him to believe the victim desired the contact was rejected as it was not unusual for a male patient to become sexually aroused while being bathed; and (5) the following day, the victim reported the incident, and as the victim made the report, he was "physically shaking," and "tears were coming down his eyes." Emerick v. Commonwealth, No. 3042-02-3, 2004 Va. App. LEXIS 152 (Ct. of Appeals Apr. 6, 2004).

Only applicable with consent of complaining witness and Commonwealth's attorney. — Trial court did not err in denying defendant's motion under subsection C of §§ 18.2-67.1 and 18.2-67.2, to be placed on probation pending completion of counseling or therapy because the provisions of subsection C of §§ 18.2-67.1 and 18.2-67.2, were only applicable with the consent of the complaining witness and the Commonwealth's attorney, and the Commonwealth's attorney clearly did not consent. Wilson v. Commonwealth, 58 Va. App. 513, 711 S.E.2d 251, 2011 Va. App. LEXIS 230 (2011).

Where spouse is complaining witness. — After defendant had a preliminary hearing in juvenile and domestic relations court, and a grand jury indicted defendant on charges of forcible sodomy and animate object sexual penetration against his wife, violations of §§ 18.2-67.1 and 18.2-67.2, defendant was not entitled under § 19.2-218.2 to return the case to the juvenile and domestic relations court for a hearing to authorize the preparation of a report to address the feasibility of counseling or therapy pursuant to § 19.2-218.1 where defendant failed to make the request for such a report at the preliminary hearing. Wilson v. Commonwealth, 58 Va. App. 513, 711 S.E.2d 251, 2011 Va. App. LEXIS 230 (2011).

Double jeopardy violated in convictions for forcible sodomy and carnal knowledge. — Convictions of both forcible sodomy and carnal knowledge violate the federal and State Constitutional protections against double jeopardy. Every instance of cunnilingus, fellatio, anallingus, or anal intercourse in violation of this section also constitutes a violation of § 18.2-361. Moreover, there is no indication that the legislature intended that two punishments be imposed for the same act. Chaine v. Commonwealth, 17 Va. App. 179, 436 S.E.2d 187 (1993), aff'd upon reh'g en banc, 18 Va. App. 301, 443 S.E.2d 924 (1994).

Impact of reporting delay in parent/child context. — When the victim is a child and the accused her father or stepfather, the failure of a child to report incidents of sodomy or other sexual offenses immediately does not render victim's testimony inherently incredible as a matter of law. Hall v. Commonwealth, No. 0699-91-3 (Ct. of Appeals July 7, 1992).

Multiple units of prosecution was authorized by the statute. — Given the legislative intent to allow multiple units of prosecution, as indicated by the language of clause (i) of subdivision A 1 of § 18.2-67.1, the trial court did not err in denying defendant's motion for merger of the indictments; the Commonwealth's evidence proved three different acts of sodomy occurred between the victim and defendant on the day alleged in the indictments. Nelson v. Commonwealth, 41 Va. App. 716, 589 S.E.2d 23, 2003 Va. App. LEXIS 615 (2003), aff'd, 268 Va. 665, 604 S.E.2d 76 (2004).

Motion to withdraw guilty plea. — In a case in which defendant pled guilty to violating §§ 18.2-90, 18.2-47, 18.2-67.1 and 18.2-53.1, he argued unsuccessfully that the circuit court abused its discretion in denying his motion to withdraw his guilty pleas prior to sentencing; defendant failed to show a good faith basis for seeking to withdraw his guilty pleas. He was clearly aware of the potential range of punishments available to the court at the time he pled guilty; as such, the fact that the sentencing guidelines recommended a higher sentence than he had hoped did not constitute a good faith basis for rescinding his pleas. Mack v. Commonwealth, 2009 Va. App. LEXIS 417 (Sept. 22, 2009).

Sexual battery not a lesser-included offense of forcible sodomy. — Because forcible sodomy required proof of penetration, while sexual battery only required proof of touching the clothing covering a victim's intimate parts, the trial court erred in finding that sexual battery under § 18.2-67.3 was a lesser-included offense of forcible sodomy under § 18.2-67.1. Bowden v. Commonwealth, 52 Va. App. 673, 667 S.E.2d 27, 2008 Va. App. LEXIS 455 (2008).

Medical evidence is not required to convict a defendant of forcible sodomy. Civitello v. Commonwealth, No. 1963-01-2, 2003 Va. App. LEXIS 2 (Ct. of Appeals Jan. 7, 2003).

Admission of evidence. — Defendant's convictions for sodomy and incest were affirmed because the trial court did not err in refusing to quash the Commonwealth's subpoena duces tecum, requesting records from a doctor who examined defendant; and in refusing to admit the evidence proffered by the defense; furthermore, there was no evidence of substantial bias on the part of the judge. Via v. Commonwealth, 42 Va. App. 164, 590 S.E.2d 583, 2004 Va. App. LEXIS 14 (2004).

Evidence obtained illegally by a hacker from defendant's computer was admissible against defendant, who was charged with sodomy, object sexual penetration, and aggravated sexual battery; the government did not know of and acquiesce in the hacker's search in a manner sufficient to transform the hacker into a government agent. Jarrett v. Commonwealth, 42 Va. App. 702, 594 S.E.2d 295, 2004 Va. App. LEXIS 127 (2004).

Trial court did not err in admitting evidence of appellant's uncharged misconduct to prove that he committed the charged crimes as the victim's testimony fell within the exception allowing evidence of prior bad acts to show the conduct and feeling of the accused toward the victim and the prior relations between the parties to prove an element of the offense charged; at trial, the victim specifically testified that, as a result of his previous attacks, she was scared that appellant was going to hurt her if she resisted him. She further testified that she continued to return to appellant's house and did not tell anyone about the attacks because she felt stuck; she believed appellant's threat that if she told anyone about his actions appellant's daughter would find out and kill herself and such testimony, if believed by the jury, would tend to demonstrate that the forcible sodomy and object sexual penetration were accomplished by actions that were tantamount to force, threat or intimidation. Lemen v. Commonwealth, 2009 Va. App. LEXIS 580 (Dec. 22, 2009).

Reversal required where evidence erroneously admitted. — Admission of similar crimes evidence was not harmless error in defendant's trial for rape and sodomy as: (1) the required intent was established upon proof that the accused knowingly and intentionally committed the acts constituting the elements of rape; (2) the required lack of consent for rape involved the victim's mental state, not the defendant's; (3) the fact that one woman was raped had no tendency to prove that another woman did not consent; and (4) the testimony of two escorts that defendant had attacked them in a manner similar to that described by the victim was highly prejudicial and encouraged the inference that defendant committed the charged crimes as he had committed similar crimes in the past. Gonzales v. Commonwealth, No. 1351-03-4, 2004 Va. App. LEXIS 337 (Ct. of Appeals July 13, 2004).

Evidence held relevant and material. — Where father, during the period of time in which it was alleged he was sexually abusing his child, showed movies to child which taught one of the very acts which he required the child to perform on him, he thereby indicated to the child that the behavior was acceptable, which made this evidence relevant and material. Stevens v. Commonwealth, No. 1056-88-3 (Ct. of Appeals, Feb. 27, 1990).

Trial court did not err in admitting doctor's testimony and photographs of victim's anus taken during medical examination. Majette v. Commonwealth, No. 2307-98-2 (Ct. of Appeals Jan. 27, 2000).

Proof of the defendant's possession of a trove of "sex toys" was admissible where it corroborated the victim's account of the defendant's attack on him and where possession and use of those items was probative of the defendant's intent toward his victims. Keller v. Commonwealth, No. 1591-99-2, 2000 Va. App. LEXIS 517 (Ct. of Appeals July 18, 2000).

Evidence held sufficient to convict defendant of sodomy. — Evidence that established that defendant's tongue penetrated at least child victim's outer vaginal lips, or labia majora, and touched but did not penetrate the vaginal opening itself, was sufficient to convict defendant of sodomy by cunnilingus. Love v. Commonwealth, 18 Va. App. 84, 441 S.E.2d 709 (1994).

Since cunnilingus involves stimulation of the vulva or clitoris and the vulva encompasses the outermost part of the female genitalia, penetration of any portion of the vulva is sufficient to prove sodomy by cunnilingus. Penetration of the vaginal opening or vagina is not required. Horton v. Commonwealth, 255 Va. 606, 499 S.E.2d 258 (1998).

Evidence was sufficient to prove that the defendant committed forcible sodomy on his eldest son, who suffered from a learning disability and Asperger's Syndrome and required specialized education, where the defendant did not challenge the child's competency as a witness but, rather, the credibility of his trial testimony when considered together with his inconsistent and oftentimes nonsensical statements to the police. Starnes v. Commonwealth, No. 0905-97-1 (Ct. of Appeals April 28, 1998).

Evidence was sufficient to support conviction of defendant for forcible sodomy arising from an incident in which 13 year old victim was awakened when the intoxicated defendant turned her over on the sofa on which she was sleeping, pulled her underpants down, and penetrated her anus with his penis, notwithstanding that the victim did not protest or resist, where she testified that she pretended to be asleep because she was scared, that she did not want it to happen, and that the defendant held her down and kept her from moving. Holden v. Commonwealth, No. 2245-97-2 (Ct. of Appeals June 30, 1998).

Evidence was sufficient to support defendant's conviction based on child victim's testimony, which was corroborated by independent evidence, including results of a physical examination. Brandon v. Commonwealth, No. 2434-98-2 (Ct. of Appeals Jan. 11, 2000).

Medical evidence was not required to convict defendant of forcible sodomy, and the evidence for conviction was sufficient given that other witnesses substantially corroborated the victims' testimony and defendant made incriminating statements to the police and at trial admitted to sexual contact with the victims. Civitello v. Commonwealth, No. 1963-01-2, 2003 Va. App. LEXIS 2 (Ct. of Appeals Jan. 7, 2003).

There was sufficient evidence to find that defendant was guilty of rape, forcible sodomy, and indecent liberties with a child for acts upon defendant's wife's four-year-old cousin because the evidence supported the victim's account of the events and defendant did have an opportunity to commit the acts on at least two occasions; the victim gave her foster mother a substantially similar account when she initially made her complaint, the victim's testimony was consistent with a drawing she did at the psychologist's instruction, and the medical evidence showed that the victim was a sexually abused child as her hymen was consistent with a painful penetrating injury. Johnson v. Commonwealth, 40 Va. App. 605, 580 S.E.2d 486, 2003 Va. App. LEXIS 303 (2003).

Trial court did not err in finding the evidence sufficient to support defendant's conviction for forcible sodomy because the jury could have reasonably concluded that defendant perpetrated the sodomy by force where the victim testified that defendant grabbed her head and turned it toward him and proceeded to hit her in the face with his penis until he shoved it into her mouth. Mohajer v. Commonwealth, 40 Va. App. 312, 579 S.E.2d 359, 2003 Va. App. LEXIS 309 (2003).

Evidence was sufficient to convict defendant of committing forcible sodomy on the victim, a mentally-retarded male, as the evidence showed that defendant knew the victim was mentally-retarded and used that disability to commit an act of sodomy on the victim because he believed that the victim "did not know what was going on." Mitchell v. Commonwealth, 41 Va. App. 598, 587 S.E.2d 727, 2003 Va. App. LEXIS 544 (2003).

Where the evidence showed that defendant made sexual contact with two boys under the age of 13, there was sufficient evidence to support convictions under §§ 18.2-67.1 and 18.2-67.3, despite the fact that the exact date of the incidents was not established. Harland v. Commonwealth, No. 0842-03-4, 2004 Va. App. LEXIS 445 (Ct. of Appeals Sept. 14, 2004).

Defendant's convictions on two counts of forcible sodomy were upheld, as sufficient evidence was presented that defendant exerted psychological pressure and emotionally dominated his employee, who was younger, smaller, and intoxicated through defendant's act of supplying him with alcohol, and intimidated him into submitting to his sexual advances. Montague v. Commonwealth, No. 2236-03-1, 2004 Va. App. LEXIS 507 (Ct. of Appeals Nov. 2, 2004).

Defendant's use of the victim's cell phone shortly after it was stolen and the undisputed DNA evidence establishing that DNA recovered from the victim matched defendant's DNA profile provided sufficient evidence to prove that defendant was the criminal agent who committed the crimes of forcible sodomy, abduction, robbery, and conspiracy to commit robbery. Hayden v. Commonwealth, — Va. App. —, — S.E.2d —, 2006 Va. App. LEXIS 275 (June 27, 2006).

Evidence that a woman lost consciousness after a blow to her head, that she was dragged to a concealed area, that she did not consent to have sex with defendant, and that spermatozoa with DNA consistent with defendant's was found in her anal cavity, was sufficient to prove that defendant used force to sodomize her, in violation of § 18.2-67.1. Molina v. Commonwealth, 272 Va. 666, 636 S.E.2d 470, 2006 Va. LEXIS 106 (2006).

Evidence admitted at defendant's bench trial sufficiently supported defendant's convictions for the rape and forcible sodomy of defendant's teenage stepdaughter. That evidence showed that defendant forcibly required defendant's teenage stepdaughter to submit to defendant's sexual advances on three occasions, that the victim credibly testified to those events, and that defendant's explanations of recorded, incriminating statements defendant made to the victim's mother, defendant's wife, were lacking in credibility. Carpenter v. Commonwealth, 51 Va. App. 84, 654 S.E.2d 345, 2007 Va. App. LEXIS 463 (2007).

Evidence was sufficient to support a conviction for sodomy of a child because defendant acknowledged that defendant had oral sex with the victim, that defendant's mouth was on the victim's vaginal area, and that the victim was 12 years old at the time. Moreover, the victim testified that defendant's tongue was both on and in the opening of the victim's vagina and that the victim contracted herpes as a result of the victim's contact with defendant. Robeson v. Commonwealth, — Va. App. —, — S.E.2d —, 2008 Va. App. LEXIS 260 (May 27, 2008).

Evidence was sufficient to support defendant's convictions involving the second victim for taking indecent liberties with a child under 14-years-old pursuant to § 18.2-370, forcible sodomy in violation of § 18.2-67.1, and aggravated sexual battery of a child less than 13 years old pursuant to § 18.2-67.3. Although the second victim could not pinpoint her exact age at the time of the incidents giving rise to the convictions, the trial court as the fact finder could determine that she was under the age of 13, as the second based her age on the relative dates of momentous events in her life, which gave the trial court a basis for determining she was less than 13 years old at the relevant times. Wood v. Commonwealth, — Va. App. —, — S.E.2d —, 2008 Va. App. LEXIS 451 (Oct. 7, 2008).

Evidence was sufficient to support defendant's convictions regarding taking indecent liberties with a child under 14 years old in violation of § 18.2-370, forcible sodomy in violation of § 18.2-67.1,

and aggravated sexual battery of a child less than 13 years old pursuant to § 18.2-67.3, all regarding the first victim. The trial court, as the fact finder because a bench trial was involved, could determine that the events that the first victim described occurred while still rejecting the first victim's timeline of the events all happening while she was in the fourth grade, which conflicted with the dates set forth in the indictment. Wood v. Commonwealth, — Va. App. —, — S.E.2d —, 2008 Va. App. LEXIS 451 (Oct. 7, 2008).

Evidence that the victim was mentally retarded; that the victim could not live independently and required constant supervision; that the victim was not told about oral sex, that was, the nature of the act; and the victim's limited ability to assess cause-effect relationships in social interaction supported defendant's conviction for forcible sodomy through use of the victim's mental incapacity under subdivision A 2 of § 18.2-67.1. Sanford v. Commonwealth, 54 Va. App. 357, 678 S.E.2d 842, 2009 Va. App. LEXIS 307 (2009).

Evidence as a whole, viewed in the light most favorable to the Commonwealth, was sufficient to support convictions for forcible sodomy, in violation of § 18.2-67.1, and attempted aggravated sexual battery, in violation of §§ 18.2-67.3 and 18.2-67.5, where the evidence included extensive corroboration of the victim's testimony and none of the arguments raised by defendant rendered the victim's testimony inherently incredible as a matter of law. Moran v. Commonwealth, 2010 Va. App. LEXIS 198 (May 11, 2010).

Evidence was sufficient to prove that defendant committed two counts of object sexual penetration and four counts of forcible sodomy as the victim's testimony established that defendant put his fingers inside her vagina more times than she could count and made her put his penis in her mouth approximately five times. Walker v. Commonwealth, 2010 Va. App. LEXIS 331 (Aug. 17, 2010).

Defendant's convictions for forcible sodomy and rape were supported by sufficient evidence as the victim's testimony showed that defendant handcuffed her, placed her face-down over a desk, pushed her down so that she could not stand up, vaginally penetrated her without her consent, and forced her to perform fellatio on him without her consent. Because defendant penetrated the victim both vaginally and orally without her consent and through the use of force, despite her resistance, the evidence was sufficient to show that defendant committed rape and forcible sodomy. Dillingham v. Commonwealth, 2011 Va. App. LEXIS 184 (2011).

Evidence was insufficient to prove oral sodomy where defendant told an investigator that he performed oral sex on the complainant, however, defendant was not asked to define "oral sex" or to indicate in any other way whether, when he performed oral sex on the complainant, he penetrated any portion of her female sexual organs. Desper v. Commonwealth, 2011 Va. App. LEXIS 343 (Nov. 8, 2011).

Testimony of the victim, which the fact finder accepted and which was corroborated by (1) the victim's statements in the immediate aftermath of the crimes to the victim's parent and the police; (2) the DNA evidence; and (3) defendant's initial denial that defendant even knew the victim, a denial that the trial court could reasonably have concluded was a lie offered to conceal defendant's guilt, when combined with defendant's later acknowledgement that defendant had consensual sexual intercourse with the victim, fully justified the trial court's conclusion that the prosecution sufficiently established defendant's guilt of the crimes of rape, object sexual penetration, and sodomy. Shepperson v. Commonwealth, 2012 Va. App. LEXIS 329 (Oct. 16, 2012).

Evidence was sufficient to convict appellant of sodomy under § 18.2-67.1 because penetration occurred as appellant had to penetrate the outermost parts of the female genitalia when he licked the victim's vagina, and appellant confirmed that he placed his mouth on the victim's vagina. Dawit Alemayehu Habtemariam v. Commonwealth, 2013 Va. App. LEXIS 10 (Jan. 15, 2013).

Sufficient evidence supported defendant's conviction for forcible sodomy, as during a child victim's videotaped forensic interview with a detective the victim did not hesitate to demonstrate with anatomically correct dolls exactly how defendant inserted defendant's penis in the victim's mouth. Klevenz v. Commonwealth, 2013 Va. App. LEXIS 45 (Feb. 5, 2013).

Evidence held insufficient to convict defendant of sodomy. — Evidence failed to support conviction of forcible sodomy on grounds of intimidation since, under circumstances, court could not conclude that victim's will was overborne by psychological or emotional domination, and there was no evidence that victim feared bodily injury if he failed to comply. Stoudt v. Commonwealth, No. 2386-98-4 (Ct. of Appeals Feb. 15, 2000).

Evidence was insufficient to support defendant's conviction for forcible sodomy under § 18.2-67.1; while there was evidence of contact in that defendant put defendant's mouth and tongue on the victim's vagina, such evidence did not establish penetration. Carter v. Commonwealth, No. 2506-01-3, 2002 Va. App. LEXIS 645 (Ct. of Appeals Oct. 29, 2002).

Although the nine-year-old victim's testimony was insufficient to prove penetration by itself, when coupled with the medical evidence, it proved that defendant penetrated the victim with his finger as a nurse testified that the victim had a tear in the "vaginal vault" beyond her hymen, and that insertion or pressure to the area caused the tear; however, the medical evidence that proved digital penetration negated penetration during sodomy, as the nurse stated that a tongue could not have created the tear that the nurse observed. Breeden v. Commonwealth, No. 0404-02-3, 2003 Va. App. LEXIS 24 (Ct. of Appeals Jan. 28, 2003).

Although the trial court properly admitted an out-of-court statement which defendant's stepdaughter gave to a detective as a recent complaint of criminal sexual assault, pursuant to § 19.2-268.2, the court erred by using the stepdaughter's statement to convict defendant of forcible sodomy because testimony which the stepdaughter gave at defendant's trial did not corroborate her out-of-court statement and there was no other evidence that established the elements of the offense. Fincham v. Commonwealth, No. 3361-02-2, 2004 Va. App. LEXIS 259 (Ct. of Appeals June 8, 2004).

Although the appellate court reversed defendant's convictions on two counts of forcible sodomy because the trial court erred when it refused to allow him to cross-examine his daughter about conversations she may have had with her mother that influenced her testimony, the court found that the daughter's testimony that defendant required her to put her mouth on his penis several years earlier, when she was five years old, was sufficient to sustain defendant's convictions and, as a result, a new trial was not barred on double jeopardy grounds. Almond v. Commonwealth, No. 0273-03-2, 2004 Va. App. LEXIS 351 (Ct. of Appeals July 20, 2004).

Given the Commonwealth's evidence that defendant's DNA was found in the victim's vaginal and anal cavity, the victim denied consenting to have sexual intercourse with defendant, and the only other person on the scene was excluded by the DNA evidence, the jury had sufficient evidence with which to convict defendant of both rape and forcible sodomy. Molina v. Commonwealth, 47 Va. App. 338, 624 S.E.2d 83, 2006 Va. App. LEXIS 6 (2006).

Evidence held sufficient to convict defendant of attempted forcible sodomy. — Evidence was sufficient to prove beyond a reasonable doubt that defendant committed attempted forcible sodomy where defendant announced the intention to commit sodomy by force and when the victim resisted, defendant proceeded to apply force to subdue the victim to defendant's will; although the acts were ineffectual, neither the ineffectuality of defendant's acts nor the prevention of performance was of a kind to rid defendant's acts of their criminal character. Smith v. Commonwealth, No. 2319-00-3, 2001 Va. App. LEXIS 640 (Ct. of Appeals Nov. 20, 2001).

Evidence was sufficient to support defendant's conviction for sodomy where the victim testified that his shorts had been lowered while he slept, that defendant was close behind the victim and was facing toward his back, and that he felt something "sticky, slimy" behind him, coupled with the medical evidence that the victim had injuries to his anus consistent with blunt force trauma directed inward. Morris v. Commonwealth, No. 2931-01-1, 2003 Va. App. LEXIS 181 (Ct. of Appeals Apr. 1, 2003).

Evidence was sufficient to support defendant's convictions for forcible sodomy even though they were based solely on the victim's testimony; that the victim could not recount in what room of the house each incident occurred and exhibited no internal physical injuries when examined by a physician over seven months later did not render his testimony inherently incredible. Gardner v. Commonwealth, No. 2192-02-3, 2004 Va. App. LEXIS 151 (Ct. of Appeals Apr. 6, 2004).

Sufficient evidence of penetration. — Where victim testified that defendant put his mouth on her vaginal area and on her vulva area, the jury could have found that during defendant's protracted assault of the victim and effort to moisten her, his mouth penetrated her vulva. Indeed, the victim testified that his mouth was on her vulva and that she could feel heat emanating from his mouth. Thus, the evidence was sufficient to prove penetration. Newby v. Commonwealth, No. 2473-95-2 (Ct. of Appeals July 1, 1997).

Evidence was sufficient to establish penetration of outermost portion of female victim's genitalia, in violation of this section. Medici v. Commonwealth, No. 0527-98-4 (Ct. of Appeals May 25, 1999).

To sustain a conviction for sodomy, the Commonwealth must prove beyond a reasonable doubt that penetration occurred; however, penetration may be proved by circumstantial evidence, and that evidence need only be slight, and in the context of a sodomy charge, evidence of the condition, position, and proximity of the parties may afford sufficient evidence of penetration. Morris v. Commonwealth, No. 2931-01-1, 2003 Va. App. LEXIS 181 (Ct. of Appeals Apr. 1, 2003).

Penetration for purposes of sodomy, like any other element, may be proved by circumstantial evidence and is not dependent on direct testimony from the victim that penetration occurred. Morris v. Commonwealth, No. 2931-01-1, 2003 Va. App. LEXIS 181 (Ct. of Appeals Apr. 1, 2003).

Defendant preserved the double jeopardy argument for appeal where defense counsel stated in a discussion with the judge that the indictments of sodomy and carnal knowledge ought to be struck, although the argument was not precisely framed as an objection, this colloquy sufficed to present the issue to the trial judge. Moreover, the trial judge's response was a clear acknowledgment that he understood the issue. Chaine v. Commonwealth, 17 Va. App. 179, 436 S.E.2d 187 (1993), aff'd upon reh'g en banc, 18 Va. App. 301, 443 S.E.2d 924 (1994).

Actual innocence not proven. — In his recantation, the minor victim stated that the prisoner never forced him to engage in any sexual act; thus, the prisoner claimed that he was actually innocent of the nolle prossed charges brought against him pursuant to §§ 18.2-67.1, 18.2-67.2, 18.2-67.3, and 18.2-370. However, the victim's statement did not demonstrate that the prisoner was actually innocent, since none of the nolle prossed charges required proof of force, threats, or intimidation where the victim was under the age of 13, or 15, or for the indecent liberties charges; thus, even if the victim, who was 11 at the time of the abuse, consented to engage in the alleged sexual acts, the conduct was still unlawful. DiCaprio-Cuozzo v. Johnson, 2010 U.S. Dist. LEXIS 108702 (E.D. Va. Oct. 12, 2010).

Jury instructions. — Inmate was properly denied habeas corpus relief on his claim that his counsel were ineffective for failing to request a jury instruction that would require unanimity on forcible sodomy because unanimity as to the means of commission of a crime was not constitutionally required for a conviction, and to the extent that the oral sodomy supported the aggravating factor that the offense was "outrageously or wantonly vile, horrible, or inhuman" there was substantial other evidence to support this aggravating factor. Moreover, the jury found the additional aggravating factor that the inmate would be a "continuing serious threat to society," which could serve as an independent basis for imposition of the death penalty. Hedrick v. True, 443 F.3d 342, 2006 U.S. App. LEXIS 7904 (4th Cir. 2006), cert. denied, 548 U.S. 928, 127 S. Ct. 10, 165 L. Ed. 2d 992 (2006).

Indefinite period of supervised probation modified. — Trial court abused its discretion in sentencing defendant to an indefinite period of supervised probation, as the period of supervised probation imposed could not extend beyond the specified period of suspension. Mason v. Commonwealth, — Va. App. —, — S.E.2d —, 2007 Va. App. LEXIS 119 (Mar. 27, 2007).

Applied in Manning v. Commonwealth, 2 Va. App. 352, 344 S.E.2d 197 (1986); Crawford v. Commonwealth, 23 Va. App. 661, 479 S.E.2d 84 (1996); Jett v. Commonwealth, 29 Va. App. 190, 510 S.E.2d 747 (1999); Anderson v. Commonwealth, 282 Va. 457, 717 S.E.2d 623, 2011 Va. LEXIS 226 (2011).

§ 18.2-67.2. Object sexual penetration; penalty.

A. An accused shall be guilty of inanimate or animate object sexual penetration if he or she penetrates the labia majora or anus of a complaining witness, whether or not his or her spouse, other than for a bona fide medical purpose, or causes such complaining witness to so penetrate his or her own body with an object or causes a complaining witness, whether or not his or her spouse, to engage in such acts with any other person or to penetrate, or to be penetrated by, an animal, and

1. The complaining witness is less than 13 years of age; or

2. The act is accomplished against the will of the complaining witness, by force, threat or intimidation of or against the complaining witness or another person, or through the use of the complaining witness's mental incapacity or physical helplessness.

B. Inanimate or animate object sexual penetration is a felony punishable by confinement in the state correctional facility for life or for any term not less than five years; and in addition:

1. For a violation of subdivision A 1, where the offender is more than three years older than the victim, if done in the commission of, or as part of the same course of conduct as, or as part of a common scheme or plan as a violation of (i) subsection A of § 18.2-47 or § 18.2-48, (ii) § 18.2-89, 18.2-90, or 18.2-91, or (iii) § 18.2-51.2, the punishment shall include a mandatory minimum term of confinement of 25 years; or

2. For a violation of subdivision A 1 where it is alleged in the indictment that the offender was 18 years of age or older at the time of the offense, the punishment shall include a mandatory minimum term of confinement for life.

The mandatory minimum terms of confinement prescribed for violations of this section shall be served consecutively with any other sentence. If the term of confinement imposed for any violation of subdivision A 1, where the offender is more than three years older than the victim, is for a term less than life imprisonment, the judge shall impose, in addition to any active sentence, a suspended sentence of no less than 40 years. This suspended sentence shall be suspended for the remainder of the defendant's life, subject to revocation by the court.

In any case deemed appropriate by the court, all or part of any sentence imposed for a violation under this section against a spouse may be suspended upon the defendant's completion of counseling or therapy, if not already provided, in the manner prescribed under § 19.2-218.1 if, after consideration of the views of the complaining witness and such other evidence as may be relevant, the court finds such action will promote maintenance of the family unit and will be in the best interest of the complaining witness.

C. Upon a finding of guilt under this section, when a spouse is the complaining witness in any case tried by the court without a jury, the court, without entering a judgment of guilt, upon motion of the defendant who has not previously had a proceeding against him for violation of this section dis-

missed pursuant to this subsection and with the consent of the complaining witness and the attorney for the Commonwealth, may defer further proceedings and place the defendant on probation pending completion of counseling or therapy, if not already provided, in the manner prescribed under § 19.2-218.1. If the defendant fails to so complete such counseling or therapy, the court may make final disposition of the case and proceed as otherwise provided. If such counseling is completed as prescribed under § 19.2-218.1, the court may discharge the defendant and dismiss the proceedings against him if, after consideration of the views of the complaining witness and such other evidence as may be relevant, the court finds such action will promote maintenance of the family unit and be in the best interest of the complaining witness.

History.
1981, c. 397; 1982, c. 508; 1986, c. 516; 1988, c. 437; 1993, c. 549; 1994, cc. 772, 794; 1999, c. 367; 2005, c. 631; 2006, cc. 853, 914; 2012, cc. 575, 605; 2013, cc. 761, 774.

Cross references.
For provision making it unlawful to work or volunteer on school grounds following convictions of certain sex offenses, see § 18.2-370.4. As to Sex Offenders and Crimes Against Minors Registry, see § 9.1-900 et seq. For provision making it unlawful for any person to operate a family day home if he, or if he knows that any other person who resides in the home, has been convicted of a felony in violation of this section, see § 63.2-1727.

Editor's note.
Acts 2012, cc. 575 and 605, cl. 2 provides: "That the provisions of this act may result in a net increase in periods of imprisonment or commitment. Pursuant to § 30-19.1:4, the estimated amount of the necessary appropriation cannot be determined for periods of imprisonment in state adult correctional facilities; therefore, Chapter 890 of the Acts of Assembly of 2011 requires the Virginia Criminal Sentencing Commission to assign a minimum fiscal impact of $50,000. Pursuant to § 30-19.1:4, the estimated amount of the necessary appropriation is $0 for periods of commitment to the custody of the Department of Juvenile Justice."
Acts 2013, cc. 761 and 774, cl. 2 provides: "That the provisions of this act may result in a net increase in periods of imprisonment or commitment. Pursuant to § 30-19.1:4, the estimated amount of the necessary appropriation cannot be determined for periods of imprisonment in state adult correctional facilities; therefore, Chapter 3 of the Acts of Assembly of 2012, Special Session I, requires the Virginia Criminal Sentencing Commission to assign a minimum fiscal impact of $50,000. Pursuant to § 30-19.1:4, the estimated amount of the necessary appropriation cannot be determined for periods of commitment to the custody of the Department of Juvenile Justice."

The 2012 amendments.
The 2012 amendments by cc. 575 and 605 are identical, and rewrote subsection B.

The 2013 amendments.
The 2013 amendments by cc. 761 and 774 are identical, and added the first sentence of the paragraph following subdivision B 2.

Law Review.
For comment, "Sexism and the Common Law: Spousal Rape in Virginia," see 8 Geo. Mason U.L. Rev. 369 (1986). For note, "Predicate Offenses for First Degree Felony Murder in Virginia," see 57 Wash. & Lee L. Rev. 561 (2000). For article surveying developments in criminal law and procedure in Virginia from July 2001 to September 2002, see 37 U. Rich. L. Rev. 45 (2002). For 2006 survey article, "Criminal Law and Procedure," see 41 U. Rich. L. Rev. 83 (2006). For 2006 survey article, "Family and Juvenile Law,"

see 41 U. Rich. L. Rev. 151 (2006). For 2007 annual survey article, "Criminal Law and Procedure," see 42 U. Rich. L. Rev. 311 (2007).

Michie's Jurisprudence.

For related discussion, see 15 M.J. Rape, § 2; 16 M.J. Sodomy, § 1.

CASE NOTES

Penetration need only be slight for purposes of this section, as well as for the statutes prohibiting rape and forcible sodomy. Jett v. Commonwealth, 27 Va. App. 759, 501 S.E.2d 457 (1998).

Evidence of penetration or stimulation of clitoris is sufficient to establish penetration under this section, since according to the anatomical description, the clitoris lies within the labia majora. Jett v. Commonwealth, 27 Va. App. 759, 501 S.E.2d 457 (1998).

Fingers as "object." — This statute makes it a crime to sexually penetrate a victim with "any object," including, as here, the defendant's finger. Bell v. Commonwealth, 22 Va. App. 93, 468 S.E.2d 114 (1996).

Any object. — The language of this section referring to penetration with "any object" is not ambiguous and includes both animate and inanimate objects. Herrel v. Commonwealth, 28 Va. App. 579, 507 S.E.2d 633 (1998).

This section criminalizes both "inanimate" and "animate object sexual penetration" and expressly states that penetration with "any object" violates the statute if all other elements have been proved; the fact that the conduct might also constitute forcible sodomy under § 18.2-67.1 did not require a different result, as where conduct permitted prosecution under either of two statutes, the selection of the charge was a matter of prosecutorial election. Gardner v. Commonwealth, No. 2192-02-3, 2004 Va. App. LEXIS 151 (Ct. of Appeals Apr. 6, 2004).

The force required to sustain a conviction is some force other than merely that force required to accomplish the unlawful touching prohibited by the statute. Adsit v. Commonwealth, No. 0882-98-2 (Ct. of Appeals Feb. 9, 1999).

Use of force shown despite lack of positive resistance. — Requisite force was proven where a male nurse committed object sexual vaginal penetration of a cerebral palsy victim whose leg had been severely injured in car accident, as defendant was in a position of trust and initiated unwanted touching and penetration, and defendant's aggressive behavior instilled fear and psychological paralysis. Wactor v. Commonwealth, 38 Va. App. 375, 564 S.E.2d 160, 2002 Va. App. LEXIS 326 (2002).

Intimidation shown. — Victim's fear of bodily harm from defendant prevented her from communicating her objections to his assault and was, therefore, sufficient to overbear her will, and evidence was sufficient to prove defendant used intimidation to accomplish animate object penetration. Mohajer v. Commonwealth, 39 Va. App. 21, 569 S.E.2d 738, 2002 Va. App. LEXIS 550 (2002).

Trial court did not err in finding the evidence sufficient to support defendant's conviction for animate object penetration because the evidence was sufficient to prove that defendant used intimidation to accomplish animate object penetration where the circumstances surrounding the assault establish that the victim was in a vulnerable position; specifically, she was naked and alone in the presence of someone she believed she could trust and whom she allowed to touch her body only because of his position as masseur. Mohajer v. Commonwealth, 40 Va. App. 312, 579 S.E.2d 359, 2003 Va. App. LEXIS 309 (2003).

Subsection C of 18.2-67.1 only applicable with consent of complaining witness and Commonwealth's attorney. — Trial court did not err in denying defendant's motion under subsection C of §§ 18.2-67.1 and 18.2-67.2, to be placed on probation pending completion of counseling or therapy because the provisions of subsection C of §§ 18.2-67.1 and 18.2-67.2, were only applicable with the consent of the complaining witness and the Commonwealth's attorney, and the Commonwealth's attorney clearly did not consent. Wilson v. Commonwealth, 58 Va. App. 513, 711 S.E.2d 251, 2011 Va. App. LEXIS 230 (2011).

Where spouse is complaining witness. — After defendant had a preliminary hearing in juvenile and domestic relations court, and a grand jury indicted defendant on charges of forcible sodomy and animate object sexual penetration against his wife, violations of §§ 18.2-67.1 and 18.2-67.2, defendant was not entitled under § 19.2-218.2 to return the case to the juvenile and domestic relations court for a hearing to authorize the preparation of a report to address the feasibility of counseling or therapy pursuant to § 19.2-218.1 where defendant failed to make the request for such a report at the preliminary hearing. Wilson v. Commonwealth, 58 Va. App. 513, 711 S.E.2d 251, 2011 Va. App. LEXIS 230 (2011).

Proof of lascivious intent not required. — A plain reading of § 18.2-67.2 establishes that the Virginia Code merely requires proof of penetration of a named sexual part, not proof of lascivious intent. Viars v. Commonwealth, — Va. App. —, — S.E.2d —, 2005 Va. App. LEXIS 147 (Apr. 12, 2005).

Amendment of indictment proper. — Pursuant to § 19.2-231, the trial court properly allowed the prosecution, after trial began, to amend an indictment charging rape (§ 18.2-61) to object sexual penetration (§ 18.2-67.2), because the amendment did not change the nature or character of the underlying conduct, penetrating victim's vagina against her will by force, only the object used to accomplish the penetration. Jackson v. Commonwealth, 2012 Va. App. LEXIS 224 (July 10, 2012).

Crimes against nature not lesser included offense. — Because every instance of object penetration does not constitute carnal knowledge under § 18.2-361 A, an offense under that statute is not a lesser-included offense of § 18.2-67.2. Smith v. Commonwealth, No. 1546-97-4 (Ct. of Appeals Dec. 1, 1998).

No double jeopardy violation. — Because the Commonwealth's evidence proved that defendant performed two separate acts on the victim while she was intoxicated to the point of unconsciousness the Double Jeopardy Clause was not implicated or violated. Jones v. Commonwealth, — Va. App. —, — S.E.2d —, 2008 Va. App. LEXIS 252 (May 27, 2008).

Admission of evidence. — Evidence obtained illegally by a hacker from defendant's computer was admissible against defendant, who was charged with sodomy, object sexual penetration, and aggravated sexual battery; the government did not know of and acquiesce in the hacker's search in a manner sufficient to transform the hacker into a government agent. Jarrett v. Commonwealth, 42 Va. App. 702, 594 S.E.2d 295, 2004 Va. App. LEXIS 127 (2004).

Trial court did not err in admitting evidence of appellant's uncharged misconduct to prove that he committed the charged crimes as the victim's testimony fell within the exception allowing evidence of prior bad acts to show the conduct and feeling of the accused toward the victim and the prior relations between the parties to prove an element of the offense charged; at trial, the victim specifically testified that, as a result of his previous attacks, she was scared that appellant was going to hurt her if she resisted him. She further testified that she continued to return to appellant's house and did not tell anyone about the attacks because she felt stuck; she believed appellant's threat that if she told anyone about his actions appellant's daughter would find out and kill herself and such testimony, if believed by the jury, would tend to demonstrate that the forcible sodomy and object sexual penetration were accomplished by actions that were tantamount to force, threat or intimidation. Lemen v. Commonwealth, 2009 Va. App. LEXIS 580 (Dec. 22, 2009).

When, in a prosecution for object sexual penetration, in violation of subdivision A 2 of § 18.2-67.2, certificates of analysis of bodily fluids for DNA evidence were admitted, along with the testimony of the author of those certificates, but two scientists involved in the analysis did not testify, defendant's right to confrontation was not violated because the witness supervised both scientists' work and was directly involved in the entire DNA analysis at issue, so only the witness could testify about the accuracy of the analysis, the laboratory's operating procedures, and any deviations from or systemic problems in those procedures. Aguilar v. Commonwealth, 280 Va. 322, 699 S.E.2d 215, 2010 Va. LEXIS 224 (2010).

When, in a prosecution for object sexual penetration, in violation of subdivision A 2 of § 18.2-67.2, certificates of analysis of bodily fluids for DNA evidence were admitted, along with the testimony of the author of those certificates, but two scientists involved in the analysis did not testify, defendant's right to confrontation was not violated because the certificates did not explain the work of one of the non-testifying scientists, contain reports that scientist might have generated, or report that scientist's factual findings, so the certificates were not that scientist's declarations, expressly or impliedly, and nothing from that scientist was presented to the fact-finder in a form functionally identical to live, in-court testimony. Aguilar v. Commonwealth, 280 Va. 322, 699 S.E.2d 215, 2010 Va. LEXIS 224 (2010).

When, in a prosecution for object sexual penetration, in violation of subdivision A 2 of § 18.2-67.2, certificates of analysis of bodily fluids for DNA evidence were admitted, along with the testimony of the author of those certificates, but two scientists involved in the analysis did not testify, defendant's right to confrontation was not violated because the witness's testimony showed one non-testifying scientist had no role in the DNA analysis, since that scientist did not find spermatozoa the witness examined, so the certificates did not contain the results of that non-testifying scientist's work. Aguilar v. Commonwealth, 280 Va. 322, 699 S.E.2d 215, 2010 Va. LEXIS 224 (2010).

Testimony concerning physical evidence. — When, in a prosecution for object sexual penetration, in violation of subdivision A 2 of § 18.2-67.2, certificates of analysis of bodily fluids for DNA evidence were admitted, along with the testimony of the author of those certificates, but two scientists involved in the analysis did not testify, defendant's right to confrontation was not violated because the only declarations in the certificates were those of the testifying witness. Aguilar v. Commonwealth, 280 Va. 322, 699 S.E.2d 215, 2010 Va. LEXIS 224 (2010).

Circumstantial evidence may be more compelling and persuasive than direct evidence, and when convincing, it is entitled to as much weight as direct evidence. Jett v. Commonwealth, 29 Va. App. 190, 510 S.E.2d 747 (1999).

Circumstantial evidence sufficient to support conviction. — Circumstantial evidence was sufficient to support conviction for attempted object sexual penetration of 8 month-old son by father where trial court implicitly found that the only reasonable hypotheses flowing from the evidence were that injuries to child's anus occurred while in father's care rather than while undergoing medical treatment and that father was the criminal agent. Marshall v. Commonwealth, 26 Va. App. 627, 496 S.E.2d 120 (1998).

Penetration may be proved by circumstantial evidence and is not dependent on direct testimony from the victim that penetration occurred. Jett v. Commonwealth, 27 Va. App. 759, 501 S.E.2d 457 (1998).

Although the child victim's testimony did not establish penetration, circumstantial evidence of the victim's pain and swollen clitoris established the element of penetration. Jett v. Commonwealth, 27 Va. App. 759, 501 S.E.2d 457 (1998).

Digital penetration shown by medical evidence. — Although the nine-year-old victim's testimony was insufficient to prove penetration by itself, when coupled with the medical evidence, it proved that defendant penetrated the victim with his finger as a nurse testified that the victim had a tear in the "vaginal vault" beyond her hymen, and that insertion or pressure to the area caused the tear; however, the medical evidence that proved digital penetration negated penetration during sodomy, as the nurse stated that a tongue could not have created the tear that the nurse observed. Breeden v. Commonwealth, No. 0404-02-3, 2003 Va. App. LEXIS 24 (Ct. of Appeals Jan. 28, 2003).

Licensed professional counselor permitted to testify as to post-traumatic stress disorder of child victim. — In a prosecution for indecent liberties with a child in defendant's custody and one count of object sexual penetration, the trial court did not abuse its discretion by allowing an expert, who was also a licensed professional counselor, to give testimony regarding a psychiatric diagnosis of the victim of sexual abuse, as the expert was both: (1) permitted by state law, and (2) qualified by her training and experience, to testify about post-traumatic stress disorder. Fitzgerald v. Commonwealth, 48 Va. App. 271, 630 S.E.2d 337, 2006 Va. App. LEXIS 249 (2006), aff'd, 643 S.E.2d 162, 2007 Va. LEXIS 63 (Va. 2007).

Evidence held sufficient to support conviction. — Testimonial evidence, along with the familial relationship, the relative ages and sizes of defendant and the victim, and the improper touching that preceded the penetration, constituted sufficient proof to support a finding that defendant committed animate sexual penetration by intimidation. Commonwealth v. Bower, 264 Va. 41, 563 S.E.2d 736, 2002 Va. LEXIS 89 (2002).

Although the trial court properly admitted an out-of-court statement which defendant's stepdaughter gave to a detective as a recent complaint of criminal sexual assault, pursuant to § 19.2-

268.2, the court erred by using the stepdaughter's statement to convict defendant of forcible sodomy because testimony which the stepdaughter gave at defendant's trial did not corroborate her out-of-court statement and there was no other evidence which established the elements of the offense. However, the stepdaughter's testimony and defendant's admission that he rubbed his stepdaughter's genitalia were sufficient to prove that he committed animate object sexual penetration and aggravated sexual battery, and the appellate court affirmed the trial court's judgment convicting defendant of those crimes. Fincham v. Commonwealth, No. 3361-02-2, 2004 Va. App. LEXIS 259 (Ct. of Appeals June 8, 2004).

There was sufficient evidence to support defendant's conviction for animate object sexual penetration of a minor under 13 years of age where defendant admitted that he had touched the victim's vagina, the victim testified that defendant's finger went "in a little bit" and that it hurt, and the child showed her mother bloodstained toilet tissue afterwards. Avalos v. Commonwealth, — Va. App. —, — S.E.2d —, 2005 Va. App. LEXIS 241 (June 21, 2005).

Sufficient evidence, including the victim's distraught demeanor and pressure marks on her upper thigh, supported defendant's conviction of animate object sexual penetration. The fact that defendant was middle-aged, had no relevant criminal past, knew the victim for two years, and that she may have been flirtatious or sexually suggestive did not render her testimony inherently incredible. Stevenson v. Commonwealth, — Va. App. —, — S.E.2d —, 2006 Va. App. LEXIS 49 (Feb. 7, 2006).

Because a child victim testified that defendant put his "thingy" "up in" "where she peed out of," which was located at her "bottom," and "started to hump her," the evidence was sufficient to convict defendant of aggravated sexual battery, animate object sexual penetration, and statutory rape under §§ 18.2-67.3, 18.2-67.2, and 18.2-61. Tinsley v. Commonwealth, 2007 Va. App. LEXIS 207 (May 15, 2007).

There was sufficient evidence that defendant was not the spouse of the victims for purposes of § 18.2-67.2 as: (1) the minimum legal age for marriage, even with parental consent, was 16 under § 20-48; (2) at the time of the offenses, the younger victim was between four and eight; the elder was between 11 and 12; and (3) any marriage between defendant and either victim would have been void pursuant to § 20-45.1. Haley v. Commonwealth, 2007 Va. App. LEXIS 402 (Nov. 6, 2007).

Given that the fact finder acted within its province to accept the Commonwealth's evidence and reject defendant's version of the facts, the absence of a suppression hearing record, no double jeopardy violation, and no error in denying a motion to strike, defendant's aggravated sexual battery and sexual penetration convictions were upheld on appeal. Jones v. Commonwealth, — Va. App. —, — S.E.2d —, 2008 Va. App. LEXIS 252 (May 27, 2008).

Defendant's convictions for object sexual penetration in violation of § 18.2-67.2 and aggravated sexual battery in violation of § 18.2-67.3 were upheld on appeal despite the 11-year-old victim's inconsistent testimony and statements to an investigator. The trial court was free to believe the victim rather than defendant. Rose v. Commonwealth, 2009 Va. App. LEXIS 385 (Sept. 1, 2009).

Evidence was sufficient to prove that defendant committed two counts of object sexual penetration and four counts of forcible sodomy as the victim's testimony established that defendant put his fingers inside her vagina more times than she could count and made her put his penis in her mouth approximately five times. Walker v. Commonwealth, 2010 Va. App. LEXIS 331 (Aug. 17, 2010).

Testimony of the victim, which the fact finder accepted and which was corroborated by (1) the victim's statements in the immediate aftermath of the crimes to the victim's parent and the police; (2) the DNA evidence; and (3) defendant's initial denial that defendant even knew the victim, a denial that the trial court could reasonably have concluded was a lie offered to conceal defendant's guilt, when combined with defendant's later acknowledgement that defendant had consensual sexual intercourse with the victim, fully justified the trial court's conclusion that the prosecution sufficiently established defendant's guilt of the crimes of rape, object sexual penetration, and sodomy. Shepperson v. Commonwealth, 2012 Va. App. LEXIS 329 (Oct. 16, 2012).

Evidence sufficient to show use of force. — Conviction for animate object sexual penetration under § 18.2-67.2 was supported by sufficient evidence, as defendant's acts of grabbing the victim and continuing to penetrate the victim's vagina after the victim told defendant to stop constituted additional and sufficient reasons, along with the "rather significant probing" of the victim's vagina and hymen found by the trial court, for the trial court to have concluded that defendant used the requisite force under § 18.2-67.2. Kanczuzewski v. Commonwealth, — Va. App. —, — S.E.2d —, 2009 Va. App. LEXIS 93 (Mar. 10, 2009).

Evidence insufficient to show use of force. — In a prosecution arising from an incident in which the 25-year-old defendant inserted his hand into the 14-year-old victim's vagina while she spent the night on the sofa in the home of a friend, in which the defendant also lived, the evidence did not establish the use of force where the victim testified that she was unable to shut her legs because of the way the defendant had his hand under her, but there was no evidence of any other use of force. Adsit v. Commonwealth, No. 0882-98-2 (Ct. of Appeals Feb. 9, 1999).

In case in which the Court of Appeals held that intimidation was not proved based on the fact that the accused was victim's parent and may have been physically larger than victim, the Virginia Supreme Court reversed, holding that those factors and the testimony of witness that she was frightened could sustain the conviction. Commonwealth v. Bower, 264 Va. 41, 563 S.E.2d 736, 2002 Va. LEXIS 89 (2002).

Defendant asserted that, in granting his motion to strike on the ground that the Commonwealth's evidence was insufficient to prove the charge of animate object sexual penetration, the trial court effectively acquitted him of that charge and dismissed the indictment, but the trial court concluded that, although the Commonwealth's evidence was insufficient to prove the element of force, threat, intimidation, or physical helplessness, the evidence was sufficient, as a matter of law, to sustain a conviction for carnal knowledge under § 18.2-63; thus, the trial court's granting of the motion to strike did not constitute a judgment of acquittal under Va. Sup. Ct. R. 3A:15. Therefore, the trial court's ruling on the motion to strike did not preclude the Commonwealth from proceeding on the amended charge of carnal knowledge; accordingly, his conviction was affirmed. Sandoval v. Commonwealth, 2006 Va. App. LEXIS 51 (Feb. 7, 2006).

Evidence of penetration held sufficient. — Despite defendant's contention that only his fingers touched the victim's clothing which covered her labia majora, and that her trousers and undergarments were between his fingers and the opening to the sexual organ and thus could not support the necessary element of penetration, the Court of Appeals of Virginia properly held that because the victim was aware of the intricate structure of her genitalia, and she testified explicitly that defendant put his finger inside the front area of the lips of her vagina, such was sufficient evidence to uphold defendant's object sexual penetration conviction; moreover, the victim's later statement that defendant's finger hit the front area of her genitalia did not detract in any way from her earlier testimony or cause the evidence to be in a state of equipoise. Davis v. Commonwealth, 272 Va. 476, 634 S.E.2d 322, 2006 Va. LEXIS 74 (2006).

Evidence of penetration held insufficient. — A defendant's conviction for object sexual penetration was not supported by the evidence where the victim's testimony was inherently incredible and so contrary to human experience as to render it unworthy of belief or to sustain guilt beyond a reasonable doubt. Davis v. Commonwealth, No. 1637-99-2, 2000 Va. App. LEXIS 612 (Ct. of Appeals Aug. 22, 2000).

Defendant's conviction for animate object sexual penetration was reversed for insufficient evidence of penetration as, even if defendant's testimony that he did not know a word other than "fingered" for touching the victim's vagina, that he did not know it meant putting his hands inside of the victim, and that he put his hand on top of her vagina on her pubic hair, but did not feel the lips of her vagina or her clitoris, was rejected as not credible, defendant's statement that he "fingered" the victim was insufficient to prove digital penetration as a detective never testified why "fingered" meant digital penetration to him, or that it was commonly accepted street slang for digital penetration. Davis v. Commonwealth, — Va. App. —, — S.E.2d —, 2006 Va. App. LEXIS 298 (July 5, 2006).

Actual innocence not proven. — In his recantation, the minor victim stated that the prisoner never forced him to engage in any sexual act; thus, the prisoner claimed that he was actually innocent of the nolle prossed charges brought against him pursuant to

§§ 18.2-67.1, 18.2-67.2, 18.2-67.3, and 18.2-370. However, the victim's statement did not demonstrate that the prisoner was actually innocent, since none of the nolle prossed charges required proof of force, threats, or intimidation where the victim was under the age of 13, or 15, or for the indecent liberties charges; thus, even if the victim, who was 11 at the time of the abuse, consented to engage in the alleged sexual acts, the conduct was still unlawful. DiCaprio-Cuozzo v. Johnson, 2010 U.S. Dist. LEXIS 108702 (E.D. Va. Oct. 12, 2010).

§ 18.2-67.2:1. Repealed by Acts 2005, c. 631, cl. 2.

§ 18.2-67.3. Aggravated sexual battery; penalty.

A. An accused shall be guilty of aggravated sexual battery if he or she sexually abuses the complaining witness, and

1. The complaining witness is less than 13 years of age, or

2. The act is accomplished through the use of the complaining witness's mental incapacity or physical helplessness, or

3. The offense is committed by a parent, stepparent, grandparent, or step-grandparent and the complaining witness is at least 13 but less than 18 years of age, or

4. The act is accomplished against the will of the complaining witness by force, threat or intimidation, and

a. The complaining witness is at least 13 but less than 15 years of age, or

b. The accused causes serious bodily or mental injury to the complaining witness, or

c. The accused uses or threatens to use a dangerous weapon.

B. Aggravated sexual battery is a felony punishable by confinement in a state correctional facility for a term of not less than one nor more than 20 years and by a fine of not more than $100,000.

History.
1981, c. 397; 1993, c. 590; 2004, c. 843; 2005, cc. 185, 406.

Cross references.
As to Sex Offenders and Crimes Against Minors Registry, see § 9.1-900 et seq. For provision making it unlawful for any person to operate a family day home if he, or if he knows that any other person who resides in the home, has been convicted of a felony in violation of this section, see § 63.2-1727.

Law Review.
For survey of Virginia criminal law and procedure for the year 2004-2005, see 40 U. Rich. L. Rev. 197 (2005). For 2006 survey article, "Criminal Law and Procedure," see 41 U. Rich. L. Rev. 83 (2006). For annual survey article, "Criminal Law and Procedure," see 46 U. Rich. L. Rev. 59 (2011).

Michie's Jurisprudence.
For related discussion, see 7B M.J. Evidence, § 267; 16 M.J. Sodomy, § 4.

CASE NOTES

Factor that elevates criminal act to felony is age of victim. — The use of identical language in these statutes defining sexual battery and aggravated sexual battery with reference to force, threat or intimidation makes it clear that the legislature did not intend for these factors to be the distinction between the two statutes. Rather, the factors that elevate the criminal act from the misdemeanor to the felony are the specific age of the victim, serious bodily or mental injury, or the use or threat of use of a dangerous weapon. Johnson v. Commonwealth, 5 Va. App. 529, 365 S.E.2d 237 (1988).

Age of complaining witness, "at least thirteen but less than fifteen," is aggravating factor which distinguishes the felonious act from a misdemeanor where force, threat or intimidation are involved. Johnson v. Commonwealth, 5 Va. App. 529, 365 S.E.2d 237 (1988).

Aggravated sexual battery is different from attempted rape in that an intent to have sexual intercourse is not required; aggravated sexual battery is markedly similar to attempted rape where the victim is female and her genitalia is touched by the perpetrator's penis. Garland v. Commonwealth, 8 Va. App. 189, 379 S.E.2d 146 (1989).

Attempted aggravated sexual battery. — General Assembly passed a law, § 18.2-67.5, stating the punishment for attempted sexual assault offenses, including attempted aggravated sexual battery, and passed § 18.2-67, permitting the deposition of a "complaining witness" in cases of sexual assault and attempted sexual assault, and, if it had intended to exclude attempt crimes from § 18.2-67.3, it would not have passed a law permitting a deposition of a "complaining witness" in attempted aggravated sexual battery and would not have passed a law stating the punishment for attempted aggravated sexual battery, so there was no evidence the General Assembly intended to abrogate common-law attempt when it passed § 18.2-67.3, and the crime of attempted aggravated sexual battery existed in Virginia. Moody v. Commonwealth, No. 1395-02-2, 2003 Va. App. LEXIS 696 (Ct. of Appeals Dec. 30, 2003).

No requirement for corroboration for aggravated sexual battery. — The reasons that support the rule that a conviction for attempted rape may be supported solely upon the testimony of the victim without further corroboration are equally applicable to prosecutions for aggravated sexual battery and there is no requirement for corroboration under this section. Garland v. Commonwealth, 8 Va. App. 189, 379 S.E.2d 146 (1989).

Impact of reporting delay in parent/child context. — When the victim is a child and the accused her father or stepfather, the failure of a child to report incidents of sodomy or other sexual offenses immediately does not render victim's testimony inherently incredible as a matter of law. Hall v. Commonwealth, No. 0699-91-3 (Ct. of Appeals July 7, 1992).

In the absence of evidence in the record explaining the extraordinary 16-month delay between the alleged molestation and the child's statements about the alleged incident to her stepmother, the evidence failed to provide a foundation from which the trial judge could have found that the complaint met the statutory requirement in § 19.2-268.2, relating to the recent complaint hearsay exception, that it was made "recently after commission of the offense." Castelow v. Commonwealth, 29 Va. App. 305, 512 S.E.2d 137 (1999).

Common-law battery compared with sexual battery. — From the language of the statutes the legislature intended some force other than merely that force required to accomplish the unlawful touching to be included within the statutorily defined criminal acts of either sexual battery or aggravated sexual battery. Where the complaining witness is at least 13 years old, unless some force is used to overcome the will of the complaining witness, the unlawful touching constitutes common-law assault and battery. Johnson v. Commonwealth, 5 Va. App. 529, 365 S.E.2d 237 (1988).

Force. — Evidence that the defendant would lie on top of his daughter at night while touching her intimate parts established force and was more force than that required to accomplish the unlawful touching. Clark v. Commonwealth, 30 Va. App. 406, 517 S.E.2d 260 (1999).

Sections 18.2-67.10 and 18.2-67.3 were harmonious, neither negated the other, and both retained a substantive meaning consistent with established caselaw; there was no requirement to show force to prove charges under § 18.2-67.3 where the victim was eight years old. Martin v. Commonwealth, — Va. App. —, — S.E.2d —, 2005 Va. App. LEXIS 337 (Sept. 6, 2005), aff'd, — Va. —, 630 S.E.2d 291 (2006).

"Force" as used in § 18.2-67.10 included actual and constructive force, and constructive force included engaging in proscribed conduct with a victim who was under age of consent; the victim's age of eight years served as proof of both the force requirement and the age requirement, which was neither improper nor incongruous in defendant's prosecution for aggravated sexual battery. Martin v. Commonwealth, 272 Va. 31, 630 S.E.2d 291, 2006 Va. LEXIS 64 (2006).

Sufficient evidence supported a conviction for aggravated sexual battery, in violation of § 18.2-67.3, although there was no evidence of actual force, because constructive force existed where the victim was mentally incapacitated under subdivision 3 of § 18.2-67.10 and was incapable of legally consenting to the sexual touching. This section did not require the use of actual force to establish sexual abuse when the complaining witness was mentally incapacitated. Consent without understanding was no consent at all. Nicholson v. Commonwealth, 56 Va. App. 491, 694 S.E.2d 788, 2010 Va. App. LEXIS 276 (2010).

Intimidation. — In a prosecution of a father for sexual battery against his daughter, the victim's testimony may support a finding that the father exercised such domination and control of her as to overcome her mind and overbear her will so as to constitute intimidation. Clark v. Commonwealth, 30 Va. App. 406, 517 S.E.2d 260 (1999).

Intimidation may be caused by the imposition of psychological pressure on one who, under the circumstances is vulnerable and susceptible to such pressure, and factors such as the paternal bond between the defendant and the victim, the victim's age and the victim's relative isolation from others may be relevant circumstances showing that the victim's ability to resist her father was impeded and that she was vulnerable and susceptible to pressure from her father. Clark v. Commonwealth, 30 Va. App. 406, 517 S.E.2d 260 (1999).

Required force not shown. — In reversing defendant's conviction for aggravated sexual battery the court noted that defendant raised the issue concerning force, threat and intimidation for the first time on appeal. Having reviewed the record the court invoked the ends of justice exception to Rule 5A:18 and considered the merits of defendant's appeal since the facts taken in the best light of the state's case did now show that defendant used the required force necessary to overcome the will of the complaining witness as required by this section. Johnson v. Commonwealth, 5 Va. App. 529, 365 S.E.2d 237 (1988).

Serious mental injury. — In order to prove the requisite element of "serious mental injury" to sustain a felony conviction for aggravated sexual battery, the record must reflect evidence proving a greater injury to the victim's mental health by way of the frequency, degree, duration or aftereffects than that which would attend any sexual battery. Any holding to the contrary would render a lesser offense of sexual battery a nullity. Gonzin v. Commonwealth, 59 Va. App. 1, 716 S.E.2d 466, 2011 Va. App. LEXIS 321 (2011).

Prosecution may be initiated by felony warrant of arrest. — This section, the provisions of Chapter 12.1 of Title 63.1 (see now Chapter 15 of Title 63.2), and §§ 16.1-259 and 16.1-260, were enacted to serve different functions in furtherance of a common goal, and when read together there are no words which specifically or inferentially prevent police authorities from initiating a prosecution for violation of this section by a felony warrant of arrest. Steele v. Commonwealth, No. 0166-90-1 (Ct. of Appeals, Oct. 8, 1991).

Sexual battery was lesser included offense of aggravated battery. — Where indictment was based on subdivision A 2 b [now see A 4 b], which required a showing that the defendant: (1) sexually abused the complaining witness; (2) against the will of the complaining witness; (3) by force, threat or intimidation or through the use of the complaining witness's mental incapacity or physical helplessness; and (4) the accused caused serious bodily or mental injury to the complaining witness, and where the misdemeanor of sexual battery consists of the first three of these elements, in this case, sexual battery was an offense which was composed entirely of elements that were also elements of the greater offense, and by listing these factors in the indictment, sexual battery was "substantially charged"; therefore, the indictment was broad enough to warrant a conviction of the lesser crime. Walker v. Commonwealth, 12 Va. App. 438, 404 S.E.2d 394 (1991).

Sexual battery not a lesser-included offense of forcible sodomy. — Because forcible sodomy required proof of penetration, while sexual battery only required proof of touching the clothing covering a victim's intimate parts, the trial court erred in finding that sexual battery under § 18.2-67.3 was a lesser-included offense of forcible sodomy under § 18.2-67.1. Bowden v. Commonwealth, 52 Va. App. 673, 667 S.E.2d 27, 2008 Va. App. LEXIS 455 (2008).

No error in permitting amendment. — Amendment of the indictment, which occurred nearly three months before trial, did not change the nature or character of the offense with which defendant was charged. The amendment affected only the manner in which the aggravated sexual battery was committed — from defendant touching the child to forcing the child to touch him — and defendant remained charged with the same crime committed against the same victim during the same period of time. He had ample opportunity to prepare a defense to the amended charge. Thus, the trial judge did not err in permitting the amendment, and in denying defendant's motion to dismiss the indictment. Atorick v. Commonwealth, No. 2934-95-4 (Ct. of Appeals July 8, 1997).

Evidence of child's prior sexual conduct properly excluded. — Trial court did not err in denying defendant's motion to present evidence of a six-year-old victim's prior sexual conduct because there was no evidence that defendant gave the notice required by § 18.2-67.7, the rape shield statute, other than the prosecutor's statement that he had received a hand-written notice. Gleason v. Commonwealth, 2010 Va. App. LEXIS 256 (June 29, 2010).

Exclusion of evidence of credibility witnesses reversible error. — Trial court committed reversible error when it excluded testimony of former neighbors that woman allegedly molested by accused had a bad reputation for truthfulness, where Commonwealth's case rested in large measure on the credibility of the accuser; where accused specifically stated in opening statement that he intended to produce witnesses to establish victim's bad reputation for truth; and where in closing argument attorney for the Commonwealth stated over accused's objection that the defense had failed to prove that the victim had a bad reputation for truth." Blaylock v. Commonwealth, 26 Va. App. 579, 496 S.E.2d 97 (1998).

Pornographic pictures, sexually explicit story from computer inadmissible where intent not in genuine dispute. — Trial court improperly admitted pornographic pictures and sexually explicit story from defendant's computer as probative of defendant's lascivious intent because neither the Commonwealth's evidence nor that developed by the appellant put the issue of intent in genuine dispute, and therefore the probative value of the evidence was outweighed by its prejudicial effect. Blaylock v. Commonwealth, 26 Va. App. 579, 496 S.E.2d 97 (1998).

Membership in association. — Defendant's membership in the North American Man-Boy Love Association and pornographic materials in his possession at the time of his arrest were admissible in order to prove that the defendant engaged in acts with the intent to sexually molest, arouse, or gratify any person when he massaged the victim's buttocks. Smith v. Commonwealth, No. 1546-97-4 (Ct. of Appeals Dec. 1, 1998).

Exclusion of evidence of prior false allegations of sexual assault, which consisted only of a denial by the prior accused of said allegations was proper, where such were uncertain, self-serving, and lacked a reasonable probability of falsity. Richardson v. Commonwealth, 42 Va. App. 236, 590 S.E.2d 618, 2004 Va. App. LEXIS 8 (2004).

Possession of pornography admissible. — Where defendant was charged with committing aggravated sexual battery, his statement that he owned pornographic videos was relevant as it heightened the likelihood that the six-year-old victim told the truth when she testified that she had watched such videos with him; the trial court properly found that the probative value of the statement outweighed its potential prejudicial effect. Croxton v. Commonwealth, — Va. App. —, — S.E.2d —, 2005 Va. App. LEXIS 166 (Apr. 26, 2005).

Admission of evidence. — Evidence obtained illegally by a hacker from defendant's computer was admissible against defendant, who was charged with sodomy, object sexual penetration, and aggravated sexual battery; the government did not know of and acquiesce in the hacker's search in a manner sufficient to transform the hacker into a government agent. Jarrett v. Commonwealth, 42 Va. App. 702, 594 S.E.2d 295, 2004 Va. App. LEXIS 127 (2004).

Motion to suppress defendant's statement properly denied. — Because defendant's statement was given in a non-custodial setting, Miranda warnings were administered to him out of an abundance of caution, and law enforcement did not apply any coercive tactics or take advantage of defendant's disability in order to obtain a statement, said statement was properly admitted. Smith v. Commonwealth, — Va. App. —, — S.E.2d —, 2008 Va. App. LEXIS 27 (Jan. 15, 2008).

Sufficient evidence of intent. — Trial court could reasonably conclude that defendant intended to sexually molest the victim by reaching his hand into the victim's underwear and rubbing his groin area for five to six seconds; hence, the evidence was sufficient on this issue. Hirst v. Commonwealth, — Va. App. —, — S.E.2d —, 2005 Va. App. LEXIS 175 (May 3, 2005).

Evidence was clearly sufficient to support appellant's conviction for aggravated sexual battery where victim testified that appellant removed her underpants and all of his own clothing, and she demonstrated with the anatomically correct dolls what transpired next, and after observing her demonstration, the prosecutor stated, "Let the record show that she's placing the hand of the doll on the private area, in the groin area, of the female doll, and furthermore, the fact that appellant removed all of his clothing before the touching took place and that the touching was of sufficient intensity and duration to hurt the prosecutrix and make her vagina including her lips and her behind red provided sufficient circumstantial evidence to support the conclusion that he acted with the requisite intent to molest or gratify either himself or the victim, or both." Hargrove v. Commonwealth, No. 2421-92-2 (Ct. of Appeals Mar. 29, 1994).

Sufficiency of evidence. — Where the only evidence was the uncorroborated testimony of the victim, there was substantial evidence in the record of the victim's poor reputation for truthfulness, and the victim failed to promptly report the incident to anyone, there was reasonable doubt as a matter of law as to the guilt of the defendant. Dailey v. Commonwealth, No. 0940-85 (Ct. of Appeals Sept. 11, 1987).

Because the victims in the instant case were over thirteen years of age, the Commonwealth had to prove that the act of aggravated sexual battery was accomplished "by force, threat or intimidation" to support the convictions; the record had to disclose that the acts of which defendant stood accused were "accomplished against the will of the complaining witness by force," which it did not. Winter v. Commonwealth, No. 0172-96-1 (Ct. of Appeals Mar. 11, 1997).

Defendant touched an "intimate part or material directly covering an intimate part", as addressed in § 18.2-67.10 6 b, where record indicated that he placed his hand at a point where victim's shirt had breast pockets. Sanderson v. Commonwealth, No. 1555-98-1 (Ct. of Appeals Jan. 11, 2000).

The evidence was sufficient to establish that the defendant touched the child victim in one of the areas specified in this section where the child testified that the defendant touched her "privates" and defined "privates" as "the area between her legs." Goode v. Commonwealth, No. 1125-00-2, 2001 Va. App. LEXIS 234 (Ct. of Appeals May 8, 2001).

The evidence was clearly sufficient to support a finding that a defendant intended to "sexually molest, arouse, or gratify" in violation of this section, where it showed that the defendant touched the intimate parts of the child victim's body with his hand and "underneath" her leg with his tongue as she and others slept in a darkened room. Goode v. Commonwealth, No. 1125-00-2, 2001 Va. App. LEXIS 234 (Ct. of Appeals May 8, 2001).

Evidence held sufficient to convict defendant of aggravated sexual battery of 9 and 12 year old sisters either during a karate class or in related circumstances. Creed v. Commonwealth, No. 0593-01-2, 2002 Va. App. LEXIS 352 (Ct. of Appeals June 18, 2002).

Although the trial court properly admitted an out-of-court statement which defendant's stepdaughter gave to a detective as a recent complaint of criminal sexual assault, pursuant to § 19.2-268.2, the court erred by using the stepdaughter's statement to convict defendant of forcible sodomy because testimony that the stepdaughter gave at defendant's trial did not corroborate her out-of-court statement and there was no other evidence that established the elements of the offense. However, the stepdaughter's testimony and defendant's admission that he rubbed his stepdaughter's genitalia were sufficient to prove that he committed animate object sexual penetration and aggravated sexual battery, and the appellate court affirmed the trial court's judgment convicting defendant of those crimes. Fincham v. Commonwealth, No.

3361-02-2, 2004 Va. App. LEXIS 259 (Ct. of Appeals June 8, 2004).

Where the evidence showed that defendant made sexual contact with two boys under the age of 13, there was sufficient evidence to support convictions under §§ 18.2-67.1 and 18.2-67.3, despite the fact that the exact date of the incidents was not established. Harland v. Commonwealth, No. 0842-03-4, 2004 Va. App. LEXIS 445 (Ct. of Appeals Sept. 14, 2004).

Convictions for aggravated sexual battery were upheld despite alleged inconsistencies in the girls' testimony at trial, at the preliminary hearing, and their earlier accounts to the principal and the police because the jury could have concluded that because of the girls' age, their immaturity, and their susceptibility to leading questions, the inconsistencies did not undermine their credibility. Defendant admitted he had been drinking, that he told the girls to come into his bedroom, that he was watching television, and that they were all on the bed; defendant also accepted one girl's testimony that the girls manipulated his hand so as to fondle two others. Hawkins v. Commonwealth, No. 0932-04-1, 2005 Va. App. LEXIS 106 (Ct. of Appeals Mar. 15, 2005).

Uncorroborated testimony supported defendant's conviction for aggravated sexual battery despite the victim's delay in reporting the assault because the delay, which was due to the victim's fear of her father, defendant, and her shame and embarrassment, was consistent with human experience and did not render her testimony inherently incredible. Wilson v. Commonwealth, 46 Va. App. 73, 615 S.E.2d 500, 2005 Va. App. LEXIS 268 (2005).

Because defendant offered no affirmative evidence of innocence to show that a criminal offense did not occur, no basis supported his miscarriage of justice argument to support reversal of his aggravated sexual battery conviction. Messina v. Commonwealth, — Va. App. —, — S.E.2d —, 2006 Va. App. LEXIS 490 (Oct. 31, 2006).

Because a child victim testified that defendant put his "thingy" "up in" "where she peed out of," which was located at her "bottom," and "started to hump her," the evidence was sufficient to convict defendant of aggravated sexual battery, animate object sexual penetration, and statutory rape under §§ 18.2-67.3, 18.2-67.2, and 18.2-61. Tinsley v. Commonwealth, 2007 Va. App. LEXIS 207 (May 15, 2007).

Given that the fact finder acted within its province to accept the Commonwealth's evidence and reject defendant's version of the facts, the absence of a suppression hearing record, no double jeopardy violation, and no error in denying a motion to strike, defendant's aggravated sexual battery and sexual penetration convictions were upheld on appeal. Jones v. Commonwealth, — Va. App. —, — S.E.2d —, 2008 Va. App. LEXIS 252 (May 27, 2008).

Evidence was sufficient to support defendant's convictions involving the second victim for taking indecent liberties with a child under 14 years old pursuant to § 18.2-370, forcible sodomy in violation of § 18.2-67.1, and aggravated sexual battery of a child less than 13 years old pursuant to § 18.2-67.3. Although the second victim could not pinpoint her exact age at the time of the incidents giving rise to the convictions, the trial court as the fact finder could determine that she was under the age of 13, as the second based her age on the relative dates of momentous events in her life, which gave the trial court a basis for determining she was less than 13 years old at the relevant times. Wood v. Commonwealth, — Va. App. —, — S.E.2d —, 2008 Va. App. LEXIS 451 (Oct. 7, 2008).

Evidence was sufficient to support defendant's convictions regarding taking indecent liberties with a child under 14 years old in violation of § 18.2-370, forcible sodomy in violation of § 18.2-67.1, and aggravated sexual battery of a child less than 13 years old pursuant to § 18.2-67.3, all regarding the first victim. The trial court, as the fact finder because a bench trial was involved, could determine that the events that the first victim described had occurred while still rejecting the first victim's timeline of the events all happening while she was in the fourth grade, which conflicted with the dates set forth in the indictment. Wood v. Commonwealth, — Va. App. —, — S.E.2d —, 2008 Va. App. LEXIS 451 (Oct. 7, 2008).

Defendant's convictions for object sexual penetration in violation of § 18.2-67.2 and aggravated sexual battery in violation of § 18.2-67.3 were upheld on appeal despite the 11-year-old victim's inconsistent testimony and statements to an investigator. The trial court was free to believe the victim rather than defendant. Rose v. Commonwealth, 2009 Va. App. LEXIS 385 (Sept. 1, 2009).

Evidence, including a child's observation of defendant's actions before, during, and after the incident, her giving a description of

defendant containing specific details, and her showing no hesitancy in identifying defendant less than 24 hours after the crime, was sufficient to convict defendant of aggravated sexual battery in violation of § 18.2-67.3. Weisel v. Commonwealth, 2009 Va. App. LEXIS 377 (Aug. 25, 2009).

Defendant's conviction of aggravated sexual battery in violation of § 18.2-67.3 was affirmed because evidence, which included victim's testimony regarding numerous touchings, and nothing in the record indicated that her testimony was inherently incredible or so contrary to human experience as to render it unworthy of belief despite defendant's attempts to impeach the victim. Martin v. Commonwealth, 2009 Va. App. LEXIS 376 (Aug. 25, 2009).

In a case in which defendant appealed his conviction for aggravated sexual battery, in violation of § 18.2-67.3, he argued unsuccessfully that the evidence was insufficient to support his conviction because the victim's testimony was inherently unbelievable. The victim's testimony was not inherently incredible, or so contrary to human experience as to render it unworthy of belief; while the record indicated discrepancies in the victim's accounts of what occurred and when, his prior inconsistent testimony was a factor in determining his credibility, but it did not automatically render the victim's testimony incredible. Levesque v. Commonwealth, 2009 Va. App. LEXIS 512 (Nov. 17, 2009).

Evidence as a whole, viewed in the light most favorable to the Commonwealth, was sufficient to support convictions for forcible sodomy, in violation of § 18.2-67.1, and attempted aggravated sexual battery, in violation of §§ 18.2-67.3 and 18.2-67.5, where the evidence included extensive corroboration of the victim's testimony and none of the arguments raised by defendant rendered the victim's testimony inherently incredible as a matter of law. Moran v. Commonwealth, 2010 Va. App. LEXIS 198 (May 11, 2010).

Defendants' convictions for aggravated sexual battery were inappropriate pursuant to subsection A of § 18.2-67.3 because the evidence failed to establish that they committed the elevated felony offense of aggravated sexual battery. The Commonwealth failed to prove serious physical or mental injury to the victim. Gonzin v. Commonwealth, 59 Va. App. 1, 716 S.E.2d 466, 2011 Va. App. LEXIS 321 (2011).

Sufficient evidence supported defendant's conviction for attempted aggravated sexual battery in violation of §§ 18.2-67.3, 18.2-67.5, and 18.2-67.10, because the trial court accepted the testimony of the child victim that defendant touched the clothing covering her breasts and private parts as she exited the school bus. In addition, the trial court viewed a video recording and found it disclosed that something happened on the bus. Gallier v. Commonwealth, 2012 Va. App. LEXIS 60 (Mar. 6, 2012).

Public policy exception to employment-at-will doctrine. — Employee who alleged that he was forced to quit his job as a result of retaliatory conduct that supervisors directed at the employee after the employee refused to engage in sexual harassment at work sufficiently stated a claim for wrongful constructive discharge in violation of public policy because the employee was a member of the class of persons that the statutes forbidding fornication, sexual battery, aggravated sexual battery, and prostitution were designed to protect. Hill v. Paramont Mfg., LLC, — F. Supp. 2d —, 2006 U.S. Dist. LEXIS 78488 (W.D. Va. Oct. 18, 2006).

Statement of child to expert was hearsay. — Where trial court permitted expert to testify that the child had told him that he had been "sexed," and where the child's statement to the psychologist went "beyond a recital of 'past pain, suffering and subjective symptoms,'" statement was hearsay, it was not subject to hearsay exception, and the trial court erred in admitting it before the jury. Jenkins v. Commonwealth, 254 Va. 333, 492 S.E.2d 131 (1997).

No double jeopardy violation. — Conviction for committing three acts of aggravated sexual battery did not violate § 19.2-294 or the double jeopardy clause of the Fifth Amendment, as defendant was convicted in a simultaneous prosecution for multiple violations of a single statute and § 19.2-294 only barred successive convictions under two or more statutes, and the trial court's segregation of offenses properly recognized the separate acts of touching separate intimate parts. De'Armond v. Commonwealth, 51 Va. App. 26, 654 S.E.2d 317, 2007 Va. App. LEXIS 460 (2007).

Because the Commonwealth's evidence proved that defendant performed two separate acts on the victim while she was intoxicated to the point of unconsciousness the Double Jeopardy Clause was not implicated or violated. Jones v. Commonwealth, — Va. App.

—, — S.E.2d —, 2008 Va. App. LEXIS 252 (May 27, 2008).

Instruction on sexual battery as lesser included offense properly denied. — The trial court properly denied the instruction on sexual battery since the difference between aggravated sexual battery and sexual battery is the age of the victim and since the evidence would not support a finding that victim was not between 13 and 15 years of age, it being uncontradicted that she was 14, a sexual battery instruction would have been inappropriate in the case. Kauffman v. Commonwealth, 8 Va. App. 400, 382 S.E.2d 279 (1989).

Instruction on contributing to the delinquency of minor as lesser included offense properly denied. — Trial court properly denied the instruction on contributing to the delinquency of a minor because it was not a lesser included offense of aggravated sexual battery since the offense of aggravated sexual battery does not require proof that the defendant was 18 years of age or older and thus, all of the elements of § 18.2-371 are not included within the offense of this section. Kauffman v. Commonwealth, 8 Va. App. 400, 382 S.E.2d 279 (1989).

Where the father, during the period of time in which it is alleged he was sexually abusing his child, showed movies to the child which taught one of the very acts which he required the child to perform on him, thereby indicating to the child that the behavior was acceptable, made this evidence relevant and material. Stevens v. Commonwealth, No. 1056-88-3 (Ct. of Appeals, Feb. 27, 1990).

Aggravated sexual assault was predicate offense for minimum sentence for child pornography under federal law. — Even if the federal statutory definition of "sexual abuse" was not congruent with the Virginia statutory definition of that term, the district court properly considered prior convictions for aggravated sexual assault, in violation of § 18.2-67.3, as predicate offenses for purposes of imposing 18 U.S.C.S. § 2252A(b)(1)'s 15-year minimum sentence against defendant for knowingly receiving child pornography because § 2252A(b)(1) clearly permits the broad inquiry into whether a prior offense "relates to" sexual abuse of a minor and was not tied to federal law definitions. United States v. Mills, — F.3d —, 2007 U.S. App. LEXIS 8780 (4th Cir. Apr. 17, 2007).

Actual innocence not proven. — In his recantation, the minor victim stated that the prisoner never forced him to engage in any sexual act; thus, the prisoner claimed that he was actually innocent of the nolle prossed charges brought against him pursuant to §§ 18.2-67.1, 18.2-67.2, 18.2-67.3, and 18.2-370. However, the victim's statement did not demonstrate that the prisoner was actually innocent, since none of the nolle prossed charges required proof of force, threats, or intimidation where the victim was under the age of 13, or 15, or for the indecent liberties charges; thus, even if the victim, who was 11 at the time of the abuse, consented to engage in the alleged sexual acts, the conduct was still unlawful. DiCaprio-Cuozzo v. Johnson, 2010 U.S. Dist. LEXIS 108702 (E.D. Va. Oct. 12, 2010).

Applied in Chrisman v. Commonwealth, 3 Va. App. 89, 348 S.E.2d 399 (1986); Seibert v. Commonwealth, 22 Va. App. 40, 467 S.E.2d 838 (1996); Jenkins v. Commonwealth, 22 Va. App. 508, 471 S.E.2d 785 (1996); M. G. v. Albemarle County Dep't of Soc. Servs., 41 Va. App. 170, 583 S.E.2d 761, 2003 Va. App. LEXIS 406 (2003).

§ 18.2-67.4. Sexual battery.

A. An accused is guilty of sexual battery if he sexually abuses, as defined in § 18.2-67.10, (i) the complaining witness against the will of the complaining witness, by force, threat, intimidation, or ruse, (ii) an inmate who has been committed to jail or convicted and sentenced to confinement in a state or local correctional facility or regional jail, and the accused is an employee or contractual employee of, or a volunteer with, the state or local correctional facility or regional jail; is in a position of authority over the inmate; and knows that the inmate is under the jurisdiction of the state or local correctional facility or regional jail, or (iii) a probationer, parolee, or a pretrial defendant or posttrial offender under the jurisdiction of the Department of Corrections, a local community-based probation services agency, a pretrial services agency, a local or regional jail for the purposes of imprisonment, a work program or any other parole/probationary or pretrial services or agency and the accused is an employee or contractual employee of, or a volunteer with, the Department of Corrections, a local community-based probation services agency, a pretrial services agency or a local or regional jail; is in a position of authority over an offender; and knows that the offender is under the jurisdiction of the Department of Corrections, a local community-based probation services agency, a pretrial services agency or a local or regional jail.

B. Sexual battery is a Class 1 misdemeanor.

History.
1981, c. 397; 1997, c. 643; 1999, c. 294; 2000, cc. 832, 1040; 2006, c. 284; 2007, c. 133.

Cross references.
As to Sex Offenders and Crimes Against Minors Registry, see § 9.1-900 et seq.

Law Review.
For note, "The Battered Woman Syndrome and Self-Defense: A Legal and Empirical Dissent," see 72 Va. L. Rev. 619 (1986).

CASE NOTES

Factor that elevates criminal act to felony is age of victim. — The use of identical language in these statutes defining sexual battery and aggravated sexual battery with reference to force, threat or intimidation makes it clear that the legislature did not intend for these factors to be the distinction between the two statutes. Rather, the factors that elevate the criminal act from the misdemeanor to the felony are the specific age of the victim, serious bodily or mental injury, or the use or threat of use of a dangerous weapon. Johnson v. Commonwealth, 5 Va. App. 529, 365 S.E.2d 237 (1988).

District court properly decided not to apply an enhancement under 18 U.S.C.S. § 2252A(b)(1) to defendant's sentence for receipt and possession of child pornography because (1) the state indictment and judicial order of conviction did not trigger the mandatory minimum sentence because the judicial order stated that defendant was found guilty of sexual battery, the statute of conviction, former Va. Code. Ann. § 18.2-67.4, did not require, as an element of the offense, that the complaining witness be a minor, and the references in the indictment suggesting that the victim was a minor must have been disregarded because they were not essential to the offense to which defendant entered his plea; and (2) the district court properly found that the state presentence report could not have been used to justify a sentence enhancement because there was not adequate evidence that defendant assented to the facts contained in the presentence report. United States v. Gardner, 2011 U.S. App. LEXIS 16621; 2011 FED App. 0214P (6th Cir.) (August 12, 2011).

Common-law battery compared with sexual battery. — The legislature imposed a greater burden on the Commonwealth to prove sexual battery than to prove common-law battery, the latter requiring only a showing of nonconsensual touching. To prove the crime of sexual battery, the Commonwealth has to establish beyond a reasonable doubt that the accused touched the intimate parts of the complaining witness, or that the complaining witness was forced to touch the intimate parts of the accused, with the intent to sexually molest, arouse or gratify any person. The acts must have been against the will of the complaining witness. Doss v. Commonwealth, No. 0019-85 (Ct. of Appeals July 30, 1986).

Sexual battery was lesser included offense of aggravated battery. — Where indictment was based on § 18.2-67.3 A 2 b [now see A 3 b], which required a showing that the defendant: (1) sexually abused the complaining witness; (2) against the will of the complaining witness; (3) by force, threat or intimidation or through the use of the complaining witness's mental incapacity or physical helplessness; and (4) the accused caused serious bodily or mental injury to the complaining witness, and where the misdemeanor of sexual battery consists of the first three of these elements, in this case, sexual battery was an offense which was composed entirely of elements that were also elements of the greater offense, and by listing these factors in the indictment, sexual battery was "substantially charged"; therefore, the indictment was broad enough to warrant a conviction of the lesser crime. Walker v. Commonwealth, 12 Va. App. 438, 404 S.E.2d 394 (1991).

Assault and battery was lesser included offense in sexual battery. — Trial court did not err in convicting defendant of lesser-included offense of assault and battery after granting motion to strike charge of sexual battery; each element of an assault and battery is encompassed within the elements of sexual battery: both offenses require a touching and the more specific and aggravated state of mind necessary to commit sexual abuse encompasses the less culpable mental state found in assault and battery. Gnadt v. Commonwealth, 27 Va. App. 148, 497 S.E.2d 887 (1998).

Role as teacher not sufficient to constitute intimidation. — Defendant's role as a teacher supervising the victim who was his student was not sufficient, standing alone, to constitute intimidation used to sexually abuse her. Clark v. Commonwealth, 12 Va. App. 1163, 408 S.E.2d 564 (1991).

Instruction on sexual battery as lesser included offense properly denied. — The trial court properly denied the instruction on sexual battery since the difference between aggravated sexual battery and sexual battery is the age of the victim and since the evidence would not support a finding that victim was not between 13 and 15 years of age, it being uncontradicted that she was 14, a sexual battery instruction would have been inappropriate in the case. Kauffman v. Commonwealth, 8 Va. App. 400, 382 S.E.2d 279 (1989).

Double jeopardy. — Sexual battery and attempted rape were separate and distinct offenses under facts in case at bar, and thus defendant could not have been twice convicted for the same offense in violation of double jeopardy. Haynes v. Commonwealth, No. 1778-98-3 (Ct. of Appeals Oct. 5, 1999).

Instruction on consent as defense was not required as there was no more than a scintilla of evidence of consent, since: (1) although there was evidence that another person entered the office in which the alleged crime occurred and that the complainant failed to seek help at that time, the defendant was fully clothed and the complainant was seated at a desk at that time and, therefore, such evidence supported the argument that a crime did not occur, but did not support the defense of consent; and (2) although there was evidence that the complainant, after leaving the defendant's office, bought cigarettes and gas and laughed at a joke, the defendant made no attempt to connect this evidence with the defense of consent. Ogungbade v. Commonwealth, No. 0991-97-2 (Ct. of Appeals May 26, 1998).

Jury instruction on defendant fleeing was improper. — Circuit court erred by instructing a jury on defendant's purported flight from an alleged victim's apartment because the record was devoid of more than a scintilla of evidence that defendant left the apartment because defendant sought to avoid detection, apprehension, arrest, or criminal prosecution. Turman v. Commonwealth, 276 Va. 558, 667 S.E.2d 767, 2008 Va. LEXIS 123 (2008).

Sufficiency of evidence. — Uncorroborated testimony supported defendant's conviction for sexual battery despite the victim's delay in reporting the assault because the delay, which was due to the victim's fear of her father, defendant, and her shame and embarrassment, was consistent with human experience and did not render her testimony inherently incredible. Wilson v. Commonwealth, 46 Va. App. 73, 615 S.E.2d 500, 2005 Va. App. LEXIS 268 (2005).

In a bench trial, evidence was sufficient to support a sexual battery conviction where the victim, whom the trial court found to be credible, testified that defendant exposed himself, tried to force her to touch his penis, and tried to reach between her legs, touch her breasts, and kiss her neck while she struggled. Patrick v. Commonwealth, 2006 Va. App. LEXIS 457 (Oct. 17, 2006).

Evidence was insufficient. — G.W. had her back to appellant and was unaware that he was behind her. Appellant employed no force beyond that necessary to squeeze G.W.'s buttocks. While the unlawful touching was patently nonconsensual, it was accomplished by surprise, not by force. Despite appellant's harassing and reprehensible conduct, the evidence in this case was insufficient to sustain a conviction under this section. Wilson v. Commonwealth, No. 2636-96-2 (Ct. of Appeals Nov. 4, 1997).

Public policy exception to employment-at-will doctrine. — Employee who alleged that he was forced to quit his job as a result of retaliatory conduct that supervisors directed at the employee after the employee refused to engage in sexual harassment at work sufficiently stated a claim for wrongful constructive discharge in violation of public policy because the employee was a member of the class of persons that the statutes forbidding fornication, sexual battery, aggravated sexual battery, and prostitution were designed to protect. Hill v. Paramont Mfg., LLC, — F. Supp. 2d —, 2006 U.S. Dist. LEXIS 78488 (W.D. Va. Oct. 18, 2006).

Applied in Woodard v. Commonwealth, 27 Va. App. 405, 499 S.E.2d 557 (1998).

§ 18.2-67.4:1. Infected sexual battery; penalty.

A. Any person who, knowing he is infected with HIV, syphilis, or hepatitis B, has sexual intercourse, cunnilingus, fellatio, anallingus or anal intercourse with the intent to transmit the infection to another person is guilty of a Class 6 felony.

B. Any person who, knowing he is infected with HIV, syphilis, or hepatitis B, has sexual intercourse, cunnilingus, fellatio, anallingus or anal intercourse with another person without having previously disclosed the existence of his infection to the other person is guilty of a Class 1 misdemeanor.

C. "HIV" means the human immunodeficiency virus or any other related virus that causes acquired immunodeficiency syndrome (AIDS).

Nothing in this section shall prevent the prosecution of any other crime against persons under Chapter 4 (§ 18.2-30 et seq.) of this title. Any person charged with a violation of this section alleging he is infected with HIV shall be subject to the testing provisions of § 18.2-62.

History.
2000, c. 831; 2004, c. 449.

Law Review.
For 2000 survey of Virginia criminal law and procedure, see 34 U. Rich. L. Rev. 749 (2000).

§ 18.2-67.4:2. Sexual abuse of a child under 15 years of age; penalty.

Any adult who, with lascivious intent, commits an act of sexual abuse, as defined in § 18.2-67.10, with any child 13 years of age or older but under 15 years of age is guilty of a Class 1 misdemeanor.

History.
2007, c. 463.

Law Review.
For 2007 annual survey article, "Criminal Law and Procedure," see 42 U. Rich. L. Rev. 311 (2007).

§ 18.2-67.5. Attempted rape, forcible sodomy, object sexual penetration, aggravated sexual battery, and sexual battery.

A. An attempt to commit rape, forcible sodomy, or inanimate or animate object sexual penetration shall be punishable as a Class 4 felony.

B. An attempt to commit aggravated sexual battery shall be a felony punishable as a Class 6 felony.

C. An attempt to commit sexual battery is a Class 1 misdemeanor.

History.

1981, c. 397; 1993, c. 549.

Cross references.

As to Sex Offenders and Crimes Against Minors Registry, see § 9.1-900 et seq. For provision making it unlawful for any person to operate a family day home if he, or if he knows that any other person who resides in the home, has been convicted of a felony in violation of this section, see § 63.2-1727.

CASE NOTES

Attempted rape consists of the intent to engage in sexual intercourse, and some direct, yet ineffectual, act towards its consummation. Siquina v. Commonwealth, 28 Va. App. 694, 508 S.E.2d 350 (1998).

Inference of specific intent. — The evidence need not show that the defendant touched the victim's sexual organs or removed the victim's clothing to reasonably infer the specific intent to rape. Siquina v. Commonwealth, 28 Va. App. 694, 508 S.E.2d 350 (1998).

Abduction and attempted rape as separate crimes. — It could not be said as a matter of law that the evidence was insufficient to support a conviction for abduction with intent to defile, where, when defendant grabbed the victim, he transported her from a location that was lighted and visible to one out of sight of potential passersby or others, as defendant's asportation of the victim substantially increased the risk of harm to the victim by decreasing the possibility of detecting his criminal activity, and as, moreover, asportation to decrease the possibility of detection is not an act inherent in or necessary to the restraint required in the commission of attempted rape. Thus, the jury could reasonably infer that the abduction was separate and apart from, and not merely incidental to the crime of attempted rape. Accordingly, multiple punishments for defendant's abduction and attempted rape of victim did not offend the double jeopardy guarantee. Coram v. Commonwealth, 3 Va. App. 623, 352 S.E.2d 532 (1987).

Attempted aggravated sexual battery. — For purposes of establishing attempted aggravated sexual battery, a direct, ineffectual act done toward the commission of the offense is not required to be the last proximate act toward the completion of the offense, but it must go beyond mere preparation and be done to produce the intended result. Tharrington v. Commonwealth, 2 Va. App. 491, 346 S.E.2d 337 (1986).

To establish the offense of attempted aggravated sexual battery, the Commonwealth is required to prove that defendant intended to sexually abuse the victim and that he did a direct, ineffectual act toward the commission of the offense. Tharrington v. Commonwealth, 2 Va. App. 491, 346 S.E.2d 337 (1986).

General assembly passed a law, § 18.2-67.5, stating the punishment for attempted sexual assault offenses, including attempted aggravated sexual battery, and passed § 18.2-67, permitting the deposition of a "complaining witness" in cases of sexual assault and attempted sexual assault, and, if it had intended to exclude attempt crimes from § 18.2-67.3, it would not have passed a law permitting a deposition of a "complaining witness" in attempted aggravated sexual battery and would not have passed a law stating the punishment for attempted aggravated sexual battery, so there was no evidence the general assembly intended to abrogate common-law attempt when it passed § 18.2-67.3, and the crime of attempted aggravated sexual battery existed in Virginia. Moody v. Commonwealth, No. 1395-02-2, 2003 Va. App. LEXIS 696 (Ct. of Appeals Dec. 30, 2003).

Sufficiency of evidence of specific intent. — The evidence that the defendant brought a five-year-old girl into the seclusion of a bathroom, suggestively kissed her on the mouth, removed his pants and underwear while he had an erection and directed the child to bend over was sufficient to infer that he possessed the specific intent to rape. Siquina v. Commonwealth, 28 Va. App. 694, 508 S.E.2d 350 (1998).

Medical evidence is not required to convict a defendant of attempted forcible sodomy. Civitello v. Commonwealth, No. 1963-01-2, 2003 Va. App. LEXIS 2 (Ct. of Appeals Jan. 7, 2003).

Reliability of expert testimony. — Where a sexual assault nurse examiner's scientific methodology did not depend upon the reliability of the procedures for the results to be sound or valid, the trial court did not have to make a reliability finding before admitting the testimony; as a result, defendant's conviction for rape and forcible sodomy was affirmed. Beale v. Commonwealth, No. 1808-03-2, 2004 Va. App. LEXIS 180 (Ct. of Appeals Apr. 20, 2004).

Evidence was sufficient to sustain the jury's verdict of attempted rape where appellant abducted the victim, detained her by force when she attempted to flee, attempted to remove her shorts, removed her blouse, and beat her. Atkins v. Commonwealth, No. 2250-91-3 (Ct. of Appeals July 13, 1993).

Evidence held sufficient for conviction for attempted aggravated sexual battery of an 11-year-old child. Tharrington v. Commonwealth, 2 Va. App. 491, 346 S.E.2d 337 (1986).

Evidence as a whole, viewed in the light most favorable to the Commonwealth, was sufficient to support convictions for forcible sodomy, in violation of § 18.2-67.1, and attempted aggravated sexual battery, in violation of §§ 18.2-67.3 and 18.2-67.5, where the evidence included extensive corroboration of the victim's testimony and none of the arguments raised by defendant rendered the victim's testimony inherently incredible as a matter of law. Moran v. Commonwealth, 2010 Va. App. LEXIS 198 (May 11, 2010).

Evidence sufficient to support conviction. — Uncorroborated testimony supported defendant's convictions for attempted rape and attempted forcible sodomy despite the victim's delay in reporting the assault because the delay, which was due to the victim's fear of her father, defendant, and her shame and embarrassment, was consistent with human experience and did not render her testimony inherently incredible. Wilson v. Commonwealth, 46 Va. App. 73, 615 S.E.2d 500, 2005 Va. App. LEXIS 268 (2005).

Sufficient evidence supported defendant's conviction for attempted aggravated sexual battery in violation of §§ 18.2-67.3, 18.2-67.5, and 18.2-67.10, because the trial court accepted the testimony of the child victim that defendant touched the clothing covering her breasts and private parts as she exited the school bus. In addition, the trial court viewed a video recording and found it disclosed that something happened on the bus. Gallier v. Commonwealth, 2012 Va. App. LEXIS 60 (Mar. 6, 2012).

§ 18.2-67.5:1. Punishment upon conviction of third misdemeanor offense.

When a person is convicted of sexual battery in violation of § 18.2-67.4, attempted sexual battery in violation of subsection C of § 18.2-67.5, a violation of § 18.2-371 involving consensual intercourse with a child, indecent exposure of himself or procuring another to expose himself in violation of § 18.2-387, or a violation of § 18.2-130, and it is alleged in the warrant, information or indictment on which the person is convicted and found by the court or jury trying the case that the person has previously been convicted within the ten-year period immediately preceding the offense charged of two or more of the offenses specified in this section, each such offense occurring on a different date, he shall be guilty of a Class 6 felony.

History.

1994, c. 468; 2006, c. 875.

Law Review.

For 2006 survey article, "Criminal Law and Procedure," see 41 U. Rich. L. Rev. 83 (2006).

CASE NOTES

Jury instructions. — In a prosecution for sexual battery, third or subsequent offense, the jury asked the trial court if it could consider defendant's prior convictions. As the jury instructions covered the issues raised by the evidence and addressed this jury question, the trial court did not abuse its discretion by referring the jury to the instructions already given with no further amplification. Minh Ngoc Tran v. Commonwealth, 2008 Va. App. LEXIS 536 (Dec. 9, 2008).

§ 18.2-67.5:2. Punishment upon conviction of certain subsequent felony sexual assault.

A. Any person convicted of (i) more than one offense specified in subsection B or (ii) one of the offenses specified in subsection B of this section and one of the offenses specified in subsection B of § 18.2-67.5:3 when such offenses were not part of a common act, transaction or scheme, and who has been at liberty as defined in § 53.1-151 between each conviction shall, upon conviction of the second or subsequent such offense, be sentenced to the maximum term authorized by statute for such offense, and shall not have all or any part of such sentence suspended, provided it is admitted, or found by the jury or judge before whom the person is tried, that he has been previously convicted of at least one of the specified offenses.

B. The provisions of subsection A shall apply to felony convictions for:

1. Carnal knowledge of a child between thirteen and fifteen years of age in violation of § 18.2-63 when the offense is committed by a person over the age of eighteen;

2. Carnal knowledge of certain minors in violation of § 18.2-64.1;

3. Aggravated sexual battery in violation of § 18.2-67.3;

4. Crimes against nature in violation of subsection B of § 18.2-361;

5. Adultery or fornication with one's own child or grandchild in violation of § 18.2-366;

6. Taking indecent liberties with a child in violation of § 18.2-370 or § 18.2-370.1; or

7. Conspiracy to commit any offense listed in subdivisions 1 through 6 pursuant to § 18.2-22.

C. For purposes of this section, prior convictions shall include (i) adult convictions for felonies under the laws of any state or the United States that are substantially similar to those listed in subsection B and (ii) findings of not innocent, adjudications or convictions in the case of a juvenile if the juvenile offense is substantially similar to those listed in subsection B, the offense would be a felony if committed by an adult in the Commonwealth and the offense was committed less than twenty years before the second offense.

The Commonwealth shall notify the defendant in writing, at least thirty days prior to trial, of its intention to seek punishment pursuant to this section.

History.

1995, c. 834; 2000, c. 333.

§ 18.2-67.5:3. Punishment upon conviction of certain subsequent violent felony sexual assault.

A. Any person convicted of more than one offense specified in subsection B, when such offenses were not part of a common act, transaction or scheme, and who has been at liberty as defined in § 53.1-151 between each conviction shall, upon conviction of the second or subsequent such offense, be sentenced to life imprisonment and shall not have all or any portion of the sentence suspended, provided it is admitted, or found by the jury or judge before whom he is tried, that he has been previously convicted of at least one of the specified offenses.

B. The provisions of subsection A shall apply to convictions for:

1. Rape in violation of § 18.2-61;

2. Forcible sodomy in violation of § 18.2-67.1;

3. Object sexual penetration in violation of § 18.2-67.2;

4. Abduction with intent to defile in violation of § 18.2-48; or

5. Conspiracy to commit any offense listed in subdivisions 1 through 4 pursuant to § 18.2-22.

C. For purposes of this section, prior convictions shall include (i) adult convictions for felonies under the laws of any state or the United States that are substantially similar to those listed in subsection B and (ii) findings of not innocent, adjudications or convictions in the case of a juvenile if the juvenile offense is substantially similar to those listed in subsection B, the offense would be a felony if committed by an adult in the Commonwealth and the offense was committed less than twenty years before the second offense.

The Commonwealth shall notify the defendant in the indictment, information, or warrant, at least thirty days prior to trial, of its intention to seek punishment pursuant to this section.

History.

1995, c. 834; 2007, c. 506.

CASE NOTES

Constitutionality. — Mandatory life sentence imposed by this section for a second or subsequent commission of violent sexual assault was not grossly disproportionate to the offense, and was therefore not unconstitutional. Medici v. Commonwealth, No. 0527-98-4 (Ct. of Appeals May 25, 1999).

Similar laws of other jurisdictions. — For purposes of identifying prior conviction under laws of another state, only that prohibition of other state's law under which defendant was convicted was required to substantially conform to Virginia law. Medici v. Commonwealth, No. 0527-98-4 (Ct. of Appeals May 25, 1999).

While it was found that the California statute, when read in its entirety, permitted a rape conviction for acts that would not necessarily constitute rape in Virginia, in making a comparison regarding the similarity of the statutes, it was only necessary to compare the Virginia rape statute with the subsection of the California statute under which the defendant was charged and convicted. Medici v. Commonwealth, 260 Va. 223, 532 S.E.2d 28, 2000 Va. LEXIS 86 (2000), overruled on other grounds by Townsend v. Commonwealth, 270 Va. 325, 619 S.E.2d 71 (2005).

Evidence of prior convictions. — Evidence of defendant's prior rape convictions was properly admitted to establish rape in question as a subsequent offense. Medici v. Commonwealth, No. 0527-98-4 (Ct. of Appeals May 25, 1999).

Admission of evidence not violation of due process rights. — The admission into evidence of a defendant's prior rape convictions during the guilt/innocence phase of his trial did not violate the defendant's due process rights where the defendant, if convicted, was subject to enhanced punishment under this section. Medici v. Commonwealth, 260 Va. 223, 532 S.E.2d 28, 2000 Va. LEXIS 86 (2000), overruled on other grounds by Townsend v. Commonwealth, 270 Va. 325, 619 S.E.2d 71 (2005).

§ 18.2-67.6. Proof of physical resistance not required.

The Commonwealth need not demonstrate that the complaining witness cried out or physically resisted the accused in order to convict the accused of an offense under this article, but the absence of such resistance may be considered when relevant to show that the act alleged was not against the will of the complaining witness.

History.

1981, c. 397.

Law Review.

For article discussing the legislative history of sexual assault law reform in Virginia, see 68 Va. L. Rev. 459 (1982).

CASE NOTES

Reasonable resistance no longer required. — The enactment of this section in 1981 eliminated the reasonable resistance requirement that previously existed under Virginia law. Farish v. Commonwealth, 2 Va. App. 627, 346 S.E.2d 736 (1986).

Victim need not believe resistance would be useless. — Under this section, the victim is not required to cry out or physically resist. The victim also does not have to reasonably believe resistance would be useless. Farish v. Commonwealth, 2 Va. App. 627, 346 S.E.2d 736 (1986).

Burden of proof not shifted to defendant. — This section does not shift the burden of proof to the defendant, but merely eliminates the requirement that the Commonwealth must prove that the victim actually resisted the attack. Farish v. Commonwealth, 2 Va. App. 627, 346 S.E.2d 736 (1986).

Assault must be shown to be against victim's will. — Under this section, the Commonwealth still must prove that the assault was against the victim's will. This section merely allows the defendant to use lack of resistance to buttress his consent defense. Farish v. Commonwealth, 2 Va. App. 627, 346 S.E.2d 736 (1986).

Instruction as to force, threat, or intimidation not required. — Since, under this section, no physical resistance is required by law, the court in a prosecution for rape was not required to instruct the jury that "there must be a show of force, threat or intimidation sufficient to overcome resistance." Farish v. Commonwealth, 2 Va. App. 627, 346 S.E.2d 736 (1986).

§ 18.2-67.7. Admission of evidence (Supreme Court Rule 2:412 derived from this section).

A. In prosecutions under this article, or under clause (iii) or (iv) of § 18.2-48, 18.2-370, 18.2-370.01, or 18.2-370.1, general reputation or opinion evidence of the complaining witness's unchaste character or prior sexual conduct shall not be admitted. Unless the complaining witness voluntarily agrees otherwise, evidence of specific instances of his or her prior sexual conduct shall be admitted only if it is relevant and is:

1. Evidence offered to provide an alternative explanation for physical evidence of the offense charged which is introduced by the prosecution, limited to evidence designed to explain the presence of semen, pregnancy, disease, or physical injury to the complaining witness's intimate parts; or

2. Evidence of sexual conduct between the complaining witness and the accused offered to support a contention that the alleged offense was not accomplished by force, threat or intimidation or through the use of the complaining witness's mental incapacity or physical helplessness, provided that the sexual conduct occurred within a period of time reasonably proximate to the offense charged under the circumstances of this case; or

3. Evidence offered to rebut evidence of the complaining witness's prior sexual conduct introduced by the prosecution.

B. Nothing contained in this section shall prohibit the accused from presenting evidence relevant to show that the complaining witness had a motive to fabricate the charge against the accused. If such evidence relates to the past sexual conduct of the complaining witness with a person other than the accused, it shall not be admitted and may not be referred to at any preliminary hearing or trial unless the party offering same files a written notice generally describing the evidence prior to the introduction of any evidence, or the opening statement of either counsel, whichever first occurs, at the preliminary hearing or trial at which the admission of the evidence may be sought.

C. Evidence described in subsections A and B of this section shall not be admitted and may not be referred to at any preliminary hearing or trial until the court first determines the admissibility of that evidence at an evidentiary hearing to be held before the evidence is introduced at such preliminary hearing or trial. The court shall exclude from the evidentiary hearing all persons except the accused, the complaining witness, other necessary witnesses, and required court personnel. If the court determines that the evidence meets the requirements of subsections A and B of this section, it shall be admissible before the judge or jury trying the case in the ordinary course of the preliminary hearing or trial. If the court initially determines that the evidence is inadmissible, but new information is discovered during the course of the preliminary hearing or trial which may make such evidence admissible, the court shall determine in an evidentiary hearing whether such evidence is admissible.

History.
1981, c. 397; 2007, c. 890; 2011, c. 785.

Editor's note.
Acts 2011, c. 785, cl. 2, provides: "That the provisions of this act may result in a net increase in periods of imprisonment or commitment. Pursuant to § 30-19.1:4, the estimated amount of the necessary appropriation cannot be determined for periods of imprisonment in state adult correctional facilities; therefore, Chapter 874 of the Acts of Assembly of 2010 requires the Virginia Criminal Sentencing Commission to assign a minimum fiscal impact of $50,000. Pursuant to § 30-19.1:4, the estimated amount of the necessary appropriation cannot be determined for periods of commitment to the custody of the Department of Juvenile Justice."

At the direction of the Virginia Code Commission, the notation to the Virginia Rules of Evidence was added to the catchline of this section. Acts 2012, cc. 688 and 708, cl. 6 provides: "That pursuant to the authority set forth in §§ 30-146 and 30-147 of the Code of Virginia, the Virginia Code Commission shall direct any party with whom the Virginia Code Commission contracts to publish the Code of Virginia to include in the catchline of every section of the Code of Virginia from which any rule contained in the Rules of Evidence has been derived a notation specifying such rule."

The 2011 amendments.
The 2011 amendment by c. 785 substituted "clause (iii) or (iv) of § 18.2-48, 18.2-370" for "§ 18.2-370" in the first sentence of subsection A.

Law Review.
For article discussing the legislative history of sexual assault law reform in Virginia, see 68 Va. L. Rev. 459 (1982). For comment on the rape shield statute in light of Winfield v. Commonwealth, 225 Va. 211, 301 S.E.2d 15 (1983), see 18 U. Rich. L. Rev. 433 (1984). For survey on evidence in Virginia for 1989, see 23 U. Rich. L. Rev. 647 (1989). For 2007 annual survey article, "Criminal Law and Procedure," see 42 U. Rich. L. Rev. 311 (2007).

CASE NOTES

Legislative intent. — The General Assembly intended to preclude evidence of general reputation or opinion of the unchaste character of the complaining witness in all circumstances. This view arises not only from the criticisms of this kind of evidence which underlay the legislative reforms of 1981, but also from the fact that the new law gives a defendant access for the first time to evidence relating to specific prior sexual conduct with third persons, if it is relevant for the purposes set forth in this section. Winfield v. Commonwealth, 225 Va. 211, 301 S.E.2d 15 (1983).

Trial court to conduct constitutional analysis of relevant evidence. — Rape shield law serves as a predicate to the constitutional analysis for the admission of evidence of a victim's prior sexual conduct in a sexual assault case; this section first directs a trial judge to make a determination of relevance, and after discarding evidence of prior sexual conduct proffered by the defendant to impugn the character of the victim or for some similarly impermissible purpose, the trial judge must then determine whether the evidence falls within one of the enumerated exceptions in the statute, which by implication is a test of materiality, or is otherwise material to an issue of the case. Finally, the trial judge must admit other relevant, material evidence, not within the enumerated exceptions, when the exclusion of such evidence would deny the defendant the constitutional right to a fair opportunity to present evidence probative of his defense of the charges against him. Neeley v. Commonwealth, 17 Va. App. 349, 437 S.E.2d 721 (1993).

This section is procedural in nature and the trial court did not violate defendant's rights under U.S. Const., Art. 1, § 10, or Va. Const., Art. 1, § 9, to be free from ex post facto laws by applying it during defendant's trial on charges that he violated former § 18.1-191 by committing fornication with his daughter in 1969 and 1970, even though § 18.2-67.7 was not enacted into law at the time

defendant committed the offenses. Pilcher v. Commonwealth, No. 2483-01-3, 2003 Va. App. LEXIS 402 (Ct. of Appeals July 15, 2003). See also, Pilcher v. Commonwealth, 41 Va. App. 158, 583 S.E.2d 70, 2003 Va. App. LEXIS 398 (2003).

Hearing must be held. — The applicability of the rape shield law and the necessity for a hearing to determine the admissibility of such evidence is not affected by the form of the inquiry. Even if the question is framed to address another's conduct, as in this case, "[d]id [the neighbor] ever touch you," the requirements of this section must be satisfied before such evidence is admissible; as no hearing was requested as required by subsection C of this section, the evidence was not admissible. McNeil v. Commonwealth, No. 1517-92-3 (Ct. of Appeals, May 17, 1994).

Court not required to conduct evidentiary hearing. — This section requires a defendant seeking to introduce evidence of a victim's prior sexual conduct to request an evidentiary hearing before such evidence can be elicited at trial, but a trial court is not required to grant a request for such a hearing; a trial court can make a threshold evaluation of a motion to hold a hearing to determine the admissibility of the evidence at issue based upon its relevance and probative value only after specific instances of sexual conduct occurring prior to the charged offense have been alleged and proffered and, where the defendant fails to proffer any specific sexual conduct occurring on any occasion prior to the offense, the defendant's request for an evidentiary hearing may be properly denied. Blackmon v. Commonwealth, 33 Va. App. 728, 536 S.E.2d 918, 2000 Va. App. LEXIS 733 (2000).

Constitutional rights of compulsory process, confrontation and due process gave defendant the right to present evidence favorable to his defense which included evidence of victim's prior sexual behavior to explain the presence of a hair fragment in her cervix, even though that evidence did not fall within the specific enumerated exception of the rape shield statute for this evidence explained the presence of the hair fragment and tended to rebut the Commonwealth's assertion that defendant was the source of it. Neeley v. Commonwealth, 17 Va. App. 349, 437 S.E.2d 721 (1993).

Relevant prior sexual conduct admissible unless barred by enumerated exceptions. — In a rape prosecution evidence of prior sexual conduct which tends to establish a matter in issue would be admissible, unless barred by the second of the three enumerated exceptions in the rape shield statute or by other evidentiary rules. League v. Commonwealth, 9 Va. App. 199, 385 S.E.2d 232 (1989).

Statute not ex post facto as applied. — Rape shield law, § 18.2-67.7, was not an ex post facto law as applied to defendant, convicted of rape of a female child under age 16 in violation of § 18.1-44 [now see § 18.2-61], and of placing his hand upon a sexual or genital part of a child under the age of 14 in violation of § 18.1-215 [now see § 18.2-370], as the law changed only procedures as to the admission of evidence; the evidence of the victim's sexual history was excluded due to defendant's failure to follow the statute's procedure by requesting a recess, as suggested by the trial court, to discuss the evidence defendant wished to admit and its relevancy. Pilcher v. Commonwealth, 41 Va. App. 158, 583 S.E.2d 70, 2003 Va. App. LEXIS 398 (2003).

Evidence of other sexual activity controlled by rape shield law. — Rape shield law, § 18.2-67.7, controls the introduction of any evidence that a victim had other sexual activity. Mott v. Commonwealth, No. 0058-03-3, 2003 Va. App. LEXIS 653 (Ct. of Appeals Dec. 16, 2003).

Evidence of prior testimony in unrelated rape prosecution, when offered to show its substantial similarity for the purpose of testing the credibility of the witness, does not fall within the scope of this section. Brown v. Commonwealth, 29 Va. App. 199, 510 S.E.2d 751 (1999).

The determination whether prior sexual conduct is reasonably proximate to the offense charged is a function not only of time, but also of the circumstances of the case, including the situation and factors surrounding the prior conduct, the relationship between the parties, and the circumstances of the alleged offense. League v. Commonwealth, 9 Va. App. 199, 385 S.E.2d 232 (1989).

Any evidence of prior sexual conduct must comply with the usual rules of evidence as well as the requirements of this section. Winfield v. Commonwealth, 225 Va. 211, 301 S.E.2d 15 (1983).

Evidence of past sexual conduct, to be admissible under the "motive to fabricate" provisions of subsection B of this section however, must show a pattern of behavior which directly relates to the conduct charged against the complaining witness in the case on trial. Winfield v. Commonwealth, 225 Va. 211, 301 S.E.2d 15 (1983).

Evidence tending to show that the complaining witness had a distinctive pattern of past sexual conduct, involving the extortion of money by threat after acts of prostitution is relevant, probative, and admissible in defense. Winfield v. Commonwealth, 225 Va. 211, 301 S.E.2d 15 (1983).

Notice insufficient. — Trial court did not err in denying defendant's motion to present evidence of a six-year-old victim's prior sexual conduct because there was no evidence that defendant gave the notice required by § 18.2-67.7, the rape shield statute, other than the prosecutor's statement that he had received a hand-written notice. Gleason v. Commonwealth, 2010 Va. App. LEXIS 256 (June 29, 2010).

The approach for determining admissibility of evidence of prior sexual conduct between a prosecutrix and defendant is two-fold; first, a trial court must determine whether it is relevant; the second prong requires the trial court to determine whether the prior sexual conduct occurred within a period of time reasonably proximate to the offense charged. League v. Commonwealth, 9 Va. App. 199, 385 S.E.2d 232 (1989).

Admissibility of prior sexual conduct must be decided on case-by-case basis. — The rape shield statute has rejected the common-law notion that once consensual sex has been shown in the past it always is relevant to prove that subsequent sexual intercourse was consensual; the rape shield statute requires the question of the admissibility of prior sexual conduct between a prosecutrix and defendant be decided on a case-by-case basis. League v. Commonwealth, 9 Va. App. 199, 385 S.E.2d 232 (1989).

Evidence of sexual contact with third party properly excluded. — The trial court properly refused to permit the introduction into evidence of a statement by the victim regarding sexual contact with someone other than the defendant where the defendant failed to proffer what the witness would have said and failed to demonstrate that the statement would have explained the medical finding that the victim had been sexually penetrated. Horsley v. Commonwealth, No. 2925-97-3 (Ct. of Appeals Dec. 22, 1998).

Prior false allegations of sexual assault, which consisted only of a denial by the prior accused of said allegations, was proper where such were uncertain, self-serving, and lacked a reasonable probability of falsity. Richardson v. Commonwealth, 42 Va. App. 236, 590 S.E.2d 618, 2004 Va. App. LEXIS 8 (2004).

Virginia's Rape Shield Statute precluded defendant from introducing evidence of the victim's alleged prior sexual conduct with a third person, wherein the victim accused the boyfriend of the victims' mother of inappropriate touching and then recanted; contrary to defendant's claim of fabrication, defendant failed to show that there was a reasonable probability that the child's allegations against the third person were false. Ortiz v. Commonwealth, 276 Va. 705, 667 S.E.2d 751, 2008 Va. LEXIS 122 (2008).

Evidence of complainant's contraction of gonorrhea admissible. — Trial court erred in applying this section to exclude evidence that complaining witness learned that she had contracted gonorrhea. Because such evidence did not directly or necessarily prove prior sexual conduct of the complaining witness within the meaning of this section, and because such evidence was otherwise relevant to show that the complaining witness may have had a motive to fabricate her allegations of rape, the evidence was admissible. Evans v. Commonwealth, 14 Va. App. 118, 415 S.E.2d 851 (1992).

Relevance of venereal disease contracted by accuser. — Regardless of whether the evidence implicates the accused as the person who purportedly transmitted the disease, evidence that a complaining witness contracted a venereal disease after the date of the alleged offense is relevant because it tends to prove that the infected person harbors bias or ill-will against a recent sexual partner. Evans v. Commonwealth, 14 Va. App. 118, 415 S.E.2d 851 (1992).

Evidence that complainant contracted venereal disease is more relevant when the victim delayed in reporting the incident of sexual assault. Evans v. Commonwealth, 14 Va. App. 118, 415 S.E.2d 851 (1992).

Evidence inadmissible to prove propensity or to impeach credibility. — Where the only purpose offered for introducing evidence of the victim's prior sexual conduct is to establish her propensity to engage in consensual sexual acts or to impeach her general credibility, such evidence is rendered inadmissible under the statute. Currie v. Commonwealth, 10 Va. App. 204, 391 S.E.2d 79 (1990).

The term "reasonably proximate" cannot be closely confined within any particular time frame. League v. Commonwealth, 9 Va. App. 199, 385 S.E.2d 232 (1989).

Whether prior sexual conduct is reasonably proximate to the offense charged must be decided based on the totality of the circumstances of each case; while the time which has elapsed between the two alleged sexual acts is an important factor to be considered, a court also must consider the nature of the prior relationship and sexual conduct, whether the relationship was a continuing one, and the circumstances surrounding the alleged offense; these factors, together with the time lapse between the alleged acts, govern whether the evidentiary value of the prior conduct is so remote that it cannot fairly be said to have probative value on the issue whether the prosecutrix consented to the sexual act with which the accused is charged. League v. Commonwealth, 9 Va. App. 199, 385 S.E.2d 232 (1989).

Remark about prior consensual intercourse justified mistrial. — Manifest necessity existed for declaring a mistrial, where defendant's counsel, ignorant of the Virginia Rape Shield Statute, in his opening statement related to the jury the alleged prior consensual sexual intercourse between defendant and the complaining witness. Graves v. Garraghty, 618 F. Supp. 1348 (E.D. Va. 1985).

Considering only lapse of time in ruling on prior sexual conduct was error. — Where the trial court refused to allow the defendant to testify about a prior act of consensual sexual intercourse between the prosecutrix and him, the trial court erred by considering only the lapse of time in ruling that the prior sexual conduct was too remote to be admissible, and by failing to consider other circumstances of the relationship; based on defendant's account of what transpired, since the alleged rape was so intertwined with the prior consensual sexual intercourse and the alleged discussion about future sex for money that to exclude that evidence deprived defendant of a meaningful opportunity to present his defense. League v. Commonwealth, 9 Va. App. 199, 385 S.E.2d 232 (1989).

Evidence of prior false accusation admissible. — In sex offense cases, however, the weight of authority recognizes more liberal rules concerning impeachment of complaining witnesses. Accordingly, a majority of jurisdictions that have considered the issue hold that evidence of prior false accusations is admissible to impeach the complaining witness' credibility or as substantive evidence tending to prove that the instant offense did not occur. Clinebell v. Commonwealth, 235 Va. 319, 368 S.E.2d 263 (1988).

Where defendant sought to prove for impeachment purposes that his daughter makes false statements concerning sexual behavior, such statements were not conduct within the meaning of this section, and, therefore, the section was inapplicable. Clinebell v. Commonwealth, 235 Va. 319, 368 S.E.2d 263 (1988).

False denial of prior intercourse not an "accusation." — While a special rule relating to impeachment in sexual assault cases has been recognized which permits evidence of prior false accusations to be admitted to impeach the alleged victim's credibility or as substantive evidence that the alleged offense did not occur, this rule does not permit introduction of a victim's false statement to the police that she had not previously engaged in intercourse; this statement could not be construed as part of a system of false accusations casting doubt on the victim's accusation against the defendant. Thompson v. Commonwealth, 28 Va. App. 543, 507 S.E.2d 110 (1998).

Exclusion of prior complaint proper. — Exclusion of evidence of the victim's prior complaint of sexual abuse against another man was proper, because the circumstances of the prior complaint were so different that the disputed evidence had no logical tendency to establish the prior incident as an alternate source of the child's sexual knowledge; the prior complaint was that when the victim was five years old, the victim's grandmother's boyfriend placed the victim's hand on the boyfriend's penis, over clothing, an incident that had no logical tendency to show the victim's prior knowledge of the physical appearance of a penis, or of the fellatio or object sexual penetration the victim described at trial. Polaski v. Commonwealth, 2009 Va. App. LEXIS 165 (Apr. 7, 2009).

Mixed question of fact and law. — Under this section the trial judge is called upon to apply a mixed question of fact and law. The trial judge must determine whether alleged sexual conduct "occurred within a period of time reasonably proximate to the offense charged under the circumstances of this case." Graves v. Garraghty, 618 F. Supp. 1348 (E.D. Va. 1985).

Exception for evidence offered to explain physical evidence. — In a prosecution for forcible anal sodomy, the exception which permits the introduction of evidence which is relevant and is offered to provide an alternative explanation for physical evidence of the offense did not permit cross-examination of a victim concerning a false statement she had made to the police denying that she had previously engaged in any kind of sexual intercourse where the physical evidence at issue was of a rectal scar and the victim's prior consensual vaginal intercourse would not have caused such a scar. Thompson v. Commonwealth, 28 Va. App. 543, 507 S.E.2d 110 (1998).

Court's ability to determine if evidence comes within section. — Only by hearing the witnesses, or by stipulation of the Commonwealth that witnesses would testify as indicated in the notice required by subsection B, could the court determine whether the proffered evidence came within this section. Johnson v. Commonwealth, 9 Va. App. 176, 385 S.E.2d 223 (1989).

Exclusion of properly excludable evidence on improper grounds. — Where the trial judge based his decision to exclude the evidence of prior sexual conduct on inappropriate grounds under Virginia law, but he unquestionably could have decided to exclude the evidence of prior sexual conduct between the complaining witness and defendant on the basis of the lack of "reasonable proximity" or upon a lack of materiality of the evidence, defendant failed to demonstrate the existence of circumstances impugning fundamental fairness or infringing specific constitutional protections. Absent such circumstances, the admissibility of the evidence at issue does not present a federal question, and, accordingly, his habeas claim that this section was unconstitutional if the trial judge's function thereunder was to admit or exclude evidence based on his credibility findings was dismissed as failing to present a federal question for consideration by the federal district court. Graves v. Garraghty, 618 F. Supp. 1348 (E.D. Va. 1985).

Victim's journal admissible for impeachment. — Exclusion of child sexual assault victim's journal, under Virginia's rape shield statute, § 18.2-67.7, was in error, as the purpose of the journals was to attack the victim's credibility, and the journals were proper impeachment; however, the error was harmless where the evidence of guilt was found to be overwhelming, and the trial court, in a bench trial, stated that the trial court had reviewed the journals, and had the journals been considered, the journals would not have changed the trial court's mind. Cairns v. Commonwealth, 40 Va. App. 271, 579 S.E.2d 340, 2003 Va. App. LEXIS 221 (2003).

Trial counsel did not err in failing to present testimony of victim's unchaste character. — Trial counsel for an inmate convicted of rape did not err in failing to present testimony regarding the victim's unchaste character because Virginia's Rape Shield statute specifically excluded such testimony. Esser v. Johnson, — F. Supp. 2d —, 2005 U.S. Dist. LEXIS 35830 (W.D. Va. July 19, 2005).

What evidence statute designed to exclude. — This statute was designed to prevent the introduction of evidence that would serve only to degrade the victim and that would be highly prejudicial; where the only purpose offered for introducing evidence of the victim's prior sexual conduct is to establish his or her propensity to engage in consensual sexual acts or to impeach his or her general credibility, such evidence is rendered inadmissible by the statute. Thompson v. Commonwealth, 28 Va. App. 543, 507 S.E.2d 110 (1998).

Trial court did not abuse its discretion. — Trial court, where defendant was accused of sodomy and incest towards his adopted teenage daughter, did not err in refusing to admit evidence concerning the daughter's prior reports of sexual abuse toward the boyfriend of her biological mother to the extent the evidence alleged that the child had sexual activity and only with respect to the sodomy charge. Via v. Commonwealth, 42 Va. App. 164, 590 S.E.2d 583, 2004 Va. App. LEXIS 14 (2004).

Evidence that a juvenile previously made reports of sexually stimulating behavior to gain attention to show that she and other complaining witnesses had a similar motive to fabricate the charges against defendant was properly excluded as: (1) the proffered evidence only showed that the juvenile had previously been exposed to sexual conduct, not that she made any false reports of sexual abuse or that she had any motive to make up the charges against defendant; (2) the evidence had no relevance to the allegations pertaining to the victim, for which defendant was convicted; and (3) the evidence involved conduct over two years prior to the issues at trial. Holcomb v. Commonwealth, 2006 Va. App. LEXIS 269 (June 20, 2006).

CIRCUIT COURT OPINIONS

Portions of videotape were admissible. — Portions of a videotape of sexual conduct between a victim and defendant was admissible as: (1) the victim and defendant were in a sexual relationship for a long period of time; (2) they engaged in what could be characterized as "rough sex"; (3) the videotape was made with the victim's consent; (4) the alleged offenses occurred approximately five weeks after the intimate relationship ended; (5) they lived in the same apartment after their intimate relationship ended; and (6) the prejudicial effect of the videotape did not outweigh its probative value. Commonwealth v. Goodwin, — Va. Cir. —, 2005 Va. Cir. LEXIS 310 (Alexandria June 15, 2005).

Evidence admissible for impeachment only. — In a rape case, evidence of two other assaults on the complaining witness allegedly occurring near the time of defendant's alleged assault on the complaining witness was admissible for impeachment purposes, but not to show that the complaining witness consented to sexual intercourse with defendant; evidence of sperm DNA from an unknown third person on the complaining witness's shirt, and evidence that the complaining witness was kissing a female friend on the night of the alleged rape was inadmissible. Commonwealth v. Sanchez-Garcia, — Va. Cir. —, 2004 Va. Cir. LEXIS 250 (Amherst County June 22, 2004).

Evidence of prior sexual conduct admissible. — Because only one to one and one-half months lapsed between the parties' prior sexual conduct and an alleged rape, because the conduct was alleged to have been consensual, and because the rape was allegedly the result of a fee dispute over the conduct, the alleged prior sexual conduct was admissible under subdivision A 2 of § 18.2-67.7. Commonwealth v. Quintanilla, 70 Va. Cir. 11, 2005 Va. Cir. LEXIS 298 (Greensville County 2005).

Evidence not admissible. — Defendant's motion to admit evidence of the prior sexual conduct of the complainant with another person was denied because the reason proffered for admission of that evidence was not enumerated in § 18.2-67.7, the Rape Shield statute, and the evidence was neither material nor probative of whether the complaining witness had sexual intercourse with defendant. Commonwealth v. Beckford, — Va. Cir. —, 2005 Va. Cir. LEXIS 312 (Alexandria Nov. 22, 2005).

§ 18.2-67.8. Closed preliminary hearings.

In preliminary hearings for offenses charged under this article or under §§ 18.2-361, 18.2-366, 18.2-370 or § 18.2-370.1, the court may, on its own motion or at the request of the Commonwealth, the complaining witness, the accused, or their counsel, exclude from the courtroom all persons except officers of the court and persons whose presence, in the judgment of the court, would be supportive of the complaining witness or the accused and would not impair the conduct of a fair hearing.

History.
1981, c. 397; 1993, c. 440.

Michie's Jurisprudence.
For related discussion, see 5B M.J. Criminal Procedure, § 20.

CASE NOTES

Mandamus not available to challenge closure order. — A writ of mandamus was improperly issued to a reporter and newspaper granting them access to records of certain preliminary proceedings; the proper procedure would have been for the petitioners to have filed motions to intervene and objections to the courts' closure orders and, if such had been rejected, to appeal those orders. Hertz v. Times-World Corp., 259 Va. 599, 528 S.E.2d 458, 2000 Va. LEXIS 81 (2000).

§ 18.2-67.9. Testimony by child victims and witnesses using two-way closed-circuit television.

A. The provisions of this section shall apply to an alleged victim who was fourteen years of age or under at the time of the alleged offense and is sixteen or under at the time of the trial and to a witness who is fourteen years of age or under at the time of the trial.

In any criminal proceeding, including preliminary hearings, involving an alleged offense against a child, relating to a violation of the laws pertaining to kidnapping (§ 18.2-47 et seq.), criminal sexual assault (§ 18.2-61 et seq.) or family offenses pursuant to Article 4 (§ 18.2-362 et seq.) of Chapter 8 of Title 18.2, or involving an alleged murder of a person of any age, the attorney for the Commonwealth or the defendant may apply for an order from the court that the testimony of the alleged victim or a child witness be taken in a room outside the courtroom and be televised by two-way closed-circuit television. The party seeking such order shall apply for the order at least seven days before the trial date or at least seven days before such other preliminary proceeding to which the order is to apply.

B. The court may order that the testimony of the child be taken by closed-circuit television as provided in subsection A if it finds that the child is unavailable to testify in open court in the presence of the defendant, the jury, the judge, and the public, for any of the following reasons:

1. The child's persistent refusal to testify despite judicial requests to do so;

2. The child's substantial inability to communicate about the offense; or

3. The substantial likelihood, based upon expert opinion testimony, that the child will suffer severe emotional trauma from so testifying.

Any ruling on the child's unavailability under this subsection shall be supported by the court with findings on the record or with written findings in a court not of record.

C. In any proceeding in which closed-circuit television is used to receive testimony, the attorney for the Commonwealth and the defendant's attorney shall be present in the room with the child, and the child shall be subject to direct and cross-examination. The only other persons allowed to be present in the room with the child during his testimony shall be those persons necessary to operate the closed-circuit equipment, and any other person whose presence is determined by the court to be necessary to the welfare and well-being of the child.

D. The child's testimony shall be transmitted by closed-circuit television into the courtroom for the defendant, jury, judge and public to view. The defendant shall be provided with a means of private, contemporaneous communication with his attorney during the testimony.

E. Notwithstanding any other provision of law, none of the cost of the two-way closed-circuit television shall be assessed against the defendant.

History.
1988, c. 846; 1999, c. 668; 2001, c. 410.

Editor's note.
Acts 2001, c. 410, cl. 2, provides: "That the provisions of this act shall not be construed so as to require the installation of permanent two-way closed-circuit television equipment in any courtroom in the Commonwealth."

Law Review.
For comment on testimony by child victims using two-way closed-circuit television, see 22 U. Rich. L. Rev. 691 (1988). For article, "Legal Issues Involving Children," see 35 U. Rich. L. Rev. 741 (2001). For annual survey article on legal issues involving children, see 38 U. Rich. L. Rev. 161 (2003).

Michie's Jurisprudence.
For related discussion, see 20 M.J. Witnesses, §§ 9, 31.

CASE NOTES

Constitutionality of the statute. — Section 18.2-67.9 comports with the requirements of the Sixth Amendment's Confrontation Clause because the use of a two-way closed-circuit television provides greater protections for a criminal defendant and more closely mirrors a courtroom environment, and the elements of effective confrontation not only permit a defendant to confound and undo the false accuser, or reveal the child coached by a malevolent adult, but may well aid a defendant in eliciting favorable testimony from the child witness. Johnson v. Commonwealth, 40 Va. App. 605, 580 S.E.2d 486, 2003 Va. App. LEXIS 303 (2003).

Substantial inability to communicate about the offense. — Testimony and demeanor of two child witnesses at the hearing on the Commonwealth's motion to allow the witnesses to testify at defendant's trial by closed-circuit television supported the trial court's finding that the witnesses had a substantial inability to communicate about the sex offenses at issue in open court in defendant's presence, and justified the trial court's decision to allow their testimony by closed-circuit television pursuant to § 18.2-67.9 B 2. Civitello v. Commonwealth, No. 1963-01-2, 2003 Va. App. LEXIS 2 (Ct. of Appeals Jan. 7, 2003).

Defendant's constitutional protections not violated. — Section 18.2-67.9, which allowed the victim to testify via a two-way closed circuit television, did not violate defendant's constitutional protections because the trial court followed the statutory requirements and applied them correctly; the statute was valid as applied to defendant as there was a finding of "necessity," which was supported by the evidence, as the trial court found that the victim was unable to testify in open court in the presence of defendant, the jury, the judge and the public, the finding was based on expert testimony that there was a substantial likelihood that the child would suffer severe emotional trauma from testifying, the trial court took the additional step of requiring the Commonwealth to have the victim undergo an independent psychological examination prior to making a decision on the necessity of using closed-circuit television at trial, and the record also proved that the "other elements" of defendant's confrontations rights were met. Johnson v. Commonwealth, 40 Va. App. 605, 580 S.E.2d 486, 2003 Va. App. LEXIS 303 (2003).

Illustrative case. — In a case in which defendant was alleged to have sexually abused his six year old daughter, the trial court did not err in finding a substantial likelihood that, based upon expert opinion testimony, the child would suffer severe emotional trauma if forced to testify in open court, and to allow her under § 18.2-67.9 B 3 to testify by closed-circuit television; because the child would suffer "severe emotional trauma" if forced to testify in open court, she was "unavailable." Parrish v. Commonwealth, 38 Va. App. 607, 567 S.E.2d 576, 2002 Va. App. LEXIS 487 (2002).

Failure to raise issue at trial barred consideration on appeal. — Appellate court did not consider defendant's argument that two-way closed-circuit testimony of the victim and her brother violated § 18.2-67.9 where defendant conceded that he had not made the statutory argument at trial. Roadcap v. Commonwealth, 50 Va. App. 732, 653 S.E.2d 620, 2007 Va. App. LEXIS 445 (2007).

§ 18.2-67.10. General definitions.

As used in this article:

1. *"Complaining witness"* means the person alleged to have been subjected to rape, forcible sodomy, inanimate or animate object sexual penetration, marital sexual assault, aggravated sexual battery, or sexual battery.

2. *"Intimate parts"* means the genitalia, anus, groin, breast, or buttocks of any person.

3. *"Mental incapacity"* means that condition of the complaining witness existing at the time of an offense under this article which prevents the complaining witness from understanding the nature or consequences of the sexual act involved in such offense and about which the accused knew or should have known.

4. *"Physical helplessness"* means unconsciousness or any other condition existing at the time of an offense under this article which otherwise rendered the complaining witness physically unable to communicate an unwillingness to act and about which the accused knew or should have known.

5. The complaining witness's *"prior sexual conduct"* means any sexual conduct on the part of the complaining witness which took place before the conclusion of the trial, excluding the conduct involved in the offense alleged under this article.

6. *"Sexual abuse"* means an act committed with the intent to sexually molest, arouse, or gratify any person, where:

a. The accused intentionally touches the complaining witness's intimate parts or material directly covering such intimate parts;

b. The accused forces the complaining witness to touch the accused's, the witness's own, or another person's intimate parts or material directly covering such intimate parts;

c. If the complaining witness is under the age of 13, the accused causes or assists the complaining witness to touch the accused's, the witness's own, or another person's intimate parts or material directly covering such intimate parts; or

d. The accused forces another person to touch the complaining witness's intimate parts or material directly covering such intimate parts.

History.
1981, c. 397; 1987, c. 277; 1993, c. 549; 1994, c. 568; 2004, c. 741.

Cross references.
As to Sex Offenders and Crimes Against Minors Registry, see § 9.1-900 et seq.

Law Review.
For 2003/2004 survey of family and juvenile law, see 39 U. Rich. L. Rev. 241 (2004). For 2007 annual survey article, "Criminal Law and Procedure," see 42 U. Rich. L. Rev. 311 (2007). For survey of Virginia law on criminal law and procedure for the year 2007-2008, see 43 U. Rich. L. Rev. 149 (2008). For article, "Construction Law," see 45 U. Rich. L. Rev. 227 (2010). For annual survey article, "Criminal Law and Procedure," see 46 U. Rich. L. Rev. 59 (2011).

CASE NOTES

Factor that elevates criminal act to felony is age of victim. — The use of identical language in these statutes defining sexual battery and aggravated sexual battery with reference to force, threat or intimidation makes it clear that the legislature did not intend for these factors to be the distinction between the two statutes. Rather, the factors that elevate the criminal act from the misdemeanor to the felony are the specific age of the victim, serious bodily or mental injury, or the use or threat of use of a dangerous weapon. Johnson v. Commonwealth, 5 Va. App. 529, 365 S.E.2d 237 (1988).

Statute did not require force against eight-year-old victim. — Sections 18.2-67.10 and 18.2-67.3 were harmonious, neither negated the other, and both retained a substantive meaning consistent with established caselaw; there was no requirement to show force to prove charges under § 18.2-67.3 where the victim was eight years old. Martin v. Commonwealth, — Va. App. —, — S.E.2d —, 2005 Va. App. LEXIS 337 (Sept. 6, 2005), aff'd, — Va. —, 630 S.E.2d 291 (2006).

"Force" as used in § 18.2-67.10 included actual and constructive force, and constructive force included engaging in proscribed conduct with a victim who was under age of consent; the victim's age of eight years served as proof of both the force requirement and the age requirement, which was neither improper nor incongruous in defendant's prosecution for aggravated sexual battery. Martin v. Commonwealth, 272 Va. 31, 630 S.E.2d 291, 2006 Va. LEXIS 64 (2006).

Statute did not require force against mentally incapacitated adult. — Sufficient evidence supported a conviction for aggravated sexual battery, in violation of § 18.2-67.3, although there was no evidence of actual force, because constructive force existed where the victim was mentally incapacitated under subdivision 3 of § 18.2-67.10 and was incapable of legally consenting to the sexual touching. Section 18.2-67.3 did not require the use of actual force to establish sexual abuse when the complaining witness was mentally incapacitated. Consent without understanding was no consent at all. Nicholson v. Commonwealth, 56 Va. App. 491, 694 S.E.2d 788, 2010 Va. App. LEXIS 276 (2010).

Burden of proving mental incapacity. — A person may passively or suggestively take advantage of a mentally retarded or incapacitated individual; however, the fact that a victim may have diminished mental capacity does not relieve the Commonwealth of its burden of proving that the "mental incapacity" is that defined by subdivision 3 of this section. Adkins v. Commonwealth, 20 Va. App. 332, 457 S.E.2d 382 (1995).

Common-law battery compared with sexual battery. — The legislature imposed a greater burden on the Commonwealth to prove sexual battery than to prove common-law battery, the latter requiring only a showing of nonconsensual touching. To prove the crime of sexual battery, the Commonwealth has to establish beyond a reasonable doubt that the accused touched the intimate parts of the complaining witness, or that the complaining witness was forced to touch the intimate parts of the accused, with the intent to sexually molest, arouse or gratify any person. The acts must have been against the will of the complaining witness. Doss v. Commonwealth, No. 0019-85 (Ct. of Appeals July 30, 1986).

Previous false statements concerning sexual behavior not conduct. — Where defendant sought to prove for impeachment purposes that his daughter makes false statements concerning sexual behavior, such statements were not conduct within the meaning of § 18.2-67.7, and, therefore, that section was inapplicable. Clinebell v. Commonwealth, 235 Va. 319, 368 S.E.2d 263 (1988).

No requirement for corroboration for aggravated sexual battery. — The reasons that support the rule that a conviction for attempted rape may be supported solely upon the testimony of the victim without further corroboration are equally applicable to prosecutions for aggravated sexual battery, and there is no requirement for corroboration under § 18.2-67.3. Garland v. Commonwealth, 8 Va. App. 189, 379 S.E.2d 146 (1989).

Aggravated sexual battery is different from attempted rape in that an intent to have sexual intercourse is not required; aggravated sexual battery is markedly similar to attempted rape where the victim is female and her genitalia is touched by the perpetrator's penis. Garland v. Commonwealth, 8 Va. App. 189, 379 S.E.2d 146 (1989).

Intent to gain sexual gratification not shown. — Disposition of founded, level-one sexual abuse was erroneous because there was no evidence that the father had an intent to sexually molest, arouse, or gratify; the father's testimony describing the occasions where he medically examined the child or administered suppositories rebutted an inference that the father intended to gain sexual gratification by touching the child on those occasions. Rice v. Va. Dep't of Soc. Servs., — Va. App. —, — S.E.2d —, 2007 Va. App. LEXIS 123 (Mar. 27, 2007).

Evidence held irrelevant to issue of intent. — Testimony of detective that videotapes seized from defendant's home during search were pornographic was irrelevant to show that defendant had criminal intent to sexually molest, arouse, or gratify himself under subdivision 6 of this section, where he was charged with the aggravated sexual battery of a seven-year old girl, as no causal relationship or logical connection existed between that characterization and the current charge; thus, such testimony should not have been admitted, was more prejudicial than probative, and was immaterial to issue of criminal intent. Quinones v. Commonwealth, 35 Va. App. 634, 547 S.E.2d 524, 2001 Va. App. LEXIS 337 (2001).

Testimony of daughter that defendant allegedly forced her to perform a sex act on him 20 years earlier was irrelevant to show that defendant had criminal intent to sexually molest, arouse, or gratify himself under subdivision 6 of this section, where he was charged with the aggravated sexual battery of a seven-year-old girl, as no causal relationship or logical connection existed between the earlier incident and the current charge; thus, such testimony should not have been admitted, was more prejudicial than probative, and was impermissible prior bad act evidence. Quinones v. Commonwealth, 35 Va. App. 634, 547 S.E.2d 524, 2001 Va. App. LEXIS 337 (2001).

Mental incapacity need not be permanent condition. — Term "mental incapacity" as used in subdivision 3 of § 18.2-67.10 may extend to a transitory circumstance such as intoxication if the nature and degree of the intoxication has gone beyond the stage of merely reduced inhibition and has reached a point where the victim does not understand "the nature or consequences of the sexual act." Molina v. Commonwealth, 272 Va. 666, 636 S.E.2d 470, 2006 Va. LEXIS 106 (2006).

Sufficient evidence of mental incapacity. — In a prosecution for rape, the evidence was clearly sufficient to support an instruction on mental incapacity at the time of the alleged rape based on the victim's intoxication. Molina v. Commonwealth, 47 Va. App. 338, 624 S.E.2d 83, 2006 Va. App. LEXIS 6 (2006).

Jury was properly instructed that defendant could be found guilty of rape in violation of subsection A of § 18.2-61 if it found he had intercourse with the victim by using her mental incapacity. The evidence showed the victim had lost consciousness after a blow to the head, and blacked-out due to aggravation of her bipolar condition by alcohol and drug abuse; as used in § 18.2-67.10, the term "mental incapacity" could extend to a transitory circumstance such as voluntary intoxication. Molina v. Commonwealth, 272 Va. 666, 636 S.E.2d 470, 2006 Va. LEXIS 106 (2006).

Evidence clearly showed the 28-year-old victim, who had a performance IQ of 57, and was not able to live outside her family home, was not capable of giving consent to defendant, who offered to take her to work, but instead drove her to his home and had sex with her. Sene v. Commonwealth, 2009 Va. App. LEXIS 333 (July 28, 2009).

There was sufficient evidence to convict appellant of rape where: (1) the victim testified that she woke up with sharp pains between her legs; (2) the sexual assault nurse examiner observed small hemorrhagic spots, abrasions, and skin breaking on the victim's genitalia, which she testified was consistent with trauma; (3) a rational trier of fact could find beyond a reasonable doubt that the degree of the victim's intoxication reached a point where she did not understand the nature or consequences of the sexual act; and (4) appellant knew of the victim's condition because he was at the party, and he was one of the people who walked her home from the party. Roberts v. Commonwealth, 2010 Va. App. LEXIS 13 (Jan. 12, 2010).

Insufficient evidence of mental incapacity. — Where complainant had advanced with her peers from middle school to high school during the period following the alleged rape, and a peer-comparison placed her only "slightly below average," the record failed to show beyond a reasonable doubt that at the time of the alleged crime that complainant suffered from a mental incapacity that prevented her from understanding the nature and consequences of the sexual act involved in such offense and about which the defendant knew or should have known. White v. Commonwealth, 23 Va. App. 593, 478 S.E.2d 713 (1996).

Proof of physical helplessness. — Evidence was sufficient to establish that defendant used his position of trust and the victim's vulnerable condition to commit forcible sodomy in violation of § 18.2-67.1 where: (1) although the victim was able to communicate and a conviction could not be based on physical helplessness, his Parkinson's disease severely limited his abilities; (2) defendant, while bathing the victim, took the victim's penis in his hand and washed him up and down, which made the victim uncomfortable; (3) defendant put the victim's penis in defendant's mouth for 15-20 seconds before the victim was able to move away from defendant; (4) defendant's claim that the victim's "body language" led him to believe the victim desired the contact was rejected as it was not unusual for a male patient to become sexually aroused while being bathed; and (5) the following day, the victim reported the incident, and as the victim made the report, he was "physically shaking," and "tears were coming down his eyes." Emerick v. Commonwealth, No. 3042-02-3, 2004 Va. App. LEXIS 152 (Ct. of Appeals Apr. 6, 2004).

Membership in association. — Defendant's membership in the North American Man-Boy Love Association and pornographic materials in his possession at the time of his arrest were admissible in order to prove that the defendant engaged in acts with the intent to sexually molest, arouse, or gratify any person when he massaged the victim's buttocks. Smith v. Commonwealth, No. 1546-97-4 (Ct. of Appeals Dec. 1, 1998).

Prior sexual conduct. — Exclusion of child sexual assault victim's journal, under Virginia's rape shield statute, § 18.2-67.7, was in error, although harmless, as the purpose of the journals was to attack the victim's credibility, and the journals were proper impeachment; prior similar testimony was not considered prior sexual conduct, under subdivision 5 of § 18.2-67.10, when offered to impeach the complaining witness by suggesting fabrication. Cairns v. Commonwealth, 40 Va. App. 271, 579 S.E.2d 340, 2003 Va. App. LEXIS 221 (2003).

"Intimate parts or material directly covering such intimate parts." — Defendant touched an "intimate part or material directly covering an intimate part" where record indicated that he placed his hand at a point where victim's shirt had breast pockets. Sanderson v. Commonwealth, No. 1555-98-1 (Ct. of Appeals Jan. 11, 2000).

Trial court properly held that the evidence, via the victim's testimony and demonstration as to how and where defendant touched him in the groin area, was sufficient as to the element of "intimate part." Hirst v. Commonwealth, — Va. App. —, — S.E.2d —, 2005 Va. App. LEXIS 175 (May 3, 2005).

Evidence sufficient to support conviction. — Sufficient evidence supported defendant's conviction for attempted aggravated sexual battery in violation of §§ 18.2-67.3, 18.2-67.5, and 18.2-67.10, because the trial court accepted the testimony of the child victim that defendant touched the clothing covering her breasts and private parts as she exited the school bus. In addition, the trial court viewed a video recording and found it disclosed that something happened on the bus. Gallier v. Commonwealth, 2012 Va. App. LEXIS 60 (Mar. 6, 2012).

Evidence was clearly sufficient to support appellant's conviction for aggravated sexual battery where victim testified that appellant removed her underpants and all of his own clothing, and she demonstrated with the anatomically correct dolls what transpired next, and after observing her demonstration, the prosecutor stated, "Let the record show that she's placing the hand of the doll on the private area, in the groin area, of the female doll," and furthermore, the fact that appellant removed all of his clothing before the touching took place and that the touching was of sufficient intensity and duration to hurt the prosecutrix and make her vagina including her lips and her behind red provides sufficient circumstantial evidence to support the conclusion that he acted with the requisite intent to molest or gratify either himself or the victim, or both. Hargrove v. Commonwealth, No. 2421-92-2 (Ct. of Appeals Mar. 29, 1994).

Applied in Walker v. Commonwealth, 12 Va. App. 438, 404 S.E.2d 394 (1991); Previtire v. Commonwealth, 16 Va. App. 869, 433 S.E.2d 515 (1993); Howard v. Commonwealth, 21 Va. App. 473, 465 S.E.2d 142 (1995); Carter v. Gordon, 28 Va. App. 133, 502 S.E.2d 697 (1998); Newton v. Commonwealth, No. 1586-99-1, 2000 Va. App. LEXIS 361 (Ct. of Appeals May 16, 2000); Wactor v. Commonwealth, 38 Va. App. 375, 564 S.E.2d 160, 2002 Va. App. LEXIS 326 (2002); M. G. v. Albemarle County Dep't of Soc. Servs., 41 Va. App. 170, 583 S.E.2d 761, 2003 Va. App. LEXIS 406 (2003); Jones v. West, 46 Va. App. 309, 616 S.E.2d 790, 2005 Va. App. LEXIS 307 (2005).

ARTICLE 8.

SEDUCTION.

§§ 18.2-68 through 18.2-70. Repealed by Acts 1994, c. 59.

ARTICLE 9.

ABORTION.

Michie's Jurisprudence.
For related discussion, see 1A M.J. Abortion, §§ 1, 2.

§ 18.2-71. Producing abortion or miscarriage, etc.; penalty.

Except as provided in other sections of this article, if any person administer to, or cause to be taken by a woman, any drug or other thing, or use means, with intent to destroy her unborn child, or to produce abortion or miscarriage, and thereby destroy such child, or produce such abortion or miscarriage, he shall be guilty of a Class 4 felony.

History.
Code 1950, § 18.1-62; 1960, c. 358; 1970, c. 508; 1975, cc. 14, 15.

Cross references.
As to limitation of prosecution, see § 19.2-8. As to prohibition against partial birth infanticide, and penalty therefor, see § 18.2-71.1.

Law Review.
For note on abortion, Medicaid and equal protection, see 62 Va. L. Rev. 788 (1976).

CASE NOTES

United States Supreme Court ruling regarding abortion. — A state criminal abortion statute that excepts from criminality only a life saving procedure on behalf of the mother without regard to pregnancy stage and without recognition of the other interests involved, is violative of the due process clause of the Fourteenth Amendment. (a) For the stage prior to approximately the end of the first trimester, the abortion decision and its effectuation must be left to the medical judgment of the pregnant woman's attending physician. (b) For the stage subsequent to approximately the end of the first trimester, the state, in promoting its interest in the health of the mother, may, if it chooses, regulate the abortion procedure in

ways that are reasonably related to maternal health. (c) For the stage subsequent to viability the state, in promoting its interest in the potentiality of human life, may, if it chooses, regulate, and even proscribe, abortion except where it is necessary, in appropriate medical judgment, for the preservation of the life or health of the mother. Roe v. Wade, 410 U.S. 113, 93 S. Ct. 705, 35 L. Ed. 2d 147 (1973). See also Webster v. Reproductive Health Servs., 492 U.S. 490, 109 S. Ct. 3040, 106 L. Ed. 2d 410 (1989) and Planned Parenthood v. Casey, 505 U.S. 833, 112 S. Ct. 2791, 120 L. Ed. 2d 674 (1992).

Constitutionality. — While it is true that a statute which imposes a duty upon a physician to take affirmative action to preserve a fetus, irrespective of the stage of pregnancy and the viability of the fetus, is constitutionally impermissible, after viability the sovereign has a compelling interest sufficient to justify regulation reasonably designed to preserve the life of the fetus. The proscription in this section against destruction of the fetus is not a command to preserve it; and, while subsection c of § 18.2-74 requires a physician to utilize fetal life support measures during the third trimester if there is any clearly visible evidence of viability, nothing in this article imposes such an affirmative duty during the pre-viable stages of pregnancy. Simopoulos v. Commonwealth, 221 Va. 1059, 277 S.E.2d 194 (1981), aff'd, 462 U.S. 506, 103 S. Ct. 2532, 76 L. Ed. 2d 755 (1983).

Section 54.1-2917 was clearly enacted in aid of and for the purpose of facilitating the standards established in the state abortion statute, § 18.2-71, et seq. Simopoulos v. Virginia State Bd. of Medicine, 644 F.2d 321 (4th Cir. 1981).

Abortion and miscarriage synonymous. — Abortion is defined as "the expulsion of the fetus at so early a period of uterogestation that it has not acquired the power of sustaining an independent life." Although there may be a technical distinction recognized in medicine between abortion and miscarriage, the words are usually synonymous in law. Coffman v. Commonwealth, 188 Va. 553, 50 S.E.2d 431 (1948); Anderson v. Commonwealth, 190 Va. 665, 58 S.E.2d 72 (1950).

Section was passed to protect child, and society. — This section was passed, not for the protection of the pregnant woman, but for the protection of the unborn child and through it society. Miller v. Bennett, 190 Va. 162, 56 S.E.2d 217 (1949).

The crime denounced is not limited to abortion in its narrow meaning of expulsion of the fetus, but includes, as it plainly declares, the use of any means with intent to destroy an unborn child, resulting in the destruction of such child. Coffman v. Commonwealth, 188 Va. 553, 50 S.E.2d 431 (1948); Simopoulos v. Commonwealth, 221 Va. 1059, 277 S.E.2d 194 (1981), aff'd, 462 U.S. 506, 103 S. Ct. 2532, 76 L. Ed. 2d 755 (1983).

The intent with which the means are used is the controlling factor. It seems clear from the language of this section that more than one intended consequence is included. If only the intent to cause an abortion, in the sense of expulsion of the fetus, and the causing of such abortion, were meant to be covered, the words "intent to destroy her unborn child," and "thereby destroy such child" would be useless. It is not to be presumed that those words were used for no purpose and mean nothing in the statute. Anderson v. Commonwealth, 190 Va. 665, 58 S.E.2d 72 (1950).

Fetus need not be living at time of act. — This section is in two parts. The first part deals with the destruction of an unborn child by administering to the woman any drug or other thing, or using any means with intent so to do. The second portion of the statute deals with performing these same acts with intent to produce and producing an abortion or miscarriage. Nowhere in the section is there any requirement that the fetus be living at the time of the act in order to constitute a violation, but under the first portion the life of the fetus at the time of the act is presupposed from the words "destroy her unborn child." Anderson v. Commonwealth, 190 Va. 665, 58 S.E.2d 72 (1950).

If the means used with the intent to destroy an unborn child result in the death of the mother and thereby the destruction of the child, the death of the mother is an agency set in motion by the means used to destroy the child. If the destruction of the child — the intended result — was accomplished by the means used, the perpetrator is guilty, under this section, of using means with intent to destroy the child, and thereby destroying the child, even though the death of the mother was not intended. Coffman v. Commonwealth, 188 Va. 553, 50 S.E.2d 431 (1948).

Medical necessity exception matter of defense. — Where defendant's indictment for violation of abortion statutes did not attempt to negate the exception of a medical necessity to treat the patient, the exception was a matter of defense for the defendant to assert and not for the indictment to deny since the exception was made in a substantive section subsequent to the enacting section of the abortion statutes. Simopoulos v. Commonwealth, 221 Va. 1059, 277 S.E.2d 194 (1981), aff'd, 462 U.S. 506, 103 S. Ct. 2532, 76 L. Ed. 2d 755 (1983).

Unnecessary to charge intent that fetus be expelled outside hospital. — Where defendant was convicted under an indictment charging that he employed procedures intended to initiate abortion during the second trimester of pregnancy and that he did so outside of a hospital licensed by the state, it was unnecessary to charge that he intended his patient to expel the fetus outside a hospital, since the proviso in § 18.2-73 applies to all procedures performed during the entire process, and since the definition of abortion is not limited to "expulsion of the fetus." Simopoulos v. Commonwealth, 221 Va. 1059, 277 S.E.2d 194 (1981), aff'd, 462 U.S. 506, 103 S. Ct. 2532, 76 L. Ed. 2d 755 (1983).

Option with respect to allegation of causation. — The Commonwealth had the option of alleging and proving that a saline injection administered by the defendant caused either the death of the fetus or the expulsion of the fetus in a prosecution for violation of the abortion statutes, since the crime is not limited to a narrow meaning of expulsion of the fetus. Simopoulos v. Commonwealth, 221 Va. 1059, 277 S.E.2d 194 (1981), aff'd, 462 U.S. 506, 103 S. Ct. 2532, 76 L. Ed. 2d 755 (1983).

Sufficiency of evidence to prove causation. — Absent evidence of any other causative factor, evidence that the defendant acknowledged administering a saline solution with intent to terminate pregnancy and that he realized that the procedure would destroy the fetus, testimony by the patient that the defendant told her the fetus was destroyed, and testimony by the medical examiner that the fetus was born dead, was sufficient to show that the saline solution destroyed the fetus. Simopoulos v. Commonwealth, 221 Va. 1059, 277 S.E.2d 194 (1981), aff'd, 462 U.S. 506, 103 S. Ct. 2532, 76 L. Ed. 2d 755 (1983).

Declaratory or injunctive relief against section. — Where plaintiff was convicted under this section, his attempt to secure either declaratory or injunctive relief against this section was foreclosed by the United States Supreme Court's decision in Roe v. Wade, 410 U.S. 113, 93 S. Ct. 705, 35 L. Ed. 2d 147 (1973); Simopoulos v. Virginia State Bd. of Medicine, 644 F.2d 321 (4th Cir. 1981).

Unprofessional conduct. — Order of the Virginia Board of Medicine suspending a physician's license for unprofessional conduct was supported by evidence that the physician initiated an abortion without performing a sonogram to determine the gestational age of the fetus because the physician's failure to correctly estimate the age of the fetus caused the physician to perform a criminal abortion, under § 18.2-71, as the fetus's age was such that the procedure had to be performed in a hospital, under § 18.2-73. Abofreka v. Va. Bd. of Med., — Va. App. —, — S.E.2d —, 2007 Va. App. LEXIS 304 (Aug. 14, 2007).

Applied in Richmond Medical Ctr. for Women v. Gilmore, 144 F.3d 326 (4th Cir. 1998); Richmond Medical Ctr. for Women v. Gilmore, 11 F. Supp. 2d 795 (E.D. Va. 1998).

§ 18.2-71.1. Partial birth infanticide; penalty.

A. Any person who knowingly performs partial birth infanticide and thereby kills a human infant is guilty of a Class 4 felony.

B. For the purposes of this section, *"partial birth infanticide"* means any deliberate act that (i) is intended to kill a human infant who has been born alive, but who has not been completely extracted or expelled from its mother, and that (ii) does kill such infant, regardless of whether death occurs before or after extraction or expulsion from its mother has been completed.

The term "partial birth infanticide" shall not under any circumstances be construed to include any of the following procedures: (i) the suction curettage abortion procedure, (ii) the suction aspiration abortion procedure, (iii) the dilation and evacuation abortion procedure involving dismemberment of the fetus prior to removal from the body of the mother, or (iv) completing delivery of a living human infant and severing the umbilical cord of any infant who has been completely delivered.

C. For the purposes of this section, *"human infant who has been born alive"* means a product of human conception that has been completely or substantially expelled or extracted from its mother, regardless of the duration of pregnancy, which after such expulsion or extraction breathes or shows any other evidence of life such as beating of the heart, pulsation of the umbilical cord, or definite movement of voluntary muscles, whether or not the umbilical cord has been cut or the placenta is attached.

D. For purposes of this section, *"substantially expelled or extracted from its mother"* means, in the case of a headfirst presentation, the infant's entire head is outside the body of the mother, or, in the case of breech presentation, any part of the infant's trunk past the navel is outside the body of the mother.

E. This section shall not prohibit the use by a physician of any procedure that, in reasonable medical judgment, is necessary to prevent the death of the mother, so long as the physician takes every medically reasonable step, consistent with such procedure, to preserve the life and health of the infant. A procedure shall not be deemed necessary to prevent the death of the mother if completing the delivery of the living infant would prevent the death of the mother.

F. The mother may not be prosecuted for any criminal offense based on the performance of any act or procedure by a physician in violation of this section.

History.

2003, cc. 961, 963.

Law Review.

For 2006 survey article, "Health Care Law," see 41 U. Rich. L. Rev. 179 (2006).

CASE NOTES

I. Decisions Under Current Law.
II. Decisions Under Prior Law.

I. DECISIONS UNDER CURRENT LAW.

Constitutionality. — Insofar as plaintiffs purported to mount an as-applied challenge to Virginia's Partial Birth Infanticide Act, the court concluded that they had not presented sufficiently concrete circumstances in which the as-applied challenge could be resolved, but recognized that the Act was open to a proper as-applied challenge in a discrete case. Richmond Med. Ctr. for Women v. Herring, 570 F.3d 165, 2009 U.S. App. LEXIS 13593 (4th Cir. 2009).

Virginia's Partial Birth Infanticide Act provides sufficient clarity as to what conduct is prohibited to enable a doctor of reasonable intelligence to avoid criminal liability under it, and therefore the Virginia Act is constitutional. Richmond Med. Ctr. for Women v. Herring, 570 F.3d 165, 2009 U.S. App. LEXIS 13593 (4th Cir. 2009).

Plaintiffs' facial challenge to Virginia's Partial Birth Infanticide Act failed, as there was little or no evidence in the record suggesting the inevitability of the "accidental" intact dilation and evacuation abortion that would have violated the Virginia Act, and to the extent that such a circumstance might have arisen in a rare case, the doctor had adequate alternatives so as to preclude a finding on a facial challenge that the statute was unconstitutional in "a large fraction" of the cases in which it was relevant (when the fetus appeared at the cervix head first and passed the anatomical landmarks, there was never a need to perform an overt act to kill it, as it could simply be removed from the woman intact, and in the rare event that the fetus appeared at the cervix in breech position and its skull became lodged in the cervix, the woman's life was in danger, and the doctor could take any step within reasonable medical judgment that was necessary to prevent the mother's death). Richmond Med. Ctr. for Women v. Herring, 570 F.3d 165, 2009 U.S. App. LEXIS 13593 (4th Cir. 2009).

Standard dilation and evacuations. — Provisions for a safe harbor and affirmative defenses, as well as the requirement of "an overt act," ensured that Virginia's Partial Birth Infanticide Act would not create a barrier or have a chilling effect on a woman's right to have a standard dilation and evacuation or her physician's ability to undertake the procedure without fear of criminal liability. Richmond Med. Ctr. for Women v. Herring, 570 F.3d 165, 2009 U.S. App. LEXIS 13593 (4th Cir. 2009).

Exclusion of evidence. — Even if the district court abused its discretion in excluding the Commonwealth's opinion evidence from the summary judgment process, it did not change the fact that § 18.2-71.1, which criminalized certain partial-birth abortion methods, was facially unconstitutional because it did not contain an exception to preserve a woman's health. The Commonwealth's evidence, at most, indicated some division of medical opinion on the question of whether banning the intact dilation and evacuation and dilation and extraction procedures could have endangered a woman's health, but a unanimity of medical opinion was not required. Richmond Med. Ctr. for Women v. Hicks, 409 F.3d 619, 2005 U.S. App. LEXIS 10186 (4th Cir. 2005) reh'g denied, 422 F.3d 160, 2005 U.S.App. LEXIS 19067 (4th Cir. 2005), vacated and remanded, Herring v. Richmond Medical Ctr. for Women, 127 S.Ct. 2094, 167 L.Ed.2d 810, 2007 U.S. LEXIS 4339 (2007) (for further consideration in light of *Gonzales v. Carhart*, 127 S.Ct. 1610, 167 L.Ed.2d 480, 2007 U.S. LEXIS 4338 (April 18, 2007)).

II. DECISIONS UNDER PRIOR LAW.

Editor's note.
The cases below were decided under former § 18.2-74.2.

Constitutionality. — Former § 18.2-74.2 was unconstitutional under the due process clause of the Fourteenth Amendment in that it impermissibly infringed upon the fundamental right to choose an abortion; because it imposed an undue burden on that right; and because it contained no health exception and an inadequate life exception. Richmond Med. Ctr. for Women v. Gilmore, 55 F. Supp. 2d 441 (E.D. Va. 1999), aff'd, 224 F.3d 337 (4th Cir. 2000).

Former § 18.2-74.2 violated the due process clause of the Fourteenth Amendment to the United States Constitution because it did not contain an exception for pre-viability or post-viability abortion procedures that were necessary, in appropriate medical judgment, for the preservation of the life or health of the mother. Richmond Med. Ctr. for Women v. Gilmore, 224 F.3d 337, 2000 U.S. App. LEXIS 19111 (4th Cir. 2000).

Vagueness. — Plaintiffs, who were Virginia physicians, medical clinics, and non-profit corporations offering reproductive health services and obstetrical and gynecological medical services, including abortions, to women in Virginia, in their request for injunctive relief, raised questions as to the vagueness of former § 18.2-74.2, going to the merits so serious, substantial, difficult and doubtful, as to make them grounds for more deliberate investigation. Richmond Medical Ctr. for Women v. Gilmore, 11 F. Supp. 2d 795 (E.D. Va. 1998).

Void for vagueness. — Plaintiffs challenging the constitutionality of former § 18.2-74.2, raised questions so serious, substantial, difficult and doubtful as to make them grounds for more deliberate investigation. Indeed, plaintiffs were likely to succeed on their challenge that the section was void for vagueness, as there were various constructions, definitions and interpretations of the term "partial birth abortion," as well as the constituent definitional elements of that term including "delivers," "living fetus" and "substantial portion thereof." Richmond Medical Ctr. for Women v. Gilmore, 144 F.3d 326 (4th Cir. 1998).

Former § 18.2-74.2 did not give a person of ordinary intelligence fair notice that his contemplated conduct was forbidden by the statute. Richmond Medical Ctr. for Women v. Gilmore, 144 F.3d 326 (4th Cir. 1998).

"Partial birth abortion" lacks medical meaning. — The term "partial birth abortion," as a whole and as defined in former § 18.2-74.2, is impermissibly vague in that the term has no medical meaning and no one, not even those charged with enforcing it, know its precise contours. Richmond Med. Ctr. for Women v. Gilmore, 55 F. Supp. 2d 441 (E.D. Va. 1999), aff'd, 224 F.3d 337 (4th Cir. 2000).

Undue burden on woman's right to seek abortion pre-viability. — On a motion for preliminary injunction, plaintiffs, who were Virginia physicians, medical clinics, and non-profit corporations offering reproductive health services and obstetrical and gynecological medical services, including abortions, to women in Virginia, established a likelihood of success in showing that, without a maternal health exception, former § 18.2-74.2 placed an undue burden on a woman's right to seek an abortion pre-viability because it had the effect of subjecting women to an appreciably greater risk of injury or death than would be the case if these women could rely upon their physician to perform the currently accepted and widely used method of abortion. Richmond Medical Ctr. for Women v. Gilmore, 11 F. Supp. 2d 795 (E.D. Va. 1998); Richmond Medical Ctr. for Women v. Gilmore, 144 F.3d 326 (4th Cir. 1998).

Former § 18.2-74.2 operated to ban dilation and evacuation procedure, indisputably the most common and safest method of abortion in the second trimester of pregnancy. Richmond Medical Ctr. for Women v. Gilmore, 144 F.3d 326 (4th Cir. 1998).

Former § 18.2-74.2 denied women seeking a late-term (but pre-viability) abortion access to a safe procedure, and instead, in those cases in which the statute was implicated, required them to undergo a statistically more risky procedure; this amounted to an undue burden. Richmond Med. Ctr. for Women v. Gilmore, 55 F. Supp. 2d 441 (E.D. Va. 1999), aff'd, 224 F.3d 337 (4th Cir. 2000).

And was unconstitutional due to lack of health exception and inadequate life exception. — The United States Supreme Court has made it clear that the state may not proscribe abortion without providing an exception for procedures that are necessary, in appropriate medical judgment, for the preservation of the life or health of the mother. Former § 18.2-74.2 contained no health exception and an inadequate life exception. Richmond Med. Ctr. for Women v. Gilmore, 55 F. Supp. 2d 441 (E.D. Va. 1999), aff'd, 224 F.3d 337 (4th Cir. 2000).

Public interest favored issuance of injunction to enjoin former § 18.2-74.2, for the public is certainly interested in the prevention of enforcement of laws which may be unconstitutional. Richmond Medical Ctr. for Women v. Gilmore, 144 F.3d 326 (4th Cir. 1998).

In granting injunctive relief, the court took into account the ambiguity in the statutory terms and the fact that the defendants were unwilling to agree that procedures regularly performed by the plaintiffs were excluded from the reach of the Act. The Court also considered the nature of the injury likely to be sustained by the plaintiffs and their patients, absent such an injunction, and the lack of harm to the defendants, as well as their unencumbered ability to enforce Virginia's existing abortion regulations. Richmond Medical Ctr. for Women v. Gilmore, 144 F.3d 326 (4th Cir. 1998).

Absent injunction, plaintiffs physicians would have suffered irreparable harm through the threat of criminal prosecution for exercising what they considered safe medical judgment in the treatment of their patients and for performing abortions which, under *Roe* and *Casey*, they were permitted to perform. Richmond Medical Ctr. for Women v. Gilmore, 144 F.3d 326 (4th Cir. 1998).

§ 18.2-72. When abortion lawful during first trimester of pregnancy.

Notwithstanding any of the provisions of § 18.2-71, it shall be lawful for any physician licensed by the Board of Medicine to practice medicine and surgery, to terminate or attempt to terminate a human pregnancy or aid or assist in the termination of a human pregnancy by performing an abortion or causing a miscarriage on any woman during the first trimester of pregnancy.

History.
    1975, cc. 14, 15.

Cross references.
    As to prohibition against partial birth infanticide, and penalty therefor, see § 18.2-71.1.

Law Review.
    For survey of Virginia criminal law for the year 1974-1975, see 61 Va. L. Rev. 1697 (1975).

CASE NOTES

This statute pertaining to first trimester abortions conforms to the constitutional principles expressed in Roe v. Wade, 410 U.S. 113, 93 S. Ct. 705, 35 L. Ed. 2d 147 (1973); Northern Va. Women's Medical Ctr. v. Balch, 617 F.2d 1045 (4th Cir. 1980).

Applied in Northern Va. Women's Medical Ctr. v. Balch, 617 F.2d 1045 (4th Cir. 1980); Richmond Medical Ctr. for Women v. Gilmore, 144 F.3d 326 (4th Cir. 1998); Richmond Medical Ctr. for Women v. Gilmore, 11 F. Supp. 2d 795 (E.D. Va. 1998).

OPINIONS OF THE ATTORNEY GENERAL

Constitutionality. — Commonwealth has authority to promulgate regulations for facilities in which first trimester abortions are performed as well as for providers of first trimester abortions, so long as the regulations adhere to constitutional limitations. See opinion of Attorney General to The Honorable Ralph K. Smith, Member, Senate of Virginia, 2010 Va. AG LEXIS 45 (8/20/10); Opinion of Attorney General to The Honorable Robert G. Marshall, Member, House of Delegates, 10-012, 2010 Va. AG LEXIS 44 (8/20/10).

§ 18.2-73. When abortion lawful during second trimester of pregnancy.

Notwithstanding any of the provisions of § 18.2-71 and in addition to the provisions of § 18.2-72, it shall be lawful for any physician licensed by the Board of Medicine to practice medicine and surgery, to terminate or attempt to terminate a human pregnancy or aid or assist in the termination of a human pregnancy by performing an abortion or causing a miscarriage on any woman during the second trimester of pregnancy and prior to the third trimester of pregnancy provided such procedure is performed in a hospital licensed by the State Department of Health or operated by the Department of Behavioral Health and Developmental Services.

History.
    1975, cc. 14, 15; 2009, cc. 813, 840.

Cross references.
    As to prohibition against partial birth infanticide, and penalty therefor, see § 18.2-71.1.

The 2009 amendments.
    The 2009 amendments by cc. 813 and 840 are identical and substituted "operated by the Department of Behavioral Health and Developmental Services" for "under the control of the State Board of

Mental Health, Mental Retardation and Substance Abuse Services."

Law Review.
    For survey of Virginia criminal law for the year 1974-1975, see 61 Va. L. Rev. 1697 (1975). For note on permissible limits of abortion regulation in light of Simopoulos v. Virginia, 462 U.S. 506, 103 S. Ct. 2532, 76 L. Ed. 2d 755 (1983), see 18 U. Rich. L. Rev. 137 (1983). For annual survey of Virginia law article, "Administrative Law," see 47 U. Rich. L. Rev. 7 (2012).

CASE NOTES

Constitutionality. — The hospital requirement contained in the proviso in this section is constitutionally permissible, since it is reasonably related to the state's compelling interest in preserving and protecting maternal health, and since it does not unreasonably limit a pregnant woman's access to medical care and thereby abridge her right to elect to abort. Simopoulos v. Commonwealth, 221 Va. 1059, 277 S.E.2d 194 (1981), aff'd, 462 U.S. 506, 103 S. Ct. 2532, 76 L. Ed. 2d 755 (1983).

Virginia's requirement that second-trimester abortions be performed in licensed clinics is not an unreasonable means of furthering the state's compelling interest in protecting the woman's own health and safety. The state has a legitimate interest in seeing to it that abortion, like any other medical procedure, is performed under circumstances that insure maximum safety for the patient. Simopoulos v. Virginia, 462 U.S. 506, 103 S. Ct. 2532, 76 L. Ed. 2d 755 (1983).

Section consistent with normal medical practice. — This section does not require that the patient be hospitalized as an inpatient or that the abortion be performed in a full-service, acute-care hospital. Rather, the state's requirement that second-trimester abortions be performed in licensed clinics appears to comport with accepted medical practice, and leaves the method and timing of the abortion precisely where they belong — with the physician and the patient. Simopoulos v. Virginia, 462 U.S. 506, 103 S. Ct. 2532, 76 L. Ed. 2d 755 (1983).

The hospital proviso applies to all procedures performed during the entire abortion process, including the means employed with intent to initiate the process. Simopoulos v. Commonwealth, 221 Va. 1059, 277 S.E.2d 194 (1981), aff'd, 462 U.S. 506, 103 S. Ct. 2532, 76 L. Ed. 2d 755 (1983).

Thus, unnecessary to charge intent that fetus be expelled outside hospital. — Where defendant was convicted under an indictment charging that he employed procedures intended to initiate abortion during the second trimester of pregnancy and that he did so outside of a hospital licensed by the state, it was unnecessary to charge that he intended his patient to expel the fetus outside a hospital. Simopoulos v. Commonwealth, 221 Va. 1059, 277 S.E.2d 194 (1981), aff'd, 462 U.S. 506, 103 S. Ct. 2532, 76 L. Ed. 2d 755 (1983).

Applied in Richmond Medical Ctr. for Women v. Gilmore, 144 F.3d 326 (4th Cir. 1998); Richmond Medical Ctr. for Women v. Gilmore, 11 F. Supp. 2d 795 (E.D. Va. 1998); Abofreka v. Va. Bd. of Med., — Va. App. —, — S.E.2d —, 2007 Va. App. LEXIS 304 (Aug. 14, 2007).

OPINIONS OF THE ATTORNEY GENERAL

Constitutionality. — Commonwealth has authority to promulgate regulations for facilities in which first trimester abortions are performed as well as for providers of first trimester abortions, so long as the regulations adhere to constitutional limitations. See opinion of Attorney General to The Honorable Ralph K. Smith, Member, Senate of Virginia, 2010 Va. AG LEXIS 45 (8/20/10); Opinion of Attorney General to The Honorable Robert G. Marshall, Member, House of Delegates, 10-012, 2010 Va. AG LEXIS 44 (8/20/10).

§ 18.2-74. When abortion or termination of pregnancy lawful after second trimester of pregnancy.

Notwithstanding any of the provisions of § 18.2-71 and in addition to the provisions of

§§ 18.2-72 and 18.2-73, it shall be lawful for any physician licensed by the Board of Medicine to practice medicine and surgery to terminate or attempt to terminate a human pregnancy or aid or assist in the termination of a human pregnancy by performing an abortion or causing a miscarriage on any woman in a stage of pregnancy subsequent to the second trimester provided the following conditions are met:

(a) Said operation is performed in a hospital licensed by the Virginia State Department of Health or operated by the Department of Behavioral Health and Developmental Services.

(b) The physician and two consulting physicians certify and so enter in the hospital record of the woman, that in their medical opinion, based upon their best clinical judgment, the continuation of the pregnancy is likely to result in the death of the woman or substantially and irremediably impair the mental or physical health of the woman.

(c) Measures for life support for the product of such abortion or miscarriage must be available and utilized if there is any clearly visible evidence of viability.

History.
1975, cc. 14, 15; 2009, cc. 813, 840.

Cross references.
As to prohibition against partial birth infanticide, and penalty therefor, see § 18.2-71.1.

The 2009 amendments.
The 2009 amendments by cc. 813 and 840 are identical and substituted "operated by the Department of Behavioral Health and Developmental Services" for "under the control of the State Board of Mental Health, Mental Retardation and Substance Abuse Services" in subdivision (a).

Law Review.
For survey of Virginia criminal law for the year 1974-1975, see 61 Va. L. Rev. 1697 (1975).

CASE NOTES

Constitutionality. — While it is true that a statute which imposes a duty upon a physician to take affirmative action to preserve a fetus, irrespective of the stage of pregnancy and the viability of the fetus, is constitutionally impermissible, after viability the sovereign has a compelling interest sufficient to justify regulation reasonably designed to preserve the life of the fetus. The proscription in § 18.2-71 against destruction of the fetus is not a command to preserve it; and, while subdivision (c) of this section requires a physician to utilize fetal life support measures during the third trimester if there is any clearly visible evidence of viability, nothing in this article imposes such an affirmative duty during the pre-viable stages of pregnancy. Simopoulos v. Commonwealth, 221 Va. 1059, 277 S.E.2d 194 (1981), aff'd, 462 U.S. 506, 103 S. Ct. 2532, 76 L. Ed. 2d 755 (1983).

Applied in Richmond Medical Ctr. for Women v. Gilmore, 144 F.3d 326 (4th Cir. 1998); Richmond Medical Ctr. for Women v. Gilmore, 11 F. Supp. 2d 795 (E.D. Va. 1998).

OPINIONS OF THE ATTORNEY GENERAL

Constitutionality. — Commonwealth has authority to promulgate regulations for facilities in which first trimester abortions are performed as well as for providers of first trimester abortions, so long as the regulations adhere to constitutional limitations. See opinion of Attorney General to The Honorable Ralph K. Smith, Member, Senate of Virginia, 2010 Va. AG LEXIS 45 (8/20/10); Opinion of Attorney General to The Honorable Robert G. Marshall, Member, House of Delegates, 10-012, 2010 Va. AG LEXIS 44 (8/20/10).

§ 18.2-74.1. Abortion, etc., when necessary to save life of woman.

In the event it is necessary for a licensed physician to terminate a human pregnancy or assist in the termination of a human pregnancy by performing an abortion or causing a miscarriage on any woman in order to save her life, in the opinion of the physician so performing the abortion or causing the miscarriage, §§ 18.2-71, 18.2-73 and 18.2-74 shall not be applicable.

History.
Code 1950, § 18.1-62.3; 1970, c. 508; 1975, cc. 14, 15.

Cross references.
As to prohibition against partial birth infanticide, and penalty therefor, see § 18.2-71.1.

Law Review.
For survey of Virginia criminal law for the year 1974-1975, see 61 Va. L. Rev. 1697 (1975). For note discussing access of minors to contraceptives, abortion, and sterilization without parental consent, see 12 U. Rich. L. Rev. 221 (1977).

Michie's Jurisprudence.
For related discussion, see 9B M.J. Indictments, Informations and Presentments, § 25.

CASE NOTES

Medical necessity exception matter of defense. — Where defendant's indictment for violation of abortion statutes did not attempt to negate the exception of a medical necessity to treat the patient, the exception was a matter of defense for the defendant to assert and not for the indictment to deny since the exception was made in a substantive section subsequent to the enacting section of the abortion statutes. Simopoulos v. Commonwealth, 221 Va. 1059, 277 S.E.2d 194 (1981), aff'd, 462 U.S. 506, 103 S. Ct. 2532, 76 L. Ed. 2d 755 (1983).

And burden of negating necessity on Commonwealth. — Once a defendant invokes this section as a defense in a prosecution for violation of the abortion statutes, the Commonwealth has the burden of negating maternal health necessity beyond a reasonable doubt. Simopoulos v. Commonwealth, 221 Va. 1059, 277 S.E.2d 194 (1981), aff'd, 462 U.S. 506, 103 S. Ct. 2532, 76 L. Ed. 2d 755 (1983).

The prosecution is not obligated to prove lack of medical necessity beyond a reasonable doubt until appellant invokes medical necessity as a defense. Simopoulos v. Virginia, 462 U.S. 506, 103 S. Ct. 2532, 76 L. Ed. 2d 755 (1983).

Evidence sufficient to refute claim of maternal health necessity. — See Simopoulos v. Commonwealth, 221 Va. 1059, 277 S.E.2d 194 (1981), aff'd, 462 U.S. 506, 103 S. Ct. 2532, 76 L. Ed. 2d 755 (1983).

Applied in Richmond Medical Ctr. for Women v. Gilmore, 11 F. Supp. 2d 795 (E.D. Va. 1998).

§ 18.2-74.2. Repealed by Acts 2003, cc. 961 and 963.

Cross references.
As to prohibition against partial birth infanticide, and penalty therefor, see § 18.2-71.1.

§ 18.2-75. Conscience clause.

Nothing in §§ 18.2-72, 18.2-73 or § 18.2-74 shall require a hospital or other medical facility or physician to admit any patient under the provisions hereof for the purpose of performing an abortion. In addition, any person who shall state in writing an objection to any abortion or all abortions on personal, ethical, moral or religious grounds shall not be required to participate in procedures which will result in such abortion, and the refusal of such person, hospital or other medical facility to participate therein shall not form the basis of any claim for damages on account of such refusal or for any disciplinary or recriminatory action against such person, nor shall any such person be denied employment because of such objection or refusal. The written objection shall remain in effect until such person shall revoke it in writing or terminate his association with the facility with which it is filed.

History.
Code 1950, § 18.1-63.1; 1974, c. 679; 1975, cc. 14, 15.

Law Review.
For note, "Patient Autonomy Versus Religious Freedom: Should State Legislatures Require Catholic Hospitals to Provide Emergency Contraception to Rape Victims," see 60 Wash. & Lee L. Rev. 1007 (2003). For article, "Taking Conscience Seriously," see 98 Va. L. Rev. 1501 (2012).

Michie's Jurisprudence.
For related discussion, see 19 M.J. Warrants, § 2.

CASE NOTES

Restrictions on abortion services not required. — While this section permits private hospital corporations to place certain restrictions on abortion services or to refuse them altogether, it does not require them to do so, and it need not forbid them to do so. Simopoulos v. Commonwealth, 221 Va. 1059, 277 S.E.2d 194 (1981), aff'd, 462 U.S. 506, 103 S. Ct. 2532, 76 L. Ed. 2d 755 (1983).

Statute of limitations. — Where plaintiffs questioned whether Virginia's Conscience Clause imbued their claims with sufficient implied contractual obligations to warrant application of Virginia's three-year contract limitation period, § 8.01-246, to a wrongful discharge claim based on the Conscience Clause, the court rejected a similar argument, holding that wrongful discharge claims fall under Virginia's catchall statute of limitations, § 8.01-248. Michael v. Sentara Health Sys., 939 F. Supp. 1220 (E.D. Va. 1996).

§ 18.2-76. Informed written consent required; civil penalty.

A. Before performing any abortion or inducing any miscarriage or terminating a pregnancy as provided in § 18.2-72, 18.2-73, or 18.2-74, the physician shall obtain the informed written consent of the pregnant woman. However, if the woman has been adjudicated incapacitated by any court of competent jurisdiction or if the physician knows or has good reason to believe that such woman is incapacitated as adjudicated by a court of competent jurisdiction, then only after permission is given in writing by a parent, guardian, committee, or other person standing in loco parentis to the woman, may the physician perform the abortion or otherwise terminate the pregnancy.

B. At least 24 hours before the performance of an abortion, a qualified medical professional trained in sonography and working under the supervision of a physician licensed in the Commonwealth shall perform fetal transabdominal ultrasound imaging on the patient undergoing the abortion for the purpose of determining gestational age. If the pregnant woman lives at least 100 miles from the facility where the abortion is to be performed, the fetal ultrasound imaging shall be performed at least two hours before the abortion. The ultrasound image shall contain the dimensions of the fetus and accurately portray the presence of external members and internal organs of the fetus, if present or viewable. Determination of gestational age shall be based upon measurement of the fetus in a manner consistent with standard medical practice in the community for determining gestational age. When only the gestational sac is visible during ultrasound imaging, gestational age may be based upon measurement of the gestational sac. If gestational age cannot be determined by a transabdominal ultrasound, then the patient undergoing the abortion shall be verbally offered other ultrasound imaging to determine gestational age, which she may refuse. A print of the ultrasound image shall be made to document the measurements that have been taken to determine the gestational age of the fetus.

The provisions of this subsection shall not apply if the woman seeking an abortion is the victim of rape or incest, if the incident was reported to law-enforcement authorities. Nothing herein shall preclude the physician from using any ultrasound imaging that he considers to be medically appropriate pursuant to the standard medical practice in the community.

C. The qualified medical professional performing fetal ultrasound imaging pursuant to subsection B shall verbally offer the woman an opportunity to view the ultrasound image, receive a printed copy of the ultrasound image and hear the fetal heart tones pursuant to standard medical practice in the community, and shall obtain from the woman written certification that this opportunity was offered and whether or not it was accepted and, if applicable, verification that the pregnant woman lives at least 100 miles from the facility where the abortion is to be performed. A printed copy of the ultrasound image shall be maintained in the woman's medical record at the facility where the abortion is to be performed for the longer of (i) seven years or (ii) the extent required by applicable federal or state law.

D. For purposes of this section:

"Informed written consent" means the knowing and voluntary written consent to abortion by a pregnant woman of any age, without undue inducement or any element of force, fraud, deceit, duress, or other form of constraint or coercion by the physician who is to perform the abortion or his agent. The basic information to effect such consent, as required by this subsection, shall be provided by telephone or in person to the woman at least 24 hours before the abortion by the physician who is to perform the abortion, by a referring physician, or by a licensed professional or practical nurse working under the direct supervision of either the physician who is to perform the abortion or the referring physician; however, the information in subdivision 5 may be provided instead by a licensed health-care professional working under the direct supervision of either the physician who is to perform the abortion or the referring physician. This basic information shall include:

1. A full, reasonable and comprehensible medical explanation of the nature, benefits, and risks of and alternatives to the proposed procedures or protocols to be followed in her particular case;

2. An instruction that the woman may withdraw her consent at any time prior to the performance of the procedure;

3. An offer for the woman to speak with the physician who is to perform the abortion so that he may answer any questions that the woman may have and provide further information concerning the procedures and protocols;

4. A statement of the probable gestational age of the fetus at the time the abortion is to be performed and that fetal ultrasound imaging shall be performed prior to the abortion to confirm the gestational age; and

5. An offer to review the printed materials described in subsection F. If the woman chooses to review such materials, they shall be provided to her in a respectful and understandable manner, without prejudice and intended to give the woman the opportunity to make an informed choice and shall be provided to her at least 24 hours before the abortion or mailed to her at least 72 hours before the abortion by first-class mail or, if the woman requests, by certified mail, restricted delivery. This offer for the woman to review the material shall advise her of the following: (i) the Department of Health publishes printed materials that describe the unborn child and list agencies that offer alternatives to abortion; (ii) medical assistance benefits may be available for prenatal care, childbirth and neonatal care, and that more detailed information on the availability of such assistance is contained in the printed materials published by the Department; (iii) the father of the unborn child is liable to assist in the support of her child, even in instances where he has offered to pay for the abortion, that assistance in the collection of such support is available, and that more detailed information on the availability of such assistance is contained in the printed materials published by the Department; (iv) she has the right to review the materials printed by the Department and that copies will be provided to her free of charge if she chooses to review them; and (v) a statewide list of public and private agencies and services that provide ultrasound imaging and auscultation of fetal

heart tone services free of charge. Where the woman has advised that the pregnancy is the result of a rape, the information in clause (iii) may be omitted.

The information required by this subsection may be provided by telephone or in person.

E. The physician need not obtain the informed written consent of the woman when the abortion is to be performed pursuant to a medical emergency or spontaneous miscarriage. "Medical emergency" means any condition which, on the basis of the physician's good faith clinical judgment, so complicates the medical condition of a pregnant woman as to necessitate the immediate abortion of her pregnancy to avert her death or for which a delay will create a serious risk of substantial and irreversible impairment of a major bodily function.

F. On or before October 1, 2001, the Department of Health shall publish, in English and in each language which is the primary language of two percent or more of the population of the Commonwealth, the following printed materials in such a way as to ensure that the information is easily comprehensible:

1. Geographically indexed materials designed to inform the woman of public and private agencies and services available to assist a woman through pregnancy, upon childbirth and while the child is dependent, including, but not limited to, information on services relating to (i) adoption as a positive alternative, (ii) information relative to counseling services, benefits, financial assistance, medical care and contact persons or groups, (iii) paternity establishment and child support enforcement, (iv) child development, (v) child rearing and stress management, (vi) pediatric and maternal health care, and (vii) public and private agencies and services that provide ultrasound imaging and auscultation of fetal heart tone services free of charge. The materials shall include a comprehensive list of the names and telephone numbers of the agencies, or, at the option of the Department of Health, printed materials including a toll-free, 24-hour-a-day telephone number which may be called to obtain, orally, such a list and description of agencies in the locality of the caller and of the services they offer;

2. Materials designed to inform the woman of the probable anatomical and physiological characteristics of the human fetus at two-week gestational increments from the time when a woman can be known to be pregnant to full term, including any relevant information on the possibility of the fetus's survival and pictures or drawings representing the development of the human fetus at two-week gestational increments. Such pictures or drawings shall contain the dimensions of the fetus and shall be realistic and appropriate for the stage of pregnancy depicted. The materials shall be objective, nonjudgmental and designed to convey only accurate scientific information about the human fetus at the various gestational ages; and

3. Materials containing objective information describing the methods of abortion procedures com-

monly employed, the medical risks commonly associated with each such procedure, the possible detrimental psychological effects of abortion, and the medical risks commonly associated with carrying a child to term.

The Department of Health shall make these materials available at each local health department and, upon request, to any person or entity, in reasonable numbers and without cost to the requesting party.

G. Any physician who fails to comply with the provisions of this section shall be subject to a $2,500 civil penalty.

History.
Code 1950, § 18.1-62.1; 1970, c. 508; 1972, c. 823; 1975, cc. 14, 15; 1979, c. 250; 1997, c. 801; 2001, cc. 473, 477; 2003, c. 784; 2012, c. 131.

The 2012 amendments.
The 2012 amendment by c. 131 substituted "§ 18.2-72, 18.2-73, or 18.2-74" for "§§ 18.2-72, 18.2-73, or § 18.2-74" in subsection A; added subsections B and C; redesignated former subsections B through E as subsections D through G; inserted "and that fetal ultrasound imaging shall be performed prior to the abortion to confirm the gestational age" in subdivision D 4; in subdivision D 5, in the first paragraph, inserted clause (v) in the next-to-last sentence and deleted "above" following "in clause (iii)" in the last sentence and rewrote the final paragraph; inserted clause (vii) in the next-to-last sentence of subdivision F 1; and made related changes.

Law Review.
For note discussing access of minors to contraceptives, abortion, and sterilization without parental consent, see 12 U. Rich. L. Rev. 221 (1977). For note on the permissible scope of parental involvement in the abortion decision of an unmarried minor, see 2 G.M.U. L. Rev. 235 (1978). For survey of Virginia law on domestic relations for the year 1978-1979, see 66 Va. L. Rev. 281 (1980). For comment on abortion and the two-parent notification requirement, see 11 G.M.U. L. Rev. 207 (1989). For survey on evidence in Virginia for 1989, see 23 U. Rich. L. Rev. 647 (1989). For 2000 survey of Virginia health law, see 34 U. Rich. L. Rev. 853 (2000). For article, "Legal Issues Involving Children," see 35 U. Rich. L. Rev. 741 (2001).

§ 18.2-76.1. Encouraging or promoting abortion.

If any person, by publication, lecture, advertisement, or by the sale or circulation of any publication, or through the use of a referral agency for profit, or in any other manner, encourage or promote the performing of an abortion or the inducing of a miscarriage in this Commonwealth which is prohibited under this article, he shall be guilty of a Class 3 misdemeanor.

History.
Code 1950, § 18.1-63; 1960, c. 358; 1972, c. 725; 1975, cc. 14, 15.

Law Review.
For survey of Virginia constitutional law for the year 1974-1975, see 61 Va. L. Rev. 1677 (1975).

CASE NOTES

Editor's note.
The case cited below was decided under this section as it read in 1971 when all encouragement for procuring of abortion by adver-

tisement was prohibited. The section has since been limited to prohibit advertisement in Virginia of practices prohibited by state law.

Unconstitutional application. — Virginia could not apply this section as it read in 1971, to appellant's publication of an advertisement without unconstitutionally infringing upon his First Amendment rights. Bigelow v. Virginia, 421 U.S. 809, 95 S. Ct. 2222, 44 L. Ed. 2d 600 (1975).

Formerly aimed at out-of-state services. — As applied, this section as it stood before the 1972 amendment was directed at the publishing of informative material relating to services offered in another state and was not directed at advertising by a referral agency or a practitioner whose activity Virginia had authority or power to regulate as the section now does. Bigelow v. Virginia, 421 U.S. 809, 95 S. Ct. 2222, 44 L. Ed. 2d 600 (1975).

State police power does not extend to legal activities in other states. — A state does not acquire power or supervision over the internal affairs of another state merely because the welfare and health of its own citizens may be affected when they travel to that state. It may seek to disseminate information so as to enable its citizens to make better informed decisions when they leave. But it may not, under the guise of exercising internal police powers, bar a citizen of another state from disseminating information about an activity that is legal in that state. Bigelow v. Virginia, 421 U.S. 809, 95 S. Ct. 2222, 44 L. Ed. 2d 600 (1975).

Section's overbreadth moot. — In view of this section's amendment since appellant's conviction in such a way as "effectively to repeal" its prior application, there is no possibility now that the statute's pre-1972 form will be applied again to appellant or will chill the rights of others. As a practical matter, the issue of its overbreadth has become moot for the future. Bigelow v. Virginia, 421 U.S. 809, 95 S. Ct. 2222, 44 L. Ed. 2d 600 (1975).

Advertising, like all public expression, may be subject to reasonable regulation that serves a legitimate public interest. Bigelow v. Virginia, 421 U.S. 809, 95 S. Ct. 2222, 44 L. Ed. 2d 600 (1975).

But is subject to First Amendment protection. — The fact that a particular advertisement in appellant's newspaper had commercial aspects or reflected the advertiser's commercial interests did not negate all First Amendment guarantees. The state was not free of constitutional restraint merely because the advertisement involved sales or "solicitations." Bigelow v. Virginia, 421 U.S. 809, 95 S. Ct. 2222, 44 L. Ed. 2d 600 (1975).

Commercial activity protected. — The existence of commercial activity, in itself, is no justification for narrowing the protection of expression secured by the First Amendment. Bigelow v. Virginia, 421 U.S. 809, 95 S. Ct. 2222, 44 L. Ed. 2d 600 (1975).

Informative aspects of advertisement. — Advertisement published in appellant's newspaper did more than simply propose a commercial transaction where it contained factual material of clear "public interest." Portions of its message, most prominently the lines, "Abortions are now legal in New York. There are no residency requirements," involved the exercise of the freedom of communicating information and disseminating opinion. Bigelow v. Virginia, 421 U.S. 809, 95 S. Ct. 2222, 44 L. Ed. 2d 600 (1975).

§ 18.2-76.2. Not set out.

History.
1975, cc. 14, 15.

Editor's note.
Section 18.2-76.2 is a severability clause. See Acts 1975, cc. 14, 15.

CHAPTER 5.

CRIMES AGAINST PROPERTY.

Article 1. Arson and Related Crimes.

Section
18.2-77.   Burning or destroying dwelling house, etc.

ARTICLE 1.

ARSON AND RELATED CRIMES.

Michie's Jurisprudence.

For related discussion, see 2A M.J. Arson, §§ 1-3, 6, 8; 8A M.J. Explosions and Explosives, § 14; 15 M.J. Railroads, § 143; 21A M.J. Words and Phrases.

§ 18.2-77. Burning or destroying dwelling house, etc.

A. If any person maliciously (i) burns, or by use of any explosive device or substance destroys, in whole or in part, or causes to be burned or destroyed, or (ii) aids, counsels or procures the burning or destruction of any dwelling house or manufactured home whether belonging to himself or another, or any occupied hotel, hospital, mental health facility, or other house in which persons usually dwell or lodge, any occupied railroad car, boat, vessel, or river craft in which persons usually dwell or lodge, or any occupied jail or prison, or any occupied church or occupied building owned or leased by a church that is immediately adjacent to a church, he shall be guilty of a felony, punishable by imprisonment for life or for any period not less than five years and, subject to subdivision g of § 18.2-10, a fine of not more than $100,000. Any person who maliciously sets fire to anything, or aids, counsels or procures the setting fire to anything, by the burning whereof such occupied dwelling house, manufactured home, hotel, hospital, mental health facility or other house, or railroad car, boat, vessel, or river craft, jail or prison, church or building owned or leased by a church that is immediately adjacent to a church, is burned shall be guilty of a violation of this subsection.

B. Any such burning or destruction when the building or other place mentioned in subsection A is unoccupied, shall be punishable as a Class 4 felony.

C. For purposes of this section, "church" shall be defined as in § 18.2-127.

History.

Code 1950, § 18.1-75; 1960, c. 358; 1975, cc. 14, 15; 1977, c. 63; 1978, c. 443; 1993, c. 406; 1997, c. 832.

Cross references.

For definition of "barrier crime" as including a conviction of arson as set out in § 18.2-77 et seq., or an equivalent offense in another state, and prohibition against assisted living facilities, adult day care centers or child welfare agencies hiring for certain compensated employment persons who have committed such an offense, see §§ 63.2-1719, 63.2-1720. As to report to children's residential facility for which a background check is being performed on whether the applicant has ever been convicted of or is the subject of pending charges for various crimes, including arson as set out in § 18.2-77 et seq., or an equivalent offense in another state, see § 63.2-1726.

Law Review.

For survey of Virginia criminal law for the year 1974-1975, see 61 Va. L. Rev. 1697 (1975). For note, "Criminal Procedure and Criminal Law: Virginia Supreme Court Decisions During the 70's," see 15 U. Rich. L. Rev. 585 (1981). For article, "Preclusion of Evidence of Criminal Conviction in Civil Action Arising from the Same Incident," see 10 G.M.U. L. Rev. 107 (1988). For note, "Predicate Offenses for First Degree Felony Murder in Virginia," see 57 Wash. & Lee L. Rev. 561 (2000).

CASE NOTES

When a building is burned, the law presumes the fire was caused by accident rather than by a deliberate act. Augustine v. Commonwealth, 226 Va. 120, 306 S.E.2d 886 (1983).

Elements of offense. — To establish arson, the Commonwealth must prove the fire was of incendiary origin and that the accused was a guilty agent in the burning. Augustine v. Commonwealth, 226 Va. 120, 306 S.E.2d 886 (1983); Avila v. Commonwealth, No. 1980-99-4, 2000 Va. App. LEXIS 472 (Ct. of Appeals June 27, 2000).

In order to support a conviction for arson, it is essential that the evidence reveal that the fire was of incendiary origin and that it point unerringly to the guilty party. Plowden v. Commonwealth, No. 1620-96-2 (Ct. of Appeals June 10, 1997).

Term "anything" in § 18.2-77 refers to the accelerant used to start the fire of a dwelling, not the object of the fire; the statutory language proscribes the setting fire to anything, by the burning whereof such occupied dwelling house is burned. Schwartz v. Commonwealth, 267 Va. 751, 594 S.E.2d 925, 2004 Va. LEXIS 72 (2004).

Corpus delicti must consist of proof that the fire was of incendiary, rather than of accidental origin. In this respect the defense is aided by a presumption that the fire was caused by accident. But this presumption is rebuttable. Cook v. Commonwealth, 226 Va. 427, 309 S.E.2d 325 (1983).

Arson may be proved by circumstantial evidence where all the circumstances of time, place, motive, means, opportunity and conduct concur in pointing out the accused as the perpetrator of the crime. Avila v. Commonwealth, No. 1980-99-4, 2000 Va. App. LEXIS 472 (Ct. of Appeals June 27, 2000).

Circumstantial evidence of criminal agency in an arson case must "point unerringly" to the defendant. But this amounts to no more and no less than a requirement that the evidence must exclude every reasonable hypothesis of innocence, the standard applicable to every criminal case. Cook v. Commonwealth, 226 Va. 427, 309 S.E.2d 325 (1983).

When the Commonwealth relies upon circumstantial evidence, it is essential not only that the evidence reveal that the fire was of incendiary origin, but it must also point unerringly to the guilty party. Augustine v. Commonwealth, 226 Va. 120, 306 S.E.2d 886 (1983).

It is sufficient where every reasonable hypothesis of innocence is excluded. — Arson stands upon no different footing than any other criminal offense. Where circumstantial evidence is sufficient to exclude every reasonable hypothesis of innocence, it is sufficient to support a conviction. The hypotheses which must be thus excluded are those which flow from the evidence itself, and not from the imaginations of defense counsel. Cook v. Commonwealth, 226 Va. 427, 309 S.E.2d 325 (1983).

Language of section should be followed in indictment. — In indictments for statutory offenses, the language of the statute defining the offense should be strictly followed. Howel v. Commonwealth, 46 Va. (5 Gratt.) 664 (1848).

Ownership need not be in indictment. — To prove the dwelling-house element under this section, the Commonwealth need not establish ownership of the premises, only routine habitation, and an allegation in an indictment that the property the defendant had set on fire was owned by a named individual was thus a circumstance immaterial to the offense and clearly unnecessary to a successful prosecution of the indictment. Alston v. Commonwealth, 32 Va. App. 661, 529 S.E.2d 851, 2000 Va. App. LEXIS 460 (2000).

Use of word "burn" is essential. — In an indictment for arson, it is not sufficient to use the words "set fire to" the house; but the word "burn" must be used, that being the word employed in this section to define the offense. Howel v. Commonwealth, 46 Va. (5 Gratt.) 664 (1848).

Time of burning must be charged. — To convict of the offense of burning at night, it seems that the indictment must charge the burning in the night. Curran's Case, 48 Va. (7 Gratt.) 619 (1850).

Though the offense of burning in the daytime may be charged in the common-law form, omitting to state whether the burning was in the night or daytime, yet it is more appropriate to charge the burning in the daytime. Curran's Case, 48 Va. (7 Gratt.) 619 (1850).

Term "dwelling house" means place which human beings regularly use for sleeping even though the occupants are temporarily absent. Marable v. Commonwealth, 27 Va. App. 505, 500 S.E.2d 233 (1998).

A dwelling referred to as "temporarily unoccupied" is one that is currently uninhabited, not one from which its occupants are merely absent at the time it is burned. Davis v. Commonwealth, 16 Va. App. 6, 427 S.E.2d 441 (1993).

Despite that legislature subsequently deleted the word "temporarily" from statute, it should not be construed to require proof that one or more people were physically present in the dwelling at the time of the burning. Marable v. Commonwealth, 27 Va. App. 505, 500 S.E.2d 233 (1998).

Use of term "unoccupied" was not intended to reduce punishment for violation of this section where the occupant or occupants are merely temporarily absent, but continue to reside there. Marable v. Commonwealth, 27 Va. App. 505, 500 S.E.2d 233 (1998).

Absence of occupants. — When the defendant burned the house in which he and others lived, he was guilty of a Class 2 felony, rather than a Class 3 felony, even though no one was in the house at the time. Davis v. Commonwealth, 16 Va. App. 6, 427 S.E.2d 441 (1993).

Question whether fire is of incendiary or of accidental origin is a question of fact which must often turn upon the weight of circumstantial evidence. Cook v. Commonwealth, 226 Va. 427, 309 S.E.2d 325 (1983).

When a fact finder has accepted the testimony of a qualified expert witness, which negates every reasonable possibility that a fire was of accidental origin, the Supreme Court cannot hold the evidence insufficient, as a matter of law, to support a finding that the fire was of incendiary origin. Cook v. Commonwealth, 226 Va. 427, 309 S.E.2d 325 (1983).

Separate offenses. — Section 18.2-77 clearly and unambiguously set forth the legislature's intent that the burning of a dwelling house, caused by igniting another item, be prosecuted as a separate and distinct offense. Schwartz v. Commonwealth, 41 Va. App. 61, 581 S.E.2d 891, 2003 Va. App. LEXIS 339 (2003), aff'd, 267 Va. 751, 594 S.E.2d 925 (2004).

By separate statutes, the legislature has criminalized the arson of an occupied dwelling, on the one hand, § 18.2-77, and the arson of personal property, § 18.2-81, on the other. Therefore, where defendant burned a dwelling and two separate vehicles, the legislature intended that there should be three units of prosecution, for the burning of the dwelling and for the burning of each vehicle. Schwartz v. Commonwealth, 267 Va. 751, 594 S.E.2d 925, 2004 Va. LEXIS 72 (2004).

When defendant was charged with multiple arson counts, the single larceny doctrine did not bar his convictions, because he was charged with the statutory offense of arson, not larceny, this doctrine was only applied to those statutory offenses for which no legislative intent to abrogate the theory of common-law larceny could be ascertained, and the plain language of §§ 18.2-77 and 18.2-81 showed the legislature's intention to allow multiple arson convictions in certain circumstances. Schwartz v. Commonwealth, 41 Va. App. 61, 581 S.E.2d 891, 2003 Va. App. LEXIS 339 (2003), aff'd, 267 Va. 751, 594 S.E.2d 925 (2004).

Insufficiency of evidence. — Evidence that a fire was of incendiary origin, that the accused had an opportunity to commit the crime, and that he cherished and had expressed ill feelings towards the owner of the property destroyed, does not warrant a conviction. Garner v. Commonwealth, 2 Va. Dec. 458, 26 S.E. 507 (1897); Jones v. Commonwealth, 103 Va. 1012, 49 S.E. 663 (1905).

Evidence sufficient. — The evidence was sufficient to support a defendant's conviction under this section where nine fires were set in the condominium occupied by the defendant's estranged husband in a manner described by the fire marshall as a classic example of a revenge fire and where the circumstantial evidence established time, means and opportunity, from which the jury could infer that the defendant was the perpetrator of the crime. Avila v. Commonwealth, No. 1980-99-4, 2000 Va. App. LEXIS 472 (Ct. of Appeals June 27, 2000).

The circumstantial evidence sufficiently supported a defendant's arson conviction, where the owner of the home that was burned testified that, on the night of the fire, the defendant entered her house upset and intoxicated and was alone in the house for approximately 20 minutes before the fire was detected, where immediately after the fire was discovered, two witnesses saw a man running from the house and attempting to leave the area hurriedly in a blue sedan bearing a particular license plate, and where the defendant was later found in possession of that car. Neblett v. Commonwealth, No. 1247-00-2, 2001 Va. App. LEXIS 282 (Ct. of Appeals May 22, 2001).

Although defendant's conviction of solicitation to commit a felony was reversed because improper impeachment evidence was admitted, the evidence that she asked another person to commit an arson against a dwelling house was sufficient to support her conviction, and thus the Commonwealth could retry her if it was so inclined. Goodson v. Commonwealth, — Va. App. —, — S.E.2d —, 2006 Va. App. LEXIS 515 (Nov. 14, 2006).

Evidence was sufficient to prove beyond a reasonable doubt that defendant set fire to defendant's wife's home intentionally and maliciously and that defendant was guilty of arson of the dwelling where defendant set fire to the couch using a cigarette lighter and left the dwelling, removing the parties' cat from the home. The obvious result of defendant's burning of the sofa was the complete destruction of the house. Bradbury v. Commonwealth, 2010 Va. App. LEXIS 421 (Nov. 2, 2010).

Trial court did not err in finding the evidence sufficient for the jury to conclude that a dwelling was occupied within the meaning of subsection A of § 18.2-77 because defendant admittedly purchased gasoline and burned the dwelling where defendant and other employees lived shortly after defendant's employment was terminated. Andelic v. Commonwealth, 2012 Va. App. LEXIS 155 (May 15, 2012).

Applied in Knight v. Commonwealth, 225 Va. 85, 300 S.E.2d 600 (1983); Creech v. Commonwealth, 242 Va. 385, 410 S.E.2d 650 (1991).

§ 18.2-78. What not deemed dwelling house.

No outhouse, not adjoining a dwelling house, nor under the same roof, although within the curtilage thereof, shall be deemed a part of such dwelling house, within the meaning of this chapter, unless some person usually lodge therein at night.

History.
Code 1950, § 18.1-77; 1960, c. 358; 1975, cc. 14, 15.

Cross references.
For sections limited by this section, see notes to §§ 18.2-90 and 18.2-91.

Law Review.
For article, "Preclusion of Evidence of Criminal Conviction in Civil Action Arising from the Same Incident," see 10 G.M.U. L. Rev. 107 (1988).

CASE NOTES

This section creates no offense. It declares nothing necessary to be noticed in pleading, either in the indictment or elsewhere. It is a mere incident to § 18.2-77, and a mere limitation of the words "dwelling house" therein mentioned. Page v. Commonwealth, 67 Va. (26 Gratt.) 943 (1875).

When outhouse deemed a dwelling house. — To make an outhouse, not adjoining a dwelling house nor under the same roof, a dwelling house, two things must appear: First, that the outhouse is within the curtilage of a dwelling house, and occupied therewith; and, second, that some person usually lodges therein at night. Page v. Commonwealth, 67 Va. (26 Gratt.) 943 (1875).

§ 18.2-79. Burning or destroying meeting house, etc.

If any person maliciously burns, or by the use of any explosive device or substance, maliciously de-

stroys, in whole or in part, or causes to be burned or destroyed, or aids, counsels, or procures the burning or destroying, of any meeting house, courthouse, townhouse, college, academy, schoolhouse, or other building erected for public use except an asylum, hotel, jail, prison or church or building owned or leased by a church that is immediately adjacent to a church, or any banking house, warehouse, storehouse, manufactory, mill, or other house, whether the property of himself or of another person, not usually occupied by persons lodging therein at night, at a time when any person is therein, or if he maliciously sets fire to anything, or causes to be set on fire, or aids, counsels, or procures the setting on fire of anything, by the burning whereof any building mentioned in this section is burned, at a time when any person is therein, he shall be guilty of a Class 3 felony. If such offense is committed when no person is in such building mentioned in this section, the offender shall be guilty of a Class 4 felony.

History.
Code 1950, § 18.1-78; 1960, c. 358; 1975, cc. 14, 15; 1997, c. 832.

Law Review.
For article, "Preclusion of Evidence of Criminal Conviction in Civil Action Arising from the Same Incident," see 10 G.M.U. L. Rev. 107 (1988). For note, "Predicate Offenses for First Degree Felony Murder in Virginia," see 57 Wash. & Lee L. Rev. 561 (2000).

Michie's Jurisprudence.
For related discussion, see 8A M.J. Explosions and Explosives, § 14.

CASE NOTES

Any burning sufficient. — The amount of burning necessary to support a conviction pursuant to this section is any amount, provided there is a perceptible wasting of the fiber of the building or object which is the subject of arson. Calderon v. Commonwealth, No. 2132-99-4, 2000 Va. App. LEXIS 475 (Ct. of Appeals June 27, 2000).

Only a slight burning is necessary for the purposes of conviction under this section. Hancock v. Commonwealth, 12 Va. App. 774, 407 S.E.2d 301 (1991).

Malice required for arson same as malice required for other common law crimes. — No Virginia case distinguishes the malice which is a necessary element of arson from the malice which has been required in other common law crimes; malice inheres in the doing of a wrongful act intentionally, or without just cause or excuse, or as a result of ill will. It may be directly evidenced by words, or inferred from acts and conduct which necessarily result in injury and its existence is a question of fact to be determined by the trier of fact. Bell v. Commonwealth, 11 Va. App. 530, 399 S.E.2d 450 (1991).

Evidence held sufficient. — Where evidence showed that defendant either doused cushion with gasoline or placed the cushion and used the match to ignite the gasoline, either act was sufficient to constitute arson in violation of this section. Hancock v. Commonwealth, 12 Va. App. 774, 407 S.E.2d 301 (1991).

Evidence was sufficient to support defendant's conviction for arson, for setting fire to an unoccupied building, in violation of § 18.2-79. Though circumstantial, the evidence showed that: (1) defendant threatened to burn down the structure after defendant was ejected from the property following a disagreement with another person; (2) defendant threatened to burn the structure down; (3) defendant was present at the time of the fire; (4) an accelerant was used to start the fire; and (5) defendant fled when defendant was confronted. Sloan v. Commonwealth, 2008 Va. App. LEXIS 452 (Oct. 7, 2008).

Applied in Knight v. Commonwealth, 225 Va. 85, 300 S.E.2d 600 (1983).

§ 18.2-80. Burning or destroying any other building or structure.

If any person maliciously, or with intent to defraud an insurance company or other person, burn, or by the use of any explosive device or substance, maliciously destroy, in whole or in part, or cause to be burned or destroyed, or aid, counsel or procure the burning or destruction of any building, bridge, lock, dam or other structure, whether the property of himself or of another, at a time when any person is therein or thereon, the burning or destruction whereof is not punishable under any other section of this chapter, he shall be guilty of a Class 3 felony. If he commits such offense at a time when no person is in such building, or other structure, and such building, or other structure, with the property therein, be of the value of $200, or more, he shall be guilty of a Class 4 felony, and if it and the property therein be of less value, he shall be guilty of a Class 1 misdemeanor.

History.
Code 1950, §§ 18.1-80, 18.1-81, 18.1-85; 1960, c. 358; 1975, cc. 14, 15; 1981, c. 197.

Law Review.
For note, "Predicate Offenses for First Degree Felony Murder in Virginia," see 57 Wash. & Lee L. Rev. 561 (2000).

Michie's Jurisprudence.
For related discussion, see 8A M.J. Explosions and Explosives, § 14.

CASE NOTES

Indictment should describe building with particularity. — An indictment under this section must describe the building with such particularity as will inform accused what building is meant. Richards v. Commonwealth, 81 Va. 110 (1885).

Accidental burning presumed. — Where a building or structure is burned, the presumption is that the fire was caused by accident, rather than by the act of the accused accompanied by a deliberate intent. Simmons v. Commonwealth, 208 Va. 778, 160 S.E.2d 569 (1968).

Burden of proof. — To establish the offense against the defendant, the Commonwealth had the burden of proving that the fire which burned the railway company's bridge was of incendiary origin and that the defendant was the guilty agent in the burning. Simmons v. Commonwealth, 208 Va. 778, 160 S.E.2d 569 (1968).

To support a conviction under this section, the Commonwealth has the burden to prove beyond a reasonable doubt both that the fire was incendiary and that the accused was the criminal agent. Jefferson v. Commonwealth, No. 2706-98-2, 2000 Va. App. LEXIS 620 (Ct. of Appeals Aug. 22, 2000).

Indictment held sufficient. — When an indictment charged that the accused "did feloniously burn a certain barn and property therein, said barn and the property therein being the property of one H.H. Dulaney, and situated in the county aforesaid, which said barn and the property therein was then and there of the value of $1,500," the indictment was sufficient under this section. Wolf v. Commonwealth, 71 Va. (30 Gratt.) 833 (1878).

Evidence as to value of building prior to fire. — It was not error for the trial court to refuse to strike the evidence of an expert who testified that the value of the burned building, before the fire, would have exceeded the minimum threshold for a felony conviction under this section, on grounds that his reasoning was faulty and

that he had no experience in this kind of appraisal. The validity of the reasoning process by which an expert reaches his opinion is within the province of the trier of fact, and goes only to the weight to be accorded to his opinion. Addison v. Commonwealth, 224 Va. 713, 299 S.E.2d 521 (1983).

Evidence held sufficient. — Evidence held sufficient where the defendant was at the location of the shed that was burned, alone and out of sight of any witness, only minutes before the fire started, she was admittedly angry at the owner and displayed this anger by intentionally denting a car just after leaving the shed, and where the defendant admitted that she was smoking just before she went to the shed and after. Jefferson v. Commonwealth, No. 2706-98-2, 2000 Va. App. LEXIS 620 (Ct. of Appeals Aug. 22, 2000).

Evidence was insufficient to sustain defendant's conviction under this section. Simmons v. Commonwealth, 208 Va. 778, 160 S.E.2d 569 (1968).

§ 18.2-81. Burning or destroying personal property, standing grain, etc.

If any person maliciously, or with intent to defraud an insurance company or other person, set fire to or burn or destroy by any explosive device or substance, or cause to be burned, or destroyed by any explosive device or substance, or aid, counsel, or procure the burning or destroying by any explosive device or substance, of any personal property, standing grain or other crop, he shall, if the thing burnt or destroyed, be of the value of $200 or more, be guilty of a Class 4 felony; and if the thing burnt or destroyed be of less value, he shall be guilty of a Class 1 misdemeanor.

History.
Code 1950, §§ 18.1-79, 18.1-85; 1960, c. 358; 1972, c. 53; 1975, cc. 14, 15; 1981, c. 197.

Law Review.
For survey of Virginia criminal law for the year 1971-1972, see 58 Va. L. Rev. 1206 (1972). For note, "Predicate Offenses for First Degree Felony Murder in Virginia," see 57 Wash. & Lee L. Rev. 561 (2000).

CASE NOTES

Construction. — Because the burning of personal property with intent to defraud as defined under § 18.2-81 substantially corresponded to the generic definition of arson for the purposes of 18 U.S.C.S. § 924(e), the district court did not err in finding that defendant's conviction under § 18.2-81 qualified as a predicate conviction for purposes of the Armed Career Criminal Act. United States v. Craig, — F.3d —, 2007 U.S. App. LEXIS 12903 (4th Cir. June 4, 2007).

Section 19.2-284 has no application to proving a violation of this section; this section is silent on the issue of ownership. This section proscribes not only burning another person's property, but the broader offense of burning any property with malice or the intent to defraud an insurance company or another person; thus, this section requires proof only of malice or intent to defraud. Proof of ownership, or of an insurable interest, is not an element of malicious burning under this section, and § 19.2-284 does not make it such. Hamm v. Commonwealth, 16 Va. App. 150, 428 S.E.2d 517 (1993).

Corpus delicti must consist of proof that the fire was of incendiary, rather than of accidental origin. In this respect the defense is aided by a presumption that the fire was caused by accident. But this presumption is rebuttable. Cook v. Commonwealth, 226 Va. 427, 309 S.E.2d 325 (1983).

Malice in the case of arson is not necessarily a feeling of ill will toward another person, but may be a purposeful intent to do a wrongful act. Consequently, malice may be inferred from the fact that a person intentionally burned insured property for the purpose of defrauding or injuring an insurance carrier. Hamm v. Commonwealth, 16 Va. App. 150, 428 S.E.2d 517 (1993).

When defendant was charged with multiple arson counts, the single larceny doctrine did not bar his convictions, because he was charged with the statutory offense of arson, not larceny, this doctrine was only applied to those statutory offenses for which no legislative intent to abrogate the theory of common law larceny could be ascertained, and the plain language of §§ 18.2-77 and 18.2-81 showed the legislature's intention to allow multiple arson convictions in certain circumstances. Schwartz v. Commonwealth, 41 Va. App. 61, 581 S.E.2d 891, 2003 Va. App. LEXIS 339 (2003), aff'd, 267 Va. 751, 594 S.E.2d 925 (2004).

Circumstantial evidence of criminal agency in an arson case must "point unerringly" to the defendant. But this amounts to no more and no less than a requirement that the evidence must exclude every reasonable hypothesis of innocence, the standard applicable to every criminal case. Cook v. Commonwealth, 226 Va. 427, 309 S.E.2d 325 (1983).

It is sufficient where every reasonable hypothesis of innocence is excluded. — Arson stands upon no different footing than any other criminal offense. Where circumstantial evidence is sufficient to exclude every reasonable hypothesis of innocence, it is sufficient to support a conviction. The hypotheses which must be thus excluded are those which flow from the evidence itself, and not from the imaginations of defense counsel. Cook v. Commonwealth, 226 Va. 427, 309 S.E.2d 325 (1983).

Question whether fire is of incendiary or of accidental origin is a question of fact which must often turn upon the weight of circumstantial evidence. Cook v. Commonwealth, 226 Va. 427, 309 S.E.2d 325 (1983).

When a fact finder has accepted the testimony of a qualified expert witness, which negates every reasonable possibility that a fire was of accidental origin, the Supreme Court cannot hold the evidence insufficient, as a matter of law, to support a finding that the fire was of incendiary origin. Cook v. Commonwealth, 226 Va. 427, 309 S.E.2d 325 (1983).

Intent to defraud insurance company may also be malicious burning. — The fact that this section includes a separate provision for "burning with intent to defraud an insurance company" does not exclude that wrongful act as being an act of malicious burning; this section separately identifies a common species of malicious burning, which, prior to the enactment of this section, was defined separately and punished differently from other acts of malicious burning. (See former Code §§ 18.1-79 and 18.1-85.) Hamm v. Commonwealth, 16 Va. App. 150, 428 S.E.2d 517 (1993).

Conviction bars recovery on insurance policy. — In an action on a fire insurance policy brought after the plaintiff had been convicted under this section, the question whether or not the plaintiff fraudulently destroyed, or connived at the destruction of, his own property for the purpose of securing the insurance is identical with that which was heard and determined against him in the criminal prosecution, and while it is not res judicata as against the insurance company, the plaintiff should not be permitted to reopen the question and avoid the legal effect of the judgment of conviction by a collateral attack upon it. If the defendant could succeed in such an action, he would thereby avoid the logical consequences of his conviction. Eagle, Star & British Dominions Ins. Co. v. Heller, 149 Va. 82, 140 S.E. 314 (1927).

Clause vitiating section is against public policy. — It would be against public policy to write into a contract of fire insurance a provision that the assured might recover even though convicted under this section of burning the property with intent to defraud the insurer. Eagle, Star & British Dominions Ins. Co. v. Heller, 149 Va. 82, 140 S.E. 314 (1927).

Unit of prosecution. — Section 18.2-81, by its plain language, created a single and separate unit of prosecution for each item of personal property destroyed as the result of arson. Schwartz v. Commonwealth, 41 Va. App. 61, 581 S.E.2d 891, 2003 Va. App. LEXIS 339 (2003), aff'd, 267 Va. 751, 594 S.E.2d 925 (2004).

By separate statutes, the legislature has criminalized the arson of an occupied dwelling, on the one hand, § 18.2-77, and the arson of personal property, § 18.2-81, on the other. Therefore, where defendant burned a dwelling and two separate vehicles, the legislature intended that there should be three units of prosecution, for

the burning of the dwelling and for the burning of each vehicle. Schwartz v. Commonwealth, 267 Va. 751, 594 S.E.2d 925, 2004 Va. LEXIS 72 (2004).

The Commonwealth's evidence was sufficient to support appellant's arson conviction. Virginia v. Commonwealth, 17 Va. App. 684, 440 S.E.2d 438 (1994).

Applied in Underwood v. Commonwealth, 218 Va. 1045, 243 S.E.2d 231 (1978).

§ 18.2-82. Burning building or structure while in such building or structure with intent to commit felony.

If any person while in any building or other structure unlawfully, with intent to commit a felony therein, shall burn or cause to be burned, in whole or in part, such building or other structure, the burning of which is not punishable under any other section of this chapter, he shall be guilty of a Class 4 felony.

History.
Code 1950, § 18.1-80.1; 1970, c. 356; 1975, cc. 14, 15.

Law Review.
For article, "Preclusion of Evidence of Criminal Conviction in Civil Action Arising from the Same Incident," see 10 G.M.U. L. Rev. 107 (1988). For note, "Predicate Offenses for First Degree Felony Murder in Virginia," see 57 Wash. & Lee L. Rev. 561 (2000).

CASE NOTES

Legislative intent. — The legislative intent was not to exclude burnings proscribed by other sections of the arson chapter, but rather to enlarge the compass of the chapter by including burnings not otherwise proscribed. Such a building, a multi-purpose structure which ill fits the limited definition of buildings mentioned elsewhere in the chapter, falls squarely within the meaning of "any building or other structure." Knight v. Commonwealth, 225 Va. 85, 300 S.E.2d 600 (1983).

This section requires the Commonwealth to prove that the burning occurred while the accused was in the building with intent to commit a felony. Knight v. Commonwealth, 225 Va. 85, 300 S.E.2d 600 (1983).

The Commonwealth has the burden of proving that the fire was of incendiary origin and that the defendant was the guilty agent in the burning. Knight v. Commonwealth, 225 Va. 85, 300 S.E.2d 600 (1983).

Whether the origin of a fire was accidental or incendiary is a question of fact, and resolution of that question may, and often must, turn upon the weight of circumstantial evidence. Knight v. Commonwealth, 225 Va. 85, 300 S.E.2d 600 (1983).

§ 18.2-83. Threats to bomb or damage buildings or means of transportation; false information as to danger to such buildings, etc.; punishment; venue.

A. Any person (a) who makes and communicates to another by any means any threat to bomb, burn, destroy or in any manner damage any place of assembly, building or other structure, or any means of transportation, or (b) who communicates to another, by any means, information, knowing the same to be false, as to the existence of any peril of bombing, burning, destruction or damage to any such place of assembly, building or other structure, or any means of transportation, shall be guilty of a Class 5 felony; provided, however, that if such person be under fifteen years of age, he shall be guilty of a Class 1 misdemeanor.

B. A violation of this section may be prosecuted either in the jurisdiction from which the communication was made or in the jurisdiction where the communication was received.

History.
Code 1950, §§ 18.1-78.1 through 18.2-78.4; 1960, c. 358; 1975, cc. 14, 15; 1982, c. 502.

Cross references.
As to denial of driving privileges to juvenile for a violation of this section, see § 16.1-278.9.

Law Review.
For article, "Preclusion of Evidence of Criminal Conviction in Civil Action Arising from the Same Incident," see 10 G.M.U. L. Rev. 107 (1988).

CASE NOTES

This section is not vague. — A threat, in the criminal context, is recognized to be a communication avowing an intent to injure another's person or property. The communication, taken in its particular context, must reasonably cause the receiver to believe that the speaker will act according to his expression of intent. Perkins v. Commonwealth, 12 Va. App. 7, 402 S.E.2d 229 (1991).

Section is not overbroad. — A claim that a statute on its face contains no requirement of mens rea or scienter is no ground for holding the statute unconstitutional since such requirement will be read into the statute by the court when it appears the legislature implicitly intended that it must be proved. Perkins v. Commonwealth, 12 Va. App. 7, 402 S.E.2d 229 (1991).

Elements of offense. — In order to sustain a conviction under the statute, the communication must be taken in context, must have been maliciously made, and must reasonably cause the receiver of the threat to believe that the speaker of the threat will act according to his expressed intent. Jones v. Commonwealth, No. 0977-98-3 (Ct. of Appeals Feb. 23, 1999).

This section can be read as requiring a criminal mens rea. Such a narrowing construction of this statute prevents overbreadth. Only an individual who maliciously makes and communicates any threat prohibited by the statute will be punished. Perkins v. Commonwealth, 12 Va. App. 7, 402 S.E.2d 229 (1991).

But intent to carry out threat not required. — The statute does not require the Commonwealth to prove that the defendant intended to carry out his threat to burn the victim's house; proof that the threat was made and communicated satisfies the statutory requirement. Wyatt v. Commonwealth, No. 0554-97-3 (Ct. of Appeals March 24, 1998).

Defendant's age is not an essential element of the offense defined in this section. Lambert v. Commonwealth, 9 Va. App. 67, 383 S.E.2d 752 (1989).

"Threat" defined. — The term "threat" is defined as an avowed present determination or intent to injure presently or in the future. Parnell v. Commonwealth, 15 Va. App. 342, 423 S.E.2d 834 (1992).

This section is not limited to unconditional threats. Henry v. Commonwealth, No. 0520-96-4 (Ct. of Appeals June 17, 1997).

Context must be considered when determining whether words were threat. — In determining whether words were uttered as a threat, the context in which they were uttered must be considered. Parnell v. Commonwealth, 15 Va. App. 342, 423 S.E.2d 834 (1992).

Instruction that Commonwealth had to prove "true threat." — Trial judge did not err in refusing to instruct the jury that the Commonwealth had to prove a "true threat" or a "serious threat." The statute requires proof of a "threat." The adjectives "true" and "serious" would have interjected an issue that was not supported by the evidence. Parnell v. Commonwealth, 15 Va. App. 342, 423 S.E.2d 834 (1992).

Jury instruction on proof of a threat. — Even if the trial judge erred in not more fully explaining to the jury the definition of "threat," the omission was harmless error. Parnell v. Commonwealth, 15 Va. App. 342, 423 S.E.2d 834 (1992).

Defendant's statement that "he will die and his house will burn" was admissible, and its probative value outweighed the incidental prejudice that it may have engendered. Parnell v. Commonwealth, 15 Va. App. 342, 423 S.E.2d 834 (1992).

Delay in reporting threat to police. — The fact that the victim did not immediately report the defendant's threat to the police did not require a finding that she did not believe that he would commit the act. Jones v. Commonwealth, No. 0977-98-3 (Ct. of Appeals Feb. 23, 1999).

Relevance of evidence. — Evidence concerning a message that was left a mere three days before a bomb threat was made was not so far removed in time from the charged offense as to render it irrelevant. Summerlin v. Commonwealth, 37 Va. App. 288, 557 S.E.2d 731, 2002 Va. App. LEXIS 17 (2002).

In light of the manifest anger and hostility expressed by defendant toward the organization he threatened to bomb, and his hostile voicemail, the evidence presented was sufficient to prove beyond a reasonable doubt that defendant made and communicated a threat to bomb a building with the requisite unlawful intent to make and communicate such a threat. Summerlin v. Commonwealth, 37 Va. App. 288, 557 S.E.2d 731, 2002 Va. App. LEXIS 17 (2002).

Applied in Dance v. Commonwealth, 32 Va. App. 466, 528 S.E.2d 723, 2000 Va. App. LEXIS 360 (2000).

§ 18.2-84. Causing, inciting, etc., commission of act proscribed by § 18.2-83.

Any person fifteen years of age or over, including the parent of any child, who shall cause, encourage, incite, entice or solicit any person, including a child, to commit any act proscribed by the provisions of § 18.2-83, shall be guilty of a Class 5 felony.

History.
Code 1950, § 18.1-78.5; 1960, c. 358; 1975, cc. 14, 15.

§ 18.2-85. Manufacture, possession, use, etc., of fire bombs or explosive materials or devices; penalties.

For the purpose of this section:

"Device" means any instrument, apparatus or contrivance, including its component parts, that is capable of producing or intended to produce an explosion but shall not include fireworks as defined in § 27-95.

"Explosive material" means any chemical compound, mechanical mixture or device that is commonly used or can be used for the purpose of producing an explosion and which contains any oxidizing and combustive agents or other ingredients in such proportions, quantities or packaging that an ignition by fire, friction, concussion, percussion, detonation or by any part of the compound or mixture may cause a sudden generation of highly heated gases. These materials include, but are not limited to, gunpowder, powders for blasting, high explosives, blasting materials, fuses (other than electric circuit breakers), detonators, and other detonating agents and smokeless powder.

"Fire bomb" means any container of a flammable material such as gasoline, kerosene, fuel oil, or other

chemical compound, having a wick composed of any material or a device or other substance which, if set or ignited, is capable of igniting such flammable material or chemical compound but does not include a similar device commercially manufactured and used solely for the purpose of illumination or cooking.

"Hoax explosive device" means any device which by its design, construction, content or characteristics appears to be or to contain a bomb or other destructive device or explosive but which is an imitation of any such device or explosive.

Any person who (i) possesses materials with which fire bombs or explosive materials or devices can be made with the intent to manufacture fire bombs or explosive materials or devices or, (ii) manufactures, transports, distributes, possesses or uses a fire bomb or explosive materials or devices shall be guilty of a Class 5 felony. Any person who constructs, uses, places, sends, or causes to be sent any hoax explosive device so as to intentionally cause another person to believe that such device is a bomb or explosive shall be guilty of a Class 6 felony.

Nothing in this section shall prohibit the authorized manufacture, transportation, distribution, use or possession of any material, substance, or device by a member of the armed forces of the United States, fire fighters or law-enforcement officers, nor shall it prohibit the manufacture, transportation, distribution, use or possession of any material, substance or device to be used solely for scientific research, educational purposes or for any lawful purpose, subject to the provisions of §§ 27-97 and 27-97.2.

History.
Code 1950, § 18.1-78.6; 1968, c. 249; 1972, c. 126; 1975, cc. 14, 15, 497; 1976, c. 526; 1977, c. 326; 1990, cc. 644, 647; 1992, c. 540; 2000, cc. 951, 1065; 2002, cc. 588, 623; 2005, c. 204.

Cross references.
As to prohibition and penalty for possession, manufacture, distribution etc. of weapons of terrorism or hoax device, see, § 18.2-46.6.

Law Review.
For survey of Virginia criminal law for the year 1971-1972, see 58 Va. L. Rev. 1206 (1972). For survey of Virginia criminal law for the year 1974-1975, see 61 Va. L. Rev. 1697 (1975). For annual survey of Virginia law article, "Criminal Law and Procedure," see 47 U. Rich. L. Rev. 143 (2012).

CASE NOTES

Burden of proof on defendant. — Trial court did not violate defendant's due process rights by requiring defendant to show that defendant possessed or manufactured explosive materials or devices for an educational purpose, a scientific purpose, or any lawful purpose, because the last clause of § 18.2-85, constituted a statutory defense for which defendant bore burden of providing supporting evidence. Flanagan v. Commonwealth, 58 Va. App. 681, 714 S.E.2d 212, 2011 Va. App. LEXIS 274 (2011).

Sufficient evidence of fire bomb possession. — There was sufficient evidence to support the trial court's finding beyond a reasonable doubt that defendant possessed the fire bomb where defendant was a passenger in vehicle; the fire bomb was found on the vehicle's passenger side floorboard; defendant was aware of the

object's presence in the vehicle; and although defendant denied knowledge that the object was a fire bomb, the trial court found his testimony to be totally incredible. The trial court was entitled to infer from defendant's "totally incredible" testimony that defendant had lied about his knowledge of the nature of the fire bomb, as well as the events surrounding his arrest, to conceal his guilt. Benton v. Commonwealth, No. 1510-96-1 (Ct. of Appeals May 13, 1997).

Defendant's felony convictions for possession of materials with which explosive materials could be made with intent to manufacture such materials in violation of clause (i) and possession of explosive materials in violation of clause (ii) did not violate the Double Jeopardy Clauses of the United States and Virginia Constitutions even though defendant had been convicted of violating Norfolk City, Va., Code §§ 17.1-43 and 17.1-44(25) because each of the misdemeanor and felony offenses required an element of proof the other offenses did not; sections 17.1-43 and 17.1-44(25) required findings of a dangerous condition liable to cause or contribute to a fire and that a defendant possessed or manufactured fireworks, convictions under clauses (i) and (ii) of this section did not, and a conviction under clause (ii) required a showing that defendant possessed prohibited items other than fireworks. Saunders v. Commonwealth, No. 1195-10-1, 2011 Va. App. LEXIS 384 (Dec. 6, 2011).

No double jeopardy bar. — Defendant's felony convictions for possession of materials with which explosive materials could be made with intent to manufacture such materials in violation of clause (i) and possession of explosive materials in violation of clause (ii) did not violate § 19.2-294 even though defendant had been convicted of violating Norfolk City, Va., Code §§ 17.1-43 and 17.1-44(25) because § 19.2-294 did not bar convictions for felony and misdemeanor charges based on the same act as long as those charges were prosecuted in a single, concurrent evidentiary hearing. Saunders v. Commonwealth, No. 1195-10-1, 2011 Va. App. LEXIS 384 (Dec. 6, 2011).

Sufficient evidence of possession of explosive materials. — Evidence established beyond a reasonable doubt that defendant clearly possessed explosive materials in violation of § 18.2-85 because among the items found in defendant's possession was gunpowder, which was, by explicit statutory designation, explosive material; the trial court explicitly found that defendant was not found guilty under the indictments with respect to firebombs or explosive devices but as to explosive materials. Saunders v. Commonwealth, No. 1195-10-1, 2011 Va. App. LEXIS 384 (Dec. 6, 2011).

CIRCUIT COURT OPINIONS

No double jeopardy bar. — Double jeopardy pursuant to Va. Const., art. I, § 8, U.S. Const., amend. V, or § 19.2-294 did not bar defendant's felony prosecution for charges stemming from the making and storing of hazardous materials for the purpose of manufacturing fireworks, violations of §§ 18.2-85, 10.1-1455, after he pleaded guilty to violations of Norfolk, Va. City Code §§ 17.1-43 and 17.1-44(25), because each of the four statutes required different elements of proof. Commonwealth v. Saunders, 78 Va. Cir. 345, 2009 Va. Cir. LEXIS 173 (Norfolk May 27, 2009).

§ 18.2-86. Setting fire to woods, fences, grass, etc.

If any person maliciously set fire to any wood, fence, grass, straw or other thing capable of spreading fire on land, he shall be guilty of a Class 6 felony.

History.
Code 1950, § 18.1-82; 1960, c. 358; 1968, c. 362; 1975, cc. 14, 15.

Law Review.
For note, "Predicate Offenses for First Degree Felony Murder in Virginia," see 57 Wash. & Lee L. Rev. 561 (2000).

CASE NOTES

Insufficient evidence. — While evidence was sufficient to prove beyond a reasonable doubt that defendant intentionally and maliciously set fire to a couch and that defendant was guilty of arson of the dwelling, the Commonwealth failed to prove that defendant intended to burn the land or, indeed, that any land was burned as a result of defendant's actions. Bradbury v. Commonwealth, 2010 Va. App. LEXIS 421 (Nov. 2, 2010).

§ 18.2-87. Setting woods, etc., on fire intentionally whereby another is damaged or jeopardized.

Any person who intentionally sets or procures another to set fire to any woods, brush, leaves, grass, straw, or any other inflammable substance capable of spreading fire, and who intentionally allows the fire to escape to lands not his own, whereby the property of another is damaged or jeopardized, shall be guilty of a Class 1 misdemeanor, and shall be liable for the full amount of all expenses incurred in fighting the fire.

History.
    Code 1950, § 18.1-83; 1960, c. 358; 1975, cc. 14, 15; 1988, c. 403.

Law Review.
    For note, "Predicate Offenses for First Degree Felony Murder in Virginia," see 57 Wash. & Lee L. Rev. 561 (2000).

Michie's Jurisprudence.
    For related discussion, see 8B M.J. Fires, § 3; 15 M.J. Railroads, § 68.

§ 18.2-87.1. Setting off chemical bombs capable of producing smoke in certain public buildings.

It shall be unlawful for any person to willfully and intentionally set off or cause to be set off any chemical bomb capable of producing smoke in any building used for public assembly or regularly used by the public including, but not limited to, schools, theaters, stores, office buildings, shopping malls, coliseums and arenas. Any person convicted of a violation of this section shall be guilty of a Class 2 misdemeanor.

History.
    1976, c. 153.

Law Review.
    For note, "Predicate Offenses for First Degree Felony Murder in Virginia," see 57 Wash. & Lee L. Rev. 561 (2000).

§ 18.2-88. Carelessly damaging property by fire.

If any person carelessly, negligently or intentionally set any woods or marshes on fire, or set fire to any stubble, brush, straw, or any other substance capable of spreading fire on lands, whereby the property of another is damaged or jeopardized, he shall be guilty of a Class 4 misdemeanor, and shall be liable for the full amount of all expenses incurred in fighting the fire.

History.
    Code 1950, § 18.1-84; 1960, c. 358; 1975, cc. 14, 15.

Law Review.
    For note, "Predicate Offenses for First Degree Felony Murder in Virginia," see 57 Wash. & Lee L. Rev. 561 (2000).

Michie's Jurisprudence.
    For related discussion, see 8B M.J. Fires, §§ 3, 8; 15 M.J. Railroads, § 68.

CASE NOTES

Anyone justified in fighting fire may recover expenses. — The clear meaning of this section is that the negligent party is liable for all expenses incurred in fighting the fire by anyone who is justified in fighting it. United States v. C & O Ry., 130 F.2d 308 (4th Cir. 1942). See also C & O Ry. v. United States, 139 F.2d 632 (4th Cir. 1944).
    That other sections provide for the recovery of expenses in the putting out of fires by state officials only does not nullify the plain provisions of this section to the effect that the negligent party "shall be liable for the full amount of all expenses incurred in fighting the fire." United States v. C & O Ry., 130 F.2d 308 (4th Cir. 1942).
    United States may recover. — The United States was held entitled to recover under this section for expenses incurred in fighting a fire which endangered a national forest. United States v. C & O Ry., 130 F.2d 308 (4th Cir. 1942); C & O Ry. v. United States, 139 F.2d 632 (4th Cir. 1944).

ARTICLE 2.
BURGLARY AND RELATED OFFENSES.

Michie's Jurisprudence.
    For related discussion, see 3A M.J. Burglary and Housebreaking, §§ 2-5, 9, 10.

§ 18.2-89. Burglary; how punished.

If any person break and enter the dwelling house of another in the nighttime with intent to commit a felony or any larceny therein, he shall be guilty of burglary, punishable as a Class 3 felony; provided, however, that if such person was armed with a deadly weapon at the time of such entry, he shall be guilty of a Class 2 felony.

History.
    Code 1950, § 18.1-86; 1960, c. 358; 1975, cc. 14, 15.

Cross references.
    For provision making it unlawful to work or volunteer on school grounds following convictions of certain sex offenses, see § 18.2-370.4. As to requirement of saliva or tissue sample for DNA analysis after arrest for a violent felony, see § 19.2-310.2:1. For definition of "barrier crime" as including a conviction of burglary as set out in § 18.2-89 et seq., or an equivalent offense in another state, and prohibition against child welfare agencies and foster and adoptive homes approved by child-placing agencies hiring for certain compensated employment persons who have committed such an offense, see §§ 63.2-1719, 63.2-1720. As to report to children's residential facility for which a background check is being performed on whether the applicant has ever been convicted of or is the subject of pending charges for various crimes, including burglary as set out in § 18.2-89 et seq., or an equivalent offense in another state, see § 63.2-1726.

Law Review.
    For note, "Reformation of Burglary," see 11 Wm. & Mary L. Rev. 211 (1969). For survey of Virginia criminal law and procedure for the year 1969-1970, see 56 Va. L. Rev. 1572 (1970). For survey of Virginia criminal law for the year 1974-1975, see 61 Va. L. Rev. 1697 (1975). For note, "Predicate Offenses for First Degree Felony Murder in Virginia," see 57 Wash. & Lee L. Rev. 561 (2000). For

2007 annual survey article, "Criminal Law and Procedure," see 42 U. Rich. L. Rev. 311 (2007).

Michie's Jurisprudence.
For related discussion, see 21A M.J. Words and Phrases.

CASE NOTES

The term "dwelling house" in this section means a place which human beings regularly use for sleeping. Turner v. Commonwealth, 33 Va. App. 88, 531 S.E.2d 619, 2000 Va. App. LEXIS 566 (2000).

Following principles demonstrate how a house must be "regularly used" to qualify as a dwelling under § 18.2-89: (1) a person may have multiple dwelling houses, and each dwelling house must have humans sleep in it and engage in other functions typically associated with habitation; (2) the house must be maintained to make it suitable for immediate or rapid habitation; (3) a person must inhabit the house on a usual or periodic basis; and (4) when the occupant is absent, he or she must intend to return to the house within a usual or periodic time. Giles v. Commonwealth, 51 Va. App. 449, 658 S.E.2d 703, 2008 Va. App. LEXIS 167 (2008), aff'd, 277 Va. 369, 672 S.E.2d 879, 2009 Va. LEXIS 42 (2009).

A dwelling is no longer a "dwelling house" for purposes of this section when its occupants leave it without any intention to return. Rash v. Commonwealth, 9 Va. App. 22, 383 S.E.2d 749 (1989).

Defendant's burglary conviction was reversed where the house that defendant broke into and entered was no longer a "dwelling house" for purposes of § 18.2-89 since the homeowner's testimony disclosed he had already left the property with no intent to return to the house. Barts v. Commonwealth, No. 0556-01-3, 2002 Va. App. LEXIS 110 (Ct. of Appeals Feb. 19, 2002).

Vacation home is dwelling house even when unoccupied. — Court of appeals did not err in affirming a circuit court's ruling that the house defendant broke into satisfied the dwelling house requirement of § 18.2-89 because the house was analogous to a vacation home; vacation homes are dwelling houses even when unoccupied at the time of a break in. Giles v. Commonwealth, 277 Va. 369, 672 S.E.2d 879, 2009 Va. LEXIS 42 (2009).

Commonwealth satisfied its burden of proving that the structure defendant broke into was used as a habitation to satisfy the "dwelling house" requirement of § 18.2-89 because the contents of the house and evidence of the owner's behavior in relation to the house were probative of whether it was used periodically for the purpose of habitation; a house is a dwelling house pursuant to § 18.2-89 when the house is used for habitation, including periodic habitation, and periodic habitation does not require that the house be used at regular intervals but rather requires that when the house is used, it is used for the purpose of habitation. Giles v. Commonwealth, 277 Va. 369, 672 S.E.2d 879, 2009 Va. LEXIS 42 (2009).

Structure does not have to be physically inhabited every day or week or month to be a dwelling house when the danger to personal safety that is sought to be protected does not dissipate simply because the structure is not occupied on a regular basis; the danger continues irrespective of frequency of habitation so long as when the structure is used, it is used for the purpose of habitation, and a dwelling house does not lose its character as such simply because a person is absent for either a regular or irregular period of time. Giles v. Commonwealth, 277 Va. 369, 672 S.E.2d 879, 2009 Va. LEXIS 42 (2009).

Evidence of "dwelling house." — Commonwealth presented sufficient evidence to show that a house was a dwelling because the owner of the house slept there about one weekend per month, and the house was maintained for immediate occupancy; habitation sufficient to constitute a dwelling house under § 18.2-89 includes maintenance for reasonably prompt habitation and at a minimum periodic habitation. Giles v. Commonwealth, 51 Va. App. 449, 658 S.E.2d 703, 2008 Va. App. LEXIS 167 (2008), aff'd, 277 Va. 369, 672 S.E.2d 879, 2009 Va. LEXIS 42 (2009).

Statutory burglary conviction under § 18.2-91 was improper as the house involved in the burglary was not a "dwelling house," as that term was defined in §§ 18.2-89, 18.2-90, and 18.2-91, in that the record contained no evidence that the house was used for habitation as no one slept there, the house was unfurnished, and no one used it for the usual activities of life. Additionally, there was no

evidence that anyone who had used the house for habitation had any intention of resuming that use. Johns v. Commonwealth, 53 Va. App. 742, 675 S.E.2d 211, 2009 Va. App. LEXIS 172 (2009).

Sufficient evidence that defendant was armed with a deadly weapon. — In a prosecution on a charge of burglary while armed with a deadly weapon, the evidence was sufficient to prove that defendant was armed with a deadly weapon when he entered the victim's home as the evidence showed that defendant admitted to the police that he obtained the knife from another home, that he entered the home through the screened-in porch, that the screen had been cut, and that a knife was recovered near the victim's keys, which were laying in a neighbor's yard. It was a reasonable inference that the recovered knife was the knife used to attack the victim, especially since the victim testified that the recovered knife did not belong to her. Morales v. Commonwealth, 2010 Va. App. LEXIS 452 (Nov. 16, 2010).

Intent constitutes an essential part of the crime of burglary and should be both alleged and proved. Vaughn v. Commonwealth, 51 Va. (10 Gratt.) 758 (1853).

Specific intent is an essential element of the crime of statutory burglary and it is necessary for the intent to be established as a matter of fact before a conviction can be had. Williams v. Peyton, 414 F.2d 776 (4th Cir. 1969).

Specific intent is an essential element of burglary. Taylor v. Commonwealth, 207 Va. 326, 150 S.E.2d 135 (1966).

Intent is almost always established by circumstantial evidence. Williams v. Peyton, 414 F.2d 776 (4th Cir. 1969).

Intent to commit felony may be inferred. — The intent to commit a felony may be inferred from the defendant's unauthorized presence in a building at night. Witt v. Commonwealth, 15 Va. App. 215, 422 S.E.2d 465 (1992).

Sufficient evidence supported a burglary conviction, although defendant was discovered in an apartment before any theft took place, where defendant's intent to commit larceny was implied when defendant entered the apartment only after witnessing its occupant leave and defendant's testimony regarding the reason for entering the apartment was not credible. Newby v. Commonwealth, 2010 Va. App. LEXIS 210 (May 18, 2010).

Conviction reversed where incorrect intent shown. — Defendant's conviction for breaking and entering with intent to commit larceny was reversed, where circumstantial evidence showing a nighttime entry and assault of a female resident reflected an intent to rape or ravish rather than an intent to steal from the victim. Maynard v. Commonwealth, 10 Va. App. 15, 389 S.E.2d 910 (1990).

Intent to do serious physical harm. — Defendant's burglary conviction in violation of § 18.2-89 was appropriate because the evidence was sufficient and the trial court was entitled to draw on all the circumstances shown by the evidence to determine what defendant's intent actually was when he entered the victim's apartment. Considering defendant's prior robbery of the victim, defendant's threat to the victim with a gun a few hours earlier, and defendant's threats to the victim as he was unlawfully entering the victim's apartment, it was appropriately determined that defendant intended to do serious physical harm to the victim at the time of entry. Young v. Commonwealth, 2010 Va. App. LEXIS 164 (Apr. 27, 2010).

Breaking which will constitute burglary may be actual or constructive. Clarke v. Commonwealth, 66 Va. (25 Gratt.) 908 (1874).

Constructive breaking includes entrance effected by threats, fraud, or conspiracy. Clarke v. Commonwealth, 66 Va. (25 Gratt.) 908 (1874).

Opening of a secured window is sufficient to constitute the element of breaking. Bright v. Commonwealth, 4 Va. App. 248, 356 S.E.2d 443 (1987).

Facts showing insufficient breaking. — D. and H. jointly rented a room, of which each has a key. C. rented an adjoining room, the doors of the two rooms entering upon the same porch near each other. They frequently interchanged visits. H. and C. conspired to steal D.'s goods in his absence, and H. opened the door with his key, and they entered the room, and took and carried away the trunk of D., with its contents. This was not such a breaking as would constitute burglary in C. Clarke v. Commonwealth, 66 Va. (25 Gratt.) 908 (1874).

The removal of a cloth from one of the nails by which it hung over a window was not a sufficient breaking to constitute burglary. Hunter v. Commonwealth, 48 Va. (7 Gratt.) 641 (1850).

Possession of stolen goods as evidence of guilt. — The law in Virginia is well settled that the possession of stolen goods is of itself not even prima facie evidence of housebreaking or of burglary. But when goods have been obtained by means of a burglary or housebreaking, the fact of such possession is a most material circumstance to be considered by the jury, and when, in addition to such possession, other inculpatory circumstances are proved, such, for example, as the refusal of the accused to give any account, or his giving a false account of how he came by the goods, such proof will warrant a conviction. Stallard v. Commonwealth, 130 Va. 769, 107 S.E. 722 (1921). See also Hall's Case, 44 Va. (3 Gratt.) 593 (1846); Walker v. Commonwealth, 69 Va. (28 Gratt.) 969 (1877); Taliaferro v. Commonwealth, 77 Va. 411 (1883); Wright v. Commonwealth, 82 Va. 183 (1886); Gravely v. Commonwealth, 86 Va. 396, 10 S.E. 431 (1889); Porterfield v. Commonwealth, 91 Va. 801, 22 S.E. 352 (1895); Henderson v. Commonwealth, 98 Va. 794, 34 S.E. 881 (1900); Williams v. Commonwealth, 193 Va. 764, 71 S.E.2d 73 (1952).

Unexplained or falsely explained possession of goods recently stolen in a burglary, coupled with other inculpatory circumstances, will sustain a conviction of burglary where the sufficiency of the evidence is challenged. Schaum v. Commonwealth, 215 Va. 498, 211 S.E.2d 73 (1975).

Under Virginia law, upon proof of a breaking and entering and a theft of goods, and if the evidence warrants an inference that the breaking and entering and the theft were committed at the same time by the same person and as part of the same transaction, the exclusive possession of the stolen goods shortly thereafter, unexplained or falsely denied, has the same efficiency to give rise to an inference that the possessor is guilty of the breaking and entering as to an inference that he is guilty of the larceny. Bright v. Commonwealth, 4 Va. App. 248, 356 S.E.2d 443 (1987).

Rational factfinder could conclude that defendant was guilty of burglary because defendant was found in possession of stolen checks shortly after the victim's son discovered the burglary of the victim's home, and that fact gave rise to the reasonable inference that defendant broke into the victim's home and took the checks from her checkbook. Delain v. Commonwealth, 2012 Va. App. LEXIS 340 (Oct. 23, 2012).

Strict proof of the identity of the articles stolen is required unless the possession is recent. Cook v. Commonwealth, 214 Va. 686, 204 S.E.2d 252 (1974).

The identity of stolen property which is incapable of strict proof is not required to be strictly proved where the possession is very recent. Cook v. Commonwealth, 214 Va. 686, 204 S.E.2d 252 (1974).

Fingerprint evidence. — A latent fingerprint found at the scene of the crime tends to show that the accused was at the scene of the crime. However, only if the circumstances regarding the fingerprint show that the accused was at the scene of the crime at the time the crime was committed, may one rationally infer that the accused committed the crime. Thus, where defendant's handprint was found outside the office broken into and near the point of entry, it established that the defendant, at some point in time, was in the dance studio, but since neither the handprint nor the circumstances surrounding its discovery established when the defendant was in the dance studio, the presence of the handprint created no inference that the defendant broke into the office and the burglary conviction should be reversed. Varker v. Commonwealth, 14 Va. App. 445, 417 S.E.2d 7 (1992).

Although the only fingerprint of defendant's was found on the back door of the house, and not at the point of entry, it was a clear and reasonable inference that the same person made efforts to enter other parts of the house by, inter alia, removing wood from around the window of the back door. That evidence, in conjunction with testimony that the victim did not know defendant, denied authorizing him to be on her property, and excluded him as a worker authorized to be there, was sufficient to support defendant's conviction for burglary. Green v. Commonwealth, — Va. App. —, — S.E.2d —, 2005 Va. App. LEXIS 266 (July 12, 2005).

Overt acts constituting crime under this section and § 18.2-91 may be the same. — The overt acts constituting the crime of burglary under this section, and constituting housebreaking with intent to commit larceny under § 18.2-91, now defined as statutory burglary, may be the same, that is, the breaking and

entering. The intent with which the particular crime is committed, the character of the house entered, and the time of the occurrence determine the nature and degree of the crime. Proof of the intent, of the character of the house entered, and of the time of the breaking and entering, or entering without breaking, are matters of evidence. Smyth v. Morrison, 200 Va. 728, 107 S.E.2d 430 (1959).

Indictment alleging burglary is good. — An indictment which charges a breaking into a house in the nighttime with intent to steal, and stealing therefrom, is an indictment for burglary, and is good. Wright v. Commonwealth, 82 Va. 183 (1886).

Allegation of actual larceny in an indictment for burglary or housebreaking is simply to show the intent to commit a felony, which intent is an essential part of these crimes. Speers v. Commonwealth, 58 Va. (17 Gratt.) 570 (1867).

One may be found guilty of larceny, though acquitted of burglary. — Where the indictment charged not only breaking and entering, but the stealing of a trunk and its contents, of a stated value, the prisoner, though acquitted of burglary, might be found guilty of larceny. Clarke v. Commonwealth, 66 Va. (25 Gratt.) 908 (1874).

And one charged with burglary and larceny may be found guilty of housebreaking or larceny. — One charged with breaking and entering a dwelling house of another in the nighttime, with intent to commit larceny, and the commission of larceny at one and the same time may, depending upon the evidence, be acquitted of burglary and found guilty of housebreaking, or guilty of larceny, as the proof justifies. Smyth v. Morrison, 200 Va. 728, 107 S.E.2d 430 (1959).

A conviction was not void on the ground that upon defendant's plea of guilty to an indictment charging burglary the court found him guilty of, and sentenced him for, housebreaking and larceny. Smyth v. Morrison, 200 Va. 728, 107 S.E.2d 430 (1959).

Robbery, burglary, grand larceny and abduction, are each treated separately and are governed by a separate statutory provision. Austin v. Peyton, 279 F. Supp. 227 (W.D. Va. 1968).

No lesser included offense of trespass. — When defendant was indicted for burglary, in violation of § 18.2-89, he could not validly be convicted of trespass, in violation of § 18.2-119, as statutory trespass was not a lesser included offense of common-law burglary, unless he acquiesced in such a conviction, and counsel's statements leading the trial court to believe it could convict defendant of trespass if it found the evidence insufficient to convict him of burglary, were such an acquiescence. Freeman v. Commonwealth, No. 0796-02-3, 2003 Va. App. LEXIS 331 (Ct. of Appeals June 10, 2003).

Statutory burglary was a lesser-included offense of common-law burglary. — Conviction for common-law burglary was vacated and the case was remanded for a new sentencing hearing on the offense of statutory burglary because statutory burglary was a lesser-included offense of common-law burglary; the additional element of requiring that the offense take place in the nighttime was the only distinction between the two forms of burglary. Wright v. Commonwealth, 49 Va. App. 312, 641 S.E.2d 119, 2007 Va. App. LEXIS 60 (2007).

Attempted burglary. — Evidence supported defendant's conviction of attempted burglary, as a rational trier of fact could conclude that defendant intended to break into a residence and, by opening an outer glass door and trying to force open an wooden inner door, committed direct acts in furtherance of that goal. Shelton v. Commonwealth, — Va. App. —, — S.E.2d —, 2008 Va. App. LEXIS 255 (May 27, 2008).

Restitution may be ordered for insurer. — The statutes declare a legislative intent to provide restitution for the victims of crimes, including corporations. One cannot conclude that the legislature intended by the most recent legislation to limit the power of the courts to order restitution. Therefore, it was proper for the court in the instant case to order burglar to pay restitution to insurance carrier of victims. Alger v. Commonwealth, 19 Va. App. 252, 450 S.E.2d 765 (1994).

Burden of proof. — When the Commonwealth's evidence proves a breaking and entering and a theft of goods and justifies an inference that both offenses were committed at the same time by the same person as a part of the same criminal enterprise, if the evidence proves further that the goods stolen were found soon thereafter in the possession of the accused, the Commonwealth has made a prima facie case that the accused broke and entered. At that point, although the ultimate burden of proof remains with the Commonwealth, the burden of going forward with the evidence shifts to the accused. Brown v. Commonwealth, 213 Va. 748, 195 S.E.2d 703 (1973); Schaum v. Commonwealth, 215 Va. 498, 211 S.E.2d 73 (1975).

When a prima facie case of breaking and entering has been established, if the accused fails to go forward with the evidence in justification of possession, his failure is an inculpatory circumstance which, considered with the circumstance of possession, is sufficient to support a conviction of breaking and entering. Brown v. Commonwealth, 213 Va. 748, 195 S.E.2d 703 (1973).

If the accused elects to go forward with the evidence, he bears the burden of proving the truth of his evidence in justification of possession, and if he fails, his failure is another such inculpatory circumstance. Brown v. Commonwealth, 213 Va. 748, 195 S.E.2d 703 (1973).

Where the record disclosed no evidence that a family member of the victim opened the secured window through which it was alleged that defendant entered burglarized dwelling, the Commonwealth was not required to examine every person who might have had access to the window in order to establish a prima facie case of burglary. Bright v. Commonwealth, 4 Va. App. 248, 356 S.E.2d 443 (1987).

Facts showing "nighttime." — Because the burglar apparently needed to turn on the lights to effectuate the burglary, the jury reasonably could have inferred that it was dark at the time of the burglary. Inman v. Commonwealth, No. 0939-88-3 (Ct. of Appeals March 27, 1990).

Where evidence proved that the residence was burglarized sometime between 8:00 p.m. on July 1, 1992, and 4:00 p.m. the following day; melted candle wax was discovered throughout the house, including the victim's bedroom, where she kept her jewelry; and further, no artificial light was necessary in the house during the daytime, the jury was entitled to infer that there was sufficient evidence to support a conviction for nighttime burglary. Pair v. Commonwealth, No. 0451-93-2 (Ct. of Appeals June 14, 1994).

Court would not take judicial notice of records. — The Commonwealth failed to establish that defendant broke and entered victims' house in the nighttime even though the Commonwealth argued that the court could take judicial notice of records (not in evidence in the case) that on June 3, 1986, the sun set at 8:19 p.m. and rose the following morning at 5:46 a.m., and that it was reasonable to assume that the family did not retire prior to 8:19 p.m. White v. Commonwealth, No. 0056-89-1 (Ct. of Appeals July 24, 1990).

Sufficiency of evidence. — The record was not so lacking in evidence of the petitioner's specific intent to commit larceny that a conviction for burglary was constitutionally precluded. Williams v. Peyton, 414 F.2d 776 (4th Cir. 1969).

Evidence that defendant broke into a victim's home by popping open a screen door and entering it armed with a knife, and that defendant attempted to kill the victim, was sufficient to sustain defendant's burglary conviction. Singleton v. Commonwealth, No. 1432-02-1, 2003 Va. App. LEXIS 185 (Ct. of Appeals Apr. 1, 2003).

Where a neighbor heard noise at the victim's house, saw defendant leaving the victim's house with a cord dangling from a pocket, defendant cursed upon realizing that the neighbor had seen defendant, and defendant gave conflicting statements as to defendant's whereabouts on the night of the incident, the Commonwealth's circumstantial evidence was sufficient to support the convictions for burglary and petit larceny. Tucker v. Commonwealth, No. 1288-02-2, 2003 Va. App. LEXIS 347 (Ct. of Appeals June 17, 2003).

Evidence was sufficient to find defendant guilty of felony burglary in violation of § 18.2-89, where defendant was identified by the victim who saw him at her window, there was blood that matched defendant's DNA on the inside windowsill of the victim's home and on a chair that defendant stood on to reach the window, and two other witnesses identified defendant; defendant's intent to commit larceny was inferable where there was no evidence of a contrary intent, and defendant's explanation that he was intoxicated and confused and thought that he was at his own home lacked merit. Carter v. Commonwealth, No. 1051-02-2, 2003 Va. App. LEXIS 390 (Ct. of Appeals July 8, 2003).

Victim's identification along with a wide range of circumstantial evidence, including the fact that defendant was acting strangely the day after the incident and had changed defendant's appearance,

that clothing matching what the victim said the attacker wore was found in defendant's home, and that duct tape like that used on the victim was found in defendant's home were sufficient to support defendant's convictions for rape, robbery, statutory burglary, malicious wounding, and unlawful wounding in the commission of a felony. Parker v. Commonwealth, 2009 Va. App. LEXIS 235 (May 19, 2009).

Evidence was sufficient to support defendant's convictions for robbery, shooting within an occupied dwelling, using a firearm in the commission of a felony, armed burglary, and malicious wounding, because ample evidence supported a finding that defendant was a perpetrator in a home invasion: three of the victims identified defendant at trial, and a co-defendant testified that defendant said he intended to rob the home, that he entered the home wearing a bullet-proof vest and armed with a handgun, and that he later told the co-defendant that he had struck one of the victim's in the head. Trial court did not abuse discretion in ruling on misidentification of accomplices by witnesses. Streater v. Commonwealth, 2009 Va. App. LEXIS 504 (Nov. 10, 2009).

Evidence was sufficient to establish that defendant entered the victim's home without permission because defendant told an investigator that he entered his uncle's home without permission and damage to plywood that fit over a window and to the outside of a door was consistent with illegal entry. Hairston v. Commonwealth, 2006 Va. App. LEXIS 612 (Nov. 20, 2006).

Defendant's confession and the corroborating DNA evidence was sufficient to support defendant's convictions for murder, rape, statutory burglary, and robbery. Farmer v. Commonwealth, 61 Va. App. 402, 737 S.E.2d 32, 2013 Va. App. LEXIS 34 (2013).

Common scheme or plan in burglary. — That three businesses, in close proximity, were burglarized within six days; that the same method of entry was used in each case; and that in each burglary, cash registers or parts of them were stolen, allowed the trial court to find that the crimes were connected or constituted parts of a common scheme or plan, Va. Sup. Ct. R. 3A:6(b), to such a degree that justice did not require that the charges be severed under Va. Sup. Ct. R. 3A:10(c). Kinnard v. Commonwealth, 2008 Va. App. LEXIS 340 (July 22, 2008).

Sentence enhancement. — Statutory burglary under § 18.2-89 qualifies as a violent felony under 18 U.S.C.S. § 924(e)(2)(B)(ii) for purposes of sentence enhancement. King v. United States, 214 F. Supp. 2d 669, 2002 U.S. Dist. LEXIS 14911 (E.D. Va. 2002).

Sentence within range set by legislature is proper. — Trial court did not abuse its discretion in imposing a 43-year sentence against defendant, as said sentence was within the ranges set by the legislature and well below the total statutory maximum for the various felony offenses for which he was convicted. Clark v. Commonwealth, — Va. App. —, — S.E.2d —, 2008 Va. App. LEXIS 234 (May 13, 2008).

Applied in Hitt v. Commonwealth, 43 Va. App. 473, 598 S.E.2d 783, 2004 Va. App. LEXIS 320 (2004).

§ 18.2-90. Entering dwelling house, etc., with intent to commit murder, rape, robbery or arson; penalty.

If any person in the nighttime enters without breaking or in the daytime breaks and enters or enters and conceals himself in a dwelling house or an adjoining, occupied outhouse or in the nighttime enters without breaking or at any time breaks and enters or enters and conceals himself in any building permanently affixed to realty, or any ship, vessel or river craft or any railroad car, or any automobile, truck or trailer, if such automobile, truck or trailer is used as a dwelling or place of human habitation, with intent to commit murder, rape, robbery or arson in violation of §§ 18.2-77, 18.2-79 or § 18.2-80, he shall be deemed guilty of statutory burglary, which offense shall be a Class 3 felony. However, if such person was armed with a deadly weapon at the time of such entry, he shall be guilty of a Class 2 felony.

History.

Code 1950, § 18.1-88; 1960, c. 358; 1970, c. 381; 1975, cc. 14, 15; 1985, c. 110; 1992, c. 546; 1997, c. 832; 2004, c. 842.

Cross references.

For provision making it unlawful to work or volunteer on school grounds following convictions of certain sex offenses, see § 18.2-370.4. As to Sex Offenders and Crimes Against Minors Registry, see § 9.1-900 et seq. As to requirement of saliva or tissue sample for DNA analysis after arrest for a violent felony, see § 19.2-310.2:1.

Law Review.

For survey of Virginia criminal law for the year 1971-1972, see 58 Va. L. Rev. 1206 (1972). For note, "Predicate Offenses for First Degree Felony Murder in Virginia," see 57 Wash. & Lee L. Rev. 561 (2000). For survey of Virginia criminal law and procedure for the year 2004-2005, see 40 U. Rich. L. Rev. 197 (2005).

Michie's Jurisprudence.

For related discussion, see 21A M.J. Words and Phrases.

CASE NOTES

I. In General.
II. Elements of Offense.
    A. Intent.
    B. Breaking and Entering.
    C. Dwelling House, etc.
III. Other Matters.

I. IN GENERAL.

The offense of housebreaking is purely statutory in Virginia. Williams v. Commonwealth, 193 Va. 764, 71 S.E.2d 73 (1952).

Offense qualifies as a generic burglary. — Defendant's offenses that were in violation of §§ 18.2-90 and 18.2-91 did qualify as generic burglaries, for purposes of 18 U.S.C.S. § 924(e). United States v. Joshua, 259 F. Supp. 2d 446, 2003 U.S. Dist. LEXIS 6963 (E.D. Va. 2003).

In a case in which defendant pled guilty to possession of a firearm by a convicted felon in violation of 18 U.S.C.S. § 922(g)(1), and he objected to the assertion in his presentence report that he qualified as an armed career criminal under the Armed Career Criminal Act, 18 U.S.C.S. § 924(e), he argued unsuccessfully that one of the offenses the probation report cited as a predicate offense failed to qualify. Under §§ 18.2-90 and 18.2-91, defendant's offense of breaking and entering a shop with the intent to commit larceny qualified as generic burglary under the Armed Career Criminal Act, and, under the modified categorical approach, the appropriate documents necessarily established that he pled guilty to and was convicted of generic burglary. United States v. Baxter, 2010 U.S. Dist. LEXIS 1678 (W.D. Va. Jan. 11, 2010), aff'd, 642 F.3d 475, 2011 U.S. App. LEXIS 8476 (4th Cir. Va. 2011).

In a case in which defendant was sentenced to 27 months of imprisonment for violating 18 U.S.C.S. § 922(g)(1), the district court incorrectly found that the Armed Career Criminal Act did not apply to defendant. Defendant had three violations of § 18.2-90, and, contrary to the district court's determination, his breaking and entering of a restaurant and a market were generic burglaries under the Armed Career Criminal Act. United States v. Foster, 662 F.3d 291, 2011 U.S. App. LEXIS 23807 (4th Cir. 2011).

This section is limited by § 18.2-78. Compton v. Commonwealth, 190 Va. 48, 55 S.E.2d 446 (1949).

Timing of offense is not essential element of offense. — Whenever there is a breaking and entering of a dwelling with a larcenous intent, the timing of the offense is not an essential element of the offense. Griffin v. Commonwealth, 13 Va. App. 409, 412 S.E.2d 709 (1991).

Since breaking and entering of a dwelling, at any time, is the essential element of the offense, the indictment's allegation that the offense occurred in the daytime was nothing more than surplusage. Griffin v. Commonwealth, 13 Va. App. 409, 412 S.E.2d 709 (1991).

Because breaking and entering a dwelling "at any time" with the requisite intent is a violation of this section, the specification "daytime" was neither "legally essential" to charge a violation of the statute nor varied the conduct which the statute proscribes. Griffin v. Commonwealth, 13 Va. App. 409, 412 S.E.2d 709 (1991).

Unnecessary words that describe, limit or qualify statutory necessary words must be proved. — Where unnecessary words in an indictment describe, limit or qualify the statutory necessary words, the unnecessary words have to be proven as charged. Griffin v. Commonwealth, 13 Va. App. 409, 412 S.E.2d 709 (1991).

The addition of the word "daytime" in the defendant's indictment more particularly defined the term "any time," the general span of time within which the conduct of breaking and entering the dwelling is statutorily described; the phrase "any time" is not, however, a statutorily necessary word. Griffin v. Commonwealth, 13 Va. App. 409, 412 S.E.2d 709 (1991).

Evidence sufficient to show that appellant entered home after sunset. — Evidence at trial was sufficient to prove beyond a reasonable doubt that appellant entered victim's home after sunset. Although victim returned home when it was not "fully dark," she put away her groceries, sat to watch television, and heard him enter after she turned the lights on. Dailey v. Commonwealth, No. 0555-97-2 (Ct. of Appeals Dec. 9, 1997).

The addition of "daytime" was surplusage that designated the general time of the offense but did not describe, limit, or qualify the conduct which is statutorily proscribed. Griffin v. Commonwealth, 13 Va. App. 409, 412 S.E.2d 709 (1991).

This section and § 18.2-91 might well have been combined, for they refer directly, though not solely, to, and define as an offense, the breaking and entering of a dwelling house in the daytime, with intent to commit murder, rape or robbery (this section) or larceny, or any felony other than murder, rape, or robbery (§ 18.2-91). The overt acts constituting the crime are the same — that is, the breaking and entering. The intent with which the particular crime is committed does not change its general nature or character, because whichever intent is shown, the crime is of the same nature — that is, a felony of the specific class denounced by these sections. Sullivan v. Commonwealth, 157 Va. 867, 161 S.E. 297 (1931).

Under this and the following section, housebreaking or store-breaking, as a consummated crime, includes both a nighttime entry without breaking and a breaking and entry in the daytime or nighttime under stated conditions, as precisely the same felony. An attempt to commit the offense may be perpetrated either by the attempt to enter without breaking or by the attempt to break and enter. Willoughby v. Smyth, 194 Va. 267, 72 S.E.2d 636 (1952).

Applied in Scott v. Commonwealth, 228 Va. 519, 323 S.E.2d 572 (1984); Martin v. Taylor, 857 F.2d 958 (4th Cir. 1988); Turner v. Commonwealth, 38 Va. App. 851, 568 S.E.2d 468, 2002 Va. App. LEXIS 525 (2002); Rowland v. Commonwealth, 281 Va. 396, 707 S.E.2d 331, 2011 Va. LEXIS 60 (2011).

II. ELEMENTS OF OFFENSE.

A. Intent.

Specific intent is an essential element of burglary. Taylor v. Commonwealth, 207 Va. 326, 150 S.E.2d 135 (1966).

Intent must be proved. — Where a statute makes an offense consist of an act combined with a particular intent, such intent is as necessary to be proved as the act itself, and it is necessary for the intent to be established as a matter of fact before a conviction can be had. Surmise and speculation as to the existence of the intent are not sufficient, and no intent in law or mere legal presumption, differing from the intent in fact, can be allowed to supply the place of the latter. Dixon v. Commonwealth, 197 Va. 380, 89 S.E.2d 344 (1955).

Intent not satisfied by showing entry contrary to will of occupier. — Even where the entry is contrary to the will of the occupier of the premises, the requirement that a person breaks and enters any banking house with intent to commit robbery under this section is not satisfied by the mere showing that the accused entered the bank with the intent to commit robbery contrary to the will of the occupier of the premises. Johns v. Commonwealth, 10 Va. App. 283, 392 S.E.2d 487 (1990).

Inference of intent to rob. — Jurors were not required to accept defendant's statement that he did not want victim to see him as indicative of intent only to commit larceny; they could reasonably infer that he broke and entered home with intent to rob. Alston v. Commonwealth, No. 0468-01-4 CHIEF, 2002 Va. App. LEXIS 252 (Ct. of Appeals Apr. 30, 2002).

A person who enters a store intending to commit robbery therein enters the store unlawfully. Clark v. Commonwealth, 22 Va. App. 673, 472 S.E.2d 663 (1996), aff'd on reh'g en banc, 24 Va. App. 253, 481 S.E.2d 495 (1997).

Sufficient evidence of intent. — There was sufficient evidence for a trial judge to infer that defendant's specific intent when he unlawfully entered an apartment with a firearm and ordered the occupant to get down was to commit one of the felonies enumerated in § 18.2-90, such as murder, even though the trial court found that the evidence was insufficient to prove a specific intent to rob as required for attempted robbery. Collins v. Commonwealth, — Va. App. —, — S.E.2d —, 2005 Va. App. LEXIS 380 (Oct. 4, 2005).

Given that the Commonwealth presented sufficient evidence that defendant burglarized an apartment with the requisite specific intent and malice to disfigure, maim, disable, or kill at least three of the victims, without provocation, his convictions based upon said actions were upheld on appeal. Slayton v. Commonwealth, — Va. App. —, — S.E.2d —, 2007 Va. App. LEXIS 180 (May 1, 2007).

Evidence was sufficient to prove that defendant intended to commit arson where defendant unlawfully entered defendant's wife's home in violation of a protective order, knowing both that defendant's wife was not there and that defendant was not permitted to be there, and where defendant intentionally and maliciously set fire to the couch and removed the parties' cat from the home. Bradbury v. Commonwealth, 2010 Va. App. LEXIS 421 (Nov. 2, 2010).

B. Breaking and Entering.

Right to possession, not ownership, determines whether entry lawful. — Where a defendant and his wife had been separated for a year and the wife had remained in the family residence, the defendant's proprietary interest was relegated to the wife's superior possessory interest and right to exclusive habitation such that the defendant's acts in breaking and entering the home, accompanied by the requisite unlawful intent, offended the wife's right of habitation and constituted burglary in violation of this section, notwithstanding his joint ownership of the property. Turner v. Commonwealth, 33 Va. App. 88, 531 S.E.2d 619, 2000 Va. App. LEXIS 566 (2000).

"Housebreaking" and "storebreaking" are proper descriptive terms. — The descriptive words "housebreaking" and "storebreaking" have long been applied to the statutory offenses defined in this and the following section and are proper descriptive terms of the statutory offense. Willoughby v. Smyth, 194 Va. 267, 72 S.E.2d 636 (1952).

The word "break," used in this section, is borrowed from the law of burglary. If then, in any case, a person by even slight force removes or displaces anything attached to the house as a part thereof, and relied on by the occupant for the safety of the house, it is a breaking within the meaning of this section, if the other constituent parts of the offense exist. Finch v. Commonwealth, 55 Va. (14 Gratt.) 643 (1858).

Slight force sufficient to constitute "breaking." — Breaking, as an element of the crime of burglary, may be either actual or constructive. Actual breaking involves the application of some force, slight though it may be, whereby the entrance is effected. Merely pushing open a door, turning the key, lifting the latch, or resort to other slight physical force is sufficient to constitute this element of the crime. Phoung v. Commonwealth, 15 Va. App. 457, 424 S.E.2d 712 (1992).

A "breaking" within the meaning of this section may be actual or constructive. Hucks v. Commonwealth, 33 Va. App. 168, 531 S.E.2d 658, 2000 Va. App. LEXIS 568 (2000), overruled in part by Velasquez v. Commonwealth, 276 Va. 326, 661 S.E.2d 454 (2008).

No breaking required where the entry occurs at night. — Defendant's burglary conviction under § 18.2-91 was supported by the evidence since no breaking was required under § 18.2-90 since defendant entered the apartment in the nighttime; intent to commit an assault and battery was shown as defendant was wearing body armor, and carrying brass knuckles and a gun. Consent was not a defense to statutory burglary. Jones v. Commonwealth, — Va. App. —, — S.E.2d —, 2009 Va. App. LEXIS 44 (Feb. 3, 2009), aff'd, 279 Va. 295, 687 S.E.2d 738 (2010).

Breaking was not a required element to support a conviction for statutory burglary under § 18.2-90 where defendant's entry occurred at night and, therefore, the fact that an occupant of the house opened the door to defendant did not render the evidence insufficient to support a conviction under § 18.2-91. Stegall v. Commonwealth, 2010 Va. App. LEXIS 137 (Apr. 6, 2010).

Entry must be contrary to will of occupier. — A breaking, either actual or constructive, to support a conviction of burglary, must have resulted in an entrance contrary to the will of the occupier of the house. Opie v. Commonwealth, No. 2173-99-1, 2000 Va. App. LEXIS 633 (Ct. of Appeals Aug. 29, 2000).

Because the Commonwealth's evidence in support of a statutory burglary offense charged under § 18.2-90 showed that defendant entered the victim's residence without first being allowed to enter, as was usually the case between the two, such was sufficient to show that defendant's entry was without permission, and any conflicts in the testimony was for the jury to resolve. Moreover, the victim's testimony that he did not have a problem with defendant's entry did not compel a different result. Sayers v. Commonwealth, — Va. App. —, — S.E.2d —, 2007 Va. App. LEXIS 438 (Dec. 11, 2007).

Actual breaking involves the application of some force, slight though it may be, whereby the entrance is effected. Williams v. Commonwealth, 193 Va. 764, 71 S.E.2d 73 (1952).

Slight touching sufficient to establish "breaking." — Actual breaking involves the application of some force, slight though it may be, whereby entrance is effected; merely pushing open a door, turning the key, lifting the latch, or resorting to other slight physical force is sufficient to constitute this element of the crime. Levenberry v. Com., No. 0979-00-4, 2001 Va. App. LEXIS 177 (Ct. of Appeals Apr. 3, 2001).

Force must be applied to something attached to premises. — While it is well settled that only slight force is required to constitute a breaking, the force must be applied to something attached to the premises and relied upon by the occupant for safety. Johns v. Commonwealth, 10 Va. App. 283, 392 S.E.2d 487 (1990).

Opening closed door may be breaking. — An entry into a dwelling house, through a door that was so closed that it came within the casing, and to open which required some degree of force, constitutes in law a breaking, though there was no fastening of any other kind on the door. Finch v. Commonwealth, 55 Va. (14 Gratt.) 643 (1858).

But door must be shown to have been closed. — Where the evidence established only that door was open when homeowner returned, and no evidence proved that the door was closed when the homeowner left for work or when his children later left for school, the record was devoid of evidence of any force, even the slight physical force necessary to establish a breaking. Levenberry v. Com., No. 0979-00-4, 2001 Va. App. LEXIS 177 (Ct. of Appeals Apr. 3, 2001).

Sliding glass door partially open. — Intruders enlarged the opening of a partially open sliding glass door in order to get inside the house; therefore, the evidence was sufficient to permit the jury to find that a breaking had occurred. Phoung v. Commonwealth, 15 Va. App. 457, 424 S.E.2d 712 (1992).

Lifting latch or opening gate may be breaking. — A breaking, for purposes of burglary, requires the application of force, however slight, to accomplish an entrance against the occupier's will. Therefore, merely lifting a latch or opening a gate, where it is contrary to the will of the occupier, is sufficient proof of breaking to support a conviction for burglary. Dalton v. Commonwealth, 14 Va. App. 544, 418 S.E.2d 563 (1992).

Screen from window removed. — The evidence established that a screen from a window had been removed. The evidence was sufficient to prove beyond a reasonable doubt that appellant entered victim's trailer by breaking. Dailey v. Commonwealth, No. 0555-97-2 (Ct. of Appeals Dec. 9, 1997).

Breaking into warehouse or store is not breach of peace. — While breaking and entering a dwelling of another may often constitute a breach of the peace, particularly when it is done for the purpose of committing rape, robbery, or murder, breaking into a warehouse or store for the purpose of committing larceny is not a breach of the peace. Taylor v. Commonwealth, 11 Va. App. 649, 400 S.E.2d 794 (1991).

Constructive breaking. — Where entry is gained by threats, fraud or conspiracy, a constructive breaking is deemed to have occurred. Opie v. Commonwealth, No. 2173-99-1, 2000 Va. App. LEXIS 633 (Ct. of Appeals Aug. 29, 2000).

Although there was no evidence that any force, however slight, was used by the defendant to gain entry into the dwelling, the evidence proved a constructive breaking where the owner testified that the defendant walked onto his porch, grabbed him by the arm, and while holding a box-cutter, forced him inside the house; the owner's testimony that he was scared and that he couldn't do anything about it proved beyond a reasonable doubt that the defendant gained entry into the residence by threat of violence to the owner. Opie v. Commonwealth, No. 2173-99-1, 2000 Va. App. LEXIS 633 (Ct. of Appeals Aug. 29, 2000).

A constructive breaking by fraud under this section requires proof of more than an entry with criminal intent. Johns v. Commonwealth, 10 Va. App. 283, 392 S.E.2d 487 (1990).

Entry while armed with deadly weapon. — To elevate statutory burglary to a Class 2 felony, the Commonwealth must prove that the defendant was armed with a deadly weapon at the time of the entry; a deadly weapon is one which is likely to produce death or great bodily injury from the manner in which it is used, and whether a weapon is to be regarded as deadly often depends more on the manner in which it has been used than on its intrinsic character. Opie v. Commonwealth, No. 2173-99-1, 2000 Va. App. LEXIS 633 (Ct. of Appeals Aug. 29, 2000).

For purposes of this section a box-cutter may constitute a "deadly weapon" in that a boxcutter is not materially different from a locked-blade knife and combines the fine-edged sharpness of a straight razor with the retracting capacity of a locked-blade knife; it is common knowledge that a box-cutter is an instrument with a sharp blade or razor that could be used as a weapon to kill or inflict serious injury on a person. Opie v. Commonwealth, No. 2173-99-1, 2000 Va. App. LEXIS 633 (Ct. of Appeals Aug. 29, 2000).

Sufficient proof of entering. — Despite defendant's claim on appeal that the evidence at his trial was insufficient to support his conviction for armed burglary, the fact that his accomplice had kicked in the door of an apartment was sufficient to prove that an "entering" of the apartment had occurred because it was reasonable for the jury to have inferred that when the door was kicked in, and it fell off its hinges and into the apartment, that the foot of the accomplice, however briefly, had entered the home as well. Further, under the theory of accomplice liability, the actions of one principal were imputed to any other, pursuant to § 18.2-18. Wilson v. Commonwealth, — Va. App. —, — S.E.2d —, 2006 Va. App. LEXIS 243 (May 30, 2006).

Insufficient evidence. — Evidence was insufficient to convict defendant as a principal in the second degree of petit larceny because, although the circumstances were highly suspicious, they did not show that the items defendant helped the principal, a known burglar, carry from the triplex containing the burgled apartment, were items belonging to the victim, which had been stolen from the apartment. Gillison v. Commonwealth, 2009 Va. App. LEXIS 477 (Oct. 27, 2009).

C. Dwelling House, etc.

A "meathouse" is a "storehouse" within the meaning of this section and § 18.2-91. Benton v. Commonwealth, 91 Va. 782, 21 S.E. 495 (1895).

Chain link fence and "storehouse." — The eight foot chain link fence, enclosing the storage area on three sides, provided some security against unwanted intruders. In the absence of an expressed legislative intent to the contrary, the court declines to hold that a wall of a structure must be composed of a particular material in order for the structure to be the subject of burglary. Accordingly, the fact that three sides of this structure were composed of a chain link fence, rather than some other material, does not exclude the structure from classification as a "storehouse" under this section. Dalton v. Commonwealth, 14 Va. App. 544, 418 S.E.2d 563 (1992).

Mill may be "house." — Whether a mill is or is not a house within the scope of this and the following section is a matter of law and fact. A mill may be a house. McDorman v. Smyth, 187 Va. 522, 47 S.E.2d 441 (1948), overruled in part on other grounds, by Carroll v. Johnson, 278 Va. 683, 685 S.E.2d 647 (2009).

A chicken house which was at least 75 feet from the dwelling house, and in which no person usually lodged at night, was not a

parcel of the dwelling house, and not within the terms of the first part of this section. But a chicken house tall enough to stand up in, and having walls and a roof, was such a structure as is included in the words of this section "or other house." Compton v. Commonwealth, 190 Va. 48, 55 S.E.2d 446 (1949); Carter v. Commonwealth, 199 Va. 466, 100 S.E.2d 681 (1957).

Burglarizing building leased to United States as post office. — Where the defendants had burglarized a building privately owned and leased to the United States for a post office, and where there had been no federal prosecution, the prosecution for burglarizing post offices was not preempted by the United States. Bowling v. Slayton, 344 F. Supp. 650 (W.D. Va. 1972).

Before breaking into a trailer can serve as the basis for statutory burglary, the Commonwealth must prove that the trailer is used as a dwelling or place of human habitation. Graybeal v. Commonwealth, 228 Va. 736, 324 S.E.2d 698 (1985).

It would violate sound principles of statutory construction and strain the clear intendment of this section to hold that a trailer not used as a dwelling nevertheless falls under the definition of "other house." Graybeal v. Commonwealth, 228 Va. 736, 324 S.E.2d 698 (1985).

Trailer used as an office is an "office" within the meaning of this section. — Although the wheels remained attached to a sixteen-foot office trailer set up on a storage lot, it was an office within the meaning of this section where it rested on a cinder block foundation, it served as a mailing address and had electrical and telephone services and it was furnished, equipped and used as the office of a towing business operating off of the lot. Rooney v. Commonwealth, 16 Va. App. 738, 432 S.E.2d 525 (1993).

"Dwelling house" does not include rooms or compartments within a private residence. — For purposes of §§ 18.2-90 and 18.2-91, the definition of "dwelling house" contemplates a residence within which human beings sleep or habituate, but it does not contemplate individual rooms or compartments within such residence that are not "dwelling houses" in and of themselves, such as a rented room within a larger dwelling, intended to be the place of habitation/residence for the individual residing there. Hitt v. Commonwealth, 43 Va. App. 473, 598 S.E.2d 783, 2004 Va. App. LEXIS 320 (2004).

The phrase "other house," in this section, is a general phrase placed at the end of a list of specific references to various structures. Those specific structures share the common element of being improvements affixed to the ground, that is, they are realty. Under the doctrine of ejusdem generis, the general phrase "other house" must look for its meaning to the specific items which precede it. Graybeal v. Commonwealth, 228 Va. 736, 324 S.E.2d 698 (1985).

A school is an "other house" and the proper subject of burglary, within the meaning of the statute. Allard v. Commonwealth, 24 Va. App. 57, 480 S.E.2d 139 (1997).

In the present case, the evidence concerning the school's physical characteristics pointed to the single, inexorable conclusion that the school was an "other house" within the meaning of the statute, despite the trial court's reference to the "school" as the situs of the alleged burglary. Allard v. Commonwealth, 24 Va. App. 57, 480 S.E.2d 139 (1997).

"Shop." — Use of the term "shop" in the indictment to which defendant pled guilty did not take his conviction in violation of § 18.2-90 outside the sweep of Taylor or the meaning of "burglary" under the Armed Career Criminal Act, 18 U.S.C.S. § 924(e). Rather the reference to "shop" necessarily established that his prior burglary conviction was based on his entry into a structure affixed to the ground, namely, "a building." United States v. Baxter, 642 F.3d 475, 2011 U.S. App. LEXIS 8476 (4th Cir. 2011).

Requirement that structure be affixed to the ground. — It is clear that in order for a structure to be the subject of burglary, the structure must be permanently affixed to the ground so as to become a part of the realty at the time of the unlawful entry. Dalton v. Commonwealth, 14 Va. App. 544, 418 S.E.2d 563 (1992).

Where the evidence did not establish that a shed was affixed to the realty, it was insufficient to prove that defendant broke into a "storehouse" as prohibited by § 18.2-90. Robinson v. Commonwealth, No. 0470-03-1, 2004 Va. App. LEXIS 90 (Ct. of Appeals Feb. 24, 2004).

Whether previously mobile property that has been rendered stationary is affixed and a part of the real estate, and thus a subject of burglary, is a factual question, and the determination of the trial court will be reversed only if unsupported by credible evidence. Buie v. Commonwealth, 21 Va. App. 526, 465 S.E.2d 596 (1996).

School bus used for storage not shown affixed to realty. — In a prosecution for burglary of a school bus and larceny of mobile home skirting stored therein, where the record revealed that the school bus was used for storage and that the back door handle was secured by a large I-bolt and security lock, but there was no other evidence of the condition of the bus, the Commonwealth failed to prove an essential fact as charged in the indictment and required by the statute, that is, that the school bus was permanently affixed to the ground as in the case of a "storehouse" or "warehouse" and thus was part of the realty. Crews v. Commonwealth, 3 Va. App. 531, 352 S.E.2d 1 (1987).

With respect to structures other than the dwelling house of another, the legislature specifically chose to impose the habitability element only for automobiles, trucks or trailers; accordingly the Commonwealth was not required to prove the school's habitability as an element of the crime in this case. Allard v. Commonwealth, 24 Va. App. 57, 480 S.E.2d 139 (1997).

"Dwelling house" not found. — Statutory burglary conviction under § 18.2-91 was improper as the house involved in the burglary was not a "dwelling house," as that term was defined in §§ 18.2-89, 18.2-90, and 18.2-91, in that the record contained no evidence that the house was used for habitation as no one slept there, the house was unfurnished, and no one used it for the usual activities of life. Additionally, there was no evidence that anyone who had used the house for habitation had any intention of resuming that use. Johns v. Commonwealth, 53 Va. App. 742, 675 S.E.2d 211, 2009 Va. App. LEXIS 172 (2009).

III. OTHER MATTERS.

Motion to withdraw guilty plea. — In a case in which defendant pled guilty to violating §§ 18.2-90, 18.2-47, 18.2-67.1 and 18.2-53.1, he argued unsuccessfully that the circuit court abused its discretion in denying his motion to withdraw his guilty pleas prior to sentencing; defendant failed to show a good faith basis for seeking to withdraw his guilty pleas. He was clearly aware of the potential range of punishments available to the court at the time he pled guilty; as such, the fact that the sentencing guidelines recommended a higher sentence than he had hoped did not constitute a good faith basis for rescinding his pleas. Mack v. Commonwealth, 2009 Va. App. LEXIS 417 (Sept. 22, 2009).

Effect of motion to require Commonwealth to elect. — Whatever the motive of the attorney for an accused in making a motion to require the attorney for the Commonwealth to elect whether the accused will be tried under this section or under § 18.2-91, the same consequences follow: The accused acquiesces in a prosecution for breaking and entering with intent to commit murder, rape or robbery. The motion, by necessary implication, conceded the right to try the accused under either section. Though the procedure may be irregular, the accused cannot be allowed to take advantage of an irregularity for which he is directly responsible. Sullivan v. Commonwealth, 157 Va. 867, 161 S.E. 297 (1931).

Alibi defense. — See Johnson v. Commonwealth, 210 Va. 16, 168 S.E.2d 97 (1969).

Section 18.2-121 is not lesser included offense of § 18.2-91 or this section. — This section, which identifies § 18.2-91's prohibited acts, includes offenses against properties not specified in § 18.2-121, i.e., ships, vessels, river craft. Thus, a violation of § 18.2-91 will not invariably and necessarily include a violation of § 18.2-121 and the misdemeanor is, consequently, not a lesser included offense of either this section or § 18.2-91. Crump v. Commonwealth, 13 Va. App. 286, 411 S.E.2d 238 (1991).

Evidence sufficient to find defendant present at scene of crimes. — Defendant's fingerprint, impressed in blood on a moveable object (a flashlight), found at the scene of the crimes was sufficient in light of attendant circumstances to find that the defendant was at the scene at the time the crimes were committed in a prosecution for murder and breaking and entering with intent to commit murder. Turner v. Commonwealth, 218 Va. 141, 235 S.E.2d 357 (1977).

Appellant's convictions for two counts of robbery, one count of statutory burglary, and three counts of use of a firearm in the commission of the felonies were affirmed because it was reasonable for the fact finder to conclude the intruder knew the victims' habits and DNA evidence indicated at some point in time, appellant had

touched the BB gun. Swinson v. Commonwealth, 2010 Va. App. LEXIS 311 (Aug. 3, 2010).

Evidence sufficient to show intent to commit rape. — See Dixon v. Commonwealth, 197 Va. 380, 89 S.E.2d 344 (1955).

Evidence of possession of stolen goods is not sufficient of itself to support a conviction of housebreaking. Williams v. Commonwealth, 193 Va. 764, 71 S.E.2d 73 (1952).

Evidence insufficient to show that breaking occurred. — Where appellant's sister had not told appellant that he could not return to the apartment, where appellant temporarily resided in the apartment, slept on the sofa, and had clothing in the apartment, and where the inference that appellant somehow broke into the apartment was no more reasonable than the inference that one of the children or the mother opened the door to give him entry to the apartment, the evidence failed to prove beyond a reasonable doubt that a breaking occurred. Mayo v. Commonwealth, No. 0293-97-2 (Ct. of Appeals Nov. 25, 1997).

Although the evidence showed that defendant entered each of two residences within minutes of each other on the same morning, the evidence was insufficient to show that defendant "broke" into either of the residences, and, thus, defendant's convictions on two counts of burglary had to be reversed and the two counts of burglary had to be dismissed. Pettey v. Commonwealth, No. 1702-03-1, 2004 Va. App. LEXIS 299 (Ct. of Appeals June 29, 2004).

Evidence that the front door of the victims' home was clearly breached, that a tracker dog picked up defendant's scent, that defendant gave conflicting stories as to why he was hiding in the woods at 4:30 in the morning, and the fact that defendant's clothes were dry despite the fact that he was found lying on the ground, which was heavily covered with dew, was sufficient to support defendant's conviction for burglary. Tucker v. Commonwealth, — Va. App. —, — S.E.2d —, 2006 Va. App. LEXIS 526 (Nov. 21, 2006).

Defendant not convicted of crime different from that in indictment. — Defendant was not convicted of a crime different in nature from that charged in the indictment where the original indictment charged the crime of breaking and entering a dwelling house with the intent to maim, and was amended to charge breaking and entering with the intent to commit murder, nor did the trial court err in permitting the amendment. Smith v. Commonwealth, 10 Va. App. 592, 394 S.E.2d 30 (1990).

Where instruction omitted requirement of violence or intimidation, error was harmless. — Where the error in the jury instruction was that the instruction omitted the requirement of violence or intimidation as an element of the offense charged in the indictment, it essentially permitted a conviction on a finding that defendant broke and entered the dwelling with only the intent to commit larceny rather than robbery, contrary to the statutory law. Because the erroneous instruction related to the elements of the crime charged, the error also was "substantial." However, the error in the jury instruction was not material because it did not affect the outcome of the trial; while error, it was harmless. Phoung v. Commonwealth, 15 Va. App. 457, 424 S.E.2d 712 (1992).

Verdict held responsive to indictment. — Where indictment charged that petitioner "feloniously did enter the storehouse" verdict finding him guilty "of attempted storebreaking" was responsive to the indictment. The charge embraced the lesser offense of attempting to enter without breaking or of attempting to break and enter and whether the act towards its commission was an attempt to enter without breaking, or an attempt to break and enter, which was a matter of evidence, the effect was the same. Willoughby v. Smyth, 194 Va. 267, 72 S.E.2d 636 (1952).

Amendment to defendant's burglary indictment, which added the aggravated circumstance of committing the felony while armed with a deadly weapon, did not change the nature or character of the offense. Hawkins v. Commonwealth, No. 0188-87-1 (Ct. of Appeals Jan. 3, 1989).

§ 18.2-91. Entering dwelling house, etc., with intent to commit larceny, assault and battery or other felony.

If any person commits any of the acts mentioned in § 18.2-90 with intent to commit larceny, or any felony other than murder, rape, robbery or arson in violation of §§ 18.2-77, 18.2-79 or § 18.2-80, or if any person commits any of the acts mentioned in § 18.2-89 or § 18.2-90 with intent to commit assault and battery, he shall be guilty of statutory burglary, punishable by confinement in a state correctional facility for not less than one or more than twenty years or, in the discretion of the jury or the court trying the case without a jury, be confined in jail for a period not exceeding twelve months or fined not more than $2,500, either or both. However, if the person was armed with a deadly weapon at the time of such entry, he shall be guilty of a Class 2 felony.

History.
Code 1950, § 18.1-89; 1960, c. 358; 1962, c. 505; 1970, c. 381; 1975, cc. 14, 15, 602; 1991, c. 710; 1992, c. 486; 1996, c. 1040; 1997, c. 832.

Cross references.
For provision making it unlawful to work or volunteer on school grounds following convictions of certain sex offenses, see § 18.2-370.4. As to requirement of saliva or tissue sample for DNA analysis after arrest for a violent felony, see § 19.2-310.2:1.

Editor's note.
The above section is § 18.2-91 as enacted by Acts 1975, c. 602. Pursuant to § 30-152, it has been substituted for § 18.2-91 as enacted by Acts 1975, cc. 14 and 15.

Law Review.
For survey of Virginia criminal law for the year 1971-1972, see 58 Va. L. Rev. 1206 (1972). For survey of Virginia criminal procedure for the year 1973-1974, see 60 Va. L. Rev. 1505 (1974). For survey of Virginia criminal law for the year 1974-1975, see 61 Va. L. Rev. 1697 (1975). For survey of Virginia criminal law for the year 1978-1979, see 66 Va. L. Rev. 241 (1980). For a note, "Predicate Offenses for First Degree Felony Murder in Virginia," see 57 Wash. & Lee L. Rev. 561 (2000). For survey of Virginia criminal law and procedure for the year 2004-2005, see 40 U. Rich. L. Rev. 197 (2005).

Michie's Jurisprudence.
For related discussion, see 1A M.J. Abduction and Kidnapping, § 3; 21A M.J. Words and Phrases.

CASE NOTES

I. In General.
II. Elements.
  A. Intent.
  B. Entering.
  C. Dwelling House, etc.
III. Deadly Weapon.
IV. Indictment.
V. Prosecution and Conviction.
VI. Illustrative Cases.

I. IN GENERAL.

Offense described in section is a felony. — Breaking and entering a house in the nighttime, with intent to commit larceny, is a felony. Benton v. Commonwealth, 91 Va. 782, 21 S.E. 495 (1895). See also Benton v. Commonwealth, 89 Va. 570, 16 S.E. 725 (1893).
Section is limited by § 18.2-78. Compton v. Commonwealth, 190 Va. 48, 55 S.E.2d 446 (1949).
Elements. — To sustain a conviction for statutory burglary under this section, the commonwealth must prove: (1) The accused entered a dwelling house in the nighttime without breaking or broke and entered the dwelling house in the daytime and (2) The accused entered with the intent to commit any felony other than murder, rape, robbery or arson. Robertson v. Commonwealth, 31 Va. App. 814, 525 S.E.2d 640 (2000).
Offense qualifies as a generic burglary. — Defendant's offenses that were in violation of §§ 18.2-90 and 18.2-91 did qualify as generic burglaries, for purposes of 18 U.S.C.S. § 924(e). United

States v. Joshua, 259 F. Supp. 2d 446, 2003 U.S. Dist. LEXIS 6963 (E.D. Va. 2003).
In a case in which defendant pled guilty to possession of a firearm by a convicted felon in violation of 18 U.S.C.S. § 922(g)(1), and he objected to the assertion in his presentence report that he qualified as an armed career criminal under the Armed Career Criminal Act, 18 U.S.C.S. § 924(e), he argued unsuccessfully that one of the offenses the probation report cited as a predicate offense failed to qualify. Under §§ 18.2-90 and 18.2-91, defendant's offense of breaking and entering a shop with the intent to commit larceny qualified as generic burglary under the Armed Career Criminal Act, and, under the modified categorical approach, the appropriate documents necessarily established that he pled guilty to and was convicted of generic burglary. United States v. Baxter, 2010 U.S. Dist. LEXIS 1678 (W.D. Va. Jan. 11, 2010), aff'd, 642 F.3d 475, 2011 U.S. App. LEXIS 8476 (4th Cir. Va. 2011).
"Shop." — Use of the term "shop" in the indictment to which defendant pled guilty did not take his conviction in violation of § 18.2-90 outside the sweep of Taylor or the meaning of "burglary" under the Armed Career Criminal Act, 18 U.S.C.S. § 924(e). Rather the reference to "shop" necessarily established that his prior burglary conviction was based on his entry into a structure affixed to the ground, namely, "a building." United States v. Baxter, 642 F.3d 475, 2011 U.S. App. LEXIS 8476 (4th Cir. 2011).
The Commonwealth can establish a prima facie case that a defendant broke and entered by: (1) proving that goods were stolen from a house which was broken into; (2) justifying the inference that both offenses were committed at the same time, by the same person, as part of the same criminal enterprise and (3) proving that the goods were found soon thereafter in the possession of the accused. Rosser v. Commonwealth, No. 2862-99-3, 2000 Va. App. LEXIS 762 (Ct. of Appeals Nov. 28, 2000).
Unnecessary words that describe, limit or qualify statutory necessary words must be proved. — Unnecessary words in an indictment describe, limit or qualify the statutory necessary words and, thus, the unnecessary words have to be proven as charged. Griffin v. Commonwealth, 13 Va. App. 409, 412 S.E.2d 709 (1991).
The addition of the word "daytime" in the defendant's indictment more particularly defined the term "any time," the general span of time within which the conduct of breaking and entering the dwelling is statutorily described; the phrase "any time" is not, however, a statutorily necessary word. Griffin v. Commonwealth, 13 Va. App. 409, 412 S.E.2d 709 (1991).
The addition of "daytime" was surplusage that designated the general time of the offense but did not describe, limit, or qualify the conduct which is statutorily proscribed. Griffin v. Commonwealth, 13 Va. App. 409, 412 S.E.2d 709 (1991).
Larceny is necessarily involved. — In a charge of entering a barn in the night and stealing property therefrom, larceny is necessarily involved. Stallard v. Commonwealth, 130 Va. 769, 107 S.E. 722 (1921).
Trespass not lesser-included offense of statutory burglary. — Trespass in violation of § 18.2-119 is not a lesser-included offense of statutory burglary and a trial court lacks the authority to convict for trespass under an indictment charging breaking and entering even if the accused fails to object. Shifflett v. Commonwealth, No. 2702-99-2, 2000 Va. App. LEXIS 843 (Ct. of Appeals Dec. 28, 2000).
Section 18.2-121 is not lesser included offense of § 18.2-90 or this section. — Section 18.2-90, which identifies this section's prohibited acts, includes offenses against properties not specified in § 18.2-121, i.e., ships, vessels, river craft. Thus, a violation of this section will not invariably and necessarily include a violation of § 18.2-121 and the misdemeanor is, consequently, not a lesser included offense of either § 18.2-90 or this section. Crump v. Commonwealth, 13 Va. App. 286, 411 S.E.2d 238 (1991).
Common-law trespass is not a lesser included offense of statutory burglary under this section. Dowell v. Commonwealth, No. 1567-87-2 (Ct. of Appeals May 21, 1991).
Common-law trespass is not a lesser included offense of statutory burglary under this section, even when the indictment specifically charges that a dwelling was burglarized. Taylor v. Commonwealth, 11 Va. App. 649, 400 S.E.2d 794 (1991).
Since statutory burglary does not contain the element of an actual or threatened breach of the peace, common-law trespass is

not a lesser included offense of statutory burglary. Taylor v. Commonwealth, 11 Va. App. 649, 400 S.E.2d 794 (1991).

Instruction as to punishment. — In a prosecution for carbreaking with intent to commit larceny, the court instructed the jury that if they found the accused guilty, his punishment should be not less than one nor more than 10 years in the penitentiary (now state correctional facility), "or, in the discretion of the jury, confinement in jail for twelve months and a fine not exceeding $500." The instruction was held error, as this section as it stood at the time of the prosecution plainly said, "or, in the discretion of the jury, confined in jail not exceeding twelve months and fined not exceeding $500." But as the jury did not exercise its discretion, but fixed a penitentiary (now state correctional facility) sentence, the error was harmless. Clark v. Commonwealth, 135 Va. 490, 115 S.E. 704 (1923).

Applied in Guynn v. Commonwealth, 220 Va. 478, 259 S.E.2d 822 (1979); Edwards v. Sasser, 462 F. Supp. 374 (E.D. Va. 1979); Knight v. Commonwealth, 225 Va. 85, 300 S.E.2d 600 (1983); Hall v. Commonwealth, 225 Va. 533, 303 S.E.2d 903 (1983); Crews v. Commonwealth, 3 Va. App. 531, 352 S.E.2d 1 (1987); Martin v. Taylor, 857 F.2d 958 (4th Cir. 1988); Buie v. Commonwealth, 21 Va. App. 526, 465 S.E.2d 596 (1996); Stinnie v. Commonwealth, 21 Va. App. 610, 466 S.E.2d 752 (1996); Crawley v. Commonwealth, 29 Va. App. 372, 512 S.E.2d 169 (1999); Turner v. Commonwealth, 38 Va. App. 851, 568 S.E.2d 468, 2002 Va. App. LEXIS 525 (2002); Jay v. Commonwealth, 275 Va. 510, 659 S.E.2d 311, 2008 Va. LEXIS 53 (2008); Rowland v. Commonwealth, 281 Va. 396, 707 S.E.2d 331, 2011 Va. LEXIS 60 (2011).

II. ELEMENTS.

A. Intent.

Specific intent is an essential element of burglary. Taylor v. Commonwealth, 207 Va. 326, 150 S.E.2d 135 (1966).

Intent must be proved. — This section makes an offense consist of an act combined with a particular intent. Therefore, proof of such intent is as necessary as proof of the act itself and must be established as a matter of fact. Ridley v. Commonwealth, 219 Va. 834, 252 S.E.2d 313 (1979).

Under this section, proof of intent is as necessary as proof of the act itself. Ridley v. Commonwealth, 219 Va. 834, 252 S.E.2d 313 (1979).

The means by which a person breaks into a store is not the determining factor as to his intent once within the store. Vincent v. Commonwealth, — Va. App. —, — S.E.2d —, 2007 Va. App. LEXIS 491 (Nov. 20, 2007).

But may be inferred from facts and circumstances. — The specific intent with which an unlawful entry into a dwelling or storehouse was made may be inferred from the surrounding facts and circumstances. Ridley v. Commonwealth, 219 Va. 834, 252 S.E.2d 313 (1979).

Intent may, and often must, be inferred from the facts and circumstances in a particular case. Ridley v. Commonwealth, 219 Va. 834, 252 S.E.2d 313 (1979).

When an unlawful entry is made into a dwelling, the presumption is that the entry was made for an unlawful purpose and the specific purpose, meaning specific intent, with which such an entry is made may be inferred from the surrounding facts and circumstances. Black v. Commonwealth, 222 Va. 838, 284 S.E.2d 608 (1981).

The fact finder may infer that a person intends the immediate, direct and necessary consequences of his voluntary acts. Robertson v. Commonwealth, 31 Va. App. 814, 525 S.E.2d 640 (2000).

Intent may be shown by the circumstances, including a person's conduct and statements. Robertson v. Commonwealth, 31 Va. App. 814, 525 S.E.2d 640 (2000).

In a prosecution for burglary under this section, proof that the accused unlawfully entered another's dwelling supports an inference that the entry was made for an unlawful purpose; the specific intent with which the unlawful entry is made may be inferred from the surrounding facts and circumstances. Robertson v. Commonwealth, 31 Va. App. 814, 525 S.E.2d 640 (2000).

Defendant's unlawful entry into complainant's residence supported inference that he entered with an unlawful purpose, and surrounding circumstances supported inference that he entered with an intent to assault complainant. Gore v. Commonwealth, No.

1393-99-1 (Ct. of Appeals Apr. 4, 2000).

Evidence was sufficient to prove beyond a reasonable doubt that defendant possessed the specific intent to commit larceny, as required by this section, when he unlawfully broke into and entered a victim's home because: (1) the evidence and reasonable inferences flowing from that evidence proved that defendant forcibly broke and entered the victim's home by breaking through a boarded-up front door and a door jamb and that he walked inside the house, where the victim's uncle saw him with something white in his hand; (2) when seen by the uncle, defendant fled and later denied entering the home, giving rise to an inference of guilt; and (3) even though the victim could not specifically identify anything missing from his home and the uncle could not identify the white object in defendant's hand, a rational fact finder could have reasonably inferred that defendant held an item in his hand that he intended to steal from the victim's home. Hairston v. Commonwealth, — Va. App. —, — S.E.2d —, 2008 Va. App. LEXIS 551 (Dec. 23, 2008).

Evidence was sufficient to prove that the defendant had formed an intent to physically harm the victim when he forced his way into her home where the recent relationship between the defendant and the victim had been adversarial and litigious, the defendant had been arguing with and "talking trash" to the victim moments before his unlawful entry, he displayed a pocket knife in his hand during the argument, and he forced his way into the victim's home as soon as she attempted to end their encounter. Donaldson v. Commonwealth, No. 1956-97-1 (Ct. of Appeals Sept. 22, 1998).

Because defendant struck the victim in the back of the head with a baseball bat after forcibly entering the victim's house with two companions who were similarly armed with weapons, the evidence was sufficient to find defendant intended an unlawful wounding; therefore, defendant was properly found guilty of violating § 18.2-91. Wilson v. Commonwealth, 2010 Va. App. LEXIS 425 (Nov. 2, 2010).

Evidence supported defendant's burglary conviction, as the surrounding facts and circumstances adequately established defendant's intent to commit larceny when defendant entered an apartment; as defendant stated to a detective and in a written statement, when defendant broke into other persons' homes, defendant's intention was always to steal property or money. Smith v. Commonwealth, 2011 Va. App. LEXIS 156 (May 10, 2011).

In a prosecution for attempted burglary with the intent to commit larceny, assault and battery, or a felony other than rape, robbery or arson in violation of §§ 18.2-91 and 18.2-26, there was sufficient evidence that defendant had the specific intent to commit larceny when he broke a window in an attempt to enter a garage. His codefendant's knowledge that the victim stored property there was imputed to defendant. Bourne v. Commonwealth, 2012 Va. App. LEXIS 171 (May 22, 2012).

Intent to commit larceny inferred from unauthorized presence. — In the absence of evidence showing a contrary intent, the trier of fact may infer that a defendant's unauthorized presence in a house or building of another in the nighttime was with intent to commit larceny. Ridley v. Commonwealth, 219 Va. 834, 252 S.E.2d 313 (1979).

Where there was no evidence showing that defendant merely intended to damage merchandise in a store rather than steal the merchandise after he broke into the store, a trial court properly adopted a Ridley inference that defendant possessed the specific intent to commit an unlawful entry into the store with intent to commit larceny. The record showed no evidence that property within the store was damaged in any way or in any amount; the only relevant evidence was that a shopping cart had been pushed into a rack of jeans and the merchandise was dispersed. Vincent v. Commonwealth, — Va. App. —, — S.E.2d —, 2007 Va. App. LEXIS 491 (Nov. 20, 2007).

Inference from possession of recently stolen property. — The reasonableness of the inference of guilty knowledge, or theft, from the unexplained possession of recently stolen property has been often upheld by the Fourth Circuit. Nevertheless, even a reasonable inference if unsupported, will not provide a basis for proof beyond a reasonable doubt. Rather, the recent possession of stolen property should be viewed as probative evidence of the crime and reviewed along with the other evidence in the case to determine whether a rational juror could find the defendant guilty beyond a reasonable doubt. Berryman v. Moore, 619 F. Supp. 853 (E.D. Va.

1985), certification of probable cause denied and dismissed, 792 F.2d 139 (4th Cir. 1986).

In a burglary prosecution, the commonwealth can establish a violation of this section by: (1) proving that goods were stolen from a house which was broken into; (2) justifying the inference that both offenses were committed at the same time, by the same person, as part of the same criminal enterprise; and (3) proving that the goods were found soon thereafter in the possession of the accused. Dickerson v. Commonwealth, No. 0090-00-1, 2001 Va. App. LEXIS 105 (Ct. of Appeals Mar. 6, 2001).

To prove beyond a reasonable doubt that the possession of stolen property was exclusive so as to give rise to the presumption that the possessor obtained the property unlawfully, the commonwealth's evidence must show that the accused was consciously asserting at least a possessory interest in the stolen property or was exercising dominion over the stolen property. Dickerson v. Commonwealth, No. 0090-00-1, 2001 Va. App. LEXIS 105 (Ct. of Appeals Mar. 6, 2001).

Where it was established that the defendant was in exclusive possession of the victims' stolen jewelry within days of the theft and he alone exercised dominion over the stolen property when he sold it to a jeweler, the defendant's exclusive possession was sufficiently recent to establish prima facie cases of larceny and burglary and to justify inferences by the trial court that the defendant was the thief and burglar who broke into both victims' homes and stole their property. Dickerson v. Commonwealth, No. 0090-00-1, 2001 Va. App. LEXIS 105 (Ct. of Appeals Mar. 6, 2001).

It is well settled that the unexplained possession of recently stolen property creates a presumption of guilt, but such possession must be exclusive on the part of the accused; the evidence must reveal that the accused was consciously asserting at least a possessory interest in or exercising dominion over the stolen property. Savage v. Commonwealth, No. 0889-00-1, 2001 Va. App. LEXIS 119 (Ct. of Appeals Mar. 13, 2001).

When evidence has been introduced, which, if believed, establishes that a house has been broken and entered and goods stolen therefrom, and warrants an inference beyond a reasonable doubt that the breaking and entering and the larceny of the goods were committed at the same time, by the same person or persons, as a part of the same transaction, upon principle and authority, the exclusive possession of the stolen goods shortly thereafter, unexplained or falsely denied, has the same efficiency to give rise to an inference that the possessor is guilty of the breaking and entering as to an inference that he is guilty of the larceny. Savage v. Commonwealth, No. 0889-00-1, 2001 Va. App. LEXIS 119 (Ct. of Appeals Mar. 13, 2001).

Upon proof of a breaking and entering and a theft of goods, and if the evidence warrants an inference that the breaking and entering and the theft were committed at the same time by the same person and as part of the same transaction, the exclusive possession of the stolen goods shortly thereafter, unexplained or falsely denied, has the same efficiency to give rise to an inference that the possessor is guilty of the breaking and entering as to an inference that he is guilty of larceny. Rosser v. Commonwealth, No. 2862-99-3, 2000 Va. App. LEXIS 762 (Ct. of Appeals Nov. 28, 2000).

Evidential value of possession of stolen goods. — In Virginia it is well settled that the possession of stolen goods is, of itself, not even prima facie evidence of housebreaking or burglary. Walters v. Commonwealth, 159 Va. 903, 165 S.E. 495 (1932); Williams v. Commonwealth, 193 Va. 764, 71 S.E.2d 73 (1952).

Bare evidence of the possession of the stolen goods is not sufficient of itself to support a conviction of housebreaking. Fields v. Commonwealth, 215 Va. 120, 207 S.E.2d 822 (1974).

Defendant's possession of single item of stolen property with no showing when burglary occurred or that a larceny and burglary occurred simultaneously do not support an inference that he burglarized the victim's home. Clark v. Commonwealth, No. 0275-85 (Ct. of Appeals Sept. 22, 1986).

Intent to commit larceny cannot be inferred from lack of other intent. — Defendant's conviction for breaking and entering with an intent to commit larceny in violation of § 18.2-91 could not stand, as the Commonwealth did not proved beyond a reasonable doubt the defendant intended to commit larceny. Larceny could not be inferred from the absence of evidence of a different intent, and defendant was neither found in the store or with any store mer-

chandise. Vincent v. Commonwealth, 276 Va. 648, 668 S.E.2d 137, 2008 Va. LEXIS 109 (2008).

Testimony concerning other items of stolen property not subject of indictment. — Trial court did not err in overruling motion to exclude testimony concerning other items of property stolen at the time of the burglary, even though such items were not the subject of the grand larceny indictment. Caccioppo v. Commonwealth, 20 Va. App. 534, 458 S.E.2d 592 (1995).

Evidence of prior conviction for burglary properly admitted. — Evidence relating to defendant's involvement in a prior burglary was properly admitted in his trial for a later burglary because defendant's statement to police raised the issue of larcenous intent, and evidence of prior bad acts was permissible in order to show absence of mistake or accident and intent. Slaughter v. Commonwealth, 49 Va. App. 659, 644 S.E.2d 89, 2007 Va. App. LEXIS 182 (2007).

B. Entering.

Under common law, an entry occurs when any part of the body enters a dwelling and the Virginia legislature has not altered this definition of entry in this section. Franklin v. Commonwealth, 28 Va. App. 719, 508 S.E.2d 362 (1998).

Entering store during business hours. — A defendant can be found guilty of burglary where he enters a store during normal business hours with the intent to commit robbery therein. Browder v. Commonwealth, No. 1499-97-2 (Ct. of Appeals Dec. 22, 1998).

Entrance must be against will of occupier. — A breaking, either actual or constructive, to support a conviction of burglary must have resulted in an entrance contrary to the will of the occupier of the house. Robertson v. Commonwealth, 31 Va. App. 814, 525 S.E.2d 640 (2000).

Presumption of entry for unlawful purpose. — When an unlawful entry is made into a dwelling of another, the presumption is that the entry was made for an unlawful purpose. This same principle is equally applicable to breaking and entering a storehouse in the nighttime with intent to commit larceny. Ridley v. Commonwealth, 219 Va. 834, 252 S.E.2d 313 (1979).

When an unlawful entry is made into the dwelling of another, the presumption is that the entry is made for an unlawful purpose. The specific purpose, meaning specific intent, with which such an entry is made may be inferred from the surrounding facts and circumstances. Scott v. Commonwealth, 228 Va. 519, 323 S.E.2d 572 (1984).

Remaining on business premises after close of business without owner's consent. — Where a store owner invites the public to enter his premises he consents for the entrant to view his merchandise for the limited purpose of purchase, or to otherwise engage in a lawful activity thereon. It is not the will of the owner that entrance be made to defraud or steal from him. The consent to entry expires at the close of business and an invitee's presence on the premises thereafter, without the knowledge or consent of the owner, constitutes a form of entry by fraud and deception when the original entry was made with intent to steal. Jones v. Commonwealth, 3 Va. App. 295, 349 S.E.2d 414 (1986).

Where defendant entered the store under the pretense that he was a prospective customer and he then secreted himself on the premises until the store closed for business at which time, without permission of the owner, he attempted to remove property from the store without paying for it, the evidence established that prior to entry defendant had formed in his mind the intent to remain on the premises and to commit the theft. Under such circumstances, an intent was sufficient to meet the requirement of this section. Jones v. Commonwealth, 3 Va. App. 295, 349 S.E.2d 414 (1986).

Where defendants entered the store before closing and secreted themselves in the storeroom where they remained until the store closed, at which time they intended to do "a little Christmas shopping," there was a "breaking and entering" within the meaning of this section despite defendant's argument that there was no attempt to steal during regular store hours. The intent to steal was formulated prior to the time defendants entered the store, and such intent, when combined with the method of entry, was sufficient to sustain the conviction. Jones v. Commonwealth, 3 Va. App. 295, 349 S.E.2d 414 (1986).

To constitute the crime of statutory burglary of a storehouse in the nighttime, an entry, with or without breaking, must be made with intent to commit larceny or a felony. Fields v.

Commonwealth, 215 Va. 120, 207 S.E.2d 822 (1974).

No breaking required where the entry occurs at night. — Defendant's burglary conviction under § 18.2-91 was supported by the evidence since no breaking was required under § 18.2-90 since defendant entered the apartment in the nighttime; intent to commit an assault and battery was shown as defendant was wearing body armor, and carrying brass knuckles and a gun. Consent was not a defense to statutory burglary. Jones v. Commonwealth, — Va. App. —, — S.E.2d —, 2009 Va. App. LEXIS 44 (Feb. 3, 2009), aff'd, 279 Va. 295, 687 S.E.2d 738 (2010).

In the daytime, both an entry and a breaking must occur with the same intent. Fields v. Commonwealth, 215 Va. 120, 207 S.E.2d 822 (1974).

Actual breaking involves the application of some force, slight though it may be, whereby the entrance is effected; merely pushing open a door, turning the key, lifting the latch or resort to other slight physical force is sufficient to constitute this element of the crime. Robertson v. Commonwealth, 31 Va. App. 814, 525 S.E.2d 640 (2000).

Evidence did not establish beyond a reasonable doubt that defendant was required to use any physical force to enter a shed and, thus, committed a breaking as required by § 18.2-91. The breaking of the shed door could have occurred at any time during the seven or eight days that the owner was away from the owner's property. Finney v. Commonwealth, 277 Va. 83, 671 S.E.2d 169, 2009 Va. LEXIS 12 (2009).

Broken refrigerator lock held insufficient evidence of breaking. — Court's reliance on evidence of damaged and broken lock on a walk-in refrigerator to show a forceful entry into the premises was misplaced as the refrigerator was not attached to the premises and there was no showing that the lock on it was intended to protect anything other than its contents. Hence, the "breaking" element of statutory burglary was not satisfied. Murphy v. Commonwealth, No. 1198-01-2, 2002 Va. App. LEXIS 399 (Ct. of Appeals July 23, 2002).

Timing of offense is not essential element of offense. — Whenever there is a breaking and entering of a dwelling with a larcenous intent, the timing of the offense is not an essential element of the offense. Griffin v. Commonwealth, 13 Va. App. 409, 412 S.E.2d 709 (1991).

Since breaking and entering of a dwelling, at any time, is the essential element of the offense, the indictment's allegation that the offense occurred in the daytime was nothing more than surplusage. Griffin v. Commonwealth, 13 Va. App. 409, 412 S.E.2d 709 (1991).

Because breaking and entering a dwelling "at any time" with the requisite intent is a violation of § 18.2-90, the specification "daytime" was neither "legally essential" to charge a violation of statute nor varied the conduct which the statute proscribes. Griffin v. Commonwealth, 13 Va. App. 409, 412 S.E.2d 709 (1991).

Right to possession, not ownership, determines whether entry lawful. — Where a defendant and his wife had been separated for a year and the wife had remained in the family residence, the defendant's proprietary interest was relegated to the wife's superior possessory interest and right to exclusive habitation such that the defendant's acts in breaking and entering the home, accompanied by the requisite unlawful intent, offended the wife's right of habitation and constituted burglary in violation of this section, notwithstanding his joint ownership of the property. Turner v. Commonwealth, 33 Va. App. 88, 531 S.E.2d 619, 2000 Va. App. LEXIS 566 (2000).

Allegation of ownership of building. — An indictment for housebreaking which described the property as "a certain mill house not adjoining to or occupied with the dwelling house of Frances Newman," was a sufficient allegation of ownership by Frances Newman. Webster v. Commonwealth, 80 Va. 598 (1885); Speers v. Commonwealth, 58 Va. (17 Gratt.) 570 (1867). See Butler v. Commonwealth, 81 Va. 159 (1885).

Entry of portion of body sufficient. — The evidence established the defendant's entry into the subject premises where, after breaking the lock and splintering the door, the defendant inserted his arm and shoulder through the opening into the victim's apartment. Franklin v. Commonwealth, 28 Va. App. 719, 508 S.E.2d 362 (1998).

Evidence sufficient to find entering. — Evidence was sufficient to support defendant's statutory burglary conviction where in entering the office, defendant had to turn the handle of the main door, which was always shut, and push the door open; the jury could properly reject defendant's theories in his burglary defense that there was no actual or constructive breaking. Sheppard v. Commonwealth, No. 3230-02-4, 2004 Va. App. LEXIS 155 (Ct. of Appeals Apr. 6, 2004).

Evidence was sufficient to support defendant's burglary conviction even though no signs of forced entry were found around the door or windows immediately after the burglary, because the evidence established that defendant and defendant's companion had no lawful authority to enter the subject residence and the detective who arrived to investigate described the interior of the residence as "ransacked"; thus, the jury was entitled to find that defendant applied some force, however slight, to gain entry into the residence. Seis v. Commonwealth, 2007 Va. App. LEXIS 432 (Nov. 27, 2007).

Evidence sufficient to find attempt to enter. — In a prosecution for attempted burglary with the intent to commit larceny, assault and battery, or a felony other than rape, robbery or arson in violation of §§ 18.2-91 and 18.2-26, the evidence was sufficient to support the theory that defendant broke the victim's window in an attempt to enter his garage. The fact finder could conclude that the victim heard the noise of a breaking glass and metallic window frame, which had been intact earlier, and that the fleeing defendant and codefendant had broken the window and frame in an attempt to gain entry to the garage. Bourne v. Commonwealth, 2012 Va. App. LEXIS 171 (May 22, 2012).

Evidence insufficient to prove breaking. — Although the evidence showed that defendant entered each of two residences within minutes of each other on the same morning, the evidence was insufficient to show that defendant "broke" into either of the residences, and, thus, defendant's convictions on two counts of burglary had to be reversed and the two counts of burglary had to be dismissed. Pettey v. Commonwealth, No. 1702-03-1, 2004 Va. App. LEXIS 299 (Ct. of Appeals June 29, 2004).

C. Dwelling House, etc.

Winnebago mobile home was "dwelling." — In a prosecution under this section as embraced by the Assimilative Crimes Act, 18 U.S.C. §§ 2 and 13, a Winnebago mobile home was a "dwelling" at the time of the theft, where evidence showed that the owner used it as a home when he was on the road and that it was appropriately equipped for that purpose. United States v. Lavender, 602 F.2d 639 (4th Cir. 1979).

"Dwelling house" does not include rooms or compartments within a private residence. — For purposes of §§ 18.2-90 and 18.2-91, the definition of "dwelling house" contemplates a residence within which human beings sleep or habituate, but it does not contemplate individual rooms or compartments within such residence that are not "dwelling houses" in and of themselves, such as a rented room within a larger dwelling, intended to be the place of habitation/residence for the individual residing there. Hitt v. Commonwealth, 43 Va. App. 473, 598 S.E.2d 783, 2004 Va. App. LEXIS 320 (2004).

Before breaking into a trailer can serve as the basis for statutory burglary, the Commonwealth must prove that the trailer is used as a dwelling or place of human habitation. Graybeal v. Commonwealth, 228 Va. 736, 324 S.E.2d 698 (1985).

It would violate sound principles of statutory construction and strain the clear intendment of § 18.2-90 to hold that a trailer not used as a dwelling nevertheless falls under the definition of "other house." Graybeal v. Commonwealth, 228 Va. 736, 324 S.E.2d 698 (1985).

The phrase "other house," in § 18.2-90, is a general phrase placed at the end of a list of specific references to various structures. Those specific structures share the common element of being improvements affixed to the ground, that is, they are realty. Under the doctrine of ejusdem generis, the general phrase "other house" must look for its meaning to the specific items which precede it. Graybeal v. Commonwealth, 228 Va. 736, 324 S.E.2d 698 (1985).

"Affixed to realty." — In a burglary conviction, the Commonwealth established that the victim's home was permanently affixed to realty because the testimony established that the structure defendant entered was the victim's dwelling, and photographs showed that the residence was affixed to realty. Arrington v. Commonwealth, 2010 Va. App. LEXIS 87 (Mar. 9, 2010).

Habitability as element of offense. — With respect to structures other than the dwelling house of another, the legislature specifically chose to impose the habitability element only for automobiles, trucks or trailers; accordingly the Commonwealth was not required to prove the school's habitability as an element of the crime in this case. Allard v. Commonwealth, 24 Va. App. 57, 480 S.E.2d 139 (1997).

Burglarizing building leased to United States as post office. — Where the defendants had burglarized a building privately owned and leased to the United States for a post office, and where there had been no federal prosecution, the prosecution for burglarizing post offices was not preempted by the United States. Bowling v. Slayton, 344 F. Supp. 650 (W.D. Va. 1972).

"Dwelling house" not found. — Statutory burglary conviction under § 18.2-91 was improper as the house involved in the burglary was not a "dwelling house," as that term was defined in §§ 18.2-89, 18.2-90, and 18.2-91, in that the record contained no evidence that the house was used for habitation as no one slept there, the house was unfurnished, and no one used it for the usual activities of life. Additionally, there was no evidence that anyone who had used the house for habitation had any intention of resuming that use. Johns v. Commonwealth, 53 Va. App. 742, 675 S.E.2d 211, 2009 Va. App. LEXIS 172 (2009).

III. DEADLY WEAPON.

Fact finder determines whether weapon deadly. — Generally, unless a weapon is per se a deadly one, the fact finder should determine whether it, and the manner of its use, place it in that category. Pritchett v. Commonwealth, 219 Va. 927, 252 S.E.2d 352 (1979).

And burden is upon Commonwealth. — The burden of showing that a weapon is deadly is upon the Commonwealth. Pritchett v. Commonwealth, 219 Va. 927, 252 S.E.2d 352 (1979).

Club made from metal pipe as deadly weapon. — A club made from a piece of metal pipe or tubing flattened at one end to provide a gripping handle with a heavy metal bolt inserted in and affixed to the opposite end of the pipe, making that end heavier than the handle end, was designed and constructed as a weapon. Where, if that weapon is used in the manner contemplated by its design and construction, as an instrument to forcefully strike or flail an object, it would be likely to cause death or great bodily harm to a human being, it would not be error to conclude that it was a deadly weapon for purposes of prosecution under this section. Pritchett v. Commonwealth, 219 Va. 927, 252 S.E.2d 352 (1979).

Proof of an act of violence not required. — A violation of this section does not require proof of an act of violence or an act likely to produce violence. Taylor v. Commonwealth, 11 Va. App. 649, 400 S.E.2d 794 (1991).

Proof of breach of the peace not required. — A breach of the peace is not a fact the government is required to prove to obtain a conviction for violation of this section. Taylor v. Commonwealth, 11 Va. App. 649, 400 S.E.2d 794 (1991).

Breaking into warehouse or store is not breach of peace. — While breaking and entering a dwelling of another may often constitute a breach of the peace, particularly when it is done for the purpose of committing rape, robbery, or murder, breaking into a warehouse or store for the purpose of committing larceny is not a breach of the peace. Taylor v. Commonwealth, 11 Va. App. 649, 400 S.E.2d 794 (1991).

IV. INDICTMENT.

Indictment may aver intent, commission of larceny, or both. — The averment of an intent to steal is sufficient under this section; so also, where the felony has actually been committed, it seems sufficient to allege the commission, as that is the strongest evidence of the intention. But the intent to commit a felony and the actual commission of it may both be alleged, and, in general, this is the better mode of statement. Speers v. Commonwealth, 58 Va. (17 Gratt.) 570 (1867); Clark v. Commonwealth, 135 Va. 490, 115 S.E. 704 (1923).

While it is good practice for a prosecutor to aver and establish the commission of larceny as proving burglarious intent, under this section only the intent, not the theft, is an integrant of burglary. Downey v. Peyton, 451 F.2d 236 (4th Cir. 1971).

It may charge housebreaking and larceny in one count. —

Housebreaking with intent to commit larceny would be complete under this section whether the larceny was actually committed or not, but it is permissible to charge not only the breaking and entering with intent to commit larceny, but also the larceny, at the same time, as one continuous act; the charge of larceny in such case being the best evidence of the intent with which the breaking was committed. Clark v. Commonwealth, 135 Va. 490, 115 S.E. 704 (1923).

Though they are distinct offenses. — Grand larceny and housebreaking with the intent to commit larceny are distinct offenses under the law, and to each is affixed its own penalty, but they may be and often are one continued act, and may be charged in the same count of an indictment. Benton v. Commonwealth, 91 Va. 782, 21 S.E. 495 (1895); Branch v. Commonwealth, 184 Va. 394, 35 S.E.2d 593 (1945).

Such an indictment is for housebreaking and not for larceny. — An indictment which charges a breaking into a house with intent to steal, and the stealing therefrom, is an indictment for housebreaking, and not for larceny, and is good. Speers v. Commonwealth, 58 Va. (17 Gratt.) 570 (1867); Vaughan v. Commonwealth, 58 Va. (17 Gratt.) 576 (1867); Butler v. Commonwealth, 81 Va. 159 (1885).

Accused may be found guilty of either offense. — Where the accused is charged with breaking and entering with intent to commit larceny, and the commission of the larceny, he may be convicted of either offense but not of both. Clark v. Commonwealth, 135 Va. 490, 115 S.E. 704 (1923).

In an indictment under this section if the actual larceny is properly stated, the prisoner may be found guilty of the larceny, though acquitted of the housebreaking. Vaughan v. Commonwealth, 58 Va. (17 Gratt.) 576 (1867). See also Speers v. Commonwealth, 58 Va. (17 Gratt.) 570 (1867).

Viewed in the light most favorable to the Commonwealth, the evidence showed both: (1) that a breaking and entering and larceny occurred and (2) that the defendant possessed one of the credit cards taken in that burglary within hours of the break-in, thereby permitting application of the inference that he was the thief; there was sufficient evidence of burglary under § 18.2-91 to support conviction. Issak v. Commonwealth, No. 1853-02-4, 2003 Va. App. LEXIS 346 (Ct. of Appeals June 17, 2003).

Except where breaking and larceny are one continuous act. — Where the breaking and entering with intent to commit larceny and the commission of the larceny are one continuous act, the accused can only be convicted of the offense of breaking and entering with intent to commit larceny. Clark v. Commonwealth, 135 Va. 490, 115 S.E. 704 (1923).

An indictment contained a single count, and charged defendant with breaking and entering a certain railroad car with intent to commit larceny therein, and the larceny from the car of certain enumerated articles. Accused asked an instruction that should the jury find the accused guilty of breaking and entering the car with intent to steal, and also guilty of stealing the property, they could bring in a verdict for only one of the offenses. It was held that it was not error to refuse this instruction, as it told the jury that if the accused broke and entered the car with intent to steal, and stole the property, they could bring in a verdict for only one of the offenses, when in fact only one offense was committed if the act was continuous. Clark v. Commonwealth, 135 Va. 490, 115 S.E. 704 (1923).

Although both burglary under this section and grand larceny under § 18.2-95 are committed in an unbroken line of misconduct, the continuity does not bar an indictment and a conviction for each of the two offenses. Downey v. Peyton, 451 F.2d 236 (4th Cir. 1971).

No fatal variance found. — Evidence was sufficient to convict defendant of breaking and entering under § 18.2-91 and there was not a fatal variance between the evidence offered at trial and the indictment, which charged defendant with breaking and entering with the intent to commit larceny, as: (1) § 18.2-91 was cited in the indictment in accordance with § 19.2-220 and Va. Sup. Ct. R. 3A:6(a); (2) the citation in the indictment to § 18.2-91 incorporated by reference the complete definition of the offense set forth in the statute and supplemented the charging language of the indictment; (3) as the statute's title reflected, the offense could be committed with the "intent to commit larceny, assault and battery or other felony"; (4) although the body of the charge omitted reference to the intent to commit assault and battery, that specific intent was alleged in the indictment; (5) in reciting an abbreviated title of the charged offense, the indictment specifically referenced the "intent to commit A and B," or assault and battery; and (6) the arrest warrant underlying the felony charge specifically accused defendant of breaking and entering in the nighttime the dwelling house of the victim with the intent to commit assault and battery. Barth v. Commonwealth, 2007 Va. App. LEXIS 56 (Feb. 20, 2007).

Sufficiency of charge in indictment. — An indictment in the usual form for housebreaking was not insufficient because it did not negative the idea that the barroom which was broken and entered adjoined any dwelling house other than that of the owner of the barroom. Lawrence v. Commonwealth, 81 Va. 484 (1886).

Insufficient indictment. — A burglary indictment which charges the accused entered the premises with the intent to commit a "felony other than murder, rape or robbery" does not set forth the element of intent specifically enough to apprise the accused of the nature and character of the offense. Sims v. Commonwealth, 28 Va. App. 611, 507 S.E.2d 648 (1998).

V. PROSECUTION AND CONVICTION.

There can be only one penalty imposed. — Upon a count charging both grand larceny and housebreaking, the accused may be found guilty of either of the offenses, but there can be only one penalty imposed. Benton v. Commonwealth, 91 Va. 782, 21 S.E. 495 (1895); Branch v. Commonwealth, 184 Va. 394, 35 S.E.2d 593 (1945).

Unless there is a separate count for larceny. — If it is desired to punish for both larceny and housebreaking a separate count for larceny must be inserted in the indictment. Benton v. Commonwealth, 91 Va. 782, 21 S.E. 495 (1895).

General verdict of guilty is deemed to be for housebreaking. — It is well settled in Virginia that when an indictment contains but one count, charging housebreaking and larceny, and the verdict is a general one of guilty, the verdict will be considered as one for the major offense of housebreaking. Walters v. Commonwealth, 159 Va. 903, 165 S.E. 495 (1932); Harris v. Commonwealth, 185 Va. 26, 37 S.E.2d 868 (1946).

Conviction is bar to further prosecution. — If there is a conviction generally, or of the grand larceny only, and it is submitted to, in either case, this is a bar to further prosecution. Benton v. Commonwealth, 91 Va. 782, 21 S.E. 495 (1895).

Double jeopardy. — The double jeopardy clause does not bar conviction and sentence at one trial for burglary under this section and grand larceny under § 18.2-95 arising from a unitary criminal transaction, since each offense rests on different necessary elements. The clause is infringed only if all the components of a crime defined under one statute must also be proved to convict under another. The test to be applied is whether each provision requires proof of an additional fact which the other does not. Downey v. Peyton, 451 F.2d 236 (4th Cir. 1971).

Whether a defendant effected an integrated transgression or two unrelated ones, where the defendant executed each fundamental burglary, i.e., a breaking and an entry with essential intent, and every ingredient of grand larceny, i.e., a taking of goods, chattels and money of the value of $50 or more, quite clearly the factors of taking, asportation and value, indispensable in larceny, are not so in burglary. By contrast, breaking and entering — the essence of burglary — are not constituents of larceny. Obviously, convictions of both burglary under this section and larceny under § 18.2-95 do not invade a defendant's constitutional protection from double jeopardy. Downey v. Peyton, 451 F.2d 236 (4th Cir. 1971).

One may be convicted of destruction of private property and burglary. — One may be convicted of destruction of private property in violation of § 18.2-137, in addition to being convicted of burglary in violation of this section, as a result of causing damage to property when breaking and entering a building because each offense requires proof of a fact not required for the other. Fitzgerald v. Commonwealth, 11 Va. App. 625, 401 S.E.2d 208 (1991).

Prosecution for breaking and entering and destroying private property not barred by § 19.2-294. — Section 19.2-294, which bars a prosecution for a violation of one statute if a defendant has been convicted of violation of another statute for the same act, is inapplicable where the "same act" involved was the breaking of the doors of the places broken into. This act, although common to both the convictions of breaking and entering and the convictions for destroying private property, was a violation of § 18.2-137,

destroying private property, but was not a violation of this section, statutory burglary. Thus, the same act was a violation of only one of the two statutes, not both. Fitzgerald v. Commonwealth, 11 Va. App. 625, 401 S.E.2d 208 (1991).

Prosecution in federal court for both breaking and entering and larceny. — A defendant charged with breaking and entering an officers' club on a United States Army post and stealing the contents of a safe in the club could be prosecuted both for breaking and entering under this section, as authorized by the federal Assimilative Crimes Act, and for larceny under the federal statute relating to larceny within the special maritime and territorial jurisdiction of the United States. Clark v. United States, 267 F.2d 99 (4th Cir. 1959).

Verdict held responsive to charge. — An indictment contained only one count, and charged the statutory offense of housebreaking, with twofold averment of intent to steal and of actual theft as one continuous act. The jury found the accused guilty of housebreaking "as charged in the indictment" and he contended that the verdict was a nullity on the ground that it found him guilty of housebreaking alone and not of housebreaking with intent to commit larceny. It was held that the verdict was responsive to the charge in the indictment. McDorman v. Smyth, 187 Va. 522, 47 S.E.2d 441 (1948).

Sentences under this section and § 18.2-95 held not excessive. — Concurrent three-year terms of imprisonment for violations of this section and § 18.2-95 are not constitutionally excessive in view of the nature of the offenses. Phennicie v. Huffman, No. 0739-85 (Ct. of Appeals Apr. 23, 1986).

Sentences of six years in the penitentiary (now state correctional facility) upon conviction of breaking and entering a dwelling house with intent to commit larceny under this section and 20 years upon conviction of grand larceny under § 18.2-95, all of the 20-year sentence being suspended, were not constitutionally excessive in view of the nature of the offenses. Phennicie v. Huffman, No. 1001-85 (Ct. of Appeals Apr. 23, 1986).

Sentences of 10 years in the penitentiary (now state correctional facility) upon conviction of breaking and entering a dwelling house with intent to commit larceny under this section and 20 years upon conviction of grand larceny under § 18.2-95, all of the 20-year sentence for grand larceny being suspended, were not constitutionally excessive in view of the nature of the offenses. Phennicie v. Huffman, No. 1000-85 (Ct. of Appeals Apr. 23, 1986).

Sentences of 10 years in the penitentiary (now state correctional facility) upon conviction of each of two charges of breaking and entering a dwelling house with intent to commit larceny under this section, two years of the sentence on each offense being suspended, 5 years upon conviction of grand larceny under § 18.2-95, two years of the sentence for the offense being suspended, 10 years in the penitentiary (now state correctional facility) for additional statutory burglary and grand larceny convictions at a later trial, four years of the sentence being suspended, were not constitutionally excessive in view of the nature of the offenses. Phennicie v. Huffman, No. 0740-85 (Ct. of Appeals Apr. 23, 1986).

No error in denying concurrent sentence. — Given that the record on appeal adequately demonstrated that the sentencing judge correctly understood his discretion and sentenced defendant within the lawful scope of that discretion, the Court of Appeals of Virginia declined to apply the ends of justice exception to Va. Sup. Ct. R. 5A:18. As a result, no error resulted in the denial of defendant's request for a concurrent sentence. Scalf v. Commonwealth, 2008 Va. App. LEXIS 230 (May 13, 2008).

Insufficient documentation to show nature of delinquent act. — As the Commonwealth failed to prove that appellant juvenile was previously adjudicated delinquent of an act that would have been a violent felony under subsection C of § 17.1-805 if committed by an adult, his conviction for possession of a firearm, in violation of Subsection A of § 18.2-308.2, could not stand; the Commonwealth's attempt to prove a prior breaking and entering conviction, in violation of § 18.2-91, was insufficient where the nature of the delinquent act for which the juvenile was adjudicated was unclear by the document in support of that conviction. Preston v. Commonwealth, 281 Va. 52, 704 S.E.2d 127, 2011 Va. LEXIS 23 (2011).

VI. ILLUSTRATIVE CASES.

Evidence sufficient to sustain conviction. — In a prosecution under this section the evidence, though conflicting, warranted the jury in finding that a saddle found near defendant's residence was the property of the prosecuting witness; that this saddle had been seen by a witness in defendant's possession; that the saddle was stolen property; that defendant's possession was recent; that defendant failed to give a reasonable account of how his possession was acquired, but gave false account; that the saddle was obtained by entry of the barn of the prosecuting witness in the nighttime, as charged in the indictment; and that defendant was guilty of the larceny of the saddle. It was held that this was sufficient to sustain a verdict of guilty. Stallard v. Commonwealth, 130 Va. 769, 107 S.E. 722 (1921). See also, United States v. Butler, 390 F.2d 620 (4th Cir. 1968), cert. denied, 392 U.S. 915, 88 S. Ct. 2078, 20 L. Ed. 2d 1375 (1968); Guynn v. Commonwealth, 220 Va. 478, 259 S.E.2d 822 (1979).

Where credible evidence proved that defendant exited the back door of the residence, leaving the door open, and moved his truck to a nearby parking lot, and re-entered the residence carrying a gun with the intent to assault the victim, this was sufficient to support his conviction. Bruce v. Commonwealth, 22 Va. App. 264, 469 S.E.2d 64 (1996), aff'd, 256 Va. 371, 506 S.E.2d 318 (1998).

Evidence was sufficient to convict defendant under this section where there was direct evidence of breaking by force, the defendant had pawned some of the stolen property, and the police found a set of tin snips at the scene bearing the defendant's first initial and last name. Cobb v. Commonwealth, 26 Va. App. 418, 494 S.E.2d 899 (1998).

Evidence was sufficient to identify the defendant as the person who broke into and entered a dwelling in violation of this section, notwithstanding the defendant's contention that the victim was mistaken in identifying him as the person inside the house because he only saw the intruder for "a couple of seconds" and his ability to see into the house was impaired by bright afternoon sunlight, where the victim testified that he had known the defendant for 20 years and that he was certain that he was the man he saw walking through his house. Wright v. Commonwealth, No. 0672-97-3.

Where the evidence placed the defendant in the office or rooms from which property was taken immediately before the thefts were discovered, where the defendant had no rationale for being in those locations, and where, when confronted, he gave each victim a false explanation of his presence and intentions, the evidence was sufficient to support his conviction. Brown v. Commonwealth, No. 0107-97-2 (Ct. of Appeals June 16, 1998).

Evidence was sufficient to convict defendant under this section where there was direct evidence of breaking by force, the defendant had pawned some of the stolen property, and the police found a set of tin snips at the scene bearing the defendant's first initial and last name. Cobb v. Commonwealth, 26 Va. App. 418, 494 S.E.2d 899 (1998).

A conviction for burglary was proper where the evidence showed that the defendant also intended to discharge a firearm in an occupied building and to commit criminal assault. Browder v. Commonwealth, No. 1499-97-2 (Ct. of Appeals Dec. 22, 1998).

The evidence was sufficient to support a defendant's conviction under this section where the defendant appeared on the victim's porch with two accomplices immediately before the break-in, supposedly looking for someone they believed lived in her home, the defendant was present in the car with the accomplices immediately following the break-in, the defendant attempted to conceal himself as the get-away car passed by a police officer and fled on foot when the car was eventually stopped, and the victim's neighbor, who witnessed the incident, testified that she observed two men leave the victim's home and her general description of the race and height of one of the men she saw leaving the victim's home fit the defendant. Perry v. Commonwealth, No. 2667-99-2, 2000 Va. App. LEXIS 749 (Ct. of Appeals Nov. 21, 2000).

Evidence was sufficient to establish intent to commit assault and battery, where defendant's conduct, both before and after he broke open apartment door, clearly manifested a continuing intent to assault his estranged wife. Moore v. Commonwealth, No. 0915-99-1 (Ct. of Appeals Feb. 29, 2000).

The evidence was sufficient to support the defendant's conviction for breaking and entering with the intent to commit assault and battery where the defendant called the owner of a home and, in threatening manner, informed the owner that he was coming to retrieve his wife, angrily demanded admittance when he arrived, entered the house, broke down the door to a bedroom and then assaulted both his wife and the owner; these circumstances supported the inference that the defendant traveled to the house with the intent to commit assault. Archer v. Commonwealth, No. 2550-99-2, 2000 Va. App. LEXIS 485 (Ct. of Appeals July 5, 2000).

The evidence was sufficient to sustain a defendant's conviction for breaking and entering with the intent to commit larceny where the defendant's unauthorized presence in an office suite before normal business hours permitted an inference that he intended to commit larceny and where, in addition to his unauthorized presence, the evidence proved that the defendant possessed a screwdriver whose tip was altered sufficiently to serve as a burglary tool and a latex glove that would prevent his fingerprints from being detected on a door he might manipulate for entry and an officer testified that several additional altered screwdrivers were found in the defendant's car. Hucks v. Commonwealth, 33 Va. App. 168, 531 S.E.2d 658, 2000 Va. App. LEXIS 568 (2000), overruled in part by Velasquez v. Commonwealth, 276 Va. 326, 661 S.E.2d 454 (2008).

Evidence that showed that defendant broke into a house, took a woman's duffel bag which had distinctive red striping on it, and was seen by several neighbors carrying the bag around the time that two neighborhood houses were burglarized was sufficient to sustain defendant's convictions for statutory burglary. Cullipher v. Commonwealth, No. 2422-01-1, 2002 Va. App. LEXIS 626 (Ct. of Appeals Oct. 15, 2002).

Circumstantial evidence, such as the defendant's statement that he possesses a firearm, was sufficient evidence to prove beyond a reasonable doubt that an accused indeed possessed a firearm during a burglary under § 18.2-91. Bell v. Commonwealth, No. 0318-02-1, 2003 Va. App. LEXIS 373 (Ct. of Appeals July 1, 2003).

Evidence was sufficient to support defendant's convictions for statutory burglary and grand larceny where: (1) defendant's DNA profile was consistent with blood drops underneath a window; (2) a partial analysis on a beer bottle did not exclude defendant; (3) defendant was not a customer or an employee of the co-op, and no evidence suggested that he had a reason to be on the premises; (4) defendant lied to police about his whereabouts at the time of the break-in; and (5) before police shared any information with defendant as to the condition of the truck, he made the spontaneous statement that "the truck was not damaged." Davis v. Commonwealth, No. 0649-03-2, 2004 Va. App. LEXIS 220 (Ct. of Appeals May 11, 2004).

Defendant's conviction for breaking and entering with the intent to commit a larceny was upheld on appeal where sufficient evidence existed to permit a rational trier of fact to have found that defendant broke into a transmission shop. Eyewitness testimony identified defendant as the perpetrator and the sequential testimony of the witnesses left no time frame unaccounted for. Green v. Commonwealth, No. 0703-04-2, 2005 Va. App. LEXIS 49 (Ct. of Appeals Feb. 8, 2005).

Defendant's convictions for grand larceny and breaking and entering with intent to commit larceny were affirmed as: (1) an employee of the victim business testified that a storeroom window was intact on the day before the burglary and that the next day he discovered his computer and other items missing and found that the window was broken; (2) the storeroom was not a place where employees regularly went; (3) defendant repeatedly told a detective that he had never been inside the storeroom; (4) it could be hypothesized that defendant's blood was left in the storeroom during the burglary and that defendant was the burglar; and (5) the fact that the burglar did not take a broken printer and that defendant knew that the printer was broken provided additional circumstantial evidence that defendant was the perpetrator. Smith v. Commonwealth, — Va. App. —, — S.E.2d —, 2006 Va. App. LEXIS 295 (July 5, 2006).

Evidence was sufficient to prove that defendant illegally entered an apartment, even though only the tenant testified on this point, because neither the owner nor the realty company could have given defendant permission to enter the apartment, as the apartment was leased; moreover, the trial court could have reasonably inferred that neither the tenant's roommate nor the owner gave defendant permission to enter the apartment given his method of entry, which was through a broken and boarded up window. Contrary to defendant's claim that there was insufficient evidence of burglary intent, defendant's statement to the police did not provide any alternative reason why he entered the home through the window off the alley, and he had a bag with him, directly below the window, which allowed the trial court to infer that defendant intended to take things from the home, put them into the bag, and steal those items. Slaughter v. Commonwealth, 49 Va. App. 659, 644 S.E.2d 89, 2007 Va. App. LEXIS 182 (2007).

Given that the Commonwealth presented sufficient evidence that defendant burglarized an apartment with the requisite specific intent and malice to disfigure, maim, disable, or kill at least three of the victims, without provocation, his convictions based upon said actions were upheld on appeal. Slayton v. Commonwealth, — Va. App. —, — S.E.2d —, 2007 Va. App. LEXIS 180 (May 1, 2007).

Evidence was sufficient to prove that defendant broke into and entered the dwelling house of another because defendant had conceded that he had no legal right to be in his former girlfriend's apartment, and his counsel conceded that defendant was not legally there; a protective order that was in place at the time of the break-in forbade defendant from having any contact with the girlfriend, who told defendant not to come over and that if he did, she would call the police. Thomas v. Commonwealth, 2008 Va. App. LEXIS 161 (Apr. 8, 2008).

Defendant's convictions on four counts of grand larceny and four counts of burglary were supported by sufficient evidence as defendant admitted that he took part in the burglaries of the first two of four homes, and the evidence supported a reasonable inference that defendant took part in the burglaries of the third and fourth homes, in that, at the fourth house, defendant's fingerprints were found on bank envelopes stolen from the third house. The similarity of the burglaries was relevant circumstantial evidence that tended to show that defendant was the criminal agent as the breaking and entering occurred by the same means each time, the same type of personal property was stolen, the master bedroom in each house was the target of each burglary, and dresser drawers were dumped in each location. Wilkins v. Commonwealth, 2008 Va. App. LEXIS 483 (Oct. 28, 2008).

Convictions of grand larceny, § 18.2-95, and statutory burglary, § 18.2-91, were supported by sufficient evidence because the trial court was not obligated to accept defendant's explanation of possession of recently stolen tools as credible, and was entitled to rely on evidence of his falsely denied recent possession as proof of his guilt; the trial court clearly rejected defendant's story of how he purchased, then pawned, the stolen tools as too coincidental, and disregarded defendant's explanation as too opposed to probabilities. Marshall v. Commonwealth, 2009 Va. App. LEXIS 318 (July 14, 2009).

In a case in which defendant appealed his convictions for breaking and entering, in violation of § 18.2-91, and grand larceny, in violation of § 18.2-95, he argued unsuccessfully that the evidence was insufficient to support his convictions. The trial court reasonably concluded from the evidence that the items stolen and those defendant sold to a pawn shop were the same items: (1) the pawn shop required a picture identification prior to purchasing property from a customer; (2) the purchase agreements issued to defendant for the purchase of a guitar and television listed the serial numbers of the items purchased; and (3) those serial numbers matched the serial numbers of the stolen guitar and television. Lunsford v. Commonwealth, 55 Va. App. 59, 683 S.E.2d 831, 2009 Va. App. LEXIS 461 (2009).

Evidence, including that defendant and another individual went to a victim's apartment while armed, went to confront the victim, and rushed out of the apartment in pursuit of the victim, who had escaped through a window, was sufficient to support defendant's conviction for burglary while armed with a deadly weapon under § 18.2-91. Jones v. Commonwealth, 279 Va. 295, 687 S.E.2d 738, 2010 Va. LEXIS 4 (2010).

Evidence was sufficient to support defendant's conviction for statutory burglary under § 18.2-91, although a companion who lived in the house opened a door to defendant, because defendant entered the house with the intent to steal and the entry occurred at night and, therefore, under § 18.2-90, breaking was not a required element. Stegall v. Commonwealth, 2010 Va. App. LEXIS 137 (Apr. 6, 2010).

Evidence that one set of victims testified that a nylon camouflaged holster found with defendant's wallet and belongings looked like one missing from their house, one of the firearms recovered from defendant's shed bore the serial number of a firearm missing from their home, and deer meat stolen from another victim and uniquely packaged was identified by another victim supported defendant's convictions for grand larceny, two counts of breaking and entering, two counts of larceny of a firearm, petit larceny, and destruction of property. Bowles v. Commonwealth, 2010 Va. App. LEXIS 275 (July 13, 2010).

Totality of the circumstances permitted a reasonable inference that defendant broke and entered two businesses and intended to commit larceny when he did so because defendant was present at an office complex for an extended period of time at night after business hours; defendant left the building carrying a concealed object and placed it in his vehicle where a duffle bag was found containing a tire iron, work gloves, a flashlight, and loose change. Baker v. Commonwealth, 2011 Va. App. LEXIS 358 (Nov. 22, 2011).

There was sufficient evidence to establish that defendant entered the pharmacy store with the intent to commit larceny or a felony other than murder, rape, robbery, or arson, upholding his conviction under the right result for the wrong reason doctrine, where the evidence showed that defendant told an informant during a controlled buy that defendant went to a pharmacy to rob it for specified drugs, and demanded money and a drug, demanded the drug from filled prescriptions when the pharmacist responded he had no access to the drug. Towler v. Commonwealth, 59 Va. App. 284, 718 S.E.2d 463, 2011 Va. App. LEXIS 402 (2011).

Because § 18.2-91 did not require the use or display of a firearm during a burglary, and because defendant's challenge to the sufficiency of the evidence under § 18.2-53.1 for use of a firearm in the commission of a breaking and entering was waived, the ends of justice exception in Va. Sup. Ct. R. 5A:18 did not apply. Blackwell v. Commonwealth, 2012 Va. App. LEXIS 9 (Jan. 17, 2012).

Where the Commonwealth demonstrated that someone broke and entered into an office one day and the next day defendant successfully cashed a forged check drawn from that company's checking account, the factfinder was permitted to determine that defendant's justification for possessing the stolen checks was not credible and the evidence was sufficient to support defendant's burglary conviction. Hopper v. Commonwealth, 2012 Va. App. LEXIS 200 (June 12, 2012).

Where defendant punched the victim, who had been blocking the entrance into his home, through the entry space and followed the victim into the house, the evidence was sufficient to allow the trial court to infer that defendant applied some force to the door in order to enter the house and to support defendant's conviction for statutory burglary with the intent to commit assault and battery. Latson v. Commonwealth, 2012 Va. App. LEXIS 207 (June 19, 2012).

Circumstantial evidence held sufficient. — See Johnson v. Commonwealth, No. 3026-02-2, 2003 Va. App. LEXIS 707 (Ct. of Appeals Dec. 30, 2003).

Evidence sufficient to convict as principal in the second degree. — In a case in which defendant was convicted of burglary, in violation of § 18.2-91, as a principal in the second degree, he argued unsuccessfully that the evidence was insufficient to show that he actually committed the burglary. The evidence established that he gave his wife the entry codes she needed to enter both the main office building in which an insurance agency was located and the agent's actual office space, and the evidence further established that when he gave her the codes he knew that she intended to use them to gain entry to the insurance office and steal property; the Commonwealth was not required to prove that he committed the actual burglary. Saunders v. Commonwealth, 2009 Va. App. LEXIS 532 (Dec. 1, 2009).

Tool marks on door and admission of burglaries in neighborhood were insufficient evidence. — Where burglary victim's testimony furnished evidence only of tool marks on his garage door, and defendant's admissions that he had committed burglaries in the neighborhood furnished no proof that an entry was actually made into the house in question by a person having the requisite intent, because he simply did not know which houses he had entered, burglary conviction would be reversed for failure to prove the corpus delicti. Caminade v. Commonwealth, 230 Va. 505, 338 S.E.2d 846 (1986).

Evidence sufficient to convict for attempted statutory burglary. — Evidence was sufficient to convict defendant of attempted statutory burglary because the evidence was sufficient to prove that defendant attempted to break into his sister's house with the intent to steal money or items from her house at a time when he needed "a fix" for his drug addiction because: (1) defendant knew his sister was not at home because no one responded to his "banging" on the door; (2) defendant pulled off the screens on some windows, but was unable to open the windows; (3) defendant then beat on the lock on the back door with a shovel; (4) a neighbor informed defendant that his sister was not at home and defendant walked to the front of the house where the neighbor heard more loud noise but did not investigate further; and (5) defendant's sister testified that she had not given defendant permission to enter her house and that he later told her he that he did try and break into her house. Perkins v. Commonwealth, No. 1025-03-1, 2004 Va. App. LEXIS 419 (Ct. of Appeals Sept. 7, 2004).

Evidence that a resident of the apartment building observed defendant, from a distance of about ten feet, with a hammer in his hand immediately after she heard banging in the vicinity, and that, five to ten minutes later, police found defendant with an object later identified as a hammer was sufficient to support defendant's conviction for attempted breaking and entering with intent to commit larceny. Barnett v. Commonwealth, — Va. App. —, — S.E.2d —, 2007 Va. App. LEXIS 2 (Jan. 9, 2007).

Evidence was sufficient to prove that defendant attempted to commit burglary of a residence, as an officer observed evidence of a break-in after receiving a call from the home, and a maintenance person described damage to screens that the maintenance person replaced during the time frame consistent with defendant's method of cutting screens to gain entry. Smith v. Commonwealth, 2011 Va. App. LEXIS 156 (May 10, 2011).

Driving the getaway car. — Evidence was sufficient to sustain a burglary conviction where defendant drove the other participants to the crime scene, waited for their return from a safe distance across the street in the dark, and then provided the transportation for their flight from the scene of the crime by driving the getaway car. Defendant admitted on cross-examination to knowing before the burglary that "something bad was going to happen at the burglary scene." Thomas v. Commonwealth, — Va. App. —, — S.E.2d —, 2006 Va. App. LEXIS 73 (Feb. 28, 2006).

Evidence held insufficient to sustain conviction. — See Williams v. Commonwealth, 193 Va. 764, 71 S.E.2d 73 (1952).

Where neighbor's testimony failed to correspond with the victim's description of her knitting bag in two pivotal respects and the neighbor did not testify as to whether or not defendant was carrying the bag when he initially walked behind the town homes towards the victim's residence, the evidence was insufficient to support the inference that defendant was the person who broke into the victim's residence and stole her property. McKinney v. Commonwealth, No. 1129-96-2 (Ct. of Appeals May 13, 1997).

Where appellant's sister had not told appellant that he could not return to the apartment, where appellant temporarily resided in the apartment, slept on the sofa, and had clothing in the apartment, and where the inference that appellant somehow broke into the apartment was no more reasonable than the inference that one of the children or the mother opened the door to give him entry to the apartment, the evidence failed to prove beyond a reasonable doubt that a breaking occurred. Mayo v. Commonwealth, No. 0293-97-2 (Ct. of Appeals Nov. 25, 1997).

Circumstantial evidence was insufficient to prove that the defendant committed grand larceny and/or burglary where: (1) there was evidence that she walked toward a business that was burglarized, but there was no evidence that she entered the business or was seen inside the business; (2) although the defendant's boots were very similar to footprints in the snow at the scene of the crime, no evidence of a match was presented; and (3) police officers saw other persons near the scene of the crime shortly after the defendant was allowed to leave, but did not examine their shoes or try to match them to the footprints in the snow. Martin v. Commonwealth, No. 1556-97-2 (Ct. of Appeals June 9, 1998).

Evidence was insufficient to prove a "breaking" into the residence of the defendant's mother and stepfather where the defendant had a key to the house, the defendant's mother testified that when he called her she gave him permission to enter the house and that he was never told that he could not enter the house, and the defendant's stepfather testified that he did not tell the defendant that he could not be in the house, that he knew that the defendant still had clothes in the house, and that the defendant did have permission to enter the house. Whitaker v. Commonwealth, No. 2050-97-4 (Ct. of Appeals July 7, 1998).

Evidence was insufficient to support a conviction where: (1) the parties stipulated that two homes were burglarized and that goods valued at more than $200 were stolen from each home; (2) although there was evidence that the defendant thereafter pawned some items, there was no evidence as to what those items were; and (3) a police officer could not recall whether the defendant admitted that he pawned "that stuff" or "some stuff." Dailey v. Commonwealth, No. 0327-98-1 (Ct. of Appeals Feb. 9, 1999).

Where the evidence established that on two occasions on the day of the burglary a stolen cell phone was used to call a cab to transport the defendant, and the defendant acknowledged that the calls were made on his behalf although he did not recall who made the actual calls, such evidence was insufficient to establish the defendant's guilt beyond a reasonable doubt. While the suspicion of the defendant's guilt was strong, it was equally plausible that the phone calls were made by a certain third parties. Savage v. Commonwealth, No. 0889-00-1, 2001 Va. App. LEXIS 119 (Ct. of Appeals Mar. 13, 2001).

Defendant's conviction of statutory burglary was reversed, because the offense of statutory burglary required an entry during the nighttime, and the evidence clearly indicated that defendant's entry into a business took place during the day, and the Commonwealth did not amend the indictment to allege breaking and entering, which would have constituted burglary where the entry occurred during the day. Scott v. Commonwealth, 49 Va. App. 68, 636 S.E.2d 893, 2006 Va. App. LEXIS 511 (2006).

Conviction for breaking and entering with the intent to commit larceny was reversed because the Commonwealth did not prove defendant committed a larceny; defendant did not tamper with cash registers, the security cameras did not record defendant concealing any property on his person, defendant did not have any property belonging to the store in his possession, and the evidence failed to show that any merchandise was missing from the store after the incident. Vincent v. Commonwealth, — Va. App. —, — S.E.2d —, 2007 Va. App. LEXIS 19 (Jan. 23, 2007).

Evidence was insufficient to sustain defendant's conviction for statutory burglary under § 18.2-91, because defendant entered the house through the open garage, which was part of the house, and only employed force to enter the utility room, once inside the house. Lacey v. Commonwealth, 54 Va. App. 32, 675 S.E.2d 846, 2009 Va. App. LEXIS 214 (2009).

Evidence was insufficient to convict defendant as a principal in the second degree of burglary because, although the circumstances were highly suspicious, they did not show that defendant knowingly contributed to the burglary committed by a principal, a known burglar, or that the principal committed a burglary since evidence that the principal came from a house containing three apartments did not show that he came from the burgled apartment or that he was the perpetrator of the burglary, particularly as the victim had been away for several days and did not know when the breaking had occurred. Gillison v. Commonwealth, 2009 Va. App. LEXIS 477 (Oct. 27, 2009).

While the evidence showed that defendant and a coconspirator entered the subject house sometime while the house was empty, between 6:30 and 11:30 p.m, there was no clarification on the time of the entry and the trial court did not take judicial notice of what time sunset occurred. Thus, the evidence was insufficient to prove that defendant entered the house in the nighttime, as required for a burglary conviction. Derrick v. Commonwealth, 2013 Va. App. LEXIS 101 (Apr. 2, 2013).

Evidence sufficient to support unlawful entry. — Evidence was sufficient to support the unlawful entry element for defendant's burglary conviction under § 18.2-91 where defendant conceded that he entered the victim's apartment at night, without her permission and contrary to her will, and the trial court had ample reason to disbelieve that defendant heard any voice, whether real or imagined, inviting him into the apartment. Menefee v. Commonwealth, No. 3188-02-2, 2004 Va. App. LEXIS 77 (Ct. of Appeals Feb. 17, 2004).

Statutory burglary conviction was upheld, where it was supported by evidence that defendant: (1) broke into the victim's home around midnight after making repeated phone calls to the victim which were eventually unanswered; (2) broke into the victim's home, initially taking some of the victim's belongings; (3) returned to the home and assaulted the victim; and (4) threatened to return to the home in order to "get the victim"; defendant's assaultive intent could be inferred by the fact finder, despite defendant's denial of the same. Hicks v. Commonwealth, No. 1421-03-3, 2004 Va. App. LEXIS 172 (Ct. of Appeals Apr. 13, 2004).

Evidence was sufficient to support defendant's conviction for statutory burglary where the Commonwealth proved that defendant broke into the victim's locked house through a back window. When the victim arrived home, defendant stepped from behind the front door with a pistol in his hand and subsequently raped her. Breeden v. Commonwealth, 43 Va. App. 169, 596 S.E.2d 563, 2004 Va. App. LEXIS 257 (2004).

District court properly applied the Armed Career Criminal Act to defendant's state conviction for burglary, even though the statute under which defendant was convicted (§ 18.2-91) encompassed unlawful entry into areas that were not buildings or structures, because the indictment charged defendant with breaking and entering a business, which necessarily ensured that defendant sought to enter a building or structure. United States v. Shelton, — F.3d —, 2006 U.S. App. LEXIS 22284 (4th Cir. Aug. 30, 2006).

CIRCUIT COURT OPINIONS

Evidence sufficient to sustain conviction. — Because photographs of a door showed extensive damage to the door and the door frame, defendant was found in the premises going through a trash can, and defendant did not have permission to enter the apartment, the evidence fully supported a conviction for statutory burglary. Commonwealth v. Abbott, 68 Va. Cir. 73, 2005 Va. Cir. LEXIS 89 (Amherst County 2005).

§ 18.2-92. Breaking and entering dwelling house with intent to commit other misdemeanor.

If any person break and enter a dwelling house while said dwelling is occupied, either in the day or nighttime, with the intent to commit any misdemeanor except assault and battery or trespass, he shall be guilty of a Class 6 felony. However, if the person was armed with a deadly weapon at the time of such entry, he shall be guilty of a Class 2 felony.

History.
Code 1950, § 18.1-88.1; 1968, c. 530; 1970, c. 381; 1975, cc. 14, 15; 1992, c. 486.

Cross references.
As to requirement of saliva or tissue sample for DNA analysis after arrest for a violent felony, see § 19.2-310.2:1.

Law Review.
For 1995 survey of criminal law and procedure, see 29 U. Rich. L. Rev. 951 (1995).

Michie's Jurisprudence.
For related discussion, see 9B M.J. Husband and Wife, § 87.

CASE NOTES

Other than by judicial extension in some jurisdictions, there was no common law equivalent to this section. Johnson v. Commonwealth, 18 Va. App. 441, 444 S.E.2d 559 (1994).

This section is a lesser included offense of § 18.2-89, the principal distinction being that under this section the crime intended upon entry is a non-theft misdemeanor rather than a felony. Johnson v. Commonwealth, 18 Va. App. 441, 444 S.E.2d 559 (1994).

"Occupied" construed. — The phrase "while said dwelling is occupied" in this section is not an element of the crime requiring the physical presence of the occupant at the time of the unlawful entry. Rather, it is language intended by the legislature to emphasize the character of the use of the dwelling as a place of current habitation rather than a dwelling that is temporarily vacant. Johnson v. Commonwealth, 18 Va. App. 441, 444 S.E.2d 559 (1994).

Evidence establishing both actual and constructive breaking and entering. — Where the prosecutrix in a case of breaking and entering with the intent to commit assault and battery testified that she opened her door only about one foot, and thus the defendant had to push the door open additionally in order to enter the apartment, and where she also stated that she expressly told the defendant to remain outside when she went to get him a glass of water, this testimony established both an actual and a constructive breaking and entering by the defendant. Johnson v. Commonwealth, 221 Va. 872, 275 S.E.2d 592 (1981).

Forcing victim to open door is constructive breaking. — Given the lack of any qualifications, the phrase "to gain entry" in a jury instruction permitted the jury to find defendant guilty of burglary under § 18.2-92 by way of a constructive breaking if defendant forced the victim to open a door no less than if defendant had forced the door open. Lay v. Commonwealth, 50 Va. App. 330, 649 S.E.2d 714, 2007 Va. App. LEXIS 326 (2007).

Evidence showing only that the defendant broke and entered an apartment as he fled from the police, entering from one side of the apartment and exiting on the other, was insufficient to show that he did this with intent to obstruct a law enforcement officer. Thomas v. Commonwealth, No. 0213-90-2 (Ct. of Appeals March 12, 1991).

Defendant's mere presence did not establish participation in the break-in; however, other circumstances surrounding his presence and his subsequent entry into the dwelling were sufficient to establish that he shared the criminal intent to break into the apartment. Johnson v. Commonwealth, 18 Va. App. 441, 444 S.E.2d 559 (1994).

Intent inferred. — Required intent to commit some misdemeanor could be inferred by defendant's participation either as the principal housebreaker or as a principal in the second degree to the breaking, and his subsequent entry into the home. Johnson v. Commonwealth, 18 Va. App. 441, 444 S.E.2d 559 (1994).

Amending the indictment to change the intent. — Trial court did not err by amending the indictment, which charged breaking and entering with the intent to commit destruction of property, by adding the phrase "or indecent exposure" where: (1) the amendment permitted the Commonwealth to satisfy its burden of proof with either of two specific alternatives; (2) the modification of the original indictment did not change the general nature or character of the crime charged; (3) only the intent changed, and as amended the indictment still charged a misdemeanor of the same general nature or class; (4) the amendment did not surprise defendant because the original indictment included a count that charged indecent exposure; (5) the amendment did not prejudice defendant because the trial court continued the case after making the amendment; and (6) the trial court convicted defendant of the charge as originally stated. Esquibele v. Commonwealth, No. 2500-03-4, 2004 Va. App. LEXIS 586 (Ct. of Appeals Nov. 30, 2004).

Evidence sufficient for breaking. — Evidence presented at trial was sufficient to show that defendant broke and entered the victim's apartment. The evidence proved that defendant was present at the scene of the break-in and that he was inside the victim's apartment immediately following the break-in. Although victim's testimony was not conclusive as to what door — the main door of the apartment building or the interior apartment door — she saw defendant push against, the trier of fact was privileged to weigh this evidence and determine whether or not defendant committed an act of breaking. Johnson v. Commonwealth, 18 Va. App. 441, 444 S.E.2d 559 (1994).

Evidence of deadly weapon sufficient. — Evidence was sufficient to convict defendant of statutory burglary while armed with a deadly weapon under § 18.2-92 where it showed that defendant entered an apartment looking for his assailants, brandished gun at the occupants, and only left when satisfied his quarry was not present; the Commonwealth did not need to prove that the gun was operable or loaded for it to be a deadly weapon. Inge v. Commonwealth, 39 Va. App. 85, 570 S.E.2d 869, 2002 Va. App. LEXIS 617 (2002).

No error in failure to instruct. — Where defendant made no effort to take any property or thing of value, reached for and tore the victim's night clothes, and attempted to quiet her and get her to her bedroom, the trial judge did not err in refusing to instruct the jury that they could find the defendant guilty of burglary with the intent to commit a misdemeanor. Lea v. Commonwealth, 16 Va. App. 300, 429 S.E.2d 477 (1993).

Evidence insufficient to show intent to obstruct justice. — Evidence did not prove that defendants had the intent to obstruct justice when they entered apartment where evidence proved that the three men entered the apartment in an apparent attempt to avoid detection or to await the end of the disturbances in which they had been involved; no evidence proved that they had any contact with police officers before they entered the apartment or even that police officers were present when they entered the apartment; and although the men peered through the windows, no facts or circumstances proved that the defendants intended by threat or force to attempt to intimidate or impede a law-enforcement officer. Dowdell v. Commonwealth, No. 1694-93-1 (Ct. of Appeals March 7, 1995).

Applied in Turner v. Commonwealth, 38 Va. App. 851, 568 S.E.2d 468, 2002 Va. App. LEXIS 525 (2002).

§ 18.2-93. Entering bank, armed, with intent to commit larceny.

If any person, armed with a deadly weapon, shall enter any banking house, in the daytime or in the nighttime, with intent to commit larceny of money, bonds, notes, or other evidence of debt therein, he shall be guilty of a Class 2 felony.

History.
Code 1950, § 18.1-90; 1960, c. 358; 1975, cc. 14, 15.

Law Review.
For survey of Virginia law on criminal law for the year 1974-1975, see 61 Va. L. Rev. 1697 (1975).

Michie's Jurisprudence.
For related discussion, see 3A M.J. Burglary and Housebreaking, § 5; 16 M.J. Robbery, §§ 3, 9.

CASE NOTES

Section recognizes robbery as crime against the person. — The enactment of this section clearly shows that it has never been the intention of the legislature to enlarge, decrease or change the common-law crime of robbery. Recognizing the doctrine that robbery is a crime against the person, and not against a house or other inanimate thing, the legislature passed this section. Falden v. Commonwealth, 167 Va. 542, 189 S.E. 326 (1937); Cox v. Commonwealth, 218 Va. 689, 240 S.E.2d 524 (1978).

Property of another need not be taken. — A person convicted under this section need not have taken the personal property of another. Hill v. Commonwealth, 2 Va. App. 683, 347 S.E.2d 913 (1986).

"Banking house." — Technical distinctions in the definitions of "bank" and "savings and loan association" provided for regulatory purposes, and found in the banking and finance title of the Code, do not bar inclusion of both types of financial institutions within the general descriptive term "banking house" as used in this section. Black v. Commonwealth, 20 Va. App. 186, 455 S.E.2d 755 (1995).

Expert improperly qualified. — In a prosecution for the use of a deadly weapon with the intent to commit larceny and the use of a firearm in the commission of a robbery, the trial court erred in qualifying a detective as an expert in firearms, as the BB gun defendant used was clearly not a "firearm." However, the error was harmless as the detective had the requisite knowledge to be classified as an expert on BB guns, and his improper classification could have only had a slight effect on the jury, if any. Justiss v. Commonwealth, 61 Va. App. 261, 734 S.E.2d 699, 2012 Va. App. LEXIS 404 (2012).

Expert's opinion went to ultimate issue. — In prosecution for the use of a firearm with the intent to commit larceny, the trial court reversibly erred in allowing a detective to testify as an expert that the BB gun defendant used was capable of causing serious injury or death, as this opinion went to the ultimate issue — whether the BB gun was a "deadly weapon" — and improperly invaded the province of the jury. Justiss v. Commonwealth, 61 Va.

App. 261, 734 S.E.2d 699, 2012 Va. App. LEXIS 404 (2012).

Evidence of deadly weapon sufficient. — Evidence was sufficient to support defendant's conviction of entering a bank with a deadly weapon, because defendant displayed the object as an offensive weapon, capable of inflicting death or great bodily injury, and the teller, who was familiar with guns, testified that she saw the handle part of the pistol. Davis v. Commonwealth, No. 1149-01-3, 2002 Va. App. LEXIS 580 (Ct. of Appeals Oct. 1, 2002).

Because there was evidence that a BB gun could cause serious injury or death, even if the trial court had given defendant's requested jury instructions, the verdict would have been the same; thus, defendant was properly convicted of entering a bank armed with a deadly weapon with the intent to commit larceny. Young v. Commonwealth, — Va. App. —, — S.E.2d —, 2005 Va. App. LEXIS 402 (Oct. 11, 2005).

In prosecution for the use of a deadly weapon with the intent to commit larceny, there was sufficient evidence for a jury to conclude that the BB gun defendant used while robbing a bank was a deadly weapon, including a detective's testimony that he knew of two incidents involving BB guns that resulted in either death or serious bodily injury. Justiss v. Commonwealth, 61 Va. App. 261, 734 S.E.2d 699, 2012 Va. App. LEXIS 404 (2012).

Pistol with wooden bullets held to be deadly. — Where the defendant entered the bank wielding a pistol in the ordinary manner contemplated by its nature and design and his brandishing of it held it out as an offensive weapon, capable of inflicting death or great bodily injury, the mere fact that the wooden bullets therein were ab initio incapable of being discharged did not make the pistol any less deadly within the meaning of this section. Cox v. Commonwealth, 218 Va. 689, 240 S.E.2d 524 (1978).

Evidence of good character of accused is admissible. — Evidence of the good character of the accused in a prosecution under this section should be admitted, not for the purpose of affecting his guilt or innocence, but for the effect it may have upon the degree of his punishment. The Commonwealth should also have the right to introduce evidence in rebuttal. Roach v. Commonwealth, 157 Va. 954, 162 S.E. 50 (1932).

Nolo contendere should not be accepted. — A charge of entering a banking house while armed with a deadly weapon with intent to commit larceny is a charge of a felony. Under the law prevailing in Virginia a plea of nolo contendere cannot be accepted in a felony case, and in a prosecution under this section the court errs in receiving the plea. Roach v. Commonwealth, 157 Va. 954, 162 S.E. 50 (1932).

Convictions under this section and § 18.2-53.1 not double jeopardy. — In order to prove the offense pursuant to this section, the commonwealth must establish that the defendant entered a bank while armed with a deadly weapon but evidence of use or display of the weapon is not an element of this crime as it is under § 18.2-53.1 and, therefore, convicting a defendant both for use of a firearm in the commission of a robbery and for entry into a banking house while armed with a deadly weapon does not violate the double jeopardy clause. Collins v. Commonwealth, No. 0253-00-1, 2001 Va. App. LEXIS 90 (Ct. of Appeals Feb. 27, 2001).

Convictions under this section and § 18.2-58 not double jeopardy. — Convictions for both robbery and entry of a banking house with the intent to commit larceny while armed with a deadly weapon did not violate the double jeopardy clause. Hill v. Commonwealth, 2 Va. App. 683, 347 S.E.2d 913 (1986).

§ 18.2-94. Possession of burglarious tools, etc.

If any person have in his possession any tools, implements or outfit, with intent to commit burglary, robbery or larceny, upon conviction thereof he shall be guilty of a Class 5 felony. The possession of such burglarious tools, implements or outfit by any person other than a licensed dealer, shall be prima facie evidence of an intent to commit burglary, robbery or larceny.

History.
Code 1950, § 18.1-87; 1960, c. 358; 1970, c. 587; 1975, cc. 14, 15.

Law Review.

For note discussing possession of burglarious tools, see 53 Va. L. Rev. 702 (1967). For survey of Virginia criminal law for the year 1972-1973, see 59 Va. L. Rev. 1458 (1973). For Fourth Circuit Review, see 35 Wash. & Lee L. Rev. 564 (1978). For survey of Virginia law on criminal law and procedure for the year 2007-2008, see 43 U. Rich. L. Rev. 149 (2008). For annual survey article, "Criminal Law and Procedure," see 44 U. Rich. L. Rev. 339 (2009). For note, "Modern Police Practices: Arizona v. Gant's Illusory Restriction of Vehicle Searches Incident to Arrest," 97 Va. L. Rev. 1727 (2011).

Michie's Jurisprudence.

For related discussion, see 21A M.J. Words and Phrases.

CASE NOTES

The presumption of criminal intent does not attach to all tools, implements, or outfits embraced by the statute but only to such offending articles innately burglarious in character, those commonly used by burglars in house breaking and safe cracking, particularly suitable and appropriate to accomplish the destruction of any ordinary hindrance of access to any building, vault or safe. Hagy v. Commonwealth, 35 Va. App. 152, 543 S.E.2d 614, 2001 Va. App. LEXIS 153 (2001).

Statute requires proof that tools, implements or outfit were intrinsically "burglarious" only when the Commonwealth relies upon the statutory presumption to establish the requisite criminal intent. Moss v. Commonwealth, 29 Va. App. 1, 509 S.E.2d 510 (1999).

Plastic bag not an "implement." — As an ordinary plastic bag is not an "implement" as proscribed by § 18.2-94 because it serves no particular purpose in furtherance of a trade, occupation, profession, or work, defendant's conviction for possession of burglarious tools was reversed. Williams v. Commonwealth, 50 Va. App. 337, 649 S.E.2d 717, 2007 Va. App. LEXIS 333 (2007).

Mere possession of burglarious tools is not a crime. — The mere possession of burglarious tools is not a crime under the statute. It is possession with intent to use them to commit a crime. The tools or implements may be, and usually are, designed and manufactured for lawful purposes. Burnette v. Commonwealth, 194 Va. 785, 75 S.E.2d 482 (1953).

The mere possession of burglarious tools, without more, is not in itself considered a crime under this section. Richards v. Cox, 303 F. Supp. 946 (W.D. Va. 1969).

Mere possession of burglarious tools is not a crime, for such may be, and usually are, designed and manufactured for lawful purposes; the gravamen of the offense arises from the possessor's intent to use these common, ordinary objects for a criminal purpose specified by statute, namely, burglary, robbery or larceny. Blaney v. Commonwealth, No. 2571-99-1, 2001 Va. App. LEXIS 174 (Ct. of Appeals Apr. 3, 2001).

This section does not require that burglarious tools actually be used in the burglary, only that they be possessed with intent to commit burglary. Watkins v. Commonwealth, 26 Va. App. 335, 494 S.E.2d 859 (1998).

All the last sentence of this section does is to create a presumption of a criminal intent from proof of possession of burglarious tools or implements. Such a presumption is not conclusive; it cuts off no defense. It interposes no obstacle to a contest of all the issues of fact, and relieves neither the court nor the jury of the duty to determine all of the questions of fact from the weight of the whole evidence. It is merely a rule of evidence and not the determination of a fact. Burnette v. Commonwealth, 194 Va. 785, 75 S.E.2d 482 (1953); Nance v. Commonwealth, 203 Va. 428, 124 S.E.2d 900 (1962).

Possession creates only a prima facie presumption of the criminal intent of the accused which is not conclusive. Richards v. Cox, 303 F. Supp. 946 (W.D. Va. 1969).

And such sentence is constitutional. — The last sentence of this section is not unconstitutional as making the mere possession of common ordinary tools of a trade or calling prima facie evidence of intent to commit a crime. The word "such," as used in the last sentence, does not refer to the phrase "any tools, etc.," used in the preceding sentence, and viewing the history and purpose of this section a proper construction requires the word "such" to be ignored

and deleted. Thus construed the statute makes the meaning of the last sentence clear and consistent with the legislative intent to adopt a rule of evidence making possession of only burglarious tools (by one other than a licensed dealer) prima facie evidence of intent to commit burglary, robbery or larceny. Burnette v. Commonwealth, 194 Va. 785, 75 S.E.2d 482 (1953).

The test of the constitutionality of a statute making proof of a certain fact presumptive evidence of another fact is whether there is a natural and rational evidentiary relation between the fact proven and the ultimate fact presumed. The last sentence of this section, making possession of burglarious tools prima facie evidence of intent to commit burglary, robbery or larceny meets this test. Burnette v. Commonwealth, 194 Va. 785, 75 S.E.2d 482 (1953).

This section couples "possession" of tools with the "intent" to commit a crime. Richards v. Cox, 303 F. Supp. 946 (W.D. Va. 1969).

State must prove "tools" were under control of accused. — It is incumbent upon the Commonwealth to prove that the "tools" were under the control of the accused. Richards v. Cox, 303 F. Supp. 946 (W.D. Va. 1969).

Pair of pants can constitute "outfit" as that term is used in this section. Mercer v. Commonwealth, 29 Va. App. 380, 512 S.E.2d 173 (1999).

Burden of proof on showing pant wearing intent. — Because a pair of pants is not necessarily "burglarious," that is, it is not an item commonly used to break into a structure, to convict defendant under Virginia's burglary statute, the Commonwealth was required to prove that defendant possessed these pants with the intent to use them to commit larceny. Mercer v. Commonwealth, 29 Va. App. 380, 512 S.E.2d 173 (1999), , overruled as stated in Edwards v. Commonwealth, 53 VA. App. 402, 672 S.E.2d 894 (2009) (overruled "to the extent that it defines 'outfit' as 'wearing apparel'").

"Outfit" not limited to wearing apparel. — The Court of Appeals of Virginia overrules Mercer v. Commonwealth, 29 Va. App. 380, 512 S.E. 2d, 173 (1999) to the extent that it defines "outfit" as "wearing apparel," and holds that, in the context of § 18.2-94, the appropriate definition of "outfit" is the articles forming equipment or the tools or instruments comprised in any special equipment; as a carpenter's or a surgeon's outfit. Edwards v. Commonwealth, 53 Va. App. 402, 672 S.E.2d 894, 2009 Va. App. LEXIS 160 (2009).

Burden of making reasonable explanation is shifted to defendant. — When a person, other than a licensed dealer, has been shown to have in his possession burglarious tools, the burden of making a reasonable explanation to overcome the statutory presumption is shifted to him, — an explanation sufficiently credible to be accepted by a jury. Nance v. Commonwealth, 203 Va. 428, 124 S.E.2d 900 (1962).

Once possession is proven, the burden of going forward with the evidence shifts to the defendant, but this does not shift the burden of ultimate proof, or deprive defendant of his right to have the jury instructed on the presumption of innocence. Richards v. Cox, 303 F. Supp. 946 (W.D. Va. 1969).

Upon proof that one not a licensed dealer is in possession of "burglarious tools," the Commonwealth is entitled to a presumption on intent, shifting the burden to the defendant to explain the possession. However, the Commonwealth is free to prove its case without the benefit of the presumption. Carter v. Commonwealth, 223 Va. 528, 290 S.E.2d 865 (1982).

Instruction held proper. — An instruction to the jury in the words of the last sentence of this section was proper where the evidence showed possession of burglarious tools. Nance v. Commonwealth, 203 Va. 428, 124 S.E.2d 900 (1962).

Vending machine keys were tools. — Where defendant admitted that he wrongfully gained possession of vending machine keys and thereafter employed them to open several vending machines and steal coins, he clearly possessed and used the keys, tools embraced by this section, with an intent to commit larceny, a violation of the statute. Moss v. Commonwealth, 29 Va. App. 1, 509 S.E.2d 510 (1999).

Sufficiency of evidence. — In prosecution under this section where evidence showed that burglarious tools were found in a car in which defendant was riding with another man, conviction was reversed because Commonwealth failed to prove beyond a reasonable doubt that defendant had actual or constructive possession and control of them. Burnette v. Commonwealth, 194 Va. 785, 75 S.E.2d 482 (1953).

Where the two defendants had been riding together in an automobile and one of them, while being hotly pursued by police officers late at night, had thrown burglarious tools from the car, a conviction of each defendant under this section was affirmed. Nance v. Commonwealth, 203 Va. 428, 124 S.E.2d 900 (1962).

Where defendant was a stranger in the neighborhood, passed by people and houses closer to his car to get to the residence in question, left his companion positioned so as to serve as a lookout, was wearing a wool coat on a hot summer day, concealing a screwdriver that could be used in a break-in and carrying a towel, and claimed that he had had car trouble and that his companion was a hitchhiker but his car was started without difficulty, the trier of fact was entitled to draw reasonable inferences from these facts. Carter v. Commonwealth, 223 Va. 528, 290 S.E.2d 865 (1982).

A trial court did not err in concluding that, in the aggregate, a defendant's possession of a ski mask, dark clothing, duct tape, a glass cutter and a long screwdriver constituted "tools, implements, or outfits innately burglarious in character." Filby v. Commonwealth, No. 2208-99-1, 2000 Va. App. LEXIS 552 (Ct. of Appeals July 25, 2000).

The evidence was sufficient to support a conviction under this section where all the tools found in the vehicle occupied by the defendant and others were prying implements or tools that could be used to forcibly open vending machines or other structures, the defendant had been seen on three separate occasions exchanging large amounts of coins for currency after vending machines in the vicinity had been vandalized, the driver of the car had a key used to enter vending machines and one of the screwdrivers in the car was found to have red paint on it that was of the same color that is on Coca-Cola vending machines Hagy v. Commonwealth, 35 Va. App. 152, 543 S.E.2d 614, 2001 Va. App. LEXIS 153 (2001).

Although a dent-puller was not innately burglarious in character, the circumstantial evidence in defendant's case was sufficient to sustain defendant's conviction of possession of burglarious tools, specifically a dent-puller, where: (1) a motorist who drove by and saw defendant walking from some vending machines toward defendant's truck noticed nothing wrong with the machines at that time, but upon returning within 10 minutes, noticed that defendant's truck was gone and the machines had been broken into; (2) the motorist's testimony regarding the timing of the damage seemed to contradict defendant's claim that defendant only went to investigate the machines after seeing some suspicious juveniles at the machines and discovered at that time that the machines had been broken into; (3) defendant's truck contained a dent-puller; (4) a police officer testified that the vending machines appeared to have been broken into using a dent-puller; and (5) the stolen money changers from the vending machines were found in a dumpster 25 yards from defendant's apartment. Sprouse v. Commonwealth, — Va. App. —, — S.E.2d —, 2002 Va. App. LEXIS 748 (Dec. 17, 2002).

Considering that defendant used rocks to assist in breaking through a door and that he intended to break and enter, the evidence was sufficient to prove he possessed burglary tools, where a police officer responded to a scene and saw defendant manipulating the victim's screen door with something in his hand, defendant fled when the officer was announced, and the officer and a neighbor chased and apprehended defendant and found two, three-inch in diameter rocks in defendant's front pants pocket. Bell v. Commonwealth, No. 3181-02-1, 2003 Va. App. LEXIS 548 (Ct. of Appeals Nov. 4, 2003).

Evidence that: (1) defendant was stopped near a parked car that had a broken window and a screwdriver in plain view in the back seat; (2) he said the screwdriver was not his but his fingerprints might be on it; (3) he later admitted using the screwdriver to break the window to gain entry into the car so as to obtain money; and (4) the car owner had not given him permission to enter her car, was sufficient to convict him of possession of burglarious tools. Ridley v. Commonwealth, — Va. App. —, — S.E.2d —, 2006 Va. App. LEXIS 156 (Apr. 25, 2006).

Evidence that a resident of the apartment building observed defendant, from a distance of about ten feet, with a hammer in his hand immediately after she heard banging in the vicinity, and that, five to ten minutes later, police found defendant with an object later identified as a hammer was sufficient to support defendant's conviction for possession of burglarious tools. Barnett v. Commonwealth, — Va. App. —, — S.E.2d —, 2007 Va. App. LEXIS 2 (Jan. 9, 2007).

Where defendant stuffed a shirt into a store clerk's mouth and bound her hands and feet with a plastic tie in the course of his robbery of the store, the evidence was sufficient to prove that defendant possessed the plastic ties with the intent to commit robbery; defendant's binding of the victim's hands and feet, during which he actually possessed the plastic ties, was part of the continuing violence against her that defendant used to accomplish the theft. Solesbee v. Commonwealth, — Va. App. —, — S.E.2d —, 2008 Va. App. LEXIS 35 (Jan. 22, 2008).

Because a purse defendant possessed at the time she committed petit larceny, and which she admitted to intending to use to conceal merchandise from a department store, was not a burglarious "tool," "implement," or "outfit" as these terms were defined under § 18.2-94, her conviction under said statute was reversed. Edwards v. Commonwealth, 52 Va. App. 70, 661 S.E.2d 488, 2008 Va. App. LEXIS 259 (2008).

Evidence was not sufficient to support defendant's conviction for possession of a tool, implement or outfit with intent to commit larceny under § 18.2-94; while the appellate court rejected defendant's argument that the evidence was insufficient merely because defendant's purse was not burglarious, it held that defendant's purse did not constitute a larcenous "outfit" within the meaning of § 18.2-94. Edwards v. Commonwealth, 53 Va. App. 402, 672 S.E.2d 894, 2009 Va. App. LEXIS 160 (2009).

When defendant's co-conspirator attempted to burglarize the subject residence with a screwdriver, defendant, who set in motion and participated in the burglary plan, was criminally liable as a principal in the second degree; thus, the evidence was sufficient to support conviction for possession of burglary tools under § 18.2-94. Owens v. Commonwealth, 54 Va. App. 99, 675 S.E.2d 879, 2009 Va. App. LEXIS 204 (2009).

Because defendant lacked permission to be at a car lot after hours or to possess a car radio, the pliers and other tools that defendant had provided sufficient evidence of intent; therefore, the evidence was sufficient to convict defendant of possession of burglary tools under § 18.2-94 and to revoke the suspension of defendant's sentence for a prior offense. Jones v. Commonwealth, 2009 Va. App. LEXIS 201 (Apr. 28, 2009).

Evidence was sufficient to support defendant's conviction for possession of burglarious tools because doors of two offices were pried open, and defendant placed an object in the passenger compartment of his car where the police found a duffle bag; only a tire iron and loose change were made exhibits, but testimony showed that the duffle bag also contained a flashlight and work gloves. Baker v. Commonwealth, 2011 Va. App. LEXIS 358 (Nov. 22, 2011).

Evidence insufficient. — As the Commonwealth provided no real basis for its contention that appellant actually intended to commit common-law larceny — as opposed to the crime for which he was charged — other than its claim that appellant vaguely intended to steal, the Commonwealth failed to establish that appellant possessed the laptop and remagging device with the intent to commit burglary, robbery, or larceny. In proving appellant had the intent to commit credit card fraud, the Commonwealth did not also prove that he intended to commit common-law larceny; consequently, appellant's conviction for possession of burglarious tools was reversed. Gheorghiu v. Commonwealth, 54 Va. App. 645, 682 S.E.2d 50, 2009 Va. App. LEXIS 424 (2009), aff'd in part, rev'd in part, 280 Va. 678, 701 S.E.2d 407 (2010).

Applied in Boone v. Stacy, 597 F. Supp. 114 (E.D. Va. 1984).

ARTICLE 3.

LARCENY AND RECEIVING STOLEN GOODS.

Michie's Jurisprudence.

For related discussion, see 12A M.J. Larceny, §§ 2, 6, 8, 9, 17, 18, 24, 31, 32; 15 M.J. Prohibition, § 14.

§ 18.2-95. Grand larceny defined; how punished.

Any person who (i) commits larceny from the person of another of money or other thing of value of

$5 or more, (ii) commits simple larceny not from the person of another of goods and chattels of the value of $200 or more, or (iii) commits simple larceny not from the person of another of any firearm, regardless of the firearm's value, shall be guilty of grand larceny, punishable by imprisonment in a state correctional facility for not less than one nor more than twenty years or, in the discretion of the jury or court trying the case without a jury, be confined in jail for a period not exceeding twelve months or fined not more than $2,500, either or both.

History.

Code 1950, § 18.1-100; 1960, c. 358; 1966, c. 247; 1975, cc. 14, 15, 603; 1980, c. 175; 1991, c. 710; 1992, c. 822; 1998, c. 821.

Cross references.

As to punishment for attempt to commit larceny, see § 18.2-26. As to charging housebreaking and larceny in one count, see § 18.2-91 and note. As to petit larceny, see § 18.2-96. As to dogs as subject to larceny, see § 18.2-97. As to computer time, services, etc., as property subject to larceny, see § 18.2-152.1 et seq. As to payment by the Department of Social Services of assistant attorney for the Commonwealth for prosecution of public assistance fraud cases, see § 63.2-525.

Editor's note.

The above section is § 18.2-95 as enacted by Acts 1975, c. 603. Pursuant to § 30-152, it has been substituted for § 18.2-95 as enacted by Acts 1975, cc. 14 and 15.

Law Review.

For survey of Virginia criminal law and procedure for the year 1969-1970, see 56 Va. L. Rev. 1572 (1970). For survey of Virginia law on criminal procedure for the year 1973-1974, see 60 Va. L. Rev. 1505 (1974). For survey of Virginia criminal law for the year 1976-1977, see 63 Va. L. Rev. 1396 (1977). For survey of Virginia criminal law for the year 1977-1978, see 64 Va. L. Rev. 1407 (1978). For note, "Criminal Procedure and Criminal Law: Virginia Supreme Court Decisions During the 70's," see 15 U. Rich. L. Rev. 585 (1981). For an article relating to all published Virginia criminal law decisions between July 1, 1997, and July 1, 1998, see 32 U. Rich. L. Rev. 1091 (1998). For a note, "Pleading for Theft Consolidation in Virginia: Larceny, Embezzlement, False Pretenses and § 19.2-284," see 55 Wash. & Lee L. Rev. 249 (1998).

CASE NOTES

I. General Consideration.
    A. In General.
    B. Elements.
    C. Value.
II. Illustrative Cases.
    A. Proof Generally.
    B. Admissibility of Evidence.
    C. Sufficiency of Evidence.
III. Prosecution, Sentencing, etc.

I. GENERAL CONSIDERATION.

A. In General.

The standards of grand and petit larceny are wholly arbitrary. The legislature may change them, and it might entirely abolish such distinctions. Bell v. Commonwealth, 167 Va. 526, 189 S.E. 441 (1937).

Robbery, burglary, grand larceny and abduction, are each treated separately and are governed by a separate statutory provision. Austin v. Peyton, 279 F. Supp. 227 (W.D. Va. 1968).

Larceny has often been defined as the wrongful or fraudulent taking of personal goods of some intrinsic value, belonging to another, without his assent, and with the intention to deprive the

owner thereof permanently. Skeeter v. Commonwealth, 217 Va. 722, 232 S.E.2d 756 (1977).

Larceny is the wrongful or fraudulent taking of personal goods belonging to another without his consent and with the intention to deprive the owner thereof permanently. Berryman v. Moore, 619 F. Supp. 853 (E.D. Va. 1985), certification of probable cause denied and dismissed, 792 F.2d 139 (4th Cir. 1986).

Larceny, robbery distinguished. — If appellant killed victim intending to steal his property, the theft was robbery. If appellant killed victim only for a purpose unrelated to theft, and as an after thought decided to steal his property, the theft was larceny. Shepperson v. Commonwealth, 19 Va. App. 586, 454 S.E.2d 5 (1995).

For theft by violence or intimidation to constitute robbery, the intent to steal must exist at the time of the violence or intimidation. Shepperson v. Commonwealth, 19 Va. App. 586, 454 S.E.2d 5 (1995).

Larceny, embezzlement distinguished. — Embezzlement and larceny are separate offenses with different elements. The key distinction between embezzlement and larceny is that larceny involves a trespassory taking of property while embezzlement involves a conversion of property received with the owner's consent. Cera v. Commonwealth, No. 0432-94-4 (Ct. of Appeals May 2, 1995).

Larceny and embezzlement are not the same offense for determining time limits under § 19.2-243. Cera v. Commonwealth, No. 0432-94-4 (Ct. of Appeals May 2, 1995).

Under Virginia law, embezzlement, false pretenses, and larceny are three separate offenses, and there is not a general "theft" statute, as there is in most states, that encompasses both types of behavior; § 18.2-95 defines grand larceny; § 18.2-111 defines embezzlement; and § 18.2-178 defines false pretenses. The Commonwealth of Virginia has always purported to treat the three basic theft crimes of larceny, embezzlement, and false pretenses as separate and distinct offenses, and maintains separate statutes for each crime. United States v. Good, 326 F.3d 589, 2003 U.S. App. LEXIS 7543 (4th Cir. Apr. 22, 2003).

Grand larceny. — Under this section, grand larceny includes the taking, not from the person of another, of goods that have a value of $200 or more. Tarpley v. Commonwealth, 261 Va. 251, 542 S.E.2d 761, 2001 Va. LEXIS 31 (2001).

The concept of larceny from the person recognizes an enhanced societal concern for conduct that implicates at least a potential for personal assault, conduct that involves the person of the victim and jeopardizes his personal security. Garland v. Commonwealth, 18 Va. App. 706, 446 S.E.2d 628 (1994).

Larceny by receiving stolen goods is a lesser offense which is included in the major one of larceny, and the lesser offense is indictable as larceny, and the accused may be convicted of the lesser offense of receiving stolen goods. Cabbler v. Commonwealth, 212 Va. 520, 184 S.E.2d 781 (1971), cert. denied, 405 U.S. 1075, 92 S. Ct. 1501, 31 L. Ed. 2d 807 (1972).

The crime of receiving stolen goods is a lesser offense included in the crime of larceny. Henderson v. Commonwealth, 215 Va. 811, 213 S.E.2d 782 (1975).

Larceny by receiving stolen goods. — Although the trial court erred by convicting defendant of violating § 18.2-95, instead of § 18.2-108, after the jury found defendant guilty of grand larceny by receiving stolen property, the trial court's failure to include a reference to § 18.2-108 in its final order was a clerical error that did not require reversal. Bazemore v. Commonwealth, No. 0103-02-1, 2003 Va. App. LEXIS 291 (Ct. of Appeals May 13, 2003).

Because larceny is a continuing offense, anyone who knows that personal property is stolen and assists in its transportation or disposition is guilty of larceny. Moehring v. Commonwealth, 223 Va. 564, 290 S.E.2d 891 (1982).

Double jeopardy. — The double jeopardy clause does not bar conviction and sentence at one trial for burglary under § 18.2-91 and grand larceny under this section arising from a unitary criminal transaction since each offense rests on different necessary elements. The clause is infringed only if all the components of a crime defined under one statute must also be proved to convict under another. The test to be applied is whether each provision requires proof of an additional fact which the other does not. Downey v. Peyton, 451 F.2d 236 (4th Cir. 1971).

Court of Appeals erred in reversing defendant's conviction of grand larceny of a person due to defendant's earlier acquittal of robbery, charged pursuant to § 18.2-58, as proof of violence or intimidation was required in a robbery prosecution, but not for grand larceny from the person, and proof of the value of the property stolen was required in a prosecution for grand larceny from the person, but not for robbery; hence, double jeopardy did not bar prosecution on the grand larceny charge upon a robbery acquittal. Commonwealth v. Hudgins, 269 Va. 602, 611 S.E.2d 362, 2005 Va. LEXIS 37 (2005), reversing 43 Va. App. 219, 597 S.E.2d 221 (2004); overruling Jones v. Commonwealth, 218 Va. 757, 240 S.E.2d 658 (1978).

Defendant did not show that defendant's Va. Const., Art. I, § 8, double jeopardy rights were violated when the trial court, after defendant pled guilty, denied defendant's motion to consolidate separate indictments charging defendant with grand larceny. The indictments charged defendant with making two separate, unauthorized purchases of various equipment parts on the same day and from the same victim, but both indictments alleged that the purchases each exceeded $200, which meant that defendant did not show a double jeopardy violation on the face of the indictments or in the record. Johns v. Commonwealth, — Va. App. —, — S.E.2d —, 2008 Va. App. LEXIS 74 (Feb. 12, 2008).

Because the General Assembly clearly and unambiguously intended that grand larceny and larceny with intent to sell or distribute (in violation of §§ 18.2-95 and 18.2-108.01, respectively) were to be punished separately, no double jeopardy violation occurred. Tharrington v. Commonwealth, 58 Va. App. 704, 715 S.E.2d 388, 2011 Va. App. LEXIS 296 (2011).

Larceny as a predicate offense. — District court's sentencing determination that a prior conviction for larceny constituted a crime of violence for purposes of determining career offender status predicate offenses, was upheld on appeal. United States v. Smith, 359 F.3d 662, 2004 U.S. App. LEXIS 3981 (4th Cir. 2004).

Defendant's Virginia conviction for grand larceny from a person in violation of § 18.2-95 qualified as a violent felony under 18 U.S.C.S. § 924(e). United States v. Rogers, — F.3d —, 2008 U.S. App. LEXIS 218 (4th Cir. Jan. 7, 2008), cert. denied, 129 S. Ct. 994, 2009 U.S. LEXIS 596, 173 L. Ed. 2d 291 (U.S. 2009).

Section 19.2-270.1 provides alternative means of establishing adequate foundation to authenticate a photograph which is offered under the independent silent witness theory in prosecutions under this section and § 18.2-96. Saunders v. Commonwealth, 1 Va. App. 396, 339 S.E.2d 550 (1986).

Applied in Ward v. Connor, 495 F. Supp. 434 (E.D. Va. 1980); Grant v. Commonwealth, 223 Va. 680, 292 S.E.2d 348 (1982); Boone v. Stacy, 597 F. Supp. 114 (E.D. Va. 1984); Salecki v. Virginia, 51 Bankr. 364 (Bankr. E.D. Va. 1985); Brown v. Booker, 622 F. Supp. 993 (E.D. Va. 1985); Kern v. Commonwealth, 2 Va. App. 84, 341 S.E.2d 397 (1986); Speight v. Commonwealth, 2 Va. App. 140, 342 S.E.2d 408 (1986); Crews v. Commonwealth, 3 Va. App. 531, 352 S.E.2d 1 (1987); Wilson v. Commonwealth, 249 Va. 95, 452 S.E.2d 669 (1995); Commonwealth v. Taylor, 256 Va. 514, 506 S.E.2d 312 (1998); Acey v. Commonwealth, 29 Va. App. 240, 511 S.E.2d 429 (1999); Jay v. Commonwealth, 275 Va. 510, 659 S.E.2d 311, 2008 Va. LEXIS 53 (2008).

B. Elements.

To sustain conviction of larceny by false pretenses, the Commonwealth must prove: (1) That the accused intended to defraud; (2) that a fraud actually occurred; (3) that the accused used false pretenses to perpetrate the fraud; and (4) that the false pretenses induced the owner to part with his property. Brown v. Commonwealth, 30 Va. App. 243, 516 S.E.2d 678 (1999).

Line of credit not subject of larceny. — At common law only the credit card itself, not the line of credit it represented, could be the subject of larceny; the same limitation applies under this section. Owolabi v. Commonwealth, 16 Va. App. 78, 428 S.E.2d 14 (1993).

There is a caption when the defendant takes possession and he takes possession when he exercises dominion and control over the property. Ellis v. Commonwealth, No. 2704-99-1, 2001 Va. App. LEXIS 82 (Ct. of Appeals Feb. 27, 2001).

What is a taking. — In every larceny there must be an actual taking, or severance of the goods from the possession of the owner. To "take" an article, signifies "to lay hold of, seize or grasp it with the hands or otherwise," and doing so, animo furandi, constitutes a felonious taking. Jones v. Commonwealth, 3 Va. App. 295, 349 S.E.2d 414 (1986).

To constitute the crime of larceny, there must have been a felonious taking of property from the possession of the owner, and the thief must, for an instant at least, have had complete and absolute possession of the stolen property, and during such possession and control he must have feloniously removed the same from the place it occupied just before he grasped, seized or laid hold of the same. Winston v. Commonwealth, No. 0431-95-2 (Ct. of Appeals April 9, 1996).

Taking from possession of owner required. — In every larceny there must be an actual taking or severance of the goods from the possession of the owner. Bruhn v. Commonwealth, 35 Va. App. 339, 544 S.E.2d 895, 2001 Va. App. LEXIS 216 (2001), aff'd, 264 Va. 597, 570 S.E.2d 866 (2002).

No larceny when property never in possession of alleged victim. — Where an employee received payment in the form of a check made payable to him personally for work allegedly done on behalf of his employer, but the employee never signed the check over to the employer and the employer never obtained possession of the funds, the employee's action in retaining the funds did not constitute larceny. Bruhn v. Commonwealth, 35 Va. App. 339, 544 S.E.2d 895, 2001 Va. App. LEXIS 216 (2001), aff'd, 264 Va. 597, 570 S.E.2d 866 (2002).

Good faith belief that property belongs to defendant. — There can be no larceny if an accused, in good faith, believes that the property taken belongs to him, since the essential element of intent is absent in that circumstance. Stanley v. Webber, 260 Va. 90, 531 S.E.2d 311, 2000 Va. LEXIS 93 (2000).

To prove that a defendant took property, the Commonwealth has to establish that there was a caption or taking of the property and an asportation or carrying away of the property. Ellis v. Commonwealth, No. 2704-99-1, 2001 Va. App. LEXIS 82 (Ct. of Appeals Feb. 27, 2001).

There is an asportation when a defendant carries away the property. Ellis v. Commonwealth, No. 2704-99-1, 2001 Va. App. LEXIS 82 (Ct. of Appeals Feb. 27, 2001).

Asportation may be imputed to defendant who acts through innocent agent. — Where defendant sold farm equipment that he did not own to an innocent buyer and authorized the buyer to remove the equipment from the actual owner's farm, the removal of the property by the buyer as defendant's "innocent agent" was properly attributed to defendant as a principal in the first degree, thereby satisfying the asportation requirement for larceny. McAlevy v. Commonwealth, 44 Va. App. 318, 605 S.E.2d 283, 2004 Va. App. LEXIS 575 (2004), aff'd, — Va. —, 620 S.E.2d 758 (2005).

Although an innocent third party took a victim's farm equipment, defendant was criminally responsible for grand larceny because the third party was acting under defendant's direction and as defendant's agent; using the third party to remove the property was no different than if defendant took it and then sold it to the third party. McAlevy v. Commonwealth, 270 Va. 378, 620 S.E.2d 758, 2005 Va. LEXIS 89 (2005).

Common-law definition. — Declared a crime by this section, larceny is also a common-law crime defined as the wrongful or fraudulent taking of personal goods of some intrinsic value, belonging to another, without his assent, and with the intention to deprive the owner thereof permanently. The animus furandi must accompany the taking, but the wrongful taking of property in itself imports the animus furandi. Winston v. Commonwealth, No. 0431-95-2 (Ct. of Appeals April 9, 1996).

Physical contact with victim not necessary. — Larceny from the person embraces not only theft of property from physical contact with the victim, but also theft of property that is in the victim's possession and within his immediate custody and control. Therefore, defendant who reached over countertop and took money out of open cash drawer, while standing within two feet and reaching to within inches of cashier, who stood just to the side of the cash register, and across the countertop from cashier and grabbed a handful of cash and ran from the restaurant, frightening the cashier, was guilty under this section. Garland v. Commonwealth, 18 Va. App. 706, 446 S.E.2d 628 (1994).

The animus furandi must accompany the taking, but the wrongful taking of the property in itself imports the animus furandi. Skeeter v. Commonwealth, 217 Va. 722, 232 S.E.2d 756 (1977).

Exclusive possession required to raise larceny presumption. — For the larceny presumption to arise, the Commonwealth must establish that the accused was in exclusive possession of property recently stolen. Best v. Commonwealth, 222 Va. 387, 282 S.E.2d 16 (1981).

The presumption of fact arising from the unexplained possession of recently stolen property requires, inter alia, a showing of exclusive possession of the stolen property by the accused, though such possession may be joint. Moehring v. Commonwealth, 223 Va. 564, 290 S.E.2d 891 (1982).

Regardless of other incriminating evidence. — The larceny presumption arises only when the accused has been shown to be in exclusive possession of recently stolen property, regardless of how much other incriminating evidence the Commonwealth has marshalled. Best v. Commonwealth, 222 Va. 387, 282 S.E.2d 16 (1981).

To prove beyond a reasonable doubt that an accused's possession of stolen property was exclusive, the Commonwealth's evidence must show that the accused was consciously asserting at least a possessory interest in the stolen property or was exercising dominion over the stolen property. Blaney v. Commonwealth, No. 2571-99-1, 2001 Va. App. LEXIS 174 (Ct. of Appeals Apr. 3, 2001).

Inference of larceny arising from exclusive possession of stolen property. — Unexplained possession of recently stolen goods permits the fact finder to infer that the possessor is the thief. In order for the fact finder to draw the inference of larceny from possession of recently stolen property, the Commonwealth must establish that the accused was in exclusive possession of the stolen property. Exclusive possession need not be sole possession; exclusive possession may be established by showing that the person jointly possessed the property with another, provided that he exerts dominion and control over the property. Edmondson v. Commonwealth, No. 1504-92-1 (Ct. of Appeals Dec. 21, 1993).

Where it was established that the defendant was in exclusive possession of the victims' stolen jewelry within days of the theft and he alone exercised dominion over the stolen property when he sold it to a jeweler, the defendant's exclusive possession was sufficiently recent to establish prima facie cases of larceny and burglary and to justify inferences by the trial court that the defendant was the thief and burglar who broke into both victims' homes and stole their property. Dickerson v. Commonwealth, No. 0090-00-1, 2001 Va. App. LEXIS 105 (Ct. of Appeals Mar. 6, 2001).

A challenged instruction which informed the jury that it might reasonably draw an inference from the defendant's exclusive possession of a recently stolen automobile that he was the thief provided that the defendant did not reasonably or satisfactorily explain his possession did not relieve the commonwealth of its burden to prove every element of the crime beyond a reasonable doubt in violation of the due process clause; the challenged instruction created only a permissive inference that the jury was free to reject, irrespective of whether the defendant offered a reasonable explanation consistent with his innocence. Dobson v. Commonwealth, 260 Va. 71, 531 S.E.2d 569, 2000 Va. LEXIS 88 (2000).

Possession of goods recently stolen is prima facie evidence of guilt of the crime of larceny and throws upon the accused the burden of accounting for that possession. Blaney v. Commonwealth, No. 2571-99-1, 2001 Va. App. LEXIS 174 (Ct. of Appeals Apr. 3, 2001).

In a burglary prosecution, the Commonwealth can establish a violation of this section by: (1) proving that goods were stolen from a house which was broken into; (2) justifying the inference that both offenses were committed at the same time, by the same person, as part of the same criminal enterprise; and (3) proving that the goods were found soon thereafter in the possession of the accused. Blaney v. Commonwealth, No. 2571-99-1, 2001 Va. App. LEXIS 174 (Ct. of Appeals Apr. 3, 2001).

In a case in which defendant appealed his convictions for uttering a forged check in violation of § 18.2-172 and attempted grand larceny in violation of §§ 18.2-95 and 18.2-26, he argued unsuccessfully that it would violate his due process rights under the Fourteenth Amendment to infer his guilty knowledge solely from the fact that he possessed the forged check. The evidence in the record rationally connected the permissive inference of guilty knowledge of the check's forgery to defendant's possession of the forged instrument, and his possession of the forged check, in conjunction with the other circumstantial evidence, allowed the inference that he knew the check was forged. Coles v. Commonwealth, 2009 Va. App. LEXIS 484 (Oct. 27, 2009).

Larceny inference not applicable. — Because the trial court erred in applying the larceny inference to the scrap metal that was not unusual in any way, and the only other evidence against defendant was defendant's statement to a detective that defendant assisted an individual in selling similar scrap metal, the evidence was insufficient to support defendant's conviction for grand larceny of scrap metal. Smith v. Commonwealth, — Va. App. —, — S.E.2d —, 2009 Va. App. LEXIS 37 (Feb. 3, 2009).

Possession of stolen property supporting inference of breaking and entering. — The unexplained or falsely denied exclusive possession of stolen goods shortly after a burglary has the same efficiency to give rise to an inference that the possessor is guilty of the breaking and entering as to an inference that he is guilty of the larceny. Blaney v. Commonwealth, No. 2571-99-1, 2001 Va. App. LEXIS 174 (Ct. of Appeals Apr. 3, 2001).

No presumption where several people had access. — The larceny presumption does not arise when the evidence merely reveals that the stolen property was found in a place to which several people, including the accused, had access. Best v. Commonwealth, 222 Va. 387, 282 S.E.2d 16 (1981).

Joint possession raising presumption. — One can be in exclusive possession of an item when he jointly possesses it with another. The evidence must reveal, however, that the accused was consciously asserting at least a possessory interest in the stolen property or was exercising dominion over the stolen property. Best v. Commonwealth, 222 Va. 387, 282 S.E.2d 16 (1981).

Larceny presumption shifts burden of persuasion. — Possession of goods recently stolen is prima facie evidence of guilt of the crime of larceny and throws upon the accused the burden of accounting for that possession. Dickerson v. Commonwealth, No. 0090-00-1, 2001 Va. App. LEXIS 105 (Ct. of Appeals Mar. 6, 2001).

Permanent loss by the owner is not a required element of larceny. Jones v. Commonwealth, 3 Va. App. 295, 349 S.E.2d 414 (1986).

Mere removal of merchandise not larceny unless intent to steal shown. — The mere removal of merchandise from a display shelf to a shopping cart, and the subsequent movement of the shopping cart to other areas of the store, is not larceny unless the evidence otherwise shows that the taking was with the intent to steal. Welch v. Commonwealth, 15 Va. App. 518, 425 S.E.2d 101 (1992).

Slightest asportation sufficient. — When an individual harbors the requisite intent to steal and permanently deprive the owner of property, acts on such intent by taking possession of the property even for an instant, and moves the targeted property, larceny has been committed. The slightest asportation is sufficient, even though the property may be abandoned immediately. Welch v. Commonwealth, 15 Va. App. 518, 425 S.E.2d 101 (1992).

Removal of property from owner's premises not required. — Removal of the targeted property from the owner's premises is not required. Welch v. Commonwealth, 15 Va. App. 518, 425 S.E.2d 101 (1992).

Testimony concerning other items of stolen property not subject of indictment. — Trial court did not err in overruling motion to exclude testimony concerning other items of property stolen at the time of the burglary, even though such items were not the subject of the grand larceny indictment. Caccioppo v. Commonwealth, 20 Va. App. 534, 458 S.E.2d 592 (1995).

It was in Commonwealth's Attorney's discretion whether to prosecute appellant under § 58.1-348 or to prosecute him under this section. Brown v. Commonwealth, 30 Va. App. 243, 516 S.E.2d 678 (1999).

Writs of prohibition and mandamus did not lie. — Writ of prohibition did not lie against a judge with jurisdiction to adjudicate and to enter any order in proceedings involving felony charges against two defendants; a writ of mandamus did not lie to fix and prescribe the judgment to be rendered. In re Commonwealth's Atty. for Roanoke, 265 Va. 313, 576 S.E.2d 458, 2003 Va. LEXIS 38 (2003).

Single intent. — Defendant's conviction for grand larceny in violation of § 18.2-95 was affirmed because a reasonable jury could find that defendant did in fact act with a single intent as the factors enumerated in Acey v. Commonwealth and defendant's methodology both supported finding single intent. Tanner v. Commonwealth, 2010 Va. App. LEXIS 23 (Jan. 19, 2010).

Venue. — In a case in which defendant appealed his conviction in a bench trial for grand larceny of a rental vehicle, he argued that Chesterfield County, Virginia, was not the proper venue in which to try the case as the Commonwealth did not prove he possessed the vehicle within the county. Venue was not an element of the offense, and the Commonwealth did not have to prove it beyond a reasonable doubt; since the evidence proved that renter last saw the vehicle outside of her Chesterfield County residence and it was from there the car was stolen, the Commonwealth presented sufficient evidence that the crime occurred within the territorial jurisdiction of the trial court and venue was proper in Chesterfield County. Williams v. Commonwealth, 2012 Va. App. LEXIS 231 (July 17, 2012).

C. Value.

Value is an essential element of the offense of grand larceny and the Commonwealth is required to prove that the value of stolen property is at least equal to the statutory amount. Berryman v. Moore, 619 F. Supp. 853 (E.D. Va. 1985), certification of probable cause denied and dismissed, 792 F.2d 139 (4th Cir. 1986).

The intent required to commit larceny, the animus furandi, is defined as the taking of property with the mental design of permanently depriving the owner of possession of the goods; the animus furandi must accompany the taking but the wrongful taking of property in itself imports the animus furandi. Briggs v. Commonwealth, No. 2917-99-2, 2001 Va. App. LEXIS 32 (Ct. of Appeals Jan. 30, 2001).

Intent to steal. — A conviction of larceny requires proof beyond a reasonable doubt of the defendant's intent to steal, which must accompany his taking of the property. Tarpley v. Commonwealth, 261 Va. 251, 542 S.E.2d 761, 2001 Va. LEXIS 31 (2001).

The value of the goods specified in this section is an essential element of the crime. Knight v. Commonwealth, 225 Va. 85, 300 S.E.2d 600 (1983).

Proof that an article has some value is sufficient to warrant a conviction of petit larceny, but where the value of the thing stolen determines the grade of the offense, the value must be alleged and the Commonwealth must prove the value to be the statutory amount. Owen v. Commonwealth, No. 1495-95-2 (Ct. of Appeals May 28, 1996).

While the original purchase price of an item may be admitted as evidence of its current value, there must also be "due allowance for elements of depreciation." Owen v. Commonwealth, No. 1495-95-2 (Ct. of Appeals May 28, 1996).

The value of the goods specified in the statute is an element of the crime which the Commonwealth must prove beyond a reasonable doubt. Parker v. Commonwealth, 254 Va. 118, 489 S.E.2d 482 (1997).

To prove grand larceny, the Commonwealth is required to prove that the items stolen had a value equal to or greater than the statutory amount. Hodges v. Commonwealth, No. 0622-99-2, 2000 Va. App. LEXIS 225 (Ct. of Appeals Mar. 28, 2000).

Value of item stolen not entire property it is part. — The monetary element of this section is measured by the value of the item actually stolen, not by the value of the entire property of which it is a part. Camden v. Commonwealth, No. 2951-96-3 (Ct. of Appeals Dec. 16, 1997).

Value of firearm. — This section makes larceny of a firearm a felony "regardless of its value." Therefore, value is not an element of the crime, and the value language in an indictment is unnecessary to the charge. Murphy v. Commonwealth, No. 0974-99-2, 2000 Va. App. LEXIS 366 (Ct. of Appeals May 16, 2000).

General consideration. — There was no need to reverse a defendant grand larceny conviction where the indictment stated that he was indicted for grand larceny of a shotgun, without regard to its value; this was also true as to the petit larceny conviction. Winkler v. Commonwealth, No. 2998-01-2, 2003 Va. App. LEXIS 353 (Ct. of Appeals June 24, 2003).

Direct proof of the value is not essential if circumstantial evidence proves the same fact and at the same time excludes every reasonable hypothesis to the contrary. Veney v. Commonwealth, 212 Va. 805, 188 S.E.2d 80 (1972).

Necessity for allegation and proof of value. — Proof that an article has some value is sufficient to warrant a conviction of petit

larceny, but where the value of the thing stolen determines the grade of the offense, the value must be alleged and the Commonwealth must prove the value to be the statutory amount. Wright v. Commonwealth, 196 Va. 132, 82 S.E.2d 603 (1954); Knight v. Commonwealth, 225 Va. 85, 300 S.E.2d 600 (1983).

While evidence that an article has some value is sufficient to sustain a conviction for petit larceny, when the value of the stolen item determines the grade of the offense, the Commonwealth must prove the value to be at least the statutory amount. Parker v. Commonwealth, 254 Va. 118, 489 S.E.2d 482 (1997).

The Commonwealth bears the burden of proving the value of the goods element beyond a reasonable doubt. Knight v. Commonwealth, 225 Va. 85, 300 S.E.2d 600 (1983).

Standard of proof regarding value. — In a grand larceny prosecution, the burden is upon the Commonwealth to prove beyond a reasonable doubt that the value of the goods stolen equals at least the amount fixed by statute in definition of the offense. Dunn v. Commonwealth, 222 Va. 704, 284 S.E.2d 792 (1981).

Testimony as to value included cigarette packs that were dropped. — Evidence was insufficient to establish grand larceny where the owner of a store, following a break-in of the store, testified that the total amount of the cigarette packs found on the floor of the store, on the ground outside of the entrance to the store, and dropped from a bag carried by defendant as defendant fled from a police officer, was $410.59. The evidence failed to prove that: (1) defendant and defendant's accomplice exercised dominion or absolute control over the cigarette packs found on the floor; (2) there was an asportation of the items found on the floor, i.e. movement of the seized items accompanied by the intent to steal; and (3) the amount of the cigarette packs dropped by defendant from the bag was at least $200. Britt v. Commonwealth, 276 Va. 569, 667 S.E.2d 763, 2008 Va. LEXIS 115 (2008).

Price tags used to determine item's value. — The Virginia Supreme Court has recognized an exception to the hearsay rule in shoplifting cases permitting the admission into evidence of price tags regularly affixed to items of personalty offered for sale or, in substitution, testimony concerning the amounts shown on such tags when there is no objection to such testimony on best evidence grounds. Robinson v. Commonwealth, 258 Va. 3, 516 S.E.2d 475 (1999).

Price tags affixed to items of merchandise, when admitted, suffice to make out a prima facie case of an item's value; and the accused retains full opportunity to cross-examine adverse witnesses and to present rebutting evidence on the issue of value. Briggs v. Commonwealth, No. 2917-99-2, 2001 Va. App. LEXIS 32 (Ct. of Appeals Jan. 30, 2001).

Testimony of security officer regarding price shown on price tags. — The value of merchandise a defendant had attempted to steal was properly established where a security officer for the store testified that, after the stolen items had been photographed and after she had examined the price tags affixed to the items, the merchandise was resold, and identified the price of each of the stolen items based on her inspection of the price tags affixed to the merchandise at the time of the theft. Pilson v. Commonwealth, No. 1051-99-3, 2000 Va. App. LEXIS 791 (Ct. of Appeals Dec. 5, 2000).

Computer generated inventory report of stolen items from a store. — Defendant's convictions for grand larceny and larceny with the intent to sell or distribute stolen property, in violation of § 18.2-108, were affirmed because the trial court did not err by admitting into evidence a computer-generated inventory report of stolen pharmaceutical items from a drug store as a business records exception to the hearsay rule. Further, the record reflected sufficient evidence from which the trial court could infer beyond a reasonable doubt that defendant stole merchandise valued at $200 or more; thus, the credible evidence before the trial court was sufficient to convict defendant of grand larceny and larceny with the intent to sell or distribute stolen property. McDowell v. Commonwealth, 48 Va. App. 104, 628 S.E.2d 542, 2006 Va. App. LEXIS 229 (2006).

Qualification of witness testifying to property's value. — Ownership of property by a corporation does not automatically qualify a company employee to testify about the value of company property. Walls v. Commonwealth, 248 Va. 480, 450 S.E.2d 363 (1994).

The general rule is that opinion testimony of a nonexpert, who is not the owner of the personal property in question, is admissible upon the subject of property value, provided the witness possesses sufficient knowledge of the value of the property or has had ample opportunity for forming a correct opinion as to value. Walls v. Commonwealth, 248 Va. 480, 450 S.E.2d 363 (1994); Owen v. Commonwealth, No. 1495-95-2 (Ct. of Appeals May 28, 1996).

The opinion testimony of the owner of personal property is competent and admissible on the question of the value of such property, regardless of the owner's knowledge of property values. Neville v. Commonwealth, No. 1228-99-2, 2000 Va. App. LEXIS 492 (Ct. of Appeals July 5, 2000).

The opinion testimony of the owner of stolen property is generally competent and admissible on the issue of the value of that property. Parker v. Commonwealth, 254 Va. 118, 489 S.E.2d 482 (1997); Lester v. Commonwealth, 30 Va. App. 495, 518 S.E.2d 318 (1999).

Victim's evidence was competent, not inherently incredible, and sufficient to prove beyond a reasonable doubt that a stolen power washer had a value of more than $200 and that defendant committed grand larceny. The victim was the owner, and for that reason alone, was competent to state the victim's opinion regardless of the victim's knowledge of property values, and the victim's testimony established a solid foundation upon which the victim based the victim's opinion. Fitzgerald v. Commonwealth, — Va. App. —, — S.E.2d —, 2007 Va. App. LEXIS 471 (Dec. 27, 2007).

Where defendant was charged with grand larceny based on his theft of over $200 worth of coins from a decedent's home, as the decedent's brother had filled jars with coins, taken them to the decedent's home, and had specific knowledge about the size and contents of each jar, the trial court did not abuse its discretion in permitting the brother's testimony that the missing coins were worth more than $200. Burton v. Commonwealth, 58 Va. App. 274, 708 S.E.2d 444, 2011 Va. App. LEXIS 177 (2011).

Property owner's testimony as to value. — Testimony of the owner of the stolen copper wire, who had operated a contracting company for eight years, was sufficient to support a finding that the stolen wire was worth about $2,000. Since the wire was not mechanical or electrical equipment that had a limited life span or was subject to deterioration from wear and tear, a depreciation analysis was not required. Tackett v. Commonwealth, — Va. App. —, — S.E.2d —, 2009 Va. App. LEXIS 81 (Feb. 24, 2009).

Evidence of value of burglarized items was sufficient to support a grand larceny conviction because the victim consistently testified that the value of the cigarettes taken from his store, which he had restocked the day before the burglary, exceeded $200, and he also testified that $50 in change left in a drawer for his employees had been taken. Fitzgerald v. Commonwealth, 2010 Va. App. LEXIS 17 (Jan. 12, 2010).

Fair market value. — The value of an object of larceny is the fair market value at the time and place of theft. Berryman v. Moore, 619 F. Supp. 853 (E.D. Va. 1985), certification of probable cause denied and dismissed, 792 F.2d 139 (4th Cir. 1986).

The test is market value, and particularly retail value. Robinson v. Commonwealth, 258 Va. 3, 516 S.E.2d 475 (1999).

Fair market value is the price property will bring when offered for sale by a seller who desires but is not obliged to sell and bought by a buyer under no necessity of purchasing. Robinson v. Commonwealth, 258 Va. 3, 516 S.E.2d 475 (1999).

Defendant's conviction for grand larceny for his theft of a leaf blower and hedge pruner could not be sustained because the Commonwealth did not prove that the fair market value of the items at the time they were taken was $200 or more; although the groundskeeper who saw defendant take the tools testified about what she thought would be the retail price of the stolen tools with new ones, her testimony was in a range and at no point in her testimony did she say that the retail price of new tools approximated the original purchase price of the stolen tools, which had shown signs of ordinary wear and tear. Brown v. Commonwealth, — Va. App. —, — S.E.2d —, 2005 Va. App. LEXIS 198 (May 17, 2005).

Value of stolen property is measured as of time of theft, and the original purchase price may be admitted as evidence of its current value. Lester v. Commonwealth, 30 Va. App. 495, 518 S.E.2d 318 (1999).

It is generally held that evidence of value a reasonable time prior and subsequent to the larceny is admissible, its weight being for the trier of fact. Lester v. Commonwealth, 30 Va. App. 495, 518 S.E.2d 318 (1999).

Although the evidence of the value of a tire and rim at the time of a theft was insufficient to support defendant's conviction of grand larceny under clause (ii) of § 18.2-95, the circumstantial evidence was sufficient to find defendant guilty of the lesser-included offense of petit larceny. Banks v. Commonwealth, — Va. App. —, — S.E.2d —, 2009 Va. App. LEXIS 27 (Jan. 27, 2009).

Allowance for depreciation in value. — While the original purchase price of an item may be admitted as evidence of its current value, there must also be due allowance for elements of depreciation. Dunn v. Commonwealth, 222 Va. 704, 284 S.E.2d 792 (1981).

Evidence was insufficient to prove requisite $200 of property value, where testimony established only that bicycles had originally cost $200, and they were purchased a year or two prior to the attempted larceny. Curry v. Commonwealth, No. 0722-99-1 (Ct. of Appeals Mar. 14, 2000).

Value. — The Commonwealth failed to present sufficient evidence to establish beyond a reasonable doubt that the value of the stolen items was equal to or over two hundred dollars where there was no evidence from the owner or persons familiar with the goods of their current values reflecting the effects of age and wear and tear on their values, and, in spite of evidence of appellant's asking prices or prices that potential buyers agreed or offered to pay for the goods, the potential buyers never bought those items. White v. Commonwealth, No. 2125-93-2 (Ct. of Appeals Feb. 28, 1995).

Where witness, who was not the owner of the tools, did not testify about the original purchase price of the tools or the effect of age and wear and tear on the value of the tools; testified only that the tools were purchased in 1986 or 1987 by someone other than herself; that she did not know the purchase price; that the tools were tools with a lifetime guaranty; and that they were in excellent working order. Although she estimated the replacement cost of the tools to be $540 and thus more than $200, this estimate did not adequately establish the current value of the stolen tools, reflecting the effects of wear and tear. Therefore, the trial court erred in finding the evidence sufficient to prove that the value of the tools was more than $200. Owen v. Commonwealth, No. 1495-95-2 (Ct. of Appeals May 28, 1996).

Value of goods taken from a store was shown to be at least $200, so as to sufficiently prove that the taking was felonious, where the items taken on one day were valued at $142 and there were five other occasions when similar or greater quantities of items were taken from the store by the defendant. Bentley v. Commonwealth, No. 1569-97-2 (Ct. of Appeals May 5, 1998).

Evidence was sufficient to establish that a cellular telephone was valued at more than $200, where two clerks working at the cellular telephone store at which the defendant obtained the telephone by fraud testified that the telephone was worth $300 when new and that it was still in good working order. Faulk v. Commonwealth, No. 0154-97-1 (Ct. of Appeals June 9, 1998).

Evidence was sufficient to establish the value of women's clothing taken from a store by the defendant where two loss prevention officers testified to such value based on price tags from identical clothing which indicated their value. Jackson v. Commonwealth, No. 1212-97-4 (Ct. of Appeals Oct. 6, 1998).

The expert testimony of a pawn shop owner regarding the value of two stolen computers was sufficient to support a defendant's conviction for grand larceny where the witness was provided with the make, model, manufacturer, age and last known working condition and features of the computers; the fact that the witness had not personally examined the computers went only to the weight of his testimony and that testimony, together with the circumstantial evidence of the computers' condition before, during, and after the theft, was sufficient to support the conviction. Hodges v. Commonwealth, No. 0622-99-2, 2000 Va. App. LEXIS 225 (Ct. of Appeals Mar. 28, 2000).

The evidence was sufficient to establish the value of a necklace stolen by the defendant where, although no evidence was offered to prove the condition of the necklace, its carat weight, or its current value, the owner testified that the necklace was worth $600 and that he had bought it for that price; without any countervailing evidence, the fact finder was entitled to infer from the evidence that the necklace, originally purchased for $600, was worth at least $200 at the time of the theft. Neville v. Commonwealth, No. 1228-99-2, 2000 Va. App. LEXIS 492 (Ct. of Appeals July 5, 2000).

Evidence was sufficient to support defendant's grand larceny conviction where defendant stole two laptop computers and a personal digital assistant that were relatively new; the jury could reasonably conclude as a matter of common knowledge and in light of the purchase prices and the purchase dates, that they were valued, in the aggregate, at more than $200, without evidence of depreciation. Sheppard v. Commonwealth, No. 3230-02-4, 2004 Va. App. LEXIS 155 (Ct. of Appeals Apr. 6, 2004).

Trial court did not err in convicting defendant of felony embezzlement and sentencing him accordingly, as the evidence sufficiently proved that the value of the material transferred from his computer at work to a third-party server was greater than $200 and embezzlement, like computer fraud, carried a greater punishment if the value of goods embezzled was more than $200. DiMaio v. Commonwealth, 46 Va. App. 755, 621 S.E.2d 696, 2005 Va. App. LEXIS 456 (2005).

Because used catalytic converters had no legal market value beyond the scrap or recycling value of their component parts, and the Commonwealth did not demonstrate that the actual value of the converters at the time of the theft exceeded the statutory threshold of $200 in § 18.2-95, defendant's conviction was reversed. Baylor v. Commonwealth, 55 Va. App. 82, 683 S.E.2d 843, 2009 Va. App. LEXIS 460 (2009).

For purposes of defendant's grand larceny conviction, the Commonwealth met its burden in showing that the depreciated value of the stolen electronics was greater than $200; the victim testified that the stolen iPod was worth around $200 because that was how much she purchased it for and camera was worth $200 to $250, which was what it was purchased for less than a year earlier. Watson v. Commonwealth, 2013 Va. App. LEXIS 32 (Jan. 29, 2013).

Intrinsic value of stock certificates. — Defendant's claim that his conviction for possessing stolen property was improper on the ground that stock certificates had no intrinsic value was defaulted where defendant failed to raise the issue in the trial court. The "ends of justice" exception could not be applied to the defaulted claim because defendant did not suffer a miscarriage of justice in that precedent held that stock certificates had significant value and were readily transferable on the open market, and the Commonwealth established the value of the stock through testimony from the owner of the stock as to the fact that the certificates had a value of approximately $21,000. Wheeler v. Commonwealth, 44 Va. App. 689, 607 S.E.2d 133, 2005 Va. App. LEXIS 8 (2005).

II. ILLUSTRATIVE CASES.

A. Proof Generally.

Where no ability to pay, jury could infer intent to steal. — Where the record showed that, when the defendant was arrested and searched, he did not possess any money or retail charge cards, this evidence indicated that the appellant had no ability to pay for the two televisions. Accordingly, the jury could reasonably have inferred that he acted with the intent to steal. Welch v. Commonwealth, 15 Va. App. 518, 425 S.E.2d 101 (1992).

Larceny "from the person." — A. was standing in the street, holding six dollars, which he was counting, in his open hand, and J. passing by took the money out of A.'s hand and walked off, no force being used beyond what was necessary to withdraw the money. A. asked J. for it several times as she walked off, but she would not return it. This was larceny from the person, within the meaning of this section, if it was done animo furandi. Johnson v. Commonwealth, 65 Va. (24 Gratt.) 555 (1873).

Purse between legs "on her person." — Where at the time the assault and the concomitant theft began the evidence established that victim had the pocketbook tucked between her legs, this qualified as being on her person for the purposes of this section. Saunders v. Commonwealth, 18 Va. App. 825, 447 S.E.2d 526 (1994).

Multiple counts supported by evidence. — Evidence was sufficient to support a conviction of two counts, rather than only one count, of grand larceny, arising from the defendant's taking of a truck in which a gun was located, where the defendant did not see the gun until he had already taken the truck, and where he then hid it so that he could later sell it to purchase crack cocaine. Atkins, Jr. v. Commonwealth, No. 1322-97-2 (Ct. of Appeals June 9, 1998).

Conduct arguably constituted two criminal offenses. — Evidence clearly and affirmatively showed that an element of one of the crimes of which defendant was convicted did not occur. Accordingly, there was error in the judgment appealed from and application of the ends of justice exception was necessary to avoid a grave injustice. Ali v. Commonwealth, 280 Va. 665, 701 S.E.2d 64, 2010 Va. LEXIS 273 (2010).

Intent to permanently deprive owner. — Despite defendant's claims to the contrary, the circumstantial evidence, particularly defendant's conduct, established that he intended to permanently deprive the victim of the car. Yancey v. Commonwealth, No. 2647-01-2, 2002 Va. App. LEXIS 428 (Ct. of Appeals July 30, 2002).

Evidence supported the trial court's finding that defendant took a victim's vehicle with the intent to permanently deprive the victim of it, supporting defendant's conviction for grand larceny of a vehicle. That defendant's murder plan never succeeded due to the victim's escape did not vitiate defendant's larcenous intent during the trespassory taking. McEachern v. Commonwealth, 52 Va. App. 679, 667 S.E.2d 343, 2008 Va. App. LEXIS 471 (2008).

Evidence properly considered as evidence of intention to commit larceny. — Where, as defendant was placed under arrest, he identified himself to the police using a false name, and provided the police with a fictitious social security number and date of birth, while this conduct ultimately gave rise to his conviction of forging a public document, this evidence also was properly considered as evidence of the appellant's intention to commit larceny. Welch v. Commonwealth, 15 Va. App. 518, 425 S.E.2d 101 (1992).

Jury could infer defendant acted with criminal intent. — Where after manager asked defendant to accompany him back inside the store, the defendant fled, where during the ensuing chase, the defendant stopped and confronted the manager, indicated that he was armed and told the manager, "don't make me shoot you," from this evidence the jury could properly infer that the defendant had acted with criminal intent when he moved televisions toward the exit gate. Welch v. Commonwealth, 15 Va. App. 518, 425 S.E.2d 101 (1992).

Intent to wound does not preclude intent to steal. — The mere fact that appellant had the intent to commit malicious wounding did not exclude the hypothesis that he also formed the intent to steal victim's property. Saunders v. Commonwealth, 18 Va. App. 825, 447 S.E.2d 526 (1994).

Possession and movement satisfied asportation element. — A jury could reasonably have concluded that the appellant actually possessed the televisions from the moment he took them from the display shelf and placed them in the shopping cart, until he abandoned the cart in the lawn and garden area outside the store building. Such possession and movement satisfied the asportation element of larceny, if such conduct was done animo furandi. The evidence clearly showed such an intent to steal. Welch v. Commonwealth, 15 Va. App. 518, 425 S.E.2d 101 (1992).

Retailers not required to wait until thief flees to attempt apprehension. — The Court of Appeals would not impose upon Virginia retailers a requirement that they must wait until a suspected thief flees the store with merchandise before they may attempt an apprehension. Where there is evidence that an individual has acted in a manner that is inconsistent with that of a prospective purchaser, and has exercised immediate dominion and control over the property, despite his continued presence within the owner's store, such conduct establishes sufficient possession to satisfy that element of larceny. Welch v. Commonwealth, 15 Va. App. 518, 425 S.E.2d 101 (1992).

Removal of goods from store display was larceny where found near store exit. — Larceny was accomplished when defendants removed the items from the locations in the store where they were displayed by the owner, where such items were adjacent to the storeroom door which led to the outside or were being worn at the time of arrest. Jones v. Commonwealth, 3 Va. App. 295, 349 S.E.2d 414 (1986).

Larceny shown despite period following break-in during which location of property uncertain. — Evidence was sufficient to prove the element of larceny, despite the almost four-week interval following the break-in during which the location of the rings was uncertain in that their owner merely assumed that they were in their usual place in the case on top of his dresser, where the rings were carefully stored, evidence presented showed that they were not removed from this box or the box disturbed save on the rare occasions when they were worn by their owner. These facts made it unlikely that the rings could have been lost through carelessness or accident. Nor was the time during which they were unaccounted for before and after the break-in so long as to dispel the reasonable inference that they were taken at that time. Berryman v. Moore, 619 F. Supp. 853 (E.D. Va. 1985), certification of probable cause denied and dismissed, 792 F.2d 139 (4th Cir. 1986).

Vehicle in repair shop. — When the victim took her vehicle to repair shop, she retained both her ownership and her right to reclaim possession, and thus defendant's conviction for grand theft from her was proper. Catterton v. Commonwealth, 23 Va. App. 407, 477 S.E.2d 748 (1996).

That defendant was in the stolen car nine days after the theft does not prove that defendant either stole the car or exercised dominion or control over the vehicle at any time. Burgess v. Commonwealth, 14 Va. App. 1018, 421 S.E.2d 664 (1992).

Although both burglary under § 18.2-91 and grand larceny under this section are committed in an unbroken line of misconduct, the continuity does not bar an indictment and a conviction for each of the two offenses. Downey v. Peyton, 451 F.2d 236 (4th Cir. 1971).

For a charge under former § 18.2-340.9, the misappropriated funds must be from gross receipts of bingo games or raffles conducted by licensed organizations; there is no minimum amount. For a charge of grand larceny not from the person under this section, there is no limitation on the source of the stolen property, but the property must be worth at least $200; thus, each offense contains an element the other does not, and defendant therefore was not punished twice for the same offense. Waldrop v. Commonwealth, No. 2094-94-2 (Ct. of Appeals Dec. 29, 1995).

Circumstances reflected intent to rape rather than intent to steal. — Where later in the morning of the crime as victim searched through her purse for a telephone number to report her absence from work, she discovered that $80 was missing from her wallet, and where the purse containing the wallet was on the floor beside the dresser in the victim's bedroom during the attack, the circumstantial evidence in this record failed to support an inference beyond a reasonable doubt that the intruder entered the victim's dwelling with the intent to commit larceny; the evidence established that the intruder entered the victim's dwelling sometime between 1:30 a.m. and 3:00 a.m. by cutting through the front door screen, and he then assaulted the victim over the course of the next two hours; these circumstances, standing alone, reflected an intent to rape or ravish rather than an intent to steal from the victim. Maynard v. Commonwealth, 11 Va. App. 437, 399 S.E.2d 635 (1990).

B. Admissibility of Evidence.

Admission of authenticated photograph of goods as substantive evidence. — A photograph of the goods or merchandise alleged to have been taken or converted, which bears the sworn writing of the arresting officer and the photographer's signature, shall be deemed competent evidence of such goods or merchandise and shall be admissible to the same extent as if such goods and merchandise had been introduced as evidence. When a photograph is so authenticated and admitted, it becomes not just an illustration of the testimony of a witness but an independent silent witness constituting substantive evidence. Saunders v. Commonwealth, 1 Va. App. 396, 339 S.E.2d 550 (1986).

Photographs admissible as illustrative evidence despite noncompliance with § 19.2-270.1. — The trial court did not err in admitting photographs of recovered, stolen property in a larceny prosecution where the Commonwealth failed to comply with § 19.2-270.1 because they were received as illustrative, rather than substantive, evidence, and, thus, were not subject to the requirements of § 19.2-270.1. Saunders v. Commonwealth, 1 Va. App. 396, 339 S.E.2d 550 (1986).

Thumbprint as evidence of dominion and control. — Where defendant's thumbprint was on the jewelry box the presence of the thumbprint was evidence that he exercised dominion and control over that item of recently stolen property found in the room, as well as the other items stolen from that residence. Edmondson v. Commonwealth, No. 1504-92-1 (Ct. of Appeals Dec. 21, 1993).

Name on personal documents in bag. — Evidence that defendant's name was on personal documents contained in the bag permitted the fact finder to infer bag belonged to defendant and thus to place the value of the stolen items at a level sufficient to support grand larceny conviction. Washington v. Commonwealth,

No. 1866-03-2, 2004 Va. App. LEXIS 246 (Ct. of Appeals June 1, 2004).

Valuation testimony. — Where store loss prevention officers took identical items of clothing, photographed them, recorded their prices and calculated their value to be over one thousand dollars and the items stolen were for sale and bore price tags indicating their value, the actions taken by the officers gave them sufficient knowledge to establish the value of the stolen merchandise, and their testimony was reliable and sufficient for that purpose. Jackson v. Commonwealth, No. 1212-97-4 (Ct. of Appeals October 6, 1998).

Admissibility of price tags. — Price tags in instant case clearly fell within the business records hearsay exception where loss prevention officers testified that the price tags arrive at the store attached to the merchandise; the tags were placed on the merchandise in the ordinary course of business by a store employee at the time their price was determined; the purpose of the tags is to record the value of the merchandise and track its sale; and tags were used by customers and cashiers to indicate the price of goods for sale and were collected when the items were sold. Jackson v. Commonwealth, No. 1212-97-4 (Ct. of Appeals October 6, 1998).

Admissibility of cash register receipts. — Cash register receipt was properly admitted into evidence under the price tag exception to the hearsay rule because the bar code on the products stolen were not readily decipherable by a judge or jury, but the receipt generated by scanning the bar codes at a cash register summarized the purchase prices of the items in a form that was comprehensible to the fact finder at trial. Twine v. Commonwealth, 48 Va. App. 224, 629 S.E.2d 714, 2006 Va. App. LEXIS 212 (2006).

Admission of murder victim's affidavit. — In a capital murder case, the trial court's admission of the victim's affidavit, which had been attached to her request for a protective order and stated that defendant, her husband, had previously threatened and raped her, in order to prove that defendant later raped and murdered his estranged wife, violated the Confrontation Clause; however, the affidavit's admission was harmless as to defendant's conviction for grand larceny because it did not affect the jury's determination of guilt as to defendant's theft of the victim's car. Crawford v. Commonwealth, 53 Va. App. 138, 670 S.E.2d 15, 2008 Va. App. LEXIS 554 (2008).

Admission of an abuse affidavit into evidence, although violative of defendant's U.S. Const., Amend. VI right to confrontation, was harmless beyond a reasonable doubt for convictions for capital murder, abduction with intent to defile, rape, grand larceny, and two counts of use of a firearm, where the evidence was sufficient to support the convictions absent the affidavit. Crawford v. Commonwealth, 281 Va. 84, 704 S.E.2d 107, 2011 Va. LEXIS 20 (2011).

Evidence properly admitted. — Defendant's convictions for murder in violation of § 18.2-32, use of a firearm in the commission of a felony in violation of § 18.2-53.1, and grand larceny in violation of § 18.2-95 were appropriate because the trial court did not err in admitting evidence of prior crimes to establish defendant's identity since he disputed his identity as the perpetrator of the instant offenses. Additionally, given the substantial evidence of prior bad acts, evidence of a damaged fence did not substantially influence the jury; its admission was therefore harmless. McMillian v. Commonwealth, 2011 Va. LEXIS 74 (Mar. 1, 2011).

Harmless error. — Admission of affidavits, although in error, was held harmless. Hutt v. Commonwealth, 2012 Va. App. LEXIS 228 (July 10, 2012).

C. Sufficiency of Evidence.

Evidence was sufficient to establish that a car was stolen, notwithstanding fact that one of its two owners did not testify that he did not give permission to the defendant to use the car, where the record contained no evidence that defendant or his codefendants had ever met either owner of the car, one owner of the car reported it as stolen, and the steering column of the car was broken open to allow it to be started without a key. Davidson, Jr. v. Commonwealth, No. 2514-97-2 (Ct. of Appeals July 7, 1998).

Evidence was sufficient to establish dominion and control of a stolen car where the defendant and his codefendants used the car to execute and escape after a robbery. Davidson, Jr. v. Commonwealth, No. 2514-97-2 (Ct. of Appeals July 7, 1998).

Fingerprint evidence alone insufficient. — Evidence that a defendant's fingerprints were found on a vehicle from which various items had been stolen was insufficient to sustain a conviction for grand larceny in the absence of other evidence indicating that the fingerprints were left on the vehicle at the time of the crime; in order to show a defendant was the criminal agent, fingerprint evidence must be coupled with evidence of other circumstances tending to reasonably exclude the hypothesis that the print was impressed at a time other than that of the crime. Watkins v. Commonwealth, No. 1975-99-1, 2000 Va. App. LEXIS 247 (Ct. of Appeals Apr. 4, 2000).

Evidence of value of stolen goods shown by Commonwealth. — Testimony that a small fraction of the property stolen was sold shortly after its theft for eight hundred and fifty dollars was an inherently reliable indication of the value of the property stolen from which the jury could have determined that its total value was at least two hundred dollars, therefore, the Commonwealth did not fail to produce evidence of theft of goods valued in excess of two hundred dollars in support of the charge of grand larceny. Bradley v. Commonwealth, No. 0260-93-3 (Ct. of Appeals May 10, 1994).

Expert's testimony, along with circumstantial evidence of stolen computers' operability before, during and after theft, established that value of stolen goods was $200 or more. Hodges v. Commonwealth, No. 0622-99-2 (Ct. of Appeals Mar. 28, 2000).

Commonwealth sufficiently proved defendant committed grand larceny where evidence showed that defendant tried to leave store with a boxed computer priced at $798 without paying for the computer and that, after the computer was retrieved with the box still sealed with the original tape, it was later sold to a customer for $798 and was not returned; given such evidence and the lack of evidence to support defendant's theories that the box defendant took was empty or contained a damaged computer, the trial court's failure to require the Commonwealth to exclude such hypothesis was not plainly wrong. Mitchell v. Commonwealth, No. 1549-01-2, 2002 Va. App. LEXIS 313 (Ct. of Appeals May 21, 2002).

Because the testimony of a victim was sufficient to prove beyond a reasonable doubt that the value of the stolen pressure washer was at least $200 and defendant failed to preserve his other claims as required by Va. Sup. Ct. R. 5A:18, defendant's conviction for grand larceny, in violation of § 18.2-95, was affirmed. Hatcher v. Commonwealth, 2010 Va. App. LEXIS 76 (Feb. 23, 2010).

In defendant's prosecution for grand larceny in which it was shown that defendant stripped siding, fixtures, electrical wiring, and plumbing from the victim's trailer, it was no error to find the evidence was sufficient to prove the value of the stolen items was $200 or more because: (1) the record did not show the victim's testimony as to value simply recited replacement cost, as, while the "figures" the victim testified to were replacement costs the victim obtained, and the victim's estimates of value used this predicate information, the estimates were stated to be the victim's appraisal of the items' value "at the time they were taken"; (2) the evidence included a receipt showing defendant was paid $101.09 for the items and defendant's statement that defendant received "approximately $200" for the scrap metal; and (3) the victim testified the victim valued the fixtures "at the time that they were taken" at $2,000, based on the information the victim gathered, stated as the victim's opinion. Denoncourt v. Commonwealth, 2010 Va. App. LEXIS 329 (Aug. 10, 2010).

In defendant's prosecution for grand larceny in which it was shown that defendant stripped siding, fixtures, electrical wiring, and plumbing from the victim's trailer, hearsay was not erroneously received as to the cost of repairing the damage, when the victim testified to estimates to repair the trailer, because the trial court could explore the victim's knowledge of the value of the stolen items to assess how much weight to attach to the victim's opinion, including the basis for the opinion. Denoncourt v. Commonwealth, 2010 Va. App. LEXIS 329 (Aug. 10, 2010).

In a grand larceny prosecution under § 18.2-95, the evidence was sufficient to prove that the value of the stolen items exceeded $200 as the victim's testimony established that the four stolen items collectively totaled at least $651 when they were purchased new, and the trial court found that the stolen items did not depreciate below $200. The victim was the sole owner of the four items and had knowledge of their use and condition. Hill v. Commonwealth, 2011 Va. App. LEXIS 196 (June 7, 2011).

Testimony that purchase price of one of two stolen items exceeded $200 held sufficient. — In a prosecution for larceny of two rings, testimony of the owner of the rings that the purchase price of only one of the rings exceeded $200, while this factor might not conclusively establish value, could certainly have given the trial judge, who saw both rings, a sufficient basis, taken with the other evidence of value, for finding that the "current value" of the rings exceed $200. Berryman v. Moore, 619 F. Supp. 853 (E.D. Va. 1985).

Value of stolen goods not shown. — The Commonwealth introduced evidence as to the age, original purchase price, and condition of each of the items taken, the owner of the items testified that all were in good working condition, and the Commonwealth introduced photographs of the items taken; however, the record contained insufficient evidence of the value of the items where there was no testimony as to the fair market value of the items, some of which were 15 years old, except for one item, a VCR valued at $50, and the record contained insufficient evidence from which the jury could determine depreciation from the original purchase prices. Davis v. Commonwealth, No. 2045-92-4 (Ct. of Appeals, May 17, 1994).

Evidence of value presented in instant case was inadequate as a matter of law to establish that element of the crime beyond a reasonable doubt where witness demonstrated insufficient knowledge of the value of the stolen items and lacked ample opportunity for forming an accurate opinion on value. Employed by the cable television company as production manager for "just over a month," witness described the items, stated their age, and said they were in "good working order." But he did not testify about the original cost or the effect of age and wear and tear on the value of the stolen equipment. He did not personally buy equipment for his employer, and merely based his estimate of fair market value on "personal experience" as a consumer and "experience as a manager for the company," neither of which afforded him a basis for giving a competent opinion of value. Walls v. Commonwealth, 248 Va. 480, 450 S.E.2d 363 (1994).

Trial court erred in permitting two of the owner's employees to testify about the value of the stolen television set where neither of the employees had examined the television set, nor knew whether it was fully functional, other than turning it on and off; did not know the make, model, or exact age of the set; and their only knowledge of television set values came from their own personal purchases. Givens v. Commonwealth, No. 0105-94-2 (Ct. of Appeals March 21, 1995).

Where there was no testimony that the cordless telephone handset was worth $200 or more, and the Commonwealth did not present other evidence to prove the value of the handset satisfied required statutory amount, the evidence was insufficient to prove this element of grand larceny beyond a reasonable doubt. Parker v. Commonwealth, 254 Va. 118, 489 S.E.2d 482 (1997).

Defendant's conviction for grand larceny was improper because the Commonwealth failed to prove that the value of the jackhammer that defendant rented was at least $200. The only evidence of the jackhammer's value that the trial court found persuasive, which was its original purchase price and replacement cost, was insufficient to prove its worth. Byrum v. Commonwealth, 2010 Va. App. LEXIS 211 (May 18, 2010).

Defendant's conviction for grand larceny in violation of § 18.2-95 was reversed because the trial court had no basis to determine the value of the copper or the air conditioning unit and thus, the evidence was insufficient to prove that the value of the goods stolen was $200 or more. Branch v. Commonwealth, 2010 Va. App. LEXIS 83 (Mar. 9, 2010).

Circumstantial evidence was sufficient to support conclusion that defendant was an aider and abetter in a purse snatching and was the driver of the "getaway" car. Powell v. Commonwealth, No. 0549-89-2 (Ct. of Appeals Aug. 28, 1990).

Circumstantial evidence was sufficient to support finding that defendant embezzled deposit money from his employer. Cassell v. Commonwealth, No. 1595-98-2 (Ct. of Appeals Sept. 28, 1999).

The only reasonable hypothesis flowing from the evidence was that the defendant took money from the cash box at a finance company where the defendant was the only person who entered the office where the cash box was kept after having observed an employee put $300 in the box, the employee had heard rattling sounds coming from the office while the defendant was in the office alone and, immediately after the defendant left the office, the employee discovered that the cash box was empty. Ellis v. Commonwealth, No. 2704-99-1, 2001 Va. App. LEXIS 82 (Ct. of Appeals Feb. 27, 2001).

When viewed in the light most favorable to the Commonwealth, the circumstantial evidence presented at trial was sufficient to sustain the defendant's conviction where such evidence established that the defendant was the only person who had the opportunity to take the missing items from the victim's bedroom, the value of the stolen property exceeded $200, the defendant had a crack habit, and the defendant had stolen from his girlfriend days before the theft in question. Hines v. Commonwealth, No. 3049-99-1, 2000 Va. App. LEXIS 782 (Ct. of Appeals Nov. 28, 2000).

The evidence was sufficient to support the defendant's conviction for grand larceny where the Commonwealth not only proved the defendant had the opportunity to steal the money and thereafter behaved furtively, in a manner suggestive of guilt, but also included anyone else as a possible thief, thereby eliminating every reasonable hypothesis consistent with innocence. Mendez v. Commonwealth, No. 0946-99-2, 2000 Va. App. LEXIS 525 (Ct. of Appeals July 18, 2000).

The circumstantial evidence was sufficient to support the defendant's conviction for grand larceny where the evidence established that, after the defendant made a delivery to an individual at the business from which a laptop computer was stolen, the defendant was observed entering the room where the recipient of the delivery had been working on the laptop five to fifteen minutes earlier, the recipient then heard the sound of a cable dropping on the floor from that room and, after hearing the defendant depart, checked and discovered that the laptop was missing but that the laptop cable remained on the floor; no one else had entered the office during the relevant time and the recipient of the delivery identified the defendant as the courier in his office. The defendant had a motive in that he owed money to the IRS in taxes and the defendant admitted that he had falsified his log sheet for the day to change the order of his deliveries. Marshall v. Commonwealth, No. 0576-99-4, 2000 Va. App. LEXIS 294 (Ct. of Appeals Apr. 25, 2000).

Circumstantial evidence was sufficient to convict defendant of grand larceny, where victim testified that she left upholstery cleaner alone for over an hour and he had had to retrieve water from kitchen for living room by passing open door to bedroom where purse containing $2,300 was located. Petteway v. Commonwealth, No. 1679-00-2, 2001 Va. App. LEXIS 344 (Ct. of Appeals June 19, 2001).

In a prosecution for grand larceny, drawing all reasonable inferences in favor of the prosecution, the jury could have reasonably concluded that the direct and circumstantial evidence presented at trial supported a finding that defendant was in joint possession of a stolen white automobile with an unidentified driver of the vehicle, such that the "possession" element of the charge of grand larceny was proved beyond a reasonable doubt. Teal v. Angelone, — F.3d —, 2003 U.S. App. LEXIS 278 (4th Cir. Jan. 9, 2003), cert. denied, 539 U.S. 948, 123 S. Ct. 2622, 156 L. Ed. 2d 639 (2003).

Where a witness saw a car leave a burglarized home, the car's license plate matched that of defendant's live-in girlfriend, defendant admitted handling unusual shotgun shells found in the car that matched shells from the home, the witness was "90 percent" sure defendant was the driver of the car, and defendant (who had eight prior felony convictions) gave numerous conflicting stories about whether, when, and where he had driven his girlfriend's car, the circumstantial evidence had been sufficient to convict him of breaking and entering. Johnson v. Commonwealth, No. 3026-02-2, 2003 Va. App. LEXIS 707 (Ct. of Appeals Dec. 30, 2003).

Only reasonable hypothesis flowing from circumstantial evidence that defendant entered an apartment at a very late hour, without permission, and that money and medication was found missing from the apartment the next morning, was that defendant took the money and medication, and the evidence sufficiently supported defendant's grand larceny conviction, despite the fact that two other maintenance workers also had keys to the apartment, as there was no evidence they entered the apartment. Freeman v. Commonwealth, No. 0796-02-3, 2003 Va. App. LEXIS 331 (Ct. of Appeals June 10, 2003).

Where the victim's car and personal belongings were taken while the house was locked and defendant was asleep on the victim's couch, nothing in the record supported the scenario suggested by defendant that someone else stole the victim's property; the trial court was not wrong in rejecting a hypothesis "from the imagina-

tion" of defendant because the circumstantial evidence was sufficient to convict defendant of grand larceny. Brown v. Commonwealth, No. 1749-03-2, 2004 Va. App. LEXIS 211 (Ct. of Appeals May 4, 2004).

Finding that defendant was the thief who committed grand larceny of three power washers was justified where said circumstances showed that: (1) he was the only one seen leaving the scene of the crime running into the woods; (2) he ran past his stolen getaway car and attempted to obtain a ride from a complete stranger; and (3) when that plan failed, he was apprehended while driving the getaway car that he had earlier abandoned. Watts v. Commonwealth, No. 2974-03-2, 2005 Va. App. LEXIS 133 (Ct. of Appeals Mar. 29, 2005).

Defendant's conviction for petit and grand larceny was supported by sufficient evidence where: (1) the items found in the rear cargo area of the car driven by defendant at the time of a traffic stop had been recently stolen from vehicles parked on a body shop lot; (2) the jury was not required to accept defendant's explanation that he was legitimately present on the lot and that either his brother or co-defendant could have placed the stolen items in the cargo compartment, unbeknownst to him; (3) there was a discrepancy between defendant's statement to a police officer as to the time defendant was on the property and the time a security officer saw defendant's car leaving the body shop lot; (4) defendant drove from the lot in a rapid manner; and (5) the jury could have reasonably inferred that defendant's denial of knowledge of the presence of the stolen goods in the car and his explanation to the police officer were not credible. Sbitan v. Commonwealth, — Va. App. —, — S.E.2d —, 2006 Va. App. LEXIS 19 (Jan. 17, 2006).

Evidence was sufficient to support a conviction for grand larceny of $1,000 from defendant's girlfriend because the circumstantial evidence taken as a whole was consistent with a finding of guilt and excluded all reasonable hypotheses of innocence. Only seven people had any access to the bedroom where the money was located, only two people knew that the victim had the money, only defendant saw the victim put the money in a Bible in her bedroom, and defendant exhibited a number of unusual behaviors. White v. Commonwealth, — Va. App. —, — S.E.2d —, 2006 Va. App. LEXIS 538 (Nov. 28, 2006).

Larceny conviction based on theft of inkjet cartridges was supported by sufficient circumstantial evidence including evidence that, when arrested, defendant attempted to conceal the whereabouts of his car and his possession of the stolen cartridges; the trial court was entitled to infer that the 56 cartridges consisting of 24 different types of cartridges found in defendant's possession was inconsistent with a normal consumer purchase. Finally, while still in possession of the stolen cartridges, defendant was arrested attempting to steal more inkjet cartridges. Brown v. Commonwealth, — Va. App. —, — S.E.2d —, 2007 Va. App. LEXIS 223 (May 29, 2007).

Defendant's convictions on four counts of grand larceny and four counts of burglary were supported by sufficient evidence as defendant admitted that he took part in the burglaries of the first two of four homes, and the evidence supported a reasonable inference that defendant took part in the burglaries of the third and fourth homes, in that, at the fourth house, defendant's fingerprints were found on bank envelopes stolen from the third house. The similarity of the burglaries was relevant circumstantial evidence that tended to show that defendant was the criminal agent as the breaking and entering occurred by the same means each time, the same type of personal property was stolen, the master bedroom in each house was the target of each burglary, and dresser drawers were dumped in each location. Wilkins v. Commonwealth, 2008 Va. App. LEXIS 483 (Oct. 28, 2008).

Evidence that defendant had the opportunity to take the copper wire, no one other than defendant had worked on the wire, defendant knew that the wire's connections had been cut, and defendant had access to the locked panel boxes where the wire had been connected at the time in question was sufficient to prove beyond a reasonable doubt that defendant was the person who stole the wire. Tackett v. Commonwealth, — Va. App. —, — S.E.2d —, 2009 Va. App. LEXIS 81 (Feb. 24, 2009).

Because the circumstantial evidence — including the owners' identification of their all terrain vehicle, a witness's identification of defendant, and defendant's DNA on a crushed beer can found in a pack on the all terrain vehicle's handlebars — excluded any reasonable hypothesis of innocence and proved beyond a reasonable doubt that defendant stole the all terrain vehicle, defendant was properly convicted of grand larceny. Dove v. Commonwealth, 2011 Va. App. LEXIS 243 (July 19, 2011).

Evidence held sufficient to sustain conviction of grand larceny. Wright v. Commonwealth, 196 Va. 132, 82 S.E.2d 603 (1950); Jordan v. Commonwealth, 207 Va. 591, 151 S.E.2d 390 (1966); Skeeter v. Commonwealth, 217 Va. 722, 232 S.E.2d 756 (1977); Shepherd v. Commonwealth, No. 2728-97-4 (Ct. of Appeals Nov. 10, 1998); Martin v. Commonwealth, No. 1556-97-2 (Ct. of Appeals Jan. 12, 1999); Brown v. Commonwealth, No. 0542-02-3, 2003 Va. App. LEXIS 22 (Jan. 21, 2003).

Evidence was sufficient to support defendant's conviction for grand larceny, as evidence that defendant broke into home and stole a woman's duffel bag with distinctive red striping, and was seen by several neighbors shortly afterwards carrying that duffel bag, allowed for the reasonable inference that defendant also stole items from the woman that she claimed were missing from her home and which supported a conviction under the grand larceny statute. Cullipher v. Commonwealth, No. 2422-01-1, 2002 Va. App. LEXIS 626 (Ct. of Appeals Oct. 15, 2002).

Where the trial court erred in admitting, over defendant's objection, hearsay testimony from two witnesses concerning information they saw displayed on a cash register computer screen, as the Commonwealth failed to admit the printout information of what was displayed, such error was harmless; defendant's inconsistent reasons for not having a receipt for a generator he had stolen, and the fact that the receipt that was attached to the generator was for a toolbox he had earlier abandoned, provided sufficient evidence to support his conviction. Baber v. Commonwealth, No. 2832-01-2, 2003 Va. App. LEXIS 212 (Ct. of Appeals Apr. 8, 2003).

Where defendant was found driving a vehicle that had been stolen 35 days earlier, defendant claimed that he didn't know that the vehicle was stolen, defendant claimed that his brother asked him to drive the vehicle, and defendant's brother denied the claim that he had asked defendant to drive the vehicle and testified that a cousin acquired the vehicle in exchange for drugs, there was uncontroverted evidence that defendant was in recent and exclusive possession of the stolen vehicle; hence, there was sufficient evidence to support defendant's conviction for grand larceny. Randolph v. Commonwealth, No. 2162-02-1, 2003 Va. App. LEXIS 511 (Ct. of Appeals Oct. 14, 2003).

Evidence was not insufficient to support larceny conviction as the trial judge was not required to believe testimony that defendant did not know that projector was stolen and there was identification evidence to support the conclusion that defendant stole the projector. Howard v. Commonwealth, No. 2166-03-2, 2004 Va. App. LEXIS 460 (Ct. of Appeals Sept. 28, 2004).

Evidence was sufficient to support defendant's conviction for grand larceny for possession of a recently stolen backhoe, as the trial court was at liberty to discount defendant's self-serving explanations as little more than lying to conceal defendant's guilt and could treat such prevarications as affirmative evidence of guilty knowledge. Burton v. Commonwealth, — Va. App. —, — S.E.2d —, 2006 Va. App. LEXIS 464 (Oct. 17, 2006).

Evidence, taken in the light most favorable to the Commonwealth, demonstrated that defendant, through defendant's own admission, took a savings withdrawal book from the residence of a person for whom defendant had performed cleaning services, presented forged withdrawal slips from the person's savings book to a teller at the bank where the relevant account was located, and received in cash the amount written on the withdrawal slip; as a result, a rational trier of fact could reasonably conclude that defendant committed grand larceny in violation of § 18.2-95. Stokes v. Commonwealth, 49 Va. App. 401, 641 S.E.2d 780, 2007 Va. App. LEXIS 89 (2007).

Because a police officer's statement of the result of an investigation did not call for objectionable matter and did not state an assertion of an out-of-court declarant, defendant's hearsay objection was properly overruled; defendant's unexplained recent possession of a stolen vehicle was sufficient to prove defendant guilty of grand larceny. Rodgers v. Commonwealth, 2007 Va. App. LEXIS 107 (Mar. 20, 2007).

Witness's testimony implicating the witness, defendant, and another person was not inherently incredible and was sufficient to prove beyond a reasonable doubt that defendant was guilty of grand larceny. Walker v. Commonwealth, — Va. App. —, — S.E.2d —, 2008 Va. App. LEXIS 475 (Oct. 21, 2008).

Victim's testimony, that defendant was only person besides the victim to enter the victim's home between the time the victim placed the victim's purse with the wallet in it on the bed and when the victim found the wallet missing, was sufficient to support defendant's conviction for grand larceny. Hollie v. Commonwealth, 2009 Va. App. LEXIS 5 (Jan. 13, 2009).

While no one saw defendant carrying the bags of stolen crab legs out of a store, the evidence showed that defendant and his two cohorts walked into the store, grabbed twelve bags of crab legs, went into a bathroom with them, returned holding nothing in their hands, exited the store without paying for anything, and ran to their car; thus, the logical inference from the evidence presented was that defendant and his two cohorts concealed the crab legs in their clothing while in the bathroom and left the store. Brown v. Commonwealth, 54 Va. App. 107, 676 S.E.2d 326, 2009 Va. App. LEXIS 226 (2009).

Because defendant acknowledged that the traveler's checks defendant executed "probably" belonged to someone else, it was immaterial whether defendant knew they were counterfeit or fake; accordingly, the evidence was sufficient to find defendant guilty of grand larceny and uttering a forged traveler's check in violation of §§ 18.2-95 and 18.2-172. McQuinn v. Commonwealth, 2009 Va. App. LEXIS 258 (June 9, 2009).

Defendant's conviction for grand larceny of a string trimmer in violation of § 18.2-95 was appropriate because the evidence proved that defendant's blood was deposited on the metal stand when it was used to commit the larceny of the string trimmer. The owner's testimony was also competent on the issue of the value of the trimmer and sufficient to establish its value of at least $200. Swiggett v. Commonwealth, 2010 Va. App. LEXIS 53 (Feb. 9, 2010).

Grand larceny conviction was supported by sufficient evidence, as a rational factfinder would easily have found the vehicle possessed by defendant belonged to the victim, as no witnesses testified that there were two identical vehicles in the mechanic's yard at the time the victim's car was stolen and it was within the trial court's province to believe the mechanic's testimony and not that of defendant, a convicted felon. Britt v. Commonwealth, 2010 Va. App. LEXIS 246 (June 22, 2010).

Evidence that one set of victims testified that a nylon camouflaged holster found with defendant's wallet and belongings looked like one missing from their house, one of the firearms recovered from defendant's shed bore the serial number of a firearm missing from their home, and deer meat stolen from another victim and uniquely packaged was identified by another victim supported defendant's convictions for grand larceny, two counts of breaking and entering, two counts of larceny of a firearm, petit larceny, and destruction of property. Bowles v. Commonwealth, 2010 Va. App. LEXIS 275 (July 13, 2010).

Evidence was sufficient to sustain defendant's conviction for grand larceny, in violation of § 18.2-95, where defendant was found in possession of the victim's vehicle, without the victim's permission, and defendant admitted that he drove the vehicle to Florida. Crawford v. Commonwealth, 281 Va. 84, 704 S.E.2d 107, 2011 Va. LEXIS 20 (2011).

Sufficient evidence supported defendant's § 18.2-95 conviction as it could be inferred that defendant acted with the intent to permanently deprive a bank of its money since: (1) defendant opened a new checking account solely to deposit a cashier's check; (2) within days, defendant cashed three checks on the newly created account using two different names and addresses; (3) when contacted by the bank, defendant did not appear surprised there was a problem with the cashier's check; (4) defendant did not show for a meeting with the bank defendant promised to attend; and (5) defendant ignored the bank representatives and decided to keep and use the money from the spurious check. Dennis v. Commonwealth, 2010 Va. App. LEXIS 377 (Sept. 21, 2010).

Conviction for grand larceny under § 18.2-95 was supported by fact finder's conclusion that defendant did not have the substantial ability to return the property at time defendant took it due to money troubles; the trial judge was not required to believe defendant's testimony that defendant intended to return jewelry the next day when defendant got paid and could retrieve the items from the pawn shop. Marsh v. Commonwealth, 57 Va. App. 645, 704 S.E.2d 624, 2011 Va. App. LEXIS 44 (2011).

Where defendant cashed in $385 worth of coins a few days after the coins, a motorcycle, and other belongings were taken from a decedent's home, defendant was seen in possession of the motorcycle, and some of the decedent's belongings were found at his home, there was sufficient evidence that the coins he cashed in were the same coins taken from the decedent's home and that the coins were worth more than $200. Burton v. Commonwealth, 58 Va. App. 274, 708 S.E.2d 444, 2011 Va. App. LEXIS 177 (2011).

Defendant's conviction for grand larceny, § 18.2-95, for taking items from a store was proper, as an innocent shopper would have produced a receipt, if the shopper still had it; when asked at trial where the receipt was, defendant first guessed it was at home, but changed defendant's story and claimed the police confiscated it from defendant's home. Gray v. Commonwealth, 2012 Va. App. LEXIS 178 (May 29, 2012).

Sufficient evidence of grand larceny by false pretenses. — Where defendant sold victims a car he had not paid for and for which he did not have legal title; victims gave defendant money for the car, ownership of which he could not legally transfer; and defendant issued victims a receipt for the car and he deceived them regarding the status of the car's title, conviction for grand larceny by false pretenses was affirmed. Wileman v. Commonwealth, 24 Va. App. 642, 484 S.E.2d 621 (1997).

Evidence sustaining conviction of attempted grand larceny. — Where the defendant was arrested while in the act of prying open the trunk of a car that contained a money bag, which he knew was in the trunk and which he thought contained money, but which was in fact empty; and the trunk also contained a camera, a movie projector and a tire having a total value of more than $200; and the indictment returned against the defendant charged him with attempted grand larceny of those three articles; the defendant was properly convicted of attempted grand larceny because the natural inference to be drawn from his actions was that he intended to steal whatever he found in the trunk. Coleman v. Commonwealth, 211 Va. 571, 179 S.E.2d 470 (1971).

Because the cash register tapes were properly admitted under the business records exception to the hearsay rule, the evidence presented was sufficient to convict cashier of attempted grand larceny. From the eyewitness testimony and the tapes, the trial judge properly inferred that out of customer's entire grocery order, totaling $426.22, cashier, in an attempt to hide the actual amount of items taken from the store, scanned only five deli items equaling $25.30. That the scanner in cashier's checkstand may have malfunctioned, not registering over $400 worth of groceries, and gone unnoticed by cashier, was a hypothesis of innocence unsupported by the evidence. Furthermore, the customer's five deli items scanned in cashier's lane exactly matched five deli items that were rescanned by head teller. Lastly, prices of certain items from the customer's cart, worth over $200 in total, were personally verified by head teller, thus supplying conclusive proof of the value of the items taken to prove a conviction of attempted grand larceny. Fitzhugh v. Commonwealth, 20 Va. App. 275, 456 S.E.2d 163 (1995).

Evidence was sufficient to sustain a conviction of grand larceny because a victim testified that defendant sold him a tow dolly, a surveillance video showed a truck similar to defendant's truck leaving a gas station's parking lot after hours with a tow dolly, and testimony showed that the tow dolly was worth more than $1,500. Berry v. Commonwealth, 2010 Va. App. LEXIS 217 (May 25, 2010).

Evidence held sufficient to prove grand larceny. — Where trial court was entitled to conclude that defendant knew that property was stolen, actively participated in its disposition, and lied about his actual role in the transaction in order to mask this fact, defendant's conviction for grand larceny would be affirmed. Speight v. Commonwealth, 4 Va. App. 83, 354 S.E.2d 95 (1987).

Considering the unique nature of the copper bus bars, the circumstances under which they were found in the defendant's possession, their location next to the plant and in close proximity to a storage bin containing similar bus bars, the time of day— approximately 11 p.m.—at which the defendant was transporting them, the matching distinctive shiny and tarnished colorations between the stockpiled copper and that possessed by the defendant, the gap in the fence enabling the copper to be removed from the plant's property, and the fact that the plant had copper of these dimensions missing from its inventory, the evidence was sufficient to identify the copper found in the defendant's possession as belonging to the plant and to prove that it was stolen. Lew v.

Commonwealth, 20 Va. App. 353, 457 S.E.2d 392 (1995).

Ample evidence supported the finding that the defendant was the criminal agent who stole the plant's copper bus bars. Unexplained or falsely explained possession of recently stolen goods is a fact sufficient for the judge or jury to infer that the person in possession of the stolen goods was the thief. Moreover, the evidence showed that as a workman inside the plant, the defendant had the means and opportunity to gain access to the secured area where the copper was stored. His explanation that he found the large amount of valuable copper alongside the roadway, next to the plant where he worked, and that he was taking his found property home late at night, was not credible, and the fact finder was entitled to disbelieve it. Lew v. Commonwealth, 20 Va. App. 353, 457 S.E.2d 392 (1995).

All of the evidence in this case indicated that the car found in the possession of the defendant was the same car that had recently been stolen. Accordingly, the conviction was affirmed. Warf v. Commonwealth, No. 1086-96-1 (Ct. of Appeals Jan. 28, 1997).

Where the victim testified that she requested the return of her motorcycle and defendant refused, and defendant's own testimony established that he had converted the motorcycle to his own use by giving it to his cousin, the trial court was entitled to conclude that he intended to permanently deprive the victim of her property. Morris v. Commonwealth, No. 1606-96-2 (Ct. of Appeals Apr. 1, 1997).

Where, when questioned by police regarding whether there were any weapons in the room, defendant said there might possibly be a gun or knife under one of the beds, where the police immediately found the gun under one of the mattresses, lying directly beside a knife that appellant admitted was his, and where although appellant denied ownership of the gun, its presence with his knife and his earlier statement indicating his awareness of its presence permitted the inference "that appellant exercised the dominion and control necessary to show constructive possession," the evidence of his constructive possession of a firearm was sufficient to support his conviction for grand larceny of the firearm and possession of a firearm by a convicted felon. Archer v. Commonwealth, 26 Va. App. 1, 492 S.E.2d 826 (1997).

Evidence was sufficient to prove that the defendant committed grand larceny of a cellular telephone where he opened a cellular account and obtained a telephone using a false name and social security number, and he was told to return the telephone after several days, but neither the defendant nor the telephone ever returned. Faulk v. Commonwealth, No. 0154-97-1 (Ct. of Appeals June 9, 1998).

Evidence was sufficient to establish that defendant had exclusive possession of stolen car, where he was found operating vehicle and in possession of its keys, his wallet was found hidden in vehicle, and he had been seen in possession of an identical car after theft but prior to his arrest. Dobson v. Commonwealth, No. 2802-97-2 (Ct. of Appeals June 15, 1999).

Evidence was sufficient to sustain defendant's conviction of grand larceny under this section where a patient observed defendant twisting her bracelet while defendant, a phlebotomist, was drawing blood which was the last time the patient saw the bracelet and the only other person who could have stolen it, an emergency room doctor, never touched the bracelet. Bailey v. Commonwealth, No. 0485-01-4, 2002 Va. App. LEXIS 146 (Ct. of Appeals Mar. 12, 2002).

Absent a credible, exculpatory explanation for his possession of a stolen check, the trial judge permissibly inferred that the evidence was sufficient to support defendant's conviction for larceny. Gilbert v. Commonwealth, No. 2128-01-3, 2002 Va. App. LEXIS 664 (Ct. of Appeals Nov. 5, 2002). See Sprouse v. Commonwealth, — Va. App. —, — S.E.2d —, 2002 Va. App. LEXIS 748 (Dec. 17, 2002); Covil v. Commonwealth, No. 2860-02-1, 2003 Va. App. LEXIS 632 (Ct. of Appeals Dec. 9, 2003), aff'd, 268 Va. 692, 604 S.E.2d 79 (2004).

Evidence was sufficient to support defendant's convictions for statutory burglary and grand larceny where: (1) defendant's DNA profile was consistent with blood drops underneath a window; (2) a partial analysis on a beer bottle did not exclude defendant; (3) defendant was not a customer or an employee of the co-op, and no evidence suggested that he had a reason to be on the premises; (4) defendant lied to police about his whereabouts at the time of the break-in; and (5) before police shared any information with defendant as to the condition of the truck, he made the spontaneous statement that "the truck was not damaged." Davis v. Commonwealth, No. 0649-03-2, 2004 Va. App. LEXIS 220 (Ct. of Appeals May 11, 2004).

Because the cash register receipt for the items defendant stole was properly admitted and established that the value of the merchandise stolen was $693.29 and because defendant offered no evidence at trial to refute the prices of the stolen items listed on the receipt, the evidence was sufficient to sustain defendant's conviction for grand larceny. Twine v. Commonwealth, 48 Va. App. 224, 629 S.E.2d 714, 2006 Va. App. LEXIS 212 (2006).

Whether defendant made unauthorized transactions from defendant's former employer's account or supplied the necessary information to defendant's spouse for the spouse to conduct the transactions, the evidence was sufficient to prove beyond a reasonable doubt that defendant committed grand larceny as either a principal in the first or second degree. The evidence showed that unauthorized transactions were paid to accounts containing the names of defendant and the spouse, and that defendant and the spouse, by retaining copies of checks drawn on the employer's bank account, had ready access to the account and routing numbers required to make transactions by telephone. Rashad Jamar Cason v. Commonwealth, — Va. App. —, — S.E.2d —, 2009 Va. App. LEXIS 46 (Feb. 3, 2009).

In a case in which defendant appealed his convictions for breaking and entering, in violation of § 18.2-91, and grand larceny, in violation of § 18.2-95, he argued unsuccessfully that the evidence was insufficient to support his convictions. The trial court reasonably concluded from the evidence that the items stolen and those defendant sold to a pawn shop were the same items: (1) the pawn shop required a picture identification prior to purchasing property from a customer; (2) the purchase agreements issued to defendant for the purchase of a guitar and television listed the serial numbers of the items purchased; and (3) those serial numbers matched the serial numbers of the stolen guitar and television. Lunsford v. Commonwealth, 55 Va. App. 59, 683 S.E.2d 831, 2009 Va. App. LEXIS 461 (2009).

Evidence that defendant secretly took a rifle without the owner's permission after she had fallen asleep, engaged the police in a high speed chase that resulted in his crashing his car, and that he abandoned the rifle, was sufficient to convict him of grand larceny in violation of § 18.2-95, as there was no evidence he intended to return the gun. Massa v. Commonwealth, 2012 Va. App. LEXIS 300 (Sept. 25, 2012).

Sufficient evidence to convict defendant as principal. — In a criminal prosecution for grand larceny, where defendant and his father deceived the owner of a car to gain access to the car and then disappeared with the car for six weeks, the evidence was sufficient to convict defendant as a principal. Tuck v. Commonwealth, No. 3376-02-3, 2003 Va. App. LEXIS 623 (Ct. of Appeals Dec. 9, 2003).

In a case in which defendant appealed his conviction in a bench trial for grand larceny of a rental vehicle, his challenge to the sufficiency of the evidence that he was the criminal agent who stole the vehicle was without merit as it ignored the credibility determinations that the court necessarily reached in support of the conviction, and it also failed to consider the competency of circumstantial evidence to establish guilt beyond a reasonable doubt. The evidence supported the conviction beyond a reasonable doubt. Williams v. Commonwealth, 2012 Va. App. LEXIS 231 (July 17, 2012).

Evidence held insufficient to prove grand larceny. — Fact that defendant, who was hitchhiking, accepted a ride from the first person who stopped, and that he knew that person was driving a stolen vehicle, raised a suspicion of guilt, but was not sufficient to establish beyond a reasonable doubt that the defendant committed grand larceny. Moehring v. Commonwealth, 223 Va. 564, 290 S.E.2d 891 (1982).

Proof that a defendant knew that an automobile was stolen and was in the automobile as a passenger did not suffice to prove the defendant guilty of larceny of the automobile. Burgess v. Commonwealth, 14 Va. App. 1018, 421 S.E.2d 664 (1992).

Where the evidence did not prove beyond a reasonable doubt that defendant exercised any degree of dominion or control over the vehicle or that he shared joint exclusive possession of the stolen vehicle with anyone, the court of appeals reversed the larceny conviction. Burgess v. Commonwealth, 14 Va. App. 1018, 421 S.E.2d 664 (1992).

In an action for grand larceny no evidence was presented of the value of credit cards, only of the lines of credit they represented;

consequently, the evidence did not support a finding that the card had a value greater than $200, and the defendant, who obtained the cards by false representation, could be convicted only of petit larceny, not grand larceny. Owolabi v. Commonwealth, 16 Va. App. 78, 428 S.E.2d 14 (1993).

Evidence failed to support conviction of grand larceny where defendant cashed an Aid to Dependent Children (now TANF) check at a convenience store, reported to the Department of Social Services that the check was stolen or lost and by affidavit swore that she had neither endorsed the check nor authorized its endorsement, and Social Services subsequently issued her another check and withdrew the amount of the first check from the bank account of the convenience store. Nothing in the evidence supported a finding that defendant intended thereby to steal from the convenience store or that, at that time, she intended to present a false claim to the Department of Social Services. Nor was there any evidence supporting a finding that defendant knew that her execution of the affidavit would cause the Department of Social Services to withdraw money from the account of the convenience store. Redd v. Commonwealth, 29 Va. App. 256, 511 S.E.2d 436 (1999).

Circumstantial evidence was insufficient to prove that the defendant committed grand larceny and/or burglary where: (1) there was evidence that she walked toward a business that was burglarized, but there was no evidence that she entered the business or was seen inside the business; (2) although the defendant's boots were very similar to footprints in the snow at the scene of the crime, no evidence of a match was presented; and (3) police officers saw other persons near the scene of the crime shortly after the defendant was allowed to leave, but did not examine their shoes or try to match them to the footprints in the snow. Martin v. Commonwealth, No. 1556-97-2 (Ct. of Appeals June 9, 1998).

Evidence was insufficient to support a conviction where: (1) the parties stipulated that two homes were burglarized and that goods valued at more than $200 were stolen from each home; (2) although there was evidence that the defendant thereafter pawned some items, there was no evidence as to what those items were; and (3) a police officer could not recall whether the defendant admitted that he pawned "that stuff" or "some stuff." Dailey v. Commonwealth, No. 0327-98-1 (Ct. of Appeals Feb. 9, 1999).

A defendant's conduct in not leaving a vehicle and moving into the front seat while it was being stolen by another was insufficient to support his conviction for grand larceny as a principal in the second degree; no evidence proved the defendant participated in the theft or aided and abetted the perpetrator by inciting, encouraging, advising or assisting him or proved the defendant was a look-out and no evidence proved the defendant shared the perpetrator's criminal intent. Hampton v. Commonwealth, 32 Va. App. 644, 529 S.E.2d 843, 2000 Va. App. LEXIS 465 (2000).

The evidence was insufficient as a matter of law to establish the defendant's larcenous intent at the time he drove a companion's car away from a fight in which the owner had been attacked where the trier of fact could not determine, without speculation, that the defendant intended to deprive the owner of his car permanently. Tarpley v. Commonwealth, 261 Va. 251, 542 S.E.2d 761, 2001 Va. LEXIS 31 (2001).

Charges that a defendant committed grand larceny by passing counterfeit checks were not sufficiently proved by evidence which failed to link him to the specific checks upon which the charges were based. Bell v. Commonwealth, No. 0139-01-2, 2002 Va. App. LEXIS 151 (Ct. of Appeals Mar. 12, 2002).

Although the evidence showed that the woman's purse and its contents, valued at more the $200, was taken from the lawyer's office where the woman worked as a paralegal, the evidence was insufficient to prove all of the elements of grand larceny beyond a reasonable doubt, and, thus defendant's grand larceny conviction was reversed. Defendant denied taking the purse, was not shown to be in possession of any of its contents, and two other people had been in the office during the two-hour time period before the woman noticed that the purse was missing. Anderson v. Commonwealth, No. 2460-02-2, 2003 Va. App. LEXIS 690 (Ct. of Appeals Dec. 23, 2003).

Defendant's conviction for grand larceny was reversed because the evidence failed to prove that the value of the lottery ticket she allegedly stole was $200 or more; under the common law, the value of the ticket was the value of the paper on which it was printed or

50 cents. Hunt v. Commonwealth, 46 Va. App. 25, 614 S.E.2d 668, 2005 Va. App. LEXIS 239 (2005).

Evidence offered to prove the corpus delicti in a trial for larceny was insufficient where the evidence failed to prove that property has been stolen from another or where property found in the accused's possession could not be identified as having been stolen. Lew v. Commonwealth, 20 Va. App. 353, 457 S.E.2d 392 (1995).

Evidence held sufficient. — Unbroken chain of events, including defendant's entry into the victim's home, taking of a VCR, carrying such away while shielding the front of his body from the victim's view, his immediate departure thereafter, and fingerprints found on a beer can within ten feet from the place where the VCR was taken, was sufficient circumstantial evidence to support petit larceny conviction. Turner v. Commonwealth, No. 1942-01-3, 2002 Va. App. LEXIS 222 (Ct. of Appeals Apr. 9, 2002).

Evidence proved beyond a reasonable doubt that defendant was the criminal agent of the charged offenses of forgery and uttering, in violation of § 18.2-172, and grand larceny of the proceeds, in violation of § 18.2-95, where only defendant had access to the victim's checkbook during the time the check in question was stolen, and defendant cashed the check. Clary v. Commonwealth, No. 3010-00-2, 2002 Va. App. LEXIS 324 (Ct. of Appeals May 28, 2002).

Evidence showing that after bingo game had concluded, witness, who had the only key, had locked the proceeds in walk-in refrigerator in kitchen, that the next day defendant was found leaving the kitchen with a box of stolen food, and that the refrigerator locks were broken and food was strewn all over the refrigerator, and that when on the following day the refrigerator and its contents were examined, the cash was missing, was sufficient for the trial court to reasonably infer that defendant, who had been seen stealing the food, had also stolen the missing cash. Murphy v. Commonwealth, No. 1198-01-2, 2002 Va. App. LEXIS 399 (Ct. of Appeals July 23, 2002).

Evidence sufficiently supported defendant's conviction for committing grand larceny in the second degree as it showed that defendant helped to select the items that were eventually stolen and handed them to defendant's sister, that defendant concealed one of the two stolen items with a garment bag defendant brought into the store, and that defendant was with defendant's sister as the sister visibly carried items out of the store in a red shopping bag despite the fact that the sister had not brought that bag into the store and had made no purchases; it was not reasonable to infer from the evidence and the circumstances that the sister acted alone in stealing the items. Falo v. Commonwealth, No. 2730-01-4, 2002 Va. App. LEXIS 753 (Ct. of Appeals Dec. 17, 2002).

Evidence that defendant wrote 142 checks worth $82,130 on a church's bank account over a 25-month period and used the money for various purposes, including as gifts to others, supported the trial court's judgment that he committed multiple, separate acts of embezzlement, in violation of §§ 18.2-111 and 18.2-95. Bragg v. Commonwealth, 42 Va. App. 607, 593 S.E.2d 558, 2004 Va. App. LEXIS 103 (2004).

Defendant's convictions for grand larceny and breaking and entering with intent to commit larceny were affirmed as: (1) an employee of the victim business testified that a storeroom window was intact on the day before the burglary and that the next day he discovered his computer and other items missing and found that the window was broken; (2) the storeroom was not a place where employees regularly went; (3) defendant repeatedly told a detective that he had never been inside the storeroom; (4) it could be hypothesized that defendant's blood was left in the storeroom during the burglary and that defendant was the burglar; and (5) the fact that the burglar did not take a broken printer and that defendant knew that the printer was broken provided additional circumstantial evidence that defendant was the perpetrator. Smith v. Commonwealth, — Va. App. —, — S.E.2d —, 2006 Va. App. LEXIS 295 (July 5, 2006).

Defendant's conviction for larceny from a person under § 18.2-95 was supported for § 8.01-680 purposes by a victim's identification of defendant that was corroborated by Deoxyribonucleic Acid from a vest defendant left at the crime scene. Gantt v. Commonwealth, 2008 Va. App. LEXIS 430 (Sept. 23, 2008).

Defendant's conviction of embezzlement in violation of § 18.2-95 was supported by the evidence, as a manager of the store where defendant worked testified that store video showed defendant print two money orders, grab them, and walk off. There was no customer at the cash register at the time. McDonald v. Commonwealth, — Va. App. —, — S.E.2d —, 2008 Va. App. LEXIS 532 (Dec. 9, 2008).

Convictions of grand larceny and statutory burglary were supported by sufficient evidence because the trial court was not obligated to accept defendant's explanation of possession of recently stolen tools as credible, and was entitled to rely on evidence of his falsely denied recent possession as proof of his guilt; the trial court clearly rejected defendant's story of how he purchased, then pawned, the stolen tools as too coincidental, and disregarded defendant's explanation as too opposed to probabilities. Marshall v. Commonwealth, 2009 Va. App. LEXIS 318 (July 14, 2009).

Evidence was sufficient to sustain defendant's conviction for grand larceny because defendant's act of removing paint from the display shelf in a store, placing it in a cart, and representing that the paint had already been purchased created a substantial risk of permanent loss of the paint to the store, and since defendant's stated intent to return the paint was entirely contingent upon the store's payment of the full value of the paint, which was a condition he had no right to impose, his intent to "sell" it back to the owner under fraudulent circumstances did not negate his intent to steal the paint at the time of the taking; the intent to return, conditioned on a future event that may or may not occur and based on a false assertion of ownership, should be disregarded as a matter of law and, as such, cannot negate the inference of intent to steal. Carter v. Commonwealth, 54 Va. App. 700, 682 S.E.2d 77, 2009 Va. App. LEXIS 386 (2009), aff'd, 280 Va. 100, 694 S.E.2d 590, 2010 Va. LEXIS 74 (2010).

Evidence supported a finding that defendant and two accomplices had agreed to commit grand larceny in violation of subsection B of § 18.2-23 and § 18.2-95 because testimony revealed that they were in a store, together, for one-and-a-half hours, taking merchandise and thereafter concealing the merchandise, and the trial court could properly infer that defendant and the accomplices, prior to entering the store, agreed upon a course of action that would provide the means to conceal the merchandise to be stolen from the store; because the evidence proved conspiracy, and the aggregate value of the merchandise concealed by defendant and the accomplices exceeded $200, the trial court did not err in convicting defendant of grand larceny. Brown v. Commonwealth, 2010 Va. App. LEXIS 299 (July 27, 2010).

Conviction for grand larceny as principal in second degree, was supported by defendant's statement that defendant had not yet been arrested and defendant's persistent use of the vehicle to accommodate a friend, meet a family member, and ride to defendant's own home rather than any attempt to stop the continued use of the vehicle. Williams v. Commonwealth, 56 Va. App. 638, 696 S.E.2d 233, 2010 Va. App. LEXIS 315 (2010).

In a prosecution for grand larceny under clause (ii) of § 18.2-95, evidence that a decedent's home was in complete disarray after his death, that coins as well as other items were missing, and that his brother had filed a police report, was sufficient to support the trial court's conclusion that the missing coins were taken without the owner's permission. Burton v. Commonwealth, 58 Va. App. 274, 708 S.E.2d 444, 2011 Va. App. LEXIS 177 (2011).

Insufficient evidence. — Where a deputy found a stolen handgun within 60 feet of where a truck in which defendant had been riding had stopped, where gun was not found until the next day, defendant did nothing to suggest he had any knowledge of, or dominion or control over the gun; further, assuming the driver of the truck stole the gun, as there was neither proof that defendant failed to oppose the theft nor proof of other circumstances upon which to find he acted as a principal in the second degree, his conviction of grand larceny on an aiding and abetting theory was not supported by sufficient evidence. Myers v. Commonwealth, 43 Va. App. 113, 596 S.E.2d 536, 2004 Va. App. LEXIS 238 (2004).

III. PROSECUTION, SENTENCING, ETC.

Trial in absentia. — Record supported the trial court's judgment that defendant was warned he could be tried in absentia if he did not appear for trial, and the trial court did not abuse its discretion when it allowed the Commonwealth to try defendant in absentia on a charge of conspiracy to commit grand larceny. Sullivan v. Commonwealth, No. 2300-02-4, 2004 Va. App. LEXIS 67 (Ct. of Appeals Feb. 10, 2004).

Larceny and venue considerations. — Even though larceny is a continuing offense and the offense of receiving stolen property is deemed larceny, an accused who receives stolen property knowing it to be stolen may be tried only in those jurisdictions in which the accused is guilty of trespassing against the owner's property right. That offense can only occur in the place where the accused received the property or possessed it. The fiction of larceny as a continuing offense does not create venue where the offense for which the accused is prosecuted occurred outside the jurisdiction of the trial court. Davis v. Commonwealth, 14 Va. App. 709, 419 S.E.2d 285 (1992).

Guilty pleas. — In a case in which defendant appealed his conviction for grand larceny, in violation of § 18.2-95, the trial court did not abuse its discretion in denying his motion to withdraw his guilty plea prior to sentencing. He had 14 prior felony convictions, several for grand larceny, and he also had numerous misdemeanor convictions for petit larceny; for him to argue that he was confused or subjected to undue influence by his attorney was nothing more than a dilatory attempt to postpone his trial. Terrell v. Commonwealth, 2012 Va. App. LEXIS 243 (July 24, 2012).

Sufficiency of indictment. — It was unnecessary that there be a specific allegation of felonious intent contained in the indictment. Skeeter v. Commonwealth, 217 Va. 722, 232 S.E.2d 756 (1977).

The charge in an indictment that defendant did steal United States currency of the value of $200 from a named person is sufficient to charge defendant with the commission of larceny of goods and chattels of the value of $100 (now $200) or more as defined in this section. Skeeter v. Commonwealth, 217 Va. 722, 232 S.E.2d 756 (1977).

Evidence that defendant's employer owned a truck and tools that were supplied to defendant but not returned by him was sufficient to sustain defendant's conviction for grand larceny, in violation of § 18.2-95, even though the indictment charged defendant with stealing the truck and tools from a corporation and the Commonwealth of Virginia did not prove that defendant's employer was a corporation. Commonwealth v. Nuckles, 266 Va. 519, 587 S.E.2d 695, 2003 Va. LEXIS 107 (2003).

Amendment of indictment. — Defendant's conviction of grand larceny under § 18.2-95 was not improper based on an alleged amendment of the indictment during his trial from § 18.2-95 to § 18.2-98 because while the amendment was granted, the indictment was not actually amended. Lucas v. Commonwealth, 2009 Va. App. LEXIS 181 (Apr. 21, 2009).

As to instructions relating to presumption of innocence of charge under this section, see Barnes v. Commonwealth, 190 Va. 732, 58 S.E.2d 12 (1950).

No basis to give petit larceny instruction. — Refusal to give a jury instruction on petit larceny as a lesser-included offense of grand larceny was proper because defendant's theory was that she had nothing to do with the theft, but that her boyfriend stole the tools and that she merely loaned her identification card to her brother to enable him to pawn some of the stolen items; the jury could have either acquitted defendant or convicted her of grand larceny, but no version of the facts supported a petit larceny instruction. Juliano v. Commonwealth, 2009 Va. App. LEXIS 321 (July 21, 2009).

Inference of larceny defined; how punished. — Defendant was properly found guilty of being an accomplice to grand larceny where he snickered and smiled while ignoring the victim's demands for his property and the stolen property was seen in the defendant's car with him right after the theft. Taylor v. Commonwealth, No. 2367-02-1, 2003 Va. App. LEXIS 355 (Ct. of Appeals June 24, 2003).

No error in denying concurrent sentence. — Given that the record on appeal adequately demonstrated that the sentencing judge correctly understood his discretion and sentenced defendant within the lawful scope of that discretion, the Court of Appeals of Virginia declined to apply the ends of justice exception to Va. Sup. Ct. R. 5A:18. As a result, no error resulted in the denial of defendant's request for a concurrent sentence. Scalf v. Commonwealth, 2008 Va. App. LEXIS 230 (May 13, 2008).

Sentences under this section and § 18.2-91 held not excessive. — Concurrent three-year terms of imprisonment for violations of § 18.2-91 and this section are not constitutionally excessive in view of the nature of the offenses. Phennicie v. Huffman, No. 0739-85 (Ct. of Appeals Apr. 23, 1986).

Sentences of six years in the penitentiary (now state correctional facility) upon conviction of breaking and entering a dwelling house with intent to commit larceny under § 18.2-91 and 20 years upon conviction of grand larceny under this section, all of the 20-year sentence being suspended, were not constitutionally excessive in view of the nature of the offenses. Phennicie v. Huffman, No. 1001-85 (Ct. of Appeals Apr. 23, 1986).

Sentences of 10 years in the penitentiary (now state correctional facility) upon conviction of breaking and entering a dwelling house with intent to commit larceny under § 18.2-91 and 20 years upon conviction of grand larceny under this section, all of the 20-year sentence for grand larceny being suspended, were not constitutionally excessive in view of the nature of the offenses. Phennicie v. Huffman, No. 1000-85 (Ct. of Appeals Apr. 23, 1986).

Sentences of 10 years in the penitentiary (now state correctional facility) upon conviction of each of two charges of breaking and entering a dwelling house with intent to commit larceny under § 18.2-91, two years of the sentence on each offense being suspended, 5 years upon conviction of grand larceny under this section, two years of the sentence for the offense being suspended, 10 years in the penitentiary (now state correctional facility) for additional statutory burglary and grand larceny convictions at a later trial, four years of the sentence being suspended, were not constitutionally excessive in view of the nature of the offenses. Phennicie v. Huffman, No. 0740-85 (Ct. of Appeals Apr. 23, 1986).

Sentence proper. — Defendant's 10-year sentence for felony embezzlement constituted half of the maximum punishment, was not in excess of the statutory maximum, and could not be reviewed on appeal since embezzlement could result in a larceny conviction under § 18.2-111, and grand larceny had a maximum sentence under § 18.2-95 of 20 years in prison. Greene v. Commonwealth, 2008 Va. App. LEXIS 319 (July 15, 2008).

Prior juvenile adjudication. — As appellant juvenile did not dispute that he was previously convicted of the non-violent felony of grand larceny, in violation of § 18.2-95, the evidence was sufficient to support his conviction for possession of a firearm after having been adjudicated delinquent, as a juvenile 14 years of age or older, of an act that would have been a non-violent felony if committed by an adult, in violation of § 18.2-308.2. Preston v. Commonwealth, 281 Va. 52, 704 S.E.2d 127, 2011 Va. LEXIS 23 (2011).

§ 18.2-96. Petit larceny defined; how punished.

Any person who:

1. Commits larceny from the person of another of money or other thing of value of less than $5, or

2. Commits simple larceny not from the person of another of goods and chattels of the value of less than $200, except as provided in subdivision (iii) of § 18.2-95, shall be deemed guilty of petit larceny, which shall be punishable as a Class 1 misdemeanor.

History.

Code 1950, § 18.1-101; 1960, c. 358; 1966, c. 247; 1975, cc. 14, 15; 1980, c. 175; 1992, c. 822.

Cross references.

As to punishment for attempt to commit petit larceny, see § 18.2-27. As to grand larceny, see § 18.2-95. As to computer time, services, etc., as property subject to larceny, see § 18.2-152.1 et seq. As to limitation on prosecution for petit larceny, see § 19.2-8. As to sentence of petit larceny on prosecution for grand larceny, see § 19.2-289. As to conviction of petit larceny though thing stolen is worth more than $50, see § 19.2-290. As to payment by the Department of Social Services of assistant attorney for the Commonwealth for prosecution of public assistance fraud cases, see § 63.2-525.

Law Review.

For survey of Virginia criminal law for the year 1977-1978, see 64 Va. L. Rev. 1407 (1978). For a note, "Pleading for Theft Consolidation in Virginia: Larceny, Embezzlement, False Pretenses and § 19.2-284," see 55 Wash. & Lee L. Rev. 249 (1998).

Michie's Jurisprudence.

For related discussion, see 3A M.J. Burglary and Housebreaking, § 12.

CASE NOTES

Larceny defined. — Larceny is the wrongful taking of the goods of another without the owner's consent and with the intention to permanently deprive the owner of possession of the goods. Bright v. Commonwealth, 4 Va. App. 248, 356 S.E.2d 443 (1987).

Larceny that was a misdemeanor was a petit larceny, there were no other possibilities for other larcenies within the context of § 18.2-181. Since § 18.2-96 had no impact upon the foregoing analysis, the one year statute of limitations under § 19.2-8, which applied to misdemeanors, did not apply to defendant's act of passing a bad check for $140.88. Foster v. Commonwealth, 271 Va. 235, 623 S.E.2d 902, 2006 Va. LEXIS 6 (2006).

The term "felonious" is not used in this section in defining petit larceny, and a charge in a warrant that the accused did unlawfully take, steal and carry away the property of another distinguishes the offense from a mere trespass, and stamps it as petit larceny. The definition of Webster and other lexicographers of the verb "to steal" is "to take and carry away feloniously"; the words "steal" and "larceny" are synonymous. Satterfield v. Commonwealth, 105 Va. 867, 52 S.E. 979 (1906).

This section does not require proof of any minimum value. Evans v. Commonwealth, 226 Va. 292, 308 S.E.2d 126 (1983).

Proof that an article has some value is sufficient to warrant a conviction of petit larceny, but where the value of the thing stolen determines the grade of the offense, the value must be alleged and the Commonwealth must prove the value to be the statutory amount. Owen v. Commonwealth, No. 1495-95-2 (Ct. of Appeals May 28, 1996).

Allowance for depreciation. — While the original purchase price of an item may be admitted as evidence of its current value, there must also be "due allowance for elements of depreciation." Owen v. Commonwealth, No. 1495-95-2 (Ct. of Appeals May 28, 1996).

No proof need be adduced to show that the subject of petit larceny has a specific value. Evans v. Commonwealth, 226 Va. 292, 308 S.E.2d 126 (1983).

Larceny by receiving stolen goods is a lesser offense which is included in the major one of larceny, and the lesser offense is indictable as larceny, and the accused may be convicted of the lesser offense of receiving stolen goods. Cabbler v. Commonwealth, 212 Va. 520, 184 S.E.2d 781 (1971).

The crime of receiving stolen goods is a lesser offense included in the crime of larceny. Henderson v. Commonwealth, 215 Va. 811, 213 S.E.2d 782 (1975).

When larceny is lesser-included offense of robbery. — Where defendant was charged initially with robbery for stealing a bicycle from an 11-year-old victim, and where the trial court, in acquitting defendant of that robbery charge, noted its belief that the evidence was sufficient to convict him of larceny from the person but did not convict him of any larceny offense, the court thereby acquitted defendant of any larceny offense that was a part of the robbery charge, and the Commonwealth was thereafter barred by the Double Jeopardy Clause from requiring him to stand trial anew for stealing the same bicycle from the same person in the same criminal act that was the basis of the robbery trial. Therefore, the trial court erred in denying defendant's motion to dismiss the indictment as violative of the Double Jeopardy Clause. Hudgins v. Commonwealth, 43 Va. App. 219, 597 S.E.2d 221, 2004 Va. App. LEXIS 264 (2004), rev'd, remanded, 269 Va. 209, 608 S.E.2d 907 (2005), as to issue of impeachment questions asked during cross-examination.

Larceny and venue considerations. — Even though larceny is a continuing offense and the offense of receiving stolen property is deemed larceny, an accused who receives stolen property knowing it to be stolen may be tried only in those jurisdictions in which the accused is guilty of trespassing against the owner's property right. That offense can only occur in the place where the accused received the property or possessed it. The fiction of larceny as a continuing offense does not create venue where the offense for which the accused is prosecuted occurred outside the jurisdiction of the trial court. Davis v. Commonwealth, 14 Va. App. 709, 419 S.E.2d 285 (1992).

The information contained in the warrant provided the defendant with sufficient notice of the charged crime, even in the absence of a clear indication of who owned the picture. Therefore, the trial court did not err in denying the defendant's motion to dismiss on grounds that the warrant was fatally defective in not naming the owner of the picture. Humphreys v. Commonwealth, No. 1324-95-4 (Ct. of Appeals Feb. 11, 1997).

Probable cause for purposes of store's right to detain suspected shoplifter. — Store was immune from liability under § 8.01-226.9 in a customer's false imprisonment and malicious prosecution action, and therefore it was entitled to summary judgment, because it had probable cause to detain customer for committing petit larceny in violation of § 18.2-96 after she attempted to leave the store with a TV and VCR for which she had no receipt. At the time the store's employees detained the customer, they knew that: (1) she had received full credit on her mother's credit card for the returned merchandise; (2) she did not pay for the new television and VCR; (3) she had stood close to her friend while the friend shoplifted twice in the store; and (4) the customer attempted to leave the store with the TV and VCR without a receipt proving that she had paid for them. Jones v. Target Corp., 341 F. Supp. 2d 583, 2004 U.S. Dist. LEXIS 21425 (E.D. Va. 2004).

Where defendant was found in possession of property of a type recently stolen, it was not necessary for the goods to have been identified by serial number or with further precision than appeared from the record. Wright v. Commonwealth, 2 Va. App. 743, 348 S.E.2d 9 (1986).

Unexplained possession of stolen goods permits inference of larceny by possessor. — Once the crime of larceny is established, the unexplained possession of recently stolen goods permits an inference of larceny by the possessor. Bright v. Commonwealth, 4 Va. App. 248, 356 S.E.2d 443 (1987).

Defendant's recent exclusive possession of stolen handgun and his conflicting or false explanation as to where he obtained it supported finding of his guilt as to petit larceny. Bright v. Commonwealth, 4 Va. App. 248, 356 S.E.2d 443 (1987).

Defendant's conviction for petit and grand larceny was supported by sufficient evidence where: (1) the items found in the rear cargo area of the car driven by defendant at the time of a traffic stop had been recently stolen from vehicles parked on a body shop lot; (2) the jury was not required to accept defendant's explanation that he was legitimately present on the lot and that either his brother or co-defendant could have placed the stolen items in the cargo compartment, unbeknownst to him; (3) there was a discrepancy between defendant's statement to a police officer as to the time defendant was on the property and the time a security officer saw defendant's car leaving a body shop lot; (4) defendant drove from the lot in a rapid manner; and (5) the jury could have reasonably inferred that defendant's denial of knowledge of the presence of the stolen goods in the car and his explanation to the police officer were not credible. Sbitan v. Commonwealth, — Va. App. —, — S.E.2d —, 2006 Va. App. LEXIS 19 (Jan. 17, 2006).

Larceny inference. — Arguments which defendant made at trial, coupled with the Commonwealth's argument and the trial court's express findings, indicated that the court was aware of and took into consideration defendant's challenge to the sufficiency of the evidence to bring the larceny inference into play, despite the fact that defendant did not specifically mention the larceny inference, as the Commonwealth clearly addressed the inference and argued that defendant's falsely explained possession of the property permitted the reasonable inference that he was the one who stole it; further, when the trial court rejected defendant's explanation for how he came into possession of the property, defendant's challenge to the applicability of the larceny inference was properly before the appellate court on appeal. Woods v. Commonwealth, — Va. App. —, — S.E.2d —, 2005 Va. App. LEXIS 142 (Apr. 12, 2005).

One month time lapse between when items were discovered missing and when they were found in defendant's bedroom was sufficiently brief to be construed as recent possession. Wright v. Commonwealth, 2 Va. App. 743, 348 S.E.2d 9 (1986).

Where some of the missing items were found in a private area of the home occupied by the defendant, the trier of fact was permitted to find that they were in his exclusive constructive possession. Wright v. Commonwealth, 2 Va. App. 743, 348 S.E.2d 9 (1986).

Disorderly conduct is not a lesser included offense of larceny. Cuthrell v. Zayre of Va., Inc., 214 Va. 427, 201 S.E.2d 779 (1974).

Charges of petit larceny and of disorderly conduct are two separate and distinct offenses, and a conviction of the one does not bar the conviction of the other. Cuthrell v. Zayre of Va., Inc., 214 Va. 427, 201 S.E.2d 779 (1974).

Invited error. — Trial court did not err in finding defendant guilty of petit larceny, a misdemeanor, when she was indicted as a principal in the second degree to third offense petit larceny, a felony under §§ 18.2-104 and 18.2-18, where defendant requested the trial court to treat her actions as misdemeanor petit larceny, and she was subject to the misdemeanor finding that her counsel requested, as she was precluded from raising the same on appeal under the invited error doctrine; additionally, misdemeanor petit larceny was a lesser-included offense of a violation of § 18.2-104. Brumfield v. Commonwealth, No. 0794-04-3, 2004 Va. App. LEXIS 625 (Ct. of Appeals Dec. 21, 2004).

Section 19.2-270.1 provides alternative means of establishing adequate foundation to authenticate a photograph which is offered under the independent silent witness theory in prosecutions under § 18.2-95 and this section. Saunders v. Commonwealth, 1 Va. App. 396, 339 S.E.2d 550 (1986).

Admission of authenticated photograph of goods as substantive evidence. — A photograph of the goods or merchandise alleged to have been taken or converted, which bears the sworn writing of the arresting officer and the photographer's signature, shall be deemed competent evidence of such goods or merchandise and shall be admissible to the same extent as if such goods and merchandise had been introduced as evidence. When a photograph is so authenticated and admitted, it becomes not just an illustration of the testimony of a witness but an independent silent witness constituting substantive evidence. Saunders v. Commonwealth, 1 Va. App. 396, 339 S.E.2d 550 (1986).

Opinion testimony of nonexpert admissible. — The general rule is that opinion testimony of a nonexpert, who is not the owner of the personal property in question, is admissible upon the subject of property value, provided the witness possesses sufficient knowledge of the value of the property or has had ample opportunity for forming a correct opinion as to value. Owen v. Commonwealth, No. 1495-95-2 (Ct. of Appeals May 28, 1996).

Department of Transportation employee off-loading stone at his residence. — Where appellant, in the course of his employment with the Virginia Department of Transportation (VDOT), was driving a truck containing approximately five tons of stone that was the property of VDOT; was instructed to take the stone back to the VDOT shop, three to four miles away—the stone was not waste material, had some value, and could have been used in the future by VDOT; but instead of returning the stone to the shop as he had been instructed to do, appellant, without permission, drove the truck to his place of residence and off-loaded the stone onto the residence's driveway, evidence was sufficient to support the jury's finding that when appellant put the stone on the driveway he intended to deprive its owner thereof permanently and, thus, to steal VDOT's property. Baylor v. Commonwealth, No. 1017-93-2 (Ct. of Appeals Dec. 6, 1994).

Evidence of violence supports burglary. — Where the victim was violently flung around as defendant forcefully pulled the victim's purse from the victim's hands and arm, the conduct was sufficiently violent to support a burglary conviction rather than a larceny conviction. Taylor v. Commonwealth, No.0735-02-1, 2003 Va. App. LEXIS 117 (Ct. of Appeals Mar. 4, 2003).

Evidence held sufficient. — Where the evidence placed the defendant in the office or rooms from which the property was taken immediately before the thefts were discovered, the defendant had no rationale for being in those locations, and where, when confronted, he gave each victim a false explanation of his presence and intentions, the evidence was sufficient to support his conviction. Brown v. Commonwealth, No. 0107-97-2 (Ct. of Appeals June 16, 1998).

Unbroken chain of events, including defendant's entry into the victim's home, taking of a VCR, carrying such away while shielding the front of his body from the victim's view, his immediate depar-

ture thereafter, and fingerprints found on a beer can within ten feet from the place where the VCR was taken, was sufficient circumstantial evidence to support petit larceny conviction. Turner v. Commonwealth, No. 1942-01-3, 2002 Va. App. LEXIS 222 (Ct. of Appeals Apr. 9, 2002).

Evidence was clearly sufficient to prove beyond a reasonable doubt that defendant took victim's credit card and also took money from her friend's cash box without permission. Warren v. Commonwealth, No. 1078-01-2, 2002 Va. App. LEXIS 275 (Ct. of Appeals May 7, 2002).

Circumstantial evidence was sufficient to prove that the cigarette cartons defendant carried beneath his jacket and discarded as he fled through store's parking lot were stolen from the store. Curtis v. Commonwealth, No. 3225-01-2, 2002 Va. App. LEXIS 380 (Ct. of Appeals July 9, 2002).

Evidence was competent, not inherently incredible, and sufficient to prove beyond a reasonable doubt that defendant was guilty of petit larceny, because the victims testified that the items recovered from defendant's truck had been taken from their vehicles, and on the same day the police officer discovered the stolen items in defendant's vehicle. Harris v. Commonwealth, 38 Va. App. 680, 568 S.E.2d 385, 2002 Va. App. LEXIS 501 (2002), rev'd on other grounds, 266 Va. 28, 581 S.E.2d 385, 2002 Va. App. LEXIS 501 (2002).

Viewing the totality of the circumstances, the trial judge could reasonably conclude that defendant aided and abetted a common plan and scheme to commit forgery, uttering, and petit larceny, using counterfeit traveler's checks. Spruill v. Commonwealth, No. 3054-01-3, 2002 Va. App. LEXIS 705 (Ct. of Appeals Nov. 26, 2002).

Where a neighbor heard noise at the victim's house, saw defendant leaving the victim's house with a cord dangling from a pocket, defendant cursed upon realizing that the neighbor had seen defendant, and defendant gave conflicting statements as to defendant's whereabouts on the night of the incident, the Commonwealth's circumstantial evidence was sufficient to support the convictions for burglary and petit larceny. Tucker v. Commonwealth, No. 1288-02-2, 2003 Va. App. LEXIS 347 (Ct. of Appeals June 17, 2003).

Defendant was properly convicted of larceny for removing two tubes of ointment from their boxes and placing them in his pocket, despite his not leaving the store with them, because his acts and his statement that he was just being "stupid" indicated criminal intent. Dance v. Commonwealth, No. 3085-02-2, 2003 Va. App. LEXIS 393 (Ct. of Appeals July 8, 2003).

Where defendant was seen entering a store with an empty bag and leaving with a full one, and thereafter, she returned with another empty bag and when she was accused of taking canned goods, due to the messy condition of the recently restocked shelf, she denied it but bent out of view and left the store, whereupon the canned goods from that shelf were left on the floor, and further, where a police deputy saw defendant's bags in her motel room and then recovered them from the woods, filled with unpaid items from the store after defendant's son threw them from the balcony, the evidence was sufficient to support defendant's conviction for petit larceny, third degree, in violation of § 18.2-96. Saunders v. Commonwealth, No. 1606-02-3, 2003 Va. App. LEXIS 394 (Ct. of Appeals July 8, 2003).

Evidence which showed that defendant did not return to a gas station within one hour to pay for gasoline she put into a car, as promised, and did not contact the station to explain her failure to return, was sufficient to uphold the trial court's judgment convicting defendant of petit larceny, third offense. Cherry v. Commonwealth, No. 3365-01-2, 2003 Va. App. LEXIS 488 (Ct. of Appeals Sept. 30, 2003).

Petit larceny conviction was upheld, where defendant continued to order drinks from a bar, despite knowing that he didn't have any money to pay for them; further, an inculpatory inference was strengthened by defendant's verbal abuse of the proprietor's wife and his later assault on the police officer, which were hardly the response of an innocent patron attempting to cope with a simple misunderstanding over a bar tab. Wheeler v. Commonwealth, No. 0860-03-3, 2004 Va. App. LEXIS 461 (Ct. of Appeals Sept. 28, 2004).

Because: (1) sufficient evidence established that defendant was in exclusive possession of multiple items taken without permission from the scene of the crime; (2) the trier of fact was entitled to apply the larceny inference to infer that he was the thief, and reject defendant's explanation for how he gained exclusive possession of the stolen items; (3) additional evidence established that someone closely resembling defendant was seen fleeing the burglarized premises shortly after defendant carted the stolen dresser off down the street; and (4) defendant admitted having in his possession several of the items missing from the premises, defendant's petit larceny and statutory burglary convictions were upheld on appeal. Woods v. Commonwealth, — Va. App. —, — S.E.2d —, 2005 Va. App. LEXIS 142 (Apr. 12, 2005).

In a prosecution of defendant for uttering two forged checks and petit larceny, the evidence was sufficient to prove beyond a reasonable doubt that defendant committed petit larceny on the basis that defendant received $50 from a bank in return for each of the forged checks. This evidence was sufficient for the trial court to conclude that defendant fraudulently induced the bank to give him this money and that he did not intend to return it. Vernon v. Commonwealth, — Va. App. —, — S.E.2d —, 2006 Va. App. LEXIS 585 (Dec. 28, 2006).

Although the evidence of the value of a tire and rim at the time of a theft was insufficient to support defendant's conviction of grand larceny under clause (ii) of § 18.2-95, the circumstantial evidence was sufficient to find defendant guilty of the lesser-included offense of petit larceny. Banks v. Commonwealth, — Va. App. —, — S.E.2d —, 2009 Va. App. LEXIS 27 (Jan. 27, 2009).

In a case in which defendant was convicted of petit larceny as a third or subsequent offense in violation of §§ 18.2-96 and 18.2-104, he argued unsuccessfully that the Commonwealth's evidence against him was circumstantial and insufficient to prove beyond a reasonable doubt that he committed larceny from a store. The assistant manager's testimony, which the trial court credited, excluded defendant's three hypotheses, and the assistant manager's delay in reporting the incident to the police did not diminish his certainty about what he witnessed. Townsend v. Commonwealth, 2009 Va. App. LEXIS 493 (Nov. 3, 2009).

Evidence was sufficient to convict defendant of two counts of petit larceny where two grocery store clerks identified photographs of defendant as the person who presented forged checks to them and the true owner of the checks testified that her checks were stolen when an unknown thief broke into her car. Shelton v. Commonwealth, 2006 Va. App. LEXIS 610 (Nov. 16, 2006).

Defendant told a detective that defendant took a pair of pants during a break-in at an apartment and threw them on the ground when defendant realized a wallet was not in the pants; this evidence was sufficient to prove a larceny of the pants. Smith v. Commonwealth, 2011 Va. App. LEXIS 156 (May 10, 2011).

Where company's owner testified that several checks were missing from his office after it was broken into and that he did not sign the check that defendant cashed, and defendant admitted to an officer that he cashed the subject check the day after the break-in, the evidence was sufficient to support a larceny inference. Hopper v. Commonwealth, 2012 Va. App. LEXIS 200 (June 12, 2012).

Evidence held insufficient. — Evidence which placed the defendant where the theft occurred and in the general area where the fruits of the crime were found created no more than a suspicion that defendant was a perpetrator of the crime and was insufficient to prove beyond a reasonable doubt that he was guilty of larceny. Duncan v. Commonwealth, 218 Va. 545, 238 S.E.2d 807 (1977).

Where witness, who was not the owner of the tools, did not testify about the original purchase price of the tools or the effect of age and wear and tear on the value of the tools; testified only that the tools were purchased in 1986 or 1987 by someone other than herself; that she did not know the purchase price; that the tools were tools with a lifetime guaranty; and that they were in excellent working order. Although she estimated the replacement cost of the tools to be $540 and thus more than $200, this estimate did not adequately establish the current value of the stolen tools, reflecting the effects of wear and tear. Therefore, the trial court erred in finding the evidence sufficient to prove that the value of the tools was more than $200. Owen v. Commonwealth, No. 1495-95-2 (Ct. of Appeals May 28, 1996).

Evidence was insufficient to prove that defendant intended to permanently deprive owner of drill defendant had borrowed, where defendant at all times acknowledged that owner was entitled to possession and that defendant intended to return drill, and where when defendant was unable to do so, he accounted for drill by paying owner for it. Huddleston v. Commonwealth, No. 2335-98-3 (Ct. of Appeals Oct. 19, 1999).

Enhanced by prior conviction. — A conviction of "petit larceny" in violation of this section may be enhanced by a prior conviction of an offense "deemed to be larceny" by former § 19.2-297. Swinson v. Commonwealth, 16 Va. App. 923, 434 S.E.2d 348 (1993).

Defendant's previous convictions of larceny were not elements of the offense for which he was convicted; evidence of the convictions, however, was evidence which, if believed, enhanced the punishment for the petit larceny for which he was on trial. Woodson v. Commonwealth, 16 Va. App. 539, 431 S.E.2d 82 (1993).

Introduction of prior convictions proper in recidivist crimes. — Defendant moved to bifurcate the guilt phase of the trial so that the jury would not be aware of his prior larceny convictions until it determined whether he was guilty of petit larceny in violation of §§ 18.2-96 and 18.2-104, but the trial court stated that there was no authority for such a procedure and that it was for the legislature to change the manner of proof in recidivist crimes. When the legislature enacted and amended § 19.2-295.1, it chose not to create a separate bifurcated procedure of the guilt phase for these offenses, thus, the trial court did not err. Elem v. Commonwealth, 55 Va. App. 55, 683 S.E.2d 830, 2009 Va. App. LEXIS 462 (2009).

Error in failing to give instruction was not harmless. — Error in failing to give the requested instruction that defendant's previous larceny conviction should not be considered in determining his guilt or innocence on petit larceny charge was not harmless, for the witness' ability to observe the defendant at the time of the offense was questionable and the defendant's statements to the police were ambiguous and thus, the evidence of the defendant's guilt was not so overwhelming and the error so insignificant by comparison that the Court of Appeals could have said that the error could not have affected the verdict. Woodson v. Commonwealth, 16 Va. App. 539, 431 S.E.2d 82 (1993).

Cautionary instruction is appropriate in trial on a charge of petit larceny. — A cautionary instruction to the jury is appropriate in a trial on a charge of petit larceny under the enhanced punishment provisions; such an instruction should direct the jury not to consider a defendant's previous convictions in determining guilt or innocence. Woodson v. Commonwealth, 16 Va. App. 539, 431 S.E.2d 82 (1993).

No basis to give petit larceny instruction. — Refusal to give a jury instruction on petit larceny, § 18.2-96, as a lesser-included offense of grand larceny was proper because defendant's theory was that she had nothing to do with the theft, but that her boyfriend stole the tools and that she merely loaned her identification card to her brother to enable him to pawn some of the stolen items; the jury could have either acquitted defendant or convicted her of grand larceny, but no version of the facts supported a petit larceny instruction. Juliano v. Commonwealth, 2009 Va. App. LEXIS 321 (July 21, 2009).

Lesser included offense of felony third offense larceny. — Defendant's conviction for petit larceny was reversed and dismissed because defendant was also convicted of felony third offense larceny, in violation of § 18.2-104, and the felony larceny offense was a greater offense of the lesser included offense of petit larceny. Farrar v. Commonwealth, 2006 Va. App. LEXIS 301 (July 5, 2006).

New trial warranted where value of goods were not proven in grand larceny case. — Defendant's conviction for grand larceny was improper because the Commonwealth failed to prove that the value of the jackhammer that defendant rented was at least $200; the only evidence of the jackhammer's value that the trial court found persuasive, which was its original purchase price and replacement cost, was insufficient to prove its worth. Thus, a remand for a new trial on a charge of petit larceny was warranted. Byrum v. Commonwealth, 2010 Va. App. LEXIS 211 (May 18, 2010).

Applied in Conkling v. Commonwealth, 45 Va. App. 518, 612 S.E.2d 235, 2005 Va. App. LEXIS 173 (2005); Smith v. Commonwealth, 59 Va. App. 710, 722 S.E.2d 310, 2012 Va. App. LEXIS 56 (2012).

OPINIONS OF THE ATTORNEY GENERAL

Theft of gasoline from self-service pump. — The actions of an individual who presses the "pay inside" button at a self-service gasoline pump to activate the pump to dispense fuel into his motor vehicle and drives away without paying for such fuel are tantamount to theft of the gasoline and such an individual is subject to criminal prosecution for petit larceny. See opinion of Attorney General to The Honorable R. Steven Landes, Member, House of Delegates, 01-090 (12/27/01).

§ 18.2-96.1. Identification of certain personalty.

A. The owner of personal property may permanently mark such property, including any part thereof, for the purpose of identification with the social security number of the owner, preceded by the letters "VA."

B. [Repealed.]

C. It shall be unlawful for any person to remove, alter, deface, destroy, conceal, or otherwise obscure the manufacturer's serial number or marks, including personalty marked with a social security number preceded by the letters "VA," from such personal property or any part thereof, without the consent of the owner, with intent to render it or other property unidentifiable.

D. It shall be unlawful for any person to possess such personal property or any part thereof, without the consent of the owner, knowing that the manufacturer's serial number or any other distinguishing identification number or mark, including personalty marked with a social security number preceded by the letters "VA," has been removed, altered, defaced, destroyed, concealed, or otherwise obscured with the intent to violate the provisions of this section.

E. A person in possession of such property which is otherwise in violation of this section may apply in writing to the Bureau of Criminal Investigation, Virginia State Police, for assignment of a number for the personal property providing he can show that he is the lawful owner of the property. If a number is issued in conformity with the provisions of this section, then the person to whom it was issued and any person to whom the property is lawfully disposed of shall not be in violation of this section. This subsection shall apply only when the application has been filed by a person prior to arrest or authorization of a warrant of arrest for that person by a court.

F. Any person convicted of an offense under this section, when the value of the personalty is less than $200, shall be guilty of a Class 1 misdemeanor and, when the value of the personalty is $200 or more, shall be guilty of a Class 5 felony.

History.
1981, c. 165; 1982, c. 382.

CASE NOTES

Applied in Clay v. Commonwealth, 36 Va. App. 433, 552 S.E.2d 369, 2001 Va. App. LEXIS 518 (2001).

§ 18.2-97. Larceny of certain animals and poultry.

Any person who shall be guilty of the larceny of a dog, horse, pony, mule, cow, steer, bull or calf shall be guilty of a Class 5 felony; and any person who shall be guilty of the larceny of any poultry of the value of $5 dollars or more, but of the value of less than $200, or of a sheep, lamb, swine, or goat, of the value of less than $200, shall be guilty of a Class 6 felony.

History.
Code 1950, § 18.1-102; 1960, c. 358; 1962, c. 15; 1966, c. 247; 1975, cc. 14, 15; 1981, c. 197.

CASE NOTES

This section makes cattle-stealing a special crime, with a special punishment, and a person charged with the commission of this crime may not be forced to answer for any other. Wolfe v. Commonwealth, 167 Va. 486, 189 S.E. 320 (1937).

And the value of the property stolen is not the measure of the offense of cattle-stealing. Wolfe v. Commonwealth, 167 Va. 486, 189 S.E. 320 (1937).

It is of no moment that "a" appears before the names of the animals embraced in this section, for it has been held that the article does not necessarily denote the singular. Wolfe v. Commonwealth, 167 Va. 486, 189 S.E. 320 (1937). See § 1-13.15.

Sufficiency of evidence. — Where no one witnessed the alleged crime of larceny of a dog, and the dog's owner testified that his dogs ran loose all the time, there was no evidence to prove that the defendant took and carried away the dog; the defendant's possession of the missing dog nine months later was insufficient evidence to establish larceny where the defendant explained that he traded dogs with another person in the spring, a fact which was corroborated by the Commonwealth's evidence. Hall v. Commonwealth, No. 0473-86-3 (Ct. of Appeals Oct. 26, 1987).

Applied in Chesson v. Commonwealth, 216 Va. 827, 223 S.E.2d 923 (1976).

§ 18.2-97.1. Removal of a transmitting device; penalty.

Any person who removes an electronic or radio transmitting device from a dog, falcon, hawk, or owl without the permission of the owner and with the intent to prevent or hinder the owner from locating the dog, falcon, hawk, or owl is guilty of a Class 1 misdemeanor. Upon a finding of guilt, the court shall order that the defendant pay as restitution the actual value of any dog, falcon, hawk, or owl lost or killed as a result of such removal. The court may also order restitution to the owner for any lost breeding revenues.

History.
2007, cc. 484, 721; 2011, c. 191.

The 2011 amendments.
The 2011 amendment by c. 191 substituted "an electronic or radio transmitting device from a dog, falcon, hawk, or owl," for "from a dog an electronic or radio transmitting collar," deleted "of the dog" following "permission of the owner," and inserted "falcon, hawk, or owl" twice.

§ 18.2-98. Larceny of bank notes, checks, etc., or any book of accounts.

If any person steal any bank note, check, or other writing or paper of value, whether the same represents money and passes as currency, or otherwise, or any book of accounts, for or concerning money or goods due or to be delivered, he shall be deemed guilty of larceny thereof, and may be charged for such larceny under § 18.2-95 or 18.2-96, and if convicted shall receive the same punishment, according to the value of the thing stolen, prescribed for the punishment of the larceny of goods and chattels. The provisions of this section shall be construed to embrace all bank notes and papers of value representing money and passing as currency, whether the same be the issue of this Commonwealth or any other state, or of the United States, or of any corporation, and shall include all other papers of value, of whatever description. In a prosecution under this section, the money due on or secured by the writing, paper or book, and remaining unsatisfied, or which in any event might be collected thereon, or the value of the property or money affected thereby, shall be deemed to be the value of the article stolen.

History.
   Code 1950, §§ 18.1-104, 18.1-105; 1960, c. 358; 1975, cc. 14, 15; 2009, c. 591.

Cross references.
   See §§ 18.2-95, 18.2-96, 18.2-111.

Editor's note.
   Acts 2009, c. 591, cl. 2, provides: "That the provisions of this act may result in a net increase in periods of imprisonment or commitment. Pursuant to § 30-19.1:4, the estimated amount of the necessary appropriation is $0 for periods of imprisonment in state adult correctional facilities and cannot be determined for periods of commitment to the custody of the Department of Juvenile Justice."

The 2009 amendments.
   The 2009 amendment by c. 591 inserted "may be charged for such larceny under § 18.2-95 or 18.2-96, and if convicted shall" in the first sentence.

Law Review.
   For article on justification as a defense to crime, see 59 Va. L. Rev. 1326 (1973). For 2006 survey article, "Criminal Law and Procedure," see 41 U. Rich. L. Rev. 83 (2006).

Michie's Jurisprudence.
   For related discussion, see 6B M.J. Embezzlement, § 4.

CASE NOTES

Travelers' checks are susceptible of larceny or embezzlement, by virtue of this section. Allen v. Commonwealth, 186 Va. 376, 42 S.E.2d 838 (1947).
   Larceny of bond by obligor. — An obligor who obtains possession of his bond by fraud lucri causa is guilty of the larceny thereof. And it is no defense that he did not know that his act amounted to larceny. Vaughn v. Commonwealth, 51 Va. (10 Gratt.) 758 (1853).
   Indictment should charge paper is property of some person. — If an indictment for stealing bank notes does not charge that they are the bank notes of, or belong to, some named person or persons, or some person to the jurors unknown, the defect is fatal, and is not cured by the statute of jeofails. Barker v. Commonwealth, 4 Va. (2 Va. Cas.) 122 (1817).
   It should describe paper. — An indictment charging the prisoner with stealing certain papers of the value of $110, without further description of the papers, is fatally defective. Robinson v. Commonwealth, 73 Va. (32 Gratt.) 866 (1879).
   Amount of note is taken as value. — In an indictment for stealing bank notes, it is sufficient to state that the notes were for a certain sum of money, without stating their value. Adams v. Commonwealth, 64 Va. (23 Gratt.) 949 (1873).
   Face value of money is its value. — The indictment here properly charged grand larceny in that it alleged the money stolen

to be $590. Since money was the subject of the larceny its face value is its value. Wright v. Commonwealth, 196 Va. 132, 82 S.E.2d 603 (1954).
   The last sentence of this section merely prescribes a rule for estimating the value of the paper, and is not a part of the necessary description of the offense prescribed by the preceding sections, although the words "remaining unsatisfied" are usually inserted in the indictment in such cases. Whalen v. Commonwealth, 90 Va. 544, 19 S.E. 182 (1894).
   Value of paper is not traversable. — In an indictment for stealing bank notes, it is sufficient to state that the notes were for a certain sum of money, without stating their value, under this section. In such a case, since the passage of this section, the value of the bank notes is not traversable. Adams v. Commonwealth, 64 Va. (23 Gratt.) 949 (1873).
   And no proof of value is necessary. — Pursuant to this section, no proof of the value of a stolen check was necessary, as the law deems it to be of the value expressed on its face. Whalen v. Commonwealth, 90 Va. 544, 19 S.E. 182 (1894).
   Enhancing punishment. — Stealing a check, in violation of this section, is "like" concealing merchandise in violation of § 18.2-103 for purposes of enhancing punishment under § 18.2-104, and is an offense deemed to be larceny for purposes of enhancing punishment under former § 19.2-297. Stamps v. Commonwealth, 12 Va. App. 862, 407 S.E.2d 337 (1991).
   Sufficient averment of property. — An indictment which charged a larceny of bank notes "of the value, etc., of the money, goods and chattels of one G.F. and from the said G.F." is a sufficient averment of property in the notes in G.F., the person from whom they were stolen, after verdict; for the words "the money, goods and chattels of" may be rejected as surplusage. Commonwealth v. Moseley, 4 Va. (2 Va. Cas.) 154 (1819).
   Evidence held sufficient to prove defendant was guilty of grand larceny. — Facts supported a reasonable inference by the trier of fact that defendant had both the opportunity and the means to obtain all of the checks and that he knew his possession of employee's check was wrongful, therefore, Commonwealth met its burden to establish guilt of grand larceny beyond a reasonable doubt. Hubbard v. Commonwealth, No. 2111-92-3 (Ct. of Appeals May 10, 1994).
   Because defendant took a check that was payable to her husband, endorsed his name to the check, and deposited it to her personal account without permission or pursuant to a good faith claim of right, she was properly convicted of grand larceny and uttering under §§ 18.2-98 and 18.2-172. Kocher v. Commonwealth, — Va. App. —, — S.E.2d —, 2009 Va. App. LEXIS 115 (Mar. 17, 2009).
   Amendment of indictment. — Defendant's conviction of grand larceny under § 18.2-95 was not improper based on an alleged amendment of the indictment during his trial from § 18.2-95 to § 18.2-98 because while the amendment was granted, the indictment was not actually amended. Lucas v. Commonwealth, 2009 Va. App. LEXIS 181 (Apr. 21, 2009).
   Applied in Morton v. Commonwealth, 225 Va. 282, 302 S.E.2d 27 (1983).

§ 18.2-98.1. Repealed by Acts 1984, c. 751.

Cross references.
   For present provisions as to computer crimes, see § 18.2-152.1 et seq.

§ 18.2-99. Larceny of things fixed to the freehold.

Things which savor of the realty, and are at the time they are taken part of the freehold, whether they be of the substance or produce thereof, or affixed thereto, shall be deemed goods and chattels of which larceny may be committed, although there be no interval between the severing and taking away.

History.
   Code 1950, § 18.1-106; 1960, c. 358; 1975, cc. 14, 15.

Law Review.

For note on crops as personalty or realty relative to larceny, see 39 Va. L. Rev. 1116 (1953). For article on justification as a defense to crime, see 59 Va. L. Rev. 1326 (1973).

Michie's Jurisprudence.

For related discussion, see 8B M.J. Fixtures, § 14.

§ 18.2-100. Removal of crop by tenant before rents and advances are satisfied.

It shall be unlawful for any person renting the lands of another, either for a share of the crop or for money consideration, to remove therefrom, without the consent of the landlord, any part of such crop until the rents and advances are satisfied. Every such offense shall be punishable as a Class 3 misdemeanor.

History.

Code 1950, § 18.1-115; 1960, c. 358; 1975, cc. 14, 15.

§ 18.2-101. Selling, etc., of goods distrained or levied on.

If any person fraudulently sell, pledge, encumber, remove, destroy, receive or secrete any goods, chattels or other personal property of any kind whatsoever that has been distrained or levied upon, with intent to defeat such distress or levy, he shall be deemed guilty of the larceny thereof.

History.

Code 1950, § 18.1-108; 1960, c. 358; 1975, cc. 14, 15.

Law Review.

For comment on cumulative remedies under article 9 of the U.C.C., see 14 Wm. & Mary L. Rev. 213 (1972). For article on justification as a defense to crime, see 59 Va. L. Rev. 1326 (1973).

CASE NOTES

Gravamen is removal with intent to defeat levy. — The gravamen of the offense created by this section is that the property was fraudulently removed, etc., with intent to defeat the levy or distress. Duff v. Commonwealth, 92 Va. 769, 23 S.E. 643 (1895).

§ 18.2-102. Unauthorized use of animal, aircraft, vehicle or boat; consent; accessories or accomplices.

Any person who shall take, drive or use any animal, aircraft, vehicle, boat or vessel, not his own, without the consent of the owner thereof and in the absence of the owner, and with intent temporarily to deprive the owner thereof of his possession thereof, without intent to steal the same, shall be guilty of a Class 6 felony; provided, however, that if the value of such animal, aircraft, vehicle, boat or vessel shall be less than $200, such person shall be guilty of a Class 1 misdemeanor. The consent of the owner of an animal, aircraft, vehicle, boat or vessel to its taking, driving or using shall not in any case be presumed or implied because of such owner's consent on a previous occasion to the taking, driving or using of such animal, aircraft, vehicle, boat or vessel by the same or a different person. Any person who assists in, or is a party or accessory to, or an accomplice in, any such unauthorized taking, driving or using shall be subject to the same punishment as if he were the principal offender.

History.

Code 1950, § 18.1-164; 1960, c. 358; 1970, c. 8; 1975, cc. 14, 15; 1981, c. 197.

Cross references.

For provision that this section shall not apply to a bona fide repossession of a vehicle, aircraft, boat or vessel by the holder of a lien thereon or his agents, see § 18.2-148.

Law Review.

For survey of Virginia criminal law and procedure for the year 1970-1971, see 57 Va. L. Rev. 1438 (1971). For survey of Virginia criminal law for the year 1972-1973, see 59 Va. L. Rev. 1458 (1973). For article, "Preclusion of Evidence of Criminal Conviction in Civil Action Arising from the Same Incident," see 10 G.M.U. L. Rev. 107 (1988). For survey of Virginia criminal law and procedure for the year 2004-2005, see 40 U. Rich. L. Rev. 197 (2005). For 2007 annual survey article, "Criminal Law and Procedure," see 42 U. Rich. L. Rev. 311 (2007).

Michie's Jurisprudence.

For related discussion, see 2B M.J. Automobiles, § 126; 2B M.J. Aviation, § 1; 12A M.J. Livery Stables, § 1.

CASE NOTES

Elements of offense. — Under this section, a conviction of unauthorized use of a vehicle requires proof of use without the consent of the owner with intent temporarily to deprive the owner of possession, without intent to steal, or proof of assistance in such use. Reese v. Commonwealth, 230 Va. 172, 335 S.E.2d 266 (1985).

Violation when scope of permitted taking exceeded. — Where an act violates the specific scope or duration of consent to use a vehicle, a trespassory taking contemplated by this section occurs. This is not to say that in every instance where a person is in possession of property with the owner's consent, an unanticipated use constitutes a trespass. The focus is strictly on acts that violate the owner's express limitations of the scope or duration of the consent given. Overstreet v. Commonwealth, 17 Va. App. 234, 435 S.E.2d 906 (1993).

Where the owner gives consent to a temporary possession or a possession for a limited purpose, the expiration of that qualification creates a constructive revestment of possession in the true owner with "bare charge or custody" in the other person. A violation of this possessory right constitutes a trespassory taking. Overstreet v. Commonwealth, 17 Va. App. 234, 435 S.E.2d 906 (1993).

Where owner had given defendant permission to use his automobile on the express condition that the car be returned by 3:00 a.m. on April 8, and defendant retained possession of the car until 11:30 p.m. on April 8, a prima facie case of unauthorized use was established since the evidence shows that the borrower's use of the vehicle exceeded the scope and duration of the owner's consent. Eley v. Commonwealth, No. 2526-95-1 (Ct. of Appeals Mar. 11, 1997).

The main difference between larceny and the statutory offense of unauthorized use of a motor vehicle is that in the former there must be an intent to deprive the owner of his property permanently, while in the latter the intent is to deprive the owner of possession of his automobile temporarily and without any intent to steal the same. The intent with which property is taken determines the offense. Slater v. Commonwealth, 179 Va. 264, 18 S.E.2d 909 (1942); Robinson v. Commonwealth, 190 Va. 134, 56 S.E.2d 367 (1949); Travelers Indem. Co. v. Ford, 208 Va. 151, 156 S.E.2d 606 (1967); Comer v. Commonwealth, 211 Va. 246, 176 S.E.2d 432 (1970).

The taking of a car, unaccompanied by an intent permanently to deprive the owner of the car, is a crime separate from the crime of larceny. A taking without the requisite intent is not within the coverage of a theft insurance policy. Travelers Indem. Co. v. Ford, 208 Va. 151, 156 S.E.2d 606 (1967).

Intent alone distinguishes larceny of a vehicle from unauthorized use. Hewitt v. Commonwealth, 213 Va. 605, 194 S.E.2d 893 (1973).

Permissive use may develop into unauthorized use where the borrower's acts exceed the scope or duration of the owner's consent to use his or her vehicle. Eley v. Commonwealth, No. 2526-95-1 (Ct. of Appeals Mar. 11, 1997).

Where, as here, an owner gives another consent to temporary possession for a limited time, the expiration of that qualification extinguishes the borrower's rightful possession. Continued possession by the borrower is a violation of the owner's possessory right and constitutes a trespassory taking. Eley v. Commonwealth, No. 2526-95-1 (Ct. of Appeals Mar. 11, 1997).

No theft if return intended. — Under the terms of an automobile insurance policy, in order to constitute a theft there must be present an intent permanently to deprive the owner of the vehicle. If it is shown that the alleged thief intended to return the vehicle after using it temporarily, there is no theft. Travelers Indem. Co. v. Ford, 208 Va. 151, 156 S.E.2d 606 (1967).

The intent temporarily to deprive the owner of his property is an essential element of this offense and that intent is just as necessary to be proved as the act itself. Blanks v. Gordon, 202 Va. 295, 117 S.E.2d 82 (1960).

Taking without intent to steal. — If defendant did unlawfully take the automobile of another, without the consent of the owner and in his absence, and with the intent to temporarily deprive the owner of his possession, but without intent to steal said vehicle, the crime is complete under this section. United States v. Schuster, 220 F. Supp. 61 (E.D. Va. 1963).

Unauthorized use is a lesser offense included under larceny. Hewitt v. Commonwealth, 213 Va. 605, 194 S.E.2d 893 (1973).

Where defendant argued that the evidence did not show he only intended to temporarily deprive the owner of the use of his car, rather, any intent shown was that he had intended to deprive permanently the owner of his car, and therefore, the evidence was insufficient to show unauthorized taking, such argument had little or no validity in view of the supreme court's decision that unauthorized use is a lesser included offense of larceny. United States v. Garcia, 868 F.2d 114 (4th Cir.), cert. denied, 490 U.S. 1094, 109 S. Ct. 2439, 104 L. Ed. 2d 995 (1989).

Unauthorized use is a lesson. — Where the defendant was found in exclusive possession of the recently stolen vehicle, the evidence was sufficient to find he was driving a stolen car and to exclude every reasonable hypothesis that he drove a different car. Montague v. Commonwealth, 40 Va. App. 430, 579 S.E.2d 667, 2003 Va. App. LEXIS 289 (2003).

Taking and abandonment constitute larceny. — Accused, who did not have the consent of the owner to take his car, testified that he had no intention of stealing the car though he never intended to return it but intended to abandon it in a neighboring town. It was held that he was guilty of larceny. Slater v. Commonwealth, 179 Va. 264, 18 S.E.2d 909 (1942).

In Reese v. Commonwealth, 230 Va. 172, 335 S.E.2d 266 (1985), the court held that the circumstances under which the car was taken, and accused's actions regarding it afterwards, including his abandoning it in a public highway, showed clearly that he was guilty of the offense of larceny and not of unauthorized use.

Defendant properly convicted of using wife's car without consent. — Defendant was properly convicted of destroying and using without consent a car that was "not his own," in violation of §§ 18.2-137 and 18.2-102, respectively, because his interest in his wife's car was an inchoate right that would vest only on entry of a decree of equitable distribution in a divorce proceeding. McDuffie v. Commonwealth, 49 Va. App. 170, 638 S.E.2d 139, 2006 Va. App. LEXIS 573 (2006).

Value of the automobile. — Where, in prosecution for the felonious unauthorized use of an automobile in violation of this section, the evidence did not clearly show that the automobile in working condition could not have a value of more than $200, the ends of justice did not require that the Supreme Court consider the issue of the sufficiency of the evidence to prove that the value of the automobile was over $200 for the first time on appeal. Mounce v. Commonwealth, 4 Va. App. 433, 357 S.E.2d 742 (1987).

Conviction under section when evidence tends to prove only larceny. — Although the evidence may tend to prove only the offense of larceny charged in the indictment, the finder of fact may nevertheless convict of a lesser offense of unauthorized use. Hewitt v. Commonwealth, 213 Va. 605, 194 S.E.2d 893 (1973).

Evidence of defendant's mere presence in stolen vehicle is not enough to support a conviction as a principal in the second degree. Reese v. Commonwealth, 230 Va. 172, 335 S.E.2d 266 (1985).

Sufficient evidence of unauthorized use. — Where defendant had the consent of the owner to use the vehicle for a limited purpose and for a limited period of time, and defendant exceeded both of these limitations, in so doing, his use of the vehicle constituted a trespassory taking. Accordingly, the Commonwealth established a prima facie case of unauthorized use of an automobile and the record supported by sufficient evidence defendant's conviction. Overstreet v. Commonwealth, 17 Va. App. 234, 435 S.E.2d 906 (1993).

Although defendant had permission to use the victim's car, defendant did not return the vehicle within the scope of the consent; consequently, the trial court properly convicted defendant of unauthorized use of a vehicle. Huber v. Commonwealth, — Va. App. —, — S.E.2d —, 2005 Va. App. LEXIS 382 (Oct. 4, 2005).

Evidence that a vehicle owner saw defendant get into the owner's vehicle and drive away, a witness saw the vehicle pass by at a "high rate of speed," and seconds later, the vehicle collided with another vehicle, was sufficient to prove that defendant was driving the vehicle at the time of the accident. Davis v. Commonwealth, 2009 Va. App. LEXIS 220 (May 12, 2009).

Evidence, including that a car owner revoked her consent allowing defendant to use her car, that defendant received a voice message regarding such revocation, and that defendant drove away with the owner's car, was sufficient to support his conviction of unauthorized use of a vehicle in violation of § 18.2-102. Butor v. Commonwealth, 2010 Va. App. LEXIS 61 (Feb. 23, 2010).

Proof of venue. — Venue was improper for defendant's trial for unauthorized use of an automobile in violation of § 19.2-244 because although the trial court found that defendant unlawfully used the car, the only evidence of that use was in jurisdictions other than the city where defendant was tried, and even though defendant was charged with the larceny of the car in the city, the trial court specifically acquitted him of that offense; the Commonwealth may not rely on a greater offense to prove venue where the evidence fails to prove the defendant committed the greater offense and the lesser-included offense could not be properly charged in the jurisdiction. Taylor v. Commonwealth, 58 Va. App. 185, 708 S.E.2d 241, 2011 Va. App. LEXIS 140 (2011).

§ 18.2-102.1. Removal of shopping cart from store premises.

(1) The term *"shopping cart"* when used in this section means those push carts of the type or types which are commonly provided by grocery stores, drugstores, or other merchant stores or markets for the use of the public in transporting commodities in stores and markets from the store to a place outside the store.

(2) It shall be unlawful for any person to remove a shopping cart from the premises, of the owner of such shopping cart without the consent, of the owner or of his agent, servant, or employee given at the time of such removal. For the purpose of this section, the premises shall include all the parking area set aside by the owner, or on behalf of the owner, for the parking of cars for the convenience of the patrons of the owner.

(3) Any person convicted of a violation under subsection (2) shall be guilty of a Class 3 misdemeanor.

History.
Code 1950, § 18.1-117.2; 1975, c. 269.

The number of this section was assigned by the Virginia Code Commission, the 1975 act having assigned no number.

§ 18.2-102.2. Unauthorized use of dairy milk cases or milk crates; penalty.

It shall be unlawful for any person to:

1. Buy, sell, or dispose of any milk case or milk crate bearing the name or label of the owner without the written consent of the owner or his designated agent;

2. Refuse, upon written demand of the owner or his designated agent, to return to the owner or his designated agent any milk case or milk crate bearing the name or label of the owner; or

3. Deface, obliterate, erase, cover up, or otherwise remove or conceal any name, label, registered trademark, insignia, or other business identification of an owner of a milk case or milk crate without the consent of the owner, for the purpose of destroying or removing from the milk case or milk crate evidence of its ownership.

A violation of this section shall be punishable as a Class 4 misdemeanor.

For purposes of this section, milk cases or milk crates shall be deemed to bear a name or label of an owner when there is imprinted or attached on the case or crate a name, insignia, mark, business identification, or label showing ownership or sufficient information to ascertain ownership. The term *"milk case"* or *"milk crate"* means a wire or plastic container which holds sixteen quarts or more of beverage and is used by distributors or retailers or their agents as a means to transport, store, or carry dairy products.

History.
1990, c. 452.

§ 18.2-103. Concealing or taking possession of merchandise; altering price tags; transferring goods from one container to another; counseling, etc., another in performance of such acts.

Whoever, without authority, with the intention of converting goods or merchandise to his own or another's use without having paid the full purchase price thereof, or of defrauding the owner of the value of the goods or merchandise, (i) willfully conceals or takes possession of the goods or merchandise of any store or other mercantile establishment, or (ii) alters the price tag or other price marking on such goods or merchandise, or transfers the goods from one container to another, or (iii) counsels, assists, aids or abets another in the performance of any of the above acts, when the value of the goods or merchandise involved in the offense is less than $200, shall be guilty of petit larceny and, when the value of the

goods or merchandise involved in the offense is $200 or more, shall be guilty of grand larceny. The willful concealment of goods or merchandise of any store or other mercantile establishment, while still on the premises thereof, shall be prima facie evidence of an intent to convert and defraud the owner thereof out of the value of the goods or merchandise.

History.
Code 1950, § 18.1-126; 1960, c. 358; 1970, c. 652; 1975, cc. 14, 15; 1994, c. 706.

Law Review.
For survey of Virginia law on criminal law and procedure for the year 1969-1970, see 56 Va. L. Rev. 1572 (1970). For article summarizing published Virginia criminal law decisions between July 1, 2002 and July 1, 2003, see 38 U. Rich. L. Rev. 87 (2003).

CASE NOTES

To convict an accused for unlawful concealment in violation of this section, the commonwealth must prove a willful concealment of merchandise done with the intent to convert the merchandise or to defraud the storekeeper. Johnson v. Commonwealth, 35 Va. App. 134, 543 S.E.2d 605, 2001 Va. App. LEXIS 133 (2001).

Goods. — "Goods" includes not only merchandise offered for sale but also any other items of tangible personal property belonging to a merchant; the Virginia Legislature intended to proscribe the concealment of both merchandise offered for sale and other types of goods not offered for sale. Hulcher v. Commonwealth, 39 Va. App. 601, 575 S.E.2d 579, 2003 Va. App. LEXIS 33 (2003).

Concealment must be "willful." — This section does not prohibit simply the concealment of merchandise; it prohibits a "willful" concealment and the word "willful" when used in a criminal statute generally means an act done with a bad purpose, without justifiable excuse, stubbornly, obstinately, perversely or without ground for believing it is lawful. Johnson v. Commonwealth, 35 Va. App. 134, 543 S.E.2d 605, 2001 Va. App. LEXIS 133 (2001).

Concealment while still on premises. — The willful concealment of goods while still on the premises is prima facie evidence of intent to defraud the owner of the value of the goods or merchandise at issue. Johnson v. Commonwealth, 35 Va. App. 134, 543 S.E.2d 605, 2001 Va. App. LEXIS 133 (2001).

Concealment on the person not required. — The plain language of this section does not require proof of concealment on the person; concealment in another area of the store may thus constitue a violation of the statute if done willfully. Johnson v. Commonwealth, 35 Va. App. 134, 543 S.E.2d 605, 2001 Va. App. LEXIS 133 (2001).

Evidence of probation violation properly admitted to prove concealment. — During defendant's trial for third offense petit larceny under §§ 18.2-103 and 18.2-104, the circuit court properly admitted into evidence an order finding defendant had previously violated probation to prove she committed the predicate offense of concealment. Defendant was not unfairly prejudiced by the admission of the order, even though it mentioned a prior conviction for drug distribution, because the record showed that the circuit court did not consider the evidence regarding drug distribution, as the law presumed; rather, the circuit court convicted defendant based on its consideration of the credibility of the witnesses, not defendant's history with law enforcement. Thornley v. Commonwealth, — Va. App. —, — S.E.2d —, 2008 Va. App. LEXIS 273 (June 10, 2008).

Evidence of value of items stolen was improperly admitted. — Defendant's felony shoplifting conviction was reversed because the admission of evidence of the value of the items defendant stole violated defendant's right to confrontation, as (1) a handwritten list of the items and the items' value, and a subsequent voided store receipt created from the list, were testimonial, as the list and receipt were created to prove the items' value to show defendant committed felony, rather than misdemeanor, shoplifting,

(2) the author and declarant of the handwritten list and the store receipt did not testify, nor was the author subject to cross-examination, (3) a testifying supervisor admitted the supervisor did not verify that the list stated each stolen item's correct quantity and price, and (4) these exhibits were the only evidence of the items taken and the items' value. Robertson v. Commonwealth, 60 Va. App. 688, 732 S.E.2d 30, 2012 Va. App. LEXIS 297 (2012).

Improperly admitting evidence of value of items stolen was not harmless. — In a felony shoplifting prosecution, the erroneous admission of a handwritten list and a voided store receipt to prove the value of the items stolen was not harmless because (1) admitting the voided receipt did not cure admitting the handwritten list, since the receipt was based on the list, and (2) these exhibits, which had the same constitutional defect, were the only evidence of the value of what defendant stole. Robertson v. Commonwealth, 60 Va. App. 688, 732 S.E.2d 30, 2012 Va. App. LEXIS 297 (2012).

Evidence supported willful concealment. — Defendant's conviction for petit larceny, third offense, in violation of § 18.2-103 was appropriate because the evidence showed that he had willfully concealed merchandise while on the store's premises, thus creating a prima facie case of an intent to steal and defraud the owner. A deputy testified that a store employee indicated to him that she suspected defendant of shoplifting and because there was no objection to that testimony, the trial court was free to consider it as evidence. Talley v. Commonwealth, 2010 Va. App. LEXIS 441 (Nov. 9, 2010).

Sufficient evidence supported conviction. — Defendant's conviction for felony shoplifting was supported by sufficient evidence that the value of the merchandise was at least $200, the minimum required by § 18.2-103, as the admission of exhibits listing the items shoplifted, their prices, and an adding machine tape adding the prices together, and a voided receipt did not violate the Confrontation Clause, U.S. Const. amend. VI, since the exhibits were jointly prepared by a store manager and an employee, under the manager's supervision and direction, and the manager testified at trial about the preparation of the exhibits. Robertson v. Commonwealth, 61 Va. App. 554, 738 S.E.2d 531, 2013 Va. App. LEXIS 97 (Mar. 19, 2013).

Insufficient evidence. — Insufficient evidence supported defendant's felony shoplifting conviction because, absent exhibits that were admitted in violation of defendant's right to confrontation, the evidence did not prove the element that the stolen items' value was at least $200. Robertson v. Commonwealth, 60 Va. App. 688, 732 S.E.2d 30, 2012 Va. App. LEXIS 297 (2012).

Enhanced punishment for repeat offenders. — An objective reading of § 18.2-104 demonstrates the General Assembly, in plain terms, has designed a system of enhanced punishment for those who repeatedly commit the "shoplifting" offenses defined in this section, whether the prior conviction resulted from charges under a comparable local ordinance or under the state statute. Scott v. Commonwealth, 217 Va. 425, 230 S.E.2d 236 (1976) (decided under former § 18.1-126).

Over defendant's objection, the district court assigned him a criminal history point for a 2005 sentence in a Virginia state court for shoplifting — or, more specifically, for altering a price tag on merchandise valued at less than $200 — and on appeal, defendant contended that he should not have received a criminal history point for his prior shoplifting sentence because the underlying offense was similar to the listed insufficient funds check offense and because his sentence did not include any term of probation or incarceration; however, the district court correctly determined that defendant's prior shoplifting offense was not similar to the listed insufficient funds check offense and properly assessed a single criminal history point for the shoplifting sentence. Under Virginia law, both shoplifting and insufficient funds check offenses could involve the acquisition of a store's merchandise without paying the full purchase price thereof but in a shoplifting offense, this was effectuated by concealing the merchandise or altering the merchandise's price tag and in an insufficient funds check offense the merchandise acquisition was carried out by issuing a bad check; because of these significant differences, the elements of the shoplifting offense and those of the insufficient funds check offense could not be deemed nearly corresponding or resembling in many respects. United States v. Osborne, 514 F.3d 377, 2008 U.S. App.

LEXIS 1871 (4th Cir. 2008), cert. denied, 128 S. Ct. 2525, 2008 U.S. LEXIS 4438 (U.S. 2008).

Satisfaction of enhancement requirements. — Because a 1999 petit larceny conviction and an NCIC report sufficiently showed defendant's two prior larceny convictions, and he could not benefit from using three different social security numbers in his prior encounters with law enforcement, defendant's third or subsequent larceny conviction was upheld on appeal as supported by sufficient evidence. Ghee v. Commonwealth, — Va. App. —, — S.E.2d —, 2008 Va. App. LEXIS 105 (Mar. 4, 2008).

Sentence not excessive. — As defendant did not raise a challenge to a petit larceny, third offense sentence under §§ 18.2-103 and 18.2-104 below, and because the sentence to five years of imprisonment with three years' suspended was not excessive on its face, there was no reason to invoke the ends of justice exception under Va. Sup. Ct. R. 5A:18. Brittle v. Commonwealth, 54 Va. App. 505, 680 S.E.2d 335, 2009 Va. App. LEXIS 359 (2009).

Qualified privilege. — The legal principles applicable to shoplifting, and to civil litigation arising from efforts to control this crime, do not include the concept of qualified privilege. Tweedy v. J.C. Penney Co., 216 Va. 596, 221 S.E.2d 152 (1976).

Stealing a check in violation of § 18.2-98 is "like" concealing merchandise in violation of this section for purpose of enhancing punishment under § 18.2-104, and is an offense deemed to be larceny for purposes of enhancing punishment under former § 19.2-297. Stamps v. Commonwealth, 12 Va. App. 862, 407 S.E.2d 337 (1991).

Appellate review precluded. — Defendant's failure to object to the introduction of the prior convictions and failure to challenge the sufficiency of the evidence precluded appellate review of defendant's third offense petit larceny conviction under §§ 18.2-103 and 18.2-104 as: (1) Va. Sup. Ct. R. 5A:18 did not apply as defendant did not dispute that defendant concealed steaks in a grocery store, or challenge a 2005 order stating that defendant pled guilty to second offense petit larceny; (2) although the two 1997 orders did not prove the convictions, they did not establish the non-existence of the predicate offenses; (3) the pre-sentence report proved that defendant was sentenced in 1993 for petit larceny; and (4) defendant did not show that an element of the offense did not occur or that he was convicted of a non-offense. Brittle v. Commonwealth, 54 Va. App. 505, 680 S.E.2d 335, 2009 Va. App. LEXIS 359 (2009).

CIRCUIT COURT OPINIONS

Right to impartial jury. — Defendant's claim that if the Commonwealth was allowed to introduce defendant's prior larceny convictions at defendant's trial for violating §§ 18.2-103 and 18.2-104 in a non-bifurcated guilt phase, defendant's constitutional right to an impartial jury under the Sixth Amendment and Va. Const., Art. I, § 8 would be abridged was not supported and was rejected. Commonwealth v. Dickens, 77 Va. Cir. 57, 2008 Va. Cir. LEXIS 124 (Fairfax County 2008).

Cruel and unusual punishment. — Defendant's claim that the Eighth Amendment and Va. Const., Art. I, § 9, applied to criminal procedure issues was unsupported and was rejected; there was no logical nexus between the Eighth Amendment's proscription against cruel and unusual punishment and the admissibility of evidence at trial concerning prior convictions of a criminal defendant charged under a recidivist statute such as §§ 18.2-103 and 18.2-104. Commonwealth v. Dickens, 77 Va. Cir. 57, 2008 Va. Cir. LEXIS 124 (Fairfax County 2008).

Bifurcated trial denied. — Commonwealth could introduce evidence of defendant's prior larceny convictions in the guilt phase of a concealment trial under §§ 18.2-103 and 18.2-104, and upon request, a limiting instruction would be given that the evidence could be considered only as proof of defendant's prior predicate convictions, and not as proof that defendant committed the concealment; defendant's request for a separate proceeding after a preliminary finding of culpability, but before defendant was convicted, was rejected as under § 19.2-295.1, a separate proceeding to determine punishment occurred only after a defendant was convicted of a felony. Commonwealth v. Dickens, 77 Va. Cir. 57, 2008 Va. Cir. LEXIS 124 (Fairfax County 2008).

OPINIONS OF THE ATTORNEY GENERAL

Theft of gasoline from self-service pump. — The actions of an individual who presses the "pay inside" button at a self-service gasoline pump to activate the pump to dispense fuel into his motor vehicle and drives away without paying for such fuel are tantamount to theft of the gasoline and such an individual is subject to criminal prosecution for petit larceny. See opinion of Attorney General to The Honorable R. Steven Landes, Member, House of Delegates, 01-090 (12/27/01).

§ 18.2-104. Punishment for conviction of misdemeanor larceny.

When a person is convicted of an offense of larceny or any offense deemed to be or punished as larceny under any provision of the Code, and it is alleged in the warrant, indictment or information on which he is convicted, and admitted, or found by the jury or judge before whom he is tried, that he has been before convicted in the Commonwealth of Virginia or in another jurisdiction for any offense of larceny or any offense deemed or punishable as larceny, or of any substantially similar offense in any other jurisdiction, regardless of whether the prior convictions were misdemeanors, felonies or a combination thereof, he shall be confined in jail not less than thirty days nor more than twelve months; and for a third, or any subsequent offense, he shall be guilty of a Class 6 felony.

History.
Code 1950, § 18.1-126.1; 1970, c. 652; 1975, cc. 14, 15; 1980, c. 174; 1987, c. 178; 1994, c. 706.

Law Review.
For 1991 survey on criminal law and procedure, see 25 U. Rich. L. Rev. 731 (1991). For an article, "Criminal Law and Procedure," see 31 U. Rich. L. Rev. 1015 (1997).

CASE NOTES

Enhanced punishment for repeat offenders. — An objective reading of this section demonstrates the General Assembly, in plain terms, has designed a system of enhanced punishment for those who repeatedly commit the "shoplifting" offenses defined in § 18.2-103, whether the prior conviction resulted from charges under a comparable local ordinance or under the state statute. Scott v. Commonwealth, 217 Va. 425, 230 S.E.2d 236 (1976) (decided under former § 18.1-126).
Trial court did not err in declining to give defendant's proffered jury instruction in defendant's case where defendant was indicted for willfully concealing or taking possession of clothing valued at less than $200 after having previously been convicted on two or more other occasions of larceny. Defendant's instruction was not a correct statement of the law because the Commonwealth was entitled to offer evidence of defendant's prior convictions to prove the recidivist part of § 18.2-104 although defendant's instruction would have prohibited the consideration of such evidence. Pcelinski v. Commonwealth, — Va. App. —, — S.E.2d —, 2008 Va. App. LEXIS 81 (Feb. 19, 2008).
Misdemeanor becomes felony showing third or subsequent commission. — A crime that on the first or second commission is a misdemeanor, becomes a felony upon proof of the additional element of its commission being a third or subsequent such occurrence. Pittman v. Commonwealth, 17 Va. App. 33, 434 S.E.2d 694 (1993).
The only restriction as to "like offenses" is geographical, that is, the conviction must have occurred in "the Commonwealth of Virginia." Scott v. Commonwealth, 217 Va. 425, 230 S.E.2d 236

(1976) (decided under former § 18.1-126.1).
Uttering bad check not "like offense." — Prior bad check convictions do not constitute a third offense under this section. The elements of uttering a bad check and of willfully concealing merchandise with intent to convert or defraud are different; the two offenses are not "like." Snead v. Commonwealth, 11 Va. App. 643, 400 S.E.2d 806 (1991).
Stealing a check in violation of § 18.2-98 is "like" concealing merchandise in violation of § 18.2-103 for purpose of enhancing punishment under this section, and is an offense deemed to be larceny for purposes of enhancing punishment under former § 19.2-297. Stamps v. Commonwealth, 12 Va. App. 862, 407 S.E.2d 337 (1991).
Robbery not larceny. — Defendant's prior robbery conviction should not have counted as a prior larceny conviction under this section, because robbery is not a larceny or an offense deemed to be larceny or punished as larceny. Harris v. Commonwealth, 23 Va. App. 311, 477 S.E.2d 3 (1996), aff'd on reh'g en banc, 24 Va. App. 613, 484 S.E.2d 170 (1997).
Consideration of violations of local ordinances. — There is no express or implied limitation in this section preventing consideration of convictions for "like offenses" which are based on comparable local ordinances. Scott v. Commonwealth, 217 Va. 425, 230 S.E.2d 236 (1976) (decided under former § 18.1-126.1).
Consideration of prior uncounseled misdemeanor conviction. — Trial court did not err by admitting evidence of an uncounseled misdemeanor conviction in order to elevate defendant's third offense of petit larceny to a felony, where despite defendant's contention to the contrary she did not have the right to counsel for a prior misdemeanor conviction, as she was only sentenced to pay a fine; moreover, any violation of the statutory right to counsel did not mandate exclusion of the conviction order. Kapoor v. Commonwealth, No. 2582-03-4, 2004 Va. App. LEXIS 557 (Ct. of Appeals Nov. 16, 2004).
Consideration of juvenile adjudications. — Defendant's prior juvenile adjudications were not proper predicate offenses for sentence enhancement purposes; thus, because § 18.2-104 did not expressly include juvenile adjudications, unlike other enhancement statutes, the statute's enhancement provisions were not implicated by juvenile adjudications. Conkling v. Commonwealth, 45 Va. App. 518, 612 S.E.2d 235, 2005 Va. App. LEXIS 173 (2005).
Proof of actual sentence for prior offense not to go to jury. — The trial court erred in allowing the complete text of the sentencing orders including the level of punishment assessed to go before the jury. Where it is alleged in the indictment on which he is convicted, and admitted, or found by the jury or judge before whom he is tried, that an accused has been before sentenced for any larceny or offense deemed to be larceny, then he shall be subject to enhancement of his sentence. The court does not read the term "sentenced" to mean that proof of the actual sentence must be shown. Rather, the fact that the accused was sentenced for a larceny crime is all that is required. Coleman v. Commonwealth, No. 1087-93-1 (Ct. of Appeals Dec. 13, 1994).
The introduction of the actual sentence may prejudice an accused in that the jurors may consider the length of his prior sentence in determining the sentence they will impose for the present offense. Accordingly, effective redaction of the sentencing order to remove the prejudicial material is required. Coleman v. Commonwealth, No. 1087-93-1 (Ct. of Appeals Dec. 13, 1994).
National Criminal Information Center report as record of prior convictions. — As defendant did not claim his two prior convictions listed in a National Criminal Information Center report were invalid, and the report's alleged incompleteness went to the weight to be given it, not its admissibility, the trial court properly admitted the report under the public records exception to the hearsay rule. Hawes v. Commonwealth, No. 1094-03-4, 2004 Va. App. LEXIS 395 (Ct. of Appeals Aug. 17, 2004).
Evidence of probation violation properly admitted to prove concealment. — During defendant's trial for third offense petit larceny under §§ 18.2-103 and 18.2-104, the circuit court properly admitted into evidence an order finding defendant had previously violated probation to prove she committed the predicate offense of concealment. Defendant was not unfairly prejudiced by the admission of the order, even though it mentioned a prior conviction for drug distribution, because the record showed that the circuit court did not consider the evidence regarding drug distribu-

tion, as the law presumed; rather, the circuit court convicted defendant based on its consideration of the credibility of the witnesses, not defendant's history with law enforcement. Thornley v. Commonwealth, — Va. App. —, — S.E.2d —, 2008 Va. App. LEXIS 273 (June 10, 2008).

Harmless error. — Defendant was properly convicted of larceny, third or subsequent offense, in violation of § 18.2-104 because assuming that the trial court erred in admitting evidence of other stolen vehicles, any such error was harmless under § 8.01-678; the jury's verdict of guilt would have been the same had evidence of the stolen vehicles been excluded because the evidence of defendant's guilt was overwhelming. Johnson v. Commonwealth, 2012 Va. App. LEXIS 239 (July 24, 2012).

Evidence held sufficient. — In a case in which defendant was convicted of petit larceny as a third or subsequent offense in violation of §§ 18.2-96 and 18.2-104, he argued unsuccessfully that the Commonwealth's evidence against him was circumstantial and insufficient to prove beyond a reasonable doubt that he committed larceny from a store. The assistant manager's testimony, which the trial court credited, excluded defendant's three hypotheses, and the assistant manager's delay in reporting the incident to the police did not diminish his certainty about what he witnessed. Townsend v. Commonwealth, 2009 Va. App. LEXIS 493 (Nov. 3, 2009).

Satisfaction of enhancement requirements. — Where copies of records of seven convictions became part of trial court's record, where the trial court found defendant guilty of the offense charged, relying on defendant's felony convictions to support the enhancement, and where defendant alleges that he did not have counsel for the three misdemeanor convictions and that the felony convictions were based on the prior uncounseled misdemeanor convictions, the record reflected that the Commonwealth satisfied the requirements § 18.2-104 by presenting evidence of seven convictions and the trial court subjected defendant to the enhanced penalty by specifically selecting two convictions for which defendant had the assistance of counsel. Webb v. Commonwealth, 17 Va. App. 188, 436 S.E.2d 284 (1993).

Evidence that defendant wrote checks belonging to his deceased father to obtain goods from people who received the checks was sufficient to sustain defendant's convictions for obtaining goods by false pretenses, in violation of § 18.2-178, and the trial court which convicted defendant did not err by admitting a National Crime Information Center printout over defendant's objection or by considering the printout as evidence that defendant had prior convictions for larceny to convict him of committing Class 6 felonies, pursuant to § 18.2-104. Argenbright v. Commonwealth, No. 3282-02-3, 2003 Va. App. LEXIS 613 (Ct. of Appeals Nov. 25, 2003).

In a prior action which was used to support defendant's conviction for unlawful concealment, third offense, there was sufficient evidence to support the enhancement despite the fact that the blanks for listing the prosecuting and defending attorneys were empty; the summons/order included a fee on the line for court appointed attorney, there was a notation at the bottom of the form with the appointed attorney's name, a "Request for Appointment of a Lawyer" form and a "Determination of Indigency" form both contained defendant's signature and the same docket number as the conviction, and the request form specifically listed the name of the court-appointed lawyer for the case. Razzaq v. Commonwealth, No. 0245-03-1, 2004 Va. App. LEXIS 113 (Ct. of Appeals Mar. 23, 2004).

Where defendant was convicted of third offense petit larceny, a court order, revoking probation on defendant's 1994 grand larceny conviction, was competent to establish a previous conviction; defendant failed to rebut the presumption of the regularity of the order. Humphries v. Commonwealth, No. 0282-04-1, 2005 Va. App. LEXIS 20 (Ct. of Appeals Jan. 11, 2005).

Because a 1999 petit larceny conviction and an NCIC report sufficiently showed defendant's two prior larceny convictions, and he could not benefit from using three different social security numbers in his prior encounters with law enforcement, defendant's third or subsequent larceny conviction was upheld on appeal as supported by sufficient evidence. Ghee v. Commonwealth, — Va. App. —, — S.E.2d —, 2008 Va. App. LEXIS 105 (Mar. 4, 2008).

Bifurcated trial denied. — Defendant moved to bifurcate the guilt phase of the trial so that the jury would not be aware of his prior larceny convictions until it determined whether he was guilty of petit larceny in violation of §§ 18.2-96 and 18.2-104, but the trial court stated that there was no authority for such a procedure and that it was for the legislature to change the manner of proof in recidivist crimes. When the legislature enacted and amended § 19.2-295.1, it chose not to create a separate bifurcated procedure of the guilt phase for these offenses, thus, the trial court did not err. Elem v. Commonwealth, 55 Va. App. 55, 683 S.E.2d 830, 2009 Va. App. LEXIS 462 (2009).

Excessive sentence. — Defendant's plea was valid because the trial court conducted an extensive colloquy with him to ensure his plea of guilty was made knowingly, intelligently, and voluntarily and defendant, at no time, raised any issues regarding the voluntary nature of his plea. During the 15 months following his plea, defendant never challenged the trial court's acceptance of his plea; there was also no merit to his contention that he had little or no opportunity to challenge the voluntary nature of his plea in the trial court. Swilling v. Commonwealth, 2009 Va. App. LEXIS 24 (Jan. 27, 2009).

Sentence not excessive. — As defendant did not raise a challenge to the a petit larceny, third offense sentence under §§ 18.2-103 and 18.2-104 below, and because the sentence to to five years of imprisonment with three years' suspended was not excessive on its face, there was no reason to invoke the ends of justice exception under Va. Sup. Ct. R. 5A:18. Brittle v. Commonwealth, 54 Va. App. 505, 680 S.E.2d 335, 2009 Va. App. LEXIS 359 (2009).

Invited error. — Trial court did not err in finding defendant guilty of petit larceny, a misdemeanor under § 18.2-96, when she was indicted as a principal in the second degree to third offense petit larceny, a felony under §§ 18.2-104 and 18.2-18, where defendant requested the trial court to treat her actions as misdemeanor petit larceny, and she was subject to the misdemeanor finding that her counsel requested, as she was precluded from raising the same on appeal under the invited error doctrine; additionally, misdemeanor petit larceny was a lesser-included offense of a violation of § 18.2-104. Brumfield v. Commonwealth, No. 0794-04-3, 2004 Va. App. LEXIS 625 (Ct. of Appeals Dec. 21, 2004).

Lesser included offenses. — Defendant's conviction for petit larceny was reversed and dismissed because defendant was also convicted of felony third offense larceny, in violation of § 18.2-104, and the felony larceny offense was a greater offense of the lesser included offense of petit larceny. Farrar v. Commonwealth, 2006 Va. App. LEXIS 301 (July 5, 2006).

Appellate review precluded. — Defendant's failure to object to the introduction of the prior convictions and failure to challenge the sufficiency of the evidence precluded appellate review of defendant's third offense petit larceny conviction under §§ 18.2-103 and 18.2-104 as: (1) Va. Sup. Ct. R. 5A:18 did not apply as defendant did not dispute that defendant concealed steaks in a grocery store, or challenge a 2005 order stating that defendant pled guilty to second offense petit larceny; (2) although the two 1997 orders did not prove the convictions, they did not establish the non-existence of the predicate offenses; (3) the pre-sentence report proved that defendant was sentenced in 1993 for petit larceny; and (4) defendant did not show that an element of the offense did not occur or that he was convicted of a non-offense. Brittle v. Commonwealth, 54 Va. App. 505, 680 S.E.2d 335, 2009 Va. App. LEXIS 359 (2009).

Applied in Hudson v. Commonwealth, 9 Va. App. 110, 383 S.E.2d 767 (1989); Dance v. Commonwealth, No. 3085-02-2, 2003 Va. App. LEXIS 393 (Ct. of Appeals July 8, 2003); Patrick v. Commonwealth, 50 Va. App. 650, 653 S.E.2d 288, 2007 Va. App. LEXIS 420 (2007).

CIRCUIT COURT OPINIONS

Cruel and unusual punishment. — Defendant's claim that the Eighth Amendment and Va. Const., Art. I, § 9 applied to criminal procedure issues was unsupported and was rejected; there was no logical nexus between the Eighth Amendment's proscription against cruel and unusual punishment and the admissibility of evidence at trial concerning prior convictions of a criminal defendant charged under a recidivist statute such as §§ 18.2-103 and 18.2-104. Commonwealth v. Dickens, 77 Va. Cir. 57, 2008 Va. Cir. LEXIS 124 (Fairfax County 2008).

Introduction of prior convictions do not impede impartial jury. — Defendant's claim that if the Commonwealth was allowed to introduce defendant's prior larceny convictions at defendant's trial for violating §§ 18.2-103 and 18.2-104 in a non-bifurcated guilt phase, defendant's constitutional right to an impartial jury under the Sixth Amendment and Va. Const., Art. I, § 8 would be abridged, was not supported and was rejected. Commonwealth v. Dickens, 77 Va. Cir. 57, 2008 Va. Cir. LEXIS 124 (Fairfax County 2008).

Bifurcated trial denied. — Commonwealth could introduce evidence of defendant's prior larceny convictions in the guilt phase of a concealment trial under §§ 18.2-103 and 18.2-104, and upon request, a limiting instruction would be given that the evidence could be considered only as proof of defendant's prior predicate convictions, and not as proof that defendant committed the concealment; defendant's request for a separate proceeding after a preliminary finding of culpability, but before defendant was convicted, was rejected as, under § 19.2-295.1, a separate proceeding to determine punishment occurred only after a defendant was convicted of a felony. Commonwealth v. Dickens, 77 Va. Cir. 57, 2008 Va. Cir. LEXIS 124 (Fairfax County 2008).

§ 18.2-104.1. Liability upon conviction under § 18.2-103.

Any person who has been convicted of violating the provisions of § 18.2-103 shall be civilly liable to the owner for the retail value of any goods and merchandise illegally converted and not recovered by the owner, and for all costs incurred in prosecuting such person under the provisions of § 18.2-103. Such costs shall be limited to actual expenses, including the base wage of one employee acting as a witness for the Commonwealth and suit costs. Provided, however, the total amount of allowable costs granted hereunder shall not exceed $250, excluding the retail value of the goods and merchandise.

History.
1976, c. 577.

Law Review.
For survey of Virginia tort law for the year 1975-1976, see 62 Va. L. Rev. 1489 (1976).

Michie's Jurisprudence.
For related discussion, see 5B M.J. Criminal Procedure, § 11.

§ 18.2-105. Repealed by Acts 2004, c. 462.

Cross references.
For current provisions relating to exemption from civil liability in connection with arrest or detention of a person suspected of shoplifting, see § 8.01-226.9.

§ 18.2-105.1. Detention of suspected shoplifter.

A merchant, agent or employee of the merchant, who has probable cause to believe that a person has shoplifted in violation of § 18.2-95 or § 18.2-96 or § 18.2-103, on the premises of the merchant, may detain such person for a period not to exceed one hour pending arrival of a law-enforcement officer.

History.
1976, c. 515.

CASE NOTES

Miranda not applicable. — An interrogation by private store security agents of a suspect detained pursuant to this section is not a custodial police interrogation, but is a confrontation between private citizens. Thus, such an interrogation is not governed by the requirements of Miranda. Vazirnezami v. Commonwealth, No. 0497-90-4 (Ct. of Appeals July 1, 1991).

CIRCUIT COURT OPINIONS

Resistance to arrest. — The court found that the employee did identify himself and therefore the detention was lawful; thus, the defendant did not have the right to use reasonable force to resist his detention, where he had shoplifted and was detained as he left the store. Commonwealth v. Patterson, 60 Va. Cir. 312, 2002 Va. Cir. LEXIS 276 (Fairfax County 2002).

§ 18.2-105.2. Manufacture, sale, etc., of devices to shield against electronic detection of shoplifting prohibited; penalty.

It shall be unlawful to manufacture, sell, offer for sale, distribute or possess any specially coated or laminated bag or other device primarily designed and intended to shield shoplifted merchandise from detection by an anti-theft electronic alarm sensor, with the intention that the same be used to aid in the shoplifting of merchandise. A violation of this section shall be punishable as a Class 1 misdemeanor.

History.
1984, c. 386; 2003, c. 831.

Law Review.
For note, "Modern Police Practices: Arizona v. Gant's Illusory Restriction of Vehicle Searches Incident to Arrest," 97 Va. L. Rev. 1727 (2011).

§ 18.2-106. "Agents of the merchant" defined.

As used in this article *"agents of the merchant"* shall include attendants at any parking lot owned or leased by the merchant, or generally used by customers of the merchant through any contract or agreement between the owner of the parking lot and the merchant.

History.
Code 1950, § 18.1-128; 1960, c. 358; 1975, cc. 14, 15.

Cross references.
As to limitations on powers of registered armed security officers, see § 9.1-146.

§ 18.2-107. Theft or destruction of public records by others than officers.

If any person steal or fraudulently secrete or destroy a public record or part thereof, including a microphotographic copy thereof, he shall, if the offense be not embraced by § 18.2-472 be guilty of a Class 6 felony.

History.
Code 1950, § 18.1-308; 1960, c. 358; 1974, c. 649; 1975, cc. 14, 15; 1977, c. 107.

§ 18.2-108. Receiving, etc., stolen goods.

A. If any person buys or receives from another person, or aids in concealing, any stolen goods or other thing, knowing the same to have been stolen, he shall be deemed guilty of larceny thereof, and may be proceeded against, although the principal offender is not convicted.

B. If any person buys or receives any goods or other thing, used in the course of a criminal investigation by law enforcement that such person believes to have been stolen, he shall be deemed guilty of larceny thereof.

History.
Code 1950, § 18.1-107; 1960, c. 358; 1975, cc. 14, 15; 2008, c. 578.

Cross references.
As to right of accused to demand statement from Commonwealth's attorney of what section he intends to rely upon to ask for conviction of larceny, see § 18.2-111.

Editor's note.
Acts 2008, c. 578, cl. 2, provides: "That the provisions of this act may result in a net increase in periods of imprisonment or commitment. Pursuant to § 30-19.1:4, the estimated amount of the necessary appropriation cannot be determined for periods of imprisonment in state adult correctional facilities and is $0 for periods of commitment to the custody of the Department of Juvenile Justice."

The 2008 amendments.
The 2008 amendment by c. 578 designated the existing provisions as subsection A and added subsection B; in subsection A, substituted "buys or receives" for "buy or receive," "aids" for "aid" and "is" for "be."

Law Review.
For article on justification as a defense to crime, see 59 Va. L. Rev. 1326 (1973).

Michie's Jurisprudence.
For related discussion, see 15 M.J. Receiving Stolen Goods, §§ 1, 2, 3, 4.

CASE NOTES

Section read in connection with §§ 18.2-95 and 18.2-96. — Since an offense against this section is made larceny, without specifying either the punishment or the degree of larceny, this section must be read in connection with §§ 18.2-95 and 18.2-96. Wright v. Commonwealth, 196 Va. 132, 82 S.E.2d 603 (1954).

Although the trial court erred by convicting defendant of violating § 18.2-95, instead of § 18.2-108, after the jury found defendant guilty of grand larceny by receiving stolen property, the trial court's failure to include a reference to § 18.2-108 in its final order was a clerical error that did not require reversal. Bazemore v. Commonwealth, No. 0103-02-1, 2003 Va. App. LEXIS 291 (Ct. of Appeals May 13, 2003).

Statute written in the disjunctive. — The statute defines the offense of larceny in the disjunctive, stating that any person who buys or receives or aids in concealing property knowing that it was the fruit of a theft is guilty of constructive larceny. Roach v. Commonwealth, No. 2783-98-2, 2000 Va. App. LEXIS 562 (Ct. of Appeals Aug. 1, 2000).

Receiving stolen goods may be charged as larceny. — Receiving stolen goods, knowing them to be stolen, may be charged as larceny. Clark v. Commonwealth, 135 Va. 490, 115 S.E. 704 (1923).

An accused may be tried for receiving stolen goods under a larceny indictment. Dove v. Peyton, 343 F.2d 210 (4th Cir. 1965); Gunter v. Peyton, 287 F. Supp. 928 (W.D. Va. 1968).

Or robbery. — The accused in an indictment for robbery is apprised of his liability to conviction as a criminal receiver. Dove v. Peyton, 343 F.2d 210 (4th Cir. 1965).

And where defendant is indicted for armed robbery, but is tried as an accessory to armed robbery and convicted for receiving stolen property and the conviction is affirmed by the Supreme Court, he cannot be retried for any crime of greater gravity than the receipt

of stolen goods. Dove v. Peyton, 343 F.2d 210 (4th Cir. 1965).

And proof of receiving sustains charge of simple larceny. — If a person is indicted for the simple larceny of a thing, and the proof is that it was stolen by some other person, and received by the accused knowing it to have been stolen, the proof will sustain the charge. Price v. Commonwealth, 62 Va. (21 Gratt.) 846 (1872); Hey v. Commonwealth, 73 Va. (32 Gratt.) 946 (1879).

Under this section, on a charge of actual larceny it is permissible to prove and obtain a conviction of constructive larceny, consisting of the receiving of stolen goods, knowing them to have been stolen. Stapleton v. Commonwealth, 140 Va. 475, 124 S.E. 237 (1924).

For offense is included in larceny. — The crime of receiving stolen goods is a lesser offense which is included in the major one of larceny. Branch v. Commonwealth, 184 Va. 394, 35 S.E.2d 593 (1945).

Larceny by receiving stolen goods is a lesser offense which is included in the major one of larceny, and the lesser offense is indictable as larceny, and the accused may be convicted of the lesser offense of receiving stolen goods. Cabbler v. Commonwealth, 212 Va. 520, 184 S.E.2d 781 (1971).

And is deemed larceny under this section. — Receiving stolen goods, knowing them to have been stolen, is deemed larceny merely by reason of this section. Stapleton v. Commonwealth, 140 Va. 475, 124 S.E. 237 (1924).

The act of receiving stolen goods is deemed to be larceny in Virginia. Gunter v. Peyton, 287 F. Supp. 928 (W.D. Va. 1968).

Effect of failure to demand statement under § 18.2-111. — The accused having been indicted for larceny and having failed to exercise his right under § 18.2-111 to demand a statement in writing from the attorney for the Commonwealth of what he intended to rely upon to ask for a conviction, the prosecuting attorney was entitled to ask for a conviction for receiving stolen bonds, or for receiving lost bonds, as might be shown by the evidence. Hutchinson v. Commonwealth, 133 Va. 710, 112 S.E. 624 (1922).

To convict an offender under this section, four things must be proved: (1) that the goods or other things were previously stolen by some other person; (2) that the accused bought or received them from another person, or aided in concealing them; (3) that at the time the accused bought or received them, or aided in concealing them, he knew that they had been stolen; and (4) that he bought or received them, or aided in concealing them, malo animo or with a dishonest intent. Hey v. Commonwealth, 73 Va. (32 Gratt.) 946 (1879); Gilland v. Commonwealth, 184 Va. 223, 35 S.E.2d 130 (1945); Starks v. Commonwealth, 225 Va. 48, 301 S.E.2d 152 (1983).

In order to convict defendant, the Commonwealth had the burden of proving: (1) guilty knowledge; (2) buying, receiving, or aiding in concealing the property; and (3) dishonest intent. Lee v. Commonwealth, No. 0352-89-1 (Ct. of Appeals Aug. 21, 1990).

In order to support defendant's conviction of grand larceny, the evidence must show beyond a reasonable doubt that he: (1) received fifty or more dollars of stolen money from another, or aided in concealing such amount of stolen money, (2) knowing the same to be stolen, and (3) so received or aided in concealing such stolen amount of money with a dishonest intent. Wright v. Commonwealth, 196 Va. 132, 82 S.E.2d 603 (1954).

To prove the corpus delicti and to establish the guilt of the defendant, the Commonwealth has the burden of showing: (1) that goods of the value of more than $50 were previously stolen by some other person; (2) the defendant aided in concealing them; (3) that at the time he so aided in concealing them, he knew they had been stolen; and (4) that he so aided in concealing them with a dishonest intent. Parish v. Commonwealth, 206 Va. 627, 145 S.E.2d 192 (1965), cert. denied, 384 U.S. 942, 86 S. Ct. 1463, 16 L. Ed. 2d 540 (1966); Pasanello v. Commonwealth, 206 Va. 640, 145 S.E.2d 200 (1965).

Evidence insufficient to prove intent. — Evidence was insufficient as a matter of law to prove the requisite intent for larceny, where the Commonwealth's uncontradicted evidence did not exclude as a reasonable hypothesis that defendant came upon a pair of stolen jet skis in the woods and used them with the intent of returning them each day to that place. Lee v. Commonwealth, No. 0352-89-1 (Ct. of Appeals Aug. 21, 1990).

Even if the evidence were sufficient to show that appellant knew the vehicle was stolen, mere presence in and subsequent flight from the vehicle was insufficient to show that the accused aided in concealing it with a dishonest intent. Reid v. Commonwealth, No. 0480-93-1 (Ct. of Appeals Oct. 4, 1994).

To convict a defendant under this section, the Commonwealth must prove that property was: (1) previously stolen by another; and (2) received by defendant; (3) with knowledge of the theft; and (4) a dishonest intent. Snow v. Commonwealth, 33 Va. App. 766, 537 S.E.2d 6, 2000 Va. App. LEXIS 754 (2000).

Conviction is dependent upon guilty knowledge. — This section makes a conviction dependent upon guilty knowledge, and the Commonwealth must show beyond a reasonable doubt that the accused received from another person "any stolen goods or other thing, knowing the same to have been stolen." Kanter v. Commonwealth, 171 Va. 524, 199 S.E. 477 (1938).

The testimony of two police officers describing the defendant's frantic efforts to evade the police in a stolen vehicle, as well as the testimony by one officer concerning the "popped" ignition and the defendant's statement that he believed one of the other occupants had stolen the vehicle, if believed by the fact finder, were sufficient to prove receipt of the stolen vehicle with the requisite knowledge required by this section. Snow v. Commonwealth, 33 Va. App. 766, 537 S.E.2d 6, 2000 Va. App. LEXIS 754 (2000).

The defendant's dishonest intent in aiding in the concealment of the goods not only may, but usually must, be shown by circumstantial evidence. Parish v. Commonwealth, 206 Va. 627, 145 S.E.2d 192 (1965), cert. denied, 384 U.S. 942, 86 S. Ct. 1463, 16 L. Ed. 2d 540 (1966); Pasanello v. Commonwealth, 206 Va. 640, 145 S.E.2d 200 (1965).

Knowledge that the goods received were stolen property is an essential element of the crime, one which the Commonwealth must prove beyond a reasonable doubt. Lewis v. Commonwealth, 225 Va. 497, 303 S.E.2d 890 (1983).

Guilty knowledge may be shown by circumstances. — The great weight of authority is to the effect that guilty knowledge need not be directly proved. It may be shown by circumstances. It is sufficiently shown if the circumstances proven are such as must have made or caused the recipient of stolen goods to believe they were stolen. Reaves v. Commonwealth, 192 Va. 443, 65 S.E.2d 559 (1951).

Absent proof of an admission against interest, knowledge that the goods received were stolen necessarily must be shown by circumstantial evidence. Lewis v. Commonwealth, 225 Va. 497, 303 S.E.2d 890 (1983).

Guilty knowledge need not be directly proved. It may be shown by circumstances. It is sufficiently shown if the circumstances proven are such as must have made or caused the recipient of stolen goods to believe they were stolen. Lewis v. Commonwealth, 225 Va. 497, 303 S.E.2d 890 (1983).

An essential element of the offense of receiving stolen property is guilty knowledge, which may be supplied by circumstantial evidence, including the circumstance that the accused was in possession of recently stolen property. Roberts v. Commonwealth, 230 Va. 264, 337 S.E.2d 255 (1985).

Guilty knowledge is an essential element of the offense as defined by the statute, but absent proof of an admission against interest, such knowledge necessarily must be shown by circumstantial evidence. Spitzer v. Commonwealth, 233 Va. 7, 353 S.E.2d 711 (1987).

Police officer's testimony describing defendant's frantic efforts to evade arrest was sufficient to prove concealment with guilty knowledge within the intendment of this section. Spitzer v. Commonwealth, 233 Va. 7, 353 S.E.2d 711 (1987).

When the evidence shows concealment of stolen property, the Commonwealth is not required to prove that the accused was the thief or that he received that property from the thief or "another person." Spitzer v. Commonwealth, 233 Va. 7, 353 S.E.2d 711 (1987).

The testimony of one who sold allegedly stolen goods to defendant is especially relevant. — Such testimony is admissible under the guilty-knowledge exception to the general rule that evidence of offenses other than those charged is inadmissible. Lewis v. Commonwealth, 225 Va. 497, 303 S.E.2d 890 (1983).

When goods are stolen and concealed, it is proper to show the connection of the accused therewith wherever they may be traced. Parish v. Commonwealth, 206 Va. 627, 145 S.E.2d 192 (1965), cert. denied, 384 U.S. 942, 86 S. Ct. 1463, 16 L. Ed. 2d 540 (1966); Pasanello v. Commonwealth, 206 Va. 640, 145 S.E.2d 200 (1965).

Where the secreting of goods is performed pursuant to a common plan and design and carried out by a combination of which the defendant was a part, defendant was "concluded and bound" by such action, regardless of the identity of the person who actually secreted the stolen goods. Pasanello v. Commonwealth, 206 Va. 640, 145 S.E.2d 200 (1965).

Evidence of recent possession is relevant. — On the prosecution of an indictment for larceny it was not error to instruct the jury in effect that they might consider the fact of recent exclusive possession of the stolen property, under the circumstances set forth in the instruction, as evidence of constructive larceny, as well as of actual larceny. Evidence of possession is relevant not only in cases of larceny, but also in prosecutions for receiving stolen goods. Stapleton v. Commonwealth, 140 Va. 475, 124 S.E. 237 (1924); Reaves v. Commonwealth, 192 Va. 443, 65 S.E.2d 559 (1951). See also Gilland v. Commonwealth, 184 Va. 223, 35 S.E.2d 130 (1945).

The mere naked possession of stolen goods, unaided by other proof, is no evidence that the possessor received the goods knowing them to have been stolen. But recent exclusive unexplained possession of stolen goods is a circumstance for the consideration of the jury. Stapleton v. Commonwealth, 140 Va. 475, 124 S.E. 237 (1924).

And possession of goods not mentioned in indictment may be shown. — In a prosecution for burglary and larceny the court did not err in admitting testimony showing that the accused had in his possession when arrested other stolen goods not mentioned in the indictment. Stapleton v. Commonwealth, 140 Va. 475, 124 S.E. 237 (1924).

Permitted inference. — Proof of recent possession of stolen property allows the trier of fact to infer that the defendant knew it to be stolen. Collins v. Commonwealth, No. 1965-96-4 (Ct. of Appeals June 3, 1997).

Trial court did not have to believe defendant's version of how defendant acquired car and was entitled to infer that defendant knew car was stolen; defendant knew of the shotgun based on its location under the passenger seat. Ridley v. Commonwealth, No. 1850-01-1, 2002 Va. App. LEXIS 387 (Ct. of Appeals July 16, 2002).

Uncharged crimes properly admitted. — When defendant was convicted of receiving stolen property, evidence that defendant possessed stolen property for which defendant was not charged was properly admitted because (1) the jury was properly instructed to consider evidence that defendant committed a crime other than that for which defendant was tried only as evidence defendant knowingly possessed stolen goods, and not as evidence that defendant stole the items, and (2) the evidence was relevant and admissible to prove guilty knowledge and an absence of mistake in possessing stolen property, as the evidence concerned events roughly contemporaneous with the charged crimes, much of the evidence was factually interwoven with evidence in the case, and defendant was not entitled to have the evidence "sanitized." Kelley v. Commonwealth, 2012 Va. App. LEXIS 305 (Oct. 2, 2012).

In a prosecution for receiving stolen property in which evidence of defendant's uncharged crimes was admitted, the Commonwealth was not limited to only admitting evidence of one uncharged crime because the jury was properly instructed as to the limited purposes for which the evidence could be considered. Kelley v. Commonwealth, 2012 Va. App. LEXIS 305 (Oct. 2, 2012).

Evidence insufficient to show possession. — Defendant was apprehended before he had even approached the stolen vehicle, and he never admitted to the police that he used the vehicle. The record was devoid of physical evidence, such as fingerprints, or testimonial evidence from witnesses that would tie defendant to the vehicle on the day in question. There was a lack of evidence to show defendant possessed the stolen vehicle as set forth in the indictment. McClary v. Commonwealth, No. 0187-97-1 (Ct. of Appeals Jan. 27, 1998).

Evidence was insufficient to establish defendant possessed stolen property in Virginia Beach, Virginia. While defendant clearly exercised dominion and control over the stolen vehicle in Williamsburg, the record did not suggest that defendant, a passenger, exercised any measure of dominion or control over the vehicle or otherwise asserted a possessory interest in the vehicle while in Virginia Beach. Ramsey v. Commonwealth, — Va. App. —, — S.E.2d —, 2008 Va. App. LEXIS 354 (July 8, 2008).

Evidence that the accused had in his possession when arrested other stolen goods, not mentioned in the indict-

ment, is admissible on a prosecution for receiving stolen goods, knowing them to have been stolen, as tending to show guilty knowledge. Stapleton v. Commonwealth, 140 Va. 475, 124 S.E. 237 (1924).

And when circumstantial evidence is of a convincing character and excludes every reasonable hypothesis other than that the accused is guilty, there is no ground upon which the Supreme Court may, or will, disturb the judgment of the trial court. Parish v. Commonwealth, 206 Va. 627, 145 S.E.2d 192 (1965), cert. denied, 384 U.S. 942, 86 S. Ct. 1463, 16 L. Ed. 2d 540 (1966); Pasanello v. Commonwealth, 206 Va. 640, 145 S.E.2d 200 (1965).

Burden of proof. — All that the Commonwealth is required to do under its burden of proof is to establish, beyond a reasonable doubt, the essential elements of the offense of concealing stolen goods. Parish v. Commonwealth, 206 Va. 627, 145 S.E.2d 192 (1965), cert. denied, 384 U.S. 942, 86 S. Ct. 1463, 16 L. Ed. 2d 540 (1966); Pasanello v. Commonwealth, 206 Va. 640, 145 S.E.2d 200 (1965).

Receiving stolen goods and larceny considerations. — Even though larceny is a continuing offense and the offense of receiving stolen property is deemed larceny, an accused who receives stolen property knowing it to be stolen may be tried only in those jurisdictions in which the accused is guilty of trespassing against the owner's property right. That offense can only occur in the place where the accused received the property or possessed it. The fiction of larceny as a continuing offense does not create venue where the offense for which the accused is prosecuted occurred outside the jurisdiction of the trial court. Davis v. Commonwealth, 14 Va. App. 709, 419 S.E.2d 285 (1992).

Insufficient evidence to show receipt of stolen property. — Appellate court incorrectly held that defendant "received" stolen property, which was brought home by the father of her child in an effort to support defendant and her child, just by proof that defendant benefited from the proceeds of the sale of this property as the fact that a defendant received a benefit from the stolen property was not an element of receiving stolen property and was insufficient to show that defendant "received" the stolen property. Thus, the trial court's judgment of conviction was plainly wrong and had to be reversed under § 8.01-680. Whitehead v. Commonwealth, 278 Va. 105, 677 S.E.2d 265, 2009 Va. LEXIS 62 (2009).

Canons of Ethics (see now the Rules of Professional Conduct) may not conflict with section. — Section 54.1-3915 authorizing the promulgation of the Canons of Ethics (see now the Rules of Professional Conduct) forbids inconsistency with this section. In re Ryder, 263 F. Supp. 360 (E.D. Va.), aff'd, 381 F.2d 713 (4th Cir. 1967).

Instructions held proper. — See Gilland v. Commonwealth, 184 Va. 223, 35 S.E.2d 130 (1945); Reaves v. Commonwealth, 192 Va. 443, 65 S.E.2d 559 (1951).

The Commonwealth's election to proceed against the defendant for the greater offenses under the general larceny statutes did not preclude the giving of instructions on, and the conviction of the defendant of, the lesser offenses of larceny by receiving stolen property, since the lesser offenses were included in the major offense of larceny. Cabbler v. Commonwealth, 212 Va. 520, 184 S.E.2d 781 (1971), cert. denied, 405 U.S. 1075, 92 S. Ct. 1501, 31 L. Ed. 2d 807 (1972).

Evidence held sufficient to sustain conviction of grand larceny. Wright v. Commonwealth, 196 Va. 132, 82 S.E.2d 603 (1954).

Sufficient evidence. — Where defendant was found in possession of the stolen automobile within hours of its theft, falsely denied any connection to the vehicle, but later admitted acquiring it from a cocaine fiend in exchange for narcotics, such evidence, together with the entire record, was sufficient to establish the guilty knowledge requisite to the conviction. Bynum v. Commonwealth, 23 Va. App. 412, 477 S.E.2d 750 (1996).

Evidence was sufficient to affirm defendant's conviction for receiving stolen property, where it showed that the owner's grandson stole a bracelet and diamond ring worth $2,950 from this grandmother, that he and a friend pawned the stolen jewelry to the defendant, who worked at a pawn shop, for $120, that defendant prepared no paperwork and that he did not file the required information with the police, and that subsequently, the defendant returned the bracelet to the grandmother and charged her nothing,

and gave conflicting explanations for his actions. Diaz v. Commonwealth, No. 2987-97-4 (Ct. of Appeals Feb. 16, 1999).

Evidence sustained defendants' convictions where a stolen all terrain vehicle (ATV) was recovered from their property, where defendants admitted possession of the ATV and claimed to have purchased it for less than half of its value from a seller they could not identify, and where defendants could not produce a receipt for the sale. Shaver v. Commonwealth, 30 Va. App. 789, 520 S.E.2d 393 (1999).

Evidence was sufficient to establish that police officer knew vehicle was stolen, and that she aided and abetted her brother's receipt and concealment of vehicle. Barnes v. Commonwealth, No. 2693-98-1 (Ct. of Appeals Mar. 21, 2000).

Where after defendant returned a clock to a retailer for cash police found nine other of the retailer's clocks in their original store wrappers in the trunk of defendant's car, evidence was sufficient to support defendant's conviction. Panajotov v. Commonwealth, No. 1054-01-4, 2002 Va. App. LEXIS 330 (Ct. of Appeals June 4, 2002).

The evidence was sufficient to support a finding beyond a reasonable doubt that the defendant was aiding in concealing property that he knew to be stolen where the defendant, although possibly not involved in the theft of a vehicle, had occupied the vehicle for a period of hours before being approached by a police officer and, when approached by the officer, falsely told the officer that the vehicle belonged to his sister in a deliberate attempt to conceal from the officer that the car was stolen. Roach v. Commonwealth, No. 2783-98-2, 2000 Va. App. LEXIS 562 (Ct. of Appeals Aug. 1, 2000).

Where the pipe that defendant sold to a scrap metal dealer was unique, had recently been stolen, and defendant's hypothesis of innocence was rejected as unreasonable, the evidence of possession of recently stolen goods was sufficient to support a conviction for receiving stolen property. Thomas v. Commonwealth, No. 0738-02-2, 2002 Va. App. LEXIS 738 (Ct. of Appeals Dec. 10, 2002).

Evidence was sufficient to prove defendant intended to permanently deprive the owner of the stolen vehicle he was driving of the vehicle, because larceny was a continuing offense, and evidence that defendant knew the vehicle was stolen and drove it with that knowledge was sufficient to establish this element. Bazemore v. Commonwealth, 42 Va. App. 203, 590 S.E.2d 602, 2004 Va. App. LEXIS 19 (2004).

Evidence was sufficient to show that the camcorder stolen from the victim was the same one defendant pawned and thus, to support his receipt of stolen property conviction. Angelina v. Commonwealth, — Va. App. —, — S.E.2d —, 2005 Va. App. LEXIS 233 (June 14, 2005).

Defendant's convictions for grand larceny, in violation of § 18.2-95, and larceny with the intent to sell or distribute stolen property, in violation of § 18.2-108, were affirmed because the trial court did not err by admitting into evidence a computer-generated inventory report of stolen pharmaceutical items from a drug store as a business records exception to the hearsay rule. Further, the record reflected sufficient evidence from which the trial court could infer beyond a reasonable doubt that defendant stole merchandise valued at $200 or more; thus, the credible evidence before the trial court was sufficient to convict defendant of grand larceny and larceny with the intent to sell or distribute stolen property. McDowell v. Commonwealth, 48 Va. App. 104, 628 S.E.2d 542, 2006 Va. App. LEXIS 229 (2006).

Defendant's admission to two witnesses that the guns defendant had were stolen, in addition to the special agent's finding that one of the shotguns in defendant's possession had been stolen from a county was sufficient to support the trial court's finding that defendant was guilty of knowingly receiving a stolen shotgun. Cooper v. Commonwealth, 54 Va. App. 558, 680 S.E.2d 361, 2009 Va. App. LEXIS 356 (2009).

Sufficient evidence supported a conviction of felony receipt of stolen property because shortly after a reported theft, which included the victim's watch and several video games and related video game items, the stolen watch was found in defendant's residence, and defendant and another person sold 50 used video games to a resale store, and the store's receipt exactly matched the victim's list of stolen games. Palmer v. Commonwealth, 2009 Va. App. LEXIS 533 (Dec. 1, 2009).

Evidence of value of goods. — Defendant's claim that his conviction for possessing stolen property was improper on the ground that stock certificates had no intrinsic value was defaulted where defendant failed to raise the issue in the trial court. The "ends of justice" exception could not be applied to the defaulted claim because defendant did not suffer a miscarriage of justice in that precedent held that stock certificates had significant value and were readily transferable on the open market, and the Commonwealth established the value of the stock through testimony from the owner of the stock as to the fact that the certificates had a value of approximately $21,000. Wheeler v. Commonwealth, 44 Va. App. 689, 607 S.E.2d 133, 2005 Va. App. LEXIS 8 (2005).

In a case in which defendant was convicted of receiving stolen property, the evidence of value regarding the stolen items ("demo" cell phones) was of such a nature that a factfinder could reasonably conclude that their replacement cost was sufficient to establish that their actual value exceeded the statutory minimum of $200. Since it was reasonable to infer that these phones were new models in good working condition, it followed that evidence of their replacement value closely approximated their actual value. Little v. Commonwealth, 59 Va. App. 725, 722 S.E.2d 317, 2012 Va. App. LEXIS 58 (2012).

Evidence was sufficient to support defendant's conviction for receiving stolen property worth more than $200, where the evidence established that approximately 75 to 80 cartons of cigarettes worth approximately $40 each were stolen and the value of the stolen cigarettes was at least $3,000; that defendant's share of the theft may have only been a few packs did not alter the fact that he received stolen goods worth more than $200. Dellinger v. Commonwealth, 2012 Va. App. LEXIS 226 (July 10, 2012).

Determination that rental truck was abandoned justified search. — Police properly concluded that a U-Haul truck rented by defendant was abandoned, and a trial court properly refused to suppress the evidence of stolen motorcycles found therein, where, after the police received a tip, it was determined that the rental agreement had expired, the truck was covered with mud and stuck, and was left on the property of defendant's aunt without her knowledge. Defendant had no expectation of privacy in the rental truck at the time and place of the search, because it was deemed abandoned. Thomas v. Commonwealth, No. 0524-03-3, 2004 Va. App. LEXIS 298 (Ct. of Appeals June 29, 2004).

Restitution. — Because defendant's plea agreement to receiving or concealing stolen property in violation of § 18.2-108 specifically waived any right of appeal from the decision of the trial court, not merely the conviction itself, the trial court did not err in ordering defendant to pay restitution pursuant to subsection B of § 19.2-305. Craig v. Commonwealth, 2011 Va. App. LEXIS 329 (Nov. 1, 2011).

Applied in Wilson v. Commonwealth, 220 Va. 26, 255 S.E.2d 464 (1979); Grant v. Commonwealth, 223 Va. 680, 292 S.E.2d 348 (1982); Fulcher v. Commonwealth, 226 Va. 96, 306 S.E.2d 874 (1983); Berryman v. Moore, 619 F. Supp. 853 (E.D. Va. 1985).

§ 18.2-108.01. Larceny with intent to sell or distribute; sale of stolen property; penalty.

A. Any person who commits larceny of property with a value of $200 or more with the intent to sell or distribute such property is guilty of a felony punishable by confinement in a state correctional facility for not less than two years nor more than 20 years. The larceny of more than one item of the same product is prima facie evidence of intent to sell or intent to distribute for sale.

B. Any person who sells, attempts to sell or possesses with intent to sell or distribute any stolen property with an aggregate value of $200 or more where he knew or should have known that the property was stolen is guilty of a Class 5 felony.

C. A violation of this section constitutes a separate and distinct offense.

History.
2003, c. 831.

CASE NOTES

Subsection B not lesser-included offense of subsection A. — Defendant's conviction under subsection B of § 18.2-108.01 was reversed because (1) defendant was charged with a violation of subsection A of § 18.2-108.01, and (2) a violation of subsection B of § 18.2-108.01 was not a lesser-included offense of subsection A of § 18.2-108.01, since subsection A prohibited a grand larceny with the intent to sell or distribute stolen goods, but did not require proof of a sale or distribution, while subsection B prohibited the sale or attempt to sell or distribute stolen property, requiring proof of an actual or attempted sale or distribution, so proof of a violation of subsection A did not encompass a violation of subsection B. Bryant v. Commonwealth, 2012 Va. App. LEXIS 222 (July 10, 2012).

Double jeopardy. — Because the General Assembly clearly and unambiguously intended that grand larceny and larceny with intent to sell or distribute (in violation of §§ 18.2-95 and 18.2-108.01, respectively) were to be punished separately, no double jeopardy violation occurred. Tharrington v. Commonwealth, 58 Va. App. 704, 715 S.E.2d 388, 2011 Va. App. LEXIS 296 (2011).

Evidence sufficient to support conviction. — Evidence that defendant's companion stole multiple packages of three different items from a store, permitting a statutory inference that the companion acted with the requisite intent to sell or distribute those items; that defendant was the sole driver of the vehicle where the goods were found and admitted that he let a companion put the stolen items in the vehicle; and that defendant knew the value of the items was greater than $200 was sufficient to support defendant's conviction for the second offense of larceny with intent to sell or distribute stolen property, in violation of § 18.2-108.01. Bunch v. Commonwealth, 2010 Va. App. LEXIS 483 (Dec. 14, 2010).

Evidence insufficient to support conviction. — Evidence was insufficient to support defendant's conviction for the first charged offense of larceny with intent to sell or distribute stolen property, in violation of § 18.2-108.01, where there was no evidence to prove that defendant acted with the requisite intent to sell the items stolen in connection with that offense. Bunch v. Commonwealth, 2010 Va. App. LEXIS 483 (Dec. 14, 2010).

§ 18.2-108.1. Receipt of stolen firearm.

Notwithstanding the provisions of § 18.2-108, any person who buys or receives a firearm from another person or aids in concealing a firearm, knowing that the firearm was stolen, shall be guilty of a Class 6 felony and may be proceeded against although the principal offender is not convicted.

History.
1988, c. 358; 1998, c. 821.

Law Review.
For an article relating to all published Virginia criminal law decisions between July 1, 1997, and July 1, 1998, see 32 U. Rich. L. Rev. 1091 (1998).

CASE NOTES

The purpose and policy of this section is to prohibit the possession of a stolen firearm. This section, in effect, is designed to deter the potential physical harm that could emanate from the acquisition of a weapon by nefarious means. Fields v. Commonwealth, No. 0437-94-3 (Ct. of Appeals Aug. 22, 1995).

The term firearm, as used in this section, refers to actual firearms only. Fields v. Commonwealth, No. 0437-94-3 (Ct. of Appeals Aug. 22, 1995).

Proof by circumstantial evidence. — Although the Commonwealth may prove that the object possessed in violation of this section is an actual firearm by presenting direct forensic evidence of its nature, as with any other element of a crime, the Commonwealth may also assert its proof by circumstantial evidence. Fields v. Commonwealth, No. 0437-94-3 (Ct. of Appeals Aug. 22, 1995).

Offense under section not lesser included offense of grand larceny. — Defendant was indicted for grand larceny pursuant to § 18.2-95 and convicted in a bench trial for larceny of a firearm in violation of this section. The trial judge erroneously ruled that § 18.2-108.1 was a lesser included offense of § 18.2-95, and the conviction was reversed. Hendrix v. Commonwealth, No. 0625-96-1 (Ct. of Appeals Mar. 18, 1997).

Evidence sufficient. — Defendant's conviction for receiving or concealing a stolen firearm was supported by sufficient evidence as the evidence showed that defendant was arrested in the area where a gun was found in the woods, that his DNA profile was recovered from the firearm, and that defendant came back later the same night, leading to an inference that he did so in order to search for the items he had previously hidden. Defendant's effort to conceal the firearm just prior to his arrest and then retrieve it just after his release permitted the reasonable inference that he knew that the firearm was stolen. Scott v. Commonwealth, 2010 Va. App. LEXIS 458 (Nov. 23, 2010).

Applied in Acey v. Commonwealth, 29 Va. App. 240, 511 S.E.2d 429 (1999).

§ 18.2-109. Receipt or transfer of possession of stolen vehicle, aircraft or boat.

Any person who, with intent to procure or pass title to a vehicle, aircraft, boat or vessel, which he knows or has reason to believe has been stolen, shall receive or transfer possession of the same from one to another or who shall with like intent have in his possession any vehicle, aircraft, boat or vessel which he knows or has reason to believe has been stolen, and who is not an officer of the law engaged at the time in the performance of his duty as an officer, shall be guilty of a Class 6 felony.

History.
Code 1950, § 18.1-165; 1960, c. 358; 1975, cc. 14, 15.

Michie's Jurisprudence.
For related discussion, see 2B M.J. Aviation, § 1; 15 M.J. Receiving Stolen Goods, § 1.

§ 18.2-110. Repealed by Acts 2004, c. 995.

Cross references.
For current provisions as to forfeiture of motor vehicles used in commission of certain crimes, see § 19.2-386.16.

ARTICLE 4.

EMBEZZLEMENT AND FRAUDULENT CONVERSIONS.

Michie's Jurisprudence.
For related discussion, see 1B M.J. Appeal and Error, § 118; 2B M.J. Automobiles, § 126; 2B M.J. Aviation, §§ 1, 11; 9B M.J. Indictments, Informations and Presentments, § 48; 12A M.J. Larceny, § 21.

§ 18.2-111. Embezzlement deemed larceny; indictment.

If any person wrongfully and fraudulently use, dispose of, conceal or embezzle any money, bill, note, check, order, draft, bond, receipt, bill of lading or any other personal property, tangible or intangible, which he shall have received for another or for his employer, principal or bailor, or by virtue of his office, trust, or employment, or which shall have been entrusted or delivered to him by another or by any court, corporation or company, he shall be guilty of embezzlement. Proof of embezzlement shall be sufficient to sustain the charge of larceny. Any person convicted hereunder shall be deemed guilty of larceny and may be indicted as for larceny and upon conviction shall be punished as provided in § 18.2-95 or § 18.2-96.

History.
Code 1950, § 18.1-109; 1960, c. 358; 1975, cc. 14, 15; 1979, c. 349; 1994, c. 555; 2003, c. 733.

Cross references.
As to computer time, services, etc., as property subject to larceny, see § 18.2-152.1 et seq. As to indictment for embezzlement, see § 19.2-223.

Law Review.
For article on justification as a defense to crime, see 59 Va. L. Rev. 1326 (1973). For survey of Virginia criminal law for the year 1977-1978, see 64 Va. L. Rev. 1407 (1978). For a note, "Pleading for Theft Consolidation in Virginia: Larceny, Embezzlement, False Pretenses and § 19.2-284," see 55 Wash. & Lee L. Rev. 249 (1998). For annual survey essay, "Rethinking Theft Crimes in Virginia," see 38 U. Rich. L. Rev. 13 (2003). For article summarizing published Virginia criminal law decisions between July 1, 2002 and July 1, 2003, see 38 U. Rich. L. Rev. 87 (2003).

Michie's Jurisprudence.
For related discussion, see 6B M.J. Embezzlement, §§ 2 - 5, 11.

CASE NOTES

This section is not by itself vague. Statutes are not read in isolation where there exists a judicial gloss on their meaning. Mechling v. Slayton, 361 F. Supp. 770 (E.D. Va. 1973).

Embezzlement is a statutory crime. Moss v. Harwood, 102 Va. 386, 46 S.E. 385 (1904).

Elements of offense. — A person entrusted with possession of another's personalty who converts such property to his own use or benefit is guilty of the statutory offense of embezzlement. Evans v. Commonwealth, 226 Va. 292, 308 S.E.2d 126 (1983).

To establish the crime of embezzlement under this section, the Commonwealth must prove that the accused wrongfully appropriated to his or her own use or benefit, with the intent to deprive the owner thereof, the property entrusted or delivered to the accused. However, proof of the misappropriation of property entrusted to the possession of the accused is insufficient, standing alone, to prove that the accused was the embezzler. Zoretic v. Commonwealth, 13 Va. App. 241, 409 S.E.2d 832 (1991).

Embezzlement, larceny distinguished. — Embezzlement and larceny are separate offenses with different elements. The key distinction between embezzlement and larceny is that larceny involves a trespassory taking of property while embezzlement involves a conversion of property received with the owner's consent. Cera v. Commonwealth, No. 0432-94-4 (Ct. of Appeals May 2, 1995).

Larceny and embezzlement are not the same offense for determining time limits under § 19.2-243. Cera v. Commonwealth, No. 0432-94-4 (Ct. of Appeals May 2, 1995).

Under Virginia law, embezzlement, false pretenses, and larceny are three separate offenses and there is not a general "theft" statute, as there is in most states, that encompasses both types of behavior, and § 18.2-95 defines grand larceny; § 18.2-111 defines embezzlement; and § 18.2-178 defines false pretenses. The Commonwealth of Virginia has always purported to treat the three basic theft crimes of larceny, embezzlement, and false pretenses as separate and distinct offenses, and maintains separate statutes for each crime. United States v. Good, 326 F.3d 589, 2003 U.S. App. LEXIS 7543 (4th Cir. Apr. 22, 2003).

Proof of embezzlement not sufficient to support larceny charge. — Proof of embezzlement does not support a conviction under an indictment alleging larceny. While prior to being amended in 1994, this section permitted a defendant to be "indicted as for larceny," and proof of embezzlement was sufficient to sustain a larceny charge, these provisions were eliminated by the 1994 amendments. By eliminating these provisions, the General Assembly intended to change the law so that proof of embezzlement is no longer sufficient to sustain a larceny charge. Bruhn v. Commonwealth, 35 Va. App. 339, 544 S.E.2d 895, 2001 Va. App. LEXIS 216 (2001), aff'd, 264 Va. 597, 570 S.E.2d 866 (2002).

General Assembly intended the current version of the statute to preclude conviction under an indictment for larceny on proof of embezzlement. Bruhn v. Commonwealth, 37 Va. App. 537, 559 S.E.2d 880, 2002 Va. App. LEXIS 127, aff'd, 264 Va. 597, 570 S.E.2d 866 (2002).

The legislature only recently eliminated the election provision in this section, supporting the conclusion that the legislature's deletion of the election provision was generated by and followed from its amendment making the crime charged and the crime underlying the conviction one and the same. Bruhn v. Commonwealth, 37 Va. App. 537, 559 S.E.2d 880, 2002 Va. App. LEXIS 127, aff'd, 264 Va. 597, 570 S.E.2d 866 (2002).

First sentence of § 18.2-111 provides that any person committing the described acts shall be guilty of embezzlement, and the only reference to larceny is in the second sentence, which now states that embezzlement shall be deemed larceny and upon conviction thereof, the person shall be punished as provided in the larceny code sections. Commonwealth v. Bruhn, 264 Va. 597, 570 S.E.2d 866, 2002 Va. LEXIS 166 (2002).

The 1994 amendments to § 18.2-111, regarding embezzlement deemed larceny, were not narrowly tailored to eliminate unneeded language, but constituted a complete reformulation of the statute, and most particularly, the elimination of the permissive provision that embezzlement could be "indicted as for larceny" evinces a clear legislative intent to require specificity in the indictment. Commonwealth v. Bruhn, 264 Va. 597, 570 S.E.2d 866, 2002 Va. LEXIS 166 (2002).

When defendant kept money given to him on behalf of his employer, the evidence was insufficient to convict him of larceny, due to the absence of a trespassory taking, and he could not be considered guilty under § 18.2-111, which, prior to its amendment, had allowed someone found guilty of the elements of embezzlement to be considered guilty of larceny, but now required that defendant be specifically charged with embezzlement. Commonwealth v. Bruhn, 264 Va. 597, 570 S.E.2d 866, 2002 Va. LEXIS 166 (2002).

Mental element of the crime of embezzlement is a fraudulent purpose to deprive the owner of his property and to appropriate the same. Bain v. Commonwealth, 215 Va. 89, 205 S.E.2d 641 (1974).

To constitute the statutory crime of embezzlement it is necessary to prove that an accused wrongfully appropriated to his own use or benefit, with the intent to deprive the owner thereof, the property of another which has been entrusted to him by reason of his employment or office. Revell v. Commonwealth, 215 Va. 708, 213 S.E.2d 756 (1975).

Section 18.2-112 emphasizes the conversion of property by someone in a position of trust who, by virtue of their position, exercises control over the property converted or has custody of the property. Ratliff v. Commonwealth, 20 Va. App. 43, 455 S.E.2d 259 (1995).

Formal fiduciary relationship not necessary. — In order to prove embezzlement, however, the existence of a formal fiduciary relationship is not necessary. Rather, the Commonwealth must prove that the defendant was entrusted with the property of another. In this case, victim entrusted defendant as his insurance agent, with $1,400 to pay over to insurance company. The court found irrespective of § 38.2-1813 that these facts established the required entrustment to sustain defendant's conviction. Chiang v. Commonwealth, 6 Va. App. 13, 365 S.E.2d 778 (1988).

Requisite intent. — To establish the requisite intent, it is not necessary to show that the defendant wrongfully appropriated the entrusted property to his or her own personal use or benefit. This section only requires that a person wrongfully and fraudulently use, dispose of, conceal or embezzle the property. Therefore, if the defendant diverts funds to benefit another, that action is sufficient to establish the wrongful appropriation of the property to his or her

own use. Chiang v. Commonwealth, 6 Va. App. 13, 365 S.E.2d 778 (1988).

Proof of embezzlement will sustain charge of larceny. — On an indictment for larceny, proof of embezzlement is sufficient to sustain the charge. Shinn v. Commonwealth, 73 Va. (32 Gratt.) 899 (1879); Pitsnogle v. Commonwealth, 91 Va. 808, 22 S.E. 351 (1895). But see Bruhn v. Commonwealth, 35 Va. App. 339, 544 S.E.2d 895, 2001 Va. App. LEXIS 216 (2001), aff'd, 264 Va. 597, 570 S.E.2d 866 (2002).

Bona fide conversion is not embezzlement. — The conversion of property under a bona fide claim of ownership is not embezzlement. To constitute embezzlement there must be a fraudulent intent to deprive the owner of his property. Wadley v. Commonwealth, 98 Va. 803, 35 S.E. 452 (1900); Whitlow v. Commonwealth, 184 Va. 910, 37 S.E.2d 18 (1946).

Proof of criminal agency. — While proof that property entrusted to the possession of the accused has been misappropriated is not enough, standing alone, to prove that the accused was the embezzler, where there is additional evidence, sufficient to show that the accused acted with the requisite criminal intent and that his conduct was designed to conceal his criminal purpose, a finding that the accused was the criminal agent will be upheld. Smith v. Commonwealth, 222 Va. 646, 283 S.E.2d 209 (1981).

Employer's retention of withheld taxes can give rise to embezzlement prosecution. — Section 58.1-474 imposes a statutorily-created trust on funds withheld by employers from employees' wages for state income tax liability purposes. Because such funds are held in trust for the benefit of the Commonwealth of Virginia and are not the property of the employer, an employer's retention of such funds can give rise to a criminal prosecution for embezzlement under § 18.2-111, which requires the fraudulent use, disposition, concealment or embezzlement of money received for another by virtue of one's employment. George v. Commonwealth, 276 Va. 767, 667 S.E.2d 779, 2008 Va. LEXIS 125 (2008).

Authority of corporate officer. — Evidence was insufficient to support embezzlement convictions where the Commonwealth failed to show that defendant, as the treasurer of a real estate development corporation, lacked authority to pay defendant for defendant's time and reimburse defendant for expenses incurred in managing the development corporation's property. Stinespring v. Commonwealth, 2009 Va. LEXIS 200 (Apr. 28, 2009).

Failure to return rented automobile. — Defendant came into lawful possession of an automobile through a rental agreement, and under its terms he had an absolute duty to return it at a stipulated time. He failed to return the automobile entrusted to him and gave no explanation of what had happened to it until sometime after his arrest. The failure of defendant to return the vehicle, coupled with the surrounding circumstances, furnished sufficient evidence from which the trial court could conclude that the defendant, after lawfully coming into possession of the automobile, formed an intent to wrongfully and fraudulently convert it to his own use. The requisite intent to commit the offense was inferred from all the facts and circumstances of the case. Stegall v. Commonwealth, 208 Va. 719, 160 S.E.2d 566 (1968).

Words not imputing crime of embezzlement. — To publish of a chief of police that he "has within the last past twelve months collected certain fines of Officer P., which fines do not appear by the records of the police court to have been reported," does not impute to him the crime of embezzlement. Moss v. Harwood, 102 Va. 386, 46 S.E. 385 (1904).

Charging embezzlement of several sums as one act. — An indictment which charges the larceny of a specific sum, although the bill of particulars sets forth various and sundry charges of smaller sums aggregating the total charged in the indictment, charges but a single act of embezzlement, and is sufficient. Commonwealth v. Brown, 11 Va. L. Reg. (n.s.) 140 (1925). See § 19.2-223.

When an indictment charges a statutory offense that is capable of being classified as either a felony or a misdemeanor, the use of the word "feloniously" is not surplusage. Instead, it indicates which grade of the offense is being charged. Thus, the inclusion of the word "feloniously" in defendant's indictment indicated the grand jury's intent to charge the felony grade of embezzlement. Davis v. Commonwealth, No. 2626-95-2 (Ct. of Appeals Apr. 1, 1997).

Finding that variance claim was waived was harmless

error. — Although an appeals court erred in concluding that defendant had waived a variance claim, because the record showed that defendant sufficiently raised the issue in the trial court, the error was harmless because no fatal variance existed in defendant's case: (1) defendant was convicted of embezzlement under § 18.2-111 based on evidence showing that he had withheld taxes from his employees' paychecks but he had not paid over the withheld amount to the Commonwealth of Virginia, as required by § 58.1-472; (2) defendant claimed a variance existed because his indictments defined the crime as embezzling funds belonging to the Commonwealth, but a jury instruction defined the crime as embezzling funds belonging to the employees; (3) the jury instruction merely identified the funds at issue and did not contradict the indictments' allegation as to the statutory owner of the withheld taxes, i.e., the Commonwealth; and (4) no fatal variance occurred because the ownership of the funds was not a matter for jury determination in defendant's case. George v. Commonwealth, 276 Va. 767, 667 S.E.2d 779, 2008 Va. LEXIS 125 (2008).

Fatal variance. — an indictment charged defendant with embezzlement from a subcontractor in violation of § 18.2-111, but the Commonwealth's evidence at trial failed to show that defendant was in a position of trust with the subcontractor, defendant's conviction was reversed due to a fatal variance between the indictment and the evidence. Bowman v. Commonwealth, 2013 Va. App. LEXIS 41 (Feb. 5, 2013).

Question of intent is for jury. — S., the secretary of a building association, was indicted for the larceny of a check, the property of the association. The check was given to S. in payment of a debt due the association. It was made payable to S., as secretary, and also to bearer. S. cashed the check but did not return or account for the proceeds at the meetings of the association. It was held that it was S.'s duty, not to collect, but to turn the check over to the treasurer of the association, but if S. had accounted for the money, that fact would, of course, show that he had no intention to appropriate the check. S. not having done so, it was a question for the jury, whether he intended to embezzle the check. And to convict him, it was necessary that the jury should be satisfied that this intention existed before, or at the time the check passed into the possession of the bank. Shinn v. Commonwealth, 73 Va. (32 Gratt.) 899 (1879).

Expert testimony. — It was error to allow an expert witness to give his opinion that certain unrecorded receipts were used to replace funds converted by defendant to her own use, for this was tantamount to his expressing an opinion on the issue in the case. Webb v. Commonwealth, 204 Va. 24, 129 S.E.2d 22 (1963).

Effect of failure to demand statement from attorney for Commonwealth. — Accused having been indicted for larceny and having failed to exercise his right under this section to demand a statement in writing from the attorney for the Commonwealth of what he intended to rely upon to ask for a conviction, the prosecuting attorney was entitled to ask for a conviction for receiving stolen bonds or for receiving lost bonds, as might be shown by the evidence. Hutchinson v. Commonwealth, 133 Va. 710, 112 S.E. 624 (1922).

Virginia is authorized by § 19.2-245 to prosecute embezzlement, even though most or all of the illegal acts took place in another state. Keselica v. Commonwealth, 24 Va. App. 115, 480 S.E.2d 756 (1997).

The trial court had jurisdiction over a prosecution for embezzlement where the defendant took a guitar amplifier belonging to the victim with him when he moved from Virginia to West Virginia and then used it as collateral for a loan he secured from a pawn shop in West Virginia, as the crime commenced when the defendant appropriated the amplifier to his own use and removed it, without authorization, to West Virginia. Bescher v. Commonwealth, No. 1489-97-4 (Ct. of Appeals April 14, 1998).

Late motion. — When a motion is made under this section, but not within the time prescribed by the statute, a designation made orally in open court is sufficient and, in the absence of a showing of prejudice, does not result in reversible error. Roberts v. Commonwealth, 230 Va. 264, 337 S.E.2d 255 (1985).

Sufficient evidence for inference of wrongful intent. — Appellant's failure to return the computer to victim, his failure to pay her for the computer, his failure to contact her after the contractual sixty day term elapsed, and his failure to provide her with an address or telephone number where he could be reached constituted sufficient evidence from which the trial judge could

infer that the appellant wrongfully intended to appropriate the computer to his own use or benefit. Jackson v. Commonwealth, No. 1552-95-2 (Ct. of Appeals Dec. 31, 1996).

There was sufficient evidence that defendants, who operated a restaurant through a limited liability company and failed to pay sales and meals taxes, had the intent to commit embezzlement. The taxes were collected but not remitted to tax authorities; defendants' inability to pay the taxes in a lump sum suggested that they no longer had the money to do so; and records suggested that tax funds had been spent on personal expenses. Neofotis v. Commonwealth, 2006 Va. App. LEXIS 406 (Aug. 29, 2006).

Value of goods taken from a store was shown to be at least $200, so as to sufficiently prove that the taking was felonious, where the items taken on one day were valued at $142 and there were five other occasions when similar or greater quantities of items were taken from the store by the defendant. Bentley v. Commonwealth, No. 1569-97-2 (Ct. of Appeals May 5, 1998).

Evidence was sufficient to show intent to commit embezzlement where subsequent to his termination of employment, the defendant was asked to return tree climbing equipment on several occasions, the employer made several attempts to collect the equipment at the defendant's home, the defendant lied about the location of the equipment, and the defendant was persuaded to return the equipment only after he was in police custody. Magouirk v. Commonwealth, No. 2768-97-1 (Ct. of Appeals Nov. 24, 1998).

Evidence was sufficient to sustain defendant's conviction of felony embezzlement where $290.29 was missing from a store's receipts on days when she worked, a video camera recorded her stealing money from a cash register and placing it in her sock, and she confessed to taking "$200 or so." Miles v. Commwealth, No. 2958-00-4, 2002 Va. App. LEXIS 147 (Ct. of Appeals Mar. 12, 2002).

Evidence sufficient to support conviction. — Defendant exercised dominion and control over plaintiff's car contrary to her express directions and the fact finder could have found beyond a reasonable doubt that he did so with the intention of obtaining either a financial benefit for himself or his employer by exacting from plaintiff towage and storage fees or a pecuniary advantage in regard to property damage that plaintiff had sustained; accordingly, the evidence was sufficient to support the embezzlement conviction. Scrivano v. Commonwealth, No. 0656-93-4 (Ct. of Appeals May 3, 1994).

Where defendant, who was president of the corporation, corrupted correct ledger entries to at once reduce by $5,000 monies previously received by the corporation from another and increase by a like sum funds she paid to the corporation in consideration for stock, defendant clearly converted corporate assets to her benefit. The creativity of her stratagem did not diminish her culpability. Carter v. Commonwealth, No. 1489-95-3 (Ct. of Appeals Dec. 31, 1996).

Circumstantial evidence was sufficient to support finding that defendant embezzled deposit money from his employer. Cassell v. Commonwealth, No. 1595-98-2 (Ct. of Appeals Sept. 28, 1999).

Evidence was sufficient to prove that defendant, as person in charge of ordering office supplies for her employer, wrongfully converted inkjet printer cartridges to her own use, and that value of cartridges wrongfully converted was greater than $200. Hillsman v. Commonwealth, No. 1658-98-4 (Ct. of Appeals Dec. 7, 1999).

There was sufficient evidence to support defendant's conviction for embezzlement as the air compressor that he sold from the garage he leased was personal property not real property; the air compressor's connection to the building was merely by wires and a hose, it was easily detached, and it was not essential to the purpose of the building, which was storage. McBride v. Commonwealth, No. 1947-02-4, 2003 Va. App. LEXIS 428 (Ct. of Appeals Aug. 5, 2003).

Evidence that defendant wrote 142 checks on a church's bank account over a 25-month period and used the money for various purposes, including as gifts to others, supported the trial court's judgment that he committed multiple, separate acts of embezzlement, and the trial court did not err when it allowed the Commonwealth to join distinct acts into five separate charges of embezzlement, each covering a period of four, five, or six months, and convicting defendant of all five charges. Bragg v. Commonwealth, 42 Va. App. 607, 593 S.E.2d 558, 2004 Va. App. LEXIS 103 (2004).

Evidence supported defendant's conviction for embezzlement on November 10, 2003, as defendant was short, no transactional errors explained the shortage, and defendant had exclusive access to her cash drawer; defendant had similar shortages in November and February, which reflected a pattern consistent with a January embezzlement that defendant acknowledged. Harris v. Commonwealth, — Va. App. —, — S.E.2d —, 2005 Va. App. LEXIS 375 (Oct. 4, 2005).

Conviction of embezzlement was supported by sufficient evidence including a videotape showing defendant, a sales clerk, undercharging a customer for a sales transaction, removing price tags from items during the transaction against store procedure, and removing sensor tags from the items before scanning the items into the register, also against store procedure. Maynor v. Commonwealth, — Va. App. —, — S.E.2d —, 2005 Va. App. LEXIS 424 (Oct. 25, 2005).

Trial court did not err in finding defendant guilty, following a bench trial, of computer fraud, computer trespass, embezzlement, and attempted extortion, as the evidence showed that defendant transferred computer files from his computer at work to a third-party server before he was terminated from his position as human resource director, that he used the removed material to threaten the company in an attempt to forgive a loan it had made to him, and that the company established the value of the material removed as required to support convictions on those offenses. DiMaio v. Commonwealth, 46 Va. App. 755, 621 S.E.2d 696, 2005 Va. App. LEXIS 456 (2005).

Convictions of computer fraud and larceny were supported by sufficient evidence, including testimony that the market value of personnel files taken by defendant exceeded $10,000, and unchallenged testimony that market value of form covenants not to compete taken by defendant was between $5,000 and $7,000. DiMaio v. Commonwealth, 272 Va. 504, 636 S.E.2d 456, 2006 Va. LEXIS 110 (2006).

Evidence was sufficient to support defendant's conviction for general embezzlement under § 18.2-111 for not paying state withholding tax that defendant withheld from defendant's employees in defendant's bank account. Pursuant to § 58.1-474, defendant was not merely a debtor of the Commonwealth when defendant withheld that money, but, instead, defendant held the property of another because that statute said that defendant held that money in trust for the Commonwealth. George v. Commonwealth, 51 Va. App. 137, 655 S.E.2d 43, 2008 Va. App. LEXIS 12, aff'd, 276 Va. 767, 667 S.E.2d 779, 2008 Va. LEXIS 125 (2008).

Evidence supported defendant's embezzlement conviction under § 18.2-111 as: (1) co-defendant and defendant informed a victim that they needed $2,295 to purchase construction materials for a project at the victim's home; (2) the victim gave them a $2,295 check with "Material Payment" on the memo line; (3) defendant cashed the check and failed to purchase the materials; (4) defendant allowed co-defendant to use $800 of the proceeds for van repairs; and (5) defendant failed to account for more than $300 of the check proceeds. Frye v. Commonwealth, — Va. App. —, — S.E.2d —, 2008 Va. App. LEXIS 380 (Aug. 12, 2008).

Defendant's evidentiary insufficiency challenge to his § 18.2-111 embezzlement convictions was properly rejected: (1) the Commonwealth of Virginia showed that defendant placed taxes withheld from his employees' wages in the bank account that he used for paying his personal and business expenses, that he failed to pay over the withheld taxes to the Commonwealth as required by § 58.1-472, and that at times the balance in defendant's bank account was less than the amount of the withheld taxes; (2) defendant argued that § 18.2-111 required proof that he lawfully acquired possession of another's property and then wrongfully converted it to his own use, but that the funds at issue were his own funds and that he had merely a debtor-creditor relationship with the Commonwealth with regard to the withheld taxes; (3) § 58.1-474 was similar to 26 U.S.C.S. § 7501, which the U.S. Supreme Court had held created a statutory trust on behalf of the federal government and deprived employers of any equitable interest that they might claim in taxes that were withheld from their employees' salaries; (4) there was nothing that limited § 58.1-474 to civil matters or prevented the Commonwealth from relying on that statute to criminally prosecute an employer who failed to pay over the withheld taxes; and (5) because § 58.1-474 imposed a statutorily-created trust on the funds that defendant withheld from his employees' wages for state income tax liability purposes, and those funds were considered to be held in trust for the benefit of the Commonwealth and were not defendant's property, his receipt of the withheld taxes could be used to prove that he had received money for another, which was a required element of embezzlement under this section. George v. Commonwealth, 276 Va. 767, 667 S.E.2d 779, 2008 Va. LEXIS 125 (2008).

Defendant's conviction of embezzlement in violation of § 18.2-111 was supported by the evidence, as a manager of the store where defendant worked testified that store video showed defendant print two money orders, grab them, and walk off. There was no customer at the cash register at the time. McDonald v. Commonwealth, — Va. App. —, — S.E.2d —, 2008 Va. App. LEXIS 532 (Dec. 9, 2008).

The appellate court found sufficient evidence to support the conclusion that the seller handed the truck over jointly to defendant and his wife, thereby delivering the truck to defendant for purposes of § 18.2-111 as there was credible evidence that the transaction was viewed as a joint "purchase" by defendant and his wife. Spain v. Commonwealth, 2012 Va. App. LEXIS 54 (Feb. 28, 2012).

Evidence was sufficient to prove embezzlement as it showed that defendant admitted to stealing her employer's property when she marked down items for a customer without the employer's authorization and when she gave the same customer eleven shirts without any payment. While defendant contended that there was no evidence of fraudulent intent, she told her employer's loss prevention officer that she was stealing and that she knew it was wrong, and she also gave away shirts to the customer in addition to the unauthorized markdowns. Wells v. Commonwealth, 60 Va. App. 111, 724 S.E.2d 225, 2012 Va. App. LEXIS 131 (2012).

Defendant was properly convicted of embezzlement, because the evidence established the wrongful taking of Social Security Administration checks received by defendant for her employer in violation of § 18.2-111. Leftwich v. Commonwealth, 61 Va. App. 422, 737 S.E.2d 42, 2013 Va. App. LEXIS 37 (2013).

Evidence insufficient to support conviction. — Defendant bookkeeper could not be convicted where the only evidence of a shortage was the fact that the deposits and cash on hand over the period in question did not equal the cash receipts shown on the books. This could have resulted as easily from certain weaknesses in the system of internal control over funds as from any defalcation by defendant. Webb v. Commonwealth, 204 Va. 24, 129 S.E.2d 22 (1963).

The evidence was insufficient as a matter of law to support a conviction for embezzlement where all that reasonably could be inferred from the evidence was that the defendant had the opportunity to commit the crime and that he fled at a time when wages were payable to him. Simmons v. Commonwealth, 219 Va. 181, 247 S.E.2d 359 (1978).

The Commonwealth failed to produce sufficient evidence to establish the defendant's criminal intent and agency, where the defendant was a temporary employee who received the envelope containing the employer's funds on her first day on the job, she was given little direction as to what to do with it, and there was no evidence that the defendant knew that the envelope contained money, or that she attempted to hide it or exert control over its contents. Waymack v. Commonwealth, 4 Va. App. 547, 358 S.E.2d 765 (1987).

Where the evidence proved that defendant was not the only employee who had access to the money in the safe, that there were numerous internal discrepancies, and the evidence failed to exclude the reasonable hypothesis that the discrepancy at issue was caused by counting errors committed by the cashiers, proof of guilt was not established beyond a reasonable doubt. Tribuzi v. Commonwealth, 25 Va. App. 289, 487 S.E.2d 870 (1997).

There was insufficient evidence to support the conviction of an assistant manager of a restaurant for embezzlement of monies that she asserted she deposited in a bank's deposit box where: (1) A witness testified that the bank's deposit box had previously malfunctioned in such a way that a deposited bag could be removed, (2) There was no evidence that the defendant attempted to conceal her alleged criminal activity or that she possessed the criminal intent necessary to sustain her conviction, and (3) In her six years of employment with the victim, the defendant had been promoted from counter personnel to assistant manager. Pettway v. Commonwealth, No. 0559-97-2 (Ct. of Appeals June 16, 1998).

Defendant's conviction for embezzlement in violation of § 18.2-111 was supported by sufficient evidence where she worked as a convenience store cashier and was seen on the store's videotape performing a cash refund, although there was no customer present, her explanation that she was correcting an earlier error was not supported by the earlier journal entry, she had failed to follow the proper procedure, including attaching the receipt and getting a manager to approve the refund, and the cash drawer was short. Simerson v. Commonwealth, No. 0637-02-1, 2003 Va. App. LEXIS 145 (Ct. of Appeals Mar. 18, 2003).

Defendant gas station lessee's embezzlement conviction was reversed, as the Commonwealth failed to prove that the money he received from gasoline sales, which he failed to remit to the lessor, was the lessor's property, or that he intended to defraud the lessor. Dove v. Commonwealth, 41 Va. App. 571, 586 S.E.2d 890, 2003 Va. App. LEXIS 502 (2003).

Where a former airline employee obtained flight vouchers without first paying for reserved airline tickets by exploiting a loophole in the airline's reservation system, the evidence was insufficient to sustain two embezzlement convictions because there was no evidence that defendant was entrusted with the airline tickets by virtue of his employment. Brown v. Commonwealth, 56 Va. App. 178, 692 S.E.2d 271, 2010 Va. App. LEXIS 177 (2010).

Evidence insufficient to impute personal criminal liability to corporate president where the only proof of his involvement with the funds was the stipulation that he was the corporation's president. Rooney v. Commonwealth, 27 Va. App. 634, 500 S.E.2d 830 (1998).

Jury questions to court. — In an embezzlement prosecution, the trial court did not err in not defining "fraud" upon the request of the jury as the term was a plain word commonly used in general discourse and as a jury instruction had already provided the jury with the definition of a fraudulent act. Wells v. Commonwealth, 60 Va. App. 111, 724 S.E.2d 225, 2012 Va. App. LEXIS 131 (2012).

Jury instructions. — In an embezzlement prosecution, the trial court did not err in failing to instruct the jury that proof of misappropriation of property was insufficient, standing alone, to prove embezzlement as the instruction was merely repetitious, in that the jury had already been instructed on the elements of embezzlement, including the fact that the jury had to find a wrongful and fraudulent conversion in addition to misappropriation. Wells v. Commonwealth, 60 Va. App. 111, 724 S.E.2d 225, 2012 Va. App. LEXIS 131 (2012).

Sentence proper. — Defendant's 10-year sentence for felony embezzlement constituted half of the maximum punishment, was not in excess of the statutory maximum, and could not be reviewed on appeal since embezzlement could result in a larceny conviction under § 18.2-111, and grand larceny had a maximum sentence under § 18.2-95 of 20 years in prison. Greene v. Commonwealth, 2008 Va. App. LEXIS 319 (July 15, 2008).

Restitution. — Following defendant's conviction for embezzlement, a trial court abused its discretion by ordering restitution based solely on figures listed in a victim impact statement, without evidence that the amount of loss alleged was actually caused by defendant's crimes. Boley v. Commonwealth, 2013 Va. App. LEXIS 118 (Apr. 16, 2013).

Applied in Gwaltney v. Commonwealth, 19 Va. App. 468, 452 S.E.2d 687 (1995); Nestle v. Commonwealth, 22 Va. App. 336, 470 S.E.2d 133 (1996); Commissary Concepts Mgmt. Corp. v. Mziguir, 267 Va. 586, 594 S.E.2d 915, 2004 Va. LEXIS 66 (2004).

§ 18.2-111.1. Repealed by Acts 2004, c. 459.

§ 18.2-111.2. Failure to pay withheld child support; embezzlement.

If any employer withholds money from the pay of his employee for the purpose of paying administrative or court-ordered child support on behalf of the employee and then wrongfully and fraudulently fails to make payment of the money withheld, the employer shall be guilty of embezzlement.

History.
1999, c. 56.

§ 18.2-112. Embezzlement by officers, etc., of public or other funds; default in paying over funds evidence of guilt.

If any officer, agent or employee of the Commonwealth or of any city, town, county, or any other political subdivision, or the deputy of any such officer having custody of public funds, or other funds coming into his custody under his official capacity, knowingly misuse or misappropriate the same or knowingly dispose thereof otherwise than in accordance with law, he shall be guilty of a Class 4 felony; and any default of such officer, agent, employee or deputy in paying over any such funds to the proper authorities when required by law to do so shall be deemed prima facie evidence of his guilt.

History.
Code 1950, § 18.1-110; 1960, c. 358; 1973, c. 15; 1975, cc. 14, 15; 1979, c. 585.

Law Review.
For survey of Virginia criminal law for the year 1972-1973, see 59 Va. L. Rev. 1458 (1973). For survey of Virginia criminal law for the year 1974-1975, see 61 Va. L. Rev. 1697 (1975).

Michie's Jurisprudence.
For related discussion, see 1B M.J. Appeal and Error, § 118; 5A M.J. Counties, § 43.

CASE NOTES

This section deals with public officials in possession of public funds and requires that they do not knowingly misuse or misappropriate such funds, or knowingly use them in a way not in accordance with the law, regardless of whether they were prompted by a criminal intent. Crider v. Commonwealth, 206 Va. 574, 145 S.E.2d 222 (1965).

Section does not create an express trust for 11 U.S.C.S. § 523(a)(4) purposes. A trust imposed ex maleficio is insufficient to give rise to the existence of a fiduciary relationship for the purposes of bankruptcy law. On the basis of these considerations, no fiduciary relationship exists between the Commonwealth and the debtors which would warrant nondischargeability in bankruptcy under 11 U.S.C.S. § 523(a)(4) as a defalcation in fiduciary duty. Virginia Comm'n of Game & Inland Fisheries v. Myers, 52 Bankr. 901 (Bankr. E.D. Va. 1985).

Section is directed against fraudulent and felonious misuse. — This section is directed against the fraudulent and felonious misuse and misappropriation of public funds by an officer of the state, and not against the mere failure to pay over such funds within the required time. Robinson v. Commonwealth, 104 Va. 888, 52 S.E. 690 (1906).

This section emphasizes the conversion of property by someone in a position of trust who, by virtue of their position, exercises control over the property converted or has custody of the property. Ratliff v. Commonwealth, 20 Va. App. 43, 455 S.E.2d 259 (1995).

An essential element of this section is the custody of the funds that are misappropriated. Ratliff v. Commonwealth, 20 Va. App. 43, 455 S.E.2d 259 (1995).

"Custody." — If a person charged with an offense under this section does not physically possess the property, the element of "custody" requires proof that the person had the authority to dispose of or distribute the funds. Ratliff v. Commonwealth, 20 Va. App. 43, 455 S.E.2d 259 (1995).

Knowingly misusing funds is embezzlement. — If a person "knowingly" misuses or misappropriates money which has once come into his hands as treasurer, or knowingly disposes thereof otherwise than in accordance with law, he is guilty of the embezzlement thereof under this section. Aetna Cas. & Sur. Co. v. Board of

Supvrs., 160 Va. 11, 168 S.E. 617 (1933).

The essence of the crime is the scienter, the guilty knowledge of the defendant that the payments obtained by her for overtime were a misuse or misappropriation of public funds, or a disposition of them not in accordance with law. Crider v. Commonwealth, 206 Va. 574, 145 S.E.2d 222 (1965).

The proof required is that the defendant used or disposed of the public funds in her charge knowing that such use or disposition was a misuse or misappropriation of the funds or not in accordance with the law. Crider v. Commonwealth, 206 Va. 574, 145 S.E.2d 222 (1965).

Fraudulent intent is not necessary. — While the detention of public funds may be done with fraudulent intent, fraudulent intent is not a necessary element of the offense created by this section. If the forbidden act or acts are done "knowingly," a violation occurs. Crider v. Commonwealth, 206 Va. 574, 145 S.E.2d 222 (1965).

Money may be detained without being misappropriated. Crider v. Commonwealth, 206 Va. 574, 145 S.E.2d 222 (1965).

The detention of the money is one of the elements constituting the offense, but it does not constitute the offense itself. Crider v. Commonwealth, 206 Va. 574, 145 S.E.2d 222 (1965).

A peace bond is in the nature of a conditional fine. As such, and until the condition is satisfied and the payor becomes entitled to reimbursement, the cash is moneys belonging to the state and its embezzlement by a public officer is a violation of this section. Healy v. Commonwealth, 213 Va. 325, 191 S.E.2d 736 (1972).

Words not imputing to officer larceny or embezzlement. — To publish of a chief of police that he "has within the last past twelve months collected certain fines of Officer P., which fines do not appear by the records of the police court to have been reported," does not impute to him the crime of larceny or embezzlement. Moss v. Harwood, 102 Va. 386, 46 S.E. 385 (1904).

Not necessary to prove embezzlement of whole sum charged. — On a charge of embezzlement of a given sum it is not necessary to prove the embezzlement of the whole sum charged in the indictment. Robinson v. Commonwealth, 104 Va. 888, 52 S.E. 690 (1906).

Indictment held sufficient. — An indictment which charges that a justice of the peace, by virtue of his office, had the custody of five dollars of the public funds of the state, which he was required to pay to the clerk of the circuit court of his county, and that he feloniously and knowingly did misuse and misappropriate, and feloniously and knowingly disposed of the same otherwise than by paying the same over to said clerk, in accordance with law, and concluding with a charge of larceny and embezzlement, is a sufficient indictment for a felony under this section. Robinson v. Commonwealth, 104 Va. 888, 52 S.E. 690 (1906).

Evidence sufficient to support conviction. — Evidence was sufficient to support defendant's conviction for knowingly misappropriating funds that came into her custody and possession by virtue of her position as an employee of the city's school system, as it established that she received a check based on the community college's purchase of an ad for her school's football program and that she knowingly misappropriated the funds because the check was made payable to the city's high school, yet she endorsed the check with her name, and deposited the funds into her personal account at a credit union rather than give the check to the school bookkeeper as her duties required her to do. Gunn v. Commonwealth, 272 Va. 580, 637 S.E.2d 324, 2006 Va. LEXIS 116 (2006).

Evidence held sufficient to support conviction of deputy treasurer for embezzlement of funds from county treasurer's office. Orr v. Commonwealth, 2 Va. App. 371, 344 S.E.2d 627 (1986).

Jury instruction. — Defendant's conviction was reversed for error in instructing the jury that they should find her guilty if she caused the overtime payments to be made "knowing that such expenditures of public funds were not authorized" by the town council or manager. Crider v. Commonwealth, 206 Va. 574, 145 S.E.2d 222 (1965).

§ 18.2-112.1. Misuse of public assets; penalty.

A. For purposes of this section, *"public assets"* means personal property belonging to or paid for by the Commonwealth, or any city, town, county, or any other political subdivision, or the labor of any person other than the accused that is paid for by the Commonwealth, or any city, town, county, or any other political subdivision.

B. Any full-time officer, agent, or employee of the Commonwealth, or of any city, town, county, or any other political subdivision who, without lawful authorization, uses or permits the use of public assets for private or personal purposes unrelated to the duties and office of the accused or any other legitimate government interest when the value of such use exceeds $1,000 in any 12-month period, is guilty of a Class 4 felony.

History.
2008, cc. 738, 755.

Editor's note.
Acts 2008, cc. 738 and 755, cl. 2, provides: "That the provisions of this act may result in a net increase in periods of imprisonment or commitment. Pursuant to § 30-19.1:4, the estimated amount of the necessary appropriation cannot be determined for periods of imprisonment in state adult correctional facilities and is $0 for periods of commitment to the custody of the Department of Juvenile Justice."

§ 18.2-113. Fraudulent entries, etc., in accounts by officers or clerks of financial institutions, joint stock companies or corporations; penalty.

If any officer or clerk of any financial institution, joint stock company or corporation makes, alters or omits to make any entry in any account kept in or by such financial institution, company or corporation, with intent, in so doing, to conceal the true state of such account, or to defraud such financial institution, company or corporation, or to enable or assist any person to obtain money to which he was not entitled, such officer or clerk shall be guilty of a Class 4 felony.

History.
Code 1950, § 18.1-111; 1960, c. 358; 1975, cc. 14, 15; 1996, c. 77; 2003, c. 740.

Michie's Jurisprudence.
For related discussion, see 8B M.J. Falsifying accounts, § 2.

CASE NOTES

This section is not directed against false entries, but against any entry made with intent to conceal, etc., so an indictment which charges that the accused made a false and fraudulent entry goes further than this section. But where such words are used they are not surplusage, and the Commonwealth is bound to prove a false and fraudulent entry. Mitchell v. Commonwealth, 141 Va. 541, 127 S.E. 368 (1925).

§ 18.2-114. Repealed by Acts 2004, c. 459.

§ 18.2-114.1. When collection of money by commissioner, etc., larceny.

If any special commissioner or receiver, appointed by any court to collect money, and required by law, or decree of the court, to give bond before collecting the same, shall collect such money, or any part thereof, without giving such bond, and fail properly to account for the same, he shall be deemed guilty of larceny of the money so collected and not so accounted for.

History.
1978, c. 718.

Michie's Jurisprudence.
For related discussion, see 15 M.J. Receivers, § 22.

§ 18.2-115. Fraudulent conversion or removal of property subject to lien or title to which is in another.

Whenever any person is in possession of any personal property, including motor vehicles or farm products, in any capacity, the title or ownership of which he has agreed in writing shall be or remain in another, or on which he has given a lien, and such person so in possession shall fraudulently sell, pledge, pawn or remove such property from the premises where it has been agreed that it shall remain, and refuse to disclose the location thereof, or otherwise dispose of the property or fraudulently remove the same from the Commonwealth, without the written consent of the owner or lienor or the person in whom the title is, or, if such writing be a deed of trust, without the written consent of the trustee or beneficiary in such deed of trust, he shall be deemed guilty of the larceny thereof.

In any prosecution hereunder, the fact that such person after demand therefor by the lienholder or person in whom the title or ownership of the property is, or his agent, shall fail or refuse to disclose to such claimant or his agent the location of the property, or to surrender the same, shall be prima facie evidence of the violation of the provisions of this section. In the case of farm products, failure to pay the proceeds of the sale of the farm products to the secured party, lienholder or person in whom the title or ownership of the property is, or his agent, within ten days after the sale or other disposition of the farm products unless otherwise agreed by the lender and borrower in the obligation of indebtedness, note or other evidence of the debt shall be prima facie evidence of a violation of the provisions of this section. The venue of prosecutions against persons fraudulently removing any such property, including motor vehicles, from the Commonwealth shall be the county or city in which such property or motor vehicle was purchased or in which the accused last had a legal residence.

This section shall not be construed to interfere with the rights of any innocent third party purchasing such property, unless such writing shall be docketed or recorded as provided by law.

History.
Code 1950, § 18.1-116; 1960, c. 358; 1975, cc. 14, 15; 1986, c. 484.

Law Review.
For article on justification as a defense to crime, see 59 Va. L. Rev. 1326 (1973).

Michie's Jurisprudence.
For related discussion, see 2B M.J. Automobiles, § 130; 3C M.J. Commercial Law, § 99; 19 M.J. Venue, § 14.

CASE NOTES

Fraud contemplated by this section is an act by a debtor intended to deprive a secured creditor of his collateral by appropriating it to the debtor's own use. Bain v. Commonwealth, 215 Va. 89, 205 S.E.2d 641 (1974).

The fraud contemplated is an act by a debtor intended to deprive a secured creditor of his collateral by appropriating it to the debtor's own use and is to be distinguished from the definition of fraud in civil cases which requires a misrepresentation of fact intended to induce another to part with something of value. Gregory v. Commonwealth, 5 Va. App. 89, 360 S.E.2d 858 (1987), aff'd, 237 Va. 354, 377 S.E.2d 405, cert. denied, 493 U.S. 845, 110 S. Ct. 137, 107 L. Ed. 2d 97 (1989).

Phrase "without the consent of the ... lienor ..." modifies the phrase "fraudulently remove the same from the state" as well as the phrase "sell, pledge, pawn ... or otherwise dispose of the property." Gregory v. Commonwealth, 5 Va. App. 89, 360 S.E.2d 858 (1987), aff'd, 237 Va. 354, 377 S.E.2d 405, cert. denied, 493 U.S. 845, 110 S. Ct. 137, 107 L. Ed. 2d 97 (1989).

Fraud directed against lienor or title holder. — This section requires proof that fraudulent intent be directed against the lienor or person in whom the title is rather than against an innocent purchaser or subsequent creditor. Bain v. Commonwealth, 215 Va. 89, 205 S.E.2d 641 (1974).

Section violated whether fraudulent intent formed within or outside state. — Where the secured property is disposed of without the consent of the lienor by the debtor appropriating it to his own use, a fraudulent disposal has occurred within the meaning of the statute, regardless of whether the fraudulent intent is formed within or outside the boundaries of Virginia. Gregory v. Commonwealth, 5 Va. App. 89, 360 S.E.2d 858 (1987), aff'd, 237 Va. 354, 377 S.E.2d 405, cert. denied, 493 U.S. 845, 110 S. Ct. 137, 107 L. Ed. 2d 97 (1989).

Proof that fraudulent intent occurred within state not required. — Nothing in the language of the statute requires proof that the fraudulent intent to dispose or the actual disposal of the secured property occurred within the boundaries of Virginia. Gregory v. Commonwealth, 5 Va. App. 89, 360 S.E.2d 858 (1987), aff'd, 237 Va. 354, 377 S.E.2d 405, cert. denied, 493 U.S. 845, 110 S. Ct. 137, 107 L. Ed. 2d 97 (1989).

Failure to return collateral upon demand by lienholder is prima facie evidence of violation of this section. Where such a failure occurs, even the existence of written permission to remove the collateral is immaterial under this section, as the creditor need not show the lack of such permission to make out a prima facie case. Lewis v. First Nat'l Bank, 645 F. Supp. 1499 (W.D. Va. 1986), aff'd, 818 F.2d 861 (4th Cir. 1987).

Debtor's sale of collateral. — Even though a bank's security interest was unrecorded and therefore unperfected as to third parties, the bank was entitled to rely upon and enforce its security agreement against defaulting debtor, and as debtor's subsequent sale deprived the bank of its right to sell the collateral upon default, the bank's security interest comes within the purview of this section. Bain v. Commonwealth, 215 Va. 89, 205 S.E.2d 641 (1974).

Where the evidence proved that defendant sold the equipment in question in contravention of the lease and that he was aware that the lease terms required written consent before the equipment could be sold, this was sufficient to convict under this statute. Compton v. Commonwealth, 22 Va. App. 751, 473 S.E.2d 95 (1996).

Evidence that defendant removed property from Virginia in violation of a security agreement and that he transferred the property to a dealer in Pennsylvania in exchange for a credit on property he purchased from that dealer was sufficient to prove fraudulent conversion in violation of this section. Landes v. Commonwealth, 37 Va. App. 710, 561 S.E.2d 37, 2002 Va. App. LEXIS 180 (2002).

Failure to leave forwarding address or to contact creditor waived right to deny that demand made. — Even assuming that the debtor did not actually receive the demand for return of the collateral, her failure to leave a functional forwarding address or contact the creditor constituted a waiver of her right to deny that the demand was made. Lewis v. First Nat'l Bank, 645 F. Supp. 1499 (W.D. Va. 1986), aff'd, 818 F.2d 861 (4th Cir. 1987).

Proceedings under this section not extreme or outrageous where probable cause exists. — The initiation of criminal proceedings against someone under this section with probable cause is not extreme or outrageous as a matter of law. If it were, any prosecution under this section that was terminated would be grounds for a suit, and the statute would be essentially useless, as lienholders would fear being liable for infliction of emotional distress. Lewis v. First Nat'l Bank, 645 F. Supp. 1499 (W.D. Va. 1986), aff'd, 818 F.2d 861 (4th Cir. 1987).

Jurisdiction proper in county where lien created and failure to obtain consent to disposal occurred. — Jurisdiction was proper in Botetourt County, where the lien was created and the failure to obtain the bank's consent to the disposal of its collateral both occurred in Botetourt County and only the formation of the intent to deprive the bank of its collateral and the actual disposal of the tractor occurred outside of this state. The harm which this section is intended to prevent is the economic injury caused to the secured party by defendant's actions and the infringement of the lien created in Virginia. Gregory v. Commonwealth, 5 Va. App. 89, 360 S.E.2d 858 (1987), aff'd, 237 Va. 354, 377 S.E.2d 405, cert. denied, 493 U.S. 845, 110 S. Ct. 137, 107 L. Ed. 2d 97 (1989).

§ 18.2-115.1. Unlawful sublease of a motor vehicle; penalty.

A. It shall be unlawful for any person, for profit in the course of business, who is not a party to a lease contract, conditional sales contract, or security agreement which transfers any right or interest in a motor vehicle, knowing that the motor vehicle is subject to a lease, security interest or lien, to:

1. Obtain or exercise control over a motor vehicle and sell, transfer, assign, or lease the motor vehicle to another person without the prior written authorization of the secured creditor, lessor, or lienholder if he receives compensation or other consideration for the sale, transfer, assignment, or lease of the motor vehicle; or

2. Assist, cause, or arrange the actual or purported sale, transfer, assignment, or lease of a motor vehicle to another person without the prior written authorization of the secured creditor, lessor, or lienholder if he receives compensation or other consideration for assisting, causing, or arranging the sale, transfer, assignment, or lease of the motor vehicle.

B. A violation of this section is punishable as a Class 3 misdemeanor.

C. This section shall not apply to any employee acting upon request of his employer.

D. This section shall not apply if the entire indebtedness owed under or secured by the lease, conditional sales contract, or security agreement through the date of payment is paid in full and received by the lessor or secured party within thirty days after the sale, transfer, assignment, or lease of the motor vehicle.

History.
1990, c. 844; 1993, c. 608.

§ 18.2-116. Failure to pay for or return goods delivered for selection or approval.

If any person shall solicit and obtain from any merchant any goods, wares or merchandise for examination or approval, and shall thereafter, upon written demand, refuse or fail to return the same to such merchant in unused condition, or to pay for the same, such person so offending shall be deemed guilty of the larceny thereof. But the provisions of this section shall not apply unless such written demand be made within five days after delivery, and unless the goods, wares or merchandise shall have attached to them or to the package in which they are contained a label, card or tag containing the words, "Delivered for selection or approval."

History.
Code 1950, § 18.1-117; 1960, c. 358; 1975, cc. 14, 15.

§ 18.2-117. Failure of bailee to return animal, aircraft, vehicle or boat.

If any person comes into the possession as bailee of any animal, aircraft, vehicle, boat or vessel, and fail to return the same to the bailor, in accordance with the bailment agreement, he shall be deemed guilty of larceny thereof and receive the same punishment, according to the value of the thing stolen, prescribed for the punishment of the larceny of goods and chattels. The failure to return to the bailor such animal, aircraft, vehicle, boat or vessel, within five days from the time the bailee has agreed in writing to return the same shall be prima facie evidence of larceny by such bailee of such animal, aircraft, vehicle, boat or vessel.

History.
Code 1950, § 18.1-163; 1960, c. 358; 1975, cc. 14, 15.

Michie's Jurisprudence.
For related discussion, see 2B M.J. Automobiles, § 126; 2B M.J. Aviation, § 1; 12A M.J. Larceny, § 8; 12A M.J. Livery Stables, § 1.

CASE NOTES

Legislative intent. — The label affixed by the legislature to the crime defined in this section, larceny after bailment, clearly indicates an intent to create a new statutory crime, incorporating some elements of the existing crime of larceny, defined as it was at common law. United States v. Parker, 522 F.2d 801 (4th Cir. 1975).

Virginia has not enacted a statutory definition of larceny, looking instead to the common law. United States v. Parker, 522 F.2d 801 (4th Cir. 1975).

This section does not codify the common-law crime of larceny but rather creates a statutory offense for failing to return the property in accordance with the terms of the agreement. Ketchum v. Commonwealth, 12 Va. App. 258, 403 S.E.2d 382 (1991).

The failure of this section to require mens rea or scienter is not fatal to its constitutionality. — A claim that a statute on its face contains no requirement of mens rea or scienter is no ground for holding the statute unconstitutional, since such requirement will be read into the statute by the court when it appears the legislature implicitly intended that it must be proved. Maye v. Commonwealth, 213 Va. 48, 189 S.E.2d 350 (1972).

Mens rea or scienter must be proven. — This section implicitly requires proof of an element of mens rea or scienter, even though the requirement does not appear in the statute. Molash v. Commonwealth, 3 Va. App. 243, 348 S.E.2d 868 (1986).

Proof of intent to permanently deprive owner of his or her property is not required to sustain a conviction under this section. Ketchum v. Commonwealth, 12 Va. App. 258, 403 S.E.2d 382 (1991).

Vagueness of section. — This section is not so vague as to deny to the average individual of ordinary intelligence fair notice that certain actions are proscribed. United States v. Parker, 522 F.2d 801 (4th Cir. 1975).

Elements of crime. — The first sentence of this section clearly sets forth two elements of the conduct prohibited thereunder: (1) the actor must be a bailee of an animal, aircraft, vehicle, boat or vessel; and (2) he must fail to return such possession in accordance with the terms of the bailment agreement. United States v. Parker, 522 F.2d 801 (4th Cir. 1975).

Elements of common-law larceny which are consistent with a taking by a bailee, such as the intent at the time of taking to permanently deprive another of his possession, would be incorporated in the crime, while elements not consistent therewith, such as a trespassory taking, would not be. United States v. Parker, 522 F.2d 801 (4th Cir. 1975).

The distinction between larceny after bailment and the common-law offense of larceny is that in the former it is not necessary to allege or prove that the original taking was trespassory. Maye v. Commonwealth, 213 Va. 48, 189 S.E.2d 350 (1972).

The statutory crime of "larceny after bailment" does not require a trespassory taking of the personal property of another. United States v. Closkey, 411 F.2d 1212 (4th Cir. 1969).

Where there was no written agreement between bailors and bailees and the bailors of the property had taken possession of it within two days of its abandonment by the bailees, that portion of the statute establishing a prima facie case was not applicable. Molash v. Commonwealth, 3 Va. App. 243, 348 S.E.2d 868 (1986).

Intent. — Nowhere in this section is there an explicit requirement of criminal intent. United States v. Parker, 522 F.2d 801 (4th Cir. 1975).

Despite defendant's claims to the contrary, the circumstantial evidence, particularly defendant's conduct, established that he intended to permanently deprive victim of car. Yancey v. Commonwealth, No. 2647-01-2, 2002 Va. App. LEXIS 428 (Ct. of Appeals July 30, 2002).

Application of prima facie presumption held proper. — Trial court properly applied the prima facie presumption under § 18.2-117 that defendant had a fraudulent intent to commit larceny for failure to return a rental car to the rental car company because the evidence showed that the car was not recovered until more than five days after the date it should have been returned. Further, the defendant's evidence did not rebut the presumption because it failed to explain why he did not return the car between the date that it was due and the date that he was hospitalized, which was four days after the due date, and defendant provided no dates or documentation to verify that he had been hospitalized at another hospital due to a suicide attempt during the four-day period. Newport v. Commonwealth, — Va. App. —, — S.E.2d —, 2005 Va. App. LEXIS 152 (Apr. 19, 2005).

Fraudulent intent held not established. — Where defendants, who were long-distance truck drivers employed to haul freight, argued that they merely left the trailer at a truck stop, told its rightful possessor of its location, and went home to Minnesota, there was no evidence that excluded the hypothesis that defendants became disillusioned with their employment and merely left the trailer where it was when they decided to quit, and the testimony that they notified the lawful possessor of the trailer of its location when they quit, was not contradicted by any other witness, fraudulent intent on the part of the defendants was not established. Molash v. Commonwealth, 3 Va. App. 243, 348 S.E.2d 868 (1986).

Probable cause found. — There was probable cause for plaintiff's arrest, imprisonment, and subsequent prosecution for failure to return a rental vehicle, because plaintiff's failure to return his rental car within five days after the date set forth in his rental agreement was prima facie evidence of a violation under the terms of the statute. Curtis v. Devlin, — F. Supp. 2d —, 2005 U.S. Dist. LEXIS 6703 (E.D. Va. Apr. 19, 2005).

Sufficiency of evidence. — Evidence was sufficient to find defendant guilty of violating § 18.2-117 where the car owner

testified that defendant kept her car for more than a day longer than agreed upon. Since the owner's testimony was not inherently incredible, the trial court's finding that the car owner was more credible than defendant controlled. James v. State, — Va. App. —, — S.E.2d —, 2007 Va. App. LEXIS 449 (Dec. 18, 2007).

§ 18.2-118. Fraudulent conversion or removal of leased personal property.

A. Whenever any person is in possession or control of any personal property, by virtue of or subject to a written lease of such property, except property described in § 18.2-117, and such person so in possession or control shall, with intent to defraud, sell, secrete, or destroy the property, or dispose of the property for his own use, or fraudulently remove the same from the Commonwealth without the written consent of the lessor thereof, or fail to return such property to the lessor thereof within 30 days after expiration of the lease or rental period for such property stated in such written lease, he shall be deemed guilty of the larceny thereof.

B. The fact that such person signs the lease or rental agreement with a name other than his own, or fails to return such property to the lessor thereof within 30 days after the giving of written notice to such person that the lease or rental period for such property has expired, shall be prima facie evidence of intent to defraud. For purposes of this section, notice mailed by certified mail and addressed to such person at the address of the lessee stated in the lease, shall be sufficient giving of written notice under this section.

C. The venue of prosecution under this section shall be the county or city in which such property was leased or in which such accused person last had a legal residence.

History.
Code 1950, § 18.1-117.1; 1966, c. 474; 1975, cc. 14, 15; 1978, c. 675; 2013, c. 536.

The 2013 amendments.
The 2013 amendment by c. 536 substituted the subsection A through C designators for the former subsection (a) through (c) designators and substituted "30 days" for "ten days" in subsection B.

Law Review.
For survey of Virginia criminal law for the year 1977-1978, see 64 Va. L. Rev. 1407 (1978).

Michie's Jurisprudence.
For related discussion, see 12A M.J. Larceny, § 8.

CASE NOTES

Value not proven. — Defendant's conviction for grand larceny was improper because the Commonwealth failed to prove that the value of the jackhammer that defendant rented was at least $200. The only evidence of the jackhammer's value that the trial court found persuasive, which was its original purchase price and replacement cost, was insufficient to prove its worth. Byrum v. Commonwealth, 2010 Va. App. LEXIS 211 (May 18, 2010).

Fraudulent intent. — "Ends of justice" exception in Va. Sup. Ct. R. 5A:18 did not apply to allow the appellate court to review defendant's contention that fraudulent intent under § 18.2-118 had not been proven because the Commonwealth was not entitled to the prima facie showing of "fraudulent intent." Defendant failed to raise this issue with the trial court, and the record did not contain evidence affirmatively proving that defendant had no intent to defraud; instead, the evidence clearly indicated that defendant leased a television set, that he did not pay for it, and that he failed to return it or contact the store to explain his failure. McDowell v. Commonwealth, 57 Va. App. 308, 701 S.E.2d 820, 2010 Va. App. LEXIS 453 (2010).

Trial court erred in convicting defendant of fraudulent conversion of leased personal property because, although defendant breached defendant's written lease agreement with a rental company, the evidence failed to prove beyond a reasonable doubt that defendant intended to defraud the company by failing to abide by the terms of the agreement. The evidence showed only that defendant failed to make rental payments or to return a leased television set to the rental company after defendant failed to make the lease payments required by the lease agreement. Bert v. Commonwealth, 2011 Va. App. LEXIS 318 (Oct. 18, 2011).

Notice sufficient. — Notice requirement of subsection B of § 18.2-118 was satisfied by a store sending defendant a notice to his apartment that his failure to return rented property might result in prosecution. Adding the apartment number and the city to the address stated in the lease agreement did not violate the notice requirements as the address was even more accurate than the one in the agreement. McDowell v. Commonwealth, 57 Va. App. 308, 701 S.E.2d 820, 2010 Va. App. LEXIS 453 (2010).

Failure to return rental property conviction under § 18.2-118 was supported by sufficient evidence. While the date testified to by the store manager as the date that defendant rented the equipment was only a day before the sheriff recovered the property, the manager's testimony that defendant had the property for a couple of months and that substantial rent charges accrued as a result of defendant's failure to return the equipment supported the trial court's resolution of the conflict in the evidence. Commonwealth v. McNeal, 282 Va. 16, 710 S.E.2d 733, 2011 Va. LEXIS 129 (2011).

ARTICLE 5.

TRESPASS TO REALTY.

§ 18.2-119. Trespass after having been forbidden to do so; penalties.

If any person without authority of law goes upon or remains upon the lands, buildings or premises of another, or any portion or area thereof, after having been forbidden to do so, either orally or in writing, by the owner, lessee, custodian, or the agent of any such person, or other person lawfully in charge thereof, or after having been forbidden to do so by a sign or signs posted by or at the direction of such persons or the agent of any such person or by the holder of any easement or other right-of-way authorized by the instrument creating such interest to post such signs on such lands, structures, premises or portion or area thereof at a place or places where it or they may be reasonably seen, or if any person, whether he is the owner, tenant or otherwise entitled to the use of such land, building or premises, goes upon, or remains upon such land, building or premises after having been prohibited from doing so by a court of competent jurisdiction by an order issued pursuant to §§ 16.1-253, 16.1-253.1, 16.1-253.4, 16.1-278.2 through 16.1-278.6, 16.1-278.8, 16.1-278.14, 16.1-278.15, 16.1-279.1, 19.2-152.8, 19.2-152.9 or § 19.2-152.10 or an ex parte order issued pursuant to § 20-103, and after having been served with such order, he shall be guilty of a Class

1 misdemeanor. This section shall not be construed to affect in any way the provisions of §§ 18.2-132 through 18.2-136.

History.
Code 1950, § 18.1-173; 1960, c. 358; 1975, cc. 14, 15; 1982, c. 169; 1987, cc. 625, 705; 1991, c. 534; 1998, cc. 569, 684; 2011, c. 195.

Cross references.
For provision authorizing the owner, lessee, custodian, or person lawfully in charge of property to designate the local law-enforcement agency as a person lawfully in charge of the property for the purpose of enforcing trespass violations, see § 15.2-1717.1.

The 2011 amendments.
The 2011 amendment by c. 195 twice inserted "or the agent of any such person" and inserted "or at the direction of."

Law Review.
For brief discussion of "sit-ins," see 47 Va. L. Rev. 1464 (1961). For survey of Virginia criminal law and procedure for the year 1969-1970, see 56 Va. L. Rev. 1572 (1970). For survey of Virginia criminal law for the year 1971-1972, see 58 Va. L. Rev. 1206 (1972). For article, "Construction Law," see 45 U. Rich. L. Rev. 227 (2010).

Michie's Jurisprudence.
For related discussion, see 11B M.J. Labor, § 9; 18 M.J. Trespass, §§ 1, 27.

CASE NOTES

Section is constitutional. — There is nothing in this section when properly applied which infringes upon any privilege or right guaranteed by the federal Constitution. Hall v. Commonwealth, 188 Va. 72, 49 S.E.2d 369 (1948), appeal dismissed, 335 U.S. 875, 69 S. Ct. 240, 93 L. Ed. 418 (1949).

The increased punishments provided by the 1958 and 1960 amendments to this section, and the addition of § 18.2-120, may fairly be said to have been enacted with an eye to the "sit-in." The legislature's motive alone, however, could not invalidate the statute. Besides, the criminal elements of the present statutes are no more expansive than were those of the 1934 trespass statute. Henderson v. Trailway Bus Co., 194 F. Supp. 423 (E.D. Va. 1961), aff'd sub nom. Robinson v. Hunter, 374 U.S. 488, 83 S. Ct. 1875, 10 L. Ed. 2d 1044 (1963).

Defendant's conviction for violating the housing authority's trespass policy did not violate his right to freedom of intimate association, as his alleged right of intimate association did not permit him to commit intentional acts of criminal trespass on the housing authority's privately-owned property. Commonwealth v. Hicks, 267 Va. 573, 596 S.E.2d 74, 2004 Va. LEXIS 75 (2004).

First Amendment right of association and right to due process not violated. — The issuance of trespass notices barring two defendants from coming onto the premises of a public housing complex and the subsequent prosecution of those defendants for trespassing on the premises did not violate the defendants' First Amendment right of association or their right to due process. Collins v. Commonwealth, 30 Va. App. 443, 517 S.E.2d 277 (1999).

Violation of Interstate Commerce Act. — Where a bus terminal and restaurant were operated as an integral part of an interstate bus company's transportation service for interstate passengers, a conviction under this section of a black patron who refused to leave the portion of the restaurant reserved for white patrons was reversed as a violation of the Interstate Commerce Act. Boynton v. Virginia, 364 U.S. 454, 81 S. Ct. 182, 5 L. Ed. 2d 206 (1960).

Housing Authority's trespass procedure not overbroad. — In reversing the Virginia Supreme Court, the United States Supreme Court held that the Richmond Redevelopment and Housing Authority's trespassing policy, which barred people with no "legitimate business or social purpose" from entering, was not overbroad. Virginia v. Hicks, 539 U.S. 113, 539 U.S. 113, 123 S. Ct. 2191, 156 L. Ed. 2d 148, 2003 U.S. LEXIS 4782 (2003), reversing Commonwealth v. Hicks, 264 Va. 48, 563 S.E.2d 674 (2002).

Trial court's entry of trespass conviction against defendant was upheld, as defendant's argument that the trespass policy was vague, had to be rejected; defendant received a hand-delivered letter, which he signed and acknowledged, that directed him not to return to the housing authority's property and he had been convicted pursuant to that statute on two prior occasions for criminal trespass on the housing authority's property, which meant the statute and trespass policy were not vague. Commonwealth v. Hicks, 267 Va. 573, 596 S.E.2d 74, 2004 Va. LEXIS 75 (2004).

Section protects property rights. — The only purpose of this section is to protect the rights of the owners or those in lawful control of private property. Hall v. Commonwealth, 188 Va. 72, 49 S.E.2d 369 (1948); Price v. Commonwealth, 209 Va. 383, 164 S.E.2d 676 (1968).

In Hall v. Commonwealth, 188 Va. 72, 49 S.E.2d 369 (1948), the statement that the only purpose of this section is to protect the rights of the owners or those in lawful control of private property was made in the context of a controversy whether the trespass statute could be applied, consistently with First and Fourth Amendment guarantees, to the use of passageways in a privately owned apartment building and the case did not involve the applicability of the trespass statute to property owned by the Commonwealth. Johnson v. Commonwealth, 212 Va. 579, 186 S.E.2d 53 (1972).

Trespass not lesser-included offense of statutory burglary. — Trespass in violation of this section is not a lesser-included offense of § 18.2-91 and a trial court lacks the authority to convict for trespass under an indictment charging breaking and entering even if the accused fails to object. Shifflett v. Commonwealth, No. 2702-99-2, 2000 Va. App. LEXIS 843 (Ct. of Appeals Dec. 28, 2000).

When defendant was indicted for burglary, in violation of § 18.2-89, he could not validly be convicted of trespass, in violation of § 18.2-119, as statutory trespass was not a lesser-included offense of common-law burglary, unless he acquiesced in such a conviction, and counsel's statements leading the trial court to believe it could convict defendant of trespass if it found the evidence insufficient to convict him of burglary, were such an acquiescence. Freeman v. Commonwealth, No. 0796-02-3, 2003 Va. App. LEXIS 331 (Ct. of Appeals June 10, 2003).

Conviction under City of Alexandria Code § 13-1-33(a) compared. — Despite defendant's claim that the trial court erred in admitting an improperly authenticated document purportedly authorizing the police to bar persons from the City of Alexandria Redevelopment Housing Authority property, given the overwhelming evidence of defendant's guilt, including his admission that he was barred from said property, but traversed it anyway in an attempt to flee police, his trespassing conviction under City of Alexandria, Va., Code § 13-1-33(a), which substantially tracked the language of § 18.2-119, was upheld on appeal. Thus, any error committed by the trial court in admitting the authorization document into evidence did not substantially influence the court's verdict, and was therefore, harmless. Cheeks v. City of Alexandria, 2007 Va. App. LEXIS 261 (June 26, 2007).

Willful trespass required. — As a penal statute, the Virginia criminal trespass statute has been uniformly construed to require a willful trespass. Reed v. Commonwealth, 6 Va. App. 65, 366 S.E.2d 274 (1988).

On land under bona fide claim of right. — One cannot be convicted of trespass when one enters or stays upon the land under a bona fide claim of right. Reed v. Commonwealth, 6 Va. App. 65, 366 S.E.2d 274 (1988).

A good faith belief that one has a right to be on the premises negates criminal intent. Reed v. Commonwealth, 6 Va. App. 65, 366 S.E.2d 274 (1988).

A bona fide claim of right is a sincere, although perhaps mistaken, good faith belief that one has some legal right to be on the property. The claim need not be one of title or ownership, but it must rise to the level of authorization. Reed v. Commonwealth, 6 Va. App. 65, 366 S.E.2d 274 (1988).

Defendant was entitled to a jury instruction on the claim of right defense to criminal trespass because he testified that he believed, based on information from the police officer who issued him the trespass notice, that his barment from the premises had lapsed, and two witnesses corroborated his account of the statements of the officer issuing the trespass notice. O'Banion v. Commonwealth, 30 Va. App. 709, 519 S.E.2d 817 (1999).

This section applies to publicly owned property other than thoroughfares. Johnson v. Commonwealth, 212 Va. 579, 186 S.E.2d 53, cert. denied, 407 U.S. 925, 92 S. Ct. 2458, 32 L. Ed. 2d 812 (1972).

The "**thoroughfares**" to which the case of *Johnson v. Commonwealth*, 212 Va. 579, 186 S.E.2d 53 (1972) reaffirms that this section does not apply, is limited to those ways or passages designated for general public access. Miller v. Commonwealth, 10 Va. App. 472, 393 S.E.2d 431 (1990).

Alley was not "thoroughfare." — Alley located on Housing Authority property, which was government property and had been clearly marked to deter trespassing, as to which the Housing Authority had an express agreement with the police to enforce the policy that access to the alley be restricted and not open it to the general public, and which had been vacated by municipal ordinance, was not intended for public use and therefore was not a "thoroughfare." Thus, this section operated to bar defendant's use of the alley. Miller v. Commonwealth, 10 Va. App. 472, 393 S.E.2d 431 (1990).

Section applies to a building which is owned by the Commonwealth. Johnson v. Commonwealth, 212 Va. 579, 186 S.E.2d 53, cert. denied, 407 U.S. 925, 92 S. Ct. 2458, 32 L. Ed. 2d 812 (1972).

This section applies only to places where a person goes "without authority of law," meaning property not at the time affected with a public interest. Racial segregation on property in private demesne has never in law been condemnable. Indeed, the occupant may lawfully forbid any and all persons, regardless of his reason or their race or religion to enter or remain upon any part of his premises which are not devoted to a public use. Assurance of this right is the entire and sole aid of this section. Henderson v. Trailway Bus Co., 194 F. Supp. 423 (E.D. Va. 1961), aff'd sub nom. Robinson v. Hunter, 374 U.S. 488, 83 S. Ct. 1875, 10 L. Ed. 2d 1044 (1963).

Trespass on Indian reservation. — Evidence supported defendant's conviction of trespassing on the Mattaponi Indian Tribe's reservation where the Mattaponi Tribal Council, at a regular tribal meeting, voted to bar defendant from the reservation, and the Supreme Court of Virginia had recognized that the Tribal Council was the governmental body of the sovereign Mattaponi Indian Tribe; Va. Acts 1894, c. 845, and its amended version, Acts 1896, c. 843, were not intended to provide the sole method by which the Mattaponi Indian Tribe could expel or forbid an individual from coming upon the reservation. Custalow v. Commonwealth, 43 Va. App. 71, 596 S.E.2d 95, 2004 Va. App. LEXIS 235 (2004).

Student protestors. — When actions of student protestors are measured against the standards of conduct immunized by the First Amendment and it is clear that their actions are not immunized since their conduct materially disrupted classwork, created substantial disorder and materially interfered with the rights of others, this section is properly invoked. Pleasants v. Commonwealth, 214 Va. 646, 203 S.E.2d 114 (1974).

As the duly authorized agent of the school board, the principal is vested with the inherent power to revoke, for good cause, the right of any student to remain upon school property when that student, alone or in concert with others, disrupts regular school activities or the maintenance of good order and discipline, and the student thus has no "authority of law" to remain on school premises. Pleasants v. Commonwealth, 214 Va. 646, 203 S.E.2d 114 (1974).

Necessity no defense to trespass on clinic to distribute anti-abortion literature. — Necessity is not a defense to a charge of trespassing on the premises of a women's medical clinic in order to give anti-abortion literature to patients considering an abortion since there were reasonable and legal alternatives to their violation of the law. Buckley v. City of Falls Church, 7 Va. App. 32, 371 S.E.2d 827 (1988).

The trial court did not err in finding that the defendant was not in the housing development under a legitimate claim of right; he did not live there, was not visiting a resident there, and had been forbidden by the "No Trespassing" signs from being there. Thus, the evidence was sufficient to support the trespass conviction. Boone v. Commonwealth, No. 2575-95-2, 1997 Va. App. LEXIS 56 (Ct. of Appeals Feb. 4, 1997).

Conviction of minister of Jehovah's Witnesses under this section for entering an apartment house and calling on the tenants contrary to a rule of the apartment house, after being informed of the rule and warned to desist, was affirmed in Hall v. Commonwealth, 188 Va. 72, 49 S.E.2d 369 (1948), appeal dismissed, 335 U.S. 875, 69 S. Ct. 240, 93 L. Ed. 418 (1949).

Entering posted property. — Entering property of Dan River Mills where signs forbidding such entry were posted was a violation of this section. Hubbard v. Commonwealth, 207 Va. 673, 152 S.E.2d 250 (1967).

Proof that authorized party posted "No Trespassing" sign required. — Evidence was insufficient to prove that defendant committed trespass in violation of § 18.2-119 because the Commonwealth was required to prove beyond a reasonable doubt that the property was posted by one of the enumerated parties having authority to do so, but the Commonwealth presented no evidence regarding who posted "no trespassing" signs on the property, and, therefore, the record contained no indication whether that person or persons had authority to post the property under § 18.2-119; the plain language of § 18.2-119 requires proof, as an element of the crime of trespass, that oral or written notice of the proscription against entry be given or a "no trespassing" sign be posted by the owner, lessee, custodian, or other person lawfully in charge of the property, or by the holder of an easement or other right-of-way who was authorized to post such a sign by the instrument creating that person's interest in the property, and proof of the existence of "no trespassing" signs on the property alone is insufficient to satisfy the elements of trespass set forth in § 18.2-119. Baker v. Commonwealth, 278 Va. 656, 685 S.E.2d 661, 2009 Va. LEXIS 97 (2009).

Right of police officer to remain on premises. — The right of a police officer to remain in a poolroom should be distinguished from the right of an ordinary citizen to remain on premises after being asked to leave. Parker v. McCoy, 212 Va. 808, 188 S.E.2d 222 (1972).

A police officer has a law-given right, rather than an owner-consensual right, in the line of his duty to enter a business establishment to observe at least what is not hidden from view in the establishment. And an officer has the same right to remain on the premises until he has discharged his duty, despite the owner's request that he leave. Parker v. McCoy, 212 Va. 808, 188 S.E.2d 222 (1972).

Sufficiency of evidence. — The evidence was sufficient to support the defendant's conviction where the victim, his estranged girlfriend, testified that, when she failed to respond to the defendant knocking on her doors and window, the defendant entered her trailer without her permission; although the victim suffered from memory loss, paranoia, and bi-polar disorder due to an earlier car crash, her testimony to the relevant events did not seem inherently incredible and the trial court had been entitled to weigh these facts in determining the victim's credibility. Whitby v. Commonwealth, No. 1343-99-1, 2000 Va. App. LEXIS 551 (Ct. of Appeals July 25, 2000).

Where an officer observed appellant at a motel after visiting hours, sufficient evidence supported appellant's trespassing conviction because the fact finder could reasonably conclude that appellant was lying when appellant claimed not to have seen any of the signs prohibiting patrons from having visitors after 10:00 p.m. Yancey v. Commonwealth, 2008 Va. App. LEXIS 29 (Jan. 15, 2008).

Defendant's conviction for trespassing was proper, as the evidence was found to be sufficient. The trial court, as the finder of fact, rejected defendant's argument that defendant entered a property owner's property in a good-faith attempt to visit defendant's children. Wyatt v. Commonwealth, — Va. App. —, — S.E.2d —, 2008 Va. App. LEXIS 203 (Apr. 29, 2008).

Defendant's conviction for trespassing under § 18.2-119 was appropriate, in part because he had informed the university registrar of his intention to withdraw from the university after completing his course work for the spring semester and he was aware that he was not permitted to occupy the apartment beyond May 31, 2009. However, he continued to occupy the apartment on June 1, 2009. Maciel v. Commonwealth, 2011 Va. App. LEXIS 9 (Jan. 11, 2011).

Where defendant was stopped outside a convenience store, the officer possessed a reasonable suspicion that defendant was trespassing because (1) the convenience store was in a high-crime area, (2) the particular location and manner in which defendant and another man were standing suggested that they may have been engaged in the specific, ongoing crime of trespassing, (3) defendant's "evasive behavior" upon seeing the officer's patrol car was a pertinent factor, and (4) defendant took a path that led defendant past the convenience store's front door but made no effort to enter. United States v. Bumpers, 705 F.3d 168, 2013 U.S. App. LEXIS 1075 (4th Cir. 2013).

Intent required. — Although this section silent as to intent, the case law in Virginia has uniformly construed the statutory offense of criminal trespass to require a willful trespass and, as such, one who enters or stays upon another's land under a bona fide claim of right cannot be convicted of trespass. O'Banion v. Commonwealth, 33 Va. App. 47, 531 S.E.2d 599, 2000 Va. App. LEXIS 536 (2000), overruled in part by Harris v. Commonwealth, 274 Va. 409, 650 S.E.2d 89 (2007), which held that a box cutter does not meet the definition of the item "razor" enumerated in § 18.2-308 A.

Defendant's argument that the housing authority's policy against criminal trespass was vague and therefore could not be applied to him, had to be rejected, as the Commonwealth had to prove that defendant meant to violate the statute because the statute had an intent requirement and it was able to do so. Commonwealth v. Hicks, 267 Va. 573, 596 S.E.2d 74, 2004 Va. LEXIS 75 (2004).

Defendant lacked requisite intent. — Where the undisputed evidence established that defendant was on island under an agreement with construction company that in exchange for his services as night watchman, defendant could stay on the island and the construction company would build him a shelter, defendant established a bona fide claim of right as a matter of law, and because he acted on that good faith belief, he could not have had the requisite intent for a criminal trespass conviction. That his belief may have been wrong or that he could have been evicted in a civil action did not render his conduct criminal. Without the criminal intent he committed no criminal trespass. Reed v. Commonwealth, 6 Va. App. 65, 366 S.E.2d 274 (1988).

Police lacked probable cause to believe defendant was trespassing at a housing project. — Defendant's evasive answers to a police sergeant's questions inside a housing project tenant's apartment did not provide the police officers with probable cause to arrest defendant for trespassing because before questioning defendant, the police sergeant had resolved any doubt as to defendant's status as a trespasser. The tenant had already related that she knew defendant, had allowed appellant into her apartment, and had previously let him into her apartment to use her telephone; therefore, defendant was no longer a suspected trespasser. Parham v. Commonwealth, — Va. App. —, — S.E.2d —, 2005 Va. App. LEXIS 381 (Oct. 4, 2005).

Search incident to lawful arrest. — Search of defendant which showed that defendant had a bag of marijuana in defendant's pants pocket was permissible as a search incident to a lawful arrest since defendant was forbidden to be on the property from which defendant had been removed shortly before police were informed that defendant was back on the property, and, thus, defendant was committing a trespass; accordingly, police officer could frisk defendant for weapons, especially since one officer noticed that defendant had a bulge in defendant's right front pocket and was entitled to pat defendant down for the officer's own personal safety. McCracken v. Commonwealth, 39 Va. App. 254, 572 S.E.2d 493, 2002 Va. App. LEXIS 696 (2002).

Upon supplying defendant's personal information (defendant's name, date of birth, and social security number) to the dispatcher and learning that defendant had been previously warned to stay off the property, the police officer possessed probable cause to believe that defendant was violating § 18.2-119; accordingly, the officer was justified in arresting defendant and in searching defendant incident to that arrest, and the trial court did not err in denying the motions to suppress and to strike the evidence. Wyatt v. Commonwealth, No. 2722-01-1, 2002 Va. App. LEXIS 781 (Ct. of Appeals Dec. 31, 2002).

Although defendant presented evidence that provided a defense to a charge of trespass under this section, the evidence did not defeat a police officer's belief of guilt; as a result, the trial court properly denied defendant's motion to suppress. McClam v. Commonwealth, No. 3349-02-2, 2004 Va. App. LEXIS 208 (Ct. of Appeals May 4, 2004).

When an officer "arrested" defendant for trespass, he did not use the correct procedure when he placed her in custody, rather than issuing her a summons, because trespass was a class 1 misdemeanor, but, if there was a statutory violation, it did not require that evidence seized from defendant in a search incident to her arrest be suppressed, because exclusion of evidence was not an available remedy for a statutory violation, where no constitutional violation occurred. Coppedge v. Commonwealth, No. 2920-03-1, 2005 Va. App. LEXIS 23 (Ct. of Appeals Jan. 18, 2005).

Police sergeant did not have probable cause to believe defendant was trespassing at a posted housing project complex even though he claimed defendant "darted" around the building and appeared to be in flight from the unmarked police car. Although the sergeant testified that after defendant saw the unmarked police vehicle, he "darted" to the rear of the building, there was no evidence of flight or "darting" in the record; furthermore, the sergeant did not see defendant outside the apartment; instead, his knowledge was limited to what the state trooper told him, and the trooper never indicated that defendant "darted." Parham v. Commonwealth, — Va. App. —, — S.E.2d —, 2005 Va. App. LEXIS 381 (Oct. 4, 2005).

Denial of defendant's motion to suppress was proper as defendant was arrested for trespassing under § 18.2-119, and the Fourth Amendment's exclusionary rule did not require the exclusion of the evidence seized from defendant during a search incident to a valid arrest for a misdemeanor violation for which § 19.2-74 required release on a summons. Simmons v. Commonwealth, 2008 Va. App. LEXIS 360 (July 29, 2008).

Evidence supported defendant's conviction of possession of cocaine with intent to distribute in violation of § 18.2-248 as defendant was aware of, had control of, and consciously possessed the cocaine found on the front passenger floorboard of a car defendant had driven on a suspended license, after defendant was arrested for trespassing under § 18.2-119 as: (1) the officers saw a clear plastic bag on the front passenger floorboard, which contained 41.1 grams of cocaine, worth about $4,100; (2) the packaging of the cocaine was consistent with "mid-level" distribution; (3) 10 grams of marijuana, $209 in cash, and a cell phone were discovered on defendant; (4) the cash was organized in a manner consistent with the sale of drugs; and (5) neither the registered owner nor any previous occupant would likely have left the cocaine sitting unsecured in the car. Simmons v. Commonwealth, 2008 Va. App. LEXIS 360 (July 29, 2008).

Applied in Northern Va. Women's Medical Ctr. v. Balch, 617 F.2d 1045 (4th Cir. 1980); Chaffinch v. C & P Tel. Co., 227 Va. 68, 313 S.E.2d 376 (1984); Beaudett v. City of Hampton, 775 F.2d 1274 (4th Cir. 1985); McAfee v. Deale, 20 F. Supp. 2d 943 (E.D. Va. 1998).

OPINIONS OF THE ATTORNEY GENERAL

Polling places on school property. — Because there is no conflict between this section and §§ 24.2-307, 24.2-310 B, and 24.2-310.1, requiring polling places to be located in public buildings such as public school buildings, an individual prohibited from entering school property may enter the portion of that property designated as a polling place solely for the purpose of casting his vote. See opinion of Attorney General to The Honorable James M. Shuler, Member, House of Delegates, 05-093 (2/8/06).

§ 18.2-119.1. Validity of signs forbidding trespass; penalty.

If any person knowingly and intentionally posts No Trespassing signs on the land of another without the permission of a person authorized to post such signs on that land, he shall be guilty of a Class 3 misdemeanor.

History.
1999, c. 274.

§ 18.2-120. Instigating, etc., such trespass by others; preventing service to persons not forbidden to trespass.

If any person shall solicit, urge, encourage, exhort, instigate or procure another or others to go upon or remain upon the lands, buildings, or premises of another, or any part, portion or area thereof, knowing such other person or persons to have been forbidden, either orally or in writing, to do so by the owner, lessee, custodian or other person lawfully in charge thereof, or knowing such other person or persons to have been forbidden to do so by a sign or signs posted on such lands, buildings, premises or part, portion or area thereof at a place or places where it or they may reasonably be seen; or if any person shall, on such lands, buildings, premises or part, portion or area thereof prevent or seek to prevent the owner, lessee, custodian, person in charge or any of his employees from rendering service to any person or persons not so forbidden, he shall be guilty of a Class 1 misdemeanor.

History.
Code 1950, § 18.1-173.1; 1960, c. 358; 1975, cc. 14, 15.

CASE NOTES

This section applies only to places where a person goes "without authority of law," meaning property not at the time affected with a public interest. Racial segregation on property in private demesne has never in law been condemnable. Indeed, the occupant may lawfully forbid any and all persons regardless of his reason or their race or religion, to enter or remain upon any part of his premises which are not devoted to a public use. Assurance of this right is the entire and sole aim of this section. Henderson v. Trailway Bus Co., 194 F. Supp. 423 (E.D. Va. 1961), aff'd sub nom. Robinson v. Hunter, 374 U.S. 488, 83 S. Ct. 1875, 10 L. Ed. 2d 1044 (1963).

It was enacted with an eye to the "sit-in." — The increased punishments provided by the 1958 and 1960 amendments to § 18.2-119, and the addition of this section, may fairly be said to have been enacted with an eye to the "sit-in." The legislature's motive alone however, could not invalidate the statute. Besides, the criminal elements of the present statutes are no more expansive than were those of the 1934 trespass statute. Henderson v. Trailway Bus Co., 194 F. Supp. 423 (E.D. Va. 1961), aff'd sub nom. Robinson v. Hunter, 374 U.S. 488, 83 S. Ct. 1875, 10 L. Ed. 2d 1044 (1963).

Applied in Northern Va. Women's Medical Ctr. v. Balch, 617 F.2d 1045 (4th Cir. 1980).

§ 18.2-121. Entering property of another for purpose of damaging it, etc.

It shall be unlawful for any person to enter the land, dwelling, outhouse or any other building of another for the purpose of damaging such property or any of the contents thereof or in any manner to interfere with the rights of the owner, user or the occupant thereof to use such property free from interference.

Any person violating the provisions of this section shall be guilty of a Class 1 misdemeanor. However, if a person intentionally selects the property entered because of the race, religious conviction, color or national origin of the owner, user or occupant of the property, the person shall be guilty of a Class 6 felony, and the penalty upon conviction shall include a term of confinement of at least six months, 30 days of which shall be a mandatory minimum term of confinement.

History.
Code 1950, § 18.1-183; 1960, c. 358; 1975, cc. 14, 15; 1994, c. 658; 1997, c. 833; 2004, c. 461.

Michie's Jurisprudence.
For related discussion, see 5B M.J. Criminal Procedure, § 78.

CASE NOTES

This section is not a lesser included offense of statutory burglary. Crump v. Commonwealth, 13 Va. App. 286, 411 S.E.2d 238 (1991).

This section is not lesser included offense of § 18.2-90 or § 18.2-91. — Section 18.2-90, which identifies § 18.2-91's prohibited acts, includes offenses against properties not specified in this section, i.e., ships, vessels, river craft. Thus, a violation of § 18.2-91 will not invariably and necessarily include a violation of this section and the misdemeanor is, consequently, not a lesser included offense of either § 18.2-90 or § 18.2-91. Crump v. Commonwealth, 13 Va. App. 286, 411 S.E.2d 238 (1991).

Applied in Northern Va. Women's Medical Ctr. v. Balch, 617 F.2d 1045 (4th Cir. 1980).

§ 18.2-121.1. Permitting certain animals to run at large.

The owner or manager of any animal mentioned in § 55-316, who shall knowingly permit such animal to run at large in any county or portion thereof, under quarantine, shall be deemed to be guilty of a Class 4 misdemeanor.

History.
Code 1950, § 8-885; 1977, c. 624.

§ 18.2-121.2. Trespass by spotlight on agricultural land.

If any person shall willfully use a spotlight or similar lighting apparatus to cast a light upon private property used for livestock or crops without the written permission of the person in legal possession of such property, he shall be guilty of a Class 3 misdemeanor.

The prohibition of this section shall not apply to light cast by (i) permanently installed outdoor lighting fixtures, (ii) headlamps on vehicles moving in normal travel on public or private roads, (iii) railroad locomotives or rolling stock being operated on the tracks or right-of-way of a railroad company, (iv) aircraft or watercraft, (v) apparatus used by employees of any public utility in maintaining the utility's lines and equipment, (vi) apparatus used by members of rescue squads or fire departments in the performance of their official duties, (vii) apparatus used by any law-enforcement officer in the performance of his official duties, or (viii) farm machinery or motor vehicles being used in normal farming operations.

History.
1981, c. 460.

§ 18.2-122. Repealed by Acts 1998, c. 6.

§ 18.2-123. Repealed by Acts 2004, c. 459.

§ 18.2-124. Jurisdiction over offenses committed in Capitol Square.

The Circuit Court of the City of Richmond shall have jurisdiction to try cases of offenses committed in Capitol Square except as hereinafter provided. The district court of the City of Richmond shall have jurisdiction to try misdemeanor cases arising under § 18.2-122, and all other offenses committed in the Capitol Square of which it would have jurisdiction if committed within the corporate limits and jurisdiction of the city; and the Capitol Police, or any member thereof, shall have the same authority to arrest and to swear out warrants for offenses committed on the Capitol Square as policemen of the City of Richmond have to arrest or to swear out warrants for offenses committed within the jurisdiction of the city.

History.
Code 1950, § 2.1-97; 1966, c. 677; 1975, cc. 14, 15; 2004, c. 459.

Editor's note.
Secton 18.2-122, referred to above, was repealed by Acts 1998, c. 6.

§ 18.2-125. Trespass at night upon any cemetery.

If any person, without the consent of the owner, proprietor or custodian, go or enter in the nighttime, upon the premises, property, driveways or walks of any cemetery, either public or private, for any purpose other than to visit the burial lot or grave of some member of his family, he shall be guilty of a Class 4 misdemeanor.

History.
Code 1950, § 18.1-181; 1960, c. 358; 1975, cc. 14, 15.

§ 18.2-126. Violation of sepulture; defilement of a dead human body; penalties.

A. If a person unlawfully disinters or displaces a dead human body, or any part of a dead human body which has been deposited in any vault, grave or other burial place, he is guilty of a Class 4 felony.

B. If a person willfully and intentionally physically defiles a dead human body he is guilty of a Class 6 felony. For the purposes of this section, the term "defile" shall not include any autopsy or the recovery of organs or tissues for transplantation, or any other lawful purpose.

History.
Code 1950, § 18.1-243; 1960, c. 358; 1975, cc. 14, 15; 1995, c. 306.

Michie's Jurisprudence.
For related discussion, see 3B M.J. Cemeteries, § 8; 5C M.J. Dead Bodies, §§ 1, 3.

§ 18.2-127. Injuries to churches, church property, cemeteries, burial grounds, etc.; penalty.

A. Any person who willfully or maliciously commits any of the following acts is guilty of a Class 1 misdemeanor:

1. Destroys, removes, cuts, breaks, or injures any tree, shrub, or plant on any church property or within any cemetery or lot of any memorial or monumental association;

2. Destroys, mutilates, injures, or removes and carries away any flowers, wreaths, vases, or other ornaments placed within any church or on church property, or placed upon or around any grave, tomb, monument, or lot in any cemetery, graveyard, or other place of burial; or

3. Obstructs proper ingress to and egress from any church or any cemetery or lot belonging to any memorial or monumental association.

B. Any person who willfully or maliciously destroys, mutilates, defaces, injures, or removes any object or structure permanently attached or affixed within any church or on church property, any tomb, monument, gravestone, or other structure placed within any cemetery, graveyard, or place of burial, or within any lot belonging to any memorial or monumental association, or any fence, railing, or other work for the protection or ornament of any tomb, monument, gravestone, or other structure aforesaid, or of any cemetery lot within any cemetery is guilty of a Class 6 felony. A person convicted under this section who is required to pay restitution by the court shall be required to pay restitution to the church, if the property damaged is property of the church, or to the owner of a cemetery, if the property damaged is located within such cemetery regardless of whether the property damaged is owned by the cemetery or by another person.

C. This section shall not apply to any work which is done by the authorities of a church or congregation in the maintenance or improvement of any church property or any burial ground or cemetery belonging to it and under its management or control and which does not injure or result in the removal of a tomb, monument, gravestone, grave marker or vault. For purposes of this section, "church" shall mean any place of worship, and "church property" shall mean any educational building or community center owned or rented by a church.

History.
Code 1950, § 18.1-244; 1960, c. 358; 1975, cc. 14, 15; 1982, c. 561; 1983, c. 579; 1990, c. 510; 2004, c. 203.

§ 18.2-128. Trespass upon church or school property.

A. Any person who, without the consent of some person authorized to give such consent, goes or enters upon, in the nighttime, the premises or property of any church or upon any school property for any purpose other than to attend a meeting or service held or conducted in such church or school property, shall be guilty of a Class 3 misdemeanor.

B. It shall be unlawful for any person, whether or not a church member or student, to enter upon or remain upon any church or school property in violation of (i) any direction to vacate the property by a person authorized to give such direction or (ii) any posted notice which contains such information, posted at a place where it reasonably may be seen. Each time such person enters upon or remains on the posted premises or after such direction that person refuses to vacate such property, it shall constitute a separate offense.

A violation of this subsection shall be punishable as a Class 1 misdemeanor, except that any person, other than a parent, who violates this subsection on school property with the intent to abduct a student shall be guilty of a Class 6 felony.

C. For purposes of this section: (i) "school property" includes a school bus as defined in § 46.2-100 and (ii) "church" means any place of worship and includes any educational building or community center owned or leased by a church.

History.
Code 1950, § 18.1-182; 1960, c. 358; 1975, cc. 14, 15; 1988, c. 497; 1989, c. 680; 1993, c. 961; 1994, c. 326; 1995, cc. 493, 642; 1997, c. 779.

Law Review.
For survey on legal issues involving children in Virginia for 1989, see 23 U. Rich. L. Rev. 705 (1989).

Michie's Jurisprudence.
For related discussion, see 3C M.J. Colleges and Universities, § 1; 16 M.J. Religious Societies, § 3.

CASE NOTES

Good faith defense not shown. — The trial court did not err in rejecting the defendant's good faith defense based upon his asserted belief that he and other anti-abortion demonstrators were not on school property while they were on the sidewalk in front of the school where several authorized persons, including the school principal and the superintendent of the school district, told the demonstrators to leave, they refused to do so, and, upon learning from police officers that they could be arrested for failing to leave, the defendant responded, "then you'll have to arrest us." Reyes v. Commonwealth, No. 0480-98-3 (Ct. of Appeals Apr. 13, 1999).

§ 18.2-129. Repealed by Acts 1989, c. 680.

Cross references.
As to trespass upon church or school property, see § 18.2-128.

§ 18.2-130. Peeping or spying into dwelling or enclosure.

A. It shall be unlawful for any person to enter upon the property of another and secretly or furtively peep, spy or attempt to peep or spy into or through a window, door or other aperture of any building, structure, or other enclosure of any nature occupied or intended for occupancy as a dwelling, whether or not such building, structure or enclosure is permanently situated or transportable and whether or not such occupancy is permanent or temporary, or to do the same, without just cause, upon property owned by him and leased or rented to another under circumstances that would violate the occupant's reasonable expectation of privacy.

B. It shall be unlawful for any person to use a peephole or other aperture to secretly or furtively peep, spy or attempt to peep or spy into a restroom, dressing room, locker room, hotel room, motel room, tanning bed, tanning booth, bedroom or other location or enclosure for the purpose of viewing any nonconsenting person who is totally nude, clad in undergarments, or in a state of undress exposing the genitals, pubic area, buttocks or female breast and the circumstances are such that the person would otherwise have a reasonable expectation of privacy.

C. The provisions of this section shall not apply to a lawful criminal investigation or a correctional official or local or regional jail official conducting surveillance for security purposes or during an investigation of alleged misconduct involving a person committed to the Department of Corrections or to a local or regional jail.

D. As used in this section, *"peephole"* means any hole, crack or other similar opening through which a person can see.

E. A violation of this section is a Class 1 misdemeanor.

History.
Code 1950, § 18.1-174; 1960, c. 358; 1975, cc. 14, 15; 1992, c. 520; 1999, c. 351; 2003, cc. 81, 87.

Michie's Jurisprudence.
For related discussion, see 1A M.J. Adultery, Fornication and Lewdness, § 2.

CASE NOTES

Prosecution not limited to those who are wholly hidden from view. Rather, it prohibits surreptitious peeping with the intent to invade the privacy of another. Copeland v. Commonwealth, 31 Va. App. 512, 525 S.E.2d 9 (2000); Morales v. Commonwealth, 31 Va. App. 541, 525 S.E.2d 23 (2000).

§ 18.2-131. Trespass upon licensed shooting preserve.

It shall be unlawful for any person to trespass on a licensed shooting preserve. Any person convicted of such trespass shall be guilty of a Class 4 misdemeanor and shall be responsible for all damage. Owners or keepers of dogs trespassing on preserves shall be responsible for all damage done by such dogs.

History.
Code 1950, § 29-49; 1975, cc. 14, 15.

Cross references.
For revocation of licenses and penalties if any person is found guilty of violating any of the hunting, trapping or inland fish laws or regulations, see § 29.1-338.

§ 18.2-132. Trespass by hunters and fishers.

Any person who goes on the lands, waters, ponds, boats or blinds of another to hunt, fish or trap without the consent of the landowner or his agent shall be deemed guilty of a Class 3 misdemeanor.

History.
Code 1950, § 29-165; 1954, c. 155; 1962, c. 469; 1975, cc. 14, 15.

Cross references.
For revocation of licenses and penalties if any person is found guilty of violating any of the hunting, trapping or inland fish laws or regulations, see § 29.1-338.

CASE NOTES

Willful intent. — State is required to prove that a defendant had a willful intent to violate this section, the trespass by a hunter statute, as the general criminal trespass statute's requirement that the state prove willful intent means that this section, which is silent on the issue of intent, has the same willful intent requirement. Lawson v. Commonwealth, 35 Va. App. 610, 547 S.E.2d 513, 2001 Va. App. LEXIS 339 (2001).

As to private ownership of stream, see Boerner v. McCallister, 197 Va. 169, 89 S.E.2d 23 (1955).

As to prosecution dependent upon right of riparian proprietor to prohibit hunting between high and low-water marks along part of his land, see Miller v. Commonwealth, 159 Va. 924, 166 S.E. 557 (1932).

§ 18.2-133. Refusal of person on land, etc., of another to identify himself.

Any person who goes on the lands, waters, ponds, boats or blinds of another to hunt, fish, or trap and willfully refuses to identify himself when requested by the landowner or his agent so to do shall be deemed guilty of a Class 4 misdemeanor.

History.
Code 1950, § 29-165.1; 1954, c. 156; 1962, c. 469; 1975, cc. 14, 15.

Cross references.
For revocation of licenses and penalties if any person is found guilty of violating any of the hunting, trapping or inland fish laws or regulations, see § 29.1-338.

§ 18.2-134. Trespass on posted property.

Any person who goes on the lands, waters, ponds, boats or blinds of another, which have been posted in accordance with the provisions of § 18.2-134.1, to hunt, fish or trap except with the written consent of or in the presence of the owner or his agent shall be guilty of a Class 1 misdemeanor.

History.
Code 1950, § 29-166; 1954, c. 155; 1962, c. 469; 1975, cc. 14, 15; 1987, c. 603.

Cross references.
For revocation of licenses and penalties if any person is found guilty of violating any of the hunting, trapping or inland fish laws or regulations, see § 29.1-338.

§ 18.2-134.1. Method of posting lands.

A. The owner or lessee of property described in § 18.2-134 may post property by (i) placing signs prohibiting hunting, fishing or trapping where they may reasonably be seen; or (ii) placing identifying paint marks on trees or posts at each road entrance and adjacent to public roadways and public waterways adjoining the property. Each paint mark shall be a vertical line of at least two inches in width and at least eight inches in length and the center of the mark shall be no less than three feet nor more than six feet from the ground or normal water surface. Such paint marks shall be readily visible to any person approaching the property.

B. The type and color of the paint to be used for posting shall be prescribed by the Department of Game and Inland Fisheries.

History.
1987, c. 603.

§ 18.2-135. Destruction of posted signs; posting land of another.

Any person who shall mutilate, destroy or take down any "posted," "no hunting" or similar sign or poster on the lands or waters of another, or who shall post such sign or poster on the lands or waters of another, without the consent of the landowner or his agent, shall be deemed guilty of a Class 3 misdemeanor and his hunting, fishing, and trapping license and privileges shall be revoked for a period of one to five years from the date of conviction.

History.
Code 1950, § 29-167; 1962, c. 469; 1975, cc. 14, 15; 2010, c. 183.

Cross references.
For revocation of licenses and penalties if any person is found guilty of violating any of the hunting, trapping or inland fish laws or regulations, see § 29.1-338.

The 2010 amendments.
The 2010 amendment by c. 183 substituted "fishing, and trapping license and privileges" for "license" and "of one to five years from the date of conviction" for "not exceeding the expiration date of such license."

§ 18.2-136. Right of certain hunters to go on lands of another; carrying firearms or bows and arrows prohibited.

Fox hunters and coon hunters, when the chase begins on other lands, may follow their dogs on prohibited lands, and hunters of all other game, when the chase begins on other lands, may go upon prohibited lands to retrieve their dogs, falcons, hawks, or owls but may not carry firearms or bows and arrows on their persons or hunt any game while thereon. The use of vehicles to retrieve dogs, falcons, hawks, or owls on prohibited lands shall be allowed only with the permission of the landowner or his agent. Any person who goes on prohibited lands to retrieve his dogs, falcons, hawks, or owls pursuant to this section and who willfully refuses to identify himself when requested by the landowner or his agent to do so is guilty of a Class 4 misdemeanor.

History.
Code 1950, § 29-168; 1964, c. 600; 1975, cc. 14, 15; 1988, c. 593; 1991, cc. 317, 327; 2007, cc. 145, 658; 2011, c. 191.

The 2011 amendments.
The 2011 amendment by c. 191 inserted "falcons, hawks, or owls" three times.

§ 18.2-136.1. Enforcement of §§ 18.2-131 through 18.2-135.

Conservation police officers, sheriffs and all other law-enforcement officers shall enforce the provisions of §§ 18.2-131, 18.2-132, 18.2-133, 18.2-134 and 18.2-135.

History.
1975, cc. 14, 15.

Editor's note.
At the direction of the Virginia Code Commission, "Conservation police officers" was substituted for "Game wardens" to conform to the name change by Acts 2007, c. 87.

ARTICLE 6.

DAMAGE TO REALTY AND PERSONALTY THEREON.

§ 18.2-137. Injuring, etc., any property, monument, etc.

A. If any person unlawfully destroys, defaces, damages or removes without the intent to steal any property, real or personal, not his own, or breaks down, destroys, defaces, damages or removes without the intent to steal, any monument or memorial for war veterans described in § 15.2-1812, any monument erected for the purpose of marking the site of any engagement fought during the War between the States, or for the purpose of designating the boundaries of any city, town, tract of land, or any tree marked for that purpose, he shall be guilty of a Class 3 misdemeanor; provided that the court may, in its discretion, dismiss the charge if the locality or organization responsible for maintaining the injured property, monument, or memorial files a written affidavit with the court stating it has received full payment for the injury.

B. If any person intentionally causes such injury, he shall be guilty of (i) a Class 1 misdemeanor if the value of or damage to the property, memorial or monument is less than $1,000 or (ii) a Class 6 felony if the value of or damage to the property, memorial or monument is $1,000 or more. The amount of loss caused by the destruction, defacing, damage or removal of such property, memorial or monument may be established by proof of the fair market cost of repair or fair market replacement value. Upon conviction, the court may order that the defendant pay restitution.

History.
Code 1950, § 18.1-172; 1960, c. 358; 1975, cc. 14, 15, 598; 1990, c. 933; 1999, c. 625.

Editor's note.

The above section is § 18.2-137 as enacted by Acts 1975, c. 598. Pursuant to § 30-152, it has been substituted for § 18.2-137 as enacted by Acts 1975, cc. 14 and 15.

Law Review.

For 2007 annual survey article, "Criminal Law and Procedure," see 42 U. Rich. L. Rev. 311 (2007).

Michie's Jurisprudence.

For related discussion, see 3A M.J. Boundaries, § 53; 12A M.J. Malicious Mischief, § 3.

CASE NOTES

One may be convicted of destruction of private property and burglary. — One may be convicted of destruction of private property in violation of this section, in addition to being convicted of burglary in violation of § 18.2-91, as a result of causing damage to property when breaking and entering a building because each offense requires proof of a fact not required for the other. Fitzgerald v. Commonwealth, 11 Va. App. 625, 401 S.E.2d 208 (1991).

Prosecution for breaking and entering and destroying private property not barred by § 19.2-294. — Section 19.2-294, which bars a prosecution for a violation of one statute if a defendant has been convicted of violation of another statute for the same act, is inapplicable where the "same act" involved was the breaking of the doors of the places broken into. This act, although common to both the convictions of breaking and entering and the convictions for destroying private property, was a violation of this section, destroying private property, but was not a violation of § 18.2-91, statutory burglary. Thus, the same act was a violation of only one of the two statutes, not both. Fitzgerald v. Commonwealth, 11 Va. App. 625, 401 S.E.2d 208 (1991).

Conviction for killing dogs. — Definition of destruction of personal property applied in prosecution for killing dogs and destroying hunting equipment, as dogs and cats are included in definition of personal property, under former § 3.1-796.127 [now § 3.2-6585], and dogs were rendered useless as a result of defendant's actions; defendant's conviction would thus be affirmed. Smith v. Commonwealth, — Va. App. —, — S.E.2d —, 2002 Va. App. LEXIS 400 (July 23, 2002).

Act done under bona fide claim of right. — A defendant cannot be convicted under this section where the act complained of was done under a bona fide claim of right. Wise v. Commonwealth, 98 Va. 837, 36 S.E. 479 (1900).

Criminal responsibility attaches to lawful act done in a criminally negligent manner. — Criminal responsibility under this section attaches when property is damaged or destroyed during the commission of an unlawful act, which includes the performance of a lawful act in a criminally negligent manner. Crowder v. Commonwealth, 16 Va. App. 382, 429 S.E.2d 893 (1993).

Interpretation regarding negligence. — Subsection B of § 18.2-137 attaches criminal liability when a person performs a volitional act that damages the property of another and the person specifically intends to cause damage to the property by that act. Subsection B does not criminalize the mere performance of a volitional act conducted in a criminally negligent manner that happens to damage the property of another. Scott v. Commonwealth, 58 Va. App. 35, 707 S.E.2d 17, 2011 Va. App. LEXIS 104 (2011).

Cost of repair cannot be established through victim's hearsay testimony as to estimate for repair. — In an action charging defendant with felony destruction of property, the victim's hearsay testimony as to the estimated cost of repairing the damage to the victim's truck did not suffice to establish the fair market cost of repairing the damage. Brown v. Commonwealth, — Va. App. —, — S.E.2d —, 2009 Va. App. LEXIS 30 (Jan. 27, 2009).

Local ordinance invalid. — Under § 15.2-1429, no punishment for violation of an ordinance may exceed the penalties prescribed by general law for like offenses; Virginia Beach, Va., Code § 23-38, which punished destruction of property by fine of up to $2,500 and up to 12 months in jail, manifested a conflict with state law because the penalty that attached exceeded the penalty under the state code destruction of property statute, § 18.2-137, a violation of which was punishable only by a fine not exceeding $500.

Strout v. City of Va. Beach, 43 Va. App. 99, 596 S.E.2d 529, 2004 Va. App. LEXIS 240 (2004).

Defendant properly convicted of destroying wife's car. — Defendant was properly convicted of destroying and using without consent a car that was "not his own," in violation of §§ 18.2-137 and 18.2-102, respectively, because his interest in his wife's car was an inchoate right that would vest only on entry of a decree of equitable distribution in a divorce proceeding. McDuffie v. Commonwealth, 49 Va. App. 170, 638 S.E.2d 139, 2006 Va. App. LEXIS 573 (2006).

Evidence sufficient to support conviction under subsection A. — Defendant's conviction for property damage under subsection B of § 18.2-137 was inappropriate because the Commonwealth implausibly read subsection B to punish the lowest mens rea with relatively high penalties; subsection B of § 18.2-137 did not criminalize the mere performance of a volitional act conducted in a criminally negligent manner that happened to damage the property of another. However, because the trial court found as a matter of fact that defendant's behavior was criminally negligent, the appellate court remanded for re-sentencing on the lesser-included offense set forth in subsection A of § 18.2-137. Scott v. Commonwealth, 58 Va. App. 35, 707 S.E.2d 17, 2011 Va. App. LEXIS 104 (2011).

Trial court was not plainly wrong in finding that defendant caused an officer's watch to break because a rational factfinder could infer that defendant's resistance to the officers' efforts to bring him to the ground and place him in handcuffs was a proximate cause of the officer's watch breaking; the basic facts were that the officer's watch was intact prior to the struggle with defendant and that the officer's watch was broken and lying on the ground after the struggle with defendant. Hyman v. Commonwealth, 2012 Va. App. LEXIS 144 (May 8, 2012).

Evidence sufficient to support conviction. — Evidence was sufficient to support a conviction for malicious destruction of property where: (1) the defendant was the victim's unfaithful lover whom she recently expelled from her apartment; (2) the defendant threatened the victim on previous occasions and intimated his desire for revenge; (3) the victim saw the defendant leave work during the time her apartment was entered and her property destroyed; and (4) property belonging to the victim was destroyed, while items belonging to the defendant were either missing or disturbed but not damaged. Johnson v. Commonwealth, No. 2498-97-4 (Ct. of Appeals Oct. 6, 1998).

The evidence was sufficient to support a finding that the defendant unlawfully damaged the Commonwealth's property in furtherance of his criminal purpose where the defendant, in an attempt to evade apprehension, ignored emergency lights and sirens of two law enforcement vehicles, together with on officer's entreaties to stop, fled along interstate highways at excessive speed, dangerously operated his truck and, in a continuing effort to escape capture, twice collided with the police vehicle operated by the trooper, intentionally driving forward on both occasions, aware that the trooper was ahead, slowing to effect a stop. Simmons v. Commonwealth, No. 1202-99-3, 2000 Va. App. LEXIS 563 (Ct. of Appeals Aug. 1, 2000).

Evidence that defendant and his friends gained unlawful access to a condominium, consumed liquor and food they found in the condominium, and caused $12,000 in damage before they left was sufficient to sustain defendant's conviction for felonious damage to property, in violation of § 18.2-137. Cobble v. Commonwealth, No. 3257-02-3, 2003 Va. App. LEXIS 633 (Ct. of Appeals Dec. 9, 2003).

Evidence that: (1) defendant was stopped near a parked car that had a broken window and a screwdriver in plain view in the back seat; (2) he said the screwdriver was not his but his fingerprints might be on it; and (3) he later admitted using the screwdriver to break the car window to gain entry into the car, was sufficient to convict him of misdemeanor damage to property. Ridley v. Commonwealth, — Va. App. —, — S.E.2d —, 2006 Va. App. LEXIS 156 (Apr. 25, 2006).

Evidence was sufficient to support defendant's conviction for felony destruction of property in violation of § 18.2-137, rather than misdemeanor destruction, as the crime was a general intent crime and the Commonwealth showed that defendant intended to damage property though defendant did not intend the consequence of damaging the property to be damage caused to a third person's property as a result of defendant chasing in defendant's vehicle another driver's vehicle, as well as the monetary amount of damage to the third person's property, necessary to prove felony destruction. Nunez v. Commonwealth, — Va. App. —, — S.E.2d —, 2007 Va. App. LEXIS 132 (Apr. 3, 2007).

Evidence that a vehicle owner saw defendant get into the owner's vehicle and drive away, a witness saw the vehicle pass by at a "high rate of speed," and seconds later, the vehicle collided with another vehicle, was sufficient to prove that defendant was driving the vehicle at the time of the accident. Davis v. Commonwealth, 2009 Va. App. LEXIS 220 (May 12, 2009).

Defendant was properly convicted of misdemeanor destruction of property as a principal in the first degree, for driving a getaway car in which those who actually damaged a victim's mailbox tried to escape, because: (1) § 18.2-18, concerning felony principals and accessories before the fact, did not abrogate the common-law rule that, in misdemeanors, all participants were principals; and (2) defendant admitted participating in this criminal episode. Wade v. Commonwealth, 56 Va. App. 689, 696 S.E.2d 258, 2010 Va. App. LEXIS 321 (2010).

Evidence that one set of victims testified that a nylon camouflaged holster found with defendant's wallet and belongings looked like one missing from their house, one of the firearms recovered from defendant's shed bore the serial number of a firearm missing from their home, and deer meat stolen from another victim and uniquely packaged was identified by another victim supported defendant's convictions for grand larceny, two counts of breaking and entering, two counts of larceny of a firearm, petit larceny, and destruction of property. Bowles v. Commonwealth, 2010 Va. App. LEXIS 275 (July 13, 2010).

Where defendant drove his girlfriend's car at speeds of 77 to 107 miles per hour, 42 to 72 miles per hour over the posted speed limit of 35 miles per hour while driving in a populated area, and he moved out of the through lane of traffic and into the left turn lane, and drove his car into another vehicle causing the two vehicles to hit a third vehicle, there was sufficient evidence to convict him of felony destruction of property in violation of § 18.2-137 as a rational fact finder could infer that, when driving at such a high rate of speed in a left turn lane, where drivers exited the road to enter a shopping plaza, defendant intended to ram into other vehicles waiting to turn into the shopping plaza. Knight v. Commonwealth, 61 Va. App. 148, 733 S.E.2d 701, 2012 Va. App. LEXIS 363 (2012).

Evidence insufficient to support conviction. — Where defendant drove his truck on the complainant's property, shattering barley and leaving ruts in the ground, the trial court erred in convicting him of felony destruction of property without evidence that the property destroyed exceeded $1,000. The case was remanded for retrial of defendant for the lesser-included offense of misdemeanor destruction of property. Crowder v. Commonwealth, 41 Va. App. 658, 588 S.E.2d 384, 2003 Va. App. LEXIS 576 (2003).

Defendant's conviction for misdemeanor destruction of property in violation of subsection B of § 18.2-137 was reversed because pursuant to § 8.01-680, the trial court was plainly wrong in finding that defendant had the specific intent to break an officer's watch; the record was devoid of any actions or statements by defendant before, during, or after the incident from which the trial court could have inferred his specific intent to damage the officer's watch. Hyman v. Commonwealth, 2012 Va. App. LEXIS 144 (May 8, 2012).

Failure to preserve issue for appeal. — In a prosecution for destroying property in violation of § 18.2-137, defendant did not raise before the trial court his claims that the evidence was insufficient to establish the value of a car and his intent to destroy it. As the evidence was sufficient to establish his intent, and there was no evidence the car was worth less than $1,000, the appellate court declined to apply Va. Sup. Ct. R. 5A:18's "ends of justice" exception to the requirement that a timely objection had to be made to preserve a claim for appeal. McDuffie v. Commonwealth, 49 Va. App. 170, 638 S.E.2d 139, 2006 Va. App. LEXIS 573 (2006).

Reversal not required by omission of intent element from instruction. — Omission of the intent element from a finding instruction did not require reversal of defendant's conviction for damaging property under § 18.2-137 because defendant did not object to the finding instruction, the verdict form, or the sentencing instruction, and the verdict correctly included the intent element; the ends of justice exception to Va. Sup. Ct. R. 5A:18 did not apply because the evidence was overwhelming that defendant acted intentionally when he threw a brick through a window. Perry v. Commonwealth, 2006 Va. App. LEXIS 270 (June 20, 2006).

Applied in Martin v. Taylor, 857 F.2d 958 (4th Cir. 1988); McCary v. Commonwealth, 36 Va. App. 27, 548 S.E.2d 239, 2001 Va. App. LEXIS 462 (2001).

§ 18.2-138. Damaging public buildings, etc.; penalty.

Any person who willfully and maliciously (i) breaks any window or door of the Capitol, any courthouse, house of public worship, college, school house, city or town hall, or other public building or library, (ii) damages or defaces the Capitol or any other public building or any statuary in the Capitol, on the Capitol Square, or in or on any other public buildings or public grounds, or (iii) destroys any property in any of such buildings shall be guilty of a Class 6 felony if damage to the property is $1,000 or more or a Class 1 misdemeanor if the damage is less than $1,000.

Any person who willfully and unlawfully damages or defaces any book, newspaper, magazine, pamphlet, map, picture, manuscript, or other property located in any library, reading room, museum, or other educational institution shall be guilty of a Class 6 felony if damage to the property is $1,000 or more or a Class 1 misdemeanor if the damage is less than $1,000.

History.
Code 1950, § 18.1-177; 1960, c. 358; 1975, cc. 14, 15; 1990, c. 454.

Law Review.
For article, "Virginia Laws Affecting Churches," see 43 Va. L. Rev. 119 (1957).

§ 18.2-138.1. Repealed by Acts 2004, c. 462.

Cross references.
For current provisions relating to willful and malicious damage to or defacement of public or private facilities, see § 15.2-1812.2.

§ 18.2-139. Injuries to trees, fences or herbage on grounds of Capitol, or in any public square.

If any person:

(1) Cut down, pull up, girdle or otherwise injure or destroy any tree growing in the grounds of the Capitol, or in any public square or grounds, without the consent of the Governor, or of the circuit court of the county or city in which such grounds or square is situated; or

(2) Willfully and maliciously injure the fences or herbage of the Capitol grounds, or of any such square or grounds,

he shall be guilty of a Class 3 misdemeanor.

History.
Code 1950, § 18.1-180; 1960, c. 358; 1975, cc. 14, 15.

§ 18.2-140. Destruction of trees, shrubs, etc.

It shall be unlawful for any person to pick, pull, pull up, tear, tear up, dig, dig up, cut, break, injure, burn or destroy, in whole or in part, any tree, shrub, vine, plant, flower or turf found, growing or being upon the land of another, or upon any land reserved, set aside or maintained by the Commonwealth as a public park, or as a refuge or sanctuary for wild animals, birds or fish, or upon any land reserved, set aside or maintained as a public park by a park authority created under the provisions of § 15.2-5702, without having previously obtained the permission in writing of such other or his agent or of the superintendent or custodian of such park, refuge or sanctuary so to do, unless the same be done under the personal direction of such owner, his agent, tenant or lessee or superintendent or custodian of such park, refuge or sanctuary.

Any person violating this section shall be guilty of a Class 3 misdemeanor; provided, however, that the approval of the owner, his agent, tenant or lessee, or the superintendent or custodian of such park or sanctuary afterwards given in writing or in open court shall be a bar to further prosecution or suit.

History.
Code 1950, § 18.1-178; 1960, c. 358; 1975, cc. 14, 15; 1976, c. 757; 1998, c. 81.

Cross references.
As to dumping trash, etc., on highways, rights of way or private property, see § 33.1-346.

§ 18.2-141. Cutting or destroying trees; carrying axe, saw, etc., while hunting.

It shall be unlawful for any person while hunting for game or wildlife on the property of another to carry any axe other than a belt axe with a handle less than twenty inches, saw or other tool or instrument customarily used for the purpose of cutting, felling, mutilating or destroying trees without obtaining prior permission of the landowner. Any person violating the provisions of this section shall be guilty of a Class 3 misdemeanor.

Conservation police officers, sheriffs and all law-enforcement officers shall enforce the provisions of this section.

History.
Code 1950, § 18.1-179; 1960, c. 358; 1975, cc. 14, 15.

Editor's note.
At the direction of the Virginia Code Commission, "Conservation police officers" was substituted for "Game wardens" to conform to the name change made by Acts 2007, c. 87.

Michie's Jurisprudence.
For related discussion, see 18 M.J. Trespass, § 1.

§ 18.2-142. Repealed by Acts 1979, c. 252.

Cross references.
For present provisions making it unlawful to damage caves, see § 10.1-1000 et seq.

§ 18.2-143. Pulling down fences or leaving open gates.

If any person, without permission of the owner, pull down the fence of another and leave the same

down, or, without permission, open and leave open the gate of another, or any gate across a public road established by order of court, or if any person other than the owner or owners of the lands through which a line of railroad runs open and leave open a gate at any public or private crossing of the right-of-way of a railroad, he shall be guilty of a Class 4 misdemeanor.

History.
Code 1950, § 18.1-176; 1960, c. 358; 1975, cc. 14, 15.

Michie's Jurisprudence.
For related discussion, see 8B M.J. Fences, § 4; 15 M.J. Railroads, § 143; 18 M.J. Trespass, § 1.

ARTICLE 7.

DAMAGE TO AND TAMPERING WITH PROPERTY.

§ 18.2-144. Maiming, killing or poisoning animals, fowl, etc.

Except as otherwise provided for by law, if any person maliciously shoot, stab, wound or otherwise cause bodily injury to, or administer poison to or expose poison with intent that it be taken by, any horse, mule, pony, cattle, swine or other livestock of another, with intent to maim, disfigure, disable or kill the same, or if he do any of the foregoing acts to any animal of his own with intent to defraud any insurer thereof, he shall be guilty of a Class 5 felony. If any person do any of the foregoing acts to any fowl or to any companion animal with any of the aforesaid intents, he shall be guilty of a Class 1 misdemeanor, except that any second or subsequent offense shall be a Class 6 felony if the current offense or any previous offense resulted in the death of an animal or the euthanasia of an animal based on the recommendation of a licensed veterinarian upon determination that such euthanasia was necessary due to the condition of the animal, and such condition was a direct result of a violation of this section.

History.
Code 1950, § 18.1-159; 1960, c. 358; 1964, c. 400; 1975, cc. 14, 15; 1977, c. 598; 1978, c. 559; 1999, c. 620.

Cross references.
As to larceny of dog, see § 18.2-97. As to comprehensive animal laws, see § 3.2-5900 et seq. As to status of dogs as personal property, see § 3.2-6585.

Michie's Jurisprudence.
For related discussion, see 1B M.J. Animals, §§ 4, 14, 15; 14B M.J. Poisons and Poisoning, § 1; 18 M.J. Trespass, § 1.

CASE NOTES

This section makes the offense consist of an act combined with a particular intent, and that intent cannot be presumed but must be proven. Thus an instruction to the effect that the law presumes a man to intend the natural and probable consequence of his act, and that if the accused struck a cow with a deadly weapon, the presumption of the law would be that he unlawfully intended to maim, disfigure and kill the cow, constituted error. Winckler v. Commonwealth, 155 Va. 1146, 156 S.E. 364 (1931).

Wounding in self-defense. — In a trial under this section it appeared from the evidence that the accused wounded a cow in an attempt to save himself or his own cow when charged by it. Accused's narrative was uncontradicted and was corroborated by other testimony. It was held that, giving to the testimony of the Commonwealth all the probative value to which it was entitled, it was wholly insufficient to sustain the verdict of guilty. Winckler v. Commonwealth, 155 Va. 1146, 156 S.E. 364 (1931).

Sufficiency of evidence. — Sufficient evidence permitted the jury to find beyond a reasonable doubt that defendant possessed a firearm and shot a dog where defendant admitted driving by the site of the shooting on the day of the shooting, one of two girls saw defendant shoot a firearm toward the barn where they were playing with the dog, the other saw him with a firearm right after the shooting, and the girls were certain defendant was the man they saw at the barn with the firearm. Ford v. Commonwealth, 48 Va. App. 262, 630 S.E.2d 332, 2006 Va. App. LEXIS 238 (2006).

§ 18.2-144.1. Prohibition against killing or injuring police animals; penalty.

It shall be unlawful for any person to maliciously shoot, stab, wound or otherwise cause bodily injury to, or administer poison to or expose poison with intent that it be taken by a dog, horse or other animal owned, used or trained by a law-enforcement agency, regional jail or the Department of Corrections while such animal is performing his lawful duties or is being kept in a kennel, pen or stable while off duty. A violation of this section shall be punishable as a Class 5 felony. The court shall order that the defendant pay restitution for the cost of any animal killed or rendered unable to perform its duties. Such cost shall include training expenses.

History.
1989, c. 558; 1998, c. 8.

§ 18.2-144.2. Prohibition against making a false representation of ownership of an animal to an animal shelter or pound; penalty.

A. It shall be unlawful for any person to deliver or release any animal not owned by that person to a pound, animal shelter or humane society, as these terms are defined in § 3.2-6500, or to any other similar facility for animals, or any agent thereof, and to falsely represent to such facility or agent that such person is the owner of the animal.

B. A violation of subsection A shall be punished as a Class 1 misdemeanor.

C. No pound, animal shelter, humane society or other similar facility for animals, or the directors or employees of any such business or facility, shall, in the absence of gross negligence, be civilly liable for accepting and disposing of any animal in good faith from a person who falsely claims to be the owner of the animal.

History.
1994, c. 885.

Editor's note.
At the direction of the Virginia Code Commission, Title 3.2 references were substituted for Title 3.1 references to conform to the title revision by Acts 2008, c. 860, effective October 1, 2008.

§ 18.2-145. Protection of homing pigeons.

It shall be unlawful for any person at any time or in any manner to hunt, pursue, take, capture, wound, maim, disfigure, or kill any homing pigeon of another person, or to make use of any pit or pitfall, scaffold, cage, snare, trap, net, baited hook or similar device or drug, poison chemical or explosive, for the purpose of injuring, capturing or killing any such homing pigeon, provided that any officer, employee or agent of a city or county acting pursuant to authority of an ordinance thereof may take, capture and kill pigeons in, on and about any building or structure devoted to business, commercial or industrial purposes when any pigeons are using such premises for roosting, resting or congregating thereon; all pigeons taken upon such premises shall be conclusively deemed not to be homing pigeons or the property of any person.

Any person violating any of the foregoing provisions shall be guilty of a Class 3 misdemeanor.

History.
Code 1950, § 18.1-160; 1960, c. 358; 1975, cc. 14, 15.

Michie's Jurisprudence.
For related discussion, see 12A M.J. Larceny, § 8.

§ 18.2-145.1. Damaging or destroying research farm product; penalty; restitution.

A. Any person or entity that (i) maliciously damages or destroys any farm product, as defined in § 3.2-4709 and (ii) knows the product is grown for testing or research purposes in the context of product development in conjunction or coordination with a private research facility or a university or any federal, state or local government agency is guilty of a Class 1 misdemeanor if the value of the farm product was less than $200, or a Class 6 felony if the value of the farm product was $200 or more.

B. The court shall order the defendant to make restitution in accordance with § 19.2-305.1 for the damage or destruction caused. For the purpose of awarding restitution under this section, the court shall determine the market value of the farm product prior to its damage or destruction and, in so doing, shall include the cost of: (i) production, (ii) research, (iii) testing, (iv) replacement and (v) product development directly related to the product damaged or destroyed.

History.
2001, cc. 547, 572.

Editor's note.
At the direction of the Virginia Code Commission, Title 3.2 references were substituted for Title 3.1 references to conform to the title revision by Acts 2008, c. 860, effective October 1, 2008.

§ 18.2-146. Breaking, injuring, defacing, destroying or preventing the operation of vehicle, aircraft or boat.

Any person who shall individually or in association with one or more others willfully break, injure, tamper with or remove any part or parts of any vehicle, aircraft, boat or vessel for the purpose of injuring, defacing or destroying said vehicle, aircraft, boat or vessel, or temporarily or permanently preventing its useful operation, or for any purpose against the will or without the consent of the owner of such vehicle, aircraft, boat or vessel, or who shall in any other manner willfully or maliciously interfere with or prevent the running or operation of such vehicle, aircraft, boat or vessel, shall be guilty of a Class 1 misdemeanor.

History.
Code 1950, § 18.1-166; 1960, c. 358; 1975, cc. 14, 15.

Cross references.
As to tampering with, etc., airplanes or markings of airports, landing fields or other aeronautical facilities, see § 5.1-16.

Michie's Jurisprudence.
For related discussion, see 2B M.J. Automobiles, § 126.3; 2B M.J. Aviation, § 1.

CASE NOTES

Willfulness does not require finding of intent and bad purpose. — The court of appeals rejected defendant's proffered instruction which would have required the jury to find both intent and bad purpose under the first element of willfulness; the particular bad purpose required under this section is specifically set forth as a separate element of the offense; an instruction requiring the jury to find bad purpose under the element of willfulness would have been redundant and not required by law. Benjamin v. Commonwealth, No. 1064-88-4 (Ct. of Appeals July 3, 1990).

Suppression of evidence. — Assuming that an investigator's actions violated §§ 18.2-146 and 19.2-249, that violation did not entitle defendant to suppression of the evidence because the statutes did not provide for the remedy of exclusion. Hill v. Commonwealth, No. 1828-11-3, 2012 Va. App. LEXIS 318 (Oct. 9, 2012).

§ 18.2-147. Entering or setting in motion, vehicle, aircraft, boat, locomotive or rolling stock of railroad; exceptions.

Any person who shall, without the consent of the owner or person in charge of a vehicle, aircraft, boat, vessel, locomotive or other rolling stock of a railroad, climb into or upon such vehicle, aircraft, boat, vessel, locomotive or other rolling stock of a railroad, with intent to commit any crime, malicious mischief, or injury thereto, or who, while a vehicle, aircraft, boat, vessel, locomotive or other rolling stock of a railroad is at rest and unattended, shall attempt to manipulate any of the levers and starting crank or other device, brakes or mechanism thereof or to set into motion such vehicle, aircraft, boat, vessel, locomotive or other rolling stock of a railroad, with the intent to commit any crime, malicious mischief, or injury thereto, shall be guilty of a Class 1 misde-

meanor, except that the foregoing provision shall not apply when any such act is done in an emergency or in furtherance of public safety or by or under the direction of an officer in the regulation of traffic or performance of any other official duty.

History.
Code 1950, § 18.1-167; 1960, c. 358; 1975, cc. 14, 15.

§ 18.2-147.1. Breaking and entering into railroad cars, motortrucks, aircraft, etc., or pipeline systems.

Any person who breaks the seal or lock of any railroad car, vessel, aircraft, motortruck, wagon or other vehicle or of any pipeline system, containing shipments of freight or express or other property, or breaks and enters any such vehicle or pipeline system with the intent to commit larceny or any felony therein shall be guilty of a Class 4 felony; provided, however, that if such person is armed with a firearm at the time of such breaking and entering, he shall be guilty of a Class 3 felony.

History.
1979, c. 336.

Michie's Jurisprudence.
For related discussion, see 3A M.J. Burglary and Housebreaking, § 2.

CASE NOTES

Vehicle of commerce. — Where victim stored tires in the trailer and also transported the tires in the trailer for sale at flea markets, the tires were property which was the subject of transportation in a vehicle in commerce. Furthermore, the tires were cargo, chattels, or goods transported by victim and were analogous to freight. Hairston v. Commonwealth, 19 Va. App. 487, 452 S.E.2d 872 (1995).

From its very tenor this section is directed to cargo theft. The particular vehicle or pipeline system is required to contain, according to the crucial clause, "shipments of freight or express or other property." Martin v. Commonwealth, 224 Va. 298, 295 S.E.2d 890 (1982).

Section may have been adopted from 18 U.S.C.S. § 2117. The purpose of the federal statute is to provide protection for interstate and foreign shipments while in transit. Martin v. Commonwealth, 224 Va. 298, 295 S.E.2d 890 (1982).

Construction of "other property." — The term "other property" cannot be viewed in the abstract and construed broadly to mean "any property," whether or not a part of a "shipment." Under the rule of ejusdem generis, when a particular class of persons or things is enumerated in a statute and general words follow, the general words are to be restricted in their meaning to a sense analogous to the less general, particular words. Likewise, according to the maxim noscitur a sociis (associated words) when general and specific words are grouped, the general words are limited by the specific and will be construed to embrace only objects similar in nature to those things identified by the specific words. Martin v. Commonwealth, 224 Va. 298, 295 S.E.2d 890 (1982).

While the meaning of "other property" does not encompass articles of personal property kept in private vehicles, "other property" does equate to shipments of things analogous to freight or express. Hairston v. Commonwealth, 19 Va. App. 487, 452 S.E.2d 872 (1995).

"Shipment" applies to the term "other property." Martin v. Commonwealth, 224 Va. 298, 295 S.E.2d 890 (1982).

Section inapplicable to personal property kept in private automobile. — The statutory term "other property" is restricted in its meaning to "shipments" of things analogous to "freight" or "express." The meaning does not encompass articles of personal property kept in a private automobile for sentimental reasons. Martin v. Commonwealth, 224 Va. 298, 295 S.E.2d 890 (1982).

§ 18.2-147.2. Devices for puncturing motor vehicle tires.

It shall be unlawful for any person to manufacture, distribute, have in his possession or place upon any highway or private property jackrocks which are primarily designed for the purpose of disabling motor vehicles by the puncturing of tires by anyone other than a law-enforcement officer. Any person convicted of unlawful manufacture, distribution, possession or use of such device shall be guilty of a Class 1 misdemeanor. A law-enforcement officer who is lawfully engaged in the discharge of his duties shall not be subject to the provisions of this section.

History.
1982, c. 253; 2007, c. 437.

§ 18.2-148. Bona fide repossession under lien.

The provisions of §§ 18.2-102, 18.2-146 and 18.2-147 shall not apply to a bona fide repossession of a vehicle, aircraft, boat or vessel by the holder of a lien on such vehicle, aircraft, boat or vessel, or by the agents or employees of such lienholder.

History.
Code 1950, § 18.1-168; 1960, c. 358; 1975, cc. 14, 15.

Michie's Jurisprudence.
For related discussion, see 2B M.J. Aviation, § 1; 12A M.J. Larceny, § 8.

§ 18.2-149. Injury to hired animal, aircraft, vehicle or boat.

If any person after having rented or leased from any other person an animal, aircraft, vehicle, boat or vessel shall willfully injure or damage the same, by hard or reckless driving or using, or by using the same in violation of any statute of this Commonwealth, or allow or permit any other person so to do, or hire the same to any other person without the consent of the bailor, such person shall be guilty of a Class 3 misdemeanor.

History.
Code 1950, § 18.1-161; 1960, c. 358; 1975, cc. 14, 15.

Cross references.
As to procuring an animal, aircraft, vehicle or boat mentioned in this section by fraud, or as to failure to pay rental for or damage to such animal, etc., see § 18.2-206.

Michie's Jurisprudence.
For related discussion, see 2B M.J. Automobiles, § .126.3; 2B M.J. Aviation, § 1; 12A M.J. Livery Stables, § 1.

§ 18.2-150. Willfully destroying vessel, etc.

If any person willfully scuttle, cast away or otherwise dispose of, or in any manner destroy, except as

otherwise provided, a ship, vessel or other watercraft, with intent to injure or defraud any owner thereof or of any property on board the same, or any insurer of such ship, vessel or other watercraft, or any part thereof, or of any such property on board the same, if the same be of the value of $200, he shall be guilty of a Class 4 felony, but if it be of less value than $200, he shall be guilty of a Class 1 misdemeanor.

History.
Code 1950, § 18.1-170; 1960, c. 358; 1975, cc. 14, 15; 1981, c. 197.

§ 18.2-151. Opening or carrying away pumps, etc., used for dispensing gasoline, etc.

If any person, with intent to commit larceny therefrom, break and open, or open, or carry away, any pump, tank, or other similar equipment or container used for dispensing or storing kerosene, gasoline or motor oils, he shall be guilty of a Class 6 felony.

History.
Code 1950, § 18.1-169; 1960, c. 358; 1975, cc. 14, 15.

§ 18.2-152. Stealing from or tampering with parking meter, vending machine, pay telephone, etc.

Any person who enters, forces or attempts to force an entrance into, tampers with, or inserts any part of an instrument into any parking meter, vending machine, pay telephone, money changing machine, or any other device designed to receive money, with intent to steal therefrom, shall for the first conviction thereof be guilty of a Class 1 misdemeanor, and for any subsequent conviction of a violation thereof shall be guilty of a Class 6 felony.

History.
Code 1950, § 18.1-125.1; 1968, c. 518; 1975, cc. 14, 15.

Law Review.
For 2007 annual survey article, "Electronic Data: A Commentary on the Law in Virginia in 2007," see 42 U. Rich. L. Rev. 355 (2007).

Michie's Jurisprudence.
For related discussion, see 18 M.J. Trespass, § 1.

ARTICLE 7.1.
COMPUTER CRIMES.

§ 18.2-152.1. Short title.

This article shall be known and may be cited as the "Virginia Computer Crimes Act."

History.
1984, c. 751.

Cross references.
As to the Attorney General's limited authority to institute or conduct criminal prosecutions under this article, see § 2.2-511.

Law Review.

For article on Virginia's response to computer abuses, see 19 U. Rich. L. Rev. 85 (1984). For an article, "Uniformity, Choice of Law and Software Sales," see 8 Geo. Mason L. Rev. 261 (1999). For a note, "Computer Network Trespasses: Solving New Problems with Old Solutions," see 57 Wash. & Lee L. Rev. 209 (2000). For 2000 survey of Virginia technology law, see 34 U. Rich. L. Rev. 1051. (2000). For 2002 survey of Virginia technology law, see 37 U. Rich. L. Rev. 341 (2002).

Michie's Jurisprudence.

For related discussion, see 12A M.J. Larceny, § 2.

CASE NOTES

Applied in DIRECTV, Inc. v. Amato, 269 F. Supp. 2d 688, 2003 U.S. Dist. LEXIS 12722 (E.D. Va. 2003); 21st Century Sys. v. Perot Sys. Gov't Servs., 284 Va. 32, 726 S.E.2d 236, 2012 Va. LEXIS 139 (2012).

§ 18.2-152.2. Definitions; computer crimes.

For purposes of this article:

"Commercial electronic mail" means electronic mail, the primary purpose of which is the advertisement or promotion of a commercial product or service.

"Computer" means a device that accepts information in digital or similar form and manipulates it for a result based on a sequence of instructions. Such term does not include simple calculators, automated typewriters, facsimile machines, or any other specialized computing devices that are preprogrammed to perform a narrow range of functions with minimal end-user or operator intervention and are dedicated to a specific task.

"Computer data" means any representation of information, knowledge, facts, concepts, or instructions which is being prepared or has been prepared and is intended to be processed, is being processed, or has been processed in a computer or computer network. "Computer data" may be in any form, whether readable only by a computer or only by a human or by either, including, but not limited to, computer printouts, magnetic storage media, punched cards, or stored internally in the memory of the computer.

"Computer network" means two or more computers connected by a network.

"Computer operation" means arithmetic, logical, monitoring, storage or retrieval functions and any combination thereof, and includes, but is not limited to, communication with, storage of data to, or retrieval of data from any device or human hand manipulation of electronic or magnetic impulses. A "computer operation" for a particular computer may also be any function for which that computer was generally designed.

"Computer program" means an ordered set of data representing coded instructions or statements that, when executed by a computer, causes the computer to perform one or more computer operations.

"Computer services" means computer time or services, including data processing services, Internet services, electronic mail services, electronic message services, or information or data stored in connection therewith.

"Computer software" means a set of computer programs, procedures and associated documentation concerned with computer data or with the operation of a computer, computer program, or computer network.

"Electronic mail service provider" (EMSP) means any person who (i) is an intermediary in sending or receiving electronic mail and (ii) provides to end-users of electronic mail services the ability to send or receive electronic mail.

"Financial instrument" includes, but is not limited to, any check, draft, warrant, money order, note, certificate of deposit, letter of credit, bill of exchange, credit or debit card, transaction authorization mechanism, marketable security, or any computerized representation thereof.

"Network" means any combination of digital transmission facilities and packet switches, routers, and similar equipment interconnected to enable the exchange of computer data.

"Owner" means an owner or lessee of a computer or a computer network or an owner, lessee, or licensee of computer data, computer programs or computer software.

"Person" shall include any individual, partnership, association, corporation or joint venture.

"Property" shall include:

1. Real property;

2. Computers and computer networks;

3. Financial instruments, computer data, computer programs, computer software and all other personal property regardless of whether they are:

a. Tangible or intangible;

b. In a format readable by humans or by a computer;

c. In transit between computers or within a computer network or between any devices which comprise a computer; or

d. Located on any paper or in any device on which it is stored by a computer or by a human; and

4. Computer services.

"Spam" means unsolicited commercial electronic mail. Spam shall not include commercial electronic mail transmitted to a recipient with whom the sender has an existing business or personal relationship.

A person *"uses"* a computer or computer network when he attempts to cause or causes a computer or computer network to perform or to stop performing computer operations.

A person is *"without authority"* when he knows or reasonably should know that he has no right, agreement, or permission or acts in a manner knowingly exceeding such right, agreement, or permission.

History.

1984, c. 751; 1999, cc. 886, 904, 905; 2000, c. 627; 2003, cc. 987, 1016; 2005, cc. 761, 812, 827; 2009, cc. 321, 376; 2010, c. 489.

Cross references.

As to the authority for certain size cities to provide computer services, see § 15.2-2109.

Editor's note.

Acts 2010, c. 489, cl. 2, provides: "Pursuant to § 30-19.1:4, the estimated amount of the necessary appropriation cannot be determined for periods of imprisonment in state adult correctional facilities; therefore, Chapter 781 of the 2009 Acts of Assembly requires the Virginia Criminal Sentencing Commission to assign a minimum fiscal impact of $50,000. Pursuant to § 30-19.1:4, the estimated amount of the necessary appropriation is $0 for periods of commitment to the custody of the Department of Juvenile Justice."

The 2009 amendments.

The 2009 amendments by cc. 321 and 376 are virtually identical, and substituted "agreement, or permission or acts in a manner exceeding such right, agreement" for "or permission or knowingly acts in a manner exceeding such right" in the last paragraph. In addition, c. 321 inserted "knowingly" preceding "exceeding such right" in the last paragraph, which has been set out in the form above at the direction of the Virginia Code Commission.

The 2010 amendments.

The 2010 amendment by c. 489 inserted "commercial electronic mail" and "spam" definitions.

Law Review.

For article on Virginia's response to computer abuses, see 19 U. Rich. L. Rev. 85 (1984). For a note, "Computer Network Trespasses: Solving New Problems with Old Solutions," see 57 Wash. & Lee L. Rev. 209 (2000). For article, "Construction Law," see 45 U. Rich. L. Rev. 227 (2010).

CASE NOTES

Documents not "computer software." — Set of documents received by defendant was not a computer program, for it was not something that could be executed by a computer, causing the computer to perform a computer operation and although the documents described a computer program proposed to be created, they did not relate to a program in existence, and, thus, were not documentation associated with a set of computer programs or procedures; therefore, the set of documents obtained by the defendant was not, by definition, computer software and did not constitute property specified in the indictment to have been obtained from computer software company and thus the defendant's conviction of obtaining software by false pretenses cannot stand. O'Connor v. Commonwealth, 16 Va. App. 416, 430 S.E.2d 567 (1993).

CIRCUIT COURT OPINIONS

Use of computer "without authority." — To the extent defendant's demurrer asserted that no claim was stated because he had authority to use his employer's computer and to download data, the demurrer was overruled because defendant had no authority to use his employer's computers for purposes not authorized by his employer and inimical to his employer's best interest. McGladrey & Pullen, L.L.P. v. Shrader, 62 Va. Cir. 401, 2003 Va. Cir. LEXIS 274 (Rockingham County 2003).

Use of Virginia computers for purposes of personal jurisdiction. — Union organizers who allegedly sent misleading e-mails to employees of an Internet service access provider were subject to personal jurisdiction under subdivision A 3 and subsection B of § 8.01-328.1 and subdivision 4 of § 18.2-152.2 because the organizers sent the allegedly tortious e-mail messages to Virginia computers over Virginia servers, thereby causing the Virginia computers and networks to perform functions for which they were generally designed. Aitken v. Communs. Workers of Am., 496 F. Supp. 2d 653, 2007 U.S. Dist. LEXIS 51434 (E.D. Va. 2007).

§ 18.2-152.3. Computer fraud; penalty.

Any person who uses a computer or computer network, without authority and:

1. Obtains property or services by false pretenses;
2. Embezzles or commits larceny; or
3. Converts the property of another;

is guilty of the crime of computer fraud.

If the value of the property or services obtained is $200 or more, the crime of computer fraud shall be punishable as a Class 5 felony. Where the value of the property or services obtained is less than $200, the crime of computer fraud shall be punishable as a Class 1 misdemeanor.

History.

1984, c. 751; 1985, c. 322; 2003, cc. 987, 1016; 2005, cc. 747, 761, 827, 837.

Law Review.

For article on Virginia's response to computer abuses, see 19 U. Rich. L. Rev. 85 (1984).

Michie's Jurisprudence.

For related discussion, see 8B M.J. Fraud and Deceit, § 30.

CASE NOTES

Proof. — The Virginia Computer Crimes Act does not require proof of elements beyond those necessary to prove copyright infringement of a computer program. Rosciszewski v. Arete Assocs., 1 F.3d 225 (4th Cir. 1993).

Unauthorized use of computer network. — The defendants violated the Computer Crimes Act by causing "aol.com" to appear in the electronic header information of e-mail messages which they sent to AOL members advertising pornographic web sites. Sending such messages through AOL's computer network was unauthorized, and the defendants intended to obtain services by false pretenses and to convert AOL's property in that, by using the false "aol.com" designation, the defendants illegally obtained the unauthorized service of AOL's mail delivery service and the defendants obtained free advertising from AOL because AOL, not the defendants, bore the cost of sending these messages. America Online, Inc. v. LCGM, Inc., 46 F. Supp. 2d 444 (E.D. Va. 1998).

Preemption. — Virginia Computer Crimes Act (VCCA) claims were dismissed because allegations of unauthorized copying of software under the Virginia Computer Crimes Act were preempted by the Copyright Act. SecureInfo Corp. v. Telos Corp., 387 F. Supp. 2d 593, 2005 U.S. Dist. LEXIS 21228 (E.D. Va. 2005).

Virginia Computer Crimes Act (VCCA), § 18.2-152.3 et seq., claim was preempted by the Copyright Act because it was difficult to see how any claim under the VCCA would have contained any elements making it qualitatively different from the Copyright Act claims because the complaint consistently alleged that each of the reports generated by a government relations and analysis firm's proprietary database bore a copyright notice, that the firm owned a copyright in the proprietary database in the organization of the information in a searchable format available in no other source, and that the firm owned copyrights in each of the bill summaries within the database that were original works of authorship. State Analysis, Inc. v. Am. Fin. Servs. Assoc., 621 F. Supp. 2d 309, 2009 U.S. Dist. LEXIS 27548 (E.D. Va. 2009).

At no point did the complaint plead specific facts giving rise to a plausible inference of larceny, false pretenses, embezzlement, or conversion, as required by the plain text of the Virginia Computer Crimes Act, § 18.2-152.3 et seq. In fact, the claim was reduced to nothing more than a copyright infringement allegation, dressed up in VCCA garb. Cvent, Inc. v. Eventbrite, Inc., 2010 U.S. Dist. LEXIS 96354 (E.D. Va. Sept. 14, 2010).

Evidence held sufficient. — Evidence was sufficient to support finding that police officer used computerized criminal information system, without authority, in order to help her brother retain stolen vehicle. Barnes v. Commonwealth, No. 2693-98-1 (Ct. of Appeals Mar. 21, 2000).

Website host demonstrated that a competitor and its employee obtained its property by false pretenses in violation of § 18.2-152.3 and subdivision A 6 of § 18.2-152.4, where the website host traced alleged hacking attacks to the competitor and its employee, and it was highly likely that the competitor and its employee converted the website host's proprietary information for their own use. Physicians Interactive v. Lathian Sys., — F. Supp. 2d —, 2003 U.S. Dist. LEXIS 22868 (E.D. Va. Dec. 5, 2003).

Trial court did not err in finding defendant guilty, following a bench trial, of computer fraud, computer trespass, embezzlement, and attempted extortion, as the evidence showed that defendant transferred computer files from his computer at work to a third-party server before he was terminated from his position as human resource director, that he used the removed material to threaten the company in an attempt to forgive a loan it had made to him, and that the company established the value of the material removed as required to support convictions on those offenses. DiMaio v. Commonwealth, 46 Va. App. 755, 621 S.E.2d 696, 2005 Va. App. LEXIS 456 (2005).

Convictions of computer fraud and larceny were supported by sufficient evidence, including testimony that the market value of personnel files taken by defendant exceeded $10,000, and unchallenged testimony that market value of form covenants not to compete taken by defendant was between $5,000 and $7,000. DiMaio v. Commonwealth, 272 Va. 504, 636 S.E.2d 456, 2006 Va. LEXIS 110 (2006).

Evidence insufficient. — Defendants were properly granted summary judgment on plaintiff corporations' Virginia Computer Crimes Act claim because the corporations produced no factual evidence that defendant used a computer to withdraw funds he was not authorized to withdraw for an illegal or unauthorized purpose; defendant was authorized to access one of the corporation's bank accounts, and defendant's use of a computer was merely incidental to the withdrawal of the money. Othentec Ltd. v. Phelan, 526 F.3d 135, 2008 U.S. App. LEXIS 10233 (4th Cir. 2008).

Where a high school student misrepresented himself as a college student in order to submit his written work as a college student for review and archiving by a company that checked students' submitted papers for plagiarism, the student was entitled to summary judgment on the company's claim that he violated the Virginia Computer Crimes Act, because the company failed to produce any evidence of actual or economic damages resulting from the student's allegedly unauthorized submissions. A.V. v. iParadigms, 544 F. Supp. 2d 473, 2008 U.S. Dist. LEXIS 19715 (E.D. Va. 2008).

CIRCUIT COURT OPINIONS

Unauthorized use of computer network. — Where defendant's demurrer asserted that no claim was stated because he had authority to use his employer's computer and to download data, the demurrer was overruled because defendant had no authority to use his employer's computers for purposes not authorized by his employer and inimical to his employer's best interest. McGladrey & Pullen, L.L.P. v. Shrader, 62 Va. Cir. 401, 2003 Va. Cir. LEXIS 274 (Rockingham County 2003).

No violation found. — Plaintiff had not shown that his former partners violated the Virginia Computer Crimes Act. Denying plaintiff access to a computer network and transferring computer systems, software, and data did not constitute computer fraud, theft of computer services, or embezzlement; moreover, plaintiff had failed to prove damages resulting from any such violation. Greenfeld v. Stitely, 2007 Va. Cir. LEXIS 7 (Fairfax County Jan. 5, 2007).

§ 18.2-152.3:1. Transmission of unsolicited commercial electronic mail (spam); penalty.

A. Any person who:

1. Uses a computer or computer network with the intent to falsify or forge electronic mail transmission information or other routing information in any manner in connection with the transmission of spam through or into the computer network of an electronic mail service provider or its subscribers; or

2. Knowingly sells, gives, or otherwise distributes or possesses with the intent to sell, give, or distribute software that (i) is primarily designed or produced for the purpose of facilitating or enabling the falsification of the transmission information or other routing information of spam; (ii) has only limited commercially significant purpose or use other than to facilitate or enable the falsification of the transmission information or other routing information of spam; or (iii) is marketed by that person acting alone or with another for use in facilitating or enabling the falsification of the transmission information or other routing information of spam is guilty of a Class 1 misdemeanor.

B. Any person who commits a violation of subdivision A 1 when (i) the volume of spam transmitted exceeded 10,000 attempted recipients in any 24-hour time period, 100,000 attempted recipients in any 30-day time period, or one million attempted recipients in any one-year time period or (ii) revenue generated from a specific transmission of spam exceeded $1,000 or the total revenue generated from all spam transmitted to any EMSP exceeded $50,000, is guilty of a Class 6 felony.

C. Any person who knowingly hires, employs, uses, or permits any minor to assist in the transmission of spam in violation of subsection B is guilty of a Class 6 felony.

History.
2003, cc. 987, 1016; 2010, c. 489.

Editor's note.
Acts 2010, c. 489, cl. 2 provides: "Pursuant to § 30-19.1:4, the estimated amount of the necessary appropriation cannot be determined for periods of imprisonment in state adult correctional facilities; therefore, Chapter 781 of the 2009 Acts of Assembly requires the Virginia Criminal Sentencing Commission to assign a minimum fiscal impact of $50,000. Pursuant to § 30-19.1:4, the estimated amount of the necessary appropriation is $0 for periods of commitment to the custody of the Department of Juvenile Justice."

The 2010 amendments.
The 2010 amendment by c. 489 rewrote the section.

Law Review.
For article, "Construction Law," see 45 U. Rich. L. Rev. 227 (2010).

CASE NOTES

Unconstitutionally overbroad. — Section 18.2-152.3:1 is unconstitutionally overbroad on its face because the statute prohibits the anonymous transmission of all unsolicited bulk e-mails including those containing political, religious or other speech protected by the First Amendment to the United States Constitution. Jaynes v. Commonwealth, 276 Va. 443, 666 S.E.2d 303, 2008 Va. LEXIS 104 (2008), cert. denied, 129 S. Ct. 1670, 2009 U.S. LEXIS 2463, 173 L. Ed. 2d 1036 (U.S. 2009).

Statute violates protected right of anonymous speech. — By prohibiting false routing information in the dissemination of e-mails, § 18.2-152.3:1 infringes on the protected right to engage in anonymous speech. Jaynes v. Commonwealth, 276 Va. 443, 666 S.E.2d 303, 2008 Va. LEXIS 104 (2008), cert. denied, 129 S. Ct. 1670, 2009 U.S. LEXIS 2463, 173 L. Ed. 2d 1036 (U.S. 2009).

Jurisdiction. — Because the use of the computer network of an e-mail service provider or its subscribers was an integral part of the crime charged and because the use of a provider's e-mail servers was the immediate result of defendant's acts, defendant was amenable to prosecution in Virginia for a violation of § 18.2-152.3:1. Jaynes v. Commonwealth, 276 Va. 443, 666 S.E.2d 303, 2008 Va. LEXIS 104 (2008), cert. denied, 129 S. Ct. 1670, 2009 U.S. LEXIS 2463, 173 L. Ed. 2d 1036 (U.S. 2009).

Not a trespass statute. — Section 18.2-152.3:1 does not prohibit the unauthorized use of privately owned e-mail servers; the statute only prohibits the intentional use of false routing information in connection with sending certain e-mail through such servers. Thus, even if an e-mail service provider specifically allowed persons using false Internet provider addresses and domain names to use its server, the sender could be prosecuted under § 18.2-152.3:1 although there was no unauthorized use or trespass; therefore, § 18.2-152.3:1 is not a trespass statute. Jaynes v. Commonwealth, 276 Va. 443, 666 S.E.2d 303, 2008 Va. LEXIS 104 (2008), cert. denied, 129 S. Ct. 1670, 2009 U.S. LEXIS 2463, 173 L. Ed. 2d 1036 (U.S. 2009).

CIRCUIT COURT OPINIONS

Constitutionality of felony provisions. — Felony provisions of the statute governing the transmission of unsolicited bulk electronic mail (TUBES), satisfies constitutionally protected due process requirements in that the volume of the transmissions is clearly delineated, and thus, the public is on notice as to the precise limitations on their conduct. Where the terms used in TUBES are given their plain meaning and are harmonized with each other, a reasonable person is able to govern his or her conduct in a way to access the Internet for the purpose of transmitting electronic mail from anywhere in the world without fear of criminal prosecution in Virginia. Commonwealth v. Jaynes, 65 Va. Cir. 355, 2004 Va. Cir. LEXIS 272 (Loudoun County 2004).

Multiple-count indictments under statute governing the transmission of unsolicited bulk electronic mail were not subject to dismissal on the grounds that conviction on all the counts would violate defendants' constitutional rights protecting them from double jeopardy where the indictments charged distinct and separate times when the discrete acts of legislatively proscribed criminal conduct are alleged to have been committed. Commonwealth v. Jaynes, 65 Va. Cir. 355, 2004 Va. Cir. LEXIS 272 (Loudoun County 2004).

Statute governing the transmission of unsolicited bulk electronic mail does not violate the dormant commerce clause because Virginia has an interest in the protection of the property interests of its citizens and the requirement that intentionally disingenuous information be deleted from the routing process does not impose a weighty burden, if a burden at all, on any person or business choosing to send bulk electronic mail or on other states and the limitations that they choose to impose upon unsolicited bulk electronic mail transmissions. Commonwealth v. Jaynes, 65 Va. Cir. 355, 2004 Va. Cir. LEXIS 272 (Loudoun County 2004).

Constitutionality of misdemeanor provisions. — While the misdemeanor provisions of the statute governing the transmission of unsolicited bulk electronic mail, are constitutionally suspect both because of their failure to qualify by type or quantify by number the meaning of "bulk" electronic mail, since defendants had not been charged with the misdemeanor violations, judgment on the constitutionality of those provisions was reserved. Commonwealth v. Jaynes, 65 Va. Cir. 355, 2004 Va. Cir. LEXIS 272 (Loudoun County 2004).

Indictment sufficient without routing information. — Defendants who were charged with violations of § 18.2-152.3:1 were not entitled to a bill of particulars when the indictment sufficiently set forth where and when the offenses were allegedly committed. Routing information, names of electronic mail service providers and their subscribers, and the identity of the recepients, did not need to be provided when the act of transmission was the act that was circumscribed by the statute. Commonwealth v. Jaynes, 64 Va. Cir. 443, 2004 Va. Cir. LEXIS 155 (Loudoun County 2004).

Statute governing the transmission of unsolicited bulk electronic mail, which criminalizes the falsification or forging of transmission or other routing information, is not an unlawful content-based prior restraint on speech because, even assuming that TUBES implicates the First Amendment, the routing information affects only the manner and speed at which the mail is conveyed, not the content of the message, and limits only the use of false or forged transmission of routing information by senders of electronic mail, leaving open other channels of communication for those seeking to get their message to the public. Commonwealth v. Jaynes, 65 Va. Cir. 355, 2004 Va. Cir. LEXIS 272 (Loudoun County 2004).

§ 18.2-152.4. Computer trespass; penalty.

A. It shall be unlawful for any person, with malicious intent, to:

1. Temporarily or permanently remove, halt, or otherwise disable any computer data, computer programs or computer software from a computer or computer network;

2. Cause a computer to malfunction, regardless of how long the malfunction persists;

3. Alter, disable, or erase any computer data, computer programs or computer software;

4. Effect the creation or alteration of a financial instrument or of an electronic transfer of funds;

5. Use a computer or computer network to cause physical injury to the property of another;

6. Use a computer or computer network to make or cause to be made an unauthorized copy, in any form, including, but not limited to, any printed or electronic form of computer data, computer programs or computer software residing in, communicated by, or produced by a computer or computer network;

7. [Repealed.]

8. Install or cause to be installed, or collect information through, computer software that records all or a majority of the keystrokes made on the computer of another without the computer owner's authorization; or

9. Install or cause to be installed on the computer of another, computer software for the purpose of (i) taking control of that computer so that it can cause damage to another computer or (ii) disabling or disrupting the ability of the computer to share or transmit instructions or data to other computers or to any related computer equipment or devices, including but not limited to printers, scanners, or fax machines.

B. Any person who violates this section is guilty of computer trespass, which shall be a Class 1 misdemeanor. If there is damage to the property of another valued at $1,000 or more caused by such person's act in violation of this section, the offense shall be a Class 6 felony. If a person installs or causes to be installed computer software in violation of this section on more than five computers of another, the offense shall be a Class 6 felony. If a person violates subdivision A 8, the offense shall be a Class 6 felony.

C. Nothing in this section shall be construed to interfere with or prohibit terms or conditions in a contract or license related to computers, computer data, computer networks, computer operations, computer programs, computer services, or computer software or to create any liability by reason of terms or conditions adopted by, or technical measures implemented by, a Virginia-based electronic mail service provider to prevent the transmission of unsolicited electronic mail in violation of this article. Nothing in this section shall be construed to prohibit the monitoring of computer usage of, the otherwise lawful copying of data of, or the denial of computer or Internet access to a minor by a parent or legal guardian of the minor.

History.
1984, c. 751; 1985, c. 322; 1990, c. 663; 1998, c. 892; 1999, cc. 886, 904, 905; 2002, c. 195; 2003, cc. 987, 1016; 2005, cc. 761, 812, 827; 2007, c. 483.

Cross references.
As to transmission of unsolicited bulk electronic mail, see now § 18.2-15.3:1.

Law Review.
For article on Virginia's response to computer abuses, see 19 U. Rich. L. Rev. 85 (1984). For an article relating to all published Virginia criminal law decisions between July 1, 1997, and July 1, 1998, see 32 U. Rich. L. Rev. 1091 (1998). For an article, "Technology and the Law," see 32 U. Rich. L. Rev. 1383 (1998). For a note, "Computer Network Trespasses: Solving New Problems with Old Solutions," see 57 Wash. & Lee L. Rev. 209 (2000). For article surveying developments in family law in Virginia, see 37 U. Rich. L. Rev. 155 (2002).

Michie's Jurisprudence.
For related discussion, see 18 M.J. Trespass, § 1.

CASE NOTES

Evidence of violation. — Website host demonstrated that a competitor and its employee obtained its property by false pretenses in violation of § 18.2-152.3 and subdivision A 6 of § 18.2-152.4, where the website host traced alleged hacking attacks to the competitor and its employee, and it was highly likely that the competitor and its employee converted the website host's proprietary information for their own use. Physicians Interactive v. Lathian Sys., — F. Supp. 2d —, 2003 U.S. Dist. LEXIS 22868 (E.D. Va. Dec. 5, 2003).

Trial court did not err in finding defendant guilty, following a bench trial, of computer fraud, computer trespass, embezzlement, and attempted extortion, as the evidence showed that defendant transferred computer files from his computer at work to a third-party server before he was terminated from his position as human resource director, that he used the removed material to threaten the company in an attempt to forgive a loan it had made to him, and that the company established the value of the material removed as required to support convictions on those offenses. DiMaio v. Commonwealth, 46 Va. App. 755, 621 S.E.2d 696, 2005 Va. App. LEXIS 456 (2005).

CIRCUIT COURT OPINIONS

Unauthorized use of computer network. — To the extent defendant's demurrer asserted that no claim was stated because he had authority to use his employer's computer and to download data, the demurrer was overruled because defendant had no authority to use his employer's computers for purposes not authorized by his employer and inimical to his employer's best interest. McGladrey & Pullen, L.L.P. v. Shrader, 62 Va. Cir. 401, 2003 Va. Cir. LEXIS 274 (Rockingham County 2003).

§ 18.2-152.5. Computer invasion of privacy; penalties.

A. A person is guilty of the crime of computer invasion of privacy when he uses a computer or computer network and intentionally examines without authority any employment, salary, credit or any other financial or identifying information, as defined in clauses (iii) through (xiii) of subsection C of § 18.2-186.3, relating to any other person. "Examination" under this section requires the offender to review the information relating to any other person after the time at which the offender knows or should know that he is without authority to view the information displayed.

B. The crime of computer invasion of privacy shall be punishable as a Class 1 misdemeanor.

C. Any person who violates this section after having been previously convicted of a violation of this section or any substantially similar laws of any other state or of the United States is guilty of a Class 6 felony.

D. Any person who violates this section and sells or distributes such information to another is guilty of a Class 6 felony.

E. Any person who violates this section and uses such information in the commission of another crime is guilty of a Class 6 felony.

F. This section shall not apply to any person collecting information that is reasonably needed to (i) protect the security of a computer, computer service, or computer business, or to facilitate diagnostics or repair in connection with such computer, computer service, or computer business or (ii) determine whether the computer user is licensed or authorized to use specific computer software or a specific computer service.

History.
1984, c. 751; 1985, c. 398; 2001, c. 358; 2005, cc. 747, 761, 827, 837.

Law Review.
For article on Virginia's response to computer abuses, see 19 U. Rich. L. Rev. 85 (1984).

Michie's Jurisprudence.
For related discussion, see 16 M.J. Right of Privacy, § 1.

CASE NOTES

Evidence sufficient. — The evidence was sufficient to support the defendant's conviction under this section where the defendant, a police dispatcher, used the Virginia Criminal Information Network to access criminal information regarding four individuals without authorization and without any request for the information. Plasters v. Commonwealth, No. 1870-99-3, 2000 Va. App. LEXIS 473 (Ct. of Appeals June 27, 2000).

CIRCUIT COURT OPINIONS

Discovery. — Virginia circuit courts may, pursuant to the powers governing discovery, grant "authority" for parties to access information otherwise protected by § 18.2-152.5. However, Va. Sup. Ct. R. 4:9 limits inspection and copying to "designated" documents; it does not allow a party to access computer files carte blanche. Albertson v. Albertson, 73 Va. Cir. 94, 2007 Va. Cir. LEXIS 132 (Fairfax County 2007).

§ 18.2-152.5:1. Using a computer to gather identifying information; penalties.

A. It is unlawful for any person, other than a law-enforcement officer, as defined in § 9.1-101, and acting in the performance of his official duties, to use a computer to obtain, access, or record, through the use of material artifice, trickery or deception, any identifying information, as defined in clauses (iii) through (xiii) of subsection C of § 18.2-186.3. Any person who violates this section is guilty of a Class 6 felony.

B. Any person who violates this section and sells or distributes such information to another is guilty of a Class 5 felony.

C. Any person who violates this section and uses such information in the commission of another crime is guilty of a Class 5 felony.

History.
2005, cc. 747, 760, 761, 827, 837.

§ 18.2-152.6. Theft of computer services; penalties.

Any person who willfully obtains computer services without authority is guilty of the crime of theft of computer services, which shall be punishable as a Class 1 misdemeanor. If the theft of computer services is valued at $2,500 or more, he is guilty of a Class 6 felony.

History.
1984, c. 751; 1985, c. 322; 2003, cc. 987, 1016; 2005, cc. 746, 761, 827.

Law Review.
For article on Virginia's response to computer abuses, see 19 U. Rich. L. Rev. 85 (1984).

Michie's Jurisprudence.
For related discussion, see 12A M.J. Larceny, § 2.

CASE NOTES

Evidence held insufficient. — Where a high school student misrepresented himself as a college student in order to submit his written work as a college student for review and archiving by a company that checked students' submitted papers for plagiarism, the student was entitled to summary judgment on the company's claim that he violated the Virginia Computer Crimes Act, because the company failed to produce any evidence of actual or economic damages resulting from the student's allegedly unauthorized submissions. A.V. v. iParadigms, 544 F. Supp. 2d 473, 2008 U.S. Dist. LEXIS 19715 (E.D. Va. 2008).

Damages. — Summary judgment was granted against the company's counterclaims under the Computer Fraud and Abuse Act (CFAA), 18 U.S.C.S. § 1030(a)(5)(A)(iii) & (B)(i), and the Virginia Computer Crimes Act (VCCA), §§ 18.2-152.1-18.2-152.16, based on the conclusion that the company failed to produce evidence that it suffered any actual or economic damages; however, the district court construed the economic damages provision too narrowly for the CFAA claim and the evidence of consequential damages presented by the company came within the any damages language of the VCCA. A.V. v. iParadigms, LLC, 562 F.3d 630, 2009 U.S. App. LEXIS 7892 (4th Cir. 2009).

§ 18.2-152.7. Personal trespass by computer; penalty.

A. A person is guilty of the crime of personal trespass by computer when he uses a computer or computer network to cause physical injury to an individual.

B. If committed maliciously, the crime of personal trespass by computer shall be punishable as a Class 3 felony. If such act is done unlawfully but not maliciously, the crime of personal trespass by computer shall be punishable as a Class 6 felony.

History.
1984, c. 751; 1985, c. 322; 2003, cc. 987, 1016; 2005, cc. 746, 761, 827.

Law Review.
For article on Virginia's response to computer abuses, see 19 U. Rich. L. Rev. 85 (1984). For a note, "Computer Network Trespasses: Solving New Problems with Old Solutions," see 57 Wash. & Lee L. Rev. 209 (2000).

Michie's Jurisprudence.
For related discussion, see 18 M.J. Trespass, § 1.

§ 18.2-152.7:1. Harassment by computer; penalty.

If any person, with the intent to coerce, intimidate, or harass any person, shall use a computer or computer network to communicate obscene, vulgar, profane, lewd, lascivious, or indecent language, or make any suggestion or proposal of an obscene nature, or threaten any illegal or immoral act, he shall be guilty of a Class 1 misdemeanor.

History.
2000, c. 849.

Law Review.
For a note, "Computer Network Trespasses: Solving New Problems with Old Solutions," see 57 Wash. & Lee L. Rev. 209 (2000). For annual survey of Virginia law article, "Criminal Law and Procedure," see 47 U. Rich. L. Rev. 143 (2012).

CASE NOTES

Employee failed to allege "intent to coerce, intimidate, or harass." — In granting a motion to dismiss a wrongful discharge claim in violation of public policy, the court found that an employee failed to state a claim for computer harassment; the employee had not alleged that her supervisor sent offensive e-mails with an intent "to coerce, intimidate, or harass" her, and moreover, there was no causal connection between the alleged conduct and her termination. Miller v. Wash. Workplace, Inc., 298 F. Supp. 2d 364, 2004 U.S. Dist. LEXIS 5773 (E.D. Va. 2004).

References in an instant message were not obscene. — Defendant's conviction for harassment by computer in violation of § 18.2-152.7:1 was reversed, as defendant's use of "whore" and repeated use of "fuck you" in an instant message to the victim was insufficient to permit a reasonable trier of fact to conclude the references were obscene; the words were used as a method to show anger with the victim and to direct the victim away from defendant's roommate. Airhart v. Commonwealth, — Va. App. —, — S.E.2d —, 2007 Va. App. LEXIS 11 (Jan. 16, 2007).

Obscenity. — Court of appeals erred in affirming defendant's conviction for harassment by computer in violation § 18.2-152.7:1 because it should not have substituted a dictionary definition of "obscene" for that provided by the general assembly in § 18.2-372;

the general assembly provided a definition of "obscene" in § 18.2-372 to comport with constitutional requirements, and there was no suggestion that the definition was constitutionally infirm. Barson v. Commonwealth, 284 Va. 67, 726 S.E.2d 292, 2012 Va. LEXIS 121 (2012).

Search and seizure. — District court properly denied defendant's motion to suppress evidence of a DVD containing child pornography in his trial for possession of child pornography in violation of 18 U.S.C.S. §§ 2252A(a)(5)(B) and 2256(8)(A) because the computer files containing child pornography did not fall outside the scope of a search warrant for purposes of U.S. Const., Amend. IV; the images of child pornography contained on the DVD were sufficiently relevant to the crimes designated in the warrant to justify their seizure under the warrant, which authorized a search for instrumentalities of computer harassment under § 18.2-152.7:1. United States v. Williams, 592 F.3d 511, 2010 U.S. App. LEXIS 1327 (4th Cir. 2010), cert. denied, 131 S. Ct. 595, 178 L. Ed. 2d 434, 2010 U.S. LEXIS 8864 (U.S. 2010).

No due process violation. — When it was found that sufficient evidence supported defendant's conviction under § 18.2-152.7:1, prohibiting harassment by computer, when applying the common definition of "obscene," rather than a definition of that term that was used in a prior appellate decision, defendant's right to due process was not violated because the criminalization of the conduct resulting in defendant's conviction predated that decision, which dealt with a different criminal statute and remained subject to the appellate court's en banc review, as well as review by the Virginia Supreme Court. Barson v. Commonwealth, 58 Va. App. 451, 711 S.E.2d 220, 2011 Va. App. LEXIS 228 (2011).

Venue. — Commonwealth established venue in Virginia Beach under subdivisions 4 and 6 of § 19.2-249.2 during defendant's trial for harassment by computer in violation of § 18.2-152.7:1 because the evidence was sufficient to prove a strong presumption that the victim received the e-mails defendant sent her while she resided in Virginia Beach, on a computer located within Virginia Beach; the victim lived in Virginia Beach, and she testified that all the offensive e-mails were sent to her e-mail account in the City of Virginia Beach. Barson v. Commonwealth, 2010 Va. App. LEXIS 427 (Nov. 2, 2010).

Evidence sufficient to support conviction. — Sufficient evidence supported defendant's conviction under § 18.2-152.7:1, prohibiting harassment by computer, arising from e-mails defendant sent to the victim, because (1) the common definition of the word "obscene" more accurately encompassed the type of communicative conduct proscribed by the statute, namely, that which was obscene, vulgar, profane, lewd, lascivious, or indecent, than did a definition in § 18.2-372, which was actually a definition of pornography, and (2) a reasonable fact finder could conclude that the language defendant used in the e-mails to the victim fit the common definition. Barson v. Commonwealth, 58 Va. App. 451, 711 S.E.2d 220, 2011 Va. App. LEXIS 228 (2011).

Defendant was properly convicted of computer harassment in violation of § 18.2-152.7:1, as many of his e-mails to the victim expressed "an appeal to the prurient interest in sex," included "shameful" sexual suggestions that went "substantially beyond customary limits," as these terms were used in the obscenity statute, § 18.2-352, and many of them made obscene proposals and implicitly threatened "illegal or immoral" acts. Moter v. Commonwealth, 61 Va. App. 471, 737 S.E.2d 538, 2013 Va. App. LEXIS 54 (2013).

Evidence insufficient to support conviction. — Trial court erred in convicting defendant of harassment by computer in violation of § 18.2-152.7:1 because the evidence was insufficient to permit a reasonable trier of fact to conclude that the e-mails defendant sent were obscene under § 18.2-372; although the e-mails contained vulgar, offensive, and sexually explicit language, defendant's use of those words, considered as a whole and in the context of the marital discord and the angry, offensive tone and purpose of the e-mails, did not establish or support a factual or legal determination that he intended an appeal to the prurient interest in sex, but rather, the evidence showed that defendant wrote the e-mails solely to convey his anger and disgust and that he forwarded them to his family and friends to embarrass the victim. Barson v. Commonwealth, 2010 Va. App. LEXIS 427 (Nov. 2, 2010).

Court of appeals erred in affirming defendant's conviction for harassment by computer in violation of § 18.2-152.7:1 because

defendant's emails to his wife, as offensive, vulgar, and disgusting as their language could have been, did not meet the standard of obscenity provided by § 18.2-372. Barson v. Commonwealth, 284 Va. 67, 726 S.E.2d 292, 2012 Va. LEXIS 121 (2012).

§ 18.2-152.8. Property capable of embezzlement.

For purposes of §§ 18.2-95, 18.2-96, 18.2-108, and 18.2-111, personal property subject to embezzlement, larceny, or receiving stolen goods shall include:

1. Computers and computer networks;

2. Financial instruments, computer data, computer programs, computer software and all other personal property regardless of whether they are:

a. Tangible or intangible;

b. In a format readable by humans or by a computer;

c. In transit between computers or within a computer network or between any devices which comprise a computer; or

d. Located on any paper or in any device on which it is stored by a computer or by a human; and

3. Computer services.

History.
1984, c. 751; 2005, cc. 746, 761, 827.

Law Review.
For article on Virginia's response to computer abuses, see 19 U. Rich. L. Rev. 85 (1984).

Michie's Jurisprudence.
For related discussion, see 6B M.J. Embezzlement, § 4.

§§ 18.2-152.9, 18.2-152.10. Repealed by Acts 2005, cc. 746, 761, and 827, cl. 2.

§ 18.2-152.11. Article not exclusive.

The provisions of this article shall not be construed to preclude the applicability of any other provision of the criminal law of this Commonwealth which presently applies or may in the future apply to any transaction or course of conduct which violates this article, unless such provision is clearly inconsistent with the terms of this article.

History.
1984, c. 751.

§ 18.2-152.12. Civil relief; damages.

A. Any person whose property or person is injured by reason of a violation of any provision of this article or by any act of computer trespass set forth in subdivisions A 1 through A 8 of § 18.2-152.4 regardless of whether such act is committed with malicious intent may sue therefor and recover for any damages sustained and the costs of suit. Without limiting the generality of the term, "damages" shall include loss of profits.

B. If the injury under this article arises from the transmission of spam in contravention of the authority granted by or in violation of the policies set by the electronic mail service provider where the defendant has knowledge of the authority or policies of the EMSP or where the authority or policies of the EMSP are available on the electronic mail service provider's website, the injured person, other than an electronic mail service provider, may also recover attorneys' fees and costs, and may elect, in lieu of actual damages, to recover the lesser of $10 for each and every spam message transmitted in violation of this article, or $25,000 per day. The injured person shall not have a cause of action against the electronic mail service provider that merely transmits the spam over its computer network. Transmission of electronic mail from an organization to its members shall not be deemed to be spam.

C. If the injury under this article arises from the transmission of spam in contravention of the authority granted by or in violation of the policies set by the electronic mail service provider where the defendant has knowledge of the authority or policies of the EMSP or where the authority or policies of the EMSP are available on the electronic mail service provider's website, an injured electronic mail service provider may also recover attorneys' fees and costs, and may elect, in lieu of actual damages, to recover $1 for each and every intended recipient of a spam message where the intended recipient is an end user of the EMSP or $25,000 for each day an attempt is made to transmit a spam message to an end user of the EMSP. In calculating the statutory damages under this provision, the court may adjust the amount awarded as necessary, but in doing so shall take into account the number of complaints to the EMSP generated by the defendant's messages, the defendant's degree of culpability, the defendant's prior history of such conduct, and the extent of economic gain resulting from the conduct. Transmission of electronic mail from an organization to its members shall not be deemed to be spam.

D. At the request of any party to an action brought pursuant to this section, the court may, in its discretion, conduct all legal proceedings in such a way as to protect the secrecy and security of the computer, computer network, computer data, computer program and computer software involved in order to prevent possible recurrence of the same or a similar act by another person and to protect any trade secrets of any party and in such a way as to protect the privacy of nonparties who complain about violations of this section.

E. The provisions of this article shall not be construed to limit any person's right to pursue any additional civil remedy otherwise allowed by law.

F. A civil action under this section must be commenced before expiration of the time period prescribed in § 8.01-40.1. In actions alleging injury arising from the transmission of spam, personal jurisdiction may be exercised pursuant to § 8.01-328.1.

History.

1984, c. 751; 1985, c. 92; 1999, cc. 886, 904, 905; 2003, cc. 987, 1016; 2005, cc. 746, 761, 827; 2010, cc. 489, 529.

Editor's note.

Acts 2010, c. 489, cl. 2 provides: "Pursuant to § 30-19.1:4, the estimated amount of the necessary appropriation cannot be determined for periods of imprisonment in state adult correctional facilities; therefore, Chapter 781 of the 2009 Acts of Assembly requires the Virginia Criminal Sentencing Commission to assign a minimum fiscal impact of $50,000. Pursuant to § 30-19.1:4, the estimated amount of the necessary appropriation is $0 for periods of commitment to the custody of the Department of Juvenile Justice."

The 2010 amendments.

The 2010 amendment by c. 489 substituted "spam" for "unsolicited bulk electonic mail" throughout the section.

The 2010 amendment by c. 529 substituted "A 8" for "A 6" in subsection A.

Law Review.

For a note, "Allocating Discovery Costs in the Computer Age: Deciding Who Should Bear the Costs of Discovery of Electronically Stored Data," see 57 Wash. & Lee L. Rev. 257 (2000). For a note, "Computer Network Trespasses: Solving New Problems with Old Solutions," see 57 Wash. & Lee L. Rev. 209 (2000).

CASE NOTES

Evidence of actual damages. — Summary judgment was granted against the company's counterclaims under the Computer Fraud and Abuse Act (CFAA), 18 U.S.C.S. § 1030(a)(5)(A)(iii) & (B)(i), and the Virginia Computer Crimes Act (VCCA), §§ 18.2-152.1-18.2-152.16, based on the conclusion that the company failed to produce evidence that it suffered any actual or economic damages; however, the district court construed the economic damages provision too narrowly for the CFAA claim and the evidence of consequential damages presented by the company came within the any damages language of the VCCA. A.V. v. iParadigms, LLC, 562 F.3d 630, 2009 U.S. App. LEXIS 7892 (4th Cir. 2009).

CIRCUIT COURT OPINIONS

No violation. — Because a company failed to show an injury that resulted from a former employee's actions in inadvertently copying two documents while clearing out personal computer files, there was no violation of § 18.2-152.12. Tryco, Inc. v. United States Med. Source, 80 Va. Cir. 619, 2010 Va. Cir. LEXIS 91 (Fairfax County Aug. 3, 2010).

Punitive damages not allowed. — Punitive damages are not permitted under the Virginia Computer Crimes Act. McGladrey & Pullen, L.L.P. v. Shrader, 62 Va. Cir. 401, 2003 Va. Cir. LEXIS 274 (Rockingham County 2003).

§ 18.2-152.13. Severability.

If any provision or clause of this article or application thereof to any person or circumstances is held to be invalid, such invalidity shall not affect other provisions or applications of this article which can be given effect without the invalid provision or application, and to this end the provisions of this article are declared to be severable.

History.

1984, c. 751.

§ 18.2-152.14. Computer as instrument of forgery.

The creation, alteration, or deletion of any computer data contained in any computer or computer network, which if done on a tangible document or instrument would constitute forgery under Article 1 (§ 18.2-168 et seq.) of Chapter 6 of this Title, will also be deemed to be forgery. The absence of a tangible writing directly created or altered by the offender shall not be a defense to any crime set forth in Article 1 (§ 18.2-168 et seq.) of Chapter 6 of this Title if a creation, alteration, or deletion of computer data was involved in lieu of a tangible document or instrument.

History.
    1984, c. 751; 1985, c. 322.

Michie's Jurisprudence.
    For related discussion, see 8B M.J. Forgery, § 9.

§ 18.2-152.15. Encryption used in criminal activity.

Any person who willfully uses encryption to further any criminal activity shall be guilty of an offense which is separate and distinct from the predicate criminal activity and punishable as a Class 1 misdemeanor.

"Encryption" means the enciphering of intelligible data into unintelligible form or the deciphering of unintelligible data into intelligible form.

History.
    1999, c. 455.

§ 18.2-152.16. Repealed by Acts 2004, c. 995.

Cross references.
    For current provisions as to forfeitures for computer crimes, see § 19.2-386.17.

ARTICLE 7.2.

FRAUDULENT PROCUREMENT, SALE, OR RECEIPT OF TELEPHONE RECORDS.

§ 18.2-152.17. Fraudulent procurement, sale, or receipt of telephone records.

A. Whoever (i) knowingly procures, attempts to procure, solicits, or conspires with another to procure a telephone record by fraudulent means; (ii) knowingly sells, or attempts to sell, a telephone record without the authorization of the customer to whom the record pertains; or (iii) receives a telephone record knowing that such record has been obtained by fraudulent means is guilty of a Class 1 misdemeanor.

B. As used in this section:

"Procure" in regard to such a telephone record means to obtain by any means, whether electronically, in writing, or in oral form, with or without consideration.

"Telecommunications carrier" means any person that provides commercial telephone services to a customer, irrespective of the communications technology used to provide such service, including, but not limited to, traditional wireline or cable telephone service; cellular, broadband PCS, or other wireless telephone service; microwave, satellite, or other terrestrial telephone service; and voice over Internet telephone service.

"Telephone record" means information retained by a telecommunications carrier that relates to the telephone number dialed by the customer or the incoming number of a call directed to a customer, or other data related to such calls typically contained on a customer telephone bill such as the time the call started and ended, the duration of the call, the time of day the call was made, and any charges applied. For purposes of this section, any information collected and retained by customers utilizing Caller I.D., or other similar technology, does not constitute a telephone record.

C. Nothing in this section shall be construed to prevent any action by a law-enforcement agency, or any officer or employee of such agency, from obtaining telephone records in connection with the performance of the official duties of the agency.

D. Nothing in this section shall be construed to prohibit a telecommunications carrier from obtaining, using, disclosing, or permitting access to any telephone record, either directly or indirectly through its agents (i) in compliance with a subpoena or subpoena duces tecum or as otherwise authorized by law; (ii) with the lawful consent of the customer or subscriber; (iii) as may be necessarily incident to the rendition of the service or to the protection of the rights or property of the provider of that service, or to protect users of those services and other carriers from fraudulent, abusive, or unlawful use of, subscription to, such services; (iv) to a governmental entity, if the telecommunications carrier reasonably believes that an emergency involving immediate danger of death or serious physical injury to any person justifies disclosure of the information; or (v) to the National Center for Missing and Exploited Children, in connection with a report submitted thereto under the Victims of Child Abuse Act of 1990.

E. Venue for the trial of any person charged with an offense under this section may be in the locality in which:

1. Any act was performed in furtherance of any course of conduct in violation of this section;

2. The accused has his principal place of business in the Commonwealth;

3. Any accused had control or possession of any proceeds of the violation or of any books, records, documents, property, financial instrument, telephone record, or other material or objects that were used in furtherance of the violation;

4. From which, to which, or through which any access to a telecommunication carrier was made whether by wires, electromagnetic waves, microwaves, optics or any other means of communication; or

5. The accused resides, or resided at the time of the offense.

History.
2006, c. 469.

ARTICLE 8.

OFFENSES RELATING TO RAILROADS AND OTHER UTILITIES.

Michie's Jurisprudence.
For related discussion, see 3A M.J. Canals and Canal Companies, §§ 2, 3; 13B M.J. Negligence, § 22.

§ 18.2-153. Obstructing or injuring canal, railroad, power line, etc.

If any person maliciously obstruct, remove or injure any part of a canal, railroad or urban, suburban or interurban electric railway, or any lines of any electric power company, or any bridge or fixture thereof, or maliciously obstruct, tamper with, injure or remove any machinery, engine, car, trolley, supply or return wires or any other work thereof, or maliciously open, close, displace, tamper with or injure any switch, switch point, switch lever, signal lever or signal of any such company, whereby the life of any person on such canal, railroad, urban, suburban or interurban electric railway, is put in peril, he shall be guilty of a Class 4 felony; and, in the event of the death of any such person resulting from such malicious act, the person so offending shall be deemed guilty of murder, the degree to be determined by the jury or the court trying the case without a jury.

If any such act be committed unlawfully, but not maliciously, the person so offending shall be guilty of a Class 6 felony; and in the event of the death of any such person resulting from such unlawful act, the person so offending shall be deemed guilty of involuntary manslaughter.

History.
Code 1950, § 18.1-147; 1960, c. 358; 1975, cc. 14, 15.

Michie's Jurisprudence.
For related discussion, see 15 M.J. Railroads, §§ 57, 143.

§ 18.2-154. Shooting at or throwing missiles, etc., at train, car, vessel, etc.; penalty.

Any person who maliciously shoots at, or maliciously throws any missile at or against, any train or cars on any railroad or other transportation company or any vessel or other watercraft, or any motor vehicle or other vehicles when occupied by one or more persons, whereby the life of any person on such train, car, vessel, or other watercraft, or in such motor vehicle or other vehicle, may be put in peril, is guilty of a Class 4 felony. In the event of the death of any such person, resulting from such malicious shooting or throwing, the person so offending is

guilty of murder in the second degree. However, if the homicide is willful, deliberate and premeditated, he is guilty of murder in the first degree.

If any such act is committed unlawfully, but not maliciously, the person so offending is guilty of a Class 6 felony and, in the event of the death of any such person, resulting from such unlawful act, the person so offending is guilty of involuntary manslaughter.

If any person commits a violation of this section by maliciously or unlawfully shooting, with a firearm, at a conspicuously marked law-enforcement, fire or rescue squad vehicle, ambulance or any other emergency medical vehicle, the sentence imposed shall include a mandatory minimum term of imprisonment of one year to be served consecutively with any other sentence.

History.
Code 1950, § 18.1-152; 1960, c. 358; 1975, cc. 14, 15; 1990, c. 426; 2004, c. 461; 2005, c. 143; 2013, cc. 761, 774.

Editor's note.
Acts 2013, cc. 761 and 774, cl. 2 provides: "That the provisions of this act may result in a net increase in periods of imprisonment or commitment. Pursuant to § 30-19.1:4, the estimated amount of the necessary appropriation cannot be determined for periods of imprisonment in state adult correctional facilities; therefore, Chapter 3 of the Acts of Assembly of 2012, Special Session I, requires the Virginia Criminal Sentencing Commission to assign a minimum fiscal impact of $50,000. Pursuant to § 30-19.1:4, the estimated amount of the necessary appropriation cannot be determined for periods of commitment to the custody of the Department of Juvenile Justice."

The 2013 amendments.
The 2013 amendments by cc. 761 and 774 are identical, and added "to be served consecutively with any other sentence" at the end of the third paragraph.

CASE NOTES

This section was not unconstitutionally vague as applied to defendant convicted of second degree murder thereafter. Willis v. Commonwealth, 10 Va. App. 430, 393 S.E.2d 405 (1990). See amendments by Acts 2005, c. 143.

Court should have declined deciding whether portion of statute unconstitutionally vague. — The aspect of this section that would allegedly allow the judge or jury unfettered discretion to determine what constitutes first degree murder is severable from those provisions of the statute which define the offense of murder, which is deemed second degree. Thus, since defendant was not convicted of first degree murder, the court should have declined deciding whether that portion of the statute was unconstitutionally vague. Willis v. Commonwealth, 10 Va. App. 430, 393 S.E.2d 405 (1990). See amendments by Acts 2005, c. 143.

Legislative intent. — The legislature, when it enacted the predecessor to this section, clearly intended to make punishable as murder the killing of an occupant of a motor vehicle resulting from a malicious shooting into the vehicle whereby the life of any person in the vehicle is put in peril. Willis v. Commonwealth, 10 Va. App. 430, 393 S.E.2d 405 (1990).

Homicide under section is presumptively second degree murder. — In Virginia, every malicious killing is prima facie second degree murder, and the burden is on the commonwealth to elevate the grade of the offense to first degree. Accordingly, a homicide resulting from maliciously shooting into an occupied vehicle is presumptively second degree murder. Willis v. Commonwealth, 10 Va. App. 430, 393 S.E.2d 405 (1990).

To constitute murder under this section, the Commonwealth must prove beyond a reasonable doubt that the accused committed:

(1) a malicious shooting, (2) at or against a motor vehicle, (3) when occupied by one or more persons, (4) whereby the life of any person in such motor vehicle may be put in peril, and (5) the death of any such person results therefrom. Willis v. Commonwealth, 10 Va. App. 430, 393 S.E.2d 405 (1990).

Murder under section does not preclude conviction under § 18.2-53.1. — Murder under this section accomplished by a "malicious shooting" does not preclude a conviction under § 18.2-53.1 for use of a firearm in the commission of murder. Willis v. Commonwealth, 10 Va. App. 430, 393 S.E.2d 405 (1990).

Allegation of violation of section sufficient to charge offenses proscribed by reference. — Although original indictment did not contain a separate averment that felonious shooting caused the death of an occupant of a vehicle, the allegation, that defendant's acts violated this section, incorporated the offenses proscribed therein by reference and was sufficient to charge him with those offenses which are proscribed by that section of the criminal code, including murder. Thus because the original indictment was sufficient to have prosecuted defendant for murder, an amendment adding language that the shooting resulted in the death of an occupant of the vehicle did not change the nature of character of the acts which the indictment alleged that defendant had committed. Willis v. Commonwealth, 10 Va. App. 430, 393 S.E.2d 405 (1990).

Assault not a lesser-included offense. — In a case in which defendant was convicted for unlawful shooting at an occupied vehicle, in violation of § 18.2-154, he unsuccessfully argued that double jeopardy barred his conviction, because he was previously tried and convicted of assault, arising out of the same events and assault was a lesser-included offense of unlawful shooting at an occupied vehicle. The plain language of § 18.2-154 simply did not require the intent to inflict bodily injury on the part of the accused, and, since the intent requirement was an essential element required to prove assault, assault was not a lesser-included offense in unlawful shooting at an occupied vehicle. Armstead v. Commonwealth, 55 Va. App. 354, 685 S.E.2d 876, 2009 Va. App. LEXIS 563 (2009).

Multiple shots constitute multiple violations. — This statute does not proscribe a continuous course of conduct; rather, each offense is complete upon the firing of one shot when the life of another is endangered and a defendant who fires multiple shots at a motor vehicle may thus be convicted of multiple violations of the statute. Stephens v. Commonwealth, 35 Va. App. 141, 543 S.E.2d 609, 2001 Va. App. LEXIS 134 (2001), aff'd, 263 Va. 58, 557 S.E.2d 227 (2002).

Evidence held sufficient. — Defendant's conviction of maliciously throwing a missile at an occupied motor vehicle in violation of § 18.2-154 was supported by sufficient evidence, where a bottle which defendant threw into the cab of a truck could have placed a person's life in peril, by causing the driver to lose control of the vehicle or to drive recklessly from the scene. Davis v. Commonwealth, No. 2480-01-2, 2003 Va. App. LEXIS 242 (Ct. of Appeals Apr. 22, 2003).

Evidence supported a defendant's conviction for deliberately throwing rocks with sufficient force to break a van's rear window and his conviction for intentional vandalism. Lamb v. Commonwealth, No. 1262-02-2, 2003 Va. App. LEXIS 252 (Ct. of Appeals Apr. 29, 2003).

Evidence held insufficient. — Evidence was insufficient to convict defendant of maliciously shooting into an occupied vehicle in violation of § 18.2-154 because the trial court erred in rejecting defendant's self-defense claim as it applied to the initial aggressor and to the innocent bystander. Defendant acted in justifiable self-defense, had no obligation to retreat, and was permitted to repel the attack by reasonable force where the initial aggressor, who one month prior had shot and injured defendant, shot at or into defendant's vehicle and, therefore, defendant was not criminally responsible for the innocent bystander's ultimate injury, which occurred when defendant returned fire. Hill v. Commonwealth, 2010 Va. App. LEXIS 219 (June 1, 2010).

Jury instructions. — Where no rational fact finder could find that a victim of an armed robbery did anything that could have provoked defendant to shoot the victim after the victim entered a vehicle, the trial court correctly ruled that the heat-of-passion instruction could not be given. Smith v. Commonwealth, No. 2992-02-3, 2004 Va. App. LEXIS 213 (Ct. of Appeals May 4, 2004).

Sentencing. — Defendant's prior Virginia conviction for throw-ing a missile at an occupied vehicle, in violation of § 18.2-154, qualified as a categorical crime of violence such that his career offender designation was proper under U.S. Sentencing Guidelines Manual §§ 4B1.1, 4B1.2, despite error in using the modified categorical approach. United States v. Light, 2012 U.S. App. LEXIS 24722 (4th Cir. Nov. 29, 2012).

§ 18.2-155. Injuring, etc., signal used by railroad.

If any person maliciously injure, destroy, molest, or remove any switchlamp, flag or other signal used by any railroad, or any line, wire, post, lamp or any other structure or mechanism used in connection with any signal on a railroad, or destroys or in any manner interferes with the proper working of any signal on a railroad, whereby the life of any person is or may be put in peril he shall be guilty of a Class 4 felony; and in the event of the death of such person resulting from such malicious injuring, destroying or removing, the person so offending shall be deemed guilty of murder, the degree to be determined by the jury or the court trying the case without a jury. If such act be done unlawfully but not maliciously the offender shall be guilty of a Class 1 misdemeanor, provided that in the event of the death of any such person resulting from such unlawful injuring, destroying or removing, the person so offending shall be deemed guilty of involuntary manslaughter.

History.
Code 1950, § 18.1-153; 1960, c. 358; 1975, cc. 14, 15.

§ 18.2-156. Taking or removing waste or packing from journal boxes.

If any person shall willfully and maliciously take or remove the waste or packing from any journal box of any locomotive, engine, tender, carriage, coach, car, caboose or truck used or operated upon any railroad, whether the same be operated by steam or electricity, he shall be guilty of a Class 6 felony.

History.
Code 1950, § 18.1-151; 1960, c. 358; 1975, cc. 14, 15.

§ 18.2-157. Injury to fences or cattle stops along line of railroad.

Any person who shall willfully or maliciously cut, break down, injure or destroy any fence erected along the line of any railroad for the purpose of fencing the track or depot grounds of such road, or shall break down, injure or destroy any cattle stop along the line of any railroad, shall be guilty of a Class 3 misdemeanor.

History.
Code 1950, § 18.1-155; 1960, c. 358; 1975, cc. 14, 15.

§ 18.2-158. Driving, etc., animal on track to recover damages.

If any person, with a view to the recovery of damages against a railroad company, willfully ride, drive, or lead any animal, or otherwise contrive for any animal to go, on the railroad track of such company, and such animal is by reason thereof killed or injured, he shall be guilty of a Class 3 misdemeanor.

History.
Code 1950, § 18.1-154; 1960, c. 358; 1975, cc. 14, 15.

Cross references.
As to trespassing on railroad track generally, see § 18.2-159.

§ 18.2-159. Trespassing on railroad track.

Any person who goes upon the track of a railroad other than to pass over such road at a public or private crossing, or who willfully rides, drives or leads any animal or contrives for any animal to go on such track except to cross as aforesaid, without the consent of the railroad company or person operating such road, shall be guilty of a Class 4 misdemeanor. A second violation of the provisions of this section occurring within two years of the first violation shall be punishable as a Class 3 misdemeanor. A third or subsequent violation of the provisions of this section occurring within two years of a second or a subsequent violation shall be punishable as a Class 1 misdemeanor. This section shall not apply to any section of track which has been legally abandoned pursuant to an order of a federal or state agency having jurisdiction over the track and is not being used for railroad service.

For purposes of this section, track shall mean the rail, ties, and ballast of the railroad.

History.
Code 1950, § 18.1-148; 1960, c. 358; 1975, cc. 14, 15; 1993, c. 845.

Cross references.
As to driving animal on railroad track with intent to recover damages, see § 18.2-158.

Michie's Jurisprudence.
For related discussion, see 1B M.J. Animals, § 17; 18 M.J. Trespass, § 1.

CASE NOTES

Railroads are entitled to the exclusive use of their tracks, and it is a violation of this section for one to be on any track without the consent of the company. Ingle v. Clinchfield R.R., 169 Va. 131, 192 S.E. 782 (1937).

Section does not affect liability of railroad to licensee. — In an action for death, it was contended that the decedent at the time of the accident could not be regarded as a licensee, because he was walking on the track, and this section makes it a misdemeanor for any person to be on a railroad track, except at a crossing, within 100 yards of a moving train. It was held that this section could not be given the effect contended for. To do so would deprive licensees of the protection which has always been accorded to them, there being many cases in which recoveries have been allowed to licensees who have been injured on the track while apparently violating this section. C & O Ry. v. Bullington's Adm'r, 135 Va. 307, 16 S.E. 237 (1923).

§ 18.2-160. Trespassing on railroad trains.

If any person, not being a passenger or employee, shall be found trespassing upon any railroad car or train of any railroad in this Commonwealth, by riding on any car, or any part thereof, on its arrival, stay or departure at or from any station or depot of such railroad, or on the passage of any such car or train over any part of any such railroad, such person shall be guilty of a Class 4 misdemeanor.

History.
Code 1950, § 18.1-150; 1960, c. 358; 1975, cc. 14, 15.

Michie's Jurisprudence.
For related discussion, see 18 M.J. Trespass, § 1.

§ 18.2-160.1. Boarding or riding transportation district train without lawful payment of fare; penalty.

A. It is unlawful for any person to board or ride a train operated by, or under contract with, a transportation district created pursuant to Chapter 45 (§ 15.2-4500 et seq.) of Title 15.2 when he fails or refuses to pay the posted fare published by the transportation district, or fails to properly validate a train ticket of the transportation district. A violation of this subsection continues from the point of boarding through termination of the train's scheduled trip. Any person who violates the provisions of this subsection is subject to a civil penalty of $100.

B. It is unlawful for any person to board or ride a train operated by, or under contract with, a transportation district created pursuant to Chapter 45 (§ 15.2-4500 et seq.) of Title 15.2 with a validated ticket and to willfully use the ticket outside the designated zone of the paid ride. A violation of this subsection continues throughout the time that such ticket is used outside the designated zone of the paid ride. Any person who violates the provisions of this subsection is subject to a civil penalty of $100.

C. It is unlawful for any person to board or ride a train operated by, or under contract with, a transportation district created pursuant to Chapter 45 (§ 15.2-4500 et seq.) of Title 15.2 when he uses a fraudulent or counterfeit ticket as a means to evade payment of the posted fare published by the transportation district. A violation of this subsection continues from the point of boarding through termination of the train's scheduled trip. A violation of this subsection is punishable as a Class 2 misdemeanor with a fine of not less than $500 for a first violation and with a fine of not less than $750 for a second or subsequent conviction when the second or subsequent conviction occurs more than 24 hours after but within 365 days of a prior violation.

D. Any person who has been convicted of violating subsection C shall be civilly liable to the Commonwealth and the transportation district for all costs incurred in prosecuting such person. The costs shall be limited to actual expenses, including the base wage of one employee acting as a witness for the Commonwealth and suit costs, but the total costs recovered shall not exceed the maximum amount of the fine that may be imposed for the offense.

History.

1988, c. 762; 1991, c. 241; 2009, c. 760; 2010, cc. 445, 837; 2012, c. 676.

The 2009 amendments.

The 2009 amendment by c. 760 inserted the subsection A and B designations; in subsection A, in the first sentence, substituted "willfully and with intent to defraud (i) fails" for "has failed or refused" and added clauses (ii) through (iv) and substituted "is punishable as a Class 2 misdemeanor" for "shall be punishable by a fine of not less than $150 nor more than $250" in the next-to-last sentence; and in subsection B, in the first sentence, substituted "this section" for "the provisions of § 18.2-160.1," inserted "Commonwealth and the" preceding "transportation district" and deleted "under the provisions of § 18.2-160.1" at the end and substituted "$500" for "$250" in the last sentence.

The 2010 amendments.

The 2010 amendments by cc. 445 and 837 are nearly identical, and designated the former second paragraph of subsection A as subsection D; added subsections B and C; and rewrote subsection A; and in subsection D, substituted "the maximum amount of the fine that may be imposed for the offense" for "$500." In addition, c. 837 substituted "subsection C" for "this section" in subsection D.

The 2012 amendments.

The 2012 amendment by c. 676 added "for a first violation and with a fine of not less than $750 for a second or subsequent conviction when the second or subsequent conviction occurs more than 24 hours after but within 365 days of a prior violation" at the end of the third sentence of subsection C.

§ 18.2-160.2. Trespassing on public transportation; penalty.

Any person who enters or remains upon or within a vehicle operated by a public transportation service without the permission of, or after having been forbidden to do so by, the owner, lessee, or authorized operator thereof is guilty of a Class 4 misdemeanor.

"Public transportation service" means passenger transportation service provided by bus, rail or other surface conveyance that provides transportation to the general public on a regular and continuing basis.

History.

2007, c. 461.

§ 18.2-161. Repealed by Acts 2004, c. 459.

§ 18.2-162. Damage or trespass to public services or utilities.

Any person who shall intentionally destroy or damage any facility which is used to furnish oil, telegraph, telephone, electric, gas, sewer, wastewater or water service to the public, shall be guilty of a Class 4 felony, provided that in the event the destruction or damage may be remedied or repaired for $200 or less such act shall constitute a Class 3 misdemeanor. On electric generating property marked with no trespassing signs, the security personnel of a utility may detain a trespasser for a period not to exceed one hour pending arrival of a law-enforcement officer.

Notwithstanding any other provisions of this title, any person who shall intentionally destroy or damage, or attempt to destroy or damage, any such facility, equipment or material connected therewith, the destruction or damage of which might, in any manner, threaten the release of radioactive materials or ionizing radiation beyond the areas in which they are normally used or contained, shall be guilty of a Class 4 felony, provided that in the event the destruction or damage results in the death of another due to exposure to radioactive materials or ionizing radiation, such person shall be guilty of a Class 2 felony; provided further, that in the event the destruction or damage results in injury to another, such person shall be guilty of a Class 3 felony.

History.

Code 1950, § 18.1-158; 1960, c. 358; 1964, c. 224; 1966, c. 446; 1975, cc. 14, 15; 1980, c. 548; 1981, c. 197; 1985, c. 299; 1992, c. 352.

Michie's Jurisprudence.

For related discussion, see 6B M.J. Electricity, § 18; 12A M.J. Larceny, § 8.

CIRCUIT COURT OPINIONS

Illegality defense to negligence based on statute. — Whether an injured excavator intentionally destroyed an underground power line was an issue properly left to the fact finder; therefore, the trial court did not grant summary judgment to a utility company that the excavator sued for negligence when the utility asserted the defense of illegality. Fulcher v. Va. Elec. & Power Co., 60 Va. Cir. 199, 2002 Va. Cir. LEXIS 267 (Norfolk 2002).

§ 18.2-162.1. Diverting wastewater line; diverting or wasting public water supply.

Any person who willfully and maliciously (i) diverts any public wastewater or sewer line or (ii) diverts or wastes any public water supply by tampering with any fire hydrant shall be guilty of a Class 2 misdemeanor.

History.

1980, c. 140; 1992, c. 352.

§ 18.2-163. Tampering with metering device; diverting service; civil liability.

A. Any person who (i) tampers with any metering device incident to the facilities set forth in § 18.2-162, or otherwise intentionally prevents such a metering device from properly registering the degree, amount or quantity of service supplied, or (ii) diverts such service, except telephonic or electronic extension service not owned or controlled by any such company without authorization from the owner of the facility furnishing the service to the public, shall be guilty of a Class 1 misdemeanor.

B. The presence of any metering device found to have been altered, tampered with, or bypassed in a manner that would cause the metering device to inaccurately measure and register the degree, amount or quantity of service supplied or which would cause the service to be diverted from the recording apparatus of the meter shall be prima facie evidence of intent to violate and of the violation of this section by the person to whose benefit it is that such service be unmetered, unregistered or diverted.

C. The court may order restitution for the value of the services unlawfully used and for all costs. Such costs shall be limited to actual expenses, including the base wages of employees acting as witnesses for the Commonwealth, and suit costs. However, the total amount of allowable costs granted hereunder shall not exceed $250, excluding the value of the service.

History.
Code 1950, § 18.1-158.1; 1966, c. 446; 1975, cc. 14, 15; 1976, c. 273; 1978, c. 813; 1992, c. 525.

Cross references.
As to action for injunctive and equitable relief, and an award of damages, to a provider of services that have been tampered with, see § 8.01-44.7.

Michie's Jurisprudence.
For related discussion, see 6B M.J. Electricity, § 18; 12A M.J. Larceny, § 8.

CASE NOTES

Meaning of "tamper," etc. — The language in this section providing that any person who tampers with any metering device or otherwise intentionally prevents such a device from properly registering the degree, amount or quantity of such service supplied would be guilty of a misdemeanor, means tampering with the metering device for a corrupt purpose of preventing its proper registration of the amount of the electrical service supplied. Cox v. Commonwealth, 220 Va. 22, 255 S.E.2d 462 (1979).

Applicability in bankruptcy. — Where a power company alleged that a debtor had tampered with a meter and sought to have the resulting debt deemed nondischargeable under 11 U.S.C.S. § 523, the power company could not rely on the presumption in § 18.2-163 or its tariffs to establish that the debtor tampered with the meter or to establish he engaged in fraudulent or willful conduct. Liability under § 523 could not be established merely by a state statutory presumption. Power v. Robinson (In re Robinson), 340 B.R. 316, 2006 Bankr. LEXIS 497 (Bankr. E.D. Va. 2006).

§ 18.2-164. Unlawful use of, or injury to, telephone and telegraph lines; copying or obstructing messages; penalty.

A. If any person commits any of the following acts, he is guilty of a Class 2 misdemeanor:

1. Maliciously injure, molest, cut down, or destroy any telephone or telegraph line, wire, cable, pole, tower, or the material or property belonging thereto;

2. Maliciously cut, break, tap, or make any connection with any telephone or telegraph line, wire, cable, or instrument of any telegraph or telephone company which has legally acquired the right-of-way by purchase, condemnation, or otherwise;

3. Maliciously copy in any unauthorized manner any message, either social, business, or otherwise, passing over any telephone or telegraph line, wire, cable, or wireless telephone transmission in the Commonwealth;

4. Willfully or maliciously prevent, obstruct, or delay by any means or contrivance whatsoever the sending, conveyance, or delivery in the Commonwealth of any authorized communication by or through any telephone or telegraph line, wire, cable, or wireless transmission device under the control of any telephone or telegraph company doing business in the Commonwealth;

5. Maliciously aid, agree with, employ, or conspire with any unauthorized person or persons unlawfully to do or cause to be done any of the acts hereinbefore mentioned.

B. If any person, with the intent to prevent another person from summoning law-enforcement, fire, or rescue services:

1. Commits any act set forth in subsection A; or

2. Maliciously prevents or interferes with telephone or telegraph communication by disabling or destroying any device that enables such communication, whether wired or wireless, he is guilty of a Class 1 misdemeanor.

History.
Code 1950, § 18.1-156; 1960, c. 358; 1975, cc. 14, 15; 2002, cc. 810, 818; 2006, c. 457.

Law Review.
For survey of Virginia criminal law for the year 1972-1973, see 59 Va. L. Rev. 1458 (1973).

§ 18.2-165. Unlawful use of, or injury to, television or radio signals and equipment.

Any person who shall willfully or maliciously break, injure or otherwise destroy or damage any of the posts, wires, towers or other materials or fixtures employed in the construction or use of any line of a television coaxial cable, or a microwave radio system, or willfully or maliciously interfere with such structure so erected, or in any way attempt to lead from its uses or make use of the electrical signal or any portion thereof properly belonging to or in use or in readiness to be made use of for the purpose of using said electrical signal from any television coaxial cable company or microwave system or owner of such property, shall be guilty of a Class 3 misdemeanor.

History.
Code 1950, § 18.1-157; 1960, c. 358; 1975, cc. 14, 15.

§ 18.2-165.1. Tampering with or unlawful use of cable television service.

Any person who (i) shall knowingly obtain or attempt to obtain cable television service from another by means, artifice, trick, deception or device without the payment to the operator of such service of all lawful compensation for each type of service obtained; (ii) shall knowingly, and with intent to profit thereby from any consideration received or expected, assist or instruct any other person in obtaining or attempting to obtain any cable television service without the payment to the operator of said service of all lawful compensation; (iii) shall knowingly tamper or otherwise interfere with or connect to by any means whether mechanical, electrical, acoustical or other, any cables, wires, or other devices used for the distribution of cable television service without authority from the operator of such service; or (iv) shall knowingly sell, rent, lend, promote, offer or advertise for sale, rental or use any device of any description or any plan for making or assembling the same to any person, with knowledge that the person intends to use such device or plan to do any of the acts hereinbefore mentioned or if the device or plan was represented either directly or indirectly by the person distributing it as having the ability to facilitate the doing of any of the acts hereinbefore mentioned, shall be guilty of a Class 6 felony if convicted under clause (ii) or (iv) above and shall be guilty of a Class 1 misdemeanor if convicted under clause (i) or (iii) above.

As used herein, cable television service shall include any and all services provided by or through the facilities of any cable television system or closed circuit coaxial cable communications system or any microwave, satellite or similar transmission service used in connection with any cable television system or other similar closed circuit coaxial cable communications system.

In any prosecution under this section, the existence on property in the actual possession of the accused, of any connection, wire, conductor, or any device whatsoever, which permits the use of cable television service without the same being reported for payment to and specifically authorized by the operator of the cable television service shall be prima facie evidence of intent to violate and of the violation of this section by the accused.

Nothing contained in this section shall be construed so as to abrogate or interfere with any contract right or remedy of any person having a contract with the owner of a television coaxial cable, or a cablevision system, or a microwave radio system.

History.
1978, c. 712; 1979, c. 500; 1981, c. 197; 1991, c. 502.

Law Review.
For survey of Virginia criminal law for the year 1977-1978, see 64 Va. L. Rev. 1407 (1978).

§ 18.2-165.2. Unlawful interference with emergency two-way radio communications; penalty.

A. It shall be unlawful for any person to knowingly and willfully (i) interfere with the transmission of a radio communication, the purpose of which is to inform or to inquire about an emergency or (ii) transmit false information about an emergency.

B. For the purposes of this section, *"emergency"* means a condition or circumstance in which an individual is or is reasonably believed by the person transmitting the communication to be in imminent danger of death or serious bodily harm or in which property is in imminent danger of damage or destruction.

C. Any person who violates the provisions of this section shall be guilty of a Class 1 misdemeanor.

History.
1985, c. 100.

§ 18.2-166. Disclosing or inducing disclosure of certain information concerning customers of telephone companies.

Any person:
(1) Who is an employee of a telephone company, or an employee of a company which prints or otherwise handles lists of telephone customers for a telephone company and who discloses to another the names, addresses, or telephone numbers of any two or more customers of telephone service, knowing that such disclosure is without the consent of the telephone company furnishing said service; or
(2) Who knowingly induces such an employee to make such disclosure by giving, offering, or promising to such employee any gift, gratuity, or thing of value, or by doing or promising to do any act beneficial to such employee; or
(3) Who takes, copies, or compiles any list containing the aforesaid information knowing that such conduct is without the consent of the telephone company furnishing said service; or
(4) Who attempts, aids or abets another, or conspires with another, to commit any of the aforesaid acts,
shall be guilty of a Class 3 misdemeanor.

History.
Code 1950, § 18.1-417.1; 1968, c. 332; 1975, cc. 14, 15.

§ 18.2-167. Selling or transferring certain telephonic instruments.

(a) It shall be unlawful for any person knowingly to make, sell, offer or advertise for sale, possess, or give or otherwise transfer to another any instrument, apparatus, equipment, or device or plans or instructions for making or assembling any instrument, apparatus, equipment or device which has been designed, adapted, used, or employed with the intent or for the purpose of (1) obtaining long distance toll telephone or telegraph service or the transmission of a long distance toll message, signal, or other communication by telephone or telegraph, or over telephone or telegraph facilities, without the payment of charges for any such long distance message, signal or other communication; or (2) concealing or assisting another to conceal from any supplier of telephone or telegraph service or from any person charged with the responsibility of enforcing this section, the existence or place of origin or of destination of any long distance toll message, signal, or other communication by telephone or telegraph, or over telephone or telegraph facilities. Persons violating any provision of this section shall be guilty of a Class 3 misdemeanor.

(b) Any such instrument, apparatus, equipment or device, or plans or instructions therefor, may be seized by court order or under a warrant; and, upon a final conviction of any person owning the seized materials, or having any ownership interest therein, for a violation of any provision of this section, the instrument, apparatus, equipment, device, or plans or instructions shall be ordered destroyed as contraband by the court in which the person is convicted.

History.
Code 1950, § 18.1-238.3; 1966, c. 445; 1975, cc. 14, 15.

§ 18.2-167.1. Interception or monitoring of customer telephone calls; penalty.

It shall be unlawful for any person, firm or corporation to intercept or monitor, or attempt to intercept or monitor, the transmission of a message, signal or other communication by telephone between an employee or other agent of such person, firm or corporation and a customer of such person, firm or corporation.

The provisions of this section shall not apply if the person, firm or corporation gives notice to such employee or agent that such monitoring may occur at any time during the course of such employment.

Any person, firm or corporation violating the provisions of this section shall be guilty of a Class 4 misdemeanor. The provisions of this section shall not apply to any wiretap or other interception of any communication authorized pursuant to Chapter 6 of Title 19.2 (§ 19.2-61 et seq.).

History.
1982, c. 380.

CHAPTER 6.

CRIMES INVOLVING FRAUD.

Section
18.2-246.14. Counterfeit cigarettes; penalty; civil penalty.
18.2-246.15. Enforcement.

ARTICLE 1.

FORGERY.

Michie's Jurisprudence.
For related discussion, see 8B M.J. Forgery, §§ 2, 6.1, 7, 9-11, 13, 24, 25.

§ 18.2-168. Forging public records, etc.

If any person forge a public record, or certificate, return, or attestation, of any public officer or public employee, in relation to any matter wherein such certificate, return, or attestation may be received as legal proof, or utter, or attempt to employ as true, such forged record, certificate, return, or attestation, knowing the same to be forged, he shall be guilty of a Class 4 felony.

History.
Code 1950, § 18.1-92; 1960, c. 358; 1975, cc. 14, 15; 1976, c. 146.

CASE NOTES

Intent to defraud is an element of the offense of forgery of public documents. Campbell v. Commonwealth, 14 Va. App. 988, 421 S.E.2d 652 (1992), aff'd, 246 Va. 1974, 431 S.E.2d 648 (1993).

Offense is against public in general or government. — It is readily apparent that violation of any of the forgery statutes other than § 18.2-172 is an offense against the public in general or, as in this case, the government itself. Campbell v. Commonwealth, 13 Va. App. 33, 409 S.E.2d 21 (1991), modified on other grounds, 14 Va. App. 988, 421 S.E.2d 652 (1992), aff'd, 246 Va. 1974, 431 S.E.2d 648 (1993).

"Public record" means, but is not limited to, all written books, papers, letters, documents, photographs, tapes, microfiche, microfilm, photostats, sound recordings, maps, other documentary materials or information in any recording medium regardless of physical form or characteristics, including electronically recorded data, made or received in pursuance of law or in connection with the transaction of public business by any agency or employee of state government or its political subdivisions. Hall v. Commonwealth, No. 1265-99-2, 2000 Va. App. LEXIS 287 (Ct. of Appeals Apr. 18, 2000).

Section 18.2-168 plainly states that a person is guilty of forgery of a public document if he forges "a public record," not public records generally. Hines v. Commonwealth, 39 Va. App. 752, 576 S.E.2d 781, 2003 Va. App. LEXIS 92 (2003).

A public record must be a written memorial, intended to serve as evidence of something written, said or done, made by a public officer authorized by law to make it, but that authority need not be derived from express statutory enactment. Coleman v. Commonwealth, 66 Va. (25 Gratt.) 865 (1874).

Includes record of transactions of public officer. — Whenever a written record of the transactions of a public officer, in his office, is a convenient and appropriate mode of discharging the duties of his office, it is not only his right but his duty to keep that written memorial, whether expressly required so to do or not; and when kept it becomes a public document, a public record, belonging to the office and not the officer. Coleman v. Commonwealth, 66 Va. (25 Gratt.) 865 (1874).

Such as warrant book of sinking fund. — The warrant book of the sinking fund, kept by the (then) second auditor in his office, of the transactions of the (then) commissioners of the sinking fund of the state, is such a public record that it may be the subject of forgery. Coleman v. Commonwealth, 66 Va. (25 Gratt.) 865 (1874).

The trial court correctly concluded that each praecipe

was a forged public record, purportedly documenting the Commonwealth's motion to nolle prosequi a pending criminal prosecution, clearly the pursuit of "public business" by a "public officer;" thus defendant's actions involving the praecipes supported his convictions. Chellman v. Commonwealth, No. 1630-95-4, 1997 Va. App. LEXIS 157 (Ct. of Appeals Mar. 25, 1997).

A confirmation of insurance document was a public record for purposes of this section in that it was completed in part by a police officer, was used by the police and the DMV, as agents of the Commonwealth, to ascertain whether the vehicle was properly insured as required by state law and the officer kept a duplicate original for a governmental and public purpose. Hall v. Commonwealth, No. 1265-99-2, 2000 Va. App. LEXIS 287 (Ct. of Appeals Apr. 18, 2000).

Forgery during jail intake. — Where defendant, during initial intake following his arrest on criminal charges, forged fingerprint card and jail classification cards, and made statements prompted by deputy's questions, such questions were biographical in nature and part of routine booking procedure, and Miranda warnings were not required. Watts v. Commonwealth, 38 Va. App. 206, 562 S.E.2d 699, 2002 Va. App. LEXIS 250 (2002).

Jail intake records. — Court of appeals declined to apply the ends of justice exception to defendant's claim that certain documents were not public records within the meaning of § 18.2-168 because jail/annex property issued/returned sheets, police department advice of rights forms, advice of right form, and written statement to the police were all public records; those documents were made in connection with transaction of public business, admitting a prisoner to jail and investigating a crime, and were made by an authorized public officer to serve as evidence of things that were written, said or done, the receipt of defendant's personal property at the jail and the distribution of jail property to defendant in the context of the property records, or legal proof that defendant had been advised of his Miranda rights and had given a statement to the police. Word v. Commonwealth, No. 2660-07-3, 2009 Va. App. LEXIS 330 (Ct. of Appeals July 21, 2009).

Fingerprint card is clearly a public record. Greene v. Commonwealth, No. 1824-94-4 (Ct. of Appeals May 30, 1995).

Traffic summons was forged "public record." — Traffic summons before the court was clearly a forged "public record" which could "be received as legal proof," a writing expressly proscribed by this section. Blake v. Commonwealth, No. 2872-96-1 (Ct. of Appeals Jan. 20, 1998).

Traffic summons was a public record as it became the charging document on which a general district court tried an accused, under § 16.1-129, and if an accused willfully violated his written promise to appear in court, given when he signed the summons, he could be convicted for failure to appear under § 19.2-128, regardless of the disposition of, and in addition to, the charge upon which he was originally arrested, under § 19.2-74 A 3, and, given this statutory scheme, each signed summons clearly could constitute a separate offense under § 18.2-168, regarding forgery of a public document. Hines v. Commonwealth, 39 Va. App. 752, 576 S.E.2d 781, 2003 Va. App. LEXIS 92 (2003).

When defendant signed five separate summonses, issued at the same time, for five separate traffic infractions with his brother's name, the "single larceny doctrine" did not apply to make him guilty of only one forgery. Hines v. Commonwealth, 39 Va. App. 752, 576 S.E.2d 781, 2003 Va. App. LEXIS 92 (2003).

Forged public documents: vehicle title and operator's license. — Evidence showed the defendant uttered a forged public document where he used faked names and records to obtain an operator's license and an application for a vehicle title and then injured an officer attempting to flee. Mohamed v. Commonwealth, No. 3439-01-1, 2003 Va. App. LEXIS 277 (Ct. of Appeals May 6, 2003).

Where evidence showed the defendant forged his brother's signature to prolong his deception of being the person whose license was given to an officer, or the person whose license was suspended was given notice, conviction for forgery was proper. Brown v. Commonwealth, No. 1189-02-2, 2003 Va. App. LEXIS 297 (Ct. of Appeals May 13, 2003).

Community service attendance sheet is public record. — Sufficient evidence supported defendant's convictions of forgery and uttering a public record, as the evidence in defendant's case showed that defendant added hours to a community service attendance sheet to show that defendant had performed all of defendant's court-ordered community service when in fact defendant had not done so; the attendance sheet qualified as a required public record to support defendant's conviction because the evidence showed that it was a document the probation officer collected pursuant to the duties that the county imposed upon her in supervising individuals on probation and the evidence also showed that defendant had added hours to it that defendant had not worked despite the fact that the sheet said not to write on it and that doing so would amount to forgery, a felony. Koch v. Commonwealth, No. 3078-05-4, 2007 Va. App. LEXIS 3 (Ct. of Appeals Jan. 9, 2007).

Juvenile and domestic relations district court guilty plea form not a public record. — Court of appeals invoked the ends of justice exception to defendant's claim that the trial court erred in convicting him of forging a juvenile and domestic relations district court guilty plea form because a miscarriage of justice took place, and defendant showed affirmative evidence in the record establishing that an element of the offense of forging a public document did not exist and that he did not commit the crime of forging a public record; the juvenile and domestic relations district court guilty plea form was not a public record because it was not prepared in connection with a legitimate legal proceeding, and that form was replaced with a general district court form before final judgment was entered in the general district court. Word v. Commonwealth, No. 2660-07-3, 2009 Va. App. LEXIS 330 (Ct. of Appeals July 21, 2009).

"Ends of justice" exception should have been invoked where erroneous jury instruction was so defective that it allowed the jury to convict defendant of forgery even if the jury concluded that defendant lacked an intent to defraud. Intent to defraud, however, is a necessary element of forgery. Campbell v. Commonwealth, 14 Va. App. 988, 421 S.E.2d 652 (1992), aff'd, 246 Va. 1974, 431 S.E.2d 648 (1993).

"To the prejudice of another" is not an element of the offense of forging a public document. The language "to the prejudice of another's right" appears only in § 18.2-172 and that statute expressly excludes this section, which criminalizes the forging of public documents; therefore, the legislature did not intend that the "prejudice to another's right" requirement be in any other sections. Campbell v. Commonwealth, 13 Va. App. 33, 409 S.E.2d 21 (1991), modified on other grounds, 14 Va. App. 988, 421 S.E.2d 652 (1992), aff'd, 246 Va. 1974, 431 S.E.2d 648 (1993).

Harm or prejudice to right of another person not element. — Harm or prejudice to the right of another person has never been and is not now an element of the crime of forgery of public records in this Commonwealth. Campbell v. Commonwealth, 246 Va. 174, 431 S.E.2d 648 (1993).

Public officer or public employee. — Strictly for the purposes of this section, where a registered security officer is engaged in a duty specifically granted by statute, that officer is a "public officer or public employee." Coston v. Commonwealth, 29 Va. App. 350, 512 S.E.2d 158 (1999).

When defendant forged the summons issued by a registered security officer, it was as if defendant had forged a summons issued to him by a police officer, and the same criminal culpability resulted. Coston v. Commonwealth, 29 Va. App. 350, 512 S.E.2d 158 (1999).

Multiple prosecutions. — Analysis of the concept of "a public record" and a summons proved the legislature intended to allow multiple prosecutions for contemporaneous forgeries of such documents. Hines v. Commonwealth, 39 Va. App. 752, 576 S.E.2d 781, 2003 Va. App. LEXIS 92 (2003).

Multiple convictions. — Language and structure of the Virginia Code proved the legislature intended to allow multiple convictions for forgery of public records. Hines v. Commonwealth, 39 Va. App. 752, 576 S.E.2d 781, 2003 Va. App. LEXIS 92 (2003).

Court of appeals declined to apply the ends of justice exception to defendant's claim that the trial court erred by convicting him of seven counts of forgery based upon multiple signatures on two documents in violation of § 18.2-168 because an allegation that defendant's guarantee against double jeopardy could have been violated was not enough to invoke the ends of justice exception to Va. Sup. Ct. R. 5A:18; each of the signatures documented a separate transaction, either the receipt or return of property, and, therefore, had a separate existence with separate consequences. Word v.

Commonwealth, No. 2660-07-3, 2009 Va. App. LEXIS 330 (Ct. of Appeals July 21, 2009).

Uttering completed simultaneously with forgery. — Uttering does not require that a forged instrument be negotiated; uttering is completed simultaneously with a forgery where the forged signature on an electronic screen at the Virginia Department of Motor Vehicles is being employed as true in order to generate a false public record. Bennett v. Commonwealth, 48 Va. App. 354, 631 S.E.2d 332, 2006 Va. App. LEXIS 278 (2006).

Admission of evidence harmless error. — In defendant's forgery case, although the appellate court accepted the Commonwealth's concession of error concerning the admission of a witness' general habit testimony and assumed without deciding that it was error, it concluded that the error was harmless because the erroneously admitted testimony did not influence the verdict of the bench trial. Asinugo v. Commonwealth, 2010 Va. App. LEXIS 280 (July 20, 2010).

Evidence was sufficient to prove defendant's false signature was a false writing with intent to defraud. — Evidence was sufficient to prove that defendant's signature as "Gray Shaw" on a fingerprint card after his arrest was a false writing made with intent to defraud in prosecution for forgery where the defendant was fingerprinted five times previously, he had reported and signed his name as "Dexter Reid," and although he reported his name as Gary Shaw during the arrest at issue, he himself misspelled "Gary" as "Gray" when signing the fingerprint card. Reid v. Commonwealth, 16 Va. App. 468, 431 S.E.2d 63 (1993).

Evidence sufficient to support conviction. — Defendant's conviction for uttering a forged public record was affirmed as defendant instituted the process that produced a fraudulent license when he stood for a photograph and signed a computer screen, even though he did not accept the fraudulent license; uttering was completed simultaneously with the forgery as the forged signature on the electronic screen was being employed as true in order to generate a false public record. Bennett v. Commonwealth, 48 Va. App. 354, 631 S.E.2d 332, 2006 Va. App. LEXIS 278 (2006).

Defendant's convictions on two counts of forging a public document and two counts of uttering a forged public document were upheld on appeal, given sufficient evidence that: (1) defendant caused a police officer to issue two forged summonses to him, by providing false information to the officer as he prepared the documents; and (2) defendant uttered them by knowingly allowing the officer to rely upon them in order to avoid further prosecution. Moreover, signing one's own name with the intent that the writing be received as written by another person, impersonating another in the signature of an instrument, or signing in such a way as to make the writing purport to be that of another, were all considered to be acts of forgery. Rodriquez v. Commonwealth, 50 Va. App. 667, 653 S.E.2d 296, 2007 Va. App. LEXIS 428 (2007).

Evidence supported the trial court's finding that defendant had the requisite intent to forge his signature because the Commonwealth presented evidence in support of its argument that defendant chose to use a certain name to conceal the criminal record existing under his actual name, and thus receive a lighter sentence, in the form of defendant's criminal record and his statement that he did not have any crimes against him under the other name. Word v. Commonwealth, No. 2660-07-3, 2009 Va. App. LEXIS 330 (Ct. of Appeals July 21, 2009).

Evidence was sufficient to support defendant's conviction for forging a public record, in violation of § 18.2-168, where defendant disclosed an alias during a traffic stop, causing the arrest warrant to be prepared under that name, and then signed the fingerprint card using the alias, without providing his legally recognized name anywhere on the card, even though the card included a space for aliases. Asinugo v. Commonwealth, 2010 Va. App. LEXIS 280 (July 20, 2010).

There was sufficient evidence to support defendant's conviction for forgery under § 18.2-168 because a subcontractor testified that he never gave defendant permission to use his contractor's number, and that evidence was supported by the fact that the subcontractor immediately had a building permit rescinded when he found out that his contractor's number was listed; defendant admitted that he filled out the permit, including the subcontractor's number, and submitted it to the secretary for the building inspection office. Williams v. Commonwealth, 2011 Va. App. LEXIS 367 (Nov. 29, 2011).

Error in admitting evidence of pending charge of grand larceny. — The fact that defendant was originally charged with a grand larceny felony charge was not a material element in the offense of forging a public document; for the defendant's willfulness and his motive for forging Central Criminal Records Exchange (CCRE) form were not in issue at the trial, and even if the Commonwealth was entitled to demonstrate the defendant's willfulness or to show his motive in forging the CCRE form, the slight probative value of nature of the offense would not outweigh its prejudicial effect, and thus the trial court abused its discretion in admitting evidence of the pending charge of grand larceny. Tucker v. Commonwealth, 17 Va. App. 520, 438 S.E.2d 492 (1993).

Jury instructions proper. — Jury instructions, one of which created a permissible inference that defendant forged the documents defendant provided to an individual seeking to erase any record of a drunk driving conviction, based on the fact that defendant handed the documents to the individual, created a permissible inference, not a mandatory presumption. Ruiz v. Commonwealth, No. 1915-07-4, 2008 Va. App. LEXIS 566 (Ct. of Appeals Dec. 23, 2008).

Applied in Frontanilla v. Commonwealth, 38 Va. App. 220, 562 S.E.2d 706, 2002 Va. App. LEXIS 272 (2002).

CIRCUIT COURT OPINIONS

Signing summons with false name as new and distinct crime for purpose of exclusionary rule. — Although off-duty police officer violated the Fourth Amendment and Va. Const. Art. 1, § 8, in ordering defendant to stop, defendant committed a new and distinct crime while in custody in signing a uniform summons with a false name, thereby purging the taint of the initial police misconduct, and defendant's motion to suppress the summons and his statements to the officer was denied. Commonwealth v. Cooper, 56 Va. Cir. 501, 2001 Va. Cir. LEXIS 491 (Charlottesville 2001).

§ 18.2-169. Forging, or keeping an instrument for forging, a seal.

If any person forge, or keep or conceal any instrument for the purpose of forging, the seal of the Commonwealth, the seal of a court, or of any public office, or body politic or corporate in this Commonwealth, he shall be guilty of a Class 4 felony.

History.
Code 1950, § 18.1-93; 1960, c. 358; 1975, cc. 14, 15.

CIRCUIT COURT OPINIONS

Seal of the Commonwealth. — The image of the seal of the Commonwealth of Virginia on drivers' licenses was merely a representation of the seal of the Commonwealth, and did not constitute the actual seal of the Commonwealth as described in this section and defined by former §§ 7.1-26 and 7.1-27 [now §§ 1-500 and 1-501] so as to support indictments for forgery stemming from defendants production of fake drivers' licenses. Commonwealth v. Bechtler, 56 Va. Cir. 186, 2001 Va. Cir. LEXIS 130 (Rockingham County 2001).

§ 18.2-170. Forging coin or bank notes.

If any person (1) forge any coin, note or bill current by law or usage in this Commonwealth or any note or bill of a banking company, (2) fraudulently make any base coin, or a note or bill purporting to be the note or bill of a banking company, when such company does not exist, or (3) utter, or attempt to employ as true, or sell, exchange, or deliver, or offer to sell, exchange, or deliver, or receive on sale, exchange, or delivery, with intent to utter or employ, or to have the same uttered or employed as true, any such false, forged, or base coin, note or bill, knowing it to be so, he shall be guilty of a Class 4 felony.

History.
Code 1950, § 18.1-94; 1960, c. 358; 1975, cc. 14, 15.

Law Review.
For survey of Virginia law on evidence for the year 1978-1979, see 66 Va. L. Rev. 293 (1980).

Michie's Jurisprudence.
For related discussion, see 5A M.J. Counterfeiting, § 2.

CASE NOTES

Constitutionality. — The difference in classification of the offense of forgery and uttering embodied in this section and § 18.2-172 is not arbitrary and unreasonable, because there are logical reasons for the distinction; thus, the sections are not unconstitutional. Tedder v. Cox, 317 F. Supp. 33 (W.D. Va. 1970).

Brightening base pieces is criminal. — One who brightens base pieces (which are brought to him ready formed, with the impression and appearance of dollars, except that they are of a dark color, like lead, and not then passable), by boiling them in a lye, and rubbing them with woolen cloth, and subjecting them to other processes, thereby rendering them by resemblance to real dollars more fit for circulation, is guilty of counterfeiting. Rasnick v. Commonwealth, 4 Va. (2 Va. Cas.) 356 (1823).

As is passing forged note of defunct bank. — It is felony to pass a counterfeit note of the bank of the United States, dated at a time when that bank was in existence, though, at the time of passing the note, the charter of the bank had expired. Buckland v. Commonwealth, 35 Va. (8 Leigh) 732 (1837).

But passing must be with guilty knowledge. — The passing of a counterfeit note may be of itself a perfectly innocent transaction; the guilt consists in passing it knowing it to be counterfeit. Finn v. Commonwealth, 26 Va. (5 Rand.) 701 (1827); Fitzgerald v. Commonwealth, 219 Va. 266, 246 S.E.2d 899 (1978).

For a defendant to be convicted of uttering a counterfeit bill, the evidence must not only show that he passed counterfeit currency, it must also show that he knew it to be counterfeit at the time he passed it. Fitzgerald v. Commonwealth, 219 Va. 266, 246 S.E.2d 899 (1978).

Time and place of passing and scienter sufficiently certain. — Where an indictment for passing a counterfeit note charges that the prisoner, on a particular day, at the county of M. and within the jurisdiction of the court, being possessed of the note, feloniously did pass the same, well knowing it to be counterfeit at the time he passed it, the time and place of passing the note and of the scienter are set forth with sufficient certainty. Buckland v. Commonwealth, 35 Va. (8 Leigh) 732 (1837).

Which must be proved. — In a prosecution for uttering counterfeit coin, the guilty knowledge of the prisoner that the coin was counterfeit is a fact to be proved. Wash v. Commonwealth, 57 Va. (16 Gratt.) 530 (1861).

Evidence that prisoner passed other counterfeit notes admissible to show scienter. — On the trial of an indictment for passing a counterfeit bank note or check, after evidence that the prisoner passed the note, and that it was counterfeit, evidence that the prisoner had in his possession and attempted to pass other counterfeit notes of the same kind to other persons, the day after he passed those in the indictment mentioned, is admissible to prove the scienter. Hendrick v. Commonwealth, 32 Va. (5 Leigh) 708 (1834). See Martin v. Commonwealth, 29 Va. (2 Leigh) 745 (1830).

Indictment valid which contains several charges in one count. — An indictment which charges a prisoner with the offenses of falsely making, forging and counterfeiting; of causing and procuring to be falsely made, forged and counterfeited, and of willingly acting and assisting in the said false making, forging and counterfeiting, is a good indictment, though all of these charges are contained in a single count. The words of the statute being pursued, and there being a general verdict of guilty, judgment ought not to be arrested on the ground that the offenses are distinct. Rasnick v. Commonwealth, 4 Va. (2 Va. Cas.) 356 (1823).

Or which does not state how accused caused note to be passed. — An indictment for causing and procuring a counterfeited bank note to be offered to be passed, without stating by whom or how the accused caused and procured it to be done, is sufficiently certain, and good. Brown v. Commonwealth, 29 Va. (2 Leigh) 769 (1839).

Or which does not state a later indorsement. — In setting out counterfeit bank note in haec verba, in an indictment for feloniously passing the same, an indorsement appearing to have been made on the note after it was passed is properly omitted and the omission is therefore no ground for the objection of variance. Buckland v. Commonwealth, 35 Va. (8 Leigh) 732 (1837).

Or that it was to the prejudice of another. — Upon an indictment of passing a counterfeit note of a bank, without alleging that the bank is a chartered bank, or that there is no such bank, and without alleging that the note was passed "to the prejudice of another's rights," or "for the prisoner's own benefit, or for the benefit of another," it was held that the offense so charged is a felony, and the indictment is good and sufficient. Murry v. Commonwealth, 32 Va. (5 Leigh) 720 (1835). See Commonwealth v. Ervin, 4 Va. (2 Va. Cas.) 337 (1823).

Or that injury was intended. — A charge that a forgery of bank notes was committed with intent to injure "divers good citizens of the Commonwealth, and others, to the jurors unknown," without setting out an intent to injure the president, directors of those banks, or of any particular person, or body politic, by name, is good after verdict. Commonwealth v. Ervin, 4 Va. (2 Va. Cas.) 337 (1823).

It is not necessary to produce the coin to convict one of passing a counterfeit coin. Kirk v. Commonwealth, 36 Va. (9 Leigh) 627 (1838).

Evidence of the passing of counterfeit notes by a confederate. — Upon the trial of an indictment for passing counterfeit bank notes, the prisoner appears clearly to have been confederated with another in passing counterfeit notes, and present when such notes were passed; the notes so passed may be produced in evidence against the prisoner. Martin v. Commonwealth, 29 Va. (2 Leigh) 745 (1830).

Evidence that a confederate, in the defendant's presence, passed counterfeit notes of the same description on other occasions is admissible against the defendant to prove scienter or guilty knowledge on his part. Fitzgerald v. Commonwealth, 219 Va. 266, 246 S.E.2d 899 (1978).

Evidence sufficient to show knowledge. — Given defendant's conduct in repeatedly attempting to get counterfeit bills back from the cashier to whom he had given the bills, the physical appearance of the bills which immediately identified them to the cashier, the store manager, and the investigating officer as counterfeit, and defendant's inconsistent statements to the cashier and the officer as to how he obtained the bills, a rational fact finder could reasonably have inferred that defendant knew the bills were counterfeit when he passed them to the cashier. Pratt v. Commonwealth, — Va. App. —, — S.E.2d —, 2006 Va. App. LEXIS 595 (Dec. 28, 2006).

Evidence was sufficient to prove the intent necessary to support a conviction for uttering where the jury was permitted to infer defendant's guilty knowledge from his possession of forged traveler's checks, where defendant provided conflicting accounts as to how he obtained the checks, and after defendant obtained the checks, he immediately negotiated each check for an inexpensive item and a large amount of cash. Richardson v. Commonwealth, 2010 Va. App. LEXIS 84 (Mar. 9, 2010).

Presumptive evidence that accused was the forger. — Upon the trial of an indictment for forging bank notes the fact, if proved, of the forged notes mentioned in the indictment, and other forged notes of like kind, and the plates, implements and materials for forging such notes being found in the prisoner's possession is prima facie or circumstantial presumptive evidence that the prisoner was the forger, proper to be given to the jury. Spencer v. Commonwealth, 29 Va. (2 Leigh) 751 (1830).

State court has jurisdiction when act also constitutes federal offense. — A state court has jurisdiction to punish the offense of attempting to pass a forged note purporting to be a note of one of the national banks of the United States, though the offense is contrary to a law of the Congress of the United States. Jet v. Commonwealth, 59 Va. (18 Gratt.) 933 (1867). See also Hendrick v. Commonwealth, 32 Va. (5 Leigh) 707 (1834).

§ 18.2-171. Making or having anything designed for forging any writing, etc.

If any person engrave, stamp, or cast, or otherwise make or mend, any plate, block, press, or other thing, adapted and designed for the forging and false making of any writing or other thing, the forging or false making whereof is punishable by this chapter, or if such person have in possession any such plate, block, press, or other thing, with intent to use, or cause or permit it to be used, in forging or false making any such writing or other thing, he shall be guilty of a Class 4 felony.

History.

Code 1950, § 18.1-95; 1960, c. 358; 1975, cc. 14, 15.

Michie's Jurisprudence.

For related discussion, see 5A M.J. Counterfeiting, § 5; 21A M.J. Words and Phrases.

CASE NOTES

"Adapted" and "designed" defined. — "Adapted" means "capable of being used; fit or suitable." "Designed" means "appropriate, fit, prepared, or suitable; also adapted, designated, or intended." Smith v. Commonwealth, 190 Va. 10, 55 S.E.2d 427 (1949).

"Such person" in the second portion of this section refers to "any person" in the first portion thereof. Smith v. Commonwealth, 190 Va. 10, 55 S.E.2d 427 (1949).

"Any such plate, block, press, or other thing," the possession of which is condemned by the second portion of the section, is such a device or instrumentality the making or mending of which is condemned by the first portion — that is, such as is "adapted and designed for the forging and false making of any writing." Smith v. Commonwealth, 190 Va. 10, 55 S.E.2d 427 (1949).

This section condemns either the making or mending of, or the possession of, the instrumentality for an unlawful purpose. It is immaterial that it was originally planned, constructed and intended to be used for a lawful purpose. Smith v. Commonwealth, 190 Va. 10, 55 S.E.2d 427 (1949).

What this section condemns is either the making or mending or the possession of the instrumentality for an evil or unlawful purpose. Hanbury v. Commonwealth, 203 Va. 182, 122 S.E.2d 911 (1961).

Proof of intent by maker or mender not needed. — Proof of intent that it be used for forgery, on the part of one who makes or mends a check-writing machine, is not necessary to sustain a conviction of unlawful possession of the instrumentality in the hands of another. Smith v. Commonwealth, 190 Va. 10, 55 S.E.2d 427 (1949).

Possession of rubber stamp for marking city tax paid on cigarette packages. — See Hanbury v. Commonwealth, 203 Va. 182, 122 S.E.2d 911 (1961).

Indictment insufficient. — An indictment charging that the prisoner did knowingly have in his custody, without lawful authority or excuse, "one die or instrument" for the purpose of producing and impressing the stamp and similitude of the current silver coin called a half dollar (no further describing the die or instrument), is insufficient. Commonwealth v. Scott, 40 Va. (1 Rob.) 695 (1842).

Sufficiency of evidence. — When accused was arrested following his purchase of a check-writing machine, he had in his possession blank checks bearing a company's printed name and the forged signature of an official of the company. The Commonwealth proved that on the day before his arrest he had cashed a forged check of the company. It was held that this evidence was sufficient to sustain his conviction under the second portion of this section. Smith v. Commonwealth, 190 Va. 10, 55 S.E.2d 427 (1949).

§ 18.2-172. Forging, uttering, etc., other writings.

If any person forge any writing, other than such as is mentioned in §§ 18.2-168 and 18.2-170, to the prejudice of another's right, or utter, or attempt to employ as true, such forged writing, knowing it to be forged, he shall be guilty of a Class 5 felony. Any person who shall obtain, by any false pretense or token, the signature of another person, to any such writing, with intent to defraud any other person, shall be deemed guilty of the forgery thereof, and shall be subject to like punishment.

History.

Code 1950, § 18.1-96; 1960, c. 358; 1975, cc. 14, 15.

Cross references.

As to obtaining a signature by false pretense, see § 18.2-178. As to substitute checks as evidence pursuant to the federal Check Clearing for the 21st Century Evidence Act, see § 8.01-391.1. As to evidence of forged instrument in prosecution for forgery, see § 19.2-224.

Law Review.

For survey of Virginia law on evidence for the year 1970-1971, see 57 Va. L. Rev. 1591 (1971).

Michie's Jurisprudence.

For related discussion, see 5B M.J. Criminal Procedure, §§ 3, 4; 5A M.J. Counterfeiting, §§ 2, 4.

CASE NOTES

I. General Consideration.
II. Elements of Forgery.
  A. In General.
  B. Particular Instruments.
III. Uttering.
IV. Indictment.
V. Evidence.
  A. Presumptions and Burden of Proof.
  B. Proof of Handwriting.
  C. Documentary Evidence.
  D. Best and Secondary Evidence.
  E. Other Matters.

I. GENERAL CONSIDERATION.

Constitutionality. — The difference in classification of the offense of forgery and uttering embodied in § 18.2-170 and this section is not arbitrary and unreasonable, because there are logical reasons for the distinction; thus, the sections are not unconstitutional. Tedder v. Cox, 317 F. Supp. 33 (W.D. Va. 1970).

Violation of forgery statutes other than this section is offense against public or government. — It is readily apparent that violation of any of the forgery statutes other than this section is an offense against the public in general or the government itself. Campbell v. Commonwealth, 13 Va. App. 33, 409 S.E.2d 21 (1991), modified on other grounds, 14 Va. App. 988, 421 S.E.2d 652 (1992), aff'd, 246 Va. 1974, 431 S.E.2d 648 (1993).

The language "to the prejudice of another's right" appears only in this section and this statute expressly excludes § 18.2-168, which criminalizes the forging of public documents; therefore, the legislature did not intend that the "prejudice to another's right" requirement be in any other sections. Campbell v. Commonwealth, 13 Va. App. 33, 409 S.E.2d 21 (1991), modified on other grounds, 14 Va. App. 988, 421 S.E.2d 652 (1992), aff'd, 246 Va. 1974, 431 S.E.2d 648 (1993).

Evidence held insufficient to prove venue. — Defendant's two grand larceny and two uttering a forged check convictions were reversed on appeal, as the trial court erred in finding the evidence insufficient to establish venue, no evidence was presented by the Commonwealth as to the location of the alleged crimes, and the Commonwealth failed to ask the court to take judicial notice of that location. Harris v. Commonwealth, — Va. App. —, — S.E.2d —, 2006 Va. App. LEXIS 493 (Oct. 31, 2006).

Evidence held sufficient to prove venue. — Trial court did not err in convicting defendant of forgery in violation of § 18.2-172 because venue was proper in Mecklenburg County, Virginia since the evidence established a strong presumption that defendant deposited or placed the forged instrument with another person or firm in Mecklenburg County pursuant to § 19.2-245.1, and the record did not suggest the involvement of an alternate jurisdiction from which defendant could reasonably have perpetrated the forgery; the victim's attorney sent an unsigned note to defendant's residence in Mecklenburg County, and although the record was silent as to who received the note, the only logical inference flowing from the evidence was that defendant passed the instrument back to either the victim, who resided in Mecklenburg, or the attorney, whose principal place of business was also in Mecklenburg. Duckworth v. Commonwealth, 2011 Va. App. LEXIS 60 (Feb. 22, 2011).

Applied in Timbers v. Commonwealth, 28 Va. App. 187, 503 S.E.2d 233 (1998); Dillard v. Commonwealth, 32 Va. App. 515, 529 S.E.2d 325, 2000 Va. App. LEXIS 399 (2000); Wadkins v. Arnold, 214 F.3d 535, 2000 U.S. App. LEXIS 12102 (4th Cir. 2000); Wadkins v. Arnold, 214 F.3d 535, 2000 U.S. App. LEXIS 12102 (4th Cir. 2000).

II. ELEMENTS OF FORGERY.

A. In General.

"Forgery" defined. — Forgery is the making of a false writing which, if genuine, would be apparently of legal efficacy. Terry v. Commonwealth, 87 Va. 672, 13 S.E. 104 (1891).

Forgery is the false making or materially altering with intent to defraud, of any writing which, if genuine, might apparently be of legal efficacy, or the foundation of legal liability. Bullock v. Commonwealth, 205 Va. 558, 138 S.E.2d 261 (1964); Bateman v. Commonwealth, 205 Va. 595, 139 S.E.2d 102 (1964); Moore v. Commonwealth, 207 Va. 838, 153 S.E.2d 231 (1967); Fitzgerald v. Commonwealth, 227 Va. 171, 313 S.E.2d 394 (1984).

Forgery is the fraudulent making or alteration of a writing to the prejudice of another man's right. Bullock v. Commonwealth, 205 Va. 558, 138 S.E.2d 261 (1964).

Forgery is the false making or materially altering with intent to defraud, of any writing which, if genuine, might apparently be of legal efficacy, or the foundation of legal liability. Gordon v. Commonwealth, No. 1717-88-1 (Ct. of Appeals Apr. 10, 1990).

While a person may adopt any name he may choose so long as it was done for an honest purpose, forgery is committed by signing an assumed name, or a fictitious name, for a dishonest purpose and with intent to defraud. Moore v. Commonwealth, 207 Va. 838, 153 S.E.2d 231 (1967).

To sustain a forgery conviction, the Commonwealth had to prove that the accused falsely made or materially altered a writing, without the authority to do so, and did so to the prejudice of another's right. Manas v. Commonwealth, No. 2789-00-1, 2001 Va. App. LEXIS 524 (Ct. of Appeals Sept. 25, 2001).

Materiality. — A fact is material when it influences a person to enter into a contract, when it deceives him and induces him to act, or when without it, the transaction would not have occurred. Beiler v. Commonwealth, 243 Va. 291, 415 S.E.2d 849 (1992).

It made no difference that appellant's alterations of the checks did not change the bank's contract with check writer. Appellant's fraudulent alterations were material because they induced the tellers to pay the larger amounts shown on the checks. Beiler v. Commonwealth, 243 Va. 291, 415 S.E.2d 849 (1992).

Extent of defendant's participation. — It is immaterial whether the defendant actually cashed the checks, or whether they were forged by one person, endorsed by the defendant, and cashed by the forger or by a third person, where the defendant's participation in the concerted action, and his fraudulent intent, are sufficiently supported by the evidence. Fitzgerald v. Commonwealth, 227 Va. 171, 313 S.E.2d 394 (1984).

Presence or absence at time of forgery. — One who procures the forgery of an instrument is an accessory before the fact if he was absent when the writing was forged, or a principal in the second degree if he was present. The distinction is of no consequence, because his guilt is the same, and he is subject to the same punishment, in either event. Fitzgerald v. Commonwealth, 227 Va. 171, 313 S.E.2d 394 (1984).

Writings, invalid on their face, are not subjects of forgery. If intrinsic circumstances are essential to the efficacy of the instrument, they must be averred in the indictment. Terry v. Commonwealth, 87 Va. 672, 13 S.E. 104 (1891).

But writing of questionable validity is. — A bail bond taken by a sheriff which has been altered in a material part may be the subject of a prosecution for forgery, although some doubts may be raised respecting the validity of the bond, arising from the recitals in the condition. Commonwealth v. Linton, 4 Va. (2 Va. Cas.) 476 (1825).

Writing must be to the prejudice of another. — This section predicates the offense of forgery only of such writings as are, or may be, to the prejudice of another. Terry v. Commonwealth, 87 Va. 672, 13 S.E. 104 (1891).

Or have a possibility of being prejudicial. — An instrument is one of legal efficacy, within the rules relating to forgery, where by any possibility, it may operate to the injury of another. Gordon v. Commonwealth, 100 Va. 825, 41 S.E. 746 (1902); Hanbury v. Commonwealth, 203 Va. 182, 122 S.E.2d 911 (1961).

Proof of actual prejudice not necessary. — This section does not require that the Commonwealth prove beyond a reasonable doubt that someone, in fact, was prejudiced by appellant's conduct. Rather, a conviction may be sustained where the evidence shows the possibility that the forged instrument may operate to the prejudice of another's right. Mitchell v. Commonwealth, No. 2528-92-2 (Ct. of Appeals June 7, 1994).

This section does not require that the forged or altered document operate to the actual prejudice of one who does or could rely on the genuineness of the document itself, but rather only that the forged document had the potential to operate to the prejudice of another. Stevenson v. Commonwealth, 27 Va. App. 453, 499 S.E.2d 580 (1998).

When defendant was prosecuted for forgery for making false entries in a nursing home patient's record, the Commonwealth did not have to show that anyone was actually prejudiced because the statute only required proof that a forged instrument might operate to the prejudice of another's right. Beshah v. Commonwealth, 60 Va. App. 161, 725 S.E.2d 144, 2012 Va. App. LEXIS 142 (2012).

A city is a "person" whose rights may be prejudiced by a forgery. Hanbury v. Commonwealth, 203 Va. 182, 122 S.E.2d 911 (1961).

The rights of a city were prejudiced by the use of a forged city cigarette tax stamp because it was thereby deprived of the tax payable to it on the cigarettes sold by defendant which bore the false stamp and potentially on the several thousand packages which defendant had imprinted with the false stamp preparatory to selling them. Hanbury v. Commonwealth, 203 Va. 182, 122 S.E.2d 911 (1961).

Possibility of prejudice evident. — Appellant's signing of parolee's name on indigent legal aid form while under arrest created a possibility of prejudice to the parolee. If her parole officer had been informed that she had been arrested, the prejudice to the parolee would have been indisputable. Additionally, appellant's false execution of the form created the possibility of prejudice to the Commonwealth. Appellant created a possibility that the wrong person would be tried, convicted, and punished for her criminal offense. Mitchell v. Commonwealth, No. 2528-92-2 (Ct. of Appeals June 7, 1994).

When defendant was prosecuted for forgery for making false entries in a nursing home patient's record, there was sufficient evidence of possible prejudice to another's right because (1) the patient was exposed to actual and potential prejudice, (2) the nursing home faced sanctions, and (3) the falsified records could prejudice the Medicaid program. Beshah v. Commonwealth, 60 Va. App. 161, 725 S.E.2d 144, 2012 Va. App. LEXIS 142 (2012).

Intent to defraud. — Intent to defraud for the purposes of a forgery conviction under § 18.2-172 was demonstrated by the fact that defendant used her best friend's identifying information on a hospital discharge form to avoid arrest for a probation violation. Pullin v. Commonwealth, — Va. App. —, — S.E.2d —, 2009 Va. App. LEXIS 139 (Mar. 24, 2009).

Defendant was properly convicted of forgery for making false entries in a nursing home patient's record because, inter alia, defendant's intent to defraud was shown by (1) the number of false entries, (2) defendant's experience, training, and knowledge of the need for accurate records, (3) defendant's perjured testimony denying the entries were false, and (4) defendant's payment for work defendant did not do. Beshah v. Commonwealth, 60 Va. App. 161, 725 S.E.2d 144, 2012 Va. App. LEXIS 142 (2012).

Forgery and larceny. — One may be found guilty of forgery and of uttering a forged check, and of the larceny of the proceeds of the check. Bateman v. Commonwealth, 205 Va. 595, 139 S.E.2d 102 (1964).

And one may attempt to employ as true a forged instrument, yet not be guilty of larceny if he obtained no money or property by his action. Bateman v. Commonwealth, 205 Va. 595, 139 S.E.2d 102 (1964).

However, evidence necessary to establish forgery or uttering a forged instrument is not the same required to establish larceny. Bateman v. Commonwealth, 205 Va. 595, 139 S.E.2d 102 (1964).

For case discussing the application of "Wharton's Rule" in forgery and conspiracy to commit a felony case, see Ramsey v. Commonwealth, 2 Va. App. 265, 343 S.E.2d 465 (1986).

B. Particular Instruments.

Forgery of indorsement of note is an offense. — The making of a negotiable note, indorsing the name of a third person on the back thereof, and passing it to the payee constitutes the offense of forgery. Powell v. Commonwealth, 52 Va. (11 Gratt.) 822 (1854).

But forging a power of attorney to recover money is not. — The forgery of a power of attorney to recover money for military services, is not a crime within an "act against forgery." Commonwealth v. Proctor, 3 Va. (1 Va. Cas.) 4 (1791).

Nor is forging of letter of introduction. — A letter of introduction was held not a writing in respect whereof forgery can be committed, either at common law or under the statute. Foulkes v. Commonwealth, 41 Va. (2 Rob.) 836 (1843).

Forgery of city cigarette tax stamps is an offense under this section. — Under a city ordinance which levied a tax on cigarettes to be paid by the wholesaler or dealer, each package sold had to be marked with a stamp or the printed mark of a meter machine. Defendant sold cigarettes through vending machines and to avoid paying the tax made and used a stamp with which he imitated the meter mark of a particular wholesaler. He was properly convicted under this section for possessing this stamp with intent to forge for forging the mark on cigarettes found in his home, and for forging and uttering cigarettes in his machines bearing this mark. Hanbury v. Commonwealth, 203 Va. 182, 122 S.E.2d 911 (1961).

But city ordinance punishing as misdemeanor forgery of city tax stamps on cigarettes was invalid, since the crime of forgery was already controlled by a general state statute making it a felony. Hanbury v. Commonwealth, 203 Va. 182, 122 S.E.2d 911 (1961).

Payroll check. — Because a payroll check that defendant cashed contained defendant's name, fraudulently written as the intended payee, defendant's handwritten endorsement, and a misspelled signature of the drawer's representative on the bottom left portion of the check's front, the check had apparent legal efficacy to find defendant guilty of forgery and uttering. Perry v. Commonwealth, — Va. App. —, — S.E.2d —, 2006 Va. App. LEXIS 426 (Sept. 19, 2006).

Hospital discharge form. — Defendant was properly convicted of forgery because a hospital discharge form defendant signed with her best friend's name had legal efficacy for the purposes of § 18.2-172 because the language of the form could have subjected the friend to financial liability for defendant's treatment. Pullin v. Commonwealth, — Va. App. —, — S.E.2d —, 2009 Va. App. LEXIS 139 (Mar. 24, 2009).

Medical clearance for light duty work form. — Evidence was sufficient to convict defendant of forgery and uttering because he deliberately falsified a medical clearance for light duty work form in order to obtain light-duty, sedentary, inside work, and he uttered the forged form when he presented it to his supervisor as good and valid. Lee v. Commonwealth, 2010 Va. App. LEXIS 181 (May 4, 2010).

III. UTTERING.

"Uttering." — Uttering is an assertion by word or action that a writing known to be forged is good and valid. Bateman v. Commonwealth, 205 Va. 595, 139 S.E.2d 102 (1964); Gordon v. Commonwealth, No. 1717-88-1 (Ct. of Appeals Apr. 10, 1990).

"Utter" is defined as to put or send, as a forged check, into circulation. Bateman v. Commonwealth, 205 Va. 595, 139 S.E.2d 102 (1964).

Uttering of forged instrument separate offense from forgery. — The forging of an instrument and the uttering of such forged instrument are distinct and substantive offenses. Page v. Commonwealth, 36 Va. (9 Leigh) 683 (1839); Mowbray v. Commonwealth, 38 Va. (11 Leigh) 643 (1841); Dowdy v. Commonwealth, 50 Va. (9 Gratt.) 727 (1852); Johnson v. Commonwealth, 102 Va. 927, 46 S.E. 789 (1904); Bateman v. Commonwealth, 205 Va. 595, 139 S.E.2d 102 (1964).

This section lists two offenses in the disjunctive: One, forgery and the other, uttering or attempting to employ as true a forged writing. Bateman v. Commonwealth, 205 Va. 595, 139 S.E.2d 102 (1964).

What constitutes the offense. — Any assertion or declaration, by word or act, directly or indirectly, that the forged writing is good, with knowledge that it is forged, is an uttering or attempting to employ as true the said writing, provided that such assertion or declaration was made in the prosecution of the purpose of obtaining the money mentioned in the said writing. Chahoon v. Commonwealth, 61 Va. (20 Gratt.) 733 (1871); Sands v. Commonwealth, 61 Va. (20 Gratt.) 800 (1871).

Knowledge that writing is forged. — Evidence was sufficient to prove that defendant knew check was forged at the time she tendered it for payment, and her conviction for uttering was therefore affirmed. Hutchings v. Commonwealth, No. 2066-98-3 (Ct. of Appeals Nov. 9, 1999).

Evidence supported the trial court's finding that defendant uttered two checks knowing them to be forged when he cashed them; defendant's possession of the forged checks, which he submitted as payee, permitted the inference that he knew they were forged. Vernon v. Commonwealth, — Va. App. —, — S.E.2d —, 2006 Va. App. LEXIS 585 (Dec. 28, 2006).

Sufficient evidence was presented to support defendant's conviction for uttering in violation of § 18.2-172 because defendant endorsed a check knowing that he did not perform "housework" as noted in the memo section; therefore, defendant knew the check was forged and presented it to a bank with the intent to defraud. Massengale v. Commonwealth, — Va. App. —, — S.E.2d —, 2007 Va. App. LEXIS 84 (Mar. 13, 2007).

In a case in which defendant appealed his convictions for uttering a forged check in violation of § 18.2-172 and attempted grand larceny in violation of §§ 18.2-95 and 18.2-26, he argued unsuccessfully that it would violate his due process rights under the Fourteenth Amendment to infer his guilty knowledge solely from the fact that he possessed the forged check. The evidence in the record rationally connected the permissive inference of guilty knowledge of the check's forgery to defendant's possession of the forged instrument, and his possession of the forged check, in conjunction with the other circumstantial evidence, allowed the inference that he knew the check was forged. Coles v. Commonwealth, 2009 Va. App. LEXIS 484 (Oct. 27, 2009).

Accused must have himself uttered or assisted another. — To convict a prisoner of uttering, or attempting to employ as true, a forged writing, it must be shown that the accused himself uttered or attempted to employ as true the said forged writing, or was present at the time such forged writing was uttered or attempted to be employed as true by some other person, aiding and assisting such person to utter or employ the same as true. Sands v. Commonwealth, 61 Va. (20 Gratt.) 800 (1871).

Counsel recovering judgment on note he knows to be forged is uttering. — The bringing of a suit at law, as counsel, upon a forged note, and recovering judgment thereon with the knowledge that the note was a forgery, is held to be an attempt to employ the said note as true, and an uttering thereof, within the meaning of the statute. Chahoon v. Commonwealth, 61 Va. (20 Gratt.) 733 (1871); Sands v. Commonwealth, 61 Va. (20 Gratt.) 800 (1871).

Passing forged checks of bank with invalid charter an offense. — Upon an indictment for passing a counterfeit check or order of a branch of the bank of the United States, on the cashier of the bank, payable to T.R. or order, and indorsed by T.R. to bearer, it was held that whether the charter of the bank be constitutional or not, and whether the charter authorizes the issue of such checks or orders or not, the counterfeiting or passing counterfeits of such checks or orders, is felony. Hendrick v. Commonwealth, 32 Va. (5 Leigh) 707 (1834).

Evidence held sufficient. — Trial court did not abuse its discretion in denying defendant's motion for appointment of a handwriting expert in a case where defendant was accused of forging the checks of defendant's friend and presenting them at the friend's bank in order to obtain funds from the friend's checking account, as defendant did not show a particularized need for such testimony since the crime of uttering did not require direct proof that defendant personally forged or altered the checks. Dickenson v. Commonwealth, No. 1095-02-1, 2003 Va. App. LEXIS 228 (Ct. of Appeals Apr. 15, 2003).

Because defendant took a check that was payable to her husband, endorsed his name to the check, and deposited it to her personal account without permission or pursuant to a good faith claim of right, she was properly convicted of grand larceny and uttering under §§ 18.2-98 and 18.2-172. Kocher v. Commonwealth, — Va. App. —, — S.E.2d —, 2009 Va. App. LEXIS 115 (Mar. 17, 2009).

Evidence was sufficient to convict defendant of three counts of uttering where two grocery store clerks identified photographs of defendant as the person who presented forged checks to them and the true owner of the checks testified that her checks were stolen when an unknown thief broke into her car. Shelton v. Commonwealth, 2006 Va. App. LEXIS 610 (Nov. 16, 2006).

IV. INDICTMENT.

Uttering and forging may be charged in separate counts. — Forging and uttering a forged paper knowing it to be forged, being separate and distinct offenses, may be charged in separate counts in the same indictment. Johnson v. Commonwealth, 102 Va. 927, 46 S.E. 789 (1904).

Utterings and forging may be charged in separate counts of the same indictment. Bateman v. Commonwealth, 205 Va. 595, 139 S.E.2d 102 (1964).

And accused may be found guilty of both forgery and uttering a forged instrument, if each offense is charged in a separate count in the same indictment. Bateman v. Commonwealth, 205 Va. 595, 139 S.E.2d 102 (1964).

And punished for each offense separately. — A jury may find a prisoner guilty upon a count of uttering and a count of forging, and ascertain the punishment for each offense separately. Bateman v. Commonwealth, 205 Va. 595, 139 S.E.2d 102 (1964).

A general description of the offense in the words of the statute is sufficient. Huffman v. Commonwealth, 27 Va. (6 Rand.) 685 (1828).

Indictment need not contain words "to the prejudice of another's right." — The words, "to the prejudice of another's right," in relation to forgeries, are descriptive not of the offense but of the writings of which forgery may be committed, and it is not therefore necessary that they shall be inserted in the indictment in describing the offense charged. Hendrick v. Commonwealth, 32 Va. (5 Leigh) 707 (1834); Murry v. Commonwealth, 32 Va. (5 Leigh) 720 (1835); Powell v. Commonwealth, 52 Va. (11 Gratt.) 822 (1854).

Nor set out indorsements on forged note. — An indictment for forgery charged that the forgery was of a negotiable note, and set it out in haec verba, without setting out the indorsements upon the back. On the trial when the note was offered in evidence, it was objected to on the ground of variance. It was held that it was not necessary to set out in the indictment the indorsements upon the note, or any other matter written upon the same paper, constituting no part of the note itself, and not entering into the essential description of that instrument. Perkins v. Commonwealth, 48 Va. (7 Gratt.) 651 (1851).

Nor that the persons accused procured to forge the instrument. — It is not necessary to set forth in the count the persons whom the prisoner procured to forge the instrument, or with whom he acted and assisted in the forgery. A general description, in the words of the statute, is sufficient. Huffman v. Commonwealth, 27 Va. (6 Rand.) 685 (1828).

Nor that forger of receipt was indebted. — On an indictment for forging a receipt, it is not necessary that it should be averred that the person charged with the offense is indebted to the individual against whom the receipt is forged in order to show that the latter stands in a situation to be defrauded by the former. The guilt or innocence of the accused is not dependent on the ultimate result of a settlement of accounts between the parties, nor can one be permitted to forge an acquittance to defeat even an unjust demand. Gordon v. Commonwealth, 100 Va. 825, 41 S.E. 746 (1902).

Forgery of check and indorsement thereon may be charged in one count. — An indictment charging in one count the forgery of a check and of the indorsement thereon, is not liable to the objection of duplicity or misjoinder. Sprouse v. Commonwealth, 81 Va. 374 (1886).

Variance. — Where the indictment described in detail the note which it was alleged that defendant had forged and uttered, and the evidence showed that the instrument, when presented to the bank, was signed in blank, there was held to be no variance between the allegations and proof, since the signing of the forged names to the note and thereafter completing the instrument constituted a forgery and there was no variance as to the uttering of the forged instrument because the evidence showed that it was negotiated with, and accepted by, the bank after it had been completed. Bullock v. Commonwealth, 205 Va. 558, 138 S.E.2d 261 (1964).

Accused may be acquitted because of variance. — The statute does not make a variance between the indictment and the forged paper immaterial. The accused must be acquitted on that ground, if no other. And if acquitted, the presumption, in the absence of evidence to the contrary, is that he was acquitted on that ground. Burress v. Commonwealth, 68 Va. (27 Gratt.) 934 (1876), overruled on another point, Keister's Ex'rs v. Philips' Ex'x, 124 Va. 585, 98 S.E. 674 (1919).

Immaterial variance. — The difference between "account" as set out in the indictment and "acct" as written in a forged order, is not a material variance which will exclude the order as evidence. Burress v. Commonwealth, 68 Va. (27 Gratt.) 934 (1876), overruled on another point, Keister's Ex'rs v. Philips' Ex'x, 124 Va. 585, 98 S.E. 674 (1919).

Description of instrument. — In a prosecution for forging, or attempting to employ as true any forged instrument, it is sufficient to describe the same in the indictment in such manner as would sustain an indictment for the larceny of such instrument. Coleman v. Commonwealth, 66 Va. (25 Gratt.) 865 (1874). See § 19.2-224.

Incomplete recital of note. — An indictment charged the forgery of an indorsement on a negotiable note which was described as to the amount, date, to whom payable and when due, but the indictment did not state who was the maker of the note or where it was payable. It was held that it was a good indictment. Cocke v. Commonwealth, 54 Va. (13 Gratt.) 750 (1855).

Inaccurate recital. — The description of the writing in the indictment as the indorsement of a person whose name is forged will not vitiate the indictment though the simulated liability might not be that of a technical indorser, but of a different character. Powell v. Commonwealth, 52 Va. (11 Gratt.) 822 (1854).

Indictment charging as principal in second degree. — An indictment which charges that the prisoner caused and procured a certain instrument to be forged, and willingly assisted in the forgery, etc., is to be understood as charging that he caused it to be done in his presence, and that he aided, being present, in other words, as charging him as principal in the second degree, and not as accessory. Huffman v. Commonwealth, 27 Va. (6 Rand.) 685 (1828). See Rasnick v. Commonwealth, 4 Va. (2 Va. Cas.) 356 (1823).

Indictment held good after verdict. — To charge that the prisoners willingly acted and assisted in false making and forging, without setting out in particular any person who was assisted; to charge them with causing and procuring the forged notes to be passed, without setting out the persons whom the prisoners caused or procured to pass them, nor to whom; to charge them with passing them to W.S. with intent to defraud the said W.S. and others; also, to charge them with causing and procuring them to be passed or exchanged, was good after verdict. Commonwealth v. Ervin, 4 Va. (2 Va. Cas.) 337 (1823).

V. EVIDENCE.

A. Presumptions and Burden of Proof.

Every presumption is in favor of innocence. — It is a fundamental principle of law that fraud must be clearly alleged and proven. Every presumption is in favor of innocence and not of guilt.

In the instant case it was alleged that a certain deed was a forgery, but there was no evidence to sustain the averment. Branham v. Clinchfield Coal Corp., 123 Va. 346, 96 S.E. 761 (1918).

Failure of accused to produce evidence may be considered. — If the jury believe that it is in the power of the accused to produce evidence in elucidation of the subject matter of the charge against him, then his failure or neglect to produce such evidence may be considered by the jury, in connection with the other facts proved in the case. Chahoon v. Commonwealth, 61 Va. (20 Gratt.) 733 (1871).

Authority. — The prosecution must prove beyond reasonable doubt that defendant was not authorized to sign the name which he allegedly forged and this burden of proof was not sustained where witness whose name was signed would not testify that defendant was unauthorized. Lawson v. Commonwealth, 201 Va. 663, 112 S.E.2d 899 (1960).

Presumption of authority. — Where one signs the name of another to a check it is presumed, in the absence of other evidence, that he or she has the authority to do so and the burden is on the Commonwealth not only to prove that the defendant signed another's name as maker of the check but the evidence must establish that this was done without authority. Bowman v. Commonwealth, 28 Va. App. 204, 503 S.E.2d 241 (1998).

The unexplained possession of a forged instrument by one who endeavors to obtain money thereon is prima facie evidence that such person forged the instrument, but such prima facie evidence may be rebutted by an explanation satisfactory to the jury as to how he came into possession of the instrument. Bullock v. Commonwealth, 205 Va. 558, 138 S.E.2d 261 (1964); Bateman v. Commonwealth, 205 Va. 595, 139 S.E.2d 102 (1964).

It was held to be reversible error to instruct the jury that defendant's possession and uttering of the forged instrument raised a presumption that he forged it, which presumption would become conclusive unless defendant explained the possession or the forgery. Bullock v. Commonwealth, 205 Va. 558, 138 S.E.2d 261 (1964); Bateman v. Commonwealth, 205 Va. 595, 139 S.E.2d 102 (1964).

Possession of a forged check by an accused, which he claims as a payee, is prima facie evidence that he either forged the instrument or procured it to be forged. Oliver v. Commonwealth, 35 Va. App. 286, 544 S.E.2d 870, 2001 Va. App. LEXIS 196 (2001).

Evidence failed to link defendant to checks upon which charges were based. — Charges that a defendant committed forgery and uttering by passing counterfeit checks were not sufficiently proved by evidence which failed to link him to the specific checks upon which the charges were based. Bell v. Commonwealth, No. 0139-01-2, 2002 Va. App. LEXIS 151 (Ct. of Appeals Mar. 12, 2002).

Evidence of intent to defraud drawee. — The fact that an instrument was forged, made payable to the defendant, and endorsed by him, is sufficient evidence of the defendant's intent to defraud the drawee. Fitzgerald v. Commonwealth, 227 Va. 171, 313 S.E.2d 394 (1984).

Physician's alteration of test date held not forgery. — is prima facie evidence that he either forged the instrument or procured it to be forged. Such a prima facie showing of guilt does not rise to the level of a conclusive presumption, and it may be rebutted, but it will warrant submission of the issue of guilt of forgery to the jury, and will support a verdict of guilty if the jury so finds. Fitzgerald v. Commonwealth, 227 Va. 171, 313 S.E.2d 394 (1984).

Where physician produced a forged writing by altering a date on patient's cardiac stress test report, but when he did so there was no possibility that the altered document did or could prejudice insurer's rights, as at that time surgery had already been completed and insurer acknowledged that its liability already existed at that time, physician was not guilty of the crime of forgery. Stevenson v. Commonwealth, 258 Va. 485, 522 S.E.2d 368 (1999).

B. Proof of Handwriting.

Writings of accused and of person whose writing is allegedly forged are admissible. — On an indictment for forgery it is not error to admit in evidence other writings of the prisoner shown to be genuine, and of the person whose writing is alleged to have been forged also shown to be genuine, for the purpose of comparing by expert testimony the genuine handwritings with the handwriting of the paper alleged to have been forged. Nor is it error to admit in evidence enlarged photographs of these genuine writings for the purpose of facilitating comparison. Johnson v. Commonwealth, 102 Va. 927, 46 S.E. 789 (1904).

Genuine specimens of handwriting admissible. — Genuine specimens of handwriting or the signature of the person whose handwriting is involved may be introduced, subject to proper control by the judge, and, without the testimony of experts, such specimens may be subjected to comparison with a disputed paper with the jury. Keister's Ex'rs v. Philips' Ex'x, 124 Va. 585, 98 S.E. 674 (1919), which involved a prosecution under this section.

As is evidence of similar mistake in spelling by accused. — At the examination of the prisoner by the mayor, the prisoner reluctantly, at the mayor's request but without threat or promise to induce him to do so, wrote the name he was suspected of having forged; in doing so he made the same mistake in spelling the name as appeared on the forged instrument. This fact was properly admitted to the jury. Sprouse v. Commonwealth, 81 Va. 374 (1886).

Expert testimony not required. — Trial court did not abuse its discretion in denying defendant's motion for appointment of a handwriting expert in a case where defendant was accused of forging the checks of defendant's friend and presenting them at the friend's bank in order to obtain funds from the friend's checking account, as defendant did not show a particularized need for such testimony since the crime of forgery did not require direct proof that defendant personally forged or altered the checks. Dickenson v. Commonwealth, No. 1095-02-1, 2003 Va. App. LEXIS 228 (Ct. of Appeals Apr. 15, 2003).

Nonexpert testimony held admissible. — Upon a trial for forgery, to prove that the paper was forged a witness was introduced who said that he knew H., the party whose signature was in question and who was dead, about two years; was his tenant; had seen him write; thought he knew his handwriting tolerably well; but could not swear to a particular signature as his, without knowing the fact; thought he had a sufficient knowledge or recollection of his signature to enable him to give an opinion as to the genuineness of his signature, though he would not swear absolutely about it. The witness then said, "I think it is not his handwriting; but at the same time, I cannot say on oath positively it is not." This is admissible evidence. Chahoon v. Commonwealth, 61 Va. (20 Gratt.) 733 (1871).

Testimony held inadmissible. — A witness who states that he is perfectly familiar with the handwriting of the accused, and states the circumstances which made him so familiar with it, expresses the confident opinion from his knowledge of the accused's handwriting that he was incapable of writing the order. This opinion is incompetent testimony, and properly excluded. Burress v. Commonwealth, 68 Va. (27 Gratt.) 934 (1876), overruled on another point, Keister's Ex'rs v. Philips' Ex'x, 124 Va. 585, 98 S.E. 674 (1919).

C. Documentary Evidence.

Bank clerk's book entries competent to prove note was as described in indictment. — Upon a trial for the forgery of an indorsement on a note, the note having been deposited in bank for collection, the original entries in the book of the note clerk of the bank, proved by the clerk to have been made by him from the note, are competent evidence to prove that the note and indorsement thereon were as described in the indictment. Cocke v. Commonwealth, 54 Va. (13 Gratt.) 750 (1855).

Forged paper admissible although when passed it varied from description in indictment. — A forged paper was passed by a prisoner bearing date in 1828; immediately after, with the knowledge of the holder, the prisoner altered the date to 1827. The indictment set forth its tenor, and described it as dated in 1827. The paper is proper evidence to go to the jury in support of the indictment, notwithstanding the proof that it bore the date of 1828, when passed. Huffman v. Commonwealth, 27 Va. (6 Rand.) 685 (1828).

Records as evidence. — C. had forged a note and employed the prisoner, an attorney, to bring suit thereon, which he did and recovered judgment. In the prosecution of the attorney for uttering the forged note the records of the civil suit and the testimony of the clerks of the court are admissible evidence to show the complicity of the prisoner in the uttering of the forged paper. Sands v. Commonwealth, 61 Va. (20 Gratt.) 800 (1871).

An action at law was brought upon the note alleged to be forged, against the curator of H., and judgment rendered without any defense. A suit in equity was then brought to subject the real estate of H. to the payment of the judgment. There was a decree for sale, and sale, in both of which suits the prisoner was counsel for the estate, and he purchased a part of the property. The record of these cases, with the testimony of the clerks of the respective courts, were admissible evidence, with other evidence, to show the uttering of the forged paper and the complicity of the prisoner in the uttering of it. Sands v. Commonwealth, 61 Va. (20 Gratt.) 800 (1871).

Evidence was clearly sufficient to support defendant's forgery and uttering convictions where defendant conceded at oral argument that the evidence was sufficient to establish the crimes if certain bank affidavits were lawfully admitted and the affidavits in question were prepared solely for a fraud investigation by the bank and, thus, were admissible business records. Wooding v. Commonwealth, 2010 Va. App. LEXIS 200 (May 18, 2010).

Harmless error. — Admission of affidavits, although in error, was held harmless. Hutt v. Commonwealth, 2012 Va. App. LEXIS 228 (July 10, 2012).

D. Best and Secondary Evidence.

Allegedly forged instrument is best evidence. — On a trial for forgery the instrument alleged to be forged is the best evidence of itself and its contents, and therefore its production can never be dispensed with unless unavoidable. Pendleton v. Commonwealth, 31 Va. (4 Leigh) 694 (1834).

Secondary evidence is admissible upon proof that original probably lost. — On the trial of an indictment for forgery of a check on a bank, if there be proof rendering it highly probable that the original paper has been lost or destroyed, though this was not done by the accused or by his procurement, secondary evidence of the contents, character and description of the paper, is admissible to sustain the prosecution. Pendleton v. Commonwealth, 31 Va. (4 Leigh) 694 (1834).

Or that accused will not produce it. — Upon a trial for the forgery of an indorsement on a note, the Commonwealth having proved that the note went into the prisoner's possession, and notice to the prisoner to produce it, may prove the note and the forgery in its absence. Cocke v. Commonwealth, 54 Va. (13 Gratt.) 750 (1855).

Foundation for admission of secondary evidence. — On a trial of indictment for forgery of a letter of credit with intent to defraud W. & W., the Commonwealth proved that a draft, presented by the prisoner to W. & W. at the same time with the letter of credit, had been filed, together with an indictment against the prisoner for forging the same, with the clerk of the court, who, on making search for the draft among the papers in his office, had been unable to find it. Thereupon the Commonwealth offered secondary evidence of the contents of the draft, no notice having been given to the prisoner before the jury was impanelled of any intention to offer such evidence. The foundation so laid for the admission of the secondary evidence is sufficient. Foulkes v. Commonwealth, 41 Va. (2 Rob.) 836 (1843).

Proof of nongenuineness of instrument. — Upon a trial for forgery of a written instrument, the Commonwealth may, without producing as a witness the party by whom the instrument purports to be signed, and without accounting for his absence, prove by the evidence of other witnesses that the instrument is not genuine; such evidence not being in its nature secondary to that of the party whose signature is in question. Foulkes v. Commonwealth, 41 Va. (2 Rob.) 836 (1843).

E. Other Matters.

Time of forgery of check. — On a charge of forgery by the addition of words to a check, the addition may be shown to have been made at any time after the delivery to the payee thereof. Gordon v. Commonwealth, 100 Va. 825, 41 S.E. 746 (1902).

Pecuniary condition of person whose note is forged is admissible. — On a trial for the forgery of a note of a person who has since died, the Commonwealth may prove that such person was prompt in the payment of his debts, and that he owned large property — real and personal — and was doing a good business. Sands v. Commonwealth, 61 Va. (20 Gratt.) 800 (1871). See also Chahoon v. Commonwealth, 61 Va. (20 Gratt.) 733 (1871).

Refreshing witness's recollection. — Trial court did not err in allowing the Commonwealth to refresh a victim's recollection because the record established that the victim forgot some portion of the facts of the matter about which she was called to testify since the substance of the victim's testimony was that she could not remember whether she said something to defendant about a forged check; the victim examined the note provided to her by the Commonwealth, indicated it was in her handwriting, testified that the content of the note was "correct," and then relinquished the note before testifying more specifically about its content, and that testimony provided the needed foundation for allowing the victim to present her refreshed recollection regarding her conversation with defendant about the check. Bell v. Commonwealth, 2010 Va. App. LEXIS 461 (Nov. 30, 2010).

Evidence that accused had notes in certain county admissible to show forgery committed there. — Evidence that the prisoner had the notes in his possession in a certain county was proper evidence to go before the jury of the fact that he committed the forgery there. Spencer v. Commonwealth, 29 Va. (2 Leigh) 751 (1830).

Reversal where Commonwealth argued other offenses made charged offenses more punishable. — Defendant's convictions of one count of forgery and one count of uttering a check were reversed, where the Commonwealth was erroneously allowed to argue to the jury that other check cashing offenses committed by defendant rendered the charged offenses "more punishable." Tomlin v. Commonwealth, No. 0558-89-3 (Ct. of Appeals Sept. 25, 1990).

Forgery conviction vacated for lack of jurisdiction. — Because defendant's brother was the victim of forgery committed by defendant, the juvenile and domestic relations district court had exclusive, original jurisdiction to determine whether there was probable cause. Therefore, since defendant was never brought before a juvenile and domestic relations district court for the purpose of determining probable cause, or for any purpose, but rather was brought before the general district court which acted in the absence of jurisdiction and thus had no power to certify the case to the circuit court, the forgery conviction is vacated. Pope v. Commonwealth, 19 Va. App. 130, 449 S.E.2d 269 (1994).

Privileges. — Section 19.2-271.2(ii) did not apply because defendant was indicted for uttering a check with insufficient funds, she was not charged with "forgery or uttering." Lindsey v. Commonwealth, 2007 Va. App. LEXIS 480 (Dec. 27, 2007).

Evidence of similar transactions. — In a prosecution under this section evidence as to similar transactions closely connected in time with the offense charged was admissible as tending to show a general scheme or guilty knowledge and intent. Sloan v. Commonwealth, 199 Va. 877, 102 S.E.2d 278 (1958).

The admission of evidence of similar offenses committed by defendant was clearly admissible as tending to show a general scheme or guilty knowledge and fraudulent intent on the part of the defendant. Bullock v. Commonwealth, 205 Va. 558, 138 S.E.2d 261 (1964).

Evidence showing or tending to show the guilt of an accused of offenses committed at other times is inadmissible when its purpose is to show the character of the accused or his disposition to commit an offense similar to that charged; but evidence of other offenses is admissible when used to show motive, intent, or guilty knowledge, or when it is connected with or leads up to the offense for which the accused is on trial. Harris v. Commonwealth, 211 Va. 742, 180 S.E.2d 520 (1971).

When guilty knowledge is an essential element of an offense charged, evidence of acts committed by the accused and of his conduct at or about the time of the offense charged which tends to establish his knowledge is admissible, even though such evidence shows or tends to show an offense other than that charged, and this rule has been applied to offenses committed before and after the date of the offense for which the accused is on trial. Harris v. Commonwealth, 211 Va. 742, 180 S.E.2d 520 (1971).

Evidence showing that both checks were forgeries; that the defendant falsely identified himself when the checks were presented; and that defendant's attempt to cash the second check occurred "shortly" after the first check was cashed, was clearly admissible as tending to show a general scheme or guilty knowledge and fraudulent intent on the part of the defendant. Harris v. Commonwealth, 211 Va. 742, 180 S.E.2d 520 (1971).

Evidence of aiding and abetting. — Viewing the totality of the circumstances, the trial judge could reasonably conclude that defendant lent her countenance and approval and, therefore, aided and abetted a common plan and scheme to commit forgery, uttering,

and petit larceny, using counterfeit traveler's checks. Spruill v. Commonwealth, No. 3054-01-3, 2002 Va. App. LEXIS 705 (Ct. of Appeals Nov. 26, 2002).

Evidence sufficient to sustain conviction. — See United States v. Bullock, 402 F.2d 476 (4th Cir. 1968).

Evidence was sufficient to support defendant's conviction of uttering a forged instrument, despite defendant's claims that she did not know that a check which she claimed to have received at a yard sale and which she completed by adding her name and then cashed was stolen or forged, given the overall circumstances of the case; the finder of fact was not required to accept defendant's bizarre and self-serving claims of innocence. Gates v. Commonwealth, No. 2728-00-2, 2001 Va. App. LEXIS 645 (Ct. of Appeals Nov. 20, 2001).

Evidence was sufficient to sustain forgery convictions where fingerprint expert testified that defendant's latent fingerprints were on the forged documents, a handwriting expert testified that defendant wrote out certain printed information on the documents, and handwriting expert testified that there were indications that defendant wrote the work hours and forged the signature of the signing supervisor; these, along with inconsistent statements by defendant, were sufficient to prove beyond a reasonable doubt that defendant forged the time sheets. Barr v. Commonwealth, No. 1150-01-3, 2002 Va. App. LEXIS 218 (Ct. of Appeals Apr. 9, 2002).

Evidence proved beyond a reasonable doubt that defendant was the criminal agent of the charged offenses of forgery and uttering, in violation of § 18.2-172, and grand larceny of the proceeds, in violation of § 18.2-95, where only defendant had access to the victim's checkbook during the time the check was stolen, and defendant cashed the check. Clary v. Commonwealth, No. 3010-00-2, 2002 Va. App. LEXIS 324 (Ct. of Appeals May 28, 2002).

Defendant's convictions on two counts of forging a public document and two counts of uttering a forged public document were upheld on appeal, given sufficient evidence that: (1) defendant caused a police officer to issue two forged summonses to him, by providing false information to the officer as he prepared the documents; and (2) defendant uttered them by knowingly allowing the officer to rely upon them in order to avoid further prosecution. Moreover, signing one's own name with the intent that the writing be received as written by another person, impersonating another in the signature of an instrument, or signing in such a way as to make the writing purport to be that of another, were all considered to be acts of forgery. Rodriquez v. Commonwealth, 50 Va. App. 667, 653 S.E.2d 296, 2007 Va. App. LEXIS 428 (2007).

Because defendant acknowledged that the traveler's checks defendant executed "probably" belonged to someone else, it was immaterial whether defendant knew they were counterfeit or fake; accordingly, the evidence was sufficient to find defendant guilty of grand larceny and uttering a forged traveler's check in violation of §§ 18.2-95 and 18.2-172. McQuinn v. Commonwealth, 2009 Va. App. LEXIS 258 (June 9, 2009).

Evidence was sufficient to convict defendant of forgery and uttering because he deliberately falsified a medical clearance for light duty work form in order to obtain light-duty, sedentary, inside work, and he uttered the forged form when he presented it to his supervisor as good and valid. Lee v. Commonwealth, 2010 Va. App. LEXIS 181 (May 4, 2010).

Evidence was sufficient to support defendant's conviction for attempting to obtain money by false pretenses and uttering a forged check drawn on the account of her employer in violation of §§ 18.2-178 and 18.2-172 because the only reasonable hypothesis flowing from the direct and circumstantial evidence was that defendant shared in an accomplice's intent to utter a forged check and to attempt to obtain money by false pretenses; defendant, who worked across the hall from the victim and had access to her office, admitted to the victim that she had possessed the check at issue, defendant accompanied the accomplice to a check cashing business and admitted knowing that the accomplice was there to cash a check, and defendant, the only one of the three people at the business that day who had a direct tie to the employer, remained in the car during the transaction, fabricated a reason to enter the business after police arrived and entered, and attempted to flee the scene alone after learning that the accomplice had been handcuffed. Bell v. Commonwealth, 2010 Va. App. LEXIS 461 (Nov. 30, 2010).

Evidence insufficient to sustain conviction. — Where a former airline employee obtained flight vouchers without first paying for reserved airline tickets by exploiting a loophole in the airline's reservation system, the evidence was insufficient to sustain four uttering convictions because there was no evidence that the vouchers were forgeries. Brown v. Commonwealth, 56 Va. App. 178, 692 S.E.2d 271, 2010 Va. App. LEXIS 177 (2010).

CIRCUIT COURT OPINIONS

Legal authority of allegedly forged instrument. — Although defendant stole a check and filled it in, because defendant signed defendant's name on the signature line, the check did not constitute a forgery as it was not signed by the maker; therefore, the check could not be the subject of prosecution for forgery or uttering. Commonwealth v. Green, 70 Va. Cir. 452, 2004 Va. Cir. LEXIS 371 (Greensville County 2004).

§ 18.2-172.1. Falsifying or altering and fraudulently using transcripts or diplomas; penalty.

Any person who materially falsifies or alters a transcript or diploma from an institution of postsecondary education and fraudulently uses the same for pecuniary gain or in furtherance of such person's education shall be guilty of a Class 3 misdemeanor.

History.
1983, c. 91.

§ 18.2-172.2. Maliciously affixing another's signature to writing; penalty.

Any person who maliciously affixes a facsimile or likeness of the signature of another person to any writing without the permission of that person and with the intent to create the false impression that the writing was signed by that person is guilty of a Class 1 misdemeanor.

History.
2008, c. 595.

§ 18.2-173. Having in possession forged coin or bank notes.

If any person have in his possession forged bank notes or forged or base coin, such as are mentioned in § 18.2-170, knowing the same to be forged or base, with the intent to utter or employ the same as true, or to sell, exchange, or deliver them, so as to enable any other person to utter or employ them as true, he shall, if the number of such notes or coins in his possession at the same time, be ten or more, be guilty of a Class 6 felony; and if the number be less than ten, he shall be guilty of a Class 3 misdemeanor.

History.
Code 1950, § 18.1-97; 1960, c. 358; 1975, cc. 14, 15.

Michie's Jurisprudence.
For related discussion, see 5A M.J. Counterfeiting, §§ 2, 5.

CASE NOTES

Felonious possession of forged coin is a distinct offense. — The forging of a coin, and the felonious having in possession of such forged coin, are distinct and substantive offenses. Scott v. Commonwealth, 55 Va. (14 Gratt.) 687 (1858).

And a prisoner examined for forgery cannot be indicted under this section. — A prisoner is examined for forging and counterfeiting 24 pieces of silver coin, and is sent on to the circuit court for further trial. He cannot be indicted for feloniously having in his possession 10 or more pieces of coin, with intent to alter and employ the same as true. Scott v. Commonwealth, 55 Va. (14 Gratt.) 687 (1858).

Indictment for the felony must allege possession "at the same time." — An indictment under the statute, for feloniously having in his possession more than 10 pieces of forged or base coin, must allege that the prisoner had them in his possession at the same time; and the charge that on a certain day he had them in his possession is not sufficient. Scott v. Commonwealth, 55 Va. (14 Gratt.) 687 (1858).

Sufficient circumstantial evidence supported conviction. — Sufficient circumstantial evidence that defendant knew that the currency was counterfeit supported defendant's § 18.2-173 conviction where: (1) defendant did not disclaim knowledge that the bills were counterfeit; (2) he admitted that he obtained the counterfeit currency from a friend; (3) he told a deputy that the $20 bills were the only counterfeit money he had; (4) he attempted to conceal his identity by giving the deputy false identification, which was evidence of guilty knowledge; and (5) the fraudulent nature of the bills was apparent to the deputy, who had no training in detecting counterfeit currency. Siharath v. Commonwealth, 2013 Va. App. LEXIS 122 (Apr. 16, 2013).

Sufficient circumstantial evidence that defendant intended to utter or employ the counterfeit currency as true supported defendant's § 18.2-173 conviction where: (1) he segregated his counterfeit currency from his genuine currency, the purpose of which was to enable the possessor to readily distinguish it from the genuine currency; (2) defendant had been unemployed for two years with no readily identifiable source of income; (3) he was traveling to a location commonly known for gambling and recreational activities; and (4) it could reasonably be concluded that defendant was carrying the $200 in counterfeit currency to supplement his $130 in genuine currency to pay his trip expenses. Siharath v. Commonwealth, 2013 Va. App. LEXIS 122 (Apr. 16, 2013).

ARTICLE 2.

IMPERSONATION.

§ 18.2-174. Impersonating law-enforcement officer; penalty.

Any person who falsely assumes or exercises the functions, powers, duties, and privileges incident to the office of sheriff, police officer, marshal, or other peace officer, or any local, city, county, state, or federal law-enforcement officer, or who falsely assumes or pretends to be any such officer, is guilty of a Class 1 misdemeanor. A second or subsequent offense is punishable as a class 6 felony.

History.
Code 1950, § 18.1-311; 1960, c. 358; 1975, cc. 14, 15; 2013, cc. 410, 431, 638.

Editor's note.
Acts 2013, c. 431, cl. 2 provides: "That the provisions of this act may result in a net increase in periods of imprisonment or commitment. Pursuant to § 30-19.1:4, the estimated amount of the necessary appropriation is $4,048 for periods of imprisonment in state adult correctional facilities and cannot be determined for periods of commitment to the custody of the Department of Juvenile Justice."
Acts 2013, c. 431, cl. 3 provides: "That the provisions of this act shall not become effective unless an appropriation of general funds effectuating the purposes of this act is included in a general

appropriation act passed by the 2013 Session of the General Assembly, which becomes law."

Acts 2013, c. 431, cl. 4 provides: "That the General Assembly determines that the requirements of the third enactment of this act have been met."

The 2013 amendments.

The 2013 amendments by cc. 410 and 638 are identical, and rewrote the section which read: "Any person who shall falsely assume or exercise the functions, powers, duties and privileges incident to the office of sheriff, police officer, marshal, or other peace officer, or who shall falsely assume or pretend to be any such officer, shall be deemed guilty of a Class 1 misdemeanor."

The 2013 amendment by c. 431 rewrote the section. The section has been set out in the form above at the direction of the Virginia Code Commission.

Law Review.

For article on model abusive debt collection statute for Virginia, see 15 Wm. & Mary L. Rev. 567 (1974).

CASE NOTES

Constitutionality. — This section was not facially unconstitutional under the First Amendment because: (1) the Virginia impersonation statute had a plainly legitimate sweep where by protecting unsuspecting citizens from those who falsely pretend to be law-enforcement officers, the statute served the Commonwealth's critical interest in public safety, and the second clause prohibited dangerous conduct, such as pretending to be a law-enforcement officer in order to board an airplane, that might not fall under the first clause; and (2) defendant was right at the core of the Virginia impersonation statute's plainly legitimate sweep since there was no question that defendant tried to dodge a traffic ticket by falsely assuming or pretending to be a law-enforcement officer. United States v. Chappell, 691 F.3d 388, 2012 U.S. App. LEXIS 16990 (4th Cir. 2012).

Under the overbreadth analysis, a law that restricts speech may be invalidated only if its realistic unconstitutional applications are substantial, not only in an absolute sense, but also relative to the statute's plainly legitimate sweep. Neither condition is satisfied with respect to § 18.2-174 since the statute's legitimate sweep was considerable. United States v. Chappell, 691 F.3d 388, 2012 U.S. App. LEXIS 16990 (4th Cir. 2012).

Fugitive recovery agent exceeded authority. — Evidence was sufficient to convict a fugitive recovery agent in connection with his stop of a vehicle in which he thought a fugitive might be riding, as he exceeded the scope of the authority granted him under § 19.2-149 by: (1) wearing a misleading badge representing that he was part of a "special investigations unit" of a law-enforcement body; (2) stating that he was with a "violent crimes unit"; and (3) interrogating the woman he stopped about her possible drunk driving after he realized that the fugitive was not in the car. English v. Commonwealth, 43 Va. App. 370, 598 S.E.2d 322, 2004 Va. App. LEXIS 294 (2004).

In this 42 U.S.C.S. § 1983 action, defendant was denied summary judgment as to the Fourth Amendment claim because no prudent person in defendant's position could conclude, even on the basis of a reasonable mistake in interpreting or applying the law, that probable cause existed to arrest plaintiff for violating § 18.2-174 under the specific constellation of facts in this record. Merchant v. Fairfax County, 2011 U.S. Dist. LEXIS 39862 (E.D. Va. 2011).

Probable cause. — Where an arrestee was arrested for impersonating a police officer under § 18.2-174 based on a conversation with an officer, the officer was properly denied summary judgment based on qualified immunity as to an unlawful seizure claim because there was a lack of probable cause since the arrestee accurately related to the officer that the arrestee was a deputy director of the county department of corrections and that the arrestee worked in public safety, the arrestee referred to the arrestee's county-issued vehicle as a "police car" by using air quotes, and the arrestee carried a lawfully-issued badge. Merchant v. Bauer, 677 F.3d 656, 2012 U.S. App. LEXIS 8469 (4th Cir. 2012).

§ 18.2-174.1. Impersonating certain public safety personnel; penalty.

Any person who willfully impersonates, with the intent to make another believe he is, a certified emergency medical services personnel, firefighter, special forest warden designated pursuant to § 10.1-1135, fire marshal, or fire chief is guilty of a Class 1 misdemeanor. A second or subsequent offense is punishable as a Class 6 felony.

History.

1993, c. 403; 2000, c. 962; 2002, c. 536; 2013, c. 431.

Editor's note.

Acts 2013, c. 431, cl. 2 provides: "That the provisions of this act may result in a net increase in periods of imprisonment or commitment. Pursuant to § 30-19.1:4, the estimated amount of the necessary appropriation is $4,048 for periods of imprisonment in state adult correctional facilities and cannot be determined for periods of commitment to the custody of the Department of Juvenile Justice."

Acts 2013, c. 431, cl. 3 provides: "That the provisions of this act shall not become effective unless an appropriation of general funds effectuating the purposes of this act is included in a general appropriation act passed by the 2013 Session of the General Assembly, which becomes law."

Acts 2013, c. 431, cl. 4 provides: "That the General Assembly determines that the requirements of the third enactment of this act have been met."

The 2013 amendments.

The 2013 amendment by c. 431 deleted "including any" following "firefighter," and added the last sentence.

§ 18.2-175. Unlawful wearing of officer's uniform or insignia; unlawful use of vehicle with word "police" shown thereon.

No person, not such an officer as is referred to in § 19.2-78, shall wear any such uniform as is designated pursuant to the provisions of such section or wear an insignia or markings containing the Seal of the Commonwealth or the insignia of any such officer's uniform, nor shall any person not such an officer, or not authorized by such officer, or not authorized by the military police of the armed forces or of the National Guard, or not authorized by the military police of other governmental agencies, use or cause to be used on the public roads or highways of this Commonwealth, any motor vehicle bearing markings with the word "police" shown thereon. However, the prohibition against wearing an insignia or markings containing the Seal of the Commonwealth shall not apply to any certified firefighter or to any certified or licensed emergency medical personnel. Any violation of this section shall be a Class 1 misdemeanor.

History.

Code 1950, § 18.1-312; 1960, c. 358; 1966, c. 420; 1968, c. 675; 1975, cc. 14, 15; 1979, c. 704; 1991, c. 424.

Cross references.

For provision prohibiting wearing of State Police officer's uniform by other person, see § 52-9.2.

Law Review.

For article on model abusive debt collection statute for Virginia, see 15 Wm. & Mary L. Rev. 567 (1974). For survey of Virginia criminal law for the year 1977-1978, see 64 Va. L. Rev. 1407 (1978).

§ 18.2-176. Unauthorized wearing or displaying on motor vehicles of any button, insignia or emblem of certain associations or societies or of Southern Cross of Honor.

(a) No person shall wear the button or insignia of any order of police, trade union or veterans' organization or display upon a motor vehicle the insignia or emblem of any automobile club, medical society, order of police, trade union or veterans' organization or use such button, insignia or emblem to obtain aid or assistance unless entitled to wear, display or use the same under the constitution, bylaws, rules or regulations of the organization concerned.

(b) No person shall wear any Southern Cross of Honor when not entitled to do so by the regulations under which such Crosses of Honor are given.

(c) A violation of this section shall be a Class 3 misdemeanor.

History.
Code 1950, § 18.1-410; 1960, c. 358; 1964, c. 124; 1975, cc. 14, 15.

§ 18.2-177. Illegal use of insignia.

Any person who shall willfully wear, exhibit, display, print, or use, for any purpose, the badge, motto, button, decoration, charm, emblem, rosette, or other insignia of any such association or organization mentioned in § 2.2-411, duly registered under Article 2 (§ 2.2-411 et seq.) of Chapter 4, Title 2.2, unless he shall be entitled to use and wear the same under the constitution and bylaws, rules and regulations of such association or organization, shall be guilty of a Class 4 misdemeanor.

History.
Code 1950, § 2.1-80; 1966, c. 677; 1975, cc. 14, 15.

ARTICLE 3.
FALSE PRETENSES.

§ 18.2-178. Obtaining money or signature, etc., by false pretense.

A. If any person obtain, by any false pretense or token, from any person, with intent to defraud, money, a gift certificate or other property that may be the subject of larceny, he shall be deemed guilty of larceny thereof; or if he obtain, by any false pretense or token, with such intent, the signature of any person to a writing, the false making whereof would be forgery, he shall be guilty of a Class 4 felony.

B. Venue for the trial of any person charged with an offense under this section may be in the county or city in which (i) any act was performed in furtherance of the offense, or (ii) the person charged with the offense resided at the time of the offense.

History.
Code 1950, § 18.1-118; 1960, c. 358; 1975, cc. 14, 15; 2001, c. 131; 2006, c. 321.

Cross references.
As to right of accused in prosecution for larceny to demand statement in writing of what statute attorney for Commonwealth intends to rely on, see § 18.2-111. As to computer time, services, etc., as property subject to larceny, see § 18.2-152.1 et seq. As to obtaining a signature by false pretense, see also § 18.2-172.

Law Review.
For article on justification as a defense to crime, see 59 Va. L. Rev. 1326 (1973). For a note, "Pleading for Theft Consolidation in Virginia: Larceny, Embezzlement, False Pretenses and § 19.2-284," see 55 Wash. & Lee L. Rev. 249 (1998). For 2007 annual survey article, "Electronic Data: A Commentary on the Law in Virginia in 2007," see 42 U. Rich. L. Rev. 355 (2007).

Michie's Jurisprudence.
For related discussion, see 8B M.J. False Pretenses and Cheats, § 2; 12A M.J. Larceny, § 19.

CASE NOTES

I. General Considerations.
II. Evidentiary Matters.

I. GENERAL CONSIDERATIONS.

In general. — Under Virginia law, embezzlement, false pretenses, and larceny are three separate offenses and there is not a general "theft" statute, as there is in most states, that encompasses both types of behavior, and § 18.2-95 defines grand larceny; § 18.2-111 defines embezzlement; and § 18.2-178 defines false pretenses. The Commonwealth of Virginia has always purported to treat the three basic theft crimes of larceny, embezzlement, and false pretenses as separate and distinct offenses, and maintains separate statutes for each crime. United States v. Good, 326 F.3d 589, 2003 U.S. App. LEXIS 7543 (4th Cir. Apr. 22, 2003).

Obtaining by false pretense may be shown under indictment for larceny. — It is the settled law of Virginia that upon an indictment simply charging larceny the state may show that the subject of the larceny was obtained by a false token or pretense. Dowdy v. Commonwealth, 50 Va. (9 Gratt.) 727 (1852); Leftwich v. Commonwealth, 61 Va. (20 Gratt.) 716 (1870); Anable v. Commonwealth, 65 Va. (24 Gratt.) 563 (1873); Fay v. Commonwealth, 69 Va. (28 Gratt.) 912 (1877); Trogdon v. Commonwealth, 72 Va. (31 Gratt.) 862 (1878); Lewis v. Commonwealth, 120 Va. 875, 91 S.E. 174 (1917). See also Hoback v. Commonwealth, 69 Va. (28 Gratt.) 922 (1877); Anthony v. Commonwealth, 88 Va. 847, 14 S.E. 834 (1892); Pitsnogle v. Commonwealth, 91 Va. 808, 22 S.E. 351 (1895); Mangus v. McClelland, 93 Va. 786, 22 S.E. 364 (1895).

Proof that the accused obtained money by false pretenses will sustain an indictment for larceny. Bateman v. Commonwealth, 205 Va. 595, 139 S.E.2d 102 (1964); Bourgeois v. Commonwealth, 217 Va. 268, 227 S.E.2d 714 (1976).

But every element of offense must be proved. — Although this section makes false pretenses equivalent to larceny, yet one cannot be found guilty under a simple count charging him with larceny any more than under one charging specifically the offense of obtaining money, etc., by false pretenses, if there is wanting in the proof any of those elements which constitute that offense. Anable v. Commonwealth, 65 Va. (24 Gratt.) 563 (1873). See also Fay v. Commonwealth, 69 Va. (28 Gratt.) 912 (1877); Trogdon v. Commonwealth, 72 Va. (31 Gratt.) 862 (1878).

Where the Commonwealth failed to prove larceny by false pretenses the conviction cannot be upheld on grounds that the evidence at trial was sufficient to sustain a conviction of the common-law crime of larceny by trick and that the jury instruction set forth all the elements of this crime. An accused is entitled to be clearly informed of the charge against him. The Commonwealth cannot retrospectively argue that defendant should be convicted of a crime for which he was not prosecuted, and on which the jury was not instructed. Baker v. Commonwealth, 225 Va. 192, 300 S.E.2d 788 (1983).

Because salesperson knew that suit was stolen when defendant returned it for cash, evidence failed to prove that any store employee was induced by false pretenses to pay money. Gaines v. Commonwealth, No. 1354-98-4 (Ct. of Appeals July 6, 1999).

Elements of offense. — To constitute the statutory offense of obtaining money under false pretenses four things must occur: (1) There must be an intent to defraud. (2) There must be an actual fraud committed. (3) False pretenses must be used for the purpose of perpetrating the fraud. (4) The fraud must be accomplished by means of false pretenses made use of for the purpose; that is, they must be in some degree the cause, if not the controlling and decisive cause, which induced the owner to part with his property. Anable v. Commonwealth, 65 Va. (24 Gratt.) 563 (1873); Hubbard v. Commonwealth, 201 Va. 61, 109 S.E.2d 100 (1959); Bourgeois v. Commonwealth, 217 Va. 268, 227 S.E.2d 714 (1976); Riegert v. Commonwealth, 218 Va. 511, 237 S.E.2d 803 (1977); Sult v. Commonwealth, 221 Va. 915, 275 S.E.2d 608 (1981); Quidley v. Commonwealth, 221 Va. 963, 275 S.E.2d 622 (1981); Millard v. Commonwealth, 34 Va. App. 202, 539 S.E.2d 84, 2000 Va. App. LEXIS 850 (2000).

Under the provisions of this section, for one to be guilty of the crime of larceny by false pretense, he must make a false representation of an existing fact with knowledge of its falsity and, on that basis, obtain from another person money or other property which may be the subject of larceny, with the intent to defraud. Lund v. Commonwealth, 217 Va. 688, 232 S.E.2d 745 (1977).

Merely showing that the accused knowingly stated what was false is not sufficient; there must also be proof that his intent was to defraud. Riegert v. Commonwealth, 218 Va. 511, 237 S.E.2d 803 (1977).

An essential element of larceny by false pretenses is that both title to and possession of property must pass from the victim to the defendant (or his nominee). The gravamen of the offense is the obtainment of ownership of property. Baker v. Commonwealth, 225 Va. 192, 300 S.E.2d 788 (1983); Davies v. Commonwealth, 15 Va. App. 350, 423 S.E.2d 839 (1992).

The victim need only rely to some degree on the false pretense in order for the Commonwealth to satisfy the fourth prong of this test. Bestwick v. Commonwealth, No. 0954-98-4, 2000 Va. App. LEXIS 222 (Ct. of Appeals Mar. 28, 2000).

Grand larceny by false pretenses conviction was reversed, and the case was dismissed, where the state failed to present evidence that defendant acquired any type of ownership interest in the vehicle he allegedly stole, such as a promissory note, sales contract, or other document that would have evidenced some type of ownership transfer. Shropshire v. Commonwealth, 40 Va. App. 34, 577 S.E.2d 521, 2003 Va. App. LEXIS 122 (2003).

Gravamen is that pretenses are false. — The gravamen of the offense is that the pretenses are false, and if the prisoner can show that the representations upon which he obtained the property from the owner are true, he cannot be convicted. Anable v. Commonwealth, 65 Va. (24 Gratt.) 563 (1873).

The gravamen of the offense is the obtainment of ownership of property, by false representations or pretenses. Quidley v. Commonwealth, 221 Va. 963, 275 S.E.2d 622 (1981).

The false pretense must be a representation as to an existing fact or a past event. Bourgeois v. Commonwealth, 217 Va. 268, 227 S.E.2d 714 (1976); Riegert v. Commonwealth, 218 Va. 511, 237 S.E.2d 803 (1977); Watson v. Commonwealth, 4 Va. App. 450, 358 S.E.2d 735 (1987).

Intent must have existed when false pretenses were made. — Unless the selling of property was by false pretense, with intent to defraud the buyer, the case is not within this section. Therefore the fraudulent intent must have existed at the time the false pretenses by which the money was obtained were made. Fay v. Commonwealth, 69 Va. (28 Gratt.) 912 (1877).

The fraudulent intent must have existed at the time the false pretenses were made, by which the property was obtained. Riegert v. Commonwealth, 218 Va. 511, 237 S.E.2d 803 (1977); Orr v. Commonwealth, 229 Va. 298, 329 S.E.2d 30 (1985).

Merely showing that the accused knowingly stated what was false is not sufficient; there must also be proof that his intent was to defraud. Orr v. Commonwealth, 229 Va. 298, 329 S.E.2d 30 (1985).

For more than a century, the law has required proof that the intent and the representation occur simultaneously; in a prosecution for larceny by false pretenses, the Commonwealth must prove the fraudulent intent existed at the time the false pretenses were made by which the property was obtained. A court's refusal of a proffered jury instruction to this effect was grounds for reversal. Lewis v. Commonwealth, 28 Va. App. 164, 503 S.E.2d 222 (1998).

Conduct of accused must be examined. — In order to determine whether the intent to defraud existed at the time the act was committed, the conduct and representations of the accused must be examined, since intent is a secret operation of the mind. Riegert v. Commonwealth, 218 Va. 511, 237 S.E.2d 803 (1977); Orr v. Commonwealth, 229 Va. 298, 329 S.E.2d 30 (1985).

Single larceny doctrine. — There is no manifest intent by the legislature in this section to abrogate the common-law doctrine of single larceny whereby a series of larcenous acts will be considered a single count of larceny if they are done pursuant to a single impulse and in execution of a general fraudulent scheme. The following factors must be considered when deciding whether the single larceny doctrine applies: (1) the location of the items taken; (2) the lapse of time between the takings; (3) the general and specific intent of the taker; (4) the number of owners of the items taken; and (5) whether intervening events occurred between the takings; the primary factor to be considered is the intent of the thief. Millard v. Commonwealth, 34 Va. App. 202, 539 S.E.2d 84, 2000 Va. App. LEXIS 850 (2000).

A defendant could only be properly convicted on one count of obtaining money by false pretenses where the evidence proved that the defendant had presented three checks to a bank teller in one transaction and that during that same transaction, the teller gave the defendant cash equaling the total of the face amount of the three checks. Millard v. Commonwealth, 34 Va. App. 202, 539 S.E.2d 84, 2000 Va. App. LEXIS 850 (2000).

Pretenses must have had decisive influence. — The false pretenses, either with or without other causes, must have had a decisive influence upon the mind of the owner, so that without their weight he would not have parted with his property. Fay v. Commonwealth, 69 Va. (28 Gratt.) 912 (1877).

The jury must believe from the evidence, beyond all reasonable doubt, that the alleged false pretenses were believed by the owner, that but for them he would not have parted with his goods, that is, that they had the prevailing and controlling influence in making the owner part with his property. Trogdon v. Commonwealth, 72 Va. (31 Gratt.) 862 (1878).

The victim of the fraudulent scheme need not be the person to whom the false pretense or misrepresentation is made. Mosteller v. Commonwealth, 222 Va. 143, 279 S.E.2d 380 (1981).

Sufficient if victim eventually may suffer loss. — The crime is complete under this section when the fraud intended is consummated by obtaining the property sought by means of the false representations, and the offense is not purged by ultimate restoration or payment to the victim; thus, it is sufficient if the fraud of the accused has put the victim in such a position that he may eventually suffer loss. Quidley v. Commonwealth, 221 Va. 963, 275 S.E.2d 622 (1981).

Ultimate victim not the intended victim no defense. — Where evidence established that defendant intentionally committed an actual fraud by use of false pretenses and obtained money thereby, the fact that the ultimate victim was not the one against whom the false pretenses were used was no defense. Grites v. Commonwealth, 9 Va. App. 51, 384 S.E.2d 328 (1989).

And ultimate financial gain or loss immaterial. — There is no requirement under this section that the intended victim suffer actual pecuniary loss; thus, the ultimate financial gain or loss to the victim is immaterial. Quidley v. Commonwealth, 221 Va. 963, 275 S.E.2d 622 (1981).

Where defendant obtained ownership of goods from a company through use of fraudulent documents, the crime charged was complete at that instant since there was no guarantee that the bogus papers would pass unchallenged through normal business channels resulting in ultimate payment by the city from its Public Assistance Fund; thus, the company was placed by defendant's fraud in a position that it might suffer loss through refusal of the city to honor the company's request for payment of the goods it had delivered to defendant, and the fact that ultimately the company suffered no loss was irrelevant. Quidley v. Commonwealth, 221 Va. 963, 275 S.E.2d 622 (1981).

When a defendant obtained money from a bank through use of a fraudulent withdrawal slip which purported to permit her to withdraw money from her grandfather's account, the crime charged was complete at that instant and the bank's later discovery of the forgery and its decision not to debit the grandfather's account did not establish a fatal variance between the terms of the indictment, which charged the defendant obtained her grandfather's money, and the evidence, which she argued proved she obtained a bank's money. Gardner v. Commonwealth, 32 Va. App. 595, 529 S.E.2 820, 2000 Va. App. LEXIS 461 (2000).

Change in ownership and possession. — False pretenses involves a change in ownership as well as possession. Bray v. Commonwealth, 9 Va. App. 417, 388 S.E.2d 837 (1990).

An essential element of larceny by false pretenses is that both title to and possession of property must pass from the victim to the defendant (or his or her nominee); this element was not established where the defendant had both title and possession of a vehicle prior to fraudulently obtaining a certificate of title that did not show the existence of the victim's lien on the vehicle. Bolden v. Commonwealth, 28 Va. App. 488, 507 S.E.2d 84 (1998).

Title to property must be obtained. — An essential element of larceny by false pretenses is that both title to and possession of property must pass from the victim to the defendant or his or her nominee; the gravamen of the offense is the obtainment of ownership of property. Lewis v. Commonwealth, 28 Va. App. 164, 503 S.E.2d 222 (1998).

Purchase of vehicle under conditional sales contract. — When a defendant, by false pretenses, obtains possession of a vehicle and a temporary certificate of ownership under a conditional sales contract pursuant to which the seller retains legal title as security and has the right to repossess the vehicle, the property interest conveyed by the delivery of possession and the completion of the temporary certificate of ownership is sufficient to support a conviction for larceny by false pretenses. Lewis v. Commonwealth, 28 Va. App. 164, 503 S.E.2d 222 (1998).

Worthless check for advance payment of first month's rent. — A person cannot be convicted of larceny by false pretenses for giving a worthless check for the advance payment of the first month's rent on residential real estate and, in return, receiving the key to the premises. Bray v. Commonwealth, 9 Va. App. 417, 388 S.E.2d 837 (1990).

Offense separate from uttering forged note. — Obtaining money by false pretense, which amounts to larceny under this section, is a separate and distinct offense from uttering a forged note for that amount. Bullock v. Commonwealth, 205 Va. 867, 140 S.E.2d 821 (1965).

One may be found guilty of forgery and of uttering a forged check, and of the larceny of the proceeds of the check. Bateman v. Commonwealth, 205 Va. 595, 139 S.E.2d 102 (1964).

Penalty is the same as for larceny. — Obtaining money by false pretenses is made larceny by this section, and the penalty for the offense is the same as in other cases of larceny. Dull v. Commonwealth, 66 Va. (25 Gratt.) 965 (1875).

Obtaining check as larceny of money. — Where an indictment alleged the larceny of money by false pretenses, and the proof showed the larceny of a check afterwards cashed by the accused, in every real sense money was paid to the accused, and, therefore, the charge in the indictment was substantially proven. Lewis v. Commonwealth, 120 Va. 875, 91 S.E. 174 (1917).

Obtaining check from bank by false representation to another. — Where defendant obtained a check from issuer under false pretenses, Commonwealth could charge defendant with obtaining money from bank under false pretenses despite the fact bank was not the one to whom the misrepresentation was made. Grites v. Commonwealth, 9 Va. App. 51, 384 S.E.2d 328 (1989).

False statements made in claiming witness' fees. — In a prosecution for petit larceny under this section, the Commonwealth contended that the accused had claimed and received a total mileage and attendance allowance, as a witness in a certain case, for a much longer trip than he had in fact made. It was held that the gravamen of the offense was that the representations made by the accused as to the distance he was compelled to travel were false and untrue. The evidence was held insufficient to warrant a conviction. Hagy v. Commonwealth, 168 Va. 663, 190 S.E. 144 (1937).

Improperly inflating vendors' bids. — The enactment of §§ 59.1-68.6 et seq. and § 18.2-498.1 et seq. did not preclude the Commonwealth from obtaining a conviction under this section of a defendant alleged to have improperly inflated vendors' bids to the detriment of the Commonwealth, where the alleged acts took place prior to the enactment of the new statutes. Mosteller v. Commonwealth, 222 Va. 143, 279 S.E.2d 380 (1981).

Claim-of-right defense properly rejected. — Appellant's conviction of larceny by false pretenses, in violation of § 18.2-178, was affirmed where the trial court properly rejected her claim-of-right defense based on its disbelief of her testimony, not because it misunderstood the law surrounding the defense. Groves v. Commonwealth, 50 Va. App. 57, 646 S.E.2d 28, 2007 Va. App. LEXIS 242 (2007).

Applied in Storey v. Patient First Corp., 207 F. Supp. 2d 431, 2002 U.S. Dist. LEXIS 10937 (E.D. Va. 2002); Burriesci v. Commonwealth, 59 Va. App. 50, 717 S.E.2d 140, 2011 Va. App. LEXIS 344 (2011).

II. EVIDENTIARY MATTERS.

Refreshing witness's recollection. — Trial court did not err in allowing the Commonwealth to refresh a victim's recollection because the record established that the victim forgot some portion of the facts of the matter about which she was called to testify since the substance of the victim's testimony was that she could not remember whether she said something to defendant about a forged check; the victim examined the note provided to her by the Commonwealth, indicated it was in her handwriting, testified that the content of the note was "correct," and then relinquished the note before testifying more specifically about its content, and that testimony provided the needed foundation for allowing the victim to present her refreshed recollection regarding her conversation with defendant about the check. Bell v. Commonwealth, 2010 Va. App. LEXIS 461 (Nov. 30, 2010).

Evidence of the difference in value, if any, between services and goods provided and the amount paid for them, is not evidence of a false representation of a past or existing fact, nor does such evidence prove that any representation made was false or was of a past or present fact, as opposed to mere promises or statements of intention relating to future events. Watson v. Commonwealth, 4 Va. App. 450, 358 S.E.2d 735 (1987).

Circumstantial evidence is as acceptable to prove guilt as direct evidence, and in some cases, such as proof of intent or knowledge, it is practically the only method of proof. Parks v. Commonwealth, 221 Va. 492, 270 S.E.2d 755 (1980), cert. denied, 450 U.S. 1029, 101 S. Ct. 1738, 68 L. Ed. 2d 224 (1981).

Harmless error in limiting cross-examination. — Defendant's convictions for obtaining $200 or more by false pretenses and giving material false testimony under oath were appropriate even though the trial court's limitation on cross-examination was erroneous because the error was harmless. The record contained extensive evidence impeaching defendant's testimony and establishing the falsified documentary evidence on other critical points and the attorney was not a witness to any of the evidence upon which the conviction for giving material false testimony was based. Lindsey v. Commonwealth, 2011 Va. App. LEXIS 72 (Mar. 1, 2011).

Refusing to instruct jury that it must find that defendant obtained title. — In prosecution for grand larceny by false pretenses, the trial court erred in refusing to instruct the jury that it must find that defendant obtained title to the property; although the trial court erred in instructing the jury regarding the elements of the offense, the error was harmless. Davies v. Commonwealth, 15 Va. App. 350, 423 S.E.2d 839 (1992).

Circumstantial evidence may prove intent. — Since direct proof of intent is often impossible, it can be shown by circumstantial evidence and the conduct or representation of the accused may thus be considered to determine whether the intent to defraud existed at the time the act was committed. Bestwick v. Commonwealth, No. 0954-98-4, 2000 Va. App. LEXIS 222 (Ct. of Appeals Mar. 28, 2000).

Circumstantial evidence held insufficient. — Circumstantial evidence that the defendant entertained an intent to defraud at the time of the act in question held insufficient to sustain the conviction. See Riegert v. Commonwealth, 218 Va. 511, 237 S.E.2d 803 (1977).

False statements not proven. — Although defendant and his girlfriend told an acquaintance of their intent to sell "fake" ecstasy pills, the statements concerned future events and were not statements of false pretenses, and because any "false" statements to a police officer were made after the exchange, the Commonwealth failed to establish all the elements of the offense of obtaining money by false pretenses. Parker v. Commonwealth, — Va. App. —, — S.E.2d —, 2006 Va. App. LEXIS 12 (Jan. 10, 2006).

Charge to jury. — When on an indictment for larceny the court charges the jury in the usual form, and on the trial it appears that the money charged to have been stolen was obtained by false pretenses, another charge by the court is neither necessary nor proper. Dull v. Commonwealth, 66 Va. (25 Gratt.) 965 (1875).

The court properly deleted a paragraph of the defendant's proposed instruction, which paragraph stated that the Commonwealth was required to prove that the defendant's false representations were used for the purpose of perpetrating the fraud, as the paragraph was duplicative of a paragraph which stated that the Commonwealth was required to prove that the representations were made with the intent to defraud. Kirk v. Commonwealth, No. 2735-97-4 (Ct. of Appeals Dec. 8, 1998).

Evidence held sufficient to sustain conviction under this section, where defendant's representations that his business was in sound condition and that he had consummated necessary financial arrangements with a bank to ensure payment of his check were false. Hubbard v. Commonwealth, 201 Va. 61, 109 S.E.2d 100 (1959).

There was sufficient evidence to support the defendant's conviction of obtaining money by false pretenses, where a check in the amount of $950 and in the victim's handwriting was dated and negotiated after the defendant was discharged from the defendant's employ, it was payable to a friend of the defendant's, and the notation on the check read "services rendered," but the friend testified that she performed no services for the victim. Watson v. Commonwealth, 4 Va. App. 450, 358 S.E.2d 735 (1987).

The misleading and false statements by appellant clearly showed his fraudulent intent. Moreover, the fact that appellant had similarly defrauded others also established his fraudulent intent. Therefore, the Commonwealth's evidence was sufficient to prove beyond a reasonable doubt that appellant made false representations and that he did so with the requisite fraudulent intent. Pope v. Commonwealth, No. 0692-96-1 (Ct. of Appeals Jan. 14, 1997).

Where defendant/appellant lied to plaintiff/appellee regarding materials in his possession to complete work under contract to construct a shed, trial court could properly infer not only that defendant intended to defraud his customer, but also that customer relied upon his false representations in paying him second installment of contract price. Bestwick v. Commonwealth, No. 0954-98-4 (Ct. of Appeals Mar. 28, 2000).

The evidence was sufficient to support the defendant's conviction for obtaining money by false pretenses where the defendant entered into a contract with the victim to build a hay barn and then lied to her about having obtained all of the materials to induce her to write a check for the second installment of the contract price. Bestwick v. Commonwealth, No. 0954-98-4, 2000 Va. App. LEXIS 222 (Ct. of Appeals Mar. 28, 2000).

Evidence which showed that defendant presented worthless checks for deposit in an account she had at a credit union, withdrew money from the account, and failed to pay a negative balance in the account was sufficient to sustain her conviction for grand larceny by false pretenses, and the trial court did not err when it rejected defendant's testimony that she was not the person who opened the account at the credit union and withdrew money from it. Johnson v. Commonwealth, No. 1764-03-4, 2004 Va. App. LEXIS 367 (Ct. of Appeals Aug. 3, 2004).

Evidence supported defendant's conviction for obtaining money in excess of $200 under false pretense under § 18.2-178, where the first words defendant's girlfriend uttered to the undercover detective, "these are the pills" was a false pretense. The detective's statement that the detective gave the girlfriend the money because of the detective's "past experience" with the girlfriend did not necessarily preclude a finding that the detective's expectation of what the girlfriend would give the detective was induced by a false representation of past or present fact; the jury could reasonably have interpreted the detective's statement to mean that the detective had chosen to believe the representations that "these are the pills" and that the pills were "real" because the detective had found the girlfriend truthful in the past. Parker v. Commonwealth, 275 Va. 150, 654 S.E.2d 580, 2008 Va. LEXIS 5 (2008).

Evidence was sufficient to prove the intent necessary to support a conviction for obtaining money by false pretenses where the jury was permitted to infer defendant's guilty knowledge from his

possession of forged traveler's checks, where defendant provided conflicting accounts as to how he obtained the checks, and where after defendant obtained the checks, he immediately negotiated each check for an inexpensive item and a large amount of cash. Richardson v. Commonwealth, 2010 Va. App. LEXIS 84 (Mar. 9, 2010).

Defendant's convictions for larceny by false pretenses and attempted larceny by false pretenses, in violation of §§ 18.2-178 and 18.2-26 were appropriate because defendant conceded that he received title to a wheelchair and the theft of that item alone was sufficient to support the allegations contained in the indictment. Additionally, defendant consistently made false representations regarding his disability and work capacity to whomever he needed to in order to gain financially. Brabson v. Commonwealth, 2010 Va. App. LEXIS 80 (Mar. 2, 2010).

Defendant's conviction for obtaining money by false pretenses after exchanging an electronic video game system at a store was affirmed. Once the trial judge concluded that testimony that defendant did not know the property was stolen was not credible, nothing remained to refute the prosecution's evidence. Sweat v. Commonwealth, 2010 Va. App. LEXIS 341 (Aug. 17, 2010).

Evidence was sufficient to support defendant's conviction for attempting to obtain money by false pretenses and uttering a forged check drawn on the account of her employer in violation of §§ 18.2-178 and 18.2-172 because the only reasonable hypothesis flowing from the direct and circumstantial evidence was that defendant shared in an accomplice's intent to utter a forged check and to attempt to obtain money by false pretenses; defendant, who worked across the hall from the victim and had access to her office, admitted to the victim that she had possessed the check at issue, defendant accompanied the accomplice to a check cashing business and admitted knowing that the accomplice was there to cash a check, and defendant, the only one of the three people at the business that day who had a direct tie to the employer, remained in the car during the transaction, fabricated a reason to enter the business after police arrived and entered, and attempted to flee the scene alone after learning that the accomplice had been handcuffed. Bell v. Commonwealth, 2010 Va. App. LEXIS 461 (Nov. 30, 2010).

Trial court did not err in finding the evidence was sufficient to convict defendant of obtaining the victim's money by false pretenses in violation of § 18.2-178 because defendant intentionally and fraudulently misled the victim to believe that the money she gave him was to purchase a trailer he owned; the victim relied on the false representation that defendant owned the trailer at the time she paid him for the purchase of the trailer, and defendant lacked the legal authority to transfer legal title of the trailer to the victim. Pettit v. Commonwealth, 2011 Va. App. LEXIS 368 (Nov. 29, 2011).

As defendant falsely claimed to be a licensed attorney, he obtained money by false pretenses in violation of § 18.2-178 when he accepted legal fees from the victims. That they could have been represented at the proceedings by a lay advocate pursuant to subsection C of § 22.1-214 was irrelevant, as they did not seek to employ one, and defendant did not represent himself to them as such. Deiner v. Commonwealth, 2012 Va. App. LEXIS 109 (Apr. 10, 2012).

Evidence that shortly after giving a check to the first victim and taking the merchandise from the store, defendant issued a stop payment on the check without explanation to the merchant and never returned the merchandise or responded to the merchant's attempt to communicate with her, and less than two months later, and while on bond for that incident, defendant repeated the same course of action at a second merchant was sufficient to support convicitons for obtaining money or property by false pretense. Austin v. Commonwealth, 60 Va. App. 60, 723 S.E.2d 633, 2012 Va. App. LEXIS 113 (2012).

Fact that bank could have protected itself from loss was immaterial. — Evidence was sufficient that defendant obtained money by false pretenses even though the bank could have protected itself from loss by asserting its rights as a holder in due course; evidence was established that the bank suffered a loss, and whether the bank could have prevented its loss or anyone's loss was immaterial. Grites v. Commonwealth, 9 Va. App. 51, 384 S.E.2d 328 (1989).

Evidence was not sufficient to establish seller's intent to defraud buyers because evidence supported the hypothesis that seller intended to use buyers' money to obtain ownership of the property and to convey the ownership to the buyers; evidence was established that seller took proceeds of buyers' check and secured a cashier's check payable to the owner of the property; furthermore, there was no direct evidence that anyone told seller that buyers no longer desired to purchase the property or that a stop payment order had been placed on the check. Grites v. Commonwealth, 9 Va. App. 51, 384 S.E.2d 328 (1989).

Evidence insufficient to support conviction. — The evidence did not establish beyond a reasonable doubt that the alleged false pretenses induced the owner to part with his property. To the contrary, the alleged victim stated that the representations made were not a determining factor in his decision to make a contribution to defendant. A majority of the court having determined that the Commonwealth failed to establish one of the necessary elements of larceny by false pretenses, defendant's conviction was reversed and the case against him was dismissed. Wynne v. Commonwealth, 18 Va. App. 459, 445 S.E.2d 160 (1994).

Evidence that defendant wrote checks belonging to his deceased father to obtain goods from people who received the checks was sufficient to sustain defendant's convictions for obtaining goods by false pretenses, in violation of § 18.2-178, and the trial court which convicted defendant did not err by admitting a National Crime Information Center printout over defendant's objection or by considering the printout as evidence that defendant had prior convictions for larceny to convict him of committing Class 6 felonies, pursuant to § 18.2-104. Argenbright v. Commonwealth, No. 3282-02-3, 2003 Va. App. LEXIS 613 (Ct. of Appeals Nov. 25, 2003).

Evidence was insufficient to support the defendant's conviction where: (1) The defendant's wife told their landlord that she was receiving an inheritance and asked if she could deposit the funds in the landlord's savings account; (2) The landlord agreed and gave her the account number so that the funds could be wired directly to the account; (3) The defendant's wife later told the landlord, in the defendant's presence, that the funds had been wired and then asked for a check for $2,500 to pay medical bills; (4) The landlord gave a blank check to the defendant's wife, who gave it to the defendant, who filled it out in the presence of the landlord; and (5) The defendant and his wife shortly thereafter disappeared; the evidence did not show that the defendant knew that the wife's money was not wired to the landlord's account and, therefore, did not show guilty knowledge on his part. Lee v. Commonwealth, No. 0770-97-2 (Ct. of Appeals February 24, 1998).

Grand larceny by false pretenses conviction was reversed, and the case was dismissed, where the State failed to present evidence that defendant acquired any type of ownership interest in the vehicle he allegedly stole, such as a promissory note, sales contract, or other document that would have evidenced some type of ownership transfer. Shropshire v. Commonwealth, 40 Va. App. 34, 577 S.E.2d 521, 2003 Va. App. LEXIS 122 (2003).

Conviction for obtaining money by false pretenses was reversed because the evidence failed to prove that defendant knew at the time of the agreement to help the alleged victim obtain refinancing that defendant would be paid by an entity other than the alleged victim. Jackson v. Commonwealth, — Va. App. —, — S.E.2d —, 2006 Va. App. LEXIS 547 (Dec. 12, 2006).

Because the Commonwealth conceded that the evidence of an intent to defraud was insufficient to sustain defendant's conviction of obtaining goods by false pretenses in violation of § 43-13, there had to be a concession that the evidence was insufficient to prove the conviction of conspiracy to commit a felony in violation of § 18.2-22; both required the intent to defraud, and the conspiracy alleged and tried was a conspiracy to violate § 18.2-178, and not a conspiracy to violate § 43-13. Hinote v. Commonwealth, No. 2570-10-2, 2011 Va. App. LEXIS 362 (Ct. of Appeals Nov. 22, 2011).

Defendant's conviction for obtaining goods by false pretenses, §§ 18.2-178 and 43-13, was reversed because the Commonwealth properly conceded that the evidence did not show that defendant intended to defraud when obtaining building materials from a builders supply company; to prove larceny by false pretenses, the intent to defraud had to exist when the property was obtained, and that could not happen based on the inference upon which the Commonwealth relied. Hinote v. Commonwealth, No. 2570-10-2, 2011 Va. App. LEXIS 362 (Ct. of Appeals Nov. 22, 2011).

Variance between indictment and proof at trial as to ownership. — When the Commonwealth alleged in an indictment that the money obtained by the defendant was the property of a named individual, her grandfather, but the evidence showed the money was the property of the bank in which the grandfather maintained a savings account, it proved a different offense, resulting in a fatal variance and requiring that the defendant's conviction be reversed. Gardner v. Commonwealth, 262 Va. 18, 546 S.E.2d 686, 2001 Va. LEXIS 80 (2001).

No variance between indictment and proof at trial. — In a prosecution for obtaining money by false pretenses, although the state lottery reimbursed merchants for money paid for winning tickets, as each of the two merchant victims sustained a loss of cash funds when they paid defendant for the stolen tickets, the cash from the merchants' till did not belong to state lottery officials even though it was contractually obligated to reimburse its agents when they paid winners. As a result, no variance existed between the warrants and the proof presented at trial. Francis v. Commonwealth, 2008 Va. App. LEXIS 216 (May 6, 2008).

§ 18.2-178.1. Financial exploitation of mentally incapacitated persons; penalty.

A. It is unlawful for any person who knows or should know that another person suffers from mental incapacity to, through the use of that other person's mental incapacity, take, obtain, or convert money or other thing of value belonging to that other person with the intent to permanently deprive him thereof. Any person who violates this section shall be deemed guilty of larceny.

B. Venue for the trial of an accused charged with a violation of this section shall be in any county or city in which (i) any act was performed in furtherance of the offense or (ii) the accused resided at the time of the offense.

C. This section shall not apply to a transaction or disposition of money or other thing of value in which the accused acted for the benefit of the person with mental incapacity or made a good faith effort to assist such person with the management of his money or other thing of value.

D. As used in this section, "mental incapacity" means that condition of a person existing at the time of the offense described in subsection A that prevents him from understanding the nature or consequences of the transaction or disposition of money or other thing of value involved in such offense.

History.
2013, cc. 419, 452.

Editor's note.
Acts 2013, cc. 419 and 452, cl. 2 provides: "That the provisions of this act may result in a net increase in periods of imprisonment or commitment. Pursuant to § 30-19.1:4, the estimated amount of the necessary appropriation cannot be determined for periods of imprisonment in state adult correctional facilities; therefore, Chapter 3 of the Acts of Assembly of 2012, Special Session I, requires the Virginia Criminal Sentencing Commission to assign a minimum fiscal impact of $50,000. Pursuant to § 30-19.1:4, the estimated amount of the necessary appropriation cannot be determined for periods of commitment to the custody of the Department of Juvenile Justice."

§ 18.2-179. Unlawful operation of coin box telephone, parking meter, vending machine, etc.

Any person who shall operate, cause to be operated, or attempt to operate or cause to be operated any coin box telephone, parking meter, vending machine or other machine that operates on the coin-in-the-slot principle, whether of like kind or not, designed only to receive lawful coin of the United States of America, in connection with the use or enjoyment of telephone or telegraph service, parking privileges or any other service, or the sale of merchandise or other property, by means of a slug, or any false, counterfeit, mutilated, sweated or foreign coin, or by any means, method, trick or device whatsoever, not authorized by the owner, lessee or licensee of such coin box telephone, parking meter, vending machine or other machine; or who shall obtain or receive telephone or telegraph service, parking privileges, merchandise, or any other service or property from any such coin box telephone, parking meter, vending machine or other machines, designed only to receive lawful coin of the United States of America, without depositing in or surrendering to such coin box telephone, parking meter, vending machine, or other machine lawful coin of the United States of America to the amount required therefor by the owner, lessee or licensee of such coin box telephone, parking meter, vending machine or other machine, shall be guilty of a Class 3 misdemeanor.

History.
Code 1950, § 28.1-124; 1960, c. 358; 1975, cc. 14, 15.

Law Review.
For article on justification as a defense to crime, see 59 Va. L. Rev. 1326 (1972).

Michie's Jurisprudence.
For related discussion, see 12A M.J. Larceny, § 8; 18 M.J. Telegraph and Telephone Companies, § 2.

CASE NOTES

Verbal deceit is not embraced by this section, because criminal statutes are to be narrowly construed, and are not to be read as encompassing every arguable interpretation of their language. United States v. Guyette, 382 F. Supp. 1266 (E.D. Va. 1974).

The enactment of former § 18.2-187 (see now § 18.2-187.1), which forbids obtaining phone services with an invalid credit card, is evidence that the General Assembly did not believe this section adequate to protect the phone company from verbal fraud. United States v. Guyette, 382 F. Supp. 1266 (E.D. Va. 1974).

This section forbids only "physical" or "mechanical" means, methods, and devices of defrauding those who own and operate pay telephones and other coin-operated machines, and not "verbal" fraud practiced upon a phone company by the artifice of giving the telephone operators false, invalid, or nonexistent credit card number. United States v. Guyette, 382 F. Supp. 1266 (E.D. Va. 1974).

Only owners of coin telephones can be verbally defrauded. — While the owners of all machines in the coin-in-the-slot category may be "mechanically" defrauded, only the owners of coin telephones can be "verbally" defrauded. United States v. Guyette, 382 F. Supp. 1266 (E.D. Va. 1974).

§ 18.2-180. Manufacture, etc., of slugs, etc., for such unlawful use.

Any person who, with intent to cheat or defraud the owner, lessee, licensee or other person entitled to the contents of any such coin box telephone, parking meter, vending machine or other machine operated on the coin-in-the-slot principle, designed only to receive lawful coin of the United States of America, in connection with the use of any such coin box telephone, parking meter, vending machine or other machine, or who, knowing or having reason to believe that the same is intended for such unlawful use, shall manufacture, sell, offer to sell, advertise for sale or give away any slug, device or substance whatsoever, intended or calculated to be placed or deposited in any such coin box telephone, parking meter, vending machine or other machine, shall be guilty of a Class 3 misdemeanor.

The manufacture, sale, offer for sale, advertisement for sale, giving away or possession of any such slug, device or substance whatsoever, intended or calculated to be placed or deposited in any such coin box telephone, parking meter, vending machine or other machine that operates on the coin-in-the-slot principle, shall be prima facie evidence of intent to cheat or defraud within the meaning of this section and § 18.2-179.

History.
Code 1950, § 18.1-125; 1960, c. 358; 1975, cc. 14, 15.

ARTICLE 4.

BAD CHECK LAW.

§ 18.2-181. Issuing bad checks, etc., larceny.

Any person who, with intent to defraud, shall make or draw or utter or deliver any check, draft, or order for the payment of money, upon any bank, banking institution, trust company, or other depository, knowing, at the time of such making, drawing, uttering or delivering, that the maker or drawer has not sufficient funds in, or credit with, such bank, banking institution, trust company, or other depository, for the payment of such check, draft or order, although no express representation is made in reference thereto, shall be guilty of larceny; and, if this check, draft, or order has a represented value of $200 or more, such person shall be guilty of a Class 6 felony. In cases in which such value is less than $200, the person shall be guilty of a Class 1 misdemeanor.

The word *"credit"* as used herein, shall be construed to mean any arrangement or understanding with the bank, trust company, or other depository for the payment of such check, draft or order.

Any person making, drawing, uttering or delivering any such check, draft or order in payment as a present consideration for goods or services for the purposes set out in this section shall be guilty as provided herein.

History.
Code 1950, § 6.1-115; 1966, c. 584; 1975, cc. 14, 15; 1978, c. 791; 1981, c. 230.

Cross references.

As to issuance of bad check being prima facie evidence of intent and knowledge, see § 18.2-183. As to recovery of costs in civil actions for bad checks, see § 17.1-626.1. As to additional recovery in certain civil actions concerning checks, see § 8.01-27.1. As to admissible evidence regarding identity of party presenting bad check, draft or order, see § 19.2-270.3.

Law Review.

For comment, "Right to Court-Appointed Counsel for Misdemeanants in Virginia," see 4 U. Rich. L. Rev. 306 (1970). For survey of Virginia law on evidence for the year 1969-1970, see 56 Va. L. Rev. 1325 (1970). For survey of Virginia criminal law for the year 1972-1973, see 59 Va. L. Rev. 1458 (1973). For survey of Virginia criminal law for the year 1977-1978, see 64 Va. L. Rev. 1407 (1978). For note, "Criminal Procedure and Criminal Law: Virginia Supreme Court Decisions During the 70's," see 15 U. Rich. L. Rev. 585 (1981). For survey of Virginia criminal law and procedure for the year 2004-2005, see 40 U. Rich. L. Rev. 197 (2005). For 2006 survey article, "Criminal Law and Procedure," see 41 U. Rich. L. Rev. 83 (2006).

Michie's Jurisprudence.

For related discussion, see 3A M.J. Banks and Banking, § 89; 12A M.J. Larceny, § 2.

CASE NOTES

Object of section. — This section is specifically aimed at discouraging the giving of a bad check for a cash purchase when the drawer has, instead of the present means, only a vague intention to make the check good at some time in the future. Cook v. Commonwealth, 178 Va. 251, 16 S.E.2d 635 (1941); Rosser v. Commonwealth, 192 Va. 813, 66 S.E.2d 851 (1951); Bagheri v. Commonwealth, 12 Va. App. 1071, 408 S.E.2d 259 (1991).

Burden of proof. — By issuing the check, the appellant impliedly represented that the account contained funds sufficient to honor the check; therefore, the burden of producing evidence that he expressly represented otherwise was with the appellant. Bolinsky v. Commonwealth, No. 2055-93-2 (Ct. of Appeals Feb. 14, 1995).

"Depository." — The "depository" language in this section refers to the institution upon which the funds are drawn, not the entity where the check is uttered. Warner v. Commonwealth, 30 Va. App. 141, 515 S.E.2d 803 (1999).

"Or." — The language "make or draw or utter or deliver" is in the disjunctive and there is nothing in the section to indicate that "or" should be read to mean "and." Thus, "or" is to be given its ordinary meaning. Patterson v. Commonwealth, 216 Va. 306, 218 S.E.2d 435 (1975).

This section encompasses a worthless check given to obtain cash as well as the giving of bad checks for what purports to be a cash purchase. Warren v. Commonwealth, 219 Va. 416, 247 S.E.2d 692 (1978).

Elements differ from common-law larceny. — The elements of the offense under this section are materially different from those of common-law larceny. Payne v. Commonwealth, 222 Va. 485, 281 S.E.2d 873 (1981).

Essential element. — False representation that a check is good is a necessary element of the offense at which the statute is directed. Hubbard v. Commonwealth, 201 Va. 61, 109 S.E.2d 100 (1959).

An essential element of the bad check offense is that the drawer or utterer falsely represent that the check is good. Bolinsky v. Commonwealth, No. 2055-93-2 (Ct. of Appeals Feb. 14, 1995).

The gravamen of the offense is the fraudulent intent, and the lack of funds creates a prima facie but not a conclusive presumption of such intent. Turner v. Brenner, 138 Va. 232, 121 S.E. 510 (1924); Rosser v. Commonwealth, 192 Va. 813, 66 S.E.2d 851 (1951).

The gravamen of the offense denounced by this section is the intent to defraud. It is an indispensable element of the crime. Cook v. Commonwealth, 178 Va. 251, 16 S.E.2d 635 (1941).

The gravamen of the offense created by this statute is the intent to defraud. Huntt v. Commonwealth, 212 Va. 737, 187 S.E.2d 183 (1972).

Under the bad check statute, the gravamen of the offense is the intent to defraud. It may be established by either direct or circumstantial evidence. Sylvestre v. Commonwealth, 10 Va. App. 253, 391 S.E.2d 336 (1990).

Intent to defraud is an indispensable element of the crime and the burden is upon the Commonwealth to prove its existence at the time of drawing or uttering the check. Huntt v. Commonwealth, 212 Va. 737, 187 S.E.2d 183 (1972).

Fraudulent intent in the mind of the drawer at the time the checks were written and negotiated is the gravamen of the offense, and an indispensable element of the crime. Absent the statutory presumption it must be proved by the Commonwealth. Rinkov v. Commonwealth, 213 Va. 307, 191 S.E.2d 731 (1972).

Under this section, the gravamen of the offense is the intent to defraud. Such intent is an essential element of the crime, and the burden is on the Commonwealth to prove that it existed at the time the checks were drawn or uttered. Patterson v. Commonwealth, 216 Va. 306, 218 S.E.2d 435 (1975).

Under this section, the gravamen of the offense is the intent to defraud, and the offense is complete when, with the requisite intent, a person utters a check he knows to be worthless. Warren v. Commonwealth, 219 Va. 416, 247 S.E.2d 692 (1978).

And the crime is committed when the drawer utters the check. Cook v. Commonwealth, 178 Va. 251, 16 S.E.2d 635 (1941); Rosser v. Commonwealth, 192 Va. 813, 66 S.E.2d 851 (1951).

Thus, payment is no bar to prosecution. — A prosecution might be carried on even if the drawer had made payment within the period specified in § 18.2-183. Such payment would constitute no bar to prosecution; it would merely negative the presumption of fraudulent intent which would otherwise obtain. Cook v. Commonwealth, 178 Va. 251, 16 S.E.2d 635 (1941).

And drawer's subsequent acts are relevant only as to intent. — The acts of the drawer in his dealings with the holder after issuing the check are relevant only insofar as they tend to prove or disprove the actual commission of the crime on the date upon which the check was drawn. Cook v. Commonwealth, 178 Va. 251, 16 S.E.2d 635 (1941).

Since the crime, if any, is committed at the time the check is drawn, subsequent acts of the drawer are of evidential value only in helping to establish the operative fact of fraudulent intent. Cook v. Commonwealth, 178 Va. 251, 16 S.E.2d 635 (1941).

The intent to defraud under this section for making or passing a bad check must be based upon a false representation that the check as written and delivered is good. Thus, the bad check offense as defined by the statute has not been committed if the payee knows at the time that the check was made and delivered that it was not then good or collectible. Bolinsky v. Commonwealth, No. 2055-93-2 (Ct. of Appeals Feb. 14, 1995).

Express representation not necessary. — This section, in terms, dispenses with the proof of "express representation." Hubbard v. Commonwealth, 201 Va. 61, 109 S.E.2d 100 (1959).

This section dispenses with proof of an extrinsic representation that check was good. Warren v. Commonwealth, 219 Va. 416, 247 S.E.2d 692 (1978).

And it need not be shown that the implied representation was relied upon or that anything was received in return for the check. Warren v. Commonwealth, 219 Va. 416, 247 S.E.2d 692 (1978).

To prove a bad-check offense, it need not be shown that anything was received in return for the check, for the offense is complete when, with the requisite intent, a person utters a check he knows to be worthless. Payne v. Commonwealth, 222 Va. 485, 281 S.E.2d 873 (1981).

Knowledge of payee that check not good. — Where, at the time a check is drawn or delivered, the payee understands that it is not then good or collectible, the offense prohibited by statutes of the character of this section has not been committed. Hubbard v. Commonwealth, 201 Va. 61, 109 S.E.2d 100 (1959).

The view that this section is not violated where the payee accepts a check knowing that it is not then good, with an understanding that it will be paid at some later time, is based not upon a theory of contributory negligence but upon the rationale that the maker does not possess the necessary fraudulent intent when he utters the check under such circumstances. Warren v. Commonwealth, 219 Va. 416, 247 S.E.2d 692 (1978).

Purpose of paragraph referring to "present consider-

ation." — The purpose of the 1978 amendment, which added the last paragraph referring to "present consideration," was simply to provide that bad checks given as a present consideration for intangible goods or services may, assuming all other provisions of the statute are met, constitute the crime of larceny. Sylvestre v. Commonwealth, 10 Va. App. 253, 391 S.E.2d 336 (1990).

The 1978 amendment, which added the last paragraph referring to "present consideration," did not make it the crime of larceny to give a bad check as payment for past debts or as gifts, nor did the amendment alter or limit the scope of the first paragraph as it existed prior to 1978. Sylvestre v. Commonwealth, 10 Va. App. 253, 391 S.E.2d 336 (1990).

This section does not "make it the crime of larceny to give a bad check as payment for past debts". Dagenhart v. Commonwealth, No. 2547-94-2 (Ct. of Appeals Dec. 29, 1995).

Evidence did not exclude hypothesis check given for past debt. — Proof that defendant passed a bad check to a grocery store, standing alone was not adequate to bring the case within the ambit of this section, where the evidence did not exclude the hypothesis that the check was given for a past debt. Sylvestre v. Commonwealth, 10 Va. App. 253, 391 S.E.2d 336 (1990).

Crime does not require anything received in return for check. — To prove a bad check offense, it is not necessary that anything be received in return for the check. The offense is complete when, with intent to defraud, a person makes or draws or utters a check he knows to be worthless. Bray v. Commonwealth, 9 Va. App. 417, 388 S.E.2d 837 (1990).

This section requires the Commonwealth to establish both intent to defraud and knowledge of insufficient funds in order to convict the defendant. Huntt v. Commonwealth, 212 Va. 737, 187 S.E.2d 183 (1972).

Discovery by the payee that a check was worthless before the transaction was completed did not preclude a conviction under this section. United States v. Sparks, 560 F.2d 1173 (4th Cir. 1977); Warren v. Commonwealth, 219 Va. 416, 247 S.E.2d 692 (1978).

Passing worthless check to one's own bank. — One can be convicted under Virginia's "Bad Check Law" of passing to his own bank a worthless check drawn on his account in that bank. Warren v. Commonwealth, 219 Va. 416, 247 S.E.2d 692 (1978).

A conviction is not precluded by a bank's failure to exercise "ordinary diligence" to ascertain from the "means available" the true status of a customer's account before cashing his worthless check. Warren v. Commonwealth, 219 Va. 416, 247 S.E.2d 692 (1978).

And refusal of bank to create overdraft no excuse. — The refusal of a bank to exercise the authority to charge a worthless check against a customer's account even though such charge would create an overdraft did not excuse the actions of a customer in presenting a worthless check, where those actions were otherwise criminally actionable under this section. Warren v. Commonwealth, 219 Va. 416, 247 S.E.2d 692 (1978).

Worthless check in payment of security deposit. — A person can be convicted under the bad check law for passing a worthless check in payment of a security deposit upon the rental of real estate. Bray v. Commonwealth, 9 Va. App. 417, 388 S.E.2d 837 (1990).

Not similar to shoplifting offense. — Over defendant's objection, the district court assigned him a criminal history point for a 2005 sentence in a Virginia state court for shoplifting — or, more specifically, for altering a price tag on merchandise valued at less than $200 — and on appeal, defendant contended that he should not have received a criminal history point for his prior shoplifting sentence because the underlying offense was similar to the listed insufficient funds check offense and because his sentence did not include any term of probation or incarceration; however, the district court correctly determined that defendant's prior shoplifting offense was not similar to the listed insufficient funds check offense and properly assessed a single criminal history point for the shoplifting sentence. Under Virginia law, both shoplifting and insufficient funds check offenses could involve the acquisition of a store's merchandise without paying the full purchase price thereof but in a shoplifting offense, this was effectuated by concealing the merchandise or altering the merchandise's price tag and in an insufficient funds check offense the merchandise acquisition was carried out by issuing a bad check; because of these significant

differences, the elements of the shoplifting offense and those of the insufficient funds check offense could not be deemed nearly corresponding or resembling in many respects. United States v. Osborne, 514 F.3d 377, 2008 U.S. App. LEXIS 1871 (4th Cir. 2008), cert. denied, 128 S. Ct. 2525, 2008 U.S. LEXIS 4438 (U.S. 2008).

Five-year statute of limitations applied. — Five-year statute of limitations for petit larceny applied to defendant's charge of uttering a bad check because uttering a bad check was a form of larceny. Foster v. Commonwealth, 44 Va. App. 574, 606 S.E.2d 518, 2004 Va. App. LEXIS 626 (2004), aff'd, — Va. —, 623 S.E.2d 902 (2006).

Larceny that was a misdemeanor was a petit larceny, there were no other possibilities for other larcenies within the context of § 18.2-181. Since § 18.2-96 had no impact upon the foregoing analysis, the one year statute of limitations under § 19.2-8, which applied to misdemeanors, did not apply to defendant's act of passing a bad check. Foster v. Commonwealth, 271 Va. 235, 623 S.E.2d 902, 2006 Va. LEXIS 6 (2006).

Privileges. — Section 19.2-271.2(ii) did not apply because defendant was indicted for uttering a check with insufficient funds, she was not charged with "forgery or uttering." Lindsey v. Commonwealth, 2007 Va. App. LEXIS 480 (Dec. 27, 2007).

Evidence of prior worthless checks held admissible. — Evidence of two prior worthless checks given by the defendant to the same payee was properly admitted in a prosecution under this section for the purpose of showing both intent and knowledge on the part of the defendant. United States v. Sparks, 560 F.2d 1173 (4th Cir. 1977).

Sufficiency of evidence. — While the opening of two checking accounts and the other circumstances shown by the evidence created a strong suspicion or probability of guilt, this is not sufficient, as the evidence must establish the guilt of the accused beyond a reasonable doubt. The guilt of a party is not proved merely because the facts are consistent with his guilt. They must be inconsistent with his innocence. Huntt v. Commonwealth, 212 Va. 737, 187 S.E.2d 183 (1972).

Only reasonable hypothesis flowing from all the evidence was that, at time he delivered check in payment of automobile, defendant acted both with intent to defraud and knowledge that account contained insufficient funds. Schrieberg v. Commonwealth, No. 1192-98-2 (Ct. of Appeals Feb. 29, 2000).

In defendant's prosecution for uttering bad checks, the Commonwealth was entitled to the rebuttable presumption under § 18.2-183, to the effect that the return of a check by a drawee bank because of lack of funds constituted prima facie evidence of intent to defraud unless the maker paid the holder the amount due within five days of receiving written notice of dishonor, because defendant did not pay the amount due to the store within five days of the store's giving notice; thus, the Commonwealth presented prima facie evidence of defendant's intent to defraud when she cashed the checks at the store. The trier of fact was entitled to discount defendant's explanations and conclude that she had failed to rebut the presumption. Charles v. Commonwealth, 2011 Va. App. LEXIS 130 (Apr. 19, 2011).

Evidence showing intent to defraud. — See Kite v. United States, 216 F.2d 802 (4th Cir. 1954).

Conviction did not violate due process. — Defendant's conviction of larceny by altering a bad check was not so totally devoid of evidentiary support as to violate due process. Alley v. Paderick, 373 F. Supp. 920 (W.D. Va. 1974).

Violation of section on federal reservation. — See Kite v. United States, 216 F.2d 802 (4th Cir. 1954).

Applied in Edwards v. Commonwealth, 227 Va. 349, 315 S.E.2d 239 (1984); Wileman v. Commonwealth, 24 Va. App. 642, 484 S.E.2d 621 (1997).

§ 18.2-181.1. Issuance of bad checks.

It shall be a Class 6 felony for any person, within a period of ninety days, to issue two or more checks, drafts or orders for the payment of money in violation of § 18.2-181, which have an aggregate represented value of $200 or more and which (i) are drawn upon the same account of any bank, banking institution, trust company or other depository and (ii) are made payable to the same person, firm or corporation.

History.
1988, c. 496.

CASE NOTES

Elements of offense. — In order to sustain a conviction, the Commonwealth must establish that: (1) the defendant wrote two or more checks on the same bank account; (2) the checks were written to the same person, firm or corporation; (3) he knew when he wrote the checks that he did not have sufficient funds in his account to cover their payment; (4) he wrote the checks with the intent to defraud; (5) the checks were written within a 90 day period; (6) the aggregate value of the checks written to each person, firm or corporation exceeded $200; and (7) the defendant received goods or services for each check. Burnett v. Commonwealth, No. 0111-98-3 (Ct. of Appeals Jan. 5, 1999).

Evidence sufficient to support conviction. — Evidence was sufficient to show that the defendant knew, when he wrote checks, that his account did not have sufficient funds and that he intended to defraud two merchants where the merchants wrote to him regarding returned checks and giving him five days to pay, and the defendant wrote the checks at issue after his account had been closed by his bank. Burnett v. Commonwealth, No. 0111-98-3 (Ct. of Appeals Jan. 5, 1999).

§ 18.2-182. Issuing bad checks on behalf of business firm or corporation in payment of wages; penalty.

Any person who shall make, draw, or utter, or deliver any check, draft, or order for the payment of money, upon any bank, banking institution, trust company or other depository on behalf of any business firm or corporation, for the purpose of paying wages to any employee of such firm or corporation, or for the purpose of paying for any labor performed by any person for such firm or corporation, knowing, at the time of such making, drawing, uttering or delivering, that the account upon which such check, draft or order is drawn has not sufficient funds, or credit with, such bank, banking institution, trust company or other depository, for the payment of such check, draft or order, although no express representation is made in reference thereto, shall be guilty of a Class 1 misdemeanor; except that if this check, draft, or order has a represented value of $200 or more, such person shall be guilty of a Class 6 felony.

The word *"credit,"* as used herein, shall be construed to mean any arrangement or understanding with the bank, banking institution, trust company, or other depository for the payment of such check, draft or order.

In addition to the criminal penalty set forth herein, such person shall be personally liable in any civil action brought upon such check, draft or order.

History.
Code 1950, § 6.1-116; 1966, c. 584; 1975, cc. 14, 15; 2005, c. 598.

Cross references.
As to admissible evidence regarding identity of party presenting bad check, draft or order, see § 19.2-270.3.

CASE NOTES

Applied in Edwards v. Commonwealth, 227 Va. 349, 315 S.E.2d 239 (1984).

§ 18.2-182.1. Issuing bad checks in payment of taxes.

Any person who shall make, draw, utter, or deliver two or more checks, drafts, or orders within a period of ninety days which have an aggregate represented value of $1,000 or more, for the payment of money upon any bank, banking institution, trust company, or other depository on behalf of any taxpayer for the payment of any state tax under § 58.1-486 or § 58.1-637, knowing, at the time of such making, drawing, uttering, or delivering, that the account upon which such check, draft, or order is drawn has not sufficient funds or credit with such bank, banking institution, trust company, or other depository for the payment of such check, draft, or order, although no express representation is made in reference thereto, shall be guilty of a Class 1 misdemeanor.

The word *"credit,"* as used herein, means any arrangement or understanding with the bank, banking institution, trust company, or other depository for the payment of such check, draft, or order.

History.
1992, c. 763.

§ 18.2-183. Issuance of bad check prima facie evidence of intent and knowledge; notice by certified or registered mail.

In any prosecution or action under the preceding sections, the making or drawing or uttering or delivery of a check, draft, or order, payment of which is refused by the drawee because of lack of funds or credit shall be prima facie evidence of intent to defraud or of knowledge of insufficient funds in, or credit with, such bank, banking institution, trust company or other depository unless such maker or drawer, or someone for him, shall have paid the holder thereof the amount due thereon, together with interest, and protest fees (if any), within five days after receiving written notice that such check, draft, or order has not been paid to the holder thereof. Notice mailed by certified or registered mail, evidenced by return receipt, to the last known address of the maker or drawer shall be deemed sufficient and equivalent to notice having been received by the maker or drawer.

If such check, draft or order shows on its face a printed or written address, home, office, or otherwise, of the maker or drawer, then the foregoing notice, when sent by certified or registered mail to such address, with or without return receipt requested, shall be deemed sufficient and equivalent to notice having been received by the maker or drawer, whether such notice shall be returned undelivered or not.

When a check is drawn on a bank in which the maker or drawer has no account, it shall be presumed that such check was issued with intent to defraud, and the five-day notice set forth above shall not be required in such case.

History.

Code 1950, § 6.1-117; 1966, c. 584; 1975, cc. 14, 15.

Law Review.

For survey of Virginia criminal law for the year 1972-1973, see 59 Va. L. Rev. 1458 (1973). For survey of Virginia criminal law for the year 1977-1978, see 64 Va. L. Rev. 1407 (1978).

Michie's Jurisprudence.

For related discussion, see 3A M.J. Banks and Banking, § 89.

CASE NOTES

This section defines a mere rule of evidence upon which the Commonwealth may rely in facilitating proof of the fraudulent intent of the drawer. Cook v. Commonwealth, 178 Va. 251, 16 S.E.2d 635 (1941); Rinkov v. Commonwealth, 213 Va. 307, 191 S.E.2d 731 (1972); Alley v. Paderick, 373 F. Supp. 920 (W.D. Va. 1974); Patterson v. Commonwealth, 216 Va. 306, 218 S.E.2d 435 (1975); Bray v. Commonwealth, 9 Va. App. 417, 388 S.E.2d 837 (1990).

And need not be charged in indictment. — Accused assigned as error the failure of the indictment to contain an allegation as to the five days' notice, mentioned in this section. It was held that this section, dealing only with a rule of evidence, is not an element of the crime and need not be charged in the indictment. Cook v. Commonwealth, 178 Va. 251, 16 S.E.2d 635 (1941).

And the Commonwealth may prosecute even though no notice of dishonor was ever given, but in such event the Commonwealth would be required to prove affirmatively the existence of a fraudulent intent in the mind of the drawer. Cook v. Commonwealth, 178 Va. 251, 16 S.E.2d 635 (1941); Alley v. Paderick, 373 F. Supp. 920 (W.D. Va. 1974).

Where petitioner was not notified pursuant to the provisions of this section, it was inapplicable to his case, and consequently, the Commonwealth could not avail itself of the statutory presumption and had to affirmatively establish petitioner's fraudulent intent. Alley v. Paderick, 373 F. Supp. 920 (W.D. Va. 1974).

The presumption is rebuttable. — Under this section, if the holder gives written notice of dishonor to the drawer, and payment is not made within five days therefrom, a presumption arises that the drawer uttered the check with fraudulent intent, but this presumption may be rebutted. Cook v. Commonwealth, 178 Va. 251, 16 S.E.2d 635 (1941).

This section creates a rebuttable presumption of the necessary intent and knowledge if a dishonored check is not paid within five days after giving of the notice specified in the statute. Huntt v. Commonwealth, 212 Va. 737, 187 S.E.2d 183 (1972).

In finding defendant guilty of presenting bad checks, the trial court properly relied on the statutory rebuttable presumption from which it could find, but was not required to find, that defendant had the intent to defraud when he presented the worthless checks for payment to the store owner and properly imposed on the Commonwealth the ultimate burden of persuasion. Cox v. Commonwealth, 2011 Va. App. LEXIS 273 (Aug. 23, 2011).

And does not arise where payee given notice of lack of funds. — Where one gives a check without funds in the bank to cover it, but informs the payee of such conditions, even if he had fraudulent intent in such transaction, it is not within the terms of this section, and there should be no prima facie presumption of an attempt to defraud. Turner v. Brenner, 138 Va. 232, 121 S.E. 510 (1924).

Proof of either actual receipt of notice or date payee sent notice not required. — The statute does not require the Commonwealth to establish either actual receipt of the notice or the date the payee sent the notice; rather, the statute only requires proof that the notice was sent by certified mail and that the accused

failed to repay the amount due within five days. Motsinger v. Commonwealth, No. 1406-98-3 (Ct. of Appeals Apr. 13, 1999).

Presumption applies where bank account was closed. — When defendant drew checks on banks at which his accounts had been closed, the statutory presumption of fraudulent intent in § 18.2-183 applied to him, even though the statute only spoke of such a presumption existing when a check was drawn on a bank at which the drawer had no account. The fact that § 18.2-184 specifically mentioned closed accounts did not mean that the legislature, in failing to mention closed accounts in § 18.2-183, did not mean for the presumption in § 18.2-183 to apply when a check was drawn on a bank at which the drawer's account was closed because when provisions in one act were omitted from another act on the same subject, the omitted provisions were applied where the purposes of the two acts were consistent. Sykes v. Commonwealth, 42 Va. App. 581, 593 S.E.2d 545, 2004 Va. App. LEXIS 98 (2004).

Language of § 18.2-200.1 plainly means that a request for a return of money advanced on a construction project is sufficient notice if sent by certified mail, return receipt requested, without proof of actual receipt, unlike the notices required by the bad check law, former § 6.1-117, now codified at § 18.2-183, Virginia Tort Claims Act, § 8.01-195.1 et seq., the Virginia Habitual Offenders Act, former § 46.2-355, repealed in 1999, and the Virginia Interstate Agreement on Detainers, art. III(b), found in § 53.1-210. Holsapple v. Commonwealth, 266 Va. 593, 587 S.E.2d 561, 2003 Va. LEXIS 96 (2003), cert. denied, 543 U.S. 826, 125 S. Ct. 164, 160 L. Ed. 2d 39 (2004).

Evidence sufficient to invoke presumption. — Where the Commonwealth introduced two returned checks stamped "insufficient funds" as well as bank statements indicating that the checks were both presented and returned on two separate occasions, and it was shown that the payee notified defendant by certified mail that the bank dishonored the checks and that the payee had demanded payment within five days but received none, the evidence was sufficient to invoke the rebuttable presumption of this section. Bagheri v. Commonwealth, 12 Va. App. 1071, 408 S.E.2d 259 (1991).

Where the defendant admitted that she wrote a check upon a bank, and the evidence showed that the check was returned with the stamp "account closed," the evidence was sufficient to invoke the presumption created by statute that the check was issued with intent to defraud. Bratton v. Commonwealth, No. 1003-97-3 (Ct. of Appeals June 9, 1998).

Where the defendant failed to pay the amount of a check within five days after being notified that the check was not paid by the bank, the evidence was sufficient to invoke the presumption created by this section that she knew she had insufficient funds in her account when she wrote the check. Bratton v. Commonwealth, No. 1003-97-3 (Ct. of Appeals June 9, 1998).

In defendant's prosecution for uttering bad checks, the Commonwealth was entitled to the rebuttable presumption under § 18.2-183, to the effect that the return of a check by a drawee bank because of lack of funds constituted prima facie evidence of intent to defraud unless the maker paid the holder the amount due within five days of receiving written notice of dishonor, because defendant did not pay the amount due to the store within five days of the store's giving notice; thus, the Commonwealth presented prima facie evidence of defendant's intent to defraud when she cashed the checks at the store. The trier of fact was entitled to discount defendant's explanations and conclude that she had failed to rebut the presumption. Charles v. Commonwealth, 2011 Va. App. LEXIS 130 (Apr. 19, 2011).

Defendant's failure to overcome the rebuttable presumption. — Trial court could properly find from the evidence of defendant's passing a check that was returned for insufficient funds and defendant's bank statements showing that his account was overdrawn that defendant failed to rebut the presumption arising under § 18.2-183 that he wrote the check with the intent to defraud the hardware seller, knowing he did not have sufficient funds in his account to pay the check. Hartman v. Commonwealth, No. 1161-02-3, 2004 Va. App. LEXIS 70 (Ct. of Appeals Feb. 10, 2004).

Evidence did not raise presumption of fraudulent intent. — Evidence showing that defendant had received actual notice by telephone that her check had been returned for insufficient funds and had agreed to repay the amount owed was nothing more than an acknowledgment that she was indebted to the payee, and did not raise a presumption of fraudulent intent. Sylvestre v. Commonwealth, 10 Va. App. 253, 391 S.E.2d 336 (1990).

Evidence insufficient to raise prima facie presumption. — Where there was no evidence before the trial court to show why payment on returned checks was refused and no evidence that defendant had no account with the drawee bank, the Commonwealth could not rely on this section for prima facie evidence of intent. Harrison v. Commonwealth, 211 Va. 8, 174 S.E.2d 783 (1970).

What constitutes payment of "amount due thereon." — Payments totaling $22.00 on a check drawn in the amount of $588.80 did not constitute the payment of "the amount due thereon" within the meaning of this section. Cook v. Commonwealth, 178 Va. 251, 16 S.E.2d 635 (1941).

Section may not be used to prove fraudulent intent in bankruptcy proceeding. — A bankruptcy court may not use this section, which makes the uttering of a check without sufficient funds prima facie evidence of intent to defraud, to infer the existence of fraudulent intent in bankruptcy. Bankruptcy law is distinct from criminal law and state statutes do not affect the burdens of proof the parties bear in dischargeability proceedings. In a bankruptcy court the creditor must prove by clear and convincing evidence the debtor intended to defraud that creditor in order for a debt based upon that transaction to be determined nondischargeable. Aircon Distribs., Inc. v. Holt, 24 Bankr. 696 (Bankr. E.D. Va. 1982).

The purpose of requiring the notice to be sent by registered or certified mail, and evidenced by a receipt, is to have not only evidence of the required mailing to the defendant, but also evidence that the notice was either received in person by the defendant (as would be shown by his signature on the return receipt), or that the letter did in fact reach the last known address of the defendant and was there accepted by someone at that address. Rinkov v. Commonwealth, 213 Va. 307, 191 S.E.2d 731 (1972).

Evidence sufficient to support conviction. — Petit larceny conviction under § 18.2-183 was supported by evidence that payee attempted numerous times, by phone and mail, to contact defendant with no response and that defendant made no efforts to repay the bad check until after she was served with a warrant, more than four months after the bad check was written. Vance v. Commonwealth, — Va. App. —, — S.E.2d —, 2007 Va. App. LEXIS 87 (Mar. 13, 2007).

Where the record reflected that defendant gave the bad checks to his mother to cash at her place of employment; defendant left Virginia shortly after presenting the checks for payment, leaving no forwarding address; and the store owner sent defendant, by certified mail, two letters notifying defendant the check were not paid and defendant thereafter did not pay the amount due within five days, as required by § 18.2-183, the evidence was sufficient to support defendant's conviction for presenting two or more bad checks in return for cash. Cox v. Commonwealth, 2011 Va. App. LEXIS 273 (Aug. 23, 2011).

§ 18.2-184. Presumption as to notation attached to check, draft or order.

In any prosecution or action under the preceding sections, any notation attached to or stamped upon a check, draft or order which is refused by the drawee because of lack of funds or credit, bearing the terms "not sufficient funds," "uncollected funds," "account closed," or "no account in this name," or words of similar import, shall be prima facie evidence that such notation is true and correct.

History.
Code 1950, § 6.1-117.1; 1970, c. 695; 1974, c. 322; 1975, cc. 14, 15.

Law Review.
For survey of recent legislation on finance — Bad checks, see 5 U. Rich. L. Rev. 194 (1970).

Evidence sufficient to invoke presumption. — Where the defendant admitted that she wrote a check upon a bank, and the evidence showed that the check was returned with the stamp "account closed," the evidence was sufficient to invoke the presumption created by this section. Bratton v. Commonwealth, No. 1003-97-3 (Ct. of Appeals June 9, 1998).

When defendant drew checks on banks at which his accounts had been closed, the statutory presumption of fraudulent intent in § 18.2-183 applied to him, even though the statute only spoke of such a presumption existing when a check was drawn on a bank at which the drawer had no account. The fact that § 18.2-184 specifically mentioned closed accounts did not mean that the legislature, in failing to mention closed accounts in § 18.2-183, did not mean for the presumption to apply when a check was drawn on a bank at which the drawer's account was closed because when provisions in one act were omitted from another act on the same subject, the omitted provisions were applied where the purposes of the two acts were consistent. Sykes v. Commonwealth, 42 Va. App. 581, 593 S.E.2d 545, 2004 Va. App. LEXIS 98 (2004).

§ 18.2-185. Evidence and presumptions in malicious prosecution actions after issuance of bad check.

In any civil action growing out of an arrest under § 18.2-181 or § 18.2-182, no evidence of statements or representations as to the status of the check, draft, order or deposit involved, or of any collateral agreement with reference to the check, draft, or order, shall be admissible unless such statements, or representations, or collateral agreement, be written upon the instrument at the time it is given by the drawer.

If payment of any check, draft, or order for the payment of money be refused by the bank, banking institution, trust company or other depository upon which such instrument is drawn, and the person who drew or uttered such instrument be arrested or prosecuted under the provisions of § 18.2-181 or § 18.2-182, for failure or refusal to pay such instrument, the one who arrested or caused such person to be arrested and prosecuted, or either, shall be conclusively deemed to have acted with reasonable or probable cause in any suit for damages that may be brought by the person who drew or uttered such instrument, if the one who arrested or caused such person to be arrested and prosecuted, or either, shall have, before doing so, presented or caused such instrument to be presented to the depository on which it was drawn where it was refused, and then waited five days after notice, as provided in § 18.2-183, without the amount due under the provisions of such instrument being paid.

History.
Code 1950, § 6.1-118; 1966, c. 584; 1975, cc. 14, 15.

Michie's Jurisprudence.
For related discussion, see 3A M.J. Banks and Banking, § 89; 12A M.J. Larceny, § 2.

ARTICLE 5.

FALSE REPRESENTATIONS TO OBTAIN PROPERTY OR CREDIT.

§ 18.2-186. False statements to obtain property or credit.

A. A person shall be guilty of a Class 1 misdemeanor if he makes, causes to be made or conspires to make directly, indirectly or through an agency, any materially false statement in writing, knowing it to be false and intending that it be relied upon, concerning the financial condition or means or ability to pay of himself, or of any other person for whom he is acting, or any firm or corporation in which he is interested or for which he is acting, for the purpose of procuring, for his own benefit or for the benefit of such person, firm or corporation, the delivery of personal property, the payment of cash, the making of a loan or credit, the extension of a credit, the discount of an account receivable, or the making, acceptance, discount, sale or endorsement of a bill of exchange or promissory note.

B. Any person who knows that a false statement has been made in writing concerning the financial condition or ability to pay of himself or of any person for whom he is acting, or any firm or corporation in which he is interested or for which he is acting and who, with intent to defraud, procures, upon the faith thereof, for his own benefit, or for the benefit of the person, firm or corporation in which he is interested or for which he is acting, any such delivery, payment, loan, credit, extension, discount making, acceptance, sale or endorsement, shall, if the value of the thing or the amount of the loan, credit or benefit obtained is $200 or more, be guilty of grand larceny or, if the value is less than $200, be guilty of petit larceny.

C. Venue for the trial of any person charged with an offense under this section may be in the county or city in which (i) any act was performed in furtherance of the offense, or (ii) the person charged with the offense resided at the time of the offense.

D. As used in this section, "in writing" shall include information transmitted by computer, facsimile, e-mail, Internet, or any other electronic medium, and shall not include information transmitted by any such medium by voice transmission.

History.
Code 1950, § 18.1-119; 1960, c. 358; 1966, c. 247; 1975, cc. 14, 15; 1981, c. 197; 1991, c. 546; 2006, c. 321; 2007, c. 518.

Michie's Jurisprudence.
For related discussion, see 8B M.J. False Pretenses and Cheats, § 4.

CASE NOTES

False writing supports conviction. — Where the indictment charged appellant with unlawfully and feloniously procuring property or credit of the value of $3500, knowing that such benefit was obtained on the basis of a false statement in writing from the Bank of Southside Virginia could support a conviction under this section. Mueller v. Commonwealth, 15 Va. App. 649, 426 S.E.2d 339 (1993).

Evidence sufficient. — Appellant applied for credit with a car dealership and supplied information supplied which was entirely fraudulent, consisting of false addresses, false telephone numbers, a non-existent insurance policy and a falsified identification card, and appellant signed a temporary registration certificate and took possession of the car, driving it off the lot. She failed to pay for the sale of the car or the extension of credit despite having acquired possession and title to the car. Accordingly, there was sufficient evidence of a failure to pay to sustain appellant's conviction under this section. Marsh v. Commonwealth, 32 Va. App. 669, 530 S.E.2d 425, 2000 Va. App. LEXIS 404 (2000).

§ 18.2-186.1. Repealed by Acts 1981, c. 255.

Cross references.
For present provisions covering similar subject matter to the repealed section, see § 32.1-310 et seq.

§ 18.2-186.2. False statements or failure to disclose material facts in order to obtain aid or benefits under any local, state or federal housing assistance program.

Any person who (i) knowingly makes or causes to be made either directly or indirectly or through any agent or agency, any false statement in writing with the intent that it shall be relied upon, or fails to disclose any material fact concerning the financial means or ability to pay of himself or of any other person for whom he is acting, for the purpose of procuring aid and benefits available under any local, state or federally funded housing assistance program, or (ii) knowingly fails to disclose a change in circumstances in order to obtain or continue to receive under any such program aid or benefits to which he is not entitled or who knowingly aids and abets another person in the commission of any such act is guilty of a Class 1 misdemeanor.

History.
1980, c. 303.

§ 18.2-186.3. Identity theft; penalty; restitution; victim assistance.

A. It shall be unlawful for any person, without the authorization or permission of the person or persons who are the subjects of the identifying information, with the intent to defraud, for his own use or the use of a third person, to:

1. Obtain, record, or access identifying information which is not available to the general public that would assist in accessing financial resources, obtaining identification documents, or obtaining benefits of such other person;

2. Obtain money, credit, loans, goods, or services through the use of identifying information of such other person;

3. Obtain identification documents in such other person's name; or

4. Obtain, record, or access identifying information while impersonating a law-enforcement officer or an official of the government of the Commonwealth.

B. It shall be unlawful for any person without the authorization or permission of the person who is the subject of the identifying information, with the intent to sell or distribute the information to another to:

1. Fraudulently obtain, record, or access identifying information that is not available to the general public that would assist in accessing financial resources, obtaining identification documents, or obtaining benefits of such other person;

2. Obtain money, credit, loans, goods, or services through the use of identifying information of such other person;

3. Obtain identification documents in such other person's name; or

4. Obtain, record, or access identifying information while impersonating a law-enforcement officer or an official of the Commonwealth.

B1. It shall be unlawful for any person to use identification documents or identifying information of another person, whether that person is dead or alive, or of a false or fictitious person, to avoid summons, arrest, prosecution, or to impede a criminal investigation.

C. As used in this section, "identifying information" shall include but not be limited to: (i) name; (ii) date of birth; (iii) social security number; (iv) driver's license number; (v) bank account numbers; (vi) credit or debit card numbers; (vii) personal identification numbers (PIN); (viii) electronic identification codes; (ix) automated or electronic signatures; (x) biometric data; (xi) fingerprints; (xii) passwords; or (xiii) any other numbers or information that can be used to access a person's financial resources, obtain identification, act as identification, or obtain money, credit, loans, goods, or services.

D. Violations of this section shall be punishable as a Class 1 misdemeanor. Any violation resulting in financial loss of greater than $200 shall be punishable as a Class 6 felony. Any second or subsequent conviction shall be punishable as a Class 6 felony. Any violation of subsection B where five or more persons' identifying information has been obtained, recorded, or accessed in the same transaction or occurrence shall be punishable as a Class 5 felony. Any violation of subsection B where 50 or more persons' identifying information has been obtained, recorded, or accessed in the same transaction or occurrence shall be punishable as a Class 4 felony. Any violation resulting in the arrest and detention of the person whose identification documents or identifying information were used to avoid summons, arrest, prosecution, or to impede a criminal investigation shall be punishable as a Class 5 felony. In any proceeding brought pursuant to this section, the crime shall be considered to have been committed in any locality where the person whose identify-

ing information was appropriated resides, or in which any part of the offense took place, regardless of whether the defendant was ever actually in such locality.

E. Upon conviction, in addition to any other punishment, a person found guilty of this offense shall be ordered by the court to make restitution as the court deems appropriate to any person whose identifying information was appropriated or to the estate of such person. Such restitution may include the person's or his estate's actual expenses associated with correcting inaccuracies or errors in his credit report or other identifying information.

F. Upon the request of a person whose identifying information was appropriated, the Attorney General may provide assistance to the victim in obtaining information necessary to correct inaccuracies or errors in his credit report or other identifying information; however, no legal representation shall be afforded such person.

History.
2000, c. 349; 2001, c. 423; 2003, cc. 847, 914, 918; 2004, c. 450; 2006, cc. 455, 496; 2007, c. 441; 2009, cc. 314, 380; 2013, cc. 420, 466.

Cross references.
As to fraudulent notification of prizes and larceny of lottery tickets, see § 58.1-4018.1.

Editor's note.
Acts 2009, cc. 314 and 380, cl. 2 provides: "That the provisions of this act may result in a net increase in periods of imprisonment or commitment. Pursuant to § 30-19.1:4, the estimated amount of the necessary appropriation cannot be determined for periods of imprisonment in state adult correctional facilities and is $ 0 for periods of commitment to the custody of the Department of Juvenile Justice."

Acts 2013, c. 420, cl. 2 provides: "That the provisions of this act may result in a net increase in periods of imprisonment or commitment. Pursuant to § 30-19.1:4, the estimated amount of the necessary appropriation is at least $30,152 for periods of imprisonment in state adult correctional facilities and cannot be determined for periods of commitment to the custody of the Department of Juvenile Justice."

Acts 2013, c. 466, cl. 2 provides: "That the provisions of this act may result in a net increase in periods of imprisonment or commitment. Pursuant to § 30-19.1:4, the estimated amount of the necessary appropriation is $30,152 for periods of imprisonment in state adult correctional facilities and cannot be determined for periods of commitment to the custody of the Department of Juvenile Justice."

The 2009 amendments.
The 2009 amendments by cc. 314 and 380 are identical, and inserted "money, credit, loans" in subdivisions A2 and B2 and subsection C.

The 2013 amendments.
The 2013 amendments by cc. 420 and 466, in subsection D, substituted "Class 5 felony" for "Class 6 felony" at the end of the fourth and sixth sentences, and "Class 4 felony" for "Class 5 felony" at the end of the fifth sentence.

Law Review.
For 2000 survey of Virginia criminal law and procedure, see 34 U. Rich. L. Rev. 749 (2000). For 2006 survey article, "Criminal Law and Procedure," see 41 U. Rich. L. Rev. 83 (2006).

CASE NOTES

Venue improper. — Based on the record, there was insufficient evidence to demonstrate a strong presumption that any part of obtaining, accessing or recording the female victim's identifying information with the intent to defraud occurred in Arlington County; there was no evidence showing where the laptop belonging to defendant was located when accessed, who accessed it, or who remagged the credit card numbers, specifically the female victim's number, onto the credit cards. The lack of such evidence made it impossible to sustain a strong presumption that any part of the crime of identity theft under§ 18.2-186.3 occurred in Arlington County, and therefore, venue in that county was improper under § 18.2-198.1. Gheorghiu v. Commonwealth, 280 Va. 678, 701 S.E.2d 407, 2010 Va. LEXIS 268 (2010).

Double jeopardy. — Although appellant accurately noted that he committed the respective crimes in a similar manner, this fact did not render the convictions improper; under the Blockburger test, offenses charged were examined in the abstract, without referring to the particular facts of the case under review. Viewed in the abstract, identity theft and credit card fraud were separate offenses punishable in a single criminal proceeding; accordingly, appellant's convictions for identity theft and for credit card fraud were proper and did not violate double jeopardy protections. Gheorghiu v. Commonwealth, 54 Va. App. 645, 682 S.E.2d 50, 2009 Va. App. LEXIS 424 (2009), aff'd in part, rev'd in part, 280 Va. 678, 701 S.E.2d 407 (2010).

Giving false identity information during traffic stop. — After defendant gave an officer false identity information during a vehicle stop, the power to arrest defendant for providing false identity information under § 18.2-186.3 authorized the officer to search the vehicle because it was reasonable to believe that the vehicle might contain evidence of that crime, specifically defendant's true identity and driving status. Armstead v. Commonwealth, 56 Va. App. 569, 695 S.E.2d 561, 2010 Va. App. LEXIS 300 (2010).

§ 18.2-186.3:1. Identity fraud; consumer reporting agencies; police reports.

A. A consumer may report a case of identity theft to the law-enforcement agency in the jurisdiction where he resides. If a consumer, as defined by the Fair Credit Reporting Act, 15 U.S.C. § 1681 et seq., submits to a consumer reporting agency, as defined by the Fair Credit Reporting Act, 15 U.S.C. § 1681 et seq., a copy of a valid police report, the consumer reporting agency shall, within 30 days of receipt thereof, block the reporting of any information that the consumer alleges appears on his credit report, as defined by the Fair Credit Reporting Act, 15 U.S.C. § 1681 et seq., as a result of a violation of § 18.2-186.3. The consumer reporting agency shall promptly notify the furnisher of the information that a police report has been filed, that a block has been requested, and the effective date of the block.

B. Consumer reporting agencies may decline to block or may rescind any block of consumer information if, in the exercise of good faith and reasonable judgment, the consumer reporting agency believes that: (i) the information was blocked due to a misrepresentation of a material fact by the consumer; (ii) the information was blocked due to fraud, in which the consumer participated, or of which the consumer had knowledge, and which may for purposes of this section be demonstrated by circumstantial evidence; (iii) the consumer agrees that portions of the blocked information or all of it were blocked in error; (iv) the consumer knowingly obtained or should have known that he obtained possession of goods, services, or moneys as a result of the blocked transaction or transactions; or (v) the consumer reporting agency, in the exercise of good faith and reasonable judgment, has substantial reason based on specific, verifiable facts to doubt the authenticity of the consumer's report of a violation of § 18.2-186.3.

C. If blocked information is unblocked pursuant to this section, the consumer shall be notified in the same manner as consumers are notified of the reinsertion of information pursuant to the Fair Credit Reporting Act at 15 U.S.C. § 1681i, as amended. The prior presence of the blocked information in the consumer reporting agency's file on the consumer is not evidence of whether the consumer knew or should have known that he obtained possession of any goods, services, or moneys.

D. A consumer reporting agency shall accept the consumer's version of the disputed information and correct the disputed item when the consumer submits to the consumer reporting agency documentation obtained from the source of the item in dispute or from public records confirming that the report was inaccurate or incomplete, unless the consumer reporting agency, in the exercise of good faith and reasonable judgment, has substantial reason based on specific, verifiable facts to doubt the authenticity of the documentation submitted and notifies the consumer in writing of that decision, explaining its reasons for unblocking the information and setting forth the specific, verifiable facts on which the decision is based.

E. A consumer reporting agency shall delete from a consumer credit report inquiries for credit reports based upon credit requests that the consumer reporting agency verifies were initiated as a result of a violation of § 18.2-186.3.

F. The provisions of this section do not apply to (i) a consumer reporting agency that acts as a reseller of credit information by assembling and merging information contained in the databases of other consumer reporting agencies, and that does not maintain a permanent database of credit information from which new consumer credit reports are produced, (ii) a check services or fraud prevention services company that issues reports on incidents of fraud or authorizations for the purpose of approving or processing negotiable instruments, electronic funds transfers, or similar payment methods, or (iii) a demand deposit account information service company that issues reports regarding account closures due to fraud, substantial overdrafts, automatic teller machine abuse or similar negative information regarding a consumer to inquiring banks or other financial institutions for use only in reviewing a consumer request for a demand deposit account at the inquiring bank or financial institution.

History.
2003, cc. 914, 918; 2006, c. 298.

§ 18.2-186.4. Use of a person's identity with the intent to coerce, intimidate, or harass; penalty.

It shall be unlawful for any person, with the intent to coerce, intimidate, or harass another person, to publish the person's name or photograph along with identifying information as defined in clauses (iii) through (ix), or clause (xii) of subsection C of § 18.2-186.3, or identification of the person's primary residence address. Any person who violates this section is guilty of a Class 1 misdemeanor.

Any person who violates this section knowing or having reason to know that person is a law-enforcement officer, as defined in § 9.1-101, is guilty of a Class 6 felony. The sentence shall include a mandatory minimum term of confinement of six months.

History.
2001, cc. 775, 782; 2007, c. 736; 2010, c. 767.

The 2010 amendments.
The 2010 amendment by c. 767 substituted "or identification of the person's primary residence" for "including identification of the person's primary residence."

§ 18.2-186.4:1. Internet publication of personal information of certain public officials.

A. The Commonwealth shall not publish on the Internet the personal information of any public official if a court has, pursuant to subsection B, ordered that the official's personal information is prohibited from publication and the official has made a demand in writing to the Commonwealth, accompanied by the order of the court, that the Commonwealth not publish such information.

B. Any public official may petition a circuit court for an order prohibiting the publication on the Internet, by the Commonwealth, of the official's personal information. The petition shall set forth the specific reasons that the official seeks the order. The court shall issue such an order only if it finds that (i) there exists a threat to the official or a person who resides with him that would result from publication of the information or (ii) the official has demonstrated a reasonable fear of a risk to his safety or the safety of someone who resides with him that would result from publication of the information on the Internet.

C. If the Commonwealth publishes the public official's personal information on the Internet prior to receipt of a written demand by the official under subsection A, it shall remove the information from publication on the Internet within 48 hours of receipt of the written demand.

D. A written demand made by any public official pursuant to this section shall be effective for four years as follows:

1. For a law-enforcement officer, if the officer remains continuously employed as a law-enforcement officer throughout the four-year period; and

2. For a federal or state judge or justice, if such public official continuously serves throughout the four-year period.

E. For purposes of this section:

"*Commonwealth*" means any agency or political subdivision of the Commonwealth of Virginia.

"*Law-enforcement officer*" means the same as that term is defined in § 9.1-101, 5 U.S.C. § 8331(20), excluding officers whose duties relate to detention as defined in 5 U.S.C. § 8331(20), and any other federal officer or agent who is credentialed with the authority to enforce federal law.

"*Personal information*" means home address, home telephone numbers, personal cell phone numbers, or personal email address.

"*Publication*" and "*publishes*" means intentionally communicating personal information to, or otherwise making personal information available to, and accessible by, the general public through the Internet or other online service.

"*Public official*" means any state or federal judge or justice and any law-enforcement officer.

F. No provision of this section shall apply to lists of registered voters and persons who voted, voter registration records, or lists of absentee voters prepared or provided under Title 24.2.

History.
2010, c. 767; 2012, c. 143.

The 2012 amendments.
The 2012 amendment by c. 143 rewrote the section.

§ 18.2-186.5. Expungement of false identity information from police and court records; Identity Theft Passport.

Any person whose name or other identification has been used without his consent or authorization by another person who has been charged or arrested using such name or identification may file a petition with the court for relief pursuant to § 19.2-392.2. A person who has petitioned the court pursuant to § 19.2-392.2 as a result of a violation of § 18.2-186.3, may submit to the Attorney General a certified copy of a court order obtained pursuant to § 19.2-392.2. Upon receipt by the Attorney General of a certified copy of the court order and upon request by such person, the Office of the Attorney General, in cooperation with the State Police, may issue an "Identity Theft Passport" stating that such an order has been submitted. The Office of the Attorney General shall provide access to identity theft information to (i) criminal justice agencies and (ii) individuals who have submitted a court order pursuant to this section. When the Office of the Attorney General issues an Identity Theft Passport, it shall transmit a record of the issuance of the passport to the Department of Motor Vehicles. The Department shall note on the individual's driver abstract that a court order was obtained pursuant to § 19.2-392.2 and that an Identity Theft Passport has been issued. The provisions of § 2.2-3808 shall not apply to this section.

History.

2003, cc. 914, 918; 2004, c. 450; 2006, c. 298; 2011, c. 619.

The 2011 amendments.

The 2011 amendment by c. 619 substituted "may issue" for "shall issue" in the third sentence and added the last sentence.

§ 18.2-186.6. Breach of personal information notification.

A. As used in this section:

"Breach of the security of the system" means the unauthorized access and acquisition of unencrypted and unredacted computerized data that compromises the security or confidentiality of personal information maintained by an individual or entity as part of a database of personal information regarding multiple individuals and that causes, or the individual or entity reasonably believes has caused, or will cause, identity theft or other fraud to any resident of the Commonwealth. Good faith acquisition of personal information by an employee or agent of an individual or entity for the purposes of the individual or entity is not a breach of the security of the system, provided that the personal information is not used for a purpose other than a lawful purpose of the individual or entity or subject to further unauthorized disclosure.

"Encrypted" means the transformation of data through the use of an algorithmic process into a form in which there is a low probability of assigning meaning without the use of a confidential process or key, or the securing of the information by another method that renders the data elements unreadable or unusable.

"Entity" includes corporations, business trusts, estates, partnerships, limited partnerships, limited liability partnerships, limited liability companies, associations, organizations, joint ventures, governments, governmental subdivisions, agencies, or instrumentalities or any other legal entity, whether for profit or not for profit.

"Financial institution" has the meaning given that term in 15 U.S.C. § 6809(3).

"Individual" means a natural person.

"Notice" means:

1. Written notice to the last known postal address in the records of the individual or entity;

2. Telephone notice;

3. Electronic notice; or

4. Substitute notice, if the individual or the entity required to provide notice demonstrates that the cost of providing notice will exceed $50,000, the affected class of Virginia residents to be notified exceeds 100,000 residents, or the individual or the entity does not have sufficient contact information or consent to provide notice as described in subdivisions 1, 2, or 3 of this definition. Substitute notice consists of all of the following:

a. E-mail notice if the individual or the entity has e-mail addresses for the members of the affected class of residents;

b. Conspicuous posting of the notice on the website of the individual or the entity if the individual or the entity maintains a website; and

c. Notice to major statewide media.

Notice required by this section shall not be considered a debt communication as defined by the Fair Debt Collection Practices Act in 15 U.S.C. § 1692a.

Notice required by this section shall include a description of the following:

(1) The incident in general terms;

(2) The type of personal information that was subject to the unauthorized access and acquisition;

(3) The general acts of the individual or entity to protect the personal information from further unauthorized access;

(4) A telephone number that the person may call for further information and assistance, if one exists; and

(5) Advice that directs the person to remain vigilant by reviewing account statements and monitoring free credit reports.

"Personal information" means the first name or first initial and last name in combination with and linked to any one or more of the following data elements that relate to a resident of the Commonwealth, when the data elements are neither encrypted nor redacted:

1. Social security number;

2. Driver's license number or state identification card number issued in lieu of a driver's license number; or

3. Financial account number, or credit card or debit card number, in combination with any required security code, access code, or password that would permit access to a resident's financial accounts.

The term does not include information that is lawfully obtained from publicly available information, or from federal, state, or local government records lawfully made available to the general public.

"Redact" means alteration or truncation of data such that no more than the following are accessible as part of the personal information:

1. Five digits of a social security number; or

2. The last four digits of a driver's license number, state identification card number, or account number.

B. If unencrypted or unredacted personal information was or is reasonably believed to have been accessed and acquired by an unauthorized person and causes, or the individual or entity reasonably believes has caused or will cause, identity theft or another fraud to any resident of the Commonwealth, an individual or entity that owns or licenses computerized data that includes personal information shall disclose any breach of the security of the system following discovery or notification of the breach of the security of the system to the Office of the Attorney General and any affected resident of the Commonwealth without unreasonable delay. Notice required by this section may be reasonably delayed to allow the individual or entity to determine the scope of the breach of the security of the system and restore the reasonable integrity of the system. Notice required by this section may be delayed if, after the individual or entity notifies a law-enforcement agency, the law-enforcement agency determines and advises the individual or entity that the notice will impede a criminal or civil investigation, or homeland or national security. Notice shall be made without unreasonable delay after the law-enforcement agency determines that the notification will no longer impede the investigation or jeopardize national or homeland security.

C. An individual or entity shall disclose the breach of the security of the system if encrypted information is accessed and acquired in an unencrypted form, or if the security breach involves a person with access to the encryption key and the individual or entity reasonably believes that such a breach has caused or will cause identity theft or other fraud to any resident of the Commonwealth.

D. An individual or entity that maintains computerized data that includes personal information that the individual or entity does not own or license shall notify the owner or licensee of the information of any breach of the security of the system without unreasonable delay following discovery of the breach of the security of the system, if the personal information was accessed and acquired by an unauthorized person or the individual or entity reasonably believes the personal information was accessed and acquired by an unauthorized person.

E. In the event an individual or entity provides notice to more than 1,000 persons at one time pursuant to this section, the individual or entity shall notify, without unreasonable delay, the Office of the Attorney General and all consumer reporting agencies that compile and maintain files on consumers on a nationwide basis, as defined in 15 U.S.C. § 1681a(p), of the timing, distribution, and content of the notice.

F. An entity that maintains its own notification procedures as part of an information privacy or security policy for the treatment of personal information that are consistent with the timing requirements of this section shall be deemed to be in compliance with the notification requirements of this section if it notifies residents of the Commonwealth in accordance with its procedures in the event of a breach of the security of the system.

G. An entity that is subject to Title V of the Gramm-Leach-Bliley Act (15 U.S.C. § 6801 et seq.) and maintains procedures for notification of a breach of the security of the system in accordance with the provision of that Act and any rules, regulations, or guidelines promulgated thereto shall be deemed to be in compliance with this section.

H. An entity that complies with the notification requirements or procedures pursuant to the rules, regulations, procedures, or guidelines established by the entity's primary or functional state or federal regulator shall be in compliance with this section.

I. Except as provided by subsections J and K, pursuant to the enforcement duties and powers of the Office of the Attorney General, the Attorney General may bring an action to address violations of this section. The Office of the Attorney General may impose a civil penalty not to exceed $150,000 per breach of the security of the system or a series of breaches of a similar nature that are discovered in a single investigation. Nothing in this section shall limit an individual from recovering direct economic damages from a violation of this section.

J. A violation of this section by a state-chartered or licensed financial institution shall be enforceable exclusively by the financial institution's primary state regulator.

K. A violation of this section by an individual or entity regulated by the State Corporation Commission's Bureau of Insurance shall be enforced exclusively by the State Corporation Commission.

L. The provisions of this section shall not apply to criminal intelligence systems subject to the restrictions of 28 C.F.R. Part 23 that are maintained by law-enforcement agencies of the Commonwealth and the organized Criminal Gang File of the Virginia Criminal Information Network (VCIN), established pursuant to Chapter 2 (§ 52-12 et seq.) of Title 52.

History.
2008, cc. 566, 801.

Editor's note.
At the direction of the Virginia Code Commission, in subsection E, "15 U.S.C. § 1681a(p)" was substituted for "15 U.S.C. § 1681(a)(p)."

§ 18.2-187. Repealed by Acts 1978, c. 807.

Cross references.
For present section covering the subject matter of the repealed section, see § 18.2-187.1.

§ 18.2-187.1. Obtaining or attempting to obtain oil, electric, gas, water, telephone, telegraph, cable television or electronic communication service without payment; penalty; civil liability.

A. It shall be unlawful for any person knowingly, with the intent to defraud, to obtain or attempt to obtain, for himself or for another, oil, electric, gas, water, telephone, telegraph, cable television or electronic communication service by the use of any false information, or in any case where such service has been disconnected by the supplier and notice of disconnection has been given.

B. It shall be unlawful for any person to obtain or attempt to obtain oil, electric, gas, water, telephone, telegraph, cable television or electronic communication service by the use of any scheme, device, means or method, or by a false application for service with intent to avoid payment of lawful charges therefor.

B1. It shall be unlawful for any person to obtain, or attempt to obtain, electronic communication service as defined in § 18.2-190.1 by the use of an unlawful electronic communication device as defined in § 18.2-190.1.

C. The word "notice" as used in subsection A shall be notice given in writing to the person to whom the service was assigned. The sending of a notice in writing by registered or certified mail in the United States mail, duly stamped and addressed to such person at his last known address, requiring delivery to the addressee only with return receipt requested, and the actual signing of the receipt for such mail by the addressee, shall be prima facie evidence that such notice was duly received.

D. Any person who violates any provisions of this section, if the value of service, credit or benefit procured is $200 or more, shall be guilty of a Class 6 felony; or if the value is less than $200, shall be guilty of a Class 1 misdemeanor. In addition, the court may order restitution for the value of the services unlawfully used and for all costs. Such costs shall be limited to actual expenses, including the base wages of employees acting as witnesses for the Commonwealth, and suit costs. However, the total amount of allowable costs granted hereunder shall not exceed $250, excluding the value of the service.

E. Any party providing oil, electric, gas, water, telephone, telegraph, cable television or electronic communication service who is aggrieved by a violation of this section may, in a civil proceeding in any court of competent jurisdiction, seek both injunctive and equitable relief, and an award of damages, including attorney's fees and costs. In addition to any other remedy provided by law, the party aggrieved may recover an award of actual damages or $500 whichever is greater for each action.

History.
1978, c. 807; 1981, c. 197; 1992, c. 525; 1993, c. 439; 2002, c. 671; 2003, c. 354.

Law Review.
For survey of Virginia administrative law for year 1977-1978, see 64 Va. L. Rev. 1365 (1978). For survey of Virginia criminal law for the year 1977-1978, see 64 Va. L. Rev. 1407 (1978). For article on developments in the field of Virginia public utility law from June 2002 through May 2003, see 38 U. Rich. L. Rev. 195 (2003).

Michie's Jurisprudence.
For related discussion, see 5A M.J. Courts, § 56; 18 M.J. Telegraph and Telephone Companies, § 2.

CASE NOTES

47 U.S.C.S. § 553 does not preempt this section. Carter v. Commonwealth, 25 Va. App. 721, 492 S.E.2d 480 (1997).

Aggregation of value allowed. — Although none of the individual calls appellant made were shown to have a value in excess of $200, aggregation of the value of individual calls made in violation of this section was permitted to prove that the unlawful conduct was a felony. The unlawful calls for which appellant was indicted all

occurred within approximately one hour of one another and were in execution of a general fraudulent scheme. JHA v. Commonwealth, 18 Va. App. 349, 444 S.E.2d 258 (1994).

Value of services, not loss to phone company, controls. — Although appellant argued that the indictment alleged that the loss of the value of the calls, $300.85, was incurred by phone company, and therefore, because the evidence disclosed that phone company's loss was only a portion of the $300.85, appellant asserted that it had not been shown that phone company sustained a loss sufficient to prove the felony, the value of the service fraudulently obtained was proved to be $300.85, and the terms of its disposition by phone company, if collected, did not reduce the value of the service so obtained. JHA v. Commonwealth, 18 Va. App. 349, 444 S.E.2d 258 (1994).

Costs. — Under this section, the offense created is a species of larceny. As such, the value of service, credit or benefit procured is to be measured at the time the services were taken. Penley v. Commonwealth, 51 Va. App. 166, 655 S.E.2d 746, 2008 Va. App. LEXIS 31 (2008).

This section makes a distinction between "value of services received" and "costs," and the latter are only recoverable as restitution. Penley v. Commonwealth, 51 Va. App. 166, 655 S.E.2d 746, 2008 Va. App. LEXIS 31 (2008).

When defendant violated § 18.2-187.1 by using an illegal electrical meter, the value of the services he took was limited to the electrical current he used and did not include the costs incurred by the power company as a result of the theft. Thus, the trial court erred in considering the costs in determining that he obtained services worth more than $200; as the elements of a misdemeanor violation of § 18.2-187.1, a lesser included offense, had been proven beyond a reasonable doubt, defendant was to be resentenced. Penley v. Commonwealth, 51 Va. App. 166, 655 S.E.2d 746, 2008 Va. App. LEXIS 31 (2008).

Notice of termination. — Evidence was sufficient to establish that defendant received the required written notice that defendant's utility service was to be disconnected, as required by subsection A of § 18.2-187.1, because the electric company mailed four termination notices to defendant pursuant to subsection C of § 18.2-187.1, and registered and certified mail was not a requirement, but merely created a rebuttable presumption. Lamb v. Commonwealth, 2013 Va. App. LEXIS 40 (Feb. 5, 2013).

Evidence of past behavior and usage. — Defendant's conviction for felony obtaining or attempting to obtain utility service by fraud was proper because, based upon the evidence of his behavior and past usage of the utility, the jury reasonably inferred that he had diverted the gas to his residence in order to continue to use the gas as he had done in the past. Robinson v. Commonwealth, 2011 Va. App. LEXIS 113 (Apr. 5, 2011).

Evidence sufficient. — Evidence supported defendant's conviction of fraudulently obtaining electric service, as the circumstantial evidence established that defendant intentionally obtained electric service by altering an electric meter, allowing defendant to obtain free electricity after defendant's service was disconnected. Lamb v. Commonwealth, 2013 Va. App. LEXIS 39 (Feb. 5, 2013).

Applied in Hall v. Commonwealth, 2 Va. App. 159, 342 S.E.2d 640 (1986).

§ 18.2-187.2. Audiovisual recording of motion pictures unlawful; penalty.

A. It shall be unlawful for any person to operate an audiovisual recording function of a device in a commercial theater, excluding the lobby and other common areas, to record a motion picture or any portion thereof without the consent of the owner or lessee of the theater. Any person who violates the provisions of this section is guilty of a Class 1 misdemeanor.

B. The owner or lessee of a commercial theater where a motion picture is being exhibited, or his authorized agent or employee, who has probable cause to believe that a person has made a recording in violation of subsection A on the premises of the owner or lessee, may detain such person for a period not to exceed one hour pending arrival of a law-enforcement officer. Such owner, lessee, agent or employee shall not be held civilly liable for unlawful detention if such detention does not exceed one hour, slander, malicious prosecution, false imprisonment, false arrest, or assault and battery of the person so arrested or detained, whether such arrest or detention takes place on the premises of the owner or lessee or after close pursuit from such premises, provided that, in causing the arrest or detention of such person, the owner, lessee, agent or employee had at the time of such arrest or detention probable cause to believe the person was making or had made an illegal recording in violation of subsection A.

C. This section shall not apply to any lawfully authorized investigative, law-enforcement, protective, or intelligence gathering activity by an agent or employee of the Commonwealth or the federal government.

D. The term *"audiovisual recording function"* means that component of an analog or digital photographic or video camera or other device developed with the capability to record or transmit a motion picture or any part thereof.

History.
2004, c. 759.

§ 18.2-188. Defrauding hotels, motels, campgrounds, boardinghouses, etc.

It shall be unlawful for any person, without paying therefor, and with the intent to cheat or defraud the owner or keeper to:

1. Put up at a hotel, motel, campground or boardinghouse;

2. Obtain food from a restaurant or other eating house;

3. Gain entrance to an amusement park; or

4. Without having an express agreement for credit, procure food, entertainment or accommodation from any hotel, motel, campground, boardinghouse, restaurant, eating house or amusement park.

It shall be unlawful for any person, with intent to cheat or defraud the owner or keeper out of the pay therefor to obtain credit at a hotel, motel, campground, boardinghouse, restaurant or eating house for food, entertainment or accommodation by means of any false show of baggage or effects brought thereto.

It shall be unlawful for any person, with intent to cheat or defraud, to obtain credit at a hotel, motel, campground, boardinghouse, restaurant, eating house or amusement park for food, entertainment or accommodation through any misrepresentation or false statement.

It shall be unlawful for any person, with intent to cheat or defraud, to remove or cause to be removed any baggage or effects from a hotel, motel, campground, boardinghouse, restaurant or eating house

while there is a lien existing thereon for the proper charges due from him for fare and board furnished.

Any person who violates any provision of this section shall, if the value of service, credit or benefit procured or obtained is $200 or more, be guilty of a Class 5 felony; or if the value is less than $200, a Class 1 misdemeanor.

History.
Code 1950, § 18.1-120; 1960, c. 358; 1974, c. 615; 1975, cc. 14, 15; 1977, c. 178; 1981, c. 197; 1993, c. 575.

Cross references.
As to lien of innkeepers, etc., see §§ 43-31, 43-34 through 43-36.

Law Review.
For article on justification as a defense to crime, see 59 Va. L. Rev. 1326 (1973).

Michie's Jurisprudence.
For related discussion, see 8B M.J. False Pretenses and Cheats, § 4; 9B M.J. Hotels, Inns and Restaurants, § 4.

CASE NOTES

Express agreement for credit. — Where an inn accepted the defendant's promissory note in satisfaction of the charges arising from accommodations procured by defendant, inarguably an express agreement for credit, the inn could not rely upon subsection 4 of § 18.2-188 when defendant subsequently defaulted. Louis v. Commonwealth, 40 Va. App. 228, 578 S.E.2d 820, 2003 Va. App. LEXIS 179 (2003).

Unlawful to fraudulently procure entertainment from restaurant. — Crime of defrauding restaurant was complete when defendant accepted benefits of band's entertainment, while concealing fact that he had stopped payment on check written to cover cost of band. Morton v. Commonwealth, No. 0864-98-4 (Ct. of Appeals July 20, 1999).

§ 18.2-188.1. Defrauding person having a lien on an animal; penalty.

It shall be unlawful to remove or cause any horse or other animal to be removed from the possession of the owner or keeper of a livery stable or other person having a lien on the horse or animal for keep, support and care pursuant to § 43-32, with intent to defraud or cheat the lienholder. A violation of this section shall be punishable as a Class 2 misdemeanor.

History.
1990, c. 639.

§ 18.2-189. Defrauding keeper of motor vehicles or watercraft.

A person shall be guilty of a Class 2 misdemeanor if he:

1. Stores a motor vehicle, boat or other watercraft with any person, firm or corporation engaged in the business of conducting a garage, marina, watercraft dealership or other facility for the (i) storage of motor vehicles, boats or other watercraft, (ii) furnishing of supplies to motor vehicles, boats or other watercraft, or (iii) alteration or repair of motor vehicles, boats or other watercraft, and obtains

storage, supplies, alterations or repairs for such motor vehicle, boat or other watercraft, without having an express agreement for credit, or procures storage, supplies, alterations or repairs on account of such motor vehicle, boat or other watercraft so stored, without paying therefor, and with the intent to cheat or defraud the owner or keeper of the garage, marina or boat repair facility; or

2. With such intent, obtains credit at the garage, marina, watercraft dealership or boat repair facility for such storage, supplies, alterations or repairs through any misrepresentation or false statement; or

3. With such intent, removes or causes to be removed any such motor vehicle, boat or other watercraft from any such garage, marina, watercraft dealership or boat repair facility while there is a lien existing thereon for the proper charges due from him for storage, supplies, alterations or repairs furnished thereon, in accordance with the provisions of § 43-32, 43-33, 46.2-644.01, or § 46.2-644.02.

History.
Code 1950, § 18.1-121; 1960, c. 358; 1975, cc. 14, 15; 1978, c. 245; 1988, c. 414; 2009, c. 664.

Editor's note.
Acts 2009, c. 664, cl. 3, provides: "That the provisions of this act shall become effective on October 1, 2009."

The 2009 amendments.
The 2009 amendment by c. 664, effective October 1, 2009, substituted "provisions of § 43-32, 43-33, 46.2-644.01, or § 46.2-644.02" for "provisions of § 43-32, or § 43-33" in subdivision 3.

Law Review.
For article on justification as a defense to crime, see 59 Va. L. Rev. 1326 (1973).

Michie's Jurisprudence.
For related discussion, see 2A M.J. Arrest, § 9.

CASE NOTES

Towing services. — While this section does not mention either the term "tow truck" or the word "services," it is common knowledge that tow-truck services are necessary in many highway accidents and that often a damaged vehicle must be towed to a garage before it can be stored, supplied with parts, altered, or repaired. Hence, in many cases, towing services are essential to the practical operation of this section. It is fairly arguable that such services are implicitly included in the statute's provisions. DeChene v. Smallwood, 226 Va. 475, 311 S.E.2d 749, cert. denied, 469 U.S. 857, 105 S. Ct. 184, 83 L. Ed. 2d 118 (1984).

§ 18.2-190. Fraudulent misrepresentation as to breed of bull or cattle.

Any person who, in the sale, gift or transfer, of any bull or cattle, knowingly shall make any false representation that such bull is registered, or entitled to registration, in some recognized standard and accredited herd of cattle, or three-quarters blood of such breed, or that such cattle are from such a herd or breed of cattle, shall be guilty of a Class 1 misdemeanor.

History.
Code 1950, §§ 18.1-185, 18.1-186; 1960, c. 358; 1975, cc. 14, 15.

Michie's Jurisprudence.
For related discussion, see 8B M.J. False Pretenses and Cheats, § 4.

ARTICLE 5.1.

OFFENSES INVOLVING TELECOMMUNICATION DEVICES.

§ 18.2-190.1. Definitions.

As used in this article, unless the context requires a different meaning:

"Electronic communication device" means (i) any type of instrument, device, machine, equipment or software that is capable of transmitting, acquiring, encrypting, decrypting or receiving any signs, signals, writings, images and sounds or intelligence of any nature by wire, radio, optical or other electromagnetic systems or (ii) any part, accessory or component of such an instrument, device, machine, equipment or software, including, but not limited to, any computer circuit, computer chip, security module, smart card, electronic mechanism, or other component, accessory or part, that is capable of facilitating the transmission, acquisition, encryption, decryption or reception of signs, signals, writings, images, and sounds or intelligence of any nature by wire, radio, optical or other electromagnetic systems.

"Electronic communication service" means any service provided for a charge or compensation to facilitate the lawful origination, transmission, emission or reception of signs, signals, writings, images and sounds or intelligence of any nature through the use of an electronic communication device as that term is defined in this section.

"Electronic communication service provider" means any person or entity providing any electronic communication service including (i) any person or entity owning or operating any cable television, satellite, Internet-based, telephone, wireless, microwave, fiber optic, data transmission or radio distribution network, system or facility; (ii) any person or entity that for a fee supplies equipment or services to an electronic communication service provider; and (iii) any person or entity providing an electronic communication service directly or indirectly using any of the systems, networks, or facilities described in clause (i).

"Equipment or materials used to manufacture an unlawful electronic communication device" means (i) a scanner capable of intercepting the electronic serial number or mobile identification number of a cellular or other wireless telephone; (ii) electronic software or hardware capable of altering or changing the factory-installed electronic serial number of a cellular or other wireless telephone or a computer containing such software; (iii) a list of cellular or other wireless telephone electronic serial numbers with their associated mobile identification numbers; or (iv) a part, accessory or component of an unlawful

electronic communications device possessed or used in the manufacture of such device including any electronic serial number, computer software, mobile identification number, service access card, account number, or personal identification number used to acquire, receive, use, decrypt or transmit an electronic communication service without the actual consent or knowledge of the electronic communication service provider.

"Manufacture of an unlawful electronic communication device" means to make, produce or assemble an unlawful electronic communication device, or to modify, alter, program or reprogram an electronic communication device to be capable of performing any of the illegal functions of an unlawful electronic communication device as that term is defined in this section.

"Sell" means to sell, exchange, lease, give or dispose of to another or to offer or agree to do the same.

"Unlawful electronic communication device" means any electronic communication device that has been manufactured, designed, developed, altered, modified, programmed or reprogrammed, alone or in conjunction with another electronic communication device, so as to be capable of facilitating the disruption, acquisition, receipt, transmission, retransmission or decryption of an electronic communication service without the actual consent or knowledge of the electronic communication service provider. Such unlawful devices include, but are not limited to (i) any device, technology, product, service, equipment, computer software, or any component or part thereof, primarily distributed, sold, designed, assembled, developed, manufactured, modified, programmed, reprogrammed or used for the purpose of facilitating the unauthorized receipt of, transmission of, disruption of, decryption of, access to, or acquisition of any electronic communication service provided by any electronic communication service provider; and (ii) any type of instrument, device, machine, equipment, technology, or software that is primarily designed, assembled, manufactured, developed, sold, distributed, possessed, used or offered, promoted or advertised for the purpose of defeating or circumventing any technology, device or software, or any component or part thereof, used by the provider, owner or licensee of any electronic communication service or of any data, audio or video programs or transmissions, to protect any such electronic communication, data, audio or video services, programs or transmissions from unauthorized receipt, acquisition, access, decryption, disclosure, communication, transmission or retransmission.

History.
1993, c. 439; 1998, c. 518; 2002, c. 671; 2003, c. 354.

Law Review.
For an article, "Technology and the Law," see 32 U. Rich. L. Rev. 1383 (1998). For article on developments in the field of Virginia public utility law from June 2002 through May 2003, see 38 U. Rich. L. Rev. 195 (2003).

Michie's Jurisprudence.
For related discussion, see 18 M.J. Telegraph and Telephone Companies, § 2.

§ 18.2-190.2. Possession of an unlawful electronic communication device or equipment etc., used to manufacture such device; penalty.

A person who knowingly possesses (i) an unlawful electronic communication device or (ii) equipment or materials used to manufacture an unlawful electronic communication device as defined in § 18.2-190.1 with the intent to manufacture an unlawful electronic communication device shall be guilty of a Class 6 felony unless such possession is by an electronic communication equipment manufacturer while lawfully acting in that capacity, or a facilities-based electronic communication service provider licensed by the Federal Communications Commission or by a law-enforcement agency.

History.
1993, c. 439; 1998, c. 518; 2002, c. 671; 2003, c. 354.

Law Review.
For an article, "Technology and the Law," see 32 U. Rich. L. Rev. 1383 (1998).

§ 18.2-190.3. Sale of an unlawful electronic communication device; penalty.

A person who (i) knowingly sells an unlawful electronic communication device or (ii) sells material, including hardware, data, computer software or other information or equipment, knowing, or having reason to know, that the purchaser or a third person intends to use such material in the manufacture of an unlawful electronic communication device, shall be guilty of a Class 6 felony.

History.
1993, c. 439; 1998, c. 518; 2002, c. 671; 2003, c. 354.

Law Review.
For an article, "Technology and the Law," see 32 U. Rich. L. Rev. 1383 (1998).

§ 18.2-190.4. Manufacture of an unlawful electronic communication device; penalty.

A person who knowingly manufactures an unlawful electronic communication device shall be guilty of a Class 6 felony.

History.
1993, c. 439; 1998, c. 518; 2002, c. 671; 2003, c. 354.

Law Review.
For an article, "Technology and the Law," see 32 U. Rich. L. Rev. 1383 (1998).

§ 18.2-190.5. Separate offenses; penalty.

For purposes of imposing criminal penalties for violations of §§ 18.2-190.3 and 18.2-190.4, the commission of the prohibited activity regarding each unlawful electronic communication device shall be deemed a separate offense.

History.
2002, c. 671; 2003, c. 354.

§ 18.2-190.6. Restitution.

The court may, in addition to any other sentence authorized by law, require a person convicted of violating § 18.2-190.3 or § 18.2-190.4 to make restitution in the manner provided in § 19.2-305.1.

History.
2002, c. 671.

§ 18.2-190.7. Repealed by Acts 2004, c. 995.

Cross references.
For current provisions as to forfeiture of unlawful electronic communication devices, see § 19.2-386.18.

§ 18.2-190.8. Civil relief; damages.

Any electronic communication service provider aggrieved by a violation of this article may seek both injunctive and equitable relief and an award of damages including attorney's fees and costs. In addition to any other remedy provided by law, the party aggrieved may recover an award of actual damages or $500, whichever is greater, for each unlawful electronic communications device involved in the action. In any case in which the court finds that the violation was committed for purposes of commercial advantage or financial gain, the award shall be increased by an amount not to exceed three times the actual damages sustained or $1,500 for each unlawful electronic communications device involved, whichever is greater.

History.
2002, c. 671; 2003, c. 354.

ARTICLE 6.

OFFENSES RELATING TO CREDIT CARDS.

§ 18.2-191. Definitions.

The following words and phrases as used in this article, unless a different meaning is plainly required by the context, shall have the following meanings:

"Acquirer" means a business organization, financial institution or an agent of a business organization or financial institution that authorizes a merchant to accept payment by credit card or credit card number for money, goods, services or anything else of value.

"Cardholder" means the person or organization named on the face of a credit card to whom or for whose benefit the credit card is issued by an issuer.

"Credit card" means any instrument or device, whether known as a credit card, credit plate, payment device number, or by any other name, issued with or without fee by an issuer for the use of the cardholder in obtaining money, goods, services or anything else of value on credit. For the purpose of this article, "credit card" shall also include a similar device, whether known as a debit card, or any other name, issued with or without fee by an issuer for the use of the cardholder in obtaining money, goods, services or anything else of value by charging the account of the cardholder with a bank or any other person even though no credit is thereby extended.

"Expired credit card" means a credit card which is no longer valid because the term shown on it has elapsed.

"Issuer" means the business organization or financial institution or its duly authorized agent which issues a credit card.

"Payment device number" means any code, account number or other means of account access, other than a check, draft or similar paper instrument, that can be used to obtain money, goods, services or anything else of value, or to initiate a transfer of funds. "Payment device number" does not include an encoded or truncated credit card number or payment device number.

"Receives" or *"receiving"* means acquiring possession or control of the credit card number or payment device number or accepting the same as security for a loan.

"Revoked credit card" means a credit card which is no longer valid because permission to use it has been suspended or terminated by the issuer.

"Sales draft" means a paper form evidencing a purchase of goods, services or anything else of value from a merchant through the use of a credit card.

"Cash advance/withdrawal draft" means a paper form evidencing a cash advance or withdrawal from a bank or other financial institution through the use of a credit card.

History.
Code 1950, § 18.1-125.2; 1968, c. 480; 1975, cc. 14, 15; 1977, c. 103; 1980, c. 99; 1985, c. 266; 1991, c. 546.

Law Review.
For survey of the Virginia law on contracts and sales for the year 1967-1968, see 54 Va. L. Rev. 1572 (1968). For survey of Virginia law on criminal law and procedure for the year 2007-2008, see 43 U. Rich. L. Rev. 149 (2008).

Michie's Jurisprudence.
For related discussion, see 2B M.J. Aviation, § 1; 3C M.J. Commercial Law, § 94; 8B M.J. False Pretenses and Cheats, § 4; 8B M.J. Fraud and Deceit, § 71.

CASE NOTES

Meaning of "credit card." — When defendant used a credit card account access number that had been issued with another person's data, he employed a credit card issued to or for the benefit of someone else; a credit card is not just a ubiquitous plastic card but is any device that allows a cardholder to obtain anything of value on credit. Hill v. Commonwealth, No. 2030-00-1, 2002 Va. App. LEXIS 256 (Ct. of Appeals Apr. 30, 2002).

§ 18.2-192. Credit card theft.

(1) A person is guilty of credit card or credit card number theft when:

(a) He takes, obtains or withholds a credit card or credit card number from the person, possession, custody or control of another without the cardholder's consent or who, with knowledge that it has been so taken, obtained or withheld, receives the credit card or credit card number with intent to use it or sell it, or to transfer it to a person other than the issuer or the cardholder; or

(b) He receives a credit card or credit card number that he knows to have been lost, mislaid, or delivered under a mistake as to the identity or address of the cardholder, and who retains possession with intent to use, to sell or to transfer the credit card or credit card number to a person other than the issuer or the cardholder; or

(c) He, not being the issuer, sells a credit card or credit card number or buys a credit card or credit card number from a person other than the issuer; or

(d) He, not being the issuer, during any twelve-month period, receives credit cards or credit card numbers issued in the names of two or more persons which he has reason to know were taken or retained under circumstances which constitute a violation of § 18.2-194 and subdivision (1) (c) of this section.

(2) Credit card or credit card number theft is grand larceny and is punishable as provided in § 18.2-95.

History.
Code 1950, § 18.1-125.3; 1968, c. 480; 1975, cc. 14, 15; 1976, c. 318; 1985, c. 266.

Law Review.
For survey of Virginia criminal law for the year 1974-1975, see 61 Va. L. Rev. 1697 (1975).

Michie's Jurisprudence.
For related discussion, see 12A M.J. Larceny, § 8.

CASE NOTES

There is no language in this section specifically creating prima facie evidence of credit card theft, although there is a provision that when a person, other than the cardholder or a person authorized by him, possesses two or more signed credit cards, such possession shall be prima facie evidence of credit card forgery. Cheatham v. Commonwealth, 215 Va. 286, 208 S.E.2d 760 (1974), overruled in part by Meeks v. Commonwealth, 274 Va. 798, 651 S.E.2d 637 (2007).

If the General Assembly had intended to create prima facie evidence of withholding a credit card from mere possession of a recently stolen credit card, it would have included specific language to accomplish that purpose. Cheatham v. Commonwealth, 215 Va. 286, 208 S.E.2d 760 (1974), overruled in part by Meeks v. Commonwealth, 274 Va. 798, 651 S.E.2d 637 (2007).

The word "withhold" must import something more than mere retention, for mere retention could be consistent with innocent intent. Cheatham v. Commonwealth, 215 Va. 286, 208 S.E.2d 760 (1974), overruled in part by Meeks v. Commonwealth, 274 Va. 798, 651 S.E.2d 637 (2007).

The gravamen of this section is the taking of a single credit card, and the taking of each card constitutes a separate statutory offense for which the perpetrator may be separately convicted and punished. Johnson v. Commonwealth, No. 1665-88-1 (Ct. of Appeals Dec. 4, 1990).

And each card taken represents a separate offense. — Trial court properly refused to merge three indictments for larceny under the single larceny doctrine, since the taking of credit cards represented separate statutory offenses for each card defendant took. Scott v. Commonwealth, 36 Va. App. 276, 549 S.E.2d 624, 2001 Va. App. LEXIS 449 (2001).

Double jeopardy. — Although appellant accurately noted that he committed the respective crimes in a similar manner, this fact did not render the convictions improper; under the Blockburger test, offenses charged were examined in the abstract, without referring to the particular facts of the case under review. Viewed in the abstract, identity theft and credit card fraud were separate offenses punishable in a single criminal proceeding; accordingly, appellant's convictions for identity theft and for credit card fraud were proper and did not violate double jeopardy protections. Gheorghiu v. Commonwealth, 54 Va. App. 645, 682 S.E.2d 50, 2009 Va. App. LEXIS 424 (2009), aff'd in part, rev'd in part, 280 Va. 678, 701 S.E.2d 407 (2010).

Sufficiency of indictment. — Defendant's convictions for credit card theft in violation of § 18.2-192 were proper because she provided no case law or authority to support her contention that time was an element of the offense of credit card theft. As time was not an element of the offense, the Commonwealth was not required to prove the exact date of the offenses, as long as the evidence established beyond a reasonable doubt that the crimes occurred and defendant committed the crimes; there was sufficient evidence to show that defendant obtained the credit cards and received the credit cards and, therefore, the trial court did not err in finding the evidence sufficient to prove the offenses. Trang Chau v. Commonwealth, 2011 Va. App. LEXIS 30 (Feb. 1, 2011).

The retention must be accompanied by an intent to deprive the owner of possession and to use the card, or to sell it, or to transfer it to a person other than the issuer or the cardholder. Cheatham v. Commonwealth, 215 Va. 286, 208 S.E.2d 760 (1974), overruled in part by Meeks v. Commonwealth, 274 Va. 798, 651 S.E.2d 637 (2007).

The statute may be violated by proof that the accused was in receipt of the card knowing that it was taken from the possession, custody or control of the cardholder without her consent. In a prosecution under those circumstances, the Commonwealth does not have to prove that the accused was the thief; however, it does have to prove that he had knowing receipt of a card with intent to use, sell or transfer it. Lyne v. Commonwealth, No. 2428-94-2 (Ct. of Appeals Mar. 26, 1996).

The taking must be with the intent to use, sell, or transfer the card to a person other than the issuer or the cardholder. Darnell v. Commonwealth, 12 Va. App. 948, 408 S.E.2d 540 (1991).

Proof of intent. — Under subdivision (1) (a), the Commonwealth is required to prove "intent to use ... or sell ... or transfer" the card. Lyne v. Commonwealth, No. 2428-94-2 (Ct. of Appeals Mar. 26, 1996).

Evidence was sufficient to support trial court's conclusion that defendant held credit cards without owner's consent, and intended to use them. Lee v. Commonwealth, No. 1170-98-4 (Ct. of Appeals June 22, 1999).

Because the trial court, which concluded that an intent to use was an element of the "first prong" of subdivision 1 of § 18.2-192 and that the intent to use or sell was applicable only to the second prong, misinterpreted, by omission, the elements of the offense proscribed by § 18.2-192(1)(a), as the taking of a credit card had to be with the intent to use, sell, or transfer the card to a person other than the issuer or the cardholder, defendant's conviction was reversed. Lassiter v. Commonwealth, — Va. App. —, — S.E.2d —, 2006 Va. App. LEXIS 531 (Nov. 21, 2006).

Misuse of properly issued card not theft. — Defendant's misuse of university motor pool gasoline card issued to him by the university to put gas into his own vehicle did not constitute credit card theft for purposes of this section. Sykes v. Commonwealth, 27 Va. App. 77, 497 S.E.2d 511 (1998).

Presumption should not be extended. — The presumption of guilt from unexplained or falsely explained possession of recently stolen goods should not be extended to the "withholding" of a credit card, thus constituting statutory grand larceny. Cheatham v. Commonwealth, 215 Va. 286, 208 S.E.2d 760 (1974), overruled in part by Meeks v. Commonwealth, 274 Va. 798, 651 S.E.2d 637 (2007).

A charge of mere possession of a stolen credit card is not sufficient to state the offense of credit card theft under subdivision (1) (a). Wilder v. Commonwealth, 217 Va. 145, 225 S.E.2d 411 (1976) (decided under former § 18.1-125.3).

Taking proved. — The statute does not require the Commonwealth to prove that defendant received the credit card number directly from the cardholder. Nor does the statute exclude individuals who obtain credit card numbers from discarded receipts, via the telephone or the Internet, or any of the myriad ways in which credit card numbers can be fraudulently acquired without possession of the credit card or without the cardholder's consent. Therefore, where defendant acquired cardholder's credit card number without his consent, the taking element of this section was proved because defendant interfered with cardholder's right to determine who shall have the right to use his credit card number. Harrison v. Commonwealth, 32 Va. App. 525, 529 S.E.2d 330, 2000 Va. App. LEXIS 401 (2000).

Mere proof of possession of a recently stolen credit card is insufficient to support a conviction for credit card theft. Sandoval v. Commonwealth, 20 Va. App. 133, 455 S.E.2d 730 (1995).

Business record exception. — Defendant's convictions for credit card theft in violation of § 18.2-192(1)(a) and credit card fraud were proper because the trial court did not err in admitting credit card statements under the business record exception to the hearsay rule. A financial investigator testified that in the course of doing business, the company maintained records in relation to the charges and payments on credit cards and that those records were made contemporaneously with the actions taken with regard to the credit accounts; according to the investigator, the statements were an accurate account of the credit card company's records at the time they were printed prior to trial. Trang Chau v. Commonwealth, 2011 Va. App. LEXIS 30 (Feb. 1, 2011).

Reversal of conviction of credit card theft. — Because the Commonwealth joined in the defendant's request for reversal of the conviction for credit card theft, the appellate court reversed and dismissed that count of the indictment without reaching the merits of that assignment of error. Issak v. Commonwealth, No. 1853-02-4, 2003 Va. App. LEXIS 346 (Ct. of Appeals June 17, 2003).

Inconsistent verdict. — Defendant's conviction of credit card fraud under § 18.2-195(1)(a) was reversed because it was inconsistent with his acquittal of credit card theft under § 18.2-192(a)(1), which was based on a trial court's finding in a bench trial that defndant did not withhold a company credit card with the intention of stealing it. Myatt v. Commonwealth, 2010 Va. App. LEXIS 97 (Mar. 16, 2010).

Evidence held sufficient. — Evidence was clearly sufficient to prove beyond a reasonable doubt that defendant took the victim's credit card and also took money from her friend's cash box without permission. Warren v. Commonwealth, No. 1078-01-2, 2002 Va. App. LEXIS 275 (Ct. of Appeals May 7, 2002).

Evidence supported defendant's conviction of credit card theft in violation of subdivision (1) (a) of § 18.2-192, as defendant's acts of: (1) entering the victim's jeep without knowing the victim or having the victim's permission; (2) ransacking the jeep; (3) taking the victim's credit card and money from the jeep; and (4) running away from a police officer who tried to question defendant, allowed the jury to infer that defendant stole the credit card with the intention of using, selling, or transferring it. Fisher v. Commonwealth, No. 2871-01-4 CHIEF, 2002 Va. App. LEXIS 639 (Ct. of Appeals Oct. 22, 2002).

Evidence proved that defendant retained the recently renewed credit cards after being expressly directed to cancel the account and then used the cards with the intent to use them for her personal benefit was sufficient to support convictions for embezzlement. Kingsley v. Commonwealth, No. 0587-03-2, 2004 Va. App. LEXIS 384 (Ct. of Appeals Aug. 10, 2004).

Despite defendant's claim that the Commonwealth failed to present sufficient evidence to prove that he had the requisite intent to use the credit cards at the time of the taking, his convictions on four counts of credit card theft were upheld on appeal, as: (1) the victim identified defendant as the perpetrator of the crimes; (2) some of the victim's stolen items were found in defendant's truck, including two of the four stolen credit cards; and (3) defendant's

wife was in possession of the victim's jacket, wallet, and the other two stolen credit cards. Hence, the evidence and the inferences drawn from it were sufficient to allow the jury to conclude that defendant had the requisite intent to use the stolen credit cards. Anderson v. Commonwealth, — Va. App. —, — S.E.2d —, 2007 Va. App. LEXIS 215 (May 22, 2007).

Defendant's convictions for credit card theft in violation of § 18.2-192 and credit card fraud were proper because a credit card fraud investigator testified that the phone numbers used to activate credit cards were automatically recorded electronically, absent the involvement of any credit card employee and there was credible evidence to support the findings that the record was prepared, and regularly relied upon, in the credit card company's ordinary course of business. Trang Chau v. Commonwealth, 2011 Va. App. LEXIS 30 (Feb. 1, 2011).

Venue, — Credit card theft, § 18.2-192, and credit card fraud, § 18.2-195, are different offenses; venue for prosecution of credit card theft was not established in the Circuit Court of the City of Alexandria because the crime was completed where the card was taken, which was outside of the city, regardless of the fact that defendant later used the credit card in Alexandria. Meeks v. Commonwealth, 274 Va. 798, 651 S.E.2d 637, 2007 Va. LEXIS 127 (2007).

Venue in Alexandria, Virginia, was established in defendant's trial for credit card theft and credit card fraud because defendant's fraudulent use of the stolen credit card at a hotel in Alexandria established an element of the crime, and raised a strong presumption that an act in furtherance of the crime occurred in Alexandria. Meeks v. Commonwealth, — Va. App. —, — S.E.2d —, 2006 Va. App. LEXIS 604 (May 10, 2006), rev'd, 274 Va. 798, 651 S.E.2d 637 (2007).

Venue, under § 18.2-198.1, was proper in Alexandria, Virginia because defendant committed credit card theft, in violation of subdivision (1)(a) of § 18.2-192, by unlawfully taking a credit card from its rightful owner, defendant's former employer in Alexandria, with the intent to use the card when defendant was terminated, thereby completing the crime of credit card theft in Alexandria, even though defendant committed the crime of credit card fraud, in violation of § 18.2-195, by using the card to make personal purchases in Maryland. Baldwin v. Commonwealth, 2011 Va. App. LEXIS 348 (Nov. 15, 2011).

Prosecution under this section barred. — Subsequent prosecution under this section was barred, where defendant had been convicted of petit larceny, of a "pocketbook, containing U.S. currency, credit cards and misc. items," which constituted the same conduct to be alleged and proved as essential elements in the credit card theft prosecution. Darnell v. Commonwealth, 12 Va. App. 948, 408 S.E.2d 540 (1991).

Applied in Bunn v. Commonwealth, 21 Va. App. 593, 466 S.E.2d 744 (1996).

§ 18.2-193. Credit card forgery.

(1) A person is guilty of credit card forgery when:

(a) With intent to defraud a purported issuer, a person or organization providing money, goods, services or anything else of value, or any other person, he falsely makes or falsely embosses a purported credit card or utters such a credit card; or

(b) He, not being the cardholder or a person authorized by him, with intent to defraud the issuer, or a person or organization providing money, goods, services or anything else of value, or any other person, signs a credit card; or

(c) He, not being the cardholder or a person authorized by him, with intent to defraud the issuer, or a person or organization providing money, goods, services or anything else of value, or any other person, forges a sales draft or cash advance/withdrawal draft, or uses a credit card number of a card of which he is not the cardholder, or utters, or attempts to employ as true, such forged draft knowing it to be forged.

(2) A person falsely makes a credit card when he makes or draws, in whole or in part, a device or instrument which purports to be the credit card of a named issuer but which is not such a credit card because the issuer did not authorize the making or drawing, or alters a credit card which was validly issued.

(3) A person falsely embosses a credit card when, without the authorization of the named issuer, he completes a credit card by adding any of the matter, other than the signature of the cardholder, which an issuer requires to appear on the credit card before it can be used by a cardholder. Conviction of credit card forgery shall be punishable as a Class 5 felony.

History.
Code 1950, § 18.1-125.4; 1968, c. 480; 1975, cc. 14, 15; 1980, c. 99; 1985, c. 266.

Michie's Jurisprudence.
For related discussion, see 3C M.J. Commercial Law, § 94.

CASE NOTES

Testimony did not implicate ultimate issue of fact. — None of the elements of this section were testified to by witness. Witness simply testified that the person in the videotape appeared to be the defendant. He did not testify that defendant used the victim's credit card, had the intent to defraud, or to any other element of the offense. Accordingly, witness's testimony did not implicate an ultimate issue of fact and the trial court did not err by allowing his testimony. Rogers v. Commonwealth, No. 2269-96-1 (Ct. of Appeals Oct. 7, 1997).

Handwriting expert testimony not necessary. — It was not necessary that a handwriting expert testify concerning the writing on the Food Lion receipt in order for the jury to conclude defendant forged the document. From the evidence of the Food Lion tape showing the actual transaction made with the victim's stolen credit card, the jury could conclude beyond a reasonable doubt that defendant, with the intent to defraud the victim, forged a sales draft or used the victim's credit card number, or uttered as true the forged draft, knowing it to be forged, in violation of subdivision (1)(c). Sabur v. Commonwealth, No. 0880-99-2, 2000 Va. App. LEXIS 456 (Ct. of Appeals June 20, 2000).

Evidence held sufficient. — When defendant used a credit card account access number that had been issued with another person's data, supplied by defendant who was representing himself as that person, he employed a device issued to someone else; it was not necessary for that person to be aware that an application for credit had been made in his name. Hill v. Commonwealth, No. 2030-00-1, 2002 Va. App. LEXIS 256 (Ct. of Appeals Apr. 30, 2002).

§ 18.2-194. Unauthorized possession of two or more signed credit cards or credit card numbers.

When a person, other than the cardholder or a person authorized by him, possesses two or more credit cards which are signed or two or more credit card numbers, such possession shall be prima facie evidence that said cards or credit card numbers were obtained in violation of § 18.2-192.

History.
Code 1950, § 18.1-125.5; 1968, c. 480; 1975, cc. 14, 15; 1985, c. 266; 2005, c. 157.

§ 18.2-195. Credit card fraud; conspiracy; penalties.

(1) A person is guilty of credit card fraud when, with intent to defraud any person, he:

(a) Uses for the purpose of obtaining money, goods, services or anything else of value a credit card or credit card number obtained or retained in violation of § 18.2-192 or a credit card or credit card number which he knows is expired or revoked;

(b) Obtains money, goods, services or anything else of value by representing (i) without the consent of the cardholder that he is the holder of a specified card or credit card number or (ii) that he is the holder of a card or credit card number and such card or credit card number has not in fact been issued;

(c) Obtains control over a credit card or credit card number as security for debt; or

(d) Obtains money from an issuer by use of an unmanned device of the issuer or through a person other than the issuer when he knows that such advance will exceed his available credit with the issuer and any available balances held by the issuer.

(2) A person who is authorized by an issuer to furnish money, goods, services or anything else of value upon presentation of a credit card or credit card number by the cardholder, or any agent or employee of such person, is guilty of a credit card fraud when, with intent to defraud the issuer or the cardholder, he:

(a) Furnishes money, goods, services or anything else of value upon presentation of a credit card or credit card number obtained or retained in violation of § 18.2-192, or a credit card or credit card number which he knows is expired or revoked;

(b) Fails to furnish money, goods, services or anything else of value which he represents or causes to be represented in writing or by any other means to the issuer that he has furnished; or

(c) Remits to an issuer or acquirer a record of a credit card or credit card number transaction which is in excess of the monetary amount authorized by the cardholder.

(3) Conviction of credit card fraud is punishable as a Class 1 misdemeanor if the value of all money, goods, services and other things of value furnished in violation of this section, or if the difference between the value of all money, goods, services and anything else of value actually furnished and the value represented to the issuer to have been furnished in violation of this section, does not exceed $200 in any six-month period; conviction of credit card fraud is punishable as a Class 6 felony if such value exceeds $200 in any six-month period.

(4) Any person who conspires, confederates or combines with another, (i) either within or without the Commonwealth to commit credit card fraud within the Commonwealth or (ii) within the Commonwealth to commit credit card fraud within or without the Commonwealth, is guilty of a Class 6 felony.

History.

Code 1950, § 18.1-125.6; 1968, c. 480; 1975, cc. 14, 15; 1978, c. 364; 1980, c. 99; 1981, c. 197; 1985, c. 266; 1991, c. 546.

Law Review.

For survey of Virginia criminal law for the year 1977-1978, see 64 Va. L. Rev. 1407 (1978). For survey of Virginia law on criminal law and procedure for the year 2007-2008, see 43 U. Rich. L. Rev. 149 (2008). For article, "Construction Law," see 45 U. Rich. L. Rev. 227 (2010).

CASE NOTES

Not aggravated felony for purposes of immigration proceeding. — Virginia's credit card fraud offense did not substantially correspond to a theft offense under 8 U.S.C.S. § 1101(a)(43)(G); additionally, the indictment did not show that the alien was convicted of all the elements of a theft offense under § 1101(a)(43)(G) because: (1) she was not charged with taking goods without the consent of the merchant; and (2) it was not conclusive from the indictment that she actually obtained any property from the cardholder. Therefore, she was not convicted of an aggravated felony within the meaning of 8 U.S.C.S. § 1101(a)(43), and the order for her removal pursuant to 8 U.S.C.S. § 1227(a)(2)(A)(iii) was vacated. Soliman v. Gonzales, 419 F.3d 276, 2005 U.S. App. LEXIS 17989 (4th Cir. 2005).

Venue. — Credit card theft, § 18.2-192, and credit card fraud, § 18.2-195, were different offenses; venue for prosecution of credit card theft was not established in the Circuit Court of the City of Alexandria because the crime was completed where the card was taken, which was outside of the city, regardless of the fact that defendant later used the credit card in Alexandria. Meeks v. Commonwealth, 274 Va. 798, 651 S.E.2d 637, 2007 Va. LEXIS 127 (2007).

Venue in Alexandria, Virginia, was established in defendant's trial for credit card theft and credit card fraud because defendant's fraudulent use of the stolen credit card at a hotel in Alexandria established an element of the crime, and raised a strong presumption that an act in furtherance of the crime occurred in Alexandria. Meeks v. Commonwealth, — Va. App. —, — S.E.2d —, 2006 Va. App. LEXIS 604 (May 10, 2006), rev'd, 274 Va. 798, 651 S.E.2d 637 (2007).

Defendant's possession of the male victim's credit card number was based on the fact that he had the number when he was arrested in Arlington County, and at that point, the credit card number had already been used to purchase a laptop computer in Fairfax and the crime of credit card fraud in violation of § 18.2-195 was complete. Therefore, possession of the credit card number in Arlington County subsequent to the commission of the crime could not further the crime, and the Court of Appeals' judgment sustaining the trial court's ruling that venue was proper in Arlington County under § 18.2-198.1 was erroneous and had to be set aside. Gheorghiu v. Commonwealth, 280 Va. 678, 701 S.E.2d 407, 2010 Va. LEXIS 268 (2010).

Venue, under § 18.2-198.1, was proper in Alexandria, Virginia because defendant committed credit card theft, in violation of subdivision (1)(a) of § 18.2-192, by unlawfully taking a credit card from its rightful owner, defendant's former employer in Alexandria, with the intent to use the card when defendant was terminated, thereby completing the crime of credit card theft in Alexandria, even though defendant committed the crime of credit card fraud, in violation of § 18.2-195, by using the card to make personal purchases in Maryland. Baldwin v. Commonwealth, 2011 Va. App. LEXIS 348 (Nov. 15, 2011).

Business record exception. — Defendant's convictions for credit card theft and credit card fraud were proper because the trial court did not err in admitting credit card statements under the business record exception to the hearsay rule. A financial investigator testified that in the course of doing business, the company maintained records in relation to the charges and payments on credit cards and that those records were made contemporaneously with the actions taken with regard to the credit accounts; according to the investigator, the statements were an accurate account of the credit card company's records at the time they were printed prior to trial. Trang Chau v. Commonwealth, 2011 Va. App. LEXIS 30 (Feb. 1, 2011).

Inconsistent verdict. — Defendant's conviction of credit card fraud under § 18.2-195(1)(a) was reversed because it was inconsistent with his acquittal of credit card theft under § 18.2-192(a)(1), which was based on a trial court's finding in a bench trial that defndant did not withhold a company credit card with the intention of stealing it. Myatt v. Commonwealth, 2010 Va. App. LEXIS 97 (Mar. 16, 2010).

Evidence did not support a conviction for attempted credit card fraud where, although there was evidence that the defendant knew that his unemployed companion had a credit card he was attempting to use to make substantial purchases, there was no evidence that the defendant knew that the credit card did not belong to his companion. Poindexter v. Commonwealth, No. 0457-98-2 (Ct. of Appeals Apr. 27, 1999).

Evidence supported a conviction for credit card fraud. — Where defendant told store clerk that the credit card number was his and then testified at trial that his girlfriend gave him the number, defendant would have no reason to tell clerk the credit card number was his if he had not known the status of the number. And where defendant gave clerk a false address when he filled out the warranty card for his purchase, this evidence was sufficient for the trial judge to find beyond a reasonable doubt that defendant had the requisite intent to defraud. Harrison v. Commonwealth, 32 Va. App. 525, 529 S.E.2d 330, 2000 Va. App. LEXIS 401 (2000).

When defendant used a credit card account access number that had been issued with another person's data, supplied by defendant who was representing himself as that person, he employed a device issued to or for the benefit of someone else; it was not necessary for that person to be aware that an application for credit had been made in his name. Hill v. Commonwealth, No. 2030-00-1, 2002 Va. App. LEXIS 256 (Ct. of Appeals Apr. 30, 2002).

Defendant's convictions for credit card fraud, under § 18.2-195, were affirmed because the evidence that defendant used ATM cards to make withdrawals from a bank account of his employer's company without permission and purchased personal items with the cash obtained from the withdrawals was sufficient to support the convictions. Abbett v. Commonwealth, — Va. App. —, — S.E.2d —, 2008 Va. App. LEXIS 115 (Mar. 11, 2008).

Evidence was sufficient to support a conviction for credit card fraud, although the cardholder, defendant's employer, had twice previously given defendant permission to possess and use the card, because defendant did not have permission to possess the card when he made four other separate and discrete purchases. Kovalaske v. Commonwealth, 56 Va. App. 224, 692 S.E.2d 641, 2010 Va. App. LEXIS 197 (2010).

Defendant's convictions for credit card theft and credit card fraud were proper because a credit card fraud investigator testified that the phone numbers used to activate credit cards were automatically recorded electronically, absent the involvement of any credit card employee and there was credible evidence to support the findings that the record was prepared, and regularly relied upon, in the credit card company's ordinary course of business. Trang Chau v. Commonwealth, 2011 Va. App. LEXIS 30 (Feb. 1, 2011).

Evidence did not support a conviction for credit card fraud. — Defendant's conviction for credit card fraud, in violation of § 18.2-195, was reversed because defendant had the cardholder's consent to possess the card when defendant engaged in the subject transactions, purchased personal items with the credit card; defendant worked as a subcontractor for the cardholder and was given the card for business purposes and thus, defendant lawfully held the card. Saponaro v. Commonwealth, 51 Va. App. 149, 655 S.E.2d 49, 2008 Va. App. LEXIS 11 (2008).

While defendant gave the victim's credit card to the friend in order to purchase certain items at a department store, there was no evidence that defendant used the card at a shoe store; consequently, the evidence was insufficient to establish the $200 threshold necessary to convict defendant of felony credit card fraud under subdivision 3 of § 18.2-195. Thompson v. Commonwealth, 2010 Va. App. LEXIS 392 (Oct. 5, 2010).

§ 18.2-195.1. Credit card factoring.

A. Any authorized person who presents to the issuer or acquirer for payment a credit card or credit card number transaction record of a sale which was not made by such person or his agent or employee, without the express authorization of the acquirer and with intent to defraud the issuer, acquirer or cardholder, is guilty of a Class 5 felony. If such act is done without authorization of the acquirer but without intent to defraud, he shall be guilty of a Class 1 misdemeanor.

B. Any person who, without the express authorization of the acquirer and with intent to defraud the issuer, acquirer or cardholder, employs or otherwise causes an authorized person to remit to an acquirer or issuer a credit card transaction record of sale that was not made by the authorized person is guilty of a Class 5 felony. If such act is done without the authorization of the acquirer but without intent to defraud, he shall be guilty of a Class 1 misdemeanor.

C. As used in this section, *"authorized person"* means a person authorized by the acquirer to furnish money, goods, services or anything else of value upon presentation of a credit card or credit card number by a cardholder and includes an agent or employee of a person having such authority.

History.
1991, c. 546.

§ 18.2-195.2. Fraudulent application for credit card; penalties.

A. A person shall be guilty of a Class 1 misdemeanor if he makes, causes to be made or conspires to make, directly, indirectly or through an agency, any materially false statement in writing concerning the financial condition or means or ability to pay of himself or of any other person for whom he is acting or any firm or corporation in which he is interested or for which he is acting, knowing the statement to be false and intending that it be relied upon for the purpose of procuring a credit card. However, if the statement is made in response to an unrequested written solicitation from the issuer or an agent of the issuer to apply for a credit card, he shall be guilty of a Class 4 misdemeanor.

B. A person who knows that a false statement has been made in writing concerning the financial condition or ability to pay of himself or of any person for whom he is acting or any firm or corporation in which he is interested or for which he is acting and who with intent to defraud, procures a credit card, upon the faith of such false statement, for his own benefit, or for the benefit of the person, firm or corporation in which he is interested or for which he is acting, and obtains by use of the credit card, money, property, services or any thing of value, is guilty of grand larceny if the value of whatever is obtained is $200 or more or petit larceny if the value is less than $200.

C. As used in this section, "in writing" shall include information transmitted by computer, facsimile, e-mail, Internet, or any other electronic medium, and shall not include information transmitted by any such medium by voice transmission.

History.
1991, c. 546; 2007, c. 518.

§ 18.2-196. Criminal possession of credit card forgery devices.

(1) A person is guilty of criminal possession of credit card forgery devices when:

(a) He is a person other than the cardholder and possesses two or more incomplete credit cards, with intent to complete them without the consent of the issuer; or

(b) He possesses, with knowledge of its character, machinery, plates or any other contrivance designed to reproduce instruments purporting to be credit cards of an issuer who has not consented to the preparation of such credit cards.

(2) A credit card is incomplete if part of the matter, other than the signature of the cardholder, which an issuer requires to appear on the credit card before it can be used by a cardholder, has not yet been stamped, embossed, imprinted or written upon.

Conviction of criminal possession of credit card forgery devices is punishable as a Class 6 felony.

History.
Code 1950, § 18.1-125.7; 1968, c. 480; 1975, cc. 14, 15.

§ 18.2-196.1. Unlawful use of payment card scanning devices and re-encoders; penalty.

A. Any person who with malicious intent uses a scanning device or a re-encoder on the payment card of another without the permission of the authorized payment card user is guilty of a Class 1 misdemeanor.

B. Any person who violates this section and sells or distributes such information to another is guilty of a Class 6 felony.

C. Any person who violates this section and uses such information in the commission of another crime is guilty of a Class 6 felony.

D. For the purposes of this section:

1. *"Authorized payment card user"* means any person with the authorization or permission to use any payment card to obtain, purchase, or receive goods, services, money, or anything else of value from a merchant.

2. *"Merchant"* means an owner or operator of any mercantile establishment or any agent, employee, lessee, consignee, officer, director, franchisee, or independent contractor of such owner or operator who receives from an authorized payment card user or someone he believes to be an authorized payment card user, a payment card or information from a payment card, or what he believes to be a payment card or information from a payment card, as the instrument for obtaining, purchasing or receiving goods, services, money, or anything else of value from him.

3. *"Payment card"* means a credit card, charge card, debit card, hotel key card, stored-value card,

white plastic, or any other card containing encoded information that allows an authorized payment card user to obtain, purchase, or receive goods, services, money, or anything else of value from a merchant.

4. *"Re-encoder"* means an electronic device that transfers encoded information from the magnetic strip or stripe of a payment card onto the magnetic strip or stripe of a different payment card.

5. *"Scanning device"* means a scanner, reader, or any other electronic device that is used to access, read, scan, obtain, memorize, temporarily store, or permanently store encoded information on the magnetic strip or stripe of a payment card.

History.
2005, c. 166.

§ 18.2-197. Criminally receiving goods and services fraudulently obtained.

A person is guilty of criminally receiving goods and services fraudulently obtained when he receives money, goods, services or anything else of value obtained in violation of subsection (1) of § 18.2-195 with the knowledge or belief that the same were obtained in violation of subsection (1) of § 18.2-195. Conviction of criminal receipt of goods and services fraudulently obtained is punishable as a Class 1 misdemeanor if the value of all money, goods, services and anything else of value, obtained in violation of this section, does not exceed $200 in any six-month period; conviction of criminal receipt of goods and services fraudulently obtained is punishable as a Class 6 felony if such value exceeds $200 in any six-month period.

History.
Code 1950, § 18.1-125.8; 1968, c. 480; 1975, cc. 14, 15; 1981, c. 197.

§ 18.2-198. Obtaining airline, railroad, steamship, etc., ticket at discount price.

A person who obtains at a discount price a ticket issued by an airline, railroad, steamship or other transportation company from other than an apparent agent of such company which was acquired in violation of subsection (1) of § 18.2-195 without reasonable inquiry to ascertain that the person from whom it was obtained had a legal right to possess it shall be presumed to know that such ticket was acquired under circumstances constituting a violation of subsection (1) of § 18.2-195.

History.
Code 1950, § 18.1-125.9; 1968, c. 480; 1975, cc. 14, 15.

§ 18.2-198.1. Venue.

Notwithstanding the provisions of § 19.2-244, a prosecution for a violation of this article may be had in any county or city in which (i) any act in furtherance of the crime was committed or (ii) an issuer or

acquirer, or an agent of either, sustained a financial loss as a result of the offense. A prosecution for a violation of § 18.2-192 may be had in any county or city where a credit card number is used, is attempted to be used, or is possessed with intent to violate § 18.2-193, 18.2-195, or 18.2-197.

History.
1991, c. 546; 2008, c. 797.

The 2008 amendments.
The 2008 amendment by c. 797 added the last sentence.

CASE NOTES

Venue established for credit card theft and fraud. — Credit card theft, § 18.2-192, and credit card fraud, § 18.2-195, were different offenses; venue for prosecution of credit card theft was not established in the Circuit Court of the City of Alexandria because the crime was completed where the card was taken, which was outside the city, regardless of the fact that defendant later used the credit card in Alexandria. Meeks v. Commonwealth, 274 Va. 798, 651 S.E.2d 637, 2007 Va. LEXIS 127 (2007).

Venue in Alexandria, Virginia, was established in defendant's trial for credit card theft and credit card fraud because defendant's fraudulent use of the stolen credit card at a hotel in Alexandria established an element of the crime, and raised a strong presumption that an act in furtherance of the crime occurred in Alexandria. Meeks v. Commonwealth, — Va. App. —, — S.E.2d —, 2006 Va. App. LEXIS 604 (May 10, 2006), rev'd, 274 Va. 798, 651 S.E.2d 637 (2007).

Based on the record, there was insufficient evidence to demonstrate a strong presumption that any part of obtaining, accessing or recording the female victim's identifying information with the intent to defraud occurred in Arlington County; there was no evidence showing where the laptop belonging to defendant was located when accessed, who accessed it, or who remagged the credit card numbers, specifically the female victim's number, onto the credit cards. The lack of such evidence made it impossible to sustain a strong presumption that any part of the crime of identity theft under § 18.2-186.3 occurred in Arlington County, and therefore, venue in that county was improper under § 18.2-198.1. Gheorghiu v. Commonwealth, 280 Va. 678, 701 S.E.2d 407, 2010 Va. LEXIS 268 (2010).

Defendant's convictions for credit card theft and credit card fraud were proper because the trial court did not err in finding that an act in furtherance of the credit card fraud occurred in Loudoun County and holding that venue was appropriate in that jurisdiction. Defendant told a postal inspector that she obtained the credit cards, an investigator testified that the credit car was activated from defendant's Loudoun County home, and another investigator testified that the credit card statements were sent to defendant's Loudoun County home. Trang Chau v. Commonwealth, 2011 Va. App. LEXIS 30 (Feb. 1, 2011).

Venue, under § 18.2-198.1, was proper in Alexandria, Virginia because defendant committed credit card theft, in violation of subdivision (1)(a) of § 18.2-192, by unlawfully taking a credit card from its rightful owner, defendant's former employer in Alexandria, with the intent to use the card when defendant was terminated, thereby completing the crime of credit card theft in Alexandria, even though defendant committed the crime of credit card fraud, in violation of § 18.2-195, by using the card to make personal purchases in Maryland. Baldwin v. Commonwealth, 2011 Va. App. LEXIS 348 (Nov. 15, 2011).

Venue improper. — Defendant's possession of the male victim's credit card number was based on the fact that he had the number when he was arrested in Arlington County, and at that point, the credit card number had already been used to purchase a laptop computer in Fairfax and the crime of credit card fraud in violation of § 18.2-195 was complete. Therefore, possession of the credit card number in Arlington County subsequent to the commission of the crime could not further the crime, and the Court of Appeals' judgment sustaining the trial court's ruling that venue was proper in Arlington County under § 18.2-198.1 was erroneous and had to be set aside. Gheorghiu v. Commonwealth, 280 Va. 678, 701 S.E.2d 407, 2010 Va. LEXIS 268 (2010).

§ 18.2-199. Penalties for violation of article.

Persons violating any provision of this article for which no other specific punishment is provided for shall be guilty of a Class 6 felony.

History.
Code 1950, § 18.1-125.10; 1968, c. 480; 1975, cc. 14, 15.

Michie's Jurisprudence.
For related discussion, see 2B M.J. Aviation, § 1; 8B M.J. False Pretenses and Cheats, § 4; 8B M.J. Fraud and Deceit, § 71.

ARTICLE 7.

MISCELLANEOUS FALSE AND FRAUDULENT ACTS.

§ 18.2-200. Failure to perform promise to deliver crop, etc., in return for advances.

If any person obtain from another an advance of money, merchandise or other thing, upon a promise in writing that he will send or deliver to such other person his crop or other property, and fraudulently fail or refuse to perform such promise, and also fail to make good such advance, he shall be deemed guilty of the larceny of such money, merchandise or other thing.

History.
Code 1950, § 18.1-113; 1960, c. 358; 1975, cc. 14, 15.

§ 18.2-200.1. Failure to perform promise for construction, etc., in return for advances.

If any person obtain from another an advance of money, merchandise or other thing, of value, with fraudulent intent, upon a promise to perform construction, removal, repair or improvement of any building or structure permanently annexed to real property, or any other improvements to such real property, including horticulture, nursery or forest products, and fail or refuse to perform such promise, and also fail to substantially make good such advance, he shall be deemed guilty of the larceny of such money, merchandise or other thing if he fails to return such advance within fifteen days of a request to do so sent by certified mail, return receipt requested, to his last known address or to the address listed in the contract.

History.
1980, c. 459; 1987, c. 358.

Law Review.
For article summarizing published Virginia criminal law decisions between July 1, 2002 and July 1, 2003, see 38 U. Rich. L. Rev. 87 (2003). For 2003/2004 survey of criminal law and procedure, see 39 U. Rich. L. Rev. 133 (2004). For article reviewing case law and

changes in legislation affecting Virginia construction law, see 40 U. Rich. L. Rev. 143 (2005).

Michie's Jurisprudence.
For related discussion, see 8B M.J. False Pretenses and Cheats, § 2; 12A M.J. Larceny, § 2.

CASE NOTES

Elements of offense. — This section consists of the following five elements: (1) obtaining an advance of money from another person; (2) a fraudulent intent at the time the advance is obtained; (3) a promise to perform construction or improvement involving real property; (4) a failure to perform the promise; and (5) a failure to return the advance within fifteen days of a request to do so by certified mail to the defendant's last known address or his address listed in the contract. Raymer v. Commonwealth, No. 0586-99-2, 2000 Va. App. LEXIS 265 (Ct. of Appeals Apr. 11, 2000); Baugh v. Commonwealth, No. 0348-00-2, 2001 Va. App. LEXIS 589 (Ct. of Appeals Oct. 23, 2001).

Fraud depends on circumstances. — Whether fraud actually existed will depend upon the circumstances of each case. Norman v. Commonwealth, 2 Va. App. 518, 346 S.E.2d 44 (1986).

And conduct and representations of defendant. — To determine whether or not there was fraudulent intent, the court will look to the conduct and representations of the defendant. Norman v. Commonwealth, 2 Va. App. 518, 346 S.E.2d 44 (1986).

Fraudulent intent. — A defendant's use of false statements is a significant factor that tends to prove fraudulent intent in construction fraud. Rader v. Commonwealth, 15 Va. App. 325, 423 S.E.2d 207 (1992).

Trial court did not err in admitting evidence that builder violated three building code provisions. Evidence of the violations was relevant and probative because it tended to show his state of mind in performing the contract and his intent to defraud. Rader v. Commonwealth, 15 Va. App. 325, 423 S.E.2d 207 (1992).

Construction fraud can occur despite the fact that a builder or contractor begins to perform on the contract. The relevant question is whether a builder or contractor, in accepting an advance based upon future work promised, had fraudulent intent not to perform or to perform only partially, not whether the contractor had performed work for which he was paid. Rader v. Commonwealth, 15 Va. App. 325, 423 S.E.2d 207 (1992).

The time for determining fraudulent intent is the time at which the defendant procures the advance, not at the time the parties enter into the contract. Rader v. Commonwealth, 15 Va. App. 325, 423 S.E.2d 207 (1992).

A trial judge could infer intent to defraud from the defendant's failure to do anything in furtherance of his promise to perform after he received payment and also could consider as evidence tending to prove intent to defraud, as well as from the defendant's pattern of conduct regarding the two victims, who were neighbors, and others. Raymer v. Commonwealth, No. 0586-99-2, 2000 Va. App. LEXIS 265 (Ct. of Appeals Apr. 11, 2000).

When a defendant is alleged to have failed to perform construction in return for an advance of money, whether a fraudulent intent existed at the time the advance was obtained depends upon the circumstances of the case; the defendant's conduct and representations must be examined in order to determine if a fraudulent intent existed at the time. A defendant's use of false statements is a significant factor that tends to prove fraudulent intent in construction fraud. Baugh v. Commonwealth, No. 0348-00-2, 2001 Va. App. LEXIS 589 (Ct. of Appeals Oct. 23, 2001).

In a construction fraud case under § 18.2-200.1, the evidence was insufficient to support a finding that defendant obtained an advance of funds with fraudulent intent where defendant's false representation and his failure to timely complete the project were the sole factors indicative of a fraudulent intent. While defendant's performance and progress were below expectations, the evidence showed that defendant was working, albeit leisurely, towards completing the contract. Davis v. Commonwealth, 2010 Va. App. LEXIS 287 (July 20, 2010).

Payment due at specified stage in project. — The fact that a payment is due at a specified stage in a project does not, without more, prove whether it is payment for work completed or an advance or draw for work to be done. Rader v. Commonwealth, 15

Va. App. 325, 423 S.E.2d 207 (1992).

Evidence probative of state of mind. — Investigator's testimony that he discussed with defendant, before the alleged construction fraud at issue occurred, his failure to return advances to several of his clients, was properly admitted as it was probative of defendant's state of mind and his intent to defraud the victims in the instant case. Mughrabi v. Commonwealth, 38 Va. App. 538, 567 S.E.2d 542, 2002 Va. App. LEXIS 446 (2002).

Evidence supported the jury's finding of fraudulent intent at the time contractor received an additional $400 for construction improvements job. Contractor's removal of equipment from the job site immediately after he obtained the $400, without performing any additional work, entitled the jury to infer that the intent not to do further work existed when appellant took the money. Fenlason v. Commonwealth, No. 1492-91-2 (Ct. of Appeals Jan. 12, 1993).

Promise to do something in the future is not the equivalent of "substantially making good such advance," even if the defendant had offered to repay the advance. Norman v. Commonwealth, 2 Va. App. 518, 346 S.E.2d 44 (1986).

Construction fraud can occur despite the fact that a builder begins work on contract; the relevant question is whether a builder or contractor obtained an advance based upon future work promised with a fraudulent intent not to perform or to perform only partially, not whether the contractor had performed work for which he was paid. Holsapple v. Commonwealth, 38 Va. App. 480, 566 S.E.2d 210, 2002 Va. App. LEXIS 376 (2002), aff'd on rehearing, 39 Va. App. 522, 574 S.E.2d 756 (2003).

A septic system falls within the scope of this section since it is a tangible object (a "structure") permanently annexed to real property. Boothe v. Commonwealth, 4 Va. App. 484, 358 S.E.2d 740 (1987).

Proof of actual receipt of notice of demand to return payment was not needed. Holsapple v. Commonwealth, 38 Va. App. 480, 566 S.E.2d 210, 2002 Va. App. LEXIS 376 (2002), aff'd on rehearing, 39 Va. App. 522, 574 S.E.2d 756 (2003).

Commonwealth did not have to prove that defendant received an actual notice from the victim requesting the return of funds that the victim advanced to defendant for construction that was never performed as § 18.2-200.1 only required that the victim send a request for return of the funds advanced via certified mail with a return receipt requested, and the evidence showed that the victim followed that requirement. Holsapple v. Commonwealth, 39 Va. App. 522, 574 S.E.2d 756, 2003 Va. App. LEXIS 76 (2003).

Commonwealth did not have to admit into evidence the return receipt of a request for return of money advanced to prove construction fraud under § 18.2-200.1; a request constituted sufficient notice if it was sent by certified mail, return receipt requested, without proof of actual receipt. Holsapple v. Commonwealth, 266 Va. 593, 587 S.E.2d 561, 2003 Va. App. LEXIS 96 (2003), cert. denied, 543 U.S. 826, 125 S. Ct. 164, 160 L. Ed. 2d 39 (2004).

Language of § 18.2-200.1 plainly means that a request for a return of money advanced on a construction project is sufficient notice if sent by certified mail, return receipt requested, without proof of actual receipt, unlike the notices required by the bad check law, former § 6.1-117, now codified at § 18.2-183, Virginia Tort Claims Act, § 8.01-195.1 et seq., the Virginia Habitual Offenders Act, former § 46.2-355, repealed in 1999, and the Virginia Interstate Agreement on Detainers, art. III(b), found in § 53.1-210. Holsapple v. Commonwealth, 266 Va. 593, 587 S.E.2d 561, 2003 Va. App. LEXIS 96 (2003), cert. denied, 543 U.S. 826, 125 S. Ct. 164, 160 L. Ed. 2d 39 (2004).

Producing receipts which show defendant expended more than he received. — Nothing in this section supports the argument that, so long as a defendant can produce receipts indicating that he expended more than the amount of money he received in advances, he cannot be prosecuted for fraud, even if he fraudulently obtained some advances. Jimenez v. Commonwealth, 10 Va. App. 277, 392 S.E.2d 827 (1990), reversed on other grounds, 241 Va. 244, 402 S.E.2d 678 (1991).

A letter sent to the defendant by the victim met the requirements of the statute, notwithstanding that it did not cite the statute and that it demanded amounts in addition to an amount advanced for construction work, where the letter informed the defendant that his contract was canceled and expressly requested return of the advance. Sensabaugh v. Commonwealth, No. 2811-97-3 (Ct. of Appeals Feb. 9, 1999).

The victim's letter to defendant demanding return of the entire amount paid for the construction project, instead of just the advance which had not been applied to the project, which was sent by certified mail, return receipt requested, was a sufficient demand. Baugh v. Commonwealth, No. 0348-00-2, 2001 Va. App. LEXIS 589 (Ct. of Appeals Oct. 23, 2001).

Certified letters sent to last known address. — The requirement that the victim demand return of the amount paid was satisfied where the evidence proved that the two victims sent certified letters, with return receipts requested, to the defendant and that both victims used the address that appeared on the defendant's contract with one of the victims; the fact that one of the letters was returned unclaimed and that the defendant denied receiving the other did not preclude a conviction where no evidence tended to prove that the address used by the victims was not the defendant's last known address. Raymer v. Commonwealth, No. 0586-99-2, 2000 Va. App. LEXIS 265 (Ct. of Appeals Apr. 11, 2000).

Incorrect zip code. — Where the customer used the correct street address, city, and state and an incorrect zip code on the envelope, but used the proper zip code on the certified mail card, the legally required notice of the customer's claim was in invalidated. McCary v. Commonwealth, 42 Va. App. 119, 590 S.E.2d 110, 2003 Va. App. LEXIS 700 (2003).

Phone conversation failed to satisfy notice requirement. — Demand to builder by homeowner for the return of the advances by telephone only six days prior to builder's arrest did not waive the statutory requirement of a written notice by certified mail. The notice requirement of this section was a material element of the offense charged, and the omission of the element in the jury instruction, as well as the failure to produce evidence thereof, constituted reversible error. Jimenez v. Commonwealth, 241 Va. 244, 402 S.E.2d 678 (1991).

Failure to assert error at trial court level. — Trial court held that appellant waived an assignment of error asserting that the trial court erred by not applying all of the necessary elements of § 18.2-200.1 when it found him guilty of construction fraud, because he never raised the issue in the trial court, thus, the issue was not preserved for review. Sexton v. Commonwealth, 2013 Va. App. LEXIS 119 (Apr. 16, 2013).

Prosecution was not in bad faith although motive debt collection. — Criminal prosecution for larceny was not a bad faith prosecution even where the motive was debt collection. Starr v. Virginia, 147 Bankr. 380 (Bankr. E.D. Va. 1991).

Testimony of witnesses on defendant's business relationships with them properly admitted. — Where defendant objected to the Commonwealth's evidence concerning defendant's failure to complete improvements for witnesses, and where the Commonwealth argued that the two witnesses contracted with defendant contemporaneously with defendant's dealings with the church and that the witnesses would tend to prove that defendant's acceptance of advance money and failure to complete the work were not isolated events and indicated fraudulent intent, the trial judge did not err in ruling that the evidence tended to cast light on defendant's business practices and intent when accepting advances of money. Moreover, the testimony of the two homeowners was not rendered inadmissible merely because it proved conduct that did not rise to the level of criminal conduct. Gilyard v. Commonwealth, No. 1188-92-2 (Ct. of Appeals Dec. 28, 1993).

Sufficiency of evidence. — The circumstantial evidence of the defendant's fraudulent intent at the time he contracted to install a septic system and driveway was insufficient to sustain the conviction, where the Commonwealth did not establish that the defendant made any false statements to the other party inducing him to enter into the contract, the defendant actually began working on the property shortly after the modification to the contract was signed, the defendant's father was taken ill and died during this period, and the contract did not require that any funds be put into an escrow account. Boothe v. Commonwealth, 4 Va. App. 484, 358 S.E.2d 740 (1987).

Evidence was sufficient to support a conviction where the defendant requested money for a subsequent third draw representing that the advance was needed to get the finishing materials and to pay his workers, but within a week of receiving the third draw, the defendant and his workers packed their tools and left the job without completing work. Sensabaugh v. Commonwealth, No. 2811-97-3 (Ct. of Appeals Feb. 9, 1999).

Evidence was sufficient to prove defendant's intent to defraud, despite his explanations for his delays in performing the work (inclement weather and his heart attack), as he had a pattern of demanding advances for supplies he never purchased and he falsely told the victims that he had several crews working for him, and the jury had the right to disbelieve his exculpatory testimony. Mughrabi v. Commonwealth, 38 Va. App. 538, 567 S.E.2d 542, 2002 Va. App. LEXIS 446 (2002).

Evidence was sufficient to prove beyond a reasonable doubt that defendant violated § 18.2-200.1 as defendant's conduct and representations demonstrated that defendant obtained advanced funds from the victim and the victim's brother-in-law with the fraudulent intent not to complete the construction project for which they had advanced funds and at a time when defendant knew defendant would have to report to jail within a matter of days. Holsapple v. Commonwealth, 39 Va. App. 522, 574 S.E.2d 756, 2003 Va. App. LEXIS 76 (2003); Holsapple v. Commonwealth, 266 Va. 593, 587 S.E.2d 561, 2003 Va. LEXIS 96 (2003), cert. denied, 543 U.S. 826, 125 S. Ct. 164, 160 L. Ed. 2d 39 (2004).

Evidence that defendant made promises to modular home customers that he failed to fulfill, failed to obtain a contractor's license, failed to communicate with customers, and failed to inform customers of the company's financial difficulties was sufficient to prove that defendant obtained advances from customers with the requisite fraudulent intent. McCary v. Commonwealth, 42 Va. App. 119, 590 S.E.2d 110, 2003 Va. App. LEXIS 700 (2003).

Because defendant admitted to a construction contract, admitted to the terms of its rescission, including an agreement to return the money within a week, and admitted to never returning the money, the evidence was sufficient to establish defendant's guilt of contractor fraud under § 18.2-200.1. Short v. Commonwealth, — Va. App. —, — S.E.2d —, 2005 Va. App. LEXIS 262 (July 5, 2005).

Homeowner's testimony that he gave defendant $1,500 after he reviewed defendant's written proposal to paint his house for $4,000, and that defendant did not paint the house and did not return the money for more than 30 days after he made a written demand for return of the money, was sufficient to sustain defendant's conviction for contractor fraud. Heywood v. Commonwealth, — Va. App. —, — S.E.2d —, 2006 Va. App. LEXIS 220 (May 23, 2006).

Sufficient evidence was presented in defendant's case from which the trial court could find defendant guilty of construction fraud in violation of § 18.2-200.1. The evidence showed that: (1) defendant obtained an advance of money to perform residential siding work for the homeowners; (2) that the advance was obtained after defendant made a fraudulent promise to the homeowners that defendant would perform such work; and (3) that defendant neither kept defendant's promise nor returned the advance despite the homeowners' request by certified mail that defendant do so. Pitts v. Commonwealth, — Va. App. —, — S.E.2d —, 2008 Va. App. LEXIS 85 (Feb. 19, 2008).

Evidence was not sufficient to support appellant's conviction for construction fraud, in violation of § 18.2-200.1, because although the combination of the circumstances did not excuse appellant from performing his contract, the record did not support the conclusion that he did not intend to complete the work when he accepted the advance; attempts were made, either by men who worked with appellant or by someone on appellant's behalf, to complete the work. Dyer v. Commonwealth, 2010 Va. App. LEXIS 34 (Jan. 26, 2010).

Insufficient evidence of fraudulent intent. — Conviction for construction fraud was not supported by sufficient evidence that defendant had fraudulently intended to induce homeowners to provide an advance of funds; he openly admitted that he was struggling financially, his wife was ill, and he was responsible for four children. His failure to perform the contract or return the advanced funds could have been due to poor management, financial distress or both. Phillips v. Commonwealth, — Va. App. —, — S.E.2d —, 2008 Va. App. LEXIS 46 (Jan. 29, 2008).

Evidence failed to show that defendant obtained a contract advance by promising to perform electrical work with fraudulent intent because defendant only failed to complete the contract work and there was no showing of any false statements to induce the victim to pay him the advance or other duplicitous conduct. Parrish v. Commonwealth, 2010 Va. App. LEXIS 125 (Mar. 30, 2010).

Jury instructions. — Defendant's conviction for construction fraud, in violation of § 18.2-200.1 was overturned where one of the jury instructions erroneously suggested the weight that should have been given to specific evidence and impermissibly commented upon the evidence. The trial court was not entitled to emphasize such evidence to the jury for use in its decision on whether defendant acted with fraudulent intent. Keefer v. Commonwealth, 56 Va. App. 520, 694 S.E.2d 802, 2010 Va. App. LEXIS 272 (2010).

Applied in Klink v. Commonwealth, 12 Va. App. 815, 407 S.E.2d 5 (1991); Bottoms v. Commonwealth, 281 Va. 23, 704 S.E.2d 406, 2011 Va. LEXIS 22 (2011); Smith v. Commonwealth, 59 Va. App. 710, 722 S.E.2d 310, 2012 Va. App. LEXIS 56 (2012).

§ 18.2-201. Advances secured by fraudulent promise to perform agricultural labor.

If any person enter into a contract of employment, oral or written, for the performance of personal service to be rendered within one year, in and about the cultivation of the soil, and, at any time during the pendency of such contract, thereby obtain from the landowner, or the person so engaged in the cultivation of the soil, advances of money or other thing of value under such contract, with intent to injure or defraud his employer, and fraudulently refuses or fails to perform such service or to refund such money or other thing of value so obtained, he shall be guilty of a Class 3 misdemeanor. But no prosecution hereunder shall be commenced more than sixty days after the breach of such contract.

History.
    Code 1950, § 18.1-114; 1960, c. 358; 1975, cc. 14, 15.

§§ 18.2-202, 18.2-203. Repealed by Acts 2004, c. 459.

§ 18.2-204. False statement for the purpose of defrauding industrial sick benefit company.

Any agent, physician or other person who shall knowingly or willfully make any false or fraudulent statement or representation of any material fact:

(1) In or with reference to any application for insurance in any industrial sick benefit company licensed, or which may be licensed, to do business in this Commonwealth,

(2) As to the death or disability of a policy or certificate holder in any such company,

(3) For the purpose of procuring or attempting to procure the payment of any false or fraudulent claim against any such company, or

(4) For the purpose of obtaining or attempting to obtain any money from or benefit in any such company,

shall be guilty of a Class 3 misdemeanor.

Any such person who shall willfully make a false statement of any material fact or thing in a sworn statement as to the death or disability of a policy or certificate holder in any such company for the purpose of procuring payment of a benefit named in the policy or certificate of such holder, shall be guilty of perjury, and shall be proceeded against and punished as provided by the statutes of this Commonwealth in relation to the crime of perjury.

History.
Code 1950, § 18.1-122; 1960, c. 358; 1975, cc. 14, 15.

Law Review.
For note, "Lying on the Stand Won't Cost You a Dime: Should Courts Recognize a Civil Action in Tort for Perjury," see 44 Wash. & Lee L. Rev. 1257 (1988).

Michie's Jurisprudence.
For related discussion, see 8B M.J. False Pretenses and Cheats, § 4.

§ 18.2-204.1. Fraudulent use of birth certificates, etc.; penalty.

A. Any person who obtains or possesses a fictitious birth certificate or the birth certificate of another for the purpose of establishing a false identity for himself is guilty of a Class 1 misdemeanor. Any person who manufactures, sells, or transfers a fictitious birth certificate or the birth certificate of another for the purpose of establishing a false identity for himself or for another person is guilty of a Class 6 felony.

B. Except as provided in subsection A, any person who obtains, possesses, sells, or transfers any document for the purpose of establishing a false status, occupation, membership, license or identity for himself or any other person is guilty of a Class 1 misdemeanor.

C. Any person who obtains, possesses, sells, or transfers such birth certificate or document with the intent that such certificate or document be used to purchase a firearm is guilty of a Class 6 felony.

D. The provisions of this section shall not apply to members of state, federal, county, city or town law-enforcement agencies in the performance of their duties.

E. The provisions of this section shall not preclude prosecution under any other statute.

History.
1978, c. 615; 1979, c. 479; 1981, c. 593; 2003, cc. 889, 914, 918; 2006, c. 271; 2011, c. 401.

Editor's note.
Acts 2011, c. 401, cl. 2, provides: "That the provisions of this act may result in a net increase in periods of imprisonment or commitment. Pursuant to § 30-19.1:4, the estimated amount of the necessary appropriation cannot be determined for periods of imprisonment in state adult correctional facilities; therefore, Chapter 874 of the Acts of Assembly of 2010 requires the Virginia Criminal Sentencing Commission to assign a minimum fiscal impact of $50,000. Pursuant to § 30-19.1:4, the estimated amount of the necessary appropriation is $0 for periods of commitment to the custody of the Department of Juvenile Justice."

The 2011 amendments.
The 2011 amendment by c. 401 rewrote subsections A, B and C.

§ 18.2-204.2. Manufacture, sale, etc., or possession of fictitious, facsimile or simulated official license or identification; penalty.

A. Except as provided in subsection D of § 18.2-204.1, it shall be unlawful for any person to manufacture, advertise for sale, sell or possess any fictitious, facsimile or simulated driver's license issued by any state, territory or possession of the United States, the District of Columbia, the Commonwealth of Puerto Rico or any foreign country or government; United States Armed Forces identification card; United States passport or foreign government visa; Virginia Department of Motor Vehicles special identification card; official identification issued by any other federal, state or foreign government agency; or official university or college student identification card, or in any way reproduce any identification card or facsimile thereof in such a manner that it could be mistaken for a valid license or identification of any type specified in this subsection.

B. Any person manufacturing, advertising for sale, selling or reproducing such card or facsimile thereof shall be guilty of a Class 1 misdemeanor.

C. Any person possessing any such card or facsimile thereof shall be guilty of a Class 2 misdemeanor.

D. The provisions of this section shall not preclude an election to prosecute under § 18.2-172, except to prosecute for forgery or uttering of such license or identification card or facsimile thereof as proof of age.

History.
1980, c. 281; 1989, c. 705; 1992, c. 531; 2006, cc. 445, 484; 2011, c. 401.

Editor's note.
Acts 2010, c. 401, cl. 2, provides: "That the provisions of this act may result in a net increase in periods of imprisonment or commitment. Pursuant to § 30-19.1:4, the estimated amount of the necessary appropriation cannot be determined for periods of imprisonment in state adult correctional facilities; therefore, Chapter 874 of the Acts of Assembly of 2010 requires the Virginia Criminal Sentencing Commission to assign a minimum fiscal impact of $50,000. Pursuant to § 30-19.1:4, the estimated amount of the necessary appropriation is $0 for periods of commitment to the custody of the Department of Juvenile Justice."

The 2011 amendments.
The 2011 amendment by c. 401 added the exception at the beginning in subsection A and made a related change.

Michie's Jurisprudence.
For related discussion, see 9B M.J. Identity, § 1; 9B M.J. Infants, § 81.

§ 18.2-204.3. Transfers for the sole or primary purpose of obtaining a lower unemployment tax rate; penalty.

A. Any person who transfers or attempts to transfer any trade or business to another person, where the sole or primary purpose of the transfer is to obtain a lower unemployment tax rate, is guilty of a Class 1 misdemeanor.

B. Any person who knowingly advises another person to transfer any trade or business to another person where the sole or primary purpose of the transfer is to obtain a lower unemployment tax rate, is guilty of a Class 1 misdemeanor.

C. Any person who is found guilty of more than two such actions under subsections A or B is guilty of a Class 6 felony.

D. It shall be the duty of the attorney for the Commonwealth to whom the Commission shall report, pursuant to subsection B of § 60.2-500, any violation of this section, to determine whether to proceed with prosecution.

History.
2005, cc. 47, 91.

§ 18.2-205. False pretense in obtaining registration of cattle and other animals and giving false pedigree.

Every person who by any false pretense shall obtain from any club, association, society or company for improving the breed of cattle, horses, sheep, swine or other domestic animals the registration of any animal in the herd register or other register of any such club, association, society or company, or a transfer of any such registration, and every person who shall knowingly give a false pedigree of any animal shall be guilty of a Class 3 misdemeanor.

History.
Code 1950, § 18.1-123; 1960, c. 358; 1975, cc. 14, 15.

Michie's Jurisprudence.
For related discussion, see 8B M.J. False Pretenses and Cheats, § 4.

§ 18.2-206. Procuring an animal, aircraft, vehicle or boat with intent to defraud.

If any person procure any such animal, aircraft, vehicle, boat or vessel mentioned in § 18.2-149 by fraud or by misrepresenting himself as some other person or with the intent to cheat or defraud such other person, he shall be guilty of a Class 1 misdemeanor. The failure to pay the rental for or damage to such animal, aircraft, vehicle, boat or vessel, or absconding without paying such rental or damage, shall be prima facie evidence of the intent to defraud at the time of renting or leasing such animal, aircraft, vehicle, boat or vessel.

History.
Code 1950, § 18.1-162; 1960, c. 358; 1975, cc. 14, 15.

Michie's Jurisprudence.
For related discussion, see 2B M.J. Automobiles, § 126; 12A M.J. Livery Stables, § 1.

CASE NOTES

Relationship to other law. — Crimes in which fraud was an ingredient had always been regarded as involving moral turpitude, and at a minimum, petitioner alien's conviction for violating § 18.2-206 by procuring a vehicle with intent to defraud qualified as a morally turpitudinous act. Kporlor v. Holder, 597 F.3d 222, 2010 U.S. App. LEXIS 4734 (4th Cir. 2010), cert. denied, 131 S. Ct. 503, 178 L. Ed. 2d 370, 2010 U.S. LEXIS 8464 (U.S. 2010).

§ 18.2-207. Making false entry, etc., in marriage register, etc.

If any clerk of a court, commissioner of the revenue, physician, surgeon, medical examiner or minister celebrating a marriage, or clerk or keeper of the records of any religious society, shall, in any book, register, record, certificate or copy which such person is by Title 20 (§ 20-13 et seq.) required to keep, make, or give, knowingly make any false, erroneous, or fraudulent entry, record, registration, or written statement, he shall, for every such offense, be guilty of a Class 3 misdemeanor.

History.
Code 1950, § 18.1-98; 1960, c. 358; 1975, cc. 14, 15.

Michie's Jurisprudence.
For related discussion, see 8B M.J. Falsifying accounts, § 2.

§ 18.2-208. Making false statement, etc., for marriage record, etc.

If any person, upon whose information or statement any record or registration may lawfully be made under Title 20 (§ 20-13 et seq.), knowingly give any false information, or make any false statement to be used for the purpose of making any such record or registration, he shall, for every such offense, be guilty of a Class 4 misdemeanor.

History.
Code 1950, § 18.1-99; 1960, c. 358; 1975, cc. 14, 15.

Michie's Jurisprudence.
For related discussion, see 8B M.J. Falsifying accounts, § 2.

§ 18.2-209. False publications.

Any person who knowingly and willfully states, delivers or transmits by any means whatever to any publisher, or employee of a publisher, of any newspaper, magazine, or other publication or to any owner, or employee of an owner, of any radio station, television station, news service or cable service, any false and untrue statement, knowing the same to be false or untrue, concerning any person or corporation, with intent that the same shall be published, broadcast or otherwise disseminated, shall be guilty of a Class 3 misdemeanor.

History.
Code 1950, § 18.1-407; 1960, c. 358; 1975, cc. 14, 15; 1978, c. 359.

Michie's Jurisprudence.
For related discussion, see 12A M.J. Libel and Slander, § 49; 13B M.J. Newspapers, § 6.

§ 18.2-209.1. Penalties for false certificate or failure to give bond.

A. If any clerk make a certificate as to any bond of a special commissioner appointed under Article 11 (§ 8.01-96 et seq.) of Chapter 3 of Title 8.01, knowing it to be false, he shall be guilty of a Class 3 misdemeanor, and shall, upon conviction, be removed from his office.

B. If any special commissioner appointed under Article 11 of Chapter 3 of Title 8.01 shall advertise property for sale or rent, and shall sell or rent the same before he shall have given bond as is required by § 8.01-99, he shall be guilty of a Class 3 misdemeanor.

History.
1978, c. 718.

§ 18.2-209.2. Failure of clerk to give notice of appointment of special commissioner to collect purchase money or rent.

If any clerk fail to give notice as required by § 8.01-103 of a special commissioner, he shall be guilty of a Class 4 misdemeanor.

History.
1978, c. 718.

§ 18.2-210. Stamping, etc., on newspapers, any word, etc., to cause belief it was done by publisher; circulating such newspapers.

No person, without first obtaining the consent of the publisher so to do, shall affix to, or place or insert in, or print, stamp or impress upon any newspaper or any part thereof, after the same shall have been issued for circulation by the publisher thereof, any word, figure, design, picture, emblem or advertisement with intent to cause, or which when so affixed, placed, inserted, printed, stamped or impressed may cause, the public to believe that such word, figure, design, picture, emblem or advertisement was affixed, placed, printed, inserted, stamped or impressed in and upon such newspaper by the publisher of the same as a part thereof.

No person shall knowingly circulate, distribute or sell, or cause to be circulated, distributed or sold, any newspaper upon which has been so affixed, placed, inserted, printed, stamped or impressed any word, figure, design, picture, emblem or advertisement in violation of the terms hereof.

Any person violating the provisions hereof shall be guilty of a Class 4 misdemeanor. Each violation shall constitute a separate offense.

History.
Code 1950, § 18.1-409; 1960, c. 358; 1964, c. 560; 1975, cc. 14, 15.

Michie's Jurisprudence.
For related discussion, see 13B M.J. Newspapers, § 6.

§ 18.2-211. Repealed by Acts 2004, c. 459.

§ 18.2-212. Calling or summoning ambulance or fire-fighting apparatus without just cause; maliciously activating fire alarms in public buildings; venue.

A. Any person who without just cause therefor, calls or summons, by telephone or otherwise, any ambulance, or fire-fighting apparatus, or any person who maliciously activates a manual or automatic fire alarm in any building used for public assembly or for other public use, including, but not limited to, schools, theaters, stores, office buildings, shopping centers and malls, coliseums and arenas, regardless of whether fire apparatus responds or not, shall be deemed guilty of a Class 1 misdemeanor.

B. A violation of this section may be prosecuted either in the jurisdiction from which the call or summons was made or in the jurisdiction where the call or summons was received.

History.
Code 1950, § 18.1-412; 1960, c. 358; 1975, cc. 14, 15; 1976, c. 75; 1982, c. 502.

Michie's Jurisprudence.
For related discussion, see 8B M.J. Fires, § 14.

§ 18.2-212.1. Unlawful for person not blind or incapacitated to carry white, white tipped with red or metallic cane.

It is unlawful for any person, unless totally or partially blind or otherwise incapacitated, while on any public street or highway to carry in a raised or extended position a cane or walking stick which is metallic or white in color or white tipped with red. Any person violating any provisions of this section shall be guilty of a Class 4 misdemeanor.

History.
Code 1950, §§ 46.1-238, 46.1-239; 1958, c. 541; 1964, c. 20; 1975, cc. 14, 15.

§ 18.2-213. Simulation of warrants, processes, writs and notices.

Any person who, for the purpose of collecting money, shall knowingly deliver, mail, send or otherwise use or cause to be used any paper or writing simulating or intended to simulate any warrant, process, writ, notice of execution lien or notice of motion for judgment shall be guilty of a Class 4 misdemeanor.

History.
Code 1950, § 18.1-313; 1960, c. 358; 1975, cc. 14, 15.

Law Review.
For article on model abusive debt collection statute for Virginia, see 15 Wm. & Mary L. Rev. 567 (1974).

§ 18.2-213.1. (Effective until January 1, 2014) Obtaining certification as small, women-owned, or minority-owned business, or disadvantaged business by deception; penalty.

A. Except as otherwise provided by § 18.2-498.3, a person shall be guilty of a Class 1 misdemeanor if, in the course of business, he:

1. Fraudulently obtains or retains certification as a small, women-owned, or minority-owned business or disadvantaged business;

2. Willfully makes a false statement knowing it to be untrue, whether by affidavit, report or other representation, to an official or employee of a public body for the purpose of influencing the certification or denial of certification of any business entity as a small, women-owned, or minority-owned business, or disadvantaged business;

3. Willfully obstructs or impedes any agency official or employee who is investigating the qualifications of a business entity which has requested certification as a small, women-owned, or minority-owned business, or disadvantaged business; or

4. Fraudulently obtains public moneys reserved for or allocated or available to small, women-, or minority-owned businesses or disadvantaged business.

B. For the purposes of this section, "minority-owned business," and "small business" and "women-owned business" shall have the same meaning as those terms are defined in § 2.2-1401 and "disadvantaged business" shall mean the same as that term is defined in § 2.2-2311.

History.
1987, c. 689; 1989, c. 570; 2006, cc. 831, 921; 2009, c. 869.

Section set out twice.
The section above is effective until January 1, 2014. For the version of this section effective January 1, 2014, see the following section, also numbered 18.2-213.1.

The 2009 amendments.
The 2009 amendment by c. 869 substituted "small, women-owned, or minority-owned" for "small, women- or minority-owned" wherever it appears, deleted "enterprise" following "business" at the end of subdivisions A 1 through A 4; and in subsection B, deleted "disadvantaged business enterprise" following "purposes of this section" and added the language beginning "and 'disadvantaged business' shall."

§ 18.2-213.1. (Effective January 1, 2014) Obtaining certification as small, women-owned, or minority-owned business, or disadvantaged business by deception; penalty.

A. Except as otherwise provided by § 18.2-498.3, a person shall be guilty of a Class 1 misdemeanor if, in the course of business, he:

1. Fraudulently obtains or retains certification as a small, women-owned, or minority-owned business or disadvantaged business;

2. Willfully makes a false statement knowing it to be untrue, whether by affidavit, report or other representation, to an official or employee of a public body for the purpose of influencing the certification or denial of certification of any business entity as a small, women-owned, or minority-owned business, or disadvantaged business;

3. Willfully obstructs or impedes any agency official or employee who is investigating the qualifications of a business entity which has requested certification as a small, women-owned, or minority-owned business, or disadvantaged business; or

4. Fraudulently obtains public moneys reserved for or allocated or available to small, women-owned, or minority-owned businesses or disadvantaged business.

B. For the purposes of this section, "minority-owned business," and "small business" and "women-owned business" shall have the same meaning as those terms are defined in § 2.2-1604 and "disadvantaged business" shall mean the same as that term is defined in § 2.2-2311.

History.
1987, c. 689; 1989, c. 570; 2006, cc. 831, 921; 2009, c. 869; 2013, c. 482.

Section set out twice.
The section above is effective January 1, 2014. For this section as in effect until January 1, 2014, see the preceding section, also numbered 18.2-213.1.

Editor's note.
Acts 2013, c. 482, cl. 7 provides: "That the provisions of this act shall become effective on January 1, 2014."

The 2013 amendments.
The 2013 amendment by c. 482, effective January 1, 2014, substituted "women-owned" for "women-" in subdivision A 4; and substituted "§ 2.2-1604" for "§ 2.2-1401" in subsection B.

§ 18.2-213.2. Filing false lien or encumbrance against another.

Any person who maliciously files a lien or encumbrance in a public record against the real or personal property of another knowing that such lien or encumbrance is false is guilty of a Class 5 felony. The court in its conviction order or in a separate order, shall direct the clerk of any jurisdiction in which a false lien or encumbrance has been filed to release from record such lien or encumbrance specifically described in the conviction order or separate order, including any notice or memorandum of lien. Such lien or encumbrance shall be deemed invalid and shall be treated as if it was never filed.

History.
2013, c. 454.

Editor's note.
Acts 2013, c. 454, cl. 2 provides: "That the provisions of this act may result in a net increase in periods of imprisonment or commitment. Pursuant to § 30-19.1:4, the estimated amount of the necessary appropriation cannot be determined for periods of imprisonment in state adult correctional facilities; therefore, Chapter 3 of the Acts of Assembly of 2012, Special Session I, requires the Virginia Criminal Sentencing Commission to assign a minimum fiscal impact of $50,000. Pursuant to § 30-19.1:4, the estimated amount of the necessary appropriation cannot be determined for periods of commitment to the custody of the Department of Juvenile Justice."

ARTICLE 8.

MISREPRESENTATIONS AND OTHER OFFENSES CONNECTED WITH SALES.

§ 18.2-214. Changing or removing, etc., trademarks, identification marks, etc.

Any person, firm, association or corporation who or which intentionally removes, defaces, alters, changes, destroys or obliterates in any manner or way or who causes to be removed, defaced, altered, changed, destroyed or obliterated in any manner or way any trademark, distinguishment or identification number, serial number or mark on or from any article or device, in order to secrete its identification with intent to defraud, shall be guilty of a Class 1 misdemeanor.

History.
Code 1950, § 59.1-42; 1968, c. 439; 1975, cc. 14, 15.

Cross references.
As to remedies for violations of this chapter, see § 59.1-68.2 et seq.

Law Review.
For survey of Virginia commercial law for the year 1969-1970, see 56 Va. L. Rev. 1387 (1970).

Michie's Jurisprudence.
For related discussion, see 3C M.J. Commercial Law, § 2; 8B M.J. False Pretenses and Cheats, § 4.

§ 18.2-214.1. Penalties for failure to report removal or alteration of identification or serial number on business machines.

It shall be unlawful for any person, firm, association, or corporation regularly engaged in the business of repairing, selling, renting or leasing of business machines to fail to report any business machine which such person, firm, association, or corporation knows has an altered or removed identification or serial number. The report shall be made to the appropriate law-enforcement agency for the county, city, or town where such business machine is located.

For purposes of this section, the term "business machines" includes, but is not limited to, typewriters, adding machines, check-writing machines, cash registers, calculators, addressing machines, copying, and accounting equipment, and recording equipment.

Any person, firm, association, or corporation violating the provisions of this section shall be guilty of a Class 4 misdemeanor.

History.
1981, c. 186; 1982, c. 154.

§ 18.2-215. Removal or alteration of identification numbers on household electrical appliances; possession of such appliances.

No person, firm, association or corporation, either individually or in association with one or more other persons, firms, associations or corporations shall remove, change or alter the serial number or other identification number stamped upon, cut into or attached as a permanent part of any household or electrical or electronic appliance where such number was stamped upon, cut into or attached to such appliance by the manufacturer thereof.

No person, firm, association or corporation shall knowingly have in his or its possession for the purpose of resale or keep in his possession for a period in excess of forty-eight hours without reporting such possession to the appropriate law-enforcement agency in his county, town or city a household or electrical or electronic appliance, with knowledge that the serial number or other identification number has been removed, changed or altered.

Any person, firm, association or corporation violating the provisions of this section shall be guilty of a Class 1 misdemeanor.

History.
Code 1950, § 59.1-43; 1968, c. 439; 1975, cc. 14, 15; 1976, c. 305.

§ 18.2-216. Untrue, deceptive or misleading advertising, inducements, writings or documents.

Any person, firm, corporation or association who, with intent to sell or in anywise dispose of merchandise, securities, service or anything offered by such person, firm, corporation or association, directly or indirectly, to the public for sale or distribution or with intent to increase the consumption thereof, or to induce the public in any manner to enter into any obligation relating thereto, or to acquire title thereto, or any interest therein, makes, publishes, disseminates, circulates or places before the public, or causes, directly or indirectly to be made, published, disseminated, circulated or placed before the public, in a newspaper or other publications, or in the form of a book, notice, handbill, poster, blueprint, map, bill, tag, label, circular, pamphlet or letter or in any other way, an advertisement of any sort regarding merchandise, securities, service, land, lot or anything so offered to the public, which advertisement contains any promise, assertion, representation or statement of fact which is untrue, deceptive or misleading, or uses any other method, device or practice which is fraudulent, deceptive or misleading to induce the public to enter into any obligation, shall be guilty of a Class 1 misdemeanor.

The actions prohibited in this section, shall be construed as including (i) the advertising in any manner by any person of any goods, wares or merchandise as a bankrupt stock, receiver's stock or trustee's stock, if such stock contains any goods, wares or merchandise put therein subsequent to the date of the purchase by such advertiser of such stock, and if such advertisement of any such stock fail to set forth the fact that such stock contains other goods, wares or merchandise put therein, subsequent to the date of the purchase by such advertiser of such stock in type as large as the type used in any other part of such advertisement, including the caption of the same, it shall be a violation of this section; and (ii) the use of any writing or document which appears to be, but is not in fact a negotiable check, negotiable draft or other negotiable instrument unless the writing clearly and conspicuously, in at least 14-point bold type, bears the phrase "THIS IS NOT A CHECK" printed on its face.

History.
Code 1950, § 59.1-44; 1968, c. 439; 1975, cc. 14, 15, 507; 2005, c. 150.

Editor's note.
The above section is § 59.1-44 as amended by Acts 1975, c. 507, except that "Class 1" has been inserted preceding "misdemeanor" at the end of the first sentence pursuant to Acts 1975, cc. 14 and 15. As required by Acts 1975, c. 589, cl. 2, the above text has been substituted for § 18.2-216 as enacted by Acts 1975, cc. 14 and 15.

Law Review.
For survey of Virginia commercial law for the year 1974-1975, see 61 Va. L. Rev. 1668 (1975). For survey of Virginia commercial law for the year 1978-1979, see 66 Va. L. Rev. 217 (1980). For 2003/2004 survey of real estate and land use law, see 39 U. Rich. L. Rev. 357 (2004).

Research references.
Rosden and Rosden, The Law of Advertising (Matthew Bender).

Michie's Jurisprudence.
For related discussion, see 3C M.J. Commercial Law, § 34.

CASE NOTES

This is a penal statute and must be construed strictly. Henry v. R.K. Chevrolet, Inc., 219 Va. 1011, 254 S.E.2d 66 (1979).
Section applicable to non-oral advertisement only. — In enacting this section, the legislature was addressing itself solely to non-oral advertisement. Henry v. R.K. Chevrolet, Inc., 219 Va. 1011, 254 S.E.2d 66 (1979).
The amendment to this section, adding the language "or uses any other method, device or practice which is fraudulent, deceptive or misleading to induce the public to enter into any obligation," was not intended to expand the statute to cover verbal practices. Henry v. R.K. Chevrolet, Inc., 219 Va. 1011, 254 S.E.2d 66 (1979).
Resulting damages. — District court erred in granting summary judgment to plaintiff on a false advertising claim because, while a marketing brochure satisfied the statutory requirements of a false advertisement, under § 18.2-216, because the brochure was an advertisement and it was, at a minimum, misleading or deceptive, the district court did not consider whether the brochure made plaintiff suffer loss. Persaud Cos. v. IBCS Group, Inc., 2011 U.S. App. LEXIS 8497 (4th Cir. Apr. 25, 2011).
Time limitations. — A cause of action for false advertising brought pursuant to § 59.1-68.3 and this section is subject to the limitation period prescribed in § 8.01-243 rather than the limitation period and accrual date for fraud set forth in §§ 8.01-243 (a) and 8.01-249 (1), respectively. McMillion v. Dryvit Sys., 262 Va. 463, 262 S.E.2d 463, 2001 Va. LEXIS 110 (2001).

Buyer of sellers' assets and trademark was precluded from claiming false advertising by the sellers under § 18.2-216 based on the sellers' use of the trademark in violation of the sale agreement, since the two-year limitations period for asserting the claims after the sellers began using the trademark expired, and the sellers' new line of products using the trademark within the limitations period was not shown to edge closer to the buyer in product similarity to warrant a new period of limitations. East West, LLC v. Rahman, 2012 U.S. Dist. LEXIS 78205 (E.D. Va. June 5, 2012).
Adequate allegations of false advertising. — Plaintiff car dealership's former owner's claim under § 8.01-221 against defendants, a car manufacturer and its financing division, failed to state a claim as § 8.01-221 did not create a separate private action for the alleged Racketeer Influenced and Corrupt Organizations Act claims' predicate acts, and while § 59.1-68.3 provided private actions for false advertising under §§ 18.2-216 and 18.2-217, there were no allegations on the nature of such advertising, and an executive's alleged false credentials in a resume was insufficient. Field v. GMAC LLC, 660 F. Supp. 2d 679, 2008 U.S. Dist. LEXIS 110164 (E.D. Va. 2008).
Applied in Koontz v. Jaffarian, 617 F. Supp. 1108 (E.D. Va. 1985); Maldonado v. Nutri/System, 776 F. Supp. 278 (E.D. Va. 1991); Parker-Smith v. Sto Corp., 262 Va. 432, 551 S.E.2d 615, 2001 Va. LEXIS 87 (2001).

CIRCUIT COURT OPINIONS

A criminal conviction is not a prerequisite to recovery under §§ 18.2-216 and 59.1-68.3. Virginia Beach Rehab Specialists, Inc. v. Augustine Med., Inc., 58 Va. Cir. 379, 2002 Va. Cir. LEXIS 155 (Norfolk 2002).
Action barred by statute of limitations. — Count asserting that defendants violated Virginia's False Advertising Statute, § 18.2-216, was barred by the statute of limitations of § 8.01-248 because more than two years had passed between the accrual of the cause of action and the filing of the motion for judgment. Fix v. Eakin/Youngtob Assocs., 61 Va. Cir. 604, 2002 Va. Cir. LEXIS 95 (Alexandria 2002).
Plaintiffs' claim that defendant violated § 18.2-216 was time-barred under § 8.01-248, as plaintiffs "suffered loss" not when they discovered damages allegedly caused by defendant's defective insulation product, but either when that product was chosen by the builders or installed by the subcontractor, as plaintiffs did not receive the quality product and construction contemplated by the contractual relationship with the builder and subcontractor. Lesner Pointe Condo. Ass'n v. Harbour Point Bldg. Corp., 61 Va. Cir. 609, 2002 Va. Cir. LEXIS 424 (Virginia Beach 2002).
Action not barred by statute of limitations. — Limited liability company's plea in bar to buyers' false advertising claim was overruled because the § 8.01-248 two-year statute of limitations began to run on date the home sale went to settlement rather than the contract date, and the suit was thus timely; the buyers did not suffer a loss until they purchased the home, and the purchase was not complete until settlement. Brown v. Labelle, 84 Va. Cir. 258, 2012 Va. Cir. LEXIS 23 (Fairfax County Feb. 2, 2012).
Intent to sell. — Home buyers who contracted to have a home built failed to sufficiently state a cause of action for a violation of § 18.2-216, where the home buyers failed to allege that the information concerning the home builder's expertise was published with the intent to sell or to induce the public to enter into an obligation. Weiss v. Cassidy Dev. Corp., 61 Va. Cir. 237, 2003 Va. Cir. LEXIS 22 (Fairfax County 2003).
Liablity of corporate agents. — In their suit against a corporation and its agents, as the plaintiffs did not establish that there was any other tort underlying the false advertising statute, § 18.2-216, the agents could not be held individually liable on the basis of the statutory language alone. 313 Freemason v. Freemason Assocs., 59 Va. Cir. 407, 2002 Va. Cir. LEXIS 365 (Norfolk Aug. 30, 2002).
Adequate allegation of false advertising. — Home purchasers adequately stated a cause of action against the development corporation in that the home purchasers alleged that the development corporation published information regarding its homebuilding expertise with the intent to sell or to induce the public to enter into an obligation, and, thus, development corpora-

tion's demurrer as to the home purchasers' demurrer had to be overruled. Weiss v. Cassidy Dev. Corp., 63 Va. Cir. 76, 2003 Va. Cir. LEXIS 183 (Fairfax County 2003).

By providing buyers with literature to induce them to purchase one of its modular homes, and inducing them to contract with a builder, a manufacturer created a nexus between the buyers and builder; therefore, the buyers could bring a false advertising claim against the manufacturer under §§ 18.2-216 and 18.2-217, even though it was not a party to the contract between the buyers and builder. Cash v. GWVA Corp., 74 Va. Cir. 243, 2007 Va. Cir. LEXIS 169 (Fairfax County 2007).

Allegations subject to proof at trial. — Demurrer was overruled because the allegations of the amended complaint that the clients suffered damages as a result of false advertising was subject to proof at trial. Foster v. Wintergreen Real Estate Co., 81 Va. Cir. 353, 2010 Va. Cir. LEXIS 252 (Nelson County Nov. 16, 2010).

False advertisement allegation insufficient to show statutory conspiracy. — Demurrer dismissing a statutory conspiracy claim against a real estate company and individual brokers was not reconsidered on the theory that § 18.2-216 false advertisement claims showed statutory conspiracy because (1) the claims only alleged false advertising, and (2) the company and the individual defendants were one entity. Foster v. Wintergreen Real Estate Co., 84 Va. Cir. 5, 2011 Va. Cir. LEXIS 209 (Nelson County Oct. 27, 2011).

§ 18.2-216.1. Unauthorized use of name or picture of any person; punishment.

A person, firm, or corporation that knowingly uses for advertising purposes, or for the purpose of trade, the name, portrait, or picture of any person resident in the Commonwealth, without having first obtained the written consent of such person, or if dead, of his surviving consort, or if none, his next of kin, or, if a minor, of his or her parent or guardian, as well as that of such minor, shall be deemed guilty of a misdemeanor and be fined not less than $50 nor more than $1,000.

History.
Code 1950, § 8-650; 1977, c. 624.

Cross references.
As to suit for injunction and damages for unauthorized use of the name or picture of any person, see § 8.01-40.

§ 18.2-217. Advertising merchandise, etc., for sale with intent not to sell at price or terms advertised; prima facie evidence of violation.

(a) Any person, firm, corporation or association who in any manner advertises or offers for sale to the public any merchandise, goods, commodity, service or thing with intent not to sell, or with intent not to sell at the price or upon the terms advertised or offered, shall be guilty of a Class 1 misdemeanor.

(b) In any prosecution or civil action under this section, the refusal by any person, firm, corporation or association or any employee, agent or servant thereof to sell, or the refusal to sell at the price or upon the terms advertised or offered, any merchandise, goods, commodity, service or thing advertised or offered for sale to the public, shall be prima facie evidence of a violation of this section; provided, that this subsection shall not apply when it is clearly stated in the advertisement or offer by which such

merchandise, goods, commodity, service or thing is advertised or offered for sale to the public, that the advertiser or offeror has a limited quantity or amount of such merchandise, goods, commodity, service or thing for sale, and the advertiser or offeror at the time of such advertisement or offer did in fact have at least such quantity or amount for sale.

History.
Code 1950, § 59.1-45; 1968, c. 439; 1972, c. 217; 1975, cc. 14, 15.

Research references.
Rosden and Rosden, The Law of Advertising (Matthew Bender).

CASE NOTES

Adequate allegations of false advertising. — Plaintiff car dealership's former owner's claim under § 8.01-221 against defendants, a car manufacturer and its financing division, failed to state a claim as § 8.01-221 did not create a separate private action for the alleged Racketeer Influenced and Corrupt Organizations Act claims' predicate acts, and while § 59.1-68.3 provided private actions for false advertising under §§ 18.2-216 and 18.2-217, there were no allegations on the nature of such advertising, and an executive's alleged false credentials in a resume was insufficient. Field v. GMAC LLC, 660 F. Supp. 2d 679, 2008 U.S. Dist. LEXIS 110164 (E.D. Va. 2008).

CIRCUIT COURT OPINIONS

Adequate allegation of false advertising. — By providing buyers with literature to induce them to purchase one of its modular homes, and inducing them to contract with a builder, a manufacturer created a nexus between the buyers and builder; therefore, the buyers could bring a false advertising claim against the manufacturer under §§ 18.2-216 and 18.2-217, even though it was not a party to the contract between the buyers and builder. Cash v. GWVA Corp., 74 Va. Cir. 243, 2007 Va. Cir. LEXIS 169 (Fairfax County 2007).

§ 18.2-218. Failure to indicate goods, etc., are "seconds," "irregulars," "secondhand," etc.

Any person, firm, corporation or association who in any manner knowingly advertises or offers for sale to the public any merchandise, goods, commodity or thing which is defective, blemished, secondhand or used, or which has been designated by the manufacturer thereof as "seconds," "irregulars," "imperfects," "not first class," or words of similar import without clearly and unequivocally indicating in the advertisement or offer of the merchandise, goods, commodity or thing or the articles, units or parts, thereof so advertised or offered for sale to the public is defective, blemished, secondhand or used or consists of "seconds," "irregulars," "imperfects" or "not first class," shall be guilty of a Class 1 misdemeanor.

History.
Code 1950, § 59.1-46; 1968, c. 439; 1975, cc. 14, 15.

§ 18.2-219. Repealed by Acts 1992, c. 768.

Cross references.
For present provisions relating to advertising former or comparative price of merchandise, etc., see § 59.1-207.40 et seq.

§ 18.2-220. Use of word "wholesale" or "wholesaler."

Any person, firm, corporation or association who in any manner in any advertisement or offer for sale to the public of any merchandise, goods, commodity or thing uses the words "wholesale" or "wholesaler" to represent or describe the nature of its business shall be guilty of a Class 1 misdemeanor, unless such person, firm, corporation or association is actually engaged in selling at wholesale the merchandise, goods, commodity or thing advertised or offered for sale.

History.
Code 1950, § 59.1-48; 1968, c. 439; 1975, cc. 14, 15.

§ 18.2-221. Advertising new or used automobiles or trucks.

Any person, firm, corporation or association engaged in selling new or used automobiles or trucks to the public shall be guilty of a Class 2 misdemeanor unless, in any printed advertisement or printed offer in which a price is stated, the following is included: (a) the make, year, and model of such automobile or truck; (b) if reference is made to items of optional equipment which are not included in the advertised price, the additional cost of each such items of optional equipment; and (c) if the manufacturer's suggested retail price is stated, whether such price is an F.O.B. factory or delivered price.

History.
Code 1950, § 59.1-49; 1968, c. 439; 1975, cc. 14, 15; 1985, c. 420.

§ 18.2-222. Misrepresentation as to source of merchandise; penalty.

No person, firm, corporation or association selling or offering for sale any article or merchandise, shall in any manner represent, contrary to fact, that the article was made for, or acquired directly or indirectly from, the United States government or its military or naval forces or any agency of the United States government, or that it has been disposed of by the United States government.

Any person, firm, corporation or association violating any provision of this section shall be guilty of a Class 3 misdemeanor.

History.
Code 1950, § 59.1-53; 1968, c. 439; 1975, cc. 14, 15; 1983, c. 290.

§ 18.2-223. "Going out of business" sales; permit required.

It shall be unlawful for any person to advertise, or conduct, a sale for the purpose of discontinuing a retail business, or to modify the word "sale" in any advertisement with the words "going out of business" or any other words which tend to insinuate that the retail business is to be discontinued and the

merchandise liquidated, unless such person obtains a permit to conduct such sale from the city, town or county, or from each city, town or county, wherein such sale is to be conducted.

A violation of the provisions of this section shall be punishable as a Class 1 misdemeanor.

History.
Code 1950, § 59.1-53.1; 1972, c. 399; 1975, cc. 14, 15.

Research references.
Rosden and Rosden, The Law of Advertising (Matthew Bender).

Michie's Jurisprudence.
For related discussion, see 8B M.J. Fraud and Deceit, § 2.

§ 18.2-224. "Going out of business" sales; counties, cities and towns to issue permits; inspections; application for permit; inventory required; commingling of other goods prohibited; duration; additional permits; inclusion of permit number and dates in advertisements; fee.

Every county, town and city shall issue permits to retail merchants for special sales as required by § 18.2-223 upon the application of such merchant and shall inspect the advertisement and conducting of such sale to insure that it is being advertised and conducted in conformity with the required permit.

All applications for special sale permits shall be accompanied by an inventory, including the kind and quantity of all goods which are to be offered for sale during the sale and only the goods specified in the inventory list may be advertised or sold during the sale period. Goods not included on the inventory of special sale goods shall not be commingled with or added to the special sale goods. Each county, city or town shall have the right to revoke a special sale permit upon proof that goods not appearing on the original inventory of special sale goods have been commingled with or added to the special sale goods.

Each special sale permit shall be valid for a period of no longer than sixty days, and any extension of that time shall constitute a new special sale and shall require an additional permit and inventory. A maximum of one permit beyond the initial sixty-day permit may be granted solely for the purpose of liquidating only those goods contained in the initial inventory list which remain unsold.

Any person who advertises such sale shall conspicuously include in the advertisement the permit number assigned for the sale by the city, town or county wherein the sale is to be conducted and the effective dates of the sale as authorized in the permit.

Each county, town and city is authorized to charge a fee for the issuance of special sale permits. Such fee shall not exceed sixty-five dollars for each permit.

History.
Code 1950, § 59.1-53.2; 1972, c. 399; 1975, cc. 14, 15; 1983, c. 445; 1988, c. 779; 1992, c. 562.

Michie's Jurisprudence.
For related discussion, see 8B M.J. Fraud and Deceit, § 2.

§ 18.2-225. Misrepresentations as to agricultural products.

Misrepresentation by advertising in the press or by radio or by television, or misrepresentation by letter, statement, mark representing grade, quality or condition, label or otherwise in handling, selling, offering or exposing for sale any agricultural commodities is hereby prohibited.

Any person, firm, association or corporation who shall violate any of the provisions of this section shall be guilty of a Class 3 misdemeanor.

The Director of the Division of Marketing, with the approval of the Commissioner of Agriculture and Consumer Services, may, in his discretion, cause prosecutions for violations of this section to be instituted through the attorneys for the Commonwealth, or otherwise, in counties or cities of the Commonwealth where in his opinion violations of this section are found.

History.
Code 1950, § 59.1-54; 1968, c. 439; 1975, cc. 14, 15.

§ 18.2-226. Fraud and misrepresentation in sale of liquid fuels, lubricating oils and similar products.

It shall be unlawful for any person, firm, association or corporation, to store, sell, expose for sale or offer for sale any liquid fuels, lubricating oils or other similar products, in any manner whatsoever, so as to deceive or tend to deceive the purchaser as to the nature, quality and identity of the product so sold or offered for sale.

History.
Code 1950, § 59.1-55; 1968, c. 439; 1975, cc. 14, 15.

§ 18.2-227. Same; sale from pump indicating other brand.

It shall be unlawful for any person, firm, association or corporation to store, keep, expose for sale, offer for sale or sell, from any tank or container, or from any pump or other distributing device or equipment, any other liquid fuels, lubricating oils or other similar products than those indicated by the name, trade name, symbol, sign or other distinguishing mark or device of the manufacturer or distributor, appearing upon the tank, container, pump or other distributing equipment from which the same are sold, offered for sale or distributed.

History.
Code 1950, § 59.1-56; 1968, c. 439; 1975, cc. 14, 15.

§ 18.2-228. Same; imitating indicia of other brands.

It shall be unlawful, for any person, firm, association or corporation to disguise or camouflage his or their own equipment by imitating the design, symbol or trade name of the equipment under which recognized brands of liquid fuels, lubricating oils and similar products are generally marketed.

History.
Code 1950, § 59.1-57; 1968, c. 439; 1975, cc. 14, 15.

§ 18.2-229. Same; false trade name or mixing brands.

It shall be unlawful for any person, firm, association or corporation to expose for sale, offer for sale or sell, under any trademark or trade name in general use, any liquid fuels, lubricating oils or other like products, except those manufactured or distributed by the manufacturer or distributor marketing liquid fuels, lubricating oils or other like products under such trademark or trade name, or to substitute, mix or adulterate the liquid fuels, lubricating oils or other similar products sold, offered for sale or distributed under such trademark or trade name.

History.
Code 1950, § 59.1-58; 1968, c. 439; 1975, cc. 14, 15.

§ 18.2-230. Same; assisting in violation of §§ 18.2-226 through 18.2-229.

It shall be unlawful for any person, firm, association or corporation to aid or assist any other person, firm, association or corporation in the violation of the provisions of §§ 18.2-226 through 18.2-229 by depositing or delivering into any tank, receptacle or other container any other liquid fuels, lubricating oils or like products than those intended to be stored therein and distributed therefrom, as indicated by the name of the manufacturer or distributor or the trademark or trade name of the product displayed on the container itself, or on the pump or other distributing device used in connection therewith.

History.
Code 1950, § 59.1-59; 1968, c. 439; 1975, cc. 14, 15.

§ 18.2-231. Same; label required.

There shall be firmly attached to or painted at or near the point of outlet from which lubricating oil is drawn or poured out for sale or delivery a sign or label consisting of the word or words in letters not less than one inch in height comprising the brand or trade name of such lubricating oil. But if any lubricating oil shall have no brand or trade name, the above sign or label shall consist of the words "lubricating oil, no brand."

History.
Code 1950, § 59.1-60; 1968, c. 439; 1975, cc. 14, 15.

§ 18.2-232. Same; punishment for violation of §§ 18.2-226 through 18.2-231.

Any person, firm, association or corporation or any officer, agent or employee thereof who shall violate any provision of §§ 18.2-226 through 18.2-231, shall be guilty of a Class 3 misdemeanor; and a second or any subsequent offense shall be punishable as a Class 1 misdemeanor.

History.
Code 1950, § 59.1-61; 1968, c. 439; 1975, cc. 14, 15.

§ 18.2-233. Sale of goods marked "sterling" and "sterling silver."

A person who makes or sells or offers to sell or dispose of or has in his possession with intent to sell or dispose of any article of merchandise marked, stamped or branded with the words "sterling" or "sterling silver," or encased or enclosed in any box, package, cover or wrapper, or other thing in or by which such article is packed, enclosed or otherwise prepared for sale or disposition, having thereon any engraving or printed label, stamp, imprint, mark or trademark indicating or denoting by such marking, stamping, branding, engraving or printing that such article is silver, sterling silver or solid silver, unless nine hundred and twenty-five one-thousandths part of the component parts of the metal of which such article is manufactured is pure silver, shall be guilty of a Class 2 misdemeanor.

History.
Code 1950, § 59.1-62; 1968, c. 439; 1975, cc. 14, 15.

§ 18.2-234. Sale of goods marked "coin" and "coin silver."

A person who makes or sells or offers to sell or dispose of, or has in his possession with intent to sell or dispose of, any article of merchandise marked, stamped or branded with words "coin" or "coin silver," or encased or enclosed in any box, package, cover, wrapper or other thing in or by which such article is packed, enclosed, or otherwise prepared for sale or disposition, having thereon any engraving or printed label, stamp, imprint, mark or trademark indicating or denoting by such marking, stamping, branding, engraving or printing that such article is coin or coin silver, unless nine hundred one-thousandths part of the component parts of the metal of which such article is manufactured is pure silver, shall be guilty of a Class 2 misdemeanor.

History.
Code 1950, § 59.1-63; 1968, c. 439; 1975, cc. 14, 15.

§ 18.2-235. Regulating sale of merchandise made of gold.

Any person who marks or sells or offers to sell or dispose of or has in his possession with intent to sell or dispose of any article of merchandise made of gold of a less carat of fineness than is stamped or marked on it or of a less carat of fineness than is engraved, stamped or imprinted on the tag, card, box, label, package, wrapper, cover or other thing in or by which such article is packed, enclosed or otherwise prepared for sale or disposition shall be guilty of a Class 2 misdemeanor.

History.
Code 1950, § 59.1-64; 1968, c. 439; 1975, cc. 14, 15.

§ 18.2-236. Repealed by Acts 2006, cc. 392 and 485, cl. 2, effective July 1, 2006.

Cross references.
For current provisions as to penalties for improperly labeling food as kosher and halal, see § 3.2-5124.

§ 18.2-237. Buying, etc., certain secondhand materials; intent; possession.

If any person buy or receive secondhand grate baskets, keys, bells and bell fixtures, gas fixtures, water fixtures, water pipes, gas pipes, or any part of such fixtures or pipes with intent to defraud, he shall be guilty of a Class 2 misdemeanor. Possession of any such secondhand baskets, keys, bells and bell fixtures, water fixtures, gas fixtures, water pipes, gas pipes, or any part of such fixtures or pipes if bought or received from any other person than the manufacturer thereof or his authorized agent or the owner thereof shall be prima facie evidence of such intent.

History.
Code 1950, § 59.1-66; 1968, c. 439; 1975, cc. 14, 15.

Michie's Jurisprudence.
For related discussion, see 15 M.J. Receiving Stolen Goods, § 1.

§ 18.2-238. Buying, etc., pig iron, etc., with intent to defraud; possession; evidence of intent.

If any person buy or receive pig iron or railroad, telephone, telegraph, coal mining, industrial, manufacturing or public utility iron, brass, copper, metal or any composition thereof with intent to defraud, he shall be guilty of a Class 6 felony. Possession of any pig iron or railroad, telephone, telegraph, coal mining, industrial, manufacturing or public utility iron, brass, copper, metal or any composition thereof, if bought or received from any other person than the manufacturer thereof or his authorized agent or of a regularly licensed dealer therein, shall be prima facie evidence of such intent.

History.
Code 1950, § 59.1-67; 1968, c. 439; 1975, cc. 14, 15.

Michie's Jurisprudence.
For related discussion, see 15 M.J. Receiving Stolen Goods, § 2.

CASE NOTES

Buying or receiving rather than possession in manner forbidden must be proved. — In a prosecution under this section it is incumbent on the Commonwealth to prove, as an essential element of the offense, that the articles were bought or received in the manner forbidden by this section before any presumption will arise from the possession of such articles. The presumption declared to arise from possession is of the intent and not of the fact that the articles were bought or received. Goldman v. Commonwealth, 100 Va. 865, 42 S.E. 923 (1902).

Dealer prosecuted for acts of subordinates. — A licensed junk dealer who receives recently stolen property, or who buys metal in violation of this section, may not escape just suspicion by merely showing that he was frank and concealed no fact within his personal knowledge, and that he did not personally receive the goods. If he closes his eyes to the criminal or suspicious acts of his subordinates and employees, and accepts the benefit of such services to him, while he may upon his trial secure an acquittal, he ought not to expect to escape prosecution. Virginia Ry. & Power Co. v. Klaff, 123 Va. 260, 96 S.E. 244 (1918).

§ 18.2-239. Pyramid promotional schemes; misdemeanor; definitions; contracts void.

Every person who contrives, prepares, sets up, operates, advertises or promotes any pyramid promotional scheme shall be guilty of a Class 1 misdemeanor. For the purposes of this section:

(1) *"Compensation"* means the transfer of money or anything of value.

"Compensation" does not mean payment based on sales of goods or services to persons who are not participants in the scheme and who are not purchasing in order to participate in the scheme;

(2) *"Consideration"* means the payment of cash or the purchase of goods, services, or intangible property;

(3) *"Promotes"* means inducing one or more other persons to become a participant; and

(4) *"Pyramid promotional scheme"* means any plan or operation by which a person gives consideration for the opportunity to receive compensation a majority of which is derived from the introduction of other persons into the plan or operation rather than from the sale or consumption of goods, services, or intangible property by a participant or other persons introduced into the plan or operation.

All contracts and agreements, now existing or hereafter formed, whereof the whole or any part of the consideration is given for the right to participate in pyramid promotional scheme programs, are against public policy, void and unenforceable.

Any violation of the provisions of this section shall constitute a prohibited practice under the provisions of § 59.1-200 and shall be subject to any and all of the enforcement provisions of the Virginia Consumer Protection Act (§ 59.1-196 et seq.).

History.
Code 1950, §§ 59.1-67.1, 59.1-67.2; 1970, c. 450; 1975, cc. 14, 15; 2008, cc. 791, 842.

The 2008 amendments.
The 2008 amendments by cc. 791 and 842 are identical, and deleted former subdivision (a), which read: "'Pyramid promotional scheme' means any program utilizing a pyramid or chain process by which a participant gives a valuable consideration for the opportunity to receive compensation or things of value in return for inducing other persons to become participants in the program";

redesignated former subdivisions (b) and (c) as subdivisions (1) and (3), respectively; added the first sentence of subdivision (1); substituted "means" for "shall mean" in subdivision (3); added subdivision (4); added the last paragraph; and made minor stylistic changes.

Law Review.
For survey of Virginia law on business associations for the year 1969-1970, see 56 Va. L. Rev. 1536 (1970). For survey of Virginia commercial law for the year 1969-1970, see 56 Va. L. Rev. 1387 (1970).

CASE NOTES

"Compensation." — Where the evidence showed that the predominant theme of the songs, cheers, printed materials, and tape recordings used at defendants' seminar and workshop was that a new recruit could utilize the marketing phase of the program to recoup any investment he might make in the program, and recruits were told they could earn a large profit simply by inducing others to invest and participate in the program, both in promise and in performance, the commissions were "compensation" within the intendment of subdivision (a) [now subdivision (4)] of this section. Bell v. Commonwealth, 236 Va. 298, 374 S.E.2d 13 (1988).

"Valuable consideration." — Although recruits were not required to pay defendant corporation their own money in order to acquire the opportunity to earn commissions, where they suffered a detriment in time and effort and conferred a benefit upon that corporation in the process of earning such opportunity, recruits were required to give "valuable consideration" within the meaning of subdivision (a) [now subdivision (4)] of this section. Bell v. Commonwealth, 236 Va. 298, 374 S.E.2d 13 (1988).

"Pyramid sales scheme" does not indicate requirement of compensation flowing to intermediate participants. — Neither the dictionary definition nor the statutory definition of a "pyramid sales scheme" indicates that there must be a multi-layered vertical chain of compensation flowing to intermediate participants from the efforts of their recruits. Love v. Durastill of Richmond, Inc., 242 Va. 186, 408 S.E.2d 892 (1991).

Company was a pyramid promotional scheme under this section where although a recruit was not required to pay company any of his own money in order to acquire the opportunity to earn commissions, he conferred a benefit, a valuable consideration, upon the company in the process of persuading others to make purchases. Bell v. Commonwealth, 236 Va. 298, 374 S.E.2d 13 (1988).

Water purification system company's scheme was within the language of the statutory definition of a pyramid promotional scheme because it utilized a pyramid or chain process that placed the company at the apex of a pyramid resting upon a base of distributors who had been enticed into paying the company $5,000 for the ever-decreasing opportunity to recoup their investment by recruiting other distributors. Love v. Durastill of Richmond, Inc., 242 Va. 186, 408 S.E.2d 892 (1991).

OPINIONS OF THE ATTORNEY GENERAL

Participation in "gifting program" is violation of statute. — Every person who participates in a "gifting program" by paying $2,000, with the expectation of advancing and ultimately receiving $16,000, is guilty of a Class 1 misdemeanor for operating a pyramid promotional scheme. See opinion of Attorney General to The Honorable William H. Fuller III, Commonwealth's Attorney for the City of Danville, 00-053 (8/29/00).

§ 18.2-240. Same; injunction.

Any attorney for the Commonwealth may petition a court of competent jurisdiction to enjoin the further prosecution of any pyramid promotional scheme as defined in § 18.2-239, and to appoint receivers to secure and distribute in an equitable manner any assets received by any participant as a result of such scheme, any such distribution to effect reimbursement, to the extent possible, for uncompensated payments made to become a participant in the scheme. The procedure in any such suit shall be similar to the procedure in other suits for equitable relief, except that no bond shall be required upon the granting of either a temporary or permanent injunction therein. Any person who organizes an endless chain scheme and, either directly or through an agent, promotes such scheme within the Commonwealth shall be deemed subject to the personal jurisdiction of such court of competent jurisdiction under §§ 8.01-328 through 8.01-330, and shall be liable for reasonable costs and attorneys' fees in such suit.

History.
Code 1950, § 59.1-67.3; 1970, c. 450; 1975, cc. 14, 15.

§ 18.2-241. Acceptance of promissory notes in payment for food sold at retail.

As used in this section, *"food"* includes food, groceries and beverages, for human consumption. *"Retailer"* means a person who sells food for consumption and not for resale.

It shall be unlawful for any retailer to accept, in payment for any food sold by him to a customer, a promissory note or notes for an amount in excess of twice the sales price of food delivered by him to the customer. As used in this section the word *"delivered"* means that actual physical delivery into the exclusive custody and control of the customer is made within seven days of the receipt of the note by the seller.

Any person who violates the provisions of this section shall be guilty of a Class 3 misdemeanor.

History.
Code 1950, § 59.1-68; 1968, c. 439; 1975, cc. 14, 15.

§ 18.2-242. Use of games, lotteries, etc., for promoting sale of certain products.

(a) No retail establishment in this Commonwealth shall use any game, contest, lottery or other scheme or device, whereby a person or persons may receive gifts, prizes or gratuities as determined by chance for the purpose of promoting, furthering or advertising the sale of any product or products having both a federal and state excise tax placed upon it, and the fact that no purchase is required in order to participate in such game, contest, lottery or scheme shall not exclude such game, contest, lottery or scheme from the provisions of this section.

(b) Any person violating the provision of this section shall be guilty of a Class 3 misdemeanor.

History.
Code 1950, § 59.1-68.01; 1970, c. 764; 1975, cc. 14, 15.

Law Review.
For survey of Virginia commercial law for the year 1969-1970, see 56 Va. L. Rev. 1387 (1970).

OPINIONS OF THE ATTORNEY GENERAL

The statute prohibits a cigarette manufacturer's sweepstakes promotion at a retail establishment. See opinion of Attorney General to The Honorable Thomas C. Wright, Jr., Member, House of Delegates, 02-006 (3/7/02).

§ 18.2-242.1. Certain referral transactions in connection with consumer sales or leases prohibited; effect of such transactions.

(a) For the purpose of this section, the term *"consumer sale or lease of goods or services"* means the sale or lease of goods or services which are purchased or leased by a natural person primarily for a personal, family or household purpose, and not for resale.

(b) With respect to a consumer sale or lease of goods or services, no seller or lessor shall give or offer to give a rebate or discount or otherwise pay or offer to pay value to the buyer or lessee as an inducement for the sale or lease in return for the buyer's giving to the seller or lessor the names of prospective buyers or lessees, or otherwise aiding the seller or lessor in entering into a transaction with another buyer or lessee, if the earning of the rebate, discount, or other value is contingent upon the occurrence of any sale, lease, appointment, demonstration, interview, conference, seminar, bailment, testimonial or endorsement subsequent to the time the buyer or lessee enters into the agreement of sale or lease.

(c) Agreements made in whole or in part pursuant to a referral transaction as above described shall be void and unenforceable by the seller or lessor. The buyer or lessee shall be entitled to retain the goods, services or money received pursuant to a referral transaction without obligation to make any further or future payments of any sort on the transaction total, or he shall be entitled to avoid the transaction and to recover from the seller or lessor any sums paid to the seller or lessor pursuant to the transaction.

History.
Code 1950, § 59.1-68.02; 1975, c. 3; 1976, c. 641.

The number of this section was assigned by the Virginia Code Commission, the number in the 1975 act having been 59.1-68.02.

Law Review.
For survey of Virginia commercial law for the year 1974-1975, see 61 Va. L. Rev. 1668 (1975).

§ 18.2-243. When issuer or distributor of advertisements not guilty of violation; inadvertent error.

A person, firm, corporation or association who or which, for compensation, issues or distributes any advertisement or offer, written, printed, oral or otherwise, in reliance upon the copy or information supplied him by the advertiser or offeror, shall not be deemed to have violated the provisions of this article, nor shall an inadvertent error on the part of any such person, firm, corporation or association be deemed a violation of such provisions.

History.
Code 1950, § 59.1-51; 1968, c. 439; 1975, cc. 14, 15.

Law Review.
For article, "Congressional Inquiry and the Federal Criminal Law," see 46 U. Rich. L. Rev. 457 (2012).

§ 18.2-244. Right to select clientele or customers not affected.

Nothing in this article shall be deemed to impair the right of any person, firm, corporation or association to select its clientele or customers.

History.
Code 1950, § 59.1-52; 1968, c. 439; 1975, cc. 14, 15.

§ 18.2-245. Enjoining violation of this article.

(a) Any person, firm, corporation or association who violates any one or more of the sections in this article, may be enjoined by any court of competent jurisdiction notwithstanding the existence of an adequate remedy at law. In any action under this section, it shall not be necessary that damages be alleged or proved.

(b) Actions for injunctive relief under this section may be brought by an attorney for the Commonwealth in the name of the Commonwealth of Virginia upon their own complaint or upon the complaint of any person, firm, corporation or association. The bringing of an action under this section shall not prevent the institution or continuation of criminal proceedings against the same defendant or defendants.

History.
Code 1950, § 59.1-50; 1968, c. 439; 1975, cc. 14, 15.

§ 18.2-246. Penalty in general for violations.

Unless otherwise provided, any person who shall violate any provision of any section in this article shall be guilty of a Class 1 misdemeanor.

History.
Code 1950, § 59.1-68.1; 1968, c. 439; 1975, cc. 14, 15.

Michie's Jurisprudence.
For related discussion, see 3C M.J. Commercial Law, § 2; 8B M.J. False Pretenses and Cheats, § 4.

ARTICLE 9.

VIRGINIA COMPREHENSIVE MONEY LAUNDERING ACT.

§ 18.2-246.1. Title.

This article shall be known and may be cited as the "Virginia Comprehensive Money Laundering Act."

History.
1999, c. 348.

§ 18.2-246.2. Definitions.

"*Conduct*" or "*conducts*" includes initiating, concluding, participating in, or assisting in a financial transaction.

"*Financial transaction*" means any purchase, sale, trade, loan, pledge, investment, gift, transfer, transmission, transportation, delivery, deposit, withdrawal, payment, transfer between accounts, exchange of currency, extension of credit, purchase or sale of monetary instruments, use of a safe-deposit box, or any other acquisition or disposition of monetary instruments by any means including the movement of funds by wire or other electronic means, which is knowingly designed in whole or in part to conceal or disguise the nature, location, source, ownership or control of the property involved in the transaction.

"*Monetary instruments*" means (i) coin or currency of the United States or of any other country, travelers' checks, personal checks, bank checks, cashier's checks, credit cards, debit cards, and money orders or (ii) securities or other negotiable instruments, in bearer form or otherwise.

"*Person*" includes any individual, partnership, association, corporation or joint venture.

"*Proceeds*" means property acquired or derived, directly or indirectly, from, produced through, realized through, or caused by an act or omission and includes property, real or personal, of any kind.

"*Property*" means anything of value, and includes any interest therein, including any benefit, privilege, claim or right with respect to anything of value, whether real or personal, tangible or intangible.

History.
1999, c. 348; 2003, cc. 541, 549.

§ 18.2-246.3. Money laundering; penalties.

A. It shall be unlawful for any person knowingly to conduct a financial transaction where the person knows the property involved in the transaction represents the proceeds of an activity which is punishable as a felony under the laws of the Commonwealth, another state or territory of the United States, the District of Columbia, or the United States. A violation of this section is punishable by imprisonment of not more than forty years or a fine of not more than $500,000 or by both imprisonment and a fine.

B. Any person who, for compensation, converts cash into negotiable instruments or electronic funds for another, knowing the cash is the proceeds of some form of activity which is punishable as a felony under the laws of the Commonwealth, another state or territory of the United States, the District of Columbia, or the United States, shall be guilty of a Class 1 misdemeanor. Any second or subsequent violation of this subsection shall be punishable as a Class 6 felony.

History.
1999, c. 348.

§ 18.2-246.4. Repealed by Acts 2004, c. 995.

Cross references.
For current provisions as to seizure of property used in connection with money laundering, see § 19.2-386.19.

§ 18.2-246.5. Forfeiture of business license or registration upon conviction of sale or distribution of imitation controlled substance; money laundering.

Any person, firm or corporation holding a license or registration to operate any business as required by either state or local law shall forfeit such license or registration upon conviction of a violation of (i) § 18.2-248 relating to an imitation controlled substance or (ii) § 18.2-246.3 relating to money laundering. Upon a conviction under this section the attorney for the Commonwealth shall notify any appropriate agency.

History.
1999, c. 348.

ARTICLE 10.
CIGARETTE DELIVERY SALE REQUIREMENTS.

§ 18.2-246.6. Definitions.

For purposes of this article:
"*Adult*" means a person who is at least the legal minimum purchasing age.
"*Board*" means the Virginia Alcoholic Beverage Control Board.
"*Consumer*" means an individual who is not permitted as a wholesaler pursuant to § 58.1-1011 or who is not a retailer.
"*Delivery sale*" means any sale of cigarettes to a consumer in the Commonwealth regardless of whether the seller is located in the Commonwealth where either (i) the purchaser submits the order for such sale by means of a telephonic or other method of voice transmission, the mails or any other delivery service, or the Internet or other online service; or (ii) the cigarettes are delivered by use of the mails or a delivery service. A sale of cigarettes not for personal consumption to a person who is a wholesale dealer or retail dealer, as such terms are defined in § 58.1-1000, shall not be a delivery sale. A delivery of cigarettes, not through the mail or by a common carrier, to a consumer performed by the owner, employee or other individual acting on behalf of a retailer authorized to sell such cigarettes shall not be a delivery sale.

"*Delivery service*" means any person who is engaged in the commercial delivery of letters, packages, or other containers.
"*Legal minimum purchasing age*" is the minimum age at which an individual may legally purchase cigarettes in the Commonwealth.
"*Mails*" or "*mailing*" means the shipment of cigarettes through the United States Postal Service.
"*Shipping container*" means a container in which cigarettes are shipped in connection with a delivery sale.
"*Shipping documents*" means bills of lading, airbills, or any other documents used to evidence the undertaking by a delivery service to deliver letters, packages, or other containers.

History.
2003, c. 1010; 2005, c. 839.

§ 18.2-246.7. Requirements for delivery sales.

A. No person shall make a delivery sale of cigarettes to any individual who is under the legal minimum purchase age in the Commonwealth.
B. Each person accepting a purchase order for a delivery sale shall comply with:
1. The age verification requirements set forth in § 18.2-246.8;
2. The disclosure requirements set forth in § 18.2-246.9;
3. The shipping requirements set forth in § 18.2-246.10;
4. The registration and reporting requirements set forth in § 18.2-246.11;
5. The tax collection requirements set forth in § 18.2-246.12; and
6. All other laws of the Commonwealth generally applicable to sales of cigarettes that occur entirely within the Commonwealth, including, but not limited to, those laws imposing: (i) excise taxes, (ii) sales taxes, and (iii) license and revenue-stamping requirements.

History.
2003, c. 1010.

§ 18.2-246.8. Age verification requirements.

A. No person shall mail, ship, or otherwise deliver cigarettes in connection with a delivery sale unless prior to the first delivery sale to a consumer such person:
1. Obtains from the prospective consumer a certification that includes (i) a reliable confirmation that the consumer is at least the legal minimum purchase age, and (ii) a statement signed by the prospective consumer in writing that certifies the prospective consumer's address and that the consumer is at least 18 years of age. Such statement shall also confirm (a) that the prospective consumer understands that signing another person's name to such certification is illegal, (b) that the sale of

cigarettes to individuals under the legal minimum purchase age is illegal, and (c) that the purchase of cigarettes by individuals under the legal minimum purchase age is illegal under the laws of the Commonwealth;

2. Makes a good faith effort to verify the information contained in the certification provided by the prospective consumer pursuant to subsection A against a commercially available database of valid, government-issued identification that contains the date of birth or age of the individual placing the order, or obtains a photocopy or other image of the valid, government-issued identification stating the date of birth or age of the individual placing the order;

3. Provides to the prospective consumer, via e-mail or other means, a notice that meets the requirements of § 18.2-246.9; and

4. Receives payment for the delivery sale from the prospective consumer by a credit or debit card that has been issued in such consumer's name or by a check drawn on the consumer's account.

B. Persons accepting purchase orders made via the Internet for delivery sales may request that prospective consumers provide their e-mail addresses.

History.
2003, c. 1010.

§ 18.2-246.9. Disclosure requirements.

The notice required under subdivision A 3 of § 18.2-246.8 shall include:

1. A prominent and clearly legible statement that cigarette sales to consumers below the legal minimum purchase age are illegal;

2. A prominent and clearly legible statement that consists of one of the warnings set forth in section 4(a)(1) of the Federal Cigarette Labeling and Advertising Act (15 U.S.C. § 1333(a)(1)) rotated on a quarterly basis;

3. A prominent and clearly legible statement that sales of cigarettes are restricted to those consumers who provide verifiable proof of age in accordance with § 18.2-246.8; and

4. A prominent and clearly legible statement that cigarette sales are subject to tax under § 58.1-1001, and an explanation of how such tax has been, or is to be, paid with respect to such delivery sale.

History.
2003, c. 1010.

§ 18.2-246.10. Shipping requirements.

Each person who mails, ships, or otherwise delivers cigarettes in connection with a delivery sale:

1. Shall include as part of the shipping documents a clear and conspicuous statement providing as follows: "Cigarettes: Virginia Law Prohibits Shipping to Individuals Under 18, and Requires the Payment of all Applicable Taxes";

2. Shall use a method of mailing, shipping, or delivery that obligates the delivery service or any party making delivery to require (i) the consumer placing the purchase order for the delivery sale, or an adult of legal minimum purchase age, to sign to accept delivery of the shipping container, and (ii) proof, in the form of a valid, government-issued identification bearing a photograph of the individual who signs to accept delivery of the shipping container, demonstrating that he is either the addressee who is of legal minimum purchase age or another adult of legal minimum purchase age. However, proof of the legal minimum purchase age shall be required only if such individual appears to be under 27 years of age; and

3. Shall provide to the delivery service retained for such delivery sale evidence of full compliance with § 18.2-246.12.

History.
2003, c. 1010.

§ 18.2-246.11. Registration and reporting requirements.

A. Prior to making delivery sales or mailing, shipping, or otherwise delivering cigarettes in connection with any such delivery sales, every person shall file with the Board and with the Attorney General a statement setting forth such person's name, trade name, and the address of such person's principal place of business and any other place of business.

B. Not later than the tenth day of each calendar month, each person that has made a delivery sale or mailed, shipped, or otherwise delivered cigarettes in connection with any such delivery sale during the previous calendar month shall file with the Board and with the Attorney General a report in the format prescribed by the Board, which may include an electronic format, that provides for each and every such delivery sale:

1. The name and address of the consumer to whom such delivery sale was made;

2. The brand or brands of the cigarettes that were sold in such delivery sale; and

3. The quantity of cigarettes that were sold in such delivery sale.

C. Any person who satisfies the requirements of § 376 of Title 15 of the United States Code shall be deemed to satisfy the requirements of this section.

D. For purposes of any penalty that may be imposed for a violation of this section, a failure to file a particular statement or report with both the Board and the Attorney General shall constitute a single violation.

History.
2003, c. 1010; 2009, c. 847.

The 2009 amendments.
The 2009 amendment by c. 847 added subsection D.

§ 18.2-246.12. Collection of taxes.

Each person accepting a purchase order for a delivery sale shall collect and remit to the Board all cigarette taxes imposed by the Commonwealth with respect to such delivery sale, except that such collection and remission shall not be required to the extent such person has obtained proof (in the form of the presence of applicable revenue stamps or otherwise) that such taxes already have been paid to the Commonwealth. In the event the Board finds that any tax imposed by the Commonwealth and administered by the Department of Taxation has not been collected and remitted, the Board shall provide the Department of Taxation with a notification of such sale which shall include:

1. The name and address of the consumer to whom such sale was made;

2. The name and address of the seller of the cigarettes;

3. The brand or brands of the cigarettes that were sold in such sale; and

4. The quantity of cigarettes that were sold in such sale.

History.
2003, c. 1010.

§ 18.2-246.13. Civil penalties; penalties.

A. In addition to any criminal penalties for violations of this article and except for civil penalties otherwise provided in this article, a first violation of any provision of this article shall be punishable by a civil penalty of no more than $1,000. A second or subsequent violation of any provision of this article shall be punishable by a civil penalty of no more than $10,000.

B. Any prospective consumer who knowingly submits a false certification under subdivision A 1 of § 18.2-246.8 shall be subject to a civil penalty of no more than $5,000 for each such offense.

C. Any person failing to collect or remit to the Board or the Department of Taxation any tax required in connection with a delivery sale shall be assessed, in addition to any other applicable penalty, a civil penalty of no more than five times the retail value of the cigarettes involved.

D. Any civil penalty collected under this article shall be paid to the general fund.

E. Any person who fails to file the statement required by subsection A of § 18.2-246.11 and thereafter makes a delivery sale is guilty of a Class 1 misdemeanor and for any second or subsequent offense is guilty of a violation of § 18.2-498.3.

F. Any person who knowingly and with the intent to defraud, mislead, or deceive makes a statement filed as required by subsection A of § 18.2-246.11 which is false is guilty of a violation of § 18.2-498.3. Each such filed statement containing one or more false statements shall constitute a separate offense.

G. Any person who fails to make the report required by subsection B of § 18.2-246.11 is guilty of a Class 1 misdemeanor and for any second or subsequent offense is guilty of a violation of § 18.2-498.3.

H. Any person who knowingly and with the intent to defraud, mislead, or deceive makes a materially false statement in any report required by subsection B of § 18.2-246.11 is guilty of a violation of § 18.2-498.3. Each such report containing one or more false statements constitutes a separate offense.

History.
2003, c. 1010; 2004, c. 995; 2009, c. 847; 2013, c. 625.

Editor's note.
Acts 2013, c. 625, cl. 2 provides: "That the provisions of this act may result in a net increase in periods of imprisonment or commitment. Pursuant to § 30-19.1:4, the estimated amount of the necessary appropriation cannot be determined for periods of imprisonment in state adult correctional facilities; therefore, Chapter 3 of the Acts of Assembly of 2012, Special Session I, requires the Virginia Criminal Sentencing Commission to assign a minimum fiscal impact of $50,000. Pursuant to § 30-19.1:4, the estimated amount of the necessary appropriation cannot be determined for periods of commitment to the custody of the Department of Juvenile Justice."

The 2009 amendments.
The 2009 amendment by c. 847 added subsections E through H.

The 2013 amendments.
The 2013 amendment by c. 625 substituted "In addition to any criminal penalties for violations of this article and except for civil penalties otherwise provided in this article" for "Except as specifically provided in § 18.2-246.14" in the first sentence of subsection A.

§ 18.2-246.14. Counterfeit cigarettes; penalty; civil penalty.

A. It is unlawful to distribute or possess counterfeit cigarettes.

B. Any person who knowingly distributes or possesses with the intent to distribute a total quantity of less than 10 cartons of counterfeit cigarettes is guilty of a Class 1 misdemeanor. Any person who is convicted of a second or subsequent offense involving a total quantity of less than 10 cartons of counterfeit cigarettes is guilty of a Class 6 felony, provided that the accused was at liberty as defined in § 53.1-151 between each conviction, and it is admitted, or found by the jury or judge before whom the person is tried, that the accused was previously convicted of a violation of this subsection. Any person who knowingly distributes or possesses with the intent to distribute a total quantity of 10 or more cartons of counterfeit cigarettes is guilty of a Class 6 felony.

C. Any person who knowingly violates subsection A with a total quantity of less than two cartons of cigarettes shall be punished by a civil penalty of no more than $1,000. Any person who knowingly violates subsection A shall, for a second or subsequent offense involving a total quantity of less than two cartons of cigarettes, be punished by a civil penalty of no more than $5,000 and, if applicable, the revocation by the Department of Taxation of his wholesale dealer license.

D. Any person who knowingly violates subsection A with a total quantity of two or more cartons of cigarettes shall be punished by a civil penalty of no more than $2,000. Any person who knowingly violates subsection A shall, for a second or subsequent offense involving a total quantity of two or more cartons of cigarettes, be punished by a civil penalty of no more than $50,000 and, if applicable, the revocation by the Department of Taxation of his wholesale dealer license.

For purposes of this section, counterfeit cigarettes shall include but not be limited to cigarettes that (i) have false manufacturing labels, (ii) are not manufactured by the manufacturer indicated on the container, or (iii) have affixed to the container a false tax stamp.

History.
2003, c. 1010; 2004, c. 995; 2013, c. 625.

Editor's note.
Acts 2013, c. 625, cl. 2 provides: "That the provisions of this act may result in a net increase in periods of imprisonment or commitment. Pursuant to § 30-19.1:4, the estimated amount of the necessary appropriation cannot be determined for periods of imprisonment in state adult correctional facilities; therefore, Chapter 3 of the Acts of Assembly of 2012, Special Session I, requires the Virginia Criminal Sentencing Commission to assign a minimum fiscal impact of $50,000. Pursuant to § 30-19.1:4, the estimated amount of the necessary appropriation cannot be determined for periods of commitment to the custody of the Department of Juvenile Justice."

The 2013 amendments.
The 2013 amendment by c. 625 substituted "is unlawful to distribute" for "shall be unlawful to sell" in subsection A; inserted subsection B and redesignated the remaining subsections accordingly.

§ 18.2-246.15. Enforcement.

The Attorney General is authorized to enforce the provisions of this article. The Attorney General may assess the civil penalties authorized by this article, with the concurrence of the attorney for the Commonwealth pursuant to § 2.2-511, may prosecute criminal violations under this article, and may bring an action in the appropriate court to collect assessed penalties or prevent or restrain violations of this article by any person, or any person controlling such person. The Board and the State Department of Taxation shall cooperate with the Attorney General in his enforcement efforts and provide to the Attorney General all information and documentation in their possession necessary for the Attorney General to accomplish such enforcement.

History.
2003, c. 1010; 2009, c. 847; 2013, c. 625.

Editor's note.
Acts 2013, c. 625, cl. 2 provides: "That the provisions of this act may result in a net increase in periods of imprisonment or commitment. Pursuant to § 30-19.1:4, the estimated amount of the necessary appropriation cannot be determined for periods of imprison-

ment in state adult correctional facilities; therefore, Chapter 3 of the Acts of Assembly of 2012, Special Session I, requires the Virginia Criminal Sentencing Commission to assign a minimum fiscal impact of $50,000. Pursuant to § 30-19.1:4, the estimated amount of the necessary appropriation cannot be determined for periods of commitment to the custody of the Department of Juvenile Justice."

The 2009 amendments.
The 2009 amendment by c. 847, in the second sentence, inserted "assess the civil penalties ... under § 18.2-246.13, and may" and substituted "to collect assessed penalties or" for "in the Commonwealth to" and added the last sentence.

The 2013 amendments.
The 2013 amendment by c. 625 substituted "this article" for "§ 18.2-246.13" in the second sentence.

CHAPTER 7.

CRIMES INVOLVING HEALTH AND SAFETY.

Article 1. Drugs.

ARTICLE 1.

DRUGS.

Michie's Jurisprudence.

For related discussion, see 6B M.J. Drugs and Druggists, §§ 2, 5.

§ 18.2-247. Use of terms "controlled substances," "marijuana," "Schedules I, II, III, IV, V and VI," "imitation controlled substance" and "counterfeit controlled substance" in Title 18.2.

A. Wherever the terms *"controlled substances"* and *"Schedules I, II, III, IV, V and VI"* are used in Title 18.2, such terms refer to those terms as they are used or defined in the Drug Control Act (§ 54.1-3400 et seq.).

B. The term *"imitation controlled substance"* when used in this article means (i) a counterfeit controlled substance or (ii) a pill, capsule, tablet, or substance in any form whatsoever which is not a controlled substance subject to abuse, and:

1. Which by overall dosage unit appearance, including color, shape, size, marking and packaging or by representations made, would cause the likelihood that such a pill, capsule, tablet, or substance in any other form whatsoever will be mistaken for a controlled substance unless such substance was introduced into commerce prior to the initial introduction into commerce of the controlled substance which it is alleged to imitate; or

2. Which by express or implied representations purports to act like a controlled substance as a stimulant or depressant of the central nervous system and which is not commonly used or recognized for use in that particular formulation for any purpose other than for such stimulant or depressant effect, unless marketed, promoted, or sold as permitted by the United States Food and Drug Administration.

C. In determining whether a pill, capsule, tablet, or substance in any other form whatsoever, is an "imitation controlled substance," there shall be considered, in addition to all other relevant factors, comparisons with accepted methods of marketing for legitimate nonprescription drugs for medicinal purposes rather than for drug abuse or any similar nonmedicinal use, including consideration of the packaging of the drug and its appearance in overall finished dosage form, promotional materials or representations, oral or written, concerning the drug, and the methods of distribution of the drug and where and how it is sold to the public.

D. The term *"marijuana"* when used in this article means any part of a plant of the genus Cannabis, whether growing or not, its seeds or resin; and every compound, manufacture, salt, derivative, mixture, or preparation of such plant, its seeds, or its resin. Marijuana shall not include any oily extract containing one or more cannabinoids unless such extract contains less than 12 percent of tetrahydrocannabinol by weight, or the mature stalks of such plant, fiber produced from such stalk, oil or cake made from the seed of such plant, unless such stalks, fiber, oil or cake is combined with other parts of plants of the genus Cannabis.

E. The term *"counterfeit controlled substance"* means a controlled substance that, without authorization, bears, is packaged in a container or wrapper that bears, or is otherwise labeled to bear, the trademark, trade name, or other identifying mark, imprint or device or any likeness thereof, of a drug manufacturer, processor, packer, or distributor other than the manufacturer, processor, packer, or distributor who did in fact so manufacture, process, pack or distribute such drug.

History.

1975, cc. 14, 15; 1979, c. 435; 1982, c. 462; 1984, c. 684; 1992, c. 756; 1999, cc. 661, 722; 2004, c. 688.

Cross references.

For Drug Dealer Liability Act, allowing parent or legal custodian to bring an action for damages incurred because of child's unlawful use of a controlled substance while under the age of 18, see § 8.01-227.4 et seq. As to presumption of no bail for illegal aliens charged with certain crimes, see § 19.2-120.1. As to report of conviction of school employees convicted under Article 1 (§ 18.2-247 et seq.) of Chapter 7 of Title 18.2, see § 19.2-291.1. As to expulsion of students for certain drug offenses, see § 22.1-277.08. For definition of "barrier crime" as including a conviction of any felony violation relating to possession or distribution of drugs as set out in § 18.2-247 et seq., or an equivalent offense in another state, and prohibition against child welfare agencies and foster and adoptive homes approved by child-placing agencies hiring for certain compensated employment persons who have committed such an offense, see §§ 63.2-1719, 63.2-1720. As to report to children's residential facility for which a background check is being performed on whether the applicant has ever been convicted of or is the subject of pending charges for various crimes, including possession or distribution of drugs as set out in § 18.2-247 et seq., or an equivalent offense in another state, see § 63.2-1726.

Law Review.

For survey of Virginia criminal law for the year 1977-1978, see 64 Va. L. Rev. 1407 (1978).

Research references.

David Bernheim, Defense of Narcotics Cases (Matthew Bender).

CASE NOTES

Meaning of "subject to abuse." — An imitation controlled substance, as defined by subsection B, must be one which has a disposition or tendency to be misused. Rhodes v. Commonwealth, 12 Va. App. 473, 404 S.E.2d 522 (1991).

Effect of 1992 amendment. — The 1992 amendment to subsection B of this section removed the comma and the words "which is" preceding the words "subject to abuse." This amendment effectively deleted the entire subordinate clause. By deleting the comma and the subordinate clause, the legislature significantly changed not only the sentence's structure, but also its meaning. The legislature thereby substantively changed the definition of the statutory offense. Werres v. Commonwealth, 19 Va. App. 744, 454 S.E.2d 36 (1995).

By eliminating the subordinate clause and by leaving in its stead the phrase, "subject to abuse," so that the phrase now modifies a different clause, "which is not a controlled substance," the legislature eliminated the requirement that the imitation substance be one that is itself subject to abuse. Thus, the change effectively broadened the definition of an imitation controlled substance to include any pill, capsule, tablet, or substance in any form whatsoever that by express or implied representation is intended or appears to imitate a controlled substance, but which is not a "controlled substance subject to abuse." Werres v. Commonwealth, 19 Va. App. 744, 454 S.E.2d 36 (1995).

Following the 1992 amendment, subsection B of this section does not require that the Commonwealth prove the identity of the imitation controlled substance. Werres v. Commonwealth, 19 Va. App. 744, 454 S.E.2d 36 (1995).

Inference of distribution permitted. — By its nature, an imitation controlled substance has little or no use other than its commercial value in being misrepresented and sold as a controlled substance. A finder of fact may infer from evidence of a recent sale of a controlled substance, related by time and place to a similar substance still in the seller's possession, that the seller intended to distribute the substance he or she still possessed. Werres v. Commonwealth, 19 Va. App. 744, 454 S.E.2d 36 (1995).

Evidence insufficient to establish substance had disposition to being misused. — Where no evidence was introduced as to the nature of the substance which the defendant sold, and where it could have been sugar, flour, or some inert substance with no particular propensity for misuse, the evidence was insufficient to establish that the substance had a disposition or tendency to being misused; therefore, the Commonwealth failed to prove that the defendant distributed an imitation controlled substance as defined by subsection B. Rhodes v. Commonwealth, 12 Va. App. 473, 404 S.E.2d 522 (1991).

§ 18.2-248. Manufacturing, selling, giving, distributing, or possessing with intent to manufacture, sell, give, or distribute a controlled substance or an imitation controlled substance prohibited; penalties.

A. Except as authorized in the Drug Control Act (§ 54.1-3400 et seq.), it shall be unlawful for any person to manufacture, sell, give, distribute, or possess with intent to manufacture, sell, give or distribute a controlled substance or an imitation controlled substance.

B. In determining whether any person intends to manufacture, sell, give or distribute an imitation controlled substance, the court may consider, in addition to all other relevant evidence, whether any distribution or attempted distribution of such pill, capsule, tablet or substance in any other form whatsoever included an exchange of or a demand for money or other property as consideration, and, if so, whether the amount of such consideration was substantially greater than the reasonable value of such pill, capsule, tablet or substance in any other form whatsoever, considering the actual chemical composition of such pill, capsule, tablet or substance in any other form whatsoever and, where applicable, the price at which over-the-counter substances of like chemical composition sell.

C. Except as provided in subsection C1, any person who violates this section with respect to a controlled substance classified in Schedule I or II shall upon conviction be imprisoned for not less than five nor more than 40 years and fined not more than $500,000. Upon a second conviction of such a violation, and it is alleged in the warrant, indictment, or information that the person has been before convicted of such an offense or of a substantially similar offense in any other jurisdiction, which offense would be a felony if committed in the Commonwealth, and such prior conviction occurred before the date of the offense alleged in the warrant, indictment, or information, any such person may, in the discretion of the court or jury imposing the sentence, be sentenced to imprisonment for life or for any period not less than five years, three years of which shall be a mandatory minimum term of imprisonment to be served consecutively with any other sentence, and he shall be fined not more than $500,000.

When a person is convicted of a third or subsequent offense under this subsection and it is alleged in the warrant, indictment or information that he has been before convicted of two or more such offenses or of substantially similar offenses in any other jurisdiction which offenses would be felonies if committed in the Commonwealth and such prior convictions occurred before the date of the offense alleged in the warrant, indictment, or information, he shall be sentenced to imprisonment for life or for a period of not less than 10 years, 10 years of which shall be a mandatory minimum term of imprisonment to be served consecutively with any other sentence, and he shall be fined not more than $500,000.

Any person who manufactures, sells, gives, distributes or possesses with the intent to manufacture, sell, give, or distribute the following is guilty of a felony punishable by a fine of not more than $1 million and imprisonment for five years to life, five years of which shall be a mandatory minimum term of imprisonment to be served consecutively with any other sentence:

1. 100 grams or more of a mixture or substance containing a detectable amount of heroin;

2. 500 grams or more of a mixture or substance containing a detectable amount of:

a. Coca leaves, except coca leaves and extracts of coca leaves from which cocaine, ecgonine, and derivatives of ecgonine or their salts have been removed;

b. Cocaine, its salts, optical and geometric isomers, and salts of isomers;

c. Ecgonine, its derivatives, their salts, isomers, and salts of isomers; or

d. Any compound, mixture, or preparation that contains any quantity of any of the substances referred to in subdivisions 2a through 2c;

3. 250 grams or more of a mixture or substance described in subdivisions 2a through 2d that contain cocaine base; or

4. 10 grams or more of methamphetamine, its salts, isomers, or salts of its isomers or 20 grams or more of a mixture or substance containing a detectable amount of methamphetamine, its salts, isomers, or salts of its isomers.

The mandatory minimum term of imprisonment to be imposed for a violation of this subsection shall not be applicable if the court finds that:

a. The person does not have a prior conviction for an offense listed in subsection C of § 17.1-805;

b. The person did not use violence or credible threats of violence or possess a firearm or other dangerous weapon in connection with the offense or induce another participant in the offense to do so;

c. The offense did not result in death or serious bodily injury to any person;

d. The person was not an organizer, leader, manager, or supervisor of others in the offense, and was not engaged in a continuing criminal enterprise as defined in subsection I; and

e. Not later than the time of the sentencing hearing, the person has truthfully provided to the Commonwealth all information and evidence the person has concerning the offense or offenses that were part of the same course of conduct or of a common scheme or plan, but the fact that the person has no relevant or useful other information to provide or that the Commonwealth already is aware of the information shall not preclude a determination by the court that the defendant has complied with this requirement.

C1. Any person who violates this section with respect to the manufacturing of methamphetamine, its salts, isomers, or salts of its isomers or less than 200 grams of a mixture or substance containing a detectable amount of methamphetamine, its salts, isomers, or salts of its isomers shall, upon conviction, be imprisoned for not less than 10 nor more than 40 years and fined not more than $500,000. Upon a second conviction of such a violation, any such person may, in the discretion of the court or jury imposing the sentence, be sentenced to imprisonment for life or for any period not less than 10 years, and be fined not more than $500,000. When a person is convicted of a third or subsequent offense under this subsection and it is alleged in the warrant, indictment, or information that he has been previously convicted of two or more such offenses or of substantially similar offenses in any other jurisdiction, which offenses would be felonies if committed in the Commonwealth and such prior convictions occurred before the date of the offense alleged in the warrant, indictment, or information, he shall be sentenced to imprisonment for life or for a period not less than 10 years, three years of which shall be a mandatory minimum term of imprisonment to be served consecutively with any other sentence and he shall be fined not more than $500,000. Upon conviction, in addition to any other punishment, a person found guilty of this offense shall be ordered by the court to make restitution, as the court deems appropriate, to any innocent property owner whose property is damaged, destroyed, or otherwise rendered unusable as a result of such methamphetamine production. This restitution shall include the person's or his estate's estimated or actual expenses associated with cleanup, removal, or repair of the affected property. If the property that is damaged, destroyed, or otherwise rendered unusable as a result of such methamphetamine production is property owned in whole or in part by the person convicted, the court shall order the person to pay to the Methamphetamine Cleanup Fund authorized in § 18.2-248.04 the reasonable estimated or actual expenses associated with cleanup, removal, or repair of the affected property or, if actual or estimated expenses cannot be determined, the sum of $10,000.

D. If such person proves that he gave, distributed or possessed with intent to give or distribute a controlled substance classified in Schedule I or II only as an accommodation to another individual who is not an inmate in a community correctional facility, local correctional facility or state correctional facility as defined in § 53.1-1 or in the custody of an employee thereof, and not with intent to profit thereby from any consideration received or expected nor to induce the recipient or intended recipient of the controlled substance to use or become addicted to or dependent upon such controlled substance, he shall be guilty of a Class 5 felony.

E. If the violation of the provisions of this article consists of the filling by a pharmacist of the prescription of a person authorized under this article to issue the same, which prescription has not been received in writing by the pharmacist prior to the filling thereof, and such written prescription is in fact received by the pharmacist within one week of the time of filling the same, or if such violation consists of a request by such authorized person for the filling by a pharmacist of a prescription which has not been received in writing by the pharmacist and such prescription is, in fact, written at the time of such request and delivered to the pharmacist within one week thereof, either such offense shall constitute a Class 4 misdemeanor.

E1. Any person who violates this section with respect to a controlled substance classified in Schedule III except for an anabolic steroid classified in Schedule III, constituting a violation of § 18.2-248.5, shall be guilty of a Class 5 felony.

E2. Any person who violates this section with respect to a controlled substance classified in Schedule IV shall be guilty of a Class 6 felony.

E3. Any person who proves that he gave, distributed or possessed with the intent to give or distribute a controlled substance classified in Schedule III or IV, except for an anabolic steroid classified in Schedule III, constituting a violation of § 18.2-248.5, only as an accommodation to another individual who is not an inmate in a community correctional facility, local correctional facility or state correctional facility as defined in § 53.1-1 or in the custody of an employee thereof, and not with the intent to profit thereby from any consideration received or expected nor to induce the recipient or intended recipient of the controlled substance to use or become addicted to or dependent upon such controlled substance, is guilty of a Class 1 misdemeanor.

F. Any person who violates this section with respect to a controlled substance classified in Schedule V or Schedule VI or an imitation controlled substance which imitates a controlled substance classified in Schedule V or Schedule VI, shall be guilty of a Class 1 misdemeanor.

G. Any person who violates this section with respect to an imitation controlled substance which imitates a controlled substance classified in Schedule I, II, III, or IV shall be guilty of a Class 6 felony. In any prosecution brought under this subsection, it is not a defense to a violation of this subsection that the defendant believed the imitation controlled substance to actually be a controlled substance.

H. Any person who manufactures, sells, gives, distributes or possesses with the intent to manufacture, sell, give or distribute the following:

1. 1.0 kilograms or more of a mixture or substance containing a detectable amount of heroin;

2. 5.0 kilograms or more of a mixture or substance containing a detectable amount of:

a. Coca leaves, except coca leaves and extracts of coca leaves from which cocaine, ecgonine, and derivatives of ecgonine or their salts have been removed;

b. Cocaine, its salts, optical and geometric isomers, and salts of isomers;

c. Ecgonine, its derivatives, their salts, isomers, and salts of isomers; or

d. Any compound, mixture, or preparation which contains any quantity of any of the substances referred to in subdivisions a through c;

3. 2.5 kilograms or more of a mixture or substance described in subdivision 2 which contains cocaine base;

4. 100 kilograms or more of a mixture or substance containing a detectable amount of marijuana; or

5. 100 grams or more of methamphetamine, its salts, isomers, or salts of its isomers or 200 grams or more of a mixture or substance containing a detectable amount of methamphetamine, its salts, isomers, or salts of its isomers shall be guilty of a felony punishable by a fine of not more than $1 million and imprisonment for 20 years to life, 20 years of which shall be a mandatory minimum sentence. Such mandatory minimum sentence shall not be applicable if the court finds that (i) the person does not have a prior conviction for an offense listed in subsection C of § 17.1-805; (ii) the person did not use violence or credible threats of violence or possess a firearm or other dangerous weapon in connection with the offense or induce another participant in the offense to do so; (iii) the offense did not result in death or serious bodily injury to any person; (iv) the person was not an organizer, leader, manager, or supervisor of others in the offense, and was not engaged in a continuing criminal enterprise as defined in subsection I of this section; and (v) not later than the time of the sentencing hearing, the person has truthfully provided to the Commonwealth all information and evidence the person has concerning the offense or offenses that were part of the same course of conduct or of a common scheme or plan, but the fact that the person has no relevant or useful other information to provide or that the Commonwealth already is aware of the information shall not preclude a determination by the court that the defendant has complied with this requirement.

H1. Any person who was the principal or one of several principal administrators, organizers or leaders of a continuing criminal enterprise shall be guilty of a felony if (i) the enterprise received at least $100,000 but less than $250,000 in gross receipts during any 12-month period of its existence from the manufacture, importation, or distribution of heroin or cocaine or ecgonine or methamphetamine or the derivatives, salts, isomers, or salts of isomers thereof or marijuana or (ii) the person engaged in the enterprise to manufacture, sell, give, distribute or possess with the intent to manufacture, sell, give or distribute the following during any 12-month period of its existence:

1. At least 1.0 kilograms but less than 5.0 kilograms of a mixture or substance containing a detectable amount of heroin;

2. At least 5.0 kilograms but less than 10 kilograms of a mixture or substance containing a detectable amount of:

a. Coca leaves, except coca leaves and extracts of coca leaves from which cocaine, ecgonine, and derivatives of ecgonine or their salts have been removed;

b. Cocaine, its salts, optical and geometric isomers, and salts of isomers;

c. Ecgonine, its derivatives, their salts, isomers, and salts of isomers; or

d. Any compound, mixture, or preparation which contains any quantity of any of the substances referred to in subdivisions a through c;

3. At least 2.5 kilograms but less than 5.0 kilograms of a mixture or substance described in subdivision 2 which contains cocaine base;

4. At least 100 kilograms but less than 250 kilograms of a mixture or substance containing a detectable amount of marijuana; or

5. At least 100 grams but less than 250 grams of methamphetamine, its salts, isomers, or salts of its isomers or at least 200 grams but less than 1.0 kilograms of a mixture or substance containing a detectable amount of methamphetamine, its salts, isomers, or salts of its isomers.

A conviction under this section shall be punishable by a fine of not more than $1 million and imprisonment for 20 years to life, 20 years of which shall be a mandatory minimum sentence.

H2. Any person who was the principal or one of several principal administrators, organizers or leaders of a continuing criminal enterprise if (i) the enterprise received $250,000 or more in gross receipts during any 12-month period of its existence from the manufacture, importation, or distribution of heroin or cocaine or ecgonine or methamphetamine or the derivatives, salts, isomers, or salts of isomers thereof or marijuana or (ii) the person engaged in the enterprise to manufacture, sell, give, distribute or possess with the intent to manufacture, sell, give or distribute the following during any 12-month period of its existence:

1. At least 5.0 kilograms of a mixture or substance containing a detectable amount of heroin;

2. At least 10 kilograms of a mixture or substance containing a detectable amount of:

a. Coca leaves, except coca leaves and extracts of coca leaves from which cocaine, ecgonine, and derivatives of ecgonine or their salts have been removed;

b. Cocaine, its salts, optical and geometric isomers, and salts of isomers;

c. Ecgonine, its derivatives, their salts, isomers, and salts of isomers; or

d. Any compound, mixture, or preparation which contains any quantity of any of the substances referred to in subdivisions a through c;

3. At least 5.0 kilograms of a mixture or substance described in subdivision 2 which contains cocaine base;

4. At least 250 kilograms of a mixture or substance containing a detectable amount of marijuana; or

5. At least 250 grams of methamphetamine, its salts, isomers, or salts of its isomers or at least 1.0 kilograms of a mixture or substance containing a detectable amount of methamphetamine, its salts, isomers, or salts of its isomers shall be guilty of a felony punishable by a fine of not more than $1 million and imprisonment for life, which shall be served with no suspension in whole or in part. Such punishment shall be made to run consecutively with any other sentence. However, the court may impose a mandatory minimum sentence of 40 years if the court finds that the defendant substantially cooperated with law-enforcement authorities.

I. For purposes of this section, a person is engaged in a continuing criminal enterprise if (i) he violates any provision of this section, the punishment for which is a felony and either (ii) such violation is a part of a continuing series of violations of this section which are undertaken by such person in concert with five or more other persons with respect to whom such person occupies a position of organizer, a supervisory position, or any other position of management, and from which such person obtains substantial income or resources or (iii) such violation is committed, with respect to methamphetamine or other controlled substance classified in Schedule I or II, for the benefit of, at the direction of, or in association with any criminal street gang as defined in § 18.2-46.1.

J. Except as authorized in the Drug Control Act (§ 54.1-3400 et seq.), any person who possesses any two or more different substances listed below with the intent to manufacture methamphetamine, methcathinone, or amphetamine is guilty of a Class 6 felony: liquified ammonia gas, ammonium nitrate, ether, hypophosphorus acid solutions, hypophosphite salts, hydrochloric acid, iodine crystals or tincture of iodine, phenylacetone, phenylacetic acid, red phosphorus, methylamine, methyl formamide, lithium, sodium metal, sulfuric acid, sodium hydroxide, potassium dichromate, sodium dichromate, potassium permanganate, chromium trioxide, methylbenzene, methamphetamine precursor drugs, trichloroethane, or 2-propanone.

K. The term "methamphetamine precursor drug," when used in this article, means a drug or product containing ephedrine, pseudoephedrine, or phenylpropanolamine or any of their salts, optical isomers, or salts of optical isomers.

History.
Code 1950, § 54-524.101:1; 1972, c. 798; 1973, c. 479; 1974, c. 586; 1975, cc. 14, 15; 1976, c. 614; 1977, c. 409; 1978, cc. 177, 779; 1979, c. 435; 1982, cc. 276, 462; 1985, c. 569; 1986, c. 453; 1988, c. 355; 1990, c. 82; 1991, c. 13; 1992, cc. 685, 737, 756; 1995, c. 538; 1999, c. 722; 2000, cc. 1020, 1041; 2004, c. 461; 2005, cc. 174, 759, 796, 923, 941; 2006, cc. 697, 759; 2008, cc. 79, 618; 2009, c. 750; 2012, cc. 219, 710, 844; 2013, c. 426.

Cross references.
As to reimbursement for methamphetamine lab cleanup costs, see § 15.2-1716.2. As to accommodation possession or distributin, see § 18.2-248.1. For penalty for possession of a controlled substance classified in Schedule VI, see § 18.2-250.

Editor's note.
Acts 2009, c. 750, cl. 2, provides: "That the provisions of this act shall not become effective unless an appropriation effectuating the purposes of this act is included in the general appropriation act passed by the 2009 Regular Session of the General Assembly that becomes law; however no appropriation shall be necessary if the corrections impact cannot be determined."
Acts 2009, c. 750, cl. 3, provides: "That the provisions of this act may result in a net increase in periods of imprisonment or commitment. Pursuant to § 30-19.1:4, the estimated amount of the necessary appropriation cannot be determined for periods of imprisonment in state adult correctional facilities and is $0 for periods of commitment to the custody of the Department of Juvenile Justice."
Acts 2012, cc. 710 and 844, cl. 2 provides: "That the provisions of this act may result in a net increase in periods of imprisonment or commitment. Pursuant to § 30-19.1:4, the estimated amount of the necessary appropriation is $5,512,531 for periods of imprisonment in state adult correctional facilities and is $0 for periods of commitment to the custody of the Department of Juvenile Justice."
Acts 2013, c. 426, cl. 2 provides: "That the provisions of this act may result in a net increase in periods of imprisonment or commitment. Pursuant to § 30-19.1:4, the estimated amount of the necessary appropriation is $0 for periods of imprisonment in state adult correctional facilities and is $0 for periods of commitment to the custody of the Department of Juvenile Justice."

The 2008 amendments.
The 2008 amendments by cc. 79 and 618 are identical, and inserted "or Schedule VI" twice in subsection F; and inserted a comma following "III" in subsection G.

The 2009 amendments.
The 2009 amendment by c. 750, in subsection C, in the second sentence of the first paragraph, deleted "or subsequent" preceding "conviction of such a violation" and inserted "and it is alleged in the warrant, indictment, or information that the person has been before convicted of such an offense or of a substantially similar offense in any other jurisdiction, which offense would be a felony is committed in the Commonwealth, and such prior conviction occurred before the date of the offense alleged in the warrant, indictment, or information." See Editor's notes.

The 2012 amendments.
The 2012 amendment by c. 219, in subsection C1, substituted "shall include" for "may include" in the next-to-last sentence and added the last sentence.
The 2012 amendments by cc. 710 and 844 are identical, and in subsection C, substituted "five years, three years of which shall be a mandatory minimum term of imprisonment to be served consecutively with any other sentence, and he shall be fined not more than $500,000" for "five years, and be fined not more than $500,000" at the end of first paragraph, and substituted "10 years" for "five years" twice in the second paragraph.

The 2013 amendments.
The 2013 amendment by c. 426, in subsection J, inserted "ammonium nitrate" and deleted "metal" following "lithium."

Law Review.

Robbs v. Commonwealth, 211 Va. 153, 176 S.E.2d 429 (1970), dealing with possession of narcotic drugs and cited under repealed § 54-524.55 was commented on in 5 U. Rich. L. Rev. 430 (1971). For survey of Virginia statutory changes in substantive criminal law for the year 1970-1971, see 57 Va. L. Rev. 1467 (1971). For survey of Virginia criminal law for the year 1971-1972, see 58 Va. L. Rev. 1206 (1972); for the year 1972-1973, see 59 Va. L. Rev. 1458 (1973); for the year 1975-1976, see 62 Va. L. Rev. 1400 (1976); for the year 1977-1978, see 64 Va. L. Rev. 1407 (1978); for the year 1978-1979, see 66 Va. L. Rev. 241 (1980). For note, "Criminal Procedure and Criminal Law: Virginia Supreme Court Decisions During the 70's," see 15 U. Rich. L. Rev. 585 (1981). For 2006 survey article, "Criminal Law and Procedure," see 41 U. Rich. L. Rev. 83 (2006).

CASE NOTES

I. General Consideration.
II. Elements.
　A. Possession.
　B. Distribution.
III. Evidence.
　A. Search and Seizure.
　B. Admission of Evidence.
　C. Sufficiency of Evidence.
　　1. Evidence of possession.
　　2. Evidence of distribution.
　　3. Evidence of conspiracy.

I. GENERAL CONSIDERATION.

Constitutionality. — See Wood v. Commonwealth, 213 Va. 363, 192 S.E.2d 762 (1972).

This section and former § 54-524.101 compared. — The same criminal sanctions which were imposed by former § 54-524.101 were generally retained in this section. The General Assembly provided, however, for a reduced penalty in certain cases. Wood v. Commonwealth, 214 Va. 97, 197 S.E.2d 200 (1973).

The legislative intent implicit in the statute is that the General Assembly established two clearly defined gradations of controlled drug distribution offenses. Gardner v. Commonwealth, 217 Va. 5, 225 S.E.2d 354 (1976) (decided under former § 54-524.101:1).

This section is intended to curtail the sale of illicit drugs as a commercial enterprise. Bentley v. Cox, 508 F. Supp. 870 (E.D. Va. 1981).

Strict construction. — Because statute is penal in nature, it must be strictly construed, and any ambiguity or reasonable doubt as to its meaning must be resolved in defendant's favor. Mason v. Commonwealth, 16 Va. App. 260, 430 S.E.2d 543 (1993).

Relationship with the federal Armed Career Criminal Act. — Defendant contended that during sentencing the district court erred when it designated him an armed career criminal; however, a defendant convicted of violating 18 U.S.C.S. § 922(g)(1) qualified as an armed career criminal under 18 U.S.C.S. § 924(e) if he had three prior convictions for a serious drug offense and in 1983, defendant had three separate Virginia convictions for distribution of cocaine under § 18.2-248 — each of those convictions carried a maximum penalty of forty years' imprisonment, satisfying the statutory requirement under 18 U.S.C.S. § 924(e). Although defendant claimed the drug offenses should not have been considered due to their age, there was no temporal restriction on prior felonies for the purposes of the Armed Career Criminal Act. United States v. Boysaw, — F.3d —, 2006 U.S. App. LEXIS 22687 (4th Cir. Sept. 6, 2006).

This section creates only a single offense, that being the unlawful manufacture, sale, transfer or distribution, or possession of certain controlled drugs. Stillwell v. Commonwealth, 219 Va. 214, 247 S.E.2d 360 (1978), decided prior to 1979 amendment.

Subsection A "creates only a single offense . . . the illegal transfer of controlled drugs." Rush v. Commonwealth, No. 2058-94-2 (Ct. of Appeals Mar. 26, 1996).

Trial court erred in denying defendant's motion to consolidate or dismiss indictments charging him with three counts of possession with the intent to distribute a Schedule II controlled substance,

oxycodone, because the Commonwealth failed to provide evidence that defendant possessed different demonstrated intents sufficient to support three separate charges of possession with the intent to distribute oxycodone. Lane v. Commonwealth, 51 Va. App. 565, 659 S.E.2d 553, 2008 Va. App. LEXIS 185 (2008).

Duplicitous indictments requires election of offense, not dismissal. — An indictment that tracks the language of subsection A charges a single offense that can be committed by several means. Even if the indictments were duplicitous, the appropriate remedy for a duplicitous indictment is to "force the government to elect the offense upon which it will proceed, . . . not require the dismissal of the indictment." Rush v. Commonwealth, No. 2058-94-2 (Ct. of Appeals Mar. 26, 1996).

Two separate offenses. — Defendant was not prosecuted twice for the same offense of distribution of cocaine in violation of § 18.2-248 because all parties were aware at all stages of the proceedings that there were two transactions that occurred on the same date, in different locations, at different times, involving different drugs, which in turn led to separate certificates of analysis. Because defendant's second trial involved separate acts, the *Blockburger* test was inapplicable. Lappegard v. Commonwealth, 2009 Va. App. LEXIS 379 (Aug. 25, 2009).

Trial court did not err in refusing to merge the indictments for distribution of cocaine and distribution of heroin, because the record proved that defendant made two separate and distinct sales of different drugs on the same day. Gay v. Commonwealth, 2010 Va. App. LEXIS 467 (Nov. 30, 2010).

Felony-murder based on underlying drug distribution. — Evidence was insufficient to sustain defendant's felony-murder conviction under § 18.2-33 where: (1) the underlying offense was the sale of ecstasy in violation of § 18.2-248; (2) the place element for felony-murder was missing because defendant sold the ecstasy to the victim in a store parking lot, and the drug transaction was completed; (3) the victim ingested the ecstasy over two hours after the drug buy, after she went to dinner, stopped at a gas station for cigarettes, and went to a friend's apartment; and (4) the place element for felony-murder was missing because the underlying felony took place in the store parking lot, and the victim did not ingest the ecstasy until she was at the apartment. Woodard v. Commonwealth, 61 Va. App. 567, 739 S.E.2d 220, 2013 Va. App. LEXIS 96 (Mar. 6, 2013).

Evidence of other crimes is properly received if it is relevant and probative of an issue on trial, such as an element of the offense charged or the required predicate for enhanced punishment; conviction of a prior like offense is an element of the charge as set forth in this indictment, and is also a necessary predicate to an enhanced penalty pursuant to this section. Berry v. Commonwealth, 22 Va. App. 209, 468 S.E.2d 685 (1996).

Forty years of good behavior not excessive punishment. — Sentence for violation of this section to a term of nine years in the penitentiary, of which four-and-one-half years were suspended conditioned on appellant's good behavior for 40 years, did not constitute excessive and unreasonable punishment. Worsham v. Commonwealth, No. 1944-93-2 (Ct. of Appeals March 14, 1995).

Life sentence not cruel and unusual punishment. — Sentence of life imprisonment for being the principal, or a principal administrator, organizer, or leader, of a continuing criminal enterprise engaged, during a one-year period, in the distribution of at least five kilograms of a mixture containing cocaine base, in violation of subsection H2 of § 18.2-248, did not amount to cruel or unusual punishment under the Virginia Constitution or U.S. Const., Amend. VIII. Dunaway v. Commonwealth, 52 Va. App. 281, 663 S.E.2d 117, 2008 Va. App. LEXIS 326 (2008).

And accommodation provisions relate only to punishment. — The provisions of subsection A, dealing with the reduced penalty contingent upon proof of an accommodation gift, distribution or possession operates only to mitigate the degree of criminality or punishment, rather than to create two different substantive offenses. Stillwell v. Commonwealth, 219 Va. 214, 247 S.E.2d 360 (1978), decided prior to 1979 amendment.

The clear intent of the legislature is to enhance punishment by proving that there has been a second conviction, or if more than a "second," then such "subsequent" convictions as there have been. Dotson v. Commonwealth, 18 Va. App. 465, 445 S.E.2d 492 (1994).

Defendant doesn't have to be convicted of first offense before committing second for enhancement. — This statute does not require that, in order for the enhanced penalty provision to obtain, the defendant must have been convicted of a first offense before committing the second offense. Able v. Commonwealth, 16 Va. App. 542, 431 S.E.2d 337 (1993).

There is no requirement in this section that the indictment must state that the offense charged is a second or subsequent offense to which the enhanced penalty provision may apply. Patterson v. Commonwealth, 17 Va. App. 644, 440 S.E.2d 412 (1994).

Amendment of indictment increasing amount of cocaine was permissible. — Amendment to an indictment, charging defendant with being the principal, or a principal administrator, organizer, or leader of a continuing criminal enterprise engaged, during a one-year period, in the distribution of at least five kilograms of a mixture containing cocaine base, which served only to change punishment by increasing amount of cocaine base possessed by defendant, and did not add a new charge or otherwise change the nature or character of the offense charged was permissible under § 19.2-231. Dunaway v. Commonwealth, 52 Va. App. 281, 663 S.E.2d 117, 2008 Va. App. LEXIS 326 (2008).

Imposition of enhanced punishment held proper. — Court did not err by applying enhanced punishment provision to second offense although defendant had not been previously convicted when he committed or was tried for the second offense; an enhanced punishment may be applied where there are multiple convictions for separate offenses in a simultaneous prosecution. Mason v. Commonwealth, 16 Va. App. 260, 430 S.E.2d 543 (1993).

This section contains no provision that, in order for the enhanced penalty provision to obtain, the defendant must have been convicted of the first offense before committing the second offense. Jones v. Commonwealth, 21 Va. App. 435, 464 S.E.2d 558 (1995).

Although appellant was previously convicted as accommodation, court correct in allowing enhanced punishment. — Because appellant was convicted previously under this section, albeit as an accommodation under subsection C, the trial court was correct in allowing the enhanced punishment stated in the second sentence of subsection C. Miller v. Commonwealth, No. 1668-91-2 (Ct. of Appeals March 30, 1993).

Applicability of § 18.2-248.1 to offenses committed prior to effective date. — Penalties provided by § 18.2-248.1 could not be applied to offenses of distribution and sale of marijuana committed prior to the effective date of § 18.2-248.1 and prosecuted under this section, though trial and sentencing occurred after that date, absent election by the Commonwealth to proceed under § 18.2-248.1 and the defendants' consent to such an election. Ruplenas v. Commonwealth, 221 Va. 972, 275 S.E.2d 628 (1981).

Legally authorized dealers are excepted from provisions of section. — Specifically excepted from the provisions of this section are those persons legally authorized under this chapter to deal in controlled drugs. Wood v. Commonwealth, 213 Va. 363, 192 S.E.2d 762 (1972).

Users and addicts, if they have gained a familiarity or experience with a drug, may identify it. Hill v. Commonwealth, 8 Va. App. 60, 379 S.E.2d 134 (1989).

Possession is a lesser-included offense of distribution. — Proof of the elements of the offense of feloniously, knowingly, and intentionally distributing a controlled substance necessarily encompasses proof of the possession of that same controlled substance and, therefore, the offense of possessing a controlled substance is a lesser-included offense of distribution of a controlled substance. Austin v. Commonwealth, 33 Va. App. 124, 531 S.E.2d 637, 2000 Va. App. LEXIS 572 (2000).

Failure to give lesser included offense instruction held error. — While the jury could have concluded that the defendant tolerated the presence of the drugs in the apartment and thus constructively shared possession, the jury could also have had a reasonable doubt as to whether the defendant shared the intent to distribute. Therefore, the evidence supporting a theory of simple possession by the defendant was "more than a scintilla" and failure to grant the instruction on the lesser included offense was error. Harrison v. Commonwealth, 12 Va. App. 581, 405 S.E.2d 854 (1991).

Mitigation of punishment. — This section provides for the mitigation of punishment in those "instances" of drug distribution not by a dealer in drugs, but by an individual citizen motivated by a desire to accommodate a friend, without any intent to profit or to induce or to encourage the use of drugs. However, to benefit from

this sentencing advantage, the statute, together with § 18.2-263, places the burden of proving the existence of an accommodation distribution on the shoulders of the defendant, by a preponderance of the evidence. Winston v. Commonwealth, 16 Va. App. 901, 434 S.E.2d 4 (1993).

Trial court did not err in refusing to apply the mitigation of the accommodation defense under this section where the defendant admitted to police he sometimes made a small profit from the sale of drugs and also received drugs as consideration for his assistance in obtaining the drugs for others. Barlow v. Commonwealth, 26 Va. App. 421, 494 S.E.2d 901 (1998).

Court not required to follow jury's recommendation for leniency. — Under this section, the jury had no authority to recommend a sentence of less than five years. Thus, in imposing sentence on appellant, the trial court was not required to follow the jury's recommendation for leniency. Carcamo v. Commonwealth, No. 1554-95-4 (Ct. of Appeals Sept. 17, 1996).

Separate trial unwarranted. — Trial court did not err in not ordering a separate trial on charges of involuntary manslaughter and unlawful distribution of a controlled substance, in violation of § 18.2-248, against a doctor, where the offenses were based on the same act or transactions, or on two or more acts or transactions that were connected or constitute parts of a common scheme or plan; moreover, defendant conceded that the evidence of the distribution was essential to the trial of the homicide charge. Jere v. Commonwealth, No. 2125-02-2, 2003 Va. App. LEXIS 465 (Ct. of Appeals Sept. 9, 2003).

Revocation of indefinitely suspended sentence. — Trial court had jurisdiction to revoke defendant's suspended sentence after he violated conditions of sentence and probation, and to resentence him to prison; under § 18.2-306 the court could revoke defendant's unspecified suspended sentence during the maximum prescribed sentence plus one year and trial court's action occurred well within the prescribed period. Derrick v. Commonwealth, No. 2722-00-3, 2002 Va. App. LEXIS 283 (Ct. of Appeals May 7, 2002).

Based on the characteristics of the area and defendant's conduct, including defendant's unprovoked flight, a motion to suppress evidence of the cocaine found on defendant's person was properly denied because the police had a reasonable suspicion of criminal activity. Whitfield v. Commonwealth, 265 Va. 358, 576 S.E.2d 463, 2003 Va. LEXIS 37 (2003).

Plea agreements and sentencing. — Because defendant never voiced any objection to the sentences imposed against him after entering guilty pleas to two indictments charging distribution of cocaine pursuant to a plea agreement, the trial court's denial of defendant's motion to modify the sentences was upheld on appeal. The appellate court found no abuse of discretion on the part of the trial court in failing to modify defendant's sentences since defendant responded to the trial court's questions regarding the plea agreement, found that it was voluntarily entered into, that defendant never voiced any objections, and because the sentences did not exceed the maximum allowable. Russell v. Commonwealth, — Va. App. —, — S.E.2d —, 2005 Va. App. LEXIS 263 (July 5, 2005).

Because defendant's conviction of possession of marijuana in a lockbox with the intent to distribute was not for the "same act or transaction" as his possession of marijuana in his pocket, his circuit court conviction of possession of marijuana with the intent to distribute did not violate double jeopardy principles; a mere overlap in proof between two prosecutions does not establish a double jeopardy violation. Peake v. Commonwealth, 46 Va. App. 35, 614 S.E.2d 672, 2005 Va. App. LEXIS 238 (2005).

Suspended sentence was legal. — Because defendant did not object to a sentence of 29 years, 11 months with a suspended sentence of 25 years, five months conditioned upon the completion of a transitional program, and because the sentence did not exceed the maximum sentence in § 18.2-248, defendant's challenge to the sentencing order was barred by Va. Sup. Ct. R. 5A:18. Johnson v. Commonwealth, 2007 Va. App. LEXIS 257 (July 3, 2007).

Applied in Rozier v. Commonwealth, 219 Va. 525, 248 S.E.2d 789 (1978); Spear v. Commonwealth, 221 Va. 450, 270 S.E.2d 737 (1980); Ketter v. Commonwealth, 222 Va. 134, 278 S.E.2d 841 (1981); Hamby v. Commonwealth, 222 Va. 257, 279 S.E.2d 163 (1981); Morton v. Commonwealth, 227 Va. 216, 315 S.E.2d 224 (1984); Rider v. Commonwealth, 8 Va. App. 595, 383 S.E.2d 25 (1989); United States v. Smith, 727 F. Supp. 1023 (W.D. Va. 1990); Belcher v. Commonwealth, 17 Va. App. 44, 435 S.E.2d 160 (1993);

Robinson v. Commonwealth, 19 Va. App. 642, 453 S.E.2d 916 (1995); White v. Commonwealth, 25 Va. App. 662, 492 S.E.2d 451 (1997); Booker v. Commonwealth, 276 Va. 37, 661 S.E.2d 461, 2008 Va. LEXIS 84 (2008); Epps v. Commonwealth, 59 Va. App. 71, 717 S.E.2d 151, 2011 Va. App. LEXIS 351 (2011); Booker v. Commonwealth, 61 Va. App. 323, 734 S.E.2d 729, 2012 Va. App. LEXIS 407 (2012).

II. ELEMENTS.

A. Possession.

"Possession." — In order to convict a defendant of "possession" of a narcotic drug, it generally is necessary to show that defendant was aware of the presence and character of the particular substance and was intentionally and consciously in possession of it. Physical possession giving the defendant "immediate and exclusive control" is sufficient. However, the possession need not always be exclusive. The defendant may share it with one or more. The duration of the possession is immaterial and need not always be actual possession. The defendant may be shown to have had constructive possession by establishing that the drugs involved were subject to his dominion or control. Robbs v. Commonwealth, 211 Va. 153, 176 S.E.2d 429 (1970).

To establish "possession" in a legal sense, it is not sufficient to simply show actual or constructive possession of the drug by the defendant. The Commonwealth must also establish that the defendant intentionally and consciously possessed it with knowledge of its nature and character. Burton v. Commonwealth, 215 Va. 711, 213 S.E.2d 757 (1975).

To convict a defendant of illegal possession of drugs, the Commonwealth must prove that the defendant was aware of the presence and character of the drugs, and that he intentionally and consciously possessed them. Andrews v. Commonwealth, 216 Va. 179, 217 S.E.2d 812 (1975).

Possession may be proved by evidence of acts and declarations of conduct of the accused from which the inference may be fairly drawn that he knew of the existence of narcotics at the place where they were found. Andrews v. Commonwealth, 216 Va. 179, 217 S.E.2d 812 (1975).

Constructive possession may be established by a showing that an accused has dominion or control over the drugs. Andrews v. Commonwealth, 216 Va. 179, 217 S.E.2d 812 (1975).

Possession of a controlled substance may be actual or constructive. Archer v. Commonwealth, 225 Va. 416, 303 S.E.2d 863 (1983).

Where the defendant acted as an intermediary between the purchaser and another, who was holding the controlled substance at the defendant's request and the defendant knew of the presence and character of the drug and it was subject to his dominion and control, there was, therefore, ample proof that he was in constructive possession of it. Archer v. Commonwealth, 225 Va. 416, 303 S.E.2d 863 (1983).

When one person is in actual possession of a drug, another may have simultaneous constructive possession. Archer v. Commonwealth, 225 Va. 416, 303 S.E.2d 863 (1983).

Possession need not always be exclusive. The defendant may share it with one or more. Hunley v. Commonwealth, 30 Va. App. 556, 518 S.E.2d 347 (1999).

Duration of possession is immaterial. Hunley v. Commonwealth, 30 Va. App. 556, 518 S.E.2d 347 (1999).

In order to convict a person of illegal possession of an illicit drug, the commonwealth must prove beyond a reasonable doubt that the accused was aware of the presence and character of the drug and that the accused consciously possessed it. Jackson v. Commonwealth, No. 2823-99-4, 2000 Va. App. LEXIS 729 (Ct. of Appeals Nov. 14, 2000).

Possession of controlled drug gives rise to inference of defendant's knowledge of its character. Hunley v. Commonwealth, 30 Va. App. 556, 518 S.E.2d 347 (1999).

Fact finder was not required to accept defendant's theory that he was unaware of nature of substance in package; based on defendant's conduct, fact finder could reasonably infer that he knowingly and intentionally possessed cocaine. Shackleford v. Commonwealth, No. 2883-98-3 (Ct. of Appeals Mar. 28, 2000).

Proximity may tend to show knowledge. — Proof that a person is in close proximity to contraband is a relevant fact that, depending on the circumstances, may tend to show that, as an

owner or occupant of property, the person necessarily knows of the presence, nature and character of the item that is found there. Young v. Commonwealth, No. 1228-00-2, 2001 Va. App. LEXIS 251 (Ct. of Appeals May 15, 2001).

Awareness of presence and character of substance. — Evidence that the defendant acted suspiciously after he exited a bus from New York, a known source for drugs, that he gave police officers inconsistent stories about the circumstances of his visit, that his behavior became more suspicious after he entered the taxi cab in which the drugs and a firearm were later found and that, after he got out of the cab at a motel and in response to an officer's request to search his bag, he remarked that "you can go ahead and search the bag, there's no drugs or anything in it," was sufficient for the fact finder to have reasonably inferred that the defendant knowingly and intentionally possessed the cocaine which he had concealed in the cab. Shackleford v. Commonwealth, 32 Va. App. 307, 528 S.E.2d 123, 2000 Va. App. LEXIS 233 (2000), aff'd, 262 Va. 196, 547 S.E.2d 899 (2001).

Where defendant's connection to the drugs was significantly greater than mere proximity, and details recounted by an officer permitted the trial court to draw the reasonable inference that defendant possessed the drugs found in the precise spot where the officer saw him reaching, and from which he quickly exited when he saw the officer, such evidence permitted the trial judge to conclude that defendant was aware of the drugs and exercised dominion and control over them. Walker v. Commonwealth, No. 1665-03-2, 2004 Va. App. LEXIS 474 (Ct. of Appeals Oct. 5, 2004).

Possession coextensive with § 18.2-250 possession. — Under the Virginia statutes, possession under this section must be coextensive with possession under § 18.2-250. Such an interpretation is required as a matter of due process of law since, otherwise, a defendant could be subject to a presumption of possession based upon his occupancy of an apartment in a prosecution under this section, whereas such a presumption would be barred in a prosecution under the lesser offense of § 18.2-250. Bentley v. Cox, 508 F. Supp. 870 (E.D. Va. 1981).

Possession of a drug need not be exclusive, but may instead be joint. Archer v. Commonwealth, 225 Va. 416, 303 S.E.2d 863 (1983).

Accommodation possession. — Court's refusal to grant accommodation instruction had no effect on verdict and was harmless error, where defendant was convicted of lesser offense of simple possession, which was less culpable than accommodation possession with intent to distribute, with a like penalty. Watford v. Commonwealth, No. 0569-99-1 (Ct. of Appeals Mar. 7, 2000).

Constructive possession may be established by circumstantial evidence provided such evidence excludes every reasonable hypothesis of innocence that flows from the evidence. Whether a hypothesis of innocence is reasonable is a question of fact. Johnson v. Commonwealth, No. 1487-99-3, 2000 Va. App. LEXIS 504 (Ct. of Appeals July 11, 2000).

To support a conviction based upon constructive possession, the Commonwealth must point to evidence of acts, statements, or conduct of the accused or other facts or circumstances which tend to show that the defendant was aware of both the presence and character of the substance and that it was subject to his dominion and control. Behrens v. Commonwealth, 3 Va. App. 131, 348 S.E.2d 430 (1986); Brown v. Commonwealth, 5 Va. App. 489, 364 S.E.2d 773 (1988).

The Commonwealth stressed that defendant had initially denied ownership of the jacket and then admitted it when the officer found receipts bearing his name. The Commonwealth suggested to the jury that, because he denied ownership, defendant must have known that the cocaine was in the jacket. The Commonwealth was required to prove that defendant intentionally and consciously possessed the cocaine. Without the denial of ownership, the Commonwealth could not have implied that defendant consciously possessed it with knowledge of its nature and character. Admission of defendant's statements was therefore reversible error. Carroll v. Commonwealth, No. 2353-95-2 (Ct. of Appeals Feb. 25, 1997).

Constructive possession may be shown by defendant's acts, declarations or conduct which support the inference that the contraband was "subject to his dominion or control." Wilkins v. Commonwealth, 18 Va. App. 293, 443 S.E.2d 440 (1994).

Constructive possession must be shown by acts, statements, or conduct. — To support a conviction based upon constructive possession, the Commonwealth must point to evidence of acts, statements, or conduct of the accused or other facts or circumstances which tend to show that the defendant was aware of both the presence and character of the substance and that it was subject to his dominion and control. Drew v. Commonwealth, 230 Va. 471, 338 S.E.2d 844 (1986); Shurbaji v. Commonwealth, 18 Va. App. 415, 444 S.E.2d 549 (1994).

Constructive possession may be established when there are acts, statements or conduct of the accused or other facts or circumstances which tend to show that the accused was aware of both the presence and character of the substance and that it was subject to his dominion and control. Jackson v. Commonwealth, No. 2823-99-4, 2000 Va. App. LEXIS 729 (Ct. of Appeals Nov. 14, 2000).

The proximity of the dispenser containing bullets and cocaine to the handgun, combined with the correspondence of the bullets in the dispenser to the bullets in the handgun, gave rise to a reasonable inference that the two items were possessed in conjunction. Further, the relative privacy of the yard in which these items, and no others, were found supported the inference that the defendant dropped both items when running from the officer. Therefore, evidence was sufficient for conviction under this section and § 18.2-308.4. Hunt v. Commonwealth, No. 0257-94-1 (Ct. of Appeals March 21, 1995).

The Commonwealth did not meet its burden to prove beyond a reasonable doubt that appellant was aware of the presence and character of the cocaine and was intentionally and consciously in physical or constructive possession of it; most notably, the Commonwealth failed to rule out the reasonable hypothesis that an unnamed person fleeing through the kitchen may have dropped the baggie(s) into the can on his way through the sliding door and onto the deck. Pemberton v. Commonwealth, 17 Va. App. 651, 440 S.E.2d 420 (1994).

Evidence that defendant "suspected" that drugs may have been inside the package failed to prove beyond a reasonable doubt that he intentionally and consciously possessed the drugs. Thus, the evidence was insufficient to support the conviction for attempted possession of cocaine with intent to distribute. Gaither v. Commonwealth, No. 0610-96-2 (Ct. of Appeals June 24, 1997).

Knowledge not inferred from having been seen with known cocaine supplier. — Defendant's knowledge of the cocaine could not be inferred from his having been seen with a known cocaine supplier shortly before his arrest, where the evidence proved only that defendant had some conversation with the supplier, but there was no evidence regarding what they discussed. Behrens v. Commonwealth, 3 Va. App. 131, 348 S.E.2d 430 (1986).

Defendant's awareness of cocaine could not be inferred from his failure to show surprise upon being arrested, even if the proposition that guilty knowledge may be inferred from a failure to show surprise at being arrested were to be accepted, where the only evidence regarding defendant's reaction to his arrest came from a police officer who testified that defendant was cooperative and made no attempt to escape. This testimony did not establish lack of surprise. Behrens v. Commonwealth, 3 Va. App. 131, 348 S.E.2d 430 (1986).

Mere proximity to a controlled substance is insufficient to establish possession, and furthermore, no presumption of possession arises from the ownership or occupancy of the premises where drugs are found. Bentley v. Cox, 508 F. Supp. 870 (E.D. Va. 1981).

Mere proximity of a defendant to packages of heroin was not sufficient to establish constructive possession, and the conviction of possession with intent to distribute could not be sustained. Wright v. Commonwealth, 217 Va. 669, 232 S.E.2d 733 (1977).

Mere proximity to a controlled drug is not sufficient to establish dominion and control. Drew v. Commonwealth, 230 Va. 471, 338 S.E.2d 844 (1986).

Based upon the appellant's admitted prior cocaine use and the location and visibility of the cocaine, the trial court could reasonably infer that the appellant was aware of the presence and character of the cocaine and his proximity to the drugs was sufficient to establish possession. Brown v. Commonwealth, 5 Va. App. 489, 364 S.E.2d 773 (1988).

While mere proximity to a controlled substance is insufficient to establish possession, it is a factor to consider when determining whether the accused constructively possessed drugs. Brown v. Commonwealth, 5 Va. App. 489, 364 S.E.2d 773 (1988).

The fact that a suspect's personal items are found in close proximity to contraband does not, in and of itself, establish ownership, knowledge or possession. Plunkett v. Commonwealth, Nos. 3002-99-3, 0257-00-3, 2000 Va. App. LEXIS 831 (Ct. of Appeals Dec. 19, 2000).

Defendant's mere proximity to cocaine found between sun visor and roof of car was not sufficient to prove constructive possession. Kindred v. Commonwealth, No. 1182-99-1 (Ct. of Appeals Mar. 7, 2000).

A person's proximity to a place where a controlled substance is present is insufficient to support a conviction, where the evidence does not prove that the person intentionally and knowingly possessed the controlled substance. Williams v. Commonwealth, No. 0289-00-1, 2001 Va. App. LEXIS 303 (Ct. of Appeals June 5, 2001).

Ownership of premises and proximity to contraband. — Proof that a person is in close proximity to contraband is a relevant fact that, depending on the circumstances, may tend to show that, as an owner or occupant of property, the person necessarily knows of the presence, nature and character of a substance that is found there. Johnson v. Commonwealth, No. 1487-99-3, 2000 Va. App. LEXIS 504 (Ct. of Appeals July 11, 2000).

Documents showing defendant claimed house as residence. — Several documents introduced to show that defendant claimed the house in which cocaine was found as his residence, though relevant, raised no presumption that he knowingly or intentionally possessed the controlled substance found there. Drew v. Commonwealth, 230 Va. 471, 338 S.E.2d 844 (1986).

Ownership of premises relevant to dominion and control. — Ownership or occupancy of premises where illicit drugs are found is a circumstance that may be considered together with other evidence tending to prove that the owner or occupant exercised dominion and control over the items on the premises in order to prove that the owner or occupant constructively possessed the contraband. Johnson v. Commonwealth, No. 1487-99-3, 2000 Va. App. LEXIS 504 (Ct. of Appeals July 11, 2000).

Occupancy of vehicle raises no presumption. — A person's occupancy of a vehicle in which a controlled substance is found raises no presumption that the person either knowingly or intentionally possessed the controlled substance. Williams v. Commonwealth, No. 0289-00-1, 2001 Va. App. LEXIS 303 (Ct. of Appeals June 5, 2001).

Ownership or occupancy alone is insufficient to prove knowing possession. — Ownership or occupancy of a vehicle or of premises where illicit drugs are found is a circumstance that may be considered together with other evidence tending to prove that the owner or occupant exercised dominion and control over items in the vehicle or on the premises in order to prove that the owner or occupant constructively possessed the contraband; however, ownership or occupancy alone is insufficient to prove knowing possession of drugs located on the premises or in a vehicle. Burchette v. Commonwealth, 15 Va. App. 432, 425 S.E.2d 81 (1992).

Items in vehicle failed to establish link between defendant and marijuana. — Commonwealth's evidence failed to establish any link between defendant and the marijuana found in his vehicle, other than defendant's ownership of the vehicle. The nature of the other items found in the vehicle that were shown to belong to defendant, the handgun and cellular phone, did not tie him to the drugs or drug paraphernalia. Those are items frequently found in vehicles where the owner or occupant has no relation to drug trafficking. To the extent that receipt for a gun purchase, phone bill, defendant's wallet and driver's license in the vehicle could prove that defendant recently occupied the vehicle, the evidence did not support an inference that the drugs were in the vehicle at the time. Burchette v. Commonwealth, 15 Va. App. 432, 425 S.E.2d 81 (1992).

Not separate drug offense for sentencing under 21 U.S.C.S. § 841(b)(1)(A). — Defendant's conviction for possession with intent to distribute cocaine was not a separate drug conviction from a federal conviction for possession with intent to distribute and distribution of cocaine for purposes of sentencing under 21 U.S.C.S. § 841(b)(1)(A) because both convictions arose from the same criminal episode and concurrent sentences were imposed for them. United States v. Gardner, 534 F. Supp. 2d 655, 2008 U.S. Dist. LEXIS 12034 (W.D. Va. 2008).

Not prior felony drug offense for purposes of sentencing under 21 U.S.C.S. § 841(b)(1)(A). — Defendant's conviction for possession with intent to distribute an imitation controlled substance under § 18.2-248 was not a felony drug conviction for purposes of sentencing under 21 U.S.C.S. § 841(b)(1)(A) because it was not within the listed felony drug offenses under 21 U.S.C.S. § 802(44), the Commonwealth was not required to prove a nexus between defendant and an actual controlled substance, and the act prohibited by § 18.2-248 was not prohibited by any federal statute. United States v. Gardner, 534 F. Supp. 2d 655, 2008 U.S. Dist. LEXIS 12034 (W.D. Va. 2008).

Possession of a modicum of an illegal drug is sufficient to sustain a conviction. Robbs v. Commonwealth, 211 Va. 153, 176 S.E.2d 429 (1970).

The modicum of heroin in the bottom of the "bottle cap cooker," if possessed by the defendant, was sufficient to support her conviction. Robbs v. Commonwealth, 211 Va. 153, 176 S.E.2d 429 (1970).

B. Distribution.

Legislative intent. — While the legislature has seen fit to make distribution of cocaine as an accommodation punishable with less severity than distribution for profit, the gravamen of the offense is possession of the drug with the intent to distribute it to another. McCoy v. Commonwealth, 9 Va. App. 227, 385 S.E.2d 628 (1989).

The plain and obvious meaning of this section and § 18.2-248.01 is to prohibit the possession or transportation of illegal substances in Virginia by a person whose intent is to distribute them anywhere. Seke v. Commonwealth, 24 Va. App. 318, 482 S.E.2d 88 (1997).

The term "distribute" as used in former § 54-524.101 has been defined by the General Assembly so as to give it the broadest possible meaning and to proscribe acts which would not fall within the more limited terms of "sale," "barter," "gift" or "exchange" which appear in the federal and state statutes underpinning the "procuring agent" rule." Wood v. Commonwealth, 214 Va. 97, 197 S.E.2d 200 (1973).

The conscious choice by the General Assembly of the word "distribute" and the broad definition given that word by it evinces a legislative intent to proscribe not only the illegal sale, barter, exchange or gift of controlled drugs but also any delivery or transfer, actual or constructive, of possession or title to such drugs from one person to another. Wood v. Commonwealth, 214 Va. 97, 197 S.E.2d 200 (1973).

The term "profit" as used in subsection D is defined as a commercial transaction in which there is a consideration involved; it does not necessarily mean that a seller of drugs has to sell his drugs to a buyer at a price in excess of the amount the seller paid for the drugs. Booker v. Commonwealth, No. 0710-99-4, 2000 Va. App. LEXIS 352 (Ct. of Appeals May 9, 2000).

"Profit" is any consideration received or expected. — A person convicted of distributing a controlled substance is not entitled to the reduced penalty afforded by subsection A if the distribution was made "with intent to profit thereby." The profit contemplated by the statute is any consideration received or expected. Heacock v. Commonwealth, 228 Va. 397, 323 S.E.2d 90 (1984).

Statutory presumption as to distribution. — No statutory presumption was included in this section before the 1973 amendment that any distribution is for profit or to induce use, addiction or dependency. Jefferson v. Commonwealth, 214 Va. 432, 201 S.E.2d 749 (1974).

Proof of intent essential to conviction. — In cases involving crimes which require an act coupled with a specific intent, such as this one, proof of intent is essential to conviction. While intent may be shown by circumstantial evidence, the existence of intent cannot be based upon speculation or surmise. Adkins v. Commonwealth, 217 Va. 437, 229 S.E.2d 869 (1976) (decided under former § 54-524.101:1).

It is firmly established under Virginia law that the existence of intent cannot be based upon speculation or surmise; thus, assuming proof of possession by the defendant, it is necessary for the Commonwealth to introduce sufficient evidence showing the drugs seized were intended for distribution and were not for the defendant's personal use. Bentley v. Cox, 508 F. Supp. 870 (E.D. Va. 1981).

In order for a defendant to be convicted of possession of a controlled substance with the intent to distribute, the Commonwealth must prove that the defendant possessed the controlled substance contemporaneously with his intention to distribute that substance. Stanley v. Commonwealth, 12 Va. App. 867, 407 S.E.2d 13 (1991).

Intent must be proved by circumstances. — Intent is not susceptible of direct proof; it must be proved by circumstances. United States v. Childs, 463 F.2d 390 (4th Cir.), cert. denied, 409 U.S. 966, 93 S. Ct. 271, 34 L. Ed. 2d 232 (1972).

Because direct proof of intent is often impossible, it must be shown by circumstantial evidence which is consistent with guilt and inconsistent with and excludes every reasonable hypothesis of innocence. Wilkins v. Commonwealth, 18 Va. App. 293, 443 S.E.2d 440 (1994).

Intent necessarily must be proved by circumstances. Hunter v. Commonwealth, 213 Va. 569, 193 S.E.2d 779 (1973).

Where crack cocaine was packaged in two plastic bags, and he possessed a large amount of cash and a loaded handgun, that along with the evidence that possession of 9.5 grams of cocaine was inconsistent with personal use, was sufficient proof that defendant was in possession of cocaine with the intent to distribute. Tinker v. Commonwealth, No. 1959-94-1 (Ct. of Appeals Oct. 31, 1995).

The intent of an accused to distribute drugs may be shown by circumstantial evidence; circumstances that shed light on the accused's specific intent regarding illegal drugs in the accused's possession include: (1) the quantity and method of packaging of the drugs possessed by the accused; (2) the presence or absence of an unusual amount of money suggesting profit from sales; and (3) the presence or absence of drug paraphernalia. Brooks v. Commonwealth, No. 0811-02-4, 2003 Va. App. LEXIS 118 (Ct. of Appeals Mar. 4, 2003).

Defendant's convictions for possession of both marijuana and cocaine with the intent to distribute were upheld, where the evidence showed that as a principal in the second degree, she allowed two known drug dealers to use her apartment to sell drugs, knew that drugs were kept in her house, and police observed hand-to-hand transactions from defendant's apartment over a two-month period of time. Edmonds v. Commonwealth, No. 2176-03-2, 2004 Va. App. LEXIS 468 (Ct. of Appeals Oct. 5, 2004).

Circumstantial evidence of intent to distribute prescription drugs. — Indicia of intent to distribute drugs must be contextualized to the specific drug at issue. For illegally distributed prescription drugs, the packaging factor takes into account the presence or absence of pharmacy pill bottles or other forms of pharmaceutical packaging. Sample v. Commonwealth, No. 2594-02-3, 2003 Va. App. LEXIS 627 (Ct. of Appeals Dec. 9, 2003).

Because direct evidence is often impossible to produce, intent may be shown by circumstantial evidence that is consistent with guilt, inconsistent with innocence, and excludes every reasonable hypothesis of innocence. Dunbar v. Commonwealth, 29 Va. App. 387, 512 S.E.2d 823 (1999).

Factors that may indicate the defendant intended to distribute the illegal drugs in his possession include the possession of a quantity of drugs greater than that ordinarily possessed for one's personal use, the method of packaging of the controlled substance, the quantity and denomination of the cash possessed, the absence of any paraphernalia suggestive of personal use, the presence of equipment related to drug distribution, and the presence of firearms. Thus, there was sufficient evidence to support defendant's conviction for distribution of cocaine under § 18.2-248 where defendant possessed, inter alia, 4.01 grams of powder cocaine packaged in seven plastic bag corners, a large amount of case, an electronic scale, and a large quantity of ammunition, and where there was no evidence in the record that defendant used cocaine or that he possessed it for his personal use. Emerson v. Commonwealth, 43 Va. App. 263, 597 S.E.2d 242, 2004 Va. App. LEXIS 274 (2004).

Provided it is sufficiently convincing to exclude every reasonable hypothesis except that of guilt. — However, the Commonwealth need only exclude reasonable hypotheses of innocence that flow from the evidence, not those that spring from the imagination of the defendant. Emerson v. Commonwealth, 43 Va. App. 263, 597 S.E.2d 242, 2004 Va. App. LEXIS 274 (2004).

Absence of claim defendant used is evidence of the possession of drugs with intent to distribute. Askew v. Commonwealth, 40 Va. App. 104, 578 S.E.2d 58, 2003 Va. App. LEXIS 135 (2003).

No geographical limitation on intent element. — The phrase "intent ... to distribute" in both this section § 18.2-248.01 contains no geographical limitation. The Commonwealth is not required to prove the place where a defendant intends to distribute illegal substances in order to obtain a conviction under either section of the Code of Virginia. Seke v. Commonwealth, 24 Va. App. 318, 482 S.E.2d 88 (1997).

Quantity alone is not determinative of intent to distribute, but rather is a circumstance to be considered together with other factors. Stanley v. Commonwealth, No. 0077-88-2 (Ct. of Appeals Sept. 25, 1990).

Quantity may be considered along with other circumstances to support an inference of intent to distribute, and quantity alone, under certain circumstances, may be sufficient to support an inference of intent to distribute. Adkins v. Commonwealth, 217 Va. 437, 229 S.E.2d 869 (1976) (decided under former § 54-524.101:1).

The quantity of a controlled substance is a factor which may indicate the purpose for which it is possessed. Possession of a small quantity creates an inference that the drug is for personal use. Possession of a small quantity of a controlled substance, however, when considered with other circumstances, may be sufficient to establish an intent to distribute. The method of packaging of the controlled substance is such a circumstance. Servis v. Commonwealth, 6 Va. App. 507, 371 S.E.2d 156 (1988).

Quantum of evidence necessary to prove an intent to distribute depends on the facts and circumstances of each case; in addition to evidence proving the quantity and type of drug possessed, the Commonwealth may introduce opinion testimony from law-enforcement officers familiar with the habits and propensities of local drug users as to what amounts are inconsistent with personal use. Askew v. Commonwealth, 40 Va. App. 104, 578 S.E.2d 58, 2003 Va. App. LEXIS 135 (2003).

Defendant's possession of a residue or trace amount of cocaine was sufficient to support his conviction of possession with intent to distribute. Stanley v. Commonwealth, No. 0077-88-2 (Ct. of Appeals Sept. 25, 1990).

Packaging as evidence of intent. — Relevant to an evaluation of intent is the manner in which the drugs were packaged when seized, and the finder of fact may consider evidence that the drugs were "packaged in distributable form." Bentley v. Cox, 508 F. Supp. 870 (E.D. Va. 1981).

Even if substance is packaged for distribution, there must be additional evidence to preclude the inference that it was purchased in the packaged form for personal use rather than being held in that fashion for distribution. The additional evidence available to preclude such an inference [may be] the presence of a large, or bulk, quantity from which smaller packages may have been made up for distribution, or the presence of paraphernalia used in the packaging process. Servis v. Commonwealth, 6 Va. App. 507, 371 S.E.2d 156 (1988).

Presence of unusual amount of money, suggesting profit from sales, is a circumstance that negates an inference of possession for personal use. Servis v. Commonwealth, 6 Va. App. 507, 371 S.E.2d 156 (1988).

Belief that substance is a "real controlled substance," rather than "imitation controlled substance" no defense. — Evidence was sufficient to prove an intent to distribute an imitation controlled substance in violation of subsection G of § 18.2-248 because a detective's testimony dismantled defendant's hypothesis, and the sole defense theory of the case, that defendant believed he possessed real, not imitation, crack and had been "ripped off," and since defendant was not "ripped off," the only remaining reasonable hypothesis was that he possessed it to distribute; the detective stated that if defendant was an experienced user, he would have purchased crack in bulk, rather than in three packages because he would have been able to obtain more of the substance, but if defendant was an inexperienced user, he would not have purchased that quantity of crack since that's a lot more than a new cocaine user would attempt. Holloway v. Commonwealth, 57 Va. App. 658, 705 S.E.2d 510, 2011 Va. App. LEXIS 94 (2011).

Accommodation defense only relevant to sentencing. — In a prosecution for distribution of cocaine, the trial court did not err by not allowing the jury to consider a juvenile's accommodation defense during the guilt phase of the trial; this defense was only relevant to sentencing, and the trial court, not the jury, determined sentence in a juvenile case. Foster v. Commonwealth, 38 Va. App. 549, 567 S.E.2d 547, 2002 Va. App. LEXIS 447 (2002).

Presumption against accommodation distribution after guilt established. — This section contains a presumption against an accommodation distribution to the extent that it is relevant to the determination of the proper degree of punishment, but only after guilt has been established. Stillwell v. Commonwealth, 219 Va. 214, 247 S.E.2d 360 (1978), decided prior to 1979 amendment.

And presumption lasts until evidence makes case for jury. — The presumption created with regard to accommodation retains its effect until opposing evidence (whether from the Commonwealth or the defendant) is sufficient to make a case for the jury, that is, to convince the judge that a jury could reasonably find that the defendant was an accommodation distributor. This is the obvious standard to be applied for overcoming the statutory presumption that operates in favor of the Commonwealth in cases prosecuted under this section, and it is unnecessary for the standard to be spelled out in the statute. Stillwell v. Commonwealth, 219 Va. 214, 247 S.E.2d 360 (1978), decided prior to 1979 amendment.

Burden on defendant to show accommodation. — The statutory scheme behind this section provides that once the guilt of the defendant has been established (a determination completely independent of the profit-accommodation distinction), a second determination of the proper punishment is to be made. This section and § 18.2-263 place the burden of proving the existence of an accommodation distribution (and the right to the lesser penalty) to the trier of fact on the shoulders of the defendant. Stillwell v. Commonwealth, 219 Va. 214, 247 S.E.2d 360 (1978), decided prior to 1979 amendment.

This section and § 18.2-263 place the burden of proving the existence of an accommodation distribution (and the right to the lesser penalty) to the trier of fact on the shoulders of the defendant. In other words, the statute contains a presumption against an accommodation distribution to the extent that it is relevant to the determination of the proper degree of punishment, but only after guilt has been established. Ulmer v. Commonwealth, No. 0369-85 (Ct. of Appeals Aug. 26, 1986).

By preponderance of evidence. — A defendant, charged with an unlawful sale of drugs, who defends on the ground that he distributed the drugs for accommodation only, is not required to establish such accommodation beyond a reasonable doubt, but only by a preponderance of the evidence. He is required to produce some evidence which satisfies the trier of the facts that his distribution was for accommodation. Stillwell v. Commonwealth, 219 Va. 214, 247 S.E.2d 360 (1978), decided prior to 1979 amendment.

Subsection D establishes a presumption against an accommodation distribution and requires a defendant to prove accommodation by a preponderance of the evidence. Booker v. Commonwealth, No. 0710-99-4, 2000 Va. App. LEXIS 352 (Ct. of Appeals May 9, 2000).

Drug party held for purpose of profit rather than as accommodation. — Defendant was properly found to have distributed drugs with the intent to profit thereby rather than simply to accommodate friends, where the drug he supplied at a party was very high quality cocaine, the quality was sufficient to distribute among a number of users, and the paraphernalia he took as he fled from the police and "stuff" later retrieved from his home and buried in the woods were indicia of commercial traffic in drugs. Heacock v. Commonwealth, 228 Va. 397, 323 S.E.2d 90 (1984).

Where defendant expected to profit from an illegal drug transaction by sharing in the drugs, not even a scintilla of evidence established an accommodation pursuant to § 18.2-248 D; thus, the trial court properly refused defendant's proffered accommodation instruction. Walker v. Commonwealth, No. 2974-01-4, 2003 Va. App. LEXIS 110 (Ct. of Appeals Mar. 4, 2003).

Factual impossibility not a defense. — Where defendant had completed every act necessary for commission of the substantive crime, and the only reason the distribution was not a crime was a defect in the substance itself, which was unknown to defendant, the impossibility was clearly factual, not legal, and as such, could not be asserted as a defense to the attempted crime. Parham v. Commonwealth, 2 Va. App. 633, 347 S.E.2d 172 (1986).

Evidence of consummation of sale. — The finder of fact may rely upon facts, including possession of currency, from which an inference may reasonably be drawn that the defendant had consummated a sale of drugs. Bentley v. Cox, 508 F. Supp. 870 (E.D. Va. 1981).

Evidence of persons using drugs. — The finder of fact may consider whether the defendant personally used the drugs which he possessed, and if it is shown that the defendant was in exclusive possession, it may also be considered whether any persons accompanying the defendant when the seizure occurred were at that time using drugs of the type seized. Bentley v. Cox, 508 F. Supp. 870 (E.D. Va. 1981).

Insufficient evidence to establish substance as cocaine. — In a prosecution for distribution of cocaine the Commonwealth had no physical evidence of the substance procured from the defendant, and therefore was not able to conduct any laboratory analysis. Their only evidence concerning the nature of the substance consisted of the testimony of a witness who testified that she had given some stolen beer to defendant in exchange for crack cocaine. To establish that it was cocaine, the Commonwealth asked witness how long she had used cocaine, how often, the manner of use, what it looked like, and what effect it had on her. Then she was asked her opinion on what the substance was that she had traded for beer. This is insufficient to prove that the substance was in fact cocaine. Furthermore, no corroborating evidence was presented to support witness' opinion. Thus, the Commonwealth's evidence failed to prove a distribution of cocaine beyond a reasonable doubt. Turner v. Commonwealth, No. 2907-95-2 (Ct. of Appeals Nov. 26, 1996).

To obtain a conviction under this section, the commonwealth is required to prove that the defendant intentionally and consciously possessed the controlled substance, either actually or constructively, with knowledge of its nature and character, together with the intent to distribute it. Jackson v. Commonwealth, No. 0684-00-1, 2001 Va. App. LEXIS 21 (Ct. of Appeals Jan. 23, 2001).

The mere presence of drugs in a room appellant used is insufficient to support a conviction for possession with intent to distribute. Powell v. Commonwealth, No. 2202-93-4 (Ct. of Appeals April 11, 1995).

No retrial after successful challenge to sufficiency of evidence. — Where a petitioner challenged the sufficiency of the evidence used to convict him of possession of marijuana and LSD with intent to distribute, and where the district court upheld his challenge, the Commonwealth could not be permitted the option to retry the petitioner, for a retrial would be in violation of the double jeopardy clause. Bentley v. Cox, 508 F. Supp. 870 (E.D. Va. 1981).

Cognizable habeas corpus issue. — Where defendant claimed that his conviction for possession of cocaine with intent to distribute in violation of § 18.2-248 was invalid because the police executed an illegal "no knock" search, it was not cognizable in a habeas corpus proceeding because it had been decided by the trial court and on direct appeal; knocking and announcing police presence would have been dangerous or futile. Henry v. Warden, 265 Va. 246, 576 S.E.2d 495, 2003 Va. LEXIS 31 (2003).

Indictment, which expressly charged possession with intent to distribute, also implicitly charged the lesser included offense of simple possession. Russell v. United States, 507 F.2d 1029 (4th Cir. 1974).

Nature of distribution is jury question. — It was peculiarly within the province of the jury to determine from the evidence whether distribution was made for profit or merely for accommodation. Brown v. Commonwealth, 215 Va. 753, 213 S.E.2d 764 (1975).

Evidence sufficient to prove lesser-included offense of simple possession. — Cocaine residue in defendant's pocket, $115 in cash, and a cell phone were insufficient to prove he possessed cocaine with intent to distribute; thus, on appeal his conviction was reduced to the lesser-included offense of simple possession of cocaine. Claiborne v. Commonwealth, No. 0279-01-2, 2002 Va. App. LEXIS 112 (Ct. of Appeals Feb. 19, 2002).

No reasonable inference of guilt. — It cannot be reasonably inferred from the mere presence of the defendant at the street intersection and the intersection's reputation as a place for trafficking in drugs that he was engaged in the illegal activity of drug distribution over the period of time defendant was observed by the detectives. This unrelated evidence tended to show defendant's "guilt by association" and it was highly prejudicial to him. Smith v. Commonwealth, 217 Va. 336, 228 S.E.2d 562 (1976).

The jury should not concern itself with background information on the prohibited substance, but should make an objective finding of guilt or innocence based on relevant evidence and punish the guilty within the limits fixed by statute. Smith v. Commonwealth, 223 Va. 721, 292 S.E.2d 362 (1982).

To permit evidence respecting extreme horrors which may result from the use of illegal substances diverts the jury from its principal inquiry and injects an element of passion into the trial prejudicial to the accused. Smith v. Commonwealth, 223 Va. 721, 292 S.E.2d 362 (1982).

A distribution for consideration precludes an accommodation instruction. See Booker v. Commonwealth, No. 0710-99-4, 2000 Va. App. LEXIS 352 (Ct. of Appeals May 9, 2000).

When accommodation instruction granted. — Where there is sufficient evidence to support a request instruction defining the offense of possession with intent to make an accommodation distribution, the request should be granted. Schindel v. Commonwealth, 219 Va. 814, 252 S.E.2d 302 (1979).

An instruction on accommodation distribution was not warranted where, according to the defendant's evidence, she was merely present during a drug sale but neither participated in nor countenanced the sale, while, under the Commonwealth's version of the facts, she arranged the drug sale, actively participated in the transaction, and expected drugs in return for her participation. Mondido v. Commonwealth, No. 0035-97-2 (Ct. of Appeals July 28, 1998).

Defendant's convictions for two counts of distribution of cocaine, third offense, in violation of § 18.2-248; three counts of distribution of marijuana; two counts of conspiracy to distribute cocaine, third offense; three counts of conspiracy to distribute marijuana; one count of possession of cocaine with intent to distribute; and one count of possession of marijuana with intent to distribute were proper because the trial court did not err in not instructing the jury on the lesser punishment of distribution for accommodation under subsection D of § 18.2-248. In each transaction, the agent was the buyer, and not the cousin, who had only arranged the meetings for the agent; additionally, the fact that defendant did not make any money on the transactions was not dispositive. Martin v. Commonwealth, 2010 Va. App. LEXIS 205 (May 18, 2010).

Error in refusal of accommodation instruction. — Where jury could find on basis of evidence presented that defendant had no intent to share in the sale proceeds, did not participate in the sale transaction except to arrange it and that sale of drugs was prompted by undercover policeman and informant, the trial court committed reversible error in refusing the accommodation instruction based on the provisos of subsection A. Gardner v. Commonwealth, 217 Va. 5, 225 S.E.2d 354 (1976) (decided under former § 54-524.101:1).

Accommodation defense was negated by evidence that the defendant stated that would be taken care for assisting an undercover officer in his purchase of cocaine, his ready availability and eagerness to procure cocaine for the undercover officer, his ongoing familiarity with the whereabouts and inventory of a dealer, and his detached relationship with the undercover officer. Ricks v. Commonwealth, No. 0432-98-1 (Ct. of Appeals Apr. 13, 1999).

Refusal of witness to reveal source of cocaine. — Where witness refused to reveal his source of cocaine in Florida, and his motive for refusing to answer was purportedly because of threats he had received against his family, but answered in detail every other question propounded to him by either the Commonwealth or the defendant and witness' source of cocaine was not relevant to the question of the defendant's guilt, and the defendant was given an opportunity on cross-examination and during closing argument to expose this infirmity, the trial court did not abuse its discretion in refusing to strike witness' direct testimony. Nichols v. Commonwealth, 6 Va. App. 426, 369 S.E.2d 218 (1988).

The trial court did not err in overruling defendant's motion for a mistrial, made when a prosecution witness testified that he had gone to the area where the drug transaction took place because it was known that drugs were sold there, where the trial court did make a factual inquiry to determine whether defendant's rights had been prejudiced, the trial judge asked each juror individually if he or she could disregard the prejudicial remark, and the record did not show that the jury failed to follow the cautionary instruction. Hines v. Commonwealth, No. 0092-86-2 (Ct. of Appeals Oct. 13, 1987).

Evidence sufficient to prove manufacture. — The defendant's statement to the police that "you don't have PCP," indicating some degree of familiarity with the chemical process, together with the other evidence, including the chemicals and paraphernalia found in the cabin with the defendant, was sufficient for the jury reasonably to have concluded that the defendant manufactured or participated in the manufacture of both PCC and PCP. McGee v.

Commonwealth, 4 Va. App. 317, 357 S.E.2d 738 (1987).

Sentencing. — Defendant's sentence was proper in defendant's case where defendant pled guilty to three counts of distributing cocaine and received a 22-year sentence on each count, to be served concurrently; the range for one offense was five to 40 years, and, thus, defendant's sentence could properly be imposed if it was between 15 years and 120 years in prison. Jackson v. Commonwealth, 2007 Va. App. LEXIS 233 (June 12, 2007).

III. EVIDENCE.

A. Search and Seizure.

Probable cause supported search warrant. — Probable cause supported search warrant, during which drugs and guns were found, where the informant was responsible for investigating embezzlements for defendant's employer and the investigating police officer corroborated the information; the search was also lawful under the good faith exception to the exclusionary rule as the police were executing an arrest warrant when they discovered marijuana on defendant's person and searched the residence with defendant's consent, discovering methamphetamine on top of a locked safe in defendant's bedroom, which also contained marijuana. Coffey v. Commonwealth, No. 2912-01-3, 2003 Va. App. LEXIS 32 (Ct. of Appeals Jan. 28, 2003).

Unlawful search and seizure. — Trial court erred in not suppressing evidence of heroin found in defendant's home pursuant to a search warrant obtained after police stopped defendant's car, as the stop of the automobile was conducted without reasonable suspicion, and was thus unlawful. Mozelle v. Commonwealth, No. 1734-00-1, 2001 Va. App. LEXIS 521 (Ct. of Appeals Sept. 25, 2001).

Combination of police interception of defendant's telephone call and their positioning police cruiser in front of his car constituted an illegal seizure of defendant; therefore, defendant's reluctant consent to a search of his vehicle was tainted and ineffective to justify the search. Bolden v. Commonwealth, 263 Va. 465, 561 S.E.2d 701, 2002 Va. LEXIS 52 (2002).

Where police officer did a lawful pat down search of defendant for weapons incident to a search of another person's house, the officer did not then have probable cause to search defendant's pockets because the character of the plastic bag as contraband was not immediately apparent from the frisk. Murphy v. Commonwealth, 264 Va. 568, 570 S.E.2d 836, 2002 Va. LEXIS 159 (2002).

Defendant's conviction for possession of a Schedule I controlled substance with intent to distribute pursuant to § 18.2-248 was reversed where the drugs subject to a motion to suppress would not inevitably have been discovered in the course of defendant's arrest; the police officer did not develop probable cause to search defendant's pocket and pants leg for weapons or drugs where no evidence indicated that the officer felt an object he could reasonably have believed was a weapon during the initial frisk. Shelton v. Commonwealth, No. 0153-02-2, 2002 Va. App. LEXIS 786 (Ct. of Appeals Dec. 31, 2002).

But where there was reasonable cause to believe that defendant was unlawfully in possession of illegal drugs or a concealed weapon, a limited pat-down search was warranted; the trial court did not err in denying defendant's motion to suppress. Pressley v. Commonwealth, No. 2710-01-2, 2003 Va. App. LEXIS 14 (Jan. 21, 2003).

Search incident to valid arrest. — In a prosecution for distribution of drugs, as defendant's bloodshot eyes, slurred speech, unsteadiness on his feet, and possession of an open can of beer gave an officer probable cause to arrest him for public drunkenness under § 18.2-388, drugs found in a search of defendant's pockets were admissible as the fruits of a search incident to an arrest. Whether the officer exceeded the permissible scope of a weapons frisk, whether he believed he had probable cause to arrest defendant before the search, and the fact that he performed the search before the arrest were irrelevant. Commonwealth v. Lasley, — Va. App. —, — S.E.2d —, 2009 Va. App. LEXIS 10 (Jan. 13, 2009).

Good faith exception. — Assuming arguendo that a search warrant was invalid, seized cocaine was admissible under the "good faith" exception to the exclusionary rule, as there was no evidence that the officers executing the warrant acted other than in good faith and with a reasonable belief that warrant was valid, and the search warrant affidavit contained some indicia of probable cause. White v. Commonwealth, — Va. App. —, — S.E.2d —, 2006 Va. App. LEXIS 95 (Mar. 21, 2006).

Good faith exception to exclusionary rule supported denial of motion to suppress. — Trial court did not err in denying defendant's motion to suppress evidence seized as a result of a search warrant, where despite the fact that the affidavit supporting the same failed to provide the issuing magistrate with a substantial basis for concluding that probable cause to search defendant's home existed, officers possessed an objectively reasonable belief in the existence of probable cause, namely, that the fruits of criminal activity would probably be found at defendant's residence, for the good faith exception to the exclusionary rule to apply. Anzualda v. Commonwealth, 44 Va. App. 764, 607 S.E.2d 749, 2005 Va. App. LEXIS 88 (2005).

Search while being processed for detention. — Where appellant was subjected to a visual body cavity search while being processed for detention into a jail and defendant was convicted of drug possession, the search was reasonable because the jail had a responsibility to find and destroy drugs; regarding appellant's argument that there was no medically trained personnel present at the time of the search, appellant was not subject to the provisions of § 19.2-59.1, because appellant had been charged with a felony. Winston v. Commonwealth, 51 Va. App. 74, 654 S.E.2d 340, 2007 Va. App. LEXIS 485 (2007).

In a case in which defendant appealed his conviction for possession of cocaine with intent to distribute, third offense, in violation of subsection C of § 18.2-248, he argued unsuccessfully that the trial court erred in denying his motion to suppress evidence seized during what he asserted was a warrantless visual body cavity search. During the search incident to his arrest, defendant removed his outer clothes, remaining clothed only in his boxer shorts, and when the contraband was discovered, only the upper portion of his buttocks was visible to the officers. Woodson v. Commonwealth, 2009 Va. App. LEXIS 451 (Oct. 6, 2009).

Police officer's safety and reasonable intrusion upon passenger. — When the state's interest in allowing police officers to take measures for their protection and safety is weighed against the de minimis intrusion on the passenger's personal liberty, the former prevails. Police officer acted reasonably when he requested the passenger exit the vehicle. Defendant was properly charged with possession of cocaine with intent to distribute. Bethea v. Commonwealth, 14 Va. App. 474, 419 S.E.2d 249 (1992).

Evidence found during a consensual encounter not suppressed. — Trial court did not err in denying defendant's motion to suppress evidence, as a police officer's questions to defendant after the officer told defendant he was free to leave involved a consensual encounter and meant that defendant was not seized in violation of his Fourth Amendment rights; thus, defendant's conviction for possession of cocaine with intent to distribute, based on defendant showing the officer an ashtray full of the remains of marijuana cigarettes, which led to the discovery of even more cocaine in defendant's car, was proper. Dickerson v. Commonwealth, 266 Va. 14, 581 S.E.2d 195, 2003 Va. LEXIS 60 (2003).

Suppression of evidence. — Where heroin was found on a defendant during an improper warrantless search where an officer intruded on the defendant's personal liberty by handcuffing him while investigating a traffic violation, a motion to suppress should have been granted. Lawrence v. Commonwealth, 40 Va. App. 95, 578 S.E.2d 54, 2003 Va. App. LEXIS 136 (2003).

Trial court properly denied defendant's suppression motion as the cocaine was discovered during a proper search incident to a lawful arrest for a concealed weapon violation; it was legally irrelevant under the Fourth Amendment that the deputy chose not to charge defendant with the lesser concealed weapon violation of § 18.2-308, upon discovering the suspected drugs during the search, enabling the deputy to charge defendant with possession of cocaine with intent to distribute under § 18.2-248, and possession of a firearm while simultaneously possessing illegal drugs under subsection A of § 18.2-308.4. Slayton v. Commonwealth, 41 Va. App. 101, 582 S.E.2d 448, 2003 Va. App. LEXIS 352 (2003).

Conversation which defendant had with a detective in the detective's car after defendant was stopped for traffic violations was consensual, and the appellate court found that trial court properly refused to suppress drugs and other evidence the detective found after defendant told him he could search his car and his apartment and upheld the trial court's judgment convicting defendant of possession of a controlled substance with intent to distribute, bribery, possession of a controlled substance while possessing a firearm, and possession of marijuana. Ouellette v. Commonwealth, No. 0776-03-2, 2004 Va. App. LEXIS 349 (Ct. of Appeals July 20, 2004).

Defendant's broad and unfocused questions to law-enforcement officers, and continuous insistence on desiring to talk to them about his passenger's involvement in suspicious activity, despite numerous warnings given to him regarding his rights under Miranda, established that police did not violate his right to counsel and right to remain silent; thus, the trial court properly denied suppression of the evidence seized and his statements, and his convictions for possession with intent to distribute and transporting more than one ounce of cocaine into the Commonwealth with the intent to distribute were affirmed. Medley v. Commonwealth, 44 Va. App. 19, 602 S.E.2d 411, 2004 Va. App. LEXIS 453 (2004).

Defendant's incriminating statements made after he received Miranda warnings were properly admitted, as said statements were not made as a result of an illegal arrest, but after a lawful detention by officers and an arrest based on probable cause of finding cocaine and a gun in the residence searched via a valid warrant; thus, defendant's suppression motion was properly denied, and his conviction was upheld. Whitaker v. Commonwealth, No. 3232-03-2, 2005 Va. App. LEXIS 34 (Ct. of Appeals Feb. 1, 2005).

Trial court did not err in denying defendant's motion to suppress, as the anticipatory warrant that was executed at his residence was valid; defendant was protected from an improper search and seizure due to fact that defendant inspected the package delivered to him, accepted it, and took it inside his house, thus lessening the possibility that the package, which contained drugs, was delivered to him as part of government misconduct. Ward v. Commonwealth, 47 Va. App. 733, 627 S.E.2d 520, 2006 Va. App. LEXIS 105 (2006).

Trial court erred in denying defendant's motion to suppress evidence obtained as a result of the lawful arrest of defendant on an outstanding warrant, as the search of defendant at a lockup violated defendant's Fourth Amendment rights in a case where defendant was later convicted of possession of cocaine with intent to distribute; contrary to the Commonwealth's argument, the search of defendant was not a less intrusive strip search, but was a more intrusive visual body cavity search where police officers had defendant bend over and spread defendant's buttock cheeks, and the search was unreasonable because police did not have a "clear indication" that evidence was located within defendant's body and the police officers did not show that they faced exigent circumstances that required such an invasive search be performed. King v. Commonwealth, 49 Va. App. 717, 644 S.E.2d 391, 2007 Va. App. LEXIS 194 (2007).

Trial court should have suppressed evidence obtained in violation of defendant's Fourth Amendment rights in a case where a police officer testified that the officer knew capsules that the officer felt in defendant's left front pants pocket contained heroin because the officer's training and experience told the officer that was how heroin was packaged. The officer also admitted at the suppression hearing that some over-the-counter medications were packaged in capsules and, thus, it was not immediately apparent to the officer when the officer felt the capsules that they contained evidence of a crime. Cost v. Commonwealth, 275 Va. 246, 657 S.E.2d 505, 2008 Va. App. LEXIS 33 (2008).

Suppression motion properly denied. — Defendant's suppression motion was properly denied, and the Fourth Amendment was not violated, where: (1) a police officer had a reasonable, articulable suspicion that defendant was the man who was wanted on the capias as defendant's physical characteristics and clothing matched the description provided by dispatch, and defendant was near the address provided by dispatch in the backseat of a taxi matching the description provided by dispatch; (2) the officer was justified in detaining defendant further as he gave obviously false identifying information; and (3) when defendant struck the officer, he had probable cause for the arrest, which led to the search incident to a lawful arrest in which the drugs were discovered. Jackson v. Commonwealth, No. 0628-02-3, 2003 Va. App. LEXIS 340 (Ct. of Appeals June 17, 2003).

Trial court properly denied defendant's motion to suppress evidence seized from his person and to exclude statements made to the police before and after his arrest, because the conversation with defendant was consensual in that one of the officer's asked defendant for permission to speak to him. Subsequently, a warrant was found outstanding on defendant and the discovery of 58 baggies of crack cocaine on his person was made during the search incident to his arrest, which was lawful. Stith v. Commonwealth, No. 2394-03-2, 2005 Va. App. LEXIS 1 (Ct. of Appeals Jan. 11, 2005).

In a case in which defendant appealed his conviction for violating § 18.2-248, he argued unsuccessfully that the trial court erred in denying his motion to suppress evidence of a crack cocaine cookie block found beneath his seat and his subsequent confession at the police precinct because the police lacked a reasonable, articulable suspicion to believe he was engaged in criminal activity rendering the evidence obtained as a result of that seizure inadmissible at trial. Defendant was a passenger in a car that matched a description of a car with expired Alabama license plates that had been reportedly driving recklessly up and down a block in a high-crime, high-drug area. Ward v. Commonwealth, 2009 Va. App. LEXIS 585 (Dec. 29, 2009).

Trial court did not err in denying defendant's motion to suppress evidence because police officers had a particularized and objective basis for suspecting that defendant was involved in criminal activity since defendant was loitering in a known open-air drug market and was talking to people whom a trained and experienced police officer knew to be drug dealers; defendant was observed waving at vehicles in the area of high drug activity, which the officer, who was an expert in street-level drug transactions, testified was behavior consistent with soliciting potential drug sales. Baker v. Commonwealth, 2010 Va. App. LEXIS 444 (Nov. 9, 2010).

Police officers patrolling a high-crime area were justified in seizing defendant because they had articulable facts that gave rise to reasonable suspicion of criminal activity where, upon approach for investigative questioning regarding his presence in an area where he did not live, defendant fled, clutching his waistband. Accordingly, contraband which fell out of defendant's pocket during the seizure was properly admitted in defendant's trial for possession of a controlled substance with intent to distribute, second or subsequent offense, in violation of § 18.2-248. Simmons v. Commonwealth, 2010 Va. App. LEXIS 418 (Oct. 26, 2010).

Motion to suppress denied. — In the prosecution of possession of cocaine with intent to distribute, the trial court did not err in denying defendant's motion to suppress evidence seized from his person, because: (1) defendant's non-verbal response to an investigating officer intimated that defendant was inviting a pat-down frisk of his person, by automatically assuming the frisk position; and (2) defendant could not be heard to complain by his voluntary acts of submitting to a pat-down frisk, given that the encounter was brief and defendant was not boxed in; moreover, the record adequately reflected that it was immediately apparent to the officer from his initial pat-down that the flat oblong, odd shaped rock he felt in defendant's pant pocket was crack cocaine. Graham v. Commonwealth, — Va. App. —, — S.E.2d —, 2005 Va. App. LEXIS 287 (July 19, 2005).

In a prosecution for possession of heroin and cocaine with intent to distribute, as neither the driver of a rental vehicle nor defendant, a passenger, was a lessee or an authorized driver, and they offered no explanation of their connection to the named lessee, defendant had no expectation of privacy in the vehicle under the Fourth Amendment and thus lacked standing to challenge a traffic stop of the vehicle. Williams v. Commonwealth, — Va. App. —, — S.E.2d —, 2006 Va. App. LEXIS 268 (June 20, 2006).

In a case in which defendant appealed his conviction for violating §§ 18.2-248 and 18.2-250.1, he argued unsuccessfully that the circuit court erred in denying his motion to suppress because he had been subjected to a strip search in violation of the Fourth Amendment. Defendant had not been subjected to a strip search, he was not naked at any time during his encounter with police, neither his genitals nor his buttocks were exposed, and, while a police officer saw defendant's underwear when he removed the marijuana and cocaine, his underwear was never removed. Bell v. Commonwealth, 2009 Va. App. LEXIS 420 (Sept. 22, 2009).

Drugs found in vehicle recently occupied by defendant. — Following an interlocutory appeal by the Commonwealth pursuant to § 19.2-398 A 2, the appellate court determined that the trial court erred in granting defendant's motion to suppress drugs found in a vehicle recently occupied by defendant in relation to charges of possession of cocaine and heroin with intent to distribute, § 18.2-248, because the automobile exception had no separate exigency requirement, and the search of the vehicle did not violate Virginia constitutional law prohibiting illegal searches and seizures. Commonwealth v. Rogers, — Va. App. —, — S.E.2d —, 2003 Va. App. LEXIS 85 (Feb. 25, 2003).

B. Admission of Evidence.

Chain of custody established. — There was no error in admitting cocaine into evidence where, although undercover agent remembered receiving two pieces of cocaine from defendant and police detective documented that he received one piece, it was mere speculation that any tampering or substitution occurred, and totality of circumstances afforded reasonable assurance that admitted cocaine was obtained from defendant. Stevens v. Commonwealth, No. 1522-98-2 (Ct. of Appeals Jan. 27, 2000).

Trial court properly admitted into evidence two certificates of analysis as evidence of the chain of custody of the drugs seized during the drug sales under § 19.2-187.01 in defendant's trial for possession with intent to distribute under § 18.2-248, and conspiring to distribute a controlled substance under § 18.2-256 where: (1) the initials on the postal receipts matched those on the Request for Laboratory Examination; (2) a police officer mailed the narcotics to the Virginia Division of Forensic Science, which verified its receipt by executing the Request for Laboratory Examination; (3) the receipt alone established prima facie evidence of the chain of custody; and (4) that the initials on the postal receipts were not consistent with the signatures on the two Requests for Laboratory Examination did not undermine the statutory inference under § 19.2-187.01. Martin v. Commonwealth, No. 1221-02-2, 2003 Va. App. LEXIS 341 (Ct. of Appeals June 17, 2003).

Fact that a person who was in charge of a police department's forensic division testified that he received drugs which defendant allegedly sold to a state trooper from another person in the division, while a detective who received the drugs from the state trooper testified that he delivered the drugs directly to the person who was in charge of the forensic division, was not enough to break the chain of custody, and the trial court did not err when it found that the Commonwealth established a valid chain of custody. Smith v. Commonwealth, No. 2268-02-2, 2004 Va. App. LEXIS 66 (Ct. of Appeals Feb. 10, 2004).

In defendant's prosecution for possession of cocaine with the intent to distribute in violation of § 18.2-248, defendant's motions to strike for a broken chain of custody and insufficiency of the evidence to establish the intent to distribute were properly denied because testimony of police officers and an evidence custodian plus the jury's observance of the cocaine, and the lack of drug paraphernalia found on defendant sufficiently proved that the seized substance was crack cocaine packaged for distribution. Hurt v. Commonwealth, — Va. App. —, — S.E.2d —, 2006 Va. App. LEXIS 507 (Nov. 7, 2006).

Court affirmed defendant's drug conviction under § 18.2-248 because defendant's objection to the chain of custody of evidence could not be sustained as the Commonwealth had established prima facie evidence that the Division of Forensic Science (DFS) properly had custody of the evidence under § 19.2-187.01; section 19.2-187.01 authorized the trial court to receive a certificate of analysis as evidence of the chain of custody of the material tested. When the Commonwealth presented a duly attested certificate of analysis, it established "prima facie evidence" that DFS had custody of the material described therein from the time such material was received by an authorized agent of such laboratory until such material was released. Mitchell v. Commonwealth, — Va. App. —, — S.E.2d —, 2006 Va. App. LEXIS 499 (Nov. 7, 2006).

Admissibility of laboratory report. — Where the defendant was seen taking money from another person, the defendant handed the other person a very small object from a container later found to hold heroin, the other person was placed under police surveillance and, after being stopped by the police, was seen to throw a foil packet from his car, these facts constituted circumstantial evidence linking the heroin observed in the defendant's possession to the foil recovered from the other person. Therefore, the laboratory analysis of the foil found in front of the vehicle was probative evidence of the defendant's intent to distribute, as well as his possession of, the heroin in question, and the trial court properly allowed the jury to consider the laboratory report and assign it whatever weight the jury deemed proper. Hines v. Commonwealth, No. 0092-86-2 (Ct. of Appeals Oct. 13, 1987).

Because defendant, charged with possession of cocaine with

intent to distribute, in violation of § 18.2-248, neglected to inform the Commonwealth of his desire to have the scientist who prepared the certificate of analysis present until the day of trial, defendant waived his Confrontation Clause rights. Thus, no error resulted in admitting the certificate of analysis without the scientist's testimony. McCray v. Commonwealth, — Va. App. —, — S.E.2d —, 2008 Va. App. LEXIS 36 (Jan. 22, 2008).

Admissibility of advertisement advocating marijuana legalization. — The trial court committed reversible error in admitting evidence, because it was irrelevant, that seven months after his arrest, the defendant placed a political advertisement in a local newspaper advocating legalization of marijuana. The "admissions" contained in the advertisement did not tend to prove that seven months earlier, the defendant grew marijuana. At most, the defendant's statement, "Pot smokers don't deserve to be in prison. How are we criminals?", admitted marijuana use, not that he might have grown or manufactured it. Further, the advertisement concerning "pot smokers" did not tend to prove knowledge and intent to grow and distribute marijuana. None of this evidence tended to prove that the defendant grew marijuana seven months before making the statement. Moore v. Commonwealth, No. 1649-93-3 (Ct. of Appeals May 9, 1995).

Tape recording admissible even if interpreted to prove guilt of other crimes. — Tape recording of a conversation between defendant and a police informant, made while the informant was making a controlled buy of cocaine from defendant, was admissible, even if interpreted to prove that defendant was guilty of other crimes, to show that he knew the substance he sold was in fact cocaine, a required element of the offense. Watkins v. Commonwealth, No. 0543-89-2 (Ct. of Appeals Oct. 23, 1990).

In a prosecution for distributing cocaine in violation of § 18.2-248, evidence of "other crimes" was admissible under the theory that defendant had "opended the door" to evidence by testifying. She had testified that she did not know what crack was, and the evidence was highly relevant because it tended to establish that she was aware of the nature and character of cocaine at the time of the alleged distribution. McGowan v. Commonwealth, 48 Va. App. 333, 630 S.E.2d 758, 2006 Va. App. LEXIS 266 (2006), rev'd, on grounds that the evidence was nevertheless unfairly prejudicial, McGowan v. Commonwealth, 274 Va. 689, 652 S.E.2d 103 (2007).

Other crimes evidence properly admitted. — In a prosecution for distributing cocaine in violation of § 18.2-248, the trial court properly allowed other crimes evidence concerning defendant's possession of crack cocaine when she was arrested, because by testifying that she did not know what crack was, she opened the door to admission of this evidence in rebuttal, knowledge being an element of the offense. McGowan v. Commonwealth, 48 Va. App. 333, 630 S.E.2d 758, 2006 Va. App. LEXIS 266 (2006), rev'd, on grounds that the evidence was nevertheless unfairly prejudicial, McGowan v. Commonwealth, 274 Va. 689, 652 S.E.2d 103 (2007).

Previous convictions. — In a case in which defendant appealed his conviction for possession of cocaine with intent to distribute, third offense, in violation of subsection C of § 18.2-248, he argued unsuccessfully that the trial court erred in finding the evidence sufficient to prove that he had previously been convicted on two prior occasions of possession of controlled substances with intent to distribute. Despite his arguments to the contrary, the prior conviction orders established that he was the same person as was in those orders. Woodson v. Commonwealth, 2009 Va. App. LEXIS 451 (Oct. 6, 2009).

Sufficient evidence of identity in prior convictions. — Virginia Criminal Information Network report on defendant that specifically stated that he used a specified alias was sufficient to establish an evidentiary link with a prior conviction involving a defendant with that alias and defendant. Joyce v. Commonwealth, 56 Va. App. 646, 696 S.E.2d 237, 2010 Va. App. LEXIS 325 (2010).

Presentence report. — In a case in which defendant appealed his sentence for violating 8 U.S.C.S. § 1326, he unsuccessfully argued that the presentence report (PSR) was absent any indication that any of his three prior Virginia drug convictions qualified under the U.S. Sentencing Guidelines as a drug trafficking offense. However, the indictments and the plea agreement for those convictions were attached to the PSR and those documents made clear that he was convicted under Va. Code Ann. § 18.2-248(A) of two counts of distribution of methamphetamine and one count of distribution of cocaine, which constituted drug trafficking offenses for purposes of § 2L1.2(b)(1)(A)(i). United States v. Sandoval-Campos, 2011 U.S. App. LEXIS 23357 (November 21, 2011).

Expert testimony. — Expert testimony, usually that of a police officer familiar with narcotics, is routinely offered to prove the significance of the weight and packaging of drugs regarding whether it is for personal use. Askew v. Commonwealth, 40 Va. App. 104, 578 S.E.2d 58, 2003 Va. App. LEXIS 135 (2003).

Impermissible expert testimony. — Trial court committed reversible error by allowing police detective who qualified as narcotics expert to express his opinion that a person who possessed 93 grams of cocaine was a person who sold cocaine. Such testimony, was an opinion upon an ultimate issue of fact and, therefore, invaded the province of the jury. Even though expert qualified his opinion by stating that the quantity of cocaine "would suggest" that defendant was a person who sold cocaine, expert clearly expressed an opinion upon an ultimate issue of fact. Llamera v. Commonwealth, 243 Va. 262, 414 S.E.2d 597 (1992).

Defendant's statements. — In defendant's trial for possession of a controlled substance with intent to distribute, the trial court did not err in determining that defendant made a knowing, intelligent, and voluntary waiver of rights when defendant gave statements after an officer read the Miranda warnings to defendant at a hospital, but before defendant received treatment, where defendant's injuries did not affect the ability to make a voluntary waiver. Simmons v. Commonwealth, 2010 Va. App. LEXIS 418 (Oct. 26, 2010).

Testimony regarding charges that were nolle prosequied. — Defendant was not deprived of due process at sentencing where Commonwealth elicited testimony regarding charges that were nolle prosequied, because there was no evidence that the Commonwealth agreed not to elicit testimony regarding defendant's drug associations at sentencing, and the testimony regarding such "associations" was admissible under subsection C of § 19.2-299. Sizer v. Commonwealth, 2010 Va. App. LEXIS 337 (Aug. 17, 2010).

C. Sufficiency of Evidence.

1. Evidence of possession.

Evidence of dominion and control. — When cocaine was found under the passenger seat in which defendant had been riding, and he acknowledged that it was within his dominion and control, sufficient circumstantial evidence showed he knew of its presence and character because: (1) it was found "just under" the front of defendant's seat; (2) defendant and the driver had borrowed the car earlier that morning to go "pick up something," and the car's owner said there were no drugs in it at that time; (3) defendant and the driver were the only people in the car when it was stopped for a traffic violation; (4) after the car was stopped, defendant, who had a significant amount of cash on his person, despite being unemployed and homeless, left it without explanation, and, when he obeyed an officer's order to return, he left the door open to provide a means of escape; and (5) an expert testified that the amount and denominations of money found on defendant were consistent with drug dealing. Coleman v. Commonwealth, — Va. App. —, — S.E.2d —, 2006 Va. App. LEXIS 111 (Mar. 28, 2006).

Combined evidence of defendant's possession of the key to the vehicle, the presence of defendant's fingerprint found on a tool to the drug trade in the glove box, the location of the scale and loaded gun next to the drugs, and the location of defendant's personal papers in the same compartment, supported the trial court's finding that defendant exercised dominion and control over the contraband items and was aware of their presence and character. Grimes v. Commonwealth, 2010 Va. App. LEXIS 378 (Sept. 21, 2010).

Sufficient evidence of constructive possession. — Evidence supported the conclusion that defendant constructively possessed cocaine where defendant occupied both the house and, in particular, the lit bedroom where the cocaine was found in plain view; before the police entered her bedroom, the bedroom door was shut; when they entered, defendant was awake and approaching the door; the cocaine was three to four feet from her on the floor and in plain view; and no other person occupied her room or was present when the officers entered. These circumstances support the inference that defendant knew of the existence of the cocaine and had dominion and control over it. McNair v. Commonwealth, No. 2080-93-1, 1994 Va. App. LEXIS 675 (Ct. of Appeals Nov. 15, 1994).

Where defendant possessed car for whole day on day in which

cocaine was found, he was arrested, he was wearing a beeper, he admitted to owning $2691 found in the car's trunk, and the bag of drugs in question was in plain view on the car's front seat, evidence was sufficient to sustain conviction for cocaine possession with intent to distribute. White v. Commonwealth, 24 Va. App. 446, 482 S.E.2d 876 (1997).

Evidence was sufficient to show that the defendant possessed methamphetamines where the drugs were found in a Marlboro cigarette package on the floor of the defendant's truck near where he had been sitting, and two passengers in the truck testified that they smoked other brands of cigarettes and that the defendant smoked Marlboros and had purchased some earlier in the evening. Summers v. Commonwealth, No. 0166-97-3 (Ct. of Appeals June 2, 1998).

Constructive possession by the defendant of cocaine found in a motel room was established where the defendant had been registered and was in occupancy of the room only briefly when the police arrived and discovered the illicit drugs and related paraphernalia already secreted in the bed, and the defendant raised the box springs and mattress together in an effort to divert police attention from drugs hidden between them. Boone v. Commonwealth, No. 1851-97-1 (Ct. of Appeals August 4, 1998).

Constructive possession by the defendant of cocaine found in a car was supported by his custody, control and use of the vehicle, while holding the only keys, together with his statements that he may have handled digital scales later found with the drugs in a locked area of the car. Boone v. Commonwealth, No. 1851-97-1 (Ct. of Appeals August 4, 1998).

The evidence was sufficient to support the defendant's conviction for possession of cocaine with the intent to distribute where the police, in executing a search warrant, found the defendant in a bedroom in which a quantity of cocaine was found, her husband was present in the room with her, the defendant and her husband were both dressed in clothing from which it could reasonably be inferred that they intended to sleep in the room and the defendant's food stamp papers were found in the room, along with a scale and a bag or purse containing $4,500. Morgan v. Commonwealth, No. 3009-99-2, 2001 Va. App. LEXIS 70 (Ct. of Appeals Feb. 20, 2001).

Where a defendant confessed to trading crack cocaine for a shotgun and making other cocaine sales during the several days immediately preceding his arrest, admitted assisting another occupant of the premises in a cocaine sale earlier that day, and admitted handling drug paraphernalia found scattered about the home, and where these statements and the defendant's continuing involvement with others in the distribution of cocaine from the premises were corroborated by the testimony of another occupant, such evidence clearly established that the defendant actually and constructively possessed cocaine. Young v. Commonwealth, No. 1228-00-2, 2001 Va. App. LEXIS 251 (Ct. of Appeals May 15, 2001).

The Commonwealth established that a defendant constructively possessed cocaine and marijuana where the defendant testified that he knew what marijuana, cocaine and a gun looked like, that he sat on a couch with a handgun between himself and another individual, that he saw the drugs on a coffee table located directly in front of the couch and the marijuana on the side of the couch near him, and that he noticed the marijuana and gun as soon as he entered the living room and where the drugs and handgun were located within the immediate vicinity of appellant and, at one point, the other individual went to the door and talked to someone else, leaving the defendant alone with the drugs and handgun. In combination, these circumstances established the defendant's knowledge of the drugs and firearm and that they were subject to his dominion and control. Jackson v. Commonwealth, No. 0684-00-1, 2001 Va. App. LEXIS 21 (Ct. of Appeals Jan. 23, 2001).

The totality of the circumstances demonstrated that it was reasonable to conclude that a container holding rocks of crack cocaine came from the defendant's person where, before retracting his statement, the defendant had admitted that he knew about the drugs and there was simply no other plausible explanation to establish how the drugs came to rest behind the rear tire of a squad car and directly in front of the defendant's feet other than to conclude that the drugs came from the defendant's person. Jackson v. Commonwealth, No. 2823-99-4, 2000 Va. App. LEXIS 729 (Ct. of Appeals Nov. 14, 2000).

Evidence was sufficient to support finding that defendant exercised dominion and control over drugs and firearm found hidden together near his feet, under box spring of bed. Mosley v. Commonwealth, No. 2477-98-3 (Ct. of Appeals Dec. 7, 1999).

The evidence was sufficient to support the defendant's conviction where the defendant was found in a room that he rented, in which illegal drugs were found in a pair of his shoes, the defendant acknowledged the shoes as his and was anxious to retrieve a pair of shoes before leaving the room, and the other individuals found in the room when the police arrived denied putting the cocaine in the shoes. Johnson v. Commonwealth, No. 1487-99-3, 2000 Va. App. LEXIS 504 (Ct. of Appeals July 11, 2000).

Evidence was sufficient to convict defendant of possession of cocaine with intent to distribute where: (1) the police found a large quantity of cocaine, marijuana, scales bearing a white residue, and one-inch plastic baggies in plain view in the same bedroom in which defendant then they would find a firearm; and (2) the fact that police found cocaine on defendant's person and cocaine and marijuana in defendant's vehicle established a familiarity with those substances and indicated an awareness of the nature and character of the cocaine and marijuana in plain view in the bedroom. Pitchford v. Commonwealth, No. 1582-01-1, 2002 Va. App. LEXIS 565 (Ct. of Appeals Sept. 24, 2002).

Evidence was sufficient to prove possession of methamphetamine in that defendant was aware of both the presence of the drug and that it was subject to his dominion and control where: (1) defendant owned the house; (2) he kept a locked safe in the closet of his master bedroom; (3) he kept his guns in a gun cabinet and the keys to the cabinet in that room; (4) he knew the combination to the safe and opened it for the police; and (5) he told the police that he kept additional marijuana in the safe, and the police found marijuana inside the safe and on top of the safe, along with methamphetamine. Coffey v. Commonwealth, No. 2912-01-3, 2003 Va. App. LEXIS 32 (Ct. of Appeals Jan. 28, 2003).

Company that rented a van to defendant properly repossessed the van after it learned that defendant rented the van without a valid driver's license, police lawfully seized drugs and other items they found inside the van after one of the company's employees gave them consent to search, and the appellate court held that evidence found inside the van, including cocaine that was wrapped in a receipt pertaining to repair work on a car which a police officer saw defendant driving, was sufficient to sustain defendant's conviction for possession of cocaine with intent to distribute. Johnson v. Commonwealth, No. 0806-02-3, 2003 Va. App. LEXIS 453 (Ct. of Appeals Aug. 26, 2003).

Evidence that the gun and the cocaine were found in very close proximity to items that defendant admitted to having in his pockets when he entered the room and within arms reach of defendant, who was found hiding in a closet, was sufficient to support convictions for possession of cocaine and possession of firearm while in possession of cocaine. Kersey v. Commonwealth, No. 3354-02-2, 2004 Va. App. LEXIS 59 (Ct. of Appeals Feb. 10, 2004).

Defendants conviction for possession of cocaine with the intent to distribute was affirmed because the evidence that after the police stopped a vehicle for erratic driving they found that defendant had cocaine in his pants pocket and cocaine on the floorboard behind the passenger seat of the car in which defendant was riding, along with an officer's testimony that the amount of cocaine found was too much for defendant's personal use and that the cocaine was packaged to be distributed was sufficient to support the conviction. Copeland v. Commonwealth, 42 Va. App. 424, 592 S.E.2d 391, 2004 Va. App. LEXIS 62 (2004).

Evidence was sufficient to support defendant's conviction for possession of cocaine with intent to distribute, including: (1) photographs of the location of the handgun and the 98 individually packaged baggies of crack cocaine, immediately adjacent to where defendant was sitting; (2) the items seized by the officer upon defendant's arrest, including a cell phone and a large amount of cash in small denominations; (3) defendant's movement away from the cocaine and handgun when he saw the officer approach; and (4) the fact that there were three individuals sitting on the porch did not negate defendant's possession as possession could be shared. Peek v. Commonwealth, No. 0340-03-1, 2004 Va. App. LEXIS 193 (Ct. of Appeals Apr. 27, 2004).

Evidence supported a trial court's finding that defendant constructively possessed illegal drugs found in his home where 14 pills were found in a plastic vial in a candy box in the living room of defendant's home, various empty pill bottles, some of which con-

tained Schedule III and IV drugs, were found in defendant's bedroom, one bottle bore the name of a different party and other bottles evidenced names that had been scratched off, a medication guide was also found in the bedroom, where defendant owned the home and lived there, where, although his elderly mother also resided in the home, she did not take pain medication, where $2,289 arranged sequentially in descending order of denominations was also found in the candy box containing the plastic vial of pills, where defendant was not employed, and where no explanation of the source of the funds was in evidence; convictions for possession of a Schedule II controlled substance and possession of a firearm while in possession of a Schedule II controlled substance were affirmed. Newsome v. Commonwealth, No. 1987-03-3, 2004 Va. App. LEXIS 456 (Ct. of Appeals Sept. 28, 2004).

Defendant's conviction for possession with the intent to distribute heroin was upheld on appeal where the evidence showed that the two heroine capsules were seized when the police came to defendant's home with a search warrant, and defendant showed the police where the drugs were on the mantel of his fireplace in his home. Gray v. Commonwealth, No. 0374-04-1, 2005 Va. App. LEXIS 52 (Ct. of Appeals Feb. 8, 2005).

Circumstantial evidence, consisting of: (1) defendant's possession of a small amount of crack cocaine on his person; and (2) the presence of 26.395 grams of crack cocaine having a street value of $2,850 inside the glove compartment of the vehicle defendant was driving, was sufficient to sustain his conviction for possession of cocaine with the intent to distribute, as the fact finder could infer, based on defendant's possession and the quantity found in the vehicle, that he was aware of the presence and character of the drugs found in the glove compartment; further, said evidence proved more than just mere proximity. Harsley v. Commonwealth, — Va. App. —, — S.E.2d —, 2006 Va. App. LEXIS 82 (Mar. 7, 2006).

Evidence was sufficient to support defendant's conviction for possession with intent to distribute heroin; police located defendant in the specific place that a confidential and reliable informant said defendant would be, at the time the informant said he would be at that location, and the police found heroin in a baggie packaged in 16 individual capsules on the floorboard directly behind where defendant was seated in the police cruiser after he was placed there and police observed him make furtive movements after informing him that they knew that he had heroin concealed in the rear of his pants. Muhammad v. Commonwealth, — Va. App. —, — S.E.2d —, 2006 Va. App. LEXIS 109 (Mar. 28, 2006).

Evidence that when police arrived at defendant's home, he left through a side door to the porch, and that police found cocaine hidden above a cabinet on the porch, along with defendant's prescription drugs, was sufficient to proved he constructively possessed the cocaine. White v. Commonwealth, — Va. App. —, — S.E.2d —, 2006 Va. App. LEXIS 95 (Mar. 21, 2006).

Defendant's conviction of possession of cocaine with intent to distribute was supported by sufficient evidence, as evidence that defendant was found near a table which contained drugs and packing equipment, and that defendant was in control of the home, provided a rational basis to conclude beyond a reasonable doubt that defendant was aware of the presence and character of the cocaine and that it was subject to his dominion and control. Stevenson v. Commonwealth, — Va. App. —, — S.E.2d —, 2006 Va. App. LEXIS 245 (May 30, 2006).

Evidence of constructive possession of cocaine was sufficient to support defendant's convictions of possession with intent to distribute cocaine and possession of a firearm while in possession of a controlled substance. Defendant went inside his bedroom when he saw police; a loaded firearm was within arm's reach when police entered the bedroom; cocaine was near defendant and in plain view; more cocaine was in a dresser drawer and drug packaging materials were on the dresser; bullets were on a windowsill; and some of defendant's belongings were in the bedroom. Cherry v. Commonwealth, — Va. App. —, — S.E.2d —, 2006 Va. App. LEXIS 358 (Aug. 8, 2006).

Where other facts provided evidence from which a fact finder could infer defendant's domination and control over the drugs that were found on the ground and where proximity was but one factor for the fact finder to consider, the evidence was sufficient to prove constructive possession. Sales v. Commonwealth, — Va. App. —, — S.E.2d —, 2008 Va. App. LEXIS 129 (Mar. 18, 2008).

There was sufficient circumstantial evidence of constructive possession to support a conviction for possession of cocaine with intent to distribute: (1) the area in which an officer saw defendant run was an alleyway, no more than 3 feet wide and there was no testimony that this was a high foot-traffic area or that people were gathered in the alleyway; (2) the officer saw defendant place his hands in his pockets, remove his sweatshirt, and then throw that on the ground; (3) the cocaine was found on the ground near the same sweatshirt; (4) evidence supported an inference that defendant reached into his pocket during a chase and threw the cocaine on the ground while running from the officer; and (5) defendant carried a large amount of cash in denominations consistent with drug distribution, and also admitted to ownership of the cocaine found on his person. Sales v. Commonwealth, — Va. App. —, — S.E.2d —, 2008 Va. App. LEXIS 129 (Mar. 18, 2008).

Where the evidence showed that defendant initially admitted owning a handgun found a few feet from where he was arrested, at most 10 feet from the handgun, under a bush, the police found a baggie of cocaine worth over $4,000 under the bush, an eyewitness saw defendant drop a dark, soft item during his flight, consistent with a bag of cocaine being discarded, and defendant admitted owning a digital scale that was found in his car and covered with cocaine residue, there was sufficient evidence to convict him of possession with intent to distribute. Sanders v. Commonwealth, 2008 Va. App. LEXIS 320 (July 15, 2008).

Defendant's conviction for possession of cocaine with intent to distribute was supported by sufficient evidence to show defendant's constructive possession of cocaine as a passenger in a vehicle involved in a police chase. Evidence that defendant was near the cocaine, that defendant stated that defendant did not have anything to do with what was in the glove compartment where the cocaine was found, and of defendant fleeing when police found the incriminating evidence was sufficient to support defendant's conviction beyond a reasonable doubt. McMillan v. Commonwealth, 277 Va. 11, 671 S.E.2d 396, 2009 Va. LEXIS 18 (2009).

Conviction of possession of cocaine with intent to distribute was proper because the evidence was sufficient to prove that defendant possessed the drugs found in his mother's residence under circumstances in which defendant had entered his mother's residence for a few minutes just prior to being stopped by the detectives, at the time he was detained, defendant had a digital scale with him, after obtaining consent to search the mother's residence, the detectives found cocaine in a back bedroom stored inside a locked footlocker, and defendant had the keys to the footlocker in his pocket; in addition, the footlocker contained various items belonging to defendant including his personal paperwork and mail and the box for the digital scale found with defendant. Moreover, the drugs recovered from defendant's shoe were packaged in a similar manner to the drugs found in the footlocker. Banks v. Commonwealth, 2009 Va. App. LEXIS 147 (Mar. 31, 2009).

The proximity of the illegal drugs to defendant's credit cards, bank cards, social security card, clothing, and bed, coupled with her efforts to prevent police from entering her home, were sufficient evidence of acts, statements, or conduct tending to show that defendant was aware of both the presence and character of the substance and that it was subject to her dominion and control. Muwwakyl v. Commonwealth, 2009 Va. App. LEXIS 237 (May 26, 2009).

Evidence supported defendant's § 18.2-248 conviction as: (1) a motel room was filled with a quantity of both powdered and crack cocaine, glasses, jars, and spoons used in mixing the cocaine, and papers on which the newly manufactured crack cocaine had been set out to dry in plain view; (2) a gym bag containing glasses and spoons of the kind used in the manufacture of crack cocaine and a manila envelope bearing defendant's name was also in the room; (3) defendant was only a few feet away from the contraband; and (4) defendant had to have walked into the motel room, past a large quantity of drugs and paraphernalia, to reach the bed in which defendant was sleeping. Adkins v. Commonwealth, 2009 Va. App. LEXIS 336 (July 28, 2009).

Evidence was sufficient to prove possession where the totality of the circumstances established that defendant was aware of both the presence and character of cocaine and marijuana and that the drugs were subject to defendant's dominion and control where defendant was the operator of the vehicle and was sitting next to the console within arm's reach of where the drugs were found, the lid to the console was not shut securely, a passenger testified that the drugs did not belong to her and were already in the vehicle when she entered it, and the drugs found in the console were the same type of drugs that defendant sought in text messages sent a few weeks before the arrest. Hicks v. Commonwealth, 2010 Va. App. LEXIS 188 (May 11, 2010).

Proof that contraband found on premises insufficient to prove constructive possession. — Under this section, proof that contraband was found in premises owned or occupied by the defendant is insufficient, standing alone, to prove constructive possession. Such evidence is probative, but it is only a circumstance which may be considered along with the other evidence. Behrens v. Commonwealth, 3 Va. App. 131, 348 S.E.2d 430 (1986).

Insufficient evidence of constructive possession. — Evidence did not support finding that defendant constructively possessed contraband, even though it was found in a house which he occupied, where evidence did not show that the defendant was in the dwelling recently enough to permit a reasonable inference that he was aware of the presence of the contraband. No direct evidence placed the defendant in the house; while police found mail addressed to him on a dresser in a bedroom, the postmark on the mail was six days before the discovery of the contraband; and they also found evidence of at least one other person living in the house. Diggs v. Commonwealth, No. 0957-93-2, 1994 Va. App. LEXIS 622 (Ct. of Appeals Oct. 11, 1994).

The evidence fell short of establishing that the defendant knew of the presence of drugs found under a crushed soda can in a gutter or that he exercised dominion and control over the drugs where the only evidence was the testimony of a police officer that he saw the defendant standing at the curb of the roadway, bent over at the waist, and that when the other returned to the area where the defendant had been standing, the officer found a bag containing heroin and cocaine under the soda can; the officer never saw the defendant put anything on the ground or put anything under the soda can and only saw the defendant's back and that he was bent over at the waist. Richards v. Commonwealth, No. 0823-00-1, 2001 Va. App. LEXIS 72 (Ct. of Appeals Feb. 20, 2001).

Defendant's presence in house where she rented a room was insufficient to prove beyond a reasonable doubt that she possessed cocaine seized in house. Harris v. Commonwealth, No. 2840-97-1 (Ct. of Appeals June 22, 1999).

Evidence was insufficient to prove possession where drugs were found on rear floor of car occupied by four persons, and defendant made no furtive movements before or after stop or did anything else to incriminate himself. Tables v. Commonwealth, No. 1419-99-1, 2000 Va. App. LEXIS 149 (Ct. of Appeals Feb. 29, 2000).

The evidence was insufficient to establish beyond a reasonable doubt that defendant possessed cocaine with the intent to distribute where the defendant, while driving a relative's car, was stopped by a police officer who discovered a covered can under the driver's seat containing cocaine, but there was no evidence that the defendant had ever touched the can or been aware of its contents; although the defendant had a significant amount of cash on his person and seemed quite nervous, this was explained by the testimony of the defendant's aunt that she had given him the cash to purchase money orders for her and by the fact that the defendant was driving on a suspended license. Williams v. Commonwealth, No. 0289-00-1, 2001 Va. App. LEXIS 303 (Ct. of Appeals June 5, 2001).

Convictions for possession of cocaine with the intent to distribute, third or subsequent offense, and possession of marijuana were reversed because defendant's only proven connection to the drugs was defendant's proximity to them; no evidence proved that the officer or anyone else saw defendant with drugs or saw defendant place the drugs in the plywood. In addition, defendant's fingerprints were not on the bags recovered, which was relevant as the Commonwealth's theory was that defendant was holding the drugs down the front of defendant's pants in ungloved hands. Maxwell v. Commonwealth, — Va. App. —, — S.E.2d —, 2006 Va. App. LEXIS 518 (Nov. 21, 2006).

Although defendant's conduct may have been suspicious no one ever saw defendant with the cocaine at issue, defendant never made any incriminating statements concerning the cocaine, and the one fingerprint found on a plastic bag in a lumberyard to which defendant had run, was not defendant's fingerprint. As a result, the State did not prove that defendant was ever in such close proximity as would support a finding that defendant was aware of both the presence and character of the cocaine, and that the cocaine was subject to defendant's dominion and control such as would support a conviction pursuant to § 18.2-248. Maxwell v. Commonwealth, 275 Va. 437, 657 S.E.2d 499, 2008 Va. LEXIS 21 (2008).

Where Commonwealth's evidence demonstrated that defendant was nervous, told the driver to turn right, and was sitting in car that contained drugs that were not visible to anyone, the evidence was insufficient to support defendant's conviction for possession of heroin with intent to distribute under § 18.2-248. Cross v. Commonwealth, 2009 Va. App. LEXIS 236 (May 19, 2009).

Defendant's conviction for possession of ecstasy with intent to distribute, second or subsequent offense, was not supported by sufficient evidence where there was no evidence that defendant ever exercised dominion and control over the vehicle or the suitcase with the drugs, or that defendant had knowledge of the presence, nature, and character of the drugs such that defendant's occupancy of the vehicle could have supported the conclusion that defendant constructively possessed them. Merritt v. Commonwealth, 55 Va. App. 719, 689 S.E.2d 757, 2010 Va. App. LEXIS 81 (2010).

Evidence was insufficient to establish that defendant possessed cocaine with intent to distribute because the only evidence linking him to cocaine found in an apartment was his proximity to the apartment, which did not show that he was aware of the cocaine or that it was within his dominion and control. Mason v. Commonwealth, 2010 Va. App. LEXIS 79 (Mar. 2, 2010).

Possession of cocaine insufficient to exclude hypothesis that purchase was for personal use. — Where evidence established that appellant possessed about six grams of crack cocaine with a street value of between $500 and $900 and that he had $232 on his person at the time of his arrest, and no evidence indicated whether these amounts of cocaine and cash were consistent with distribution or personal use, and where although a blue gym bag containing drug paraphernalia and razor blades was discovered on a bed in the motel room where appellant was arrested, no evidence established that these items belonged to appellant rather than to one of the room's other two occupants, based on these circumstances, the mere possession of the cocaine and cash by appellant was insufficient to exclude the reasonable hypothesis that appellant had purchased cocaine for personal use from one of the other occupants of the room prior to the officers' arrival. Wright v. Commonwealth, No 2528-96-3 (Ct. of Appeals Dec. 9, 1997).

Defendant's conviction for possession of an imitation controlled substance with the intent to distribute in violation of § 18.2-248 was reversed because the evidence did not preclude the reasonable hypothesis of possession for personal use. There was nothing in the record suggesting that defendant knew that the substance he possessed was not cocaine, and there was no proffer by the Commonwealth that the quantify of imitation substance, standing alone, was inconsistent with personal use. Holloway v. Commonwealth, 55 Va. App. 609, 687 S.E.2d 557, 2010 Va. App. LEXIS 32 (2010).

Contraband found in hotel room. — A defendant need not be found inside a hotel room in order to establish that he constructively possessed contraband found therein. However, something more than mere rental of the room must be shown. Behrens v. Commonwealth, 3 Va. App. 131, 348 S.E.2d 430 (1986).

Where the defendant paid for the motel room, and he was given the only key to the room, which was found in his pocket the following day when he was detained in the motel's parking lot, the cocaine found in the motel room was subject to the defendant's dominion and control, thus permitting a finding of constructive possession. Thorne v. Commonwealth, No. 1011-86-2 (Ct. of Appeals Sept. 30, 1987).

Suspicious circumstances, including proximity to a controlled drug, are insufficient to support a conviction. Behrens v. Commonwealth, 3 Va. App. 131, 348 S.E.2d 430 (1986).

Suspicion, no matter how strong, is insufficient to sustain a criminal conviction. Thus, where, at most, the evidence created a suspicion that defendant was aware of the presence of the cocaine in the residence, the evidence was insufficient to support a conviction of possession of cocaine with intent to distribute. Torian v. Commonwealth, No. 1770-96-2 (Ct. of Appeals May 27, 1997).

Under the totality of the circumstances, defendant, who was convicted of possession of cocaine with intent to distribute under § 18.2-248 and possession of a firearm while in possession of drugs under § 18.2-308.4, was not illegally seized under the Fourth

Amendment as the police officer had a particularized and objective basis for suspecting that defendant was involved in criminal activity where: (1) defendant fled a consensual encounter with the officer; (2) the officer had a reasonable suspicion to detain defendant where he suspiciously, while in a high-crime area, leaned toward a car tire as the officer approached; (3) defendant could not provide an address in the housing area, which had been posted as a "no trespassing" area, without squinting at a building behind him and giving the officer that address; and (4) defendant's placement of his hands underneath him and his unusual movements after he fell suggested that he was attempting to remove something from his clothing. White v. Commonwealth, No. 2091-02-1, 2003 Va. App. LEXIS 367 (Ct. of Appeals June 24, 2003).

Evidence insufficient to prove possession. — Evidence was insufficient to establish that defendant jointly possessed the ecstasy found in the possession of a passenger in defendant's vehicle; the evidence did not establish either that defendant was aware of the character and presence of the ecstasy or that the ecstasy was under defendant's dominion and control. Even though defendant admitted that a roll of cash belonged to him, it was rolled sequentially according to denomination rather than in amounts corresponding to the price of an ecstasy pill; the evidence was all circumstantial and, at most, created mere suspicion. Jordan v. Commonwealth, 273 Va. 639, 643 S.E.2d 166, 2007 Va. LEXIS 59 (2007).

Evidence proving aiding and abetting. — Conviction for possession of ecstasy, a Schedule I controlled substance, with intent to distribute was supported by evidence that defendant served as the "muscle" or "lookout" in a drug transportation scheme and thus, was aware of the presence and character of the ecstasy and that defendant aided and abetted his companions in their possession and intent to distribute the ecstasy. Merritt v. Commonwealth, 57 Va. App. 542, 704 S.E.2d 158, 2011 Va. App. LEXIS 25 (2011).

Defendant's statements to undercover officer prove intent to purchase and possess. — Defendant's statement to the undercover officer that he wanted to purchase "ready rock" and his statement after his arrest that he intended to purchase "crack" cocaine proved that he intended to purchase and possess cocaine. Grant v. Commonwealth, No. 1546-91-1 (Ct. of Appeals April 20, 1993).

Evidence was sufficient to support defendant's conviction for possession of cocaine with intent to distribute it, where a box containing 83.7 grams of cocaine was found on the front seat of a car driven by defendant and occupied by only one passenger, seated next to defendant. Aquila v. Commonwealth, No. 0748-88-2 (Ct. of Appeals Apr. 17, 1990).

Where defendant was the sole occupant of the vehicle in which the drugs were found, he had given his car keys to his girlfriend after seeing the police and when his girlfriend spoke with the police, he yelled to her, "don't give them the keys," his actions and the words directed to her bespoke a guilty knowledge that drugs were present in the vehicle's trunk; given that the car doors were unlocked and its windows were open, the keys were needed only if the police wanted to search the car's trunk and the fact finder could infer that he had given the girlfriend the keys to prevent the officers from obtaining access to the vehicle's trunk, knowing that he had placed illicit drugs there; these facts supported the trial court's finding that defendant knowingly and voluntarily possessed cocaine. Hardy v. Commonwealth, 17 Va. App. 677, 440 S.E.2d 434 (1994).

Where detective described the physical appearance of the item purchased by appellant, causing the detective to believe that, based on his experience, it was cocaine; a high price was paid in cash for the small amount of substance; the transaction between appellant and the seller, like the one between the detective and the seller, was carried on with secrecy or deviousness; and appellant referred to the substance by its street name, a "20," indicating a twenty dollar rock of crack cocaine, the fact finder could reasonably find beyond a reasonable doubt that appellant possessed cocaine. Thomas v. Commonwealth, No. 2352-92-4 (Ct. of Appeals June 14, 1994).

Where a plastic bag containing cocaine was clearly visible on the floor of the driver's side of a vehicle operated by defendant; defendant was alone in the car, provided police with a false Social Security number, and was in possession of $242 in cash; and defendant fled upon learning particulars of the informant's report and at the moment officer spotted the bag of cocaine and proceeded to investigate, conduct indicative of a guilty mind; there was sufficient evidence of knowing possession. Robertson v. Commonwealth, No. 1807-96-2 (Ct. of Appeals June 24, 1997).

Evidence was sufficient to support defendant's conviction for possession with the intent to distribute cocaine in violation of § 18.2-248, where the drugs were found in plain view within defendant's reach, it was unlikely anyone other than defendant left $1,900 worth of cocaine on the back floor of the taxi defendant was riding in, and defendant made a furtive gesture when police stopped the taxi. Richardson v. Commonwealth, No. 2610-00-1, 2001 Va. App. LEXIS 625 (Ct. of Appeals Nov. 13, 2001).

Circumstances which tended to prove possession, including identification of the premises defendant lived in, linking defendant therein, as well as belongings found in the same safe in which cocaine was found, supported the conviction. Norrell v. Commonwealth, No. 0978-02-2, 2003 Va. App. LEXIS 233 (Ct. of Appeals Apr. 22, 2003).

Police detective's testimony that he saw defendant throw an object under a car and that he found a bag containing cocaine under the car 15 seconds later was sufficient to sustain defendant's conviction for possession of cocaine with intent to distribute, even though another detective testified that he did not see defendant make a throwing motion and that the bag of cocaine was found beside the car, not under it. Sawyer v. Commonwealth, No. 1917-03-1, 2004 Va. App. LEXIS 366 (Ct. of Appeals Aug. 3, 2004).

Defendant's conviction for possession of cocaine with intent to distribute was affirmed, as the evidence showed that he intentionally and consciously possessed the cocaine inside the package delivered to him, as he took that package into his home even after he returned misdirected mail to the delivery person and despite the fact that the package he took inside was not addressed to him. Ward v. Commonwealth, 47 Va. App. 733, 627 S.E.2d 520, 2006 Va. App. LEXIS 105 (2006).

Since defendant had not assigned error to the sufficiency of the evidence to support his conviction for possession of cocaine while possessing a firearm, he had conceded the factual finding that he was in actual or constructive possession of cocaine. Thus, defendant had waived his challenge to the sufficiency of evidence of possession of cocaine with regard to the charge of possession with intent to distribute cocaine. Wilson v. Commonwealth, 272 Va. 19, 630 S.E.2d 326, 2006 Va. LEXIS 60 (2006).

Evidence was sufficient to convict defendant of possession of cocaine because defendant was the only occupant of his vehicle when an officer found a baggie of cocaine wedged between the door of the car and the window, and there was no evidence that someone other than defendant could have put the baggie there; the baggie was only slightly wedged between the window and the weather stripping, and it took almost no effort for the officer to pull the baggie out. Smith v. Commonwealth, — Va. App. —, — S.E.2d —, 2008 Va. App. LEXIS 164 (Apr. 8, 2008).

Evidence was sufficient to support defendant's convictions for possessing both marijuana and the cocaine found in a vehicle where the drugs were found in the front passenger compartment of the vehicle, which was occupied solely by defendant. While seated in the police vehicle, defendant emphatically shouted that everything in the vehicle belonged to him, as defendant's fiance came up on foot and claimed that the vehicle belonged to her. Even though defendant later denied the statements, the trial court was at liberty to judge defendant's credibility. Armstead v. Commonwealth, 56 Va. App. 569, 695 S.E.2d 561, 2010 Va. App. LEXIS 300 (2010).

Evidence was sufficient to support defendant's conviction for possession of cocaine with intent to distribute because: (1) when the police intercepted a package, which they suspected of containing contraband, at a FedEx distribution facility, a drug dog indicated the presence of illegal drugs in the package; (2) the police obtained a search warrant, opened the package, and discovered cocaine inside; (3) the police placed a small amount of the cocaine inside a new package and transferred the air bill that indicated the recipient and return addresses onto the new package; (4) a police officer disguised as a FedEx employee delivered the package to defendant's apartment; (5) defendant identified the recipient as defendant's cousin and accepted the package on behalf of the cousin; and (6) not long after, the police executed a search warrant and found defendant, the unopened package, and drug paraphernalia in the apartment. Thus, the evidence was sufficient to prove that defendant knew the unopened FedEx box contained cocaine, that defen-

dant had arranged for a second person in another state to sell defendant cocaine, and that defendant was a principal in the second degree to the transportation of cocaine into the Commonwealth of Virginia. Clark v. Commonwealth, 2011 Va. App. LEXIS 219 (July 5, 2011).

Defendant's conviction for possession of cocaine with intent to distribute was appropriate because the evidence was sufficient. The Commonwealth proved that a portion of the substance seized from the bedroom was cocaine, and the fact-finder was free to make the reasonable inference that the remaining untested portion of that solid, homogenous substance was also cocaine; that, along with defendant's possession of a digital scale, baggies, an "owe sheet" that matched names to amounts of money, and a detective's testimony that defendant's possession of the cocaine was inconsistent with personal use, was sufficient. Burrell v. Commonwealth, 58 Va. App. 417, 710 S.E.2d 509, 2011 Va. App. LEXIS 211 (2011).

Evidence that defendant was in actual possession of cocaine and that a plastic bag containing 11 knotted plastic bags with crack cocaine inside was observed in plain view on the floorboard of the vehicle, directly behind the driver's seat, was sufficient to show defendant's knowledge of the cocaine recovered. Willoughby v. Commonwealth, 2012 Va. App. LEXIS 73 (Mar. 13, 2012).

2. Evidence of distribution.

Circumstances establishing intent to distribute in a narcotic prosecution may properly consist of the quantity of the product involved, the nature of its packaging, and other relevant facts. United States v. Childs, 463 F.2d 390 (4th Cir.), cert. denied, 409 U.S. 966, 93 S. Ct. 271, 34 L. Ed. 2d 232 (1972).

Quantity, when considered in context with other circumstances, is a circumstance which may have significant probative value. Indeed, quantity, when greater than the supply ordinarily possessed by a narcotics user for his personal use, is a circumstance which, standing alone, may be sufficient to support a finding of intent to distribute. Hunter v. Commonwealth, 213 Va. 569, 193 S.E.2d 779 (1973); Adkins v. Commonwealth, 217 Va. 437, 229 S.E.2d 869 (1976); Dutton v. Commonwealth, 220 Va. 762, 263 S.E.2d 52 (1980).

Where in addition to defendant's possession of a quantity of drugs greater than the supply ordinarily possessed for one's personal use, no paraphernalia for personal use were found on defendant when he was arrested, and furthermore, defendant did not appear to be under the influence of narcotics, these facts tend to discount defendant's argument that he might merely have been a heavy user of cocaine. The finder of fact was entitled to consider whether a heavy user with a bag containing four ounces and another bag with only a residue of cocaine, would not show some sign of being under the influence of the drug. The absence of evidence of personal use is a circumstance supporting the inference that the possession is for distribution. Herndon v. Commonwealth, No. 0440-85 (Ct. of Appeals Apr. 21, 1987).

Where the arresting officer testified that, based on his training and experience, he believed that possession of 3.4 grams of cocaine was consistent with distribution, not personal use, and although on cross-examination he stated that it was conceivable that an individual with a serious addiction could consume around three grams of cocaine in two days, this was still sufficient to prove intent to distribute. Gregory v. Commonwealth, 22 Va. App. 100, 468 S.E.2d 117 (1996).

In proving intent, various types of circumstantial evidence may be appropriate, including evidence concerning the quantity of drugs and cash possessed, the method of packaging, whether the defendant himself used drugs and the absence of evidence suggestive of personal use. Jackson v. Commonwealth, No. 2823-99-4, 2000 Va. App. LEXIS 729 (Ct. of Appeals Nov. 14, 2000).

Circumstantial proof of a defendant's intent to distribute includes quantity of drugs discovered, packaging of drugs, and presence or absence of drug paraphernalia. Shackleford v. Commonwealth, No. 2883-98-3 (Ct. of Appeals Mar. 28, 2000).

Proof of the intent to distribute drugs may be established by circumstantial evidence, including the quantity of drugs and cash possessed and whether the accused is a drug user; large sums of money, particularly in small denominations, and the absence of drug paraphernalia supporting personal drug use, have been commonly accepted as factors indicating intent to distribute. Johnson v.

Commonwealth, No. 1487-99-3, 2000 Va. App. LEXIS 504 (Ct. of Appeals July 11, 2000).

Factors which may be considered to determine intent to distribute include the quantity of drugs found, the presence of an unusual amount of money, the presence of drug paraphernalia consistent with involvement in the drug trade rather than personal use, such as a scale or a pager, and the presence of firearms, which are also recognized as tools of the drug trade, the possession of which are probative of intent to distribute. McCain v. Commonwealth, No. 2368-99-3, 2000 Va. App. LEXIS 512 (Ct. of Appeals July 18, 2000), aff'd, 261 Va. 483, 545 S.E.2d 541, (2001).

Several factors may constitute probative evidence of intent to distribute a controlled substance, including the quantity of the drugs seized, the manner in which they were packaged and the presence of an unusual amount of cash, equipment related to drug distribution or firearms. McCain v. Commonwealth, 261 Va. 483, 545 S.E.2d 541, 2001 Va. LEXIS 42 (2001).

In cases lacking direct evidence of drug distribution, intent to distribute must be shown by circumstantial evidence; among the circumstances that tend to prove an intent to distribute are: (1) the quantity of the drugs seized; (2) the manner in which they were packaged; (3) the presence of equipment related to drug distribution, including pagers and firearms; (4) the absence of paraphernalia suggestive of personal use; and (5) possession of a quantity greater than that ordinarily possessed for one's personal use. Askew v. Commonwealth, 40 Va. App. 104, 578 S.E.2d 58, 2003 Va. App. LEXIS 135 (2003).

Possession of a large sum of money, especially in small denominations, and the absence of any paraphernalia suggestive of personal use, are regularly recognized as factors indicating an intent to distribute. Ford v. Commonwealth, Nos. 0446-03-1, 0455-03-1, 2003 Va. App. LEXIS 651 (Ct. of Appeals Dec. 16, 2003).

Defendant's convictions for possession with an intent to distribute heroin within 1000 feet of a school were upheld, as the evidence sufficiently showed that defendant had actual possession of the plastic bag containing the 38 heroin capsules before giving them to his companion, who discarded them while being pursued by the police; moreover, the State properly posed a hypothetical to its expert, despite the fact that the expert's testimony tended to prove an ultimate fact in issue, where the hypothetical posed had some relationship to the evidence in the record. Lewis v. Va., No. 3111-03-1, 2004 Va. App. LEXIS 595 (Ct. of Appeals Dec. 7, 2004).

Sufficient evidence existed to support a defendant's convictions for possession of marijuana with intent to distribute and possession of cocaine with intent to distribute where the evidence showed that defendant was found in an apartment outfitted as a headquarters of a major drug operation, with a large amount of cash in his pocket, and a loaded weapon in his belt. Defendant's convictions were not based on his mere incidental presence in the apartment when the search warrant was executed and the drugs were found; rather, the evidence established him as an active drug dealer present at the headquarters of a major drug operation of which he was a part. Wilson v. Commonwealth, 46 Va. App. 408, 617 S.E.2d 431, 2005 Va. App. LEXIS 324 (2005), rev'd, remanded as to issue of recusal, 630 S.E.2d 326, 2006 Va. LEXIS 60 (2006).

Defendant's conviction for possessing cocaine with the intent to distribute was upheld on appeal, as the state presented sufficient circumstantial evidence of the element of intent through the expert testimony of a police detective, who testified as to the quantity of cocaine found, the characteristics of the same, and the significance of the absence of both cash and a smoking device on defendant's person. Thorogood v. Commonwealth, — Va. App. —, — S.E.2d —, 2007 Va. App. LEXIS 25 (Jan. 30, 2007).

Defendant's consent to a fiance's drug sales from their home, defendant's reliance on the income from the marijuana sales for defendant's livelihood, and defendant's reliance on the pinches from the methamphetamine to support defendant's drug habit provided other circumstances from which it could be inferred defendant assented to the possession of the methamphetamine and marijuana with intent to distribute under § 18.2-248 as an aider and abettor. Dunn v. Commonwealth, 52 Va. App. 611, 665 S.E.2d 868, 2008 Va. App. LEXIS 418 (2008).

There was sufficient circumstantial evidence to show that defendant intended to distribute methadone as the evidence showed that defendant possessed three disparate drugs, a factor leading to the conclusion that he was engaging in the business of drug distribution, and the quantity of heroin alone found in defendant's possession was inconsistent with personal use, as was the packaging of the methadone. While only one of the ten alleged methadone tablets was tested and found to contain methadone, the trial court was entitled to consider all the evidence and was not limited to relying on the number of methadone tablets in defendant's possession. Williams v. Commonwealth, 278 Va. 190, 677 S.E.2d 280, 2009 Va. LEXIS 71 (2009).

Evidence indicating possession and intent to distribute. — Possession of significant sums of cash and drugs, items routinely classified as tools of the drug trade, the manner in which the drugs are packaged and testimony that the quantity and packaging of the drugs in question is consistent with dealing in the local drug trade are all significant factors when determining whether the evidence supports a finding of both possession and an intent to distribute. Wilson v. Commonwealth, No. 1072-00-1, 2001 Va. App. LEXIS 121 (Ct. of Appeals Mar. 13, 2001).

Based on the evidence of the amount of cocaine, the size of the unwrapped rock, the lack of a smoking device on defendant's person, and the absence of any signs of chronic drug use, the trial court did not err in convicting defendant of possession of cocaine with the intent to distribute under § 18.2-248. Robinson v. Commonwealth, — Va. App. —, — S.E.2d —, 2009 Va. App. LEXIS 64 (Feb. 10, 2009).

Defendant's conviction for possession of cocaine with intent to distribute in violation of § 18.2-248 was proper because the evidence was sufficient. Verifying the quantity of the drugs, and the officer's testimony regarding the location of the drugs and lack of smoking or ingestion paraphernalia, combined with the detective's expert testimony regarding the typical operating procedures of drug dealers as opposed to drug users, the trial court did not err in rejecting defendant's hypothesis of innocence. Trimmer v. Commonwealth, 2010 Va. App. LEXIS 189 (May 11, 2010).

Evidence was sufficient to support defendant's convictions for possession with the intent to distribute Methadone and Diazepamin and attempt to deliver to a prisoner a controlled substance in violation of §§ 18.2-248 and 18.2-474.1 because defendant knew of the procedures to turn in prescription medication at a jail annex, and not only did he fail to follow those procedures, but he also concealed the pills in his underwear and told a sergeant that he brought the pills into the jail to give to other inmates so his stay would "go a lot easier;" defendant took all the necessary steps to accomplish his objective of delivering drugs to others in the jail annex because in preparation for reporting to jail, he concealed drugs, for which he had no prescription, he entered the jail with those drugs, and he failed to report the drugs to jail personnel, and but for a strip search, he would have completed his crimes. Hounshell v. Commonwealth, 2010 Va. App. LEXIS 443 (Nov. 9, 2010).

Evidence was sufficient to prove intent to distribute. — The manner in which cocaine was packaged, its location in more than one place in defendant's home, the presence of packaging paraphernalia and cocaine residue, and expert testimony explaining the uses of the paraphernalia, constituted sufficient evidence to establish defendant's intent to distribute cocaine. Early v. Commonwealth, 10 Va. App. 219, 391 S.E.2d 340 (1990).

Although defendant contended the presence of drug paraphernalia was probative of his intent to personally use cocaine, and not to distribute, such evidence did not conclusively refute a finding of intent to distribute. Dunbar v. Commonwealth, 29 Va. App. 387, 512 S.E.2d 823 (1999).

Where defendant acted suspiciously as she and her companion disembarked the train from New York, a known source for drugs entering Richmond, and defendant consented to the search of both bags, the actions and statements of the two permitted an inference that their trip was a joint enterprise and that the defendant was worried that the police knew they were transporting drugs. Yancey v. Commonwealth, 30 Va. App. 510, 518 S.E.2d 325 (1999).

Where the defendant acted suspiciously as he and his companion disembarked a train from New York, a known source for drugs, walked very quickly from the train through the parking lot, and the defendant consented to a search of the bag which contained cocaine, the Commonwealth proved beyond a reasonable doubt that the defendant possessed the bag and knew the drugs were inside it. Hunley v. Commonwealth, 30 Va. App. 556, 518 S.E.2d 347 (1999).

Evidence was sufficient to show intent to distribute, where an informant purchased crack cocaine at the defendant's house with a marked bill and the defendant was found, on the next day, in possession of 15 rocks of crack cocaine, a significant amount of cash, and the marked bill, notwithstanding the defendant's assertion that the cocaine was for personal use, that he had just cashed a Social Security check, and that the marked bill was given to him by a friend for allowing the use of his apartment to entertain a guest. Jones v. Commonwealth, No. 0830-97-3 (Ct. of Appeals May 5, 1998).

Evidence was sufficient to establish the defendant's intent to distribute methamphetamines found in his truck where: (1) A passenger testified that the defendant had distributed methamphetamines to her and her sister earlier in the evening; (2) The drugs were in cut-corner baggies closed with twist ties; (3) Baggies with corners cut off, cut-corner baggies, and twist ties were found in the truck; and (4) An officer testified that, although the amount of drugs found was consistent with personal use, the presence of the baggies and twist ties was not, and that people that buy for personal use don't usually repackage their own supply. Summers v. Commonwealth, No. 0166-97-3 (Ct. of Appeals June 2, 1998).

Evidence was sufficient to establish the defendant's intent to distribute 13 grams of cocaine found on his person, notwithstanding fact that such amount was not inconsistent with personal use, where no paraphernalia connected with personal use was found. Faulk v. Commonwealth, No. 0154-97-1 (Ct. of Appeals June 9, 1998).

Evidence to the effect that the quantity of cocaine in defendant's possession (26.2 grams) was inconsistent with personal use, coupled with the fact that the drug was found together with a large sum of money (over $500) and electronic scales suitable for weighing like contraband in furtherance of distribution, was sufficient to support conviction for possession of cocaine with intent to distribute, despite defendant's attempt to offer explanations refuting intent. Barksdale v. Commonwealth, 31 Va. App. 205, 522 S.E.2d 388 (1999).

Circumstantial evidence was sufficient to support a conviction for possession of cocaine with intent to distribute despite the fact that the defendant did not complete the transaction. Morse v. Commonwealth, No. 2395-97-2 (Ct. of Appeals Oct. 20, 1998).

Evidence established the defendant's intent to distribute where: (1) He possessed 7.5 grams of cocaine, an amount inconsistent with personal use, but had no paraphernalia to personally use the cocaine; and (2) Although unemployed, he carried $565 in two pants pockets and two pagers. Drummond v. Commonwealth, No. 3043-97-1 (Ct. of Appeals Jan. 26, 1999).

The evidence was sufficient to establish that the defendant possessed cocaine with the intent to distribute where the defendant had several smaller bags containing cocaine in another bag, had dropped a scale on the ground when he was stopped by the police, was carrying a pager and was carrying currency in small bills. Ingram v. Commonwealth, No. 2996-99-2, 2001 Va. App. LEXIS 15 (Ct. of Appeals Jan. 16, 2001).

The evidence was sufficient to establish that a defendant possessed rocks of crack cocaine with the intent to distribute where the defendant possessed a quantity of drugs that a police officer testified was inconsistent with personal use, the drugs were individually packaged, the defendant had five twenty-dollar bills on his person, the defendant told a police officer that he didn't do cocaine but admitted he smoked marijuana, which admission was supported by a marijuana pipe found on the defendant's person and, finally, the defendant effectively admitted to a police officer that he intended to sell the cocaine, even though the defendant later retracted this statement. Jackson v. Commonwealth, No. 2823-99-4, 2000 Va. App. LEXIS 729 (Ct. of Appeals Nov. 14, 2000).

Evidence was sufficient to establish that defendant possessed cocaine with requisite intent to distribute, where he was apprehended with 2.3 grams of cocaine, a pager, $935 dollars grouped in nine $100 bundles, and a firearm, all circumstances inconsistent with personal use. Christian v. Commonwealth, No. 0558-98-1 (Ct. of Appeals Aug. 3, 1999).

The evidence was sufficient to establish that the defendant possessed cocaine with the intent to distribute where the defendant claimed he was not a drug user, yet was found in possession of over six grams of cocaine, and had a pager and $150, although he was unemployed. Johnson v. Commonwealth, No. 1487-99-3, 2000 Va. App. LEXIS 504 (Ct. of Appeals July 11, 2000).

The evidence was sufficient to establish that the defendant possessed cocaine with the intent to distribute where, of the approximately 60 grams of cocaine found on the defendant and in his car, 55 grams were packaged in two individually wrapped blocks in a single plastic bag, a relatively large amount of cash was found in the defendant's possession, and, at the time of his arrest, the defendant possessed digital scales, a semi-automatic handgun and a pager; there was also no evidence in the record that the defendant was a user of cocaine. McCain v. Commonwealth, 261 Va. 483, 545 S.E.2d 541, 2001 Va. LEXIS 42 (2001).

Evidence was sufficient to support defendant's intent to distribute charge where: (1) a cigarette box in the car defendant was driving contained 24 individually packaged rocks of crack cocaine; (2) defendant did not possess drug paraphernalia; (3) defendant thanked the officer charging him with possession of cocaine for not charging him with possession with intent to distribute; and (4) an expert testified that the cocaine from the glove box was inconsistent with personal use. Williams v. Commonwealth, 42 Va. App. 723, 594 S.E.2d 305, 2004 Va. App. LEXIS 156 (2004).

Defendant's motion to strike the evidence was properly denied as the evidence was sufficient to support defendant's conviction of possession of heroin with the intent to distribute, second or subsequent offense and possession with the intent to distribute heroin within 1,000 feet of school property where: (1) defendant's claim that he could have been taking something out of the girl's pocket when the officer approached was rejected; (2) defendant's nervousness and heavy breathing allowed the reasonable inference that defendant knew that he possessed illegal drugs; (3) the Commonwealth's expert testified that the amount of heroin, the lack of devices to ingest the heroin, and defendant's unemployment, made his possession of 49 capsules, worth approximately $500, inconsistent with personal use; and (4) the quantity of heroin, alone, was sufficient to support the conviction. Walker v. Commonwealth, 42 Va. App. 782, 595 S.E.2d 30, 2004 Va. App. LEXIS 169 (2004).

Evidence was sufficient to prove defendant's possession of cocaine intent to distribute charge where: (1) defendant hurried inside upon seeing police officers arrive; (2) defendant was in the bathroom immediately before the cocaine was found in the toilet, and the officer following him heard him close the lid to the toilet; (3) defendant was present and in the immediate vicinity of the drugs that were found in plain view; (4) even though he denied ownership, defendant admitted that he knew there was cocaine in the toilet; and (5) other items indicative of distribution, including a clear plastic baggy, a cellular phone, $155, and flakes of marijuana, were found on defendant. Hicks v. Commonwealth, No. 0760-03-1, 2004 Va. App. LEXIS 161 (Ct. of Appeals Apr. 6, 2004).

Where defendant admitted to handing some marijuana to a passenger, the evidence permitted a finding that defendant intended to distribute the marijuana held in his hands. Brooks v. Commonwealth, No. 3399-01-3, 2002 Va. App. LEXIS 666 (Ct. of Appeals Nov. 5, 2002).

Evidence was sufficient to support defendant's conviction of possession of heroin with the intent to distribute where 1.89 grams of heroin was found in defendant's vehicle and $2,148 and a digital scale were found in defendant's residence; consideration of the entirety of the evidence supported the trial court's finding of guilt. Patterson v. Commonwealth, No. 3330-01-2, 2002 Va. App. LEXIS 714 (Ct. of Appeals Dec. 3, 2002).

There was sufficient evidence to convict defendant of possession with the intent to distribute cocaine where over six grams of cocaine as well as cash were found in defendant's pockets and a digital scale with a razor blade were found nearby and because the finder of fact chose not to believe defendant's testimony that the cocaine was for personal use. Gregory v. Commonwealth, No. 0441-02-1, 2003 Va. App. LEXIS 63 (Ct. of Appeals Feb. 11, 2003).

Evidence of the method of cutting and packaging of cocaine as $20 rocks, coupled with a quantity of cash and crumpled $20 bills and the absence of a smoking device or other evidence that defendant possessed the drugs for personal use, supported the finding that defendant possessed the cocaine with an intent to distribute it. Brooks v. Commonwealth, No. 0811-02-4, 2003 Va. App. LEXIS 118 (Ct. of Appeals Mar. 4, 2003).

Evidence was sufficient to support defendant's conviction for possession of cocaine with intent to distribute where: (1) a detective testified that 7.36 grams of cocaine was inconsistent with personal use; (2) the cocaine was packaged in seven packages, and had a street value of $700; (3) defendant carried $65 when he was arrested; (4) defendant carried a pager; and (5) defendant did not carry a device with which to consume crack cocaine, and although he testified at the trial, he never admitted to using crack cocaine, and denied possessing it. Askew v. Commonwealth, 40 Va. App. 104, 578 S.E.2d 58, 2003 Va. App. LEXIS 135 (2003).

Where an officer reasonably suspected a defendant was operating his vehicle in violation of the law and lawfully stopped him and the odor of marijuana and other observations gave probable cause for a search his conviction for possession of cocaine with the intent to distribute under § 18.2-248 was affirmed. Savage v. Commonwealth, No. 0799-02-1, 2003 Va. App. LEXIS 187 (Ct. of Appeals Apr. 1, 2003).

Police acted reasonably when they conducted a strip search of defendant who was arrested for failure to appear in court on a felony narcotics charge before they placed defendant in a detention facility, and the trial court's judgments denying defendant's motion to suppress 12 pieces of cocaine which police found in a plastic bag defendant had placed between his buttocks, and convicting defendant of possession of cocaine with the intent to distribute and obstruction of justice for fighting with police when they attempted to conduct their search, were upheld. Craddock v. Commonwealth, 40 Va. App. 539, 580 S.E.2d 454, 2003 Va. App. LEXIS 296 (2003).

Trial court did not err in convicting defendant of possessing cocaine with intent to distribute in violation of subsection A of § 18.2-248 because: (1) defendant constructively possessed the cocaine where defendant made a movement towards the center of the vehicle, and moments later, the officers discovered the narcotics there in plain view; and (2) the evidence was sufficient to prove defendant intended to distribute the drugs defendant possessed where defendant's bag contained 12 individually wrapped cocaine "rocks" commonly distributed in the retail drug trade, and an officer explained that such an amount was inconsistent with personal use. Spratley v. Commonwealth, No. 0533-02-2, 2003 Va. App. LEXIS 310 (Ct. of Appeals May 20, 2003).

Evidence was sufficient to support defendant's conviction for possession of cocaine with intent to distribute, in violation of § 18.2-248, where: (1) defendant possessed nearly 10 times the amount a typical cocaine user would possess; (2) the cocaine was packaged in a manner typically used for distribution; (3) defendant had $140 in $20 bills on his person, and typical cocaine users paid with $20 bills; (4) defendant had no smoking device on his person, and the Commonwealth's expert testified that a typical cocaine user would have a pipe or papers on him to smoke the cocaine; and (5) the trial court was entitled to conclude that defendant had given false testimony regarding his intended use of the cocaine and that he had done so to conceal his guilt. Jackson v. Commonwealth, No. 0628-02-3, 2003 Va. App. LEXIS 340 (Ct. of Appeals June 17, 2003).

Where an officer saw defendant lean inside a vehicle, hand something to the driver and then place a plastic bag in the waistband of his shorts, the officer placed defendant under arrest. Defendant was properly convicted of possession of cocaine with intent to distribute and possession of heroin with intent to distribute, based on evidence of 55 capsules of heroin weighing approximately 3.9 grams and 3.8 grams of cocaine seized from his person during the arrest. Moody v. Commonwealth, No. 3183-02-1, 2003 Va. App. LEXIS 624 (Ct. of Appeals Dec. 9, 2003).

Circumstantial proof of a defendant's intent to distribute includes the quantity of the drugs discovered, the packaging of the drugs, and the presence or absence of drug paraphernalia. Sample v. Commonwealth, No. 2594-02-3, 2003 Va. App. LEXIS 627 (Ct. of Appeals Dec. 9, 2003).

Evidence was sufficient to show defendant's intent to distribute cocaine when (1) 3.6 grams of cocaine packaged in 48 separate baggies was found on defendant's person; (2) an officer qualified as an expert in the field of street-level narcotic sales testified this amount was inconsistent with personal use, as was the manner in which it was packaged; and (3) no paraphernalia for the ingestion of cocaine was found on defendant. Baker v. Commonwealth, No. 1311-03-2, 2004 Va. App. LEXIS 222 (Ct. of Appeals May 11, 2004).

Evidence was sufficient to support defendant's conviction for possession of cocaine with intent to distribute where: (1) the officer found eight, individually wrapped, aluminum packets of an off-white rock, found to be 1.284 grams of cocaine, in defendant's pants pocket; (2) the officer also recovered currency; (3) defendant waived his Miranda rights, and told the officer that he used cocaine in

exchange for rides; (4) there was testimony as to how crack cocaine was packaged for sale, which was consistent with the way the cocaine was packaged; and (5) the amount of crack cocaine found on defendant was inconsistent with personal use. Muse v. Commonwealth, No. 1556-03-2, 2004 Va. App. LEXIS 290 (Ct. of Appeals June 22, 2004).

Circumstantial evidence of intent, including defendant's statement that the substance found on his person was not for his own use, that he believed that substance was cocaine, and his presence in an open air drug market prior to his apprehension and arrest, was sufficient to support his conviction for possessing an imitation controlled substance with the intent to distribute it. Spinner v. Commonwealth, No. 2548-03-3, 2004 Va. App. LEXIS 490 (Ct. of Appeals Oct. 12, 2004).

Where: (1) an informant arranged to buy cocaine from a person later identified as defendant at a specific time, date, and place; (2) defendant arrived in the precise manner expected; (3) defendant possessed a quantity of cocaine inconsistent with personal use, a large amount of cash, and a firearm; and (4) defendant was present precisely as arranged, ready, and able to sell cocaine, this evidence permitted the reasonable inference that the defendant was willing and intended to sell cocaine; thus, such evidence was sufficient to support a possession with intent to distribute cocaine conviction. McNeal v. Commonwealth, No. 0668-04-2, 2005 Va. App. LEXIS 128 (Ct. of Appeals Mar. 29, 2005).

Considering the quantity of the heroin and the manner of packaging when it was seized, which was backed by the testimony of a detective who qualified as an expert in heroin distribution, the trial court was entitled to conclude that the only reasonable hypothesis flowing from the evidence was that defendant intended to distribute the heroin found when police conducted a search of an apartment he was in. Fitzgerald v. Commonwealth, — Va. App. —, — S.E.2d —, 2005 Va. App. LEXIS 258 (July 5, 2005).

The cocaine was found in her mattress, there was also a large amount of cash in the mattress, there was no evidence of personal use by defendant, and defendant admitted to a detective that she had the cocaine for the purpose of distribution. McClain v. Commonwealth, 2005 Va. App. LEXIS 453 (Nov. 15, 2005).

Because 12 "baggies" of cocaine, a revolver, and currency in small denominations were found on defendant, and because no personal smoking devise was found, the circumstantial evidence was sufficient to conclude that defendant possessed the cocaine with the intent to distribute it. Murray v. Commonwealth, — Va. App. —, — S.E.2d —, 2006 Va. App. LEXIS 52 (Feb. 7, 2006).

Conviction of possession of cocaine with intent to distribute was supported by sufficient evidence, including, inter alia, expert testimony that the amount of cocaine recovered from defendant, some seven grams with a street value of approximately $700, and "unsmokeable" in the form recovered, was inconsistent with personal use; further, no paraphernalia typically associated with personal drug use was recovered from defendant, and in addition, defendant possessed a firearm and two cellular phones, which the expert testified were considered "tools of the trade in narcotics." Cokley v. Commonwealth, — Va. App. —, — S.E.2d —, 2006 Va. App. LEXIS 116 (Mar. 28, 2006).

Evidence that 12 grams of cocaine seized from defendant's home had been cut into pieces for easy sale; that defendant had a firearm, a tool of the drug trade, in his bedroom; and that he had no devices that would indicate the drugs were for his personal consumption, was sufficient to show his intent to distribute. White v. Commonwealth, — Va. App. —, — S.E.2d —, 2006 Va. App. LEXIS 95 (Mar. 21, 2006).

Defendant's conviction of possession of drugs with intent to distribute was upheld on appeal as the Commonwealth presented sufficient evidence of the element of intent, including: (1) that the quantity of the drugs found near defendant was inconsistent with personal use; (2) that no drug-use paraphernalia was found; and (3) defendant's own testimony that he was not a user, which was corroborated by his brother. Harper v. Commonwealth, 49 Va. App. 517, 642 S.E.2d 779, 2007 Va. App. LEXIS 144 (2007).

Evidence that defendant had two-and-a-half grams of cocaine on defendant's person, consisting of one large piece and eight smaller individually wrapped pieces, a manner of packaging not consistent with personal use, was sufficient to support a conviction for possession of cocaine with the intent to distribute, in violation of § 18.2-248. Watson v. Commonwealth, — Va. App. —, — S.E.2d —,

2007 Va. App. LEXIS 408 (Nov. 13, 2007).

Convictions for possession of cocaine with intent to distribute and possession of methadone with intent to distribute under § 18.2-248 were supported by a detective's testimony that the large amounts of drugs possessed by defendant were not consistent with personal use and the certificate of analysis that indicated the ten tablets, one of which was tested and found to be methadone, all appeared to be the same and had identical markings. Williams v. Commonwealth, 52 Va. App. 194, 662 S.E.2d 627, 2008 Va. App. LEXIS 301 (2008), aff'd, 677 S.E.2d 280, 2009 Va. LEXIS 71 (Va. 2009).

Evidence supported defendant's conviction of possession of cocaine with intent to distribute in violation of § 18.2-248 as defendant was aware of, had control of, and consciously possessed the cocaine found on the front passenger floorboard of a car defendant had driven on a suspended license, after defendant was arrested for trespassing under § 18.2-119 as: (1) the officers saw a clear plastic bag on the front passenger floorboard, which contained 41.1 grams of cocaine, worth about $4,100; (2) the packaging of the cocaine was consistent with "mid-level" distribution; (3) 10 grams of marijuana, $209 in cash, and a cell phone were discovered on defendant; (4) the cash was organized in a manner consistent with the sale of drugs; and (5) neither the registered owner nor any previous occupant would likely have left the cocaine sitting unsecured in the car. Simmons v. Commonwealth, 2008 Va. App. LEXIS 360 (July 29, 2008).

Evidence that defendant possessed six clear, empty baggies that were cut up for distribution, that no rolling papers or smoking pipes typically found on a marijuana user were present, and that defendant possessed two cell phones, taken together, supported defendant's conviction for possession of marijuana with intent to distribute under § 18.2-248. Boone v. Commonwealth, — Va. App. —, — S.E.2d —, 2008 Va. App. LEXIS 434 (Sept. 23, 2008).

The evidence was sufficient to support a conviction of possession with intent to distribute cocaine when a detective gave expert testimony that the over 20 grams of powdered cocaine found on defendant's person was inconsistent with personal use and that it had a street value of over $2,000. Aydlett v. Commonwealth, — Va. App. —, — S.E.2d —, 2008 Va. App. LEXIS 514 (Nov. 25, 2008).

Testimony by a police detective that 7.5 grams of cocaine in five bags recovered from defendant was inconsistent with personal use based on the amount in bags and fact that cocaine was packaged in plastic bag corners was sufficient to show that defendant possessed the cocaine with the intent to distribute and supported defendant's conviction for possession of cocaine with the intent to distribute in violation of § 18.2-248. Wyatt v. Commonwealth, — Va. App. —, — S.E.2d —, 2009 Va. App. LEXIS 53 (Feb. 10, 2009).

Detective's expert testimony indicating that the amount of cocaine, 0.898 grams, was inconsistent with personal use; the lack of drug paraphernalia indicative of personal use; the fact that defendant did not appear to be under the influence of drugs at the time of defendant's arrest; and the fact that the drugs were individually packaged was sufficient to support a finding that defendant intended to distribute the cocaine rocks received by the detective. Kearney v. Commonwealth, — Va. App. —, — S.E.2d —, 2009 Va. App. LEXIS 56 (Feb. 10, 2009).

While the cocaine in defendant's possession was not packaged for distribution, the officer's testimony, as an expert, that the amount was inconsistent with personal use and that scales and packaging were found at defendant's residence, was sufficient to support defendant's conviction for possession with intent to distribute. Samy v. Commonwealth, 2009 Va. App. LEXIS 194 (Apr. 28, 2009).

Evidence that defendant fled to the bathroom where the drugs were found upon seeing the officer enter the residence, that defendant stated that defendant did not smoke crack cocaine, and the testimony of a narcotics expert that the amount of cocaine founds was inconsistent with personal use, a fact supported by the absence of smoking devices, supported defendant's conviction for possession of cocaine with intent to distribute under § 18.2-248. Phelps v. Commonwealth, 2009 Va. App. LEXIS 320 (July 14, 2009).

Evidence that two clear plastic bags containing a total of fourteen heroin capsules was found in defendant's car, along with a detective's testimony that the amount of heroin and the packaging were inconsistent with personal use, was sufficient to support defendant's conviction for possession of heroin with intent to distribute in violation of § 18.2-248. Brooks v. Commonwealth, 2009 Va. App. LEXIS 311 (July 14, 2009).

In a case in which defendant appealed his conviction for possession of cocaine with intent to distribute, third offense, in violation of subsection C of § 18.2-248, he argued unsuccessfully that the trial court erred in finding the evidence sufficient to prove he possessed cocaine with intent to distribute. Defendant conceded the evidence, if lawfully seized, was sufficient to prove he possessed cocaine, but contended the evidence failed to prove he intended to distribute that cocaine; an officer, who had witnessed several hundred drug transactions, observed defendant take an individually wrapped rock of suspected cocaine out of a bag and receive money in exchange for that item, and the officers later recovered that same bag, containing individually packaged cocaine, from defendant's person. Woodson v. Commonwealth, 2009 Va. App. LEXIS 451 (Oct. 6, 2009).

In a case in which defendant appealed his conviction for possession of cocaine with intent to distribute in violation of § 18.2-248, he argued unsuccessfully that the evidence was insufficient to support the conviction. Not only did defendant possess cocaine, he possessed multiple drugs that were packaged individually in baggie corners, making them easier, more profitable to sell, he was carrying a firearm, and he possessed no paraphernalia consistent with personal use of cocaine. Scott v. Commonwealth, 55 Va. App. 166, 684 S.E.2d 833, 2009 Va. App. LEXIS 513 (2009).

Evidence was sufficient to show that defendant possessed heroin and cocaine with intent to distribute because he had numerous individual packages containing either the drugs or drug residue, he had no individual use paraphernalia, and he had two cell phones and $61 in cash. Murphy v. Commonwealth, 2010 Va. App. LEXIS 103 (Mar. 23, 2010).

Evidence was sufficient to prove an intent to distribute an imitation controlled substance in violation of subsection G of § 18.2-248 since the evidence did not support defendant's suggestion that he purchased three packages of crack cocaine because a bulk quantity was not available at the time; the absence of a smoking device was evidence of an intent to distribute, and it was reasonable for the fact finder to conclude that since one could not "smoke" an imitation drug, there was no need for defendant to possess a smoking device. Holloway v. Commonwealth, 57 Va. App. 658, 705 S.E.2d 510, 2011 Va. App. LEXIS 94 (2011).

Sufficient evidence supported defendant's conviction for possession with intent to distribute, as the evidence established a buyer gave defendant a $20 bill received from a detective, and in return defendant gave the buyer crack cocaine the buyer intended to transmit to the detective; when the police searched defendant's person, they recovered the $20 bill. Miles v. Commonwealth, 2011 Va. App. LEXIS 283 (Sept. 20, 2011).

Evidence was sufficient for a rational fact finder to concluded that defendant and his passenger shared an intent to distribute the cocaine that was recovered, where defendant exercised dominion and control over the cocaine, yet no smoking or ingestion devices were found and defendant denied being a drug user, and the detective testified that the behavior of defendant and the passenger, driving to an apartment complex known for drug transactions where passenger went inside for a short period before returning and driving off, suggested their engagement in a drug transaction. Willoughby v. Commonwealth, 2012 Va. App. LEXIS 73 (Mar. 13, 2012).

Evidence sufficient to prove distribution. — See Hulett v. Commonwealth, No. 0328-98-4 (Ct. of Appeals Mar. 9, 1999).

Evidence was sufficient to establish that the defendant was distributing cocaine where: (1) the defendant and his companion repeatedly approached cars; (2) the defendant received money from the companion; (3) the defendant disappeared behind a dumpster in the vicinity of a hidden stash of cocaine, return to the waiting car and effect an exchange; and (4) he also opened the trunk of his wife's car, which was parked adjacent to the dumpster and contained substantial cash in denominations consistent with the sale of cocaine rocks like those found near the dumpster. Uzzle, Jr. v. Commonwealth, No. 0192-98-1 (Ct. of Appeals Apr. 13, 1999).

Defendant's conviction of distribution of cocaine in violation of § 18.2-248 was supported by sufficient evidence where defendant was present in an open air drug market engaging in several hand-to-hand transactions, defendant removed an off-white substance wrapped in plastic from his mouth, which a buyer retrieved, defendant's transaction with the buyer took less than a minute, defendant ran from an officer even before the officer announced the reason for his approach, and cocaine was found in the possession of the buyer. Brown v. Commonwealth, No. 3458-01-3, 2003 Va. App. LEXIS 18 (Jan. 21, 2003).

Evidence, although mostly circumstantial, supported the trial court's finding that a paid, confidential informant purchased cocaine from the defendant on each of the four occasions where the informant met the defendant for controlled buys of cocaine. Jackson v. Commonwealth, No. 0113-02-2, 2003 Va. App. LEXIS 41 (Ct. of Appeals Feb. 4, 2003).

Where a witness testified he purchased crack cocaine from the defendant, at the conclusion of the evidence the jury properly evaluated the testimony of the witnesses, including the defendant's alibi witnesses, and determined that the testimony of the Commonwealth's witnesses was more credible than the testimony of the alibi witnesses. Mander v. Commonwealth, No. 1310-02-1, 2003 Va. App. LEXIS 188 (Ct. of Appeals Apr. 1, 2003).

Conviction for distribution of cocaine was supported by sufficient evidence showing that, during the course of a controlled drug buy, an informant drove a seller to defendant's home, the seller took designated money from the informant, the seller entered the residence, and shortly thereafter, the seller returned with cocaine; additionally, the seller was seen talking to defendant inside the house, and defendant was found with the designated money, six $100 bills that had been marked beforehand by officers and given to the informant. The evidence also revealed that defendant had been involved in the sale of drugs on prior occasions, and had large sums of cash on him despite being unemployed for two years. Taylor v. Commonwealth, — Va. App. —, — S.E.2d —, 2007 Va. App. LEXIS 159 (Apr. 17, 2007).

Evidence supported a finding that defendant supplied the heroin sold to an officer as: (1) if the runner possessed heroin when the runner approached the officer, the runner would have immediately sold it to the officer, and there would have been no reason for the runner to interact with defendant; (2) there was a hand-to-hand transaction between the runner and defendant; and (3) the runner immediately went to the officer's car, and sold the officer the heroin. Peoples v. Commonwealth, — Va. App. —, — S.E.2d —, 2007 Va. App. LEXIS 403 (Nov. 6, 2007).

Defendant's convictions for possession of cocaine with intent to distribute, in violation of § 18.2-248, was supported by sufficient evidence as the evidence showed that eleven small, plastic baggies containing crack cocaine were found on defendant. A rational fact finder could conclude that defendant possessed the crack cocaine with intent to distribute as, though defendant claimed that he intended only to smoke the drugs, he had no user paraphernalia and no lighter, match, or other igniter for burning the crack, and defendant could not recall the name of the dealer from whom he purchased the crack. Barnes v. Commonwealth, — Va. App. —, — S.E.2d —, 2009 Va. App. LEXIS 66 (Feb. 10, 2009).

Defendant's continued possession of imitation drugs after learning they were not real and having had opportunities to dispose of them supported the trial court's finding that defendant intended to distribute the imitation drugs and, therefore, the evidence was sufficient to support defendant's conviction for possession with intent to distribute. Boxley v. Commonwealth, — Va. App. —, — S.E.2d —, 2009 Va. App. LEXIS 99 (Mar. 10, 2009).

Defendant's convictions for distributing cocaine were proper because the evidence was sufficient. Defendant's admission that she sold cocaine in the county corroborated the informant purchaser's testimony and the jury was permitted to find the informant's testimony credible; that was a finding that the appellate court would not disturb on appeal. Terry v. Commonwealth, 2010 Va. App. LEXIS 216 (May 25, 2010).

Sufficiency of the evidence. — Where the evidence reflected that defendant's accomplice was a minor and that the cocaine found in a vehicle was given to the driver by the accomplice, who received it from defendant, the evidence was sufficient to support defendant's convictions for possession and distribution of cocaine, in violation of §§ 18.2-248, 18.2-255, and 18.2-255.2. Battle v. Commonwealth, No. 2934-02-1, 2004 Va. App. LEXIS 124 (Ct. of Appeals Mar. 23, 2004).

Because the record clearly established that the term "twenty" referred to cocaine and not marijuana, the trial judge correctly found that a police video and a police officer's testimony were sufficient to convict defendant of attempted distribution of cocaine under § 8.01-680. Turner v. Commonwealth, — Va. App. —, —

S.E.2d —, 2005 Va. App. LEXIS 368 (Sept. 27, 2005).

Given the three-minute time period between a police officer's observation of the hand-to-hand exchange of a heroin capsule between defendant and a man and the seizure of the capsule from the man, the trial court could have reasonably inferred that the capsule retrieved was the same capsule defendant handed to the man three minutes earlier. Wooden v. Commonwealth, 2006 Va. App. LEXIS 47 (Feb. 7, 2006).

Evidence was sufficient to sustain a conviction for possession of heroin with intent to distribute where, during a transaction, the buyer gave money to defendant, and he asked "how many," and the co-conspirator returned from the tree and handed capsules containing a white substance to the buyer. After police confronted the buyer, he threw away five capsules containing heroin. Banks v. Commonwealth, — Va. App. —, — S.E.2d —, 2006 Va. App. LEXIS 60 (Feb. 14, 2006).

Evidence that "dime" rock sold to defendant for $10 came out of a bag containing four other rocks of crack cocaine was sufficient to support defendant's conviction for possession of cocaine with intent to distribute. Bailey v. Commonwealth, — Va. App. —, — S.E.2d —, 2008 Va. App. LEXIS 7 (Jan. 8, 2008).

There was clear and convincing evidence that defendant was engaged in both the distribution of a controlled substance and possession with the intent to distribute a controlled substance where: (1) the drug transactions were directly observed by the police; (2) an officer observed defendant take the suspected heroin capsules out of the bag and receive money in exchange for those capsules; (3) an officer also observed defendant place the money in his pocket; (4) defendant fled when alerted by persons that police were in the area; (5) an officer observed defendant drop the bag and never lost sight of the bag until retrieved by another officer; (6) no one else came into that area until the bag was recovered; and (7) a laboratory analysis proved the capsules in the bag contained heroin. The evidence was sufficient to prove that defendant engaged in a drug transaction and was sufficient to support his conviction of distribution of or possession with intent to distribute a controlled substance. Parker v. Commonwealth, — Va. App. —, — S.E.2d —, 2008 Va. App. LEXIS 223 (May 6, 2008).

Evidence supported defendant's conviction of possession of cocaine with intent to distribute in violation of § 18.2-248 as defendant was the sole occupant of a car in which cocaine was found on the front passenger floorboard, and defendant did not tell the police that defendant was with anyone standing on the sidewalk, or that there had been passengers in the car; the cocaine was under defendant's dominion and control. Simmons v. Commonwealth, 2008 Va. App. LEXIS 360 (July 29, 2008).

Where evidence showed that a paid confidential informant engaged in a series of "buy-walk" controlled purchases of illegal narcotics from defendant while outfitted with audio and video recording equipment that recorded the transactions was sufficient to sustain convictions for two counts of distribution of cocaine and two counts of distribution of heroin in violation of subsection C of § 18.2-248. Gay v. Commonwealth, 2010 Va. App. LEXIS 467 (Nov. 30, 2010).

Evidence was sufficient to convict appellant of possession of the cocaine with intent to distribute under § 18.2-248 as he possessed the keys to the gold car, which contained the cocaine, the gun and clothing similar to appellant's, from which it could be inferred that the contraband in the car was subject to his dominion and control. Womack v. Commonwealth, 2013 Va. App. LEXIS 38 (Feb. 5, 2013).

Evidence sufficient to support conviction as principal administrator, organizer or leader of a continuing criminal enterprise. — Evidence was sufficient to support defendant's conviction under subsection H2 of § 18.2-248; there was testimony that the substance defendant possessed was bought and sold in countless transactions over the course of a year without complaint, supporting an inference that it was real crack; the testimony of witnesses as to the amount of crack purchased and sold by defendant was credible evidence that defendant possessed with intent to distribute as much as 13 kilograms of crack; and the evidence supported a finding that defendant organized, supervised, or managed five others, including a bodyguard and a chauffeur. Dunaway v. Commonwealth, 52 Va. App. 281, 663 S.E.2d 117, 2008 Va. App. LEXIS 326 (2008).

Evidence insufficient to exclude every reasonable hypothesis of innocence. — Evidence that cocaine was found in a gym bag that also contained various personal items belonging to the defendant simply did not exclude the very real possibility that someone other than the defendant used or had access to the gym bag and had left the drugs there unbeknownst to him. Plunkett v. Commonwealth, Nos. 3002-99-3, 0257-00-3, 2000 Va. App. LEXIS 831 (Ct. of Appeals Dec. 19, 2000).

There was insufficient evidence to support defendant's convictions for possession of cocaine and possession of cocaine with intent to distribute because the evidence that linked the passenger to the drugs and established his guilt did not also link defendant to the drugs and establish defendant's guilt. Defendant did not arouse suspicion when stopped, he was cooperative, he consented to both searches, and he had no drugs on his person or in his bedroom. No acts, statements, or conduct of defendant suggested that he knew the drugs were present or consciously exercised dominion and control over them. The evidence never placed defendant in the presence of drugs in plain view. It did not show any joint action or effort that permitted an inference of joint enterprise or possession. Silencieux v. Commonwealth, No. 2701-03-2, 2004 Va. App. LEXIS 355 (Ct. of Appeals July 20, 2004).

Evidence insufficient to prove intent to distribute. — In a prosecution of defendant for possession of LSD with intent to distribute, the evidence was insufficient to establish defendant's intent to distribute those drugs where there was no showing by the prosecution that the amount of LSD possessed was incompatible with the hypothesis that the defendant had it for his own use; that his party guests at the time of the raid had recently used LSD; or that any other person seen coming out of the defendant's apartment was found in possession of LSD. Bentley v. Cox, 508 F. Supp. 870 (E.D. Va. 1981).

The Commonwealth failed to prove beyond a reasonable doubt intent to distribute, where the police found in a dresser drawer a bag which contained seven sandwich baggies, each containing ten baggie corners, for a total of seventy plastic corners containing a total of 4.2 ounces of marijuana, no unusual amounts of money or marijuana related paraphernalia were found during the search of the apartment or on the person of defendant upon her arrest, and an officer testified that the mode of packaging was as consistent with purchase as with distribution. Wells v. Commonwealth, 2 Va. App. 549, 347 S.E.2d 139 (1986).

Because the quantity of residue found in the defendant's possession was too small to be distributed, even assuming that the trier of fact could infer from the evidence introduced at trial that the defendant had in the past distributed cocaine, there was no basis on which the trier of fact could infer that the residue introduced at trial was part of that larger supply. Moreover, no evidence was presented as to when or where the supply had been either possessed or distributed. Thus, the Commonwealth failed to prove contemporaneous possession and intent to distribute. Stanley v. Commonwealth, 12 Va. App. 867, 407 S.E.2d 13 (1991).

Where evidence showed that the police found a film canister containing 8.17 grams of chunky cocaine in a duffle bag in the defendant's bedroom; that no paraphernalia was found; that no evidence indicated that the amount possessed was consistent with distribution or personal use; that neither a large sum of money nor packaging materials were seized; and that evidence of the defendant's intent was limited to the suspicions of those who lived in the same building, the evidence was insufficient to support a finding that the defendant possessed cocaine with the intent to distribute it. Taylor v. Commonwealth, No. 0610-93-2 (Ct. of Appeals Oct. 11, 1994).

The testimony of those living in the building with the defendant expressing suspicion about his activities amounted to no more than surmise or speculation, an inadequate basis for finding the defendant's intent to distribute cocaine beyond a reasonable doubt. Taylor v. Commonwealth, No. 0610-93-2 (Ct. of Appeals Oct. 11, 1994).

Although evidence established that defendant possessed cocaine, it failed to exclude all reasonable hypotheses of defendant's innocence on charge of distribution or intent to distribute. Ramsey v. Commonwealth, No. 2958-98-2 (Ct. of Appeals Oct. 19, 1999).

The evidence was insufficient to exclude every reasonable hypothesis except that of guilt where the evidence established only that the defendant possessed a small quantity of cocaine; no evidence proved that he owned or constructively possessed other items of contraband found by the police in executing a search warrant at the defendant's aunt's house. Leftwich v. Commonwealth, No. 2466-99-3, 2000 Va. App. LEXIS 761 (Ct. of Appeals Nov. 28, 2000).

Evidence was insufficient to support defendant's conviction for possession of cocaine with the intent to distribute; there was no evidence presented at defendant's bench trial that the cocaine residue that police found in a raid on the residence where defendant lived with other people was the remainder of a larger supply that was intended for distribution. Lunceford v. Commonwealth, — Va. App. —, — S.E.2d —, 2006 Va. App. LEXIS 98 (Mar. 21, 2006).

Evidence was insufficient to support defendant's conviction for possession with the intent to distribute cocaine, as a principal in the second degree, because, given that the principal in the first degree was unknown, and it was not proven that defendant had exclusive control and authority over the residence where the drugs were found, defendant resided with other people, the circumstantial evidence that was presented by the Commonwealth of Virginia failed to exclude all reasonable inferences inconsistent with defendant's guilt as a principal in the second degree. Brickhouse v. Commonwealth, 276 Va. 682, 668 S.E.2d 160, 2008 Va. LEXIS 113 (2008).

Sufficient evidence of felony murder. — Commonwealth proved an unbroken chain of events leading from appellant's sale of the heroin to victim's death where evidence established that: (1) appellant sold the heroin to buyer at 9:00 p.m.; (2) appellant knew buyer was going to resell the heroin to victim and warned her of the strength of the drugs; (3) 30 to 45 minutes later, buyer sold the heroin to victim; (4) victim remained in her kitchen with the bag of heroin and cotton, which is used for injecting heroin; and (5) victim fell asleep on her sofa and died. Hillman v. Commonwealth, No. 2194-93-4 (Ct. of Appeals May 16, 1995).

Insufficient evidence of knowledge of intended illegal use. — Where no testimony was introduced to prove buyer's level of personal consumption, how often he consumed LSD, how powerful one LSD dose is, how long unused LSD can be stored before it loses its potency, or why his purchase of 2,000 hits differed from the quantities purchased earlier in the year-long series of transactions, without more compelling evidence in the record, expert testimony on these issues was necessary to establish that appellant knew or should have known that buyer was distributing LSD. Hudak v. Commonwealth, 19 Va. App. 260, 450 S.E.2d 769 (1994).

Evidence insufficient to prove possession. — In a prosecution of defendant for possession of LSD with the intent to distribute, the proof of the defendant's possession of the substance was defective since the prosecution established only that 31 tablets of LSD were found in an envelope behind a garbage can in the kitchen, there was no evidence that the defendant, by his statements or conduct during the search, indicated his awareness of the existence of the LSD at the place where it was found, and it was not in plain view; thus, the evidence was merely that LSD was found in the defendant's kitchen on the night of a party at his premises. Bentley v. Cox, 508 F. Supp. 870 (E.D. Va. 1981).

Evidence failed to sufficiently relate any cocaine to either defendant or the alleged offense, and therefore, the requisite corpus delicti of the crime was not proven; witness' testimony was simply insufficient to prove that defendant distributed cocaine to her. Hinton v. Commonwealth, 15 Va. App. 64, 421 S.E.2d 35 (1992).

3. Evidence of conspiracy.

Accomplice testimony sufficiently corroborated to support conviction. — In a criminal prosecution for two counts of distribution of morphine and one count of conspiracy to distribute morphine, an accomplice's testimony was sufficiently corroborated by a police investigator and a confidential informant who taped a sales transaction. The court of appeals affirmed defendant's convictions. Johnson v. Commonwealth, 42 Va. App. 46, 590 S.E.2d 75, 2003 Va. App. LEXIS 673 (2003).

Insufficient evidence of conspiracy to distribute. — Neither the ongoing relationship between appellant and LSD buyer, nor the extension of credit from buyer to appellant, provided sufficient evidence with which the jury could have reasonably concluded that a conspiracy to distribute existed. The transactions between appellant and buyer simply lacked the essential element of an agreement between two parties to commit a subsequent distribution offense together. Hudak v. Commonwealth, 19 Va. App. 260, 450 S.E.2d 769 (1994).

Defendant's conviction for conspiracy to distribute a controlled substance was reversed, as the Commonwealth did not establish through sufficient corroborating evidence the corpus delicti; rather, the Commonwealth relied on mere conjecture and speculation that defendant was involved in an agreement with another person to distribute drugs. Corsaro v. Commonwealth, — Va. App. —, — S.E.2d —, 2006 Va. App. LEXIS 516 (Nov. 14, 2006).

Possession by more than one party. — Where the drugs at issue are possessed by more than one person, the commonwealth may not rely upon the quantity and packaging of drugs to establish a defendant's intent to distribute because one party in possession may intend to distribute the drugs while another person who constructively possesses the same substances because they are subject to his dominion and control may not share the intent to distribute the substances. Jackson v. Commonwealth, No. 0684-00-1, 2001 Va. App. LEXIS 21 (Ct. of Appeals Jan. 23, 2001).

Evidence held sufficient to establish conspiracy. — Where by selling cocaine to co-conspirator and receiving partial payment of less than agreed price, defendant retained interest in and maintained continuing participation in co-conspirator's venture, where by advancing cocaine on credit, and insuring that co-conspirator could perform his obligations, defendant actively became partner in venture and where evidence supported finding that defendant was drug dealer who agreed to credit arrangement with co-conspirator, another drug dealer, in hope of promoting future dealings, acts evinced agreement between and concert of action by parties sufficient to prove conspiracy beyond reasonable doubt. Zuniga v. Commonwealth, 7 Va. App. 523, 375 S.E.2d 381 (1988).

Evidence held sufficient to support conviction of conspiracy to sell, give, or distribute cocaine in violation of this section and § 18.2-256. Hodge v. Commonwealth, 7 Va. App. 351, 374 S.E.2d 76 (1988).

The Commonwealth's evidence was competent, not inherently incredible and sufficient to prove beyond a reasonable doubt that the defendant and a third party had a pre-offense agreement to distribute cocaine and engaged in a conspiracy to distribute cocaine, where the co-conspirator flagged down an unmarked police vehicle containing undercover officers, inquired as to the occupants' interest in purchasing drugs, told the driver to drive down the street to a known drug area, then instructed the driver to return to their original location and told the driver to pull up by the defendant and where, without prompting from the co-conspirator, the defendant walked over to the vehicle and asked the co-conspirator what the occupants of the vehicle wanted and the co-conspirator told the defendant the type and quantity of drug; unless there was a prearranged agreement to sell drugs, there was no reason for the defendant to approach the vehicle and to spontaneously ask the co-conspirator what the occupants wanted. Taylor v. Commonwealth, No. 1728-00-1, 2001 Va. App. LEXIS 310 (Ct. of Appeals June 5, 2001).

Defendant's convictions for conspiracy to distribute cocaine under §§ 18.2-248 and 18.2-256 were affirmed; the evidence established that defendant's associate and defendant conspired to distribute cocaine to an undercover police officer, and the jury could reasonably infer from a detective's testimony and use of the term "employ" that there was an agreement between the associate and defendant that the associate would provide certain services for defendant. Walker v. Commonwealth, — Va. App. —, — S.E.2d —, 2006 Va. App. LEXIS 491 (Oct. 31, 2006).

Sufficient evidence supported defendant's conviction for conspiracy to possess cocaine with intent to distribute, as the close timeframe and coordinated efforts of two individuals and defendant supported the reasonable inference that one of the individuals and defendant had a prearranged plan to sell cocaine; that individual's attempt to conceal the arrangement to sell cocaine undermined the individual's testimony that the individual was merely present during the transaction. Miles v. Commonwealth, 2011 Va. App. LEXIS 283 (Sept. 20, 2011).

Circumstantial evidence supported defendant's convictions for conspiracy to distribute drugs in violation of §§ 18.2-256 and 18.2-248 because a reasonable fact-finder could conclude that defendant and her boyfriend agreed to meet an informant in order to sell him cocaine and that defendant's part in the conspiracy was neither innocent nor inadvertent; On two separate occasions defendant drove her boyfriend to the same parking lot, where the boyfriend made a quick transaction with the informant, who had purchased drugs from him in the past. Foster v. Commonwealth, 2012 Va. App. LEXIS 310 (Oct. 2, 2012).

Evidence of conspiracy held insufficient. — In prosecution for violation of this section and § 18.2-256, sufficient evidence was not presented to establish prima facie case of conspiracy where Commonwealth introduced no evidence, direct or circumstantial, to prove existence of agreement between defendant and unidentified man apart from statements made by unidentified man, and where Commonwealth's independent evidence of conspiracy consisted merely of testimony that two men met on street corner for 15 to 20 seconds and their hands came together in air for 3 to 5 seconds. Poole v. Commonwealth, 7 Va. App. 510, 375 S.E.2d 371 (1988).

Evidence was sufficient to establish that defendant was principal in the second degree. — Evidence was sufficient to support defendant's conviction as a principal in the second degree in the distribution of cocaine, even though defendant was not actually present when the cocaine was transferred by another, and defendant was a couple hundred yards away; as actual presence at the scene of the commission of a crime was not required to convict an accused as a principal in the second degree, and defendant, in the instant case, was constructively present at the crime's commission and was aiding and abetting in the commission of the crime, under § 18.2-18. Paige v. Commonwealth, No. 1444-02-4, 2003 Va. App. LEXIS 492 (Ct. of Appeals Sept. 30, 2003).

Defendant's convictions for distribution of cocaine and conspiracy to distribute cocaine were affirmed because sufficient evidence, in the form of the intermediaries testimony and telephone logs, supported the jury's finding that defendant was guilty of distribution of cocaine and conspiracy to distribute cocaine through sales by the intermediaries to an undercover officer on defendant's behalf. Franco v. Commonwealth, No. 0222-03-4, 2004 Va. App. LEXIS 73 (Ct. of Appeals Feb. 10, 2004).

Possession and assisting a person to sell does not prove conspiracy. — While certain overt conduct may be sufficient to prove the existence of an agreement, simply proving the act of constructively possessing cocaine and assisting a person to sell it is not sufficient to establish a conspiracy. The evidence must show an agreement between the parties, and that is not shown by proving that one party decides or undertakes to assist the other. Woodley v. Commonwealth, No. 2122-93-2 (Ct. of Appeals Feb. 21, 1995).

Knowledge of nature of drug. — Defendant's conviction for possession of ecstasy with intent to distribute in violation of § 18.2-248 was affirmed because evidence of defendant's acts, statements, and conduct established his knowledge of the nature and character of the drug. Robinson v. Commonwealth, 2010 Va. App. LEXIS 21 (Jan. 19, 2010).

CIRCUIT COURT OPINIONS

Motion to suppress evidence. — Police officer who saw defendant's vehicle weaving in traffic and make a right-hand turn without using a turn signal had reason to believe that defendant was driving under the influence, and the officer lawfully seized drugs which the officer saw in defendant's vehicle after the officer stopped defendant's vehicle. Commonwealth v. Brock, — Va. Cir. —, 2002 Va. Cir. LEXIS 270 (Newport News July 22, 2002).

Because a reasonable person in defendant's position would have believed that after an officer's explanation regarding defendant's failure to possess a city and county tax sticker, and after defendant's registration and license were cleared the traffic stop was over and defendant was free to leave, defendant's consent to search thereafter was involuntary, warranting suppression of the marijuana and cocaine seized from his person. Commonwealth v. Cooper, 68 Va. Cir. 515, 2004 Va. Cir. LEXIS 367 (Charlottesville Dec. 6, 2004).

Granting of defendant's motion to suppress charges under § 18.2-248 was appropriate because the Commonwealth failed to prove that defendant's consent was voluntary. In view of a lieutenant's accusation that defendant was transporting illegal drugs in her vehicle, no reasonable person in defendant's position would have felt free to withhold consent. Commonwealth v. Johnston, 82 Va. Cir. 381, 2011 Va. Cir. LEXIS 196 (Martinsville Mar. 22, 2011).

Imposition of enhanced punishment. — Enhanced punishment was properly applied for multiple convictions on separate offenses in a simultaneous prosecution, because by sufficiently establishing each offense, the Commonwealth necessarily proved the second or subsequent offense for purposes of subsection C of this section. Commonwealth v. Sanderson, 55 Va. Cir. 135, 2001 Va. Cir. LEXIS 255 (Norfolk 2001).

OPINIONS OF THE ATTORNEY GENERAL

Food stamp benefits. — The federal Personal Responsibility and Work Opportunity Reconciliation Act encompasses felony convictions for manufacturing controlled substances or for obtaining controlled substances by false pretenses; those persons with such convictions are disqualified from receiving food stamp benefits because § 63.2-505.2 does not exempt such convictions from the application of the federal law. See opinion of Attorney General to The Honorable Gerald E. Mabe, II, Commonwealth's Attorney, 11-112, 2012 Va. AG LEXIS 5 (1/27/12).

§ 18.2-248.01. Transporting controlled substances into the Commonwealth; penalty.

Except as authorized in the Drug Control Act (§ 54.1-3400 et seq.) it is unlawful for any person to transport into the Commonwealth by any means with intent to sell or distribute one ounce or more of cocaine, coca leaves or any salt, compound, derivative or preparation thereof as described in Schedule II of the Drug Control Act or one ounce or more of any other Schedule I or II controlled substance or five or more pounds of marijuana. A violation of this section shall constitute a separate and distinct felony. Upon conviction, the person shall be sentenced to not less than five years nor more than 40 years imprisonment, three years of which shall be a mandatory minimum term of imprisonment, and a fine not to exceed $1,000,000. A second or subsequent conviction hereunder shall be punishable by a mandatory minimum term of imprisonment of 10 years, which shall be served consecutively with any other sentence.

History.

1992, c. 723; 2000, cc. 1020, 1041; 2004, c. 461.

CASE NOTES

Constitutionality. — This section does not violate the Commerce Clause by prohibiting the transportation of certain controlled substances either into or through the Commonwealth. Seke v. Commonwealth, 24 Va. App. 318, 482 S.E.2d 88 (1997).

The plain and obvious meaning of § 18.2-248 and this section is to prohibit the possession or transportation of illegal substances in Virginia by a person whose intent is to distribute them anywhere. Seke v. Commonwealth, 24 Va. App. 318, 482 S.E.2d 88 (1997).

Venue. — Venue properly exists in each jurisdiction through which the statutory minimum quantity of a controlled substance was transported but not in those jurisdictions where less than the required amount was transported; venue was, accordingly, not appropriate in the city in which a package containing one gram of cocaine was delivered to the defendant where the package in question had contained a much larger quantity when it had been transported to another city but all but one gram had been removed prior to the controlled delivery to the defendant. Green v. Commonwealth, 32 Va. App. 438, 528 S.E.2d 187, 2000 Va. App. LEXIS 335 (2000).

No geographical limitation on intent element. — The phrase "intent . . . to distribute" in both § 18.2-248 and this section

contains no geographical limitation. The Commonwealth is not required to prove the place where a defendant intends to distribute illegal substances in order to obtain a conviction under either section of the Code of Virginia. Seke v. Commonwealth, 24 Va. App. 318, 482 S.E.2d 88 (1997).

Virginia not required to be final destination. — The Commonwealth is not required to prove that a defendant's intended final destination is Virginia in order to obtain a conviction under this section. Instead, a violation of this section is proved when a person enters the Commonwealth while transporting any of the illegal substances set forth in this section. Seke v. Commonwealth, 24 Va. App. 318, 482 S.E.2d 88 (1997).

Defendant's convictions for transporting into the Commonwealth more than one ounce of heroin with intent to distribute and for conspiring to transport into the Commonwealth more than one ounce of heroin with intent to distribute, after heroin was found in a bag during a consensual search of the defendant's railroad sleeper car room and the defendant confessed to transporting the heroin for another person from Florida to New York, were affirmed as the trial court did not err in denying the defendant's motion to dismiss on the ground that he had already been prosecuted for the same conduct and acts in federal court, in denying defendant's motion to suppress on the grounds he was illegally seized in violation of his Fourth Amendment rights, and in denying defendant's motion to exclude evidence previously suppressed in federal court under the doctrines of res judicata and collateral estoppel. Londono v. Commonwealth, 40 Va. App. 377, 579 S.E.2d 641, 2003 Va. App. LEXIS 257 (2003).

Importation shown by circumstantial evidence. — Evidence was sufficient to support conviction for importing narcotics into Virginia with intent to distribute, in violation of § 18.2-248.01, where defendant was driving and owned car in which the marijuana was found, as possession could be actual or constructive; when stopped by a trooper, defendant's vehicle was traveling southbound away from Maryland and toward Norfolk, Virginia, and defendant twice informed the trooper that defendant had just come from Maryland, which constituted circumstantial evidence relating to the entry of the marijuana into Virginia and defendant's role in that entry, and such evidence reasonably supported a determination that when defendant was stopped, defendant had just transported the drugs from Maryland into Virginia. Kelly v. Commonwealth, 41 Va. App. 250, 584 S.E.2d 444, 2003 Va. App. LEXIS 419 (2003).

Receiving a package through the mail was sufficient for conviction. — Motion to strike was properly denied because there was sufficient evidence to find that defendant participated as a principal in the second degree in transporting the drugs into the Commonwealth with intent to distribute. Defendant was constructively present at the crime's commission and he committed overt acts in furtherance of the offense because he received the package containing four pounds of marijuana from a mail box company. Washington v. Commonwealth, 43 Va. App. 291, 597 S.E.2d 256, 2004 Va. App. LEXIS 268 (2004).

Evidence was sufficient to prove defendant's connection with a package left on his front stoop such that when he began to open the package, his act of accepting delivery of the package was part of the parcel's transportation for purposes of sustaining his conviction for transporting more than five pounds of marijuana into the Commonwealth with intent to distribute in violation of § 18.2-248.01. Ford v. Commonwealth, 55 Va. App. 598, 687 S.E.2d 551, 2010 Va. App. LEXIS 27 (2010).

Commonwealth not required to prove purity of substance. — The language of the statute mandates that the quantity of the mixture — the "compound" or "preparation" — rather than the purity of the cocaine in the mixture be used to determine the weight of the substance. Shackleford v. Commonwealth, 32 Va. App. 307, 528 S.E.2d 123, 2000 Va. App. LEXIS 233 (2000), aff'd, 262 Va. 196, 547 S.E.2d 899 (2001).

Proof of weight. — Commonwealth was not required to prove purity of controlled substance in order to establish its weight. Shackleford v. Commonwealth, No. 2883-98-3 (Ct. of Appeals Mar. 28, 2000).

Quantity of mixture, not amount of pure cocaine, determines weight. — The plain terms of this section mandate that the quantity of the mixture — the "compound" or "preparation" — rather than the purity of the cocaine in the mixture be used to determine the weight of the substance transported into the Commonwealth. Shackleford v. Commonwealth, 262 Va. 196, 547 S.E.2d 899, 2001 Va. LEXIS 78 (2001).

Possession not lesser included offense of transporting. — The offense of possessing a controlled substance is not a lesser included offense of transporting a controlled substance; a defendant may thus be convicted both of transporting marijuana under this section and of possessing marijuana under § 18.2-248. Bolden v. Commonwealth, No. 1951-00-4, 2001 Va. App. LEXIS 269 (Ct. of Appeals May 22, 2001), rev'd on other grounds, 263 Va. 465, 561 S.E. 2d 701, 2002 Va. LEXIS 52 (2002).

Evidence sufficient. — Conviction for transporting ecstasy into the Commonwealth with intent to distribute was supported by evidence that defendant served as the "muscle" or "lookout" in a drug transportation scheme, that a drug notebook contained an entry associating defendant to a drug transaction by its designation, and by Western Union receipts for cash wired to defendant in New York, allowing a jury to infer that defendant was in New York to arrange for the purchase of the ecstasy for transportation to Virginia. Merritt v. Commonwealth, 57 Va. App. 542, 704 S.E.2d 158, 2011 Va. App. LEXIS 25 (2011).

Conviction for transporting five or more pounds of marijuana into Virginia with intent to distribute was supported by evidence defendant had driven from Maryland into Virginia on the day he was stopped by the police; defendant rented a vehicle in Maryland following a trip to Boston, and was heading toward his home in Florida; defendant had proceeded south through the length of the Commonwealth and nearly reached the border with North Carolina; and the quantity of marijuana was found concealed in suitcases with routing tags indicating the bags had traveled to Boston. Jhurital v. Commonwealth, 2011 Va. App. LEXIS 302 (Oct. 4, 2011).

Evidence was sufficient to support defendant's conviction for transporting one or more ounces of cocaine into the Commonwealth of Virginia because (1) when the police intercepted a package, which they suspected of containing contraband, at a FedEx distribution facility, a drug dog indicated the presence of illegal drugs in the package; (2) the police obtained a search warrant, opened the package, and discovered cocaine inside; (3) the police placed a small amount of the cocaine inside a new package and transferred the air bill that indicated the recipient and return addresses onto the new package; (4) a police officer disguised as a FedEx employee delivered the package to defendant's apartment; (5) defendant identified the recipient as defendant's cousin and accepted the package on behalf of the cousin; and (6) not long after, the police executed a search warrant and found defendant, the unopened package, and drug paraphernalia in the apartment. Thus, the evidence was sufficient to prove that defendant knew the unopened FedEx box contained cocaine, that defendant had arranged for a second person in another state to sell defendant cocaine, and that defendant was a principal in the second degree to the transportation of cocaine into the Commonwealth of Virginia. Clark v. Commonwealth, 2011 Va. App. LEXIS 219 (July 5, 2011).

Insufficient evidence. — Defendant's conviction for transporting into the Commonwealth one ounce or more of a Schedule I or II controlled substance with the intent to distribute was not supported by sufficient evidence where any inference that defendant shared the criminal intent of his companions to import ecstasy into the Commonwealth was based upon sheer speculation and certainly did not rise to the level of proof beyond a reasonable doubt. Merritt v. Commonwealth, 55 Va. App. 719, 689 S.E.2d 757, 2010 Va. App. LEXIS 81 (2010).

§ 18.2-248.02. Allowing a minor or incapacitated person to be present during manufacture or attempted manufacture of methamphetamine prohibited; penalties.

Any person 18 years of age or older who knowingly allows (i) a minor under the age of 15, (ii) a minor 15 years of age or older with whom he maintains a custodial relationship, including but not limited to as a parent, step-parent, grandparent, step-grandparent, or who stands in loco parentis with respect to such minor, or (iii) a mentally incapacitated or physically helpless person of any age, to be present in the same dwelling, apartment as defined by § 55-79.2, unit of a hotel as defined in § 35.1-1, garage, shed, or vehicle during the manufacture or attempted manufacture of methamphetamine as prohibited by subsection C1 of § 18.2-248 is guilty of a felony punishable by imprisonment for not less than 10 nor more than 40 years. This penalty shall be in addition to and served consecutively with any other sentence.

History.
2005, cc. 923, 941; 2013, c. 743.

Editor's note.
Acts 2013, c. 743, cl. 2 provides: "That the provisions of this act may result in a net increase in periods of imprisonment or commitment. Pursuant to § 30-19.1:4, the estimated amount of the necessary appropriation cannot be determined for periods of imprisonment in state adult correctional facilities; therefore, Chapter 3 of the Acts of Assembly of 2012, Special Session I, requires the Virginia Criminal Sentencing Commission to assign a minimum fiscal impact of $50,000. Pursuant to § 30-19.1:4, the estimated amount of the necessary appropriation is $0 for periods of commitment to the custody of the Department of Juvenile Justice."

Acts 2013, c. 743, cl. 3 provides: "That the provisions of this act shall not become effective unless an appropriation of general funds effectuating the purposes of this act is included in a general appropriation act passed by the 2013 Session of the General Assembly, which becomes law."

Acts 2013, c. 743, cl. 4 provides: "That the General Assembly determines that the requirements of the third enactment of this act have been met."

The 2013 amendments.
The 2013 amendment by c. 743, in the first sentence, inserted "knowingly allows (i) a minor under the age of 15, (ii) a minor 15 years of age or older with whom he," deleted "over a child under the age of 18" following "custodial relationship," and substituted "such minor, or (iii) a mentally incapacitated or physically helpless person of any age, to be present" for "such child, and who knowingly allows that child to be present."

§ 18.2-248.03. Manufacturing, selling, giving, distributing, or possessing with intent to manufacture, sell, give, or distribute methamphetamine; penalty.

A. Notwithstanding any other provision of law, any person who manufactures, sells, gives, distributes, or possesses with intent to manufacture, sell, give, or distribute 28 grams or more of a mixture or substance containing a detectable amount of methamphetamine, its salts, isomers, or salts of its isomers is guilty of a felony punishable by a fine of not more than $500,000 and imprisonment for not less than five nor more than 40 years, three years of which shall be a mandatory minimum term of imprisonment to be served consecutively with any other sentence.

B. Notwithstanding any other provision of law, any person who manufactures, sells, gives, distributes, or possesses with intent to manufacture, sell, give, or distribute 227 grams or more of a mixture or substance containing a detectable amount of methamphetamine, its salts, isomers, or salts of its isomers is guilty of a felony punishable by a fine of not more than $1 million and imprisonment for not less than five years nor more than life, five years of which shall be a mandatory minimum term of imprisonment to be served consecutively with any other sentence.

History.
2008, cc. 858, 874.

Cross references.
As to reimbursement for methamphetamine lab cleanup costs, see § 15.2-1716.2.

Editor's note.
Acts 2008, cc. 858 and 874, cl. 2, provides: "That the provisions of this act may result in a net increase in periods of imprisonment or commitment. Pursuant to § 30-19.1:4, the estimated amount of the necessary appropriation is $260,310 for periods of imprisonment in state adult correctional facilities and cannot be determined for periods of commitment to the custody of the Department of Juvenile Justice."

§ 18.2-248.04. Methamphetamine Cleanup Fund established.

There is hereby created in the state treasury a special nonreverting fund to be known as the Methamphetamine Cleanup Fund, hereafter referred to as "the Fund." The Fund shall be established on the books of the Comptroller. All moneys assessed against a person convicted of manufacture of methamphetamine as methamphetamine cleanup funds pursuant to subsection C1 of § 18.2-248 shall be paid into the state treasury and credited to the Fund. Interest earned on moneys in the Fund shall remain in the Fund and be credited to it. Any moneys remaining in the Fund, including interest thereon, at the end of each fiscal year shall not revert to the general fund but shall remain in the Fund. Moneys in the Fund shall be used solely for the purposes of restoration to an environmentally sound state sites used for the criminal manufacture of methamphetamine. Expenditures and disbursements from the Fund shall be made by the State Treasurer on warrants issued by the Comptroller upon written request signed by any agency of the Commonwealth, law-enforcement agency, or locality with the responsibility for and engaged in a specific methamphetamine site cleanup.

History.
2012, c. 219.

§ 18.2-248.1. Penalties for sale, gift, distribution or possession with intent to sell, give or distribute marijuana.

Except as authorized in the Drug Control Act, Chapter 34 of Title 54.1, it shall be unlawful for any person to sell, give, distribute or possess with intent to sell, give or distribute marijuana.

(a) Any person who violates this section with respect to:

(1) Not more than one-half ounce of marijuana is guilty of a Class 1 misdemeanor;

(2) More than one-half ounce but not more than five pounds of marijuana is guilty of a Class 5 felony;

(3) More than five pounds of marijuana is guilty of a felony punishable by imprisonment of not less than five nor more than 30 years.

If such person proves that he gave, distributed or possessed with intent to give or distribute marijuana only as an accommodation to another individual and not with intent to profit thereby from any consideration received or expected nor to induce the recipient or intended recipient of the marijuana to use or become addicted to or dependent upon such marijuana, he shall be guilty of a Class 1 misdemeanor.

(b) Any person who gives, distributes or possesses marijuana as an accommodation and not with intent to profit thereby, to an inmate of a state or local correctional facility as defined in § 53.1-1, or in the custody of an employee thereof shall be guilty of a Class 4 felony.

(c) Any person who manufactures marijuana, or possesses marijuana with the intent to manufacture such substance, not for his own use is guilty of a felony punishable by imprisonment of not less than five nor more than 30 years and a fine not to exceed $10,000.

(d) When a person is convicted of a third or subsequent felony offense under this section and it is alleged in the warrant, indictment or information that he has been before convicted of two or more felony offenses under this section or of substantially similar offenses in any other jurisdiction which offenses would be felonies if committed in the Commonwealth and such prior convictions occurred before the date of the offense alleged in the warrant, indictment or information, he shall be sentenced to imprisonment for life or for any period not less than five years, five years of which shall be a mandatory minimum term of imprisonment to be served consecutively with any other sentence and he shall be fined not more than $500,000.

History.
1979, c. 435; 1986, c. 467; 2000, cc. 819, 1020, 1041; 2004, c. 461; 2006, cc. 697, 759.

Law Review.
For survey of Virginia criminal law for the year 1978-1979, see 66 Va. L. Rev. 241 (1980).

CASE NOTES

I. General Considerations.
II. Illustrative Cases.

I. GENERAL CONSIDERATIONS.

Constitutionality. — Since there is no fundamental right to the private use, possession or trade in marijuana or cocaine, and since governments have the power to enact and enforce sumptuary laws in this area, § 18.2-248, now amended and cited as this section and § 18.2-250 do not violate the Ninth and Tenth Amendments to the United States Constitution. Wolkind v. Selph, 495 F. Supp. 507 (E.D. Va. 1980), aff'd, 649 F.2d 865 (4th Cir. 1981).

Private possession of marijuana is not a fundamental constitutional right and the private possession of cocaine is not a fundamental constitutional right, accordingly, Virginia's statutory framework establishing criminal penalties for the possession with the intent to distribute marijuana and for the simple possession of cocaine need bear only a rational relationship to a legitimate interest of the Commonwealth. Wolkind v. Selph, 495 F. Supp. 507 (E.D. Va. 1980), aff'd, 649 F.2d 865 (4th Cir. 1981).

The statutory punishment for possession of marijuana with the intent to distribute is not irrational and does not violate the due process and equal protection provisions of the Fourteenth Amendment. Wolkind v. Selph, 495 F. Supp. 507 (E.D. Va. 1980), aff'd, 649 F.2d 865 (4th Cir. 1981).

Constitutionality of prior provision relating to accommodation distribution of marijuana. — The portion of § 18.2-248, as it stood prior to the 1979 amendment and prior to the enactment of this section, which related to a penalty for giving, distributing or possessing marijuana as an accommodation was not in violation of the decision in *Mullaney v. Wilbur*, 421 U.S. 684, 95 S. Ct. 1881, 49 L. Ed. 2d 508 (1975), nor was it unconstitutionally vague or a violation of due process. Stillwell v. Commonwealth, 219 Va. 214, 247 S.E.2d 360 (1978).

Applicability to offenses committed prior to effective date. — Penalties provided by this section could not be applied to offenses of distribution and sale of marijuana committed prior to the effective date of this section and prosecuted under § 18.2-248, though trial and sentencing occurred after that date, absent election by the Commonwealth to proceed under this section and the defendants' consent to such an election. Ruplenas v. Commonwealth, 221 Va. 972, 275 S.E.2d 628 (1981).

Predecessor to section created single offense. — Section 18.2-248 A, as it stood prior to the 1979 amendment and prior to the enactment of this section, created only a single offense, that being the unlawful manufacture, sale, transfer, distribution or possession of certain controlled drugs. Stillwell v. Commonwealth, 219 Va. 214, 247 S.E.2d 360 (1978).

And accommodation provisions related only to punishment. — The provisions of § 18.2-248 A, as it stood prior to the 1979 amendment and the enactment of this section, which dealt with the reduced penalty contingent upon proof of an accommodation gift, distribution or possession of marijuana, operated only to mitigate the degree of criminality or punishment, rather than to create two different substantive offenses. Stillwell v. Commonwealth, 219 Va. 214, 247 S.E.2d 360 (1978).

Nature of illegal substance need not be proved by direct evidence. — The nature of an illegal substance transferred can be demonstrated by circumstantial evidence and the types of circumstantial evidence that may be considered include the following: Evidence of the physical appearance of the substance involved in the transaction, evidence that the substance produced the expected effects when sampled by someone familiar with the illicit drug, evidence that the substance was used in the same manner as the illicit drug, testimony that a high price was paid in cash for the substance, evidence that the transactions involving the substance were carried on with secrecy or deviousness, and evidence that the substance was called by the name of the illegal narcotic by the defendant or others in his presence. Bareford v. Commonwealth, No. 0564-00-2, 2001 Va. App. LEXIS 155 (Ct. of Appeals Mar. 27, 2001).

Defendant could be retried for same or greater offense upon vacation of conviction. — When the defendant appealed her misdemeanor possession conviction to the circuit court, as she had a right to do under § 16.1-132, her conviction was vacated; therefore, the defendant could be retried for the same or a greater offense without double jeopardy being violated. Peterson v. Commonwealth, 5 Va. App. 389, 363 S.E.2d 440 (1987).

The acceptance of the guilty plea to misdemeanor possession did not constitute an inferential finding of not guilty of the greater charge of felony possession. Consequently, the defendant was not impliedly acquitted of felony possession, and she could be retried for felony possession unless some other double jeopardy principle barred reprosecution. Peterson v. Commonwealth, 5 Va. App. 389, 363 S.E.2d 440 (1987).

"Manufacture" and "production" used synonymously. — With respect to violations of this section, the words manufacture and production are used synonymously. Manufacture, as defined by

§ 54.1-3401, "means the production, preparation, propagation, compounding, conversion or processing of any item." Section 54.1-3401 states that "'production' includes the manufacture, planting, cultivation, growing or harvesting of a controlled substance or marijuana." By these definitions, the legislature has clearly expressed its intent that the term manufacturing includes the planting, cultivating, growing, or harvesting of marijuana. Although the definition of "manufacture" as used in the context of the manufacture of marijuana may not precisely comport with the present day lay meaning of the term, that does not give the appellate court license to find error in the trial court's instruction. The court's function is to interpret the legislature's meaning of words in statutes. King v. Commonwealth, 2 Va. App. 708, 347 S.E.2d 530 (1986).

Definition of "manufacture" in Drug Control Act still relevant. — The offense of manufacturing marijuana was once a part of the Drug Control Act, § 54.1-3400 et seq. (see § 54.1-3400 et seq.). In 1975, marijuana related offenses were recodified in Title 18.2; however, the Drug Control Act's definition of "manufacture" continues to be relevant to marijuana-related offenses. King v. Commonwealth, 2 Va. App. 708, 347 S.E.2d 530 (1986).

Instruction as to definition of "manufacture" in § 54.1-3401. — Although defendant was convicted of a violation of subdivision (c) of this section, and the term "manufacture" is not defined in that title, the court did not err in giving the jury the definition of "manufacture" contained in § 54.1-3401 of the Drug Control Act. King v. Commonwealth, 2 Va. App. 708, 347 S.E.2d 530 (1986).

Ownership, specific time of possession not mandated. — This section does not require that the accused have title to the contraband, only possession; also, the duration of the possession is immaterial. Kilfeather v. Commonwealth, No. 0494-90-2 (Ct. of Appeals June 16, 1992).

The possession need not be exclusive. Ekhart v. Commonwealth, 222 Va. 447, 281 S.E.2d 853 (1981).

Possession need not be actual, exclusive, or lengthy in order to support a conviction; instead, this section criminalizes constructive or joint possession of illegal drugs of any duration. Wells v. Commonwealth, 32 Va. App. 775, 531 S.E.2d 16, 2000 Va. App. LEXIS 498 (2000).

To convict a person of possession of illegal drugs the Commonwealth must prove that the defendant was aware of the presence and character of the drugs and that he intentionally and consciously possessed them. Wells v. Commonwealth, 32 Va. App. 775, 531 S.E.2d 16, 2000 Va. App. LEXIS 498 (2000).

Proof of constructive possession. — Constructive possession may be shown by establishing that the marijuana was known to and subject to the dominion and control of the accused. Eckhart v. Commonwealth, 222 Va. 447, 281 S.E.2d 853 (1981).

Constructive possession of illegal drugs may be proven by evidence of acts, statements or conduct of the accused or other facts or circumstances which tend to show that the accused was aware of both the presence and character of the substance and that it was subject to his dominion and control. Wells v. Commonwealth, 32 Va. App. 775, 531 S.E.2d 16, 2000 Va. App. LEXIS 498 (2000).

Evidence was sufficient to support conviction for possession of marijuana with intent to distribute, in violation of § 18.2-248.1, where defendant was driving and owned car in which the marijuana was found, as possession could be actual or constructive. Kelly v. Commonwealth, 41 Va. App. 250, 584 S.E.2d 444, 2003 Va. App. LEXIS 419 (2003).

Defendant's constructive possession of marijuana found in his residence was sufficiently shown by his request for money and guns, made after original charges were nolle prossed, which were taken out of a locked gun case in his home from where marijuana was also found, and a reasonable inference that flowed from this statement was that defendant claimed ownership of the same; further, the trial court was entitled to reject defendant's alternative theories as to the placement of the drugs in the home by his aunt's sister, out of her disdain for him. Cason v. Commonwealth, No. 1433-04-2, 2005 Va. App. LEXIS 137 (Ct. of Appeals Apr. 5, 2005).

Proximity insufficient to show possession. — Knowledge of the presence and character of the controlled substance may be shown by evidence of the acts, statements or conduct of the accused. Mere proximity to the controlled substance, however, is insufficient to establish possession. Eckhart v. Commonwealth, 222 Va. 447, 281 S.E.2d 853 (1981).

Neither close proximity to illegal drugs nor occupancy of an automobile in which they are found, standing alone, is sufficient to prove possession of such drugs; however, both are factors that may be considered in determining whether possession occurred in a particular case. Wells v. Commonwealth, 32 Va. App. 775, 531 S.E.2d 16, 2000 Va. App. LEXIS 498 (2000).

Probative value of occupancy of residence where marijuana found. — While there is no presumption of knowing or intentional possession of the marijuana from a defendant's occupancy of a residence, her occupancy of the premises as a cotenant is a factor to be considered with other evidence in determining whether she had constructive possession. Eckhart v. Commonwealth, 222 Va. 447, 281 S.E.2d 853 (1981).

Where marijuana was found in defendant's bedroom underneath his bed, and his fingerprints were found on two of the plastic bags containing the marijuana, the evidence was sufficient to convict defendant of possession of marijuana. Wright v. Commonwealth, 2 Va. App. 743, 348 S.E.2d 9 (1986).

Evidence that just prior to police entry, defendant was sitting in his kitchen where marijuana was located, in conjunction with defendant's admission that the drugs belonged to him, supported a finding that the marijuana was known to him and subject to his control. Hambury v. Commonwealth, 3 Va. App. 435, 350 S.E.2d 524 (1986).

Evidence proved that defendant conspired to purchase more than five pounds of marijuana where evidence showed that she joined with another defendant to pool their resources to purchase eleven pounds of marijuana, and that she was only to receive an amount less than the whole when they made the later division of the marijuana did not change the nature of the initial agreement to buy more than five pounds. Estrada v. Commonwealth, No. 1777-92-1 (Ct. of Appeals July 12, 1994).

Proof of agreement to distribute. — Where the indictment charged defendant with a conspiracy to distribute more than one-half ounce of marijuana, one of the felonies defined in this section, the Commonwealth was required to prove an agreement to distribute a proscribed substance and to prove both the identity and the quantity of the substance contemplated by the agreement. Graves v. Commonwealth, 234 Va. 578, 363 S.E.2d 705 (1988).

Packaging of substance to be considered when evidence of intent to distribute is circumstantial. — The method of packaging of the controlled substance is a factor which may be considered in determining the purpose for which it is being held. Monroe v. Commonwealth, 4 Va. App. 154, 355 S.E.2d 336 (1987).

Even if the substance is packaged for distribution, there must be additional evidence to preclude the inference that it was purchased in the packaged form for personal use rather than being held in that fashion for distribution. Monroe v. Commonwealth, 4 Va. App. 154, 355 S.E.2d 336 (1987).

Presence of unusual amount of money, suggesting profit from sales, is a circumstance that negates an inference of possession for personal use. Servis v. Commonwealth, 6 Va. App. 507, 371 S.E.2d 156 (1988).

Quantity possessed to be considered when evidence of intent to distribute is circumstantial. — When the proof of intent to distribute narcotics rests upon circumstantial evidence, the quantity which the defendant possesses is a circumstance to be considered. Indeed, quantity, alone, may be sufficient to establish such intent if it is greater than the supply ordinarily possessed for one's personal use. However, possession of a small quantity creates an inference that the drug was for the personal use of the defendant. Dukes v. Commonwealth, 227 Va. 119, 313 S.E.2d 382 (1984).

The quantity of a controlled substance is a factor which may indicate the purpose for which it is possessed. Possession of a small quantity creates an inference that the drug is for personal use. On the other hand, possession of a quantity greater than that ordinarily possessed for one's personal use may be sufficient to establish an intent to distribute. Monroe v. Commonwealth, 4 Va. App. 154, 355 S.E.2d 336 (1987).

Possession of a quantity greater than that ordinarily possessed for one's personal use may be sufficient to establish an intent to distribute it. Josephs v. Commonwealth, 10 Va. App. 87, 390 S.E.2d 491 (1990). But see Young v. Commonwealth, 275 Va. 587, 659 S.E.2d 308, 2008 Va. LEXIS 54 (2008), which overruled the holding in *Josephs* to the extent that it can be read to mean that mere possession, without more, can prove guilty knowledge .

The evidence of the presence of growing marijuana plants may have precluded an inference that the smaller bags of marijuana were purchased in that form for personal use rather than being held in that manner to facilitate distribution. The supervised growth of many marijuana plants indicates a continuing enterprise in the production and distribution of marijuana. Monroe v. Commonwealth, 4 Va. App. 154, 355 S.E.2d 336 (1987).

Permissible yield testimony. — Investigator's estimations of the potential yield of the immature plants and dose divisibility of that yield were permissible assertions based upon his knowledge in response to appropriate hypothetical questions. The weight and credence given to that testimony were matters for the jury to consider. Taylor v. Commonwealth, No. 0963-93-3 (Ct. of Appeals Feb. 7, 1995).

To convict defendant of possession with intent to distribute more than one-half ounce but less than five pounds of marijuana, Commonwealth had the burden of proving beyond a reasonable doubt that the plant material, exclusive of mature stalk and sterilized seeds, weighed more than one-half ounce. Hill v. Commonwealth, 17 Va. App. 480, 438 S.E.2d 296 (1993).

The intent to personally use a portion of the whole does not negate a person's intent to also distribute some of the drug. Thornton v. Commonwealth, No. 1882-93-2 (Ct. of Appeals March 21, 1995).

Sufficient proof of weight. — The evidence was sufficient to prove that the defendant possessed the requisite quantity of marijuana where two bags of marijuana weighing a combined one pound, six ounces, were found together and the defendant's fingerprints were found on the larger of the bags. Although the commonwealth never proved the weight of the bag that bore the defendant's fingerprints without the weight of the other bag, the trial judge was free to conclude that the defendant was in constructive possession of both bags. Cutler v. Commonwealth, No. 0194-00-1, 2001 Va. App. LEXIS 137 (Ct. of Appeals Mar. 20, 2001).

Weight, excluding certain stalks and seeds, determines offense grade. — Under this section, the weight of the proscribed marijuana, excluding mature stalks and sterilized seeds, determines the grade of the offense. Guzman v. Commonwealth, No. 1211-93-2 (Ct. of Appeals June 7, 1994).

Evidence failed to prove, beyond a reasonable doubt, weight of marijuana or that it exceeded one-half ounce, where forensic chemist testified that he did not weigh leafy material separate from seeds and stems, and that he could not visually determine weight of seeds and stems at trial. Hinton v. Commonwealth, No. 1616-98-2 (Ct. of Appeals June 29, 1999).

Where expert testified that removal of seeds and stems from marijuana similar to that seized from defendant normally reduced its weight by one third, fact finder could permissibly infer that 9.59 ounces of marijuana, exclusive of seeds and mature stalks, exceeded one-half ounce. Neale v. Commonwealth, No. 1822-98-3 (Ct. of Appeals Sept. 28, 1999).

Evidence was sufficient to convict for possession of more than one-half ounce but less than five pounds of marijuana because the definition of marijuana included mature stalks and seeds in determining the total weight of the substance. Brown v. Commonwealth, 56 Va. App. 8, 690 S.E.2d 301, 2010 Va. App. LEXIS 92 (2010).

Failure to prove weight warranted reversal of felony conviction. — The trial court erred in convicting appellant of the felony of possession of more than one-half ounce but less than five pounds of marijuana with intent to distribute since the Commonwealth failed to prove that the marijuana weighed more than one-half ounce absent the seeds and stems. At trial, the police officer who executed the search warrant testified that the bags contained leaves, stems or twigs, and seeds, but the officer stated that he did not instruct the division of forensic science laboratory to weigh only the leafy parts contained in the bags, nor did the laboratory personnel ever indicate to him that they weighed only the leafy parts of the plant material. Guzman v. Commonwealth, No. 1211-93-2 (Ct. of Appeals June 7, 1994).

The commonwealth has the burden of proving beyond a reasonable doubt that the plant material, exclusive of mature stalk and sterilized seeds, weighs more than one-half ounce and that burden is not met when the quantity of material is of small weight and the trier of fact merely infers that the weight of the marijuana, less the stems, sterilized seeds and twigs, exceeds one-half ounce. Hughes v.

Commonwealth, No. 2604-99-1, 2000 Va. App. LEXIS 817 (Ct. of Appeals Dec. 19, 2000).

When a trial judge decided by visual inspection the comparative weights of the contents of two bags of marijuana, which included seeds, stems and twigs, she did no more than draw a mere inference of the necessary facts and any such inference was purely speculative because no facts were proved that would have supported such an inference. Hughes v. Commonwealth, No. 2604-99-1, 2000 Va. App. LEXIS 817 (Ct. of Appeals Dec. 19, 2000).

Quantity and other circumstances may establish intent to distribute. — The quantity of a controlled substance is a factor which may indicate the purpose for which it is possessed. Possession of a small quantity creates an inference that the drug is for personal use. Possession of a small quantity of a controlled substance, however, when considered with other circumstances, may be sufficient to establish an intent to distribute. The method of packaging of the controlled substance is such a circumstance. Servis v. Commonwealth, 6 Va. App. 507, 371 S.E.2d 156 (1988).

Circumstantial evidence used to convict defendant supported conviction for possession with intent to distribute marijuana where defendant had a pound of drugs and $3000 in cash; defendant's objection to probation was unpreserved and barred. Park v. Commonwealth, No. 2578-02-4, 2003 Va. App. LEXIS 620 (Ct. of Appeals Dec. 2, 2003).

Officer's testimony regarding intent held proper. — The officer's testimony that the amount of 6.88 ounces of marijuana was inconsistent with an individual's personal use, based on what a user would normally buy or use at one time, did not constitute an opinion of the ultimate issue of fact that the defendant had an intent to distribute the marijuana found in his house. Davis v. Commonwealth, 12 Va. App. 728, 406 S.E.2d 922 (1991).

Presumption against accommodation distribution after guilt established. — Section 18.2-248, as it stood prior to the 1979 amendment and the enactment of this section, contained a presumption against an accommodation distribution to the extent that it is relevant to the determination of the proper degree of punishment, but only after guilt has been established. Stillwell v. Commonwealth, 219 Va. 214, 247 S.E.2d 360 (1978).

And presumption lasts until evidence makes case for jury. — The presumption created with regard to accommodation retains its effect until opposing evidence (whether from the Commonwealth or the defendant) is sufficient to make a case for the jury, that is, to convince the judge that a jury could reasonably find that the defendant was an accommodation distributor. This is the obvious standard to be applied for overcoming the statutory presumption that operated in favor of the Commonwealth in cases prosecuted under § 18.2-248, as it stood prior to 1979 amendment and the enactment of this section, and it was unnecessary for the standard to be spelled out in the statute. Stillwell v. Commonwealth, 219 Va. 214, 247 S.E.2d 360 (1978).

Burden on defendant to show accommodation. — The statutory scheme behind § 18.2-248 as it stood prior to the 1979 amendment and the enactment of this section provided that once the guilt of the defendant has been established (a determination completely independent of the profit-accommodation distinction), a second determination of the proper punishment is to be made. That statute and § 18.2-263 placed the burden of proving the existence of an accommodation distribution (and the right to the lesser penalty) to the trier of fact on the shoulders of the defendant. Stillwell v. Commonwealth, 219 Va. 214, 247 S.E.2d 360 (1978).

Defendant not entitled to accommodation instruction. — Evidence, in trial of defendant for distributing more than one-half ounce but not more than five pounds of marijuana, failed to support an accommodation instruction where defendant admitted that she sold marijuana to detective but denied that she had profited from the sale — she testified that she had purchased the marijuana from "a friend" for $120 and had sold it to the detective for $120 — the fact that the defendant did not sell the drugs for more than she paid for them was of no consequence for the evidence clearly showed that the distribution was a commercial transaction where consideration was involved. Hudspith v. Commonwealth, 17 Va. App. 136, 435 S.E.2d 588 (1993).

Even assuming that the trial court's refusal to instruct the jury during the penalty phase of defendant's trial as to "accommodation conspiracy" on the charge against defendant of conspiracy to possess marijuana with intent to distribute was error, the error was harmless beyond a reasonable doubt; since the jury rejected an accommodation claim regarding the charge against defendant of possession of marijuana with intent to distribute, the appellate court could confidently conclude that the jury would have rejected an accommodation claim with regard to the "conspiracy to possess" charge as well. McPherson v. Commonwealth, — Va. App. —, S.E.2d —, 2006 Va. App. LEXIS 88 (Mar. 14, 2006).

Defendant's convictions for two counts of distribution of cocaine, third offense; three counts of distribution of marijuana; two counts of conspiracy to distribute cocaine, third offense; three counts of conspiracy to distribute marijuana; one count of possession of cocaine with intent to distribute; and one count of possession of marijuana with intent to distribute were proper because the trial court did not err in not instructing the jury on the lesser punishment of distribution for accommodation. In each transaction, the agent was the buyer, and not the cousin, who had only arranged the meetings for the agent; additionally, the fact that defendant did not make any money on the transactions was not dispositive. Martin v. Commonwealth, 2010 Va. App. LEXIS 205 (May 18, 2010).

Even if substance is packaged for distribution, there must be additional evidence to preclude the inference that it was purchased in the packaged form for personal use rather than being held in that fashion for distribution. The additional evidence available to preclude such an inference may be the presence of a large, or bulk, quantity from which smaller packages may have been made up for distribution, or the presence of paraphernalia used in the packaging process. Servis v. Commonwealth, 6 Va. App. 507, 371 S.E.2d 156 (1988).

By preponderance of evidence. — A defendant, charged with an unlawful sale of drugs, who defends on the ground that he distributed the drugs for accommodation only, is not required to establish such accommodation beyond a reasonable doubt, but only by a preponderance of the evidence. He is required to produce some evidence which satisfies the trier of the facts that his distribution was for accommodation. Stillwell v. Commonwealth, 219 Va. 214, 247 S.E.2d 360 (1978), decided under § 18.2-248 as it stood prior to the 1979 amendment and the enactment of this section.

Applied in Morton v. Commonwealth, 227 Va. 216, 315 S.E.2d 224 (1984); Stamper v. Commonwealth, 228 Va. 707, 324 S.E.2d 682 (1985); Arnold v. Commonwealth, 4 Va. App. 275, 356 S.E.2d 847 (1987); Barber v. Commonwealth, 5 Va. App. 172, 360 S.E.2d 888 (1987); Reynolds v. Commonwealth, 9 Va. App. 430, 388 S.E.2d 659 (1990); Wolfe v. Commonwealth, 265 Va. 193, 576 S.E.2d 471, 2003 Va. LEXIS 32.

II. ILLUSTRATIVE CASES.

Evidence of prior bad acts. — Defendant's convictions for possession with intent to distribute marijuana under § 18.2-248.1 and conspiracy to distribute marijuana under §§ 18.2-256 and 18.2-248.1 were proper because the trial court did not abuse its discretion in admitting evidence of defendant's other bad acts as part of a common scheme or plan to support his current convictions. The evidence was relevant and admissible to show a course of conduct entered into by defendant to sell marijuana through his middleman and it proved that he committed similar acts with similar results. Pinnix v. Commonwealth, 2011 Va. App. LEXIS 149 (May 3, 2011).

Suppression of evidence. — Defendant's motion to suppress was denied because the marijuana residue found during the justified pat-down search was a valid basis for arrest, as possession of less than one-half ounce of marijuana was a class one misdemeanor; therefore, the evidence seized as a result of the arrest was admissible. United States v. Akers, — F. Supp. 2d —, 2005 U.S. Dist. LEXIS 19920 (W.D. Va. Sept. 13, 2005).

Considering the totality of circumstances, and the evidence and all reasonable inferences flowing from that evidence in defendant's favor because defendant prevailed on defendant's motion to suppress in the trial court, the seizure of marijuana from a knotted plastic baggie inside defendant's purse located in defendant's vehicle had to be suppressed. The evidence, used to charge defendant with possession of marijuana with the intent to distribute in violation of § 18.2-248.1, did not establish probable cause to believe there was marijuana inside the baggie in the purse. Commonwealth v. Anderson, — Va. App. —, — S.E.2d —, 2008 Va. App. LEXIS 130 (Mar. 18, 2008).

As defendant appeared to shove something under the driver's

seat after an officer activated his overhead lights, the office's search for weapons in the area of defendant's movement was objectively reasonable. And as the officer found a cooler from which emanated the odor of marijuana, he had both reasonable suspicion to look inside the cooler for a weapon and probable cause to check it for marijuana; therefore, the marijuana did not have to be suppressed. Johnson v. Commonwealth, 2011 Va. App. LEXIS 173 (May 17, 2011).

Certificates of analysis. — Where certificates of analysis pertaining to drugs and a firearm had been admissible at the time defendant was initially found guilty in a bench trial, since he had not availed himself of his right under former § 19.2-187.1 to call the scientists who prepared the certificates as witnesses, the trial court did not err in reopening the case to allow the scientists to testify and defendant to cross-examine them, because Confrontation Clause law had changed in the interim, and this procedure protected defendant's constitutional rights to confrontation and a fair trial. Morgan v. Commonwealth, 61 Va. App. 58, 733 S.E.2d 151, 2012 Va. App. LEXIS 336 (2012).

Sufficient evidence of awareness and dominion. — Where evidence showed that the marijuana was being grown in an area accessible only from the backyard of the house where defendant was living by himself; that a watering hose ran from the house to the area of cultivation; and inside the house police found weighing scales and plastic baggies surrounded by marijuana debris, giving rise to the fair inference that marijuana was being weighed and packaged for distribution, evidence was sufficient to show that defendant was aware of the presence and character of the marijuana and exercised dominion and control over it. Taylor v. Commonwealth, No. 0963-93-3 (Ct. of Appeals Feb. 7, 1995).

Sufficient circumstantial evidence. — Where evidence was presented at trial from which it could be fairly deduced that the other persons living in the vicinity actually utilized their potential access to the marijuana plot, the jury did not err in finding the circumstantial evidence adduced by the Commonwealth sufficient for conviction. Taylor v. Commonwealth, No. 0963-93-3 (Ct. of Appeals Feb. 7, 1995).

The circumstantial evidence was sufficient to support the defendant's conviction where, from the evidence presented, the fact finder could have inferred beyond a reasonable doubt that the defendant was aware of the presence and character of marijuana contained inside a backpack in his vehicle and that it was subject to his dominion and control. Although there were other people in the vehicle with the defendant when the backpack containing the marijuana was thrown from the vehicle while the occupants were fleeing from the police, the defendant's fingerprints were on one of the two bags of marijuana in the backpack and his flight from and inconsistent statements to the police about that flight and the location of the vehicle provide the "other circumstances" which reasonably excluded innocence. Cutler v. Commonwealth, No. 0194-00-1, 2001 Va. App. LEXIS 137 (Ct. of Appeals Mar. 20, 2001).

Based on the totality of the circumstances, including a police surveillance and "buy money" on defendant's person, defendant was aware of the quantity of packaged marijuana and firearms and was in a position to exercise dominion and control over the marijuana. Collins v. Commonwealth, No. 1920-01-1, 2002 Va. App. LEXIS 429 (Ct. of Appeals July 30, 2002).

Defendant's conviction for manufacturing marijuana, pursuant to § 18.2-248.1 (c), was upheld, where circumstances including the tremendous volume of production, the sophistication of the equipment and the operation, the elaborate security and monitoring system in place, and the presence of a a large, hidden, underground room, accessed through a closet in the den, which served as a main growing room helped to discount and disprove defendant's theory that he grew for his own personal use. Floyd v. Commonwealth, — Va. App. —, — S.E.2d —, 2003 Va. App. LEXIS 239 (Apr. 22, 2003).

Sufficient evidence of intent to distribute. — Considered together, the method of packaging (there were 26 bags of marijuana in defendant's residence) and the quantity of marijuana found (cumulatively, the marijuana weighed almost 2 ½ ounces) proved an intent to distribute. Additionally, defendant's lack of credibility provided an additional ground upon which the trier of fact could infer his guilt. Therefore, the evidence sufficiently supported the trial court's finding that defendant intended to distribute the marijuana. Hansell v. Commonwealth, No. 1986-96-1 (Ct. of Appeals June 24, 1997).

Evidence was sufficient to show defendant's intent to distribute marijuana, where defendant was found in possession of .935 ounces of marijuana, the marijuana was in a plastic baggie inside a box with similar plastic baggies, and, although defendant stated that the marijuana was for personal use, no paraphernalia consistent with personal consumption was found. Ward v. Commonwealth, No. 1164-97-3 (Ct. of Appeals May 19, 1998).

Because a deputy's experience and an advanced narcotics course provided the knowledge needed to give an expert opinion on the packaging and distribution of marijuana, the evidence was sufficient to support defendant's conviction for possession with intent to distribute under § 18.2-248.1. Brooks v. Commonwealth, — Va. App. —, — S.E.2d —, 2007 Va. App. LEXIS 237 (June 19, 2007).

There was sufficient evidence to support appellant's conviction for possession with the intent to distribute of more than one-half ounce but less than five pounds of marijuana where: (1) the expert witness considered the quantity of drugs in concluding appellant's possession of 1.59 ounces of marijuana was inconsistent with personal use; and (2) the expert testified that a typical marijuana user would carry less than one-half ounce. Cratch v. Commonwealth, 2009 Va. App. LEXIS 433 (Sept. 29, 2009).

Evidence did not prove defendant aware of drugs. — Defendant's conviction of possession of more than five pounds of marijuana with intent to distribute was reversed, where the evidence fell short of proving that she was aware of the drugs found in the parked automobile in which she was seated, or that the drugs were subject to her dominion and control. Winfield v. Commonwealth, No. 1373-88-2 (Ct. of Appeals Apr. 24, 1990).

Evidence insufficient to support conviction. — Where although 90 grams of marijuana was found in plastic bags, packaged for distribution, in defendants' car, there was no evidence to preclude the inference that the quantity seized was for defendants' personal use, the evidence was insufficient to support a conviction for possession of marijuana with intent to distribute. Dutton v. Commonwealth, 220 Va. 762, 263 S.E.2d 52 (1980).

Where the Commonwealth failed to prove beyond a reasonable doubt that the defendant was in the garden area where young marijuana plants were found, and that defendant had seen the plants, or acknowledged their presence, the evidence did not establish that he was aware of the presence and character of the marijuana or that he intentionally and consciously possessed it or exercised dominion and control over it. Williams v. Commonwealth, No. 0550-90-2 (Ct. of Appeals June 11, 1991).

Where sergeant stated that he had not asked the state forensic laboratory to weigh the marijuana without the stems, seeds, or stalks and that he did not know if the marijuana had been weighed without that material, and where he further testified that it was the state lab's procedure to weigh marijuana with the seeds, stalks, and stems, the Commonwealth failed to prove that the marijuana was properly weighed or that, less the weight of the stems and sterilized seeds, it weighed more than one-half ounce. Rather, the testimony of the Commonwealth's witnesses permitted the reasonable inference that the marijuana was weighed with stems and seeds. Therefore, the evidence was not sufficient to prove that the marijuana weighed more than one-half ounce. Newton v. Commonwealth, No. 1708-96-3 (Ct. of Appeals Oct. 7, 1997).

A defendant's conviction was reversed where the evidence established that the defendant had supplied marijuana to those present at a third party's house, individuals at the house wanting to smoke marijuana usually obtained the marijuana from a table and did not see who put it there, and no other witnesses were able to provide an affirmative link between the defendant and the marijuana taken from the table; because other witnesses admitted to providing marijuana for use at the house during that time, the evidence was insufficient to establish that the defendant distributed marijuana in the county where he was charged and tried. Bareford v. Commonwealth, No. 0564-00-2, 2001 Va. App. LEXIS 155 (Ct. of Appeals Mar. 27, 2001).

Commonwealth's circumstantial evidence failed to eliminate the reasonable hypothesis that someone other than defendant brought the pots of marijuana to the home on the day they were discovered; thus, the evidence was insufficient, as a matter of law, to prove that defendant manufactured the marijuana. Lowe v. Commonwealth, 36 Va. App. 163, 548 S.E.2d 904, 2001 Va. App. LEXIS 404 (2001).

Appellant's conviction for possession with intent to distribute marijuana was reversed because there was no evidence that the odor detected by the officers was coming from appellant's person, that appellant showed any physical signs of having recently used marijuana, or that appellant possessed any drugs on his person. Ervin v. Commonwealth, 2010 Va. App. LEXIS 249 (June 22, 2010).

Evidence was insufficient to convict defendant of possession of more than one-half ounce of marijuana with intent to sell; while the evidence established that eight plastic bags containing marijuana weighed 0.92 ounce, as the Commonwealth did not establish the weight of bags, it failed to prove that the marijuana alone weighed more than one-half ounce. Johnson v. Commonwealth, 2011 Va. App. LEXIS 173 (May 17, 2011).

Defendant's conviction for possession of marijuana with the intent to distribute in violation of § 18.2-248.1 was reversed because the facts were insufficient to prove that defendant possessed the marijuana since the only facts were that defendant was the owner of the parked car and that he had custody of a set of keys to that car; there was no timeline for when defendant was last in the vehicle or if he was in fact the last person in the vehicle, although defendant had possession of the key to the vehicle, nothing indicated that he had possession of the only key, and defendant was cooperative in providing the key to the glove compartment upon request. Lewis v. Commonwealth, 2011 Va. App. LEXIS 136 (Apr. 26, 2011).

Evidence that defendant was in close proximity to two bags of marijuana that the trial court found to be a "significant amount" and was clearly visible to anyone in the car and was within arm's reach of the marijuana was sufficient to support defendant's conviction for possession with intent to distribute marijuana under § 18.2-248.1. Ferebee v. Commonwealth, 2012 Va. App. LEXIS 388 (Dec. 4, 2012).

Sufficient evidence to support conviction. — Evidence was sufficient to sustain defendant's conviction for manufacturing marijuana not for his own use, in violation of subsection (c) of § 18.2-248.1, where: (1) when video surveillance began, 11 well cared for marijuana plants were growing in a wooded area; (2) an expert testified that the recovered plants had a potential yield of six pounds of saleable marijuana, which was inconsistent with personal use; (3) defendant was the only person seen on the videotapes exercising dominion and control over the plants; (4) defendant's systematic removal of the more mature plants, mid-way through the growing season, was consistent with the manufacturing of marijuana; and (5) the fact that no lighting devices, packing materials, or distribution equipment were found did not discount the conclusion that the marijuana plants were being manufactured for distribution. Dolan v. Commonwealth, — Va. App. —, — S.E.2d —, 2002 Va. App. LEXIS 778 (Dec. 31, 2002).

Evidence that defendant was observed packaging marijuana from a large bag into many smaller one and that another man was also seek doing the same and then selling it to passersby was sufficient to support the trial court's determination of guilty beyond a reasonable doubt that defendant possessed marijuana with the intent to distribute it and conspired to do so. Williams v. Commonwealth, No. 1842-02-2, 2003 Va. App. LEXIS 699 (Ct. of Appeals Dec. 30, 2003).

Defendant's incriminating statements made after he received Miranda warnings were properly admitted, as said statements were not made as a result of an illegal arrest, but after a lawful detention by officers and an arrest based on probable cause of finding cocaine and a gun in the residence searched via a valid warrant; thus, defendant's suppression motion was properly denied, and his conviction was upheld. Whitaker v. Commonwealth, No. 3232-03-2, 2005 Va. App. LEXIS 34 (Ct. of Appeals Feb. 1, 2005).

Sufficient evidence existed to support defendant's conviction for possession with intent to distribute marijuana because while police found defendant in the kitchen and the marijuana, a bag of cocaine, and a gun were in plain view in the living room, defendant had to walk through the living room to reach the kitchen; therefore, it was reasonable to infer that defendant was aware of the presence and character of the drugs in the living room. Additionally, a scale, multiple baggies of marijuana, and cash all found in the kitchen cabinets and a large sum of cash and a gun found on defendant's person proved sufficient dominion and control over the illicit drugs to establish constructive possession. Wilson v. Commonwealth, 272 Va. 19, 630 S.E.2d 326, 2006 Va. LEXIS 60 (2006).

Evidence that defendant owned the car where officers found a significant quantity of the drug, a key on defendant's key chain opened the closet in defendant's home where drugs were found, and packaging material and a scale were found in defendant's room was sufficient to support conviction for possession of marijuana. Richards v. Commonwealth, — Va. App. —, — S.E.2d —, 2007 Va. App. LEXIS 22 (Jan. 23, 2007).

There was no error in the trial court's conviction of defendant for possession of more than five pounds of marijuana with intent to distribute, as defendant admitted to a detective that defendant took possession of a package, which defendant knew contained marijuana, and that defendant intended to transfer the package and its contents to another. An expert witness testified that the amount of marijuana recovered from defendant's residence, almost nine pounds, was very inconsistent with personal use. Hargrove v. Commonwealth, 53 Va. App. 545, 673 S.E.2d 896, 2009 Va. App. LEXIS 123 (2009).

Ample evidence supported the trial court's finding that defendant intended to use the marijuana for purposes other than defendant's own use, including the discovery of electronic digital scales, hemostats, baggies, and individually packaged methamphetamine — items that were part of defendant's ongoing operations. Cooper v. Commonwealth, 54 Va. App. 558, 680 S.E.2d 361, 2009 Va. App. LEXIS 356 (2009).

Evidence, including that police found over $3,000 in varied denominations in defendant's care and on his person and that he was in possession of cocaine and marijuana without paraphernalia, was sufficient to overcome the presumption of personal use and was sufficient to convict him of possession of marijuana with intent to distribute, in violation of § 18.2-248.1. Johnson v. Commonwealth, 2010 Va. App. LEXIS 69 (Feb. 23, 2010).

Evidence was sufficient to prove possession where the totality of the circumstances established that defendant was aware of both the presence and character of cocaine and marijuana and that the drugs were subject to defendant's dominion and control where defendant was the operator of the vehicle and was sitting next to the console within arm's reach of where the drugs were found, the lid to the console was not shut securely, a passenger testified that the drugs did not belong to her and were already in the vehicle when she entered it, and the drugs found in the console were the same type of drugs that defendant sought in text messages sent a few weeks before the arrest. Hicks v. Commonwealth, 2010 Va. App. LEXIS 188 (May 11, 2010).

Defendant's conviction for possession of marijuana with intent to distribute was appropriate because, at the traffic stop, defendant was in sole possession of the vehicle and possessed the key to the glove compartment, which contained marijuana valued at over $200. At that same time, the vehicle smelled strongly of the distinctive odor of marijuana, which the trial court found had been recently burnt; an expert further testified that the packaging of the marijuana was inconsistent with personal use. Ervin v. Commonwealth, 57 Va. App. 495, 704 S.E.2d 135, 2011 Va. App. LEXIS 24 (2011).

Sufficient evidence of more than personal use possession. — Evidence disclosed that the quantity of marijuana being manufactured was greater than that ordinarily possessed for one's personal use where it showed that the following items were discovered at defendant's house: 15 green marijuana plants, 14 growing inside appellant's residence, one growing outside; a 12-gauge shotgun; shotgun shells; .105 ounce of dried marijuana; a fluorescent light that is frequently used to assist in marijuana growth; and a copper smoking device. Bailey v. Commonwealth, No. 0886-93-4 (Ct. of Appeals Nov. 22, 1994).

Defendant held not entrapped by fear of reprisal if he did not complete sale. — In a prosecution for distribution of marijuana, the court could reasonably infer that the defendant continued in the transaction for personal benefit and not out of fear of reprisal, and therefore rejected his entrapment defense, where the defendant conceded that he was a willing participant in arranging the drug transaction and despite defendant's contention that the person for whom he procured the marijuana, an undercover officer, threatened reprisal. Schneider v. Commonwealth, 230 Va. 379, 337 S.E.2d 735 (1985).

Improper admission of direct evidence of sale not harmless despite sufficiency of circumstantial evidence. — Where the Commonwealth presented sufficient circumstantial evidence on the element of intent from which the jury could have inferred an intent to distribute, but the only direct evidence of a sale was the inadmissible testimony of the detective who stated that the "search warrant [for defendant and defendant's car] was based on a controlled buy made by a confidential reliable informant," the error was not harmless beyond a reasonable doubt. Accordingly, the trial court erred in denying the motion for a mistrial and defendant was entitled to a new trial. Terry v. Commonwealth, 5 Va. App. 167, 360 S.E.2d 880 (1987).

Sentencing error. — Defendant's sentence on his conviction for possession of marijuana with intent to distribute was excessive and, thus, the sentence for that offense had to be corrected on remand of defendant's case to the trial court; a 15-year sentence was imposed for that offense, but since it was a Class 5 felony, the maximum punishment that could be imposed was 10 years. Lathram v. Commonwealth, — Va. App. —, — S.E.2d —, 2006 Va. App. LEXIS 168 (May 2, 2006).

Dismissal of lesser-included offense not required upon vacation of felony conviction. — Dismissal of lesser-included offense of misdemeanor distribution was not required where the appellant was not acquitted of that charge for double jeopardy purposes by the trial court's post-trial ruling which set aside original guilty verdict because of trial error; jury's verdict of guilty on the felony charge established that sufficient evidence was presented at trial to sustain a verdict for misdemeanor distribution and the trial judge committed reversible error in not granting the initial motion to strike the felony charge and allowing the matter to be submitted to the jury only on the lesser-included charge. Therefore, jeopardy continues on the lesser-included charge until the matter is completed in a defect-free proceeding. Gorham v. Commonwealth, 15 Va. App. 673, 426 S.E.2d 493 (1993).

Convictions under this section not considered under enhancement provision of § 18.2-250.1 A. — The scheme of punishment under subsection A of § 18.2-250.1 does not envision that felony convictions under this section, which carries its own severe punishments, be considered under its enhancement provision. Pierce v. Commonwealth, 2 Va. App. 383, 345 S.E.2d 1 (1986).

Motion to suppress granted. — Trial court's denial of defendant's motion to suppress was error and, thus, the finding that defendant was guilty of possession of marijuana with intent to distribute had to be reversed; police did not have probable cause to seize CDs found in defendant's car, pursuant to §§ 59.1-41.5 and 59.1-41.4, since the items they thought were bogus CDs could have been legitimate, homemade CDs, and, thus, since the search for more CDs in his car led to the discovery of marijuana, the motion to suppress the marijuana evidence should have been granted because the seizure of that evidence was not reasonable given the lack of probable cause to search. McLaughlin v. Commonwealth, 48 Va. App. 243, 629 S.E.2d 724, 2006 Va. App. LEXIS 218 (2006).

CIRCUIT COURT OPINIONS

Motion to suppress. — Defendant's motion to suppress, pursuant to § 19.2-266.2, drugs found in defendant's pocket in relation to a charge of possession of marijuana with intent to distribute, § 18.2-248.1, was denied; the circumstances provided an officer with an objective basis for suspecting that defendant was armed and dangerous, so a pat-down search of defendant was legal. Commonwealth v. St. Louis, 61 Va. Cir. 384, 2003 Va. Cir. LEXIS 151 (Charlottesville 2003).

Habeas corpus. — Petitioner inmate was granted a writ of habeas corpus vacating his state conviction for misdemeanor possession with intent to distribute marijuana in violation of § 18.2-248.1, which was the sole basis of his incarceration in a federal jail, because the matter remained in actual controversy and was not moot since petitioner was restrained as the result of his Virginia conviction and had an extraordinary stake in the outcome of his petition; the order vacating petitioner's conviction would directly impact the duration of his current confinement because the Virginia conviction was the sole cause of petitioner's pending immigration proceedings under 8 U.S.C.S. § 1227(a)(2)(A)(iii). Ibrahim v. Superintendent, Rappahannock Reg'l Jail, 82 Va. Cir. 353, 2011 Va. Cir. LEXIS 81 (Fairfax County May 16, 2011).

§ 18.2-248.1:1. Penalties for possession, sale, gift, or distribution of or possession with intent to sell, give, or distribute synthetic cannabinoids; manufacturing.

A. For the purposes of this title, synthetic cannabinoids means any substance that contains one or more cannabimimetic agents or that contains their salts, isomers, and salts of isomers whenever the existence of such salts, isomers, and salts of isomers is possible within the specific chemical designation, and any preparation, mixture, or substance containing, or mixed or infused with, any detectable amount of one or more cannabimimetic agents.

1. "Cannabimimetic agents" means any substance that is within any of the following structural classes:

a. 2-(3-hydroxycyclohexyl)phenol with substitution at the 5-position of the phenolic ring by alkyl or alkenyl, whether or not substituted on the cyclohexyl ring to any extent;

b. 3-(1-naphthoyl)indole or 1H-indol-3-yl-(1-naphthyl)methane with substitution at the nitrogen atom of the indole ring, whether or not further substituted on the indole ring to any extent, whether or not substituted on the naphthoyl or naphthyl ring to any extent;

c. 3-(1-naphthoyl)pyrrole with substitution at the nitrogen atom of the pyrrole ring, whether or not further substituted in the pyrrole ring to any extent, whether or not substituted on the naphthoyl ring to any extent;

d. 1-(1-naphthylmethyl)indene with substitution of the 3-position of the indene ring, whether or not further substituted in the indene ring to any extent, whether or not substituted on the naphthyl ring to any extent;

e. 3-phenylacetylindole or 3-benzoylindole with substitution at the nitrogen atom of the indole ring, whether or not further substituted in the indole ring to any extent, whether or not substituted on the phenyl ring to any extent;

f. 3-cyclopropoylindole with substitution at the nitrogen atom of the indole ring, whether or not further substituted on the indole ring to any extent, whether or not substituted on the cyclopropyl ring to any extent;

g. 3-adamantoylindole with substitution at the nitrogen atom of the indole ring, whether or not further substituted on the indole ring to any extent, whether or not substituted on the adamantyl ring to any extent;

h. N-(adamantyl)-indole-3-carboxamide with substitution at the nitrogen atom of the indole ring, whether or not further substituted on the indole ring to any extent, whether or not substituted on the adamantyl ring to any extent; or

i. N-(adamantyl)-indazole-3-carboxamide with substitution at a nitrogen atom of the indazole ring, whether or not further substituted on the indazole ring to any extent, whether or not substituted on the adamantyl ring to any extent.

2. The term cannabimimetic agents includes:

5-(1,1-Dimethylheptyl)-2-[3-hydroxycyclohexyl]-phenol (other name: CP 47,497);

5-(1,1-Dimethylhexyl)-2-[3-hydroxycyclohexyl]-phenol (other name: CP 47,497 C6 homolog);

5-(1,1-Dimethyloctyl)-2-[3-hydroxycyclohexyl]-phenol (other name: CP 47,497 C8 homolog);

5-(1,1-Dimethylnonyl)-2-[3-hydroxycyclohexyl]-phenol (other name: CP 47,497 C9 homolog);

1-pentyl-3-(1-naphthoyl)indole (other names: JWH-018, AM-678);

1-butyl-3-(1-naphthoyl)indole (other name: JWH-073);

1-pentyl-3-(2-methoxyphenylacetyl)indole (other name: JWH-250);

1-hexyl-3-(naphthalen-1-oyl)indole (other name: JWH-019);

1-[2-(4-morpholinyl)ethyl]-3-(1-naphthoyl)indole (other name: JWH-200);

(6aR,10aR)-9-(hydroxymethyl)-6,6-dimethyl-3-(2-methyloctan-2-yl)-6a,7,10,10a-tetrahydrobenzo[c]chromen-1-ol (other name: HU-210);

1-pentyl-3-(4-methoxy-1-naphthoyl)indole (other name: JWH-081);

1-pentyl-3-(4-methyl-1-naphthoyl)indole (other name: JWH-122);

1-pentyl-3-(2-chlorophenylacetyl)indole (other name: JWH-203);

1-pentyl-3-(4-ethyl-1-naphthoyl)indole (other name: JWH-210);

1-pentyl-3-(4-chloro-1-naphthoyl)indole (other name: JWH-398);

1-(5-fluoropentyl)-3-(2-iodobenzoyl)indole (other name: AM-694);

1-((N-methylpiperidin-2-yl)methyl)-3-(1-naphthoyl)indole (other name: AM-1220);

1-(5-fluoropentyl)-3-(1-naphthoyl)indole (other name: AM-2201);

1-[(N-methylpiperidin-2-yl)methyl]-3-(2-iodobenzoyl)indole (other name: AM-2233);

Pravadoline (4-methoxyphenyl)-[2-methyl-1-(2-(4-morpholinyl)ethyl)indol-3-yl]methanone (other name: WIN 48,098);

1-pentyl-3-(4-methoxybenzoyl)indole (other names: RCS-4, SR-19);

1-(2-cyclohexylethyl)-3-(2-methoxyphenylacetyl)indole (other names: RCS-8, SR-18);

1-pentyl-3-(2,2,3,3-tetramethylcyclopropylmethanone)indole (other name: UR-144);

1-(5-fluoropentyl)-3-(2,2,3,3-tetramethylcyclopropylmethanone)indole (other name: XLR-11);

N-adamantyl-1-fluoropentylindole-3-carboxamide (other name: STS-135);

N-adamantyl-1-pentylindazole-3-carboxamide (other name: AKB48);

1-pentyl-3-(1-adamantoyl)indole (other name: AB-001);

(8-quinolinyl)(1-pentylindol-3-yl)carboxylate (other name: PB-22);

(8-quinolinyl)(1-(5-fluoropentyl)indol-3-yl)carboxylate (other name: 5-fluoro-PB-22).

B. It is unlawful for any person to knowingly or intentionally possess synthetic cannabinoids. Any person who violates this subsection is guilty of a Class 1 misdemeanor.

C. It is unlawful for any person to sell, give, distribute, or possess with intent to sell, give, or distribute synthetic cannabinoids. Any person who violates this subsection is guilty of a Class 6 felony.

D. If a person proves that he gave, distributed or possessed with intent to give or distribute synthetic cannabinoids only as an accommodation to another individual and not with intent to profit thereby from any consideration received or expected nor to induce the recipient or intended recipient of the synthetic cannabinoids to use or become addicted to or dependent upon such synthetic cannabinoids, he is guilty of a Class 1 misdemeanor. Any person who gives, distributes or possesses synthetic cannabinoids as an accommodation and not with intent to profit thereby, to an inmate of a state or local correctional facility as defined in § 53.1-1, or in the custody of an employee thereof is guilty of a Class 4 felony.

E. Any person who manufactures synthetic cannabinoids or possesses synthetic cannabinoids with intent to manufacture such substance is guilty of a felony punishable by imprisonment of not less than five nor more than 30 years and a fine not to exceed $10,000.

F. Any drug not listed in this section or the Drug Control Act (§ 54.1-3400 et seq.), which is privately compounded, with the specific intent to circumvent the criminal penalties for synthetic cannabinoids, to emulate or simulate the effects of synthetic cannabinoids through chemical changes such as the addition, subtraction or rearranging of a radical or the addition, subtraction or rearranging of a substituent, shall be subject to the same criminal penalties as for synthetic cannabinoids.

G. Upon conviction, in addition to any other punishment, a person found guilty of a violation of this section shall be ordered by the court to make restitution, as the court deems appropriate, to any innocent property owner whose property is damaged, destroyed, or otherwise rendered unusable as a result of such synthetic cannabinoid production. This restitution may include the person's or his estate's estimated or actual expenses associated with cleanup, removal, or repair of the affected property.

History.

2011, cc. 384, 410; 2012, cc. 762, 816; 2013, cc. 295, 785.

Editor's note.

Acts 2011, cc. 384 and 410, cl. 2 made this section effective March 23, 2011.

Acts 2011, cc. 384 and 410, cl. 3 provides: "That the provisions of this act may result in a net increase in periods of imprisonment or commitment. Pursuant to § 30-19.1:4, the estimated amount of the necessary appropriation cannot be determined for periods of imprisonment in state adult correctional facilities; therefore, Chapter 874 of the Acts of Assembly of 2010 requires the Virginia Criminal Sentencing Commission to assign a minimum fiscal impact of $50,000. Pursuant to § 30-19.1:4, the estimated amount of the necessary appropriation cannot be determined for periods of commitment to the custody of the Department of Juvenile Justice."

Acts 2012, cc. 762 and 816, cl. 2 provides: "That the provisions of this act may result in a net increase in periods of imprisonment or commitment. Pursuant to § 30-19.1:4, the estimated amount of the necessary appropriation cannot be determined for periods of imprisonment in state adult correctional facilities; therefore, Chapter 890 of the Acts of Assembly of 2011 requires the Virginia Criminal Sentencing Commission to assign a minimum fiscal impact of $50,000. Pursuant to § 30-19.1:4, the estimated amount of the necessary appropriation cannot be determined for periods of commitment to the custody of the Department of Juvenile Justice."

Acts 2013, cc. 295 and 785, cl. 2 provides: "That the provisions of this act may result in a net increase in periods of imprisonment or commitment. Pursuant to § 30-19.1:4, the estimated amount of the necessary appropriation cannot be determined for periods of imprisonment in state adult correctional facilities; therefore, Chapter 3 of the Acts of Assembly of 2012, Special Session I, requires the Virginia Criminal Sentencing Commission to assign a minimum fiscal impact of $50,000. Pursuant to § 30-19.1:4, the estimated amount of the necessary appropriation cannot be determined for periods of commitment to the custody of the Department of Juvenile Justice."

The 2012 amendments.

The 2012 amendments by cc. 762 and 816 are identical, and rewrote subsection A.

The 2013 amendments.

The 2013 amendment by c. 295, effective March 13, 2013, added subdivisions A 1 f through subdivisions A 1 i; and added the language beginning "1-pentyl-3-(2,2,3,3-tetramethylcyclopropylmethanone)indole (other name: UR-144)" and ending "N-adamantyl-1-pentylindazole-3-carboxamide (other name: AKB48)" at the end; and made minor spelling changes and added other names throughout.

The 2013 amendment by c. 785, in subdivision A 1, added subdivisions A 1 f through A 1 i; and in subdivision A 2 added the entries beginning with "1-pentyl-3-(2,2,3,3-tetramethylcyclopropylmethanone)indole (other name: UR-144)" to the end; and made minor spelling changes and added other names throughout.

CASE NOTES

Applied in Epps v. Commonwealth, 59 Va. App. 71, 717 S.E.2d 151, 2011 Va. App. LEXIS 351 (2011).

§ 18.2-248.2. Repealed by Acts 1981, c. 598.

Cross references.

For present provisions concerning drug paraphernalia, see §§ 18.2-265.1 through 18.2-265.5.

§ 18.2-248.3. Professional use of imitation controlled substances.

No civil or criminal liability shall be imposed by virtue of this article on any person licensed under the Drug Control Act, Chapter 34 of Title 54.1, who manufactures, sells, gives or distributes an imitation controlled substance for use as a placebo by a licensed practitioner in the course of professional practice or research.

History.

1982, c. 462.

§ 18.2-248.4. Advertisement of imitation controlled substances prohibited; penalty.

It shall be a Class 1 misdemeanor for any person knowingly to sell or display for sale, or to distribute, whether or not any charge is made therefor, any book, pamphlet, handbill or other printed matter which he knows is intended to promote the distribution of an imitation controlled substance.

History.

1982, c. 462.

§ 18.2-248.5. Illegal stimulants and steroids; penalty.

A. Except as authorized in the Drug Control Act (§ 54.1-3400 et seq.), Chapter 34 of Title 54.1, it shall be unlawful for any person to knowingly manufacture, sell, give, distribute or possess with intent to manufacture, sell, give or distribute any anabolic steroid.

A violation of subsection A shall be punishable by a term of imprisonment of not less than one year nor more than 10 years or, in the discretion of the jury or the court trying the case without a jury, confinement in jail for not more than 12 months or a fine of not more than $20,000, either or both. Any person violating the provisions of this subsection shall, upon conviction, be incarcerated for a mandatory minimum term of six months to be served consecutively with any other sentence.

B. It shall be unlawful for any person to knowingly sell or otherwise distribute, without prescription, to a minor any pill, capsule or tablet containing any combination of caffeine and ephedrine sulfate.

A violation of this subsection B shall be punishable as a Class 1 misdemeanor.

History.

1984, c. 620; 1988, c. 428; 1989, c. 567; 2000, cc. 1020, 1041; 2004, c. 461.

§§ 18.2-248.6, 18.2-248.7. Repealed by Acts 1999, c. 348, cl. 2.

§ 18.2-248.8. Repealed by Acts 2012, cc. 160 and 252, cl. 2, effective January 1, 2013.

Cross references.

For current provisions related to penalty for sale of methamphetamine precursors ephedrine and pseudoephedrine, see § 18.2-265.7.

Editor's note.

Acts 2012, cc. 160 and 252, cl. 3 provides: "That the provisions of this act shall become effective on January 1, 2013."

Former §18.2-248.8, sale of the methamphetamine precursors ephedrine and pseudoephedrine; penalty, derived from Acts 2006, cc. 865, 893.

§ 18.2-249. Repealed by Acts 2004, c. 995.

Cross references.

For current provisions as to seizure of property used in connection with or derived from illegal drug transactions, see § 19.2-386.22.

§ 18.2-250. Possession of controlled substances unlawful.

A. It is unlawful for any person knowingly or intentionally to possess a controlled substance unless the substance was obtained directly from, or pursuant to, a valid prescription or order of a practitioner while acting in the course of his professional practice, or except as otherwise authorized by the Drug Control Act (§ 54.1-3400 et seq.).

Upon the prosecution of a person for a violation of this section, ownership or occupancy of premises or vehicle upon or in which a controlled substance was found shall not create a presumption that such person either knowingly or intentionally possessed such controlled substance.

(a) Any person who violates this section with respect to any controlled substance classified in Schedule I or II of the Drug Control Act shall be guilty of a Class 5 felony.

(b) Any person other than an inmate of a penal institution as defined in § 53.1-1 or in the custody of an employee thereof, who violates this section with respect to a controlled substance classified in Schedule III shall be guilty of a Class 1 misdemeanor.

(b1) Violation of this section with respect to a controlled substance classified in Schedule IV shall be punishable as a Class 2 misdemeanor.

(b2) Violation of this section with respect to a controlled substance classified in Schedule V shall be punishable as a Class 3 misdemeanor.

(c) Violation of this section with respect to a controlled substance classified in Schedule VI shall be punishable as a Class 4 misdemeanor.

B. The provisions of this section shall not apply to members of state, federal, county, city or town law-enforcement agencies, jail officers, or correctional officers, as defined in § 53.1-1, certified as handlers of dogs trained in the detection of controlled substances when possession of a controlled substance or substances is necessary in the performance of their duties.

History.

Code 1950, § 54-524.101:2; 1972, c. 798; 1973, c. 64; 1975, cc. 14, 15; 1976, c. 614; 1978, cc. 151, 177, 179; 1979, c. 435; 1980, c. 285; 1991, c. 649; 1998, c. 116.

Cross references.

As to penalty for sale, possession, etc., of controlled substance or marijuana by inmate in penal institution or in custody of employee thereof, see § 53.1-203.

Law Review.

For survey of Virginia criminal law for the year 1971-1972, see 58 Va. L. Rev. 1206 (1972); for the year 1972-1973, see 59 Va. L. Rev. 1458 (1973); for the year 1974-1975, see 61 Va. L. Rev. 1697 (1975); for the year 1975-1976, see 62 Va. L. Rev. 1400 (1976); for the year 1976-1977, see 63 Va. L. Rev. 1396 (1977); for the year 1977-1978, see 64 Va. L. Rev. 1407 (1978). For annual survey article, "Criminal Law and Procedure," see 46 U. Rich. L. Rev. 59 (2011). For annual survey of Virginia law article, "Criminal Law and Procedure," see 47 U. Rich. L. Rev. 143 (2012).

CASE NOTES

I. General Consideration.
II. Evidence.
     A. Admission of Evidence.
     B. Evidence of Knowledge.
     C. Evidence of Constructive Possession Generally.

I. GENERAL CONSIDERATION.

Constitutionality. — Since there is no fundamental right to the private use, possession or trade in marijuana or cocaine, and since governments have the power to enact and enforce sumptuary laws in this area, § 18.2-248, now amended and cited as § 18.2-248.1 and this section do not violate the Ninth and Tenth Amendments to the United States Constitution. Wolkind v. Selph, 495 F. Supp. 507 (E.D. Va. 1980), aff'd, 649 F.2d 865 (4th Cir. 1981).

Since the classification of cocaine as a narcotic drug passes constitutional muster under the rational basis test, the penalty imposed by this section for the possession of cocaine as a Schedule II drug is not irrational, arbitrary or unjust and does not deny equal protection of the laws. Wolkind v. Selph, 495 F. Supp. 507 (E.D. Va. 1980), aff'd, 649 F.2d 865 (4th Cir. 1981).

Private possession of marijuana is not a fundamental constitutional right and the private possession of cocaine is not a fundamental constitutional right; accordingly, Virginia's statutory framework establishing criminal penalties for the possession with the intent to distribute marijuana and for the simple possession of cocaine need bear only a rational relationship to a legitimate interest of the Commonwealth. Wolkind v. Selph, 495 F. Supp. 507 (E.D. Va. 1980), aff'd, 649 F.2d 865 (4th Cir. 1981).

Subjective intent to purchase. — Purchase of a noncontrolled substance that defendant subjectively believes to be a controlled substance can constitute an attempt to possess provided the government proves the defendant's subjective intent to purchase actual narcotics beyond a reasonable doubt. Smith v. Commonwealth, 16 Va. App. 626, 432 S.E.2d 1 (1993).

Possession coextensive with § 18.2-248 possession. — Under the Virginia statutes, possession under this section is coextensive with possession under § 18.2-248. Such an interpretation is required as a matter of due process of law since, otherwise, a defendant could be subject to a presumption of possession based upon occupancy of an apartment in a prosecution under the greater offense of § 18.2-248, whereas such a presumption would be barred in a prosecution under this section. Bentley v. Cox, 508 F. Supp. 870 (E.D. Va. 1981).

Double jeopardy. — Two convictions for possession of drugs with intent to distribute within 1,000 feet of a school under § 18.2-255.2 did not violate the Double Jeopardy Clause under U.S. Const., Amend. V and Va. Const., Art. I, § 8 as marijuana and cocaine were treated in the Virginia Code as separate and discrete illegal substances under §§ 18.2-250, 18.2-250.1, and 54.1-3448. Fullwood v. Commonwealth, 54 Va. App. 153, 676 S.E.2d 348, 2009 Va. App. LEXIS 224 (2009), aff'd, 279 Va. 531, 689 S.E.2d 742, 2010 Va. LEXIS 39 (2010).

Possession is a lesser-included offense of distribution. — Proof of the elements of the offense of feloniously, knowingly, and intentionally distributing a controlled substance necessarily encompasses proof of the possession of that same controlled substance and, therefore, the offense of possessing a controlled substance is a lesser-included offense of distribution of a controlled substance. Austin v. Commonwealth, 33 Va. App. 124, 531 S.E.2d 637, 2000 Va. App. LEXIS 572 (2000).

Evidence was insufficient to support defendant's conviction for possession of cocaine with the intent to distribute pursuant to § 18.2-248; there was no evidence presented at defendant's bench trial that the cocaine residue that police found in a raid on the residence where defendant lived with other people was the remainder of a larger supply that was intended for distribution; accordingly, the judgment of conviction had to be reversed and the case had to be remanded to allow the trial court to enter an order finding defendant guilty of possession of cocaine. Lunceford v. Commonwealth, — Va. App. —, — S.E.2d —, 2006 Va. App. LEXIS 98 (Mar. 21, 2006).

Violation of this section is crime involving moral turpitude and oil company could reasonably terminate cocaine user's franchise. Portaluppi v. Shell Oil Co., 684 F. Supp. 900 (E.D. Va. 1988), aff'd, 869 F.2d 245 (4th Cir. 1989).

The jury should not concern itself with background information on the prohibited substance, but should make an objective finding of guilt or innocence based on relevant evidence and punish the guilty within the limits fixed by statute. Smith v. Commonwealth, 223 Va. 721, 292 S.E.2d 362 (1982).

To permit evidence respecting extreme horrors which may result from the use of illegal substances diverts the jury from its principal inquiry and injects an element of passion into the trial prejudicial to the accused. Smith v. Commonwealth, 223 Va. 721, 292 S.E.2d 362 (1982).

In determining whether a defendant constructively possessed drugs, defendant's proximity to the drugs and his occupancy of the vehicle must also be considered. Although mere proximity to the drugs is insufficient to establish possession, and occupancy of the vehicle does not give rise to a presumption of possession, § 18.2-250, both are factors which may be considered in determining whether a defendant possessed drugs. Castaneda v. Commonwealth, 7 Va. App. 574, 376 S.E.2d 82 (1989).

Defendant's proximity to cocaine found on a kitchen counter in a home which was being searched, combined with evidence that nothing else was located on the counter and no one else was in close proximity of the same, provided sufficient evidence for the trial court to conclude that defendant was aware that drugs were present, and his proximity to the counter supported a finding that he exercised dominion and control over the cocaine. Dawson v. Commonwealth, No. 1687-02-1, 2003 Va. App. LEXIS 237 (Ct. of Appeals Apr. 22, 2003).

Ownership or occupancy may be considered in determining constructive possession. — Although the mere ownership or occupancy of premises in which an illegal drug is found does not create a presumption of conscious or intentional possession, such evidence is probative and may be considered in determining if defendant constructively possessed the offending substance. Allen v. Commonwealth, No. 1478-91-1 (Ct. of Appeals Nov. 10, 1992).

Occupancy of the premises on which drugs are found does not give rise to a presumption of possession; instead, it is only one factor to be considered along with other evidence in determining whether a defendant constructively possessed drugs. Tucker v. Commonwealth, 18 Va. App. 141, 442 S.E.2d 419 (1994).

Showing necessary for conviction. — In order to convict a defendant of "possession" of a narcotic drug, it generally is necessary to show that defendant was aware of the presence and character of the particular substance and was intentionally and consciously in possession of it. Clodfelter v. Commonwealth, 218 Va. 619, 238 S.E.2d 820 (1977); Hairston v. Commonwealth, 5 Va. App. 183, 360 S.E.2d 893 (1987).

Physical possession giving the defendant immediate and exclusive control of a drug is sufficient to satisfy the requirements of this section. Hornbaker v. Commonwealth, No. 1332-88-4 (Ct. of Appeals March 27, 1990).

To convict an accused of possession of a particular unlawful substance, the Commonwealth must prove the accused was aware of the character of the particular substance at issue. Smith v. Commonwealth, 16 Va. App. 626, 432 S.E.2d 1 (1993).

In order to justify appellant's conviction under this section, the Commonwealth had to prove beyond a reasonable doubt that he possessed the cocaine, either actually or constructively, with an awareness of its presence and character. Tucker v. Commonwealth, 18 Va. App. 141, 442 S.E.2d 419 (1994).

To convict a person of possession of illegal drugs the Commonwealth must prove that the defendant was aware of the presence and character of the drugs and that the defendant intentionally and consciously possessed them; physical possession giving the defendant immediate and exclusive control is sufficient. Brooks v. Commonwealth, No. 0811-02-4, 2003 Va. App. LEXIS 118 (Ct. of Appeals Mar. 4, 2003).

What must be included. — Although in a circumstantial

evidence case the Commonwealth must exclude every reasonable hypothesis of innocence, the Commonwealth is not required to prove that there is no possibility that someone else may have planted, discarded, abandoned or placed the drugs or paraphernalia where they were found near an accused. Brinkley v. Commonwealth, No. 1895-96-1, 1997 Va. App. LEXIS 498 (Ct. of Appeals July 22, 1997).

Knowledge. — While knowledge is an essential ingredient in the crime of possession of narcotics, such knowledge may be proved by evidence of acts, declarations or conduct of the accused from which the inference may be fairly drawn that he knew of the existence of narcotics at the place where they were found. Clodfelter v. Commonwealth, 218 Va. 619, 238 S.E.2d 820 (1977); Hairston v. Commonwealth, 5 Va. App. 183, 360 S.E.2d 893 (1987).

Knowledge may be proved by evidence of acts, declarations or conduct of the accused from which the inference may be fairly drawn that the accused knew of the existence of narcotics at the place where they were found. Therefore, where the evidence showed that defendant told the police that he was "an addict" and he directed their attention to the cocaine in his shirt pocket, from these acts and declarations, the jury could reasonably have found that defendant knew of the presence and character of the substance and that he was intentionally and consciously in possession of it. Woodson v. Commonwealth, 14 Va. App. 787, 421 S.E.2d 1 (1992), aff'd, 245 Va. 401, 429 S.E.2d 27 (1993).

Police officer's observation of defendant tossing a small bottle in the air, placing it on a church windowsill, and then abandoning it, was insufficient to prove that defendant knew the bottle contained cocaine residue. Rather, it supported the conclusion that he attached no value or significance to the bottle. Whitehead v. Commonwealth, No. 0908-93-1, 1995 Va. App. LEXIS 191 (Ct. of Appeals Feb. 28, 1995).

Defendant's statement that he picked the bottle up thinking that it might contain cocaine, but discarded it when he perceived that it did not, failed to prove that he knew the bottle contained cocaine residue. His mere hope that it might did not rise to the level of knowledge that it did. Whitehead v. Commonwealth, No. 0908-93-1, 1995 Va. App. LEXIS 191 (Ct. of Appeals Feb. 28, 1995).

Knowledge of the presence and character of the controlled substance is required but such knowledge may be shown by evidence of the acts, statements or conduct of the accused. Harrison v. Commonwealth, No. 1973-99-1, 2000 Va. App. LEXIS 581 (Ct. of Appeals Aug. 8, 2000).

Because actual or constructive possession alone was not sufficient for a conviction under § 18.2-250 and the ambiguous circumstantial evidence concerning the appearance of a bottle and its contents was as consistent with a hypothesis of innocence as it was with that of guilt in regard to knowledge, it was insufficient to support the conviction. Young v. Commonwealth, 275 Va. 587, 659 S.E.2d 308, 2008 Va. LEXIS 54 (2008).

The court overruled the holding in *Josephs v. Commonwealth* to the extent that it can be read to mean that mere possession, without more, can prove guilty knowledge. Young v. Commonwealth, 275 Va. 587, 659 S.E.2d 308, 2008 Va. LEXIS 54 (2008).

To establish possession, the Commonwealth was required to show that defendant intentionally and consciously possessed cocaine with knowledge of its nature and character. Askew v. Commonwealth, No. 0866-88-1 (Ct. of Appeals Oct. 9, 1990).

Physical possession giving the defendant "immediate and exclusive control" is sufficient for conviction. Clodfelter v. Commonwealth, 218 Va. 619, 238 S.E.2d 820 (1977).

Proof of close proximity is relevant fact. — Proof that a person is in close proximity to contraband is a relevant fact that, depending on the circumstances, may tend to show that, as an owner or occupant of property or of a vehicle, the person necessarily knows of the presence, nature and character of a substance that is found there. Burchette v. Commonwealth, 15 Va. App. 432, 425 S.E.2d 81 (1992).

Mere proximity to a controlled substance is insufficient to establish possession, and, furthermore, no presumption of possession arises from the ownership or occupancy of the premises where drugs are found. Bentley v. Cox, 508 F. Supp. 870 (E.D. Va. 1981).

Mere proximity to a controlled drug is not sufficient to establish dominion and control. Drew v. Commonwealth, 230 Va. 471, 338 S.E.2d 844 (1986).

Although proximity to drugs and the occupancy of a vehicle in which they are found are factors that may be considered in determining whether defendant possessed drugs, these factors, standing alone, do not give rise to a presumption of possession. Tomasinski v. Commonwealth, No. 1338-91-4 (Ct. of Appeals Oct. 13, 1992).

Evidence merely that accused was in the proximity of controlled substances was insufficient to prove that the accused was aware of the presence and character of a controlled substance. Jones v. Commonwealth, 17 Va. App. 572, 439 S.E.2d 863 (1994).

Although mere proximity to drugs is insufficient to establish possession, it is a circumstance that may be probative in determining whether an accused possessed such drugs. Bright v. Commonwealth, No. 2794-99-1, 2000 Va. App. LEXIS 747 (Ct. of Appeals Nov. 21, 2000).

Ownership of a vehicle where drugs are found and mere proximity to the drugs, though factors which the fact finder may consider, are insufficient alone to prove possession. Scruggs v. Commonwealth, 19 Va. App. 58, 448 S.E.2d 663 (1994).

The duration of the possession is immaterial. Clodfelter v. Commonwealth, 218 Va. 619, 238 S.E.2d 820 (1977).

Ownership or occupancy of the vehicle in which drugs are found is a circumstance probative of possession. Bright v. Commonwealth, No. 2794-99-1, 2000 Va. App. LEXIS 747 (Ct. of Appeals Nov. 21, 2000).

Possession need not always be exclusive. The defendant may share it with one or more. Clodfelter v. Commonwealth, 218 Va. 619, 238 S.E.2d 820 (1977).

Or actual. — See Clodfelter v. Commonwealth, 218 Va. 619, 238 S.E.2d 820 (1977).

Possession of a controlled substance may be exclusive or joint, actual or constructive. Woodfin v. Commonwealth, 218 Va. 458, 237 S.E.2d 777 (1977).

Possession of a controlled substance need not be exclusive and may be shared; moreover, possession of a controlled substance may be actual or constructive. McGee v. Commonwealth, 4 Va. App. 317, 357 S.E.2d 738 (1987).

Predicate conviction for 18 U.S.C.S. § 922(g)(1). — Dismissal of indictments for possession of a firearm after having been convicted of a crime punishable by more than one year of imprisonment in violation of 18 U.S.C.S. § 922(g)(1) was affirmed, where the predicate convictions were juvenile adjudications in Virginia state court; a juvenile adjudication was not a conviction under Virginia law, so such an adjudication could not serve as the underlying conviction. United States v. Walters, 359 F.3d 340, 2004 U.S. App. LEXIS 3021 (4th Cir. 2004).

Conviction following revocation of first-offender status was improper. — Circuit court should not have revoked defendant's first-offender status under § 18.2-251 and convicted her of possessing cocaine, in violation of § 18.2-250, after her stated period of probation ended: (1) the circuit court's order imposing first-offender status explicitly stated that defendant's probation ended on December 21, 2005; (2) although the circuit court continued defendant's case after December 21, 2005, it did so only to ensure that defendant paid court costs, as required under the first-offender order; (3) the circuit court did not explicitly extend defendant's probation beyond December 21, 2005, and such an extension could not occur de facto; and (4) it would not be appropriate to assume that defendant was subject to a continuing, implicit condition of good behavior after her case was continued given that a good behavior condition had been explicitly imposed on her as part of her probation. White v. Commonwealth, 276 Va. 725, 667 S.E.2d 564, 2008 Va. LEXIS 119 (2008).

Convictions under former § 54-524.76 and this section violated double jeopardy. — Where defendant was convicted under former § 54-524.76 of obtaining a drug by presenting a forged prescription, and for the same transaction was subsequently convicted under this section of possession of a controlled substance, his rights under the double jeopardy clause were violated, since the evidence necessarily used in the first prosecution would totally have sufficed to sustain the second conviction. Jordan v. Virginia, 653 F.2d 870 (4th Cir. 1980).

Simple possession of a controlled substance is a felony. — Enhancement of defendant's sentence pursuant to U.S. Sentencing Guidelines Manual § 2L1.2(b)(1)(C) was proper; while the Controlled Substances Act, 21 U.S.C.S. § 801 et seq., would not punish

defendant's conduct as a felony, it did define it as a felony given the punishment it received under subsection A of § 18.2-250. United States v. Wilson, 316 F.3d 506, 2003 U.S. App. LEXIS 616 (4th Cir. 2003), cert. denied, 538 U.S. 1025, 123 S. Ct. 1959, 155 L. Ed. 2d 871 (2003); overruled in part by Lopez v. Gonzales, 127 S.Ct. 625, 166 L.Ed.2d 462 (U.S. 2006).

Severance. — Trial court did not err in refusing to sever felon in possession of a firearm indictment from possession of cocaine and possession of firearm charges, as nothing in the record rebutted the presumption that the trial court considered only the evidence relevant to each offense when reaching its decision. Vanhook v. Commonwealth, 40 Va. App. 130, 578 S.E.2d 71, 2003 Va. App. LEXIS 149 (2003).

Revocation of deferred disposition. — Trial court did not abuse its discretion in finding that defendant violated the terms of the plea agreement, as well as its order, by failing to submit to two drug screens, and in convicting him for possession of methamphetamine after having deferred judgment on the charge pursuant to § 18.2-251. Vogt v. Commonwealth, 2012 Va. App. LEXIS 170 (May 22, 2012).

Applied in Lawson v. Commonwealth, 217 Va. 354, 228 S.E.2d 685 (1976); Womack v. Commonwealth, 220 Va. 5, 255 S.E.2d 351 (1979); Spear v. Commonwealth, 221 Va. 450, 270 S.E.2d 737 (1980); Livingston v. Commonwealth, 21 Va. App. 621, 466 S.E.2d 757 (1996); Price v. Commonwealth, 24 Va. App. 496, 483 S.E.2d 496 (1997); Perry v. Commonwealth, 55 Va. App. 122, 684 S.E.2d 227, 2009 Va. App. LEXIS 490 (2009); Hicks v. Commonwealth, 281 Va. 353, 706 S.E.2d 339, 2011 Va. LEXIS 44 (2011); Epps v. Commonwealth, 59 Va. App. 71, 717 S.E.2d 151, 2011 Va. App. LEXIS 351 (2011).

II. EVIDENCE.

A. Admission of Evidence.

Certificate of analysis properly admitted. — On appeal from a conviction of possession of cocaine, the appeals court found that no error resulted from the trial court's admission of a certificate of analysis, as such was turned over to defendant's first counsel, but lost as a result of transferring defendant's case file to his second counsel, and absent evidence to the contrary, such did not impute fault to the Commonwealth. Hobson v. Commonwealth, — Va. App. —, — S.E.2d —, 2007 Va. App. LEXIS 388 (Oct. 23, 2007).

In a prosecution on a charge of possession of cocaine, the trial court properly admitted into evidence the certificate of analysis establishing that the substance defendant possessed was cocaine. While there was an inconsistency in the description of the evidence submitted for testing and the description in the certificate, all features on the request for examination form and the certificate matched, including the date of the offense, the identity of the suspect, the identity of the officer, the case numbers assigned, and the certified mail numbers; thus, the request for examination form and the certificate coincided to connect the data analyzed and subjected the certificate to the evidence retrieved by the officer. Herndon v. Commonwealth, 2009 Va. App. LEXIS 242 (May 26, 2009), aff'd, 280 Va. 138, 694 S.E.2d 618, 2010 Va. LEXIS 70 (2010).

Where Court of Appeals was unable to say what effect inadmissible evidence had on the fact finder's decision, despite independent evidence of the nature of the controlled substance, defendant's conviction would be reversed. Payne v. Commonwealth, No. 2870-95-4, 1997 Va. App. LEXIS 166 (Ct. of Appeals Mar. 25, 1997).

Admission of a toxicologist's testimony regarding the effects of a prohibited substance was error as the defendant was on trial solely for the illegal possession of such substances; however, reversal was not required where the testimony was not such as to excite the passions of the jury. Lane v. Commonwealth, 223 Va. 713, 292 S.E.2d 358 (1982).

Involuntary consent. — When officer questioned defendant about suspected drug violations after learning that a traffic citation would not be issued, the officer effected a separate detention without reasonable articulable suspicion and defendant's consent to the search of his person was involuntary. Perry v. Commonwealth, No. 2466-00-2, 2002 Va. App. LEXIS 430 (Ct. of Appeals July 30, 2002).

Refusal to consent to search. — Evidence that defendant refused to consent to the search of his parked vehicle, assuming that the refusal was admissible evidence, did not tend to prove that defendant was exercising dominion and control over the vehicle with knowledge that it contained drugs. His refusal to consent to a search no more established the exercise of dominion and control over the contraband in the vehicle than did his ownership of the vehicle, which was insufficient to prove constructive possession. Burchette v. Commonwealth, 15 Va. App. 432, 425 S.E.2d 81 (1992).

As police officer had no basis to suspect that defendant was engaged in criminal activity or that he was armed, when defendant withdrew his consent to be searched, the officer had no legal basis to continue the encounter. Ellison v. Commonwealth, No. 1619-01-2, 2002 Va. App. LEXIS 337 (Ct. of Appeals June 11, 2002).

Valid search incident to lawful arrest. — Even if the officers had initiated the trespass investigation as a pretext to allow them to further investigate whether the defendant was involved in drug activity, once the officers had probable cause to believe that the defendant was trespassing the legality of seizing and charging him with that offense satisfied the Fourth Amendment requirement that the seizure be reasonable. Thereafter, the officer had the right to search the defendant incident to the arrest and the cocaine found as a result of that search was legally seized. Accordingly, the trial court did not err by overruling the motion to suppress the cocaine. Boone v. Commonwealth, No. 2575-95-2, 1997 Va. App. LEXIS 56 (Ct. of Appeals Feb. 4, 1997).

The totality of circumstances, viewed objectively, was clearly sufficient to provide probable cause to believe that defendant possessed heroin, justifying an immediate warrantless arrest and related search. Jones v. Commonwealth, No. 1586-01-2, 2002 Va. App. LEXIS 355 (Ct. of Appeals June 18, 2002).

The trial court properly denied defendant's motion to suppress the cocaine seized from defendant's person, as a deputy, in conducting an investigatory stop of defendant on foot, observed that defendant smelled of alcohol, had a flushed face, and was unsteady on his feet, supplying the officer with probable cause to arrest defendant for public intoxication. Thus, given the validity of the stop, the trial court correctly denied defendant's suppression motion. Croson v. Commonwealth, — Va. App. —, — S.E.2d —, 2007 Va. App. LEXIS 276 (July 24, 2007).

Defendant was properly convicted of possession of cocaine because trial court correctly denied defendant's motion to suppress a crack pipe a police officer seized from his person when the officer was conducting a reasonable search incident to arrest when he removed the crack pipe from defendant's pocket; because defendant refused to allow a police officer to conduct a pat-down search and struggled with the officer, the officer had probable cause to arrest defendant for obstruction of justice. Pettaway v. Commonwealth, 2009 Va. App. LEXIS 178 (Apr. 21, 2009).

Court of appeals properly applied the right result for the wrong reason doctrine to deny defendant's motion to suppress and affirm his conviction because the facts in the record established that the police officer had probable cause to arrest defendant for possession of PCP in violation of § 18.2-250 before the pat-down search since the officer noted the smell of drugs in the vehicle, verified the existence of PCP in the vial thrown on the ground, and identified defendant's behavior as being consistent with that of an individual under the influence of PCP. At that point, based on his training and experience as a police officer, the officer had probable cause to believe that defendant possessed PCP; as a result, the subsequent search of defendant was a lawful search incident to arrest under the Fourth Amendment. Perry v. Commonwealth, 280 Va. 572, 701 S.E.2d 431, 2010 Va. LEXIS 271 (2010).

Probable cause to stop followed by consensual search established proper seizure. — Where § 46.2-1054 prohibits driving a vehicle "with any object . . . suspended from any part of the motor vehicle in such a manner as to obstruct the driver's clear view of the highway through the windshield," and police officer has the authority to detain a vehicle upon his belief that the vehicle is being operated in violation of the law, the trial judge did not err in finding that the trooper had authority to stop the vehicle and to issue a summons. Thus, defendants' Fourth Amendment rights were not violated by detaining them and their vehicle, and any illegal drugs then obtained from a consensual search were properly seized. Pegram v. Commonwealth, Nos. 1041-95-2, 1042-95-2, 1996 Va. App. LEXIS 611 (Ct. of Appeals Sept. 24, 1996).

Evidence sufficient for probable cause. — Facts and circumstances available to the officers when they arrested and searched defendant provided them with probable cause to believe defendant constructively possessed the cocaine found in the center console of the vehicle. Among other things, the vehicle's registered owner, the only other occupant of the car, admitted possessing the homemade smoking devices found in a purse in the car, but specifically denied knowing anything about the separate container in which the drugs were found; the officers were also armed with the additional knowledge that defendant had just engaged in suspicious behavior suggestive of a drug transaction with a person traveling in a rental vehicle, and they observed a large bulge in defendant's pants pocket that defendant admitted was a roll of cash. Dodd v. Commonwealth, 50 Va. App. 301, 649 S.E.2d 222, 2007 Va. App. LEXIS 316 (2007).

Where, based on observations and a woman's statement that defendant hit her, an officer had probable cause to arrest defendant for assault, and upon seeing white powder on defendant's face and in his nose, the officer had probable cause to arrest him for cocaine possession, the officer's actions in handcuffing defendant and placing him in the police car did not violate U.S. Const., Amend. IV. Davis v. Commonwealth, 2010 Va. App. LEXIS 281 (July 20, 2010).

Terry stop. — Defendant's suppression motion was improperly denied as police searched defendant for illegal substances, not for weapons, in Terry stop, and were not following leads prior to their misconduct, making the doctrine of inevitable discovery inapplicable; the white powder found on defendant during the search should have been suppressed. Jones v. Commonwealth, No. 1077-02-2, 2003 Va. App. LEXIS 189 (Ct. of Appeals Apr. 1, 2003).

Detention in police vehicle not an illegal seizure. — Officer's direction to defendant to have a seat in the vehicle was reasonable as her presence on the roadside, in the rain, endangered her and the officers; defendant's detention was reasonable and did not taint her consent to a purse search which revealed her illegal possession of cocaine. Austin v. Commonwealth, No. 0082-03-1, 2003 Va. App. LEXIS 587 (Ct. of Appeals Nov. 12, 2003).

Valid search under plain view doctrine. — Trial court erred in suppressing evidence pertaining to defendant's indictment for unlawful possession of controlled substances; as a police officer lawfully seized ammunition under a search warrant for a gun, the officer was in a lawful position to view the crack pipe and the bottles of prescription drugs, and therefore, lawfully seized the crack pipe and drugs under the plain view doctrine. Commonwealth v. Marek, No. 2123-02-4, 2003 Va. App. LEXIS 46 (Ct. of Appeals Feb. 5, 2003).

Because an informant's identification, coupled with the police officers' corroboration, provided probable cause to approach a vehicle, and because cocaine was in plain view on defendant's lap in the passenger seat, there was probable cause to arrest defendant for possession of cocaine; therefore, the trial court properly denied defendant's motion to suppress. Turner v. Commonwealth, — Va. App. —, — S.E.2d —, 2006 Va. App. LEXIS 314 (July 18, 2006).

Suppression motion properly denied. — Where a police officer acted appropriately in removing defendant from a car and restraining him after defendant failed to comply with an order to show defendant's hands, the discovery of the drugs resulted from that removal and restraint; accordingly, the trial court correctly denied defendant's motion to suppress and convicted defendant of possession of drugs under §§ 18.2-250 and 18.2-250.1. Smith v. Commonwealth, No. 1947-03-1, 2004 Va. App. LEXIS 243 (Ct. of Appeals May 25, 2004).

In a case in which defendant had been convicted of violating §§ 18.2-250, 18.2-308.2, 18.2-308.4, and subsection C of § 18.2-57, he argued unsuccessfully that the Court of Appeals of Virginia erroneously upheld the circuit court's denial of his motion to suppress the evidence because his encounter with the police officers was not consensual, and the officers lacked any reasonable suspicion to believe that he was engaged in criminal activity. During the encounter, which lasted only two or three minutes, the police checked the "ban list" but did not engage in any show of force or use language indicating that defendant was required to remain at that location, the police did not tell him that he was required to stay, and defendant did not make any attempt to leave; instead, defendant remained in the area, standing about five feet away from the officers while his companion moved to sit on some nearby steps. Montague v. Commonwealth, 278 Va. 532, 684 S.E.2d 583, 2009 Va. LEXIS 113 (2009), cert. denied, 130 S. Ct. 1537, 176 L. Ed. 2d 133, 2010 U.S. LEXIS 1456 (U.S. 2010).

Entry of a knowing and voluntary, but non-conditional

plea waived appeal from denial of motion to suppress. — Because defendant did not enter a conditional guilty plea pursuant to § 19.2-254, to a charge of possession of Oxycodone, but he entered said plea voluntarily and intelligently, he waived his right to appeal from the judgment denying his motion to suppress the evidence seized against him. Hill v. Commonwealth, 47 Va. App. 667, 626 S.E.2d 459, 2006 Va. App. LEXIS 63 (2006).

B. Evidence of Knowledge.

When ownership of property sufficient to support possession inference. — In order for ownership or occupancy of property or of a vehicle to be sufficient to support the inference that the owner or occupant also possessed contraband that was located on the property or in the vehicle, the owner or occupant must be shown to have exercised dominion and control over the premises and to have known of the presence, nature, and character of the contraband at the time of such ownership or occupancy. Burchette v. Commonwealth, 15 Va. App. 432, 425 S.E.2d 81 (1992).

Ownership or occupancy alone is insufficient to prove knowing possession. — Ownership or occupancy of a vehicle or of premises where illicit drugs are found is a circumstance that may be considered together with other evidence tending to prove that the owner or occupant exercised dominion and control over items in the vehicle or on the premises in order to prove that the owner or occupant constructively possessed the contraband; however, ownership or occupancy alone is insufficient to prove knowing possession of drugs located on the premises or in a vehicle. Burchette v. Commonwealth, 15 Va. App. 432, 425 S.E.2d 81 (1992).

Items in vehicle failed to establish link between defendant and marijuana. — Commonwealth's evidence failed to establish any link between defendant and the marijuana found in his vehicle, other than defendant's ownership of the vehicle. The nature of the other items found in the vehicle that were shown to belong to defendant, the handgun and cellular phone, did not tie him to the drugs or drug paraphernalia. Those are items frequently found in vehicles where the owner or occupant has no relation to drug trafficking. To the extent that receipt for a gun purchase, phone bill, defendant's wallet and driver's license in the vehicle could prove that defendant recently occupied the vehicle, the evidence did not support an inference that the drugs were in the vehicle at the time. Burchette v. Commonwealth, 15 Va. App. 432, 425 S.E.2d 81 (1992).

Evidence was insufficient to prove beyond a reasonable doubt that defendant was aware of the presence and character of the cocaine where automobile was owned by the driver, no evidence established how long defendant had been in the automobile or that he was the person in the automobile when the police received the report, likewise, no evidence proved that the defendant saw the small pieces of cocaine among the other items on the accessory tray on the console or that he recognized the items to be cocaine, and the evidence also failed to prove that the defendant knew that the can with cocaine residue was under the seat where he sat. Jones v. Commonwealth, 17 Va. App. 572, 439 S.E.2d 863 (1994).

Defendant's mere occupancy of a hotel room, standing alone, was insufficient to establish knowing and intentional possession of cocaine residue. Askew v. Commonwealth, No. 0866-88-1 (Ct. of Appeals Oct. 9, 1990).

Sufficiency of evidence of awareness of presence and character of drugs. — There was insufficient evidence that defendant was aware of the presence and character of the cocaine because the automobile where the cocaine was found was not registered to him, and despite the fact that he owned some of the other property found therein; furthermore, while defendant did not dispute that he exercised dominion and control over the vehicle in order to drive it, his proximity in the car to the cocaine was insufficient to support the conviction. Patterson v. Commonwealth, — Va. App. —, — S.E.2d —, 2006 Va. App. LEXIS 253 (June 6, 2006).

Despite the fact that the Commonwealth's attorney conceded at trial that the Commonwealth had not proved that defendant knowingly or intentionally possessed cocaine found in defendant's pocket, the evidence was sufficient to support defendant's conviction of possession of cocaine under circumstances in which, in his statement to the officer, defendant did not deny knowledge of the cocaine's presence in his pocket, but merely claimed the cocaine was not his and that his brother had put it there; the trial judge disbelieved this statement and disbelieved the testimony of defendant's brother. Castilloux v. Commonwealth, 2007 Va. App. LEXIS 358 (Oct. 2, 2007).

Sufficient evidence supported a conviction for possession of a controlled substance under subsivision A(a) of § 18.2-250, where defendant admitted to an officer that he thought the substance in a bag he found was drugs and that he might be able to sell it. This clearly showed that defendant was aware of the nature and character of the substance. Christian v. Commonwealth, 59 Va. App. 603, 721 S.E.2d 809, 2012 Va. App. LEXIS 47 (2012).

Insufficient evidence of knowledge. — There was insufficient evidence to support defendant's convictions for possession of cocaine and possession of cocaine with intent to distribute because the evidence that linked the passenger to the drugs and established his guilt did not also link defendant to the drugs and establish defendant's guilt. Defendant did not arouse suspicion when stopped, he was cooperative, he consented to both searches, and he had no drugs on his person or in his bedroom. No acts, statements, or conduct of defendant suggested that he knew the drugs were present or consciously exercised dominion and control over them. The evidence never placed defendant in the presence of drugs in plain view. It did not show any joint action or effort that permitted an inference of joint enterprise or possession. Silencieux v. Commonwealth, No. 2701-03-2, 2004 Va. App. LEXIS 355 (Ct. of Appeals July 20, 2004).

Sufficient evidence of knowledge of presence of contraband. — Where pipe was found under the driver's seat of the defendant's small car; when he was asked whether he knew what it was, he answered that it was a crack pipe, demonstrating that he was aware of the character of the contraband; and pipe's location — immediately under the driver's seat, uncovered, in a very clean car — combined with the defendant's statement at trial that he had done drugs with the passenger in the past, evidence supported the trial judge's conclusion that the defendant knew of the presence of the contraband. Brinkley v. Commonwealth, No. 1895-96-1, 1997 Va. App. LEXIS 498 (Ct. of Appeals July 22, 1997).

Evidence was sufficient to support a conviction for possession of cocaine where the defendant admitted that he owned and smoked marijuana in a pipe seized by the police from his person, notwithstanding his statement that the only drug he was aware of in the pipe was marijuana. Sellick v. Commonwealth, No. 2702-97-3, 1998 Va. App. LEXIS 621 (Ct. of Appeals Dec. 8, 1998).

Evidence that the drugs were found in a vehicle owned and occupied by defendant, that the officer retrieved the drugs from right on top of a console located next to defendant's seat and within defendant's reach, and that 10 syringes were found beneath defendant's seat, permitted an inference that defendant had knowledge of the presence of the drugs. The trial judge was entitled to infer that defendant's explanation was an effort to conceal guilt. Throckmorton v. Commonwealth, — Va. App. —, — S.E.2d —, 2007 Va. App. LEXIS 196 (May 15, 2007).

Presence of white powder on a dollar bill in defendant's pocket, which was clearly visible and of sufficient size to be sampled, supported the finding that defendant knowingly possessed heroin in violation of § 18.5-250. Jordan v. Commonwealth, — Va. App. —, — S.E.2d —, 2007 Va. App. LEXIS 259 (June 26, 2007).

Defendant's conviction for possession of heroin under § 18.2-250 was supported by the evidence since defendant did not raise below an alternate hypothesis that someone put a heroin capsule in defendant's hand while defendant was unconscious; the hypothesis of innocence relied solely on the "imagination of defense counsel" rather than any specific evidentiary support. Spivey v. Commonwealth, — Va. App. —, — S.E.2d —, 2007 Va. App. LEXIS 467 (Dec. 27, 2007).

Sufficient evidence supported defendant's conviction for possession of cocaine and, thus, the revocation of a previously suspended sentence, where a rock of crack cocaine was found in a pocket of pants that defendant was wearing. The jury was entitled to reject the testimony of two witnesses claiming that defendant was wearing a pair of borrowed pants. Horne v. Commonwealth, 2010 Va. App. LEXIS 220 (June 1, 2010).

Evidence was sufficient to support defendant's conviction for possession of a controlled substance, in violation of § 18.2-250, because the plain language of § 18.2-250 required defendant to now that the substance he possessed was in fact a controlled substance, but did not require defendant to know precisely what controlled substance it was. Sierra v. Commonwealth, 59 Va. App. 770, 722 S.E.2d 656, 2012 Va. App. LEXIS 74 (Mar. 20, 2012).

Knowledge not inferred from having been seen with known cocaine supplier. — Defendant's knowledge of the cocaine could not be inferred from his having been seen with a known cocaine supplier shortly before his arrest, where the evidence proved only that defendant had some conversation with the supplier, but there was no evidence regarding what they discussed. Behrens v. Commonwealth, 3 Va. App. 131, 348 S.E.2d 430 (1986).

Defendant's awareness of the cocaine could not be inferred from his failure to show surprise upon being arrested, even if the proposition that guilty knowledge may be inferred from a failure to show surprise at being arrested were to be accepted, where the only evidence regarding defendant's reaction to his arrest came from a police officer who testified that defendant was cooperative and made no attempt to escape. This testimony did not establish lack of surprise. Behrens v. Commonwealth, 3 Va. App. 131, 348 S.E.2d 430 (1986).

C. Evidence of Constructive Possession Generally.

Circumstantial evidence of possession. — Possession may be proved by evidence of acts, declarations or conduct of the accused from which the inference may be fairly drawn that he knew of the existence of narcotics at the place where they were found. Bentley v. Cox, 508 F. Supp. 870 (E.D. Va. 1981).

Circumstantial evidence of possession is sufficient to establish possession, provided it excludes every reasonable hypothesis of innocence. However, the Commonwealth need only exclude reasonable hypotheses of innocence that flow from the evidence, not those that spring from the imagination of the defendant. Whether a hypothesis of innocence is reasonable is a question of fact, and a finding by the trial court is binding on appeal unless plainly wrong. Holland v. Commonwealth, No. 0664-96-1, 1997 Va. App. LEXIS 93 (Ct. of Appeals Feb. 25, 1997).

Circumstantial evidence is sufficient to support a conviction as long as it excludes every reasonable hypothesis of innocence. Tucker v. Commonwealth, 18 Va. App. 141, 442 S.E.2d 419 (1994).

That one is merely present at the scene of a crime or in the company of a person engaging in criminal activity is not, by itself, sufficient to establish probable cause. Seemingly innocent activity, though not conclusive of probable cause, may provide the basis for a showing of probable cause when considered in the context of all the surrounding circumstances. Taylor v. Waters, 81 F.3d 429 (4th Cir. 1996).

The Commonwealth need not affirmatively disprove all theories which might negate the conclusion that the defendant possessed a controlled substance, but the conviction will be sustained if the evidence excludes every reasonable hypothesis of innocence. Harrison v. Commonwealth, No. 1973-99-1, 2000 Va. App. LEXIS 581 (Ct. of Appeals Aug. 8, 2000).

Where the evidence showed that defendant was in a high drug area, defendant was sitting on a bag of cocaine, no one else was sitting near defendant, and defendant would have noticed the bag due to a large knot, there was sufficient circumstantial evidence to support the conviction; the reasonable-hypothesis rule did not impose a higher burden of proof on the Commonwealth. Haskins v. Commonwealth, 44 Va. App. 1, 602 S.E.2d 402, 2004 Va. App. LEXIS 438 (2004).

To support a conviction based upon constructive possession, the Commonwealth must point to evidence of acts, statements, or conduct of the accused or other facts or circumstances which tend to show that the defendant was aware of both the presence and character of the substance and that it was subject to his dominion and control. Behrens v. Commonwealth, 3 Va. App. 131, 348 S.E.2d 430 (1986).

How constructive possession may be shown. — Constructive possession may be shown by evidence establishing that the contraband was subject to defendant's dominion or control. Woodfin v. Commonwealth, 218 Va. 458, 237 S.E.2d 777 (1977).

The defendant may be shown to have had constructive possession by establishing that the drugs involved were subject to his dominion or control. Clodfelter v. Commonwealth, 218 Va. 619, 238 S.E.2d 820 (1977).

Constructive possession may be shown by establishing that the contraband was known and subject to the dominion and control of the accused. Harrison v. Commonwealth, No. 1973-99-1, 2000 Va.

App. LEXIS 581 (Ct. of Appeals Aug. 8, 2000).

Insufficient evidence of constructive possession. — Evidence did not support finding that defendant constructively possessed contraband, even though it was found in a house which he occupied, where evidence did not show that the defendant was in the dwelling recently enough to permit a reasonable inference that he was aware of the presence of the contraband. No direct evidence placed the defendant in the house; while police found mail addressed to him on a dresser in a bedroom, the postmark on the mail was six days before the discovery of the contraband; and they also found evidence of at least one other person living in the house. Diggs v. Commonwealth, No. 0957-93-2, 1994 Va. App. LEXIS 622 (Ct. of Appeals Oct. 11, 1994).

Under this section, proof that contraband was found in premises owned or occupied by the defendant is insufficient, standing alone, to prove constructive possession. Such evidence is probative, but it is only a circumstance which may be considered along with the other evidence. Behrens v. Commonwealth, 3 Va. App. 131, 348 S.E.2d 430 (1986); Wynn v. Commonwealth, 5 Va. App. 283, 362 S.E.2d 193 (1987).

Defendant was found showering in a bath accessed by a hallway in the apartment, and the evidence established only that he entered the living room and bathroom. No drugs or firearms were found on or near his person, and he engaged in no conduct suggestive of an awareness that contraband was present on the premises. No evidence proved that he had an ownership or possessory interest in the apartment. Thus, save defendant's presence, the proximity of his property to contraband, and a key to the apartment on his key ring, nothing in the record related him to the offenses. While highly suspicious, these circumstances are insufficient to prove, to the exclusion of every reasonable hypothesis of innocence, that the drugs and weapons were subject to defendant's dominion and control. Boley v. Commonwealth, No. 1943-95-1, 1996 Va. App. LEXIS 521 (Ct. of Appeals July 23, 1996).

Evidence was insufficient to prove possession where drugs were found on rear floor of car occupied by four persons, and defendant made no furtive movements before or after stop or did anything else to incriminate himself. Tables v. Commonwealth, No. 1419-99-1, 2000 Va. App. LEXIS 149 (Ct. of Appeals Feb. 29, 2000).

Officer's observation of passenger's movement during traffic stop raised only a suspicion that his movement bore a connection to cocaine found in vehicle, and passenger's warning to other occupant not to "tell a lie" likewise established no inference connecting passenger to cocaine. McCray v. Commonwealth, No. 0200-99-2, 2000 Va. App. LEXIS 208 (Ct. of Appeals Mar. 21, 2000).

The evidence failed to establish that the defendant had the requisite knowledge of the presence and character of the offending contents of a bag found on the floor of the vehicle she was operating where the vehicle was owned by a third party, no evidence established the duration of the defendant's possession or familiarity with the vehicle, the bag containing drug paraphernalia and attendant residue, although in plain view on the floorboard, was opaque and closed, its contents hidden from casual observation and, apart from the defendant's nervousness, a response consistent with anxiety attributable to her suspended license, the record revealed no furtive movements, statements or other circumstances suggestive of an awareness that the bag contained contraband. Wallman v. Commonwealth, No. 0169-99-1, 2000 Va. App. LEXIS 314 (Ct. of Appeals May 2, 2000).

Even if it was assumed that the Commonwealth's suggestion that the defendant's appearance at a residence where narcotic sales were suspected to occur and his possession of stolen property were factors that indicated he was a drug user, the Commonwealth failed to establish that the defendant ever used the coffee straw containing heroin residue, that was found in the vehicle he was driving, to consume heroin or was aware that it had been used by anyone else for such a purpose; the evidence when viewed in the light most favorable to the Commonwealth, established nothing more than mere proximity to the coffee straw containing heroin residue and fell short of removing every reasonable hypothesis consistent with innocence. Harrison v. Commonwealth, No. 1973-99-1, 2000 Va. App. LEXIS 581 (Ct. of Appeals Aug. 8, 2000).

There was insufficient evidence that defendant, a front-seat passenger in a car where a bag of cocaine was found in between the driver's seat and the passenger's seat, possessed the cocaine. Defendant had not tried to hide the bag as an officer approached the car and had not exhibited any other signs of guilty knowledge; there was no evidence regarding how long he had been in the car; and although the officer could see the bag with the illumination he provided, there was no evidence that the bag would have been visible in the darkness of the passenger compartment without such additional lighting. Coward v. Commonwealth, 48 Va. App. 653, 633 S.E.2d 752, 2006 Va. App. LEXIS 397 (2006).

Evidence was insufficient to support defendant's possession of cocaine conviction under § 18.2-250 as the Commonwealth proved only that defendant was within mere proximity to the cocaine found on the ground; neither officer saw defendant make a throwing motion prior to being handcuffed and neither officer heard anything land on the ground. Davis v. Commonwealth, — Va. App. —, — S.E.2d —, 2009 Va. App. LEXIS 57 (Feb. 10, 2009).

Evidence was insufficient to establish defendant's constructive possession of cocaine because, while the circumstantial evidence may have been sufficient to raise a suspicion of guilt, it did not support a conclusion beyond a reasonable doubt by a rational trier of fact, that cocaine found in the bedroom of the home of defendant's uncle was subject to defendant's dominion and control. The evidence consisted of defendant's repeated references to the bedroom as defendant's bedroom and subsequent denial that defendant was living at the house when the police told defendant that drugs were found in the room, along with defendant's personal effects and a police detective's business card, which had been given to defendant two days previously, that were found in the room. Cordon v. Commonwealth, 280 Va. 691, 701 S.E.2d 803, 2010 Va. LEXIS 275 (2010).

Defendant's conviction for possession of marijuana with the intent to distribute in violation of § 18.2-248.1 was reversed because the facts were insufficient to prove that defendant possessed the marijuana since the only facts were that defendant was the owner of the parked car and that he had custody of a set of keys to that car; there was no timeline for when defendant was last in the vehicle or if he was in fact the last person in the vehicle, although defendant had possession of the key to the vehicle, nothing indicated that he had possession of the only key, and defendant was cooperative in providing the key to the glove compartment upon request. Lewis v. Commonwealth, 2011 Va. App. LEXIS 136 (Apr. 26, 2011).

Sufficient evidence of constructive possession. — Evidence supported the conclusion that defendant constructively possessed cocaine where defendant occupied both the house and, in particular, the lit bedroom where the cocaine was found in plain view; before the police entered her bedroom, the bedroom door was shut; when they entered, defendant was awake and approaching the door; the cocaine was three to four feet from her on the floor and in plain view; and no other person occupied her room or was present when the officers entered. These circumstances support the inference that defendant knew of the existence of the cocaine and had dominion and control over it. McNair v. Commonwealth, No. 2080-93-1, 1994 Va. App. LEXIS 675 (Ct. of Appeals Nov. 15, 1994).

Evidence that defendant was present where drugs were found in plain view, circumstances suggesting that he could have easily exercised dominion and control over those drugs, and the circumstances not suggesting that the drugs were presently or had recently been in the exclusive possession of one of the other persons in the room, was sufficient to prove constructive possession. Thrasher v. Commonwealth, No. 1773-92-3, 1994 Va. App. LEXIS 283 (Ct. of Appeals May 10, 1994).

Here, the evidence disclosed that appellant was more than in "mere proximity" to the cocaine. He was present at the table to smoke cocaine. The pipe containing cocaine residue necessary to complete that intent was within an arm's length of his reach. The chunks of cocaine on the table were in plain view. Therefore, the trial court could reasonably infer that the cocaine was jointly possessed by the four men seated at the table and that it was possessed for their exclusive use. Henry v. Commonwealth, No. 1205-95-3, 1996 Va. App. LEXIS 352 (Ct. of Appeals May 14, 1996).

Evidence was sufficient to establish constructive possession of an antenna section containing cocaine residue where: (1) defendant was the sole occupant of vehicle approached by officer; (2) when the officer approached, defendant immediately exited the vehicle; (3) the antenna section, with visible residue, together with the cigarette lighter, were found in plain view on the driver's floorboard; and (4) defendant gave inconsistent statements about his owner-

ship of the vehicle, the time he had control of the car and its contents, and his reason for being stopped. Jones v. Commonwealth, No. 1398-97-1, 1998 Va. App. LEXIS 174 (Ct. of Appeals March 24, 1998).

Evidence was sufficient to show constructive possession of cocaine found in an automobile where, upon seeing police officers, the defendant reached toward the center console and made a "pushing" action at the point where the cocaine was found, and papers found in the glove box supported the finding that the automobile was in the defendant's possession and under his control. Thomas v. Commonwealth, No. 2561-97-1, 1998 Va. App. LEXIS 607 (Ct. of Appeals Dec. 1, 1998).

Evidence was sufficient to prove constructive possession of cocaine where the police found a rock of unwrapped cocaine lying in plain view on the headboard of the defendant's bed while executing a search warrant in the apartment; the defendant kept his personal property in the room where police found the drugs, readily identified the hidden location of a gun, evidencing his familiarity with the room and its contents, and there was no evidence that anyone other than the defendant had been in the bedroom prior to the discovery of drugs within it. Wyche v. Commonwealth, No. 2729-97-1, 1999 Va. App. LEXIS 55 (Ct. of Appeals Jan. 26, 1999).

Evidence was sufficient to establish constructive possession of cocaine where: (1) an officer stopped the defendant in a car registered in his name; (2) at the time of the stop, the defendant was the sole occupant of his vehicle, which contained a multitude of papers bearing his name; (3) after observing the defendant "digging through" the bags and papers in the rear seat, ostensibly in response to the officer's request for his driver's license and registration, the officer asked the defendant to step out of the car; (4) upon searching the car, the officer found two cans containing cocaine residue hidden from plain view in separate places within the passenger compartment, which cans were noticeably modified for the purpose of using them as a smoking device; and (5) the defendant admitted that he knew of their presence. Clark v. Commonwealth, No. 0918-98-1, 1999 Va. App. LEXIS 237 (Ct. of Appeals Apr. 27, 1999).

Evidence was sufficient to prove that defendant constructively possessed cocaine found in vehicle in his shoe. Roundy v. Commonwealth, No. 2695-98-1, 1999 Va. App. LEXIS 682 (Ct. of Appeals Dec. 21, 1999).

Evidence was sufficient to find defendant in constructive possession of the cocaine where an object fell from defendant's pocket as his hand was withdrawn from the pocket; defendant disobeyed the officer's direction to remove his hands from his pockets; and a pipe, which contained cocaine, was found exactly where the object had fallen, where defendant's foot had been. Gunn v. Commonwealth, No. 1788-99-3, 2000 Va. App. LEXIS 441 (Ct. of Appeals June 13, 2000).

The evidence sufficiently supported defendant's conviction for possession of heroin in light of the fact that the defendant resided in a home where the heroin was found, the defendant was an admitted heroin user, heroin residue and other drug paraphernalia were found in plain view in the kitchen, a room of common access and use within the home, and the defendant was found in a room near the kitchen; the trial judge could find beyond a reasonable doubt from the totality of these circumstances that the defendant knew of the presence and character of the heroin and that he intentionally and consciously had constructive possession of it. Gray v. Commonwealth, No. 0669-00-2, 2001 Va. App. LEXIS 227 (Ct. of Appeals May 1, 2001).

The evidence was sufficient to support defendant's conviction where the Commonwealth proved that the defendant was the sole person in the room at the time a police officer arrived, that the defendant had been sleeping in the room, that the drugs were found in the bathroom on top of the toilet seat and that the drug paraphernalia was in the plain view of someone standing at or near the doorway to the room; viewed in the light most favorable to the Commonwealth, this evidence supported the reasonable inference that the defendant was aware of the presence and character of the paraphernalia and contraband. DeVaul v. Commonwealth, No. 1345-00-1, 2001 Va. App. LEXIS 306 (Ct. of Appeals June 5, 2001).

Totality of the evidence sufficiently proved that defendant constructively possessed the contraband, which was in plain sight and within defendant's reach in a place where defendant's personal belongings were also found. Harris v. Commonwealth, No. 2183-

01-1, 2002 Va. App. LEXIS 432 (Ct. of Appeals July 30, 2002).

Evidence was sufficient to sustain defendant's conviction of possession of cocaine where the totality of the evidence supported a finding that defendant knew of the presence and character of cocaine that was found in a suitcase in a residence, and intentionally and consciously had constructive possession of it given that defendant's wallet was found with drug paraphernalia in the bedroom where the suitcase was found; the suitcase contained men's clothing, including the pair of men's socks in which the cocaine was hidden; no men other than defendant were observed in the house; and defendant had told the police officer who found the suitcase that he wanted to retrieve his suitcase from the house. Mabry v. Commonwealth, No. 1069-01-2, 2002 Va. App. LEXIS 630 (Ct. of Appeals Oct. 22, 2002).

Evidence that defendant owned scales on which cocaine residue was found and that defendant had two rifles in a trailer where the scales were found was sufficient to sustain defendant's convictions for possession of cocaine, in violation of § 18.2-250, and simultaneous possession of cocaine and firearms, in violation of subsection A of § 18.2-308.4. Chism v. Commonwealth, No. 2892-01-2, 2002 Va. App. LEXIS 745 (Ct. of Appeals Dec. 17, 2002).

Evidence, viewed in the light most favorable to the Commonwealth, was sufficient to prove that the defendant exercised at least joint constructive possession over cocaine residue found on a spoon in the defendant's boots. Graves v. Commonwealth, No. 3348-01-1, 2003 Va. App. LEXIS 10 (Ct. of Appeals Jan. 14, 2003).

Evidence was sufficient to supporting conviction for possession of cocaine, in violation of § 18.2-250, where the trial court could have reasonably concluded that defendant was aware of the presence and character of the drugs found in the console and that he exercised dominion and control over them. Gillard v. Commonwealth, No. 0037-02-2, 2003 Va. App. LEXIS 437 (Ct. of Appeals Aug. 19, 2003).

Where defendant recently possessed a vehicle, knew of the presence and character the items hidden therein, and the items were subject to defendant's dominion and control, the evidence was sufficient to prove defendant's constructive possession of the cocaine and marijuana found in the vehicle. White v. Commonwealth, No. 0591-03-2, 2003 Va. App. LEXIS 539 (Ct. of Appeals Oct. 28, 2003).

Evidence that defendant had possession of a car for two months before police found cocaine in the car, that he was the only occupant of the car at the time the cocaine was discovered, and that the cocaine was in plain view on the driver's side of the car was sufficient to sustain a jury's verdict that defendant knowingly possessed cocaine. Hogston v. Commonwealth, No. 3232-02-3, 2003 Va. App. LEXIS 611 (Ct. of Appeals Nov. 25, 2003).

Evidence was sufficient to support defendant's conviction for possession of cocaine, as a reasonable inference could be drawn that cocaine found in several packets near him following his arrest was his since the homeowner of the home he ran into testified that no such drugs were present when she left her home shortly before defendant's arrest and the police arrested defendant because a reliable, confidential informant provided a tip to the police that defendant was in possession of cocaine. Payne v. Commonwealth, No. 3339-02-3, 2003 Va. App. LEXIS 616 (Ct. of Appeals Dec. 2, 2003).

Evidence that six to seven persons knocked on the door at various times, that on each of those occasions defendant answered the door, that defendant and the person who had knocked on the door then walked to the back of the house, in close proximity to where the cocaine was ultimately found, where they stayed for a brief time, before returning to the front of the house, where the person who had knocked on the door left, was sufficient to support defendant's conviction for possession of cocaine with intent to distribute. Brock v. Commonwealth, No. 0271-04-1, 2004 Va. App. LEXIS 617 (Ct. of Appeals Dec. 14, 2004).

Finding of constructive possession was not plainly wrong or without evidence to support it where: (1) defendant resided in the trailer where the contraband was found, and was inside the trailer when the officers executed the search warrant; (2) when the officers arrived to execute the warrant, they heard defendant announce the presence of the police, which was followed by an attempt to destroy the drugs; (3) the trial court reasonably inferred that defendant's notice of the presence of the police was notice to the others to dispose of the drugs before the officers entered the trailer; and (4)

officers found cocaine on the bathroom floor and in the toilet, and cocaine paraphernalia in the rear bedroom and hallway. Ruffin v. Commonwealth, No. 0081-04-2, 2005 Va. App. LEXIS 111 (Ct. of Appeals Mar. 22, 2005).

In defendant's prosecution for possession of cocaine, the evidence established that defendant was aware of the presence of cocaine found in her motel room and that the substance was subject to her dominion and control since the cocaine was found in a motel room registered to defendant and was specifically found in a box among items belonging to defendant. Defendant also admitted to having been caught with cocaine in the past, thus confirming her familiarity with the character of the substance. Scott v. Commonwealth, — Va. App. —, — S.E.2d —, 2006 Va. App. LEXIS 85 (Mar. 7, 2006).

Evidence was sufficient to support defendant's conviction for possession of cocaine, in violation of § 18.2-250, because: (1) defendant told a police officer that he had smoked crack and that his DNA would be found on one of the two crack pipes that the officer found on the ground near a car; (2) at trial, the Commonwealth presented a certificate of analysis, which proved that the pipes contained cocaine residue; and (3) the presence of cocaine residue on the pipes sufficiently corroborated defendant's confession that he had smoked cocaine from one of the pipes earlier that evening. Wood v. Commonwealth, — Va. App. —, — S.E.2d —, 2007 Va. App. LEXIS 236 (June 19, 2007).

Defendant's conviction for possession of cocaine with intent to distribute was supported by sufficient evidence and was not plainly wrong under § 8.01-680 as defendant's flight from police, the discovery of the cocaine in the exact area where he had fled, and an incriminating statement were sufficient to establish constructive possession; further, the quantity of cocaine found was inconsistent with personal use. Smith v. Commonwealth, 2007 Va. App. LEXIS 457 (Dec. 18, 2007).

Evidence was sufficient to convict defendant of possession of cocaine because defendant was the only occupant of his vehicle when an officer found a baggie of cocaine wedged between the door of the car and the window, and there was no evidence that someone other than defendant could have put the baggie there; the baggie was only slightly wedged between the window and the weather stripping, and it took almost no effort for the officer to pull the baggie out. Smith v. Commonwealth, — Va. App. —, — S.E.2d —, 2008 Va. App. LEXIS 164 (Apr. 8, 2008).

Appellant's conviction for possession of cocaine was upheld because an officer found cocaine in the exact location in a couch where appellant, moments earlier, had inserted a hand; also, it could be reasonably concluded from the evidence that appellant knew the nature and character of the cocaine that appellant attempted to conceal in the corner of the couch. Whitaker v. Commonwealth, 2008 Va. App. LEXIS 288 (June 17, 2008).

As the evidence, which consisted of testimony by another occupant of a car in which defendant was a passenger, established that defendant exercised dominion and control over a pipe containing cocaine residue that was found in a car, even if her possession of it was not always exclusive, which was not required, the evidence was sufficient to support defendant's conviction under § 18.2-250. Haskins v. Commonwealth, — Va. App. —, — S.E.2d —, 2008 Va. App. LEXIS 531 (Dec. 9, 2008).

From defendant's statement and the contents of a hand-rolled cigarette, the fact finder could reasonably conclude defendant knew a cigarette that defendant hand rolled contained cocaine; moreover, when officers approached defendant as defendant smoked this cigarette, defendant fled. This evidence enabled the fact finder to conclude that defendant was aware of the illegal nature and character of the substance, and, therefore, the evidence was sufficient to support defendant's conviction for possession of cocaine. Boxley v. Commonwealth, — Va. App. —, — S.E.2d —, 2009 Va. App. LEXIS 99 (Mar. 10, 2009).

Sufficient evidence existed to convict defendant of felony possession of cocaine in violation of § 18.2-250 because constructive possession of the cocaine was demonstrated by the facts that defendant was the sole occupant of the vehicle in which a glass smoking device with cocaine residue was found in plain view, defendant admitted to possession of the vehicle for 30 minutes, and the glass stem of the smoking device was still warm to the touch. Etheridge v. Commonwealth, 2009 Va. App. LEXIS 134 (Mar. 24, 2009).

Evidence was sufficient to prove defendant's constructive possession of cocaine found in his bedroom, as it established that he was the sole resident of his home; that he controlled access to the residence; and that his companion, who had been in the bedroom, did not use drugs. Little v. Commonwealth, 2009 Va. App. LEXIS 315 (July 14, 2009).

Evidence was sufficient to show that defendant constructively possessed cocaine with intent to distribute because cocaine was found on the person of a passenger, who had been in defendant's car immediately prior to the arrest, defendant had a large amount of cash, and a duffle bag in the back seat of the car contained drug paraphernalia, including a scale with cocaine residue. Colbert v. Commonwealth, 2010 Va. App. LEXIS 45 (Feb. 9, 2010).

Evidence was sufficient to prove that defendant constructively possessed cocaine and a firearm simultaneously, in violation of §§ 18.2-250 and 18.2-308.4, although defendant denied knowing about the cocaine, because defendant admitted seeing the firearm on the floor of a car and placing it under a seat, and the cocaine was found next to the firearm. The fact finder could have found it unreasonable to believe that defendant knew of the presence of the firearm, but did not know of the cocaine next to it. Wilson v. Commonwealth, 2010 Va. App. LEXIS 38 (Feb. 2, 2010).

Defendant's conviction for possession of methadone, a Schedule II controlled substance was appropriate because the evidence established that defendant constructively possessed the methadone found in his car. He admitted that he knew the bottle in his car contained methadone and he acknowledged that he had recently driven his car alone from his friend's house when the police officer discovered the methadone; that activity demonstrated that the substance was subject to his dominion and control. Thornton v. Commonwealth, 2011 Va. App. LEXIS 375 (Nov. 29, 2011).

Contraband found in hotel room. — A defendant need not be found inside a hotel room in order to establish that he constructively possessed contraband found therein. However, something more than mere rental of the room must be shown. Behrens v. Commonwealth, 3 Va. App. 131, 348 S.E.2d 430 (1986).

Occupancy of room where drugs are found. — While the defendant's occupancy of a room where drugs are found does not create a presumption that he either knowingly or intentionally possessed the drug, it is a circumstance which could be considered by the court, along with the other evidence, in determining his guilt or innocence. Clodfelter v. Commonwealth, 218 Va. 619, 238 S.E.2d 820 (1977).

Where the defendant was found inside the cabin ten feet from a container of PCP treated parsley flakes, four jars containing PCP residue, and various other chemicals and paraphernalia, including buckets, plastic bags, bongs and two triple beam balance scales, and the defendant's statements to the police indicated his awareness of the presence of the chemicals as well as their criminal import, there was sufficient circumstantial evidence for the jury to conclude that the PCP found in the cabin was within the defendant's constructive possession. McGee v. Commonwealth, 4 Va. App. 317, 357 S.E.2d 738 (1987).

Evidence was insufficient to prove that the defendant either actually or constructively possessed cocaine found in a $50 bill on a chest of drawers in his mother's house since, although circumstantial evidence presented by the Commonwealth raised a suspicion that he placed the bill containing the cocaine on the chest of drawers along with a pile of change, keys, and papers after he arrived at his mother's house and before he went to sleep, the evidence failed to exclude the reasonable hypothesis that his brother placed the cocaine on the chest of drawers and that he had no knowledge of the cocaine's presence when it was discovered by a detective. Thomas v. Commonwealth, No. 1618-97-2 (Ct. of Appeals June 16, 1998).

Cocaine in automobile insufficient to prove constructive possession. — Proof that cocaine was found in an automobile owned and occupied by defendant is insufficient, standing alone, to prove constructive possession. Nonnemacker v. Commonwealth, No. 0367-88-2 (Ct. of Appeals Sept. 11, 1990).

Failing to prove exclusive access to the automobile and failing to account for all those who may possibly have had access to the location in the car where the drugs were found, the Commonwealth could not rely on an inference from these circumstances that the defendant knew of the presence of the drugs. Brown v. Commonwealth, No. 0627-89-2 (Ct. of Appeals Aug. 13, 1991).

Although the defendant was in close proximity to the drugs found on the seat of the pickup truck he was operating and was clearly the sole occupant of the truck, which had been assigned to him by his employer, the evidence established no more than a mere suspicion that the defendant possessed the drugs where, while the drugs were in "plain view" to a police officer, who was trained in the recognition of drugs, the drugs were described as "crumbs" and the larger piece was described as being about the size of a piece of rice, there was no evidence the defendant ever saw the cocaine, knew it was present or exercised dominion and control over it, there was no evidence that the defendant was nervous, fidgety or made furtive gestures, the defendant made no statements indicating he was aware of the presence and character of the drugs, there was no evidence the defendant engaged in any illegal drug activity while in the area in which he was stopped, it was unknown whether the defendant only drove the truck to and from work or also during the workday and it was also unknown how many times the defendant actually had possession of the truck within the three weeks it had been assigned to him. Bright v. Commonwealth, No. 2794-99-1, 2000 Va. App. LEXIS 747 (Ct. of Appeals Nov. 21, 2000).

Cocaine found in police cruiser supported conviction. — Where the evidence showed that the officer conducted a thorough search of his police cruiser at the beginning of his shift, that no one but appellant was placed in the back of the cruiser that day, and that when appellant shifted his body so that the officer could handcuff him, the drugs were immediately found on the floorboard of the cruiser, evidence was sufficient to sustain the conviction. Williams v. Commonwealth, No. 1655-91-1 (Ct. of Appeals Jan. 19, 1993).

Where officer's inspection of the police vehicle immediately prior to his encounter with defendant disclosed no contraband, and only defendant and Jarrett were thereafter inside the car, and the offending drugs were discovered hidden in the area occupied by defendant, from such evidence, the jury could conclude that defendant removed the cocaine from his person and placed it beneath the seat cushion, attempting to conceal the drugs from the arresting officer. Martin v. Commonwealth, No. 2861-95-1 (Ct. of Appeals Sept. 24, 1996).

Absence of evidence as "other evidence" of possession. — Proof that LSD was found in premises or a vehicle owned or occupied by the defendant was insufficient, standing alone, to prove constructive possession. Such evidence was probative, but it was only a circumstance to be considered along with the other evidence. The "other evidence" was, in fact, an absence of evidence, where the Commonwealth relied on there being no evidence that anyone else had possessions in the house. This merely tended to reinforce the conclusion that the defendant and his wife were the sole residents of the premises; it did not foreclose the possibility that the LSD was owned and hidden by another. Powers v. Commonwealth, 227 Va. 474, 316 S.E.2d 739 (1984).

Suspicious circumstances, including proximity to a controlled drug, are insufficient to support a conviction. Behrens v. Commonwealth, 3 Va. App. 131, 348 S.E.2d 430 (1986).

Although evidence was suspicious, or may even have made it probable that defendant knew of the presence of the cocaine, such circumstantial evidence was not sufficient to support a criminal conviction for possession of the cocaine. Nelson v. Commonwealth, 17 Va. App. 708, 440 S.E.2d 627 (1994).

Suspicious circumstances, including proximity to a controlled drug, are insufficient to support a conviction. However, while mere proximity to the drugs is insufficient to establish possession, and occupancy of the premises does not give rise to a presumption of possession, both are factors which may be considered in determining whether a defendant possessed drugs. Boley v. Commonwealth, No. 1943-95-1, 1996 Va. App. LEXIS 521 (Ct. of Appeals July 23, 1996).

Documents showing defendant claimed house as residence. — Several documents introduced to show that defendant claimed the house in which cocaine was found as his residence, though relevant, raised no presumption that he knowingly or intentionally possessed the controlled substance found there. Drew v. Commonwealth, 230 Va. 471, 338 S.E.2d 844 (1986).

Failure to instruct on lesser-included offense held error. — While the jury could have concluded that the defendant tolerated the presence of the drugs in the apartment and thus constructively shared possession, the jury could also have had a reasonable doubt as to whether the defendant shared the intent to distribute.

Therefore, the evidence supporting a theory of simple possession by the defendant was "more than a scintilla" and failure to grant the instruction on the lesser included offense was error. Harrison v. Commonwealth, 12 Va. App. 581, 405 S.E.2d 854 (1991).

The evidence was sufficient. — There was ample evidence upon which the trial court could base the determination that the defendant was knowingly in possession of phencyclidine (PCP) where the defendant was in exclusive possession of the drug at the time that he was stopped and his actions in resisting the police officers were inconsistent with the actions of a person merely in possession of innocuous plant material. Hornbaker v. Commonwealth, No. 1332-88-4 (Ct. of Appeals March 27, 1990).

Where there was evidence of ownership of the vehicle by appellant in which the drugs were found and other uncontradicted evidence, viewed in its totality, fairly inferred that appellant knew of the existence of the drugs at the place where they were found and in the absence of contrary evidence, appellant's possession of the car keys was significant evidence from which, when considered with the other evidence, it could be inferred that the drugs were subject to his dominion and control, no other hypotheses could be reasonably inferred from the record, evidence was sufficient to prove appellant unlawfully possessed cocaine. Jetter v. Commonwealth, 17 Va. App. 745, 440 S.E.2d 633 (1994).

Evidence supported the defendant's conviction for possession of cocaine found in a vehicle where: (1) the defendant was the sole occupant of the vehicle and the only evidence to the contrary came from his own incredible statements; (2) cocaine and drug paraphernalia were found in plain sight and within inches of the defendant's seat; and (3) the defendant testified that he cleaned the car earlier in the evening. Graves v. Commonwealth, No. 2046-97-3 (Ct. of Appeals Jan. 12, 1999).

See Jones v. Commonwealth, No. 2670-97-2 (Ct. of Appeals Feb. 16, 1999).

Evidence was sufficient to prove that defendant had actual possession of cocaine and had thrown it on ground during chase by police through vacant lot. McHerrin v. Commonwealth, No. 0217-99-1 (Ct. of Appeals Mar. 14, 2000).

Direct and circumstantial evidence supported a finding that defendant had actual possession of cocaine a police officer retrieved from the ground when the officer testified, and a videotape confirmed, that defendant appeared nervous while he waited at the rear of the car, and the videotape showed defendant making a throwing motion before placing both hands on the rear of the car. Brooks v. Commonwealth, No. 0811-02-4, 2003 Va. App. LEXIS 118 (Ct. of Appeals Mar. 4, 2003).

Where the "totality" of the evidence showed that defendant was aware of the presence and character of the contraband, which was subject to his dominion and control, the evidence was sufficient to convict defendant of possession. Fawehimni v. Commonwealth, No. 0389-02-4, 2003 Va. App. LEXIS 125 (Ct. of Appeals Mar. 11, 2003).

Circumstantial evidence, including the fact that defendant was the only person in the home and the proximity of the clothes to defendant, clearly supported the trial court's finding that the clothing contained drugs and belonged to defendant, and that defendant knew the nature and character of the drugs. Adkins v. Commonwealth, No. 3267-01-3, 2002 Va. App. LEXIS 646 (Ct. of Appeals Oct. 29, 2002).

Defendant's flight from traffic checkpoint, defendant's presence on the side of the road next to the car defendant had been driving, and defendant's presence near heroin found in credit card receipt with numbers matching the numbers of a credit card in defendant's name were sufficient to support defendant's conviction for heroin possession as all of the evidence could lead the trial court to conclude that defendant possessed heroin but threw it to the ground to avoid detection. Blowe v. Commonwealth, No. 2201-01-2, 2002 Va. App. LEXIS 708 (Ct. of Appeals Nov. 26, 2002).

Evidence was sufficient to support defendant's conviction for possession of cocaine, where defendant was found in a closet with the cocaine; the totality of the circumstances was sufficient to support the trial court's finding that defendant exercised sufficient dominion and control over the cocaine to constitute joint constructive possession, and the fact that the evidence proved co-defendant likely possessed the same cocaine that was found in the closet did not preclude defendant from also possessing the drug. Hunter v. Commonwealth, No. 1483-01-3, 2002 Va. App. LEXIS 581 (Ct. of Appeals Oct. 1, 2002).

Evidence was sufficient to support possession of cocaine conviction under § 18.2-250, where cocaine pipe was found between defendant's seat and the seat belt harness in plain view and in close proximity to defendant, and was within the area of defendant's immediate control. Ausby v. Commonwealth, No. 2541-01-1, 2002 Va. App. LEXIS 611 (Ct. of Appeals Oct. 8, 2002).

Evidence was sufficient to support defendant's conviction for possession of cocaine where: (1) a deputy sheriff found a spoon in defendant's pocket coated with a powdery cocaine residue, (2) the cocaine on the spoon was "crystallized" and clearly visible, (3) when the deputy seized the spoon, defendant "just sort of hung his head," and (4) the evidence that defendant had a spoon coated in cocaine and that he "hung his head" when the deputy found the spoon was sufficient for the jury to find that defendant had knowledge of the substance on the spoon. Day v. Commonwealth, No. 0193-03-2, 2004 Va. App. LEXIS 50 (Ct. of Appeals Feb. 3, 2004).

Where defendant admitted that he packed the tin box and placed it in his duffle bag, facts corroborated by the presence of his personal belongings inside the bag, it was rational for the fact finder to conclude, beyond reasonable doubt, that the drug paraphernalia found in the tin box likewise belonged to defendant and thus, to support convictions for possession of cocaine and heroin. Porter v. Commonwealth, No. 0419-04-2, 2005 Va. App. LEXIS 62 (Ct. of Appeals Feb. 15, 2005).

Evidence was sufficient to support defendant's conviction for possession of heroin, as the evidence showed that at the time of defendant's arrest, police recovered two plastic bags defendant had concealed in his underwear that contained less than a gram of heroin; accordingly, the evidence showed that defendant knowingly possessed heroin. Fraierson v. Commonwealth, No. 1147-04-2, 2005 Va. App. LEXIS 135 (Ct. of Appeals Mar. 29, 2005).

As the fact finder could infer that both defendant and defendant's passenger possessed a modified pill bottle knowing it contained cocaine residue, or at the very least, defendant knew the passenger had brought or placed the smoking device in the car, evidence was sufficient to convict defendant of possessing cocaine. Furthermore, the fact that the smoking device was in the automobile, which defendant claimed defendant drove frequently, and the fact that it was near defendant in the front seat further supported the inference that defendant possessed the device and knew it contained cocaine. McCollum v. Commonwealth, — Va. App. —, — S.E.2d —, 2006 Va. App. LEXIS 240 (May 30, 2006).

Evidence that defendant fled toward the fence when defendant saw the police, made a pushing or throwing motion over the fence, and immediately thereafter, the police found marijuana and cocaine on the other side of the fence in the line of defendant's arm motion was sufficient to support conclusion defendant possessed the marijuana and cocaine. Debroux v. Commonwealth, — Va. App. —, — S.E.2d —, 2007 Va. App. LEXIS 40 (Feb. 6, 2007).

Evidence that the drugs were in a clear plastic bag located beside defendant's seat and that the officer who stopped defendant found defendant more nervous than a normal person during a traffic stop, talking rapidly, not completing sentences, and being on verge of whole body shaking, was sufficient to support defendant's conviction for cocaine possession under subsection A of § 18.2-250. Burton v. Commonwealth, — Va. App. —, — S.E.2d —, 2007 Va. App. LEXIS 222 (May 29, 2007).

Trial court did not err in convicting defendant of possession of the cocaine found in defendant's wallet at an airport, as all portions of the airport in which a person would lose a wallet were in Loudoun County, and defendant conceded that the contents of a bag of cocaine were defendant's. Hockensmith v. Commonwealth, 2008 Va. App. LEXIS 500 (Nov. 12, 2008).

Because of defendant's proximity to the drugs, defendant's occupancy of a vehicle, defendant's possession of the cocaine found on defendant's person, and defendant's participation in driving the vehicle on a trip over a known drug trafficking route, there was sufficient evidence to convict defendant of possession of cocaine with the intent to distribute under § 18.2-250. Green v. Commonwealth, — Va. App. —, — S.E.2d —, 2009 Va. App. LEXIS 127 (Mar. 24, 2009).

The evidence was insufficient to establish that the cocaine was subject to defendant's dominion or control or to show that defendant was aware of the presence and character of the particular substance where the evidence showed that defendant was present in the apartment in which the substance was found on several occasions, once during the week preceding the search, but there was utterly no evidence that he spent the night there or ever entered the bedroom where the cocaine was found. Woodfin v. Commonwealth, 218 Va. 458, 237 S.E.2d 777 (1977).

Evidence showing that the defendant had rented the hotel room, that he had deposited some of his personal effects there, and that, when questioned by the police, he had given a false identity, created a strong suspicion of guilt but fell short of showing beyond a reasonable doubt that the drugs found in the hotel room were ever actually or constructively possessed by the defendant with an awareness of their character. Clodfelter v. Commonwealth, 218 Va. 619, 238 S.E.2d 820 (1977).

While the evidence proved that the defendant was in proximity to the drugs and, thus, created a suspicion of guilt, it fell far short of proving beyond a reasonable doubt that she constructively possessed the drugs found in codefendant's tractor-trailer or on codefendant's person. Harris v. Commonwealth, 13 Va. App. 593, 413 S.E.2d 354 (1992).

Where record disclosed no statements or conduct which established that defendant was consciously involved in the accused criminal activity and the only substantive evidence of defendant's dominion and control over the heroin and related paraphernalia was his presence in his vehicle, which had also been occupied by another adult passenger, such evidence, while suspicious, was insufficient to support his conviction for possession of heroin. Smith v. Commonwealth, No. 0339-91-4 (Ct. of Appeals July 28, 1992).

Evidence that the defendant was not present when police searched the trailer where he and another man lived and found cocaine residue in a baggie discarded in a trash can in the defendant's bedroom; that later, in response to a police officer's question, the defendant admitted that everything in his bedroom belonged to him except the dresser and the carpet; and that while the record reflected that the defendant was aware that the police were investigating a cocaine-related offense, but did not reveal that the defendant knew that the residue had been found in his room when he responded to the question, was not sufficient to support a conviction for possession of cocaine. Morris v. Commonwealth, No. 0765-93-2 (Ct. of Appeals Oct. 11, 1994).

The Commonwealth presented no evidence that narcotics were actually present, that the observed behavior was consistent with a narcotics transaction, or that any of the participants were connected in any way with narcotics. The testifying officer gave no objective reason why her observations led her to the conclusion that a sale of narcotics had occurred. Based on the record, the trial judge was not plainly wrong in his ruling, and the order of suppression was affirmed. Commonwealth v. Mays, No. 2790-95-3 (Ct. of Appeals April 30, 1996).

The evidence did not support the defendant's conviction for possession of cocaine based on a test tube of crack cocaine found in his home where: He reported a robbery in the home, police found the test tube on the floor of a bedroom that was in disarray while searching for evidence relating to the robbery, defendant denied knowledge of the test tube, no other drug paraphernalia was found in the house, and no evidence other than its location tied it to the defendant; the circumstantial evidence did not exclude the reasonable hypothesis that the robbers left the test tube behind. McNair v. Commonwealth, 31 Va. App. 76, 521 S.E.2d 303 (1999).

Evidence was insufficient to establish that appellant possessed or knowingly exercised dominion and control over cocaine found in the glove box of a vehicle where it was shown only that he occupied the vehicle and was in proximity to the cocaine, but he engaged in no furtive behavior and made no statements tending to show he was aware that cocaine was present anywhere in the car. Banks v. Commonwealth, No. 1405-98-2, 1999 Va. App. LEXIS 244 (Ct. of Appeals Apr. 27, 1999).

The evidence that the defendant possessed a small piece of cocaine found in the console of the car in which he was a passenger was insufficient to support a conviction under this section where the cocaine was not in plain view and no evidence was presented that the defendant put the cocaine in the console or was aware of its presence; although the arresting officer saw the defendant's upper body moving after she stopped the driver, that observation raised only a suspicion that his movement bore a connection to the cocaine and the suspicion that the defendant may have been the guilty agent is never enough to sustain a conviction. McCray v. Common-

wealth, No. 0200-99-2, 2000 Va. App. LEXIS 208 (Ct. of Appeals Mar. 21, 2000).

Evidence was insufficient to support possession of cocaine conviction, as the Commonwealth failed to present any evidence of acts, statements, or conduct that tended to show defendant was aware of the presence of cocaine in a brown bottle found on the floor of defendant's car. Jordan v. Commonwealth, No. 3084-01-1, 2002 Va. App. LEXIS 612 (Ct. of Appeals Oct. 8, 2002).

Appellant's conviction for possession with intent to distribute marijuana was reversed because there was no evidence that the odor detected by the officers was coming from appellant's person, that appellant showed any physical signs of having recently used marijuana, or that appellant possessed any drugs on his person. Ervin v. Commonwealth, 2010 Va. App. LEXIS 249 (June 22, 2010).

CIRCUIT COURT OPINIONS

Mere proximity to a controlled substance is insufficient to establish possession, where drugs found in a vehicle driven by defendant were packaged differently than those found on defendant and a passenger had equal access to the drugs. Commonwealth v. Baker, 62 Va. Cir. 278, 2003 Va. Cir. LEXIS 294 (Norfolk 2003).

Possession illegal. — Although the estranged husband, a licensed psychiatrist, did not obtain the Fentanyl patches, on which decedent wife overdosed, legally because the estranged husband removed them from the apartment of his mother, who had a legal prescription covering his practice did not protect the insurer from liability after decedent's estate obtained a medical malpractice judgment against him; the relevant professional liability policy that covered his practice required that the criminal act directly cause the relevant harm and it was not his illegal possession of the patches that caused her to die, but, instead, it was his breach of the standard of care in failing to write a proper prescription, failing to perform a physical exam on her, failing to give proper warnings to her, and failing to do a follow-up exam on her that caused her death. Estate of Feury v. Princeton Ins. Co., 68 Va. Cir. 330, 2005 Va. Cir. LEXIS 84 (Fredericksburg 2005).

Motion to suppress allowed. — As an officer did not and could not arrest defendant for the misdemeanor offense of possession of marijuana based on the marijuana found in defendant's car pursuant to a consent search, and as defendant withdrew his consent to a search of his person (including his wallet) before the officer found any incriminating evidence, the officer's search of defendant's wallet violated defendant's rights under U.S. Const., Amend. IV, and the methampetamine tablets found in the wallet were suppressed. Commonwealth v. Johnson, 84 Va. Cir. 518, 2012 Va. Cir. LEXIS 108 (Augusta County June 15, 2012).

Certificate of analysis properly admitted. — Chemists' method for identifying cathinone, a controlled substance, using a gas chromatograph equipped with a mass spectrometer and a flame ionization detector, was sufficiently reliable to warrant admission of the test results at trial, notwithstanding defendant's suggestion that computer-assisted technology was superior to graphic comparison. Defendant's motion to exclude the chemists' certificate of analysis was denied. Commonwealth v. Isse, 80 Va. Cir. 493, 2010 Va. Cir. LEXIS 87 (Fairfax June 29, 2010).

Evidence was insufficient. — Despite defendant's admission that everything in his bedroom was his, where illegal drugs were found in said room and in other room of the house, and because others lived in the home with defendant, there were just not enough facts, statements, or conduct that tended to show defendant was aware of both the presence and the character of the drugs found and that such were subject to his dominion and control. Commonwealth v. Carter, 66 Va. Cir. 8, 2004 Va. Cir. LEXIS 264 (Nelson County 2004).

Motion to dismiss denied. — Because the question of whether or not defendant attempted to possess cocaine could only be determined from all of the evidence presented at a trial, defendant's pretrial motion to dismiss was denied. Commonwealth v. Sheely, 68 Va. Cir. 245, 2005 Va. Cir. LEXIS 252 (Salem July 8, 2005).

OPINIONS OF THE ATTORNEY GENERAL

Food stamp benefits. — The federal Personal Responsibility and Work Opportunity Reconciliation Act encompasses felony convictions for manufacturing controlled substances or for obtaining controlled substances by false pretenses; those persons with such convictions are disqualified from receiving food stamp benefits because § 63.2-505.2 does not exempt such convictions from the application of the federal law. See opinion of Attorney General to The Honorable Gerald E. Mabe, II, Commonwealth's Attorney, 11-112, 2012 Va. AG LEXIS 5 (1/27/12).

§ 18.2-250.1. Possession of marijuana unlawful.

A. It is unlawful for any person knowingly or intentionally to possess marijuana unless the substance was obtained directly from, or pursuant to, a valid prescription or order of a practitioner while acting in the course of his professional practice, or except as otherwise authorized by the Drug Control Act (§ 54.1-3400 et seq.).

Upon the prosecution of a person for violation of this section, ownership or occupancy of the premises or vehicle upon or in which marijuana was found shall not create a presumption that such person either knowingly or intentionally possessed such marijuana.

Any person who violates this section shall be guilty of a misdemeanor, and be confined in jail not more than thirty days and a fine of not more than $500, either or both; any person, upon a second or subsequent conviction of a violation of this section, shall be guilty of a Class 1 misdemeanor.

B. The provisions of this section shall not apply to members of state, federal, county, city or town law-enforcement agencies, jail officers, or correctional officers, as defined in § 53.1-1, certified as handlers of dogs trained in the detection of controlled substances when possession of marijuana is necessary for the performance of their duties.

History.
1979, c. 435; 1991, c. 649; 1998, c. 116.

Cross references.
As to sale, possession, etc., of controlled substance or marijuana by inmate in penal institution or in custody of employee, see § 53.1-203.

Law Review.
For survey of Virginia criminal law for the year 1978-1979, see 66 Va. L. Rev. 241 (1980).

Michie's Jurisprudence.
For related discussion, see 5B M.J. Criminal Procedure, § 86.

CASE NOTES

Double jeopardy. — Two convictions for possession of drugs with intent to distribute within 1,000 feet of a school under § 18.2-255.2 did not violate the Double Jeopardy Clause under U.S. Const., Amend. V and Va. Const., Art. I, § 8 as marijuana and cocaine were treated in the Virginia Code as separate and discrete illegal substances under §§ 18.2-250, 18.2-250.1, and 54.1-3448. Fullwood v. Commonwealth, 54 Va. App. 153, 676 S.E.2d 348, 2009 Va. App. LEXIS 224 (2009), aff'd, 279 Va. 531, 689 S.E.2d 742, 2010 Va. LEXIS 39 (2010).

Proof of constructive possession. — Constructive possession may be shown by establishing that the marijuana was known to and subject to the dominion and control of the accused. Hambury v. Commonwealth, 3 Va. App. 435, 350 S.E.2d 524 (1986).

Knowledge of presence and character of controlled substance may be shown by evidence of the acts, statements or conduct of the accused. Hambury v. Commonwealth, 3 Va. App. 435, 350 S.E.2d 524 (1986).

Proximity and occupancy as circumstances to be considered. — While mere proximity to contraband is insufficient to establish possession, and an accused's occupancy of the premises does not give rise to a presumption of possession, these factors are circumstances to be considered by the jury with other evidence in determining whether a defendant constructively possessed drugs. Lane v. Commonwealth, 223 Va. 713, 292 S.E.2d 358 (1982); Hambury v. Commonwealth, 3 Va. App. 435, 350 S.E.2d 524 (1986).

Totality of the evidence sufficiently proved that defendant constructively possessed the contraband, which was in plain sight and within defendant's reach in a place where defendant's personal belongings were also found. Harris v. Commonwealth, No. 2183-01-1, 2002 Va. App. LEXIS 432 (Ct. of Appeals July 30, 2002).

Search proper. — Where the officer detected a strong odor of marijuana coming from the car and the defendant, saw the defendant furtively stash a black object beneath the seat, fumble suspiciously through looking for his license, and fail to produce any identification, there was probable cause to search the defendant. Savage v. Commonwealth, No. 0799-02-1, 2003 Va. App. LEXIS 187 (Ct. of Appeals Apr. 1, 2003).

Suppression motion properly denied. — Defendant's suppression motion was properly denied, and the Fourth Amendment was not violated, where: (1) a police officer had a reasonable, articulable suspicion that defendant was the man who was wanted on the capias as defendant's physical characteristics and clothing matched the description provided by dispatch, and defendant was near the address provided by dispatch in the backseat of a taxi matching the description provided by dispatch; (2) the officer was justified in detaining defendant further as he gave obviously false identifying information; and (3) when defendant struck the officer, he had probable cause for the arrest, which led to the search incident to a lawful arrest in which the drugs were discovered. Jackson v. Commonwealth, No. 0628-02-3, 2003 Va. App. LEXIS 340 (Ct. of Appeals June 17, 2003).

Where a police officer acted appropriately in removing defendant from a car and restraining him after defendant failed to comply with an order to show defendant's hands, the discovery of the drugs resulted from that removal and restraint; accordingly, the trial court correctly denied defendant's motion to suppress and convicted defendant of possession of drugs under §§ 18.2-250 and 18.2-250.1. Smith v. Commonwealth, No. 1947-03-1, 2004 Va. App. LEXIS 243 (Ct. of Appeals May 25, 2004).

In a case in which defendant appealed his conviction for violating §§ 18.2-248 and 18.2-250.1, he argued unsuccessfully that the circuit court erred in denying his motion to suppress because he had been subjected to a strip search in violation of the Fourth Amendment. Defendant had not been subjected to a strip search, he was not naked at any time during his encounter with police, neither his genitals nor his buttocks were exposed, and, while a police officer saw defendant's underwear when he removed the marijuana and cocaine, his underwear was never removed. Bell v. Commonwealth, 2009 Va. App. LEXIS 420 (Sept. 22, 2009).

Subsequent conviction under this section required for enhanced punishment. — In order for the Commonwealth to take advantage of the enhanced punishment provided in this section, it must prove a second or subsequent conviction for unlawful possession of marijuana under this section. Any other interpretation would be contrary to the express language of the statute. Pierce v. Commonwealth, 2 Va. App. 383, 345 S.E.2d 1 (1986).

Conviction of first offense before committing second offense not required. — Subsection A of this section contains no provision requiring that, in order to trigger the enhanced penalty provision, a defendant be convicted of the first offense before committing the second offense. Napier v. Commonwealth, No. 0775-90-3 (Ct. of Appeals April 27, 1993).

Convictions under § 18.2-248.1 may not be used to enhance punishment. — The scheme of punishment under this section does not envision that felony convictions under § 18.2-248.1, which carries its own severe punishments, be considered under its enhancement provision. Pierce v. Commonwealth, 2 Va. App. 383, 345 S.E.2d 1 (1986).

Possession of marijuana not a lesser-included offense of delivering marijuana to a prisoner. — Circuit court was not precluded by double jeopardy principles from trying defendant for delivering marijuana to a prisoner, in violation of § 18.2-474.1, after she pled guilty in a district court to a charge alleging that she possessed the same marijuana, in violation of this section, because possession of marijuana was not a lesser-included offense of delivering marijuana to a prisoner. Logan v. Commonwealth, 43 Va. App. 504, 600 S.E.2d 133, 2004 Va. App. LEXIS 374 (2004).

Defendant could be retried for same or greater offense where conviction vacated. — When the defendant appealed her misdemeanor possession conviction to the circuit court, as she had a right to do under § 16.1-132, her conviction was vacated; therefore, the defendant could be retried for the same or a greater offense without double jeopardy being violated. Peterson v. Commonwealth, 5 Va. App. 389, 363 S.E.2d 440 (1987).

The acceptance of the guilty plea to misdemeanor possession did not constitute an inferential finding of not guilty of the greater charge of felony possession. Consequently, the defendant was not impliedly acquitted of felony possession, and she could be retried for felony possession unless some other double jeopardy principle barred reprosecution. Peterson v. Commonwealth, 5 Va. App. 389, 363 S.E.2d 440 (1987).

Refusal to allow search. — As police officer had no basis to suspect that defendant was engaged in criminal activity or that he was armed, when defendant withdrew his consent to be searched, the officer had no legal basis to continue the encounter. Ellison v. Commonwealth, No. 1619-01-2, 2002 Va. App. LEXIS 337 (Ct. of Appeals June 11, 2002).

Evidence sufficient to show possession of marijuana. — Evidence fully supported trial court's finding that defendant knowingly and intentionally possessed marijuana, where police found it growing near the entrance to defendant's house; the marijuana plant was in a flower bed that defendant had planted; it was the only plant in the flower bed that had been watered recently; police found a tray containing hemostats, rolling paper, and enough marijuana to roll a cigarette; and defendant was a longtime smoker of marijuana who had smoked a joint just before the police arrived at his home. Walton v. Commonwealth, 255 Va. 422, 497 S.E.2d 869 (1998).

Evidence was sufficient to support convictions for possession of marijuana, in violation of § 18.2-250.1, where the trial court could have reasonably concluded that defendant was aware of the presence and character of the drugs found in the console and that he exercised dominion and control over them. Gillard v. Commonwealth, No. 0037-02-2, 2003 Va. App. LEXIS 437 (Ct. of Appeals Aug. 19, 2003).

Where defendant recently possessed a vehicle, knew of the presence and character the items hidden therein, and the items were subject to defendant's dominion and control, the evidence was sufficient to prove defendant's constructive possession of the cocaine and marijuana found in the vehicle. White v. Commonwealth, No. 0591-03-2, 2003 Va. App. LEXIS 539 (Ct. of Appeals Oct. 28, 2003).

Evidence was sufficient to support defendants conviction for possession of marijuana where defendant admitted to possessing marijuana that was found inside his home. Breeden v. Commonwealth, 43 Va. App. 169, 596 S.E.2d 563, 2004 Va. App. LEXIS 257 (2004).

Evidence was sufficient to support his convictions for possession of a firearm by a felon and possession of marijuana because defendant stated the car where the contraband was found was his car, and defendant provided a key to the officer who found several items with defendant's name in addition to the pistol, bullets, loose marijuana and digital scale. Patterson v. Commonwealth, 2006 Va. App. LEXIS 361 (Aug. 8, 2006).

Evidence was sufficient to prove that defendant constructively possessed marijuana found in a van he owned and was driving. As a bag of marijuana and a smoking device were within arm's reach of the driver's seat, the trial court could infer that defendant knew about the marijuana and intentionally possessed it, and was entitled to reject his theory that someone else placed valuable drugs in the van while it was unlocked at a job site. Wilson v. Commonwealth, — Va. App. —, — S.E.2d —, 2006 Va. App. LEXIS 437 (Oct. 3, 2006).

Evidence that defendant fled toward the fence when defendant saw the police, made a pushing or throwing motion over the fence, and immediately thereafter the police found marijuana and cocaine on the other side of the fence in the line of defendant's arm motion was sufficient to support conclusion defendant possessed the marijuana and cocaine. Debroux v. Commonwealth, — Va. App. —, — S.E.2d —, 2007 Va. App. LEXIS 40 (Feb. 6, 2007).

Evidence that the drugs were found in a vehicle owned and occupied by defendant, that the officer retrieved the drugs from right on top of a console located next to defendant's seat and within defendant's reach, and that 10 syringes were found beneath defendant's seat, permitted an inference that defendant had knowledge of the presence of the drugs. The trial judge was entitled to infer that defendant's explanation was an effort to conceal guilt. Throckmorton v. Commonwealth, — Va. App. —, — S.E.2d —, 2007 Va. App. LEXIS 196 (May 15, 2007).

Evidence was sufficient to support defendant's convictions for possessing both marijuana and the cocaine found in a vehicle where the drugs were found in the front passenger compartment of the vehicle, which was occupied solely by defendant. While seated in the police vehicle, defendant emphatically shouted that everything in the vehicle belonged to him, as defendant's fiance came up on foot and claimed that the vehicle belonged to her. Even though defendant later denied the statements, the trial court was at liberty to judge defendant's credibility. Armstead v. Commonwealth, 56 Va. App. 569, 695 S.E.2d 561, 2010 Va. App. LEXIS 300 (2010).

Insufficient evidence of constructive possession. — Convictions for possession of cocaine with the intent to distribute, third or subsequent offense, and possession of marijuana were reversed because defendant's only proven connection to the drugs was defendant's proximity to them; no evidence proved that the officer or anyone else saw defendant with drugs or saw defendant place the drugs in the plywood. In addition, defendant's fingerprints were not on the bags recovered, which was relevant as the Commonwealth's theory was that defendant was holding the drugs down the front of defendant's pants in ungloved hands. Maxwell v. Commonwealth, — Va. App. —, — S.E.2d —, 2006 Va. App. LEXIS 518 (Nov. 21, 2006).

While defendant's conduct may have been suspicious, no one ever saw defendant with the marijuana at issue, defendant never made any incriminating statements concerning the drugs, and the one fingerprint lifted from a bag containing cocaine, not marijuana, did not belong to defendant but belonged to someone else. As a result, the State did not show that defendant was ever in such close proximity as would support a finding that defendant was aware of both the presence and the character of the marijuana, and that it was subject to defendant's dominion and control, such that defendant could be convicted pursuant to § 18.2-250.1. Maxwell v. Commonwealth, 275 Va. 437, 657 S.E.2d 499, 2008 Va. LEXIS 21 (2008).

Applied in Dukes v. Commonwealth, 227 Va. 119, 313 S.E.2d 382 (1984); Livingston v. Commonwealth, 21 Va. App. 621, 466 S.E.2d 757 (1996); Peake v. Commonwealth, 46 Va. App. 35, 614 S.E.2d 672, 2005 Va. App. LEXIS 238 (2005); Wilson v. Commonwealth, 272 Va. 19, 630 S.E.2d 326, 2006 Va. LEXIS 60 (2006); Epps v. Commonwealth, 59 Va. App. 71, 717 S.E.2d 151, 2011 Va. App. LEXIS 351 (2011).

CIRCUIT COURT OPINIONS

Motion to suppress evidence. — Because a reasonable person in defendant's position would have believed that after an officer's explanation regarding defendant's failure to possess a city and county tax sticker, and after defendant's registration and license were cleared the traffic stop was over and defendant was free to leave, defendant's consent to search thereafter was involuntary, warranting suppression of the marijuana and cocaine seized from his person. Commonwealth v. Cooper, 68 Va. Cir. 515, 2004 Va. Cir. LEXIS 367 (Charlottesville Dec. 6, 2004).

Suppression motion properly denied. — Because a pat-down search of defendant, after defendant had already told the searching officer that he had two knives on him, did not move out of the bounds of a reasonable *Terry* stop and could not be characterized as custody associated with a formal arrest, defendant was not entitled to *Miranda* warnings; hence, without any custody, defendant's statement that the hard tube-like mound in his pocket was marijuana, as well as the marijuana seized as a result, were both admissible. Commonwealth v. Herring, — Va. Cir. —, 2006 Va. Cir. LEXIS 8 (Charlottesville Feb. 13, 2006).

§ 18.2-251. Persons charged with first offense may be placed on probation; conditions; substance abuse screening, assessment treatment and education programs or services; drug tests; costs and fees; violations; discharge.

Whenever any person who has not previously been convicted of any offense under this article or under any statute of the United States or of any state relating to narcotic drugs, marijuana, synthetic cannabinoids, or stimulant, depressant, or hallucinogenic drugs, or has not previously had a proceeding against him for violation of such an offense dismissed as provided in this section, pleads guilty to or enters a plea of not guilty to possession of a controlled substance under § 18.2-250 or to possession of marijuana under § 18.2-250.1, or to possession of synthetic cannabinoids under subsection B of § 18.2-248.1:1, the court, upon such plea if the facts found by the court would justify a finding of guilt, without entering a judgment of guilt and with the consent of the accused, may defer further proceedings and place him on probation upon terms and conditions.

As a term or condition, the court shall require the accused to undergo a substance abuse assessment pursuant to § 18.2-251.01 or 19.2-299.2, as appropriate, and enter treatment and/or education program or services, if available, such as, in the opinion of the court, may be best suited to the needs of the accused based upon consideration of the substance abuse assessment. The program or services may be located in the judicial district in which the charge is brought or in any other judicial district as the court may provide. The services shall be provided by (i) a program licensed by the Department of Behavioral Health and Developmental Services, by a similar program which is made available through the Department of Corrections, (ii) a local community-based probation services agency established pursuant to § 9.1-174, or (iii) an ASAP program certified by the Commission on VASAP.

The court shall require the person entering such program under the provisions of this section to pay all or part of the costs of the program, including the costs of the screening, assessment, testing, and treatment, based upon the accused's ability to pay unless the person is determined by the court to be indigent.

As a condition of probation, the court shall require the accused (i) to successfully complete treatment or education program or services, (ii) to remain drug and alcohol free during the period of probation and submit to such tests during that period as may be necessary and appropriate to determine if the accused is drug and alcohol free, (iii) to make reasonable efforts to secure and maintain employment, and (iv) to comply with a plan of at least 100 hours of community service for a felony and up to 24 hours of community service for a misdemeanor. Such testing shall be conducted by personnel of the supervising probation agency or personnel of any program or agency approved by the supervising probation agency.

The court shall, unless done at arrest, order the accused to report to the original arresting law-enforcement agency to submit to fingerprinting.

Upon violation of a term or condition, the court may enter an adjudication of guilt and proceed as otherwise provided. Upon fulfillment of the terms and conditions, the court shall discharge the person and dismiss the proceedings against him. Discharge and dismissal under this section shall be without adjudication of guilt and is a conviction only for the purposes of applying this section in subsequent proceedings.

Notwithstanding any other provision of this section, whenever a court places an individual on probation upon terms and conditions pursuant to this section, such action shall be treated as a conviction for purposes of §§ 18.2-259.1, 22.1-315 and 46.2-390.1, and the driver's license forfeiture provisions of those sections shall be imposed. The provisions of this paragraph shall not be applicable to any offense for which a juvenile has had his license suspended or denied pursuant to § 16.1-278.9 for the same offense.

History.
Code 1950, § 54-524.101:3; 1972, c. 798; 1975, cc. 14, 15; 1976, c. 181; 1979, c. 435; 1983, c. 513; 1991, c. 482; 1992, cc. 58, 833; 1993, c. 410; 1997, c. 380; 1998, cc. 688, 783, 840; 2000, cc. 1020, 1041; 2001, cc. 430, 450, 827; 2007, c. 133; 2009, cc. 813, 840; 2011, cc. 384, 410.

Editor's note.
Acts 2011, cc. 384 and 410, cl. 3 provides: "That the provisions of this act may result in a net increase in periods of imprisonment or commitment. Pursuant to § 30-19.1:4, the estimated amount of the necessary appropriation cannot be determined for periods of imprisonment in state adult correctional facilities; therefore, Chapter 874 of the Acts of Assembly of 2010 requires the Virginia Criminal Sentencing Commission to assign a minimum fiscal impact of $50,000. Pursuant to § 30-19.1:4, the estimated amount of the necessary appropriation cannot be determined for periods of commitment to the custody of the Department of Juvenile Justice."

The 2009 amendments.
The 2009 amendments by cc. 813 and 840 are identical, and in the second paragraph, deleted the § symbol preceding "19.2-299.2" in the first sentence, and substituted "Behavioral Health and Developmental Services" for "Mental Health, Mental Retardation and Substance Abuse Services" in clause (i) of the third sentence.

The 2011 amendments.
The 2011 amendments by cc. 384 and 410, and effective March 23, 2011, are identical, and inserted "synthetic cannabinoids" and "or to possession of synthetic cannabinoids under subsection B of § 18.2-248.1:1" in the first paragraph.

Law Review.
For survey of Virginia law on criminal law for the year 1971-9172, 1971-1972, 58 Va. L. Rev. 1206 (1972). For survey of Virginia law on criminal law for the year 1972-1973, see 59 Va. L. Rev. 1458 (1973). For survey of Virginia criminal law and procedure for the

year 2004-2005, see 40 U. Rich. L. Rev. 197 (2005). For note, "New Theories of Guilt on Appeal in Virginia Criminal Cases," see 50 Wm. and Mary L. Rev. 2177 (2009).

CASE NOTES

First-offender status properly denied by trial court. — Trial court did not make an arbitrary decision and abuse its discretion in denying defendant first-offender status where defendant did not have a regular address, had a prior criminal record of two assault convictions and numerous traffic-related offenses, was suffering from depression and post-traumatic stress syndrome, and had demonstrated an uncooperative attitude by being reluctant to provide the medical release forms that would have enabled the court to obtain information about his drug use and treatment. Montalvo v. Commonwealth, 27 Va. App. 95, 497 S.E.2d 519 (1998).

Probation is a disposition intended to "reform" the offender, appropriate in "mitigating circumstances" or to promote the "public interest." It provides an "opportunity" for an accused to "repent and reform," which may be withdrawn for "unreasonable cause," determined in the sound discretion of the trial court. Connelly v. Commonwealth, 14 Va. App. 888, 420 S.E.2d 244 (1992).

Charge dismissed under this section is not "otherwise dismissed" for purpose of expungement statute. — Section 19.2-392.2 applies to innocent persons, not to those who are guilty. Under this section, probation and ultimate dismissal is conditioned on a plea of guilty or a finding of guilt. One who is "guilty" cannot occupy the status of "innocent" so as to qualify under the expungement statute as a person whose charge has been "otherwise dismissed." Gregg v. Commonwealth, 227 Va. 504, 316 S.E.2d 741 (1984).

Because defendant's possession charge was not "otherwise dismissed" within the meaning of the expungement statute, subsection A of § 19.2-392.2, as the trial court had to find defendant guilty before disposing of her case pursuant to the first offender statute, defendant was not entitled to have the charge expunged from her record. Commonwealth v. Dotson, 276 Va. 278, 661 S.E.2d 473, 2008 Va. LEXIS 80 (2008).

Trial court bound by plea agreement. — Where a plea agreement, which the trial court accepted, explicitly referred to this section and required dismissal of the charge after one year if defendant committed no further violations of law, and defendant committed no further violations, the trial court was bound to enforce the plea agreement, to discharge defendant and to dismiss the charge against him. Calvillo v. Commonwealth, 19 Va. App. 433, 452 S.E.2d 363 (1994).

Condition of good behavior implicit. — Although a court might appropriately conclude that a good behavior condition is implicit when first-offender status is imposed under § 18.2-251, just as that condition is implicit when a sentence is suspended, there is no need to rely on such an implicit condition when an order imposing first-offender status specifically imposes good behavior as a condition of the defendant's probation. In such a case, whether defendant's first-offender status is properly revoked depends on whether the defendant has violated the explicit terms of the order imposing the first-offender status, not on whether the defendant has violated an implicit good behavior condition. White v. Commonwealth, 276 Va. 725, 667 S.E.2d 564, 2008 Va. LEXIS 119 (2008).

First offender status was improperly revoked. — Circuit court should not have revoked defendant's first-offender status under § 18.2-251 and convicted her of possessing cocaine, in violation of § 18.2-250, after her stated period of probation ended: (1) the circuit court's order imposing first-offender status explicitly stated that defendant's probation ended on December 21, 2005; (2) although the circuit court continued defendant's case after December 21, 2005, it did so only to ensure that defendant paid court costs, as required under the first-offender order; (3) the circuit court did not explicitly extend defendant's probation beyond December 21, 2005, and such an extension could not occur de facto; and (4) it would not be appropriate to assume that defendant was subject to a continuing, implicit condition of good behavior after her case was continued given that a good behavior condition had been explicitly imposed on her as part of her probation. White v. Commonwealth, 276 Va. 725, 667 S.E.2d 564, 2008 Va. LEXIS 119 (2008).

Revocation of deferred disposition. — Because the appellate court affirmed defendant's underlying convictions, the trial court was undoubtedly justified in revoking the deferred disposition of a cocaine possession charge and entering "an adjudication of guilt" under § 18.2-251; this conclusion mooted defendant's complaint about the trial court's failure to take the deferred disposition under advisement. Whitfield v. Commonwealth, 57 Va. App. 396, 702 S.E.2d 590, 2010 Va. App. LEXIS 502 (2010).

Between the time when defendant pleaded guilty of possessing a controlled drug in violation of § 18.2-250 and the time of defendant's sentencing hearing, defendant was convicted of possession of marijuana which rendered defendant ineligible for a deferred disposition under § 18.2-251. Epps v. Commonwealth, 59 Va. App. 71, 717 S.E.2d 151, 2011 Va. App. LEXIS 351 (2011).

Trial court did not abuse its discretion in finding that defendant violated the terms of the plea agreement, as well as its order, by failing to submit to two drug screens, and in convicting him for possession of methamphetamine after having deferred judgment on the charge pursuant to § 18.2-251. Vogt v. Commonwealth, 2012 Va. App. LEXIS 170 (May 22, 2012).

CIRCUIT COURT OPINIONS

Defendant was not a convicted felon under statute. — Defendant's motion to strike the State's evidence as to count 2 of the indictment charging possession of a firearm by a convicted felon, in violation of § 18.2-308.2, was granted, as he was not a convicted felon, pursuant to § 18.2-251 on the date said charge was alleged in the information; moreover, the fact that he might have later been found to have violated his probation had no retroactive effect since a conviction occurred only after the court conducted a hearing, received evidence of a violation, and then entered a final appealable judgment of conviction. Commonwealth v. Cross, 71 Va. Cir. 272, 2006 Va. Cir. LEXIS 120 (Portsmouth 2006).

§ 18.2-251.01. Substance abuse screening and assessment for felony convictions.

A. When a person is convicted of a felony, not a capital offense, committed on or after January 1, 2000, he shall be required to undergo a substance abuse screening and, if the screening indicates a substance abuse or dependence problem, an assessment by a certified substance abuse counselor as defined in § 54.1-3500 employed by the Department of Corrections or by an agency employee under the supervision of such counselor. If the person is determined to have a substance abuse problem, the court shall require him to enter treatment and/or education program or services, if available, which, in the opinion of the court, is best suited to the needs of the person. The program or services may be located in the judicial district in which the conviction was had or in any other judicial district as the court may provide. The treatment and/or education program or services shall be licensed by the Department of Behavioral Health and Developmental Services or shall be a similar program or services which are made available through the Department of Corrections if the court imposes a sentence of one year or more or, if the court imposes a sentence of 12 months or less, by a similar program or services available through a local or regional jail, a local community-based probation services agency established pursuant to § 9.1-174, or an ASAP program certified by the Commission on VASAP. The services agency or program may require the person entering such program or services under the provisions of this section to pay a fee for the education and treatment component, or both, based upon the defendant's ability to pay.

B. As a condition of any suspended sentence and probation, the court shall order the person to undergo periodic testing and treatment for substance abuse, if available, as the court deems appropriate based upon consideration of the substance abuse assessment.

History.
1998, cc. 783, 840; 1999, cc. 891, 913; 2000, cc. 1020, 1041; 2007, c. 133; 2009, cc. 813, 840.

The 2009 amendments.
The 2009 amendments by cc. 813 and 840 are identical and substituted "Behavioral Health and Developmental Services" for "Mental Health, Mental Retardation and Substance Abuse Services" in the fourth sentence of subsection A.

§ 18.2-251.02. Drug Offender Assessment and Treatment Fund.

There is hereby established in the state treasury the Drug Offender Assessment and Treatment Fund which shall consist of moneys received from fees imposed on certain drug offense convictions pursuant to subdivisions A 10 and A 11 of § 17.1-275 and § 16.1-69.48:3. All interest derived from the deposit and investment of moneys in the Fund shall be credited to the Fund. Any moneys not appropriated by the General Assembly shall remain in the Drug Offender Assessment and Treatment Fund and shall not be transferred or revert to the general fund at the end of any fiscal year. All moneys in the Fund shall be subject to annual appropriation by the General Assembly to the Department of Corrections, the Department of Juvenile Justice, and the Commission on VASAP to implement and operate the offender substance abuse screening and assessment program; the Department of Criminal Justice Services for the support of community-based probation and local pretrial services agencies; and the Office of the Executive Secretary of the Supreme Court of Virginia for the support of drug treatment court programs.

History.
1998, cc. 783, 840; 2003, c. 606; 2004, c. 1004.

§ 18.2-251.1. Possession or distribution of marijuana for medical purposes permitted.

A. No person shall be prosecuted under § 18.2-250 or § 18.2-250.1 for the possession of marijuana or tetrahydrocannabinol when that possession occurs pursuant to a valid prescription issued by a medical doctor in the course of his professional practice for treatment of cancer or glaucoma.

B. No medical doctor shall be prosecuted under § 18.2-248 or § 18.2-248.1 for dispensing or distributing marijuana or tetrahydrocannabinol for medical purposes when such action occurs in the course of

his professional practice for treatment of cancer or glaucoma.

C. No pharmacist shall be prosecuted under §§ 18.2-248 to 18.2-248.1 for dispensing or distributing marijuana or tetrahydrocannabinol to any person who holds a valid prescription of a medical doctor for such substance issued in the course of such doctor's professional practice for treatment of cancer or glaucoma.

History.
1979, c. 435.

CASE NOTES

Necessity defense. — In restricting the legitimate medicinal uses of marijuana to cases involving cancer and glaucoma, the legislature evinced its intent to circumscribe the value judgment an individual can make with respect to its use for treating other conditions and, to that extent, abrogated the common-law defense of necessity. Murphy v. Commonwealth, 31 Va. App. 70, 521 S.E.2d 301 (1999).

§ 18.2-251.2. Possession and distribution of flunitrazepam; enhanced penalty.

Notwithstanding the provisions of §§ 54.1-3446 and 54.1-3452, the drug flunitrazepam shall be deemed to be listed on Schedule I for the purposes of penalties for violations of the Drug Control Act (§ 54.1-3400 et seq.). Any person knowingly manufacturing, selling, giving, distributing or possessing the drug flunitrazepam shall be punished under the penalties prescribed for such violations in accordance with §§ 18.2-248 and 18.2-250.

History.
1997, c. 595.

§ 18.2-251.3. Possession and distribution of gamma-butyrolactone; 1, 4-butanediol; enhanced penalty.

Any person who knowingly manufactures, sells, gives, distributes or possesses with the intent to distribute the substances gamma-butyrolactone; or 1, 4-butanediol, when intended for human consumption shall be guilty of a Class 3 felony.

History.
2000, c. 348.

Law Review.
For 2000 survey of Virginia criminal law and procedure, see 34 U. Rich. L. Rev. 749 (2000).

§ 18.2-251.4. Defeating drug and alcohol screening tests; penalty.

A. It is unlawful for a person to:
1. Sell, give away, distribute, transport or market human urine in the Commonwealth with the intent of using the urine to defeat a drug or alcohol screening test;

2. Attempt to defeat a drug or alcohol screening test by the substitution of a sample;

3. Adulterate a urine or other bodily fluid sample with the intent to defraud a drug or alcohol screening test.

B. A violation of this section is a Class 1 misdemeanor.

History.
2001, c. 379.

§ 18.2-252. Suspended sentence conditioned upon substance abuse screening, assessment, testing, and treatment or education.

The trial judge or court trying the case of any person found guilty of violating any law concerning the use, in any manner, of drugs, controlled substances, narcotics, marijuana, noxious chemical substances and like substances, shall condition any suspended sentence by first requiring such person to agree to undergo a substance abuse screening pursuant to § 18.2-251.01 and to submit to such periodic substance abuse testing, to include alcohol testing, as may be directed by the court. Such testing shall be conducted by the supervising probation agency or by personnel of any program or agency approved by the supervising probation agency. The cost of such testing ordered by the court shall be paid by the Commonwealth and taxed as a part of the costs of such criminal proceedings. The judge or court shall order the person, as a condition of any suspended sentence, to undergo such treatment or education for substance abuse, if available, as the judge or court deems appropriate based upon consideration of the substance abuse assessment. The treatment or education shall be provided by a program or agency licensed by the Department of Behavioral Health and Developmental Services, by a similar program or services available through the Department of Corrections if the court imposes a sentence of one year or more or, if the court imposes a sentence of 12 months or less, by a similar program or services available through a local or regional jail, a local community-based probation services agency established pursuant to § 9.1-174, or an ASAP program certified by the Commission on VASAP.

History.
Code 1950, § 54-524.101:4; 1973, c. 473; 1975, cc. 14, 15; 1979, c. 435; 1998, cc. 783, 840; 2000, cc. 1020, 1041; 2007, c. 133; 2009, cc. 813, 840.

The 2009 amendments.
The 2009 amendments by cc. 813 and 840 are identical, and substituted "Behavioral Health and Developmental Services" for "Mental Health, Mental Retardation and Substance Abuse Services" in the fifth sentence.

Law Review.
For survey of Virginia criminal law for the year 1972-1973, see 59 Va. L. Rev. 1458 (1973).

§§ 18.2-253 through 18.2-253.2. Repealed by Acts 2004, c. 995.

Cross references.
For current provisions as to seizure and custody of controlled substances, see §§ 19.2-386.23 through 19.2-386.25.

§ 18.2-254. Commitment of convicted person for treatment for substance abuse.

A. Whenever any person who has not previously been convicted of any offense under this article or under any statute of the United States or of any state relating to narcotic drugs, marijuana, stimulant, depressant, or hallucinogenic drugs or has not previously had a proceeding against him for violation of such an offense dismissed as provided in § 18.2-251 is found guilty of violating any law concerning the use, in any manner, of drugs, controlled substances, narcotics, marijuana, noxious chemical substances, and like substances, the judge or court shall require such person to undergo a substance abuse screening pursuant to § 18.2-251.01 and to submit to such periodic substance abuse testing, to include alcohol testing, as may be directed by the court. The cost of such testing ordered by the court shall be paid by the Commonwealth and taxed as a part of the costs of the criminal proceedings. The judge or court shall also order the person to undergo such treatment or education for substance abuse, if available, as the judge or court deems appropriate based upon consideration of the substance abuse assessment. The treatment or education shall be provided by a program or agency licensed by the Department of Behavioral Health and Developmental Services or by a similar program or services available through the Department of Corrections if the court imposes a sentence of one year or more or, if the court imposes a sentence of 12 months or less, by a similar program or services available through a local or regional jail, a local community-based probation services agency established pursuant to § 9.1-174, or an ASAP program certified by the Commission on VASAP.

B. The court trying the case of any person alleged to have committed any offense designated by this article or by the Drug Control Act (§ 54.1-3400 et seq.) or in any other criminal case in which the commission of the offense was motivated by or closely related to the use of drugs and determined by the court, pursuant to a substance abuse screening and assessment, to be in need of treatment for the use of drugs may commit, based upon a consideration of the substance abuse assessment, such person, upon his conviction, to any facility for the treatment of persons with substance abuse, licensed by the Department of Behavioral Health and Developmental Services, if space is available in such facility, for a period of time not in excess of the maximum term of imprisonment specified as the penalty for conviction of such offense or, if sentence was determined by a jury, not in excess of the term of imprisonment as set by such jury. Confinement under such commitment shall be, in all regards, treated as confinement in a penal institution and the person so committed may be convicted of escape if he leaves the place of commitment without authority. A charge of escape may be prosecuted in either the jurisdiction where the treatment facility is located or the jurisdiction where the person was sentenced to commitment. The court may revoke such commitment at any time and transfer the person to an appropriate state or local correctional facility. Upon presentation of a certified statement from the director of the treatment facility to the effect that the confined person has successfully responded to treatment, the court may release such confined person prior to the termination of the period of time for which such person was confined and may suspend the remainder of the term upon such conditions as the court may prescribe.

C. The court trying a case in which commission of the offense was related to the defendant's habitual abuse of alcohol and in which the court determines, pursuant to a substance abuse screening and assessment, that such defendant is in need of treatment, may commit, based upon a consideration of the substance abuse assessment, such person, upon his conviction, to any facility for the treatment of persons with substance abuse licensed by the Department of Behavioral Health and Developmental Services, if space is available in such facility, for a period of time not in excess of the maximum term of imprisonment specified as the penalty for conviction. Confinement under such commitment shall be, in all regards, treated as confinement in a penal institution and the person so committed may be convicted of escape if he leaves the place of commitment without authority. The court may revoke such commitment at any time and transfer the person to an appropriate state or local correctional facility. Upon presentation of a certified statement from the director of the treatment facility to the effect that the confined person has successfully responded to treatment, the court may release such confined person prior to the termination of the period of time for which such person was confined and may suspend the remainder of the term upon such conditions as the court may prescribe.

History.

Code 1950, § 54-524.102; 1972, c. 758; 1974, c. 447; 1975, cc. 14, 15; 1978, c. 640; 1979, cc. 413, 435; 1992, c. 852; 1998, c. 724; 2000, cc. 1020, 1041; 2004, c. 130; 2005, c. 716; 2007, c. 133; 2009, cc. 813, 840.

The 2009 amendments.

The 2009 amendments by cc. 813 and 840 are identical, and substituted "Behavioral Health and Developmental Services" for "Mental Health, Mental Retardation and Substance Abuse Services" in the fourth sentence of subsection A, and in the first sentences of subsections B and C.

Law Review.

For survey of Virginia criminal law for the year 1971-1972, see 58 Va. L. Rev. 1206 (1972); for the year 1977-1978, see 64 Va. L. Rev. 1407 (1978); for the year 1978-1979, see 66 Va. L. Rev. 241 (1980).

CASE NOTES

Applied in Ziats v. Commonwealth, 42 Va. App. 133, 590 S.E.2d 117, 2003 Va. App. LEXIS 701 (2003).

§ 18.2-254.1. Drug Treatment Court Act.

A. This section shall be known and may be cited as the "Drug Treatment Court Act."

B. The General Assembly recognizes that there is a critical need in the Commonwealth for effective treatment programs that reduce the incidence of drug use, drug addiction, family separation due to parental substance abuse, and drug-related crimes. It is the intent of the General Assembly by this section to enhance public safety by facilitating the creation of drug treatment courts as means by which to accomplish this purpose.

C. The goals of drug treatment courts include: (i) reducing drug addiction and drug dependency among offenders; (ii) reducing recidivism; (iii) reducing drug-related court workloads; (iv) increasing personal, familial and societal accountability among offenders; and, (v) promoting effective planning and use of resources among the criminal justice system and community agencies.

D. Drug treatment courts are specialized court dockets within the existing structure of Virginia's court system offering judicial monitoring of intensive treatment and strict supervision of addicts in drug and drug-related cases. Local officials must complete a recognized planning process before establishing a drug treatment court program.

E. Administrative oversight for implementation of the Drug Treatment Court Act shall be conducted by the Supreme Court of Virginia. The Supreme Court of Virginia shall be responsible for (i) providing oversight for the distribution of funds for drug treatment courts; (ii) providing technical assistance to drug treatment courts; (iii) providing training for judges who preside over drug treatment courts; (iv) providing training to the providers of administrative, case management, and treatment services to drug treatment courts; and (v) monitoring the completion of evaluations of the effectiveness and efficiency of drug treatment courts in the Commonwealth.

F. A state drug treatment court advisory committee shall be established to (i) evaluate and recommend standards for the planning and implementation of drug treatment courts; (ii) assist in the evaluation of their effectiveness and efficiency; and (iii) encourage and enhance cooperation among agencies that participate in their planning and implementation. The committee shall be chaired by the Chief Justice of the Supreme Court of Virginia or his designee and shall include a member of the Judicial Conference of Virginia who presides over a drug treatment court; a district court judge; the Executive Secretary or his designee; the directors of the following executive branch agencies: Department of Corrections, Department of Criminal Justice Services, Department of Juvenile Justice, Department of Behavioral Health and Developmental Services, Department of Social Services; a representative of the following entities: a local community-based probation and pretrial services agency, the Commonwealth's Attorney's Association, the Virginia Indigent Defense Commission, the Circuit Court Clerk's Association, the Virginia Sheriff's Association, the Virginia Association of Chiefs of Police, the Commission on VASAP, and two representatives designated by the Virginia Drug Court Association.

G. Each jurisdiction or combination of jurisdictions that intend to establish a drug treatment court or continue the operation of an existing one shall establish a local drug treatment court advisory committee. Jurisdictions that establish separate adult and juvenile drug treatment courts may establish an advisory committee for each such court. Each advisory committee shall ensure quality, efficiency, and fairness in the planning, implementation, and operation of the drug treatment court or courts that serve the jurisdiction or combination of jurisdictions. Advisory committee membership shall include, but shall not be limited to the following people or their designees: (i) the drug treatment court judge; (ii) the attorney for the Commonwealth, or, where applicable, the city or county attorney who has responsibility for the prosecution of misdemeanor offenses; (iii) the public defender or a member of the local criminal defense bar in jurisdictions in which there is no public defender; (iv) the clerk of the court in which the drug treatment court is located; (v) a representative of the Virginia Department of Corrections, or the Department of Juvenile Justice, or both, from the local office which serves the jurisdiction or combination of jurisdictions; (vi) a representative of a local community-based probation and pretrial services agency; (vii) a local law-enforcement officer; (viii) a representative of the Department of Behavioral Health and Developmental Services or a representative of local drug treatment providers; (ix) the drug court administrator; (x) a representative of the Department of Social Services; (xi) county administrator or city manager; and (xii) any other people selected by the drug treatment court advisory committee.

H. Each local drug treatment court advisory committee shall establish criteria for the eligibility and participation of offenders who have been determined to be addicted to or dependent upon drugs. Subject to the provisions of this section, neither the establishment of a drug treatment court nor anything herein shall be construed as limiting the discretion of the attorney for the Commonwealth to prosecute any criminal case arising therein which he deems advisable to prosecute, except to the extent the participating attorney for the Commonwealth agrees to do so. As defined in § 17.1-805 or 19.2-297.1, adult offenders who have been convicted of a violent criminal offense within the preceding 10 years, or juvenile offenders who previously have been adjudicated not innocent of any such offense within the preceding 10 years, shall not be eligible for participation in any drug treatment court established or continued in operation pursuant to this section.

I. Each drug treatment court advisory committee shall establish policies and procedures for the operation of the court to attain the following goals: (i) effective integration of drug and alcohol treatment services with criminal justice system case processing; (ii) enhanced public safety through intensive offender supervision and drug treatment; (iii) prompt identification and placement of eligible participants; (iv) efficient access to a continuum of alcohol, drug, and related treatment and rehabilitation services; (v) verified participant abstinence through frequent alcohol and other drug testing; (vi) prompt response to participants' noncompliance with program requirements through a coordinated strategy; (vii) ongoing judicial interaction with each drug court participant; (viii) ongoing monitoring and evaluation of program effectiveness and efficiency; (ix) ongoing interdisciplinary education and training in support of program effectiveness and efficiency; and (x) ongoing collaboration among drug treatment courts, public agencies, and community-based organizations to enhance program effectiveness and efficiency.

J. Participation by an offender in a drug treatment court shall be voluntary and made pursuant only to a written agreement entered into by and between the offender and the Commonwealth with the concurrence of the court.

K. Nothing in this section shall preclude the establishment of substance abuse treatment programs and services pursuant to the deferred judgment provisions of § 18.2-251.

L. Each offender shall contribute to the cost of the substance abuse treatment he receives while participating in a drug treatment court pursuant to guidelines developed by the drug treatment court advisory committee.

M. Nothing contained in this section shall confer a right or an expectation of a right to treatment for an offender or be construed as requiring a local drug treatment court advisory committee to accept for participation every offender.

N. The Office of the Executive Secretary shall, with the assistance of the state drug treatment court advisory committee, develop a statewide evaluation model and conduct ongoing evaluations of the effectiveness and efficiency of all local drug treatment courts. A report of these evaluations shall be submitted to the General Assembly by December 1 of each year. Each local drug treatment court advisory committee shall submit evaluative reports to the Office of the Executive Secretary as requested.

O. Notwithstanding any other provision of this section, no drug treatment court shall be established subsequent to March 1, 2004, unless the jurisdiction or jurisdictions intending or proposing to establish such court have been specifically granted permission under the Code of Virginia to establish such court. The provisions of this subsection shall not apply to any drug treatment court established on or before March 1, 2004, and operational as of July 1, 2004.

P. Subject to the requirements and conditions established by the state Drug Treatment Court Advisory Committee, there shall be established a drug treatment court in the following jurisdictions: the City of Chesapeake and the City of Newport News.

Q. Subject to the requirements and conditions established by the state Drug Treatment Court Advisory Committee, there shall be established a drug treatment court in the Juvenile and Domestic Relations District Court for the County of Franklin, provided that such court is funded solely through local sources.

R. Subject to the requirements and conditions established by the state Drug Treatment Court Advisory Committee, there shall be established a drug treatment court in the City of Bristol and the County of Tazewell, provided that the court is funded within existing state and local appropriations.

History.
2004, c. 1004; 2005, cc. 519, 602; 2006, cc. 175, 341; 2007, c. 133; 2009, cc. 205, 281, 294, 813, 840; 2010, c. 258.

Editor's note.
At the direction of the Virginia Code Commission, subsection Q as added by Acts 2009, c. 294 has been redesignated as subsection R.

Acts 2012, Sp. Sess. I, c. 3, as amended by Acts 2013, c. 806, effective for the biennium ending June 30, 2014, Item 40 H provides: "H. 1. No state funds used to support the operation of drug court programs shall be provided to programs that serve first-time substance abuse offenders only or do not include probation violators. This restriction shall not apply to juvenile drug court programs.

"2. Notwithstanding the provisions of subsection O. of § 18.2-254.1, Code of Virginia, any locality is authorized to establish a drug treatment court supported by existing state resources and by federal or local resources that may be available. This authorization is subject to the requirements and conditions regarding the establishment and operation of a local drug treatment court advisory committee as provided by § 18.2-254.1 and the requirements and conditions established by the state Drug Treatment Court Advisory Committee. Any drug court treatment progam established after July 1, 2012, shall limit participation in the program to offenders who have been determined, through the use of a nationally recognized, validated assessment tool, to be addicted to or dependent on drugs. However, no such drug court treatment program shall limit its participation to first-time substance abuse offenders only; nor shall it exclude probation violators from participation.

"3. The evaluation of drug treatment court programs required by § 18.2-254.1 shall include the collection of data needed for outcome measures, including recidivism. Drug treatment court programs shall provide to the Office of the Executive Secretary of the Supreme Court the information needed to conduct such an evaluation."

The 2009 amendments.
The 2009 amendments by cc. 205 and 281 are identical, and added subsection Q.
The 2009 amendment by c. 294 added subsection R.
The 2009 amendments by cc. 813 and 840 are identical, and substituted "Behavioral Health and Developmental Services" for

"Mental Health, Mental Retardation and Substance Abuse Services" in the second sentence of subsection F, and in clause (viii) of subsection G.

The 2010 amendments.
The 2010 amendment by c. 258 inserted "City of Bristol and the" in subsection R.

Law Review.
For essay, "The Chesterfield/Colonial Heights Drug Court: A Partnership Between the Criminal Justice System and the Treatment Community," see 43 U. Rich. L. Rev. 5 (2008).

CASE NOTES

Failure to raise issue at trial barred consideration on appeal. — Trial court did not err in failing to reverse defendant's termination from a drug court program because defendant's contention that the termination violated defendant's due process rights under the Fourteenth Amendment was procedurally barred by Va. Sup. Ct. R. 5A:18 where the trial court did not have the opportunity to address that contention. Harris v. Commonwealth, — Va. App. —, — S.E.2d —, 2009 Va. App. LEXIS 90 (Mar. 10, 2009).

§ 18.2-255. Distribution of certain drugs to persons under 18 prohibited; penalty.

A. Except as authorized in the Drug Control Act, Chapter 34 (§ 54.1-3400 et seq.) of Title 54.1, it shall be unlawful for any person who is at least 18 years of age to knowingly or intentionally (i) distribute any drug classified in Schedule I, II, III or IV, marijuana or synthetic cannabinoids to any person under 18 years of age who is at least three years his junior or (ii) cause any person under 18 years of age to assist in such distribution of any drug classified in Schedule I, II, III or IV, marijuana or synthetic cannabinoids. Any person violating this provision shall upon conviction be imprisoned in a state correctional facility for a period not less than 10 nor more than 50 years, and fined not more than $100,000. Five years of the sentence imposed for a conviction under this section involving a Schedule I or II controlled substance or one ounce or more of marijuana shall be a mandatory minimum sentence. Two years of the sentence imposed for a conviction under this section involving synthetic cannabinoids or involving less than one ounce of marijuana shall be a mandatory minimum sentence.

B. It shall be unlawful for any person who is at least 18 years of age to knowingly or intentionally (i) distribute any imitation controlled substance to a person under 18 years of age who is at least three years his junior or (ii) cause any person under 18 years of age to assist in such distribution of any imitation controlled substance. Any person violating this provision shall be guilty of a Class 6 felony.

History.
Code 1950, § 54-524.103; 1970, c. 650; 1972, c. 798; 1975, cc. 14, 15; 1976, c. 614; 1979, c. 435; 1982, c. 462; 1990, cc. 720, 864, 866; 1992, cc. 708, 724; 2000, cc. 1020, 1041; 2004, c. 461; 2011, cc. 384, 410.

Editor's note.
Acts 2011, cc. 384 and 410, cl. 3 provides: "That the provisions of this act may result in a net increase in periods of imprisonment or

commitment. Pursuant to § 30-19.1:4, the estimated amount of the necessary appropriation cannot be determined for periods of imprisonment in state adult correctional facilities; therefore, Chapter 874 of the Acts of Assembly of 2010 requires the Virginia Criminal Sentencing Commission to assign a minimum fiscal impact of $50,000. Pursuant to § 30-19.1:4, the estimated amount of the necessary appropriation cannot be determined for periods of commitment to the custody of the Department of Juvenile Justice."

The 2011 amendments.

The 2011 amendments by cc. 384 and 410, effective March 23, 2011, are identical, and in subsection A, substituted "marijuana or synthetic cannabinoids" for "or, marijuana" in clauses (i) and (ii) of the first sentence, and inserted "synthetic cannabinoids or involving" in the last sentence.

Michie's Jurisprudence.

For related discussion, see 9B M.J. Infants, § 90.

CASE NOTES

Authenticated court order reliable evidence of juvenile status. — The recommended and customary practice of circuit courts in determining and recording in the authenticated conviction order a criminal defendant's age or date of birth gives the recorded fact sufficient reliability and trustworthiness to render the order competent to prove accomplice's age in prosecution under this section. Parker v. Commonwealth, No. 0406-93-1 (Ct. of Appeals Aug. 16, 1994).

No requirement that defendant know age of drug purchaser. — Trial court was correct in refusing to grant defendant's motion to strike the charge of knowing or intentional distribution of cocaine to persons under 18 years of age even though defendant did not have actual knowledge of drug purchaser's age; the Commonwealth was required to prove that the defendant knowingly or intentionally distributed a controlled drug, and the statute does not require proof that the defendant knew the age of his drug purchaser. Pannell v. Commonwealth, 9 Va. App. 170, 384 S.E.2d 344 (1989).

Proof of age of purchaser. — The trial court did not err in allowing the Commonwealth to prove the age of the juvenile to whom the defendant sold cocaine by means of his driving record, and it was not necessary to call the juvenile in order to establish his age. Hurley v. Commonwealth, No. 2794-97-3 (Ct. of Appeals Mar. 2, 1999).

"Distribute." — Defendant was guilty of distributing controlled substance to a minor because he accomplished an actual transfer of drug to her, and fact that minor possessed drug for only a brief period of time did not undermine or diminish fact that she actually possessed it. Morris v. Commonwealth, No. 1141-98-4 (Ct. of Appeals Nov. 9, 1999).

Attempt to distribute marijuana. — Where evidence showed: (1) discussions were held on three separate occasions between defendant/seller and juvenile/purchaser regarding when and how much marijuana could be obtained; (2) parties met at a prearranged location for transfer of marijuana; (3) defendant/seller had some marijuana on hand; (4) but a misunderstanding regarding the amount of drugs to be sold prevented consummation of the sale, evidence was sufficient to prove that defendant intended and attempted to distribute marijuana to juvenile for further distribution. Wescoat v. Commonwealth, No. 1256-98-2 (Ct. of Appeals Feb. 15, 2000).

Parent giving prescription drug to child. — Parent's conviction for giving a controlled substance that had been prescribed for her to her minor children was upheld where the defendant told a detective that she gave the medication to her children in orange juice, described the specific amount she gave to each child and said that she knew that the dosage she gave the children would not harm them but would make them drowsy, and where the corroborating testimony of the children was that the defendant gave them pills mixed with orange juice and one child stated that she had told him that the drug would make him sleepy and take things off his mind. Moellar v. Commonwealth, No. 2896-99-1, 2000 Va. App. LEXIS 685 (Ct. of Appeals Oct. 3, 2000).

Hearsay testimony as to defendant's age was harmless. — Defendant's challenge to an arresting officer's hearsay testimony as to defendant's age for purposes of this section was harmless as defense counsel conceded that defendant identified his date of birth during the preliminary proceedings; further, defendant's presence during the trial afforded the trial court an opportunity to determine defendant's approximate age. Eley v. Va., No. 1776-03-1, 2004 Va. App. LEXIS 532 (Ct. of Appeals Nov. 9, 2004).

Juvenile court petition was properly admitted as evidence of a minor's age for purposes of § 18.2-255 conviction as the legislature had determined that official records were admissible as prima facie evidence if properly authenticated; defendant did not challenge the authenticity of the petition or contend that it was not an official or judicial record. Eley v. Va., No. 1776-03-1, 2004 Va. App. LEXIS 532 (Ct. of Appeals Nov. 9, 2004).

Sufficiency of the evidence. — Where the evidence reflected that defendant's accomplice was a minor and that the cocaine found in a vehicle was given to the driver by the accomplice, who received it from defendant, the evidence was sufficient to support defendant's convictions for possession and distribution of cocaine. Battle v. Commonwealth, No. 2934-02-1, 2004 Va. App. LEXIS 124 (Ct. of Appeals Mar. 23, 2004).

There was sufficient evidence to sustain defendant's convictions for violating § 18.2-255 for knowingly giving defendant's daughter and her friend morphine and another drug. Symptoms experienced by the daughter and her friend were consistent with the side effects often experienced after taking those drugs, according to a toxicologist. Wiley v. Commonwealth, — Va. App. —, — S.E.2d —, 2008 Va. App. LEXIS 106 (Mar. 4, 2008).

Venue. — Because causing a juvenile to assist in the distribution of marijuana in violation of clause (ii) of subsection A of § 18.2-255 was a continuing offense, venue was proper in the county where the juvenile sold the marijuana pursuant to § 19.2-244. Kelso v. Commonwealth, 57 Va. App. 30, 698 S.E.2d 263, 2010 Va. App. LEXIS 350 (2010), aff'd, 282 Va. 134, 710 S.E.2d 470, 2011 Va. LEXIS 128 (2011).

Venue over charges for three counts of causing a juvenile to assist in the distribution of marijuana to a third party, in violation of clause (ii) of subsection A of § 18.2-255, was proper in Hanover County where the nature of the crime was not that of a continuing crime, but one in which different elements of a single crime occur in different jurisdictions, and the record clearly showed that the juvenile distributed the marijuana he received from defendant to a third party in Hanover County. Kelso v. Commonwealth, 282 Va. 134, 710 S.E.2d 470, 2011 Va. LEXIS 128 (2011).

§ 18.2-255.1. Distribution, sale or display of printed material advertising instruments for use in administering marijuana, synthetic cannabinoids, or controlled substances to minors; penalty.

It shall be a Class 1 misdemeanor for any person knowingly to sell, distribute, or display for sale to a minor any book, pamphlet, periodical or other printed matter which he knows advertises for sale any instrument, device, article, or contrivance for advertised use in unlawfully ingesting, smoking, administering, preparing or growing marijuana, synthetic cannabinoids, or a controlled substance.

History.

1980, c. 737; 2011, cc. 384, 410.

Editor's note.

Acts 2011, cc. 384 and 410, cl. 3 provides: "That the provisions of this act may result in a net increase in periods of imprisonment or commitment. Pursuant to § 30-19.1:4, the estimated amount of the necessary appropriation cannot be determined for periods of imprisonment in state adult correctional facilities; therefore, Chapter 874 of the Acts of Assembly of 2010 requires the Virginia Criminal Sentencing Commission to assign a minimum fiscal impact of $50,000. Pursuant to § 30-19.1:4, the estimated amount of the necessary appropriation cannot be determined for periods of commitment to the custody of the Department of Juvenile Justice."

The 2011 amendments.

The 2011 amendments by cc. 384 and 410, effective March 23, 2011, are identical, and inserted "synthetic cannabinoids."

Law Review.

For note on the policing of head shops, see Wash. & Lee L. Rev. 183 (1981).

§ 18.2-255.2. Prohibiting the sale or manufacture of drugs on or near certain properties; penalty.

A. It shall be unlawful for any person to manufacture, sell or distribute or possess with intent to sell, give or distribute any controlled substance, imitation controlled substance, marijuana or synthetic cannabinoids while:

1. Upon the property, including buildings and grounds, of any public or private elementary, secondary, or post secondary school, or any public or private two-year or four-year institution of higher education, or any clearly marked licensed child day center as defined in § 63.2-100;

2. Upon public property or any property open to public use within 1,000 feet of the property described in subdivision 1;

3. On any school bus as defined in § 46.2-100;

4. Upon a designated school bus stop, or upon either public property or any property open to public use which is within 1,000 feet of such school bus stop, during the time when school children are waiting to be picked up and transported to or are being dropped off from school or a school-sponsored activity;

5. Upon the property, including buildings and grounds, of any publicly owned or publicly operated recreation or community center facility or any public library; or

6. Upon the property of any state facility as defined in § 37.2-100 or upon public property or property open to public use within 1,000 feet of such an institution. It is a violation of the provisions of this section if the person possessed the controlled substance, imitation controlled substance, marijuana or synthetic cannabinoids on the property described in subdivisions 1 through 6, regardless of where the person intended to sell, give or distribute the controlled substance, imitation controlled substance, marijuana, or synthetic cannabinoids. Nothing in this section shall prohibit the authorized distribution of controlled substances.

B. Violation of this section shall constitute a separate and distinct felony. Any person violating the provisions of this section shall, upon conviction, be imprisoned for a term of not less than one year nor more than five years and fined not more than $100,000. A second or subsequent conviction hereunder for an offense involving a controlled substance classified in Schedule I, II, or III of the Drug Control Act (§ 54.1-3400 et seq.) or synthetic cannabinoids or more than one-half ounce of marijuana shall be punished by a mandatory minimum term of imprisonment of one year to be served consecutively with any other sentence. However, if such person proves that he sold such controlled substance, marijuana, or synthetic cannabinoids only as an accommodation to another individual and not with intent to profit thereby from any consideration received or expected nor to induce the recipient or intended recipient of the controlled substance, marijuana, or synthetic cannabinoids to use or become addicted to or dependent upon such controlled substance, marijuana, or synthetic cannabinoids, he shall be guilty of a Class 1 misdemeanor.

C. If a person commits an act violating the provisions of this section, and the same act also violates another provision of law that provides for penalties greater than those provided for by this section, then nothing in this section shall prohibit or bar any prosecution or proceeding under that other provision of law or the imposition of any penalties provided for thereby.

History.

1982, c. 594; 1989, cc. 619, 682, 709; 1990, cc. 617, 622; 1991, c. 268; 1991, 1st Sp. Sess., c. 14; 1993, cc. 30, 708, 729; 1999, c. 873; 2000, cc. 1020, 1041; 2003, cc. 80, 91; 2004, c. 461; 2005, c. 716; 2006, c. 325; 2011, cc. 384, 410.

Editor's note.

Acts 2011, cc. 384 and 410, cl. 3 provides: "That the provisions of this act may result in a net increase in periods of imprisonment or commitment. Pursuant to § 30-19.1:4, the estimated amount of the necessary appropriation cannot be determined for periods of imprisonment in state adult correctional facilities; therefore, Chapter 874 of the Acts of Assembly of 2010 requires the Virginia Criminal Sentencing Commission to assign a minimum fiscal impact of $50,000. Pursuant to § 30-19.1:4, the estimated amount of the necessary appropriation cannot be determined for periods of commitment to the custody of the Department of Juvenile Justice."

The 2011 amendments.

The 2011 amendments by cc. 384 and 410, effective March 23, 2011, are identical, and in subsection A, substituted "marijuana or synthetic cannabinoids" for "or, marijuana" in the introductory language, redesignated former clauses (i) to (vi) as subdivisions 1 to 6, made related changes, and twice substituted "marijuana, or synthetic cannabinoids" for "or, marijuana" in the last sentence; in subsection B, inserted "synthetic cannabinoids" four times; and made minor stylistic changes.

Law Review.

For survey on legal issues involving children in Virginia for 1989, see 23 U. Rich. L. Rev. 705 (1989). For article summarizing published Virginia criminal law decisions between July 1, 2002 and July 1, 2003, see 38 U. Rich. L. Rev. 87 (2003).

CASE NOTES

Intent requirement defined. — This section does not state that it prohibits possession of a controlled substance while upon school property, or within 1,000 feet thereof, with the intent to sell, give, or distribute the substance elsewhere. Toliver v. Commonwealth, 38 Va. App. 27, 561 S.E.2d 743, 2002 Va. App. LEXIS 191 (2002).

Defendant's conviction of possession of a controlled substance with the intent to distribute within 1,000 feet of school property, this section was not supported by sufficient evidence, because the statute did not prohibit possession on school property with intent to distribute elsewhere, and the Commonwealth failed to present any evidence indicating that defendant intended to distribute drugs on or within 1,000 feet of school property, as defendant only came within the specified distance of the school while being chased by police. Toliver v. Commonwealth, 38 Va. App. 27, 561 S.E.2d 743, 2002 Va. App. LEXIS 191 (2002).

"Property." — This section does not limit the word "property" to the term "campus"; therefore, arrest for possession of marijuana which took place within 1,000 feet of Hampton University property fell under this section. Hughes v. Commonwealth, 33 Va. App. 405, 533 S.E.2d 649, 2000 Va. App. LEXIS 648 (2000).

"Public property." — A public thoroughfare is "public property" under subdivision A(ii) of this section. Hughes v. Commonwealth, 33 Va. App. 405, 533 S.E.2d 649, 2000 Va. App. LEXIS 648 (2000).

"Property open to public use." — Given plain meaning and legislative intent of statute, "property open to public use" is not limited to property owned by or associated with state or local government; therefore trial court properly convicted defendant who sold cocaine to undercover agent in convenience store parking lot within 1,000 feet of a school. Smith v. Commonwealth, 26 Va. App. 620, 496 S.E.2d 117 (1998).

Although persons on private property owned by a housing authority could be cited for trespassing, that did not negate an officer's unequivocal testimony that the property was open to public use, as contemplated by § 18.2-255.2, to those who followed the authority's rules. The high drug area was not inaccessible to the public and participants had full access, and it was irrelevant whether children were likely to congregate there. Parker v. Commonwealth, — Va. App. —, — S.E.2d —, 2008 Va. App. LEXIS 223 (May 6, 2008).

Meaning of the phrase "property open to public use" in § 18.2-255.2 has never been interpreted by an appellate court, most likely due to the relatively clear import of its language. Parker v. Commonwealth, — Va. App. —, — S.E.2d —, 2008 Va. App. LEXIS 223 (May 6, 2008).

Defendant's convictions of one count of possessing marijuana and one count of possessing cocaine with intent to distribute within 1,000 feet of a school while upon public property or property open to public use in violation of § 18.2-255.2 were affirmed because the parking lot where defendant possessed the drugs was property open to the public. The parking lot was readily accessible to members of the public and there was no evidence of any posted restrictions on accessing the parking lot. Fullwood v. Commonwealth, 279 Va. 531, 689 S.E.2d 742, 2010 Va. LEXIS 39 (2010).

Section creates separate and distinct felony with additional punishment. — This section creates no presumptions, but rather, creates a separate and distinct felony, with additional punishment. Commonwealth v. Burns, 240 Va. 171, 395 S.E.2d 456 (1990).

Due process does not bar application when school not in session. — Due process does not bar the application of this section to a sale of cocaine made within the prescribed distance when school is not in session and no children are present. Commonwealth v. Burns, 240 Va. 171, 395 S.E.2d 456 (1990).

Legislative finding that threat present whether or not school in session. — Implicit in the General Assembly's enactment of this section is the legislative finding that the threat of harm to children is present whether or not school is in session, school-related activities are being held, or children are present when drug transactions take place within 1,000 feet of a school. By its finding, the General Assembly has settled once and for all that such drug transactions do cause harm to children, whether or not children are present when the transactions take place. Commonwealth v. Burns, 240 Va. 171, 395 S.E.2d 456 (1990).

There was no merit to defendant's argument that, since he was in a moving vehicle and his arrest occurred after eleven o'clock at night, he did not violate intent of statute prohibiting possession of cocaine with intent to distribute within 1,000 feet of a school. Williams v. Commonwealth, No. 1156-98-1 (Ct. of Appeals Sept. 21, 1999).

Double jeopardy. — Two convictions for possession of drugs with intent to distribute within 1,000 feet of a school under § 18.2-255.2 did not violate the Double Jeopardy Clause under U.S. Const., Amend. V and Va. Const., Art. I, § 8 as marijuana and cocaine were treated in the Virginia Code as separate and discrete illegal substances under §§ 18.2-250, 18.2-250.1, and 54.1-3448. Fullwood v. Commonwealth, 54 Va. App. 153, 676 S.E.2d 348, 2009 Va. App. LEXIS 224 (2009), aff'd, 279 Va. 531, 689 S.E.2d 742, 2010 Va. LEXIS 39 (2010).

Defendant's convictions of one count of possessing marijuana and one count of possessing cocaine with intent to distribute within 1,000 feet of a school while upon public property or property open to public use in violation of § 18.2-255.2 did not violate his rights against double jeopardy because there was one transaction involving marijuana in defendant's encounter in the parking lot with a driver of the pickup truck and a second transaction involving cocaine in defendant's meeting in the parking lot with the driver wearing a Hoyas jacket. Fullwood v. Commonwealth, 279 Va. 531, 689 S.E.2d 742, 2010 Va. LEXIS 39 (2010).

Evidence sufficient to support conviction. — Defendant's motion to strike the evidence was properly denied as the evidence was sufficient to support defendant's conviction of possession of heroin with the intent to distribute, second or subsequent offense, in violation of § 18.2-248, and possession with the intent to distribute heroin within 1,000 feet of school property, where: (1) defendant's claim that he could have been taking something out of the girl's pocket when the officer approached was rejected; (2) defendant's nervousness and heavy breathing allowed the reasonable inference that defendant knew he possessed illegal drugs; (3) the Commonwealth's expert testified that the amount of heroin, the lack of devices to ingest the heroin, and defendant's unemployment, made his possession of 49 capsules, worth approximately $500, inconsistent with personal use; and (4) the quantity of heroin, alone, was sufficient to support the conviction. Walker v. Commonwealth, 42 Va. App. 782, 595 S.E.2d 30, 2004 Va. App. LEXIS 169 (2004).

Evidence supported a finding that defendant supplied the heroin sold to an officer as: (1) if the runner possessed heroin when the runner approached the officer, the runner would have immediately sold it to the officer, and there would have been no reason for the runner to interact with defendant; (2) there was a hand-to-hand transaction between the runner and defendant; and (3) the runner immediately went to the officer's car, and sold the officer the heroin. Peoples v. Commonwealth, — Va. App. —, — S.E.2d —, 2007 Va. App. LEXIS 403 (Nov. 6, 2007).

Testimony by a police detective that 7.5 grams of cocaine in five bags recovered from defendant was inconsistent with personal use based on the amount in bags and fact that cocaine was packaged in plastic bag corners was sufficient to show that defendant possessed the cocaine with the intent to distribute and supported defendant's conviction for possession of cocaine with the intent to distribute on public property within 1,000 feet of a day care center in violation of § 18.2-255.2. Wyatt v. Commonwealth, — Va. App. —, — S.E.2d —, 2009 Va. App. LEXIS 53 (Feb. 10, 2009).

Defendant's convictions for possession of cocaine with intent to distribute near school property, in violation of § 18.2-255.2, was supported by sufficient evidence as the evidence showed that eleven small, plastic baggies containing crack cocaine were found on defendant. A rational fact finder could conclude that defendant possessed the crack cocaine with intent to distribute as, though defendant claimed that he intended only to smoke the drugs, he had no user paraphernalia and no lighter, match, or other igniter for burning the crack, and defendant could not recall the name of the dealer from whom he purchased the crack. Barnes v. Commonwealth, — Va. App. —, — S.E.2d —, 2009 Va. App. LEXIS 66 (Feb. 10, 2009).

Evidence supported defendant's § 18.2-255.2 conviction as: (1) a motel room was filled with a quantity of both powdered and crack cocaine, glasses, jars, and spoons used in mixing the cocaine, and papers on which the newly manufactured crack cocaine had been set out to dry in plain view; (2) a gym bag containing glasses and spoons of the kind used in the manufacture of crack cocaine and a manila envelope bearing defendant's name was also in the room; (3) defendant was only a few feet away from the contraband; and (4) defendant had to have walked into the motel room, past a large quantity of drugs and paraphernalia, to reach the bed in which defendant was sleeping. Adkins v. Commonwealth, 2009 Va. App. LEXIS 336 (July 28, 2009).

Defendant's conviction for possession with intent to distribute heroin within 1,000 feet of school property was not reversed when officers used an aerial photograph when testifying that the place where defendant was observed distributing heroin was within 1,000 feet of school property because, if markings on the photograph showing the limits of school property were hearsay, the admission of the testimony of an officer who did not rely on a means other than the markings to establish that defendant was within 1,000 feet of school property was harmless error, as the testimony was cumulative of the testimony of another officer who did rely on other means. Bynum v. Commonwealth, 57 Va. App. 487, 704 S.E.2d 131, 2011 Va. App. LEXIS 16 (2011).

Defendant's conviction for possession with intent to distribute heroin within 1,000 feet of school property was not reversed when officers used an aerial photograph when testifying that the place where defendant was observed distributing heroin was within 1,000 feet of school property because, if markings on the photograph showing the limits of school property were hearsay, the officers did not rely on the markings, as an officer testified that the officer was able to testify as to the distance between the school boundary and the point where defendant was observed with heroin without relying on the markings. Bynum v. Commonwealth, 57 Va. App. 487, 704 S.E.2d 131, 2011 Va. App. LEXIS 16 (2011).

Defendant's conviction for possession with intent to distribute heroin within 1,000 feet of school property was not reversed when officers used an aerial photograph when testifying that the place where defendant was observed distributing heroin was within 1,000 feet of school property because the photograph was not hearsay as there was no out-of-court declarant, as an aerial photograph of a geographic area was not the repetition of prior recorded human input or observation, nor was the photograph the recordation or compilation of another human being's assertions or a communication of input from another person but was simply a technological reproduction of an existing reality, so the photograph's reliability did not depend on an out-of-court declarant's veracity or perceptive abilities, and a witness using the photograph was not "reading" the "assertions" of an out-of-court declarant. Bynum v. Commonwealth, 57 Va. App. 487, 704 S.E.2d 131, 2011 Va. App. LEXIS 16 (2011).

Sufficiency of the evidence. — Where the evidence reflected that defendant's accomplice was a minor and that the cocaine found in a vehicle was given to the driver by the accomplice, who received it from defendant, the evidence was sufficient to support defendant's convictions for possession and distribution of cocaine. Battle v. Commonwealth, No. 2934-02-1, 2004 Va. App. LEXIS 124 (Ct. of Appeals Mar. 23, 2004).

Applied in Copeland v. Commonwealth, 42 Va. App. 424, 592 S.E.2d 391, 2004 Va. App. LEXIS 62 (2004).

CIRCUIT COURT OPINIONS

"Property open to public use." — While possession of drugs inside a house is illegal, the interior of the house, although it may be located within 1,000 feet of school property, is not what is meant by "property open to public use;" therefore, the there was insufficient to convict defendant of a second firearm charge and the possession of drugs with intent to distribute within 1,000 feet of a school. Commonwealth v. Capers, 57 Va. Cir. 79, 2001 Va. Cir. LEXIS 521 (Norfolk 2001).

§ 18.2-256. Conspiracy.

Any person who conspires to commit any offense defined in this article or in the Drug Control Act (§ 54.1-3400 et seq.) is punishable by imprisonment or fine or both which may not be less than the minimum punishment nor exceed the maximum punishment prescribed for the offense, the commission of which was the object of the conspiracy.

History.
Code 1950, § 54-524.104; 1970, c. 650; 1972, c. 798; 1975, cc. 14, 15; 1978, c. 130.

Cross references.
As to exception of offenses defined in this chapter from the provisions of the general statute governing conspiracy to commit felony, see § 18.2-22 (d).

Law Review.
For survey of Virginia criminal law for the year 1972-1973, see 59 Va. L. Rev. 1458 (1973).

CASE NOTES

A single agreement can form the basis for multiple violations of this section. Otherwise, criminals would be encouraged to plot a number of drug-related crimes simultaneously, because only one conspiracy would exist. This could not have been the intention of the General Assembly. Wooten v. Commonwealth, 235 Va. 89, 368 S.E.2d 693 (1988).

Proof. — Existence of conspiracy to distribute between seller and buyer, has been proved if, evidence demonstrates: (1) that seller knows buyer's intended illegal use; and (2) that by the sale the seller intends to further, promote and cooperate in venture. Zuniga v. Commonwealth, 7 Va. App. 523, 375 S.E.2d 381 (1988).

Second element of conspiracy to distribute must be proved since not every instance of sale of restricted goods, harmful as are opiates, in which seller knows buyer intends to use them unlawfully, will support charge of conspiracy, and proof of second element establishes necessary preconcert and connivance which places conduct beyond aiding and abetting. Zuniga v. Commonwealth, 7 Va. App. 523, 375 S.E.2d 381 (1988).

Defendant need only know essential nature of conspiracy. — Where defendant knew that coconspirator was planning to go into Virginia to sell narcotics and that sale would enable coconspirator to return following night and pay amount advanced on credit evidence for conspiracy to distribute cocaine did not need to show defendant knew entire scope or details of plan of distribution; evidence needed only to show that he knew of essential nature of scheme. Zuniga v. Commonwealth, 7 Va. App. 523, 375 S.E.2d 381 (1988).

No need to prove sustained course of conduct in conspiracy. — Where case involved conspiracy to distribute cocaine, although evidence did not establish that there was "regular, sustained and prolonged" course of conduct between defendant and coconspirator, such course of conduct did not need to be proved, since commodity was per se unlawful. Zuniga v. Commonwealth, 7 Va. App. 523, 375 S.E.2d 381 (1988).

Conspiring with police officer and officer's informant. — An accused may not be convicted under this section for conspiring to distribute cocaine with a police officer and the officer's confidential informant. Fortune v. Commonwealth, 12 Va. App. 643, 406 S.E.2d 47 (1991).

Conspiring with informant who was agent of police. — The evidence was insufficient to prove the existence of a conspiracy between appellant and A. During both transactions for which appellant with charged with conspiracy, A was working as a confidential informant — an agent of the police. Because A was not a "bona fide co-conspirator," there could be no "meeting of the minds" as a matter of law between him and appellant to distribute heroin to detective. Levi v. Commonwealth, No. 2640-96-2 (Ct. of Appeals Sept. 16, 1997).

Evidence of acts of co-conspirators. — Where the Commonwealth's evidence established a prima facie case of conspiracy, the trial court did not err in admitting evidence of acts of co-conspirators in furtherance of that conspiracy. Barber v. Commonwealth, 5 Va. App. 172, 360 S.E.2d 888 (1987).

Evidence of another conspiracy was properly admitted to prove defendant's intent and to show that both conspiracies were part of a common scheme or plan. Barber v. Commonwealth, 5 Va. App. 172, 360 S.E.2d 888 (1987).

Evidence that defendants constructively possessed cocaine was probative of the object of the conspiracy. Hodge v. Commonwealth, 7 Va. App. 351, 374 S.E.2d 76 (1988).

Acts in furtherance of conspiracy held shown. — Where each transaction involved defendant, alleged co-conspirator, and others and occurred at approximately the same time, and resulted in the commingling of the two loads of marijuana, the nature and scope of the activities set forth in the indictment involved the identical offenses of possession and distribution of marijuana, a pattern of mutual cooperation took place among the various parties, and both transactions involved an agreement between defendant and alleged co-conspirator in which alleged co-conspirator agreed to store marijuana for defendant until defendant distributed it, the evidence was sufficient as a matter of law to establish that the activities relating to the marijuana obtained from another alleged co-conspirator's residence were acts in furtherance of a single conspiracy. Barber v. Commonwealth, 5 Va. App. 172, 360 S.E.2d 888 (1987).

All drug conspiracies not same. — The legislature, in enacting this section, determined that all drug conspiracies are not the same. Conspiracies to commit more serious drug offenses are to be punished more severely. Wooten v. Commonwealth, 235 Va. 89, 368 S.E.2d 693 (1988).

In order to convict defendant of conspiring to distribute a controlled drug, the Commonwealth had to prove beyond a reasonable doubt that an agreement existed between the two men by some concerted action to distribute the drugs. Reed v. Commonwealth, 213 Va. 593, 194 S.E.2d 746 (1973). See Johnson v. Commonwealth, 42 Va. App. 46, 590 S.E.2d 75, 2003 Va. App. LEXIS 673 (2003).

Chain of custody established. — Trial court properly admitted into evidence two certificates of analysis as evidence of the chain of custody of the drugs seized during the drug sales under § 19.2-187.01 in defendant's trial for possession with intent to distribute under § 18.2-248, and conspiring to distribute a controlled substance under § 18.2-256 where: (1) the initials on the postal receipts matched those on the Request for Laboratory Examination; (2) a police officer mailed the narcotics to the Virginia Division of Forensic Science, which verified its receipt by executing the Request for Laboratory Examination; (3) the receipt alone established prima facie evidence of the chain of custody; and (4) that the initials on the postal receipts were not consistent with the signatures on the two Requests for Laboratory Examination did not undermine the statutory inference under § 19.2-187.01. Martin v. Commonwealth, No. 1221-02-2, 2003 Va. App. LEXIS 341 (Ct. of Appeals June 17, 2003).

Evidence of prior bad acts. — Defendant's convictions for possession with intent to distribute marijuana under § 18.2-248.1 and conspiracy to distribute marijuana under §§ 18.2-256 and 18.2-248.1 were proper because the trial court did not abuse its discretion in admitting evidence of defendant's other bad acts as part of a common scheme or plan to support his current convictions. The evidence was relevant and admissible to show a course of conduct entered into by defendant to sell marijuana through his middleman and it proved that he committed similar acts with similar results. Pinnix v. Commonwealth, 2011 Va. App. LEXIS 149 (May 3, 2011).

Proof of agreement to distribute. — Where the indictment charged defendant with a conspiracy to distribute more than one-half ounce of marijuana, one of the felonies defined in § 18.2-248.1, the Commonwealth was required to prove an agreement to distribute a proscribed substance and to prove both the identity and the quantity of the substance contemplated by the agreement. Graves v. Commonwealth, 234 Va. 578, 363 S.E.2d 705 (1988).

Accomplice testimony was sufficiently corroborated to support conviction. — An accomplice's testimony was sufficiently corroborated by a police investigator and a confidential informant who taped a sales transaction. Johnson v. Commonwealth, 42 Va. App. 46, 590 S.E.2d 75, 2003 Va. App. LEXIS 673 (2003).

Evidence held sufficient to support conviction of conspiracy to sell, give, or distribute cocaine in violation of § 18.2-248 and this section. Hodge v. Commonwealth, 7 Va. App. 351, 374 S.E.2d 76 (1988); Gonzales-Loya v. Commonwealth, No. 1670-99-4, 2000 Va. App. LEXIS 458 (Ct. of Appeals June 20, 2000).

Both parts of the Zuniga test (see *Zuniga v. Commonwealth,* 7 Va. App. 523, 375 S.E.2d 381 (1988)) for determining the presence of a conspiracy in a sale of a controlled substance were met where from the two statements the defendant made during the transaction concerning his knowledge of what partner intended to do with the marijuana and his expectation of sharing in the profits of partner's sale of the marijuana. Edwards v. Commonwealth, 18 Va. App. 45, 441 S.E.2d 351 (1994).

Evidence was sufficient to support defendant's conviction of aiding and abetting prescription fraud in violation of § 18.2-258.1 where: (1) defendant's girlfriend falsely told the pharmacist that she had not had received the pain medication, including a Schedule II controlled substance under § 54.1-3448, and the pharmacist relied on the misrepresentation when she refilled them, which constituted prescription fraud under clauses (i) and (iii) of subsection A of § 18.2-258.1; (2) defendant was present at the time, and incited, encouraged, advised, or assisted in the crime; (3) defendant was with his girlfriend on both occasions that the prescriptions

were filled, stood silently beside her when she lied about having not received them, and injected himself into the conversation, in a belligerent and distracting manner, when the pharmacist attempted to find out the truth; and (4) defendant said nothing when they were given a second set of medications, which they used to "get high" as soon as they got home. Comeau v. Commonwealth, No. 1290-02-2, 2003 Va. App. LEXIS 342 (Ct. of Appeals June 17, 2003).

Defendant's convictions for distribution of cocaine and conspiracy to distribute cocaine were affirmed because sufficient evidence, in the form of the intermediaries testimony and telephone logs, supported the jury's finding that defendant was guilty of distribution of cocaine and conspiracy to distribute cocaine through sales by the intermediaries to an undercover officer on defendant's behalf. Franco v. Commonwealth, No. 0222-03-4, 2004 Va. App. LEXIS 73 (Ct. of Appeals Feb. 10, 2004).

Defendant's convictions for conspiracy to distribute cocaine under §§ 18.2-248 and 18.2-256 were affirmed; the evidence established that defendant's associate and defendant conspired to distribute cocaine to an undercover police officer, and the jury could reasonably infer from a detective's testimony and use of the term "employ" that there was an agreement between the associate and defendant that the associate would provide certain services for defendant. Walker v. Commonwealth, — Va. App. —, — S.E.2d —, 2006 Va. App. LEXIS 491 (Oct. 31, 2006).

Evidence was sufficient to support defendant's conviction for conspiring to distribute methamphetamine in violation of § 18.2-256. Circumstantial evidence in the case showed that: (1) defendant knew that an acquaintance had placed drugs in a manila envelope at defendant's house because defendant promised to safeguard the contents, methamphetamine, with defendant's life; (2) defendant knew that the acquaintance intended to distribute the methamphetamine in the envelope given the markings the acquaintance made on the envelope; and (3) defendant acted in concert with the acquaintance to aid in the methamphetamine distribution. Brown v. Commonwealth, — Va. App. —, — S.E.2d —, 2008 Va. App. LEXIS 121 (Mar. 11, 2008).

Conviction for conspiracy to possess ecstasy with intent to distribute was supported by evidence that defendant served as the "muscle" or "lookout" in a drug transportation scheme, that defendant arrived at the bus depot to meet a bus from New York for the purpose of providing security as the drugs were removed from a bus and carried to a vehicle, there were numerous phone calls between defendant and two others involved, and defendant received money via wire while in New York days before the transaction. Merritt v. Commonwealth, 57 Va. App. 542, 704 S.E.2d 158, 2011 Va. App. LEXIS 25 (2011).

Circumstantial evidence supported defendant's convictions for conspiracy to distribute drugs in violation of §§ 18.2-256 and 18.2-248 because a reasonable fact-finder could conclude that defendant and her boyfriend agreed to meet an informant in order to sell him cocaine and that defendant's part in the conspiracy was neither innocent nor inadvertent; On two separate occasions defendant drove her boyfriend to the same parking lot, where the boyfriend made a quick transaction with the informant, who had purchased drugs from him in the past. Foster v. Commonwealth, 2012 Va. App. LEXIS 310 (Oct. 2, 2012).

Evidence of conspiracy held insufficient. — In prosecution for violation of § 18.2-248 and this section sufficient evidence was not presented to establish prima facie case of conspiracy where Commonwealth introduced no evidence, direct or circumstantial, to prove existence of agreement between defendant and unidentified man apart from statements made by unidentified man, and where Commonwealth's independent evidence of conspiracy consisted merely of testimony that two men met on street corner for 15 to 20 seconds and their hands came together in air for three to five seconds. Poole v. Commonwealth, 7 Va. App. 510, 375 S.E.2d 371 (1988).

Evidence was insufficient to prove that defendant conspired to distribute cocaine where the evidence established only that he knew that others were selling out of his house, but failed to establish his prior agreement to participate in the offense; although defendant may have aided and abetted the distribution of cocaine, the evidence fell short of establishing the concert of action necessary for conspiracy. Yates, Jr. v. Commonwealth, No. 1962-97-2 (Ct. of Appeals June 30, 1998).

Defendant's conviction for conspiracy to distribute ecstasy was not supported by sufficient evidence where any inference that defendant shared the criminal intent of his companions to import ecstasy into the Commonwealth was based upon sheer speculation and certainly did not rise to the level of proof beyond a reasonable doubt. Merritt v. Commonwealth, 55 Va. App. 719, 689 S.E.2d 757, 2010 Va. App. LEXIS 81 (2010).

Insufficient evidence of conspiracy to distribute. — Neither the ongoing relationship between appellant and LSD buyer, nor the extension of credit from buyer to appellant, provided sufficient evidence with which the jury could have reasonably concluded that a conspiracy to distribute existed. The transactions between appellant and buyer simply lacked the essential element of an agreement between two parties to commit a subsequent distribution offense together. Hudak v. Commonwealth, 19 Va. App. 260, 450 S.E.2d 769 (1994).

Where evidence merely showed that appellant agreed to pick up the package at the bus station, that he picked up the package, that he suspected drugs, and that the package contained a large quantity of cocaine; no evidence proved that he agreed to distribute cocaine or that he was aware of the nature of the contents of the package; and no evidence proved that he had opened that package or any other package; the evidence was insufficient to support the conviction for conspiracy to distribute cocaine. Gaither v. Commonwealth, No. 0610-96-2 (Ct. of Appeals June 24, 1997).

Proof that defendant and another person sold drugs from the same house, standing alone, did not constitute a conspiracy, because evidence of a distribution offense absent an agreement could not suffice to support a conspiracy conviction. Harris v. Commonwealth, No. 2840-97-1 (Ct. of Appeals June 22, 1999).

Evidence was insufficient to support defendant's conviction for conspiracy to distribute cocaine because (1) when the police intercepted a package, which they suspected of containing contraband, at a FedEx distribution facility, a drug dog indicated the presence of illegal drugs in the package; (2) the police obtained a search warrant, opened the package, and discovered cocaine inside; (3) the police placed a small amount of the cocaine inside a new package and transferred the air bill that indicated the recipient and return addresses onto the new package; (4) a police officer disguised as a FedEx employee delivered the package to defendant's apartment; (5) defendant identified the recipient as defendant's cousin and accepted the package on behalf of the cousin; and (6) not long after, the police executed a search warrant and found defendant, the unopened package, and drug paraphernalia in the apartment. Thus, the evidence was insufficient to prove that defendant conspired with a second person to distribute cocaine because the evidence failed to demonstrate anything beyond a mere sale of drugs, which was legally insufficient to support the charge. Clark v. Commonwealth, 2011 Va. App. LEXIS 219 (July 5, 2011).

Insufficient evidence of knowledge of intended illegal use. — Where no testimony was introduced to prove buyer's level of personal consumption, how often he consumed LSD, how powerful one LSD dose is, how long unused LSD can be stored before it loses its potency, or why his purchase of 2,000 hits differed from the quantities purchased earlier in the year-long series of transactions, without more compelling evidence in the record, expert testimony on these issues was necessary to establish that appellant knew or should have known that buyer was distributing LSD. Hudak v. Commonwealth, 19 Va. App. 260, 450 S.E.2d 769 (1994).

Evidence of assistance insufficient to establish conspiracy. — While certain overt conduct may be sufficient to prove the existence of an agreement, simply proving the act of constructively possessing cocaine and assisting a person to sell it is not sufficient to establish a conspiracy. The evidence must show an agreement between the parties, and that is not shown by proving that one party decides or undertakes to assist the other. Woodley v. Commonwealth, No. 2122-93-2 (Ct. of Appeals Feb. 21, 1995).

Defendant not entitled to accommodation instruction. — Even assuming that the trial court's refusal to instruct the jury during the penalty phase of defendant's trial as to "accommodation conspiracy" on the charge against defendant of conspiracy to possess marijuana with intent to distribute was error, the error was harmless beyond a reasonable doubt; since the jury rejected an accommodation claim regarding the charge against defendant of possession of marijuana with intent to distribute, the appellate court could confidently conclude that the jury would have rejected an accommodation claim with regard to the "conspiracy to possess"

charge as well. McPherson v. Commonwealth, — Va. App. —, — S.E.2d —, 2006 Va. App. LEXIS 88 (Mar. 14, 2006).

Defendant's convictions for two counts of distribution of cocaine, third offense; three counts of distribution of marijuana; two counts of conspiracy to distribute cocaine, third offense; three counts of conspiracy to distribute marijuana; one count of possession of cocaine with intent to distribute; and one count of possession of marijuana with intent to distribute were proper because the trial court did not err in not instructing the jury on the lesser punishment of distribution for accommodation. In each transaction, the agent was the buyer, and not the cousin, who had only arranged the meetings for the agent; additionally, the fact that defendant did not make any money on the transactions was not dispositive. Martin v. Commonwealth, 2010 Va. App. LEXIS 205 (May 18, 2010).

Applied in Wolfe v. Commonwealth, 265 Va. 193, 576 S.E.2d 471, 2003 Va. LEXIS 32 (2003).

§ 18.2-257. Attempts.

(a) Any person who attempts to commit any offense defined in this article or in the Drug Control Act (§ 54.1-3400 et seq.) which is a felony shall be imprisoned for not less than one nor more than ten years; provided, however, that any person convicted of attempting to commit a felony for which a lesser punishment may be imposed may be punished according to such lesser penalty.

(b) Any person who attempts to commit any offense defined in this article or in the Drug Control Act which is a misdemeanor shall be guilty of a Class 2 misdemeanor; provided, however, that any person convicted of attempting to commit a misdemeanor for which a lesser punishment may be imposed may be punished according to such lesser penalty.

History.
Code 1950, § 54-524.104:1; 1972, c. 798; 1973, c. 447; 1975, cc. 14, 15; 1979, c. 435.

CASE NOTES

Proof. — In a prosecution for an attempt to commit a crime, the Commonwealth must prove the accused had a specific intent to commit that crime. Smith v. Commonwealth, 16 Va. App. 626, 432 S.E.2d 1 (1993).

Purchase of a noncontrolled substance that defendant subjectively believes to be a controlled substance can constitute an attempt to possess provided the government proves the defendant's subjective intent to purchase actual narcotics beyond a reasonable doubt. Smith v. Commonwealth, 16 Va. App. 626, 432 S.E.2d 1 (1993).

Second element of conspiracy to distribute must be proved since not every instance of sale of restricted goods, harmful as are opiates, in which seller knows buyer intends to use them unlawfully, will support charge of conspiracy, and proof of second element establishes necessary preconcert and connivance which places conduct beyond aiding and abetting. Zuniga v. Commonwealth, 7 Va. App. 523, 375 S.E.2d 381 (1988).

Defendant need only know essential nature of conspiracy. — Where defendant knew that coconspirator was planning to go into Virginia to sell narcotics and that sale would enable coconspirator to return following night and pay amount advanced on credit evidence for conspiracy to distribute cocaine did not need to show defendant knew entire scope or details of plan of distribution; evidence needed only to show that he knew of essential nature of scheme. Zuniga v. Commonwealth, 7 Va. App. 523, 375 S.E.2d 381 (1988).

No need to prove sustained course of conduct in conspiracy. — Where case involved conspiracy to distribute cocaine, although evidence did not establish that there was "regular, sustained and prolonged" course of conduct between defendant and coconspirator, such course of conduct did not need to be proved, since commodity was per se unlawful. Zuniga v. Commonwealth, 7 Va. App. 523, 375 S.E.2d 381 (1988).

Factual impossibility not a defense. — Where defendant had completed every act necessary for commission of the substantive crime, and the only reason the distribution was not a crime was a defect in the substance itself, which was unknown to defendant, the impossibility was clearly factual, not legal, and as such, could not be asserted as a defense to the attempted crime. Parham v. Commonwealth, 2 Va. App. 633, 347 S.E.2d 172 (1986).

No error in amendment which substituted this section for § 18.2-26. — Where prior to trial, the trial court granted the Commonwealth's motion to amend second count of indictment, and where the nature of the amendment changed the attempt statute on which the Commonwealth was relying from § 18.2-26, the general attempt statute, to this section, which covers attempts to violate the Drug Control Act, the trial court did not err in granting the Commonwealth's motion to amend the indictment against defendant. The amendment did not change the "nature or character of the offense charged"; it merely substituted reference to this section, the specific provision covering attempts to commit drug offenses, for § 18.2-26, the general provision covering attempts to commit general, non-capital felonies. Robinson v. Commonwealth, No. 1840-90-1 (Ct. of Appeals July 21, 1992).

Evidence held sufficient to prove second element. — Evidence demonstrated that by sale defendant intended to further, promote and cooperate in coconspirator's venture, where defendant had stake in venture because, by extending credit, defendant stood to make profits which came from encouragement of coconspirator's illicit operations. Zuniga v. Commonwealth, 7 Va. App. 523, 375 S.E.2d 381 (1988).

Where by selling cocaine to coconspirator and receiving partial payment of less than agreed price, defendant retained interest in and maintained continuing participation in coconspirator's venture, where by advancing cocaine on credit and insuring that coconspirator could perform his obligations, defendant actively became partner in venture, and where evidence supported finding that defendant was drug dealer who agreed to credit arrangement with coconspirator, another drug dealer, in hope of promoting future dealings, acts evinced agreement between and concert of action by parties sufficient to prove conspiracy beyond reasonable doubt. Zuniga v. Commonwealth, 7 Va. App. 523, 375 S.E.2d 381 (1988).

Sufficiency of the evidence. — Because the record clearly established that the term "twenty" referred to cocaine and not marijuana, the trial judge correctly found that a police video and a police officer's testimony were sufficient to convict defendant of attempted distribution of cocaine. Turner v. Commonwealth, — Va. App. —, — S.E.2d —, 2005 Va. App. LEXIS 368 (Sept. 27, 2005).

Illegal search. — Defendant's suppression motion was improperly denied as police searched defendant for illegal substances, not for weapons, in Terry stop, and were not following leads prior to their misconduct, making the doctrine of inevitable discovery inapplicable; the white powder found on defendant during the search should have been suppressed. Jones v. Commonwealth, No. 1077-02-2, 2003 Va. App. LEXIS 189 (Ct. of Appeals Apr. 1, 2003).

§ 18.2-258. Certain premises deemed common nuisance; penalty.

Any office, store, shop, restaurant, dance hall, theater, poolroom, clubhouse, storehouse, warehouse, dwelling house, apartment, building of any kind, vehicle, vessel, boat, or aircraft, which with the knowledge of the owner, lessor, agent of any such lessor, manager, chief executive officer, operator, or tenant thereof, is frequented by persons under the influence of illegally obtained controlled substances or marijuana, as defined in § 54.1-3401, or synthetic cannabinoids, or for the purpose of illegally obtaining possession of, manufacturing or distributing controlled substances, marijuana, or synthetic cannabinoids, or is used for the illegal possession, manufacture or distribution of controlled substances, marijuana, or synthetic cannabinoids shall be deemed a common nuisance. Any such owner, lessor, agent of any such lessor, manager, chief executive officer, operator, or tenant who knowingly permits, establishes, keeps or maintains such a common nuisance is guilty of a Class 1 misdemeanor and, for a second or subsequent offense, a Class 6 felony.

History.

Code 1950, § 54-524.104:2; 1972, c. 736; 1973, c. 400; 1975, cc. 14, 15; 1979, c. 435; 1990, c. 948; 1992, cc. 248, 538; 2004, c. 462; 2011, cc. 384, 410.

Editor's note.

Acts 2011, cc. 384 and 410, cl. 3 provides: "That the provisions of this act may result in a net increase in periods of imprisonment or commitment. Pursuant to § 30-19.1:4, the estimated amount of the necessary appropriation cannot be determined for periods of imprisonment in state adult correctional facilities; therefore, Chapter 874 of the Acts of Assembly of 2010 requires the Virginia Criminal Sentencing Commission to assign a minimum fiscal impact of $50,000. Pursuant to § 30-19.1:4, the estimated amount of the necessary appropriation cannot be determined for periods of commitment to the custody of the Department of Juvenile Justice."

The 2011 amendments.

The 2011 amendments by cc. 384 and 410, effective March 23, 2011, are identical, and inserted "synthetic cannabinoids" three times and made related changes.

CASE NOTES

Use of premises for possession and distribution of marijuana. — This section very clearly requires: (1) That the owner of the premises have knowledge that it is being frequented for the purpose of the illegal possession and distribution of marijuana and (2) That the owner knowingly permit, keep or maintain the nuisance. Peace v. Commonwealth, No. 2651-99-2, 2000 Va. App. LEXIS 725 (Ct. of Appeals Nov. 14, 2000).

Insufficient evidence that activity "permitted" by defendant. — The mother of a 15 year-old son did not "establish," "keep," or "maintain" the family home for the purpose of allowing the son and his friends to smoke marijuana in the garage. By knowing about the illegal activity and allowing it to continue the defendant did not "permit" the activity in that the evidence showed no affirmative act or decided assent and very clearly indicated that the defendant became upset and discouraged the activity when she was confronted with it. Peace v. Commonwealth, No. 2651-99-2, 2000 Va. App. LEXIS 725 (Ct. of Appeals Nov. 14, 2000).

§ 18.2-258.01. Enjoining nuisances involving illegal drug transactions.

The attorney for the Commonwealth, or any citizen of the county, city, or town, where such a nuisance as is described in § 18.2-258 exists, may, in addition to the remedies given in and punishment imposed by this chapter, maintain a suit in equity in the name of the Commonwealth to enjoin the same; provided, however, the attorney for the Commonwealth shall not be required to prosecute any suit brought by a citizen under this section. In every case where the bill charges, on the knowledge or belief of complainant, and is sworn to by two witnesses, that a nuisance exists as described in § 18.2-258, a temporary injunction may be granted as soon as the bill is presented to the court provided reasonable notice has been given. The injunction shall enjoin and restrain any owners, tenants, their agents, employees, and any other person from contributing to or maintaining the nuisance and may impose such other requirements as the court deems appropriate. If, after hearing, the court finds that the material allegations of the bill are true, although the premises complained of may not then be unlawfully used, it shall continue the injunction against such persons or premises for such period of time as it deems appropriate, with the right to dissolve the injunction upon a proper showing by the owner of the premises.

History.
  1990, c. 948.

§ 18.2-258.02. Maintaining a fortified drug house; penalty.

Any office, store, shop, restaurant, dance hall, theater, poolroom, clubhouse, storehouse, warehouse, dwelling house, apartment or building or structure of any kind which is (i) substantially altered from its original status by means of reinforcement with the intent to impede, deter or delay lawful entry by a law-enforcement officer into such structure, (ii) being used for the purpose of manufacturing or distributing controlled substances, marijuana, or synthetic cannabinoids, and (iii) the object of a valid search warrant, shall be considered a fortified drug house. Any person who maintains or operates a fortified drug house is guilty of a Class 5 felony.

History.
  1996, c. 913; 2011, cc. 384, 410.

Editor's note.
  Acts 2011, cc. 384 and 410, cl. 3 provides: "That the provisions of this act may result in a net increase in periods of imprisonment or commitment. Pursuant to § 30-19.1:4, the estimated amount of the necessary appropriation cannot be determined for periods of imprisonment in state adult correctional facilities; therefore, Chapter 874 of the Acts of Assembly of 2010 requires the Virginia Criminal Sentencing Commission to assign a minimum fiscal impact of $50,000. Pursuant to § 30-19.1:4, the estimated amount of the necessary appropriation cannot be determined for periods of commitment to the custody of the Department of Juvenile Justice."

The 2011 amendments.
  The 2011 amendments by cc. 384 and 410, effective March 23, 2011, are identical, and inserted "synthetic cannabinoids" in clause (ii), and made a related change.

Law Review.
  For survey of Virginia law on criminal law and procedure for the year 2007-2008, see 43 U. Rich. L. Rev. 149 (2008).

CASE NOTES

Substantially altered from its original status. — Supreme Court of Virginia does not set forth an all-encompassing definition of the phrase "substantially altered from its original status" as set forth in § 18.2-258.02, but, instead, recognizes that each case will turn upon its own peculiar facts. Jones v. Commonwealth, 276 Va.

121, 661 S.E.2d 412, 2008 Va. LEXIS 63 (2008).
  Insufficient evidence that structure was substantially altered from its original status. — Evidence was not sufficient to sustain defendant's conviction for maintaining or operating a fortified drug house in violation of § 18.2-258.02 where although the use of a stove and a 2x4 board wedged between a door and stairway, and a screwdriver inserted into the door's latch impeded the police, that use did not substantially alter the structure from its original status. Jones v. Commonwealth, 276 Va. 121, 661 S.E.2d 412, 2008 Va. LEXIS 63 (2008).

§ 18.2-258.1. Obtaining drugs, procuring administration of controlled substances, etc., by fraud, deceit or forgery.

A. It shall be unlawful for any person to obtain or attempt to obtain any drug or procure or attempt to procure the administration of any controlled substance, marijuana, or synthetic cannabinoids: (i) by fraud, deceit, misrepresentation, embezzlement, or subterfuge; or (ii) by the forgery or alteration of a prescription or of any written order; or (iii) by the concealment of a material fact; or (iv) by the use of a false name or the giving of a false address.

B. It shall be unlawful for any person to furnish false or fraudulent information in or omit any information from, or willfully make a false statement in, any prescription, order, report, record, or other document required by Chapter 34 (§ 54.1-3400 et seq.) of Title 54.1.

C. It shall be unlawful for any person to use in the course of the manufacture or distribution of a controlled substance, marijuana, or synthetic cannabinoids a license number which is fictitious, revoked, suspended, or issued to another person.

D. It shall be unlawful for any person, for the purpose of obtaining any controlled substance, marijuana, or synthetic cannabinoids to falsely assume the title of, or represent himself to be, a manufacturer, wholesaler, pharmacist, physician, dentist, veterinarian or other authorized person.

E. It shall be unlawful for any person to make or utter any false or forged prescription or false or forged written order.

F. It shall be unlawful for any person to affix any false or forged label to a package or receptacle containing any controlled substance.

G. This section shall not apply to officers and employees of the United States, of this Commonwealth or of a political subdivision of this Commonwealth acting in the course of their employment, who obtain such drugs for investigative, research or analytical purposes, or to the agents or duly authorized representatives of any pharmaceutical manufacturer who obtain such drugs for investigative, research or analytical purposes and who are acting in the course of their employment; provided that such manufacturer is licensed under the provisions of the Federal Food, Drug and Cosmetic Act; and provided further, that such pharmaceutical manufacturer, its agents and duly authorized representatives file with the Board such information as the Board may deem appropriate.

H. Except as otherwise provided in this subsection, any person who shall violate any provision herein shall be guilty of a Class 6 felony.

Whenever any person who has not previously been convicted of any offense under this article or under any statute of the United States or of any state relating to narcotic drugs, marijuana, or stimulant, depressant, or hallucinogenic drugs, or has not previously had a proceeding against him for violation of such an offense dismissed, or reduced as provided in this section, pleads guilty to or enters a plea of not guilty to the court for violating this section, upon such plea if the facts found by the court would justify a finding of guilt, the court may place him on probation upon terms and conditions.

As a term or condition, the court shall require the accused to be evaluated and enter a treatment and/or education program, if available, such as, in the opinion of the court, may be best suited to the needs of the accused. This program may be located in the judicial circuit in which the charge is brought or in any other judicial circuit as the court may provide. The services shall be provided by a program certified or licensed by the Department of Behavioral Health and Developmental Services. The court shall require the person entering such program under the provisions of this section to pay all or part of the costs of the program, including the costs of the screening, evaluation, testing and education, based upon the person's ability to pay unless the person is determined by the court to be indigent.

As a condition of supervised probation, the court shall require the accused to remain drug free during the period of probation and submit to such tests during that period as may be necessary and appropriate to determine if the accused is drug free. Such testing may be conducted by the personnel of any screening, evaluation, and education program to which the person is referred or by the supervising agency.

Unless the accused was fingerprinted at the time of arrest, the court shall order the accused to report to the original arresting law-enforcement agency to submit to fingerprinting.

Upon violation of a term or condition, the court may enter an adjudication of guilt upon the felony and proceed as otherwise provided. Upon fulfillment of the terms and conditions of probation, the court shall find the defendant guilty of a Class 1 misdemeanor.

History.
1977, c. 558; 1979, c. 435; 1992, c. 76; 1997, c. 542; 2009, cc. 813, 840; 2011, cc. 384, 410.

Editor's note.
Acts 2011, cc. 384 and 410, cl. 3 provides: "That the provisions of this act may result in a net increase in periods of imprisonment or commitment. Pursuant to § 30-19.1:4, the estimated amount of the necessary appropriation cannot be determined for periods of imprisonment in state adult correctional facilities; therefore, Chapter 874 of the Acts of Assembly of 2010 requires the Virginia Criminal Sentencing Commission to assign a minimum fiscal impact of $50,000. Pursuant to § 30-19.1:4, the estimated amount of the necessary appropriation cannot be determined for periods of commitment to the custody of the Department of Juvenile Justice."

The 2009 amendments.
The 2009 amendments by cc. 813 and 840 are identical, and substituted "Behavioral Health and Developmental Services" for "Mental Health, Mental Retardation and Substance Abuse Services" in the third sentence of the third paragraph of subsection H.

The 2011 amendments.
The 2011 amendments by cc. 384 and 410, effective March 23, 2011, are identical, and inserted "synthetic cannabinoids" in subsection A, subsection C, and subsection D, and made related changes.

Law Review.
For note on criminal procedure and preventing multiple punishments, see 38 Wash. & Lee L. Rev. 598 (1981).

CASE NOTES

Constitutionality. — A statute passes constitutional muster if it specifies with reasonable certainty and definiteness the conduct which is commanded or prohibited, so that a person of ordinary intelligence may know what is thereby required of him. This section passes this test; it tells any person of ordinary intelligence not to use a false name when he obtains or attempts to obtain drugs. McCutcheon v. Commonwealth, 224 Va. 30, 294 S.E.2d 808 (1982).

Purpose of clause (iv) of subsection A of this section is not to protect physicians and pharmacists from fraud or deceit in their issuance and filling of prescriptions, although this protection may be an incidental result of the statute's enforcement. Rather, the statute's purpose is to aid in curbing the excessive use of drugs and the obtaining of drugs unlawfully. McCutcheon v. Commonwealth, 224 Va. 30, 294 S.E.2d 808 (1982).

The language of this section does not exempt pharmacists from the class of persons covered, and there is no reason to read such limitation into the statute's plain language. Hill v. Commonwealth, No. 2345-93-3 (Ct. of Appeals July 5, 1995).

Emphasis is on motivation for using name. — The emphasis should be placed where it was intended, that is, upon the motivation of the person using a false name, and the inquiry should be whether the motivation is culpable or innocent. McCutcheon v. Commonwealth, 224 Va. 30, 294 S.E.2d 808 (1982).

Not motivation of physician or pharmacist to write or fill prescription. — Legislative intent would be subverted by requiring the Commonwealth to prove that a prescription would not have been written or filled but for the use of a false name. The adoption of this requirement would render clause (iv) of subsection A of this section virtually inoperative against a person with a seemingly legitimate complaint who is wont to use a different name in any number of physician's office or pharmacies in an effort to obtain a supply of drugs. Such a person is an obvious target of the statute's focus. Application of a "but for" rule, however, would place the statute's emphasis upon a physician's or pharmacist's motivation to write or fill a prescription. Where the doctor's motivation is to heal the sick, the user of a false name would go unpunished. McCutcheon v. Commonwealth, 224 Va. 30, 294 S.E.2d 808 (1982).

It was unnecessary for the Commonwealth to produce drug analysis reports to prove that the substances appellant obtained were actually Cephalexin and Lomotil. Circumstantial evidence is sufficient to allow the fact finder to infer the nature of the substance in question. In this case, proof of the substances was provided by appellant, a pharmacist himself, who, during testimony, identified the Cephalexin and Lomotil by name and admitted to obtaining the drugs to treat certain illnesses. Hill v. Commonwealth, No. 2345-93-3 (Ct. of Appeals July 5, 1995).

Construction with the Drug Control Act. — Provisions of the Drug Control Act, such as §§ 54.1-3404, 54.1-3405, and 54.1-3406 indicate that the General Assembly has established a system of record-keeping designed to reflect the identity of all persons to whom controlled drugs are sold, administered, or dispensed. These records, the Act states, shall be complete and accurate and, as the Act permits, their contents may be divulged for law-enforcement purposes. In determining legislative intent, clause (iv) of subsection A of this section and the Act should be read together. This reading reveals the intent to ensure the accuracy and completeness of drug-control records and to aid their law-enforcement role by penalizing the use of a false name in obtaining or attempting to obtain a controlled drug. McCutcheon v. Commonwealth, 224 Va. 30, 294 S.E.2d 808 (1982).

Use of false name is prima facie violation. — When the Commonwealth shows that the accused has used a false name in obtaining or attempting to obtain a drug, a prima facie violation is established. The burden then shifts to the accused to go forward with evidence showing that his motivation to use a false name was innocent. McCutcheon v. Commonwealth, 224 Va. 30, 294 S.E.2d 808 (1982); Pancoast v. Commonwealth, 2 Va. App. 28, 340 S.E.2d 833 (1986).

Extent of control. — While appellant exercised some form of legal control over pharmacy's stock of drugs by nature of his employment, this control did not extend to appropriating specific drugs for his own personal use in violation of state law. Hill v. Commonwealth, No. 2345-93-3 (Ct. of Appeals July 5, 1995).

The fact that defendant did not obtain any drugs for herself and that she apparently was not present when the prescription was filled does not vitiate the felonious intent established by the Commonwealth. At most, such evidence relates to whether she was a principal in the second degree or an accessory before the fact. However, principals in the second degree and accessories before the fact are held accountable to the same extent as principals in the first degree. Pancoast v. Commonwealth, 2 Va. App. 28, 340 S.E.2d 833 (1986).

Jury may infer intent. — Where appellant admitted that he dispensed Cephalexin and Lomotil without permission from authorized medical personnel; that he increased the dosage of the Cephalexin and used a nurse's name without her consent to obtain a refill; that he increased the amount of refills allowed; that he never contacted the original prescribing doctors to notify them of his actions; and that he used another physician to "cover" the prescriptions that he filled, despite the fact that appellant testified that none of his actions were committed with the intent to defraud, misrepresent, deceive, or use subterfuge, it was within the jury's province to draw reasonable inferences from the proven facts. Hill v. Commonwealth, No. 2345-93-3 (Ct. of Appeals July 5, 1995).

Admissibility of evidence. — In a case in which defendant was convicted of attempting to fraudulently obtain a controlled substance, in violation of clause (i) of subsection A of § 18.2-258.1, she unsuccessfully challenged the trial court's admission of a nurse practitioner's testimony as expert testimony. Given the narrow scope of the nurse practitioner's testimony, the evidence before the court sufficiently established his expert qualifications, and there was no merit in defendant's suggestion that the Commonwealth did not lay a proper foundation to render his opinion admissible. Quesenberry v. Commonwealth, 2009 Va. App. LEXIS 546 (Dec. 8, 2009).

Sufficiency of evidence. — Fact that defendant delivered forged prescription to pharmacy to be filled, and completed patient profile on his girlfriend's behalf, using same name that appeared on prescription, supported finding that he intended to obtain a drug by fraud, in violation of this section. Maxey v. Commonwealth, No. 1856-98-3 (Ct. of Appeals June 29, 1999).

Conviction for obtaining a drug or controlled substance by fraud was upheld where defendant's contention that she never received certain prescriptions filled the day before, where the log indicated receipt of refills of those same prescriptions and established that defendant acted with the requisite intent to obtain the refills by fraud, deceit, misrepresentation or subterfuge. Nuzzo v. Elder, No. 1394-02-2, 2003 Va. App. LEXIS 517 (Ct. of Appeals Oct. 14, 2003).

The evidence demonstrated that the prescription defendant presented to the pharmacy was altered after doctor wrote it and before pharmacy technician received it. Weis v. Commonwealth, No. 1481-02-2, 2003 Va. App. LEXIS 518 (Ct. of Appeals Oct. 14, 2003).

Sufficient evidence to convict a defendant of prescription fraud included the testimony of a pharmacist, a detective, a friend who recanted her alibi testimony, and defendant. Dasey v. Commonwealth, 2005 Va. App. LEXIS 454 (Nov. 15, 2005).

In a case in which defendant was convicted of attempting to fraudulently obtain a controlled substance, in violation of clause (i) of subsection A of § 18.2-258.1, and she framed her attack on the sufficiency of the evidence upon the assumption that the trial court erred in allowing a nurse practitioner to offer his dissimilar-donors

opinion as to two urine samples, since the appellate court rejected her challenge to the admission of the nurse practitioner's testimony, her sufficiency of the evidence challenge failed. Quesenberry v. Commonwealth, 2009 Va. App. LEXIS 546 (Dec. 8, 2009).

Defendant's conviction for attempt to commit prescription fraud was appropriate because the evidence was sufficient; the doctor that allegedly wrote the prescription had terminated his medical practice in May of 2008 and the prescription was purportedly written on August 14, 2008; the doctor's longtime employee also identified the prescription as fraudulent. Tiggs v. Commonwealth, 2011 Va. App. LEXIS 365 (Nov. 29, 2011).

Insufficient evidence. — Evidence did not support obtaining a prescription drug by fraud where it was not proven that the defendant knew or should have known that a doctor had not prescribed the drug and that he had not simply helped a bad friend by picking up a prescription. Mulligan v. Commonwealth, No. 2905-01-1, 2002 Va. App. LEXIS 704 (Ct. of Appeals Nov. 26, 2002).

Defendant could not rely on defense of duress, where she relented and wrote the prescription after being constantly harassed by her husband, for whom she was obtaining the drugs. While she may have been in great need of sleep, there was nothing in the record to indicate that she was in fear of imminent death or serious bodily harm, or that she had no alternative other than to commit an illegal act. Pancoast v. Commonwealth, 2 Va. App. 28, 340 S.E.2d 833 (1986).

Examining the plain meaning of subsection E, the term "prescription" refers to "an order for drugs or medical supplies." Thomas v. Commonwealth, No. 0671-95-2 (Ct. of Appeals Mar. 26, 1996).

Convictions under former § 54-524.76 and § 18.2-250 violated double jeopardy. — Where defendant was convicted under former § 54-524.76 of obtaining a drug by presenting a forged prescription, and for the same transaction was subsequently convicted under § 18.2-250 of possession of a controlled substance, his rights under the double jeopardy clause were violated, since the evidence necessarily used in first prosecution would totally have sufficed to sustain the second conviction. Jordan v. Virginia, 653 F.2d 870 (4th Cir. 1980).

Applied in Williams v. Commonwealth, 14 Va. App. 666, 418 S.E.2d 346 (1992).

OPINIONS OF THE ATTORNEY GENERAL

Fingerprinting by pharmacists. — A pharmacist may provide to law-enforcement officials the fingerprint of any customer suspected of prescription fraud. See opinion of Attorney General to The Honorable K. Mike Fleenor Jr., Commonwealth's Attorney for Pulaski County, 00-086 (1/11/02).

Food stamp benefits. — The federal Personal Responsibility and Work Opportunity Reconciliation Act encompasses felony convictions for manufacturing controlled substances or for obtaining controlled substances by false pretenses; those persons with such convictions are disqualified from receiving food stamp benefits because § 63.2-505.2 does not exempt such convictions from the application of the federal law. See opinion of Attorney General to The Honorable Gerald E. Mabe, II, Commonwealth's Attorney, 11-112, 2012 Va. AG LEXIS 5 (1/27/12).

§ 18.2-258.2. Assisting individuals in unlawfully procuring prescription drugs; penalty.

Unless otherwise specifically authorized by law, any person who, for compensation, knowingly assists another in unlawfully procuring prescription drugs from a pharmacy or other source he knows is not licensed, registered or permitted by the licensing authority of the Commonwealth, any other state or territory of the United States, or the United States, is guilty of a Class 1 misdemeanor and, upon a second or subsequent conviction, a Class 6 felony.

History.
2004, c. 620.

§ 18.2-259. Penalties to be in addition to civil or administrative sanctions.

Any penalty imposed for violation of this article or of the Drug Control Act (§ 54.1-3400 et seq.) shall be in addition to, and not in lieu of, any civil or administrative penalty or sanction authorized by law.

History.
Code 1950, § 54-524.105; 1970, c. 650; 1975, cc. 14, 15.

§ 18.2-259.1. Forfeiture of driver's license for violations of article.

A. In addition to any other sanction or penalty imposed for a violation of this article, the (i) judgment of conviction under this article or (ii) placement on probation following deferral of further proceedings under § 18.2-251 or subsection H of § 18.2-258.1 for any such offense shall of itself operate to deprive the person so convicted or placed on probation after deferral of proceedings under § 18.2-251 or subsection H of § 18.2-258.1 of the privilege to drive or operate a motor vehicle, engine, or train in the Commonwealth for a period of six months from the date of such judgment or placement on probation. Such license forfeiture shall be in addition to and shall run consecutively with any other license suspension, revocation or forfeiture in effect or imposed upon the person so convicted or placed on probation. However, a juvenile who has had his license suspended or denied pursuant to § 16.1-278.9 shall not have his license forfeited pursuant to this section for the same offense.

B. The court trying the case shall order any person so convicted or placed on probation to surrender his driver's license to be disposed of in accordance with the provisions of § 46.2-398 and shall notify the Department of Motor Vehicles of any such conviction entered and of the license forfeiture to be imposed.

C. In those cases where the court determines there are compelling circumstances warranting an exception, the court may provide that any individual be issued a restricted license to operate a motor vehicle for any of the purposes set forth in subsection E of § 18.2-271.1. No restricted license issued pursuant to this subsection shall permit any person to operate a commercial motor vehicle as defined in the Virginia Commercial Driver's License Act (§ 46.2-341.1 et seq.). The court shall order the surrender of such person's license in accordance with the provisions of subsection B and shall forward to the Commissioner of the Department of Motor Vehicles a copy of its order entered pursuant to this subsection. This order shall specifically enumerate the restrictions imposed and contain such information regarding the person to whom such a permit is issued as is reasonably necessary to identify such person. The court shall also provide a copy of its order to such person who may operate a motor vehicle on the order until receipt from the Commissioner of the Department of Motor Vehicles of a restricted license, but only if the order provides for a restricted license for that period. A copy of the order and, after receipt thereof, the restricted license shall be carried at all times by such person while operating a motor vehicle. The court may require a person issued a restricted permit under the provisions of this subsection to be monitored by an alcohol safety action program during the period of license suspension. Any violation of the terms the restricted license or of any condition set forth by the court related thereto, or any failure to remain drug-free during such period shall be reported forthwith to the court by such program. Any person who operates a motor vehicle in violation of any restriction imposed pursuant to this section shall be guilty of a violation of § 46.2-301.

History.
1992, cc. 58, 833; 1993, c. 920; 1994, cc. 403, 545; 1999, c. 45; 2000, c. 325; 2001, cc. 645, 779.

Law Review.
For an article relating to all published Virginia criminal law decisions between July 1, 1997, and July 1, 1998, see 32 U. Rich. L. Rev. 1091 (1998).

CASE NOTES

Proper purposes. — The desire to deter the use of illegal drugs and the operation of motor vehicles by persons under the influence of controlled substances constitute proper purposes which reasonably relate to this section's mandatory suspension of driver's license. Walton v. Commonwealth, 24 Va. App. 757, 485 S.E.2d 641 (1997), aff'd, 255 Va. 422, 497 S.E.2d 869 (1998).

Causal relationship between the purposes of this section and its text exist even where the drug offense does not relate to or involve the use of a motor vehicle. The legislature could reasonably assume that a person who possesses illegal substances would use those substances and could operate a motor vehicle while under the influence of said substances. Likewise, the legislature could reasonably conclude that a person who possesses illegal substances would use a motor vehicle to transport those substances. Walton v. Commonwealth, 24 Va. App. 757, 485 S.E.2d 641 (1997), aff'd, 255 Va. 422, 497 S.E.2d 869 (1998).

Suspension of driver's license proper even though conviction did not involve the operation of a motor vehicle. — Suspension of driver's license of defendant convicted of possession of marijuana did not violate his substantive due process rights; although defendant's drug offense did not involve the operation of a motor vehicle, the General Assembly in enacting this section acted in the interest of public safety and could reasonably have assumed that a person who possesses illegal substances would use those substances and could operate a motor vehicle while under their influence. Walton v. Commonwealth, 255 Va. 422, 497 S.E.2d 869 (1998).

§ 18.2-260. Prescribing, dispensing, etc., drug except as authorized in article and Drug Control Act; violations for which no penalty provided.

It shall be unlawful for any person to prescribe, administer or dispense any drug except as authorized in the Drug Control Act (§ 54.1-3400 et seq.) or in this article. Any person who violates any provision of the Drug Control Act or of this article, for which no penalty is elsewhere specified in this article or in Article 7 (§ 54.1-3466 et seq.) of the Drug Control Act, shall be guilty of a Class 1 misdemeanor.

History.
Code 1950, § 54-524.106; 1970, c. 650; 1973, c. 548; 1975, cc. 14, 15.

§ 18.2-260.1. Falsifying patient records.

Any person who, with the intent to defraud, falsifies any patient record shall be guilty of a Class 1 misdemeanor.

History.
1997, c. 619; 2011, c. 204.

The 2011 amendments.
The 2011 amendment by c. 204 substituted "with the intent to defraud" for "fraudulently" and "Class 1 misdemeanor" for "Class 3 misdemeanor."

Michie's Jurisprudence.
For related discussion, see 14B M.J. Physicians and Surgeons, §§ 2, 5.

CASE NOTES

Applied in Storey v. Patient First Corp., 207 F. Supp. 2d 431, 2002 U.S. Dist. LEXIS 10937 (E.D. Va. 2002).

§ 18.2-261. Monetary penalty.

Any person licensed by the State Board of Pharmacy who violates any of the provisions of the Drug Control Act (§ 54.1-3400 et seq.) or of this article, and who is not criminally prosecuted, shall be subject to the monetary penalty provided in this section. If, by a majority vote, the Board shall determine that the respondent is guilty of the violation complained of, the Board shall proceed to determine the amount of the monetary penalty for such violation, which shall not exceed the sum of $1,000 for each violation. Such penalty may be sued for and recovered in the name of the Commonwealth.

History.
Code 1950, § 54-524.107; 1970, c. 650; 1975, cc. 14, 15; 1980, c. 678.

§ 18.2-262. Witnesses not excused from testifying or producing evidence because of self-incrimination.

No person shall be excused from testifying or from producing books, papers, correspondence, memoranda or other records for the Commonwealth as to any offense alleged to have been committed by another under this article or under the Drug Control Act (§ 54.1-3400 et seq.) by reason of his testimony or other evidence tending to incriminate himself, but the testimony given and evidence so produced by such person on behalf of the Commonwealth when called for by the trial judge or court trying the case, or by the attorney for the Commonwealth, or when summoned by the Commonwealth and sworn as a witness by the court or the clerk and sent before the grand jury, shall be in no case used against him nor shall he be prosecuted as to the offense as to which he testifies. Any person who refuses to testify or produce books, papers, correspondence, memoranda or other records, shall be guilty of a Class 2 misdemeanor.

History.
Code 1950, § 54-524.107:1; 1971, Ex. Sess., c. 170; 1975, cc. 14, 15; 1984, c. 667.

Law Review.
For annual survey article, "Criminal Law and Procedure," see 44 U. Rich. L. Rev. 339 (2009).

Michie's Jurisprudence.
For related discussion, see 20 M.J. Witnesses, § 81.

CASE NOTES

This section does not extend transactional immunity to nondrug offenses. since, while the statute extends use immunity to all prosecutions against a witness, this section provides transactional immunity only "as to the offense as to which he testifies" and the word "offense" as used in this context does not refer to any offense to which he may have at any time testified; it refers only to the offense or offenses for which he was compelled to testify under the terms of the statute. Caldwell v. Commonwealth, 8 Va. App. 86, 379 S.E.2d 368 (1989).

The transactional immunity from prosecution provided for in this section does not extend to nondrug related offenses about which a person may not be compelled to testify. Caldwell v. Commonwealth, 8 Va. App. 86, 379 S.E.2d 368 (1989).

The statute applies only to crimes involving illegal drugs and, therefore, did not apply in a robbery prosecution. Walton v. Commonwealth, No. 2471-97-1 (Ct. of Appeals Mar. 30, 1999); Saab v. Commonwealth, No. 2472-97-1 (Ct. of Appeals Mar. 30, 1999).

Transactional immunity waived. — Trial court did not err in denying defendant's motion to dismiss charges of possession with intent to distribute more than five pounds of marijuana and transporting more than five pounds of marijuana into the Commonwealth because defendant implicitly waived any transactional immunity he could have had under § 18.2-262 by agreeing to voluntarily testify for the Commonwealth; a waiver of the statutory right need not be a "knowing and intelligent" express waiver, but instead, a waiver of the provisions of this statute may be made implicitly. Murphy v. Commonwealth, 51 Va. App. 535, 659 S.E.2d 538, 2008 Va. App. LEXIS 180 (2008), aff'd, 277 Va. 221, 672 S.E.2d 884, 2009 Va. LEXIS 38 (2009).

Controlling effect of § 19.2-215.1 et seq. — In order to give full force and effect both to § 19.2-215.1 et seq., addressing the narrow, specific exemption for multi-jurisdictional grand juries, and to this section, addressing grand juries generally, the later enacted statutory scheme (§ 19.2-215.1 et seq.) is construed to control testimony before multi-jurisdictional grand juries. Tharpe v. Commonwealth, 18 Va. App. 37, 441 S.E.2d 228 (1994).

The word "offense" refers to the earlier language in this section describing the offense for which a defendant was compelled to testify and this includes "any offense alleged to have been committed by another under this article or under the Drug Control Act (§§ 54.1-3400 et seq.)" but it is illogical to conclude that the General Assembly intended to provide immunity for any crime about which a person may at any time testify even if he was not compelled to do so. Caldwell v. Commonwealth, 8 Va. App. 86, 379 S.E.2d 368 (1989).

The only offenses for which defendant was entitled to be

immune from prosecution were the two drug offenses for which her friend was being prosecuted when defendant testified since these two offenses were the only ones alleged to have been committed by another and for which defendant's testimony was for the Commonwealth. Dunmyer v. Commonwealth, No. 0091-89-4 (Ct. of Appeals Mar. 13, 1990).

Only compelled testimony afforded immunity. — Immunity protections of § 18.2-262 apply only to witnesses whose testimony is compelled. Murphy v. Commonwealth, 277 Va. 221, 672 S.E.2d 884, 2009 Va. LEXIS 38 (2009).

As defendant's testimony at co-defendant's preliminary hearing was voluntarily given in return for the prosecution's agreement to dismiss one of two pending charges, the transactional immunity provisions of § 18.2-2 62 did not entitle him to dismissal of another charge to which he had agreed to plead guilty. Murphy v. Commonwealth, 277 Va. 221, 672 S.E.2d 884, 2009 Va. LEXIS 38 (2009).

Applied in Thornton v. Commonwealth, 22 Va. App. 2, 467 S.E.2d 820 (1996); Newton v. Commonwealth, 29 Va. App. 433, 512 S.E.2d 846.

§ 18.2-263. Unnecessary to negative exception, etc.; burden of proof of exception, etc.

In any complaint, information, or indictment, and in any action or proceeding brought for the enforcement of any provision of this article or of the Drug Control Act (§ 54.1-3400 et seq.), it shall not be necessary to negative any exception, excuse, proviso, or exemption contained in this article or in the Drug Control Act, and the burden of proof of any such exception, excuse, proviso, or exemption shall be upon the defendant.

History.
Code 1950, § 54-524.108; 1970, c. 650; 1975, cc. 14, 15.

Law Review.
For survey of Virginia law on evidence for the year 1971-1972, see 58 Va. L. Rev. 1268 (1972). For annual survey article, "Criminal Law and Procedure," see 46 U. Rich. L. Rev. 59 (2011).

CASE NOTES

Burden of proving accommodation. — Section 18.2-248 and this section place the burden of proving the existence of an accommodation distribution (and the right to the lesser penalty) to the trier of fact on the shoulders of the defendant. In other words, the statute contains a presumption against an accommodation distribution to the extent that it is relevant to the determination of the proper degree of punishment, but only after guilt has been established. Ulmer v. Commonwealth, No. 0369-85 (Ct. of Appeals Aug. 26, 1986).

Section relieves Commonwealth of impossible burden. — This section takes note of the fact that a defendant is the person with the greatest knowledge and easiest access to evidence to show, for example, that his sale or distribution of a controlled substance was one of accommodation and not a commercial transaction, and therefore relieves the Commonwealth of what would amount to an impossible burden of affirmatively negating every exception, excuse, proviso or exemption claimed by a defendant. Stillwell v. Commonwealth, 219 Va. 214, 247 S.E.2d 360 (1978).

Presumption against accommodation continues until there is proof by a preponderance of the evidence that the transaction was an accommodation distribution. Ulmer v. Commonwealth, No. 0369-85 (Ct. of Appeals Aug. 26, 1986).

Failure to meet burden of proof for accommodation instruction. — Defendant's convictions for two counts of distribution of cocaine, third offense; three counts of distribution of marijuana; two counts of conspiracy to distribute cocaine, third offense; three

counts of conspiracy to distribute marijuana; one count of possession of cocaine with intent to distribute; and one count of possession of marijuana with intent to distribute were proper because the trial court did not err in not instructing the jury on the lesser punishment of distribution for accommodation. In each transaction, the agent was the buyer, and not the cousin, who had only arranged the meetings for the agent; additionally, the fact that defendant did not make any money on the transactions was not dispositive. Martin v. Commonwealth, 2010 Va. App. LEXIS 205 (May 18, 2010).

Burden of proof of any exception, excuse, proviso, or exemption on defendant. — This section did not impermissibly shift the burden of proof to defendant, as the presence of a valid prescription was an affirmative defense, peculiarly within knowledge of defendant, for which defendant had the burden of going forward with supporting evidence. Williams v. Commonwealth, 57 Va. App. 341, 702 S.E.2d 260, 2010 Va. App. LEXIS 481 (2010).

No exemption, etc. — Where the defendant made no claim that he possessed a drug of unknown properties, or that it was a legal drug, or that he came into possession of it in a legal manner, he did not have any burden to prove that his possession, sale, or dispensing was lawful as an exemption to this chapter. He was under no burden to prove anything, and he could rely on his plea of not guilty. Walker v. Commonwealth, 212 Va. 289, 183 S.E.2d 739 (1971).

Where the defendant made no claim that he possessed a drug of unknown properties, or that it was a legal drug, or that he came into possession of it in a legal manner, but rather he denied that he possessed or sold any drug, there was no "exception, excuse, proviso or exemption" involved in the case, and no occasion for any resort by the Commonwealth to the provisions of this section. Walker v. Commonwealth, 212 Va. 289, 183 S.E.2d 739 (1971).

Applied in Heacock v. Commonwealth, 228 Va. 397, 323 S.E.2d 90 (1984).

§ 18.2-264. Inhaling drugs or other noxious chemical substances or causing, etc., others to do so.

A. It shall be unlawful, except under the direction of a practitioner as defined in § 54.1-3401, for any person deliberately to smell or inhale any drugs or any other noxious chemical substances including but not limited to fingernail polish or model airplane glue, containing any ketones, aldehydes, organic acetates, ether, chlorinated hydrocarbons or vapors, with the intent to become intoxicated, inebriated, excited, stupefied or to dull the brain or nervous system.

Any person violating the provisions of this subsection shall be guilty of a Class 1 misdemeanor.

B. It shall be unlawful for any person, other than one duly licensed, deliberately to cause, invite or induce any person to smell or inhale any drugs or any other noxious substances or chemicals containing any ketone, aldehydes, organic acetates, ether, chlorinated hydrocarbons or vapors with the intent to intoxicate, inebriate, excite, stupefy or to dull the brain or nervous system of such person.

Any person violating the provisions of this subsection shall be guilty of a Class 2 misdemeanor.

History.
Code 1950, § 18.1-70.1; 1968, c. 391; 1969, Ex. Sess., c. 19; 1973, c. 27; 1975, cc. 14, 15; 1993, c. 416.

Law Review.
For comment on state's power to require an individual to protect himself, see 26 Wash. & Lee L. Rev. 112 (1969).

§ 18.2-264.01. Repealed by Acts 2002, c. 831, cl. 2, effective July 1, 2003.

§ 18.2-264.1. Repealed by Acts 1994, c. 432.

§ 18.2-265. Repealed by Acts 1979, c. 638.

ARTICLE 1.1.

DRUG PARAPHERNALIA.

§ 18.2-265.1. Definition.

As used in this article, the term *"drug paraphernalia"* means all equipment, products, and materials of any kind which are either designed for use or which are intended by the person charged with violating § 18.2-265.3 for use in planting, propagating, cultivating, growing, harvesting, manufacturing, compounding, converting, producing, processing, preparing, strength testing, analyzing, packaging, repackaging, storing, containing, concealing, injecting, ingesting, inhaling, or otherwise introducing into the human body marijuana or a controlled substance. It includes, but is not limited to:

1. Kits intended for use or designed for use in planting, propagating, cultivating, growing or harvesting of marijuana or any species of plant which is a controlled substance or from which a controlled substance can be derived;

2. Kits intended for use or designed for use in manufacturing, compounding, converting, producing, processing, or preparing marijuana or controlled substances;

3. Isomerization devices intended for use or designed for use in increasing the potency of marijuana or any species of plant which is a controlled substance;

4. Testing equipment intended for use or designed for use in identifying or in analyzing the strength or effectiveness of marijuana or controlled substances;

5. Scales and balances intended for use or designed for use in weighing or measuring marijuana or controlled substances;

6. Diluents and adulterants, such as quinine hydrochloride, mannitol, or mannite, intended for use or designed for use in cutting controlled substances;

7. Separation gins and sifters intended for use or designed for use in removing twigs and seeds from, or in otherwise cleaning or refining, marijuana;

8. Blenders, bowls, containers, spoons, and mixing devices intended for use or designed for use in compounding controlled substances;

9. Capsules, balloons, envelopes, and other containers intended for use or designed for use in packaging small quantities of marijuana or controlled substances;

10. Containers and other objects intended for use or designed for use in storing or concealing marijuana or controlled substances;

11. Hypodermic syringes, needles, and other objects intended for use or designed for use in parenterally injecting controlled substances into the human body;

12. Objects intended for use or designed for use in ingesting, inhaling, or otherwise introducing marijuana, cocaine, hashish, or hashish oil into the human body, such as:

a. Metal, wooden, acrylic, glass, stone, plastic, or ceramic pipes with or without screens, permanent screens, hashish heads, or punctured metal bowls;

b. Water pipes;

c. Carburetion tubes and devices;

d. Smoking and carburetion masks;

e. Roach clips, meaning objects used to hold burning material, such as a marijuana cigarette, that has become too small or too short to be held in the hand;

f. Miniature cocaine spoons, and cocaine vials;

g. Chamber pipes;

h. Carburetor pipes;

i. Electric pipes;

j. Air-driven pipes;

k. Chillums;

l. Bongs;

m. Ice pipes or chillers.

History.
1981, c. 598; 1983, c. 535.

Law Review.
For note on Virginia's drug paraphernalia law, see 16 U. Rich. L. Rev. 161 (1982).

Michie's Jurisprudence.
For related discussion, see 6B M.J. Drugs and Druggists, §§ 2, 5.

CASE NOTES

Sale of items that are drug paraphernalia per se. — The General Assembly intended the objects listed in subdivision 12 to be drug paraphernalia per se. Under circumstances where items sold are listed in that section, the trial court need not consider the factors set forth in § 18.2-265.2 to determine whether a defendant was selling drug paraphernalia. Other items that are sometimes labeled drug paraphernalia have multiple uses, some legal and some illegal. When the Commonwealth's case is based on the sale of such items, a trial court may consider the factors in § 18.2-265.2 to determine whether the ambiguous object is drug paraphernalia. Morrison v. Commonwealth, 37 Va. App. 273, 557 S.E.2d 724, 2002 Va. App. LEXIS 1 (2002).

§ 18.2-265.2. Evidence to be considered in cases under this article.

In determining whether an object is drug paraphernalia, the court may consider, in addition to all other relevant evidence, the following:

1. Constitutionally admissible statements by the accused concerning the use of the object;

2. The proximity of the object to marijuana or controlled substances, which proximity is actually known to the accused;

3. Instructions, oral or written, provided with the object concerning its use;

4. Descriptive materials accompanying the object which explain or depict its use;

5. National and local advertising within the actual knowledge of the accused concerning its use;

6. The manner in which the object is displayed for sale;

7. Whether the accused is a legitimate supplier of like or related items to the community, such as a licensed distributor or dealer of tobacco products;

8. Evidence of the ratio of sales of the objects defined in § 18.2-265.1 to the total sales of the business enterprise;

9. The existence and scope of legitimate uses for the object in the community;

10. Expert testimony concerning its use or the purpose for which it was designed;

11. Relevant evidence of the intent of the accused to deliver it to persons who he knows, or should reasonably know, intend to use the object with an illegal drug. The innocence of an owner, or of anyone in control of the object, as to a direct violation of this article shall not prevent a finding that the object is intended for use or designed for use as drug paraphernalia.

History.
1981, c. 598; 1983, c. 535.

Law Review.
For note on Virginia's drug paraphernalia law, see 16 U. Rich. L. Rev. 161 (1982).

CASE NOTES

Sale of items that are drug paraphernalia per se. — The General Assembly intended the objects listed in subdivision 12 of § 18.2-265.1. to be drug paraphernalia per se. Under circumstances where items sold are listed in that section, the trial court need not consider the factors set forth in this section to determine whether a defendant was selling drug paraphernalia. Other items that are sometimes labeled drug paraphernalia have multiple uses, some legal and some illegal. When the Commonwealth's case is based on the sale of such items, a trial court may consider the factors in § 18.2-265.2 to determine whether the ambiguous object is drug paraphernalia. Morrison v. Commonwealth, 37 Va. App. 273, 557 S.E.2d 724, 2002 Va. App. LEXIS 1 (2002).

§ 18.2-265.3. Penalties for sale, etc., of drug paraphernalia.

A. Any person who sells or possesses with intent to sell drug paraphernalia, knowing, or under circumstances where one reasonably should know, that it is either designed for use or intended by such person for use to illegally plant, propagate, cultivate, grow, harvest, manufacture, compound, convert, produce, process, prepare, test, analyze, pack, repack, store, contain, conceal, inject, ingest, inhale, or otherwise introduce into the human body marijuana or a controlled substance, shall be guilty of a Class 1 misdemeanor.

B. Any person eighteen years of age or older who violates subsection A hereof by selling drug paraphernalia to a minor who is at least three years junior to the accused in age shall be guilty of a Class 6 felony.

C. Any person eighteen years of age or older who distributes drug paraphernalia to a minor shall be guilty of a Class 1 misdemeanor.

History.
1981, c. 598; 1983, c. 535; 1984, c. 31.

Law Review.
For note on Virginia's drug paraphernalia law, see 16 U. Rich. L. Rev. 161 (1982).

CASE NOTES

Scienter requirement. — The scienter requirement for a conviction for selling drug paraphernalia is either actual knowledge or constructive knowledge (under circumstances where one reasonably should know) that the item is either designed for use or intended by the accused for use to illegally ingest, inhale, or otherwise introduce into the human body marijuana or a controlled substance. Morrison v. Commonwealth, 37 Va. App. 273, 557 S.E.2d 724, 2002 Va. App. LEXIS 1 (2002).

For a conviction for selling drug paraphernalia, the Commonwealth need prove only that defendant was aware when he sold the items, or possessed them with the intent to sell, that buyers in general are likely to use the items with illegal drugs, not that a particular buyer intended to use the items in this fashion. Morrison v. Commonwealth, 37 Va. App. 273, 557 S.E.2d 724, 2002 Va. App. LEXIS 1 (2002).

Sale of paraphernalia per se. — Once the evidence proves a defendant offered any of the per se paraphernalia items for sale, the Commonwealth has made a prima facie case the defendant sold drug paraphernalia. Morrison v. Commonwealth, 37 Va. App. 273, 557 S.E.2d 724, 2002 Va. App. LEXIS 1 (2002).

Quantity and other circumstances may establish intent to distribute. — The quantity of a controlled substance is a factor which may indicate the purpose for which it is possessed. Possession of a small quantity creates an inference that the drug is for personal use. Possession of a small quantity of a controlled substance, however, when considered with other circumstances, may be sufficient to establish an intent to distribute. The method of packaging of the controlled substance is such a circumstance. Servis v. Commonwealth, 6 Va. App. 507, 371 S.E.2d 156 (1988).

Even if substance is packaged for distribution, there must be additional evidence to preclude the inference that it was purchased in the packaged form for personal use rather than being held in that fashion for distribution. The additional evidence available to preclude such an inference [may be] the presence of a large, or bulk, quantity from which smaller packages may have been made up for distribution, or the presence of paraphernalia used in the packaging process. Servis v. Commonwealth, 6 Va. App. 507, 371 S.E.2d 156 (1988).

Presence of unusual amount of money, suggesting profit from sales, is a circumstance that negates an inference of possession for personal use. Servis v. Commonwealth, 6 Va. App. 507, 371 S.E.2d 156 (1988).

§ 18.2-265.4. Repealed by Acts 2004, c. 995.

Cross references.
For current provisions as to seizure and forfeiture of drug paraphernalia, see § 19.2-386.26.

§ 18.2-265.5. Advertisement of drug paraphernalia prohibited; penalty.

It shall be unlawful for any person to place in any newspaper, magazine, handbill or other publication any advertisement, knowing or under circumstances where one reasonably should know, that the purpose of the advertisement, in whole or in part, is to promote the sale of objects designed or intended by such person for use as drug paraphernalia. A violation of this section shall be punishable as a Class 1 misdemeanor.

History.
  1983, c. 535.

ARTICLE 1.2.

SALE OF EPHEDRINE OR RELATED COMPOUNDS.

§ 18.2-265.6. Definitions.

As used in this article, unless the context requires a different meaning:

"*Department*" means the Department of State Police.

"*Ephedrine or related compounds*" means ephedrine and pseudoephedrine base or their salts, isomers, or salts of isomers.

"*Pharmacy*" means any establishment or institution from which drugs, medicines, or medicinal chemicals are dispensed or offered for sale or on which a sign is displayed bearing the words "apothecary," "druggist," "drugs," "drug store," "drug sundries," "medicine store," "pharmacist," "pharmacy," or "prescriptions filled" or any similar words intended to indicate that the practice of pharmacy is being conducted pursuant to a license issued under Chapter 33 (§ 54.1-3300 et seq.) of Title 54.1.

"*Retail distributor*" means an entity licensed to conduct business in the Commonwealth that offers for sale to the public at a retail outlet any nonprescription compound, mixture, or preparation containing ephedrine or related compounds.

"*System*" or "*electronic system*" means a real-time electronic recordkeeping and monitoring system for the sale of ephedrine or related compounds.

History.
  2012, cc. 160, 252.

Editor's note.
  Acts 2012, cc. 160 and 252, cl. 3 provides: "That the provisions of this act shall become effective on January 1, 2013."

§ 18.2-265.7. Sale of the methamphetamine precursors ephedrine or related compounds; penalty.

A. The sale of any product containing ephedrine or related compounds sold by a pharmacy or retail distributor shall be limited to no more than 3.6 grams per day and 9 grams per 30-day period per individual customer. The limits shall apply to the total amount of base ephedrine or related compounds contained in the products and not to the overall weight of the products.

B. Ephedrine or related compounds shall only be displayed for sale behind a store counter that is not accessible to consumers or in a locked case that requires assistance by a store employee for customer access.

C. Any person purchasing, receiving, or otherwise acquiring ephedrine or related compounds shall, prior to taking possession, present photo identification issued by a government or an educational institution.

D. The pharmacy or retail distributor shall maintain a written log or electronic system with the purchaser's name and address, birth date, and signature; the product name and quantity sold; and the date and time of the transaction. Unless exempt under subsection B of § 18.2-265.8 or § 18.2-265.11, the pharmacy or retail distributor shall use the electronic recordkeeping and monitoring system to report all nonprescription sales of any product containing ephedrine or related compounds.

E. The purchaser shall sign the record acknowledging an understanding of the applicable sales limit and that providing false statements or misrepresentations may subject the purchaser to criminal penalties under § 1001 of Title 18 of the United States Code.

F. The pharmacy or retail distributor shall maintain records of all sales required to be entered into the electronic system or written log for a period of two years from the date of the last entry.

G. The provisions of this article do not apply to sales of ephedrine or related compounds pursuant to a valid prescription.

H. Any person who willfully violates this section is guilty of a Class 1 misdemeanor.

History.
  2012, cc. 160, 252.

Editor's note.
  Acts 2012, cc. 160 and 252, cl. 3 provides: "That the provisions of this act shall become effective on January 1, 2013."

§ 18.2-265.8. Real-time electronic recording of sales of ephedrine or related compounds; memorandum of understanding.

A. The Department shall enter into a memorandum of understanding with an appropriate entity to establish the Commonwealth's participation in a real-time electronic recordkeeping and monitoring system for the sale of ephedrine or related compounds. The memorandum of understanding shall include the following:

1. A real-time electronic recordkeeping and monitoring system shall be provided at no charge to the Commonwealth or to participating pharmacies and retail distributors and shall be approved by the Department.

2. The system shall provide, at no charge to participating pharmacies and retail distributors, appropriate training, 24-hour online support, and a toll-free telephone help line that is staffed 24 hours a day.

3. The system shall be able to communicate in real time with similar systems operated in other states and the District of Columbia and similar systems containing information submitted by more than one state.

4. The system shall comply with information exchange standards adopted by the National Information Exchange Model.

5. The system shall include a stop sales alert, which shall be a notification that completion of the sale would result in the seller or purchaser violating the quantity limits set forth in § 18.2-265.7, with an override function that may be used by a pharmacy or retail distributor under the circumstances set forth in § 18.2-265.9 and shall record each instance in which the override function is utilized.

6. The system shall provide for the recording of the following:

a. The date and time of the transaction;

b. The name, address, date of birth, and photo identification number of the purchaser; the type of identification; and the government or educational institution of issuance;

c. The number of packages purchased; the total number of grams of ephedrine or related compounds per package; and the name of the compound, mixture, or preparation containing ephedrine or related compounds; and

d. The signature of the purchaser or unique number connecting the transaction to a paper signature maintained at the retail premises.

7. The system shall ensure that submitted data is retained within the system for at least two years from the date of submission.

B. The Department shall provide a process for a pharmacy or retail distributor to apply for, obtain, and periodically renew an exemption from the requirement to report transactions to the electronic system if the pharmacy or retail distributor lacks broadband access or maintains a sales volume of less than 72 grams of ephedrine or related compounds in a 30-day period.

C. The Superintendent of State Police shall promulgate regulations pursuant to the Administrative Process Act (§ 2.2-4000 et seq.) for the implementation of this section. Regulations adopted under this section shall be deemed a customary police function for purposes of subdivision B 6 of § 2.2-4002.

History.
2012, cc. 160, 252.

Editor's note.
Acts 2012, cc. 160 and 252, cl. 3 provides: "That the provisions of this act shall become effective on January 1, 2013."

§ 18.2-265.9. Stop sales alerts; interruption of electronic system.

A. A pharmacy or retail distributor shall not complete the sale if the system generates a stop sales alert unless the individual distributing the ephedrine or related compound has a reasonable

fear of imminent bodily harm if the sale is not completed.

B. In the event of a mechanical or electronic interruption of the system, the pharmacy or retail establishment shall maintain a written log of sales of ephedrine or related compounds until the system is restored. The information written in the log shall be transmitted to the system as soon as practicable after the system is restored.

History.
2012, cc. 160, 252.

Editor's note.
Acts 2012, cc. 160 and 252, cl. 3 provides: "That the provisions of this act shall become effective on January 1, 2013."

§ 18.2-265.10. Exemption from participation in electronic system; requirement to maintain log.

Any pharmacy or retail distributor that has been granted an exemption from participation in the system pursuant to subsection B of § 18.2-265.8 shall forward to the Department every seven days by fax or electronic means a legible copy of the log required by § 18.2-265.7.

History.
2012, cc. 160, 252.

Editor's note.
Acts 2012, cc. 160 and 252, cl. 3 provides: "That the provisions of this act shall become effective on January 1, 2013."

§ 18.2-265.11. Exemption from participation in electronic system and maintenance of a written log.

A. The following entities shall not be required to participate in the electronic system and shall not be required to maintain a written log:

1. Licensed manufacturers that manufacture and lawfully distribute products in the channels of commerce.

2. Wholesalers that lawfully distribute products in the channels of commerce.

3. Inpatient pharmacies of health care facilities licensed in the Commonwealth.

4. Licensed long-term health care facilities.

5. Government-operated health care clinics or departments or centers.

6. Physicians who dispense drugs pursuant to § 54.1-3304.

7. Pharmacies located in correctional facilities.

8. Government-operated or industry-operated medical facilities serving the employees of the Commonwealth or local or federal government.

B. Purchases of ephedrine or related compounds pursuant to a valid prescription are not required to be reported to the system or entered into a written log.

C. The sale of a single package containing no more than 60 milligrams of ephedrine or related compounds to an individual is not required to be reported to the system or entered into a log provided it is an isolated sale.

History.
2012, cc. 160, 252.

Editor's note.
Acts 2012, cc. 160 and 252, cl. 3 provides: "That the provisions of this act shall become effective on January 1, 2013."

§ 18.2-265.12. Authority to access data, records, and reports.

The Department or other law-enforcement agency of the Commonwealth or any federal agency conducting a criminal investigation involving the manufacture of methamphetamine consistent with state or federal law may access data, records, and reports regarding the sale of ephedrine or related compounds. In addition, such information may be accessed if relevant to proceedings in any court, investigatory grand jury, or special grand jury that has been impaneled in accordance with the provisions of Chapter 13 (§ 19.2-191 et seq.) of Title 19.2.

The Superintendent of State Police shall promulgate regulations, pursuant to the Administrative Process Act (§ 2.2-4000 et seq.), for the implementation of this section. Regulations adopted under this section shall be deemed a customary police function for purposes of subdivision B 6 of § 2.2-4002.

History.
2012, cc. 160, 252.

Editor's note.
Acts 2012, cc. 160 and 252, cl. 3 provides: "That the provisions of this act shall become effective on January 1, 2013."

§ 18.2-265.13. Confidentiality of data in possession of Department.

All data, records, and reports related to the sale of ephedrine or related compounds to retail customers and any abstracts of such data, records, and reports that are in the possession of the Department pursuant to this article shall be confidential and exempt from the Virginia Freedom of Information Act (§ 2.2-3700 et seq.) and the Government Data Collection and Dissemination Practices Act (§ 2.2-3800 et seq.).

History.
2012, cc. 160, 252.

Editor's note.
Acts 2012, cc. 160 and 252, cl. 3 provides: "That the provisions of this act shall become effective on January 1, 2013."

§ 18.2-265.14. Prohibition on disclosure of information by entity operating the system.

The entity operating the system pursuant to the memorandum of understanding with the Depart-

ment shall not use or disclose the information collected on behalf of the Department from a pharmacy or retail distributor for any purpose other than (i) to ensure compliance with this article or the federal Combat Methamphetamine Epidemic Act of 2005, (ii) to comply with the United States government or a political subdivision thereof for law-enforcement purposes pursuant to state or federal law, or (iii) to facilitate a product recall necessary to protect public health and safety.

History.
2012, cc. 160, 252.

Editor's note.
Acts 2012, cc. 160 and 252, cl. 3 provides: "That the provisions of this act shall become effective on January 1, 2013."

§ 18.2-265.15. Prohibition on disclosure of information by pharmacy or retail distributor; civil immunity.

A pharmacy or retail distributor that sells any product containing ephedrine or related compounds shall not use or disclose the information in the system or a written log for any purpose other than (i) to ensure compliance with this article or the federal Combat Methamphetamine Epidemic Act of 2005, (ii) to comply with the United States government or a political subdivision thereof for law-enforcement purposes pursuant to state or federal law, or (iii) to facilitate a product recall necessary to protect public health and safety. A pharmacy or retail distributor shall report information in the written log or electronic system to law-enforcement personnel upon request, and any pharmacy or retail distributor that in good faith releases such information to federal, state, or local law-enforcement officers, or to any person acting on behalf of such officers, shall be immune from civil liability for the release unless the release constitutes gross negligence or intentional, wanton, or willful misconduct.

History.
2012, cc. 160, 252.

Editor's note.
Acts 2012, cc. 160 and 252, cl. 3 provides: "That the provisions of this act shall become effective on January 1, 2013."

§ 18.2-265.16. Compliance with statutory provisions; civil immunity.

Absent gross negligence, recklessness, or willful misconduct, any pharmacy or retail distributor utilizing the system or written log in compliance with this article shall be immune from civil liability as a result of actions or omissions in carrying out such statutory duties.

History.
2012, cc. 160, 252.

Editor's note.
Acts 2012, cc. 160 and 252, cl. 3 provides: "That the provisions of this act shall become effective on January 1, 2013."

§ 18.2-265.17. Exemption of information systems from provisions related to the Virginia Information Technologies Agency.

The provisions of Chapter 20.1 (§ 2.2-2005 et seq.) of Title 2.2 shall not apply to this article.

History.
2012, cc. 160, 252.

Editor's note.
Acts 2012, cc. 160 and 252, cl. 3 provides: "That the provisions of this act shall become effective on January 1, 2013."

§ 18.2-265.18. Failure to report certain sales; penalty.

Any person subject to the recordkeeping and reporting requirements set forth in this article that willfully fails to report nonprescription sales of ephedrine or related compounds is guilty of a Class 1 misdemeanor.

History.
2012, cc. 160, 252.

Editor's note.
Acts 2012, cc. 160 and 252, cl. 3 provides: "That the provisions of this act shall become effective on January 1, 2013."

ARTICLE 2.

DRIVING MOTOR VEHICLE, ETC., WHILE INTOXICATED.

§ 18.2-266. Driving motor vehicle, engine, etc., while intoxicated, etc.

It shall be unlawful for any person to drive or operate any motor vehicle, engine or train (i) while such person has a blood alcohol concentration of 0.08 percent or more by weight by volume or 0.08 grams or more per 210 liters of breath as indicated by a chemical test administered as provided in this article, (ii) while such person is under the influence of alcohol, (iii) while such person is under the influence of any narcotic drug or any other self-administered intoxicant or drug of whatsoever nature, or any combination of such drugs, to a degree which impairs his ability to drive or operate any motor vehicle, engine or train safely, (iv) while such person is under the combined influence of alcohol and any drug or drugs to a degree which impairs his ability to drive or operate any motor vehicle, engine or train safely, or (v) while such person has a blood concentration of any of the following substances at a level that is equal to or greater than: (a) 0.02 milligrams of cocaine per liter of blood, (b) 0.1 milligrams of methamphetamine per liter of blood, (c) 0.01 milligrams of phencyclidine per liter of blood, or (d) 0.1 milligrams of 3,4-methylenedioxymethamphetamine per liter of blood. A charge alleging a violation of this section shall support a conviction under clauses (i), (ii), (iii), (iv), or (v).

For the purposes of this article, the term "*motor vehicle*" includes mopeds, while operated on the public highways of this Commonwealth.

History.
Code 1950, § 18.1-54; 1960, c. 358; 1975, cc. 14, 15; 1977, c. 637; 1984, c. 666; 1986, c. 635; 1987, c. 661; 1992, c. 830; 1994, cc. 359, 363; 1996, c. 439; 2005, cc. 616, 845.

Cross references.
For authorization for locality to provide by ordinance for reimbursement of certain expenses incurred in responding to DUI and other traffic incidents related to violation of §§ 18.2-51.4, 18.2-266, 29.1-738, 46.2-852 et seq., 46.2-300 et seq., and 46.2-894, see § 15.2-1716. As to presumption of no bail for illegal aliens charged with certain crimes, see § 19.2-120.1. As to admissibility of written results of blood alcohol tests conducted in the regular course of providing emergency medical treatment, see § 19.2-187.02. As to dismissal of one of dual charges for driving while intoxicated and reckless driving upon conviction of other charge, see § 19.2-294.1. As to revocation of license upon fourth conviction, see § 46.2-394. As to incorporation of provisions of this article in local ordinances, see § 46.2-1313.

Editor's note.
Acts 2002, c. 811, cl. 2, provides: "That a court shall not transmit to the Department of Motor Vehicles (i) an order of conviction or abstract of conviction for a second violation of § 18.2-266 or a substantially similar local ordinance, as described in subsection B of § 18.2-271, unless the defendant was tried and convicted on a process alleging such a second offense, nor (ii) an order of conviction or abstract of conviction for a third or subsequent violation of § 18.2-266 or substantially similar local ordinance, as described in subsection C of § 18.2-271, unless the defendant was tried and convicted on a process alleging such a third or subsequent offense. However, when such conviction is upon a process other than as described in subsection B or C of § 18.2-271, the court shall transmit such order or abstract as an initial violation. Upon receipt of a conviction of a second offense transmitted pursuant to subsection B of § 18.2-271, the Commissioner of Motor Vehicles shall revoke the driver's license of an individual in accordance with subsection A of § 46.2-391. Upon receipt of a conviction of a third or subsequent offense transmitted pursuant to subsection C of § 18.2-271, the Commissioner shall revoke the driver's license of an individual in accordance with subsection B of § 46.2-391.

"The Commissioner shall not revoke the driver's license of an individual under subsections A or B of § 46.2-391 if the court fails to comply with the requirements set forth in the above paragraph."

Acts 2004, c. 937, cl. 2, provides: "That the Department of Motor Vehicles shall determine the impact on its recordkeeping system if the penalties currently applicable to a third conviction of § 18.2-266 were applicable without regard to the time period in which the offenses were committed."

Law Review.
For survey of Virginia criminal law for the year 1975-1976, see 62 Va. L. Rev. 1400 (1976). For note discussing the defendant's right to independent analysis of the breathalyzer ampoule, see 21 Wm. & Mary L. Rev. 219 (1979). For note, "Criminal Procedure and Criminal Law: Virginia Supreme Court Decisions During the 70's," see 15 U. Rich. L. Rev. 585 (1981). For survey on legal issues involving children in Virginia for 1989, see 23 U. Rich. L. Rev. 705 (1989). For 1991 survey on criminal law and procedure, see 25 U. Rich. L. Rev. 731 (1991). For note, "Drunk Driving, Administrative License Suspension, and Double Jeopardy in Virginia", see 4 Geo. Mason L. Rev. 521 (1996). For an article, "Criminal Law and Procedure," see 31 U. Rich. L. Rev. 1015 (1997). For survey of Virginia law on criminal law and procedure for the year 2007-2008, see 43 U. Rich. L. Rev. 149 (2008). For annual survey article, "Criminal Law and Procedure," see 44 U. Rich. L. Rev. 339 (2009).

Research references.
Cohen and Green, Apprehending and Prosecuting the Drunk Driver: A Manual for Police and Prosecution (Matthew Bender).

James F. Mosher, Liquor Liability Law (Matthew Bender).

Richard E. Erwin, Defense of Drunk Driving Cases: Criminal - Civil (Matthew Bender).

Michie's Jurisprudence.

For related discussion, see 2B M.J. Automobiles, §§ 47, 112, 118, 122; 5A M.J. Courts, § 58.

CASE NOTES

I. GENERAL CONSIDERATION.

Constitutionality. — This section does not offend the due process clause as it does not establish a mandatory presumption but allows only a permissive inference that the fact finder is free to reject. The trial court properly treated § 18.2-266 as a permissive inference, explicitly stating so. Yap v. Commonwealth, 49 Va. App. 622, 643 S.E.2d 523, 2007 Va. App. LEXIS 171 (2007).

Construction. — In construing this section and §§ 18.2-270 through 18.2-273 consideration must be given to the words used, their relation to the subject matter in which they are used, the purposes for which the statute was intended, and the mischief sought to be suppressed. Commonwealth v. Ellett, 174 Va. 403, 4 S.E.2d 762 (1939).

To determine the proper interpretation of this section, the court must focus on the specific language used in this section, and the appropriate evidentiary weight of the results of the subsequently administered blood alcohol test. Davis v. Commonwealth, 8 Va. App. 291, 381 S.E.2d 11 (1989).

Construction with other law. — Reckless driving and speeding are separate and distinct offenses; nothing in the language of § 19.2-294.1 precludes the Commonwealth or a locality from convicting a person for both DUI and speeding. White v. Commonwealth, 26 Va. App. 410, 494 S.E.2d 896 (1998).

A conviction under § 18.2-36.1 requires proof both that the accused violated clauses (ii), (iii), or (iv) of this section and that such misconduct caused the death of another, elements not necessary to common-law involuntary manslaughter. Section 18.2-36.1 C expressly provides that the provisions of § 18.2-36.1 shall not preclude prosecution under any other homicide statute. Stover v. Commonwealth, 31 Va. App. 225, 522 S.E.2d 397 (1999), upholding defendant's conviction under § 18.2-36 for involuntary manslaughter.

Definitions in § 46.2-100 do not control Title 18.2, and therefore, the definition of operator pursuant to § 46.2-100 was inapplicable where defendant was convicted of driving a motor vehicle while under the influence of alcohol. Reynolds v. City of Va. Beach, 31 Va. App. 629, 525 S.E.2d 65 (2000).

The Virginia legislature intended to permit the imposition of multiple punishments for involuntary manslaughter while driving under the influence, under § 18.2-36.1, and driving under the influence, under clauses (ii), (iii) or (iv) of this section upon convictions obtained in a single trial. Goodman v. Commonwealth, 37 Va. App. 374, 558 S.E.2d 555, 2002 Va. App. LEXIS 45 (2002).

Trial court did not err in denying defendant's motion to strike, which alleged that he could not have been prosecuted for felony child abuse for transporting his son while driving under the influence, since § 18.2-270 simply provides an additional penalty for driving under the influence while transporting a person 17 years

of age or younger and does not include within its parameters the elements of the child abuse and neglect offense; furthermore, this section did not require proof of those elements for a conviction of DUI. Wolfe v. Commonwealth, 42 Va. App. 776, 595 S.E.2d 27, 2004 Va. App. LEXIS 168 (2004).

Section 19.2-294.1 required the dismissal of defendant's indictment for felony driving under the influence, fourth offense, in violation of §§ 18.2-266 and 18.2-270 because defendant had been previously convicted of reckless driving in the general district court arising out of the same act or acts that were the basis of the felony indictment for driving under the influence. Lawson v. Commonwealth, 61 Va. App. 292, 734 S.E.2d 714, 2012 Va. App. LEXIS 402 (2012).

Assimilative Crimes Act. — Virginia offense of driving while intoxicated is assimilated as federal law in certain federal enclaves within the Commonwealth, including Fort Eustis, 18 U.S.C.S. § 7, pursuant to the Assimilative Crimes Act (ACA), 18 U.S.C.S. § 13. United States v. Clark, 361 F. Supp. 2d 502, 2005 U.S. Dist. LEXIS 4230 (E.D. Va. 2005).

Defendant's sentence of 27 months imprisonment for drunk driving and for driving with a suspended license fell below the midpoint of the range prescribed by § 18.2-266 and subdivision C 1 of § 18.2-270, and because the sentence fell within the state-prescribed range, it was consonant with the Assimilative Crimes Act's "like punishment" requirement. United States v. Finley, 531 F.3d 288, 2008 U.S. App. LEXIS 13762 (4th Cir. 2008).

This section defines a single offense, commonly referred to as DUI, and the clauses merely set forth the means by which the offense of driving under the influence may be proved. Graham v. Commonwealth, No. 2292-91-3 (Ct. of Appeals June 22, 1993).

The gravamen of the offense is driving while under the influence of alcohol, and the Commonwealth must establish both essential facts beyond a reasonable doubt to carry the burden of proof. Clemmer v. Commonwealth, 208 Va. 661, 159 S.E.2d 664 (1968).

The issue under clause (i) of this section is not whether a driver was in fact under the influence of alcohol to a degree that his ability to drive safely was affected; rather, the issue is whether at the time he was driving his blood alcohol concentration was at least .10 (now .08) percent. Lemond v. Commonwealth, 19 Va. App. 687, 454 S.E.2d 31 (1995).

Clause (i), the per se statute. — The presumptions contained in § 18.2-269 are not applicable to an offense under clause (i) as a result of the 1986 amendment to this code section and thus, the inquiry under this section is not whether a driver was in fact "under the influence of alcohol" to a degree that his ability to drive safely was affected; rather, the issue is whether at the time he was driving his blood alcohol concentration was at least .10 (now .08) percent as measured by a subsequently administered chemical test pursuant to former § 18.2-268 (now § 18.2-268.1 et seq.) and it is for this reason that clause (i) has come to be known as the "per se" statute. Davis v. Commonwealth, 8 Va. App. 291, 381 S.E.2d 11 (1989).

While the clause (i) proscribes no time limit within which the chemical test must be administered after driving, it is axiomatic that there can be no prosecution under this section without the existence of a chemical test obtained under the provisions of § 18.2-268(B). Davis v. Commonwealth, 8 Va. App. 291, 381 S.E.2d 11 (1989).

City ordinance successfully incorporated clause (i). — City ordinance successfully incorporated this section by reference; the words in the city ordinance adopting provisions of the statute "pertaining to driving motor vehicles while intoxicated" are words of description and do not act to exclude clause (i) from incorporation. Reardon v. City of Manassas, 11 Va. App. 244, 397 S.E.2d 544 (1990).

Ordinance against driving under influence of alcohol paralleled and substantially conformed to state statute and thus conviction under ordinance could be considered in determining whether defendant was habitual offender. Although ordinance adopted prior version of statute and did not provide for incorporation of future amendments, and statute was amended, adding a per se offense of operating a vehicle with a blood alcohol level of 0.15 percent or more, the ordinance nonetheless met the requirement that it parallel and substantially conform to this section. West v. Commonwealth, 14 Va. App. 350, 416 S.E.2d 50 (1992).

This section and the "implied consent" statute are sepa-

rate. — Former "implied consent" statute § 18.2-268 (now § 18.2-268.2 et seq.) and the drunken driving statute (this section) are not intricately related, but rather completely separate offenses with separate penalties. United States v. Gholson, 319 F. Supp. 499 (E.D. Va. 1970).

The defendant's contention at the trial that this section and former § 18.2-268 (now § 18.2-268.1 et seq.) should be read together by virtue of the decision of *Russell v. Hammond,* 200 Va. 600, 106 S.E.2d 626 (1959) has no merit. This section is a separate statute and is not cited in *Russell v. Hammond* as being read together with the blood test statutes. United States v. Gholson, 319 F. Supp. 499 (E.D. Va. 1970).

One committing a homicide while violating this section may be convicted of involuntary manslaughter. Massie v. Commonwealth, 177 Va. 883, 15 S.E.2d 30 (1941).

Right to jury trial. — Article I, § 8, of the Virginia Constitution and Rule 3A:13(a) guaranteed defendant a right to a jury in the trial court on both charges of driving under the influence and driving on a revoked operator's license. McCormick v. City of Virginia Beach, 5 Va. App. 369, 363 S.E.2d 124 (1987).

For a discussion of the applicability of Miranda warnings to motor vehicle offenses, see Clay v. Riddle, 541 F.2d 456 (4th Cir. 1976). See also Berkemer v. McCarty, 468 U.S. 420, 104 S. Ct. 3138, 82 L. Ed. 2d 317 (1984).

Warrant invalid where based on county code provision containing obsolete statutory reference. — Driving under the influence of alcohol was not an offense at common law. It exists solely as a creature of statute. Therefore, a warrant stating that the defendant did unlawfully in violation of the county code operate a motor vehicle while under the influence of alcohol or other self-administered drug or intoxicants had no effect, where it cited a county code provision which was invalid because it referred to former § 18.1-54 et seq., rather than the current driving under the influence law, § 18.2-266 et seq. This was not altered by the fact that the wording on the warrant described a violation of § 18.2-266 et seq., since defendant was not charged with violating a provision of the Virginia Code. The existence of a state statute defining the same crime does not form a basis for conviction where a defendant has not been so charged. Mitchell v. County of Hanover, 1 Va. App. 486, 340 S.E.2d 173 (1986).

State court criminal DUI proceedings barred a hearing in federal district court of claims against officer for violation of petitioner's fourth, fifth, and fourteenth amendment rights during the course of his arrest and for violation of 42 U.S.C.S. § 1983 for alleged unconstitutional application of state statutory scheme for DUI offenses. Grochowski v. Virginia, 741 F. Supp. 1230 (W.D. Va. 1990), aff'd sub nom. Grochowski v. Dewitt-Rickards, 928 F.2d 399 (4th Cir.), cert. denied, 502 U.S. 859, 112 S. Ct. 176, 116 L. Ed. 2d 139 (1991).

Applied in Davis v. Commonwealth, 219 Va. 808, 252 S.E.2d 299 (1979); Sargent v. Commonwealth, 5 Va. App. 143, 360 S.E.2d 895 (1987); Rosenbaum v. Commonwealth, 12 Va. App. 61, 402 S.E.2d 498 (1991); Farmer v. Commonwealth, 12 Va. App. 337, 404 S.E.2d 371 (1991); Nash v. Commonwealth, 12 Va. App. 550, 404 S.E.2d 743 (1991); Sos v. Commonwealth, 14 Va. App. 862, 419 S.E.2d 426 (1992); Wallace v. Commonwealth, 32 Va. App. 497, 528 S.E.2d 739, 2000 Va. App. LEXIS 387 (2000); Woods v. Mendez, 265 Va. 68, 574 S.E.2d 263, 2003 Va. LEXIS 18 (2003); Smith v. Commonwealth, 44 Va. App. 189, 604 S.E.2d 108, 2004 Va. App. LEXIS 509 (2004); United States v. Montigue, 357 F. Supp. 2d 939, 2005 U.S. Dist. LEXIS 2450 (E.D. Va. 2005); Thomas v. Commonwealth, 59 Va. App. 496, 720 S.E.2d 157, 2012 Va. App. LEXIS 14 (2012).

II. ELEMENTS.

A. Drive or Operate.

Driving an automobile means putting it in motion. Gallagher v. Commonwealth, 205 Va. 666, 139 S.E.2d 37 (1964).

But the word "operate" is not limited to moving the vehicle from one place to another. Gallagher v. Commonwealth, 205 Va. 666, 139 S.E.2d 37 (1964); Lyons v. City of Petersburg, 221 Va. 10, 266 S.E.2d 880 (1980).

The meaning of the word "operate" as used in this section is not limited to the movement of the vehicle. Nicolls v. Commonwealth, 212 Va. 257, 184 S.E.2d 9 (1971).

The word "operate" is not defined in this section, but the word

"operator" is defined, in part, in § 46.1-1 (17) (see now § 46.2-100) as "every person who drives or is in actual physical control of a motor vehicle," and this definition is approved for the purpose of determining whether one "operates" a motor vehicle within the meaning of this section. Nicolls v. Commonwealth, 212 Va. 257, 184 S.E.2d 9 (1971); Lyons v. City of Petersburg, 221 Va. 10, 266 S.E.2d 880 (1980).

The language of this section is to be construed to mean that a vehicle need not be functional in the sense of being able to move from place to place in order to be "operated." Keesee v. Commonwealth, 32 Va. App. 263, 527 S.E.2d 473, 2000 Va. App. LEXIS 295 (2000).

It is the commonality of the underlying offending conduct, the continuous, uninterrupted operation of a motor vehicle, that invokes the preclusive effect of this section. Harris v. City of Va. Beach, 19 Va. App. 214, 450 S.E.2d 401 (1994).

"Operating" inoperable vehicle. — The contention that a defendant cannot be convicted of operating an inoperable vehicle is without merit, since a motor vehicle is defined in § 46.1-1 (15) (see now § 46.2-100) as "every vehicle as herein defined which is self-propelled or designed for self-propulsion." Nicolls v. Commonwealth, 212 Va. 257, 184 S.E.2d 9 (1971).

Where defendant was arrested after the officer found him sitting at the steering wheel of his car, which was stuck in a ditch, with the motor running and the right rear wheel spinning, it was held that he was operating the vehicle and that his conviction was proper under this section, for it prohibits operation as well as driving of a vehicle while intoxicated. Gallagher v. Commonwealth, 205 Va. 666, 139 S.E.2d 37 (1964).

No bright line rule for "operating" or "driving." — Neither the court of appeals nor the state supreme court has fashioned a bright line rule that a vehicle's motor must be running or its ignition switch must be in the "on" position for a defendant to be convicted of driving or operating a motor vehicle while intoxicated in violation of this section. Propst v. Commonwealth, 24 Va. App. 791, 485 S.E.2d 657 (1997).

Breath test certificate was irrelevant to prove driving and was improperly admitted. — Where the statement of facts stated that appellant was drinking "during the stop," because the evidence did not exclude the reasonable hypothesis that appellant was drinking after the driving and operation of the vehicle, the breath certificate was irrelevant to prove appellant's driving or operating the car and should not have been admitted. Foster v. Commonwealth, No. 1593-91-2 (Ct. of Appeals March 16, 1993).

Circumstances sufficient to show that drunken driver was "operating" his truck. — Evidence was sufficient to prove that defendant convicted of second offense of driving motor vehicle while under the influence of alcohol was "operating" his truck when approached by police officer: truck's engine was running and its headlights and taillights were illuminated; defendant, though standing on the road, was bending his body into the interior space of the truck; and defendant admitted that he had just left his house to ride around the block and was going straight home. Leake v. Commonwealth, 27 Va. App. 101, 497 S.E.2d 522 (1998).

Evidence sufficient to prove defendant "operated" vehicle. — The evidence was sufficient to prove that the defendant was "operating" the vehicle where the police officer who was dispatched to the scene of an accident found the defendant alone in the vehicle with his legs pinned under the steering wheel and dashboard, the defendant was conscious but was unable to move because he was trapped inside the car, and the car was in gear and the key was in the ignition. Keesee v. Commonwealth, 32 Va. App. 263, 527 S.E.2d 473, 2000 Va. App. LEXIS 295 (2000).

The evidence, although circumstantial, was sufficient to prove that the defendant was the driver of the car where, immediately after a witness heard the squealing of the tires and a loud boom, she observed the defendant lying on the ground on the driver's side of the car and the other occupant climb from the front passenger side of the vehicle and exit from the driver's side door, when a second witness arrived at the scene he observed the defendant sitting in the driver's seat with his legs out the side door, the defendant sustained injuries to the left side of his body, which were consistent with the damage to only the driver's side of the car, while the other occupant did not sustain any injuries and, finally, the vehicle was registered in the name of the defendant's father. McCain v. Commonwealth, No. 1789-99-3, 2000 Va. App. LEXIS 345 (Ct. of Appeals May 9, 2000).

Even though defendant's car did not start when defendant turned the key in the ignition, the evidence was sufficient to prove that defendant "operated" a motor vehicle within the meaning of § 18.2-266 because, by operating the car's ignition switch, defendant manipulated the mechanical or electrical equipment of the car and engaged the machinery of the car that, alone or in sequence, would activate the car's motive power. Floyd v. Commonwealth, No. 0568-01-2, 2002 Va. App. LEXIS 440 (Ct. of Appeals July 30, 2002).

Even though defendant's attempt to start defendant's disabled vehicle was in response to a request by a state trooper who did not know at the time that defendant was intoxicated, the fact that defendant was responding to the trooper's request did not render the evidence insufficient to prove that defendant "operated" the car within the meaning of § 18.2-266 because defendant, knowing of defendant's own intoxication, could and should have declined the trooper's request. Floyd v. Commonwealth, No. 0568-01-2, 2002 Va. App. LEXIS 440 (Ct. of Appeals July 30, 2002).

Defendant who was intoxicated when he grabbed the steering wheel of a vehicle his sister was driving, and caused his sister to lose control of the vehicle, was properly convicted of driving under the influence of alcohol (second or subsequent offense), in violation of §§ 18.2-266 and 18.2-270 B, and operating a vehicle as an habitual offender, in violation of § 46.2-357. Dugger v. Commonwealth, 40 Va. App. 586, 580 S.E.2d 477, 2003 Va. App. LEXIS 305 (2003).

Sufficient evidence established that defendant was the operator of a car where he was still in the driver's seat with the key in the ignition when an officer arrived on the scene, and defendant admitted that he was the driver; no Miranda warnings were required during the Terry stop. Pruitt v. Commonwealth, — Va. App. —, —, S.E.2d —, 2008 Va. App. LEXIS 57 (Feb. 5, 2008).

Even though defendant was found unconscious in a parked vehicle, the evidence was sufficient to convict him of operating a vehicle while intoxicated because the key was in the vehicle's ignition, it was turned so that the vehicle's electrical system would work, and the vehicle's radio was on. Nelson v. Commonwealth, 2010 Va. App. LEXIS 42 (2010), aff'd, 281 Va. 212, 707 S.E.2d 815, 2011 Va. LEXIS 27 (2011).

In a prosecution on a charge of driving while intoxicated under § 18.2-266, the evidence showed that defendant "operated" his vehicle. Defendant was found inside the vehicle, and the key was in the "on" or "accessory" position, although the motor was not running; defendant's action in turning on the radio by placing the key in the "on" position of the ignition constituted manipulating the vehicle's electrical equipment. Nelson v. Commonwealth, 281 Va. 212, 707 S.E.2d 815, 2011 Va. LEXIS 27 (2011).

Because time is not an element of a charge of driving under the influence, the Commonwealth was not required to prove the exact date of defendant's arrest in order to convict him of the same. Raikes v. Commonwealth, 2007 Va. App. LEXIS 386 (Oct. 23, 2007).

Prosecution in federal court for driving while intoxicated on federal land. — The Assimilative Crimes Act of 1948, 18 U.S.C.S. § 13, makes applicable to a prosecution in a federal court for driving while intoxicated on a federal parkway within the territorial limits of Virginia the Virginia statute which prohibits one from driving an automobile while under the influence of alcohol and the Virginia statute (§ 18.2-270) which prescribes penalties for the offense. Kay v. United States, 255 F.2d 476 (4th Cir.), cert. denied, 358 U.S. 825, 79 S. Ct. 42, 3 L. Ed. 2d 65 (1958), commented on in 16 Wash. & Lee L. Rev. 62 (1959).

In a prosecution under the Assimilative Crimes Act for drunken driving on a military post in Virginia, the magistrate need not consider both the Virginia statutes, this section and former § 18.2-268 (now § 18.2-268.1 et seq.) together, but may consider this section as a separate offense and disregard any evidence as to blood tests with respect to a drunken driving charge. United States v. Gholson, 319 F. Supp. 499 (E.D. Va. 1970).

Special assessment inapplicable to offense committed on federal enclave. — As drunken driving offenses are excepted from Virginia's "additional cost" provision in § 19.2-368.18, no punishment exists in state law similar to the federal assessments in the Assimilative Crimes Act, 18 U.S.C.S. § 13, and for that reason the special assessment cannot apply to drunken driving offenses committed in Virginia on a federal enclave. United States v. Robertson,

638 F. Supp. 1202 (E.D. Va. 1986).

Applicability to driving on private roads. — In Valentine v. County of Brunswick, 202 Va. 696, 119 S.E.2d 486 (1961), it was held that a county ordinance similar to this section applied to driving on private roads as well as public highways.

Public ownership of the property upon which the vehicle is driven or operated is not an element the Commonwealth must prove in a prosecution for driving in violation of this section. Mitchell v. Commonwealth, 26 Va. App. 27, 492 S.E.2d 839 (1997).

Violation may occur in parking lot. — This statute does not specify that the driving or operating that it criminalizes must occur on a public highway; thus defendant could properly be convicted of drunk driving for such conduct in a parking lot. Gray v. Commonwealth, 23 Va. App. 351, 477 S.E.2d 301 (1996).

Fact that defendant operated vehicle while trying to extricate it from a ditch, off the traveled portion of the public highway, was of no importance. Reynolds v. City of Va. Beach, 31 Va. App. 629, 525 S.E.2d 65 (2000).

Defendant did not drive or operate car since key in ignition did not engage car. — Because the presence of the key in the ignition switch in the off position did not engage the mechanical or electrical equipment of the car, the defendant did not "drive or operate" the car within the meaning of the statutes that were incorporated by reference in a city ordinance. Stevenson v. City of Falls Church, 243 Va. 434, 416 S.E.2d 435 (1992).

No error in refusing proffered jury instruction. — Trial court did not err in refusing defendant's proffered jury instruction defining "operating a motor vehicle" because the instruction was not an accurate statement of the law when it was not necessary that the jury find that defendant acted with the purpose of putting a car in motion to find that he operated a car within the meaning of § 18.2-266. The instruction the trial court granted fully and fairly covered the principles of law relevant to the question of whether he operated the car in which he was found. Ngomondjami v. Commonwealth, 54 Va. App. 310, 678 S.E.2d 281, 2009 Va. App. LEXIS 296 (2009).

B. Negligence and Causation.

Violation of section as negligence. — If defendant was driving his car while under the influence of intoxicants, he violated this section and that was negligence. Yet it was not his intoxication but his negligence that had to be the proximate cause of the mishap before there could be a finding against him because of his conduct in that respect. Bogstad v. Hope, 199 Va. 453, 100 S.E.2d 745 (1957).

There can be no conviction unless there is evidence tending to establish the agency responsible for the erratic behavior of the accused. Miller v. Commonwealth, 214 Va. 689, 204 S.E.2d 268 (1974).

Intoxication is relevant to determination of degree of defendant's negligence whether ordinary, gross or wanton. It may serve to elevate the defendant's conduct to the level of negligence so gross, wanton and culpable as to show a reckless disregard of human life, a requisite element for a conviction of involuntary manslaughter. Essex v. Commonwealth, 228 Va. 273, 322 S.E.2d 216 (1984).

The degree of intoxication is a circumstance relevant to a determination of the question whether, in light of all other circumstances, the act of driving an automobile was such an improper performance of a lawful act as to constitute negligence so gross and culpable as to indicate a callous disregard to human life. Beck v. Commonwealth, 216 Va. 1, 216 S.E.2d 8 (1975).

Where driver was driving a car and he admitted on the scene that he had been drinking before getting behind the wheel that night, and defendant said that he could smell alcohol on plaintiff, probable cause existed to arrest driver for DUI. Cooper v. City of Va. Beach, 817 F. Supp. 1310 (E.D. Va. 1993).

Criminal negligence. — Even when the evidence shows a level of intoxication lower than that necessary to a conviction for violation of this section, such evidence is germane to the question of criminal negligence. Beck v. Commonwealth, 216 Va. 1, 216 S.E.2d 8 (1975).

Conduct rather than degree of intoxication determines malice. — The defendant's degree of intoxication, however great, neither enhances nor impairs the set of facts relied upon to establish implied malice. In making the determination whether malice exists, the fact finder must be guided by the quality of the defendant's conduct, its likelihood of causing death or great bodily harm, and whether it was volitional or inadvertent; not by the defendant's blood-alcohol level. Essex v. Commonwealth, 228 Va. 273, 322 S.E.2d 216 (1984).

C. Under the Influence.

1. Under the influence of alcohol.

The burden is on the Commonwealth to prove that the defendant was under the influence of intoxicants, not on the defendant to prove that he was not. The Commonwealth's evidence must exclude every reasonable hypothesis of innocence. Until that is done the defendant is not required to explain or to offer evidence of his innocence. Clemmer v. Commonwealth, 208 Va. 661, 159 S.E.2d 664 (1968).

In order to convict the defendant, it is necessary that the Commonwealth establish two things: (1) that the defendant was operating or driving a motor vehicle, and (2) that he was under the influence of intoxicants at the time he was driving or operating it. Nicolls v. Commonwealth, 212 Va. 257, 184 S.E.2d 9 (1971).

The Commonwealth bears the burden of proving that the accused was driving under the influence of alcohol or other self-administered intoxicant. Miller v. Commonwealth, 214 Va. 689, 204 S.E.2d 268 (1974).

Consumption of alcohol after driving. — Where there is evidence that alcohol has been consumed after driving the chemical test cannot accurately reflect the blood alcohol concentration at the time of driving since the chemical test simply cannot distinguish between two sources of alcohol, and where no alcohol is consumed between the time of driving and the time the chemical test is administered, the test results can reflect only that alcohol consumed before or during driving, and clause (i) is applicable only in these latter circumstances. Davis v. Commonwealth, 8 Va. App. 291, 381 S.E.2d 11 (1989).

Where the issue of whether defendant drank after an accident was disputed, and the trial court ruled that the credible evidence was insufficient to prove as a matter of law that the defendant drank after the accident, its submission of the issue to the jury was proper, as the jury was entitled to discredit defendant's evidence; when it did so, the Commonwealth could rely on the presumption that defendant was under the influence at the time of the accident. Acheson v. Commonwealth, No. 1706-03-4, 2004 Va. App. LEXIS 566 (Ct. of Appeals Nov. 16, 2004).

The prescribed measurement is an evidentiary fact which creates a rebuttable presumption that the measurement accurately reflects the blood alcohol concentration at the time of driving. Davis v. Commonwealth, 8 Va. App. 291, 381 S.E.2d 11 (1989).

Presumption of blood alcohol concentration at time of driving. — Where it is undisputed that appellant's blood alcohol concentration at the time of testing registered at 0.17 percent, there is a presumption that appellant's blood alcohol concentration was also 0.17 percent at the time of driving. Kehl v. Commonwealth, 15 Va. App. 602, 426 S.E.2d 127 (1993).

The prescribed measurement is an evidentiary fact which creates a rebuttable presumption. — Results of a chemical test showing that blood alcohol concentration was .10 (now .08) percent or more creates a rebuttable presumption that the measurement accurately reflects the blood alcohol concentration at the time of driving. Nelson v. Commonwealth, 16 Va. App. 266, 430 S.E.2d 553 (1993).

Being "under the influence of alcohol" is established when any person has consumed enough alcoholic beverages to so affect his manner, disposition, speech, muscular movement, general appearance or behavior, as to be apparent to observation. Moore v. Commonwealth, No. 0264-99-4, 2000 Va. App. LEXIS 538 (Ct. of Appeals July 25, 2000).

Test is as to whether defendant was under influence of intoxicants. — Under this section the burden is not upon the Commonwealth to prove that, while he was driving an automobile, accused was under the influence of intoxicants to such an extent that his ability to drive with safety to himself and others was thereby materially impaired. The test to be applied, in a prosecution under this section, is not merely the ability of the driver to operate the automobile with safety to himself and others, but whether or not he was under the influence of intoxicants at the time he was driving or running an automobile. Owens v. Commonwealth,

147 Va. 624, 136 S.E. 765 (1927).

Question for jury. — In a prosecution for operating a motor vehicle while under the influence of intoxicants, there was evidence for the State that the defendant was intoxicated. The evidence given by the defendant and his witnesses was to the effect that he was not intoxicated. The resulting conflict in the evidence was for the jury to settle. Rodgers v. Commonwealth, 197 Va. 527, 90 S.E.2d 257 (1955).

Improper jury instruction. — Jury instruction, that evidence was present of the amount of alcohol in blood of defendant at time of the accident, was factually incorrect and contrary to unrefuted, expert testimony that the test measures the amount of alcohol in the blood at the time of the test; thus, reversible error occurred. Taylor v. Commonwealth, 12 Va. App. 419, 404 S.E.2d 78 (1991).

2. Narcotics or drugs.

Narcotic not self-administered. — Trial and appellate courts should not have found that defendant violated § 18.2-266, driving under the influence of a narcotic drug, after defendant drove defendant's vehicle into a telephone pole following defendant's release from a hospital where defendant had been treated for severe pain; pursuant to the plain language of that statute, the narcotic had to be self-administered and no dispute existed but that the narcotics that influenced the accident were administered by medical personnel at the hospital. Jackson v. Commonwealth, 274 Va. 630, 652 S.E.2d 111, 2007 Va. LEXIS 128 (2007).

Under the influence of drugs. — Reading §§ 18.2-51.4 and 18.2-266(iii) together, their plain meaning is that a person violates § 18.2-51.4 when he or she recklessly causes serious bodily injury to another person resulting in permanent and significant physical impairment to that person while operating a vehicle under the influence of any narcotic drug which impairs the driver's ability to operate a motor vehicle in violation of § 18.2-266(iii). Ratliff v. Commonwealth, 53 Va. App. 443, 672 S.E.2d 913, 2009 Va. App. LEXIS 83 (2009).

Defendant was properly convicted of recklessly causing serious and permanent bodily injury to another person while driving under the influence of narcotic drugs, as she admitted having controlled substances in her system, and § 18.2-51.4 did not apply only to those who operated a vehicle under the influence of alcohol. Ratliff v. Commonwealth, 53 Va. App. 443, 672 S.E.2d 913, 2009 Va. App. LEXIS 83 (2009).

Driving under the influence of any drug that impairs ability to drive prohibited. — Conviction of driving under the influence, § 18.2-266, was supported by sufficient evidence under circumstances in which defendant drove while under the influence of a drug administered to him at a hospital by a nurse because the statute prohibited driving while under the influence of any drug that impaired the ability to drive. Jackson v. Commonwealth, — Va. App. —, — S.E.2d —, 2006 Va. App. LEXIS 603 (Dec. 22, 2006), rev'd on grounds that drug must be self-administered, 274 Va. 630, 652 S.E.2d 111 (2007).

Involuntary unconsciousness defense properly rejected. — Trial court properly convicted a defendant of driving while intoxicated and did not err by rejecting his involuntary unconsciousness defense since the trial court made no factual finding that he was sleepwalking at the time of the accident due to taking prescription medication. Contrary to the defendant's contention on appeal, the trial court found that proof beyond a reasonable doubt existed that the defendant was driving under the influence based on having a blood alcohol level greater than .15, but less than .20, thus, there was a sufficient independent basis to find that he was intoxicated while driving to defeat his involuntary unconsciousness defense claim. Bradley v. Commonwealth, 2009 Va. App. LEXIS 347 (Aug. 4, 2009).

III. EVIDENCE.

A. Admissibility, Burden of Proof, Presumptions.

Rebuttable presumption. — Where the presence of an open container of alcohol and defendant's appearance gave rise to a rebuttable presumption under § 18.2-323.1 that defendant consumed alcohol while driving, the fact that an officer did not perceive defendant to be drunk or driving under the influence did not negate the presumption because a driver did not have to be intoxicated to the extent necessary to support a conviction under § 18.2-266 in order to be found guilty of drinking while operating a motor vehicle in violation of § 18.2-323.1. United States v. Washington, 439 F. Supp. 2d 589, 2006 U.S. Dist. LEXIS 52064 (E.D. Va. 2006), aff'd, 2009 U.S. App. LEXIS 16364 (4th Cir. Va. 2009).

Doctor's testimony was not sufficient to rebut presumption. — Doctor's testimony that it was just as likely that appellant's blood alcohol concentration at the time of driving exceeded 0.17 as it was that his blood alcohol concentration was below 0.17 percent, and that his feeling was that appellant's blood alcohol concentration was below a .10 but that his stronger feeling was that he did not think anybody can say what it was, was not sufficient to rebut the presumption that appellant's blood alcohol concentration at the time of the breathalyzer test was the same as it was at the time of the offense, one hour and 28 minutes earlier. Kehl v. Commonwealth, 15 Va. App. 602, 426 S.E.2d 127 (1993).

No presumption of intoxication where certificate inadmissible. — Where the certificate of analysis of the breath test is inadmissible, the Commonwealth is not entitled to a rebuttable presumption that defendant was intoxicated at the time of the alleged offense (where his blood-alcohol content was greater than 0.10%). Such defendant's guilt or innocence must therefore be determined from the other evidence of his condition at the time of the alleged offense. Overbee v. Commonwealth, 227 Va. 238, 315 S.E.2d 242 (1984).

Presumption not applied. — Trial court did not err in convicting defendant of driving under the influence of alcohol in violation of § 18.2-266 because the trial court considered the totality of the evidence and did not apply any statutory presumption set forth in § 18.2-269 to defendant's blood alcohol test result shown on the certificate of analysis; the trial court emphasized its reliance on the photographs of the accident taken at the scene and the circumstantial evidence, in particular but not limited to, defendant's admission that he had consumed four twenty-two ounce beers before the accident. Bilger v. Commonwealth, 2011 Va. App. LEXIS 371 (Nov. 29, 2011).

Validity of arrest. — Officer had probable cause to arrest defendant for driving under the influence of alcohol, because a reasonable person could have properly inferred from the totality of the circumstances that defendant had drunk enough alcohol, at the time of the accident, to observably affect his manner, disposition, speech, muscular movement, general appearance, or behavior, since: (1) the officer knew that defendant had been in a bar until nearly closing time; (2) the officer knew that defendant struck the victim while driving his motorcycle; (3) the officer observed at the hospital that defendant had a quite strong odor of alcohol about his person; and (4) the officer saw that, although defendant's only apparent injuries were scrapes and bruises, defendant's speech was slurred. Bristol v. Commonwealth, 47 Va. App. 584, 625 S.E.2d 676, 2006 Va. App. LEXIS 53 (2006), reversed, remanded, 272 Va. 568, 636 S.E.2d 460 (2006), as to validity of arrest. See note following.

Because defendant was not validly arrested within three hours of the offenses, as required by subsection A of § 18.2-268.2, and an officer's act of telling defendant that he was under arrest and advising him of the implied consent law was insufficient to satisfy the restraint requirement to assert his lawful authority to arrest defendant, defendant did not impliedly consent to have his blood drawn; thus, the certificate of analysis containing defendant's blood test results was inadmissible. Bristol v. Commonwealth, 272 Va. 568, 636 S.E.2d 460, 2006 Va. LEXIS 115 (2006).

Validity of amended warrant. — Because a warrant provided defendant with notice of the nature and character of the offense with which defendant was charged, and because §§ 16.1-137 and 19.2-226 authorized the trial court to amend the warrant to delete reference to a city code, which was mere surplusage, the trial court properly denied defendant's motion to dismiss, and found defendant guilty of a second offense of driving under the influence under § 18.2-266. Dennis v. Commonwealth, 2008 Va. App. LEXIS 530 (Dec. 9, 2008).

Certificate not admissible where arrest took place after blood test. — Trial court erred in admitting a certificate of analysis at defendant's trial pursuant to § 18.2-268.2, because the purported arrest for driving under the influence took place after the blood test was administered. Sprouse v. Commonwealth, 53 Va. App. 488, 673 S.E.2d 481, 2009 Va. App. LEXIS 109 (2009).

Certificate inadmissible where arrest not timely made. —

Where there is no evidence that defendant was arrested within two hours of the alleged offense, the certificate showing the alcohol content of defendant's blood is inadmissible. Overbee v. Commonwealth, 227 Va. 238, 315 S.E.2d 242 (1984).

Sobriety checkpoint. — The seizure of defendant upon the initial stop at a license and sobriety checkpoint in question was constitutionally valid, where uniformed police officers, wearing reflector vests, were assigned to the scene, the area and the warning sign were well-lighted, there were two marked police vehicles present with red lights flashing, the geography of the site permitted adequate space for the momentary initial detention to check licenses and to afford space for vehicles, whose operators required further evaluation, to pull aside, the officers at the checkpoint had no discretion regarding which vehicles to stop and every southbound vehicle was halted, if congestion occurred, vehicles were permitted to move through the checkpoint until the congestion cleared, and the police endeavored to detain a motorist no more than 30 seconds for the license check. Balancing the state's strong interest in protecting the public from the grave risk presented by drunk drivers, against the minimal inconvenience caused motorists approaching the roadblock, the action of the police was not an impermissible infringement upon defendant's reasonable expectation of privacy. Lowe v. Commonwealth, 230 Va. 346, 337 S.E.2d 273 (1985), cert. denied, 475 U.S. 1084, 106 S. Ct. 1464, 89 L. Ed. 2d 720 (1986).

Admission of refusal to perform test did not violate constitutions. — Neither the Fifth Amendment nor Va. Const., Art. I, § 8 were violated by the admission in evidence of defendant's refusal to take a field sobriety test. Farmer v. Commonwealth, 12 Va. App. 337, 404 S.E.2d 371 (1991).

But inferring an admission did violate Constitutions. — In a prosecution for driving under the influence in violation of § 18.2-266 as assimilated under 18 U.S.C.S. §§ 7 and 13, the trial court violated defendant's Fifth Amendment right against self-incrimination by inferring an admission of culpability from defendant's silence when defendant was advised of Virginia's implied consent statute, § 18.2-268.2; however, the error was harmless because sufficient independent evidence established defendant's identity as the driver of the vehicle involved in the accident in question. United States v. Hagedorn, — F.3d —, 2002 U.S. App. LEXIS 25762 (4th Cir. Dec. 16, 2002).

In prosecution for driving under the influence on a military base in violation of § 18.2-266, as assimilated under 18 U.S.C.S. §§ 7, 13, the appellate court determined that the district court violated defendant's Fifth Amendment right against self-incrimination by inferring an admission that defendant was the driver of the vehicle by remaining silent in the face of being advised of Virginia's implied consent statute applicable to drivers under § 18.2-268.2, and defendant's silence under such circumstances did not constitute an admission of culpability; however, the error was harmless because unrelated evidence established defendant's identity as the driver. United States v. Hagedorn, — F.3d —, 2003 U.S. App. LEXIS 1805 (4th Cir. Feb. 3, 2003).

Physical performance during field sobriety tests not protected by Fifth Amendment. — Trial court did not err in denying defendant's motion to suppress testimony regarding his field sobriety tests because an officer's failure to read defendant his *Miranda* warnings prior to administering the tests did not require the suppression of the results since defendant's physical performance during the tests was not protected by the Fifth Amendment; neither the physical components of the field sobriety tests nor defendant's inability to perform them constituted a testimonial communication because none of the three tests compelled defendant to reveal his knowledge, thoughts, or beliefs, but rather, they only required him to exhibit certain physical characteristics. Gibson v. Commonwealth, 57 Va. App. 772, 706 S.E.2d 541, 2011 Va. App. LEXIS 95 (2011).

Checkpoint constitutionality. — Field officer's control over the timing of a checkpoint did not constitute unbridled discretion sufficient to render the checkpoint unconstitutional; although the field officer was allowed to designate the timing of the traffic checking detail, he had no discretion to decide the location of the assigned roadblock, and he was required to obtain approval from a supervisor before he began stopping vehicles. Crouch v. Commonwealth, 26 Va. App. 214, 494 S.E.2d 144 (1997).

Field officer's limited authority to determine the specific time of a sobriety checkpoint roadblock during a particular workweek did not constitute unbridled discretion sufficient to render the checkpoint unconstitutional. Crouch v. Commonwealth, 26 Va. App. 214, 494 S.E.2d 144 (1997).

Adequate foundation for blood test results. — Defendant's conviction for DUI, third offense, was appropriate because the admitted blood test did not lack an adequate foundation, defendant admitted to an officer that she had consumed alcohol on the night of the incident, and open containers were found in her car. The hospital's record keeper testified that a member of the hospital's trauma team drew blood from defendant, that defendant received a patient record number, and that the number was a unique number that stayed with the patient throughout his or her stay; defendant's patient record number matched the patient trauma number that a member of the fire department testified that he recorded when defendant arrived at the hospital; and a forensic toxicologist provided detailed testimony about the procedure for drawing blood in a hospital setting. Barlow v. Commonwealth, 2011 Va. App. LEXIS 112 (Apr. 5, 2011).

Admission of certificate into evidence does not implicate right to confrontation. — Trial court, in defendant's driving while intoxicated case did not err in admitting into evidence a certificate of blood alcohol analysis based on the result, contained in a certificate of analysis, from a breath test; the breath test result contained in the certificate of analysis was not hearsay evidence, pursuant to § 18.2-268.9, and, therefore the admission into evidence of that result did not implicate defendant's constitutional right to confrontation. Luginbyhl v. Commonwealth, 46 Va. App. 460, 618 S.E.2d 347, 2005 Va. App. LEXIS 329 (2005), substituted op., on reh'g, 48 Va. App. 58, 628 S.E.2d 74 (2006) (wherein the court held that error was harmless while declining to address the constitutional issue) .

Defendant waived her Sixth Amendment rights to confrontation by failing to avail herself of her statutory right under § 19.2-187.1 to subpoena the operator of a breath test in her driving under the influence trial under § 18.2-266. Thus, it was proper to admit the certificate of the blood alcohol analysis without live testimony of the operator pursuant to §§ 18.2-268.9 and 19.2-187. McKeel v. Commonwealth, — Va. App. —, — S.E.2d —, 2006 Va. App. LEXIS 575 (Dec. 19, 2006).

Trial court did not err in admitting a certificate of blood alcohol analysis into evidence because the statements in the certificate did not implicate the Confrontation Clause; the breath test result was not a statement made by a witness, a state trooper's testimony in the attestation clause of the certificate merely stated the trooper's opinion that he complied with approved methods in conducting the breath test, and the maintenance log for the breathalyzer was essentially a business record. Wimbish v. Commonwealth, 51 Va. App. 474, 658 S.E.2d 715, 2008 Va. App. LEXIS 168 (2008).

Defendant was properly convicted of driving while intoxicated because the trial court did not violate defendant's constitutional right to confrontation when it admitted his blood alcohol breath analysis into evidence in accordance with the terms of § 19.2-187; because defendant did not subpoena the booking tech who administered the blood alcohol breath analysis, he waived his opportunity to cross-examine potential witnesses. Ki-Ho Min v. Commonwealth, — Va. App. —, — S.E.2d —, 2008 Va. App. LEXIS 144 (Mar. 25, 2008).

Admission of certificate violated Confrontation Clause. — Trial court erred in admitting into evidence a certificate of blood alcohol analysis because the attestation clause included in the certificate was testimonial in nature, and its admission, over the objection of defendant, constituted a violation of the Confrontation Clause when the facts establishing the validity and admissibility of the breath test result had to be proved by live, in-court testimony; while there is no constitutional requirement that the factual predicates in § 18.2-268.9 be established prior to the admission of the results of the test, once the General Assembly conditions the validity and admissibility of the breath-test results on the proof of those facts, the Commonwealth must prove those facts through live, in-court testimony and not by affidavit. Grant v. Commonwealth, 54 Va. App. 714, 682 S.E.2d 84, 2009 Va. App. LEXIS 390 (2009).

Admission of certificate an error. — Officer made an invalid warrantless arrest for a misdemeanor not committed in his presence as the single-vehicle accident occurred on or beside a private road in a gated, guarded residential complex; thus, the exceptions

to the warrant requirement in § 19.2-81 did not apply. Therefore, the implied consent law did not apply to permit the certificate of analysis of defendant's breath test to be admitted into evidence. Roseborough v. Commonwealth, 281 Va. 233, 704 S.E.2d 414, 2011 Va. LEXIS 13 (2011).

Admission of certificate not harmless error. — Trial court's error in admitting into evidence a certificate of blood alcohol analysis was not harmless beyond a reasonable doubt because in order to convict defendant of a per se violation under clause (i) of § 18.2-266 or invoke the presumption of intoxication afforded by subdivision A 3 of § 18.2-269 the trial court had to rely on the facts recited in the attestation clause in order to conclude that the test was conducted in accordance with the relevant statutes; the only evidence that the breath test was administered either as provided by Title 18.2, Chapter Seven, Article Two of the Virginia Code or in accordance with the provisions of §§ 18.2-268.1 through 18.2-268.12, as required by § 18.2-269, was in the attestation clause on the certificate of analysis, and because the use of the attestation clause in the case violated the Confrontation Clause, it could not be used to prove that the breath test was administered in accordance with the relevant statutes. Grant v. Commonwealth, 54 Va. App. 714, 682 S.E.2d 84, 2009 Va. App. LEXIS 390 (2009).

No Brady violation. — Trial court did not err by refusing to dismiss a driving under the influence of alcohol charge against defendant because assuming, without deciding, that repair records and testing logs for two Intoxilyzers were exculpatory evidence, there was no Brady violation when defendant was able to utilize that evidence at trial. Newman v. Commonwealth, 2009 Va. App. LEXIS 360 (Aug. 11, 2009).

Breath test certificate filed prior to trial. — Defendant was properly convicted of driving under the influence, as the Commonwealth proved that the breath test certificate was filed seven days prior to trial with the clerk of the trial court as required by § 19.2-187. Cephas v. Commonwealth, No. 3359-01-4, 2003 Va. App. LEXIS 114 (Ct. of Appeals Mar. 4, 2003).

Certificate not provided. — As defendant's request to the Commonwealth for a copy of the analysis of his breath alcohol content was in proper form, but the certificate was not provided as required by § 19.2-187, his conviction of driving under the influence was reversed; and since the trial court expressly ruled that the remaining evidence was by itself insufficient to convict, the warrant was dismissed. Dotson v. Commonwealth, No. 1416-02-2, 2003 Va. App. LEXIS 282 (Ct. of Appeals May 6, 2003).

Certificate of blood withdrawal. — In a DWI trial, the Commonwealth was permitted to introduce evidence of a certificate of analysis of a blood vial drawn shortly after defendant's arrest, even though the certificate of blood withdrawal had become detached from the vial. Defendant was convicted based on evidence that the blood in the vial had a blood alcohol content of 0.14% by weight by volume. Williams v. Commonwealth, No. 2451-02-4, 2003 Va. App. LEXIS 597 (Ct. of Appeals Nov. 18, 2003).

Preliminary breath test results properly admitted at suppression hearing. — Where an officer read defendant an "implied consent card" and told him he was not required to take the preliminary breath test (PBT), that it was strictly "for the benefit of probable cause," and that the result of the PBT "could not be used against him in court," the advisement, though inartful, was sufficient to allow admission of the result at a suppression hearing to establish probable cause to arrest. Neatrour v. Commonwealth, No. 2090-03-4, 2004 Va. App. LEXIS 462 (Ct. of Appeals Sept. 28, 2004).

Admission of Department of Motor Vehicle record at sentencing phase proper. — Trial court did not err by admitting defendant's Department of Motor Vehicle (DMV) record into evidence at the sentencing phase of his trial for driving under the influence of alcohol (DUI) in violation of § 18.2-266 because when the jury found defendant guilty of DUI, § 46.2-943 authorized the admission of his DMV record into evidence during the sentencing phase as evidence of his prior traffic record; a DMV record is admissible as evidence of a defendant's prior traffic record. Ngomondjami v. Commonwealth, 54 Va. App. 310, 678 S.E.2d 281, 2009 Va. App. LEXIS 296 (2009).

Burden of proof. — Under § 18.2-268.9, the Commonwealth is not required to introduce evidence showing the Virginia Department of Forensic Science's compliance with subdivision B 3 of § 9.1-1101 before a certificate of blood alcohol analysis becomes admissible; rather, the substantial compliance provisions of § 18.2-

268.11 indicate that the defendant has the burden of producing evidence showing noncompliance with procedural requirements like that contained in subdivision B 3 of § 9.1-1101. Fitzgerald v. Commonwealth, 61 Va. App. 279, 734 S.E.2d 708, 2012 Va. App. LEXIS 398 (2012).

B. Scientific Tests.

Blood test results not required. — State's failure to comply with the implied consent law procedural requirements did not forbid a prosecution for aggravated manslaughter, blood test results were not required for a conviction under either § 18.2-266 or 18.2-36.1. Stevens v. Commonwealth, 46 Va. App. 234, 616 S.E.2d 754, 2005 Va. App. LEXIS 407 (2005), aff'd, — Va. —, 634 S.E.2d 305 (2006).

No automatic right to blood test. — It does not appear that a person arrested for driving under the influence has the automatic right to a blood test. United States v. Gholson, 319 F. Supp. 499 (E.D. Va. 1970).

Former § 18.2-268 (now § 18.2-268.1 et seq.) did not entitle one charged with a violation of this section to an automatic blood test. United States v. Fletcher, 344 F. Supp. 332 (E.D. Va. 1972).

No right to alcohol tests where original arrest was for public drunkeness. — Where defendant was arrested for public drunkenness, but an off-duty officer from another county who had observed his driving later swore out a criminal complaint and persuaded a magistrate to issue a warrant against defendant for driving under the influence, defendant had not been entitled to blood or breath tests under § 18.2-268.2. Wilson v. Commonwealth, 45 Va. App. 193, 609 S.E.2d 612, 2005 Va. App. LEXIS 84 (2005).

Effect of refusal to take blood test. — The concept of the law is that a driver, if arrested under this section, may be asked to consent to taking the blood test and for an unreasonable refusal, the penalty of a suspended license would be imposed. United States v. Gholson, 319 F. Supp. 499 (E.D. Va. 1970).

Imposition of criminal penalties for refusal to take a breath test did not transform the refusal into testimonial evidence; admission of defendant's statement of refusal to take a breath test was proper. The refusal constituted the crime, not the statement in response to an officer's question, and admission of the statement did not violate the Fifth Amendment. Acuna v. Commonwealth, 2006 Va. App. LEXIS 306 (July 11, 2006).

Blood sample from unconscious defendant. — Implied consent law did not require an officer to obtain a blood sample from an unconscious defendant in order to be able to prosecute him for driving under the influence. Oliver v. Commonwealth, 40 Va. App. 20, 577 S.E.2d 514, 2003 Va. App. LEXIS 98 (2003).

While the taking of a blood sample from an unconscious defendant alleged to have been driving under the influence was permitted, it was not mandatory in order to prosecute defendant for driving under the influence. Oliver v. Commonwealth, 40 Va. App. 20, 577 S.E.2d 514, 2003 Va. App. LEXIS 98 (2003).

Test must relate to alcohol consumption before or during act of driving. — Because the evil which this section is intended to prohibit is driving with a specified blood alcohol concentration and because the language employed in the statute refers to driving while having a specified blood alcohol concentration, the after-administered blood alcohol concentration test results must be related to the consumption of alcohol before or during the act of driving. Davis v. Commonwealth, 8 Va. App. 291, 381 S.E.2d 11 (1989).

Test results presumptive. — Because the blood alcohol concentration reflected by the chemical test necessarily resulted from alcohol consumed prior to or during driving, the test results are presumptive evidence of the blood alcohol concentration at the time of driving and as such, the accused may challenge the test results by competent evidence, such as, for example, that he had not consumed enough alcohol in the relevant time to reach the level indicated by the chemical test results. Davis v. Commonwealth, 8 Va. App. 291, 381 S.E.2d 11 (1989).

Trial court did not err in treating defendant's California driving under the influence conviction as a predicate offense for a recidivism enhancement to her Virginia DUI punishment under subdivision B 3 of § 18.2-270 because the California's DUI statute was substantially similar to § 18.2-266 where in neither statute were the blood alcohol concentration presumptions mandatory or conclu-

sive. Taylor v. Commonwealth, 2010 Va. App. LEXIS 96 (Mar. 16, 2010).

Chemical analysis of blood alcohol content as evidence. — There is no reason why the results of a chemical analysis of blood alcohol content should not be admissible if based upon a foundation which tends to ensure the reliability of the test equipment and procedures, the integrity of the chain of custody of the blood specimen, and the technical competence of the person who performed the analysis. Whether the foundation is sufficient is a question within the sound discretion of the trial judge. If the judge finds the foundation sufficient, the credibility of the witnesses and the weight to be accorded the evidence are matters within the province of the jury. Essex v. Commonwealth, 228 Va. 273, 322 S.E.2d 216 (1984).

Upon a conviction under § 18.2-266 where proof of a defendant's blood alcohol level is by a valid chemical breath or blood test, § 18.2-270 applies; to hold otherwise would defeat the purpose of § 18.2-270. Thus, the enhanced penalty provided for in § 18.2-270 A for defendants with breath alcohol readings in excess of 0.15 applied to defendant's sentence for driving while intoxicated in violation of § 18.2-266. United States v. Barber, 360 F. Supp. 2d 784, 2005 U.S. Dist. LEXIS 4640 (E.D. Va. 2005).

Defendant's conviction of driving while intoxicated was affirmed because the certificate of blood alcohol analysis was admissible under § 18.2-268.9 regardless of any alleged error in admitting the certificate of instrument accuracy, and, correspondingly, any error in admitting the certificate of instrument accuracy was harmless. Fitzgerald v. Commonwealth, 61 Va. App. 279, 734 S.E.2d 708, 2012 Va. App. LEXIS 398 (2012).

Defendant may contest reliability of blood alcohol concentration test. — Defendant who was convicted of operating a motor vehicle while having a blood alcohol concentration of .10 (now .08) percent may contest reliability of a blood alcohol concentration test results by proving in an appropriate case that the margin of error of a particular device was in excess of the margin deemed scientifically acceptable; however, merely proving the margin of error in a particular breathalyzer test, without more, does not as a matter of law, negate its reliability. Nelson v. Commonwealth, 16 Va. App. 266, 430 S.E.2d 553 (1993).

Requirements in order to implicate §§ 18.2-268.2 through 18.2-268.8. — Sections 18.2-268.2 through 18.2-268.8 provide the procedural requirements for taking, handling, identifying and disposing of blood samples under Virginia's implied consent law. To implicate the statutes the driver must have operated a motor vehicle upon a public highway in this Commonwealth and have been arrested for a violation of this section (or a similar ordinance) within two hours of the alleged offense of driving under the influence of alcohol. Thurston v. City of Lynchburg, 15 Va. App. 475, 424 S.E.2d 701 (1992).

Applicability of testing requirements. — While the statutory requirements of § 18.2-268 (see now § 18.2-268.1 et seq.) are to be strictly applied, they apply only to DUI prosecutions under this section, and not to an involuntary manslaughter prosecution under § 18.2-36. Taylor v. Commonwealth, No. 1977-94-4 (Ct. of Appeals July 18, 1995).

Need for cleansing procedures to comply with statute. — Because the driving under the influence (DUI) statutes specify the means for cleansing the puncture area, failure to comply with the statutory requirement would necessitate that the prosecution be dismissed. Taylor v. Commonwealth, No. 1977-94-4 (Ct. of Appeals July 18, 1995).

Calibration after administration of test. — Trial court did not err in admitting breath test certificate in prosecution for driving under the influence, where calibration of breath test machine was conducted before the breath test was administered and not afterwards as required by former 1 VAC § 30-50-90 (presently 6 VAC § 20-190-110(3)); regulation was procedural, not substantive, and substantial rather than strict compliance with its provisions was all that was necessary for the test result certificate to be admissible. Hegedus v. Commonwealth, No. 2732-00-3, 2001 Va. App. LEXIS 598 (Ct. of Appeals Oct. 30, 2001).

When breathalyzer not prerequisite to warrant. — Where an officer has probable cause to obtain an arrest warrant for driving under the influence, there is no legal requirement that the officer administer a breathalyzer test before obtaining the arrest warrant.

Leonard v. County of Spotsylvania, No. 2089-96-2 (Ct. of Appeals June 3, 1997).

A chemical analysis of one's blood provides a scientifically accurate method of determining whether a person is intoxicated, removes the question from the field of speculation, and supplies the best evidence for that determination. Thurston v. City of Lynchburg, 15 Va. App. 475, 424 S.E.2d 701 (1992).

Chemical analysis relevant to degree of intoxication. — Proof by chemical analysis of the percentage of alcohol in the blood is relevant to a determination of the degree of intoxication. Essex v. Commonwealth, 228 Va. 273, 322 S.E.2d 216 (1984).

Error to admit blood test results where failure to follow statutory mandates. — Where the government has failed in its responsibilities to follow the statutory mandates in the taking, handling, identification and disposition of blood samples under the statutory scheme, it is error to admit at trial the results of tests concerning such blood samples. Thurston v. City of Lynchburg, 15 Va. App. 475, 424 S.E.2d 701 (1992).

Although a nurse and police officer committed technical violations of former § 18.2-268.6 when they packaged a sample of defendant's blood for transportation to a laboratory, the violations were trivial and the trial court did not err by finding that there was substantial compliance with the statute and admitting the results of the blood test into evidence. Jones v. Commonwealth, No. 2967-02-2, 2004 Va. App. LEXIS 64 (Ct. of Appeals Feb. 10, 2004).

Waiver of right to separate sample where accused voluntarily interrupts procedure. — The government's failure to comply strictly with the statutory mandate to provide the accused with a sample of blood for independent testing resulted from the voluntary act of the accused in interrupting the completion of the blood removal process; where an accused voluntarily interrupts the blood removal procedure before the physician, nurse or technician completes that procedure, the accused, by his conduct, shall be deemed to have waived his right to an independent analysis of a separate sample as provided by §§ 18.2-268.6 and 18.2-268.7. Thurston v. City of Lynchburg, 15 Va. App. 475, 424 S.E.2d 701 (1992) (decided prior to 2003 amendments to §§ 18.2-268.6 and 18.2-268.7.)

Where defendant disrupted blood removal procedure, no error in admitting one sample. — Defendant's voluntary act in disrupting the blood removal procedure constituted a waiver of his right to a separate sample for independent testing. Thus, it was not error for the trial court to admit the results of the blood test analyzed from the one sample sent to the state laboratory by the arresting officer. Thurston v. City of Lynchburg, 15 Va. App. 475, 424 S.E.2d 701 (1992).

Where defendant disrupted breathalyzer test, sufficient evidence supported the trial court's finding that defendant deliberately refused to cooperate in giving a breath sample where defendant, who had two prior DUI convictions, barely blew into the breathalyzer machine during a first attempt, resulting in the apparatus not being activated, and failed a second time to blow as instructed after the arresting officer informed defendant that defendant was not performing the test properly and gave defendant another chance; defendant did not give a medical reason for not giving a valid breath sample and it was reasonable for the officer to conclude from defendant's conduct during the two attempts that defendant was not cooperating and that defendant would continue such non-cooperation if further tests were attempted. Lee Banks Walker v. Commonwealth, No. 0349-02-1, 2003 Va. App. LEXIS 246 (Ct. of Appeals Apr. 22, 2003).

Physical inability to take breath test. — Trial court erred in convicting defendant of driving under the influence in violation of § 18.2-266 because the trial court failed to rule on whether defendant was physically unable to take the breath test required by § 18.2-268.2, and it did not resolve the conflict in the testimony; defendant testified he suffered from acid reflux, causing him to burp involuntarily, and if believed, defendant could not comply with the twenty-minute observation period, but an officer testified that he spoke with defendant for approximately thirty minutes at the scene and heard no burping, nor did he hear burping from the time of arrest until defendant was taken to jail. Packard v. Commonwealth, 2011 Va. App. LEXIS 107 (Mar. 29, 2011).

Breath test properly performed although clerical mistake in certificate. — While the certificate of blood alcohol analysis

indicated an alcohol content of ".10% grams per 210 liters of breath," deputy testified that he mistakenly included the percent sign on the certificate, that it was a clerical mistake, and that appellant's true "reading from the machine was .10" grams per 210 liters of breath. The evidence established that deputy properly performed the breath test, and the actual result comported with the statutory requirements. Murray v. Commonwealth, No. 2142-96-4 (Ct. of Appeals Nov. 4, 1997).

Absence of evidence establishing when breath test was administered went to the weight of the evidence and was a factor, as was other evidence, for jury to consider. Killingsworth v. Commonwealth, No. 2447-98-3 (Ct. of Appeals Nov. 9, 1999).

Certificate of analysis properly admitted. — Trial court did not err by admitting the certificate of analysis into evidence because the evidence established that the breath test was administered in compliance with the twenty-minute observation period required by § 18.2-268.9; the attestation clause that was part of the certificate of analysis admitted into evidence stated that appellant's breath test "was conducted in accordance with Department of Forensic Science specifications, one of which provided for the twenty-minute period of observation, and the testimony of the person who administered the breath test established that a police officer observed defendant for the required twenty minutes prior to the attempted test on the first Intoxilyzer before she was immediately moved to the second Intoxilyzer only a few feet away. Newman v. Commonwealth, 2009 Va. App. LEXIS 360 (Aug. 11, 2009).

C. Other Evidence of Intoxication.

Other evidence of intoxication. — Where the Commonwealth offers no chemical test results of an accused's blood or breath, the issue becomes whether the accused is under the influence, which has to be determined from all of the evidence of his condition at the time of the alleged offense. Moore v. Commonwealth, No. 0264-99-4, 2000 Va. App. LEXIS 538 (Ct. of Appeals July 25, 2000).

Detention by off-duty officer from another jurisdiction. — Off-duty officer from another county who briefly detained but did not arrest defendant for driving under the influence had not acted improperly under color of office but only did what a citizen could have done. Assuming arguendo that administering field sobriety tests implicated the "color of office" doctrine, as defendant refused to submit to the tests, there was nothing to suppress. Wilson v. Commonwealth, 45 Va. App. 193, 609 S.E.2d 612, 2005 Va. App. LEXIS 84 (2005).

Officer's question necessarily attendant to legitimate police procedure. — Trial court did not err in denying defendant's motion to suppress testimony regarding his field sobriety tests because the arresting officer's question about whether defendant had any physical problems, and defendant's response thereto, were necessarily attendant to a legitimate police procedure, administering the field sobriety tests, and the question was designed to assure the validity of the tests and not to elicit, nor did it elicit, an incriminating response; the "physical problems" question was sufficiently analogous to asking whether defendant understood the officer's instructions as to how each test was to be performed, and both questions were clearly meant to assure the validity of the test and not to elicit an incriminatory response. Gibson v. Commonwealth, 57 Va. App. 772, 706 S.E.2d 541, 2011 Va. App. LEXIS 95 (2011).

Evidence was sufficient to prove that defendant was intoxicated at the time of the accident, although the officer did not conclude that defendant was intoxicated until some 55 to 85 minutes after the accident had occurred, where defendant told officer that he had consumed six to eight beers that day and he stated that he had not had anything alcoholic to drink since the accident. Wheeling v. City of Roanoke, 2 Va. App. 42, 341 S.E.2d 389 (1986).

Where defendant told the arresting officer, at the time of his arrest, that he had consumed six to eight beers that day and stated that he had not had anything alcoholic to drink since the accident, but at trial he testified that he drank a half pint of whiskey following the accident and further testified that he did not remember telling the arresting officer that he had not had anything alcoholic to drink since the accident, the jury was entitled to assess the credibility of these conflicting statements and testimony in arriving at its verdict. Wheeling v. City of Roanoke, 2 Va. App. 42, 341 S.E.2d 389 (1986).

Despite defendant's contention that the Commonwealth failed to comply with the procedural requirements of a DUI charge, where given defendant's admission to being intoxicated and his statements asking what he had hit, even without a blood test, the jury properly convicted defendant on all other evidence showing he was intoxicated. Stevens v. Commonwealth, 44 Va. App. 122, 603 S.E.2d 642, 2004 Va. App. LEXIS 496 (2004).

Where results of defendant's breath test were properly admitted, and an officer testified as to defendant's conduct at the scene leading to his arrest, the evidence was sufficient to support a finding defendant was intoxicated at the time of the accident and, thus, operated his vehicle while intoxicated. Pruitt v. Commonwealth, — Va. App. —, — S.E.2d —, 2008 Va. App. LEXIS 57 (Feb. 5, 2008).

Other evidence of intoxication. — Even if admission of blood test results in a case was error because defendant was not arrested within three hours and, thus, defendant did not give implied consent to such a test, defendant could still be convicted of driving under the influence as a fourth or subsequent offense, in violation of § 18.2-266. Admission of such evidence was harmless where other compelling evidence was admitted of defendant driving while intoxicated. Lyle v. Commonwealth, 2008 Va. App. LEXIS 205 (Apr. 29, 2008).

Repeated weaving within lane created reasonable suspicion. — Officer who had experience with intoxicated drivers had a reasonable and articulable suspicion to stop defendant's vehicle and investigate further, where the officer observed defendant's vehicle for 25 seconds weaving repeatedly within its lane between five and ten times over a distance of one-half mile. Neal v. Commonwealth, 27 Va. App. 233, 498 S.E.2d 422 (1998).

Evidence was sufficient to prove that defendant's intoxication caused erratic driving observed by police officer. — Although defendant claimed that an anxiety attack caused the erratic driving observed by a police officer, the trial court was not required to accept defendant's explanation, especially since there was credible evidence that defendant was intoxicated at the time. Cousins v. Commonwealth, No. 2140-02-2, 2003 Va. App. LEXIS 354 (Ct. of Appeals June 24, 2003).

Trial court's verdict was reasonable under § 8.01-680 and the evidence was sufficient to support defendant's driving under influence conviction under § 18.2-266 where: (1) defendant admitted consuming vodka that afternoon; (2) he had a half-empty bottle of vodka under the driver's seat of his wrecked car, and he attempted to get rid of the bottle before the police discovered it; (3) he attempted to flee from the scene of the accident; (4) he smelled of alcohol; and (5) he had no disabling medical condition. Rorech v. Commonwealth, No. 1085-02-4, 2003 Va. App. LEXIS 388 (Ct. of Appeals July 8, 2003).

Harmless error in admission of evidence that defendant was offered breath tests. — Although, pursuant to § 18.2-267, the trial court erred in a DUI trial in allowing testimony that defendant was offered breath tests following a traffic stop, that evidence was harmless because there was overwhelming evidence that defendant drove while intoxicated; under § 4.1-100, "intoxicated" meant a condition in which a person had drunk enough alcoholic beverages to observably affect his manner, disposition, speech, muscular movement, general appearance, or behavior. The evidence at trial proved that defendant drove his car at a reckless speed and that, when stopped, he had an odor of alcohol about his breath, red and glassy eyes, and slurred speech, and performed poorly on field sobriety tests. Reid v. Commonwealth, 2009 Va. App. LEXIS 308 (July 14, 2009).

D. Sufficiency of Evidence.

The evidence was sufficient to support defendant's conviction of driving under influence of intoxicants where defendant admitted having had two drinks, drove his car onto the shoulder of the road and again into the center lane, veered across the road when the trooper signalled him to stop then back again into a telephone pole, was unsteady on his feet when arrested and proposed to the officer that the charge be fixed. Doughty v. Commonwealth, 204 Va. 240, 129 S.E.2d 664 (1963).

Conviction was supported by the evidence where it was proved defendant drove his vehicle into the rear of a bus stopped for a red light, gave no explanation for the occurrence, denied he was driving his vehicle and made conflicting statements as to who was driving, had a strong odor of alcohol on his breath, and could not satisfactorily complete certain coordination tests administered by police at the scene. Holt v. City of Richmond, 204 Va. 364, 131 S.E.2d 394 (1963), cert. denied, 376 U.S. 917, 84 S. Ct. 672, 11 L. Ed. 2d 613 (1964).

Evidence of defendant's consumption of alcohol prior to operating his car, the manner in which he operated his car, his inability to recite accurately the alphabet, and his conduct during the testing procedure all combined to establish beyond a reasonable doubt his guilt. Thurston v. City of Lynchburg, 15 Va. App. 475, 424 S.E.2d 701 (1992).

Where defendant, the sole occupant of the locked vehicle stopped in the middle of the road, was asleep, slumped across the front seat with his head on the passenger side and his lower torso in the seat behind the steering wheel and although the motor was not running and the vehicle's lights were off, the key was in the ignition, turned to the on position, and the transmission mechanism was in drive, the evidence was sufficient to prove that defendant operated a motor vehicle while under the influence of alcohol. Rivers v. Commonwealth, No. 1222-92-1 (Ct. of Appeals May 24, 1994).

A defendant's admission that he consumed several alcoholic beverages, together with the testimony of the arresting officer regarding the defendant's appearance and lack of coordination, was sufficient to support a conviction for driving under the influence of alcohol. Lemond v. Commonwealth, 19 Va. App. 687, 454 S.E.2d 31 (1995).

Evidence was sufficient to prove beyond a reasonable doubt that defendant was intoxicated where he stopped his vehicle in the travel lane of a public road in the middle of the night and got out to clean it; staggered as he walked; had an odor of alcohol about him; slurred his speech; failed a sobriety test; and admitted earlier alcohol consumption. Leake v. Commonwealth, 27 Va. App. 101, 497 S.E.2d 522 (1998).

Evidence was sufficient to support defendant's conviction of driving under the influence of alcohol (DUI), third or subsequent offense, in violation of §§ 18.2-266, 18.2-270, where defendant was stopped after a police officer saw defendant's vehicle weaving on the road; defendant had two prior DUI convictions; defendant admitted that defendant had consumed alcohol two hours before the stop; and defendant had a strong odor of alcohol, gave incoherent responses, was unsteady, and failed three field sobriety tests. Lee Banks Walker v. Commonwealth, No. 0349-02-1, 2003 Va. App. LEXIS 246 (Ct. of Appeals Apr. 22, 2003).

Where the form provided defendant listed only one approved laboratory where defendant could have second vial of blood tested, trial court properly refused to dismiss driving under the influence charges because a deputy's observations of defendant's movements would have supported a conviction even without blood tests. Cutright v. Commonwealth, 43 Va. App. 593, 601 S.E.2d 1, 2004 Va. App. LEXIS 398 (2004).

Sufficient evidence, including defendant's extreme intoxication that could be detected by an officer; his admissions; and act of driving while ignoring traffic signals and running a red light, striking a vehicle without slowing down or braking and questioning what he hit, even absent admission of a hospital toxicology report, supported his aggravated involuntary manslaughter conviction. Stevens v. Commonwealth, 44 Va. App. 122, 603 S.E.2d 642, 2004 Va. App. LEXIS 496 (2004).

Defendant's aggravated involuntary manslaughter conviction was upheld on appeal, as the trial court did not err by: (1) failing to foreclose prosecution of the aggravated involuntary manslaughter charge on the ground that the Commonwealth did not comply with the procedural requirements of a driving under the influence charge; (2) failing to exclude a hospital toxicology report based on insufficient proof of reliability; (3) failing to instruct the jury on criminal negligence; and (4) finding the evidence sufficient to prove he was guilty of aggravated involuntary manslaughter, as (a) evidence of defendant's intoxication was overwhelming without the need for blood test results, given defendant's admissions and eyewitness testimony about strong odor of alcohol on his person; (b) the State's failure to substantially comply with the procedural requirements for testing blood and breath samples under the implied consent law did not apply to a prosecution under § 18.2-36.1 or 18.2-266; (c) trial court did not abuse its discretion in refusing to admit one instruction on grounds that it might have confused the jury, and two other instructions, as redundant; and (d) along with defendant's intoxication, the combination of defendant's act of ignoring traffic signals and running a red light and the lack of skid marks showing no evidence of him braking or attempting to slow down, provided sufficient evidence to establish his gross, wanton, and culpable conduct. Stevens v. Commonwealth, 46 Va. App. 234, 616 S.E.2d 754, 2005 Va. App. LEXIS 407 (2005), aff'd, — Va. —, 634 S.E.2d 305 (2006).

Because a witness saw defendant spinning a truck around a pasture in an effort to get onto a road and defendant, who was later found on foot, admitted ownership of the truck and that defendant was intoxicated, the evidence was sufficient to convict defendant of driving while intoxicated. Pickard v. Commonwealth, — Va. App. —, — S.E.2d —, 2005 Va. App. LEXIS 195 (May 17, 2005).

In a DWI case, even if the admission of a written breath test analysis result and the accompanying certificate violated the Confrontation Clause because the evidence was "testimonial," the error was harmless. The other evidence, including defendant's statement that he was drunk and that he was an alcoholic, his glassy, bloodshot eyes, his smell of alcohol, his admission that he had had six to eight drinks of vodka, and his failure of field sobriety tests, proved guilt beyond a reasonable doubt without the test result. Luginbyhl v. Commonwealth, 48 Va. App. 58, 628 S.E.2d 74, 2006 Va. App. LEXIS 170 (2006).

Where defendant's vehicle struck a barricade near a military base's gate, defendant's convictions for operating a motor vehicle on a military reservation while impaired by an intoxicant and operating a motor vehicle as an habitual offender while impaired by an intoxicant were upheld because substantial evidence supported the finding that defendant was intoxicated since it was clear that defendant's alcohol consumption so affected defendant's manner, disposition, speech, muscular movement, general appearance or behavior as to be apparent to observation. United States v. Scott, 188 Fed. Appx. 213, 2006 U.S. App. LEXIS 16899 (4th Cir. July 6, 2006).

Defendant's challenge to the sufficiency of the evidence to support a conviction under § 18.2-266 (i), failed because, inter alia, the jury could have discounted the Commonwealth's evidence of a .20 blood alcohol concentration (BAC), while also discounting the toxicologist's low-ball BAC as naively reliant on defendant's self-serving claim that defendant had no more than five beers that night; further, evidence of defendant's erratic driving, the smell of alcohol on defendant's breath, defendant's glassy eyes, defendant's slurred speech, and defendant's failure of three field sobriety tests eliminated any challenge to the sufficiency of the evidence. Morin v. Commonwealth, 2007 Va. App. LEXIS 346 (Sept. 18, 2007).

Trial court did not err in finding defendant guilty of driving under the influence of alcohol, second offense within ten years, in violation of clause (ii) of § 18.2-266 because a rational trier of fact could have found that defendant was operating her vehicle while under the influence of alcohol; defendant admitted to a police officer that she had been drinking alcohol, and she failed to perform her field sobriety tests correctly. Brown v. Commonwealth, — Va. App. —, — S.E.2d —, 2008 Va. App. LEXIS 158 (Apr. 8, 2008).

Evidence in the record supported the trial court's finding that defendant was guilty of driving under the influence of alcohol because the trial court did not arbitrarily reject evidence that defendant's breath test result was elevated as a result of her earlier use of spackle, paint, and cleaner and by the deployment of her airbag after her collision; the trial court was free to accept or reject all or part of defendant's testimony regarding her use of specific painting and spackle products. Newman v. Commonwealth, 2009 Va. App. LEXIS 360 (Aug. 11, 2009).

Evidence was sufficient to prove defendant was under the influence of alcohol pursuant to clause (ii) of § 18.2-266 because the trial court was entitled to reject defendant's statements concerning a physical disability regarding his legs, and defendant performed three additional field sobriety tests that did not involve use of his legs, failing all three. Newcomb v. Commonwealth, 2009 Va. App. LEXIS 422 (Sept. 22, 2009).

Evidence was sufficient to support defendant's DUI conviction where defendant ingested unprescribed narcotic pills prior to driving, drove well below the posted speed limit and swerved twice between the traffic lane and the shoulder, pulled over into a residential driveway and overshot the driveway leaving the vehicle teetering on three wheels, appeared intoxicated, confused, disoriented, and unsteady on her feet, and failed two field sobriety tests.

Taylor v. Commonwealth, 2010 Va. App. LEXIS 96 (Mar. 16, 2010).

While it was undisputed that defendant did not put the vehicle in motion so as to drive it, defendant's conviction for driving or operating a vehicle under the influence of alcohol was supported by evidence that defendant seized actual control of the vehicle when defendant switched seats with another individual in an effort to represent herself as the operator of the vehicle. Rix v. Commonwealth, 56 Va. App. 749, 697 S.E.2d 33, 2010 Va. App. LEXIS 332 (2010).

Defendant's conviction for driving under influence under § 18.2-266 was supported by the reporting witness' testimony that the witness saw people exit the car fight after hearing a "loud bang," shortly thereafter the witness found defendant lying in the front seat of the vehicle, and defendant attempted to leave scene of the accident. Shorter v. Commonwealth, 2010 Va. App. LEXIS 327 (Aug. 10, 2010).

Appellant's conviction for operating a motor vehicle while under the influence of alcohol, a second or subsequent offense, was affirmed where: (1) the police found appellant alone, heavily intoxicated, behind the wheel of his own car minutes after a report that the car was traveling in the wrong lane of traffic; and (2) appellant admitted he was traveling to Crewe, and he further stated he pulled off the road because the lights from oncoming traffic frightened him. Thompson v. Commonwealth, 2010 Va. App. LEXIS 265 (July 6, 2010).

Conviction for driving while under influence of drugs under § 18.2-266 was upheld, as defendant failed to prove the affirmative defense of involuntary intoxication where the evidence showed that defendant drove around two vehicles before hitting a third, defendant successfully pulled over and stopped his car after striking the vehicle, defendant used a cell phone while in his car roadside, and defendant was able to communicate with the investigating officer and, albeit unsuccessfully, attempt to perform field sobriety tests. Shortt v. Commonwealth, 2010 Va. App. LEXIS 442 (Nov. 9, 2010).

Totality of the evidence supported the trial court's finding that defendant was under the influence of alcohol in violation of § 18.2-266 when he overturned his vehicle because a deputy testified that when he arrived at the scene of the accident he detected a strong odor of alcohol emanating from defendant, defendant admitted that he had consumed four twenty-two ounce beers before the accident, and a blood sample taken shortly after the accident revealed alcohol in defendant's blood; the trial court was entitled to evaluate and either accept or reject defendant's assertion that placing chewing tobacco in his mouth and catching his flip-flop on the accelerator caused him to overturn his vehicle. Bilger v. Commonwealth, 2011 Va. App. LEXIS 371 (Nov. 29, 2011).

Evidence that showed beyond a reasonable doubt that defendant was drunk, that he was seated behind the steering wheel of his vehicle on a public street, and that the key was in the ignition switch of the car was sufficient to support defendant's conviction for driving or operating a motor vehicle while under the influence of alcohol under § 18.2-266. Enriquez v. Commonwealth, 283 Va. 511, 722 S.E.2d 252, 2012 Va. LEXIS 49 (2012).

Evidence was sufficient to find defendant guilty of driving under the influence as it showed that defendant had a blood alcohol content level of 0.23 per 210 liters of breath according to a breathalyzer test taken shortly after defendant was apprehended, which was 15 minutes after an officer saw defendant flee the scene of a DUI checkpoint. Defendant did not object to the admission of the blood alcohol content certificate, and the Commonwealth's own evidence did not rebut the permissible inference. Simmons v. Commonwealth, 2012 Va. App. LEXIS 204 (June 19, 2012).

Evidence held insufficient to support conviction of driving under the influence of intoxicants. Fowlkes v. Commonwealth, 194 Va. 676, 74 S.E.2d 683 (1953).

Evidence establishing that defendant was intoxicated fifty-five minutes after being involved in an accident was not sufficient to support a jury finding that he was intoxicated at the time of the accident. Coffey v. Commonwealth, 202 Va. 185, 116 S.E.2d 257 (1960).

The manner in which the accident occurred, the appearance and behavior of defendant, and his bizarre conduct generally, constituted sufficient evidence to engender a probability of guilt. However, the evidence failed to establish that the drinking of alcohol or the self-administering of drugs caused this conduct, and, in its absence, the court of appeals was unable to conclude that beyond a reasonable doubt defendant operated his automobile under the influence of alcohol or some self-administered drug. Clemmer v. Commonwealth, 208 Va. 661, 159 S.E.2d 664 (1968).

The evidence was not such that one could infer from it a tacit admission by defendant that he had been drinking, or was under the influence of alcohol. Clemmer v. Commonwealth, 208 Va. 661, 159 S.E.2d 664 (1968).

Probable cause for arrest found. — Trial court's entry of an order granting defendant's motion to suppress was reversed as the police had probable cause to arrest defendant for driving under the influence, making the search incident to a lawful arrest constitutional, where: (1) defendant failed to stop at an intersection controlled by a stop sign and did not signal a turn; (2) the officer smelled alcohol as defendant rolled down his window and defendant denied consuming any alcohol; (3) his movements were slow, his speech was somewhat slurred, and his eyes were glassy and bloodshot; (4) defendant successfully completed the counting field sobriety test; and (5) defendant did not follow the officer's instructions on the alphabet sobriety test, and put his foot down and used his arms to maintain balance on the stork stand sobriety test. Commonwealth v. Elliott, No. 1000-03-2, 2003 Va. App. LEXIS 467 (Ct. of Appeals Sept. 4, 2003).

IV. PUNISHMENT.

A. Convictions, Sentencing, etc.

Degree of intoxication relevant to punishment. — The defendant's degree of intoxication is relevant to a determination of the appropriate quantum of punishment. Voluntary intoxication, in the case of a driver, is an aggravating factor properly considered for this purpose. Essex v. Commonwealth, 228 Va. 273, 322 S.E.2d 216 (1984).

Intoxication relevant as aggravating factor bearing on culpability of conduct. — The same reckless driving is more dangerous at the hands of a drunken driver than it would be if he were sober, and his conduct is therefore more culpable. Intoxication, therefore, is relevant as an aggravating factor, increasing with its degree, bearing upon the relative culpability of the defendant's conduct, even though it is irrelevant to the determination of malice. Essex v. Commonwealth, 228 Va. 273, 322 S.E.2d 216 (1984).

Degree of intoxication is aggravating factor when death is proximate result. — When death is the proximate result of criminal negligence in the operation of a motor vehicle, the degree of a driver's intoxication is relevant as an aggravating factor, tending to show the relative dangerousness of his conduct. Essex v. Commonwealth, 228 Va. 273, 322 S.E.2d 216 (1984).

Sentence found to be reasonable. — District court's 15-month sentence imposed upon defendant's guilty plea to driving under the influence (third offense), a violation of 18 U.S.C.S. § 13, assimilating §§ 18.2-266 and 18.2-270, and driving on a suspended driver's license (third offense), a violation of 18 U.S.C.S. §§ 7, 13, assimilating § 46.2-301, was proper because (1) the sentence was not plainly unreasonable under 18 U.S.C.S. § 3742(e) given the district court's consideration of defendant's three drunk driving convictions in a short time frame; (2) the district court also considered the provisions under 18 U.S.C.S. § 3553 in imposing sentence; and (3) allowing the 15-month sentence to run consecutive to the sentence he was serving for violating his probation was not plain error under U.S. Sentencing Guidelines Manual. United States v. Floresdelgado, 2005 U.S. App. LEXIS 6121 (4th Cir. Apr. 13, 2005).

Discretion to impose fine. — Jury had the discretion under subsection C of § 18.2-270 to fine defendant $2,500 for his fourth offense under this section. By setting a mandatory minimum fine of $1,000, § 18.2-270 C gave a jury the discretion to impose a larger fine, and as the more specific statute, it controlled over § 18.2-10, which applied to Class 6 felonies in general. Neria v. Commonwealth, — Va. App. —, — S.E.2d —, 2009 Va. App. LEXIS 136 (Mar. 24, 2009).

Double jeopardy established. — Although a circuit court had discretion under § 16.1-137 to amend a defective warrant, defendant's double jeopardy rights were violated when the circuit court, in an appeal de novo under § 16.1-136, improperly amended the warrant to charge driving under the influence (DUI) second offense under § 18.2-266 after defendant had been acquitted of that charge by a district court, which had then convicted defendant of a lesser offense of DUI first offense. Turner v. Commonwealth, 49 Va. App.

381, 641 S.E.2d 771, 2007 Va. App. LEXIS 78 (2007).

Although a circuit court had discretion under § 16.1-137 to amend a defective warrant, defendant's double jeopardy rights were violated when the circuit court, in an appeal de novo under § 16.1-136, improperly amended the warrant to charge driving under the influence (DUI) second offense under § 18.2-266 after defendant had been acquitted of that charge by a district court, which had then convicted defendant of a lesser offense of DUI first offense. Turner v. Commonwealth, 49 Va. App. 381, 641 S.E.2d 771, 2007 Va. App. LEXIS 78 (2007).

Multiple convictions arising out of same act not barred. — Section 19.2-294 does not bar multiple convictions arising out of the same act if they are prosecuted simultaneously. Thus where warrants for involuntary manslaughter and driving while under the influence of alcohol were issued at the same time, although the charges were heard at different times in different courts, because the charges were initiated simultaneously, the proceedings were concurrent, not successive, and thus, both convictions were permitted under § 19.2-294. Doss v. Commonwealth, No. 2003-93-3, 1995 Va. App. LEXIS 425 (May 9, 1995).

Although defendant had already been convicted of driving under the influence under § 18.2-266 from the same incident, his conviction for eluding a police officer under subsection B of § 46.2-817 was not barred by § 19.2-294 because the specific acts serving as basis for prosecution of the offenses were separate and distinct in that the same evidence would not produce a conviction for both offenses. Wolford v. Commonwealth, 2006 Va. App. LEXIS 513 (Nov. 14, 2006).

Person acquitted under section could be prosecuted for involuntary manslaughter. — The doctrine of collateral estoppel may not bar the prosecution for involuntary manslaughter of a person previously acquitted of driving under the influence of intoxicants, since the issue of intoxication is not necessarily dispositive of the crime of involuntary manslaughter. Simon v. Commonwealth, 220 Va. 412, 258 S.E.2d 567 (1979).

But evidence of intoxication would be barred. — Although the defendant could be tried for involuntary manslaughter, even though he previously had been acquitted of driving under the influence of intoxicants based upon failure of the Commonwealth to prove legal intoxication, since the issue of intoxication is not necessarily dispositive of the crime of involuntary manslaughter, the Commonwealth should have been barred, under the doctrine of collateral estoppel, from introducing in the manslaughter trial evidence to show that the defendant was intoxicated while operating the motor vehicle. Simon v. Commonwealth, 220 Va. 412, 258 S.E.2d 567 (1979).

Though consumption of alcohol could be shown. — If the Commonwealth elected to try a defendant who previously had been acquitted of the offense under this section for involuntary manslaughter, the Commonwealth would not be estopped from introducing evidence to show that the defendant consumed alcohol shortly before the accident in question, since the quantity of alcohol consumed by an automobile driver, even though not enough to cause legal intoxication, may be sufficient to impair his capacity to perceive the dangers with the clarity, make decisions with the prudence, and operate the vehicle with the skill and caution required by law. Simon v. Commonwealth, 220 Va. 412, 258 S.E.2d 567 (1979).

Denial of bifurcation not error. — Where defendant was charged with operating a motor vehicle while intoxicated, the fourth offense in 10 years, the trial court did not abuse its discretion in denying a motion to bifurcate the guilt phase of the trial from the evidence of recidivism because any potential prejudice was resolved by a limiting instruction. Nelson v. Commonwealth, 2010 Va. App. LEXIS 42 (2010), aff'd, 281 Va. 212, 707 S.E.2d 815, 2011 Va. LEXIS 27 (2011).

Where defendant was charged with operating a motor vehicle while intoxicated, the fourth offense in 10 years, the trial court did not abuse its discretion in denying a motion to bifurcate the guilt phase of the trial from the evidence of recidivism because any potential prejudice was resolved by a limiting instruction. Nelson v. Commonwealth, 2010 Va. App. LEXIS 42 (2010), aff'd, 281 Va. 212, 707 S.E.2d 815, 2011 Va. LEXIS 27 (2011).

Reversal of subsequent conviction necessitated. — Where defendant was charged and convicted of both § 19.2-294.1 offenses, driving under the influence (DUI) and reckless driving, and the evidence was undisputed that the alleged misconduct was intimately related in time and distance, arising from and connected by one continuous, uninterrupted operation of defendant's motor vehicle, under such circumstances, the legislature clearly intended that a conviction of one offense result in a dismissal of the other. Accordingly, defendant's subsequent conviction for DUI should have been reversed. Harris v. City of Va. Beach, 19 Va. App. 214, 450 S.E.2d 401 (1994).

Confusing instruction properly refused. — It was not error to refuse an instruction that defendant might be thought guilty of reckless driving yet not be guilty of driving while drunk. This would have been confusing to the jury, directing their attention to an offense with which defendant was not charged. Mawyer v. Commonwealth, 203 Va. 898, 128 S.E.2d 433 (1962).

No error in denying motion for mistrial based on attorney's statements. — Trial court did not err in denying defendant's motion for a mistrial based on improper statements made by the Commonwealth's attorney. The factual basis for the argument arose when the Commonwealth's attorney referred to defendant as an "alcoholic" during the cross-examination of one of defendant's witnesses and referred to defendant's "ability to throw back quite a few [alcoholic drinks] at a time" during the cross-examination of another defense witness. These statements were clearly improper. However, it is just as clear that the trial court sustained defendant's objections, gave no consideration to the objectionable statements, and "[tried] the case just on the evidence that [came] before [it] and nothing else." Accordingly, no prejudice resulted. Thurston v. City of Lynchburg, 15 Va. App. 475, 424 S.E.2d 701 (1992).

B. Habitual Offender Rules.

Evidence of prior conviction. — In convicting defendant of driving under the influence, the trial court did not err in admitting evidence of prior DUI conviction, as the arrest warrant constituted an official document, and the trial court properly consulted the warrant as evidence of the ordinance under which defendant was previously convicted in taking judicial notice of its provisions. Webb v. Commonwealth, No. 2749-01-2, 2003 Va. App. LEXIS 138 (Ct. of Appeals Mar. 18, 2003).

Extent of out-of-state conviction conformance necessary. — In order to adjudicate a defendant an habitual offender based upon a conviction from another state, only that prohibition of the other state's law under which the person was convicted must substantially conform to this section. Honaker v. Commonwealth, 19 Va. App. 682, 454 S.E.2d 29 (1995).

It is not required that another state's law regarding driving while under the influence of intoxicants or drugs conform in every respect to this section in order for an out-of-state conviction to be used as a predicate offense; only that portion of the other state's law under which the person was convicted must substantially conform. Commonwealth v. Lowe, 31 Va. App. 806, 525 S.E.2d 636 (2000).

Where defendant's charging documents and records of conviction referred to Md. Code Ann., Transp. § 21-902(a), the record did not give rise to a reasonable inference that the statutes on which defendant's prior convictions were based substantially conformed to this section, and on the contrary, the record left open the possibility that defendant was convicted under Md. Code Ann., Transp. § 21-902(a), which was not substantially similar to § 18.2-266, the appellate court found that the district court abused its discretion in accepting defendant's guilty plea to fourth offense DWI. United States v. Thomas, 367 F.3d 194, 2004 U.S. App. LEXIS 8734 (4th Cir. 2004).

Predicate conviction. — A conviction under clause (i) of this section is a predicate conviction to a finding of habitual offender status under former § 46.2-351. Flaherty v. Commonwealth, 14 Va. App. 148, 415 S.E.2d 867 (1992).

Where an enhanced driving under the influence (DUI) punishment was statutorily activated by a conviction or an offense within 10 years pursuant to former § 18.2-270, defendant could be convicted of a third offense DUI in violation of § 18.2-266 even though a trial was pending on a second offense. Williams v. Commonwealth, 265 Va. 268, 576 S.E.2d 468, 2003 Va. LEXIS 22 (2003).

Trial court erred by imposing an enhanced sentence, pursuant to subsection C of § 18.2-270, against a defendant based upon his prior conviction for DWI under 36 C.F.R. § 4.23(a)(2) where said regulation was not substantially similar to a conviction under § 18.2-266, as a conviction under federal law did not translate into

a conviction under the state law. Corey v. Commonwealth, No. 0421-02-4, 2003 Va. App. LEXIS 582 (Ct. of Appeals Nov. 12, 2003).

Evidence of prior driving under the influence (DUI) convictions does not constitute the "traffic record" as contemplated by § 46.2-943 where the offense charged under this section is a subsequent offense of DUI punishable under § 18.2-270. Proof of such charge requires proof of the prior DUI convictions, and a trial court, therefore, does not err in admitting evidence of a defendant's prior DUI convictions independent of his prior traffic record during the guilt stage of the trial. Farmer v. Commonwealth, 10 Va. App. 175, 390 S.E.2d 775 (1990).

In a DUI second offense trial, the burden is on the Commonwealth to prove the prior conviction beyond a reasonable doubt. McBride v. Commonwealth, 24 Va. App. 30, 480 S.E.2d 126 (1997).

Because the Commonwealth offered no evidence to rebut the presumption that defendant was not found guilty of violating this section in the prior proceeding, the trial court's conclusion that he had a prior conviction lacked evidence to support it. McBride v. Commonwealth, 24 Va. App. 30, 480 S.E.2d 126 (1997).

To be considered under Habitual Offender Statute, conviction in another state must be based on conduct which violates this section. — If a conviction in another state is based on conduct which is not a violation of this section, then to consider it under former § 46.2-351 would, without authority, expand the scope of the convictions which could be considered beyond that which the General Assembly specifically authorized. Cox v. Commonwealth, 13 Va. App. 328, 411 S.E.2d 444 (1991).

To allow a conviction in another state to be the basis for a finding that a person is an habitual offender would expand former § 46.2-351 beyond its stated limits if the conviction in the other state was based on an act which would not be a violation of this section. Cox v. Commonwealth, 13 Va. App. 328, 411 S.E.2d 444 (1991).

Another state's law permitting a conviction for an act not constituting an offense under this section is not substantially conforming under former § 46.2-351. Cox v. Commonwealth, 13 Va. App. 328, 411 S.E.2d 444 (1991).

Notice of charges. — Defendant's argument that, despite his failure to give proper notice of his challenge to the constitutionality of a local DUI code section, the trial court should have considered the challenge in the "interests of justice" failed; notwithstanding the validity of any provision of the local code, each warrant, the one charging the instant DUI offense, and the one charging the underlying 1998 prior DUI offense, described the offense charged and cited both the state code section, § 18.2-266, and the local code section, Newport News, Va., City Code § 26-72. Accordingly, in each instance, defendant was properly informed of the nature and character of the charge against him and he was in fact, convicted and sentenced for DUI in violation of § 18.2-266, the state statute, which he did not challenge. Artis v. Commonwealth, 2008 Va. App. LEXIS 502 (Nov. 12, 2008).

Conviction for third offense upheld. — Defendant who had one conviction for driving under the influence (DUI) and was awaiting trial on a second DUI charge when he was arrested and charged with a third DUI was properly convicted of felony DUI for the third incident, pursuant to §§ 18.2-266 and 18.2-270, once he was also convicted of the second DUI charge. Williams v. Commonwealth, 38 Va. App. 414, 565 S.E.2d 328, 2002 Va. App. LEXIS 369 (2002), aff'd, 265 Va. 268, 576 S.E.2d 468 (2003).

Evidence of prior conviction allowed. — Trial court properly rejected an attempt defendant made during his trial on a charge that he drove under the influence a third or subsequent time within 10 years, to suppress two prior DUI convictions, because his argument that his earlier convictions were obtained in violation of his right to effective assistance of counsel did not rise to the level of a constitutional violation that negated those convictions, and they were not subject to collateral attack. Vester v. Commonwealth, 42 Va. App. 592, 593 S.E.2d 551, 2004 Va. App. LEXIS 99 (2004).

Under § 46.2-384, a Department of Motor Vehicles transcript, certified pursuant to § 46.2-215, was prima facie evidence of the facts stated therein and was therefore sufficient to prove defendant's prior DUI offenses and support his conviction under §§ 18.2-266 and 18.2-270. Mitchem v. Commonwealth, 2010 Va. App. LEXIS 18 (Jan. 12, 2010).

Convictions did not violate double jeopardy clause. — Convictions for driving under the influence, this section, and driving after having been declared an habitual offender, § 46.2-357, did not violate the double jeopardy clause because the charges at issue required proof of a fact the other did not. Dowless v. Commonwealth, No. 0687-91-1 (Ct. of Appeals Feb. 2, 1993).

Conviction after suspension of driving privilege did not violate double jeopardy. — Defendant's conviction for driving under the influence after the suspension of her driving privileges pursuant to § 46.2-391.2 did not violate her double jeopardy rights because, notwithstanding any incidental punitive effect it may have had, the 60-day administrative suspension was a civil sanction and, thus, did not offend double jeopardy protections. Depsky v. Commonwealth, 50 Va. App. 454, 650 S.E.2d 867, 2007 Va. App. LEXIS 372 (2007).

Determination of whether foreign state law "substantially conforms" to Virginia law. — In determining whether North Carolina DUI law under which appellant was twice convicted "substantially conforms" to Virginia's DUI law, courts look to the elements of the two statutes rather than to the offender's conduct; mere fact that both provisions are loosely referred to as per se statutes is insufficient to show substantial conformity in using out of state convictions for habitual offender adjudication in Virginia. Commonwealth v. Ayers, 17 Va. App. 401, 437 S.E.2d 580 (1993).

Permissible use of out-of-state predicate conviction. — Notwithstanding the fact that there are substantial differences between West Virginia Code § 17C-5-2 and this section, because the prohibition of West Virginia law under which appellant was convicted substantially conformed to this section, it could be used as a predicate offense for appellant's adjudication as an habitual offender pursuant to § 46.2-351 et seq. Honaker v. Commonwealth, 19 Va. App. 682, 454 S.E.2d 29 (1995).

Trial judge could have concluded that the conviction in West Virginia was based on conduct which is also a violation of this section, and thus to consider it under former § 46.2-351 would not expand the scope of the convictions which could be considered in making his ruling. Honaker v. Commonwealth, 19 Va. App. 682, 454 S.E.2d 29 (1995).

Under the Driver License Compact, which has been codified in identical form in Virginia and Maryland, any conviction reported from Maryland to the Virginia Department of Motor Vehicles must, of necessity, be limited to motor vehicle use while intoxicated and, therefore, the Maryland statutes governing the offense of driving while intoxicated substantially conform to Virginia law and a defendant's conviction in Maryland may be considered as a predicate offense for purposes of Virginia's habitual offender law. Commonwealth v. Lowe, 31 Va. App. 806, 525 S.E.2d 636 (2000).

Record indicating convictions for drunk driving satisfied requirements of habitual offender statute. — Where the defendant claimed that the record indicating "drunk driving" was insufficient to satisfy the requirement of former § 46.2-351 in that it failed to establish that the conviction was for a violation of this section or a local ordinance conforming to the provision of this section, the DMV record and abstract of conviction showing the defendant had been convicted of "drunk driving" or "driving while intoxicated" satisfied the requirement of § 46.2-351. Danielson v. Commonwealth, No. 0951-89-2 (Ct. of Appeals Dec. 26, 1990).

CIRCUIT COURT OPINIONS

Constitutionality. — Because defendant started the engine of a vehicle while intoxicated, defendant's behavior fell well within the well-established definition of "operate"; in addition, because § 18.2-266 did not contain a mens rea requirement, defendant lacked standing to complain that the statute was unconstitutionally vague under the Fifth and Fourteenth Amendments. Commonwealth v. McConnell, 68 Va. Cir. 471, 2005 Va. Cir. LEXIS 194 (Charlottesville Sept. 29, 2005).

Presumptions of §§ 18.2-266 and 18.2-269 are permissible inferences because they do not remove the element of alcohol content from the case and do not shift the burden of persuasion to the defendant; thus, they do not violate due process or the right to confrontation. Furthermore, § 18.2-270, which relies on a violation of § 18.2-266, is not unconstitutional, as the burden of persuasion is with the Commonwealth at all times. Commonwealth v. Stump, 69 Va. Cir. 433, 2006 Va. Cir. LEXIS 95 (Roanoke 2006).

Construction. — Court denied defendant's motion to declare

certain parts of § 18.2-269 unconstitutional because the Virginia General Assembly was well within its authority to find that a blood alcohol level of 0.08 and above created a permissive inference that an individual was "under the influence of alcohol" as that term was used in clause (ii) of § 18.2-266. Commonwealth v. Pattarasok, 69 Va. Cir. 423, 2006 Va. Cir. LEXIS 15 (Fairfax County 2006).

Only if § 18.2-269 could reasonably be read to provide a permissible inference could it satisfy due process requirements; the circuit court found that due process required § 18.2-269 be treated as creating a permissible inference, rather than as a mandatory rebuttable presumption, and, so construed, the statute was constitutional, both facially and as applied to defendants. Commonwealth v. Padilla, 69 Va. Cir. 409, 2006 Va. Cir. LEXIS 16 (Fairfax County 2006), aff'd, Yap v. Commonwealth, 49 Va. App. 622, 643 S.E.2d 523, 2007 Va. App. LEXIS 171 (2007).

In a driving under the influence of alcohol violation, the circuit court found that § 18.2-269 would violate due process if interpreted as shifting the burden to defendants to rebut an element of the offense that the fact finder would otherwise be required to conclude; when the charge was driving under the influence of alcohol, a mandatory rebuttable presumption that required the fact finder upon the presentation of a certain blood alcohol level to conclude that defendants were under the influence of alcohol, unless rebutted by them, would adversely affect their right to trial by jury and their right to remain silent, and it would diminish the requirement of the state to prove defendants' guilt beyond a reasonable doubt. Commonwealth v. Padilla, 69 Va. Cir. 409, 2006 Va. Cir. LEXIS 16 (Fairfax County 2006), aff'd, Yap v. Commonwealth, 49 Va. App. 622, 643 S.E.2d 523, 2007 Va. App. LEXIS 171 (2007).

Revocation of a driver's driving privilege was not a manifest injustice after he was convicted of two violations of § 18.2-266, arising from two separate incidents, and a violation of 36 C.F.R. § 4.23(a)(2), arising from a third incident, all occurring within 10 years, because 36 C.F.R. § 4.23(a)(2) was substantially similar to § 18.2-266. Sayler v. Commonwealth, 71 Va. Cir. 258, 2006 Va. Cir. LEXIS 117 (Albemarle County 2006).

Officer must be present. — Sections 18.2-266, 19.2-81 and 46.2-100, read together, require that an individual drive or operate or be in actual physical control of a motor vehicle in the presence of the arresting officer for an arrest to be valid. Commonwealth v. Coakley, 56 Va. Cir. 99, 2001 Va. Cir. LEXIS 446 (Norfolk 2001).

Sobriety checkpoint. — Field officer's broad and unchecked discretion under the Albemarle County, Va., Police Dep't Gen. Ord. No. 4-6, Subject: Traffic/Sobriety Checkpoints (Sept. 28, 2001) runs afoul of the Fourth Amendment; therefore, a court granted a motion to suppress evidence in a driving under the influence case. Commonwealth v. Pearson, 64 Va. Cir. 488, 2004 Va. Cir. LEXIS 173 (Albemarle County 2004).

Suppression of evidence from investigatory stop. — Defendant's motion to suppress the evidence obtained after an investigatory stop should have been granted since defendant's vehicle was not making erratic movements; rather, the movements constituted an isolated instance of mild weaving. Commonwealth v. Webb, 56 Va. Cir. 419, 2001 Va. Cir. LEXIS 481 (Danville 2001).

Rebuttable presumption does not violate due process. — Rebuttable presumptions in §§ 18.2-266(i) and 18.2-269 did not violate defendant's due process rights, because the court was required to analyze the rebuttable presumptions as permissive inferences, as to which defendant had no standing to make a facial constitutional challenge. Commonwealth v. Draper, 72 Va. Cir. 111, 2006 Va. Cir. LEXIS 315 (Martinsville 2006).

Double jeopardy. — Where defendant was convicted of driving under the influence (DUI) and operating a motor vehicle after having been adjudicated a habitual offender and while under the influence of alcohol, defendant's plea in bar asserting double jeopardy was overruled, as the punishment for the habitual offender offense could be enhanced, and defendant could be punished for both the habitual offender offense and the DUI. Commonwealth v. Lloyd, 61 Va. Cir. 114, 2003 Va. Cir. LEXIS 4 (Warren County 2003).

Administrative license suspension did not bar prosecution. — Sixty-day administrative license suspension requirement in § 46.2-391.2 is civil, and not criminal, like its seven-day counterpart, and a subsequent driving under the influence (DUI) prosecution thus does not violate double jeopardy or § 19.2-294. Accordingly, such a suspension did not bar a DUI prosecution under

§ 18.2-266. Commonwealth v. Stump, 69 Va. Cir. 433, 2006 Va. Cir. LEXIS 95 (Roanoke 2006).

Out-of-state convictions. — In a case in which a driver's Virginia driver's license was revoked due to a driving while intoxicated (DWI) conviction in Arkansas, and the driver, pursuant to § 46.2-410.1, sought judicial review of that revocation, arguing that there was a manifest injustice because the Commissioner of Motor Vehicles made an error in law as Arkansas DWI law, Ark. Code Ann. § 5-65-103, was not substantially parallel and substantially conforming to the Virginia DWI statute, § 18.2-266, that argument failed. The Arkansas DWI statute was substantially parallel and substantially conforming to the Virginia DWI statute because under both code sections, the ultimate fact that the government had to prove in order to obtain a conviction for DWI was that the alcohol content at the time of the driving was 0.08 percent or more. Hunt v. Commonwealth, 2009 Va. Cir. LEXIS 44 (Fairfax June 15, 2009).

Evidence excluded. — Certificate of blood alcohol analysis was ordered excluded as evidence in defendant's driving under the influence case, where the breath testing operator reversed the sequence of machine testing procedures required by 1 VAC § 30-50-90(c) and it was clear that substantial compliance with the procedures, established to insure the accuracy of the breath test equipment, did not occur. Commonwealth v. Lizazu-Arias, 57 Va. Cir. 478, 2000 Va. Cir. LEXIS 512 (Fairfax County Oct. 23, 2000).

In a prosecution for driving while intoxicated, results of a blood test should not be admitted where evidence rebutted a presumption that a parking lot was a public highway; the lot was clearly designed to facilitate entrance to and egress from a store, ample signage made clear that the owners of the parking lot offered it to patrons alone, the owners exercised their right to revoke permission to park on the lot, the lot was accessible 24 hours a day and the store was open for business commensurately. Evidence did not lead to a conclusion that the owners of the roadway could not or would not close their doors and bar the public from vehicular traffic at will. Commonwealth v. Wood, 73 Va. Cir. 333, 2007 Va. Cir. LEXIS 215 (Charlottesville May 9, 2007).

Sufficiency of evidence. — Even though defendant was not on a public highway when approached by a police officer, the implied consent statute was inappropriately applied, defendant was not obliged to submit to a breath test, and the results of that test were inadmissible against him, there was sufficient evidence to find defendant guilty of driving while intoxicated, given the totality of the circumstances; defendant was passed out in the driver's seat of a car while it was running, he failed the field sobriety tests, and he had a strong odor of alcohol that was detected by the officer. Commonwealth v. Wood, 73 Va. Cir. 333, 2007 Va. Cir. LEXIS 215 (Charlottesville May 9, 2007).

License suspension for second offense held improper. — Defendant who was not charged with second offense DUI could not have his license suspended as a second offender, and commissioner's order of suspension was manifestly unjust and improperly conflicted with the order of trial court, as defendant had not been adjudged to be a second offender. Richardson v. Commonwealth, 2002 Va. Cir. LEXIS 63 (Roanoke Apr. 16, 2002).

OPINIONS OF THE ATTORNEY GENERAL

There is no statutory time limit within which a magistrate must grant bond for an intoxicated person charged with a misdemeanor offense, such as driving under the influence or public intoxication. See opinion of Attorney General to The Honorable Gary W. Waters, Sheriff for the City of Portsmouth, 04-49 (7/15/04).

Authority of Commissioner of the Department of Motor Vehicles. — The Commissioner of the Department of Motor Vehicles is both authorized and mandated to impose an ignition interlock system upon an individual seeking reinstatement of a driver's license after the three-year license revocation period resulting from a conviction for driving under the influence, second or subsequent offense, when the convicting court fails to order the installation of such system. See opinion of Attorney General to The Honorable Joseph P. Johnson, Jr., Member, House of Delegates, 10-018, 2010 Va. AG LEXIS 17 (4/20/10).

§ 18.2-266.1. Persons under age 21 driving after illegally consuming alcohol; penalty.

A. It shall be unlawful for any person under the age of 21 to operate any motor vehicle after illegally consuming alcohol. Any such person with a blood alcohol concentration of 0.02 percent or more by weight by volume or 0.02 grams or more per 210 liters of breath but less than 0.08 by weight by volume or less than 0.08 grams per 210 liters of breath as indicated by a chemical test administered as provided in this article shall be in violation of this section.

B. A violation of this section is a Class 1 misdemeanor. Punishment shall include (i) forfeiture of such person's license to operate a motor vehicle for a period of one year from the date of conviction and (ii) a mandatory minimum fine of $500 or performance of a mandatory minimum of 50 hours of community service. This suspension period shall be in addition to the suspension period provided under § 46.2-391.2. The penalties and license forfeiture provisions set forth in §§ 16.1-278.9, 18.2-270 and 18.2-271 shall not apply to a violation of this section. Any person convicted of a violation of this section shall be eligible to attend an Alcohol Safety Action Program under the provisions of § 18.2-271.1 and may, in the discretion of the court, be issued a restricted license during the term of license suspension.

C. Notwithstanding §§ 16.1-278.8 and 16.1-278.9, upon adjudicating a juvenile delinquent based upon a violation of this section, the juvenile and domestic relations district court shall order disposition as provided in subsection B.

History.
1994, cc. 359, 363; 1995, c. 31; 2003, c. 605; 2008, c. 729; 2009, c. 660; 2011, cc. 134, 683.

Editor's note.
Acts 2008, c. 729, which rewrote the first sentence and added the second sentence in subsection B, expired July 1, 2010, pursuant to Acts 2008, c. 729, cl. 2.

Acts 2008, c. 729, cl. 3, provides: "That the Department of Criminal Justice Services shall submit to the Chairmen of the House and Senate Committees for Courts of Justice an interim report not later than January 15, 2009, and a final report not later than November 1, 2009, on the number of detentions pursuant to § 18.2-266.1 of the Code of Virginia that are in violation of the federal Juvenile Justice and Delinquency Prevention Act."

Acts 2009, c. 660 substituted "shall include" for "shall be" in the first sentence of subsection B as amended by Acts 2008, c. 729, which expired July 1, 2010. Therefore, the amendments by Acts 2009, c. 660 are no longer reflected in this section.

The 2011 amendments.
The 2011 amendments by cc. 134 and 683 are identical, and rewrote the first sentence in subsection B, which read: "A violation of this section shall be punishable by forfeiture of such person's license to operate a motor vehicle for a period of six months from the date of conviction and by a fine of not more than $500."

Michie's Jurisprudence.
For related discussion, see 2B M.J. Automobiles, § 118.

CASE NOTES

Construction of subsection A. — The offense defined by the first sentence of subsection A is proved if the Commonwealth proves that a person under the age of twenty-one years operates a motor vehicle after consuming alcohol, in any amount, and that the consumption was illegal. The second sentence provides for the establishment of a prima facie case upon proof that a person under twenty-one years of age operates a motor vehicle while having the prescribed level of blood alcohol concentration, casting upon the accused against whom such a prima facie case is established the burden of going forward with evidence raising a reasonable doubt as to the illegality of his alcohol consumption. Mejia v. Commonwealth, 23 Va. App. 173, 474 S.E.2d 866 (1996).

This section creates a rebuttable presumption that a defendant's blood alcohol content while driving was the same as indicated by the results of a subsequently administered test. Charles v. Commonwealth, 23 Va. App. 161, 474 S.E.2d 860 (1996).

Evidence defendant may present. — In cases involving prosecutions under this section, a defendant may introduce evidence to show that, despite his blood alcohol concentration of at least 0.10 percent on a subsequently administered test, his blood alcohol concentration at the time of driving was less than 0.10 percent. However, evidence tending to prove that the defendant was not under the influence, such as adequate performance on field sobriety tests, is irrelevant and inadmissible. Charles v. Commonwealth, 23 Va. App. 161, 474 S.E.2d 860 (1996).

§ 18.2-267. Preliminary analysis of breath to determine alcoholic content of blood.

A. Any person who is suspected of a violation of § 18.2-266, 18.2-266.1, subsection B of § 18.2-272, or a similar ordinance shall be entitled, if such equipment is available, to have his breath analyzed to determine the probable alcoholic content of his blood. The person shall also be entitled, upon request, to observe the process of analysis and to see the blood-alcohol reading on the equipment used to perform the breath test. His breath may be analyzed by any police officer of the Commonwealth, or of any county, city or town, or by any member of a sheriff's department in the normal discharge of his duties.

B. The Department of Forensic Science shall determine the proper method and equipment to be used in analyzing breath samples taken pursuant to this section and shall advise the respective police and sheriff's departments of the same.

C. Any person who has been stopped by a police officer of the Commonwealth, or of any county, city or town, or by any member of a sheriff's department and is suspected by such officer to be guilty of an offense listed in subsection A, shall have the right to refuse to permit his breath to be so analyzed, and his failure to permit such analysis shall not be evidence in any prosecution for an offense listed in subsection A.

D. Whenever the breath sample analysis indicates that alcohol is present in the person's blood, the officer may charge the person with a violation of an offense listed in subsection A. The person so charged shall then be subject to the provisions of §§ 18.2-268.1 through 18.2-268.12, or of a similar ordinance.

E. The results of the breath analysis shall not be admitted into evidence in any prosecution for an offense listed in subsection A, the purpose of this section being to permit a preliminary analysis of the alcoholic content of the blood of a person suspected of having committed an offense listed in subsection A.

F. Police officers or members of any sheriff's department shall, upon stopping any person suspected of having committed an offense listed in subsection A, advise the person of his rights under the provisions of this section.

G. Nothing in this section shall be construed as limiting the provisions of §§ 18.2-268.1 through 18.2-268.12.

History.
Code 1950, § 18.1-54.1; 1970, c. 511; 1975, cc. 14, 15; 1979, c. 717; 1985, cc. 355, 609; 1990, c. 825; 1992, c. 830; 1994, cc. 359, 363; 1996, cc. 154, 952; 2004, c. 1013; 2005, cc. 757, 840, 868, 881.

Cross references.
As to provisions relating to the transfer of duties from Division of Forensic Science in Department of Criminal Justice Services to Department of Forensic Science, see Editor's notes under § 9.1-1100.

Law Review.
For comment on the admissibility of documentary evidence and the right to confrontation, see 12 Wm. & Mary L. Rev. 440 (1970). For survey of recent legislation on criminal law — breath test to determine alcoholic content of blood, see 5 U. Rich. L. Rev. 189 (1970). For survey of Virginia criminal law and procedure for the year 1969-1970, see 56 Va. L. Rev. 1572 (1970).

Michie's Jurisprudence.
For related discussion, see 2B M.J. Automobiles, § 118.

CASE NOTES

Admission of taking of alcosensor test, without admission of results of test. — It was not error for the court to permit the introduction of evidence that the defendant was offered and agreed to take an alcosensor test, that the arresting officer saw the results of the test, and that the results formed a part of his basis for arresting the defendant, where the actual results of the test were not admitted into evidence. Crewey v. Commonwealth, No. 1288-97-3 (Ct. of Appeals Dec. 22, 1998).

Results of preliminary breath test inadmissible in prosecution under § 18.2-36.1. — By express wording of statute, a prosecution for violation of § 18.2-36.1 was necessarily a "prosecution under § 18.2-266," and thus this section applied to bar results of preliminary breath test in prosecution under § 18.2-36.1. Hall v. Commonwealth, No. 1280-98-4 (Ct. of Appeals Sept. 28, 1999).

Admission of refusal to perform test did not violate constitutions. — Neither the Fifth Amendment nor Va. Const., Art. I, § 8 were violated by the admission in evidence of defendant's refusal to take a field sobriety test. Farmer v. Commonwealth, 12 Va. App. 337, 404 S.E.2d 371 (1991).

Evidence of refusal, to show defendant believed he might fail, violates constitution. — Evidence of a refusal to submit to field sobriety tests, when used by the finder of fact as evidence that the accused refused to submit to the test because he believed he might fail, violates the accused's right, under Article I, § 8 of the Constitution of Virginia, not to "be compelled...to give evidence against himself." Farmer v. Commonwealth, 10 Va. App. 175, 390 S.E.2d 775 (1990).

Defendant who refused to give proper breath sample was not entitled to dismissal based on lack of breath analysis. — Sufficient evidence supported the trial court's finding that defendant deliberately refused to cooperate in giving a breath sample where defendant, who had two prior DUI convictions, barely blew into the breathalyzer machine during a first attempt, resulting in the apparatus not being activated, and failed a second time to blow as instructed after the arresting officer informed defendant that defendant was not performing the test properly and gave defendant another chance; defendant did not give a medical reason for not giving a valid breath sample and it was reasonable for the officer to conclude from defendant's conduct during the two attempts that defendant was not cooperating and that defendant would continue such non-cooperation if further tests were attempted. Lee Banks Walker v. Commonwealth, No. 0349-02-1, 2003 Va. App. LEXIS 246 (Ct. of Appeals Apr. 22, 2003).

Failure to offer test does not result in constitutional prejudice. — A defendant may not claim that he or she was constitutionally prejudiced by not having a preliminary breath test administered in that he or she was denied evidence that may have tended to corroborate the defendant's testimony contesting the breathalyzer result; this section expressly provides that the results of such a test are not admissible in any prosecution but are intended instead to resolve disputes at the scene regarding probable cause to arrest. Jones v. Town of Marion, 28 Va. App. 791, 508 S.E.2d 921 (1999), aff'd, 259 Va. 7, 524 S.E.2d 866 (2000).

The purpose of this section is to permit a preliminary analysis of the alcohol content of the blood of a person suspected of driving while intoxicated and to authorize the officer to charge an accused who tests positive, but not to allow the test results to be admitted as evidence of guilt. Stacy v. Commonwealth, 22 Va. App. 417, 470 S.E.2d 584 (1996).

This section provides a mechanism to resolve a potential on-the-scene dispute between the police and the accused concerning the alcoholic content of the blood of the accused. Jones v. Town of Marion, 28 Va. App. 791, 508 S.E.2d 921 (1999), aff'd, 259 Va. 7, 524 S.E.2d 866 (2000).

Failure to comply with subsection F of this section does not render breath test results obtained pursuant to former § 18.2-268 (now § 18.2-268.1 et seq.) inadmissible. Wohlford v. Commonwealth, 3 Va. App. 467, 351 S.E.2d 47 (1986).

Advisement held sufficient. — Where an officer read defendant an "implied consent card" and told him he was not required to take the preliminary breath test (PBT), that it was strictly "for the benefit of probable cause," and that the result of the PBT "could not be used against him in court," the advisement, though inartful, was sufficient to allow admission of the result at a suppression hearing to establish probable cause to arrest. Neatrour v. Commonwealth, No. 2090-03-4, 2004 Va. App. LEXIS 462 (Ct. of Appeals Sept. 28, 2004).

Defendant opened door for admission of alka-sensor results. — Although alka-sensor results are otherwise inadmissible, defendant opened the door for such admission by testifying that he had performed "fine" on the field test, thereby urging the court to find that he had acted reasonably. Nichols v. Commonwealth, No. 0006-88-3 (Ct. of Appeals May 2, 1989).

Limitation on use. — The results of the preliminary breath test may be admitted into evidence at a pretrial probable cause or suppression hearing, but the results shall not be admitted into evidence in any prosecution which determines guilt or innocence. Woolridge v. Commonwealth, 29 Va. App. 339, 512 S.E.2d 153 (1999).

Use in suppression hearing proper. — "Prosecution" as it is used in this section does not include a pretrial suppression hearing to determine the legality of the arrest; "prosecution" is limited to the proceedings devoted to determining the guilt or innocence of a person charged with a crime. Stacy v. Commonwealth, 22 Va. App. 417, 470 S.E.2d 584 (1996).

Alka-sensor test inadmissible to show reasonable refusal of former § 18.2-268 (now § 18.2-268.1 et seq.) tests. — Result of a preliminary alka-sensor test which allegedly read .00 and which was taken pursuant to this section was not admissible to show whether driver reasonably refused to submit to a blood or breath test as required by former § 18.2-268 (now § 18.2-268.1 et seq.). Northup v. Commonwealth, No. 0290-89-2 (Ct. of Appeals Sept. 11, 1990).

Test results inadmissible in aggravated manslaughter prosecution. — Since § 18.2-36.1, relating to causing the death of another while intoxicated, expressly references a violation of § 18.2-266 as the predicate for the prosecution of aggravated manslaughter, and since this section bars the admission of preliminary breath analysis results in a prosecution under § 18.2-266, so also is the admission of such results barred in a prosecution for aggravated manslaughter. Hall v. Commonwealth, 32 Va. App. 616, 529 S.E.2d 829, 2000 Va. App. LEXIS 466 (2000).

Failure to offer preliminary test did not invalidate arrest. — Where the record established that the arresting officer had probable cause to arrest the defendant for driving while intoxicated based on the fact that the defendant had been driving erratically, smelled strongly of alcohol, would have fallen had the officer not caught him as he got out of his van and was unable to stand, the fact that the officer had not offered the defendant a preliminary breath test because he believed the defendant was incapable of performing any sobriety test did not invalidate the defendant's arrest. Jones v. Town of Marion, 28 Va. App. 791, 508 S.E.2d 921 (1999), aff'd, 259 Va. 7, 524 S.E.2d 866 (2000).

Harmless error in admission of evidence that defendant was offered breath tests. — Although, pursuant to § 18.2-267, the trial court erred in a DUI trial in allowing testimony that defendant was offered breath tests following a traffic stop, that evidence was harmless because there was overwhelming evidence that defendant drove while intoxicated; under § 4.1-100, "intoxicated" meant a condition in which a person had drunk enough alcoholic beverages to observably affect his manner, disposition, speech, muscular movement, general appearance, or behavior. The evidence at trial proved that defendant drove his car at a reckless speed and that, when stopped, he had an odor of alcohol about his breath, red and glassy eyes, and slurred speech, and performed poorly on field sobriety tests. Reid v. Commonwealth, 2009 Va. App. LEXIS 308 (July 14, 2009).

Applied in Stevens v. Commonwealth, 44 Va. App. 122, 603 S.E.2d 642, 2004 Va. App. LEXIS 496 (2004); Stevens v. Commonwealth, 46 Va. App. 234, 616 S.E.2d 754, 2005 Va. App. LEXIS 407 (2005).

§ 18.2-268. Repealed by Acts 1992, c. 830.

Cross references.

For present provisions relating to chemical testing to determine alcohol or drug content of blood, see § 18.2-268.1 et seq.

Editor's note.

The repealed section was amended by Acts 1992, c. 561.

Acts 1992, c. 830, cl. 3 provides: "That whenever any of the conditions, requirements, provisions, or contents of § 18.2-268 or § 46.2-341.26 of the Code of Virginia, as such sections existed before July 1, 1992, are revised and renumbered, all references to such former sections, conditions, requirements, provisions, contents, or portions thereof shall apply to the renumbered section."

Acts 1992, c. 830, cl. 4 provides: "That references to actions taken pursuant to or offenses under any of the new sections shall be read to include actions taken or offenses under the corresponding provisions of old § 18.2-268 or § 46.2-341.26."

§ 18.2-268.1. Chemical testing to determine alcohol or drug content of blood; definitions.

As used in §§ 18.2-268.2 through 18.2-268.12, unless the context clearly indicates otherwise:

The phrase *"alcohol or drug"* means alcohol, a drug or drugs, or any combination of alcohol and a drug or drugs.

The phrase *"blood or breath"* means either or both.

"Chief police officer" means the sheriff in any county not having a chief of police, the chief of police of any county having a chief of police, the chief of police of the city, or the sergeant or chief of police of the town in which the charge will be heard, or their authorized representatives.

"Department" means the Department of Forensic Science.

"Director" means the Director of the Department of Forensic Science.

"License" means any driver's license, temporary driver's license, or instruction permit authorizing the operation of a motor vehicle upon the highways.

"Ordinance" means a county, city or town ordinance.

History.
1992, c. 830; 2005, cc. 868, 881.

Cross references.
As to a law-enforcement officer's right to require that his blood or urine specimen be sent to a laboratory of their choice for independent testing to determine blood or alcohol content, see § 9.1-501.

Editor's note.
Acts 1992, c. 830, cl. 3 provides: "That whenever any of the conditions, requirements, provisions, or contents of § 18.2-268 or § 46.2-341.26 of the Code of Virginia, as such sections existed before July 1, 1992, are revised and renumbered, all references to such former sections, conditions, requirements, provisions, contents, or portions thereof shall apply to the renumbered section."

Acts 1992, c. 830, cl. 4 provides: "That references to actions taken pursuant to or offenses under any of the new sections shall be read to include actions taken or offenses under the corresponding provisions of old § 18.2-268 or § 46.2-341.26."

CASE NOTES

Section that is specific governs over one that covers subject in a general way. — When one statute speaks to a subject in a general way and another deals with a part of the same subject in a more specific manner, the two should be harmonized, if possible, and where they conflict, the latter prevails; this Code section is more specific than § 19.2-187.01 statute and directly applies to blood alcohol test results, and thus this section is applicable to the facts of this case. Hilberath v. Commonwealth, No. 0351-92-4 (Ct. of Appeals Mar. 8, 1994).

CIRCUIT COURT OPINIONS

Refusal to submit to test when not legally under arrest. — Court found the driving under the influence (DUI) defendant was improperly charged with refusing to submit to a breath or blood test since the defendant was not legally under arrest for DUI, as the defendant's arrest was in violation of § 19.2-81; therefore, when the defendant was read his implied consent rights, requiring him to have been lawfully arrested in order to be subject to the mandate to submit, the defendant's refusal to submit did not constitute a violation of the statute, and his refusal to submit was not admissible since the test itself, even if he had consented to the test, was inadmissible. Commonwealth v. Coakley, 56 Va. Cir. 99, 2001 Va. Cir. LEXIS 446 (Norfolk 2001).

§ 18.2-268.2. Implied consent to post-arrest testing to determine drug or alcohol content of blood.

A. Any person, whether licensed by Virginia or not, who operates a motor vehicle upon a highway, as defined in § 46.2-100, in the Commonwealth shall be deemed thereby, as a condition of such operation, to have consented to have samples of his blood, breath, or both blood and breath taken for a chemical test to determine the alcohol, drug, or both alcohol and drug content of his blood, if he is arrested for violation of § 18.2-266, 18.2-266.1, or subsection B of § 18.2-272 or of a similar ordinance within three hours of the alleged offense.

B. Any person so arrested for a violation of clause (i) or (ii) of § 18.2-266 or both, § 18.2-266.1 or subsection B of § 18.2-272 or of a similar ordinance shall submit to a breath test. If the breath test is unavailable or the person is physically unable to submit to the breath test, a blood test shall be given. The accused shall, prior to administration of the test, be advised by the person administering the test that he has the right to observe the process of analysis and to see the blood-alcohol reading on the equipment used to perform the breath test. If the equipment automatically produces a written printout of the breath test result, the printout, or a copy, shall be given to the accused.

C. A person, after having been arrested for a violation of clause (iii), (iv), or (v) of § 18.2-266 or § 18.2-266.1 or subsection B of § 18.2-272 or of a similar ordinance, may be required to submit to a blood test to determine the drug or both drug and alcohol content of his blood. When a person, after having been arrested for a violation of § 18.2-266 (i) or (ii) or both, submits to a breath test in accordance with subsection B or refuses to take or is incapable of taking such a breath test, he may be required to submit to tests to determine the drug or both drug and alcohol content of his blood if the law-enforcement officer has reasonable cause to believe the person was driving under the influence of any drug or combination of drugs, or the combined influence of alcohol and drugs.

History.
1992, c. 830; 1993, c. 746; 1994, cc. 359, 363; 1995, c. 23; 2002, c. 748; 2004, c. 1013; 2005, cc. 616, 757, 840.

Editor's note.
Acts 1994, cc. 359 and 363, which amended this section, in cl. 2 provide that "the provisions of this act contained in §§ 18.2-268.2 through 18.2-268.5, 18.2-271, 18.2-271.1 and 46.2-391.2 through 46.2-391.5 shall become effective January 1, 1995, except to the extent that the amendments merely reflect the enactment by this act of § 18.2-266.1."

Law Review.
For survey of Virginia criminal law and procedure for the year 2004-2005, see 40 U. Rich. L. Rev. 197 (2005). For survey of Virginia law on criminal law and procedure for the year 2007-2008, see 43 U. Rich. L. Rev. 149 (2008).

Michie's Jurisprudence.
For related discussion, see 2B M.J. Automobiles, § 118; 17 M.J. Streets and Highways, § 2.

CASE NOTES

I. General Consideration.
II. Unavailability of test or inability to take test.

I. GENERAL CONSIDERATION.

Construction with other law. — Even if the State's failure to comply with the implied consent law procedural requirements did not forbid a prosecution for aggravated manslaughter, blood test results were not required for a conviction under either § 18.2-266 or 18.2-36.1. Stevens v. Commonwealth, 46 Va. App. 234, 616 S.E.2d 754, 2005 Va. App. LEXIS 407 (2005), aff'd, — Va. —, 634 S.E.2d 305 (2006).

In its 1995 revision, legislature eliminated driver's option

to elect which test to take and mandated that a driver accused of DUI shall submit to a breath test. Lamay v. Commonwealth, 29 Va. App. 461, 513 S.E.2d 411 (1999).

Limitation on blood test availability. — Only when a breath test is unavailable or the accused is physically unable to take one, is a blood test to be given. Lamay v. Commonwealth, 29 Va. App. 461, 513 S.E.2d 411 (1999).

Trial court did not err in admitting the certificate of analysis generated from defendant's blood test after the police officer who arrested defendant for driving under the influence of alcohol, second offense, had defendant take a blood test because the officer determined defendant was physically unable to take the breath test as a result of his having recently eaten chili which was giving him indigestion; the evidence supported the officer's determination that the blood test had to be taken due to defendant's inability to take the breath test. Pearson v. Commonwealth, 43 Va. App. 317, 597 S.E.2d 269, 2004 Va. App. LEXIS 272 (2004).

No mandatory duty on arresting officer to obtain blood test. — Trial court did not improperly refuse to dismiss defendant's driving under the influence charge because of the arresting officer's failure to obtain a blood test because nothing in the implied consent statute imposed a mandatory duty on the arresting officer to obtain blood testing for drivers, like defendant, suspected of being under the influence of drugs. Taylor v. Commonwealth, 2010 Va. App. LEXIS 96 (Mar. 16, 2010).

This section protects one who has the odor of alcohol on his breath but has not been drinking to excess, and one whose conduct may create the appearance of intoxication when he is suffering from some physical condition over which he has no control. Thurston v. City of Lynchburg, 15 Va. App. 475, 424 S.E.2d 701 (1992).

Requirements in order to implicate this section through § 18.2-268.8. — This section through § 18.2-268.8 provide the procedural requirements for taking, handling, identifying and disposing of blood samples under Virginia's implied consent law. To implicate the statutes the driver must have operated a motor vehicle upon a public highway in this Commonwealth and have been arrested for a violation of § 18.2-266 (or a similar ordinance) within two hours of the alleged offense of driving under the influence of alcohol. Thurston v. City of Lynchburg, 15 Va. App. 475, 424 S.E.2d 701 (1992).

Because defendant was not validly arrested within three hours of the offenses, as required by subsection A of § 18.2-268.2, and an officer's act of telling defendant that he was under arrest and advising him of the implied consent law was insufficient to satisfy the restraint requirement to assert his lawful authority to arrest defendant, defendant did not impliedly consent to have his blood drawn; thus, the certificate of analysis containing defendant's blood test results was inadmissible. Bristol v. Commonwealth, 272 Va. 568, 636 S.E.2d 460, 2006 Va. LEXIS 115 (2006).

Lawful arrest required to imply consent. — For an arrestee to be deemed to have given implied consent under this section, the arrest must have been lawful; if the arrest was not lawful, consent for blood alcohol testing is not implied, and the results of any such test are not admissible for the purpose of providing a rebuttable presumption of intoxication. Smith v. Commonwealth, 32 Va. App. 228, 527 S.E.2d 456, 2000 Va. App. LEXIS 281 (2000).

Arrest followed by a release on a summons. — In a trial on the offense of driving under the influence, the circuit court properly admitted results of a blood test from a sample collected while defendant was in the hospital. Subsection B of § 19.2-73 authorized issuance of a summons, and an arrest followed by a release on a summons satisfied the requirement of "constraining" the arrestee's liberty under the implied consent statutes. Reading §§ 19.2-73 and 19.2-74 in pari materia with the implied consent statute, an arrest followed by a release on summons satisfies the requirement of "constraining" the arrestee's personal liberty, for purposes of implicating the statutory duty to provide a blood or breath sample. Young v. Commonwealth, 57 Va. App. 731, 706 S.E.2d 53, 2011 Va. App. LEXIS 77 (2011).

Criminal and civil actions independent. — Operation of a motor vehicle while under the influence of alcohol or drugs may give rise to two separate and distinct proceedings — one a criminal action for DUI and the other a civil, administrative proceeding on the refusal charge. "Each action proceeds independently of the other and the outcome of one is of no consequence to the other."

Cash v. Commonwealth, 251 Va. 46, 466 S.E.2d 736 (1996).

Road was "highway" as defined in § 46.2-100. — Where evidence proved that appellant drove into a ditch alongside a parking lot, and where evidence demonstrated that road upon which appellant traveled when deputy approached him was open for use by the public, and it provided unrestricted vehicular access to a store and campground from a thoroughfare, the road was a "highway" as defined in § 46.2-100, and Virginia's implied consent statute applied to appellant when he drove upon it. Murray v. Commonwealth, No. 2142-96-4 (Ct. of Appeals Nov. 4, 1997).

Law applies to any place in § 46.2-100's definition of "highway." — The implied consent law applies to any way or place encompassed within the two-prong definition of "highway" contained in § 46.2-100. Mitchell v. Commonwealth, 26 Va. App. 27, 492 S.E.2d 839 (1997).

Parking lot not a "highway." — Parking lot of apartment complex was not a "highway" for purposes of implied consent statute. White v. City of Lynchburg, No. 0591-99-3 (Ct. of Appeals Feb. 15, 2000).

Since this section is restricted by its terms to a "highway," a defendant's contention that the section afforded him the right to a breathalyzer test failed where the defendant was stopped in a restaurant parking lot, which was not considered a highway. Edwards v. City of Virginia Beach, No. 2751-00-1, 2001 Va. App. LEXIS 522 (Ct. of Appeals Sept. 25, 2001).

Law applied to roads of mobile home complex. — Where no evidence in the record proved that the streets in the mobile home complex were restricted exclusively to the private use of the mobile home dwellers or those persons who visited them, and, indeed, the evidence proved that the roads in the mobile home complex were open to the unrestricted use of the public, the implied consent law applied to defendant when he operated his vehicle on the roads of the mobile home complex. Mitchell v. Commonwealth, 26 Va. App. 27, 492 S.E.2d 839 (1997).

Consent not qualified or conditional. — The consent to submit to a blood or breath test, granted when a person operates a motor vehicle upon the highways, "is not a qualified consent and it is not a conditional consent, and therefore there can be no qualified refusal or conditional refusal to take the test." The mere fact that under the statute "an accused is afforded an opportunity to establish the reasonableness of his refusal does not operate to dilute the consent previously given, or convert that consent into a qualified or conditional one." Cash v. Commonwealth, 251 Va. 46, 466 S.E.2d 736 (1996).

Where an arresting officer has probable cause to believe an incoherent or unconscious driver has violated § 18.2-266, prohibiting driving under the influence of alcohol, the implied consent law, this section, operates to permit the taking and testing of blood from that driver and that incoherence or unconsciousness does not constitute a refusal, reasonable or unreasonable, because consent is continuing. Goodman v. Commonwealth, 37 Va. App. 374, 558 S.E.2d 555, 2002 Va. App. LEXIS 45 (2002).

Accused's silence was not an admission of guilt. — In a prosecution for driving under the influence in violation of § 18.2-266, as assimilated under 18 U.S.C.S. §§ 7 and 13, the trial court violated defendant's Fifth Amendment right against self-incrimination by inferring an admission of culpability from defendant's silence when defendant was advised of Virginia's implied consent statute, § 18.2-268.2; as defendant's consent to a breath test demonstrated, defendant's silence did not constitute a refusal to taking a blood or breath test. United States v. Hagedorn, — F.3d —, 2002 U.S. App. LEXIS 25762 (4th Cir. Dec. 16, 2002).

In prosecution for driving under the influence on a military base in violation of § 18.2-266, as assimilated under 18 U.S.C.S. §§ 7, 13, the appellate court determined that the district court violated defendant's Fifth Amendment right against self-incrimination by inferring an admission that defendant was the driver of the vehicle by remaining silent in the face of being advised of Virginia's implied consent statute applicable to drivers under § 18.2-268.2, and defendant's silence under such circumstances did not constitute an admission of culpability; however, the error was harmless because unrelated evidence established defendant's identity as the driver. United States v. Hagedorn, — F.3d —, 2003 U.S. App. LEXIS 1805 (4th Cir. Feb. 3, 2003).

The measurement of a blood alcohol test creates a rebuttable presumption that the measurement accurately reflects the blood alcohol concentration at the time of driving. The defendant is entitled to challenge this presumption through evidence calling into question the accuracy of the test results. Terpstra v. Commonwealth, No. 0716-95-4 (Ct. of Appeals April 9, 1996).

Accused holds the option to take blood or breath test. — When the legislature enacted this statute, it granted to the accused, not the Commonwealth, the option to take a blood or breath test. That election, whether based on the accused's perception of the reliability of these tests or their invasive nature, is one that this court must honor. Breeden v. Commonwealth, 15 Va. App. 148, 421 S.E.2d 674 (1992) (decided under former § 18.2-268).

Driver has right to receive benefits of test. — Once the Commonwealth has elected to have a driver take a blood or breath test pursuant to this statute, the driver has a right to receive the benefits of the test. Breeden v. Commonwealth, 15 Va. App. 148, 421 S.E.2d 674 (1992) (decided under former § 18.2-268).

Does not give the operator of a motor vehicle the right to request a breathalyzer or blood test. — Plaintiff failed to state a due process claim against defendant police officer because § 18.2-268.2 did not, as plaintiff alleged, give the operator of a motor vehicle the right to request a breathalyzer or blood test. Edwards v. Oberndorf, 309 F. Supp. 2d 780, 2003 U.S. Dist. LEXIS 26012 (E.D. Va. 2003).

Defendant arrested for public drunkenness but later charged with driving under the influence not entitled to blood or breath tests. — Where defendant was originally arrested for public drunkenness, but an off-duty officer from another county who had observed his driving later swore out a criminal complaint and persuaded a magistrate to issue a warrant against defendant for driving under the influence, defendant had not been entitled to blood or breath tests under § 18.2-268.2. Wilson v. Commonwealth, 45 Va. App. 193, 609 S.E.2d 612, 2005 Va. App. LEXIS 84 (2005).

Scope of accused's right to view results. — The term "process of analysis" does not enlarge the scope of what the accused is entitled to review under this section; the accused is not entitled to view the results obtained from each breath sample, but only the results printed out by the equipment used to perform the breath test. Rasmussen v. Commonwealth, 31 Va. App. 233, 522 S.E.2d 401 (1999).

Nothing in this section or in § 18.2-268.9 indicates any intention on the part of the legislature to give an accused the right to immediately view results of a breath test other than those actually printed out by the equipment used to conduct the test. Rasmussen v. Commonwealth, 31 Va. App. 233, 522 S.E.2d 401 (1999).

Where an accused is afforded the opportunity to view the print-out of the blood-alcohol reading taken by the breathalyzer machine, the requirements of this section and § 18.2-268.9 have been met. Carey v. Commonwealth, No. 1888-98-4, 2000 Va. App. LEXIS 303 (Ct. of Appeals Apr. 25, 2000).

Where defendant only saw certificate with printout of lower of two blood alcohol readings, the only evidence not made immediately available to him was evidence of an inculpatory nature; as he was afforded the opportunity to view the print-out of the blood-alcohol reading taken by the breathalyzer machine, the requirements of this section and § 18.2-268.9 were met. Kauffman v. Commonwealth, No. 1725-98-2, 2000 Va. App. LEXIS 452 (Ct. of Appeals June 20, 2000).

Scope of accused's right to a copy of results. — The plain language of subsection B provides that an individual who is given a breath test is entitled to a printout of the result only if the machine automatically produces a printout. Where no printout is produced, there is no copy to give the test taker. Wing v. Commonwealth, No. 1760-03-4, 2004 Va. App. LEXIS 368 (Ct. of Appeals Aug. 3, 2004).

Agreement to take test does not mean belief in one's innocence. — Upon being arrested for DUI, one is required either to take the blood or breath test or suffer additional consequences, thus, the agreement to take the blood or breath test, as opposed to suffering the consequences of taking neither, does not carry with it the same indicia of belief in one's innocence as does the willingness to take a voluntary field sobriety test. Hammond v. Commonwealth, 17 Va. App. 565, 439 S.E.2d 877 (1994).

A driver's subjective belief that he was not under the influence of alcohol is not a reasonable basis for refusing the test, nor is the fact that he could and did operate his vehicle in a proficient manner. Thus, evidence of his state of sobriety or proficiency in operating the vehicle is not admissible in a case involving refusal to take a blood or breath test. Cash v. Commonwealth, 251 Va. 46, 466 S.E.2d 736 (1996).

Waiver of right to separate sample where accused voluntarily interrupts procedure. — The government's failure to comply strictly with the statutory mandate to provide the accused with a sample of blood for independent testing resulted from the voluntary act of the accused in interrupting the completion of the blood removal process; where an accused voluntarily interrupts the blood removal procedure before the physician, nurse or technician completes that procedure, the accused, by his conduct, shall be deemed to have waived his right to an independent analysis of a separate sample as provided by §§ 18.2-268.6 and 18.2-268.7. Thurston v. City of Lynchburg, 15 Va. App. 475, 424 S.E.2d 701 (1992) (decided prior to 2003 amendments to §§ 18.2-268.6 and 18.2-268.7.)

Where defendant disrupted blood removal procedure, no error in admitting one sample. — Defendant's voluntary act in disrupting the blood removal procedure constituted a waiver of his right to a separate sample for independent testing. Thus, it was not error for the trial court to admit the results of the blood test analyzed from the one sample sent to the state laboratory by the arresting officer. Thurston v. City of Lynchburg, 15 Va. App. 475, 424 S.E.2d 701 (1992).

Credibility issues. — The factual determinations involved in evaluating a witness' credibility are necessary predicates to a legal ruling on the admissibility of that witness' testimony and, as such, are questions for the trial judge and not the jury. Bennett v. Commonwealth, 31 Va. App. 30, 520 S.E.2d 845 (1999).

Error to admit blood test results where failure to follow statutory mandates. — Where the government has failed in its responsibilities to follow the statutory mandates in the taking, handling, identification and disposition of blood samples under the statutory scheme, it is error to admit at trial the results of tests concerning such blood samples. Thurston v. City of Lynchburg, 15 Va. App. 475, 424 S.E.2d 701 (1992).

Purpose. — The purpose of the implied consent law requiring the test to be taken is to determine the concentration of alcohol in a driver's blood or breath sample, and thereby determine the driver's state of intoxication or sobriety and whether defendant was sober or intoxicated, in fact. Quinn v. Commonwealth, 9 Va. App. 321, 388 S.E.2d 268 (1990) (decided under former § 18.2-268).

Under the implied consent law, any person who operates a motor vehicle upon a highway in the Commonwealth is deemed, as a condition of such operation, to have consented to have samples of blood, breath, or both, taken for a chemical test to determine alcohol content of the person's blood, if that person is arrested for DUI in violation of the applicable statutes or of a similar local ordinance. Cash v. Commonwealth, 251 Va. 46, 466 S.E.2d 736 (1996).

Implied consent not part of penalty. — The implied consent of one who operates a vehicle on the public highways of Virginia to take a blood test, in event he be charged with drunk driving, is not a part of the penalty or punishment inflicted for drunk driving. It is a measure flowing from the police power of the state designed to protect other users of state highways. Deaner v. Commonwealth, 210 Va. 285, 170 S.E.2d 199 (1969) (decided under former § 18.2-268).

Implied consent law did not require an officer to obtain a blood sample from an unconscious defendant in order to be able to prosecute him for driving under the influence. Oliver v. Commonwealth, 40 Va. App. 20, 577 S.E.2d 514, 2003 Va. App. LEXIS 98 (2003).

Absence of independent laboratory test. — Where attorney for the Commonwealth made no attempt to explain the absence of the independent laboratory test results, merely stating that he "didn't have anything to do with it. It's up to the defendant," the trial judge erred by admitting the Commonwealth's certificate of analysis without an explanation for the absence of the results. The Commonwealth receives the vial that is to be mailed to the independent laboratory, is responsible for mailing it, and for receiving and filing the test results. Taffe v. Commonwealth, No. 1938-93-3 (Ct. of Appeals March 14, 1995).

No right to consult counsel. — For the Supreme Court to uphold the contention of defendant that his right to consult counsel before refusing or taking the blood test is a constitutional right, would virtually nullify the implied consent law. Deaner v. Commonwealth, 210 Va. 285, 170 S.E.2d 199 (1969) (decided under former § 18.2-268).

The blood test prescribed by this section is a part of a civil and administrative proceeding and defendant had no right to condition his taking the test upon his ability first to consult with counsel. Deaner v. Commonwealth, 210 Va. 285, 170 S.E.2d 199 (1969) (decided under former § 18.2-268).

A person charged with operating a motor vehicle while under the influence of intoxicants does not have a constitutional right to consult an attorney before deciding whether to take a blood test. Coleman v. Commonwealth, 212 Va. 684, 187 S.E.2d 172 (1972) (decided under former § 18.2-268).

Denial of the right to consult with counsel before an accused decides whether to take a blood test does not impair an accused's right to a trial "by the law of the land" guaranteed by Art. I, § 8, of the State Constitution. Law v. City of Danville, 212 Va. 702, 187 S.E.2d 197 (1972) (decided under former § 18.2-268).

Because a proceeding relative to refusal to take a blood test is civil in nature, a person arrested for driving under the influence does not have a constitutional right to consult with counsel before deciding whether to submit to the test. Bailey v. Commonwealth, 215 Va. 130, 207 S.E.2d 828 (1974) (decided under former § 18.2-268).

A person's unwillingness to take the test without prior consultation with counsel does not constitute a reasonable basis for the refusal. Cash v. Commonwealth, 251 Va. 46, 466 S.E.2d 736 (1996).

Because defendant's unwillingness to submit to a breath test without access to counsel amounted to an unreasonable refusal under subsection A of § 18.2-268.3, the trial court properly instructed the jury on said issue. Thus, defendant's conviction of unreasonably refusing to submit to a breath test, after having been convicted of two predicate offenses within ten years, in violation of § 18.2-268.3, was upheld on appeal. Brothers v. Commonwealth, 50 Va. App. 468, 650 S.E.2d 874, 2007 Va. App. LEXIS 370 (2007).

Failure to make valid arrest within two hours. — Where the accident happened and the offense occurred just before 3:00 p.m., and an invalid arrest was made at 4:35 p.m., but the accused was not properly arrested until 6:15 p.m., since the arrest was untimely, the defendant is not deemed to have consented to the testing of his breath under the "implied consent" law. Thomas v. Town of Marion, 226 Va. 251, 308 S.E.2d 120 (1983) (decided under former § 18.2-268).

Because police failed to arrest appellant for driving under the influence of alcohol within two hours of the accident, the certificate of analysis was inadmissible at trial. Castillo v. Commonwealth, 21 Va. App. 482, 465 S.E.2d 146 (1995) (decided under former § 18.2-268).

Valid arrest found. — Court found that defendant was arrested for purposes of this section, even though the officer issued the summons for DUI after defendant had been transported to the hospital and more than three hours after the alleged offense; the certificate of analysis containing the results of the blood test were therefore admissible against him at trial. Varner v. Commonwealth, No. 2354-03-1, 2004 Va. App. LEXIS 609 (Ct. of Appeals Dec. 14, 2004).

Valid arrest not found. — Officer made an invalid warrantless arrest for a misdemeanor not committed in his presence as the single-vehicle accident occurred on or beside a private road in a gated, guarded residential complex; thus, the exceptions to the warrant requirement in § 19.2-81 did not apply. Therefore, the implied consent law did not apply to permit the certificate of analysis of defendant's breath test to be admitted into evidence. Roseborough v. Commonwealth, 281 Va. 233, 704 S.E.2d 414, 2011 Va. LEXIS 13 (2011).

Probable cause for arrest found. — Deputy had sufficient probable cause to justify arresting defendant for unreasonable refusal to provide a breath sample based on the smell of alcohol on defendant, defendant's red and glassy eyes, the fact that defendant was argumentative, and the fact that defendant refused to perform field sobriety tests. Jones v. Commonwealth, 51 Va. App. 730, 660 S.E.2d 343, 2008 Va. App. LEXIS 213 (2008), aff'd in part and vacated in part, 279 Va. 52, 688 S.E.2d 269, 2010 Va. LEXIS 20 (Va. 2010), , concluding that refusal to perform field sobriety tests is not evidence of "consciousness of guilt".

A warrantless search of a blood sample for alcohol level analysis will be upheld only if: (1) the process is a reasonable one which is performed in a reasonable manner; (2) there was in advance a clear indication that in fact the evidence sought will be found; and (3) there were exigent circumstances, such as a need to take the test before the percentage of alcohol in the blood diminished. Tipton v. Commonwealth, 18 Va. App. 370, 444 S.E.2d 1 (1994). But see Bristol v. Commonwealth, 272 Va. 568, 636 S.E.2d 460 (2006), which overruled the *Tipton* court as to the existence of exigent circumstances.

The defendant may not unilaterally abrogate the agreement or withdraw that consent by refusing the test unless there is a reasonable basis for the refusal. A fear of being "framed" is not such a basis; it is not "reasonable" in the sense that evidence of endangerment of the health of the accused by withdrawal of blood furnishes a "reasonable" basis for refusal. That type of evidence should have been offered in the trial of the DUI charge because it may relate to the question whether the police officer's stop of the accused was lawful; certainly such evidence is not probative in the trial of the refusal charge. Cash v. Commonwealth, 251 Va. 46, 466 S.E.2d 736 (1996).

Where the defendant's warrantless arrest was unlawful, he was not bound under this section to submit to a breathalyzer test; therefore the result of the breathalyzer test administered to the defendant should not have been admitted in evidence at his trial. Durant v. City of Suffolk, 4 Va. App. 445, 358 S.E.2d 732 (1987) (decided under former § 18.2-268).

No error in admission of certificate of analysis. — Based on a deputy's observations of defendant as she sat in her car in her driveway and her admission that she had consumed alcohol and then had driven her car and picked her daughter up from school, the trial court could reasonably have found that defendant pulled into her driveway after driving on a public highway, while under the influence of alcohol, with minors in the vehicle, and did so within one hour of her arrest; thus, the evidentiary requirements of the implied consent statute were satisfied and the trial court did not err in admitting a certificate of analysis. Easton v. Commonwealth, — Va. App. —, — S.E.2d —, 2005 Va. App. LEXIS 248 (June 28, 2005).

There was sufficient evidence that the three-hour testing requirement of the implied consent statute was satisfied where: (1) an officer first received a call at 6:20 a.m. and reported to the accident scene at a busy intersection by 6:26 a.m.; (2) when the officer arrived, defendant was still inside his vehicle, seated behind the steering wheel, with the keys in the ignition; and (3) it was reasonable for the trial court to conclude that the accident had occurred shortly prior to the call. Since defendant's arrest at 6:35 a.m. was well within three hours of the time the evidence established that the accident happened (and thus the time he committed the offense of driving while intoxicated), the trial court did not abuse its discretion in admitting the certificate of analysis of his breathalyzer test. Pruitt v. Commonwealth, — Va. App. —, — S.E.2d —, 2008 Va. App. LEXIS 57 (Feb. 5, 2008).

Even assuming, without deciding, that the officer did not have the statutory authority to arrest defendant for driving while intoxicated, it was not error for the trial court to admit the certificate of analysis into evidence, because the implied consent statute was not used to obtain the breath sample where defendant expressly volunteered to provide the sample before the officer mentioned the implied consent statute to defendant. Roseborough v. Commonwealth, 53 Va. App. 451, 672 S.E.2d 917, 2009 Va. App. LEXIS 84 (2009).

Certificate not admissible where arrest took place after blood test. — Trial court erred in admitting a certificate of analysis at defendant's trial pursuant to § 18.2-268.2, because the purported arrest for driving under the influence took place after the blood test was administered. Sprouse v. Commonwealth, 53 Va. App. 488, 673 S.E.2d 481, 2009 Va. App. LEXIS 109 (2009).

Section not construed to alter or expand federal implied consent statute. — This section should not be relied upon by federal district court to alter or expand 18 U.S.C.S. § 3117, the federal implied consent statute. United States v. Jerge, 738 F. Supp. 181 (E.D. Va. 1990) (decided under former § 18.2-268).

Test results admissible even though original DUI charge was dismissed. — Defendant's argument that the results of a breath test defendant took within two hours of the time defendant was arrested and charged by police with misdemeanor driving under the influence (DUI) could not be used at defendant's trial for felony DUI because defendant's original arrest was vacated when the Commonwealth moved successfully to nolle prosequi the misdemeanor charge so it could seek a felony indictment was without merit. Williams v. Commonwealth, 38 Va. App. 414, 565 S.E.2d 328, 2002 Va. App. LEXIS 369 (2002), aff'd, 265 Va. 268, 576 S.E.2d 468 (2003).

Blood alcohol tests properly admitted. — In a prosecution for aggravated involuntary manslaughter, the trial court did not commit reversible error in allowing into evidence the results of a blood alcohol content test performed on a blood sample taken from a defendant in violation of his Fourth, Fifth, and Fourteenth Amendment rights, as: (1) a test conducted by hospital personnel had been independently performed and the written report thereof was admissible under § 19.2-187.02; (2) defendant consented to a second blood test administered by a deputy sheriff under the implied consent law; (3) evidence of defendant's intoxication was overwhelming despite testing over three times the legal limit; and (4) it was unreasonable to believe that the jury would have rejected the hospital-administered test and accepted, instead, the implied consent law test. Stevens v. Commonwealth, 272 Va. 481, 634 S.E.2d 305, 2006 Va. LEXIS 87 (2006), cert. denied, 549 U.S. 1350, 127 S. Ct. 2053, 167 L. Ed. 2d 784, 2007 U.S. LEXIS 4119 (U.S. 2007).

Harmless error. — Even if a trial court errs in admitting an analysis of the blood test results where defendant was not arrested within three hours of driving under the influence and, thus, did not give implied consent pursuant to subsection A of § 18.2-268.2 to have blood drawn, the error in admitting such evidence may be harmless. Admission of such evidence is harmless where there is other, compelling evidence that defendant was operating a vehicle while intoxicated. Lyle v. Commonwealth, 2008 Va. App. LEXIS 205 (Apr. 29, 2008).

Refusal to submit to test can factor into probable cause. — Defendant's conviction for unreasonably refusing to submit to a blood or breath test after being arrested for driving under the influence of alcohol in violation of § 18.2-268.2 was affirmed because his refusal to submit could be considered in a police officer's assessment of probable cause to arrest him. Jones v. Commonwealth, 279 Va. 52, 688 S.E.2d 269, 2010 Va. LEXIS 20 (2010).

Sufficient evidence of refusal to take breath test. — Evidence was sufficient to prove defendant's refusal to take a breath test in violation of § 18.2-268.3 because the only reasonable hypothesis flowing from the evidence was that defendant intentionally failed to give adequate effort to produce a test result determined by the machine to be valid and, thus, that he unreasonably refused to have a sample of his breath taken for the purpose of having its alcohol content analyzed; § 18.2-268.3 contemplates the cooperation reasonably necessary to generate a result deemed valid by the testing equipment and its licensed operator. Chisman v. Commonwealth, 2011 Va. App. LEXIS 189 (May 31, 2011).

Applied in Weaver v. Commonwealth, 29 Va. App. 487, 513 S.E.2d 423 (1999); Stevens v. Commonwealth, 44 Va. App. 122, 603 S.E.2d 642, 2004 Va. App. LEXIS 496 (2004); Rowley v. Commonwealth, 48 Va. App. 181, 629 S.E.2d 188, 2006 Va. App. LEXIS 167 (2006); Brown v. Commonwealth, — Va. App. —, — S.E.2d —, 2008 Va. App. LEXIS 158 (Apr. 8, 2008).

II. UNAVAILABILITY OF TEST OR INABILITY TO TAKE TEST.

Commonwealth must establish valid reason for lack of availability of test. — Once a driver elects to take either the blood test or the breath test, if the election is not honored because of unavailability, the Commonwealth must establish a valid reason for the lack of availability of a test. Mason v. Commonwealth, 15 Va. App. 583, 425 S.E.2d 544 (1993).

Reasonable basis for unavailability of test. — Where the officer was the only state police officer in the county that night and was under orders not to leave the jurisdiction of the county, the trial court did not err in finding that the Commonwealth established a reasonable basis for the unavailability of the blood test. Mason v. Commonwealth, 15 Va. App. 583, 425 S.E.2d 544 (1993).

Burden of proving physical inability to take breath test is on the accused driver. Lamay v. Commonwealth, 29 Va. App. 461, 513 S.E.2d 411 (1999).

Where the arresting police officer contended that defendant refused to take a breath test, under subsection B of § 18.2-268.2, by refusing to properly blow into the machine, and defendant contended that defendant was physically unable to do so, due to a medical condition involving defendant's lungs, the burden rested upon defendant to present evidence that defendant was physically unable to take the test, and physical inability was a condition precedent to any finding that the Commonwealth was required to offer a blood test; defendant's conviction for refusing to submit to a breath test, in violation of § 18.2-268.3, was affirmed. Hudson v. Commonwealth, 266 Va. 371, 585 S.E.2d 583, 2003 Va. LEXIS 84 (2003).

Inability to take breath test question of law. — The question of whether a person suspected of driving under the influence was physically unable to take a breath test and, therefore, was entitled to a blood test is a question of law to be resolved by the trial court even where the resolution of this matter requires the court to decide issues of credibility. Bennett v. Commonwealth, 33 Va. App. 335, 533 S.E.2d 22, 2000 Va. App. LEXIS 645 (2000).

Trial court erred in failing to rule on whether defendant was physically unable to take the breath test required by § 18.2-268.2 because the evidence of defendant's condition was conflicting since defendant testified he suffered from acid reflux, causing him to burp involuntarily, and if believed, defendant could not comply with the twenty-minute observation period, but an officer testified that he spoke with defendant for approximately thirty minutes at the scene and heard no burping, nor did he hear burping from the time of arrest until defendant was taken to jail; the trial court did not resolve the conflict in testimony and made no finding, that defendant failed to prove he was physically unable to take the breath test, and such a ruling would be inconsistent with the trial court's finding that defendant was not entitled to a breath or blood test. Packard v. Commonwealth, 2011 Va. App. LEXIS 107 (Mar. 29, 2011).

After an accused presents evidence of his physical inability, the Commonwealth is entitled to present evidence in rebuttal, after which it rests upon the trial court to determine whether the accused satisfied his or her burden. Lamay v. Commonwealth, 29 Va. App. 461, 513 S.E.2d 411 (1999).

Defendant's need to use an inhaler. — Where an officer only had to provide a blood test if he chose to compel submission to chemical testing and a breath test was unavailable or an arrestee was physically unable to submit to the breath test, an asthmatic defendant, who used her inhaler while being transported to a detention center and after her arrival there, had no statutory right to require the officer to give her a breath test under subsection B of § 18.2-268.2. Brown-Fitzgerald v. Commonwealth, 51 Va. App. 232, 656 S.E.2d 422, 2008 Va. App. LEXIS 53 (2008).

When refusal charge to be dismissed. — Numerous, often competing considerations must be taken into account in scheduling work shifts in a law-enforcement agency. However, if these considerations are allowed to take precedence so as to subvert the availability of either test authorized by subsection B of this section, any refusal charge resulting from the application of such procedures must be dismissed. Commonwealth v. Gray, 248 Va. 633, 449 S.E.2d 807 (1994) (decision prior to 1994 amendment).

Reasonable explanation of breath test unavailability found. — Where there was no basis for concluding that the sheriff's procedures were applied in an arbitrary or capricious manner on the date of defendant's arrest, or that the breath test was available on the date, the Commonwealth met its burden of establishing a reasonable explanation as to why the breath test was unavailable. Commonwealth v. Gray, 248 Va. 633, 449 S.E.2d 807 (1994) (decision prior to 1994 amendment).

When the breathalyzer machine at the county jail malfunctioned it became "unavailable" within the meaning of this section and the commonwealth was not required to search surrounding areas for an otherwise available machine before requesting the defendant submit to a blood test. Herring v. Commonwealth, 28 Va. App. 588, 507 S.E.2d 638 (1998).

Denial of right to blood test warranted dismissal. — Defendant's right to a blood test was denied when she was refused such a test without a showing that it was unavailable. The charge of driving while under the influence of alcohol should have been dismissed because the denial of defendant's right to a blood test deprived her of an opportunity to prove her innocence. A driver cannot be convicted of unreasonably refusing to take a blood or breath test "without an adequate explanation from the government as to why one of the tests was unavailable." Breeden v. Commonwealth, 15 Va. App. 148, 421 S.E.2d 674 (1992) (decided under former § 18.2-268).

If chosen test unavailable, available test must be taken. — Although this section permits the accused to elect between a breath or blood test, if the chosen test is unavailable, then the available test must be taken. United States v. Jerge, 738 F. Supp. 181 (E.D. Va. 1990) (decided under former § 18.2-268).

Burden of explaining why defendant deprived of choice of tests. — If the Commonwealth or locality deprives a defendant of the choice of tests provided by this statute, it has the burden of explaining why. Driver v. Commonwealth, 6 Va. App. 583, 371 S.E.2d 27 (1988) (decided under former § 18.2-268).

Once a driver elects to take either the blood test or the breath test, if the election is not honored because of unavailability, the Commonwealth must establish a valid reason for the lack of availability of the test; here, a valid reason was provided when three attempts to take blood from the defendant were unsuccessful. Walker v. City of Lynchburg, 22 Va. App. 197, 468 S.E.2d 164 (1996).

Record must disclose reasons for unavailability of test. — This section contemplates the existence of both a blood and breath test, and when one of the tests is unavailable, the record must contain evidence disclosing the reasons for its unavailability. Driver v. Commonwealth, 6 Va. App. 583, 371 S.E.2d 27 (1988) (decided under former § 18.2-268).

When the evidence establishes that either the blood test or the breath test is unavailable, a defendant cannot be convicted of "unreasonably" refusing to submit to testing without an adequate explanation from the government as to why that test was unavailable. Driver v. Commonwealth, 6 Va. App. 583, 371 S.E.2d 27 (1988) (decided under former § 18.2-268).

Admissibility of physical inability to take test. — Evidence of physical inability to take breath test is admissible in a prosecution for DUI. Whereas evidence unique to a refusal charge has historically been precluded at a DUI trial, and vice versa, the changes in this section require a different evidentiary result. Lamay v. Commonwealth, 29 Va. App. 461, 513 S.E.2d 411 (1999).

Evidence of unavailability of blood test held insufficient. — Where no reason was given in the record for why the two people certified to take blood were not available, there was insufficient evidence to establish that the blood test was not available to the defendant and thus, that his refusal to take the breath test was unreasonable. Driver v. Commonwealth, 6 Va. App. 583, 371 S.E.2d 27 (1988) (decided under former § 18.2-268).

The defendant's need to use nitroglycerin for his heart condition during the 20 minute waiting period did not meet the "physical inability" requirement necessitating the use of a blood test. St. Clair v. City of Lynchburg, No. 1649-97-3 (Ct. of Appeals Nov. 24, 1998).

Issue preserved for appeal. — Defendant preserved the issue of whether the trial court erred in not making a factual determination of whether he was physically unable to perform the breathalyzer test required by § 18.2-268.2 because the trial court never ruled on defendant alleged inability since the trial court thought it did not need to do so when it concluded defendant was not entitled to either a breath test or a blood test; the issue of whether defendant was physically able to take the breath test was squarely before the trial court. Packard v. Commonwealth, 2011 Va. App. LEXIS 107 (Mar. 29, 2011).

CIRCUIT COURT OPINIONS

Lawful arrest required to imply consent. — As defendant's arrest for driving under the influence was made by an officer who did not have the statutory authority to make an arrest outside of a university's jurisdiction, the arrest was not a lawful arrest sufficient to implement the implied consent law. Defendant's motion to suppress a certificate of the breath test analysis therefore had to be granted. Commonwealth v. Thompson, 69 Va. Cir. 283, 2005 Va. Cir. LEXIS 321 (Charlottesville 2005).

Arrest for purpose of administering blood test. — Defendant was arrested for purposes of administration of a blood alcohol test because he was taken to a hospital after a vehicular collision,

and he was not free to leave the hospital of his own accord, but rather, he remained under uninterrupted police supervision until he was discharged from the hospital. Commonwealth v. Isaac, 81 Va. Cir. 508, 2009 Va. Cir. LEXIS 196 (Fairfax County Dec. 31, 2009).

Parking lot not a "highway." — Implied consent law did not apply and defendant should not have been forced to take a breath test where defendant's car was parked in a marked parking space outside a store in a shopping center parking lot; signs were posted at the entrance to the lot indicating that the lot was to be used for customers when shopping and was not open to off-site, commuter, or overnight parking; the signs prohibited loitering, soliciting and handbilling; and an officer noticed that the car was running and the driver's side door was open, but defendant appeared to be passed out in the driver's seat. Commonwealth v. Wood, 73 Va. Cir. 333, 2007 Va. Cir. LEXIS 215 (Charlottesville May 9, 2007).

§ 18.2-268.3. Refusal of tests; penalties; procedures.

A. It shall be unlawful for a person who is arrested for a violation of § 18.2-266, 18.2-266.1, or subsection B of § 18.2-272 or of a similar ordinance to unreasonably refuse to have samples of his blood or breath or both blood and breath taken for chemical tests to determine the alcohol or drug content of his blood as required by § 18.2-268.2 and any person who so unreasonably refuses is guilty of a violation of this section.

B. When a person is arrested for a violation of § 18.2-51.4, 18.2-266, 18.2-266.1 or, subsection B of § 18.2-272 or of a similar ordinance and such person refuses to permit blood or breath or both blood and breath samples to be taken for testing as required by § 18.2-268.2, the arresting officer shall advise the person, from a form provided by the Office of the Executive Secretary of the Supreme Court, that (i) a person who operates a motor vehicle upon a highway in the Commonwealth is deemed thereby, as a condition of such operation, to have consented to have samples of his blood and breath taken for chemical tests to determine the alcohol or drug content of his blood, (ii) a finding of unreasonable refusal to consent may be admitted as evidence at a criminal trial, (iii) the unreasonable refusal to do so constitutes grounds for the revocation of the privilege of operating a motor vehicle upon the highways of the Commonwealth, (iv) the criminal penalty for unreasonable refusal within 10 years of a prior conviction for driving while intoxicated or unreasonable refusal is a Class 2 misdemeanor, and (v) the criminal penalty for unreasonable refusal within 10 years of any two prior convictions for driving while intoxicated or unreasonable refusal is a Class 1 misdemeanor. The form from which the arresting officer shall advise the person arrested shall contain a brief statement of the law requiring the taking of blood or breath samples, a statement that a finding of unreasonable refusal to consent may be admitted as evidence at a criminal trial, and the penalties for refusal. The Office of the Executive Secretary of the Supreme Court shall make the form available on the Internet and the form shall be considered an official publication of the Commonwealth for the purposes of § 8.01-388.

C. The arresting officer shall, under oath before the magistrate, execute the form and certify, (i) that the defendant has refused to permit blood or breath or both blood and breath samples to be taken for testing; (ii) that the officer has read the portion of the form described in subsection B to the arrested person; (iii) that the arrested person, after having had the portion of the form described in subsection B read to him, has refused to permit such sample or samples to be taken; and (iv) how many, if any, violations of this section, § 18.2-266, or any offense described in subsection E of § 18.2-270 the arrested person has been convicted of within the last 10 years. Such sworn certification shall constitute probable cause for the magistrate to issue a warrant or summons charging the person with unreasonable refusal. The magistrate shall attach the executed and sworn advisement form to the warrant or summons. The warrant or summons for a first offense under this section shall be executed in the same manner as a criminal warrant or summons. If the person arrested has been taken to a medical facility for treatment or evaluation of his medical condition, the arresting officer may read the advisement form to the person at the medical facility, and issue, on the premises of the medical facility, a summons for a violation of this section in lieu of securing a warrant or summons from the magistrate. The magistrate or arresting officer, as the case may be, shall forward the executed advisement form and warrant or summons to the appropriate court.

D. A first violation of this section is a civil offense and subsequent violations are criminal offenses. For a first offense the court shall suspend the defendant's privilege to drive for a period of one year. This suspension period is in addition to the suspension period provided under § 46.2-391.2.

If a person is found to have violated this section and within 10 years prior to the date of the refusal he was found guilty of any of the following: a violation of this section, a violation of § 18.2-266, or a violation of any offense listed in subsection E of § 18.2-270, arising out of separate occurrences or incidents, he is guilty of a Class 2 misdemeanor and the court shall suspend the defendant's privilege to drive for a period of three years. This suspension period is in addition to the suspension period provided under § 46.2-391.2.

If a person is found guilty of a violation of this section and within 10 years prior to the date of the refusal he was found guilty of any two of the following: a violation of this section, a violation of § 18.2-266, or a violation of any offense listed in subsection E of § 18.2-270 arising out of separate occurrences or incidents, he is guilty of a Class 1 misdemeanor and the court shall suspend the defendant's privilege to drive for a period of three years. This suspension period is in addition to the suspension period provided under § 46.2-391.2.

History.
1992, c. 830; 1994, cc. 359, 363; 1997, c. 691; 2001, cc. 654, 779; 2004, cc. 985, 1013, 1022; 2004, Sp. Sess. I, c. 2; 2005, cc. 757, 840; 2009, c. 239.

Editor's note.
Acts 1994, cc. 359 and 363, cls. 2, provide that "the provisions of this act contained in §§ 18.2-268.2 through 18.2-268.5, 18.2-271, 18.2-271.1 and 46.2-391.2 through 46.2-391.5 shall become effective January 1, 1995, except to the extent that the amendments merely reflect the enactment by this act of § 18.2-266.1."

The 2009 amendments.
The 2009 amendment by c. 239 added the last sentence in subsection B.

Law Review.
For article, "Criminal Law and Procedure," see 35 U. Rich. L. Rev. 537 (2001). For 2003/2004 survey of criminal law and procedure, see 39 U. Rich. L. Rev. 133 (2004). For survey of Virginia criminal law and procedure for the year 2004-2005, see 40 U. Rich. L. Rev. 197 (2005).

Michie's Jurisprudence.
For related discussion, see 2B M.J. Automobiles, § 118.

CASE NOTES

Constitutionality. — Defendant's conviction for unlawfully refusing to provide a breath sample after being arrested for driving under the influence of alcohol was affirmed as § 18.2-268.3 did not compel testimonial evidence in breach of the Fifth Amendment or authorize an unlawful search or seizure in violation of the Fourth Amendment. Rowley v. Commonwealth, 48 Va. App. 181, 629 S.E.2d 188, 2006 Va. App. LEXIS 167 (2006).

"Trial." — As used in this section, "trial" refers to the hearing of the evidence on the charge. Farren v. Commonwealth, 30 Va. App. 234, 516 S.E.2d 253 (1999).

An accused may not pick and choose the specific sample he wants withdrawn; he or she either consents or refuses. Thurston v. City of Lynchburg, 15 Va. App. 475, 424 S.E.2d 701 (1992).

Admission of refusal to perform test did not violate constitutions. — Neither the Fifth Amendment nor Va. Const., Art. I, § 8 were violated by the admission in evidence of defendant's refusal to take a field sobriety test. Farmer v. Commonwealth, 12 Va. App. 337, 404 S.E.2d 371 (1991) (decided under former § 18.2-268).

Evidence of refusal, to show defendant believed he might fail, violates constitution. — Evidence of a refusal to submit to field sobriety tests, when used by the finder of fact as evidence that the accused refused to submit to the test because he believed he might fail, violates the accused's right, under Va. Const., Art. I, § 8, not to "be compelled ... to give evidence against himself." Farmer v. Commonwealth, 10 Va. App. 175, 390 S.E.2d 775 (1990) (decided under former § 18.2-268).

Blood test as Fourth Amendment search. — A blood test administered to defendant driver two hours after automobile accident was a search within the meaning of the Fourth Amendment. Tipton v. Commonwealth, 18 Va. App. 370, 444 S.E.2d 1 (1994) But see Bristol v. Commonwealth, 272 Va. 568, 636 S.E.2d 460 (2006), which overruled the Tipton court as to the existence of exigent circumstances.

Taking of blood sample from unconscious defendant. — While the taking of a blood sample from an unconscious defendant alleged to have been driving under the influence was permitted, it was not mandatory in order to prosecute defendant for driving under the influence. Oliver v. Commonwealth, 40 Va. App. 20, 577 S.E.2d 514, 2003 Va. App. LEXIS 98 (2003).

Consent not qualified or conditional. — The consent to submit to a blood or breath test, granted when a person operates a motor vehicle upon the highways, "is not a qualified consent and it is not a conditional consent, and therefore there can be no qualified refusal or conditional refusal to take the test." The mere fact that under the statute "an accused is afforded an opportunity to establish the reasonableness of his refusal does not operate to dilute the consent previously given, or convert that consent into a qualified or conditional one." Cash v. Commonwealth, 251 Va. 46, 466 S.E.2d 736 (1996).

The fact that under this section an accused is afforded an opportunity to establish the reasonableness of his refusal to consent to the taking of a sample of his blood or breath does not operate to dilute the consent previously given, under the implied consent law in § 18.2-268.2, or convert that consent into a qualified or conditional one, so the fact that an accused is unconscious at the time of an incident is not a refusal to take the test. Goodman v. Commonwealth, 37 Va. App. 374, 558 S.E.2d 555, 2002 Va. App. LEXIS 45 (2002).

Because defendant's unwillingness to submit to a breath test without access to counsel amounted to an unreasonable refusal under subsection A of § 18.2-268.3, the trial court properly instructed the jury on said issue. Thus, defendant's conviction of unreasonably refusing to submit to a breath test, after having been convicted of two predicate offenses within ten years, in violation of § 18.2-268.3, was upheld on appeal. Brothers v. Commonwealth, 50 Va. App. 468, 650 S.E.2d 874, 2007 Va. App. LEXIS 370 (2007).

The concept of the law is that a driver, if arrested under the drunk driving statute (§ 18.2-266), may be asked to consent to taking the test and for an unreasonable refusal, the penalty of a suspended license would be imposed. United States v. Gholson, 319 F. Supp. 499 (E.D. Va. 1970) (decided under former § 18.2-268).

The fact that under the Virginia statute an accused is afforded an opportunity to establish the reasonableness of his refusal does not operate to dilute the consent previously given, or convert that consent into a qualified or conditional one. The statute does excuse from taking the test one whose refusal is reasonable. An illustration is where a person's health would be endangered by the withdrawal of blood. Deaner v. Commonwealth, 210 Va. 285, 170 S.E.2d 199 (1969) (decided under former § 18.2-268).

When the evidence establishes that either the blood test or the breath test is unavailable, a defendant cannot be convicted of "unreasonably" refusing to submit to testing without an adequate explanation from the government as to why that test was unavailable. Driver v. Commonwealth, 6 Va. App. 583, 371 S.E.2d 27 (1988) (decided under former § 18.2-268).

The court of appeals does not have jurisdiction over an appeal from a conviction of refusal to take a blood or breath test. Thomas v. Commonwealth, 22 Va. App. 735, 473 S.E.2d 87 (1996), rev'd on other grounds, on reh'g, en banc, 24 Va. App. 49, 480 S.E.2d 135 (1997).

Construction of license suspension with other punishments. — The one year license suspension pursuant to this section for refusing a blood/breath test is no part of the punishment for drunk driving nor is it added punishment for the offense committed; it is a measure flowing from the police power of the state designed to protect other users of the state highways. Brame v. Commonwealth, 252 Va. 122, 476 S.E.2d 177 (1996).

Defendant's administrative license suspension was not a criminal proceeding, and hence, could not serve as a bar to a proceeding under this section for refusing to submit to a blood or breath test. Brame v. Commonwealth, 252 Va. 122, 476 S.E.2d 177 (1996).

A person arrested must be advised by the arresting officer of the implied consent condition and that "the unreasonable refusal" to submit to a test constitutes grounds for revocation of driving privileges. If the person refuses to permit the testing, the person shall be taken before a magistrate, who must advise the person again of the implied consent law's requirements. If the person declares the refusal in writing on a prescribed form, or refuses to so declare, then no samples shall be taken. Cash v. Commonwealth, 251 Va. 46, 466 S.E.2d 736 (1996).

Evidence of unavailability of blood test held insufficient. — Where no reason was given in the record for why the two people certified to take blood were not available, there was insufficient evidence to establish that the blood test was not available to the defendant and thus, that his refusal to take the breath test was unreasonable. Driver v. Commonwealth, 6 Va. App. 583, 371 S.E.2d 27 (1988) (decided under former § 18.2-268).

Unlawful refusal charges are administrative and civil in nature, and therefore, the Commonwealth can appeal from a finding of not guilty in a prosecution for unreasonably refusing to submit to a blood or breath alcohol test. Commonwealth v. Rafferty, 241 Va. 319, 402 S.E.2d 17 (1991) (decided under former § 18.2-268).

There must be some reasonable factual basis for refusal to take the blood test, for example, endangerment of the health of

the accused by the withdrawal of blood. Bailey v. Commonwealth, 215 Va. 130, 207 S.E.2d 828 (1974) (decided under former § 18.2-268).

Defendant required to present evidence of claimed physical inability to take breath test. — Where the arresting police officer contended that defendant refused to take a breath test by refusing to properly blow into the machine, and defendant contended that defendant was physically unable to do so, due to a medical condition involving defendant's lungs, the burden rested upon defendant to present evidence that defendant was physically unable to take the test, and physical inability was a condition precedent to any finding that the Commonwealth was required to offer a blood test. Hudson v. Commonwealth, 266 Va. 371, 585 S.E.2d 583, 2003 Va. LEXIS 84 (2003).

Adequate reason for refusal. — Whether defendant's reason for refusing the test was adequate, depended, not upon his subjective reason, but rather upon whether his explanation for refusing the test constituted a legally cognizable reason for doing so and that determination depended largely upon the purpose of the test and defendant's explanation was material, and thus admissible. Quinn v. Commonwealth, 9 Va. App. 321, 388 S.E.2d 268 (1990) (decided under former § 18.2-268).

Sufficient evidence of refusal to take breath test. — Evidence was sufficient to prove defendant's refusal to take a breath test in violation of § 18.2-268.3 because the only reasonable hypothesis flowing from the evidence was that defendant intentionally failed to give adequate effort to produce a test result determined by the machine to be valid and, thus, that he unreasonably refused to have a sample of his breath taken for the purpose of having its alcohol content analyzed; § 18.2-268.3 contemplates the cooperation reasonably necessary to generate a result deemed valid by the testing equipment and its licensed operator. Chisman v. Commonwealth, 2011 Va. App. LEXIS 189 (May 31, 2011).

Trial court to determine "reasonableness." — At trial of the refusal charge, the declaration of refusal or the magistrate's certificate is prima facie evidence that the defendant refused to submit to the testing. "However, this shall not prohibit the defendant from introducing on his behalf evidence of the basis for his refusal. The court shall determine the reasonableness of such refusal." Cash v. Commonwealth, 251 Va. 46, 466 S.E.2d 736 (1996).

It is not reasonable to refuse a blood analysis solely because counsel advises not to take the test. Bailey v. Commonwealth, 215 Va. 130, 207 S.E.2d 828 (1974) (decided under former § 18.2-268).

Nor due to lack of consultation with counsel. — An unwillingness to take the blood test without prior consultation with counsel is not a reasonable refusal. Coleman v. Commonwealth, 212 Va. 684, 187 S.E.2d 172 (1972); Bailey v. Commonwealth, 215 Va. 130, 207 S.E.2d 828 (1974) (decided under former § 18.2-268).

Nor belief that test is unwarranted. — It is not reasonable to refuse to take a blood or breath test which is designed for the very purpose of determining a driver's state of sobriety, and which the driver is deemed to have impliedly consented to take, on the ground that the driver believes that the test is unwarranted. Quinn v. Commonwealth, 9 Va. App. 321, 388 S.E.2d 268 (1990) (decided under former § 18.2-268).

A driver's subjective belief that he was not under the influence of alcohol is not a reasonable basis for refusing the test, nor is the fact that he could and did operate his vehicle in a proficient manner. Thus, evidence of his state of sobriety or proficiency in operating the vehicle is not admissible in a case involving refusal to take a blood or breath test. Cash v. Commonwealth, 251 Va. 46, 466 S.E.2d 736 (1996).

The defendant may not unilaterally abrogate the agreement or withdraw that consent by refusing the test unless there is a reasonable basis for the refusal. A fear of being "framed" is not such a basis; it is not "reasonable" in the sense that evidence of endangerment of the health of the accused by withdrawal of blood furnishes a "reasonable" basis for refusal. That type of evidence should have been offered in the trial of the DUI charge because it may relate to the question whether the police officer's stop of the accused was lawful; certainly such evidence is not probative in the trial of the refusal charge. Cash v. Commonwealth, 251 Va. 46, 466 S.E.2d 736 (1996).

Refusal based on reluctance to sign document implying agency. — A defendant's refusal, following an automobile accident, to sign the consent form required by a hospital before administration of a blood test did not constitute a refusal to submit to the blood test within the contemplation of subsection (c) (now this section) of this section, where his refusal was based upon his reluctance to sign his name to a printed document whose contents implied that he had been the driver of the automobile, and not upon his unwillingness to submit to a blood test. Simon v. Commonwealth, 220 Va. 412, 258 S.E.2d 567 (1979) (decided under former § 18.2-268).

Alka-sensor test inadmissible to show reasonable refusal of section's tests. — Result of a preliminary alka-sensor test which allegedly read .00 and which was taken pursuant to § 18.2-267 was not admissible to show whether driver reasonably refused to submit to a blood or breath test as required by this section. Northup v. Commonwealth, No. 0290-89-2 (Ct. of Appeals Sept. 11, 1990) (decided under former § 18.2-268).

No right to consult counsel. — For the Supreme Court to uphold the contention of defendant that his right to consult counsel before refusing or taking the blood test is a constitutional right, would virtually nullify the implied consent law. Deaner v. Commonwealth, 210 Va. 285, 170 S.E.2d 199 (1969) (decided under former § 18.2-268).

The blood test prescribed by this section is a part of a civil and administrative proceeding and defendant had no right to condition his taking the test upon his ability first to consult with counsel. Deaner v. Commonwealth, 210 Va. 285, 170 S.E.2d 199 (1969) (decided under former § 18.2-268).

A person charged with operating a motor vehicle while under the influence of intoxicants does not have a constitutional right to consult an attorney before deciding whether to take a blood test. Coleman v. Commonwealth, 212 Va. 684, 187 S.E.2d 172 (1972) (decided under former § 18.2-268).

Denial of the right to consult with counsel before an accused decides whether to take a blood test does not impair an accused's right to a trial "by the law of the land" guaranteed by Art. I, § 8, of the State Constitution. Law v. City of Danville, 212 Va. 702, 187 S.E.2d 197 (1972) (decided under former § 18.2-268).

Because a proceeding relative to refusal to take a blood test is civil in nature, a person arrested for driving under the influence does not have a constitutional right to consult with counsel before deciding whether to submit to the test. Bailey v. Commonwealth, 215 Va. 130, 207 S.E.2d 828 (1974) (decided under former § 18.2-268).

Although an action brought by the Commonwealth for refusal to submit to a blood or a breath test is a civil proceeding, the Commonwealth is required to prove its case beyond a reasonable doubt. Cash v. Commonwealth, 5 Va. App. 506, 364 S.E.2d 769 (1988) (decided under former § 18.2-268).

A person's unwillingness to take the test without prior consultation with counsel does not constitute a reasonable basis for the refusal. Cash v. Commonwealth, 251 Va. 46, 466 S.E.2d 736 (1996).

Officer not required to advise defendant of consequences where he has agreed to test. — An officer was not required to advise the defendant of the consequences of his refusal to take a breath test where, after being advised that drivers on Virginia highways are required to take a breath test, the defendant agreed to take such a test. Whibley v. Commonwealth, No. 1515-97-4 (Ct. of Appeals Oct. 27, 1998).

Certificate of committing justice that defendant refused to submit to test. — Under subsection (m) (now subsection E), the certificate of the committing justice is made "prima facie evidence that the defendant refused to submit to the taking of a sample of his blood to determine the alcoholic content thereof." Lacking a certificate, the Commonwealth is not entitled to the benefit of subsection (m) (now subsection E) of the statute; it may, however, prove the refusal by other evidence. Boggs v. Commonwealth, 212 Va. 658, 187 S.E.2d 204 (1972) (decided under former § 18.2-268).

Upon refusal, the magistrate shall certify to such fact and that the person was advised of the law's requirements, and shall charge the person with a violation of § 18.2-268.2 for refusing the test. Cash v. Commonwealth, 251 Va. 46, 466 S.E.2d 736 (1996).

Jurisdiction where offense occurred, not where refusal was executed, had authority to prosecute. — Jurisdiction in which the driving offense occurred had authority to prosecute individual for refusal to give a breath or blood sample even though the declaration of refusal was executed before a magistrate in

another jurisdiction; the requirement that the declaration be before a magistrate is a procedural, not a substantive, requirement of the implied consent statute; the magistrate only verifies the arrested individual's initial refusal to the arresting officer, and refusal is deemed under the implied consent statute to have occurred where the act of driving occurred. Robertie v. City of Fairfax, 10 Va. App. 400, 392 S.E.2d 503 (1990) (decided under former § 18.2-268).

This section does not require that different judge hear unreasonable refusal charge, nor does it suggest that knowledge of that charge mandates recusal. Farren v. Commonwealth, 30 Va. App. 234, 516 S.E.2d 253 (1999).

Although unreasonable refusal charge must be tried subsequent to trial of a related charge of driving under the influence, it does not follow that the two charges were tried together in violation of the statutory mandate if arraignment was held on the refusal charge before the trial court heard any evidence on the charge of driving under the influence. The hearing of the evidence must be what is subsequent to the hearing of the evidence on the first charge. Farren v. Commonwealth, 30 Va. App. 234, 516 S.E.2d 253 (1999).

The warrant referred to by this section is obviously not a criminal warrant. It is in the nature of a writ or precept from a competent authority in pursuance of law, directing the doing of an act, and addressed to the officer or person competent to do the act. Deaner v. Commonwealth, 210 Va. 285, 170 S.E.2d 199 (1969) (decided under former § 18.2-268).

This section directs that the warrant "be executed" in the same manner as a criminal warrant. This is to prescribe an appropriate method of serving notice on the accused. Deaner v. Commonwealth, 210 Va. 285, 170 S.E.2d 199 (1969) (decided under former § 18.2-268).

Prosecution by Commonwealth Attorney. — Trial court properly denied defendant's motion to remove the Commonwealth of Virginia Attorney from the trial of defendant's case for refusal of a breath test, in violation of § 18.2-268.3, because, despite the fact that first-offense refusal cases under § 18.2-268.3 were civil in nature, the Commonwealth and Assistant Commonwealth Attorneys were vested with the authority to prosecute them under § 18.2-268.4 in that the Virginia Legislature in subsection B directed that the procedure for appeal and trial under the code section was to be the same as provided by law for misdemeanors. Under subsection B of § 15.2-1627, misdemeanors were prosecuted by Commonwealth Attorneys and their assistants. Kozmina v. Commonwealth, 281 Va. 347, 706 S.E.2d 860, 2011 Va. LEXIS 53 (2011).

Criminal and civil actions independent. — Operation of a motor vehicle while under the influence of alcohol or drugs may give rise to two separate and distinct proceedings — one a criminal action for DUI and the other a civil, administrative proceeding on the refusal charge. "Each action proceeds independently of the other and the outcome of one is of no consequence to the other." Cash v. Commonwealth, 251 Va. 46, 466 S.E.2d 736 (1996).

Offense may not be prosecuted under federal Assimilative Crimes Act. — The offense of refusing to take a breathalyzer test may not be prosecuted under the federal Assimilative Crimes Act, since the proceeding under this section to suspend a driver's license for his refusal to submit to a test is administrative and civil, not criminal, in nature. United States v. Rowe, 599 F.2d 1319 (4th Cir. 1979) (decided under former § 18.2-268).

Applied in Lamay v. Commonwealth, 29 Va. App. 461, 513 S.E.2d 411 (1999); Stevens v. Commonwealth, 44 Va. App. 122, 603 S.E.2d 642, 2004 Va. App. LEXIS 496 (2004).

§ 18.2-268.4. Trial and appeal for refusal.

A. Venue for the trial of the warrant or summons shall lie in the court of the county or city in which the offense of driving under the influence of intoxicants or other offense listed in subsection A of § 18.2-268.3 is to be tried.

B. The procedure for appeal and trial of a first offense of § 18.2-268.3 shall be the same as provided by law for misdemeanors; if requested by either party on appeal to the circuit court, trial by jury shall be as provided in Article 4 (§ 19.2-260 et seq.) of Chapter 15 of Title 19.2, and the Commonwealth shall be required to prove its case beyond a reasonable doubt.

C. If the defendant pleads guilty to a violation of § 18.2-266, 18.2-266.1, or subsection B of § 18.2-272 or of a similar ordinance, the court may dismiss the warrant or summons.

The court shall dispose of the defendant's license in accordance with the provisions of § 46.2-398; however, the defendant's license shall not be returned during any period of suspension imposed under § 46.2-391.2.

History.
1992, c. 830; 1994, cc. 151, 359, 363; 2004, cc. 985, 1013; 2005, cc. 757, 840, 943.

Law Review.
For 2003/2004 survey of criminal law and procedure, see 39 U. Rich. L. Rev. 133 (2004).

Michie's Jurisprudence.
For related discussion, see 2B M.J. Automobiles, § 118.

CASE NOTES

Defendant's substantive right of appeal regulated by § 8.01-670. — Although subsection V (now the first paragraph of this section) regulates the procedure on appeal, a defendant's substantive right of appeal is regulated by § 8.01-670, which authorizes an appeal to the Supreme Court by any person aggrieved by a final judgment in any other civil case. Thus, the Supreme Court had jurisdiction in a refusal to submit to a blood or breath alcohol test case. Commonwealth v. Rafferty, 241 Va. 319, 402 S.E.2d 17 (1991) (decided under former § 18.2-268).

Trial court did not err in holding that neither res judicata nor collateral estoppel bars a court from suspending a person's operator's license for one year for his refusal to take a blood or breath alcohol test when he has already suffered a seven-day administrative suspension for the same refusal. Simmons v. Commonwealth, 252 Va. 118, 475 S.E.2d 806 (1996).

Unlawful refusal charges are administrative and civil in nature, and therefore, the Commonwealth can appeal from a finding of not guilty in a prosecution for unreasonably refusing to submit to a blood or breath alcohol test. Commonwealth v. Rafferty, 241 Va. 319, 402 S.E.2d 17 (1991) (decided under former § 18.2-268).

Entitled to new trial in circuit court. — By incorporating the "procedure for appeal" set forth in § 16.1-136 into this section, the General Assembly has declared that a person convicted in a court not of record of unreasonable refusal is entitled, on appeal, to a new trial by jury in the circuit court. Eames v. Town of Rocky Mount, 217 Va. 16, 225 S.E.2d 197 (1976) (decided under former § 18.2-268).

Prosecution by Commonwealth Attorney. — Trial court properly denied defendant's motion to remove the Commonwealth of Virginia's Attorney from the trial of defendant's case for refusal of a breath test, in violation of § 18.2-268.3, because, despite the fact that first-offense refusal cases under § 18.2-268.3 were civil in nature, the Commonwealth and Assistant Commonwealth Attorneys were vested with the authority to prosecute them under § 18.2-268.4 in that the Virginia Legislature in subsection B directed that the procedure for appeal and trial under the code section was to be the same as provided by law for misdemeanors. Under subsection B of § 15.2-1627, misdemeanors were prosecuted by Commonwealth Attorneys and their assistants. Kozmina v. Commonwealth, 281 Va. 347, 706 S.E.2d 860, 2011 Va. LEXIS 53 (2011).

§ 18.2-268.5. Qualifications and liability of persons authorized to take blood sample; procedure for taking samples.

For purposes of this article, only a physician, registered nurse, licensed practical nurse, phlebotomist, graduate laboratory technician or a technician or nurse designated by order of a circuit court acting upon the recommendation of a licensed physician, using soap and water, polyvinylpyrrolidone iodine, pvp iodine, povidone iodine or benzalkonium chloride to cleanse the part of the body from which the blood is taken and using instruments sterilized by the accepted steam sterilizer or some other sterilizer which will not affect the accuracy of the test, or using chemically clean sterile disposable syringes, shall withdraw blood for the purpose of determining its alcohol or drug or both alcohol and drug content. It is a Class 3 misdemeanor to reuse single-use-only needles or syringes. No civil liability shall attach to any person authorized to withdraw blood as a result of the act of withdrawing blood as provided in this section from any person submitting thereto, provided the blood was withdrawn according to recognized medical procedures. However, the person shall not be relieved from liability for negligence in the withdrawing of any blood sample.

No person arrested for a violation of § 18.2-266, 18.2-266.1, or subsection B of § 18.2-272, or a similar ordinance shall be required to execute in favor of any person or corporation a waiver or release of liability in connection with the withdrawal of blood and as a condition precedent to the withdrawal of blood as provided for in this section.

History.
1992, c. 830; 1994, cc. 359, 363; 2004, cc. 150, 440, 1013; 2005, cc. 757, 840.

Michie's Jurisprudence.
For related discussion, see 2B M.J. Automobiles, § 118.

CASE NOTES

Applicability of testing requirements. — While the statutory requirements of § 18.2-268 (see now § 18.2-268.1 et seq.) are to be strictly applied, they apply only to DUI prosecutions under § 18.2-266, and not to an involuntary manslaughter prosecution under § 18.2-36. Taylor v. Commonwealth, No. 1977-94-4 (Ct. of Appeals July 18, 1995).

Where blood tests were performed by medical personnel in a hospital emergency room, and the toxicology report was shown to be a business record, recorded in the regular course of hospital business, contemporaneously made, and authenticated by its authorized custodian, such acted as sufficient foundation for the admissibility of the hospital blood test as a business record; further, blood tests performed by medical personnel in a hospital emergency room are not subject to the requirements of § 18.2-268.5. Stevens v. Commonwealth, 44 Va. App. 122, 603 S.E.2d 642, 2004 Va. App. LEXIS 496 (2004).

Admission of hospital toxicology report held proper. — Blood tests performed by medical personnel in a hospital emergency room are not subject to the requirements of this section; further, the statute applies only to blood drawn under the implied consent law. Stevens v. Commonwealth, 46 Va. App. 234, 616 S.E.2d 754, 2005 Va. App. LEXIS 407 (2005), aff'd, — Va. —, 634 S.E.2d 305 (2006).

Need for cleansing to comply with statute. — Because the driving under the influence (DUI) statutes specify the means for cleansing the puncture area, failure to comply with the statutory requirement would necessitate that the prosecution be dismissed. Taylor v. Commonwealth, No. 1977-94-4 (Ct. of Appeals July 18, 1995).

Language in order specifying laboratory technician's place of employment was surplusage. — Where record proved that order appointing person who withdrew blood was entered by the circuit court, that this person was a laboratory technician, that the laboratory technician was recommended by a licensed physician, and that the order authorized the laboratory technician to withdraw blood pursuant to former § 18.2-268 F, the language in the order specifying laboratory technician's place of employment was not statutorily required and had no substantive bearing on the technician's qualifications. The specification of technician's place of employment was surplusage and did not limit his authority. Duggan v. Commonwealth, No. 1258-91-4 (Ct. of Appeals Feb. 23, 1993) (decided under former § 18.2-268(F)).

An accused may not pick and choose the specific sample he wants withdrawn; he or she either consents or refuses. Thurston v. City of Lynchburg, 15 Va. App. 475, 424 S.E.2d 701 (1992).

Relevant questions going to weight of certificate as evidence. — The questions as to the qualification of the person taking the sample, the possibility of contamination from the fact that the defendant's arm was wiped with alcohol before the needle was inserted into his vein and the effect, if any, of the presence of a white powder, described as an anti-coagulant, in the vial, are all relevant. Such questions, however, go to the weight of the evidence rather than to the initial admissibility of the certificate. If the proof established a material failure to follow the procedure required by statute, it may be that the certificate should be stricken from the record, but the proof here established no such failure. Kay v. United States, 255 F.2d 476 (4th Cir.), cert. denied, 358 U.S. 825, 79 S. Ct. 42, 3 L. Ed. 2d 65 (1958) (decided under former § 18.2-268).

Failure to comply with blood-taking procedure goes to weight of evidence. — The question of how blood is taken is procedural, and a failure to comply with the directed procedures goes to the weight of the evidence and is to be considered with all the evidence in the case, with the right to the defendant to show noncompliance and resulting prejudice. Shumate v. Commonwealth, 207 Va. 877, 153 S.E.2d 257 (1967) (decided under former § 18.2-268).

Where the statute requires that when the Commonwealth draws blood for the purposes of an alcohol or drug test, the part of the body from which the blood is taken must be cleaned with "soap and water, polyvinylpyrrolidone iodine or benzalkonium chloride," but the record stated that "benadine" was used to clean appellant's arm, and nothing in the record supported the argument that using "benadine" substantially complied with the statute, then a finding of substantial compliance could not be supported. Hudson v. Commonwealth, 21 Va. App. 184, 462 S.E.2d 913 (1995).

Given substantial compliance by Commonwealth with procedures for blood extraction, absence of evidence establishing whether a solution was used to prepare defendant's arm goes to the weight of the evidence, not to its admissibility; therefore, trial judge did not abuse his discretion by admitting in evidence certificate of blood analysis showing defendant to have been intoxicated, there being no evidence in the record to prove that nurse's failure to cleanse defendant's arm caused a contamination which affected the accuracy of the test. Snider v. Commonwealth, 26 Va. App. 729, 496 S.E.2d 665 (1998).

Reasonable proof that the instrument was properly sterilized is essential in establishing the reliability of the test itself. Brush v. Commonwealth, 205 Va. 312, 136 S.E.2d 864 (1964) (decided under former § 18.2-268).

In the absence of proof showing that the instrument used to withdraw defendant's blood was sterilized pursuant to the requirements of this section, the Commonwealth has not met the burden imposed upon it, and the certificates setting forth the alcoholic content of defendant's blood are not admissible. Brush v. Common-

wealth, 205 Va. 312, 136 S.E.2d 864 (1964) (decided under former § 18.2-268).

§ 18.2-268.6. Transmission of blood samples.

The blood sample withdrawn pursuant to § 18.2-268.5 shall be placed in vials provided or approved by the Department of Forensic Science. The vials shall be sealed by the person taking the sample or at his direction. The person who seals the vials shall complete the prenumbered certificate of blood withdrawal forms and attach one form to each vial. The completed withdrawal certificate for each vial shall show the name of the accused, the name of the person taking the blood sample, the date and time the blood sample was taken and information identifying the arresting or accompanying officer. The vials shall be placed in a container provided by the Department, and the container shall be sealed to prevent tampering with the vials. The arresting or accompanying officer shall take possession of the container as soon as the vials are placed in the container and sealed, and shall promptly transport or mail the container to the Department.

History.
1992, c. 830; 2001, c. 561; 2003, cc. 933, 936; 2005, cc. 868, 881.

Cross references.
As to the powers and duties of the Department of Criminal Justice Services and the Criminal Justice Services Board, see § 9.1-102.

Law Review.
For article summarizing published Virginia criminal law decisions between July 1, 2002 and July 1, 2003, see 38 U. Rich. L. Rev. 87 (2003).

CASE NOTES

Editor's note.
Most of the cases below were decided prior to the 2003 amendment to this section.

Applicability. — Destruction of DNA evidence did not warrant dismissal of the indictment against defendant, as defendant was not entitled to an independent DNA analysis pursuant to this section, as this section particularly applies to DUI cases; furthermore, the record contained no evidence of bad faith by the police, and defendant failed to show that the evidence would have been exculpatory. Hayden v. Commonwealth, — Va. App. —, — S.E.2d —, 2006 Va. App. LEXIS 275 (June 27, 2006).

Merely showing form to an accused at the time a blood sample is taken is insufficient to comply with the requirement of this section that the independent analysis designation form be given to the accused. Artis v. City of Suffolk, 19 Va. App. 168, 450 S.E.2d 165 (1994).

Non-compliance with form delivery requirement negates possibility of substantial compliance. — Assuming without deciding that the delivery of the independent analysis designation form is a step relating to taking, handling, identifying, and disposing of blood samples, the failure to comply with that requirement of the statute negates the possibility of substantial compliance. Artis v. City of Suffolk, 19 Va. App. 168, 450 S.E.2d 165 (1994).

Waiver of right to separate sample where accused voluntarily interrupts procedure. — The government's failure to comply strictly with the statutory mandate to provide the accused with a sample of blood for independent testing resulted from the voluntary act of the accused in interrupting the completion of the blood removal process; where an accused voluntarily interrupts the blood removal procedure before the physician, nurse or technician completes that procedure, the accused, by his conduct, shall be deemed to have waived his right to an independent analysis of a separate sample as provided by this section and § 18.2-268.7. Thurston v. City of Lynchburg, 15 Va. App. 475, 424 S.E.2d 701 (1992).

Where defendant disrupted blood removal procedure, no error in admitting one sample. — Defendant's voluntary act in disrupting the blood removal procedure constituted a waiver of his right to a separate sample for independent testing. Thus, it was not error for the trial court to admit the results of the blood test analyzed from the one sample sent to the state laboratory by the arresting officer. Thurston v. City of Lynchburg, 15 Va. App. 475, 424 S.E.2d 701 (1992).

Relevant questions going to weight of certificate as evidence. — The questions as to the qualification of the person taking the sample, the possibility of contamination from the fact that the defendant's arm was wiped with alcohol before the needle was inserted into his vein and the effect, if any, of the presence of a white powder, described as an anti-coagulant, in the vial, are all relevant. Such questions, however, go to the weight of the evidence rather than to the initial admissibility of the certificate. If the proof established a material failure to follow the procedure required by statute, it may be that the certificate should be stricken from the record, but the proof here established no such failure. Kay v. United States, 255 F.2d 476 (4th Cir.), cert. denied, 358 U.S. 825, 79 S. Ct. 42, 3 L. Ed. 2d 65 (1958) (decided under former § 18.2-268).

Attachment of certificate is not essential to validity of proceeding. — In a DWI trial, the Commonwealth was permitted to introduce evidence of a certificate of analysis of a blood vial drawn shortly after defendant's arrest, even though the certificate of blood withdrawal had become detached from the vial. These facts otherwise established substantial compliance with the procedures governing the taking and handling of defendant's blood. Williams v. Commonwealth, No. 2451-02-4, 2003 Va. App. LEXIS 597 (Ct. of Appeals Nov. 18, 2003).

Failure to comply with blood-taking procedure goes to weight of evidence. — The question of how blood is taken is procedural, and a failure to comply with the directed procedures goes to the weight of the evidence and is to be considered with all the evidence in the case, with the right to the defendant to show noncompliance and resulting prejudice. Shumate v. Commonwealth, 207 Va. 877, 153 S.E.2d 257 (1967) (decided under former § 18.2-268).

Unexplained loss of blood vial sent to the independent laboratory of appellant's own choosing required dismissal of his driving under the influence conviction. Smith v. Commonwealth, No. 0868-93-2 (Ct. of Appeals Aug. 30, 1994).

The Commonwealth failed to prove that it substantially complied with the requirements of this section where the trooper gave appellant an out-of-date list of laboratories that included laboratories that were no longer approved by the Division of Forensic Science, appellant selected from the list a facility that was no longer a laboratory approved by the division, the hospital returned the container to the court, unopened and untested, with the notation: "Refused," the Commonwealth took no further action to have the sample tested and in addition, trooper testified that he thought the list used was last corrected in 1989, over two years prior to the date of arrest. Shoemaker v. Commonwealth, 18 Va. App. 61, 441 S.E.2d 354 (1994).

The trial court's attempt to fashion a remedy for the Commonwealth's failure to update the approved list of laboratories by refusing to admit the Commonwealth's test results, and proceeding to try the case based only on the arresting officer's testimony was inadequate because the independent test results could have been exculpatory. Shoemaker v. Commonwealth, 18 Va. App. 61, 441 S.E.2d 354 (1994).

Guilty pleas. — Court of Appeals of Virginia refused to hear defendant's appeal from a circuit court's judgment denying her motion to dismiss a charge of driving under the influence of alcohol (DUI), based on a claim that the Commonwealth failed to comply with § 18.2-268.6 when it submitted a sample of her blood for testing, because defendant pled guilty to DUI after her motion was denied. Conrad v. Commonwealth, No. 3076-02-3, 2003 Va. App. LEXIS 608 (Ct. of Appeals Nov. 25, 2003).

Substantial compliance with statutory requirements. —

Where certificate of analysis produced by laboratory indicated that the laboratory had been unable to test the blood sample contained in the box because the vial when received was smashed and blood had leaked out, where Commonwealth produced uncontradicted evidence that vials were in good condition when received by officer, and where boxes containing the vials were maintained in a refrigerator by property clerk for police department, and the boxes remained sealed and were not leaking when property clerk mailed them to the respective laboratories, the Commonwealth's evidence demonstrated that it substantially complied with the statutory procedures relating to the taking and handling of blood samples, and sufficiently explained the unavailability of the independent blood test. Amaya-Portillo v. Commonwealth, No. 2559-96-4 (Ct. of Appeals Dec. 9, 1997).

Although a nurse and police officer committed technical violations of former § 18.2-268.6 when they packaged a sample of defendant's blood for transportation to a laboratory, the violations were trivial and the trial court did not err by finding that there was substantial compliance with the statute and admitting the results of the blood test into evidence. Jones v. Commonwealth, No. 2967-02-2, 2004 Va. App. LEXIS 64 (Ct. of Appeals Feb. 10, 2004) (applying former version of § 18.2-268.6).

As defendant received independent blood alcohol content testing, which produced the same results as the Commonwealth's lab, and there was no evidence suggests that these results were invalid or that additional testing elsewhere might have produced different findings, the trial court properly refused to dismiss driving under the influence charges simply because the form provided defendant listed only one independent lab. Cutright v. Commonwealth, 43 Va. App. 593, 601 S.E.2d 1, 2004 Va. App. LEXIS 398 (2004) (applying former version of § 18.2-268.6).

Insufficient compliance with statutory requirements. — Officer's action of showing the independent analysis designation form to defendant and then returning the form to the arrest file was insufficient to comply substantially with the requirements of this section. Artis v. City of Suffolk, 19 Va. App. 168, 450 S.E.2d 165 (1994).

Evidence introduced at the suppression hearing showed that the officer merely showed defendant the form stating that defendant could use a procedure outlined on the form for having an independent chemical analysis performed, and had defendant read and sign the form, which defendant then returned to the officer; the officer's failure to give defendant a copy of the form, as required by § 18.2-268.6, meant the officer did not substantially comply with that statutory provision and meant the motion to suppress should have been granted. Ingram v. Commonwealth, No. 2015-02-3, 2003 Va. App. LEXIS 479 (Ct. of Appeals Sept. 16, 2003).

Blood alcohol tests properly admitted. — In a prosecution for aggravated involuntary manslaughter, the trial court did not commit reversible error in allowing into evidence the results of a blood alcohol content test performed on a blood sample taken from a defendant in violation of his Fourth, Fifth, and Fourteenth Amendment rights, as: (1) a test conducted by hospital personnel had been independently performed and the written report thereof was admissible under § 19.2-187.02; (2) defendant consented to a second blood test administered by a deputy sheriff under the implied consent law; (3) evidence of defendant's intoxication was overwhelming despite testing over three times the legal limit; and (4) it was unreasonable to believe that the jury would have rejected the hospital-administered test and accepted, instead, the implied consent law test. Stevens v. Commonwealth, 272 Va. 481, 634 S.E.2d 305, 2006 Va. LEXIS 87 (2006), cert. denied, 549 U.S. 1350, 127 S. Ct. 2053, 167 L. Ed. 2d 784, 2007 U.S. LEXIS 4119 (U.S. 2007).

Applied in Stevens v. Commonwealth, 44 Va. App. 122, 603 S.E.2d 642, 2004 Va. App. LEXIS 496 (2004); Stevens v. Commonwealth, 46 Va. App. 234, 616 S.E.2d 754, 2005 Va. App. LEXIS 407 (2005).

§ 18.2-268.7. Transmission of blood test samples; use as evidence.

A. Upon receipt of a blood sample forwarded to the Department for analysis pursuant to § 18.2-268.6, the Department shall have it examined for its alcohol or drug or both alcohol and drug content and the Director shall execute a certificate of analysis indicating the name of the accused; the date, time and by whom the blood sample was received and examined; a statement that the seal on the vial had not been broken or otherwise tampered with; a statement that the container and vial were provided or approved by the Department and that the vial was one to which the completed withdrawal certificate was attached; and a statement of the sample's alcohol or drug or both alcohol and drug content. The Director shall remove the withdrawal certificate from the vial, attach it to the certificate of analysis and state in the certificate of analysis that it was so removed and attached. The certificate of analysis with the withdrawal certificate shall be returned to the clerk of the court in which the charge will be heard.

B. After completion of the analysis, the Department shall preserve the remainder of the blood until 90 days have lapsed from the date the blood was drawn. During this 90-day period, the accused may, by motion filed before the court in which the charge will be heard, with notice to the Department, request an order directing the Department to transmit the remainder of the blood sample to an independent laboratory retained by the accused for analysis. The Department shall destroy the remainder of the blood sample if no notice of a motion to transmit the remaining blood sample is received during the 90-day period.

C. When a blood sample taken in accordance with the provisions of §§ 18.2-268.2 through 18.2-268.6 is forwarded for analysis to the Department, a report of the test results shall be filed in that office. Upon proper identification of the certificate of withdrawal, the certificate of analysis, with the withdrawal certificate attached, shall, when attested by the Director, be admissible in any court as evidence of the facts therein stated and of the results of such analysis (i) in any criminal proceeding, provided the requirements of subsection A of § 19.2-187.1 have been satisfied and the accused has not objected to the admission of the certificate pursuant to subsection B of § 19.2-187.1, or (ii) in any civil proceeding. On motion of the accused, the report of analysis prepared for the remaining blood sample shall be admissible in evidence provided the report is duly attested by a person performing such analysis and the independent laboratory that performed the analysis is accredited or certified to conduct forensic blood alcohol/drug testing by one or more of the following bodies: American Society of Crime Laboratory Directors/Laboratory Accreditation Board (ASCLD/LAB); College of American Pathologists (CAP); United States Department of Health and Human Services Substance Abuse and Mental Health Services Administration (SAMHSA); or American Board of Forensic Toxicology (ABFT).

Upon request of the person whose blood was analyzed, the test results shall be made available to him.

The Director may delegate or assign these duties to an employee of the Department.

History.
1992, c. 830; 1993, c. 688; 1994, cc. 337, 359, 363; 2003, cc. 933, 936; 2005, cc. 868, 881; 2009, Sp. Sess. I, cc. 1, 4.

The 2009 amendments.
The 2009 amendments by Sp. Sess. I, c. 1, effective August 21, 2009, and Sp. Sess. I, c. 4, effective September 15, 2009, are identical, and added the subsection B designator to the former second paragraph of subsection A; redesignated former subsection B as subsection C, and rewrote the second sentence thereof.

CASE NOTES

Editor's note.
Most of the cases below were decided prior to the 2003 amendment to this section.

Error to admit blood test results where failure to follow statutory mandates. — Where the government has failed in its responsibilities to follow the statutory mandates in the taking, handling, identification and disposition of blood samples under the statutory scheme, it is error to admit at trial the results of tests concerning such blood samples. Thurston v. City of Lynchburg, 15 Va. App. 475, 424 S.E.2d 701 (1992).

Unavailability of independent test results. — When an accused asks that his blood sample be sent to an independent laboratory for testing and an independent analysis is not available at trial, the Commonwealth has the burden to explain the absence of independent test results and show that it substantially complied with the steps relating to the taking, handling, identification, and disposition of defendant's blood and/or breath samples. The Commonwealth must prove that the unavailability of the independent test results is not due to unreasonable conduct by the Commonwealth or its agents. Kemp v. Commonwealth, 16 Va. App. 360, 429 S.E.2d 875 (1993).

Subsection M, regarding the availability of results to the person tested, is mandatory. Wendel v. Commonwealth, 12 Va. App. 958, 407 S.E.2d 690 (1991) (decided under former § 18.2-268).

Subsection Z (see now § 18.2-268.11) does not deal with or address the handling of test results, and it does not relieve the Commonwealth of its responsibility under subsection M to provide an accused with the test results when they have been requested. Wendel v. Commonwealth, 12 Va. App. 958, 407 S.E.2d 690 (1991) (decided under former § 18.2-268).

Test results presumptive. — Because the blood alcohol concentration reflected by the chemical test necessarily resulted from alcohol consumed prior to or during driving, the test results are presumptive evidence of the blood alcohol concentration at the time of driving and as such, the accused may challenge the test results by competent evidence, such as, for example, that he had not consumed enough alcohol in the relevant time to reach the level indicated by the chemical test results. Davis v. Commonwealth, 8 Va. App. 291, 381 S.E.2d 11 (1989) (decided under former § 18.2-268).

Commonwealth's failure to produce test results. — When the accused requests the Commonwealth's results, and the Commonwealth does not possess and/or cannot produce the results, the Commonwealth must explain the absence of test results. Wendel v. Commonwealth, 12 Va. App. 958, 407 S.E.2d 690 (1991) (decided under former § 18.2-268).

Absence of proof that no test results were obtained. — Since the test results are "but auxiliary proof" and are not a necessary prerequisite to a conviction, a prosecution should not fail merely because the accused makes a formal request for the results and they are either unavailable or inadmissible. When, however, a sample has been taken for testing, the Commonwealth is required to adhere to those statutory procedures designed to yield test results. In the absence of proof explaining that no results were obtained, trial courts must presume that test results were obtained and can be made available. Wendel v. Commonwealth, 12 Va. App. 958, 407 S.E.2d 690 (1991) (decided under former § 18.2-268).

Because Fifth Amendment is limited in application. — The

Fifth Amendment to the federal Constitution, even if applicable to the states, is limited to oral testimony and does not preclude the use of one's body or secretions therefrom or proof of the results of their chemical analyses. Walton v. City of Roanoke, 204 Va. 678, 133 S.E.2d 315 (1963) (decided under former § 18.2-268).

Admission of the certificate does not deprive defendant of his right of confrontation by witnesses. Kay v. United States, 255 F.2d 476 (4th Cir.), cert. denied, 358 U.S. 825, 79 S. Ct. 42, 3 L. Ed. 2d 65 (1958) (decided under former § 18.2-268).

And is admissible in federal court. — In a federal court, the certificate would be admissible under the provisions of 28 U.S.C.S. § 1732, as a writing made, pursuant to statutory requirement, in the regular performance of the official duty of the Chief Medical Examiner of Virginia (now the Director of the Division of Forensic Science). Kay v. United States, 255 F.2d 476 (4th Cir.), cert. denied, 358 U.S. 825, 79 S. Ct. 42, 3 L. Ed. 2d 65 (1958) (decided under former § 18.2-268).

Certificate self-authenticating. — The General Assembly intended to spare the Commonwealth the prosecutorial and financial burdens of calling two public officers to testify in every drunk driving case involving breathalyzer test evidence. When the certificate contains what this section requires, this section makes the certificate self-authenticating for purposes of admissibility, and once the certificate is admitted, this section makes it evidence of the alcoholic content of the blood to be considered with all other evidence in the case. Stroupe v. Commonwealth, 215 Va. 243, 207 S.E.2d 894 (1974) (decided under former § 18.2-268).

But the certificate is not conclusive evidence of the statutory regularity of the test. Stroupe v. Commonwealth, 215 Va. 243, 207 S.E.2d 894 (1974) (decided under former § 18.2-268).

Procedural violations did not require suppression of blood test results. — Where the form provided defendant listed only one approved laboratory where defendant could have the second vial of blood tested, as defendant did receive independent blood alcohol content testing, the trial court was not obliged to suppress the blood test results. The legislative remedy for a procedural violation of the driving under the influence statutes was not suppression of the evidence, but a full and fair opportunity for both sides to prove or disprove any prejudicial effect of the violation. Cutright v. Commonwealth, 43 Va. App. 593, 601 S.E.2d 1, 2004 Va. App. LEXIS 398 (2004).

Admissibility of certificate of blood analysis governed by § 19.2-187. — The admissibility of a certificate of blood analysis prepared pursuant to this section is governed by the requirements of § 19.2-187. Basfield v. Commonwealth, No. 0291-89-2 (Ct. of Appeals Oct. 2, 1990); Basfield v. Commonwealth, 11 Va. App. 122, 398 S.E.2d 80 (1990) (decided under former § 18.2-268).

Attachment of certificate is not essential to validity of proceeding. — A statute directing the mode of proceeding by public officers is to be deemed directory, and a precise compliance is not to be deemed essential to the validity of the proceedings, unless so declared by statute; use of the word "shall" is not a sufficient legislative declaration making attachment of the certificate essential to the validity of the proceeding. Commonwealth v. Rafferty, 241 Va. 319, 402 S.E.2d 17 (1991) (decided under former § 18.2-268).

In a DWI trial, the Commonwealth was permitted to introduce evidence of a certificate of analysis of a blood vial drawn shortly after defendant's arrest, even though the certificate of blood withdrawal had become detached from the vial. These facts otherwise established substantial compliance with the procedures governing the taking and handling of defendant's blood. Williams v. Commonwealth, No. 2451-02-4, 2003 Va. App. LEXIS 597 (Ct. of Appeals Nov. 18, 2003).

Relevant questions going to weight of certificate as evidence. — The questions as to the qualification of the person taking the sample, the possibility of contamination from the fact that the defendant's arm was wiped with alcohol before the needle was inserted into his vein and the effect, if any, of the presence of a white powder, described as an anti-coagulant, in the vial, are all relevant. Such questions, however, go to the weight of the evidence rather than to the initial admissibility of the certificate. If the proof established a material failure to follow the procedure required by statute, it may be that the certificate should be stricken from the record, but the proof here established no such failure. Kay v. United States, 255 F.2d 476 (4th Cir.), cert. denied, 358 U.S. 825, 79 S. Ct.

42, 3 L. Ed. 2d 65 (1958) (decided under former § 18.2-268).

Failure to comply with blood-taking procedure goes to weight of evidence. — The question of how blood is taken is procedural, and a failure to comply with the directed procedures goes to the weight of the evidence and is to be considered with all the evidence in the case, with the right to the defendant to show noncompliance and resulting prejudice. Shumate v. Commonwealth, 207 Va. 877, 153 S.E.2d 257 (1967) (decided under former § 18.2-268).

With respect to regularity of the test, the defendant has the right to prove noncompliance with test procedures, but such proof would not defeat admissibility of the certificate but only affect its weight as evidence of the alcoholic content of his blood. Stroupe v. Commonwealth, 215 Va. 243, 207 S.E.2d 894 (1974) (decided under former § 18.2-268).

Failure to make valid arrest within two hours. — Where the accident happened and the offense occurred just before 3:00 p.m., and an invalid arrest was made at 4:35 p.m., but the accused was not properly arrested until 6:15 p.m., since the arrest was untimely, the defendant is not deemed to have consented to the testing of his breath under the "implied consent" law. Thomas v. Town of Marion, 226 Va. 251, 308 S.E.2d 120 (1983) (decided under former § 18.2-268).

Certificate inadmissible where arrest not timely made. — Where there is no evidence that defendant was arrested within two hours of the alleged offense, the certificate showing the alcohol content of defendant's blood is inadmissible. Overbee v. Commonwealth, 227 Va. 238, 315 S.E.2d 242 (1984) (decided under former § 18.2-268).

Certificate of blood alcohol analysis erroneously admitted. — Drunk driving defendant's certificate of blood alcohol analysis was erroneously admitted into evidence where the certificate stated that the container into which the vial of defendant's blood was placed was not sealed, even though the certificate indicated that the seal on the vial itself had not been broken or tampered with. Williams v. Commonwealth, 10 Va. App. 636, 394 S.E.2d 728 (1990) (decided under former § 18.2-268).

Applied in Durrette v. County of Spotsylvania, 22 Va. App. 122, 468 S.E.2d 128 (1996).

OPINIONS OF THE ATTORNEY GENERAL

Certificate of analysis of the defendant's blood alcohol level is the proper evidence in a prosecution for driving while intoxicated. See opinion of Attorney General to The Honorable Christopher K. Peace, Member, House of Delegates 08-065 (9/22/08).

§ 18.2-268.8. Fees.

Payment for withdrawing blood shall not exceed $25, which shall be paid out of the appropriation for criminal charges. If the person whose blood sample was withdrawn is subsequently convicted for a violation of § 18.2-266, 18.2-266.1, or subsection B of § 18.2-272 or of a similar ordinance, or is placed under the purview of a probational, educational, or rehabilitational program as set forth in § 18.2-271.1, the amount charged by the person withdrawing the sample shall be taxed as part of the costs of the criminal case and shall be paid into the general fund of the state treasury.

If the person whose blood sample was withdrawn is subsequently convicted for violation of § 18.2-266, 18.2-266.1, or subsection B of § 18.2-272 or a similar ordinance, a fee of $25 for testing the first blood sample by the Department shall be taxed as part of the costs of the criminal case and shall be paid into the general fund of the state treasury.

History.

1992, c. 830; 1994, cc. 359, 363; 2001, c. 561; 2003, cc. 933, 936; 2004, c. 1013; 2005, cc. 757, 840, 868, 881.

§ 18.2-268.9. Assurance of breath-test validity; use of breath-test results as evidence.

A. To be capable of being considered valid as evidence in a prosecution under § 18.2-266, 18.2-266.1, or subsection B of § 18.2-272, or a similar ordinance, chemical analysis of a person's breath shall be performed by an individual possessing a valid license to conduct such tests, with a type of equipment and in accordance with methods approved by the Department.

B. The Department shall establish a training program for all individuals who are to administer the breath tests. Upon a person's successful completion of the training program, the Department may license him to conduct breath-test analyses. Such license shall identify the specific types of breath test equipment upon which the individual has successfully completed training. Any individual conducting a breath test under the provisions of § 18.2-268.2 shall issue a certificate which will indicate that the test was conducted in accordance with the Department's specifications, the name of the accused, that prior to administration of the test the accused was advised of his right to observe the process and see the blood alcohol reading on the equipment used to perform the breath test, the date and time the sample was taken from the accused, the sample's alcohol content, and the name of the person who examined the sample. This certificate, when attested by the individual conducting the breath test on equipment maintained by the Department, shall be admissible in any court as evidence of the facts therein stated and of the results of such analysis (i) in any criminal proceeding, provided that the requirements of subsection A of § 19.2-187.1 have been satisfied and the accused has not objected to the admission of the certificate pursuant to subsection B of § 19.2-187.1, or (ii) in any civil proceeding. Any such certificate of analysis purporting to be signed by a person authorized by the Department shall be admissible in evidence without proof of seal or signature of the person whose name is signed to it. A copy of the certificate shall be promptly delivered to the accused. Copies of Department records relating to any breath test conducted pursuant to this section shall be admissible provided such copies are authenticated as true copies either by the custodian thereof or by the person to whom the custodian reports.

The officer making the arrest, or anyone with him at the time of the arrest, or anyone participating in the arrest of the accused, if otherwise qualified to conduct such test as provided by this section, may administer the breath test and analyze the results.

History.

1992, c. 830; 1994, cc. 359, 363; 1996, cc. 154, 952; 1997, c. 256; 1999, c. 273; 2004, c. 1013; 2005, cc. 757, 840, 868, 881; 2006, c. 101; 2009, Sp. Sess. I, cc. 1, 4.

Cross references.

As to the authority of the Department of Criminal Justice Services to adopt regulations for the administration of this section, see § 9.1-102.

The 2009 amendments.

The 2009 amendments by Sp. Sess. I, c. 1, effective August 21, 2009, and Sp. Sess. I, c. 4, effective September 15, 2009, are identical, and added the subsection designators; deleted the former second sentence of subsection A, which read: "The Department shall test the accuracy of the breath-testing equipment at least once every six months."; and in the first paragraph of subsection B, deleted "the equipment on which the breath test was conducted has been tested within the past six months and has been found to be accurate" following "Department's specifications" in the fourth sentence and rewrote the fifth sentence.

Law Review.

For an article, "Criminal Law and Procedure," see 31 U. Rich. L. Rev. 1015 (1997). For survey of Virginia criminal law and procedure for the year 2004-2005, see 40 U. Rich. L. Rev. 197 (2005). For 2006 survey article, "Criminal Law and Procedure," see 41 U. Rich. L. Rev. 83 (2006). For essay, "The Confrontation Clause and the High Stakes of the Court's Consideration of Briscoe v. Virginia," see 95 Va. L. Rev. In Brief 97 (2010).

CASE NOTES

Because Fifth Amendment is limited in application. — The Fifth Amendment to the federal Constitution, even if applicable to the states, is limited to oral testimony and does not preclude the use of one's body or secretions therefrom or proof of the results of their chemical analyses. Walton v. City of Roanoke, 204 Va. 678, 133 S.E.2d 315 (1963) (decided under former § 18.2-268).

Requirement as to time of test is procedural. — The requirement in subsection (r1) of § 18.2-268 (now § 18.2-268.9) of the time of the test on a certificate, as subsection (s) (now § 18.2-268.11) makes clear, is procedural in nature. United States v. Robertson, 638 F. Supp. 1202 (E.D. Va. 1986) (decided under former § 18.2-268).

This section does not require proof of the accuracy of an individual test as a prerequisite to admissibility of the resulting certificate. Woolridge v. Commonwealth, 29 Va. App. 339, 512 S.E.2d 153 (1999).

Instruction on particular type of equipment not required. — This section requires that the person conducting the test have received forty hours of training in general and does not mandate that the instruction have been given with respect to the particular make or model of breath analyzer used in the defendant's case. Reynolds v. Commonwealth, 30 Va. App. 153, 515 S.E.2d 808 (1999).

Failure to comply with storage requirements of machine. — Failure to comply with the required procedure for storing a breath analysis machine did not, by itself, require suppression of defendant's breath test results, where no evidence established that the police failed to comply with any of the regulations governing the "taking, handling, identification, and disposition of breath samples" other than the improper placement of the breath analysis machine, where the machine had a self-correcting mechanism, where there was no allegation that the machine was tampered with or that the results were incorrect, and defendant failed to show that the failure to comply with the storage methods prejudiced his rights. Henry v. Commonwealth, 44 Va. App. 702, 607 S.E.2d 140, 2005 Va. App. LEXIS 6 (2005).

Officer's training found sufficient. — Officer who received 40 hours of training on Breathalyzer 900-A, and an additional eight hours on Intoxilyzer 5000, met requirements of this section. Castro v. Commonwealth, No. 0216-99-4 (Ct. of Appeals Jan. 11, 2000).

Sufficient evidence of time notation. — Although the certificate that the deputy sheriff gave to defendant did not specify the time defendant took the test, the deputy sheriff testified as to the time and the events that occurred during and after the test. His testimony proved that the notes he made contemporaneously with the test contained the time the breath sample was taken. This evidence proved substantial compliance with the requirements of this section. Price v. Commonwealth, No. 0460-95-2 (Ct. of Appeals May 28, 1996).

Permissible analysis tool. — The Intoximeter 3000 performs a chemical analysis of a breath sample within the meaning of this section, and the trial judge did not err in denying appellant's motion to suppress the results of the test. Lemond v. Commonwealth, 19 Va. App. 687, 454 S.E.2d 31 (1995).

Intoxilyzer reliable. — Trial court did not arbitrarily accept the result of an unreliable Intoxilyzer because the breath test was conducted on an Intoxilyzer certified to be accurate pursuant to § 18.2-268.9, and attested as being operated in accordance with Department of Forensic Science specifications; therefore, the Intoxilyzer used to test the alcohol content of defendant breath was reliable. Newman v. Commonwealth, 2009 Va. App. LEXIS 360 (Aug. 11, 2009).

Breath analysis properly admitted where omission as to time of test later corrected. — Certificate of defendant's breath alcohol analysis was properly admitted where it was regular in all respects except that the time of the test had been omitted, when defendant was given a copy, but this omission was subsequently corrected. United States v. Robertson, 638 F. Supp. 1202 (E.D. Va. 1986) (decided under former § 18.2-268).

Physical inability to take breath test. — Trial court erred in convicting defendant of driving under the influence in violation of § 18.2-266 because the trial court failed to rule on whether defendant was physically unable to take the breath test required by § 18.2-268.2, and it did not resolve the conflict in the testimony; defendant testified he suffered from acid reflux, causing him to burp involuntarily, and if believed, defendant could not comply with the twenty-minute observation period, but an officer testified that he spoke with defendant for approximately thirty minutes at the scene and heard no burping, nor did he hear burping from the time of arrest until defendant was taken to jail. Packard v. Commonwealth, 2011 Va. App. LEXIS 107 (Mar. 29, 2011).

Where the defendant's warrantless arrest was unlawful, he was not bound under this section to submit to a breathalyzer test; therefore the result of the breathalyzer test administered to the defendant should not have been admitted in evidence at his trial. Durant v. City of Suffolk, 4 Va. App. 445, 358 S.E.2d 732 (1987) (decided under former § 18.2-268).

Scope of accused's right to view results. — Nothing in this section or in § 18.2-268.2 indicates any intention on the part of the legislature to give an accused the right to immediately view results of a breath test other than those actually printed out by the equipment used to conduct the test. Rasmussen v. Commonwealth, 31 Va. App. 233, 522 S.E.2d 401 (1999).

Where an accused is afforded the opportunity to view the print-out of the blood-alcohol reading taken by the breathalyzer machine, the requirements of this section and § 18.2-268.2 have been met. Carey v. Commonwealth, No. 1888-98-4, 2000 Va. App. LEXIS 303 (Ct. of Appeals Apr. 25, 2000).

Where defendant only saw certificate with printout of lower of two blood alcohol readings, the only evidence not made immediately available to him was evidence of an inculpatory nature; as he was afforded the opportunity to view the print-out of the blood-alcohol reading taken by the breathalyzer machine, the requirements of this section and § 18.2-268.2 were met. Kauffman v. Commonwealth, No. 1725-98-2, 2000 Va. App. LEXIS 452 (Ct. of Appeals June 20, 2000).

Opportunity to view read out from breathalyzer machine satisfies requirements. — Giving defendant an opportunity to view the print out of the blood-alcohol reading taken by the breathalyzer machine satisfied the requirements of this section; moreover, the appeals court agreed with the trial judge that since the breath test procedure did not contemplate defendant having his breath sample analyzed by an independent party, then the fact that he was shown the result, but not actually given a paper copy of the result, could hardly have had any effect on his substantive rights at trial. Shelton v. Commonwealth, 45 Va. App. 175, 609 S.E.2d 89, 2005 Va. App. LEXIS 78 (2005).

Guilt or innocence determined from all evidence of defendant's condition. — The statutory mandate is that the guilt or innocence of the accused be determined from all the evidence of his condition at the time of the alleged offense, with or without a breath analysis. Brooks v. City of Newport News, 224 Va. 311, 295 S.E.2d

801 (1982) (decided under former § 18.2-268).

Result of breath analysis is but auxiliary proof which may tend to corroborate evidence of objective symptoms. Brooks v. City of Newport News, 224 Va. 311, 295 S.E.2d 801 (1982) (decided under former § 18.2-268).

Error to admit certificate indicating that license is invalid. — This section requires the test to be administered by an operator with a valid license. The qualification of the operator is a matter of substance, not procedure, and is not waived by subsection (s) of § 18.2-268 (now § 18.2-268.11). A court, therefore, is in error in admitting the certificate into evidence where it indicates that the license is invalid. Brooks v. City of Newport News, 224 Va. 311, 295 S.E.2d 801 (1982) (decided under former § 18.2-268).

Qualifications of person conducting test. — Officer who was licensed to conduct tests on Intoxilyzer 5000, who had completed forty hours of training on Breathalyzer 900A, and who had later completed an eight-hour course on the Intoxilyzer 5000, met requirements of this section. Killingsworth v. Commonwealth, No. 2447-98-3 (Ct. of Appeals Nov. 9, 1999).

Other evidence may render erroneous admission of certificate harmless. — Where the testimony at the trial clearly showed that there was no room for reasonable doubt about defendant's actual condition at the time of his arrest, and the evidence of his guilt was clear and compelling, the erroneous ruling of the trial court in admitting a certificate which showed that the operator's license was invalid was harmless. Brooks v. City of Newport News, 224 Va. 311, 295 S.E.2d 801 (1982) (decided under former § 18.2-268).

Admission of certificate not error. — Officer's personal knowledge of the required test for accuracy affected, if anything, the weight of the certificate of breath analysis as evidence, not its admissibility. Thus, admission of the certificate was not error, even though officer had no personal knowledge of the breath analysis machine's performance testing. Anderson v. Commonwealth, 25 Va. App. 26, 486 S.E.2d 115 (1997).

Trial court did not err in admitting results of breathalyzer test into evidence, despite defendant's having chewed cigarette tobacco between time of his arrest and time of analysis; evidence permitted a finding that any alcohol in defendant's mouth did not skew test results, and therefore that test substantially complied with statutory requirements for its admission. Pollard v. Commonwealth, No. 2638-98-2 (Ct. of Appeals Sept. 21, 1999).

The admission of a certificate of breath analysis was not error where the test used complied with the procedures in 1 VAC 30-50-90(A) (now 6 VAC 20-190-110(3)(A)) but not with 1 VAC 30-50-90(C) (now 6 VAC 20-190-110(3)(C)), because the procedure used substantially complied with the breath-test methods approved by the Virginia Department of Criminal Justice Services, Division of Forensic Science. Rollins v. Commonwealth, 37 Va. App. 73, 554 S.E.2d 99, 2001 Va. App. LEXIS 593 (2001).

Officer who arrested defendant for driving under the influence of alcohol, second offense, properly determined that defendant was physically unable to complete a breath test due to defendant's recent ingestion of chili, which was giving defendant indigestion at the time of the breath test, and, thus, the certificate of analysis from the blood test that the officer had defendant take was admissible, as no showing was made that the officer violated Virginia's implied consent law. Pearson v. Commonwealth, 43 Va. App. 317, 597 S.E.2d 269, 2004 Va. App. LEXIS 272 (2004).

Trial court did not err when it found that a police officer substantially complied with the requirements of this section when she administered a breath test to defendant who was coughing, and that expert testimony which defendant offered did not rebut the presumption created by § 18.2-269 that defendant was under the influence of alcohol, and the appellate court affirmed the trial court's judgment admitting the results of the test and using them to convict defendant of driving under the influence of alcohol. Wing v. Commonwealth, No. 1760-03-4, 2004 Va. App. LEXIS 368 (Ct. of Appeals Aug. 3, 2004).

Trial court, in defendant's driving while intoxicated case, did not err in admitting into evidence a certificate of blood alcohol analysis based on the result, contained in a certificate of analysis, from a breath test; the breath test result contained in the certificate of analysis was not hearsay evidence and therefore the admission into evidence of that result did not implicate defendant's constitutional right to confrontation. Luginbyhl v. Commonwealth, 46 Va. App.

460, 618 S.E.2d 347, 2005 Va. App. LEXIS 329 (2005), substituted op., on reh'g, 48 Va. App. 58, 628 S.E.2d 74 (2006) (wherein the court held the error was harmless while declining to address the constitutional issue).

Defendant waived her Sixth Amendment rights to confrontation by failing to avail herself of her statutory right under § 19.2-187.1 to subpoena the operator of a breath test in her driving under the influence trial under § 18.2-266. Thus, it was proper to admit the certificate of the blood alcohol analysis without live testimony of the operator pursuant to §§ 18.2-268.9 and 19.2-187. McKeel v. Commonwealth, — Va. App. —, — S.E.2d —, 2006 Va. App. LEXIS 575 (Dec. 19, 2006).

Trial court's error in admitting into evidence a certificate of blood alcohol analysis was not harmless beyond a reasonable doubt because in order to convict defendant of a per se violation under clause (i) of § 18.2-266 or invoke the presumption of intoxication afforded by subdivision A 3 of § 18.2-269 the trial court had to rely on the facts recited in the attestation clause in order to conclude that the test was conducted in accordance with the relevant statutes; the only evidence that the breath test was administered either as provided by Title 18.2, Chapter Seven, Article Two of the Virginia Code or in accordance with the provisions of §§ 18.2-268.1 through 18.2-268.12, as required by § 18.2-269, was in the attestation clause on the certificate of analysis, and because the use of the attestation clause in the case violated the Confrontation Clause, it could not be used to prove that the breath test was administered in accordance with the relevant statutes. Grant v. Commonwealth, 54 Va. App. 714, 682 S.E.2d 84, 2009 Va. App. LEXIS 390 (2009).

Trial court did not err by admitting the certificate of analysis into evidence because the evidence established that the breath test was administered in compliance with the twenty-minute observation period required by § 18.2-268.9; the attestation clause that was part of the certificate of analysis admitted into evidence stated that appellant's breath test "was conducted in accordance with Department of Forensic Science specifications, one of which provided for the twenty-minute period of observation, and the testimony of the person who administered the breath test established that a police officer observed defendant for the required twenty minutes prior to the attempted test on the first Intoxilyzer before she was immediately moved to the second Intoxilyzer only a few feet away. Newman v. Commonwealth, 2009 Va. App. LEXIS 360 (Aug. 11, 2009).

Defendant's conviction of driving while intoxicated was affirmed because the certificate of blood alcohol analysis was admissible under § 18.2-268.9 regardless of any alleged error in admitting the certificate of instrument accuracy, and, correspondingly, any error in admitting the certificate of instrument accuracy was harmless. Fitzgerald v. Commonwealth, 61 Va. App. 279, 734 S.E.2d 708, 2012 Va. App. LEXIS 398 (2012).

Admission of breath test analysis harmless error. — In a DWI case, even if the admission of a written breath test analysis result and the accompanying certificate violated the Confrontation Clause because the evidence was "testimonial," the error was harmless. The other evidence, including defendant's statement that he was drunk and that he was an alcoholic, his glassy, bloodshot eyes, his smell of alcohol, his admission that he had had six to eight drinks of vodka, and his failure of field sobriety tests, proved guilt beyond a reasonable doubt without the test result. Luginbyhl v. Commonwealth, 48 Va. App. 58, 628 S.E.2d 74, 2006 Va. App. LEXIS 170 (2006).

Admission of certificate violated Confrontation Clause. — Trial court erred in admitting into evidence a certificate of blood alcohol analysis because the attestation clause included in the certificate was testimonial in nature, and its admission, over the objection of defendant, constituted a violation of the Confrontation Clause when the facts establishing the validity and admissibility of the breath-test result had to be proved by live, in-court testimony; while there is no constitutional requirement that the factual predicates in § 18.2-268.9 be established prior to the admission of the results of the test, once the General Assembly conditions the validity and admissibility of the breath-test results on the proof of those facts, the Commonwealth must prove those facts through live, in-court testimony and not by affidavit. Grant v. Commonwealth, 54 Va. App. 714, 682 S.E.2d 84, 2009 Va. App. LEXIS 390 (2009).

Burden of proof. — Under § 18.2-268.9, the Commonwealth is not required to introduce evidence showing the Virginia Department of Forensic Science's compliance with subdivision B 3 of § 9.1-1101 before a certificate of blood alcohol analysis becomes admissible; rather, the substantial compliance provisions of § 18.2-268.11 indicate that the defendant has the burden of producing evidence showing noncompliance with procedural requirements like that contained in subdivision B 3 of § 9.1-1101. Fitzgerald v. Commonwealth, 61 Va. App. 279, 734 S.E.2d 708, 2012 Va. App. LEXIS 398 (2012).

Applied in Stevens v. Commonwealth, 44 Va. App. 122, 603 S.E.2d 642, 2004 Va. App. LEXIS 496 (2004).

CIRCUIT COURT OPINIONS

Admission of certificate of blood alcohol analysis did not violate right of confrontation. — Admission of the certificate of blood alcohol analysis did not violate defendant's right of confrontation because the attestation clause of the certificate of blood alcohol analysis was non-testimonial hearsay and the statements of the breath test operator in the attestation clause did not accuse defendant of any wrongdoing but simply laid the foundation for the admission of the certificate under the statute. Commonwealth v. Draper, 72 Va. Cir. 111, 2006 Va. Cir. LEXIS 315 (Martinsville 2006).

Compliance with regulatory procedure for validating. — Court denied the defendant's motion to dismiss the driving under the influence charges against him because under § 18.2-268.9 and 1 VAC 30-50-90(C), the officer was required to, and did, follow Commonwealth-approved guidelines in The Virginia Register of Regulations, Vol. 16, Issue 11, p. 1505, to administer the new breath test (the Intoxilyzer Model 5000) based upon its operating manual, rather than 1 VAC 30-50-90(C)'s unmodified provisions governing the old breath test (the Smith & Wesson 900A). Commonwealth v. Fox, 68 Va. Cir. 489, 2001 Va. Cir. LEXIS 532 (Amherst County 2001).

OPINIONS OF THE ATTORNEY GENERAL

Compliance with regulatory procedure for validating breath test device. — A person holding a valid license from the Division of Forensic Science to perform a breath test need only comply substantially with the regulatory procedure for validating a breath test device prior to conducting a test to determine the alcohol or drug content of a person's blood. See opinion of Attorney General to The Honorable George W. Grayson, Member, House of Delegates, 00-100 (1/12/01).

is the proper evidence in a prosecution for driving while intoxicated. See opinion of Attorney General to The Honorable Christopher K. Peace, Member, House of Delegates 08-065 (9/22/08).

§ 18.2-268.10. Evidence of violation of driving under the influence offenses.

A. In any trial for a violation of § 18.2-266, 18.2-266.1, or subsection B of § 18.2-272 or a similar ordinance, the admission of the blood or breath test results shall not limit the introduction of any other relevant evidence bearing upon any question at issue before the court, and the court shall, regardless of the result of any blood or breath tests, consider other relevant admissible evidence of the condition of the accused. If the test results indicate the presence of any drug other than alcohol, the test results shall be admissible, except in a prosecution under clause (v) of § 18.2-266, only if other competent evidence has been presented to relate the presence of the drug or drugs to the impairment of the accused's ability to drive or operate any motor vehicle, engine or train safely.

B. The failure of an accused to permit a blood or breath sample to be taken to determine the alcohol or drug content of his blood is not evidence and shall not be subject to comment by the Commonwealth at the trial of the case, except in rebuttal or pursuant to subsection C; nor shall the fact that a blood or breath test had been offered the accused be evidence or the subject of comment by the Commonwealth, except in rebuttal or pursuant to subsection C.

C. Evidence of a finding against the defendant under § 18.2-268.3 for his unreasonable refusal to permit a blood or breath sample to be taken to determine the alcohol or drug content of his blood shall be admissible into evidence, upon the motion of the Commonwealth or the defendant, for the sole purpose of explaining the absence at trial of a chemical test of such sample. When admitted pursuant to this subsection such evidence shall not be considered evidence of the accused's guilt.

D. The court or jury trying the case involving a violation of clause (ii), (iii) or (iv) of § 18.2-266 or § 18.2-266.1, or a similar ordinance shall determine the innocence or guilt of the defendant from all the evidence concerning his condition at the time of the alleged offense.

History.
1992, c. 830; 1994, cc. 359, 363; 2001, c. 654; 2004, c. 1013; 2005, cc. 616, 757, 840.

Law Review.
For article, "Criminal Law and Procedure," see 35 U. Rich. L. Rev. 537 (2001).

Michie's Jurisprudence.
For related discussion, see 2B M.J. Automobiles, §§ 118, 122; 7B M.J. Evidence, § 49.

CASE NOTES

Determination of guilt or innocence of accused. — The statutory mandate is that the guilt or innocence of the accused be determined from all the evidence of his condition at the time of the alleged offense, with or without a blood analysis. Thurston v. City of Lynchburg, 15 Va. App. 475, 424 S.E.2d 701 (1992).

Refusal to permit blood or breath test immaterial. — This section makes evidence of an accused's refusal to permit a blood or breath sample to be taken immaterial, or not a proper issue, in a driving under the influence prosecution, except where a defendant raises the issue, in which case evidence of a refusal to take a test becomes material for rebuttal, but evidence of the refusal must be relevant to the material issue raised by the defendant's evidence. Calhoun v. Commonwealth, 35 Va. App. 506, 546 S.E.2d 239, 2001 Va. App. LEXIS 279 (2001).

And refusal to take test is not probative except in rebuttal. — A defendant's refusal to take a blood or breath test has no probative value as to guilt or innocence and is not relevant or material, except in rebuttal when the defendant raises an issue pertaining to the offer of, or failure to take, the test. Calhoun v. Commonwealth, 35 Va. App. 506, 546 S.E.2d 239, 2001 Va. App. LEXIS 279 (2001).

Evidence of refusal held not admissible in rebuttal. — Evidence that a defendant refused to take a blood or breath test did not disprove or contradict his testimony that he was not intoxicated, nor did it prove he consumed a greater amount of alcohol than he had admitted, and accordingly, evidence of such refusal was not relevant to the material issues raised by his testimony; only evidence bearing on the facts asserted in the defendant's testimony, such as evidence of his performance on field sobriety tests or the arresting officer's common observations of the defendant's speech and physical appearance, would be admissible as tending to rebut or disprove the defendant's testimony. Calhoun v. Commonwealth, 35 Va. App. 506, 546 S.E.2d 239, 2001 Va. App. LEXIS 279 (2001).

Commonwealth cannot comment on accused's failure to take blood or breath test. — This section only prohibits the Commonwealth, not the accused, from commenting on the failure of the accused to take a blood or breath test, except in rebuttal; furthermore, this section does not prohibit the accused from offering evidence of the willingness to take a blood or breath test. Hammond v. Commonwealth, 17 Va. App. 565, 439 S.E.2d 877 (1994).

Comment on absence of chemical test results permitted. — A prosecutor's comment that there would be no testimony of any chemical test was an accurate and valid statement to prospective jurors advising them that chemical tests and the statutory rebuttable presumption of intoxication were not going to be used to prove that the defendant was under the influence of alcohol; the trial court properly denied the defendant's motion for a mistrial because the prosecutor made no reference whatsoever to the defendant's refusal to submit to the chemical test as an explanation for the need to resort to other evidence. Moore v. Commonwealth, No. 0264-99-4, 2000 Va. App. LEXIS 538 (Ct. of Appeals July 25, 2000).

Evidence of willingness to take blood or breath test must be relevant. — This section does not prohibit the accused from offering evidence of the willingness to take a blood or breath test. However, notwithstanding the court's interpretation of this section, the evidence offered by the accused surrounding the administration of the breath or blood test must be relevant in order to be admissible. Hammond v. Commonwealth, 16 Va. App. 347, 429 S.E.2d 631 (1993), aff'd upon reh'g en banc, 17 Va. App. 565, 439 S.E.2d 877 (1994).

Refusal of alkasensor test inadmissible in manslaughter trial. — Where a defendant is charged with aggravated involuntary manslaughter and it is alleged as an element of that charge that the defendant was driving while intoxicated, the trial on the manslaughter charge would also be trial of a charge under § 18.2-266 (ii) and, therefore, evidence that the defendant refused an alkasensor test would be inadmissible under this section. Maddox v. Commonwealth, No. 1129-99-4, 2000 Va. App. LEXIS 575 (Ct. of Appeals Aug. 1, 2000).

Admission of refusal to perform test did not violate constitutions. — Neither the Fifth Amendment nor Va. Const., Art. I, § 8 were violated by the admission in evidence of defendant's refusal to take a field sobriety test. Farmer v. Commonwealth, 12 Va. App. 337, 404 S.E.2d 371 (1991) (decided under former § 18.2-168).

Evidence of refusal, to show defendant believed he might fail, violates constitution. — Evidence of a refusal to submit to field sobriety tests, when used by the finder of fact as evidence that the accused refused to submit to the test because he believed he might fail, violates the accused's right, under Va. Const., Art. I, § 8, not to "be compelled ... to give evidence against himself." Farmer v. Commonwealth, 10 Va. App. 175, 390 S.E.2d 775 (1990) (decided under former § 18.2-168).

Test results presumptive. — Because the blood alcohol concentration reflected by the chemical test necessarily resulted from alcohol consumed prior to or during driving, the test results are presumptive evidence of the blood alcohol concentration at the time of driving and as such, the accused may challenge the test results by competent evidence, such as, for example, that he had not consumed enough alcohol in the relevant time to reach the level indicated by the chemical test results. Davis v. Commonwealth, 8 Va. App. 291, 381 S.E.2d 11 (1989) (decided under former § 18.2-168).

Consumption of alcohol after driving. — Where there is evidence that alcohol has been consumed after driving the chemical test cannot accurately reflect the blood alcohol concentration at the time of driving since the chemical test simply cannot distinguish between two sources of alcohol and where no alcohol is consumed between the time of driving and the time the chemical test is administered the test results can reflect only that alcohol consumed before or during driving and § 18.2-266 (i) is applicable only in these latter circumstances. Davis v. Commonwealth, 8 Va. App. 291, 381 S.E.2d 11 (1989) (decided under former § 18.2-168).

Chemical analysis of blood alcohol content as evidence. —

There is no reason why the results of a chemical analysis of blood alcohol content should not be admissible if based upon a foundation which tends to ensure the reliability of the test equipment and procedures, the integrity of the chain of custody of the blood specimen, and the technical competence of the person who performed the analysis. Whether the foundation is sufficient is a question within the sound discretion of the trial judge. If the judge finds the foundation sufficient, the credibility of the witnesses and the weight to be accorded the evidence are matters within the province of the jury. Essex v. Commonwealth, 228 Va. 273, 322 S.E.2d 216 (1984) (decided under former § 18.2-268).

Evidence of results of hospital test of blood alcohol content, competent because supported by a proper foundation, constituted "other relevant evidence" within the intendment of this section and was properly admitted as proof of drunken driving. However, this evidence, though probative, raised no legal presumption of intoxication, where it was not conducted in accordance with the provisions of this section. Essex v. Commonwealth, 228 Va. 273, 322 S.E.2d 216 (1984) (decided under former § 18.2-268).

Guilt or innocence determined from all evidence of defendant's condition. — The statutory mandate is that the guilt or innocence of the accused be determined from all the evidence of his condition at the time of the alleged offense, with or without a breath analysis. Brooks v. City of Newport News, 224 Va. 311, 295 S.E.2d 801 (1982) (decided under former § 18.2-268).

Any error caused in a bench trial by the admission of evidence of defendant's evasive behavior concerning the taking of a breathalyzer test, and the prosecutor's comment thereon, was harmless, where other evidence of defendant's inebriated condition was overwhelming. Foster v. Commonwealth, No. 1964-00-1, 2001 Va. App. LEXIS 378 (Ct. of Appeals June 26, 2001).

Result of breath analysis is but auxiliary proof which may tend to corroborate evidence of objective symptoms. Brooks v. City of Newport News, 224 Va. 311, 295 S.E.2d 801 (1982) (decided under former § 18.2-268).

Other evidence may render erroneous admission of certificate harmless. — Where the testimony at the trial clearly showed that there was no room for reasonable doubt about defendant's actual condition at the time of his arrest, and evidence of his guilt was clear and compelling, the erroneous ruling of the trial court in admitting a certificate which showed that the operator's license was invalid was harmless. Brooks v. City of Newport News, 224 Va. 311, 295 S.E.2d 801 (1982) (decided under former § 18.2-268).

Harmless error in admission of evidence that defendant was offered breath tests. — Although the trial court erred in a DUI trial in allowing testimony that defendant was offered breath tests following a traffic stop, that evidence was harmless because there was overwhelming evidence that defendant drove while intoxicated; under § 4.1-100, "intoxicated" meant a condition in which a person had drunk enough alcoholic beverages to observably affect his manner, disposition, speech, muscular movement, general appearance, or behavior. The evidence at trial proved that defendant drove his car at a reckless speed and that, when stopped, he had an odor of alcohol about his breath, red and glassy eyes, and slurred speech, and performed poorly on field sobriety tests. Reid v. Commonwealth, 2009 Va. App. LEXIS 308 (July 14, 2009).

§ 18.2-268.11. Substantial compliance.

The steps set forth in §§ 18.2-268.2 through 18.2-268.9 relating to taking, handling, identifying, and disposing of blood or breath samples are procedural and not substantive. Substantial compliance shall be sufficient. Failure to comply with any steps or portions thereof shall not of itself be grounds for finding the defendant not guilty, but shall go to the weight of the evidence and shall be considered with all the evidence in the case; however, the defendant shall have the right to introduce evidence on his own behalf to show noncompliance with the aforesaid procedures or any part thereof, and that as a result his rights were prejudiced.

History.
1992, c. 830; 2003, cc. 933, 936.

Michie's Jurisprudence.
For related discussion, see 2B M.J. Automobiles, § 118.

CASE NOTES

Construction with § 18.2-268.9. — This section applies to the provisions of § 18.2-268.9. Joseph v. Commonwealth, No. 0607-95-3 (Ct. of Appeals Dec. 10, 1996).

Unavailability of independent test results forecloses prosecution. — When an accused asks that his blood sample be sent to an independent laboratory for testing and an independent analysis is not available at trial, the Commonwealth has the burden to explain the absence of independent test results and show that it substantially complied with the steps relating to the taking, handling, identification, and disposition of defendant's blood sample, and when the Commonwealth cannot prove that it substantially complied with the statutory procedures referred to in this section the Commonwealth is foreclosed from prosecution. Gray v. Commonwealth, No. 1972-91-2 (Ct. of Appeals July 27, 1993).

Subsection Z (now § 18.2-268.11) does not deal with or address the handling of test results, and it does not relieve the Commonwealth of its responsibility under subsection M to provide an accused with the test results when they have been requested. Wendel v. Commonwealth, 12 Va. App. 958, 407 S.E.2d 690 (1991) (decided under former § 18.2-268).

Non-compliance with form delivery requirement negates possibility of substantial compliance. — Assuming without deciding that the delivery of the independent analysis designation form is a step relating to taking, handling, identifying, and disposing of blood samples, the failure to comply with that requirement of the statute negates the possibility of substantial compliance. Artis v. City of Suffolk, 19 Va. App. 168, 450 S.E.2d 165 (1994).

Failure to comply with blood-taking procedure goes to weight of evidence. — The question of how blood is taken is procedural, and a failure to comply with the directed procedures goes to the weight of the evidence and is to be considered with all the evidence in the case, with the right to the defendant to show noncompliance and resulting prejudice. Shumate v. Commonwealth, 207 Va. 877, 153 S.E.2d 257 (1967) (decided under former § 18.2-268).

With respect to regularity of the test, the defendant has the right to prove noncompliance with test procedures, but such proof would not defeat admissibility of the certificate but only affect its weight as evidence of the alcoholic content of his blood. Stroupe v. Commonwealth, 215 Va. 243, 207 S.E.2d 894 (1974) (decided under former § 18.2-268).

Where the statute requires that when the Commonwealth draws blood for the purposes of an alcohol or drug test, the part of the body from which the blood is taken must be cleaned with "soap and water, polyvinylpyrrolidone iodine or benzalkonium chloride," but the record stated that "benadine" was used to clean appellant's arm, and nothing in the record supported the argument that using "benadine" substantially complied with the statute, then a finding of substantial compliance could not be supported. Hudson v. Commonwealth, 21 Va. App. 184, 462 S.E.2d 913 (1995).

Failure to introduce evidence of test equipment calibration. — Lack of statutorily mandated evidence of test equipment calibration affected integrity of result, and was a matter of substance. Brown v. Commonwealth, No. 0787-98-4 (Ct. of Appeals July 6, 1999).

But this section does not change the ultimate burden of proof in a prosecution under this section. Shumate v. Commonwealth, 207 Va. 877, 153 S.E.2d 243 (1967) (decided under former § 18.2-268).

Requirement as to time of test is procedural. — The requirement in subsection (r1) of § 18.2-268 (now § 18.2-268.9) of the time of the test on a certificate, as subsection (s) (now § 18.2-268.11) of this section makes clear, is procedural in nature. United States v. Robertson, 638 F. Supp. 1202 (E.D. Va. 1986) (decided under former § 18.2-268).

Error to admit certificate indicating that license is invalid. — This section requires the test to be administered by an operator with a valid license. The qualification of the operator is a matter of substance, not procedure, and is not waived by former § 18.2-268. A court, therefore, is in error in admitting the certificate into evidence where it indicates that the license is invalid. Brooks v. City of Newport News, 224 Va. 311, 295 S.E.2d 801 (1982) (decided under former § 18.2-268).

Chemical analysis properly admitted. — Defendant's conviction of driving while intoxicated was affirmed because the certificate of blood alcohol analysis was admissible under § 18.2-268.9 regardless of any alleged error in admitting the certificate of instrument accuracy, and, correspondingly, any error in admitting the certificate of instrument accuracy was harmless. Fitzgerald v. Commonwealth, 61 Va. App. 279, 734 S.E.2d 708, 2012 Va. App. LEXIS 398 (2012).

Burden of proof. — Under § 18.2-268.9, the Commonwealth is not required to introduce evidence showing the Virginia Department of Forensic Science's compliance with subdivision B 3 of § 9.1-1101 before a certificate of blood alcohol analysis becomes admissible; rather, the substantial compliance provisions of § 18.2-268.11 indicate that the defendant has the burden of producing evidence showing noncompliance with procedural requirements like that contained in subdivision B 3 of § 9.1-1101. Fitzgerald v. Commonwealth, 61 Va. App. 279, 734 S.E.2d 708, 2012 Va. App. LEXIS 398 (2012).

Substantial compliance with statutory requirements shown. — Where certificate of analysis produced by laboratory indicated that the laboratory had been unable to test the blood sample contained in the box because the vial when received was smashed and blood had leaked out, where Commonwealth produced uncontradicted evidence that vials were in good condition when received by officer, and where boxes containing the vials were maintained in a refrigerator by property clerk for police department, and the boxes remained sealed and were not leaking when property clerk mailed them to the respective laboratories, the Commonwealth's evidence demonstrated that it substantially complied with the statutory procedures relating to the taking and handling of blood samples, and sufficiently explained the unavailability of the independent blood test. Amaya-Portillo v. Commonwealth, No. 2559-96-4 (Ct. of Appeals Dec. 9, 1997).

The court properly found that the procedures used by a police officer in administering a breathalyzer test substantially complied with the applicable statutes and regulations, notwithstanding that the officer did not wait 20 minutes after the defendant ingested two prescription nitroglycerin tablets before administering the test, where an expert testified that the nitroglycerin probably would not technically invalidate the breathalyzer test. St. Clair v. City of Lynchburg, No. 1649-97-3 (Ct. of Appeals Nov. 24, 1998).

Trial court did not err in admitting results of breathalyzer test into evidence, despite defendant's having chewed cigarette tobacco between time of his arrest and time of analysis; evidence permitted a finding that any alcohol in defendant's mouth did not skew test results, and therefore that test substantially complied with statutory requirements for its admission. Pollard v. Commonwealth, No. 2638-98-2 (Ct. of Appeals Sept. 21, 1999).

In a DWI trial, the Commonwealth was permitted to introduce evidence of a certificate of analysis of a blood vial drawn shortly after defendant's arrest, even though the certificate of blood withdrawal had become detached from the vial. These facts otherwise established substantial compliance with the procedures governing the taking and handling of defendant's blood. Williams v. Commonwealth, No. 2451-02-4, 2003 Va. App. LEXIS 597 (Ct. of Appeals Nov. 18, 2003).

Although a nurse and police officer committed technical violations of former § 18.2-268.6 when they packaged a sample of defendant's blood for transportation to a laboratory, the violations were trivial and the trial court did not err by finding that there was substantial compliance with the statute and admitting the results of the blood test into evidence. Jones v. Commonwealth, No. 2967-02-2, 2004 Va. App. LEXIS 64 (Ct. of Appeals Feb. 10, 2004).

Officer who arrested defendant for driving under the influence of alcohol, second offense, properly determined that defendant was physically unable to complete a breath test due to defendant's recent ingestion of chili, which was giving defendant indigestion at the time of the breath test, and, thus, the certificate of analysis from the blood test that the officer had defendant take was admissible, as no showing was made that the officer violated Virginia's implied consent law. Pearson v. Commonwealth, 43 Va.

App. 317, 597 S.E.2d 269, 2004 Va. App. LEXIS 272 (2004).

Trial court did not err when it found that a police officer substantially complied with the requirements of § 18.2-268.9 when she administered a breath test to defendant who was coughing and that expert testimony which defendant offered did not rebut the presumption created by § 18.2-269 that defendant was under the influence of alcohol, and the appellate court affirmed the trial court's judgment admitting the results of the test and using them to convict defendant of driving under the influence of alcohol. Wing v. Commonwealth, No. 1760-03-4, 2004 Va. App. LEXIS 368 (Ct. of Appeals Aug. 3, 2004).

Where the form provided listed only one approved laboratory for independent testing, as defendant did receive independent blood alcohol content testing, the trial court was not obliged to suppress the blood test results. The legislative remedy for a procedural violation of the driving under the influence statutes was not suppression of the evidence, but a full and fair opportunity for both sides to prove or disprove any prejudicial effect of the violation. Cutright v. Commonwealth, 43 Va. App. 593, 601 S.E.2d 1, 2004 Va. App. LEXIS 398 (2004).

Failure to comply with the required procedure for storing a breath analysis machine did not, by itself, require suppression of defendant's breath test results, where no evidence established that the police failed to comply with any of the regulations governing the "taking, handling, identification, and disposition of breath samples" other than the improper placement of the breath analysis machine, where the machine had a self-correcting mechanism, where there was no allegation that the machine was tampered with or that the results were incorrect, and defendant failed to show that the failure to comply with the storage methods prejudiced his rights. Henry v. Commonwealth, 44 Va. App. 702, 607 S.E.2d 140, 2005 Va. App. LEXIS 6 (2005).

Giving defendant an opportunity to view the print out of the blood-alcohol reading taken by the breathalyzer machine satisfied the requirements of § 18.2-268.9; moreover, the appeals court agreed with the trial judge that since the breath test procedure did not contemplate defendant having his breath sample analyzed by an independent party, then the fact that he was shown the result, but not actually given a paper copy of the result, could hardly have had any effect on his substantive rights at trial. Shelton v. Commonwealth, 45 Va. App. 175, 609 S.E.2d 89, 2005 Va. App. LEXIS 78 (2005).

Applied in Stevens v. Commonwealth, 44 Va. App. 122, 603 S.E.2d 642, 2004 Va. App. LEXIS 496 (2004).

§ 18.2-268.12. Ordinances.

The governing bodies of counties, cities and towns are authorized to adopt ordinances paralleling the provisions of §§ 18.2-268.1 through 18.2-268.11.

History.
1992, c. 830.

CASE NOTES

Applied in Stevens v. Commonwealth, 44 Va. App. 122, 603 S.E.2d 642, 2004 Va. App. LEXIS 496 (2004).

§ 18.2-269. Presumptions from alcohol or drug content of blood.

A. In any prosecution for a violation of § 18.2-36.1 or clause (ii), (iii) or (iv) of § 18.2-266, or any similar ordinance, the amount of alcohol or drugs in the blood of the accused at the time of the alleged offense as indicated by a chemical analysis of a sample of the accused's blood or breath to determine the alcohol or drug content of his blood in accordance with the provisions of §§ 18.2-268.1 through 18.2-

268.12 shall give rise to the following rebuttable presumptions:

(1) If there was at that time 0.05 percent or less by weight by volume of alcohol in the accused's blood or 0.05 grams or less per 210 liters of the accused's breath, it shall be presumed that the accused was not under the influence of alcohol intoxicants at the time of the alleged offense;

(2) If there was at that time in excess of 0.05 percent but less than 0.08 percent by weight by volume of alcohol in the accused's blood or 0.05 grams but less than 0.08 grams per 210 liters of the accused's breath, such facts shall not give rise to any presumption that the accused was or was not under the influence of alcohol intoxicants at the time of the alleged offense, but such facts may be considered with other competent evidence in determining the guilt or innocence of the accused;

(3) If there was at that time 0.08 percent or more by weight by volume of alcohol in the accused's blood or 0.08 grams or more per 210 liters of the accused's breath, it shall be presumed that the accused was under the influence of alcohol intoxicants at the time of the alleged offense; or

(4) If there was at that time an amount of the following substances at a level that is equal to or greater than: (a) 0.02 milligrams of cocaine per liter of blood, (b) 0.1 milligrams of methamphetamine per liter of blood, (c) 0.01 milligrams of phencyclidine per liter of blood, or (d) 0.1 milligrams of 3,4-methylenedioxymethamphetamine per liter of blood, it shall be presumed that the accused was under the influence of drugs at the time of the alleged offense to a degree which impairs his ability to drive or operate any motor vehicle, engine or train safely.

B. The provisions of this section shall not apply to and shall not affect any prosecution for a violation of § 46.2-341.24.

History.

Code 1950, § 18.1-57; 1960, c. 358; 1964, c. 240; 1966, c. 636; 1972, c. 757; 1973, c. 459; 1975, cc. 14, 15; 1977, c. 638; 1983, c. 504; 1986, c. 635; 1989, cc. 554, 574, 705; 1992, c. 830; 1994, cc. 359, 363; 2005, c. 616.

Law Review.

For note on the Virginia blood test statute discussing statistical methods of evaluating blood samples, see 56 Va. L. Rev. 349 (1970). For survey of Virginia criminal law for the year 1971-1972, see 58 Va. L. Rev. 1206 (1972). For survey of Virginia law on evidence for the year 1972-1973, see 59 Va. L. Rev. 1526 (1973). For survey of Virginia law on evidence for the year 1973-1974, see 60 Va. L. Rev. 1543 (1974). For note discussing the defendant's right to independent analysis of the breathalyzer ampoule, see 21 Wm. & Mary L. Rev. 219 (1979). For note, "The Constitutionality of Sobriety Checkpoints," see 43 Wash. & Lee L. Rev. 1469 (1986).

Michie's Jurisprudence.

For related discussion, see 2B M.J. Automobiles, § 118.

CASE NOTES

Constitutionality. — Consideration by the jury of the statutory presumptions created by this section does not deprive the defendant of any protected right. Kay v. United States, 255 F.2d 476 (4th Cir.), cert. denied, 358 U.S. 825, 79 S. Ct. 42, 3 L. Ed. 2d 65 (1958).

This section did not create a mandatory presumption, but allowed a permissive inference that the fact finder was free to reject; § 18.2-269 simply shifted the burden of producing evidence, while the burden of proof remained with the Commonwealth. The trial court analyzed the statute as a permissive inference, noting that it must be read to contain permissive inferences in order to satisfy due process requirements. Yap v. Commonwealth, 49 Va. App. 622, 643 S.E.2d 523, 2007 Va. App. LEXIS 171 (2007).

Trial court did not err in refusing to declare §§ 18.2-269 and 18.2-270 unconstitutional in a case where defendant was charged with and later convicted of driving under the influence of alcohol; there did not exist an evidentiary presumption relieving the Commonwealth of the burden of proof beyond a reasonable doubt in those two statutes, as § 18.2-269 did not have a mandatory presumption but a rebuttable presumption and § 18.2-270 had no presumption at all. Lawrence v. Commonwealth, — Va. App. —, — S.E.2d —, 2007 Va. App. LEXIS 150 (Apr. 10, 2007).

Defendant's challenge to the constitutionality of the "rebuttable presumptions" employed by § 18.2-269 failed because the jury was not instructed on them and the presumptions clearly did not apply to the per se violations defendant claimed to have been convicted under. Morin v. Commonwealth, 2007 Va. App. LEXIS 346 (Sept. 18, 2007).

Presumptions inapplicable where defendant refuses tests. — The presumptions established by this section apply only when a blood or breath test is administered; this section does not apply where the defendant refused to take either a blood or breath test and no test was given under the implied consent law. Groggins v. Commonwealth, 34 Va. App. 19, 537 S.E.2d 605, 2000 Va. App. LEXIS 764 (2000).

Evidence of results of hospital test of blood alcohol content, competent because supported by a proper foundation, constituted "other relevant evidence" within the intendment of former § 18.2-268 (now § 18.2-268.1 et seq.) and was properly admitted as proof of drunken driving. However, this evidence, though probative, raised no legal presumption of intoxication, where it was not conducted in accordance with the provisions of former § 18.2-268. Essex v. Commonwealth, 228 Va. 273, 322 S.E.2d 216 (1984).

Expert testimony. — Trial court did not err in allowing blood alcohol test results into evidence, where exigent circumstances justified warrantless arrest and search of defendant, and Commonwealth relied on expert opinion to explain significance of defendant's blood alcohol level and did not rely on statutory presumption contained in this section. Felts v. Commonwealth, No. 1997-98-3 (Ct. of Appeals Oct. 5, 1999).

Trial court did not err when it found that a police officer substantially complied with the requirements of § 18.2-268.9 when she administered a breath test to defendant who was coughing, and that expert testimony that defendant offered did not rebut the presumption created by § 18.2-269 that defendant was under the influence of alcohol, and the appellate court affirmed the trial court's judgment admitting the results of the test and using them to convict defendant of driving under the influence of alcohol. Wing v. Commonwealth, No. 1760-03-4, 2004 Va. App. LEXIS 368 (Ct. of Appeals Aug. 3, 2004).

North Carolina statute not substantially similar to this section. — Under subdivision A (3) of this section, an accused may present evidence to rebut the presumption, and if such evidence creates a reasonable doubt as to his guilt, the fact finder must acquit. In North Carolina, however, mere proof that an accused's blood alcohol is 0.10 percent is conclusive as to guilt. With such a fundamental difference, the North Carolina statute (§ 20-138.1 of the General Statutes of North Carolina) is not substantially similar within the meaning of § 18.2-270. Shinault v. Commonwealth, 228 Va. 269, 321 S.E.2d 652 (1984).

Certificates allowed for presumption supporting conviction. — Evidence, viewed in the light most favorable to the Commonwealth, was sufficient to show that defendant was under the influence of alcohol at the time he crashed his vehicle into the back end of a pickup truck and caused the death of its driver; the trial court had several certificates of analysis indicating defendant was driving with a blood-alcohol level of over .08 grams, which permitted the trial court to presume that defendant was under the influence of alcohol intoxicants at the time of the alleged offense, and other evidence in the form of eyewitness testimony also supported that conviction. West v. Commonwealth, 43 Va. App. 327, 597 S.E.2d 274, 2004 Va. App. LEXIS 276 (2004).

Trial court did not err in denying defendant's motion to exclude from evidence a blood alcohol content certificate showing his state of intoxication because defendant introduced substantially similar evidence during his case in chief, thereby waiving his objection and rendering harmless any alleged error; defendant's evidence, a 0.14 percent blood alcohol content certificate of analysis, dealt with the same subject as, and was sufficiently similar to, the Commonwealth's 0.16 percent blood alcohol content certificate, and both established blood alcohol content levels in excess of 0.08 percent, thereby triggering the inference of subdivision A 3 of § 18.2-269 that defendant was under the influence of alcohol intoxicants at the time of the alleged offense. Isaac v. Commonwealth, 58 Va. App. 255, 708 S.E.2d 435, 2011 Va. App. LEXIS 164 (2011).

Certificate inadmissible where arrest not timely made. — Where there is no evidence that defendant was arrested within two hours of the alleged offense, the certificate showing the alcohol content of defendant's blood is inadmissible. Overbee v. Commonwealth, 227 Va. 238, 315 S.E.2d 242 (1984).

Because defendant was not validly arrested within three hours of the offenses, as required by subsection A of § 18.2-268.2, and an officer's act of telling defendant that he was under arrest and advising him of the implied consent law was insufficient to satisfy the restraint requirement to assert his lawful authority to arrest defendant, defendant did not impliedly consent to have his blood drawn; thus, the certificate of analysis containing defendant's blood test results was inadmissible. Bristol v. Commonwealth, 272 Va. 568, 636 S.E.2d 460, 2006 Va. LEXIS 115 (2006).

No presumption of intoxication where certificate inadmissible. — Where the certificate of analysis of the breath test is inadmissible, the Commonwealth is not entitled to a rebuttable presumption that defendant was intoxicated at the time of the alleged offense (where his blood-alcohol content was greater than 0.10%). Such defendant's guilt or innocence must therefore be determined from the other evidence of his condition at the time of the alleged offense. Overbee v. Commonwealth, 227 Va. 238, 315 S.E.2d 242 (1984).

Where defendant's breath certificate of analysis showed unexplained results of ".10 percent" grams per 210 liters, without evidence explaining the error, the trial judge could not assume that "%" was simply inserted by error and that the correct measurement for alcohol content was .10 grams per 210 liters of the accused's breath, the statutory presumption of intoxication under this section. Van Lear v. Commonwealth, No. 1924-94-3 (Ct. of Appeals Feb. 20, 1996).

The presumption created by this section is rebuttable. It neither restricts the defendant in the presentation of his defense nor deprives him of the presumptions of innocence. Since wide experience has demonstrated the close connection between the presumed fact and the alcoholic content of the blood, there is no constitutional objection to the jury's consideration, with all of the other evidence, of the statutory presumption. Kay v. United States, 255 F.2d 476 (4th Cir.), cert. denied, 358 U.S. 825, 79 S. Ct. 42, 3 L. Ed. 2d 65 (1958).

Presumption not applied. — Trial court did not err in convicting defendant of driving under the influence of alcohol in violation of § 18.2-266 because the trial court considered the totality of the evidence and did not apply any statutory presumption set forth in § 18.2-269 to defendant's blood alcohol test result shown on the certificate of analysis; the trial court emphasized its reliance on the photographs of the accident taken at the scene and the circumstantial evidence, in particular but not limited to, defendant's admission that he had consumed four twenty-two ounce beers before the accident. Bilger v. Commonwealth, 2011 Va. App. LEXIS 371 (Nov. 29, 2011).

Where the appellate court was unable to determine whether the trial court applied this section's rebuttable presumption of intoxication to prove appellant's intoxication, since the Commonwealth presented other independent evidence of appellant's intoxication but where the trial court wrongly admitted the certificate after ruling that the Commonwealth had complied with the implied consent law, and subsequent to the certificate's admission, the Commonwealth failed to offer evidence on the significance of the test results in the certificate, reversal was required. Castillo v. Commonwealth, 21 Va. App. 482, 465 S.E.2d 146 (1995).

Admission of certificate not harmless error. — Trial court's error in admitting into evidence a certificate of blood alcohol analysis was not harmless beyond a reasonable doubt because in order to convict defendant of a per se violation under clause (i) of § 18.2-266 or invoke the presumption of intoxication afforded by subdivision A 3 of § 18.2-269 the trial court had to rely on the facts recited in the attestation clause in order to conclude that the test was conducted in accordance with the relevant statutes; the only evidence that the breath test was administered either as provided by Title 18.2, Chapter Seven, Article Two of the Virginia Code or in accordance with the provisions of §§ 18.2-268.1 through 18.2-268.12, as required by § 18.2-269, was in the attestation clause on the certificate of analysis, and because the use of the attestation clause in the case violated the Confrontation Clause, it could not be used to prove that the breath test was administered in accordance with the relevant statutes. Grant v. Commonwealth, 54 Va. App. 714, 682 S.E.2d 84, 2009 Va. App. LEXIS 390 (2009).

Applied in United States v. Robertson, 638 F. Supp. 1202 (E.D. Va. 1986); Stevens v. Commonwealth, 46 Va. App. 234, 616 S.E.2d 754, 2005 Va. App. LEXIS 407 (2005); Stevens v. Commonwealth, 272 Va. 481, 634 S.E.2d 305, 2006 Va. LEXIS 87 (2006).

CIRCUIT COURT OPINIONS

Constitutionality. — Court denied defendant's motion to declare certain parts of § 18.2-269 unconstitutional because the Virginia General Assembly was well within its authority to find that a blood alcohol level of 0.08 and above created a permissive inference that an individual was "under the influence of alcohol" as that term was used in § 18.2-266. Commonwealth v. Pattarasok, 69 Va. Cir. 423, 2006 Va. Cir. LEXIS 15 (Fairfax County 2006).

Court denied defendant's motion to declare certain parts of § 18.2-269 unconstitutional because its rebuttable presumptions were to be given permissive or burden-of-production shifting effect only. Commonwealth v. Pattarasok, 69 Va. Cir. 423, 2006 Va. Cir. LEXIS 15 (Fairfax County 2006).

Only if this section could reasonably be read to provide a permissible inference could it satisfy due process requirements; the circuit court found that due process required that § 18.2-269 be treated as creating a permissible inference, rather than as a mandatory rebuttable presumption, and, so construed, the statute was constitutional, both facially and as applied to defendants. Commonwealth v. Padilla, 69 Va. Cir. 409, 2006 Va. Cir. LEXIS 16 (Fairfax County 2006), aff'd, Yap v. Commonwealth, 49 Va. App. 622, 643 S.E.2d 523, 2007 Va. App. LEXIS 171 (2007).

In a driving under the influence of alcohol in violation of § 18.2-266, the circuit court found that this section would violate due process if interpreted as shifting the burden to defendants to rebut an element of the offense that the fact finder would otherwise be required to conclude; when the charge was driving under the influence of alcohol, a mandatory rebuttable presumption that required the fact finder upon the presentation of a certain blood alcohol level to conclude that defendants were under the influence of alcohol, unless rebutted by them, would adversely affect their right to trial by jury and their right to remain silent, and it would diminish the requirement of the state to prove defendants' guilt beyond a reasonable doubt. Only if § 18.2-269 could reasonably be read to provide a permissible inference could it satisfy due process requirements; the circuit court found that due process required that § 18.2-269 be treated as creating a permissible inference, rather than as a mandatory rebuttable presumption, and, so construed, the statute was constitutional, both facially and as applied to defendants. Commonwealth v. Padilla, 69 Va. Cir. 409, 2006 Va. Cir. LEXIS 16 (Fairfax County 2006), aff'd, Yap v. Commonwealth, 49 Va. App. 622, 643 S.E.2d 523, 2007 Va. App. LEXIS 171 (2007).

Presumptions of §§ 18.2-266 and 18.2-269 are permissive inferences because they do not remove the element of alcohol content from the case and do not shift the burden of persuasion to the defendant; thus, they do not violate due process or the right to confrontation. Furthermore, § 18.2-270, which relies on a violation of § 18.2-266, is not unconstitutional, as the burden of persuasion is with the Commonwealth at all times. Commonwealth v. Stump, 69 Va. Cir. 433, 2006 Va. Cir. LEXIS 95 (Roanoke 2006).

Rebuttable presumption does not violate due process. — Rebuttable presumptions in §§ 18.2-266(i) and 18.2-269 did not violate defendant's due process rights, because the court was required to analyze the rebuttable presumptions as permissive inferences, as to which defendant had no standing to make a facial constitutional challenge. Commonwealth v. Draper, 72 Va. Cir. 111, 2006 Va. Cir. LEXIS 315 (Martinsville 2006).

§ 18.2-270. Penalty for driving while intoxicated; subsequent offense; prior conviction.

A. Except as otherwise provided herein, any person violating any provision of § 18.2-266 shall be guilty of a Class 1 misdemeanor with a mandatory minimum fine of $250. If the person's blood alcohol level as indicated by the chemical test administered as provided in this article or by any other scientifically reliable chemical test performed on whole blood under circumstances reliably establishing the identity of the person who is the source of the blood and the accuracy of the results (i) was at least 0.15, but not more than 0.20, he shall be confined in jail for an additional mandatory minimum period of five days or, (ii) if the level was more than 0.20, for an additional mandatory minimum period of 10 days.

B. 1. Any person convicted of a second offense committed within less than five years after a prior offense under § 18.2-266 shall upon conviction of the second offense be punished by a mandatory minimum fine of $500 and by confinement in jail for not less than one month nor more than one year. Twenty days of such confinement shall be a mandatory minimum sentence.

2. Any person convicted of a second offense committed within a period of five to 10 years of a prior offense under § 18.2-266 shall upon conviction of the second offense be punished by a mandatory minimum fine of $500 and by confinement in jail for not less than one month. Ten days of such confinement shall be a mandatory minimum sentence.

3. Upon conviction of a second offense within 10 years of a prior offense, if the person's blood alcohol level as indicated by the chemical test administered as provided in this article or by any other scientifically reliable chemical test performed on whole blood under circumstances reliably establishing the identity of the person who is the source of the blood and the accuracy of the results (i) was at least 0.15, but not more than 0.20, he shall be confined in jail for an additional mandatory minimum period of 10 days or, (ii) if the level was more than 0.20, for an additional mandatory minimum period of 20 days. In addition, such person shall be fined a mandatory minimum fine of $500.

C. 1. Any person convicted of three offenses of § 18.2-266 committed within a 10-year period shall upon conviction of the third offense be guilty of a Class 6 felony. The sentence of any person convicted of three offenses of § 18.2-266 committed within a 10-year period shall include a mandatory minimum sentence of 90 days, unless the three offenses were committed within a five-year period, in which case the sentence shall include a mandatory minimum

sentence of confinement for six months. In addition, such person shall be fined a mandatory minimum fine of $1,000.

2. A person who has been convicted of § 18.2-36.1, 18.2-36.2, 18.2-51.4, 18.2-51.5, or a felony violation of § 18.2-266 shall upon conviction of a subsequent violation of § 18.2-266 be guilty of a Class 6 felony. The punishment of any person convicted of such a subsequent violation of § 18.2-266 shall include a mandatory minimum term of imprisonment of one year and a mandatory minimum fine of $1,000.

3. The punishment of any person convicted of a fourth or subsequent offense of § 18.2-266 committed within a 10-year period shall, upon conviction, include a mandatory minimum term of imprisonment of one year. In addition, such person shall be fined a mandatory minimum fine of $1,000. Unless otherwise modified by the court, the defendant shall remain on probation and under the terms of any suspended sentence for the same period as his operator's license was suspended, not to exceed three years.

4. The vehicle solely owned and operated by the accused during the commission of a felony violation of § 18.2-266 shall be subject to seizure and forfeiture. After an arrest for a felony violation of § 18.2-266, the Commonwealth may file an information in accordance with § 19.2-386.34.

D. In addition to the penalty otherwise authorized by this section or § 16.1-278.9, any person convicted of a violation of § 18.2-266 committed while transporting a person 17 years of age or younger shall be (i) fined an additional minimum of $500 and not more than $1,000 and (ii) sentenced to a mandatory minimum period of confinement of five days.

E. For the purpose of determining the number of offenses committed by, and the punishment appropriate for, a person under this section, an adult conviction of any person, or finding of guilty in the case of a juvenile, under the following shall be considered a conviction of § 18.2-266: (i) the provisions of § 18.2-36.1 or the substantially similar laws of any other state or of the United States, (ii) the provisions of §§ 18.2-51.4, 18.2-266, former § 18.1-54 (formerly § 18-75), the ordinance of any county, city or town in this Commonwealth or the laws of any other state or of the United States substantially similar to the provisions of § 18.2-51.4, or § 18.2-266, or (iii) the provisions of subsection A of § 46.2-341.24 or the substantially similar laws of any other state or of the United States.

F. Mandatory minimum punishments imposed pursuant to this section shall be cumulative, and mandatory minimum terms of confinement shall be served consecutively. However, in no case shall punishment imposed hereunder exceed the applicable statutory maximum Class 1 misdemeanor term of confinement or fine upon conviction of a first or second offense, or Class 6 felony term of confinement or fine upon conviction of a third or subsequent offense.

History.

Code 1950, § 18.1-58; 1960, c. 358; 1962, c. 302; 1975, cc. 14, 15; 1982, c. 301; 1983, c. 504; 1989, c. 705; 1991, cc. 370, 710; 1992, c. 891; 1993, c. 972; 1997, c. 691; 1999, cc. 743, 945, 949, 987; 2000, cc. 784, 956, 958, 980, 982; 2002, c. 759; 2003, cc. 573, 591; 2004, cc. 461, 937, 946, 950, 957, 958, 962; 2006, cc. 82, 314; 2009, c. 229; 2012, cc. 283, 756; 2013, cc. 415, 655.

Cross references.

As to application of this section in federal court, see note to § 18.2-266.

Editor's note.

Acts 2004, c. 937, cl. 2, provides: "That the Department of Motor Vehicles shall determine the impact on its recordkeeping system if the penalties currently applicable to a third conviction of § 18.2-266 were applicable without regard to the time period in which the offenses were committed."

Acts 2009, c. 229, cl. 2, provides: "That the provisions of this act may result in a net increase in periods of imprisonment or commitment. Pursuant to § 30-19.1:4, the estimated amount of the necessary appropriation is $0 for periods of imprisonment in state adult correctional facilities and is $0 for periods of commitment to the custody of the Department of Juvenile Justice."

Acts 2013, cc. 415 and 655, cl. 2 provides: "That the provisions of this act may result in a net increase in periods of imprisonment or commitment. Pursuant to § 30-19.1:4, the estimated amount of the necessary appropriation cannot be determined for periods of imprisonment in state adult correctional facilities; therefore, Chapter 3 of the Acts of Assembly of 2012, Special Session I, requires the Virginia Criminal Sentencing Commission to assign a minimum fiscal impact of $50,000. Pursuant to § 30-19.1:4, the estimated amount of the necessary appropriation is $0 for periods of commitment to the custody of the Department of Juvenile Justice."

The 2009 amendments.

The 2009 amendment by c. 229, in subsection A and in subdivision B 3, inserted "or by any other scientifically reliable chemical test performed on whole blood under circumstances reliably establishing the identity of the person who is the source of the blood and the accuracy of the results" and inserted the clauses (i) and (ii) designations.

The 2012 amendments.

The 2012 amendments by cc. 283 and 756 are identical, and rewrote subdivision C 3 by substituting "§ 19.2-386.34" for "§ 19.2-386.1" at the end of the second sentence and deleting the remainder of the paragraph and the former two paragraphs following.

The 2013 amendments.

The 2013 amendments by cc. 415 and 655 are identical, and added subdivision C 2 and redesignated former subdivisions C 2 and C 3 as subdivisions C 3 and C 4.

Law Review.

For note on the Virginia blood test statute discussing statistical methods of evaluating blood samples, see 56 Va. L. Rev. 349 (1970). For comment on 1982 amendments to Virginia's driving while intoxicated laws, see 17 U. Rich. L. Rev. 189 (1982). For 2000 survey of Virginia criminal law and procedure, see 34 U. Rich. L. Rev. 749 (2000). For article summarizing published Virginia criminal law decisions between July 1, 2002 and July 1, 2003, see 38 U. Rich. L. Rev. 87 (2003). For 2003/2004 survey of criminal law and procedure, see 39 U. Rich. L. Rev. 133 (2004). For 2006 survey article, "Criminal Law and Procedure," see 41 U. Rich. L. Rev. 83 (2006).

Michie's Jurisprudence.

For related discussion, see 2B M.J. Automobiles, § 118; 5B M.J. Criminal Procedure, §§ 3, 86.

CASE NOTES

Constitutionality. — Trial court did not err in refusing to declare §§ 18.2-269 and 18.2-270 unconstitutional in a case where defendant was charged with and later convicted of driving under the influence of alcohol; there did not exist an evidentiary presumption relieving the Commonwealth of the burden of proof beyond a reasonable doubt in those two statutes, as § 18.2-269 did not have a mandatory presumption but a rebuttable presumption and § 18.2-270 had no presumption at all. Lawrence v. Commonwealth, — Va. App. —, — S.E.2d —, 2007 Va. App. LEXIS 150 (Apr. 10, 2007).

Trial court properly sentenced defendant to a mandatory term of ten days in jail for driving a motor vehicle while intoxicated in violation of § 18.2-266 because § 18.2-270 was constitutional and did not contain an unconstitutional mandatory presumption; sentencing pursuant to § 18.2-270 does not require proof of the accused's blood alcohol level at the time of the offense but simply mandates a minimum sentence if the accused has been convicted of driving while intoxicated and his blood alcohol level, as indicated by the chemical test, exceeded the threshold level. Wimbish v. Commonwealth, 51 Va. App. 474, 658 S.E.2d 715, 2008 Va. App. LEXIS 168 (2008).

The purpose of this statute is to enable the court or jury to impose a heavier punishment when the accused is tried for and convicted of an offense charged as a second or subsequent offense. To effect this purpose, the prior offense must be charged and proven by the Commonwealth. Meredith v. Commonwealth, No. 1117-93-3 (Ct. of Appeals Jan. 10, 1995).

Trial court or jury has discretion to set amount of fine. — Subsection C of § 18.2-270 sets a mandatory minimum fine of $1,000. The plain, obvious, and rational meaning of "mandatory minimum fine of $1,000" is that the trial court or jury has the discretion to impose a pecuniary punishment greater than $1,000, and nothing in the statute supports a different conclusion. Neria v. Commonwealth, — Va. App. —, — S.E.2d —, 2009 Va. App. LEXIS 136 (Mar. 24, 2009).

Jury had the discretion under subsection C of § 18.2-270 to fine defendant $2,500 for his fourth offense under § 18.2-266. By setting a mandatory minimum fine of $1,000, subsection C gave a jury the discretion to impose a larger fine, and as the more specific statute, it controlled over § 18.2-10, which applied to Class 6 felonies in general. Neria v. Commonwealth, — Va. App. —, — S.E.2d —, 2009 Va. App. LEXIS 136 (Mar. 24, 2009).

Specific fine provisions prevail over general provisions. — Fine provisions of subsection C of § 18.2-270 and subdivision (f) of § 18.2-10 directly conflict with each other. Because the provisions cannot be harmonized, the more specific statute, subsection C of § 18.2-270, prevails. Neria v. Commonwealth, — Va. App. —, — S.E.2d —, 2009 Va. App. LEXIS 136 (Mar. 24, 2009).

The provisions of this section are dependent upon the nature of the charge contained in the warrant or indictment, and deal with the punishment to be fixed by the court or jury. Commonwealth v. Ellett, 174 Va. 403, 4 S.E.2d 762 (1939).

And to impose the heavier punishment prior offense must be charged. — The purpose of this section is to enable the court or jury to impose a heavier punishment when the accused is tried for and convicted of an offense charged as a second or subsequent offense. To effect this purpose, the prior offense must be charged and proven. Commonwealth v. Ellett, 174 Va. 403, 4 S.E.2d 762 (1939).

For the heavier punishment to be imposed by jury or a court trying a case without a jury, the prior offenses must be charged and proven. Calfee v. Commonwealth, 215 Va. 253, 208 S.E.2d 740 (1974).

Trial court's judgment of conviction was reversed and defendant's case was remanded to the trial court for resentencing in a case where defendant had been convicted of a third DWI within a 10-year period and had been sentenced in accordance with the enhanced punishment provisions of § 18.2-270; the Commonwealth did not prove that defendant had been previously convicted of a second offense of driving while intoxicated within a five-year period, as the evidence at most disclosed that defendant had been arraigned in the earlier proceeding and found guilty of "DWI, 2nd offense," and not the second offense of driving while intoxicated within a five-year period that would be needed to enhance the punishment in the current case. Stewart v. Commonwealth, 2007 Va. App. LEXIS 104 (Mar. 20, 2007).

Applicability of mandatory incarceration periods. — Upon a conviction under § 18.2-266 where proof of a defendant's blood alcohol level is by a valid chemical breath or blood test, § 18.2-270 applies; to hold otherwise would defeat the purpose of § 18.2-270. Thus, the enhanced penalty provided for in § 18.2-270(A) for defendants with breath alcohol readings in excess of 0.15 applied to defendant's sentence for driving while intoxicated in violation of § 18.2-266. United States v. Barber, 360 F. Supp. 2d 784, 2005 U.S. Dist. LEXIS 4640 (E.D. Va. 2005).

County ordinance held invalid. — County ordinance which provided for a lesser punishment than that provided by general law was invalid. Commonwealth v. Holtz, 12 Va. App. 1151, 408 S.E.2d 561 (1991).

County ordinance held valid. — In adopting by reference all provisions of state statute prohibiting driving while under the influence, the county effectively adopted the same penalty provided in the state statute, and the county ordinance was valid. Commonwealth v. Howell, 20 Va. App. 732, 460 S.E.2d 614 (1995).

Judicial notice of city ordinances. — Defendant's assertion that subsection C of § 18.2-270 was void for vagueness, failed because the disputed levels of punishment for driving while intoxicated were clearly proscribed by the statute. Cubitt v. Commonwealth, No. 3462-01-1, 2002 Va. App. LEXIS 747 (Ct. of Appeals Dec. 17, 2002).

Sufficiency of reference to subsequent offense. — The charge of "SUBSEQUENT OFFENSE" DUI in violation of § 18.2-266 and the pretrial notice from the commonwealth's attorney that the prosecution was for third offense were sufficient to notify a defendant that the charge against him was for a third offense or subsequent offense. Thieman v. Commonwealth, No. 1404-99-3, 2000 Va. App. LEXIS 713 (Ct. of Appeals Nov. 7, 2000).

The purposes of an allegation in a warrant or indictment that an accused has been previously convicted of a similar offense are to put him on notice that proof of his prior conviction will be introduced in evidence and to permit the imposition of a heavier punishment if the second or subsequent offense is proved. Calfee v. Commonwealth, 215 Va. 253, 208 S.E.2d 740 (1974).

Conviction under statute which might not result in conviction under this section not "substantially conforming." — If a person may be convicted of an offense under another jurisdiction's statute for conduct which might not result in a conviction under this section, the statutes are not "substantially conforming." Cox v. Commonwealth, 13 Va. App. 328, 411 S.E.2d 444 (1991).

Assimilation of sentencing ranges under the Assimilative Crimes Act. — District court applied federal sentencing policy and law in imposing a home detention as defendant's sentence for driving while his blood alcohol was in excess of 0.08 grams per 210 liters of breath on a military base, but § 18.2-270 was assimilated under the Assimilative Crimes Act, 18 U.S.C.S. § 13 and dictated the minimum and maximum statutory terms of confinement. United States v. Montigue, 357 F. Supp. 2d 939, 2005 U.S. Dist. LEXIS 2450 (E.D. Va. 2005).

Defendant's sentence of 27 months imprisonment for drunk driving and for driving with a suspended license fell below the midpoint of the range prescribed by § 18.2-266 and subdivision C 1 of § 18.2-270, and because the sentence fell within the state-prescribed range, it was consonant with the Assimilative Crimes Act's "like punishment" requirement. United States v. Finley, 531 F.3d 288, 2008 U.S. App. LEXIS 13762 (4th Cir. 2008).

Magistrate was bound by the mandatory minimum sentence. — In the context of the Assimilated Crimes Act, 18 U.S.C.S. § 13, defendant did not point to a single federal policy that Virginia's driving while intoxicated offense and its associated penalties conflicted with and as there was no justification for casting aside the mandatory minimum sentence prescribed by Virginia law, defendant was subject to the mandatory minimum sentence of twenty days imprisonment. United States v. Clark, 361 F. Supp. 2d 502, 2005 U.S. Dist. LEXIS 4230 (E.D. Va. 2005).

Defendant argued that, even if federal courts were bound by the mandatory minimum penalty, the sentence imposed by the magistrate judge was a lawful substitute for imprisonment under the Schedule of Substitute Punishments contained in U.S. Sentencing Guidelines Manual § 5C1.1(e); defendant's contention that confinement to the enclave qualified as home confinement was rejected as confinement to the enclave was not confinement at all; when a person was free to go where he pleased, he was not detained. United States v. Clark, 361 F. Supp. 2d 502, 2005 U.S. Dist. LEXIS 4230 (E.D. Va. 2005).

Jury instructions omitting minimum fine did not require new sentencing proceeding. — Although a jury instruction erroneously left out the mandatory minimum fine of $1,000 under subsection C of § 18.2-270, defendant, who was fined $2,500, was not entitled to a new sentencing proceeding. The punishment fit within the statutory requirements of subsection C, which required a fine of at least $1,000, and did not prejudice defendant. Neria v. Commonwealth, — Va. App. —, — S.E.2d —, 2009 Va. App. LEXIS 136 (Mar. 24, 2009).

Burden of proving conviction under substantially similar law. — The Commonwealth bears the burden of proving that an out-of-state conviction was obtained under laws substantially similar to those of the Commonwealth. Shinault v. Commonwealth, 228 Va. 269, 321 S.E.2d 652 (1984).

Substantially similar law proven. — Trial court did not err in treating defendant's California driving under the influence conviction as a predicate offense for a recidivism enhancement to her Virginia DUI punishment under subdivision B 3 of § 18.2-270 because the California's DUI statute was substantially similar to § 18.2-266 where in neither statute were the blood alcohol concentration presumptions mandatory or conclusive. Taylor v. Commonwealth, 2010 Va. App. LEXIS 96 (Mar. 16, 2010).

North Carolina statute not substantially similar to § 18.2-269 A 3. — Under subdivision A 3 of § 18.2-269 of the Code of Virginia, an accused may present evidence to rebut the presumption, and if such evidence creates a reasonable doubt as to his guilt, the fact finder must acquit. In North Carolina, however, mere proof that an accused's blood alcohol is 0.10 percent is conclusive as to guilt. With such a fundamental difference, the North Carolina statute (§ 20-138.1 of the General Statutes of North Carolina) is not substantially similar within the meaning of this section. Shinault v. Commonwealth, 228 Va. 269, 321 S.E.2d 652 (1984).

Insufficient showing of similarity of foreign law. — Where defendant was convicted for a second and subsequent offense of driving under the influence of intoxicants, a prior conviction for drunk driving in North Carolina which was shown on a certified transcript of the defendant's driving record prepared by the Virginia Division of Motor Vehicles (now Department of Motor Vehicles) was insufficient to carry the Commonwealth's burden of proving substantial similarity and to shift to the defendant the burden of going forward with the evidence of dissimilarity. Rufty v. Commonwealth, 221 Va. 836, 275 S.E.2d 584 (1981).

Trial court erred by imposing an enhanced sentence, pursuant to subsection C of § 18.2-270, against a defendant based upon his prior conviction for DWI under 36 C.F.R. § 4.23(a)(2) where said regulation was not substantially similar to a conviction under § 18.2-266, as a conviction under federal law did not translate into a conviction under the state law. Corey v. Commonwealth, No. 0421-02-4, 2003 Va. App. LEXIS 582 (Ct. of Appeals Nov. 12, 2003).

In a DUI second offense trial, the burden is on the Commonwealth to prove the prior conviction beyond a reasonable doubt. McBride v. Commonwealth, 24 Va. App. 30, 480 S.E.2d 126 (1997).

Prior conviction could be used where Commonwealth presented proof of representation by appointed counsel. — Defendant's second conviction for driving under the influence of alcohol was properly considered in applying the enhanced sentencing provisions of subdivision C 1 because the Commonwealth, in addition to relying on the presumption of regularity of court proceedings, presented evidence that the court had appointed counsel to represent defendant at the second prosecution and introduced a time sheet signed by appointed counsel, requesting compensation for in-court and out-of-court services rendered during counsel's representation of defendant. Tweedy v. Commonwealth, 2009 Va. App. LEXIS 192 (Apr. 28, 2009).

Prior conviction arose out of same act or acts. — Section 19.2-294.1 required the dismissal of defendant's indictment for felony driving under the influence, fourth offense, in violation of §§ 18.2-266 and 18.2-270 because defendant had been previously convicted of reckless driving in the general district court arising out of the same act or acts that were the basis of the felony indictment for driving under the influence. Lawson v. Commonwealth, 61 Va. App. 292, 734 S.E.2d 714, 2012 Va. App. LEXIS 402 (2012).

Conviction of third offense upheld. — Defendant who had one conviction for driving under the influence (DUI) and was awaiting trial on a second DUI charge when he was arrested and charged with a third DUI was properly convicted of felony DUI for the third incident, pursuant to §§ 18.2-266 and 18.2-270, after he was also convicted of the second DUI charge. Williams v. Commonwealth, 38 Va. App. 414, 565 S.E.2d 328, 2002 Va. App. LEXIS 369 (2002), aff'd, 265 Va. 268, 576 S.E.2d 468 (2003).

Where an enhanced driving under the influence (DUI) punishment was statutorily activated by a conviction or an offense within 10 years pursuant to § 18.2-270, defendant could be convicted of a third offense DUI in violation of § 18.2-266 even though a trial was pending on a second offense. Williams v. Commonwealth, 265 Va. 268, 576 S.E.2d 468, 2003 Va. LEXIS 22 (2003).

Transporting child under the age of 17. — Trial court did not err in denying defendant's motion to strike, which alleged that he could not have been prosecuted for felony child abuse under subsection B of § 18.2-371.1, based on the act of transporting his son while driving under the influence, as this section simply provides an additional penalty for driving under the influence while transporting a person 17 years of age or younger and does not include within its parameters the elements of the child abuse and neglect offense. Wolfe v. Commonwealth, 42 Va. App. 776, 595 S.E.2d 27, 2004 Va. App. LEXIS 168 (2004).

Jury instructions necessary before prior conviction admissible. — A previous conviction of a similar offense is admissible when the jury is told that such evidence is admitted only for the purpose of fixing the quantum of punishment if the accused is found guilty and is not to be considered by them as evidence of guilt in the second or subsequent offense for which he is on trial. Calfee v. Commonwealth, 215 Va. 253, 208 S.E.2d 740 (1974).

Where a final order sentenced accused to thirty days instead of one month as stated in the verdict and presumably prescribed, in accordance with this section, by the town ordinance under which he was prosecuted, the judgment should be made to accord with the verdict in all necessary particulars on a retrial. Dickerson v. Town of Christiansburg, 201 Va. 342, 111 S.E.2d 292 (1959).

Evidence of prior conviction properly admitted. — Where the trial court instructed the jury that although the defendant had been previously convicted of a similar offense they should not consider this in determining his guilt or innocence of the charge they were then trying, and they were further instructed that in the event they found the defendant guilty as charged in the warrant they could consider the prior conviction in determining the quantum of his punishment, the trial court did not err in admitting evidence of defendant's prior conviction. Calfee v. Commonwealth, 215 Va. 253, 208 S.E.2d 740 (1974).

Because defendant offered no evidence rebutting the presumption of regularity attaching to previous conviction for driving under the influence of alcohol, and because evidence supported finding that defendant was represented by counsel in previous trial, the trial court did not err in admitting evidence of prior conviction to enhance penalties against defendant under "third offense" provision for DUI. Samuels v. Commonwealth, 27 Va. App. 119, 497 S.E.2d 873 (1998).

In convicting defendant of driving under the influence (DUI), the trial court did not err in admitting evidence of prior DUI conviction, as the arrest warrant constituted an official document, and the trial court properly consulted the warrant as evidence of the ordinance under which defendant was previously convicted in taking judicial notice of its provisions. Webb v. Commonwealth, No. 2749-01-2, 2003 Va. App. LEXIS 138 (Ct. of Appeals Mar. 18, 2003).

Trial court properly rejected an attempt defendant made during his trial on a charge that he drove under the influence a third or subsequent time within 10 years, to suppress two prior DUI convictions, because his argument that his earlier convictions were obtained in violation of his right to effective assistance of counsel did not rise to the level of a constitutional violation that negated those convictions, and they were not subject to collateral attack. Vester v. Commonwealth, 42 Va. App. 592, 593 S.E.2d 551, 2004 Va. App. LEXIS 99 (2004).

Under § 46.2-384, a Department of Motor Vehicles transcript, certified pursuant to § 46.2-215, was prima facie evidence of the facts stated therein and was therefore sufficient to prove defendant's prior DUI offenses and support his conviction under §§ 18.2-266 and 18.2-270. Mitchem v. Commonwealth, 2010 Va. App. LEXIS 18 (Jan. 12, 2010).

Prior convictions could not be used absent proof of rep-

resentation or waiver thereof. — Where the Commonwealth failed to prove defendant was represented by counsel in either of the prior misdemeanor DUI convictions, and failed to prove he waived his right to counsel, the two prior uncounseled misdemeanor convictions, although valid convictions since no jail time was imposed, could not be used under an enhanced penalty statute such as this section. The Commonwealth could not rely on these prior uncounseled convictions to enhance the punishment, causing defendant to be imprisoned for his third DUI conviction even though he was represented by counsel on the third offense. Sargent v. Commonwealth, 5 Va. App. 143, 360 S.E.2d 895 (1987).

Record of prior misdemeanor conviction silent on incarceration or representation. — The record of a prior misdemeanor conviction, silent with respect to related incarceration or representation of the accused by counsel, is entitled to a presumption of regularity on collateral attack in a recidivist proceeding and may provide sufficient evidence to support the imposition of enhanced punishment for a second offense DUI within five years. Nicely v. Commonwealth, 25 Va. App. 579, 490 S.E.2d 281 (1997).

Evidence of prior driving under the influence (DUI) convictions does not constitute the "traffic record" as contemplated by § 46.2-943 where the offense charged under § 18.2-266 is a subsequent offense of DUI punishable under this section. Proof of such charge requires proof of the prior DUI convictions, and a trial court, therefore, does not err in admitting evidence of a defendant's prior DUI convictions independent of his prior traffic record during the guilt stage of the trial. Farmer v. Commonwealth, 10 Va. App. 175, 390 S.E.2d 775 (1990).

Since evidence of prior driving under the influence of alcohol (DUI) convictions does not constitute the "traffic record" as contemplated by § 46.2-943 where the offense charged under § 18.2-266 is a subsequent offense of DUI punishable under this section, and since proof of such charge requires proof of prior DUI convictions, the trial court did not err in admitting evidence of defendant's prior DUI convictions independent of his prior traffic record during the guilt stage of the trial. Farmer v. Commonwealth, 12 Va. App. 337, 404 S.E.2d 371 (1991).

Evidence sufficient to prove defendant "operated" vehicle. — Defendant, who was intoxicated when he grabbed the steering wheel of a vehicle his sister was driving and caused his sister to lose control of the vehicle, was properly convicted of driving under the influence of alcohol (second or subsequent offense), in violation of § 18.2-266 and subsection B of § 18.2-270, and operating a vehicle as an habitual offender, in violation of § 46.2-357. Dugger v. Commonwealth, 40 Va. App. 586, 580 S.E.2d 477, 2003 Va. App. LEXIS 305 (2003).

Even though defendant was found unconscious in a parked vehicle, the evidence was sufficient to convict him of operating a vehicle while intoxicated because the key was in the vehicle's ignition, it was turned so that the vehicle's electrical system would work, and the vehicle's radio was on. Nelson v. Commonwealth, 2010 Va. App. LEXIS 42 (2010), aff'd, 281 Va. 212, 707 S.E.2d 815, 2011 Va. LEXIS 27 (2011).

In a prosecution on a charge of driving while intoxicated under § 18.2-266, the evidence showed that defendant "operated" his vehicle. Defendant was found inside the vehicle, and the key was in the "on" or "accessory" position, although the motor was not running; defendant's action in turning on the radio by placing the key in the "on" position of the ignition constituted manipulating the vehicle's electrical equipment. Nelson v. Commonwealth, 281 Va. 212, 707 S.E.2d 815, 2011 Va. LEXIS 27 (2011).

Sentence found to be reasonable. — District court's 15-month sentence imposed upon defendant's guilty plea to driving under the influence (third offense), a violation of 18 U.S.C.S. § 13, assimilating § 18.2-266 and subdivision B 3 of § 18.2-270, and driving on a suspended driver's license (third offense), a violation of 18 U.S.C.S. §§ 7, 13, assimilating § 46.2-301, was proper because (1) the sentence was not plainly unreasonable under 18 U.S.C.S. § 3742(e) given the district court's consideration of defendant's three drunk driving convictions in short time frame; (2) the district court also considered the provisions under 18 U.S.C.S. § 3553 in imposing sentence; and (3) allowing the 15-month sentence to run consecutive to the sentence he was serving for violating his probation was not plain error under U.S. Sentencing Guidelines Manual § 5G1.3, cmt., application n. 3(C). United States v. Floresdelgado, 2005 U.S. App. LEXIS 6121 (4th Cir. Apr. 13, 2005).

Electronic home monitoring not available for mandatory minimum sentence. — Defendant was not entitled to serve a 90-day mandatory minimum sentence on electronic home monitoring, pursuant to § 53.1-131.2, upon conviction of driving under the influence, third offense, because the mandatory minimum could not have been served on probation or suspended and, thus, electronic home monitoring was not available. McNeil v. Commonwealth, 2009 Va. App. LEXIS 427 (Sept. 29, 2009).

Denial of bifurcation not error — Where defendant was charged with operating a motor vehicle while intoxicated, the fourth offense in 10 years, the trial court did not abuse its discretion in denying a motion to bifurcate the guilt phase of the trial from the evidence of recidivism because any potential prejudice was resolved by a limiting instruction. Nelson v. Commonwealth, 2010 Va. App. LEXIS 42 (2010), aff'd, 281 Va. 212, 707 S.E.2d 815, 2011 Va. LEXIS 27 (2011).

Applied in Nash v. Commonwealth, 12 Va. App. 550, 404 S.E.2d 743 (1991); Commonwealth v. Carter, 21 Va. App. 150, 462 S.E.2d 582 (1995); Barrett v. Commonwealth, 250 Va. 243, 462 S.E.2d 109 (1995); Conkling v. Commonwealth, 45 Va. App. 518, 612 S.E.2d 235, 2005 Va. App. LEXIS 173 (2005); Roseborough v. Commonwealth, 281 Va. 233, 704 S.E.2d 414, 2011 Va. LEXIS 13 (2011).

CIRCUIT COURT OPINIONS

Constitutionality. — Presumptions of §§ 18.2-266 and 18.2-269 are permissive inferences because they do not remove the element of alcohol content from the case and do not shift the burden of persuasion to the defendant; thus, they do not violate due process or the right to confrontation. Furthermore, § 18.2-270, which relies on a violation of § 18.2-266, is not unconstitutional, as the burden of persuasion is with the Commonwealth at all times. Commonwealth v. Stump, 69 Va. Cir. 433, 2006 Va. Cir. LEXIS 95 (Roanoke 2006).

Test results. — Though alka-sensor test results were not excluded from consideration, where a defendant had no evidence showing the reliability of the 0.19 alka-sensor test that rebutted the 0.20 breathalyzer test which was confirmed, the defendant was sentenced accordingly. Commonwealth v. Pettey, 56 Va. Cir. 265, 2001 Va. Cir. LEXIS 456 (Charlottesville 2001).

§ 18.2-270.01. Multiple offenders; payment to Trauma Center Fund.

A. The court shall order any person convicted of a violation of §§ 18.2-36.1, 18.2-51.4, 18.2-266, 18.2-266.1 or § 46.2-341.24 who has been convicted previously of one or more violations of any of those sections or any ordinance, any law of another state, or any law of the United States substantially similar to the provisions of those sections within 10 years of the date of the current offense to pay $50 to the Trauma Center Fund for the purpose of defraying the costs of providing emergency medical care to victims of automobile accidents attributable to alcohol or drug use.

B. There is hereby established in the state treasury a special nonreverting fund to be known as the Trauma Center Fund. The Fund shall consist of any moneys paid into it by virtue of operation of subsection A hereof and any moneys appropriated thereto by the General Assembly and designated for the Fund. Any moneys deposited to or remaining in the Fund during or at the end of each fiscal year or biennium, including interest thereon, shall not revert to the general fund but shall remain in the Fund and be available for allocation in ensuing fiscal years. The Department of Health shall award and administer grants from the Trauma Center Fund to appropriate trauma centers based on the cost to provide emergency medical care to victims of automobile accidents. The Department of Health shall develop, on or before October 1, 2004, written criteria for the awarding of such grants that shall be evaluated and, if necessary, revised on an annual basis.

History.
2004, c. 999.

OPINIONS OF THE ATTORNEY GENERAL

Constitutionality. — Acts 2010, c. 874, as amended by Acts 2011, c. 890, § 3-6.03, is consistent with Article IV, § 12 of the Constitution of Virginia. See opinion of Attorney General to The Honorable Robert G. Marshall, Member, Virginia House of Delegates, 11-049, 2011 Va. AG LEXIS 28 (5/13/11).

§ 18.2-270.1. Ignition interlock systems; penalty.

A. For purposes of this section and § 18.2-270.2:

"*Commission*" means the Commission on VASAP.

"*Department*" means the Department of Motor Vehicles.

"*Ignition interlock system*" means a device that (i) connects a motor vehicle ignition system to an analyzer that measures a driver's blood alcohol content; (ii) prevents a motor vehicle ignition from starting if a driver's blood alcohol content exceeds 0.02 percent; and (iii) is equipped with the ability to perform a rolling retest and to electronically log the blood alcohol content during ignition, attempted ignition and rolling retest.

"*Rolling retest*" means a test of the vehicle operator's blood alcohol content required at random intervals during operation of the vehicle, which triggers the sounding of the horn and flashing of lights if (i) the test indicates that the operator has a blood alcohol content which exceeds 0.02 percent or (ii) the operator fails to take the test.

B. In addition to any penalty provided by law for a conviction under § 18.2-51.4 or 18.2-266 or a substantially similar ordinance of any county, city or town, any court of proper jurisdiction shall, as a condition of a restricted license, prohibit an offender from operating a motor vehicle that is not equipped with a functioning, certified ignition interlock system for any period of time not to exceed the period of license suspension and restriction, not less than six consecutive months without alcohol-related violations of the interlock requirements. The court shall, for a conviction under § 18.2-51.4, a second or subsequent offense of § 18.2-266 or a substantially similar ordinance of any county, city or town, or as a condition of license restoration pursuant to subsection C of § 18.2-271.1 or § 46.2-391, require that such a system be installed on each motor vehicle, as defined in § 46.2-100, owned by or registered to the offender, in whole or in part, for such period of time.

Such condition shall be in addition to any purposes for which a restricted license may be issued pursuant to § 18.2-271.1. The court may order the installation of an ignition interlock system to commence immediately upon conviction. A fee of $20 to cover court and administrative costs related to the ignition interlock system shall be paid by any such offender to the clerk of the court. The court shall require the offender to install an electronic log device with the ignition interlock system on a vehicle designated by the court to measure the blood alcohol content at each attempted ignition and random rolling retest during operation of the vehicle. The offender shall be enrolled in and supervised by an alcohol safety action program pursuant to § 18.2-271.1 and to conditions established by regulation under § 18.2-270.2 by the Commission during the period for which the court has ordered installation of the ignition interlock system. The offender shall be further required to provide to such program, at least quarterly during the period of court ordered ignition interlock installation, a printout from such electronic log indicating the offender's blood alcohol content during such ignitions, attempted ignitions, and rolling retests, and showing attempts to circumvent or tamper with the equipment.

C. In any case in which the court requires the installation of an ignition interlock system, the court shall order the offender not to operate any motor vehicle that is not equipped with such a system for the period of time that the interlock restriction is in effect. The clerk of the court shall file with the Department of Motor Vehicles a copy of the order, which shall become a part of the offender's operator's license record maintained by the Department. The Department shall issue to the offender for the period during which the interlock restriction is imposed a restricted license which shall appropriately set forth the restrictions required by the court under this subsection and any other restrictions imposed upon the offender's driving privilege, and shall also set forth any exception granted by the court under subsection F.

D. The offender shall be ordered to provide the appropriate ASAP program, within 30 days of the effective date of the order of court, proof of the installation of the ignition interlock system. The Program shall require the offender to have the system monitored and calibrated for proper operation at least every 30 days by an entity approved by the Commission under the provisions of § 18.2-270.2 and to demonstrate proof thereof. The offender shall pay the cost of leasing or buying and monitoring and maintaining the ignition interlock system. Absent good cause shown, the court may revoke the offender's driving privilege for failing to (i) timely install such system or (ii) have the system properly monitored and calibrated.

E. No person shall start or attempt to start a motor vehicle equipped with an ignition interlock system for the purpose of providing an operable motor vehicle to a person who is prohibited under this section from operating a motor vehicle that is not equipped with an ignition interlock system. No person shall tamper with, or in any way attempt to circumvent the operation of, an ignition interlock system that has been installed in the motor vehicle of a person under this section. Except as authorized in subsection G, no person shall knowingly furnish a motor vehicle not equipped with a functioning ignition interlock system to any person prohibited under subsection B from operating any motor vehicle which is not equipped with such system. A violation of this subsection is punishable as a Class 1 misdemeanor.

F. Any person prohibited from operating a motor vehicle under subsection B may, solely in the course of his employment, operate a motor vehicle which is owned or provided by his employer without installation of an ignition interlock system, if the court expressly permits such operation as a condition of a restricted license at the request of the employer, but such person may not operate a school bus, school vehicle, or a commercial motor vehicle as defined in § 46.2-341.4. This subsection shall not apply if such employer is an entity wholly or partially owned or controlled by the person otherwise prohibited from operating a vehicle without an ignition interlock system.

G. The Commission shall promulgate such regulations and forms as are necessary to implement the procedures outlined in this section.

History.
1995, c. 486; 1996, c. 841; 1997, c. 691; 1998, cc. 783, 840; 1999, c. 734; 2000, cc. 958, 980; 2004, c. 961; 2007, c. 686; 2008, c. 862; 2012, cc. 141, 570.

Editor's note.
Acts 2008, c. 862, which amended subsection F, in cl. 2 provides: "That the provisions of this act shall become effective on October 1, 2008."

Acts 2008, c. 862, cl. 3, provides: "That no general fund appropriations shall be used by any agency or program to cover the costs of leasing, buying, monitoring, maintaining, or installing ignition interlock systems on vehicles owned or operated by persons found by the court to be indigent."

The 2008 amendments.
The 2008 amendment by c. 862, effective October, 1, 2008, inserted "school bus, school vehicle, or a" preceding "commerical motor vehicle" in the first sentence in subsection F.

The 2012 amendments.
The 2012 amendments by cc. 141 and 570 are identical, and in subsection B, divided the former first sentence into the present first and second sentences by substituting "The court shall, for a conviction under § 18.2-51.4, a second or subsequent offense under § 18.2-266 or a substantially similar ordinance of any county, city or town, or as a condition of license restoration pursuant to subsection C of § 18.2-271.1 or § 46.2-391" for "and shall" and substituted "shall, as a condition of a restricted license" for "(i) may, for a first offense, (ii) shall, for a second or subsequent offense and, (iii) shall, for an offense where an offender's blood alcohol content equals or exceeds 0.15 percent, as a condition of a restricted license or as a condition of license restoration under subsection C of § 18.2-271.1 or 46.2-391" near the beginning of the first sentence; and in subsection C, in the first sentence, substituted "shall order" for "shall direct," "that" for "which," and "the interlock restriction is in effect" for "installation is ordered" and "period during which the

interlock restriction is imposed" for "installation period required by the court" in the last sentence.

CASE NOTES

Engaging ignition interlock system constituted operation of motor vehicle. — Defendant violated a condition of probation that required that defendant be free from alcohol while operating a motor vehicle, by committing three ignition interlock violations; "operating" a motor vehicle included engaging the ignition interlock system. Gravely v. Commonwealth, No. 0430-02-3, 2003 Va. App. LEXIS 19 (Jan. 21, 2003).

OPINIONS OF THE ATTORNEY GENERAL

Authority of Commissioner of the Department of Motor Vehicles. — The Commissioner of the Department of Motor Vehicles is both authorized and mandated to impose an ignition interlock system upon an individual seeking reinstatement of a driver's license after the three-year license revocation period resulting from a conviction for driving under the influence, second or subsequent offense, when the convicting court fails to order the installation of such system. See opinion of Attorney General to The Honorable Joseph P. Johnson, Jr., Member, House of Delegates, 10-018, 2010 Va. AG LEXIS 17 (4/20/10).

§ 18.2-270.2. Ignition interlock system; certification by Commission on VASAP; regulations; sale or lease; monitoring use; reports.

A. The Executive Director of the Commission on VASAP or his designee shall, pursuant to approval by the Commission, certify ignition interlock systems for use in this Commonwealth and adopt regulations and forms for the installation, maintenance and certification of such ignition interlock systems.

The regulations adopted shall include requirements that ignition interlock systems:

1. Do not impede the safe operation of the vehicle;

2. Minimize opportunities to be bypassed, circumvented or tampered with, and provide evidence thereof;

3. Correlate accurately with established measures of blood alcohol content and be calibrated according to the manufacturer's specifications;

4. Work accurately and reliably in an unsupervised environment;

5. Have the capability to provide an accurate written measure of blood alcohol content for each ignition, attempted ignition, and rolling retest, and record each attempt to circumvent or tamper with the equipment;

6. Minimize inconvenience to other users;

7. Be manufactured or distributed by an entity responsible for installation, user training, service, and maintenance, and meet the safety and operational requirements promulgated by the National Highway Transportation Safety Administration;

8. Operate reliably over the range of motor vehicle environments or motor vehicle manufacturing standards;

9. Be manufactured by an entity which is adequately insured against liability, in an amount established by the Commission, including product liability and installation and maintenance errors;

10. Provide for an electronic log of the driver's experience with the system with an information management system capable of electronically delivering information to the agency supervising the interlock user within twenty-four hours of the collection of such information from the datalogger; and

11. Provide for a rolling retest of the operator's blood alcohol content.

Such regulations shall also provide for the establishment of a fund, using a percentage of fees received by the manufacturer or distributor providing ignition interlock services, to afford persons found by the court to be indigent all or part of the costs of an ignition interlock system.

The Commission shall design and adopt a warning label to be affixed to an ignition interlock system upon installation. The warning label shall state that a person tampering with, or attempting to circumvent the ignition interlock system shall be guilty of a Class 1 misdemeanor and, upon conviction, shall be subject to a fine or incarceration or both.

The Commission shall publish a list of certified ignition interlock systems and shall ensure that such systems are available throughout the Commonwealth. The local alcohol safety action program shall make the list available to eligible offenders, who shall have the responsibility and authority to choose which certified ignition interlock company will supply the offender's equipment. A manufacturer or distributor of an ignition interlock system that seeks to sell or lease the ignition interlock system to persons subject to the provisions of § 18.2-270.1 shall pay the reasonable costs of obtaining the required certification, as set forth by the Commission.

B. A person may not sell or lease or offer to sell or lease an ignition interlock system to any person subject to the provisions of § 18.2-270.1 unless:

1. The system has been certified by the Commission; and

2. The warning label adopted by the Commission is affixed to the system.

C. A manufacturer or distributor of an ignition interlock system shall provide such services as may be required at no cost to the Commonwealth. Such services shall include a toll free, twenty-four-hour telephone number for the users of ignition interlock systems.

History.
1995, c. 486; 2000, cc. 341, 362.

OPINIONS OF THE ATTORNEY GENERAL

Regulations to govern the certification of ignition interlock systems must be adopted by the Commission on the Virginia Alcohol Safety Action Program. Any regulatory scheme must allow for multiple vendors of ignition interlock systems if in fact their systems meet such certification requirements. See opinion of Attorney General to The Honorable H. Morgan Griffith, Member, House of Delegates, 08-026 (5/5/08).

Authority of Commissioner of the Department of Motor Vehicles. — The Commissioner of the Department of Motor Vehicles is both authorized and mandated to impose an ignition interlock system upon an individual seeking reinstatement of a driver's license after the three-year license revocation period resulting from a conviction for driving under the influence, second or subsequent offense, when the convicting court fails to order the installation of such system. See opinion of Attorney General to The Honorable Joseph P. Johnson, Jr., Member, House of Delegates, 10-018, 2010 Va. AG LEXIS 17 (4/20/10).

§ 18.2-271. Forfeiture of driver's license for driving while intoxicated.

A. Except as provided in § 18.2-271.1, the judgment of conviction if for a first offense under § 18.2-266 or for a similar offense under any county, city, or town ordinance, or for a first offense under subsection A of § 46.2-341.24, shall of itself operate to deprive the person so convicted of the privilege to drive or operate any motor vehicle, engine or train in the Commonwealth for a period of one year from the date of such judgment. This suspension period shall be in addition to the suspension period provided under § 46.2-391.2.

B. If a person (i) is tried on a process alleging a second offense of violating § 18.2-266 or subsection A of § 46.2-341.24, or any substantially similar local ordinance, or law of any other jurisdiction, within ten years of a first offense for which the person was convicted, or found guilty in the case of a juvenile, under § 18.2-266 or subsection A of § 46.2-341.24 or any valid local ordinance or any law of any other jurisdiction substantially similar to § 18.2-266 or subsection A of § 46.2-341.24 and (ii) is convicted thereof, such conviction shall of itself operate to deprive the person so convicted of the privilege to drive or operate any motor vehicle, engine or train in the Commonwealth for a period of three years from the date of the judgment of conviction and such person shall have his license revoked as provided in subsection A of § 46.2-391. The court trying such case shall order the surrender of the person's driver's license, to be disposed of in accordance with § 46.2-398, and shall notify such person that his license has been revoked for a period of three years and that the penalty for violating that revocation is as set out in § 46.2-391. This suspension period shall be in addition to the suspension period provided under § 46.2-391.2. Any period of license suspension or revocation imposed pursuant to this section, in any case, shall run consecutively with any period of suspension for failure to permit a blood or breath sample to be taken as required by §§ 18.2-268.1 through 18.2-268.12 or §§ 46.2-341.26:1 through 46.2-341.26:11 or any period of suspension for a previous violation of § 18.2-266, 18.2-266.1, or 46.2-341.24.

C. If a person (i) is tried on a process alleging (a) a felony conviction of § 18.2-266 or (b) a third or subsequent offense of violating § 18.2-266 or subsection A of § 46.2-341.24, or any substantially

similar local ordinance, or law of any other jurisdiction, within 10 years of two other offenses for which the person was convicted, or found not innocent in the case of a juvenile, under § 18.2-266 or subsection A of § 46.2-341.24 or any valid local ordinance or any law of any other jurisdiction substantially similar to § 18.2-266 or subsection A of § 46.2-341.24 and (ii) is convicted thereof, such conviction shall of itself operate to deprive the person so convicted of the privilege to drive or operate any motor vehicle, engine or train in the Commonwealth and such person shall not be eligible for participation in a program pursuant to § 18.2-271.1 and shall, upon such conviction, have his license revoked as provided in subsection B of § 46.2-391. The court trying such case shall order the surrender of the person's driver's license, to be disposed of in accordance with § 46.2-398, and shall notify such person that his license has been revoked indefinitely and that the penalty for violating that revocation is as set out in § 46.2-391.

D. Notwithstanding any other provision of this section, the period of license revocation or suspension shall not begin to expire until the person convicted has surrendered his license to the court or to the Department of Motor Vehicles.

E. The provisions of this section shall not apply to, and shall have no effect upon, any disqualification from operating a commercial motor vehicle imposed under the provisions of the Commercial Driver's License Act (§ 46.2-341.1 et seq.).

History.

Code 1950, § 18.1-59; 1960, c. 358; 1962, c. 625; 1964, c. 240; 1972, c. 757; 1975, cc. 14, 15; 1982, c. 301; 1983, c. 504; 1984, cc. 623, 673; 1989, c. 705; 1990, c. 949; 1992, cc. 722, 830, 891; 1994, cc. 359, 363; 2000, cc. 956, 982; 2001, c. 739; 2002, c. 873; 2010, c. 521; 2013, cc. 415, 655.

Cross references.

For authority of court to suspend the driver's license of an individual upon the conviction of a traffic offense that causes the death of a person under certain circumstances, and where appropriate to issue a restricted license for the purposes set forth in § 18.2-271.1 E, see § 46.2-396.1.

Editor's note.

Acts 2002, c. 811, cl. 2, provides: "That a court shall not transmit to the Department of Motor Vehicles (i) an order of conviction or abstract of conviction for a second violation of § 18.2-266 or a substantially similar local ordinance, as described in subsection B of § 18.2-271, unless the defendant was tried and convicted on a process alleging such a second offense, nor (ii) an order of conviction or abstract of conviction for a third or subsequent violation of § 18.2-266 or substantially similar local ordinance, as described in subsection C of § 18.2-271, unless the defendant was tried and convicted on a process alleging such a third or subsequent offense. However, when such conviction is upon a process other than as described in subsection B or C of § 18.2-271, the court shall transmit such order or abstract as an initial violation. Upon receipt of a conviction of a second offense transmitted pursuant to subsection B of § 18.2-271, the Commissioner of Motor Vehicles shall revoke the driver's license of an individual in accordance with subsection A of § 46.2-391. Upon receipt of a conviction of a third or subsequent offense transmitted pursuant to subsection C of § 18.2-271, the Commissioner shall revoke the driver's license of an individual in accordance with subsection B of § 46.2-391.

"The Commissioner shall not revoke the driver's license of an individual under subsections A or B of § 46.2-391 if the court fails to comply with the requirements set forth in the above paragraph."

Acts 2013, cc. 415 and 655, cl. 2 provides: "That the provisions of this act may result in a net increase in periods of imprisonment or commitment. Pursuant to § 30-19.1:4, the estimated amount of the necessary appropriation cannot be determined for periods of imprisonment in state adult correctional facilities; therefore, Chapter 3 of the Acts of Assembly of 2012, Special Session I, requires the Virginia Criminal Sentencing Commission to assign a minimum fiscal impact of $50,000. Pursuant to § 30-19.1:4, the estimated amount of the necessary appropriation is $0 for periods of commitment to the custody of the Department of Juvenile Justice."

The 2010 amendments.

The 2010 amendment by c. 521 inserted "or any period of suspension for a previous violation of § 18.2-266, 18.2-266.1, or 46.2-341.24" at the end of subsection B.

The 2013 amendments.

The 2013 amendments by cc. 415 and 655 are identical, and inserted "(a) a felony conviction of § 18.2-266 or (b)" near the beginning of subsection C, and made a minor stylistic change.

Law Review.

For survey of Virginia criminal law and procedure for the year 1969-1970, see 56 Va. L. Rev. 1572 (1970). For survey of Virginia criminal law for the year 1971-1972, see 58 Va. L. Rev. 1206 (1972). For comment on 1982 amendments to Virginia's driving while intoxicated laws, see 17 U. Rich. L. Rev. 189 (1982). For 2007 annual survey article, "Criminal Law and Procedure," see 42 U. Rich. L. Rev. 311 (2007).

Michie's Jurisprudence.

For related discussion, see 2B M.J. Automobiles, § 118; 5B M.J. Criminal Procedure, § 75.

CASE NOTES

Editor's note.

The cases below were decided prior to subsequent amendments to this section.

Purpose. — The purpose of this section is to deprive the convicted person of the right to secure a permit to operate a vehicle for a specified time after he has been convicted once or more than once. Commonwealth v. Ellett, 174 Va. 403, 4 S.E.2d 762 (1939).

The purpose of §§ 18.2-266 and 18.2-270 through 18.2-273 is not only to punish drunken drivers, but to prevent such drivers from using the highways to the hazard of other citizens. Commonwealth v. Ellett, 174 Va. 403, 4 S.E.2d 762 (1939).

Provisions self-executing. — The provisions of this section become effective only after judgments of conviction, and then are self-executing. Commonwealth v. Ellett, 174 Va. 403, 4 S.E.2d 762 (1939).

Procedure after ordering suspension of license. — While a court suspends a driver's license under the provisions of § 18.2-271, the court must follow the procedure mandated in § 46.2-398 after ordering the suspension of the license. Corbin v. Commonwealth, 44 Va. App. 196, 604 S.E.2d 111, 2004 Va. App. LEXIS 516 (2004).

The loss of the right to operate a vehicle is no part of the judgment of conviction, or the punishment fixed by the court or jury, and no action or order of the court or other officer is required to put it into effect. It is not dependent upon evidence necessary to convict. Evidence of conviction alone is essential. Commonwealth v. Ellett, 174 Va. 403, 4 S.E.2d 762 (1939).

No equal protection violation. — Prohibition against granting defendant, who was found guilty of driving while his blood alcohol concentration was in excess of .10, a restricted driving permit to operate a commercial motor vehicle, as defined in the Virginia Commercial Driver's License Act, during his employment hours did not deny him equal protection of the laws although other persons may be permitted to drive noncommercial motor vehicles during the hours of such person's employment if the operation of a motor vehicle is a necessary incident of such employment, even if defendant was similarly situated to a person who drives as a part of his or her employment but does not hold a commercial driver's

license. Lockett v. Commonwealth, 17 Va. App. 488, 438 S.E.2d 497 (1993).

"Subsequent offense" need not have been tried as a "second offense." — This section makes a conviction under § 18.2-266 following a conviction for the former violation of a similar act a "subsequent offense," whether or not it was tried as a "second offense." Commonwealth v. Ellett, 174 Va. 403, 4 S.E.2d 762 (1939).

Error in imposing penalty for second offense DUI when conviction was first offense DUI. — Trial court erred when it imposed the penalty for second offense driving under the influence of alcohol (DUI) when, although he was charged with second offense, his conviction was for first offense DUI. Snead v. County of Chesterfield, No. 0865-90-2 (Ct. of Appeals June 4, 1991).

Correction of sentence after grant of appeal. — Where an appeal from conviction for driving under the influence was granted in part to consider the legality of the court's sentence, it was proper for the circuit court subsequent to granting an appeal, to correct the sentence to conform with this section by entering an order nunc pro tunc changing the license revocation period from 12 to six months. Wheeling v. City of Roanoke, 2 Va. App. 42, 341 S.E.2d 389 (1986).

Sufficient evidence for conviction. — Defendant's conviction for driving on a revoked operator's license was upheld where: (1) there was no evidence that the general district court did not forward notice of the conviction to the Department of Motor Vehicles (DMV) or that the DMV did not revoke defendant's driver's license; (2) defendant pled guilty to two prior convictions under § 18.2-266 and signed a DC-210 form that gave him notice that he was unable to operate a motor vehicle for three years and listed the possible penalties for driving after the conviction; and (3) it was undisputed that defendant knew he was forbidden to drive. Smith v. Commonwealth, 44 Va. App. 189, 604 S.E.2d 108, 2004 Va. App. LEXIS 509 (2004).

Applied in Wheeling v. City of Roanoke, 2 Va. App. 42, 341 S.E.2d 389 (1986).

OPINIONS OF THE ATTORNEY GENERAL

Calculation of 20-year period for revocation of driver's license upon second conviction. — The 10-year period specified in subsection B for revocation of a driver's license upon a second conviction of driving under the influence of alcohol or drugs is calculated from the first to the second conviction, in the case of an adult, or between two findings of guilt, in the case of a juvenile. See opinion of Attorney General to The Honorable Harry J. Parrish, Member, House of Delegates, 00-102 (1/16/01).

§ 18.2-271.1. Probation, education and rehabilitation of person charged or convicted; person convicted under law of another state.

A. Any person convicted of a first or second offense of § 18.2-266 (i), (ii), (iii), or (iv), or any ordinance of a county, city, or town similar to the provisions thereof, or provisions of subsection A of § 46.2-341.24, shall be required by court order, as a condition of probation or otherwise, to enter into and successfully complete an alcohol safety action program in the judicial district in which such charge is brought or in any other judicial district upon such terms and conditions as the court may set forth. However, upon motion of a person convicted of any such offense following an assessment of the person conducted by an alcohol safety action program, the court, for good cause, may decline to order participation in such a program if the assessment by the alcohol safety action program indicates that intervention is not appropriate for such person. In no event shall such persons be permitted to enter any such program which is not certified as meeting minimum standards and criteria established by the Commission on the Virginia Alcohol Safety Action Program (VASAP) pursuant to subsection H of this section and to § 18.2-271.2. However, any person charged with a violation of a first or second offense of § 18.2-266 (i), (ii), (iii), or (iv), or any ordinance of a county, city, or town similar to the provisions thereof, or provisions of subsection A of § 46.2-341.24, may, at any time prior to trial, enter into an alcohol safety action program in the judicial district in which such charge is brought or in any other judicial district. Any person who enters into such program prior to trial may pre-qualify with the program to have an ignition interlock system installed on any motor vehicle owned or operated by him. However, no ignition interlock company shall install an ignition interlock system on any such vehicle until a court issues to the person a restricted license with the ignition interlock restriction.

B. The court shall require the person entering such program under the provisions of this section to pay a fee of no less than $250 but no more than $300. A reasonable portion of such fee, as may be determined by the Commission on VASAP, but not to exceed 10 percent, shall be forwarded monthly to be deposited with the State Treasurer for expenditure by the Commission on VASAP, and the balance shall be held in a separate fund for local administration of driver alcohol rehabilitation programs. Upon a positive finding that the defendant is indigent, the court may reduce or waive the fee. In addition to the costs of the proceeding, fees as may reasonably be required of defendants referred for intervention under any such program may be charged.

C. Upon conviction of a violation of § 18.2-266 or any ordinance of a county, city or town similar to the provisions thereof, or subsection A of § 46.2-341.24, the court shall impose the sentence authorized by § 18.2-270 or 46.2-341.28 and the license revocation as authorized by § 18.2-271. In addition, if the conviction was for a second offense committed within less than 10 years after a first such offense, the court shall order that restoration of the person's license to drive be conditioned upon the installation of an ignition interlock system on each motor vehicle, as defined in § 46.2-100, owned by or registered to the person, in whole or in part, for a period of six months beginning at the end of the three year license revocation, unless such a system has already been installed for six months prior to that time pursuant to a restricted license order under subsection E of this section. Upon a finding that a person so convicted is required to participate in the program described herein, the court shall enter the conviction on the warrant, and shall note that the person so convicted has been referred to such program. The court may then proceed to issue an order in accordance with subsection E of this section, if the court finds that the person so convicted is eligible for a restricted license. If the court finds good cause for a

person not to participate in such program or subsequently that such person has violated, without good cause, any of the conditions set forth by the court in entering the program, the court shall dispose of the case as if no program had been entered, in which event the revocation provisions of § 46.2-389 and subsection A of § 46.2-391 shall be applicable to the conviction. The court shall, upon final disposition of the case, send a copy of its order to the Commissioner of the Department of Motor Vehicles. If such order provides for the issuance of a restricted license, the Commissioner of the Department of Motor Vehicles, upon receipt thereof, shall issue a restricted license. Appeals from any such disposition shall be allowed as provided by law. The time within which an appeal may be taken shall be calculated from the date of the final disposition of the case or any motion for rehearing, whichever is later.

D. Any person who has been convicted in another state of the violation of a law of such state substantially similar to the provisions of § 18.2-266 or subsection A of § 46.2-341.24, and whose privilege to operate a motor vehicle in this Commonwealth is subject to revocation under the provisions of § 46.2-389 and subsection A of § 46.2-391, may petition the general district court of the county or city in which he resides that he be given probation and assigned to a program as provided in subsection A of this section and that, upon entry into such program, he be issued an order in accordance with subsection E of this section. If the court finds that such person would have qualified therefor if he had been convicted in this Commonwealth of a violation of § 18.2-266 or subsection A of § 46.2-341.24, the court may grant the petition and may issue an order in accordance with subsection E of this section as to the period of license suspension or revocation imposed pursuant to § 46.2-389 or subsection A of § 46.2-391. Such order shall be conditioned upon the successful completion of a program by the petitioner. If the court subsequently finds that such person has violated any of the conditions set forth by the court, the court shall dispose of the case as if no program had been entered and shall notify the Commissioner, who shall revoke the person's license in accordance with the provisions of § 46.2-389 or subsection A of § 46.2-391. A copy of the order granting the petition or subsequently revoking or suspending such person's license to operate a motor vehicle shall be forthwith sent to the Commissioner of the Department of Motor Vehicles.

No period of license suspension or revocation shall be imposed pursuant to this subsection which, when considered together with any period of license suspension or revocation previously imposed for the same offense in any state, results in such person's license being suspended for a period in excess of the maximum periods specified in this subsection.

E. Except as otherwise provided herein, whenever a person enters a certified program pursuant to this section, and such person's license to operate a motor vehicle, engine or train in the Commonwealth has been suspended or revoked, the court may, in its discretion and for good cause shown, provide that such person be issued a restricted permit to operate a motor vehicle for any of the following purposes: (i) travel to and from his place of employment; (ii) travel to and from an alcohol rehabilitation or safety action program; (iii) travel during the hours of such person's employment if the operation of a motor vehicle is a necessary incident of such employment; (iv) travel to and from school if such person is a student, upon proper written verification to the court that such person is enrolled in a continuing program of education; (v) travel for health care services, including medically necessary transportation of an elderly parent or, as designated by the court, any person residing in the person's household with a serious medical problem upon written verification of need by a licensed health professional; (vi) travel necessary to transport a minor child under the care of such person to and from school, day care, and facilities housing medical service providers; (vii) travel to and from court-ordered visitation with a child of such person; (viii) travel to a screening, evaluation and education program entered pursuant to § 18.2-251 or subsection H of § 18.2-258.1; (ix) travel to and from court appearances in which he is a subpoenaed witness or a party and appointments with his probation officer and to and from any programs required by the court or as a condition of probation; (x) travel to and from a place of religious worship one day per week at a specified time and place; (xi) travel to and from appointments approved by the Division of Child Support Enforcement of the Department of Social Services as a requirement of participation in a court-ordered intensive case monitoring program for child support for which the participant maintains written proof of the appointment, including written proof of the date and time of the appointment, on his person; (xii) travel to and from jail to serve a sentence when such person has been convicted and sentenced to confinement in jail and pursuant to § 53.1-131.1 the time to be served is on weekends or nonconsecutive days; or (xiii) travel to and from the facility that installed or monitors the ignition interlock in the person's vehicle. No restricted license issued pursuant to this subsection shall permit any person to operate a commercial motor vehicle as defined in the Virginia Commercial Driver's License Act (§ 46.2-341.1 et seq.). The court shall order the surrender of such person's license to operate a motor vehicle to be disposed of in accordance with the provisions of § 46.2-398 and shall forward to the Commissioner of the Department of Motor Vehicles a copy of its order entered pursuant to this subsection, which shall specifically enumerate the restrictions imposed and contain such information regarding the person to whom such a permit is issued as is reasonably necessary to identify such person. The court shall also provide a copy of its order to the person so

convicted who may operate a motor vehicle on the order until receipt from the Commissioner of the Department of Motor Vehicles of a restricted license, if the order provides for a restricted license for that time period. A copy of such order and, after receipt thereof, the restricted license shall be carried at all times while operating a motor vehicle. Any person who operates a motor vehicle in violation of any restrictions imposed pursuant to this section shall be guilty of a violation of § 18.2-272. Such restricted license shall be conditioned upon enrollment within 15 days in, and successful completion of, a program as described in subsection A of this section. No restricted license shall be issued during the first four months of a revocation imposed pursuant to subsection B of § 18.2-271 or subsection A of § 46.2-391 for a second offense of the type described therein committed within 10 years of a first such offense. No restricted license shall be issued during the first year of a revocation imposed pursuant to subsection B of § 18.2-271 or subsection A of § 46.2-391 for a second offense of the type described therein committed within five years of a first such offense. No restricted license shall be issued during any revocation period imposed pursuant to subsection C of § 18.2-271 or subsection B of § 46.2-391. Notwithstanding the provisions of § 46.2-411, the fee charged pursuant to § 46.2-411 for reinstatement of the driver's license of any person whose privilege or license has been suspended or revoked as a result of a violation of § 18.2-266, subsection A of § 46.2-341.24 or of any ordinance of a county, city or town, or of any federal law or the laws of any other state similar to the provisions of § 18.2-266 or subsection A of § 46.2-341.24 shall be $105. Forty dollars of such reinstatement fee shall be retained by the Department of Motor Vehicles as provided in § 46.2-411, $40 shall be transferred to the Commission on VASAP, and $25 shall be transferred to the Commonwealth Neurotrauma Initiative Trust Fund.

F. The court shall have jurisdiction over any person entering such program under any provision of this section until such time as the case has been disposed of by either successful completion of the program, or revocation due to ineligibility or violation of a condition or conditions imposed by the court, whichever shall first occur. Revocation proceedings shall be commenced by notice to show cause why the court should not revoke the privilege afforded by this section. Such notice shall be made by first-class mail to the last known address of such person, and shall direct such person to appear before the court in response thereto on a date contained in such notice, which shall not be less than 10 days from the date of mailing of the notice. Failure to appear in response to such notice shall of itself be grounds for revocation of such privilege. Notice of revocation under this subsection shall be sent forthwith to the Commissioner of the Department of Motor Vehicles.

G. For the purposes of this section, any court which has convicted a person of a violation of § 18.2-

266, subsection A of § 46.2-341.24 or any ordinance of a county, city or town similar to the provisions of § 18.2-266 shall have continuing jurisdiction over such person during any period of license revocation related to that conviction, for the limited purposes of (i) referring such person to a certified alcohol safety action program, (ii) providing for a restricted permit for such person in accordance with the provisions of subsection E, and (iii) imposing terms, conditions and limitations for actions taken pursuant to clauses (i) and (ii), whether or not it took either such action at the time of the conviction. This continuing jurisdiction is subject to the limitations of subsection E that provide that no restricted license shall be issued during a revocation imposed pursuant to subsection C of § 18.2-271 or subsection B of § 46.2-391 or during the first four months or first year, whichever is applicable, of the revocation imposed pursuant to subsection B of § 18.2-271 or subsection A of § 46.2-391. The provisions of this subsection shall apply to a person convicted of a violation of § 18.2-266, subsection A of § 46.2-341.24 or any ordinance of a county, city or town similar to the provisions of § 18.2-266 on, after and at any time prior to July 1, 2003.

H. The State Treasurer, the Commission on VASAP or any city or county is authorized to accept any gifts or bequests of money or property, and any grant, loan, service, payment or property from any source, including the federal government, for the purpose of driver alcohol education. Any such gifts, bequests, grants, loans or payments shall be deposited in the separate fund provided in subsection B.

I. The Commission on VASAP, or any county, city, town, or any combination thereof may establish and, if established, shall operate, in accordance with the standards and criteria required by this subsection, alcohol safety action programs in connection with highway safety. Each such program shall operate under the direction of a local independent policy board chosen in accordance with procedures approved and promulgated by the Commission on VASAP. Local sitting or retired district court judges who regularly hear or heard cases involving driving under the influence and are familiar with their local alcohol safety action programs may serve on such boards. The Commission on VASAP shall establish minimum standards and criteria for the implementation and operation of such programs and shall establish procedures to certify all such programs to ensure that they meet the minimum standards and criteria stipulated by the Commission. The Commission shall also establish criteria for the administration of such programs for public information activities, for accounting procedures, for the auditing requirements of such programs and for the allocation of funds. Funds paid to the Commonwealth hereunder shall be utilized in the discretion of the Commission on VASAP to offset the costs of state programs and local programs run in conjunction with any county, city or town and costs incurred by

the Commission. The Commission shall submit an annual report as to actions taken at the close of each calendar year to the Governor and the General Assembly.

J. Notwithstanding any other provisions of this section or of § 18.2-271, nothing in this section shall permit the court to suspend, reduce, limit, or otherwise modify any disqualification from operating a commercial motor vehicle imposed under the provisions of the Virginia Commercial Driver's License Act (§ 46.2-341.1 et seq.).

History.
1975, c. 601; 1976, cc. 612, 691; 1977, c. 240; 1978, c. 352; 1979, c. 353; 1980, c. 589; 1981, c. 195; 1982, c. 301; 1983, c. 504; 1984, c. 778; 1986, cc. 552, 590; 1987, cc. 465, 663; 1988, cc. 781, 858, 859, 888; 1989, c. 705; 1990, c. 949; 1991, cc. 131, 491; 1992, c. 559; 1993, cc. 527, 919; 1994, cc. 359, 363, 870; 1996, c. 984; 1997, cc. 472, 508; 1998, c. 703; 1999, c. 743; 2000, cc. 958, 970, 980; 2001, cc. 182, 645, 779; 2002, c. 806; 2003, c. 290; 2004, c. 720; 2007, cc. 194, 553; 2009, c. 295; 2010, cc. 446, 682; 2011, c. 592; 2012, cc. 141, 570.

Cross references.
As to issuance of restricted licenses in cases where court has suspended a minor's driver's license for unexcused absences from school, see § 46.2-334.001.

The 2009 amendments.
The 2009 amendment by c. 295 substituted "ten years" for "five years" in the second sentence of subsection C.

The 2010 amendments.
The 2010 amendment by c. 446 added clause (x) in subsection E.
The 2010 amendment by c. 682 added another clause (x) in subsection E, which was subsequently redesignated as clause (xi) at the direction of the Virginia Code Commission.

The 2011 amendments.
The 2011 amendment by c. 592 added clause (xii) in the first sentence in subsection E and made minor stylistic changes.

The 2012 amendments.
The 2012 amendments by cc. 141 and 570 are identical, and added the last two sentences in subsection A; and in subsection E, inserted clause (xiii) and made related changes.

Law Review.
For comment on 1982 amendments to Virginia's driving while intoxicated laws, see 17 U. Rich. L. Rev. 189 (1982).

Michie's Jurisprudence.
For related discussion, see 2B M.J. Automobiles, § 118.

CASE NOTES

Section does not limit referral to those not previously referred. — The first sentence of subsection A defines the eligibility for a referral. The second sentence merely requires that special consideration be given in the case of one who has not been referred previously. The statute does not limit eligibility for a VASAP referral to those who have not previously been so referred. Turner v. Commonwealth, 13 Va. App. 29, 408 S.E.2d 586 (1991).

Recognition of the right of municipalities to deal with the subject. — This section clearly recognizes the power, which theretofore existed in the municipalities, to adopt ordinances declaring the offense of driving vehicles or conveyances, while intoxicated, as an offense against the municipality. Shaw v. City of Norfolk, 167 Va. 346, 189 S.E. 335 (1937).

Discretion in assignments to alcohol programs. — The language "the court shall give mature consideration to the needs of such person in determining whether he be allowed to enter such program" imposes upon a court in a drunk-driving case the duty to give "good faith consideration" to a motion to assign the accused to an alcohol program authorized by this section. Midkiff v. Commonwealth, 223 Va. 1, 286 S.E.2d 150 (1982); Blevins v. Town of Marion, 226 Va. 200, 308 S.E.2d 105 (1983).

The ultimate decision whether to admit a person to a program rests in the trial court's discretion, but that discretion may only be exercised after the court gives "mature consideration to the needs of such person." Blevins v. Town of Marion, 226 Va. 200, 308 S.E.2d 105 (1983).

This section did not require the trial court to grant defendants' motions for VASAP referral. Whether to grant either motion lay within the sound discretion of the trial court. Turner v. Commonwealth, 13 Va. App. 29, 408 S.E.2d 586 (1991).

No equal protection violation. — Prohibition against granting defendant, who was found guilty of driving while his blood alcohol concentration was in excess of .10, a restricted driving permit to operate a commercial motor vehicle, as defined in the Virginia Commercial Driver's License Act, during his employment hours did not deny him equal protection of the laws although other persons may be permitted to drive noncommercial motor vehicles during the hours of such person's employment if the operation of a motor vehicle is a necessary incident of such employment, even if defendant was similarly situated to a person who drives as a part of his or her employment but does not hold a commercial driver's license. Lockett v. Commonwealth, 17 Va. App. 488, 438 S.E.2d 497 (1993).

Notice for show cause summons. — Court did not abuse its discretion by revoking three months of defendant's suspended sentence for driving under the influence because the court began the revocation proceedings by issuing a show cause summons that it mailed by first-class mail to defendant's last known address; such actions followed the exact procedure mandated by this section. Whitt v. Commonwealth, No. 0600-04-3, 2005 Va. App. LEXIS 40 (Ct. of Appeals Feb. 1, 2005).

Drinking problem not prerequisite for VASAP program. — Nothing in this section supports the view expressed by the trial judge that the VASAP program is only for people who have a drinking problem. This section is not limited to people who have a drinking problem; thus, the trial judge abused his discretion when using that view of the statute as a disqualifying factor for admission. Taylor v. Commonwealth, 12 Va. App. 419, 404 S.E.2d 78 (1991).

Ambit of the alcohol rehabilitation statute is not limited to those who plead guilty. It requires the court to give good faith consideration to a motion to be admitted to an alcohol rehabilitation program made by any convicted defendant who is a first or second offender and who has not previously entered a similar program. Blevins v. Town of Marion, 226 Va. 200, 308 S.E.2d 105 (1983).

Record disclosed no indication that the trial court gave good faith consideration to defendant's motion for admission to an alcohol rehabilitation program, where the court's remarks indicated that it deemed the defendant to be an unsuitable candidate and denied his motion upon the sole ground that he had availed himself of his constitutional right to stand upon a plea of not guilty, thus putting the prosecution to its proof. Blevins v. Town of Marion, 226 Va. 200, 308 S.E.2d 105 (1983).

Trial court should have conditioned issuance of restricted license upon enrollment in, and successful completion of, a certified Virginia Alcohol Safety Action Program (VASAP), although defendant had previously completed a VASAP program. Commonwealth v. Meadows, 17 Va. App. 624, 440 S.E.2d 154 (1994).

Effect on driving privileges. — Defendant asserted that the government's evidence constructively amended the indictment, resulting in a fatal variance; however, defendant's contention that because he received a restricted license, his license was no longer suspended, lacked merit. Even though the license was restricted, he was suspended with the restrictions and the government's evidence that defendant had a restricted license did not amount to a fatal variance from the offense charged in the indictment. United States v. Arias, — F.3d —, 2007 U.S. App. LEXIS 711 (4th Cir. Jan. 12, 2007).

OPINIONS OF THE ATTORNEY GENERAL

No authority to issue restricted operator's permit two and one-half years after conviction. — A general district court had no statutory authority to issue a restricted operator's permit to an individual whose conviction of a second offense of driving while intoxicated occurred two and one-half years earlier. See opinion of Attorney General to The Honorable Timothy S. Fisher, Judge, Seventh Judicial District of Virginia, 01-031 (12/28/01).

Authority of Commissioner of the Department of Motor Vehicles. — The Commissioner of the Department of Motor Vehicles is both authorized and mandated to impose an ignition interlock system upon an individual seeking reinstatement of a driver's license after the three-year license revocation period resulting from a conviction for driving under the influence, second or subsequent offense, when the convicting court fails to order the installation of such system. See opinion of Attorney General to The Honorable Joseph P. Johnson, Jr., Member, House of Delegates, 10-018, 2010 Va. AG LEXIS 17 (4/20/10).

§ 18.2-271.2. Commission on VASAP; purpose; membership; terms; meetings; staffing; compensation and expenses; chairman's executive summary.

A. There is hereby established in the legislative branch of state government the Commission on the Virginia Alcohol Safety Action Program (VASAP). The Commission shall administer and supervise the state system of local alcohol and safety action programs, develop and maintain operation and performance standards for local alcohol and safety action programs, and allocate funding to such programs. The Commission shall have a total membership of 15 members that shall consist of six legislative members and nine nonlegislative citizen members. Members shall be appointed as follows: four current or former members of the House Committee for Courts of Justice, to be appointed by the Speaker of the House of Delegates; two members of the Senate Committee for Courts of Justice, to be appointed by the Senate Committee on Rules; three sitting or retired judges, one each from the circuit, general district and juvenile and domestic relations district courts, who regularly hear or heard cases involving driving under the influence and are familiar with their local alcohol safety action programs, to be appointed by the Chairman of the Committee on District Courts; two directors of local alcohol safety action programs, to be appointed by the legislative members of the Commission; one representative from the law-enforcement profession, to be appointed by the Speaker of the House and one nonlegislative citizen at large, to be appointed by the Senate Committee on Rules; one representative from the Virginia Department of Motor Vehicles whose duties are substantially related to matters to be addressed by the Commission to be appointed by the Commissioner of the Department of Motor Vehicles, and one representative from the Department of Behavioral Health and Developmental Services whose duties also substantially involve such matters, to be appointed by the Commissioner of Behavioral Health and Developmental Services. Legislative members shall serve terms coincident with their terms of office. In accordance with the staggered terms previously established, nonlegislative citizen members shall serve two-year terms. All members may be reappointed. Appointments to fill vacancies, other than by expiration of a term, shall be made for the unexpired terms. Any appointment to fill a vacancy shall be made in the same manner as the original appointment.

B. The Commission shall meet at least four times each year at such places as it may from time to time designate. A majority of the members shall constitute a quorum. The Commission shall elect a chairman and vice-chairman from among its membership.

The Commission shall be empowered to establish and ensure the maintenance of minimum standards and criteria for program operations and performance, accounting, auditing, public information and administrative procedures for the various local alcohol safety action programs and shall be responsible for overseeing the administration of the statewide VASAP system. Such programs shall be certified by the Commission in accordance with procedures set forth in the Commission on VASAP Certification Manual. The Commission shall also oversee program plans, operations and performance and a system for allocating funds to cover deficits that may occur in the budgets of local programs.

C. The Commission shall appoint and employ and, at its pleasure, remove an executive director and such other persons as it may deem necessary, and determine their duties and fix their salaries or compensation.

D. The Commission shall appoint a Virginia Alcohol Safety Action Program Advisory Board to make recommendations to the Commission regarding its duties and administrative functions. The membership of such Board shall be appointed in the discretion of the Commission and include personnel from (i) local safety action programs, (ii) the State Board of Behavioral Health and Developmental Services, community services boards, or behavioral health authorities and (iii) other community mental health services organizations. An assistant attorney general who provides counsel in matters relating to driving under the influence shall also be appointed to the Board.

E. Legislative members of the Commission shall receive compensation as provided in § 30-19.12. Funding for the costs of compensation of legislative members shall be provided by the Commission. All members shall be reimbursed for all reasonable and necessary expenses as provided in §§ 2.2-2813 and 2.2-2825 to be paid out of that portion of moneys paid in VASAP defendant entry fees which is forwarded to the Virginia Alcohol Safety Action Program.

F. The chairman of the Commission shall submit to the Governor and the General Assembly an annual executive summary of the interim activity and work of the Commission no later than the first day of each regular session of the General Assembly. The executive summary shall be submitted as provided in the procedures of the Division of Legislative Automated Systems for the processing of legislative documents and reports and shall be posted on the General Assembly's website.

History.
1986, c. 580; 1988, cc. 781, 859, 888; 1990, cc. 1, 317; 1992, c. 560; 1993, c. 757; 2003, c. 885; 2005, c. 758; 2009, cc. 813, 840.

Cross references.
As to the certification of criminal justice agencies under this section see, § 9.1-101.

The 2009 amendments.
The 2009 amendments by cc. 813 and 840 are identical, and substituted "Behavioral Health and Developmental" for "Mental Health, Mental Retardation and Substance Abuse" and "Commissioner of Behavorial Health and Developmental Services" for "Commissioner of the Department of Mental Health, Mental Retardation, and Substance Abuse Services" in subsection A; and rewrote clause (ii) of subsection D, which read "state or local boards of mental health and mental retardation."

§ 18.2-271.3. Repealed by Acts 1999, c. 734.

§ 18.2-271.4. Oath of office.

Every case manager, and any other employee who is designated by the director of any VASAP-certified local alcohol safety action program operated pursuant to this article to provide probation and related services, shall take an oath of office as prescribed in § 49-1, by a person authorized to administer oaths pursuant to § 49-3, before entering the duties of his office.

History.
2001, cc. 380, 396.

§ 18.2-272. Driving after forfeiture of license.

A. Any person who drives or operates any motor vehicle, engine or train in the Commonwealth during the time for which he was deprived of the right to do so (i) upon conviction of a violation of § 18.2-268.3 or of an offense set forth in subsection E of § 18.2-270, (ii) by § 18.2-271 or 46.2-391.2, (iii) after his license has been revoked pursuant to § 46.2-389 or 46.2-391, or (iv) in violation of the terms of a restricted license issued pursuant to subsection E of § 18.2-271.1, is guilty of a Class 1 misdemeanor except as otherwise provided in § 46.2-391, and is subject to administrative revocation of his driver's license pursuant to §§ 46.2-389 and 46.2-391. Any person convicted of three violations of this section committed within a 10-year period is guilty of a Class 6 felony.

Nothing in this section or § 18.2-266, 18.2-270 or 18.2-271, shall be construed as conflicting with or repealing any ordinance or resolution of any city, town or county which restricts still further the right of such persons to drive or operate any such vehicle or conveyance.

B. Regardless of compliance with any other restrictions on his privilege to drive or operate a motor vehicle, it shall be a violation of this section for any person whose privilege to drive or operate a motor vehicle has been restricted, suspended or revoked because of a violation of § 18.2-36.1, 18.2-51.4, 18.2-266, 18.2-268.3, 46.2-341.24, or a similar ordinance or law of another state or the United States to drive or operate a motor vehicle while he has a blood alcohol content of 0.02 percent or more.

Any person suspected of a violation of this subsection shall be entitled to a preliminary breath test in accordance with the provisions of § 18.2-267, shall be deemed to have given his implied consent to have samples of his blood, breath or both taken for analysis pursuant to the provisions of § 18.2-268.2, and, when charged with a violation of this subsection, shall be subject to the provisions of §§ 18.2-268.1 through 18.2-268.12.

C. Any person who drives or operates a motor vehicle without a certified ignition interlock system as required by § 46.2-391.01 is guilty of a Class 1 misdemeanor and is subject to administrative revocation of his driver's license pursuant to §§ 46.2-389 and 46.2-391.

History.
Code 1950, § 18.1-60; 1960, c. 358; 1975, cc. 14, 15; 1988, c. 859; 1991, c. 64; 2004, cc. 948, 1013; 2005, cc. 757, 840; 2006, c. 390; 2007, c. 258; 2009, cc. 71, 255.

Editor's note.
Acts 2006, c. 390, which amended subsection A, in cl. 3 provides: "That the provisions of this act shall not become effective unless an appropriation of general funds effectuating the purposes of this act is included in the general appropriations act passed by the 2006 Session of the General Assembly, which becomes law." The funding was provided in the 2006 appropriation act. See Acts 2006, Sp. Sess. I, c. 3, Item 387 F.

The 2009 amendments.
The 2009 amendments by cc. 71 and 255 are identical, and added subsection C.

Law Review.
For 2003/2004 survey of criminal law and procedure, see 39 U. Rich. L. Rev. 133 (2004). For 2006 survey article, "Criminal Law and Procedure," see 41 U. Rich. L. Rev. 83 (2006). For 2007 annual survey article, "Criminal Law and Procedure," see 42 U. Rich. L. Rev. 311 (2007).

CASE NOTES

Right to jury trial. — Virginia Const., Art. I, § 8, and Rule 3A:13(a) guaranteed defendant a right to a jury in the trial court on both charges of driving under the influence and driving on a revoked operator's license. McCormick v. City of Virginia Beach, 5 Va. App. 369, 363 S.E.2d 124 (1987).

Effect on driving privileges. — Defendant asserted that the government's evidence constructively amended the indictment resulting in a fatal variance; however, defendant's contention that because he received a restricted license, his license was no longer suspended, lacked merit. Even though the license was restricted, he was suspended with the restrictions and the government's evidence that defendant had a restricted license did not amount to a fatal variance from the offense charged in the indictment. United States

v. Arias, — F.3d —, 2007 U.S. App. LEXIS 711 (4th Cir. Jan. 12, 2007).

Punishment provisions of this section are superseded by provisions directly related to cases involving habitual offenders— the provisions contained in § 46.2-357 under which appellant was charged. Travis v. Commonwealth, 20 Va. App. 410, 457 S.E.2d 420 (1995).

CIRCUIT COURT OPINIONS

Moped. — A "moped" is not a "motor vehicle" under § 8.2-272. Archer v. Fink, 57 Va. Cir. 354, 2002 Va. Cir. LEXIS 215 (Charlottesville 2002).

Administrative suspension of license. — Because a trial court's criminal order was not in conflict with the legislatively imposed civil suspension of driver's privilege to drive, the administrative suspension of the driver's privilege to drive was not overturned. Huff v. DMV, 58 Va. Cir. 517, 2002 Va. Cir. LEXIS 171 (Danville 2002).

OPINIONS OF THE ATTORNEY GENERAL

When vehicle may be impounded. — Because the offense of driving during a suspension period may be considered a violation of either § 46.2-301 or § 18.2-272, the vehicle being driven by an individual who commits such offense should be impounded pursuant to the former statute, without regard to whether the individual was arrested and charged under either statute. See opinion of Attorney General to The Honorable Norman deV. Morrison, Judge, Clarke County General District Court, 02-007 (4/29/02).

Arrest warrant is not sufficient for impoundment of vehicle. — An arrest warrant issued to a driver for violation of this section is not sufficient under § 46.2-301.1 for the administrative impoundment of the driver's vehicle. See opinion of Attorney General to The Honorable Archer L. Yeatts III, Chief Judge, Henrico County General District Court, 99-085 (3/10/00).

§ 18.2-273. Report of conviction to Department of Motor Vehicles.

The clerk of every court of record and the judge of every court not of record shall, within thirty days after final conviction of any person in his court under the provisions of this article, report the fact thereof and the name, post-office address and street address of such person, together with the license plate number on the vehicle operated by such person to the Commissioner of the Department of Motor Vehicles who shall preserve a record thereof in his office.

History.
Code 1950, § 18.1-61; 1960, c. 358; 1975, cc. 14, 15.

Michie's Jurisprudence.
For related discussion, see 2B M.J. Automobiles, § 118.

CASE NOTES

The Commissioner of the Division of Motor Vehicles (now Department of Motor Vehicles) has no power to hear evidence to fix the measure of guilt, nor has he the right to disregard a judgment of conviction. Commonwealth v. Ellett, 174 Va. 403, 4 S.E.2d 762 (1939).

Applied in Smith v. Commonwealth, 44 Va. App. 189, 604 S.E.2d 108, 2004 Va. App. LEXIS 509 (2004).

ARTICLE 3.

TRANSPORTING DANGEROUS ARTICLES.

§§ 18.2-274 through 18.2-278. Repealed by Acts 1980, c. 759.

Cross references.

For present provisions as to transportation of hazardous materials, see § 10.1-1450 et seq.

ARTICLE 3.1.

TRANSPORTATION OF HAZARDOUS MATERIALS.

§§ 18.2-278.1 through 18.2-278.7. Repealed by Acts 1986, c. 492.

Cross references.

As to the transportation of hazardous materials, see now § 10.1-1450 et seq.

Editor's note.

Acts 1986, c. 492 purported to repeal Article 3.1 of Chapter 7 of this title, "consisting of §§ 18.2-278.2 through 18.2-278.7." Since, however, this article also contained § 18.2-278.1, and since the language contained within this section is incorporated in § 10.1-1400, it appears that this section was also intended to have been repealed by Acts 1986, c. 492.

ARTICLE 4.

DANGEROUS USE OF FIREARMS OR OTHER WEAPONS.

Michie's Jurisprudence.

For related discussion, see 20 M.J. Weapons, §§ 4.1, 9, 12.

§ 18.2-279. Discharging firearms or missiles within or at building or dwelling house; penalty.

If any person maliciously discharges a firearm within any building when occupied by one or more persons in such a manner as to endanger the life or lives of such person or persons, or maliciously shoots at, or maliciously throws any missile at or against any dwelling house or other building when occupied by one or more persons, whereby the life or lives of any such person or persons may be put in peril, the person so offending is guilty of a Class 4 felony. In the event of the death of any person, resulting from such malicious shooting or throwing, the person so offending is guilty of murder in the second degree. However, if the homicide is willful, deliberate and premeditated, he is guilty of murder in the first degree.

If any such act be done unlawfully, but not maliciously, the person so offending is guilty of a Class 6

felony; and, in the event of the death of any person resulting from such unlawful shooting or throwing, the person so offending is guilty of involuntary manslaughter. If any person willfully discharges a firearm within or shoots at any school building whether occupied or not, he is guilty of a Class 4 felony.

History.

Code 1950, §§ 18.1-66, 18.1-152; 1960, c. 358; 1975, cc. 14, 15; 1992, c. 738; 2005, c. 143.

Cross references.

As to presumption of no bail for illegal aliens charged with certain crimes, see § 19.2-120.1.

Law Review.

For annual survey article, "Criminal Law and Procedure," see 46 U. Rich. L. Rev. 59 (2011).

CASE NOTES

Offense is a general intent offense. — The offense as defined by the statute is not a specific intent crime; rather, it is a general intent offense. Fleming v. Commonwealth, 13 Va. App. 349, 412 S.E.2d 180 (1991).

A violation of the statute may be established upon proof that a person unlawfully discharged a firearm at or in the direction of an occupied dwelling if the person knew or should have known that the dwelling was in the line of fire, even if the person did not specifically intend to shoot at or into the dwelling. Fleming v. Commonwealth, 13 Va. App. 349, 412 S.E.2d 180 (1991).

All that is required of the Commonwealth to prove a violation of this section is that it prove beyond a reasonable doubt that the principal in the first degree intended to shoot at or toward an occupied dwelling. Fleming v. Commonwealth, 13 Va. App. 349, 412 S.E.2d 180 (1991).

Prosecution, to support a conviction for the lesser included offense of unlawfully discharging a firearm at or against an occupied building, in violation of § 18.2-279, was not required to prove that defendant had the specific intent to fire at or against a convenience store that was behind the person at whom defendant was shooting. Ellis v. Commonwealth, 281 Va. 499, 706 S.E.2d 849, 2011 Va. LEXIS 46 (2011).

Commonwealth relieved of burden of proving endangerment. — The language of this statute is a legislative declaration that human lives may be endangered when a deadly weapon is maliciously discharged at or against a building occupied by people and that such conduct is felonious. This legislative determination relieves the Commonwealth of the burden of proving that human life was, in fact, endangered. Dowdy v. Commonwealth, 220 Va. 114, 255 S.E.2d 506 (1979).

At or toward occupied dwelling. — In construing the plain meaning of the second prong of § 18.2-279, regarding maliciously shooting at a dwelling house, the word "at" had a common and easily understood meaning and was defined as a function word used to indicate that toward which an action is directed, so all that was required of the Commonwealth to prove a violation of § 18.2-279 was that it prove beyond a reasonable doubt that the principal in the first degree intended to shoot at or toward an occupied dwelling. King v. Commonwealth, 40 Va. App. 193, 578 S.E.2d 803, 2003 Va. App. LEXIS 61 (2003).

No limitation on locale of shots. — Section 18.2-279, prohibiting the discharge of a firearm within or at an occupied dwelling, did not specify where the shooter had to be located in relation to the occupied dwelling, and there was no legislative directive implicating such a limitation, thus, when read together, the first prong of the statute dealt with the locale of the shot, (i.e., "within the building"), and the second prong concerned the destination of the shot, (i.e., "at the building") and did not specify the locale of the shooter. King v. Commonwealth, 40 Va. App. 193, 578 S.E.2d 803, 2003 Va. App. LEXIS 61 (2003).

Failure to instruct on essential elements. — In prosecution under this section, it was reversible error on the part of the trial court to fail to instruct the jury on the essential elements of the offense. Dowdy v. Commonwealth, 220 Va. 114, 255 S.E.2d 506 (1979).

Evidence of shooting similar to shooting charged. — While acquittal of a charge of a similar crime on the same night may lessen its probative value, it does not make it inadmissible and evidence of a shooting similar to shooting defendant was charged with had probative value. Tomlinson v. Commonwealth, 8 Va. App. 218, 380 S.E.2d 26 (1989).

The throwing of a bottle from close range with sufficient force to break the storm door and to injure homeowner is sufficient to support a finding that lives were "put in peril" within the meaning of this section. Waller v. Commonwealth, No. 1696-89-3 (Ct. of Appeals Nov. 20, 1990).

No probable cause to enter without a warrant. — When police received a call that someone had been shooting a weapon on a certain street, and, when they contacted the person who made the call, that person pointed out defendant, who was not engaged in any criminal behavior, they did not have probable cause allowing them to enter defendant's back yard without a warrant, because the call did not state or reasonably imply that a weapon had been fired "within" or "at" an occupied dwelling, so a person of reasonable caution was not warranted in believing that an offense had been or was being committed. Quente v. Commonwealth, No. 1517-03-1, 2004 Va. App. LEXIS 212 (Ct. of Appeals May 4, 2004).

Evidence sufficient to show lives endangered. — Evidence that defendant shot a gun into the ceiling of a hospital while in close proximity to seventy-five persons and that there was a possibility that the bullet might have ricocheted, was sufficient to prove the firearm was discharged in such a manner as to endanger lives. Strickland v. Commonwealth, 16 Va. App. 180, 428 S.E.2d 507 (1993).

Evidence was sufficient to establish that the defendant discharged a firearm in a manner that endangered the lives of persons in a store, notwithstanding that the shells which he fired from a shotgun had no pellets or other shot, where a detective testified that the weapon discharged a wad that would enter a person standing nearby "just like a bullet." Browder v. Commonwealth, No. 1499-97-2 (Ct. of Appeals Dec. 22, 1998).

Evidence that defendant fired weapon inside house showed that defendant endangered spouse's life, as defendant fired the weapon in the bedroom and the spouse was sitting in the nearby living room, close enough to be endangered had the ammunition deflected. Kirby v. Commonwealth, 264 Va. 440, 570 S.E.2d 832, 2002 Va. LEXIS 164 (2002).

Evidence was sufficient to prove beyond a reasonable doubt that defendant committed the offense of shooting into an occupied dwelling in violation of § 18.2-279, where: (1) in addition to blood evidence, primer residue from a gunshot was found on defendant's hand; (2) defendant's own written statement placed him at the scene; (3) a letter from defendant was intercepted, which indicated that a witness had seen defendant on the back porch during the shooting, and suggested testimony to explain the events; and (4) although the shootings might not have been part of the original plan, since defendant participated in the planned enterprise, he could be held accountable for the incidental crimes. Paxton v. Commonwealth, No. 3063-01-2, 2002 Va. App. LEXIS 785 (Ct. of Appeals Dec. 31, 2002).

When defendant was indicted for shooting at or against an occupied building or dwelling house, putting the lives of the occupants in peril, proof that he fired a weapon from inside the building at a fleeing victim did not fatally vary from the indictment as defendant fired "at" a part of the building, and the portion of the statute referenced in defendant's indictment did not specify where the shooter had to be located in reference to the building. King v. Commonwealth, 40 Va. App. 193, 578 S.E.2d 803, 2003 Va. App. LEXIS 61 (2003).

Defendant was properly convicted of both murder and malicious discharge of a firearm, where there was testimony that another person was about three to four feet from the murder victim at the time of the killing, and the other person was knocked back and could not hear; defendant clearly endangered this other person, and the crime took place within a dwelling. Proctor v. Commonwealth, 40 Va. App. 233, 578 S.E.2d 822, 2003 Va. App. LEXIS 182 (2003).

In a case in which defendant appealed his conviction for discharging a firearm within an occupied building, in violation of § 18.2-279, he argued unsuccessfully that the evidence was insufficient to support his conviction. The testimony of two witnesses was sufficient to support the conviction; one witnessed the event and was in the house when it occurred, and the other witness, a police investigator, testified that defendant admitted firing the weapon. Berger v. Commonwealth, 2006 Va. App. LEXIS 609 (Nov. 17, 2006).

Evidence sufficient to support conviction. — Evidence was sufficient to support defendant's convictions for robbery, shooting within an occupied dwelling, using a firearm in the commission of a felony, armed burglary, and malicious wounding, because ample evidence supported a finding that defendant was a perpetrator in a home invasion: three of the victims identified defendant at trial, and a co-defendant testified that defendant said he intended to rob the home, that he entered the home wearing a bullet-proof vest and armed with a handgun, and that he later told the co-defendant that he had struck one of the victim's in the head. Trial court did not abuse discretion in ruling on misidentification of accomplices by witnesses. Streater v. Commonwealth, 2009 Va. App. LEXIS 504 (Nov. 10, 2009).

Prosecution's case was legally sufficient and the trial court, as the fact finder, could reasonably have inferred from the character of the neighborhood, the presence of others in the vicinity, and the density of the surrounding development, that defendant knew or should of known that an occupied building was in defendant's line of fire when defendant unlawfully discharged a weapon toward the victim. Ellis v. Commonwealth, 281 Va. 499, 706 S.E.2d 849, 2011 Va. LEXIS 46 (2011).

Suspended sentence and post-release supervision properly imposed. — Defendant's sentence to three years of incarceration plus an additional six months, suspended upon a condition of six months of post-release supervision, for unlawfully throwing a missile at or against an occupied building pursuant to § 18.2-279, was not in error on the ground that it exceeded the jury's recommendation of three years; subsection A of § 19.2-295.2 permits a trial court to impose a suspended term of incarceration and post-release supervision when a jury's sentence includes an active term of incarceration, and the trial court did not make additional fact findings in imposing the sentence beyond those found by the jury. Perry v. Commonwealth, 2006 Va. App. LEXIS 270 (June 20, 2006).

Failure to present argument barred decision on appeal. — In a case in which defendant argued on appeal that he lacked the mens rea to violate § 18.2-279, he had not presented that argument to the trial court, and he did not argue that the appellate court should invoke the good cause or to meet the ends of justice exceptions, the appellate court would not consider that argument. Berger v. Commonwealth, 2006 Va. App. LEXIS 609 (Nov. 17, 2006).

Applied in Parnell v. Commonwealth, 15 Va. App. 342, 423 S.E.2d 834 (1992); King v. Commonwealth, 264 Va. 576, 570 S.E.2d 863, 2002 Va. LEXIS 168 (2002); Armstead v. Commonwealth, 55 Va. App. 354, 685 S.E.2d 876, 2009 Va. App. LEXIS 563 (2009).

§ 18.2-280. Willfully discharging firearms in public places.

A. If any person willfully discharges or causes to be discharged any firearm in any street in a city or town, or in any place of public business or place of public gathering, and such conduct results in bodily injury to another person, he shall be guilty of a Class 6 felony. If such conduct does not result in bodily injury to another person, he shall be guilty of a Class 1 misdemeanor.

B. If any person willfully discharges or causes to be discharged any firearm upon the buildings and grounds of any public, private or religious elementary, middle or high school, he shall be guilty of a Class 4 felony, unless he is engaged in a program or curriculum sponsored by or conducted with permission of a public, private or religious school.

C. If any person willfully discharges or causes to be discharged any firearm upon any public property within 1,000 feet of the property line of any public, private or religious elementary, middle or high school property he shall be guilty of a Class 4 felony, unless he is engaged in lawful hunting.

D. This section shall not apply to any law-enforcement officer in the performance of his official duties nor to any other person whose said willful act is otherwise justifiable or excusable at law in the protection of his life or property, or is otherwise specifically authorized by law.

E. Nothing in this statute shall preclude the Commonwealth from electing to prosecute under any other applicable provision of law instead of this section.

History.
Code 1950, § 18.1-69; 1960, c. 358; 1975, cc. 14, 15; 1992, c. 735; 1999, c. 996; 2001, c. 712; 2005, c. 928.

Law Review.
For article, "Legal Issues Involving Children," see 35 U. Rich. L. Rev. 741 (2001). For annual survey article, "Criminal Law and Procedure," see 44 U. Rich. L. Rev. 339 (2009).

CASE NOTES

Definition of "school property" in subsection C. — Evidence that defendant discharged a firearm within 1,000 feet of the property line of "school property" was sufficient to support defendant's conviction under subsection C of this section, because there was nothing in subsection C that distinguished between schools that lease facilities and those that did not, or limited its application to schools that were in session or occupied. King v. Commonwealth, 53 Va. App. 257, 670 S.E.2d 767, 2009 Va. App. LEXIS 1 (2009).

Public property. — Proof that a defendant fired a firearm from property owned by the government is required under subsection C of § 18.2-280. Cuffee v. Commonwealth, 61 Va. App. 353, 735 S.E.2d 693, 2013 Va. App. LEXIS 7 (2013).

Testimony that defendant shot from the rear of a vehicle parked on a street supported the trial court's conclusion that defendant shot from the street, which was public property; therefore, defendant's conviction under subsection C of § 18.2-280 was proper. Cuffee v. Commonwealth, 61 Va. App. 353, 735 S.E.2d 693, 2013 Va. App. LEXIS 7 (2013).

Relationship with other law. — District court did not clearly err in enhancing defendant's sentence on the ground that he possessed the firearm in connection with another felony offense; the testimonial and forensic evidence supported the finding that defendant fired the series of shots outside a nightclub, wounding a witness, which constituted a felony under Virginia law. United States v. Wallace, 2012 U.S. App. LEXIS 10423 (4th Cir. May 22, 2012).

Applied in United States v. Smith, 727 F. Supp. 1023 (W.D. Va. 1990); Ellis v. Commonwealth, 281 Va. 499, 706 S.E.2d 849, 2011 Va. LEXIS 46 (2011).

§ 18.2-281. Setting spring gun or other deadly weapon.

It shall be unlawful for any person to set or fix in any manner any firearm or other deadly weapon so that it may be discharged or activated by a person coming in contact therewith or with any string, wire, spring, or any other contrivance attached thereto or designed to activate such weapon remotely. Any person violating this section shall be guilty of a Class 6 felony.

History.
Code 1950, § 18.1-69.1; 1966, c. 422; 1975, cc. 14, 15.

§ 18.2-282. Pointing, holding, or brandishing firearm, air or gas operated weapon or object similar in appearance; penalty.

A. It shall be unlawful for any person to point, hold or brandish any firearm or any air or gas operated weapon or any object similar in appearance, whether capable of being fired or not, in such manner as to reasonably induce fear in the mind of another or hold a firearm or any air or gas operated weapon in a public place in such a manner as to reasonably induce fear in the mind of another of being shot or injured. However, this section shall not apply to any person engaged in excusable or justifiable self-defense. Persons violating the provisions of this section shall be guilty of a Class 1 misdemeanor or, if the violation occurs upon any public, private or religious elementary, middle or high school, including buildings and grounds or upon public property within 1,000 feet of such school property, he shall be guilty of a Class 6 felony.

B. Any police officer in the performance of his duty, in making an arrest under the provisions of this section, shall not be civilly liable in damages for injuries or death resulting to the person being arrested if he had reason to believe that the person being arrested was pointing, holding, or brandishing such firearm or air or gas operated weapon, or object that was similar in appearance, with intent to induce fear in the mind of another.

C. For purposes of this section, the word "*firearm*" means any weapon that will or is designed to or may readily be converted to expel single or multiple projectiles by the action of an explosion of a combustible material. The word "*ammunition,*" as used herein, shall mean a cartridge, pellet, ball, missile or projectile adapted for use in a firearm.

History.
Code 1950, § 18.1-69.2; 1968, c. 513; 1975, cc. 14, 15; 1990, cc. 588, 599; 1992, c. 735; 2003, c. 976; 2005, c. 928.

Law Review.
For annual survey article, "Criminal Law and Procedure," see 46 U. Rich. L. Rev. 59 (2011).

Michie's Jurisprudence.
For related discussion, see 20 M.J. Weapons, § 2.

CASE NOTES

Elements of offense. — There are two elements of the offense: (1) pointing or brandishing a firearm; and (2) doing so in such a manner as to reasonably induce fear in the mind of a victim. Kelsoe v. Commonwealth, 226 Va. 197, 308 S.E.2d 104 (1983).

Gravamen of offense is inducement of fear. — In this section, the General Assembly clearly proscribed an offense against the person. The gravamen of the offense is the inducement of fear in another. Kelsoe v. Commonwealth, 226 Va. 197, 308 S.E.2d 104 (1983).

Defining "firearm." — Whether the term "firearm" when used in a statute without being defined is to be given its traditional meaning or a more expansive meaning depends upon the purpose and policy underlying the particular statute. When the statute is designed not only to deter physical harm, a more expansive definition of "firearm" is required in order to effectuate that purpose. On the other hand, when a statute is designed only to proscribe the act of possessing a firearm or the conduct of a felon in order to reduce a real threat of harm to the public, a narrower, more traditional definition of "firearm" is required. Jones v. Commonwealth, 16 Va. App. 354, 429 S.E.2d 615 (1993), overruled in part, Armstrong v. Commonwealth, 36 Va. App. 312, 549 S.E.2d 641 (2001).

Where there is no evidence that fear by victim was intended or resulted, this section is not applicable. Bailey v. Commonwealth, 5 Va. App. 331, 362 S.E.2d 750 (1987).

Multiple punishment for pointing firearm at several people is not double jeopardy. — Where defendant pointed the pistol toward three men and each was afraid and backed away from the defendant, imposition of three punishments did not constitute double jeopardy. Kelsoe v. Commonwealth, 226 Va. 197, 308 S.E.2d 104 (1983).

Conviction for brandishing a firearm and assault did not violate double jeopardy. — Because defendant's commission of an assault and the brandishing of a firearm were two distinct and separate acts, separated in time and space, and each conviction was sustained by different evidence, his double jeopardy rights were not violated. Jackson v. Commonwealth, — Va. App. —, — S.E.2d —, 2008 Va. App. LEXIS 251 (May 27, 2008).

Privilege to protect property is defense to section. — The trial judge erred in not permitting defendant, charged under this section, from asserting the defense of privilege to protect property from an armed trespasser. Diffendal v. Commonwealth, 8 Va. App. 417, 382 S.E.2d 24 (1989).

Brandishing shotgun disproportionate force where cable workers unarmed. — The brandishing of the shotgun by defendant was disproportionate to any threat posed by the unarmed cable workers, irrespective of the legality of the cable company's conduct. Pike v. Commonwealth, 24 Va. App. 373, 482 S.E.2d 839 (1997).

Inadvertent sighting insufficient. — The elements of this section are not proved beyond a reasonable doubt when the evidence merely proved that a person holding a firearm was inadvertently seen by another. Thus, the evidence did not prove beyond a reasonable doubt that defendant held the gun in such a manner as to reasonably induce fear in the mind of another. Crewe v. Commonwealth, No. 2709-95-2 (Ct. of Appeals Oct. 29, 1996).

Sufficient evidence of brandishing. — Where record disclosed that defendant's sister excitedly called upon defendant to "give her the gun," prompting him to rush toward the residence, armed with a .44 or .45 caliber pistol; a "clicking sound" was heard as defendant loaded a "clip" of ammunition into the weapon, and he yelled "I'll F[ ] all you M[ ] F[ ]ers up."; defendant entered the home, waving the gun about and pointing it at people inside, and demanded, "Who in the f[ ] hit my sister?"; and four persons present during the offenses identified the weapon as a "gray gun," with a long barrel; the jury properly concluded that the defendant possessed an actual firearm and brandished it at those present in the residence. Britt v. Commonwealth, No. 0679-96-1 (Ct. of Appeals Apr. 15, 1997).

Defendant's conviction of brandishing a firearm was supported by sufficient evidence, as defendant's act of showing the victim a flare gun in defendant's waistband constituted brandishing, and the action induced fear in the victim. Morris v. Commonwealth, 269 Va. 127, 607 S.E.2d 110, 2005 Va. LEXIS 3 (2005).

Evidence was sufficient to prove that defendant violated subsection A of § 18.2-282 as to the owner of a house because the owner's request of defendant to put his gun away was sufficient evidence of the owner's requisite apprehension of bodily harm; the owner's apprehension was further confirmed by her testimony that defendant was only deterred from brandishing his gun by the threat of police intervention. Huffman v. Commonwealth, 51 Va. App. 469, 658 S.E.2d 713, 2008 Va. App. LEXIS 165 (2008).

Sufficient evidence supported defendant's conviction for brandishing a firearm because the trial court's finding that he did not act in self-defense was not plainly wrong, as (1) neither victim displayed or threatened to use a firearm or other weapon on the date of the crime, (2) a statement of facts indicated the victims were not armed, (3) there was no evidence that the victims' shouts at defendant evidenced an intent to inflict bodily harm on defendant, (4) while defendant fled when the victims arrived at the crime's location, the fact-finder could conclude that defendant did not prove

defendant reasonably apprehended a danger to defendant, (5) while a victim had held defendant at gunpoint two years earlier, which would have supported a finding that defendant could reasonably have feared for defendant's safety when the victims confronted defendant at the time of the crime, the trier of fact could conclude defendant did not prove defendant harbored such fear on that date. Swilling v. Commonwealth, 2011 Va. App. LEXIS 169 (May 17, 2011).

Privilege to protect property no defense. — A deadly weapon may not be brandished solely in defense of personal property. Commonwealth v. Alexander, 260 Va. 238, 531 S.E.2d 567 (2000).

A defendant was properly convicted of brandishing a firearm where he had retrieved a rifle from his house and pointed it at an agent who had been sent by a lienholder to repossess the defendant's motor vehicle; the defendant's threat to use deadly force constituted assault and as such, was an illegal response to a threat to property. Commonwealth v. Alexander, 260 Va. 238, 531 S.E.2d 567 (2000).

Defendant's motion to suppress was denied where the officers had sufficient probable cause to arrest defendant on the charge of brandishing a firearm once they had: (i) arrived at the mall parking lot in response to a reported brandishing incident; (ii) been directed to the purported suspect by the victim of the offense, who remained present at the scene, still on the telephone with the 911 emergency operator; (iii) corroborated the detailed description of the suspect and vehicle that had been provided earlier by the victim in the course of the 911 telephone call; and (iv) observed defendant engaging in evasive and agitated behavior at the scene, i.e., attempting to drive his vehicle out of the parking lot upon spotting the officers, moving his arms and hands about in an animated manner and repeatedly reaching for the driver's side rear door once standing outside the vehicle. United States v. Beckham, 325 F. Supp. 2d 678, 2004 U.S. Dist. LEXIS 13848 (E.D. Va. 2004).

Elements of offense in relation to federal RICO indictment. — Defendants sought dismissal of counts under 18 U.S.C.S. §§ 1959 and 924(c), of the indictment on the ground that the elements of Virginia's malicious or unlawful wounding statute, § 18.2-51, and brandishing statute, § 18.2-282, the state laws that the charged assaults allegedly violated, did not match — element-by-element — with the elements of assault with a dangerous weapon under federal law, but, the elements of malicious or unlawful wounding under Virginia law were adequately similar to those of assault with a dangerous weapon and aggravated assault as generically defined, the indictment charging assault with a dangerous weapon was sufficient, and the motion to dismiss was denied. United States v. Cuong Gia Le, 316 F. Supp. 2d 355, 2004 U.S. Dist. LEXIS 7786 (E.D. Va. 2004).

Not a lesser included offense. — Brandishing a firearm is not a lesser included offense of robbery given that robbery did not require the use of a firearm, and brandishing did not require the taking of property; thus, it was clear that robbery could be committed without brandishing and brandishing could be committed without the taking of property. Morris v. Commonwealth, 45 Va. App. 181, 609 S.E.2d 92, 2005 Va. App. LEXIS 79 (2005).

Brandishing not lesser-included offense of use of firearm in commission of felony. — Word "threaten" means to utter threats against, promise punishment, reprisal, or other distress to, whereas the word "induce" means to move and lead, to bring in, or to bring on or bring about: effect, cause; thus, in cases involving the threatening display of a firearm under § 18.2-53.1, the defendant must display his or her firearm to promise punishment, reprisal or other distress to the victim, whereas in cases involving brandishing under § 18.2-282, the defendant must merely brandish or display a firearm in such a manner as to reasonably bring about or cause fear in the mind of the victim, and while the concepts are concededly similar, they are not the same. Nasser Nasser Ghalambor Dezfuli v. Commonwealth, 58 Va. App. 1, 707 S.E.2d 1, 2011 Va. App. LEXIS 105 (2011).

It is possible to brandish a firearm during a violation for § 18.2-53.1 because brandishing often does occur when one uses or displays a firearm in the commission of a felony; nevertheless, the prosecution is not required to prove a criminal defendant actually brandished his or her firearm in order to obtain a conviction under § 18.2-53.1 because § 18.2-53.1 is written in the disjunctive, prohibiting either the actual use of a firearm, or the display of a firearm in a threatening manner, and thus, the Commonwealth can obtain a conviction under § 18.2-53.1 if it proves the defendant "used or attempted to use" his or her firearm, even in the absence of evidence that the defendant brandished it, but the prosecution is not required to prove the defendant displayed his or her firearm in a threatening manner to obtain a conviction for brandishing a firearm under § 18.2-282. Nasser Nasser Ghalambor Dezfuli v. Commonwealth, 58 Va. App. 1, 707 S.E.2d 1, 2011 Va. App. LEXIS 105 (2011).

Because it is possible to commit a violation of § 18.2-53.1 without brandishing a firearm, and because one can brandish a firearm without also committing a violation of § 18.2-53.1, the act of brandishing is not a lesser-included offense of use of a firearm in the commission of a felony; viewed in the abstract, these code sections each require proof of a fact that the other does not because the offense of using a firearm in the commission of a felony requires proof that the defendant either used or attempted to use a firearm or that he or she displayed a firearm in a threatening manner during the commission or attempt to commit one of the felonies enumerated in the statute, and thus, in such cases, the Commonwealth must prove that the defendant used or threateningly displayed the firearm expressly to assist him or her in attempting or completing a specified underlying criminal act, but, in a prosecution for the act of brandishing, the Commonwealth must merely prove that the defendant pointed, held or brandished a firearm in a manner that reasonably induced fear in the mind of some nearby person. Nasser Nasser Ghalambor Dezfuli v. Commonwealth, 58 Va. App. 1, 707 S.E.2d 1, 2011 Va. App. LEXIS 105 (2011).

Trial court erred in convicting defendant of brandishing a firearm in violation of § 18.2-282 as a lesser-included offense of use of a firearm in the commission of a felony, § 18.2-53.1, because brandishing under § 18.2-282 was not a lesser-included offense of use of a firearm in the commission of a felony under § 18.2-53.1; the Commonwealth can obtain a conviction for use of a firearm during the commission of a felony without proof that the defendant brandished the firearm, and a conviction for brandishing without also proving use of the firearm in the commission of a felony, and although the evidence presented to prove the former offense may overlap with the evidence used to prove the latter, the Commonwealth must submit proof of completely different elements for a finding of guilt as to each separate offense, and thus, these offenses are different for purposes of *Blockburger*. Nasser Nasser Ghalambor Dezfuli v. Commonwealth, 58 Va. App. 1, 707 S.E.2d 1, 2011 Va. App. LEXIS 105 (2011).

Severance not required. — Trial court did not abuse its discretion when it declined to sever the charges of possession of a firearm by a felon, in violation of § 18.2-308.2, from the charges of carrying a concealed weapon and felony brandishing of a firearm, because the brandishment charges required the Commonwealth to also show a prior felony conviction, and defendant was thus not prejudiced by the introduction of the prior convictions at trial. Ellis v. Commonwealth, — Va. App. —, — S.E.2d —, 2006 Va. App. LEXIS 235 (Apr. 18, 2006).

Jury instructions. — Because the jury instructions on concert of action fully and fairly covered the principle of law, and because defendant acted with an accomplice pursuant to a scheme that involved robbing the victim with a gun, defendant was accountable for the victim's death; consequently, defendant was properly convicted of first-degree murder and use of a firearm during the commission of a felony. Baker v. Commonwealth, 2010 Va. App. LEXIS 507 (Mar. 31, 2010).

Applied in Jackson v. Commonwealth, 39 Va. App. 624, 576 S.E.2d 206, 2003 Va. App. LEXIS 37 (2003); Myers v. Shaver, 245 F. Supp. 2d 805, 2003 U.S. Dist. LEXIS 2547 (W.D. Va. 2003).

CIRCUIT COURT OPINIONS

No evidence of fear. — In an action involving an eye injury sustained when a BB pellet was fired from a car, demurrers to two negligence per se counts were sustained because there was no allegation that the BB gun was brandished or held in a manner to reasonably induce fear in the mind of anyone, as required to sustain a cause of action under § 18.2-282. Selph v. Elbourn, 79 Va. Cir. 536, 2009 Va. Cir. LEXIS 139 (Lancaster County Nov. 25, 2009).

§ 18.2-282.1. Brandishing a machete or other bladed weapon with intent to intimidate; penalty.

It shall be unlawful for any person to point, hold, or brandish a machete or any weapon, with an exposed blade 12 inches or longer, with the intent of intimidating any person or group of persons and in a manner that reasonably demonstrates that intent. This section shall not apply to any person engaged in excusable or justifiable self-defense. A person who violates this section is guilty of a Class 1 misdemeanor or, if the violation occurs upon any public, private, or religious elementary, middle, or high school, including buildings and grounds or upon public property within 1,000 feet of such school property, he is guilty of a Class 6 felony.

History.
2006, cc. 844, 895.

Law Review.
For 2006 survey article, "Criminal Law and Procedure," see 41 U. Rich. L. Rev. 83 (2006).

§ 18.2-283. Carrying dangerous weapon to place of religious worship.

If any person carry any gun, pistol, bowie knife, dagger or other dangerous weapon, without good and sufficient reason, to a place of worship while a meeting for religious purposes is being held at such place he shall be guilty of a Class 4 misdemeanor.

History.
Code 1950, § 18.1-241; 1960, c. 358; 1962, c. 411; 1975, cc. 14, 15.

OPINIONS OF THE ATTORNEY GENERAL

Personal protection constitutes a good and sufficient reason. — Carrying a weapon for personal protection constitutes a good and sufficient reason under § 18.2-283 to carry a weapon into a place of worship while a meeting for religious purposes is being held there, but places of worship can restrict or ban firearms from their premises. See opinion of Attorney General to The Honorable Mark L. Cole, Member, House of Delegates, 11-043, 2011 Va. AG LEXIS 23 (4/8/11).

§ 18.2-283.1. Carrying weapon into courthouse.

It shall be unlawful for any person to possess in or transport into any courthouse in this Commonwealth any (i) gun or other weapon designed or intended to propel a missile or projectile of any kind, (ii) frame, receiver, muffler, silencer, missile, projectile or ammunition designed for use with a dangerous weapon and (iii) any other dangerous weapon, including explosives, stun weapons as defined in § 18.2-308.1, and those weapons specified in subsection A of § 18.2-308. Any such weapon shall be subject to seizure by a law-enforcement officer. A violation of this section is punishable as a Class 1 misdemeanor.

The provisions of this section shall not apply to any police officer, sheriff, law-enforcement agent or official, conservation police officer, conservator of the peace, magistrate, court officer, judge, or city or county treasurer while in the conduct of such person's official duties.

History.
1988, c. 615; 2004, c. 995; 2007, cc. 87, 519; 2012, c. 295.

The 2012 amendments.
The 2012 amendment by c. 295, in the last paragraph, inserted "or city or county treasurer" and made a related change.

Michie's Jurisprudence.
For related discussion, see 20 M.J. Weapons, § 4.

§ 18.2-284. Selling or giving toy firearms.

No person shall sell, barter, exchange, furnish, or dispose of by purchase, gift or in any other manner any toy gun, pistol, rifle or other toy firearm, if the same shall, by action of an explosion of a combustible material, discharge blank or ball charges. Any person violating the provisions of this section shall be guilty of a Class 4 misdemeanor. Each sale of any of the articles hereinbefore specified to any person shall constitute a separate offense.

Nothing in this section shall be construed as preventing the sale of what are commonly known as cap pistols.

History.
Code 1950, § 18.1-347; 1960, c. 348; 1975, cc. 14, 15; 2003, c. 976.

CASE NOTES

Defining "firearm." — Whether the term "firearm" when used in a statute without being defined is to be given its traditional meaning or a more expansive meaning depends upon the purpose and policy underlying the particular statute. When the statute is designed not only to deter physical harm, a more expansive definition of "firearm" is required in order to effectuate that purpose. On the other hand, when a statute is designed only to proscribe the act of possessing a firearm or the conduct of a felon in order to reduce a real threat of harm to the public, a narrower, more traditional definition of "firearm" is required. Jones v. Commonwealth, 16 Va. App. 354, 429 S.E.2d 615 (1993), overruled in part, Armstrong v. Commonwealth, 36 Va. App. 312, 549 S.E.2d 641 (2001).

§ 18.2-285. Hunting with firearms while under influence of intoxicant or narcotic drug; penalty.

It shall be unlawful for any person to hunt wildlife with a firearm, bow and arrow, or crossbow in the Commonwealth of Virginia while he is (i) under the influence of alcohol; (ii) under the influence of any narcotic drug or any other self-administered intoxicant or drug of whatsoever nature, or any combination of such drugs, to a degree that impairs his ability to hunt with a firearm, bow and arrow, or crossbow safely; or (iii) under the combined influence of alcohol and any drug or drugs to a degree that impairs his ability to hunt with a firearm, bow

and arrow, or crossbow safely. Any person who violates the provisions of this section is guilty of a Class 1 misdemeanor. Conservation police officers, sheriffs and all other law-enforcement officers shall enforce the provisions of this section.

History.
Code 1950, § 29-140.1; 1952, c. 96; 1962, c. 469; 1975, cc. 14, 15; 1999, c. 543; 2005, c. 507.

Editor's note.
At the direction of the Virginia Code Commission, "Conservation police officers" was substituted for "Game wardens" in the last sentence, to conform to the name change by Acts 2007, c. 87.

CASE NOTES

Applied in Fredericksburg Constr. Co. v. J.W. Wyne Excavating, Inc., 260 Va. 137, 530 S.E.2d 148, 2000 Va. LEXIS 106 (2000).

§ 18.2-286. Shooting in or across road or in street.

If any person discharges a firearm, crossbow or bow and arrow in or across any road, or within the right-of-way thereof, or in a street of any city or town, he shall, for each offense, be guilty of a Class 4 misdemeanor.

The provisions of this section shall not apply to firing ranges or shooting matches maintained, and supervised or approved, by law-enforcement officers and military personnel in performance of their lawful duties.

History.
Code 1950, § 33.1-349; 1970, c. 322; 1975, cc. 14, 15; 1993, c. 322; 1994, c. 18.

Michie's Jurisprudence.
For related discussion, see 20 M.J. Weapons, § 8.

OPINIONS OF THE ATTORNEY GENERAL

Forfeiture of weapons. — With very rare possible exceptions, subsection A of § 29.1-521.2 establishes the procedure to be used in forfeiting a firearm used by a person convicted of violating this section. The court convicting the violator has the discretion to declare a forfeiture of the firearm used in the crime. See opinion of Attorney General to The Honorable Phillip C. Steele, Commonwealth's Attorney for Giles County, 05-047 (8/19/05).

The Commonwealth's attorney of the county or city wherein the forfeiture of a firearm was incurred must file an information to enforce that forfeiture in the circuit court of his county or city. See opinion of Attorney General to The Honorable Phillip C. Steele, Commonwealth's Attorney for Giles County, 05-047 (8/19/05).

§ 18.2-286.1. Shooting from vehicles so as to endanger persons; penalty.

Any person who, while in or on a motor vehicle, intentionally discharges a firearm so as to create the risk of injury or death to another person or thereby cause another person to have a reasonable apprehension of injury or death shall be guilty of a Class 5 felony. Nothing in this section shall apply to a law-enforcement officer in the performance of his duties.

History.
1990, c. 951.

Cross references.
For definition of "barrier crime" as including a conviction of drive by shooting as set out in § 18.2-286.1, or an equivalent offense in another state, and prohibition against assisted living facilities, adult day care centers or child welfare agencies hiring for certain compensated employment persons who have committed such an offense, see §§ 63.2-1719, 63.2-1720.

CASE NOTES

Multiple shots constitute multiple violations. — This statute does not proscribe a continuous course of conduct; rather, each offense is complete upon the firing of one shot when the life of another is endangered and a defendant who fires multiple shots from one motor vehicle may thus be convicted of multiple violations of the statute. Stephens v. Commonwealth, 35 Va. App. 141, 543 S.E.2d 609, 2001 Va. App. LEXIS 134 (2001), aff'd, 263 Va. 58, 557 S.E.2d 227 (2002).

Evidence insufficient. — The evidence was held insufficient to sustain the convictions under this statute. Morris v. Commonwealth, 21 Va. App. 306, 464 S.E.2d 169 (1995).

Lack of jurisdiction. — In a case in which defendant appealed his conviction for violating §§ 18.2-51, 18.2-53.1, and 18.2-286.1, he argued that evidence of other crimes was inadmissible. The appellate court lacked jurisdiction to consider his argument as it was not presented in the assignment of error on his brief, as required by Va. Sup. Ct. R. 5A:12(c)(1), and was not included as part of the assignment of error on which the appeal was granted at the petition stage. Wyche v. Commonwealth, 2012 Va. App. LEXIS 227 (July 10, 2012).

§ 18.2-287. Repealed by Acts 2004, c. 462.

Cross references.
For current provisions authorizing counties to regulate carrying of loaded firearms on public highways, see § 15.2-1209.1.

§ 18.2-287.01. Carrying weapon in air carrier airport terminal.

It shall be unlawful for any person to possess or transport into any air carrier airport terminal in the Commonwealth any (i) gun or other weapon designed or intended to propel a missile or projectile of any kind, (ii) frame, receiver, muffler, silencer, missile, projectile or ammunition designed for use with a dangerous weapon, and (iii) any other dangerous weapon, including explosives, stun weapons as defined in § 18.2-308.1, and those weapons specified in subsection A of § 18.2-308. Any such weapon shall be subject to seizure by a law-enforcement officer. A violation of this section is punishable as a Class 1 misdemeanor. Any weapon possessed or transported in violation of this section shall be forfeited to the Commonwealth and disposed of as provided in § 19.2-386.28.

The provisions of this section shall not apply to any police officer, sheriff, law-enforcement agent or official, or conservation police officer, or conservator of the peace employed by the air carrier airport, nor shall the provisions of this section apply to any passenger of an airline who, to the extent otherwise permitted by law, transports a lawful firearm, weapon, or ammunition into or out of an air carrier airport terminal for the sole purposes, respectively, of (i) presenting such firearm, weapon, or ammunition to U.S. Customs agents in advance of an international flight, in order to comply with federal law, (ii) checking such firearm, weapon, or ammunition with his luggage, or (iii) retrieving such firearm, weapon, or ammunition from the baggage claim area.

Any other statute, rule, regulation, or ordinance specifically addressing the possession or transportation of weapons in any airport in the Commonwealth shall be invalid, and this section shall control.

History.
2004, c. 894; 2007, cc. 87, 519; 2013, c. 746.

Editor's note.
Acts 2013, c. 746, cl. 2 provides: "That the provisions of this act are declaratory of existing law."

The 2013 amendments.
The 2013 amendment by c. 746 substituted "§ 19.2-386.28" for "subsection A of § 18.2-308" at the end of the first paragraph.

Law Review.
For 2003/2004 survey of criminal law and procedure, see 39 U. Rich. L. Rev. 133 (2004).

§ 18.2-287.1. Repealed by Acts 2004, c. 462.

Cross references.
For current provisions concerning regulation of transportation of loaded rifle or shotgun, see § 15.2-915.2.

§ 18.2-287.2. Wearing of body armor while committing a crime; penalty.

Any person who, while committing a crime of violence as defined in § 18.2-288 (2) or a felony violation of § 18.2-248 or subdivision (a) 2 or 3 of § 18.2-248.1, has in his possession a firearm or knife and is wearing body armor designed to diminish the effect of the impact of a bullet or projectile shall be guilty of a Class 4 felony.

History.
1990, c. 936; 1997, c. 311.

CASE NOTES

Sufficient evidence. — Sufficient evidence supported defendant's conviction for wearing body armor while committing a crime, as a police officer testified without objection that defendant was wearing a bulletproof vest, and defendant stated that the vest was body armor. Jones v. Commonwealth, — Va. App. —, — S.E.2d —, 2009 Va. App. LEXIS 44 (Feb. 3, 2009), aff'd, 279 Va. 295, 687 S.E.2d 738 (2010).

Not only was there no dispute that defendant was wearing a bulletproof vest when he committed statutory burglary, but the finder of fact was entitled to rely on the uncontested and uncontradicted testimony in determining whether defendant violated § 18.2-287.2. Jones v. Commonwealth, 279 Va. 295, 687 S.E.2d 738, 2010 Va. LEXIS 4 (2010).

§ 18.2-287.3. Repealed by Acts 1993, cc. 467, 494.

Cross references.
As to present provisions relating to possession or transportation

of certain firearms by persons under the age of eighteen, see § 18.2-308.7.

§ 18.2-287.4. Carrying loaded firearms in public areas prohibited; penalty.

It shall be unlawful for any person to carry a loaded (a) semi-automatic center-fire rifle or pistol that expels single or multiple projectiles by action of an explosion of a combustible material and is equipped at the time of the offense with a magazine that will hold more than 20 rounds of ammunition or designed by the manufacturer to accommodate a silencer or equipped with a folding stock or (b) shotgun with a magazine that will hold more than seven rounds of the longest ammunition for which it is chambered on or about his person on any public street, road, alley, sidewalk, public right-of-way, or in any public park or any other place of whatever nature that is open to the public in the Cities of Alexandria, Chesapeake, Fairfax, Falls Church, Newport News, Norfolk, Richmond, or Virginia Beach or in the Counties of Arlington, Fairfax, Henrico, Loudoun, or Prince William.

The provisions of this section shall not apply to law-enforcement officers, licensed security guards, military personnel in the performance of their lawful duties, or any person having a valid concealed handgun permit or to any person actually engaged in lawful hunting or lawful recreational shooting activities at an established shooting range or shooting contest. Any person violating the provisions of this section shall be guilty of a Class 1 misdemeanor.

The exemptions set forth in § 18.2-308 shall apply, mutatis mutandis, to the provisions of this section.

History.
1991, c. 570; 1992, c. 790; 2003, c. 976; 2004, c. 995; 2005, c. 160; 2007, c. 813.

Editor's note.
Acts 2007, c. 813, cl. 2, provides: "That the provisions of this act shall not affect the powers of any locality with respect to any ordinance, resolution or bylaw validly adopted and not repealed or rescinded prior to July 1, 2007."

CASE NOTES

Defining "firearm." — Whether the term "firearm" when used in a statute without being defined is to be given its traditional meaning or a more expansive meaning depends upon the purpose and policy underlying the particular statute. When the statute is designed not only to deter physical harm, a more expansive definition of "firearm" is required in order to effectuate that purpose. On the other hand, when a statute is designed only to proscribe the act of possessing a firearm or the conduct of a felon in order to reduce a real threat of harm to the public, a narrower, more traditional definition of "firearm" is required. Jones v. Commonwealth, 16 Va. App. 354, 429 S.E.2d 615 (1993), overruled in part, Armstrong v. Commonwealth, 36 Va. App. 312, 549 S.E.2d 641 (2001).

OPINIONS OF THE ATTORNEY GENERAL

Carrying concealed handguns in state parks with permit. — The Department of Conservation and Recreation does not have the authority to issue regulations prohibiting, within state parks, the carrying of concealed handguns by valid permit holders. See opinion of Attorney General to The Honorable Richard H. Black, Member, House of Delegates, 02-074 (9/9/02).

Carrying and possession of firearms within state parks. — The Department of Conservation and Recreation does not have the authority to prohibit the carrying and possession of firearms within state parks beyond that currently prohibited by law. See opinion of Attorney General to The Honorable Ken T. Cuccinelli, II, Member, Senate of Virginia, 08-043 (9/26/08).

ARTICLE 5.

UNIFORM MACHINE GUN ACT.

Michie's Jurisprudence.
For related discussion, see 20 M.J. Weapons, §§ 4.1, 9.

§ 18.2-288. Definitions.

When used in this article:

(1) *"Machine gun"* applies to any weapon which shoots or is designed to shoot automatically more than one shot, without manual reloading, by a single function of the trigger.

(2) *"Crime of violence"* applies to and includes any of the following crimes or an attempt to commit any of the same, namely, murder, manslaughter, kidnapping, rape, mayhem, assault with intent to maim, disable, disfigure or kill, robbery, burglary, housebreaking, breaking and entering and larceny.

(3) *"Person"* applies to and includes firm, partnership, association or corporation.

History.
Code 1950, § 18.1-258; 1960, c. 358; 1975, cc. 14, 15.

Uniform law cross references.
For other signatory state provisions, see:
Arkansas: A.C.A. §§ 5-73-201 to 5-73-211.
Maryland: Md. Ann. Code, CR §§ 4-401 et seq.
Montana: Mont. Ann. Code, § 45-8-301 et seq.

Michie's Jurisprudence.
For related discussion, see 20 M.J. Weapons, § 4.

OPINIONS OF THE ATTORNEY GENERAL

Nonexempt persons. — The Uniform Machine Gun Act does not prevent the discharge or firing of a machine gun by a nonexempt person. See opinion of Attorney General to Colonel W. Gerald Massengill, Superintendent, Department of State Police, 02-056 (7/30/02).

A nonexempt person may transport a machine gun away from his registered bona fide permanent residence or business address. See opinion of Attorney General to Colonel W. Gerald Massengill, Superintendent, Department of State Police, 02-056 (7/30/02).

§ 18.2-289. Use of machine gun for crime of violence.

Possession or use of a machine gun in the perpetration or attempted perpetration of a crime of violence is hereby declared to be a Class 2 felony.

History.
Code 1950, § 18.1-259; 1960, c. 358; 1975, cc. 14, 15.

§ 18.2-290. Use of machine gun for aggressive purpose.

Unlawful possession or use of a machine gun for an offensive or aggressive purpose is hereby declared to be a Class 4 felony.

History.

Code 1950, § 18.1-260; 1960, c. 358; 1968, c. 229; 1975, cc. 14, 15.

§ 18.2-291. What constitutes aggressive purpose.

Possession or use of a machine gun shall be presumed to be for an offensive or aggressive purpose:

(1) When the machine gun is on premises not owned or rented for bona fide permanent residence or business occupancy by the person in whose possession the machine gun may be found;

(2) When the machine gun is in the possession of, or used by, a person who has been convicted of a crime of violence in any court of record, state or federal, of the United States of America, its territories or insular possessions;

(3) When the machine gun has not been registered as required in § 18.2-295; or

(4) When empty or loaded shells which have been or are susceptible of use in the machine gun are found in the immediate vicinity thereof.

History.

Code 1950, § 18.1-261; 1960, c. 358; 1975, cc. 14, 15.

OPINIONS OF THE ATTORNEY GENERAL

Individual may display historic machine guns at the Virginia War Memorial without violating the Uniform Machine Gun Act, provided that the machine guns are registered pursuant to the Act and federal law and are not used for offensive or aggressive purposes. See opinion of Attorney General to The Honorable Frank D. Hargrove Sr., Member, House of Delegates, 04-065 (10/7/04).

§ 18.2-292. Presence prima facie evidence of use.

The presence of a machine gun in any room, boat or vehicle shall be prima facie evidence of the possession or use of the machine gun by each person occupying the room, boat, or vehicle where the weapon is found.

History.

Code 1950, § 18.1-262; 1960, c. 358; 1975, cc. 14, 15.

§ 18.2-293. What article does not apply to.

The provisions of this article shall not be applicable to:

(1) The manufacture for, and sale of, machine guns to the armed forces or law-enforcement officers of the United States or of any state or of any political subdivision thereof, or the transportation required for that purpose; and

(2) Machine guns and automatic arms issued to the national guard of Virginia by the United States or such arms used by the United States army or navy or in the hands of troops of the national guards of other states or territories of the United States passing through Virginia, or such arms as may be provided for the officers of the State Police or officers of penal institutions.

History.

Code 1950, § 18.1-263; 1960, c. 358; 1975, cc. 14, 15.

§ 18.2-293.1. What article does not prohibit.

Nothing contained in this article shall prohibit or interfere with:

(1) The possession of a machine gun for scientific purposes, or the possession of a machine gun not usable as a weapon and possessed as a curiosity, ornament, or keepsake; and

(2) The possession of a machine gun for a purpose manifestly not aggressive or offensive.

Provided, however, that possession of such machine guns shall be subject to the provisions of § 18.2-295.

History.

Code 1950, § 18.1-263; 1960, c. 358; 1975, cc. 14, 15.

§ 18.2-294. Manufacturer's and dealer's register; inspection of stock.

Every manufacturer or dealer shall keep a register of all machine guns manufactured or handled by him. This register shall show the model and serial number, date of manufacture, sale, loan, gift, delivery or receipt of every machine gun, the name, address, and occupation of the person to whom the machine gun was sold, loaned, given or delivered, or from whom it was received. Upon demand every manufacturer or dealer shall permit any marshal, sheriff or police officer to inspect his entire stock of machine guns, parts, and supplies therefor, and shall produce the register, herein required, for inspection. A violation of any provisions of this section shall be punishable as a Class 3 misdemeanor.

History.
Code 1950, § 18.1-264; 1960, c. 358; 1975, cc. 14, 15.

§ 18.2-295. Registration of machine guns.

Every machine gun in this Commonwealth shall be registered with the Department of State Police within twenty-four hours after its acquisition or, in the case of semi-automatic weapons which are converted, modified or otherwise altered to become machine guns, within twenty-four hours of the conversion, modification or alteration. Blanks for registration shall be prepared by the Superintendent of State Police, and furnished upon application. To comply with this section the application as filed shall be notarized and shall show the model and serial number of the gun, the name, address and occupation of the person in possession, and from whom and the purpose for which, the gun was acquired or altered. The Superintendent of State Police shall upon registration required in this section forthwith furnish the registrant with a certificate of registration, which shall be valid as long as the registrant remains the same. Certificates of registration shall be retained by the registrant and produced by him upon demand by any peace officer. Failure to keep or produce such certificate for inspection shall be a Class 3 misdemeanor, and any peace officer, may without warrant, seize the machine gun and apply for its confiscation as provided in § 18.2-296. Upon transferring a registered machine gun, the transferor shall forthwith notify the Superintendent in writing, setting forth the date of transfer and name and address of the transferee. Failure to give the required notification shall constitute a Class 3 misdemeanor. Registration data shall not be subject to inspection by the public.

History.
Code 1950, § 18.1-265; 1960, c. 358; 1972, c. 199; 1975, cc. 14, 15; 1978, c. 618; 1988, c. 460.

Law Review.
For survey of Virginia criminal law for the year 1971-1972, see 58 Va. L. Rev. 1206 (1972).

§ 18.2-296. Search warrants for machine guns.

Warrant to search any house or place and seize any machine gun possessed in violation of this article may issue in the same manner and under the same restrictions as provided by law for stolen property, and any court of record, upon application of the attorney for the Commonwealth, a police officer or conservator of the peace, may order any machine gun, thus or otherwise legally seized, to be confiscated and either destroyed or delivered to a peace officer of the Commonwealth or a political subdivision thereof.

History.
Code 1950, § 18.1-266; 1960, c. 358; 1975, cc. 14, 15.

§ 18.2-297. How article construed.

This article shall be so interpreted and construed as to effectuate its general purpose to make uniform the law of those states which enact it.

History.
Code 1950, § 18.1-267; 1960, c. 358; 1975, cc. 14, 15.

§ 18.2-298. Short title of article.

This article may be cited as the "Uniform Machine Gun Act."

History.
Code 1950, § 18.1-268; 1960, c. 358; 1975, cc. 14, 15.

ARTICLE 6.

"SAWED-OFF" SHOTGUN AND "SAWED-OFF" RIFLE ACT.

Michie's Jurisprudence.
For related discussion, see 20 M.J. Weapons, §§ 4.1, 9.

§ 18.2-299. Definitions.

When used in this article:

"Sawed-off shotgun" means any weapon, loaded or unloaded, originally designed as a shoulder weapon, utilizing a self-contained cartridge from which a number of ball shot pellets or projectiles may be fired simultaneously from a smooth or rifled bore by a single function of the firing device and which has a barrel length of less than 18 inches for smooth bore weapons and 16 inches for rifled weapons. Weapons of less than .225 caliber shall not be included.

"Sawed-off rifle" means a rifle of any caliber, loaded or unloaded, which expels a projectile by action of an explosion of a combustible material and is designed as a shoulder weapon with a barrel or barrels length of less than 16 inches or which has been modified to an overall length of less than 26 inches.

"Crime of violence" applies to and includes any of the following crimes or an attempt to commit any of the same, namely, murder, manslaughter, kidnapping, rape, mayhem, assault with intent to maim, disable, disfigure or kill, robbery, burglary, housebreaking, breaking and entering and larceny.

"Person" applies to and includes firm, partnership, association or corporation.

History.
Code 1950, § 18.1-268.1; 1968, c. 661; 1975, cc. 14, 15; 1992, c. 580; 2004, c. 930.

Cross references.
As to presumption of no bail for illegal aliens charged with certain crimes, see § 19.2-120.1.

Law Review.

For survey of Virginia criminal law for the year 1972-1973, see 59 Va. L. Rev. 1458 (1973).

CASE NOTES

Commonwealth must prove defendant used "sawed-off" shotgun" in commission of crime. — Trial judge committed reversible error by giving an instruction to the jury which read: "Under the law, the weapon in this case was a sawed-off shotgun" since the Commonwealth must prove beyond a reasonable doubt that the defendant used a sawed-off shotgun in the commission of the crime of murder or manslaughter. Bruce v. Commonwealth, 9 Va. App. 298, 387 S.E.2d 279 (1990).

Jury must decide whether gun is a "sawed-off shotgun." — Whether the weapon met the statutory definition of a "sawed-off shotgun" was a factual issue for the jury to decide. Bruce v. Commonwealth, 9 Va. App. 298, 387 S.E.2d 279 (1990).

Jury properly used their reason, common sense, knowledge, experience, and examination of the gun at issue to determine whether it met the statutory definition of "sawed-off shotgun" under § 18.2-299 because the gun was admitted into evidence and the trial court properly instructed the jury on the definition. Person v. Commonwealth, 60 Va. App. 549, 729 S.E.2d 782, 2012 Va. App. LEXIS 255 (2012).

Evidence was sufficient to prove that "sawed-off shotgun" was used in commission of offense. — Evidence proved that appellant was one of two men who chased victim and fired upon him with the intent to kill, and while appellant and his coconspirators actually intended to kill the victim's son, appellant mistakenly believed that the victim was in fact his son during the pursuit, and accordingly, when the two men fired upon the victim with the intent to kill his son, their murderous intent was transferred to the killing of the victim, and evidence supported the conclusion that the sawed-off shotgun was used in the commission of this offense for the victim testified that he observed appellant "cocking something" as appellant exited car and began to run towards him. Henderson v. Commonwealth, 17 Va. App. 444, 438 S.E.2d 292 (1993).

Effect of absence of firing pin. — Possession of a weapon that would have become a completely operable sawed-off shotgun after a moment's delay to insert a firing pin satisfies the statutory definition of "sawed-off" shotgun. The absence of a firing pin in such a weapon does not exempt it from prohibition. Rogers v. Commonwealth, 14 Va. App. 774, 418 S.E.2d 727 (1992).

The absence of a firing pin in a weapon does not exempt it from the definition of "any weapon . . . from which a number of ball shot pellets or projectiles may be fired" as provided in the definition of "sawed-off" shotgun." Robinson v. Commonwealth, No. 0934-91-2 (Ct. of Appeals Oct. 6, 1992).

Caliber requirement is an element of the crime. — In prosecutions for possession of a sawed-off shotgun, the Commonwealth must prove that the subject weapon falls within the statutory definition, including the requirement that it be not less than a specified caliber; the statutory requirement relating to the weapon's caliber defines an element of the crime and not an affirmative defense. Dillard v. Commonwealth, 28 Va. App. 340, 504 S.E.2d 411 (1998).

Applied in Taylor v. Commonwealth, 10 Va. App. 260, 391 S.E.2d 592 (1990).

§ 18.2-300. Possession or use of "sawed-off" shotgun or rifle.

A. Possession or use of a "sawed-off" shotgun or "sawed-off" rifle in the perpetration or attempted perpetration of a crime of violence is a Class 2 felony.

B. Possession or use of a "sawed-off" shotgun or "sawed-off" rifle for any other purpose, except as permitted by this article and official use by those persons permitted possession by § 18.2-303, is a Class 4 felony.

History.

Code 1950, § 18.1-268.2; 1968, c. 661; 1975, cc. 14, 15; 1978, c. 710; 1992, c. 580.

Cross references.

For definition of "barrier crime" as including a conviction of use of a sawed-off shotgun in a crime of violence as set out in subsection A of § 18.2-300, or an equivalent offense in another state, and prohibition against assisted living facilities, adult day care centers or child welfare agencies hiring for certain compensated employment persons who have committed such an offense, see §§ 63.2-1719, 63.2-1720.

Law Review.

For survey of Virginia criminal law for the year 1972-1973, see 59 Va. L. Rev. 1458 (1973). For survey of Virginia criminal law for the year 1974-1975, see 61 Va. L. Rev. 1697 (1975).

CASE NOTES

Actual knowledge of the weapon's specific physical characteristics is not required. Rather, sufficient intent is established if the defendant is shown to have possessed an item which he knew to be a firearm within the general meaning of the term. It is the dangerous character of the object that obviates proof of scienter. Pierce v. Commonwealth, No. 1622-88-4 (Ct. of Appeals Apr. 10, 1990).

Defendant's conviction for use of a sawed-off shotgun during the commission of rape was not error even though he was acquitted of the underlying rape charge. Finney v. Commonwealth, No. 1089-87-3 (Ct. of Appeals Apr. 25, 1989).

Evidence was sufficient for jury to have found that a sawed-off shotgun was used by appellant in the attempted murder of victim where appellant and his companions discussed all of the plans for the killing in appellant's home, the sawed-off shotgun that was to be used to shoot intended victim was obtained from a room in appellant's home, there was no evidence that any other weapon was discussed, available or used in the subsequent attempted murder of victim, and in addition, appellant and coconspirator purchased ammunition for the shotgun, and coconspirator placed the weapon under the hood of the Chevrolet before the vehicle left for intended victim's neighborhood, appellant chased victim, mistaking him for intended victim, and that during chase two shots was fired, and only weapon recovered was sawed-off shotgun obtained from appellant's home, and further the only ammunition recovered were shotgun shells. Henderson v. Commonwealth, 17 Va. App. 444, 438 S.E.2d 292 (1993).

Commonwealth must prove defendant used "sawed-off" shotgun" in commission of crime. — Trial judge committed reversible error by giving an instruction to the jury which read: "Under the law, the weapon in this case was a sawed-off shotgun" since the Commonwealth must prove beyond a reasonable doubt that the defendant used a sawed-off shotgun in the commission of the crime of murder or manslaughter. Bruce v. Commonwealth, 9 Va. App. 298, 387 S.E.2d 279 (1990).

Jury must decide whether gun is a "sawed-off shotgun." — Whether the weapon met the statutory definition of a "sawed-off shotgun" was a factual issue for the jury to decide. Bruce v. Commonwealth, 9 Va. App. 298, 387 S.E.2d 279 (1990).

Caliber requirement is an element of the crime. — In prosecutions for possession of a sawed-off shotgun, the Commonwealth must prove that the subject weapon falls within the statutory definition, including the requirement that it be not less than a specified caliber; the statutory requirement relating to the weapon's caliber defines an element of the crime and not an affirmative defense. Dillard v. Commonwealth, 28 Va. App. 340, 504 S.E.2d 411 (1998).

Applied in Turner v. Commonwealth, 221 Va. 513, 273 S.E.2d 36

(1980); Hall v. Commonwealth, 8 Va. App. 350, 381 S.E.2d 512 (1989); Taylor v. Commonwealth, 10 Va. App. 260, 391 S.E.2d 592 (1990).

§§ 18.2-301, 18.2-302. Repealed by Acts 1978, c. 710.

§ 18.2-303. What article does not apply to.

The provisions of this article shall not be applicable to:

(1) The manufacture for, and sale of, "sawed-off" shotguns or "sawed-off" rifles to the armed forces or law-enforcement officers of the United States or of any state or of any political subdivision thereof, or the transportation required for that purpose; and

(2) "Sawed-off" shotguns, "sawed-off" rifles and automatic arms issued to the National Guard of Virginia by the United States or such arms used by the United States Army or Navy or in the hands of troops of the national guards of other states or territories of the United States passing through Virginia, or such arms as may be provided for the officers of the State Police or officers of penal institutions.

History.
Code 1950, § 18.1-268.5; 1968, c. 661; 1975, cc. 14, 15; 1992, c. 580.

Law Review.
For survey of Virginia criminal law for the year 1972-1973, see 59 Va. L. Rev. 1458 (1973).

§ 18.2-303.1. What article does not prohibit.

Nothing contained in this article shall prohibit or interfere with the possession of a "sawed-off" shotgun or "sawed-off" rifle for scientific purposes, the possession of a "sawed-off" shotgun or "sawed-off" rifle possessed in compliance with federal law or the possession of a "sawed-off" shotgun or "sawed-off" rifle not usable as a firing weapon and possessed as a curiosity, ornament, or keepsake.

History.
Code 1950, § 18.1-268.5; 1968, c. 661; 1975, cc. 14, 15; 1976, c. 351; 1992, c. 580; 1993, c. 449.

CASE NOTES

The only exceptions to the proscription of civilian possession of sawed-off shotguns are the defenses set forth in this section. In order for a defendant to rely on these defenses, he must prove either that he possessed the shotgun for scientific purposes, or that the shotgun was both unusable and possessed as a curiosity, ornament, or keepsake. The conjunctive language of the second exception means that a weapon merely unusable as a firing weapon does not fall within the provisions of this section. Rogers v. Commonwealth, 14 Va. App. 774, 418 S.E.2d 727 (1992).

§ 18.2-304. Manufacturer's and dealer's register; inspection of stock.

Every manufacturer or dealer shall keep a register of all "sawed-off" shotguns and "sawed-off" rifles

manufactured or handled by him. This register shall show the model and serial number, date of manufacture, sale, loan, gift, delivery or receipt of every "sawed-off" shotgun and "sawed-off" rifle, the name, address, and occupation of the person to whom the "sawed-off" shotgun or "sawed-off" rifle was sold, loaned, given or delivered, or from whom it was received. Upon demand every manufacturer or dealer shall permit any marshal, sheriff or police officer to inspect his entire stock of "sawed-off" shotguns and "sawed-off" rifles, and "sawed-off" shotgun or "sawed-off" rifle barrels, and shall produce the register, herein required, for inspection. A violation of any provision of this section shall be punishable as a Class 3 misdemeanor.

History.
Code 1950, § 18.1-268.6; 1968, c. 661; 1975, cc. 14, 15; 1992, c. 580.

Law Review.
For survey of Virginia criminal law for the year 1972-1973, see 59 Va. L. Rev. 1458 (1973).

§ 18.2-305. Repealed by Acts 1976, c. 351.

§ 18.2-306. Search warrants for "sawed-off" shotguns and rifles; confiscation and destruction.

Warrant to search any house or place and seize any "sawed-off" shotgun or "sawed-off" rifle possessed in violation of this article may issue in the same manner and under the same restrictions as provided by law for stolen property, and any court of record, upon application of the attorney for the Commonwealth, a police officer or conservator of the peace, may order any "sawed-off" shotgun or "sawed-off" rifle thus or otherwise legally seized, to be confiscated and either destroyed or delivered to a peace officer of the Commonwealth or a political subdivision thereof.

History.
Code 1950, § 18.1-268.8; 1968, c. 661; 1975, cc. 14, 15; 1992, c. 580.

§ 18.2-307. Short title of article.

This article may be cited as the "Sawed-Off Shotgun and Sawed-Off Rifle Act."

History.
Code 1950, § 18.1-268.9; 1968, c. 661; 1975, cc. 14, 15; 1992, c. 580.

ARTICLE 6.1.

CONCEALED WEAPONS AND CONCEALED HANDGUN PERMITS.

Editor's note.
Acts 2013, c. 746, which recodified former § 18.2-308 as Article 6.1 (§ 18.2-307.1 et seq.), in cl. 2 provides: "That the provisions of this act are declaratory of existing law."

§ 18.2-307.1. Definitions.

As used in this article, unless the context requires a different meaning:

"Ballistic knife" means any knife with a detachable blade that is propelled by a spring-operated mechanism.

"Handgun" means any pistol or revolver or other firearm, except a machine gun, originally designed, made, and intended to fire a projectile by means of an explosion of a combustible material from one or more barrels when held in one hand.

"Law-enforcement officer" means those individuals defined as a law-enforcement officer in § 9.1-101, law-enforcement agents of the armed forces of the United States and the Naval Criminal Investigative Service, and federal agents who are otherwise authorized to carry weapons by federal law. "Law-enforcement officer" also means any sworn full-time law-enforcement officer employed by a law-enforcement agency of the United States or any state or political subdivision thereof, whose duties are substantially similar to those set forth in § 9.1-101.

"Lawfully admitted for permanent residence" means the status of having been lawfully accorded the privilege of residing permanently in the United States as an immigrant in accordance with the immigration laws, such status not having changed.

"Personal knowledge" means knowledge of a fact that a person has himself gained through his own senses, or knowledge that was gained by a law-enforcement officer or prosecutor through the performance of his official duties.

"Spring stick" means a spring-loaded metal stick activated by pushing a button that rapidly and forcefully telescopes the weapon to several times its original length.

History.
2013, c. 746.

§ 18.2-308. Carrying concealed weapons; exceptions; penalty.

A. If any person carries about his person, hidden from common observation, (i) any pistol, revolver, or other weapon designed or intended to propel a missile of any kind by action of an explosion of any combustible material; (ii) any dirk, bowie knife, switchblade knife, ballistic knife, machete, razor, slingshot, spring stick, metal knucks, or blackjack; (iii) any flailing instrument consisting of two or more rigid parts connected in such a manner as to allow them to swing freely, which may be known as a nun chahka, nun chuck, nunchaku, shuriken, or fighting chain; (iv) any disc, of whatever configuration, having at least two points or pointed blades which is designed to be thrown or propelled and which may be known as a throwing star or oriental dart; or (v) any weapon of like kind as those enumerated in this subsection, he is guilty of a Class 1 misdemeanor. A second violation of this section or a conviction under this section subsequent to any conviction under any substantially similar ordinance of any county, city, or town shall be punishable as a Class 6 felony, and a third or subsequent such violation shall be punishable as a Class 5 felony. For the purpose of this section, a weapon shall be deemed to be hidden from common observation when it is observable but is of such deceptive appearance as to disguise the weapon's true nature. It shall be an affirmative defense to a violation of clause (i) regarding a handgun, that a person had been issued, at the time of the offense, a valid concealed handgun permit.

B. This section shall not apply to any person while in his own place of abode or the curtilage thereof.

C. Except as provided in subsection A of § 18.2-308.012, this section shall not apply to:

1. Any person while in his own place of business;

2. Any law-enforcement officer, wherever such law-enforcement officer may travel in the Commonwealth;

3. Any person who is at, or going to or from, an established shooting range, provided that the weapons are unloaded and securely wrapped while being transported;

4. Any regularly enrolled member of a weapons collecting organization who is at, or going to or from, a bona fide weapons exhibition, provided that the weapons are unloaded and securely wrapped while being transported;

5. Any person carrying such weapons between his place of abode and a place of purchase or repair, provided the weapons are unloaded and securely wrapped while being transported;

6. Any person actually engaged in lawful hunting, as authorized by the Board of Game and Inland Fisheries, under inclement weather conditions necessitating temporary protection of his firearm from those conditions, provided that possession of a handgun while engaged in lawful hunting shall not be construed as hunting with a handgun if the person hunting is carrying a valid concealed handgun permit;

7. Any State Police officer retired from the Department of State Police, any officer retired from the Division of Capitol Police, any local law-enforcement officer, auxiliary police officer or animal control officer retired from a police department or sheriff's office within the Commonwealth, any special agent retired from the State Corporation Commission or the Alcoholic Beverage Control Board, any conservation police officer retired from the Department of Game and Inland Fisheries, any Virginia Marine Police officer retired from the Law Enforcement Division of the Virginia Marine Resources Commission, any campus police officer appointed under Chapter 17 (§ 23-232 et seq.) of Title 23 retired from a campus police department, and any retired investigator of the security division of the State Lottery Department, other than an officer or agent terminated for cause, (i) with a service-related disability;

(ii) following at least 15 years of service with any such law-enforcement agency, board or any combination thereof; (iii) who has reached 55 years of age; or (iv) who is on long-term leave from such law-enforcement agency or board due to a service-related injury, provided such officer carries with him written proof of consultation with and favorable review of the need to carry a concealed handgun issued by the chief law-enforcement officer of the last such agency from which the officer retired or the agency that employs the officer or, in the case of special agents, issued by the State Corporation Commission or the Alcoholic Beverage Control Board. A copy of the proof of consultation and favorable review shall be forwarded by the chief or the Board to the Department of State Police for entry into the Virginia Criminal Information Network. The chief law-enforcement officer shall not without cause withhold such written proof if the retired law-enforcement officer otherwise meets the requirements of this section. An officer set forth in clause (iv) who receives written proof of consultation to carry a concealed handgun shall surrender such proof of consultation upon return to work or upon termination of employment with the law-enforcement agency. Notice of the surrender shall be forwarded to the Department of State Police for entry into the Virginia Criminal Information Network. However, if such officer retires on disability because of the service-related injury, and would be eligible under clause (i) for written proof of consultation to carry a concealed handgun, he may retain the previously issued written proof of consultation. A retired law-enforcement officer who receives proof of consultation and favorable review pursuant to this subdivision is authorized to carry a concealed handgun in the same manner as a law-enforcement officer authorized to carry a concealed handgun pursuant to subdivision 2.

7a. Any person who is eligible for retirement with at least 20 years of service with a law-enforcement agency or board mentioned in subdivision 7 who has resigned in good standing from such law-enforcement agency or board to accept a position covered by a retirement system that is authorized under Title 51.1, provided such person carries with him written proof of consultation with and favorable review of the need to carry a concealed handgun issued by the chief law-enforcement officer of the agency from which he resigned or, in the case of special agents, issued by the State Corporation Commission or the Alcoholic Beverage Control Board. A copy of the proof of consultation and favorable review shall be forwarded by the chief, Board or Commission to the Department of State Police for entry into the Virginia Criminal Information Network. The chief law-enforcement officer shall not without cause withhold such written proof if the law-enforcement officer otherwise meets the requirements of this section.

For purposes of applying the reciprocity provisions of § 18.2-308.014, any person granted the privilege to carry a concealed handgun pursuant to subdivision 7 or this subdivision, while carrying the proof of consultation and favorable review required, shall be deemed to have been issued a concealed handgun permit.

For purposes of complying with the federal Law Enforcement Officers Safety Act of 2004, a retired or resigned law-enforcement officer who receives proof of consultation and review pursuant to subdivision 7 or this subdivision shall have the opportunity to annually participate, at the retired or resigned law-enforcement officer's expense, in the same training and testing to carry firearms as is required of active law-enforcement officers in the Commonwealth. If such retired or resigned law-enforcement officer meets the training and qualification standards, the chief law-enforcement officer shall issue the retired or resigned officer certification, valid one year from the date of issuance, indicating that the retired or resigned officer has met the standards of the agency to carry a firearm;

8. Any State Police officer who is a member of the organized reserve forces of any of the armed services of the United States, national guard, or naval militia, while such officer is called to active military duty, provided such officer carries with him written proof of consultation with and favorable review of the need to carry a concealed handgun issued by the Superintendent of State Police. The proof of consultation and favorable review shall be valid as long as the officer is on active military duty and shall expire when the officer returns to active law-enforcement duty. The issuance of the proof of consultation and favorable review shall be entered into the Virginia Criminal Information Network. The Superintendent of State Police shall not without cause withhold such written proof if the officer is in good standing and is qualified to carry a weapon while on active law-enforcement duty.

For purposes of applying the reciprocity provisions of § 18.2-308.014, any person granted the privilege to carry a concealed handgun pursuant to this subdivision, while carrying the proof of consultation and favorable review required, shall be deemed to have been issued a concealed handgun permit;

9. Any attorney for the Commonwealth or assistant attorney for the Commonwealth, wherever such attorney may travel in the Commonwealth;

10. Any person who may lawfully possess a firearm and is carrying a handgun while in a personal, private motor vehicle or vessel and such handgun is secured in a container or compartment in the vehicle or vessel; and

11. Any enrolled participant of a firearms training course who is at, or going to or from, a training location, provided that the weapons are unloaded and securely wrapped while being transported.

D. This section shall also not apply to any of the following individuals while in the discharge of their official duties, or while in transit to or from such duties:

1. Carriers of the United States mail;

2. Officers or guards of any state correctional institution;

3. Conservators of the peace, except that an attorney for the Commonwealth or assistant attorney for the Commonwealth may carry a concealed handgun pursuant to subdivision C 9. However, the following conservators of the peace shall not be permitted to carry a concealed handgun without obtaining a permit as provided in this article: (i) notaries public; (ii) registrars; (iii) drivers, operators or other persons in charge of any motor vehicle carrier of passengers for hire; or (iv) commissioners in chancery;

4. Noncustodial employees of the Department of Corrections designated to carry weapons by the Director of the Department of Corrections pursuant to § 53.1-29; and

5. Harbormaster of the City of Hopewell.

History.
Code 1950, § 18.1-269; 1960, c. 358; 1964, c. 130; 1975, cc. 14, 15, 594; 1976, c. 302; 1978, c. 715; 1979, c. 642; 1980, c. 238; 1981, c. 376; 1982, cc. 71, 553; 1983, c. 529; 1984, cc. 360, 720; 1985, c. 427; 1986, cc. 57, 451, 625, 641; 1987, cc. 592, 707; 1988, cc. 359, 793; 1989, cc. 538, 542; 1990, cc. 640, 648, 825; 1991, c. 637; 1992, cc. 510, 705; 1993, cc. 748, 861; 1994, cc. 375, 697; 1995, c. 829; 1997, cc. 916, 921, 922; 1998, cc. 662, 670, 846, 847; 1999, cc. 628, 666, 679; 2001, cc. 25, 384, 657; 2002, cc. 699, 728, 826; 2004, cc. 355, 423, 462, 876, 885, 900, 901, 903, 905, 926, 995, 1012; 2005, cc. 344, 420, 424, 441, 839; 2006, c. 886; 2007, cc. 87, 272, 408, 455; 2008, cc. 69, 75, 80, 309, 464, 742; 2009, cc. 235, 779, 780; 2010, cc. 387, 433, 576, 586, 602, 677, 700, 709, 740, 741, 754, 841, 863; 2011, cc. 231, 234, 384, 410; 2012, cc. 132, 175, 291, 557, 776; 2013, cc. 559, 746.

Cross references.
As to carrying weapon to place of religious worship or on Sunday, see § 18.2-283. As to prohibiting possession of blackjacks, brass knuckles, etc., see § 18.2-311. As to presumption of no bail for illegal aliens charged with certain crimes, see § 19.2-120.1. As to carrying weapons by penitentiary guards and officials, see § 53.1-29.

Editor's note.
The above section is § 18.2-308 as enacted by Acts 1975, c. 594. Pursuant to § 30-152, it has been substituted for § 18.2-308 as enacted by Acts 1975, cc. 14 and 15.

Acts 2006, c. 886, cl. 2, provides: "That the provisions of this act creating subdivisions D1 and J5, amending subsection I, and amending subsection D, eliminating the five-year permit and subsection H referencing expiration of such a permit shall not become effective unless an appropriation of funds effectuating the purposes of these provisions is included in the general appropriations act for the period of July 1, 2006, through June 30, 2008, passed during the 2007 Session of the General Assembly, which become law; if such funds are appropriated, then such provisions of this act shall become effective on July 1, 2007." The appropriation of funds was not included in the general appropriations act passed during the 2007 session. The section is set out above without the above referenced amendments made by Acts 2006, c. 886.

Acts 2011, cc. 384 and 410, cl. 3 provides: "That the provisions of this act may result in a net increase in periods of imprisonment or commitment. Pursuant to § 30-19.1:4, the estimated amount of the necessary appropriation cannot be determined for periods of imprisonment in state adult correctional facilities; therefore, Chapter 874 of the Acts of Assembly of 2010 requires the Virginia Criminal Sentencing Commission to assign a minimum fiscal impact of $50,000. Pursuant to § 30-19.1:4, the estimated amount of the necessary appropriation cannot be determined for periods of commitment to the custody of the Department of Juvenile Justice."

Acts 2012, c. 776, cl. 2, provides: "That the provisions of this act may result in a net increase in periods of imprisonment or commit-

ment. Pursuant to § 30-19.1:4, the estimated amount of the necessary appropriation is $0 for periods of imprisonment in state adult correctional facilities and is $0 for periods of commitment to the custody of the Department of Juvenile Justice."

Acts 2013, c. 746, which recodified former § 18.2-308 as Article 6.1 (§ 18.2-307.1 et seq.) in cl. 2 provides: "That the provisions of this act are declaratory of existing law." Acts 2013, cc. 135, 559, and 659 also amended this section. Pursuant to § 30-152 those amendments have been given effect in §§ 18.2-308.02 and 18.2-308.03.

The 2006 amendments.
The 2006 amendment by c. 886, in subsection D, deleted "five-year" preceding "permit" in the first, seventeenth and nineteenth sentences and inserted "and notify the State Police of the issuance of the permit" in the thirteenth sentence; inserted subsections D1, H1, J1, J5 and S; in subsection E 13, inserted "a disqualifying conviction or upon" in the second sentence and "of such individual or of a deputy sheriff, police officer, or assistant attorney for the Commonwealth" in the third sentence; in the first sentence in subsection H, deleted "and the expiration date" following "issuance" and made a related change; deleted the former first sentence, relating to new concealed handgun permits for previous permitees in subsection I; and added the paragraph defining "Personal knowledge" in subsection M. See Editor's note for contingent effective date for certain amendments.

The 2007 amendments.
The 2007 amendment by c. 87 substituted "conservation police officer" for "game warden" in the first sentence of subdivision B 7.
The 2007 amendment by c. 272 inserted the present seventh sentence in subsection D.
The 2007 amendment by c. 408 added the third paragraph in subdivision B 7.
The 2007 amendment by c. 455 deleted "and" at the end of subdivision B 6; substituted "; and" for the period at the end of subdivision B 7; and added subdivision B 8.

The 2008 amendments.
The 2008 amendment by c. 69 inserted the present second sentence of subsection I, and added subsection K1.
The 2008 amendment by c. 75 inserted "any officer retired from the Division of Capitol Police" near the beginning of the first sentence of the first paragraph of subdivision B 7.
The 2008 amendment by c. 80, in subdivision B 7, inserted "or (iv) who is on long-term leave from such law-enforcement agency or board due to a service-related injury" and "or the agency that employs the officer" and made a related change in the first sentence, and added the present fourth through sixth sentences.
The 2008 amendment by c. 309 added "nor shall any proof of demonstrated competence expire" to the end of the introductory paragraph in subsection G.
The 2008 amendment by c. 464 added subdivision B 9; inserted "an attorney for the Commonwealth or assistant attorney for the Commonwealth may carry a concealed handgun pursuant to subdivision B 9. However" in subdivision C 4; and made minor stylistic changes.
The 2008 amendment by c. 742 added the last sentence in subsection J; and rewrote subsection J4, which read: "Any individual for whom it would be unlawful to purchase, possess or transport a firearm under § 18.2-308.1:2 or 18.2-308.1:3, who holds a concealed handgun permit, may have the permit suspended by the court that issued the permit during the period of incompetency, incapacity or disability."

The 2009 amendments.
The 2009 amendment by c. 235 added the last two sentences in subsection K.
The 2009 amendment by c. 779 inserted "or any retired law-enforcement officer ... required by such statute" in subsection J3.
The 2009 amendment by c. 780 inserted "including an electronic, video, or on-line course" in subdivisions G 7 and P1 7.

The 2010 amendments.
The 2010 amendment by c. 387 inserted "or of a substantially similar offense under the laws of any other state, the District of Columbia, the United States, or its territories" in subdivision E 9.
The 2010 amendment by c. 433 added the last sentence of subdivision B 7.

The 2010 amendment by c. 576, in subsection D, inserted the present fifteenth through seventeenth paragraphs and the nineteenth paragraph; and in subsection H, in the first sentence, inserted "or of the clerk of court who has been authorized to issue such permits pursuant to subsection D" and made a related change.

The 2010 amendments by cc. 586 and 741, are identical, and in subsection I, in the first sentence, inserted "and upon receipt by the circuit court of criminal history record information as provided in subsection D" following "subsection D" and substituted "it is found that the applicant is subject to any of the disqualifications set forth in subsection E" for "there is good cause shown for refusing to reissue a permit" and added the present second and third sentences.

The 2010 amendments by cc. 602 and 709, are identical, and rewrote subsection J3.

The 2010 amendments by cc. 677 and 700 are identical, and inserted the nineteenth through twenty-second sentences in subsection D.

The 2010 amendments by cc. 740 and 841 are identical, and added subdivision B 10 and made a related change.

The 2010 amendment by c. 754 added subdivision K (vi) and made a related change.

The 2010 amendment by c. 863 inserted the subdivision B 7a designation and therein added the first paragraph; and in the following two paragraphs (the former last two paragraphs in subdivision B 7), twice inserted "subdivision 7 or" and inserted "or resigned" throughout.

The 2011 amendments.

The 2011 amendment by c. 231, in subsection D, substituted "the clerk shall certify on the application that the 45-day period has expired, and mail or send via electronic mail a copy of the certified application to the applicant within five business days of the expiration of the 45-day period" for "the clerk shall certify on the application that the 45-day period has expired, and send a copy of the certified application to the applicant" near the end.

The 2011 amendment by c. 234 added subsection K2.

The 2011 amendments by cc. 384 and 410, effective March 23, 2011, are identical, and inserted "synthetic cannabinoids" in subdivision E 8, subdivision E 19, subdivision E 20, and made a minor stylistic change.

The 2012 amendments.

The 2012 amendment by c. 132 added the last sentence in subsection A; and in subsection H, substituted "photo identification" for "photo-identification" in the third sentence and added the last four sentences.

The 2012 amendments by cc. 175 and 557 are identical, and deleted the former sixth through thirteenth sentences of subsection D relating to fingerprinting.

The 2012 amendment by c. 291, in subsection B, substituted "person" for "regularly enrolled member of a target shooting organization" in subdivision B 3, added subdivision B 11, and made related changes; in subsection D, inserted the fourth sentence and "via United States mail" in the seventh sentence; added "including, if applicable, any reason under subsection E which is the basis of the denial" at the end of the fifth sentence in subsection I; in subsection K, substituted "receives the application" for "accepts the application" in the sixth sentence and "received by the court" for "accepted by the court" in the ninth sentence; and substituted "receives the information" for "accepts the information" in the last sentence of subsection K1.

The 2012 amendment by c. 776 inserted "any campus police officers appointed under Chapter 17 (§ 23-232 et seq.) of Title 23 retired from a campus police department" in subdivision A 7; deleted "campus police officers appointed pursuant to Chapter 17 (§ 23-232 et seq.) of Title 23" in the definition of "law-enforcement officer" in subsection M.

The 2013 amendments.

The 2013 amendment by c. 559 substituted "armed forces" for "Armed Forces" throughout the section; in subdivision C 7, deleted "and" following "Marine Resources Commission," inserted "and any retired investigator of the security division of the State Lottery Department" in the first sentence, and made minor stylistic changes.

The 2013 amendment by c. 746 redesignated most of the former

provisions of subsection B as C; redesignated former subsection C as subsection D; deleted former subsections D through S and transferred provisions to § 18.2-307.1 et seq.; substituted "subsection A of § 18.2-308.012" for "subsection J1" in the introductory paragraph of subsection C; substituted "§ 18.2-308.014" for "subsection P" in the second paragraphs of subdivisions C 7a and C 8; deleted the formerly repealed subdivision 3 and redesignated the following accordingly in subsection C; in subdivision C 3, substituted "subdivision C 9" for "subdivision B 9" in the first sentence, and substituted "this article" for "subsection D hereof" and clause (i) through (iv) designators for clause (a) through (d) designators in the second sentence; and made minor stylistic changes.

Law Review.

For survey of Virginia criminal law for the year 1973-1974, see 60 Va. L. Rev. 1499 (1974). For article, "Legal Issues Involving Children," see 35 U. Rich. L. Rev. 741 (2001). For article surveying developments in criminal law and procedure in Virginia from July 2001 to September 2002, see 37 U. Rich. L. Rev. 45 (2002). For survey of Virginia criminal law and procedure for the year 2004-2005, see 40 U. Rich. L. Rev. 197 (2005). For 2007 annual survey article, "Criminal Law and Procedure," see 42 U. Rich. L. Rev. 311 (2007). For survey of Virginia law on criminal law and procedure for the year 2007-2008, see 43 U. Rich. L. Rev. 149 (2008). For annual survey article, "Criminal Law and Procedure," see 44 U. Rich. L. Rev. 339 (2009). For article, "Construction Law," see 45 U. Rich. L. Rev. 227 (2010).

Michie's Jurisprudence.

For related discussion, see 20 M.J. Weapons, § 4; 21A M.J. Words and Phrases.

CASE NOTES

This section is sufficiently plain, when read in the light of its history. Withers v. Commonwealth, 109 Va. 837, 65 S.E. 16 (1909).

Issues for fact finder. — Whether a weapon is upon a person or is readily accessible are largely questions of fact that must be left to reasonable inferences drawn by the fact finder from the facts and circumstances of the case. Leith v. Commonwealth, 17 Va. App. 620, 440 S.E.2d 152 (1994).

The determination of whether a particular knife falls within the meaning of a term used in the statute is a question of fact to be determined by the trier of fact. Delcid v. Commonwealth, 32 Va. App. 14, 526 S.E.2d 273 (2000).

Motion to suppress denied. — Trial court properly denied defendant's suppression motion as the cocaine was discovered during a proper search incident to a lawful arrest for a concealed weapon violation; it was legally irrelevant under the Fourth Amendment that the deputy chose not to charge defendant with the lesser concealed weapon violation of § 18.2-308, upon discovering the suspected drugs during the search, enabling the deputy to charge defendant with possession of cocaine with intent to distribute under § 18.2-248, and possession of a firearm while simultaneously possessing illegal drugs under subsection A of § 18.2-308.4. Slayton v. Commonwealth, 41 Va. App. 101, 582 S.E.2d 448, 2003 Va. App. LEXIS 352 (2003).

Trial court did not err in denying defendant's motion to suppress; even assuming the arrest and search violated state law requiring release on a summons, the officers had probable cause to believe defendant committed the misdemeanor of possessing a concealed weapon and, thus, the arrest and search were not unconstitutional. An officer testified that the officer saw what the officer thought was the butt of a firearm protruding from defendant's rear pant's pocket. Coleman v. Commonwealth, 2008 Va. App. LEXIS 463 (Oct. 14, 2008).

Accessibility of a concealed weapon. — Prompt and immediate use is clearly the evil proscribed by this section. But while the location of a weapon is a significant circumstance for the court to consider in weighing accessibility, a weapon is not inaccessible as a matter of law if available only upon noticeable body motion. Watson v. Commonwealth, 17 Va. App. 124, 435 S.E.2d 428 (1993).

Accessibility of a concealed weapon for "prompt and immediate use" is clearly the evil proscribed by this section. Leith v. Commonwealth, 17 Va. App. 620, 440 S.E.2d 152 (1994).

A defendant's argument that a weapon was not "hidden from

common observation" because it was covered only by a readily movable windbreaker jacket lacked foundation in that this section requires only that the weapon be hidden from common observation, not that the covering be difficult to remove. Accessibility of a concealed weapon for prompt and immediate use is clearly the evil proscribed by the statute and the fact that the windbreaker was readily movable supported rather than weakened the defendant's conviction. Barley v. Commonwealth, No. 0117-00-3, 2000 Va. App. LEXIS 765 (Ct. of Appeals Nov. 28, 2000).

Appellate court's judgment that affirmed the trial court's judgment finding defendant guilty of concealing a weapon "about his person" as a second offense was plainly wrong and had to be reversed; once defendant exited defendant's car and closed the door to the car in which defendant had concealed a pistol in the car's center console compartment, defendant no longer had the pistol "about his person," as was required for a conviction on the charged offense because the pistol was no longer accessible to defendant so as to afford "prompt and immediate use." Pruitt v. Commonwealth, 274 Va. 382, 650 S.E.2d 684, 2007 Va. LEXIS 109 (2007).

Concealment of firearm not requisite under § 18.2-308.4. — Section 18.2-308.4 is not an extension of this section. The clear wording of § 18.2-308.4 prohibits unlawful possession of cocaine "simultaneously with" knowingly and intentionally possessing any firearm. No language in § 18.2-308.4 requires proof of concealment of weapons. Jefferson v. Commonwealth, 14 Va. App. 77, 414 S.E.2d 860 (1992).

Exception for conservators of the peace. — In interpreting this criminal statute, the court is bound by the statutory definition of "conservator of the peace" adopted by the legislature and codified in § 19.2-12 and is not permitted to ignore or rewrite the statute in favor of a broader common-law definition. Frias v. Commonwealth, 34 Va. App. 193, 538 S.E.2d 374, 2000 Va. App. LEXIS 838 (2000).

Former § 9-183.8, concerning the licensing and registration of security guards, expressly states that compliance with the provisions of that article does not authorize any person to exercise any powers of a conservator of the peace and it necessarily follows that a registered security guard does not, by virtue of that status alone, fall within the exemption from the prohibition on carrying concealed weapons for conservators of the peace. Frias v. Commonwealth, 34 Va. App. 193, 538 S.E.2d 374, 2000 Va. App. LEXIS 838 (2000).

Availability of weapon contemplated by this section means in a ready manner or without much difficulty. Watson v. Commonwealth, 17 Va. App. 124, 435 S.E.2d 428 (1993).

No application to convicted felon who has not had rights restored. — This section allows a person to place his firearm under his coat, hunting jacket or other outer garment to protect it from the weather, but it has no application to a convicted felon who has not had his rights to possess a weapon restored. United States v. Etheridge, 932 F.2d 318 (4th Cir.), cert. denied, 502 U.S. 917, 112 S. Ct. 323, 116 L. Ed. 2d 264 (1991).

Hidden from common view. — A weapon is hidden from common view under this section when it is hidden from all except those with an unusual or exceptional opportunity to view it. Clarke v. Commonwealth, 32 Va. App. 286, 527 S.E.2d 484, 2000 Va. App. LEXIS 299 (2000).

A gun found in the pocket on the back of the vehicle seat in which the defendant was seated was concealed from common view where it became visible to the investigating officer only when he approached the front passenger seat of the vehicle close enough for him to peer down into the seat's pocket compartment from directly above. Clarke v. Commonwealth, 32 Va. App. 286, 527 S.E.2d 484, 2000 Va. App. LEXIS 299 (2000).

Deputy had probable cause under the Fourth Amendment to believe that defendant was carrying a concealed weapon in violation of § 18.2-308 where: (1) except for a "couple of inches" of the butt of the handgun protruding from defendant's pocket, the rest of the weapon was completely hidden, and even those "couple of inches" were observed by the deputy only during the close-quarters encounter of a weapons frisk, not beforehand; (2) a reasonable probability existed that the firearm, both at the time of the pat-down and during the few moments immediately preceding it, was hidden from all except those with an unusual or exceptional opportunity to observe it; and (3) an equally reasonable probability supported the inference that defendant, having lied about having a firearm on him when directly questioned by the deputy, did not

possess a permit issued under subsection D of § 18.2-308 authorizing him to carry a concealed weapon. Slayton v. Commonwealth, 41 Va. App. 101, 582 S.E.2d 448, 2003 Va. App. LEXIS 352 (2003).

Pistol under car floor mat warranted conviction. — Defendant was properly convicted of carrying a concealed weapon where police inventory revealed a fully loaded pistol under the driver's floor mat completely out of sight. Watson v. Commonwealth, 17 Va. App. 124, 435 S.E.2d 428 (1993).

Pellet gun protruding above vehicle seat. — Fact finder could infer beyond a reasonable doubt that a pellet gun was concealed from public view under § 18.2-308 A, where police officer could only see the back of the grip of the gun protruding above the driver's seat of defendant's vehicle. Fountain v. Commonwealth, No. 0262-01-2, 2002 Va. App. LEXIS 276 (Ct. of Appeals May 7, 2002).

Gun placed in vehicle console. — Evidence that defendant placed his gun in the console of his vehicle after a traffic accident was sufficient to support his conviction of concealment of a weapon, because, from his position next to the driver's door, defendant could have easily obtained his gun from the console, and thus the gun was concealed about his person. Pruitt v. Commonwealth, 2006 Va. App. LEXIS 597 (May 24, 2006).

"Secured in a container or compartment." — Defendant's gun was in compliance with the exception to the concealed weapon prohibition in subdivision B 10 of § 18.2-308 because was "secured" in a closed, latched, and well-fastened glove compartment, and the General Assembly specifically chose to omit the term "locked" from the exception. Doulgerakis v. Commonwealth, 61 Va. App. 417, 737 S.E.2d 40, 2013 Va. App. LEXIS 36 (2013).

Evidence proved that weapon was concealed "about the person." — Pistol was certainly close to defendant where it was in console compartment of car that was located adjacent to the area that he was sitting, and thus, the evidence supported judge's finding that the weapon was concealed "about the person" within the meaning of this section. Leith v. Commonwealth, 17 Va. App. 620, 440 S.E.2d 152 (1994).

Evidence was sufficient to prove that a concealed weapon was "about" defendant's "person" under § 18.2-308 even though defendant was standing outside the car when the gun was discovered inside the car. Since no one returned to the vehicle after the four occupants exited the car, the only explanation was that the weapon was concealed prior to defendant leaving the back seat; thus, it was reasonable for the trial court to infer that the weapon was concealed while defendant sat in close proximity to it. Johnson v. Commonwealth, 2010 Va. App. LEXIS 475 (Dec. 14, 2010).

Insufficient evidence that weapon was "about the person" of defendant. — Defendant's conviction for carrying a concealed weapon, second offense, under subsection A of § 18.2-308, was improper because the evidence was insufficient to permit a reasonable trier of fact to conclude that the gun was "about the person" of defendant when he hid it under the rain catch and walked away. His gun had not been concealed prior to his placing it under the rain catch and no evidence showed that he remained in the proximity of the rain catch and the hidden gun for any appreciable length of time beyond that necessary to place his pistol under the rain catch. Ruth v. Commonwealth, 2011 Va. App. LEXIS 317 (Oct. 18, 2011).

Pistol in handbag warranted conviction. — Defendant was properly convicted of carrying a concealed weapon where she carried a pistol in a brown, zippered handbag. Schaaf v. Commonwealth, 220 Va. 429, 258 S.E.2d 574 (1979).

A pistol carried in a handbag is not only near and about the carrier's person, hidden from common observation, but in some handbags it is so accessible that it could be fired without being removed therefrom. It is so connected with the person as to be readily accessible for use or surprise if desired. Schaaf v. Commonwealth, 220 Va. 429, 258 S.E.2d 574 (1979).

Defendant violated this section by carrying a handgun in a gym bag. Hall v. Commonwealth, 12 Va. App. 559, 389 S.E.2d 921 (1990).

And *Sutherland v. Commonwealth*, 109 Va. 834, 65 S.E. 15 (1909), held overruled to the extent that it may be in conflict with holding approving conviction for concealing pistol in handbag. See Schaaf v. Commonwealth, 220 Va. 429, 258 S.E.2d 574 (1979).

Sufficient reasons to deny permit and authority to grant limited permit. — Trial court sufficiently stated reasons for its denial of an application to carry a concealed weapon, and the court had authority to grant a limited permit; where the trial court stated that applicant failed to give reasons for the issuance of a permit which demonstrated a need to carry a concealed weapon and that there were suitable alternatives to carrying a concealed weapon available to applicant, the court sufficiently complied with the requirement that specific reasons for the denial be stated; furthermore, permit restrictions of the limited permit were consistent with the court's authority to issue such a permit. In re Gatti, No. 0083-89-4 (Ct. of Appeals May 9, 1989).

When weapon concealed. — Carrying a weapon in one's back pocket, covered by a duffle bag, constitutes carrying a concealed weapon if the handle of the weapon, the only part of the weapon extending outside of the pocket, is concealed by the duffle bag. Main v. Commonwealth, 20 Va. App. 370, 457 S.E.2d 400 (1995) (decision prior to 1995 amendment).

Evidence was sufficient to prove that handgun carried by defendant was concealed, where police office who viewed defendant from the back and front observed no visible sign that defendant was carrying a weapon and later saw defendant retrieve a handgun from his right coat pocket and drop it on the ground. Winston v. Commonwealth, 26 Va. App. 746, 497 S.E.2d 141 (1998).

It did not appear that defendant's conduct was in compliance with subsection A of § 18.2-308, which prohibited carrying a concealed firearm about the person without a permit. Virginia case law suggested that defendant, whose concealed-carry permit had expired, carried the firearm at issue "about his person" and in a concealed manner when he held a messenger bag (in which the firearm was hidden) in the backseat of his vehicle. United States v. Masciandaro, 648 F. Supp. 2d 779, 2009 U.S. Dist. LEXIS 76802 (E.D. Va. 2009), aff'd, 638 F.3d 458, 2011 U.S. App. LEXIS 5964 (4th Cir. Va. 2011).

Sufficiency of evidence of intent to conceal. — Assuming that this statute requires proof of intent to conceal, the circumstantial evidence, viewed in the light most favorable to the commonwealth, supported a finding that the defendant did, in fact, intentionally place a weapon beneath a jacket on the passenger seat next to him where the defendant told a police officer the weapon was in the passenger seat, the officer found the weapon there, positioned beneath the jacket, the defendant himself testified that the weapon could not have fallen from the console to a location beneath the jacket and, finally, no evidence indicated that anyone besides the defendant approached the car and put the weapon beneath the jacket. Barley v. Commonwealth, No. 0117-00-3, 2000 Va. App. LEXIS 765 (Ct. of Appeals Nov. 28, 2000).

Sufficient evidence of concealment. — Conviction for carrying a concealed weapon was supported by testimony that defendant sometimes carried the dagger in his pants pocket; in addition, the trial judge could have reasonably concluded that the officer saw defendant when he came from the public street into the hallway and thus, could have inferred that the dagger, which was concealed when the officer searched defendant, was likewise concealed before defendant entered the building. Edwards v. Commonwealth, No. 1960-02-4, 2004 Va. App. LEXIS 36 (Ct. of Appeals Jan. 28, 2004).

Evidence was sufficient to convict defendant of possession of a concealed weapon by a convicted felon, in violation of § 18.2-308.2, where defendant admitted that he possessed a razor and any razor was explicitly included as a weapon in subsection A of § 18.2-308. The manner in which defendant used the razor was irrelevant to the analysis. Uzzle v. Commonwealth, 2010 Va. App. LEXIS 239 (2010).

Insufficient evidence of concealment. — Although the police officers testified that they did not observe the gun in the police wagon before putting appellant inside, that testimony did not exclude the hypothesis that the gun was in the wagon and hidden from common observation. Moreover, the evidence proved that two police officers searched appellant after he was captured and arrested. Both officers testified that they found nothing on his person when they searched him. This evidence failed to prove beyond a reasonable doubt that the gun was hidden on his person when he was placed in the wagon. Glaze v. Commonwealth, No. 0822-94-2 (Ct. of Appeals April 25, 1995) (decision prior to 1995 amendment).

Evidence was insufficient to convict defendant of carrying a concealed weapon under subsection A of § 18.2-308 because the weapon was not on defendant's person, but it was located in a locked glove compartment of a car in which he was a front seat passenger, and defendant did not possess a key to the locked glove compartment. Hunter v. Commonwealth, 56 Va. App. 50, 690 S.E.2d

792, 2010 Va. App. LEXIS 130 (2010).

Physical characteristics of knife and not purpose for carrying determine whether the knife is a weapon contemplated by this section. Ricks v. Commonwealth, 27 Va. App. 442, 499 S.E.2d 575 (1998).

Not all knives prohibited. — Defendant's knife, which was described by the arresting officer as a steak knife, was not a weapon "of like kind" to a dirk, despite the prosecutor's allegation that it satisfied the definition because it had a sharp end at the bottom edge and an extreme point that would certainly cut straight through flesh if propelled with any type of force. Goodwin v. Commonwealth, — Va. App. —, — S.E.2d —, 2005 Va. App. LEXIS 265 (July 12, 2005).

Defendant's conviction for possession of a concealed weapon by a convicted felon in violation of subsection A of § 18.2-308.2 was vacated because the evidence did not establish that the knife defendant possessed was one of the items enumerated in subsection A of § 18.2-308 or that it was a weapon of like kind to one enumerated, and the record was devoid of any facts on which one could find that the knife was either designed for fighting purposes or commonly understood to be a weapon. McMillan v. Commonwealth, 55 Va. App. 392, 686 S.E.2d 525, 2009 Va. App. LEXIS 571 (2009).

Circumstances surrounding possession relevant to determining nature of bladed instrument. — The determination of whether a given bladed instrument is an implement or a weapon requires consideration not only of the physical character of the instrument itself but also of the circumstances surrounding its possession and use. Delcid v. Commonwealth, 32 Va. App. 14, 526 S.E.2d 273 (2000).

Carrying a concealed non-weapon does not violate this section even though that non-weapon may be "of like kind" to a dirk; for the offense to be committed, the object carried concealed must be a weapon and the purpose for which it is created and employed is a critical distinction between an implement and a weapon. Thus, while the specific purpose for which the item is possessed is not itself an element of the crimes defined by this section, that purpose is one of the defining characteristics of the item in question. Delcid v. Commonwealth, 32 Va. App. 14, 526 S.E.2d 273 (2000).

Box cutter is not a weapon within the meaning of this section. — Appellate court erred in upholding the trial court's conviction finding defendant guilty of possessing a concealed weapon, a box cutter, after having been convicted of a felony, in violation of subsection A of § 18.2-308.2; the box cutter was not a weapon enumerated in subsection A of § 18.2-308 and did not fit in the category in that statute that included weapons of any kind like the weapons enumerated in subsection A of § 18.2-308. Harris v. Commonwealth, 274 Va. 409, 650 S.E.2d 89, 2007 Va. LEXIS 103 (2007).

Razor blade. — Razor blade found in defendant's pocket was a concealed weapon within the definition in § 18.2-308 A, and there was no requirement that a handle be attached to the blade to bring it within the statute's definition. Sykes v. Commonwealth, 37 Va. App. 262, 556 S.E.2d 794, 2001 Va. App. LEXIS 697 (2001).

Sufficient evidence. — Evidence was sufficient to support conviction for possession of a concealed weapon, in violation of § 18.2-308, because the trial court could have reasonably concluded that defendant was aware of the presence and character of the gun under the driver's seat of his car and it was subject to his dominion and control based on its location. Gillard v. Commonwealth, No. 0037-02-2, 2003 Va. App. LEXIS 437 (Ct. of Appeals Aug. 19, 2003).

Shotgun discovered on the floorboard between the center console and the passenger seat of defendant's vehicle, hidden from common view and observation, provided sufficient evidence to support defendant's conviction for possession of a concealed weapon, despite fact defendant alerted officer to weapons' presence. Weatherford v. Commonwealth, — Va. App. —, — S.E.2d —, 2005 Va. App. LEXIS 251 (June 28, 2005).

Because the police found a concealed weapon in defendant's possession that, as a convicted felon, defendant could not lawfully carry in a concealed manner, and because defendant failed to prove that a miscarriage of justice had occurred after failing to preserve a claim, Va. Sup. Ct. R. 5A:18 barred review of the issue. Davis v. Commonwealth, 2006 Va. App. LEXIS 444 (Oct. 10, 2006).

Defendant's convictions for illegal possession of a firearm under §§ 18.2-308.2, 18.2-308.4, and 18.2-308 were affirmed as defendant constructively possessed a handgun since: (1) defendant was convicted of possession of cocaine and marijuana with intent to distribute; (2) a handgun was found in the driver's seat of defendant's vehicle; (3) defendant was either sitting on the handgun or just next to it when an officer first saw defendant; and (4) a handgun was as much a tool of the illegal drug trade as the drugs, digital scales, and plastic distribution bags found in defendant's vehicle. Bolden v. Commonwealth, 49 Va. App. 285, 640 S.E.2d 526, 2007 Va. App. LEXIS 52 (2007).

Conviction for possession of a concealed weapon was supported by evidence showing that defendant was aware of the presence and character of the firearm and it was within defendant's dominion and control. Among other things, defendant exited vehicle along with the only other passenger and attempted to contact the officer before the officer could get to the vehicle, and the gun was in proximity to where defendant had been sitting. Bolden v. Commonwealth, 275 Va. 144, 654 S.E.2d 584, 2008 Va. LEXIS 6 (2008), cert. denied, 129 S. Ct. 284, 2008 U.S. LEXIS 6378, 172 L. Ed. 2d 208 (U.S. 2008).

Knife constituted a "weapon of like kind." — A convicted felon's knife constituted a "weapon of like kind" where the knife was not a common pocketknife, but had physical features making it similar to several of the prohibited knives listed in clause A (ii) of this section, and the blade came to a point like a bowie knife, with one side sharpened and the other side shaped with a concave curvature. There was no error in the trial court's denial of his motion to strike the evidence. Ohin v. Commonwealth, 47 Va. App. 194, 622 S.E.2d 784, 2005 Va. App. LEXIS 509 (2005).

Conviction under § 18.2-308.2 for possessing a concealed weapon after having been convicted of a felony was proper because a knife found on defendant's person had similar characteristics to a bowie knife, such as a single sharp edge, a dull flat edge, and point, to constitute a "weapon of like kind" under subsection A of § 18.2-308. Gilliam v. Commonwealth, 49 Va. App. 508, 642 S.E.2d 774, 2007 Va. App. LEXIS 143 (2007).

Kitchen knife did not constitute a "weapon of like kind." — Although the kitchen knife possessed by defendant was a potentially dangerous object, it was not a "weapon," because it was not designed for fighting purposes nor was it commonly understood to be a "weapon"; therefore, defendant's conviction for possession of a concealed weapon by a felon under § 18.2-308 was vacated. Farrakhan v. Commonwealth, 273 Va. 177, 639 S.E.2d 227, 2007 Va. LEXIS 10 (2007).

Because there was no evidence that defendant's kitchen steak knife was designed for fighting purposes, nor was it commonly understood to be a weapon, it was not a weapon as defined in subsection A of § 18.2-308; therefore, the court did not need to consider whether it was a weapon of like kind. Defendant's conviction for being a convicted felon in possession of a weapon under subsection A of § 18.2-308.2 was reversed. Green v. Commonwealth, 2009 Va. App. LEXIS 573 (Dec. 22, 2009).

Butterfly knife. — Defendant's knife was a weapon "of like kind" to a dirk and was therefore a deadly weapon, where it was a butterfly knife which, when opened, most closely resembled a dirk, and it was described by arresting officer as a "fighting knife." Kingrey v. Commonwealth, No. 2202-97-2 (Ct. of Appeals July 13, 1999).

In order to prove an item found in a defendant's possession is "of like kind," the Commonwealth must prove that it is substantially similar to one of the weapons enumerated in subsection A. Thompson v. Commonwealth, 277 Va. 280, 673 S.E.2d 469, 2009 Va. LEXIS 35 (2009).

Investigative detention. — Evidence was sufficient to provide a reasonable suspicion that defendant was engaged, or was about to engage, in a criminal activity which justified brief investigative detention, where police officers observed defendant's behavior as being consistent with a drive-up drug transaction and where they discovered a gun in defendant's coat pocket. Brown v. Commonwealth, No. 0178-01-1, 2001 Va. App. LEXIS 653 (Ct. of Appeals Dec. 4, 2001).

Lawful search and seizure. — Officer had reasonable basis for belief that defendant was carrying a concealed weapon where: (1) he saw defendant walk away from his friends when other officers questioned them; (2) defendant's answers to questions about his age and location of residence appeared suspicious; and (3) officer noticed heavy object in pocket of defendant's jacket, thus, the court

properly denied defendant's motion to suppress handgun which officer discovered when he conducted pat-down. Andrews v. Commonwealth, 37 Va. App. 479, 559 S.E.2d 401, 2002 Va. App. LEXIS 89 (2002).

Petition not timely filed. — Petition to Court of Appeals was considered a review pursuant to subsection D of this section, and thus its filing more than 30 days after the decision was untimely. It was not treated as a "petition for appeal" under Rule 5A:12 whereby the filing would have followed the record within 40 days and been timely. In re Cummins, 19 Va. App. 128, 449 S.E.2d 263 (1994).

Possession of a firearm by a convicted felon is not lesser included offense of carrying a concealed weapon. — Sections 18.2-308.2, 18.2-308, and 18.2-282 each require proof of an element that the others do not. Morris v. Commonwealth, 45 Va. App. 181, 609 S.E.2d 92, 2005 Va. App. LEXIS 79 (2005).

Conviction not based on same evidence as later conviction of being a felon in possession of a handgun. — Defendant's conviction of possession of a firearm by a felon, § 18.2-308.2, was affirmed; the possession by a felon conviction was based on different evidence than the conviction for carrying a concealed weapon, which was based on the same incident, and therefore § 19.2-294 did not bar the possession by a felon conviction. Jefferson v. Commonwealth, 43 Va. App. 361, 597 S.E.2d 290, 2004 Va. App. LEXIS 277 (2004).

Preservation for review. — As defendant did not move to strike the charge of possession of a concealed weapon by a felon, he failed to preserve his claim that the evidence was insufficient to convict him. And as he claimed the prosecution failed to prove an element of the crime, i.e., that the knives he possessed were not of "like kind" to those enumerated weapons in § 18.2-308, not that there was affirmative evidence that an element of the crime did not occur, he did not show that the ends of justice exception to Va. Sup. Ct. R. 5A:18 should apply to his conviction. Massa v. Commonwealth, 2012 Va. App. LEXIS 300 (Sept. 25, 2012).

Applied in Jones v. Commonwealth, No. 2079-03-2, 2004 Va. App. LEXIS 353 (Ct. of Appeals July 20, 2004).

CIRCUIT COURT OPINIONS

Proof of residency a reasonable requirement for issuance of concealed handgun permit. — Trial court granted a police department's demurrer in a declaratory judgment action pursuant to § 8.01-184, and determined that the department could require applicants for concealed handgun permits to present evidence of residency in addition to a State application, as subsection D of § 18.2-308 only allowed the court to grant such a permit to a resident of the county, and the submission of corroborating proof of residence was a reasonable request. Merkel v. Manger, — Va. Cir. —, 2003 Va. Cir. LEXIS 80 (Fairfax County May 5, 2003).

Exception for conservators of the peace. — Former police officer who resigned was not entitled to proof of consultation and review (police credentials) under subdivision B 8 [now subdivision B 7] because his resignation could not be equated with retirement, which would have entitled him to the credentials. Fey v. Rappoport, 58 Va. Cir. 190, 2002 Va. Cir. LEXIS 32 (Fairfax County 2002).

Former police officer seeking mandamus relief to require the issuance to him of proof of consultation and review, which would allow him to carry a concealed weapon, under subdivision B 8 [now subdivision B 7], had an adequate remedy at law in that he could apply for a concealed weapons permit under subdivision D, and the fact that such permit would only allow him to carry a handgun and would require payment of a fee did not render this remedy inadequate. Fey v. Rappoport, 58 Va. Cir. 190, 2002 Va. Cir. LEXIS 32 (Fairfax County 2002).

Permit revoked. — Defendant's gun permit was revoked for defendant's convictions of obstructing justice and brandishing a firearm; subsection J of § 18.2-308 did not only refer to a felony conviction, as the phrase "an offense" referred to the second misdemeanor offense, which triggered a disqualification under subsection E of § 18.2-308. Commonwealth v. Campbell, 60 Va. Cir. 232, 2002 Va. Cir. LEXIS 259 (Spotsylvania County 2002).

Simultaneous prosecutions not barred. — Requirements for proving a concealed weapons misdemeanor under this section were distinct from the requirements of § 18.2-308.2, although the two charges were commenced at the same or concurrent time, and the prosecutions were not sequential in nature simply because the misdemeanor was more amenable to an expeditious resolution than the felony; thus, no violation of § 19.2-294 resulted. Commonwealth v. Turner, 62 Va. Cir. 209, 2003 Va. Cir. LEXIS 312 (Charlottesville 2003).

OPINIONS OF THE ATTORNEY GENERAL

Applicant for concealed handgun permit who is denied a permit based on submission of an incomplete application should not have his application dismissed with prejudice and may reapply by submitting a complete application pursuant to subsection D of this section. See opinion of Attorney General to The Honorable David F. Pugh, Judge, Seventh Judicial Circuit, 04-40 (7/13/04).

Concealed weapon prohibited on school property. — A person with a valid concealed weapons permit may not carry a gun onto school property or a school bus and keep the weapon on or about his or her person at all times. See opinion of Attorney General to The Honorable Robert G. Marshall, Member, House of Delegates, 00-022 (11/9/00).

Concealed weapons not permitted on lands controlled by the Department of Conservation and Recreation. — A person with a concealed weapons permit is prohibited from carrying a concealed weapon onto lands controlled by the Department of Conservation and Recreation. See opinion of Attorney General to The Honorable Richard H. Black, Member, House of Delegates, 01-080 (12/6/01).

The sheriff is the chief law-enforcement officer of the office of the sheriff for the purposes of subdivision B 8 [now subdivision B 7]. See opinion of Attorney General to the Honorable John R. Newhart, Sheriff for the City of Chesapeake, 01-065 (3/26/02).

Retired deputy sheriff's identification card satisfied subdivision B 8. — A retired deputy sheriff's identification card, which was issued by the sheriff and identified the holder as a retired deputy sheriff, satisfied the requirement of subdivision B 8 [now subdivision B 7]. See opinion of Attorney General to the Honorable John R. Newhart, Sheriff for the City of Chesapeake, 01-065 (3/26/02).

Duty of clerk of court when issuing concealed weapon permit. — When issuing a concealed weapon permit, the clerk of court has no duty to verify with the general district or the juvenile and domestic relations district court whether the applicant has any criminal charges or protective orders pending against him in those courts. The failure of a clerk to detect any existing protective orders or criminal charges does not constitute gross negligence, provided the clerk has followed the statutory requirements governing the issuance of a concealed weapon permit. See opinion of Attorney General to The Honorable Jack Kennedy, Clerk of the Circuit Court, Wise County and City of Norton, 11-018, 2011 Va. AG LEXIS 26 (5/13/11).

Carrying concealed weapons. — Governing boards of colleges and universities may not impose a general prohibition on the carrying of concealed weapons by permitted individuals. Pursuant to specific grants of statutory authority, however, colleges and universities may regulate the conduct of students and employees to prohibit them from carrying concealed weapons on campus. See opinion of Attorney General to The Honorable R. Creigh Deeds, Member, Senate of Virginia, 05-078 (1/4/06).

Under current law, a university lawfully may promulgate a policy that prohibits persons from openly carrying a firearm in the buildings that are subject to the policy. However, where a university adopted a policy rather than a regulation, it has not "otherwise prohibited by law" persons with a concealed carry permit from possessing a handgun, and, therefore, the policies may not be used to prohibit persons with such a permit from carrying a concealed firearm into the buildings covered by the policy. See opinion of Attorney General to The Honorable Emmett W. Hanger, Jr., Member, Senate of Virginia, 11-078, 2011 Va. AG LEXIS 54 (7/1/11).

Carrying concealed handguns in state parks. — The Department of Conservation and Recreation does not have the authority to issue regulations prohibiting, within state parks, the carrying of concealed handguns by valid permit holders. See opinion of Attorney General to The Honorable Richard H. Black, Member, House of Delegates, 02-074 (9/9/02).

Carrying concealed weapon in car. — An individual may not keep a firearm stored in his vehicle at a place of employment if there is a company policy or signage prohibiting firearms on the premises. See opinion of Attorney General to The Honorable Stephen D. Newman, Member, Senate of Virginia, 11-111, 2012 Va. AG LEXIS 18 (5/25/12).

Provided the handgun is properly secured in a container or compartment within the vehicle, persons who may lawfully possess a firearm but have not been issued a concealed weapons permit may possess, in a vehicle, a handgun that is loaded and the handgun may remain within reach of a driver or passenger under such conditions; Furthermore, for a handgun to be "secured in a container or compartment," such storage tool need not be locked. See opinion of Attorney General to The Honorable Stephen D. Newman, Member, Senate of Virginia, 11-111, 2012 Va. AG LEXIS 18 (5/25/12).

Deferred finding of guilt relating to first-offense assault and battery under § 18.2-57.3 is not a "conviction" in the legal sense of the word, such a deferred finding is considered a "conviction" for purposes of applying that section in subsequent proceedings and for purposes of this section during a defendant's term of probation; also, the person's "conviction" terminates once the person completes probation and the deferred finding proceedings against him are dismissed, except for purposes of applying § 18.2-57.3 in any future proceeding under that section. See opinion of Attorney General to The Honorable Gary A. Mills, Judge, Seventh Judicial District, 04-066 (9/27/04).

Release of names of concealed handgun carry permittees. — The Department of State Police possesses the discretionary authority to release the names of concealed handgun carry permittees pursuant to a request under the The Virginia Freedom of Information Act. See opinion of Attorney General to The Honorable Dave Nutter, Member, House of Delegates, 07-027 (4/6/07).

Attorney for the Commonwealth or assistant attorney for the Commonwealth. — The 2008 amendments to § 18.2-308 clearly exempt Commonwealth's attorneys and assistant Commonwealth's attorneys from the general prohibitions on carrying concealed handguns, subject only to the restrictions in subsection J1 of § 18.2-308. Therefore, pursuant to state law such individuals may carry concealed handguns on school property. See opinion of Attorney General to The Honorable R. Lee Ware, Member, House of Delegates, 08-111, 2009 Va. AG LEXIS 23 (7/13/09).

§ 18.2-308.01. Carrying a concealed handgun with a permit.

A. The prohibition against carrying a concealed handgun in clause (i) of subsection A of § 18.2-308 shall not apply to a person who has a valid concealed handgun permit issued pursuant to this article. The person issued the permit shall have such permit on his person at all times during which he is carrying a concealed handgun and shall display the permit and a photo identification issued by a government agency of the Commonwealth or by the U.S. Department of Defense or U.S. State Department (passport) upon demand by a law-enforcement officer. A person to whom a nonresident permit is issued shall have such permit on his person at all times when he is carrying a concealed handgun in the Commonwealth and shall display the permit on demand by a law-enforcement officer. A person whose permit is extended due to deployment shall carry with him and display, upon request of a law-enforcement officer, a copy of the documents required by subsection B of § 18.2-308.010.

B. Failure to display the permit and a photo identification upon demand by a law-enforcement officer shall be punishable by a $25 civil penalty, which shall be paid into the state treasury. Any attorney for the Commonwealth of the county or city in which the alleged violation occurred may bring an action to recover the civil penalty. A court may waive such penalty upon presentation to the court of a valid permit and a government-issued photo identification. Any law-enforcement officer may issue a summons for the civil violation of failure to display the concealed handgun permit and photo identification upon demand.

C. The granting of a concealed handgun permit pursuant to this article shall not thereby authorize the possession of any handgun or other weapon on property or in places where such possession is otherwise prohibited by law or is prohibited by the owner of private property.

History.
2013, c. 746.

§ 18.2-308.02. Application for a concealed handgun permit; Virginia resident or domiciliary.

A. Any person 21 years of age or older may apply in writing to the clerk of the circuit court of the county or city in which he resides, or if he is a member of the United States armed forces, the county or city in which he is domiciled, for a five-year permit to carry a concealed handgun. There shall be no requirement regarding the length of time an applicant has been a resident or domiciliary of the county or city. The application shall be made under oath before a notary or other person qualified to take oaths and shall be made only on a form prescribed by the Department of State Police, in consultation with the Supreme Court, requiring only that information necessary to determine eligibility for the permit. No information or documentation other than that which is allowed on the application in accordance with this section may be requested or required by the clerk or the court.

B. The court shall require proof that the applicant has demonstrated competence with a handgun and the applicant may demonstrate such competence by one of the following, but no applicant shall be required to submit to any additional demonstration of competence, nor shall any proof of demonstrated competence expire:

1. Completing any hunter education or hunter safety course approved by the Department of Game and Inland Fisheries or a similar agency of another state;

2. Completing any National Rifle Association firearms safety or training course;

3. Completing any firearms safety or training course or class available to the general public offered by a law-enforcement agency, junior college, college, or private or public institution or organization or firearms training school utilizing instructors certified by the National Rifle Association or the Department of Criminal Justice Services;

4. Completing any law-enforcement firearms safety or training course or class offered for security guards, investigators, special deputies, or any division or subdivision of law enforcement or security enforcement;

5. Presenting evidence of equivalent experience with a firearm through participation in organized shooting competition or current military service or proof of an honorable discharge from any branch of the armed services;

6. Obtaining or previously having held a license to carry a firearm in the Commonwealth or a locality thereof, unless such license has been revoked for cause;

7. Completing any firearms training or safety course or class, including an electronic, video, or online course, conducted by a state-certified or National Rifle Association-certified firearms instructor;

8. Completing any governmental police agency firearms training course and qualifying to carry a firearm in the course of normal police duties; or

9. Completing any other firearms training which the court deems adequate.

A photocopy of a certificate of completion of any of the courses or classes; an affidavit from the instructor, school, club, organization, or group that conducted or taught such course or class attesting to the completion of the course or class by the applicant; or a copy of any document that shows completion of the course or class or evidences participation in firearms competition shall constitute evidence of qualification under this subsection.

C. The making of a materially false statement in an application under this article shall constitute perjury, punishable as provided in § 18.2-434.

D. The clerk of court shall withhold from public disclosure the applicant's name and any other information contained in a permit application or any order issuing a concealed handgun permit, except that such information shall not be withheld from any law-enforcement officer acting in the performance of his official duties.

E. An application is deemed complete when all information required to be furnished by the applicant, including the fee for a concealed handgun permit as set forth in § 18.2-308.03, is delivered to and received by the clerk of court before or concomitant with the conduct of a state or national criminal history records check.

History.
2013, cc. 659, 746.

Editor's note.
Acts 2013, c. 746 recodified § 18.2-308 as Article 6 (§§ 18.2-307.1 through 18.2-308.015). The last sentence in subsection D of § 18.2-308, was rewritten as subsection D of this section. Pursuant to § 30-152, amendments by Acts 2013, c. 659, were given effect in this section by substituting "shall" for "may," "applicant's name and any other information" for "social security number," "or any order issuing a concealed weapon handgun permit" for "in response to a request to inspect or copy any such permit application" and "information" for "social security number" in subsection D.

§ 18.2-308.03. Fees for concealed handgun permits.

A. The clerk shall charge a fee of $10 for the processing of an application or issuing of a permit, including his costs associated with the consultation with law-enforcement agencies. The local law-enforcement agency conducting the background investigation may charge a fee not to exceed $35 to cover the cost of conducting an investigation pursuant to this article. The $35 fee shall include any amount assessed by the U.S. Federal Bureau of Investigation for providing criminal history record information, and the local law-enforcement agency shall forward the amount assessed by the U.S. Federal Bureau of Investigation to the State Police with the fingerprints taken from any nonresident applicant. The State Police may charge a fee not to exceed $5 to cover its costs associated with processing the application. The total amount assessed for processing an application for a permit shall not exceed $50, with such fees to be paid in one sum to the person who receives the application. Payment may be made by any method accepted by that court for payment of other fees or penalties. No payment shall be required until the application is received by the court as a complete application.

B. No fee shall be charged for the issuance of such permit to a person who has retired from service (i) as a magistrate in the Commonwealth; (ii) as a special agent with the Alcoholic Beverage Control Board or as a law-enforcement officer with the Department of State Police, the Department of Game and Inland Fisheries, or a sheriff or police department, bureau, or force of any political subdivision of the Commonwealth, after completing 15 years of service or after reaching age 55; (iii) as a law-enforcement officer with the U.S. Federal Bureau of Investigation, Bureau of Alcohol, Tobacco and Firearms, Secret Service Agency, Drug Enforcement Administration, United States Citizenship and Immigration Services, U.S. Customs and Border Protection, Department of State Diplomatic Security Service, U.S. Marshals Service, or Naval Criminal Investigative Service, after completing 15 years of service or after reaching age 55; (iv) as a law-enforcement officer with any police or sheriff's department within the United States, the District of Columbia, or any of the territories of the United States, after completing 15 years of service; (v) as a law-enforcement officer with any combination of the agencies listed in clauses (ii) through (iv), after completing 15 years of service; (vi) as a designated boarding team member or boarding officer of the United States Coast Guard, after completing 15 years of service or after reaching age 55; or (vii) as a correctional officer as defined in § 53.1-1 after completing 15 years of service.

History.
2013, cc. 135, 559, 746.

Editor's note.
Acts 2013, c. 746 recodified § 18.2-308 as Article 6 (§§ 18.2-307.1 through 18.2-308.015). Subsection K of § 18.2-308, was rewritten

as subsection B of this section. Pursuant to § 30-152, amendments by Acts 2013, c. 135, were given effect in this section by substituting "U.S. Customs and Border Protection" for "Customs Service" in clause (iii) and inserting clause (vii) at the end of subsection B.

Subsection K of § 18.2-308, was rewritten as subsection B of this section by Acts 2013, c. 746. Pursuant to § 30-152, amendments by Acts 2013, c. 559, were given effect in this section by substituting "U.S. Customs and Border Protection" for "Customs Service" in clause (iii) of subsection B.

§ 18.2-308.04. Processing of the application and issuance of a concealed handgun permit.

A. The clerk of court shall enter on the application the date on which the application and all other information required to be submitted by the applicant is received.

B. Upon receipt of the completed application, the court shall consult with either the sheriff or police department of the county or city and receive a report from the Central Criminal Records Exchange.

C. The court shall issue the permit via United States mail and notify the State Police of the issuance of the permit within 45 days of receipt of the completed application unless it is determined that the applicant is disqualified. Any order denying issuance of the permit shall be in accordance with § 18.2-308.08. If the applicant is later found by the court to be disqualified after a five-year permit has been issued, the permit shall be revoked.

D. A court may authorize the clerk to issue concealed handgun permits, without judicial review, to applicants who have submitted complete applications, for whom the criminal history records check does not indicate a disqualification and, after consulting with either the sheriff or police department of the county or city, about which application there are no outstanding questions or issues. The court clerk shall be immune from suit arising from any acts or omissions relating to the issuance of concealed handgun permits without judicial review pursuant to this section unless the clerk was grossly negligent or engaged in willful misconduct. This section shall not be construed to limit, withdraw, or overturn any defense or immunity already existing in statutory or common law, or to affect any cause of action accruing prior to July 1, 2010.

E. The permit to carry a concealed handgun shall specify only the following information: name, address, date of birth, gender, height, weight, color of hair, color of eyes, and signature of the permittee; the signature of the judge issuing the permit, of the clerk of court who has been authorized to sign such permits by the issuing judge, or of the clerk of court who has been authorized to issue such permits pursuant to subsection D; the date of issuance; and the expiration date. The permit to carry a concealed handgun shall be no larger than two inches wide by three and one-fourth inches long and shall be of a uniform style prescribed by the Department of State Police.

History.
2013, c. 746.

§ 18.2-308.05. Issuance of a de facto permit.

If the court has not issued the permit or determined that the applicant is disqualified within 45 days of the date of receipt noted on the application, the clerk shall certify on the application that the 45-day period has expired, and mail or send via electronic mail a copy of the certified application to the applicant within five business days of the expiration of the 45-day period. The certified application shall serve as a de facto permit, which shall expire 90 days after issuance, and shall be recognized as a valid concealed handgun permit when presented with a valid government-issued photo identification pursuant to subsection A of § 18.2-308.01, until the court issues a five-year permit or finds the applicant to be disqualified. If the applicant is found to be disqualified after the de facto permit is issued, the applicant shall surrender the de facto permit to the court and the disqualification shall be deemed a denial of the permit and a revocation of the de facto permit.

History.
2013, c. 746.

§ 18.2-308.06. Nonresident concealed handgun permits.

A. Nonresidents of the Commonwealth 21 years of age or older may apply in writing to the Virginia Department of State Police for a five-year permit to carry a concealed handgun. Every applicant for a nonresident concealed handgun permit shall submit two photographs of a type and kind specified by the Department of State Police for inclusion on the permit and shall submit fingerprints on a card provided by the Department of State Police for the purpose of obtaining the applicant's state or national criminal history record. As a condition for issuance of a concealed handgun permit, the applicant shall submit to fingerprinting by his local or state law-enforcement agency and provide personal descriptive information to be forwarded with the fingerprints through the Central Criminal Records Exchange to the U.S. Federal Bureau of Investigation for the purpose of obtaining criminal history record information regarding the applicant and obtaining fingerprint identification information from federal records pursuant to criminal investigations by state and local law-enforcement agencies. The application shall be made under oath before a notary or other person qualified to take oaths on a form provided by the Department of State Police, requiring only that information necessary to determine eligibility for the permit. If the permittee is later found by the Department of State Police to be disqualified, the permit shall be revoked and the person shall return the permit after being so notified by the Department of State Police. The permit requirement and restriction provisions of subsection C of § 18.2-308.02 and § 18.2-308.09 shall apply, mutatis mutandis, to the provisions of this subsection.

B. The applicant shall demonstrate competence with a handgun by one of the following:

1. Completing a hunter education or hunter safety course approved by the Virginia Department of Game and Inland Fisheries or a similar agency of another state;

2. Completing any National Rifle Association firearms safety or training course;

3. Completing any firearms safety or training course or class available to the general public offered by a law-enforcement agency, junior college, college, or private or public institution or organization or firearms training school utilizing instructors certified by the National Rifle Association or the Department of Criminal Justice Services or a similar agency of another state;

4. Completing any law-enforcement firearms safety or training course or class offered for security guards, investigators, special deputies, or any division or subdivision of law enforcement or security enforcement;

5. Presenting evidence of equivalent experience with a firearm through participation in organized shooting competition approved by the Department of State Police or current military service or proof of an honorable discharge from any branch of the armed services;

6. Obtaining or previously having held a license to carry a firearm in the Commonwealth or a locality thereof, unless such license has been revoked for cause;

7. Completing any firearms training or safety course or class, including an electronic, video, or on-line course, conducted by a state-certified or National Rifle Association-certified firearms instructor;

8. Completing any governmental police agency firearms training course and qualifying to carry a firearm in the course of normal police duties; or

9. Completing any other firearms training that the Virginia Department of State Police deems adequate.

A photocopy of a certificate of completion of any such course or class; an affidavit from the instructor, school, club, organization, or group that conducted or taught such course or class attesting to the completion of the course or class by the applicant; or a copy of any document that shows completion of the course or class or evidences participation in firearms competition shall satisfy the requirement for demonstration of competence with a handgun.

C. The Department of State Police may charge a fee not to exceed $100 to cover the cost of the background check and issuance of the permit. Any fees collected shall be deposited in a special account to be used to offset the costs of administering the nonresident concealed handgun permit program.

D. The permit to carry a concealed handgun shall contain only the following information: name, address, date of birth, gender, height, weight, color of hair, color of eyes, and photograph of the permittee; the signature of the Superintendent of the Virginia Department of State Police or his designee; the date of issuance; and the expiration date.

E. The Superintendent of the State Police shall promulgate regulations, pursuant to the Administrative Process Act (§ 2.2-4000 et seq.), for the implementation of an application process for obtaining a nonresident concealed handgun permit.

History.
  2013, c. 746.

§ 18.2-308.07. Entry of information into the Virginia Criminal Information Network.

A. An order issuing a concealed handgun permit pursuant to § 18.2-308.04, or the copy of the permit application certified by the clerk as a de facto permit pursuant to § 18.2-308.05, shall be provided to the State Police and the law-enforcement agencies of the county or city by the clerk of the court. The State Police shall enter the permittee's name and description in the Virginia Criminal Information Network so that the permit's existence and current status will be made known to law-enforcement personnel accessing the Network for investigative purposes.

B. The Department of State Police shall enter the name and description of a person issued a nonresident permit pursuant to § 18.2-308.06 in the Virginia Criminal Information Network so that the permit's existence and current status are known to law-enforcement personnel accessing the Network for investigative purposes.

C. The State Police shall withhold from public disclosure permittee information submitted to the State Police for purposes of entry into the Virginia Criminal Information Network, except that such information shall not be withheld from any law-enforcement agency, officer, or authorized agent thereof acting in the performance of official law-enforcement duties, nor shall such information be withheld from an entity that has a valid contract with any local, state, or federal law-enforcement agency for the purpose of performing official duties of the law-enforcement agency. However, nothing in this subsection shall be construed to prohibit the release of (i) records by the State Police concerning permits issued to nonresidents of the Commonwealth pursuant to § 18.2-308.06 or (ii) statistical summaries, abstracts, or other records containing information in an aggregate form that does not identify any individual permittees.

History.
  2013, c. 746.

Editor's note.
  Acts 2013, c. 746, cl. 2 provides: "That the provisions of this act are declaratory of existing law."

§ 18.2-308.08. Denial of a concealed handgun permit; appeal.

A. Only a circuit court judge may deny issuance of a concealed handgun permit to a Virginia resident or domiciliary who has applied for a permit pursuant to § 18.2-308.04. Any order denying issuance of a concealed handgun permit shall state the basis for the denial of the permit, including, if applicable, any reason under § 18.2-308.09 that is the basis of the denial, and the clerk shall provide notice, in writing, upon denial of the application, of the applicant's right to an ore tenus hearing and the requirements for perfecting an appeal of such order.

B. Upon request of the applicant made within 21 days, the court shall place the matter on the docket for an ore tenus hearing. The applicant may be represented by counsel, but counsel shall not be appointed, and the rules of evidence shall apply. The final order of the court shall include the court's findings of fact and conclusions of law.

C. Any person denied a permit to carry a concealed handgun by the circuit court may present a petition for review to the Court of Appeals. The petition for review shall be filed within 60 days of the expiration of the time for requesting an ore tenus hearing, or if an ore tenus hearing is requested, within 60 days of the entry of the final order of the circuit court following the hearing. The petition shall be accompanied by a copy of the original papers filed in the circuit court, including a copy of the order of the circuit court denying the permit. Subject to the provisions of subsection B of § 17.1-410, the decision of the Court of Appeals or judge shall be final. Notwithstanding any other provision of law, if the decision to deny the permit is reversed upon appeal, taxable costs incurred by the person shall be paid by the Commonwealth.

History.
  2013, c. 746.

§ 18.2-308.09. Disqualifications for a concealed handgun permit.

The following persons shall be deemed disqualified from obtaining a permit:

1. An individual who is ineligible to possess a firearm pursuant to § 18.2-308.1:1, 18.2-308.1:2, or 18.2-308.1:3 or the substantially similar law of any other state or of the United States.

2. An individual who was ineligible to possess a firearm pursuant to § 18.2-308.1:1 and who was discharged from the custody of the Commissioner pursuant to § 19.2-182.7 less than five years before the date of his application for a concealed handgun permit.

3. An individual who was ineligible to possess a firearm pursuant to § 18.2-308.1:2 and whose competency or capacity was restored pursuant to § 64.2-2012 less than five years before the date of his application for a concealed handgun permit.

4. An individual who was ineligible to possess a firearm under § 18.2-308.1:3 and who was released from commitment less than five years before the date of this application for a concealed handgun permit.

5. An individual who is subject to a restraining order, or to a protective order and prohibited by § 18.2-308.1:4 from purchasing or transporting a firearm.

6. An individual who is prohibited by § 18.2-308.2 from possessing or transporting a firearm, except that a permit may be obtained in accordance with subsection C of that section.

7. An individual who has been convicted of two or more misdemeanors within the five-year period immediately preceding the application, if one of the misdemeanors was a Class 1 misdemeanor, but the judge shall have the discretion to deny a permit for two or more misdemeanors that are not Class 1. Traffic infractions and misdemeanors set forth in Title 46.2 shall not be considered for purposes of this disqualification.

8. An individual who is addicted to, or is an unlawful user or distributor of, marijuana, synthetic cannabinoids, or any controlled substance.

9. An individual who has been convicted of a violation of § 18.2-266 or a substantially similar local ordinance, or of public drunkenness, or of a substantially similar offense under the laws of any other state, the District of Columbia, the United States, or its territories within the three-year period immediately preceding the application, or who is a habitual drunkard as determined pursuant to § 4.1-333.

10. An alien other than an alien lawfully admitted for permanent residence in the United States.

11. An individual who has been discharged from the armed forces of the United States under dishonorable conditions.

12. An individual who is a fugitive from justice.

13. An individual who the court finds, by a preponderance of the evidence, based on specific acts by the applicant, is likely to use a weapon unlawfully or negligently to endanger others. The sheriff, chief of police, or attorney for the Commonwealth may submit to the court a sworn, written statement indicating that, in the opinion of such sheriff, chief of police, or attorney for the Commonwealth, based upon a disqualifying conviction or upon the specific acts set forth in the statement, the applicant is likely to use a weapon unlawfully or negligently to endanger others. The statement of the sheriff, chief of police, or the attorney for the Commonwealth shall be based upon personal knowledge of such individual or of a deputy sheriff, police officer, or assistant attorney for the Commonwealth of the specific acts, or upon a written statement made under oath before a notary public of a competent person having personal knowledge of the specific acts.

14. An individual who has been convicted of any assault, assault and battery, sexual battery, discharging of a firearm in violation of § 18.2-280 or 18.2-286.1 or brandishing of a firearm in violation of § 18.2-282 within the three-year period immediately preceding the application.

15. An individual who has been convicted of stalking.

16. An individual whose previous convictions or adjudications of delinquency were based on an offense that would have been at the time of conviction a felony if committed by an adult under the laws of any state, the District of Columbia, the United States or its territories. For purposes of this disqualifier, only convictions occurring within 16 years following the later of the date of (i) the conviction or adjudication or (ii) release from any incarceration imposed upon such conviction or adjudication shall be deemed to be "previous convictions."

17. An individual who has a felony charge pending or a charge pending for an offense listed in subdivision 14 or 15.

18. An individual who has received mental health treatment or substance abuse treatment in a residential setting within five years prior to the date of his application for a concealed handgun permit.

19. An individual not otherwise ineligible pursuant to this article, who, within the three-year period immediately preceding the application for the permit, was found guilty of any criminal offense set forth in Article 1 (§ 18.2-247 et seq.) or of a criminal offense of illegal possession or distribution of marijuana, synthetic cannabinoids, or any controlled substance, under the laws of any state, the District of Columbia, or the United States or its territories.

20. An individual, not otherwise ineligible pursuant to this article, with respect to whom, within the three-year period immediately preceding the application, upon a charge of any criminal offense set forth in Article 1 (§ 18.2-247 et seq.) or upon a charge of illegal possession or distribution of marijuana, synthetic cannabinoids, or any controlled substance under the laws of any state, the District of Columbia, or the United States or its territories, the trial court found that the facts of the case were sufficient for a finding of guilt and disposed of the case pursuant to § 18.2-251 or the substantially similar law of any other state, the District of Columbia, or the United States or its territories.

History.
2013, c. 746.

§ 18.2-308.010. Renewal of concealed handgun permit.

A. 1. Persons who previously have held a concealed handgun permit shall be issued, upon application as provided in § 18.2-308.02, a new five-year permit unless it is found that the applicant is subject to any of the disqualifications set forth in § 18.2-308.09. Persons who previously have been issued a concealed handgun permit pursuant to this article shall not be required to appear in person to apply for a new five-year permit pursuant to this section, and the application for the new permit may be submitted via the United States mail. The circuit court that receives the application shall promptly notify an applicant if the application is incomplete or if the fee submitted for the permit pursuant to § 18.2-308.03 is incorrect.

2. If a new five-year permit is issued while an existing permit remains valid, the new five-year permit shall become effective upon the expiration date of the existing permit, provided that the application is received by the court at least 90 days but no more than 180 days prior to the expiration of the existing permit.

3. Any order denying issuance of the new permit shall be in accordance with subsection A of § 18.2-308.08.

B. If a permit holder is a member of the Virginia National Guard, armed forces of the United States, or the Armed Forces Reserves of the United States, and his five-year permit expires during an active-duty military deployment outside of the permittee's county or city of residence, such permit shall remain valid for 90 days after the end date of the deployment. In order to establish proof of continued validity of the permit, such a permittee shall carry with him and display, upon request of a law-enforcement officer, a copy of the permittee's deployment orders or other documentation from the permittee's commanding officer that order the permittee to travel outside of his county or city of residence and that indicate the start and end date of such deployment.

History.
2013, c. 746.

§ 18.2-308.011. Replacement permits.

A. The clerk of a circuit court that issued a valid concealed handgun permit shall, upon presentation of the valid permit and proof of a new address of residence by the permit holder, issue a replacement permit specifying the permit holder's new address. The clerk of court shall forward the permit holder's new address of residence to the State Police. The State Police may charge a fee not to exceed $5, and the clerk of court issuing the replacement permit may charge a fee not to exceed $5. The total amount assessed for processing a replacement permit pursuant to this subsection shall not exceed $10, with such fees to be paid in one sum to the person who receives the information for the replacement permit.

B. The clerk of a circuit court that issued a valid concealed handgun permit shall, upon submission of a notarized statement by the permit holder that the permit was lost or destroyed, issue a replacement permit. The replacement permit shall have the same expiration date as the permit that was lost or destroyed. The clerk shall issue the replacement permit within 10 business days of receiving the

notarized statement, and may charge a fee not to exceed $5.

History.
2013, c. 746.

§ 18.2-308.012. Prohibited conduct.

A. Any person permitted to carry a concealed handgun who is under the influence of alcohol or illegal drugs while carrying such handgun in a public place is guilty of a Class 1 misdemeanor. Conviction of any of the following offenses shall be prima facie evidence, subject to rebuttal, that the person is "under the influence" for purposes of this section: manslaughter in violation of § 18.2-36.1, maiming in violation of § 18.2-51.4, driving while intoxicated in violation of § 18.2-266, public intoxication in violation of § 18.2-388, or driving while intoxicated in violation of § 46.2-341.24. Upon such conviction that court shall revoke the person's permit for a concealed handgun and promptly notify the issuing circuit court. A person convicted of a violation of this subsection shall be ineligible to apply for a concealed handgun permit for a period of five years.

B. No person who carries a concealed handgun onto the premises of any restaurant or club as defined in § 4.1-100 for which a license to sell and serve alcoholic beverages for on-premises consumption has been granted by the Virginia Alcoholic Beverage Control Board under Title 4.1 may consume an alcoholic beverage while on the premises. A person who carries a concealed handgun onto the premises of such a restaurant or club and consumes alcoholic beverages is guilty of a Class 2 misdemeanor. However, nothing in this subsection shall apply to a federal, state, or local law-enforcement officer.

History.
2013, c. 746.

§ 18.2-308.013. Suspension or revocation of permit.

A. Any person convicted of an offense that would disqualify that person from obtaining a permit under § 18.2-308.09 or who violates subsection C of § 18.2-308.02 shall forfeit his permit for a concealed handgun and surrender it to the court. Upon receipt by the Central Criminal Records Exchange of a record of the arrest, conviction, or occurrence of any other event that would disqualify a person from obtaining a concealed handgun permit under § 18.2-308.09, the Central Criminal Records Exchange shall notify the court having issued the permit of such disqualifying arrest, conviction, or other event. Upon receipt of such notice of a conviction, the court shall revoke the permit of a person disqualified pursuant to this subsection, and shall promptly notify the State Police and the person whose permit was revoked of the revocation.

B. An individual who has a felony charge pending or a charge pending for an offense listed in subdivision 14 or 15 of § 18.2-308.09, holding a permit for a concealed handgun, may have the permit suspended by the court before which such charge is pending or by the court that issued the permit.

C. The court shall revoke the permit of any individual for whom it would be unlawful to purchase, possess, or transport a firearm under § 18.2-308.1:2 or 18.2-308.1:3, and shall promptly notify the State Police and the person whose permit was revoked of the revocation.

History.
2013, c. 746.

§ 18.2-308.014. Reciprocity.

A. A valid concealed handgun or concealed weapon permit or license issued by another state shall authorize the holder of such permit or license who is at least 21 years of age to carry a concealed handgun in the Commonwealth, provided (i) the issuing authority provides the means for instantaneous verification of the validity of all such permits or licenses issued within that state, accessible 24 hours a day, and (ii) except for the age of the permit or license holder and the type of weapon authorized to be carried, the requirements and qualifications of that state's law are adequate to prevent possession of a permit or license by persons who would be denied a permit in the Commonwealth under this article. The Superintendent of State Police shall (a) in consultation with the Office of the Attorney General determine whether states meet the requirements and qualifications of this subsection, (b) maintain a registry of such states on the Virginia Criminal Information Network (VCIN), and (c) make the registry available to law-enforcement officers for investigative purposes. The Superintendent of the State Police, in consultation with the Attorney General, may also enter into agreements for reciprocal recognition with any state qualifying for recognition under this subsection.

B. A valid concealed handgun permit issued by Maryland shall be valid in the Commonwealth, provided (i) the holder of the permit is licensed in Maryland to perform duties substantially similar to those performed by Virginia branch pilots licensed pursuant to Chapter 9 (§ 54.1-900 et seq.) of Title 54.1 and is performing such duties while in the Commonwealth, and (ii) the holder of the permit is 21 years of age or older.

C. For the purposes of participation in concealed handgun reciprocity agreements with other jurisdictions, the official government-issued law-enforcement identification card issued to an active-duty law-enforcement officer in the Commonwealth who is exempt from obtaining a concealed handgun permit under this article shall be deemed a concealed handgun permit.

History.
2013, c. 746.

§ 18.2-308.015. Inclusion of Supreme Court website on application.

For the purposes of understanding the law relating to the use of deadly and lethal force, the Department of State Police, in consultation with the Supreme Court on the development of the application for a concealed handgun permit under this article, shall include a reference to the Virginia Supreme Court website address or the Virginia Reports on the application.

History.
2013, c. 746.

ARTICLE 7.

OTHER ILLEGAL WEAPONS.

Michie's Jurisprudence.
For related discussion, see 20 M.J. Weapons, §§ 2, 4, 4.1, 7.2, 9, 12, 13.

§ 18.2-308.1. Possession of firearm, stun weapon, or other weapon on school property prohibited.

A. If any person possesses any (i) stun weapon as defined in this section; (ii) knife, except a pocket knife having a folding metal blade of less than three inches; or (iii) weapon, including a weapon of like kind, designated in subsection A of § 18.2-308, other than a firearm; upon (a) the property of any public, private or religious elementary, middle or high school, including buildings and grounds; (b) that portion of any property open to the public and then exclusively used for school-sponsored functions or extracurricular activities while such functions or activities are taking place; or (c) any school bus owned or operated by any such school, he shall be guilty of a Class 1 misdemeanor.

B. If any person possesses any firearm designed or intended to expel a projectile by action of an explosion of a combustible material while such person is upon (i) any public, private or religious elementary, middle or high school, including buildings and grounds; (ii) that portion of any property open to the public and then exclusively used for school-sponsored functions or extracurricular activities while such functions or activities are taking place; or (iii) any school bus owned or operated by any such school, he shall be guilty of a Class 6 felony.

C. If any person possesses any firearm designed or intended to expel a projectile by action of an explosion of a combustible material within a public, private or religious elementary, middle or high school building and intends to use, or attempts to use, such firearm, or displays such weapon in a threatening manner, such person shall be guilty of a Class 6 felony and sentenced to a mandatory minimum term of imprisonment of five years to be served consecutively with any other sentence.

The exemptions set out in § 18.2-308 shall apply, mutatis mutandis, to the provisions of this section. The provisions of this section shall not apply to (i) persons who possess such weapon or weapons as a part of the school's curriculum or activities; (ii) a person possessing a knife customarily used for food preparation or service and using it for such purpose; (iii) persons who possess such weapon or weapons as a part of any program sponsored or facilitated by either the school or any organization authorized by the school to conduct its programs either on or off the school premises; (iv) any law-enforcement officer; (v) any person who possesses a knife or blade which he uses customarily in his trade; (vi) a person who possesses an unloaded firearm that is in a closed container, or a knife having a metal blade, in or upon a motor vehicle, or an unloaded shotgun or rifle in a firearms rack in or upon a motor vehicle; (vii) a person who has a valid concealed handgun permit and possesses a concealed handgun while in a motor vehicle in a parking lot, traffic circle, or other means of vehicular ingress or egress to the school; or (viii) an armed security officer, licensed pursuant to Article 4 (§ 9.1-138 et seq.) of Chapter 1 of Title 9.1, hired by a private or religious school for the protection of students and employees as authorized by such school. For the purposes of this paragraph, "weapon" includes a knife having a metal blade of three inches or longer and "closed container" includes a locked vehicle trunk.

As used in this section:

"*Stun weapon*" means any device that emits a momentary or pulsed output, which is electrical, audible, optical or electromagnetic in nature and which is designed to temporarily incapacitate a person.

History.

1979, c. 467; 1988, c. 493; 1990, cc. 635, 744; 1991, c. 579; 1992, cc. 727, 735; 1995, c. 511; 1999, cc. 587, 829, 846; 2001, c. 403; 2003, cc. 619, 976; 2004, cc. 128, 461; 2005, cc. 830, 928; 2007, c. 519; 2011, c. 282; 2013, c. 416.

Cross references.

As to expulsion from school attendance for not less than one year of a student who has brought a firearm onto school property or to a school-sponsored activity as prohibited by this section, see § 22.1-277.07.

Editor's note.

Acts 2011, c. 282, cl. 2, provides: "That the provisions of this act may result in a net increase in periods of imprisonment or commitment. Pursuant to § 30-19.1:4, the estimated amount of the necessary appropriation is $0 for periods of imprisonment in state adult correctional facilities and cannot be determined for periods of commitment to the custody of the Department of Juvenile Justice."

The 2011 amendments.

The 2011 amendment by c. 282 added the subsection C designation and in subsection C, substituted "If any person possesses any firearm designed or intended to expel a projectile by action of an explosion of a combustible material" for "however, if the person possesses any firearm" and inserted "guilty of a Class 6 felony and."

The 2013 amendments.

The 2013 amendment by c. 416 inserted "or (viii) an armed security officer, licensed pursuant to Article 4 (§ 9.1-138 et seq.) of

Chapter 1 of Title 9.1, hired by a private or religious school for the protection of students and employees as authorized by such school" in the second paragraph of subsection C, and made a related change.

Law Review.

For a review of Virginia legal issues involving children, see 33 U. Rich. L. Rev. 1001 (1999). For annual survey article on legal issues involving children, see 38 U. Rich. L. Rev. 161 (2003). For 2003/2004 survey of family and juvenile law, see 39 U. Rich. L. Rev. 241 (2004).

Michie's Jurisprudence.

For related discussion, see 16 M.J. Schools, § 1.

CASE NOTES

Section 18.2-308.1 creates strict criminal liability and the trial court properly refused to instruct the jury that, to find a teacher who was accused of bringing a handgun onto school property, it had to find she knew she had the gun in her possession. Esteban v. Commonwealth, 266 Va. 605, 587 S.E.2d 523, 2003 Va. LEXIS 106 (2003).

Exception for conservators of the peace. — In interpreting this criminal statute, the court is bound by the statutory definition of "conservator of the peace" adopted by the legislature and codified in § 19.2-12 and is not permitted to ignore or rewrite the statute in favor of a broader common-law definition. Frias v. Commonwealth, 34 Va. App. 193, 538 S.E.2d 374, 2000 Va. App. LEXIS 838 (2000).

This section incorporates the exceptions set forth in § 18.2-308, which includes the exception for "conservators of the peace." Frias v. Commonwealth, 34 Va. App. 193, 538 S.E.2d 374, 2000 Va. App. LEXIS 838 (2000).

Section 9-183.8, concerning the licensing and registration of security guards, expressly states that compliance with the provisions of that article does not authorize any person to exercise any powers of a conservator of the peace and it necessarily follows that a registered security guard does not, by virtue of that status alone, fall within the exemption from the prohibition on carrying weapons on school grounds for conservators of the peace. Frias v. Commonwealth, 34 Va. App. 193, 538 S.E.2d 374, 2000 Va. App. LEXIS 838 (2000).

Proof of prior juvenile adjudication of illegal firearm possession. — Evidence was sufficient to convict defendant of violating § 18.2-308.2 by possessing a firearm after having been adjudicated delinquent as a juvenile of an act that would have been a felony if committed by an adult, as a certified record of a juvenile probation order stated that the juvenile had been found to be delinquent of carrying a pistol into a public school in violation of § 18.2-308.1, a Class 6 felony. Under § 8.01-389, that certified order was prima facie proof of the facts stated therein. Wilder v. Commonwealth, 2008 Va. App. LEXIS 350 (July 8, 2008).

Felons may possess stun weapons and tasers. — The 2001 amendments to subsection A of § 18.2-308.2 expanded the class of weapons that a felon could not possess to include stun weapons and tasers within its proscription, and the amendment created an exception to the general prohibition of possession of a stun weapon or taser as defined in § 18.2-308.1 by allowing possession of those weapons in the home; clearly the legislative intent was that the exception apply only to stun weapons and tasers, firearms that are limited in their ability to injure. Alger v. Commonwealth, 40 Va. App. 89, 578 S.E.2d 51, 2003 Va. App. LEXIS 137 (2003) (decided under § 18.2-308.2 as it read prior to later amendments).

Possession of machete. — Defendant's possession of a machete with a seventeen-and-one-half-inch, curved, metal blade on school grounds did not violate § 18.2-308.1 because the machete was a type of knife within the meaning of clause (vi) of subsection B of § 18.2-308.1 and, therefore, defendant's possession of the machete in his automobile fell within the statutory exception. McNamara v. Commonwealth, 56 Va. App. 238, 692 S.E.2d 648, 2010 Va. App. LEXIS 204 (2010).

Applied in Wofford v. Evans, 390 F.3d 318, 2004 U.S. App. LEXIS 24181 (4th Cir. 2004).

OPINIONS OF THE ATTORNEY GENERAL

Unattended weapon prohibited on school property. — A person with a valid concealed weapons permit who carries a gun to school and leaves it unattended, and not on his or her person, is in violation of the statute. See opinion of Attorney General to The Honorable Robert G. Marshall, Member, House of Delegates, 00-022 (11/9/00).

Concealed weapon prohibited on school property. — A person with a valid concealed weapons permit may not carry a gun onto school property or a school bus and keep the weapon on or about his or her person at all times. See opinion of Attorney General to The Honorable Robert G. Marshall, Member, House of Delegates, 00-022 (11/9/00).

A school board has authority to discipline a student whose action is in conformance with the language of the 2003 amendment of subsection B of this section, pertaining to the possession of an unloaded firearm in a locked vehicle trunk. See opinion of Attorney General to The Honorable Kevin G. Miller, Member, Senate of Virginia, 03-083 (10/15/03).

County school board does not have authority to prohibit the possession of firearms at school board meetings that are not held on school property. See opinion of Attorney General to Mr. James E. Barnett, County Attorney for York County, 06-072 (1/29/07).

Attorney for the Commonwealth or assistant attorney for the Commonwealth. — The 2008 amendments to § 18.2-308 clearly exempt Commonwealth's attorneys and assistant Commonwealth's attorneys from the general prohibitions on carrying concealed handguns, subject only to the restrictions in subsection J1 of § 18.2-308. Therefore, pursuant to state law such individuals may carry concealed handguns on school property. See opinion of Attorney General to The Honorable R. Lee Ware, Member, House of Delegates, 08-111, 2009 Va. AG LEXIS 23 (7/13/09).

§ 18.2-308.1:1. Purchase, possession or transportation of firearms by persons acquitted by reason of insanity; penalty.

A. It shall be unlawful for any person acquitted by reason of insanity and committed to the custody of the Commissioner of Behavioral Health and Developmental Services, pursuant to Chapter 11.1 (§ 19.2-182.2 et seq.) of Title 19.2, on a charge of treason, any felony or any offense punishable as a misdemeanor under Title 54.1 or a Class 1 or Class 2 misdemeanor under this title, except those misdemeanor violations of (i) Article 2 (§ 18.2-266 et seq.) of Chapter 7 of this title, (ii) Article 2 (§ 18.2-415 et seq.) of Chapter 9 of this title, or (iii) § 18.2-119, or (iv) an ordinance of any county, city, or town similar to the offenses specified in (i), (ii), or (iii), to knowingly and intentionally purchase, possess, or transport any firearm. A violation of this subsection shall be punishable as a Class 1 misdemeanor.

B. Any person so acquitted may, upon discharge from the custody of the Commissioner, petition the general district court in the city or county in which he resides to restore his right to purchase, possess or transport a firearm. A copy of the petition shall be mailed or delivered to the attorney for the Commonwealth for the jurisdiction where the petition was filed who shall be entitled to respond and represent the interests of the Commonwealth. The court shall conduct a hearing if requested by either party. If the court determines, after receiving and considering evidence concerning the circumstances regarding the disability referred to in subsection A and the person's criminal history, treatment record, and reputation as developed through character witness

statements, testimony, or other character evidence, that the person will not be likely to act in a manner dangerous to public safety and that the granting of the relief would not be contrary to the public interest, the court shall grant the petition. Any person denied relief by the general district court may petition the circuit court for a de novo review of the denial. Upon a grant of relief in any court, the court shall enter a written order granting the petition, in which event the provisions of subsection A do not apply. The clerk of court shall certify and forward forthwith to the Central Criminal Records Exchange, on a form provided by the Exchange, a copy of any such order.

C. As used in this section, "treatment record" shall include copies of health records detailing the petitioner's psychiatric history, which shall include the records pertaining to the commitment or adjudication that is the subject of the request for relief pursuant to this section.

History.
1990, c. 692; 2008, cc. 788, 854, 869; 2009, cc. 813, 840; 2010, c. 781; 2011, c. 775.

Editor's note.
Acts 2008, cc. 854 and 869, cl. 2 provides: "That the provisions of this act may result in a net increase in periods of imprisonment or commitment. Pursuant to § 30-19.1:4, the estimated amount of the necessary appropriation cannot be determined for periods of imprisonment in state adult correctional facilities and is $0 for periods of commitment to the custody of the Department of Juvenile Justice."

The 2008 amendments.
The 2008 amendment by c. 788, in subsection B, substituted "general district court" for "circuit court" in the first sentence; inserted the present second and third sentences; substituted the present provisions of the fourth sentence for "The court may, in its discretion and for good cause shown, grant the petition and issue a permit, in which event the provisions of subsection A do not apply" and added the last sentence.

The 2008 amendments by cc. 854 and 869 are identical, and inserted "purchase" following "to knowingly and intentionally" near the end of the first sentence in subsection A.

The 2009 amendments.
The 2009 amendments by cc. 813 and 840 are identical and substituted "Behavioral Health and Developmental Services" for "Mental Health, Mental Retardation and Substance Abuse Services" in subsection A.

The 2010 amendments.
The 2010 amendment by c. 781 added the second and third sentences of subsection B.

The 2011 amendments.
The 2011 amendment by c. 775, in subsection B, substituted "the city or county in which he resides to restore his right to purchase, possess or transport" for "which he resides for a permit to possess or carry" in the first sentence, substituted "after receiving and considering evidence concerning the circumstances regarding the disability referred to in subsection A and the person's criminal history, treatment record, and reputation as developed through character witness statements, testimony, or other character evidence" for "that the circumstances regarding the disability referred to in subsection A and the person's criminal history, treatment record, and reputation are such" in the fourth sentence, and deleted "and issue a permit" following "petition" in the sixth sentence; added subsection C; and made a minor stylistic change.

CASE NOTES

Applied in Eastlack v. Commonwealth, 282 Va. 120, 710 S.E.2d 723, 2011 Va. LEXIS 126 (2011).

§ 18.2-308.1:2. Purchase, possession or transportation of firearm by persons adjudicated legally incompetent or mentally incapacitated; penalty.

A. It shall be unlawful for any person who has been adjudicated (i) legally incompetent pursuant to former § 37.1-128.02 or former § 37.1-134, (ii) mentally incapacitated pursuant to former § 37.1-128.1 or former § 37.1-132 or (iii) incapacitated pursuant to Chapter 20 (§ 64.2-2000 et seq.) of Title 64.2 to purchase, possess, or transport any firearm. A violation of this subsection shall be punishable as a Class 1 misdemeanor.

B. Any person whose competency or capacity has been restored pursuant to former § 37.1-134.1, former § 37.2-1012, or § 64.2-2012 may petition the general district court in the city or county in which he resides to restore his right to purchase, possess or transport a firearm. A copy of the petition shall be mailed or delivered to the attorney for the Commonwealth for the jurisdiction where the petition was filed who shall be entitled to respond and represent the interests of the Commonwealth. The court shall conduct a hearing if requested by either party. If the court determines, after receiving and considering evidence concerning the circumstances regarding the disability referred to in subsection A and the person's criminal history, treatment record, and reputation as developed through character witness statements, testimony, or other character evidence, that the person will not be likely to act in a manner dangerous to public safety and that the granting of the relief would not be contrary to the public interest, the court shall grant the petition. Any person denied relief by the general district court may petition the circuit court for a de novo review of the denial. Upon a grant of relief in any court, the court shall enter a written order granting the petition, in which event the provisions of subsection A do not apply. The clerk of court shall certify and forward forthwith to the Central Criminal Records Exchange, on a form provided by the Exchange, a copy of any such order.

C. As used in this section, "treatment record" shall include copies of health records detailing the petitioner's psychiatric history, which shall include the records pertaining to the commitment or adjudication that is the subject of the request for relief pursuant to this section.

History.
1994, c. 907; 1997, c. 921; 2004, c. 995; 2011, c. 775.

Editor's note.
Section 37.1-134.1 referred to in this section, was repealed by Acts 1997, c. 921, effective January 1, 1998.

At the direction of the Virginia Code Commission, the reference to "Chapter 10 (§ 37.2-1000 et seq.) of Title 37.2" was changed to "Chapter 20 (§ 64.2-2000 et seq.) of Title 64.2" and the reference to "former § 37.1-134.1 or § 37.2-1012" was changed to "former § 37.1-134.1, former § 37.2-1012, or § 64.2-2012" to conform to the recodification of Title 64.1 by Acts 2012, c. 614, effective October 1, 2012.

The 2011 amendments.
The 2011 amendment by c. 775 rewrote the section, which read: "It shall be unlawful for any person who has been adjudicated (i) legally incompetent pursuant to former § 37.1-128.02 or former § 37.1-134, (ii) mentally incapacitated pursuant to former § 37.1-128.1 or former § 37.1-132 or (iii) incapacitated pursuant to Chapter 10 (§ 37.2-1000 et seq.) of Title 37.2 and whose competency or capacity has not been restored pursuant to former § 37.1-134.1 or § 37.2-1012, to purchase, possess, or transport any firearm. A violation of this section shall be punishable as a Class 1 misdemeanor."

§ 18.2-308.1:3. Purchase, possession or transportation of firearm by persons involuntarily admitted or ordered to outpatient treatment; penalty.

A. It shall be unlawful for any person involuntarily admitted to a facility or ordered to mandatory outpatient treatment pursuant to § 19.2-169.2, involuntarily admitted to a facility or ordered to mandatory outpatient treatment as the result of a commitment hearing pursuant to Article 5 (§ 37.2-814 et seq.) of Chapter 8 of Title 37.2, or who was the subject of a temporary detention order pursuant to § 37.2-809 and subsequently agreed to voluntary admission pursuant to § 37.2-805 to purchase, possess or transport a firearm. A violation of this subsection shall be punishable as a Class 1 misdemeanor.

B. Any person prohibited from purchasing, possessing or transporting firearms under this section may, at any time following his release from involuntary admission to a facility, his release from an order of mandatory outpatient treatment, or his release from voluntary admission pursuant to § 37.2-805 following the issuance of a temporary detention order, petition the general district court in the city or county in which he resides to restore his right to purchase, possess or transport a firearm. A copy of the petition shall be mailed or delivered to the attorney for the Commonwealth for the jurisdiction where the petition was filed who shall be entitled to respond and represent the interests of the Commonwealth. The court shall conduct a hearing if requested by either party. If the court determines, after receiving and considering evidence concerning the circumstances regarding the disabilities referred to in subsection A and the person's criminal history, treatment record, and reputation as developed through character witness statements, testimony, or other character evidence, that the person will not likely act in a manner dangerous to public safety and that granting the relief would not be contrary to the public interest, the court shall grant the petition. Any person denied relief by the general district court may petition the circuit court for a de novo review of the denial. Upon a grant of relief in any court, the court shall enter a written order granting the petition, in which event the provisions of subsection A do not apply. The clerk of court shall certify and forward forthwith to the Central Criminal Records Exchange, on a form provided by the Exchange, a copy of any such order.

C. As used in this section, "treatment record" shall include copies of health records detailing the petitioner's psychiatric history, which shall include the records pertaining to the commitment or adjudication that is the subject of the request for relief pursuant to this section.

History.

1994, c. 907; 2004, c. 995; 2008, cc. 751, 788; 2010, c. 781; 2011, c. 775.

The 2008 amendments.

The 2008 amendments by cc. 751 and 788 are identical and, substituted the present provisions of the first sentence in subsection A for "It shall be unlawful for any person involuntarily committed pursuant to Article 5 (§ 37.2-814 et seq.) of Chapter 8 of Title 37.2 to purchase, possess or transport a firearm during the period of such person's commitment"; and in subsection B, substituted the present provisions of the first and second sentences for "Any person prohibited from purchasing, possessing or transporting firearms under this section may, at any time following his release from commitment, petition the circuit court in the city or county in which he resides to restore his right to purchase, possess or transport a firearm. The court may, in its discretion and for good cause shown, grant the petition" and inserted the third and fourth sentences.

The 2010 amendments.

The 2010 amendment by c. 781 added the second and third sentences of subsection B.

The 2011 amendments.

The 2011 amendment by c. 775, in subsection B, substituted "after receiving and considering evidence concerning" for "that" and "as developed through character witness statements, testimony, or other character evidence" for "are such" in the fourth sentence, substituted "do not apply" for "shall no longer apply" at the end of the sixth sentence; and added subsection C.

§ 18.2-308.1:4. Purchase or transportation of firearm by persons subject to protective orders; penalty.

It is unlawful for any person who is subject to (i) a protective order entered pursuant to § 16.1-253.1, 16.1-253.4, 16.1-278.2, 16.1-279.1, 19.2-152.8, 19.2-152.9, or 19.2-152.10; (ii) an order issued pursuant to subsection B of § 20-103; (iii) an order entered pursuant to subsection E of § 18.2-60.3; (iv) a preliminary protective order entered pursuant to subsection F of § 16.1-253 where a petition alleging abuse or neglect has been filed; or (v) an order issued by a tribunal of another state, the United States or any of its territories, possessions or commonwealths, or the District of Columbia pursuant to a statute that is substantially similar to those cited in clauses (i), (ii), (iii), or (iv) to purchase or transport any firearm while the order is in effect. Any person with a concealed handgun permit shall be prohibited from carrying any concealed firearm, and shall surrender his permit to the court entering the order, for the duration of any protective order referred to

herein. A violation of this section is a Class 1 misdemeanor.

History.

1994, c. 907; 1996, c. 866; 1998, c. 569; 2001, c. 357; 2002, cc. 783, 865; 2004, c. 995; 2011, cc. 373, 402; 2013, c. 759.

Editor's note.

Acts 2013, c. 759, cl. 2 provides: "That the provisions of this act may result in a net increase in periods of imprisonment or commitment. Pursuant to § 30-19.1:4, the estimated amount of the necessary appropriation is at least $23,197 for periods of imprisonment in state adult correctional facilities and cannot be determined for periods of commitment to the custody of the Department of Juvenile Justice."

The 2011 amendments.

The 2011 amendments by cc. 373 and 402 are identical, and in clause (i) of the first sentence, deleted "§ 16.1-253" following "pursuant to" and inserted "16.1-278.2"; added present clause (iv) and redesignated former clause (iv) as clause (v); substituted "(iii), or (iv)" for "or (iii)" in the second sentence; and made stylistic changes.

The 2013 amendments.

The 2013 amendment by c. 759 substituted "It is unlawful" for "It shall be unlawful" at the beginning, and "subsection E" for "subsection D" in clause (iii) of the first sentence.

Law Review.

For article, "Family Law," see 35 U. Rich. L. Rev. 651 (2001). For article surveying developments in family law in Virginia, see 37 U. Rich. L. Rev. 155 (2002).

OPINIONS OF THE ATTORNEY GENERAL

Issuance of concealed weapon permit. — When issuing a concealed weapon permit, the clerk of court has no duty to verify with the general district or the juvenile and domestic relations district court whether the applicant has any criminal charges or protective orders pending against him in those courts. See opinion of Attorney General to The Honorable Jack Kennedy, Clerk of the Circuit Court, Wise County and City of Norton, 11-018, 2011 Va. AG LEXIS 26 (5/13/11).

§ 18.2-308.1:5. Purchase or transportation of firearm by persons convicted of certain drug offenses prohibited.

Any person who, within a thirty-six consecutive month period, has been convicted of two misdemeanor offenses under subsection B of § 18.2-248.1:1, § 18.2-250, or 18.2-250.1 shall be ineligible to purchase or transport a handgun. However, upon expiration of a period of five years from the date of the second conviction and provided the person has not been convicted of any such offense within that period, the ineligibility shall be removed.

History.

1995, c. 577; 2011, cc. 384, 410.

Editor's note.

Acts 2011, cc. 384 and 410, cl. 3 provides: "That the provisions of this act may result in a net increase in periods of imprisonment or commitment. Pursuant to § 30-19.1:4, the estimated amount of the necessary appropriation cannot be determined for periods of imprisonment in state adult correctional facilities; therefore, Chapter 874 of the Acts of Assembly of 2010 requires the Virginia Criminal Sentencing Commission to assign a minimum fiscal impact of $50,000. Pursuant to § 30-19.1:4, the estimated amount of the necessary appropriation cannot be determined for periods of commitment to the custody of the Department of Juvenile Justice."

The 2011 amendments.
The 2011 amendments by cc. 384 and 410, effective March 23, 2011, are identical, and inserted "subsection B of § 18.2-248.1:1" and made a minor stylistic change.

§ 18.2-308.2. Possession or transportation of firearms, firearms ammunition, stun weapons, explosives or concealed weapons by convicted felons; penalties; petition for permit; when issued.

A. It shall be unlawful for (i) any person who has been convicted of a felony; (ii) any person adjudicated delinquent as a juvenile 14 years of age or older at the time of the offense of murder in violation of § 18.2-31 or 18.2-32, kidnapping in violation of § 18.2-47, robbery by the threat or presentation of firearms in violation of § 18.2-58, or rape in violation of § 18.2-61; or (iii) any person under the age of 29 who was adjudicated delinquent as a juvenile 14 years of age or older at the time of the offense of a delinquent act which would be a felony if committed by an adult, other than those felonies set forth in clause (ii), whether such conviction or adjudication occurred under the laws of the Commonwealth, or any other state, the District of Columbia, the United States or any territory thereof, to knowingly and intentionally possess or transport any firearm or ammunition for a firearm, any stun weapon as defined by § 18.2-308.1, or any explosive material, or to knowingly and intentionally carry about his person, hidden from common observation, any weapon described in subsection A of § 18.2-308. However, such person may possess in his residence or the curtilage thereof a stun weapon as defined by § 18.2-308.1. Any person who violates this section shall be guilty of a Class 6 felony. However, any person who violates this section by knowingly and intentionally possessing or transporting any firearm and who was previously convicted of a violent felony as defined in § 17.1-805 shall be sentenced to a mandatory minimum term of imprisonment of five years. Any person who violates this section by knowingly and intentionally possessing or transporting any firearm and who was previously convicted of any other felony within the prior 10 years shall be sentenced to a mandatory minimum term of imprisonment of two years. The mandatory minimum terms of imprisonment prescribed for violations of this section shall be served consecutively with any other sentence.

B. The prohibitions of subsection A shall not apply to (i) any person who possesses a firearm, ammunition for a firearm, explosive material or other weapon while carrying out his duties as a member of the Armed Forces of the United States or of the National Guard of Virginia or of any other state, (ii) any law-enforcement officer in the performance of his duties, or (iii) any person who has been pardoned or whose political disabilities have been removed pursuant to Article V, Section 12 of the Constitution of Virginia provided the Governor, in the document granting the pardon or removing the person's political disabilities, may expressly place conditions upon the reinstatement of the person's right to ship, transport, possess or receive firearms.

C. Any person prohibited from possessing, transporting or carrying a firearm or stun weapon under subsection A, may petition the circuit court of the jurisdiction in which he resides for a permit to possess or carry a firearm or stun weapon; however, no person who has been convicted of a felony shall be qualified to petition for such a permit unless his civil rights have been restored by the Governor or other appropriate authority. A copy of the petition shall be mailed or delivered to the attorney for the Commonwealth for the jurisdiction where the petition was filed who shall be entitled to respond and represent the interests of the Commonwealth. The court shall conduct a hearing if requested by either party. The court may, in its discretion and for good cause shown, grant such petition and issue a permit. The provisions of this section relating to firearms, ammunition for a firearm, and stun weapons shall not apply to any person who has been granted a permit pursuant to this subsection.

C1. Any person who was prohibited from possessing, transporting or carrying explosive material under subsection A may possess, transport or carry such explosive material if his right to possess, transport or carry explosive material has been restored pursuant to federal law.

D. For the purpose of this section:
"Ammunition for a firearm" means the combination of a cartridge, projectile, primer, or propellant designed for use in a firearm other than an antique firearm as defined in § 18.2-308.2:2.

"Explosive material" means any chemical compound mixture, or device, the primary or common purpose of which is to function by explosion; the term includes, but is not limited to, dynamite and other high explosives, black powder, pellet powder, smokeless gun powder, detonators, blasting caps and detonating cord but shall not include fireworks or permissible fireworks as defined in § 27-95.

History.
1979, c. 474; 1982, c. 515; 1983, c. 233; 1986, cc. 409, 641; 1987, c. 108; 1988, c. 237; 1989, cc. 514, 531; 1993, cc. 468, 926; 1994, cc. 859, 949; 1999, cc. 829, 846; 2001, cc. 811, 854; 2002, c. 362; 2003, c. 110; 2004, cc. 429, 461, 995; 2005, cc. 600, 833; 2007, c. 519; 2008, c. 752; 2009, c. 236; 2010, c. 781.

Editor's note.
Acts 2008, c. 752, cl. 2 provides: "That the provisions of this act may result in a net increase in periods of imprisonment or commitment. Pursuant to § 30-19.1:4, the estimated amount of the necessary appropriation cannot be determined for periods of imprisonment in state adult correctional facilities and is $0 for periods of commitment to the custody of the Department of Juvenile Justice."
Acts 2009, c. 236, cl. 2, provides: "That the provisions of this act may result in a net increase in periods of imprisonment or commitment. Pursuant to § 30-19.1:4, the estimated amount of the necessary appropriation cannot be determined for periods of imprison-

ment in state adult correctional facilities and cannot be determined for periods of commitment to the custody of the Department of Juvenile Justice."

The 2008 amendments.

The 2008 amendment by c. 752 deleted "on or after July 1, 2005" in clause (ii) in subsection A.

The 2009 amendments.

The 2009 amendment by c. 236, in subsection A, inserted "ammunition for a firearm, any"; in clause (i) in subsection B and in the last sentence of subsection C inserted "ammunition for a firearm"; and divided subsection D into the introductory language of subsection D and the definition of "Explosive material" and added the definition of "Ammunition for a firearm."

The 2010 amendments.

The 2010 amendment by c. 781 added the second and third sentences in subsection C.

Law Review.

For note, "The Clemency Process in Virginia", see 27 U. Rich. L. Rev. 241 (1993). For article surveying developments in criminal law and procedure in Virginia from July 2001 to September 2002, see 37 U. Rich. L. Rev. 45 (2002). For 2003/2004 survey of criminal law and procedure, see 39 U. Rich. L. Rev. 133 (2004). For survey of Virginia criminal law and procedure for the year 2004-2005, see 40 U. Rich. L. Rev. 197 (2005). For 2006 survey article, "Criminal Law and Procedure," see 41 U. Rich. L. Rev. 83 (2006). For note, "Modern Police Practices: Arizona v. Gant's Illusory Restriction of Vehicle Searches Incident to Arrest," 97 Va. L. Rev. 1727 (2011).

Michie's Jurisprudence.

For related discussion, see 20 M.J. Weapons, §§ 4.1, 7.2, 13.

CASE NOTES

I. IN GENERAL.

Constitutionality. — This section does not criminalize an act previously committed, and in the instant case, the attempted firearm purchase occurred several years after this section was amended to prohibit the possession of a firearm by any convicted felon. The prohibition of firearm possession by convicted felons comes about as a relevant incident to the state regulation of firearms, and thus is not an unconstitutional ex post facto law. Dodson v. Commonwealth, 23 Va. App. 286, 476 S.E.2d 512 (1996).

Imposition of a five-year mandatory minimum sentence for defendant's conviction of possession of a firearm by a convicted felon under § 18.2-308.2 did not violate the constitutional provision of Va. Const., Art. III, § 1, requiring the separation of powers because the power of punishment was vested in the legislative, not the judicial department. Johnson v. Commonwealth, 56 Va. App. 244, 692 S.E.2d 651, 2010 Va. App. LEXIS 201 (2010).

Age classification did not violate due process and equal protection. — Defendant's conviction for possessing a firearm while under the age of 29 after being convicted of a felony as a juvenile was affirmed where the appellate court found the age classification in this section did not discriminate against defendant by violating his equal protection and due process rights. The permissible public safety concern of keeping firearms out of the hands of convicted felons and keeping firearms out of the hands of young adults who were convicted of what would have been a felony if they had been tried as adults was a legitimate governmental objective. Pulley v. Commonwealth, No. 0415-01-1, 2002 Va. App. LEXIS 75 (Ct. of Appeals Feb. 5, 2002).

Double jeopardy violation. — State conceded that defendant's convictions for possession of a firearm after having been convicted of a felony, as well as carrying a concealed weapon after having been convicted of a felony, both in violation of subsection A of § 18.2-308.2, violated defendant's double jeopardy rights since the

convictions were predicated on the same act; as a result, one of the convictions had to be reversed. Perez v. Commonwealth, — Va. App. —, — S.E.2d —, 2006 Va. App. LEXIS 436 (Oct. 3, 2006).

Purpose. — Mischief at which subsection A of § 18.2-308.2 is directed is the possession of firearms by convicted felons in an attempt to prevent indiscriminate use of dangerous weapons by one previously convicted of a serious crime; section 18.2-308.2 expresses a legislative intent of keeping firearms out of the hands of convicted felons. Alger v. Commonwealth, 40 Va. App. 89, 578 S.E.2d 51, 2003 Va. App. LEXIS 137 (2003).

Construction with § 16.1-308. — Regarding defendant's unlawful possession of a firearm, any ambiguity over juvenile protections between § 16.1-308 and this section, which applies to adult felons and juveniles of a certain age convicted of acts that would be felonies for adults, must be resolved in favor of this section, which is the more specific statute and prevails over the general statute concerning collateral disabilities for convicted juveniles. Griffin v. Commonwealth, 33 Va. App. 413, 533 S.E.2d 653, 2000 Va. App. LEXIS 649 (2000).

Juvenile conviction under Virginia law was not a criminal conviction for purposes of defining "prohibited person" under 18 U.S.C.S. § 922 and U.S. Sentencing Guidelines Manual § 2K2.1(a)(6); the fact that defendant was considered a "prohibited person" under subsection A of § 18.2-308.2 was irrelevant for purposes of a federal firearms conviction. United States v. Bugg, 248 F. Supp. 2d 507, 2003 U.S. Dist. LEXIS 3215 (E.D. Va. 2003).

Appeal dismissed under fugitive disentitlement doctrine. — Appeal of a conviction for possession of a firearm while under age 29 after a felonious juvenile adjudication, § 18.2-308.2, was dismissed because defendant was a fugitive from justice, there was a sufficient nexus between the appeal and his fugitive status, and dismissal furthered the goals of the Fugitive Disentitlement Doctrine. Reid v. Commonwealth, 57 Va. App. 42, 698 S.E.2d 269, 2010 Va. App. LEXIS 349 (2010).

Sufficiency of indictment. — Indictment was sufficient to inform defendant of weapon possession offense he committed under this section and that he could receive the mandatory minimum sentence of five years in prison if evidence was introduced showing he had previously convicted of a violent felony, and since the Commonwealth made the required showing, defendant's argument that the indictment insufficiently alleged the offense was without merit. Thomas v. Commonwealth, 37 Va. App. 748, 561 S.E.2d 56, 2002 Va. App. LEXIS 176 (2002).

Original indictment did not charge a nonoffense where: (1) by its reference to § 18.2-308.2, the indictment provided defendant with notice of the nature and character of the offense with which he was charged; (2) the amended indictment tracked the language of § 18.2-308.2 to charge that defendant carried in a concealed manner a dirk, bowie knife, switchblade knife, ballistic knife, machete, or razor or any weapon of like kind; (3) the nature of the charged offense was not changed; and (4) defendant did not claim surprise regarding the charged offense or request a continuance of the trial date. Thompson v. Commonwealth, 51 Va. App. 205, 656 S.E.2d 409, 2008 Va. App. LEXIS 59 (2008), rev'd, 277 Va. 280, 673 S.E.2d 469 (2009) (as to whether butterfly knife was weapon of like kind).

Sufficient identification of defendant. — Trial court did not err in finding that a witness's identification of defendant as the person who robbed the convenience store where she worked was sufficiently reliable. The witness observed the robber's eyes, forehead, and nose during the robbery for about 10 to 15 minutes; she saw his full facial profile for about five seconds; she identified defendant as the robber in photographic and "live" lineups and at trial; and although she acknowledged that the robber had a mark and pimples on his face and defendant at trial did not, this went to the weight of the evidence. Fells v. Commonwealth, — Va. App. —, — S.E.2d —, 2006 Va. App. LEXIS 162 (May 2, 2006).

Identification evidence supported defendant's conviction of possession of a firearm by a convicted felon, as the victims' identification of defendant was sufficient to prove defendant's identity as the shooter; one victim reliably identified defendant as the person with whom the victim argued on the night of the subject shooting and another victim testified unequivocally that the same person who argued with the first victim was the shooter. Cuffee v. Commonwealth, 61 Va. App. 353, 735 S.E.2d 693, 2013 Va. App. LEXIS 7 (2013).

Number of violations based on number of occasions weapons possessed. — The unit of prosecution for this offense is the number of occasions on which a defendant "possesses" one or more weapons; when the evidence establishes that a defendant exercised dominion and control over a firearm on two separate occasions, the defendant has committed two distinct violations of a single criminal proscription. Brown v. Commonwealth, No. 1438-00-1, 2001 Va. App. LEXIS 336 (Ct. of Appeals June 12, 2001).

Number of occasions appropriately delineates the unit of prosecution constituting one offense of "possession" under § 18.2-308.2; the word "occasion," as employed in the context, refers to a discrete unit of time, and not to an open-ended, perpetual, and ongoing period, and thus, the use of the term "occasion" to determine the statutory proscription of a convicted felon's possession of a firearm delineates a distinct unit of time, a specific unit of prosecution. Baker v. Commonwealth, 59 Va. App. 146, 717 S.E.2d 442, 2011 Va. App. LEXIS 373 (2011).

Trial court did not err in convicting defendant of three counts of possession of a firearm in violation of § 18.2-308.2 because defendant exercised dominion and control over a firearm on three separate occasions; accordingly, the evidence established that defendant committed three distinct violations of possession of a firearm in violation of § 18.2-308.2. Baker v. Commonwealth, 59 Va. App. 146, 717 S.E.2d 442, 2011 Va. App. LEXIS 373 (2011).

Collateral estoppel. — Defendant was properly convicted of possession of a firearm by a felon under § 18.2-308.2, even though a jury had acquitted defendant of five related felonies, as collateral estoppel did not apply since the charges were brought simultaneously, with the jury hearing five counts and the court hearing the possession count. Rice v. Commonwealth, 57 Va. App. 437, 703 S.E.2d 254, 2011 Va. App. LEXIS 2 (2011).

Miranda warning. — Where a defendant had carried gun which was fired at his home, it followed that he discarded it between his home and where he was stopped; the public threat justified invoking the public safety exception to Miranda requirements. Benton v. Commonwealth, 40 Va. App. 136, 578 S.E.2d 74, 2003 Va. App. LEXIS 150 (2003).

Possession of three firearms. — When defendant possessed three firearms, he committed a single offense under this section, not three. Acey v. Commonwealth, 29 Va. App. 240, 511 S.E.2d 429 (1999).

Acquittal of defendant of murder charges and use of a firearm in the commission of murder based on a finding of self-defense did not require a finding that the trial court erroneously convicted defendant of the possession of a firearm by a convicted felon, as he possessed the firearm before becoming embroiled in the altercation which led to the shooting. Wilson v. Commonwealth, No. 0962-97-1 (Ct. of Appeals April 7, 1998).

Unlawful search and seizure. — Trial court erred in not suppressing evidence of weapon and ammunition, discovered when defendant's automobile was unlawfully stopped by police, and a search warrant was obtained, as this evidence was the fruit of an unlawful stop and seizure. Mozelle v. Commonwealth, No. 1734-00-1, 2001 Va. App. LEXIS 521 (Ct. of Appeals Sept. 25, 2001).

Motion to suppress properly denied. — Trial court properly admitted evidence of gun because defendant was not initially seized when he pulled his car into a gas station of his own volition and not in response to an officer's lights as his decision to turn into the gas station was not in submission to the officer's authority, therefore when an officer saw defendant reach into his waistband, and refuse to show his hands when asked, it was reasonable for the officer to believe that defendant was reaching for a gun. Pannell v. Commonwealth, — Va. App. —, — S.E.2d —, 2008 Va. App. LEXIS 136 (Mar. 18, 2008).

In a case in which defendant had been convicted of violating §§ 18.2-250, 18.2-308.2, 18.2-308.4, and subsection C of § 18.2-57, he argued unsuccessfully that the Court of Appeals of Virginia erroneously upheld the circuit court's denial of his motion to suppress the evidence because his encounter with the police officers was not consensual, and the officers lacked any reasonable suspicion to believe that he was engaged in criminal activity. During the encounter, which lasted only two or three minutes, the police checked the "ban list" but did not engage in any show of force or use language indicating that defendant was required to remain at that location, the police did not tell him that he was required to stay, and defendant did not make any attempt to leave; instead, defendant

remained in the area, standing about five feet away from the officers while his companion moved to sit on some nearby steps. Montague v. Commonwealth, 278 Va. 532, 684 S.E.2d 583, 2009 Va. LEXIS 113 (2009), cert. denied, 130 S. Ct. 1537, 176 L. Ed. 2d 133, 2010 U.S. LEXIS 1456 (U.S. 2010).

Defense of necessity remains available. — Common-law defense of necessity remains available, upon an appropriate factual predicate, as a defense to a charge of possessing a firearm after having been convicted of a felony under § 18.2-308.2. Alger v. Commonwealth, 40 Va. App. 89, 578 S.E.2d 51, 2003 Va. App. LEXIS 137 (2003).

Severance. — Trial court did not err in refusing to sever felon in possession of a firearm indictment from possession of cocaine and possession of firearm charges, as nothing in the record rebutted the presumption that the trial court considered only the evidence relevant to each offense when reaching its decision. Vanhook v. Commonwealth, 40 Va. App. 130, 578 S.E.2d 71, 2003 Va. App. LEXIS 149 (2003).

Trial court did not abuse its discretion when it declined to sever the charges of possession of a firearm by a felon from the charges of carrying a concealed weapon and felony brandishing of a firearm, because the brandishment charges, in violation of § 18.2-282, required the Commonwealth to also show a prior felony conviction, and defendant was thus not prejudiced by the introduction of the prior convictions at trial. Ellis v. Commonwealth, — Va. App. —, — S.E.2d —, 2006 Va. App. LEXIS 235 (Apr. 18, 2006).

Motion for continuance. — Denial of defendant's motion for a continuance so that he could secure the testimony of his brother did not warrant reversal, as: (1) defendant could not show that the absence of the brother's proffered testimony could not have prejudiced defendant's defense because it addressed a subject on which he needed no defense; and (2) the Commonwealth never contested the assertion that the brother brought the handgun defendant was charged with possessing into defendant's apartment during defendant's last move, but instead focused on what happened to the handgun after the move. Spruill v. Commonwealth, — Va. App. —, — S.E.2d —, 2005 Va. App. LEXIS 476 (Nov. 29, 2005).

Instruction on necessity. — Trial court erred in refusing convicted felon's requested jury instruction as to necessity when he was tried for possession of a firearm that he used solely to defend himself and his girlfriend from assailants. Humphrey v. Commonwealth, 37 Va. App. 36, 553 S.E.2d 546, 2001 Va. App. LEXIS 573 (2001).

Defendant was not entitled to a jury instruction on the defense of necessity due to his fear that an individual who shot him would attack him again, where he only had a generalized fear of such an attack, rather than evidence that a real and specific threat existed at the time he possessed the firearm. Byers v. Commonwealth, 37 Va. App. 174, 554 S.E.2d 714, 2001 Va. App. LEXIS 636 (2001).

Jury instruction on self-defense proper. — Trial court properly instructed the jury that defendant, a convicted felon, had to show that she reasonably feared "serious" bodily injury or death at the hands of the victim to have acted in self-defense in possessing a firearm. Walker v. Commonwealth, No. 1686-03-2, 2004 Va. App. LEXIS 282 (Ct. of Appeals June 15, 2004).

Trial court properly refused to give defendant's proffered instruction on self-defense in the face of an assault as defendant's son refused to leave her home, and although defendant obtained a rifle during the incident, she testified she did not point the gun at her son or "use" the gun in order to get her son out of her house; thus, the rifle was not necessary to repel the son from defendant's home. There was no evidence that the son threatened defendant with death or serious bodily harm, and defendant's response to obtain a deadly weapon exceeded the use of reasonable force to repel the assault. Walker v. Commonwealth, No. 1686-03-2, 2004 Va. App. LEXIS 282 (Ct. of Appeals June 15, 2004).

Reliance on advice of probation officer as affirmative defense. — Under the Interstate Compact Relating to Juveniles, where a juvenile's probation was transferred to North Carolina, a probation officer in that state became an adjunct officer of Virginia's probation system. Thus, defendant could assert, pursuant to *Miller v. Commonwealth*, his alleged reasonable reliance on such a probation officer's advice as an affirmative defense to a charge of possession of a firearm by a convicted felon. Palmer v. Commonwealth, 48 Va. App. 457, 632 S.E.2d 611, 2006 Va. App. LEXIS 344 (2006).

Mandatory two-year sentence. — Trial court properly instructed the jury to recommend a sentence no lower than the two-year mandatory minimum term required by § 18.2-308.2 for the defendant's conviction of possessing a firearm after having been convicted of a felony, and the trial court also did not err in imposing the two-year sentence recommended by the jury, as the trial court had no discretion to do otherwise. Mouberry v. Commonwealth, 39 Va. App. 576, 575 S.E.2d 567, 2003 Va. App. LEXIS 17 (2003).

Mandatory sentence of five years. — Jury was required to fix defendant's sentence for possession of a firearm by a convicted felon in violation of subsection A of § 18.2-308.2 to a mandatory sentence of five years of imprisonment as: (1) defendant possessed a handgun found in a pillowcase located at defendant's feet in a car in which defendant was a passenger; and (2) defendant had been previously convicted of possession of a firearm by a felon, which was classified as a violent felony under § 17.1-805. Lee v. Commonwealth, 2008 Va. App. LEXIS 324 (July 15, 2008).

Sentence appropriate. — Defendant's sentence of five years in the penitentiary after he was convicted of possession of a firearm by a felon was proper because eliminating the five-year mandate would not have affected the total sentence. On defendant's motion to reconsider, the trial court indicated that eliminating the five-year mandate would not have affected the total sentence because it would have imposed the five-year sentence in the exercise of its discretion given defendant's serious and extensive criminal history. Marshall v. Commonwealth, 2010 Va. App. LEXIS 68 (Feb. 23, 2010).

Lesser included offenses. — Possession of a firearm by a convicted felon was not barred as a lesser included offense of brandishing a firearm and carrying a concealed weapon; Sections 18.2-308.2, 18.2-308, and 18.2-282 each require proof of an element that the others do not. Morris v. Commonwealth, 45 Va. App. 181, 609 S.E.2d 92, 2005 Va. App. LEXIS 79 (2005).

Although defendant's conviction for possession of a firearm after having been convicted of a violent felony in violation of subsection A of § 18.2-308.2 was reversed because the circuit court orders showing his prior convictions were not properly authenticated, defendant could be sentenced under § 19.2-285 for possession after committing a felony because he admitted to being a convicted felon. Waller v. Commonwealth, 278 Va. 731, 685 S.E.2d 48, 2009 Va. LEXIS 100 (2009).

Applied in Allen v. Commonwealth, 3 Va. App. 657, 353 S.E.2d 162 (1987); United States v. Walters, 225 F. Supp. 2d 684, 2002 U.S. Dist. LEXIS 19028 (E.D. Va. 2002); United States v. Davis, 234 F. Supp. 2d 601, 2002 U.S. Dist. LEXIS 24781 (E.D. Va. 2002); Conkling v. Commonwealth, 45 Va. App. 518, 612 S.E.2d 235, 2005 Va. App. LEXIS 173 (2005); Banks v. Commonwealth, 280 Va. 612, 701 S.E.2d 437, 2010 Va. LEXIS 274 (2010); Epps v. Commonwealth, 59 Va. App. 71, 717 S.E.2d 151, 2011 Va. App. LEXIS 351 (2011); Booker v. Commonwealth, 61 Va. App. 323, 734 S.E.2d 729, 2012 Va. App. LEXIS 407 (2012).

II. CONVICTED FELON STATUS.

"Convicted felon" status. — A defendant was not a convicted felon for purposes of this section where, at the time of the offense in question, the final order of conviction in the previous felony case had not yet been entered. Archer v. Commonwealth, No. 2550-99-2, 2000 Va. App. LEXIS 485 (Ct. of Appeals July 5, 2000).

Because of his prior conviction in the military for housebreaking the defendant was guilty of possession of a firearm by a convicted felon; however, the trial court improperly sentenced the defendant because the crime was not a violent felony. Turner v. Commonwealth, 38 Va. App. 851, 568 S.E.2d 468, 2002 Va. App. LEXIS 525 (2002).

Criminal docket entries were properly admissible as prima facie evidence of the public record of defendant's criminal convictions in Maryland and, as public records, the contents of the records fell under an exception to the hearsay rule, § 8.01-389 A1 and, a witness saw defendant with guns in his truck; thus, the evidence was sufficient to convict defendant of possession of a firearm after being convicted of a felony in violation of subsection A of § 18.2-308.2. Broward v. Commonwealth, No. 0743-02-3, 2003 Va. App. LEXIS 370 (Ct. of Appeals July 1, 2003).

In a prosecution for possession of a firearm by a convicted felon, sufficient evidence was introduced to allow the trial court to infer that defendant had been convicted of a felony, despite the lack of an order imposing sentence for the prior felony, because the Commonwealth introduced an order of conviction of the prior felony, as well as the testimony of a probation officer that defendant was on probation at the time he possessed a firearm, and defendant testified that he had been convicted of a felony. Nichols v. Commonwealth, — Va. App. —, — S.E.2d —, 2007 Va. App. LEXIS 1 (Jan. 9, 2007).

Defendant's conviction pursuant to § 18.2-308.2 of possession of a firearm after having previously been convicted of a felony could not stand since it was not properly supported by evidence that defendant had a prior felony conviction. The Commonwealth's exhibit indicating that defendant had been convicted of attempted arson when defendant was a 14-year-old juvenile was not conclusive on the point about whether defendant had been convicted of a felony. McMillan v. Commonwealth, 277 Va. 11, 671 S.E.2d 396, 2009 Va. LEXIS 18 (2009).

Restoration of civil rights after serving time for predicate felony does not affect convicted felon status. — Defendant's conviction of possession of a firearm by a convicted felon was proper, as defendant's prior felony conviction from West Virginia constituted the requisite predicate felony; despite the fact that defendant served his time for the West Virginia crime and thereafter, his civil rights were restored in West Virginia, that restoration had no bearing on defendant's legal ability to possess a firearm in Virginia. Farnsworth v. Commonwealth, 43 Va. App. 490, 599 S.E.2d 482, 2004 Va. App. LEXIS 358 (2004), aff'd, 270 Va. 1, 613 S.E.2d 459 (2005).

Exemptions limited to those in statute. — Section 18.2-308.2 expressly provides two specific methods by which a convicted felon may be exempted from the prohibition against possessing a firearm in Virginia, and accordingly, the Court of Appeals of Virginia holds that § 18.2-308.2 B (iii) and C constitute the exclusive means by which a convicted felon may obtain the exemption; nothing in the section automatically exempts from its application a convicted felon whose civil rights have been restored by another state following the felon's completion of his sentence in that state. Farnsworth v. Commonwealth, 43 Va. App. 490, 599 S.E.2d 482, 2004 Va. App. LEXIS 358 (2004), aff'd, 270 Va. 1, 613 S.E.2d 459 (2005).

Defendant's possession of a firearm in Virginia violated § 18.2-308.2, even though the State of West Virginia restored his civil rights, because he failed to obtain relief as one who had his political disabilities removed or his civil rights restored by the Governor, pursuant to Va. Const., Art. V, § 12 and § 18.2-308.2, the only exemptions under Virginia laws. Farnsworth v. Commonwealth, 270 Va. 1, 613 S.E.2d 459, 2005 Va. LEXIS 63 (2005), cert. denied, — U.S. —, 126 S. Ct. 1628, 164 L. Ed. 2d 342, 2006 U.S. LEXIS 2589 (2006).

Prior juvenile adjudication. — The mandatory sentencing provision of § 18.2-308.2 is implicated by a prior juvenile adjudication. Carter v. Commonwealth, 38 Va. App. 116, 562 S.E.2d 331, 2002 Va. App. LEXIS 230 (2002).

Evidence was sufficient to convict defendant of possessing a firearm after having been convicted of a felony, in violation of § 18.2-308.2 where defendant was not charged under a specific subsection of § 18.2-308.2, and was given fair notice of the charges against him; defendant conceded that he was in possession of a weapon and the Commonwealth presented evidence that defendant was under 29 when the present offense was committed, and that defendant was 14 or older when adjudicated guilty of unlawful wounding, an offense that would have been a felony if committed by an adult. Jones v. Commonwealth, No. 1077-02-2, 2003 Va. App. LEXIS 189 (Ct. of Appeals Apr. 1, 2003).

Defendant's sentence to a mandatory five-year term under § 18.2-308.2 for possession of a firearm by a convicted felon, was affirmed as he had been convicted of possessing a firearm after conviction of a felony in violation of § 18.2-308.2 when he was 14, which would have been classified as a violent felony under subsections B and C of § 17.1-805, if he had been tried as an adult; defendant's argument that his juvenile conviction could not serve as the necessary predicate act for § 18.2-308.2 because he was not convicted under an indictment was rejected, and § 19.2-217, relied upon by defendant, was inapplicable. Parks v. Commonwealth, No. 2780-02-1, 2003 Va. App. LEXIS 385 (Ct. of Appeals July 8, 2003).

Convictions for possession of a firearm when under the age of 29 and after having been convicted of a delinquent act as a juvenile that would have been a felony if committed by an adult were reversed because the juvenile court's records did not establish the fact and nature of the adjudication and thus, the Commonwealth failed to prove that defendant had been convicted as a juvenile of a delinquent act that was felonious in nature. Palmer v. Commonwealth, 269 Va. 203, 609 S.E.2d 308, 2005 Va. LEXIS 25 (2005).

Trial court erred in convicting defendant on a charge of possession of a firearm by a convicted felon, because the Commonwealth failed to show that defendant had a prior felony conviction, as notes from a juvenile proceeding against defendant were ambiguous as to whether defendant was convicted of felony burglary. Overbey v. Commonwealth, 271 Va. 231, 623 S.E.2d 904, 2006 Va. LEXIS 10 (2006).

Trial court's judgment of conviction finding defendant guilty of possessing a firearm while under the age of 29, after having been convicted of a delinquent act that would have been a felony if committed by an adult, had to be reversed, as the juvenile court order that the trial court relied on did not make clear to which offense, or both, it was referring to when it stated "found guilty" in regard to charges against him when he was 15-years-old of grand larceny and petit larceny; accordingly, the juvenile court's judgment order was not sufficiently clear, as required by § 19.2-307, and the Commonwealth could not definitively show that defendant had been adjudicated guilty of a delinquent act that would have been a felony had he been an adult. Johnson v. Commonwealth, — Va. App. —, — S.E.2d —, 2006 Va. LEXIS 91 (Mar. 14, 2006).

There was no merit to appellant's argument that the mandatory punishment provision of § 18.2-308.2 did not apply to adjudications of delinquency; the complete reference to the charge in appellant's disposition order and the disposition notice, when read together, were sufficient to prove that appellant's prior adjudication was a felony. Ghee v. Commonwealth, — Va. App. —, — S.E.2d —, 2006 Va. App. LEXIS 477 (Oct. 24, 2006).

Evidence was sufficient to convict defendant of possession of a firearm after having been convicted of a felony, as an undated juvenile adjudication order stating that a "child" was found guilty of breaking and entering and larceny and was committed to the Virginia Department of Juvenile Justice (DJJ) was adequate proof that defendant, while a juvenile, committed two acts that would have been felonies if committed by an adult. Under § 16.1-228, "child" meant a person less than 18 years of age; and under § 16.1-278.7, only a juvenile 11 years or older could be committed to DJJ. Perez v. Commonwealth, 274 Va. 724, 652 S.E.2d 95, 2007 Va. LEXIS 129 (2007).

As a judge's notes clearly complied with the substance of § 19.2-307 in that they listed defendant's guilty plea, the judge's finding of guilt, the sentence, and conditional suspension of the sentence, and it was immaterial that the judge did not list whether the case was tried by a judge or jury, as all cases of that type in juvenile and domestic relations district court were tried by a judge, there was sufficient evidence to establish defendant's prior delinquency for purposes of § 18.2-308.2. Sanders v. Commonwealth, 2008 Va. App. LEXIS 320 (July 15, 2008).

Evidence was sufficient to convict defendant of violating § 18.2-308.2 by possessing a firearm after having been adjudicated delinquent as a juvenile of an act that would have been a felony if committed by an adult, as a certified record of a juvenile probation order stated that the juvenile had been found to be delinquent of carrying a pistol into a public school in violation of § 18.2-308.1, a Class 6 felony. Under § 8.01-389, that certified order was prima facie proof of the facts stated therein. Wilder v. Commonwealth, 2008 Va. App. LEXIS 350 (July 8, 2008).

As appellant juvenile did not dispute that he was previously convicted of the non-violent felony of grand larceny, in violation of § 18.2-95, the evidence was sufficient to support his conviction for possession of a firearm after having been adjudicated delinquent, as a juvenile 14 years of age or older, of an act that would have been a non-violent felony if committed by an adult, in violation of § 18.2-308.2. Preston v. Commonwealth, 281 Va. 52, 704 S.E.2d 127, 2011 Va. LEXIS 23 (2011).

As the Commonwealth failed to prove that appellant juvenile was previously adjudicated delinquent of an act that would have been a violent felony under subsection C of § 17.1-805 if committed by an adult, his conviction for possession of a firearm, in violation of clause (iii) of subsection A of § 18.2-308.2, could not stand; the Commonwealth's attempt to prove a prior breaking and entering

conviction, in violation of § 18.2-91, was insufficient where the nature of the delinquent act for which the juvenile was adjudicated was unclear by the document in support of that conviction. Preston v. Commonwealth, 281 Va. 52, 704 S.E.2d 127, 2011 Va. LEXIS 23 (2011).

In light of the presumption of regularity, the absence of a mark on a prior juvenile adjudication indicating that a Boykin-type colloquy had been given, especially when there was no requirement in § 19.2-307 that the information be on the adjudication, defendant was properly convicted of violating § 18.2-308.2. Isaac v. Commonwealth, 2010 Va. App. LEXIS 423 (Nov. 2, 2010).

Evidence of adjudication of delinquency. — Adjudication order was relevant of an adjudication of delinquency under § 18.2-308.2(A)(iii) since the order described an adjudicatory hearing based on a subsection A of § 18.2-308.2 charge and stated that defendant pled guilty and that the juvenile court accepted the plea; the order tended to prove that defendant had been previously adjudicated delinquent. Perry v. Commonwealth, 61 Va. App. 502, 737 S.E.2d 922, 2013 Va. App. LEXIS 66 (2013).

Sufficient evidence of a prior adjudication of delinquency supported defendant's conviction of possession of a firearm after having been adjudicated delinquent of an act which would be a felony if committed by an adult under § 18.2-308.2 where; (1) an adjudication order was admitted that described an adjudicatory hearing based on a § 18.2-308.2 A felony charge and stated that defendant pled guilty and that the juvenile court accepted the plea; (2) the adjudication order tended to prove that defendant had been previously adjudicated delinquent; and (3) although the disposition order was not admitted, there was no evidence that defendant's conviction changed after the adjudication hearing, and the juvenile court could not have dismissed the prior charge under subdivision A 5 of § 16.1-278.8 because an adjudication of guilt had been made. Perry v. Commonwealth, 61 Va. App. 502, 737 S.E.2d 922, 2013 Va. App. LEXIS 66 (2013).

Not arresting or charging felons not basis for due process claim. — Mother alleged that the city police department maintained and enforced a policy of not arresting or charging felons found in possession of a firearm, but instead, referred such cases to federal authorities for prosecution and that, pursuant to this policy, the officers did not arrest or charge an individual with being a felon in possession of a firearm; thus, from the date that one officer observed the individual in possession of a firearm through the date that the decedent was shot and killed, defendants did not arrest or charge the individual. While the mother alleged that defendants created the danger by affirmatively deciding not to arrest the individual, it was clear that defendants took no affirmative action and such an "omission claim" failed as a matter of law. Mills v. City of Roanoke, 518 F. Supp. 2d 815, 2007 U.S. Dist. LEXIS 76082 (W.D. Va. 2007).

Prosecution allowed to introduce specific nature of prior felony. — Allowing the Commonwealth to introduce the specific nature of defendant's prior felony conviction was not in contravention of the long established principle that evidence of specific prior criminal acts should be excluded because of its prejudicial effect on the defendant, since the Commonwealth is entitled to prove the elements set forth in the indictment, and proof of the handgun charge under subsection A required proof of the previous conviction for robbery. The evidence was, therefore, offered and admitted for a legitimate purpose and not for the prohibited purpose of showing a predisposition on the part of the accused to commit crime. If the result were otherwise, the Commonwealth would be precluded from introducing sufficient evidence against any defendant to obtain a conviction under subsection A. Glover v. Commonwealth, 3 Va. App. 152, 348 S.E.2d 434 (1986), aff'd sub nom. Johnson v. Commonwealth, 236 Va. 48, 372 S.E.2d 134 (1988).

Proper instruction on prior felony. — Despite the fact that the indictment was unclear about which of defendant's two prior convictions was being used to show his status as a convicted felon, defendant failed to present his claim that the evidence varied to the trial court and also failed to file a bill of particulars; the Commonwealth limited its proof of defendant's status as a felon to his prior conviction for unlawful wounding and the trial court, therefore, properly instructed the jury accordingly. Miles v. Commonwealth, No. 0074-01-2, 2002 Va. App. LEXIS 251 (Ct. of Appeals Apr. 30, 2002).

Due process defense. — Trial court erroneously concluded that defendant's probation officer was not a source legally sufficient to invoke the Due Process Clause as a bar to his prosecution and conviction. Based on the totality of the circumstances, defendant's reliance on the advice of his probation officer was reasonable and in good faith. Miller v. Commonwealth, 25 Va. App. 727, 492 S.E.2d 482 (1997).

Bureau of Alcohol, Tobacco and Firearms (ATF) and Virginia Department of Game and Inland Fisheries (VDGIF) agents were not legally sufficient to invoke the due process defense. Miller v. Commonwealth, 25 Va. App. 727, 492 S.E.2d 482 (1997).

Defendant's due process defense to his conviction was properly rejected as defendant failed to show that his parole officer ever affirmatively assured him that he could possess a firearm before he was 29 years old or that he sought such affirmative assurance; rather, the parole officer only told defendant that he could not lawfully possess a firearm while on parole, which fell far short of constituting an affirmative assurance that defendant could possess a firearm before he reached age 29. Bowen v. Commonwealth, 2006 Va. App. LEXIS 119 (Mar. 28, 2006).

Commonwealth not required to prove defendant knowingly or intentionally violated statute for conviction. — Trial court did not err in finding the evidence to support defendant's conviction for possession of a firearm after having been convicted of a felony despite the Commonwealth's failure to establish that defendant intended to violate § 18.2-308.2 since § 18.2-308.2 contained no scienter or mens rea element for a conviction; thus, whether defendant was confused about his status as a convicted felony, whether he intended to mislead the gun dealer, or whether he intended to knowingly violate the statute was of no moment. Branch v. Commonwealth, 42 Va. App. 665, 593 S.E.2d 835, 2004 Va. App. LEXIS 114 (2004).

Forgetfulness no defense. — One may not lose possession or dispossess oneself of property by mere forgetfulness. Therefore, defendant's argument on appeal that he later lost awareness of the presence of the gun which had gathered dust on top of friend's kitchen cabinet and was not discovered by police until two years after its placement there was to no avail. Bond v. Commonwealth, No. 2476-95-1 (Ct. of Appeals Dec. 31, 1996).

A defendant cannot dictate which felony conviction the Commonwealth may offer into evidence to prove his felon status; although it is true that the Commonwealth could have proven the prior felony conviction element of the indictment by tendering a copy of defendant's prior burglary conviction order instead of the murder charge, an accused cannot, without stipulation of guilt, require the Commonwealth to pick and choose among its proofs, and to elect which to present and which to forego. Essex v. Commonwealth, 18 Va. App. 168, 442 S.E.2d 707 (1994).

Defendant guilty where prior conviction was involuntary manslaughter. — Trial court properly found defendant guilty of possession of a handgun after having been previously convicted of a felony involving the use of a firearm, where it was stipulated that the prior conviction was for involuntary manslaughter which was a reduction of a charge of murder and was based on defendant's having killed another person with a shotgun. Lindsey v. Commonwealth, No. 0137-89-2 (Ct. of Appeals Oct. 9, 1990).

An authenticated court order which proves that an accused has been convicted of a specific felony is relevant and admissible to prove an essential element of a violation of this section. Essex v. Commonwealth, 18 Va. App. 168, 442 S.E.2d 707 (1994).

Failure to authenticate prior convictions. — Defendant's conviction for possession of a firearm after having been convicted of a violent felony in violation of subsection A of § 18.2-308.2 was reversed because the circuit court orders showing his prior convictions were not authenticated by a judge's signature as required by subsection A of § 17.1-123. Waller v. Commonwealth, 278 Va. 731, 685 S.E.2d 48, 2009 Va. LEXIS 100 (2009).

Certified transfer order from city. — Trial court properly admitted a prior certified transfer order from a city indicating that the defendant had been convicted for burglary and a sentencing order describing the sentenced imposed for a burglary conviction because the city court's attestation proclaimed that each document was a true copy of a record in the court and the documents certified were part of that court's record. In addition, the court had sufficient evidence to conclude that defendant was a convicted felon and that he possessed contraband because the transfer order recited that the defendant had been found guilty of violating § 18.2-89. Wilson v. Commonwealth, No. 1229-03-1, 2005 Va. App. LEXIS 26 (Ct. of Appeals Jan. 18, 2005).

Evidence of prior conviction admissible despite defendant's stipulation thereto. — Evidence of defendant's prior conviction for robbery was properly received for the purpose of showing a prior conviction, although defendant stipulated that he had a prior conviction of a type which satisfied subsection A, since the Commonwealth is not obliged to enter into an agreement whereby it is precluded from putting on its evidence simply because the defendant is willing to make a qualified stipulation. Glover v. Commonwealth, 3 Va. App. 152, 348 S.E.2d 434 (1986), aff'd sub nom. Johnson v. Commonwealth, 236 Va. 48, 372 S.E.2d 134 (1988).

Felon's claims that disability had been removed were unavailing. — In prosecution of felon for possession of a firearm where felon did not proceed under this section or the federal statute to remove his disability against possession of firearms, his claims that the disability had been removed by the Virginia Parole Board, the purchase of a hunting license, or statements by a Virginia state court judge were unavailing. United States v. Etheridge, 932 F.2d 318 (4th Cir.), cert. denied, 502 U.S. 917, 112 S. Ct. 323, 116 L. Ed. 2d 264 (1991).

Insufficient evidence of defendant's age at time of predicate. — Defendant's conviction of possession of a firearm by a convicted felon, in violation of § 18.2-308.2, was reversed where the Commonwealth failed to prove that defendant was at least 14 years old at the time of defendant's predicate juvenile adjudication for grand larceny, as was required by subdivision A (ii) of § 18.2-308.2; evidence of defendant's age at the time of the prior adjudication as opposed to the date of the prior offense itself was insufficient. Green v. Commonwealth, No. 2945-01-1, 2002 Va. App. LEXIS 667 (Ct. of Appeals Nov. 5, 2002).

Evidence of prior felony. — Defendant's conviction of knowingly and intentionally possessing a firearm after previously having been convicted of a felony, § 18.2-308.2, was affirmed; any error by the trial court in admitting an exhibit showing prior felony convictions was harmless. Murrow v. Commonwealth, No. 2659-02-2, 2004 Va. App. LEXIS 23 (Ct. of Appeals Jan. 20, 2004).

Sufficient evidence was introduced to support a finding that defendant had a felony conviction entered prior to his felony convictions in the present case, and, thus, that he could properly be convicted of a statutory violation that involved having a gun while he was a felon; the evidence showed that defendant, when he was 15-years-old, was charged with and convicted of offenses as a juvenile that if committed by an adult would be a felony and, thus, that such conduct occurred before his conduct in the present case. Perez v. Commonwealth, — Va. App. —, — S.E.2d —, 2006 Va. App. LEXIS 436 (Oct. 3, 2006).

Evidence was sufficient to establish that defendant possessed a firearm, and since defendant did not dispute that he was previously convicted of a violent felony, the supreme court further held that the jury verdict convicting defendant of possession of a firearm by a convicted felon under subsection A of § 18.2-308.2 was not plainly wrong. When police arrived at defendant's residence, defendant was alone in the bedroom in which the firearm was found, and the bedroom contained defendant's clothes and personal effects. Rawls v. Commonwealth, 272 Va. 334, 634 S.E.2d 697, 2006 Va. LEXIS 77 (2006).

In a prosecution for possession of a firearm by a convicted felon, in violation of § 18.2-308.2, because an printout from the National Crime Information Network was properly admitted as a business record, and the officer testifying about the same provided sufficient foundation for its admission over a hearsay objection, when such evidence was combined with two other exhibits, regarding a New Jersey conviction and an accusation, respectively, said conviction was upheld on appeal; further, trial counsel's relevancy argument as to the latter two was rejected, as such went more to the weight of the evidence rather than to its admissibility. Guerara-Sandoval v. Commonwealth, 2007 Va. App. LEXIS 296 (Aug. 7, 2007).

Commonwealth entitled to offer whatever evidence was available. — Circuit court did not abuse its discretion in admitting five conviction orders during defendant's trial for knowingly and intentionally possessing or transporting a firearm after having previously been convicted of a violent felony in violation of subsection A of § 18.2-308.2 because the Commonwealth was not limited to adducing evidence of only one prior conviction for a violent felony.

Boone v. Commonwealth, 2013 Va. LEXIS 47 (Apr. 18, 2013).

Subsection A of § 18.2-308.2 does not provide a rule of evidence constraining the Commonwealth's prerogative to prove the elements of their respective offenses with its choice of the available evidence because the phrase "previously convicted of a violent felony" in subsection A merely sets forth an additional element the Commonwealth is required to prove beyond a reasonable doubt to obtain an enhanced sentence; accordingly, while the article "a" in subsection A does reflect legislative intent that proof of only one violent felony is necessary to obtain the enhanced sentence, that article does not limit the evidence the Commonwealth may adduce to prove it. Boone v. Commonwealth, 2013 Va. LEXIS 47 (Apr. 18, 2013).

Because subsection A of § 18.2-308.2 establishes the elements of the offense rather than a rule of evidence by which the elements may be proven, the statute does not limit the Commonwealth's prerogative to meet its burden of proof using whatever available evidence it chooses. Boone v. Commonwealth, 2013 Va. LEXIS 47 (Apr. 18, 2013).

Subsequent prosecution not barred. — In the instant case, the trial court dismissed the indictment under § 18.2-308.2:2, because the criminal history consent form did not comply with statutory requirements. Thus, the dismissal was not an acquittal for double jeopardy purposes, and double jeopardy did not bar prosecution of the defendant under this section. Dodson v. Commonwealth, 23 Va. App. 286, 476 S.E.2d 512 (1996).

Conviction not based on same evidence as earlier conviction of carrying a concealed weapon. — Defendant's conviction of possession of a firearm by a felon was affirmed; the possession by a felon conviction was based on different evidence than the conviction for carrying a concealed weapon under § 18.2-308, which was based on the same incident, and therefore § 19.2-294 did not bar the possession by a felon conviction. Jefferson v. Commonwealth, 43 Va. App. 361, 597 S.E.2d 290, 2004 Va. App. LEXIS 277 (2004).

III. WEAPONS.

What constitutes deadly weapon. — Defendant's knife was a weapon "of like kind" to a dirk and was therefore a deadly weapon, where it was a butterfly knife which, when opened, most closely resembled a dirk, and it was described by arresting officer as a "fighting knife." Kingrey v. Commonwealth, No. 2202-97-2 (Ct. of Appeals July 13, 1999).

Defendant's knife, which was described by the arresting officer as a steak knife, was not a weapon "of like kind" to a dirk despite the prosecutor's allegation that it satisfied the definition because it had a sharp end at the bottom edge and an extreme point that would certainly cut straight through flesh if propelled with any type of force. Goodwin v. Commonwealth, — Va. App. —, — S.E.2d —, 2005 Va. App. LEXIS 265 (July 12, 2005).

Conviction under § 18.2-308.2 for possessing a concealed weapon after having been convicted of a felony was proper because a knife found on defendant's person had similar characteristics to a bowie knife, such as a single sharp edge, a dull flat edge, and point, to constitute a "weapon of like kind" under subsection A of § 18.2-308. Gilliam v. Commonwealth, 49 Va. App. 508, 642 S.E.2d 774, 2007 Va. App. LEXIS 143 (2007).

Evidence was sufficient to convict defendant of possession of a concealed weapon by a convicted felon, in violation of § 18.2-308.2, where defendant admitted that he possessed a razor and any razor was explicitly included as a weapon in subsection A of § 18.2-308. The manner in which defendant used the razor was irrelevant to the analysis. Uzzle v. Commonwealth, 2010 Va. App. LEXIS 239 (2010).

Kitchen knife did not constitute a "weapon of like kind." — Although the kitchen knife possessed by defendant was a potentially dangerous object, it was not a "weapon," because it was not designed for fighting purposes nor was it commonly understood to be a "weapon"; therefore, defendant's conviction for possession of a concealed weapon by a felon under § 18.2-308 was vacated. Farrakhan v. Commonwealth, 273 Va. 177, 639 S.E.2d 227, 2007 Va. LEXIS 10 (2007).

Because there was no evidence that defendant's kitchen steak knife was designed for fighting purposes, nor was it commonly understood to be a weapon, it was not a weapon as defined in subsection A of § 18.2-308; because it was not a weapon, the court did not need to consider whether it was a weapon of like kind.

Defendant's conviction for being a convicted felon in possession of a weapon under subsection A of § 18.2-308.2 was reversed. Green v. Commonwealth, 2009 Va. App. LEXIS 573 (Dec. 22, 2009).

Jury instruction failed to require determination as to whether pneumatic gun was a weapon of like kind. — Defendant was barred from challenging the sufficiency of the evidence to support his carrying a concealed weapon as a convicted felon, arguing that the pneumatic gun that he used did not fall within the weapons of like kind classification under this section, as defendant admitted that the gun was a weapon while arguing a motion to strike, and defendant agreed to a jury instruction that did not require the jury to determine whether the unique characteristics of the pneumatic gun placed it within the weapon of like kind catch-all; to the extent that the agreed instruction misstated the law by failing to qualify the use of the term weapon, defendant could not challenge it. Aylor v. Commonwealth, No. 3366-02-2, 2004 Va. App. LEXIS 183 (Ct. of Appeals Mar. 2, 2004).

"Butterfly knife" a prohibited weapon. — A "butterfly knife," consisting of a single blade with a two-part hinged handle which folded to enclose the blade and which could be flipped open to create a straight-bladed knife, sharpened on one side, approximately nine inches long with a blade four inches long and a sharp point, was a weapon of like kind to a dirk under § 18.2-308 A and a convicted felon's possession of such a knife was, therefore, a violation of this section. Delcid v. Commonwealth, 32 Va. App. 14, 526 S.E.2d 273 (2000).

"Butterfly knife" was not "weapon of like kind." — Defendant was improperly convicted of violating subsection A of § 18.2-308.2 by carrying a weapon concealed about his person, after having been convicted of a felony, because the evidence was insufficient to establish that his "butterfly knife" was a "weapon of like kind" to a dirk or any other weapon enumerated in subsection A of § 18.2-308. Thompson v. Commonwealth, 277 Va. 280, 673 S.E.2d 469, 2009 Va. LEXIS 35 (2009).

Scuba knife not weapon of like kind. — Possession of a scuba knife could not support a conviction under § 18.2-308.2, because the scuba knife was a safety device and a tool, and was not designed for fighting purposes or commonly understood to be a weapon. McMillan v. Commonwealth, 2009 Va. App. LEXIS 118 (Mar. 17, 2009).

Defendant's conviction for possession of a concealed weapon by a convicted felon in violation of subsection A of § 18.2-308.2 was vacated because the evidence did not establish that the knife defendant possessed was one of the items enumerated in subsection A of § 18.2-308 or that it was a weapon of like kind to one enumerated, and the record was devoid of any facts on which one could find that the knife was either designed for fighting purposes or commonly understood to be a weapon. McMillan v. Commonwealth, 55 Va. App. 392, 686 S.E.2d 525, 2009 Va. App. LEXIS 571 (2009).

"Firearm" defined. — Statute prohibiting a felon from being in possession of a firearm did not indicate that the legislature meant to limit the term "firearm" to only presently-operable instruments; rather, the Commonwealth only had to prove that the instrument was designed, made, and intended to expel a projectile by an explosion, and where the Commonwealth proved that the rifle that defendant, a convicted felon, possessed had those characteristics, it proved defendant possessed a "firearm" as contemplated by the statute. Armstrong v. Commonwealth, 263 Va. 573, 562 S.E.2d 139, 2002 Va. LEXIS 67 (2002).

Trial court properly convicted defendant of being a felon in the possession of a firearm when witnesses had testified that defendant had used a plastic flare launcher in a threatening manner, which was precisely the type of behavior the statute was designed to prevent. Quesenberry v. Commonwealth, 41 Va. App. 126, 583 S.E.2d 55, 2003 Va. App. LEXIS 395 (2003).

Because a certificate of analysis excluding the item tested from the statutory definition of "firearm" under subsection A of § 18.2-308.2 was issued after defendant's conviction became final, defendant's petition for a writ of actual innocence under § 19.2-327.10 et seq., was granted, and the conviction was ordered expunged pursuant to § 19.2-327.13. Copeland v. Commonwealth, 52 Va. App. 529, 664 S.E.2d 528, 2008 Va. App. LEXIS 381 (2008).

Neither a commemorative replica of a handgun, which does not include a firing pin or other mechanical device necessary to fire a projectile by explosion, nor a BB gun, which fires BBs by the force of a spring, would be sufficient to convict a person under § 18.2-308.2 for possession of a firearm by a convicted felon because they are not designed, made, and intended to fire or expel a projectile by means of an explosion. Startin v. Commonwealth, 281 Va. 374, 706 S.E.2d 873, 2011 Va. LEXIS 57 (2011).

The term "firearm" as used in this section is used in its traditional sense. The statute does not seek to protect the public from fear of harm caused by the display of weapons; rather, it is concerned with preventing a person, who is known to have committed a serious crime in the past, from becoming dangerously armed, regardless of whether that person uses, displays, or conceals the firearm. Accordingly, this section does not include a BB handgun, which is a device that propels a projectile by pneumatic pressure. Jones v. Commonwealth, 16 Va. App. 354, 429 S.E.2d 615 (1993), overruled in part, Armstrong v. Commonwealth, 36 Va. App. 312, 549 S.E.2d 641 (2001).

Flare gun is firearm. — Defendant's conviction of possessing a firearm after having been convicted of a felony was supported by sufficient evidence, because the flare gun found in defendant's possession satisfied the statutory definition of a firearm. Morris v. Commonwealth, 269 Va. 127, 607 S.E.2d 110, 2005 Va. LEXIS 3 (2005).

Exception limited to stun weapons and tasers. — The 2001 amendments to subsection A of § 18.2-308.2 expanded the class of weapons that a felon could not possess to include stun weapons and tasers within its proscription, and the amendment created an exception to the general prohibition of possession of a stun weapon or taser as defined in § 18.2-308.1 by allowing possession of those weapons in the home; clearly the legislative intent was that the exception apply only to stun weapons and tasers, firearms that are limited in their ability to injure. Alger v. Commonwealth, 40 Va. App. 89, 578 S.E.2d 51, 2003 Va. App. LEXIS 137 (2003) (decided under § 18.2-308.2 as it read prior to later amendments).

Trial court did not err in convicting defendant on a charge of possession of a firearm after having been previously convicted of a felony, as defendant's contention that the relevant statute contained an exception allowing for his possession of a firearm at his residence had to be rejected since the exception applied only to stun weapons and tasers at one's residence, and an absurd result would occur if it were read to also include firearms. Hundley v. Commonwealth, No. 1184-02-03, 2003 Va. App. LEXIS 530 (Ct. of Appeals Oct. 21, 2003).

Phrase "stun weapon or taser as defined in § 18.2-308.1" was the last antecedent before the "except clause," and as such, "stun weapon or taser" was the referential and qualifying phrase; thus, according to the last antecedent rule of construction, the "except" clause in former § 18.2-308.2 modified only "stun weapon or taser" and not "firearm," and did not permit defendant, as a convicted felon, to possess a firearm within her home, the curtilage thereof, or anywhere else. Alger v. Commonwealth, 267 Va. 255, 590 S.E.2d 563, 2004 Va. LEXIS 21 (2004) (decided under § 18.2-308.2 as it read prior to later amendments).

It is impossible to decipher whether the word "any" is intended to include the possession of a firearm or ammunition as a singular activity or as a "plural activity." Acey v. Commonwealth, 29 Va. App. 240, 511 S.E.2d 429 (1999).

Firearm that could be readily or easily restored to operability. — A defendant who had previously been convicted of a felony was properly convicted of violating this section notwithstanding the fact that the firearm in question was not presently operable where the firearm could be readily or easily restored to operability. Armstrong v. Commonwealth, No. 1388-99-3, 2000 Va. App. LEXIS 753 (Ct. of Appeals Nov. 21, 2000), aff'd, on reh'g, en banc, 36 Va. App. 312, 549 S.E.2d 641 (2001), aff'd, remanded, 263 Va. 573, 562 S.E.2d 139 (2002).

Evidence supported a conviction for possession of a firearm by a convicted felon, in violation of § 18.2-308.2, was affirmed because the Commonwealth of Virginia met its burden of proving the subject weapon was designed, made, and intended to expel a projectile by means of an explosion, and there was no evidence that the weapon was in such a state of disrepair that it lost that characteristic. Barlow v. Commonwealth, 61 Va. App. 668, 739 S.E.2d 269, 2013 Va. App. LEXIS 107 (Apr. 2, 2013).

Inoperable firearm. — Because the trial court's factual determination that a handgun was a firearm was not plainly wrong or without evidence to support it, defendant's conviction for possession

of a firearm by a convicted felon was affirmed; the evidence of inoperability because of missing parts indicated that the handgun could have been repaired, and defendant's testimony that the chambers of the handgun "just fell off of it" was insufficient to support a finding that the handgun lost its characteristic as a firearm. Kingsbur v. Commonwealth, 267 Va. 348, 593 S.E.2d 208, 2004 Va. LEXIS 32 (2004).

Firearms not permitted to felons in their residences. — 2001 amendments to former § 18.2-308.2 A do not permit convicted felons to possess firearms in their residence or the curtilage thereof. Alger v. Commonwealth, 40 Va. App. 89, 578 S.E.2d 51, 2003 Va. App. LEXIS 137 (2003) (decided under § 18.2-308.2 as it read prior to later amendments).

Commonwealth of Virginia met its burden of proving that defendant violated § 18.2-308.2 by showing that defendant was convicted on attempted armed robbery in 1982, and that police saw defendant place a bag containing a handgun next to a trash receptacle in 2002, and the appellate court affirmed the trial court's judgment that the handgun defendant possessed was a "firearm" within the meaning of § 18.2-308.2, even though it was missing its firing pin and other parts and could not be fired. Kingsbur v. Commonwealth, 40 Va. App. 307, 579 S.E.2d 357, 2003 Va. App. LEXIS 217 (2003), aff'd, 267 Va. 348, 593 S.E.2d 208 (2004).

Amendment to subsection A of § 18.2-308.2 which allowed persons convicted of a felony to possess a stun weapon or taser in their residence or the curtilage of their residence did not apply to other weapons, and the trial court properly convicted defendant of violating former subsection A of § 18.2-308.2 because he possessed a revolver in the backyard of his home. Robinson v. Commonwealth, No. 0563-02-3, 2003 Va. App. LEXIS 293 (Ct. of Appeals May 13, 2003).

Exception allowing possession of a firearm inside the home or curtilage, set forth in subsection A of § 18.2-308.2, did not permit defendant to possess firearms in his residence or the curtilage thereof. Plumley v. Commonwealth, No. 1799-02-3, 2003 Va. App. LEXIS 501 (Ct. of Appeals Oct. 7, 2003).

Required proof. — In a prosecution under this section, the Commonwealth is required to prove that the purported firearm had the actual ability to expel a projectile by the power of an explosion. Moore v. Commonwealth, No. 2755-95-3 (Ct. of Appeals Dec. 31, 1996).

This section requires the Commonwealth to prove, as an essential element of the offense, that the accused possessed an actual firearm, not merely an object of similar appearance. Redd v. Commonwealth, 29 Va. App. 256, 511 S.E.2d 436 (1999).

This section prohibits felons from possessing actual firearms that are presently operable or that can readily or easily be made operable or capable of being fired with minimal effort and expertise. Armstrong v. Commonwealth, No. 1388-99-3, 2000 Va. App. LEXIS 753 (Ct. of Appeals Nov. 21, 2000), aff'd, on reh'g, en banc, 36 Va. App. 312, 549 S.E.2d 641 (2001), aff'd, remanded, 263 Va. 573, 562 S.E.2d 139 (2002).

This section prohibits a felon from possessing a device that has the actual capacity to do serious harm because of its ability to expel a projectile by the power of an explosion, and it is not concerned with the use or display of a device that may have the appearance of a firearm. Redd v. Commonwealth, 29 Va. App. 256, 511 S.E.2d 436 (1999).

Direct evidence of operability not required. — While the best method of proving the ability of a firearm to discharge shot by gunpowder is to introduce the testimony of a ballistics expert who test-fired the weapon, the Commonwealth is not required to offer direct evidence that the firearm is operable. Instead, the operability of a firearm may be proved by circumstantial evidence. Moore v. Commonwealth, No. 2755-95-3 (Ct. of Appeals Dec. 31, 1996).

A reasonable fact finder may infer operability from an object which looks like, feels like, sounds like or is like, a firearm. Such an inference would be reasonable without direct proof of operability. Moore v. Commonwealth, No. 2755-95-3 (Ct. of Appeals Dec. 31, 1996).

Under this section, the Commonwealth was only required to prove that a convicted felon knowingly and intentionally possessed or transported any firearm and that the firearm was made with the purpose of expelling a projectile by gunpowder or other explosion; it was not required to prove that the gun was operable, because the statute's plain language does not require such proof. Armstrong v.

Commonwealth, 36 Va. App. 312, 549 S.E.2d 641, 2001 Va. App. LEXIS 503 (2001).

Commonwealth proved a handgun found in defendant's residence was loaded and seemed to be fully functional. As the Commonwealth was not obliged under § 18.2-308.2 to prove that the firearm was operable, the evidence was sufficient to support defendant's conviction. Williams v. Commonwealth, — Va. App. —, — S.E.2d —, 2006 Va. App. LEXIS 94 (Mar. 14, 2006).

Because the prosecution did not have to prove that a weapon that was found in plain site during a warrantless search of defendant's residence was operable under § 18.2-308.2, the trial court properly denied defendant's motion to strike. Williams v. Commonwealth, 49 Va. App. 439, 642 S.E.2d 295, 2007 Va. App. LEXIS 113 (2007).

Physical inability to operate firearm no defense. — The plain language of § 18.2-308.2 prohibits "possession" of any firearm by a convicted felon and provides no exception from that requirement related to the felon's physical ability to use the firearm at a particular time. Byers v. Commonwealth, 37 Va. App. 174, 554 S.E.2d 714, 2001 Va. App. LEXIS 636 (2001).

Evidence supporting "firearm." — The fact that shots were fired, striking the car, corroborating other testimony, was relevant evidence because it established that appellant possessed a weapon, capable of firing bullets. McCloud v. Commonwealth, No. 2343-94-1 (Ct. of Appeals Dec. 5, 1995).

Sufficient evidence of firearm. — Store clerk's description of the object brandished by defendant as "a long black gun" was insufficient, alone, to prove that the object possessed the ability to expel a projectile by the power of an explosion. However, defendant's threat, upon presenting the weapon, to kill the clerk was an implied assertion that the object was a functioning weapon, being in fact the firearm that it appeared to be and possessing the power to kill. This implied assertion, which was corroborated by the appearance of the object and was uncontradicted by any other evidence, was evidence sufficient to support the trial court's finding that the object was a firearm. Redd v. Commonwealth, 29 Va. App. 256, 511 S.E.2d 436 (1999).

Evidence was sufficient to prove that the defendant possessed a firearm where, after a fight, the defendant retreated to his trailer and returned with his brother, three witnesses believed the defendant possessed a firearm, two witnesses saw him raise his arm as if to shoot, all three ducked instinctively to protect themselves, and bullets damaged property in the line of fire. Martin v. Commonwealth, No. 0678-98-3 (Ct. of Appeals Jan. 12, 1999).

Where, in a pat-down search of defendant's person, police recovered a magazine to a semi-automatic Bersa handgun containing seven rounds of .380 ammunition from his left front pants pocket and a .380 caliber Bersa semi-automatic handgun from a nearby closet shelf, even though at the time of its recovery, this weapon did not have a clip loaded into the frame, the contemporaneous possession of the magazine with the possession of the weapon found in the closet provided a substantial nexus to become a functional firearm with the ability to fire by explosion. Hunter v. Commonwealth, No. 1904-99-1, 2000 Va. App. LEXIS 439 (Ct. of Appeals June 13, 2000).

Sufficient evidence permitted the jury to find beyond a reasonable doubt that defendant possessed a firearm and shot a dog where defendant admitted driving by the site of the shooting on the day of the shooting, one of two girls saw defendant shoot a firearm toward the barn where they were playing with the dog, the other saw him with a firearm right after the shooting, and the girls were certain defendant was the man they saw at the barn with the firearm. Ford v. Commonwealth, 48 Va. App. 262, 630 S.E.2d 332, 2006 Va. App. LEXIS 238 (2006).

Evidence was sufficient to support his convictions for possession of a firearm by a felon and possession of marijuana because defendant stated the car where the contraband was found was his car, and defendant provided a key to the officer who found several items with defendant's name in addition to the pistol, bullets, loose marijuana and digital scale. Patterson v. Commonwealth, 2006 Va. App. LEXIS 361 (Aug. 8, 2006).

Evidence was sufficient to support defendant's conviction of possession of a firearm by a convicted felon, § 18.2-308.2, because an eyewitness testified that he saw defendant with a gun, that the witness worked for the federal Department of Justice as a firearms instructor and had use of firearms everyday, that he observed defendant's hand for two minutes in a lighted area, that he observed the barrel of the gun and the firing mechanism, and that

the item was a Glock 9mm, an object that the parties agreed was designed to expel a projectile by means of an explosion. Elder v. Commonwealth, — Va. App. —, — S.E.2d —, 2007 Va. App. LEXIS 375 (Oct. 9, 2007).

Sufficient evidence supported defendant's § 18.2-308.2 conviction as a victim testified that a small, silver, semi-automatic pistol was pointed at his temple; defendant's concurrent demand that the victim part with possession of a vehicle supported the victim's conclusion that a gun and not a toy was pointed at the victim's head. Jordan v. Commonwealth, 60 Va. App. 675, 731 S.E.2d 622, 2012 Va. App. LEXIS 281 (2012).

There was sufficient evidence that defendant possessed a firearm to support defendant's conviction under subsection A of § 18.2-308.2 where: (1) a police officer with training on firearms testified that the instrument was a revolver, and that in revolvers, when the trigger was pulled, the firing pin hit the strike plate on the round and sent the round out of the barrel by force; (2) another officer testified that she removed six rounds of ammunition from the instrument when she retrieved the instrument from the street; and (3) the firearm itself was admitted. Perry v. Commonwealth, 61 Va. App. 502, 737 S.E.2d 922, 2013 Va. App. LEXIS 66 (2013).

Insufficient evidence of firearm. — Commonwealth failed to prove that defendant possessed a device having ability to expel a projectile by power of an explosion. Gates v. Commonwealth, No. 0502-98-4 (Ct. of Appeals July 13, 1999).

Evidence was not sufficient to support defendant's conviction for possession of a firearm by a convicted felon under § 18.2-308.2, because it only showed that the object used by defendant gave the appearance of having firing capability, it did not demonstrate that the object defendant possessed was designed, made, and intended to expel a projectile by means of an explosion. Jamar v. Commonwealth, 2011 Va. App. LEXIS 387 (Dec. 6, 2011).

Sufficient evidence for inference of operability. — Where detective testified that he examined the rifle, tested the trigger mechanism, and that the rifle was a .50 caliber black powder rifle; a photograph of the rifle was introduced; and the detective testified in detail how the rifle functioned to discharge a bullet by an explosion of gunpowder, a reasonable fact finder could infer that the rifle was operable and therefore a firearm under this section. Moore v. Commonwealth, No. 2755-95-3 (Ct. of Appeals Dec. 31, 1996).

A convicted felon had constructive possession of a firearm where he was carrying a clip and ammunition for a particular rifle on his person, he exercised control over the trailer where the rifle was found and he directed his wife to the precise location of the rifle in the trailer and directed her to produce it. Gregory v. Commonwealth, 28 Va. App. 393, 504 S.E.2d 886 (1998), overruled in part, Armstrong v. Commonwealth, 36 Va. App. 312, 549 S.E.2d 641 (2001).

Pointing a gun at the victim while demanding the contents of his pockets was an implied assertion by the defendant that the weapon was operable. By pointing a gun at the victim and demanding money, the defendant was, indeed, making a statement equivalent to "I will shoot you if you do not comply with my demand." Kirby v. Commonwealth, No. 0076-00-3, 2000 Va. App. LEXIS 783 (Ct. of Appeals Dec. 5, 2000).

Insufficient evidence for inference that gun was real. — Witness's testimony clearly proved that he was intimidated by an object that had the appearance of a gun. However, his testimony that he could not say whether the object "was a real gun or not" left uncertain whether appellant possessed a toy or an actual gun. Witness admitted that he "was not a gun person." From witness's testimony, the trier of fact could not infer beyond a reasonable doubt that the device was indeed a "real gun." Williams v. Commonwealth, No. 2584-96-1 (Ct. of Appeals Feb. 10, 1998).

The description of the firearm in a juvenile petition was excess language because the precise type of firearm was not an element of the offense. Toliver v. Commonwealth, No. 2880-99-2, 2000 Va. App. LEXIS 716 (Ct. of Appeals Nov. 7, 2000).

Ammunition was explosive material. — Not only was .25 caliber ammunition an explosive material for purposes of § 18.2-308.2, but evidence, including that defendant had a commercially labeled box containing 42 cartridges and common knowledge recognized that firearm ammunitions contained gunpowder and functioned by explosion, was sufficient to sustain his conviction thereunder. Davis v. Commonwealth, 2010 Va. App. LEXIS 29 (Jan. 26, 2010).

Evidence sufficient to prove cartridges were ammunition.
— Contrary to defendant's claim, the evidence was not insufficient to prove that the cartridges found on defendant's person contained propellant, as nothing in subsection D of § 18.2-308.2 indicated that it was the obvious intention of the legislature that the disjunctive "or" was meant to mean "and." Williams v. Commonwealth, 61 Va. App. 1, 733 S.E.2d 124, 2012 Va. App. LEXIS 332 (2012).

IV. POSSESSION, TRANSPORTATION, AND CONCEALMENT.

A conviction for knowingly and intentionally possessing a firearm after having been convicted of a felony requires proof beyond a reasonable doubt of either actual or constructive possession of the firearm. Hancock v. Commonwealth, 21 Va. App. 466, 465 S.E.2d 138 (1995).

Sufficient evidence of knowledge. — In a prosecution on a charge of possessing a firearm after having been convicted of a felony, in violation of § 18.2-308.2, the evidence was sufficient to show that defendant knew of the presence of the guns on the premises where he resided as they were in plain view. Redmond v. Commonwealth, 57 Va. App. 254, 701 S.E.2d 81, 2010 Va. App. LEXIS 446 (2010).

Sufficient evidence of defendant's identity. — Facts, considered in their totality, could have led a reasonable fact finder to conclude that defendant was, in fact, the masked man in camouflage carrying a rifle, as defendant testified he knew that the twins had beaten his son on the day in question; the masked man told the person at the door "they beat my son"; the man told another person it's "Uncle Horace," and defendant's first name was Horace; defendant was spotted just moments later, near the vicinity of the crime, wearing camouflage clothing; and defendant changed his clothes immediately after an investigator drove by. Henderson v. Commonwealth, 2011 Va. App. LEXIS 301 (Oct. 4, 2011).

Evidence of drug distribution a factor in motive to possess firearm. — Trial court did not abuse its discretion in admitting into evidence the 46 plastic baggies or the police officer's expert testimony about their use in the illegal drug trade. Both individually and collectively, the facts tended to show just what the prosecutor argued: that defendant was still engaged in the distribution of marijuana; while not alone dispositive, evidence linking a defendant to drug distribution could be considered as one factor in determining whether he may have had a motive to possess a firearm. Thomas v. Commonwealth, 44 Va. App. 741, 607 S.E.2d 738, 2005 Va. App. LEXIS 31 (2005).

Proof that a firearm was located close to defendant was not sufficient to prove the elements of the offense beyond a reasonable doubt. Hancock v. Commonwealth, 21 Va. App. 466, 465 S.E.2d 138 (1995).

Convictions for three seperate offenses proper. — In accordance with the gravamen of the offense, a new offense of possession of a firearm could be established with each separate act or occurrence. Under that analysis, each of defendant's three convictions derived from distinct offenses; the first on the day defendant stole the weapon, the second on the day he attempted to sell it, and the third on the day he sold it. Baker v. Commonwealth, 284 Va. 572, 733 S.E.2d 642, 2012 Va. LEXIS 188 (Nov. 1, 2012).

Sufficient evidence of possession. — Evidence was sufficient to find that defendant had been in actual possession of handgun recovered from area where he fell while running from police. Hill v. Commonwealth, No. 2336-98-1 (Ct. of Appeals Nov. 23, 1999).

Evidence was sufficient to support finding that defendant, a convicted felon, intentionally possessed a firearm; while defendant's paralysis may have precluded him from personally dispossessing the gun hidden under his bedding, nothing prevented him from calling friends, family, or neighbors to remove the gun, and his paralysis did not explain why he secreted the gun with its ammunition back under the bedding. Baker v. Commonwealth, No. 1142-00-3, 2001 Va. App. LEXIS 343 (Ct. of Appeals June 19, 2001).

Evidence was sufficient to prove that defendant, a convicted felon, possessed a firearm, where defendant kept guns in his bedroom, defendant forbade the children from "messing with" the guns, and defendant went hunting with his boys and the guns. Donnelly v. Commonwealth, No. 2070-00-2, 2001 Va. App. LEXIS 621 (Ct. of Appeals Nov. 13, 2001).

Trial court did not have to believe defendant's version of how defendant acquired car and was entitled to infer that defendant knew car was stolen; defendant knew of the shotgun based on its location under the passenger seat. Ridley v. Commonwealth, No. 1850-01-1, 2002 Va. App. LEXIS 387 (Ct. of Appeals July 16, 2002).

Evidence showed that defendant, a felon, was in unlawful possession of a weapon as defendant's spouse testified that while they were home alone defendant obtained a pistol she owned and fired it twice, which caused the spouse to grab her keys and flee since defendant talked about that day being the day the spouse was going to die. Kirby v. Commonwealth, 264 Va. 440, 570 S.E.2d 832, 2002 Va. LEXIS 164 (2002).

Where defendant told police officers that defendant found firearm, evidence was sufficient to support defendant's conviction of possession of a firearm by a convicted felon, as defendant admitted picking up the firearm, thus exercising dominion and control over the firearm. Greene v. Commonwealth, No. 3343-01-2, 2002 Va. App. LEXIS 717 (Ct. of Appeals Dec. 3, 2002).

Defendant's had knowing possession of guns, where the defendant's wife confessed that she had shot at the defendant with a gun in their home, the defendant complained to the police that the defendant's wife had shot at him with a gun in their home, and the defendant led the police to the guns kept in the defendant's locked bedroom in their home. Nowlin v. Commonwealth, 40 Va. App. 327, 579 S.E.2d 367, 2003 Va. App. LEXIS 218 (2003), . But see Crawford v. Washington, 541 U.S. 36, 124 S. Ct. 1354, 158 L. Ed. 2d 177 (2004).

Testimonial evidence from the victim of an assault committed by defendant, a convicted felon, and officers who recovered the gun used to commit the same, provided sufficient evidence for a jury to convicted defendant of possession of a firearm by a convicted felon; a requisite logical connection between defendant's possession of the weapon and the crime charged was highly probative and, with the limiting instructions given to the jury as to the gun's recovery by police, outweighed any incidental prejudice. McDaniel v. Commonwealth, No. 3317-01-4, 2003 Va. App. LEXIS 349 (Ct. of Appeals June 17, 2003).

Evidence was sufficient to support defendant's conviction for possession of a firearm by a convicted felon, as the evidence showed that defendant armed himself with a gun he had purchased during the previous month and confronted another man at defendant's residence who had threatened defendant because the other man had started residing with defendant's wife while defendant was in jail; the jury was entitled to reject defendant's necessity defense, as the evidence showed that defendant had purchased the gun at least several days before the shooting occurred and, thus, defendant was not under an imminent threat at the time he came into possession of the gun. Hood v. Commonwealth, No. 2419-02-2, 2004 Va. App. LEXIS 33 (Ct. of Appeals Jan. 28, 2004).

Sufficient evidence of possession of a firearm after having been previously convicted of a violent felony, where: (1) photographs of the location of the handgun immediately adjacent to where defendant was sitting, (2) defendant's movement away from the cocaine and handgun when he saw the officer approach, and (3) the fact that there were three individuals sitting on the porch did not negate defendant's possession as possession could be shared. Peek v. Commonwealth, No. 0340-03-1, 2004 Va. App. LEXIS 193 (Ct. of Appeals Apr. 27, 2004).

Although defendant denied knowing that there was a handgun in a bag which contained items belonging to him and the driver of the truck stopped by police testified that he put the gun in the bag and did not tell defendant he had done so, the trial court did not err when it refused to believe defendant's claim of innocence and the driver's testimony and convicted defendant of possession of a firearm after having been convicted of a felony. Bailey v. Commonwealth, No. 0617-03-4, 2004 Va. App. LEXIS 369 (Ct. of Appeals Aug. 3, 2004).

Evidence that defendant bought the gun with another, handled the gun on occasion, and was within reach of the gun was sufficient to support his conviction for possession of a firearm. Maye v. Commonwealth, 44 Va. App. 463, 605 S.E.2d 353, 2004 Va. App. LEXIS 590 (2004).

Where a firearm was found beneath a mattress in the single bedroom of a home of which defendant was the sole occupant, the evidence showed that defendant constructively possessed the gun and was sufficient to support his conviction for possession of a firearm by a convicted felon. Ricks v. Commonwealth, No. 2534-

03-1, 2005 Va. App. LEXIS 19 (Ct. of Appeals Jan. 11, 2005).

Because the police found a concealed weapon in defendant's possession that, as a convicted felon, defendant could not lawfully carry in a concealed manner, and because defendant failed to prove that a miscarriage of justice had occurred after failing to preserve a claim, Va. Sup. Ct. R. 5A:18 barred review of the issue. Davis v. Commonwealth, 2006 Va. App. LEXIS 444 (Oct. 10, 2006).

Evidence was sufficient to prove that defendant constructively possessed a handgun found in a van he owned and was driving. An officer found an empty holster within reach of the driver's seat, and a gun beneath the van's second row of seating; defendant's delay in pulling over after the officer activated his overhead lights permitted the inference that defendant, a convicted felon, removed the gun from the holster and slipped it under the second seat before pulling over. Wilson v. Commonwealth, — Va. App. —, — S.E.2d —, 2006 Va. App. LEXIS 437 (Oct. 3, 2006).

Fact that defendant's grandmother did not tell the officers that defendant lived elsewhere and the presence of defendant's official identifications and clothing in the same room as the closet containing the subject firearms provided sufficient evidence to support defendant's conviction for possession of a firearm after having been previously convicted of a felony under § 18.2-308.2. Blake v. Commonwealth, — Va. App. —, — S.E.2d —, 2007 Va. App. LEXIS 311 (Aug. 21, 2007).

Conviction for possession of a firearm by a convicted felon was supported by evidence showing that defendant was aware of the presence and character of the firearm and it was within defendant's dominion and control. Among other things, defendant exited vehicle along with the only other passenger and attempted to contact the officer before the officer could get to the vehicle, and the gun was in proximity to where defendant had been sitting. Bolden v. Commonwealth, 275 Va. 144, 654 S.E.2d 584, 2008 Va. LEXIS 6 (2008), cert. denied, 129 S. Ct. 284, 2008 U.S. LEXIS 6378, 172 L. Ed. 2d 208 (U.S. 2008).

Defendant possessed a handgun found by an officer in a pillowcase located at defendant's feet in a car in which defendant was a passenger for purposes of subsection A of § 18.2-308.2 as: (1) defendant admitted that defendant owned jewelry in the same pillowcase as the loaded handgun; and (2) defendant possessed five rocks of crack cocaine in one sock, $1,380 in the other sock, and almost one-half kilo of cocaine in another bag adjacent to the pillowcase. Lee v. Commonwealth, 2008 Va. App. LEXIS 324 (July 15, 2008).

Evidence was sufficient to support defendant's conviction for possession of a firearm, after having been previously convicted of a felony, under § 18.2-308.2, where the trial court could have found beyond a reasonable doubt that, while in possession of another person's vehicle, defendant was aware of the presence and character of the rifle in the vehicle and exercised dominion and control over the weapon, using the weapon to teach defendant's seven-year-old son to shoot. Falls v. Commonwealth, — Va. App. —, — S.E.2d —, 2008 Va. App. LEXIS 491 (Nov. 4, 2008).

Rational factfinder could conclude beyond a reasonable doubt that defendant possessed a firearm in violation of subsection A of § 18.2-308.2 even though no gun was found at the time of his arrest because the arresting officer discovered primer residue on defendant's right hand shortly after his apprehension, which suggested that defendant had recently fired a firearm; the trial court had ample grounds to reject defendant's hypothesis that the primer residue on his hand came from a police officer because the arresting officer testified that he had not recently fired a firearm, and he made it clear that police officers in his department were specifically trained to sanitize their hands after firing a firearm because of the risk of lead poisoning. Peterson v. Commonwealth, — Va. App. —, — S.E.2d —, 2009 Va. App. LEXIS 142 (Mar. 24, 2009).

Because the circumstantial evidence was sufficient to conclude that a gun found in defendant's vehicle was real, defendant was properly convicted of possessing a firearm by a convicted felon, a violation of § 18.2-308.2. Jones v. Commonwealth, 2007 Va. App. LEXIS 499 (Oct. 30, 2007), aff'd, 277 Va. 171, 670 S.E.2d 727 (2009).

Evidence was sufficient to convict defendant of possessing a firearm after a felony conviction because one victim testified that defendant brandished an automatic firearm, rather than a revolver, and the other victim testified that defendant threatened to shoot him if he did not comply with defendant's demands. Eley v.

Commonwealth, 2009 Va. App. LEXIS 480 (Oct. 27, 2009).

In a case in which defendant appealed his conviction for possessing firearms, in violation of § 18.2-308.2, he argued unsuccessfully that the evidence was insufficient to support that conviction. Since there had been sufficient evidence to convict defendant of discharging a firearm within an occupied building, in violation of § 18.2-279, there was sufficient evidence that he also violated § 18.2-308.2. Berger v. Commonwealth, 2006 Va. App. LEXIS 609 (Nov. 17, 2006).

In a case in which defendant appealed his conviction for possessing firearms, in violation of § 18.2-308.2, he argued unsuccessfully that the evidence was insufficient to support that conviction. A witness testified that she took at least four guns from her property and put them in a shed located behind defendant's house, and defendant was home at the time, and the witness told him that she did not want the guns on her property so she was placing them in his shed; that testimony was sufficient to prove that defendant was aware of the presence and character of the guns in his outbuilding and that they were subject to his dominion and control. Berger v. Commonwealth, 2006 Va. App. LEXIS 609 (Nov. 17, 2006).

Appellant's conviction for possession of a firearm by a convicted felon was affirmed; in light of appellant's admission that the bag and the mail inside were his, there was ample support for the reasonable inference that he was aware of the other contents of the backpack, including the firearm, and that it was subject to his dominion and control. Morris v. Commonwealth, 2009 Va. App. LEXIS 432 (Sept. 29, 2009).

Evidence was sufficient for a rational factfinder to convict defendant of being a convicted felon in possession of a firearm in violation of § 18.2-308.2 because there was credible testimony that defendant possessed what certainly appeared to be a firearm and that shots were fired, and that testimony was corroborated by physical evidence that shots indeed were fired, such as bullet holes found in the house and empty shell casings found around the home after the home invasion was over; a rational factfinder was permitted to infer from the evidence that defendant carried an actual firearm, rather than a toy gun or water pistol, as defendant claimed on appeal. Streater v. Commonwealth, 2009 Va. App. LEXIS 504 (Nov. 10, 2009).

Evidence was sufficient to find appellant knowingly and intentionally possessed the shotgun as a convicted felon, in violation of § 18.2-308.2, where: (1) the shotgun was found resting against appellant's leg; (2) the evidence showed that police were called to appellant's house earlier in the day, based on reports of shots fired outside the residence; (3) spent shell casings, which appeared new, were found in appellant's backyard; and (4) appellant admitted to owning the jacket found in the vehicle that contained 12-gauge shotgun ammunition. Reynolds v. Commonwealth, 2009 Va. App. LEXIS 587 (Dec. 29, 2009).

Evidence was sufficient to prove that defendant, a convicted violent felon found in possession of cocaine, possessed a firearm within the meaning of §§ 18.2-308.2 and 18.2-308.4 when he was driving a car that contained the frame, cylinder pin, and cylinder with ammunition for a revolver, which was successfully test-fired. Seward v. Commonwealth, 2009 Va. App. LEXIS 579 (Dec. 22, 2009).

Appellant's conviction for of being a felon in possession of a firearm was affirmed because items related to the firearm were mixed in with items belonging to appellant, his girlfriend, and their child, allowing the trial court to infer that appellant had dominion and control over the firearm. Davis v. Commonwealth, 2010 Va. App. LEXIS 273 (July 13, 2010).

Conviction for possession of a firearm by a convicted felon, in violation of § 18.2-308.2, was supported by the fact that the evidence in the record did not indicate that anyone else had access to the gun to exclusion of defendant and that defendant's contention that he got the car from his cousin was not supported by the evidence. Lamb v. Commonwealth, 2011 Va. App. LEXIS 46 (Feb. 8, 2011).

Sufficient evidence supported defendant's conviction for possession of a firearm after having been convicted of a violent felony, in violation of § 18.2-308.2, because it was fired from the passenger side of a vehicle before being tossed from the side where defendant was seated. Because the weapon was fired in close proximity to defendant, the evidence was sufficient to prove beyond a reasonable doubt his constructive possession of the firearm. Benguche v.

Commonwealth, 2012 Va. App. LEXIS 313 (Oct. 9, 2012).

Evidence was sufficient to find defendant guilty of at least constructive possession of a firearm in violation of § 18.2-308.2, because after police stopped the car in which he was riding, a officer saw him standing next to the area where a handgun was found on the ground. Berry v. Commonwealth, 2012 Va. App. LEXIS 385 (Nov. 27, 2012).

Insufficient evidence of possession. — Where a handgun had been hidden in a blanket on the front floorboard of a truck in which defendant was a passenger, defendant made no furtive gestures toward the firearm nor were there any acts, statements, or conduct indicating he exercised dominion and control over it, that had been in close proximity to the firearm was legally insufficient to prove possession. Myers v. Commonwealth, 43 Va. App. 113, 596 S.E.2d 536, 2004 Va. App. LEXIS 238 (2004).

Evidence was sufficient to show constructive possession of a handgun where defendant was driving a car when it was pulled over; the car was registered to his wife, only they possessed keys to it, and only he and his wife ever drove the car; the handgun was found in the glove compartment; defendant reached into the glove compartment to retrieve the registration while the gun was in that glove compartment; and defendant admitted he saw the gun and yet said nothing to the police officer about it. Gore v. Commonwealth, No. 1776-97-1 (Ct. of Appeals June 23, 1998).

There was insufficient evidence that defendant constructively possessed ammunition. There was no evidence that defendant was aware of the ammunition in the car in which she was riding or had any interest in the car; mere proximity to the ammunition was insufficient without more to show constructive possession. Swann v. Commonwealth, 2012 Va. App. LEXIS 380 (Nov. 27, 2012).

Sufficient evidence of constructive possession. — Evidence was sufficient to show constructive possession of a gun found behind the brake pedal of a vehicle where the defendant had six rounds of ammunition for the gun in his actual possession, notwithstanding his innocent explanations for his possession of ammunition. Loney v. Commonwealth, No. 1147-98-2 (Ct. of Appeals Mar. 2, 1999).

Evidence was sufficient to show constructive possession of a gun where the defendant conceded knowledge of the weapon by revealing to the arresting officer its presence and location; the defendant also conceded exercise of dominion and control when he admitted at trial that he had "probably" retrieved the gun from its hidden location and looked at it. Baker v. Commonwealth, No. 1142-00-3, 2001 Va. App. LEXIS 343 (Ct. of Appeals June 19, 2001).

The evidence clearly supported a finding that the defendant, a convicted felon, exercised dominion and control over a bag of capsules containing heroin and a firearm found on the floor on the passenger side of a vehicle, where the operator of the vehicle and the defendant, the sole passenger, were observed by police exchanging capsules and unidentified small items from the window of the car for cash and where, as police stopped the vehicle within minutes of such a transaction, the defendant furtively leaned forward and back very fast. Grier v. Commonwealth, 35 Va. App. 560, 546 S.E.2d 743, 2001 Va. App. LEXIS 297 (2001).

Where a detective saw defendant appear to drop something, heard something hit the floor, and saw a firearm on the floor near defendant, the evidence was sufficient to show that defendant possessed the firearm. Ellis v. Commonwealth, No. 2977-01-1, 2002 Va. App. LEXIS 427 (Ct. of Appeals July 30, 2002).

Even though defendant was not immediately in possession of a firearm, the evidence was sufficient to show he constructively possessed one in the home he ran into when he saw the police, as the homeowner testified that the gun found in the bucket at the time of defendant's arrest was not there when the homeowner left moments before defendant was arrested by police in the house. Payne v. Commonwealth, No. 3339-02-3, 2003 Va. App. LEXIS 616 (Ct. of Appeals Dec. 2, 2003).

Defendant's temporal and physical proximity to the firearm, the fact that a female was the only other adult living at the residence, and defendant's statement that the firearm was not hers, provided sufficient circumstantial evidence to permit a finding that the defendant possessed the firearm. McCray v. Commonwealth, — Va. App. —, — S.E.2d —, 2008 Va. App. LEXIS 220 (May 6, 2008).

Evidence was sufficient to convict defendant of possession of a firearm by a non-violent felon where a gun was found on a car seat next to him; his behavior appeared suspicious to a trained officer;

he gave a false name; and DNA evidence indicated it was highly likely that he had handled the gun. Glasgow v. Commonwealth, — Va. App. —, — S.E.2d —, 2008 Va. App. LEXIS 529 (Dec. 9, 2008).

Sufficient evidence of dominion and control. — Though not in defendant's residence, the gun was in an apartment that defendant frequented on a regular basis and often stayed overnight. He admitted placing the firearm there without asking the consent of the apartment's owner, and when asked by the apartment's owner what he planned to do with it, he stated that he was going to hold it until he decided to return it to the gun's owner. He thereafter had unrestricted access to the firearm. Therefore, the evidence presented at trial sufficiently proved his dominion and control over the firearm. Bond v. Commonwealth, No. 2476-95-1 (Ct. of Appeals Dec. 31, 1996).

Where, when questioned by police regarding whether there were any weapons in the room, defendant said there might possibly be a gun or knife under one of the beds, where the police immediately found the gun under one of the mattresses, lying directly beside a knife that appellant admitted was his, and where although appellant denied ownership of the gun, its presence with his knife and his earlier statement indicating his awareness of its presence permitted the inference "that appellant exercised the dominion and control necessary to show constructive possession," the evidence of his constructive possession of a firearm was sufficient to support his conviction for grand larceny of the firearm and possession of a firearm by a convicted felon. Archer v. Commonwealth, 26 Va. App. 1, 492 S.E.2d 826 (1997).

Evidence was sufficient to support finding that defendant exercised dominion and control over drugs and firearm found hidden together near his feet, under box spring of bed. Mosley v. Commonwealth, No. 2477-98-3 (Ct. of Appeals Dec. 7, 1999).

Where defendant was traveling alone, it was reasonable to concluded that he was aware of the firearm protruding from under the front seat of the vehicle that he was driving and that it was subject to his dominion and control. Shelton v. Commonwealth, No. 3012-03-2, 2005 Va. App. LEXIS 87 (Ct. of Appeals Mar. 1, 2005).

Because defendant occupied a dwelling in which a firearm was found, admitted knowledge of the presence of the gun in the house, and possessed the trigger lock keys, which rendered the firearm subject to defendant's dominion and control, the evidence was sufficient to find that defendant constructively possessed the firearm; accordingly, the evidence was also sufficient to convict defendant of possession of a firearm after having been convicted of a felony and possession of a firearm while in possession of drugs. Herndon v. Commonwealth, — Va. App. —, — S.E.2d —, 2009 Va. App. LEXIS 129 (Mar. 24, 2009).

Defendant was properly convicted of possession of a firearm by a felon in violation of § 18.2-308.2, because the weapon lay on a console between the driver's seat where defendant sat and his passenger. Although the passenger owned both the vehicle and the weapon, defendant knew it was there and his access to it was unrestricted. Smallwood v. Commonwealth, 278 Va. 625, 688 S.E.2d 154, 2009 Va. LEXIS 105 (2009).

Evidence was sufficient to support defendant's conviction for possession of a firearm by a convicted felon, although defendant raised the affirmative defense of good faith reliance on a probation officer's assurance that defendant could keep firearms in a gun cabinet at home if the cabinet was locked, because defendant, a convicted felon, possessed the key to a locked gun cabinet containing firearms and the trial court clearly did not believe defendant's testimony concerning the content of the conversation with the probation officer where another probation officer testified that convicted felons were advised under the office's former policy that they could keep firearms in their homes only if they did not have access to the key used to lock the firearms. Torian v. Commonwealth, 2010 Va. App. LEXIS 193 (May 11, 2010).

In a prosecution on a charge of possessing a firearm after having been convicted of a felony, in violation of § 18.2-308.2, the evidence was sufficient to prove that defendant owned the property where the guns were found jointly with his girlfriend on the date of the search as his name was provided when the property was listed for sale, the girlfriend made attempts to contact defendant when the police arrived to execute the search warrant, and defendant exercised dominion and control over the premises where the guns were found. Redmond v. Commonwealth, 57 Va. App. 254, 701 S.E.2d 81, 2010 Va. App. LEXIS 446 (2010).

Insufficient evidence of dominion and control. — Evidence failed to prove beyond a reasonable doubt that appellant knowingly and intentionally exercised dominion and control over weapon at the time charged in the indictment. The evidence disclosed that appellant worked in a small office where a gun had been kept at an undetermined time. The gun belonged to one of the owners of the grill and was kept for the benefit of the night mangers. No evidence proved that appellant was a night manager. The evidence revealed that the office in which appellant worked when he was on the premises was one of three places the gun may have been kept, but it was not shown to have been in the office on or about the date of appellant's arrest. Flowers v. Commonwealth, No. 0128-97-1 (Ct. of Appeals Jan. 27, 1998).

Because the circumstances did not exclude a reasonable hypothesis that someone else placed gun in car, unbeknownst to defendant, the trial court was plainly wrong in finding the evidence sufficient as matter of law to support the conviction. Branch v. Commonwealth, No. 1077-01-2, 2002 Va. App. LEXIS 273 (Ct. of Appeals May 7, 2002).

Where defendant was convicted of possession of a firearm by a convicted felon, there was insufficient evidence that defendant constructively possessed the weapon that was hidden under the floor mat of the car beneath where defendant was seated; there was no evidence that defendant owned or had ever used the gun, the bulge from the gun was difficult to see at night, there was no evidence as to whether defendant would have been able to feel the gun under the mat, and defendant made no furtive movements toward the gun. Gadsden v. Commonwealth, — Va. App. —, — S.E.2d —, 2005 Va. App. LEXIS 459 (Nov. 15, 2005).

Search and seizure based on anonymous tip held lawful. — Trial court properly denied defendant's motion to suppress firearm seized from him through a warrantless pat down, despite the fact that the involved officers' suspicion that defendant was shooting at a vehicle was provided by an anonymous tip, as: (1) the police dispatcher and the investigating officers had objective reasons to believe the caller was reliable; (2) the caller's continued presence on the telephone as the encounter unfolded established this reliability; and (3) the caller provided updated information at the time the officers actually approached defendant, and the officers corroborated this information. Williams v. Commonwealth, No. 0783-04-1, 2005 Va. App. LEXIS 129 (Ct. of Appeals Mar. 29, 2005).

Probable cause to arrest. — Granting of defendant's motion to suppress was improper because a reasonable officer had probable cause to arrest defendant for the possession of a firearm after having been convicted of a felony. The officer had knowledge that defendant was a felon convicted of a drug offense; that defendant was a passenger in the vehicle driven by a female; that during the search of that vehicle based on an alert by a drug dog, a gun was discovered in a bag containing men's clothing that appeared to fit defendant; and that the female acknowledged that she knew that defendant owned a gun, but that she did not know it was in the vehicle in which she was transporting defendant's belongings. Commonwealth v. Sanford, 2011 Va. App. LEXIS 206 (June 21, 2011).

Sufficient evidence to prove attempt to purchase. — Defendant attempted to purchase a firearm in contravention of subdivision A ii where defendant visited a gun shop, selected a gun he wanted to buy, and submitted the required Virginia Criminal History Check Form; submission of the form was a direct act done toward the completion of a felony, which was not materially different from the payment of the sale price of the gun. Both acts moved beyond arranging the means to purchase the gun and effectively invoked action on the part of the vendor, thereby commencing the consummation of the intended unlawful act. Parsons v. Commonwealth, 32 Va. App. 576, 529 S.E.2d 810, 2000 Va. App. LEXIS 426 (2000).

Sufficient evidence of concealment. — Gun located under front passenger seat of vehicle was properly determined to be "hidden from common observation." Williams v. Commonwealth, No. 1156-98-1 (Ct. of Appeals Sept. 21, 1999).

CIRCUIT COURT OPINIONS

Constitutionality. — This section, prohibiting persons convicted of a felony as a juvenile from possessing firearms until age 29, did not violate the equal protection and due process clauses of the United States Constitution, nor was its mandatory sentence scheme illegal. The age classification was rationally related to the legitimate governmental purpose of keeping firearms out of the hands of felons and extending the prohibition to those who committed a felony as a juvenile. The mandatory sentencing provision was not inconsistent with its classification as a Class 6 felony. Commonwealth v. Pulley, 54 Va. Cir. 461, 2001 Va. Cir. LEXIS 203 (Norfolk 2001).

Simultaneous prosecutions not barred. — Requirements for proving a concealed weapons misdemeanor under § 18.2-308 were distinct from the requirements of § 18.2-308.2, although the two charges were commenced at the same or concurrent time, and the prosecutions were not sequential in nature simply because the misdemeanor was more amenable to an expeditious resolution than the felony; thus, no violation of § 19.2-294 resulted. Commonwealth v. Turner, 62 Va. Cir. 209, 2003 Va. Cir. LEXIS 312 (Charlottesville 2003).

Collateral estoppel. — Defendant's trial for possession of a firearm after having been convicted of a felony was barred by collateral estoppel after his acquittal of murder, use of a firearm in the commission of a felony, and the willful discharge of a firearm within 1,000 feet of an elementary school; in light of the standard malice instruction that was given, the only way a rational juror could have acquitted defendant was to have found a failure by the Commonwealth to prove that defendant was the gunman. Commonwealth v. Cappell, 58 Va. Cir. 324, 2002 Va. Cir. LEXIS 149 (Rockingham County 2002).

"Convicted felon" status. — Defendant's motion to strike the State's evidence as to count 2 of the indictment charging possession of a firearm by a convicted felon, in violation of § 18.2-308.2, was granted, as he was not a convicted felon, pursuant to § 18.2-251 on the date said charge was alleged in the information; moreover, the fact that he might have later been found to have violated his probation had no retroactive effect since a conviction occurred only after the court conducted a hearing, received evidence of a violation, and then entered a final appealable judgment of conviction. Commonwealth v. Cross, 71 Va. Cir. 272, 2006 Va. Cir. LEXIS 120 (Portsmouth 2006).

Restoration of civil rights did not include right to possess and transport firearms. — In a case in which a convicted felon petitioned for a permit to possess and carry firearms, while the Governor of Virginia had restored the convicted felon's rights to vote, hold public office, serve on a jury and to be a notary public, the order expressly declined to restore the convicted felon's right to possess firearms. Contrary to the convicted felon's argument, the term civil rights, as used in subsection C of § 18.2-308.2, did not encompass all civil rights, notwithstanding the fact that in his case, the Governor excluded the restoration of his civil right to possess and transport firearms. Chisholm v. Commonwealth, 2009 Va. Cir. LEXIS 116 (Fairfax County Oct. 20, 2009).

§ 18.2-308.2:01. Possession or transportation of certain firearms by certain persons.

A. It shall be unlawful for any person who is not a citizen of the United States or who is not a person lawfully admitted for permanent residence to knowingly and intentionally possess or transport any assault firearm or to knowingly and intentionally carry about his person, hidden from common observation, an assault firearm.

B. It shall be unlawful for any person who is not a citizen of the United States and who is not lawfully present in the United States to knowingly and intentionally possess or transport any firearm or to knowingly and intentionally carry about his person, hidden from common observation, any firearm. A violation of this section shall be punishable as a Class 6 felony.

C. For purposes of this section, *"assault firearm"* means any semi-automatic center-fire rifle or pistol that expels single or multiple projectiles by action of an explosion of a combustible material and is equipped at the time of the offense with a magazine which will hold more than 20 rounds of ammunition or designed by the manufacturer to accommodate a silencer or equipped with a folding stock.

History.
1993, c. 674; 2003, c. 976; 2004, cc. 347, 995; 2008, c. 408.

Editor's note.
Acts 2008, c. 408, cl. 2, provides: "That the provisions of this act may result in a net increase in periods of imprisonment or commitment. Pursuant to § 30-19.1:4, the estimated amount of the necessary appropriation cannot be determined for periods of imprisonment in state adult correctional facilities and cannot be determined for periods of commitment to the custody of the Department of Juvenile Justice."

The 2008 amendments.
The 2008 amendment by c. 408 designated the existing paragraphs as subsections A through C.

§ 18.2-308.2:1. Prohibiting the selling, etc., of firearms to certain persons.

Any person who sells, barters, gives or furnishes, or has in his possession or under his control with the intent of selling, bartering, giving or furnishing, any firearm to any person he knows is prohibited from possessing or transporting a firearm pursuant to § 18.2-308.1:1, 18.2-308.1:2, 18.2-308.1:3, 18.2-308.2, subsection B of § 18.2-308.2:01, or § 18.2-308.7 shall be guilty of a Class 4 felony. However, this prohibition shall not be applicable when the person convicted of the felony, adjudicated delinquent or acquitted by reason of insanity has (i) been issued a permit pursuant to subsection C of § 18.2-308.2 or been granted relief pursuant to subsection B of § 18.2-308.1:1, or § 18.2-308.1:2 or 18.2-308.1:3 (ii) been pardoned or had his political disabilities removed in accordance with subsection B of § 18.2-308.2 or (iii) obtained a permit to ship, transport, possess or receive firearms pursuant to the laws of the United States.

History.
1988, c. 327; 1990, c. 692; 1993, cc. 467, 494, 882, 926; 2004, c. 995; 2008, c. 408; 2011, c. 775; 2013, c. 797.

Editor's note.
Acts 2008, c. 408, cl. 2, provides: "That the provisions of this act may result in a net increase in periods of imprisonment or commitment. Pursuant to § 30-19.1:4, the estimated amount of the necessary appropriation cannot be determined for periods of imprisonment in state adult correctional facilities and cannot be determined for periods of commitment to the custody of the Department of Juvenile Justice."
Acts 2013, c. 797, cl. 2 provides: "That the provisions of this act may result in a net increase in periods of imprisonment or commitment. Pursuant to § 30-19.1:4, the estimated amount of the necessary appropriation is $46,773 for periods of imprisonment in state adult correctional facilities and cannot be determined for periods of commitment to the custody of the Department of Juvenile Justice."

The 2008 amendments.
The 2008 amendment by c. 408 inserted "subsection B of § 18.2-308.2:01" and made a minor stylistic change.

The 2011 amendments.
The 2011 amendment by c. 775 inserted "been granted relief pursuant to" in clause (i) of the second sentence.

The 2013 amendments.
The 2013 amendment by c. 797 inserted "18.2-308.1:2, 18.2-308.1:3," and substituted "Class 4 felony" for "Class 6 felony" in the first sentence; and inserted "or § 18.2-308.1:2 or 18.2-308.1:3" at the end of clause (i) of the second sentence.

Michie's Jurisprudence.
For related discussion, see 20 M.J. Weapons, § 4.

CASE NOTES

Convicted felon must take affirmative action to restore rights. — A convicted felon in Virginia retains the civil disabilities resulting from his conviction until he himself takes affirmative action to have his civil rights restored. Almond v. United States, 854 F. Supp. 439 (W.D. Va. 1994).

§ 18.2-308.2:2. Criminal history record information check required for the transfer of certain firearms.

A. Any person purchasing from a dealer a firearm as herein defined shall consent in writing, on a form to be provided by the Department of State Police, to have the dealer obtain criminal history record information. Such form shall include only the written consent; the name, birth date, gender, race, citizenship, and social security number and/or any other identification number; the number of firearms by category intended to be sold, rented, traded, or transferred; and answers by the applicant to the following questions: (i) has the applicant been convicted of a felony offense or found guilty or adjudicated delinquent as a juvenile 14 years of age or older at the time of the offense of a delinquent act that would be a felony if committed by an adult; (ii) is the applicant subject to a court order restraining the applicant from harassing, stalking, or threatening the applicant's child or intimate partner, or a child of such partner, or is the applicant subject to a protective order; and (iii) has the applicant ever been acquitted by reason of insanity and prohibited from purchasing, possessing or transporting a firearm pursuant to § 18.2-308.1:1 or any substantially similar law of any other jurisdiction, been adjudicated legally incompetent, mentally incapacitated or adjudicated an incapacitated person and prohibited from purchasing a firearm pursuant to § 18.2-308.1:2 or any substantially similar law of any other jurisdiction, or been involuntarily admitted to an inpatient facility or involuntarily ordered to outpatient mental health treatment and prohibited from purchasing a firearm pursuant to § 18.2-308.1:3 or any substantially similar law of any other jurisdiction.

B. 1. No dealer shall sell, rent, trade or transfer from his inventory any such firearm to any other person who is a resident of Virginia until he has (i) obtained written consent and the other information on the consent form specified in subsection A, and provided the Department of State Police with the name, birth date, gender, race, citizenship, and social security and/or any other identification number and the number of firearms by category intended to be sold, rented, traded or transferred and (ii) requested criminal history record information by a telephone call to or other communication authorized by the State Police and is authorized by subdivision 2 to complete the sale or other such transfer. To establish personal identification and residence in Virginia for purposes of this section, a dealer must require any prospective purchaser to present one photo-identification form issued by a governmental agency of the Commonwealth or by the United States Department of Defense, and other documentation of residence. Except where the photo-identification was issued by the United States Department of Defense, the other documentation of residence shall show an address identical to that shown on the photo-identification form, such as evidence of currently paid personal property tax or real estate tax, or a current (a) lease, (b) utility or telephone bill, (c) voter registration card, (d) bank check, (e) passport, (f) automobile registration, or (g) hunting or fishing license; other current identification allowed as evidence of residency by Part 178.124 of Title 27 of the Code of Federal Regulations and ATF Ruling 2001-5; or other documentation of residence determined to be acceptable by the Department of Criminal Justice Services, that corroborates that the prospective purchaser currently resides in Virginia. Where the photo-identification was issued by the Department of Defense, permanent orders assigning the purchaser to a duty post in Virginia, including the Pentagon, shall be the only other required documentation of residence. For the purposes of this section and establishment of residency for firearm purchase, residency of a member of the armed forces shall include both the state in which the member's permanent duty post is located and any nearby state in which the member resides and from which he commutes to the permanent duty post. When the photo-identification presented to a dealer by the prospective purchaser is a driver's license or other photo-identification issued by the Department of Motor Vehicles, and such identification form contains a date of issue, the dealer shall not, except for a renewed driver's license or other photo-identification issued by the Department of Motor Vehicles, sell or otherwise transfer a firearm to the prospective purchaser until 30 days after the date of issue of an original or duplicate driver's license unless the prospective purchaser also presents a copy of his Virginia Department of Motor Vehicles driver's record showing that the original date of issue of the driver's license was more than 30 days prior to the attempted purchase.

In addition, no dealer shall sell, rent, trade or transfer from his inventory any assault firearm to any person who is not a citizen of the United States or who is not a person lawfully admitted for permanent residence. To establish citizenship or lawful admission for a permanent residence for purposes of purchasing an assault firearm, a dealer shall require a prospective purchaser to present a certified birth certificate or a certificate of birth abroad issued by the United States State Department, a certificate of citizenship or a certificate of naturalization issued by the United States Citizenship and Immigration Services, an unexpired U.S. passport, a United States citizen identification card, a current voter registration card, a current selective service registration card, or an immigrant visa or other documentation of status as a person lawfully admitted for permanent residence issued by the United States Citizenship and Immigration Services.

Upon receipt of the request for a criminal history record information check, the State Police shall (1) review its criminal history record information to determine if the buyer or transferee is prohibited from possessing or transporting a firearm by state or federal law, (2) inform the dealer if its record indicates that the buyer or transferee is so prohibited, and (3) provide the dealer with a unique reference number for that inquiry.

2. The State Police shall provide its response to the requesting dealer during the dealer's request, or by return call without delay. If the criminal history record information check indicates the prospective purchaser or transferee has a disqualifying criminal record or has been acquitted by reason of insanity and committed to the custody of the Commissioner of Behavioral Health and Developmental Services, the State Police shall have until the end of the dealer's next business day to advise the dealer if its records indicate the buyer or transferee is prohibited from possessing or transporting a firearm by state or federal law. If not so advised by the end of the dealer's next business day, a dealer who has fulfilled the requirements of subdivision 1 may immediately complete the sale or transfer and shall not be deemed in violation of this section with respect to such sale or transfer. In case of electronic failure or other circumstances beyond the control of the State Police, the dealer shall be advised immediately of the reason for such delay and be given an estimate of the length of such delay. After such notification, the State Police shall, as soon as possible but in no event later than the end of the dealer's next business day, inform the requesting dealer if its records indicate the buyer or transferee is prohibited from possessing or transporting a firearm by state or federal law. A dealer who fulfills the requirements of subdivision 1 and is told by the State Police that a response will not be available by the end of the dealer's next business day may immediately complete the sale or transfer and shall not be deemed in violation of this section with respect to such sale or transfer.

3. Except as required by subsection D of § 9.1-132, the State Police shall not maintain records longer than 30 days, except for multiple handgun transactions for which records shall be maintained for 12 months, from any dealer's request for a

criminal history record information check pertaining to a buyer or transferee who is not found to be prohibited from possessing and transporting a firearm under state or federal law. However, the log on requests made may be maintained for a period of 12 months, and such log shall consist of the name of the purchaser, the dealer identification number, the unique approval number and the transaction date.

4. On the last day of the week following the sale or transfer of any firearm, the dealer shall mail or deliver the written consent form required by subsection A to the Department of State Police. The State Police shall immediately initiate a search of all available criminal history record information to determine if the purchaser is prohibited from possessing or transporting a firearm under state or federal law. If the search discloses information indicating that the buyer or transferee is so prohibited from possessing or transporting a firearm, the State Police shall inform the chief law-enforcement officer in the jurisdiction where the sale or transfer occurred and the dealer without delay.

5. Notwithstanding any other provisions of this section, rifles and shotguns may be purchased by persons who are citizens of the United States or persons lawfully admitted for permanent residence but residents of other states under the terms of subsections A and B upon furnishing the dealer with proof of citizenship or status as a person lawfully admitted for permanent residence and one photo-identification form issued by a governmental agency of the person's state of residence and one other form of identification determined to be acceptable by the Department of Criminal Justice Services.

6. For the purposes of this subsection, the phrase "dealer's next business day" shall not include December 25.

C. No dealer shall sell, rent, trade or transfer from his inventory any firearm, except when the transaction involves a rifle or a shotgun and can be accomplished pursuant to the provisions of subdivision B 5 to any person who is not a resident of Virginia unless he has first obtained from the Department of State Police a report indicating that a search of all available criminal history record information has not disclosed that the person is prohibited from possessing or transporting a firearm under state or federal law. The dealer shall obtain the required report by mailing or delivering the written consent form required under subsection A to the State Police within 24 hours of its execution. If the dealer has complied with the provisions of this subsection and has not received the required report from the State Police within 10 days from the date the written consent form was mailed to the Department of State Police, he shall not be deemed in violation of this section for thereafter completing the sale or transfer.

D. Nothing herein shall prevent a resident of the Commonwealth, at his option, from buying, renting or receiving a firearm from a dealer in Virginia by obtaining a criminal history record information check through the dealer as provided in subsection C.

E. If any buyer or transferee is denied the right to purchase a firearm under this section, he may exercise his right of access to and review and correction of criminal history record information under § 9.1-132 or institute a civil action as provided in § 9.1-135, provided any such action is initiated within 30 days of such denial.

F. Any dealer who willfully and intentionally requests, obtains, or seeks to obtain criminal history record information under false pretenses, or who willfully and intentionally disseminates or seeks to disseminate criminal history record information except as authorized in this section shall be guilty of a Class 2 misdemeanor.

G. For purposes of this section:

"Actual buyer" means a person who executes the consent form required in subsection B or C, or other such firearm transaction records as may be required by federal law.

"Antique firearm" means:

1. Any firearm (including any firearm with a matchlock, flintlock, percussion cap, or similar type of ignition system) manufactured in or before 1898;

2. Any replica of any firearm described in subdivision 1 of this definition if such replica (i) is not designed or redesigned for using rimfire or conventional centerfire fixed ammunition or (ii) uses rimfire or conventional centerfire fixed ammunition that is no longer manufactured in the United States and that is not readily available in the ordinary channels of commercial trade;

3. Any muzzle-loading rifle, muzzle-loading shotgun, or muzzle-loading pistol that is designed to use black powder, or a black powder substitute, and that cannot use fixed ammunition. For purposes of this subdivision, the term "antique firearm" shall not include any weapon that incorporates a firearm frame or receiver, any firearm that is converted into a muzzle-loading weapon, or any muzzle-loading weapon that can be readily converted to fire fixed ammunition by replacing the barrel, bolt, breech-block, or any combination thereof; or

4. Any curio or relic as defined in this subsection.

"Assault firearm" means any semi-automatic center-fire rifle or pistol which expels single or multiple projectiles by action of an explosion of a combustible material and is equipped at the time of the offense with a magazine which will hold more than 20 rounds of ammunition or designed by the manufacturer to accommodate a silencer or equipped with a folding stock.

"Curios or relics" means firearms that are of special interest to collectors by reason of some quality other than is associated with firearms intended for sporting use or as offensive or defensive weapons. To be recognized as curios or relics, firearms must fall within one of the following categories:

1. Firearms that were manufactured at least 50 years prior to the current date, which use rimfire or

conventional centerfire fixed ammunition that is no longer manufactured in the United States and that is not readily available in the ordinary channels of commercial trade, but not including replicas thereof;

2. Firearms that are certified by the curator of a municipal, state, or federal museum that exhibits firearms to be curios or relics of museum interest; and

3. Any other firearms that derive a substantial part of their monetary value from the fact that they are novel, rare, bizarre, or because of their association with some historical figure, period, or event. Proof of qualification of a particular firearm under this category may be established by evidence of present value and evidence that like firearms are not available except as collectors' items, or that the value of like firearms available in ordinary commercial channels is substantially less.

"Dealer" means any person licensed as a dealer pursuant to 18 U.S.C. § 921 et seq.

"Firearm" means any handgun, shotgun, or rifle that will or is designed to or may readily be converted to expel single or multiple projectiles by action of an explosion of a combustible material.

"Handgun" means any pistol or revolver or other firearm originally designed, made and intended to fire single or multiple projectiles by means of an explosion of a combustible material from one or more barrels when held in one hand.

"Lawfully admitted for permanent residence" means the status of having been lawfully accorded the privilege of residing permanently in the United States as an immigrant in accordance with the immigration laws, such status not having changed.

H. The Department of Criminal Justice Services shall promulgate regulations to ensure the identity, confidentiality and security of all records and data provided by the Department of State Police pursuant to this section.

I. The provisions of this section shall not apply to (i) transactions between persons who are licensed as firearms importers or collectors, manufacturers or dealers pursuant to 18 U.S.C. § 921 et seq.; (ii) purchases by or sales to any law-enforcement officer or agent of the United States, the Commonwealth or any local government, or any campus police officer appointed under Chapter 17 (§ 23-232 et seq.) of Title 23; or (iii) antique firearms, curios or relics.

J. The provisions of this section shall not apply to restrict purchase, trade or transfer of firearms by a resident of Virginia when the resident of Virginia makes such purchase, trade or transfer in another state, in which case the laws and regulations of that state and the United States governing the purchase, trade or transfer of firearms shall apply. A National Instant Criminal Background Check System (NICS) check shall be performed prior to such purchase, trade or transfer of firearms.

J1. All licensed firearms dealers shall collect a fee of $2 for every transaction for which a criminal history record information check is required pursu-

ant to this section, except that a fee of $5 shall be collected for every transaction involving an out-of-state resident. Such fee shall be transmitted to the Department of State Police by the last day of the month following the sale for deposit in a special fund for use by the State Police to offset the cost of conducting criminal history record information checks under the provisions of this section.

K. Any person willfully and intentionally making a materially false statement on the consent form required in subsection B or C or on such firearm transaction records as may be required by federal law, shall be guilty of a Class 5 felony.

L. Except as provided in § 18.2-308.2:1, any dealer who willfully and intentionally sells, rents, trades or transfers a firearm in violation of this section shall be guilty of a Class 6 felony.

L1. Any person who attempts to solicit, persuade, encourage, or entice any dealer to transfer or otherwise convey a firearm other than to the actual buyer, as well as any other person who willfully and intentionally aids or abets such person, shall be guilty of a Class 6 felony. This subsection shall not apply to a federal law-enforcement officer or a law-enforcement officer as defined in § 9.1-101, in the performance of his official duties, or other person under his direct supervision.

M. Any person who purchases a firearm with the intent to (i) resell or otherwise provide such firearm to any person who he knows or has reason to believe is ineligible to purchase or otherwise receive from a dealer a firearm for whatever reason or (ii) transport such firearm out of the Commonwealth to be resold or otherwise provided to another person who the transferor knows is ineligible to purchase or otherwise receive a firearm, shall be guilty of a Class 4 felony and sentenced to a mandatory minimum term of imprisonment of one year. However, if the violation of this subsection involves such a transfer of more than one firearm, the person shall be sentenced to a mandatory minimum term of imprisonment of five years. The prohibitions of this subsection shall not apply to the purchase of a firearm by a person for the lawful use, possession, or transport thereof, pursuant to § 18.2-308.7, by his child, grandchild, or individual for whom he is the legal guardian if such child, grandchild, or individual is ineligible, solely because of his age, to purchase a firearm.

N. Any person who is ineligible to purchase or otherwise receive or possess a firearm in the Commonwealth who solicits, employs or assists any person in violating subsection M shall be guilty of a Class 4 felony and shall be sentenced to a mandatory minimum term of imprisonment of five years.

O. Any mandatory minimum sentence imposed under this section shall be served consecutively with any other sentence.

P. All driver's licenses issued on or after July 1, 1994, shall carry a letter designation indicating whether the driver's license is an original, duplicate or renewed driver's license.

History.

1989, c. 745; 1990, cc. 594, 692; 1991, cc. 515, 525, 716; 1992, cc. 637, 872; 1993, cc. 451, 461, 486, 493, 674; 1994, c. 624; 1997, c. 341; 1998, c. 844; 2002, c. 695; 2003, cc. 833, 976; 2004, cc. 354, 461, 837, 904, 922; 2005, cc. 578, 859; 2007, c. 509; 2008, cc. 854, 869; 2009, cc. 813, 840; 2011, c. 235; 2012, cc. 37, 257, 776; 2013, cc. 450, 662, 761, 774, 797.

Editor's note.

Acts 2008, cc. 854 and 869, cl. 2 provides: "That the provisions of this act may result in a net increase in periods of imprisonment or commitment. Pursuant to § 30-19.1:4, the estimated amount of the necessary appropriation cannot be determined for periods of imprisonment in state adult correctional facilities and is $0 for periods of commitment to the custody of the Department of Juvenile Justice."

Acts 2012, c. 776, cl. 2, provides: "That the provisions of this act may result in a net increase in periods of imprisonment or commitment. Pursuant to § 30-19.1:4, the estimated amount of the necessary appropriation is $0 for periods of imprisonment in state adult correctional facilities and is $0 for periods of commitment to the custody of the Department of Juvenile Justice."

Acts 2013, cc. 761 and 774, cl. 2 provides: "That the provisions of this act may result in a net increase in periods of imprisonment or commitment. Pursuant to § 30-19.1:4, the estimated amount of the necessary appropriation cannot be determined for periods of imprisonment in state adult correctional facilities; therefore, Chapter 3 of the Acts of Assembly of 2012, Special Session I, requires the Virginia Criminal Sentencing Commission to assign a minimum fiscal impact of $50,000. Pursuant to § 30-19.1:4, the estimated amount of the necessary appropriation cannot be determined for periods of commitment to the custody of the Department of Juvenile Justice."

Acts 2013, c. 797, cl. 2 provides: "That the provisions of this act may result in a net increase in periods of imprisonment or commitment. Pursuant to § 30-19.1:4, the estimated amount of the necessary appropriation is $46,773 for periods of imprisonment in state adult correctional facilities and cannot be determined for periods of commitment to the custody of the Department of Juvenile Justice."

The 2008 amendments.

The 2008 amendments by cc. 854 and 869 are identical, and in subsection A, added clause (iii) and made related changes.

The 2009 amendments.

The 2009 amendments by cc. 813 and 840 are identical, and substituted "Commissioner of Behavioral Health and Developmental Services" for "Commissioner of Mental Health, Mental Retardation and Substance Abuse Services" in subdivision B 2.

The 2011 amendments.

The 2011 amendment by c. 235 inserted "including the Pentagon" in the fifth sentence in the first paragraph in subdivision B 1.

The 2012 amendments.

The 2012 amendments by cc. 37 and 257 are identical, and repealed subsection P, relating to the limitation on handgun purchases to no more than one per month.

The 2012 amendment by c. 776 inserted "or any campus police officer appointed under Chapter 17 (§ 23-232 et seq.) of Title 23" in subsection I and subdivision P 2 j [now repealed], and made minor stylistic changes.

The 2013 amendments.

The 2013 amendments by cc. 450 and 662 are identical, and in subdivision B 1, deleted "shall be deemed to be the permanent duty post" preceding "of a member" and inserted "shall include both the state in which the member's permanent duty post is located and any nearby state in which the member resides and from which he commutes to the permanent duty post" in the fifth sentence of the first paragraph.

The 2013 amendments by cc. 761 and 774 are identical, and added "to be served consecutively with any other sentence" at the end of the second sentence of subsection M and at the end of subsection N. Subsections M and N have been set out in the form above at the direction of the Virginia Code Commission.

The 2013 amendment by c. 797, in subsection M, substituted "Class 4 felony and sentenced to a mandatory minimum term of imprisonment of one year" for "Class 5 felony" at the end of the first sentence, and added the second sentence; inserted subsection O and redesignated former subsection O as P; and deleted former subsection P, which was previously repealed.

Law Review.

For 2007 annual survey article, "Criminal Law and Procedure," see 42 U. Rich. L. Rev. 311 (2007).

Michie's Jurisprudence.

For related discussion, see 20 M.J. Weapons, §§ 2, 12.

CASE NOTES

Purpose. — This section is a part of a statutory scheme reflecting a legislative purpose to interdict the availability and use of firearms by persons previously convicted of felony offenses. That purpose finds its justification from the lessons of common experience that possession of firearms by felons presents a high risk of harm to others. Mayhew v. Commonwealth, 20 Va. App. 484, 458 S.E.2d 305 (1995).

The specific legislative purpose underpinning subsection L of this section, consistent with the general legislative purpose of interdicting the availability and use of firearms by convicted felons, is to prohibit licensed firearms dealers from failing to make the appropriate criminal background check required by subsections B and C of this section. Mayhew v. Commonwealth, 20 Va. App. 484, 458 S.E.2d 305 (1995).

Exemptions. — The exemptions found in subsection I of this section are not negative elements of the offense that must be proven by the Commonwealth. Rather, they are circumstances, within the knowledge of the accused, which may be raised as statutory defenses to the charge that the dealer has unlawfully failed to obtain the criminal background check required by subsections B and C of this section. In short, these exemptions are affirmative defenses for which the accused has the burden of going forward with supporting evidence. Mayhew v. Commonwealth, 20 Va. App. 484, 458 S.E.2d 305 (1995).

In construing subsections I and L of this section, there is an implicit requirement that the application of the exemption found in the former is limited to circumstances where the dealer knows the purchaser is a police officer at the time of the sale. Mayhew v. Commonwealth, 20 Va. App. 484, 458 S.E.2d 305 (1995).

In order for firearms dealer to assert that his or her failure to conduct the requisite background check was permitted pursuant to clause I (ii) of this section, he or she must demonstrate actual knowledge that the exemption applied at the time of the sale. Mayhew v. Commonwealth, 20 Va. App. 484, 458 S.E.2d 305 (1995).

Limitation on consent form inquiries. — Subsection A of this section explicitly and unambiguously limits the inquiries of the consent form "only ... to information required by subdivision B 1 [of this section]" and the federally mandated "firearms transaction record." Brooks v. Commonwealth, 19 Va. App. 563, 454 S.E.2d 3 (1995).

Information not required on consent form. — Neither subdivision B 1 of this section nor the referenced federal ATF Form 4473 and attendant regulations require information from a prospective firearms purchaser pertaining to criminal charges. Therefore, such information is not included in the "criminal history record" contemplated by the statute, is not "required" on the consent form, and is not subject to the criminal sanctions of subsection K of this section. Brooks v. Commonwealth, 19 Va. App. 563, 454 S.E.2d 3 (1995).

Conviction as juvenile. — The evidence established that the defendant gave a materially false response to the question of whether he had been convicted in any court of a crime for which the judge could have imprisoned him for more than one year where the defendant had been convicted of grand larceny, attempted grand larceny, petit larceny, possession of a firearm by one under the age of eighteen, attempted robbery and use of a firearm in the commission of a felony when he was seventeen years of age and it was clear that the judge could have imposed more than a one-year sentence for those convictions and, in fact, had imposed a sentence of twenty-four months to be served at a juvenile detention center. Kirby v. Commonwealth, No. 3015-99-2, 2000 Va. App. LEXIS 846 (Ct. of Appeals Dec. 28, 2000).

Commonwealth need not prove that materially false statement was made to a federally licensed firearm dealer. — Under plain language of this section, Commonwealth was not required to prove that defendant, who intentionally made a materially false statement on a criminal background investigation consent form required of prospective firearm purchasers, made the statement to a federally licensed firearms dealer. Adkins v. Commonwealth, 27 Va. App. 166, 497 S.E.2d 896 (1998).

Failure to prove defendant knew information to be false. — Defendant's conviction for a violation of subsection K of § 18.2-308.2:2 was inappropriate because there was no evidence to support a finding that he knew that he had been indicted when he signed the ATF form. The Commonwealth thus failed to prove an element of the crime. Smith v. Commonwealth, 282 Va. 449, 718 S.E.2d 452, 2011 Va. LEXIS 220 (2011).

Construction with § 18.2-308.2. — In this case, the trial court dismissed the indictment under this section, because the criminal history consent form did not comply with statutory requirements. Thus, the dismissal was not an acquittal for double jeopardy purposes, and double jeopardy did not bar prosecution of the defendant under § 18.2-308.2. Dodson v. Commonwealth, 23 Va. App. 286, 476 S.E.2d 512 (1996).

Jurisdiction. — Suit brought by a man convicted of misdemeanor conviction of domestic violence as defined in the Gun Control Act of 1968, 18 U.S.C.S. § 922(g)(9), against the state police under subsection E of § 18.2-308.2:2 and § 9.1-135, after his request to buy a firearm was rejected, was a civil action not an appeal of an administrative agency decision, thereby vesting appellate jurisdiction with the Supreme Court of Virginia rather than the Court of Appeals under § 17.1-405. Foltz v. Dep't of State Police, 55 Va. App. 182, 684 S.E.2d 841, 2009 Va. App. LEXIS 510 (2009).

Standing to challenge statute. — Because any injury to plaintiffs, persons who wanted to purchase hand guns from out of state, resulted from decisions made by third parties rather than the application of the challenged laws to them directly, plaintiffs lacked standing to bring their Second Amendment challenges to 18 U.S.C.S. § 922(b)(3), 27 C.F.R. § 478.99 and § 18.2-308.2:2, laws and a regulation that placed restriction on the interstate transfers of handguns. Lane v. Holder, 703 F.3d 668, 2012 U.S. App. LEXIS 26640 (4th Cir. Dec. 31, 2012).

Sale from own inventory shown. — Where evidence showed that defendant was operating the table under his business name, he exercised control and authority over the firearm and its display—this is so even if someone else owned the firearm—and defendant held the firearm for sale and negotiated the sale, accordingly, defendant was conducting a sale from his inventory as contemplated by the statute. Mayhew v. Commonwealth, 20 Va. App. 484, 458 S.E.2d 305 (1995).

Violation established. — Even though he claimed that he did not know he had been indicted, defendant made a false statement on a firearm purchase form, in violation of § 18.2-308.2:2, because he declared on the form that he was not under indictment when he was on bail awaiting trial on a felony drug charge that had been pending for nearly a year and a half. Smith v. Commonwealth, 56 Va. App. 166, 692 S.E.2d 265, 2010 Va. App. LEXIS 168 (2010).

Evidence supported the trial court's finding that defendant willfully and intentionally made a false statement in violation of subsection K of § 18.2-308.2:2 because ATF Form 4473 issued by the Bureau of Alcohol, Tobacco, Firearms, and Explosives explicitly warned defendant that making a false statement constituted a crime, but despite that warning, defendant affirmatively declared he was not under indictment, while all along knowing he had no idea what the word "indictment" meant; by doing so, defendant displayed a deliberate disregard for its truth or falsity with a conscious purpose to avoid learning the truth, and if defendant did not know what an indictment was, he should not have affirmatively represented on the ATF Form that he was not under indictment. Smith v. Commonwealth, 57 Va. App. 319, 701 S.E.2d 826, 2010 Va. App. LEXIS 468 (Nov. 23, 2010).

§ 18.2-308.2:3. Criminal background check required for employees of a gun dealer to transfer firearms; exemptions; penalties.

A. No person, corporation or proprietorship licensed as a firearms dealer pursuant to 18 U.S.C. § 921 et seq. shall employ any person to act as a seller, whether full-time or part-time, permanent, temporary, paid or unpaid, for the transfer of firearms under § 18.2-308.2:2, if such employee would be prohibited from possessing a firearm under §§ 18.2-308.1:1, 18.2-308.1:2, 18.2-308.1:3, 18.2-308.2, or § 18.2-308.2:01 or is an illegal alien, or is prohibited from purchasing or transporting a firearm pursuant to § 18.2-308.1:4 or § 18.2-308.1:5.

B. Prior to permitting an applicant to begin employment, the dealer shall obtain a written statement or affirmation from the applicant that he is not disqualified from possessing a firearm and shall submit the applicant's fingerprints and personal descriptive information to the Central Criminal Records Exchange to be forwarded to the Federal Bureau of Investigation (FBI) for the purpose of obtaining national criminal history record information regarding the applicant.

C. Prior to August 1, 2000, the dealer shall obtain written statements or affirmations from persons employed before July 1, 2000, to act as a seller under § 18.2-308.2:2 that they are not disqualified from possessing a firearm. Within five working days of the employee's next birthday, after August 1, 2000, the dealer shall submit the employee's fingerprints and personal descriptive information to the Central Criminal Records Exchange to be forwarded to the Federal Bureau of Investigation (FBI) for the purpose of obtaining national criminal history record information regarding the request.

C1. In lieu of submitting fingerprints pursuant to this section, any dealer holding a valid federal firearms license (FFL) issued by the Bureau of Alcohol, Tobacco and Firearms (ATF) may submit a sworn and notarized affidavit to the Department of State Police on a form provided by the Department, stating that the dealer has been subjected to a record check prior to the issuance and that the FFL was issued by the ATF. The affidavit may also contain the names of any employees that have been subjected to a record check and approved by the ATF. This exemption shall apply regardless of whether the FFL was issued in the name of the dealer or in the name of the business. The affidavit shall contain the valid FFL number, state the name of each person requesting the exemption, together with each person's identifying information, including their social security number and the following statement: "I hereby swear, under the penalty of perjury, that as a condition of obtaining a federal firearms license, each person requesting an exemption in this affidavit has been subjected to a fingerprint identification check by the Bureau of Alcohol, Tobacco and Firearms and the Bureau of Alcohol, Tobacco and Firearms subsequently determined that each person satisfied the requirements of 18 U.S.C. § 921 et seq. I understand that any person convicted of making a false statement in this affidavit is guilty of a Class 5 felony and that in addition to any other penalties imposed by law, a conviction under this section shall result in the forfeiture of my federal firearms license."

D. The Department of State Police, upon receipt of an individual's record or notification that no record exists, shall submit an eligibility report to the requesting dealer within 30 days of the applicant beginning his duties for new employees or within 30 days of the applicant's birthday for a person employed prior to July 1, 2000.

E. If any applicant is denied employment because of information appearing on the criminal history record and the applicant disputes the information upon which the denial was based, the Central Criminal Records Exchange shall, upon written request, furnish to the applicant the procedures for obtaining a copy of the criminal history record from the Federal Bureau of Investigation. The information provided to the dealer shall not be disseminated except as provided in this section.

F. The applicant shall bear the cost of obtaining the criminal history record unless the dealer, at his option, decides to pay such cost.

G. Upon receipt of the request for a criminal history record information check, the State Police shall establish a unique number for that firearm seller. Beginning September 1, 2001, the firearm seller's signature, firearm seller's number and the dealer's identification number shall be on all firearm transaction forms. The State Police shall void the firearm seller's number when a disqualifying record is discovered. The State Police may suspend a firearm seller's identification number upon the arrest of the firearm seller for a potentially disqualifying crime.

H. This section shall not restrict the transfer of a firearm at any place other than at a dealership or at any event required to be registered as a gun show.

I. Any person who willfully and intentionally requests, obtains, or seeks to obtain criminal history record information under false pretenses, or who willfully and intentionally disseminates or seeks to disseminate criminal history record information except as authorized by this section and § 18.2-308.2:2, shall be guilty of a Class 2 misdemeanor.

J. Any person willfully and intentionally making a materially false statement on the personal descriptive information required in this section shall be guilty of a Class 5 felony. Any person who offers for transfer any firearm in violation of this section shall be guilty of a Class 1 misdemeanor. Any dealer who willfully and knowingly employs or permits a person to act as a firearm seller in violation of this section shall be guilty of a Class 1 misdemeanor.

K. There is no civil liability for any seller for the actions of any purchaser or subsequent transferee of a firearm lawfully transferred pursuant to this section.

L. The provisions of this section requiring a seller's background check shall not apply to a licensed dealer.

M. Any person who willfully and intentionally makes a false statement in the affidavit as set out in subdivision C 1 shall be guilty of a Class 5 felony.

N. For purposes of this section:

"Dealer" means any person, corporation or proprietorship licensed as a dealer pursuant to 18 U.S.C. § 921 et seq.

"Firearm" means any handgun, shotgun, or rifle that will or is designed to or may readily be converted to expel single or multiple projectiles by action of an explosion of a combustible material.

"Place of business" means any place or premises where a dealer may lawfully transfer firearms.

"Seller" means for the purpose of any single sale of a firearm any person who is a dealer or an agent of a dealer, who may lawfully transfer firearms and who actually performs the criminal background check in accordance with the provisions of § 18.2-308.2:2.

"Transfer" means any act performed with intent to sell, rent, barter, trade or otherwise transfer ownership or permanent possession of a firearm at the place of business of a dealer.

History.
2000, c. 794; 2002, c. 880; 2003, c. 976.

§ 18.2-308.3. Use or attempted use of restricted ammunition in commission or attempted commission of crimes prohibited; penalty.

A. When used in this section:

"Restricted firearm ammunition" applies to bullets, projectiles or other types of ammunition that are: (i) coated with or contain, in whole or in part, polytetrafluoroethylene or a similar product, (ii) commonly known as "KTW" bullets or "French Arcanes," or (iii) any cartridges containing bullets coated with a plastic substance with other than lead or lead alloy cores, jacketed bullets with other than lead or lead alloy cores, or cartridges of which the bullet itself is wholly comprised of a metal or metal alloy other than lead. This definition shall not be construed to include shotgun shells or solid plastic bullets.

B. It shall be unlawful for any person to knowingly use or attempt to use restricted firearm ammunition while committing or attempting to commit a crime. Violation of this section shall constitute a separate and distinct felony and any person found guilty thereof shall be guilty of a Class 5 felony.

History.
1983, c. 602; 1988, c. 530.

Michie's Jurisprudence.
For related discussion, see 3A M.J. Burglary and Housebreaking, § 2; 9B M.J. Homicide, §§ 17, 28; 12B M.J. Mayhem, § 2; 15 M.J. Rape, § 2; 16 M.J. Robbery, § 2; 20 M.J. Weapons, § 9.

CASE NOTES

Right to counsel not violated. — Defendant's aggravated malicious wounding and use of a firearm in the commission of a felony convictions were not subject to reversal on appeal, as the trial court did not violate his right to counsel by erroneously disqualifying his retained trial counsel prior to trial, and appoint substitute counsel to defend him, based on an existing conflict of interest due to counsel's representation of a Commonwealth's witness. Johnson v. Commonwealth, 50 Va. App. 600, 652 S.E.2d 156, 2007 Va. App. LEXIS 406 (2007).

Sufficient evidence. — Defendant's convictions for illegal possession of a firearm under §§ 18.2-308.2, 18.2-308.4, and 18.2-308 were affirmed as defendant constructively possessed a handgun since: (1) defendant was convicted of possession of cocaine and marijuana with intent to distribute; (2) a handgun was found in the driver's seat of defendant's vehicle; (3) defendant was either sitting on the handgun or just next to it when an officer first saw defendant; and (4) a handgun was as much a tool of the illegal drug trade as the drugs, digital scales, and plastic distribution bags found in defendant's vehicle. Bolden v. Commonwealth, 49 Va. App. 285, 640 S.E.2d 526, 2007 Va. App. LEXIS 52 (2007).

§ 18.2-308.4. Possession of firearms while in possession of certain substances.

A. It shall be unlawful for any person unlawfully in possession of a controlled substance classified in Schedule I or II of the Drug Control Act (§ 54.1-3400 et seq.) of Title 54.1 to simultaneously with knowledge and intent possess any firearm. A violation of this subsection is a Class 6 felony and constitutes a separate and distinct felony.

B. It shall be unlawful for any person unlawfully in possession of a controlled substance classified in Schedule I or II of the Drug Control Act (§ 54.1-3400 et seq.) to simultaneously with knowledge and intent possess any firearm on or about his person. A violation of this subsection is a Class 6 felony and constitutes a separate and distinct felony and any person convicted hereunder shall be sentenced to a mandatory minimum term of imprisonment of two years. Such punishment shall be separate and apart from, and shall be made to run consecutively with, any punishment received for the commission of the primary felony.

C. It shall be unlawful for any person to possess, use, or attempt to use any pistol, shotgun, rifle, or other firearm or display such weapon in a threatening manner while committing or attempting to commit the illegal manufacture, sale, distribution, or the possession with the intent to manufacture, sell, or distribute a controlled substance classified in Schedule I or Schedule II of the Drug Control Act (§ 54.1-3400 et seq.), synthetic cannabinoids or more than one pound of marijuana. A violation of this subsection is a Class 6 felony, and constitutes a separate and distinct felony and any person convicted hereunder shall be sentenced to a mandatory minimum term of imprisonment of five years. Such punishment shall be separate and apart from, and shall be made to run consecutively with, any punishment received for the commission of the primary felony.

History.
1987, c. 285; 1990, c. 625; 1992, c. 707; 1993, c. 831; 1999, cc. 829, 846; 2003, c. 949; 2004, cc. 461, 995; 2011, cc. 384, 410.

Editor's note.
Acts 2011, cc. 384 and 410, cl. 3 provides: "That the provisions of this act may result in a net increase in periods of imprisonment or commitment. Pursuant to § 30-19.1:4, the estimated amount of the necessary appropriation cannot be determined for periods of imprisonment in state adult correctional facilities; therefore, Chapter 874 of the Acts of Assembly of 2010 requires the Virginia Criminal Sentencing Commission to assign a minimum fiscal impact of $50,000. Pursuant to § 30-19.1:4, the estimated amount of the necessary appropriation cannot be determined for periods of commitment to the custody of the Department of Juvenile Justice."

The 2011 amendments.
The 2011 amendments by cc. 384 and 410, effective March 23, 2011, are identical, and inserted "synthetic cannabinoids" in the first sentence of subsection C and made a minor stylistic change.

Law Review.
For article summarizing published Virginia criminal law decisions between July 1, 2002 and July 1, 2003, see 38 U. Rich. L. Rev. 87 (2003).

Michie's Jurisprudence.
For related discussion, see 5B M.J. Criminal Procedure, § 72; 6B M.J. Drugs and Druggists, § 2; 20 M.J. Weapons, § 4.1.

CASE NOTES

Constitutionality. — Defendant did not show that subsection C of § 18.2-308.4, prohibiting possession of a firearm while possessing a Schedule I or II controlled substance with intent to distribute, was void for vagueness as applied to defendant, in violation of defendant's Fourteenth Amendment rights. The plain language of the statute did not require that the Commonwealth prove a nexus between the firearm and the controlled substance and, thus, defendant did not show that a Fourteenth Amendment violation occurred. Johnson v. Commonwealth, — Va. App. —, — S.E.2d —, 2008 Va. App. LEXIS 97 (Feb. 26, 2008).

Retrospective application of amendment not allowed. — The statutorily mandated five-year term of imprisonment proscribed in this section is neither vague nor unconstitutional. By amending the statute to proscribe a mandatory minimum sentence for either violation of the statute, the legislature merely determined that it was removing from a trial court's discretion the power to sentence the defendant within a statutorily proscribed range of punishments. Quarles v. Commonwealth, No. 0943-00-2, 2001 Va. App. LEXIS 65 (Ct. of Appeals Feb. 13, 2001).

The concept of individualized sentencing in criminal cases generally is not constitutionally required; hence, the trial court's imposition of the mandatory minimum sentence under this section did not violate defendant's constitutional rights. Harris v. Commonwealth, No. 0687-00-2, 2001 Va. App. LEXIS 413 (Ct. of Appeals July 10, 2001).

Trial court properly denied defendant's motion to be sentenced under a version of this section that became effective after the crime was committed; the language of the statute did not clearly allow for retroactive application of the amendment, and the statute also could not be applied retroactively pursuant to §§ 1-13.39:3 and 1-16 [see now §§ 1-238 and 1-239]. Taylor v. Commonwealth, 44 Va. App. 179, 604 S.E.2d 103, 2004 Va. App. LEXIS 512 (2004).

Effective date of amendments. — Where law in effect at the time that defendant committed the offense of possessing a firearm while possessing cocaine provided for a mandatory, minimum penalty of five years in prison, the trial court properly determined that it had no discretion to impose another sentence despite the fact that the law changed to establish gradations for the offense and to fix new punishments before defendant was sentenced. The law in effect at the time of the offense determines the penalty that the trial court must impose. Presbury v. Commonwealth, No. 0206-04-3, 2004 Va. App. LEXIS 628 (Ct. of Appeals Dec. 21, 2004).

Construction with § 18.2-10. — Contention that the mandatory minimum sentence provided in this section conflicts with the Class 6 felony sentencing range found in § 18.2-10 (f) was without merit; by describing the offense as a Class 6 felony, this section limits the sentence that the trial judge may impose, and additionally, precludes the imposition of a fine, because the jail term exceeds 12 months. Harris v. Commonwealth, No. 0687-00-2, 2001 Va. App. LEXIS 413 (Ct. of Appeals July 10, 2001).

Concealment of firearm not requisite. — This section is not an extension of the concealed weapons statute, § 18.2-308. The clear wording of this section prohibits unlawful possession of cocaine "simultaneously with" knowingly and intentionally possessing any firearm. No language in this section requires proof of concealment of weapons. Jefferson v. Commonwealth, 14 Va. App. 77, 414 S.E.2d 860 (1992).

Display of firearm in threatening manner not requisite. — To convict defendant of violating subsection C of § 18.2-308.4, the prosecution had not been required to prove that defendant possessed a firearm "in a threatening manner," as that phrase modifies only the verb "display" immediately preceding it. Wright v. Commonwealth, 53 Va. App. 266, 670 S.E.2d 772, 2009 Va. App. LEXIS 2, aff'd, 278 Va. 754, 685 S.E.2d 655, 2009 Va. LEXIS 111 (2009).

Possession of firearm on or about defendant's person. — Evidence was insufficient to convict defendant of possessing a controlled substance while simultaneously possessing a firearm on or about his person under subsection B of § 18.2-308.4 because even though defendant constructively possessed a firearm located in a locked glove compartment of a car in which he was a front seat passenger, he did not have ready access to use of the firearm, which was required to show possession on or about his person, because the firearm was in a locked glove compartment and defendant did not possess a key to the glove compartment. Hunter v. Commonwealth, 56 Va. App. 50, 690 S.E.2d 792, 2010 Va. App. LEXIS 130 (2010).

Severance. — Trial court did not err in refusing to sever felon in possession of a firearm indictment from possession of cocaine and possession of firearm charges, as nothing in the record rebutted the presumption that the trial court considered only the evidence relevant to each offense when reaching its decision. Vanhook v. Commonwealth, 40 Va. App. 130, 578 S.E.2d 71, 2003 Va. App. LEXIS 149 (2003).

Only constructive possession necessary. — Actual possession of both firearm and controlled substance is not required by the wording of this section. Constructive possession of either or both is sufficient for conviction. Jefferson v. Commonwealth, 14 Va. App. 77, 414 S.E.2d 860 (1992); Samuels v. Commonwealth, No. 1364-94-2 (Ct. of Appeals Aug. 1, 1995).

Defendant's conviction for possession of a firearm while in the possession of a controlled substance was upheld on appeal where the evidence showed that defendant constructively possessed a 9 mm gun, because he admitted to the police that he received the handgun from his son and showed the police where he had hidden it, wrapped in plastic bags inside a vacuum cleaner, so his grandchildren would not find it. Gray v. Commonwealth, No. 0374-04-1, 2005 Va. App. LEXIS 52 (Ct. of Appeals Feb. 8, 2005).

To obtain a conviction under subsection C of § 18.2-308.4, it is sufficient to prove that the defendant had constructive, rather than actual, possession of drugs and a firearm. Wright v. Commonwealth, 53 Va. App. 266, 670 S.E.2d 772, 2009 Va. App. LEXIS 2, aff'd, 278 Va. 754, 685 S.E.2d 655, 2009 Va. LEXIS 111 (2009).

In a case in which defendant was convicted of violating subsection C of § 18.2-308.4, he argued unsuccessfully that a conviction required the Commonwealth to prove actual, simultaneous possession of both the drugs and the firearm. A violation of subsection C could be proven by constructive possession. Wright v. Commonwealth, 278 Va. 754, 685 S.E.2d 655, 2009 Va. LEXIS 111 (2009).

Proof of nexus between drug offense and firearm possession. — To obtain a conviction under subsection C of § 18.2-308.4, the prosecution must prove a nexus between the drug offense and the firearm possession — proof that actual or constructive possession of the firearm somehow furthers, advances, or helps the defendant to commit the offense of actually or constructively possessing a controlled substance with an intent to distribute it. Wright v. Commonwealth, 53 Va. App. 266, 670 S.E.2d 772, 2009 Va. App. LEXIS 2, aff'd, 278 Va. 754, 685 S.E.2d 655, 2009 Va. LEXIS 111 (2009).

As defendant admitted owning a loaded handgun and 114 grams of crack cocaine found in his bedroom, and the detective who arrested him had encountered him in his car two days earlier, at which time he had the loaded firearm with him, the evidence established that defendant's gun protected his drugs, thereby providing the necessary nexus between his constructive possession of the handgun and drugs. Therefore, the evidence had been sufficient to convict him of possessing a firearm while possessing cocaine with the intent to distribute. Wright v. Commonwealth, 53 Va. App. 266, 670 S.E.2d 772, 2009 Va. App. LEXIS 2, aff'd, 278 Va. 754, 685 S.E.2d 655, 2009 Va. LEXIS 111 (2009).

In a case in which defendant was convicted of violating subsection C of § 18.2-308.4, he argued unsuccessfully that the evidence was insufficient to establish a nexus between the possession of the firearm and the unlawful activity. Nothing in subsection C contained such a requirement. Wright v. Commonwealth, 278 Va. 754, 685 S.E.2d 655, 2009 Va. LEXIS 111 (2009).

Valid search under plain view doctrine. — Trial court erred in suppressing evidence pertaining to defendant's indictment for possession of a firearm while in possession of a controlled substance; as a police officer lawfully seized ammunition under a search warrant for a gun, the officer was in a lawful position to view the crack pipe and the bottles of prescription drugs, and therefore, lawfully seized the crack pipe and drugs under the plain view doctrine. Commonwealth v. Marek, No. 2123-02-4, 2003 Va. App. LEXIS 46 (Ct. of Appeals Feb. 5, 2003).

Verdict not "illegal." — Although verdict incorrectly combined a penitentiary term and a fine for crimes of possession of cocaine with intent to distribute and possession of a firearm while in possession of cocaine, entire verdict was not "illegal" for trial court may impose a valid sentence in substitution for one that is void. Barksdale v. Commonwealth, 17 Va. App. 456, 438 S.E.2d 761 (1993).

Multiple convictions and punishments. — Where defendant made two sales of cocaine and had ready access to firearms while retrieving the drugs, the evidence was sufficient to show multiple violations of the same offense that warranted separate punishments. Hamlett v. Commonwealth, No. 1903-02-3, 2003 Va. App. LEXIS 369 (Ct. of Appeals June 24, 2003).

Under the totality of the circumstances, defendant, who was convicted of possession of cocaine with intent to distribute under § 18.2-248 and possession of a firearm while in possession of drugs under § 18.2-308.4, was not illegally seized under the Fourth Amendment as the police officer had a particularized and objective basis for suspecting that defendant was involved in criminal activity where: (1) defendant fled a consensual encounter with the officer; (2) the officer had a reasonable suspicion to detain defendant where he suspiciously, while in a high-crime area, leaned toward a car tire as the officer approached; (3) defendant could not provide an address in the housing area, which had been posted as a "no trespassing" area, without squinting at a building behind him and giving the officer that address; and (4) defendant's placement of his hands underneath him and his unusual movements after he fell suggested that he was attempting to remove something from his clothing. White v. Commonwealth, No. 2091-02-1, 2003 Va. App. LEXIS 367 (Ct. of Appeals June 24, 2003).

Trial court properly denied defendant's suppression motion as the cocaine was discovered during a proper search incident to a lawful arrest for a concealed weapon violation; it was legally irrelevant under the Fourth Amendment that the deputy chose not to charge defendant with the lesser concealed weapon violation of § 18.2-308, upon discovering the suspected drugs during the search, enabling the deputy to charge defendant with possession of cocaine with intent to distribute under § 18.2-248, and possession of a firearm while simultaneously possessing illegal drugs under subsection A of § 18.2-308.4. Slayton v. Commonwealth, 41 Va. App. 101, 582 S.E.2d 448, 2003 Va. App. LEXIS 352 (2003).

To sustain a conviction pursuant to the provisions of this section, the Commonwealth must prove not only that the accused possessed cocaine, but that the firearm was "knowingly" and "simultaneously" possessed. Each of these factors must be proved beyond reasonable doubt and, when proof is by circumstantial evidence, the circumstances proved must be consistent with guilt, inconsistent with innocence, and exclude all reasonable hypothesis of innocence. Cooper v. Commonwealth, No. 1083-89-2 (Ct. of Appeals Sept. 3, 1991).

Controlled substance and firearm need not be introduced. — To obtain a conviction under this section, the commonwealth must prove that the defendant possessed a controlled substance with intent to distribute it while simultaneously possessing a firearm but it may do this without introducing either the controlled substance or the firearm. Users and addicts may testify as to the nature of a drug and, in a similar manner, the commonwealth can prove the existence of a firearm without offering the tangible object as evidence. Adams v. Commonwealth, No. 0138-00-3, 2001 Va. App. LEXIS 128 (Ct. of Appeals Mar. 13, 2001).

Failure of indictment to allege all material facts. — Even though defendant had also been charged with possession of and intent to distribute cocaine, it was error for sentencing judge to assume that defendant had been convicted under subsection B of this section rather than subsection A, because the indictment did not allege that defendant had the intent to manufacture, sell, or distribute cocaine in his possession while simultaneously possessing a firearm. Moore v. Commonwealth, 27 Va. App. 192, 497 S.E.2d 908 (1998).

Suppression of evidence. — Defendant's incriminating statements made after he received Miranda warnings were properly admitted, as said statements were not made as a result of an illegal arrest, but after a lawful detention by officers and an arrest based on probable cause of finding cocaine and a gun in the residence searched via a valid warrant; thus, his convictions under §§ 18.2-248.1, 18.2-248, and 18.2-308.4, were upheld. Whitaker v. Commonwealth, No. 3232-03-2, 2005 Va. App. LEXIS 34 (Ct. of Appeals Feb. 1, 2005).

In a case in which defendant had been convicted of violating §§ 18.2-250, 18.2-308.2, 18.2-308.4, and subsection C of § 18.2-57, he argued unsuccessfully that the Court of Appeals of Virginia erroneously upheld the circuit court's denial of his motion to suppress the evidence because his encounter with the police officers was not consensual, and the officers lacked any reasonable suspicion to believe that he was engaged in criminal activity. During the encounter, which lasted only two or three minutes, the police checked the "ban list" but did not engage in any show of force or use language indicating that defendant was required to remain at that location, the police did not tell him that he was required to stay, and defendant did not make any attempt to leave; instead, defendant remained in the area, standing about five feet away from the officers while his companion moved to sit on some nearby steps. Montague v. Commonwealth, 278 Va. 532, 684 S.E.2d 583, 2009 Va. LEXIS 113 (2009), cert. denied, 130 S. Ct. 1537, 176 L. Ed. 2d 133, 2010 U.S. LEXIS 1456 (U.S. 2010).

Sufficient evidence. — Ample evidence supported the findings that appellant constructively possessed a weapon or weapons with knowledge and intent while constructively possessing cocaine where the trial record established that he stayed at house where arrest was made several nights a week, he was discovered leaving the master bedroom where drugs and money were found mixed with his personal papers and property, cocaine was found in close proximity to two weapons, and both the drugs and the guns were easily accessible to appellant. Jefferson v. Commonwealth, 14 Va. App. 77, 414 S.E.2d 860 (1992).

The proximity of the dispenser containing bullets and cocaine to the handgun, combined with the correspondence of the bullets in the dispenser to the bullets in the handgun, gave rise to a reasonable inference that the two items were possessed in conjunction. Further, the relative privacy of the yard in which these items, and no others, were found supported the inference that the defendant dropped both items when running from the officer. Therefore, evidence was sufficient for conviction under § 18.2-248 and this section. Hunt v. Commonwealth, No. 0257-94-1 (Ct. of Appeals March 21, 1995).

Appellant told the police that the handguns found under his bed were not his, but that his brother had entrusted them to him. This evidence alone was sufficient to prove that appellant was aware of the presence and character of the firearms, and that they were subject to his dominion and control; thus, establishing constructive possession. Accordingly, appellant's conviction was affirmed. Morris v. Commonwealth, No. 1507-95-3 (Ct. of Appeals May 14, 1996).

Evidence was sufficient to support finding that defendant exercised dominion and control over drugs and firearm found hidden together near his feet, under box spring of bed. Mosley v. Commonwealth, No. 2477-98-3 (Ct. of Appeals Dec. 7, 1999).

Only reasonable hypothesis flowing from evidence was that defendant exercised at least joint possession of firearm found in dresser drawer of bedroom he shared with girlfriend, and thus evidence was sufficient to prove defendant's constructive possession of weapon. Vest v. Commonwealth, No. 0803-99-3 (Ct. of Appeals Feb. 15, 2000).

Circumstantial evidence held sufficient to show that the defendant had a handgun on his person when he initially refused to consent to a pat-down and that, after his unsuccessful attempt to enter a friend's house, he walked to the side of the house, deposited the gun in a shopping cart behind a concrete wall, returned and

then consented to the pat-down, knowing the police officer would find nothing on his person; the defendant's flight when confronted with the gun the officer found in the grocery cart was itself evidence of his guilt. McCain v. Commonwealth, No. 2368-99-3, 2000 Va. App. LEXIS 512 (Ct. of Appeals July 18, 2000), aff'd, 261 Va. 483, 545 S.E.2d 541, (2001).

The evidence was sufficient to support an inference that the defendant possessed a functional firearm where, during a drug sale, the defendant told a story of being stopped by a state trooper when he possessed a pistol and, as he told of the gun, he displayed the handle of a pistol concealed under his shirt; given the context of the events, the only reasonable hypothesis flowing from this evidence was that the defendant possessed an actual firearm. Where there was no evidence to suggest the weapon did not function, it would be unreasonable to conclude that the defendant talked about, carried and displayed something that looked like a gun but could not function as one. Taylor v. Commonwealth, 33 Va. App. 735, 536 S.E.2d 922, 2000 Va. App. LEXIS 736 (2000).

The evidence was sufficient to support defendant's conviction under this section where the defendant, after refusing to permit a pat-down search, began walking away from two police officers to an area behind a wall, one of the officers saw the shadow of an arm reach from the wall into an area where a metal grocery cart was located, the officer heard the sound of one metal object hitting against another metal object, the defendant then consented to a pat-down search, no one else was present in the area where the grocery cart was located, and a handgun was found in the cart; this evidence, combined with the evidence of the defendant's flight when confronted with the handgun and the evidence of his possession of cocaine with the intent to distribute, was sufficient to establish the defendant's guilt beyond a reasonable doubt on the firearm charge. McCain v. Commonwealth, 261 Va. 483, 545 S.E.2d 541, 2001 Va. LEXIS 42 (2001).

Where a defendant confessed to trading crack cocaine for a shotgun on the day preceding his arrest and to handling firearms found scattered about the home where various items associated with cocaine distribution were found, and where these statements and the defendant's continuing involvement with others in the distribution of cocaine from the premises were corroborated by the testimony of another occupant, such evidence clearly established that defendant actually and constructively possessed the firearms. Young v. Commonwealth, No. 1228-00-2, 2001 Va. App. LEXIS 251 (Ct. of Appeals May 15, 2001).

Presence of the firearm in defendant's house, coupled with the statement to the police that they could find it beneath the mattress in the back bedroom, was sufficient to establish that defendant had knowledge of the presence of the firearm, and that it was subject to his dominion and control and hence was sufficient to sustain his conviction for possession of a firearm; the trial court could reject defendant's statement that the firearm belonged to his wife. Pitchford v. Commonwealth, No. 1582-01-1, 2002 Va. App. LEXIS 565 (Ct. of Appeals Sept. 24, 2002).

Evidence that defendant owned scales on which cocaine residue was found and that defendant had two rifles in a trailer where the scales were found was sufficient to sustain defendant's convictions for possession of cocaine, in violation of § 18.2-250, and simultaneous possession of cocaine and firearms, in violation of subsection A of § 18.2-308.4. Chism v. Commonwealth, No. 2892-01-2, 2002 Va. App. LEXIS 745 (Ct. of Appeals Dec. 17, 2002).

Where an officer reasonably suspected a defendant was operating his vehicle in violation of the law and lawfully stopped him and the odor of marijuana and other observations gave probable cause for a search and his conviction possession of a firearm while in possession of a controlled substance under § 18.2-308.4 was affirmed. Savage v. Commonwealth, No. 0799-02-1, 2003 Va. App. LEXIS 187 (Ct. of Appeals Apr. 1, 2003).

Only reasonable hypothesis flowing from the evidence was that defendant actually or constructively possessed a firearm and drugs found outside a bedroom window where an officer saw defendant standing with his torso and arms out the open bedroom window, and although the officer did not see anything in defendant's hand and did not see him make any sort of throwing motion as he leaned out the window, the officer immediately found drugs and a firearm outside the bedroom window. That the sister might also have had actual or constructive possession of the drugs and firearm before defendant attempted to dispose of them through the open window did not diminish defendant's guilt. Smithers v. Commonwealth, No. 2144-02-2, 2003 Va. App. LEXIS 510 (Ct. of Appeals Oct. 14, 2003).

Evidence was sufficient to support conviction for possession of a firearm while in possession of drugs, in violation of § 18.2-308.4, where the trial court could have reasonably concluded that defendant was aware of the presence and character of the gun under the driver's seat of his car and it was subject to his dominion and control based on its location and that defendant was aware of the presence and character of the drugs found in the console and that he exercised dominion and control over them as well. Gillard v. Commonwealth, No. 0037-02-2, 2003 Va. App. LEXIS 437 (Ct. of Appeals Aug. 19, 2003).

Evidence was sufficient to show that defendant possessed cocaine, and, simultaneously, with knowledge and intent, possessed any firearm even though the cocaine was not located in his pants pocket until he had been taken to jail following a traffic stop more than one hour after the initial traffic stop for speeding revealed he was carrying the gun without a permit. The trial court's finding that he possessed both simultaneously, for the purpose of conviction, excluded every other reasonable hypothesis that flowed from the evidence. Bailey v. Commonwealth, No. 2767-02-1, 2003 Va. App. LEXIS 610 (Ct. of Appeals Nov. 25, 2003).

Evidence was sufficient to show that defendant was in possession of cocaine at the same time he possessed a firearm, as reasonable inferences existed that the cocaine packets found beneath defendant in the house he ran into when he saw police and the gun found in a nearby bucket belonged to defendant. The homeowner testified that neither the cocaine nor gun belonged to her and were not in the house when she left it shortly before defendant's arrest, and a reliable, confidential informant reported to police that defendant was in possession of cocaine shortly before defendant was arrested. Payne v. Commonwealth, No. 3339-02-3, 2003 Va. App. LEXIS 616 (Ct. of Appeals Dec. 2, 2003).

Evidence that the gun and the cocaine were found in very close proximity to items that defendant admitted to having in his pockets when he entered the room and within arms reach of defendant, who was found hiding in a closet, was sufficient to support convictions for possession of cocaine and possession of firearm while in possession of cocaine. Kersey v. Commonwealth, No. 3354-02-2, 2004 Va. App. LEXIS 59 (Ct. of Appeals Feb. 10, 2004).

There was sufficient evidence to support the jury's finding that defendant was guilty beyond a reasonable doubt of possession of a firearm while possessing cocaine in violation of § 18.2-308.4 where the arresting officer saw the blue plastic cap from a vial which contained cocaine in defendant's hand and it was thereafter retrieved from a cushion where the gun was found, the driver did not appear to have an opportunity to have placed the gun under a cushion where it was later found, and defendant was sitting on the cushion where the gun was hidden; the jury's determination that defendant possessed the firearm and its rejection of the hypothesis that the driver placed the firearm under the cushion was not plainly wrong. Artis v. Commonwealth, No. 3305-02-1, 2004 Va. App. LEXIS 131 (Ct. of Appeals Mar. 30, 2004).

Evidence was sufficient to support defendant's conviction possession of a firearm while in the possession of drugs, including: (1) photographs of the location of the handgun and the 98 individually packaged baggies of crack cocaine, immediately adjacent to where defendant was sitting; (2) defendant's movement away from the cocaine and handgun when he saw the officer approach; and (3) the fact that there were three individuals sitting on the porch did not negate defendant's possession as possession could be shared. Peek v. Commonwealth, No. 0340-03-1, 2004 Va. App. LEXIS 193 (Ct. of Appeals Apr. 27, 2004).

Evidence supported a trial court's finding that defendant constructively possessed illegal drugs found in his home where 14 pills were found in a plastic vial in a candy box in the living room of defendant's home, various empty pill bottles, some of which contained Schedule III and IV drugs, were found in defendant's bedroom, one bottle bore the name of a different party and other bottles evidenced names that had been scratched off, a medication guide was also found in the bedroom, where defendant owned the home and lived there, where, although his elderly mother also resided in the home, she did not take pain medication, where $2,289 arranged sequentially in descending order of denominations was also found in the candy box containing the plastic vial of pills, where defendant was not employed, and where no explanation of

the source of the funds was in evidence; convictions for possession of a Schedule II controlled substance and possession of a firearm while in possession of a Schedule II controlled substance were affirmed. Newsome v. Commonwealth, No. 1987-03-3, 2004 Va. App. LEXIS 456 (Ct. of Appeals Sept. 28, 2004).

Defendant's convictions for illegal possession of a firearm under §§ 18.2-308.2, 18.2-308.4, and 18.2-308 were affirmed as defendant constructively possessed a handgun since: (1) defendant was convicted of possession of cocaine and marijuana with intent to distribute; (2) a handgun was found in the driver's seat of defendant's vehicle; (3) defendant was either sitting on the handgun or just next to it when an officer first saw defendant; and (4) a handgun was as much a tool of the illegal drug trade as the drugs, digital scales, and plastic distribution bags found in defendant's vehicle. Bolden v. Commonwealth, 49 Va. App. 285, 640 S.E.2d 526, 2007 Va. App. LEXIS 52 (2007).

Evidence was sufficient to prove that defendant was aware of both the presence and character of a set of scales and that the scales were subject to defendant's dominion and control, to support defendant's conviction for possession of a firearm while in possession of cocaine. Defendant admitted that defendant knew of the safe's contents and that defendant had accessed the safe; from this, the trial court, as fact finder, could infer that defendant knew the scales were in the safe. Banks v. Commonwealth, — Va. App. —, — S.E.2d —, 2007 Va. App. LEXIS 43 (Feb. 13, 2007).

Conviction for possession of a firearm while in possession of cocaine was supported by evidence showing that defendant was aware of the presence and character of the firearm and it was within defendant's dominion and control. Among other things, defendant exited vehicle along with the only other passenger and attempted to contact the officer before the officer could get to the vehicle, and the gun was in proximity to where defendant had been sitting. Bolden v. Commonwealth, 275 Va. 144, 654 S.E.2d 584, 2008 Va. LEXIS 6 (2008), cert. denied, 129 S. Ct. 284, 2008 U.S. LEXIS 6378, 172 L. Ed. 2d 208 (U.S. 2008).

Trial court did not err in finding the Commonwealth's evidence sufficient to prove beyond a reasonable doubt that defendant possessed a firearm while in possession of more than one pound of marijuana with intent to distribute, violating subsection C of § 18.2-308.4. Defendant admitted to a detective that a pistol located on a kitchen table, adjacent to the pantry where defendant placed a marijuana package, belonged to defendant, and that defendant used it for protection; at trial defendant testified that the pistol belonged to defendant. Hargrove v. Commonwealth, 53 Va. App. 545, 673 S.E.2d 896, 2009 Va. App. LEXIS 123 (2009).

In a case in which defendant was convicted of violating subsection C of § 18.2-308.4, he argued unsuccessfully that the trial court and the Court of Appeals of Virginia erred in concluding that sufficient evidence was produced to show that he possessed the firearm while committing the offense of possession of cocaine with the intent to distribute or to show a nexus between the possession of the firearm and the criminal act. The indictment charging a violation of subsection C of § 18.2-308.4 did not limit the charge to defendant's possession of cocaine with intent to distribute while in his automobile; trial testimony established that both the cocaine recovered from him at the time of his initial arrest and everything combined, which included the cocaine recovered at his home, the gun, the packaging material, and the scale, along with the absence of items to use cocaine, supported the conclusion that the cocaine was not for personal use. Wright v. Commonwealth, 278 Va. 754, 685 S.E.2d 655, 2009 Va. LEXIS 111 (2009).

Although defendant claimed no knowledge of the exact location of a gun in his car, evidence was sufficient to convict defendant of possession of a firearm while in possession of certain controlled substances where defendant knew of the presence of the gun somewhere in the car, the gun was found underneath defendant's seat, and defendant was the car's sole occupant. Gholston v. Commonwealth, 2010 Va. App. LEXIS 202 (2010).

Evidence was sufficient to prove that defendant constructively possessed cocaine and a firearm simultaneously, in violation of § 18.2-308.4, although defendant denied knowing about the cocaine, because defendant admitted seeing the firearm on the floor of a car and placing it under a seat, and the cocaine was found next to the firearm. The fact finder could have found it unreasonable to believe that defendant knew of the presence of the firearm, but did not know of the cocaine next to it. Wilson v. Commonwealth, 2010

Va. App. LEXIS 38 (Feb. 2, 2010).

Combined evidence of defendant's possession of the key to the vehicle, the presence of defendant's fingerprint found on a tool to the drug trade in the glove box, the location of the scale and loaded gun next to the drugs, and the location of defendant's personal papers in the same compartment, supported the trial court's finding that defendant exercised dominion and control over the contraband items and was aware of their presence and character. Grimes v. Commonwealth, 2010 Va. App. LEXIS 378 (Sept. 21, 2010).

Evidence was sufficient to convict appellant of possession of a firearm while in possession of cocaine under § 18.2-308.4 because, upon concluding that appellant had recently occupied the gold car and possessed the cocaine, the trial court was entitled to find that he possessed the firearm found next to the console containing cocaine and to find that the gun was subject to his dominion and control. Womack v. Commonwealth, 2013 Va. App. LEXIS 38 (Feb. 5, 2013).

Sufficient evidence of possession. — Evidence that defendant bought the gun with another, handled the gun on occasion, and was within reach of the gun was sufficient to support his conviction for possession of a firearm. Maye v. Commonwealth, 44 Va. App. 463, 605 S.E.2d 353, 2004 Va. App. LEXIS 590 (2004).

Where defendant was traveling alone, it was reasonable to concluded that he was aware of the firearm protruding from under the front seat of the vehicle that he was driving and that it was subject to his dominion and control. Shelton v. Commonwealth, No. 3012-03-2, 2005 Va. App. LEXIS 87 (Ct. of Appeals Mar. 1, 2005).

Evidence of constructive possession of cocaine was sufficient to support defendant's convictions of possession with intent to distribute cocaine and possession of a firearm while in possession of a controlled substance. Defendant went inside his bedroom when he saw police; a loaded firearm was within arm's reach when police entered the bedroom; cocaine was near defendant and in plain view; more cocaine was in a dresser drawer and drug packaging materials were on the dresser; bullets were on a windowsill; and some of defendant's belongings were in the bedroom. Cherry v. Commonwealth, — Va. App. —, — S.E.2d —, 2006 Va. App. LEXIS 358 (Aug. 8, 2006).

Testimony of defendant's mother that the mother gave defendant the car where the gun was found and that the mother had not used the car in about a year was sufficient to support a finding that defendant knowingly possessed the firearm found in the car. Jordan v. Commonwealth, — Va. App. —, — S.E.2d —, 2007 Va. App. LEXIS 259 (June 26, 2007).

Commonwealth was not required to prove that defendant possessed the firearm in a threatening manner in order to prove that he possessed a firearm in violation of subsection C of § 18.2-308.4. Clark v. Commonwealth, — Va. App. —, — S.E.2d —, 2008 Va. App. LEXIS 269 (June 3, 2008).

Because defendant occupied a dwelling in which a firearm was found, admitted knowledge of the presence of the gun in the house, and possessed the trigger lock keys, which rendered the firearm subject to defendant's dominion and control, the evidence was sufficient to find that defendant constructively possessed the firearm; accordingly, the evidence was also sufficient to convict defendant of possession of a firearm after having been convicted of a felony and possession of a firearm while in possession of drugs. Herndon v. Commonwealth, — Va. App. —, — S.E.2d —, 2009 Va. App. LEXIS 129 (Mar. 24, 2009).

Evidence was sufficient to prove that defendant, a convicted violent felon found in possession of cocaine, possessed a firearm within the meaning of §§ 18.2-308.2 and 18.2-308.4 when he was driving a car that contained the frame, cylinder pin, and cylinder with ammunition for a revolver, which was successfully test-fired. Seward v. Commonwealth, 2009 Va. App. LEXIS 579 (Dec. 22, 2009).

Insufficient evidence of constructive possession. — Evidence did not support finding that defendant constructively possessed contraband, even though it was found in a house which he occupied, where evidence did not show that the defendant was in the dwelling recently enough to permit a reasonable inference that he was aware of the presence of the contraband. No direct evidence placed the defendant in the house; while police found mail addressed to him on a dresser in a bedroom, the postmark on the mail was six days before the discovery of the contraband; and they also found evidence of at least one other person living in the house.

Diggs v. Commonwealth, No. 0957-93-2, 1994 Va. App. LEXIS 622 (Ct. of Appeals Oct. 11, 1994).

Evidence was insufficient to prove possession of the firearm where no other evidence linked the defendant to the firearm and evidence did not exclude the theory, suggested by the defendant, that someone else put the firearm under her mattress. Lawrence v. Commonwealth, No. 1153-02-1, 2003 Va. App. LEXIS 190 (Ct. of Appeals Apr. 1, 2003).

Evidence of operability not needed. — There was no error in the judgment appealed from since the World War I era handgun possessed by defendant, a felon, was designed, made, and intended to expel a projectile by means of an explosion; the state did not have to show that the handgun was "operable," "capable" of being fired, or had the "actual capacity to do serous harm." McDaniel v. Commonwealth, 264 Va. 429, 574 S.E.2d 234, 2002 Va. LEXIS 150 (2002).

Trial court properly convicted defendant on a charge of possession of a firearm while simultaneously possessing cocaine; the Commonwealth was only required to prove, and did prove, that the firearm was designed, made, and intended to expel a projectile by means of an explosion, and not that the firearm was operable. Sprouse v. Commonwealth, No. 2438-03-2, 2005 Va. App. LEXIS 59 (Ct. of Appeals Feb. 8, 2005).

Applied in Jackson v. Commonwealth, 39 Va. App. 624, 576 S.E.2d 206, 2003 Va. App. LEXIS 37 (2003); Booker v. Commonwealth, 61 Va. App. 323, 734 S.E.2d 729, 2012 Va. App. LEXIS 407 (2012).

§ 18.2-308.5. Manufacture, import, sale, transfer or possession of plastic firearm prohibited.

It shall be unlawful for any person to manufacture, import, sell, transfer or possess any plastic firearm. As used in this section, *"plastic firearm"* means any firearm, including machine guns and sawed-off shotguns as defined in this chapter, containing less than 3.7 ounces of electromagnetically detectable metal in the barrel, slide, cylinder, frame or receiver of which, when subjected to inspection by X-ray machines commonly used at airports, does not generate an image that accurately depicts its shape. A violation of this section shall be punishable as a Class 5 felony.

History.
1989, c. 663; 2004, c. 995.

§ 18.2-308.6. Repealed by Acts 2009, c. 288, cl. 1.

§ 18.2-308.7. Possession or transportation of certain firearms by persons under the age of 18; penalty.

It shall be unlawful for any person under 18 years of age to knowingly and intentionally possess or transport a handgun or assault firearm anywhere in the Commonwealth. For the purposes of this section, "handgun" means any pistol or revolver or other firearm originally designed, made and intended to fire single or multiple projectiles by means of an explosion of a combustible material from one or more barrels when held in one hand and "assault firearm" means any (i) semi-automatic centerfire rifle or pistol which expels single or multiple projectiles by action of an explosion of a combustible material and is equipped at the time of the offense with a magazine which will hold more than 20 rounds of ammunition or designed by the manufacturer to accommodate a silencer or equipped with a folding stock or (ii) shotgun with a magazine which will hold more than seven rounds of the longest ammunition for which it is chambered. A violation of this section shall be a Class 1 misdemeanor.

This section shall not apply to:

1. Any person (i) while in his home or on his property; (ii) while in the home or on the property of his parent, grandparent, or legal guardian; or (iii) while on the property of another who has provided prior permission, and with the prior permission of his parent or legal guardian if the person has the landowner's written permission on his person while on such property;

2. Any person who, while accompanied by an adult, is at, or going to and from, a lawful shooting range or firearms educational class, provided that the weapons are unloaded while being transported;

3. Any person actually engaged in lawful hunting or going to and from a hunting area or preserve, provided that the weapons are unloaded while being transported; and

4. Any person while carrying out his duties in the Armed Forces of the United States or the National Guard of this Commonwealth or any other state.

History.
1993, cc. 467, 494; 2003, c. 976; 2004, c. 995.

§ 18.2-308.8. Importation, sale, possession or transfer of Striker 12's prohibited; penalty.

It shall be unlawful for any person to import, sell, possess or transfer the following firearms: the Striker 12, commonly called a *"streetsweeper,"* or any semi-automatic folding stock shotgun of like kind with a spring tension drum magazine capable of holding twelve shotgun shells. A violation of this section shall be punishable as a Class 6 felony.

History.
1993, c. 888.

The number of this section was assigned by the Virginia Code Commission, the number in the 1993 act having been 18.2-308.7.

Law Review.
For note, "Modern Police Practices: Arizona v. Gant's Illusory Restriction of Vehicle Searches Incident to Arrest," 97 Va. L. Rev. 1727 (2011).

§ 18.2-309. Furnishing certain weapons to minors; penalty.

A. If any person sells, barters, gives or furnishes, or causes to be sold, bartered, given or furnished, to any minor a dirk, switchblade knife or bowie knife, having good cause to believe him to be a minor, such person shall be guilty of a Class 1 misdemeanor.

B. If any person sells, barters, gives or furnishes, or causes to be sold, bartered, given or furnished, to any minor a handgun, having good cause to believe him to be a minor, such person shall be guilty of a Class 6 felony. This subsection shall not apply to any transfer made between family members or for the purpose of engaging in a sporting event or activity.

History.
Code 1950, § 18.1-344; 1960, c. 358; 1975, cc. 14, 15; 1992, c. 487; 1993, c. 855.

Michie's Jurisprudence.
For related discussion, see 9B M.J. Infants, § 89; 20 M.J. Weapons, § 12.

§ 18.2-310. Repealed by Acts 2004, c. 995.

Cross references.
For current provisions as to forfeiture of certain weapons used in commission of criminal offense, see § 19.2-386.29.

§ 18.2-311. Prohibiting the selling or having in possession blackjacks, etc.

If any person sells or barters, or exhibits for sale or for barter, or gives or furnishes, or causes to be sold, bartered, given or furnished, or has in his possession, or under his control, with the intent of selling, bartering, giving or furnishing, any blackjack, brass or metal knucks, any disc of whatever configuration having at least two points or pointed blades which is designed to be thrown or propelled and which may be known as a throwing star or oriental dart, switchblade knife, ballistic knife as defined in § 18.2-307.1, or like weapons, such person is guilty of a Class 4 misdemeanor. The having in one's possession of any such weapon shall be prima facie evidence, except in the case of a conservator of the peace, of his intent to sell, barter, give or furnish the same.

History.
Code 1950, § 18.1-271; 1960, c. 358; 1975, cc. 14, 15; 1985, c. 394; 1988, c. 359; 2013, c. 746.

Cross references.
As to sale, etc., of toy firearms, see § 18.2-284. As to sale, etc., of weapons to minors, see § 18.2-309.

Editor's note.
Acts 2013, c. 746, cl. 2 provides: "That the provisions of this act are declaratory of existing law."

The 2013 amendments.
The 2013 amendment by c. 746 substituted "ballistic knife as defined in § 18.2-307.1, or like weapons, such person is guilty" for "ballistic knife, or like weapons, such person shall be guilty" near the end of the first sentence.

§ 18.2-311.1. Removing, altering, etc., serial number or other identification on firearm.

Any person, firm, association or corporation who or which intentionally removes, defaces, alters, changes, destroys or obliterates in any manner or way or who or which causes to be removed, defaced, altered, changed, destroyed or obliterated in any manner or way the name of the maker, model, manufacturer's or serial number, or any other mark or identification on any pistol, shotgun, rifle, machine gun or any other firearm shall be guilty of a Class 1 misdemeanor.

History.
1975, c. 590.

Law Review.
For survey of Virginia criminal law and procedure for the year 2004-2005, see 40 U. Rich. L. Rev. 197 (2005).

CASE NOTES

Venue. — Defendant's conviction of altering the serial number of a firearm in violation of § 18.2-311.1 was reversed; as there was no evidence he removed the serial number in Brunswick County, the Commonwealth failed to meet its burden under § 19.2-244 to show that venue was proper in that county. Bonner v. Commonwealth, 61 Va. App. 247, 734 S.E.2d 692, 2012 Va. App. LEXIS 399 (2012).

As the offense of altering or removing a serial number of a firearm, § 18.2-311.1, constitutes a discrete act rather than a continuing offense, under § 19.2-244, venue is proper where the alteration or removal was done. Bonner v. Commonwealth, 61 Va. App. 247, 734 S.E.2d 692, 2012 Va. App. LEXIS 399 (2012).

§ 18.2-311.2. Third conviction of firearm offenses; penalty.

On a third or subsequent conviction of any offense contained in Article 4, 5, 6, or 7 of Chapter 7 (§ 18.2-247 et seq.) of Title 18.2, which would ordinarily be punished as a Class 1 misdemeanor, where it is alleged in the information or indictment on which the person is convicted, that (i) such person has been twice previously convicted of a violation of any Class 1 misdemeanor or felony offense contained in either Article 4, 5, 6, or 7 of Chapter 7 of Title 18.2 or § 18.2-53.1, or of a substantially similar offense under the law of any other jurisdiction of the United States, and (ii) each such violation occurred on a different date, such person shall be guilty of a Class 6 felony.

History.
1994, c. 731.

ARTICLE 8.

MISCELLANEOUS DANGEROUS CONDUCT.

§ 18.2-312. Illegal use of tear gas, phosgene and other gases.

If any person maliciously release or cause or procure to be released in any private home, place of business or place of public gathering any tear gas, mustard gas, phosgene gas or other noxious or nauseating gases or mixtures of chemicals designed to, and capable of, producing vile or injurious or nauseating odors or gases, and bodily injury results to any person from such gas or odor, the offending person shall be guilty of a Class 3 felony.

If such act be done unlawfully, but not maliciously, the offending person shall be guilty of a Class 6 felony.

Nothing herein contained shall prevent the use of tear gas or other gases by police officers or other peace officers in the proper performance of their duties, or by any person or persons in the protection of person, life or property.

History.
Code 1950, § 18.1-70; 1960, c. 358; 1975, cc. 14, 15.

Law Review.
For survey of Virginia criminal law for the year 1974-1975, see 61 Va. L. Rev. 1697 (1975).

CASE NOTES

Construction. — When defendant sprayed a store manager with mace on the sidewalk between the front of the store and the store's parking lot, he violated the statute by discharging a noxious gas in a place of public gathering. Bolton v. Commonwealth, 36 Va. App. 358, 550 S.E.2d 342, 2001 Va. App. LEXIS 477 (2001).

§ 18.2-313. Handling or using snakes so as to endanger human life or health.

It shall be unlawful for any person, or persons, to display, exhibit, handle or use any poisonous or dangerous snake or reptile in such a manner as to endanger the life or health of any person.

Any person violating the provisions of this section shall be guilty of a Class 4 misdemeanor.

History.
Code 1950, § 18.1-72; 1960, c. 358; 1975, cc. 14, 15.

Law Review.
For comment on state's power to require an individual to protect himself, see 26 Wash. & Lee L. Rev. 112 (1969).

§ 18.2-313.1. Withholding information about possibly rabid animal; penalty.

It shall be unlawful for any person to (i) knowingly withhold information from, or knowingly give false information to, any lawfully authorized governmental agent which would reasonably lead to the discovery or location and capture of any animal reasonably identifiable as one that has potentially exposed a human being to rabies; (ii) upon the request of an animal control officer, a law-enforcement officer, or an official of the Department of Health, willfully fail to grant access to any animal owned, harbored, or kept by that person that is suspected of having caused a rabies exposure to a human being; or (iii) upon notice by an animal control officer, a law-enforcement officer, or an official of the Department of Health, willfully fail to comply with a confinement, isolation, or quarantine order.

Any person violating the provisions of this section shall be guilty of a Class 2 misdemeanor.

History.
1989, c. 491; 2010, c. 834.

The 2010 amendments.
The 2010 amendment by c. 834, in the first paragraph, inserted the clause (i) designation and therein substituted "that has potentially exposed a human being to rabies" for "which has bitten a human being," and added clauses (ii) and (iii).

Michie's Jurisprudence.
For related discussion, see 1B M.J. Animals, § 10.

§ 18.2-313.2. Introduction of snakehead fish or zebra mussel; penalty.

Any person who knowingly introduces into the Commonwealth any snakehead fish of the family Channidae, or knowingly places or causes to be placed into state waters any zebra mussel (Dreissena polymorpha) or the larvae thereof, without a permit from the Director of Game and Inland Fisheries issued pursuant to § 29.1-575 is guilty of a Class 1 misdemeanor.

History.
2005, c. 916.

§ 18.2-314. Failing to secure medical attention for injured child.

Any parent or other person having custody of a minor child which child shows evidence of need for medical attention as the result of physical injury inflicted by an act of any member of the household, whether the injury was intentional or unintentional, who knowingly fails or refuses to secure prompt and adequate medical attention, or who conspires to prevent the securing of such attention, for such minor child, shall be guilty of a Class 1 misdemeanor; provided, however, that any parent or other person having custody of a minor child that is being furnished Christian Science treatment by a duly accredited Christian Science practitioner shall not, for that reason alone, be considered in violation of this section.

History.
Code 1950, § 18.1-74.2; 1966, c. 578; 1975, cc. 14, 15.

Cross references.
For definition of "barrier crime" as including a conviction of failure to secure medical attention for an injured child as set out in § 18.2-314, or an equivalent offense in another state, and prohibition against assisted living facilities, adult day care centers or child welfare agencies hiring for certain compensated employment persons who have committed such an offense, see §§ 63.2-1719, 63.2-1720. As to report to children's residential facility for which a background check is being performed on whether the applicant has ever been convicted of or is the subject of pending charges for various crimes, including failure to secure medical attention for an injured child as set out in § 18.2-314, or an equivalent offense in another state, see § 63.2-1726.

§ 18.2-315. Repealed by Acts 1980, c. 173.

§ 18.2-316. Duty of persons causing well or pit to be dug to fill it before abandonment.

Any person who has caused to be dug on his own land or the land of another any well or pit, shall fill such well or pit with earth so that the same shall not be dangerous to human beings, animals or fowls before such well or such pit is abandoned; and any person owning land whereon any such well or pit is located shall in the same manner fill with earth any such well or pit which has been abandoned, provided such person has knowledge of the existence of such well or pit.

But in the case of mining operations in lieu of filling the shaft or pit the owner or operator thereof on ceasing operations in such shaft or pit shall securely fence the same and keep the same at all times thereafter securely fenced.

Any person violating any provision of this section shall be deemed guilty of a Class 3 misdemeanor.

History.
Code 1950, § 18.1-73; 1960, c. 358; 1975, cc. 14, 15.

Michie's Jurisprudence.
For related discussion, see 1A M.J. Abandonment, § 1; 13B M.J. Negligence, § 16.

CASE NOTES

A "well," as the term is commonly used, means a cylindrical shaft of a relatively small diameter. Certainly, an excavation covering three-fourths of an acre is not within the commonly accepted definition of a well. Polesky v. Northern Va. Constr. Co., 196 Va. 532, 84 S.E.2d 443 (1954).

Second paragraph applies only to persons engaged in mining operations. — The provision in the second paragraph of this section requiring the fencing of an abandoned "shaft or pit" applies only to one engaged in "mining operations." Polesky v. Northern Va. Constr. Co., 196 Va. 532, 84 S.E.2d 443 (1954).

Section held inapplicable. — Plaintiff sued for the wrongful death of her twelve-year-old son who drowned in water which had collected in an abandoned hole where defendant had dug sand and gravel. Her action was predicated on a violation of this section. This section, however, has no application to an excavation of the size of defendant's, which covered nearly an acre. Therefore the trial court correctly dismissed the action. Polesky v. Northern Va. Constr. Co., 196 Va. 532, 84 S.E.2d 443 (1954).

§ 18.2-317. Covers to be kept on certain wells.

Every person owning or occupying any land on which there is a well having a diameter greater than six inches and which is more than ten feet deep shall at all times keep the same covered in such a manner as not to be dangerous to human beings, animals or fowls.

Any person violating the provisions of this section shall be guilty of a Class 3 misdemeanor.

History.
Code 1950, § 18.1-74; 1960, c. 358; 1975, cc. 14, 15.

§ 18.2-318. Authority of counties, cities and towns to require and regulate well covers.

Notwithstanding the provisions of § 18.2-317, the governing body of any county, city or town may adopt ordinances requiring persons owning or occupying any land within such county, city or town on which there is a well having a diameter greater than six inches and which is more than ten feet deep to keep the same covered in such a manner as not to be dangerous to human beings, animals or fowls.

Any such ordinance may specify and require reasonable minimum standards for the construction, installation and maintenance of such covers, including the manner in which any concrete used in connection therewith shall be reinforced, and may prescribe punishment for violations not inconsistent with general law.

History.
Code 1950, § 18.1-74.1; 1962, c. 525; 1975, cc. 14, 15.

§ 18.2-319. Discarding or abandoning iceboxes, etc.; precautions required.

It shall be unlawful for any person, firm or corporation to discard, abandon, leave or allow to remain in any place any icebox, refrigerator or other container, device or equipment of any kind with an interior storage area of more than two cubic feet of clear space which is airtight, without first removing the door or doors or hinges from such icebox, refrigerator, container, device or equipment.

This section shall not apply to any icebox, refrigerator, container, device or equipment which is being used for the purpose for which it was originally designed, or is being used for display purposes by any retail or wholesale merchant, or is crated, strapped or locked to such an extent that it is impossible for a child to obtain access to any airtight compartment thereof.

Any violation of the provisions of this section shall be punishable as a Class 3 misdemeanor.

History.
Code 1950, § 18.1-415; 1960, c. 358; 1975, cc. 14, 15.

Michie's Jurisprudence.
For related discussion, see 1A M.J. Abandonment, § 1.

§ 18.2-320. Sale, etc., of plastic bags; warning required.

(a) No person shall sell, offer for sale, or deliver, or offer for delivery, or give away any plastic bag or partial plastic bag intended to enclose freshly cleaned clothing, the length of which totals twenty-five inches or more and the material of which is less than one mil (1/1000 inch) in thickness; unless such plastic bag bears the following warning statement, or a warning statement which the Commissioner of Health has approved as the equivalent thereof:

"WARNING: To avoid danger of suffocation, keep this plastic bag away from babies and children. Do not use this bag in cribs, beds, carriages or playpens."

(b) Such warning statement shall be imprinted in a prominent place on the plastic bag or shall appear on a label securely attached to the bag in a promi-

nent place, and shall be printed in legible type of at least thirty-six point type.

(c) Violators of this section shall be guilty of a Class 3 misdemeanor.

History.
Code 1950, § 18.1-415.1; 1968, c. 340; 1975, cc. 14, 15.

§ 18.2-321. Using X ray, fluoroscope, etc., in the fitting of footwear.

It shall be unlawful for any person to use any X ray, fluoroscope, or other equipment or apparatus employing roentgen rays, in the fitting of shoes or other footwear. This section shall not apply to any licensed physician or surgeon in the practice of his profession. Any person violating the provisions of this section shall be guilty of a Class 3 misdemeanor.

History.
Code 1950, § 18.1-416; 1960, c. 358; 1975, cc. 14, 15.

§ 18.2-322. Expectorating in public places.

No person shall spit, expectorate, or deposit any sputum, saliva, mucus, or any form of saliva or sputum upon the floor, stairways, or upon any part of any public building or place where the public assemble, or upon the floor of any part of any public conveyance, or upon any sidewalk abutting on any public street, alley or lane of any town or city.

Any person violating any provision of this section shall be guilty of a Class 4 misdemeanor.

History.
Code 1950, § 32-69; 1975, cc. 14, 15.

§ 18.2-322.1. Repealed by Acts 1997, c. 391.

§ 18.2-323. Leaving disabled or dead animal in road, or allowing dead animal to remain unburied.

If any person cast any dead animal into a road or knowingly permit any dead animal to remain unburied upon his property when offensive to the public or, having in custody any maimed, diseased, disabled or infirm animal, leave it to lie or be in a street, road or public place, he shall be guilty of a Class 3 misdemeanor.

History.
Code 1950, § 32-70.1; 1958, c. 548; 1970, c. 72; 1975, cc. 14, 15.

§ 18.2-323.01. Prohibition against disposal of dead body; penalty.

It shall be unlawful for any person to dispose of a dead body as defined in § 32.1-249 (i) on private property without the written permission of the landowner or (ii) on public property.

A violation of this section shall be punishable as a Class 1 misdemeanor.

History.
1992, c. 883.

§ 18.2-323.02. Prohibition against concealment of dead body; penalty.

Any person who transports, secretes, conceals or alters a dead body, as defined in § 32.1-249, with malicious intent and to prevent detection of an unlawful act or to prevent the detection of the death or the manner or cause of death is guilty of a Class 6 felony.

History.
2007, c. 436.

§ 18.2-323.1. Drinking while operating a motor vehicle; possession of open container while operating a motor vehicle and presumption; penalty.

A. It shall be unlawful for any person to consume an alcoholic beverage while driving a motor vehicle upon a public highway of this Commonwealth.

B. A rebuttable presumption that the driver has consumed an alcoholic beverage in violation of this section shall be created if (i) an open container is located within the passenger area of the motor vehicle, (ii) the alcoholic beverage in the open container has been at least partially removed and (iii) the appearance, conduct, odor of alcohol, speech or other physical characteristic of the driver of the motor vehicle may be reasonably associated with the consumption of an alcoholic beverage.

For the purposes of this section:

"Open container" means any vessel containing an alcoholic beverage, except the originally sealed manufacturer's container.

"Passenger area" means the area designed to seat the driver of any motor vehicle, any area within the reach of the driver, including an unlocked glove compartment, and the area designed to seat passengers. This term shall not include the trunk of any passenger vehicle, the area behind the last upright seat of a passenger van, station wagon, hatchback, sport utility vehicle or any similar vehicle, the living quarters of a motor home, or the passenger area of a motor vehicle designed, maintained or used primarily for the transportation of persons for compensation, including a bus, taxi, or limousine, while engaged in the transportation of such persons.

C. A violation of this section is punishable as a Class 4 misdemeanor.

History.
1989, c. 343; 2002, c. 890.

Law Review.
For article surveying developments in criminal law and procedure in Virginia from July 2001 to September 2002, see 37 U. Rich. L. Rev. 45 (2002).

Michie's Jurisprudence.
For related discussion, see 2B M.J. Automobiles, § 118.

CASE NOTES

Relationship with offense of driving under the influence. — Where the presence of an open container of alcohol and defendant's appearance gave rise to a rebuttable presumption that defendant consumed alcohol while driving, the fact that an officer did not perceive defendant to be drunk or driving under the influence did not negate the presumption because a driver did not have to be intoxicated to the extent necessary to support a conviction under § 18.2-266 in order to be found guilty of drinking while operating a motor vehicle in violation of § 18.2-323.1. United States v. Washington, 439 F. Supp. 2d 589, 2006 U.S. Dist. LEXIS 52064 (E.D. Va. 2006), aff'd, 2009 U.S. App. LEXIS 16364 (4th Cir. Va. 2009).

Open container and defendant's appearance justified vehicle search. — Officer who observed a partially empty bottle of alcohol inside defendant's vehicle during a traffic stop did not violate the Fourth Amendment by retrieving the bottle because the presence of the open container of alcohol combined with the officer's observation that defendant's eyes were watery and bloodshot and that defendant's hands were shaking gave rise to a rebuttable presumption that defendant consumed alcohol while driving. United States v. Washington, 439 F. Supp. 2d 589, 2006 U.S. Dist. LEXIS 52064 (E.D. Va. 2006), aff'd, 2009 U.S. App. LEXIS 16364 (4th Cir. Va. 2009).

§ 18.2-324. Throwing or depositing certain substances upon highway; removal of such substances.

No person shall throw or deposit or cause to be deposited upon any highway any glass bottle, glass, nail, tack, wire, can, or any other substance likely to injure any person or animal, or damage any vehicle upon such highway, nor shall any person throw or deposit or cause to be deposited upon any highway any soil, sand, mud, gravel or other substances so as to create a hazard to the traveling public. Any person who drops, or permits to be dropped or thrown, upon any highway any destructive, hazardous or injurious material shall immediately remove the same or cause it to be removed. Any person removing a wrecked or damaged vehicle from a highway shall remove any glass or other injurious substance dropped upon the highway from such vehicle. Any persons violating the provisions of this section shall be guilty of a Class 1 misdemeanor.

This section shall not apply to the use, by a law-enforcement officer while in the discharge of official duties, of any device designed to deflate tires. The Division of Purchase and Supply shall, pursuant to § 2.2-1112, set minimum standards for such devices and shall give notice of such standards to law-enforcement offices in the Commonwealth. No such device shall be used which does not meet or exceed the standards.

History.
Code 1950, § 33.1-350; 1970, c. 322; 1975, cc. 14, 15; 1997, c. 136.

CASE NOTES

Applied in Coleman v. Blankenship Oil Corp., 221 Va. 124, 267 S.E.2d 143 (1980).

§ 18.2-324.1. Punishment for violation of §§ 55-298.1 through 55-298.5, relating to electric fences.

The violation of any provision of §§ 55-298.1 through 55-298.5 shall constitute a Class 1 misdemeanor.

History.

Code 1950, § 8-868.2; 1960, c. 384; 1977, c. 624.

CHAPTER 8.
CRIMES INVOLVING MORALS AND DECENCY.

Article 1. Gambling.

ARTICLE 1.

GAMBLING.

Michie's Jurisprudence.

For related discussion, see 9A M.J. Gaming and Gaming Contracts, §§ 2 - 6, 8 - 10, 12, 3, 19; 9B M.J. Horse and Dog Racing, § 1; 12A M.J. Lotteries, §§ 2, 4.

§ 18.2-325. Definitions.

1. "Illegal gambling" means the making, placing or receipt of any bet or wager in the Commonwealth of money or other thing of value, made in exchange for a chance to win a prize, stake or other consideration or thing of value, dependent upon the result of any game, contest or any other event the outcome of which is uncertain or a matter of chance, whether such game, contest or event occurs or is to occur inside or outside the limits of the Commonwealth.

For the purposes of this subdivision and notwithstanding any provision in this section to the contrary, the making, placing, or receipt of any bet or wager of money or other thing of value shall include the purchase of a product, Internet access, or other thing, which purchase credits the purchaser with free points or other measurable units that may be (i) risked by the purchaser for an opportunity to win additional points or other measurable units that are redeemable by the purchaser for money or (ii) redeemed by the purchaser for money, and but for the free points or other measurable units, with regard to clauses (i) and (ii), the purchase of the product, Internet access, or other thing (a) would be of insufficient value in and of itself to justify the purchase or (b) is merely incidental to the chance to win money.

2. "Interstate gambling" means the conduct of an enterprise for profit which engages in the purchase or sale within the Commonwealth of any interest in a lottery of another state or country whether or not such interest is an actual lottery ticket, receipt, contingent promise to pay, order to purchase, or other record of such interest.

3. "Gambling device" includes:

a. Any device, machine, paraphernalia, equipment, or other thing, including books, records and other papers, which are actually used in an illegal gambling operation or activity, and

b. Any machine, apparatus, implement, instrument, contrivance, board or other thing, or electronic or video versions thereof, including but not limited to those dependent upon the insertion of a coin or other object for their operation, which operates, either completely automatically or with the aid of some physical act by the player or operator, in such a manner that, depending upon elements of chance, it may eject something of value or determine the prize or other thing of value to which the player is entitled; provided, however, that the return to the user of nothing more than additional chances or the right to use such machine is not deemed something of value within the meaning of this subsection; and provided further, that machines that only sell, or entitle the user to, items of merchandise of equivalent value that may differ from each other in composition, size, shape or color, shall not be deemed gambling devices within the meaning of this subsection.

Such devices are no less gambling devices if they indicate beforehand the definite result of one or more operations but not all the operations. Nor are they any less a gambling device because, apart from their use or adaptability as such, they may also sell or deliver something of value on a basis other than chance.

4. "Operator" includes any person, firm or association of persons, who conducts, finances, manages, supervises, directs or owns all or part of an illegal gambling enterprise, activity or operation.

History.
1975, cc. 14, 15; 1992, c. 423; 2010, c. 877; 2011, cc. 879, 887.

Cross references.
As to witnesses in prosecutions for gaming, see § 18.2-337. As to recovery back of gaming losses, see §§ 11-14 through 11-16.

Editor's note.
Acts 2010, c. 877, cl. 2 provides: "That the provisions of this act are declaratory of existing law."

Acts 2011, cc. 879 and 887, cl. 3 provides: "That the provisions of this act may result in a net increase in periods of imprisonment or commitment. Pursuant to § 30-19.1:4, the estimated amount of the necessary appropriation is $0 for periods of imprisonment in state adult correctional facilities and is $0 for periods of commitment to the custody of the Department of Juvenile Justice."

The 2010 amendments.
The 2010 amendment by c. 877 added subdivisions 1 a and 1 b and made minor stylistic changes.

The 2011 amendments.
The 2011 amendments by cc. 879 and 887 are identical, and deleted the a designation from the second paragraph of subdivision 1, and in the second paragraph of subdivision 1, inserted "Internet access, or other thing," added clause (i) designator, and added clause (ii); deleted subdivision 1 b which read: "Nothing in this section shall be construed or interpreted to prohibit the conduct of any lawful game, contest, lottery, scheme, or promotional offering that complies with the requirements contained in § 18.2-325.1"; and inserted "or electronic or video versions thereof" in subdivision 3 b.

Law Review.
For annual survey article, "Local Government Law," see 46 U. Rich. L. Rev. 175 (2011).

CASE NOTES

What are bets. — While a bet implies a risk, it does not necessarily imply risk in both parties. There must be between them a chance of gain and a chance of loss; but it does not follow that each of the parties to the bet must have both these chances. Shumate v. Commonwealth, 56 Va. (15 Gratt.) 653 (1860).

"Conducts, finances, manages, supervises, directs, or owns," as used in subdivision (3) [now subdivision 4], construed. — See Turner v. Commonwealth, 226 Va. 456, 309 S.E.2d 337 (1983).

The phrase "all or part of" in the definition of "operator" is intended to bring within the sweep of the statute a co-commander, co-leader, or co-manager. It is not intended as a mechanism for bootstrapping a defendant who played no leadership role in the operation into one who did. The phrase simply means that where there is proof that a defendant played even a partial leadership role in the illegal gambling enterprise then he can be convicted under § 18.2-328. Turner v. Commonwealth, 226 Va. 456, 309 S.E.2d 337 (1983).

"Bagman" in numbers operation held not to be an "operator." — See Turner v. Commonwealth, 226 Va. 456, 309 S.E.2d 337 (1983).

Section not applicable to ticket purchases made outside Virginia. — Because of the "lag time" necessary to assure that the agents in other states could purchase the foreign lottery tickets and return them to Virginia prior to the drawing, all orders were for prospective, not present, wagers; therefore, a wager did not occur until the agents purchased the lottery tickets, and since those purchases occurred outside the Commonwealth of Virginia, § 18.2-330 and this section, as then in force, were inapplicable. Chavis v. Commonwealth, No. 1547-92-2 (Ct. of Appeals Feb. 15, 1994).

Pull-tab cards were "gambling devices." — Pull-tab cards which required a purchasing player to match symbols in perforated windows in order to be a "winner" were "gambling devices" within the meaning of this section. Virginia ABC Bd. v. VFW Ocean View Post-3160, 10 Va. App. 165, 390 S.E.2d 202 (1990).

Applied in Daniels v. Mobley, 285 Va. 402, 737 S.E.2d 895, 2013 Va. LEXIS 27 (2013).

OPINIONS OF THE ATTORNEY GENERAL

Poker tournaments. — Questions whether poker tournament and related business activities constitute gambling and whether the office of the Commissioner of the Revenue should issue business licenses authorizing such activities and whether admissions and other taxes should be assessed and collected in connection therewith require factual determinations. See opinion of Attorney General to The Honorable Franklin D. Edmondson, Commissioner of the Revenue for the City of Portsmouth, 07-084 (1/22/08).

The element of consideration is missing, and therefore no illegal gambling occurs, when the opportunity to win a prize is offered both with a purchase and without the requirement of a purchase. See opinion of Attorney General to The Honorable Bill Janis, Member, House of Delegates, 10-064, 2010 Va. AG LEXIS 41 (7/30/10).

Whether scenarios involving charitable donations at computer terminals, political contributions made from computers in business establishments, or sale of prepaid, rechargeable telephone card and/or computer work station time constitute legal sweepstakes or illegal gambling, depends on whether the element of consideration is missing. The question is whether the sweepstakes is the product, i.e., individuals are paying to participate in a game of chance, or whether it is a charitable donation, political contribution or marketing tool. See opinion of Attorney General to The Honorable G. Manoli Loupassi, Member, House of Delegates, 11-086, 2011 Va. AG LEXIS 58 (8/12/11).

Illegal gambling. — Hypothetical examples that center on payment of money in exchange for a product, such as a phone card or a DVD, where the product offered to the consumer is not in fact the object of the transaction, instead, the consumer disregards the item "purchased" and seeks the opportunity to play a game of chance in order to win prizes or money, would constitute illegal gambling because the elements of prize, chance and consideration are present. See opinion of Attorney General to The Honorable R.

Edward Houck, Member, Senate of Virginia, 10-095, 2010 Va. AG LEXIS 60 (10/15/10).

§ 18.2-325.1. Repealed by Acts 2011, cc. 879 and 887, cl. 2.

Editor's note.

Former § 18.2-325.1, pertaining to lawful games, contests, etc.; methods of entry; and requirements, derived from Acts 2010, c. 877.

§ 18.2-326. Penalty for illegal gambling.

Except as otherwise provided in this article, any person who illegally gambles or engages in interstate gambling as defined in § 18.2-325 shall be guilty of a Class 3 misdemeanor. If an association or pool of persons illegally gamble, each person therein shall be guilty of illegal gambling.

However, if any person makes, places, or receives any bet or wager of money or other thing of value on a horse race in the Commonwealth, whether the race is inside or outside the limits of the Commonwealth at any place or through any means other than (i) at a racetrack licensed by the Virginia Racing Commission pursuant to Chapter 29 (§ 59.1-364 et seq.) of Title 59.1 or (ii) at a satellite facility or through advance deposit account wagering, as those terms are defined in § 59.1-365, licensed by the Virginia Racing Commission pursuant to Chapter 29 (§ 59.1-364 et seq.) of Title 59.1, such person shall be guilty of a Class 1 misdemeanor. For the purposes of this paragraph, venue shall be in any county or city in which any act was performed in furtherance of any course of conduct constituting illegal gambling.

History.

Code 1950, § 18.1-316; 1960, c. 358; 1973, c. 463; 1975, cc. 14, 15; 1992, c. 423; 2011, c. 732.

Editor's note.

Acts 2011, c. 732, cl. 2, provides: "That the Virginia Racing Commission shall promulgate regulations to implement the provisions of this act to be effective within 280 days of its enactment."

The 2011 amendments.

The 2011 amendment by c. 732 added the second paragraph.

CASE NOTES

Application. — There was sufficient proof that through his activities, defendant knowingly aided and abetted the illegal gambling among spectators of the cockfighting operation, and insomuch as § 18.2-326 made gambling on cockfighting illegal, and thus encompassed within 18 U.S.C.S. § 1955(b)(1), defendant's statutory argument failed; although § 18.2-333 clarified that participants in a contest of skill, where they may win a prize or purse, were not guilty of gambling, nothing in that made it lawful for any person to wager on the outcome of such events. United States v. Kingrea, 567 F.3d 119, 2009 U.S. App. LEXIS 11505 (4th Cir. 2009).

Malum prohibitum. — In this State gambling is mala prohibita. Parr v. Commonwealth, 198 Va. 721, 96 S.E.2d 160 (1957).

Gambling is not an offense at common law. Parr v. Commonwealth, 198 Va. 721, 96 S.E.2d 160 (1957).

It is unlawful to bet at any game at a public place. Neal v. Commonwealth, 63 Va. (22 Gratt.) 917 (1872).

Applied in Turner v. Commonwealth, 226 Va. 456, 309 S.E.2d

337 (1983); Resorts Int'l Hotel, Inc. v. Agresta, 569 F. Supp. 24 (E.D. Va. 1983).

OPINIONS OF THE ATTORNEY GENERAL

The element of consideration is missing, and therefore no illegal gambling occurs, when the opportunity to win a prize is offered both with a purchase and without the requirement of a purchase. See opinion of Attorney General to The Honorable Bill Janis, Member, House of Delegates, 10-064, 2010 Va. AG LEXIS 41 (7/30/10).

Whether scenarios involving charitable donations at computer terminals, political contributions made from computers in business establishments, or sale of prepaid, rechargeable telephone card and/or computer work station time constitute legal sweepstakes or illegal gambling, depends on whether the element of consideration is missing. The question is whether the sweepstakes is the product, i.e., individuals are paying to participate in a game of chance, or whether it is a charitable donation, political contribution or marketing tool. See opinion of Attorney General to The Honorable G. Manoli Loupassi, Member, House of Delegates, 11-086, 2011 Va. AG LEXIS 58 (8/12/11).

Illegal gambling. — Hypothetical examples that center on payment of money in exchange for a product, such as a phone card or a DVD, where the product offered to the consumer is not in fact the object of the transaction, instead, the consumer disregards the item "purchased" and seeks the opportunity to play a game of chance in order to win prizes or money, would constitute illegal gambling because the elements of prize, chance and consideration are present. See opinion of Attorney General to The Honorable R. Edward Houck, Member, Senate of Virginia, 10-095, 2010 Va. AG LEXIS 60 (10/15/10).

§ 18.2-327. Winning by fraud; penalty.

If any person while gambling cheats or by fraudulent means wins or acquires for himself or another money or any other valuable thing, he shall be fined not less than five nor more than ten times the value of such winnings. This penalty shall be in addition to any other penalty imposed under this article.

History.

Code 1950, § 18.1-318; 1960, c. 358; 1975, cc. 14, 15.

§ 18.2-328. Conducting illegal gambling operation; penalties.

The operator of an illegal gambling enterprise, activity or operation shall be guilty of a Class 6 felony. However, any such operator who engages in an illegal gambling operation which (i) has been or remains in substantially continuous operation for a period in excess of thirty days or (ii) has gross revenue of $2,000 or more in any single day shall be fined not more than $20,000 and imprisoned not less than one year nor more than ten years.

As used in this section, the term *"gross revenue"* means the total amount of illegal gambling transactions handled, dealt with, received by or placed with such operation, as distinguished from any net figure or amount from which deductions are taken, without regard to whether money or any other thing of value actually changes hands.

History.

Code 1950, § 18.1-318.1; 1972, c. 364; 1975, cc. 14, 15; 1983, c. 331.

CASE NOTES

Constitutionality. — Even if the definition of illegal gambling in § 18.2-325 was "read" as not having an exception for games of skill, § 18.2-333 provided that skill be considered in determining whether § 18.2-328 had been violated. The ruling of the circuit court concerning § 18.2-325 could not have rendered an otherwise valid § 18.2-328 void for vagueness. Daniels v. Mobley, 285 Va. 402, 737 S.E.2d 895, 2013 Va. LEXIS 27 (2013).

Legislative intent. — The General Assembly intended to allow the Commonwealth to elect to charge a defendant with multiple counts of violating this section, where the evidence proves that the statute was violated at separate and distinct times. Dingus v. Commonwealth, 23 Va. App. 382, 477 S.E.2d 303 (1996).

Construction. — While this section is penal in nature and must be strictly construed and any ambiguity as to its meaning resolved in the defendant's favor, that does not mean that the defendant is entitled to a favorable result based on an unreasonably restrictive interpretation of the Code. Dingus v. Commonwealth, 23 Va. App. 382, 477 S.E.2d 303 (1996).

This section is in pari materia with several other provisions on gambling, which calls into play the rule of construction that statutes relating to the same subject should be read and construed together. Turner v. Commonwealth, 226 Va. 456, 309 S.E.2d 337 (1983).

Defendant need not be only person in charge. — In order to bring defendant within the ambit of this section it was not necessary to show that he was the only person in charge. The statute was intended to bring within its sweep a co-commander, co-leader, or co-manager; moreover, where there is proof that a defendant played even a partial leadership role in the illegal gambling enterprise then he can be convicted under this section. Walton v. Commonwealth, No. 0388-85 (Ct. of Appeals Nov. 12, 1986).

"Bagman" in numbers operation held not to be an "operator." — See Turner v. Commonwealth, 226 Va. 456, 309 S.E.2d 337 (1983).

Proof requirements. — To convict under this section, the Commonwealth need only prove that the defendant operated an illegal gambling enterprise, activity or operation. Dingus v. Commonwealth, 23 Va. App. 382, 477 S.E.2d 303 (1996).

Evidence of leadership role in gambling operation. — Evidence that defendant arranged to lease the building where the gambling occurred, made the necessary renovations to the building, paid the monthly rent, handled the "overhead" for the club, gave instructions to handlers of the house money and personally handled and collected money from the dice games, showed that defendant played a leadership or management role in the gambling operation and the trier of fact could properly have found beyond a reasonable doubt that defendant actively conducted, managed, supervised or directed all or part of the gambling enterprise. Walton v. Commonwealth, No. 0388-85 (Ct. of Appeals Nov. 12, 1986).

Sports publications were hearsay evidence. — Where sports publications were admitted into evidence to show that the betting sheets written by defendant corresponded with the season's football and basketball schedules and win-loss records, the publications were hearsay and did not fall within any recognized exception to the hearsay rule, and the trial court erred in admitting them. Papuchis v. Commonwealth, 15 Va. App. 281, 422 S.E.2d 419 (1992).

Sufficiency of evidence. — Where the evidence was examined without the improperly admitted taped telephone conversation, the evidence was insufficient to show that the defendant was operating a gambling enterprise, as no physical evidence was identified by the expert witness linking the defendant to the illegal activity in the house. Snead v. Commonwealth, 4 Va. App. 493, 358 S.E.2d 750 (1987).

Applied in Turner v. Commonwealth, 226 Va. 456, 309 S.E.2d 337 (1983); Resorts Int'l Hotel, Inc. v. Agresta, 569 F. Supp. 24 (E.D. Va. 1983).

OPINIONS OF THE ATTORNEY GENERAL

Illegal gambling. — Hypothetical examples that center on payment of money in exchange for a product, such as a phone card or a DVD, where the product offered to the consumer is not in fact the object of the transaction, instead, the consumer disregards the item "purchased" and seeks the opportunity to play a game of chance in order to win prizes or money, would constitute illegal gambling because the elements of prize, chance and consideration are present. See opinion of Attorney General to The Honorable R. Edward Houck, Member, Senate of Virginia, 10-095, 2010 Va. AG LEXIS 60 (10/15/10).

§ 18.2-329. Owners, etc., of gambling place permitting its continuance; penalty.

If the owner, lessee, tenant, occupant or other person in control of any place or conveyance, knows, or reasonably should know, that it is being used for illegal gambling, and permits such gambling to continue without having notified a law-enforcement officer of the presence of such illegal gambling activity, he shall be guilty of a Class 1 misdemeanor.

History.
Code 1950, §§ 18.1-319, 18.1-324, 18.1-337, 18.1-339; 1960, c. 358; 1968, c. 401; 1975, cc. 14, 15.

§ 18.2-330. Accessories to gambling activity; penalty.

Any person, firm or association of persons, other than those persons specified in other sections of this article, who knowingly aids, abets or assists in the operation of an illegal gambling enterprise, activity or operation, shall be guilty of a Class 1 misdemeanor.

History.
Code 1950, §§ 18.1-319, 18.1-325; 1960, c. 358; 1968, c. 401; 1975, cc. 14, 15; 1984, c. 625.

Cross references.
As to gaming contracts being void, see § 11-14.

CASE NOTES

Section not applicable to ticket purchases made outside Virginia. — Because of the "lag time" necessary to assure that the agents in other states could purchase the foreign lottery tickets and return them to Virginia prior to the drawing, all orders were for prospective, not present, wagers; therefore, a wager did not occur until the agents purchased the lottery tickets, and since those purchases occurred outside the Commonwealth of Virginia, § 18.2-325 and this section, as then in force, were inapplicable. Chavis v. Commonwealth, No. 1547-92-2 (Ct. of Appeals Feb. 15, 1994).

Applied in Turner v. Commonwealth, 226 Va. 456, 309 S.E.2d 337 (1983).

§ 18.2-331. Illegal possession, etc., of gambling device; penalty.

A person is guilty of illegal possession of a gambling device when he manufactures, sells, transports, rents, gives away, places or possesses, or conducts or negotiates any transaction affecting or designed to affect ownership, custody or use of any gambling device, believing or having reason to believe that the same is to be used in the advancement of unlawful gambling activity. Violation of any provision of this section shall constitute a Class 1 misdemeanor.

History.

Code 1950, §§ 18.1-323, 18.1-329, 18.1-330; 1960, c. 358; 1962, c. 633; 1964, c. 371; 1975, cc. 14, 15.

CASE NOTES

Gambling device illustrated. — A slot machine operated by the player depositing a nickel or token and then turning a crank, whereupon the machine will automatically pay a reward, which will always contain a package of mint of the retail value of five cents and sometimes in addition thereto one or more tokens which may be used in playing the machine, is a gambling device within the meaning of this section against slot machines, though by means of an indicator the player was informed as to what the machine will play before each play but there is no method of knowing what the reward will be as to subsequent plays. Ferris v. Jones, 13 Va. L. Reg. (n.s.) 235 (1927).

Applied in Resorts Int'l Hotel, Inc. v. Agresta, 569 F. Supp. 24 (E.D. Va. 1983).

OPINIONS OF THE ATTORNEY GENERAL

Illegal gambling. — Hypothetical examples that center on payment of money in exchange for a product, such as a phone card or a DVD, where the product offered to the consumer is not in fact the object of the transaction, instead, the consumer disregards the item "purchased" and seeks the opportunity to play a game of chance in order to win prizes or money, would constitute illegal gambling because the elements of prize, chance and consideration are present. See opinion of Attorney General to The Honorable R. Edward Houck, Member, Senate of Virginia, 10-095, 2010 Va. AG LEXIS 60 (10/15/10).

Consideration. — Whether scenarios involving charitable donations at computer terminals or political contributions made from computers in business establishments constitute legal sweepstakes or illegal gambling, depends on whether the element of consideration is missing. The question is whether the sweepstakes is the product, i.e., individuals are paying to participate in a game of chance, or whether it is a charitable donation or political contribution. See opinion of Attorney General to The Honorable G. Manoli Loupassi, Member, House of Delegates, 11-086, 2011 Va. AG LEXIS 58 (8/12/11).

§ 18.2-332. Certain acts not deemed "consideration" in prosecution under this article.

In any prosecution under this article, no consideration shall be deemed to have passed or been given because of any person's attendance upon the premises of another; his execution, mailing or delivery of an entry blank; his answering of questions, verbally or in writing; his witnessing of a demonstration or other proceeding; or any one or more thereof, where no charge is made to, paid by, or any purchase required of him in connection therewith.

History.

Code 1950, § 18.1-340.1; 1960, c. 226; 1975, cc. 14, 15.

OPINIONS OF THE ATTORNEY GENERAL

The element of consideration is missing, and therefore no illegal gambling occurs, when the opportunity to win a prize is offered both with a purchase and without the requirement of a purchase. See opinion of Attorney General to The Honorable Bill Janis, Member, House of Delegates, 10-064, 2010 Va. AG LEXIS 41 (7/30/10).

§ 18.2-333. Exceptions to article; certain sporting events.

Nothing in this article shall be construed to prevent any contest of speed or skill between men, animals, fowl or vehicles, where participants may receive prizes or different percentages of a purse, stake or premium dependent upon whether they win or lose or dependent upon their position or score at the end of such contest.

Any participant who, for the purpose of competing for any such purse, stake or premium offered in any such contest, knowingly and fraudulently enters any contestant other than the contestant purported to be entered or knowingly and fraudulently enters a contestant in a class in which it does not belong, shall be guilty of a Class 3 misdemeanor.

History.

Code 1950, §§ 18.1-319, 18.1-322; 1960, c. 358; 1968, c. 401; 1975, cc. 14, 15.

CASE NOTES

Application. — There was sufficient proof that through his activities, defendant knowingly aided and abetted the illegal gambling among spectators of the cockfighting operation, and insomuch as § 18.2-326 made gambling on cockfighting illegal, and thus encompassed within 18 U.S.C.S. § 1955(b)(1), defendant's statutory argument failed; although § 18.2-333 clarified that participants in a contest of skill, where they may win a prize or purse, were not guilty of gambling, nothing in that made it lawful for any person to wager on the outcome of such events. United States v. Kingrea, 567 F.3d 119, 2009 U.S. App. LEXIS 11505 (4th Cir. 2009).

Applied in Daniels v. Mobley, 285 Va. 402, 737 S.E.2d 895, 2013 Va. LEXIS 27 (2013).

§ 18.2-334. Exception to article; private residences.

Nothing in this article shall be construed to make it illegal to participate in a game of chance conducted in a private residence, provided such private residence is not commonly used for such games of chance and there is no operator as defined in subsection 4 of § 18.2-325.

History.

Code 1950, § 18.1-327; 1960, c. 358; 1975, cc. 14, 15; 1992, c. 423.

§ 18.2-334.1. Defeated at referendum.

Editor's note.

This section, relating to horse racing and pari-mutuel betting, was enacted by Acts 1978, c. 600. The 1978 act, which also enacted §§ 59.1-216 through 59.1-254, was made subject to referendum held Nov. 7, 1978, and provided that, if approved, the act would become effective Jan. 1, 1979. The act was defeated at the referendum, and therefore never went into effect.

§ 18.2-334.2. (Effective until January 1, 2014) Same; bingo games, raffles and duck races conducted by certain organizations.

Nothing in this article shall apply to any bingo game, instant bingo, raffle, or duck race conducted solely by organizations as defined in § 18.2-340.16 which have received a permit as set forth in § 18.2-340.25, or which are exempt from the permit requirement under § 18.2-340.23.

History.
1979, c. 420; 1993, c. 513; 1995, c. 837.

Section set out twice.
The section above is effective until January 1, 2014. For the version of this section effective January 1, 2014, see the following section, also numbered 18.2-334.2.

§ 18.2-334.2. (Effective January 1, 2014) Same; bingo games, raffles and duck races conducted by certain organizations.

Nothing in this article shall apply to any bingo game, instant bingo, network bingo, raffle, or duck race conducted solely by organizations as defined in § 18.2-340.16 which have received a permit as set forth in § 18.2-340.25, or which are exempt from the permit requirement under § 18.2-340.23.

History.
1979, c. 420; 1993, c. 513; 1995, c. 837; 2013, cc. 36, 350.

Section set out twice.
The section above is effective January 1, 2014. For this section as in effect until January 1, 2014, see the preceding section, also numbered 18.2-334.2.

Editor's note.
Acts 2013, cc. 36 and 350, cl. 2 provides: "That the provisions of this act shall become effective on January 1, 2014, except that the provisions of § 18.2-340.19 of this act shall become effective on July 1, 2013."

The 2013 amendments.
The 2013 amendments by cc. 36 and 350, effective January 1, 2014, are identical and inserted "network bingo."

§ 18.2-334.3. Exemptions to article; state lottery.

Nothing in this article shall apply to any lottery conducted by the Commonwealth of Virginia pursuant to Chapter 40 of Title 58.1.

History.
1987, c. 531.

CASE NOTES

Section 11-14 is not a part of Chapter 8, Art. 1, of Title 18.2 of the Code and, therefore, the operation of § 11-14 is unaffected by the provisions of this section. Hughes v. Cole, 251 Va. 3, 465 S.E.2d 820 (1996).

§ 18.2-334.4. Exemptions to article; pari-mutuel wagering.

Nothing in this article shall be construed to make it illegal to participate in any race meeting or pari-mutuel wagering conducted in accordance with Chapter 29 (§ 59.1-364 et seq.) of Title 59.1.

History.
1988, c. 855.

§ 18.2-335. Repealed by Acts 1979, c. 420.

Cross references.
For present provisions as to bingo games and raffles, see § 18.2-334.2 and Article 1.1:1 (§ 18.2-340.15 et seq.) of this chapter.

§ 18.2-336. Repealed by Acts 2004, c. 995.

Cross references.
For current provisions as to forfeiture of money, gambling devices, etc., seized from illegal gambling enterprise, see § 19.2-386.30.

§ 18.2-337. Immunity of witnesses from prosecution.

No witness called by the Commonwealth or by the court, giving evidence either before the grand jury or in any prosecution under this article, shall ever be prosecuted for the offense being prosecuted concerning which he testifies. Such witness shall be compelled to testify and for refusing to do so may be punished for contempt.

History.
Code 1950, § 19.1-266; 1960, c. 366; 1975, cc. 14, 15.

Cross references.
For other provisions as to immunity of witnesses, see §§ 18.2-445 and 48-15.

CASE NOTES

This section secures full protection to witnesses testifying in prosecutions for unlawful gaming, and one is not justified in refusing to testify on the ground that his answer will tend to criminate and disgrace him. Kendrick v. Commonwealth, 78 Va. 490 (1884). See also Flanary v. Commonwealth, 113 Va. 775, 75 S.E. 289 (1912).

§ 18.2-338. Enforcement of § 18.2-331 by Governor and Attorney General.

If it shall come to the knowledge of the Governor that § 18.2-331 is not being enforced in any county, city or town, the Governor may call upon the Attorney General to direct its enforcement in such county, city or town, and thereupon the Attorney General may instruct the attorney for the Commonwealth, sheriff and chief of police, if any, of such county, or the attorney for the Commonwealth and chief of police of such city, or the attorney for the Commonwealth of the county in which such town is located and the chief of police or sergeant of such town, to take such steps as may be necessary to insure the enforcement of such section in such county, city or town, and if any such officers, after receiving such instructions, shall thereafter fail or refuse to exercise diligence in the enforcement of § 18.2-331, the Attorney General shall make report thereof in writing to the Governor and to the judge of the circuit court having jurisdiction over the acts thereby prohibited, and thereupon the Attorney General upon being directed so to do by the Governor, shall take such steps as he may deem proper in directing the institution and prosecution of criminal proceedings, to secure the enforcement of § 18.2-331.

History.
Code 1950, § 18.1-334; 1960, c. 358; 1975, cc. 14, 15.

§ 18.2-339. Enjoining offenses relating to gambling.

Whenever any person shall be engaged in committing, or in permitting to be committed, or shall be about to commit, or permit, any act prohibited by any one or more of the sections in this article, the attorney for the Commonwealth of the county or city in which such act is being, or is about to be, committed or permitted, or the Attorney General of the Commonwealth, may institute and maintain a suit in equity in the appropriate court, in the name of the Commonwealth, upon the relation of such attorney for the Commonwealth, or the Attorney General, to enjoin and restrain such person from committing, or permitting, such prohibited act or acts. The procedure in any such suit shall be similar to the procedure in other suits for injunctions, except that no bond shall be required upon the granting of either a temporary or permanent injunction therein.

History.
Code 1950, § 18.1-343; 1960, c. 358; 1975, cc. 14, 15.

§ 18.2-340. County ordinances prohibiting illegal gambling.

The governing body of any county may adopt ordinances prohibiting illegal gambling, including a provision for forfeiture proceedings in accordance with Chapter 22.1 (§ 19.2-386.1 et seq.) of Title 19.2. Such ordinances shall not conflict with the provisions of this article or with other state laws and any penalties provided for violation of such ordinances shall not exceed a fine of $2,500 or confinement in jail for 12 months, either or both.

History.
Code 1950, § 18.1-344; 1960, c. 358; 1975, cc. 14, 15; 1991, c. 710; 2012, cc. 283, 756.

The 2012 amendments.
The 2012 amendments by cc. 283 and 756 are identical, and substituted "gambling, including a provision for forfeiture proceedings in accordance with Chapter 22.1 (§ 19.2-386.1 et seq.) of Title 19.2" for "gambling and other illegal activity related thereto, including provision for forfeiture proceedings in the name of the county" at the end of the first sentence and "12 months" for "twelve months" in the second sentence.

ARTICLE 1.1.
BINGO AND RAFFLES.

§§ 18.2-340.1 through 18.2-340.14. Repealed by Acts 1995, c. 837, effective July 1, 1996.

Editor's note.
Acts 1995, c. 837, cl. 5, provides: "That the provisions of Article 1.1 (§ 18.2-340.1 et seq.) of Chapter 8 of Title 18.2 and any ordinances adopted pursuant thereto by local governing bodies shall remain in effect until July 1, 1996, when the Charitable Gaming Commission shall be vested with control of all charitable gaming in the Commonwealth and implement its regulations in accordance with Article 1.1:1 (§ 18.2-340.15 et seq.) of Chapter 8 of Title 18.2. No local governing body shall collect, in advance, any audit fee for the review of charitable gaming financial reports required to be filed by Article 2 (§ 18.2-340.1 et seq.) of Chapter 8 of Title 18.2."

ARTICLE 1.1:1.
CHARITABLE GAMING.

§ 18.2-340.15. State control of charitable gaming.

A. Charitable gaming as authorized herein shall be permitted in the Commonwealth as a means of funding qualified organizations but shall be conducted only in strict compliance with the provisions of this article. The Department of Agriculture and Consumer Services is vested with control of all charitable gaming in the Commonwealth. The Charitable Gaming Board shall have the power to prescribe regulations and conditions under which such gaming shall be conducted to ensure that it is conducted in a manner consistent with the purpose for which it is permitted.

B. The conduct of any charitable gaming is a privilege that may be granted or denied by the Department of Agriculture and Consumer Services or its duly authorized representatives in its discretion in order to effectuate the purposes set forth in this article.

History.
1995, c. 837; 2003, c. 884; 2006, c. 644; 2008, cc. 387, 689.

Cross references.
As to the Charitable Gaming Board, see § 2.2-2452 et seq.

Editor's note.
Acts 2008, cc. 387 and 689, cl. 3 provides: "That as of July 1, 2008, the Department of Agriculture and Consumer Services shall be deemed successor in interest to the Department of Charitable Gaming to the extent that this act transfers powers and duties. All right, title, and interest in and to any real or tangible personal property vested in the Department of Charitable Gaming shall be

transferred to and taken as standing in the name of the Department of Agriculture and Consumer Services."

Acts 2008, cc. 387 and 689, cl. 4 provides: "That the Governor may transfer an appropriation or any portion thereof within a state agency established, abolished, or otherwise affected by the provisions of this act, or from one such agency to another, to support the changes in organization or responsibility resulting from or required by the provisions of this act."

Acts 2008, cc. 387 and 689, cl. 5 provides: "That all rules and regulations adopted by the Department of Charitable Gaming or the Charitable Gaming Board that are in effect as of July 1, 2008, and that pertain to the subject of this act, shall remain in full force and effect until altered, amended, or rescinded by the Department of Agriculture and Consumer Services or the Charitable Gaming Board."

The 2008 amendments.

The 2008 amendments by cc. 387 and 689 are nearly the same, and substituted "Department of Agriculture and Consumer Services" for "Department of Charitable Gaming" in the second sentence in subsection A and in subsection B. In addition, c. 387 substituted "Board of Agriculture and Consumer Services" for "Charitable Gaming Board" in the third sentence of subsection A.

§ 18.2-340.16. (Effective until January 1, 2014) Definitions.

As used in this article, unless the context requires a different meaning:

"*Bingo*" means a specific game of chance played with (i) individual cards having randomly numbered squares ranging from one to seventy-five, (ii) Department-approved electronic devices that display facsimiles of bingo cards and are used for the purpose of marking and monitoring players' cards as numbers are called, or (iii) Department-approved cards, in which prizes are awarded on the basis of designated numbers on such cards conforming to a predetermined pattern of numbers selected at random.

"*Board*" means the Charitable Gaming Board created pursuant to § 2.2-2455.

"*Bona fide member*" means an individual who participates in activities of a qualified organization other than such organization's charitable gaming activities.

"*Charitable gaming*" or "*charitable games*" means those raffles and games of chance explicitly authorized by this article.

"*Charitable gaming supplies*" includes bingo cards or sheets, devices for selecting bingo numbers, instant bingo cards, pull-tab cards and seal cards, and any other equipment or product manufactured for or intended to be used in the conduct of charitable games. However for the purposes of this article, charitable gaming supplies shall not include items incidental to the conduct of charitable gaming such as markers, wands or tape.

"*Commissioner*" means the Commissioner of the Department of Agriculture and Consumer Services.

"*Conduct*" means the actions associated with the provision of a gaming operation during and immediately before or after the permitted activity, which may include, but not be limited to, (i) selling bingo cards or packs, electronic devices, instant bingo or pull-tab cards, or raffle tickets, (ii) calling bingo games, (iii) distributing prizes, and (iv) any other services provided by volunteer workers.

"*Department*" means the Department of Agriculture and Consumer Services.

"*Fair market rental value*" means the rent that a rental property will bring when offered for lease by a lessor who desires to lease the property but is not obligated to do so and leased by a lessee under no necessity of leasing.

"*Gaming expenses*" means prizes, supplies, costs of publicizing gaming activities, audit and administration or permit fees, and a portion of the rent, utilities, accounting and legal fees and such other reasonable and proper expenses as are directly incurred for the conduct of charitable gaming.

"*Gross receipts*" means the total amount of money generated by an organization from charitable gaming before the deduction of expenses, including prizes.

"*Instant bingo*," "*pull tabs*," or "*seal cards*" means specific games of chance played by the random selection of one or more individually prepacked cards, including Department-approved electronic versions thereof, with winners being determined by the preprinted or predetermined appearance of concealed letters, numbers or symbols that must be exposed by the player to determine wins and losses and may include the use of a seal card which conceals one or more numbers or symbols that have been designated in advance as prize winners. Such cards may be dispensed by electronic or mechanical equipment.

"*Jackpot*" means a bingo game that the organization has designated on its game program as a jackpot game in which the prize amount is greater than $100.

"*Landlord*" means any person or his agent, firm, association, organization, partnership, or corporation, employee, or immediate family member thereof, which owns and leases, or leases any premises devoted in whole or in part to the conduct of bingo games, and any person residing in the same household as a landlord.

"*Management*" means the provision of oversight of a gaming operation, which may include, but is not limited to, the responsibilities of applying for and maintaining a permit or authorization, compiling, submitting and maintaining required records and financial reports, and ensuring that all aspects of the operation are in compliance with all applicable statutes and regulations.

"*Operation*" means the activities associated with production of a charitable gaming activity, which may include, but not be limited to (i) the direct on-site supervision of the conduct of charitable gaming; (ii) coordination of volunteers; and (iii) all responsibilities of charitable gaming designated by the organization's management.

"*Organization*" means any one of the following:

1. A volunteer fire department or rescue squad or auxiliary unit thereof which has been recognized in

accordance with § 15.2-955 by an ordinance or resolution of the political subdivision where the volunteer fire department or rescue squad is located as being a part of the safety program of such political subdivision;

2. An organization operated exclusively for religious, charitable, community or educational purposes;

3. An athletic association or booster club or a band booster club established solely to raise funds for school-sponsored athletic or band activities for a public school or private school accredited pursuant to § 22.1-19 or to provide scholarships to students attending such school;

4. An association of war veterans or auxiliary units thereof organized in the United States;

5. A fraternal association or corporation operating under the lodge system;

6. A local chamber of commerce; or

7. Any other nonprofit organization that raises funds by conducting raffles that generate annual gross receipts of $40,000 or less, provided such gross receipts from the raffle, less expenses and prizes, are used exclusively for charitable, educational, religious or community purposes.

"*Qualified organization*" means any organization to which a valid permit has been issued by the Department to conduct charitable gaming or any organization that is exempt pursuant to § 18.2-340.23.

"*Raffle*" means a lottery in which the prize is won by (i) a random drawing of the name or prearranged number of one or more persons purchasing chances or (ii) a random contest in which the winning name or preassigned number of one or more persons purchasing chances is determined by a race involving inanimate objects floating on a body of water, commonly referred to as a "duck race."

"*Reasonable and proper business expenses*" means business expenses actually incurred by a qualified organization in the conduct of charitable gaming and not otherwise allowed under this article or under Board regulations on real estate and personal property tax payments, travel expenses, payments of utilities and trash collection services, legal and accounting fees, costs of business furniture, fixtures and office equipment and costs of acquisition, maintenance, repair or construction of an organization's real property. For the purpose of this definition, salaries and wages of employees whose primary responsibility is to provide services for the principal benefit of an organization's members shall not qualify as a business expense. However, payments made pursuant to § 51.1-1204 to the Volunteer Firefighters' and Rescue Squad Workers' Service Award Fund shall be deemed a reasonable and proper business expense.

"*Supplier*" means any person who offers to sell, sells or otherwise provides charitable gaming supplies to any qualified organization.

History.
1995, c. 837; 1996, c. 919; 1997, cc. 777, 838; 1998, cc. 57, 398; 1999, c. 534; 2002, cc. 282, 340; 2003, c. 884; 2006, c. 644; 2007, cc. 160, 264; 2008, cc. 387, 689; 2009, c. 121; 2010, c. 429.

Section set out twice.
The section above is effective until January 1, 2014. For the version of this section effective January 1, 2014, see the following section, also numbered 18.2-340.16.

Editor's note.
Acts 1998, c. 398, cl. 3, effective October 1, 1998, provides: "That none of the provisions of this act shall be construed to reduce the potential lawful uses of gross receipts from charitable gaming derived by qualified organizations from what they were interpreted to be by the Charitable Gaming Commission [now the Agriculture and Consumer Services] as of January 14, 1998."

Acts 2008, cc. 387 and 689, cl. 3 provides: "That as of July 1, 2008, the Department of Agriculture and Consumer Services shall be deemed successor in interest to the Department of Charitable Gaming to the extent that this act transfers powers and duties. All right, title, and interest in and to any real or tangible personal property vested in the Department of Charitable Gaming shall be transferred to and taken as standing in the name of the Department of Agriculture and Consumer Services."

Acts 2008, cc. 387 and 689, cl. 4 provides: "That the Governor may transfer an appropriation or any portion thereof within a state agency established, abolished, or otherwise affected by the provisions of this act, or from one such agency to another, to support the changes in organization or responsibility resulting from or required by the provisions of this act."

Acts 2008, cc. 387 and 689, cl. 5 provides: "That all rules and regulations adopted by the Department of Charitable Gaming or the Charitable Gaming Board that are in effect as of July 1, 2008, and that pertain to the subject of this act, shall remain in full force and effect until altered, amended, or rescinded by the Department of Agriculture and Consumer Services or the Charitable Gaming Board."

Acts 2010, c. 429, cl. 3, provides: "That the Department of Agriculture and Consumer Services shall report to the chairs of the House Committee on General Laws and the Senate Committee on General Laws and Technology on or before December 1, 2010 concerning the Department's efforts to increase the number of Department-approved independent laboratory testers in order to expedite the Department's approval process for new charitable games authorized by Article 1:1 (§ 18.2-340.15 et seq.) of Chapter 6 of Title 18.2 and regulations of the Charitable Gaming Board."

The 2008 amendments.
The 2008 amendments by cc. 387 and 689 are identical, and added the definition of "Commissioner"; in the definition of "Department," substituted "Agriculture and Consumer Services" for "Charitable Gaming created in accordance with Chapter 9.1 (§ 2.2-905 et seq.) of Title 2.2"; and deleted the definition for "Director."

The 2009 amendments.
The 2009 amendment by c. 121 substituted "$40,000" for "$25,000" in subdivision 7 in the definition of "Organization."

The 2010 amendments.
The 2010 amendment by c. 429, in the definition of "jackpot," deleted "exclusive of a 'winner-take-all' bingo game" following "as a jackpot game"; and in the definition of "landlord," substituted "any premises devoted" for "any premise devoted."

CASE NOTES

The term "raffle" does not encompass a system whereby, to win, a purchaser must match bars, cherries or lemons in triple sequence. Virginia ABC Bd. v. VFW Ocean View Post-3160, 10 Va. App. 165, 390 S.E.2d 202 (1990) (decided under former § 18.2-340.1).

Single, double, and triple bingo lines do not satisfy the definition of "jackpot" in subdivision 5. Therefore, prizes awarded for those accomplishments are not "jackpot" prizes. Only prizes awarded for success at "coverall" qualify as "jackpot" prizes. Regular Veterans Ass'n v. Commonwealth, 18 Va. App. 683, 446 S.E.2d 621 (1994) (decided under former § 18.2-340.1).

OPINIONS OF THE ATTORNEY GENERAL

Definition of "instant bingo" and "pull tabs" does not authorize the use of electronic devices that display facsimiles of instant bingo cards or pull tabs. Such games may not be played using equipment that merely dispenses a receipt showing the amount of winnings due to the player upon completion of the game. See opinion of Attorney General to Mr. Harry M. Durham, Interim Director, Department of Charitable Gaming, 06-093 (6/20/07).

§ 18.2-340.16. (Effective January 1, 2014) Definitions.

As used in this article, unless the context requires a different meaning:

"Bingo" means a specific game of chance played with (i) individual cards having randomly numbered squares ranging from one to 75, (ii) Department-approved electronic devices that display facsimiles of bingo cards and are used for the purpose of marking and monitoring players' cards as numbers are called, or (iii) Department-approved cards, in which prizes are awarded on the basis of designated numbers on such cards conforming to a predetermined pattern of numbers selected at random.

"Board" means the Charitable Gaming Board created pursuant to § 2.2-2455.

"Bona fide member" means an individual who participates in activities of a qualified organization other than such organization's charitable gaming activities.

"Charitable gaming" or *"charitable games"* means those raffles and games of chance explicitly authorized by this article.

"Charitable gaming supplies" includes bingo cards or sheets, devices for selecting bingo numbers, instant bingo cards, pull-tab cards and seal cards, and any other equipment or product manufactured for or intended to be used in the conduct of charitable games. However for the purposes of this article, charitable gaming supplies shall not include items incidental to the conduct of charitable gaming such as markers, wands or tape.

"Commissioner" means the Commissioner of the Department of Agriculture and Consumer Services.

"Conduct" means the actions associated with the provision of a gaming operation during and immediately before or after the permitted activity, which may include, but not be limited to, (i) selling bingo cards or packs, electronic devices, instant bingo or pull-tab cards, or raffle tickets, (ii) calling bingo games, (iii) distributing prizes, and (iv) any other services provided by volunteer workers.

"Department" means the Department of Agriculture and Consumer Services.

"Fair market rental value" means the rent that a rental property will bring when offered for lease by a lessor who desires to lease the property but is not obligated to do so and leased by a lessee under no necessity of leasing.

"Gaming expenses" means prizes, supplies, costs of publicizing gaming activities, audit and administration or permit fees, and a portion of the rent, utilities, accounting and legal fees and such other reasonable and proper expenses as are directly incurred for the conduct of charitable gaming.

"Gross receipts" means the total amount of money generated by an organization from charitable gaming before the deduction of expenses, including prizes.

"Instant bingo," "pull tabs," or *"seal cards"* means specific games of chance played by the random selection of one or more individually prepacked cards, including Department-approved electronic versions thereof, with winners being determined by the preprinted or predetermined appearance of concealed letters, numbers or symbols that must be exposed by the player to determine wins and losses and may include the use of a seal card which conceals one or more numbers or symbols that have been designated in advance as prize winners. Such cards may be dispensed by electronic or mechanical equipment.

"Jackpot" means a bingo game that the organization has designated on its game program as a jackpot game in which the prize amount is greater than $100.

"Landlord" means any person or his agent, firm, association, organization, partnership, or corporation, employee, or immediate family member thereof, which owns and leases, or leases any premises devoted in whole or in part to the conduct of bingo games, and any person residing in the same household as a landlord.

"Management" means the provision of oversight of a gaming operation, which may include, but is not limited to, the responsibilities of applying for and maintaining a permit or authorization, compiling, submitting and maintaining required records and financial reports, and ensuring that all aspects of the operation are in compliance with all applicable statutes and regulations.

"Network bingo" means a specific bingo game in which pari-mutuel play is permitted.

"Network bingo provider" means a person licensed by the Department to operate network bingo.

"Operation" means the activities associated with production of a charitable gaming activity, which may include, but not be limited to (i) the direct on-site supervision of the conduct of charitable gaming; (ii) coordination of volunteers; and (iii) all responsibilities of charitable gaming designated by the organization's management.

"Organization" means any one of the following:

1. A volunteer fire department or rescue squad or auxiliary unit thereof which has been recognized in accordance with § 15.2-955 by an ordinance or resolution of the political subdivision where the volunteer fire department or rescue squad is located as being a part of the safety program of such political subdivision;

2. An organization operated exclusively for religious, charitable, community or educational purposes;

3. An athletic association or booster club or a band booster club established solely to raise funds for school-sponsored athletic or band activities for a public school or private school accredited pursuant to § 22.1-19 or to provide scholarships to students attending such school;

4. An association of war veterans or auxiliary units thereof organized in the United States;

5. A fraternal association or corporation operating under the lodge system;

6. A local chamber of commerce; or

7. Any other nonprofit organization that raises funds by conducting raffles that generate annual gross receipts of $40,000 or less, provided such gross receipts from the raffle, less expenses and prizes, are used exclusively for charitable, educational, religious or community purposes.

"*Pari-mutuel play*" means an integrated network operated by a licensee of the Department comprised of participating charitable organizations for the conduct of network bingo games in which the purchase of a network bingo card by a player automatically includes the player in a pool with all other players in the network, and where the prize to the winning player is awarded based on a percentage of the total amount of network bingo cards sold in a particular network.

"*Qualified organization*" means any organization to which a valid permit has been issued by the Department to conduct charitable gaming or any organization that is exempt pursuant to § 18.2-340.23.

"*Raffle*" means a lottery in which the prize is won by (i) a random drawing of the name or prearranged number of one or more persons purchasing chances or (ii) a random contest in which the winning name or preassigned number of one or more persons purchasing chances is determined by a race involving inanimate objects floating on a body of water, commonly referred to as a "duck race."

"*Reasonable and proper business expenses*" means business expenses actually incurred by a qualified organization in the conduct of charitable gaming and not otherwise allowed under this article or under Board regulations on real estate and personal property tax payments, travel expenses, payments of utilities and trash collection services, legal and accounting fees, costs of business furniture, fixtures and office equipment and costs of acquisition, maintenance, repair or construction of an organization's real property. For the purpose of this definition, salaries and wages of employees whose primary responsibility is to provide services for the principal benefit of an organization's members shall not qualify as a business expense. However, payments made pursuant to § 51.1-1204 to the Volunteer Firefighters' and Rescue Squad Workers' Service Award Fund shall be deemed a reasonable and proper business expense.

"*Supplier*" means any person who offers to sell, sells or otherwise provides charitable gaming supplies to any qualified organization.

History.

995, c. 837; 1996, c. 919; 1997, cc. 777, 838; 1998, cc. 57, 398; 1999, c. 534; 2002, cc. 282, 340; 2003, c. 884; 2006, c. 644; 2007, cc. 160, 264; 2008, cc. 387, 689; 2009, c. 121; 2010, c. 429; 2013, cc. 36, 350.

Section set out twice.

The section above is effective January 1, 2014. For this section as in effect until January 1, 2014, see the preceding section, also numbered 18.2-340.16.

Editor's note.

Acts 2013, cc. 36 and 350, cl. 2 provides: "That the provisions of this act shall become effective on January 1, 2014, except that the provisions of § 18.2-340.19 of this act shall become effective on July 1, 2013."

The 2013 amendments.

The 2013 amendments by cc. 36 and 350, effective January 1, 2014, are identical and in the paragraph defining "Bingo," substituted "75" for "seventy-five" in clause (i); and added the paragraphs defining "Network bingo," "Network bingo provider" and "Pari-mutuel pay."

§ 18.2-340.17. Repealed by Acts 2003, c. 884, cl. 2.

Cross references.

As to the Charitable Gaming Board, see § 2.2-2452 et seq.

Editor's note.

Acts 2003, c. 884, cl. 3, provides: "That all rules and regulations of the Virginia Charitable Gaming Commission that are in effect as of the effective date of this act shall remain in full force and effect until altered, amended, or rescinded by the Charitable Gaming Board created in accordance with this act."

Acts 2003, c. 884, cl. 4, provides: "That as of July 1, 2003, the Department of Charitable Gaming shall be deemed successor in interest to the Virginia Charitable Gaming Commission to the extent that this act transfers powers and duties. All right, title, and interest in and to any real or tangible personal property vested in the Virginia Charitable Gaming Commission shall be transferred to and taken as standing in the name of the Department of Charitable Gaming." Pursuant to Acts 2008, cc. 387 and 689, the Department of Agriculture and Consumer Services is the successor in interest to the Department of Charitable Gaming. See Editor's notes under § 18.2-340.16.

Acts 2003, c. 884, cl. 5, provides: "That the Charitable Gaming Board shall examine regulations, including the computation and percentage of gross receipts that are required to be used for charitable purposes by qualified organizations, and provide a report to the Governor and the 2004 Session of the General Assembly. The report shall include the Board's plans regarding regulatory action on these issues, and anticipated timetable for such action."

§ 18.2-340.18. Powers and duties of the Department.

The Department shall have all powers and duties necessary to carry out the provisions of this article and to exercise the control of charitable gaming as set forth in § 18.2-340.15. Such powers and duties shall include but not be limited to the following:

1. The Department is vested with jurisdiction and supervision over all charitable gaming authorized under the provisions of this article and including all persons that conduct or provide goods, services or premises used in the conduct of charitable gaming. It may employ such persons as are necessary to ensure that charitable gaming is conducted in conformity with the provisions of this article and the regulations of the Board. The Department shall

designate such agents and employees as it deems necessary and appropriate who shall be sworn to enforce the provisions of this article and the criminal laws of the Commonwealth and who shall be law-enforcement officers as defined in § 9.1-101.

2. The Department, its agents and employees and any law-enforcement officers charged with the enforcement of charitable gaming laws shall have free access to the offices, facilities or any other place of business of any organization, including any premises devoted in whole or in part to the conduct of charitable gaming. These individuals may enter such places or premises for the purpose of carrying out any duty imposed by this article, securing records required to be maintained by an organization, investigating complaints, or conducting audits.

3. The Department may compel the production of any books, documents, records, or memoranda of any organizations or supplier involved in the conduct of charitable gaming for the purpose of satisfying itself that this article and its regulations are strictly complied with. In addition, the Department may require the production of an annual balance sheet and operating statement of any person granted a permit pursuant to the provisions of this article and may require the production of any contract to which such person is or may be a party.

4. The Department may issue subpoenas for the attendance of witnesses before it, administer oaths, and compel production of records or other documents and testimony of such witnesses whenever, in the judgment of the Department, it is necessary to do so for the effectual discharge of its duties.

5. The Department may compel any person conducting charitable gaming to file with the Department such documents, information or data as shall appear to the Department to be necessary for the performance of its duties.

6. The Department may enter into arrangements with any governmental agency of this or any other state or any locality in the Commonwealth or any agency of the federal government for the purposes of exchanging information or performing any other act to better ensure the proper conduct of charitable gaming.

7. The Department may issue interim certification of tax-exempt status and collect a fee therefor in accordance with subsection B of § 18.2-340.24.

8. The Department shall report annually to the Governor and the General Assembly, which report shall include a financial statement of the operation of the Department and any recommendations for legislation applicable to charitable gaming in the Commonwealth.

9. The Department, its agents and employees may conduct such audits, in addition to those required by § 18.2-340.31, as they deem necessary and desirable.

10. The Department may limit the number of organizations for which a person may manage, operate or conduct charitable games.

11. The Department may report any alleged criminal violation of this article to the appropriate attorney for the Commonwealth for appropriate action.

History.
1995, c. 837; 1997, cc. 777, 838; 2003, c. 884; 2006, c. 644.

§ 18.2-340.19. Regulations of the Board.

A. The Board shall adopt regulations that:

1. Require, as a condition of receiving a permit, that the applicant use a predetermined percentage of its gross receipts for (i) those lawful religious, charitable, community or educational purposes for which the organization is specifically chartered or organized or (ii) those expenses relating to the acquisition, construction, maintenance or repair of any interest in real property involved in the operation of the organization and used for lawful religious, charitable, community or educational purposes. The regulation may provide for a graduated scale of percentages of gross receipts to be used in the foregoing manner based upon factors the Board finds appropriate to and consistent with the purpose of charitable gaming.

2. Specify the conditions under which a complete list of the organization's members who participate in the management, operation or conduct of charitable gaming may be required in order for the Board to ascertain the percentage of Virginia residents in accordance with subdivision A 3 of § 18.2-340.24. Membership lists furnished to the Board or Department in accordance with this subdivision shall not be a matter of public record and shall be exempt from disclosure under the provisions of the Freedom of Information Act (§ 2.2-3700 et seq.).

3. Prescribe fees for processing applications for charitable gaming permits. Such fees may reflect the nature and extent of the charitable gaming activity proposed to be conducted.

4. Establish requirements for the audit of all reports required in accordance with § 18.2-340.30.

5. Define electronic and mechanical equipment used in the conduct of charitable gaming. Board regulations shall include capacity for such equipment to provide full automatic daubing as numbers are called. For the purposes of this subdivision, electronic or mechanical equipment for instant bingo, pull tabs, or seal cards shall include such equipment that displays facsimiles of instant bingo, pull tabs, or seal cards and are used solely for the purpose of dispensing or opening such paper or electronic cards, or both; but shall not include (i) devices operated by dropping one or more coins or tokens into a slot and pulling a handle or pushing a button or touchpoint on a touchscreen to activate one to three or more reels marked into horizontal segments by varying symbols, where the predetermined prize amount depends on how and how many of the symbols line up when the rotating reels come to rest, or (ii) other similar devices that display

flashing lights or illuminations, or bells, whistles, or other sounds, solely intended to entice players to play.

6. Prescribe the conditions under which a qualified organization may (i) provide food and nonalcoholic beverages to its members who participate in the management, operation or conduct of bingo; (ii) permit members who participate in the management, operation or conduct of bingo to play bingo; and (iii) subject to the provisions of subdivision 13 of § 18.2-340.33, permit nonmembers to participate in the conduct of bingo so long as the nonmembers are under the direct supervision of a bona fide member of the organization during the bingo game.

7. Prescribe the conditions under which a qualified organization may sell raffle tickets for a raffle drawing that will be held outside the Commonwealth pursuant to subsection B of § 18.2-340.26.

8. Prescribe the conditions under which persons who are bona fide members of a qualified organization or a child, above the age of 13 years, of a bona fide member of such organization may participate in the conduct or operation of bingo games.

9. Prescribe the conditions under which a person below the age of 18 years may play bingo, provided such person is accompanied by his parent or legal guardian.

10. Require all qualified organizations that are subject to Board regulations to post in a conspicuous place in every place where charitable gaming is conducted a sign which bears a toll-free telephone number for "Gamblers Anonymous" or other organization which provides assistance to compulsive gamblers.

11. Prescribe the conditions under which a qualified organization may sell network bingo cards in accordance with § 18.2-340.28:1 and establish a percentage of proceeds derived from network bingo sales to be allocated to (i) prize pools, (ii) the organization conducting the network bingo, and (iii) the network bingo provider. The regulations shall also establish procedures for the retainage and ultimate distribution of any unclaimed prize.

B. In addition to the powers and duties granted pursuant to § 2.2-2456 and this article, the Board may, by regulation, approve variations to the card formats for bingo games provided such variations result in bingo games that are conducted in a manner consistent with the provisions of this article. Board-approved variations may include, but are not limited to, bingo games commonly referred to as player selection games and 90-number bingo.

History.
1995, c. 837; 1996, c. 919; 1997, cc. 777, 838; 1998, c. 845; 2001, c. 833; 2003, c. 884; 2006, c. 644; 2010, cc. 429, 572; 2013, cc. 36, 350.

Editor's note.
Acts 2010, c. 429, cl. 3, provides: "That the Department of Agriculture and Consumer Services shall report to the chairs of the House Committee on General Laws and the Senate Committee on General Laws and Technology on or before December 1, 2010 concerning the Department's efforts to increase the number of Department-approved independent laboratory testers in order to expedite the Department's approval process for new charitable games authorized by Article 1:1 (§ 18.2-340.15 et seq.) of Chapter 6 of Title 18.2 and regulations of the Charitable Gaming Board."

Acts 2013, cc. 36 and 350, cl. 2 provides: "That the provisions of this act shall become effective on January 1, 2014, except that the provisions of § 18.2-340.19 of this act shall become effective on July 1, 2013."

The 2010 amendments.
The 2010 amendment by c. 429, in subdivision A 1, deleted "excluding winner-take-all games" following "its gross receipts"; in subdivision A 5, added the second sentence; and in subdivision A 6, added clause (iii) and made related changes.

The 2010 amendment by c. 572 inserted the last sentence of subdivision A 5.

The 2013 amendments.
The 2013 amendments by cc. 36 and 350 are identical, and added subdivision A 11.

§ 18.2-340.20. Denial, suspension or revocation of permit; hearings and appeals.

A. The Department may deny, suspend or revoke the permit of any organization found not to be in strict compliance with the provisions of this article and the regulations of the Board only after the proposed action by the Department has been reviewed and approved by the Board. The action of the Department in denying, suspending or revoking any permit shall be subject to the Administrative Process Act (§ 2.2-4000 et seq.).

B. Except as provided in §§ 18.2-340.25, 18.2-340.30 and 18.2-340.36, no permit to conduct charitable gaming shall be denied, suspended or revoked except upon notice stating the proposed basis for such action and the time and place for the hearing. At the discretion of the Department, hearings may be conducted by hearing officers who shall be selected from the list prepared by the Executive Secretary of the Supreme Court. After a hearing on the issues, the Department may refuse to issue or may suspend or revoke any such permit if it determines that the organization has not complied with the provisions of this article or the regulations of the Board.

C. Any person aggrieved by a refusal of the Department to issue any permit, the suspension or revocation of a permit, or any other action of the Department may seek review of such action in accordance with Article 4 (§ 2.2-4025 et seq.) of the Administrative Process Act.

History.
1995, c. 837; 1996, c. 573; 1997, cc. 777, 838; 2000, c. 1000; 2001, c. 813; 2002, c. 282; 2003, c. 884; 2004, c. 213; 2006, c. 644; 2010, c. 711.

Editor's note.
Acts 2000, c. 1000, which added former subsection D, provided in cl. 3, as amended by Acts 2001, c. 813: "That the provisions of this act shall expire on July 1, 2002."

The section is set out above without the change by Acts 2000, c. 1000, as amended by Acts 2001, c. 813, but with the amendment by Acts 2002, c. 282.

Acts 2004, c. 213, cl. 2, provides: "That the provisions of subsection D of § 18.2-340.20 of the Code of Virginia shall expire when replacement regulations are adopted pursuant to subdivision 1 of § 18.2-340.19 by the Charitable Gaming Board." Subsection D was subsequently repealed by Acts 2006, c. 644.

The 2010 amendments.
The 2010 amendment by c. 711 inserted "only after the proposed action by the Department has been reviewed and approved by the Board" in subsection A and made minor stylistic changes.

§ 18.2-340.21. Repealed by Acts 2003, c. 884, cl. 2.

Cross references.
As to the Charitable Gaming Board, see § 2.2-2452 et seq.

§ 18.2-340.22. (Effective until January 1, 2014) Only raffles, bingo and instant bingo games permitted; prizes not gaming contracts.

A. This article permits qualified organizations to conduct raffles, bingo and instant bingo games. All games not explicitly authorized by this article or Board regulations adopted in accordance with § 18.2-340.18 are prohibited.

B. The award of any prize money for any charitable game shall not be deemed to be part of any gaming contract within the purview of § 11-14.

C. Nothing in this article shall prohibit an organization from using the State Lottery Department's Pick-3 number or any number or other designation selected by the State Lottery Department in connection with any lottery, as the basis for determining the winner of a raffle.

History.
1995, c. 837; 1997, cc. 777, 838; 2003, c. 884.

Section set out twice.
The section above is effective until January 1, 2014. For the version of this section effective January 1, 2014, see the following section, also numbered 18.2-340.22.

§ 18.2-340.22. (Effective January 1, 2014) Only raffles, bingo, network bingo, and instant bingo games permitted; prizes not gaming contracts.

A. This article permits qualified organizations to conduct raffles, bingo, network bingo, and instant bingo games. All games not explicitly authorized by this article or Board regulations adopted in accordance with § 18.2-340.18 are prohibited.

B. The award of any prize money for any charitable game shall not be deemed to be part of any gaming contract within the purview of § 11-14.

C. Nothing in this article shall prohibit an organization from using the State Lottery Department's Pick-3 number or any number or other designation selected by the State Lottery Department in connection with any lottery, as the basis for determining the winner of a raffle.

History.
1995, c. 837; 1997, cc. 777, 838; 2003, c. 884; 2013, cc. 36, 350.

Section set out twice.
The section above is effective January 1, 2014. For this section as in effect until January 1, 2014, see the preceding section also numbered 18.2-340.22.

Editor's note.
Acts 2013, cc. 36 and 350, cl. 2 provides: "That the provisions of this act shall become effective on January 1, 2014, except that the provisions of § 18.2-340.19 of this act shall become effective on July 1, 2013."

The 2013 amendments.
The 2013 amendments by cc. 36 and 350, effective January 1, 2014, are identical, and inserted "network bingo," in the first sentence of subsection A.

§ 18.2-340.23. Organizations exempt from certain permits and fees.

A. No organization that reasonably expects, based on prior charitable gaming annual results or any other quantifiable method, to realize gross receipts of $40,000 or less in any 12-month period shall be required to (i) notify the Department of its intention to conduct charitable gaming, or (ii) comply with Board regulations. If any organization's actual gross receipts for the 12-month period exceed $40,000, the Department may require the organization to file by a specified date the report required by § 18.2-340.30.

B. Any volunteer fire department or rescue squad or auxiliary unit thereof which has been recognized in accordance with § 15.2-955 by an ordinance or resolution of the political subdivision where the volunteer fire department or rescue squad is located as being part of the safety program of such political subdivision shall be exempt from the payment of application fees required by § 18.2-340.25 and the payment of audit fees required by § 18.2-340.31. Nothing in this subsection shall be construed as exempting volunteer fire departments and rescue squads from any other provisions of this article or other Board regulations.

C. Nothing in this section shall prevent the Department from conducting any investigation or audit it deems appropriate to ensure an organization's compliance with the provisions of this article and, to the extent applicable, Board regulations.

History.
1995, c. 837; 1997, cc. 777, 838; 2003, c. 884; 2006, c. 644; 2009, c. 121.

The 2009 amendments.
The 2009 amendment by c. 121, in subsection A, substituted "$40,000" for "$25,000" in the first and last sentences.

§ 18.2-340.24. Eligibility for permit; exceptions; where valid.

A. To be eligible for a permit to conduct charitable gaming, an organization shall:

1. Have been in existence and met on a regular basis in the Commonwealth for a period of at least three years immediately prior to applying for a permit.

The three-year residency requirement shall not apply (i) to any lodge or chapter of a national or international fraternal order or of a national or international civic organization which is exempt under § 501(c) of the United States Internal Revenue Code and which has a lodge or chapter holding a charitable gaming permit issued under the provisions of this article anywhere within the Commonwealth; (ii) to booster clubs which have been operating for less than three years and which have been established solely to raise funds for school-sponsored activities in public schools or private schools accredited pursuant to § 22.1-19; (iii) to recently established volunteer fire and rescue companies or departments, after county, city or town approval; or (iv) to an organization which relocates its meeting place on a permanent basis from one jurisdiction to another, complies with the requirements of subdivision 2 of this section, and was the holder of a valid permit at the time of its relocation.

2. Be operating currently and have always been operated as a nonprofit organization.

3. Have at least 50% of its membership consist of residents of the Commonwealth; however, if an organization (i) does not consist of bona fide members and (ii) is exempt under § 501(c)(3) of the United States Internal Revenue Code, the Board shall exempt such organizations from the requirements of this subdivision.

B. Any organization whose gross receipts from all charitable gaming exceeds or can be expected to exceed $40,000 in any calendar year shall have been granted tax-exempt status pursuant to § 501(c) of the United States Internal Revenue Code. At the same time tax-exempt status is sought from the Internal Revenue Service, the same documentation may be filed with the Department for an interim certification of tax-exempt status. If such documentation is filed, the Department may, after reviewing such documentation it deems necessary, issue its determination of tax-exempt status within 60 days of receipt of such documentation. The Department shall charge a fee of $500 for such determination. This interim certification of tax-exempt status shall be valid until the Internal Revenue Service issues its determination of tax-exempt status, or for 18 months, whichever is earlier.

C. A permit shall be valid only for the locations, dates, and times designated in the permit.

History.

1995, c. 837; 1996, c. 919; 2003, c. 884; 2006, c. 644; 2009, c. 121.

The 2009 amendments.

The 2009 amendment by c. 121 substituted "$40,000" for "$25,000" in the first sentence of subsection B.

§ 18.2-340.25. Permit required; application fee; form of application.

A. Except as provided for in § 18.2-340.23, prior to the commencement of any charitable game, an organization shall obtain a permit from the Department.

B. All complete applications for a permit shall be acted upon by the Department within 45 days from the filing thereof. Upon compliance by the applicant with the provisions of this article, and at the discretion of the Department, a permit may be issued. All permits when issued shall be valid for the period specified in the permit unless it is sooner suspended or revoked. No permit shall be valid for longer than two years. The application shall be a matter of public record.

All permits shall be subject to regulation by the Department to ensure the public safety and welfare in the operation of charitable games. The permit shall only be granted after a reasonable investigation has been conducted by the Department. The Department may require any prospective employee, permit holder or applicant to submit to fingerprinting and to provide personal descriptive information to be forwarded along with employee's, licensee's or applicant's fingerprints through the Central Criminal Records Exchange to the Federal Bureau of Investigation for the purposes of obtaining criminal history record information regarding such prospective employee, permit holder or applicant. The Central Criminal Records Exchange upon receipt of a prospective employee, licensee or applicant record or notification that no record exists, shall forward the report to the Commissioner of the Department or his designee, who shall belong to a governmental entity. However, nothing in this subsection shall be construed to require the routine fingerprinting of volunteer bingo workers.

C. In no case shall an organization receive more than one permit allowing it to conduct charitable gaming; however, nothing in this section shall be construed to prohibit granting special permits pursuant to § 18.2-340.27.

D. Application for a charitable gaming permit shall be made on forms prescribed by the Department and shall be accompanied by payment of the fee for processing the application.

E. Applications for renewal of permits shall be made in accordance with Board Regulations. If a complete renewal application is received 45 days or more prior to the expiration of the permit, the permit shall continue to be effective until such time as the Department has taken final action. Otherwise, the permit shall expire at the end of its term.

F. The failure to meet any of the requirements of § 18.2-340.24 shall cause the automatic denial of the permit, and no organization shall conduct any charitable gaming until the requirements are met and a permit is obtained.

History.

1995, c. 837; 1997, cc. 777, 838; 1999, c. 361; 2003, c. 884; 2006, cc. 211, 644; 2008, cc. 387, 689.

The 2008 amendments.

The 2008 amendments by cc. 387 and 689 are identical, and substituted "Commissioner" for "director" preceding "of the Department" near the end of the fourth sentence in the second paragraph of subsection B.

OPINIONS OF THE ATTORNEY GENERAL

Exemption from permit requirement. — By removing the proceeds from pull tabs in determining the gross receipts from charitable gaming conducted under the conditions specified in § 18.2-340.26:1, an organization is exempt from the permit requirement of this section, provided the gross receipts' annual results still do not exceed $25,000. See opinion of Attorney General to The Honorable Donald L. Moseley, Secretary of Administration, 01-076 (8/30/01).

§ 18.2-340.26. Sale of raffle tickets; drawings.

A. Except as provided in subsection B, a qualified organization may sell raffle tickets both in and out of the jurisdiction designated in its permit and shall conduct the drawing within the Commonwealth.

B. A qualified organization may sell raffle tickets for a raffle drawing which will be held outside the Commonwealth, provided the raffle is conducted in accordance with (i) the regulations of the Board and (ii) the laws and regulations of the jurisdiction in which the raffle drawing will be held.

C. Before a prize drawing, each stub or other detachable section of each ticket sold or won through some other authorized charitable game conducted by the same organization holding the raffle, shall be placed into a receptacle from which the winning tickets are drawn. The receptacle shall be designed so that each ticket placed in it has an equal chance of being drawn.

History.
1995, c. 837; 1997, cc. 777, 838; 2001, c. 833; 2003, c. 884; 2006, c. 644; 2008, c. 573.

The 2008 amendments.
The 2008 amendment by c. 573 added subsection C.

§ 18.2-340.26:1. Sale of instant bingo, pull tabs or seal cards; proceeds not counted as gross receipts.

A. Instant bingo, pull tabs or seal cards may be sold only upon the premises owned or exclusively leased by the organization and at such times as the portion of the premises in which the instant bingo, pull tabs or seal cards are sold is open only to members and their guests. Nothing in this article shall be construed to prohibit the conduct of games of chance involving the sale of pull tabs or seal cards, commonly known as last sale games, conducted in accordance with this section.

B. The proceeds from instant bingo, pull tabs or seal cards shall not be included in determining the gross receipts for a qualified organization provided the gaming (i) is limited exclusively to members of the organization and their guests, (ii) is not open to the general public, and (iii) there is no public solicitation or advertisement made regarding such gaming.

History.
2001, c. 833; 2006, c. 644; 2007, c. 196.

OPINIONS OF THE ATTORNEY GENERAL

Gaming organizations are subject to audit, inspection, and enforcement. — Qualified gaming organizations that sell pull tabs in private social quarters are subject to audit, inspection, and enforcement by the Charitable Gaming Commission [now the Department of Agriculture and Consumer Services]. See opinion of Attorney General to The Honorable Donald L. Moseley, Secretary of Administration, 01-076 (8/30/01).

No restrictions on uses of proceeds of games described in statute. — The charitable gaming statutes impose no restriction on the uses to which the proceeds of the games described in the statute may be put, or any requirement that such proceeds be used for any particular purpose, including charitable purposes. See opinion of Attorney General to The Honorable Donald L. Moseley, Secretary of Administration, 01-076 (8/30/01).

Exemption from permit requirement. — By removing the proceeds from pull tabs in determining the gross receipts from charitable gaming conducted under the conditions specified in this section, an organization is exempt from the permit requirement of § 18.2-340.25, provided the gross receipts' annual results still do not exceed $25,000. See opinion of Attorney General to The Honorable Donald L. Moseley, Secretary of Administration, 01-076 (8/30/01).

§ 18.2-340.26:2. Sale of instant bingo, pull tabs, or seal cards by certain booster clubs.

As a part of its annual fund-raising event, any qualified organization that is an athletic association or booster club or a band booster club may sell instant bingo, pull tabs, or seal cards provided that (i) the sale is limited to a single event in a calendar year and (ii) the event is open to the public. The Department may require organizations authorized under this section to make such financial reporting as it deems necessary.

Nothing in this section shall be construed as exempting organizations authorized to sell instant bingo, pull tabs, or seal cards under this section from any other provisions of this article or other Board regulations.

History.
2007, c. 160.

§ 18.2-340.27. Conduct of bingo games; special permits.

A. A qualified organization shall accept only cash or, at its option, checks or debit cards in payment of any charges or assessments for players to participate in bingo games. However, no such organization shall accept postdated checks in payment of any charges or assessments for players to participate in bingo games.

B. No qualified organization or any person on the premises shall extend lines of credit or accept any credit or other electronic fund transfer other than debit cards in payment of any charges or assessments for players to participate in bingo games.

C. Bingo games may be held by qualified organizations no more frequently than two calendar days in any calendar week, except in accordance with subsection E.

D. No more than two sessions of bingo games may be held by qualified organizations in any calendar day, nor shall there be more than 55 bingo games per session.

E. A special permit may be granted a qualified organization which entitles it to conduct more frequent operations of bingo games during carnivals, fairs and state, federal or religious holidays, which shall be designated in the permit.

F. Any organization may conduct bingo games only in the county, city or town or in any adjoining county, city or town in which they regularly have been in existence or met. The Department may approve exceptions to this requirement where there is a special circumstance or documented need.

History.
    1995, c. 837; 2006, c. 644; 2010, c. 429.

Editor's note.
    Acts 2010, c. 429, cl. 3, provides: "That the Department of Agriculture and Consumer Services shall report to the chairs of the House Committee on General Laws and the Senate Committee on General Laws and Technology on or before December 1, 2010 concerning the Department's efforts to increase the number of Department-approved independent laboratory testers in order to expedite the Department's approval process for new charitable games authorized by Article 1:1 (§ 18.2-340.15 et seq.) of Chapter 6 of Title 18.2 and regulations of the Charitable Gaming Board."

The 2010 amendments.
    The 2010 amendment by c. 429 added "nor shall there be more than 55 bingo games per session" to the end of subsection D.

§ 18.2-340.28. (Effective until January 1, 2014) Conduct of instant bingo, pull tabs and seal cards.

A. Any organization qualified to conduct bingo games pursuant to the provisions of this article may play instant bingo, pull tabs, or seal cards as a part of such bingo game and, if a permit is required pursuant to § 18.2-340.25, such games shall be played only at such location and at such times as designated in the permit for regular bingo games.

B. Any organization conducting instant bingo, pull tabs, or seal cards shall maintain a record of the date, quantity and card value of instant bingo supplies purchased as well as the name and address of the supplier of such supplies. The organization shall also maintain a written invoice or receipt from a nonmember of the organization verifying any information required by this subsection. Such supplies shall be paid for only by check drawn on the gaming account of the organization. A complete inventory of all such gaming supplies shall be maintained by the organization on the premises where the gaming is being conducted.

C. No qualified organization shall sell any instant bingo, pull tabs, or seal cards to any individual under 18 years of age. No individual under 18 years of age shall play or redeem any instant bingo, pull tabs, or seal cards.

History.
    1995, c. 837; 1997, cc. 777, 838; 2006, c. 644.

Section set out twice.
    The section above is effective until January 1, 2014. For the version of this section effective January 1, 2014, see the following section, also numbered 18.2-340.28.

§ 18.2-340.28. (Effective January 1, 2014) Conduct of instant bingo, network bingo, pull tabs and seal cards.

A. Any organization qualified to conduct bingo games pursuant to the provisions of this article may play instant bingo, network bingo, pull tabs, or seal cards as a part of such bingo game and, if a permit is required pursuant to § 18.2-340.25, such games shall be played only at such location and at such times as designated in the permit for regular bingo games.

B. Any organization conducting instant bingo, network bingo, pull tabs, or seal cards shall maintain a record of the date, quantity and card value of instant bingo supplies purchased as well as the name and address of the supplier of such supplies. The organization shall also maintain a written invoice or receipt from a nonmember of the organization verifying any information required by this subsection. Such supplies shall be paid for only by check drawn on the gaming account of the organization. A complete inventory of all such gaming supplies shall be maintained by the organization on the premises where the gaming is being conducted.

C. No qualified organization shall sell any instant bingo, network bingo, pull tabs, or seal cards to any individual younger than 18 years of age. No individual younger than 18 years of age shall play or redeem any instant bingo, network bingo, pull tabs, or seal cards.

History.
    1995, c. 837; 1997, cc. 777, 838; 2006, c. 644; 2013, cc. 36, 350.

Section set out twice.
    The section above is effective January 1, 2014. For this section as in effect until January 1, 2014, see the preceding section, also numbered 18.2-340.28.

Editor's note.
    Acts 2013, cc. 36 and 350, cl. 2 provides: "That the provisions of this act shall become effective on January 1, 2014, except that the provisions of § 18.2-340.19 of this act shall become effective on July 1, 2013."

The 2013 amendments.
    The 2013 amendments by cc. 36 and 350, effective January 1, 2014, are identical and inserted "network bingo," throughout the section; and substituted "younger than 18" for "under 18" twice in subsection C.

§ 18.2-340.28:1. (Effective January 1, 2014) Conduct of network bingo.

A. Any organization qualified to conduct bingo games pursuant to the provisions of this article may sell network bingo cards as a part of a regular bingo game and, if a permit is required pursuant to

§ 18.2-340.25, network bingo shall be sold only at such location and at such times as designated in the permit for regular bingo games.

B. Any organization selling network bingo cards shall maintain a record of the date and quantity of network bingo cards purchased from a licensed network bingo provider. The organization shall also maintain a written invoice or receipt from a licensed supplier verifying any information required by this subsection. Such supplies shall be paid for only by check drawn on the gaming account of the organization or by electronic fund transfer. A complete inventory of all such gaming supplies shall be maintained by the organization on the premises where network bingo cards are sold.

C. No qualified organization shall sell any network bingo cards to any individual younger than 18 years of age. No individual younger than 18 years of age shall play or redeem any network bingo cards.

D. A qualified organization shall accept only cash or, at its option, checks or debit cards in payment of any charges or assessments for players to participate in any network bingo game. However, no such organization shall accept postdated checks in payment of any charges or assessments for players to participate in network bingo games.

E. No qualified organization or any person on the premises shall extend lines of credit or accept any credit or other electronic fund transfer other than debit cards in payment of any charges or assessments for players to participate in network bingo games.

F. No qualified organization shall conduct network bingo more frequently than one day in any calendar week, which shall not be the same day of each week.

G. No network bingo games shall be permitted in the social quarters of an organization that are open only to the organization's members and their guests.

H. No qualified organization shall sell network bingo cards on the Internet or other online service or allow the play of network bingo on the Internet or other online service. However, the location where network bingo games are conducted shall be equipped with a video monitor, television, or video screen, or any other similar means of visually displaying a broadcast or signal, that relays live, real-time video of the numbers as they are called by a live caller. The Internet or other online service may be used to relay information about winning players.

I. Qualified organizations may award network bingo prizes on a graduated scale; however, no single network bingo prize shall exceed $25,000.

J. Nothing in this section shall be construed to prohibit an organization from participating in more than one network bingo network.

History.
2013, cc. 36, 350.

Editor's note.
Acts 2013, cc. 36 and 350, cl. 2 provides: "That the provisions of this act shall become effective on January 1, 2014, except that the provisions of § 18.2-340.19 of this act shall become effective on July 1, 2013."

§ 18.2-340.29. Joint operation of bingo games; written reports; joint permit required.

A. Any two or more qualified organizations may jointly organize and conduct bingo games provided both have fully complied with all other provisions of this article.

B. Any two or more qualified organizations jointly conducting such games shall be (i) subject to the same restrictions and prohibitions contained in this article that would apply to a single organization conducting bingo games and (ii) required to furnish to the Department a written report setting forth the location where such games will be held, the division of manpower, costs, and proceeds for each game to be jointly conducted.

Upon a finding that the division of manpower and costs for each game bears a reasonable relationship to the division of proceeds, the Department shall issue a joint permit.

C. No bingo game shall be jointly conducted until the joint permit issued pursuant to subsection B is obtained by the organizations.

History.
1995, c. 837; 2003, c. 884; 2006, c. 644.

§ 18.2-340.30. Reports of gross receipts and disbursements required; form of reports; failure to file.

A. Each qualified organization shall keep a complete record of all inventory of charitable gaming supplies purchased, all receipts from its charitable gaming operation, and all disbursements related to such operation. Except as provided in § 18.2-340.23, each qualified organization shall file at least annually, on a form prescribed by the Department, a report of all such receipts and disbursements, the amount of money on hand attributable to charitable gaming as of the end of the period covered by the report and any other information related to its charitable gaming operation that the Department may require. In addition, the Board, by regulation, may require any qualified organization whose net receipts exceed a specified amount during any three-month period to file a report of its receipts and disbursements for such period. All reports filed pursuant to this section shall be a matter of public record.

B. All reports required by this section shall be filed on or before the date prescribed by the Department. The Board, by regulation, shall establish a schedule of late fees to be assessed for any organization that fails to submit required reports by the due date.

C. Except as provided in § 18.2-340.23, each qualified organization shall designate or compensate an outside individual or group who shall be responsible for filing an annual, and, if required, quarterly, financial report if the organization goes out of business or otherwise ceases to conduct charitable gaming activities. The Department shall require such reports as it deems necessary until all proceeds of any charitable gaming have been used for the purposes specified in § 18.2-340.19 or have been disbursed in a manner approved by the Department.

D. Each qualified organization shall maintain for three years a complete written record of (i) all charitable gaming sessions using Department prescribed forms or reasonable facsimiles thereof approved by the Department; (ii) the name and address of each individual to whom any prize or jackpot in excess of $599 from any charitable gaming is awarded, as well as the amount of the award; and (iii) an itemized record of all receipts and disbursements, including operating costs and use of proceeds incurred in operating bingo games.

E. The failure to file reports within 30 days of the time such reports are due shall cause the automatic revocation of the permit, and no organization shall conduct any bingo game or raffle thereafter until the report is properly filed and a new permit is obtained. However, the Department may grant an extension of time for filing such reports for a period not to exceed 45 days if requested by an organization, provided the organization requests an extension within 15 days of the time such reports are due and all projected fees are paid. For the term of any such extension, the organization's permit shall not be automatically revoked, such organization may continue to conduct charitable gaming, and no new permit shall be required.

History.
1995, c. 837; 1997, cc. 777, 838; 1999, c. 360; 2003, c. 884; 2006, c. 644; 2007, c. 541.

§ 18.2-340.30:1. Repealed by Acts 2010, c. 429, cl. 2.

Editor's note.
Former § 18.2-340.30:1, establishing that proceeds from "winner-take-all" games are not counted as gross receipts, was enacted by Acts 2007, c. 550.

§ 18.2-340.31. Audit of reports; exemption; audit and administration fee.

A. All reports filed pursuant to § 18.2-340.30 shall be subject to audit by the Department in accordance with Board regulations. The Department may engage the services of independent certified public accountants to perform any audits deemed necessary to fulfill the Department's responsibilities under this article.

B. The Department shall prescribe a reasonable audit and administration fee to be paid by any organization conducting charitable gaming under a permit issued by the Department unless the organization is exempt from such fee pursuant to § 18.2-340.23. Such fee shall not exceed one and one-quarter percent of the gross receipts which an organization reports pursuant to § 18.2-340.30. The audit and administration fee shall accompany each report for each calendar quarter.

C. The audit and administration fee shall be payable to the Treasurer of Virginia. All such fees received by the Treasurer of Virginia shall be separately accounted for and shall be used only by the Department for the purposes of auditing and regulating charitable gaming.

History.
1995, c. 837; 1997, cc. 777, 838; 2003, c. 884; 2006, c. 644.

Editor's note.
Acts 2012, Sp. Sess. I, c. 3, as amended by Acts 2013, c. 806, effective for the biennium ending June 30, 2014, Item 100 B provides: "Notwithstanding § 18.2-340.31, Code of Virginia, any and all fees paid by any organization conducting charitable gaming under a permit issued by the department, including audit and administrative fees and permit fees, shall be deposited to the general fund."

§ 18.2-340.32. Repealed by Acts 2004, c. 462.

Cross references.
For current provisions as to regulation of bingo and instant bingo, see § 15.2-912.2.

§ 18.2-340.33. Prohibited practices.

In addition to those other practices prohibited by this article, the following acts or practices are prohibited:

1. No part of the gross receipts derived by a qualified organization may be used for any purpose other than (i) reasonable and proper gaming expenses, (ii) reasonable and proper business expenses, (iii) those lawful religious, charitable, community or educational purposes for which the organization is specifically chartered or organized, and (iv) expenses relating to the acquisition, construction, maintenance, or repair of any interest in the real property involved in the operation of the organization and used for lawful religious, charitable, community or educational purposes. For the purposes of clause (iv), such expenses may include the expenses of a corporation formed for the purpose of serving as the real estate holding entity of a qualified organization, provided (a) such holding entity is qualified as a tax exempt organization under § 501(c) of the Internal Revenue Code and (b) the membership of the qualified organization is identical to such holding entity.

2. Except as provided in § 18.2-340.34:1, no qualified organization shall enter into a contract with or otherwise employ for compensation any person for the purpose of organizing, managing, or conducting any charitable games. However, organizations composed of or for deaf or blind persons may use a part of their gross receipts for costs associated

with providing clerical assistance in the management and operation but not the conduct of charitable gaming.

The provisions of this subdivision shall not prohibit the joint operation of bingo games held in accordance with § 18.2-340.29.

3. No person shall pay or receive for use of any premises devoted, in whole or in part, to the conduct of any charitable games, any consideration in excess of the current fair market rental value of such property. Fair market rental value consideration shall not be based upon or determined by reference to a percentage of the proceeds derived from the operation of any charitable games or to the number of people in attendance at such charitable games.

4. No building or other premises shall be utilized in whole or in part for the purpose of conducting charitable gaming more frequently than two calendar days in any one calendar week. However, no building or other premises owned by (i) a qualified organization which is exempt from taxation pursuant to § 501(c) of the Internal Revenue Code or (ii) any county, city or town shall be utilized in whole or in part for the purpose of conducting bingo games more frequently than four calendar days in any one calendar week.

The provisions of this subdivision shall not apply to the playing of bingo games pursuant to a special permit issued in accordance with § 18.2-340.27.

5. No person shall participate in the management or operation of any charitable game unless such person is and, for a period of at least 30 days immediately preceding such participation, has been a bona fide member of the organization. For any organization that is not composed of members, a person who is not a bona fide member may volunteer in the conduct of a charitable game as long as that person is directly supervised by a bona fide official member of the organization.

The provisions of this subdivision shall not apply to (i) persons employed as clerical assistants by qualified organizations composed of or for deaf or blind persons; (ii) employees of a corporate sponsor of a qualified organization, provided such employees' participation is limited to the management, operation or conduct of no more than one raffle per year; (iii) the spouse or family member of any such bona fide member of a qualified organization provided at least one bona fide member is present; or (iv) persons employed by a qualified organization authorized to sell pull tabs or seal cards in accordance with § 18.2-340.16, provided (a) such sales are conducted by no more than two on-duty employees, (b) such employees receive no compensation for or based on the sale of the pull tabs or seal cards, and (c) such sales are conducted in the private social quarters of the organization.

6. No person shall receive any remuneration for participating in the management, operation or conduct of any charitable game, except that:

a. Persons employed by organizations composed of or for deaf or blind persons may receive remuneration not to exceed $30 per event for providing clerical assistance in the management and operation but not the conduct of charitable games only for such organizations;

b. Persons under the age of 19 who sell raffle tickets for a qualified organization to raise funds for youth activities in which they participate may receive nonmonetary incentive awards or prizes from the organization;

c. Remuneration may be paid to off-duty law-enforcement officers from the jurisdiction in which such bingo games are played for providing uniformed security for such bingo games even if such officer is a member of the sponsoring organization, provided the remuneration paid to such member is in accordance with off-duty law-enforcement personnel work policies approved by the local law-enforcement official and further provided that such member is not otherwise engaged in the management, operation or conduct of the bingo games of that organization, or to private security services businesses licensed pursuant to § 9.1-139 providing uniformed security for such bingo games, provided that employees of such businesses shall not otherwise be involved in the management, operation, or conduct of the bingo games of that organization;

d. A member of a qualified organization lawfully participating in the management, operation or conduct of a bingo game may be provided food and nonalcoholic beverages by such organization for on-premises consumption during the bingo game provided the food and beverages are provided in accordance with Board regulations; and

e. Remuneration may be paid to bingo managers or callers who have a current registration certificate issued by the Department in accordance with § 18.2-340.34:1, or who are exempt from such registration requirement. Such remuneration shall not exceed $100 per session.

7. No landlord shall, at bingo games conducted on the landlord's premises, (i) participate in the conduct, management, or operation of any bingo games; (ii) sell, lease or otherwise provide for consideration any bingo supplies, including, but not limited to, bingo cards, instant bingo cards, or other game pieces; or (iii) require as a condition of the lease or by contract that a particular manufacturer, distributor or supplier of bingo supplies or equipment be used by the organization.

The provisions of this subdivision shall not apply to any qualified organization conducting bingo games on its own behalf at premises owned by it.

8. No qualified organization shall enter into any contract with or otherwise employ or compensate any member of the organization on account of the sale of bingo supplies or equipment.

9. **(Effective until January 1, 2014)** No organization shall award any bingo prize money or any merchandise valued in excess of the following amounts:

a. No bingo door prize shall exceed $50 for a single door prize or $250 in cumulative door prizes in any one session;

b. No regular bingo or special bingo game prize shall exceed $100;

c. No instant bingo, pull tab, or seal card prize for a single card shall exceed $599; and

d. No bingo jackpot of any nature whatsoever shall exceed $1,000, nor shall the total amount of bingo jackpot prizes awarded in any one session exceed $1,000. Proceeds from the sale of bingo cards and the sheets used for bingo jackpot games shall be accounted for separately from the bingo cards or sheets used for any other bingo games.

9. **(Effective January 1, 2014)** No organization shall award any bingo prize money or any merchandise valued in excess of the following amounts:

a. No bingo door prize shall exceed $50 for a single door prize or $250 in cumulative door prizes in any one session;

b. No regular bingo or special bingo game prize shall exceed $100;

c. No instant bingo, pull tab, or seal card prize for a single card shall exceed $1,000;

d. Except as provided in subdivision 9, no bingo jackpot of any nature whatsoever shall exceed $1,000, nor shall the total amount of bingo jackpot prizes awarded in any one session exceed $1,000. Proceeds from the sale of bingo cards and the sheets used for bingo jackpot games shall be accounted for separately from the bingo cards or sheets used for any other bingo games; and

e. No single network bingo prize shall exceed $25,000. Proceeds from the sale of network bingo cards shall be accounted for separately from bingo cards and sheets used for any other bingo game.

10. The provisions of subdivision 9 shall not apply to:

Any progressive bingo game, in which (a) a regular or special prize, not to exceed $100, is awarded on the basis of predetermined numbers or patterns selected at random and (b) a progressive prize, not to exceed $500 for the initial progressive prize and $5,000 for the maximum progressive prize, is awarded if the predetermined numbers or patterns are covered when a certain number of numbers is called, provided (i) there are no more than six such games per session per organization, (ii) the amount of increase of the progressive prize per session is no more than $100, (iii) the bingo cards or sheets used in such games are sold separately from the bingo cards or sheets used for any other bingo games, (iv) the organization separately accounts for the proceeds from such sale, and (v) such games are otherwise operated in accordance with the Department's rules of play.

11. No organization shall award any raffle prize valued at more than $100,000.

The provisions of this subdivision shall not apply to a raffle conducted no more than once per calendar year by a qualified organization qualified as a tax-exempt organization pursuant to § 501(c) of the Internal Revenue Code for a prize consisting of a lot improved by a residential dwelling where 100 per-cent of the moneys received from such a raffle, less deductions for the fair market value for the cost of acquisition of the land and materials, are donated to lawful religious, charitable, community, or educational organizations specifically chartered or organized under the laws of the Commonwealth and qualified as a § 501(c) tax-exempt organization.

12. No qualified organization composed of or for deaf or blind persons which employs a person not a member to provide clerical assistance in the management and operation but not the conduct of any charitable games shall conduct such games unless it has in force fidelity insurance, as defined in § 38.2-120, written by an insurer licensed to do business in the Commonwealth.

13. No person shall participate in the management or operation of any charitable game if he has ever been convicted of any felony or if he has been convicted of any misdemeanor involving fraud, theft, or financial crimes within the preceding five years. No person shall participate in the conduct of any charitable game if, within the preceding 10 years, he has been convicted of any felony or if, within the preceding five years he has been convicted of any misdemeanor involving fraud, theft, or financial crimes. In addition, no person shall participate in the management, operation or conduct of any charitable game if that person, within the preceding five years, has participated in the management, operation, or conduct of any charitable game which was found by the Department or a court of competent jurisdiction to have been operated in violation of state law, local ordinance or Board regulation.

14. Qualified organizations jointly conducting bingo games pursuant to § 18.2-340.29 shall not circumvent any restrictions and prohibitions which would otherwise apply if a single organization were conducting such games. These restrictions and prohibitions shall include, but not be limited to, the frequency with which bingo games may be held, the value of merchandise or money awarded as prizes, or any other practice prohibited under this section.

15. A qualified organization shall not purchase any charitable gaming supplies for use in the Commonwealth from any person who is not currently registered with the Department as a supplier pursuant to § 18.2-340.34.

16. Unless otherwise permitted in this article, no part of an organization's charitable gaming gross receipts shall be used for an organization's social or recreational activities.

History.

1995, c. 837; 1996, c. 919; 1997, cc. 777, 838; 1998, cc. 57, 398; 1999, c. 534; 2000, c. 1000; 2001, c. 754; 2002, c. 282; 2003, c. 884; 2004, c. 275; 2005, cc. 776, 826; 2006, c. 644; 2007, cc. 226, 790; 2008, c. 352; 2010, c. 429; 2013, cc. 36, 350.

Subdivision 9 set out twice. — The first version of subdivision 9 above is effective until January 1, 2014. The second version of subdivision 9 is effective January 1, 2014.

Editor's note.

Acts 1998, c. 398, cl. 3, effective October 1, 1998, provides: "That none of the provisions of this act shall be construed to reduce the potential lawful uses of gross receipts from charitable gaming derived by qualified organizations from what they were interpreted to be by the Charitable Gaming Commission [now the Department of Agriculture and Consumer Services] as of January 14, 1998."

The 2000 amendment by c. 1000 added the former second paragraph of subdivision 3. Acts 2001, c. 813, cl. 3 extended the expiration date for this amendment to July 1, 2002. The section is set out above without the change by Acts 2000, c. 1000.

Acts 2005, cc. 776 and 826, cl. 2, provide: "That notwithstanding the provisions of subsection A (ii) of § 15.2-912.2, the Charitable Gaming Board shall establish the hours during which bingo games may be conducted."

Acts 2010, c. 429, cl. 3, provides: "That the Department of Agriculture and Consumer Services shall report to the chairs of the House Committee on General Laws and the Senate Committee on General Laws and Technology on or before December 1, 2010 concerning the Department's efforts to increase the number of Department-approved independent laboratory testers in order to expedite the Department's approval process for new charitable games authorized by Article 1:1 (§ 18.2-340.15 et seq.) of Chapter 6 of Title 18.2 and regulations of the Charitable Gaming Board."

Acts 2013, cc. 36 and 350, cl. 2 provides: "That the provisions of this act shall become effective on January 1, 2014, except that the provisions of § 18.2-340.19 of this act shall become effective on July 1, 2013."

The 2008 amendments.
The 2008 amendment by c. 352 rewrote the second sentence in subparagraph 9 d, which read: "Bingo cards and the sheets used for bingo jackpot games shall be sold separately from the bingo cards or sheets used for any other bingo games, and the organization shall separately account for the proceeds from such sales."

The 2010 amendments.
The 2010 amendment by c. 429 rewrote subdivision 10.

The 2013 amendments.
The 2013 amendments by cc. 36 and 350, effective January 1, 2014, are identical and in subdivision 9, substituted "$1,000" for "$599" in subdivision 9 c, added the exception at the beginning of subdivision 9 d, added subdivision 9 e, and made related changes.

CASE NOTES

Editor's note.
The cases annotated below were decided under prior law.

Single, double, and triple bingo lines do not satisfy the definition of "jackpot" in subdivision 5 of former § 18.2-340.1. Therefore, prizes awarded for those accomplishments are not "jackpot" prizes. Only prizes awarded for success at "coverall" qualify as "jackpot" prizes. Regular Veterans Ass'n v. Commonwealth, 18 Va. App. 683, 446 S.E.2d 621 (1994) (decided under former § 18.2-340.9).

If the total prizes awarded in the game equal or exceed the gross receipts from the sale of cards, those prizes will accomplish the repayment of all the gross receipts as prize money back to the players, and that game will fall within the exemption of subsection H of this section (see now subsection I). Regular Veterans Ass'n v. Commonwealth, 18 Va. App. 683, 446 S.E.2d 621 (1994) (decided under former § 18.2-340.9).

Prize/receipts ratio not within statutory provisions. — Where commander of veteran's organization acknowledged that no financial records showed equal receipts and disbursements for games, that on some days receipts exceeded prizes, and that on other days prizes exceeded receipts, and he opined that on an ongoing basis, it was "basically an averaging situation," the games as described did not satisfy the definition in subsection H of this section (see now subsection I). Regular Veterans Ass'n v. Commonwealth, 18 Va. App. 683, 446 S.E.2d 621 (1994) (decided under former § 18.2-340.9).

Evidence sufficient for violation. — Where witness's testimony did not relate specifically to games in question, receipts/prize ratio analysis did not meet burden of proof, where the records that were produced refuted a consistent return of gross receipts to the players, and where the announcement of the prize values before the

sale of cards established that no relationship existed between gross receipts and prize value determination, the evidence supported the jury's determination that games did not fall within the definition in subsection H of this section (see now subsection I) and that the ladies auxiliary and veteran's organization on the respective occasions charged against them, awarded jackpot prizes exceeding $1,000 in violation of subsection G of this section (see now subsection H). Regular Veterans Ass'n v. Commonwealth, 18 Va. App. 683, 446 S.E.2d 621 (1994) (decided under former § 18.2-340.9).

Double jeopardy inapplicable. — For a charge under this section, the misappropriated funds must be from gross receipts of bingo games or raffles conducted by licensed organizations; there is no minimum amount. For a charge of grand larceny not from the person under § 18.2-95, there is no limitation on the source of the stolen property, but the property must be worth at least $200; thus, each offense contains an element the other does not, and defendant therefore was not punished twice for the same offense. Waldrop v. Commonwealth, No. 2094-94-2 (Ct. of Appeals Dec. 29, 1995) (decided under former § 18.2-340.9).

§ 18.2-340.34. Suppliers of charitable gaming supplies; manufacturers of electronic games of chance systems; permit; qualification; suspension, revocation or refusal to renew certificate; maintenance, production, and release of records.

A. No person shall offer to sell, sell or otherwise provide charitable gaming supplies to any qualified organization and no manufacturer shall distribute electronic games of chance systems for charitable gaming in the Commonwealth unless and until such person has made application for and has been issued a permit by the Department. An application for permit shall be made on forms prescribed by the Department and shall be accompanied by a fee in the amount of $1,000. Each permit shall remain valid for a period of one year from the date of issuance. Application for renewal of a permit shall be accompanied by a fee in the amount of $1,000 and shall be made on forms prescribed by the Department.

B. The Board shall have authority to prescribe by regulation reasonable criteria consistent with the provisions of this article for the registration of suppliers and manufacturers of electronic games of chance systems for charitable gaming. The Department may refuse to issue a permit to any supplier or manufacturer who has, or which has any officer, director, partner, or owner who has (i) been convicted of or pleaded nolo contendere to a felony in any state or federal court or has been convicted of any offense which, if committed in the Commonwealth, would be a felony; (ii) been convicted of or pleaded nolo contendere to a crime involving gambling; (iii) had any license, permit, certificate or other authority related to activities defined as charitable gaming in the Commonwealth suspended or revoked in the Commonwealth or in any other jurisdiction; (iv) failed to file or has been delinquent in excess of one year in the filing of any tax returns or the payment of any taxes due the Commonwealth; or (v) failed to establish a registered office or registered agent in the Commonwealth if so required by § 13.1-634 or 13.1-763.

C. The Department may suspend, revoke or refuse to renew the permit of any supplier or manufacturer for any conduct described in subsection B or for any violation of this article or regulation of the Board. Before taking any such action, the Department shall give the supplier or manufacturer a written statement of the grounds upon which it proposes to take such action and an opportunity to be heard. Every hearing in a contested case shall be conducted in accordance with the Administrative Process Act (§ 2.2-4000 et seq.).

D. Each supplier shall document each sale of charitable gaming supplies, including electronic games of chance systems, and other items incidental to the conduct of charitable gaming, such as markers, wands or tape, to a qualified organization on an invoice which clearly shows (i) the name and address of the qualified organization to which such supplies or items were sold; (ii) the date of the sale; (iii) the name or form and serial number of each deal of instant bingo cards and pull-tab raffle cards, the quantity of deals sold and the price per deal paid by the qualified organization; (iv) the serial number of the top sheet in each packet of bingo paper, the serial number for each series of uncollated bingo paper, and the cut, color and quantity of bingo paper sold; and (v) any other information with respect to charitable gaming supplies, including electronic games of chance systems, or other items incidental to the conduct of charitable gaming as the Board may prescribe by regulation. A legible copy of the invoice shall accompany the charitable gaming supplies when delivered to the qualified organization.

Each manufacturer of electronic games of chance systems shall document each distribution of such systems to a qualified organization or supplier on an invoice which clearly shows (i) the name and address of the qualified organization or supplier to which such systems were distributed; (ii) the date of distribution; (iii) the serial number of each such system; and (iv) any other information with respect to electronic games of chance systems as the Board may prescribe by regulation. A legible copy of the invoice shall accompany the electronic games of chance systems when delivered to the qualified organization or supplier.

E. Each supplier and manufacturer shall maintain a legible copy of each invoice required by subsection D for a period of three years from the date of sale. Each supplier and manufacturer shall make such documents immediately available for inspection and copying to any agent or employee of the Department upon request made during normal business hours. This subsection shall not limit the right of the Department to require the production of any other documents in the possession of the supplier or manufacturer which relate to its transactions with qualified organizations. All documents and other information of a proprietary nature furnished to the Department in accordance with this subsection shall not be a matter of public record and

shall be exempt from disclosure under the provisions of the Freedom of Information Act (§ 2.2-3700 et seq.).

History.
1995, c. 837; 1996, c. 919; 1997, cc. 777, 838; 1999, c. 534; 2003, c. 884; 2006, c. 644; 2007, c. 264.

Cross references.
As to records which are excluded from the provisions of the Virginia Freedom of Information Act, see § 2.2-3705.1 et seq.

§ 18.2-340.34:1. Bingo managers and callers; remuneration; registration; qualification; suspension, revocation or refusal to renew certificate; exceptions.

A. No person shall receive remuneration as a bingo manager or caller from any qualified organization unless and until such person has made application for and has been issued a registration certificate by the Department. Application for registration shall be made on forms prescribed by the Department and shall be accompanied by a fee in the amount of $75. Each registration certificate shall remain valid for a period of one year from the date of issuance. Application for renewal of a registration certificate shall be accompanied by a fee in the amount of $75 and shall be made on forms prescribed by the Department.

B. As a condition of registration as a bingo manager, the applicant shall (i) have been a bona fide member of the qualified organization for at least 12 consecutive months prior to making application for registration and (ii) be required to complete a reasonable training course developed and conducted by the Department.

As a condition of registration as a bingo caller, the applicant shall be required to complete a reasonable training course developed and conducted by the Department.

The Department may refuse to register any bingo manager or caller who has (a) been convicted of or pleaded nolo contendere to a felony in any state or federal court or has been convicted of any offense which, if committed in the Commonwealth, would be a felony; (b) been convicted of or pleaded nolo contendere to a crime involving gambling; (c) had any license, permit, certificate, or other authority related to activities defined as charitable gaming in the Commonwealth suspended or revoked in the Commonwealth or in any other jurisdiction; or (d) failed to file or has been delinquent in excess of one year in the filing of any tax returns or the payment of any taxes due the Commonwealth.

C. The Department may suspend, revoke, or refuse to renew the registration certificate of any bingo manager or caller for any conduct described in subsection B or for any violation of this article or regulations of the Board. Before taking any such action, the Department shall give the bingo manager or caller a written statement of the grounds upon which it proposes to take such action and an opportunity to be heard. Every hearing in a contested case shall be conducted in accordance with the Administrative Process Act (§ 2.2-4000 et seq.).

D. The provisions of subsection A requiring registration for bingo callers with the Department shall not apply to a bingo caller for a volunteer fire department or rescue squad or auxiliary unit thereof that has been recognized in accordance with § 15.2-955 by an ordinance or resolution of the political subdivision where the volunteer fire department or rescue squad is located as being a part of the safety program of such political subdivision.

History.
2005, cc. 776, 826; 2007, cc. 226, 347.

Editor's note.
Acts 2005, cc. 776 and 826, cl. 2, provide: "That notwithstanding the provisions of subsection A (ii) of § 15.2-912.2, the Charitable Gaming Board shall establish the hours during which bingo games may be conducted."

§ 18.2-340.34:2. (Effective January 1, 2014) Licensing of network bingo providers; qualification; suspension, revocation, or refusal to renew license; maintenance, production, and release of records.

A. No person shall sell or offer to sell or otherwise provide access to a network bingo network to any qualified organization unless and until such person has made application for and has been issued a license by the Department. An application for license shall be made on forms prescribed by the Department and shall be accompanied by a fee in the amount of $500. Each license shall remain valid for a period of two years from the date of issuance. Application for renewal of a license shall be accompanied by a fee in the amount of $500 and shall be made on forms prescribed by the Department.

B. The Board shall have authority to prescribe by regulation reasonable criteria consistent with the provisions of this article for the licensure of network bingo providers. The Department may refuse to issue a license to any network bingo provider that has any officer, director, partner, or owner who has (i) been convicted of or pleaded nolo contendere to a felony in any state or federal court or has been convicted of any offense that, if committed in the Commonwealth, would be a felony; (ii) been convicted of or pleaded nolo contendere to a crime involving gambling; (iii) had any license, permit, certificate, or other authority related to activities defined as charitable gaming in the Commonwealth suspended or revoked in the Commonwealth or in any other jurisdiction; (iv) failed to file or been delinquent in excess of one year in the filing of any tax returns or the payment of any taxes due the Commonwealth; or (v) failed to establish a registered office or registered agent in the Commonwealth if so required by § 13.1-634 or 13.1-763.

C. The Department may suspend, revoke, or refuse to renew the license of any network bingo provider for any conduct described in subsection B or for any violation of this article or regulation of the Board. Before taking any such action, the Department shall give the network bingo provider a written statement of the grounds upon which it proposes to take such action and an opportunity to be heard. Every hearing in a contested case shall be conducted in accordance with the Administrative Process Act (§ 2.2-4000 et seq.).

D. The Department by regulation shall require network bingo providers to have onsite independent supervision of network bingo games as the numbers are called.

E. Each network bingo provider shall document each sale of network bingo supplies and other items incidental to the conduct of network bingo to a qualified organization on an invoice that clearly shows (i) the name and address of the qualified organization to which such supplies or items were sold; (ii) the date of the sale; (iii) the name or form and serial number of each network bingo card, the quantity of cards sold, and the price per card paid by the qualified organization; and (iv) any other information required by the Department. A legible copy of the invoice shall accompany the network bingo supplies when delivered to the qualified organization.

F. Each network bingo provider shall maintain a legible copy of each invoice required by subsection E for a period of three years from the date of sale. Each network bingo provider shall make such documents immediately available for inspection and copying to any agent or employee of the Department upon request made during normal business hours. This subsection shall not limit the right of the Department to require the production of any other documents in the possession of the network bingo provider that relate to its transactions with qualified organizations. All documents and other information of a proprietary nature furnished to the Department in accordance with this subsection shall be exempt from disclosure under the provisions of the Freedom of Information Act (§ 2.2-3700 et seq.).

History.
2013, cc. 36, 350.

Editor's note.
Acts 2013, cc. 36 and 350, cl. 2 provides: "That the provisions of this act shall become effective on January 1, 2014, except that the provisions of § 18.2-340.19 of this act shall become effective on July 1, 2013."

§ 18.2-340.35. Assistance from Department of State Police.

The Department of the State Police, upon request of the Department, shall assist in the conduct of investigations by the Department.

History.
1995, c. 837; 2003, c. 884.

§ 18.2-340.36. Suspension of permit.

A. When any officer charged with the enforcement of the charitable gaming laws of the Commonwealth has reasonable cause to believe that the conduct of charitable gaming is being conducted by an organization in violation of this article or the regulations of the Board, he may apply to any judge, magistrate, or other person having authority to issue criminal warrants for the immediate suspension of the permit of the organization conducting the bingo game or raffle. If the judge, magistrate, or person to whom such application is presented is satisfied that probable cause exists to suspend the permit, he shall suspend the permit. Immediately upon such suspension, the officer shall notify the organization in writing of such suspension.

B. Written notice specifying the particular basis for the immediate suspension shall be provided by the officer to the organization within one business day of the suspension and a hearing held thereon by the Department or its designated hearing officer within 10 days of the suspension unless the organization consents to a later date. No charitable gaming shall be conducted by the organization until the suspension has been lifted by the Department or a court of competent jurisdiction.

History.

1995, c. 837; 2003, c. 884.

§ 18.2-340.37. Criminal penalties.

A. Any person who violates the provisions of this article or who willfully and knowingly files, or causes to be filed, a false application, report or other document or who willfully and knowingly makes a false statement, or causes a false statement to be made, on any application, report or other document required to be filed with or made to the Department shall be guilty of a Class 1 misdemeanor.

B. Each day in violation shall constitute a separate offense.

C. Any person who converts funds derived from any charitable gaming to his own or another's use, when the amount of funds is less than $200, shall be guilty of petit larceny and, when the amount of funds is $200 or more, shall be guilty of grand larceny. The provisions of this section shall not preclude the applicability of any other provision of the criminal law of the Commonwealth that may apply to any course of conduct that violates this section.

History.

1995, c. 837; 1996, c. 919; 2003, c. 884; 2006, c. 644.

§ 18.2-340.38. Repealed by Acts 2001, c. 754, cl. 2.

ARTICLE 2.
SUNDAY OFFENSES.

§§ 18.2-341 through 18.2-343. Repealed by Acts 2004, c. 608.

ARTICLE 3.
SEXUAL OFFENSES, PROSTITUTION, ETC.

§ 18.2-344. Fornication.

Any person, not being married, who voluntarily shall have sexual intercourse with any other person, shall be guilty of fornication, punishable as a Class 4 misdemeanor.

History.

Code 1950, §§ 18.1-188, 18.1-190; 1960, c. 358; 1975, cc. 14, 15.

Law Review.

For survey of Virginia law on evidence for the year 1974-1975, see 61 Va. L. Rev. 1752 (1975). For an article, "Sex and Guilt," see 84 Va. L. Rev 1 (1998). For note, "Toward a More Balanced Treatment of the Negligent Transmission of Sexually Transmitted Diseases and Aids," see 12 Geo. Mason. L. Rev. 481 (2003). For 2006 survey article, "Family and Juvenile Law," see 41 U. Rich. L. Rev. 151 (2006).

Michie's Jurisprudence.

For related discussion, see 1A M.J. Actions, § 6; 1A M.J. Adultery, Fornication and Lewdness, §§ 2, 3, 8.

CASE NOTES

Constitutionality. — Where the decision on the constitutionality of § 18.2-344 was to determine the injured party's right to pursue the tort claim for damages against the boyfriend who allegedly passed herpes to the injured party during consensual sex, this presented a justiciable issue, as a decision by the state's high court would not have been an advisory opinion. Martin v. Ziherl, 269 Va. 35, 607 S.E.2d 367, 2005 Va. LEXIS 7 (2005).

Where the injured party sued the injured party's boyfriend after allegedly contracting herpes from the boyfriend, the boyfriend was unable to rely on a defense that the injured party consented to an illegal act. Martin v. Ziherl, 269 Va. 35, 607 S.E.2d 367, 2005 Va. LEXIS 7 (2005).

Section violates the Due Process Clause under U.S. Const., Amend. XIV because it impairs the liberty of unmarried persons to make decisions concerning the intimacies of their physical relationship. Martin v. Ziherl, 269 Va. 35, 607 S.E.2d 367, 2005 Va. LEXIS 7 (2005).

Action challenging constitutionality dismissed where threat of prosecution not shown. — Action seeking injunctive and declaratory relief on the grounds that this section and § 18.2-345 violated plaintiffs' rights to privacy was dismissed where plaintiffs, who sought to determine whether the state, consistent with the Constitution, may restrict the non-prostitutional, heterosexual activities of two unmarried, consenting adults when such activities occur in the privacy of one's home, failed to show even a remote chance that they were threatened with prosecution under these provisions. Doe v. Duling, 782 F.2d 1202 (4th Cir. 1986).

There is no crime in Virginia of entreat to commit fornication. The word "entreat" is found in § 18.2-29 — Criminal Solicitation. A key element of solicitation is that the substantive crime solicited be a felony; fornication is a misdemeanor. Weatherford v. Commonwealth, No. 1489-90-1 (Ct. of Appeals, March 3, 1992).

One credible witness is sufficient to authorize a conviction for fornication. Commonwealth v. Cregor, 48 Va. (7 Gratt.) 591 (1850).

Crime does not fall within definition of moral turpitude. — The crime of cohabitation and fornication does not fall within the meaning of the Virginia Supreme Court's definition of moral turpitude; therefore, song was not defamatory per se. Freedlander v. Edens Broadcasting, Inc., 734 F. Supp. 221 (E.D. Va.), aff'd, 923 F.2d 848 (4th Cir. 1990).

Participation bars recovery in tort for injuries resulting from act. — Participation in the crime of fornication, in violation of this section, bars recovery in tort for injuries (the Herpes Simplex Type 2 virus) resulting from that criminal act. Zysk v. Zysk, 239 Va. 32, 404 S.E.2d 721 (1990).

A plaintiff whose consent is obtained by duress is not subject to the general rule that consensual participation in an illegal or immoral act bars a participant from seeking monetary reward for injuries resulting from that act. Therefore, where the amended motion for judgment alleged that plaintiff participated in the act of sexual intercourse under duress and coercion caused by defendant's exploitative treatment of him, allegations of duress and coercion, as factually supported by the motion for judgment, brought plaintiff's action within the "fraud or duress" exception. Trotter v. Okawa, 248 Va. 212, 445 S.E.2d 121 (1994).

Violation of section barred recovery in tort for Herpes infection. — Plaintiff's participation in the crime of fornication, in violation of this section, barred her recovery in tort for injuries resulting from that criminal act, specifically, infection with the Herpes Simplex Type 2 virus. Zysk v. Zysk, 239 Va. 32, 404 S.E.2d 721 (1990).

Public policy exception to employment-at-will doctrine. — The public policies inherent in this section prohibiting fornication provide the basis for a narrow exception to the employment-at-will doctrine, and an employee who was a member of the class of persons the section is designed to protect may bring a common-law action for wrongful termination based on these public policies. Mitchem v. Counts, 259 Va. 179, 523 S.E.2d 246 (2000).

Employee who alleged that he was forced to quit his job as a result of retaliatory conduct that supervisors directed at the employee after the employee refused to engage in sexual harassment at work sufficiently stated a claim for wrongful constructive discharge in violation of public policy because the employee was a member of the class of persons that the statutes forbidding fornication, sexual battery, aggravated sexual battery, and prostitution were designed to protect. Hill v. Paramont Mfg., LLC, — F. Supp. 2d —, 2006 U.S. Dist. LEXIS 78488 (W.D. Va. Oct. 18, 2006).

Employee's proposed amendment (amending her complaint to allege that her discharge followed from her refusal to commit fornication, lewd and lascivious behavior and sexual assault under Virginia law) would have been futile because the Virginia Supreme Court had struck down § 18.2-344 as unconstitutional, the hug the employee complained of did not even begin to approach the sort of "open and gross lewdness" § 18.2-345 prohibited, and it was legally impossible to consent to sexual assault. Balas v. Huntington Ingalls Indus., 711 F.3d 401, 2013 U.S. App. LEXIS 5199 (4th Cir. Mar. 15, 2013).

CIRCUIT COURT OPINIONS

Violation of public policy supported constructive discharge claim. — Defendants' demurrer to three women employees' claim for constructive discharge was overruled as the women alleged that their continued employment was contingent upon their involvement in acts that violated the public policies set forth in § 18.2-344, prohibiting fornication, and § 18.2-345, prohibiting

lewd and lascivious cohabitation; additionally, the frequency and extent of one of the male employee's actions supported an inference of deliberateness and intolerable working conditions, notwithstanding defendants' assertion that the sole purpose of the man's actions was for the women to succumb to their sexual advances. Padilla v. Silver Diner, 63 Va. Cir. 50, 2003 Va. Cir. LEXIS 169 (Virginia Beach 2003).

§ 18.2-345. Repealed by Acts 2013, c. 621.

Editor's note.

Former § 18.2-345, pertaining to lewd and lascivious cohabitation, derived from Code 1950, § 18.1-193; 1960, c. 358; 1975, cc. 14, 15.

§ 18.2-346. Prostitution; commercial sexual conduct; commercial exploitation of a minor; penalties.

A. Any person who, for money or its equivalent, (i) commits adultery, fornication, or any act in violation of § 18.2-361 or (ii) offers to commit adultery, fornication, or any act in violation of § 18.2-361 and thereafter does any substantial act in furtherance thereof is guilty of prostitution, which is punishable as a Class 1 misdemeanor.

B. Any person who offers money or its equivalent to another for the purpose of engaging in sexual acts as enumerated in subsection A and thereafter does any substantial act in furtherance thereof is guilty of solicitation of prostitution, which is punishable as a Class 1 misdemeanor. However, any person who solicits prostitution from a minor (i) 16 years of age or older is guilty of a Class 6 felony or (ii) younger than 16 years of age is guilty of a Class 5 felony.

History.

Code 1950, § 18.1-194; 1960, c. 358; 1975, cc. 14, 15; 1980, c. 534; 1993, c. 609; 2013, cc. 417, 467.

Editor's note.

Acts 2013, cc. 417 and 467, cl. 2 provides: "That the provisions of this act may result in a net increase in periods of imprisonment or commitment. Pursuant to § 30-19.1:4, the estimated amount of the necessary appropriation cannot be determined for periods of imprisonment in state adult correctional facilities; therefore, Chapter 3 of the Acts of Assembly of 2012, Special Session I, requires the Virginia Criminal Sentencing Commission to assign a minimum fiscal impact of $50,000. Pursuant to § 30-19.1:4, the estimated amount of the necessary appropriation cannot be determined for periods of commitment to the custody of the Department of Juvenile Justice."

The 2013 amendments.

The 2013 amendments by cc. 417 and 467 are identical, and in subsection A, added the clause (i) and (ii) designators, substituted "is guilty of" for "shall be guilty of being a prostitute, or," and "is punishable" for "shall be punishable"; in subsection B, substituted "in subsection A" for "above," "is guilty" for "shall be guilty," and "which is punishable as" for "and shall be guilty of," and added the last sentence.

Michie's Jurisprudence.

For related discussion, see 6A M.J. Disorderly Houses and Houses of Ill Fame, §§ 2, 3.

CASE NOTES

Statutory scheme did not violate Equal Protection Clause. — The fact that solicitation to commit prostitution is a misdemeanor and is, therefore, considered a less serious crime than solicitation to commit a felony, § 18.2-29, which includes solicitation to commit sodomy, does not create an impermissible classification between groups of people similarly situated. Therefore, the court rejected the defendant's claim that the statutory scheme violated the Equal Protection Clause. Branche v. Commonwealth, 25 Va. App. 480, 489 S.E.2d 692 (1997).

No discrimination of one gender in absence of attempts to apprehend other gender. — The police do not intentionally discriminate against one gender by the absence of attempts to detect and apprehend offenders of the other gender, when no evidence is presented that offenders of the other gender are engaged in similar criminal behavior; the defendant offered no evidence that similarly situated females could have been prosecuted but were not. Branche v. Commonwealth, 25 Va. App. 480, 489 S.E.2d 692 (1997).

Attempted prostitution defined solely by section. — Attempted prostitution, unlike attempts to commit crimes generally, is defined solely by this section. Adams v. Commonwealth, 215 Va. 257, 208 S.E.2d 742 (1974).

And, as so defined, is incorporated within the offense of prostitution itself. Adams v. Commonwealth, 215 Va. 257, 208 S.E.2d 742 (1974).

Requirements for attempt to commit prostitution. — An attempt to commit prostitution requires an offer to engage in sexual intercourse for pay and a substantial act performed in furtherance of the offer. Adams v. Commonwealth, 215 Va. 257, 208 S.E.2d 742 (1974).

Evidence was sufficient to prove beyond a reasonable doubt that defendant used a vehicle to promote prostitution in violation of § 18.2-349, and the vehicle was also used to aid or promote prostitution in violation of § 18.2-348 because defendant not only committed substantial acts in furtherance of prostitution while in the vehicle by driving himself in the vehicle to the parking lot of the motel for the purpose of engaging the services of a prostitute, he used his vehicle to transport himself to a place to be used for the purpose of prostitution; the evidence proved that defendant initiated a conversation with an undercover officer concerning a "blow job," how much money he had, and whether she was a "cop," and in addition, defendant asked the officer to take a ride at the outset of the conversation and engaged in substantial acts in furtherance of completing the sexual transaction. Bakran v. Commonwealth, 57 Va. App. 197, 700 S.E.2d 471, 2010 Va. App. LEXIS 410 (2010).

How conviction sustained where no act occurred. — Where no act of adultery or fornication has occurred, a conviction under this section can be sustained only if the evidence shows an attempt to commit prostitution. Adams v. Commonwealth, 215 Va. 257, 208 S.E.2d 742 (1974).

Attempt to commit act of sodomy for money. — The General Assembly, by its amendment of this section to include within its proscription an act of sodomy for money, precluded prosecution of an attempt to commit such act under the general statutory scheme under which attempts to commit felonies are prosecuted. McFadden v. Commonwealth, 3 Va. App. 226, 348 S.E.2d 847 (1986).

Application of abstention doctrine of *Younger v. Harris*, 401 U.S. 37, 91 S. Ct. 746, 27 L. Ed. 2d 669 (1971), to action brought by corporation engaged in business of providing escort and dating services seeking order enjoining prosecution of itself or its employees under this section and § 18.2-347. See Hanpar, Inc. v. Atkinson, 496 F. Supp. 112 (E.D. Va. 1980).

Public policy exception to employment-at-will doctrine. — Employee who alleged that he was forced to quit his job as a result of retaliatory conduct that supervisors directed at the employee after the employee refused to engage in sexual harassment at work sufficiently stated a claim for wrongful constructive discharge in violation of public policy because the employee was a member of the class of persons that the statutes forbidding fornication, sexual battery, aggravated sexual battery, and prostitution were designed to protect. Hill v. Paramont Mfg., LLC, — F. Supp. 2d —, 2006 U.S. Dist. LEXIS 78488 (W.D. Va. Oct. 18, 2006).

Applied in Fine v. Commonwealth, 31 Va. App. 636, 525 S.E.2d 69 (2000); Wolfe v. Commonwealth, 42 Va. App. 776, 595 S.E.2d 27, 2004 Va. App. LEXIS 168 (2004).

§ 18.2-346.1. Testing of convicted prostitutes and injection drug users for infection with human immunodeficiency viruses and hepatitis C; limited disclosure.

A. As soon as practicable following conviction of any person for violation of § 18.2-346 or 18.2-361, or any violation of Article 1 (§ 18.2-247 et seq.) or 1.1 (§ 18.2-265.1 et seq.) of Chapter 7 involving the possession, sale, or use of a controlled substance in a form amenable to intravenous use; or the possession, sale, or use of hypodermic syringes, needles, or other objects designed or intended for use in parenterally injecting controlled substances into the human body, such person shall be required to submit to testing for infection with human immunodeficiency viruses and hepatitis C. The convicted person shall receive counseling from personnel of the Department of Health concerning (i) the meaning of the test, (ii) acquired immunodeficiency syndrome and hepatitis C, and (iii) the transmission and prevention of infection with human immunodeficiency viruses and hepatitis C.

B. Tests for human immunodeficiency viruses shall be conducted to confirm any initial positive test results before any test result shall be determined to be positive for infection. The results of such test shall be confidential as provided in § 32.1-36.1 and shall be disclosed to the person who is the subject of the test and to the Department of Health as required by § 32.1-36. The Department shall conduct surveillance and investigation in accordance with the requirements of § 32.1-39.

C. Upon receiving a report of a positive test for hepatitis C, the State Health Commissioner may share protected health information relating to such positive test with relevant sheriffs' offices, the state police, local police departments, adult or youth correctional facilities, salaried or volunteer firefighters, paramedics or emergency medical technicians, officers of the court, and regional or local jails (i) to the extent necessary to advise exposed individuals of the risk of infection and to enable exposed individuals to seek appropriate testing and treatment, and (ii) as may be needed to prevent and control disease and is deemed necessary to prevent serious harm and serious threats to the health and safety of individuals and the public.

The disclosed protected health information shall be held confidential; no person to whom such information is disclosed shall redisclose or otherwise reveal the protected health information without first obtaining the specific authorization from the individual who was the subject of the test for such redisclosure.

Such protected health information shall only be used to protect the health and safety of individuals and the public in conformance with the regulations concerning patient privacy promulgated by the federal Department of Health and Human Services, as such regulations may be amended.

D. The results of the tests shall not be admissible in any criminal proceeding related to prostitution or drug use.

The cost of the tests shall be paid by the Commonwealth and taxed as part of the cost of such criminal proceedings.

History.
1990, c. 913; 2005, c. 438.

Michie's Jurisprudence.
For related discussion, see 9A M.J. Health and Sanitation, § 1.

§ 18.2-347. Keeping, residing in or frequenting a bawdy place; "bawdy place" defined.

It shall be unlawful for any person to keep any bawdy place, or to reside in or at or visit, for immoral purposes, any such bawdy place. Each and every day such bawdy place shall be kept, resided in or visited, shall constitute a separate offense. In a prosecution under this section the general reputation of the place may be proved.

As used in this Code, *"bawdy place"* shall mean any place within or without any building or structure which is used or is to be used for lewdness, assignation or prostitution.

History.
Code 1950, §§ 18.1-195, 18.1-196; 1960, c. 358; 1975, cc. 14, 15.

Cross references.
As to pandering, see §§ 18.2-355 through 18.2-360. As to houses of prostitution, etc., as nuisances, see §§ 48-7 through 48-15.

Michie's Jurisprudence.
For related discussion, see 3C M.J. Commercial Law, § 99; 4A M.J. Contracts, § 124; 6A M.J. Disorderly Houses and Houses of Ill Fame, §§ 3, 6, ; 21A M.J. Words and Phrases.

CASE NOTES

This section and § 18.2-349 are broad and comprehensive. Dorchincoz v. Commonwealth, 191 Va. 33, 59 S.E.2d 863 (1950).

The purpose of this section is to suppress commercial prostitution and to put a ban on any place where persons may meet for the purpose of illicit intercourse without fear of being molested or interfered with by the keeper thereof. Trent v. Commonwealth, 181 Va. 338, 25 S.E.2d 350 (1943); Bennett v. Commonwealth, 182 Va. 7, 28 S.E.2d 13 (1943).

What constitutes house of prostitution. — Every house where illicit sexual intercourse is indulged between a man and a woman is not necessarily a house of prostitution. In order to constitute such a house, it must have the elements of a public house; a house which many people may frequent for immoral purposes or a house where a person may go for immoral purposes without an invitation. Trent v. Commonwealth, 181 Va. 338, 25 S.E.2d 350 (1943).

A house of ill fame is not measured by the number of its rooms or inhabitants. It is not necessary that more than one woman inhabit or resort to a place for the purpose of prostitution in order for such place to constitute a house of ill fame. Trent v. Commonwealth, 181 Va. 338, 25 S.E.2d 350 (1943).

"Bawdyhouse" and "house of ill fame" are synonymous

terms used in the law. Wilson v. Commonwealth, 132 Va. 824, 111 S.E. 96 (1922).

Also "house of prostitution" is synonymous with "house of ill fame." Trent v. Commonwealth, 181 Va. 338, 25 S.E.2d 350 (1943).

And "brothel." — A "bawdyhouse" is also spoken of as a "brothel." Wilson v. Commonwealth, 132 Va. 824, 111 S.E. 96 (1922).

Motel parking lot was bawdy place. — Evidence was sufficient to show that the motel parking lot was a bawdy place as defined by this section and city code § 29-24. Once contract had been made to go to a reputed bawdy place for an immoral purpose, the ordinance was violated when the parties arrived at the parking lot. They were then visiting a bawdy place for the specific immoral purpose that the statute and ordinance were intended to suppress. Harrison v. City of Norfolk, 16 Va. App. 572, 431 S.E.2d 658 (1993).

Prostitution defined. — Prostitution means common, indiscriminate, illicit intercourse for hire, or the practice by a female in offering her body to an indiscriminate intercourse with men for money or its equivalent. Trent v. Commonwealth, 181 Va. 338, 25 S.E.2d 350 (1943). See § 18.2-346.

Maintenance of a house of ill fame is a continuing offense. Foster v. Commonwealth, 179 Va. 96, 18 S.E.2d 314 (1942).

"General character" means "general reputation." — The words "general character," are used in the sense of "general reputation." Wilson v. Commonwealth, 132 Va. 824, 111 S.E. 96 (1922); Mitchell v. Commonwealth, 192 Va. 205, 64 S.E.2d 713 (1951).

Necessity for proving reputation. — In a prosecution for keeping a bawdyhouse it is not necessary to prove that the house had a general reputation as a bawdyhouse, where it is shown that it was in fact such a house. Wilson v. Commonwealth, 132 Va. 824, 111 S.E. 96 (1922).

Accused must know of illegal practices in house. — Before one charged with violation of this section can be found guilty, he must possess knowledge of the illegal practices that are carried on in such place. Warshaw v. City of Norfolk, 190 Va. 862, 58 S.E.2d 884 (1950).

Proof of knowledge of character of place. — In a prosecution for keeping a place where persons may meet for the purpose of illicit or illegal intercourse, it is not necessary for the state to prove actual knowledge on the part of the accused of the character of his place, or of the inmates, or of those who resorted there, but such facts and circumstances may be shown as will convince a jury beyond a reasonable doubt that the accused was bound to have cognizance, or knowledge, of the inmates of the house, or of those who resorted there. Bennett v. Commonwealth, 182 Va. 7, 28 S.E.2d 13 (1943).

Res gestae. — In a prosecution for violating this section, raiding officers could testify as to the names given them by the occupants of the cabins at a tourist camp of which accused was night manager, such evidence being admissible as a part of the res gestae. Bennett v. Commonwealth, 182 Va. 7, 28 S.E.2d 13 (1943).

Sufficiency of evidence. — Evidence held sufficient to support conviction for keeping a house of ill fame, that is, a bawdyhouse or brothel. Foster v. Commonwealth, 179 Va. 96, 18 S.E.2d 314 (1942); Wilson v. Commonwealth, 132 Va. 824, 111 S.E. 96 (1922).

Evidence sufficient to support conviction for operating a bawdyhouse. Gaskill v. Commonwealth, 206 Va. 486, 144 S.E.2d 293 (1965).

Instruction. — In a prosecution for violating this section, there was no error in the giving of an instruction that if the jury believed that accused kept a place "where persons may meet for the purpose of illegal or illicit intercourse" they should find him guilty. Bennett v. Commonwealth, 182 Va. 7, 28 S.E.2d 13 (1943).

Application of abstention doctrine of *Younger v. Harris,* 401 U.S. 37, 91 S. Ct. 746, 27 L. Ed. 2d 669 (1971), to action brought by corporation engaged in business of providing escort and dating services seeking order enjoining prosecution of itself or its employees under § 18.2-346 and this section. See Hanpar, Inc. v. Atkinson, 496 F. Supp. 112 (E.D. Va. 1980).

Applied in Stewart v. Commonwealth, 225 Va. 473, 303 S.E.2d 877 (1983).

§ 18.2-348. Aiding prostitution or illicit sexual intercourse.

It shall be unlawful for any person or any officer, employee or agent of any firm, association or corporation, with knowledge of, or good reason to believe, the immoral purpose of such visit, to take or transport or assist in taking or transporting, or offer to take or transport on foot or in any way, any person to a place, whether within or without any building or structure, used or to be used for the purpose of lewdness, assignation or prostitution within this Commonwealth; or procure or assist in procuring for the purpose of illicit sexual intercourse, or any act violative of § 18.2-361, or to give any information or direction to any person with intent to enable such person to commit an act of prostitution.

History.
Code 1950, § 18.1-197; 1960, c. 358; 1975, cc. 14, 15; 1980, c. 534.

CASE NOTES

Contents of tape recording not protected from disclosure. — The contents of a tape recording of an office conversation between complainant and an attorney were not protected from disclosure in a prosecution of the attorney for procuring for the purpose of prostitution under this section, and that disclosure did not violate the attorney's right to privacy vouch-safed by the Fourth Amendment. Cogdill v. Commonwealth, 219 Va. 272, 247 S.E.2d 392 (1978).

Evidence failed to prove van was used to aid prostitution. — See Fine v. Commonwealth, 31 Va. App. 636, 525 S.E.2d 69 (2000).

Evidence sufficient to prove vehicle was used to aid or promote prostitution. — Evidence was sufficient to prove beyond a reasonable doubt that defendant used a vehicle to promote prostitution in violation of § 18.2-349, and the vehicle was also used to aid or promote prostitution in violation of § 18.2-348 because defendant not only committed substantial acts in furtherance of prostitution while in the vehicle by driving himself in the vehicle to the parking lot of the motel for the purpose of engaging the services of a prostitute, he used his vehicle to transport himself to a place to be used for the purpose of prostitution; the evidence proved that defendant initiated a conversation with an undercover officer concerning a "blow job," how much money he had, and whether she was a "cop," and in addition, defendant asked the officer to take a ride at the outset of the conversation and engaged in substantial acts in furtherance of completing the sexual transaction. Bakran v. Commonwealth, 57 Va. App. 197, 700 S.E.2d 471, 2010 Va. App. LEXIS 410 (2010).

Applied in Edwards v. Commonwealth, 218 Va. 994, 243 S.E.2d 834 (1978); Stewart v. Commonwealth, 225 Va. 473, 303 S.E.2d 877 (1983).

§ 18.2-349. Using vehicles to promote prostitution or unlawful sexual intercourse.

It shall be unlawful for any owner or chauffeur of any vehicle, with knowledge or reason to believe the same is to be used for such purpose, to use the same or to allow the same to be used for the purpose of prostitution or unlawful sexual intercourse, or to aid or promote such prostitution or unlawful sexual intercourse by the use of any such vehicle.

History.
Code 1950, § 18.1-198; 1960, c. 358; 1975, cc. 14, 15.

CASE NOTES

Construction. — As this section is penal in nature, it must be strictly construed against the state and limited in application to cases falling clearly within the language of the section. Fine v. Commonwealth, 31 Va. App. 636, 525 S.E.2d 69 (2000).

Evidence failed to prove van was used to aid prostitution. — See Fine v. Commonwealth, 31 Va. App. 636, 525 S.E.2d 69 (2000).

Evidence sufficient to support conviction. — Evidence was sufficient to prove beyond a reasonable doubt that defendant used a vehicle to promote prostitution in violation of § 18.2-349, and the vehicle was also used to aid or promote prostitution in violation of § 18.2-348 because defendant not only committed substantial acts in furtherance of prostitution while in the vehicle by driving himself in the vehicle to the parking lot of the motel for the purpose of engaging the services of a prostitute, he used his vehicle to transport himself to a place to be used for the purpose of prostitution; the evidence proved that defendant initiated a conversation with an undercover officer concerning a "blow job," how much money he had, and whether she was a "cop," and in addition, defendant asked the officer to take a ride at the outset of the conversation and engaged in substantial acts in furtherance of completing the sexual transaction. Bakran v. Commonwealth, 57 Va. App. 197, 700 S.E.2d 471, 2010 Va. App. LEXIS 410 (2010).

Applied in Stewart v. Commonwealth, 225 Va. 473, 303 S.E.2d 877 (1983).

§ 18.2-350. Confinement of convicted prostitutes and persons violating §§ 18.2-347 through 18.2-349.

Every person convicted of being a prostitute and every person convicted of violating any of the provisions of §§ 18.2-347 through 18.2-349 shall be guilty of a Class 1 misdemeanor; provided, however, that in any case in which a city or county farm or hospital is available for the confinement of persons so convicted, confinement may be in such farm or hospital, in the discretion of the court or judge.

History.
Code 1950, § 18.1-199; 1960, c. 358; 1975, cc. 14, 15.

Michie's Jurisprudence.
For related discussion, see 6A M.J. Disorderly Houses and Houses of Ill Fame, § 6.

§§ 18.2-351 through 18.2-353. Repealed by Acts 2004, c. 459.

§ 18.2-354. Reserved.

§ 18.2-355. Taking, detaining, etc., person for prostitution, etc., or consenting thereto.

Any person who:

(1) For purposes of prostitution or unlawful sexual intercourse, takes any person into, or persuades, encourages or causes any person to enter, a bawdy place, or takes or causes such person to be taken to any place against his or her will for such purposes; or,

(2) Takes or detains a person against his or her will with the intent to compel such person, by force, threats, persuasions, menace or duress, to marry him or her or to marry any other person, or to be defiled; or,

(3) Being parent, guardian, legal custodian or one standing in loco parentis of a person, consents to

such person being taken or detained by any person for the purpose of prostitution or unlawful sexual intercourse; is guilty of pandering, and shall be guilty of a Class 4 felony.

History.
Code 1950, § 18.1-204; 1960, c. 358; 1975, cc. 14, 15; 1980, c. 534; 1997, c. 555.

Cross references.
For definition of "barrier crime" as including a conviction of pandering as set out in § 18.2-355, or an equivalent offense in another state, and prohibition against assisted living facilities, adult day care centers or child welfare agencies hiring for certain compensated employment persons who have committed such an offense, see §§ 63.2-1719, 63.2-1720. As to report to children's residential facility for which a background check is being performed on whether the applicant has ever been convicted of or is the subject of pending charges for various crimes, including pandering as set out in § 18.2-355, or an equivalent offense in another state, see § 63.2-1726. For provision making it unlawful for any person to operate a family day home if he, or if he knows that any other person who resides in the home, has been convicted of a felony in violation of this section, see § 63.2-1727.

Michie's Jurisprudence.
For related discussion, see 6A M.J. Disorderly Houses and Houses of Ill Fame, § 2.

CASE NOTES

Sections 18.2-355 through 18.2-360 considered together. — This section and §§ 18.2-356 through 18.2-360 are designed to prohibit illicit prostitution and procurement. Over a long period of time these sections have been considered together because they are all designed to accomplish the same purpose, to prohibit any act of exploiting the prostitution of a female. It is immaterial whether the act be called pandering or pimping. Edwards v. Commonwealth, 218 Va. 994, 243 S.E.2d 834 (1978).

Female concerned need not be immoral. — Under the provisions of §§ 18.2-355 through 18.2-360 there is no requirement that the female concerned must be either a prostitute or willing to engage in illicit sexual relations. The statute covers a situation where the woman is immoral, as well as where she is an innocent virgin. Martin v. Commonwealth, 195 Va. 1107, 81 S.E.2d 574 (1954).

Applied in Stewart v. Commonwealth, 225 Va. 473, 303 S.E.2d 877 (1983).

§ 18.2-356. Receiving money for procuring person.

Any person who receives any money or other valuable thing for or on account of (i) procuring for or placing in a house of prostitution or elsewhere any person for the purpose of causing such person to engage in unlawful sexual intercourse or any act in violation of § 18.2-361 or (ii) causing any person to engage in forced labor or services, concubinage, prostitution, or the manufacture of any obscene material or child pornography shall be guilty of a Class 4 felony.

History.
Code 1950, § 18.1-206; 1960, c. 358; 1975, cc. 14, 15; 1980, c. 534; 2011, c. 785.

Editor's note.
Acts 2011, c. 785, cl. 2, provides: "That the provisions of this act may result in a net increase in periods of imprisonment or commitment. Pursuant to § 30-19.1:4, the estimated amount of the neces-

sary appropriation cannot be determined for periods of imprisonment in state adult correctional facilities; therefore, Chapter 874 of the Acts of Assembly of 2010 requires the Virginia Criminal Sentencing Commission to assign a minimum fiscal impact of $50,000. Pursuant to § 30-19.1:4, the estimated amount of the necessary appropriation cannot be determined for periods of commitment to the custody of the Department of Juvenile Justice."

The 2011 amendments.
The 2011 amendment by c. 785 substituted "receives" for "shall receive" inserted the clause (i) designation, and added clause (ii).

CASE NOTES

Sections 18.2-355 through 18.2-360 considered together. — Sections 18.2-355 through 18.2-360 are designed to prohibit illicit prostitution and procurement. Over a long period of time these sections have been considered together because they are all designed to accomplish the same purpose, to prohibit any act of exploiting the prostitution of a female. It is immaterial whether the act be called pandering or pimping. Edwards v. Commonwealth, 218 Va. 994, 243 S.E.2d 834 (1978).

This section and § 18.2-357 accomplish same purpose. — This section prohibits pandering. It reaches the person who receives money for procuring any female to engage in unlawful sexual intercourse. But § 18.2-357 also prohibits pandering. The two sections were enacted to accomplish the same purpose, prohibit commercial prostitution. Edwards v. Commonwealth, 218 Va. 994, 243 S.E.2d 834 (1978).

The conduct punished under this section and § 18.2-357 and the conduct sought to be reached by a conspiracy charge under these sections is sufficiently congruent to require the application of Wharton's Rule, which is applicable where there exists a general congruence of the agreement and the completed substantive offense and under which the conspiracy and substantive offense merge when the substantive offense is proved, at least where only the potential panderer and the potential prostitute are parties to the agreement alleged. Stewart v. Commonwealth, 225 Va. 473, 303 S.E.2d 877 (1983).

The only difference between this section and § 18.2-357 is that under this section the source of the money paid is immaterial and it can be received either before or after the procuring or the placing of the female. A violation does not depend upon an act of sexual intercourse having occurred. Under § 18.2-357 the money must be knowingly received from the earnings of the female, and therefore after the act of prostitution. Edwards v. Commonwealth, 218 Va. 994, 243 S.E.2d 834 (1978).

A bellman in a hotel who is given $10 by a guest to procure for him a prostitute, and does so, violates this section. If he also receives from the prostitute a portion of her fee for the service she rendered the guest, he violates § 18.2-357. Edwards v. Commonwealth, 218 Va. 994, 243 S.E.2d 834 (1978).

One who effects a criminal act through an innocent agent is a principal in the first degree. Collins v. Commonwealth, 226 Va. 223, 307 S.E.2d 884 (1983).

A defendant may not escape criminal responsibility for a crime which he arranges to have committed by an unwitting agent. Collins v. Commonwealth, 226 Va. 223, 307 S.E.2d 884 (1983).

It is not the prostitute that this section and § 18.2-357 seek to reach but the one who profits from an act of prostitution by another. Edwards v. Commonwealth, 218 Va. 994, 243 S.E.2d 834 (1978).

Permissible amendment of indictment. — This section and § 18.2-357 are so interrelated that an indictment drawn under one could be subsequently amended to charge a violation of the other section if the evidence showed such a violation. Edwards v. Commonwealth, 218 Va. 994, 243 S.E.2d 834 (1978).

Because of the similarity of purpose and subject matter of this section and § 18.2-357, an amendment to an indictment which changes the provision under which a defendant is charged from § 18.2-357 to this section does not change the nature or character of the offense charged and is permissible under the provisions of § 19.2-231. Edwards v. Commonwealth, 218 Va. 994, 243 S.E.2d 834 (1978).

An indictment following the language of this section was sufficient, and the contention that the words "to cohabit with male persons" do not imply sexual intercourse or connote sexual relations was without merit. Martin v. Commonwealth, 195 Va. 1107, 81 S.E.2d 574 (1954).

Defendant was properly convicted of the attempt to commit the crime of pandering where he had placed a female in his room and solicited males to have intercourse with her, and was prevented from receiving the money only by the intervention of the police. Martin v. Commonwealth, 195 Va. 1107, 81 S.E.2d 574 (1954).

§ 18.2-357. Receiving money from earnings of male or female prostitute.

Any person who shall knowingly receive any money or other valuable thing from the earnings of any male or female engaged in prostitution, except for a consideration deemed good and valuable in law, shall be guilty of pandering, punishable as a Class 4 felony.

History.
Code 1950, § 18.1-208; 1960, c. 358; 1975, cc. 14, 15; 1980, c. 534.

Law Review.
For survey of Virginia evidence for the year 1972-1973, see 59 Va. L. Rev. 1526 (1973). For annual survey article, "Criminal Law and Procedure," see 44 U. Rich. L. Rev. 339 (2009).

Michie's Jurisprudence.
For related discussion, see 1A M.J. Accomplices and Accessories, § 12.

CASE NOTES

Sections 18.2-355 through 18.2-360 considered together. — Sections 18.2-355 through 18.2-360 are designed to prohibit illicit prostitution and procurement. Over a long period of time these sections have been considered together because they are all designed to accomplish the same purpose, to prohibit any act of exploiting the prostitution of a female. It is immaterial whether the act be called pandering or pimping. Edwards v. Commonwealth, 218 Va. 994, 243 S.E.2d 834 (1978).

Section 18.2-356 and this section accomplish same purpose. — Section 18.2-356 prohibits pandering. It reaches the person who receives money for procuring any female to engage in unlawful sexual intercourse. But this section also prohibits pandering. The two sections were enacted to accomplish the same purpose, prohibit commercial prostitution. Edwards v. Commonwealth, 218 Va. 994, 243 S.E.2d 834 (1978).

The conduct punished under this section and § 18.2-356 and the conduct sought to be reached by a conspiracy charge under these sections is sufficiently congruent to require the application of Wharton's Rule, which is applicable where there exists a general congruence of the agreement and the completed substantive offense and under which the conspiracy and substantive offense merge when the substantive offense is proved, at least where only the potential panderer and the potential prostitute are parties to the agreement alleged. Stewart v. Commonwealth, 225 Va. 473, 303 S.E.2d 877 (1983).

The only difference between § 18.2-356 and this section is that under § 18.2-356 the source of the money paid is immaterial and it can be received either before or after the procuring or the placing of the female. A violation does not depend upon an act of sexual intercourse having occurred. Under this section the money must be knowingly received from the earnings of the female, and therefore after the act of prostitution. Edwards v. Commonwealth, 218 Va. 994, 243 S.E.2d 834 (1978).

A bellman in a hotel who is given $10.00 by a guest to procure for him a prostitute, and does so, violates § 18.2-356. If he also receives from the prostitute a portion of her fee for the service she rendered the guest, he violates this section. Edwards v. Commonwealth, 218 Va. 994, 243 S.E.2d 834 (1978).

It is not the prostitute that § 18.2-356 and this section seek

to reach but the one who profits from an act of prostitution by another. Edwards v. Commonwealth, 218 Va. 994, 243 S.E.2d 834 (1978).

Prostitute is not accomplice. — In a prosecution under this section, the testimony of the prostitute was not that of an accomplice since the prostitute herself could not have been indicted under this section for receiving money from her own earnings. Clinton v. Commonwealth, 204 Va. 275, 130 S.E.2d 437 (1963), rev'd on other grounds, 377 U.S. 158, 84 S. Ct. 1186, 12 L. Ed. 2d 213 (1964).

Evidence that an accused received a part of the earnings of a prostitute on other occasions not too remote in time to the offense charged is admissible as tending to show a system or uniform plan from which motive, criminal intent or knowledge may be inferred. Minor v. Commonwealth, 213 Va. 278, 191 S.E.2d 825 (1972).

Permissible amendment of indictment. — Section 18.2-356 and this section are so interrelated that an indictment drawn under one could be subsequently amended to charge a violation of the other section if the evidence showed such a violation. Edwards v. Commonwealth, 218 Va. 994, 243 S.E.2d 834 (1978).

Because of the similarity of purpose and subject matter of § 18.2-356 and this section, an amendment to an indictment which changes the provision under which a defendant is charged from this section to § 18.2-356 does not change the nature or character of the offense charged and is permissible under the provisions of § 19.2-231. Edwards v. Commonwealth, 218 Va. 994, 243 S.E.2d 834 (1978).

An indictment was sufficient though it charged that money received by the accused from the earnings of a prostitute was not for a consideration deemed "good and valuable at law" instead of charging that it was not for a consideration deemed "good or valuable at law," which was the language of former § 18-97. Saunders v. Commonwealth, 186 Va. 1000, 45 S.E.2d 307 (1947).

Exception language creates an affirmative defense. — Exception language in § 18.2-357 creates an affirmative defense that places the burden of production on a defendant to show that there was some consideration given in exchange for the earnings of the prostitute. Tart v. Commonwealth, 52 Va. App. 272, 663 S.E.2d 113, 2008 Va. App. LEXIS 318 (2008).

Jury instruction as to exception language not required. — Because the exception language in § 18.2-357 was not an element of the offense, but rather an affirmative defense, defendant was required to satisfy the defendant's burden of producing or pointing to evidence that would allow the defendant to invoke the exception. Because the defendant failed to meet that threshold burden, the trial court did not err by refusing the defendant's proposed jury instruction that placed the burden on the Commonwealth to prove that defendant did not give "consideration deemed good and valuable in law" in exchange for earnings the defendant received from a roommate's prostitution. Tart v. Commonwealth, 52 Va. App. 272, 663 S.E.2d 113, 2008 Va. App. LEXIS 318 (2008).

§ 18.2-358. Repealed by Acts 2004, c. 459.

§ 18.2-359. Venue for criminal sexual assault or where any person transported for criminal sexual assault, attempted criminal sexual assault, or purposes of unlawful sexual intercourse, crimes against nature, and indecent liberties with children; venue for such crimes when coupled with a violent felony.

A. Any person transporting or attempting to transport through or across this Commonwealth, any person for the purposes of unlawful sexual intercourse or prostitution, or for the purpose of committing any crime specified in § 18.2-361 or 18.2-370, or for the purposes of committing or attempting to commit criminal sexual assault under

Article 7 (§ 18.2-61 et seq.) of Chapter 4, may be presented, indicted, tried, and convicted in any county or city in which any part of such transportation occurred.

B. Venue for the trial of any person charged with committing or attempting to commit any crime specified in § 18.2-361 or 18.2-370 or sexual assault under Article 7 (§ 18.2-61 et seq.) of Chapter 4 may be had in the county or city in which such crime is alleged to have occurred or, with the concurrence of the attorney for the Commonwealth in the county or city in which the crime is alleged to have occurred, in any county or city through which the victim was transported by the defendant prior to the commission of such offense.

C. Venue for the trial of any person charged with committing or attempting to commit criminal sexual assault under Article 7 (§ 18.2-61 et seq.) of Chapter 4 against a person under 18 years of age may be had in the county or city in which such crime is alleged to have occurred or, when the county or city where the offense is alleged to have occurred cannot be determined, then in the county or city where the person under 18 years of age resided at the time of the offense.

D. Venue for the trial of any person charged with committing or attempting to commit (i) any crime specified in § 18.2-361 or 18.2-370 or criminal sexual assault under Article 7 (§ 18.2-61 et seq.) of Chapter 4 and (ii) any violent felony as defined in § 17.1-805 or any act of violence as defined in § 19.2-297.1 arising out of the same incident, occurrence, or transaction may be had in the county or city in which any such crime is alleged to have occurred or, with the concurrence of the attorney for the Commonwealth in the county or city in which the crime is alleged to have occurred, in any county or city through which the victim was transported by the defendant in the commission of such offense.

History.
Code 1950, § 18.1-210; 1960, c. 358; 1975, cc. 14, 15; 1976, c. 54; 1978, c. 610; 1981, c. 397; 2004, c. 869; 2011, c. 763.

The 2011 amendments.
The 2011 amendment by c. 763, in subsection B, substituted "any crime specified in § 18.2-361 or 18.2-370 or" for "criminal" following "attempting to commit" and inserted "with the concurrence of the attorney for the Commonwealth in the county or city in which the crime is alleged to have occurred" preceding "in any county"; added subsection D; and made minor stylistic changes.

Law Review.
For 2003/2004 survey of family and juvenile law, see 39 U. Rich. L. Rev. 241 (2004).

CASE NOTES

Sections 18.2-355 through 18.2-360 considered together. — Sections 18.2-355 through 18.2-360 are designed to prohibit illicit prostitution and procurement. Over a long period of time these sections have been considered together because they are all designed to accomplish the same purpose, to prohibit any act of exploiting the prostitution of a female. It is immaterial whether the act be called pandering or pimping. Edwards v. Commonwealth, 218 Va. 994, 243 S.E.2d 834 (1978).

Prosecution did not violate the double jeopardy clause of the United States Constitution by indicting defendant on rape charge in Portsmouth, in addition to the murder charge tried in Norfolk for no evidence was presented that the rape occurred in Norfolk or that the victim was transported to Norfolk by the defendant prior to the commission of such offense, and the Norfolk court did not have jurisdiction to try appellant for rape. Vanegas v. Commonwealth, 17 Va. App. 451, 438 S.E.2d 289 (1993).

§ 18.2-360. Competency of persons to testify in prosecutions under §§ 18.2-355 through 18.2-361.

Any male or female referred to in §§ 18.2-355 through 18.2-361 shall be a competent witness in any prosecution under such sections to testify to any and all matters, including conversations by or with the accused with third persons in his or her presence, notwithstanding he or she may have married the accused either before or after the violation of any of the provisions of this section; but such witness shall not be compelled to testify after such marriage.

History.
Code 1950, § 18.1-211; 1960, c. 358; 1975, cc. 14, 15; 1980, c. 534.

Michie's Jurisprudence.
For related discussion, see 6A M.J. Disorderly Houses and Houses of Ill Fame, § 2.

CASE NOTES

Sections 18.2-355 through 18.2-360 considered together. — Sections 18.2-355 through 18.2-359 and this section are designed to prohibit illicit prostitution and procurement. Over a long period of time these sections have been considered together because they are all designed to accomplish the same purpose, to prohibit any act of exploiting the prostitution of a female. It is immaterial whether the act be called pandering or pimping. Edwards v. Commonwealth, 218 Va. 994, 243 S.E.2d 834 (1978).

§ 18.2-361. Crimes against nature; penalty.

A. If any person carnally knows in any manner any brute animal, or carnally knows any male or female person by the anus or by or with the mouth, or voluntarily submits to such carnal knowledge, he or she shall be guilty of a Class 6 felony, except as provided in subsection B.

B. Any person who performs or causes to be performed cunnilingus, fellatio, anilingus or anal intercourse upon or by his daughter or granddaughter, son or grandson, brother or sister, or father or mother is guilty of a Class 5 felony. However, if a parent or grandparent commits any such act with his child or grandchild and such child or grandchild is at least 13 but less than 18 years of age at the time of the offense, such parent or grandparent is guilty of a Class 3 felony.

C. For the purposes of this section, parent includes step-parent, grandparent includes step-grandparent, child includes step-child and grandchild includes step-grandchild.

History.
Code 1950, § 18.1-212; 1960, c. 358; 1968, c. 427; 1975, cc. 14, 15; 1977, c. 285; 1981, c. 397; 1993, c. 450; 2005, c. 185.

Cross references.

As to forcible sodomy, see § 18.2-67.1. As to Sex Offenders and Crimes Against Minors Registry, see § 9.1-900 et seq. For definition of "barrier crime" as including a conviction of crimes against nature involving children as set out in § 18.2-361, or an equivalent offense in another state, and prohibition against assisted living facilities, adult day care centers or child welfare agencies hiring for certain compensated employment persons who have committed such an offense, see §§ 63.2-1719, 63.2-1720. As to report to children's residential facility for which a background check is being performed on whether the applicant has ever been convicted of or is the subject of pending charges for various crimes, including crimes against nature involving children as set out § 18.2-361, or an equivalent offense in another state, see § 63.2-1726. For provision making it unlawful for any person to operate a family day home if he, or if he knows that any other person who resides in the home, has been convicted of a felony in violation of this section, see § 63.2-1727.

Law Review.

For note, "Sodomy and the Married Man," see 3 U. Rich. L. Rev. 344 (1969). For survey of constitutional law in Virginia for the year 1975-1976, see 62 Va. L. Rev. 1389 (1976). For article reviewing United States Supreme Court privacy decisions and focusing on John Doe v. Commonwealth's Att'y, 425 U.S. 985, 96 S. Ct. 2192, 48 L. Ed. 2d 810 (1976), see 12 U. Rich. L. Rev. 627 (1978). For article discussing the legislative history of sexual assault law reform in Virginia, see 68 Va. L. Rev. 459 (1982). For note on constitutionality of Virginia's sodomy statute, see 26 Wm. & Mary L. Rev. 645 (1985). For note, "Homosexuality and the Custodial Parent in Virginia — The Effects of Roe v. Roe," see 8 G.M.U. U.L. Rev. 389 (1986). For note on state's authority to proscribe certain sexual activities, see 9 G.M.U. L. Rev. 185 (1986). For survey of Virginia criminal law and procedure for the year 2004-2005, see 40 U. Rich. L. Rev. 197 (2005). For 2006 survey article, "Family and Juvenile Law," see 41 U. Rich. L. Rev. 151 (2006). For 2007 annual survey article, "Family and Juvenile Law," see 42 U. Rich. L. Rev. 417 (2007). For article, "The Equal Protection Implications of Government's Hateful Speech," see 54 Wm. & Mary L. Rev. 159 (2012).

Michie's Jurisprudence.

For related discussion, see 6A M.J. Disorderly Houses and Houses of Ill Fame, § 3; 16 M.J. Sodomy, § 1.

CASE NOTES

Constitutionality. — Although this section may have a basis in religious values, it is not contrary to the establishment clause of the state or federal constitution in that its primary effect is not to advance or inhibit religion and it does not foster excessive governmental entanglement with religion but rests plainly on long established secular values concerning sexual conduct. DePriest v. Commonwealth, 33 Va. App. 754, 537 S.E.2d 1, 2000 Va. App. LEXIS 752 (2000).

Court rejected defendant's claim that § 18.2-361 violated the Equal Protection Clause of the Fourteenth Amendment because § 18.2-361, on its face, did not draw distinctions between homosexual and heterosexual individuals. Section 18.2-361 applies equally to all citizens, regardless of sexual orientation, and all persons, male or female, whether heterosexual or homosexual, who solicit another to commit an act of sodomy are guilty of a class 6 felony. Tjan v. Commonwealth, 46 Va. App. 698, 621 S.E.2d 669, 2005 Va. App. LEXIS 447 (2005).

Defendant's convictions for four counts of sodomy were affirmed because subsection A of § 18.2-361 was constitutional as applied to defendant as his violations involved 16 and 17 year-old minors and therefore merited no protection under the Due Process Clause of the Fourteenth Amendment. McDonald v. Commonwealth, 48 Va. App. 325, 630 S.E.2d 754, 2006 Va. App. LEXIS 259 (2006), aff'd, 645 S.E.2d 918, 2007 Va. LEXIS 87 (Va. 2007).

Nothing in the United States Supreme Court opinion in Lawrence or the Supreme Court of Virginia's opinion in Martin facially invalidates subsection A of § 18.2-361. McDonald v. Commonwealth, 48 Va. App. 325, 630 S.E.2d 754, 2006 Va. App. LEXIS 259 (2006), aff'd, 645 S.E.2d 918, 2007 Va. LEXIS 87 (Va. 2007).

As defendant's victims, 16 and 17, were "minors" as defined by § 1-207, his as-applied constitutional challenge to the sodomy

statute, § 18.2-361, failed because nothing in Lawrence v. Texas, 539 U.S. 558 (2003), or Martin v. Ziherl, 607 S.E.2d 367 (2005), prohibited the application of the sodomy statute to conduct between adults and minors. McDonald v. Commonwealth, 274 Va. 249, 645 S.E.2d 918, 2007 Va. LEXIS 87 (2007).

Anti-sodomy provision of § 18.2-361 facially violates the Due Process Clause of the Fourteenth Amendment. Macdonald v. Moose, 710 F.3d 154, 2013 U.S. App. LEXIS 4921 (4th Cir. 2013).

Section is not unconstitutional on its face. Doe v. Commonwealth's Att'y ex rel. City of Richmond, 403 F. Supp. 1199 (E.D. Va. 1975), aff'd, 425 U.S. 901, 96 S. Ct. 1489, 47 L. Ed. 2d 751, reh'g denied, 425 U.S. 985, 96 S. Ct. 2192, 48 L. Ed. 2d 810 (1976).

It cannot be said that this section offends the Bill of Rights or any other of the amendments to the federal Constitution, and the wisdom or policy is a matter for the state's resolve. Doe v. Commonwealth's Att'y ex rel. City of Richmond, 403 F. Supp. 1199 (E.D. Va. 1975), aff'd, 425 U.S. 901, 96 S. Ct. 1489, 47 L. Ed. 2d 751, reh'g denied, 425 U.S. 985, 96 S. Ct. 2192, 48 L. Ed. 2d 810 (1976).

Defendant's conviction was proper in a case where he solicited an act of oral sodomy from an undercover police officer in a public place, a men's restroom at a local department store; that statute did not violate defendant's substantive due process rights and was not unconstitutional on its face, as it did not violate the protection in Lawrence given to private consensual sodomy, but did outlaw defendant's conduct, which involved a request for an act of sodomy in a public place. Singson v. Commonwealth, 46 Va. App. 724, 621 S.E.2d 682, 2005 Va. App. LEXIS 452 (2005).

Prosecution under statute with more severe penalty held not denial of equal protection. — Prosecution under § 18.2-29 and this section for a crime committed on federal land does not violate the Fourteenth Amendment right of equal protection even though similar conduct is proscribed by federal law and is punishable by lesser penalties. Fletcher v. Commonwealth, No. 0405-85 (Ct. of Appeals Oct. 10, 1986).

Lacked standing to assert that statute was unconstitutional. — Adult defendant who unsuccessfully solicited oral sex from a 17-year-old girl lacked standing to assert that § 18.2-361 was facially unconstitutional in violation of the Due Process Clause, as the statute was not unconstitutional as it applied to him. MacDonald v. Commonwealth, 2007 Va. App. LEXIS 7 (Jan. 9, 2007).

Married couples remain protected in their expectation of privacy within their own bedroom though they converse with friends or write books about their sexual relations, recounting in explicit detail their own intimacies and techniques. Lovisi v. Slayton, 539 F.2d 349 (4th Cir.), cert. denied, 429 U.S. 977, 97 S. Ct. 485, 50 L. Ed. 2d 585 (1976) (decided under former § 18.1-212).

But once married couple admits strangers as onlookers to sexual acts, federal protection of privacy dissolves. Lovisi v. Slayton, 539 F.2d 349 (4th Cir.), cert. denied, 429 U.S. 977, 97 S. Ct. 485, 50 L. Ed. 2d 585 (1976) (decided under former § 18.1-212).

If the couple performs sexual acts for the excitation or gratification of welcome onlookers, they cannot selectively claim that the state is an intruder. Lovisi v. Slayton, 539 F.2d 349 (4th Cir.), cert. denied, 429 U.S. 977, 97 S. Ct. 485, 50 L. Ed. 2d 585 (1976) (decided under former § 18.1-212).

Married couples possess the freedom to follow their own inclinations in privacy, but once they accept onlookers, whether they are close friends, chance acquaintances, observed "Peeping Toms" or paying customers, they may not exclude the state as a constitutionally forbidden intruder. Lovisi v. Slayton, 539 F.2d 349 (4th Cir.), cert. denied, 429 U.S. 977, 97 S. Ct. 485, 50 L. Ed. 2d 585 (1976) (decided under former § 18.1-212).

The presence of an onlooker in the married couple's bedroom dissolved the reasonable expectation of privacy shared by the married couple when alone. Lovisi v. Slayton, 539 F.2d 349 (4th Cir.), cert. denied, 429 U.S. 977, 97 S. Ct. 485, 50 L. Ed. 2d 585 (1976) (decided under former § 18.1-212).

Section poses threat to right of privacy of consenting adults. — While the condition of marriage would doubtless make more difficult an attempt by government to justify an intrusion upon sexual behavior, this condition is not a prerequisite to the operation of the right of privacy. Accordingly, this section poses a threat to the right of privacy possessed by consenting adults. Lovisi v. Slayton, 363 F. Supp. 620 (E.D. Va. 1973), aff'd, 539 F.2d 349 (4th

Cir.), cert. denied, 429 U.S. 977, 97 S. Ct. 485, 50 L. Ed. 2d 585 (1976).

And invades marriage bed. — This section regulates no less than the actual form of sexual expression between husband and wife. It invades the marital bed, informing the couple of the conduct in which they may or may not engage. As it applies to a married couple, this law doubtless threatens an invasion of the right of privacy. Lovisi v. Slayton, 363 F. Supp. 620 (E.D. Va. 1973), aff'd, 539 F.2d 349 (4th Cir.), cert. denied, 429 U.S. 977, 97 S. Ct. 485, 50 L. Ed. 2d 585 (1976).

Those preserving privacy may attack this section. — There is no obstacle to prevent those who have preserved the privacy surrounding their acts from asserting their constitutional rights to attack this section. Lovisi v. Slayton, 363 F. Supp. 620 (E.D. Va. 1973), aff'd, 539 F.2d 349 (4th Cir.), cert. denied, 429 U.S. 977, 97 S. Ct. 485, 50 L. Ed. 2d 585 (1976).

In order for sexual relations to be constitutionally protected, the participants have the responsibility of ensuring that the seclusion surrounding their acts was preserved. Lovisi v. Slayton, 363 F. Supp. 620 (E.D. Va. 1973), aff'd, 539 F.2d 349 (4th Cir.), cert. denied, 429 U.S. 977, 97 S. Ct. 485, 50 L. Ed. 2d 585 (1976).

But those voluntarily relinquishing it may not. — The right to privacy inherent in the federal Constitution may well extend to heterosexual relations involving oral-genital contact between consenting adults, but persons who voluntarily relinquish the privacy that would normally surround their acts are not themselves protected by such a right. They can, therefore, be prosecuted for the acts in which they engaged. Lovisi v. Slayton, 363 F. Supp. 620 (E.D. Va. 1973), aff'd, 539 F.2d 349 (4th Cir.), cert. denied, 429 U.S. 977, 97 S. Ct. 485, 50 L. Ed. 2d 585 (1976).

No privacy defense for solicitation in public parks. — The defendants' acts and their proposed conduct were clothed with no circumstance giving rise to a supportable claim of privacy where the defendants where charged with soliciting strangers in public parks to commit oral sodomy in the parks. DePriest v. Commonwealth, 33 Va. App. 754, 537 S.E.2d 1, 2000 Va. App. LEXIS 752 (2000).

Defendants failed to establish that this section is unconstitutional in so many of its applications that it could not have been intended by the legislature to be left standing to cover persons who have not preserved their privacy. Lovisi v. Slayton, 363 F. Supp. 620 (E.D. Va. 1973), aff'd, 539 F.2d 349 (4th Cir.), cert. denied, 429 U.S. 977, 97 S. Ct. 485, 50 L. Ed. 2d 585 (1976).

Although this section was designed to cover all acts of sodomy, public and private, the federal district court could not say that a prohibition against the application of this section to private acts prevents it from applying in the vast majority of its intended applications. Lovisi v. Slayton, 363 F. Supp. 620 (E.D. Va. 1973), aff'd, 539 F.2d 349 (4th Cir.), cert. denied, 429 U.S. 977, 97 S. Ct. 485, 50 L. Ed. 2d 585 (1976).

Even if this section could not constitutionally be applied to private sexual relations between consenting adults, the federal district court found that where the relations were not private, the defendants had no right which they can assert, and their conduct was not constitutionally protected. Lovisi v. Slayton, 363 F. Supp. 620 (E.D. Va. 1973), aff'd, 539 F.2d 349 (4th Cir.), cert. denied, 429 U.S. 977, 97 S. Ct. 485, 50 L. Ed. 2d 585 (1976).

There is no authoritative judicial bar to the proscription of homosexuality, since it is obviously no portion of marriage, home or family life. Doe v. Commonwealth's Att'y ex rel. City of Richmond, 403 F. Supp. 1199 (E.D. Va. 1975), aff'd, 425 U.S. 901, 96 S. Ct. 1489, 47 L. Ed. 2d 751, reh'g denied, 425 U.S. 985, 96 S. Ct. 2192, 48 L. Ed. 2d 810 (1976).

If a state determines that punishment for homosexual acts, even when committed in the home, is appropriate in the promotion of morality and decency, it is not for the federal courts to say that a state is not free to do so. Doe v. Commonwealth's Att'y ex rel. City of Richmond, 403 F. Supp. 1199 (E.D. Va. 1975), aff'd, 425 U.S. 901, 96 S. Ct. 1489, 47 L. Ed. 2d 751, reh'g denied, 425 U.S. 985, 96 S. Ct. 2192, 48 L. Ed. 2d 810 (1976).

Section reflects state's legitimate interest. — The longevity of this section testifies to the state's interest and its legitimacy. It is not an upstart notion; it has ancestry going back to Judaic and Christian law. Doe v. Commonwealth's Att'y ex rel. City of Richmond, 403 F. Supp. 1199 (E.D. Va. 1975), aff'd, 425 U.S. 901, 96 S.

Ct. 1489, 47 L. Ed. 2d 751, reh'g denied, 425 U.S. 985, 96 S. Ct. 2192, 48 L. Ed. 2d 810 (1976).

The sodomy statute, so long in force in Virginia, has a rational basis of state interest, demonstrably legitimate and mirrored in cited decisional law of the Supreme Court. Doe v. Commonwealth's Att'y ex rel. City of Richmond, 403 F. Supp. 1199 (E.D. Va. 1975), aff'd, 425 U.S. 901, 96 S. Ct. 1489, 47 L. Ed. 2d 751, reh'g denied, 425 U.S. 985, 96 S. Ct. 2192, 48 L. Ed. 2d 810 (1976).

Effect of homosexuality on moral delinquency. — To sustain this section, the state is not required to show that moral delinquency actually results from homosexuality. It is enough for upholding the legislation to establish that the conduct is likely to end in a contribution to moral delinquency. Doe v. Commonwealth's Att'y ex rel. City of Richmond, 403 F. Supp. 1199 (E.D. Va. 1975), aff'd, 425 U.S. 901, 96 S. Ct. 1489, 47 L. Ed. 2d 751, reh'g denied, 425 U.S. 985, 96 S. Ct. 2192, 48 L. Ed. 2d 810 (1976).

Double jeopardy violation in convictions for sodomy and carnal knowledge. — Convictions of both forcible sodomy and carnal knowledge violate the federal and state constitutional protections against double jeopardy. Every instance of cunnilingus, fellatio, anallingus, or anal intercourse in violation of § 18.2-67.1 A also constitutes a violation of this section. Moreover, there is no indication that the legislature intended that two punishments be imposed for the same act. Chaine v. Commonwealth, 17 Va. App. 179, 436 S.E.2d 187 (1993), aff'd upon reh'g en banc, 18 Va. App. 301, 443 S.E.2d 924 (1994).

Offense not lesser included offense of sexual penetration by object. — Because every instance of object penetration does not constitute carnal knowledge under § 18.2-361 A, an offense under that statute is not a lesser-included offense of § 18.2-67.2. Smith v. Commonwealth, No. 1546-97-4 (Ct. of Appeals Dec. 1, 1998).

Criminality of lesbianism factor in custody determination. — A lesbian mother is not per se an unfit parent. However, conduct inherent in lesbianism is punishable as a Class 6 felony in the Commonwealth, pursuant to this section; thus, that conduct is another important consideration in determining custody. Bottoms v. Bottoms, 249 Va. 410, 457 S.E.2d 102 (1995).

Sodomy "with the mouth" is another term for cunnilingus. Lankford v. Foster, 546 F. Supp. 241 (W.D. Va. 1982), aff'd, 716 F.2d 896 (4th Cir. 1983), cert. denied, 467 U.S. 1214, 104 S. Ct. 2655, 81 L. Ed. 2d 362 (1984).

Whereas sodomy "by the mouth" indicates fellatio. Lankford v. Foster, 546 F. Supp. 241 (W.D. Va. 1982), aff'd, 716 F.2d 896 (4th Cir. 1983), cert. denied, 467 U.S. 1214, 104 S. Ct. 2655, 81 L. Ed. 2d 362 (1984).

Cunnilingus, fellatio, anallingus, and anal intercourse are acts of carnal knowledge of any male or female person by the anus or by or with the mouth. Chaine v. Commonwealth, 17 Va. App. 179, 436 S.E.2d 187 (1993), aff'd upon reh'g en banc, 18 Va. App. 301, 443 S.E.2d 924 (1994).

Penetration is necessary. — To constitute the offense of buggery or other "carnal copulation" there must be a penetration (res in re), as in rape. Wise v. Commonwealth, 135 Va. 757, 115 S.E. 508 (1923).

Penetration is an essential element of the crime of sodomy so a conviction of sodomy should be reversed because there was no evidence that defendant's penis penetrated a child's mouth. Ashby v. Commonwealth, 208 Va. 443, 158 S.E.2d 657 (1968).

The Commonwealth must demonstrate that penetration occurred. Lankford v. Foster, 546 F. Supp. 241 (W.D. Va. 1982), aff'd, 716 F.2d 896 (4th Cir. 1983), cert. denied, 467 U.S. 1214, 104 S. Ct. 2655, 81 L. Ed. 2d 362 (1984).

To sustain a sodomy conviction, evidence of penetration is required. The evidence of penetration, however, may be circumstantial. Chrisman v. Commonwealth, 3 Va. App. 371, 349 S.E.2d 899 (1986).

And must be proved. — Evidence of penetration is necessary to establish sodomy, and while this may be and generally can only be shown by circumstantial evidence, such evidence must be convincing to a moral certainty and sufficient to exclude every reasonable doubt. Proof that accused had his head upon the stomach of another with the penis in his hand is insufficient. It was therefore error to charge under such circumstances that if the jury believe beyond a reasonable doubt that the accused actually indulged in such carnal copulation by taking the penis in the mouth, it is their duty to find him guilty. Hudson v. Commonwealth, 141 Va. 525, 127 S.E. 89 (1925).

To sustain a conviction for sodomy, the Commonwealth must prove beyond a reasonable doubt that penetration occurred. However, penetration may be proved by circumstantial evidence, and that evidence need only be slight. Lawson v. Commonwealth, 13 Va. App. 109, 409 S.E.2d 466 (1991).

But emission is not necessary. — The penetration of a beast by a man, against the order of nature, without emission, constitutes buggery. Commonwealth v. Thomas, 3 Va. (1 Va. Cas.) 307 (1812).

Penetration need only be slight. — In a prosecution for carnally knowing a victim with the mouth, the penetration that must be shown be only slight. Ryan v. Commonwealth, 219 Va. 439, 247 S.E.2d 698 (1978).

Penetration issue for jury. — In a prosecution for carnally knowing a victim with the mouth, the issue of penetration is a question for the jury upon the evidence in the case. Ryan v. Commonwealth, 219 Va. 439, 247 S.E.2d 698 (1978).

And may be proved by circumstantial evidence. — As in rape, penetration in sodomy can be proved by circumstantial evidence. Ryan v. Commonwealth, 219 Va. 439, 247 S.E.2d 698 (1978).

Thus, evidence of the condition, position and proximity of the parties may afford sufficient evidence of penetration to support a charge of sodomy by cunnilingus. Ryan v. Commonwealth, 219 Va. 439, 247 S.E.2d 698 (1978).

Penetration inferred from victim's account. — In a prosecution for carnally knowing a victim with the mouth, it could reasonably be inferred that penetration had occurred from the victim's account of the defendant's protracted assault upon her, extending over a period of at least 45 minutes. Ryan v. Commonwealth, 219 Va. 439, 247 S.E.2d 698 (1978).

Where victim specifically stated that penetration did not occur, there is reasonable doubt on an element essential to support defendant's conviction of sodomy. In this case, to permit the jury to draw an inference which would contradict the direct evidence given by the person whose testimony created the circumstantial evidence was error. Chrisman v. Commonwealth, 3 Va. App. 371, 349 S.E.2d 899 (1986).

Proof that accused knew victim did not consent not required. — The language of subsection A of this section requires proof only that the accused intended to "carnally know" the victim by mouth; the statute does not require proof that the accused knew the victim did not consent. Paris v. Commonwealth, 35 Va. App. 377, 545 S.E.2d 557, 2001 Va. App. LEXIS 241 (2001).

Forcing act of sodomy on wife. — See Towler v. Peyton, 303 F. Supp. 581 (W.D. Va. 1969).

When enhanced punishment available. — The offense proscribed by the "provided" clause is precisely the same offense that is proscribed by the main portion of the statute that precedes the word "provided." The legislature has provided for an enhanced punishment when the characteristics specified in the proviso are applicable to the persons prosecuted for violating the offense defined in the main portion of the statute. Chaine v. Commonwealth, 17 Va. App. 179, 436 S.E.2d 187 (1993), aff'd upon reh'g en banc, 18 Va. App. 301, 443 S.E.2d 924 (1994).

The misdemeanor of indecent exposure is not included within the offense of sodomy because the elements of indecent exposure are not included within the elements of sodomy. Similarly, the elements of indecent exposure with lascivious intent are not included within the offense of sodomy, nor are the elements of sodomy included within the offense of indecent exposure with lascivious intent. So even if a prior conviction of indecent exposure with lascivious intent was based on the same evidence as a later prosecution for sodomy, § 19.2-294 is not applicable. Ashby v. Commonwealth, 208 Va. 443, 158 S.E.2d 657 (1968).

Uncorroborated confession insufficient. — Defendant's conviction could not be sustained where the corpus delicti was proven only by his extrajudicial confession. Phillips v. Commonwealth, 202 Va. 207, 116 S.E.2d 282 (1960).

The separate confessions of co-defendants are each admissible only against the defendant who made the confession. Phillips v. Commonwealth, 202 Va. 207, 116 S.E.2d 282 (1960).

Evidence was clearly sufficient to support jury's verdict against defendant. Lewis v. Commonwealth, 209 Va. 602, 166 S.E.2d 248 (1969).

Evidence was sufficient to convict defendant of non-forcible sodomy in violation of subsection A of § 18.2-361 because the victim testified that she engaged in oral sex with defendant at his request on the date in question. Mervin-Frazier v. Commonwealth, 2010 Va. App. LEXIS 134 (Apr. 6, 2010).

Defendant's nonjury trial conviction was supported by positive evidence of the victim that the two men engaged in crimes against nature in a deserted area, and by a doctor's stipulated testimony that upon examination of the victim on the day of the incident he found the victim's rectum irritated, with a red abrasion, but without a tear or bruises. Hahn v. Commonwealth, No. 1303-89-1 (Ct. of Appeals Sept. 11, 1990).

Conviction of boy set aside. — When defendant, charged with buggery, was under twelve years of age, and no complaint was made for two years, his conviction was set aside. Williams v. Commonwealth, 2 Va. Dec. 201, 22 S.E. 859 (1895).

Failure to record preliminary hearing where credibility of prosecutrix at issue. — In a prosecution under this section, defense counsel's failure to record the preliminary hearing constitutes a serious error of judgment in a case where the credibility of the prosecutrix is at issue. Lankford v. Foster, 546 F. Supp. 241 (W.D. Va. 1982), aff'd, 716 F.2d 896 (4th Cir. 1983), cert. denied, 467 U.S. 1214, 104 S. Ct. 2655, 81 L. Ed. 2d 362 (1984).

Child's best interests are not promoted by award of custody to parent who carries on active homosexual relationship in the same residence as the child. An award of custody to such a parent constitutes an abuse of judicial discretion. Roe v. Roe, 228 Va. 722, 324 S.E.2d 691 (1985).

Failure to voir dire jury constitutes serious tactical error. — In determining whether the jury was indeed impartial in a prosecution under this section, counsel should have examined them to determine whether they or their families had ever been victims of a sex crime and whether they had young daughters. Failure to seize upon this opportunity constitutes a serious tactical error and poor judgment. Lankford v. Foster, 546 F. Supp. 241 (W.D. Va. 1982), aff'd, 716 F.2d 896 (4th Cir. 1983), cert. denied, 467 U.S. 1214, 104 S. Ct. 2655, 81 L. Ed. 2d 362 (1984).

Jury instructions in forcible sodomy case. — See Lankford v. Foster, 546 F. Supp. 241 (W.D. Va. 1982), aff'd, 716 F.2d 896 (4th Cir. 1983), cert. denied, 467 U.S. 1214, 104 S. Ct. 2655, 81 L. Ed. 2d 362 (1984).

Jury instruction gave undue prominence to duration of act. — A jury instruction which commented on a piece of circumstantial evidence tending to establish a key element of the offense charged gave undue prominence to the duration of the alleged sexual act which was but one of many pieces of circumstantial evidence the jury could have considered in reaching a verdict. Thus, there existed a danger that the jury would be misled because the instruction permitted the jury to base its decision on an inference or presumption that duration alone was sufficient to prove penetration. Simmons v. Commonwealth, No. 0460-94-3 (Ct. of Appeals Aug. 29, 1995).

Sentences for solicitation to commit oral sodomy. — Neither the five-year maximum sentence for solicitation to commit oral sodomy nor the actual sentences imposed on defendants convicted of such offense constituted a punishment in quantum so severe for a comparatively trivial offense that it would be so out of proportion to the crime as to shock the conscience and to constitute cruel and unusual punishment. DePriest v. Commonwealth, 33 Va. App. 754, 537 S.E.2d 1, 2000 Va. App. LEXIS 752 (2000).

Defendant preserved the double jeopardy argument for appeal where defense counsel stated in a discussion with the judge that the indictments of sodomy and carnal knowledge should have been struck; although the argument was not precisely framed as an objection, this colloquy sufficed to present the issue to the trial judge. Moreover, the trial judge's response was a clear acknowledgment that he understood the issue. Chaine v. Commonwealth, 17 Va. App. 179, 436 S.E.2d 187 (1993), aff'd upon reh'g en banc, 18 Va. App. 301, 443 S.E.2d 924 (1994).

Sufficiency of evidence. — General Assembly intended by its use of the phrase "carnally knows in any manner any brute animal," to include any sexual bodily connection between humans and animals because subsection A of § 18.2-361 is the only code section to prohibit carnal knowledge "in any manner," and uses that term specifically as it relates to prohibited sexual conduct with "any brute animal." Ward v. Commonwealth, 2011 Va. App. LEXIS 81 (Mar. 8, 2011).

Contention barred from appellate review. — Contention by appellant, who was convicted of pandering, regarding the erroneous use of the term "sexual acts" instead of "unlawful sexual intercourse" or one of the acts specified in this section, was barred from appellate review because it was never raised in the trial court. Haitham Shurbaji v. Commonwealth, No. 1822-92-4 (Ct. of Appeals Mar. 29, 1994).

Where defendant failed to preserve a constitutional claim that the state was precluded from enforcing § 18.2-361 because it criminalized consensual sexual acts, the appellate court held that the case did not raise either a good cause or ends of justice basis to forego the primary preservation requirements of Va. Sup. Ct. R. 5A:18. Askew v. Commonwealth, No. 0235-03-1, 2004 Va. App. LEXIS 72 (Ct. of Appeals Feb. 10, 2004).

Applied in Pedersen v. City of Richmond, 219 Va. 1061, 254 S.E.2d 95 (1979); Howard v. Commonwealth, 221 Va. 904, 275 S.E.2d 602 (1981); Nemetz v. Immigration & Naturalization Serv., 647 F.2d 432 (4th Cir. 1981); Wolfe v. Commonwealth, 42 Va. App. 776, 595 S.E.2d 27, 2004 Va. App. LEXIS 168 (2004).

ARTICLE 4.

FAMILY OFFENSES; CRIMES AGAINST CHILDREN, ETC.

§ 18.2-362. Person marrying when husband or wife is living; penalty; venue.

If any person, being married, shall, during the life of the husband or wife, marry another person in this Commonwealth, or if the marriage with such other person take place out of the Commonwealth, shall thereafter cohabit with such other person in this Commonwealth, he or she shall be guilty of a Class 4 felony. Venue for a violation of this section may be in the county or city where the subsequent marriage occurred or where the parties to the subsequent marriage cohabited.

History.
Code 1950, § 20-41; 1975, cc. 14, 15; 2003, c. 99.

Law Review.
For note, "Estop in the Name of Love: A Case for Constructive Marriage in Virginia," see 49 Wm. & Mary L. Rev. 973 (2007).

Michie's Jurisprudence.
For related discussion, see 1A M.J. Accomplices and Accessories, § 8; 2B M.J. Autrefois, Acquit and Convict, § 7; 3A M.J. Bigamy, §§ 2, 4, 9.

CASE NOTES

Section compared with § 20-38.1. — While the felony (this section) applies only to a person who, while already married, marries again, the misdemeanor (§ 20-38.1) is broader in scope and applies to any person, whether married or not, who enters into a marriage before the dissolution of an earlier marriage of one of the parties. Stuart v. Commonwealth, 11 Va. App. 216, 397 S.E.2d 533 (1990).

Commonwealth could choose to charge defendant with felony rather than misdemeanor. — Attorney for the Commonwealth could choose to charge the defendant with a felony (this section) instead of a misdemeanor (§ 20-38.1); the mere fact that the defendant may also have committed a lesser offense does not preclude the Commonwealth from charging a greater offense arising out of the same act or transaction. Stuart v. Commonwealth, 11 Va. App. 216, 397 S.E.2d 533 (1990).

Marriage while still married to another is void ab initio. —

Where parties took part in a marriage ceremony in South Carolina and at the time of the ceremony, husband had not secured a final decree of divorce from his first wife, which he subsequently obtained, the parties' marriage in South Carolina was void ab initio, not merely voidable. Hager v. Hager, 3 Va. App. 415, 349 S.E.2d 908 (1986).

Elements of offense of bigamy. — In order for a second marriage to constitute the crime of bigamy it is, of course, essential that the first marriage should have been a valid marriage, and that the marital relation should have been subsisting between the parties thereto at the time the defendant entered into the second marriage. Warner v. Commonwealth, 4 Va. (2 Va. Cas.) 95 (1817); Moore v. Commonwealth, 36 Va. (9 Leigh) 639 (1838); Oneale v. Commonwealth, 58 Va. (17 Gratt.) 582 (1867); Bird v. Commonwealth, 62 Va. (21 Gratt.) 800 (1871).

The subsequent marriage of the accused is of course an essential element of the crime. Farewell v. Commonwealth, 167 Va. 475, 189 S.E. 321 (1937).

Under this section, the crime of bigamy is complete in this state if under an invalid marriage in another state there is thereafter cohabitation under such marriage in this state. Corvin v. Commonwealth, 131 Va. 649, 108 S.E. 651 (1921); Farewell v. Commonwealth, 167 Va. 475, 189 S.E. 321 (1937).

Proof of validity of out-of-state marriage. — Where a prior marriage is alleged to have taken place in another state it must be shown that the marriage was valid where contracted. Warner v. Commonwealth, 4 Va. (2 Va. Cas.) 95 (1817); Oneale v. Commonwealth, 58 Va. (17 Gratt.) 582 (1867); Bird v. Commonwealth, 62 Va. (21 Gratt.) 800 (1871).

Unmarried party to second marriage guilty of aiding and abetting. — An unmarried person who marries another, knowing that the latter is already married, may be convicted of aiding and abetting the commission of bigamy by the latter even though this section does not in terms make the competent party to the bigamous marriage punishable. Adkins v. Commonwealth, 175 Va. 590, 9 S.E.2d 349 (1940).

What is necessary to give court jurisdiction. — Either the second unlawful marriage, or the cohabitation after the second unlawful marriage has been entered into out of this state, must take place within this state to give our courts jurisdiction. Neither the place of marriage nor the place of cohabitation is an element of the nature or character of the crime. Farewell v. Commonwealth, 167 Va. 475, 189 S.E. 321 (1937).

Reasonable belief that one is divorced is no defense. — Because the unambiguous language of this section does not require proof of a specific intent, reasonable belief that a prior marriage has been ended by divorce is not a defense to the charge of bigamy. Stuart v. Commonwealth, 11 Va. App. 216, 397 S.E.2d 533 (1990).

As to evidence to prove former marriage, see Warner v. Commonwealth, 4 Va. (2 Va. Cas.) 95 (1817); Moore v. Commonwealth, 36 Va. (9 Leigh) 639 (1838); Oneale v. Commonwealth, 58 Va. (17 Gratt.) 582 (1867); Bird v. Commonwealth, 62 Va. (21 Gratt.) 800 (1871); Womack v. Tankersley, 78 Va. 242 (1883).

Bigamy both illegal and void. — Because defendant married a second wife while married to his first wife, because this section clearly condemned bigamy as both illegal and void, and because defendant's two-year minimum prison term fell far short of implicating any Eighth Amendment issue, there was no merit in any of defendant's statutory or constitutional challenges. Cole v. Commonwealth, 58 Va. App. 642, 712 S.E.2d 759, 2011 Va. App. LEXIS 255 (2011).

§ 18.2-363. Leaving Commonwealth to evade law against bigamy.

If any persons, resident in this Commonwealth, one of whom has a husband or wife living, shall, with the intention of returning to reside in this Commonwealth, go into another state or country and there intermarry and return to and reside in this Commonwealth cohabiting as man and wife, such marriage shall be governed by the same law, in all respects, as if it had been solemnized in this Commonwealth.

History.

Code 1950, § 20-44; 1975, cc. 14, 15.

§ 18.2-364. Exceptions to preceding sections.

Sections 18.2-362 and 18.2-363 shall not extend to a person whose husband or wife shall have been continuously absent from such person for seven years next before marriage of such person to another, and shall not have been known by such person to be living within that time; nor to a person who can show that the second marriage was contracted in good faith under a reasonable belief that the former consort was dead; nor to a person who shall, at the time of the subsequent marriage, have been divorced from the bond of the former marriage; nor to a person whose former marriage was void.

History.

Code 1950, § 20-42; 1975, cc. 14, 15.

Michie's Jurisprudence.

For related discussion, see 1A M.J. Accomplices and Accessories, § 8; 2B M.J. Autrefois, Acquit and Convict, § 7; 3A M.J. Bigamy, § 2.

CASE NOTES

Void foreign decree of divorce renders second marriage bigamous. — If the accused did not go to West Virginia with the determination to make it his legal domicile, or if he went there merely for the purpose of obtaining a divorce, intending to remain no longer than was necessary to accomplish his purpose, or if the divorce was obtained by fraud, the decree of the West Virginia court is void, and the accused in marrying another woman and thereafter cohabiting with her in this state, while his former wife still was living, is guilty of bigamy. Corvin v. Commonwealth, 131 Va. 649, 108 S.E. 651 (1921).

Evidence of fraud in obtaining decree. — Where a divorce decree in another state was relied upon by accused as a defense, the material facts which culminated in the divorce suit, as well as his conduct immediately thereafter, are admissible to determine whether the decree had been obtained in good faith or by deceit and fraud. Corvin v. Commonwealth, 131 Va. 649, 108 S.E. 651 (1921).

Indictment for bigamy need not negative provisions of this section. — In a prosecution for bigamy, it is not necessary that the indictment should negative the provisions of this section, as this section constitutes no part of the description of the offense, but is disconnected with the statutory description of the crime and only affords the accused certain grounds of defense, among them a divorce from the bond of a previous marriage. Corvin v. Commonwealth, 131 Va. 649, 108 S.E. 651 (1921).

§ 18.2-365. Adultery defined; penalty.

Any person, being married, who voluntarily shall have sexual intercourse with any person not his or her spouse shall be guilty of adultery, punishable as a Class 4 misdemeanor.

History.

Code 1950, §§18.1-187, 18.1-190; 1960, c. 358; 1975, cc. 14, 15.

Law Review.

For an article, "Sex and Guilt," see 84 Va. L. Rev. 1 (1998). For 2006 survey article, "Family and Juvenile Law," see 41 U. Rich. L. Rev. 151 (2006). For note, "Estop in the Name of Love: A Case for Constructive Marriage in Virginia," see 49 Wm. & Mary L. Rev. 973 (2007).

Michie's Jurisprudence.

For related discussion, see 1A M.J. Adultery, Fornication and Lewdness, §§ 2, 3, 8.

CASE NOTES

Adultery is not protected by the First or Fourteenth Amendments to the United States Constitution particularly as the Commonwealth prohibits it by this section. Suddarth v. Slane, 539 F. Supp. 612 (W.D. Va. 1982).

State trooper who admitted to adulterous conduct could not claim wrongful dismissal pursuant to 42 U.S.C.S. § 1983, as his conduct was clearly in violation of Virginia law and the Department of State Police regulations. Suddarth v. Slane, 539 F. Supp. 612 (W.D. Va. 1982).

Applied in Roe v. Roe, 228 Va. 722, 324 S.E.2d 691 (1985).

§ 18.2-366. Adultery and fornication by persons forbidden to marry; incest.

A. Any person who commits adultery or fornication with any person whom he or she is forbidden by law to marry shall be guilty of a Class 1 misdemeanor except as provided by subsection B.

B. Any person who commits adultery or fornication with his daughter or granddaughter, or with her son or grandson, or her father or his mother, shall be guilty of a Class 5 felony. However, if a parent or grandparent commits adultery or fornication with his or her child or grandchild, and such child or grandchild is at least thirteen years of age but less than eighteen years of age at the time of the offense, such parent or grandparent shall be guilty of a Class 3 felony.

History.

Code 1950, § 18.1-191; 1960, c. 358; 1975, cc. 14, 15; 1981, c. 397; 1993, c. 703.

Cross references.

As to Sex Offenders and Crimes Against Minors Registry, see § 9.1-900 et seq. For provision that consent to adoption shall not be required of the birth father when the father has been convicted of a violation of § 18.2-61 A, § 18.2-63, or § 18.2-366 B, see § 63.2-1202 F. As to validity of an entrustment agreement for termination of parental rights, despite lack of birth father's signature, when the father has been convicted of a violation of § 18.2-61 A, § 18.2-63, or § 18.2-366 B, and the child in question was conceived as a result of such violation, see § 63.2-903 C and § 63.2-1222. As to execution of consent for parental placement adoptions, and exceptions to consent requirements, see § 63.2-1233. For definition of "barrier crime" as including a conviction of incest as set out in § 18.2-366, or an equivalent offense in another state, and prohibition against assisted living facilities, adult day care centers or child welfare agencies hiring for certain compensated employment persons who have committed such an offense, see §§ 63.2-1719, 63.2-1720. For provision making it unlawful for any person to operate a family day home if he, or if he knows that any other person who resides in the home, has been convicted of a felony in violation of this section, see § 63.2-1727.

Michie's Jurisprudence.

For related discussion, see 1A M.J. Adultery, Fornication and Lewdness, § 2; 9B M.J. Incest, § 2.

CASE NOTES

Evidence of incestuous intercourse admissible. — It is well settled that in a prosecution for incest, evidence of acts of incestuous intercourse between the parties other than those charged in the indictment or information, whether prior or subsequent thereto, is, if not too remote in point of time, admissible for the purpose of throwing light upon the relations of the parties and the incestuous disposition of the defendant toward the other party, and to corroborate the proof of the act relied upon for conviction. Brown v. Commonwealth, 208 Va. 512, 158 S.E.2d 663 (1968).

HLA test results are insufficient to prove incest. — Where the alleged victim testifies as a witness for the Commonwealth and denies the act of incest, the Human Leucocyte Antigen (HLA) test result alone may not suffice to prove incest beyond a reasonable doubt. Bridgeman v. Commonwealth, 3 Va. App. 523, 351 S.E.2d 598 (1986).

Circumstantial evidence in the nature of Human Leucocyte Antigen (HLA) test results showing a probability of paternity was insufficient as a matter of law to find defendant guilty of incest, where the Commonwealth's own evidence, including the testimony of expert regarding the lack of statistical information concerning the effect which incestuous relationships have on increasing the probability of the HLA results indicating paternity, and the denial by the alleged victim that intercourse occurred between her and defendant, created a reasonable doubt that defendant was guilty of the crime charged. Bridgeman v. Commonwealth, 3 Va. App. 523, 351 S.E.2d 598 (1986).

Evidence sufficient to prove paternity. — Where an alleged incest victim and her mother identified defendant as the victim's father, he was listed as her father on the birth certificate, the victim was born during defendant's marriage to the victim's mother, and the victim used defendant's surname throughout her life, the evidence was sufficient to prove defendant's paternity. Dowdy v. Commonwealth, No. 2509-02-3, 2003 Va. App. LEXIS 705 (Ct. of Appeals Dec. 30, 2003).

CIRCUIT COURT OPINIONS

Incest is not a lesser included offense of rape, as under this section, the incest statute, the Commonwealth has to prove a familial relationship and there is no requirement that it be nonconsensual, while lack of consent is an element of rape, and not every commission of rape was a commission of incest. Commonwealth v. Levin, 55 Va. Cir. 229, 2001 Va. Cir. LEXIS 275 (Norfolk 2001).

§ 18.2-367. Repealed by Acts 2004, c. 459.

§ 18.2-368. Placing or leaving wife for prostitution.

Any person who, by force, fraud, intimidation or threats, places or leaves, or procures any other person to place or leave his wife in a bawdy place for the purpose of prostitution or unlawful sexual intercourse, shall be guilty of pandering, punishable as a Class 4 felony.

History.
Code 1950, § 18.1-207; 1960, c. 358; 1975, cc. 14, 15.

§ 18.2-369. Abuse and neglect of incapacitated adults; penalty.

A. It shall be unlawful for any responsible person to abuse or neglect any incapacitated adult as defined in this section. Any responsible person who abuses or neglects an incapacitated adult in violation of this section and the abuse or neglect does not result in serious bodily injury or disease to the incapacitated adult is guilty of a Class 1 misdemeanor. Any responsible person who is convicted of a second or subsequent offense under this subsection is guilty of a Class 6 felony.

B. Any responsible person who abuses or neglects an incapacitated adult in violation of this section and the abuse or neglect results in serious bodily injury or disease to the incapacitated adult is guilty of a Class 4 felony. Any responsible person who abuses or neglects an incapacitated adult in violation of this section and the abuse or neglect results in the death of the incapacitated adult is guilty of a Class 3 felony.

C. For purposes of this section:

"Abuse" means (i) knowing and willful conduct that causes physical injury or pain or (ii) knowing and willful use of physical restraint, including confinement, as punishment, for convenience or as a substitute for treatment, except where such conduct or physical restraint, including confinement, is a part of care or treatment and is in furtherance of the health and safety of the incapacitated person.

"Incapacitated adult" means any person 18 years of age or older who is impaired by reason of mental illness, intellectual disability, physical illness or disability, advanced age or other causes to the extent the adult lacks sufficient understanding or capacity to make, communicate or carry out reasonable decisions concerning his well-being.

"Neglect" means the knowing and willful failure by a responsible person to provide treatment, care, goods or services which results in injury to the health or endangers the safety of an incapacitated adult.

"Responsible person" means a person who has responsibility for the care, custody or control of an incapacitated person by operation of law or who has assumed such responsibility voluntarily, by contract or in fact.

"Serious bodily injury or disease" shall include but not be limited to (i) disfigurement, (ii) a fracture, (iii) a severe burn or laceration, (iv) mutilation, (v) maiming, or (vi) life-threatening internal injuries or conditions, whether or not caused by trauma.

D. No responsible person shall be in violation of this section whose conduct was (i) in accordance with the informed consent of the incapacitated person or a person authorized to consent on his behalf; (ii) in accordance with a declaration by the incapacitated person under the Natural Death Act of Virginia (§ 54.1-2981 et seq.) or with the provisions of a valid medical power of attorney; (iii) in accordance with the wishes of the incapacitated person or a person authorized to consent on behalf of the incapacitated person and in accord with the tenets and practices of a church or religious denomination; (iv) incident to necessary movement of, placement of or protection from harm to the incapacitated person; or (v) a bona fide, recognized or approved practice to provide medical care.

History.
1992, c. 551; 1994, c. 620; 2000, c. 796; 2001, c. 181; 2004, c. 863; 2007, cc. 562, 653; 2012, cc. 476, 507.

Cross references.

For definition of "barrier crime" as including a conviction of abuse and neglect of incapacitated adults as set out in § 18.2-369, or an equivalent offense in another state, and prohibition against assisted living facilities, adult day care centers or child welfare agencies hiring for certain compensated employment persons who have committed such an offense, see §§ 63.2-1719, 63.2-1720. As to report to children's residential facility for which a background check is being performed on whether the applicant has ever been convicted of or is the subject of pending charges for various crimes, including abuse and neglect of incapacitated adults as set out in § 18.2-369, or an equivalent offense in another state, see § 63.2-1726. For provision making it unlawful for any person to operate a family day home if he, or if he knows that any other person who resides in the home, has been convicted of a felony in violation of this section, see § 63.2-1727.

The 2012 amendments.

The 2012 amendments by cc. 476 and 507 are identical, and in subsection C, substituted "any person 18 years of age or older who is impaired by reason of mental illness, intellectual disability, physical illness" for "any person 18 years or older who is impaired by reason of mental illness, mental retardation, physical illness" in the paragraph defining "Incapacitated adult."

Law Review.

For 2007 annual survey article, "Criminal Law and Procedure," see 42 U. Rich. L. Rev. 311 (2007).

Michie's Jurisprudence.

For related discussion, see 9A M.J. Guardian and Ward, § 1.

CASE NOTES

Failure to provide medical treatment. — Evidence that defendant knowingly and willfully failed to provide medical treatment to her incapacitated mother even though the doctor instructed defendant to bring her mother to his office if she experiences any problems, was sufficient to support her conviction for felonious abuse or neglect of her mother that resulted in serious bodily injury or disease. Correll v. Commonwealth, 269 Va. 3, 607 S.E.2d 119, 2005 Va. LEXIS 14 (2005).

Evidence was sufficient to establish that defendant knowingly, willfully or maliciously caused any injuries or failed to provide treatment, care, goods or services to her mother. — Among other things, defendant's failure to provide her mother with the appropriate food and/or care, including medical care, amounted to more than bad judgment, and defendant's conduct amounted to a voluntary, knowing omission which defendant could not have reasonably believed was lawful or excusable as she was clearly capable of comprehending the seriousness of her mother's condition given the fact that she had cared for her mother over the years. Correll v. Commonwealth, 42 Va. App. 311, 591 S.E.2d 712, 2004 Va. App. LEXIS 30 (2004), aff'd, 269 Va. 3, 607 S.E.2d 119 (2005).

Motion to suppress denied. — In a case of abuse or neglect of an incapacitated adult, a motion to suppress the evidence because the officer entered the house without a warrant or probable cause, was denied as the officer had consent to enter. Arms v. Commonwealth, — Va. App. —, — S.E.2d —, 2008 Va. App. LEXIS 256 (May 27, 2008).

Evidence sufficient to find neglect of incapacitated adult. — Trial court did not err in convicting defendant of felony neglect of an incapacitated adult in violation of subsection B of § 18.2-369 because defendant had a sufficient relationship with the victim by contract or in fact through her employment as a home health aide with a home health care company to make her a "responsible person" under § 18.2-369, and the Commonwealth clearly established that defendant accepted the company's offer to employ her as the victim's home health aide and that she accepted compensation for the care that she claimed to provide the victim; the evidence adduced at trial proved that defendant knowingly and willfully neglected the victim in violation of § 18.2-369 because as the victim's health care worker, who saw the victim five days a week in his home and claimed to regularly move and wash him, defendant certainly should have been aware of the victim's condition and should have acted to address it. Williams v. Commonwealth, 2009 Va. App. LEXIS 408 (Sept. 15, 2009).

§ 18.2-370. Taking indecent liberties with children; penalties.

A. Any person 18 years of age or over, who, with lascivious intent, knowingly and intentionally commits any of the following acts with any child under the age of 15 years is guilty of a Class 5 felony:

(1) Expose his or her sexual or genital parts to any child to whom such person is not legally married or propose that any such child expose his or her sexual or genital parts to such person; or

(2) [Repealed.]

(3) Propose that any such child feel or fondle his own sexual or genital parts or the sexual or genital parts of such person or propose that such person feel or fondle the sexual or genital parts of any such child; or

(4) Propose to such child the performance of an act of sexual intercourse or any act constituting an offense under § 18.2-361; or

(5) Entice, allure, persuade, or invite any such child to enter any vehicle, room, house, or other place, for any of the purposes set forth in the preceding subdivisions of this section.

B. Any person 18 years of age or over who, with lascivious intent, knowingly and intentionally receives money, property, or any other remuneration for allowing, encouraging, or enticing any person under the age of 18 years to perform in or be a subject of sexually explicit visual material as defined in § 18.2-374.1 or who knowingly encourages such person to perform in or be a subject of sexually explicit material; shall be guilty of a Class 5 felony.

C. Any person who is convicted of a second or subsequent violation of this section shall be guilty of a Class 4 felony; provided that (i) the offenses were not part of a common act, transaction or scheme; (ii) the accused was at liberty as defined in § 53.1-151 between each conviction; and (iii) it is admitted, or found by the jury or judge before whom the person is tried, that the accused was previously convicted of a violation of this section.

D. Any parent, step-parent, grandparent, or step-grandparent who commits a violation of either this section or clause (v) or (vi) of subsection A of § 18.2-370.1 (i) upon his child, step-child, grandchild, or step-grandchild who is at least 15 but less than 18 years of age is guilty of a Class 5 felony or (ii) upon his child, step-child, grandchild, or step-grandchild less than 15 years of age is guilty of a Class 4 felony.

History.

Code 1950, §§ 18.1-213 through 18.1-215; 1960, c. 358; 1973, c. 131; 1975, cc. 14, 15; 1979, c. 348; 1981, c. 397; 1986, c. 503; 2000, c. 333; 2001, cc. 776, 840; 2005, cc. 185, 762; 2013, cc. 423, 470.

Cross references.

As to aggravated sexual battery, see § 18.2-67.3. As to Sex Offenders and Crimes Against Minors Registry, see § 9.1-900 et seq. For definition of "barrier crime" as including a conviction of taking indecent liberties with children as set out in § 18.2-370 or

§ 18.2-370.1, or an equivalent offense in another state, and prohibition against assisted living facilities, adult day care centers or child welfare agencies hiring for certain compensated employment persons who have committed such an offense, see §§ 63.2-1719, 63.2-1720. As to report to children's residential facility for which a background check is being performed on whether the applicant has ever been convicted of or is the subject of pending charges for various crimes, including taking indecent liberties with children as set out in § 18.2-370 or § 18.2-370.1, or an equivalent offense in another state, see § 63.2-1726. For provision making it unlawful for any person to operate a family day home if he, or if he knows that any other person who resides in the home, has been convicted of a felony in violation of this section, see § 63.2-1727.

Editor's note.

Acts 2013, cc. 423 and 470, cl. 2 provides: "That the provisions of this act may result in a net increase in periods of imprisonment or commitment. Pursuant to § 30-19.1:4, the estimated amount of the necessary appropriation cannot be determined for periods of imprisonment in state adult correctional facilities; therefore, Chapter 3 of the Acts of Assembly of 2012, Special Session I, requires the Virginia Criminal Sentencing Commission to assign a minimum fiscal impact of $50,000. Pursuant to § 30-19.1:4, the estimated amount of the necessary appropriation cannot be determined for periods of commitment to the custody of the Department of Juvenile Justice."

The 2013 amendments.

The 2013 amendments by cc. 423 and 470 are identical, and inserted "his own sexual or genital parts or" in subdivision A (3).

Law Review.

For survey of Virginia law on evidence for the year 1969-1970, see 56 Va. L. Rev. 1325 (1970). For survey of Virginia criminal law for the year 1978-1979, see 66 Va. L. Rev. 241 (1980). For a review of criminal law in Virginia for year 1999, see 33 U. Rich. L. Rev. 857 (1999). For article, "Legal Issues Involving Children," see 35 U. Rich. L. Rev. 741 (2001). For article surveying developments in criminal law and procedure in Virginia from July 2001 to September 2002, see 37 U. Rich. L. Rev. 45 (2002). For survey of Virginia criminal law and procedure for the year 2004-2005, see 40 U. Rich. L. Rev. 197 (2005). For 2006 survey article, "Criminal Law and Procedure," see 41 U. Rich. L. Rev. 83 (2006). For 2007 annual survey article, "Criminal Law and Procedure," see 42 U. Rich. L. Rev. 311 (2007). For article, "Protecting Virtual Playgrounds: Children, Law, and Play Online: Sex Play in Virtual Worlds," see 66 Wash. & Lee L. Rev. 1127 (2009). For annual survey article, "Criminal Law and Procedure," see 46 U. Rich. L. Rev. 59 (2011).

Michie's Jurisprudence.

For related discussion, see 1A M.J. Adultery, Fornication and Lewdness, §§ 11, 15; 2B M.J. Autrefois, Acquit and Convict, § 16; 15 M.J. Rape, § 12; 16 M.J. Sodomy, § 4.

CASE NOTES

The word "lascivious" is not defined in this section and must therefore be given its ordinary meaning. As so determined, the word "lascivious" describes a state of mind that is eager for sexual indulgence, desirous of inciting to lust or of inciting sexual desire and appetite. McKeon v. Commonwealth, 211 Va. 24, 175 S.E.2d 282 (1970); Campbell v. Commonwealth, 227 Va. 196, 313 S.E.2d 402 (1984).

Actual touching not within section. — This section does not encompass situations where the accused has actually touched the victim or the victim was caused to touch the accused. Mason v. Commonwealth, No. 0309-97-2 (Ct. of Appeals May 5, 1998).

This section and § 18.2-68 deal with different approaches to a sexual offense. Black v. Peyton, 292 F. Supp. 45 (W.D. Va. 1968).

And different evidence is required to support convictions under this section and former § 18.2-68. Black v. Peyton, 292 F. Supp. 45 (W.D. Va. 1968).

Former § 18.1-215 contemplated an intentional act of a person over 21 [now 18] years of age placing the hands upon or in any manner fondling or feeling the sexual or genital parts of a child

under 14 years of age with lascivious intent. Black v. Peyton, 292 F. Supp. 45 (W.D. Va. 1968).

Unnecessary that victim perceive display. — This section proscribes the intentional display by an adult, with lascivious intent, of his or her genitals in the presence of a child where a reasonable probability exists that they might be seen by that child, regardless of the child's actual perception of such a display. Siquina v. Commonwealth, 28 Va. App. 694, 508 S.E.2d 350 (1998).

Indecent exposure is not included within the offense of sodomy because the elements of indecent exposure are not included within the elements of sodomy. Similarly, the elements of indecent exposure with lascivious intent are not included within the offense of sodomy, nor are the elements of sodomy included within the offense of indecent exposure with lascivious intent. So even if a prior conviction of indecent exposure with lascivious intent was based on the same evidence as a later prosecution for sodomy, § 19.2-294 is not applicable. Ashby v. Commonwealth, 208 Va. 443, 158 S.E.2d 657 (1968).

Indecent exposure not lesser offense of indecent liberties. — Indecent exposure, as proscribed by § 18.2-387, was not a lesser included offense of indecent liberties, as proscribed by subdivision A 1 of § 18.2-370, because all the elements of indecent exposure were not included in the offense charged, and, thus, failure to instruct the jury on indecent exposure was not error. Simon v. Commonwealth, 58 Va. App. 194, 708 S.E.2d 245, 2011 Va. App. LEXIS 153 (2011).

When physical appearance may determine age. — When proof is required that a person is above or below a given age, physical appearance may be considered as proof of that fact; if a criminal defendant's physical appearance indicates an age well above that required to be proven and the trial court determines that the fact finder is able to conclude beyond a reasonable doubt from the defendant's physical appearance that he exceeds the age required to be proven, then the defendant's physical appearance alone is sufficient evidence of his age, and the fact finder may resolve that issue based only on the defendant's physical appearance; however, in less obvious cases, where the defendant's physical appearance does not establish beyond a reasonable doubt that his age exceeds that required, then physical appearance alone is insufficient evidence of his age and must be corroborated. Jewell v. Commonwealth, 8 Va. App. 353, 382 S.E.2d 259 (1989).

Defendant's conviction of taking indecent liberties was affirmed because the trial court found that defendant was 18 years old or older based on his appearance in court, stated its finding, and that finding was proper; contrary to defendant's claim, the trial court did not base its finding on defendant's answers to its questions posed during arraignment. Winn v. Commonwealth, — Va. App. —, — S.E.2d —, 2009 Va. App. LEXIS 141 (Mar. 24, 2009).

Physical appearance was sufficient to prove age. — The physical appearance of the defendant, according to the comments of the trial judge, was sufficient as a matter of law to determine that the defendant was over 18 years old; the trial court did not err, in denying the defendant's motion to strike the evidence. Jewell v. Commonwealth, 8 Va. App. 353, 382 S.E.2d 259 (1989).

Where the statute requires that an accused be "eighteen years of age or over" at the time of the offense, and victim testified that, at the time of the instant offense, defendant was married and had two children, the oldest of whom was four years old, and where defendant was present at trial, such that his "physical appearance may be considered" by the court as evidence of his age at the time of the offense, this evidence sufficiently established that defendant was no less than 18 years of age at the time of the offenses. Gardner v. Commonwealth, No. 1050-95-1 (Ct. of Appeals Mar. 19, 1996).

Where the defendant told the victim he was twenty-eight years old and the defendant's physical appearance at trial corroborated this statement, the evidence was sufficient to prove that the defendant was more than eighteen years of age. Bloom v. Commonwealth, 34 Va. App. 364, 542 S.E.2d 18, 2001 Va. App. LEXIS 91, aff'd, 262 Va. 814, 554 S.E.2d 84 (2001).

Use of Internet in establishing attempt. — Where evidence showed that defendant knew that he was chatting with a 13-year-old girl, who was actually a detective, in an internet chat room, based on the so-called victim's statement telling him her age and that she was in the seventh grade, lived at home, and had little, if any, sexual experience, and that defendant turned on his webcam and exposed himself to the victim, such was sufficient to support his convictions of attempting to take indecent liberties with a child under the age of 14, in violation of §§ 18.2-370 and 18.2-26. Deecheandia v. Commonwealth, No. 1885-03-2, 2004 Va. App. LEXIS 266 (Ct. of Appeals June 8, 2004).

Evidence presented at trial that defendant tried to meet with a person for sex that he perceived to be a 13-year-old female from his conversations with "her" between their computers was sufficient to support his conviction of attempted indecent liberties with a minor; his defense that he could not be convicted of violating that statute because no child existed, since the "female" turned out to be a police officer, was a defense of factual, not legal, impossibility and factual impossibility was not a recognized defense to that offense. Hix v. Commonwealth, 270 Va. 335, 619 S.E.2d 80, 2005 Va. LEXIS 84 (2005).

Although defendant argued he could not be convicted of a violation of 18 U.S.C.S. § 2422(b) because the Government did not prove he was guilty of § 18.2-370 since his victim was not a child under fourteen years of age, but rather an adult posing as a child online, defendant's argument was meritless as the absence of an actual child had no bearing on the crime of attempt under § 18.2-370. United States v. Kaye, — F.3d —, 2007 U.S. App. LEXIS 16114 (4th Cir. July 6, 2007).

Reliance not on physical appearance but on documents not in evidence. — Although defendant's physical appearance was sufficient evidence that he was over 18 years of age, the trial court did not rely on the defendant's physical appearance but relied on documents which were not in evidence, therefore the case was reversed and remanded for a new trial. Jewell v. Commonwealth, 8 Va. App. 353, 382 S.E.2d 259 (1989).

Recent complaint exception to hearsay rule unavailable. — The recent complaint exception to the hearsay rule must be confined to cases involving rape. Thus, in a prosecution under this section, where the incident involved occurred some time between 2 p.m. and 3:30 p.m., the complaint by the alleged victim to his mother was not made until approximately 8 p.m., the mother was not present, and her only knowledge of the alleged crime was that gained from her four-and-a-half-year-old son, her testimony was hearsay and inadmissible. Leybourne v. Commonwealth, 222 Va. 374, 282 S.E.2d 12 (1981).

Admissibility of prior bad acts. — Defendant's convictions for using electronic means to solicit sex with a minor and attempted indecent liberties in violation of subsection B of § 18.2-374.3 and § 18.2-370 were appropriate because evidence of defendant's relationship with another female prior to the current events fell within the general exceptions to the general rule of exclusion of other bad acts evidence. The evidence was relevant to show some of the elements of the crimes charged and demonstrated not only defendant's knowledge that minors were present in the adult chat rooms but also his intent to engage in sexual acts with the current victim, just as he had done in the past. Detzler v. Commonwealth, 2010 Va. App. LEXIS 132 (Apr. 6, 2010).

Evidence of child's prior sexual conduct properly excluded. — Trial court did not err in denying defendant's motion to present evidence of a six-year-old victim's prior sexual conduct because there was no evidence that defendant gave the notice required by § 18.2-67.7, the rape shield statute, other than the prosecutor's statement that he had received a hand-written notice. Gleason v. Commonwealth, 2010 Va. App. LEXIS 256 (June 29, 2010).

Factors to be considered in determining lascivious intent are disjunctive. — When the evidence was sufficient to show defendant improperly gestured toward himself, this was sufficient to show his lascivious intent and sustain his conviction for taking indecent liberties, even though the evidence was not sufficient to show that he was sexually aroused, that he made any improper remarks, or that he asked the victims to do anything wrong, because the factors considered in determining whether lascivious intent was shown were disjunctive, so the demonstration of any one factor was sufficient. Viney v. Commonwealth, No. 0559-03-1, 2004 Va. App. LEXIS 214 (Ct. of Appeals May 4, 2004), aff'd, — Va. —, 609 S.E.2d 26 (2005).

Evidence was sufficient to prove lascivious intent where defendant asked 11 and 13 year old victims if they had ever seen a "dick" and if they wanted to see one; such questions were improper remarks and constituted competent, circumstantial evidence of

lascivious intent. Penley v. Commonwealth, No. 1880-97-2 (Ct. of Appeals Sept. 8, 1998).

Evidence of defendant's conduct during encounters with child was sufficient to prove that defendant exposed his genitals to child with lascivious intent. Brandon v. Commonwealth, No. 2434-98-2 (Ct. of Appeals Jan. 11, 2000).

Admitted telephone conversations between defendant and her incarcerated husband plainly demonstrated that they shared an intent to incite sexual desire and appetite in each other by taking sexually explicit photographs of defendant and a minor girl, who in one photograph was posed with a vibrator, and the tone of the discussions indicated the photographs were being made for husbands sexual enjoyment while defendant admittedly became sexually aroused in the process. Upon this evidence, the jury was entitled to conclude beyond a reasonable doubt that defendant possessed lascivious intent at the time the photographs were produced and that defendant was guilty of taking indecent liberties with a child in violation of § 18.2-370. Mason v. Commonwealth, 49 Va. App. 39, 636 S.E.2d 480, 2006 Va. App. LEXIS 505 (2006).

There was sufficient evidence to prove lasciviousness in support of defendant's indecent liberties conviction, a violation of subdivision A 1 of § 18.2-370, where defendant, on two different occasions within the span of three days, wore intentionally modified shorts, into the crotch of which he had cut a golf ball-sized hole, and exposed himself to a minor. Simon v. Commonwealth, 58 Va. App. 194, 708 S.E.2d 245, 2011 Va. App. LEXIS 153 (2011).

Evidence insufficient to prove lascivious intent. — See Breeding v. Commonwealth, 213 Va. 344, 192 S.E.2d 807 (1972).

Membership in association. — Defendant's membership in the North American Man-Boy Love Association and pornographic materials in his possession at the time of his arrest were admissible in order to show lascivious intent. Smith v. Commonwealth, No. 1546-97-4 (Ct. of Appeals Dec. 1, 1998).

Evidence held sufficient to show that defendant wrote letter. — Commonwealth proved sufficiently that defendant was the one who wrote letter proposing sexual acts to a 12-year-old girl since the letter came in an envelope with the defendant's return address on it and one of the comments in the letter was directly responsive to a statement made in the girl's earlier letter to the defendant. Jewell v. Commonwealth, 8 Va. App. 353, 382 S.E.2d 259 (1989).

Acts sufficient to uphold conviction. — Any one of the following factors can be sufficient to uphold a conviction under the statute: the defendant was sexually aroused; that he made any gestures toward himself or to the child; that he made any improper remarks to the child, or that he asked the child to do anything wrong. Campbell v. Commonwealth, 227 Va. 196, 313 S.E.2d 402 (1984).

Evidence showing that defendant twice transmitted to someone, whom he believed was a minor, live images of his genital parts by means of a computer and a web camera so that the minor could see his genital parts at the time of the exposure was sufficient for the trial judge to have inferred that defendant knowingly and intentionally exposed his genitals to a person whom he believed to be a minor. Brooker v. Commonwealth, 41 Va. App. 609, 587 S.E.2d 732, 2003 Va. App. LEXIS 543 (2003).

Evidence sufficient to uphold conviction. — Evidence that defendant pulled his pants down, exposed his genitalia, and beckoned to a young girl to get her attention was sufficient to show that he intentionally exposed himself, and that he did so with lascivious intent in violation of § 18.2-370. Campbell v. Commonwealth, 227 Va. 196, 313 S.E.2d 402, 1984 Va. LEXIS 282 (1984).

Evidence that defendant exposed his genitals, while it was reasonably probable that he could be seen by children, with the intent to sexually arouse himself, was sufficient to uphold conviction for indecent liberties with a child under § 18.2-370 A 1; the distance between defendant's property and that of the complainant was irrelevant. Holley v. Commonwealth, 38 Va. App. 158, 562 S.E.2d 351, 2002 Va. App. LEXIS 240 (2002).

Appellate court's judgment that affirmed the trial court's judgment finding defendant guilty of two counts of taking indecent liberties with a child was affirmed, as the trial court's judgment was not shown to be plainly wrong or without evidence to support it, as the evidence was sufficient to show that defendant had the lascivious intent required to support convictions on those charges given the fact that he looked down at his groin and adjusted his clothing in such a way as to expose his penis to two young girls riding by on bicycles. Viney v. Commonwealth, 269 Va. 296, 609 S.E.2d 26, 2005 Va. LEXIS 20 (2005).

There was sufficient evidence to support defendant's conviction for indecent liberties with a minor, because the evidence showed that defendant exposed himself with lascivious intent, both knowingly and intentionally, when he had his erect penis exposed underneath a public pier on a public beach in view of children playing in the surf nearby. Frenzel v. Commonwealth, — Va. App. —, — S.E.2d —, 2008 Va. App. LEXIS 274 (June 10, 2008).

Evidence was sufficient to support defendant's convictions involving the second victim for taking indecent liberties with a child under 14 years old pursuant to § 18.2-370, forcible sodomy in violation of § 18.2-67.1, and aggravated sexual battery of a child less than 13 years old pursuant to § 18.2-67.3. Although the second victim could not pinpoint her exact age at the time of the incidents giving rise to the convictions, the trial court as the fact finder could determine that she was under the age of 13, as the second based her age on the relative dates of momentous events in her life, which gave the trial court a basis for determining she was less than 13 years old at the relevant times. Wood v. Commonwealth, — Va. App. —, — S.E.2d —, 2008 Va. App. LEXIS 451 (Oct. 7, 2008).

Evidence was sufficient to support defendant's convictions regarding taking indecent liberties with a child under 14 years old in violation of § 18.2-370, forcible sodomy in violation of § 18.2-67.1, and aggravated sexual battery of a child less than 13 years old pursuant to § 18.2-67.3, all regarding the first victim. The trial court, as the fact finder because a bench trial was involved, could determine that the events that the first victim described occurred while still rejecting the first victim's timeline of the events all happening while she was in the fourth grade, which conflicted with the dates set forth in the indictment. Wood v. Commonwealth, — Va. App. —, — S.E.2d —, 2008 Va. App. LEXIS 451 (Oct. 7, 2008).

Defendant was properly convicted of computer solicitation of a minor in violation of § 18.2-374.3 and attempted indecent liberties with a minor in violation of § 18.2-370 because if the trial court erred in precluding defendant from inquiring of his witnesses what they said concerning the victim's age, any error was harmless, and defendant told the police after his arrest that he believed the victim was only fourteen to fifteen years old; that evidence plainly rebutted any inference that defendant thought he was pursuing an adult, and given defendant's admission that he thought the victim could have been fourteen, along with repeated references during internet chats to the victim's age of thirteen, any error did not affect the jury verdict. Mahmoudzedeh v. Commonwealth, 2009 Va. App. LEXIS 268 (June 16, 2009).

The evidence was sufficient to convict defendant of feloniously taking indecent liberties with a minor, where the evidence included testimony from the victim and the fact that defendant was aroused, which was corroborated by a lifeguard. Robertson v. Commonwealth, 2010 Va. App. LEXIS 75 (Feb. 23, 2010).

Evidence was insufficient to support a conviction under this section, where the victims asserted either that defendant tried to put his penis in their vaginas or that he touched their breasts and vaginas, but there was no evidence that he exposed his genitalia to them or made any propositions or suggestions of sexual intercourse. Mason v. Commonwealth, No. 0309-97-2 (Ct. of Appeals May 5, 1998).

Evidence was sufficient to establish an attempt to take indecent liberties with children where: (1) after passing the victims, defendant turned his car around in a driveway and returned to the location where they were standing; and (2) he then asked them twice if they had ever seen a "dick," and when they responded "no," asked if they wanted to see one; the latter inquiry reasonably could be interpreted as an attempt by defendant to entice the victims to approach his car and supported an inference that the crime would have been consummated had a neighbor not approached. Penley v. Commonwealth, No. 1880-97-2 (Ct. of Appeals Sept. 8, 1998).

The evidence was sufficient to support a conviction for attempting to take indecent liberties with a minor where the defendant established a plan to pick up the victim at a particular time and location and to take her to his house, the defendant then went to the designated location at the designated time, driving the vehicle that he had identified for the victim, and the defendant had clearly stated an intention to have the victim come to his house and engage in sexual acts. Bloom v. Commonwealth, 34 Va. App. 364, 542

S.E.2d 18, 2001 Va. App. LEXIS 91, aff'd, 262 Va. 814, 554 S.E.2d 84 (2001).

Adding "to whom he was not married" to indictment was permissible amendment. — Clearly, an element of the offense of indecent exposure is that the defendant not be married to the child. Supported by the reference to the statute, the indictments adequately informed the accused of the nature and character of the offenses charged and satisfied the requirement of a definite written statement. Thus, adding the words "to whom he was not married" was a permissible, although unnecessary, amendment. The amendment neither changed the nature or character of the offense charged nor resulted in surprise or prejudice to the accused. Cantwell v. Commonwealth, 2 Va. App. 606, 347 S.E.2d 523 (1986).

Lascivious need not be defined in jury instruction. — Because the Supreme Court of Virginia has not held that proof of one of the four factors of lasciviousness is a prerequisite to a finding of lascivious intent under § 18.2-370, defendant's suggested supplemental language defining lascivious was not required to guide the jury regarding the issue of lascivious intent. Accordingly, the trial court did not err in denying defendant's proposed instruction. Mason v. Commonwealth, 49 Va. App. 39, 636 S.E.2d 480, 2006 Va. App. LEXIS 505 (2006).

Actual innocence not proven. — In his recantation, the minor victim stated that the prisoner never forced him to engage in any sexual act; thus, the prisoner claimed that he was actually innocent of the nolle prossed charges brought against him pursuant to §§ 18.2-67.1, 18.2-67.2, 18.2-67.3, and 18.2-370. However, the victim's statement did not demonstrate that the prisoner was actually innocent, since none of the nolle prossed charges required proof of force, threats, or intimidation where the victim was under the age of 13, or 15, or for the indecent liberties charges; thus, even if the victim, who was 11 at the time of the abuse, consented to engage in the alleged sexual acts, the conduct was still unlawful. DiCaprio-Cuozzo v. Johnson, 2010 U.S. Dist. LEXIS 108702 (E.D. Va. Oct. 12, 2010).

Sentence was proper. — Sentence for taking indecent liberties with a minor was affirmed where, before passing sentence, the trial court emphasized the seriousness of the offense committed, addressed two of the arguments made by the defense in mitigation of the offense, explained that it did not feel either of those claims undermined the seriousness of the criminal acts committed against the victim, and gave reasons for exceeding the sentencing guidelines: "gravity of the offense" and "failure to truly accept responsibility"; contrary to defendant's contention, the record did not reflect that the trial court refused to consider any of the mitigating facts or circumstances presented on his behalf. The sentence imposed by the trial court was within the range set by the legislature. Harmon v. Commonwealth, 2012 Va. App. LEXIS 107 (Apr. 10, 2012).

Applied in Howard v. Commonwealth, 221 Va. 904, 275 S.E.2d 602 (1981); Chrisman v. Commonwealth, 3 Va. App. 89, 348 S.E.2d 399 (1986); Chrisman v. Commonwealth, 3 Va. App. 371, 349 S.E.2d 899 (1986); Frantz v. Commonwealth, 9 Va. App. 348, 388 S.E.2d 273 (1990); Nuckoles v. Commonwealth, 12 Va. App. 1083, 407 S.E.2d 355 (1991); Jackson v. Commonwealth, 29 Va. App. 418, 512 S.E.2d 838 (1999).

§ 18.2-370.01. Indecent liberties by children; penalty.

Any child over the age of thirteen years but under the age of eighteen who, with lascivious intent, knowingly and intentionally exposes his or her sexual or genital parts to any other child under the age of fourteen years who, measured by actual dates of birth, is five or more years the accused's junior, or proposes that any such child expose his or her sexual or genital parts to such person, shall be guilty of a Class 1 misdemeanor.

History.
1998, c. 825.

Law Review.
For an article relating to all published Virginia criminal law decisions between July 1, 1997 and July 1, 1998, see 32 U. Rich. L.

Rev. 1091 (1998). For an article, "Legal Issues Involving Children," see 32 U. Rich. L. Rev. 1345 (1998).

§ 18.2-370.1. Taking indecent liberties with child by person in custodial or supervisory relationship; penalties.

A. Any person 18 years of age or older who, except as provided in § 18.2-370, maintains a custodial or supervisory relationship over a child under the age of 18 and is not legally married to such child and such child is not emancipated who, with lascivious intent, knowingly and intentionally (i) proposes that any such child feel or fondle the sexual or genital parts of such person or that such person feel or handle the sexual or genital parts of the child; or (ii) proposes to such child the performance of an act of sexual intercourse or any act constituting an offense under § 18.2-361; or (iii) exposes his or her sexual or genital parts to such child; or (iv) proposes that any such child expose his or her sexual or genital parts to such person; or (v) proposes to the child that the child engage in sexual intercourse, sodomy or fondling of sexual or genital parts with another person; or (vi) sexually abuses the child as defined in § 18.2-67.10 (6), shall be guilty of a Class 6 felony.

B. Any person who is convicted of a second or subsequent violation of this section shall be guilty of a Class 5 felony; provided that (i) the offenses were not part of a common act, transaction or scheme; (ii) the accused was at liberty as defined in § 53.1-151 between each conviction; and (iii) it is admitted, or found by the jury or judge before whom the person is tried, that the accused was previously convicted of a violation of this section.

History.

1982, c. 521; 1986, c. 503; 1991, c. 517; 2001, c. 840; 2005, c. 185.

Cross references.

As to Sex Offenders and Crimes Against Minors Registry, see § 9.1-900 et seq. For definition of "barrier crime" as including a conviction of taking indecent liberties with children as set out in § 18.2-370 or § 18.2-370.1, or an equivalent offense in another state, and prohibition against assisted living facilities, adult day care centers or child welfare agencies hiring for certain compensated employment persons who have committed such an offense, see §§ 63.2-1719, 63.2-1720. As to report to children's residential facility for which a background check is being performed on whether the applicant has ever been convicted of or is the subject of pending charges for various crimes, including taking indecent liberties with children as set out in § 18.2-370 or § 18.2-370.1, or an equivalent offense in another state, see § 63.2-1726. For provision making it unlawful for any person to operate a family day home if he, or if he knows that any other person who resides in the home, has been convicted of a felony in violation of this section, see § 63.2-1727.

Law Review.

For 2006 survey article, "Criminal Law and Procedure," see 41 U. Rich. L. Rev. 83 (2006).

CASE NOTES

This section is clear and unambiguous is requiring proof of a "custodial or supervisory relationship" over the victim.

Krampen v. Commonwealth, 29 Va. App. 163, 510 S.E.2d 276 (1999).

"Custodial or supervisory relationship." — The "custodial or supervisory relationship" required under this section is not limited to those situations where legal custody exists. Krampen v. Commonwealth, 29 Va. App. 163, 510 S.E.2d 276 (1999).

In addition to the specific provision that such a relationship includes but is not limited to the parent, step-parent, grandparent or step-grandparent, the term also includes those individuals eighteen years or older who have a temporary, custodial relationship with a child, such as teachers, athletic instructors and baby-sitters. The child in each instance has been entrusted to the care and control of the supervising adult. Krampen v. Commonwealth, 29 Va. App. 163, 510 S.E.2d 276 (1999).

The "custodial or supervisory relationship" contemplated by this section is not limited to those situations where legal custody exists. The term also includes those individuals eighteen years or older who have a temporary, custodial relationship with a child, such as, teachers, athletic instructors and baby-sitters. DeAmicis v. Commonwealth, 29 Va. App. 751, 514 S.E.2d 788 (1999).

For a custodial or supervisory relationship to exist, the custodian or supervisor must hold some form of legal or actual authority over the child. Kisling v. Commonwealth, No. 0169-98-3 (Ct. of Appeals Dec. 22, 1998).

For a school security officer to be convicted of taking indecent liberties with a student at the school where he worked by a person in a custodial or supervisory relationship, it was not required that his victim's parents specifically entrust her to his care. Guda v. Commonwealth, 42 Va. App. 453, 592 S.E.2d 748, 2004 Va. App. LEXIS 84 (2004).

Sufficient evidence demonstrated defendant's custodial or supervisory relationship with defendant's victim because the evidence showed defendant implicitly agreed to the victim's mother's request to supervise the child while the mother was away by (1) staying at the mother's house until the mother's friend returned, and (2) ordering the mother's children to play outside and cooking dinner for the children. Nicholson v. Commonwealth, 2011 Va. App. LEXIS 405 (Dec. 20, 2011).

The requirement of a custodial relationship is not merely a basis for enhancing punishment; rather, the custodial relationship the accused maintains with respect to the victim is a predicate to guilt. Krampen v. Commonwealth, 29 Va. App. 163, 510 S.E.2d 276 (1999).

Only those persons who maintain a custodial relationship with their victim can be convicted under this section; thus defendant's taking indecent liberties convictions were not lesser included offenses of aggravated sexual battery, of which he was also found guilty. Seibert v. Commonwealth, 22 Va. App. 40, 467 S.E.2d 838 (1996).

Athletic coach. — Evidence proved beyond a reasonable doubt that when defendant sexually abused the victim defendant maintained a custodial or supervisory relationship over the victim as the victim's athletic coach; having coached the victim's high school softball team defendant was an authority figure who oversaw and supervised the victim's athletic activities for two years, and as such was in a position of trust from a young person's perspective. Accordingly, the evidence was sufficient to sustain defendant's conviction for violating § 18.2-370.1. Sadler v. Commonwealth, 51 Va. App. 17, 654 S.E.2d 313, 2007 Va. App. LEXIS 462 (2007), aff'd, 276 Va. 762, 667 S.E.2d 783, 2008 Va. LEXIS 112 (2008).

Because defendant was the coach of the victim's softball team at the time defendant took indecent liberties with the victim, even though they were not involved in team-related activities at the time, the evidence was sufficient to support a finding that at the time of the incident, defendant maintained a custodial or supervisory relationship with the victim as required by § 18.2-370.1. Sadler v. Commonwealth, 276 Va. 762, 667 S.E.2d 783, 2008 Va. LEXIS 112 (2008).

School security officer. — School security officer exercised sufficient control and care over the students at the school where he worked, including his victim, for a jury to reasonably find beyond a reasonable doubt that he had the requisite custodial or supervisory relationship with the victim to allow his conviction for taking indecent liberties with her by a person in a custodial or supervisory relationship. Guda v. Commonwealth, 42 Va. App. 453, 592 S.E.2d 748, 2004 Va. App. LEXIS 84 (2004).

Teachers' assistant has supervisory or custodial relationship to student. — Defendant was properly convicted of violating § 18.2-370.1 as he clearly maintained a supervisory or custodial relationship over the victims at the time of defendant's proposals to the victims as a teacher's assistant in the victims' math class. Dunnings v. Commonwealth, — Va. App. —, — S.E.2d —, 2008 Va. App. LEXIS 107 (Mar. 4, 2008).

Temporary custodial relationship created. — Where mother entrusted her child to the care, custody and control of defendant for purposes of professional counseling, and at defendant's suggestion, mother agreed to photography and modeling sessions during which time the defendant demanded complete control of the child, circumstances created a temporary custodial relationship between defendant and child for the duration of each session. DeAmicis v. Commonwealth, 29 Va. App. 751, 514 S.E.2d 788 (1999).

Physical appearance sufficient to prove age. — There was sufficient evidence that defendant was 18 years old at the time of the offenses for purposes of §§ 18.2-370 and 18.2-370.1 as the trial court did not commit an impermissible act of judicial notice since it specifically referred to *Jewell v. Commonwealth,* 382 S.E.2d 259 (1989), and did not state that it took judicial notice of defendant's age; the trial judge's comments regarding defendant's physical appearance and the related conclusions regarding defendant's age came in the course of the trial court's lawful duty to determine the facts. Haley v. Commonwealth, 2007 Va. App. LEXIS 402 (Nov. 6, 2007).

Exposure of buttocks. — Buttocks are not "sexual parts" within the meaning of this statute, but evidence properly presented might establish that one who exposes his or her buttocks exposed his or her genitalia as well. Moyer v. Commonwealth, 30 Va. App. 744, 520 S.E.2d 371 (1999).

Non-reproductive parts such as buttocks may be sexual if accompanied by the proper intent and, therefore, buttocks are "sexual parts" under this section if the accused, acting with the requisite lascivious intent, exposes his buttocks to a juvenile or proposes that a juvenile expose the juvenile's buttocks to the accused. Moyer v. Commonwealth, 33 Va. App. 8, 531 S.E.2d 580, 2000 Va. App. LEXIS 557 (July 25, 2000).

Delay of over a year in reporting abuse was credibly explained in a prosecution arising from the abuse of three sisters by their foster father, where defendant threatened one child and all feared separation if his actions were reported. Ingram, Sr. v. Commonwealth, No. 2720-96-2 (Ct. of Appeals March 3, 1998).

Lascivious intent. — The word "lascivious" describes a state of mind that is eager for sexual indulgence, desirous of inciting to lust or of inciting sexual desire and appetite; circumstantial evidence of lasciviousness may include evidence that the defendant was sexually aroused, that he made gestures toward himself or to the victim, that he made improper remarks to the victim or that he asked the victim to do anything wrong. Moyer v. Commonwealth, 33 Va. App. 8, 531 S.E.2d 580, 2000 Va. App. LEXIS 557 (July 25, 2000).

Sufficient evidence demonstrated defendant's lascivious intent because the evidence showed defendant (1) touched the victim's genitals while defendant and the victim were alone in a bedroom, (2) asked the victim if the victim enjoyed pornography, (3) touched the victim's genitals after the victim objected, and (4) gave self-serving testimony which could be used as evidence of defendant's guilt. Nicholson v. Commonwealth, 2011 Va. App. LEXIS 405 (Dec. 20, 2011).

No right to have psychiatric exam of child victim. — Trial court judge lacked authority to order a medical examination of the complaining witness and, therefore, did not err by denying defendant's motion for a psychiatric examination of the child victim, namely his daughter, though, as a matter of law, the trial court judge erred by denying the motion for incorrect reasons. Nobrega v. Commonwealth, — Va. App. —, — S.E.2d —, 2005 Va. App. LEXIS 189 (May 10, 2005), aff'd, 271 Va. 508, 628 S.E.2d 922 (2006).

In a prosecution for sexual abuse of a child in violation of § 18.2-370.1, the trial court properly denied defendant's motion for a psychiatric or psychological evaluation of the complaining witness, as no Virginia statute or rule authorized the trial court to do so, even where the witness had a history of mental illness and her testimony was uncorroborated. Nobrega v. Commonwealth, 271 Va. 508, 628 S.E.2d 922, 2006 Va. LEXIS 48 (2006).

Licensed professional counselor permitted to testify as to post-traumatic stress disorder of child victim. — In a pros-

ecution for indecent liberties with a child in defendant's custody and object sexual penetration, the trial court did not abuse its discretion by allowing an expert, who was also a licensed professional counselor, to give testimony regarding a psychiatric diagnosis of the victim of sexual abuse, as the expert was both: (1) permitted by state law; and (2) qualified by her training and experience to testify about post-traumatic stress disorder. Fitzgerald v. Commonwealth, 48 Va. App. 271, 630 S.E.2d 337, 2006 Va. App. LEXIS 249 (2006), aff'd, 643 S.E.2d 162, 2007 Va. LEXIS 63 (Va. 2007).

Defendant's membership in the North American Man-Boy Love Association and pornographic materials in his possession at the time of his arrest were admissible in order to show lascivious intent. Smith v. Commonwealth, No. 1546-97-4 (Ct. of Appeals Dec. 1, 1998).

Possession of pornography admissible. — Where defendant was charged with taking indecent liberties with his six-year-old stepdaughter, his statement that he owned pornographic videos was relevant as it heightened the likelihood that the child told the truth when she testified that she had watched such videos with him; the trial court properly found that the probative value of the statement outweighed its potential prejudicial effect. Croxton v. Commonwealth, — Va. App. —, — S.E.2d —, 2005 Va. App. LEXIS 166 (Apr. 26, 2005).

Sufficient evidence of custodial or supervisory relationship. — Where evidence showed that by inviting the two minor victims to his home to watch movies with their mother's permission, defendant: (1) assumed responsibility for them; and (2) had the authority to monitor and direct the victims' activities while they remained in his home, said evidence was sufficient to prove that he exercised a custodial or supervisory relationship over them; further, as the sole adult alone in his home with the victims, defendant tacitly agreed he would oversee their safety and well-being while they were in his presence. Beazley v. Commonwealth, No. 2505-03-2, 2005 Va. App. LEXIS 76 (Ct. of Appeals Feb. 22, 2005).

Where defendant, as an adult and parent hosting a 14-year old girl overnight in his home to baby sit his children, was responsible for the control of the victim's safety and well-being, and thus stood in loco parentis to the victim when he sexually assaulted her, the Commonwealth presented sufficient evidence showing that defendant was in a custodial or supervisory relationship with said victim; whether the victim's mother explicitly entrusted her to defendant's care and supervision was not dispositive. Marchioli-Acra v. Commonwealth, No. 0671-04-2, 2005 Va. App. LEXIS 101 (Ct. of Appeals Mar. 15, 2005).

Because defendant was the victim's employer, defendant maintained a "supervisory" relationship over the victim; therefore, based on defendant's admission of inappropriately touching and manipulating the victim, the trial court properly convicted defendant of taking indecent liberties with a child over whom defendant maintained a custodial or supervisory relationship. Gilbert v. Commonwealth, 47 Va. App. 266, 623 S.E.2d 428, 2005 Va. App. LEXIS 518 (2005).

Evidence was insufficient to prove that the defendant had a custodial or supervisory relationship with the victim where the victim lived with the defendant as a guest after she was evicted from her apartment after the landlord learned that her mother was in prison and that she was living in the apartment unsupervised. Kisling v. Commonwealth, No. 0169-98-3 (Ct. of Appeals Dec. 22, 1998).

Evidence was sufficient to find that defendant maintained the required "custodial or supervisory relationship" over the child where the defendant was the only adult present during trips from church. He had the responsibility for and control of the victim's safety and well-being while she was in his care, and as such, his contact with the victim was in the nature of a baby-sitter, i.e., one entrusted with the care of the child for a limited period of time. Krampen v. Commonwealth, 29 Va. App. 163, 510 S.E.2d 276 (1999).

Juvenile was under the care, custody and control of the defendant where her mother entrusted her to the defendant for the purposes of professional counseling, the defendant demanded complete control of the juvenile free from questions or interference by the mother, and he was alone with the juvenile during his sessions with her. DeAmicis v. Commonwealth, 31 Va. App. 437, 524 S.E.2d 151 (2000).

Evidence was sufficient to sustain a conviction where the victims testified they had suffered abuse from defendant, defendant denied abusing them, and the court, after due consideration, determined that the Commonwealth had proved its case beyond a reasonable doubt. Ingram, Sr. v. Commonwealth, No. 2720-96-2 (Ct. of Appeals March 3, 1998).

There was sufficient evidence to find that defendant was guilty of rape, forcible sodomy, and indecent liberties with a child for acts upon defendant's wife's four-year-old cousin because the evidence supported the victim's account of the events and defendant did have an opportunity to commit the acts on at least two occasions; the victim gave her foster mother a substantially similar account when she initially made her complaint, the victim's testimony was consistent with a drawing she did at the psychologist's instruction, and the medical evidence showed that the victim was a sexually abused child as her hymen was consistent with a painful penetrating injury. Johnson v. Commonwealth, 40 Va. App. 605, 580 S.E.2d 486, 2003 Va. App. LEXIS 303 (2003).

In a prosecution for sexual abuse of a child, the child's detailed account of two acts of sexual intercourse was sufficient to convict, despite minor inconsistencies in her testimony, her history of mental illness, and the lack of corroborating physical evidence. Nobrega v. Commonwealth, 271 Va. 508, 628 S.E.2d 922, 2006 Va. LEXIS 48 (2006).

Evidence that defendant had a long standing relationship with the victim's family and asserted authority over the victim, showing that defendant maintained a custodial or supervisory relationship with the victim, and that defendant admitted touching the victim's erect penis out of some sort of morbid curiosity was sufficient to support a conviction for custodial indecent liberties, in violation of § 18.2-370.1. Kolesnikoff v. Commonwealth, 54 Va. App. 396, 679 S.E.2d 559, 2009 Va. App. LEXIS 342 (2009).

Sufficient evidence of lascivious intent. — Although the evidence of any particular offense, standing alone, might have been insufficient to establish that the defendant acted with lascivious intent, his course of conduct in using his position as an adult role model to gain the trust of two boys and establish close personal relationships with them, coupled with detailed diary accounts of the defendant's repeated nude paddlings, nude wrestling and other encounters with these children and the testimony of one of the boys that the defendant was sexually aroused during two of the boy's encounters with him, was sufficient to support a finding that the defendant acted with the requisite lascivious intent in exposing his sexual or genital parts to both boys or proposing that they expose their sexual or genital parts to him. Moyer v. Commonwealth, 33 Va. App. 8, 531 S.E.2d 580, 2000 Va. App. LEXIS 557 (July 25, 2000).

Evidence held irrelevant to issue of intent. — Testimony of criminal defendant's daughter that defendant allegedly forced her to perform a sex act on him 20 years earlier was irrelevant to show that defendant had "lascivious intent" under this section, where he was charged with taking indecent liberties with a minor over whom he maintained a custodial or supervisory relationship, as no causal relationship or logical connection existed between the earlier incident and the current charge; thus, such testimony should not have been admitted, was more prejudicial than probative, and was impermissible prior bad act evidence. Quinones v. Commonwealth, 35 Va. App. 634, 547 S.E.2d 524, 2001 Va. App. LEXIS 337 (2001).

Testimony of detective that videotapes seized from defendant's home during search were pornographic was irrelevant to show that defendant had "lascivious intent" under this section, where he was charged with taking indecent liberties with a minor over whom he maintained a custodial or supervisory relationship, as no causal relationship or logical connection existed between that characterization and the current charge; thus, such testimony should not have been admitted, was more prejudicial than probative, and was immaterial to the issue of criminal intent. Quinones v. Commonwealth, 35 Va. App. 634, 547 S.E.2d 524, 2001 Va. App. LEXIS 337 (2001).

Amendment of charge allowed. — The Commonwealth was properly permitted to amend the indictment charging defendant with taking indecent liberties with a child, from one requiring proof of a "supervisory relationship" to another which did not, since the amendment did not add elements to the charges or otherwise jeopardize his opportunity to adequately defend himself, and defendant already had proper notice of the essential elements from the initial charge. Bottenfield v. Commonwealth, 25 Va. App. 316, 487 S.E.2d 883 (1997).

Sex offender reclassification. — Amendment of former § 19.2-298.1 that reclassified a violation of § 18.2-370.1 as a "sexually violent offense" and changed the reregistration requirements did not violate a sex offender's equal protection rights as subsection A of § 9.1-901 provided that the registration requirements applied to all persons convicted of an offense set out in § 9.1-902 "on or after July 1, 1994," and the registration distinction based on the timing of the conviction asserted by the offender did not exist. McCabe v. Commonwealth, 274 Va. 558, 650 S.E.2d 508, 2007 Va. LEXIS 112 (2007).

Amendment of former § 19.2-298.1 that reclassified a violation of § 18.2-370.1 as a "sexually violent offense" and changed the reregistration requirements did not violate a sex offender's procedural due process rights as: (1) a "sexually violent offense" under the Virginia statute was based solely on the nature of the crime, not on a determination of current dangerousness; (2) § 9.1-902 specifically defined the term "sexually violent offense" for purposes of the civil registry scheme, and § 18.2-370.1 did not incorporate the term "sexually violent offense," nor did it incorporate any other descriptive term, such as "sexual offense"; (3) it was inaccurate for the offender to claim the offender was convicted of only a "sexual offense" as the offender was convicted of a violation of § 18.2-370.1, and that conviction was the only fact relevant to the classification determination; and (4) the offender failed to allege that a hearing on the reclassification would have established facts relevant to the Virginia legislature's statutory scheme. McCabe v. Commonwealth, 274 Va. 558, 650 S.E.2d 508, 2007 Va. LEXIS 112 (2007).

Amendment of former § 19.2-298.1 that reclassified a violation of § 18.2-370.1 as a "sexually violent offense" and changed the reregistration requirements did not violate a sex offender's substantive due process rights as a personal appearance was not required for a periodic reregistration, subsection A of § 9.1-909 allowed the offender to petition for relief from the 90-day reregistration requirement, the lifetime quarterly reregistration requirement was not a liberty interest specially protected by the Due Process Clause, and the offender had no recognized fundamental right to rely on the civil legislative scheme in existence at the time of the offender's guilty plea. McCabe v. Commonwealth, 274 Va. 558, 650 S.E.2d 508, 2007 Va. LEXIS 112 (2007).

Applied in Sutton v. Commonwealth, 228 Va. 654, 324 S.E.2d 665 (1985); Kauffman v. Commonwealth, 8 Va. App. 400, 382 S.E.2d 279 (1989).

CIRCUIT COURT OPINIONS

Section 8.01-221 does not create cause of action. — Demurrer filed by a counselor and his employer as to the count of patient's complaint alleging taking indecent liberties with a minor while the accused is in a supervisory relationship was sustained because the factual allegations could be properly included in a claim for sexual assault and battery, but they did not generate a separate civil claim for a violation of § 18.2-370.1; § 8.01-221 does not create, or recognize, that a cause of action exists for a violation of the indecent liberties statute in the criminal code. B.E.L. v. Price, 81 Va. Cir. 391, 2010 Va. Cir. LEXIS 138 (Culpeper Dec. 2, 2010).

§ 18.2-370.2. Sex offenses prohibiting proximity to children; penalty.

A. *"Offense prohibiting proximity to children"* means a violation or an attempt to commit a violation of (i) subsection A of § 18.2-47, clause (ii) or (iii) of § 18.2-48, subsection B of § 18.2-361, or subsection B of § 18.2-366, where the victim of one of the foregoing offenses was a minor, or (ii) subsection A (iii) of § 18.2-61, §§ 18.2-63, 18.2-64.1, subdivision A 1 of § 18.2-67.1, subdivision A 1 of § 18.2-67.2, or subdivision A 1 or A 4 (a) of § 18.2-67.3, or §§ 18.2-370, 18.2-370.1, clause (ii) of § 18.2-371, §§ 18.2-374.1, 18.2-374.1:1 or § 18.2-379. As of July 1, 2006, "offense prohibiting proximity to children" shall include a violation of § 18.2-472.1, when the offense requiring registration was one of the foregoing offenses.

B. Every adult who is convicted of an offense prohibiting proximity to children when the offense occurred on or after July 1, 2000, shall as part of his sentence be forever prohibited from loitering within 100 feet of the premises of any place he knows or has reason to know is a primary, secondary or high school. In addition, every adult who is convicted of an offense prohibiting proximity to children when the offense occurred on or after July 1, 2006, shall as part of his sentence be forever prohibited from loitering within 100 feet of the premises of any place he knows or has reason to know is a child day program as defined in § 63.2-100.

C. Every adult who is convicted of an offense prohibiting proximity to children, when the offense occurred on or after July 1, 2008, shall as part of his sentence be forever prohibited from going, for the purpose of having any contact whatsoever with children that are not in his custody, within 100 feet of the premises of any place owned or operated by a locality that he knows or should know is a playground, athletic field or facility, or gymnasium.

A violation of this section is punishable as a Class 6 felony.

History.
2000, c. 770; 2006, cc. 857, 914; 2008, c. 579.

Editor's note.
Acts 2008, c. 579, cl. 2 provides: "That the provisions of this act may result in a net increase in periods of imprisonment or commitment. Pursuant to § 30-19.1:4, the estimated amount of the necessary appropriation is cannot be determined for periods of imprisonment in state adult correctional facilities and $0 for periods of commitment to the custody of the Department of Juvenile Justice."

The 2008 amendments.
The 2008 amendment by c. 579 inserted the first paragraph in subsection C.

Law Review.
For 2000 survey of Virginia criminal law and procedure, see 34 U. Rich. L. Rev. 749 (2000).

§ 18.2-370.3. Sex offenses prohibiting residing in proximity to children; penalty.

A. Every adult who is convicted of an offense occurring on or after July 1, 2006, where the offender is more than three years older than the victim, of one of the following qualifying offenses: (i) clause (iii) of subsection A of § 18.2-61, (ii) subdivision A 1 of § 18.2-67.1, or (iii) subdivision A 1 of § 18.2-67.2, shall be forever prohibited from residing within 500 feet of the premises of any place he knows or has reason to know is a child day center as defined in § 63.2-100, or a primary, secondary, or high school. A violation of this section is a Class 6 felony. The provisions of this section shall only apply if the qualifying offense was done in the commission of, or as a part of the same course of conduct as, or as

part of a common scheme or plan as a violation of (i) subsection A of § 18.2-47 or § 18.2-48, (ii) § 18.2-89, 18.2-90, or 18.2-91, or (iii) § 18.2-51.2.

B. An adult who is convicted of an offense as specified in subsection A of this section and has established a lawful residence shall not be in violation of this section if a child day center or a primary, secondary, or high school is established within 500 feet of his residence subsequent to his conviction.

C. Every adult who is convicted of an offense occurring on or after July 1, 2008, where the offender is more than three years older than the victim, of one of the following qualifying offenses: (i) clause (iii) of subsection A of § 18.2-61, (ii) subdivision A 1 of § 18.2-67.1, or (iii) subdivision A 1 of § 18.2-67.2, shall be forever prohibited from residing within 500 feet of the boundary line of any place he knows is a public park when such park (i) is owned and operated by a county, city or town, (ii) shares a boundary line with a primary, secondary, or high school and (iii) is regularly used for school activities. A violation of this section is a Class 6 felony. The provisions of this section shall only apply if the qualifying offense was done in the commission of, or as a part of the same course of conduct as, or as part of a common scheme or plan as a violation of (i) subsection A of § 18.2-47 or § 18.2-48, (ii) § 18.2-89, 18.2-90, or 18.2-91, or (iii) § 18.2-51.2.

D. An adult who is convicted of an offense as specified in subsection C and has established a lawful residence shall not be in violation of this section if a public park that (i) is owned and operated by a county, city or town, (ii) shares a boundary line with a primary, secondary, or high school, and (iii) is regularly used for school activities, is established within 500 feet of his residence subsequent to his conviction.

History.
2006, cc. 857, 914; 2008, c. 726.

Editor's note.
Acts 2008, c. 726, cl. 2, provides: "That the provisions of this act may result in a net increase in periods of imprisonment or commitment. Pursuant to § 30-19.1:4, the estimated amount of the necessary appropriation cannot be determined for periods of imprisonment in state adult correctional facilities and is $0 for periods of commitment to the custody of the Department of Juvenile Justice."

The 2008 amendments.
The 2008 amendment by c. 726 added subsections C and D.

§ 18.2-370.4. Sex offenses prohibiting working on school property; penalty.

A. Every adult who has been convicted of an offense occurring on or after July 1, 2006, where the offender is more than three years older than the victim, of one of the following qualifying offenses: (i) clause (iii) of subsection A of § 18.2-61, (ii) subdivision A 1 of § 18.2-67.1, or (iii) subdivision A 1 of § 18.2-67.2, shall be forever prohibited from working or engaging in any volunteer activity on property he knows or has reason to know is public or private elementary or secondary school or child day center property. A violation of this section is punishable as a Class 6 felony. The provisions of this section shall only apply if the qualifying offense was done in the commission of, or as a part of the same course of conduct of, or as part of a common scheme or plan as a violation of (i) subsection A of § 18.2-47 or 18.2-48, (ii) § 18.2-89, 18.2-90, or 18.2-91, or (iii) § 18.2-51.2.

B. An employer of a person who violates this section, or any person who procures volunteer activity by a person who violates this section, and the school or child day center where the violation of this section occurred, are immune from civil liability unless they had actual knowledge that such person had been convicted of an offense listed in subsection A.

History.
2006, cc. 853, 857, 914.

The number of this section was assigned by the Virginia Code Commission, the number in Acts 2006, c. 853, having been § 18.2-370.3.

§ 18.2-370.5. Sex offenses prohibiting entry onto school or other property; penalty.

A. Every adult who is convicted of a sexually violent offense, as defined in § 9.1-902, shall be prohibited from entering or being present (i) during school hours, and during school-related or school-sponsored activities upon any property he knows or has reason to know is a public or private elementary or secondary school or child day center property; (ii) on any school bus as defined in § 46.2-100; or (iii) upon any property, public or private, during hours when such property is solely being used by a public or private elementary or secondary school for a school-related or school-sponsored activity.

B. The provisions of clauses (i) and (iii) of subsection A shall not apply to such adult if (i) he is a lawfully registered and qualified voter, and is coming upon such property solely for purposes of casting his vote; (ii) he is a student enrolled at the school; or (iii) he has obtained a court order pursuant to subsection C allowing him to enter and be present upon such property, has obtained the permission of the school board or of the owner of the private school or child day center or their designee for entry within all or part of the scope of the lifted ban, and is in compliance with such school board's, school's or center's terms and conditions and those of the court order.

C. Every adult who is prohibited from entering upon school or child day center property pursuant to subsection A may after notice to the attorney for the Commonwealth and either (i) the proprietor of the child day center, (ii) the superintendent of public instruction of the school division in which the school is located, or (iii) the chief administrator of the school if such school is not a public school, petition the circuit court in the county or city where the school or child day center is located for permission to enter such property. For good cause shown, the court may issue an order permitting the petitioner to enter and be present on such property, subject to whatever restrictions of area, reasons for being present, or time limits the court deems appropriate.

D. A violation of this section is punishable as a Class 6 felony.

History.
2007, cc. 284, 370; 2008, c. 781; 2010, c. 402; 2011, cc. 648, 796, 855.

Editor's note.
Acts 2008, c. 781, cl. 2, provides: "That the provisions of this act may result in a net increase in periods of imprisonment or commitment. Pursuant to § 30-19.1:4, the estimated amount of the necessary appropriation cannot be determined for periods of imprisonment in state adult correctional facilities and is $0 for periods of commitment to the custody of the Department of Juvenile Justice."

Acts 2011, c. 648, cl. 2, provides: "That the provisions of this act may result in a net increase in periods of imprisonment or commitment. Pursuant to § 30-19.1:4, the estimated amount of the necessary appropriation is $0 for periods of imprisonment in state adult correctional facilities and is $0 for periods of commitment to the custody of the Department of Juvenile Justice."

Acts 2011, cc. 796 and 855, cl. 2 provides: "That the provisions of this act may result in a net increase in periods of imprisonment or commitment. Pursuant to § 30-19.1:4, the estimated amount of the necessary appropriation cannot be determined for periods of imprisonment in state adult correctional facilities; therefore, Chapter 874 of the Acts of Assembly of 2010 requires the Virginia Criminal Sentencing Commission to assign a minimum fiscal impact of $50,000. Pursuant to § 30-19.1:4, the estimated amount of the necessary appropriation is $0 for periods of commitment to the custody of the Department of Juvenile Justice."

The 2008 amendments.
The 2008 amendment by c. 781 inserted "and during school-related and school-sponsored activities" following "during school hours" in subsection A.

The 2010 amendments.
The 2010 amendment by c. 402, in subsection A, inserted "has obtained the permission of the school board or of the owner of the private school or child day center or their designee for entry within all or part of the scope of the lifted ban," "such school board's, school's or center's"; in clause B (iii), deleted "the juvenile and domestic relations district court or"; and made stylistic changes.

The 2011 amendments.
The 2011 amendment by c. 648 substituted "prohibited from entering or being present during school hours, and shall be prohibited from entering or being present during school-related or school-sponsored activities" for "prohibited from entering and being present, during school hours, and during school-related and school sponsored activities" in the first sentence in subsection A.

The 2011 amendments by cc. 796 and 855 are identical, and in subsection A, inserted the clause (i) designator and added clause (ii); in subsection B, inserted the subsection designator, "The provisions of clauses (i) and (iii) of subsection A shall not apply to such adult if" at the beginning and "pursuant to subsection C"; redesignated subsection B as C; and transferred the last sentence of former subsection A to be new subsection D.

Subsection A is set out in the form above at the direction of the Virginia Code Commission.

Law Review.
For 2007 annual survey article, "Criminal Law and Procedure," see 42 U. Rich. L. Rev. 311 (2007).

CASE NOTES

Standing to bring federal claim. — Because plaintiff, classified as a sexually violent offender, alleged harm from not being able to access church property (due to Sunday schools) or the property of defendant school board under subsection A of § 18.2-370.5, but she had not attempted to petition a state court (which she could have done anonymously), the board, or the churches, for access as provided in §§ 8.01-15.1 and 18.2-370.5, she lacked standing to bring claims of constitutional violations under U.S. Const. amend. I and XIV, based on not being able to associate with the school community and not being able to attend churches of her choosing. Doe v. Va. Dep't of State Police, 2013 U.S. App. LEXIS 7403 (4th Cir. Apr. 12, 2013).

School board has authority to determine whether to allow convicted sex offender onto school property. — Circuit court erred in granting a convicted sex offender's petition for an order permitting him to enter onto city school property to attend school events involving his stepson pursuant to § 18.2-370.5 because the circuit court improperly divested the local school board of its authority under Va. Const., Art. VIII, § 7 to supervise public schools; subsection B of § 18.2-370.5 provides circuit courts and juvenile and domestic relations district courts the authority to remove the statutory ban imposed by subsection A of § 18.2-370.5, which prohibits a violent sex offender from entering onto school property, and implicitly leaves to a school board the ultimate decision whether to allow the convicted offender entry, and § 18.2-370.5 does not restrict the supervisory authority granted by Va. Const., Art. VIII, § 7 to local school boards to determine under what, if any, circumstances a previously convicted sex offender may enter onto school property. Commonwealth v. Doe, 278 Va. 223, 682 S.E.2d 906, 2009 Va. LEXIS 88 (2009).

§ 18.2-370.6. Penetration of mouth of child with lascivious intent; penalty.

Any person 18 years of age or older who, with lascivious intent, kisses a child under the age of 13 on the mouth while knowingly and intentionally penetrating the mouth of such child with his tongue is guilty of a Class 1 misdemeanor.

History.
2008, c. 772.

Editor's note.
Acts 2008, c. 772, cl. 2, provides: "That the provisions of this act may result in a net increase in periods of imprisonment or commitment. Pursuant to § 30-19.1:4, the estimated amount of the necessary appropriation cannot be determined for periods of imprisonment in state adult correctional facilities and is $0 for periods of commitment to the custody of the Department of Juvenile Justice."

§ 18.2-371. Causing or encouraging acts rendering children delinquent, abused, etc.; penalty; abandoned infant.

Any person 18 years of age or older, including the parent of any child, who (i) willfully contributes to, encourages, or causes any act, omission, or condition which renders a child delinquent, in need of services, in need of supervision, or abused or neglected as defined in § 16.1-228, or (ii) engages in consensual sexual intercourse with a child 15 or older not his spouse, child, or grandchild, shall be guilty of a Class 1 misdemeanor. This section shall not be construed as repealing, modifying, or in any way affecting §§ 18.2-18, 18.2-19, 18.2-61, 18.2-63, and 18.2-347.

If the prosecution under this section is based solely on the accused parent having left the child at a hospital or rescue squad, it shall be an affirmative defense to prosecution of a parent under this section that such parent safely delivered the child to a hospital that provides 24-hour emergency services or to an attended rescue squad that employs emergency medical technicians, within the first 14 days of the child's life. In order for the affirmative defense to apply, the child shall be delivered in a manner reasonably calculated to ensure the child's safety.

History.
Code 1950, § 18.1-14; 1960, c. 358; 1975, cc. 14, 15; 1981, cc. 397, 568; 1990, c. 797; 1991, c. 295; 1993, c. 411; 2003, cc. 816, 822; 2006, c. 935; 2008, cc. 174, 206.

Cross references.
As to jurisdiction of Juvenile and Domestic Relations District Court, see § 16.1-241. For provision that records involving complaints of sexual abuse of a child, including the display of the child in sexually explicit visual material, as defined in § 18.2-374.1, and contributing to the delinquency of a minor in violation of § 18.2-371, be made available to the attorney for the Commonwealth and the local law-enforcement agency, see § 63.2-1503 D.

The 2008 amendments.
The 2008 amendments by cc. 174 and 206 are identical, and deleted "18.2-66" following "18.2-63" in the first paragraph.

Law Review.
For survey of Virginia law on criminal procedure for the year 1972-1973, see 59 Va. L. Rev. 1478 (1973). For article summarizing published Virginia criminal law decisions between July 1, 2002 and July 1, 2003, see 38 U. Rich. L. Rev. 87 (2003). For annual survey article on legal issues involving children, see 38 U. Rich. L. Rev. 161 (2003). For 2006 survey article, "Family and Juvenile Law," see 41 U. Rich. L. Rev. 151 (2006). For 2007 annual survey article, "Criminal Law and Procedure," see 42 U. Rich. L. Rev. 311 (2007). For 2007 annual survey article, "Family and Juvenile Law," see 42 U. Rich. L. Rev. 417 (2007).

Michie's Jurisprudence.
For related discussion, see 2A M.J. Attempts and Solicitations, § 7; 9B M.J. Infants, § 90; 15 M.J. Rape, § 23.

CASE NOTES

Not essential that accused caused the commission of the misdemeanor. — It is not an essential element of the offense that accused should have caused the prosecutrix to commit a misdemeanor. If he encouraged her to commit a misdemeanor, he was guilty of the statutory offense. Bibbs v. Commonwealth, 129 Va. 768, 106 S.E. 363 (1921).

For a child to be "in need of services" as an element of this section, circumstances specified in either § 16.1-228 (i) or (ii) must have rendered court intervention essential to resolve the difficulty. DeAmicis v. Commonwealth, 29 Va. App. 751, 514 S.E.2d 788 (1999).

It is not an essential element of the offense under this section that the accused should have "caused" the juvenile to commit the misdemeanor. It is sufficient if he "encouraged" such commission. This is so because the prohibition in the section is in the disjunctive against any person who shall cause or encourage the commission of a misdemeanor. Hubbard v. Commonwealth, 207 Va. 673, 152 S.E.2d 250 (1967).

Evidence that defendant encouraged smoking of marijuana insufficient. — The evidence was insufficient to support the conviction of the mother of a 15 year-old boy under this section where, although the mother knew her son and his friends smoked marijuana in the garage, there was no evidence that the mother affirmatively encouraged this activity and the mother attempted, although unsuccessfully and perhaps ineffectually, to discourage the activity. Peace v. Commonwealth, No. 2651-99-2, 2000 Va. App. LEXIS 725 (Ct. of Appeals Nov. 14, 2000).

Examples of "encouragement." — Where in a prosecution under this section accused admitted that he had carnal intercourse with the prosecutrix and was, therefore, a willing participant with her in the commission of the misdemeanor, such participation, in itself alone, encouraged the prosecutrix to commit such misdemeanor and made the accused guilty under the statute. Bibbs v. Commonwealth, 129 Va. 768, 106 S.E. 363 (1921).

In a prosecution under this section for encouraging a child to commit a misdemeanor, namely, fornication, even if it were true that the prosecutrix made the first advance, that did not justify the accused in encouraging her to commit the misdemeanor by yielding to her solicitation. Bibbs v. Commonwealth, 129 Va. 768, 106 S.E. 363 (1921).

Contributing to the delinquency of a minor. — Reasonable officer would have had a basis for suspecting that plaintiff visitor was contributing to the delinquency of a minor, pursuant to § 18.2-371, because a stepfather had identified his missing stepson as one of the young men in the window of the house and the visitor's actions could have led a reasonable officer to believe that the visitor sought to unlawfully conceal the stepson from his concerned stepfather. Smith v. Ray, 2011 U.S. App. LEXIS 2191 (4th Cir. Feb. 2, 2011).

Solicitation of oral sex. — By unsuccessfully soliciting oral sex from a minor, defendant willfully encouraged her to engage in a criminal act in violation of § 18.2-29. As his solicitation was clearly designed to encourage her to commit that act, which would have rendered her delinquent under § 16.1-228, the evidence established that he contributed to the delinquency of a minor in violation of § 18.2-371. MacDonald v. Commonwealth, 2007 Va. App. LEXIS 7 (Jan. 9, 2007).

Compared to § 18.2-371.1. — Felony child neglect conviction was upheld, as evidence of defendant's gross, wanton and willful conduct was presented by his act of brutally beating his mother in front of his eight-year-old son, leaving the son alone with his unconscious grandmother at night, and instructing his son not to call for help; the fact that the risks in doing so had not yet materialized did not mean that the risks were absent and did not serve to remove defendant's conduct from the prohibitions of the statute. Jones v. Commonwealth, No. 1670-03-1, 2004 Va. App. LEXIS 561 (Ct. of Appeals Nov. 16, 2004).

Defendant sufficiently preserved for review the claim that defendant could not be convicted of violating § 18.2-371, misdemeanor child abuse and neglect, because defense counsel made numerous arguments that defendant had not been charged with violating it and it was not a lesser-included offense of § 18.2-371.1, felony child abuse and neglect. Since the Commonwealth conceded that it was not a lesser-included offense and defendant had not procedurally defaulted the issue, the conviction had to be dismissed. Brown v. Commonwealth, 2008 Va. App. LEXIS 94 (Feb. 26, 2008).

Conviction hereunder not necessarily basis for impeachment of witness. — A conviction under this section does not, as a matter of law, involve moral turpitude, so as to permit cross-examination thereof for impeachment purposes. Unless the record of conviction plainly shows that the specific act constituting the ground for the conviction is one involving moral turpitude, the fact of such conviction cannot be shown. Tasker v. Commonwealth, 202 Va. 1019, 121 S.E.2d 459 (1961).

Admissibility of evidence. — The particulars of statements made by the prosecutrix in a prosecution under this section, to police officers when taken from the house of accused, would be generally inadmissible. In the instant case, however, the accused had testified that the whole case was a conspiracy against him by the police, and this authorized the Commonwealth to introduce evidence in rebuttal tending to show that there had been no such conspiracy against the accused. But it is doubtful whether the Commonwealth should have been permitted to introduce the evidence of the policeman as to all of the details of the statement. Gottlieb v. Commonwealth, 126 Va. 807, 101 S.E. 872 (1920).

Once an officer observed the seemingly underage individuals holding beer bottles and then fleeing from the police presence, he had probable cause to believe that a crime was being committed. Because the development of probable cause and the creation of the exigencies were virtually contemporaneous, the officer had no meaningful opportunity in which to obtain a search warrant for the property before exigent circumstances necessitated his further intrusion onto the premises; thus, the trial court did not err in concluding that the officer had both probable cause and exigent circumstances sufficient to justify his warrantless entry into defen-

dant's backyard, the denial of his motion to suppress was affirmed, and his convictions for contributing to the delinquency of a minor were affirmed. Robinson v. Commonwealth, 47 Va. App. 533, 625 S.E.2d 651, 2006 Va. App. LEXIS 54 (2006).

On the night of a party, defendant impliedly consented to have members of the public, including law-enforcement officers, enter her driveway, and the officer that did enter her driveway did not exceed the scope of that implied consent because, by driving up the driveway and parking in the parking area, he went no further than an ordinary member of the public would have gone in an attempt to contact the occupants of the premises; accordingly, because defendant extended an implied invitation to enter the property, and because the officer did not exceed the scope of that implied consent, the Fourth Amendment had not been implicated at the point in time when the officer observed the individuals drinking beer and then fleeing into the woods. Because the officer was legitimately present on the property when he viewed the illegal activity of minors drinking alcohol, and because defendant presented no further arguments in support of her position that the trial court should have granted her motion to suppress, the trial court did not err in denying the motion to suppress; thus, her convictions for contributing to the delinquency of a minor were affirmed. Robinson v. Commonwealth, 47 Va. App. 533, 625 S.E.2d 651, 2006 Va. App. LEXIS 54 (2006).

Character of prosecuting witness province of jury. — In the instant case defendant was charged with unlawfully and knowingly permitting prosecutrix, a child under the age of 18 years, to remain in his boarding house for the commission and permitting and encouraging her to commit immoral and vicious acts. Accused asked for an instruction that in cases of this character the testimony of the prosecuting witness should be cautiously scrutinized. The court properly refused this instruction, because it invaded the province of the jury. Gottlieb v. Commonwealth, 126 Va. 807, 101 S.E. 872 (1920).

A third party does not have a claim for relief against seller of intoxicating beverages for injuries sustained as a result of the intoxication of the vendor's patron, even if the patron is a minor. Byrd v. Gate Petro. Co., 845 F.2d 86 (4th Cir. 1988).

Conduct which renders a child abused and neglected as defined in § 16.1-228 is sufficient for a conviction under this statute and defendant's acts in photographing a juvenile's sexual or genital parts clearly constituted abusive and neglectful behavior. DeAmicis v. Commonwealth, 31 Va. App. 437, 524 S.E.2d 151 (2000).

Trial court properly denied the instruction on contributing to the delinquency of a minor since it was not a lesser included offense of aggravated sexual battery; the offense of aggravated sexual battery does not require proof that the defendant was 18 years of age or older, and thus, all of the elements of this section are not included within the offense of § 18.2-67.3. Kauffman v. Commonwealth, 8 Va. App. 400, 382 S.E.2d 279 (1989).

Advertisements for telephone sex lines. — Evidence supported a conviction where the defendant threw magazines at minors which invited them to engage in unlawful sexual acts with the pictured models, notwithstanding that their primary purpose was to advertise telephone sex lines and that the invitations to engage in unlawful sexual acts were fantasies designed to market the telephone sex lines. Hartman v. Commonwealth, No. 0569-98-3 (Ct. of Appeals Mar. 30, 1999).

Evidence sufficient to sustain conviction. — Defendant's indifference in the face of overwhelming evidence of inappropriate and illegal sexual contact between defendant's daughter and older sons led directly to the older son being found delinquent and the younger son and the daughter being found abused and neglected; the evidence, consequently, was sufficient to sustain defendant's convictions on three counts of contributing to the delinquency of a minor. Kilby v. Commonwealth, No. 1426-06-4, 2007 Va. App. LEXIS 357 (Ct. of Appeals Oct. 2, 2007).

Evidence was sufficient to convict defendant of consensual intercourse with a child 15 years or older because the victim, who was 17 years old, testified that she had consensual sexual intercourse with defendant on the date in question. Mervin-Frazier v. Commonwealth, 2010 Va. App. LEXIS 134 (Apr. 6, 2010).

Relationship to immigration laws. — Because the only document that could be considered under the modified approach to determine if petitioner alien was convicted of a crime involving moral turpitude did not state under which subsection of § 18.2-371 the alien was convicted, finding that he was subject to removal under 8 U.S.C.S. § 1227(a)(2)(A)(i) was error. Prudencio v. Holder, 669 F.3d 472, 2012 U.S. App. LEXIS 1693 (4th Cir. Jan. 30, 2012).

Applied in McDonald v. Commonwealth, 48 Va. App. 325, 630 S.E.2d 754, 2006 Va. App. LEXIS 259 (2006).

§ 18.2-371.1. Abuse and neglect of children; penalty; abandoned infant.

A. Any parent, guardian, or other person responsible for the care of a child under the age of 18 who by willful act or omission or refusal to provide any necessary care for the child's health causes or permits serious injury to the life or health of such child shall be guilty of a Class 4 felony. For purposes of this subsection, *"serious injury"* shall include but not be limited to (i) disfigurement, (ii) a fracture, (iii) a severe burn or laceration, (iv) mutilation, (v) maiming, (vi) forced ingestion of dangerous substances, or (vii) life-threatening internal injuries.

B. 1. Any parent, guardian, or other person responsible for the care of a child under the age of 18 whose willful act or omission in the care of such child was so gross, wanton and culpable as to show a reckless disregard for human life shall be guilty of a Class 6 felony.

2. If a prosecution under this subsection is based solely on the accused parent having left the child at a hospital or rescue squad, it shall be an affirmative defense to prosecution of a parent under this subsection that such parent safely delivered the child to a hospital that provides 24-hour emergency services or to an attended rescue squad that employs emergency medical technicians, within the first 14 days of the child's life. In order for the affirmative defense to apply, the child shall be delivered in a manner reasonably calculated to ensure the child's safety.

C. Any parent, guardian or other person having care, custody, or control of a minor child who in good faith is under treatment solely by spiritual means through prayer in accordance with the tenets and practices of a recognized church or religious denomination shall not, for that reason alone, be considered in violation of this section.

History.
1981, c. 568; 1988, c. 228; 1990, c. 638; 1993, c. 628; 2003, cc. 816, 822; 2006, c. 935.

Cross references.
For requirement that a valid report of child abuse or neglect involving abuse or neglect resulting in serious injury as defined in § 18.2-371.1 be investigated by a local department of social services that has been designated as a child-protective services differential response agency, see § 63.2-1506 C. For definition of "barrier crime" as including a conviction of abuse and neglect of children as set out in § 18.2-371.1, or an equivalent offense in another state, and prohibition against assisted living facilities, adult day care centers or child welfare agencies hiring for certain compensated employment persons who have committed such an offense, see §§ 63.2-1719, 63.2-1720. As to report to children's residential facility for which a background check is being performed on whether the applicant has ever been convicted of or is the subject of pending charges for various crimes, including abuse and neglect of children as set out in § 18.2-371.1, or an equivalent offense in another state, see § 63.2-1726. For provision making it unlawful

for any person to operate a family day home if he, or if he knows that any other person who resides in the home, has been convicted of a felony in violation of this section, see § 63.2-1727.

Law Review.
For annual survey article on legal issues involving children, see 38 U. Rich. L. Rev. 161 (2003). For 2006 survey article, "Family and Juvenile Law," see 41 U. Rich. L. Rev. 151 (2006).

CASE NOTES

I. General Consideration.
II. Sufficiency of Evidence.

I. GENERAL CONSIDERATION.

Person "responsible for the care of a child." — One may become a person "responsible for the care of a child" by a voluntary course of conduct and without explicit parental delegation of supervisory responsibility or court order. Snow v. Commonwealth, 33 Va. App. 766, 537 S.E.2d 6, 2000 Va. App. LEXIS 754 (2000).

"Willful" defined. — "Willful" generally means an act done with a bad purpose, without justifiable excuse or without ground for believing it is lawful and the terms "bad purpose" or "without justifiable excuse," while facially unspecific, necessarily imply knowledge that particular conduct will likely result in injury or illegality; the term "willful" denotes an act which is intentional, or knowing, or voluntary, as distinguished from accidental. Collado v. Commonwealth, 33 Va. App. 356, 533 S.E.2d 625, 2000 Va. App. LEXIS 635 (2000).

"Willful" generally means an act done with bad purpose, without justifiable excuse, or without ground for believing it is lawful. Ellis v. Commonwealth, 29 Va. App. 548, 513 S.E.2d 453 (1999).

The term "willful" denotes an act which is intentional, or knowing, or voluntary, as distinguished from accidental. Ellis v. Commonwealth, 29 Va. App. 548, 513 S.E.2d 453 (1999).

Willful omission or refusal must be proven. — To sustain a conviction under this section, the evidence must prove beyond a reasonable doubt a willful act or willful omission or willful refusal regarding the proscribed conduct. Dotson v. Commonwealth, No. 1507-99-3, 2000 Va. App. LEXIS 484 (Ct. of Appeals July 5, 2000).

Willful omissions. — Willful omissions require an awareness that the conduct would cause or permit serious injury; where the evidence against defendant did not establish that he knew danger ensued from only ordering his son to put a gun away rather than taking it from him, and failed to establish defendant's knowledge and consciousness that an injury would result from the act done, his child abuse and reckless handling of a firearm convictions were reversed. Mangano v. Commonwealth, 44 Va. App. 210, 604 S.E.2d 118, 2004 Va. App. LEXIS 511 (2004).

Implication of "bad purpose" or "without justifiable excuse." — The terms "bad purpose" or "without justifiable excuse," while facially unspecific, necessarily imply knowledge that particular conduct will likely result in injury or illegality. Ellis v. Commonwealth, 29 Va. App. 548, 513 S.E.2d 453 (1999).

Inattention and inadvertence have not been heretofore equated with actions taken willfully, thus making them subject to criminal penalty. Ellis v. Commonwealth, 29 Va. App. 548, 513 S.E.2d 453 (1999).

"Reckless disregard." — Although child's injuries were serious and painful, they were not life-threatening, and mother's approach to injuries was not so gross, wanton or culpable as to show a reckless disregard for human life. McBeth v. Commonwealth, No. 1096-98-2 (Ct. of Appeals June 29, 1999).

Duty on parent to actively monitor child's health and well-being. — This section not only precludes a parent or custodian from committing "willful acts," but also mandates that a parent or custodian may not stand idle while the child's life or health is seriously threatened. The statute imposes upon the parent the duty to make herself aware of her child's physical and mental condition and to actively monitor his health and well-being in order to insure his safety. Lester v. Commonwealth, No. 0538-89-1 (Ct. of Appeals June 12, 1990).

Double jeopardy. — Defendant's convictions for child abuse and child endangerment under §§ 18.2-371.1 and 40.1-103 were appropriate because his double-jeopardy rights were not violated since each statute required proof of additional facts not found in the other and thus constituted two distinct offenses. Child endangerment did not require serious injury, or any injury at all; child endangerment, but not child abuse, required that the child's life, health, or morals be endangered; and endangerment of a child's moral well-being was not a violation of the child abuse statute. King v. Commonwealth, 56 Va. App. 133, 692 S.E.2d 249, 2010 Va. App. LEXIS 166 (2010).

Expert testimony unnecessary to prove dangers. — Where defendant was convicted of criminal abuse and neglect for, in part, preparing a bottle for defendant's six-month-old child that contained nearly three percent alcohol, the Commonwealth was not required to produce expert testimony showing that consumption of alcohol by a six-month-old child who had not had any food or liquids for at least seven hours presented a substantial risk of serious injury or risk of death to the child, as the dangers inherent in such a situation could be inferred by the fact finder as a matter of common knowledge. Commonwealth v. Duncan, 267 Va. 377, 593 S.E.2d 210, 2004 Va. LEXIS 38 (2004), reversing 2002 Va. App. LEXIS 530 (Va. Cir. App. 2002).

Knowledge conduct would likely cause serious injury. — To obtain a conviction under this section, the commonwealth is required to prove only that the defendant knew his conduct would likely result in serious injury; an intent to cause a serious injury or any specific injury is not an element of the offense. Collado v. Commonwealth, 33 Va. App. 356, 533 S.E.2d 625, 2000 Va. App. LEXIS 635 (2000).

Where defendant, while intoxicated, allowed an eight-year old child to sit on defendant's lap and drive a van, the evidence was sufficient to convict defendant of felony child abuse and neglect under subsection B of § 18.2-371.1. Kenyon v. Commonwealth, No. 2383-02-1, 2003 Va. App. LEXIS 542 (Ct. of Appeals Oct. 28, 2003).

Expert opinion as to intent not allowed. — An expert witness was properly not allowed to give his opinion as to whether an injury sustained by a four month old child was necessarily intentionally inflicted; the expert could, and did, testify as to the mechanics of how such an injury occurs, but it was the province of the fact finder to determine whether an intentional act necessarily caused the injury. Towns v. Commonwealth, No. 0346-98-3 (Ct. of Appeals Mar. 30, 1999).

Recent childbirth alone does not excuse legal duty to care for child. — Although a court may consider the mother's condition in determining the degree of criminal culpability arising from a failure to attend to her newborn baby, the sole fact that she has recently experienced childbirth does not excuse her from a legal duty to care for the baby. Vaughan v. Commonwealth, 7 Va. App. 665, 376 S.E.2d 801 (1989).

Severity of injuries. — Subsection does not require proof that injuries inflicted by the defendant were life threatening. Woodson v. Commonwealth, No. 0140-98-2 (Ct. of Appeals Mar. 2, 1999).

An injury may be serious because of the nature and extent of the injury, the effect the injury has upon the victim or the extent to which the injury may require medical treatment. Tate v. Commonwealth, No. 0042-99-2, 2000 Va. App. LEXIS 522 (Ct. of Appeals July 18, 2000).

A child had suffered "serious injuries" within the meaning of this section where the evidence proved that the child suffered from numerous bruises of various ages on her entire body, the child had a large bruise on her forehead that was several days old and numerous small bruises and lacerations on her face, she had a scab on her shoulder in the shape of two linear lines and a bruise in the shape of a thumbprint on her thigh, an MRI showed scattered petechial hemorrhages throughout the child's brain that were approximately three to four days old, the child also had an area of bruising on the right occiput of the head and, when the child was taken to the hospital, she appeared to be lethargic; the child's injuries, although not life threatening, were indicative of multiple and repetitive trauma. Tate v. Commonwealth, No. 0042-99-2, 2000 Va. App. LEXIS 522 (Ct. of Appeals July 18, 2000).

Specifications of "serious injury" in § 18.2-371.1 do not limit the court's consideration of the term "serious bodily injury" in a case under § 16.1-253.2. They relate to a specific legislative concern, the protection of children in custodial relationships; furthermore, the statute expressly provides that the term "serious injury" is not limited to the enumerated specifications. Nolen v. Commonwealth,

53 Va. App. 593, 673 S.E.2d 920, 2009 Va. App. LEXIS 138 (2009).

Although death is not listed as a "serious injury" in this section, a defendant's argument that she could not be convicted of felony child abuse for causing her child's death by shaken baby syndrome ignored the fact that the victim suffered grievous injuries that caused death; the violent shaking caused brain injury, which produced the shock, which affected vital organs, and death resulted. Cotton v. Commonwealth, 35 Va. App. 511, 546 S.E.2d 241, 2001 Va. App. LEXIS 277 (2001).

Failure to place baby for adoption before birth not supportive of mother's plan to kill baby. — That mother never took active steps towards placing the baby for adoption before the birth was not a fact which would support a reasonable inference that she intended to kill the baby since making adoption arrangements prior to a birth may be advisable, but it is not reasonable to infer that the failure to do so indicates a plan to kill a baby. Vaughan v. Commonwealth, 7 Va. App. 665, 376 S.E.2d 801 (1989).

Transporting his son while driving under the influence. — Trial court did not err in denying defendant's motion to strike, which alleged that he could not have been prosecuted under under this section, based upon his act of transporting his son while driving under the influence, as subsection D of § 18.2-270 simply provided an additional penalty for driving under the influence while transporting a person 17 years of age or younger and did not include within its parameters the elements of the child abuse and neglect offense. Wolfe v. Commonwealth, 42 Va. App. 776, 595 S.E.2d 27, 2004 Va. App. LEXIS 168 (2004).

Unsecured handgun. — Defendant's conviction for felony child neglect under subsection A of § 18.2-371.1 was appropriate because she was aware that the handgun was in the gym bag; she was aware that the gym bag with the handgun was on the floor easily within the reach of children; and directed the children to stay in the same bedroom with the unsecured handgun. Wright v. Commonwealth, 2011 Va. App. LEXIS 309 (Oct. 11, 2011).

Compared to § 18.2-371. — Defendant sufficiently preserved for review the claim that defendant could not be convicted of violating § 18.2-371, misdemeanor child abuse and neglect, because defense counsel made numerous arguments that defendant had not been charged with violating it and it was not a lesser-included offense of § 18.2-371.1, felony child abuse and neglect. Since the Commonwealth conceded that it was not a lesser-included offense and defendant had not procedurally defaulted the issue, the conviction had to be dismissed. Brown v. Commonwealth, 2008 Va. App. LEXIS 94 (Feb. 26, 2008).

As evidence to support termination of residual parental rights. — Trial court did not err in entering a judgment that terminated the parental rights of the mother in her two minor children and found it was in the best interests of the children to do so; the mother pled guilty to one count of felony abuse and neglect in violation of § 18.2-371.1 and one count of felony cruelty and injury to children in violation of § 40.1-103, which was sufficient to establish that the mother committed a felony assault causing serious bodily injury and served as a ground for terminating her parental rights in the two minor children. Canter v. City of Bristol Dep't of Soc. Servs., No. 0507-05-3, 2005 Va. App. LEXIS 501 (Ct. of Appeals Dec. 13, 2005).

Applied in Commonwealth v. Carter, 21 Va. App. 150, 462 S.E.2d 582 (1995).

II. SUFFICIENCY OF EVIDENCE.

Evidence was sufficient to sustain conviction where the defendant frequently beat the victim, routinely confined the victim to the basement, without regard for his health, physical comfort or nutrition, and eventually ordered the victim, a 12 year old child, to leave the house permanently without making any alternative arrangements for his care. Woodson v. Commonwealth, No. 0140-98-2 (Ct. of Appeals Mar. 2, 1999).

Felony child neglect shown where the mother willfully, wantonly and culpably allowed in her home activities that exposed her six-year-old daughter to drug activity, loaded weapons and risk of death and where, by smoking marijuana in the apartment and by allowing the air in the apartment to be saturated with smoke, the mother showed a reckless and wanton disregard for the child's life and health in that the child suffered from severe asthma. Taylor v.

Commonwealth, No. 0411-99-2, 2000 Va. App. LEXIS 353 (Ct. of Appeals May 9, 2000).

The evidence was sufficient to support the defendant's conviction where her infant son had been drowned by her daughter and where it was established that, by staying out all night drinking beer, the defendant rendered herself unable to give proper attention to her children, that having slept only one and one-half hours, she made no effort to obtain assistance or to keep herself awake, that she sat on the couch where she succumbed to sleep, that knowing of her daughter's previous, potentially lethal, conduct toward her son, she nonetheless left the children unattended with no provision to protect her son from her daughter's known aggressiveness and that she did all these things knowingly and intentionally. Barrett v. Commonwealth, 32 Va. App. 693, 530 S.E.2d 437, 2000 Va. App. LEXIS 480 (2000).

The evidence was sufficient to support a trial court's finding that the defendant knew her child was at risk but, by "omission or refusal" to act, allowed the abuse to continue by entrusting her child to her boyfriend when the defendant had observed extensive cuts and bruises on the child's face and body after she had been left in the boyfriend's care several days before. Tate v. Commonwealth, No. 0042-99-2, 2000 Va. App. LEXIS 522 (Ct. of Appeals July 18, 2000).

The evidence was sufficient to support a jury's finding that the defendant was the criminal agent who inflicted the life threatening injuries to a child where the child was criminally assaulted during a period when the defendant had sole custody and control of the child. Collado v. Commonwealth, 33 Va. App. 356, 533 S.E.2d 625, 2000 Va. App. LEXIS 635 (2000).

Conviction was affirmed where, although an order showing the conviction for second degree murder of the person with whom the defendant left her deceased child was hearsay, it was admissible at the defendant's trial for abuse and neglect of her child as it fell within the scope of § 8.01-389 A, the judicial records exception to the hearsay rule. Furthermore, although the trial court erred in admitting the order into evidence as the order was irrelevant because it provided no proof of any element of defendant's trial, the admission of the order was harmless error as the evidence overwhelmingly and compellingly established defendant's guilt. Palmer v. Commonwealth, No. 3265-01-1, 2003 Va. App. LEXIS 245 (Ct. of Appeals Apr. 22, 2003).

Evidence, which included expert testimony by two physicians, showed that defendant was the only adult present with the baby several hours prior to the appearance of her symptoms of limpness and unresponsiveness, and that the injuries were inflicted by defendant in rudeness or anger, with force and violence, and with reckless disregard for the baby's well-being. Given the totality of the evidence, the appellate court found that the jury was entitled to reject defendant's explanations of innocence and to conclude that the evidence was sufficient to establish she inflicted the baby's injuries with the requisite state of mind. Morton v. Commonwealth, No. 2677-02-2, 2004 Va. App. LEXIS 40 (Ct. of Appeals Jan. 28, 2004).

Conviction for felony child neglect was supported by evidence proving that defendant showed utter disregard for the safety and well-being of her children by leaving them unsupervised for several days and nights, thereby exposing them to injury and risk of harm or death; evidence proved that defendant was the mother of the children and that she left them alone for several days and nights, all of which constituted a "willful act or omission of care" of the children and constituted criminal negligence. Ascencio v. Commonwealth, No. 3357-02-2, 2004 Va. App. LEXIS 42 (Ct. of Appeals Feb. 3, 2004).

Evidence that defendant left the child in the van and casually instructed other children to get all the children out of the van and into the house without ensuring that his instructions were obeyed, and that, over a period of more than seven hours, defendant assumed but never ascertained that the child was asleep in the house was sufficient to show defendant's total and utter disregard for her well-being, safety, and life and thus, to support convictions for involuntary manslaughter and felony child neglect. Kelly v. Commonwealth, 42 Va. App. 347, 592 S.E.2d 353, 2004 Va. App. LEXIS 47 (2004).

Reviewing court found that there was sufficient evidence to convict defendant of criminal abuse and neglect where defendant left defendant's six-month-old child with three women defendant barely knew, defendant did not give them food for the baby, the child did not receive food or liquids for more than seven hours, and defendant, more than eight hours later, prepared for the child a bottle that contained alcohol in it, which was fed to the child. Commonwealth v. Duncan, 267 Va. 377, 593 S.E.2d 210, 2004 Va. LEXIS 38 (2004), reversing 2002 Va. App. LEXIS 530 (Va. Cir. App. 2002).

Felony child abuse and neglect conviction was upheld where the evidence against defendant sufficiently proved beyond a reasonable doubt that his act of repeatedly beating his son was not negligent or non-criminal, but was reasonably calculated to produce injury and done with an indifferent disregard of the rights of others. Abshire v. Commonwealth, No. 2441-02-3, 2004 Va. App. LEXIS 119 (Ct. of Appeals Mar. 23, 2004).

Defendant's conduct in placing his 14-month-old son's feet in hot water resulting in the soles of the son's feet being burned, which defendant did because he wanted to teach the baby a lesson about "dirtying the baby's diaper" was the kind of gross, wanton, and culpable act that showed reckless disregard for his son's life; the Commonwealth was not required to show that defendant's conduct caused an actual risk of death, as the "reckless disregard" could be shown by conduct subjecting a child to a substantial risk of serious injury, which defendant's conduct did. Gray v. Commonwealth, No. 2720-02-2, 2004 Va. App. LEXIS 173 (Ct. of Appeals Apr. 13, 2004).

Where a mother had knowledge that her daughter was very jealous of her younger sibling, had tried to harm him and kill him, and that the daughter was capable of turning the water on in the bathtub, which was her favorite place to play, and of pulling the younger sibling into the bathtub, the mother's conviction for criminal neglect of both her son and her daughter was supported by the evidence; the mother had been out all night drinking alcohol, had come home and fallen asleep on the couch, and the daughter had pulled the younger sibling into the bathtub, which had two inches of water in it, covered him with toys, a laundry basket, and a blanket, and he had drowned. Barrett v. Commonwealth, 268 Va. 170, 597 S.E.2d 104, 2004 Va. LEXIS 105 (2004).

Felony child neglect conviction was upheld, as evidence of defendant's gross, wanton and willful conduct was presented by his act of brutally beating his mother in front of his eight-year-old son, leaving the son alone with his unconscious grandmother at night, and instructing his son not to call for help; the fact that the risks in doing so had not yet materialized did not mean that the risks were absent and did not serve to remove defendant's conduct from the prohibitions of the statute. Jones v. Commonwealth, No. 1670-03-1, 2004 Va. App. LEXIS 561 (Ct. of Appeals Nov. 16, 2004).

Evidence that defendant stayed up too late, that she did not take prescribed medication, and that she failed to respond to her premature infant's breathing and heart rate monitor for 27 minutes early one morning even though an alarm attached to the monitor was sounding the whole time was sufficient to support defendant's conviction; the jury was free to disbelieve her testimony that she did not hear the alarm, especially after the alarm was played for the jury and they heard how loud the alarm sounded. Wimmer v. Commonwealth, — Va. App. —, — S.E.2d —, 2005 Va. App. LEXIS 305 (Aug. 2, 2005).

The fact that defendant dealt drugs out of her apartment placed the child at risk of harm from accidental ingestion of harmful drugs, and at risk of harm from drug-related violence, and was sufficient to constitute a gross, wanton, and willful disregard for human life. Jones v. Commonwealth, 46 Va. App. 713, 621 S.E.2d 676, 2005 Va. App. LEXIS 448 (2005).

Jury's finding that a child's injuries resulted from repetitive and forceful shaking was sufficient to support its conclusion that defendant was guilty of felony child neglect. Blackmon v. Commonwealth, — Va. App. —, — S.E.2d —, 2006 Va. App. LEXIS 23 (Jan. 24, 2006).

Defendant's conviction of felony child neglect in violation of subdivision B 1 of § 18.2-371.1 was affirmed, because defendant knew or should have known that placing heroin and cocaine in the same room as her unattended son created a substantial risk of serious injury, even though the child did not ingest the drugs, and thus the totality of the evidence proved that a substantial or probable risk of harm to the child existed. Jones v. Commonwealth, 272 Va. 692, 636 S.E.2d 403, 2006 Va. LEXIS 109 (2006).

Defendant's willful act of failing to secure prompt medical attention for juveniles in her charge when one of them took sleeping pills, despite defendant's recognition that ingesting drugs could pose a substantial risk of serious injury or death, satisfied the requirement of a "willful act" in "reckless disregard for human life," as required by § 18.2-371.1. Flowers v. Commonwealth, 49 Va. App. 241, 639 S.E.2d 313, 2007 Va. App. LEXIS 14 (2007).

Evidence that the two younger children were not properly dressed before being left out in cold at night for five hours to guard against possible criminal activity supported felony neglect charges; by barring the children from seeking refuge in the building where defendant was sleeping, defendant compounded the exposure of the children to danger evidencing a reckless disregard for the rights of the children that would probably result in an injury. Ferguson v. Commonwealth, 50 Va. App. 351, 649 S.E.2d 724, 2007 Va. App. LEXIS 338 (2007).

Defendant's conviction for felony child abuse was supported by the evidence, as defendant fell within the purview of subsection A of § 18.2-371.1 during those times in which defendant was left alone with the child. Defendant's girlfriend testified that when she returned, the child was very ill, had a high fever, and had a bruise on the chest. Miller v. Commonwealth, — Va. App. —, — S.E.2d —, 2008 Va. App. LEXIS 73 (Feb. 12, 2008).

In a case in which defendant appealed her conviction for felony child neglect in violation of subsection B of § 18.2-371.1, she argued unsuccessfully that the evidence was insufficient because it failed to show that: (1) she withheld her son's medication; (2) her behavior caused a substantial risk to his life or health; and (3) she knew withholding his medication was likely to cause such a risk. The record on appeal failed to establish the defendant preserved any of her arguments for appeal as required by Va. Sup. Ct. R. 5A:18. Thornton v. Commonwealth, 2009 Va. App. LEXIS 413 (Sept. 15, 2009).

Evidence was sufficient to support defendant's conviction for felony child neglect in violation of § 18.2-371.1 because under the facts and circumstances, the trial court could determine that defendant, who had specialized medical training in pediatrics, acted in a willful manner with full knowledge of the consequences of his actions, and not only did defendant cause an infant's affliction, he did not timely offer information that could have sped her recovery; therefore, the trial court could find that defendant acted with a "bad purpose" or "without justifiable excuse" because he knew his conduct would result in injury to the infant. Gainov v. Commonwealth, 2009 Va. App. LEXIS 387 (Sept. 1, 2009).

Convictions of involuntary manslaughter, § 18.2-36, and felony child neglect, § 18.2-371.1 were supported by sufficient evidence under circumstances in which defendant, a daycare van driver, left a child in the van for a full day, and the child died of heat exposure; defendant failed to look for the child after unloading the other children from the van, despite having personally strapped the child into his car seat, did not use the van logbook designed to prevent this kind of tragedy, took the child's diaper bag inside the daycare without confirming that the child was also safely inside, failed to use the logbook inside the daycare, and then drove home, completely oblivious to the child sitting behind him. After returning home, defendant did not check to make sure the van was empty, silenced his phone, making it impossible for anyone to reach him when questions later arose concerning the child's delivery, and then slept all day leading to the reasonable inference that lack of sleep compromised his alertness that morning. Whitfield v. Commonwealth, 57 Va. App. 396, 702 S.E.2d 590, 2010 Va. App. LEXIS 502 (2010).

Evidence was sufficient to support defendant's conviction for child neglect under subsection A of § 18.2-371.1, where there was sufficient evidence to support a finding that defendant, who was dating and living with the child's mother, was a person responsible for the child's care through a voluntary course of conduct; among other things, defendant held himself out as the father, "looked out" for the child, and even helped feed, bathe, and put the child to sleep. Carrington v. Commonwealth, 59 Va. App. 614, 721 S.E.2d 815, 2012 Va. App. LEXIS 46 (Feb. 14, 2012).

Where defendant and her boyfriend were the only ones that took care of the child on the day in question and the jury accepted the boyfriend's denial, testifying that he did not cause the injuries and has never shaken the child, and the jury reasonably could have inferred that defendant fatally injured the child. Burnette v. Commonwealth, 60 Va. App. 462, 729 S.E.2d 740, 2012 Va. App. LEXIS 246 (2012).

Evidence was sufficient to permit the jury to find defendant guilty of felony child abuse or neglect, where an expert in pediatric care opined that the child's complex skull fracture could not have been caused by a fall into a playpen, but that it occurred from something with a more significant amount of force, and that since there was an absence of an explanation of an accident with the requisite degree of force, the injury was an "inflicted" head injury. The trial court was entitled to conclude that defendant lied to the police in order to conceal her guilt and that her testimony at trial was untrue, as it was not until more than a month after the incident that defendant told the police officers that she fell and caused the child to land in the playpen with a "thud." O'Berry v. Commonwealth, 2012 Va. App. LEXIS 412 (Dec. 18, 2012).

Evidence insufficient to sustain conviction. — Because defendant took significant steps to prevent the recurrence of a prior event that had placed her son at risk of harm, the fact that her actions, though significant, did not eliminate all risk to her child was insufficient to prove criminal negligence; therefore, despite her admitted alcohol consumption and failing to check the door and re-lock the same in order to prevent her child from escaping into harm's way, defendant's actions, which amounted at best to bad judgment and simple negligence, did not amount to the level of criminal negligence necessary to support a conviction under § 18.2-371.1. Frey v. Commonwealth, — Va. App. —, — S.E.2d —, 2005 Va. App. LEXIS 153 (Apr. 19, 2005).

The fact that defendant's actions in chaining and locking the door did not eliminate all risk to her children was insufficient to prove criminal negligence where there was no evidence that, on some prior occasion, the children opened a locked and chained door in order to leave the residence or that defendant was under the influence of drugs or other intoxicants causing her to sleep so soundly or for so long that she was unable to render adequate supervision. Morris v. Commonwealth, — Va. App. —, — S.E.2d —, 2005 Va. App. LEXIS 190 (May 10, 2005) Although different results were reached on rehearing at 47 Va. App. 34, 622 S.E.2d 243 (2005), the Virginia Supreme Court reversed. See the following case note.

Where defendant's young children were found in the woods near their home, unattended, while she napped, the evidence was insufficient to convict her of felonious child neglect in violation of subsection B of § 18.2-371.1. As there was no evidence that defendant was under the influence of drugs or alcohol at the time she and the children went to sleep, the prosecution did not prove that she willfully failed to care for her sons in a manner so gross, wanton, and culpable as to show a reckless disregard for their lives. Morris v. Commonwealth, 272 Va. 732, 636 S.E.2d 436, 2006 Va. LEXIS 100 (2006).

Evidence was insufficient to sustain defendant's conviction for felony child neglect, under subdivision B 1 of § 18.2-371.1, when the victim stood outside in cold weather because: (1) the evidence showed the victim was 17 years, 7 months old; (2) the victim was appropriately dressed for the winter temperature; and (3) the victim had complete access to a building with no restrictions, so the victim was not continually exposed to harsh winter conditions outside, nor was the victim required to guard against potential criminal activity outside the building, so it could not be found that defendant demonstrated a reckless disregard for the victim's health and safety. Ferguson v. Commonwealth, 51 Va. App. 427, 658 S.E.2d 692, 2008 Va. App. LEXIS 367 (2008).

Evidence was insufficient to support defendant's conviction for child neglect under subdivision B 1, where the evidence failed to show that defendant's conduct constituted a willful act or omission that was so gross, wanton, and culpable as to show a reckless disregard for human life; the burns the child had received prior to coming into defendant's care were covered with gauze and duct tape and the child's lethargy was insufficient to make defendant aware that the child needed medical attention. Shanklin v. Commonwealth, 53 Va. App. 683, 674 S.E.2d 577, 2009 Va. App. LEXIS 158 (2009).

Evidence that defendant left her children in the care of her boyfriend's parents when she and her boyfriend went out for the night; that upon returning home, defendant checked on the children and went to sleep in another room, with the door open; defendant was unaware that the other adults had left; and defendant was not aware that her three-year-old twins, who defendant knew were capable of climbing the child gate on the trailer's deck, were capable of opening the door to her trailer to gain access to the outside was insufficient to support a conviction for felony child neglect. Clark v. Commonwealth, 2012 Va. App. LEXIS 158 (May 15, 2012).

While defendant could have expected that sniffing dust remover would result in her incapacitation, thereby leaving the children unattended in the home for that period of time, without additional evidence in the record of a substantial risk or probability of serious injury or death to the children arising from environmental or human factors in that time frame, defendant's actions did not rise to the level required for a felony conviction under subdivision B 1 of § 18.2-371.1. Shifflett v. Commonwealth, 2012 Va. App. LEXIS 391 (Dec. 4, 2012).

Evidence did not support defendant's conviction of felony child neglect, as the record reflected that at no time did defendant simply disregard the care and needs of defendant's child; defendant made attempts to care for the child once defendant realized the child was in distress, including washing the child in the bathtub, calling regular caregivers for advice, and ultimately calling 911. Davis v. Commonwealth, 2012 Va. App. LEXIS 343 (Oct. 31, 2012).

Evidence of "willfulness" sufficient. — Defendant's forty-hour delay in seeking medical attention for her four-year-old son, after recognizing that he suffered extensive abuse, amounted to a violation of this section, and her fear of her boyfriend did not justify her failure to take action. Roberts v. Commonwealth, No. 1594-98-3 (Ct. of Appeals June 8, 1999).

Circumstantial evidence was sufficient to establish willfulness in child abuse case, where medical experts' opinions cast doubt upon all of defendant's multiple accounts of how the child "accidentally" sustained a fatal head injury, and indicated that the injury was consistent with abuse. Hickson v. Commonwealth, Nos. 1205-10-3, 1869-01-3, 2002 Va. App. LEXIS 243 (Ct. of Appeals Apr. 23, 2002).

Evidence that defendant was a licensed child care provider who routinely chose to allow the older children in her care to provide extended supervision for the children entrusted to defendant's care, most of whom were infants, toddlers, and preschoolers, was sufficient to prove a "willful act or omission" and thus, supported defendant's conviction for child neglect under subsection B of § 18.2-371.1. Bean-Brewer v. Commonwealth, 49 Va. App. 3, 635 S.E.2d 680, 2006 Va. App. LEXIS 469 (2006).

Evidence was sufficient to show that defendant willfully abused or neglected a child whom defendant was responsible for providing care for and, thus, defendant's conviction for a violation of subsection A of § 18.2-371.1 had to be upheld. The evidence showed that after defendant tried to clean the child with a sink sprayer shooting hot water, defendant failed to obtain the medical help that the child obviously needed and that defendant instead spent the time trying to figure ways to keep defendant from getting in trouble. Carter v. Commonwealth, — Va. App. —, — S.E.2d —, 2008 Va. App. LEXIS 447 (Oct. 7, 2008).

Evidence sufficient to establish willfulness. — The evidence was sufficient to show a willful act or omission in the care of children where the defendant, while driving a vehicle occupied by three of his brother's children, led the police on a chase at speeds exceeding 100 miles per hour until the engine of the car blew and the defendant was forced to stop. Snow v. Commonwealth, 33 Va. App. 766, 537 S.E.2d 6, 2000 Va. App. LEXIS 754 (2000).

Defendant was properly convicted of felony child abuse arising from the drowning death of her youngest child; she intentionally created a situation where a two-year-old child, who had known aggressive tendencies toward the youngest child, was left completely unsupervised, and she exposed both children to injury and/or the risk of death. Barrett v. Commonwealth, 41 Va. App. 377, 585 S.E.2d 355, 2003 Va. App. LEXIS 446 (2003), aff'd, 268 Va. 170, 597 S.E.2d 104 (2004).

Evidence that defendant placed her nine-month-old daughter in an empty hot tub for use as a bed, that the daughter became wet because the daughter was able to turn on the water faucet leading into the hot tub, that defendant turned off the water and put the child back in the hot tub and left her unattended, where the child was later found drowned was sufficient to show defendant acted so grossly, wantonly, and culpably as to demonstrate a reckless disregard for human life because the evidence showed that defendant willfully returned the daughter to a place of imminent danger despite defendant's knowledge that the child could turn on the water faucet leading to the hot tub but could not climb out of the hot tub; accordingly, defendant's conviction for felony child neglect was

affirmed. Ratliffe v. Commonwealth, No. 0532-02-3, 2003 Va. App. LEXIS 481 (Ct. of Appeals Sept. 23, 2003).

"Willfulness" was shown for purposes of a mother's convictions for neglect of two of her children where the mother's knowledge that her daughter was extremely jealous of the mother's son, and that the daughter had harmed the son and tried to kill him on prior occasions went beyond "ordinary negligence," to the point where it showed the mother's reckless disregard for the relationship between her two children; the mother was neglectful of her duty to protect both of her children, and her conduct in going to sleep and leaving both children otherwise unattended was willful and was accompanied by acts of omission of a wanton nature that showed a reckless or indifferent disregard for the life and health of both children. Barrett v. Commonwealth, 268 Va. 170, 597 S.E.2d 104, 2004 Va. LEXIS 105 (2004).

Evidence of willfull refusal to provide necessary medical care. — As there was an abundance of evidence from which the trial court could conclude that defendant willfully refused to provide necessary medical care for her child, who had third and second degree burns on his face and chest, as she clearly appreciated the severity of her baby's injuries, but did not take the baby to the hospital or otherwise seek medical care, did not care for her baby all night, and repeatedly put her baby in the care of an irresponsible caretaker, defendant was properly convicted under subsection A of § 18.2-371.1. Magno v. Commonwealth, — Va. App. —, — S.E.2d —, 2008 Va. App. LEXIS 528 (Dec. 9, 2008).

Evidence sufficient to show intent. — In a prosecution arising from a spiral fracture of the femur of a four month old child, the evidence was sufficient to show intent where the baby slept next to the defendant and the mother, and that shortly after the baby awoke at 4:20, the mother discovered that the baby's leg was limp and motionless, and that the fracture injury was one that is extremely rare, usually associated with abuse. Towns v. Commonwealth, No. 0346-98-3 (Ct. of Appeals Mar. 30, 1999).

The defendant's actions were "willful" where the evidence was sufficient to establish that the defendant, a professional daycare provider, shook a five-month-old infant so violently as to cause brain injury; the defendant's spoken intent to force the child to conform to her idea of an appropriate schedule would not justify shaking her, nor would the crying of a five-month-old infant justify such treatment and the jury was entitled to conclude from the evidence that the child did not conform to the defendant's expectations for behavior and the defendant responded by brutally shaking her into submission. Collado v. Commonwealth, 33 Va. App. 356, 533 S.E.2d 625, 2000 Va. App. LEXIS 635 (2000).

Evidence was insufficient to prove defendant's actions constituted "willful" act or omission under this section where, although defendant was negligent in forgetting to turn off a gas jet and in failing to check the operability of smoke detectors, and defendant, without question, purposefully and intentionally left her apartment to visit a friend in another residential building, the evidence failed to support the conclusion that she acted with knowledge or consciousness that her children would be injured as a likely result of her departure. Ellis v. Commonwealth, 29 Va. App. 548, 513 S.E.2d 453 (1999).

CIRCUIT COURT OPINIONS

Exclusion of certain evidence. — Photographic evidence of defendant's horrible housekeeping practices had only tangential value with respect to the issue of "willful" neglect and protecting a child from a loaded gun hanging on a wall in the home, and the prejudicial effect was potentially extreme in that jurors could conclude that defendant was a bad mother and lose sight of the issue; therefore, the evidence could be excluded. Commonwealth v. Phillips, 59 Va. Cir. 394, 2002 Va. Cir. LEXIS 229 (Spotsylvania County 2002).

OPINIONS OF THE ATTORNEY GENERAL

Members' petition for a special meeting of the board of directors of a property owners' association is not a "communication" that requires the board to provide a reasonable, effective, and free method of exchange with other owners. See opinion of Attorney

General to The Honorable Vincent F. Callahan, Jr., Member, House of Delegates, 03-107 (2/17/04).

The defense provided where a child is left at a hospital or rescue squad creates an affirmative defense to criminal acts of child abuse and neglect, but does not provide an affirmative defense to civil findings of child abuse and neglect. See opinion of Attorney General to The Honorable Martin E. Williams, Member, Senate of Virginia, 03-105 (12/16/03).

§ 18.2-371.2. Prohibiting purchase or possession of tobacco products by minors or sale of tobacco products to minors.

A. No person shall sell to, distribute to, purchase for or knowingly permit the purchase by any person less than 18 years of age, knowing or having reason to believe that such person is less than 18 years of age, any tobacco product, including but not limited to cigarettes, cigars, bidis, and wrappings.

Tobacco products may be sold from a vending machine only if the machine is (i) posted with a notice, in a conspicuous manner and place, indicating that the purchase or possession of tobacco products by minors is unlawful and (ii) located in a place which is not open to the general public and is not generally accessible to minors. An establishment which prohibits the presence of minors unless accompanied by an adult is not open to the general public.

B. No person less than 18 years of age shall attempt to purchase, purchase or possess any tobacco product, including but not limited to cigarettes, cigars, bidis, and wrappings. The provisions of this subsection shall not be applicable to the possession of tobacco products, including wrappings, by a person less than 18 years of age making a delivery of tobacco products, including wrappings, in pursuance of his employment. This subsection shall not apply to purchase, attempt to purchase or possession by a law-enforcement officer or his agent when the same is necessary in the performance of his duties.

C. No person shall sell a tobacco product, including but not limited to cigarettes, cigars, bidis, and wrappings, to any individual who does not demonstrate, by producing a driver's license or similar photo identification issued by a government agency, that the individual is at least 18 years of age. Such identification is not required from an individual whom the person has reason to believe is at least 18 years of age or who the person knows is at least 18 years of age. Proof that the person demanded, was shown, and reasonably relied upon a photo identification stating that the individual was at least 18 years of age shall be a defense to any action brought under this subsection. In determining whether a person had reason to believe an individual is at least 18 years of age, the trier of fact may consider, but is not limited to, proof of the general appearance, facial characteristics, behavior and manner of the individual.

This subsection shall not apply to mail order sales.

D. A violation of subsection A or C by an individual or by a separate retail establishment that involves a tobacco product other than a bidi shall be punishable by a civil penalty not to exceed $100 for a first violation, a civil penalty not to exceed $200 for a second violation, and a civil penalty not to exceed $500 for a third or subsequent violation.

A violation of subsection A or C by an individual or by a separate retail establishment that involves the sale, distribution or purchase of a bidi shall be punishable by a civil penalty in the amount of $500 for a first violation, a civil penalty in the amount of $1,000 for a second violation, and a civil penalty in the amount of $2,500 for a third or subsequent violation. Where a defendant retail establishment offers proof that it has trained its employees concerning the requirements of this section, the court shall suspend all of the penalties imposed hereunder. However, where the court finds that a retail establishment has failed to so train its employees, the court may impose a civil penalty not to exceed $1,000 in lieu of any penalties imposed hereunder for a violation of subsection A or C involving a tobacco product other than a bidi.

A violation of subsection B shall be punishable by a civil penalty not to exceed $100 for a first violation and a civil penalty not to exceed $250 for a second or subsequent violation. A court may, as an alternative to the civil penalty, and upon motion of the defendant, prescribe the performance of up to 20 hours of community service for a first violation of subsection B and up to 40 hours of community service for a second or subsequent violation. If the defendant fails or refuses to complete the community service as prescribed, the court may impose the civil penalty. Upon a violation of subsection B, the judge may enter an order pursuant to subdivision A 9 of § 16.1-278.8.

Any attorney for the Commonwealth of the county or city in which an alleged violation occurred may bring an action to recover the civil penalty, which shall be paid into the state treasury. Any law-enforcement officer may issue a summons for a violation of subsection A, B, or C.

E. 1. Cigarettes shall be sold only in sealed packages provided by the manufacturer, with the required health warning. The proprietor of every retail establishment which offers for sale any tobacco product, including but not limited to cigarettes, cigars, and bidis, shall post in a conspicuous manner and place a sign or signs indicating that the sale of tobacco products, including wrappings, to any person under 18 years of age is prohibited by law. Any attorney for the county, city or town in which an alleged violation of this subsection occurred may enforce this subsection by civil action to recover a civil penalty not to exceed $50. The civil penalty shall be paid into the local treasury. No filing fee or other fee or cost shall be charged to the county, city or town which instituted the action.

2. For the purpose of compliance with regulations of the Substance Abuse and Mental Health Services

Administration published at 61 Federal Register 1492, the Department of Agriculture and Consumer Services may promulgate regulations which allow the Department to undertake the activities necessary to comply with such regulations.

3. Any attorney for the county, city or town in which an alleged violation of this subsection occurred may enforce this subsection by civil action to recover a civil penalty not to exceed $100. The civil penalty shall be paid into the local treasury. No filing fee or other fee or cost shall be charged to the county, city or town which instituted the action.

F. Nothing in this section shall be construed to create a private cause of action.

G. Agents of the Virginia Alcoholic Beverage Control Board designated pursuant to § 4.1-105 may issue a summons for any violation of this section.

H. As used in this section:

"*Bidi*" means a product containing tobacco that is wrapped in temburni leaf (diospyros melanoxylon) or tendu leaf (diospyros exculpra), or any other product that is offered to, or purchased by, consumers as a bidi or beedie; and

"*Wrappings*" includes papers made or sold for covering or rolling tobacco or other materials for smoking in a manner similar to a cigarette or cigar.

History.
1986, c. 406; 1991, c. 558; 1993, c. 631; 1994, c. 305; 1995, c. 675; 1996, cc. 509, 517; 1997, cc. 812, 882; 1998, c. 363; 1999, c. 1020; 2000, c. 883; 2003, cc. 114, 615.

Law Review.
For annual survey article on legal issues involving children, see 38 U. Rich. L. Rev. 161 (2003). For note, "Modern Police Practices: Arizona v. Gant's Illusory Restriction of Vehicle Searches Incident to Arrest," 97 Va. L. Rev. 1727 (2011).

§ 18.2-371.3. Tattooing or body piercing of minors.

No person shall tattoo or perform body piercing for hire or consideration on a person less than eighteen years of age, knowing or having reason to believe such person is less than eighteen years of age except (i) in the presence of the person's parent or guardian, or (ii) when done by or under the supervision of a medical doctor, registered nurse or other medical services personnel licensed pursuant to Title 54.1 in the performance of their duties.

In addition, no person shall tattoo or perform body piercing on any client unless he complies with the Centers for Disease Control and Prevention's guidelines for "Universal Blood and Body Fluid Precautions" and provides the client with the following disclosure:

1. Tattooing and body piercing are invasive procedures in which the skin is penetrated by a foreign object.

2. If proper sterilization and antiseptic procedures are not followed by tattoo artists and body piercers, there is a risk of transmission of bloodborne pathogens and other infections, includ-

ing, but not limited to, human immunodeficiency viruses and hepatitis B or C viruses.

3. Tattooing and body piercing may cause allergic reactions in persons sensitive to dyes or the metals used in ornamentation.

4. Tattooing and body piercing may involve discomfort or pain for which appropriate anesthesia cannot be legally made available by the person performing the tattoo or body piercing unless such person holds the appropriate license from a Virginia health regulatory board.

A person who violates this section is guilty of a Class 1 misdemeanor.

For the purposes of this section:

"*Body-piercing*" means the act of penetrating the skin to make a hole, mark, or scar, generally permanent in nature. "Body piercing" does not include the use of a mechanized, presterilized ear-piercing system that penetrates the outer perimeter or lobe of the ear or both.

"*Tattoo*" means to place any design, letter, scroll, figure, symbol or any other mark upon or under the skin of any person with ink or any other substance resulting in the permanent coloration of the skin, including permanent make-up or permanent jewelry, by the aid of needles or any other instrument designed to touch or puncture the skin.

History.
1997, c. 586; 2000, c. 842; 2001, c. 270; 2006, c. 692.

Cross references.
As to regulation of tattoo parlors and body-piercing salons, see § 15.2-912.

Law Review.
For an article, "Legal Issues Involving Children," see 32 U. Rich. L. Rev. 1345 (1998). For 2000 survey of Virginia health law, see 34 U. Rich. L. Rev. 853 (2000).

CIRCUIT COURT OPINIONS

Ordinance banning tattooing. — City ordinance's total ban on tattooing violated § 1-248, as it conflicted with Virginia's policy of restricting but not banning tattooing, as expressed in §§ 15.2-912 and 18.2-371.3. Thus, the city's demurrer to petitioner's claim that the ordinance was inconsistent with state law was denied. Blue Horseshoe Tattoo, V, Ltd. v. City of Norfolk, 72 Va. Cir. 388, 2007 Va. Cir. LEXIS 151 (Norfolk 2007).

§ 18.2-371.4. Prohibiting the sale of novelty lighters to juveniles.

A. "Novelty lighter" means a mechanical or electrical device containing a combustible fuel typically used for lighting cigarettes, cigars, or pipes that is (i) designed to resemble a cartoon character, toy, gun, watch, musical instrument, vehicle, animal, food, or beverage, or (ii) a fanciful article that plays musical notes, has flashing lights, or has other entertaining features that are appealing to or intended for use by juveniles. A novelty lighter may operate on any fuel, including butane, isobutene, or liquid fuel.

B. "Novelty lighter" does not include (i) a lighter without fuel and that is incapable of being fueled, (ii) a lighter lacking a device necessary to produce combustion or a flame, (iii) a mechanical or electrical device primarily used to ignite fuel for fireplaces or for charcoal or gas grills, (iv) a lighter manufactured prior to 1980, or (v) a standard disposable lighter that is printed or decorated with logos, labels, decals, or artwork, or heat shrinkable sleeves.

C. Novelty lighters that are available for purchase at a retail establishment shall be located in a place that is not open to the general public.

D. Any individual who sells a novelty lighter to a person he knows or has reason to know is a juvenile is subject to a civil penalty of no more than $100.

E. This section may be enforced by the State Fire Marshal's Office, local fire marshals appointed pursuant to § 27-34.2 or 27-34.2:1, or law-enforcement officers.

History.
2009, c. 668.

ARTICLE 5.

OBSCENITY AND RELATED OFFENSES.

§ 18.2-372. "Obscene" defined.

The word *"obscene"* where it appears in this article shall mean that which, considered as a whole, has as its dominant theme or purpose an appeal to the prurient interest in sex, that is, a shameful or morbid interest in nudity, sexual conduct, sexual excitement, excretory functions or products thereof or sadomasochistic abuse, and which goes substantially beyond customary limits of candor in description or representation of such matters and which, taken as a whole, does not have serious literary, artistic, political or scientific value.

History.
Code 1950, § 18.1-227; 1960, c. 233; 1975, cc. 14, 15.

Cross references.
As to public and private schools blocking Internet access to material defined in this section as obscene, see § 22.1-70.2. As to inspections and disclosure requirements involving barbershops, barber schools, cosmetology salons and schools, nail care salons and schools, tattoo parlors and schools, and body-piercing salons and schools, see § 54.1-705. For definition of "barrier crime" as including a conviction of employing or permitting a minor to assist in an act constituting an offense under § 18.2-372 et seq. as set out in § 18.2-379, or an equivalent offense in another state, and prohibition against assisted living facilities, adult day care centers or child welfare agencies hiring for certain compensated employment persons who have committed such an offense, see §§ 63.2-1719, 63.2-1720. As to report to children's residential facility for which a background check is being performed on whether the applicant has ever been convicted of or is the subject of pending charges for various crimes, including employing or permitting a minor to assist in an act constituting an offense under § 18.2-372 et seq., as set out in § 18.2-379, or an equivalent offense in another state, see § 63.2-1726.

Law Review.
For comment on the law of obscenity in Virginia, see 17 Wash. & Lee L. Rev. 322 (1960). For article on written obscenity, see 11 Wm. & Mary L. Rev. 106 (1969). For survey of Virginia criminal law and procedure for the year 1969-1970, see 56 Va. L. Rev. 1572 (1970). For survey of proposed changes in statutory regulation of obscenity in Virginia for the year 1970-1971, see 57 Va. L. Rev. 1636 (1971). For article, "Construction Law," see 45 U. Rich. L. Rev. 227 (2010). For annual survey of Virginia law article, "Criminal Law and Procedure," see 47 U. Rich. L. Rev. 143 (2012).

CASE NOTES

This section has passed constitutional muster. It has been found to give "adequate warning of the conduct proscribed" so as to permit the law to be fairly administered. United States v. Pryba, 674 F. Supp. 1504 (E.D. Va. 1987).

Exercise of police power. — The Commonwealth of Virginia, in the exercise of its police power, may properly determine that public exhibition of or traffic in obscenity may be contrary to the public interest. The Commonwealth, acting through the General Assembly, has made such a determination in enacting the state obscenity laws and authorizing local governing bodies to adopt similar local ordinances. KMA, Inc. v. City of Newport News, 228 Va. 365, 323 S.E.2d 78 (1984), cert. denied, 471 U.S. 1100, 105 S. Ct. 2324, 85 L. Ed. 2d 842 (1985).

Interpretation by Supreme Court. — For the purpose of testing the constitutionality of Virginia's statute, the interpretation by the Supreme Court is as definitive as if the statute had been amended by the legislature. Grove Press, Inc. v. Evans, 306 F. Supp. 1084 (E.D. Va. 1969).

The definition of obscenity adopted by Virginia courts fully complies with the constitutional standards prescribed by the Supreme Court. Grove Press, Inc. v. Evans, 306 F. Supp. 1084 (E.D. Va. 1969).

The definition of obscenity approved by Virginia's highest court is binding upon the state's trial courts and magistrates. Grove Press, Inc. v. Evans, 306 F. Supp. 1084 (E.D. Va. 1969).

The Supreme Court has narrowed the definition of obscenity by judicial construction. Price v. Commonwealth, 214 Va. 490, 201 S.E.2d 798 (1974).

"Obscenity." — Obscenity is defined in the following terms: Whether to the average person, applying contemporary community standards, the dominant theme of the material taken as a whole appeals to the prurient interest. Under this definition, as elaborated in subsequent cases, three elements must coalesce: It must be established that (a) the dominant theme of the material taken as a whole appeals to a prurient interest in sex; (b) the material is patently offensive because it affronts contemporary community standards relating to the description or representation of sexual matters; and (c) the material is utterly without redeeming social value. Grove Press, Inc. v. Evans, 306 F. Supp. 1084 (E.D. Va. 1969).

In the definition of obscenity three elements must coalesce: it must be established that (a) the dominant theme of the material taken as a whole appeals to a prurient interest in sex; (b) the material is patently offensive because it affronts contemporary community standards relating to the description or representation of sexual matters; and (c) the material is utterly without redeeming social value. Price v. Commonwealth, 213 Va. 113, 189 S.E.2d 324 (1972).

In *House v. Commonwealth*, 210 Va. 121, 169 S.E.2d 572 (1969), the Supreme Court expressly recognized that in determining whether a publication was constitutionally protected, Virginia courts were bound by the Supreme Court's definition of obscenity found in *Roth v. United States*, 354 U.S. 476, 77 S. Ct. 1304, 1 L. Ed. 2d 1498 (1957) as amplified and explained in *A Book Named "John Cleland's Memoirs of a Woman of Pleasure" v. Attorney Gen.*, 383 U.S. 413, 86 S. Ct. 975, 16 L. Ed. 2d 1 (1966). Consequently, in a prosecution charging the sale of obscene magazines, the Supreme Court found the evidence to be insufficient to support a conviction when measured by the following test: "Whether to the average person, applying contemporary community standards: (1) the dominant theme of the material taken as a whole appeals to a prurient interest; (2) that is a shameful or morbid interest because it affronts contemporary community standards relating to the description or representation of sexual matters; and (3) the material is utterly without redeeming social value." Grove Press, Inc. v. Evans, 306 F. Supp. 1084 (E.D. Va. 1969).

Sufficient evidence supported defendant's conviction under

§ 18.2-152.7:1, prohibiting harassment by computer, arising from e-mails defendant sent to the victim, because: (1) the common definition of the word "obscene" more accurately encompassed the type of communicative conduct proscribed by the statute, namely, that which was obscene, vulgar, profane, lewd, lascivious, or indecent, than did a definition in § 18.2-372, which was actually a definition of pornography; and (2) a reasonable fact finder could conclude that the language defendant used in the e-mails to the victim fit the common definition. Barson v. Commonwealth, 58 Va. App. 451, 711 S.E.2d 220, 2011 Va. App. LEXIS 228 (2011).

Court of appeals erred in affirming defendant's conviction for harassment by computer in violation § 18.2-152.7:1 because it should not have substituted a dictionary definition of "obscene" for that provided by the general assembly in § 18.2-372; the general assembly provided a definition of "obscene" in § 18.2-372 to comport with constitutional requirements, and there was no suggestion that the definition was constitutionally infirm. Barson v. Commonwealth, 284 Va. 67, 726 S.E.2d 292, 2012 Va. LEXIS 121 (2012).

Although defendant's behavior was inappropriate, it did not rise to the level of obscenity required under § 18.2-387, as defined in § 18.2-372, and defendant's conviction of indecent exposure was improper; nothing in the record suggested that defendant invited any sexual conduct with the victim, hinted at any sexual excitement on defendant's part, or, when defendant dropped defendant's pants upon exiting a bus (with defendant's back to the victim and running away from the victim), displayed defendant's sexual organs to the victim or to anyone else. A. M. v. Commonwealth, 2013 Va. App. LEXIS 46 (Feb. 12, 2013).

A prurient interest is a shameful or morbid interest, in sex. Price v. Commonwealth, 213 Va. 113, 189 S.E.2d 324 (1972).

Virginia juries have traditionally relied on local rather than statewide community standards. Price v. Commonwealth, 214 Va. 490, 201 S.E.2d 798 (1974).

It would be difficult, if not impossible, for a Virginia jury to formulate a statewide standard of obscenity, for the state comprises communities with a vast diversity of life styles. Materials which do not offend the community standards of the metropolitan areas might well be regarded as obscene by the standards of some rural communities. Price v. Commonwealth, 214 Va. 490, 201 S.E.2d 798 (1974).

To be obscene, conduct must violate contemporary community standards of sexual candor. Copeland v. Commonwealth, 31 Va. App. 512, 525 S.E.2d 9 (2000).

Expert testimony regarding community standards is not required because the fact finder may apply his or her knowledge in ascertaining the acceptable standard in the community. Copeland v. Commonwealth, 31 Va. App. 512, 525 S.E.2d 9 (2000).

Language held not obscene. — Where defendant left a voice mail message calling an attorney a "pussy," as he meant to thereby characterize the attorney as a cowardly or effeminate man, the word had no sexual connotations attached to it, and his references to excretory functions merely served to emphasize his belief in the attorney's cowardice, the message did not have as its dominant theme an appeal to the prurient interest in sex, nor did it go substantially beyond the customary limits of candor in the description or representation of such matters. Therefore, as a matter of law, defendant's language was not obscene. Allman v. Commonwealth, 43 Va. App. 104, 596 S.E.2d 531, 2004 Va. App. LEXIS 236 (2004), overruled in part by Barson v. Commonwealth, 58 Va. App. 451, 711 S.E.2d 220, 2011 Va. App. LEXIS 228 (Va. Ct. App. 2011).

Using the § 18.2-372 definition of "obscene," defendant's use of "whore" and repeated use of "fuck you" in an instant message were insufficient to permit a reasonable trier of fact to conclude the references were obscene. Although the words were sexually explicit, defendant's usage of the words was not erotic and did not have the purpose to appeal to a prurient interest in sex, but was used in a communication where defendant told the victim to leave defendant's roommate alone; use of the words, while offensive and coarse, was a method to show anger, contempt, or disgust with the victim and to direct the victim away from the roommate. Airhart v. Commonwealth, — Va. App. —, — S.E.2d —, 2007 Va. App. LEXIS 11 (Jan. 16, 2007).

While defendant used words which could be obscene in certain contexts, defendant used the offensive words as vulgar curse or swear words to communicate his frustration, anger, contempt or disgust with the victim. Accordingly, defendant's language failed to

meet the definition of obscene as required by case law and § 18.2-372 and defendant's conviction under § 18.2-427 was reversed. Lofgren v. Commonwealth, 55 Va. App. 116, 684 S.E.2d 223, 2009 Va. App. LEXIS 491 (2009).

Trial court erred in convicting defendant of harassment by computer in violation of § 18.2-152.7:1 because the evidence was insufficient to permit a reasonable trier of fact to conclude that the e-mails defendant sent were obscene under § 18.2-372; although the e-mails contained vulgar, offensive, and sexually explicit language, defendant's use of those words, considered as a whole and in the context of the marital discord and the angry, offensive tone and purpose of the e-mails, did not establish or support a factual or legal determination that he intended an appeal to the prurient interest in sex, but rather, the evidence showed that defendant wrote the e-mails solely to convey his anger and disgust and that he forwarded them to his family and friends to embarrass the victim. Barson v. Commonwealth, 2010 Va. App. LEXIS 427 (Nov. 2, 2010).

Court of appeals erred in affirming defendant's conviction for harassment by computer in violation of § 18.2-152.7:1 because defendant's emails to his wife, as offensive, vulgar, and disgusting their language could have been, did not meet the standard of obscenity provided by § 18.2-372. Barson v. Commonwealth, 284 Va. 67, 726 S.E.2d 292, 2012 Va. LEXIS 121 (2012).

Public obscenity is not constitutionally protected. Tyrone, Inc. v. Wilkinson, 410 F.2d 639 (4th Cir.), cert. denied, 396 U.S. 985, 90 S. Ct. 477, 24 L. Ed. 2d 449 (1969).

A portrayal of nudity is not, as a matter of law, a sufficient basis for a finding that a work is obscene. Price v. Commonwealth, 214 Va. 490, 201 S.E.2d 798 (1974).

Computer harassment. — Defendant was properly convicted of computer harassment in violation of § 18.2-152.7:1, as his e-mails to the victim expressed "an appeal to the prurient interest in sex," included "shameful" sexual suggestions that went "substantially beyond customary limits," made obscene proposals, and implicitly threatened "illegal or immoral" acts. Moter v. Commonwealth, 61 Va. App. 471, 737 S.E.2d 538, 2013 Va. App. LEXIS 54 (2013).

Seizure of copy of film for use as evidence. — In the enforcement of obscenity laws, a state or locality may seize single copies of films to preserve them for use as evidence, particularly where the seizure does not prevent continued exhibition of the films. KMA, Inc. v. City of Newport News, 228 Va. 365, 323 S.E.2d 78 (1984), cert. denied, 471 U.S. 1100, 105 S. Ct. 2324, 85 L. Ed. 2d 842 (1985).

Evidence held sufficient. — Evidence that defendant exposed his genitals, that he was clearly aroused, and that he was masturbating supported the jury's findings that his conduct went "substantially beyond" acceptable community standards, and were obscene under this section. Copeland v. Commonwealth, 31 Va. App. 512, 525 S.E.2d 9 (2000).

Despite a trial court expressing uncertainty as to whether the applicable standard under § 18.2-387 was one of indecency or one of obscenity, any error was harmless because the verdict convicting defendant would have been the same as a result of defendant's conduct of exposing his buttocks and breasts (he was a transvestite), in the early morning hours, on a street known for illegal prostitution, which was conduct that was intentional and done with the purpose of appealing to the prurient interest in sex. Willis v. Commonwealth, No. 0173-04-2, 2005 Va. App. LEXIS 58 (Ct. of Appeals Feb. 8, 2005).

§ 18.2-373. Obscene items enumerated.

Obscene items shall include:

(1) Any obscene book;

(2) Any obscene leaflet, pamphlet, magazine, booklet, picture, painting, bumper sticker, drawing, photograph, film, negative, slide, motion picture, videotape recording;

(3) Any obscene figure, object, article, instrument, novelty device, or recording or transcription used or intended to be used in disseminating any obscene song, ballad, words, or sounds; or

(4) Any obscene writing, picture or similar visual representation, or sound recording, stored in an electronic or other medium retrievable in a perceivable form.

History.

Code 1950, § 18.1-229; 1960, c. 233; 1975, cc. 14, 15; 1981, c. 293; 1989, c. 546; 2000, c. 1009.

Law Review.

For 2000 survey of Virginia criminal law and procedure, see 34 U. Rich. L. Rev. 749 (2000).

CASE NOTES

Applied in Educational Books, Inc. v. Commonwealth, 228 Va. 392, 323 S.E.2d 84 (1984).

§ 18.2-374. Production, publication, sale, possession, etc., of obscene items.

It shall be unlawful for any person knowingly to:

(1) Prepare any obscene item for the purposes of sale or distribution; or

(2) Print, copy, manufacture, produce, or reproduce any obscene item for purposes of sale or distribution; or

(3) Publish, sell, rent, lend, transport in intrastate commerce, or distribute or exhibit any obscene item, or offer to do any of these things; or

(4) Have in his possession with intent to sell, rent, lend, transport, or distribute any obscene item. Possession in public or in a public place of any obscene item as defined in this article shall be deemed prima facie evidence of a violation of this section.

For the purposes of this section, *"distribute"* shall mean delivery in person, by mail, messenger or by any other means by which obscene items as defined in this article may pass from one person, firm or corporation to another.

History.

Code 1950, § 18.1-228; 1960, c. 233; 1962, c. 289; 1970, c. 204; 1975, cc. 14, 15.

Cross references.

As to enhanced penalty for using a computer in connection with a violation of §§ 18.2-374, 18.2-375, or 18.2-376, see § 18.2-376.1.

Law Review.

For survey of Virginia criminal law and procedure for the year 1969-1970, see 56 Va. L. Rev. 1572 (1970). For survey of proposed changes in statutory regulation of obscenity in Virginia for the year 1970-1971, see 57 Va. L. Rev. 1636 (1971). For survey of Virginia criminal law and procedure for the year 1970-1971, see 57 Va. L. Rev. 1438 (1971).

Michie's Jurisprudence.

For related discussion, see 14B M.J. Photographs and Photographers, § 4; 16 M.J. Searches and Seizures, § 6; 18 M.J. Theaters, Shows and Fairs, § 2.

CASE NOTES

This section does not contravene Art. I, § 12 of the Constitution of Virginia. Star News, Inc. v. Commonwealth, No. 1785-96-1 (Ct. of Appeals Jan. 6, 1998).

Provision in subdivision (4) unconstitutional. — In 1962, subdivision (4) was amended by the addition of a presumption, which renders the statute unconstitutional. Grove Press, Inc. v. Evans, 306 F. Supp. 1084 (E.D. Va. 1969).

But severable. — The presumption is unconstitutional, but severable. The remaining portion of subdivision (4) is valid. Grove Press, Inc. v. Evans, 306 F. Supp. 1084 (E.D. Va. 1969).

This section frames offenses in language that conveys sufficiently definite warning as to the proscribed conduct when measured by common understanding and practices and gives adequate warning of the conduct proscribed and mark the boundaries sufficiently distinct for judges and juries fairly to administer the law. United States v. Pryba, 674 F. Supp. 1504 (E.D. Va. 1987).

"Obscenity." — Obscenity is defined in *Roth v. United States*, 354 U.S. 476, 77 S. Ct. 1304, 1 L. Ed. 2d 1498 (1957) in the following terms: Whether to the average person, applying contemporary community standards, the dominant theme of the material taken as a whole appeals to prurient interest. Under this definition, as elaborated in subsequent cases, three elements must coalesce: It must be established that (a) the dominant theme of the material taken as a whole appeals to a prurient interest in sex; (b) the material is patently offensive because it affronts contemporary community standards relating to the description or representation of sexual matters; and (c) the material is utterly without redeeming social value. House v. Commonwealth, 210 Va. 121, 169 S.E.2d 572 (1969).

Section does not prohibit private possession of obscene material. — This section has not been construed to prohibit the private possession of obscene material, and there is no basis for concluding that Virginia courts would endow it with such a strained and unnatural meaning. Grove Press, Inc. v. Evans, 306 F. Supp. 1084 (E.D. Va. 1969).

Writing which proposes sexual conduct in violation of law. — It is not a per se violation of community standards for a writing to propose an act of sexual conduct that is in violation of the law. Hartman v. Commonwealth, No. 0569-98-3 (Ct. of Appeals Mar. 30, 1999).

Movie films are to be accorded the same constitutional protection as books. Greenmount Sales, Inc. v. Davila, 344 F. Supp. 860 (E.D. Va. 1972), aff'd in part and rev'd in part, 479 F.2d 591 (4th Cir. 1973).

Nudity is not necessarily obscenity. House v. Commonwealth, 210 Va. 121, 169 S.E.2d 572 (1969).

The determination whether a particular motion picture, book, or other work of expression is obscene is not merely a factual matter on which a jury's verdict is conclusive, but also involves an issue of constitutional law which must ultimately be decided by the court. House v. Commonwealth, 210 Va. 121, 169 S.E.2d 572 (1969).

It cannot be assumed that jurors in themselves necessarily express or reflect community standards. House v. Commonwealth, 210 Va. 121, 169 S.E.2d 572 (1969).

Expert evidence. — To sanction convictions without expert evidence of community standards encourages the jury to condemn as obscene such conduct or material as is personally distasteful or offensive to the particular juror. House v. Commonwealth, 210 Va. 121, 169 S.E.2d 572 (1969).

Burden of proof. — Since this section provides punishment for "every person who knowingly ... distributes ... any obscene item," the burden is on the Commonwealth to show that magazines are obscene and that a defendant knew they were obscene when he distributed them to retail dealers. House v. Commonwealth, 210 Va. 121, 169 S.E.2d 572 (1969).

Necessity for judicial determination that matter is in fact obscene. — A person may not be forced to go through the hardship of defending himself against a criminal prosecution — with its consequent chilling effect on him and the community at large — for possessing, selling, or promoting, etc., publications or film without the government first having judicially ascertained whether the matter for the possession, etc., of which he is being prosecuted is, in fact, obscene. Greenmount Sales, Inc. v. Davila, 344 F. Supp. 860 (E.D. Va. 1972), aff'd in part and rev'd in part, 479 F.2d 591 (4th Cir. 1973).

Unconstitutional seizure. — A seizure of allegedly obscene books on the authority of a warrant issued on the strength of the conclusory assertion of a single police officer, without any scrutiny by the judge of any materials considered obscene, is an unconstitutional seizure. Lee Art Theatre, Inc. v. Commonwealth, 210 Va. 315, 170 S.E.2d 769 (1969).

Conviction of possessing and exhibiting lewd and obscene motion pictures in violation of this section was reversed because of admission in evidence of films in question which were seized under authority of warrant issued by justice of the peace solely upon conclusory assertions of police officer without any inquiry by the justice of the peace into the factual basis for the officer's conclusions. Lee Art Theatre, Inc. v. Virginia, 392 U.S. 636, 88 S. Ct. 2103, 20 L. Ed. 2d 1313 (1968).

A city is simply entitled to retain single copies of allegedly obscene material for purposes of prosecution. Greenmount Sales, Inc. v. Davila, 479 F.2d 591 (4th Cir. 1973).

Where only single copies of allegedly obscene materials were seized and others were left on the shelves, neither the author's First Amendment right to expression nor the public's right to know is infringed. Such seizure by the police is a procedure justified by the requirements of effective law enforcement and is not prohibited by the First Amendment as a prior restraint on the circulation and dissemination of books in violation of the constitutional restrictions against abridgment of freedom of speech and press. Greenmount Sales, Inc. v. Davila, 479 F.2d 591 (4th Cir. 1973).

Evidence of probable cause for arrest. — There was no evidence of probable cause upon which the officers could have lawfully arrested defendant for violation of the obscenity law, when in searching for marijuana, one of the officers opened a chest of drawers belonging to defendant and found in it seven "nude" pictures. There was no prima facie evidence that defendant was violating the law. Upton v. Commonwealth, 211 Va. 445, 177 S.E.2d 528 (1970).

Evidence was insufficient to support a conviction where the evidence showed that the defendant threw a magazine at a minor, but the magazine was destroyed before trial, and the only evidence of its content was the minor's testimony that he thought it was a Playboy magazine and that it had photographs of "like dirty stuff." Hartman v. Commonwealth, No. 0569-98-3 (Ct. of Appeals Mar. 30, 1999).

Evidence that defendant mailed an envelope containing obscene photographs to a television station office in Hampton, that the photographs depicted defendant in various stages of undress, and that defendant included personal information as an invitation for a news anchor to contact defendant, supported defendant's conviction for distributing obscene material under § 18.2-374. Newby v. Commonwealth, 2009 Va. App. LEXIS 231 (May 19, 2009).

Applied in Wall Distribs., Inc. v. City of Newport News, 228 Va. 358, 323 S.E.2d 75 (1984); Educational Books, Inc. v. Commonwealth, 228 Va. 392, 323 S.E.2d 84 (1984); Educational Books, Inc. v. Commonwealth, 3 Va. App. 384, 349 S.E.2d 903 (1986).

§ 18.2-374.1. Production, publication, sale, financing, etc., of child pornography; presumption as to age; severability.

A. For purposes of this article and Article 4 (§ 18.2-362 et seq.) of this chapter, "child pornography" means sexually explicit visual material which utilizes or has as a subject an identifiable minor. An identifiable minor is a person who was a minor at the time the visual depiction was created, adapted, or modified; or whose image as a minor was used in creating, adapting or modifying the visual depiction; and who is recognizable as an actual person by the person's face, likeness, or other distinguishing characteristic, such as a unique birthmark or other recognizable feature; and shall not be construed to require proof of the actual identity of the identifiable minor.

For the purposes of this article and Article 4 (§ 18.2-362 et seq.) of this chapter, the term "sexu-ally explicit visual material" means a picture, photograph, drawing, sculpture, motion picture film, digital image, including such material stored in a computer's temporary Internet cache when three or more images or streaming videos are present, or similar visual representation which depicts sexual bestiality, a lewd exhibition of nudity, as nudity is defined in § 18.2-390, or sexual excitement, sexual conduct or sadomasochistic abuse, as also defined in § 18.2-390, or a book, magazine or pamphlet which contains such a visual representation. An undeveloped photograph or similar visual material may be sexually explicit material notwithstanding that processing or other acts may be required to make its sexually explicit content apparent.

B. A person shall be guilty of production of child pornography who:

1. Accosts, entices or solicits a person less than 18 years of age with intent to induce or force such person to perform in or be a subject of child pornography; or

2. Produces or makes or attempts or prepares to produce or make child pornography; or

3. Who knowingly takes part in or participates in the filming, photographing, or other production of child pornography by any means; or

4. Knowingly finances or attempts or prepares to finance child pornography.

5. [Repealed.]

B1. [Repealed.]

C1. Any person who violates this section, when the subject of the child pornography is a child less than 15 years of age, shall be punished by not less than five years nor more than 30 years in a state correctional facility. However, if the person is at least seven years older than the subject of the child pornography the person shall be punished by a term of imprisonment of not less than five years nor more than 30 years in a state correctional facility, five years of which shall be a mandatory minimum term of imprisonment. Any person who commits a second or subsequent violation of this section where the person is at least seven years older than the subject shall be punished by a term of imprisonment of not less than 15 years nor more than 40 years, 15 years of which shall be a mandatory minimum term of imprisonment.

C2. Any person who violates this section, when the subject of the child pornography is a person at least 15 but less than 18 years of age, shall be punished by not less than one year nor more than 20 years in a state correctional facility. However, if the person is at least seven years older than the subject of the child pornography the person shall be punished by term of imprisonment of not less than three years nor more than 30 years in a state correctional facility, three years of which shall be a mandatory minimum term of imprisonment. Any person who commits a second or subsequent violation of this section when he is at least seven years older than the subject shall be punished by a term of imprisonment of not less than 10 years nor more than 30 years, 10 years of which shall be a mandatory minimum term of imprisonment.

C3. The mandatory minimum terms of imprisonment prescribed for violations of this section shall be served consecutively with any other sentence.

D. For the purposes of this section it may be inferred by text, title or appearance that a person who is depicted as or presents the appearance of being less than 18 years of age in sexually explicit visual material is less than 18 years of age.

E. Venue for a prosecution under this section may lie in the jurisdiction where the unlawful act occurs or where any sexually explicit visual material associated with a violation of this section is produced, reproduced, found, stored, or possessed.

F. The provisions of this section shall be severable and, if any of its provisions shall be held unconstitutional by a court of competent jurisdiction, then the decision of such court shall not affect or impair any of the remaining provisions.

History.

1979, c. 348; 1983, c. 524; 1986, c. 585; 1992, c. 234; 1995, c. 839; 2007, cc. 418, 759, 823; 2013, cc. 761, 774.

Cross references.

As to Sex Offenders and Crimes Against Minors Registry, see § 9.1-900 et seq. As to the Child Pornography Images Registry, see § 19.2-390.3. For provision that records involving complaints of sexual abuse of a child, including the display of the child in sexually explicit visual material, as defined in § 18.2-374.1, and contributing to the delinquency of a minor in violation of § 18.2-371, be made available to the attorney for the Commonwealth and the local law-enforcement agency, see § 63.2-1503 D. For definition of "barrier crime" as including a conviction of obscenity offenses as set out in § 18.2-374.1, and prohibition against assisted living facilities, adult day care centers or child welfare agencies hiring for certain compensated employment persons who have committed such an offense, see §§ 63.2-1719, 63.2-1720. As to report to children's residential facility for which a background check is being performed on whether the applicant has ever been convicted of or is the subject of pending charges for various crimes, including obscenity offenses as set out in § 18.2-374.1, or an equivalent offense in another state, see § 63.2-1726. For provision making it unlawful for any person to operate a family day home if he, or if he knows that any other person who resides in the home, has been convicted of a felony in violation of this section, see § 63.2-1727.

Editor's note.

Acts 2013, cc. 761 and 774, cl. 2 provides: "That the provisions of this act may result in a net increase in periods of imprisonment or commitment. Pursuant to § 30-19.1:4, the estimated amount of the necessary appropriation cannot be determined for periods of imprisonment in state adult correctional facilities; therefore, Chapter 3 of the Acts of Assembly of 2012, Special Session I, requires the Virginia Criminal Sentencing Commission to assign a minimum fiscal impact of $50,000. Pursuant to § 30-19.1:4, the estimated amount of the necessary appropriation cannot be determined for periods of commitment to the custody of the Department of Juvenile Justice."

The 2013 amendments.

The 2013 amendments by cc. 761 and 774 are identical, and added subsection C3.

Law Review.

For survey of Virginia criminal law for the year 1978-1979, see 66 Va. L. Rev. 241 (1980). For annual survey article on legal issues involving children, see 38 U. Rich. L. Rev. 161 (2003). For 2007 annual survey article, "Criminal Law and Procedure," see 42 U. Rich. L. Rev. 311 (2007). For annual survey article, "Criminal Law

and Procedure," see 46 U. Rich. L. Rev. 59 (2011). For note, "Sex, Cells, and SORNA: Applying Sex Offender Registration Laws to Sexting Cases," see 52 Wm. & Mary L. Rev. 1717 (2011).

Michie's Jurisprudence.

For related discussion, see 9B M.J. Infants, §§ 81, 89.

CASE NOTES

Objectionable provisions of subsection A held severable. — The phrase "obscene for children," and the definition thereof, were severable from the remainder of the definition of "sexually explicit visual material" set forth in subsection A as it read in 1979, and the remainder of the section met all of the requirements of New York v. Ferber, 458 U.S. 747, 102 S. Ct. 3348, 73 L. Ed. 2d 1113 (1982) and was constitutional. Foster v. Commonwealth, 6 Va. App. 313, 369 S.E.2d 688 (1988) (decided under section as it read in 1979).

Elements set forth in the 1979 version of subdivisions B 1 and B 2 met the scienter requirement of New York v. Ferber, 458 U.S. 747, 102 S. Ct. 3348, 73 L. Ed. 2d 1113 (1982). Foster v. Commonwealth, 6 Va. App. 313, 369 S.E.2d 688 (1988) (decided under section as it read in 1979).

The paramount legislative goal of this section was to protect children from the harm they suffer when they are induced to become models for such materials, irrespective of the motive or intent of the offender. Freeman v. Commonwealth, 223 Va. 301, 288 S.E.2d 461 (1982).

Compelling interest of state in protecting children. — The state has a compelling interest, one central to its right to survive, in protecting its children from treatment it determines is physically or psychologically injurious to youth, and this section is intended to further the state's interest by punishing and deterring such treatment. Freeman v. Commonwealth, 223 Va. 301, 288 S.E.2d 461 (1982).

Relationship with federal sentencing laws. — Because defendant's prior 1984 conviction under subdivision B 2 of § 18.2-374.1 categorically qualified as the type of conviction Congress sought to include as a predicate conviction within 18 U.S.C.S. § 2252A(b)(1)'s broadly phrased sentencing enhancement, defendant's sentence was affirmed. United States v. Colson, 683 F.3d 507, 2012 U.S. App. LEXIS 12936 (4th Cir. 2012).

Effect on adult's First Amendment rights incidental. — The process of production from which the harm flows cannot effectively be curtailed unless the profit motive is contained. Whatever restriction the distribution penalties impose upon the First Amendment rights of adults who want to sell or view child pornography is merely an effect incidental to the achievement of the goal this section pursues. Freeman v. Commonwealth, 223 Va. 301, 288 S.E.2d 461 (1982).

No constitutional requirement to define obscenity by adult standards. — In the enactment of this section to protect children exploited by adults in the production of pornography, the legislature is not constitutionally required to define obscenity by adult standards. Freeman v. Commonwealth, 223 Va. 301, 288 S.E.2d 461 (1982).

Material depicting lewd exhibition of a juvenile's genitals is "hard core" obscenity for children. Freeman v. Commonwealth, 223 Va. 301, 288 S.E.2d 461 (1982).

Photographing of exposed nipples, while within the literal definition of nudity under § 18.2-390, is not, without more, the lewd exhibition of nudity required under this section as it read in 1979. Foster v. Commonwealth, 6 Va. App. 313, 369 S.E.2d 688 (1988) (decided under section as it read in 1979).

In a prosecution under this section, the inquiry is whether the material in issue is obscene for children. If the evidence shows that it is, the offense is complete, and how the defendant may have regarded it is irrelevant. Freeman v. Commonwealth, 223 Va. 301, 288 S.E.2d 461 (1982).

The scienter requirement of this section is satisfied if the defendant was aware of the nature of the material in issue, even if he did not know it was illegal. Freeman v. Commonwealth, 223 Va. 301, 288 S.E.2d 461 (1982).

Jurors are qualified to judge a picture from a child's viewpoint and decide what effects it may have and whether it has any redeeming social value for the average member of the juvenile community. Freeman v. Commonwealth, 223 Va. 301, 288 S.E.2d 461 (1982).

Each instance of reproduction of child pornography is a separate offense. — Where defendant was observed over a period of hours printing four distinct images of child pornography from the Internet at a public library, double jeopardy protection did not preclude defendant's conviction for each of the four instances of reproduction of child pornography under § 18.2-374.1, since the intent of the legislature was to consider each reproduction of an item of sexually explicit visual material as a unit of prosecution. Slavek v. Hinkle, 359 F. Supp. 2d 473, 2005 U.S. Dist. LEXIS 4107 (E.D. Va. 2005).

By using the word "a" followed by a succession of singular nouns in the definition of sexually explicit visual material in subsection A of § 18.2-374.1, the Virginia legislature has demonstrated its clear intent that possession of a single photograph could constitute an offense under § 18.2-374.1 and that multiple punishments would result from multiple violations of the statute. Accordingly, the permissible unit of prosecution for possession of child pornography under subdivision B 4 of § 18.2-374.1 corresponds to the number of individual items of sexually explicit visual material, and the trial court correctly ruled that appellant's convictions on the child pornography charges were not multiplicitous. Mason v. Commonwealth, 49 Va. App. 39, 636 S.E.2d 480, 2006 Va. App. LEXIS 505 (2006).

Three separate images not required. — Defendant's convictions for possession of child pornography and possession of child pornography second or subsequent offense was appropriate because subsection A of § 18.2-374.1, which defined "child pornography," did not require that each conviction be supported by three separate images containing child pornography. Chapman v. Commonwealth, 56 Va. App. 725, 697 S.E.2d 20, 2010 Va. App. LEXIS 340 (2010).

Evidence of prior sexual conduct between photographer and child admissible. — In a prosecution under this section for photographing a nude five-year-old in prurient positions, evidence of prior sexual conduct between the photographer and the child was admissible to show a motive or purpose which the photographer might have had in taking such pictures. Freeman v. Commonwealth, 223 Va. 301, 288 S.E.2d 461 (1982).

Photographs of nude daughter failed to prove violation of subdivision B 3. — Because the photographs of defendant's nude daughter did not constitute lewd exhibitions of nudity, the evidence failed to establish that defendant sought to reproduce sexually explicit material involving a minor within the purview of subdivision B 3. Foster v. Commonwealth, No. 0369-87-2 (Ct. of Appeals Nov. 21, 1989).

Photographs considered sexually explicit. — Photographs, which contained as their primary focus the close-up views of the teenager's genitalia, depicted the teenager sitting with her knees up to her breast and her legs widely spread to expose a frontal view of her genitalia were sexually explicit within the meaning of this section. Asa v. Commonwealth, 17 Va. App. 714, 441 S.E.2d 26 (1994).

Mere presence of nudity in a photograph, even child nudity, does not constitute child pornography as that term is defined by Virginia law; instead, the picture must contain a lewd exhibition of nudity. United States v. Doyle, 650 F.3d 460, 2011 U.S. App. LEXIS 10361 (4th Cir. 2011).

Evidence was sufficient to show defendant intended to induce child to be the subject of sexually explicit visual material from his actions in showing child close-up photographs of male and female genitalia; in telling her not to tell anyone what had happened the day he showed her the pictures; in defendant's handwritten account asking her to model as his corpse; and in asking her to accompany him when he took pictures of dead children. Foster v. Commonwealth, 6 Va. App. 313, 369 S.E.2d 688 (1988) (decided under section as it read in 1979).

Evidence was insufficient to show that defendant intended to induce or force child to perform in or be the subject of sexually explicit visual material since the evidence only showed that defendant photographed child in a bathing suit and showed her pictures of nude children he had taken and had another child read a typewritten introduction to a photograph album that stated the album contained nude pictures. Foster v. Commonwealth, 6 Va. App. 313, 369 S.E.2d 688 (1988) (decided under section as it read in 1979).

Evidence was sufficient to sustain conviction. — Evidence was sufficient to support defendant's convictions for forcible sodomy, in violation § 18.2-67.1 A, rape, in violation of § 18.2-61, and producing sexually explicit material, in violation of § 18.2-374.1, where evidence showed that a victim and defendant engaged in oral sex while the victim's mother was at work, during a strip poker game in which the victim ran out of clothes and had to do favors for defendant, which included putting defendant's penis in the victim's mouth and defendant putting defendant's penis in the victim's vagina; in addition, there was testimony that a victim made videos at defendant's direction and that these were termed a type of punishment, and the videos detailed various instances of sexual abuse, at least one of which was seen by the victims' 13-year-old brother. Cairns v. Commonwealth, 40 Va. App. 271, 579 S.E.2d 340, 2003 Va. App. LEXIS 221 (2003).

Concurrent sentences proper. — Trial court followed the clear mandate of subdivision C1 of § 18.2-374.1 in convicting defendant of six counts of production of child pornography, first offense, for taking six sexually explicit photographs within a two-minute window and sentenced defendant to six minimum terms to be served concurrently with each other as *Bullock v. Commonwealth*, 631 S.E.2d 334 (Va. App. 2006), was not a predicate for the application of stare decisis here as *Bullock's* holding was limited to the imposition of multiple mandatory minimum sentences under § 18.2-53.1, and § 18.2-53.1 specified that the punishment for violating the statute was to be separate and apart from, and was to be made to run consecutively with, any punishment received for the primary felony. Commonwealth v. Jefferson, 60 Va. App. 749, 732 S.E.2d 728, 2012 Va. App. LEXIS 323 (2012).

Subdivision C1 of § 18.2-374.1 does not prohibit mandatory minimum sentences imposed under that section from running concurrently as: (1) § 18.2-12.1, defining mandatory minimum, does not require that mandatory minimum sentences run consecutively; (2) § 19.2-308 provides that when any person is convicted of two or more offenses, and sentenced to confinement, such sentences shall not run concurrently, unless expressly ordered by the court; and (3) if subdivision C1 of § 18.2-374.1 were interpreted to require the mandatory minimum sentences to run consecutively, it would render superfluous the words the Virginia General Assembly used in at least 11 other criminal statutes explicitly requiring that mandatory minimum sentences run consecutively. Commonwealth v. Jefferson, 60 Va. App. 749, 732 S.E.2d 728, 2012 Va. App. LEXIS 323 (2012).

Trial court did not abuse its discretion in ordering defendant's six subdivision C1 sentences to run concurrently with each other as: (1) § 18.2-12.1, defining mandatory minimum, did not require that mandatory minimum sentences run consecutively; (2) § 19.2-308 provided that when any person was convicted of two or more offenses, and sentenced to confinement, such sentences were not to run concurrently, unless expressly ordered by the court; and (3) if subdivision C1 of § 18.2-374.1 were interpreted to require the mandatory minimum sentences to run consecutively, it would render superfluous the words the Virginia general assembly used in at least 11 other criminal statutes explicitly requiring that mandatory minimum sentences run consecutively. Commonwealth v. Jefferson, 60 Va. App. 749, 732 S.E.2d 728, 2012 Va. App. LEXIS 323 (2012).

Actual innocence not proven. — Despite the child victim's recantation, the prisoner failed to establish actual innocence with respect to two charges against him that were nolle prossed — i.e., producing sexually explicit material involving a person under the age of 18, in violation of subdivisions B 2 and B 3 of § 18.2-374.1. At best, the new evidence the prisoner offered indicated that he was actually innocent of producing any pornographic material utilizing the child victim, but the evidence failed to demonstrate that it was more likely than not that no reasonable juror would have found the prisoner guilty beyond a reasonable doubt of producing pornographic material depicting a person, other than the child victim, who was under the age of 18. DiCaprio-Cuozzo v. Johnson, 2010 U.S. Dist. LEXIS 108702 (E.D. Va. Oct. 12, 2010).

Applied in Frantz v. Commonwealth, 9 Va. App. 348, 388 S.E.2d 273 (1990).

CIRCUIT COURT OPINIONS

Not overbroad or vague. — Rebuttable permissive presumption contained in subsection D does not appear to contain any constitutional infirmity, because it is neither vague nor overbroad. Commonwealth v. Simone, 63 Va. Cir. 216, 2003 Va. Cir. LEXIS 362 (Portsmouth 2003).

Severability. — Under subsection E [now subsection F], even if the court were to find that some sections of the Virginia Child Pornography statute overbroad or vague and thus unconstitutional, the remaining provisions would not be affected or impaired because the provisions were severable. Commonwealth v. Simone, 63 Va. Cir. 216, 2003 Va. Cir. LEXIS 362 (Portsmouth 2003).

Images must be of actual children. — Virginia child pornography statute applies to images that utilize, or have as their subject, an actual male or female child. Commonwealth v. Simone, 63 Va. Cir. 216, 2003 Va. Cir. LEXIS 362 (Portsmouth 2003).

Definition of "sexually explicit visual material." — The plain language of the definition encompasses something less than the 100 percent mirror image of an actual child. Commonwealth v. Simone, 63 Va. Cir. 216, 2003 Va. Cir. LEXIS 362 (Portsmouth 2003).

Evidence insufficient to show lewd exhibition of nudity. — In a case in which defendant was charged with possession of child pornography, in violation of § 18.2-374.1:1, and defendant moved to dismiss, the evidence failed to support a finding that the offending material satisfied the element of a sexually explicit showing of a lewd exhibition of nudity required under § 18.2-374.1. The photograph depicted a female from the top of the breasts to mid thigh, she had her arms clasped across the breasts, exposing a small portion of the areola of one and possibly two breasts, and due to the grainy nature of the photograph, it was unclear whether one nipple was visible; while the photograph satisfied the definition of nudity set forth in § 18.2-390, a photograph of a young girl's exposed nipples was not, without more, a lewd exhibition of nudity. Commonwealth v. Ting Yi Oei, 2009 Va. Cir. LEXIS 115 (Loudoun County Mar. 31, 2009).

Motion to dismiss. — Defendant failed to show that trial counsel's arguments to support a motion to dismiss under § 19.2-294 fell below an objective standard of reasonableness state charges for producing child pornography under § 18.2-374.1 and federal charges for possession of images of child pornography under 18 U.S.C.S. 2252A(a)(5)(B) involved two distinct acts and required different evidence to sustain them; the federal possession charge required only a showing that the pornographic images defendant possessed in 2004 were produced by someone using materials that had entered interstate commerce, and the state charge of production required the Commonwealth to show that defendant created the pornographic images in 2003. Allen v. Johnson, 2012 Va. Cir. LEXIS 72 (Fairfax County July 20, 2012).

§ 18.2-374.1:1. Possession, reproduction, distribution, solicitation, and facilitation of child pornography; penalty.

A. Any person who knowingly possesses child pornography is guilty of a Class 6 felony.

B. Any person who commits a second or subsequent violation of subsection A is guilty of a Class 5 felony.

C. Any person who (i) reproduces by any means, including by computer, sells, gives away, distributes, electronically transmits, displays with lascivious intent, purchases, or possesses with intent to sell, give away, distribute, transmit, or display child pornography with lascivious intent or (ii) commands, entreats, or otherwise attempts to persuade another person to send, submit, transfer or provide to him any child pornography in order to gain entry into a group, association, or assembly of persons engaged in trading or sharing child pornography shall be punished by not less than five years nor more than 20 years in a state correctional facility. Any person who commits a second or subsequent violation under this subsection shall be punished by

a term of imprisonment of not less than five years nor more than 20 years in a state correctional facility, five years of which shall be a mandatory minimum term of imprisonment. The mandatory minimum terms of imprisonment prescribed for violations of this section shall be served consecutively with any other sentence.

D. Any person who intentionally operates an Internet website for the purpose of facilitating the payment for access to child pornography is guilty of a Class 4 felony.

E. All child pornography shall be subject to lawful seizure and forfeiture pursuant to § 19.2-386.31.

F. For purposes of this section it may be inferred by text, title or appearance that a person who is depicted as or presents the appearance of being less than 18 years of age in sexually explicit visual material is less than 18 years of age.

G. Venue for a prosecution under this section may lie in the jurisdiction where the unlawful act occurs or where any child pornography is produced, reproduced, found, stored, received, or possessed in violation of this section.

H. The provisions of this section shall not apply to any such material that is possessed for a bona fide medical, scientific, governmental, law-enforcement, or judicial purpose by a physician, psychologist, scientist, attorney, employee of a law-enforcement agency, or judge who possesses such material in the course of conducting his professional duties as such.

History.

1992, c. 745; 1993, c. 853; 1994, c. 511; 1999, c. 659; 2003, cc. 935, 938; 2004, c. 995; 2007, cc. 759, 823; 2009, c. 379; 2011, cc. 399, 416; 2012, c. 369; 2013, cc. 761, 774.

Cross references.

As to Sex Offenders and Crimes Against Minors Registry, see § 9.1-900 et seq. As to the Child Pornography Images Registry, see § 19.2-390.3. As to public and private schools blocking Internet access to child pornography as set out in this section, see § 22.1-70.2. For definition of "barrier crime" as including a conviction of possession of child pornography as set out in § 18.2-374.1:1, or an equivalent offense in another state, and prohibition against assisted living facilities, adult day care centers or child welfare agencies hiring for certain compensated employment persons who have committed such an offense, see §§ 63.2-1719, 63.2-1720.

Editor's note.

Acts 2012, c. 369, cl. 2, provides: "That the provisions of this act may result in a net increase in periods of imprisonment or commitment. Pursuant to § 30-19.1:4, the estimated amount of the necessary appropriation cannot be determined for periods of imprisonment in state adult correctional facilities; therefore, Chapter 890 of the Acts of Assembly of 2011 requires the Virginia Criminal Sentencing Commission to assign a minimum fiscal impact of $50,000. Pursuant to § 30-19.1:4, the estimated amount of the necessary appropriation cannot be determined for periods of commitment to the custody of the Department of Juvenile Justice."

Acts 2013, cc. 761 and 774, cl. 2 provides: "That the provisions of this act may result in a net increase in periods of imprisonment or commitment. Pursuant to § 30-19.1:4, the estimated amount of the necessary appropriation cannot be determined for periods of imprisonment in state adult correctional facilities; therefore, Chapter 3 of the Acts of Assembly of 2012, Special Session I, requires the Virginia Criminal Sentencing Commission to assign a minimum fiscal impact of $50,000. Pursuant to § 30-19.1:4, the estimated amount of the necessary appropriation cannot be determined for periods of commitment to the custody of the Department of Juvenile Justice."

The 2009 amendments.

The 2009 amendment by c. 379 added subsection G and redesignated former subsection G as subsection H; and substituted "material that is possessed" for "material which is possessed" in subsection H.

The 2011 amendments.

The 2011 amendments by cc. 399 and 416 are identical, and in subsection H, inserted "law-enforcement" and "employee of a law-enforcement agency."

The 2012 amendments.

The 2012 amendment by c. 369, in the first sentence of subsection C, added the clause (i) designator and clause (ii), and made a related change.

The 2013 amendments.

The 2013 amendments by cc. 761 and 774 are identical, and added the third sentence of subsection C.

Law Review.

For annual survey article on legal issues involving children, see 38 U. Rich. L. Rev. 161 (2003). For annual survey, "A Look Back and Forward: Legislative and Regulatory Highlights for 2008 and 2009 and a Discussion of Juvenile Transfer," see 44 U. Rich. L. Rev. 53 (2009).

CASE NOTES

Venue proper in county where unlawful act occurred. — Because appellant admitted to viewing the nude images of the victim in her Lebanon residence, which was located in Russell County, Virginia, the evidence established a strong presumption that the offense of child pornography was committed within that jurisdiction and that, under § 18.2-374.1:1, venue was proper in that county. Klewer v. Commonwealth, 2012 Va. App. LEXIS 315 (Oct. 9, 2012).

No ex post facto violation found. — Despite defendant's contention on appeal that the child pornography material he was convicted of possessing was either created or last accessed at a time when such offense was a Class 1 misdemeanor, and hence, his conviction violated his constitutional right to be free from ex post facto punishment, because the Commonwealth adequately showed that two months after the crime became a felony, defendant was aware of, and knowingly possessed said materials on his computer and accessories, his conviction for the same was upheld. Moreover, the mere fact that some of defendant's acts proving his possession in September, 2003 occurred before the change in the law did not preclude application of the new law, and the trial court properly found that defendant continued to possess the child pornographic images at the time of his arrest, notwithstanding the date the pornographic images were originally downloaded. Bodine v. Commonwealth, — Va. App. —, — S.E.2d —, 2006 Va. App. LEXIS 509 (Nov. 7, 2006).

Evidence found in temporary internet cache sufficient. — Defendant's convictions for possession of child pornography, in violation of subsection A of § 18.2-374.1:1, and possession of child pornography, second or subsequent offense, in violation of subsection B of § 18.2-374.1:1, were appropriate because the Commonwealth's introduction of 20 examples of child pornography, which were found in the temporary internet cache of defendant's computer, was certainly sufficient to prove 10 counts of possession of child pornography. Chapman v. Commonwealth, 56 Va. App. 725, 697 S.E.2d 20, 2010 Va. App. LEXIS 340 (2010).

Evidence at trial. — In a prosecution for possession of child pornography under this section, the best evidence rule did not govern digital images because an expert testified that a bit for bit copy of defendant's hard drive was considered forensically to be an original, and defendant did not assert that the admitted photographs or video clips admitted into evidence had been manipulated or altered. Midkiff v. Commonwealth, 280 Va. 216, 694 S.E.2d 576, 2010 Va. LEXIS 61 (2010).

Evidence insufficient to show dominion and control. — Convictions for possession of child pornography were reversed because defendant, as a prior tenant, did not have sufficient dominion and control over the computer on the alleged date to permit the conclusion that he possessed the images contained thereon on that date; among other things, there was no evidence to suggest he made any effort to retrieve the computer or that he retained a key to the apartment. Simone v. Commonwealth, No. 0551-04-1, 2005 Va. App. LEXIS 99 (Ct. of Appeals Mar. 15, 2005).

Evidence sufficient to support conviction. — Evidence that the computer, located in a residence over which defendant had exclusive control, contained "quick desktop access" to a folder containing the subject images, that defendant was the registered user of the computer's operating system, and that there was a software setting that had been manually set to disallow file sharing was sufficient to support defendant's conviction for misdemeanor possession of child pornography. Kromer v. Commonwealth, 45 Va. App. 812, 613 S.E.2d 871, 2005 Va. App. LEXIS 227 (2005).

Evidence was sufficient to convict appellant of possession of child pornography under § 18.2-374.1:1 because it was clear from appellant's text conversations with the victim's mother and her own statements to the police that she accessed nude images of the minor victim. Klewer v. Commonwealth, 2012 Va. App. LEXIS 315 (Oct. 9, 2012).

Jury instructions. — Defendant's convictions for possession of child pornography, in violation of subsection A of § 18.2-374.1:1, and possession of child pornography, second or subsequent offense, in violation of subsection B of § 18.2-374.1:1, were appropriate because the trial court informed the jurors as to the essential elements of the offense by instructing them that the evidence must prove beyond a reasonable doubt that defendant "knowingly possessed" child pornography in order to convict him under subsection A; thus, the trial court did not err in granting that instruction. Chapman v. Commonwealth, 56 Va. App. 725, 697 S.E.2d 20, 2010 Va. App. LEXIS 340 (2010).

CIRCUIT COURT OPINIONS

Does not apply to images that "appear to be" of children. — Neither the Virginia Code section criminalizing possession of child pornography, nor the definition of "sexually explicit visual material," refer to images that appear to be of children, as did the constitutionally objectionable portions of the Child Pornography Prevention Act of 1996 (CPPA), 18 U.S.C.S. § 2256; furthermore, the statute specifically requires that the material at issue utilize or have as its subject a "person." Commonwealth v. Simone, 63 Va. Cir. 216, 2003 Va. Cir. LEXIS 362 (Portsmouth 2003).

This section is not overly broad because the clear language of the statute reveals that it only applies to images utilizing actual children; the Virginia General Assembly not only included language in the statute to limit its application to images utilizing actual children, it also included language providing that the statute does not apply to any material having a bona fide artistic, medical, scientific, educational, religious, government, judicial, or other proper purpose; therefore the statute was narrowly tailored to achieve its purpose, as required by the strict scrutiny standard applied to governmental restrictions on speech. Commonwealth v. Simone, 63 Va. Cir. 216, 2003 Va. Cir. LEXIS 362 (Portsmouth 2003).

Nor does it apply to morphed images. — Prohibition on possession of morphed images in the Virginia child pornography statute is not unconstitutionally vague because a reasonable person is able to determine what speech is permitted and what speech is prohibited, thereby providing adequate notice to the public; furthermore, the prohibition on such morphed images is not unconstitutionally overbroad. The statute does not regulate substantially more speech than the Constitution allows to be regulated, and the statute actually contains a provision excluding from its coverage images that have bona fide purposes. Commonwealth v. Simone, 63 Va. Cir. 216, 2003 Va. Cir. LEXIS 362 (Portsmouth 2003).

In determining whether a defendant knowingly possessed sexually explicit images of children under 18 in a computer, the issue is whether defendant "reached out for and controlled" the images at issue. Commonwealth v. Simone, 63 Va. Cir. 216, 2003 Va. Cir. LEXIS 215 (Portsmouth 2003).

"Knowingly." — Pending charges of possession of child pornography in violation of § 18.2-374.1:1 were not dismissed because the "knowing" element of the charge was shown as defendant stated "I don't have too much" when asked by the police about the presence of child pornography on defendant's computer. Commonwealth v. Gardner, 72 Va. Cir. 497, 2007 Va. Cir. LEXIS 15 (Norfolk 2007).

Statute prohibits possession. — It was clear that defendant acquired mastery of and had control of pornographic images involving children, which were discovered in his temporary internet files and computer screen saver wallpaper; his Internet search terms, stories involving graphic juvenile sexual activity, and the child pornography image manually displayed on his computer wall paper proved, beyond a reasonable doubt, that he reached out for and controlled the three images contained in his computer's cache/temporary internet file. Commonwealth v. Simone, 63 Va. Cir. 216, 2003 Va. Cir. LEXIS 362 (Portsmouth 2003).

Computer images. — Defendant was convicted of possessing child pornography on his computer, where Internet searches he conducted (using the terms "Lolitas," "pedophelia," and "pre-teen pictures"), and his possession of a child pornography image that had to be manually downloaded, showed that he was reaching out for images involving child pornography with the intent to control and have dominion over them. Commonwealth v. Simone, 63 Va. Cir. 216, 2003 Va. Cir. LEXIS 215 (Portsmouth 2003).

Distinct violations for each image possessed. — If proven, each child pornography image possessed by a defendant may properly form the basis for a distinct violation of this section. Commonwealth v. Simone, 63 Va. Cir. 216, 2003 Va. Cir. LEXIS 362 (Portsmouth 2003).

Applicability of statute to offenses committed before 2003 amendment. — Counsel for defendant and the Commonwealth stipulated that the applicable version of § 18.2-374.1:1, which was amended during the Virginia legislature's 2003 session, was that in existence at the time of the crimes alleged, June 29, 2002; the stipulation was consistent with the statutory mandate embodied in § 1-16 [see now § 1-239] that no new law shall be construed to repeal a former law, as to any offense committed against the former law. Commonwealth v. Simone, 63 Va. Cir. 216, 2003 Va. Cir. LEXIS 362 (Portsmouth 2003).

§ 18.2-374.1:2. Repealed by Acts 2007, cc. 759 and 823, cl. 2.

§ 18.2-374.2. Repealed by Acts 2004, c. 995.

Cross references.
For current provisions as to seizure and forfeiture of property used in connection with production of sexually explicit items involving children, see § 19.2-386.31.

§ 18.2-374.3. Use of communications systems to facilitate certain offenses involving children.

A. As used in subsections C, D, and E "use a communications system" means making personal contact or direct contact through any agent or agency, any print medium, the United States mail, any common carrier or communication common carrier, any electronic communications system, the Internet, or any telecommunications, wire, computer network, or radio communications system.

B. It shall be unlawful for any person to use a communications system, including but not limited to computers or computer networks or bulletin boards, or any other electronic means for the purposes of procuring or promoting the use of a minor for any activity in violation of § 18.2-370 or 18.2-374.1. A violation of this subsection is a Class 6 felony.

C. It shall be unlawful for any person 18 years of age or older to use a communications system, includ-

ing but not limited to computers or computer networks or bulletin boards, or any other electronic means, for the purposes of soliciting, with lascivious intent, any person he knows or has reason to believe is a child younger than 15 years of age to knowingly and intentionally:

1. Expose his sexual or genital parts to any child to whom he is not legally married or propose that any such child expose his sexual or genital parts to such person;

2. Propose that any such child feel or fondle his own sexual or genital parts or the sexual or genital parts of such person or propose that such person feel or fondle the sexual or genital parts of any such child;

3. Propose to such child the performance of an act of sexual intercourse or any act constituting an offense under § 18.2-361; or

4. Entice, allure, persuade, or invite any such child to enter any vehicle, room, house, or other place, for any purposes set forth in the preceding subdivisions.

Any person who violates this subsection is guilty of a Class 5 felony. However, if the person is at least seven years older than the child he knows or has reason to believe is less than 15 years of age, the person shall be punished by a term of imprisonment of not less than five years nor more than 30 years in a state correctional facility, five years of which shall be mandatory minimum term of imprisonment. Any person who commits a second or subsequent violation of this subsection when the person is at least seven years older than the child he knows or has reason to believe is less than 15 years of age shall be punished by a term of imprisonment of not less than 10 years nor more than 40 years, 10 years of which shall be a mandatory minimum term of imprisonment.

D. Any person who uses a communications system, including but not limited to computers or computer networks or bulletin boards, or any other electronic means, for the purposes of soliciting, with lascivious intent, any child he knows or has reason to believe is at least 15 years of age but younger than 18 years of age to knowingly and intentionally commit any of the activities listed in subsection C if the person is at least seven years older than the child is guilty of a Class 5 felony. Any person who commits a second or subsequent violation of this subsection shall be punished by a term of imprisonment of not less than one nor more than 20 years, one year of which shall be a mandatory minimum term of imprisonment.

E. Any person 18 years of age or older who uses a communications system, including but not limited to computers or computer networks or bulletin boards, or any other electronic means, for the purposes of soliciting any person he knows or has reason to believe is a child younger than 18 years of age for (i) any activity in violation of § 18.2-355 or 18.2-361, (ii) any activity in violation of § 18.2-374.1, or (iii) a violation of § 18.2-374.1:1 is guilty of a Class 5 felony.

History.

1992, c. 699; 1999, c. 659; 2003, cc. 935, 938; 2004, cc. 414, 444, 459, 864; 2007, cc. 759, 823; 2013, cc. 423, 470.

Editor's note.

Acts 2013, cc. 423 and 470, cl. 2 provides: "That the provisions of this act may result in a net increase in periods of imprisonment or commitment. Pursuant to § 30-19.1:4, the estimated amount of the necessary appropriation cannot be determined for periods of imprisonment in state adult correctional facilities; therefore, Chapter 3 of the Acts of Assembly of 2012, Special Session I, requires the Virginia Criminal Sentencing Commission to assign a minimum fiscal impact of $50,000. Pursuant to § 30-19.1:4, the estimated amount of the necessary appropriation cannot be determined for periods of commitment to the custody of the Department of Juvenile Justice."

The 2013 amendments.

The 2013 amendments by cc. 423 and 470 are identical, and substituted "younger" for "less" in the introductory paragraph of subsection C, and in subsections D and E; and inserted "his own sexual or genital parts or" in subdivision C 2.

Law Review.

For 2003/2004 survey of family and juvenile law, see 39 U. Rich. L. Rev. 241 (2004).

Michie's Jurisprudence.

For related discussion, see 9B M.J. Infants, §§ 81, 89.

CASE NOTES

First Amendment does not bar conviction. — First Amendment to the United States Constitution did not bar defendant's conviction for using a communications system to solicit a person defendant knew, or had reason to believe, was a minor, for certain sexual offenses, in violation of subsection B of § 18.2-374.3. Although defendant claimed the statute was facially overbroad in that it barred free speech using a computer, the First Amendment did not prohibit the Commonwealth from enacting a statute to prohibit defendant from using a computer to commit a crime, that of soliciting sex from minors. Podracky v. Commonwealth, 52 Va. App. 130, 662 S.E.2d 81, 2008 Va. App. LEXIS 284 (2008).

Venue proper in county where personal contracts received. — Trial court did not err in denying defendant's challenge to venue because pursuant to §§ 18.2-374.3 and 19.2-244, venue was proper in Louisa County since a detective, who was posing as 13-year-old girl, received defendant's personal electronic contacts there; defendant chose to communicate online with the undercover officer, and the victim actually received his communications, which was a critical portion of the offense proscribed by subsection A of § 18.2-374.3, while in Louisa County. Spiker v. Commonwealth, 58 Va. App. 466, 711 S.E.2d 228, 2011 Va. App. LEXIS 221 (2011).

Because the evidence established that both individuals were in Russell County, Virginia, throughout the entire conversation in which appellant solicited the minor victim to meet her in the park, under § 18.2-374.3, the trial court correctly held that Russell County was the proper venue in which to prosecute the offense. Klewer v. Commonwealth, 2012 Va. App. LEXIS 315 (Oct. 9, 2012).

Offense not complete until victim receives contact. — Subsection A of § 18.2-374.3, by its plain terms, does not proscribe the mere act of sending a communication such as an instant message or e-mail, but it requires, in addition, that the perpetrator, by means of that communication, makes personal or direct contact with any person he knows or has reason to believe is a child less than 15 years of age. The offense, therefore, is not complete until the victim receives the personal or direct contact. Spiker v. Commonwealth, 58 Va. App. 466, 711 S.E.2d 228, 2011 Va. App. LEXIS 221 (2011).

Evidence of intent to solicit a minor via a communications device. — From the content of the three conversations that defendant had with a person whom he believed was a minor, which included defendant asking the minor if she wanted to "see and feel the real thing," and the evidence of the images defendant transmitted, the trial judge could have inferred that defendant intended to solicit a minor to commit illegal sexual acts in violation of the statute and via a communications device. Brooker v. Commonwealth, 41 Va. App. 609, 587 S.E.2d 732, 2003 Va. App. LEXIS 543 (2003).

Registration as sex offender properly required. — Trial court did not err in requiring defendant to register as a sex offender pursuant to § 9.1-902 based on defendant's conviction of computer solicitation for sex with a minor based on defendant's actions in using his computer to solicit sex from someone he thought was a 13-year-old girl, but who was, in fact, a police officer posing as a 13-year-old girl. Colbert v. Commonwealth, 47 Va. App. 390, 624 S.E.2d 108, 2006 Va. App. LEXIS 7 (2006).

Admissibility of prior bad acts. — Defendant's convictions for using electronic means to solicit sex with a minor and attempted indecent liberties in violation of subsection B of § 18.2-374.3 and § 18.2-370 were appropriate because evidence of defendant's relationship with another female prior to the current events fell within the general exceptions to the general rule of exclusion of other bad acts evidence. The evidence was relevant to show some of the elements of the crimes charged and demonstrated not only defendant's knowledge that minors were present in the adult chat rooms but also his intent to engage in sexual acts with the current victim, just as he had done in the past. Detzler v. Commonwealth, 2010 Va. App. LEXIS 132 (Apr. 6, 2010).

Evidence sufficient to uphold conviction. — Evidence was sufficient to support defendant's conviction for use of a computer to solicit a minor, as it showed that defendant used a computer to entice the "victim" to meet with him at a restaurant parking lot even though the "victim" turned out to be a police officer. Hix v. Commonwealth, 270 Va. 335, 619 S.E.2d 80, 2005 Va. LEXIS 84 (2005).

Defendant was properly convicted of computer solicitation of a minor in violation of § 18.2-374.3 and attempted indecent liberties with a minor in violation of § 18.2-370 because if the trial court erred in precluding defendant from inquiring of his witnesses what they said concerning the victim's age, any error was harmless, and defendant told the police after his arrest that he believed the victim was only fourteen to fifteen years old; that evidence plainly rebutted any inference that defendant thought he was pursuing an adult, and given defendant's admission that he thought the victim could have been fourteen, along with repeated references during internet chats to the victim's age of thirteen, any error did not affect the jury verdict. Mahmoudzadeh v. Commonwealth, 2009 Va. App. LEXIS 268 (June 16, 2009).

Because, based on the prior conversations about sex, the jury could reasonably infer that appellant intended to act on her previously-stated desire to perform various sex acts on the minor victim when she went to meet him in the park, the evidence was sufficient to convict her of electronic solicitation of a minor under subdivision C 3 of § 18.2-374.3. Klewer v. Commonwealth, 2012 Va. App. LEXIS 315 (Oct. 9, 2012).

Enhanced sentence applied even if victim was not an actual child. — Mandatory minimum sentencing provision in subsection C of § 18.2-374.3 applied to defendant even though the person that he contacted by email and telephone was an adult policewoman, not a 13-year-old girl as defendant believed. The victim of the crime need not be an actual child for the mandatory minimum sentence to apply. Grafmuller v. Commonwealth, 57 Va. App. 58, 698 S.E.2d 276, 2010 Va. App. LEXIS 348 (2010).

§ 18.2-374.4. Display of child pornography or grooming video or materials to a child unlawful; penalty.

A. Any person 18 years of age or older who displays child pornography or a grooming video or materials to a child under 13 years of age with the intent to entice, solicit, or encourage the child to engage in the fondling of the sexual or genital parts of another or the fondling of his sexual or genital parts by another, sexual intercourse, cunnilingus, fellatio, anilingus, anal intercourse, or object sexual penetration is guilty of a Class 6 felony.

B. "Grooming video or materials" means a cartoon, animation, image, or series of images depicting a child engaged in the fondling of the sexual or genital parts of another or the fondling of his sexual or genital parts by another, masturbation, sexual intercourse, cunnilingus, fellatio, anilingus, anal intercourse, or object sexual penetration.

History.
2012, c. 624.

Editor's note.
Acts 2012, c. 624, cl. 2, provides: "That the provisions of this act may result in a net increase in periods of imprisonment or commitment. Pursuant to § 30-19.1:4, the estimated amount of the necessary appropriation cannot be determined for periods of imprisonment in state adult correctional facilities; therefore, Chapter 890 of the Acts of Assembly of 2011 requires the Virginia Criminal Sentencing Commission to assign a minimum fiscal impact of $50,000. Pursuant to § 30-19.1:4, the estimated amount of the necessary appropriation is $0 for periods of commitment to the custody of the Department of Juvenile Justice."

§ 18.2-375. Obscene exhibitions and performances.

It shall be unlawful for any person knowingly to:

(1) Produce, promote, prepare, present, manage, direct, carry on or participate in, any obscene exhibitions or performances, including the exhibition or performance of any obscene motion picture, play, drama, show, entertainment, exposition, tableau or scene; provided, that no employee of any person or legal entity operating a theatre, garden, building, structure, room or place which presents such obscene exhibition or performance shall be subject to prosecution under this section if the employee is not the manager of the theatre or an officer of such entity, and has no financial interest in such theatre other than receiving salary and wages; or

(2) Own, lease or manage any theatre, garden, building, structure, room or place and lease, let, lend or permit such theatre, garden, building, structure, room or place to be used for the purpose of presenting such obscene exhibition or performance or to fail to post prominently therein the name and address of a person resident in the locality who is the manager of such theatre, garden, building, structure, room or place.

History.
Code 1950, § 18.1-230; 1960, c. 233; 1971, Ex. Sess., c. 191; 1975, cc. 14, 15.

Cross references.
As to enhanced penalty for using a computer in connection with a violation of §§ 18.2-374, 18.2-375, or 18.2-376, see § 18.2-376.1.

Law Review.
For survey of Virginia criminal law and procedure for the year 1969-1970, see 56 Va. L. Rev. 1572 (1970). For survey of Virginia statutory changes in substantive criminal law for the year 1970-1971, see 57 Va. L. Rev. 1467 (1971). For survey of Virginia constitutional law for the year 1972-1973, see 59 Va. L. Rev. 1445 (1973). For 2006 survey article, "Family and Juvenile Law," see 41 U. Rich. L. Rev. 151 (2006).

Michie's Jurisprudence.
For related discussion, see 18 M.J. Theaters, Shows and Fairs, § 2.

CASE NOTES

This section is constitutional. Grove Press, Inc. v. Evans, 306 F. Supp. 1084 (E.D. Va. 1969).

It is not unconstitutionally vague or overbroad in light of the new test of obscenity promulgated in *Miller v. California*, 413 U.S. 15, 93 S. Ct. 2607, 37 L. Ed. 2d 419 (1973), which established the following guidelines for the trier of fact to use in determining whether a work is obscene: (a) whether the average person, applying contemporary community standards would find that the work, taken as a whole, appeals to the prurient interest, (b) whether the work depicts or describes in a patently offensive way, sexual conduct specifically defined by the applicable state law, and (c) whether the work, taken as a whole, lacks serious literary, artistic, political, or scientific value. Price v. Commonwealth, 214 Va. 490, 201 S.E.2d 798 (1974).

But gives fair notice of the meaning of obscenity. Price v. Commonwealth, 214 Va. 490, 201 S.E.2d 798 (1974).

A person of ordinary understanding would have no difficulty in determining what sorts of material would be regarded as obscene under this section. Price v. Commonwealth, 214 Va. 490, 201 S.E.2d 798 (1974).

The conduct whose portrayal is proscribed must be specifically defined by statute, as written or as authoritatively construed. Price v. Commonwealth, 214 Va. 490, 201 S.E.2d 798 (1974).

Examples of descriptions that are sufficiently specific are patently offensive representations or descriptions of ultimate sexual acts, normal or perverted, actual or simulated and patently offensive representations or descriptions of masturbation, excretory functions, and lewd exhibition of the genitals. Price v. Commonwealth, 214 Va. 490, 201 S.E.2d 798 (1974).

This section prohibits only hard core pornography such as these examples, delineated by the United States Supreme Court in Miller v. California, 413 U.S. 15, 93 S. Ct. 2607, 37 L. Ed. 2d 419 (1973); Price v. Commonwealth, 214 Va. 490, 201 S.E.2d 798 (1974).

And does not restrict constitutionally protected speech and writing. Price v. Commonwealth, 214 Va. 490, 201 S.E.2d 798 (1974).

This section limits the class of works which might be found obscene to portrayals of sexual activity or excretion, not including mere nudity, which go beyond the customary limits of candor in representing such matters. Price v. Commonwealth, 214 Va. 490, 201 S.E.2d 798 (1974).

This section applies only to persons who "knowingly" violate its provisions, but all that is required is to show that the defendant exhibited the film knowing its content. Price v. Commonwealth, 213 Va. 113, 189 S.E.2d 324 (1972).

It would be difficult, if not impossible, for a Virginia jury to formulate a statewide standard of obscenity, for the state comprises communities with a vast diversity of life styles. Materials which do not offend the community standards of the metropolitan areas might well be regarded as obscene by the standards of some rural communities. Price v. Commonwealth, 214 Va. 490, 201 S.E.2d 798 (1974).

Since under *Miller v. California*, 413 U.S. 15, 93 S. Ct. 2607, 37 L. Ed. 2d 419 (1973), national standards are not constitutionally required in obscenity cases, neither are statewide standards compelled. Price v. Commonwealth, 214 Va. 490, 201 S.E.2d 798 (1974).

Local governing bodies not prevented from enacting public nudity ordinances. — State laws do not prevent a local governing body, under its police power, from enacting public nudity ordinances not inconsistent with the state law prohibiting conduct which the local governing body reasonably deems to be contrary to the morals, health, safety and general welfare of the community. Wayside Restaurant, Inc. v. City of Virginia Beach, 215 Va. 231, 208 S.E.2d 51 (1974).

Motion picture held to lack serious literary, artistic, political, or scientific value. — See Price v. Commonwealth, 214 Va. 490, 201 S.E.2d 798 (1974).

Applied in Wall Distribs., Inc. v. City of Newport News, 228 Va. 358, 323 S.E.2d 75 (1984).

§ 18.2-376. Advertising, etc., obscene items, exhibitions or performances.

It shall be unlawful for any person knowingly to prepare, print, publish, or circulate, or cause to be prepared, printed, published or circulated, any notice or advertisement of any obscene item proscribed in § 18.2-373, or of any obscene performance or exhibition proscribed in § 18.2-375, stating or indicating where such obscene item, exhibition, or performance may be purchased, obtained, seen or heard.

History.
Code 1950, § 18.1-231; 1960, c. 233; 1975, cc. 14, 15.

Cross references.
As to enhanced penalty for using a computer in connection with a violation of §§ 18.2-374, 18.2-375, or 18.2-376, see § 18.2-376.1.

Law Review.
For survey of proposed changes in statutory regulation of obscenity in Virginia for the year 1970-1971, see 57 Va. L. Rev. 1636 (1971).

§ 18.2-376.1. Enhanced penalties for using a computer in certain violations.

Any person who uses a computer in connection with a violation of §§ 18.2-374, 18.2-375, or § 18.2-376 is guilty of a separate and distinct Class 1 misdemeanor, and for a second or subsequent such offense within 10 years of a prior such offense is guilty of a Class 6 felony, the penalties to be imposed in addition to any other punishment otherwise prescribed for a violation of any of those sections.

History.
2003, cc. 987, 1016.

§ 18.2-377. Placards, posters, bills, etc.

It shall be unlawful for any person knowingly to expose, place, display, post up, exhibit, paint, print, or mark, or cause to be exposed, placed, displayed, posted, exhibited, painted, printed or marked, in or on any building, structure, billboard, wall or fence, or on any street, or in or upon any public place, any placard, poster, banner, bill, writing, or picture which is obscene, or which advertises or promotes any obscene item proscribed in § 18.2-373 or any obscene exhibition or performance proscribed in § 18.2-375, or knowingly to permit the same to be displayed on property belonging to or controlled by him.

History.
Code 1950, § 18.1-232; 1960, c. 233; 1975, cc. 14, 15.

Law Review.
For survey of proposed changes in statutory regulation of obscenity in Virginia for the year 1970-1971, see 57 Va. L. Rev. 1636 (1971).

§ 18.2-378. Coercing acceptance of obscene articles or publications.

It shall be unlawful for any person, firm, association or corporation, as a condition to any sale, allocation, consignment or delivery for resale of any paper, magazine, book, periodical or publication to require that the purchaser or consignee receive for resale any other article, book, or other publication which is obscene; nor shall any person, firm, association or corporation deny or threaten to deny any franchise or impose or threaten to impose any penalty, financial or otherwise, by reason of the failure or refusal of any person to accept such articles, books, or publications, or by reason of the return thereof.

History.
Code 1950, § 18.1-233; 1960, c. 233; 1975, cc. 14, 15.

Law Review.
For survey of proposed changes in statutory regulation of obscenity in Virginia for the year 1970-1971, see 57 Va. L. Rev. 1636 (1971).

§ 18.2-379. Employing or permitting minor to assist in offense under article.

It shall be unlawful for any person knowingly to hire, employ, use or permit any minor to do or assist in doing any act or thing constituting an offense under this article.

History.
Code 1950, § 18.1-234; 1960, c. 233; 1975, cc. 14, 15.

Cross references.
As to report to children's residential facility for which a background check is being performed on whether the applicant has ever been convicted of or is the subject of pending charges for various crimes, including employing or permitting a minor to assist in an act constituting an offense under § 18.2-372 et seq., as set out in § 18.2-379, or an equivalent offense in another state, see § 63.2-1726.

§ 18.2-380. Punishment for first offense.

Any person, firm, association or corporation convicted for the first time of an offense under §§ 18.2-374, 18.2-375, 18.2-376, 18.2-377, 18.2-378 or § 18.2-379, shall be guilty of a Class 1 misdemeanor.

History.
Code 1950, § 18.1-235.1; 1968, c. 662; 1975, cc. 14, 15; 1983, c. 412; 1985, c. 279.

§ 18.2-381. Punishment for subsequent offenses; additional penalty for owner.

Any person, firm, association or corporation convicted of a second or other subsequent offense under §§ 18.2-374 through 18.2-379 shall be guilty of a Class 6 felony. However, if the person, firm, association or corporation convicted of such subsequent offense is the owner of the business establishment where each of the offenses occurred, a fine of not more than $10,000 shall be imposed in addition to the penalties otherwise prescribed by this section.

History.
Code 1950, § 18.1-236.1; 1960, c. 233; 1968, c. 662; 1975, cc. 14, 15; 1983, c. 412.

CASE NOTES

Enhanced punishment for multiple convictions of separate offenses in simultaneous prosecution. — An enhanced punishment may be applied where there are multiple convictions for separate offenses in a simultaneous prosecution. Star News, Inc. v. Commonwealth, No. 1785-96-1 (Ct. of Appeals Jan. 6, 1998).

Applied in Educational Books, Inc. v. Commonwealth, 228 Va. 392, 323 S.E.2d 84 (1984).

§ 18.2-382. Photographs, slides and motion pictures.

Every person who knowingly:

(1) Photographs himself or any other person, for purposes of preparing an obscene film, photograph, negative, slide or motion picture for purposes of sale or distribution; or

(2) Models, poses, acts, or otherwise assists in the preparation of any obscene film, photograph, negative, slide or motion picture for purposes of sale or distribution;

shall be guilty of a Class 3 misdemeanor.

History.
Code 1950, § 18.1-235; 1960, c. 233; 1970, c. 204; 1975, cc. 14, 15.

CASE NOTES

The Constitution requires an adversary hearing to determine obscenity before seizure of a movie. Tyrone, Inc. v. Wilkinson, 410 F.2d 639 (4th Cir.), cert. denied, 396 U.S. 985, 90 S. Ct. 477, 24 L. Ed. 2d 449 (1969).

§ 18.2-383. Exceptions to application of article.

Nothing contained in this article shall be construed to apply to:

(1) The purchase, distribution, exhibition, or loan of any book, magazine, or other printed or manuscript material by any library, school, or institution of higher learning, supported by public appropriation;

(2) The purchase, distribution, exhibition, or loan of any work of art by any museum of fine arts, school, or institution of higher learning, supported by public appropriation;

(3) The exhibition or performance of any play, drama, tableau, or motion picture by any theatre, museum of fine arts, school or institution of higher learning, supported by public appropriation.

History.
Code 1950, § 18.1-236.2; 1960, c. 233; 1966, c. 516; 1975, cc. 14, 15.

§ 18.2-384. Proceeding against book alleged to be obscene.

(1) Whenever he has reasonable cause to believe that any person is engaged in the sale or commercial distribution of any obscene book, any citizen or the attorney for the Commonwealth of any county or city, or city attorney, in which the sale or commercial distribution of such book occurs may institute a proceeding in the circuit court in said city or county for adjudication of the obscenity of the book.

(2) The proceeding shall be instituted by filing with the court a petition:

(a) Directed against the book by name or description;

(b) Alleging the obscene nature of the book; and

(c) Listing the names and addresses, if known, of the author, publisher, and all other persons interested in its sale or commercial distribution.

(3) Upon the filing of a petition pursuant to this article, the court in term or in vacation shall forthwith examine the book alleged to be obscene. If the court find no probable cause to believe the book obscene, the judge thereof shall dismiss the petition; but if the court find probable cause to believe the book obscene, the judge thereof shall issue an order to show cause why the book should not be adjudicated obscene.

(4) The order to show cause shall be:

(a) Directed against the book by name or description;

(b) Published once a week for two successive weeks in a newspaper of general circulation within the county or city in which the proceeding is filed;

(c) If their names and addresses are known, served by registered mail upon the author, publisher, and all other persons interested in the sale or commercial distribution of the book; and

(d) Returnable twenty-one days after its service by registered mail or the commencement of its publication, whichever is later.

(5) When an order to show cause is issued pursuant to this article, and upon four days' notice to be given to the persons and in the manner prescribed by the court, the court may issue a temporary restraining order against the sale or distribution of the book alleged to be obscene.

(6) On or before the return date specified in the order to show cause, the author, publisher, and any person interested in the sale or commercial distribution of the book may appear and file an answer. The court may by order permit any other person to appear and file an answer amicus curiae.

(7) If no one appears and files an answer on or before the return date specified in the order to show cause, the court, upon being satisfied that the book is obscene, shall order the clerk of court to enter judgment that the book is obscene, but the court in its discretion may except from its judgment a restricted category of persons to whom the book is not obscene.

(8) If an appearance is entered and an answer filed, the court shall order the proceeding set on the calendar for a prompt hearing. The court shall conduct the hearing in accordance with the rules of civil procedure applicable to the trial of cases by the court without a jury. At the hearing, the court shall receive evidence, including the testimony of experts, if such evidence be offered, pertaining to:

(a) The artistic, literary, medical, scientific, cultural and educational values, if any, of the book considered as a whole;

(b) The degree of public acceptance of the book, or books of similar character, within the county or city in which the proceeding is brought;

(c) The intent of the author and publisher of the book;

(d) The reputation of the author and publisher;

(e) The advertising, promotion, and other circumstances relating to the sale of the book;

(f) The nature of classes of persons, including scholars, scientists, and physicians, for whom the book may not have prurient appeal, and who may be subject to exception pursuant to subsection (7).

(9) In making a decision on the obscenity of the book, the court shall consider, among other things, the evidence offered pursuant to subsection (8), if any, and shall make a written determination upon every such consideration relied upon in the proceeding in his findings of fact and conclusions of law or in a memorandum accompanying them.

(10) If he finds the book not obscene, the court shall order the clerk of court to enter judgment accordingly. If he finds the book obscene, the court shall order the clerk of court to enter judgment that the book is obscene, but the court, in its discretion, may except from its judgment a restricted category of persons to whom the book is not obscene.

(11) While a temporary restraining order made pursuant to subsection (5) is in effect, or after the entry of a judgment pursuant to subsection (7), or after the entry of judgment pursuant to subsection (10), any person who publishes, sells, rents, lends, transports in intrastate commerce, or commercially distributes or exhibits the book, or has the book in his possession with intent to publish, sell, rent, lend, transport in intrastate commerce, or commercially distribute or exhibit the book, is presumed to have knowledge that the book is obscene under §§ 18.2-372 through 18.2-378 of this article.

(12) Any party to the proceeding, including the petitioner, may appeal from the judgment of the court to the Supreme Court of Virginia, as otherwise provided by law.

(13) It is expressly provided that the petition and proceeding authorized under this article, relating to books alleged to be obscene, shall be intended only to establish scienter in cases where the establishment of such scienter is thought to be useful or desirable by the petitioner; and the provisions of § 18.2-384 shall in nowise be construed to be a necessary prerequisite to the filing of criminal charges under this article.

History.
Code 1950, § 18.1-236.3; 1960, c. 233; 1975, cc. 14, 15.

Law Review.
For survey of Virginia constitutional law for the year 1971-1972, see 58 Va. L. Rev. 1197 (1972).

Michie's Jurisprudence.
For related discussion, see 10A M.J. Injunctions, § 88; 11B M.J. Jury, § 10; 13B M.J. Newspapers, § 6; 18 M.J. Theaters, Shows and Fairs, § 2.

CASE NOTES

Constitutionality. — This section provides a sufficiently definite procedure for determining whether certain materials alleged to be obscene are, in fact, obscene, and is therefore not unconstitutionally vague. Alexander v. Commonwealth, 214 Va. 539, 203 S.E.2d 441 (1974).

Movie films are to be accorded the same constitutional protection as books. Greenmount Sales, Inc. v. Davila, 344 F. Supp. 860 (E.D. Va. 1972), aff'd in part and rev'd in part, 479 F.2d 591 (4th Cir. 1973).

No distinction can be made between seizure for condemnation and seizure for evidence. — No distinction can rationally be made between the seizure of publications and film for condemnation, and seizure for evidence in a criminal prosecution. Both types of seizure must be treated the same, for to do otherwise would sanction indiscriminate police fishing expeditions. Greenmount Sales, Inc. v. Davila, 344 F. Supp. 860 (E.D. Va. 1972), aff'd in part and rev'd in part, 479 F.2d 591 (4th Cir. 1973).

The magnitude of a particular seizure of allegedly obscene materials is not a viable determinant of whether a person's or society's right to freedom of speech and press has been abridged. Greenmount Sales, Inc. v. Davila, 344 F. Supp. 860 (E.D. Va. 1972), aff'd in part and rev'd in part, 479 F.2d 591 (4th Cir. 1973).

The community standard for obscenity is that of the locality rather than that of the State or nation. Alexander v. Commonwealth, 214 Va. 539, 203 S.E.2d 441 (1974).

Prior judicial determination of obscenity required. — A prior adversary judicial hearing must be conducted before allegedly obscene books can be seized by government authorities. Greenmount Sales, Inc. v. Davila, 344 F. Supp. 860 (E.D. Va. 1972), aff'd in part and rev'd in part, 479 F.2d 591 (4th Cir. 1973).

A person may not be forced to go through the hardship of defending himself against a criminal prosecution — with its consequent chilling effect on him and the community at large — for possessing, selling, or promoting, etc., publications or film, without the government first having judicially ascertained whether the matter for the possession, etc., of which he is being prosecuted is, in fact, obscene. Greenmount Sales, Inc. v. Davila, 344 F. Supp. 860 (E.D. Va. 1972), aff'd in part and rev'd in part, 479 F.2d 591 (4th Cir. 1973).

Nothing on the face of this section denies a prompt adversary hearing on the issue of obscenity after temporary seizure or restraint. Alexander v. Commonwealth, 214 Va. 539, 203 S.E.2d 441 (1974).

There is no absolute First or Fourteenth Amendment right to a prior adversary hearing applicable to all cases where allegedly obscene material is seized. Alexander v. Commonwealth, 214 Va. 539, 203 S.E.2d 441 (1974).

A trial by jury is not constitutionally required in a state civil obscenity proceeding pursuant to this section. Alexander v. Virginia, 413 U.S. 836, 93 S. Ct. 2803, 37 L. Ed. 2d 993 (1973); Alexander v. Commonwealth, 214 Va. 539, 203 S.E.2d 441 (1974).

The object of an adversary hearing is to ensure that expression will not be suppressed without contest and justification. An adversary proceeding contemplates an opportunity for one to be afforded the protection of the First Amendment to the Constitution of the United States. Allegedly obscene publications or movies are not to be treated the same way as narcotics, gambling paraphernalia and other contraband. The legal rules governing the former are different from the latter. Tyrone, Inc. v. Wilkinson, 294 F. Supp. 1330 (E.D. Va.), aff'd, 410 F.2d 639 (4th Cir.), cert. denied, 396 U.S. 985, 90 S. Ct. 477, 24 L. Ed. 2d 449 (1969).

Sufficiency of evidence. — See *Alexander v. Commonwealth*, 214 Va. 539, 203 S.E.2d 441 (1974).

§ 18.2-385. Section 18.2-384 applicable to motion picture films.

The provisions of § 18.2-384 shall apply mutatis mutandis in the case of motion picture film.

History.
Code 1950, § 18.1-236.4; 1966, c. 516; 1975, cc. 14, 15.

Michie's Jurisprudence.
For related discussion, see 18 M.J. Theaters, Shows and Fairs, § 2.

§ 18.2-386. Showing previews of certain motion pictures.

It shall be unlawful for any person to exhibit any trailer or preview of any motion picture which has a motion picture industry rating which would not permit persons in the audience viewing the feature motion picture to see the complete motion picture from which the trailer or preview is taken. Persons violating the provisions of this section shall be guilty of a Class 1 misdemeanor.

History.
Code 1950, § 18.1-246.1; 1970, c. 504; 1975, cc. 14, 15.

§ 18.2-386.1. Unlawful filming, videotaping or photographing of another; penalty.

A. It shall be unlawful for any person to knowingly and intentionally videotape, photograph, or film any nonconsenting person or create any videographic or still image record by any means whatsoever of the nonconsenting person if (i) that person is totally nude, clad in undergarments, or in a state of undress so as to expose the genitals, pubic area, buttocks or female breast in a restroom, dressing room, locker room, hotel room, motel room, tanning bed, tanning booth, bedroom or other location; or (ii) the videotape, photograph, film or videographic or still image record is created by placing the lens or image-gathering component of the recording device in a position directly beneath or between a person's legs for the purpose of capturing an image of the person's intimate parts or undergarments covering those intimate parts when the intimate parts or undergarments would not otherwise be visible to the general public; and when the circumstances set forth in clause (i) or (ii) are otherwise such that the person being videotaped, photographed, filmed or otherwise recorded would have a reasonable expectation of privacy.

B. The provisions of this section shall not apply to filming, videotaping or photographing or other still image or videographic recording by (i) law-enforcement officers pursuant to a criminal investigation which is otherwise lawful or (ii) correctional officials and local or regional jail officials for security purposes or for investigations of alleged misconduct involving a person committed to the Department of Corrections or to a local or regional jail, or to any sound recording of an oral conversation made as a result of any videotaping or filming pursuant to Chapter 6 (§ 19.2-61 et seq.) of Title 19.2.

C. A violation of subsection A shall be punishable as a Class 1 misdemeanor.

D. A violation of subsection A involving a nonconsenting person under the age of 18 shall be punishable as a Class 6 felony.

E. Where it is alleged in the warrant, information, or indictment on which the person is convicted and found by the court or jury trying the case that the person has previously been convicted within the 10-year period immediately preceding the offense charged of two or more of the offenses specified in this section, each such offense occurring on a different date, and when such offenses were not part of a common act, transaction, or scheme, and such person has been at liberty as defined in § 53.1-151 between each conviction, he shall be guilty of a Class 6 felony.

History.
1994, c. 640; 2004, c. 844; 2005, c. 375; 2008, c. 732.

Editor's note.
Acts 2008, c. 732, cl. 2, provides: "That the provisions of this act may result in a net increase in periods of imprisonment or commitment. Pursuant to § 30-19.1:4, the estimated amount of the necessary appropriation cannot be determined for periods of imprisonment in state adult correctional facilities and cannot be determined for periods of commitment to the custody of the Department of Juvenile Justice."

The 2008 amendments.
The 2008 amendment by c. 732 added subsection E.

Law Review.
For annual survey article on legal issues involving children, see 38 U. Rich. L. Rev. 161 (2003). For 2003/2004 survey of family and juvenile law, see 39 U. Rich. L. Rev. 241 (2004). For survey of Virginia criminal law and procedure for the year 2004-2005, see 40 U. Rich. L. Rev. 197 (2005). For annual survey article, "Criminal Law and Procedure," see 44 U. Rich. L. Rev. 339 (2009).

CASE NOTES

Expectation of privacy. — Because the victim was wearing clothing covering her undergarments while shopping in a public location, the trial court did not err in finding that she had a reasonable expectation of privacy as to those undergarments for purposes of § 18.2-386.1; under § 18.2-386.1, a person can possess a reasonable expectation of privacy when being victimized in public, and the requirement in clause (ii) of subsection A that the victim's intimate parts or undergarments covering those intimate parts not otherwise be visible to the general public is simply a standard by which to assess whether the victim's "intimate parts or undergarments" were reasonably out of view, as a prerequisite to finding that the accused has viewed them unlawfully. *Wilson v. Commonwealth*, 53 Va. App. 599, 673 S.E.2d 923, 2009 Va. App. LEXIS 137 (2009).

"Other location" does not include public forum. — The general words, "other location," as used in the statute did not apply to the defendant's videotaping from under the dress of a fully clothed person standing at a public forum, i.e., a county fairgrounds. *C'Debaca v. Commonwealth*, No. 2754-97-4 (Ct. of Appeals Feb. 2, 1999) (decided prior to 2005 amendment which added A(ii)).

Evidence sufficient. — Evidence was sufficient for the trial court to rationally find defendant guilty of attempting to photograph a victim in violation of § 18.2-386.1 because defendant was charged with and convicted of attempting to photograph the victim in violation of §§ 18.2-27 and 18.2-386.1, not the completed crime; therefore, it was not necessary for the Commonwealth to prove that defendant, in fact, accomplished "directly" photographing the victim in the proscribed manner under the statute or that defendant actually photographed anything. Wilson v. Commonwealth, 53 Va. App. 599, 673 S.E.2d 923, 2009 Va. App. LEXIS 137 (2009).

CIRCUIT COURT OPINIONS

Multiple contemporaneous convictions required sex offender registration. — Defendant was required to register as a sex offender pursuant to subdivision B 1 of § 9.1-902 after he was convicted of nine violations of § 18.2-386.1 because he had accumulated at least three convictions of § 18.2-386.1 and the contemporaneousness of his convictions was not a bar to enforcement of the registration requirement. Commonwealth v. Schneider, 78 Va. Cir. 320, 2009 Va. Cir. LEXIS 160 (Hanover County May 7, 2009).

§ 18.2-387. Indecent exposure.

Every person who intentionally makes an obscene display or exposure of his person, or the private parts thereof, in any public place, or in any place where others are present, or procures another to so expose himself, shall be guilty of a Class 1 misdemeanor. No person shall be deemed to be in violation of this section for breastfeeding a child in any public place or any place where others are present.

History.
Code 1950, § 18.1-236; 1960, c. 233; 1975, cc. 14, 15; 1994, c. 398.

Law Review.
For survey of proposed changes in statutory regulation of obscenity in Virginia for the year 1970-1971, see 57 Va. L. Rev. 1636 (1971). For article on the constitutionality of local ordinances banning nude sunbathing, see 20 U. Rich. L. Rev. 589 (1986).

Michie's Jurisprudence.
For related discussion, see 1A M.J. Adultery, Fornication and Lewdness, § 11.

CASE NOTES

"Public place." — "Public place" comprises places and circumstances where an offender does not have a reasonable expectation of privacy because of the foreseeability of a non-consenting public witness, thus, the evidence supported defendant's indecent exposure conviction. Defendant had no expectation of privacy when he masturbated while standing at the front bars of his cell, in open view of the staff, other inmates, and members of the public with authorized access. Barnes v. Commonwealth, 61 Va. App. 495, 737 S.E.2d 919, 2013 Va. App. LEXIS 65 (2013).

Indecent exposure not lesser offense of sodomy. — Indecent exposure, though it may occur in almost all cases of sodomy where two persons are involved, is not a fact that must be charged or proved to sustain a conviction of sodomy in any case. Therefore, indecent exposure is not a lesser offense included in the offense of sodomy. Ashby v. Commonwealth, 208 Va. 443, 158 S.E.2d 657 (1968).

But is lesser offense of exposure with lascivious intent. — While not a lesser offense included under sodomy because the facts to be proven are not the same, indecent exposure is a lesser offense included under the statutory felony of exposure to certain infants with lascivious intent, because only the intent differs. Hewitt v. Commonwealth, 213 Va. 605, 194 S.E.2d 893 (1973).

Local governing bodies not prevented from enacting public nudity ordinances. — State laws do not prevent a local governing body, under its police power, from enacting public nudity ordinances not inconsistent with the state law prohibiting conduct which the local governing body reasonably deems to be contrary to the morals, health, safety and general welfare of the community. Wayside Restaurant, Inc. v. City of Virginia Beach, 215 Va. 231, 208 S.E.2d 51 (1974).

Exposure of groin and buttocks clearly, fall within the proscriptions of this section. Hart v. Commonwealth, 18 Va. App. 77, 441 S.E.2d 706 (1994).

Exposure of defendant's penis violated the proscription of this section. Morales v. Commonwealth, 31 Va. App. 541, 525 S.E.2d 23 (2000).

More than indecent exposure proven. — While defendant was correct in asserting that absent proof of lascivious intent, he could only be found guilty of misdemeanor indecent exposure, defendant's conduct in looking down at his groin and then adjusting his shorts so that his previously unexposed penis was exposed to two young girls riding by on bicycles involved sufficient conduct to show his lascivious intent and support his taking indecent liberties with a child in violation of § 18.2-370. Viney v. Commonwealth, 269 Va. 296, 609 S.E.2d 26, 2005 Va. App. LEXIS 20 (2005).

Indecent exposure not lesser offense of indecent liberties. — Indecent exposure, as proscribed by § 18.2-387, was not a lesser included offense of indecent liberties, as proscribed by § 18.2-370, because all the elements of indecent exposure were not included in the offense charged, and, thus, failure to instruct the jury on indecent exposure was not error. Simon v. Commonwealth, 58 Va. App. 194, 708 S.E.2d 245, 2011 Va. App. LEXIS 153 (2011).

Evidence was clearly sufficient to support the trial court's conclusion that defendant's exposure of his "private parts" was obscene, where defendant dropped his shorts in front of a clerk in an office supply store, so that he was clad in a skimpy G-string which covered only his penis and anus, leaving his pubic area and buttocks exposed; the trial court was entitled to conclude that defendant's statements, in conjunction with his actions, clearly established that his actions had as their dominant purpose an appeal to the prurient interest in sex. Hart v. Commonwealth, 18 Va. App. 77, 441 S.E.2d 706 (1994).

Evidence that defendant exposed his genitals, that he was clearly aroused, and that he was masturbating established that defendant's actions had as their dominant purpose an appeal to the prurient interest in sex and were therefore obscene. Copeland v. Commonwealth, 31 Va. App. 512, 525 S.E.2d 9 (2000).

Proof that defendant was exposing his genitals, that he was in a visibly aroused state, and that he was masturbating satisfied the requirement that defendant's conduct violated contemporary community standards of sexual candor. Morales v. Commonwealth, 31 Va. App. 541, 525 S.E.2d 23 (2000).

Because a man masturbating in public could still display his "person" or "private parts" while not exposing his penis to sight, defendant's public masturbation in front of children was an obscene "display" of his person or private parts even though he was fully clothed. Moses v. Commonwealth, 45 Va. App. 357, 611 S.E.2d 607, 2005 Va. App. LEXIS 220 (2005).

Uncorroborated testimony supported defendant's conviction for indecent exposure despite the victim's delay in reporting the assault because the delay, which was due to the victim's fear of her father, defendant, and her shame and embarrassment, was consistent with human experience and did not render her testimony inherently incredible. Wilson v. Commonwealth, 46 Va. App. 73, 615 S.E.2d 500, 2005 Va. App. LEXIS 268 (2005).

Evidence insufficient. — Defendant was erroneously convicted of indecent exposure under § 18.2-387, where defendant's conduct in exposing her breasts to two 11- and 12-year-old boys who were family friends was not obscene; defendant's conduct was always done in a joking manner and defendant did not exhibit signs of sexual interest, such as visible arousal or masturbatory behavior. Neice v. Commonwealth, 2010 Va. App. LEXIS 231 (June 8, 2010).

Although defendant's behavior was inappropriate, it did not rise to the level of obscenity required under § 18.2-387, as defined in § 18.2-372, and defendant's conviction of indecent exposure was improper; nothing in the record suggested that defendant invited any sexual conduct with the victim, hinted at any sexual excitement on defendant's part, or, when defendant dropped defendant's pants upon exiting a bus (with defendant's back to the victim and running away from the victim), displayed defendant's sexual organs to the victim or to anyone else. A. M. v. Commonwealth, 2013 Va. App. LEXIS 46 (Feb. 12, 2013).

Harmless error. — Despite a trial court expressing uncertainty as to whether the applicable standard was one of indecency or one of obscenity, any error was harmless because the verdict convicting defendant would have been the same as a result of defendant's conduct of exposing his buttocks and breasts (he was a transvestite), in the early morning hours, on a street known for illegal prostitution, which was conduct that was intentional and done with the purpose of appealing to the prurient interest in sex. Willis v. Commonwealth, No. 0173-04-2, 2005 Va. App. LEXIS 58 (Ct. of Appeals Feb. 8, 2005).

Intent not established. — While the evidence amply established that defendant exposed his private parts while standing at his bedroom window, the Commonwealth failed to bear its burden of proving beyond a reasonable doubt that the exposure was intentional. Stiftar v. Commonwealth, No. 0431-87-4 (Ct. of Appeals Dec. 6, 1988).

Applied in Chrisman v. Commonwealth, 3 Va. App. 89, 348 S.E.2d 399 (1986).

§ 18.2-387.1. Obscene sexual display; penalty.

Any person who, while in any public place where others are present, intending that he be seen by others, intentionally and obscenely as defined in § 18.2-372, engages in actual or explicitly simulated acts of masturbation, is guilty of a Class 1 misdemeanor.

History.
2005, c. 422.

Law Review.
For survey of Virginia criminal law and procedure for the year 2004-2005, see 40 U. Rich. L. Rev. 197 (2005).

CASE NOTES

"Public place." — "Public place" comprises places and circumstances where an offender does not have a reasonable expectation of privacy because of the foreseeability of a non-consenting public witness, thus, the evidence supported defendant's sexual display conviction. Defendant had no expectation of privacy when he masturbated while standing at the front bars of his cell, in open view of the staff, other inmates, and members of the public with authorized access. Barnes v. Commonwealth, 61 Va. App. 495, 737 S.E.2d 919, 2013 Va. App. LEXIS 65 (2013).

§ 18.2-388. Profane swearing and intoxication in public; penalty; transportation of public inebriates to detoxification center.

If any person profanely curses or swears or is intoxicated in public, whether such intoxication results from alcohol, narcotic drug or other intoxicant or drug of whatever nature, he shall be deemed guilty of a Class 4 misdemeanor. In any area in which there is located a court-approved detoxification center a law-enforcement officer may authorize the transportation, by police or otherwise, of public inebriates to such detoxification center in lieu of arrest; however, no person shall be involuntarily detained in such center.

History.
Code 1950, § 18.1-237; 1960, c. 358; 1964, c. 434; 1975, cc. 14, 15; 1979, c. 654; 1982, c. 666; 1983, c. 187; 1990, c. 965.

Cross references.
As to running automobiles, engines, etc., while intoxicated, see §§ 18.2-266 through 18.2-273. As to detoxification center programs, see § 9.1-163 et seq.

Law Review.
For article, "Drunkenness and Reform of the Criminal Law," see 54 Va. L. Rev. 1135 (1968). For survey of Virginia criminal law for the year 1973-1974, see 60 Va. L. Rev. 1499 (1974).

Michie's Jurisprudence.
For related discussion, see 3A M.J. Breach of the Peace, § 5; 6B M.J. Drunkenness, § 13; 17 M.J. Statutes, § 60.

CASE NOTES

Arrest for violation of this section is authorized. — Under the plain language of this section, an officer is authorized to arrest a public inebriate. Carrasquillo v. Commonwealth, No. 0372-00-2, 2001 Va. App. LEXIS 274 (Ct. of Appeals May 22, 2001).

Intoxication on private property shielded from public view not grounds for arrest. — Police officers did not have the right to arrest an individual for public intoxication where it was clearly established at the time of the arrest that by consuming alcohol in his own yard, shielded from public view, at the end of a private road, the individual arrested did not commit the offense of public intoxication within the meaning of Virginia law. Rogers v. Pendleton, 249 F.3d 279, 2001 U.S. App. LEXIS 8157 (4th Cir. 2001).

The plain meaning of "in public" for purposes of § 18.2-388 was a place in open view, visible to the community, and could include a defendant's private property. Crislip v. Commonwealth, 37 Va. App. 66, 554 S.E.2d 96, 2001 Va. App. LEXIS 592 (2001).

Defendant should not have been arrested absent physical impairment. — Granting of a defendant's motion to suppress evidence in the form of a gun seized from his person and statements made to officers, where the officers lacked sufficient justification under the Fourth Amendment to perform a Terry v. Ohio stop, and to arrest and search defendant based on an uncorroborated anonymous tip, and where defendant admitted he had been drinking but was not intoxicated, was affirmed on appeal. United States v. Brown, 401 F.3d 588, 2005 U.S. App. LEXIS 4859 (4th Cir. 2005).

Alcoholism is not a defense to a prosecution for public drunkenness. Rakes v. Coleman, 359 F. Supp. 370 (E.D. Va. 1973).

A claim that it is cruel and unusual punishment to incarcerate an alcoholic without rehabilitation was not supported by the record. Rakes v. Coleman, 359 F. Supp. 370 (E.D. Va. 1973).

When pending prosecutions may be enjoined. — A federal court may enjoin pending prosecutions for violation of this section only upon a showing of bad faith harassment by the state or abridgement of First Amendment freedoms in addition to a showing that the alleged injuries are immediate, real and irreparable. Rakes v. Coleman, 359 F. Supp. 370 (E.D. Va. 1973).

Self-defense argument prohibited. — Defendant's conviction for assault and battery of a law-enforcement officer was appropriate because the trial court did not err in refusing to accept defendant's self-defense argument. Whether the police had probable cause to arrest defendant for disorderly conduct was immaterial because police did have probable cause to arrest him for public intoxication under § 18.2-388; thus, the police officers were acting properly when they arrested defendant and he had no legal justification for head-butting a law-enforcement officer who was carrying out his lawful duties. Davis v. Commonwealth, 2010 Va. App. LEXIS 209 (May 18, 2010).

As to standing of chronic alcoholics to seek declaratory relief on allegations of denial of defense of alcoholism and incarceration without rehabilitative treatment, see Rakes v. Coleman, 359 F. Supp. 370 (E.D. Va. 1973).

Evidence held sufficient. — Evidence was sufficient to support a finding that officer possessed probable cause to believe that defendant was drunk in public where the officer testified that defendant slurred his speech and swayed from side to side, smelled of alcohol, and had bloodshot and glassy eyes; additionally, another witness testified that he saw defendant shortly after his arrest and also noticed that he slurred his speech, stumbled, and smelled of alcohol. Wilson v. Commonwealth, No. 2850-00-2, 2002 Va. App. LEXIS 322 (Ct. of Appeals May 28, 2002).

Probable cause to arrest. — Because defendant's initial arrest for being drunk in public under § 18.2-388 was supported by probable cause, defendant had no right to resist; consequently, defendant was properly convicted of assault and battery of a police officer under § 18.2-57 when defendant later fled and then struggled with and injured a police officer. Brower v. Commonwealth, — Va. App. —, — S.E.2d —, 2008 Va. App. LEXIS 83 (Feb. 19, 2008).

As defendant's bloodshot eyes, slurred speech, unsteadiness on his feet, and possession of an open can of beer in a truck parked at a motel parking lot gave an officer probable cause to arrest him for public drunkenness under § 18.2-388, drugs found in a search of defendant's pockets were admissible as the fruits of a search incident to an arrest. Whether the officer exceeded the permissible scope of a weapons frisk, whether he believed he had probable cause to arrest defendant before the search, and the fact that he performed the search before the arrest were irrelevant. Commonwealth v. Lasley, — Va. App. —, — S.E.2d —, 2009 Va. App. LEXIS 10 (Jan. 13, 2009).

Although there was a compelling argument that § 18.2-388, which criminalized cursing at an officer, was unconstitutional, plaintiff arrestee failed to show that it was so grossly and flagrantly unconstitutional that defendant police officer should have anticipated its invalidation, thus, the arrest of the arrestee for calling the officer a bitch was supported by probable cause and the arrestee's First and Fourth Amendment claims failed. Harrison v. Deane, 2011 U.S. App. LEXIS 8873 (4th Cir. Apr. 29, 2011).

Search incident to arrest for public drunkenness. — Cocaine found on defendant during a search incident to defendant's arrest for public drunkenness was erroneously suppressed as a police officer had probable cause to arrest defendant for public drunkenness under § 18.2-388, since defendant was found drunk and sleeping in a car in a parking lot open to the public and routinely used by apartment residents and guests; it did not matter for Fourth Amendment purposes that defendant was charged under a City ordinance with a more narrow scope than the state public drunkenness statute. Commonwealth v. Carter, — Va. App. —, — S.E.2d —, 2007 Va. App. LEXIS 344 (Sept. 14, 2007).

Cocaine found in defendant's vehicle was admissible because a police officer had probable cause under subsection B of § 19.2-81 to arrest defendant for public intoxication, in violation of § 18.2-388, as the officer testified that as the officer approached defendant's parked vehicle and spoke with defendant there was a very strong odor of alcohol coming from defendant's breath, defendant's speech was slurred, and defendant's eyes were very bloodshot. Furthermore, the officer's search of defendant's vehicle was a proper search incident to arrest under then existing law, as defendant was in custody and an occupant of the vehicle. McGhee v. Commonwealth, 280 Va. 620, 701 S.E.2d 58, 2010 Va. LEXIS 260 (2010).

OPINIONS OF THE ATTORNEY GENERAL

There is no statutory time limit within which a magistrate must grant bond for an intoxicated person charged with a misdemeanor offense, such as driving under the influence or public intoxication. See opinion of Attorney General to The Honorable Gary W. Waters, Sheriff for the City of Portsmouth, 04-49 (7/15/04).

§ 18.2-389. Repealed by Acts 2004, c. 462.

Cross references.
For current provisions as to adoption of ordinances prohibiting obscenity, see § 15.2-926.2.

ARTICLE 6.

PROHIBITED SALES AND LOANS TO JUVENILES.

§ 18.2-390. Definitions.

As used in this article:

(1) *"Juvenile"* means a person less than 18 years of age.

(2) *"Nudity"* means a state of undress so as to expose the human male or female genitals, pubic area or buttocks with less than a full opaque covering, or the showing of the female breast with less than a fully opaque covering of any portion thereof below the top of the nipple, or the depiction of covered or uncovered male genitals in a discernibly turgid state.

(3) *"Sexual conduct"* means actual or explicitly simulated acts of masturbation, homosexuality, sexual intercourse, or physical contact in an act of apparent sexual stimulation or gratification with a person's clothed or unclothed genitals, pubic area, buttocks or, if such be female, breast.

(4) *"Sexual excitement"* means the condition of human male or female genitals when in a state of sexual stimulation or arousal.

(5) *"Sadomasochistic abuse"* means actual or explicitly simulated flagellation or torture by or upon a person who is nude or clad in undergarments, a mask or bizarre costume, or the condition of being fettered, bound or otherwise physically restrained on the part of one so clothed.

(6) *"Harmful to juveniles"* means that quality of any description or representation, in whatever form, of nudity, sexual conduct, sexual excitement, or sadomasochistic abuse, when it (a) predominantly appeals to the prurient, shameful or morbid interest of juveniles, (b) is patently offensive to prevailing standards in the adult community as a whole with respect to what is suitable material for juveniles, and (c) is, when taken as a whole, lacking in serious literary, artistic, political or scientific value for juveniles.

(7) *"Knowingly"* means having general knowledge of, or reason to know, or a belief or ground for belief which warrants further inspection or inquiry of both (a) the character and content of any material described herein which is reasonably susceptible of examination by the defendant, and (b) the age of the juvenile, provided however, that an honest mistake shall constitute an excuse from liability hereunder if the defendant made a reasonable bona fide attempt to ascertain the true age of such juvenile.

(8) *"Video or computer game"* means an object or device that stores recorded data or instructions, receives data or instructions generated by a person who uses it, and, by processing the data or instructions, creates an interactive game capable of being played, viewed, or experienced on or through a computer, television gaming system, console, or other technology.

History.
Code 1950, § 18.1-236.6; 1970, c. 560; 1975, cc. 14, 15, 492; 1976, c. 504; 2006, c. 463.

Cross references.
As to restrictions on state employee access to information infrastructure, see § 2.2-2827. As to public and private schools blocking

Internet access to material deemed harmful to juveniles, see § 22.1-70.2.

Editor's note.

The above section is § 18.1-236.6 as amended by Acts 1975, c. 492. Pursuant to § 30-152, it has been substituted for § 18.2-390 as enacted by Acts 1975, cc. 14 and 15.

Law Review.

For survey of proposed changes in statutory regulation of obscenity in Virginia for the year 1970-1971, see 57 Va. L. Rev. 1636 (1971). For survey of constitutional law in Virginia for the year 1975-1976, see 62 Va. L. Rev. 1389 (1976). For note, "Sex, Cells, and SORNA: Applying Sex Offender Registration Laws to Sexting Cases," see 52 Wm. & Mary L. Rev. 1717 (2011).

CASE NOTES

Virginia Code's current definition of "harmful to juveniles" is modification of Miller v. California, 413 U.S. 15, 93 S. Ct. 2607, 37 L. Ed. 2d 419 (1973) definition of obscenity, adapted for juveniles. Virginia v. American Booksellers Ass'n, 484 U.S. 383, 108 S. Ct. 636, 98 L. Ed. 2d 782 (1988).

In defining "harmful to juveniles" in subdivision (6)(c), the General Assembly interpreted the statutory definition of "harmful to juveniles" in accordance with the current United States Supreme Court definition of obscenity. American Booksellers Ass'n v. Virginia, 882 F.2d 125 (4th Cir. 1989), cert. denied, 494 U.S. 1056, 110 S. Ct. 1525, 108 L. Ed. 2d 764 (1990).

Material depicting the lewd exhibition of a juvenile's genitals is "hard core" obscenity for children. Freeman v. Commonwealth, 223 Va. 301, 288 S.E.2d 461 (1982).

Photographing of exposed nipples, while within the literal definition of nudity under this section, is not, without more, the lewd exhibition of nudity required under § 18.2-374.1 as it read in 1979. Foster v. Commonwealth, 6 Va. App. 313, 369 S.E.2d 688 (1988).

Books not shown to be "harmful to juveniles." — Where none of the 16 books in question in a certification procedure met the third prong of the tripartite test established in Ginsberg v. New York, 390 U.S. 629, 88 S. Ct. 1274 (1968), for determination of materials harmful to minors, none of the books was "harmful to juveniles" within the meaning of this section and § 18.2-391. Commonwealth v. American Booksellers Ass'n, 236 Va. 168, 372 S.E.2d 618 (1988), cert. denied, 494 U.S. 1056, 110 S. Ct. 1525, 108 L. Ed. 2d 764 (1990).

"Sexually explicit visual material" not found. — Where in photographs, the teenager's breasts, buttocks, and genitals were pictured but were not the central focus of the photographs, they did not meet the statutory requirement of "sexually explicit visual material." Asa v. Commonwealth, 17 Va. App. 714, 441 S.E.2d 26 (1994).

Applied in American Booksellers Ass'n v. Strobel, 617 F. Supp. 699 (E.D. Va. 1985); Frantz v. Commonwealth, 9 Va. App. 348, 388 S.E.2d 273 (1990); Mainstream Loudoun v. Board of Trustees, 2 F. Supp. 2d 783 (E.D. Va. 1998); Urofsky v. Gilmore, 167 F.3d 191 (4th. Cir. 1999).

§ 18.2-391. Unlawful acts; penalties.

A. It shall be unlawful for any person to sell, rent or loan to a juvenile, knowing or having reason to know that such person is a juvenile, or to knowingly display for commercial purpose in a manner whereby juveniles may examine and peruse:

1. Any picture, photography, drawing, sculpture, motion picture in any format or medium, video or computer game, electronic file or message containing an image, or similar visual representation or image of a person or portion of the human body which depicts sexually explicit nudity, sexual conduct or sadomasochistic abuse and which is harmful to juveniles, or

2. Any book, pamphlet, magazine, printed matter however reproduced, electronic file or message containing words, or sound recording which contains any matter enumerated in subdivision 1 of this subsection, or explicit and detailed verbal descriptions or narrative accounts of sexual excitement, sexual conduct or sadomasochistic abuse and which, taken as a whole, is harmful to juveniles.

However, if a person uses services of an Internet service provider or an electronic mail service provider in committing acts prohibited under this subsection, such Internet service provider or electronic mail service provider shall not be held responsible for violating this subsection.

B. It shall be unlawful for any person knowingly to sell to a juvenile an admission ticket or pass, or knowingly to admit a juvenile to premises whereon there is exhibited a motion picture, show or other presentation which, in whole or in part, depicts sexually explicit nudity, sexual conduct or sadomasochistic abuse and which is harmful to juveniles or to exhibit any such motion picture at any such premises which are not designed to prevent viewing from any public way of such motion picture by juveniles not admitted to any such premises.

C. It shall be unlawful for any juvenile falsely to represent to any person mentioned in subsection A or subsection B hereof, or to his agent, that such juvenile is 18 years of age or older, with the intent to procure any material set forth in subsection A, or with the intent to procure such juvenile's admission to any motion picture, show or other presentation, as set forth in subsection B.

D. It shall be unlawful for any person knowingly to make a false representation to any person mentioned in subsection A or subsection B hereof or to his agent, that he is the parent or guardian of any juvenile, or that any juvenile is 18 years of age, with the intent to procure any material set forth in subsection A, or with the intent to procure such juvenile's admission to any motion picture, show or other presentation, as set forth in subsection B.

E. No person shall sell, rent, or loan any item described in subdivision A 1 or A 2 to any individual who does not demonstrate his age in accordance with the provisions of subsection C of § 18.2-371.2.

F. A violation of subsection A, B, C, or D is a Class 1 misdemeanor. A person or separate retail establishment who violates subsection E shall be liable for a civil penalty not to exceed $100 for a first violation, a civil penalty not to exceed $200 for a second violation, and a civil penalty not to exceed $500 for a third or subsequent violation.

History.

Code 1950, § 18.1-236.7; 1970, c. 560; 1972, c. 421; 1975, cc. 14, 15; 1976, c. 504; 1985, c. 506; 1987, c. 356; 1999, c. 936; 2000, c. 1009; 2001, c. 451; 2006, c. 463.

Law Review.

For survey of proposed changes in statutory regulations of obscenity in Virginia for the year 1970-1971, see 57 Va. L. Rev. 1636

(1971). For survey of Virginia criminal law for the year 1971-1972, see 58 Va. L. Rev. 1206 (1972). For survey of constitutional law in Virginia for the year 1975-1976, see 62 Va. L. Rev. 1389 (1976). For 2000 survey of Virginia criminal law and procedure, see 34 U. Rich. L. Rev. 749 (2000). For 2000 survey of Virginia technology law, see 34 U. Rich. L. Rev. 1051. (2000). For article, "Legal Issues Involving Children," see 35 U. Rich. L. Rev. 741 (2001). For 2002 survey of Virginia technology law, see 37 U. Rich. L. Rev. 341 (2002). For 2003/2004 survey of family and juvenile law, see 39 U. Rich. L. Rev. 241 (2004).

CASE NOTES

Constitutionality. — Section 18.2-391, as amended by Acts 1999, c. 936, violates the First Amendment to the United States Constitution, because given the current state of Internet technology, enforcement of the statute would restrict the access of both adults and children to material considered "harmful to minors," and because the statute is not narrowly drawn. PSINet, Inc. v. Chapman, 167 F. Supp. 2d 878, 2001 U.S. Dist. LEXIS 16352 (W.D. Va. 2001), aff'd, 362 F.3d 227 (4th Cir. 2004).

Section 18.2-391, as amended by Acts 1999, c. 936, violates the Commerce Clause of the United States Constitution because it is technologically infeasible for a Web site operator to limit access to online materials by geographic location, and therefore, in order to avoid prosecution, an adult Web site operator must comply with the most restrictive state obscenity regulations if it is to make its content available on the Web at all. PSINet, Inc. v. Chapman, 167 F. Supp. 2d 878, 2001 U.S. Dist. LEXIS 16352 (W.D. Va. 2001), aff'd, 362 F.3d 227 (4th Cir. 2004).

Section 18.2-391 is unconstitutionally overbroad and violates the First Amendment; the district court's entry of summary judgment in favor of plaintiff businesses, membership organizations, and individuals which entered a permanent injunction against the statute was upheld. Psinet, Inc. v. Chapman, 362 F.3d 227, 2004 U.S. App. LEXIS 5599 (4th Cir. 2004).

Section 18.2-391 violates the Commerce Clause; given the broad reach of the Internet, it was difficult for the court to see how such a blanket regulation could be construed to have only a local effect. Psinet, Inc. v. Chapman, 362 F.3d 227, 2004 U.S. App. LEXIS 5599 (4th Cir. 2004).

Injunction issued on basis of possible unconstitutionality. — Plaintiffs representing a spectrum of businesses, membership organizations and individuals who used the Internet to communicate, disseminate, display and to seek access to a broad range of speech were entitled to a preliminary injunction enjoining the enforcement of this section on the grounds that if no injunction issued, plaintiffs faced the choice of self-censorship or subjecting themselves to criminal liability, that plaintiffs were likely to succeed on the merits in that the statute in question was not narrowly tailored, did not provide the most effective means of preventing juveniles from viewing sexually explicit and harmful materials, and unduly burdened interstate commerce, and that it was in the public interest to prevent enforcement of an unconstitutional statute. PSINet, Inc. v. Chapman, 108 F. Supp. 2d 611, 2000 U.S. Dist. LEXIS 11621 (W.D. Va. 2000).

Virginia Code's current definition of "harmful to juveniles" is modification of Miller v. California, 413 U.S. 15, 93 S. Ct. 2607, 37 L. Ed. 2d 419 (1973) definition of obscenity, adapted for juveniles. Virginia v. American Booksellers Ass'n, 484 U.S. 383, 108 S. Ct. 636, 98 L. Ed. 2d 782 (1988).

Intent of 1985 amendment to subsection (a). — The 1985 amendment to subsection (a) of this section, which added "or to knowingly display for commercial purpose in a manner whereby juveniles may examine and peruse," is aimed not at the method chosen by the bookseller to display his wares for sale, but at the opportunity he may afford to juveniles to take off the shelves books which they are unable to buy, and to read them in the store. Commonwealth v. American Booksellers Ass'n, 236 Va. 168, 372 S.E.2d 618 (1988), cert. denied, 494 U.S. 1056, 110 S. Ct. 1525, 108 L. Ed. 2d 764 (1990).

If a work is found to have serious literary, artistic, political or scientific value for a legitimate minority of normal, older adolescents, then it cannot be said to lack such value for the entire class of juveniles taken as a whole. Commonwealth v.

American Booksellers Ass'n, 236 Va. 168, 372 S.E.2d 618 (1988), cert. denied, 494 U.S. 1056, 110 S. Ct. 1525, 108 L. Ed. 2d 764 (1990).

Books not shown to be "harmful to juveniles." — Where none of the 16 books in question in a certification procedure met the third prong of the tripartite test established in Ginsberg v. New York, 390 U.S. 629, 88 S. Ct. 1274 (1968), for determination of materials harmful to minors, none of the books was "harmful to juveniles" within the meaning of § 18.2-390 and this section. Commonwealth v. American Booksellers Ass'n, 236 Va. 168, 372 S.E.2d 618 (1988), cert. denied, 494 U.S. 1056, 110 S. Ct. 1525, 108 L. Ed. 2d 764 (1990).

§ 18.2-391.1. Exceptions to application of article.

Nothing contained in this article shall be construed to apply to:

1. The purchase, distribution, exhibition, or loan of any work of art, book, magazine, or other printed or manuscript material by any accredited museum, library, school, or institution of higher learning.

2. The exhibition or performance of any play, drama, tableau, or motion picture by any theatre, museum, school or institution of higher learning, either supported by public appropriation or which is an accredited institution supported by private funds.

History.
1977, c. 480.

ARTICLE 7.

CRUELTY TO ANIMALS.

§§ 18.2-392 through 18.2-403. Repealed by Acts 1984, c. 492.

Cross references.
For the comprehensive animal laws, see now § 3.2-5900 et seq. As to offenses involving animals, see now § 18.2-403.1 et seq.

ARTICLE 8.

OFFENSES INVOLVING ANIMALS.

§ 18.2-403.1. Offenses involving animals — Class 1 misdemeanors.

The following unlawful acts and offenses against animals shall constitute and be punished as a Class 1 misdemeanor:

1. Violation of subsection A of § 3.2-6570 pertaining to cruelty to animals, except as provided for second or subsequent violations in that section.

2. Violation of § 3.2-6508 pertaining to transporting animals under certain conditions.

3. Making a false claim or receiving money on a false claim under § 3.2-6553 pertaining to compensation for livestock and poultry killed by dogs.

4. Violation of § 3.2-6518 pertaining to boarding establishments and groomers as defined in § 3.2-6500.

History.

1984, c. 492; 1992, c. 177; 1993, c. 174; 1996, c. 249; 1999, c. 620.

Editor's note.

At the direction of the Virginia Code Commission, Title 3.2 references were substituted for Title 3.1 references to conform to the title revision by Acts 2008, c. 860.

Michie's Jurisprudence.

For related discussion, see 1B M.J. Animals, § 14.

§ 18.2-403.2. Offenses involving animals — Class 3 misdemeanors.

The following unlawful acts and offenses against animals shall constitute and be punished as a Class 3 misdemeanor:

1. Violation of § 3.2-6511 pertaining to the failure of a shopkeeper or pet dealer to provide adequate care to animals.

2. Violation of § 3.2-6509 pertaining to the misrepresentation of an animal's condition by the shopkeeper or pet dealer.

3. Violation of § 3.2-6504 pertaining to the abandonment of animals.

4. Violation of § 3.2-6510 pertaining to the sale of baby fowl.

5. Violation of clause (iii) of subsection A of § 3.2-6570 pertaining to soring horses.

6. Violation of § 3.2-6519 pertaining to notice of consumer remedies required to be supplied by boarding establishments.

History.

1984, c. 492; 1992, c. 177; 1993, c. 174; 1999, c. 620; 2003, c. 787; 2008, cc. 543, 707.

Editor's note.

At the direction of the Virginia Code Commission, Title 3.2 references were substituted for Title 3.1 references to conform to the title revision by Acts 2008, c. 860.

Acts 2008, cc. 543 and 707, in cl. 3 provide: "That the provisions of this act may result in a net increase in periods of imprisonment or commitment. Pursuant to § 30-19.1:4, the estimated amount of the necessary appropriation cannot be determined for periods of imprisonment in state adult correctional facilities and cannot be determined for periods of commitment to the custody of the Department of Juvenile Justice."

The 2008 amendments.

The 2008 amendments by cc. 543 and 707 are identical, and deleted former subdivision 5, which read: "Violation of § 3.1-796.125 pertaining to fighting cocks, dogs and other animals"; and redesignated former subdivisions 6 and 7 as subdivisions 5 and 6, respectively.

Law Review.

For annual survey article, "Animal Law," see 44 U. Rich. L. Rev. 185 (2009).

§ 18.2-403.3. Offenses involving animals — Class 4 misdemeanors.

The following unlawful acts and offenses against animals shall constitute and be punished as a Class 4 misdemeanor:

1. Violation of § 3.2-6566 pertaining to interference of agents charged with preventing cruelty to animals.

2. Violation of § 3.2-6573 pertaining to shooting pigeons.

3. Violation of § 3.2-6554 pertaining to disposing of the body of a dead companion animal.

4. Violation of ordinances passed pursuant to §§ 3.2-6522 and 3.2-6525 pertaining to rabid dogs and preventing the spread of rabies and the running at large of vicious dogs.

5. Violation of an ordinance passed pursuant to § 3.2-6539 requiring dogs to be on a leash.

6. Failure by any person to secure and exhibit the permits required by § 29.1-422 pertaining to field trails, night trails and foxhounds.

7. Diseased dogs. — For the owner of any dog with a contagious or infectious disease to permit such dog to stray from his premises if such disease is known to the owner.

8. License application. — For any person to make a false statement in order to secure a dog or cat license to which he is not entitled.

9. License tax. — For any dog or cat owner to fail to pay any license tax required by § 3.2-6530 before February 1 for the year in which it is due. In addition, the court may order confiscation and the proper disposition of the dog or cat.

10. Concealing a dog or cat. — For any person to conceal or harbor any dog or cat on which any required license tax has not been paid.

11. Removing collar and tag. — For any person, except the owner or custodian, to remove a legally acquired license tag from a dog or cat without the permission of the owner or custodian.

12. Violation of § 3.2-6503 pertaining to care of animals by owner.

History.

1984, c. 492; 1993, cc. 174, 817.

Editor's note.

At the direction of the Virginia Code Commission, Title 3.2 references were substituted for Title 3.1 references to conform to the title revision by Acts 2008, c. 860.

§ 18.2-403.4. Unauthorized release of animals; penalty.

Any person who intentionally releases an animal, as defined in § 3.2-6500, lawfully confined for scientific, research, commercial, agricultural or educational purposes without the consent of the owner or custodian of the animal and with the intent to impede or obstruct any such lawful purpose shall be guilty of a Class 1 misdemeanor.

History.

1992, c. 307.

Editor's note.

At the direction of the Virginia Code Commission, Title 3.2 references were substituted for Title 3.1 references to conform to the title revision by Acts 2008, c. 860.

Michie's Jurisprudence.

For related discussion, see 1B M.J. Animals, § 17.

CHAPTER 9.

CRIMES AGAINST PEACE AND ORDER.

ARTICLE 1.

RIOT AND UNLAWFUL ASSEMBLY.

§ 18.2-404. Obstructing free passage of others.

Any person or persons who in any public place or on any private property open to the public unreasonably or unnecessarily obstructs the free passage of other persons to and from or within such place or property and who shall fail or refuse to cease such obstruction or move on when requested to do so by the owner or lessee or agent or employee of such owner or lessee or by a duly authorized law-enforcement officer shall be guilty of a Class 1 misdemeanor. Nothing in this section shall be construed to prohibit lawful picketing.

History.
Code 1950, § 18.1-254.01; 1968, c. 608; 1975, cc. 14, 15.

Cross references.
As to disorderly conduct on grounds of state hospital, see § 37.2-429.

Law Review.
For survey of Virginia statutory changes in substantive criminal law for the year 1970-1971, see 57 Va. L. Rev. 1467 (1971). For survey of Virginia law on criminal law and procedure for the year 2007-2008, see 43 U. Rich. L. Rev. 149 (2008).

Michie's Jurisprudence.
For related discussion, see 2A M.J. Arrest, § 4; 13A M.J. Mobs, Riots and Lynchings, §§ 1, 4.

CASE NOTES

Elements. — The adverbs "unreasonably" and "unnecessarily" modify the verb "obstruct" and are an element required for conviction under this section. Juares v. Commonwealth, 26 Va. App. 154, 493 S.E.2d 677 (1997).

Under this section, the accused must be proved to have obstructed the free passage of other persons either unreasonably OR unnecessarily (emphasis in original). Juares v. Commonwealth, 26 Va. App. 154, 493 S.E.2d 677 (1997).

Determining whether an obstruction is unreasonable or unnecessary requires an examination of the facts and circumstances of each case. Juares v. Commonwealth, 26 Va. App. 154, 493 S.E.2d 677 (1997).

Sufficient evidence. — Defendant obstructed the free passage of others to and from private property open to the public where she positioned herself outside a medical center so that people were required to walk around her, and vehicles entering the center were required to stop. Juares v. Commonwealth, 26 Va. App. 154, 493 S.E.2d 677 (1997).

§ 18.2-405. What constitutes a riot; punishment.

Any unlawful use, by three or more persons acting together, of force or violence which seriously jeopardizes the public safety, peace or order is riot.

Every person convicted of participating in any riot shall be guilty of a Class 1 misdemeanor.

If such person carried, at the time of such riot, any firearm or other deadly or dangerous weapon, he shall be guilty of a Class 5 felony.

History.

Code 1950, §§ 18.1-254.1, 18.1-254.2; 1968, c. 460; 1971, Ex. Sess., c. 251; 1975, cc. 14, 15.

Law Review.

For discussion of Virginia's legislative response to riots and their underlying causes, see 54 Va. L. Rev. 1031 (1968). For article, "Injunctive Control of Disruptive Student Demonstrations," see 56 Va. L. Rev. 215 (1970). For survey of Virginia criminal law procedure for the year 1969-1970, see 56 Va. L. Rev. 1572 (1970). For survey of Virginia law on evidence for the year 1969-1970, see 56 Va. L. Rev. 1325 (1970). For note, "The Clear and Present Danger Standard: Its Present Viability," see 6 U. Rich. L. Rev. 93 (1971). For survey of constitutional law in Virginia for the year 1970-1971, see 57 Va. L. Rev. 1476 (1971). For survey of Virginia statutory changes in substantive criminal law for the year 1970-1971, see 57 Va. L. Rev. 1467 (1971).

CASE NOTES

The common-law definition of unlawful assembly expressly requires clear and present danger of violent conduct. Owens v. Commonwealth, 211 Va. 633, 179 S.E.2d 477 (1971).

Mere presence is not enough to support a conviction. Jones v. Commonwealth, 210 Va. 299, 170 S.E.2d 779 (1969).

Evidence insufficient to convict. — See Corbett v. Commonwealth, 210 Va. 304, 171 S.E.2d 251 (1969).

Any action under § 18.2-407 can only be taken in conjunction with this section or § 18.2-406. Thus, before § 18.2-407 can be invoked, the public peace and order must be in jeopardy. United Steelworkers v. Dalton, 544 F. Supp. 282 (E.D. Va. 1982).

§ 18.2-406. What constitutes an unlawful assembly; punishment.

Whenever three or more persons assembled share the common intent to advance some lawful or unlawful purpose by the commission of an act or acts of unlawful force or violence likely to jeopardize seriously public safety, peace or order, and the assembly actually tends to inspire persons of ordinary courage with well-grounded fear of serious and immediate breaches of public safety, peace or order, then such assembly is an unlawful assembly. Every person who participates in any unlawful assembly shall be guilty of a Class 1 misdemeanor. If any such person carried, at the time of his participation in an unlawful assembly, any firearm or other deadly or dangerous weapon, he shall be guilty of a Class 5 felony.

History.

Code 1950, §§ 18.1-254.1, 18.1-254.3; 1968, c. 460; 1971, Ex. Sess., c. 251; 1975, cc. 14, 15.

Michie's Jurisprudence.

For related discussion, see 3A M.J. Breach of the Peace, § 2; 13A M.J. Mobs, Riots and Lynchings, §§ 1, 4.

CASE NOTES

Constitutionality. — On its face, this section does not impermissibly infringe upon rights under U.S. Const., Amend. I. United

Steelworkers v. Dalton, 544 F. Supp. 282 (E.D. Va. 1982).

Language of this section closely follows common-law definition of unlawful assembly. That definition requires the existence of circumstances evidencing a present threat of violence or breach of public order. United Steelworkers v. Dalton, 544 F. Supp. 282 (E.D. Va. 1982).

States have right to maintain public order. — There is no doubt that the states retain the right to maintain public order. When clear and present danger of riot, disorder, interference with traffic upon the public streets, or other immediate threat to public safety, peace or order, appears, the power of the state to prevent or punish is obvious. This section does no more than exercise that power. United Steelworkers v. Dalton, 544 F. Supp. 282 (E.D. Va. 1982).

Any action under § 18.2-407 can only be taken in conjunction with § 18.2-405 or this section. Thus, before § 18.2-407 can be invoked, the public peace and order must be in jeopardy. United Steelworkers v. Dalton, 544 F. Supp. 282 (E.D. Va. 1982).

§ 18.2-407. Remaining at place of riot or unlawful assembly after warning to disperse.

Every person, except the owner or lessee of the premises, his family and nonrioting guests, and public officers and persons assisting them, who remains at the place of any riot or unlawful assembly after having been lawfully warned to disperse, shall be guilty of a Class 3 misdemeanor.

History.

Code 1950, § 18.1-254.4; 1968, c. 460; 1971, Ex. Sess., c. 251; 1975, cc. 14, 15.

Cross references.

As to arrest for violation of this section, see § 19.2-74.

Michie's Jurisprudence.

For related discussion, see 13A M.J. Mobs, Riots and Lynchings, § 1.

CASE NOTES

Constitutionality. — Although this section can be applied to cause the removal from the streets of persons engaged in wholly lawful activities, that fact does not require a holding that this section is unconstitutional on its face. United Steelworkers v. Dalton, 544 F. Supp. 282 (E.D. Va. 1982).

Police must act quickly against clear and present danger. — When the public peace and order are in jeopardy, it is not unreasonable to authorize the police to clear the streets. This is not a long term measure. Once order is restored, those engaged in lawful activity may return to the streets. But at the time of a disturbance, or when there is a clear and present danger of an immediate disturbance, the Commonwealth requires that the police be able to take quick action. To require individual determinations of who is acting lawfully and who unlawfully would prove unduly burdensome. The ability of the police to restore order would be impaired; the restoration of order, unnecessarily slowed. United Steelworkers v. Dalton, 544 F. Supp. 282 (E.D. Va. 1982).

Any action under this section can only be taken in conjunction with § 18.2-405 or § 18.2-406. Thus, before this section can be invoked, the public peace and order must be in jeopardy. United Steelworkers v. Dalton, 544 F. Supp. 282 (E.D. Va. 1982).

§ 18.2-408. Conspiracy; incitement, etc., to riot.

Any person who conspires with others to cause or produce a riot, or directs, incites, or solicits other persons who participate in a riot to acts of force or violence, shall be guilty of a Class 5 felony.

History.
Code 1950, § 18.1-254.5:1; 1971, Ex. Sess., c. 251; 1975, cc. 14, 15.

§ 18.2-409. Resisting or obstructing execution of legal process.

Every person acting jointly or in combination with any other person to resist or obstruct the execution of any legal process shall be guilty of a Class 1 misdemeanor.

History.
Code 1950, § 18.1-254.6; 1968, c. 460; 1975, cc. 14, 15.

§ 18.2-410. Power of Governor to summon law-enforcement agencies, national guard, etc., to execute process or preserve the peace.

If it appears to the Governor that the power of the locality is not sufficient to enable the sheriff or other officer to execute process delivered to him or to suppress riots and to preserve the peace, he may order law-enforcement agencies, national guard, militia or other agencies of the Commonwealth or localities as may be necessary to execute such process and to preserve the peace. All persons so ordered or summoned by the Governor are required to attend and act. Any person who, without lawful cause, refuses or neglects to obey the command, shall be guilty of a Class 1 misdemeanor.

History.
Code 1950, § 18.1-254.7; 1968, c. 460; 1975, cc. 14, 15.

§ 18.2-411. Dispersal of unlawful or riotous assemblies; duties of officers.

When any number of persons, whether armed or not, are unlawfully or riotously assembled, the sheriff of the county and his deputies, the police officials of the county, city or town, and any assigned militia, or any of them, shall go among the persons assembled or as near to them as safety will permit and command them in the name of the Commonwealth immediately to disperse. If upon such command the persons unlawfully assembled do not disperse immediately, such sheriff, officer or militia may use such force as is reasonably necessary to disperse them and to arrest those who fail or refuse to disperse. To accomplish this end, the sheriff or other law-enforcement officer may request and use the assistance and services of private citizens. Every endeavor shall be used, both by such sheriff or other officers and by the officer commanding any other force, which can be made consistently with the preservation of life, to induce or force those unlawfully assembled to disperse before an attack is made upon those unlawfully assembled by which their lives may be endangered.

History.
Code 1950, §§ 18.1-254.8, 18.1-254.9; 1968, c. 460; 1975, cc. 14, 15.

Michie's Jurisprudence.
For related discussion, see 13A M.J. Mobs, Riots and Lynchings, § 2.

§ 18.2-412. Immunity of officers and others in quelling a riot or unlawful assembly.

No liability, criminal or civil, shall be imposed upon any person authorized to disperse or assist in dispersing a riot or unlawful assembly for any action of such person which was taken after those rioting or unlawfully assembled had been commanded to disperse, and which action was reasonably necessary under all the circumstances to disperse such riot or unlawful assembly or to arrest those who failed or refused to disperse.

History.
Code 1950, §§ 18.1-254.8, 18.1-254.9; 1968, c. 460; 1975, cc. 14, 15.

Michie's Jurisprudence.
For related discussion, see 13A M.J. Mobs, Riots and Lynchings, § 2.

§ 18.2-413. Commission of certain offenses in county, city or town declared by Governor to be in state of riot or insurrection.

Any person, who after the publication of a proclamation by the Governor, or who after lawful notice to disperse and retire, resists or aids in resisting the execution of process in any county, city or town declared to be in a state of riot or insurrection, or who aids or attempts the rescue or escape of another from lawful custody or confinement, or who resists or aids in resisting a force ordered out by the Governor or any sheriff or other officer to quell or suppress an insurrection or riot, shall be guilty of a Class 5 felony.

History.
Code 1950, § 18.1-254.10; 1968, c. 460; 1975, cc. 14, 15.

§ 18.2-414. Injury to property or persons by persons unlawfully or riotously assembled.

If any person or persons, unlawfully or riotously assembled, pull down, injure, or destroy, or begin to pull down, injure or destroy any dwelling house or other building, or assist therein, or perpetrate any premeditated injury on the person of another, he shall be guilty of a Class 6 felony.

History.
Code 1950, § 18.1-254.11; 1968, c. 460; 1975, cc. 14, 15.

§ 18.2-414.1. Obstructing members of rescue squad in performance of mission; penalty.

Any person or persons who unreasonably or unnecessarily obstruct a member or members of a rescue squad, whether governmental, private or volunteer, in the performance of their rescue mission or who shall fail or refuse to cease such obstruction or move on when requested to do so by a member of a rescue squad going to or at the site of a rescue mission, shall be guilty of a Class 2 misdemeanor.

History.
1976, c. 233; 2002, c. 560.

§ 18.2-414.2. Crossing established police lines, perimeters or barricades.

It shall be unlawful for any person to cross or remain within police lines or barricades which have been established pursuant to § 15.2-1714 without proper authorization.

Any person violating the provisions of this section shall be guilty of a Class 3 misdemeanor.

History.
1984, c. 533; 1990, c. 327.

Michie's Jurisprudence.
For related discussion, see 2A M.J. Arrest, § 4.

ARTICLE 2.

DISORDERLY CONDUCT.

§ 18.2-415. Disorderly conduct in public places.

A person is guilty of disorderly conduct if, with the intent to cause public inconvenience, annoyance or alarm, or recklessly creating a risk thereof, he:

A. In any street, highway, public building, or while in or on a public conveyance, or public place engages in conduct having a direct tendency to cause acts of violence by the person or persons at whom, individually, such conduct is directed; or

B. Willfully or being intoxicated, whether willfully or not, and whether such intoxication results from self-administered alcohol or other drug of whatever nature, disrupts any funeral, memorial service, or meeting of the governing body of any political subdivision of this Commonwealth or a division or agency thereof, or of any school, literary society or place of religious worship, if the disruption (i) prevents or interferes with the orderly conduct of the funeral, memorial service, or meeting or (ii) has a direct tendency to cause acts of violence by the person or persons at whom, individually, the disruption is directed; or

C. Willfully or while intoxicated, whether willfully or not, and whether such intoxication results from self-administered alcohol or other drug of whatever nature, disrupts the operation of any school or any activity conducted or sponsored by any school, if the disruption (i) prevents or interferes with the orderly conduct of the operation or activity or (ii) has a direct tendency to cause acts of violence by the person or persons at whom, individually, the disruption is directed.

However, the conduct prohibited under subdivision A, B or C of this section shall not be deemed to include the utterance or display of any words or to include conduct otherwise made punishable under this title.

The person in charge of any such building, place, conveyance, meeting, operation or activity may eject therefrom any person who violates any provision of this section, with the aid, if necessary, of any persons who may be called upon for such purpose.

The governing bodies of counties, cities and towns are authorized to adopt ordinances prohibiting and punishing the acts and conduct prohibited by this section, provided that the punishment fixed therefor shall not exceed that prescribed for a Class 1 misdemeanor. A person violating any provision of this section shall be guilty of a Class 1 misdemeanor.

History.
Code 1950, §§ 18.1-239, 18.1-240, 18.1-253.1 through 18.1-253.3; 1960, c. 358; 1968, c. 639; 1969, Ex. Sess., c. 2; 1970, c. 374; 1975, cc. 14, 15; 1976, c. 244; 1990, c. 627; 2006, c. 250.

Law Review.
For survey of recent legislation on criminal law — riotous or disorderly conduct at public meetings, see 5 U. Rich. L. Rev. 191 (1970). For survey of Virginia criminal law and procedure for the year 1969-1970, see 56 Va. L. Rev. 1572 (1970). For survey of Virginia criminal law for the year 1973-1974, see 60 Va. L. Rev. 1499 (1974); for the year 1974-1975, see 61 Va. L. Rev. 1697 (1975); for the year 1975-1976, see 62 Va. L. Rev. 1400 (1976). For note on case declaring former Virginia disorderly conduct statute, § 18.1-253.2, unconstitutional, see 33 Wash. & Lee L. Rev. 499 (1976). For survey of Virginia law on criminal law and procedure for the year 2007-2008, see 43 U. Rich. L. Rev. 149 (2008). For annual survey article, "Criminal Law and Procedure," see 44 U. Rich. L. Rev. 339 (2009).

Michie's Jurisprudence.
For related discussion, see 3B M.J. Carriers, §§ 70, 97; 6A M.J. Disorderly Conduct, § 1; 6A M.J. Disturbing Public Meetings, § 1; 13A M.J. Mobs, Riots and Lynchings, §§ 1, 4; 16 M.J. Religious Societies, § 3; 21A M.J. Words and Phrases.

CASE NOTES

Constitutionality of former section. — For case declaring the former Virginia disorderly conduct statute, § 18.1-253.2 unconstitutional, see Squire v. Pace, 380 F. Supp. 269 (W.D. Va. 1974), aff'd, 516 F.2d 250 (4th Cir.), cert. denied, 423 U.S. 840, 96 S. Ct. 68, 46 L. Ed. 2d 58 (1975).

As to meaning of "intoxicated," see Gardner v. Commonwealth, 195 Va. 945, 81 S.E.2d 614 (1954).

This section applies, not only to disturbances which are made while the religious services are progressing, but also to disturbances made while the congregation is assembled for religious worship; though it be at night after the religious services are closed for the day, and the congregation has retired to rest. Commonwealth v. Jennings, 44 Va. (3 Gratt.) 624 (1846).

Disorderly conduct is not a lesser included offense of larceny. Cuthrell v. Zayre of Va., Inc., 214 Va. 427, 201 S.E.2d 779 (1974).

Charges of petit larceny and of disorderly conduct are two separate and distinct offenses, and a conviction of the one did not bar the conviction of the other. Cuthrell v. Zayre of Va., Inc., 214 Va. 427, 201 S.E.2d 779 (1974).

An indictment for disturbing a religious congregation need not set out the means by which the disturbance and disquieting was effected. Commonwealth v. Daniels, 4 Va. (2 Va. Cas.) 402 (1824).

Lack of probable cause to arrest. — Because the police lacked probable cause to arrest defendant for either falsely summoning police or for disorderly conduct, the trial court erred in denying his motion to suppress the drugs obtained from his arrest and defendant's conviction for the possession of cocaine was improper. Thor v. Commonwealth, 2010 Va. App. LEXIS 88 (Mar. 9, 2010).

Conviction of disorderly conduct was upheld where evidence showed that defendant defied the police officer's order to remain seated in his automobile while he prepared the traffic summons, "jumped out," and became loud and uncooperative, refusing to calm down; such willful, intemperate and provocative conduct, in response to proper law enforcement activity, audible for several blocks and visible from a public street, clearly evinced the intent or recklessness contemplated by the ordinance. Keyes v. City of Va. Beach, 16 Va. App. 198, 428 S.E.2d 766 (1993).

Defendant was properly convicted for disorderly conduct at a county board of supervisors meeting where he persisted in inappropriate questioning, refused to leave the podium, disrupted the meeting, prevented the board from hearing the comments of other citizens, and forced the board to forcibly remove him from the room. Mannix v. Commonwealth, 31 Va. App. 271, 522 S.E.2d 885 (2000).

Defendant, upset about being ejected from the bar, got louder and abusive, and attracted a crowd; when officer warned the defendant he would be arrested for that behavior, the defendant started waving his arms around and continued yelling. Believing that the defendant was in the beginning stages of combative behavior and that he wanted to fight, the officer arrested the defendant. It was reasonable to infer from those facts that the defendant was not going to stop causing a scene until he was permitted to re-enter the premises, which he was not entitled to do. Jolinski v. Commonwealth, No. 2083-99-3, 2000 Va. App. LEXIS 449 (Ct. of Appeals June 20, 2000).

Defendant's conviction of disorderly conduct under this section was supported by sufficient evidence, as defendant's acts of taking pictures of the victims, the grandparents of defendant's fiance's children and others, created a risk of violence in instigating a confrontation between defendant and the children's grandmother. Potter v. Commonwealth, No. 0921-01-2, 2002 Va. App. LEXIS 98 (Ct. of Appeals Feb. 12, 2002).

Defendant's conviction of disorderly conduct under § 18.2-415 was supported by sufficient evidence; the situs of the offense, a drug store, was a public place as required by the statute, and defendant's acts of threatening a store manager with physical violence after defendant was fired from his job at the store had a direct tendency to cause acts of violence. Williams v. Commonwealth, No. 0127-02-1, 2002 Va. App. LEXIS 689 (Ct. of Appeals Nov. 19, 2002).

Defendant's conviction for disorderly conduct was affirmed where, when a police officer approached defendant, defendant became angry and loudly cursed the officer, repeatedly called the officer a "bitch" and said she did not have to do what the officer requested, attempted to evade the officer, and when the officer blocked defendant's route of escape, defendant raised her cup above her shoulder and threw the cup at the officer. Davis v. Commonwealth, No. 2638-03-2, 2004 Va. App. LEXIS 489 (Ct. of Appeals Oct. 12, 2004).

Rational jury could have concluded that defendant's threat to the officer, made when he came within striking distance of her, constituted disorderly conduct. Defendant's conduct, including her screaming profanities and demanding entrance to her boyfriend's apartment, evidenced a disintegrating situation requiring intervention of the officer. Brown v. Commonwealth, — Va. App. —, — S.E.2d —, 2005 Va. App. LEXIS 50 (Feb. 8, 2005).

Evidence was sufficient to support defendant's conviction for misdemeanor disorderly conduct in violation of § 18.2-415 in a case stemming from defendant's refusal to leave an off-site betting center even though defendant was asked to do so; defendant's belligerent words and conduct regarding attempts to evict defendant from the betting center had a direct tendency to cause acts of violence necessitating that a reasonable person respond with physical force. Collier v. Commonwealth, — Va. App. —, — S.E.2d —, 2007 Va. App. LEXIS 111 (Mar. 20, 2007).

Case involved a police officer attempting to investigate an accident in the midst of snarled traffic at a busy intersection and over a sustained period of time, appellant screamed profanities at the officer, refused to obey any of his commands or answer any of his questions, and loudly cursed at her husband; the tumult reached such a level that passing vehicles stopped in a nearby parking lot to find out the cause of alarm. It became obvious to the officer that he would have to use physical force to subdue appellant both for his own safety and the safety of those vulnerably stopped at the intersection while she carried on her tirade; under the circumstances, the trial court had a sufficient evidentiary basis to find appellant guilty of disorderly conduct. Tokora-Mansary v. Commonwealth, 2009 Va. App. LEXIS 586 (Dec. 29, 2009).

Other-crimes proviso. — Because the other-crimes proviso of § 18.2-415 applied as a matter of law to the disorderly conduct charge upon which defendant was convicted, even after giving the Commonwealth the benefit of all reasonable inferences, as his actions could either be punishable under §§ 18.2-57, 18.2-416, or 18.2-404, said conviction was reversed and the corresponding arrest warrant dismissed. Battle v. Commonwealth, 50 Va. App. 135, 647 S.E.2d 499, 2007 Va. App. LEXIS 271 (2007).

Because Hampton, Va., City Code § 24-12 was enacted pursuant to the authority of § 18.2-415, prior appellate decisions interpreting § 18.2-415 were relevant in the application of the disorderly conduct ordinance; however, while the other crimes proviso in § 18.2-415 precluded a conviction if the disorderly conduct was comprised solely of conduct punishable under Title 18.2, § 24-12(b) only applied to a subset of those offenses made punishable under Hampton, Virginia, City Code chapter 24, and defendant's conduct constituting indecent exposure was punishable under Hampton, Virginia, City Code chapter 23. Thomas v. City of Hampton, — Va. App. —, — S.E.2d —, 2008 Va. App. LEXIS 431 (Sept. 23, 2008).

Other-crimes proviso reserves disorderly conduct convictions only for conduct not punishable elsewhere in the criminal code; sometimes mistaken as a broad limitation on the statute, the other-crimes proviso has a narrow, finely calibrated scope. It is not enough that the defendant could merely be prosecuted for a Title 18.2 crime because that requires only a showing of probable cause, rather, the conduct exempted by the other-crimes proviso includes only Title 18.2 crimes for which the defendant could be found guilty beyond a reasonable doubt; equally important, the other-crimes proviso precludes a conviction only when the convictable disorderly conduct is comprised solely of conduct otherwise made punishable under this title, each distinct act that, in the aggregate, constitutes disorderly conduct must be otherwise punishable under Title 18.2 for the proviso to apply. Tokora-Mansary v. Commonwealth, 2009 Va. App. LEXIS 586 (Dec. 29, 2009).

Although appellant claimed the other-crimes proviso applied because she could have been charged under § 18.2-464, which punished refusal or neglect to obey a conservator of the peace, or § 18.2-416, which was the abusive language statute, the issue was not whether she could have been charged with other Title 18.2 offenses, it was whether she could have been found guilty beyond a reasonable doubt for such offenses. She could not be convicted under § 18.2-464 because law-enforcement officers were not listed as conservators of the peace in that statute and while she arguably could have been found guilty under § 18.2-416 for using abusive language, a conviction under that section would have punished only one of the distinct acts that, in the aggregate, constituted the basis for her disorderly conduct conviction; in short, appellant's disorderly conduct was not comprised solely of conduct otherwise made punishable under Title 18.2. Tokora-Mansary v. Commonwealth, 2009 Va. App. LEXIS 586 (Dec. 29, 2009).

Sufficiency of the evidence. — Sufficient evidence of defendant's confrontational demeanor and refusal to comply with a deputy's orders was presented to allow the jury to reasonably conclude that a sheriff deputy's concern that he might have to take physical action to subdue defendant was reasonable and supported by the evidence presented; moreover, defendant's conduct had a direct tendency to cause acts of violence by the persons at whom it was directed. Bennett v. Commonwealth, 2007 Va. App. LEXIS 155 (Apr. 17, 2007).

ARTICLE 3.

ABUSIVE AND INSULTING LANGUAGE.

Michie's Jurisprudence.

For related discussion, see 3A M.J. Breach of the Peace, §§ 2, 4; 12A M.J. Libel and Slander, § 49.

§ 18.2-416. Punishment for using abusive language to another.

If any person shall, in the presence or hearing of another, curse or abuse such other person, or use any violent abusive language to such person concerning himself or any of his relations, or otherwise use such language, under circumstances reasonably calculated to provoke a breach of the peace, he shall be guilty of a Class 3 misdemeanor.

History.
Code 1950, § 18.1-255; 1960, c. 358; 1975, cc. 14, 15.

Law Review.
For article on model abusive debt collection statute for Virginia, see 15 Wm. & Mary L. Rev. 567 (1974). For survey of Virginia criminal law for the year 1973-1974, see 60 Va. L. Rev. 1499 (1974); for the year 1975-1976, see 62 Va. L. Rev. 1400 (1976). For survey of Virginia tort law for the year 1975-1976, see 62 Va. L. Rev. 1489 (1976).

CASE NOTES

Application of this section is limited to words that have a direct tendency to cause acts of violence by the person to whom, individually, the remark is addressed. Mercer v. Winston, 214 Va. 281, 199 S.E.2d 724 (1973), cert. denied, 416 U.S. 988, 94 S. Ct. 2393, 40 L. Ed. 2d 765 (1974).

This section addresses itself to a direct confrontation of individuals in which one curses or abuses the other or uses violent abusive language concerning the other or his or her relations under circumstances which would precipitate an immediate, forceful and violent reaction by a reasonable person. It envisions words of a kind and nature spoken under such circumstances as by their utterance reasonably tend to provoke a breach of the peace. Mercer v. Winston, 214 Va. 281, 199 S.E.2d 724 (1973), cert. denied, 416 U.S. 988, 94 S. Ct. 2393, 40 L. Ed. 2d 765 (1974).

In light of such construction this section is not constitutionally vague and overbroad under the First and Fourteenth Amendments to the United States Constitution. Mercer v. Winston, 214 Va. 281, 199 S.E.2d 724 (1973), cert. denied, 416 U.S. 988, 94 S. Ct. 2393, 40 L. Ed. 2d 765 (1974).

This section serves a valid and proper purpose for it is aimed at preventing personal, face-to-face, abusive and insulting language likely to provoke a violent reaction and retaliation. Mercer v. Winston, 214 Va. 281, 199 S.E.2d 724 (1973), cert. denied, 416 U.S. 988, 94 S. Ct. 2393, 40 L. Ed. 2d 765 (1974).

Remarks designed to provoke violence. — Application of this section is limited to words that have a direct tendency to cause acts of violence by the person to whom, individually, the remark is addressed. Hershfield v. Commonwealth, 14 Va. App. 381, 417 S.E.2d 876 (1992).

A conviction under this section must be supported by evidence that abusive language is spoken to or about another in his presence or hearing and under circumstances reasonably calculated to provoke a breach of peace. Hershfield v. Commonwealth, 14 Va. App. 381, 417 S.E.2d 876 (1992).

Remarks not uttered in a "face-to-face" confrontation. — In the context of a private incident between two neighbors separated by a front yard and a fence, the language "go f——— yourself" was not uttered in a "face-to-face" confrontation. Since parties were separated by at least 55 feet and by chain link fence, this was not likely to provoke a breach of peace. Hershfield v. Commonwealth, 14 Va. App. 381, 417 S.E.2d 876 (1992).

Insulting words need not be used in presence of third person. — In order to constitute an offense under this section, the insulting words need not be used in the presence of some third person as well as in the presence of the person to or about whom they were spoken. The expression "such person," in the section refers to the person "in the presence or hearing of" whom the insult is offered; and the offense is complete whenever insulting language is spoken to or about another, or about his female relations, in his

presence and under circumstances reasonably calculated to provoke a breach of the peace, regardless of the presence or absence of third persons. Byrd v. Commonwealth, 124 Va. 833, 98 S.E. 632 (1919).

Evidence of truth is admissible in mitigation of punishment. — In a prosecution under this section, evidence that the offense words spoken were true was held not admissible in bar of the prosecution, but admissible in mitigation of the punishment. Byrd v. Commonwealth, 124 Va. 833, 98 S.E. 632 (1919).

While in many cases the insulting words spoken to or in the presence of another about his female relations, may be of such a character as that their truth would not be accorded very much, if any, weight in mitigation of the offense; yet such evidence should be received for what it is worth as an aid in fixing the punishment. Byrd v. Commonwealth, 124 Va. 833, 98 S.E. 632 (1919).

And rejection is not harmless error. — In a prosecution under this section error in rejecting evidence of the truth of the insulting words offered in mitigation of the punishment was not harmless where the amount of the fine imposed was materially larger than the minimum fixed by the statute. Byrd v. Commonwealth, 124 Va. 833, 98 S.E. 632 (1919).

"Fighting words" is jury question. — If the unlawful conduct relied upon consists of the use by a defendant of violent abusive language to another, it is for the jury to determine whether the words used are "fighting" words and whether the use of such words under the circumstances are reasonably calculated to provoke a violent reaction and retaliation. If so, their utterance constitutes an offense under this section. Mercer v. Winston, 214 Va. 281, 199 S.E.2d 724 (1973), cert. denied, 416 U.S. 988, 94 S. Ct. 2393, 40 L. Ed. 2d 765 (1974).

Venue must be established. — In a prosecution under this section, the Commonwealth is bound to establish the venue, and, regardless of instructions, if there is no proof at all as to where the offense was committed, the verdict of guilty should be set aside and a new trial awarded. Byrd v. Commonwealth, 124 Va. 833, 98 S.E. 632 (1919).

Applied in Smith v. Commonwealth, 30 Va. App. 737, 519 S.E.2d 831 (1999).

§ 18.2-417. Slander and libel.

Any person who shall falsely utter and speak, or falsely write and publish, of and concerning any female of chaste character, any words derogatory of such female's character for virtue and chastity, or imputing to such female acts not virtuous and chaste, or who shall falsely utter and speak, or falsely write and publish, of and concerning another person, any words which from their usual construction and common acceptation are construed as insults and tend to violence and breach of the peace or shall use grossly insulting language to any female of good character or reputation, shall be guilty of a Class 3 misdemeanor.

The defendant shall be entitled to prove upon trial in mitigation of the punishment, the provocation which induced the libelous or slanderous words, or any other fact or circumstance tending to disprove malice, or lessen the criminality of the offense.

History.
Code 1950, § 18.1-256; 1960, c. 358; 1973, c. 526; 1975, cc. 14, 15.

Law Review.
For survey of Virginia tort law for the year 1975-1976, see 62 Va. L. Rev. 1489 (1976). For article on modern defamation law in Virginia, see 21 U. Rich. L. Rev. 3 (1986).

CIRCUIT COURT OPINIONS

Actionable words. — Words that falsely speak towards a woman's chastity and character are actionable as defamation in

Virginia, under § 18.2-417; the words "slut," "whore," "prostitute," and "bitch" fit this meaning under the Virginia Code. Magallon v. Wireless Unlimited Inc., 2012 Va. Cir. LEXIS 98 (Fairfax County Oct. 23, 2012).

Defamation claim properly pleaded. — Employee claimed that an account manager called her a slut, bitch, whore, and prostitute, and her complaint also contained phrases including "bitch, I (expletive) fired you," and "bitch, get away from the store or I am going to call the police," which might infer that the employee had been fired for a criminal offense, which inference could harm her reputation and be prejudicial to her; the employee's complaint properly pleaded a claim for defamation for the manager's actions, for which the business might be held liable. Magallon v. Wireless Unlimited Inc., 2012 Va. Cir. LEXIS 98 (Fairfax County Oct. 23, 2012).

ARTICLE 4.

PICKETING OF DWELLING PLACES.

Michie's Jurisprudence.
For related discussion, see 11B M.J. Labor, § 9.

§ 18.2-418. Declaration of policy.

It is hereby declared that the protection and preservation of the home is the keystone of democratic government; that the public health and welfare and the good order of the community require that members of the community enjoy in their homes a feeling of well-being, tranquility, and privacy, and when absent from their homes carry with them the sense of security inherent in the assurance that they may return to the enjoyment of their homes; that the practice of picketing before or about residences and dwelling places causes emotional disturbance and distress to the occupants; that such practice has as its object the harassing of such occupants; and without resort to such practice, full opportunity exists, and under the terms and provisions of this article will continue to exist, for the exercise of freedom of speech and other constitutional rights; and that the provisions hereinafter enacted are necessary in the public interest, to avoid the detrimental results herein set forth.

History.
Code 1950, § 18.1-367.1; 1970, c. 711; 1975, cc. 14, 15.

Law Review.
For survey of recent legislation on criminal law — picketing of dwelling places prohibited, see 5 U. Rich. L. Rev. 189 (1970). For survey of Virginia criminal law and procedure for the year 1969-1970, see 56 Va. L. Rev. 1572 (1970).

§ 18.2-419. Picketing or disrupting tranquility of home.

Any person who shall engage in picketing before or about the residence or dwelling place of any individual, or who shall assemble with another person or persons in a manner which disrupts or threatens to disrupt any individual's right to tranquility in his home, shall be guilty of a Class 3 misdemeanor. Each day on which a violation of this section occurs shall constitute a separate offense.

Nothing herein shall be deemed to prohibit (1) the picketing in any lawful manner, during a labor dispute, of the place of employment involved in such labor dispute; (2) the picketing in any lawful manner of a construction site; or (3) the holding of a meeting or assembly on any premises commonly used for the discussion of subjects of general public interest.

Notwithstanding the penalties herein provided, any court of general equity jurisdiction may enjoin conduct, or threatened conduct, proscribed by this article, and may in any such proceeding award damages, including punitive damages, against the persons found guilty of actions made unlawful by this section.

History.
Code 1950, §§ 18.1-367.2 through 18.1-367.6; 1970, c. 711; 1975, cc. 14, 15.

ARTICLE 5.

ACTIVITIES TENDING TO CAUSE VIOLENCE.

§ 18.2-420. "Clandestine organization" defined.

"Clandestine organization" means: any organization (1) which conceals, or attempts to conceal, its name, activities or membership, or the names, activities or membership of any chapter, branch, unit or affiliate thereof, by the use of cover-names, codes, or any deceptive practice or other means, or (2) whose members shall be required, urged, or instructed, or shall adopt any practice, to conceal their membership or affiliation and that of others in or with such organization, or (3) whose members shall take any oath or pledge, or shall administer any such oath or pledge to those associated with them, to maintain in secrecy any matter or knowledge committed to them by the organization or by any member thereof, or (4) which shall transact business or advance any purpose at any secret meeting or meetings which are guarded or secured against intrusion by persons not associated with it, and (5) whose purpose, policy or activity includes the unlawful use of violence, threats, or intimidation in accomplishing any of its objectives.

History.
Code 1950, § 18.1-380.1; 1968, c. 792; 1975, cc. 14, 15.

§ 18.2-421. Information to be filed by clandestine organization with State Corporation Commission.

Every existing membership corporation and every existing unincorporated association which is a clandestine organization as defined in § 18.2-420, shall file with the clerk of the State Corporation Commission a sworn copy of its constitution, bylaws, rules, regulations, and oath of membership, together with a roster of its membership and a list of its officers for the current year. Every such corporation and association shall, in case its constitution, bylaws, rules, regulations or oath of membership or any part thereof be revised, changed or amended, within ten days after such revision or amendment, file with the clerk of the State Corporation Commission a sworn copy of such revised, changed or amended constitution, bylaw, rule, regulation or oath of membership. Every such corporation or association shall, within thirty days after a change has been made in its officers, file with the clerk of the State Corporation Commission a sworn statement showing such change. Every such corporation or association shall, at intervals of six months, file with the clerk of the State Corporation Commission, a sworn statement showing the names and addresses of such additional members as have been received in such corporation or association during such interval.

The violation of any provision of this section shall constitute a Class 3 misdemeanor.

The provisions of §§ 18.2-420 and 18.2-421 shall not apply to fraternal organizations which are organized for charitable, benevolent, and educational objectives and whose transactions and list of members are open for public inspection.

History.
Code 1950, § 18.1-380.2; 1968, c. 792; 1975, cc. 14, 15.

§ 18.2-422. Prohibition of wearing of masks in certain places; exceptions.

It shall be unlawful for any person over sixteen years of age while wearing any mask, hood or other device whereby a substantial portion of the face is hidden or covered so as to conceal the identity of the wearer, to be or appear in any public place, or upon any private property in this Commonwealth without first having obtained from the owner or tenant thereof consent to do so in writing. However, the provisions of this section shall not apply to persons (i) wearing traditional holiday costumes; (ii) engaged in professions, trades, employment or other activities and wearing protective masks which are deemed necessary for the physical safety of the wearer or other persons; (iii) engaged in any bona fide theatrical production or masquerade ball; or (iv) wearing a mask, hood or other device for bona fide medical reasons upon (a) the advice of a licensed physician or osteopath and carrying on his person an affidavit from the physician or osteopath specifying the medical necessity for wearing the device and the date on which the wearing of the device will no longer be necessary and providing a brief description of the device, or (b) the declaration of a disaster or state of emergency by the Governor in response to a public health emergency where the emergency declaration expressly waives this section, defines the mask appropriate for the emergency, and provides for the duration of the waiver. The violation of any

provisions of this section shall constitute a Class 6 felony.

History.
Code 1950, §§ 18.1-364, 18.1-367; 1960, c. 358; 1975, cc. 14, 15; 1986, c. 19; 2010, cc. 262, 420.

The 2010 amendments.
The 2010 amendments by cc. 262 and 420 are identical, and inserted the clause (iv) (a) designator and clause (iv) (b).

CASE NOTES

Constitutionality. — This section is not unconstitutional on its face. Hernandez v. Commonwealth, 12 Va. App. 669, 406 S.E.2d 398 (1991), aff'd sub nom. Hernandez v. Superintendent, Fredericksburg-Rappahannock Joint Sec. Ctr., 800 F. Supp. 1344 (E.D. Va. 1992); appeal dismissed, 8 F.3d 818 (4th Cir. 1993), cert. denied, 510 U.S. 1119, 114 S. Ct. 1071, 127 L. Ed. 2d 390 (1994).

In 28 U.S.C.S. § 2254 action, federal district court held this section constitutional. Virginia's mask-wearing prohibition did not violate the First nor Fourteenth Amendment guarantees of freedom of speech, due process, and equal protection as applied to habeas petitioner, a Ku Klux Klan member. Hernandez v. Superintendent, Fredericksburg-Rappahannock Joint Sec. Ctr., 800 F. Supp. 1344 (E.D. Va. 1992), appeal dismissed, 8 F.3d 818 (4th Cir. 1993), cert. denied, 510 U.S. 1119, 114 S. Ct. 1071, 127 L. Ed. 2d 390 (1994).

Section held constitutional as applied to member of Ku Klux Klan. — This section was not unconstitutional as applied to a Ku Klux Klan member who, in addition to the Klan's traditional white robe and hood, wore a mask covering his entire face except for his eyes. Hernandez v. Commonwealth, 12 Va. App. 669, 406 S.E.2d 398 (1991), aff'd sub nom. Hernandez v. Superintendent, Fredericksburg-Rappahannock Joint Sec. Ctr., 800 F. Supp. 1344 (E.D. Va. 1992); appeal dismissed, 8 F.3d 818 (4th Cir. 1993), cert. denied, 510 U.S. 1119, 114 S. Ct. 1071, 127 L. Ed. 2d 390 (1994).

Klan hood not entitled to First Amendment protection. — Ku Klux Klan member's mask-wearing did not constitute expressive conduct entitled to First Amendment protection because it did not convey a particularized message. Hernandez v. Superintendent, Fredericksburg-Rappahannock Joint Sec. Ctr., 800 F. Supp. 1344 (E.D. Va. 1992), appeal dismissed, 8 F.3d 818 (4th Cir. 1993), cert. denied, 510 U.S. 1119, 114 S. Ct. 1071, 127 L. Ed. 2d 390 (1994).

Requisite intent to conceal identity. — The words "so as to conceal the identity" express a requirement of intent; therefore, to violate this section, an individual must intend to conceal his identity by covering his face. Hernandez v. Commonwealth, 12 Va. App. 669, 406 S.E.2d 398 (1991), aff'd sub nom. Hernandez v. Superintendent, Fredericksburg-Rappahannock Joint Sec. Ctr., 800 F. Supp. 1344 (E.D. Va. 1992); appeal dismissed, 8 F.3d 818 (4th Cir. 1993), cert. denied, 510 U.S. 1119, 114 S. Ct. 1071, 127 L. Ed. 2d 390 (1994).

Actions not prohibited by section. — This section does not prohibit the masking of one's face for a purpose other than concealing one's identity, such as protection from cold weather, expression of grief, or practice of a religion. Hernandez v. Commonwealth, 12 Va. App. 669, 406 S.E.2d 398 (1991), aff'd sub nom. Hernandez v. Superintendent, Fredericksburg-Rappahannock Joint Sec. Ctr., 800 F. Supp. 1344 (E.D. Va. 1992); appeal dismissed, 8 F.3d 818 (4th Cir. 1993), cert. denied, 510 U.S. 1119, 114 S. Ct. 1071, 127 L. Ed. 2d 390 (1994).

Evidence sufficiently supported defendant's conviction for wearing a mask in a public place where police officer testified he saw defendant with his face covered by a mask in parking lot of a convenience store which was open to the public for business. Hopson v. Commonwealth, 15 Va. App. 749, 427 S.E.2d 221 (1993).

The evidence was sufficient to support a defendant's conviction under this section where a participant in a robbery identified the defendant and stated that the defendant was wearing a mask when the crime was committed and where an employee of the theatre that was robbed testified that all three men involved in the crime were wearing masks and carrying guns. Kingsberry v. Commonwealth, No. 0142-99-1, 2000 Va. App. LEXIS 622 (Ct. of Appeals Aug. 22, 2000).

See Young v. Commonwealth, No. 0363-03-1, 2003 Va. App. LEXIS 588 (Ct. of Appeals Nov. 12, 2003).

Evidence was sufficient to support a jury's verdict convicting defendant of robbery, use of a firearm in the commission of a felony, § 18.2-53.1, and wearing a mask in public, § 18.2-422, under circumstances in which defendant did not contest the victim's testimony that a robbery occurred, defendant and another individual were identified when the victim's purse was found in a creek near the other individual's residence and the other individual's fingerprint was found on the victim's credit card still inside the purse, when the other individual was arrested, defendant was with him, and, in a subsequent videotaped confession, defendant told a detective that he was the robber and gave numerous specific details about the offense, his subsequent flight from the scene, and the disposal of the purse in the creek; defendant admitted wearing a mask and using a BB gun to commit the offense. Defendant's actions did not support his claim that he confessed to prevent the other individual from being held responsible for the robbery. Sears v. Commonwealth, 2009 Va. App. LEXIS 319 (July 14, 2009).

Although no witness was able to identify defendant by facial recognition, as the robber was wearing a mask during the robbery, there was sufficient evidence to convict defendant of unlawfully wearing a mask during a robbery where the surveillance camera photographs showed the robber wearing a dark, hooded jacket or sweatshirt of some type, with a tag or label on the lower left front side, as well as distinctively marked gloves, the store owner testified that defendant's height was about the same as the height of the robber and the robber was African-American, as was defendant, a police officer later encountered defendant wearing a dark jacket, zipped up, with a knit cap on his head and the hood of his jacket pulled over his head, with a tag or label on the lower left front side, and the officer discovered a pair of gloves and a handgun lying on the ground in a haphazard fashion, as if someone had quickly or carelessly tossed them there, defendant's DNA profile was consistent with that found on the gloves, and the gloves had the same color and distinctive markings as the gloves worn by the robber. Spence v. Commonwealth, 60 Va. App. 355, 727 S.E.2d 786, 2012 Va. App. LEXIS 221 (2012).

Sufficient evidence of principal in the second degree. — Where evidence clearly showed that defendant shared co-defendant's criminal intent; committed an overt act in furtherance of their plans when he supplied mask to co-defendant so that co-defendant could not be identified; and then in a vehicle the defendant controlled, drove co-defendant to the places where the crimes were committed, evidence supported the trial court findings that defendant was guilty as a principal in the second degree of three violations of this section. McGill v. Commonwealth, 24 Va. App. 728, 485 S.E.2d 173 (1997).

Harsher sentence improper. — Judgment was reversed and the case was remanded for a new sentencing hearing on defendant's robbery, conspiracy, and wearing a mask in public convictions as the ends of justice exception in Va. Sup. Ct. R. 5A:18 applied because defendant was sentenced to a maximum total sentence of 33 years in violation of § 19.2-295, when the jury imposed a maximum total sentence of 15 years of imprisonment. Gibbs v. Commonwealth, No. 1726-11-1, 2012 Va. App. LEXIS 324 (Oct. 16, 2012).

§ 18.2-423. Burning cross on property of another or public place with intent to intimidate; penalty; prima facie evidence of intent.

It shall be unlawful for any person or persons, with the intent of intimidating any person or group of persons, to burn, or cause to be burned, a cross on the property of another, a highway or other public place. Any person who shall violate any provision of this section shall be guilty of a Class 6 felony.

Any such burning of a cross shall be prima facie evidence of an intent to intimidate a person or group of persons.

History.
Code 1950, §§ 18.1-365 through 18.1-367; 1960, c. 358; 1968, c. 350; 1975, cc. 14, 15; 1983, c. 337.

Law Review.
For 2003/2004 survey of criminal law and procedure, see 39 U. Rich. L. Rev. 133 (2004).

CASE NOTES

Constitutionality. — Section 18.2-423 violates the First Amendment to the United States Constitution, because it is impermissible to punish intimidation based solely upon the content of otherwise protected symbolic speech, and because the statute is overbroad in that it permits arrest and prosecution for both protected and unprotected speech. Black v. Commonwealth, 262 Va. 764, 553 S.E.2d 738, 2001 Va. LEXIS 144 (2001).

Statutory prohibition of cross burning with the intent to intimidate does not violate the right to freedom of speech, since the statute bans intentional intimidating conduct rather than expression. Virginia v. Black, 538 U.S. 343, 123 S. Ct. 1536, 155 L. Ed. 2d 535, 2003 U.S. LEXIS 2715 (2003).

On remand from the United States Supreme Court, the court declined to interpret a model jury instruction to save the prima facie evidence provision of § 18.2-423 from unconstitutionality because the instruction, taken in context of the other instructions, properly interpreted the provision. Thus, the court affirmed its prior holding that the prima facie evidence provision of § 18.2-423 was unconstitutionally overbroad because of its chilling effect upon the exercise of free speech under the First Amendment. Elliott v. Commonwealth, 267 Va. 464, 593 S.E.2d 263, 2004 Va. LEXIS 41 (2004).

Because Va. Const., art. I, § 12, was coextensive with the First Amendment's free speech provisions, after severance of the provision concerning prima facie evidence of intent, § 18.2-423 did not violate the First Amendment or Va. Const., art. I, § 12. Elliott v. Commonwealth, 267 Va. 464, 593 S.E.2d 263, 2004 Va. LEXIS 41 (2004).

Severability of prima facie evidence provision. — Because § 18.2-423 did not fall within either of the exceptions to the rule of severability established in § 1-17.1 [see now § 1-243], the court held that the statute was severable and that the provisions of the statute that remained did not violate the First Amendment or Va. Const., art. I, § 12. Elliott v. Commonwealth, 267 Va. 464, 593 S.E.2d 263, 2004 Va. LEXIS 41 (2004).

§ 18.2-423.01. Burning object on property of another or a highway or other public place with intent to intimidate; penalty.

A. Any person who, with the intent of intimidating any person or group of persons, burns an object on the private property of another without permission, is guilty of a Class 6 felony.

B. Any person who, with the intent of intimidating any person or group of persons, burns an object on a highway or other public place in a manner having a direct tendency to place another person in reasonable fear or apprehension of death or bodily injury is guilty of a Class 6 felony.

History.
2002, cc. 589, 600.

§ 18.2-423.1. Placing swastika on certain property with intent to intimidate; penalty; prima facie evidence of intent.

It shall be unlawful for any person or persons, with the intent of intimidating another person or group of persons, to place or cause to be placed a swastika on any church, synagogue or other building or place used for religious worship, or on any school, educational facility or community center owned or operated by a church or religious body.

A violation of this section shall be punishable as a Class 6 felony.

For the purposes of this section, any such placing of a swastika shall be prima facie evidence of an intent to intimidate another person or group of persons.

History.
1983, c. 337.

Law Review.
For article surveying developments in criminal law and procedure in Virginia from July 2001 to September 2002, see 37 U. Rich. L. Rev. 45 (2002).

§ 18.2-423.2. Displaying noose on property of another or a highway or other public place with intent to intimidate; penalty.

A. Any person who, with the intent of intimidating any person or group of persons, displays a noose on the private property of another without permission is guilty of a Class 6 felony.

B. Any person who, with the intent of intimidating any person or group of persons, displays a noose on a highway or other public place in a manner having a direct tendency to place another person in reasonable fear or apprehension of death or bodily injury is guilty of a Class 6 felony.

History.
2009, c. 277.

Editor's note.
Acts 2009, c. 277, cl. 2 provides: "That the provisions of this act may result in a net increase in periods of imprisonment or commitment. Pursuant to § 30-19.1:4, the estimated amount of the necessary appropriation cannot be determined for periods of imprisonment in state adult correctional facilities and cannot be determined for periods of commitment to the custody of the Department of Juvenile Justice."

ARTICLE 6.
UNLAWFUL USE OF TELEPHONES.

§§ 18.2-424, 18.2-425. Repealed by Acts 2007, c. 467, cl. 2.

§ 18.2-425.1. Repealed by Acts 2009, c. 699, cl. 2.

Cross references.
For current provisions restricting certain solicitation calls, see Automatic Dialing-Announcing Devices, Chapter 44.1 (§ 59.1-518.1 et seq.) of Title 59.1.

§ 18.2-426. "Emergency call" and "emergency personnel" defined.

As used in this article:

"*Emergency call*" means a call to report a fire or summon police, or for medical aid or ambulance service, in a situation where human life or property is in jeopardy and the prompt summoning of aid is essential.

"*Emergency personnel*" means any persons, paid or volunteer, who receive calls for dispatch of police, fire, or emergency medical service personnel, and includes law-enforcement officers, firefighters, including special forest wardens designated pursuant to § 10.1-1135, and emergency medical service personnel.

History.
Code 1950, § 18.1-370; 1960, c. 358; 1975, cc. 14, 15; 1995, c. 791; 2000, c. 962; 2007, c. 467.

Law Review.
For comment, "'911' Emergency Assistance Call Systems: Should Local Governments Be Liable for Negligent Failure to Respond?," see 8 Geo. Mason U.L. Rev. 103 (1985).

§ 18.2-427. Use of profane, threatening, or indecent language over public airways or by other methods.

Any person who uses obscene, vulgar, profane, lewd, lascivious, or indecent language, or makes any suggestion or proposal of an obscene nature, or threatens any illegal or immoral act with the intent to coerce, intimidate, or harass any person, over any telephone or citizens band radio, in this Commonwealth, is guilty of a Class 1 misdemeanor.

"Over any telephone" includes, for purposes of this section, any electronically transmitted communication producing a visual or electronic message that is received or transmitted by cellular telephone or other wireless telecommunications device.

History.
Code 1950, § 18.1-238; 1960, c. 358; 1964, c. 577; 1975, cc. 14, 15; 1976, c. 312; 1984, c. 592; 2010, c. 565; 2011, c. 246.

The 2010 amendments.
The 2010 amendment by c. 565 rewrote the section.

The 2011 amendments.
The 2011 amendment by c. 246 substituted "communication producing a visual or electronic message that is received or transmitted by cellular telephone or other wireless telecommunications device" for "message that is received or transmitted by telephone" in the last paragraph.

Law Review.
For survey of Virginia criminal law for the year 1972-1973, see 59 Va. L. Rev. 1458 (1973). For article on model abusive debt collection statute for Virginia, see 15 Wm. & Mary L. Rev. 567 (1974). For survey of Virginia criminal law for the year 1974-1975, see 61 Va. L. Rev. 1697 (1975); for the year 1975-1976, see 62 Va. L. Rev. 1400 (1976). For note on case holding predecessor § 18.1-238 unconstitutional, see 33 Wash. & Lee L. Rev. 499 (1976). For article, "Construction Law," see 45 U. Rich. L. Rev. 227 (2010). For annual survey of Virginia law article, "Criminal Law and Procedure," see 47 U. Rich. L. Rev. 143 (2012).

Michie's Jurisprudence.
For related discussion, see 12A M.J. Libel and Slander, § 49; 18 M.J. Telegraph and Telephone Companies, § 2.

CASE NOTES

Section as it stood prior to 1975 and 1976 amendments held facially overbroad and impermissibly sweeping. — See Walker v. Dillard, 523 F.2d 3 (4th Cir.), cert. denied, 423 U.S. 906, 96 S. Ct. 208, 46 L. Ed. 2d 136 (1975).

Section is not overbroad. — This section is not overbroad because it can be construed so that the phrase "with the intent to coerce, intimidate, or harass" applies to the words that it directly follows and also applies to the use of "obscene, vulgar, profane, lewd, lascivious, or indecent language." Perkins v. Commonwealth, 12 Va. App. 7, 402 S.E.2d 229 (1991).

In view of the legislature's amendments to the statute following the decision in *Walker v. Dillard*, 523 F.2d 3 (4th Cir.), cert. denied, 423 U.S. 906, 96 S. Ct. 208, 46 L. Ed. 2d 136 (1975), the legislature intended to address harassing conduct as the evil to be proscribed and intended to narrow the scope of the speech phrases to that which is obscene. This construction is not strained and removes protected speech from within the statute's sweep. Perkins v. Commonwealth, 12 Va. App. 7, 402 S.E.2d 229 (1991).

Section is not void for vagueness. — By requiring that the language be used with the intent to "coerce, intimidate, or harass," the statute gives a person of ordinary intelligence a reasonable opportunity to know what is prohibited. The police cannot make arbitrary arrests under the statute. By requiring a criminal mens rea, any alleged vagueness has been remedied. Perkins v. Commonwealth, 12 Va. App. 7, 402 S.E.2d 229 (1991).

Words "vulgar," "profane" and "indecent" are capable of overbroad interpretation. Walker v. Dillard, 523 F.2d 3 (4th Cir.), cert. denied, 423 U.S. 906, 96 S. Ct. 208, 46 L. Ed. 2d 136 (1975), decided prior to the 1975 and 1976 amendments to this section.

Words like "vulgar," "profane" and "indecent" have sometimes been interpreted as meaning "obscene," but only when they have been used in conjunction with other, more specific adjectives like "obscene," "lewd" and "lascivious." Walker v. Dillard, 523 F.2d 3 (4th Cir.), cert. denied, 423 U.S. 906, 96 S. Ct. 208, 46 L. Ed. 2d 136 (1975), decided prior to the 1975 and 1976 amendments to this section.

"Threat" must be narrowly defined in order to avoid punishing constitutionally protected speech. Walker v. Dillard, 523 F.2d 3 (4th Cir.), cert. denied, 423 U.S. 906, 96 S. Ct. 208, 46 L. Ed. 2d 136 (1975), decided prior to the 1975 and 1976 amendments to this section.

State has a legitimate interest in prohibiting obscene, threatening and harassing phone calls, none of which are generally thought of as protected by the First Amendment. Walker v. Dillard, 523 F.2d 3 (4th Cir.), cert. denied, 423 U.S. 906, 96 S. Ct. 208, 46 L. Ed. 2d 136 (1975), decided prior to the 1975 and 1976 amendments to this section.

Proscription of section must not be one that unduly impinges on protected expression. Walker v. Dillard, 523 F.2d 3 (4th Cir.), cert. denied, 423 U.S. 906, 96 S. Ct. 208, 46 L. Ed. 2d 136 (1975), decided prior to the 1975 and 1976 amendments to this section.

Use of expert testimony to explain caller identification device was not necessary to Commonwealth's case. The user of the caller identification device could testify as to facts establishing the reliability of the device, including that it had accurately displayed and identified telephone numbers on other occasions. Blackstone v. Commonwealth, No. 1077-96-3 (Ct. of Appeals Oct. 7, 1997).

No error in allowing manager for telephone company to testify. — Trial judge did not err in allowing regional security manager for telephone company to testify where he did not know the type of caller identification device used and claimed no expertise as to the operation of such devices. Although manager did not claim to be an expert, he had knowledge and personal experience with caller identification devices. On this record, the trial judge did abuse his discretion in concluding that manager had sufficient knowledge of this matter to give value to his opinion. Blackstone v. Commonwealth, No. 1077-96-3 (Ct. of Appeals Oct. 7, 1997).

Language held not obscene. — Where defendant left a voice mail message calling an attorney a "pussy," as he meant to thereby characterize the attorney as a cowardly or effeminate man, the word had no sexual connotations attached to it, and his references to excretory functions merely served to emphasize his belief in the

attorney's cowardice, the message did not have as its dominant theme an appeal to the prurient interest in sex, nor did it go substantially beyond the customary limits of candor in the description or representation of such matters. Therefore, as a matter of law, defendant's language was not obscene. Allman v. Commonwealth, 43 Va. App. 104, 596 S.E.2d 531, 2004 Va. App. LEXIS 236 (2004), overruled in part by Barson v. Commonwealth, 58 Va. App. 451, 711 S.E.2d 220, 2011 Va. App. LEXIS 228 (Va. Ct. App. 2011).

While defendant used words which could be obscene in certain contexts, defendant used the offensive words as vulgar curse or swear words to communicate his frustration, anger, contempt or disgust with the victim. Accordingly, defendant's language failed to meet the definition of obscene as required by case law and § 18.2-372 and defendant's conviction under § 18.2-427 was reversed. Lofgren v. Commonwealth, 55 Va. App. 116, 684 S.E.2d 223, 2009 Va. App. LEXIS 491 (2009).

Sufficient evidence of violation. — Statement to school personnel officer by employee facing termination that "I have some fireworks for you" followed by a statement that "I am going to bring all three down," supported the finding of the trial court that appellant violated this section. Witts v. Commonwealth, No. 0078-94-1 (Ct. of Appeals April 4, 1995).

Defendant was properly convicted of violating former § 18.2-427 by leaving threatening messages on the victim's answering machine because (1) defendant's language was sufficient to enable a rational fact-finder to conclude defendant threatened the victim with physical injury in the form of a sexual offense, with the obvious intent to intimidate and harass the victim, (2) such speech fell outside the protection of the First Amendment, so state law could proscribe the language, obscene or not, and (3) whether the language was obscene was immaterial, since the statutory offense of threatening illegal or immoral acts was not qualified by the word "obscene." Rives v. Commonwealth, 284 Va. 1, 726 S.E.2d 248, 2012 Va. LEXIS 126 (2012).

Admission of call trap evidence. — Results of a call trap, which is an electronic device programmed into the telephone company's computer to trace calls, may be admitted only after the particular device in question has been proven reliable. Penny v. Commonwealth, 6 Va. App. 494, 370 S.E.2d 314 (1988).

OPINIONS OF THE ATTORNEY GENERAL

Conspiracy is not a criminal act punishable under this section. See opinion of Attorney General to The Honorable J. Brandon Bell, II, Member, Senate of Virginia, 04-020 (4/16/04).

§ 18.2-428. Giving certain false information to another by telephone.

If any person maliciously advises or informs another over any telephone in this Commonwealth of the death of, accident to, injury to, illness of, or disappearance of some third party, knowing the same to be false, he shall be guilty of a Class 1 misdemeanor.

History.
Code 1950, § 18.1-238.1; 1962, c. 225; 1975, cc. 14, 15.

§ 18.2-429. Causing telephone or pager to ring with intent to annoy.

A. Any person who, with or without intent to communicate but with intent to annoy any other person, causes any telephone or digital pager, not his own, to ring or to otherwise signal, and any person who permits or condones the use of any telephone under his control for such purpose, is guilty of a Class 3 misdemeanor. A second or subsequent conviction under this subsection is punishable as a Class 2 misdemeanor if such prior conviction occurred before the date of the offense charged.

B. Any person who, with or without intent to converse, but with intent to annoy, harass, hinder or delay emergency personnel in the performance of their duties as such, causes a telephone to ring, which is owned or leased for the purpose of receiving emergency calls by a public or private entity providing fire, police or emergency medical service, and any person who knowingly permits the use of a telephone under his control for such purpose, is guilty of a Class 1 misdemeanor.

History.
Code 1950, § 18.1-238.2; 1962, c. 495; 1975, cc. 14, 15; 1989, c. 59; 1995, cc. 410, 478, 791; 2012, c. 133.

The 2012 amendments.
The 2012 amendment by c. 133 designated the existing provisions of the section as subsections A and B; substituted "is guilty" for "shall be guilty" in subsections A and B; and added the last sentence in subsection A.

§ 18.2-430. Venue for offenses under this article.

Any person violating any of the provisions of this article may be prosecuted either in the county or city from which he called or in the county or city in which the call was received.

History.
Code 1950, § 18.1-238; 1960, c. 358; 1964, c. 577; 1975, cc. 14, 15.

§ 18.2-431. Duty of telephone companies; notices in directories.

(1) It shall be the duty, on pain of contempt of court, of each telephone company in this Commonwealth to furnish immediately in response to a subpoena issued by a circuit court such information as it, its officers and employees may possess which, in the opinion of the court, may aid in the apprehension of persons suspected of violating the provisions of this article or the provisions of § 18.2-83 or § 18.2-212.

(2) Every telephone directory distributed to the public which lists the calling numbers of telephones or of any telephone exchange located in this Commonwealth shall contain a notice which explains the offenses made punishable under this article, such notice to be printed in type which conforms with and is comparable to other type on the same page, and to be placed in a prominent place in such directory. Any violation of this subsection shall be punishable as a Class 4 misdemeanor.

History.
Code 1950, §§ 18.1-238, 18.1-371; 1960, c. 358; 1964, c. 577; 1975, cc. 14, 15; 1982, c. 502.

§ 18.2-431.1. Illegal conveyance or possession of cellular telephone by prisoner or committed person; penalty.

A. It shall be unlawful for any person without authorization to provide or cause to be provided a cellular telephone to an incarcerated prisoner or person committed to the Department of Juvenile Justice in any juvenile correctional center.

B. It shall be unlawful for an incarcerated prisoner or person committed to the Department of Juvenile Justice in any juvenile correctional center without authorization to possess a cellular telephone during the period of his incarceration.

C. Any violation of this section is a Class 6 felony.

History.
2005, c. 171; 2013, cc. 707, 782.

Editor's note.
Acts 2013, c. 707, cl. 2 provides: "That the provisions of this act may result in a net increase in periods of imprisonment or commitment. Pursuant to § 30-19.1:4, the estimated amount of the necessary appropriation cannot be determined for periods of imprisonment in state adult correctional facilities; therefore, Chapter 3 of the Acts of Assembly of 2012, Special Session I, requires the Virginia Criminal Sentencing Commission to assign a minimum fiscal impact of $50,000. Pursuant to § 30-19.1:4, the estimated amount of the necessary appropriation cannot be determined for periods of commitment to the custody of the Department of Juvenile Justice."

Acts 2013, c. 782, cl. 2 provides: "Pursuant to § 30-19.1:4, the estimated amount of the necessary appropriation is at least $299,513 for periods of imprisonment in state adult correctional facilities and cannot be determined for periods of commitment to the custody of the Department of Juvenile Justice."

The 2013 amendments.
The 2013 amendments by cc. 707 and 782 are identical, and inserted "or person committed to the Department of Juvenile Justice in any juvenile correctional center" in subsections A and B; and substituted "is" for "shall be" in subsection C.

CASE NOTES

Applicability. — Section 18.2-431.1's prohibition on unauthorized cell phones encompasses incarcerated persons in both state and local correctional facilities. Lewis v. Commonwealth, 2012 Va. App. LEXIS 414 (Dec. 18, 2012).

Evidence sufficient. — Defendant's convictions for possession of a cell phone by a prisoner was supported by sufficient evidence as, in the first instance, the evidence showed that defendant handed the cell phone to the correctional officerr, establishing that he had actual possession of the phone. With regard to the second conviction, the evidence that defendant was lying on the cot moments before the officer searched the cell and that the phone could be easily felt from the outside of the mattress supported the trial court's finding that defendant constructively possessed the phone. Lewis v. Commonwealth, 2012 Va. App. LEXIS 414 (Dec. 18, 2012).

ARTICLE 7.

PLACES OF AMUSEMENT AND DANCE HALLS.

§§ 18.2-432, 18.2-433. Repealed by Acts 2004, c. 462.

Cross references.
For current provisions as to regulation of dance halls by counties, cities and towns, see § 15.2-912.3.

ARTICLE 8.

UNLAWFUL PARAMILITARY ACTIVITY.

§ 18.2-433.1. Definitions.

As used in this article:

"Civil disorder" means any public disturbance within the United States or any territorial possessions thereof involving acts of violence by assemblages of three or more persons, which causes an immediate danger of or results in damage or injury to the property or person of any other individual.

"Explosive or incendiary device" means (i) dynamite and all other forms of high explosives, (ii) any explosive bomb, grenade, missile, or similar device, or (iii) any incendiary bomb or grenade, fire bomb, or similar device, including any device which consists of or includes a breakable container including a flammable liquid or compound, and a wick composed of any material which, when ignited, is capable of igniting such flammable liquid or compound, and can be carried or thrown by one individual acting alone.

"Firearm" means any weapon that will or is designed to or may readily be converted to expel single or multiple projectiles by the action of an explosion of a combustible material; or the frame or receiver of any such weapon.

"Law-enforcement officer" means any officer as defined in § 9.1-101 or any such officer or member of the armed forces of the United States, any state, any political subdivision of a state, or the District of Columbia, and such term shall specifically include, but shall not be limited to, members of the National Guard, as defined in § 101(c) of Title 10, United States Code, members of the organized militia of any state or territory of the United States, the Commonwealth of Puerto Rico, or the District of Columbia, not included within the definition of National Guard as defined by such § 101(c), and members of the Armed Forces of the United States.

History.
1987, c. 720; 2003, c. 976; 2004, c. 263.

Editor's note.
At the direction of the Virginia Code Commission, "§ 101(c)" was twice substituted for "101(9)" in the definition of "law-enforcement officer."

Michie's Jurisprudence.
For related discussion, see 3A M.J. Breach of the Peace, § 2.

§ 18.2-433.2. Paramilitary activity prohibited.

A person shall be guilty of unlawful paramilitary activity, punishable as a Class 5 felony if he:

1. Teaches or demonstrates to any other person the use, application, or making of any firearm, explosive or incendiary device, or technique capable of causing injury or death to persons, knowing or having reason to know or intending that such train-

ing will be employed for use in, or in furtherance of, a civil disorder; or

2. Assembles with one or more persons for the purpose of training with, practicing with, or being instructed in the use of any firearm, explosive or incendiary device, or technique capable of causing injury or death to persons, intending to employ such training for use in, or in furtherance of, a civil disorder.

History.
1987, c. 720.

§ 18.2-433.3. Exceptions.

Nothing contained in this article shall be construed to apply to:

1. Any act of a law-enforcement officer performed in the otherwise lawful performance of the officer's official duties;

2. Any activity, undertaken without knowledge of or intent to cause or further a civil disorder, which is intended to teach or practice self-defense or self-defense techniques such as karate clubs or self-defense clinics, and similar lawful activity;

3. Any facility, program or lawful activity related to firearms instruction and training intended to teach the safe handling and use of firearms; or

4. Any other lawful sports or activities related to the individual recreational use or possession of firearms, including but not limited to hunting activities, target shooting, self-defense and firearms collection.

Notwithstanding any language contained herein, no activity of any individual, group, organization or other entity engaged in the lawful display or use of firearms or other weapons or facsimiles thereof shall be deemed to be in violation of this statute.

History.
1987, c. 720.

CHAPTER 10.

CRIMES AGAINST THE ADMINISTRATION OF JUSTICE.

Article 1. Perjury.

ARTICLE 1.

PERJURY.

Michie's Jurisprudence.

For related discussion, see 9B M.J. Indictments, Informations and Presentments, § 57; 12B M.J. Marriage, § 7; 21A M.J. Words and Phrases.

§ 18.2-434. What deemed perjury; punishment and penalty.

If any person to whom an oath is lawfully administered on any occasion willfully swears falsely on such occasion touching any material matter or thing, or if a person falsely make oath that any other person is 18 years of age or older in order to obtain a marriage license for such other person, or if any person in any written declaration, certificate, verification, or statement under penalty of perjury pursuant to § 8.01-4.3 willfully subscribes as true any material matter which he does not believe is true, he is guilty of perjury, punishable as a Class 5 felony. Upon the conviction of any person for perjury, such person thereby shall be adjudged forever incapable of holding any office of honor, profit or trust under the Constitution of Virginia, or of serving as a juror.

History.

Code 1950, §§ 18.1-273 through 18.1-275; 1960, c. 358; 1972, c. 823; 1975, cc. 14, 15; 2005, c. 423.

Cross references.

As to the Attorney General's limited authority to institute or conduct criminal prosecutions under this section, see § 2.2-511. As to competence of one convicted of perjury or subornation as a witness, see § 19.2-269. As to application of this section to one making a false application for welfare assistance or otherwise swearing falsely in connection with welfare, see § 63.2-502. As to application of this section to false statements made on registration form under Mutual Consent Adoption Registry, see § 63.2-1258. As to submissions to the Screened Family Day Home Provider List, see § 63.2-1704.2.

Law Review.

For note, "Lying on the Stand Won't Cost You a Dime: Should Courts Recognize a Civil Action in Tort for Perjury," see 44 Wash. & Lee L. Rev. 1257 (1988). For article reviewing recent developments and changes in legislation, case law, and Virginia Supreme Court Rules affecting civil litigation, "Civil Practice and Procedure," see 40 U. Rich. L. Rev. 95 (2005). For survey of Virginia criminal law and procedure for the year 2004-2005, see 40 U. Rich. L. Rev. 197 (2005).

Michie's Jurisprudence.

For related discussion, see 1A M.J. Acknowledgments, § 2; 14B M.J. Perjury, §§ 2, 5, 8, 10, 11.

CASE NOTES

Fifth amendment does not shield perjury. — Although the amendment grants a privilege to remain silent without risking contempt, it does not endow the person who testifies with a license to commit perjury. The warnings simply inform the witness that the privilege is available in order to eliminate the dilemma of self-incrimination or perjury. Shifflett v. Commonwealth, 5 Va. App. 277, 361 S.E.2d 783 (1987).

Failure to give fifth amendment warnings is not defense to perjury charge. Shifflett v. Commonwealth, 5 Va. App. 277, 361 S.E.2d 783 (1987).

Statements made in suppression hearing in prosecution of another. — Defendant's incriminating statements made at a suppression hearing in the prosecution of another person were constitutionally admissible as evidence against him at his trial for perjury. Because the crime of perjury had not yet been committed at the time defendant took the stand and began to testify at the suppression hearing, his sixth amendment right to counsel did not attach as to that charge. Therefore, the evidence obtained during his testimony was not required to be excluded simply because other charges were pending at that time. Shifflett v. Commonwealth, 5 Va. App. 277, 361 S.E.2d 783 (1987).

Failure to include words not fatal. — Trial court did not err in refusing to quash indictment because it failed to specifically include words "any material matter " contained in this section since body of indictment contained words "in violation of Code § 18.2-434, " and thus, appellant was fully informed of charge he was required to defend. Tomlinson v. Commonwealth, No. 0798-87-2 (Ct. of Appeals Mar. 7, 1989).

Two witnesses or other corroborating evidence required. — A perjury conviction under this section requires proof of falsity from the testimony of at least two witnesses or other corroborating evidence of falsity in the event the case is supported by the testimony of only one witness. Donowa v. Commonwealth, No. 1579-95-2 (Ct. of Appeals May 28, 1996).

The law as stated in Schwartz v. Commonwealth, 68 Va. (27 Gratt.) 1025 (1876) remains in effect, and a perjury conviction under this section requires proof of falsity from the testimony of at least two witnesses or other corroborating evidence of falsity in the event the case is supported by the testimony of only one witness. Keffer v. Commonwealth, 12 Va. App. 545, 404 S.E.2d 745 (1991).

Videotape evidence alone sufficient to convict. — Defendant's perjury conviction for denying under oath that he had masturbated in a public place was affirmed, as a videotape of him performing the act spoke for itself, and the Schwartz rule's requirement of corroborating testimony was inapplicable. Piatkowski v. Ralph D. Kaiser Co., 219 Va. 1015, 254 S.E.2d 68 (1979).

This section is to be construed strictly as a penal statute. Commonwealth v. Simon, 11 Va. L. Reg. (n.s.) 349 (1925).

Oath must be lawfully administered. — By this section "any occasion " suffices, but it is required that the oath shall be lawfully administered. Thus where there was no requirement or provision of law for a notary's administering the oath of loss of an automobile for the purpose of collecting on an insurance policy, and as under § 49-4 the notary was only authorized to take such affidavits as are required by law, such an affidavit was not lawfully administered as required by this section. Commonwealth v. Simon, 11 Va. L. Reg. (n.s.) 349 (1925).

Where the court which administered an oath had no jurisdiction to do so, one who swore falsely before it was not guilty of perjury. Commonwealth v. Calvert, 3 Va. (1 Va. Cas.) 265 (1809).

Oath must be willful and false. — To constitute the crime of perjury, the oath must have been willful and false. Falsity is the main ingredient of the crime. Thomas v. Commonwealth, 41 Va. (2 Rob.) 795 (1843); Fitch v. Commonwealth, 92 Va. 824, 24 S.E. 272 (1896).

It does not apply to gratuitous affidavit. — A "gratuitous" affidavit, that is, one unprovided for or unauthorized by law, though false, does not fall within the requirements of this section as being an oath "lawfully administered on any occasion ... touching any material matter or thing, " so as to constitute a perjury. Commonwealth v. Simon, 11 Va. L. Reg. (n.s.) 349 (1925).

Knowledge of falsity must be proved. — Perjury can only be established upon proof of knowledge of falsity of the alleged statements. It cannot be predicated where wilfulness and corrup-

tion are not proven. Rothfuss v. Commonwealth, 198 Va. 461, 94 S.E.2d 532 (1956).

And false statement must be material. — To convict one of perjury, the alleged false statement must have been material in the judicial proceeding in which it is proved to have been made. Commonwealth v. Pickering, 49 Va. (8 Gratt.) 628 (1851); Crump v. Commonwealth, 75 Va. 922 (1882); Rhodes v. Commonwealth, 78 Va. 692 (1884). See also Fitch v. Commonwealth, 92 Va. 824, 24 S.E. 272 (1896); Commonwealth v. Roach, 42 Va. (1 Gratt.) 561 (1844).

Where person makes false statements under oath regarding a material fact, he can be prosecuted for perjury for the false statement. Ganzie v. Commonwealth, 24 Va. App. 422, 482 S.E.2d 863 (1997).

R. swore that M. had stolen bacon and offered to sell it to him on November 15th, 1875. Later, R. swore that M. had stolen bacon and offered to sell it to him just before Christmas, 1875. On indictment against R. for perjury, it was not proved that M. did not steal bacon, but it was proved that R. made contradictory statements as to the date. R. was convicted. It was held that the stealing of the bacon was the material matter of the charge; that the date of the offer to sell was not material to the offense; that the oath as to the date was not material to the issue, and was not likely to induce the jury to give the readier credit to the substantial part of the evidence; and that R. was not guilty of perjury. Rhodes v. Commonwealth, 78 Va. 692 (1884).

If the untrue representation does not touch any material matter or thing in the trial, the mere falsity of the statement alone will not sustain a perjury conviction. The testimony must be relevant in the trial of the case, either to the main issue or some collateral issue. Holz v. Commonwealth, 220 Va. 876, 263 S.E.2d 426 (1980).

Defendant's perjury conviction was not upheld where the inquiry to which defendant falsely swore was not material to a proper matter of inquiry. Trotman v. Commonwealth, 10 Va. App. 403, 392 S.E.2d 685 (1990).

This section does not require the Commonwealth to establish that the false testimony was essential to the outcome of the case in order to prove that it was material. Rather, the testimony is material if it was relevant in the trial of the case, either to the main issue or some collateral issue. Donowa v. Commonwealth, No. 1579-95-2 (Ct. of Appeals May 28, 1996).

"Testimony is material if it is relevant to a main or collateral issue on trial," for purposes of this section. Ganzie v. Commonwealth, 24 Va. App. 422, 482 S.E.2d 863 (1997).

Defendant was properly convicted of perjury, as defendant's testimony at the trial of a friend who was a suspect in a murder investigation that defendant had not received a letter from the friend and had never before seen the letter from the friend addressed to him that the prosecuting attorney produced at the friend's trial was material because the letter contained statements indicating the friend's consciousness of guilt and, thus, was central to the issue of the friend's guilt or innocence. Fritter v. Commonwealth, 45 Va. App. 345, 610 S.E.2d 887, 2005 Va. App. LEXIS 124 (2005).

Multiple acts. — Separate false statements give rise to separate violations of this section; multiple acts of perjury can occur from a single occasion. Ganzie v. Commonwealth, 24 Va. App. 422, 482 S.E.2d 863 (1997).

Juror swearing falsely on voir dire commits perjury. — A circuit court has the right and power, on the trial of an indictment for felony, to compel a venireman or bystander called to serve as a juror on the trial, to be sworn on his voir dire, and to answer proper questions touching his fitness as a juror in the particular case, and the juror may be convicted of perjury because of false answers of his voir dire. Commonwealth v. Stockley, 37 Va. (10 Leigh) 678 (1840).

Corroboration. — While the code has never expressly required corroboration to sustain a perjury conviction, from an early date Virginia courts have imposed a corroboration requirement. Keffer v. Commonwealth, 12 Va. App. 545, 404 S.E.2d 745 (1991).

A perjury conviction under this section requires proof of falsity from the testimony of at least two witnesses or other corroborating evidence of falsity in the event the case is supported by the testimony of only one witness. Stewart v. Commonwealth, 22 Va. App. 117, 468 S.E.2d 126 (1996).

A detective's testimony that the defendant was driving a particular car in a particular location on a certain day was sufficiently corroborated so as to support a conviction for perjury based on the defendant's original statement that he was driving the car in a particular location on that day and his subsequent denial under oath that he made such statement as the defendant's original statement was an admission of such facts and Gibbs v. Commonwealth, No. 1117-98-3 (Ct. of Appeals Apr. 6, 1999).

Testimony of friend who was on trial and a detective that defendant talked to was sufficient to show that defendant committed perjury when he testified at the friend's trial that he had not received a letter from jail that the friend sent to him, which defendant subsequently turned over to the detective, as the testimony of the friend and detective was sufficient to satisfy the "two witness" rule necessary to sustain defendant's perjury conviction. Fritter v. Commonwealth, 45 Va. App. 345, 610 S.E.2d 887, 2005 Va. App. LEXIS 124 (2005).

Harmless error in limiting cross-examination. — Defendant's convictions for obtaining $200 or more by false pretenses and giving material false testimony under oath were appropriate even though the trial court's limitation on cross-examination was erroneous because the error was harmless. The record contained extensive evidence impeaching defendant's testimony and establishing the falsified documentary evidence on other critical points and the attorney was not a witness to any of the evidence upon which the conviction for giving material false testimony was based. Lindsey v. Commonwealth, 2011 Va. App. LEXIS 72 (Mar. 1, 2011).

Burden on Commonwealth. — In a prosecution under this section, the burden was on the Commonwealth to prove beyond a reasonable doubt not only that the statements the accused made under oath were false, but that they were known by him to be false at the time. Rothfuss v. Commonwealth, 198 Va. 461, 94 S.E.2d 532 (1956).

The Commonwealth must prove beyond a reasonable doubt, inter alia, that defendant willfully swore falsely. This burden includes not only a showing that the statements made under oath by the defendant were false, but were known by the accused to be false at the time. If the defendant believes the facts stated by him to be true, he may not properly be said to have willfully sworn falsely to such facts. Holz v. Commonwealth, 220 Va. 876, 263 S.E.2d 426 (1980).

In order to obtain a conviction for perjury, the Commonwealth must prove that the defendant made a false statement under oath, that he did so willfully, and that the statement was material to an issue involved in the trial. Donowa v. Commonwealth, No. 1579-95-2 (Ct. of Appeals May 28, 1996).

Section does not apply to perjury before federal tribunals. — A witness who gives his testimony, pursuant to the Constitution and laws of the United States, in a case pending in a court or other judicial tribunal of the United States, whether he testifies in the presence of that tribunal, or before any magistrate or officer, either of the nation or of the state, designated by act of Congress for the purpose, is accountable for the truth of his testimony to the United States only, and cannot be punished by the laws of Virginia under this section. In re Loney, 134 U.S. 372, 10 S. Ct. 584, 33 L. Ed. 949 (1890).

False affidavit for polygraph examination not perjury. — An affidavit which was a condition imposed upon the defendant by the Commonwealth's attorney as a condition precedent to obtaining a polygraph examination requested by the defendant, was not one required by law but, instead, was a gratuitous one. Such an affidavit, however false it may be, cannot sustain a conviction for perjury under this section. Mendez v. Commonwealth, 220 Va. 97, 255 S.E.2d 533 (1979).

Evidence of defendant swearing to co-applicant's age which was false. — Evidence showing that defendant was lawfully under oath and that he swore to the material fact of his co-applicant's age, which was falsely represented in the joint marriage application of the parties, was sufficient to establish defendant's guilt under this section. McKay v. Commonwealth, No. 1721-88-4 (Ct. of Appeals May 8, 1990).

Evidence of conflicting statements is insufficient to sustain conviction. — Statements made by a witness off the stand, which conflicted with his testimony, were insufficient to convict him of perjury. Schwartz v. Commonwealth, 68 Va. (27 Gratt.) 1025 (1876).

Ends of justice exception not applied. — Defendant's perjury conviction was affirmed where: (1) he was convicted under § 18.2-435, but the parties and the trial court proceeded at trial and on appeal as if defendant had been convicted for perjury under § 18.2-434; (2) defendant's claim that there was not sufficient evidence to convict him of perjury because the evidence of falsity was uncorroborated was irrelevant as it was premised on the common-law rule that perjury required proof of the falsity from at least two witnesses or one witness and corroborating evidence that did not apply to perjury under § 18.2-435; and (3) although there was no indication that defendant ever testified under oath on more than one occasion, the appellate court refused to apply the ends of justice exception to Va. Sup. Ct. R. 5A:18 sua sponte. Sutphin v. Commonwealth, 61 Va. App. 315, 734 S.E.2d 725, 2012 Va. App. LEXIS 405 (2012).

Applied in Williams v. Commonwealth, 8 Va. App. 336, 381 S.E.2d 361 (1989); N. Va. Real Estate, Inc. v. Martins, 283 Va. 86, 720 S.E.2d 121, 2012 Va. LEXIS 11 (2012).

CIRCUIT COURT OPINIONS

Knowledge of falsity must be proved. — While being examined under oath pursuant to § 8.01-358, a juror had a duty to not willfully swear falsely in her responses to questions posed to her by the court and counsel during voir dire; however, the evidence was insufficient to establish that the juror swore falsely by her silence in response to questioning by the court. Lester v. Allied Concrete Co., 38 Va. Cir. 308, 2011 Va. Cir. LEXIS 245 (Charlottesville Sept. 6, 2011).

OPINIONS OF THE ATTORNEY GENERAL

Service on jury. — A person convicted of perjury may serve as a juror after his political rights have been restored by the governor. See opinion of Attorney General to The Honorable J. Jack Kennedy, Jr., Clerk of the Circuit Court, Wise County & City of Norton, 12-095, 2012 Va. AG LEXIS 42 (11/16/2012).

Hold public office. — A person convicted of perjury may seek election to public office after his political rights have been restored by the governor. See opinion of Attorney General to The Honorable Ronald K. Elkins, Commonwealth's Attorney, Wise County & City of Norton, 12-080, 2012 Va. AG LEXIS 41 (11/16/2012).

§ 18.2-435. Giving conflicting testimony on separate occasions as to same matter; indictment; sufficiency of evidence.

It shall likewise constitute perjury for any person, with the intent to testify falsely, to knowingly give testimony under oath as to any material matter or thing and subsequently to give conflicting testimony under oath as to the same matter or thing. In any indictment for such perjury, it shall be sufficient to allege the offense by stating that the person charged therewith did, knowingly and with the intent to testify falsely, on one occasion give testimony upon a certain matter and, on a subsequent occasion, give different testimony upon the same matter. Upon the trial on such indictment, it shall be sufficient to prove that the defendant, knowingly and with the intent to testify falsely, gave such differing testimony and that the differing testimony was given on two separate occasions.

History.
Code 1950, § 18.1-276; 1960, c. 358; 1975, cc. 14, 15.

Law Review.
For note, "Lying on the Stand Won't Cost You a Dime: Should Courts Recognize a Civil Action in Tort for Perjury," see 44 Wash. & Lee L. Rev. 1257 (1988).

Michie's Jurisprudence.

For related discussion, see 9B M.J. Indictments, Informations and Presentments, § 57.

CASE NOTES

The term, "give testimony," as used in this section encompasses any material declaration made under oath, whether ex parte or in an adversary proceeding subject to cross-examination. Scott v. Commonwealth, 14 Va. App. 294, 416 S.E.2d 47 (1992).

Burden to show that testimony was not conflicting. — Where the defendant testified at a criminal proceeding that he could not read, but subsequently denied at a child custody hearing that he had testified as such, the defendant bore the burden of producing some evidence to show that his testimony was not conflicting. Henson, Jr. v. Commonwealth, No. 1741-97-2 (Ct. of Appeals Dec. 22, 1998).

Knowing use of perjured testimony. — Although witness' testimony at defendant's trial partially conflicted with the testimony he gave at a co-defendant's trial, there was no evidence indicating the witness gave partially conflicting testimony with the intent to testify falsely, that the witness had any prior negative association with defendant, or had any other motive to testify falsely at defendant's trial, thus defendant's claim that the prosecutor made knowing use of perjured testimony was insufficient as a matter of law. Angelone v. Dabney, 263 Va. 323, 560 S.E.2d 253, 2002 Va. LEXIS 43 (2002).

Conviction affirmed. — Defendant's perjury conviction was affirmed where: (1) he was convicted under § 18.2-435, but the parties and the trial court proceeded at trial and on appeal as if defendant had been convicted for perjury under § 18.2-434; (2) defendant's claim that there was not sufficient evidence to convict him of perjury because the evidence of falsity was uncorroborated was irrelevant as it was premised on the common-law rule that perjury required proof of the falsity from at least two witnesses or one witness and corroborating evidence that did not apply to perjury under § 18.2-435; and (3) although there was no indication that defendant ever testified under oath on more than one occasion, the appellate court refused to apply the ends of justice exception to Va. Sup. Ct. R. 5A:18 sua sponte. Sutphin v. Commonwealth, 61 Va. App. 315, 734 S.E.2d 725, 2012 Va. App. LEXIS 405 (2012).

Applied in Williams v. Commonwealth, 8 Va. App. 336, 381 S.E.2d 361 (1989).

§ 18.2-436. Inducing another to give false testimony; sufficiency of evidence.

If any person procure or induce another to commit perjury or to give false testimony under oath in violation of any provision of this article, he shall be punished as prescribed in § 18.2-434.

In any prosecution under this section, it shall be sufficient to prove that the person alleged to have given false testimony shall have been procured, induced, counselled or advised to give such testimony by the party charged.

History.

Code 1950, § 18.1-277; 1960, c. 358; 1975, cc. 14, 15.

Law Review.

For note, "Lying on the Stand Won't Cost You a Dime: Should Courts Recognize a Civil Action in Tort for Perjury," see 44 Wash. & Lee L. Rev. 1257 (1988).

CASE NOTES

Sufficiency of the evidence. — Trial court committed reversible error in ruling that prosecutor had laid proper foundation to admit into evidence witness's statement under the past recorded recollection exception where witness himself testified that his

memory was not good more than one or two days past the happening of an event. Scearce v. Commonwealth, 38 Va. App. 98, 561 S.E.2d 777, 2002 Va. App. LEXIS 215 (2002).

§ 18.2-437. Immunity of witnesses.

No witness called by the attorney for the Commonwealth, or by the court, and required to give evidence for the prosecution in a proceeding under this article shall ever be proceeded against for the offense concerning which he testified. Such witness shall be compelled to testify and may be punished for contempt for refusing to do so.

History.

Code 1950, § 18.1-277; 1960, c. 358; 1975, cc. 14, 15.

Law Review.

For note, "Lying on the Stand Won't Cost You a Dime: Should Courts Recognize a Civil Action in Tort for Perjury," see 44 Wash. & Lee L. Rev. 1257 (1988).

ARTICLE 2.

BRIBERY AND RELATED OFFENSES.

Michie's Jurisprudence.

For related discussion, see 3A M.J. Bribery, §§ 2, 4 — 6.

§ 18.2-438. Bribes to officers or candidates for office.

If any person corruptly give, offer or promise to any executive, legislative or judicial officer, sheriff or police officer, or to any candidate for such office, either before or after he shall have taken his seat, any gift or gratuity, with intent to influence his act, vote, opinion, decision or judgment on any matter, question, cause or proceeding, which is or may be then pending, or may by law come or be brought before him in his official capacity, he shall be guilty of a Class 4 felony and shall forfeit to the Commonwealth any such gift or gratuity given. This section shall also apply to a resident of this Commonwealth who, while temporarily absent therefrom for that purpose, shall make such gift, offer or promise.

History.

Code 1950, § 18.1-278; 1960, c. 358; 1975, cc. 14, 15; 1978, c. 123.

Cross references.

As to bribery of participant in game, contest or sport, see § 18.2-442. As to solicitation or acceptance of bribe by participant in game or by coach, etc., see § 18.2-443. As to this section in relation to the Virginia Public Procurement Act, see § 2.2-4367.

CASE NOTES

This section is not invalid because it does not in terms require that one accused thereunder have knowledge that the bribe was offered to one in his official capacity. Livingston v. Commonwealth, 184 Va. 830, 36 S.E.2d 561 (1946).

Bribery defined. — Bribery is the offering, giving, receiving, or soliciting of anything of value with intent to influence the recipient's action as a public official. Ford v. Commonwealth, 177 Va. 889, 15 S.E.2d 50 (1941).

The gist of the offense of bribery is the criminal intent to undermine the proper and orderly administration of justice. Ford v. Commonwealth, 177 Va. 889, 15 S.E.2d 50 (1941).

Offense is complete with offer or promise of bribe. — Under this section, an attempt to corrupt, evidenced by an offer or promise of a gift, constitutes bribery on the part of the offeror or promisor as fully and completely as if a corrupt gift had been made and accepted. Ford v. Commonwealth, 177 Va. 889, 15 S.E.2d 50 (1941).

Section embraces offer to pay for future protection. — In a prosecution for bribery, a constable testified that the accused had offered him six dollars a week if he would give her protection in the sale of whiskey. The accused contended that this section did not embrace an offer to pay for protection for an offense to be thereafter committed, or to pay an officer for his failure to perform his duty in the future. It was held that the comprehensive and inclusive language of this section negatived the contention of the accused. Ford v. Commonwealth, 177 Va. 889, 15 S.E.2d 50 (1941).

Indictment need not set out amount of bribe. — An indictment for attempting to bribe a deputy sheriff to summon designated persons upon a jury to try a felony was held to be good, though the amount of the bribe was not set forth, and though the offense is not an offense at common law. Commonwealth v. Chapman, 3 Va. (1 Va. Cas.) 138 (1803).

Nor state that accused had knowledge of official character of officer. — An indictment need not state that the accused had knowledge of the official character of the person to whom the bribe was offered, where the indictment necessarily implied that the accused was being charged with knowledge that he was offering a bribe to a police officer. Livingston v. Commonwealth, 184 Va. 830, 36 S.E.2d 561 (1946).

And it need not be in identical words of this section. — An indictment was held sufficient although it was not in the identical words of this section, as it gave the accused notice of the nature and character of the offense charged so that he could make his defense. Livingston v. Commonwealth, 184 Va. 830, 36 S.E.2d 561 (1946).

Evidence. — On an indictment for attempting to bribe an officer by offering to pay him a sum of money to release the accused and drop a proceeding against her for maintaining a disorderly house, it was not admissible to show that a young girl had been given whiskey to drink, and had had intercourse with a man at the house of the accused the previous night. Such evidence was entirely collateral to, and had no connection with, the alleged attempt to bribe the officer. Haynes v. Commonwealth, 104 Va. 854, 52 S.E. 358 (1905).

CIRCUIT COURT OPINIONS

Offer of $50,000 to drop out of political race not bribery. — Political candidate's claims of libel arising out of a rival's alleged accusation of bribery were subject to demurrer because the statement made, that the candidate offered a rival $50,000 to drop out of the race, did not constitute an allegation that the candidate gave money to influence her as a candidate in any official governmental decision. Borgenicht v. Norment, 75 Va. Cir. 382, 2008 Va. Cir. LEXIS 269 (Richmond Aug. 19, 2008).

§ 18.2-439. Acceptance of bribe by officer or candidate.

If any executive, legislative or judicial officer, sheriff or police officer, or any candidate for such office, accept in this Commonwealth, or if, being resident in this Commonwealth, such officer or candidate shall go out of this Commonwealth and accept and afterwards return to and reside in this Commonwealth, any gift or gratuity or any promise to make a gift or do any act beneficial to such officer or candidate under an agreement, or with an understanding, that his vote, opinion or judgment shall be given on any particular side of any question, cause or proceeding which is or may be by law brought before him in his official capacity or that in such

capacity he shall make any particular nomination or appointment or take or fail to take any particular action or perform any duty required by law, he shall be guilty of a Class 4 felony and shall forfeit his office and be forever incapable of holding any office of honor, profit or trust under the Constitution of Virginia. The word candidate as used in this section and § 18.2-438, shall mean anyone who has filed his candidacy with the appropriate electoral official or who is a candidate as defined in § 24.2-101.

History.
Code 1950, § 18.1-279; 1960, c. 358; 1975, cc. 14, 15.

Editor's note.
At the direction of the Virginia Code Commission, "§ 24.2-101" was substituted for "subdivision (2) of § 24.1-1."

§ 18.2-440. Bribes to officers to prevent service of process.

If any officer authorized to serve legal process receive any money or other thing of value for omitting or delaying to perform any duty pertaining to his office, he shall be guilty of a Class 2 misdemeanor.

History.
Code 1950, § 18.1-281; 1960, c. 358; 1975, cc. 14, 15.

CASE NOTES

The offense punishable by this section is the omitting or delaying to perform any duty, etc., not the doing of any act. Old v. Commonwealth, 59 Va. (18 Gratt.) 915 (1867).

And not merely the duty to serve legal process. — This section punishes the omitting or delaying to perform any duty pertaining to the office of one who is authorized to serve legal process, and not merely the omitting or delaying to perform the duty to serve legal process. Old v. Commonwealth, 59 Va. (18 Gratt.) 915 (1867).

The presentment should follow the terms of this section, or must use terms which show conclusively, or beyond any rational doubt to the contrary, that the accused is guilty of the offense described in this section. Unless this is done, the addition that "so the accused did receive money for omitting and delaying to perform a duty pertaining to his office of constable," etc., will not cure the defect. Old v. Commonwealth, 59 Va. (18 Gratt.) 915 (1867).

The natural and proper mode of charging a violation of this section is to aver that the accused was an officer authorized to serve legal process, as for example, a constable; that while he was such officer, it became his duty, as such, to perform a certain act, as for example, to warrant for a claim entrusted to him for that purpose and recoverable by warrant, or to serve a warrant which had been issued on such claim, and placed in his hands for execution, etc., and that he unlawfully received a certain sum of money, or a certain other thing of value, for omitting or delaying to perform his said duty. While this would be the natural and proper mode of making the charge, and would conform to the very terms of this section, it might be sufficiently made in other terms which are substantially the same with those used in this section or which show conclusively or beyond a rational doubt to the contrary, that the accused is guilty of the offense described in this section at least such a defect would be cured by the verdict. Old v. Commonwealth, 59 Va. (18 Gratt.) 915 (1867).

§ 18.2-441. Giving bribes to, or receiving bribes by, commissioners, jurors, etc.

If any person give, offer or promise to give any money or other thing of value to a commissioner appointed by a court, auditor, arbitrator, umpire or juror (although not impaneled), with intent to bias his opinion or influence his decision in relation to any matter in which he is acting or is to act, or if any such commissioner, auditor, arbitrator, umpire or juror corruptly take or receive such money or other thing, he shall be guilty of a Class 4 felony.

History.
Code 1950, § 18.1-282; 1960, c. 358; 1975, cc. 14, 15.

§ 18.2-441.1. Bribery of witnesses.

If any person give, offer, or promise to give any money or other thing of value to anyone with intent to prevent such person from testifying as a witness in any civil or criminal proceeding or with intent to cause that person to testify falsely, he shall be guilty of a Class 6 felony.

History.
1978, c. 612.

Law Review.
For article summarizing published Virginia criminal law decisions between July 1, 2002 and July 1, 2003, see 38 U. Rich. L. Rev. 87 (2003).

Michie's Jurisprudence.
For related discussion, see 5B M.J. Criminal Procedure, § 56.

CASE NOTES

Statement did not constitute bribery. — Defendant's statement that he would give the witness $500 to "squash" the case did not constitute a bribe under § 18.2-441.1 as neither the statement, nor the surrounding circumstances, demonstrated anything more than that he offered the witness money in an attempt to persuade her to dismiss the case. Law v. Commonwealth, 39 Va. App. 154, 571 S.E.2d 893, 2002 Va. App. LEXIS 671 (2002).

§ 18.2-442. Bribery of participants in games, contests or sports.

Whoever gives, promises or offers any valuable thing to any professional or amateur participant or prospective participant in any game, contest or sport, with intent to influence him to lose or try to lose or cause to be lost or to limit his or his team's margin of victory in any professional or amateur game, contest or sport in which such participant is taking part or expects to take part, or has any duty or connection therewith, shall be guilty of a Class 5 felony.

History.
Code 1950, § 18.1-402; 1960, c. 358; 1975, cc. 14, 15.

§ 18.2-443. Solicitation or acceptance of bribes by participants or by managers, coaches or trainers.

A professional or amateur participant or prospective participant in any game, contest or sport or a manager, coach or trainer of any team or individual participant or prospective participant in any such game, contest or sport, who solicits or accepts any valuable thing to influence him to lose or try to lose or cause to be lost or to limit his or his team's margin of victory in any game, contest or sport in which he is taking part, or expects to take part, or has any duty or connection therewith, shall be guilty of a Class 5 felony.

History.
Code 1950, § 18.1-403; 1960, c. 358; 1975, cc. 14, 15.

§ 18.2-444. Corruptly influencing, or being influenced as, agents, etc.

(1) Any person who gives, offers or promises to an agent, employee or servant any gift or gratuity whatever, without the knowledge and consent of the principal, employer or master of such agent, employee or servant, with intent to influence his action to the prejudice of his principal's, employer's or master's business; or

(2) An agent, employee or servant who, without the knowledge and consent of his principal, employer or master requests or accepts a gift or gratuity or a promise to make a gift or to do an act beneficial to himself, under an agreement or with an understanding that he shall act in any particular manner as to his principal's, employer's or master's business; or

(3) An agent, employee or servant who, being authorized to procure materials, supplies or other articles either by purchase or contract for his principal, employer or master or to employ service or labor for his principal, employer or master receives directly or indirectly, for himself or for another, a commission, discount or bonus from the person who makes such sale or contract, or furnishes such materials, supplies or other articles, or from a person who renders such service or labor; or

(4) Any person who gives or offers such an agent, employee or servant such commission, discount or bonus;

shall be guilty of a Class 3 misdemeanor.

History.
Code 1950, § 18.1-404; 1960, c. 358; 1975, cc. 14, 15.

CIRCUIT COURT OPINIONS

Conspiracy. — Investor's allegation for statutory conspiracy under §§ 18.2-444 and 18.2-500 was defective because: (1) there was no allegation of malice; and (2) an allegation of conspiracy, whether criminal or civil, had to at least allege an unlawful act or an unlawful purpose, and the investor failed to do so. Furthermore, a conspiracy merely to breach a contract that did not involve an independent duty arising outside the contract was insufficient to establish a civil claim under § 18.2-500. Schur v. Sprenkle, 84 Va. Cir. 418, 2012 Va. Cir. LEXIS 132 (Richmond Apr. 11, 2012).

§ 18.2-444.1. Reserved.

§ 18.2-444.2. Giving or accepting a fee or gift for purposes of influencing decisions of financial institution.

A. No officer, director, or employee of a financial institution or subsidiary, affiliate or holding company thereof, or stockholder owning ten percent or more of the issued capital stock of any such financial institution or holding company, shall accept, receive or acquire any fee, gift, property interest, or other thing of value with the intent to influence the decision of the financial institution, subsidiary, affiliate or holding company with regard to any extension of credit, investment, or purchase or sale of assets by such financial institution, subsidiary, affiliate or holding company. No person shall give, provide or cause to be transferred to any such officer, director, employee or stockholder, any fee, gift, property interest or other thing of value with the intent to influence the decision of the financial institution, subsidiary, affiliate or holding company with regard to any extension of credit, investment or purchase or sale of assets by the financial institution, subsidiary, affiliate or holding company. The foregoing provisions shall not apply to salary, wages, fees or other compensation or consideration paid by, or expenses paid or reimbursed by, such financial institution, subsidiary, affiliate or holding company. The violation of this section shall be punishable as a Class 6 felony.

B. The provisions of this section shall not apply to any such officer, director, employee or stockholder who is a member of a firm of licensed brokers, in buying for or from or selling to, or for the account of, the financial institution, in the ordinary course of business, real estate or bonds, stocks, or other evidences of debt at the usual rate of commission for such service, if the officer, director, employee or stockholder notifies the board of directors of the financial institution, its cashier or secretary, in writing, that such services will be rendered for compensation prior to the rendition of the services or within five business days following the commencement of the services. If a continuing business relationship exists, an annual disclosure may be made.

C. The provisions of this section shall not apply to fees paid to any such officer, director, employee, or stockholder who renders services to a borrower outside of his relationship with the financial institution in connection with the preparation of a loan application, or in connection with the closing of a loan, in evaluating the security or affecting a lien on the collateral, where the fact of rendition of such services for compensation is disclosed in writing to the board of directors of the financial institution, or its cashier or secretary, prior to the time such services are rendered or within five business days following the commencement of the services. If a continuing business relationship exists, an annual disclosure may be made.

History.
Code 1950, § 6.1-121; 1966, c. 584; 1981, c. 339; 1991, c. 501; 1992, c. 318.

§ 18.2-445. Immunity of witnesses.

No witness called by the court or attorney for the Commonwealth and giving evidence for the prosecution, either before the grand jury or the court in any prosecution, under this article shall ever be proceeded against for any offense of giving, or offering to give, or accepting a bribe committed by him at the time and place indicated in such prosecution; but such witness shall be compelled to testify, and for refusing to answer questions may, by the court, be punished for contempt.

History.
Code 1950, §§ 18.1-280, 18.1-405; 1960, c. 358; 1975, cc. 14, 15.

ARTICLE 3.

BRIBERY OF PUBLIC SERVANTS AND PARTY OFFICIALS.

Michie's Jurisprudence.
For related discussion, see 3A M.J. Bribery, § 5.

§ 18.2-446. Definitions.

The following words and phrases when used in this article shall have the meanings respectively ascribed to them in this section except where the context clearly requires a different meaning:

(1) *"Benefits"* means a gain or advantage, or anything regarded by the beneficiary as a gain or advantage, including a benefit to any other person or entity in whose welfare he is interested, but shall not mean an advantage promised generally to a group or class of voters as a consequence of public measures which a candidate engages to support or oppose;

(2) *"Party official"* means a person who holds an elective or appointive post in a political party in the United States by virtue of which he directs or conducts, or participates in directing or conducting party affairs at any level of responsibility;

(3) *"Pecuniary benefit"* means a benefit in the form of money, property, commercial interest or anything else the primary significance of which is economic gain;

(4) *"Public servant"* means any officer or employee of this Commonwealth or any political subdivision thereof, including members of the General Assembly and judges, and any person participating as a juror, advisor, consultant or otherwise, in performing any governmental function; but the term does not include witnesses;

(5) *"Administrative proceeding"* means any proceeding other than a judicial proceeding, the outcome of which is required to be based on a record or documentation prescribed by law including specifi-

cally, but not limited to, proceedings before a planning commission and board of zoning appeals.

History.
Code 1950, § 18.1-282.1; 1968, c. 552; 1975, cc. 14, 15.

Cross references.
As to this section in relation to the Virginia Public Procurement Act, see § 2.2-4367.

Law Review.
For article on the law of inchoate crimes, see 59 Va. L. Rev. 1235 (1973).

§ 18.2-447. When person guilty of bribery.

A person shall be guilty of bribery under the provisions of this article:

(1) If he offers, confers or agrees to confer upon another (a) any pecuniary benefit as consideration for or to obtain or influence the recipient's decision, opinion, recommendation, vote or other exercise of discretion as a public servant or party official, or (b) any benefit as consideration for or to obtain or influence either the recipient's decision, opinion, recommendation, vote or other exercise of official discretion in a judicial or administrative proceeding or the recipient's violation of a known legal duty as a public servant or party official; or

(2) If he accepts or agrees to accept from another (a) any pecuniary benefit offered, conferred or agreed to be conferred as consideration for or to obtain or influence the recipient's decision, opinion, recommendation, vote or other exercise of discretion as a public servant or party official, or (b) any benefit offered, conferred or agreed to be conferred as consideration for or to obtain or influence either the recipient's decision, opinion, recommendation, vote or other exercise of official discretion in a judicial or administrative proceeding or the recipient's violation of a known legal duty as a public servant or party official; or

(3) If he solicits from another (a) any pecuniary benefit or promise of pecuniary benefit as consideration for or in exchange for his decision, opinion, recommendation, vote or other exercise of discretion as a public servant or party official, or (b) any benefit or promise of benefit as consideration for or in exchange for his decision, opinion, recommendation, vote or other exercise of official discretion in a judicial or administrative proceeding or his violation of a known legal duty as a public servant or party official.

History.
Code 1950, § 18.1-282.2; 1968, c. 552; 1975, cc. 14, 15.

CASE NOTES

Willingness to pay money implied through another. — Where the evidence showed that the defendant, through another, implied a willingness to pay money to a corrections officer to induce him to change his testimony in a pending marijuana case, the evidence was sufficient to sustain a bribery conviction even though no specific sum was ever mentioned. Mendez v. Commonwealth, 220 Va. 97, 255 S.E.2d 533 (1979).

§ 18.2-448. Certain matters not to constitute defenses.

It shall be no defense to any prosecution under § 18.2-447 that a person whom the actor sought to influence was not qualified to act in the desired way, whether because he had not yet assumed office, or lacked jurisdiction, or for any other reason. Also it shall be no defense to a prosecution under § 18.2-447 that a resident of this Commonwealth charged with committing an act of bribery was temporarily absent from this Commonwealth at the time such act was committed.

History.
Code 1950, § 18.1-282.3; 1968, c. 552; 1975, cc. 14, 15.

§ 18.2-449. Punishment.

Any person found guilty of bribery under the provisions of this article shall be guilty of a Class 4 felony, and if such person be a public servant he shall in addition forfeit his public office and shall be forever incapable of holding any public office in this Commonwealth.

History.
Code 1950, § 18.1-282.4; 1968, c. 552; 1975, cc. 14, 15.

Law Review.
For article on the law of inchoate crimes, see 59 Va. L. Rev. 1235 (1973).

§ 18.2-450. Immunity of witnesses.

No witness called by the court or attorney for the Commonwealth and giving evidence for the prosecution, either before the grand jury or the court in any prosecution under this article shall ever be proceeded against for any offense of giving, or offering to give, or accepting a bribe committed by him at the time and place indicated in such prosecution; but such witness shall be compelled to testify, and for refusing to answer questions, may by the court, be punished for contempt.

History.
Code 1950, § 18.1-282.3; 1968, c. 552; 1975, cc. 14, 15.

ARTICLE 4.

BARRATRY.

§ 18.2-451. Definitions; application and construction of article.

(a) *"Barratry"* is the offense of stirring up litigation.

(b) A *"barrator"* is an individual, partnership, association or corporation who or which stirs up litigation.

(c) *"Stirring up litigation"* means instigating or attempting to instigate a person or persons to institute a suit at law or equity.

(d) *"Instigating"* means bringing it about that all or part of the expenses of the litigation are paid by the barrator or by a person or persons (other than the plaintiffs) acting in concert with the barrator, unless the instigation is justified.

(e) *"Justified"* means that the instigator is related by blood or marriage to the plaintiff whom he instigates, or that the instigator is entitled by law to share with the plaintiff in money or property that is the subject of the litigation or that the instigator has a direct interest in the subject matter of the litigation or occupies a position of trust in relation to the plaintiff; or that the instigator is acting on behalf of a duly constituted legal aid society approved by the Virginia State Bar which offers advice or assistance in all kinds of legal matters to all members of the public who come to it for advice or assistance and are unable because of poverty to pay legal fees.

(f) *"Direct interest"* means a personal right or a pecuniary right or liability.

This article shall not be applicable to attorneys who are parties to contingent fee contracts with their clients where the attorney does not protect the client from payment of the costs and expense of litigation, nor shall this article apply to any matter involving annexation, zoning, bond issues, or the holding or results of any election or referendum, nor shall this article apply to suits pertaining to or affecting possession of or title to real or personal property, regardless of ownership, nor shall this article apply to suits involving the legality of assessment or collection of taxes or the rates thereof, nor shall this article apply to suits involving rates or charges or services by common carriers or public utilities, nor shall this article apply to criminal prosecutions, nor to the payment of attorneys by legal aid societies approved by the Virginia State Bar, nor to proceedings to abate nuisances. Nothing herein shall be construed to be in derogation of the constitutional rights of real parties in interest to employ counsel or to prosecute any available legal remedy under the laws of this Commonwealth.

History.
Code 1950, § 18.1-388; 1960, c. 358; 1975, cc. 14, 15.

CASE NOTES

Legislative committee. — As to powers of legislative committee, created by Acts 1956, Ex. Sess., c. 34, to investigate laws relating to administration of justice with special reference to promotion or support of litigation by persons not parties thereto, see NAACP v. Committee on Offenses Against Admin. of Justice, 199 Va. 665, 101 S.E.2d 631 (1958).

Constitutionality of article. — This article was held to violate the due process and equal protection clauses of the Fourteenth Amendment to the United States Constitution in *NAACP v. Patty,* 159 F. Supp. 503 (E.D. Va. 1958). This decision was reversed by the United States Supreme Court, on the ground that the federal district court should have abstained from deciding the merits of the issues tendered it, so as to afford the Virginia courts a reasonable

opportunity to construe the statutes in question. Harrison v. NAACP, 360 U.S. 167, 79 S. Ct. 1025, 3 L. Ed. 2d 1152 (1959).

§ 18.2-452. Barratry unlawful.

Any person, if an individual, who shall engage in barratry shall be guilty of a Class 1 misdemeanor; and if a corporation, may be fined not more than $10,000. If the corporation be a foreign corporation, its certificate of authority to transact business in Virginia shall be revoked by the State Corporation Commission.

History.
Code 1950, §§ 18.1-389, 18.1-390; 1960, c. 358; 1975, cc. 14, 15.

§ 18.2-453. Aiders and abettors.

A person who aids and abets a barrator by giving money or rendering services to or for the use or benefit of the barrator for committing barratry shall be guilty of barratry and punished as provided in § 18.2-452.

History.
Code 1950, § 18.1-391; 1960, c. 358; 1975, cc. 14, 15.

§ 18.2-454. Enjoining barratry.

Suits to enjoin barratry may be brought by the Attorney General or the attorney for the Commonwealth in the appropriate circuit court.

History.
Code 1950, § 18.1-392; 1960, c. 358; 1975, cc. 14, 15.

§ 18.2-455. Unprofessional conduct; revocation of license.

Conduct that is made illegal by this article on the part of an attorney at law or any person holding license from the Commonwealth to engage in a profession is unprofessional conduct. Upon hearing pursuant to the provisions of § 54.1-3935, or other statute applicable to the profession concerned, if the defendant be found guilty of barratry, his license to practice law or any other profession shall be revoked for such period as provided by law.

History.
Code 1950, § 18.1-393; 1960, c. 358; 1975, cc. 14, 15.

ARTICLE 5.
CONTEMPT OF COURT.

Michie's Jurisprudence.
For related discussion, see 4A M.J. Contempt, §§ 2, 4 — 6, 8, 13, 15, 22, 27, 30; 9A M.J. Grand Jury, § 16.

§ 18.2-456. Cases in which courts and judges may punish summarily for contempt.

The courts and judges may issue attachments for contempt, and punish them summarily, only in the cases following:

(1) Misbehavior in the presence of the court, or so near thereto as to obstruct or interrupt the administration of justice;

(2) Violence, or threats of violence, to a judge or officer of the court, or to a juror, witness or party going to, attending or returning from the court, for or in respect of any act or proceeding had or to be had in such court;

(3) Vile, contemptuous or insulting language addressed to or published of a judge for or in respect of any act or proceeding had, or to be had, in such court, or like language used in his presence and intended for his hearing for or in respect of such act or proceeding;

(4) Misbehavior of an officer of the court in his official character;

(5) Disobedience or resistance of an officer of the court, juror, witness or other person to any lawful process, judgment, decree or order of the court.

History.
Code 1950, § 18.1-292; 1960, c. 358; 1975, cc. 14, 15.

Cross references.
As to refusal of witness to attend or to testify before court in criminal case, see §§ 18.2-445, 19.2-253. As to limitation on fine and imprisonment unless jury be impaneled, see § 18.2-457. As to power of State Corporation Commission to punish for contempt, see § 12.1-34. As to enforcing certification of examination and recognizance to clerk of court by contempt, see § 19.2-190. As to writ of error to judgment for contempt, see § 19.2-318. As to punishment as for contempt where defendant fails to pay fine or installment thereof, see § 19.2-358. As to enforcement by contempt of temporary orders for support in domestic relations court, see § 20-71. As to power to compel witnesses to testify before fire marshal, see § 27-32. As to contempt proceedings for violation of injunction against disorderly house, see §§ 48-10, 48-11. As to contempt for waste in violation of order during pendency of suit, see § 55-216. As to constitutional provision allowing legislature to regulate right of courts to punish for contempt, see Va. Const., Art. IV, § 14.

Law Review.
For note on contempt by publication and the limitations on indirect contempt of court, see 48 Va. L. Rev. 556 (1962). For case note on contempt, see 49 Va. L. Rev. 341 (1963). For comment, "Lack of Due Process in Virginia Contempt Proceeding for Failure to Comply With Order for Support and Alimony," see 4 U. Rich. L. Rev. 128 (1969). For survey of Virginia law on practice and pleading for the year 1973-1974, see 60 Va. L. Rev. 1572 (1974). For 2003/2004 survey of criminal law and procedure, see 39 U. Rich. L. Rev. 133 (2004). For annual survey of Virginia labor and employment law, see 40 U. Rich. L. Rev. 241 (2005). For article, "Construction Law," see 45 U. Rich. L. Rev. 227 (2010).

CASE NOTES

I. GENERAL CONSIDERATION.

This section is constitutional. It is a reasonable regulation of the exercise by the courts of the power to punish for contempt. Yoder v. Commonwealth, 107 Va. 823, 57 S.E. 581 (1907); Robertson v. Commonwealth, 181 Va. 520, 25 S.E.2d 352 (1943).

As is subdivision (4). — In the context of lawyers, subdivision (4) is sufficiently definite to provide the notice requisite to constitutionality under the due process clause. Greene v. Tucker, 375 F. Supp. 892 (E.D. Va. 1974).

And subdivision (5). — There is nothing unconstitutionally vague about the language of subdivision (5). Greene v. Tucker, 375 F. Supp. 892 (E.D. Va. 1974).

Classes of contempt. — Proceedings for contempt of court are of two classes, — those prosecuted to preserve the power and vindicate the dignity of the court and those to preserve and enforce the rights of private parties. The former are criminal and punitive in their nature; the latter are civil, remedial and coercive in their nature, and the parties chiefly interested in their conduct and prosecution are those individuals for the enforcement of whose private rights and remedies the original suit was instituted. Local 333B, United Marine Div. of Int'l Longshoremen's Ass'n v. Commonwealth ex rel. Va. Ferry Corp., 193 Va. 773, 71 S.E.2d 159 (1952); Holt v. Commonwealth, 205 Va. 332, 136 S.E.2d 809 (1964), rev'd on other grounds, 381 U.S. 131, 85 S. Ct. 1375, 14 L. Ed. 2d 290 (1965).

A contempt of court is in the nature of a criminal offense, and the proceeding for its punishment is criminal in its character. B & O R. R. v. City of Wheeling, 54 Va. (13 Gratt.) 40 (1855).

The purpose of a civil contempt proceeding is to procure the imposition of a punishment, which will afford remedial relief to an injured party, and in appropriate cases to preserve and enforce the rights and administer the remedies to which the court has found the persons for whose protection an injunction was granted to be entitled, and to require the violator of an injunction to restore the status quo as far as may be possible. French v. Town of Clintwood ex rel. Johnson, 203 Va. 562, 125 S.E.2d 798 (1962), cert. denied, 371 U.S. 962, 83 S. Ct. 542, 9 L. Ed. 2d 510 (1963).

Common-law contempt not bound within statutory sentencing guidelines. — Attorney's scheduling of various matters in different courts on the same day, and then his failure to call one of the courts to report that he would be tardy, was found to be sufficient to support the court's finding that he was guilty of common-law indirect criminal contempt; the court was not obligated to sentence him within the limits of §§ 18.2-456 and 18.2-457 because he was not charged with summary or direct contempt, and he had a plenary hearing prior to being found guilty. Robinson v. Commonwealth, 41 Va. App. 137, 583 S.E.2d 60, 2003 Va. App. LEXIS 397 (2003).

Necessary adjuncts to administration of justice. — The dignity of the courts and the duty of the citizens to respect them are necessary adjuncts to the administration of justice. Salyer v. Commonwealth, 209 Va. 662, 166 S.E.2d 110 (1969).

Scope of authority of Workers' Compensation Commission. — Workers' Compensation Commission has the same authority as a court to punish for noncompliance with its discovery orders and it has the inherent authority to strike a party's defenses for failure to comply with a discovery order. Jeff Coal, Inc. v. Phillips, 16 Va. App. 271, 430 S.E.2d 712 (1993).

Virginia Workers' Compensation Commission abused its discretion in assessing 34 separate contempt fines for a professional employer organization's failure to appear at a show cause hearing, one for each of its 34 client companies, as there was no statute or rule that vested the Commission with the authority to summarily divide one case into 34. Cura Group, Inc. v. Va. Workers' Comp. Comm'n, 45 Va. App. 559, 612 S.E.2d 735, 2005 Va. App. LEXIS 181 (2005).

Applied in Davis v. Commonwealth, 219 Va. 395, 247 S.E.2d 681 (1978); Bennett v. Commonwealth, 35 Va. App. 442, 546 S.E.2d 209, 2001 Va. App. LEXIS 262 (2001).

II. POWER OF COURTS.

A. In General.

The power to punish for contempt is inherent in the nature and constitution of a court. Carter v. Commonwealth, 96 Va. 791, 32 S.E. 780 (1899); Burdett v. Commonwealth, 103 Va.

838, 48 S.E. 878 (1904); Bryant v. Commonwealth, 198 Va. 148, 93 S.E.2d 130 (1956); French v. Town of Clintwood ex rel. Johnson, 203 Va. 562, 125 S.E.2d 798 (1962), cert. denied, 371 U.S. 962, 83 S. Ct. 542, 9 L. Ed. 2d 510 (1963).

The power to fine and imprison for contempt is incident to every court of record. The courts ex necessitate rei, have the power of protecting the administration of justice, with a promptitude calculated to meet the exigency of the particular case. Board of Supvrs. v. Bazile, 195 Va. 739, 80 S.E.2d 566 (1954).

A court is invested with power to punish for contempt, both by the inherent nature and constitution of the court and by this section. Higginbotham v. Commonwealth, 206 Va. 291, 142 S.E.2d 746 (1965).

Sentence and injunction imposed on a property owner for violating a Montgomery County Zoning Ordinance, which ordered defendant to clean up a defined area of his property by a specific deadline, ultimately derived from subdivision A 5 of § 15.2-2286; as the mandatory injunction was valid, the trial court had the inherent, discretionary authority to fashion reasonable remedial sanctions as punishment after finding defendant in contempt for failing to comply with the injunction, which allowed a county to enter on defendant's property, to abate the zoning violation, and to impose a lien on the property for the costs incurred. Epperly v. County of Montgomery, 46 Va. App. 546, 620 S.E.2d 125, 2005 Va. App. LEXIS 373 (2005).

The power to punish for contempt is discretionary and not mandatory under this section. Higginbotham v. Commonwealth, 206 Va. 291, 142 S.E.2d 746 (1965).

The word "summarily" used in this section does not refer to the time the adjudication of contempt must be made, but to the form of procedure which dispenses with any further proof or examination and a formal hearing. Higginbotham v. Commonwealth, 206 Va. 291, 142 S.E.2d 746 (1965).

The court's power to punish a contemner is not lost by a short delay during the course of the trial. Higginbotham v. Commonwealth, 206 Va. 291, 142 S.E.2d 746 (1965).

A delay of five days before advising defendant that he is being held in contempt for violating a ruling is not in itself prejudicial to the defendant. Higginbotham v. Commonwealth, 206 Va. 291, 142 S.E.2d 746 (1965).

The fact that a decree is final does not render the court powerless to enforce it by contempt proceedings. Rinehart & Dennis Co. v. McArthur, 123 Va. 556, 96 S.E. 829 (1918).

Power to punish violation of verbal command. — A trial court has the authority to hold an offending party in contempt for acting in bad faith or for willful disobedience of its order, and this principle applies to the oral orders, commands and directions of the court as well as written ones. Lalik v. Commonwealth, No. 1855-99-3, 2000 Va. App. LEXIS 348 (Ct. of Appeals May 9, 2000).

Trial court's power does not include power to impose attorneys' fees and costs as a sanction. — In the absence of authority granted by a statute, a trial court's inherent power to supervise the conduct of attorneys practicing before it and to discipline an attorney who engages in misconduct does not include the power to impose as a sanction an award of attorneys' fees and costs to the opposing parties. If an attorney's conduct is disruptive of court processes or disrespectful of the court itself, there is ample power to punish the misconduct as contempt. Nusbaum v. Berlin, 273 Va. 385, 641 S.E.2d 494, 2007 Va. LEXIS 26 (2007).

B. Abridgement by Legislature.

The distinction between legislative and constitutional courts should be made in the cases covered by this section. Carter v. Commonwealth, 96 Va. 791, 32 S.E. 780 (1899); Burdett v. Commonwealth, 103 Va. 838, 48 S.E. 878 (1904).

Legislature does not have absolute power over subject. — The constitutional provision, Va. Const., Art. IV, § 14, that the General Assembly "may regulate the exercise by courts of the right to punish for contempt" was not intended to clothe the legislature with absolute power over the subject. Yoder v. Commonwealth, 107 Va. 823, 57 S.E. 581 (1907).

It may regulate constitutional courts but not deprive them of the power. — There is an inherent power of self defense and self preservation in the courts of this state created by the Constitution. This power may be regulated by the legislature, but cannot be destroyed or so far diminished as to be rendered ineffec-

tual. It is a power necessarily resident in and to be exercised by the power of the court itself, and the legislature cannot deprive such courts of the power to summarily punish for contempts by providing for a jury trial in such case. Carter v. Commonwealth, 96 Va. 791, 32 S.E. 780 (1899).

Statute providing for jury trial cannot deprive courts of power. — The legislature cannot deprive the courts of the power to summarily punish for contempt by providing for a jury trial in such case. Burdett v. Commonwealth, 103 Va. 838, 48 S.E. 878 (1904).

The act of 1897, securing the defendant a jury trial in cases of direct contempt, was held unconstitutional. Carter v. Commonwealth, 96 Va. 791, 32 S.E. 780 (1899).

Nor can statute giving justices jurisdiction of misdemeanors. — A Virginia statute giving to justices of the peace exclusive jurisdiction of all misdemeanors, if intended to interfere with the jurisdiction of courts of record to punish for contempts, is void as an unwarranted invasion of the judicial by the legislative department of the government. Elam v. Commonwealth, 4 Va. L. Reg. 520 (1898).

III. ACTS CONSTITUTING CONTEMPT.

A. Contemptuous Conduct Towards Judge.

1. In General.

The "clear and present danger" standard does not apply to misconduct in the presence of the court. Williams v. Commonwealth, No. 1503-89-2 (Ct. of Appeals Feb. 12, 1991).

Contempt includes any act which is calculated to embarrass, hinder, or obstruct the court in the discharge of its responsibilities. Baugh v. Commonwealth, 14 Va. App. 368, 417 S.E.2d 891 (1992), overruled in part by Gilman v. Commonwealth, 275 Va. 222, 657 S.E.2d 474, 2008 Va. LEXIS 23 (2008).

False statement to obtain continuance is contempt. — The effort of a party to obtain a continuance of his cause by means of a statement as to his health which he knew to be false tended directly to impede and obstruct the administration of justice and was contempt. Carter v. Commonwealth, 96 Va. 791, 32 S.E. 780 (1899).

This section is broad enough to include insulting language delivered at a public meeting or published in a newspaper. Boorde v. Commonwealth, 134 Va. 625, 114 S.E. 731 (1922).

No defense that defendant thought court had adjourned. — In a prosecution for contempt in publishing an insulting libel concerning the judge of a court, the fact that the defendant thought that the court had adjourned at the time of the publication, or that the judge had in fact directed the sheriff to make the proclamation of adjournment, constitutes no defense. Burdett v. Commonwealth, 103 Va. 838, 48 S.E. 878 (1904).

No defense that defendant addressed statement to the "court" system. — The defendant violated this section although she contended that the statement was addressed to the "court" system and not the judge; the judge is a part of the court system. Williams v. Commonwealth, No. 1503-89-2 (Ct. of Appeals Feb. 12, 1991).

No obstruction of justice occurred. — Trial court erred in convicting defendant of contempt for obstructing or interrupting the administration of justice in violation of subdivision 1 of § 18.2-456 because no obstruction to the administration of justice occurred when defendant spoke with a jury administrator and a supervisor for the circuit judges' office, and although the evidence was sufficient to prove that defendant was loud and rude, it was not clear that his conduct constituted contempt under § 18.2-456; neither the administrator nor the supervisor specified how defendant behavior obstructed the administration of justice, but instead, they performed their respective jobs addressing his concerns, and no evidence showed that any court proceedings were interrupted or delayed because of defendant's conduct or that any judicial officer was prevented from performing his or her administrative duties. Henderson v. Commonwealth, 2010 Va. App. LEXIS 451 (Nov. 16, 2010).

2. Criticisms of Official Conduct.

Latitude of criticism. — Considerable latitude is permissible in the criticism of judicial decisions already rendered, but when such criticism necessarily involves the future action of the court in pending causes, a stricter rule, for obvious reasons, must be applied. Boorde v. Commonwealth, 134 Va. 625, 114 S.E. 731 (1922).

To find the line where the right of free speech ends and its abuse begins is not always an easy task. In contempt proceedings, this line must usually be defined by the courts themselves, and in such cases its location is to be established with especial care and caution. Boorde v. Commonwealth, 143 Va. 625, 114 S.E. 731 (1922).

Charging bias. — Neither an attorney charged with contempt nor his counsel could consistently with due process be convicted for contempt for filing motions for a change of venue and disqualification of the judge because of alleged bias, where the words used in the motions were plain English, in no way offensive in themselves, and wholly appropriate to charge bias in the community and bias of the presiding judge. Holt v. Virginia, 381 U.S. 131, 85 S. Ct. 1375, 14 L. Ed. 2d 290 (1965).

Utterances as to judge's conduct of an ended case. — False and libelous utterances as to a judge's conduct of an ended case may or may not be punishable contempt, depending upon whether such utterances present a clear and present danger to the administration of justice. Weston v. Commonwealth, 195 Va. 175, 77 S.E.2d 405 (1953); Salyer v. Commonwealth, 209 Va. 662, 166 S.E.2d 110 (1969).

The provisions of subdivision (3) of this section when applied to statements regarding a "proceeding had," that is, a proceeding which had been terminated, are not violative of the right of freedom of speech. Weston v. Commonwealth, 195 Va. 175, 77 S.E.2d 405 (1953).

"A clear and present danger" exists if it appears that the attack probably will affect the course of justice in future litigation and impair, if not destroy, the judicial efficiency of the court or judge subjected to attack. Salyer v. Commonwealth, 209 Va. 662, 166 S.E.2d 110 (1969).

Courts are not required to tolerate critical comments. — Courts are not required to tolerate the spontaneous expression aloud in the courtroom of critical comments by litigants or witnesses disappointed with the decision. Williams v. Commonwealth, No. 1503-89-2 (Ct. of Appeals Feb. 12, 1991).

A criticism in good faith of the practice of a judge in presiding over cases in which his sons were counsel, without imputing to the judge conscious and intentional bias and improper judgments in specific cases, is within the constitutional right of free speech. Boorde v. Commonwealth, 134 Va. 625, 114 S.E. 731 (1922).

Assertions of good faith in scheduling conflicting matters in different courts did not negate inference of contempt. — Attorney's actions in scheduling multiple matters for trial in different courts in different jurisdictions at the same time supported trial court's finding of contempt; attorney's assertions of good faith did not negate the reasonable inference that he recklessly or willfully failed timely to advise the court of his conflicting schedule. Brown v. Commonwealth, 26 Va. App. 758, 497 S.E.2d 147 (1998).

Determining whether language used constitutes contempt. — In determining whether the language used by the defendant constitutes contempt it must be borne in mind that since a summary proceeding for contempt is a proceeding "to preserve the power and vindicate the dignity of the court," it is criminal and punitive in character, and the guilt of the alleged contemner must be established beyond a reasonable doubt. Weston v. Commonwealth, 195 Va. 175, 77 S.E.2d 405 (1953).

Words held contemptuous. — A charge that a judge was a "wet judge" and that his decisions were influenced both by this fact and the appearance of his son as counsel was contempt within the meaning of this section. Boorde v. Commonwealth, 134 Va. 625, 114 S.E. 731 (1922).

The trial court found that the statement "crooked court" was contemptuous and that the statement was "addressed to or published of a judge" where the defendant made the statement immediately after she talked to the judge and she made the statement loud enough for the judge to hear. Williams v. Commonwealth, No. 1503-89-2 (Ct. of Appeals Feb. 12, 1991).

Language held not "obscene, contemptuous or insulting". — See Weston v. Commonwealth, 195 Va. 175, 77 S.E.2d 405 (1953).

B. Misconduct.

The "clear and present danger" standard in subdivision (1) of this section does not apply to misconduct in the presence of

the court. Williams v. Commonwealth, No. 1503-89-2 (Ct. of Appeals Feb. 12, 1991).

An attorney's failure to attend court is not contempt. — An attorney failing to attend court at the time of a trial previously fixed with his consent was not guilty of a contempt of court. Wise v. Commonwealth, 97 Va. 779, 34 S.E. 453 (1899).

Attorney's conduct was not contempt. — Defendant attorney's conduct did not amount to criminal contempt in violation of the statute where the record failed to reflect any evidence of intent on the part of defendant to obstruct justice and/or interrupt the administration of justice; the record did not establish that defendant's request for a continuance was unreasonable in light of the discovery he had received. Weaver v. Commonwealth, No. 1056-01-1, 2002 Va. App. LEXIS 170 (Ct. of Appeals Mar. 19, 2002).

In two cases in which the Appeals Court of Virginia affirmed the convictions of two attorneys for criminal contempt, nothing in either record suggested an intent on the part of the two attorneys to obstruct or interrupt the administration of justice as required by subdivision 1 of § 18.2-456. Unquestionably, attorney A's absence on the scheduled trial date and his release of his client was entirely consistent with his asserted good faith belief that the circuit court would grant the mutually requested continuance because of the Commonwealth's inability to proceed to trial on the scheduled trial date; likewise, the evidence was entirely consistent with attorney B's assertion that he excused his client from appearing on the scheduled trial date on the reasonable expectation that the court would grant the mutually requested continuance because of the Commonwealth's inability to proceed to trial without its necessary witness. Singleton v. Commonwealth, 278 Va. 542, 685 S.E.2d 668, 2009 Va. LEXIS 104 (2009).

There was insufficient evidence that defendant, a defense counsel, intended to be contemptuous or to interrupt or obstruct the administration of justice to support his summary contempt conviction under subdivision 1 of § 18.2-456 as defendant did not notify the court earlier of his client's wish to revoke his waiver of a jury trial because he was still discussing the pros and cons of the revocation of the waiver and the plea agreement with the client. Cartier v. Commonwealth, 2013 Va. App. LEXIS 68 (Mar. 5, 2013).

Where counsel scheduled multiple cases in different jurisdictions for the same time and failed to appear at an agreed upon trial date, the evidence was sufficient to constitute contempt. Robinson v. Commonwealth, No. 2901-01-1, 2003 Va. App. LEXIS 183 (Ct. of Appeals Apr. 1, 2003).

Failure to appear for pretrial conference. — The appellant was properly found in contempt for a violation of subdivision (1) of this section where she did not appear for a pretrial conference as ordered and later successfully objected to the testimony of an expert witness as primarily containing hearsay statements, as such objection was more properly the subject for a motion in limine which should have been settled at the pretrial conference. Roberts v. Haiar, No. 2096-97-1 (Ct. of Appeals February 24, 1998).

Conduct in what is perceived as a client's interest may also be conduct contemptuous of the court. The two are not mutually exclusive. Greene v. Tucker, 375 F. Supp. 892 (E.D. Va. 1974).

Refusal to surrender or pay over money as directed by court. — Where money is in the hands of an officer of the court, subject to the order of the court, it is clearly a contempt of the court to refuse to surrender and pay over the money as directed by the court, and obedience to the order may be enforced by contempt proceedings involving the imprisonment of the officer. French v. Pobst, 203 Va. 704, 127 S.E.2d 137 (1962).

The act of witnesses avoiding service of subpoena to appear before a grand jury did not constitute a contempt, under this statute, punishable by the court in a summary manner. Commonwealth v. Deskins, 31 Va. (4 Leigh) 685 (1834). But see Kendrick v. Commonwealth, 78 Va. 490 (1884).

Delay in request for jury trial held not contempt. — Evidence held insufficient to find defendant guilty of criminal contempt for failing, without offering an excuse, to notify the trial court of his request for a jury prior to the morning he was scheduled to be tried by the trial judge without a jury. To support a finding of the willful intent necessary for conviction of contempt, the record had to contain evidence that the delayed request was made for the purpose of obstructing or interrupting the administration of justice and not just for the purpose of exercising a right guaranteed by the Constitutions of the United States and the Commonwealth of

Virginia. Carter v. Commonwealth, 2 Va. App. 392, 345 S.E.2d 5 (1986).

Use of profanity toward prosecutor. — Where defendant used profanity toward the prosecutor at defendant's sentencing hearing, and the trial court opined that this conduct in the presence of the court disrupted the court and was in contempt of the court's process, such conduct and findings supported a contempt finding under subdivision (1) of § 18.2-456. Middlebrooks v. Commonwealth, No. 1516-01-1, 2002 Va. App. LEXIS 433 (Ct. of Appeals July 30, 2002).

Profanity not intended for trial judge to hear. — Where defendant used profanity toward the prosecutor at defendant's sentencing hearing for other offenses, but there was no evidence that defendant intended the trial judge to hear defendant's statement to the prosecutor, such evidence did not support a contempt finding under § 18.2-456 (3). Middlebrooks v. Commonwealth, No. 1516-01-1, 2002 Va. App. LEXIS 433 (Ct. of Appeals July 30, 2002).

Contempt conviction supported by evidence of defendant's intoxication in court. — Because the results of an Alcosensor test for blood alcohol content were properly admitted and considered by the circuit court as the fact finder, and defendant did not object to the admission of the general district court certificate of the conviction, filed pursuant to § 18.2-459, which he himself introduced into evidence, his contempt conviction was upheld on appeal. Rozario v. Commonwealth, 50 Va. App. 142, 647 S.E.2d 502, 2007 Va. App. LEXIS 272 (2007).

Failure to preserve assignments of error for appeal. — Ends of justice exception to Va. Sup. Ct. R. 5A:18 did not apply, as defendant knowingly falsely asserted that defendant's former husband violated probation, misbehavior sufficiently near the presence of the trial court that the court could consider it in support of defendant's contempt conviction. Amos v. Commonwealth, 2012 Va. App. LEXIS 253 (Aug. 7, 2012).

Actions held contemptuous. — Defendant's summary contempt conviction under subdivision 1 of § 18.2-456 was supported by sufficient evidence as when defendant balled up a summons and later the juvenile and domestic relations court's written orders, defendant intended to display to the court and all others in the courtroom her contemptuous disrespect for the court and its child custody decision; defendant committed misbehavior in the presence of the court, and, although no finding that her misbehavior obstructed or interrupted justice was required, her acts obstructed and interrupted justice. Parham v. Commonwealth, 60 Va. App. 450, 729 S.E.2d 734, 2012 Va. App. LEXIS 248 (2012).

C. Disobedience of Orders or Decrees.

Willful disobedience to any lawful process or order of court is contempt and summarily punishable as such. Board of Supvrs. v. Bazile, 195 Va. 739, 80 S.E.2d 566 (1954).

When one shows by his conduct a deliberate and studied effort to disobey a valid order of a court, he subjects himself to punishment for contempt. Laing v. Commonwealth, 205 Va. 511, 137 S.E.2d 896 (1964).

Disobedience of the decree of the court comes plainly within the fifth subdivision of this section. Forbes v. State Council, 107 Va. 853, 60 S.E. 81 (1908), appeal dismissed, 216 U.S. 396, 30 S. Ct. 295, 54 L. Ed. 534 (1909).

Finding of contempt rests upon four elements. — A finding of contempt for such disobedience must rest upon four elements: (1) Issuance of "lawful process"; (2) valid service of the process by one of the modes prescribed by law; (3) timely knowledge of the process by the person upon whom service is sought, where service was not personal; and (4) willful disobedience of the process. Bellis v. Commonwealth, 241 Va. 257, 402 S.E.2d 211 (1991).

Decree must contain express command or prohibition. — There is a conflict of authority on the question whether a decree or order which merely declares the rights of the parties without an express command or prohibition may be the basis of a contempt proceeding. The better and safer rule is that there must be an express command or prohibition. French v. Pobst, 203 Va. 704, 127 S.E.2d 137 (1962).

A person is in contempt of a court order only if it is shown that he or she has violated its express terms; process for contempt lies for disobedience of what is decreed, not for what may be decreed. Michaels v. Commonwealth, 32 Va. App. 601, 529 S.E.2d 822, 2000 Va. App. LEXIS 463 (2000).

Before a person may be held in contempt for violating a court order, the order must be in definite terms as to the duties thereby imposed upon him and the command must be expressed rather than implied. Michaels v. Commonwealth, 32 Va. App. 601, 529 S.E.2d 822, 2000 Va. App. LEXIS 463 (2000).

A deputy sheriff was improperly held in criminal contempt for failing to transport a prisoner where the underlying order did not expressly impose a duty on the defendant or any other personnel from the sheriff's office to transport the prisoner. Michaels v. Commonwealth, 32 Va. App. 601, 529 S.E.2d 822, 2000 Va. App. LEXIS 463 (2000).

Where there was no prior court order prohibiting an attorney from deposing a party, a finding of civil contempt under subdivision 5 of § 18.2-456 was erroneous; therefore, an attorney should not have been ordered to pay monetary sanctions to an animal rights organization. Any prohibition on such was merely an implication from the general remarks made by a circuit court, which was not a proper basis for a contempt judgment. Petrosinelli v. People for the Ethical Treatment of Animals, Inc., 273 Va. 700, 643 S.E.2d 151, 2007 Va. LEXIS 50 (2007).

This section applicable to disobeying a subpoena. — Disobedience to "any lawful process" is made subject to summary punishment or contempt by subdivision (5); "process" includes a subpoena directed to a witness. Bellis v. Commonwealth, 241 Va. 257, 402 S.E.2d 211 (1991).

Section applies to erroneous orders. — Where the court has jurisdiction of the parties and of the subject matter of the suit and the legal authority to make the order, a party refusing to obey it, however erroneously made, is liable for contempt. Such order, though erroneous, is lawful within the meaning of contempt statutes until it is reversed by an appellate court. Robertson v. Commonwealth, 181 Va. 520, 25 S.E.2d 352 (1943); Local 333B, United Marine Div. of Int'l Longshoremen's Ass'n v. Commonwealth ex rel. Va. Ferry Corp., 193 Va. 773, 71 S.E.2d 159, cert. denied, 344 U.S. 893, 73 S. Ct. 212, 97 L. Ed. 690 (1952); French v. Town of Clintwood ex rel. Johnson, 203 Va. 562, 125 S.E.2d 798 (1962), cert. denied, 371 U.S. 962, 83 S. Ct. 542, 9 L. Ed. 2d 510 (1963).

While trial court erred in ordering attorney to produce a written statement made by an employee of his client for the purpose of contradicting the latter, which statement was not admissible under § 8.01-404, it did not follow that such order was void and could be disobeyed with impunity, and attorney was therefore liable for contempt for refusal to obey order. Robertson v. Commonwealth, 181 Va. 520, 25 S.E.2d 352 (1943).

And without regard to constitutionality of act under which order issued. — An order issued by a court with jurisdiction over the subject matter and person must be obeyed by the parties until it is reversed by orderly and proper proceedings. This is true without regard even for the constitutionality of the act under which the order is issued. Local 333B, United Marine Div. of Int'l Longshoremen's Ass'n v. Commonwealth ex rel. Va. Ferry Corp., 193 Va. 773, 71 S.E.2d 159, cert. denied, 344 U.S. 893, 73 S. Ct. 212, 97 L. Ed. 690 (1952).

Judgment or order need not be in writing. — It was not the purpose of subdivision (5) of this section, in providing for summary punishment by a court for disobedience or resistance to any lawful order, to limit or confine such "order" to one which has been reduced to writing, and thereby exclude and leave unpunishable in summary contempt proceedings the verbal commands, directions or orders of the court. Robertson v. Commonwealth, 181 Va. 520, 25 S.E.2d 352 (1943).

No evidence of disobeying or resisting lawful process. — Trial court erred in convicting defendant of contempt for being disobedient or resistant to lawful process of the trial court in violation of subdivision 5 of § 18.2-456 because the record contained no evidence that defendant failed to appear on any date that he was summoned or required to report for jury duty; at most, defendant expressed his intention to disobey the jury summons in the future, but the record did not establish whether he actually did so. Henderson v. Commonwealth, 2010 Va. App. LEXIS 451 (Nov. 16, 2010).

Attorney conduct. — Attorney's continued disobedience to court's directive that he treat witnesses politely and refrain from sarcasm was sufficient to support his convictions for contempt. Crandley v. Commonwealth, No. 1694-98-1 (Ct. of Appeals Aug. 10, 1999).

A witness who left the court house before his testimony was complete was properly held to have been in contempt for disobeying an order of the court where the court had instructed the witness to step down and wait outside the courtroom while the judge conferred briefly with the attorneys; although the court did not designate the instruction as an order that the witness wait, the import of the words was made manifest by both definition and context and there was clearly nothing to suggest to the witness that he was free to elect whether to go or stay. Lalik v. Commonwealth, No. 1855-99-3, 2000 Va. App. LEXIS 348 (Ct. of Appeals May 9, 2000).

Courthouse security. — Trial court did not err in finding defendant, acting in his role as sheriff, in contempt for his conduct in threatening courthouse security by reassigning a deputy posted inside the courthouse's front entrance to a jail and taking down signs the trial court had posted regarding access to the courthouse; the trial court found that his conduct interrupted the orderly flow of the court's business and defendant's contention that he did not intend to impede the administration of justice under § 18.2-456 was belied by his conduct. Epps v. Commonwealth, 47 Va. App. 687, 626 S.E.2d 912, 2006 Va. App. LEXIS 102 (2006).

Person not a party and without notice not liable. — A seller of intoxicants who had no actual knowledge or notice of an interdiction order entered against the purchaser cannot be held in contempt for violating such order. Calamos v. Commonwealth, 184 Va. 397, 35 S.E.2d 397 (1945).

A person cannot be punished for contempt for disobedience or resistance to a decree appointing a receiver, when he was not a party to suit, had no knowledge of its existence or of the appointment of the receiver, and where the decree appointing the receiver contained no direction, mandate, or prohibition to or against him. Kidd v. Virginia Safe Deposit & Trust Corp., 113 Va. 612, 75 S.E. 145 (1912).

The disobedience of a void order is not contempt. Laing v. Commonwealth, 205 Va. 511, 137 S.E.2d 896 (1964).

Illustrative case. — Defendants were properly held in contempt for violating an injunction notwithstanding their contention that they in good faith relied upon a subsequent irregular amendment to the zoning regulation on which the injunction had been based. French v. Town of Clintwood ex rel. Johnson, 203 Va. 562, 125 S.E.2d 798 (1962), cert. denied, 371 U.S. 962, 83 S. Ct. 542, 9 L. Ed. 2d 510 (1963).

Where a trial court found that appellant was in violation of a zoning ordinance and gave him 10 days to abate the violation, it properly exercised its power to enforce its orders and did not act without jurisdiction when it found him in contempt for violating the abatement order. Miller v. Bd. of Supervisors, No. 1050-03-2, 2004 Va. App. LEXIS 71 (Ct. of Appeals Feb. 10, 2004).

Trial judge properly appointed a conservator in a domestic matter where said services were required because the husband was continually violating the court's orders, refusing to respond to discovery, and dissipating the estate; therefore, the court had the power to appoint the conservator to determine the information wife requested in discovery and to preserve the estate. However, death of the payor spouse, which abates the divorce action, also renders the pendente lite order void. Estate of Hackler v. Hackler, 44 Va. App. 51, 602 S.E.2d 426, 2004 Va. App. LEXIS 454 (2004).

The trial court properly found a landowner in contempt for violating the county code in operating his junkyard, and no violation of his rights occurred, as the county was authorized to enter his property and make whatever changes were necessary to the landscape of the property to bring such within code and protect the county's interests. Phelps v. Bd. of County Supervisors, 2007 Va. App. LEXIS 262 (July 3, 2007).

Wrongful death settlement. — Where a dock owner agreed to remove a boat dock pursuant to a wrongful death settlement agreement that was included in the court order approving the settlement, the dock owner was properly found in contempt because: (1) the dock owner used structures or objects on the property to moor or dock a boat; (2) the Wrongful Death Act, §§ 8.01-50 through 8.01-56, did not preclude the contempt proceeding; and (3) when the trial court included the settlement terms in its court order, it retained the right to enforce the obligations imposed upon the dock owner under subdivision 5 of § 18.2-456. Fisher v. Salute, 51 Va. App. 293, 657 S.E.2d 169, 2008 Va. App. LEXIS 99 (2008).

Failure to pay spousal support. — Trial court properly found a husband in contempt for failing to pay spousal support, as

previously ordered by the court, where the trial court found that the husband had failed to comply with the terms and conditions of the final divorce decree, and in addition, it found that husband had ignored two subsequent orders regarding the amount of the husband's retirement to be paid to the wife. Mihnovets v. Mihnovets, No. 2087-03-4, 2004 Va. App. LEXIS 410 (Ct. of Appeals Aug. 31, 2004).

Where at the time of circuit court trial de novo, defendant had completed alcohol abuse treatment and was not shown to have willfully disobeyed the court's order, the evidence was insufficient for the circuit court to find that defendant was in contempt of the juvenile court order. Hanson v. Commonwealth, No. 2899-95-3 (Ct. of Appeals Apr. 1, 1997).

As to the September 1994 order, the evidence was sufficient to support the trial court's finding that defendant willfully disobeyed that order, where defendant admitted at trial that she knew she was violating the order by removing her daughter from the Presbyterian home before the end of the program. Hanson v. Commonwealth, No. 2899-95-3 (Ct. of Appeals Apr. 1, 1997).

Inability to obey an order of court may be a complete defense. Camden v. Virginia Safe Deposit & Trust Corp., 115 Va. 20, 78 S.E. 596 (1913).

The inability of an alleged contemner, without fault on his part, to render obedience to an order of court, is a good defense to a charge of contempt. Laing v. Commonwealth, 205 Va. 511, 137 S.E.2d 896 (1964).

But not if disability voluntary. — But where an alleged contemner has voluntarily and contumaciously brought on himself disability to obey an order, he cannot avail himself of a plea of inability to obey as a defense to the charge of contempt. Laing v. Commonwealth, 205 Va. 511, 137 S.E.2d 896 (1964).

IV. PURGING CONTEMPTS.

Effect of want of intention. — A contempt may be purged where the defendant denies any evil intention, as where a party in his answer under oath to a rule to show cause why he should not be punished for contempt, states that he acted in good faith, without any design, wish or expectation of committing any contempt of court. Wells v. Commonwealth, 62 Va. (21 Gratt.) 500 (1871); Trimble v. Commonwealth, 96 Va. 818, 32 S.E. 786 (1899).

When disclaimer of intention unavailing. — Where an attack upon a judge is unmistakably contemptuous and insulting, disclaimer of any intention to insult the court or the judge is unavailing. Carter v. Commonwealth, 96 Va. 791, 32 S.E. 780 (1899); Boorde v. Commonwealth, 134 Va. 625, 114 S.E. 731 (1922).

Effect when language or acts bear two constructions. — If the intent with which a thing is said or done gives color and character to the act or words a disclaimer of any purpose to be guilty of a contempt, or to destroy or impair the authority due to the court, is a good defense to a charge of contempt, but this is true only of language or acts of doubtful import, and which may reasonably bear two constructions. Carter v. Commonwealth, 96 Va. 791, 32 S.E. 780 (1899); Board of Supvrs. v. Bazile, 195 Va. 739, 80 S.E.2d 566 (1954).

The advice of counsel may, under some circumstances, be a palliation of the offense of his client in disobeying the lawful orders of the court, but the extent of such palliation must depend upon the circumstances of the case and the character of the advice given. Wells v. Commonwealth, 62 Va. (21 Gratt.) 500 (1871); Trimble v. Commonwealth, 96 Va. 818, 32 S.E. 786 (1899); Trimble v. Commonwealth, 5 Va. L. Reg. 92 (1899).

Where an attorney has acted in good faith, although he may err in judgment, he is not guilty of contempt. Wells v. Commonwealth, 62 Va. (21 Gratt.) 500 (1871).

Violating a habeas corpus for the custody of a child may be purged by disclaimer by defendant of any purpose to be guilty of contempt. Trimble v. Commonwealth, 96 Va. 818, 32 S.E. 786 (1899).

V. SUMMARY PROCEEDINGS.

This section, which enlarges the classes of cases in which there may be summary punishment, is constitutional. Yoder v. Commonwealth, 107 Va. 823, 57 S.E. 581 (1907).

The power of courts of record to punish summarily for

contempts, is generally conceded to be inherent, and applies as well to constructive as to direct contempts. Carter v. Commonwealth, 96 Va. 791, 32 S.E. 780 (1899).

Limited to classes set forth in statute. — The power given to the court and judge by this section to punish "summarily" for contempt is a power to punish without the intervention of a jury and is limited to the classes of contempt set forth in this section. Yoder v. Commonwealth, 107 Va. 823, 57 S.E. 581 (1907); Kidd v. Virginia Safe Deposit & Trust Corp., 113 Va. 612, 75 S.E. 145 (1912).

For violations of subdivision (1) of this section, the General Assembly has limited the maximum punishment to a $50 fine or 10 days in jail, "without a jury." Baugh v. Commonwealth, 14 Va. App. 368, 417 S.E.2d 891 (1992), overruled in part by Gilman v. Commonwealth, 275 Va. 222, 657 S.E.2d 474, 2008 Va. LEXIS 23 (2008).

Basis for exception to requirement of full fact-finding hearing. — The exception to the general requirement of a full fact-finding hearing in cases of contempt committed directly under the eye or within the view of the court is not grounded solely in the need for immediate vindication of the court's integrity, but is also supported by the fact that there is no need of evidence or assistance of counsel before punishment, because the court has seen the offense. Greene v. Tucker, 375 F. Supp. 892 (E.D. Va. 1974).

Right of confrontation and contempt. — Defendant's constitutional right of confrontation was not violated by admission into evidence in criminal proceeding of certificate prepared by general district court judge, which detailed circumstances of offense. Baugh v. Commonwealth, 14 Va. App. 368, 417 S.E.2d 891 (1992), overruled in part by Gilman v. Commonwealth, 275 Va. 222, 657 S.E.2d 474, 2008 Va. LEXIS 23 (2008).

Summary conviction for criminal contempt has been effectively limited to cases where the contempt is judged by the court not to constitute "serious" criminal conduct. Greene v. Tucker, 375 F. Supp. 892 (E.D. Va. 1974).

Penalty imposed is evidence of seriousness of offense. — Since Virginia does not specify sentencing limits for cases of contempt, the court must look to the penalty actually imposed as the best evidence of the seriousness of the offense. Greene v. Tucker, 375 F. Supp. 892 (E.D. Va. 1974).

What are "serious" crimes for jury trial purposes. — Contempts punishable by more than six months' imprisonment or a greater than $500.00 fine or both appear to constitute "serious" crimes for jury trial purposes. Greene v. Tucker, 375 F. Supp. 892 (E.D. Va. 1974).

Jury trial not unreasonable safeguard for certain subdivision (1) contempts. — Since subdivision (1) is not statutorily restricted in terms of highly specific conduct or specific persons as are the other subsections, it cannot be considered unreasonable for the legislature to have deemed it in the interest of justice to provide a slightly greater procedural safeguard, in the form of jury trial as provided by § 18.2-457, for those contempts of subdivision (1) which will be punished by a fine exceeding $50.00 or imprisonment of more than 10 days. Greene v. Tucker, 375 F. Supp. 892 (E.D. Va. 1974).

Due process rights violated. — Trial court erred in conducting a plenary criminal contempt hearing without affording a husband in a divorce proceeding the protections to which he was entitled. Therefore, the husband's conviction for criminal contempt was reversed and vacated, including the fine and assessment of attorney's fees made against him. Clugston v. Commonwealth, 2009 Va. App. LEXIS 344 (Aug. 4, 2009).

In a summary contempt proceeding under § 18.2-456, defendants were not afforded the due process rights to which they were entitled as nothing indicated that any of the defendants' conduct was such an open, serious threat to orderly procedure that instant and summary punishment, as distinguished from due and deliberate procedures, was necessary. Scialdone v. Commonwealth, 279 Va. 422, 689 S.E.2d 716, 2010 Va. LEXIS 27 (2010).

Due process not denied. — Trial court's denial of a plenary hearing to determine guilt for certain specific acts of contempt where acts by petitioner were not only committed in the presence of the court but were elaborated upon to the court each step of the way was not a denial of due process. Greene v. Tucker, 375 F. Supp. 892 (E.D. Va. 1974).

VI. PRACTICE.

The substantial difference between a direct and constructive contempt is one of procedure. Burdett v. Commonwealth, 103 Va. 838, 48 S.E. 878 (1904).

Direct contempts. — An attachment for contempt has no other object than to bring the party into court. When the contempt is in open court, the party being present, there is no need of any process to bring him into court. Burdett v. Commonwealth, 103 Va. 838, 48 S.E. 878 (1904).

Rules of evidence in criminal law apply. — In a proceeding to punish for a criminal, or quasi criminal contempt, the rules of evidence applicable in criminal cases prevail, and a mere preponderance of evidence is not sufficient to convict, but the offense charged must be proved beyond a reasonable doubt. Kidd v. Virginia Safe Deposit & Trust Corp., 113 Va. 612, 75 S.E. 145 (1912).

The guilt of the alleged contemner must be established beyond a reasonable doubt. Salyer v. Commonwealth, 209 Va. 662, 166 S.E.2d 110 (1969).

In criminal contempt proceedings, the rules of evidence applicable in criminal cases prevail. Carter v. Commonwealth, 2 Va. App. 392, 345 S.E.2d 5 (1986).

Burden of proof. — A person charged with criminal contempt is entitled to the benefit of the presumption of innocence, and the burden is on the prosecution to prove the guilt of the accused. Carter v. Commonwealth, 2 Va. App. 392, 345 S.E.2d 5 (1986).

Mere preponderance of evidence is not sufficient to convict one of criminal contempt; the offense charged must be proved beyond a reasonable doubt. Carter v. Commonwealth, 2 Va. App. 392, 345 S.E.2d 5 (1986).

Punishment for criminal contempt is punitive in its nature and is imposed for the purpose of preserving the power and vindicating the dignity of the court. Local 333B, United Marine Div. of Int'l Longshoremen's Ass'n v. Commonwealth ex rel. Va. Ferry Corp., 193 Va. 773, 71 S.E.2d 159, cert. denied, 344 U.S. 893, 73 S. Ct. 212, 97 L. Ed. 690 (1952).

And degree of punishment is within discretion of court. — The degree of punishment for contempt is within the sound discretion of the trial court. Local 333B, United Marine Div. of Int'l Longshoremen's Ass'n v. Commonwealth ex rel. Va. Ferry Corp., 193 Va. 773, 71 S.E.2d 159, cert. denied, 344 U.S. 893, 73 S. Ct. 212, 97 L. Ed. 690 (1952).

In imposing a fine for criminal contempt, the trial judge may properly take into consideration the extent of the willful and deliberate defiance of the court's order, the seriousness of the consequences of the contumacious behavior, the necessity of effectively terminating the defendant's defiance as required by the public interest, and the importance of deterring such acts in the future. Because of the nature of these standards, great reliance must be placed upon the discretion of the trial judge. Local 333B, United Marine Div. of Int'l Longshoremen's Ass'n v. Commonwealth ex rel. Va. Ferry Corp., 193 Va. 773, 71 S.E.2d 159, cert. denied, 344 U.S. 893, 73 S. Ct. 212, 97 L. Ed. 690 (1952).

Limitation on punishment by § 18.2-457 applies only to first class. — The limitation of the duration of imprisonment for contempt imposed by § 18.2-457 applies only to contempts mentioned in the first class of this section, and not to those mentioned in the remaining four classes of the section. Yoder v. Commonwealth, 107 Va. 823, 57 S.E. 581 (1907).

Where the contempt is not established, it is error to seek to enforce the return of money improperly paid by an order directing the imprisonment of the defendant if the money be not paid. Kidd v. Virginia Safe Deposit & Trust Corp., 113 Va. 612, 75 S.E. 145 (1912).

Due process. — Reviewing court did not violate defendant's due process right to confrontation by admitting into evidence the juvenile and domestic relations court's certificate of the summary contempt conviction and particular circumstances of the offense under § 18.2-459 as no litigant in a summary contempt case had a right to cross-examine the judge under the Sixth Amendment, U.S. Const. amend. VI, and the Due Process Clause, U.S. Const. amend. XIV, did not afford a right of confrontation where the Sixth Amendment did not. Parham v. Commonwealth, 60 Va. App. 450, 729 S.E.2d 734, 2012 Va. App. LEXIS 248 (2012).

VII. APPEAL AND ERROR.

A writ of error will now lie to an order punishing for contempt. Lindsey v. Lindsey, 158 Va. 647, 164 S.E. 551 (1932).

Appeal from judgment for contempt must be by statute. — "A commitment for contempt ... is a commitment in execution; and the judgment of conviction, unless the power to supervise is given by statute, is not subject to review in any other court, not even upon a writ of habeas corpus." Forbes v. State Council, 107 Va. 853, 60 S.E. 81 (1908), cert. denied, 216 U.S. 396, 30 S. Ct. 295, 54 L. Ed. 534 (1909). See also Wells v. Commonwealth, 62 Va. (21 Gratt.) 500 (1871).

The judgment in contempt proceeding can be reviewed by a superior tribunal only by writ of error, and not always in that way. B & O R. R. v. City of Wheeling, 54 Va. (13 Gratt.) 40 (1855).

Cannot be reviewed by writ of habeas corpus. — Proceedings for contempt cannot be reviewed in the Supreme Court on application for a writ of habeas corpus. Wells v. Commonwealth, 62 Va. (21 Gratt.) 500 (1871); Cromwell v. Commonwealth, 95 Va. 254, 28 S.E. 1023 (1897).

Preservation for review. — Attorney's arguments challenging the trial court's finding the attorney to be in contempt of court were barred by Va. Sup. Ct. R. 5A:18, as they were not raised in the circuit court, providing no ruling to review on appeal. Further, the record failed to disclose anything that would allow the appellate court to invoke the ends of justice exception to Rule 5A:18. Stroupe v. Rivero, No. 1936-02-4, 2003 Va. App. LEXIS 630 (Ct. of Appeals Dec. 9, 2003).

Defendant did not adequately preserve for review his claim that there was insufficient evidence to support the trial court's finding that he committed criminal contempt of court; defendant did not object in the trial court and the appellate court could not review the claim under either the "good cause shown" or "ends of justice" exceptions contained in Va. Sup. Ct. R. 5A:18, as neither exception applied. Forbes v. Commonwealth, — Va. App. —, — S.E.2d —, 2005 Va. App. LEXIS 230 (June 14, 2005).

Husband's appeal of an order finding him in contempt and sentencing him to one day in jail was dismissed because the husband failed to timely file a transcript or written statement of facts regarding the hearing that led to the order; a transcript of that hearing, which would show the events that gave rise to the contempt finding and sentence, was indispensable to addressing the husband's argument that the trial court's contempt finding and sentence violated § 18.2-456 and constituted reversible error. Smith v. Smith, 2008 Va. App. LEXIS 184 (Apr. 15, 2008).

Arguments waived on appeal. — Attorney's failure to object to his summary conviction of criminal contempt and never having the trial court rule on any of his violation of due process claims caused such claims to be deemed waived on appeal. Nusbaum v. Berlin, 273 Va. 385, 641 S.E.2d 494, 2007 Va. LEXIS 26 (2007).

No right to cross-examine Juvenile and Domestic Relations District Court Judge. — Virginia legislature does not intend to give birth to a constitutional right to cross-examine a juvenile and domestic relations district court (JDR court) judge at an appeal of a petty direct summary contempt proceeding, a right that a defendant does not otherwise have in the JDR court or the circuit court, as: (1) a JDR court proceeding is not a criminal prosecution within the scope of the Sixth Amendment; (2) there is no constitutional right to trial at the JDR court and no constitutional right of appeal; (3) there is a statutory prohibition against calling a judge as a witness; and (4) the Virginia general assembly provides a statutory right of appeal with the caveat that a certificate from the JDR court can be used in such an appeal. Gilman v. Commonwealth, 48 Va. App. 16, 628 S.E.2d 54, 2006 Va. App. LEXIS 130 (2006), rehearing granted, 48 Va. App. 236, 629 S.E.2d 720 (2006), opinion withdrawn, vacated by 2006 Va. App. LEXIS 456 (Oct. 10, 2006).

Confrontation clause rights not violated. — Defendant's rights under the Confrontation Clause were not violated by the use of a certificate from a juvenile and domestic relations district court (JDR court) judge in her appeal from a conviction for petty direct summary contempt as the Virginia legislature did not intend to give birth to a constitutional right to cross-examine a JDR court judge at an appeal of a petty direct summary contempt proceeding as: (1) a JDR court proceeding was not a criminal prosecution within the scope of the Sixth Amendment; (2) there was no constitutional right to trial at the JDR court and no constitutional right of appeal; (3)

there was a statutory prohibition against calling a judge as a witness; and (4) the Virginia general assembly provided a statutory right of appeal with the caveat that a certificate from the JDR court could be used in such an appeal. Gilman v. Commonwealth, 48 Va. App. 16, 628 S.E.2d 54, 2006 Va. App. LEXIS 130 (2006), rehearing granted, 48 Va. App. 236, 629 S.E.2d 720 (2006), opinion withdrawn, vacated by 2006 Va. App. LEXIS 456 (Oct. 10, 2006).

CIRCUIT COURT OPINIONS

Contempt proceeding deemed civil in nature. — Because the purpose of a contempt hearing was remedial in nature, seeking compliance with the court order regarding child support payments, the contempt was not filed to punish a husband for his past transgressions, and no sanctions would be issued if he complied with the court-ordered payments, the proceeding was deemed civil in nature, allowing the wife to appeal from an order rendered therein and have a trial de novo. Zaret v. Zaret, 68 Va. Cir. 241, 2005 Va. Cir. LEXIS 236 (Norfolk July 8, 2005).

Contempt found. — Attorney's actions in purposefully rescheduling sentencing in federal trial court so that it conflicted with trial setting for defendant he represented in state trial court warranted a finding that the attorney was in contempt of the state court, as attorney's conduct was an attempt to hinder justice because attorney had already delayed the case several times by obtaining continuances. Commonwealth v. Foulks, 56 Va. Cir. 449, 2001 Va. Cir. LEXIS 89 (Suffolk 2001).

Contempt not found. — Because an owner's § 18.2-456 request for a show cause was not grounded in law or fact and was brought for the purpose of punishing the citizens who opposed his rezoning application and cost him "a lot of money," the citizens were awarded their attorneys' fees and costs under § 8.01-271.1. Sowers v. Bd. of Supervisors, 71 Va. Cir. 324, 2006 Va. Cir. LEXIS 155 (Nottoway County 2006).

Bond. — Sentence of mother for contempt to a fixed and determinant time to serve in jail without the ability to purge herself of contempt was a criminal sanction and the bond the mother posted was to release her from jail pending her appeal; no performance bond was necessary. Div. of Child Support Enforcement v. Overstreet, 58 Va. Cir. 355, 2002 Va. Cir. LEXIS 153 (Roanoke 2002).

Child in need of supervision. — Under either § 18.2-456 or subsection E of § 16.1-292, there can be multiple confinement orders for violations of orders to attend school, issued under the same Child In Need of Supervision petition. Commonwealth v. May, 62 Va. Cir. 360, 2003 Va. Cir. LEXIS 275 (Rockingham County 2003).

Court could not waive consent decree's agreed-to sanction. — Property owner and a county zoning administrator had entered into consent decree providing that the owner would be sanctioned by a fine of $100 for each day that he failed to remove a storage structure. The court that entered the decree lacked authority to waive the fine after it found the owner in contempt of court for failing to timely remove structure, since it was obliged to enforce the consent decree entered into by the parties and could not vary its terms. Shoup v. Jerro, 70 Va. Cir. 109, 2005 Va. Cir. LEXIS 282 (Fairfax County 2005).

§ 18.2-457. Fine and imprisonment by court limited unless jury impaneled.

No court shall, without a jury, for any such contempt as is mentioned in the first class embraced in § 18.2-456, impose a fine exceeding $250 or imprison more than ten days; but in any such case the court may, without an indictment, information or any formal pleading, impanel a jury to ascertain the fine or imprisonment proper to be inflicted and may give judgment according to the verdict.

History.
Code 1950, § 18.1-295; 1960, c. 358; 1975, cc. 14, 15; 1999, c. 626.

Law Review.

For survey of Virginia law on practice and pleading for the year 1973-1974, see 60 Va. L. Rev. 1572 (1974). For 2003/2004 survey of criminal law and procedure, see 39 U. Rich. L. Rev. 133 (2004).

CASE NOTES

This section only applies to first class of § 18.2-456. — The limitation of the duration of the imprisonment for contempt imposed by this section applies only to contempts mentioned in the first class of § 18.2-456, and not to those mentioned in the remaining four classes of that section. Yoder v. Commonwealth, 107 Va. 823, 57 S.E. 581 (1907). See Stroupe v. Rivero, No. 1936-02-4, 2003 Va. App. LEXIS 630 (Ct. of Appeals Dec. 9, 2003).

Jury trial not unreasonable safeguard for certain § 18.2-456 (1) contempts. — Since subdivision (1) of § 18.2-456 is not statutorily restricted in terms of highly specific conduct or specific persons as are the other subdivisions of that statute, it cannot be considered unreasonable for the legislature to have deemed it in the interest of justice to provide a slightly greater procedural safeguard, in the form of jury trial as provided by this section, for those contempts of this more general subdivision which will be punished by a fine exceeding $50 or imprisonment of more than 10 days. Greene v. Tucker, 375 F. Supp. 892 (E.D. Va. 1974).

What are "serious" crimes for jury trial purposes. — Contempts punishable by more than six months' imprisonment or a greater than $500 fine both appear to constitute "serious" crimes for jury trial purposes. Greene v. Tucker, 375 F. Supp. 892 (E.D. Va. 1974).

Penalty imposed is evidence of seriousness of offense. — Since Virginia does not specify sentencing limits for cases of contempt, the court must look to the penalty actually imposed as the best evidence of the seriousness of the offense. Greene v. Tucker, 375 F. Supp. 892 (E.D. Va. 1974).

Fine limited to $50 (now $250). — Fine of $400 for contempt was excessive: where punishment is by fine and determined without a jury, amount of fine is limited to $50 (now $250). Brown v. Commonwealth, 26 Va. App. 758, 497 S.E.2d 147 (1998).

Where the appellant was held in contempt for failure to appear at a pretrial conference and there was nothing in the record to indicate that she failed to comply with a discovery order, the court's contempt power did not flow from Rule 4:12, and instead, the fine was limited to $50 (now $250) under this section. Roberts v. Haiar, No. 2096-97-1 (Ct. of Appeals February 24, 1998).

Excessive sentence. — Where defendant's use of profanity toward the prosecutor at defendant's sentencing hearing supported a contempt finding under § 18.2-456 (1), defendant's sentence, imposed without a jury, of 12 months in jail and a $1,000 fine was excessive under the applicable sentencing statute, § 18.2-457, to the extent that it exceeded a jail term of 10 days and a $250 fine; the sentence was vacated and a sentence of 10 days in jail and a $250 fine was imposed. Middlebrooks v. Commonwealth, No. 1516-01-1, 2002 Va. App. LEXIS 433 (Ct. of Appeals July 30, 2002).

Common-law contempt not bound within statutory sentencing guidelines. — Attorney's scheduling of various matters in different courts on the same day, and then his failure to call one of the courts to report that he would be tardy, was found to be sufficient to support the court's finding that he was guilty of common-law indirect criminal contempt; the court was not obligated to sentence him within the limits of §§ 18.2-456 and 18.2-457 because he was not charged with summary or direct contempt, and he had a plenary hearing prior to being found guilty. Robinson v. Commonwealth, 41 Va. App. 137, 583 S.E.2d 60, 2003 Va. App. LEXIS 397 (2003).

No right to jury. — Trial court did not err in the manner it conducted defendant's proceedings involving civil and criminal contempt charges for his conduct in making courthouse security decisions in his role as sheriff; the record indicated that defendant was afforded all rights and privileges due him in a criminal proceeding and he was not permitted to have a jury because the Commonwealth proceeded under § 18.2-457, which allowed a punishment of no more than 10 days in jail. Epps v. Commonwealth, 47 Va. App. 687, 626 S.E.2d 912, 2006 Va. App. LEXIS 102 (2006).

Impermissible sanction. — In the absence of authority granted by a statute, a trial court's inherent power to supervise the conduct of attorneys practicing before it and to discipline an attorney who engages in misconduct does not include the power to impose as a sanction an award of attorneys' fees and costs to the opposing parties. If an attorney's conduct is disruptive of court processes or disrespectful of the court itself, there is ample power to punish the misconduct as contempt. Nusbaum v. Berlin, 273 Va. 385, 641 S.E.2d 494, 2007 Va. LEXIS 26 (2007).

§ 18.2-458. Power of judge of district court to punish for contempt.

A judge of a district court shall have the same power and jurisdiction as a judge of a circuit court to punish summarily for contempt, but in no case shall the fine exceed $250, or the imprisonment exceed ten days, for the same contempt.

History.

Code 1950, § 18.1-293; 1960, c. 358; 1975, cc. 14, 15; 1999, c. 626.

Law Review.

For comment, "Lack of Due Process in Virginia Contempt Proceeding for Failure to Comply with Order for Support and Alimony," see 4 U. Rich. L. Rev. 128 (1969).

CASE NOTES

Right of confrontation and contempt. — Defendant's constitutional right of confrontation was not violated by admission into evidence in criminal proceeding of certificate prepared by general district court judge, which detailed circumstances of offense. Baugh v. Commonwealth, 14 Va. App. 368, 417 S.E.2d 891 (1992), overruled in part by Gilman v. Commonwealth, 275 Va. 222, 657 S.E.2d 474, 2008 Va. LEXIS 23 (2008).

OPINIONS OF THE ATTORNEY GENERAL

Verbal direction to sheriff's deputies to take defendant into custody for a specified number of hours, is equivalent to a written order and therefore is binding upon the sheriff's office, and sheriff's deputies carrying out such orders enjoy the same qualified sovereign immunity they have when others are in their custody. See opinion of Attorney General to The Honorable Dennis S. Proffitt, Sheriff, County of Chesterfield, 10-069, 2010 Va. AG LEXIS 52 (8/30/10).

Prefiling review. — A district court may, pursuant to § 8.01-271.1, impose a pre-filing review requirement if such a sanction is appropriate. Further, a district court has the inherent authority to limit or prevent an attorney or a litigant from practicing before it in the event the court determines, after a hearing, that the attorney or litigant has engaged in the unauthorized practice of law or otherwise has engaged in unprofessional or unethical conduct. See opinion of Attorney General to The Honorable Barbara J. Gaden, Judge, Richmond General District Court, 10-068, 2010 Va. AG LEXIS 51 (8/30/10).

§ 18.2-459. Appeal from sentence of such judge.

Any person sentenced to pay a fine, or to confinement, under § 18.2-458, may appeal therefrom to the circuit court of the county or city in which the sentence was pronounced, upon entering into recognizance before the sentencing judge, with surety and in penalty deemed sufficient, to appear before such circuit court to answer for the offense. If such appeal be taken, a certificate of the conviction and the particular circumstances of the offense, together with the recognizance, shall forthwith be transmitted by the sentencing judge to the clerk of such circuit court, who shall immediately deliver the same to the judge thereof. Such judge, sitting without a jury, shall hear the case upon the certificate and any legal testimony adduced on either side, and make such order therein as may seem to him proper.

History.
Code 1950, § 18.1-294; 1960, c. 358; 1975, cc. 14, 15; 2013, c. 615.

The 2013 amendments.
The 2013 amendment by c. 615 substituted "sitting without a jury, shall" for "may" in the last sentence.

CASE NOTES

Construction with other laws. — Where the provisions of §§ 16.1-69.24 and 18.2-459 address the specific subject of appeals from summary contempt adjudications in the district courts, and the provisions of §§ 16.1-132 and 16.1-136 address the general subject of appeals from the district courts, to the extent that the more specific provisions of §§ 16.1-69.24 and § 18.2-459 are in conflict with the general provisions of §§ 16.1-132 and 16.1-136, the more specific statutes prevail. Gilman v. Commonwealth, 275 Va. 222, 657 S.E.2d 474, 2008 Va. LEXIS 23 (2008).

No rights under confrontation clause. — Virginia legislature does not intend to give birth to a constitutional right to cross-examine a juvenile and domestic relations district court (JDR court) judge at an appeal of a petty direct summary contempt proceeding, a right that a defendant does not otherwise have in the JDR court or the circuit court, as: (1) a JDR court proceeding is not a criminal prosecution within the scope of the Sixth Amendment; (2) there is no constitutional right to trial at the JDR court and no constitutional right of appeal; (3) there is a statutory prohibition against calling a judge as a witness; and (4) the Virginia general assembly provides a statutory right of appeal with the caveat that a certificate from the JDR court can be used in such an appeal. Gilman v. Commonwealth, 48 Va. App. 16, 628 S.E.2d 54, 2006 Va. App. LEXIS 130 (2006), rehearing granted, 48 Va. App. 236, 629 S.E.2d 720 (2006), opinion withdrawn, vacated by 2006 Va. App. LEXIS 456 (Oct. 10, 2006).

Confrontation clause rights not violated. — Defendant's rights under the Confrontation Clause were not violated by the use of a certificate from a juvenile and domestic relations district court (JDR court) judge in her appeal from a conviction for petty direct summary contempt as the Virginia legislature did not intend to give birth to a constitutional right to cross-examine a JDR court judge at an appeal of a petty direct summary contempt proceeding as: (1) a JDR court proceeding was not a criminal prosecution within the scope of the Sixth Amendment; (2) there was no constitutional right to trial at the JDR court and no constitutional right of appeal; (3) there was a statutory prohibition against calling a judge as a witness; and (4) the Virginia general assembly provided a statutory right of appeal with the caveat that a certificate from the JDR court could be used in such an appeal. Gilman v. Commonwealth, 48 Va. App. 16, 628 S.E.2d 54, 2006 Va. App. LEXIS 130 (2006), rehearing granted, 48 Va. App. 236, 629 S.E.2d 720 (2006), opinion withdrawn, vacated by 2006 Va. App. LEXIS 456 (Oct. 10, 2006).

Because the provisions of § 16.1-69.24 and § 18.2-459 had to prevail over the more general provisions of §§ 16.1-132 and 16.1-136, a contemnor appealing an adjudication of summary contempt does not receive a trial de novo in the circuit court with attendant Sixth Amendment protections and, thus, does not have a Sixth Amendment right of confrontation in that summary contempt adjudication in the circuit court. Gilman v. Commonwealth, 275 Va. 222, 657 S.E.2d 474, 2008 Va. LEXIS 23 (2008).

Reviewing court did not violate defendant's due process right to confrontation by admitting into evidence the juvenile and domestic relations court's certificate of the summary contempt conviction and particular circumstances of the offense under § 18.2-459 as no litigant in a summary contempt case had a right to cross-examine the judge under the Sixth Amendment, U.S. Const. amend. VI, and the Due Process Clause, U.S. Const. amend. XIV, did not afford a right of confrontation where the Sixth Amendment did not. Parham

v. Commonwealth, 60 Va. App. 450, 729 S.E.2d 734, 2012 Va. App. LEXIS 248 (2012).

Error to allow judge's testimony. — Trial court erred in allowing the sitting circuit judge to testify in defendant's civil and criminal contempt case where defendant defied the trial court's order to have a deputy at the courthouse entrance during weekly business hours, and he took down signs ordered to be posted by the trial court about when the courthouse would be closed absent a deputy at the front entrance despite at least one request by the trial court that a sign and corresponding order be returned; the court itself, and not the trial judge, was the victim of defendant's contemptuous conduct and other statutory authority, such as § 18.2-459, did not permit a judicial officer who simply witnesses contemptuous behavior to testify. Epps v. Commonwealth, 47 Va. App. 687, 626 S.E.2d 912, 2006 Va. App. LEXIS 102 (2006).

Defendant could not complain on appeal of evidence that he introduced at trial. — Because the results of an Alcosensor test for blood alcohol content were properly admitted and considered by the circuit court as the fact finder, and defendant did not object to the admission of the general district court certificate of the conviction, filed pursuant to § 18.2-459, which he himself introduced into evidence, his contempt conviction was upheld on appeal. Rozario v. Commonwealth, 50 Va. App. 142, 647 S.E.2d 502, 2007 Va. App. LEXIS 272 (2007).

CIRCUIT COURT OPINIONS

Confrontation clause rights not violated. — Defendant's constitutional right of confrontation was not violated when a certificate of conviction and particular circumstances of an offense prepared by a juvenile and domestic relations district court judge was admitted into evidence against her where the court was exercising its contempt jurisdiction; the basic confrontation rights only applied when a court exercised its criminal jurisdiction. Commonwealth v. Tanner, 73 Va. Cir. 434, 2007 Va. Cir. LEXIS 214 (Roanoke County July 17, 2007).

ARTICLE 6.

INTERFERENCE WITH ADMINISTRATION OF JUSTICE.

§ 18.2-460. Obstructing justice; penalty.

A. If any person without just cause knowingly obstructs a judge, magistrate, justice, juror, attorney for the Commonwealth, witness, any law-enforcement officer, or animal control officer employed pursuant to § 3.2-6555 in the performance of his duties as such or fails or refuses without just cause to cease such obstruction when requested to do so by such judge, magistrate, justice, juror, attorney for the Commonwealth, witness, law-enforcement officer, or animal control officer employed pursuant to § 3.2-6555, he shall be guilty of a Class 1 misdemeanor.

B. Except as provided in subsection C, any person who, by threats or force, knowingly attempts to intimidate or impede a judge, magistrate, justice, juror, attorney for the Commonwealth, witness, any law-enforcement officer, or an animal control officer employed pursuant to § 3.2-6555 lawfully engaged in his duties as such, or to obstruct or impede the administration of justice in any court, is guilty of a Class 1 misdemeanor.

C. If any person by threats of bodily harm or force knowingly attempts to intimidate or impede a judge, magistrate, justice, juror, attorney for the Commonwealth, witness, any law-enforcement officer, lawfully engaged in the discharge of his duty, or to obstruct or impede the administration of justice in any court relating to a violation of or conspiracy to violate § 18.2-248 or subdivision (a) (3), (b) or (c) of § 18.2-248.1, or § 18.2-46.2 or § 18.2-46.3, or relating to the violation of or conspiracy to violate any violent felony offense listed in subsection C of § 17.1-805, he shall be guilty of a Class 5 felony.

D. Any person who knowingly and willfully makes any materially false statement or representation to a law-enforcement officer or an animal control officer employed pursuant to § 3.2-6555 who is in the course of conducting an investigation of a crime by another is guilty of a Class 1 misdemeanor.

History.

Code 1950, § 18.1-310; 1960, c. 358; 1975, cc. 14, 15; 1976, c. 269; 1984, c. 571; 1989, c. 506; 1993, c. 747; 1996, c. 718; 1999, cc. 770, 800; 2002, cc. 527, 810, 818; 2003, cc. 111, 149; 2004, cc. 396, 435; 2007, cc. 220, 282; 2009, c. 242.

Cross references.

As to interference in arrest of keeper of gaming table, see § 18.2-330. As to competency of persons having the power to issue warrants to testify in any criminal proceeding wherein the defendant is charged pursuant to this section, see § 19.2-271.

The 2009 amendments.

The 2009 amendment by c. 242 inserted "or animal control officer employed pursuant to § 3.2-6555" twice in subsection A and in subsections B and D and made related changes.

Law Review.

For comment, "Spoliation: Civil Liability for Destruction of Evidence," see 20 U. Rich. L. Rev. 191 (1985). For article surveying developments in labor and employment law in Virginia, see 37 U. Rich. L. Rev. 241 (2002). For annual survey of Virginia labor and employment law, see 40 U. Rich. L. Rev. 241 (2005). For 2007 annual survey article, "Criminal Law and Procedure," see 42 U. Rich. L. Rev. 311 (2007). For article summarizing Virginia labor and employment law cases from 2007, see 43 U. Rich. L. Rev. 211 (2008). For annual survey article, "Animal Law," see 44 U. Rich. L. Rev. 185 (2009).

Michie's Jurisprudence.

For related discussion, see 14A M.J. Obstructing Justice, § 2.

CASE NOTES

Editor's note.

The cases below were decided prior to the 2002 amendment, which added subsection D, relating to the making of materially false statements to the officer conducting an investigation.

Constitutionality. — This section was not unconstitutional in granting the prosecutor discretion to charge a defendant's conduct as either a misdemeanor under subsection B or as a felony under subsection C, where there was no principled basis for differentiating between prosecutorial discretion afforded the government when a defendant had violated more than one criminal statute and prosecutorial discretion when the charging decision involved two subsections of the same statute. Bishop v. Commonwealth, 49 Va. App. 251, 639 S.E.2d 683, 2007 Va. App. LEXIS 20 (2007), rev'd, in part, on other grounds, 275 Va. 9, 654 S.E.2d 906, 2008 Va. LEXIS 19 (2008).

Because defendant threatened to kill a police officer, and because the speech proscribed by subsection C of § 18.2-460 encompassed only "threats of bodily harm," the statute was not unconstitutional either facially or as applied to defendant; "fighting words" were not necessary for a conviction under the statute. Wise v. Commonwealth, 49 Va. App. 344, 641 S.E.2d 134, 2007 Va. App. LEXIS 68 (2007).

Subsection C of § 18.2-460 does not reach a substantial amount of constitutionally protected speech and is not facially violative of the First Amendment; "fighting words" are not necessary for a conviction under § 18.2-460. Wise v. Commonwealth, 49 Va. App. 344, 641 S.E.2d 134, 2007 Va. App. LEXIS 68 (2007).

Legislative intent. — The absence of language in this section relating to use of a weapon indicates the legislative intent to include in the misdemeanor offense of obstructing justice less violent types of conduct, and to make conduct accompanied by the use of a weapon subject to prosecution for greater offenses, such as attempted murder. Martin v. Commonwealth, 242 Va. 1, 406 S.E.2d 15, cert. denied, 502 U.S. 945, 112 S. Ct. 388, 116 L. Ed. 2d 339 (1991).

The statute was enacted for the purpose of deterring those who intimidate any witness lawfully engaged in his duties as such. Fleming v. Commonwealth, 13 Va. App. 349, 412 S.E.2d 180 (1991).

Violation of subsection C. — Commonwealth failed to prove that defendant violated subsection C of § 18.2-460, because it had presented no proof that, at the time a threatening statement was made to a deputy, the deputy was engaged in the discharge of any duty "relating to a violation of or conspiracy to violate" one of the felony offenses listed in § 18.2-460. Washington v. Commonwealth, 273 Va. 619, 643 S.E.2d 485, 2007 Va. LEXIS 61 (2007).

Where defendant refused police officers' commands to stop running, and, once caught, refused commands to give officers his hands, there was insufficient evidence of "force" to convict defendant of felony obstruction of justice. But as defendant intended to impede the officers in the performance of their duties, defendant committed misdemeanor obstruction. Belton v. Commonwealth, — Va. App. —, — S.E.2d —, 2007 Va. App. LEXIS 391 (Oct. 23, 2007).

Defendant's conviction of felony obstruction of justice under subsection C of § 18.2-460 had to be reversed as none of the statutorily enumerated felony offenses were at issue. Roach v. Commonwealth, 51 Va. App. 741, 660 S.E.2d 348, 2008 Va. App. LEXIS 212 (2008).

Section does not articulate public policy exception to employment-at-will. — There is no established public policy underlying this section that would support a police officer's wrongful discharge action based on the public policy exception to the employment-at-will doctrine. City of Va. Beach v. Harris, 259 Va. 220, 523 S.E.2d 239 (2000).

Statute did not create any statutory right or a corresponding public policy of the type that would support an exception to the employment-at-will doctrine and, thus, allow a common-law action for wrongful termination. Rowan v. Tractor Supply Co., 263 Va. 209, 559 S.E.2d 709, 2002 Va. LEXIS 38 (2002).

Public policy behind the obstruction of justice statute is not to protect individuals from intimidation, but to protect the public from a flawed legal system due to impaired prosecution of criminals. Hence, an employer did not violate the public policy behind the obstruction of justice statute by terminating an employee for pursuing criminal assault charges against a fellow employee. Rowan v. Tractor Supply Co., — F.3d —, 2004 U.S. App. LEXIS 18594 (4th Cir. Sept. 2, 2004).

It is the threats made by the offender, coupled with his intent, that constitute the offense under subsection A of this section; the resulting effect of the offender's threats, such as fear, apprehension, or delay, is not an element of the crime. Polk v. Commonwealth, 4 Va. App. 590, 358 S.E.2d 770 (1987).

"Threat" defined. — The defendant's statement that he would kill the police officer was a threat as contemplated by subsection A of this section. Polk v. Commonwealth, 4 Va. App. 590, 358 S.E.2d 770 (1987).

Although words alone can support a conviction for obstruction of justice, those words generally must contain some manner of a threat intended to intimidate a police officer. Brown v. City of Danville, 44 Va. App. 586, 606 S.E.2d 523, 2004 Va. App. LEXIS 627 (2004).

It is not necessary that there be an assault or physical threat in order to find criminal intent under this statute. Woodson v. Commonwealth, 14 Va. App. 787, 421 S.E.2d 1 (1992), aff'd, 245 Va. 401, 429 S.E.2d 27 (1993).

The actual assault of a police officer is not prerequisite to a finding obstruction of justice in Virginia. Smith v. Tolley, 960 F. Supp. 977 (E.D. Va. 1997).

Intent to impede a police officer. — It is not defendant's intent to use a gun in an offensive manner that is prohibited by the statute; rather, it is his intent to impede a police officer in the performance of his duties that is the gravamen of the statute. Woodson v. Commonwealth, 14 Va. App. 787, 421 S.E.2d 1 (1992), aff'd, 245 Va. 401, 429 S.E.2d 27 (1993).

Where defendant injected himself between police officers and man they sought to question, he plainly intended and accomplished interference with proper performance of officers' duties. Mason v. Commonwealth, No. 1189-98-2 (Ct. of Appeals Aug. 3, 1999).

Trial court correctly denied defendant's motion to suppress evidence a police officer seized from his person because the officer was conducting a reasonable search incident to arrest when he removed a crack pipe from defendant's pocket; because defendant refused to allow a police officer to conduct a pat-down search and struggled with the officer, the officer had probable cause to arrest defendant for obstruction of justice. Pettaway v. Commonwealth, 2009 Va. App. LEXIS 178 (Apr. 21, 2009).

Even if an officer lacked probable cause to arrest a defendant for public intoxication, there was probable cause to support an arrest for obstruction of justice where the defendant's acts of agitation, aggression, and shouldering himself into an officer impeded the officer's ability to conduct an investigation. Thomas v. Commonwealth, 2010 Va. App. LEXIS 117 (Mar. 30, 2010).

Intent to prevent officer's performance of duty required. — A conviction for violation of this section requires proof of acts clearly indicating an intention on the part of the accused to prevent the officer from performing his duty, as to "obstruct" ordinarily implies opposition or resistance by direct action; it means to obstruct the officer himself, not merely to oppose or impede the process with which the officer is armed. Rogers v. Pendleton, 249 F.3d 279, 2001 U.S. App. LEXIS 8157 (4th Cir. 2001).

Focus is on defendant's intent, not the officer's intent. — When evaluating whether a defendant's actions fall within the ambit of § 18.2-460, a court's focus is not on the intent of the police officer but, rather, on the intent of the defendant to commit an act of violence or force. Ishtiwi v. Commonwealth, No. 0734-04-4, 2005 Va. App. LEXIS 11 (Ct. of Appeals Jan. 11, 2005).

Even assuming that a police officer had no present intent to visit defendant at the time that defendant threatened the officer that if he came to defendant's house, he would get a dog bite, defendant could not rely on the officer's lack of present intent to negate his own intent to commit an act of violence or force. Ishtiwi v. Commonwealth, No. 0734-04-4, 2005 Va. App. LEXIS 11 (Ct. of Appeals Jan. 11, 2005).

This section requires actual hindrance or obstruction of the officer, opposition or resistance by direct action; obstruction of justice does not occur when a person fails to cooperate fully with an officer or when the person's conduct merely renders the officer's task more difficult or frustrates his investigation. Rogers v. Pendleton, 249 F.3d 279, 2001 U.S. App. LEXIS 8157 (4th Cir. 2001).

Peaceful criticism directed at police officer during an arrest did not constitute "direct action" for purposes of subsection A of § 18.2-460, and police officers had no probable cause to arrest attorney under this section for advising an arrestee of his constitutional rights while officers were in the process of making the arrest; and the fact that the attorney refused to leave the scene after one of the officers told the attorney to do so did not provide a basis for probable cause because the attorney was required to have been obstructing the officer in order to have violated the order to leave under the statute. Wilson v. Kittoe, 229 F. Supp. 2d 520, 2002 U.S. Dist. LEXIS 21532 (W.D. Va. 2002), aff'd, 337 F.3d 392 (4th Cir. 2003).

The ability to peacefully criticize the police as a right of a free society has been recognized in Virginia, and police officers had no probable cause to arrest attorney under subsection A of § 18.2-460 for advising an arrestee of his constitutional rights while officers were in the process of making the arrest. Wilson v. Kittoe, 229 F. Supp. 2d 520, 2002 U.S. Dist. LEXIS 21532 (W.D. Va. 2002), aff'd, 337 F.3d 392 (4th Cir. 2003).

District court properly denied an officer's motion for summary judgment on qualified immunity grounds where an attorney's inquiry into a neighbor's son's well-being during an arrest, inquiries to the arresting and assisting officers requesting permission to talk with the son after the arrest was completed, and peaceful attempts to remind the officer of the son's constitutional rights did not give the arresting officer probable cause to arrest the attorney

for obstruction of justice under subsection A of § 18.2-460. Wilson v. Kittoe, 337 F.3d 392, 2003 U.S. App. LEXIS 14609 (4th Cir. 2003).

Sufficiency of force to constitute offense. — To constitute obstruction of an officer in the performance of his duty it is not necessary that there be an actual or technical assault upon the officer, but there must be acts clearly indicating an intention on the part of the accused to prevent the officer from performing his duty, as to "obstruct" ordinarily implies opposition or resistance by direct action and forcible or threatened means. It means to obstruct the officer himself; not merely to oppose or impede the process with which the officer is armed. Jones v. Commonwealth, 141 Va. 471, 126 S.E. 74 (1925); Love v. Commonwealth, 212 Va. 492, 184 S.E.2d 769 (1971).

Failing to cooperate fully with an officer or engaging in conduct which merely renders the officer's task more difficult is not proscribed by this section. Piela v. Commonwealth, No. 0550-99-1, 2000 Va. App. LEXIS 260 (Ct. of Appeals Apr. 4, 2000).

Running away from officer. — Commonwealth did not prove beyond a reasonable doubt that defendant "obstructed" a law-enforcement officer pursuant to subsection A of § 18.2-460 because defendant's failure to stop running away from an officer did not constitute obstruction of justice, and the officer testified at trial that he was never able to touch defendant and that defendant never threw anything at or near the officer to impede his progress, nor was there evidence that defendant threatened the officer in any manner; evidence that a suspect ran away from the police, without doing anything else, is insufficient as a matter of law to convict a person under subsection A. Brandon Jarell Love v. Commonwealth, 2010 Va. App. LEXIS 409 (Oct. 26, 2010).

Defendant's resistance, running from officers, did not prevent or significantly impede the officers in the performance of their duties and thus, required reversal of the conviction for obstruction of justice. Roberts v. Commonwealth, 2011 Va. App. LEXIS 303 (Oct. 4, 2011).

Force may be used to repel illegal arrest. — One who is illegally arrested may use a reasonable amount of force to repel the assault. United States v. Moore, 332 F. Supp. 919 (E.D. Va. 1971).

Officers' mistaken belief that defendant was the person named in the capias did not make the capias an instrument upon which they could lawfully arrest her, even if that mistake was made in good faith, and therefore defendant had the right to use reasonable force to resist arrest. Brown v. Commonwealth, 27 Va. App. 111, 497 S.E.2d 527 (1998).

By persons in close relationship. — Persons in close relationship of affinity or consanguinity may resist an officer in making an unlawful arrest. United States v. Moore, 332 F. Supp. 919 (E.D. Va. 1971).

Lawful resistance to unlawful arrest or detention not established. — Where the evidence was sufficient to convict defendant of obstruction of justice under subsection A of § 18.2-460 because she interfered with an officer's issuance of a summons to a driver of a car, in which defendant was a passenger, by making inappropriate comments and by approaching and assaulting the officer as he tried to issue the summons, defendant could not justify her conduct as lawful resistance to an unlawful arrest or detention because she was not detained or arrested when the interference occurred. Bennett v. Commonwealth, 2010 Va. App. LEXIS 12 (Jan. 12, 2010).

Solicitation not use of threat or force. — An indictment for soliciting one to use his influence with a grand juror to persuade the juror to vote against the finding of the indictment against the defendant does not charge the offense as defined by this section. In order to charge an offense under this section it is necessary to allege an attempted intimidation by threats or force. Wiseman v. Commonwealth, 143 Va. 631, 130 S.E. 249 (1925).

Conviction need not be based on proof defendant committed underlying felony. — A defendant's conviction for obstruction need not be based on proof that he committed the underlying felony. It is sufficient that the Commonwealth proved that the lawful activity of a state trooper related to an offense specified in subsection C. of this section. Turner v. Commonwealth, 20 Va. App. 713, 460 S.E.2d 605 (1995).

Neither subsection A. nor subsection B. requires a conviction for an underlying offense as an element of the alleged obstruction of justice. Subsection C. evinces legislative intent to make the punishment for obstructing justice as to certain drug offenses more severe than for obstructing justice generally. Turner v. Commonwealth, 20 Va. App. 713, 460 S.E.2d 605 (1995).

Trial court erred in imposing a sentence of 30 days in jail, where appellant was convicted for obstruction of justice in violation of subsection A, a Class 4 misdemeanor. The punishment for a Class 4 misdemeanor is a fine of not more than $250. Nesbit v. Commonwealth, 15 Va. App. 391, 424 S.E.2d 239 (1992).

Defendant convicted under this section could also be prosecuted for attempted murder. — Where defendant was first convicted of, inter alia, obstruction of justice by threats or force (a misdemeanor) and later convicted of attempted murder (a felony), the "same conduct" rule enunciated in Grady v. Corbin, 495 U.S. —, 110 S. Ct. 2084, 109 L. Ed. 2d 548 (1990), did not apply to bar prosecution of the charge of attempted murder on principles of double jeopardy. Martin v. Commonwealth, 242 Va. 1, 406 S.E.2d 15, cert. denied, 502 U.S. 945, 112 S. Ct. 388, 116 L. Ed. 2d 339 (1991).

Suppression of evidence. — In a case in which defendant was convicted for misdemeanor obstruction of justice, in violation of subsection B of § 18.2-460, for threatening two deputies with violence if they attempted to arrest him, he argued unsuccessfully that the trial court should have suppressed the evidence of his threats because, prior to making his threats against the deputies, they should have advised him of his right to remain silent under the Miranda decision. The Miranda exclusionary rule need not be pushed so far that crimes-by-words could not be proved and punished. Testa v. Commonwealth, 55 Va. App. 275, 685 S.E.2d 213, 2009 Va. App. LEXIS 534 (2009).

Sufficiency of evidence. — The defendant's threat to kill the police officer demonstrated his intent to intimidate the police officer from completion of the post-arrest processing; therefore, the evidence presented was sufficient to establish the defendant's criminal intent. Polk v. Commonwealth, 4 Va. App. 590, 358 S.E.2d 770 (1987).

By brandishing shovel and approaching officer in a threatening manner while officer attempted to serve summons, defendant attempted to intimidate or impede officer in the performance of her duties, and thus his actions amounted to obstruction of justice. Fredriksen v. Commonwealth, No. 0732-98-4 (Ct. of Appeals June 22, 1999).

The evidence was sufficient to support a defendant's conviction under this section where the defendant, who was a prisoner in the county jail, after intentionally disabling his cell door, which prevented a proper lockdown, refused to exit his cell on command and physically resisted the efforts of law-enforcement officers to remove him, while cursing and threatening one of the officers. Such behavior did not simply burden the task of a law-enforcement officer but necessitated affirmative and violent intervention to allow the proper performance of his duties, circumstances clearly contemplated by this section. Piela v. Commonwealth, No. 0550-99-1, 2000 Va. App. LEXIS 260 (Ct. of Appeals Apr. 4, 2000).

Inmate's action in intentionally disabling his cell door, which prevented a proper lockdown, and resisting officers' attempts to remove him from his cell constituted action calculated to impede law-enforcement officers in lawful discharge of their duties, and evidence was thus sufficient to sustain defendant's conviction. Piela v. Commonwealth, No. 0550-99-1 (Ct. of Appeals Apr. 4, 2000).

Evidence was sufficient to support defendant's conviction for obstruction of justice under subsection C of § 18.2-460 where: (1) defendant put items in his mouth as police approached, after observing a drug transaction; (2) defendant knew of the police presence, as the officer approached wearing a gunbelt, a shirt marked "police," and his badge around his neck; (3) defendant struggled with the officer; and (4) defendant refused to spit the items out of his mouth when ordered to do so by the officer. Ward v. Commonwealth, No. 1773-01-1, 2002 Va. App. LEXIS 624 (Ct. of Appeals Oct. 15, 2002).

Evidence was sufficient to support defendant's conviction for obstruction of justice, as it showed that defendant refused the commands of law-enforcement officers to get down on the ground so that he could be arrested and that he also refused to take his hands out of his jacket when ordered to do so, resulting in his struggle with police officers while he was being handcuffed and taken into custody. Payne v. Commonwealth, No. 3339-02-3, 2003 Va. App. LEXIS 616 (Ct. of Appeals Dec. 2, 2003).

Police acted reasonably when they conducted a strip search of defendant who was arrested for failure to appear in court on a felony narcotics charge before they placed defendant in a detention facility, and the trial court's judgments denying defendant's motion to suppress 12 pieces of cocaine which police found in a plastic bag defendant had placed between his buttocks, and convicting defendant of possession of cocaine with the intent to distribute and obstruction of justice for fighting with police when they attempted to conduct their search, were upheld. Craddock v. Commonwealth, 40 Va. App. 539, 580 S.E.2d 454, 2003 Va. App. LEXIS 296 (2003).

Where defendant, a physically imposing man, was loud, confrontational, stood within an arm's length of a police officer, and kept repeating that a police officer "better" fix or "needed to fix" a malicious wounding charge for which the officer had arrested defendant, defendant's actions constituted a "threat of bodily harm or force" and defendant acted with the requisite intent to intimidate a police officer; as a result, the evidence was sufficient to support defendant's conviction for obstructing justice under subsection C. Jones v. Commonwealth, No. 3288-02-2, 2004 Va. App. LEXIS 187 (Ct. of Appeals Mar. 2, 2004).

Where the evidence showed that defendant slipped out of his coat and ran when officers initially attempted to detain him, struggled, kicked, and was uncooperative after a group of officers were able to subdue him, and refused to move his hands into view, but had his hands on top of a loaded firearm, said facts and circumstances proved beyond a reasonable doubt that defendant was guilty of obstructing justice; moreover, defendant was not justified in using force against the officers in order to resist an investigative detention. Spinner v. Commonwealth, No. 2548-03-3, 2004 Va. App. LEXIS 490 (Ct. of Appeals Oct. 12, 2004).

Because defendant refused to spit out a suspected narcotic that defendant had ingested, the evidence was sufficient to find that defendant obstructed justice in violation of subsection A of § 18.2-460. Jones v. Commonwealth, — Va. App. —, — S.E.2d —, 2007 Va. App. LEXIS 29 (Jan. 30, 2007).

Because defendant's post-entry assaults on police officers were outside the scope of the exclusionary rule, and because police officers had probable cause under § 19.2-81 to make a warrantless arrest for public intoxication, the Fourth Amendment was irrelevant; since defendant had no right to resist the arrest, defendant's motion to suppress was properly denied and defendant was properly convicted of assault and battery on a police officer and obstruction of justice. Messier v. Commonwealth, 2007 Va. App. LEXIS 201 (May 15, 2007).

Evidence was sufficient to prove that defendant obstructed justice in violation of subsection A of § 18.2-460 as defendant's refusal to obey an officer's order to get out of defendant's car, defendant's walking away after having been told defendant was under arrest, and defendant's "pulling" and "tugging" from the officer's grasp obstructed the officer's execution of defendant's arrest. Collins v. Commonwealth, — Va. App. —, — S.E.2d —, 2007 Va. App. LEXIS 468 (Dec. 27, 2007).

Where defendant grabbed an officer's hand as the officer was trying to handcuff him, and was thrashing and pulling away so hard that he bent the handcuffs, the evidence was sufficient to prove that he obstructed justice in violation of § 18.2-460. Solorzano v. Commonwealth, — Va. App. —, — S.E.2d —, 2008 Va. App. LEXIS 39 (Jan. 22, 2008).

Appellant's obstruction of justice conviction was reversed because, although appellant failed to properly preserve the issue for appellate review, the "ends of justice" exception applied since a miscarriage of justice occurred because appellant could not have been convicted of violating subsection A of § 18.2-460 based solely upon appellant's flight from the scene. Yancey v. Commonwealth, 2008 Va. App. LEXIS 29 (Jan. 15, 2008).

Evidence was sufficient to support the trial court's finding that defendant knowingly and without just cause obstructed officers in the performance of their duties within the meaning of § 18.2-460. Defendant not only refused the officers' order to defendant to get out of the vehicle in which defendant was a passenger, but also attempted to flee by breaking away after the officers placed their hands on defendant to remove defendant from the car, and defendant physically resisted the officers' efforts to put defendant's hands behind defendant's back and handcuff defendant in order to effect an arrest for the offense of carrying a concealed firearm. Coleman v. Commonwealth, 2008 Va. App. LEXIS 463 (Oct. 14, 2008).

Evidence was sufficient to support defendant's conviction for obstruction of justice, as defendant ran from officers, twisted away from the officers, and repeatedly tried to put defendant's hands in defendant's pockets. Defendant also kicked defendant's legs as officers tried to arrest defendant. Boxley v. Commonwealth, — Va. App. —, — S.E.2d —, 2009 Va. App. LEXIS 99 (Mar. 10, 2009).

In a case in which defendant was convicted for misdemeanor obstruction of justice, in violation of subsection B of § 18.2-460, for threatening two deputies with violence if they attempted to arrest him, he argued unsuccessfully that the evidence was insufficient to support his conviction. There was ample evidence that defendant attempted to intimidate the deputies by threatening them with violence; behind a closed, locked door, he told the deputies that he would pick them off one by one if they tried to arrest him and he added that if he was going back to jail, he was bringing them down with him. Testa v. Commonwealth, 55 Va. App. 275, 685 S.E.2d 213, 2009 Va. App. LEXIS 534 (2009).

Evidence was sufficient to convict defendant of misdemeanor obstruction of justice in violation of subsection B of § 18.2-460 because he interposed himself between an officer investigating a noise complaint and the homeowner, he refused to leave, and he lunged at an officer with his hands in the air prior to being arrested. Bennett v. Commonwealth, 2009 Va. App. LEXIS 566 (Dec. 22, 2009).

Evidence showing that defendant forcibly removed his arm from the grip of a police officer arresting him and then fled from the officer did not merely represent avoidance of the officer but rather was sufficient to support defendant's conviction of obstruction of justice in violation of subsection A of § 18.2-460. Brown v. Commonwealth, 2010 Va. App. LEXIS 20 (Jan. 19, 2010).

The evidence failed to establish a violation of this section. Rhodes v. Commonwealth, 182 Va. 39, 27 S.E.2d 899 (1943).

Evidence showing only that the defendant broke and entered an apartment as he fled from the police, entering from one side of the apartment and exiting on the other, was insufficient to show that he did this with intent to obstruct a law-enforcement officer. Thomas v. Commonwealth, No. 0213-90-2 (Ct. of Appeals March 12, 1991).

Evidence did not prove that defendants had the intent to obstruct justice when they entered apartment where evidence proved that the three men entered the apartment in an apparent attempt to avoid detection or to await the end of the disturbances in which they had been involved; no evidence proved that they had any contact with police officers before they entered the apartment or even that police officers were present when they entered the apartment; and although the men peered through the windows, no facts or circumstances proved that the defendants intended by threat or force to attempt to intimidate or impede a law-enforcement officer. Dowdell v. Commonwealth, No. 1694-93-1 (Ct. of Appeals March 7, 1995).

Defendant did not use unreasonable force to resist an unlawful arrest whether she sat on the sofa and cursed and kicked or jumped from the sofa and kicked, not aiming the kick at any of the officers. Brown v. Commonwealth, 27 Va. App. 111, 497 S.E.2d 527 (1998).

Defendant, involved in automobile accident, who first told officer that he was too drunk to have been driving and later told officer that he did not remember who was driving did not obstruct the officer in the performance of his duties because, although his statements may have frustrated the officer, they did not oppose, impede, or resist the officer's efforts to investigate the accident. Ruckman v. Commonwealth, 28 Va. App. 428, 505 S.E.2d 388 (1998).

Defendant's false statements to investigating officer were insufficient to support conviction for obstruction of justice. Dobson v. Commonwealth, No. 2802-97-2 (Ct. of Appeals June 15, 1999) (decided prior to the 2002 amendment adding subsection D).

Individual's evidence showed that the individual had not committed any crime, did not at any time reach for or appear to reach for a weapon or threaten the officers in any way, and cooperated fully with the officers. Assuming these facts, the officer's arrest for obstruction of justice, was not protected by qualified immunity and the individual's Fourth Amendment claims brought under 42 U.S.C.S. § 1983 survived summary judgment. Veney v. Ojeda, 321 F. Supp. 2d 733, 2004 U.S. Dist. LEXIS 11259 (E.D. Va. 2004).

Removal of cash from police car did not involve use of force necessary to sustain conviction for obstructing justice under subsection C of § 18.2-460. Jordan v. Commonwealth, 273 Va. 639, 643 S.E.2d 166, 2007 Va. LEXIS 59 (2007).

Evidence was insufficient to support defendant's conviction for obstruction of justice, in violation of subsection D of § 18.2-460, as that statutory section was inapplicable when the police were investigating defendant and not the crime of another; defendant provided false statements to police concerning his identity when he was questioned by them. Atkins v. Commonwealth, 54 Va. App. 340, 678 S.E.2d 834, 2009 Va. App. LEXIS 310 (2009).

Evidence was insufficient to support defendant's conviction for obstruction of justice, in violation of subsection A of § 18.2-460, as his mere flight from police did not constitute obstruction of justice; defendant's action of running away when police officers indicated an intent to detain him did not "obstruct" the officers from performing their duties, but instead, merely impeded the process. Atkins v. Commonwealth, 54 Va. App. 340, 678 S.E.2d 834, 2009 Va. App. LEXIS 310 (2009).

Providing conflicting or incorrect statements to an investigating officer does not "obstruct" the officer in the performance of his duties as contemplated by this section. Wilson v. Commonwealth, No. 1072-00-1, 2001 Va. App. LEXIS 121 (Ct. of Appeals Mar. 13, 2001) (decided prior to the 2002 amendment adding subsection D).

No violation of Fourth Amendment as there was probable cause for arrest. — Following an accident in a store parking lot, at the time of the claimant's arrest, the officers had probable cause to believe that the claimant had violated numerous laws, including obstruction of justice and failure to provide the customer whose car she had damaged with her name, address, driver's license number, and vehicle registration number in violation of §§ 18.2-460 and 46.2-896. Because they had probable cause to believe that the claimant had violated the law, the officers did not violate the claimant's Fourth Amendment rights when they arrested her without a warrant. Durney v. Doss, 2004 U.S. App. LEXIS 15545 (4th Cir. July 28, 2004).

Because defendant officer's order for plaintiff passenger to remain in an automobile that was the subject of a traffic stop was lawful, the officer's belief that the passenger was violating the obstruction of justice statute by getting out of the car was likewise reasonable, as was his use of force to effectuate the resulting arrest; accordingly, the officer's arrest of the passenger and his use of force were shielded under the doctrine of qualified immunity. Coffey v. Morris, 401 F. Supp. 2d 542, 2005 U.S. Dist. LEXIS 29544 (W.D. Va. 2005).

Arresting officer was entitled to qualified immunity in an arrestee's suit alleging a Fourth Amendment violation from his arrest because there was probable cause to arrest for obstruction of justice since the arrestee lunged at the officer, pointed his finger in the officer's face, and threatened the officer when the officer attempted to talk to the arrestee in response to a call. Ware v. James City County, 652 F. Supp. 2d 693, 2009 U.S. Dist. LEXIS 83263 (E.D. Va. 2009), aff'd, 2010 U.S. App. LEXIS 11145 (4th Cir. Va. 2010).

Probable cause to arrest. — Police had probable cause to arrest defendant for obstruction of justice, where the record clearly demonstrated that detectives had a reasonable belief that defendant was not telling them the truth based on the fact that defendant's version of events differed significantly from statements the detectives received from a witness, and defendant was coy and deceptive during questioning, which served to convince the detectives that defendant was holding back information about the shooting. Commonwealth v. Helvenston, 2010 Va. App. LEXIS 237 (2010).

No probable cause to arrest. — Court was unable to conclude that there was probable cause to arrest for obstruction of justice, under subsection A of § 18.2-460, because, while the arrestee acknowledged that he was initially unable to hear the deputies due to the wind and the initial distance between him and the deputies, he alleged that upon comprehending what the deputies were yelling, he promptly followed their instructions, removed a clip and placed a pistol on the ground and then followed further instructions to lay down on the ground as well, and the arrestee further alleged that at no time did his acts indicate an intention to oppose or resist the deputies. Botkin v. Fisher, 2009 U.S. Dist. LEXIS 24554 (W.D. Va. Mar. 25, 2009).

Arrestee presented sufficient allegations to support a claim that his arrest for obstruction of justice under § 18.2-460 lacked probable cause, and therefore the officer was denied summary judgment on the issue of qualified immunity, because at the time of the arrest, the arrestee had engaged in relatively little interaction with the officer; the arrestee alleged that he waved to signal his approach, walked to the police cruiser at a measured and even pace, and respectfully contested the officer's assessment of the arrestee's son's speed. The arrestee's personal refusal to obey the officer's order to go back in the house at best raised triable issues as to probable cause. Jackson v. Brickey, 2011 U.S. Dist. LEXIS 13964 (W.D. Va. Feb. 11, 2011).

Applied in Henry v. Commonwealth, 21 Va. App. 141, 462 S.E.2d 578 (1995).

CIRCUIT COURT OPINIONS

No private right of action. — Police officer, who claimed that other police officers conspired to conceal events surrounding the death of a suspect and compelled him to testify falsely about those events, did not have a private right of action against a city or its employees to recover damages he sustained when he was terminated from the city's police department. Young v. City of Norfolk, 62 Va. Cir. 307, 2003 Va. Cir. LEXIS 296 (Norfolk 2003).

Probation officers not law-enforcement officers. — Because probation officers were not considered law-enforcement officers under the Virginia Code, an employee's allegation that the employee was directed to obstruct justice in violation of § 18.2-460 by lying to a supervisor's probation officer did not constitute a valid retaliatory discharge claim under the Bowman line of cases. Carr v. Bus. Sys. Mgmt., 73 Va. Cir. 459, 2007 Va. Cir. LEXIS 114 (Fairfax County 2007).

OPINIONS OF THE ATTORNEY GENERAL

Arrest for obstruction of justice not authorized. — Law-enforcement officer conducting a lawful investigative stop may not arrest a suspect for obstruction of justice under subsection A of this section, when the suspect refuses to identify himself to the officer; depending on the circumstances, however, there may be justification to detain a suspect for the purpose of determining his identity. See opinion of Attorney General to The Honorable Marsha L. Garst, Commonwealth's Attorney for the City of Harrisonburg, 02-082 (10/10/02).

§ 18.2-460.1. Unlawful disclosure of existence of order authorizing wire or oral interception of communication.

Except as provided in Chapter 6 (§ 19.2-61 et seq.) of Title 19.2, it shall be unlawful for any person who, by virtue of his position of authority or in the course of his employment by a court, a public utility, a law-enforcement agency, or by any other agency of state or local government, obtains knowledge of the fact that an order authorizing interception of wire or oral communication has been entered or is sought to be entered, intentionally to disclose such information to any person, except in the performance of his duties. Persons violating this section shall be guilty of a Class 1 misdemeanor.

Nothing herein precludes a court authorizing an interception under this chapter from prohibiting any other person from disclosing the existence of an order, interception, or device and imposing contempt sanctions for any willful disclosure.

History.
  1980, c. 339.

§ 18.2-461. Falsely summoning or giving false reports to law-enforcement officials.

It shall be unlawful for any person (i) to knowingly give a false report as to the commission of any crime to any law-enforcement official with intent to mislead, or (ii) without just cause and with intent to interfere with the operations of any law-enforcement official, to call or summon any law-enforcement official by telephone or other means, including engagement or activation of an automatic emergency alarm. Violation of the provisions of this section shall be punishable as a Class 1 misdemeanor.

History.
  Code 1950, § 18.1-401; 1960, c. 358; 1975, cc. 14, 15; 1996, cc. 753, 815.

CASE NOTES

Lack of probable cause to arrest. — Because the police lacked probable cause to arrest defendant for either falsely summoning police or for disorderly conduct, the trial court erred in denying his motion to suppress the drugs obtained from his arrest and defendant's conviction for the possession of cocaine was improper. Thor v. Commonwealth, 2010 Va. App. LEXIS 88 (Mar. 9, 2010).

Evidence sufficient. — Evidence was sufficient to show that defendant intended to mislead police by falsely reporting an incident to them, and to sustain his conviction under § 18.2-461(i), where defendant rode with a driver and passenger in a gray Camaro for an extended period of time on the night in question, where, having tired of defendant's repeated requests for her to drive him to various locations, the driver told defendant she wanted to take him home, where defendant was verbally abusive to the driver and tried to prevent her from driving to his residence, where, once they reached defendant's residence, defendant told the driver he would "get her back," where defendant immediately called the police and reported two women had shot at his residence from a gray Camaro and that the women possessed cocaine, and where, stopped by the police within minutes of defendant's call, the driver and her passenger possessed neither firearms nor drugs. Kimberlin v. Commonwealth, — Va. App. —, — S.E.2d —, 2005 Va. App. LEXIS 148 (Apr. 12, 2005).

Evidence was sufficient to show that defendant provided false information to a law-enforcement officer because defendant falsely told a Department of Motor Vehicles agent information about a license applicant, including that she was his wife and that she worked at two particular stores. Melendez v. Commonwealth, 2010 Va. App. LEXIS 171 (May 4, 2010).

Passenger not an informant. — Trial court did not err in denying defendant's motion to suppress cocaine the police discovered in defendant's vehicle incident to an arrest on a separate charge because the police did not rely on the passenger of the vehicle as an informant since the passenger was not an informant, and his reliability and basis of knowledge were not factors in determining whether the police had probable cause to arrest defendant; unlike an anonymous tipster, the passenger was known to the police and personally spoke with them, and by telling the police that defendant was the driver and possessed the cocaine, the passenger was subjecting himself to possible arrest if the information proved false under § 18.2-461, and placed his credibility at risk and could not lie with impunity. Jones v. Commonwealth, 2011 Va. App. LEXIS 98 (Mar. 22, 2011).

Applied in Henderson v. Commonwealth, 59 Va. App. 641, 722 S.E.2d 275, 2012 Va. App. LEXIS 116 (2012).

CIRCUIT COURT OPINIONS

No private right of action. — Police officer, who claimed that other police officers conspired to conceal events surrounding the death of a suspect and compelled him to testify falsely about those events, did not have a private right of action against a city or its employees to recover damages he sustained when he was terminated from the city's police department. Young v. City of Norfolk, 62 Va. Cir. 307, 2003 Va. Cir. LEXIS 296 (Norfolk 2003).

§ 18.2-462. Concealing or compounding offenses; penalties.

A. Except as provided in subsection B, if any person knowing of the commission of an offense takes any money or reward, or an engagement therefor, upon an agreement or understanding, expressed or implied, to compound or conceal such offense, or not to prosecute therefor, or not to give evidence thereof, he shall, if such offense is a felony, be guilty of a Class 2 misdemeanor; and if such offense is not a felony, unless it is punishable merely by forfeiture to him, he shall be guilty of a Class 4 misdemeanor.

B. Any person, other than the victim of the crime or the husband, wife, parent, grandparent, child, grandchild, brother, or sister, by consanguinity or affinity of the offender, who with actual knowledge of the commission by another of any felony offense under Chapter 4 (§ 18.2-30 et seq.) of this title, willfully conceals, alters, dismembers, or destroys any item of physical evidence with the intent to delay, impede, obstruct, prevent, or hinder the investigation, apprehension, prosecution, conviction, or punishment of any person regarding such offense is guilty of a Class 6 felony.

History.
Code 1950, § 18.1-303; 1960, c. 358; 1975, cc. 14, 15; 2005, c. 408.

Law Review.
For article on criminal restitution, a survey of its past history and an analysis of its present usefulness, see 5 U. Rich. L. Rev. 71 (1970).

Michie's Jurisprudence.
For related discussion, see 4A M.J. Compounding Offenses, §§ 2, 3, 4; 4A M.J. Contracts, § 123; 21A M.J. Words and Phrases.

CASE NOTES

Application of section. — Defendants, tobacco warehousemen, procured plaintiff's arrest upon a warrant for a misdemeanor under act which provides that it shall be a misdemeanor to procure a loan from a tobacco warehouseman upon a written promise or pledge to sell tobacco through such warehouseman, and fail to comply with such pledge, or repay the amount borrowed. Defendants upon obtaining a settlement of their claim against plaintiff, had him released and the warrant dismissed. It was held that the transaction did not fall within the condemnation of this section, but rather within the spirit, if not within the terms, of § 19.2-151. Glidewell v. Murray-Lacy & Co., 124 Va. 563, 98 S.E. 665 (1919).

Plaintiffs, who sought to recover money claimed to have been paid to prevent prosecuting of kinsman for embezzlement, contended that because this section imposes a penalty for receiving a consideration to compound a felony, but not upon the person paying the consideration, the parties were not in pari delicto and therefore plaintiffs should be permitted to recover. It was held that such contracts are illegal regardless of statute, as they tend to suppress evidence and impede the due course of public justice. Ellis v. Peoples Nat'l Bank, 166 Va. 389, 186 S.E. 9 (1936).

The evidence established a prima facie case of conspiracy between defendant and his wife where she played an active role in

the concealment of the crime by agreement with her husband and received money from the robbery in violation of this section. Stumpf v. Commonwealth, 8 Va. App. 200, 379 S.E.2d 480 (1989).

CIRCUIT COURT OPINIONS

No private right of action. — Police officer, who claimed that other police officers conspired to conceal events surrounding the death of a suspect and compelled him to testify falsely about those events, did not have a private right of action against a city or its employees to recover damages he sustained when he was terminated from the city's police department. Young v. City of Norfolk, 62 Va. Cir. 307, 2003 Va. Cir. LEXIS 296 (Norfolk 2003).

§ 18.2-462.1. Use of police radio during commission of crime.

Any person who has in his possession or who uses a device capable of receiving a police radio signal, message, or transmission, while in the commission of a felony, is guilty of a Class 1 misdemeanor. A prosecution for or conviction of the crime of use or possession of a police radio is not a bar to conviction for any other crime committed while possessing or using the police radio.

History.
1992, c. 499.

§ 18.2-463. Refusal to aid officer in execution of his office.

If any person on being required by any sheriff or other officer refuse or neglect to assist him: (1) in the execution of his office in a criminal case, (2) in the preservation of the peace, (3) in the apprehending or securing of any person for a breach of the peace, or (4) in any case of escape or rescue, he shall be guilty of a Class 2 misdemeanor.

History.
Code 1950, § 18.301; 1960, c. 358; 1975, cc. 14, 15.

§ 18.2-464. Failure to obey order of conservator of the peace.

If any person, being required by a conservator of the peace on view of a breach of the peace or other offense to bring before him the offender, refuse or neglect to obey the conservator of the peace, he shall be guilty of a Class 2 misdemeanor; and if the conservator of the peace declare himself or be known to be such to the person so refusing or neglecting, ignorance of his office shall not be pleaded as an excuse.

History.
Code 1950, § 18.1-302; 1960, c. 358; 1975, cc. 14, 15.

§ 18.2-465. Officer summoning juror to act impartially.

If any sheriff or other officer corruptly, or through favor or ill-will, summon a juror, with intent that such juror shall find a verdict for or against either party, he shall be guilty of a Class 3 misdemeanor, and forfeit his office; and he shall be forever incapable of holding any office of honor, profit or trust under the Constitution of Virginia.

History.
Code 1950, § 18.1-296; 1960, c. 358; 1975, cc. 14, 15.

§ 18.2-465.1. Penalizing employee for court appearance or service on jury panel.

Any person who is summoned to serve on jury duty or any person, except a defendant in a criminal case, who is summoned or subpoenaed to appear in any court of law or equity when a case is to be heard or who, having appeared, is required in writing by the court to appear at any future hearing, shall neither be discharged from employment, nor have any adverse personnel action taken against him, nor shall he be required to use sick leave or vacation time, as a result of his absence from employment due to such jury duty or court appearance, upon giving reasonable notice to his employer of such court appearance or summons. No person who is summoned and appears for jury duty for four or more hours, including travel time, in one day shall be required to start any work shift that begins on or after 5:00 p.m. on the day of his appearance for jury duty or begins before 3:00 a.m. on the day following the day of his appearance for jury duty. Any employer violating the provisions of this section is guilty of a Class 3 misdemeanor.

History.
1981, c. 609; 1985, c. 436; 1988, c. 415; 2000, c. 295; 2002, c. 423; 2004, c. 800; 2005, c. 931.

Law Review.
For 2003/2004 survey of state labor and employment law, see 39 U. Rich. L. Rev. 285 (2004). For annual survey of Virginia labor and employment law, see 40 U. Rich. L. Rev. 241 (2005).

CASE NOTES

Public policy. — Employee's claim for wrongful discharge in violation of the public policy expressed in § 18.2-465.1 was subject to dismissal because § 18.2-465.1 did not create any specific statutory right or set forth any specific public policy and the Virginia Supreme Court had not addressed whether § 18.2-465.1 provided a cause of action for wrongful discharge. Sewell v. Macado's, Inc., 2004 U.S. Dist. LEXIS 19950 (W.D. Va. Oct. 4, 2004).

§ 18.2-466. Corruptly procuring juror to be summoned.

If any person procure or attempt to procure a juror to be summoned, with intent that such juror shall find a verdict for or against either party, he shall be guilty of a Class 3 misdemeanor.

History.
Code 1950, § 18.1-297; 1960, c. 358; 1975, cc. 14, 15.

§ 18.2-467. Fraud in drawing jurors, etc.

If any person be guilty of any fraud, either by tampering with the jury box prior to a draft, or in drawing a juror, or in returning into the jury box the name of any person which has lawfully been drawn out and drawing and substituting another in his stead, or in any other way in drawing of jurors, he shall be guilty of a Class 1 misdemeanor.

History.
Code 1950, § 18.1-298; 1960, c. 358; 1975, cc. 14, 15.

§ 18.2-468. Making sound recordings of jury deliberations.

If any person shall install or cause to be installed or use or cause to be used any microphone or device designed for recording or transmitting for recording sound in any jury room in this Commonwealth for the purpose of recording the deliberations of any jury or for the purpose of preparing a summary of such deliberations, he shall be guilty of a Class 6 felony.

History.
Code 1950, § 18.1-299; 1960, c. 358; 1975, cc. 14, 15.

§ 18.2-469. Officer refusing, delaying, etc., to execute process for criminal.

If any officer willfully and corruptly refuse to execute any lawful process requiring him to apprehend or confine a person convicted of, or charged with, an offense, or willfully and corruptly omit or delay to execute such process, whereby such person shall escape and go at large, such officer shall be guilty of a Class 3 misdemeanor.

History.
Code 1950, § 18.1-300; 1960, c. 358; 1975, cc. 14, 15.

CASE NOTES

Section does not articulate public policy exception to employment-at-will. — There is no established public policy underlying this section that would support a police officer's wrongful discharge action based on the public policy exception to the employment-at-will doctrine. City of Va. Beach v. Harris, 259 Va. 220, 523 S.E.2d 239 (2000).

§ 18.2-470. Extortion by officer.

If any officer, for performing an official duty for which a fee or compensation is allowed or provided by law, knowingly demand and receive a greater fee or compensation than is so allowed or provided, he shall be guilty of a Class 4 misdemeanor.

History.
Code 1950, § 18.1-304; 1960, c. 358; 1975, cc. 14, 15.

Law Review.
For article on justification as a defense to crime, see 59 Va. L. Rev. 1326 (1973).

§ 18.2-471. Fraudulent issue of fee bills.

If any person authorized by law to charge fees for services performed by him and issue bills therefor fraudulently issue a fee bill for a service not performed by him, or for more than he is entitled to, he shall be guilty of a Class 3 misdemeanor and shall forfeit his office and be forever incapable of holding office of honor, profit or trust under the Constitution of Virginia.

History.
Code 1950, §§ 18.1-305, 18.1-307; 1960, c. 358; 1975, cc. 14, 15.

§ 18.2-471.1. Destruction of human biological evidence; penalty.

Any clerk of court or other public official who willfully violates an order entered pursuant to § 19.2-270.4:1 is guilty of a Class 6 felony.

History.
2006, c. 913.

§ 18.2-472. False entries or destruction of records by officers.

If a clerk of any court or other public officer fraudulently make a false entry, or erase, alter, secrete or destroy any record, including a microphotographic copy, in his keeping and belonging to his office, he shall be guilty of a Class 1 misdemeanor and shall forfeit his office and be forever incapable of holding any office of honor, profit or trust under the Constitution of Virginia.

History.
Code 1950, §§ 18.1-306, 18.1-307; 1960, c. 358; 1975, cc. 14, 15; 1977, c. 107.

§ 18.2-472.1. Providing false information or failing to provide registration information; penalty; prima facie evidence.

A. Any person subject to Chapter 9 (§ 9.1-900 et seq.) of Title 9.1, other than a person convicted of a sexually violent offense or murder as defined in § 9.1-902, who knowingly fails to register or reregister, or who knowingly provides materially false information to the Sex Offender and Crimes Against Minors Registry is guilty of a Class 1 misdemeanor. A second or subsequent conviction for an offense under this subsection is a Class 6 felony.

B. Any person convicted of a sexually violent offense or murder, as defined in § 9.1-902, who knowingly fails to register or reregister, or who knowingly provides materially false information to the Sex Offender and Crimes Against Minors Registry is guilty of a Class 6 felony. A second or subsequent conviction for an offense under this subsection is a Class 5 felony.

C. A prosecution pursuant to this section shall be brought in the city or county where the offender can be found or where the offender last registered or reregistered or, if the offender failed to comply with the duty to register, where the offender was last convicted of an offense for which registration or reregistration is required.

D. At any preliminary hearing pursuant to this section, an affidavit from the State Police issued as required in § 9.1-907 shall be admitted into evidence as prima facie evidence of the failure to comply with the duty to register or reregister. A copy of such affidavit shall be provided to the registrant or his counsel seven days prior to hearing or trial by the attorney for the Commonwealth.

E. The accused in any preliminary hearing in which an affidavit from the State Police issued as required in § 9.1-907 is offered into evidence pursuant to this section shall have the right to summon and call a custodian of records issuing the affidavit and examine him in the same manner as if he had been called as an adverse witness. Such witness shall appear at the cost of the Commonwealth.

F. At any trial or hearing other than a preliminary hearing conducted pursuant to this section, an affidavit from the State Police issued as required in § 9.1-907 shall constitute prima facie evidence of the failure to comply with the duty to register or reregister, provided the requirements of subsection G have been satisfied and the accused has not objected to the admission of the affidavit pursuant to subsection H.

G. If the attorney for the Commonwealth intends to offer the affidavit into evidence in lieu of testimony at a trial or hearing, other than a preliminary hearing, he shall:

1. Provide by mail, delivery, or otherwise, a copy of the affidavit to counsel of record for the accused, or to the accused if he is proceeding pro se, at no charge, no later than 28 days prior to the hearing or trial;

2. Provide simultaneously with the copy of the affidavit so provided under subdivision 1 a notice to the accused of his right to object to having the affidavit admitted without the presence and testimony of a custodian of the records; and

3. File a copy of the affidavit and notice with the clerk of the court hearing the matter on the day that the affidavit and notice are provided to the accused.

H. In any trial or hearing, other than a preliminary hearing, the accused may object in writing to admission of the affidavit, in lieu of testimony, as evidence of the facts stated therein. Such objection shall be filed with the court hearing the matter, with a copy to the attorney for the Commonwealth, no more than 14 days after the affidavit and notice were filed with the clerk by the attorney for the Commonwealth, or the objection shall be deemed waived. If timely objection is made, the affidavit shall not be admissible into evidence unless (i) the objection is waived by the accused or his counsel in writing or before the court, or (ii) the parties stipulate before the court to the admissibility of the affidavit.

I. Where a custodian of the records is not available for hearing or trial and the attorney for the Commonwealth has used due diligence to secure the presence of the person, the court shall order a continuance. Any continuances ordered pursuant to this subsection shall total not more than 90 days if the accused has been held continuously in custody and not more than 180 days if the accused has not been held continuously in custody.

J. Any objection by counsel for the accused, or the accused if he is proceeding pro se, to timeliness of the receipt of notice required by subsection G shall be made before hearing or trial upon his receipt of actual notice unless the accused did not receive actual notice prior to hearing or trial. A showing by the Commonwealth that the notice was mailed, delivered, or otherwise provided in compliance with the time requirements of this section shall constitute prima facie evidence that the notice was timely received by the accused. If the court finds upon the accused's objection made pursuant to this subsection, that he did not receive timely notice pursuant to subsection G, the accused's objection shall not be deemed waived and if the objection is made prior to hearing or trial, a continuance shall be ordered if requested by either party. Any continuance ordered pursuant to this subsection shall be subject to the time limitations set forth in subsection I.

K. For the purposes of this section any conviction for a substantially similar offense under the laws of (i) any foreign country or any political subdivision thereof, or (ii) any state or territory of the United States or any political subdivision thereof, the District of Columbia, or the United States shall be considered a prior conviction.

History.
1997, c. 747; 1999, c. 845; 2001, c. 365; 2003, c. 584; 2006, cc. 857, 914, 931; 2008, c. 218; 2009, Sp. Sess. I, cc. 1, 4; 2010, c. 656; 2011, c. 285.

The 2008 amendments.
The 2008 amendment by c. 218 inserted present subsection E and redesignated former subsection E as subsection F.

The 2009 amendments.
The 2009 amendments by Sp. Sess. I, c. 1, effective August 21, 2009, and Sp. Sess. I, c. 4, effective September 15, 2009, are identical, and substituted "preliminary hearing" for "trial" near the beginning of subsection D; substituted "any preliminary hearing in which" for "any hearing or trial in which," "is offered" for "is admitted" and "a custodian" for "the custodian" in subsection E; added subsections F through J; and redesignated former subsection F as K.

The 2010 amendments.
The 2010 amendment by c. 656 inserted "in lieu of testimony" in subsection G; and substituted "Provide simultaneously with" for "Attach to" in subdivision G 2.

The 2011 amendments.
The 2011 amendment by c. 285, substituted "reregister. A copy" for "reregister and a copy" in subsection D; in subsection E, inserted

"summon and" in the first sentence, and deleted "be summoned and" following "Such witness shall" in the second sentence; and inserted "In any trial or hearing, other than a preliminary hearing" at the beginning of subsection H.

Law Review.
For article, "Legal Issues Involving Children," see 35 U. Rich. L. Rev. 741 (2001). For 2006 survey article, "Criminal Law and Procedure," see 41 U. Rich. L. Rev. 83 (2006).

CASE NOTES

Affidavit not "testimonial." — Admission of an affidavit regarding defendant's sex offender registration history, prepared by the Virginia Department of State Police and reflecting records kept by the Department pursuant to statute, was not "testimonial" in nature and thus, its admission did not violate defendant's right to confrontation. Harris v. Commonwealth, 53 Va. App. 494, 673 S.E.2d 483, 2009 Va. App. LEXIS 104 (2009).

"Knowingly" means knowledge of duty to register. — Defendant was convicted of failing to register as a sex offender in violation of § 18.2-472.1, although he was delayed in California and tried to call the State Police to register from there. The term "knowingly" meant that defendant had knowledge of his duty to register; § 18.2-472.1 was not a specific intent crime. Marshall v. Commonwealth, 58 Va. App. 211, 708 S.E.2d 253, 2011 Va. App. LEXIS 154 (2011).

Fatal variance between indictment and proof. — Defendant's convictions for failing to register or re-register as a violent sexual offender in violation of § 18.2-472.1 were reversed because a fatal variance existed between the indictments and the proof offered at trial since the indictments charged defendant with failing to register or re-register in violation of § 18.2-472.1, but defendant was convicted on the assertion that he knowingly provided materially false information on his re-registration forms in violation of subsection B of § 18.2-472.1; lying on a re-registration form is different from failing to reregister in the first place because one was a crime of commission, the other of omission. Purvy v. Commonwealth, 59 Va. App. 260, 717 S.E.2d 847, 2011 Va. App. LEXIS 389 (2011).

Evidence sufficient to convict. — Evidence was sufficient to prove that defendant intentionally failed to reregister with the sexual offender registry, in violation of subsection B of § 18.2-472.1, because defendant admitted that he knew he was required to reregister every 90 days, and he had received prior reregistration forms by certified mail, although the registered mail for the underlying reregistration notice had been returned as unclaimed. Lyons v. Commonwealth, 2010 Va. App. LEXIS 54 (Feb. 9, 2010).

Evidence was sufficient to convict defendant for knowingly providing materially false information on his re-registration forms in violation of subsection B of § 18.2-472.1 because a rational factfinder could conclude that defendant did not reside at the address he provided and thus violated subsection B of § 18.2-472.1 by knowingly providing materially false information on his re-registration forms. Purvy v. Commonwealth, 59 Va. App. 260, 717 S.E.2d 847, 2011 Va. App. LEXIS 389 (2011).

Applied in Dickens v. Commonwealth, 52 Va. App. 412, 663 S.E.2d 548, 2008 Va. App. LEXIS 356 (2008).

CIRCUIT COURT OPINIONS

Affidavit violated Confrontation Clause. — Affidavit filed pursuant to subsection D of § 18.2-472.1 in a failure to register case, which affidavit stated that state police records showed that no sex offender registration or re-registration form was filed for defendant, was accusatory, resembled "ex-parte examination," was a core testimonial statement, and thus violated the Confrontation Clause. Commonwealth v. Dickens, 72 Va. Cir. 533, 2007 Va. Cir. LEXIS 17 (Norfolk 2007).

ARTICLE 7.

ESCAPE OF, COMMUNICATIONS WITH AND DELIVERIES TO PRISONERS.

Michie's Jurisprudence.
For related discussion, see 7A M.J. Escape, § 1 - 3.

§ 18.2-473. Persons aiding escape of prisoner or child.

When a person is lawfully detained as a prisoner in any jail or prison or held in custody, or when a child is placed in a local juvenile detention home, or committed to the Department of Juvenile Justice in any juvenile correctional center, or Reception and Diagnostic Center for Children or held in custody, if any person: (1) conveys anything into the jail, prison, juvenile detention home, juvenile correctional center or Reception and Diagnostic Center for Children with intent to facilitate a person's escape therefrom, (2) in any way aids such prisoner or child to escape, or in an attempt to escape, from such jail, prison, juvenile detention home, juvenile correctional center, Reception and Diagnostic Center for Children or custody, or (3) forcibly takes, or attempts to take him therefrom, such person, if the taking or escape is effected, shall, if the prisoner or child was detained on conviction, commitment or charge of felony, be confined in a state correctional facility not less than one year nor more than five years. If the same is not effected, or if the prisoner or child was not detained on such conviction, commitment or charge, he shall be guilty of a Class 1 misdemeanor.

History.
Code 1950, § 18.1-284; 1960, c. 358; 1975, cc. 14, 15; 1984, c. 587; 1989, c. 733; 1996, cc. 755, 914.

§ 18.2-473.1. Communication with prisoners or committed person; penalty.

It shall be unlawful for any person outside of any state or local correctional facility or any juvenile correctional center, other than the jailers or custodial officers in charge of the prisoners or in charge of the persons committed to the Department of Juvenile Justice, to communicate without authority by word or sign with the intent to disrupt institutional operations with any prisoner confined within a state or local correctional facility or with any person committed to the Department of Juvenile Justice in any juvenile correctional center. Any person violating this section is guilty of a Class 4 misdemeanor.

History.
1982, c. 636; 2000, c. 286; 2013, cc. 707, 782.

Editor's note.
Acts 2013, c. 707, cl. 2 provides: "That the provisions of this act may result in a net increase in periods of imprisonment or commitment. Pursuant to § 30-19.1:4, the estimated amount of the necessary appropriation cannot be determined for periods of imprisonment in state adult correctional facilities; therefore, Chapter 3 of the Acts of Assembly of 2012, Special Session I, requires the Virginia Criminal Sentencing Commission to assign a minimum fiscal impact of $50,000. Pursuant to § 30-19.1:4, the estimated amount of the necessary appropriation cannot be determined for periods of commitment to the custody of the Department of Juvenile Justice."
Acts 2013, c. 782, cl. 2 provides: "Pursuant to § 30-19.1:4, the estimated amount of the necessary appropriation is at least $299,513 for periods of imprisonment in state adult correctional facilities and cannot be determined for periods of commitment to the custody of the Department of Juvenile Justice."

The 2013 amendments.
The 2013 amendments by cc. 707 and 782 are identical, and rewrote the section.

§ 18.2-474. Delivery of articles to prisoners or committed person.

No person shall willfully in any manner deliver, or attempt to deliver, to any prisoner confined under authority of the Commonwealth of Virginia, or of any political subdivision thereof, or to any person committed to the Department of Juvenile Justice in any juvenile correctional center, any article of any nature whatsoever, without first securing the permission of the person in whose charge such prisoner or committed person is, and who may in his discretion grant or refuse permission. Any person violating this section is guilty of a Class 1 misdemeanor.

Nothing herein contained shall be construed to repeal or amend § 18.2-473.

History.
Code 1950, § 18.1-285; 1960, c. 358; 1975, cc. 14, 15; 2013, cc. 707, 782.

Editor's note.
Acts 2013, c. 707, cl. 2 provides: "That the provisions of this act may result in a net increase in periods of imprisonment or commitment. Pursuant to § 30-19.1:4, the estimated amount of the necessary appropriation cannot be determined for periods of imprisonment in state adult correctional facilities; therefore, Chapter 3 of the Acts of Assembly of 2012, Special Session I, requires the Virginia Criminal Sentencing Commission to assign a minimum fiscal impact of $50,000. Pursuant to § 30-19.1:4, the estimated amount of the necessary appropriation cannot be determined for periods of commitment to the custody of the Department of Juvenile Justice."
Acts 2013, c. 782, cl. 2 provides: "Pursuant to § 30-19.1:4, the estimated amount of the necessary appropriation is at least $299,513 for periods of imprisonment in state adult correctional facilities and cannot be determined for periods of commitment to the custody of the Department of Juvenile Justice."

The 2013 amendments.
The 2013 amendments by cc. 707 and 782 are identical, and in the first paragraph, inserted "or to any person committed to the Department of Juvenile Justice in any juvenile correctional center" and "or committed person," and substituted "is" for "shall be."

§ 18.2-474.1. Delivery of drugs, firearms, explosives, etc., to prisoners or committed persons.

Notwithstanding the provisions of § 18.2-474, any person who shall willfully in any manner deliver, attempt to deliver, or conspire with another to deliver to any prisoner confined under authority of the Commonwealth of Virginia, or of any political subdivision thereof, or to any person committed to the Department of Juvenile Justice in any juvenile correctional center, any drug which is a controlled substance regulated by the Drug Control Act in Chapter 34 (§ 54.1-3400 et seq.) of Title 54.1, synthetic cannabinoids or marijuana, is guilty of a Class 5 felony. Any person who shall willfully in any manner so deliver or attempt to deliver or conspire to deliver to any such prisoner or confined or committed person, firearms, ammunitions, or explosives of any nature is guilty of a Class 3 felony.

Nothing herein contained shall be construed to repeal or amend § 18.2-473.

History.

1975, c. 608; 1982, c. 490; 2011, cc. 384, 410; 2013, cc. 707, 782.

Cross references.

As to penalty for sale, possession, etc., of controlled substance or marijuana by inmate in penal institution or in custody of employee thereof, see § 53.1-203. For definition of "barrier crime" as including a conviction of delivery of drugs to prisoners as set out in § 18.2-474.1, or an equivalent offense in another state, and prohibition against assisted living facilities, adult day care centers or child welfare agencies hiring for certain compensated employment persons who have committed such an offense, see §§ 63.2-1719, 63.2-1720.

Editor's note.

Acts 2011, cc. 384 and 410, cl. 3 provides: "That the provisions of this act may result in a net increase in periods of imprisonment or commitment. Pursuant to § 30-19.1:4, the estimated amount of the necessary appropriation cannot be determined for periods of imprisonment in state adult correctional facilities; therefore, Chapter 874 of the Acts of Assembly of 2010 requires the Virginia Criminal Sentencing Commission to assign a minimum fiscal impact of $50,000. Pursuant to § 30-19.1:4, the estimated amount of the necessary appropriation cannot be determined for periods of commitment to the custody of the Department of Juvenile Justice."

Acts 2013, c. 707, cl. 2 provides: "That the provisions of this act may result in a net increase in periods of imprisonment or commitment. Pursuant to § 30-19.1:4, the estimated amount of the necessary appropriation cannot be determined for periods of imprisonment in state adult correctional facilities; therefore, Chapter 3 of the Acts of Assembly of 2012, Special Session I, requires the Virginia Criminal Sentencing Commission to assign a minimum fiscal impact of $50,000. Pursuant to § 30-19.1:4, the estimated amount of the necessary appropriation cannot be determined for periods of commitment to the custody of the Department of Juvenile Justice."

Acts 2013, c. 782, cl. 2 provides: "Pursuant to § 30-19.1:4, the estimated amount of the necessary appropriation is at least $299,513 for periods of imprisonment in state adult correctional facilities and cannot be determined for periods of commitment to the custody of the Department of Juvenile Justice."

The 2011 amendments.

The 2011 amendments by cc. 384 and 410, effective March 23, 2011, are identical, and inserted "synthetic cannabinoids" in the first sentence of the first paragraph.

The 2013 amendments.

The 2013 amendments cc. 707 and 782 are identical, and rewrote the first paragraph, which read: "Notwithstanding the provisions of § 18.2-474, any person who shall willfully in any manner deliver, attempt to deliver, or conspire with another to deliver to any prisoner confined under authority of the Commonwealth of Virginia, or of any political subdivision thereof, any drug which is a controlled substance regulated by the Drug Control Act in Chapter 34 of Title 54.1, synthetic cannabinoids or marijuana, shall be guilty of a Class 5 felony. Any person who shall willfully in any manner so deliver or attempt to deliver or conspire to deliver to any such prisoner, firearms, ammunitions, or explosives of any nature shall be guilty of a Class 3 felony."

Law Review.

For survey of Virginia criminal law for the year 1977-1978, see 64 Va. L. Rev. 1407 (1978).

CASE NOTES

Not precluded by double jeopardy principles. — Circuit court was not precluded by double jeopardy principles from trying defendant for delivering marijuana to a prisoner, in violation of § 18.2-474.1, after she pled guilty in a district court to a charge alleging that she possessed the same marijuana, in violation of § 18.2-250.1, because possession of marijuana was not a lesser-included offense of delivering marijuana to a prisoner. Logan v. Commonwealth, 43 Va. App. 504, 600 S.E.2d 133, 2004 Va. App. LEXIS 374 (2004).

Compared to § 18.2-474.1. — In order to manufacture, sell, give, distribute, or possess a controlled drug, which is an element of the crime of distribution under § 18.2-248, a defendant must possess that controlled substance. The same analysis does not apply to the crime of delivering a controlled substance to a prisoner, in violation of § 18.2-474.1. Logan v. Commonwealth, 43 Va. App. 504, 600 S.E.2d 133, 2004 Va. App. LEXIS 374 (2004).

Evidence sufficient to affirm conviction for attempting to deliver marijuana to a prisoner where the testimony of the deputies showed that no one other than defendant entered the restroom before one of the deputies found the marijuana. Gilliam v. Commonwealth, No. 2455-02-2, 2003 Va. App. LEXIS 515 (Ct. of Appeals Oct. 14, 2003).

Evidence sufficiently supported defendant's conviction for delivery of marijuana to her husband, a prisoner at a correctional facility, as the testimony of correctional officers and expert witnesses, as well as videotape evidence and still photographs, was sufficient to show that defendant transferred marijuana to her husband while visiting him at the correctional facility where he was incarcerated. Rodgers v. Commonwealth, — Va. App. —, — S.E.2d —, 2005 Va. App. LEXIS 257 (July 5, 2005).

Evidence was sufficient to support defendant's convictions for possession with the intent to distribute Methadone and Diazepamin and attempt to deliver to a prisoner a controlled substance in violation of §§ 18.2-248 and 18.2-474.1 because defendant knew of the procedures to turn in prescription medication at a jail annex, and not only did he fail to follow those procedures, but he also concealed the pills in his underwear and told a sergeant that he brought the pills into the jail to give to other inmates so his stay would "go a lot easier;" defendant took all the necessary steps to accomplish his objective of delivering drugs to others in the jail annex because in preparation for reporting to jail, he concealed drugs, for which he had no prescription, he entered the jail with those drugs, and he failed to report the drugs to jail personnel, and but for a strip search, he would have completed his crimes. Hounshell v. Commonwealth, 2010 Va. App. LEXIS 443 (Nov. 9, 2010).

Evidence was insufficient to prove that defendant attempted to deliver marijuana to prisoner, where the proof concerning defendant's conduct was equivocal and did not establish more than mere preparation. Lewis v. Commonwealth, 15 Va. App. 337, 423 S.E.2d 371 (1992).

Applied in Henry v. Commonwealth, 2 Va. App. 194, 342 S.E.2d 655 (1986).

§ 18.2-475. Officers, etc., voluntarily allowing person convicted, charged, or adjudicated delinquent of felony to escape; penalty.

If any sheriff, jailer, or other officer, or any guard or other person summoned or employed by any such sheriff, jailer, or other officer, voluntarily allows a prisoner or person committed to the Department of Juvenile Justice convicted of, charged with, or adjudicated delinquent of a felony to escape from his custody, he is guilty of a Class 4 felony.

History.

Code 1950, § 18.1-286; 1960, c. 358; 1975, cc. 14, 15; 1983, c. 360; 2013, cc. 707, 782.

Editor's note.

Acts 2013, c. 707, cl. 2 provides: "That the provisions of this act may result in a net increase in periods of imprisonment or commitment. Pursuant to § 30-19.1:4, the estimated amount of the necessary appropriation cannot be determined for periods of imprisonment in state adult correctional facilities; therefore, Chapter 3 of the Acts of Assembly of 2012, Special Session I, requires the Virginia Criminal Sentencing Commission to assign a minimum fiscal impact of $50,000. Pursuant to § 30-19.1:4, the estimated amount of the necessary appropriation cannot be determined for periods of commitment to the custody of the Department of Juvenile Justice."

Acts 2013, c. 782, cl. 2 provides: "Pursuant to § 30-19.1:4, the estimated amount of the necessary appropriation is at least $299,513 for periods of imprisonment in state adult correctional facilities and cannot be determined for periods of commitment to the custody of the Department of Juvenile Justice."

The 2013 amendments.

The 2013 amendments by cc. 707 and 782 are identical, and rewrote the section, which read: "If any sheriff, jailer or other officer, or any guard or other person summoned or employed by any such sheriff, jailer or other officer, voluntarily allows a prisoner convicted of or charged with felony to escape from his custody, he shall be guilty of a Class 4 felony."

CASE NOTES

Sheriff is not liable for conduct of deputy. — A sheriff is not criminally liable for an escape due to the conduct of his deputy. Commonwealth v. Lewis, 31 Va. (4 Leigh) 664 (1833).

§ 18.2-476. Officers, etc., willfully and deliberately permitting person convicted of, charged with, or adjudicated delinquent of a nonfelonious offense to escape or willfully refusing to receive person; penalty.

If any sheriff, jailer, or other officer, or any guard or other person summoned or employed by such sheriff, jailer, or other officer, willfully and deliberately permits a prisoner or person committed to the Department of Juvenile Justice convicted of, charged with, or adjudicated delinquent of an offense not a felony, to escape from his custody, or willfully refuses to receive into his custody a person lawfully committed thereto, he is guilty of a Class 2 misdemeanor.

History.

Code 1950, § 18.1-287; 1960, c. 358; 1975, cc. 14, 15; 1983, c. 360; 2013, cc. 707, 782.

Editor's note.

Acts 2013, c. 707, cl. 2 provides: "That the provisions of this act may result in a net increase in periods of imprisonment or commitment. Pursuant to § 30-19.1:4, the estimated amount of the necessary appropriation cannot be determined for periods of imprisonment in state adult correctional facilities; therefore, Chapter 3 of the Acts of Assembly of 2012, Special Session I, requires the Virginia Criminal Sentencing Commission to assign a minimum fiscal impact of $50,000. Pursuant to § 30-19.1:4, the estimated amount of the necessary appropriation cannot be determined for periods of commitment to the custody of the Department of Juvenile Justice."

Acts 2013, c. 782, cl. 2 provides: "Pursuant to § 30-19.1:4, the estimated amount of the necessary appropriation is at least $299,513 for periods of imprisonment in state adult correctional facilities and cannot be determined for periods of commitment to the custody of the Department of Juvenile Justice."

The 2013 amendments.

The 2013 amendments by cc. 707 and 782 are identical, and rewrote the section, which read: "If any sheriff, jailer or other officer, or any guard or other person summoned or employed by such sheriff, jailer or other officer, willfully and deliberately permits a prisoner convicted of or charged with an offense not a felony, to escape from his custody, or willfully refuses to receive into his custody a person lawfully committed thereto, he shall be guilty of a Class 2 misdemeanor."

CASE NOTES

Sheriff is not liable for escape permitted by deputy. — The sheriff in Virginia is ex officio jailer of his county, but may devolve the duties of jailer on a deputy, and will not be criminally liable for a negligent escape permitted by him. If, however, a prisoner is permitted to go at large with the knowledge and approval of the sheriff, and by his direction and authority, and while so at large the prisoner escapes, the sheriff is himself criminally liable for the escape. Watts v. Commonwealth, 99 Va. 872, 39 S.E. 706 (1901).

Indictment held insufficient. — An indictment against a jailer, for permitting a prisoner in his custody to have an instrument in his room with which he might break the jail and escape, and for failing carefully to examine at short intervals the condition of the jail, and what the prisoner was engaged at in said jail, in consequence of which the prisoner escaped, does not state an indictable offense. Commonwealth v. Connell, 44 Va. (3 Gratt.) 587 (1846).

Venue. — A criminal prosecution against a sheriff cannot be maintained in another county for his act in wilfully permitting the escape of a prisoner in the sheriff's own county. Commonwealth v. Lewis, 31 Va. (4 Leigh) 664 (1833).

§ 18.2-477. Prisoner escaping from jail; how punished.

If any person confined in jail or in custody after conviction of a criminal offense shall escape by force or violence, other than by setting fire thereto, he shall be guilty of a Class 6 felony. The term of confinement under this section shall commence from the expiration of the former sentence.

History.

Code 1950, § 18.1-288; 1960, c. 358; 1962, c. 506; 1975, cc. 14, 15; 1985, c. 555.

Cross references.

For definition of "barrier crime" as including a conviction of escape from jail as set out in § 18.2-477, or an equivalent offense in another state, and prohibition against assisted living facilities, adult day care centers or child welfare agencies hiring for certain compensated employment persons who have committed such an offense, see §§ 63.2-1719, 63.2-1720.

Michie's Jurisprudence.

For related discussion, see 9A M.J. Habeas Corpus, § 11.

CASE NOTES

Mistakenly indicating that prosecution is under this section. — Where, prior to the defendant's arraignment and plea, in response to an inquiry by defense counsel, the Commonwealth's attorney mistakenly indicated that he was proceeding against the defendant under this section, the defendant's claim that this was an election by the Commonwealth, which limited his punishment to the maximum provided by this section, was without merit since the defendant, prior to his plea, was advised by both his counsel and the trial court that the prosecution was being conducted under former § 53-291, and was also advised that he, as an inmate of a penal institution, was subject to a maximum penalty of 20 years imprisonment if he had inflicted bodily injury on the guard from whose custody he escaped, a fact that was later established by uncontroverted evidence. Guthrie v. Commonwealth, 212 Va. 550, 186 S.E.2d 26 (1972).

When former sentence expires. — Where a party has been indicted and the verdict of the jury finds him guilty and orders that he be imprisoned for a certain time, and before that time has expired the party escapes from jail and is afterwards retaken, he is to be kept in prison beyond the prescribed period for the length of time he was out when he escaped, and this though he has already been indicted for the escape. Cleek v. Commonwealth, 62 Va. (21 Gratt.) 777 (1871).

§ 18.2-477.1. Escapes from juvenile facility; penalty.

A. It shall be unlawful for any person to escape or remain away without proper authority from a group home or other residential care facility for children in need of services, delinquent or alleged delinquent youths in which he had been placed by the juvenile and domestic relations court or as a result of his commitment as a juvenile to the Department of Juvenile Justice. Any person violating this subsection shall be taken into custody and brought before the juvenile and domestic relations court. The court may find the person in violation of § 16.1-292 or, if the court finds the person amenable to further treatment in a juvenile facility, the court may return him to the custody of the Department.

B. It shall be unlawful for any person to escape or remain away without proper authority from a secure facility operated by or under contract with the Department of Juvenile Justice or from a secure juvenile detention facility in which he had been placed by the juvenile and domestic relations court or as a result of his commitment as a juvenile to the Department of Juvenile Justice. Any person who escapes from a facility specified in this subsection by force or by violence shall be guilty of a Class 6 felony or, if violation of this subsection occurs other than by force or violence, a Class 1 misdemeanor.

History.
1985, c. 435; 1989, c. 733; 1993, c. 840; 1994, c. 490; 1997, c. 749.

Editor's note.
Acts 1993, c. 930, cl. 3, as amended by Acts 1994, c. 564, cl. 2, and Acts 1996, c. 616, cl. 4, provides that the amendment to this section by Acts 1993, c. 930, cl. 1, shall become effective June 1, 1998, "if state funds are provided, including all local costs, to carry out the purposes of this bill by the General Assembly." The funding was not provided.

Law Review.
For an article, "Legal Issues Involving Children," see 32 U. Rich. L. Rev. 1345 (1998).

Michie's Jurisprudence.
For related discussion, see 9B M.J. Infants, § 86.

CASE NOTES

Appellant was detained pursuant to detention order. — Evidence established that appellant was a resident of a juvenile facility pursuant to an order of the juvenile and domestic relations district court. Since appellant had an upcoming detention review hearing, then a fortiori, he was being detained pursuant to an order of detention. Furthermore, according to chief correctional officer for the sheriff's office, the only persons detained in the juvenile interim holding facility were juveniles ordered there by the juvenile and

domestic relations district court judge. Testa v. Commonwealth, No. 1496-96-4 (Ct. of Appeals Dec. 9, 1997).

§ 18.2-477.2. Punishment for certain offenses committed within a secure juvenile facility or detention home.

It shall be unlawful for a person committed to the Department of Juvenile Justice in any juvenile correctional center or detained in a secure juvenile facility or detention home to commit any of the offenses enumerated in § 53.1-203. A violation of this section shall be punishable as a Class 6 felony, except that a violation of subdivision 6 of § 53.1-203 is a Class 5 felony.

History.
1999, c. 21; 2007, c. 521; 2013, cc. 707, 782.

Editor's note.
Acts 2013, c. 707, cl. 2 provides: "That the provisions of this act may result in a net increase in periods of imprisonment or commitment. Pursuant to § 30-19.1:4, the estimated amount of the necessary appropriation cannot be determined for periods of imprisonment in state adult correctional facilities; therefore, Chapter 3 of the Acts of Assembly of 2012, Special Session I, requires the Virginia Criminal Sentencing Commission to assign a minimum fiscal impact of $50,000. Pursuant to § 30-19.1:4, the estimated amount of the necessary appropriation cannot be determined for periods of commitment to the custody of the Department of Juvenile Justice."

Acts 2013, c. 782, cl. 2 provides: "Pursuant to § 30-19.1:4, the estimated amount of the necessary appropriation is at least $299,513 for periods of imprisonment in state adult correctional facilities and cannot be determined for periods of commitment to the custody of the Department of Juvenile Justice."

The 2013 amendments.
The 2013 amendment by 707 rewrote the section, which read: "It shall be unlawful for a person detained in a secure juvenile facility or detention home to commit any of the offenses enumerated in § 53.1-203. A violation of this section shall be punishable as a Class 1 misdemeanor."

The 2013 amendment by c. 782 inserted "committed to the Department of Juvenile Justice in any juvenile correctional center or" in the first sentence; and substituted "Class 6 felony, except that a violation of subdivision 6 of § 53.1-203 is a Class 5 felony" for "Class 1 misdemeanor" in the second sentence.

§ 18.2-478. Escape from jail or custody by force or violence without setting fire to jail.

If any person lawfully imprisoned in jail and not tried or sentenced on a criminal offense escapes from jail by force or violence, other than by setting fire thereto or if any person lawfully in the custody of any police officer on a charge of criminal offense escapes from such custody by force or violence, he shall be guilty of a Class 6 felony.

History.
Code 1950, § 18.1-289; 1960, c. 358; 1975, cc. 14, 15; 1985, c. 555.

Law Review.
For survey of Virginia law on criminal law and procedure for the year 2007-2008, see 43 U. Rich. L. Rev. 149 (2008).

CASE NOTES

Elements. — Because assault of an officer is not a lesser included offense of escape from a police officer by use of force or violence under the statute and because defendant's act of obstructing justice was a separate and distinct act from his escape, which the Commonwealth's evidence supported, defendant's escape conviction was well founded. Henry v. Commonwealth, 21 Va. App. 141, 462 S.E.2d 578 (1995).

Evidence that defendant ran away from an officer who was escorting him to a police wagon and was subsequently caught and subdued by three officers did not prove beyond a reasonable doubt that defendant used force to attempt to escape. Bell v. Commonwealth, No. 0139-01-2, 2002 Va. App. LEXIS 151 (Ct. of Appeals Mar. 12, 2002).

Evidence of "custody." — Because the Commonwealth had to prove that the appellant was in custody and that the custody was "on a charge of criminal offense," the existence of warrant for appellant's arrest was relevant to prove that appellant was being arrested on criminal charges. Johnson v. Commonwealth, 21 Va. App. 102, 462 S.E.2d 125 (1995).

A person is in custody for the purposes of escape under this statute when by physical force, words, or actions, that person becomes subject to the officer's control; thus, if a person of ordinary intelligence and understanding would not feel free to leave under the circumstances, then he or she is in "custody" for purposes of this section. Johnson v. Commonwealth, 21 Va. App. 102, 462 S.E.2d 125 (1995).

Because a police officer grabbed defendant's wrist in an attempt to handcuff him and told him that he was under arrest, before defendant struggled free and escaped moments later, defendant was under arrest and therefore in custody for purposes of the escape statute. Hall v. Commonwealth, 55 Va. App. 451, 686 S.E.2d 554, 2009 Va. App. LEXIS 567 (2009), aff'd, 280 Va. 566, 701 S.E.2d 68, 2010 Va. LEXIS 263 (Va. 2010).

Evidence showed that the officer went to defendant's residence and advised defendant that he had a warrant for his arrest, that after directing defendant to step onto the front porch, the officer lawfully advised defendant that he was under arrest and grabbed defendant's left wrist to handcuff him, and that the officer spoke words of arrest and actually touched defendant for the stated purpose of arrest; therefore, at that moment, notwithstanding defendant's subsequent flight, the arrest was effected and defendant was in custody since an individual under arrest was always in custody. Accordingly, the evidence was sufficient to prove that defendant was in custody pursuant to § 18.2-478 prior to his forcibly wrestling free of the officer's grasp, and that defendant escaped from custody by force or violence in violation of § 18.2-478. Hall v. Commonwealth, 280 Va. 566, 701 S.E.2d 68, 2010 Va. LEXIS 263 (2010).

Defendant not charged with a criminal offense. — Charge of escape by force from the custody of a police officer should have been dismissed where there was no evidence that defendant was charged with a criminal offense; the evidence showed that police stopped defendant because they had report that the car he was driving was stolen, not because he was charged with a criminal offense. Coles v. Commonwealth, 44 Va. App. 549, 605 S.E.2d 784, 2004 Va. App. LEXIS 612 (2004).

No evidence of written charge. — Evidence was insufficient to sustain defendant's conviction of felonious escape from custody, in violation of § 18.2-478, where the Commonwealth did not introduce any evidence that there was a written charge against him at the time he was allegedly taken into custody by an officer following an attempted traffic stop and foot chase. Hubbard v. Commonwealth, 276 Va. 292, 661 S.E.2d 464, 2008 Va. LEXIS 61 (2008).

To sustain a conviction under § 18.2-478, the evidence must show a defendant was taken into custody pursuant to a written charge; probable cause to arrest will not suffice to satisfy the "on a charge of criminal offense" element stated in § 18.2-478. Hubbard v. Commonwealth, 276 Va. 292, 661 S.E.2d 464, 2008 Va. LEXIS 61 (2008).

Sufficiency of the evidence claim not preserved. — Defendant failed to preserve his sufficiency of the evidence claim as to his escape conviction under § 18.2-478 where: (1) he failed to renew his motion to strike made at the close of the Commonwealth's case, and proceeded to put on his own evidence, thereby waiving his right to stand on the motion made at the conclusion of the Commonwealth's case; (2) renewing the arguments made in support of his motion to strike in his closing argument did not preserve a sufficiency argument for purposes of an appeal; and (3) he made a different

argument in support of his motion to set aside the verdict in the trial court than he made on appeal, which under Va. Sup. Ct. R. 5A:18, precluded the appellate court from considering the argument on appeal. Anthony v. Commonwealth, No. 0986-02-3, 2003 Va. App. LEXIS 654 (Ct. of Appeals Dec. 16, 2003).

Applied in Thomas v. Commonwealth, 56 Va. App. 1, 690 S.E.2d 298, 2010 Va. App. LEXIS 93 (2010).

§ 18.2-479. Escape without force or violence or setting fire to jail.

A. Except as provided in subsection B, any person lawfully confined in jail or lawfully in the custody of any court, officer of the court, or of any law-enforcement officer for violation of his probation or parole or on a charge or conviction of a misdemeanor, who escapes, other than by force or violence or by setting fire to the jail, is guilty of a Class 1 misdemeanor.

B. Any person, lawfully confined in jail or lawfully in the custody of any court, officer of the court, or of any law-enforcement officer on a charge or conviction of a felony, who escapes, other than by force or violence or by setting fire to the jail, is guilty of a Class 6 felony.

History.
Code 1950, § 18.1-290; 1960, c. 358; 1975, cc. 14, 15; 1985, c. 555; 2005, c. 573.

Cross references.
As to crimes by prisoners, see § 53.1-203 et seq.

Law Review.
For 2003/2004 survey of criminal law and procedure, see 39 U. Rich. L. Rev. 133 (2004). For survey of Virginia criminal law and procedure for the year 2004-2005, see 40 U. Rich. L. Rev. 197 (2005). For article, "Construction Law," see 45 U. Rich. L. Rev. 227 (2010).

Michie's Jurisprudence.
For related discussion, see 5B M.J. Criminal Procedure, § 83; 9A M.J. Habeas Corpus, § 11.

CASE NOTES

Proof of underlying offense for which accused is in custody is irrelevant to the determination of guilt, except in those cases in which the Commonwealth seeks enhanced punishment under subsection B. Williams v. Commonwealth, 29 Va. App. 696, 514 S.E.2d 381 (1999).

Arrest does not equate to being "in custody on a charge of a felony." — Probable cause to arrest will not satisfy the requirement that the Commonwealth of Virginia prove beyond a reasonable doubt that the defendant was "in custody on a charge of a felony." A criminal charge exists only when a formal written complaint has been made against the accused, and a prosecution initiated. Boone v. Commonwealth, — Va. App. —, — S.E.2d —, 2005 Va. App. LEXIS 95 (Mar. 8, 2005).

For case distinguishing offenses in this section and former § 53-291, see Wood v. Cox, 333 F. Supp. 1064 (W.D. Va. 1971).

Nothing in this section indicates it establishes the exclusive offense for persons who escape before conviction or assignment to the penitentiary (now state correctional facility) system, and nothing in former § 53-291 indicates it is applicable only to those who escape after conviction and assignment to the penitentiary system. Mason v. Commonwealth, 217 Va. 321, 228 S.E.2d 683 (1976) (decided under § 18.1-290, predecessor to this section).

Conviction under this section or former § 53-291 bars prosecution under the other. Mason v. Commonwealth, 217 Va. 321, 228 S.E.2d 683 (1976) (decided under § 18.1-290, predecessor to this section).

It is a matter of prosecutorial election whether the Com-

monwealth proceeds under this section or former § 53-291 against an accused. Mason v. Commonwealth, 217 Va. 321, 228 S.E.2d 683 (1976) (decided under § 18.1-290, predecessor to this section).

For case comparing punishment provisions of this section and former § 53-208, see Durkin v. Davis, 390 F. Supp. 249 (E.D. Va. 1975), rev'd on other grounds, 538 F.2d 1037 (4th Cir. 1976).

Attempted crimes are specific intent crimes, and therefore, where the Commonwealth charges a defendant with attempted escape, it is required to prove that: (1) the defendant intended to escape from custody; and (2) he engaged in some act in furtherance of escaping. Bennett v. Commonwealth, 35 Va. App. 442, 546 S.E.2d 209, 2001 Va. App. LEXIS 262 (2001).

Violent felony for federal sentencing purposes. — Despite its title, a conviction for escape under subsection B of § 18.2-479, constituted a violent felony for purposes of sentencing under the Armed Career Criminal Act, 18 U.S.C.S § 924(e), because the title was irrelevant to this determination, particularly as every escape, no matter how conducted, involved conduct that presented a serious potential risk of physical injury, and § 18.2-479, by its plain text, punished those who unlawfully and feloniously escaped from confinement. United States v. Mathias, 482 F.3d 743, 2007 U.S. App. LEXIS 8524 (4th Cir. 2007).

No felony escape if occurred during custody for misdemeanor. — Defendant's conviction for felony escape under subsection B of § 18.2-479 was reversed because at the time of his escape he had only been arrested for a misdemeanor and the arresting officer did not yet know that he had prior petit larceny convictions. Johnson v. Commonwealth, No. 2870-02-2, 2003 Va. App. LEXIS 513 (Ct. of Appeals Oct. 14, 2003).

Application of force to complete arrest. — Where a police officer clearly stated that defendant could not drive her truck based on a felony capias for her arrest, and applied physical force to complete the arrest, the evidence supported defendant's escape conviction. Harris v. Commonwealth, No. 0795-02-3, 2003 Va. App. LEXIS 25 (Ct. of Appeals Jan. 28, 2003).

Lesser-included offense of escape by force or violence. — Defendant's conviction of nonviolent escape from custody, as a lesser-included offense of escape by force or violence, was upheld, as the jury was authorized to conclude from the evidence presented that defendant disappeared while in custody, was left alone in an interview room, and was never found by law-enforcement officials; further, because he was convicted of a lesser-included offense, the indictment did not require the Commonwealth to prove he used force when he escaped. McBrayer v. Commonwealth, No. 1929-03-2, 2004 Va. App. LEXIS 467 (Ct. of Appeals Oct. 5, 2004).

The evidence was sufficient for a jury to have found that defendant knew he was "in custody" and not free to leave where, although the defendant arrived the police station voluntarily, he came there for the purpose of having two felony arrest warrants served on him, a deputy testified that by the time the defendant had attempted to leave, he had already served the warrants on the defendant, when the defendant began to leave, the deputy ordered the defendant to stop, the defendant ignored the deputy's request to stop and the defendant had to be physically restrained. Bennett v. Commonwealth, 35 Va. App. 442, 546 S.E.2d 209, 2001 Va. App. LEXIS 262 (2001).

Appellant was not in officer's custody. — Officer did not effectuate his legal authority to arrest appellant; he neither touched appellant nor obtained appellant's submission to his authority. Each time officer spoke to appellant, appellant responded with profanity. When officer told appellant not to run, appellant responded that he was going to run, and he did. In short, the evidence showed that appellant did not submit, in any respect, to a show of authority. Appellant was not in officer's custody at the time he ran, and accordingly, the court reversed his escape conviction. Cavell v. Commonwealth, 26 Va. App. 82, 493 S.E.2d 382 (1997).

When officer determined to place defendant in custody, he did not have physical control over defendant, and defendant fled before the officer could obtain that degree of control; thus, defendant was not in custody and his flight was not an escape under subsection B of § 18.2-479. White v. Commonwealth, 267 Va. 96, 591 S.E.2d 662, 2004 Va. LEXIS 9 (2004).

Whether a person is "in custody" for purposes of the statute depends upon whether the officer has applied direct physical restraint or, in the absence of restraint, whether the person has submitted to a show of authority. Towns v. Commonwealth, No. 1720-97-3 (Ct. of Appeals Nov. 10, 1998).

An individual is in "custody," as contemplated by § 18.2-479, when a law enforcement officer has lawfully curtailed the individual's freedom of movement to a degree associated with a formal arrest, even when a formal custodial arrest has not been effected. Applying an objective standard, the inquiry is whether the officer, with proper authority to do so, had by his words or use of physical force, curtailed the individual's freedom of movement beyond that required for a temporary investigative detention. White v. Commonwealth, 267 Va. 96, 591 S.E.2d 662, 2004 Va. LEXIS 9 (2004).

"Custody" not shown. — Whether a person is "in custody" for the purposes of this section depends upon whether the officer has applied direct physical restraint, or in the absence of restraint, whether the person has submitted to a show of authority. Thus, where defendant was present in the courthouse on another matter; officer did not physically touch or restrain defendant; and while defendant admitted that he walked to officer when his name was called, he never submitted to a show of authority, rather it was undisputed the moment officer began to read from warrant, defendant ran away, defendant was not in custody at the time he fled and therefore his conviction of escape was reversed. Towns v. Commonwealth, No. 1720-97-3 (Ct. of Appeals November 10, 1998).

Where defendant was arrested for a probation violation, and then escaped, since defendant was not in custody for a misdemeanor, escape conviction would be reversed. Khaliq v. Commonwealth, No. 1588-01-2, 2002 Va. App. LEXIS 277 (Ct. of Appeals May 7, 2002).

Defendant's escape from custody conviction was reversed, where the Commonwealth failed to show sufficient evidence that he was in the custody of the court when he failed to report to jail after being released on bond pending sentencing; thus, at the time he failed to report a sufficient restraint of physical control over him did not exist. Davis v. Commonwealth, 45 Va. App. 12, 608 S.E.2d 482, 2005 Va. App. LEXIS 43 (2005).

Where defendant failed to raise his objection before the trial court, the "ends of justice" exception was established because the record affirmatively demonstrated that the Commonwealth failed to prove an essential element for a conviction of escape from custody on a charge or conviction of a felony under subsection B of § 18.2-479 since there was no written complaint against defendant and he was not in custody on a felony conviction when he escaped from the police. Thomas v. Commonwealth, 56 Va. App. 1, 690 S.E.2d 298, 2010 Va. App. LEXIS 93 (2010).

Insufficient evidence. — Commonwealth failed to prove an essential element for a conviction of escape from custody on a charge or conviction of a felony under subsection B because the evidence affirmatively showed that there was no written complaint against defendant and he was not in custody on a felony conviction when he escaped from the police. Thomas v. Commonwealth, 56 Va. App. 1, 690 S.E.2d 298, 2010 Va. App. LEXIS 93 (2010).

Identity sufficiently established. — The testimony of the two police officers involved in the defendant's apprehension was sufficient to establish her identity as the person who had escaped from custody where, although the record did not reflect that either officer physically pointed a finger at the defendant in court, it clearly established that immediately prior to the taking of evidence, the defendant identified herself to the trial judge by name and that during their testimony, both officers identified the defendant by name as the person they had detained and stated that she was in their custody and presence when the escape and recapture occurred. Wiglesworth v. Commonwealth, No. 1291-99-2, 2000 Va. App. LEXIS 276 (Ct. of Appeals Apr. 11, 2000).

No meritorious issues were raised with regard to resisting arrest conviction. — Defendant failed to raise meritorious issues on appeal with regard to his conviction for resisting arrest in violation of 18 U.S.C.S. §§ 7 and 13, assimilating § 18.2-479; based upon the evidence presented by the government, any rational trier of fact could have found defendant guilty of resisting arrest under § 18.2-479, the Virginia statute for escape, and his acquittal on obstruction of justice charges did not bar his conviction on the resisting arrest count. United States v. Wells, — F.3d —, 2005 U.S. App. LEXIS 4829 (4th Cir. Mar. 24, 2005).

Applied in Cavell v. Commonwealth, 28 Va. App. 484, 506 S.E.2d 552 (1998).

§ 18.2-479.1. Resisting arrest; fleeing from a law-enforcement officer; penalty.

A. Any person who intentionally prevents or attempts to prevent a law-enforcement officer from lawfully arresting him, with or without a warrant, is guilty of a Class 1 misdemeanor.

B. For purposes of this section, intentionally preventing or attempting to prevent a lawful arrest means fleeing from a law-enforcement officer when (i) the officer applies physical force to the person, or (ii) the officer communicates to the person that he is under arrest and (a) the officer has the legal authority and the immediate physical ability to place the person under arrest, and (b) a reasonable person who receives such communication knows or should know that he is not free to leave.

History.
2003, cc. 112, 805.

Editor's note.
At the direction of the Virginia Code Commission, the section heading, as set out above, has been changed from "Resisting lawful arrest; penalty" to "Resisting arrest; fleeing from a law-enforcement officer; penalty."

Law Review.
For article summarizing published Virginia criminal law decisions between July 1, 2002 and July 1, 2003, see 38 U. Rich. L. Rev. 87 (2003).

§ 18.2-480. Escape, etc., by setting fire to jail.

If any person lawfully imprisoned in jail escape, or attempt to escape therefrom, by setting fire thereto, he shall be guilty of a Class 4 felony.

History.
Code 1950, § 18.1-291; 1960, c. 358; 1975, cc. 14, 15.

Michie's Jurisprudence.
For related discussion, see 9A M.J. Habeas Corpus, § 11.

§ 18.2-480.1. Admissibility of records of Department of Corrections in escape cases.

In any prosecution for, or preliminary hearing for, the offense of escape under this article or Title 53.1, the records maintained by the Department of Corrections or the Department of Juvenile Justice, when such records are duly attested by the custodian of such records, shall be admissible in evidence as evidence of the fact, location and dates of confinement, provided that the records shall be filed with the clerk of the court hearing the case at least seven days prior to the trial or preliminary hearing. On motion of the accused, the court may require the custodian to appear as a witness and be subject to cross-examination; provided such motion is made within a reasonable time prior to the day on which the case is set for trial; and provided further, that the custodian so appearing shall be considered the Commonwealth's witness.

History.
1976, c. 394; 1989, c. 733.

CHAPTER 11.

OFFENSES AGAINST THE SOVEREIGNTY OF THE COMMONWEALTH.

Article 1. Treason and Related Offenses.

ARTICLE 1.

TREASON AND RELATED OFFENSES.

§ 18.2-481. Treason defined; how proved and punished.

Treason shall consist only in:

(1) Levying war against the Commonwealth;

(2) Adhering to its enemies, giving them aid and comfort;

(3) Establishing, without authority of the legislature, any government within its limits separate from the existing government;

(4) Holding or executing, in such usurped government, any office, or professing allegiance or fidelity to it; or

(5) Resisting the execution of the laws under color of its authority.

Such treason, if proved by the testimony of two witnesses to the same overt act, or by confession in court, shall be punishable as a Class 2 felony.

History.
Code 1950, § 18.1-418; 1960, c. 358; 1975, cc. 14, 15.

Cross references.
As to amendment of indictment for treason, see § 19.2-231. As to arrest of member of General Assembly for treason, see § 30-7, and Va. Const., Art. IV, § 9.

Law Review.
For survey of Virginia criminal law for the year 1974-1975, see 61 Va. L. Rev. 1697 (1975).

Michie's Jurisprudence.

For related discussion, see 18 M.J. Treason, § 1; 21A M.J. Words and Phrases.

§ 18.2-482. Misprision of treason.

If any person knowing of such treason shall not, as soon as may be, give information thereof to the Governor, or some conservator of the peace, he shall be guilty of a Class 6 felony.

History.

Code 1950, § 18.1-419; 1960, c. 358; 1975, cc. 14, 15.

§ 18.2-483. Attempting, or instigating others, to establish usurped government.

If any person attempt to establish any such usurped government and commit any overt act therefor or by writing or speaking endeavor to instigate others to establish such government, he shall be guilty of a Class 1 misdemeanor.

History.

Code 1950, § 18.1-420; 1960, c. 358; 1975, cc. 14, 15.

Michie's Jurisprudence.

For related discussion, see 4A M.J. Conspiracy, § 2.

§ 18.2-484. Advocacy of change in government by force, violence or other unlawful means.

It shall be unlawful for any person, group, or organization to advocate any change, by force, violence, or other unlawful means in the government of the Commonwealth of Virginia or any of its subdivisions or in the government of the United States of America.

It shall be unlawful for any person to join, assist or otherwise contribute to any group or organization which, to the knowledge of such person, advocates or has as its purpose, aim or objective, any change, by force, violence, or other unlawful means in the government of the Commonwealth of Virginia or any of its subdivisions or in the government of the United States of America.

Violation of this section shall be punishable as a Class 6 felony.

Nothing herein shall be construed to limit or prohibit the advocacy, orally or otherwise, of any change, by peaceful means, in the government of the Commonwealth or any of its subdivisions or in the government of the United States.

History.

Code 1950, § 18.1-421; 1960, c. 358; 1962, c. 343; 1975, cc. 14, 15.

§ 18.2-485. Conspiring to incite one race to insurrection against another race.

If any person conspire with another to incite the population of one race to acts of violence and war against the population of another race, he shall, whether such acts of violence and war be made or not, be guilty of a Class 4 felony.

History.

Code 1950, § 18.1-422; 1960, c. 358; 1975, cc. 14, 15.

Michie's Jurisprudence.

For related discussion, see 4A M.J. Conspiracy, § 2.

ARTICLE 2.

UNIFORM FLAG ACT.

Michie's Jurisprudence.

For related discussion, see 8B M.J. Flags and Emblems, § 1.

§ 18.2-486. Definition of flag, standard, etc.

The words flag, standard, color, ensign or shield, as used in this article, shall include any flag, standard, color, ensign or shield, or copy, picture or representation thereof, made of any substance or represented or produced thereon, and of any size, evidently purporting to be such flag, standard, color, ensign or shield of the United States, or of this Commonwealth, or a copy, picture or representation thereof.

History.

Code 1950, § 18.1-423; 1960, c. 358; 1975, cc. 14, 15.

Uniform law cross references.

For other signatory state provisions, see:
Maine: 1 M.R.S. §§ 251 to 256.
Maryland: Md. Ann. Code, CR §§ 10-701 et seq.
Vermont: 13 V.S.A. §§ 1901 to 1906.

Law Review.

For survey of Virginia criminal law for the year 1971-1972, see 58 Va. L. Rev. 1206 (1972).

CASE NOTES

What is United States flag. — A flag with red and white stripes and a blank blue field in the upper left corner is admittedly similar to a United States flag, but even to a casual observer it would not purport to be a flag of the United States. Herrick v. Commonwealth, 212 Va. 789, 188 S.E.2d 209 (1972).

A flag which is approximately three feet by five feet and has 13 stripes, six white and seven red, appearing alternately, and has in the upper left corner a blue field with 26 stars of two different sizes arranged in the configuration of a peace symbol, and which was at no time an actual or official flag of the United States, does not come under this section. Herrick v. Commonwealth, 212 Va. 789, 188 S.E.2d 209 (1972).

§ 18.2-487. Exhibition or display.

No person shall, in any manner, for exhibition or display:

(1) Place or cause to be placed any word, figure, mark, picture, design, drawing or advertisement of any nature upon any flag, standard, color, ensign or shield of the United States or of this Commonwealth, or authorized by any law of the United States or of this Commonwealth;

(2) Expose to public view any such flag, standard, color, ensign or shield upon which shall have been

printed, painted or otherwise produced, or to which shall have been attached, appended, affixed or annexed, any such word, figure, mark, picture, design, drawing or advertisement; or

(3) Expose to public view for sale, manufacture or otherwise, or sell, give or have in possession for sale, for gift or for use for any purpose, any substance, being an article of merchandise, or receptacle, or thing for holding or carrying merchandise, upon or to which shall have been produced or attached any such flag, standard, color, ensign or shield, in order to advertise, call attention to, decorate, mark or distinguish such article or substance.

History.
Code 1950, § 18.1-424; 1960, c. 358; 1975, cc. 14, 15.

CASE NOTES

The purpose of this law is to prohibit any disfiguration of the United States flag. It is the flag itself which the law seeks to protect from desecration. Herrick v. Commonwealth, 212 Va. 789, 188 S.E.2d 209 (1972).

Displaying flag which is not actual or official flag of United States. — A flag which is approximately three feet by five feet and has 13 stripes, six white and seven red, appearing alternately, and has in the upper left corner a blue field with 26 stars of two different sizes arranged in the configuration of a peace symbol, and which was at no time an actual or official flag of the United States, does not come under this section. Herrick v. Commonwealth, 212 Va. 789, 188 S.E.2d 209 (1972).

§ 18.2-488. Mutilating, defacing, etc.

No person shall publicly burn with contempt, mutilate, deface, defile, trample upon, or wear with intent to defile any such flag, standard, color, ensign or shield.

History.
Code 1950, § 18.1-425; 1960, c. 358; 1968, c. 349; 1975, cc. 14, 15, 493.

Editor's note.
The above section is § 18.1-425 as amended by Acts 1975, c. 493. Pursuant to § 30-152, it has been substituted for § 18.2-488 as enacted by Acts 1975, cc. 14 and 15.

CASE NOTES

Public act. — An act done in the radio room of a public university, a place frequented by students and others who have business there, and which is visible to persons passing on the outside, is plainly an act publicly done. Franz v. Commonwealth, 212 Va. 587, 186 S.E.2d 71 (1972).

§ 18.2-488.1. Flag at half mast for certain public safety personnel killed in the line of duty.

A. As used in this section, unless the context requires a different meaning:

"Emergency medical services provider" means the same as that term is defined in § 32.1-111.1, and any member of a volunteer lifesaving crew or rescue squad.

"Firefighter" means the same as that term is defined in § 9.1-300, and any member of a volunteer fire department.

"Police officer" means any full-time or part-time employee of a police department or sheriff's office which is a part of or administered by the Commonwealth or any political subdivision thereof and who is responsible for the prevention and detection of crime and the enforcement of the penal, traffic, or highway laws of the Commonwealth.

"Service member" means a member of the United States armed forces, Virginia National Guard, or Virginia Defense Force.

B. Whenever a service member, police officer, firefighter, or emergency medical services provider who is a resident of Virginia is killed in the line of duty, all flags, state and local, flown at any building owned and operated by the Commonwealth shall be flown at half staff or mast for one day to honor and acknowledge respect for those who made the supreme sacrifice.

C. The Department of General Services shall develop procedures to effectuate the purposes of this section.

History.
2012, c. 767.

§ 18.2-489. To what article applies.

This article shall not apply to any act permitted by the statutes of the United States or by the laws of this Commonwealth, or by the United States armed forces regulations, nor shall it apply to any printed or written document or production, stationery, ornament, picture or jewelry whereon shall be depicted such flag, standard, color, ensign or shield, with no design or words thereon and disconnected with any advertisement.

History.
Code 1950, § 18.1-426; 1960, c. 358; 1975, cc. 14, 15.

§ 18.2-490. Penalty.

Any violation of this article shall be punishable as a Class 1 misdemeanor.

The provisions of this section shall not apply to § 18.2-488.1.

History.
Code 1950, § 18.1-427; 1960, c. 358; 1968, c. 349; 1975, cc. 14, 15; 2012, c. 767.

The 2012 amendments.
The 2012 amendment by c. 767 added the second sentence.

§ 18.2-491. Construction.

This article shall be so construed as to effectuate its general purpose, and to make uniform the laws of the states which enact it.

History.
Code 1950, § 18.1-428; 1960, c. 358; 1975, cc. 14, 15.

§ 18.2-492. Short title.

This article may be cited as the Uniform Flag Act.

History.
Code 1950, § 18.1-429; 1960, c. 358; 1975, cc. 14, 15.

CHAPTER 12.

MISCELLANEOUS.

ARTICLE 1.

LIQUEFIED PETROLEUM GAS CONTAINERS.

§ 18.2-493. Definitions.

As used in this article, unless the text indicates otherwise:

(a) *"Person"* shall mean any person, firm or corporation.

(b) *"Owner"* shall mean any person who holds a written bill of sale under which title or ownership to a container was transferred to such person, or any manufacturer of a container who has not sold or transferred ownership thereof by written bill of sale.

(c) *"Liquefied petroleum gas"* shall mean any material which is composed predominately of any of the following hydrocarbons or mixtures of the same: propane, propylene, butanes (normal butane and isobutane) and butylenes.

History.
Code 1950, § 18.1-400.1; 1970, c. 442; 1975, cc. 14, 15.

§ 18.2-494. Unlawful use of, filling or refilling or trafficking in containers.

No person except the owner thereof or person authorized in writing by the owner shall fill or refill with liquefied petroleum gas, or any other gas or compound, a liquefied petroleum gas container; or buy, sell, offer for sale, give, take, loan, deliver or permit to be delivered, or otherwise use, dispose of, or traffic in a liquefied petroleum gas container or containers if the container bears upon the surface thereof in plainly legible characters the name, initials, mark or other device of the owner; nor shall any person other than the owner of a liquefied petroleum gas container or a person authorized in writing by the owner deface, erase, obliterate, cover up, or otherwise remove or conceal any name, mark, initial or device thereon.

History.
Code 1950, § 18.1-400.2; 1970, c. 442; 1975, cc. 14, 15.

§ 18.2-495. Presumptive evidence.

The use of a liquefied petroleum gas container or containers by any person other than the person whose name, mark, initial or device is on the liquefied petroleum gas container or containers, without written consent, or purchase of the marked and distinguished liquefied petroleum gas container for the sale of liquefied petroleum gas or filling or refilling with liquefied petroleum gas, or possession of the liquefied petroleum gas containers by any person other than the person having his name, mark, initial or other device thereon, without the written consent of such owner, is presumptive evidence of the unlawful use, filling or refilling, or trafficking in of such liquefied petroleum gas containers.

History.
Code 1950, § 18.1-400.3; 1970, c. 442; 1975, cc. 14, 15.

§ 18.2-496. Punishment for violation.

Any person who fails to comply with any of the foregoing provisions of this article is guilty of a Class 3 misdemeanor for each separate offense.

History.
Code 1950, § 18.1-400.4; 1970, c. 442; 1975, cc. 14, 15.

§ 18.2-497. Fines and costs.

The costs incurred in the enforcement of this article shall be assessed and collected in the same manner as in criminal cases, and all fines collected by virtue of this article shall be turned over in the same manner and for the same purposes as criminal and misdemeanor fines are disposed of by law.

History.
Code 1950, § 18.1-400.5; 1970, c. 442; 1975, cc. 14, 15.

§ 18.2-498. Exempt containers.

Nothing in this article applies to or shall be construed to affect a liquefied petroleum gas container having a total capacity of five gallons or less.

History.
Code 1950, § 18.1-400.6; 1970, c. 442; 1975, cc. 14, 15.

ARTICLE 1.1.

VIRGINIA GOVERNMENTAL FRAUDS ACT.

§ 18.2-498.1. Short title.

This article shall be known and cited as the Virginia Governmental Frauds Act.

History.
1980, c. 472.

Cross references.
As to the violation of this article as grounds for denying prequalification of contractors under the Virginia Public Procurement Act, see § 2.2-4317. As to this article in relation to the Ethics in Public Contracting article of the Virginia Public Procurement Act, see § 2.2-4367.

CASE NOTES

Conviction under § 18.2-178 for inflated vendors' bids. — The enactment of § 59.1-68.6 et seq. and this article did not preclude the Commonwealth from obtaining a conviction under § 18.2-178 of a defendant alleged to have improperly inflated vendors' bids to the detriment of the Commonwealth, where the alleged acts took place prior to the enactment of the new statutes. Mosteller v. Commonwealth, 222 Va. 143, 279 S.E.2d 380 (1981).

§ 18.2-498.2. Definitions.

When used in this article, the term:

1. *"Person"* includes any natural person, any trust or association of persons, formal or otherwise, or any corporation, partnership, company or other legal or commercial entity.

2. *"Commercial dealing"* shall mean any offer, acceptance, agreement, or solicitation to sell or offer to sell or distribute goods, services or construction, to the Commonwealth of Virginia, or any local government within the Commonwealth or any department or agency thereof.

History.
1980, c. 472.

§ 18.2-498.3. Misrepresentations prohibited.

Any person, in any commercial dealing in any matter within the jurisdiction of any department or agency of the Commonwealth of Virginia, or any local government within the Commonwealth or any department or agency thereof, who knowingly falsifies, conceals, misleads, or covers up by any trick, scheme, or device a material fact, or makes any false, fictitious or fraudulent statements or representations, or makes or uses any false writing or document knowing the same to contain any false, fictitious or fraudulent statement or entry, shall be guilty of a Class 6 felony.

History.
1980, c. 472.

§ 18.2-498.4. Duty to provide certified statement.

A. The Commonwealth, or any department or agency thereof, and any local government or any department or agency thereof, may require that any person seeking, offering or agreeing to transact business or commerce with it, or seeking, offering or agreeing to receive any portion of the public funds or moneys, submit a certification that the offer or agreement or any claim resulting therefrom is not the result of, or affected by, any act of collusion with another person engaged in the same line of business or commerce; or any act of fraud punishable under this article.

B. Any person required to submit a certified statement as provided in subsection A above who knowingly makes a false statement shall be guilty of a Class 6 felony.

History.
1980, c. 472.

§ 18.2-498.5. Actions on behalf of Commonwealth or localities.

The Attorney General on behalf of the Commonwealth, or the attorney for the Commonwealth, on behalf of the county or city as the case may be may institute actions and proceedings for any and all violations occurring within their jurisdictions.

History.
1980, c. 472.

ARTICLE 2.

CONSPIRACY TO INJURE ANOTHER IN TRADE, BUSINESS OR PROFESSION.

Michie's Jurisprudence.

For related discussion, see 4A M.J. Conspiracy, §§ 2, 8, 13; 5B M.J. Criminal Procedure, §§ 6, 7.

§ 18.2-499. Combinations to injure others in their reputation, trade, business or profession; rights of employees.

A. Any two or more persons who combine, associate, agree, mutually undertake or concert together for the purpose of (i) willfully and maliciously injuring another in his reputation, trade, business or profession by any means whatever or (ii) willfully and maliciously compelling another to do or perform any act against his will, or preventing or hindering another from doing or performing any lawful act, shall be jointly and severally guilty of a Class 1 misdemeanor. Such punishment shall be in addition to any civil relief recoverable under § 18.2-500.

B. Any person who attempts to procure the participation, cooperation, agreement or other assistance of any one or more persons to enter into any combination, association, agreement, mutual understanding or concert prohibited in subsection A of this section shall be guilty of a violation of this section and subject to the same penalties set out in subsection A.

C. This section shall not affect the right of employees lawfully to organize and bargain concerning wages and conditions of employment, and take other steps to protect their rights as provided under state and federal laws.

History.

Code 1950, § 18.1-74.1:1; 1964, c. 623; 1972, c. 469; 1975, cc. 14, 15; 1994, c. 534.

Law Review.

For survey of Virginia criminal law for the year 1971-1972, see 58 Va. L. Rev. 1206 (1972). For article on injuries to business under the Virginia Conspiracy Act, see 38 Wash. & Lee L. Rev. 377 (1981). For article on the Virginia Conspiracy Statute, see 38 Wash. & Lee L. Rev. 1147 (1981). For an article, "Preserving Competition: Economic Analysis, Legal Standards, and Microsoft," see 8 Geo. Mason L. Rev. 1 (1999). For a review of antitrust and trade regulation law in Virginia for year 1999, see 33 U. Rich. L. Rev. 769 (1999). For article, "Antitrust and Trade Regulation," see 35 U. Rich. L. Rev. 453 (2001). For annual survey article discussing antitrust and trade regulation law, see 38 U. Rich. L. Rev. 39 (2003). For 2003/2004 survey of civil practice and procedure, see 39 U. Rich. L. Rev. 87 (2004).

Research references.

Stanley S. Arkin, Business Crime: Criminal Liability of the Business Community (Matthew Bender).

CASE NOTES

I. General Consideration.
II. Elements of Offense.
    A. Conspiracy.
    B. Injury.

I. GENERAL CONSIDERATION.

The focus of this section and § 18.2-500 is upon conspiracies resulting in business-related damages. Ward v. Connor, 495 F. Supp. 434 (E.D. Va. 1980), rev'd on other grounds, 657 F.2d 45 (4th Cir. 1981), cert. denied, 455 U.S. 907, 102 S. Ct. 1253, 71 L. Ed. 2d 445 (1982).

The elements of a statutory conspiracy claim under the Virginia Conspiracy Act are: (1) concerted action; (2) legal malice; and (3) causally-related injury. Virginia Vermiculite, Ltd. v. W.R. Grace & Co.-Conn., 144 F. Supp. 2d 558, 2001 U.S. Dist. LEXIS 7006 (W.D. Va. 2001), aff'd sub nom. Va. Vermiculite Ltd. v. Historic Green Springs, Inc., 307 F.3d 277 (4th Cir. 2002).

Section not applicable to injury to one's employment interests. — Where former postmaster alleged that co-workers conspired to injure him in his reputation, trade, business and profession and as a result he was demoted, the claim was dismissed for failure to state a claim for relief because this section addresses only injuries to one's business, not injuries to one's employment interests. Jordan v. Hudson, 690 F. Supp. 502 (E.D. Va. 1988), aff'd, 879 F.2d 98 (4th Cir. 1989).

To the extent a plaintiff attempts to base his conspiracy claim on injury to his personal reputation or employment, as opposed to business, interests, he fails to state a claim under this section and § 18.2-500. Warner v. Buck Creek Nursery, Inc., 149 F. Supp. 2d 246, 2001 U.S. Dist. LEXIS 7025 (W.D. Va. 2001).

The statute only applies to injury to a "business," rather than merely to employment or employment reputation. Proffit v. Ring, No. 1:01CV00121, 2002 U.S. Dist. LEXIS 1316 (W.D. Va. Jan. 28, 2002).

Where claims were brought for malicious prosecution and statutory conspiracy, under §§ 18.2-499 and 18.2-500, alleging conspiracy to injure reputation, trade, business, and profession, the trial court properly granted summary judgment to defendants on the statutory conspiracy claims, as §§ 18.2-499 and 18.2-500 applied to business and property interests, not to personal or employment interests. Andrews v. Ring, 266 Va. 311, 585 S.E.2d 780, 2003 Va. LEXIS 86 (2003).

Physician's claimed injuries (the termination of the physician's employment with an anesthesiology group and a hospital and the potential difficulty the physician faced in obtaining future employment with another hospital or anesthesiology group) did not fall within the scope of §§ 18.2-499 and 18.2-500. Mansfield v. Anesthesia Assocs., — F. Supp. 2d —, 2008 U.S. Dist. LEXIS 34732 (E.D. Va. Apr. 28, 2008).

Employment not within scope of section. — Summary judgment was granted for a defendant doctor who was chair of a hospital executive committee board and was alleged to be liable for a conspiracy under §§ 18.2-499 and 18.2-500, because defendant could not be liable for a conspiracy arising from a personal employment relationship. Payman v. Mirza, No. 2:02CV00023, 2002 U.S. Dist. LEXIS 21489 (W.D. Va. Nov. 1, 2002).

Unspecified future business prospect insufficient to support claim. — This section does not apply to a claim of injury to an unspecified future business endeavor. Warner v. Buck Creek Nursery, Inc., 149 F. Supp. 2d 246, 2001 U.S. Dist. LEXIS 7025 (W.D. Va. 2001).

Federal preemption. — Because copyright and the infringement thereof is an area controlled exclusively by the federal government, any state causes of action under this section and § 18.2-500 must be preempted in this area. Hoey v. Dexel Sys. Corp., 716 F. Supp. 222 (E.D. Va. 1989).

The Federal Airline Deregulation Act preempts any state enforcement actions having a connection with or reference to airline rates, routes, or services, and an action under this section in which the plaintiff airline alleged that the defendants entered into a business conspiracy to restrict the size of carry-on luggage was thus preempted and subject to dismissal. Continental Airlines, Inc. v. United Air Lines, Inc., 120 F. Supp. 2d 556, 2000 U.S. Dist. LEXIS 16262 (E.D. Va. 2000).

Mandatory abstention where claim was related to bankruptcy proceeding. — Where plaintiffs' claims for defamation and violation of the Virginia Business Conspiracy Act, § 18.2-499, were removed pursuant to 28 U.S.C.S. §§ 1334(b) and 1452 on the ground that the claims were related to defendant's bankruptcy proceeding, mandatory abstention was required under 28 U.S.C.S. § 1334(c)(2) because: (1) plaintiffs filed a timely motion to abstain;

(2) the case was based on state law; (3) the proceeding did not arise under Title 11; (4) the case could not have been commenced in federal court absent 28 U.S.C.S. § 1334; (5) an action was commenced and could be timely adjudicated in state court; and (6) 28 U.S.C.S. § 157(b)(4)'s "personal injury tort" exception to mandatory abstention did not apply to claims that did not involve physical injury. Massey Energy Co. v. W. Va. Consumers for Justice, 351 B.R. 348, 2006 U.S. Dist. LEXIS 73695 (E.D. Va. 2006).

Not preempted by Virginia Wine Franchise Act. — Virginia Wine Franchise Act did not preempt common-law or statutory conspiracy claims under § 18.2-499 by a wholesaler against a winery; a violation of the Act was covered by the Act, but a conspiracy to violate the Act was not. As the wholesaler had also brought an administrative proceeding before the Virginia Department of Alcoholic Beverage Control (ABC Board), however, the doctrine of primary jurisdiction meant that the ABC Board should determine whether the wrongful acts underlying the conspiracy claims had occurred. Country Vintner, Inc. v. Louis Latour, Inc., 272 Va. 402, 634 S.E.2d 745, 2006 Va. LEXIS 86 (2006).

Not preempted by Virginia Uniform Trade Secrets Act. — Plaintiff plainly articulated claims for conspiracy under § 18.2-499 that were independent of the claim for misappropriation of trade secrets and thus were not preempted under the Virginia Uniform Trade Secrets Act. E.I. Dupont De Nemours & Co. v. Kolon Indus., 2009 U.S. Dist. LEXIS 76795 (E.D. Va. Aug. 27, 2009).

Choice of law. — Under Virginia's doctrine of lex loci delicti, Georgia law governed plaintiff's claim for breach of Virginia's business conspiracy statute, because the wrong alleged and the first causally related injury occurred in Georgia and the doctrine of legislative jurisdiction was inapplicable where plaintiff raised no constitutional challenge to the application of Virginia's choice-of-law rules. Hilb Rogal & Hobbs Co. v. Risk Strategy Partners, Inc., — F.3d —, 2007 U.S. App. LEXIS 9332 (4th Cir. Apr. 24, 2007).

Exclusive distributorship arrangements do not violate the antitrust laws unless they foreclose competition in the relevant market. Thompson Everett, Inc. v. National Cable Adv., 850 F. Supp. 470 (E.D. Va. 1994), aff'd, 57 F.3d 1317 (4th Cir. 1995).

"Without lawful justification" means that the defendants contrived to accomplish some criminal or unlawful purpose, or to accomplish some purpose, not in itself criminal or unlawful, by criminal or unlawful means. Virginia Vermiculite, Ltd. v. W.R. Grace & Co.-Conn., 108 F. Supp. 2d 549, 2000 U.S. Dist. LEXIS 10513 (W.D. Va 2000).

"Without lawful justification" means that the defendants contrived to accomplish some criminal or unlawful purpose, or to accomplish some purpose, not in itself criminal or unlawful, by criminal or unlawful means; the statute thus requires that the plaintiff prove that at least one of the co-conspirators acted either with an unlawful purpose or by unlawful means. Virginia Vermiculite, Ltd. v. W.R. Grace & Co.-Conn., 144 F. Supp. 2d 558, 2001 U.S. Dist. LEXIS 7006 (W.D. Va. 2001), aff'd sub nom. Va. Vermiculite Ltd. v. Historic Green Springs, Inc., 307 F.3d 277 (4th Cir. 2002).

Required proof. — The conspiracy statutes do not require proof of actual malice, the statutes merely require proof of legal malice, i.e., that defendant acted intentionally, purposely, and without lawful justification. Commercial Bus. Sys. v. Bellsouth Servs., Inc., 249 Va. 39, 453 S.E.2d 261 (1995).

This section and § 18.2-500 do not require a plaintiff to prove that a conspirator's primary and overriding purpose is to injure another in his trade or business. Advanced Marine Enters., Inc. v. PRC, Inc., 256 Va. 106, 501 S.E.2d 148 (1998).

Although plaintiff need not prove personal spite, the alleged conduct must at least be aimed at damaging another's business. Peterson v. Cooley, 142 F.3d 181 (4th Cir. 1998).

In order to sustain a claim for statutory conspiracy under this section and § 18.2-500 the plaintiff must prove by clear and convincing evidence that the conspirators acted with legal malice, that is, that the defendant acted intentionally, purposefully and without lawful justification; these statutes do not require a plaintiff to prove that a conspirator's primary and overriding purpose was to injure another in his trade or business. Simmons v. Miller, 261 Va. 561, 544 S.E.2d 666, 2001 Va. LEXIS 48 (2001).

Because the jury instructions required the jury to find proof of injury and proof that the injured party suffered damages as a predicate to a verdict on a business conspiracy claim, the jury's finding of such a conspiracy without damages in each instance was

contrary to the jury instructions; hence, under *Rome v. Kelly Springfield Tire Co.*, 217 Va. 943, 948, 234 S.E. 2d 277, 281 (1977), the verdicts were invalid as a matter of law. Ulloa v. QSP, Inc., 271 Va. 72, 624 S.E.2d 43, 2006 Va. LEXIS 21 (2006).

Since plaintiffs provided no evidence of an agreement or an intent to injure, both of which were required to establish a business conspiracy under §§ 18.2-499 and 18.2-500, a reasonable jury could not conclude that the company and the third party were criminally and civilly liable under the theory of business conspiracy; therefore, summary judgment was granted against the claim. DAG Petroleum Suppliers L.L.C. v. BP P.L.C., 452 F. Supp. 2d 641, 2006 U.S. Dist. LEXIS 67438 (E.D. Va. 2006).

An employer sufficiently pled a claim for statutory conspiracy in violation of § 18.2-499, as it need not allege that the former employee's primary purpose was to injure the employer's business. The claims that the employee tortiously interfered with contract and violated a noncompete clause were insufficient and were dismissed. Nortec Communs., Inc. v. Lee-Llacer, 548 F. Supp. 2d 226, 2008 U.S. Dist. LEXIS 34350 (E.D. Va. 2008).

Standard of proof. — Proof of civil conspiracy must be shown by clear and convincing evidence. Multi-Channel TV Cable Co. v. Charlottesville Quality Cable Operating Co., 108 F.3d 522 (4th Cir. 1997).

Investigative-administrative arms of state not inhibited. — This section and § 18.2-500 do not create a protected interest against investigative-administrative arms of the state, as officials of a public body who act within the scope of their employment are not considered to be conspiring together for the purposes of this statute. Becker v. Russek, 518 F. Supp. 1040 (W.D. Va. 1981), aff'd, 679 F.2d 876 (4th Cir. 1982).

Dismissal of state conspiracy law claims against judge and clerk required. — Judge and deputy clerk were immune from damage claims with regards to their actions in revoking bondsman's certificate and that immunity required dismissal of the state conspiracy law claim that they conspired to injure the bondsman in her trade or business against them. Battle v. Whitehurst, 831 F. Supp. 522 (E.D. Va. 1993), aff'd, 36 F.3d 1091 (4th Cir. 1994).

Officials of the Department of Education, acting within the scope of their employment could not "combine, associate, agree, mutually undertake or concert together" to injure another in his trade or business within the meaning of this section. Fowler v. Department of Educ., 472 F. Supp. 121 (E.D. Va. 1978).

No conspiracy claim. — Any alleged conspiracy to injure a doctor's employment was not actionable under § 18.2-499 because individual defendants all served as employees or agents of a corporation; no conspiracy claim could lie against a single entity. Baylor v. Comprehensive Pain Mgmt. Ctrs., 2011 U.S. Dist. LEXIS 37699 (W.D. Va. Apr. 6, 2011).

Applied in Federated Graphics Cos. v. Napotnik, 424 F. Supp. 291 (E.D. Va. 1976); Human Resources Inst. of Norfolk, Inc. v. Blue Cross, 484 F. Supp. 520 (E.D. Va. 1980); Picture Lake Campground, Inc. v. Holiday Inns, Inc., 497 F. Supp. 858 (E.D. Va. 1980); Sun Publishing Co. v. Mecklenburg News, Inc., 594 F. Supp. 1512 (E.D. Va. 1984); Reasor v. City of Norfolk, 606 F. Supp. 788 (E.D. Va. 1984); Merrill Lynch, Pierce, Fenner & Smith, Inc. v. Bradley, 756 F.2d 1048 (4th Cir. 1985); Eshbaugh v. Amoco Oil Co., 234 Va. 74, 360 S.E.2d 350 (1987); Haigh v. Matsushita Elec. Corp. of Am., 676 F. Supp. 1332 (E.D. Va. 1987); Catercorp, Inc. v. Catering Concepts, Inc., 246 Va. 22, 431 S.E.2d 277 (1993); Derthick v. Bassett-Walker, Inc., 904 F. Supp. 510 (W.D. Va. 1995).

II. ELEMENTS OF OFFENSE.

A. Conspiracy.

Elements of offense. — To recover in an action for conspiracy to harm a business, the plaintiff must prove: (1) a combination of two or more persons for the purpose of willfully and maliciously injuring plaintiff in his business; and (2) resulting damage to plaintiff. Allen Realty Corp. v. Holbert, 227 Va. 441, 318 S.E.2d 592 (1984).

To recover in an action under this section, plaintiff must prove: (1) a combination of two or more persons for the purpose of willfully and maliciously injuring plaintiff in his business; and (2) resulting damage to plaintiff. Saliba v. Exxon Corp., 865 F. Supp. 306 (W.D. Va. 1994), aff'd, 52 F.3d 322 (4th Cir. 1995).

Company failed to present any evidence either of a conspiracy between the corporation and the non-minority owned company or legal malice on behalf of either; therefore, any injury the company might have suffered was not actionable under the Virginia Business Conspiracy Act, §§ 18.2-499 and 18.2-500. DAG Petroleum Suppliers, L.L.C. v. BP P.L.C., — F.3d —, 2008 U.S. App. LEXIS 1293 (4th Cir. Jan. 23, 2008).

Proof of malice required. — The element of legal malice requires the plaintiff to prove that the concerted action was undertaken by one conspirator to injure the plaintiff intentionally, purposefully and without lawful justification, but the statute does not require that the the co-conspirator act with legal malice; rather, the statute simply requires that one party, acting with legal malice, conspire with another party to injure the plaintiff. Virginia Vermiculite, Ltd. v. W.R. Grace & Co.-Conn., 144 F. Supp. 2d 558, 2001 U.S. Dist. LEXIS 7006 (W.D. Va. 2001), aff'd sub nom. Va. Vermiculite Ltd. v. Historic Green Springs, Inc., 307 F.3d 277 (4th Cir. 2002).

Showing of malice. — When the fact finder is satisfied from the evidence that the defendant's primary and overriding purpose is to injure his victim in his reputation, trade, business or profession, motivated by hatred, spite or ill-will, the element of malice required by this section is established, notwithstanding any additional motives entertained by the defendant to benefit himself or persons other than the victim. Greenspan v. Osheroff, 232 Va. 388, 351 S.E.2d 28 (1986).

Legal malice not found. — Defendant former employee did not engage in a conspiratorial act of legal malice in violation of § 18.2-499 by accepting future employment with an employment broker while the employee was still employed by plaintiff former employer, another employment firm that had arranged for the employee, pursuant to a contract with the employment broker, to perform temporary services for a certain manufacturer, even though the employee expected to be placed by the employment broker for an extended period with the same manufacturer, as the employee was an at-will employee, neither the employee nor the employment broker violated any contract by their conduct, and the employee did not rob the former employer of any objective or tangible business opportunity or expectancy; therefore, there was no basis for the jury's verdict in the former employer's favor on its claim against the former employee for civil liability under § 18.2-500 for allegedly violating § 18.2-499. Williams v. Dominion Tech. Partners, L.L.C., 265 Va. 280, 576 S.E.2d 752, 2003 Va. LEXIS 29 (2003).

Conduct directed at person not covered. — This section does not codify common-law actions. Rather, statutory coverage is afforded only when malicious conduct is directed at one's business, not one's person. Moore v. Allied Chem. Corp., 480 F. Supp. 364 (E.D. Va. 1979); Ward v. Connor, 495 F. Supp. 434 (E.D. Va. 1980), rev'd on other grounds, 657 F.2d 45 (4th Cir. 1981), cert. denied, 455 U.S. 907, 102 S. Ct. 1253, 71 L. Ed. 2d 445 (1982).

Where the plaintiff claimed that the alleged conspiracy caused damage to his investment and claimed monetary losses in connection with his business, he was advancing a common-law claim for libel and slander to his personal reputation. This type of claim is not actionable under this section. Moore v. Allied Chem. Corp., 480 F. Supp. 364 (E.D. Va. 1979).

But individuals who own and operate business protected. — This section does not restrict its coverage to corporations; by speaking of injury to "another in his reputation, trade, business or profession," this section also protects individuals who own and operate a business. Moore v. Allied Chem. Corp., 480 F. Supp. 364 (E.D. Va. 1979).

The two categories of "persons" protected by this section are corporations and individuals who own or operate a business. Welch v. Kennedy Piggly Wiggly Stores, Inc., 63 Bankr. 888 (W.D. Va. 1986).

Sanctions error where there was possibility city could be sued under act. — Where district judge awarded sanctions to city since plaintiffs should have known that the city was incapable of forming the criminal intent necessary for liability under the Virginia Conspiracy Act, where the Virginia Conspiracy Act itself does not clearly state whether cities can be subjected to liability, where the Virginia Supreme Court has not been confronted directly with whether a city is a person within the meaning of the Virginia Conspiracy Act, and where a recent pronouncement of the Supreme Court in a Virginia Conspiracy Act case seemed to have left open

the possibility that a city could be sued under that act, the district court abused its discretion in sanctioning plaintiffs since the court of appeals was unable to say that plaintiffs had "absolutely no chance of success" in bringing a Virginia Conspiracy Act claim against the city. Brubaker v. City of Richmond, 943 F.2d 1363 (4th Cir. 1991).

Sanctions error where Supreme Court had not rejected vicarious liability concept. — Where district court awarded sanctions to city on the ground that plaintiffs had no evidence to support their allegations that the city was involved in a scheme to prevent them from obtaining Minority Business Enterprises certification or securing investment business, when plaintiffs filed their complaint, the Virginia Supreme Court had not rejected the concept of vicarious liability in the Virginia Conspiracy Act context, and in fact, seemed to leave open at least the possibility of this theory; because plaintiffs had a sufficient factual basis for implicating the city in the scheme, the district court abused its discretion in awarding sanctions to the city on the Virginia Conspiracy Act count. Brubaker v. City of Richmond, 943 F.2d 1363 (4th Cir. 1991).

Conspiracy between corporation and its agents as legal impossibility. — Although plaintiff's allegations were initially sufficient to satisfy the threshold demands of Virginia's civil conspiracy statute, they were not sufficient to overcome the obstacle provided by the intracorporate immunity doctrine, which holds that because at least two persons must be present to form a conspiracy, a corporation cannot conspire with itself; therefore, a conspiracy between a corporation and the agents of that corporation who are acting in the scope of their employment is a legal impossibility. Selman v. American Sports Underwriters, Inc., 697 F. Supp. 225 (W.D. Va. 1988).

Where plaintiff claimed that defendant corporation and two of its employees acted in concert to interfere with plaintiff's business, no conspiracy could be established because a corporation is a legal fiction capable of acting only through its officers and employees and is considered to be essentially only one actor. Sunsport, Inc. v. Barclay Leisure Ltd., 984 F. Supp. 418 (E.D. Va. 1997).

Defendant health care insurer was entitled to summary judgment on plaintiff chiropractic providers and patients' state law conspiracy claims brought under §§ 18.2-499 and 18.2-500, for the same reasons that their antitrust claims failed; Virginia had adopted the intracorporate immunity doctrine which barred the majority of the claims and the facts did not show that a violation of the conspiracy law had occurred. Am. Chiropractic Ass'n v. Trigon Healthcare, Inc., 258 F. Supp. 2d 461, 2003 U.S. Dist. LEXIS 6961 (W.D. Va. 2003), aff'd, 367 F.3d 212 (4th Cir. 2004).

Where plaintiff, a polybutylene (PB) replacement company, alleged that defendants, former employees and a competing PB replacement company, violated § 18.2-499 by conspiring to infringe plaintiff's copyrighted consumer contract, plaintiff's business conspiracy claim failed under the doctrine of intracorporate immunity because the employees were agents of the competing company, the agents acted within the scope of their agency, and there was no evidence indicating that the employees conspired to use plaintiff's consumer contract before they formed the competing company. Accordingly, plaintiff could not establish concerted activity by two or more persons. Phoenix Renovation Corp. v. Rodriguez, — F.3d —, 2007 U.S. App. LEXIS 29253 (4th Cir. Dec. 17, 2007).

Corporate officers and directors as separate entities. — Where the directors and officers of a corporation can be shown to have a personal stake in achieving a corporation's illegal objective, they can be treated as separate entities for conspiracy purposes. Levine v. McLeskey, 881 F. Supp. 1030 (E.D. Va. 1995), vacated in part on other grounds, 164 F.3d 210 (4th Cir. 1998).

Agent could not conspire with his principal. — Claim under § 18.2-499 failed because: (1) plaintiff presented factual allegations that the individual defendant was an agent of the copyright defendants; (2) plaintiff incorporated all prior allegations into the Count alleging violation of § 18-2-499; and (3) an agent could not conspire with its principal under the intracorporate immunity doctrine. SecureInfo Corp. v. Telos Corp., 387 F. Supp. 2d 593, 2005 U.S. Dist. LEXIS 21228 (E.D. Va. 2005).

Personal-stake exception to intracorporate immunity. — The doctrine of intracorporate immunity is excepted when an agent of the corporation has an independent personal stake in achieving the corporation's impermissible objectives; such personal stake must be wholly separable from the more general and indirect corporate benefit. Hence, on defendant's motion to dismiss, plaintiffs pleaded sufficient facts to satisfy the personal stake exception, namely, that the agents of insurer, as competing physicians, had a direct interest in the market for healthcare services which was distinct and independent from their roles as agents of insurer. American Chiropractic Ass'n v. Trigon Healthcare, Inc., 151 F. Supp. 2d 723, 2001 U.S. Dist. LEXIS 10348 (W.D. Va. 2001).

A single entity cannot conspire with itself, thus, a corporation cannot conspire with its wholly owned subsidiary. Saliba v. Exxon Corp., 865 F. Supp. 306 (W.D. Va. 1994), aff'd, 52 F.3d 322 (4th Cir. 1995).

Where the record is clear that the bank's agent was retained to service "problem" loans, and that it acted within the scope of its agency, a conspiracy was a legal impossibility because a principal and an agent are not separate persons for purposes of the conspiracy statute. One entity existed, the bank, and a single entity cannot conspire with itself. Charles E. Brauer Co. v. NationsBank, 251 Va. 28, 466 S.E.2d 382 (1996).

Because an attorney was an agent of client, attorney could not conspire with the client in violation of the Virginia Business Conspiracy Statute, § 18.2-499 et seq.; thus, a federal district court properly dismissed for failure to state a claim an attorney's lawsuit alleging, inter alia, that individuals (presumably clients and one or more attorneys) who had filed disciplinary complaints against the attorney conspired to harm the attorney's reputation and trade. Prousalis v. Jamgochian, — F.3d —, 2002 U.S. App. LEXIS 12255 (4th Cir. June 20, 2002).

Former president alleged that the actions of the individual defendants that led to the association's redefinition of his job responsibilities and nonrenewal of his employment contract constituted a civil conspiracy; however, the alleged co-conspirators were all agents of the association acting within the scope of their employment and as the individual defendants were acting within the scope of their employment, the alleged conspiracy was performed by a single entity. Therefore, summary judgment was granted as to the civil conspiracy claim. Huizenga v. Am. Int'l Auto. Dealers Ass'n, 2005 U.S. Dist. LEXIS 30972 (E.D. Va. Nov. 22, 2005).

In an action in which a debtor filed suit against defendants based on their allegedly fraudulent conduct surrounding the placement of one creditor's Second Deed of Trust on the debtor's apartment complex, there was no business conspiracy because the debtor failed to show that at least two people had combined intentionally for the nefarious purpose of harming the debtor's business. Wellington Apt., LLC v. Clotworthy (In re Wellington Apt., LLC), 350 B.R. 213, 2006 Bankr. LEXIS 2362 (Bankr. E.D. Va. 2006).

Former subcontractors of a contractor were not liable for conspiracy to wilfully and maliciously injure a contractor in its business where the evidence presented indicated that the subcontractors, through their company, which competed with the contractor's, did infringe copyrighted material, but at the time before and after the contractor copyrighted its material, the subcontractors had already formed their competing company and were acting as agents of that company in infringing the copyright. Because the subcontractors were acting as agents of the same principal, within the scope of their agency relationship, a conspiracy was legally impossible. Phoenix Renovation Corp. v. Rodriguez, 461 F. Supp. 2d 411, 2006 U.S. Dist. LEXIS 79724 (E.D. Va. 2006).

Plaintiff car dealership's former owner's claim under § 18.2-499 against defendants, a car manufacturer and its financing division, failed to state a claim as the car manufacturer and its subsidiary financing division were considered a single entity and a single entity could not conspire with itself, and further, while other entities were also identified, there was no factual basis to discern the method of the alleged conspiracy or how it was carried out. Field v. GMAC LLC, 660 F. Supp. 2d 679, 2008 U.S. Dist. LEXIS 110164 (E.D. Va. 2008).

Allegations sufficient to withstand motion to dismiss. — Telecommunications provider's allegations of a business conspiracy (that defendant and another entity acted together to divert the telecommunications provider's earned commissions, and to injure or destroy the telecommunications provider's business, and that the conspiratorial conduct was willful and malicious, and resulted in substantial money damages to the telecommunications provider) were sufficient to withstand defendant's motion to dismiss. While the allegations were arguably conclusory, the complaint, in its

entirety, contained sufficient factual content to permit the court to reasonably infer that the required elements of concerted action, legal malice and causally related injury, could be met. All Bus. Solutions, Inc. v. NationsLine, Inc., 629 F. Supp. 2d 553, 2009 U.S. Dist. LEXIS 54693 (W.D. Va. 2009).

Cause of action not stated. — The plaintiff failed to state a cause of action for conspiracy to injure its business where the plaintiff provided no specific factual basis, other than the conclusory allegation that the defendants conspired with others, to support the cause of action. Stone Castle Fin., Inc. v. Friedman, Billings, Ramsey & Co., 191 F. Supp. 2d 652, 2002 U.S. Dist. LEXIS 3764 (E.D. Va. 2002).

Where a vermiculite miner sued a landowner and a preservation organization for violation of the Virginia Civil Conspiracy Act (VCCA) by reason of a gift of the owner's vermiculite-containing land to the organization, with a covenant prohibiting mining of vermiculite, because the basis for violating the VCCA was the wrong done by the conspiracy, and there was no underlying Sherman Act § 1 wrong, there was no liability under the VCCA. Va. Vermiculite, Ltd. v. Historic Green Springs, Inc., 307 F.3d 277, 2002 U.S. App. LEXIS 20877 (4th Cir. 2002), cert. denied, 538 U.S. 998, 123 S. Ct. 1900, 155 L. Ed. 2d 824 (2003).

In a brand owner's suit against a distributor alleging that the manufacturer secretly entered into a manufacturing agreement with the competing distributor and that the distributor told customers that the brand owner was going out of business, the conspiracy claim was dismissed because the brand owner failed to aver an unlawful act or an attempt by the distributor to interfere with the agreement between the brand owner and manufacturer. Bay Tobacco, LLC v. Bell Quality Tobacco Prods., LLC, 261 F. Supp. 2d 483, 2003 U.S. Dist. LEXIS 12709 (E.D. Va. 2003).

Plaintiff's claim for statutory business conspiracy under § 18.2-499 failed to state a claim for purposes of Fed. R. Civ. P. 12(b)(6), because the facts alleged were not sufficiently specific to support the conclusory language that defendants entered into an agreement with the purpose of injuring plaintiff in its business, and therefore did not satisfy the statute's heightened pleading standard. At best, plaintiff's claim alleged that defendants had agreements to sell advertising to plaintiff's competitors; none of the facts pled supported a claim that defendants were entering into the advertising agreements with the intent to maliciously injure plaintiff. Gov't Emples. Ins. Co. v. Google, Inc., 330 F. Supp. 2d 700, 2004 U.S. Dist. LEXIS 18415 (E.D. Va. 2004).

Taking all the evidence in the light most favorable to plaintiff, it would have taken more than a stretch to conclude that plaintiff's evidence supported an inference that defendants acted in concert for the specific purpose of injuring plaintiff. Waytec Elecs. Corp. v. Rohm & Haas Elec. Materials, LLC, 459 F. Supp. 2d 480, 2006 U.S. Dist. LEXIS 77673 (W.D. Va. 2006), aff'd, 2007 U.S. App. LEXIS 28113 (4th Cir. Va. 2007).

Corporate president did not state a cause of action for civil conspiracy against a bank due to one of its officer's erroneous transmission of funds from the corporation's account and the failure to transfer the funds back to the corporation's account because: (1) the president did not allege any concerted action as there was no showing of any agreement, and § 18.2-499 was not so broad as to encompass a conspiracy where there was no agreement and "but for" the bank's actions, the president would not have been damaged; (2) he failed to allege malice; and (3) the alleged business conspiracy was not pleaded with the requisite malice. Schlegel v. Bank of Am., N.A., 505 F. Supp. 2d 321, 2007 U.S. Dist. LEXIS 42551 (W.D. Va. 2007).

Amended complaint failed to set forth sufficient facts that plausibly suggested a conspiracy under § 18.2-499 and the parties' Consultant Agreement allowed defendant company to terminate its contract with plaintiff individual at will; the amended complaint was devoid of factual allegations suggesting when or how defendants entered into an agreement to act jointly to maliciously injure plaintiffs. Scharpenberg v. Carrington, 686 F. Supp. 2d 655, 2010 U.S. Dist. LEXIS 14356 (E.D. Va. 2010).

Conspiracy merely to breach a contract that did not involve an independent duty arising outside the contract was insufficient to establish a civil claim under § 18.2-499 because to permit a mere breach of contract to constitute an "unlawful act" for the purposes of the conspiracy statute would have been inconsistent with the diligence courts exercised to prevent turning every breach of contract into an actionable claim for fraud. Therefore, because the company's agreements with the owners and with the developer and the principal did not implicate statutory or independent common-law duties, merely alleging breach of those contracts was insufficient to establish a claim of statutory conspiracy under §§ 18.2-499 and 18.2-500, and the circuit court did not err in sustaining the demurrers to that claim. Station # 2, LLC v. Lynch, 280 Va. 166, 695 S.E.2d 537, 2010 Va. LEXIS 64 (2010).

Terminated subcontractor's claim under Virginia's business conspiracy statute, §§ 18.2-499 to 18.2-500, failed because the subcontractor did not prove the defendants had combined to accomplish some purpose by criminal or unlawful means. Neither could he demonstrate an injury to a business interest. Shirvinski v. United States Coast Guard, 673 F.3d 308, 2012 U.S. App. LEXIS 5106 (4th Cir. 2012).

Former employee was unable to state a civil conspiracy claim under §§ 18.2-499 and 18.2-500 because these statutes afforded a right of action only when the malicious conduct was directed at a business, and the employee's claims exclusively concerned her employment prospects. Conyers v. Va. Hous. Dev. Auth., 2012 U.S. Dist. LEXIS 134908 (E.D. Va. Sept. 19, 2012).

No authority to act as agent. — Bank's claims against a title insurance company under § 18.2-499 failed because a title agent that was alleged to have fraudulently closed mortgage loans did not act as an agent of the title company; an agreement between the title company and the title agent expressly prohibited the title agent from acting as a settlement agent on behalf of the title company. Wells Fargo Bank, N.A. v. Old Republic Title Ins. Co., 2011 U.S. App. LEXIS 4030 (4th Cir. Mar. 1, 2011).

Cause of action stated. — Plaintiff's claim for violation of the Virginia Business Conspiracy Statute survived a motion to dismiss, where it alleged that the conspirators included defendants and the credit reporting bureaus, it alleged that defendants and the three credit bureaus agreed to withhold certain information from plaintiff, and it alleged that the agreement was for the purpose of maliciously causing injury to plaintiff; the fact that the last element of malice was not pled by specifically alleging particular facts supporting the legal standard of malice was not fatal to the complaint because malice could be averred generally. College Loan Corp. v. SLM Corp., — F. Supp. 2d —, 2002 U.S. Dist. LEXIS 27744 (E.D. Va. Dec. 10, 2002).

Defendants' and a "partner's" actions constituted a prima facie case of business conspiracy; such examples were defendants' and the partner's structure of plaintiff company's settlement agreement, the purchase of a jet against plaintiffs' directions, the purchase of the eight acre parcel next to a store although the price was too high and the site was not suitable, and a stock subscription agreement that negatively impacted plaintiffs. These actions were all evidence that defendants and the partner worked together to damage plaintiffs and that damaging plaintiffs might not have been their primary purpose was immaterial under Virginia law. Atlas Partners II v. Brumberg, Mackey & Wall, PLC, — F. Supp. 2d —, 2006 U.S. Dist. LEXIS 983 (W.D. Va. Jan. 6, 2006).

Where a liquidating trustee of corporate bankruptcy debtors alleged that insiders of the debtors combined, agreed, and/or mutually undertook to willfully and maliciously loot the debtors, and described the unlawful acts that were taken in furtherance of the conspiracy, the trustee stated a viable claim under Virginia law for statutory conspiracy. Schnelling v. Crawford (In re James River Coal Co.), 360 B.R. 139, 2007 Bankr. LEXIS 159 (Bankr. E.D. Va. 2007).

Persons acting within scope of employment as agents of city do not constitute conspiracy. — If defendants, who were charged with having conspired to injure producer and promoter of shows and concerts in his trade, business, or occupation in violation of this section and § 18.2-500, were acting within the scope of their employment and, therefore, were agents of the city, then only one entity exists — the city. By definition, a single entity cannot conspire with itself. Fox v. Deese, 234 Va. 412, 362 S.E.2d 699 (1987).

This section does not mention employment as a protected activity. The section is aimed at conduct which injures a "business." Campbell v. Board of Supvrs., 553 F. Supp. 644 (E.D. Va. 1982).

Section not applicable to employment interests. — In a former employee's suit against his former employer, alleging a civil conspiracy to divest him of his stock ownership in the employer and

to injure his professional reputation and business by terminating him, in violation of §§ 18.2-499 and 18.2-500, the employee failed to state a claim because his professional reputation and stock ownership in the company were employment interests, and not business interests, which were not covered by these laws. Inman v. Klockner-Pentaplast of Am., Inc., 467 F. Supp. 2d 642, 2006 U.S. Dist. LEXIS 93620 (W.D. Va. 2006).

Covered conduct must be directly aimed toward damaging business, etc. — The Virginia Conspiracy Statute applies to any malicious conduct that injures business. However, such conduct must be directly aimed toward damaging the business, trade, reputation or profession: the injury must not be a result or secondary effect of an action taken for mere personal gain. Nationwide Mut. Fire Ins. Co. v. Jones, 577 F. Supp. 968 (W.D. Va. 1984).

But primary purpose need not be injury to another's trade or business. — Under §§ 18.2-499 and 18.2-500, plaintiffs may only recover for business conspiracy if they prove by clear and convincing evidence that: (1) a combination of two or more persons; (2) acted for the purpose of willful and malicious injury to plaintiffs by any means whatever; and (3) that act resulted in damage to plaintiffs. To prove malice, plaintiffs must show that defendants acted intentionally, purposefully, and without legal justification. Significantly, the statute does not require a plaintiff to prove that a conspirator's primary and overriding purpose is to injure another in his trade or business. Atlas Partners II v. Brumberg, Mackey & Wall, PLC, — F. Supp. 2d —, 2006 U.S. Dist. LEXIS 983 (W.D. Va. Jan. 6, 2006).

Right of action arises from conduct directed at business, not person. — A right of action is afforded under this section and § 18.2-500 only when malicious conduct is directed at one's business, not one's person, and the statutes focus upon conduct directed at property, i.e., one's business and apply only to conspiracies resulting in business-related damages. Buschi v. Kirven, 775 F.2d 1240 (4th Cir. 1985).

To recover damages for conspiracy a plaintiff must show that the defendants have combined to accomplish some criminal or unlawful purpose, or to accomplish some purpose, not in itself criminal or unlawful, by criminal or unlawful means. Potomac Valve & Fitting, Inc. v. Crawford Fitting Co., 829 F.2d 1280 (4th Cir. 1987).

Statute does not require a co-conspirator to act with legal malice, only that one party conspire with another to injure plaintiff. Multi-Channel TV Cable Co. v. Charlottesville Quality Cable Operating Co., 108 F.3d 522 (4th Cir. 1997).

Conspiracy found in banks' actions toward debtor. — There was credible evidence to support a finding that two banks acted in concert and agreed, associated, or combined for the purpose of willfully and maliciously damaging debtor in its trade or business in light of the extensive and unusual actions they undertook to eliminate any ability of debtor to continue operating or to file a reorganization plan under chapter 11 by removing the debtor's access to cash flow, inventory, or other financing. Tazewell Oil Co. v. United Va. Bank/Crestar Bank, 243 Va. 94, 413 S.E.2d 611 (1992).

Evidence sufficient to show conspiracy. — There is sufficient circumstantial evidence that conspiracy existed to injure plaintiffs where the strike was long and the lawlessness pervasive, union officials were regularly on the scene and there was no evidence that any member of the union was disciplined, or that there was any serious, comprehensive effort to stop the violence. Ramar Coal Co. v. International Union, UMW, 814 F. Supp. 502 (W.D. Va. 1993).

Evidence supported conspiracy finding where defendant attempted to drive competitor out of business by use of negative advertising campaign, damaged competitor's property, cut off competitor's service to customers without notice, and offered illegal kickbacks to apartment manager for substituting defendant's service for competitor's. Multi-Channel TV Cable Co. v. Charlottesville Quality Cable Operating Co., 108 F.3d 522 (4th Cir. 1997).

The evidence was sufficient to establish a violation of this section where a group of officers and directors informed the principal owner of their employer that they intended to resign en masse as a means of exerting leverage against the owner to accept the group's buyout offer and thus facilitate a merger of their employer with a rival firm; injury to the plaintiff employer was a known and intended result of the plan. Feddeman & Co. v. Langan Assocs., P.C., 260 Va. 35, 530 S.E.2d 668, 2000 Va. LEXIS 92 (2000).

Plaintiff's allegations that defendant individuals, prior to forming defendant corporation, and while still employed by plaintiff, conspired to misappropriate and copy plaintiff's trade secrets and proprietary information, lure away plaintiff's employees, copy plaintiff's business format, and imitate and infringe plaintiff's trademarks had sufficiently pled a conspiracy under §§ 18.2-499 and 18.2-500. Buffalo Wings Factory, Inc. v. Mohd, 622 F. Supp. 2d 325, 2007 U.S. Dist. LEXIS 91324 (E.D. Va. 2007).

Evidence insufficient to show conspiracy. — Where an insurance company ceased doing business with a flood insurance agent, the insurance company was entitled to summary judgment as to the agent's business conspiracy claim because evidence of a conversation between a general agent and the insurance company did not establish the presence of a conspiracy to injure the agent in the agent's business. Hecht v. Am. Bankers Ins. Co., 2005 U.S. Dist. LEXIS 25883 (W.D. Va. Oct. 21, 2005).

No factual basis existed to support the plaintiffs' allegation that the defendants formed an agreement to harm the plaintiffs and no evidence existed that the defendants acted with malice during their telephone conversations. To the contrary, both of the defendants denied any agreement to cut one of the plaintiffs out of the sale of a property, and one of the defendants testified that the calls were specifically prompted by the fact that the one plaintiff only presented the defendants with one offer for the property and did not present them with another offer for the property. N. Va. Real Estate, Inc. v. Martins, 283 Va. 86, 720 S.E.2d 121, 2012 Va. LEXIS 11 (2012).

Relationship terminable at-will. — In a suit stemming from the termination of a 20 year relationship for the sale and distribution of certain delicatessen products, which was based on an oral agreement, which was terminable by either party at-will, the buyers' counterclaim against the sellers for business conspiracy in violation of § 18.2-499 failed as a matter of law due to the fact that the parties had the right to terminate their at-will relationship. Frank Brunckhorst Co., L.L.C. v. Coastal Atl., Inc., 542 F. Supp. 2d 452, 2008 U.S. Dist. LEXIS 6748 (E.D. Va. 2008).

B. Injury.

No proximate cause between defendants' actions and former employer's lost profits. — Despite the testimony of an expert witness, who was a forensic accountant, as to a former employer's loss of profits from the alleged wrongful conduct of defendants, its former salesman and his new store, defendants' motion to strike, which tested sufficiency of the evidence, should have been granted. The expert used a "but-for" damages calculation, which presumed an injury to the former employer from the mere fact that the salesman, who had been an at-will employee, had stopped working at the former employer's store and had begun working at the new store; the expert did not demonstrate that defendants' wrongful conduct, including a breach of fiduciary duties and violation of §§ 18.2-499 and 18.2-500, had proximately caused any injury to the former employer. Saks Fifth Ave., Inc. v. James, Ltd., 272 Va. 177, 630 S.E.2d 304, 2006 Va. LEXIS 54 (2006).

Calculation of damages, and lost profits in particular, was speculative as it assumed future business from customers who had no duty to shop at the former employer's store; the expert also did not show that the conduct of the salesman or his new store had proximately caused any of the loss of the former employer's customers, and the expert's damages calculation, which was based on a "but-for" analysis, had focused solely on the fact that the salesman had stopped working for the former employer and did not focus on any wrongful conduct by defendants. Saks Fifth Ave., Inc. v. James, Ltd., 272 Va. 177, 630 S.E.2d 304, 2006 Va. LEXIS 54 (2006).

Consequential injury not covered. — Injury to an insurance company's business, trade or reputation which the insurance company suffered as a result of defendants' denial of responsibility for the fire which destroyed their home and false statements regarding their loss was a consequential loss from the defendants' action to recover the insurance proceeds. The statute is not aimed at this type of loss. Nationwide Mut. Fire Ins. Co. v. Jones, 577 F. Supp. 968 (W.D. Va. 1984).

Right to performance of contract and right to reap profits therefrom are property rights which are entitled to protection in the courts. Consequently, suits for procuring breach of contract proceed on this basis. Chaves v. Johnson, 230 Va. 112, 335 S.E.2d 97 (1985).

Publication of interview in magazine no offense. — Allegations that defendant journalists and magazine conspired to obtain and publish an interview with plaintiff minister and that plaintiff's fund raising activities were adversely affected as a result of the publication, failed to state a claim upon which relief could be granted under this section and § 18.2-500, since there was no basis for the general allegation that any of the defendants conspired for the specific purpose of injuring the plaintiff. Falwell v. Penthouse Int'l, Ltd., 521 F. Supp. 1204 (W.D. Va. 1981).

Hiring accountant without intent no offense. — Evidence that plaintiff's associate employed accountant to review certain financial records to determine if there was any financial mismanagement of company and that until review was made, it was totally unknown whether company was mismanaged did not support contention that plaintiff's associate employed accountant with intent to injure plaintiff, as he could not have had requisite intent when he had no knowledge of result. Semida v. Rice, 863 F.2d 1156 (4th Cir. 1988).

Agreement to stall payment to bank until customer obtained writ. — Issuing bank, account customer, and president of account customer did not conspire, in violation of this section, to injure confirming bank by agreeing to stall payment to confirming bank until account customer had obtained and had served a writ of attachment; at most, confirming bank's allegations amounted to a claim that issuing bank, account customer, and president of account customer fraudulently conspired to cause confirming bank to rest on its legal rights while account customer obtained and served the writ of attachment; such a conspiracy, even if true, was manifestly for the purpose of protecting the parties from the loss of $95,904, not for the purpose of injuring confirming bank's business; any injury to confirming bank was a "secondary" or "consequential" result of the parties' attempt to protect themselves. Petra Int'l Banking Corp. v. First Am. Bank, 758 F. Supp. 1120 (E.D. Va. 1991), aff'd sub nom. Petra Int'l Banking Corp. v. Dameron Int'l, Inc., 953 F.2d 1383 (4th Cir. 1992).

No double recovery. — Because a company's claim asserting violation of Virginia's Uniform Trade Secret Act did not require the same proof as the civil conspiracy claim, the award of both punitive and treble damages in favor of the company did not constitute an impermissible double recovery. 21st Century Sys. v. Perot Sys. Gov't Servs., 284 Va. 32, 726 S.E.2d 236, 2012 Va. LEXIS 139 (2012).

Injury to personal reputation and employment interest not covered. — Any alleged conspiracy to injure a doctor's employment was not actionable under § 18.2-499 because injury to the doctor's personal reputation and interest in employment were clearly excluded from the scope of the statute's coverage. Baylor v. Comprehensive Pain Mgmt. Ctrs., 2011 U.S. Dist. LEXIS 37699 (W.D. Va. Apr. 6, 2011).

CIRCUIT COURT OPINIONS

Unspecified future business prospect insufficient to support claim. — Where a subcontractor's expectation that it would be allowed to bid on a project did not rise to a level of a reasonable expectation of further contractual relations, the subcontractor did not show that an engineer company and its employees were involved in a conspiracy or employed "improper means." Commercial Roofing & Sheet Metal Co. v. Gardner Eng'g, Inc., 60 Va. Cir. 384, 2002 Va. Cir. LEXIS 275 (Fairfax County 2002).

Right of action arises from conduct directed at business, not person. — Trial court dismissed a police officer's claim alleging that two homebuyers and a homeowner violated this section when they conspired to have him indicted because they were unhappy with work he did on their houses while operating a private construction business, and that he was fired from his job as a police officer after he was indicted, but overruled demurrers that the homebuyers and homeowner filed to the officer's claims seeking recovery for malicious prosecution, interference with a contract, breach of contract, and fraud. Fitzgerald v. Farrell, 63 Va. Cir. 1, 2003 Va. Cir. LEXIS 340 (Loudoun County 2003).

Plaintiff's claim was dismissed as plaintiff did not allege any injury to his business, relief was only proper when malicious conduct was directed at one's business, not one's person, and §§ 18.2-499 and 18.2-500 applied only to conspiracies resulting in business-related damages. Orantes v. Pollo Ranchero, Inc., 70 Va.

Cir. 277, 2006 Va. Cir. LEXIS 52 (Fairfax County 2006).

Police officer had no cause of action for unlawful conspiracy to injure the officer's reputation or employment as a police officer because § 18.2-499 applied to business and property interests, not to personal or employment interests. Hueston v. Kizer, 2008 Va. Cir. LEXIS 280 (Hanover County May 29, 2008).

Some claims of conspiracy subject to demurrer. — Claims of conspiracy to injure a trade, business or profession, with no explainable factual basis, were subject to demurrer with leave to amend as one did not file a claim, especially one as serious as this, with no explainable factual basis, intending to "flesh it out" during discovery. Mut. Funding, Inc. v. Collins, 62 Va. Cir. 34, 2003 Va. Cir. LEXIS 68 (Spotsylvania County 2003).

Where a non-solicitation clause was not limited in duration or geography and the clause's language, requiring a newly formed competing business, did not support a bill of complaint, and where there was no business conspiracy under § 18.2-499 or 18.2-500, or common-law conspiracy because the former employer did not show that a former employee acted with malice or that there was a concerted action to accomplish an unlawful purpose, the former employee's demurrers were sustained. Int'l Paper Co. v. Brooks, 63 Va. Cir. 494, 2003 Va. Cir. LEXIS 248 (Roanoke 2003).

The *Buschi* decision, which construes §§ 18.2-499 and 18.2-500 to limit recovery to damages to a plaintiff's business, profession, or trade, and not to allow damages to a plaintiff's reputation or employment interests, is persuasive. Young v. City of Norfolk, 62 Va. Cir. 307, 2003 Va. Cir. LEXIS 296 (Norfolk 2003).

Although an owners' association claimed that sellers were motivated by personal gain to enter into a conspiracy, there were no facts alleged to indicate that the individual and corporate defendants actually agreed to engage in unlawful conduct with the purpose of injuring the association, and no conspiracy could exist without an agreement. Carlton Bridge Owners Ass'n v. Keyser, 72 Va. Cir. 565, 2007 Va. Cir. LEXIS 163 (Charlottesville 2007).

Demurrer denied as to claim of business conspiracy. — Former employee's demurrer pursuant to § 8.01-273 A was denied as to a company's claim that the former employee was involved in a business conspiracy pursuant to §§ 18.2-499 and 18.2-500, because a company adequately alleged that the former employee and others conspired to injure the company by leaving the company en masse to work for a competitor, and to take the accounts for which they were responsible, and by taking and using documents that were alleged to be confidential trade secrets. Int'l Paper Co. v. Gilliam, 63 Va. Cir. 485, 2003 Va. Cir. LEXIS 249 (Roanoke 2003).

Demurrer denied. — Former employee's and competitors' demurrers to contractor's claim of civil conspiracy were not sustained as the contractor's complaint alleged the necessary elements of a civil conspiracy, and, while the contractor alleged that the former employee and competitors acted as agents of each other, it alternatively alleged that the employee and competitors acted individually, and, while one competitor was only alleged to be affiliated with another competitor, conspiracy was pled against him as acts by all the individual competitors satisfying the elements of civil conspiracy were alleged. H.E.R.C. Prods. v. Turlington, 62 Va. Cir. 489, 2003 Va. Cir. LEXIS 305 (Norfolk 2003).

Because a retailer pleaded: (1) a concerted action by a manufacturer and a former employee; and (2) the manufacturer's unequal application of a marketing and resale policy, the retailer's claims under the Virginia Business Conspiracy Act survived demurrer. Atl. Futon v. Tempur-Pedic, Inc., 67 Va. Cir. 269, 2005 Va. Cir. LEXIS 165 (Charlottesville Apr. 26, 2005).

Because a company raised facts that, if considered as true, provided an adequate legal basis for its claims of violation of the Virginia Uniform Trade Secrets Act, breach of contract, fraud, and conspiracy, the demurrer and plea in bar of a competitor and its successor were overruled. VMC Satellite, Inc. v. Stevens & Assocs., 68 Va. Cir. 103, 2005 Va. Cir. LEXIS 231 (Loudoun County May 19, 2005).

Defendants' demurrers were denied as to an engineer's claim of business conspiracy under § 18.2-499 et seq., because the engineer alleged that defendants intentionally conspired to harm him by imputing to him an unfitness to perform his job, a lack of integrity in the discharge of his job, and prejudiced him in his profession. Rohrbaugh v. Kreidler, 71 Va. Cir. 298, 2006 Va. Cir. LEXIS 245 (Arlington County 2006).

Claim alleging that defendants conspired with one another to injure a company in its reputation, trade, business and profession in violation of §§ 18.2-499 and 18.2-500 was sufficient under Va. Sup. Ct. R. 1:4(d) to survive a demurrer as the intracorporate immunity doctrine did not apply to a conspiracy claim against employees, officers or agents who combined to harm their corporation. Colgate v. Disthene Group, Inc., 2013 Va. Cir. LEXIS 9 (Buckingham County Feb. 4, 2013).

Violation found. — Plaintiff's former partners and their new company violated §§ 18.2-499 and 18.2-500 by pursuing the unlawful purpose of forcing plaintiff out of the former partnership without compensating him for his interest and by accomplishing this purpose by unlawful means, including purporting to withdraw from the partnership while actually seizing control of its assets, converting partnership assets and plaintiff's property, inducing former partnership employees to accept employment with them, and breaching their fiduciary duties. Greenfeld v. Stitely, 2007 Va. Cir. LEXIS 7 (Fairfax County Jan. 5, 2007).

Failure to show conspiracy. — Trial court dismissed a claim which a software company filed against a professional corporation and a doctor who owned the corporation, alleging that they conspired to steal information the company compiled while performing work under a contract for the corporation, because the company did not allege that the doctor acted outside the scope of her duties as an officer of the corporation. Softwise, Inc. v. Goodrich, 63 Va. Cir. 576, 2004 Va. Cir. LEXIS 6 (Roanoke 2004).

Because a provider failed to allege adequate facts to support its claim that a company and a competitor sought to willfully and maliciously injure its business with the company, the provider failed to state a claim for civil conspiracy or a violation of §§ 18.2-499 and 18.2-500. George K. Degnon Assocs. v. Acad. for Eating Disorders, — Va. Cir. —, 2005 Va. Cir. LEXIS 202 (Fairfax County Nov. 29, 2005).

No conspiracy to interfere with the trade, business, and profession of the buyers existed between a corporation, the sellers, and the sellers' limited liability company (LLC) when the sellers sold their stock in the corporation to the buyers. There was no evidence that the LLC conspired with anyone; the intra-corporate immunity doctrine defeated a claim of conspiracy between the corporation and the sellers, who were the principals of the corporation; and the purpose of the sellers' misconduct was to induce the buyers to purchase a business based on false and fraudulent representations regarding the nature of that business, not to injure them in the operation of that business. Arias v. Jokers Wild, 73 Va. Cir. 281, 2007 Va. Cir. LEXIS 82 (Fairfax County 2007).

Plaintiff had not pleaded facts sufficient to maintain a statutory conspiracy claim; to the extent plaintiff was pleading that defendants were alleged to have conspired after the employee was employed by each entity, the intra-corporate immunity doctrine applied and a conspiracy claim could not be maintained. TradeStaff & Co. v. Nogiec, 77 Va. Cir. 77, 2008 Va. Cir. LEXIS 226 (Chesapeake 2008).

Single entity cannot conspire with itself. — Disbarred attorney could not sustain his claims that a state bar association's disciplinary board and its prosecutor caused injury when they conspired against him, either during the course of or as the result of disciplinary hearings, where the board members and the prosecutor were all part of one entity. Leach v. Va. State Bar, 73 Va. Cir. 362, 2007 Va. Cir. LEXIS 221 (Richmond June 8, 2007).

Evidence sufficient to show conspiracy. — Former employee and a retailer were held liable for violating § 18.2-499 et seq., with regard to enticing the former employee from his employ with a clothier, with the former employee purposefully taking the clothier's clientele list and the retailer having full knowledge of the same and, in fact, encouraging it. The restrictive covenant in the clothier's handbook prohibiting employment with a competitor within one mile for a period of three years was not overly harsh or oppressive and, therefore, in addition to compensatory damages in the amount of $548,611, trebled to $1,654,833, the trial court enjoined the former employee from working for the retailer for a period of three years from the date of the trial court's opinion. James, Ltd. v. Saks Fifth Ave., Inc., 67 Va. Cir. 126, 2005 Va. Cir. LEXIS 150 (Arlington County Mar. 8, 2005), rev'd in part as to treble damages, 630 S.E.2d 404, 2006 Va. LEXIS 54 (Va. 2006).

As to unenforceability of contract due to lack of valid compensation term in a business conspiracy claim, see Boy Blue,

Inc. v. Brown, 74 Va. Cir. 4, 2007 Va. Cir. LEXIS 165 (Essex County 2007).

Claim time-barred. — Plaintiff's conspiracy claim was time-barred as: (1) plaintiff asserted a claim for trebled money damages, so he did not seek purely equitable remedies; (2) a claim for conspiracy under §§ 18.2-499 and 18.2-500 was a legal cause of action, whether the claim was brought on the law or chancery side; (3) the basis of the claim was fraud and fraud was a wrongful act aimed at the person; (4) as fraud invariably acted upon the person of the victim, its consequence was personal damage; and (5) the conspiracy claim was therefore time-barred whether subsection A of § 8.01-243, which applied to fraud claims, or § 8.01-248, which applied to personal actions for which no other limitation was specified, applied. Orantes v. Pollo Ranchero, Inc., 70 Va. Cir. 277, 2006 Va. Cir. LEXIS 52 (Fairfax County 2006).

Proper pleading. — Defendants' argument that a § 8.01-499 claim should be dismissed was rejected as plaintiff alleged that defendant individuals conspired with each other, not with defendant corporation; under § 8.01-499, all that is required is two or more persons combining to injure a plaintiff's reputation, trade, business, or profession. Orantes v. Pollo Ranchero, Inc., 70 Va. Cir. 277, 2006 Va. Cir. LEXIS 52 (Fairfax County 2006).

Messages on internet message board. — Messages posted on an internet message board did not support the company's claim that the customers conspired to willfully and intentionally injure the company in reputation, trade, or business as they were non-defamatory or matters of opinion — both protected by First Amendment. Xtreme 4x4 Ctr., Inc. v. Howery, 65 Va. Cir. 469, 2004 Va. Cir. LEXIS 229 (Roanoke 2004).

Cause of action stated. — Lessee's conspiracy claim against the building owners and a contractor survived demurrer where the lessee alleged that the building owners conspired with the owners of the upper story condominiums with the intent to bar the lessee from providing live entertainment vital to its restaurants profits, violated an enforceable contract and their breach of fiduciary duties in order to achieve the end goal, and the plan culminated in a directive prohibiting the lessee from providing live entertainment, thereby damaging its profits. Station # 2, LLC v. Lynch, 75 Va. Cir. 179, 2008 Va. Cir. LEXIS 51 (Norfolk 2008).

Property owners alleged defendants wrote to government agents falsely accusing the owners of diverting a stream flow and removing wetlands. The owners' complaint sufficiently alleged legal malice — that defendants acted intentionally, purposely, and without lawful justification — to state claims of statutory conspiracy under §§ 18.2-499 and 18.2-500. Mathre v. Schweichert, — Va. Cir. —, 2007 Va. Cir. LEXIS 310 (Nelson County Aug. 9, 2007).

Development company and associate's demurrer to the restaurant operator's claim against them for conspiracy to injure a business, pursuant to §§ 18.2-499 and 18.2-500, had to be denied as the restaurant operator stated a claim under both sections. The restaurant operator alleged that: (1) they combined with others to willfully and maliciously injure the restaurant operator by preventing the restaurant operator from presenting live entertainment at its restaurant; and (2) as a result, the restaurant operator lost profits vital to the operation of the restaurant. Station # 2, LLC v. Lynch, 75 Va. Cir. 179, 2008 Va. Cir. LEXIS 52 (Norfolk 2008).

Pleadings stated claims for common-law and statutory conspiracy where an employer alleged that former employees willfully and maliciously combined together to help a competitor acquire premier partner status so that it could compete with the employer's business. Innovative Sys. & Solutions, Inc. v. Hannah, 75 Va. Cir. 363, 2008 Va. Cir. LEXIS 270 (Norfolk July 31, 2008).

In a case in which: (1) a fencing school alleged that a former employee was an officer or director of a competitor; (2) the competitor and the other defendants knew of the employee's contractual obligations to the school; (3) the competitor and the other individual defendants encouraged the employee to breach a non-competition agreement, both while he was employed and after his employment was terminated; (4) the competitor and the other individual defendants directly or indirectly provided him facilities to coach the school's students in violation of his agreement; and (5) the employee, competitor, and the individual defendants advised students to break their agreements with the school and seek instruction from the employee or the competitor, the school sufficiently stated a claim for statutory conspiracy under § 18.2-499. Va. Academy of

Fencing, Inc. v. Sintchinov, 2009 Va. Cir. LEXIS 81 (Fairfax Aug. 27, 2009).

Cause of action not stated. — Stock assignee's claim that defendants conspired to take control of a corporation did not sufficiently allege that they conspired "for the purpose of" injuring the assignee's predecessors; the complaint alleged damage to the corporation, which could only be remedied by a derivative suit. Lexcadia Capital, L.L.C. v. Next Generation Fund, L.L.C., 71 Va. Cir. 83, 2006 Va. Cir. LEXIS 104 (Fairfax County 2006).

Defendants' demurrers were granted as to a company's claim for statutory business conspiracy under §§ 18.2-499 and 18.2-500, because the company failed to allege how defendants conspired with a sublandlord to terminate a sublease, and the company failed to allege a criminal or unlawful purpose or means on the part of defendants. R & D 2001, L.L.C. v. Collins, — Va. Cir. —, 2006 Va. Cir. LEXIS 131 (Fairfax County July 12, 2006).

Counterclaim contending that a real estate agent and an administrative assistant conspired to oust defendant from a partnership alleged they took "overt steps" in furtherance of the conspiracy, but failed to specify what those steps were, and thus did not state a claim of statutory conspiracy in violation of §§ 18.2-499 and 18.2-500. Poco Loco, LLC v. Barnes, 72 Va. Cir. 165, 2006 Va. Cir. LEXIS 202 (Fairfax County 2006).

No facts were alleged by purchasers to indicate that sellers actually agreed to engage in fraudulent conduct with the purpose of injuring the purchasers. While it was true that due to the nature of conspiracy, all details may not have been known at the time of pleading, in order to survive a demurrer, a plaintiff needed to at least plead the requisite concert of action and unity of purpose in more than mere conclusory language, and no conspiracy existed without an agreement. Kayes v. Keyser, 72 Va. Cir. 549, 2007 Va. Cir. LEXIS 160 (Charlottesville 2007).

Former employer failed to sufficiently plead statutory business conspiracy in violation of §§ 18.2-499 and 18.2-500 where an underlying employment agreement was rendered invalid by a blue-pencil provision and by overbroad noncompetition and confidentiality provisions and where the employer failed to allege malice. BB&T Ins. Servs. v. Thomas Rutherfoord, Inc., 80 Va. Cir. 174, 2010 Va. Cir. LEXIS 25 (Richmond Feb. 9, 2010).

Economic loss doctrine applied to the statutory conspiracy claim, as any misstatement of facts alleged to the claim were merely contractual issues. Foster v. Wintergreen Real Estate Co., 81 Va. Cir. 353, 2010 Va. Cir. LEXIS 252 (Nelson County Nov. 16, 2010).

Demurrer dismissing a statutory conspiracy claim against a real estate company and individual brokers was not reconsidered on the theory that § 18.2-216 false advertisement claims showed statutory conspiracy because (1) the claims only alleged false advertising, and (2) the company and the individual defendants were one entity. Foster v. Wintergreen Real Estate Co., 84 Va. Cir. 5, 2011 Va. Cir. LEXIS 209 (Nelson County Oct. 27, 2011).

Demurrer dismissing a statutory conspiracy claim against a real estate company and individual brokers was not reconsidered on the theory that alleged breaches of statutory and fiduciary duties constituted statutory conspiracy because statutes and regulations allegedly violated were part of each client's contract. Foster v. Wintergreen Real Estate Co., 84 Va. Cir. 5, 2011 Va. Cir. LEXIS 209 (Nelson County Oct. 27, 2011).

Demurrer dismissing a statutory conspiracy claim was not reconsidered on the theory that an alleged tortious interference with contract fell under the conspiracy statutes because a defendant company and individual defendants were one entity, under the intracorporate immunity doctrine. Foster v. Wintergreen Real Estate Co., 84 Va. Cir. 5, 2011 Va. Cir. LEXIS 209 (Nelson County Oct. 27, 2011). Plaintiff's action for statutory conspiracy, brought against her former partner and paramour failed because the statutory business requirement was not satisfied; plaintiff complained about matters involving a deed, deed of trust, and a payment agreement, all of which involved a real estate, not a business transaction. In re Whalen, 2011 Va. Cir. LEXIS 277 (Nelson County Nov. 16, 2011).

Attorney's fees. — Where plaintiffs prevailed on defendant's counterclaim alleging conspiracy under § 18.2-499, they were not entitled to attorneys' fees under § 18.2-500, as § 18.2-500 limited recovery of such fees to the victims of conspiracies to injure them in their trade or business, and plaintiffs were accused of participating in such a conspiracy. Bhagat v. Diamond Info. Sys., L.L.C., 83 Va. Cir. 233, 2012 Va. Cir. LEXIS 79 (Loudoun County Jan. 23, 2012).

§ 18.2-500. Same; civil relief; damages and counsel fees; injunctions.

A. Any person who shall be injured in his reputation, trade, business or profession by reason of a violation of § 18.2-499, may sue therefor and recover three-fold the damages by him sustained, and the costs of suit, including a reasonable fee to plaintiff's counsel, and without limiting the generality of the term, "damages" shall include loss of profits.

B. Whenever a person shall duly file a civil action in the circuit court of any county or city against any person alleging violations of the provisions of § 18.2-499 and praying that such party defendant be restrained and enjoined from continuing the acts complained of, such court shall have jurisdiction to hear and determine the issues involved, to issue injunctions pendente lite and permanent injunctions and to decree damages and costs of suit, including reasonable counsel fees to complainants' and defendants' counsel.

History.
Code 1950, § 18.1-74.1:2; 1964, c. 623; 1975, cc. 14, 15; 2003, c. 578; 2005, c. 681.

Law Review.
For article on injuries to business under the Virginia Conspiracy Act, see 38 Wash. & Lee L. Rev. 377 (1981). For article on the Virginia Conspiracy Statute, see 38 Wash. & Lee L. Rev. 1147 (1981). For a review of antitrust and trade regulation law in Virginia for year 1999, see 33 U. Rich. L. Rev. 769 (1999). For 2003/2004 survey of civil practice and procedure, see 39 U. Rich. L. Rev. 87 (2004).

CASE NOTES

The focus of § 18.2-499 and this section is upon conspiracies resulting in business-related damages. Ward v. Connor, 495 F. Supp. 434 (E.D. Va. 1980), rev'd on other grounds, 657 F.2d 45 (4th Cir. 1981), cert. denied, 455 U.S. 907, 102 S. Ct. 1253, 71 L. Ed. 2d 445 (1982).

Section 18.2-499 not applicable to injury to one's employment interests. — Where former postmaster alleged that co-workers conspired to injure him in his reputation, trade, business and profession and as a result he was demoted, the claim was dismissed for failure to state a claim for relief because § 18.2-499 addresses only injuries to one's business, not injuries to one's employment interests. Jordan v. Hudson, 690 F. Supp. 502 (E.D. Va. 1988), aff'd, 879 F.2d 98 (4th Cir. 1989).

In a former employee's suit against his former employer, alleging a civil conspiracy to divest him of his stock ownership in the employer and to injure his professional reputation and business by terminating him, in violation of §§ 18.2-499 and 18.2-500, the employee failed to state a claim because his professional reputation and stock ownership in the company were employment interests, and not business interests, which were not covered by these laws. Inman v. Klockner-Pentaplast of Am., Inc., 467 F. Supp. 2d 642, 2006 U.S. Dist. LEXIS 93620 (W.D. Va. 2006).

Physician's claimed injuries (the termination of the physician's employment with an anesthesiology group and a hospital and the potential difficulty the physician faced in obtaining future employment with another hospital or anesthesiology group) did not fall within the scope of §§ 18.2-499 and 18.2-500. Mansfield v. Anesthesia Assocs., — F. Supp. 2d —, 2008 U.S. Dist. LEXIS 34732 (E.D. Va. Apr. 28, 2008).

Federal preemption. — Because copyright and the infringement thereof is an area controlled exclusively by the federal government, any state causes of action under § 18.2-499 and this section must be preempted in this area. Hoey v. Dexel Sys. Corp., 716 F. Supp. 222 (E.D. Va. 1989).

This section and 18 U.S.C.S. § 1961 et seq., compared. — The elements and purposes of Virginia business conspiracy statute, this section, and RICO, 18 U.S.C.S. § 1961 et seq., diverge. Where the Virginia act required a combination of two or more persons for the purpose of willfully and maliciously injuring plaintiff in his business, a RICO § 1962(c) cause of action is made out by proof of: (1) conduct (2) of an enterprise (3) through a pattern (4) of racketeering activity. Thus, the Virginia business conspiracy act is not an appropriate state statute from which to borrow a statute of limitations for RICO. HMK Corp. v. Walsey, 637 F. Supp. 710 (E.D. Va. 1986), aff'd, 828 F.2d 1071 (4th Cir. 1987), cert. denied, 484 U.S. 1009, 108 S. Ct. 706, 98 L. Ed. 2d 657 (1988).

Exclusive distributorship arrangements do not violate the antitrust laws unless they foreclose competition in the relevant market. Thompson Everett, Inc. v. National Cable Adv., 850 F. Supp. 470 (E.D. Va. 1994), aff'd, 57 F.3d 1317 (4th Cir. 1995).

This statutory action provides a remedy for wrongful conduct directed to the business. An injury to one's business is clearly an injury to one's property interest. Federated Graphics Cos. v. Napotnik, 424 F. Supp. 291 (E.D. Va. 1976); Picture Lake Campground, Inc. v. Holiday Inns, Inc., 497 F. Supp. 858 (E.D. Va. 1980).

The elements of a statutory conspiracy claim under the Virginia Conspiracy Act are: (1) concerted action; (2) legal malice; and (3) causally-related injury. Virginia Vermiculite, Ltd. v. W.R. Grace & Co.-Conn., 144 F. Supp. 2d 558, 2001 U.S. Dist. LEXIS 7006 (W.D. Va. 2001), aff'd sub nom. Va. Vermiculite Ltd. v. Historic Green Springs, Inc., 307 F.3d 277 (4th Cir. 2002).

Elements of a statutory civil conspiracy claim require a plaintiff to allege that two or more persons combined, associated, agreed, or mutually undertook together to willfully and maliciously injure the plaintiff in his reputation, trade, business, or profession; a district court erred when it dismissed a real estate broker's statutory conspiracy claim pursuant to Fed. R. Civ. P. 12(b)(6) because the broker had sufficiently alleged: (1) that a limited liability company and its agents had conspired and acted together to complete the sale of a farm without paying the broker a commission for the work that it had performed in connection with the sale; (2) that the conduct of the company and its agents was intentional, purposeful, and without lawful justification; and (3) that the conduct resulted in substantial monetary damages to the broker. T.G. Slater & Son v. Donald P. & Patricia A. Brennan LLC, 385 F.3d 836, 2004 U.S. App. LEXIS 20572 (4th Cir. 2004).

Elements of offense. — To recover in an action for conspiracy to harm a business, the plaintiff must prove: (1) a combination of two or more persons for the purpose of willfully and maliciously injuring plaintiff in his business; and (2) resulting damage to plaintiff. Allen Realty Corp. v. Holbert, 227 Va. 441, 318 S.E.2d 592 (1984); Meadow Ltd. Partnership v. Heritage Sav. & Loan Ass'n, 639 F. Supp. 643 (E.D. Va. 1986).

In order to prove a conspiracy under the Virginia Conspiracy Act, at least two people had to have combined intentionally for the nefarious purpose of harming the victim's business, but unfortunately for debtor, it did not make it over this initial hurdle. The only remaining defendant could not conspire alone. Wellington Apt., LLC v. Clotworthy (In re Wellington Apt., LLC), 2006 Bankr. LEXIS 1954 (Bankr. E.D. Va. July 27, 2006).

Company failed to present any evidence either of a conspiracy between the corporation and the non-minority owned company or legal malice on behalf of either; therefore, any injury the company might have suffered was not actionable under the Virginia Business Conspiracy Act, §§ 18.2-499 and 18.2-500. DAG Petroleum Suppliers, L.L.C. v. BP P.L.C., — F.3d —, 2008 U.S. App. LEXIS 1293 (4th Cir. Jan. 23, 2008).

Proof of malice required. — The element of legal malice requires the plaintiff to prove that the concerted action was undertaken by one conspirator to injure the plaintiff intentionally, purposefully and without lawful justification, but the statute does not require that the the co-conspirator act with legal malice; rather, the statute simply requires that one party, acting with legal malice, conspire with another party to injure the plaintiff. Virginia Vermiculite, Ltd. v. W.R. Grace & Co.-Conn., 144 F. Supp. 2d 558, 2001 U.S. Dist. LEXIS 7006 (W.D. Va. 2001), aff'd sub nom. Va. Vermiculite Ltd. v. Historic Green Springs, Inc., 307 F.3d 277 (4th Cir. 2002).

To prove malice, plaintiffs must show that defendants acted intentionally, purposefully, and without legal justification; significantly, the statute does not require a plaintiff to prove that a conspirator's primary and overriding purpose is to injure another in his trade or business. Atlas Partners II v. Brumberg, Mackey & Wall, PLC, — F. Supp. 2d —, 2006 U.S. Dist. LEXIS 983 (W.D. Va. Jan. 6, 2006).

Legal malice element of cause of action not found. — Defendant former employee did not engage in a conspiratorial act of legal malice in violation of § 18.2-499 by accepting future employment with an employment broker while the employee was still employed by plaintiff former employer, another employment firm that had arranged for the employee, pursuant to a contract with the employment broker, to perform temporary services for a certain manufacturer, even though the employee expected to be placed by the employment broker for an extended period with the same manufacturer, as the employee was an at-will employee, neither the employee nor the employment broker violated any contract by their conduct, and the employee did not rob the former employer of any objective or tangible business opportunity or expectancy; therefore, there was no basis for the jury's verdict in the former employer's favor on its claim against the former employee for civil liability under § 18.2-500 for allegedly violating § 18.2-499. Williams v. Dominion Tech. Partners, L.L.C., 265 Va. 280, 576 S.E.2d 752, 2003 Va. LEXIS 29 (2003).

Since plaintiffs provided no evidence of an agreement or an intent to injure, both of which were required to establish a business conspiracy under §§ 18.2-499 and 18.2-500, a reasonable jury could not conclude that the company and the third party were criminally and civilly liable under the theory of business conspiracy; therefore, summary judgment was granted against the claim. DAG Petroleum Suppliers L.L.C. v. BP P.L.C., 452 F. Supp. 2d 641, 2006 U.S. Dist. LEXIS 67438 (E.D. Va. 2006).

"Without lawful justification" means that the defendants contrived to accomplish some criminal or unlawful purpose, or to accomplish some purpose, not in itself criminal or unlawful, by criminal or unlawful means; the statute thus requires that the plaintiff prove that at least one of the co-conspirators acted either with an unlawful purpose or by unlawful means. Virginia Vermiculite, Ltd. v. W.R. Grace & Co.-Conn., 144 F. Supp. 2d 558, 2001 U.S. Dist. LEXIS 7006 (W.D. Va. 2001), aff'd sub nom. Va. Vermiculite Ltd. v. Historic Green Springs, Inc., 307 F.3d 277 (4th Cir. 2002).

Proof of injury required. — Under the Virginia Conspiracy Act, the plaintiff must show that the defendants' concerted action caused it injury in order to be entitled either to damages or to injunctive relief. Virginia Vermiculite, Ltd. v. W.R. Grace & Co.-Conn., 144 F. Supp. 2d 558, 2001 U.S. Dist. LEXIS 7006 (W.D. Va. 2001), aff'd sub nom. Va. Vermiculite Ltd. v. Historic Green Springs, Inc., 307 F.3d 277 (4th Cir. 2002).

To the extent a plaintiff attempts to base his conspiracy claim on injury to his personal reputation or employment, as opposed to business interests, he fails to state a claim under this section and § 18.2-499. Warner v. Buck Creek Nursery, Inc., 149 F. Supp. 2d 246, 2001 U.S. Dist. LEXIS 7025 (W.D. Va. 2001).

In a diversity action that alleged a violation of Virginia's business conspiracy statute, § 18.2-500, which permits a suit for civil relief based on a violation of § 18.2-499, the appellate court held dismissal pursuant to Fed. R. Civ. P. 12(b)(6) was warranted, where the complaint did not allege a violation of § 18.2-499 and Michigan law applied to the suit anyway. Beydoun v. Clark Constr. Int'l, LLC, — F.3d —, 2003 U.S. App. LEXIS 14838 (4th Cir. July 25, 2003).

Because the jury instructions required the jury to find proof of injury and proof that the injured party suffered damages as a predicate to a verdict on a business conspiracy claim, the jury's finding of such a conspiracy without damages in each instance was contrary to the jury instructions; hence, under *Rome v. Kelly Springfield Tire Co.*, 217 Va. 943, 948, 234 S.E. 2d 277, 281 (1977), the verdicts were invalid as a matter of law. Ulloa v. QSP, Inc., 271 Va. 72, 624 S.E.2d 43, 2006 Va. LEXIS 21 (2006).

In an action for damages by an information technology company and its sole owner against a former partner, his wife, and their new corporation, the trial court erred in conducting a retrial on damages

on a civil conspiracy claim under § 18.2-500 because the jury's verdict form awarding zero dollars clearly indicated that no injury was sustained. In addition, because an award of attorney's fees and costs was made pursuant to § 18.2-500, that award was also erroneous. Syed v. Zh Techs., Inc., 280 Va. 58, 694 S.E.2d 625, 2010 Va. LEXIS 73 (2010).

Proof of unlawful act required. — In a brand owner's suit against a distributor alleging that the manufacturer secretly entered into a manufacturing agreement with the competing distributor and that the distributor told customers that the brand owner was going out of business, the conspiracy claim was dismissed because the brand owner failed to aver an unlawful act or an attempt by the distributor to interfere with the agreement between the brand owner and manufacturer. Bay Tobacco, LLC v. Bell Quality Tobacco Prods., LLC, 261 F. Supp. 2d 483, 2003 U.S. Dist. LEXIS 12709 (E.D. Va. 2003).

Breach of contract not "unlawful act." — Conspiracy merely to breach a contract that does not involve an independent duty arising outside the contract is insufficient to establish a civil claim under § 18.2-500. Station # 2, LLC v. Lynch, 280 Va. 166, 695 S.E.2d 537, 2010 Va. LEXIS 64 (2010).

No proximate cause between defendants' actions and former employer's lost profits. — Despite the testimony of an expert witness, who was a forensic accountant, as to a former employer's loss of profits from the alleged wrongful conduct of defendants, its former salesman and his new store, defendants' motion to strike, which tested sufficiency of the evidence, should have been granted. The expert used a "but-for" damages calculation, which presumed an injury to the former employer from the mere fact that the salesman, who had been an at-will employee, had stopped working at the former employer's store and had begun working at the new store; the expert did not demonstrate that defendants' wrongful conduct, including a breach of fiduciary duties and a violation of §§ 18.2-499 and 18.2-500, had proximately caused any injury to the former employer. Saks Fifth Ave., Inc. v. James, Ltd., 272 Va. 177, 630 S.E.2d 304, 2006 Va. LEXIS 54 (2006).

Calculation of damages, and lost profits in particular, was speculative as it assumed future business from customers who had no duty to shop at the former employer's store; the expert also did not show that the conduct of the salesman or his new store had proximately caused any of the loss of the former employer's customers, and the expert's damages calculation, which was based on a "but-for" analysis, had focused solely on the fact that the salesman had stopped working for the former employer and did not focus on any wrongful conduct by defendants. Saks Fifth Ave., Inc. v. James, Ltd., 272 Va. 177, 630 S.E.2d 304, 2006 Va. LEXIS 54 (2006).

Loss of goodwill. — Because a company introduced no evidence demonstrating a diminution in value of either its fair market value or identifiable assets during the relevant time period, nor did it demonstrate that its sale price to another company was affected by the employees' actions, it introduced no evidence demonstrating a diminution in value of its goodwill; thus, the evidence was insufficient to support an award of lost goodwill damages because of the conspiracy. 21st Century Sys. v. Perot Sys. Gov't Servs., 284 Va. 32, 726 S.E.2d 236, 2012 Va. LEXIS 139 (2012).

Personal-stake exception to intracorporate immunity. — The doctrine of intracorporate immunity is excepted when an agent of the corporation has an independent personal stake in achieving the corporation's impermissible objectives; such personal stake must be wholly separable from the more general and indirect corporate benefit. Hence, on defendant's motion to dismiss, plaintiffs pleaded sufficient facts to satisfy the personal stake exception, namely, that the agents of insurer, as competing physicians, had a direct interest in the market for healthcare services which was distinct and independent from their roles as agents of insurer. American Chiropractic Ass'n v. Trigon Healthcare, Inc., 151 F. Supp. 2d 723, 2001 U.S. Dist. LEXIS 10348 (W.D. Va. 2001).

Standard of proof. — Proof of civil conspiracy must be shown by clear and convincing evidence. Multi-Channel TV Cable Co. v. Charlottesville Quality Cable Operating Co., 108 F.3d 522 (4th Cir. 1997).

Conspiracy between corporation and its agents as legal impossibility. — Although plaintiff's allegations were initially sufficient to satisfy the threshold demands of Virginia's civil conspiracy statute, they were not sufficient to overcome the obstacle provided by the intracorporate immunity doctrine, which holds that because at least two persons must be present to form a conspiracy, a corporation cannot conspire with itself; therefore, a conspiracy between a corporation and the agents of that corporation who are acting in the scope of their employment is a legal impossibility. Selman v. American Sports Underwriters, Inc., 697 F. Supp. 225 (W.D. Va. 1988).

Applicable limitation. — An action brought under this section and § 18.2-499 survives, and hence, was subject to the five-year limitation in former § 8-24. Federated Graphics Cos. v. Napotnik, 424 F. Supp. 291 (E.D. Va. 1976).

Malicious prosecution distinguished. — Malicious prosecution involves wrongful conduct directed at a person which may indirectly damage property. The statutory action under this section and § 18.2-499, on the other hand, focuses upon conduct directed at property, i.e., one's business. Accordingly, the nature of the two actions differs. Federated Graphics Cos. v. Napotnik, 424 F. Supp. 291 (E.D. Va. 1976).

If a competitor is in fact about to cease marketing a competing product, it is not unlawful to state that fact truthfully to customers. Hechler Chevrolet, Inc. v. GMC, 230 Va. 396, 337 S.E.2d 744 (1985).

Right of action arises from conduct directed at business, not person. — A right of action is afforded under § 18.2-499 and this section only when malicious conduct is directed at one's business, not one's person, and the statutes focus upon conduct directed at property, i.e., one's business and apply only to conspiracies resulting in business-related damages. Buschi v. Kirven, 775 F.2d 1240 (4th Cir. 1985).

Employee failed to allege how the alleged conspiracy hurt her in her business, instead, she alleged in conclusory terms that defendants harmed her reputation, harmed her in her profession, and in her ability to find comparable trade or business work; as such, her civil conspiracy claim failed. Bowers v. Rector, — F. Supp. 2d —, 2006 U.S. Dist. LEXIS 78114 (W.D. Va. Oct. 24, 2006).

Plaintiff's employment reputation is an employment interest and employment interests are not covered by § 18.2-500. Bowers v. Rector, — F. Supp. 2d —, 2006 U.S. Dist. LEXIS 78114 (W.D. Va. Oct. 24, 2006).

Former employee was unable to state a civil conspiracy claim under §§ 18.2-499 and 18.2-500 because these statutes afforded a right of action only when the malicious conduct was directed at a business, and the employee's claims exclusively concerned her employment prospects. Conyers v. Va. Hous. Dev. Auth., 2012 U.S. Dist. LEXIS 134908 (E.D. Va. Sept. 19, 2012).

Right of action accrues when any damage, however slight, is sustained. Eshbaugh v. Amoco Oil Co., 234 Va. 74, 360 S.E.2d 350 (1987).

Term "damages" in subsection B refers to "three-fold" recovery Advanced Marine Enters., Inc. v. PRC, Inc., 256 Va. 106, 501 S.E.2d 148 (1998).

Chancery court is permitted to award treble damages on law claim under the provisions of this section. Rather than limiting the relief available in chancery, subsection B grants complainant the additional right to seek and obtain injunctive relief, as well as damages and costs of suit. Advanced Marine Enters., Inc. v. PRC, Inc., 256 Va. 106, 501 S.E.2d 148 (1998).

Treble damage award nondischargeable in bankruptcy. — Treble damages awarded by a state court in favor of a limited liability company and its remaining members against a debtor, who was also a member, by a state court pursuant to § 18.2-500 were nondischargeable under 11 U.S.C.S. § 523(a)(4) to the extent the treble damage award was based on damages for knowing embezzlement and knowing and wrongful theft, but not to the extent the treble damages were based on other portions of the damage award that the court found dischargeable. Credit Experts, LLC v. Santos (In re Santos), 2012 Bankr. LEXIS 3076 (Bankr. E.D. Va. July 2, 2012).

Conspiracy action accrued to warehouse operator when freight forwarder demanded lower rates and staffing changes, not later when operators abandoned their contract. Detrick v. Panalpina, Inc., 108 F.3d 529 (4th Cir.), cert. denied, 522 U.S. 810, 118 S. Ct. 52, 139 L. Ed. 2d 17 (1997).

Right to performance of contract and right to reap profits therefrom are property rights which are entitled to protection

in the courts. Consequently, suits for procuring breach of contract proceed on this basis. Chaves v. Johnson, 230 Va. 112, 335 S.E.2d 97 (1985).

It is not unlawful to entice employee of competitor to leave his employment provided no wrongful means are used, and the employment is terminable at will. Hechler Chevrolet, Inc. v. GMC, 230 Va. 396, 337 S.E.2d 744 (1985).

Relationship terminable at-will. — In a suit stemming from the termination of a 20-year relationship for the sale and distribution of certain delicatessen products, which was based on an oral agreement, which was terminable by either party at-will, the buyers' counterclaim against the sellers for business conspiracy in violation of § 18.2-499 failed as a matter of law due to the fact that the parties had the right to terminate their at-will relationship. Frank Brunckhorst Co., L.L.C. v. Coastal Atl., Inc., 542 F. Supp. 2d 452, 2008 U.S. Dist. LEXIS 6748 (E.D. Va. 2008).

Employment not within scope of section. — This section is aimed at conduct which injures a "business" and the statute is to be construed to exclude employment from its scope. Buschi v. Kirven, 775 F.2d 1240 (4th Cir. 1985).

Where claims were brought for malicious prosecution and statutory conspiracy, under §§ 18.2-499 and 18.2-500, alleging conspiracy to injure reputation, trade, business, and profession, the trial court properly granted summary judgment to defendants on the statutory conspiracy claims, as §§ 18.2-499 and 18.2-500 applied to business and property interests, not to personal or employment interests. Andrews v. Ring, 266 Va. 311, 585 S.E.2d 780, 2003 Va. LEXIS 86 (2003).

Persons acting within scope of employment as agents of city do not constitute conspiracy. — If defendants, who were charged with having conspired to injure producer and promoter of shows and concerts in his trade, business, or occupation in violation of § 18.2-499 and this section, were acting within the scope of their employment and, therefore, were agents of the city, then only one entity exists — the city. By definition, a single entity cannot conspire with itself. Fox v. Deese, 234 Va. 412, 362 S.E.2d 699 (1987).

Parent corporation and its wholly-owned subsidiary are equally incapable of conspiring under this statute or the federal Sherman Act. Ray Dobbins Lincoln-Mercury, Inc. v. Ford Motor Co., 604 F. Supp. 203 (W.D. Va. 1984), aff'd, 813 F.2d 402 (4th Cir. 1985).

Investigative-administrative arms of state not inhibited. — Section 18.2-499 and this section do not create a protected interest against investigative-administrative arms of the state, as officials of a public body who act within the scope of their employment are not considered to be conspiring together for the purposes of this statute. Becker v. Russek, 518 F. Supp. 1040 (W.D. Va. 1981), aff'd, 679 F.2d 876 (4th Cir. 1982).

Dismissal of state conspiracy law claims against judge and clerk required. — Judge and deputy clerk were immune from damage claims with regards to their actions in revoking bondsman's certificate, and that immunity required dismissal of the state conspiracy law claim that they conspired to injure the bondsman in her trade or business against them. Battle v. Whitehurst, 831 F. Supp. 522 (E.D. Va. 1993), aff'd, 36 F.3d 1091 (4th Cir. 1994).

Expert testimony not always necessary to support fees and costs award. — While expert testimony ordinarily is necessary to assist determination of the attorney's fees and expenses award in action under this section, such testimony is not required in every case. Thus, where plaintiff submitted to the trial court almost 300 pages of contemporaneous time records detailing the activities for which fees were sought and also submitted affidavits of its attorneys upon the reasonableness of the hourly rates charged and the accuracy of the time billed while defendant presented nothing to contradict the affidavits, trial court's award of $472,000 was amply supported by the evidence. Tazewell Oil Co. v. United Va. Bank/Crestar Bank, 243 Va. 94, 413 S.E.2d 611 (1992).

Costs. — With the exception of reasonable attorney's fees, this section makes no provision for award of costs other than those ordinarily awarded under the general statutes of Title 14.1 (now repealed) addressing the taxing of costs. Advanced Marine Enters., Inc. v. PRC, Inc., 256 Va. 106, 501 S.E.2d 148 (1998).

Costs not recoverable. — While a prevailing party in a suit involving libelous statements about his pet care business was entitled to a fee award, he was not entitled to costs for travel and lodging because such costs were like those that the Virginia Supreme Court had not permitted in similar cases. Ebersole v. Kline-Perry, 2012 U.S. Dist. LEXIS 138659 (E.D. Va. Sept. 26, 2012).

Publication of interview in magazine no offense. — Allegations that defendant journalists and magazine conspired to obtain and publish an interview with plaintiff minister and that plaintiff's fund raising activities were adversely affected as a result of the publication, failed to state a claim upon which relief could be granted under § 18.2-499 and this section, since there was no basis for the general allegation that any of the defendants conspired for the specific purpose of injuring the plaintiff. Falwell v. Penthouse Int'l, Ltd., 521 F. Supp. 1204 (W.D. Va. 1981).

Reasonable attorneys' fees. — Prevailing party in a suit involving libelous statements about his pet care business was entitled to a fee award of $75,833 because the amount was reasonable based on the time spent on the litigation, after reductions for the hourly rate and for time spent on certain matters, such as the fee application, jury instructions, proposed stipulations, and block billing for a motion to quash. Ebersole v. Kline-Perry, 2012 U.S. Dist. LEXIS 138659 (E.D. Va. Sept. 26, 2012).

Evidence sufficient to show conspiracy. — Defendants' and a "partner's" actions constituted a prima facie case of business conspiracy; such examples were defendants' and the partner's structure of plaintiff company's settlement agreement, the purchase of a jet against plaintiffs' directions, the purchase of the eight acre parcel next to a store although the price was too high and the site was not suitable, and a stock subscription agreement that negatively impacted plaintiffs. These actions were all evidence that defendants and the partner worked together to damage plaintiffs and that damaging plaintiffs might not have been their primary purpose was immaterial under Virginia law. Atlas Partners II v. Brumberg, Mackey & Wall, PLC, — F. Supp. 2d —, 2006 U.S. Dist. LEXIS 983 (W.D. Va. Jan. 6, 2006).

Plaintiff's allegations that defendant individuals, prior to forming defendant corporation, and while still employed by plaintiff, conspired to misappropriate and copy plaintiff's trade secrets and proprietary information, lure away plaintiff's employees, copy plaintiff's business format, and imitate and infringe plaintiff's trademarks had sufficiently pled a conspiracy under §§ 18.2-499 and 18.2-500. Buffalo Wings Factory, Inc. v. Mohd, 622 F. Supp. 2d 325, 2007 U.S. Dist. LEXIS 91324 (E.D. Va. 2007).

Evidence insufficient to show conspiracy. — Where an insurance company ceased doing business with a flood insurance agent, the insurance company was entitled to summary judgment as to the agent's business conspiracy claim because evidence of a conversation between a general agent and the insurance company did not establish the presence of a conspiracy to injure the agent in the agent's business. Hecht v. Am. Bankers Ins. Co., 2005 U.S. Dist. LEXIS 25883 (W.D. Va. Oct. 21, 2005).

Allegations sufficient to withstand motion to dismiss. — Telecommunications provider's allegations of a business conspiracy (that defendant and another entity acted together to divert the telecommunications provider's earned commissions, and to injure or destroy the telecommunications provider's business, and that the conspiratorial conduct was willful and malicious, and resulted in substantial money damages to the telecommunications provider) were sufficient to withstand defendant's motion to dismiss. While the allegations were arguably conclusory, the complaint, in its entirety, contained sufficient factual content to permit the court to reasonably infer that the required elements of concerted action, legal malice and causally related injury, could be met. All Bus. Solutions, Inc. v. NationsLine, Inc., 629 F. Supp. 2d 553, 2009 U.S. Dist. LEXIS 54693 (W.D. Va. 2009).

Applied in Fowler v. Department of Educ., 472 F. Supp. 121 (E.D. Va. 1978); Evans v. Commonwealth, 226 Va. 292, 308 S.E.2d 126 (1983); Reasor v. City of Norfolk, 606 F. Supp. 788 (E.D. Va. 1984); Hechler Chevrolet, Inc. v. GMC, 230 Va. 396, 337 S.E.2d 744 (1985); Greenspan v. Osheroff, 232 Va. 388, 351 S.E.2d 28 (1986); Oksanen v. Page Mem. Hosp., 945 F.2d 696 (4th Cir. 1991); Catercorp, Inc. v. Catering Concepts, Inc., 246 Va. 22, 431 S.E.2d 277 (1993); Lansdowne Dev. Co., L.L.C. v. Xerox Realty Corp., 257 Va. 392, 514 S.E.2d 157 (1999); Feddeman & Co. v. Langan Assocs., P.C., 260 Va. 35, 530 S.E.2d 668, 2000 Va. LEXIS 92 (2000).

CIRCUIT COURT OPINIONS

Construction. — The *Buschi* decision, which construes §§ 18.2-499 and 18.2-500 to limit recovery of damages to a plaintiff's business, profession, or trade, and not to allow damages to a plaintiff's reputation or employment interests, is persuasive. Young v. City of Norfolk, 62 Va. Cir. 307, 2003 Va. Cir. LEXIS 296 (Norfolk 2003).

Failure to show a conspiracy. — Where a subcontractor's expectation that it would be allowed to bid on a project did not rise to a level of a reasonable expectation of further contractual relations, the subcontractor did not show that an engineer company and its employees were involved in a conspiracy or employed "improper means." Commercial Roofing & Sheet Metal Co. v. Gardner Eng'g, Inc., 60 Va. Cir. 384, 2002 Va. Cir. LEXIS 275 (Fairfax County 2002).

Messages posted on an internet message board did not support the company's claim that the customers conspired to willfully and intentionally injure the company in reputation, trade, or business as they were non-defamatory or matters of opinion — both protected by First Amendment. Xtreme 4x4 Ctr., Inc. v. Howery, 65 Va. Cir. 469, 2004 Va. Cir. LEXIS 229 (Roanoke 2004).

Because a provider failed to allege adequate facts to support its claim that a company and a competitor sought to willfully and maliciously injure its business with the company, the provider failed to state a claim for civil conspiracy or a violation of §§ 18.2-499 and 18.2-500. George K. Degnon Assocs. v. Acad. for Eating Disorders, — Va. Cir. —, 2005 Va. Cir. LEXIS 202 (Fairfax County Nov. 29, 2005).

Counterclaim contending that a real estate agent and an administrative assistant conspired to oust defendant from a partnership alleged they took "overt steps" in furtherance of the conspiracy, but failed to specify what those steps were, and thus did not state a claim of statutory conspiracy in violation of §§ 18.2-499 and 18.2-500. Poco Loco, LLC v. Barnes, 72 Va. Cir. 165, 2006 Va. Cir. LEXIS 202 (Fairfax County 2006).

Disbarred attorney could not recover damages on his claims that a state bar association's disciplinary board and its prosecutor caused injury when they conspired against him, either during the course of or as the result of disciplinary hearings, where the board members and the prosecutor were all part of one entity and no specific allegations of bad faith barred their entitlement to prosecutorial and judicial immunity. Leach v. Va. State Bar, 73 Va. Cir. 362, 2007 Va. Cir. LEXIS 221 (Richmond June 8, 2007).

Plaintiff had not pleaded facts sufficient to maintain a statutory conspiracy claim; to the extent plaintiff was pleading that defendants were alleged to have conspired after the employee was employed by each entity, the intra-corporate immunity doctrine applied and a conspiracy claim could not be maintained. TradeStaff & Co. v. Nogiec, 77 Va. Cir. 77, 2008 Va. Cir. LEXIS 226 (Chesapeake 2008).

In an action for damages by a company against a former employee, a limited liability company, its members, and others, defendants did not employ any unlawful means or act maliciously in setting up a competing business and, consequently, they did not violate § 18.2-500. Tryco, Inc. v. United States Med. Source, 80 Va. Cir. 619, 2010 Va. Cir. LEXIS 91 (Fairfax County Aug. 3, 2010).

Elements of offense. — Investor's allegation for statutory conspiracy under §§ 18.2-444 and 18.2-500 was defective because: (1) there was no allegation of malice; and (2) an allegation of conspiracy, whether criminal or civil, had to at least allege an unlawful act or an unlawful purpose, and the investor failed to do so. Furthermore, a conspiracy merely to breach a contract that did not involve an independent duty arising outside the contract was insufficient to establish a civil claim under § 18.2-500. Schur v. Sprenkle, 84 Va. Cir. 418, 2012 Va. Cir. LEXIS 132 (Richmond Apr. 11, 2012).

Proof of injury required. — Claims of conspiracy to injure a trade, business or profession, with no explainable factual basis, were subject to demurrer with leave to amend as one did not file a claim, especially one as serious as this, with no explainable factual basis, intending to "flesh it out" during discovery. Mut. Funding, Inc. v. Collins, 62 Va. Cir. 34, 2003 Va. Cir. LEXIS 68 (Spotsylvania County 2003).

Trial court dismissed a claim which a software company filed against a professional corporation and a doctor who owned the corporation, alleging that they conspired to steal information the company compiled while performing work under a contract for the corporation, because the company did not allege that the doctor acted outside the scope of her duties as an officer of the corporation. Softwise, Inc. v. Goodrich, 63 Va. Cir. 576, 2004 Va. Cir. LEXIS 6 (Roanoke 2004).

Plaintiff's claim was dismissed as plaintiff did not allege any injury to his business, relief was only proper when malicious conduct was directed at one's business, not one's person, and §§ 18.2-499 and 18.2-500 applied only to conspiracies resulting in business-related damages. Orantes v. Pollo Ranchero, Inc., 70 Va. Cir. 277, 2006 Va. Cir. LEXIS 52 (Fairfax County 2006).

Proof of unlawful act required. — Defendants' demurrers were granted as to a company's claim for statutory business conspiracy under §§ 18.2-499 and 18.2-500, because the company failed to allege how defendants conspired with a sublandlord to terminate a sublease, and the company failed to allege a criminal or unlawful purpose or means on the part of defendants. R & D 2001, L.L.C. v. Collins, — Va. Cir. —, 2006 Va. Cir. LEXIS 131 (Fairfax County July 12, 2006).

Business expectancy. — Whether the contractor had a business expectancy in a public contract was not appropriately disposed of on demurrer as the contractor alleged that, absent the employee's and competitors' conduct, it would have been awarded the contract as a sole source provider, and a preference, in 48 C.F.R. §§ 16.500(a) and 16.504(c)(i), for multiple providers did not establish an absolute mandate for multiple providers, and the contractor alleged it had a business expectancy in a certain public contract, the employee and the competitors knew of this expectancy, facts showed there was a reasonable certainty that the contractor would otherwise have realized this expectancy, and the contractor was damaged by the employee's and competitors' interference. However, a competitor who was only alleged to be affiliated with another competitor, with no indication of the nature of the affiliation, could not be held liable under this theory. H.E.R.C. Prods. v. Turlington, 62 Va. Cir. 489, 2003 Va. Cir. LEXIS 305 (Norfolk 2003).

Failure to show malice. — Where a non-solicitation clause was not limited in duration or geography and the clause's language, requiring a newly formed competing business, did not support a bill of complaint, and where there was no business conspiracy under §§ 18.2-499 and 18.2-500 or common-law conspiracy because the former employer did not show that a former employee acted with malice or that there was a concerted action to accomplish an unlawful purpose, the former employee's demurrers were sustained. Int'l Paper Co. v. Brooks, 63 Va. Cir. 494, 2003 Va. Cir. LEXIS 248 (Roanoke 2003).

Violation found. — Plaintiff's former partners and their new company violated §§ 18.2-499 and 18.2-500 by pursuing the unlawful purpose of forcing plaintiff out of the former partnership without compensating him for his interest and by accomplishing this purpose by unlawful means, including purporting to withdraw from the partnership while actually seizing control of its assets, converting partnership assets and plaintiff's property, inducing former partnership employees to accept employment with them, and breaching their fiduciary duties. Greenfeld v. Stitely, 2007 Va. Cir. LEXIS 7 (Fairfax County Jan. 5, 2007).

Employment not within scope of section. — Trial court dismissed a police officer's claim alleging that two homebuyers and a homeowner violated this section when they conspired to have him indicted because they were unhappy with work he did on their houses while operating a private construction business, and that he was fired from his job as a police officer after he was indicted, but overruled demurrers which the homebuyers and homeowner filed to the officer's claims seeking recovery for malicious prosecution, interference with a contract, breach of contract, and fraud. Fitzgerald v. Farrell, 63 Va. Cir. 1, 2003 Va. Cir. LEXIS 340 (Loudoun County 2003).

Evidence sufficient to show conspiracy. — Former employee and a retailer were held liable for violating § 18.2-499 et seq., with regard to enticing the former employee from his employ with a clothier, with the former employee purposefully taking the clothier's clientele list and the retailer having full knowledge of the same and, in fact, encouraging it. The restrictive covenant in the clothier's handbook prohibiting employment with a competitor within

one mile for a period of three years was not overly harsh or oppressive and, therefore, in addition to compensatory damages in the amount of $548,611, trebled to $1,654,833, the trial court enjoined the former employee from working for the retailer for a period of three years from the date of the trial court's opinion. James, Ltd. v. Saks Fifth Ave., Inc., 67 Va. Cir. 126, 2005 Va. Cir. LEXIS 150 (Arlington County Mar. 8, 2005), rev'd in part as to treble damages, 630 S.E.2d 404, 2006 Va. LEXIS 54 (Va. 2006).

Demurrer denied as to claim of business conspiracy. — Former employee's demurrer pursuant to subsection A of § 8.01-273 was denied as to a company's claim that the former employee was involved in a business conspiracy pursuant to §§ 18.2-499 and 18.2-500, because a company adequately alleged that the former employee and others conspired to injure the company by leaving the company en masse to work for a competitor, and to take the accounts for which they were responsible, and by taking and using documents that were alleged to be confidential trade secrets. Int'l Paper Co. v. Gilliam, 63 Va. Cir. 485, 2003 Va. Cir. LEXIS 249 (Roanoke 2003).

Development company and associate's demurrer to the restaurant operator's claim against them for conspiracy to injure a business, pursuant to §§ 18.2-499 and 18.2-500, had to be denied as the restaurant operator stated a claim under both sections. The restaurant operator alleged that: (1) they combined with others to willfully and maliciously injure the restaurant operator by preventing the restaurant operator from presenting live entertainment at its restaurant; and (2) as a result, the restaurant operator lost profits vital to the operation of the restaurant. Station # 2, LLC v. Lynch, 75 Va. Cir. 179, 2008 Va. Cir. LEXIS 52 (Norfolk 2008).

Claim alleging that defendants conspired with one another to injure a company in its reputation, trade, business and profession in violation of §§ 18.2-499 and 18.2-500 was sufficient under Va. Sup. Ct. R. 1:4(d) to survive a demurrer as the intracorporate immunity doctrine did not apply to a conspiracy claim against employees, officers or agents who combined to harm their corporation. Colgate v. Disthene Group, Inc., 2013 Va. Cir. LEXIS 9 (Buckingham County Feb. 4, 2013).

Claim time-barred. — Plaintiff's conspiracy claim was time-barred as: (1) plaintiff asserted a claim for trebled money damages, so he did not seek purely equitable remedies; (2) a claim for conspiracy under §§ 18.2-499 and 18.2-500 was a legal cause of action, whether the claim was brought on the law or chancery side; (3) the basis of the claim was fraud and fraud was a wrongful act aimed at the person; (4) as fraud invariably acted upon the person of the victim, its consequence was personal damage; and (5) the conspiracy claim was therefore time-barred whether subsection A of § 8.01-243, which applied to fraud claims, or § 8.01-248, which applied to personal actions for which no other limitation was specified, relied on. Orantes v. Pollo Ranchero, Inc., 70 Va. Cir. 277, 2006 Va. Cir. LEXIS 52 (Fairfax County 2006).

Cause of action stated. — Property owners alleged defendants wrote to government agents falsely accusing the owners of diverting a stream flow and removing wetlands. The owners' complaint sufficiently alleged legal malice — that defendants acted intentionally, purposely, and without lawful justification — to state claims of statutory conspiracy under §§ 18.2-499 and 18.2-500. Mathre v. Schweichert, — Va. Cir. —, 2007 Va. Cir. LEXIS 310 (Nelson County Aug. 9, 2007).

Cause of action not stated. — Stock assignee's claim that defendants conspired to take control of a corporation did not sufficiently allege that they conspired "for the purpose of" injuring the assignee's predecessors; the complaint alleged damage to the corporation, which could only be remedied by a derivative suit. Lexcadia Capital, L.L.C. v. Next Generation Fund, L.L.C., 71 Va. Cir. 83, 2006 Va. Cir. LEXIS 104 (Fairfax County 2006).

Former employer failed to sufficiently plead statutory business conspiracy in violation of §§ 18.2-499 and 18.2-500 where an underlying employment agreement was rendered invalid by a blue-pencil provision and by overbroad noncompetition and confidentiality provisions and where the employer failed to allege malice. BB&T Ins. Servs. v. Thomas Rutherford, Inc., 80 Va. Cir. 174, 2010 Va. Cir. LEXIS 25 (Richmond Feb. 9, 2010).

Demurrer dismissing a statutory conspiracy claim against a real estate company and individual brokers was not reconsidered on the theory that § 18.2-216 false advertisement claims showed statutory conspiracy because (1) the claims only alleged false advertising, and (2) the company and the individual defendants were one entity. Foster v. Wintergreen Real Estate Co., 84 Va. Cir. 5, 2011 Va. Cir. LEXIS 209 (Nelson County Oct. 27, 2011).

Demurrer dismissing a statutory conspiracy claim against a real estate company and individual brokers was not reconsidered on the theory that alleged breaches of statutory and fiduciary duties constituted statutory conspiracy because statutes and regulations allegedly violated were part of each client's contract. Foster v. Wintergreen Real Estate Co., 84 Va. Cir. 5, 2011 Va. Cir. LEXIS 209 (Nelson County Oct. 27, 2011).

Demurrer dismissing a statutory conspiracy claim was not reconsidered on the theory that an alleged tortious interference with contract fell under the conspiracy statutes because a defendant company and individual defendants were one entity, under the intracorporate immunity doctrine. Foster v. Wintergreen Real Estate Co., 84 Va. Cir. 5, 2011 Va. Cir. LEXIS 209 (Nelson County Oct. 27, 2011). Plaintiff's action for statutory conspiracy, brought against her former partner and paramour failed because the statutory business requirement was not satisfied; plaintiff complained about matters involving a deed, deed of trust, and a payment agreement, all of which involved a real estate, not a business transaction. In re Whalen, 2011 Va. Cir. LEXIS 277 (Nelson County Nov. 16, 2011).

Attorney's fees. — Where plaintiffs prevailed on defendant's counterclaim alleging conspiracy under § 18.2-499, they were not entitled to attorneys' fees under § 18.2-500, as § 18.2-500 limited recovery of such fees to the victims of conspiracies to injure them in their trade or business, and plaintiffs were accused of participating in such a conspiracy. Bhagat v. Diamond Info. Sys., L.L.C., 83 Va. Cir. 233, 2012 Va. Cir. LEXIS 79 (Loudoun County Jan. 23, 2012).

§ 18.2-501. Same; protection of persons testifying or producing evidence.

(a) No natural person shall be prosecuted or be subjected to any penalty or forfeiture for or on account of any transaction, matter or thing concerning which he may testify or produce evidence, documentary or otherwise, in any action, suit, or prosecution authorized by this article; provided, that no person so testifying shall be exempt from prosecution or punishment for perjury committed in so testifying.

(b) As used in this article a *"person"* is any person, firm, corporation, partnership or association.

History.
Code 1950, § 18.1-74.1:3; 1964, c. 623; 1975, cc. 14, 15.

Michie's Jurisprudence.
For related discussion, see 6B M.J. Embezzlement, § 12.

CASE NOTES

Conspiracy between corporation and its agents as legal impossibility. — Although plaintiff's allegations were initially sufficient to satisfy the threshold demands of Virginia's civil conspiracy statute, they were not sufficient to overcome the obstacle provided by the intracorporate immunity doctrine, which holds that because at least two persons must be present to form a conspiracy, a corporation cannot conspire with itself; therefore, a conspiracy between a corporation and the agents of that corporation who are acting in the scope of their employment is a legal impossibility. Selman v. American Sports Underwriters, Inc., 697 F. Supp. 225 (W.D. Va. 1988).

Waiver of immunity. — This section does not operate to withdraw subject matter jurisdiction. Rather, it affords the defense of immunity, and immunity may of course be waived by failure to invoke the immunity when prosecution is begun. Evans v. Commonwealth, 226 Va. 292, 308 S.E.2d 126 (1983).

Applied in Reasor v. City of Norfolk, 606 F. Supp. 788 (E.D. Va. 1984).

ARTICLE 2.1.
SPORTS AGENTS REGULATION ACT.

Editor's note.
Acts 1989, c. 530, cl. 2 provided that this article (§§ 18.2-501.1 through 18.2-501.5) would not become effective until reenacted by the 1990 Session of the General Assembly. The article was not reenacted, and therefore, never became effective.

ARTICLE 3.
MISCELLANEOUS OFFENSES IN GENERAL.

§ 18.2-502. Medical referral for profit.

(a) No person, firm, partnership, association or corporation, or agent or employee thereof, shall for profit engage in any business which in whole or in part includes the referral or recommendation of persons to a physician, hospital, health related facility, or dispensary for any form of medical care or treatment of any ailment or physical condition unless the person is advised of the criteria of selection of the physicians, hospitals, health-related facilities or dispensaries considered for the referral or recommendation. The acceptance of a fee or charge for any such referral or recommendation shall create a presumption that the business is engaged in such service for profit. A violation of the provisions of this section shall be punishable as a Class 1 misdemeanor.

(b) Whenever there is a violation of this section, in addition to the criminal sanctions, an application may be made by the Attorney General to the circuit court of the city or county in which the offense occurred, to issue an injunction, and upon notice to the defendant of not less than five days, to enjoin and restrain the continuance of such violation. If it appears to the satisfaction of the court or judge that the defendant has, in fact, violated this section, an injunction may be issued by such court or judge enjoining and restraining any further violation, without requiring proof that any person has, in fact, been injured or damaged thereby. Nothing in this section shall be construed to limit, prohibit, forbid or prevent any licensed physician or practitioner of the healing arts in the ordinary course of his professional practice from making referrals or recommendations to other members of such groups, so long as no fee is received for such referral or recommendation.

The criminal and civil provisions of this section shall not apply to any individual association or corporation not organized or incorporated for pecuniary profit or financial gain, or to any organization or association which is exempt from taxation pursuant to § 501 (c) of Title 26 of the United States Code (Int. Rev. Code of 1954).

(c) Nothing in this section shall be construed to authorize any division of fees prohibited by § 54.1-

2962 or any remuneration for referral prohibited by federal law or regulation.

History.
Code 1950, § 18.1-417.2; 1972, c. 642; 1975, cc. 14, 15; 1986, c. 632.

Law Review.
For survey of Virginia criminal law for the year 1971-1972, see 58 Va. L. Rev. 1206 (1972).

§ 18.2-502.1. Weight loss centers or clinics; disclosure.

No weight loss center or clinic shall, in its name or advertisements, use the words "physicians" or "doctors" or refer to its clients as "patients" or indicate that "medical teams" are available in its facility unless (i) the facility employs at least one registered nurse full-time and employs or contracts with at least one physician licensed by the Board of Medicine for services or consultation in connection with the facility's activities; or (ii) the facility is under the full-time supervision of a physician; or (iii) the clinic or program is operated by or in conjunction with a licensed hospital. Any physician affiliated with a weight loss center or clinic for purposes of consultation or supervision shall have primary responsibility for decisions made within the scope of that affiliation relating to the provision of medical services or care to persons using the services of that facility and shall have primary responsibility for medical decisions relating to the evaluation of the appropriateness of the admission of persons to the weight loss program. Any person who violates the provisions of this section shall be guilty of a Class 1 misdemeanor.

History.
1988, c. 765.

§ 18.2-502.2. Warning required for certain medical tests; penalty.

No commercial medical testing kit designed for consumer home use shall be sold in this Commonwealth unless a warning is provided to the consumer to the effect that such tests may produce erroneous results and that medical testing is more accurate when performed by professionals within the controlled conditions of a laboratory. The consumer shall be advised to seek professional medical consultation and, if recommended, another test for validation of such test results.

Any person who violates the provisions of this section shall be guilty of a Class 4 misdemeanor.

History.
1989, c. 142.

§ 18.2-503. Possession or duplication of certain keys.

(a) No person shall knowingly possess any key to the lock of any building or other property owned by the Commonwealth of Virginia, or a department, division, agency or political subdivision thereof, without receiving permission from a person duly authorized to give such permission to possess such key.

(b) No person, without receiving permission from a person duly authorized to give such permission, shall knowingly duplicate, copy or make a facsimile of any key to a lock of a building or other property owned by the Commonwealth of Virginia, or a department, division, agency or political subdivision thereof.

Violation of this section shall constitute a Class 3 misdemeanor.

History.
Code 1950, § 18.1-408.1; 1972, c. 139; 1975, cc. 14, 15; 1984, c. 61.

Law Review.
For survey of Virginia criminal law for the year 1971-1972, see 58 Va. L. Rev. 1206 (1972).

§ 18.2-504. Destroying or concealing wills.

If any person fraudulently destroy or conceal any will or codicil, with intent to prevent the probate thereof, he shall be guilty of a Class 6 felony.

History.
Code 1950, § 18.1-309; 1960, c. 358; 1975, cc. 14, 15.

§ 18.2-504.1. Unlawful change of name; punishment.

If any person residing in this Commonwealth changes his name or assumes another name, unlawfully, he shall be guilty of a Class 3 misdemeanor.

History.
Code 1950, § 8-577.1; 1956, c. 402; 1973, c. 401; 1976, c. 115; 1977, c. 624.

Cross references.
As to civil proceedings for change of name, see § 8.01-217.

§ 18.2-505. Preparation, etc., of papers to be submitted for academic credit.

(a) No person shall prepare, cause to be prepared or sell any term paper, thesis, dissertation or other written material for another person, for profit, with the knowledge, or under circumstances in which he should reasonably have known, that such term paper, thesis, dissertation or other written material is to be submitted by any other person for academic credit at any public or private college, university or other institution of higher learning in this Commonwealth.

(b) No person shall make or disseminate, with the intent to induce any other person to enter into any obligation relating thereto, any statement, written or oral, that he will prepare or cause to be prepared, any term paper, thesis, dissertation or other written material, to be sold for profit, for or on behalf of any person who has been assigned the written preparation of such term paper, thesis, dissertation or other written material for academic credit at any public or private college, university or other institution of higher learning in this Commonwealth.

History.
Code 1950, § 18.1-371.1; 1974, c. 342; 1975, cc. 14, 15.

§ 18.2-506. "Person" and "prepare" defined.

(a) As used in this article, *"person"* means any individual, partnership, corporation or association.

(b) As used in this article, *"prepare"* means to put into condition for intended use. "Prepare" does not include the mere typing or assembling of papers, nor the mere furnishing of information or research.

History.
Code 1950, § 18.1-371.2; 1974, c. 342; 1975, cc. 14, 15.

§ 18.2-507. Injunctions against violation of § 18.2-505.

Whenever a college, university or other institution of higher learning in this Commonwealth shall duly file a civil action in the circuit court of any county or city against any person alleging violations of the provisions of § 18.2-505, and praying that such party defendant be restrained and enjoined from continuing the acts complained of, such court shall have jurisdiction to hear and determine the issues involved, to issue injunctions pendente lite and permanent injunctions and to decree damages and costs of suit, including reasonable counsel fees to complainants' counsel.

History.
Code 1950, § 18.1-371.3; 1974, c. 342; 1975, cc. 14, 15; 2005, c. 681.

§ 18.2-508. Penalties.

Any person found guilty of violating any provision of § 18.2-505 shall be guilty of a misdemeanor and shall be punished by a fine not to exceed $1,000.

History.
Code 1950, § 18.1-371.4; 1974, c. 342; 1975, cc. 14, 15.

§ 18.2-509. Employment of lights under certain circumstances.

Any person in any motor vehicle or otherwise who, between a half hour after sunset on any day and a half hour before sunrise the following day, employs a light attached to such vehicle, or employs a spotlight to cast a light beyond the surface of the roadway upon any poultry house or other building inhabited by animals that causes such animals to panic or become injured, except upon his own land or upon private land on which he has permission, shall be guilty of a Class 4 misdemeanor.

History.
1976, c. 332.

§ 18.2-510. Burial or cremation of animals or fowls which have died.

When the owner of any animal or grown fowl which has died knows of such death, such owner shall forthwith have its body cremated or buried or request such service from an officer or other person designated for the purpose. If the owner fails to do so, any judge of a general district court, after notice to the owner if he can be ascertained, shall cause any such dead animal or fowl to be cremated or buried by an officer or other person designated for the purpose. Such officer or other person shall be entitled to recover of the owner of every such animal or fowl that is cremated or buried the actual cost of the cremation or burial and a reasonable fee to be recovered in the same manner as officers' fees are recovered, free from all exemptions in favor of such owner. Any person violating the provisions of this section shall be guilty of a Class 4 misdemeanor.

Nothing in this section shall be deemed to require the burial or cremation of the whole or portions of any animal or fowl which is to be used for food or in any commercial manner.

This section shall not apply to any county until the governing body thereof shall adopt the same.

History.
Code 1950, § 32-70; 1979, c. 716; 1981, c. 578; 2008, c. 345.

The 2008 amendments.
The 2008 amendment by c. 345 rewrote the first and second sentences which read: "When the owner of any animal or grown fowl which has died knows of such death, such owner shall forthwith have its body cremated or buried, and, if he fails to do so, any judge of a general district court, after notice to the owner if he can be ascertained, shall cause any such dead animal or fowl to be cremated or buried by an officer or other person designated for the purpose. Such officer or other person shall be entitled to recover of the owner of every such animal so cremated or buried the actual cost of the cremation or burial, not to exceed seventy-five dollars, and of the owner of every such fowl so cremated or buried the actual cost of the cremation or burial, not to exceed five dollars, to be recovered in the same manner as officers' fees are recovered, free from all exemptions in favor of such owner" in the first paragraph.

§ 18.2-511. Sale of certain military grave markers prohibited.

Any person who sells or offers for sale any military grave marker of one or more deceased persons who served in the military service of the Commonwealth, the United States, or any of the states thereof, shall be assessed a $100 civil penalty payable to the Literary Fund.

The provisions of this section shall not apply to the sale or offer for sale of such grave marker if it was (i) conveyed with real property to which it remains affixed, (ii) sold or offered for sale following manufacture or fabrication and prior to initial installation or dedication, or (iii) lawfully acquired.

History.
2004, c. 299.

§ 18.2-511.1. Smoking in proximity to a medical oxygen source in a health care facility; penalty.

Any person who smokes or uses an open flame within 25 feet of a medical oxygen source in a health care facility, as defined in § 15.2-2820, when the area is posted as an area where smoking and open flame are prohibited is guilty of a Class 2 misdemeanor.

History.
2007, c. 430; 2009, cc. 153, 154.

Editor's note.
Acts 2009, cc. 153 and 154, cl. 3 provides: "That the provisions of this act shall become effective on December 1, 2009."

The 2009 amendments.
The 2009 amendment by cc. 153 and 154, effective December 1, 2009, are identical and substituted "§ 15.2-2820" for "§ 15.2-2800."

Law Review.
For 2007 annual survey article, "Health Care Law," see 42 U. Rich. L. Rev. 441 (2007).

CHAPTER 13.

VIRGINIA RACKETEER INFLUENCED AND CORRUPT ORGANIZATION ACT.

Section
18.2-512. Short title.
18.2-513. Definitions.
18.2-514. Racketeering offenses.
18.2-515. Criminal penalties; forfeiture.
18.2-516. Prohibition of illegal money transmitting.
18.2-517. Venue for prosecution.

§ 18.2-512. Short title.

This chapter may be cited as the "Virginia Racketeer Influenced and Corrupt Organization (RICO) Act."

History.
2004, cc. 883, 996.

The numbers of §§ 18.2-512 to 18.2-517 were assigned by the Virginia Code Commission, the numbers in the 2004 act having been §§ 18.2-511 to 18.2-516.

Law Review.
For 2003/2004 survey of criminal law and procedure, see 39 U. Rich. L. Rev. 133 (2004).

§ 18.2-513. Definitions.

As used in this chapter, the term:
"*Criminal street gang*" shall be as defined in § 18.2-46.1.
"*Enterprise*" includes any of the following: sole proprietorship, partnership, corporation, business trust, criminal street gang; or other group of three or more individuals associated for the purpose of criminal activity.
"*Proceeds*" shall be as defined in § 18.2-246.2.

"*Racketeering activity*" means to commit, attempt to commit, conspire to commit, or to solicit, coerce, or intimidate another person to commit two or more of the following offenses: Article 2.1 (§ 18.2-46.1 et seq.) of Chapter 4 of this title, § 18.2-460; a felony offense of §§ 3.2-4212, 3.2-4219, 10.1-1455, 18.2-31, 18.2-32, 18.2-32.1, 18.2-33, 18.2-35, Article 2.2 (§ 18.2-46.4 et seq.) of Chapter 4 of this title, §§ 18.2-47, 18.2-48, 18.2-48.1, 18.2-49, 18.2-51, 18.2-51.2, 18.2-52, 18.2-53, 18.2-55, 18.2-58, 18.2-59, 18.2-77, 18.2-79, 18.2-80, 18.2-89, 18.2-90, 18.2-91, 18.2-92, 18.2-93, 18.2-95, Article 4 (§ 18.2-111 et seq.) of Chapter 5 of this title, Article 1 (§ 18.2-168 et seq.) of Chapter 6 of this title, §§ 18.2-178, 18.2-186, Article 6 (§ 18.2-191 et seq.) of Chapter 6 of this title, Article 9 (§ 18.2-246.1 et seq.) of Chapter 6 of this title, § 18.2-246.13, Article 1 (§ 18.2-247 et seq.) of Chapter 7 of this title, §§ 18.2-279, 18.2-286.1, 18.2-289, 18.2-300, 18.2-308.2, 18.2-308.2:1, 18.2-328, 18.2-348, 18.2-355, 18.2-356, 18.2-357, 18.2-368, 18.2-369, 18.2-374.1, Article 8 (§ 18.2-433.1 et seq.) of Chapter 9 of this title, Article 1 (§ 18.2-434 et seq.) of Chapter 10 of this title, Article 2 (§ 18.2-438 et seq.) of Chapter 10 of this title, Article 3 (§ 18.2-446 et seq.) of Chapter 10 of this title, Article 1.1 (§ 18.2-498.1 et seq.) of Chapter 12 of this title, § 3.2-6571, 18.2-516, 32.1-314, 58.1-1008.2, 58.1-1017, or 58.1-1017.1; or any substantially similar offenses under the laws of any other state, the District of Columbia, the United States or its territories.

History.
2004, cc. 883, 996; 2008, c. 681; 2009, cc. 662, 847; 2013, c. 626.

Editor's note.
Acts 2008, c. 681, cl. 2, provides: "That the provisions of this act may result in a net increase in periods of imprisonment or commitment. Pursuant to § 30-19.1:4, the estimated amount of the necessary appropriation cannot be determined for periods of imprisonment in state adult correctional facilities and is $0 for periods of commitment to the custody of the Department of Juvenile Justice."
Acts 2009, c. 662, cl. 2, provides: "That the provisions of this act may result in a net increase in periods of imprisonment or commitment. Pursuant to § 30-19.1:4, the estimated amount of the necessary appropriation cannot be determined for periods of imprisonment in state adult correctional facilities and cannot be determined for periods of commitment to the custody of the Department of Juvenile Justice."
Acts 2013, c. 626, cl. 2, provides: "That the provisions of this act may result in a net increase in periods of imprisonment or commitment. Pursuant to § 30-19.1:4, the estimated amount of the necessary appropriation cannot be determined for periods of imprisonment in state adult correctional facilities; therefore, Chapter 3 of the Acts of Assembly of 2012, Special Session I, requires the Virginia Criminal Sentencing Commission to assign a minimum fiscal impact of $50,000. Pursuant to § 30-19.1:4, the estimated amount of the necessary appropriation cannot be determined for periods of commitment to the custody of the Department of Juvenile Justice."

The 2008 amendments.
The 2008 amendment by c. 681, under the definition for "Racketeering activity," inserted "3.1-796.124" preceding "18.2-516" near the end of the paragraph, and made stylistic changes.

The 2009 amendments.
The 2009 amendment by c. 662, inserted "18.2-59," "18.2-348," "18.2-356," and "18.2-368" in the definition of "Racketeering activity."

The 2009 amendment by c. 847, in the definition of "Racketeering activity," inserted "3.2-4212, 3.2-4219," "§ 18.2-246.13," and "58.1-1008.2."

The 2013 amendments.

The 2013 amendment by c. 626 inserted "or 58.1-1017.1" and made a related change.

§ 18.2-514. Racketeering offenses.

A. It shall be unlawful for an enterprise, or for any person who occupies a position of organizer, supervisor, or manager of an enterprise, to receive any proceeds known to have been derived directly from racketeering activity and to use or invest an aggregate of $10,000 or more of such proceeds in the acquisition of any title to, or any right, interest, or equity in, real property, or in the establishment or operation of any enterprise.

B. It shall be unlawful for any enterprise, or for any person who occupies a position of organizer, supervisor, or manager of an enterprise, to directly acquire or maintain any interest in or control of any enterprise or real property through racketeering activity.

C. It shall be unlawful for any person employed by, or associated with, any enterprise to conduct or participate, directly or indirectly, in such enterprise through racketeering activity.

D. It shall be unlawful for any person to conspire to violate any of the provisions of subsection A, B, or C.

E. Each violation of this section is a separate and distinct felony punishable in accordance with § 18.2-515.

History.

2004, cc. 883, 996; 2009, c. 847.

The 2009 amendments.

The 2009 amendment by c. 847 added subsections C and D; and redesignated former subsection C as subsection E.

§ 18.2-515. Criminal penalties; forfeiture.

A. Any person or enterprise convicted of engaging in activity in violation of the provisions of § 18.2-514 is guilty of a felony punishable by imprisonment for not less than five years nor more than 40 years and a fine of not more than $1 million. A second or subsequent offense shall be punishable as a Class 2 felony and a fine of not more than $2 million.

The court may order any such person or enterprise to be divested of any interest in any enterprise or real property identified in § 18.2-514; order the dissolution or reorganization of such enterprise; and order the suspension or revocation of any license, permit, or prior approval granted to such enterprise or person by any agency of the Commonwealth or political subdivision thereof.

B. All property, real or personal, including money, together with any interest or profits derived from the investment of such money, used in substantial connection with, intended for use in the course of, or

traceable to, conduct in violation of any provision of § 18.2-514 is subject to civil forfeiture to the Commonwealth. The forfeiture proceeding shall be conducted pursuant to the provisions of Chapter 22.1 (§ 19.2-386.1 et seq.) of Title 19.2.

History.

2004, cc. 883, 996; 2012, c. 511.

The 2012 amendments.

The 2012 amendment by c. 511 inserted "together with any interest or profits derived from the investment of such money," in the first sentence of subsection B.

§ 18.2-516. Prohibition of illegal money transmitting.

A. Any person who controls, manages, or owns all or part of an enterprise, engaged in money transmission as defined in § 6.2-1900, and transmits money, which he knows or should have known was derived from or traceable to racketeering activity, is guilty of a Class 6 felony.

B. All property, real or personal, including money, used in substantial connection with, intended for use in the course of, or traceable to, conduct in violation of any provision of subsection A is subject to civil forfeiture to the Commonwealth. The forfeiture proceeding shall be conducted pursuant to the provisions of Chapter 22.1 (§ 19.2-386.1 et seq.) of Title 19.2.

History.

2004, cc. 883, 996.

Editor's note.

In subsection A, "§ 6.2-1900" was substituted for "§ 6.1-370," effective October 1, 2010, to conform to the recodification of Title 6.1 by Acts 2010, c. 794.

§ 18.2-517. Venue for prosecution.

For the purposes of venue, any violation of this chapter shall be considered to have been committed in any county or city:

1. In which any act was performed in furtherance of any course of conduct that violates this chapter;

2. That is the principal place of the enterprise in the Commonwealth;

3. In which any offender had control or possession of any proceeds of a violation of this chapter, or of any records, or any other material or objects, which were used in furtherance of a violation;

4. In which any offender resides; or

5. Any place of venue under Article 2 (§ 19.2-244 et seq.) of Chapter 15 of Title 19.2.

History.

2004, cc. 883, 996.

TITLE 19.2.

CRIMINAL PROCEDURE.

Chapter

CHAPTER 1.

GENERAL PROVISIONS.

§ 19.2-1. Repealing clause.

All acts and parts of acts, all sections of this Code, and all provisions of municipal charters, inconsistent with the provisions of this title, are, except as herein otherwise provided, repealed to the extent of such inconsistency.

History.
1975, c. 495.

Editor's note.
At its special session of 1971 the General Assembly directed the Code Commission to make a thorough study of the criminal laws of the State and make recommendations for the review and recodification of all statutes of the State relating to crime and criminal procedure. In December of 1974 the Commission sent to the Governor and General Assembly its report containing a proposed revision of Title 19.2, which was published as House Document 20 of the 1975 session. This report contains revisor's notes and other explanatory matter, which, while valuable, are too lengthy for inclusion here. The Commission's draft of the revision of Title 19.2, as amended by the General Assembly, became Chapter 495 of the Acts of 1975. Effective October 1, 1975, it repeals Title 19.1 of the Code and enacts in lieu thereof a new Title 19.2. In addition to its

revision by Chapter 495, former Title 19.1 was also amended by certain other acts passed at the 1975 session. As required by former statute (see § 30-152), the Code Commission has incorporated these amendments into new Title 19.2.

The cases prior to 1975 cited in the notes under the various sections of this title were decided under corresponding provisions of former Title 19.1.

Law Review.

For survey of the Virginia law on criminal law for the year 1961-1962, see 48 Va. L. Rev. 1342 (1962); for the year 1963-1964, see 50 Va. L. Rev. 1287 (1964). For survey of Virginia law on criminal law and procedure for the year 1967-1968, see 54 Va. L. Rev. 1579 (1968); for the year 1968-1969, see 55 Va. L. Rev. 1581 (1969). For survey of Virginia law on evidence for the year 1967-1968, see 54 Va. L. Rev. 1611 (1968). For article, "Criminal Law and Procedure," see 26 U. Rich. L. Rev. 701 (1992).

Research references.

Cipes, Bernstein, and Hall, Criminal Defense Techniques (Matthew Bender).

Criminal Law Advocacy Reporter (Matthew Bender).

Erickson, Neighbors, and George, United States Supreme Court Cases and Comments: Criminal Law and Procedure (Matthew Bender).

Kadish, Brofman, Criminal Law Advocacy (Matthew Bender).

McCloskey and Schoenberg, Criminal Law Deskbook (Matthew Bender).

Robert M. Cipes, Rules of Criminal Procedure (Matthew Bender)

Rudstein, Erlinder, and Thomas, Criminal Constitutional Law (Matthew Bender).

§ 19.2-2. Effect of repeal of Title 19.1 and enactment of this title.

The repeal of Title 19.1 effective as of October 1, 1975, shall not affect any act or offense done or committed, or any penalty or forfeiture incurred, or any right established, accrued, or accruing on or before such date, or any prosecution, suit or action pending on that day. Except as herein otherwise provided, neither the repeal of Title 19.1 nor the enactment of this title shall apply to offenses committed prior to October 1, 1975, and prosecutions for such offenses shall be governed by the prior law, which is continued in effect for that purpose. For the purposes of this section, an offense was committed prior to October 1, 1975, if any of the essential elements of the offense occurred prior thereto.

History.

1975, c. 495.

§ 19.2-3. Certain notices, recognizances and processes validated.

Any notice given, recognizance taken, or process or writ issued before October 1, 1975, shall be valid although given, taken or to be returned to a day after such date, in like manner as if this title had been effective before the same was given, taken or issued.

History.

1975, c. 495.

§ 19.2-3.1. Personal appearance by two-way electronic video and audio communication; standards.

A. Where an appearance is required or permitted before a magistrate, intake officer or, prior to trial, before a judge, the appearance may be by (i) personal appearance before the magistrate, intake officer or judge or (ii) use of two-way electronic video and audio communication. If two-way electronic video and audio communication is used, a magistrate, intake officer or judge may exercise all powers conferred by law and all communications and proceedings shall be conducted in the same manner as if the appearance were in person. If two-way electronic video and audio communication is available for use by a district court for the conduct of a hearing to determine bail or to determine representation by counsel, the court shall use such communication in any such proceeding that would otherwise require the transportation of a person from outside the jurisdiction of the court in order to appear in person before the court. Any documents transmitted between the magistrate, intake officer, or judge and the person appearing before the magistrate, intake officer, or judge may be transmitted by electronically transmitted facsimile process or other electronic method. The facsimile or other electronically generated document may be served or executed by the officer or person to whom sent, and returned in the same manner, and with the same force, effect, authority, and liability as an original document. All signatures thereon shall be treated as original signatures.

B. Any two-way electronic video and audio communication system used for an appearance shall meet the following standards:

1. The persons communicating must simultaneously see and speak to one another;

2. The signal transmission must be live, real time;

3. The signal transmission must be secure from interception through lawful means by anyone other than the persons communicating; and

4. Any other specifications as may be promulgated by the Chief Justice of the Supreme Court.

History.

1991, c. 41; 1996, cc. 755, 914; 2006, c. 285; 2009, cc. 94, 623; 2010, c. 800.

Cross references.

As to use of telephonic communication systems or electronic video and audio communication systems to conduct hearings, see §§ 16.1-93.1, 16.1-276.3, 17.1-513.2. As to the use of two-way electronic video and audio communication system used for an appearance by juvenile before an intake officer, see § 16.1-255.

Editor's note.

Acts 1996, cc. 755 and 914, cls. 7, provide: "[t]hat the provisions of this act shall apply to offenses committed and to records created and proceedings held with respect to those offenses on or after July 1, 1996."

The 2009 amendments.

The 2009 amendments by cc. 94 and 623 are identical, and in subsection A, divided the former second sentence into the second and fourth sentences by deleting "and any" at the end of the second sentence and adding "Any" at the beginning of the fourth sentence, and inserted the third sentence.

The 2010 amendments.

The 2010 amendment by c. 800 inserted "or other electronic method" and "or other electronically generated document" in subsection A.

Michie's Jurisprudence.

For related discussion, see 2A M.J. Appearances, § 11.

CASE NOTES

Annual assessment hearing for sexually violent predators. — Conducting an annual assessment hearing under § 37.2-910 of the Virginia Sexually Violent Predator Act, § 37.2-900 et seq., by video conference did not violate respondent's rights to counsel and to due process; as he was able to participate in the hearing and confer with his counsel, he was not prejudiced by the trial court's denial of his request to attend the hearing in person. Shellman v. Commonwealth, 284 Va. 711, 733 S.E.2d 242, 2012 Va. LEXIS 197 (2012).

§ 19.2-4. References to former sections, articles or chapters of Titles 18.1 and 19.1.

Whenever in this title any of the conditions, requirements, provisions or contents of any section, article or chapter of Titles 18.1 and 19.1, as such titles existed prior to October 1, 1975, are transferred in the same or in modified form to a new section, article or chapter of this title or of Title 18.2, and whenever any such former section, article or chapter is given a new number in this title or in Title 18.2, all references to any such former section, article or chapter of Title 19.1 or of Title 18.1 appearing elsewhere in this Code than in this title or in Title 18.2, shall be construed to apply to the new or renumbered section, article or chapter containing such conditions, requirements, provisions or contents or portions thereof.

History.

1975, c. 495.

§ 19.2-5. Meaning of certain terms.

As used in this title, unless otherwise clearly indicated by the context in which it appears:

"Court" means any court vested with appropriate jurisdiction under the Constitution and laws of the Commonwealth.

"Court not of record" and *"district court"* shall have the respective meanings assigned to them in Chapter 4.1 (§ 16.1-69.1 et seq.) of Title 16.1.

"Judge" means any judge, associate judge or substitute judge of any court or any magistrate.

History.

Code 1950, § 19.1-5; 1960, c. 366; 1975, c. 495; 2005, c. 839; 2008, cc. 551, 691.

The 2008 amendments.

The 2008 amendments by cc. 551 and 691 are nearly identical, and substituted "judge of any court or any magistrate" for "judge, or magistrate, of any court" in the definition of "Judge."

§ 19.2-6. Appointive power of circuit courts.

Unless otherwise specifically provided, whenever an appointive power is given to the judge of a circuit court, that power shall be exercised by a majority of the judges of the circuit. In case of a tie, such fact shall be communicated to the Chief Justice of the Supreme Court, who shall appoint a circuit judge from another circuit who shall act as a tie breaker. Where the power of appointment is to be exercised by a majority of the judges of the Second Judicial Circuit and such appointment is to a local post, board or commission in Accomack or Northampton County, the resident judge or judges of the County of Accomack or Northampton shall exercise such appointment power as if he or they comprise the majority of the judges of the Circuit.

History.

1975, c. 495; 1977, c. 288; 1994, c. 407.

§ 19.2-7. Rewards for arrest of persons convicted of or charged with offenses; rewards for conviction of unknown offenders.

The Governor may offer a reward for apprehending and securing any person convicted of an offense or charged therewith, who shall have escaped from lawful custody or confinement, or for apprehending and securing any person charged with an offense, who, there is reason to fear, cannot be arrested in the common course of proceeding. The Governor may also offer a reward for the detection and conviction of the person guilty of an offense when such offense has been committed but the person guilty thereof is unknown.

Any sheriff, deputy sheriff, sergeant, deputy sergeant or any other officer may claim and receive any reward which may be offered for the arrest and detention of any offender against the criminal laws of this or any other state or nation.

History.

Code 1950, §§ 19.1-6, 19.1-6.1; 1960, c. 366; 1962, c. 513; 1964, c. 171; 1975, c. 495.

Cross references.

As to right of police officer to receive rewards, see § 15.2-1710. As to authority of localities to offer rewards, see § 15.2-1713. As to right of officers enforcing the motor vehicle laws to receive rewards, see § 46.2-218. As to right of State Police officers to receive rewards, see § 52-10.

Law Review.

For comment, "Effect of Public Policy upon Reward Offers," see 20 Wash. & Lee L. Rev. 395 (1963).

Michie's Jurisprudence.

For related discussion, see 3A M.J. Bounties or Rewards, § 2; 13B M.J. Municipal Corporations, § 80; 15 M.J. Public Officers, § 45; 16 M.J. Sheriffs, § 7.

CASE NOTES

This section illustrates the legislative policy on the subject of rewards to public officers. Buek v. Nance, 112 Va. 28, 70 S.E. 515 (1911), wherein this section was held not applicable.

§ 19.2-8. Limitation of prosecutions.

A prosecution for a misdemeanor, or any pecuniary fine, forfeiture, penalty or amercement, shall be commenced within one year next after there was cause therefor, except that a prosecution for petit larceny may be commenced within five years, and for an attempt to produce abortion, within two years after commission of the offense.

A prosecution for any misdemeanor violation of § 54.1-3904 shall be commenced within two years of the discovery of the offense.

A prosecution for violation of laws governing the placement of children for adoption without a license pursuant to § 63.2-1701 shall be commenced within one year from the date of the filing of the petition for adoption.

A prosecution for making a false statement or representation of a material fact knowing it to be false or knowingly failing to disclose a material fact, to obtain or increase any benefit or other payment under the Virginia Unemployment Compensation Act (§ 60.2-100 et seq.) shall be commenced within three years next after the commission of the offense.

A prosecution for any violation of § 10.1-1320, 62.1-44.32 (b), 62.1-194.1, or Article 11 (§ 62.1-44.34:14 et seq.) of Chapter 3.1 of Title 62.1 that involves the discharge, dumping or emission of any toxic substance as defined in § 32.1-239 shall be commenced within three years next after the commission of the offense.

Prosecution of Building Code violations under § 36-106 shall commence within one year of discovery of the offense by the building official; provided that such discovery occurs within two years of the date of initial occupancy or use after construction of the building or structure, or the issuance of a certificate of use and occupancy for the building or structure, whichever is later. However, prosecutions under § 36-106 relating to the maintenance of existing buildings or structures as contained in the Uniform Statewide Building Code shall commence within one year of the discovery of the offense by the building official.

Prosecution of any misdemeanor violation of § 54.1-111 shall commence within one year of the discovery of the offense by the complainant, but in no case later than five years from occurrence of the offense.

Prosecution of any misdemeanor violation of any professional licensure requirement imposed by a locality shall commence within one year of the discovery of the offense by the complainant, but in no case later than five years from occurrence of the offense.

Prosecution of nonfelonious offenses which constitute malfeasance in office shall commence within two years next after the commission of the offense.

Prosecution of any violation of § 55-79.87, 55-79.88, 55-79.89, 55-79.90, 55-79.93, 55-79.94, 55-79.95, 55-79.103, or any rule adopted under or order issued pursuant to § 55-79.98, shall commence within three years next after the commission of the offense.

Prosecution of illegal sales or purchases of wild birds, wild animals and freshwater fish under § 29.1-553 shall commence within three years after commission of the offense.

Prosecution of violations under Title 58.1 for offenses involving false or fraudulent statements, documents or returns, or for the offense of willfully attempting in any manner to evade or defeat any tax or the payment thereof, or for the offense of willfully failing to pay any tax, or willfully failing to make any return at the time or times required by law or regulations shall commence within three years next after the commission of the offense, unless a longer period is otherwise prescribed.

Prosecution of violations of subsection A or B of § 3.2-6570 shall commence within five years of the commission of the offense, except violations regarding agricultural animals shall commence within one year of the commission of the offense.

A prosecution for a violation of § 18.2-386.1 shall be commenced within five years of the commission of the offense.

A prosecution for any violation of the Campaign Finance Disclosure Act, Chapter 9.3 (§ 24.2-945 et seq.) of Title 24.2, shall commence within one year of the discovery of the offense but in no case more than three years after the date of the commission of the offense.

A prosecution of a crime that is punishable as a misdemeanor pursuant to the Virginia Computer Crimes Act (§ 18.2-152.1 et seq.) or pursuant to § 18.2-186.3 for identity theft shall be commenced before the earlier of (i) five years after the commission of the last act in the course of conduct constituting a violation of the article or (ii) one year after the existence of the illegal act and the identity of the offender are discovered by the Commonwealth, by the owner, or by anyone else who is damaged by such violation.

Nothing in this section shall be construed to apply to any person fleeing from justice or concealing himself within or without the Commonwealth to avoid arrest or be construed to limit the time within which any prosecution may be commenced for desertion of a spouse or child or for neglect or refusal or failure to provide for the support and maintenance of a spouse or child.

History.
Code 1950, § 19.1-8; 1960, c. 366; 1974, c. 466; 1975, c. 495; 1976, cc. 114, 620; 1977, c. 108; 1978, c. 730; 1979, c. 243; 1980, c. 496; 1981, c. 31; 1984, c. 601; 1987, c. 488; 1990, cc. 575, 976; 1992, cc. 177, 435, 650; 1996, c. 484; 1998, c. 566; 1999, c. 620; 2005, cc. 746,

761, 827; 2006, cc. 193, 787, 892; 2008, c. 769; 2011, cc. 118, 143, 494, 553.

Editor's note.

Effective October 1, 2008, the reference to "subsection A or B of § 3.1-796.122" was changed to "subsection A or B of § 3.2-6570" to conform to Acts 2008, c. 860.

Acts 1976, c. 620, cl. 3 provides: "That the amended period of limitation for prosecutions provided for by this act shall apply only to offenses committed subsequent to the effective date of this act [April 9, 1976]."

The 2008 amendments.

The 2008 amendment by c. 769 inserted "or pursuant to § 18.2-186.3 for identity theft" in the fourteenth paragraph.

The 2011 amendments.

The 2011 amendments by cc. 118 and 143 are identical, and in the sixth paragraph, deleted "by the owner or" following "discovery of the offense" in the first sentence, and added "by the building official" in the last sentence.

The 2011 amendment by c. 494 added the eighth paragraph.

The 2011 amendment by c. 553 added the second paragraph.

Law Review.

For a discussion of statutory changes in child placement by the 1978 session of the General Assembly, see 12 U. Rich. L. Rev. 739 (1978). For 2006 survey article, "Criminal Law and Procedure," see 41 U. Rich. L. Rev. 83 (2006). For 2007 annual survey article, "Electronic Data: A Commentary on the Law in Virginia in 2007," see 42 U. Rich. L. Rev. 355 (2007).

Michie's Jurisprudence.

For related discussion, see 1A M.J. Adultery, Fornication and Lewdness, § 5; 2A M.J. Assault and Battery, § 10; 12A M.J. Larceny, § 32; 12A M.J. Limitation of Actions, §§ 1, 21.

CASE NOTES

Applicability. — Larceny that was a misdemeanor was a petit larceny, there were no other possibilities for other larcenies within the context of § 18.2-181. Since § 18.2-96 had no impact upon the foregoing analysis, the one year statute of limitations, which applied to misdemeanors, did not apply to defendant's act of passing a bad check for $140.88. Foster v. Commonwealth, 271 Va. 235, 623 S.E.2d 902, 2006 Va. LEXIS 6 (2006).

This section prescribes the limitation of criminal prosecution generally. Quillin v. Commonwealth, 105 Va. 874, 54 S.E. 333 (1906).

It has no application to a civil contempt proceeding against a husband for his refusal to obey decrees directing him to pay counsel fees and court costs incurred by his wife in a divorce suit. Eddens v. Eddens, 188 Va. 511, 50 S.E.2d 397 (1948).

This section is not applicable to a civil action based on common-law fraud. Reid v. Madison, 455 F. Supp. 1066 (E.D. Va. 1978).

This section is inapplicable to habitual offender proceedings under former § 46.1-387.1 et seq. (see now § 46.2-356 et seq.), because the habitual offender proceedings are civil in nature and not criminal. Furthermore, the Habitual Offender Act itself contemplates certification after more than five years. Bouldin v. Commonwealth, 4 Va. App. 166, 355 S.E.2d 352 (1987).

A presentment for a misdemeanor is the commencement of the prosecution; and unless the prosecution is then barred by the statute of limitations, it will not be barred by the failure to file an information or indictment upon the presentment before the time of limitations runs out. Commonwealth v. Christian, 48 Va. (7 Gratt.) 631 (1850).

Issuance of warrant commences prosecution for misdemeanor. — The issuance of a warrant commences prosecution within meaning of the provision that "a prosecution for a misdemeanor ... shall be commenced within one year next after there was cause therefor." Hall v. Commonwealth, 2 Va. App. 159, 342 S.E.2d 640 (1986).

Felony warrant does not bar prosecution for lesser included misdemeanor. — The fact that the warrant (and subsequent indictment) charged a felony does not bar prosecution for a lesser included misdemeanor so long as the prosecution was commenced within the applicable limitation period. Hall v. Commonwealth, 2 Va. App. 159, 342 S.E.2d 640 (1986).

The duty to pay a penalty for the violation of a legal regulation is a legal obligation not contractual in its nature and the limitation applicable is one year. Director Gen. of R.Rs. v. E.W. Gates & Son Co., 7 Va. L. Reg. (n.s.) 253 (1921).

Information in nature of writ of quo warranto. — An early act which limited the prosecution of certain indictments or informations to one year was held not to apply to an information in the nature of a writ of quo warranto. Commonwealth v. Birchett, 4 Va. (2 Va. Cas.) 51 (1816).

Indictment should show offense committed within statutory period. — Where there is a limitation barring the prosecution after a certain time, such facts should be stated in the indictment as will show that the offense charged was committed within the statutory period. Shiflett v. Commonwealth, 114 Va. 876, 77 S.E. 606 (1913).

Presentments issued by grand jury charging defendant with causing or creating a public nuisance and of permitting the continuation of a public nuisance were not fatally defective after the trial court amended the presentments to cover a one-year time period, which was the allotted time-period for prosecution of a misdemeanor, instead of the two-year time period that had been set forth; the trial court's amendment merely narrowed the time alleged in the presentments and did not change the nature of the offenses charged against defendant. Niazi v. Commonwealth, No. 2283-02-2, 2004 Va. App. LEXIS 102 (Ct. of Appeals Mar. 9, 2004).

Presumption on appeal. — After a verdict of conviction for a misdemeanor, an appellate court will presume that the offense was proved to have been within the period of limitation, where the record does not show the contrary. Earhart v. Commonwealth, 36 Va. (9 Leigh) 671 (1839).

Prosecution of misdemeanor brought after dismissal of manslaughter indictment. — On a trial for involuntary manslaughter, the trial court, after hearing the evidence, dismissed the manslaughter indictment, issued a bench warrant charging defendant with driving under the influence of alcohol, and found him guilty as charged. It was held that, since the warrant was issued more than one year after the accident upon which the prosecution was based occurred, and charged a specific misdemeanor for which defendant could not have been convicted under the indictment for which he was then being tried, the prosecution was barred by the statute of limitations. Ange v. Commonwealth, 217 Va. 861, 234 S.E.2d 64 (1977).

Prosecution for Building Code violations held timely. — Violations of § 119.2 of the Uniform Statewide Building Code are not continuing ones. Nevertheless, prosecution commenced within the applicable limitation period, where the building inspector did not "discover" the violations until January of 1984 when he concluded his investigation and then notified the construction company of the offenses, and prosecution began on October 16, 1984, within one year of discovery of the statutory violations. Granny's Cottage Inc. v. Town of Occoquan, 3 Va. App. 577, 352 S.E.2d 10 (1987) (decided under prior law).

CIRCUIT COURT OPINIONS

Privilege against self-incrimination inapplicable to husband's alleged adulterous affairs occurring more than a year prior to his deposition. — Because the statute of limitations in § 19.2-8 did not apply to a husband's alleged adulterous affairs occurring more than a year prior to his deposition, the husband could not invoke the privilege against self-incrimination found in U.S. Const., Amend. V and Va. Const., Art. I, § 8. Brubach v. Hystad, 68 Va. Cir. 181, 2005 Va. Cir. LEXIS 68 (Greene County 2005).

§ 19.2-8.1. Prosecution for murder or manslaughter; passage of time not a limitation.

A prosecution for murder or manslaughter, whether at common law or under the Code of Virginia, may be instituted regardless of the time elapsed between the act or omission causing the death of the victim and the death of the victim.

History.
2009, c. 278.

Editor's note.
Acts 2009, c. 278, cl. 2, provides: "That the provisions of this act may result in a net increase in periods of imprisonment or commitment. Pursuant to § 30-19.1:4, the estimated amount of the necessary appropriation cannot be determined for periods of imprisonment in state adult correctional facilities and is $0 for periods of commitment to the custody of the Department of Juvenile Justice."

§ 19.2-9. Prosecution of certain criminal cases removed from state to federal courts; costs.

When any person indicted in the courts of this Commonwealth for a violation of its laws, has his case removed to the district court of the United States under 28 U.S.C. § 1442, it shall be the duty of the attorney for the Commonwealth for the county or city in which any such indictment is found to prosecute any such case in the United States district court to which the same shall be so removed, and for his services in this behalf he shall be paid a fee of $100 for each case tried by him in such United States district court, and mileage at the rate now allowed by law to the members of the General Assembly for all necessary travel in going to and returning from such court, to be paid on his account when approved by the Attorney General.

A per diem of one dollar and fifty cents for each day of actual attendance upon such United States district court and mileage at a rate as provided by law for every mile of necessary travel in going to and returning from such court shall be paid out of the state treasury to each witness for the Commonwealth in every such case upon accounts therefor against the Commonwealth, certified by the attorney for the Commonwealth prosecuting such case and approved by the Attorney General.

It shall not be the duty of the Attorney General to appear for the Commonwealth in such cases unless he can do so without interfering with the efficient discharge of the duties imposed upon him by law; but he may appear with the attorney for the Commonwealth prosecuting such case in any case when the interests of the Commonwealth may in his judgment require his presence.

The Comptroller shall from time to time draw his warrants upon the state treasury in favor of the parties entitled to be paid the above compensation and expenses, or their assigns, upon bills certified and approved as above prescribed.

History.
Code 1950, § 19.1-14; 1960, c. 366; 1975, c. 495.

§ 19.2-9.1. Written notice required for complaining witness who is requested to take polygraph test.

A. For offenses not specified in subsection B, if a complaining witness is requested to submit to a polygraph examination during the course of a criminal investigation, such witness shall be informed in writing prior to the examination that (i) the examination is voluntary, (ii) the results thereof are inadmissible as evidence and (iii) the agreement of the complaining witness to submit thereto shall not be the sole condition for initiating or continuing the criminal investigation.

B. No law-enforcement officer, attorney for the Commonwealth, or other government official shall ask or require a victim of an alleged sex offense to submit to a polygraph examination or other truthtelling device as a condition for proceeding with the investigation of such an offense. If a victim is requested to submit to a polygraph examination during the course of a criminal investigation, such victim shall be informed in writing of the provisions of subsection A and that the refusal of a victim to submit to such an examination shall not prevent the investigation, charging, or prosecution of the offense.

C. A *"sex offense,"* for the purposes of this section, shall mean any offense set forth in Article 7 (§ 18.2-61 et seq.) of Chapter 4 of Title 18.2.

History.
1994, c. 336; 2008, cc. 512, 748.

Cross references.
As to response policies and procedures in sexual assault cases, see § 9.1-1301.

The 2008 amendments.
The 2008 amendments by cc. 512 and 748 are nearly identical, and designated the existing provisions of this section as subsection A; in subsection A, substituted "For offenses not specified in subsection B, if" for "If" at the beginning; and added subsections B and C.

§ 19.2-10. Outlawry abolished.

No proceeding of outlawry shall hereafter be instituted or prosecuted.

History.
Code 1950, § 19.1-15; 1960, c. 366; 1975, c. 495.

§ 19.2-10.1. Subpoena duces tecum for obtaining records concerning banking and credit cards.

A. A financial institution as defined in § 6.2-604, money transmitter as defined in § 6.2-1900, or commercial businesses providing credit history or credit reports; or an issuer as defined in § 6.2-424 shall disclose a record or other information pertaining to a customer, to a law-enforcement officer pursuant to a subpoena duces tecum issued pursuant to this section.

1. In order to obtain such records, the law-enforcement official shall provide a statement of the facts documenting the reasons that the records or other information sought are relevant to a legitimate law-enforcement inquiry, relating to a named person or persons, to the attorney for the Commonwealth. A court shall issue a subpoena duces tecum upon motion of the Commonwealth only if the court finds that there is probable cause to believe that a crime has been committed and to believe the records sought or other information sought, including electronic data and electronic communications, are relevant to a legitimate law-enforcement inquiry into that offense. The court may issue a subpoena duces tecum under this section regardless of whether any criminal charges have been filed.

2. A court issuing an order pursuant to this section, on a motion made promptly by the financial institution or credit card issuer, or enterprise may quash or modify the subpoena duces tecum, if the information or records requested are unusually voluminous in nature or compliance with such subpoena duces tecum would otherwise cause an undue burden on such provider.

B. No cause of action shall lie in any court against a financial institution or credit card issuer, or enterprise, its officers, employees, agents, or other specified persons for providing information, facilities, or assistance in accordance with the terms of a subpoena duces tecum under this section.

C. Upon issuance of a subpoena duces tecum under this section, the statement shall be temporarily sealed by the court upon application of the attorney for the Commonwealth for good cause shown in an ex parte proceeding. Any individual arrested and claiming to be aggrieved by the order may move the court for the unsealing of the statement, and the burden of proof with respect to continued sealing shall be upon the Commonwealth.

D. Any and all records received by law enforcement pursuant to this section shall be utilized only for a reasonable amount of time and only for a legitimate law-enforcement purpose. Upon the completion of the investigation the records shall be submitted to the court by the attorney for the Commonwealth along with a proposed order requiring the records to be sealed. Upon entry of such order, the court shall seal the records in accordance with the requirements contained in subsection C.

History.
2003, cc. 223, 541, 549; 2004, cc. 883, 996; 2010, cc. 702, 794.

The 2010 amendments.
The 2010 amendment by c. 702 inserted "including electronic data and electronic communications" in the second sentence of subdivision A 1.

The 2010 amendment by c. 794, effective October 1, 2010, in subsection A, substituted "6.2-604" for "6.1-125.1," "6.2-1900" for

"6.1-370," and "an issuer as defined in § 6.2-424" for "a credit card issuer as defined in § 11-30."

Law Review.
For article summarizing published Virginia criminal law decisions between July 1, 2002 and July 1, 2003, see 38 U. Rich. L. Rev. 87 (2003).

§ 19.2-10.2. Administrative subpoena issued for record from provider of electronic communication service or remote computing service.

A. A provider of electronic communication service or remote computing service that is transacting or has transacted any business in the Commonwealth shall disclose a record or other information pertaining to a subscriber to or customer of such service, excluding the contents of electronic communications as required by § 19.2-70.3, to an attorney for the Commonwealth pursuant to an administrative subpoena issued under this section.

1. In order to obtain such records or other information, the attorney for the Commonwealth shall certify on the face of the subpoena that there is reason to believe that the records or other information being sought are relevant to a legitimate law-enforcement investigation concerning violations of §§ 18.2-374.1, 18.2-374.1:1, former § 18.2-374.1:2, and § 18.2-374.3.

2. On a motion made promptly by the electronic communication service or remote computing service provider, a court of competent jurisdiction may quash or modify the administrative subpoena if the records or other information requested are unusually voluminous in nature or if compliance with the subpoena would otherwise cause an undue burden on the service provider.

B. All records or other information received by an attorney for the Commonwealth pursuant to an administrative subpoena issued under this section shall be used only for a reasonable length of time not to exceed 30 days and only for a legitimate law-enforcement purpose. Upon completion of the investigation the records or other information held by the attorney for the Commonwealth shall be destroyed if no prosecution is initiated.

C. No cause of action shall lie in any court against an electronic communication service or remote computing service provider, its officers, employees, agents, or other specified persons for providing information, facilities, or assistance in accordance with the terms of an administrative subpoena issued under this section.

D. Records or other information pertaining to a subscriber to or customer of such service means name, address, local and long distance telephone connection records, or records of session times and durations, length of service, including start date, and types of service utilized, telephone or instrument number or other subscriber number or identity, including any temporarily assigned network address, and means and source of payment for such service.

E. Nothing in this section shall require the disclosure of information in violation of any federal law.

History.
2007, cc. 802, 814.

§ 19.2-11. Procedure in contempt cases.

No court or judge shall impose a fine upon a juror, witness or other person for disobedience of its process or any contempt, unless he either be present in court at the time, or shall have been served with a rule, returnable to a certain time, requiring him to show cause why the fine should not be imposed and shall have failed to appear and show cause.

History.
Code 1950, § 19.1-16; 1960, c. 366; 1968, c. 639; 1975, c. 495.

Cross references.
For general provisions relating to contempt, see §§ 18.2-456 through 18.2-459 and notes thereto.

Michie's Jurisprudence.
For related discussion, see 4A M.J. Contempt, §§ 22, 29; 9A M.J. Grand Jury, § 16.

CASE NOTES

When contempt to be adjudicated. — This section does not require the trial judge to adjudicate a contempt committed in his presence at the very instant of the alleged misbehavior or disobedience of the court's ruling. He may do so under § 18.2-456, but he is not required to. Higginbotham v. Commonwealth, 206 Va. 291, 142 S.E.2d 746 (1965).

Death of the contemnor. — Punishment may not be imposed in a civil contempt proceeding when it is established that the contemnor is unable to comply with the terms of the order or to purge himself; therefore when contemnor spouse has died, the court's personal jurisdiction ends. Estate of Hackler v. Hackler, 44 Va. App. 51, 602 S.E.2d 426, 2004 Va. App. LEXIS 454 (2004).

Concealment of witnesses. — Where a court orders a subpoena for witnesses to attend the grand jury and they intentionally conceal themselves, and so prevent the process from being served until the grand jury is discharged, this is not a contempt punishable by the court in a summary manner. Commonwealth v. Deskins, 31 Va. (4 Leigh) 685 (1834).

CHAPTER 1.1.

CRIME VICTIM AND WITNESS RIGHTS ACT.

§ 19.2-11.01. Crime victim and witness rights.

A. In recognition of the Commonwealth's concern for the victims and witnesses of crime, it is the purpose of this chapter to ensure that the full impact of crime is brought to the attention of the courts of the Commonwealth; that crime victims and witnesses are treated with dignity, respect and sensitivity; and that their privacy is protected to the extent permissible under law. It is the further purpose of this chapter to ensure that victims and witnesses are informed of the rights provided to them under the laws of the Commonwealth; that they receive authorized services as appropriate; and that they have the opportunity to be heard by law-enforcement agencies, attorneys for the Commonwealth, corrections agencies and the judiciary at all critical stages of the criminal justice process to the extent permissible under law. Unless otherwise stated and subject to the provisions of § 19.2-11.1, it shall be the responsibility of a locality's crime victim and witness assistance program to provide the information and assistance required by this chapter, including verification that the standardized form listing the specific rights afforded to crime victims has been received by the victim.

As soon as practicable after identifying a victim of a crime, the investigating law-enforcement agency shall provide the victim with a standardized form listing the specific rights afforded to crime victims. The form shall include a telephone number by which the victim can receive further information and assistance in securing the rights afforded crime victims, the name, address and telephone number of the office of the attorney for the Commonwealth, the name, address and telephone number of the investigating law-enforcement agency, and a summary of the victim's rights under § 40.1-28.7:2.

1. Victim and witness protection and law-enforcement contacts.

a. In order that victims and witnesses receive protection from harm and threats of harm arising out of their cooperation with law-enforcement, or prosecution efforts, they shall be provided with information as to the level of protection which may be available pursuant to § 52-35 or to any other federal, state or local program providing protection, and shall be assisted in obtaining this protection from the appropriate authorities.

b. Victims and witnesses shall be provided, where available, a separate waiting area during court proceedings that affords them privacy and protection from intimidation, and that does not place the victim in close proximity to the defendant or the defendant's family.

2. Financial assistance.

a. Victims shall be informed of financial assistance and social services available to them as victims of a crime, including information on their possible right to file a claim for compensation from the Crime Victims' Compensation Fund pursuant to Chapter 21.1 (§ 19.2-368.1 et seq.) of this title and on other available assistance and services.

b. Victims shall be assisted in having any property held by law-enforcement agencies for evidentiary purposes returned promptly in accordance with §§ 19.2-270.1 and 19.2-270.2.

c. Victims shall be advised that restitution is available for damages or loss resulting from an offense and shall be assisted in seeking restitution in accordance with §§ 19.2-305, 19.2-305.1, Chapter 21.1 (§ 19.2-368.1 et seq.) of this title, Article 21 (§ 58.1-520 et seq.) of Chapter 3 of Title 58.1, and other applicable laws of the Commonwealth.

3. Notices.

a. Victims and witnesses shall be (i) provided with appropriate employer intercession services to ensure that employers of victims and witnesses will cooperate with the criminal justice process in order to minimize an employee's loss of pay and other benefits resulting from court appearances and (ii) advised that pursuant to § 18.2-465.1 it is unlawful for an employer to penalize an employee for appearing in court pursuant to a summons or subpoena.

b. Victims shall receive advance notification when practicable from the attorney for the Commonwealth of judicial proceedings relating to their case and shall be notified when practicable of any change in court dates in accordance with § 19.2-265.01 if they have provided their names, current addresses and telephone numbers.

c. Victims shall receive notification, if requested, subject to such reasonable procedures as the Attorney General may require pursuant to § 2.2-511, from the Attorney General of the filing and disposition of any appeal or habeas corpus proceeding involving their case.

d. Victims shall be notified by the Department of Corrections or a sheriff or jail superintendent (i) in whose custody an escape, change of name, transfer, release or discharge of a prisoner occurs pursuant to the provisions of §§ 53.1-133.02 and 53.1-160 or (ii) when an accused is released on bail, if they have provided their names, current addresses and telephone numbers in writing. Such notification may be provided through the Virginia Statewide VINE (Victim Information and Notification Everyday) System or other similar electronic or automated system.

e. Victims shall be advised that, in order to protect their right to receive notices and offer input, all agencies and persons having such duties must have current victim addresses and telephone numbers given by the victims. Victims shall also be advised that any such information given shall be confidential as provided by § 19.2-11.2.

4. Victim input.

a. Victims shall be given the opportunity, pursuant to § 19.2-299.1, to prepare a written victim impact statement prior to sentencing of a defendant and may provide information to any individual or agency charged with investigating the social history of a person or preparing a victim impact statement under the provisions of §§ 16.1-273 and 53.1-155 or any other applicable law.

b. Victims shall have the right to remain in the courtroom during a criminal trial or proceeding pursuant to the provisions of § 19.2-265.01.

c. On motion of the attorney for the Commonwealth, victims shall be given the opportunity, pursuant to §§ 19.2-264.4 and 19.2-295.3, to testify prior to sentencing of a defendant regarding the impact of the offense.

d. In a felony case, the attorney for the Commonwealth, upon the victim's written request, shall consult with the victim either verbally or in writing (i) to inform the victim of the contents of a proposed plea agreement and (ii) to obtain the victim's views about the disposition of the case, including the victim's views concerning dismissal, pleas, plea negotiations and sentencing. However, nothing in this section shall limit the ability of the attorney for the Commonwealth to exercise his discretion on behalf of the citizens of the Commonwealth in the disposition of any criminal case. The court shall not accept the plea agreement unless it finds that, except for good cause shown, the Commonwealth has complied with clauses (i) and (ii). Good cause shown shall include, but not be limited to, the unavailability of the victim due to incarceration, hospitalization, failure to appear at trial when subpoenaed, or change of address without notice.

Upon the victim's written request, the victim shall be notified in accordance with subdivision A 3 b of any proceeding in which the plea agreement will be tendered to the court.

The responsibility to consult with the victim under this subdivision shall not confer upon the defendant any substantive or procedural rights and shall not affect the validity of any plea entered by the defendant.

5. Courtroom assistance.

a. Victims and witnesses shall be informed that their addresses and telephone numbers may not be disclosed, pursuant to the provisions of §§ 19.2-11.2 and 19.2-269.2, except when necessary for the conduct of the criminal proceeding.

b. Victims and witnesses shall be advised that they have the right to the services of an interpreter in accordance with §§ 19.2-164 and 19.2-164.1.

c. Victims and witnesses of certain sexual offenses shall be advised that there may be a closed preliminary hearing in accordance with § 18.2-67.8 and, if a victim was 14 years of age or younger on the date of the offense and is 16 or under at the time of the trial, or a witness to the offense is 14 years of age or younger at the time of the trial, that two-way closed-circuit television may be used in the taking of testimony in accordance with § 18.2-67.9.

6. Post trial assistance.

a. Within 30 days of receipt of a victim's written request after the final trial court proceeding in the case, the attorney for the Commonwealth shall notify the victim in writing, of (i) the disposition of the case, (ii) the crimes of which the defendant was convicted, (iii) the defendant's right to appeal, if known, and (iv) the telephone number of offices to contact in the event of nonpayment of restitution by the defendant.

b. If the defendant has been released on bail pending the outcome of an appeal, the agency that had custody of the defendant immediately prior to his release shall notify the victim as soon as practicable that the defendant has been released.

c. If the defendant's conviction is overturned, and the attorney for the Commonwealth decides to retry the case or the case is remanded for a new trial, the victim shall be entitled to the same rights as if the first trial did not take place.

B. For purposes of this chapter, *"victim"* means (i) a person who has suffered physical, psychological or economic harm as a direct result of the commission of a felony or of assault and battery in violation of § 18.2-57 or § 18.2-57.2, stalking in violation of § 18.2-60.3, sexual battery in violation of § 18.2-67.4, attempted sexual battery in violation of § 18.2-67.5, maiming or driving while intoxicated in violation of § 18.2-51.4 or § 18.2-266, (ii) a spouse or child of such a person, (iii) a parent or legal guardian of such a person who is a minor, (iv) for the purposes of subdivision A 4 of this section only, a current or former foster parent or other person who has or has had physical custody of such a person who is a minor, for six months or more or for the majority of the minor's life, or (v) a spouse, parent, sibling or legal guardian of such a person who is physically or mentally incapacitated or was the victim of a homicide; however, "victim" does not mean a parent, child, spouse, sibling or legal guardian who commits a felony or other enumerated criminal offense against a victim as defined in clause (i).

C. Officials and employees of the judiciary, including court services units, law-enforcement agencies, the Department of Corrections, attorneys for the Commonwealth and public defenders, shall be provided with copies of this chapter by the Department of Criminal Justice Services or a crime victim and witness assistance program. Each agency, officer or employee who has a responsibility or responsibilities to victims under this chapter or other applicable law shall make reasonable efforts to become informed about these responsibilities and to ensure that victims and witnesses receive such information and services to which they may be entitled under applicable law, provided that no liability or cause of action shall arise from the failure to make such efforts or from the failure of such victims or witnesses to receive any such information or services.

History.
1995, c. 687; 1996, c. 546; 1997, c. 691; 1998, c. 485; 1999, cc. 668, 702, 844; 2000, cc. 272, 827; 2001, cc. 410, 530, 549; 2002, cc. 310, 810, 818; 2003, cc. 103, 751, 764; 2006, c. 241; 2007, cc. 94, 109, 423.

Cross references.
As to a victim of crime or a representative of a crime victims' organization serving as a member on the Criminal Justice Services Board, see § 9.1-108.

Editor's note.
Acts 2001, c. 410, cl. 2, provides: "That the provisions of this act shall not be construed so as to require the installation of permanent

two-way closed-circuit television equipment in any courtroom in the Commonwealth."

The 2007 amendments.
The 2007 amendments by cc. 94 and 109 are identical, and added the last sentence in subdivision A 3 d.
The 2007 amendment by c. 423 in the second paragraph of subsection A, deleted "and" preceding "the name," and inserted "and a summary of the victim's rights under § 40.1-28.7:2" at the end.

Law Review.
For 1995 survey of legal issues involving children, see 29 U. Rich. L. Rev. 1117 (1995). For 2000 survey of Virginia criminal law and procedure, see 34 U. Rich. L. Rev. 749 (2000). For article, "Criminal Law and Procedure," see 35 U. Rich. L. Rev. 537 (2001). For article, "Legal Issues Involving Children," see 35 U. Rich. L. Rev. 741 (2001). For annual survey article on legal issues involving children, see 38 U. Rich. L. Rev. 161 (2003). For annual survey of Virginia labor and employment law, see 40 U. Rich. L. Rev. 241 (2005). For article, "Prosecutorial Power: A Transnational Symposium: The Worldwide Accountability Deficit for Prosecutors," see 67 Wash & Lee L. Rev. 1587 (2010).

Michie's Jurisprudence.
For related discussion, see 5B M.J. Criminal Procedure, § 38; 20 M.J. Witnesses, § 35.

CASE NOTES

The statutes do not limit evidence of victim impact to that received from the victim's family members; rather, the circumstances of the individual case will dictate what evidence will be necessary and relevant, and from what sources it may be drawn. Beck v. Commonwealth, 253 Va. 373, 484 S.E.2d 898, cert. denied, 522 U.S. 1018, 118 S. Ct. 608, 139 L. Ed. 2d 495 (1997).

Relevant statutes, including this section, did not limit the evidence of victim impact to that received from the victim's family members since the circumstance of the individual case dictated what victim impact evidence would be relevant and necessary, and from what source it would be drawn; thus, victim impact statements from the victim's cousin and fiance were admissible at sentencing phase on defendant's capital murder conviction. Thomas v. Commonwealth, 263 Va. 216, 559 S.E.2d 652, 2002 Va. LEXIS 27 (2002).

Former girlfriend's psychological harm was the "direct result" of the felonies committed by defendant during a home intrusion, and the victim impact statement of the girlfriend was properly included in the pre-sentence report under subsection B of § 19.2-11.01 and § 19.2-299.1 as the goal of the home intrusion of the girlfriend's sibling was to force the girlfriend to come to that home and bring their child so that defendant could "blow her head off" with a shotgun defendant possessed; the girlfriend clearly suffered "psychological" harm as she "was scared to death" and "was waiting in horror to hear what happened" to her sibling and the sibling's family. Myers v. Commonwealth, 2008 Va. App. LEXIS 385 (Aug. 12, 2008).

Family member statements were properly admitted since the murder was determined to be a direct consequence of the conspiracy to commit robbery. — Since it could not be said that the trial court was plainly wrong when it determined that a murder was a direct consequence of a conspiracy to commit a robbery, the victim impact testimony was properly admitted even though defendant was acquitted of the murder. Furthermore, the admissibility of the victim impact testimony was relevant and within the sound discretion of the trial court even if the witnesses were not deemed "victims" under subsection B of § 19.2-11.01. Rock v. Commonwealth, 45 Va. App. 254, 610 S.E.2d 314, 2005 Va. App. LEXIS 107 (2005).

Relevant evidence not limited by statute. — There is no sound reason why relevant victim impact testimony that may be considered by a jury in a capital case should not likewise be considered in a noncapital case, §§ 19.2-295.3 and 19.2-11.01(B) do not limit the admission of relevant evidence. Rock v. Commonwealth, 45 Va. App. 254, 610 S.E.2d 314, 2005 Va. App. LEXIS 107 (2005).

No abuse of discretion in allowing victim witness to stay

in courtroom. — Circuit court did not abuse its discretion under § 19.2-265.01 by allowing a murder victim's son, who was a victim within the meaning of subsection B of § 19.2-11.01, to remain in the courtroom after he testified during the guilt phase of the trial because the circuit court correctly concluded that the victim's son did not learn anything while he was present in the court that would have changed or affected his victim impact testimony during the penalty phase, and, thus, defendant was not prejudiced by the fact that the son testified during the penalty phase after having heard much of the testimony during the guilt phase. Jackson v. Commonwealth, 267 Va. 178, 590 S.E.2d 520, 2004 Va. LEXIS 8 (2004), cert. denied, 543 U.S. 891, 125 S. Ct. 168, 160 L. Ed. 2d 155 (2004).

Because defendant provided no specific reason for finding that a victim witness's presence in the courtroom during the testimony of other witnesses would impair the fairness of the trial, the trial court did not abuse its discretion by allowing the victim witness to remain in the courtroom. Hernandez-Guerrero v. Commonwealth, 46 Va. App. 366, 617 S.E.2d 410, 2005 Va. App. LEXIS 311 (2005).

Circuit court properly found a probationer in violation of his probation, as testimony from a victim-witness in a city prosecution, which was underlying basis for the issuance of a capias in the revocation matter, was relevant; and further, that witness was exempt from sequestration, as she could not have shaped her testimony to correspond to the contents of the probationer's letter to the judge or the testimony of the probation officer. Osborne v. Commonwealth, — Va. App. —, — S.E.2d —, 2005 Va. App. LEXIS 376 (Oct. 4, 2005).

Relevance of victim impact testimony in capital case. — Trial court did not err in refusing to allow defendant to call the father of one of the decedents as a witness to testify about remarks attributed to him by the news media to the effect that as a Christian he could not hope that jurors imposed the death penalty because the testimony did not fall within the scope of victim impact testimony authorized under § 19.2-299.1 and witness opinion on what the jury should decide as the appropriate sentence in a given case was not admissible. Juniper v. Commonwealth, 271 Va. 362, 626 S.E.2d 383, 2006 Va. LEXIS 29 (2006).

With regard to defendant's convictions on two capital murder counts and the imposition of two death sentences against him, the trial court did not abuse its discretion in refusing to grant a mistrial or bar subsequent testimony from the sister of one of the murder/rape victims because no reasonable juror could conclude from the sister's testimony that she was attempting to implicate defendant in her own rape that occurred years prior in any way and the trial judge promptly, explicitly and carefully instructed the jury to disregard the inappropriate testimony that the sister made that her rapist "got away with it." Prieto v. Commonwealth, 283 Va. 149, 721 S.E.2d 484, 2012 Va. LEXIS 20 (2012).

Evidence admissible during Commonwealth's case-in-chief. — Pursuant to § 19.2-295.3, the victim was properly permitted to testify during the Commonwealth's case-in-chief of the sentencing phase of defendant's rape trial; the victim had a qualified, statutorily protected right to be heard at sentencing, and it was within the trial judge's ultimate discretion to decide when the victim would be heard on motion of the Commonwealth. Washington v. Commonwealth, 48 Va. App. 486, 632 S.E.2d 625, 2006 Va. App. LEXIS 349 (2006).

Presence of victim held not prejudicial. — Under version of §§ 19.2-11.01 and 19.2-265.01 in effect prior to July 1, 1999, defendant failed to show any prejudice resulting from the trial court's decision permitting rape victim to remain in the courtroom during malicious wounding victim's testimony; while rape victim heard malicious wounding victim's testimony, his testimony addressed the malicious wounding charge and concerned his actions prior to the time when defendant and rape victim went into the bedroom; rape victim's testimony was not influenced by malicious wounding victim's, since her testimony did not mirror his testimony; defendant's defense to the rape charge was that rape victim consented to the intercourse; and malicious wounding victim's testimony did not address the issue of whether she consented to the intercourse. Hague v. Commonwealth, No. 1274-99-2, 2000 Va. App. LEXIS 390 (Ct. of Appeals May 23, 2000).

OPINIONS OF THE ATTORNEY GENERAL

Computerized system to notify crime victims could not be used for inmates who were juveniles when crimes were committed. — Because the statutes relating to rights of victims involved in juvenile matters contained in Chapter 11 of Title 16.1 control over the general statutes relating to rights of victims as set forth in the Crime Victim and Witness Rights Act, a computerized system by which registered crime victims would be updated with information regarding future court dates, transfers, and releases of active inmates incarcerated in the city jail could not be used to provide information to victims in cases where the inmate was a juvenile when the crime was committed. See opinion of Attorney General to The Honorable Robert J. McCabe, Sheriff for the City of Norfolk, 01-058 (12/17/01).

§ 19.2-11.1. Establishment of crime victim-witness assistance programs; funding; minimum standards.

Any local governmental body which establishes, operates and maintains a crime victim and witness assistance program, whose funding is provided in whole or part by grants administered by the Department of Criminal Justice Services pursuant to § 9.1-104, shall operate the program in accordance with guidelines which shall be established by the Department to implement the provisions of this chapter and other applicable laws establishing victims' rights.

History.
1988, c. 542; 1994, cc. 361, 598; 1995, c. 687; 1996, c. 545.

Editor's note.
At the direction of the Code Commission, Acts 1994, c. 361, which amended this section, was not given effect due to a conflict. The amendment added a subdivision 10 similar to that added by Acts 1994, c. 598. The subdivisions were subsequently deleted by Acts 1995, c. 687, which enacted § 19.2-11.01.

§ 19.2-11.2. Crime victim's right to nondisclosure of certain information; exceptions; testimonial privilege.

Upon request of any witness in a criminal prosecution under § 18.2-46.2 or 18.2-46.3, or any crime victim, neither a law-enforcement agency, the attorney for the Commonwealth, the counsel for a defendant, a court nor the Department of Corrections, nor any employee of any of them, may disclose, except among themselves, the residential address, telephone number, or place of employment of the witness or victim or a member of the witness' or victim's family, except to the extent that disclosure is (i) of the site of the crime, (ii) required by law or Rules of the Supreme Court, (iii) necessary for law-enforcement purposes or preparation for court proceedings, or (iv) permitted by the court for good cause.

Except with the written consent of the victim, a law-enforcement agency may not disclose to the public information which directly or indirectly identifies the victim of a crime involving any sexual assault, sexual abuse or family abuse, except to the extent that disclosure is (i) of the site of the crime, (ii) required by law, (iii) necessary for law-enforcement purposes, or (iv) permitted by the court for good cause. In addition, at the request of the victim to the Court of Appeals of Virginia or the Supreme Court of Virginia hearing, on or after July 1, 2007, the case of a crime involving any sexual assault or sexual abuse, no appellate decision shall contain the first or last name of the victim.

Nothing herein shall limit the right to examine witnesses in a court of law or otherwise affect the conduct of any criminal proceeding.

History.
1994, cc. 845, 931; 2002, cc. 810, 818; 2005, cc. 764, 813; 2007, c. 503.

Cross references.
As to limitations on the release of criminal incident information, see § 2.2-3706.

The 2007 amendments.
The 2007 amendment by c. 503 added the last sentence in the second paragraph.

§ 19.2-11.3. Virginia Crime Victim-Witness Fund.

There is hereby established the Virginia Crime Victim-Witness Fund as a special nonreverting fund to be administered by the Department of Criminal Justice Services to support victim and witness services that meet the minimum standards prescribed for such programs under § 19.2-11.1. A portion of the sum collected pursuant to §§ 16.1-69.48:1, 17.1-275.1, 17.1-275.2, 17.1-275.3, 17.1-275.4, 17.1-275.7, 17.1-275.8, and 17.1-275.9, as specified in these sections, shall be deposited into the state treasury to the credit of this Fund. The Fund shall be distributed according to grant procedures adopted pursuant to § 9.1-104 and shall be established on the books of the Comptroller. Any funds remaining in such Fund at the end of the biennium shall not revert to the general fund, but shall remain in the Fund. Interest earned on the Fund shall be credited to the Fund.

History.
1995, c. 371; 2002, c. 831.

§ 19.2-11.4. Establishment of victim-offender reconciliation program.

A. Any Crime Victim and Witness Assistance Program may establish a victim-offender reconciliation program to provide an opportunity after conviction for a victim, at his request and upon the subsequent agreement of the offender, to:

1. Meet with the offender in a safe, controlled environment in accordance with the policies established pursuant to subsection B of § 53.1-30;

2. Give to the offender, either orally or in writing, a summary of the financial, emotional, and physical effects of the offense on the victim or the victim's family; and

3. Discuss a proposed restitution agreement which may be submitted for consideration by the sentencing court for damages incurred by the victim as a result of the offense.

B. If the victim chooses to participate in a victim-offender reconciliation program under this section,

the victim shall execute a waiver releasing the Crime Victim and Witness Assistance Program, attorney for the offender and the attorney for the Commonwealth from civil and criminal liability for actions taken by the victim or offender as a result of participation by the victim or the offender in a victim-offender reconciliation program.

C. A victim shall not be required to participate in a victim-offender reconciliation program under this section.

D. The failure of any person to participate in a reconciliation program pursuant to this section shall not be used directly or indirectly at sentencing.

History.
1995, c. 628; 2010, c. 844.

The number of this section was assigned by the Code Commission, the section number in the 1995 act having been § 19.2-11.3.

The 2010 amendments.
The 2010 amendment by c. 844 added "in accordance with the policies established pursuant to subsection B of § 53.1-30" in subdivision A 1.

CHAPTER 2.

CONSERVATORS OF THE PEACE AND SPECIAL POLICEMEN.

Article 1. Appointment.

ARTICLE 1.

APPOINTMENT.

§ 19.2-12. Who are conservators of the peace.

Every judge and attorney for the Commonwealth throughout the Commonwealth and every magistrate within the geographical area for which he is appointed or elected, shall be a conservator of the peace. In addition, every commissioner in chancery, while sitting as such commissioner; any special agent or law-enforcement officer of the United States Department of Justice, National Marine Fisheries Service of the United States Department of Commerce, Department of Treasury, Department of Agriculture, Department of Defense, Department of State, Office of the Inspector General of the Department of Transportation, Department of Homeland Security, and Department of Interior; any inspector, law-enforcement official or police personnel of the United States Postal Inspection Service; any United States marshal or deputy United States marshal whose duties involve the enforcement of the criminal laws of the United States; any officer of the Virginia Marine Police; any criminal investigator of the Department of Professional and Occupational Regulation, who meets the minimum law-enforcement training requirements established by the Department of Criminal Justice Services for in-service training; any criminal investigator of the United States Department of Labor; any special agent of the United States Naval Criminal Investigative Service, any special agent of the National Aeronautics and Space Administration, and any sworn municipal park ranger, who has completed all requirements under § 15.2-1706, shall be a conservator of the peace, while engaged in the performance of their official duties.

History.
Code 1950, § 19.1-20; 1960, c. 366; 1968, c. 639; 1972, c. 549; 1975, c. 495; 1978, c. 697; 1981, cc. 572, 587; 1990, c. 558; 1991, cc. 74, 338; 1994, cc. 375, 569, 626; 1997, c. 34; 2001, cc. 3, 31; 2002, cc. 86, 605, 789; 2004, c. 1009; 2005, c. 372; 2006, c. 88; 2007, c. 224.

Cross references.
As to inclusion of special conservators of the peace or special policemen in definition of "Criminal Justice Agency" under Chapter 9.1, see § 9.1-101.

The 2007 amendments.
The 2007 amendment by c. 224 inserted "and any sworn municipal park ranger, who has completed all requirements under § 15.2-1706" near the end of the section, and made a related change.

Michie's Jurisprudence.
For related discussion, see 2A M.J. Arrest, § 4; 2B M.J. Bail and Recognizance, § 8; 3A M.J. Breach of the Peace, § 6; 14A M.J. Notary Public, § 3.

CASE NOTES

Commissioner in chancery is conservator of peace only when performing duties of office within his county or corporation. Parker v. Commonwealth, 215 Va. 281, 208 S.E.2d 757 (1974).

Application of definition to § 18.2-308.1. — In interpreting § 18.2-308.1, which contains an exemption from the prohibition on carrying weapons on school grounds for conservators of the peace, the court is bound by the statutory definition of "conservator of the peace" adopted by the legislature and codified in this section and is not permitted to ignore or rewrite the statute in favor of a broader common-law definition. Frias v. Commonwealth, 34 Va. App. 193, 538 S.E.2d 374, 2000 Va. App. LEXIS 838 (2000).

CIRCUIT COURT OPINIONS

Park ranger. — Park rangers were permitted to exercise the powers of a conservator of the peace when engaged in the performance of their official duties; as a conservator of the peace, a ranger was permitted to make an arrest for a misdemeanor committed in his presence. A ranger's arrest of defendant for driving under the influence based on the ranger's observations of defendant was proper. Commonwealth v. Stickle, 72 Va. Cir. 494, 2007 Va. Cir. LEXIS 154 (Loudoun County 2007).

§ 19.2-13. Special conservators of the peace; authority; jurisdiction; registration; bond; liability of employers; penalty; report.

A. Upon the application of (i) any sheriff or chief of police of any county, city, or town; (ii) any corporation authorized to do business in the Commonwealth; (iii) the owner, proprietor, or authorized custodian of any place within the Commonwealth; or (iv) any museum owned and managed by the Commonwealth, a circuit court judge of any county or city shall appoint special conservators of the peace who shall serve as such for such length of time as the court may designate, but not exceeding four years under any one appointment, upon a showing by the applicant of a necessity for the security of property or the peace and presentation of evidence that the person or persons to be appointed as a special conservator of the peace possess a valid registration issued by the Department of Criminal Justice Services in accordance with the provisions of subsection B. However, a judge may deny the appointment for good cause, and shall state the specific reasons for the denial in writing in the order denying the appointment. The order of appointment may provide that a special conservator of the peace shall have all the powers, functions, duties, responsibilities and authority of any other conservator of the peace within such geographical limitations as the court may deem appropriate within the confines of the county, city or town that makes application or within the county, city or town where the corporate applicant is located, limited, except as provided in subsection E, to the judicial circuit wherein application has been made, whenever such special conservator of the peace is engaged in the performance of his duties as such. The order may also provide that the special conservator of the peace is a "law-enforcement officer" for the purposes of Article 4 (§ 37.2-808 et seq.) of Chapter 8 of Title 37.2 or Article 16 (§ 16.1-335 et seq.) of Chapter 11 of Title 16.1. The order may also provide that the special conservator of the peace is authorized to use the seal of the Commonwealth in a badge or other credential of office as the court may deem appropriate. The order may also provide that the special conservator of the peace may use the title "police" on any badge or uniform worn in the performance of his duties as such. The order may also provide that a special conservator of the peace who has completed the minimum training standards established by the Department of Criminal Justice Services, has the authority to affect arrests, using up to the same amount of force as would be allowed to a law-enforcement officer employed by the Commonwealth or any of its political subdivisions when making a lawful arrest. The order also may (a) require the local sheriff or chief of police to conduct a background investigation which may include a review of the applicant's school records, employment records, or interviews with persons possessing general knowledge of the applicant's character and fitness for such appointment and (b) limit the use of flashing lights and sirens on personal vehicles used by the conservator in the performance of his duties. Prior to granting an application for appointment, the circuit court shall ensure that the applicant has met the registration requirements established by the Criminal Justice Services Board.

B. Effective September 15, 2004, no person shall seek appointment as a special conservator of the peace from a circuit court judge without possessing a valid registration issued by the Department of Criminal Justice Services, except as provided in this section. Applicants for registration may submit an application on or after January 1, 2004. A temporary registration may be issued in accordance with regulations established by the Criminal Justice Services Board while awaiting the results of a state and national fingerprint search. However, no person shall be issued a temporary registration until he has (i) complied with, or been exempted from the compulsory minimum training standards as set forth in this section, (ii) submitted his fingerprints on a form provided by the Department to be used for the conduct of a national criminal records search and a Virginia criminal history records search, and (iii) met all other requirements of this article and Board regulations. No person with a criminal conviction for a misdemeanor involving (a) moral turpitude, (b) assault and battery, (c) damage to real or personal property, (d) controlled substances or imitation controlled substances as defined in Article 1 (§ 18.2-247 et seq.) of Chapter 7 of Title 18.2, (e) prohibited sexual behavior as described in Article 7 (§ 18.2-61 et seq.) of Chapter 4 of Title 18.2, (f) firearms, or (g) any felony, shall be registered as a special conservator of the peace. All appointments for special conservators of the peace shall become void on September 15, 2004, unless they have obtained a valid registration issued by the Department of Criminal Justice Services.

C. Each person registered as or seeking registration as a special conservator of the peace shall be covered by (i) a cash bond, or a surety bond executed by a surety company authorized to do business in the Commonwealth, in a reasonable amount to be fixed by the Board, not to be less than $10,000, conditioned upon the faithful and honest conduct of his business or employment; or (ii) evidence of a policy of liability insurance or self-insurance in an amount and with coverage as fixed by the Board. Any person who is aggrieved by the misconduct of any person registered as a special conservator of the peace and recovers a judgment against the registrant, which is unsatisfied in whole or in part, may bring an action in his own name against the bond or insurance policy of the registrant.

D. Individuals listed in § 19.2-12, individuals who have complied with or been exempted pursuant to subsection A of § 9.1-141, individuals employed as law-enforcement officers as defined in § 9.1-101 who have met the minimum qualifications set forth in § 15.2-1705 shall be exempt from the requirements in subsections A through C. Further, individuals appointed under subsection A and employed by a private corporation or entity that meets the requirements of subdivision (ii) of the definition of criminal justice agency in § 9.1-101, shall be exempt from the registration requirements of subsection A and from subsections B and C provided they have met the minimum qualifications set forth in § 15.2-1705. The Department of Criminal Justice Services shall, upon request by the circuit court, provide evidence to the circuit court of such employment prior to appointing an individual special conservator of the peace. The employing agency shall notify the circuit court within 30 days after the date such individual has left employment and all powers of the special conservator of the peace shall be void. Failure to provide such notification shall be punishable by a fine of $250 plus an additional $50 per day for each day such notice is not provided.

E. When the application is made, the circuit court shall specify in the order of appointment the name of the applicant authorized under subsection A and the geographic jurisdiction of the special conservator of the peace. Court appointments shall be limited to the judicial circuit wherein application has been made. In the case of a corporation or other business, the court appointment may also include, for good cause shown, any real property owned or leased by the corporation or business, including any subsidiaries, in other specifically named cities and counties, but shall provide that the powers of the special conservator of the peace do not extend beyond the boundaries of such real property. Effective July 1, 2004, the clerk of the appointing circuit court shall transmit a copy of the order of appointment that shall specify the following information: the person's complete name, address, date of birth, social security number, gender, race, height, weight, color of hair, color of eyes, firearm authority or limitation as set forth in subsection F, date of the order, and other information as may be required by the Department of State Police. The Department of State Police shall enter the person's name and other information into the Virginia Criminal Information Network established and maintained by the Department pursuant to Chapter 2 (§ 52-12 et seq.) of Title 52. The Department of State Police may charge a fee not to exceed $10 to cover its costs associated with processing these orders. Each special conservator of the peace so appointed on application shall present his credentials to the chief of police or sheriff or his designee of all jurisdictions where he has conservator powers. If his powers are limited to certain areas owned or leased by a corporation or business, he shall also provide notice of the exact physical addresses of those areas. Each special conservator shall provide a temporary registration letter issued by the Department of Criminal Justice Services prior to seeking an appointment by the circuit court. Once the applicant receives the appointment from the circuit court the applicant shall file the appointment order with the Department of Criminal Justice Services in order to receive his special conservator of the peace photo registration card.

If any such special conservator of the peace is the employee, agent or servant of another, his appointment as special conservator of the peace shall not relieve his employer, principal or master, from civil liability to another arising out of any wrongful action or conduct committed by such special conservator of the peace while within the scope of his employment.

Effective July 1, 2002, no person employed by a local school board as a school security officer, as defined in § 9.1-101, shall be eligible for appointment as a conservator for purposes of maintaining safety in a public school in the Commonwealth. All appointments of special conservators of the peace granted to school security officers as defined in § 9.1-101 prior to July 1, 2002 are void.

F. The court may limit or prohibit the carrying of weapons by any special conservator of the peace initially appointed on or after July 1, 1996, while the appointee is within the scope of his employment as such.

History.
Code 1950, § 19.1-28; 1960, c. 366; 1974, cc. 44, 45; 1975, c. 495; 1976, c. 220; 1982, c. 523; 1989, c. 455; 1996, cc. 850, 956; 2001, c. 249; 2002, cc. 605, 836, 868; 2003, c. 922; 2004, c. 401; 2005, c. 498; 2006, c. 290; 2007, cc. 380, 481; 2008, c. 795; 2010, cc. 530, 778, 825; 2013, cc. 105, 122.

Cross references.
As to special conservators of the peace, see § 9.1-150.1 et seq.

The 2007 amendments.
The 2007 amendments by cc. 380 and 481 are identical, and inserted "except as provided in subsection E," in the second sentence of subsection A; and in subsection E, inserted "business or other applicant" near the end of the first sentence, deleted "and to those cities and counties wherein the corporate applicant or its subsidiary holds title to real property" at the end of the second sentence, added the present third sentence, substituted "all jurisdictions where he has conservator powers" for "the jurisdiction" at the end of the seventh sentence, and added the present eighth sentence.

The 2008 amendments.
The 2008 amendment by c. 795, in subsection A, deleted "and the showing of a necessity for the security of property or the peace" following "within the Commonwealth," substituted "or city shall appoint special" for "or city, in his discretion, may appoint one or more special" and added the language beginning "upon a showing by the applicant" to the end of the first sentence and inserted the second sentence.

The 2010 amendments.
The 2010 amendment by c. 530 inserted "The order may also provide that the special conservator of the peace is authorized to use the seal of the Commonwealth in a badge or other credential of office as the court may deem appropriate." in subsection A.

The 2010 amendments by cc. 778 and 825 are identical, and inserted "or Article 16 (§ 16.1-335 et seq.) of Chapter 11 of Title 16.1" in subsection A.

The 2013 amendments.
The 2013 amendments by cc. 105 and 122 are identical, and near the beginning of the first sentence of subsection A, inserted the clause (i), (ii), and (iii) designators and clause (iv), and made related changes; and in subsection E, substituted "name of the applicant authorized under subsection A and" for "name of the sheriff or chief of police of the applicant county, city, town or the name of the corporation, business or other applicant authorized under subsection A and."

Michie's Jurisprudence.
For related discussion, see 2B M.J. Aviation, § 1.

OPINIONS OF THE ATTORNEY GENERAL

Private police officers. — The term "private police officers" in subsection D of this section refers to the category of officers appointed for the purposes described in subsection A; therefore, private police officers, who constitute special conservators of the peace and meet the training standards established by the Criminal Justice Services Board, are exempt from registration and bonding requirements. See opinion of Attorney General to The Honorable Emmett W. Hanger Jr., Member, Senate of Virginia, 04-059 (9/7/04).

§ 19.2-14. Conservators of the peace for fairgrounds and cemeteries; bond required.

The superintendent or other person in charge of any fairgrounds or any public or private cemetery shall, for the purpose of maintaining order and enforcing the criminal and police laws of the Commonwealth, or the county or city in which such fairgrounds or cemetery is situated, have all the powers, functions, duties, responsibilities and authority of a conservator of the peace within the fairgrounds or cemetery over which he may have charge and within one-half of a mile around the same.

The provisions of § 19.2-13 relative to the giving of bond and the liability of an employer, principal or master, shall be applicable to every person exercising any powers of a conservator of the peace under this section.

History.
Code 1950, § 19.1-32; 1960, c. 366; 1975, c. 495.

§ 19.2-15. When conservator appointed under § 19.2-13 need not be a citizen.

Any such conservator appointed under the provisions of § 19.2-13 whose jurisdiction is limited to the grounds attached to an airport, need not be a citizen of the Commonwealth if the proprietors of such airport shall, before any such conservator shall enter upon the duties of the office, enter into bond with approved surety before the clerk of the circuit court having jurisdiction over such airport in the penalty of $1,000 for each conservator so appointed, with condition for the faithful discharge of his official duties.

History.
Code 1950, § 19.1-29; 1960, c. 366; 1975, c. 495.

Michie's Jurisprudence.
For related discussion, see 2B M.J. Aviation, § 1.

§ 19.2-16. Repealed by Acts 1994, c. 205.

Editor's note.
Acts 1994, c. 205, cl. 2, provides that all commissions or appointments of conservators of the peace pursuant to this section shall be null and void except for appointment of persons currently employed by the Department of Conservation and Recreation. Any Commission or appointment issued pursuant to this section to persons currently employed by the Department of Conservation and Recreation shall continue in full force and effect until it is replaced by a conservation officer commission issued pursuant to § 10.1-115 or until the individual ceases to be employed by the Department.

§ 19.2-17. Repealed by Acts 1996, c. 850.

ARTICLE 2.

POWERS AND DUTIES.

§ 19.2-18. Powers and duties generally.

Every conservator of the peace shall have authority to arrest without a warrant in such instances as are set out in §§ 19.2-19 and 19.2-81. Upon making an arrest without a warrant, the conservator of the peace shall proceed in accordance with the provisions of § 19.2-22 or § 19.2-82 as the case may be.

History.
Code 1950, § 19.1-20; 1960, c. 366; 1968, c. 639; 1972, c. 549; 1975, c. 495.

Cross references.
For provision appointing directors of state hospitals and other hospital employees as conservators, see § 37.2-426.

Michie's Jurisprudence.
For related discussion, see 2A M.J. Arrest, § 4.

CASE NOTES

Conservators of the peace may carry concealed weapons. — By § 19.2-12, commissioners in chancery are conservators of the peace, and as such may carry concealed weapons, although not at the time acting in the discharge of official duty. Withers v. Commonwealth, 109 Va. 837, 65 S.E. 16 (1909).

Warrantless arrest of defendant was invalid. — Warrantless arrest of defendant in the hospital at 4:35 p.m. was invalid, where the motor vehicle accident occurred at 3:00 p.m. The officer had no authority without a warrant to arrest the accused except at the scene of the motor vehicle accident for driving under the influence and after his driver's license had been revoked, offenses which were committed not in his presence. Thomas v. Town of Marion, 226 Va. 251, 308 S.E.2d 120 (1983).

§ 19.2-19. Recognizance to keep the peace; when required.

If any person threatens to kill or injure another or to commit violence or injury against his person or property, or to unlawfully trespass upon his property, he shall be required to give a recognizance to keep the peace for such period not to exceed one year as the court hearing the complaint may determine.

History.
Code 1950, §§ 19.1-26, 19.1-27; 1960, c. 366; 1975, c. 495; 1978, c. 500.

CASE NOTES

The power of conservators of the peace to require security from persons for their good behavior and to require a recognizance to keep the peace originated in the common law of England and was crystallized in two ancient English statutes [1 Edw. 3, Stat. 2, c. 16 (1327); 34 Edw. 3, c. 1 (1360)]. Fedele v. Commonwealth, 205 Va. 551, 138 S.E.2d 256 (1964).

A proceeding under this section is a quasi-criminal case. Fedele v. Commonwealth, 205 Va. 551, 138 S.E.2d 256 (1964).

A proceeding in which security is required to be given for good behavior and to keep the peace is more in the nature of criminal or quasi-criminal, rather than civil, procedure. Fedele v. Commonwealth, 205 Va. 551, 138 S.E.2d 256 (1964).

The requirement to give security is in the nature of a conditional fine, and if an accused is unable to provide it he "shall be" committed to jail. Fedele v. Commonwealth, 205 Va. 551, 138 S.E.2d 256 (1964).

Peace bond is moneys belonging to State until payor entitled to reimbursement. — A peace bond is in the nature of a conditional fine. As such, and until the condition is satisfied and the payor becomes entitled to reimbursement, the cash is moneys belonging to the State and its embezzlement by a public officer is a violation of § 18.2-112. Healy v. Commonwealth, 213 Va. 325, 191 S.E.2d 736 (1972).

§ 19.2-20. Same; complaint and issuance of warrant therefor.

If complaint be made to any magistrate or judge that a person should be required to give a recognizance to keep the peace due to any of the reasons set forth in § 19.2-19, such magistrate or judge shall examine on oath the complainant, and any witness who may be produced, reduce the complaint to writing, and cause it to be signed by the complainant; and if probable cause is established, such magistrate or judge shall issue a warrant, reciting the complaint, and requiring the person complained of forthwith to be apprehended and brought before the district court having appropriate jurisdiction.

History.
Code 1950, § 19.1-21; 1960, c. 366; 1975, c. 495; 1978, c. 500; 1979, c. 708.

Michie's Jurisprudence.
For related discussion, see 3A M.J. Breach of the Peace, § 7.

CASE NOTES

It is doubtful whether an arrest without a warrant may be made. Jones v. Peyton, 411 F.2d 857 (4th Cir.), cert. denied, 396 U.S. 942, 90 S. Ct. 373, 24 L. Ed. 2d 243 (1969).

Warrant against "associates" of persons named is void. — A warrant, directing the "associates" of persons named to be arrested, without mentioning the names of such associates, is illegal and void as to them. Wells v. Jackson, 17 Va. (3 Munf.) 458 (1811).

Warrant held illegal. — A warrant to arrest a person of whom surety for the peace is demanded, being executed neither by a sworn officer, nor the person to whom it was directed by the magistrate, but by an individual selected by the prosecutor, who erased the name of the person appointed by the magistrate, and substituted that of the person selected by himself, is thereby rendered altogether illegal and void as a justification for arrest. Wells v. Jackson, 17 Va. (3 Munf.) 458 (1811).

§ 19.2-21. Same; procedure when accused appears.

When such person appears, if the judge, on hearing the parties, considers that there is not good cause for the complaint, he shall discharge such person, and may give judgment in his favor against the complainant for his costs. If he considers that there is good cause therefor, he may require a recognizance of the person against whom it is, and give judgment against him for the costs of the prosecution, or any part thereof; and, unless such recognizance be given, he shall commit him to jail by a warrant, stating the sum and time in and for which the recognizance is directed. The person given judgment under this section for costs may issue a writ of fieri facias thereon, if an appeal be not allowed; and proceedings thereupon may be according to §§ 16.1-99 through 16.1-101.

History.
Code 1950, § 19.1-22; 1960, c. 366; 1975, c. 495; 1978, c. 500.

CASE NOTES

A justice should take care to show cause with sufficient certainty if a party is committed for want of sureties. Fedele v. Commonwealth, 205 Va. 551, 138 S.E.2d 256 (1964).

Security as punishment. — The plight of the impecunious defendant who is committed to jail for failure to give the security required of him is apparently not considered in arriving at the conclusion that the requirement to give security is not punishment. Fedele v. Commonwealth, 205 Va. 551, 138 S.E.2d 256 (1964).

Even though the commendable procedure adopted to prevent crime was not intended to be punishment for a past offense, nevertheless the result is punishment for those persons who are unable to give security and must bear the stigma arising from commitment to jail. Fedele v. Commonwealth, 205 Va. 551, 138 S.E.2d 256 (1964).

Supreme Court has jurisdiction to consider an appeal under the provisions of § 19.2-317. Fedele v. Commonwealth, 205 Va. 551, 138 S.E.2d 256 (1964).

§ 19.2-22. Same; arrest without a warrant.

A person arrested without a warrant by any conservator of the peace or other law-enforcement officer for any of the acts set forth in § 19.2-19 committed in the presence of such conservator of the peace or law-enforcement officer, shall be brought forthwith before a magistrate or judge, and proceedings shall be had in accordance with §§ 19.2-20 and 19.2-21.

History.
1975, c. 495.

Michie's Jurisprudence.
For related discussion, see 2A M.J. Arrest, § 5.

§ 19.2-23. Payment of fees or mileage allowances into county or city treasury.

Any conservator or policeman appointed under the provisions of this chapter shall not be entitled to fees or mileage for performance of his duties as such conservator or policeman.

History.
Code 1950, § 19.1-31; 1960, c. 366; 1975, c. 495.

Michie's Jurisprudence.
For related discussion, see 2B M.J. Aviation, § 1.

ARTICLE 3.
APPEALS.

Michie's Jurisprudence.
For related discussion, see 2B M.J. Bail and Recognizance, §§ 3, 8; 3A M.J. Breach of the Peace, §§ 6, 7; 5B M.J. Criminal Procedure, § 64.

§ 19.2-24. When appeal may be taken; witnesses recognized; bail.

Any person from whom a recognizance is required under the provisions of this chapter or who has been committed to jail for failure to give security therefor, may appeal to the circuit court of the county or city, and, in such case, the judge from whose judgment the appeal is taken shall recognize such of the witnesses as he thinks proper; provided, however, that the person taking the appeal may be required to give bail, with good security, for his appearance at the circuit court of the county or city.

History.
Code 1950, § 19.1-23; 1960, c. 366; 1975, c. 495; 1978, c. 500.

CASE NOTES

Right of appeal is absolute. — Where a magistrate requires surety of the peace of any person, such person has an absolute right of appeal to the circuit court of the county or the corporation court of the corporation. In the court the case is to be heard de novo upon the evidence. Read v. Commonwealth, 65 Va. (24 Gratt.) 618 (1873).

Case may not be remanded to magistrate. — In such a case it is error to reverse the judgment of the magistrate and remand the case to the magistrate to be tried by him. Any subsequent trial of the case by the magistrate is null and void. Read v. Commonwealth, 65 Va. (24 Gratt.) 618 (1873).

§ 19.2-25. Power of court on appeal.

The court may dismiss the complaint or affirm the judgment, and make what order it sees fit as to the costs. If it award costs against the appellant, the recognizance which he may have given shall stand as security therefor. When there is a failure to prosecute the appeal, such recognizance shall remain in force, although there be no order of affirmance. On any appeal the court may require of the appellant a new recognizance if it see fit.

Any person committed to jail under this chapter may be discharged by the circuit court of the county or city on such terms as it may deem reasonable.

History.
Code 1950, §§ 19.1-24, 19.1-25; 1960, c. 366; 1975, c. 495.

CASE NOTES

Under this section the case is heard de novo. Rohanna v. Commonwealth, 168 Va. 696, 190 S.E. 171 (1937); Fedele v. Commonwealth, 205 Va. 551, 138 S.E.2d 256 (1964).

After end of term, court may not alter duration of recognizance. — In the absence of statute, after the end of the term at which final judgment was entered, the court had no power or authority to alter the final judgment by requiring appellant to give a recognizance for an entirely different duration from that fixed by the final judgment. Rohanna v. Commonwealth, 168 Va. 696, 190 S.E. 171 (1937).

Punishment cannot be increased. — This section is obviously intended for the benefit and not for the disadvantage of the accused, and its purpose is to permit the court to relieve the accused from too harsh a situation theretofore placed upon him. Certainly it was not intended to give the court authority to increase the punishment fixed by a final judgment. Rohanna v. Commonwealth, 168 Va. 696, 190 S.E. 171 (1937).

CHAPTER 3.

MAGISTRATES.

ARTICLE 1.

TRANSITION PROVISIONS.

§ 19.2-26. Repeal of inconsistent statutes, municipal charters, etc.

All acts and parts of acts, all sections of this Code, and all provisions of municipal charters, inconsistent with the provisions of this title, are, except as herein otherwise provided, repealed to the extent of such inconsistency.

History.
Code 1950, § 19.1-374; 1973, c. 545; 1975, c. 495.

§ 19.2-27. Effect of repeal of Title 39.1 on prior acts, offenses, etc.

The repeal of Title 39.1 effective as of January 1, 1974, shall not affect any act or offense done or committed or any penalty or forfeiture incurred, or any right established, accrued, or accruing on or before such date, or any prosecution, suit or action pending on that day.

History.
Code 1950, § 19.1-375; 1973, c. 545; 1975, c. 495.

§ 19.2-28. Certain notices, recognizances and processes validated.

Any notice given, recognizance taken, or process or writ issued, before January 1, 1974, shall be valid although given, taken or to be returned to a day after such date, in like manner as if this title had been effective before the same was given, taken or issued.

History.
Code 1950, § 19.1-376; 1973, c. 545; 1975, c. 495.

§ 19.2-29. References to former sections, articles and chapters in Title 39.1.

Whenever in Chapter 3 (§ 19.2-26 et seq.) of this title any of the conditions, requirements, provisions or contents of any section, article or chapter of Title 39.1, as such title existed prior to January 1, 1974, are transferred in the same or modified form to a new section, article or chapter, and whenever any such former section, article or chapter is given a new number in Chapter 3 of this title all references to any such former section, article or chapter of Title 39.1 appearing elsewhere in this Code than in Chapter 3 of this title shall be construed to apply to the new or renumbered section, article or chapter containing such conditions, requirements, provisions or contents or portions thereof.

History.
Code 1950, § 19.1-377; 1973, c. 545; 1975, c. 495; 2002, c. 310.

ARTICLE 2.

ABOLITION OF JUSTICE OF THE PEACE SYSTEM.

§ 19.2-30. Repealed by Acts 2008, cc. 551 and 691, cl. 2.

§ 19.2-31. Abolition of office of issuing justice.

Effective January 1, 1974, the office of issuing justice as provided for in Chapter 2 (§ 39.1-20 et seq.) of Title 39.1 having been abolished, nevertheless, any such special justice of the peace in office December 31, 1973, and elected by the town council for a specific term to expire after that date, may continue in office for the remainder of that term. If he continues in office as provided herein, such justice shall exercise the same powers, perform the same duties, and receive such compensation as he was receiving as of December 31, 1973.

History.
Code 1950, § 19.1-379; 1973, c. 545; 1975, c. 495.

Cross references.
For provisions as to magistrates, see § 19.2-33 et seq.

Law Review.
For survey of Virginia law on pleading and practice for the year 1972-1973, see 59 Va. L. Rev. 1559 (1973).

Michie's Jurisprudence.
For related discussion, see 5B M.J. Criminal Procedure, § 19; 11B M.J. Justices and Magistrates, § 31.

§ 19.2-32. References to justices of the peace.

References in law to justices of the peace shall be deemed to apply to magistrates unless the provisions of Chapter 3 (§ 19.2-26 et seq.) of this title shall render such reference inapplicable.

History.
Code 1950, § 19.1-380; 1973, c. 545; 1975, c. 495; 2002, c. 310.

ARTICLE 3.

THE MAGISTRATE SYSTEM.

Michie's Jurisprudence.
For related discussion, see 5B M.J. Criminal Procedure, § 19; 11B M.J. Justices and Magistrates, § 32 — 34.

§ 19.2-33. Office of magistrate.

The office of magistrate shall be vested with all the authority, duties and obligations previously vested in the office of justice of the peace prior to January 1, 1974.

History.
Code 1950, § 19.1-381; 1973, c. 545; 1975, c. 495.

Cross references.
For provisions concerning compensation of magistrates, see § 19.2-46 et seq. As to the issuance of special license plates to magistrates, pharmacists, registered nurses, general registrars or postmasters, see § 46.2-746.9.

OPINIONS OF THE ATTORNEY GENERAL

Execution of orders subjecting a person to emergency custody under § 37.2-808, or temporary detention under § 37.2-810, or providing for the transportation of such persons. — When a magistrate orders a law-enforcement agency to execute an order subjecting a person to emergency custody under § 37.2-808, or temporary detention under § 37.2-810, or providing for the transportation of such persons, the magistrate should specify the police department of the town as the "primary law-enforcement agency of the jurisdiction" when a town is served by its own police department. If the town is not served by its own police department, the sheriff's office of the surrounding county is tasked with executing such orders and with transporting persons subject to such orders. See opinion of Attorney General to Karen T. Mullins, Esquire, County Attorney, Wise County, 11-123, 2011 Va. AG LEXIS 44 (10/21/11).

§ 19.2-34. Number of magistrates.

There shall be appointed as many magistrates as are necessary for the effective administration of justice. The positions of all employees of the magistrate system shall be authorized by the Committee on District Courts established pursuant to § 16.1-69.33.

History.
Code 1950, § 19.1-382; 1973, c. 545; 1974, c. 484; 1975, c. 495; 1976, c. 138; 1977, c. 198; 1981, c. 4; 1992, c. 55; 2008, cc. 551, 691.

The 2008 amendments.
The 2008 amendments by cc. 551 and 691 are identical, and deleted "for each judicial district" following "shall be appointed," and deleted "such magistrates and any other personnel in the office of the magistrates" following "administration of justice" in the first sentence, and inserted "The positions of all employees of the magistrate system" in the second sentence.

§ 19.2-35. Appointment; supervision generally.

Magistrates and any other personnel in the office of the magistrate shall be appointed by the Executive Secretary of the Supreme Court of Virginia in consultation with the chief judges of the circuit courts having jurisdiction within the region. Each magistrate shall be appointed to serve one or more of the magisterial regions created by the Executive Secretary. Each magisterial region shall be comprised of one or more judicial districts. The Executive Secretary shall have full supervisory authority over the magistrates so appointed. Notwithstanding any other provision of law, the only methods for the selection of magistrates shall be as set out in this section.

No person shall be appointed under this section until he has submitted his fingerprints to be used for the conduct of a national criminal records search and a Virginia criminal history records search. No person with a criminal conviction for a felony shall be appointed as a magistrate.

History.
Code 1950, § 19.1-383; 1973, c. 545; 1974, c. 484; 1975, c. 495; 1976, c. 138; 1981, c. 4; 1988, c. 511; 2002, c. 310; 2004, cc. 370, 452; 2008, cc. 551, 691.

The 2008 amendments.
The 2008 amendments by cc. 551 and 691 are identical, and rewrote the first paragraph, and deleted the second and third paragraphs relating to the appointment of substitute magistrates and replacement of magistrates due to absence.

Law Review.
For survey of Virginia law on pleading and practice for the year 1972-1973, see 59 Va. L. Rev. 1559 (1973).

§ 19.2-36. Chief magistrates.

A. The Executive Secretary of the Supreme Court of Virginia may appoint chief magistrates, for the purpose of assisting in the training of the magistrates and being responsible to the Executive Secretary for the conduct of the magistrates and to further assist the Office of the Executive Secretary in the operation of one or more of the magisterial regions. The chief magistrate shall exercise direct daily supervision over the magistrates he supervises and shall have the power to suspend without pay a magistrate after consultation and with the concurrence of the Executive Secretary.

B. To be eligible for appointment as chief magistrate, a person shall meet all of the qualifications of a magistrate under § 19.2-37 and must be a member in good standing of the Virginia State Bar. His appointment as chief magistrate shall terminate effective on the date on which his membership in good standing ceases. The requirements of this subsection relating to membership in the Virginia State Bar shall not apply to any person appointed as a chief magistrate before July 1, 2008, who continues in that capacity without a break in service.

History.
Code 1950, § 19.1-384; 1973, c. 545; 1974, c. 484; 1975, c. 495; 1984, c. 37; 2004, c. 370; 2008, cc. 551, 691.

The 2008 amendments.
The 2008 amendments by cc. 551 and 691 are identical, and inserted the subsection A designation, rewrote the first paragraph, and added subsection B.

§ 19.2-37. Magistrates; eligibility for appointment; restrictions on activities.

A. Any person who is a United States citizen and resident of the Commonwealth may be appointed to the office of magistrate under this title subject to the limitations of Chapter 28 (§ 2.2-2800 et seq.) of Title 2.2 and of this section.

B. Every person appointed as a magistrate on and after July 1, 2008, shall be required to have a bachelor's degree from an accredited institution of higher education. A person initially appointed as a magistrate prior to July 1, 2008, who continues in office without a break in service is not required to have a bachelor's degree from an accredited institution of higher education.

C. A person shall not be eligible for appointment as a magistrate under the provisions of this title: (a) if such person is a law-enforcement officer; (b) if such person or his spouse is a clerk, deputy or assistant clerk, or employee of any such clerk of a district or circuit court, provided that the Committee on District Courts may authorize a magistrate to assist in the district court clerk's office on a part-time basis; (c) if the parent, child, spouse, or sibling of such person is a district or circuit court judge in the magisterial region where he will serve; or (d) if such person is the chief executive officer, or a member of the board of supervisors, town or city council, or other governing body for any political subdivision of the Commonwealth.

D. No magistrate shall issue any warrant or process in complaint of his spouse, child, grandchild, parent, grandparent, parent-in-law, child-in-law, brother, sister, brother-in-law or sister-in-law, nephew, niece, uncle, aunt, first cousin, guardian or ward.

E. A magistrate may not engage in any other activity for financial gain during the hours that he is serving on duty as a magistrate. A magistrate may not be employed outside his duty hours without the prior written approval of the Executive Secretary.

F. No person appointed as a magistrate on or after July 1, 2008, may engage in the practice of law.

G. A magistrate who is designated as a marriage celebrant under § 20-25 may not accept a fee, a gratuity, or any other thing of value for exercise of authority as a marriage celebrant.

History.
Code 1950, § 19.1-385; 1973, c. 545; 1975, c. 495; 1976, c. 138; 1978, cc. 463, 760; 1984, c. 41; 1985, c. 45; 1986, c. 202; 1996, c. 112; 1999, c. 267; 2004, c. 830; 2008, cc. 551, 691.

The 2008 amendments.
The 2008 amendments by cc. 551 and 691 are identical, and designated former first, second, and third paragraphs as subsections A, C, and D, respectively; added subsections B, E, F, and G; in subsection A, inserted "who is a United States citizen and resident of the Commonwealth"; rewrote subsection C; and in subsection D, deleted the last sentence, which read: "The residence provisions contained in this section shall not be a bar to the reappointment of any magistrate in office on July 1, 1973, provided he is otherwise eligible to serve under the provisions of this chapter."

Law Review.
For survey of Virginia law on pleading and practice for the year 1972-1973, see 59 Va. L. Rev. 1559 (1973).

OPINIONS OF THE ATTORNEY GENERAL

Warrant may not be issued to family member. — A magistrate may not issue a warrant to a sheriff who is a first cousin of the magistrate, but may issue a warrant to that sheriff's deputy. See opinion of Attorney General to The Honorable Claude Meinhard, Sheriff for Cumberland County, 00-036 (6/7/00).

§ 19.2-38. Probationary period; compensation and benefits; vacancies; revocation of appointment.

Persons appointed as magistrates under the provisions of this chapter shall serve at the pleasure of the Executive Secretary. Upon appointment by the Executive Secretary, every magistrate shall serve initially for a nine-month probationary period during which the magistrate must complete the minimum training program as established by the Committee on District Courts and satisfactorily complete a certification examination. Any magistrate who fails to successfully pass the certification examination shall not serve beyond the nine-month probationary period. The probationary period described in this section shall not apply to any magistrate serving on July 1, 2008, who has successfully completed the minimum training program and passed the certification examination, provided there is no break in service after July 1, 2008. Magistrates shall be entitled to compensation and other benefits only from the time they take office.

History.
Code 1950, § 19.1-386; 1973, c. 545; 1974, c. 484; 1975, c. 495; 1980, c. 505; 2004, c. 370; 2008, cc. 551, 691.

The 2008 amendments.
The 2008 amendments by cc. 551 and 691 are identical, and substituted "shall serve at the pleasure of the Executive Secretary. Upon appointment by the Executive Secretary, every magistrate shall serve initially for a nine-month probationary period" for "shall serve for a term of four years. Such term shall commence upon appointment and qualification, provided that any magistrate appointed for the first time to any term commencing after July 1, 1980, shall serve initially for a six-month probationary period" in the first two sentences, substituted the third sentence for "Failure to successfully pass the certification examination shall preclude the magistrate from serving beyond the six-month probationary period," inserted the fourth sentence, and deleted the last sentence, which read: "Appointments made under the provisions of this chapter shall be revocable at the pleasure of the chief circuit court judge."

§ 19.2-38.1. Training standards; training prerequisite to reappointment; waiver.

The Committee on District Courts shall establish minimum training and certification standards for magistrates in accordance with such rules and regulations as may be established by the Committee. Every magistrate shall comply with these standards and shall complete the minimum training standards as a prerequisite for continuing to serve as magistrate beyond the nine-month probationary period as established by § 19.2-38. The Committee on District Courts upon request may waive any portion of the minimum training standards for an individual magistrate.

History.
1980, c. 505; 1985, c. 132; 1995, c. 611; 2008, cc. 551, 691.

The 2008 amendments.
The 2008 amendments by cc. 551 and 691 are identical and rewrote the section.

§ 19.2-39. Bond.

Every magistrate appointed under the provisions of this chapter shall enter into bond in the sum of $5,000, made payable to the Commonwealth, before a clerk of a circuit court, for the faithful performance of his duties. The premium for such bond shall be paid by the Commonwealth. Provided, however, that in lieu of specific bonds, the Committee on District Courts may in its discretion procure faithful performance of duty blanket bonds for all magistrates and for the penalty contained in this section, unless in the discretion of the Committee, bonds with a larger penalty should be obtained. Such blanket bonds shall be made payable to the Commonwealth and shall cover all funds handled by a magistrate whether such funds belong to the Commonwealth or any political subdivision thereof. Provided further, that in those instances where specific bonds for magistrates are in effect, the Committee on District Courts may, whenever it deems it advisable, terminate such specific bonds upon obtaining a blanket bond covering such magistrates with appropriate refunds or credit being made for the unearned premiums on the specific bonds terminated. A copy of any such blanket bond so procured shall be filed with the State Comptroller and with the clerk of the respective circuit courts. The premiums for such blanket bonds shall be paid by the Commonwealth.

History.
Code 1950, § 19.1-387; 1973, c. 545; 1974, c. 484; 1975, c. 495; 2008, cc. 551, 691.

The 2008 amendments.
The 2008 amendments by cc. 551 and 691 are identical, and substituted "before a clerk of a circuit court" for "before the clerk of the circuit court which exercises jurisdiction over the political subdivision wherein such magistrate shall serve" in the first sentence, substituted "blanket bonds for all magistrates" for "blanket bonds for any or all of the districts enumerated in § 16.1-69.6 covering all magistrates included in such districts" in the third sentence, and substituted "respective circuit courts" for "respective circuit court which exercises jurisdiction over the district wherein such magistrate shall serve" in the sixth sentence.

§ 19.2-40. Repealed by Acts 1980, c. 758.

Editor's note.
Acts 1980, c. 758, cl. 3, which provided that the act should not be effective within the Nineteenth Judicial Circuit, was repealed by Acts 1981, c. 403, cl. 2.

ARTICLE 4.

SUPERVISION.

§ 19.2-41. Repealed by Acts 2008, cc. 551 and 691, cl. 2.

§ 19.2-42. Repealed by Acts 2004, c. 327.

§ 19.2-43. Duty of Executive Secretary of Supreme Court.

It shall be the duty of the Executive Secretary of the Supreme Court to exercise general supervisory power over the administration of magistrates and adopt such policies as are deemed necessary to supplement or clarify the provisions of this chapter with respect to such magistrates, to include fixing the time and place such magistrates shall serve. The Executive Secretary shall conduct training sessions and meetings for magistrates and provide information and materials for their use. He may appoint one or more magistrates to assist him and, in addition, require annual reports to be filed by the magistrates on their work as such, fees associated therewith and other information pertinent to their office, on forms to be furnished by him. The Executive Secretary may appoint and employ such personnel as are needed to manage the magistrate system and carry out the duties and responsibilities conferred upon the Executive Secretary by this chapter.

History.
Code 1950, § 19.1-392; 1973, c. 545; 1974, c. 484; 1975, c. 495; 2008, cc. 551, 691.

The 2008 amendments.
The 2008 amendments by cc. 551 and 691 are identical, and substituted "exercise general supervisory power over the administration of magistrates and adopt such policies as are deemed necessary to supplement or clarify the provisions of this chapter with respect to such magistrates, to include fixing the time and place such magistrates shall serve. The Executive Secretary shall conduct" for "assist the chief general district judges and general district courts in the supervision and mandatory training of magistrates for which purpose he shall be authorized to conduct" in the first two sentences, deleted "with the approval of the Chief Justice" preceding "required annual reports" in the third sentence, and added the last sentence.

ARTICLE 5.

JURISDICTION AND POWERS.

Michie's Jurisprudence.
For related discussion, see 11B M.J. Justices and Magistrates, §§ 2, 33, 37.

§ 19.2-44. Territorial jurisdiction.

A magistrate shall be authorized to exercise the powers conferred by this title only in the magisterial region or regions for which he is appointed. However, a magistrate may exercise these powers throughout the Commonwealth when so authorized by the Executive Secretary upon a determination that such assistance is necessary.

History.
Code 1950, § 19.1-393; 1973, c. 545; 1974, c. 484; 1975, c. 495; 1976, c. 138; 1995, c. 551; 2008, cc. 551, 691.

The 2008 amendments.
The 2008 amendments by cc. 551 and 691 are identical, and in the first sentence, inserted "be authorized to" preceding "exercise the powers" near the beginning and substituted "magisterial region or regions" for "judicial district" near the end; and in the second sentence, substituted "throughout the Commonwealth" for "in a contiguous political subdivision" and substituted "the Executive Secretary upon a determination that such assistance is necessary" for "his appointing authority and the chief circuit court judge of the district to which assistance is to be provided" at the end.

§ 19.2-44.1. Repealed by Acts 1976, c. 138.

Cross references.
For present provisions as to substitute magistrates, see § 19.2-35.

§ 19.2-45. Powers enumerated.

A magistrate shall have the following powers only:

(1) To issue process of arrest in accord with the provisions of §§ 19.2-71 to 19.2-82 of the Code;

(2) To issue search warrants in accord with the provisions of §§ 19.2-52 to 19.2-60 of the Code;

(3) To admit to bail or commit to jail all persons charged with offenses subject to the limitations of and in accord with general laws on bail;

(4) The same power to issue warrants and subpoenas as is conferred upon district courts and as limited by the provisions of §§ 19.2-71 through 19.2-82. A copy of all felony warrants issued at the request of a citizen shall be promptly delivered to the attorney for the Commonwealth for the county or city in which the warrant is returnable. Upon the request of the attorney for the Commonwealth, a copy of any misdemeanor warrant issued at the request of a citizen shall be delivered to the attorney for the Commonwealth for such county or city. All attachments, warrants and subpoenas shall be returnable before a district court or any court of limited jurisdiction continued in operation pursuant to § 16.1-70.1;

(5) To issue civil warrants directed to the sheriff or constable of the county or city wherein the defendant resides, together with a copy thereof, requiring him to summon the person against whom the claim is, to appear before a district court on a certain day, not exceeding 30 days from the date thereof to answer such claim. If there be two or more defendants and any defendant resides outside the jurisdiction in which the warrant is issued, the summons for such defendant residing outside the jurisdiction may be directed to the sheriff of the county or city of his residence, and such warrant may be served and returned as provided in § 16.1-80;

(6) To administer oaths and take acknowledgments;

(7) To act as conservators of the peace;

(8), (9) [Repealed.]

(10) To perform such other acts or functions specifically authorized by law.

History.

Code 1950, § 19.1-394; 1973, c. 545; 1974, c. 484; 1975, c. 495; 1976, c. 471; 1977, c. 332; 1978, cc. 500, 605; 1985, c. 77; 2007, cc. 122, 373; 2008, cc. 551, 691; 2009, cc. 291, 344.

The 2007 amendments.

The 2007 amendments by cc. 122 and 373 are identical, and in subdivision (4), inserted the second sentence and substituted "All" for "Such" at the beginning of the last sentence.

The 2008 amendments.

The 2008 amendments by cc. 551 and 691 are identical, and in subdivision 4, deleted "within such county or city" following "warrants and subpoenas" in the first sentence, inserted the second sentence and substituted "misdemeanor warrant" for "criminal warrant" in the third sentence.

The 2009 amendments.

The 2009 amendments by cc. 291 and 344 are identical, and in subsection (4), inserted "and as limited by the provisions of §§ 19.2-71 through 19.2-82"; and in subsection (5), made a minor stylistic change.

CASE NOTES

Immunity for acts in judicial capacity. — As judicial officers, magistrates are entitled to absolute immunity for acts performed in their judicial capacity. That immunity is vitiated only when the judicial officer acts in the clear absence of all jurisdiction. Pressly v. Gregory, 831 F.2d 514 (4th Cir. 1987).

Warrant issued after arrest irrelevant in false arrest action. — In an action under 42 U.S.C. § 1983 alleging that defendant officer denied plaintiff due process by subjecting him to a false arrest for being drunk in public, the arrest warrant issued by the magistrate subsequent to the arrest did not establish as a matter of law that probable cause existed for the defendant to arrest the plaintiff. Robinson v. Goff, 517 F. Supp. 350 (W.D. Va. 1981).

When a defendant officer in a civil action relies upon probable cause as a defense to a charge of illegal arrest under 42 U.S.C. § 1983, he must establish that probable cause existed at the time the arrest was made. A warrant, subsequently issued by a magistrate, is irrelevant to the determination of whether the officer arresting an individual without a warrant had probable cause to arrest. Robinson v. Goff, 517 F. Supp. 350 (W.D. Va. 1981).

"No-knock entry." — Under Virginia law, the authority to effect a no-knock entry stems from exigent circumstances reasonably appearing to the officers to be in existence at the time the entry is made, and not at the time the warrant is obtained; thus, under Virginia law a magistrate lacks authority to "command" a no-knock entry in advance of the entry. Fenner v. Dawes, 748 F. Supp. 404 (E.D. Va. 1990).

Applied in Tross v. Commonwealth, 21 Va. App. 362, 464 S.E.2d 523 (1995).

ARTICLE 6.

COMPENSATION AND FEES.

§ 19.2-46. Compensation.

The salaries of all magistrates shall be fixed and paid as provided in § 19.2-46.1. The salaries referred to herein shall be in lieu of all fees which may accrue to the recipient by virtue of his office.

History.

Code 1950, § 19.1-395; 1973, c. 545; 1974, c. 484; 1975, c. 495; 1980, c. 139; 2008, cc. 551, 691.

The 2008 amendments.

The 2008 amendments by cc. 551 and 691 are identical, and deleted the former second paragraph, which read: "Each substitute magistrate shall receive for his services a per diem compensation as may be established by the Committee on District Courts."

Law Review.

For survey of Virginia law on pleading and practice for the year 1972-1973, see 59 Va. L. Rev. 1559 (1973).

Michie's Jurisprudence.

For related discussion, see 11B M.J. Justices and Magistrates, §§ 34, 36.

§ 19.2-46.1. Salaries to be fixed by the Executive Secretary; limitations; mileage allowance.

Salaries of magistrates and any other personnel in the office of the magistrate shall be fixed by the Executive Secretary of the Supreme Court. Such salaries shall be fixed by the Executive Secretary at least annually at such time as he deems proper and as soon as practicable thereafter certified to the Comptroller.

In determining the salary of any magistrate, the Executive Secretary shall consider the work load of and territory and population served by the magistrate and such other factors he deems relevant.

The governing body of any county or city may add to the fixed compensation of magistrates such amount as the governing body may appropriate with the total amount not to exceed 50 percent of the amount paid by the Commonwealth to magistrates provided such additional compensation was in effect on June 30, 2008, for such magistrates and any magistrate receiving such additional compensation continues in office without a break in service. However, the total amount of additional compensation may not be increased after June 30, 2008. No additional amount paid by a local governing body shall be chargeable to the Executive Secretary of the Supreme Court, nor shall it remove or supersede any authority, control or supervision of the Executive Secretary or Committee on District Courts.

History.

1973, c. 545, § 14.1-44.2; 1974, c. 484; 1975, c. 334; 1981, c. 4; 1995, cc. 331, 378; 1998, c. 872; 2008, cc. 551, 691.

The 2008 amendments.

The 2008 amendments by cc. 551 and 691 are nearly identical, and in the first paragraph, substituted "Executive Secretary of the Supreme Court" for "Committee on District Courts established pursuant to § 16.1-69.33" in the first sentence, substituted "Executive Secretary" for "Committee" and deleted "and the Executive Secretary of the Supreme Court" from the end of the second sentence; deleted the former second paragraph, which read: "In addition to the salary authorized by this section, a magistrate may be reimbursed by the county or city for reasonable mileage expenses actually incurred in the performance of his duties"; in the second paragraph, substituted "Executive Secretary" for "Committee" and deleted the last sentence, which read: "It may require of any magistrate or district judge information on the operation of the office of the magistrate"; in the third paragraph, inserted the proviso at the end of the first sentence and added the second sentence.

§ 19.2-46.2. Full-time magistrates; certification for retirement coverage.

The Committee on District Courts shall certify to the director of the Virginia Retirement System the names of those magistrates serving on a regular full-time basis. Certification by the Committee shall qualify a magistrate as a state employee, for purposes of §§ 51.1-124.3 and 51.1-152 of the Virginia Retirement System (§ 51.1-124.1 et seq.), effective on the date given in the certificate as the date on which such magistrate first served on a regular full-time basis on or after January 1, 1974.

History.
1974, c. 353, § 14.1-44.2:1; 1998, c. 872.

§ 19.2-47. Magistrate not to receive claims or evidence of debt for collection.

No magistrate shall receive claims or evidence of debt for collection; and it shall be unlawful for any magistrate to receive claims of any kind for collection, or to accept or receive money or any other things of value by way of commission or compensation for or on account of any collection made by or through him on any such claim, either before or after judgment. Any magistrate violating this section shall be guilty of a Class 1 misdemeanor.

History.
Code 1950, § 19.1-396; 1973, c. 545; 1975, c. 495.

Cross references.
As to punishment for Class 1 misdemeanors, see § 18.2-11.

§ 19.2-47.1. Disposition of funds.

All funds paid to and collected by or on behalf of a magistrate shall be paid promptly to the appropriate district court clerk, circuit court clerk, commissioner in chancery, department of the Commonwealth, federal agency or as otherwise authorized by statute.

History.
1973, c. 545, § 14.1-44.4; 1980, c. 356; 1987, c. 22; 1998, c. 872.

§ 19.2-48. Audits.

The Auditor of Public Accounts shall audit the records of all magistrates who serve any county or city when auditing the records of the district courts of such county or city or upon request of the chief district judge of the district in which such county or city is located.

History.
Code 1950, § 19.1-397; 1973, c. 545; 1975, c. 495; 1980, c. 195; 2008, cc. 551, 691.

The 2008 amendments.
The 2008 amendments by cc. 551 and 691 are identical and substituted "serve any county" for "serve in any county."

§ 19.2-48.1. Quarters for magistrates.

A. The counties and cities served by a magistrate or magistrates shall provide suitable quarters for such magistrates, including a site for any videoconferencing equipment necessary to provide remote access to such magistrates. Insofar as possible, such quarters should be located in a public facility and should be appropriate to conduct the affairs of a judicial officer as well as provide convenient access to the public and law-enforcement officers. The county or city shall also provide all furniture and other equipment necessary for the efficient operation of the office.

B. Wherever practical, the office of magistrate shall be located at the county seat. However, offices may be located at other locations in the county, or city adjacent thereto, whenever such additional offices are necessary to effect the efficient administration of justice.

History.
1975, c. 495; 1981, c. 5; 1988, c. 510; 2008, cc. 551, 691.

Editor's note.
Acts 1993, c. 930, cl. 3, as amended by Acts 1994, c. 564, cl. 2, and Acts 1996, c. 616, cl. 4, provides that the amendment to this section by Acts 1993, c. 930, cl. 1, shall become effective June 1, 1998, "if state funds are provided, including all local costs, to carry out the purposes of this bill by the General Assembly." The funding was not provided.

The 2008 amendments.
The 2008 amendments by cc. 551 and 691 are identical, and in subsection A, rewrote the first sentence, which read: "Each county and city having a general district court or juvenile and domestic relations district court and having one or more magistrates appointed pursuant to Article 3 (§ 19.2-33 et seq.) of this chapter, shall provide suitable quarters for such magistrates."

CHAPTER 4.

SPECIAL MAGISTRATES.

§§ 19.2-49 through 19.2-51. Repealed by Acts 1980, c. 758.

Editor's note.
Acts 1980, c. 758, cl. 3, which provided that the act should not be effective within the Nineteenth Judicial Circuit, was repealed by Acts 1981, c. 403, cl. 2.

CHAPTER 5.

SEARCH WARRANTS.

Michie's Jurisprudence.

For related discussion, see 16 M.J. Searches and Seizures, §§ 3 — 10.

§ 19.2-52. When search warrant may issue.

Except as provided in § 19.2-56.1, search warrants, based upon complaint on oath supported by an affidavit as required in § 19.2-54, may be issued by any judge, magistrate or other person having authority to issue criminal warrants, if he be satisfied from such complaint and affidavit that there is reasonable and probable cause for the issuance of such search warrant.

History.

Code 1950, § 19.1-83; 1960, c. 366; 1975, c. 495; 1986, c. 636.

Cross references.

For constitutional provision, see Va. Const., Art. I, § 10. As to special police officers acting under this section, see § 15.2-1745.

Law Review.

For note, "Criminal Procedure and Criminal Law: Virginia Supreme Court Decisions During the 70's," see 15 U. Rich. L. Rev. 585 (1981). For note, "The Role of Police Culpability in Leon and Youngblood," see 76 Va. L. Rev. 1213 (1990).

CASE NOTES

What is a reasonable search is purely a judicial question, and in determining it the court must look to all the circumstances. Johnson v. Commonwealth, 213 Va. 102, 189 S.E.2d 678 (1972), cert. denied, 409 U.S. 1116, 93 S. Ct. 918, 34 L. Ed. 2d 700 (1973).

§ 19.2-53. What may be searched and seized.

Search warrants may be issued for the search of or for specified places, things or persons, and seizure therefrom of the following things as specified in the warrant:

(1) Weapons or other objects used in the commission of crime;

(2) Articles or things the sale or possession of which is unlawful;

(3) Stolen property or the fruits of any crime;

(4) Any object, thing, or person, including without limitation, documents, books, papers, records or body fluids, constituting evidence of the commission of crime. Notwithstanding any other provision in this chapter to the contrary, no search warrant may be issued as a substitute for a witness subpoena.

History.

Code 1950, § 19.1-84; 1960, c. 366; 1962, c. 519; 1966, c. 363; 1970, c. 650; 1974, c. 113; 1975, c. 495; 1981, c. 559.

Cross references.

As to search warrants relating to alcoholic beverages, see § 4.1-337. As to special police officers acting under this section, see § 15.2-1745.

Law Review.

For survey of Virginia criminal law for the year 1973-1974, see 60 Va. L. Rev. 1499 (1974). For survey of Virginia law on criminal procedure for the year 1973-1974, see 60 Va. L. Rev. 1505 (1974). For survey of Virginia law on criminal procedure for the year 1974-1975, see 61 Va. L. Rev. 1713 (1975). For survey of Virginia law on arrests in private dwellings for the year 1979-1980, see 67 Va. L. Rev. 275 (1981). For article, "Unreasonable Searches and Seizures of Papers," see 71 Va. L. Rev. 869 (1985). For 2007 annual survey article, "Electronic Data: A Commentary on the Law in Virginia in 2007," see 42 U. Rich. L. Rev. 355 (2007).

Michie's Jurisprudence.

For related discussion, see 12A M.J. Lotteries, § 4.

CASE NOTES

Papers of an evidential nature. — No search warrant can be issued for the search and seizure of papers of an evidential nature. Rees v. Commonwealth, 203 Va. 850, 127 S.E.2d 406 (1962), cert. denied, 372 U.S. 964, 83 S. Ct. 1088, 10 L. Ed. 2d 128, rehearing denied, 373 U.S. 947, 83 S. Ct. 1533, 10 L. Ed. 2d 702 (1963).

Warrant not authorized for discovery purposes. — This section does not authorize a search warrant to be issued for a criminal defendant for the purpose of discovery. Henshaw v. Commonwealth, 19 Va. App. 338, 451 S.E.2d 415 (1994).

Additional seizures under warrant. — Where appellant's address was identified in the warrant as the place to be searched, and "marijuana" was specified as the item to be seized, a search was not invalid merely because officers seized items not named in the warrant. Cherry v. Commonwealth, 21 Va. App. 132, 462 S.E.2d 574 (1995).

§ 19.2-54. Affidavit preliminary to issuance of search warrant; general search warrant prohibited; effect of failure to file affidavit.

No search warrant shall be issued until there is filed with the officer authorized to issue the same an affidavit of some person reasonably describing the place, thing, or person to be searched, the things or persons to be searched for thereunder, alleging briefly material facts, constituting the probable cause for the issuance of such warrant and alleging substantially the offense in relation to which such search is to be made and that the object, thing, or person searched for constitutes evidence of the commission of such offense. The affidavit may be filed by electronically transmitted (i) facsimile process or (ii) electronic record as defined in § 59.1-480. Such affidavit shall be certified by the officer who issues such warrant and delivered in person; mailed by certified mail, return receipt requested; or delivered by electronically transmitted facsimile process or by use of filing and security procedures as defined in the Uniform Electronic Transactions Act (§ 59.1-479 et seq.) for transmitting signed documents, by such officer or his designee or agent, to the clerk of the circuit court of the county or city wherein the search is made, with a copy of the affidavit also being delivered to the clerk of the circuit court of the county or city where the warrant is issued, if in a different county or city, within seven days after the issuance of such warrant and shall by such clerks be preserved as a record and shall at all times be subject to inspection by the public after the warrant that is the subject of the affidavit has been executed or 15 days after issuance of the warrant, whichever is earlier; however, such affidavit, any warrant issued pursuant thereto, any return made thereon, and any order sealing the affidavit, warrant, or return may be temporarily sealed for a specific period of time by the appropriate court upon application of the attorney for the Commonwealth for good cause shown in an ex parte hearing. Any individual arrested and claiming to be aggrieved by such search and seizure or any person who claims to be entitled to lawful possession of such property seized may move the appropriate court for the unsealing of such affidavit, warrant, and return. The burden of proof with respect to continued sealing shall be upon the Commonwealth. Each such clerk shall maintain an index of all such affidavits filed in his office in order to facilitate inspection. No such warrant shall be issued on an affidavit omitting such essentials, and no general warrant for the search of a house, place, compartment, vehicle or baggage shall be issued. The term "affidavit" as used in this section, means statements made under oath or affirmation and preserved verbatim.

Failure of the officer issuing such warrant to file the required affidavit shall not invalidate any search made under the warrant unless such failure shall continue for a period of 30 days. If the affidavit is filed prior to the expiration of the 30-day period, nevertheless, evidence obtained in any such search shall not be admissible until a reasonable time after the filing of the required affidavit.

History.
    Code 1950, § 19.1-85; 1960, c. 366; 1973, c. 502; 1975, c. 495; 1976, c. 552; 1977, c. 109; 1979, c. 583; 1980, c. 362; 1981, c. 559; 1989, c. 719; 2006, c. 285; 2007, c. 212; 2008, cc. 147, 183; 2011, cc. 196, 219; 2012, c. 5.

The 2007 amendments.
    The 2007 amendment by c. 212 inserted "in person or mailed by certified mail, return receipt requested" in the third sentence.

The 2008 amendments.
    The 2008 amendments by cc. 147 and 183 are identical and rewrote the third sentence of the first paragraph and made minor stylistic changes.

The 2011 amendments.
    The 2011 amendment by c. 196, inserted "after the warrant that is the subject of the affidavit has been executed or 15 days after issuance of the warrant, whichever is earlier" in the third sentence in the first paragraph.
    The 2011 amendment by c. 219, in the first paragraph, in the third sentence, inserted "any warrant issued pursuant thereto, any return made thereon, and any order sealing the affidavit, warrant, or return" and "for a specific period of time," and subdivided the former fourth sentence and therein added "warrant, and return."

The 2012 amendments.
    The 2012 amendment by c. 5, in the first paragraph, inserted the (i) designator and clause (ii) of the second sentence, added "or by use of filing and security procedures as defined in the Uniform Electronic Transactions Act (§ 59.1-479 et seq.) for transmitting signed documents" in the third sentence, and made minor stylistic changes.

Law Review.
    For survey of Virginia criminal law and procedure for the year 1970-1971, see 57 Va. L. Rev. 1438 (1971). For survey of Virginia law on criminal procedure for the year 1972-1973, see 59 Va. L. Rev. 1478 (1973). For note on reasonable suspicion and probable cause in automobile searches, see 40 Wash. & Lee L. Rev. 361 (1983). For note, "The Constitutionality of the Use of Unrecorded Oral Testimony to Establish Probable Cause for Search Warrants," see 70 Va. L. Rev. 1603 (1984). For 1985 survey of Virginia criminal procedure, see 19 U. Rich. L. Rev. 697 (1985).

CASE NOTES

I. General Consideration.
II. Probable Cause.

I. GENERAL CONSIDERATION.

The requirements of this section are the same as those of the Fourth Amendment to the federal Constitution. Wiles v. Commonwealth, 209 Va. 282, 163 S.E.2d 595 (1968).
    The requirements of the Virginia statutes controlling the issuance of search warrants and forbidding searches without a warrant (§§ 19.2-54 and 19.2-56) are in substance the same as those contained in the Fourth Amendment. Kirby v. Commonwealth, 209 Va. 806, 167 S.E.2d 411 (1969).
    General warrants are proscribed by both the Fourth Amendment and this section. The requirements of state law controlling the issuance of search warrants have been interpreted to impose the same search warrant requirements as the Fourth Amendment. The Fourth Amendment requires neither that a search warrant be elaborately detailed nor that authorities minutely identify every item for which they are searching. So long as the search warrant describes the objects of the search with reasonable specificity, it complies with the dictates of the Fourth Amendment. Morke v. Commonwealth, 14 Va. App. 496, 419 S.E.2d 410 (1992).
    The purpose of this and the following sections of this chapter is to protect and enforce the rights of citizens guaranteed to them by Va. Const., Art. I, § 10. Hall v. Commonwealth ex rel. Town of South Boston, 138 Va. 727, 121 S.E. 154 (1924).
    The purpose of this section is to give the defendant reasonable opportunity to determine that the affidavit on file is the same one upon which the determination of probable cause was based. Robertson v. Rogers, 2 Va. App. 503, 346 S.E.2d 41 (1986), aff'd, 360 S.E.2d 715 (1987).
    This section and § 19.2-250 must also be read together and harmonized. Robertson v. Rogers, 2 Va. App. 503, 346 S.E.2d 41 (1986), aff'd, 360 S.E.2d 715 (1987).
    General warrants proscribed. — Plain view doctrine may not be used only as a pretext to extend a general exploratory search from one object to another until something incriminating at last emerges as general warrants are proscribed by § 19.2-54. Commonwealth v. Marek, No. 2123-02-4, 2003 Va. App. LEXIS 46 (Ct. of Appeals Feb. 5, 2003).
    This section does not preclude the introduction of an affidavit in support of a search warrant. Lane v. Commonwealth, 223 Va. 713, 292 S.E.2d 358 (1982).
    An affidavit submitted for a warrant may be supplemented with additional affidavits. — An affidavit submitted for a warrant under this section may be supplemented or rehabilitated with additional affidavits which contain collective facts relevant to the same offenses when those affidavits are presented, simultaneously, to the issuing magistrate by the same officer. Derr v.

Commonwealth, 410 Va. 662, 410 S.E.2d 662 (1991).

Constitutional requirements as to affidavit. — "The required affidavit" means the affidavit required to support issuance of a search warrant. Under the Fourth Amendment warrant requirement, the content of that affidavit must be sufficient to support a finding of probable cause by a neutral and detached magistrate. The Constitution does not require the magistrate to certify an affidavit. The purpose of that requirement in this section is to ensure that the affidavit filed with the clerk for the information of the accused is the same affidavit upon which the finding of probable cause was based. Quintana v. Commonwealth, 224 Va. 127, 295 S.E.2d 643 (1982), cert. denied, 460 U.S. 1029, 103 S. Ct. 1280, 75 L. Ed. 2d 501 (1983).

Affidavit must include any supplementary facts presented to the magistrate to establish probable cause. McCary v. Commonwealth, 228 Va. 219, 321 S.E.2d 637 (1984).

Magistrate must be informed of some of the underlying circumstances. — Although an affidavit may be based on hearsay information and need not reflect the direct personal observations of the affiant, the magistrate must be informed of some of the underlying circumstances from which the informant concluded that the narcotics were where he claimed they were, and some of the underlying circumstances from which the officer concluded that the informant, whose identity need not be disclosed, was "credible" or his information "reliable." Wiles v. Commonwealth, 209 Va. 282, 163 S.E.2d 595 (1968).

Offense to be identified briefly and in general terms. — This section and Rule 3A:27 (now repealed) of the Supreme Court contemplate that both in the affidavit for a search warrant, and in the warrant itself, the offense in relation to which the search was to be made should be identified briefly and in general terms rather than in the precise and legalistic language usually found in an indictment, a presentment or an arrest warrant. Carratt v. Commonwealth, 215 Va. 55, 205 S.E.2d 653 (1974), cert. denied, 420 U.S. 973, 95 S. Ct. 1394, 43 L. Ed. 2d 652 (1975).

The object in identifying the offense in the affidavit for a search warrant and in the warrant is to apprise the subject of the search of the offense being investigated and the evidence sought, and to advise the officers in advance as to what they are to be searching for. Carratt v. Commonwealth, 215 Va. 55, 205 S.E.2d 653 (1974), cert. denied, 420 U.S. 973, 95 S. Ct. 1394, 43 L. Ed. 2d 652 (1975).

Omitting to allege "substantially the offense in relation to which such search is to be made" rendered the affidavit defective, the search warrant invalid, and the evidence secured in the ensuing search inadmissible. Moore v. Commonwealth, 211 Va. 569, 179 S.E.2d 458 (1971).

The mere fact that the warrant did not refer to the same Code section as the affidavit is of no consequence. What is important is that the warrant clearly and substantially described and identified the criminal violation in relation to which the search was being made. Carratt v. Commonwealth, 215 Va. 55, 205 S.E.2d 653 (1974), cert. denied, 420 U.S. 973, 95 S. Ct. 1394, 43 L. Ed. 2d 652 (1975).

Facts must be closely related to time of issuance of warrant. — Virginia's statutes fix no maximum time interval between the date of the events and circumstances recited in the affidavit and the date of the affidavit and issuance of the warrant. However, the proof must be of facts so closely related to the time of the issue of the warrant as to justify a finding of probable cause at that time. Huff v. Commonwealth, 213 Va. 710, 194 S.E.2d 690 (1973).

Search without warrant based in part on information in affidavit. — Information contained in an affidavit that supported a search warrant for defendant's residence and automobile was sufficient for the police to search the defendant without the warrant, where the police had independent information about defendant's recent, sexually deviant, behavior and numerous verifications that his car had been seen in the vicinity of the crime. Drumheller v. Commonwealth, 223 Va. 695, 292 S.E.2d 602, cert. denied, 459 U.S. 913, 103 S. Ct. 224, 74 L. Ed. 2d 178 (1982).

Statement of affiant's information source not required. — A statement of the source of the affiant's information, while required by U.S. Const., Amend. 14, is not mandated by this section. McCary v. Commonwealth, 228 Va. 219, 321 S.E.2d 637 (1984).

Affidavit based on unnamed informant's tip. — The test for determining probable cause in those many instances where the affidavit is based solely or substantially upon an informer's tip is set forth as follows: (1) The affidavit must describe some of the underlying circumstances necessary to enable a neutral and detached magistrate to judge the validity of the informant's conclusion that the narcotics were where he claimed they were; and (2) the affidavit must describe some of the underlying circumstances from which such magistrate can determine that the affiant officer's unnamed informant, whose identity need not be disclosed, was "credible" or his information "reliable." Manley v. Commonwealth, 211 Va. 146, 176 S.E.2d 309 (1970), cert. denied, 403 U.S. 936, 91 S. Ct. 2245, 29 L. Ed. 2d 716 (1971).

An affidavit for a search warrant based solely or substantially upon information from an informant must describe (1) sufficient underlying circumstances to enable a neutral and detached magistrate to judge the validity of the informant's conclusion as to the location of the contraband, and (2) some of the circumstances which would permit the magistrate to judge the credibility of the unnamed informant or the reliability of his information. Wheeler v. Commonwealth, 217 Va. 95, 225 S.E.2d 400 (1976).

To establish probable cause based upon an informant's tip, the prosecution must show underlying circumstances sufficient to support the informant's conclusions and the conclusion of the police that the informant was credible or his information reliable. This standard applies to a search or arrest made by an officer without benefit of a warrant as well as to a search or arrest made pursuant to a warrant issued by a magistrate. Wright v. Commonwealth, 222 Va. 188, 278 S.E.2d 849 (1981).

Affiant must present factual basis for crediting informant's story. — Where the accuracy of the information received from a confidential informant is not supported by other sources known or stated to be accurate or from corroborated facts known or discovered by the affiant personally or from other official or reliable reports, the officer-affiant must present in his affidavit a substantial factual basis for crediting the informant's story. Manley v. Commonwealth, 211 Va. 146, 176 S.E.2d 309 (1970), cert. denied, 403 U.S. 936, 91 S. Ct. 2245, 29 L. Ed. 2d 716 (1971).

Substantiation of informant's reliability. — The most commonly accepted and approved allegation to substantiate reliability is that the informer is a person of known and proven reliability and has furnished information to law-enforcement officers which has been instrumental in procuring convictions. But the credibility of the informer or the reliability of his information may be shown in other ways. Manley v. Commonwealth, 211 Va. 146, 176 S.E.2d 309 (1970), cert. denied, 403 U.S. 936, 91 S. Ct. 2245, 29 L. Ed. 2d 716 (1971).

Reliability may be found in an informant's statement of facts as an "eyewitness." Manley v. Commonwealth, 211 Va. 146, 176 S.E.2d 309 (1970), cert. denied, 403 U.S. 936, 91 S. Ct. 2245, 29 L. Ed. 2d 716 (1971).

The reliability standard is met where the affidavit in sufficient detail establishes that the informer is speaking with personal knowledge and relating his own participation with that of the suspects in their illegal activities. Manley v. Commonwealth, 211 Va. 146, 176 S.E.2d 309 (1970), cert. denied, 403 U.S. 936, 91 S. Ct. 2245, 29 L. Ed. 2d 716 (1971).

Informer's hearsay as admission against interest. — If the informer's hearsay comes from one of the actors in the crime in the nature of an admission against interest, the affidavit giving this information should be held sufficient. Manley v. Commonwealth, 211 Va. 146, 176 S.E.2d 309 (1970), cert. denied, 403 U.S. 936, 91 S. Ct. 2245, 29 L. Ed. 2d 716 (1971).

Mere allegation of informant's reliability is insufficient. — A mere allegation that the affiant has "received information from a reliable informant" has been held insufficient to show that the informant was credible, or that his information was reliable. Manley v. Commonwealth, 211 Va. 146, 176 S.E.2d 309 (1970), cert. denied, 403 U.S. 936, 91 S. Ct. 2245, 29 L. Ed. 2d 716 (1971).

Where a reliable informant's information is based on personal observation and participation in the illegal activity, a neutral and detached magistrate could find that the allegations in support of the affidavit are based on fact and not upon supposition and rumor. Wheeler v. Commonwealth, 217 Va. 95, 225 S.E.2d 400 (1976).

An affidavit which is merely a statement of the conclusion of the affiant, or that of the informant, that the defendant was in possession of narcotics at that time, is not a sufficient allegation of "material facts, constituting the probable cause for the issuance" of a search warrant, required by this section and the provisions of the Fourth Amendment. Wiles v. Commonwealth, 209 Va. 282, 163 S.E.2d 595 (1968).

Affidavit need not show how informant knew substance was narcotic. — A search warrant affidavit is not insufficient because it fails to show how the informant knew that the substance that he observed was a narcotic. Wheeler v. Commonwealth, 217 Va. 95, 225 S.E.2d 400 (1976).

Search warrant must describe the place to be searched. — Under the Constitution of the United States and the statutory law of Virginia it is essential to the validity of a search warrant that it describe with particularity the place to be searched. All that is required, however, is that the description be such that the officer charged with executing the search warrant can, with reasonable effort, ascertain and identify the place intended. Manley v. Commonwealth, 211 Va. 146, 176 S.E.2d 309 (1970), cert. denied, 403 U.S. 936, 91 S. Ct. 2245, 29 L. Ed. 2d 716 (1971).

A search warrant must describe with particularity the place to be searched. Brown v. Commonwealth, 212 Va. 672, 187 S.E.2d 160 (1972).

Warrant directed against multiple-occupancy structure must describe particular subunit. — A search warrant directed against a multiple-occupancy structure is invalid if it fails to describe the particular subunit to be searched with sufficient definiteness to preclude search of other units located in the larger structure and occupied by innocent persons. Manley v. Commonwealth, 211 Va. 146, 176 S.E.2d 309 (1970), cert. denied, 403 U.S. 936, 91 S. Ct. 2245, 29 L. Ed. 2d 716 (1971).

As a general rule, a search warrant directed against a multiple-occupancy building will be invalidated if it fails to specify the particular subunit to be searched. Brown v. Commonwealth, 212 Va. 672, 187 S.E.2d 160 (1972).

Or specify name of occupant. — Even though a search warrant directed against a multiple-occupancy structure fails to describe the particular subunit to be searched, it will ordinarily not be held invalid where it adequately specifies the name of the occupant of the subunit against which it is directed and provides the searching officers with sufficient information to identify, without confusion or excessive effort, such apartment unit. Manley v. Commonwealth, 211 Va. 146, 176 S.E.2d 309 (1970), cert. denied, 403 U.S. 936, 91 S. Ct. 2245, 29 L. Ed. 2d 716 (1971).

Defendant must challenge the search at trial. — If a defendant wishes to preserve his right to challenge on appeal the constitutionality of a search and seizure through which certain evidence has been obtained, he must take timely steps in the lower court, either through a motion to suppress the evidence before trial or by sufficient objection to the use of the evidence when offered at trial. Manley v. Commonwealth, 211 Va. 146, 176 S.E.2d 309 (1970), cert. denied, 403 U.S. 936, 91 S. Ct. 2245, 29 L. Ed. 2d 716 (1971).

An objection that a search warrant was not supported by an affidavit as required by statute cannot be raised for the first time on appeal from a conviction. Manley v. Commonwealth, 211 Va. 146, 176 S.E.2d 309 (1970), cert. denied, 403 U.S. 936, 91 S. Ct. 2245, 29 L. Ed. 2d 716 (1971).

Applied in Garza v. Commonwealth, 228 Va. 559, 323 S.E.2d 127 (1984).

II. PROBABLE CAUSE.

Establishing reasonable cause. — Virginia's search and seizure statutes require the judge issuing the warrant to be satisfied that there is a reasonable cause for the search. Generally, reasonable cause can be established from an affidavit, but the judge need not accept the affidavit alone, and nothing in the statutes prohibits him from conducting an adversary hearing, as the Constitution requires. Tyrone, Inc. v. Wilkinson, 410 F.2d 639 (4th Cir.), cert. denied, 396 U.S. 985, 90 S. Ct. 477, 24 L. Ed. 2d 449 (1969).

The standard for determining probable cause is probability, and not a prima facie showing, of criminal activity. Manley v. Commonwealth, 211 Va. 146, 176 S.E.2d 309 (1970), cert. denied, 403 U.S. 936, 91 S. Ct. 2245, 29 L. Ed. 2d 716 (1971).

The evidence upon which the issuance of a search warrant is based does not have to be sufficient to establish the fact that the thing sought is on the premises, but merely that the belief of the person making the affidavit that it is there is based on facts which furnish a probable or reasonable cause for such belief. The requirement is practically the same as that contained in the Fourth Amendment of the federal Constitution. Zimmerman v. Town of Bedford, 134 Va. 787, 115 S.E. 362 (1922); Tri-Pharmacy, Inc. v. United States, 203 Va. 723, 127 S.E.2d 89 (1962), cert. denied, 371 U.S. 962, 83 S. Ct. 542, 9 L. Ed. 2d 509 (1963).

Sufficient underlying circumstances. — Where a neutral magistrate could determine from statements made in an affidavit that the informant was familiar with drugs and "the drug culture" whereby he could readily recognize LSD and where a common-sense reading of the affidavit as a whole revealed the address at which the drugs were located, there were sufficient underlying circumstances to enable the magistrate to judge the validity of the informant's conclusion as to the location of the contraband. Wheeler v. Commonwealth, 217 Va. 95, 225 S.E.2d 400 (1976).

Facts in affidavit held sufficient. — Where officer failed to include in affidavit all facts verbally related to magistrate, omission did not violate requirements of this section since affidavit contained facts sufficient to support probable cause determination. Slayton v. Commonwealth, No. 0817-87-2 (Ct. of Appeals Mar. 7, 1989).

The fact that the affidavit for the search of defendant's house did not accurately describe the lots adjacent to the victim's house or state that the address of defendant's house was obtained from his DMV record was no more fatal to the warrant for the search under this section than under the Constitution. Commonwealth v. Derr, No. 0053-89-2 (Ct. of Appeals June 14, 1989).

Requirement that affidavit in support of search warrant substantially allege the offense in relation to which the search is made was satisfied where the affidavit specifically described the offenses being investigated as breaking and entering, grand larceny, and possession of stolen property; furthermore, the affidavit described the items to be searched for to include bacon and cigarettes, which were identified by quantity and name brand and stated that these items were stolen during "two business break-ins" currently under investigation; thus the affidavit substantially alleged the offenses so as to apprise adequately the defendant of the offenses and the evidence sought, and to inform those conducting the search of the items sought. West v. Commonwealth, 16 Va. App. 679, 432 S.E.2d 730 (1993).

Magistrate had probable cause to issue a search warrant to search defendant's apartment where the affidavit supporting the warrant provided a detailed description of a confidential, reliable informant who, after giving "buy money" to an unwitting informant, saw the unwitting informant knock on defendant's door, walk in with money, and return to hand the reliable informant cocaine that was purchased. Totality of the circumstances, therefore, provided the magistrate with a substantial basis to find that probable cause justified the search. Slade v. Commonwealth, 43 Va. App. 61, 596 S.E.2d 90, 2004 Va. App. LEXIS 231 (2004).

Affidavit deficiently vague. — Search warrant was issued and executed based on an affidavit that was deficiently vague and did not support probable cause where the affidavit: (1) did not specify any dates, but merely related that an unidentified suspect told a friend, who was an unidentified informant, that the suspect traded a pistol to defendant; (2) did not disclose when the conversation occurred, when the trade occurred, or whether the trade was before or after the homicide; (3) did not assert that the pistol was ever seen in the residence searched or where the trade occurred; (4) did not disclose whether the pistol was a "nine millimeter" firearm or was believed to be capable of discharging "nine millimeter" rounds; and (5) did not allege that the traded pistol was connected with the homicide. Anzualda v. Commonwealth, 42 Va. App. 481, 592 S.E.2d 761, 2004 Va. App. LEXIS 91 (2004).

Affidavit not providing sufficient basis for finding of probable cause for issuance of search warrant. — See, Riggan v. Virginia, 384 U.S. 152, 86 S. Ct. 1378, 16 L. Ed. 2d 431 (1966); Morris v. Commonwealth, 208 Va. 331, 157 S.E.2d 191 (1967).

Magistrate considered facts contained in several affidavits. — A magistrate did not violate this section when she considered the collective facts contained in several affidavits submitted at different times in the course of an on-going investigation in determining probable cause to search. Derr v. Commonwealth, 410 Va. 662, 410 S.E.2d 662 (1991).

Evidence inadmissible. — The evidence obtained as a result of a search warrant issued upon an insufficient affidavit was inadmissible. Wiles v. Commonwealth, 209 Va. 282, 163 S.E.2d 595 (1968).

Where the affidavit fails to uphold a determination of probable cause, then such failure renders the warrant void and the search illegal and any evidence secured through an illegal search becomes inadmissible at trial. Drumheller v. Commonwealth, 223 Va. 695, 292 S.E.2d 602, cert. denied, 459 U.S. 913, 103 S. Ct. 224, 74 L. Ed. 2d 178 (1982).

State procedural requirements must be respected in determining whether a state criminal conviction is constitutionally permissible because of the admission of evidence obtained as a result of an illegal search and seizure. Manley v. Commonwealth, 211 Va. 146, 176 S.E.2d 309 (1970), cert. denied, 403 U.S. 936, 91 S. Ct. 2245, 29 L. Ed. 2d 716 (1971).

Plain view exception. — Trial court erred in suppressing evidence pertaining to defendant's indictment for unlawful possession of controlled substances where a police officer lawfully seized ammunition under a search warrant for a gun, the officer was in a lawful position to view the crack pipe and the bottles of prescription drugs, and therefore, lawfully seized the crack pipe and drugs under the plain view doctrine. Commonwealth v. Marek, No. 2123-02-4, 2003 Va. App. LEXIS 46 (Ct. of Appeals Feb. 5, 2003).

"Good faith" exception. — The Supreme Court of Virginia embraces the "good faith" exception to the exclusionary rule. McCary v. Commonwealth, 228 Va. 219, 321 S.E.2d 637 (1984).

Trial court did not err in denying defendant's motion to suppress evidence seized as a result of a search warrant, where despite the fact that the affidavit supporting the same failed to provide the issuing magistrate with a substantial basis for concluding that probable cause to search defendant's home existed to issue said warrant, officers possessed an objectively reasonable belief in the existence of probable cause, namely, that the fruits of criminal activity would probably be found at defendant's residence, for the good faith exception to the exclusionary rule to apply. Anzualda v. Commonwealth, 44 Va. App. 764, 607 S.E.2d 749, 2005 Va. App. LEXIS 88 (2005).

Trial court properly denied defendant's motion to suppress despite the fact that the affidavit in support of the search warrant may have been stale, because the officers conducting the search did so in good-faith reliance on the validity of the warrant. The officer who executed the warrant testified that, based on the officer's experience and training, the officer knew that individuals who possess, manufacture, or distribute child pornography were collectors and tended to keep their collection and thus, the officer was not unreasonable in believing that there was probable cause that the images downloaded 16 months earlier could still have been in defendant's possession. Midkiff v. Commonwealth, 54 Va. App. 323, 678 S.E.2d 287, 2009 Va. App. LEXIS 294 (2009), aff'd, 280 Va. 216, 694 S.E.2d 576, 2010 Va. LEXIS 61 (2010).

Filing of affidavits was appropriate. — Filing of affidavits required by this section in the City of Danville, rather than defendant's residence of Pittsylvania County, was appropriate where the Circuit Court of the City of Danville, pursuant to § 19.2-250, had jurisdiction over the crime and the area where the search was made. Robertson v. Rogers, 2 Va. App. 503, 346 S.E.2d 41 (1986), aff'd, 360 S.E.2d 715 (1987).

Insufficient probable cause for search warrant. — Although a search warrant was facially valid, given the informant's motive to lie and the absence of evidence corroborating his allegations or establishing his reliability in some other way, probable cause was lacking; therefore, defendant's motion to suppress was properly granted. Commonwealth v. Thomas, 2011 Va. App. LEXIS 267 (Aug. 16, 2011).

CIRCUIT COURT OPINIONS

Search warrant must describe the place to be searched. — Where the description of the unit to be searched in a warrant directly conflicted with its actual location, there was insufficient evidence for the police to determine which unit to search; as a result, defendant was entitled to suppress the evidence found. Commonwealth v. Carr, 61 Va. Cir. 491, 2003 Va. Cir. LEXIS 224 (Charlottesville 2003).

Oral statement sufficient to provide information supporting probable cause. — Sworn statement, taken together with a written affidavit, supported a magistrate's finding of probable cause to issue a search warrant since U.S. Const., Amend. IV, did not require that the sworn statement be written; also, there was a nexus between drugs and defendant's home where a credible informant alleged that he purchased drugs there the previous day. Since the search warrant was properly supported, firearms found on defendant in a search of his home were not suppressed. Commonwealth v. Alger, 66 Va. Cir. 332, 2005 Va. Cir. LEXIS 37 (Page County Jan. 18, 2005).

Insufficient probable cause for search warrant. — Magistrate did not have a substantial basis for finding probable cause to issue a search warrant where the affidavit simply stated that the informant observed stolen property in defendant's residence and included no information as to when the informant observed the stolen property, what specific items of stolen property the informant observed, or how the informant knew that the property was stolen. Commonwealth v. Fuller, 78 Va. Cir. 385, 2009 Va. Cir. LEXIS 167 (Norfolk June 17, 2009).

OPINIONS OF THE ATTORNEY GENERAL

Airport searches. — Fourth Amendment protections are rights attaching to persons that can be asserted only by them either directly or through an association. The Attorney General lacks standing to bring suit against the federal government claiming a violation of the Fourth Amendment for searches conducted at airports. See opinion of Attorney General to The Honorable Robert B. Bell, Member, House of Delegates, 12-046, 2012 Va. AG LEXIS 27 (6/29/2012).

§ 19.2-55. Issuing general search warrant or search warrant without affidavit deemed malfeasance.

Any person having authority to issue criminal warrants who wilfully and knowingly issues a general search warrant or a search warrant without the affidavit required by § 19.2-54 shall be deemed guilty of a malfeasance.

History.
Code 1950, § 19.1-89; 1960, c. 366; 1975, c. 495.

§ 19.2-56. To whom search warrant directed; what it shall command; warrant to show date and time of issuance; copy of affidavit to be part of warrant and served therewith; warrants not executed within 15 days.

The judge, magistrate or other official authorized to issue criminal warrants, shall issue a search warrant if he finds from the facts or circumstances recited in the affidavit that there is probable cause for the issuance thereof.

Every search warrant shall be directed to (i) the sheriff, sergeant, or any policeman of the county, city or town in which the place to be searched is located, (ii) any law-enforcement officer or agent employed by the Commonwealth and vested with the powers of sheriffs and police, or (iii) jointly to any such sheriff, sergeant, policeman or law-enforcement officer or agent and an agent, special agent or officer of the Federal Bureau of Investigation, the Bureau of Alcohol, Tobacco and Firearms of the United States Treasury, the United States Naval Criminal Investigative Service, the United States Department of Homeland Security, any inspector, law-enforcement official or police personnel of the United States Postal Inspection Service, or the Drug Enforcement Administration. The warrant shall (i) name the affiant, (ii) recite the offense in relation to which the search is to be made, (iii) name or describe the place to be searched, (iv) describe the property or person to be searched for, and (v) recite that the magistrate has found probable cause to believe that the property or person constitutes evidence of a crime (identified in the warrant) or tends to show that a person (named or described therein) has committed or is committing a crime.

The warrant shall command that the place be forthwith searched, either in day or night, and that the objects or persons described in the warrant, if found there, be seized. An inventory shall be produced before a court having jurisdiction of the offense in relation to which the warrant was issued as provided in § 19.2-57.

Any such warrant as provided in this section shall be executed by the policeman or other law-enforcement officer or agent into whose hands it shall come or be delivered. If the warrant is directed jointly to a sheriff, sergeant, policeman or law-enforcement officer or agent of the Commonwealth and a federal agent or officer as otherwise provided in this section, the warrant may be executed jointly or by the policeman, law-enforcement officer or agent into whose hands it is delivered. No other person may be permitted to be present during or participate in the execution of a warrant to search a place except (i) the owners and occupants of the place to be searched when permitted to be present by the officer in charge of the conduct of the search and (ii) persons designated by the officer in charge of the conduct of the search to assist or provide expertise in the conduct of the search.

Any search warrant for records or other information pertaining to a subscriber to, or customer of, an electronic communication service or remote computing service, whether a domestic corporation or foreign corporation, that is transacting or has transacted any business in the Commonwealth, to be executed upon such service provider may be executed within or without the Commonwealth by hand, United States mail, commercial delivery service, facsimile, or other electronic means upon the service provider. Notwithstanding the provisions of § 19.2-57, the officer executing a warrant pursuant to this paragraph shall endorse the date of execution thereon and shall file the warrant, with the inventory attached (or a notation that no property was seized) and the accompanying affidavit, unless such affidavit was made by voice or videotape recording, within three days after the materials ordered to be produced are received by the officer from the service provider. The return shall be made in the circuit court clerk's office for the jurisdiction wherein the warrant was issued. Saturdays, Sundays, or any federal or state legal holiday shall not be used in computing the three-day filing period.

Electronic communication service or remote computing service providers, whether a foreign or domestic corporation, shall also provide the contents of electronic communications pursuant to a search warrant issued under this section and § 19.2-70.3 using the same process described in the preceding paragraph.

Every search warrant shall contain the date and time it was issued. However, the failure of any such search warrant to contain the date and time it was issued shall not render the warrant void, provided that the date and time of issuing of said warrant is established by competent evidence.

The judge, magistrate, or other official authorized to issue criminal warrants shall attach a copy of the affidavit required by § 19.2-54, which shall become a part of the search warrant and served therewith. However, this provision shall not be applicable in any case in which the affidavit is made by means of a voice or videotape recording or where the affidavit has been sealed pursuant to § 19.2-54.

Any search warrant not executed within 15 days after issuance thereof shall be returned to, and voided by, the officer who issued such search warrant.

For the purposes of this section:

"*Foreign corporation*" means any corporation or other entity, whose primary place of business is located outside of the boundaries of the Commonwealth, that makes a contract or engages in a terms of service agreement with a resident of the Commonwealth to be performed in whole or in part by either party in the Commonwealth, or a corporation that has been issued a certificate of authority pursuant to § 13.1-759 to transact business in the Commonwealth. The making of the contract or terms of service agreement or the issuance of a certificate of authority shall be considered to be the agreement of the foreign corporation or entity that a search warrant or subpoena, which has been properly served on it, has the same legal force and effect as if served personally within the Commonwealth.

"*Properly served*" means delivery of a search warrant or subpoena by hand, by United States mail, by commercial delivery service, by facsimile or by any other manner to any officer of a corporation or its general manager in the Commonwealth, to any natural person designated by it as agent for the service of process, or if such corporation has designated a corporate agent, to any person named in the latest annual report filed pursuant to § 13.1-775.

History.

Code 1950, § 19.1-86; 1960, c. 366; 1968, c. 572; 1975, c. 495; 1977, c. 289; 1979, c. 584; 1980, c. 573; 1981, c. 559; 1984, cc. 491, 598; 1988, c. 50; 1989, c. 719; 2000, c. 783; 2001, cc. 183, 205; 2007, c. 416; 2009, c. 725.

The 2007 amendments.

The 2007 amendment by c. 416 substituted "15 days" for "fifteen days" in the section catchline and the last paragraph and inserted "the United States Department of Homeland Security, any inspector, law-enforcement official or police personnel of the United States

Postal Inspection Service," in clause (iii) in the first sentence of the second paragraph.

The 2009 amendments.

The 2009 amendment by c. 725 added the fifth, sixth, tenth, eleventh, and twelfth paragraphs.

Law Review.

For comment on the reasonableness of no knock entry when exigencies are present, see 7 U. Rich. L. Rev. 565 (1973). For survey of Virginia law on criminal procedure for the year 1974-1975, see 61 Va. L. Rev. 1713 (1975). For survey of Virginia law on arrests in private dwellings for the year 1979-1980, see 67 Va. L. Rev. 275 (1981).

Michie's Jurisprudence.

For related discussion, see 1B M.J. Appeal and Error, § 240.

CASE NOTES

Requirements same as those of Fourth Amendment. — The requirements of the Virginia statutes controlling the issuance of search warrants and forbidding searches without a warrant (§§ 19.2-54 and 19.2-56) are in substance the same as those contained in the Fourth Amendment. Kirby v. Commonwealth, 209 Va. 806, 167 S.E.2d 411 (1969).

"Probable cause" defined. — Probable cause exists where the totality of the circumstances set forth in the affidavit supports a common sense decision by the magistrate that there is a fair probability that contraband or evidence of a crime will be found in a particular place. Turner v. Commonwealth, 14 Va. App. 737, 420 S.E.2d 235 (1992).

Because probable cause is a fluid concept based on probabilities, the continued existence of probable cause at a particular time is dependent upon the circumstances. So long as probable cause continues to exist, the search will be valid. Turner v. Commonwealth, 14 Va. App. 737, 420 S.E.2d 235 (1992).

Facts must be closely related to time of issuance of warrant. — Virginia's statutes fix no maximum time interval between the date of the events and circumstances recited in the affidavit and the date of the affidavit and issuance of the warrant. However, the proof must be of facts so closely related to the time of the issue of the warrant as to justify a finding of probable cause at that time. Huff v. Commonwealth, 213 Va. 710, 194 S.E.2d 690 (1973).

When a warrant has been issued based upon probable cause, whether probable cause continues to exist at the time the warrant is executed depends on the length of delay and the nature of the observed criminal activity, that is, whether the activity is an ongoing enterprise or an isolated incident. Turner v. Commonwealth, 14 Va. App. 737, 420 S.E.2d 235 (1992).

The fact that the officers delay executing a search warrant until a time the officer determines will be most opportune to yield a successful result does not invalidate the warrant so long as probable cause continued to exist at the time of execution. Turner v. Commonwealth, 14 Va. App. 737, 420 S.E.2d 235 (1992).

Sufficient probable cause for issuance of search warrant. — Motion to suppress evidence that was found in a search of defendant's home was denied because a police detective's affidavit, which was based upon the observations of the detective and another police detective and a confidential informant as to drug transactions occurring in defendant's home, presented sufficient probable cause for issuance of a search warrant. Hicks v. Commonwealth, 281 Va. 353, 706 S.E.2d 339, 2011 Va. LEXIS 44 (2011).

The provision in this section that a search warrant be executed "forthwith" is a directive to police officers to execute the warrant with reasonable dispatch and without undue delay. Turner v. Commonwealth, 14 Va. App. 737, 420 S.E.2d 235 (1992).

"Forthwith" requirement complied with. — Under the circumstances in this case, the police officers, by waiting 11 days to execute the warrant, did not violate the "forthwith" provision of the statute or the Fourth Amendment. The officers executed the warrant as soon as reasonably practicable under the circumstances. The warrant identified both a residence and its occupants as targets to be searched. The officers checked the residence at least six times, only to find the person who was also the object of the search not present. Immediately after learning that the described

occupant had returned, the officers executed the search warrant. Based on these circumstances, the officers executed the warrant as soon as reasonably practicable and, thus, that they complied with the directory component of the "forthwith" language in this section. Turner v. Commonwealth, 14 Va. App. 737, 420 S.E.2d 235 (1992).

Statutory requirement that search warrant be executed "forthwith" was satisfied where warrant was executed five days after issuance; the search was delayed to permit the warrant to be executed concurrently with search warrant for another apartment in same building; there was no basis for deeming that circumstances providing probable cause for search had grown stale by time warrant was executed. Commonwealth v. Moss, 14 Va. App. 750, 420 S.E.2d 242 (1992).

A six-day delay between a warrant's issuance and its execution did not violate the "forthwith" requirement of § 19.2-56, where the delay did not, standing alone, vitiate the reasonable belief that contraband would still be on the premises six days later, the description of the quantity of the remaining drugs as significant enough for continued sale suggested a continuing enterprise, defendant was absent from the premises the entire six days, and officers were informed that defendant kept two attack dogs in the house. Whitaker v. Commonwealth, 37 Va. App. 21, 553 S.E.2d 539, 2001 Va. App. LEXIS 568 (2001).

In a criminal prosecution for possession with intent to distribute crack cocaine, the district court denied defendant's motion to suppress evidence seized subsequent to the execution of search warrants. The ten-day delay in service of the warrants was within the time limits set forth in § 19.2-56. United States v. Davis, 276 F. Supp. 2d 522, 2003 U.S. Dist. LEXIS 13834 (E.D. Va. 2003).

Lapse of 11 days between when the search warrants were obtained and when they were executed did not violate defendant's rights under this section or the Fourth Amendment since the lapse was due to the officer's competing law-enforcement interests and there was no evidence that probable cause had dissipated by the time the warrants were executed. Maye v. Commonwealth, 44 Va. App. 463, 605 S.E.2d 353, 2004 Va. App. LEXIS 590 (2004).

Motion to suppress evidence that was found in a search of defendant's home was denied because the warrant was timely executed 13 days after its issuance pursuant to § 19.2-56, and the search was conducted forthwith in compliance with the requirements of § 19.2-56 and the Fourth Amendment. Hicks v. Commonwealth, 281 Va. 353, 706 S.E.2d 339, 2011 Va. LEXIS 44 (2011).

Scope of search not exceeded. — Defendant's motion to suppress was properly denied; a safe located during a search of his residence was in plain view, and officers could reasonably expect to find the items listed on a search warrant within the safe. The officers did not exceed the scope of the search authorized by the warrant by delaying some fifteen days to open the safe after it was seized and removed to police property. Dotson v. Commonwealth, 47 Va. App. 237, 623 S.E.2d 414, 2005 Va. App. LEXIS 514 (2005).

Where defendant conceded that probable cause to search an apartment still existed when an "all persons present" warrant was executed at an apartment twelve days after its issuance, the court assumed that the warrant was lawfully issued and a presumption of validity attached to the search. Felton v. Commonwealth, 56 Va. App. 43, 690 S.E.2d 318, 2010 Va. App. LEXIS 128 (2010).

"No knock entry." — In Virginia there is no specific statute relating to "no knock entry" in executing a search warrant. The court must therefore consider whether an unannounced search is reasonable within the meaning of the Fourth Amendment to the United States Constitution and the Constitution of Virginia. Johnson v. Commonwealth, 213 Va. 102, 189 S.E.2d 678 (1972), cert. denied, 409 U.S. 1116, 93 S. Ct. 918, 34 L. Ed. 2d 700 (1973).

Under Virginia law, the authority to effect a no-knock entry stems from exigent circumstances reasonably appearing to the officers to be in existence at the time the entry is made, and not at the time the warrant is obtained; thus, under Virginia law a magistrate lacks authority to "command" a no-knock entry in advance of the entry. Fenner v. Dawes, 748 F. Supp. 404 (E.D. Va. 1990).

Recitation of offense. — A search warrant sufficiently recites the offense if it is attached to an affidavit which specifies the offense to which the warrant pertains; however, a search warrant does not recite the offense and is fatally defective where the evidence establishes that the deficient warrant and affidavit that did recite the offense were not attached until after the execution of the search warrant. Lebedun v. Commonwealth, No. 0233-97-4 (Ct. of Appeals July 7, 1998).

Failure of warrant to state offense. — Items seized pursuant to a search warrant were inadmissible into evidence because of the failure of the warrant to state the offense in relation to which the search was to be conducted, despite the fact that the affidavit contained the offense in relation to which the search was to be conducted, where the affidavit was not attached to the warrant until after the search warrant had been executed and the disputed items seized. Gilluly v. Commonwealth, 221 Va. 38, 267 S.E.2d 105 (1980).

The failure of a warrant to state the related offense renders the warrant fatally defective and the evidence seized in the execution of the warrant inadmissible. Lebedun v. Commonwealth, 27 Va. App. 697, 501 S.E.2d 427 (1998).

Where a search is conducted pursuant to a judicially sanctioned warrant, the defendant must rebut the presumption of validity by proving that the warrant is illegal or invalid. Thus, where a warrant failed to recite the offense, the burden was on the defendant to prove that the affidavit, which expressly stated that the search pertained to charges of robbery and abduction, was not attached to the deficient warrant at the time the search occurred. Lebedun v. Commonwealth, 27 Va. App. 697, 501 S.E.2d 427 (1998).

Additional seizures under warrant. — Where appellant's address was identified in the warrant as the place to be searched, and "marijuana" was specified as the item to be seized, a search was not invalid merely because officers seized items not named in the warrant. Cherry v. Commonwealth, 21 Va. App. 132, 462 S.E.2d 574 (1995).

Applied in United States v. Belcher, 577 F. Supp. 1241 (E.D. Va. 1983).

CIRCUIT COURT OPINIONS

When a warrant has been issued based upon probable cause, whether probable cause continues to exist. — When a search warrant was used based upon probable cause, whether probable cause continued to exist at the time the warrant was executed depended on the length of delay after the warrant was issued and the nature of the observed criminal activity, that is whether the activity was an ongoing enterprise or an isolated incident. Commonwealth v. Robinson, — Va. Cir. —, 2002 Va. Cir. LEXIS 274 (Newport News May 6, 2002).

The "forthwith" requirement. — By establishing a 15-day limitation period in § 19.2-56, the General Assembly did not intend to provide that search warrants executed within that time were conclusively presumed to have been executed timely, as such an interpretation would render the "forthwith" language of the statute meaningless, a result that could not be attributed to the legislature, and "forthwith," within the context of § 19.2-56, did not mean immediately or as soon as physically possible; the fact that the statute provided that the warrant expired if not executed within 15 days meant that some latitude was provided for the time within which the search could be conducted. Commonwealth v. Robinson, — Va. Cir. —, 2002 Va. Cir. LEXIS 274 (Newport News May 6, 2002).

Under § 19.2-56, it was necessary that search warrants be executed with promptness in order to lessen the possibility that the facts upon which probable cause was initially based did not become dissipated, and the statute included a codification of the constitutional requirement that a search must be conducted while probable cause continued to exist, but it went beyond that as the "forthwith" requirement defined the policy of the state that search warrants, which were the foremost safeguard to protect against unreasonable searches proscribed by the Fourth Amendment, were to be executed with reasonable dispatch. Commonwealth v. Robinson, — Va. Cir. —, 2002 Va. Cir. LEXIS 274 (Newport News May 6, 2002).

Various relevant considerations to whether a search warrant was executed "forthwith" could include the safety of the officers executing the warrant, the safety of others in the area and other competing law-enforcement interests which precluded immediate execution of the warrant. Commonwealth v. Robinson, — Va. Cir. —, 2002 Va. Cir. LEXIS 274 (Newport News May 6, 2002).

Forthwith standard complied with. — Where police waited

five days from the issuance of a search warrant before executing it in order to wait for defendant to obtain a new supply of drugs, the warrant was executed in accordance with the forthwith standard under § 19.2-56, because defendant was engaged in an ongoing drug sale enterprise, and the delay was reasonable, as it gave the officers a more favorable chance of obtaining better results. Commonwealth v. Prosser, — Va. Cir. —, 1999 Va. Cir. LEXIS 767 (Newport News Dec. 16, 1999).

Despite an eight-day delay in executing a search warrant, its underlying probable cause was not stale because it suggested a continuing enterprise of drug sales; because no constitutional violation existed and defendant was not prejudiced, defendant's motion to suppress was denied. Commonwealth v. Roy, 55 Va. Cir. 299, 2001 Va. Cir. LEXIS 522 (Richmond 2001).

Officers did not execute a search warrant "forthwith," as required by § 19.2-56, when the delay was attributed to assisting security in a courtroom, moving office furniture, and being off duty for a few days, and no reason was given why other officers could not have served the warrant, nor was an unusual amount of official business shown. Commonwealth v. Robinson, — Va. Cir. —, 2002 Va. Cir. LEXIS 274 (Newport News May 6, 2002).

Limitations period. — Where the search warrant was executed five days after it was issued, the search warrant was executed within the 15-day limitations period under § 19.2-56 and the 10-day limitations period under Fed. R. Crim. P. 41(c)(1). Commonwealth v. Prosser, — Va. Cir. —, 1999 Va. Cir. LEXIS 767 (Newport News Dec. 16, 1999).

Suppression of evidence. — Violation of the requirement of § 19.2-56 that a search warrant be executed "forthwith" warranted suppression of any evidence seized only where defendant could show prejudice attributable to the unreasonable delay. Commonwealth v. Robinson, — Va. Cir. —, 2002 Va. Cir. LEXIS 274 (Newport News May 6, 2002).

§ 19.2-56.1. Warrant issued for search of attorney's office.

A. Any warrant sought for the search of a premises or the contents thereof belonging to or under the control of any licensed attorney-at-law to search for evidence of any crime solely involving a client of such attorney shall be issued only by a circuit court judge. Any evidence seized pursuant to this section shall be inventoried forthwith by the clerk of the issuing court and sealed by the issuing judge. As soon thereafter as is practicable, the issuing judge shall conduct an in camera inspection of the seized evidence in the presence of the attorney from whom the evidence was seized. Following such inspection the issuing judge shall return any evidence so seized which is determined to be within the scope of the attorney-client privilege and not otherwise subject to seizure.

B. Nothing herein shall bar the standing of the client to challenge the admissibility of any evidence seized pursuant to this section in any trial or proceeding.

History.
1986, c. 636.

§ 19.2-56.2. Application for and issuance of search warrant for a tracking device; installation and use.

A. As used in this section, unless the context requires a different meaning:

"*Judicial officer*" means a judge, magistrate, or other person authorized to issue criminal warrants.

"Law-enforcement officer" shall have the same meaning as in § 9.1-101.

"Tracking device" means an electronic or mechanical device that permits a person to remotely determine or track the position or movement of a person or object. "Tracking device" includes devices that store geographic data for subsequent access or analysis and devices that allow for the real-time monitoring of movement.

"Use of a tracking device" includes the installation, maintenance, and monitoring of a tracking device but does not include the interception of wire, electronic, or oral communications or the capture, collection, monitoring, or viewing of images.

B. A law-enforcement officer may apply for a search warrant from a judicial officer to permit the use of a tracking device. Each application for a search warrant authorizing the use of a tracking device shall be made in writing, upon oath or affirmation, to a judicial officer for the circuit in which the tracking device is to be installed, or where there is probable cause to believe the offense for which the tracking device is sought has been committed, is being committed, or will be committed.

The law-enforcement officer shall submit an affidavit, which may be filed by electronically transmitted (i) facsimile process or (ii) electronic record as defined in § 59.1-480, and shall include:

1. The identity of the applicant and the identity of the law-enforcement agency conducting the investigation;

2. The identity of the vehicle, container, item, or object to which, in which, or on which the tracking device is to be attached, placed, or otherwise installed; the name of the owner or possessor of the vehicle, container, item, or object described, if known; and the jurisdictional area in which the vehicle, container, item, or object described is expected to be found, if known;

3. Material facts constituting the probable cause for the issuance of the search warrant and alleging substantially the offense in relation to which such tracking device is to be used and a showing that probable cause exists that the information likely to be obtained will be evidence of the commission of such offense; and

4. The name of the county or city where there is probable cause to believe the offense for which the tracking device is sought has been committed, is being committed, or will be committed.

C. 1. If the judicial officer finds, based on the affidavit submitted, that there is probable cause to believe that a crime has been committed, is being committed, or will be committed and that there is probable cause to believe the information likely to be obtained from the use of the tracking device will be evidence of the commission of such offense, the judicial officer shall issue a search warrant authorizing the use of the tracking device. The search warrant shall authorize the use of the tracking device from within the Commonwealth to track a person or property for a reasonable period of time, not to exceed 30 days from the issuance of the search warrant. The search warrant shall authorize the collection of the tracking data contained in or obtained from the tracking device but shall not authorize the interception of wire, electronic, or oral communications or the capture, collection, monitoring, or viewing of images.

2. The affidavit shall be certified by the judicial officer who issues the search warrant and shall be delivered to and preserved as a record by the clerk of the circuit court of the county or city where there is probable cause to believe the offense for which the tracking device has been sought has been committed, is being committed, or will be committed. The affidavit shall be delivered by the judicial officer in person; mailed by certified mail, return receipt requested; or delivered by electronically transmitted facsimile process or by use of filing and security procedures as defined in the Uniform Electronic Transactions Act (§ 59.1-479 et seq.) for transmitting signed documents.

3. By operation of law, the affidavit, search warrant, return, and any other related materials or pleadings shall be sealed. Upon motion of the Commonwealth or the owner or possessor of the vehicle, container, item, or object that was tracked, the circuit court may unseal such documents if it appears that the unsealing is consistent with the ends of justice or is necessary to reasonably inform such person of the nature of the evidence to be presented against him or to adequately prepare for his defense.

4. The circuit court may, for good cause shown, grant one or more extensions, not to exceed 30 days each.

D. 1. The search warrant shall command the law-enforcement officer to complete the installation authorized by the search warrant within 15 days after issuance of the search warrant.

2. The law-enforcement officer executing the search warrant shall enter on it the exact date and time the device was installed and the period during which it was used.

3. Law-enforcement officers shall be permitted to monitor the tracking device during the period authorized in the search warrant, unless the period is extended as provided for in this section.

4. Law-enforcement officers shall remove the tracking device as soon as practical, but not later than 10 days after the use of the tracking device has ended. Upon request, and for good cause shown, the circuit court may grant one or more extensions for such removal for a period not to exceed 10 days each.

5. In the event that law-enforcement officers are unable to remove the tracking device as required by subdivision 4, the law-enforcement officers shall disable the device, if possible, and all use of the tracking device shall cease.

6. Within 10 days after the use of the tracking device has ended, the executed search warrant shall be returned to the circuit court of the county or city

where there is probable cause to believe the offense for which the tracking device has been sought has been committed, is being committed, or will be committed, as designated in the search warrant, where it shall be preserved as a record by the clerk of the circuit court.

E. Within 10 days after the use of the tracking device has ended, a copy of the executed search warrant shall be served on the person who was tracked and the person whose property was tracked. Service may be accomplished by delivering a copy to the person who, or whose property, was tracked or by leaving a copy with any individual found at the person's usual place of abode who is a member of the person's family, other than a temporary sojourner or guest, and who is 16 years of age or older and by mailing a copy to the person's last known address. Upon request, and for good cause shown, the circuit court may grant one or more extensions for such service for a period not to exceed 30 days each. Good cause shall include, but not be limited to, a continuing criminal investigation, the potential for intimidation, the endangerment of an individual, or the preservation of evidence.

F. The disclosure or publication, without authorization of a circuit court, by a court officer, law-enforcement officer, or other person responsible for the administration of this section of the existence of a search warrant issued pursuant to this section, application for such search warrant, any affidavit filed in support of such warrant, or any return or data obtained as a result of such search warrant that is sealed by operation of law is punishable as a Class 1 misdemeanor.

History.
2012, cc. 636, 679.

Editor's note.
Acts 2012, cc. 636 and 679, cl. 2 provides: "That an emergency exists and this act is in force from its passage." Acts 2012, c. 636 was approved April 5, 2012, and Acts 2012, c. 679 was approved April 6, 2012.

§ 19.2-57. Execution and return of warrant; list of property seized.

The warrant shall be executed by the search of the place described in the warrant and, if property described in the warrant is found there, by the seizure of the property. The officer who seizes any property shall prepare an inventory thereof, under oath. An inventory of any seized property shall be produced before the circuit court of the county or city where the search was conducted. The officer executing the warrant shall endorse the date of execution thereon and the officer or his designee shall file the warrant, with the inventory attached (or a notation that no property was seized) and the accompanying affidavit, unless such affidavit was made by voice or videotape recording, within three days after the execution of such search warrant in the circuit court clerk's office, wherein the search was made, as

provided in § 19.2-54. Saturdays, Sundays, or any federal or state legal holiday shall not be used in computing the three-day filing period. The officer, or his designee or agent, may file the warrant, inventory, and accompanying affidavit by delivering them in person, or by mailing them certified mail, return receipt requested, or delivering them by electronically transmitted facsimile process.

History.
Code 1950, § 19.1-87.1; 1970, c. 416; 1973, c. 11; 1975, c. 495; 1976, cc. 142, 552; 1977, c. 109; 1980, c. 573; 1984, c. 491; 2008, cc. 147, 183.

The 2008 amendments.
The 2008 amendments by cc. 147 and 183 are identical, and substituted "is found" for "be found" in the first sentence and "the circuit court of the county or city where the search was conducted" for "the court designated in the warrant" in the third sentence; inserted "the officer or his designee" in the fourth sentence; and added the last sentence.

CASE NOTES

Addendum to inventory filed satisfied requirements of this section. — Although deputy sheriff had to supplement, original inventory and return were filed within three days after execution of the search warrant, as required by the terms of this section, thus defendant's contention in requiring property seized in the inventory that was filed with the return had no basis, for this section does not prohibit filing of an addendum to inventory where filing of the original inventory been satisfied. West v. Commonwealth, 16 Va. App. 679, 432 S.E.2d 730 (1993).

Defendant not entitled to suppression of evidence. — Even if the filing of the inventory and return was not in compliance with this section, defendant was not entitled to suppression of evidence seized from his home, for this section regarding the filing of inventory after execution of warrant did not expressly command the suppression or exclusion of evidence for a violation of this section; and moreover, the defendant did not allege that his constitutional rights were violated. West v. Commonwealth, 16 Va. App. 679, 432 S.E.2d 730 (1993).

Although two seized documents were omitted from the inventory prepared and filed by police officer, noncompliance with this section did not require suppression of the remaining documents. Spivey v. Commonwealth, 23 Va. App. 715, 479 S.E.2d 543 (1997), overruled on other grounds, Henry v. Commonwealth, 32 Va. App. 547, 529 S.E.2d 796 (2000).

§ 19.2-58. Disposition of property seized.

If any such warrant be executed by the seizure of property, or of any other of the things aforesaid, the same shall be safely kept by the direction of such judge or court, to be used as evidence, and thereafter be disposed of as provided by law; provided, however, that any such property seized under such warrant which is not used in evidence and any property which is stolen or embezzled property shall be restored to its owner, and the things mentioned in § 19.2-53 may be burnt or otherwise destroyed, under such direction, as soon as there is no further need for its use as evidence unless it is otherwise expressly provided by law.

History.
Code 1950, § 19.1-87; 1960, c. 366; 1975, c. 495.

CASE NOTES

Transfer of evidence to federal authorities. — Defendant's motion to suppress evidence was properly denied; although defendant's property was transferred to federal authorities, it never lost its status as evidence, and defendant failed to formally move for the return of his property as required by §§ 19.2-58 and 19.2-60, so defendant's prostitution-related convictions were appropriate. United States v. Jenkins, — F.3d —, 2005 U.S. App. LEXIS 18376 (4th Cir. Aug. 25, 2005), cert. denied, — U.S. —, 126 S. Ct. 1092, 163 L. Ed. 2d 907 (2006).

§ 19.2-59. Search without warrant prohibited; when search without warrant lawful.

No officer of the law or any other person shall search any place, thing or person, except by virtue of and under a warrant issued by a proper officer. Any officer or other person searching any place, thing or person otherwise than by virtue of and under a search warrant, shall be guilty of malfeasance in office. Any officer or person violating the provisions of this section shall be liable to any person aggrieved thereby in both compensatory and punitive damages. Any officer found guilty of a second offense under this section shall, upon conviction thereof, immediately forfeit his office, and such finding shall be deemed to create a vacancy in such office to be filled according to law.

Provided, however, that any officer empowered to enforce the game laws or marine fisheries laws as set forth in Title 28.2 may without a search warrant enter for the purpose of enforcing such laws, any freight yard or room, passenger depot, baggage room or warehouse, storage room or warehouse, train, baggage car, passenger car, express car, Pullman car or freight car of any common carrier, or any boat, automobile or other vehicle; but nothing in this proviso contained shall be construed to permit a search of any occupied berth or compartment on any passenger car or boat or any baggage, bag, trunk, box or other closed container without a search warrant.

History.

Code 1950, § 19.1-88; 1960, c. 366; 1975, c. 495; 1976, c. 293; 1978, c. 721; 1997, c. 147.

Law Review.

For note, "Arson Investigations and the Fourth Amendment," see 30 Wash. & Lee L. Rev. 133 (1973). For survey of Virginia law on criminal procedure for the year 1974-1975, see 61 Va. L. Rev. 1713 (1975). For survey of Virginia criminal procedure for the year 1975-1976, see 62 Va. L. Rev. 1412 (1976). For comment on warrantless searches of automobiles in Virginia, see 12 U. Rich. L. Rev. 563 (1978). For article, "Warrantless Searches and Seizures in Virginia," see 17 U. Rich. L. Rev. 721 (1983). For article, "Unreasonable Searches and Seizures of Papers," see 71 Va. L. Rev. 869 (1985).

CASE NOTES

Section affords Fourth Amendment protection. — This section affords in substance only the same protection as that afforded by the Fourth Amendment. Carter v. Commonwealth, 209

Va. 317, 163 S.E.2d 589 (1968), cert. denied, 394 U.S. 991, 89 S. Ct. 1479, 22 L. Ed. 2d 766 (1969); Thompson v. Slayton, 334 F. Supp. 352 (W.D. Va. 1971).

This section was originally enacted during prohibition in response to widespread complaints concerning unreasonable searches. The statute protects against unreasonable searches and seizures, which are forbidden by the common law, and by the Fourth Amendment which is but declaratory of the common law on the subject. Burnham v. West, 681 F. Supp. 1169 (E.D. Va. 1988).

This section provides the same protection as the Fourth Amendment of the Constitution of the United States. Amato v. City of Richmond, 875 F. Supp. 1124 (E.D. Va. 1994), aff'd, 78 F.3d 578 (4th Cir. 1996), cert. denied, 519 U.S. 862, 117 S. Ct. 167, 136 L. Ed. 2d 109 (1996).

Trial court erred in denying defendant's motion to suppress evidence obtained as a result of the lawful arrest of defendant on an outstanding warrant, as the search of defendant at a lockup violated defendant's Fourth Amendment rights in a case where defendant was later convicted of possession of cocaine with intent to distribute; contrary to the Commonwealth's argument, the search of defendant was not a less intrusive strip search, but was a more intrusive visual body cavity search where police officers had defendant bend over and spread defendant's buttock cheeks, and the search was unreasonable because police did not have a "clear indication" that evidence was located within defendant's body and the police officers did not show that they faced exigent circumstances that required such an invasive search be performed. King v. Commonwealth, 49 Va. App. 717, 644 S.E.2d 391, 2007 Va. App. LEXIS 194 (2007).

Town officer was entitled to qualified immunity in a homeowner's action that alleged civil rights and illegal search claims under 42 U.S.C.S. § 1983 and § 19.2-59 because the homeowner's Fourth Amendment rights were not clearly established under the law since courts were divided on the question of whether a drunk driving offense justified a warrantless home arrest; the town was properly granted summary judgment because the homeowner did not set forth sufficient facts to establish that the supervising officials had knowledge, actual or constructive, that town police officers were engaged in conduct that posed a pervasive and unreasonable risk of constitutional injury to citizens like the homeowner. Cilman v. Reeves, 2011 U.S. App. LEXIS 22483 (4th Cir. Nov. 4, 2011).

This section does not afford greater protection than that provided under the Fourth Amendment. Gordon v. Commonwealth, No. 1717-88-1 (Ct. of Appeals Apr. 10, 1990).

Evidence obtained in violation of United States Constitution is inadmissible. — Mapp v. Ohio, 367 U.S. 643, 81 S. Ct. 1684, 6 L. Ed. Ct. 23, 7 L. Ed. 2d 72 (1961), holds that all evidence obtained by search and seizure in violation of the United States Constitution is, by that same authority inadmissible in a state court. Rees v. Commonwealth, 203 Va. 850, 127 S.E.2d 406 (1962), cert. denied, 372 U.S. 964, 83 S. Ct. 1088, 10 L. Ed. 2d 128, rehearing denied, 373 U.S. 947, 83 S. Ct. 1533, 10 L. Ed. 2d 702 (1963).

Construction of section prior to 1976 amendment. — This section, as in force in 1975 with its provision for search incident to arrest, provided no greater restriction on warrantless searches than the Fourth Amendment, the provision for warrantless search incident to arrest having been added in 1975 to bring the statute in line with Carter v. Commonwealth, 209 Va. 317, 163 S.E.2d 589 (1968), cert. denied, 394 U.S. 991, 89 S. Ct. 1479, 22 L. Ed. 2d 766 (1969), and subsequent removal of the provision in 1976 showing merely that statute should be broadly worded to avoid necessity for frequent amendments. Thims v. Commonwealth, 218 Va. 85, 235 S.E.2d 443 (1977).

It may be conceded that the language of this section is perhaps too broad in its scope. But this fault, if fault it be, is not to be corrected by the court, as correction lies within the exclusive province of the legislature. Durham Bros. & Co. v. Woodson, 155 Va. 93, 154 S.E. 485 (1930).

It was enacted to prevent searches upon mere suspicion. — It is a matter of common knowledge that for some years prior to 1920 there were complaints that many citizens were being harassed and humiliated by having their houses, vehicles and baggage searched, upon mere suspicion, by officers and other persons seeking to discover infractions of certain laws. It was primarily in response to these complaints that the Legislature enacted this section. Durham Bros. & Co. v. Woodson, 155 Va. 93, 154 S.E. 485 (1930).

And to protect personal liberty and privacy. — The prime object of the statute is the protection of the personal liberty and privacy of the citizen and the prevention of the unreasonable invasion of personal rights in the course of the administration of the law. The protection which is given by the statute to property is purely incidental. McClannan v. Chaplain, 136 Va. 1, 116 S.E. 495 (1923).

The statute has a wider scope than the common-law rule on the subject, in that it designates other places and things for the search of which search warrants are required, for which the common law does not require search warrants. McClannan v. Chaplain, 136 Va. 1, 116 S.E. 495 (1923).

And it was the legislative intent to extend the right of search to vehicles, baggage and things. This provision is found for the first time in the Acts of 1920 and clearly indicates the intention to depart from the general rule at common law and also to enlarge the right of search conferred by the Code of 1919, as well as to impose upon one who violates its provisions both a penal and a civil liability. Durham Bros. & Co. v. Woodson, 155 Va. 93, 154 S.E. 485 (1930).

No creation of action against private entity or individual. — This section does not create a cause of action against a private entity or an individual. Buonocore v. C & P Tel. Co., 254 Va. 469, 492 S.E.2d 439 (1997).

This section makes a warrant the prerequisite of a search. Carter v. Commonwealth, 209 Va. 317, 163 S.E.2d 589 (1968), cert. denied, 394 U.S. 991, 89 S. Ct. 1479, 22 L. Ed. 2d 766 (1969).

Not applicable to mine inspections. — Because subsection B of § 45.1-161.292:54 informed appellant mine operator that inspections to which he was subject were not discretionary acts but were conducted pursuant to statute, it satisfied the Burger test requiring a constitutionally adequate substitute for a warrant, and, if § 19.2-59 applied to surface mine inspections, much of the Virginia Mineral Mine Safety Act would be rendered meaningless, thus, § 19.2-59 did not apply to searches under the Virginia Mineral Mine Safety Act. Lesueur-Richmond Slate Corp. v. Fehrer, 666 F.3d 261, 2012 U.S. App. LEXIS 786 (4th Cir. 2012).

Reasonableness of search is test. — Like the Fourth Amendment, this section proscribes only an unreasonable search without a warrant. The relevant test is not whether it is reasonable to procure a search warrant, but whether the search was reasonable. Carter v. Commonwealth, 209 Va. 317, 163 S.E.2d 589 (1968), cert. denied, 394 U.S. 991, 89 S. Ct. 1479, 22 L. Ed. 2d 766 (1969).

Search and seizure incident to lawful arrest. — A search and seizure is not unlawful despite the absence of a search warrant if it occurs incident to a lawful arrest. Kirby v. Commonwealth, 209 Va. 806, 167 S.E.2d 411 (1969).

Officer exceeding his authority is a trespasser. — In an action of trespass on the case against special police officers appointed under § 15.1-144 (see now § 15.2-1737), even if the entry of the defendants upon the farm of plaintiff in search of a still was lawful, if, after the entry, they exceeded their authority by doing some act which they had no right to do, the law will consider them as trespassers ab initio. McClannan v. Chaplain, 136 Va. 1, 116 S.E. 495 (1923).

Protective sweep. — Under the Fourth Amendment, exigent circumstances justified a warrantless "protective sweep" of an apartment, even though defendant had already been arrested outside the residence, because police had reason to believe that there were other persons and a loaded weapon in the apartment. Williams v. Commonwealth, — Va. App. —, — S.E.2d —, 2006 Va. App. LEXIS 94 (Mar. 14, 2006).

Where officers, in conducting a protective sweep of an apartment after arresting, did not look into closed containers or cabinets, their quick and limited minimal intrusion did not violate the Fourth Amendment, and since they were lawfully in the apartment, they were entitled to seize a gun that was in plain view. Williams v. Commonwealth, — Va. App. —, — S.E.2d —, 2006 Va. App. LEXIS 94 (Mar. 14, 2006).

Who may be liable for punitive damages. — Although the entry of officers upon the farm of plaintiff to make a search was lawful, yet if while on the premises they were guilty of disorderly conduct injurious to the plaintiff, which was malicious or wanton, or conduct in violation of the statute, they were liable for punitive damages. McClannan v. Chaplain, 136 Va. 1, 116 S.E. 495 (1923).

Only the constitutional standard of conduct, therefore, should apply for purposes of determining sovereign immunity in actions brought under this section. Burnham v. West, 681 F. Supp. 1169 (E.D. Va. 1988).

Investigatory stop. — Suppression of evidence obtained during an investigatory stop was not required because the factual circumstances justified reasonable suspicion that defendant may have been trespassing; posted signs warned that permission to use the parking lot was reserved for patrons, and at 12:40 a.m., when the restaurant was closed, defendant was a non-patron subject to the restriction on access to the parking lot. Raab v. Commonwealth, 49 Va. App. 638, 644 S.E.2d 78, 2007 Va. App. LEXIS 179 (2007).

The trial court properly denied defendant's motion to suppress the cocaine seized from defendant's person, as a deputy, in conducting an investigatory stop of defendant on foot, observed that defendant smelled of alcohol, had a flushed face, and was unsteady on his feet, supplying the officer with probable cause to arrest defendant for public intoxication. Thus, given the validity of the stop, the trial court correctly denied defendant's suppression motion. Croson v. Commonwealth, — Va. App. —, — S.E.2d —, 2007 Va. App. LEXIS 276 (July 24, 2007).

Reasonable suspicion to stop vehicle. — Trial court erred in granting defendant's motion to suppress evidence because the officer had reasonable suspicion to stop the vehicle in which defendant was traveling based on the officer's observation of the vehicle violating two traffic laws, following too closely and exceeding the posted speed limit by at least five miles per hour; thus, the stop did not violate the Fourth Amendment. Commonwealth v. Beyene, — Va. App. —, — S.E.2d —, 2007 Va. App. LEXIS 368 (Oct. 2, 2007).

Evidence seized during pat down. — Evidence seized during pat down of defendant was inadmissible because the seizure and subsequent pat down of defendant violated defendant's rights under the Fourth Amendment. The officer did not have an objectively reasonable basis for suspecting defendant was armed and dangerous; among other things, the officer did not see a gun or anything that looked like a gun, there was no evidence defendant appeared nervous or behaved in threatening manner in placing his hands in his pockets, and the officer never asked defendant to remove his hands from his pockets or attempted to secure his own safety by less intrusive means. Roulhac v. Commonwealth, 50 Va. App. 8, 646 S.E.2d 4, 2007 Va. App. LEXIS 228 (2007).

Suppression of weapon found on defendant during a police search was erroneous because defendant was not "seized" within the meaning of the Fourth Amendment when the officer approached defendant and asked to speak to defendant; only after learning that defendant had outstanding felony warrants for robbery and firearms charges did the officer conduct a pat-down search of defendant. Commonwealth v. Collins, — Va. App. —, — S.E.2d —, 2007 Va. App. LEXIS 367 (Sept. 28, 2007).

Emergency exception to warrant requirement. — Motion to suppress evidence first seen when police entered defendant's home without a warrant to check on the welfare of defendant in response to an anonymous call was improperly granted as the warrantless entry was permissible under the emergency exception to the warrant requirement; the police conduct was not pretextual, and the police first canvassed the outside of the house, knocked on the door, and tried to contact defendant. Commonwealth v. Purnell, No. 1761-02-1, 2002 Va. App. LEXIS 767 (Ct. of Appeals Dec. 23, 2002).

Community caretaker exception to warrant requirement. — Where the trial court found that the actions of the officers were not pretextual, the officers' warrantless entry into the residence was constitutionally permissible pursuant to the community caretaker exception to the warrant requirement. Kyer v. Commonwealth, 43 Va. App. 603, 601 S.E.2d 6, 2004 Va. App. LEXIS 396 (2004).

Based on the totality of the circumstances, especially defendant's attempt to flee the scene, a police officer had reasonable, articulable facts upon which to stop defendant and investigate further; consequently, the stop did not violate the Fourth Amendment and the trial court did not err in denying defendant's motion to suppress. Higgs v. Commonwealth, — Va. App. —, — S.E.2d —, 2006 Va. App. LEXIS 216 (May 16, 2006).

Warrantless inspection of mines. — Because warrantless inspections of plaintiff's mines by defendant state inspectors were constitutional, since the state had a substantial interest in protecting worker health and safety and the scope of any inspections did not run afoul of the Fourth Amendment, plaintiff mining company failed to state a claim under 42 U.S.C.S. § 1983 and state law. The inspectors' actions were authorized by Virginia's Mineral Mine Safety Act, § 45.1-161.292:1 et seq., and Chapters 14.5 (§ 45.1-151.293 et seq.) and 14.6 (§ 45.1-161.304 et seq.) of Title 45.1, and the inspectors were entitled to qualified immunity. Lesueur-Richmond Slate Corp. v. Fehrer, 752 F. Supp. 2d 713, 2010 U.S. Dist. LEXIS 118081 (W.D. Va. 2010), aff'd, 666 F.3d 261, 2012 U.S. App. LEXIS 786 (4th Cir. 2012).

Standard for determination of sovereign immunity. — Only the Constitutional standard of conduct should apply for purposes of determining sovereign immunity in actions brought under this section. Amato v. City of Richmond, 875 F. Supp. 1124 (E.D. Va. 1994), aff'd, 78 F.3d 578 (4th Cir. 1996), cert. denied, 519 U.S. 862, 117 S. Ct. 167, 136 L. Ed. 2d 109 (1996).

Teachers and school principal entitled to sovereign immunity. — Teachers and school principal who ordered, directed and searched students were entitled to the protection of sovereign immunity from damages liability under this section. Burnham v. West, 681 F. Supp. 1169 (E.D. Va. 1988).

Articles of clothing were not obtained by illegal search and seizure, and were properly admitted into evidence. Duffield v. Peyton, 209 Va. 178, 162 S.E.2d 915 (1968).

Where defendant had impliedly consented to needed medical treatment, and the removal of his clothing and the removal of a bullet were necessary incidents thereof, as evidence of criminal agency the clothing and bullet were seizable objects and were appropriate objects to be voluntarily surrendered by the doctor who was in lawful control thereof. Craft v. Commonwealth, 221 Va. 258, 269 S.E.2d 797 (1980).

Statute of limitations for unlawful searches and seizures. — An unlawful search and seizure is characterized as a personal injury, rather than an injury to property and the applicable statute of limitations provision is contained in subsection A of § 8.01-243, which sets a two-year time limit for filing an action. Cramer v. Crutchfield, 496 F. Supp. 949 (E.D. Va. 1980), aff'd, 648 F.2d 943 (4th Cir. 1981).

Consent to search given by one with common authority over property is valid as against the absent, nonconsenting person with whom the authority is shared. Black v. Commonwealth, 223 Va. 277, 288 S.E.2d 449 (1982).

Passenger lacked standing to challenge car owner's consent. — Because defendant, as a passenger, did not have standing to challenge the search of a car or the owner's consent thereto, the trial court erred in granting defendant's motion to suppress the physical evidence obtained from the investigative traffic stop. Commonwealth v. Blevins, — Va. App. —, — S.E.2d —, 2007 Va. App. LEXIS 153 (Apr. 16, 2007).

Burden is on the Commonwealth to prove the voluntariness of a consent to search, but whether the consent was voluntarily given is a question of fact to be determined from the totality of all the circumstances. Black v. Commonwealth, 223 Va. 277, 288 S.E.2d 449 (1982).

The burden is on the Commonwealth to show that consent to a warrantless search is freely and voluntarily given. Fitzgerald v. Commonwealth, 223 Va. 615, 292 S.E.2d 798 (1982).

Inadvertent discovery of incriminating evidence. — Where a police officer, with justification for being on the premises, is not searching for evidence against the accused but inadvertently comes across incriminating evidence, he may seize it without a warrant. Fitzgerald v. Commonwealth, 223 Va. 615, 292 S.E.2d 798 (1982).

Commonwealth's limited right of appeal. — The legislature has narrowly limited the Commonwealth's right to appeal suppression orders of the trial courts to orders which are based on constitutional violations; therefore, where the Commonwealth appealed an order suppressing certain evidence solely on the grounds that the evidence was obtained in violation of this section and § 19.2-60, the court of appeals would not entertain the Commonwealth's appeal. Commonwealth v. Ragland, 7 Va. App. 452, 374 S.E.2d 183 (1988).

Anonymous tip. — Trial court properly denied defendant's motion to suppress a firearm seized from him through a warrantless pat down, despite the fact that the involved officers' suspicion that defendant was shooting at a vehicle was provided by an anonymous tip, as: (1) the police dispatcher and the investigating officers had objective reasons to believe the caller was reliable; (2) the caller's continued presence on the telephone as the encounter unfolded established this reliability; and (3) the caller provided updated information at the time the officers actually approached defendant, and the officers corroborated this information. Williams v. Commonwealth, No. 0783-04-1, 2005 Va. App. LEXIS 129 (Ct. of Appeals Mar. 29, 2005).

Damages. — This section concerns a common-law tort that has achieved constitutional dimensions, and the statute specifies the familiar tort law remedy of damages. Sovereign immunity, which is primarily applied to bar damages liability in tort suits, applies to action brought under this section. Burnham v. West, 681 F. Supp. 1169 (E.D. Va. 1988).

Motion to suppress properly granted. — Evidence found in a frisk of defendant was properly suppressed as the frisk was unconstitutional where the police did not have reason to believe that defendant was armed and dangerous at the time he was frisked since: (1) there were no facts linking defendant, a former occupant of a car, with the theft of the car or the driver's possession of a gun; (2) there was no evidence establishing that defendant and the driver were on a common mission; (3) when arrested, defendant was a pedestrian and had not been in the car for 10 minutes; and (4) there were no factors in which suspicion had been imputed to the companion of a legally detained suspect as, inter alia, defendant did not have invalid identification, the police were not outnumbered, and the encounter did not occur in a high crime area, at night, or under poor lighting conditions. Commonwealth v. Riggins, No. 2001-03-4, 2004 Va. App. LEXIS 48 (Ct. of Appeals Jan. 30, 2004).

CIRCUIT COURT OPINIONS

No cause of action for unreasonable seizures. — This section, which creates a cause of action for unreasonable searches, creates no such cause for unreasonable seizures. Gray v. Rhoads, 55 Va. Cir. 362, 2001 Va. Cir. LEXIS 300 (Charlottesville 2001), remanded on other grounds, 268 Va. 81, 597 S.E.2d 93 (2004).

Reasonableness of search is test. — Defendant's motion to suppress evidence located as a result of the officer's search was denied, as the officer's finding of cocaine on defendant's person due to a pat-down search was based on a reasonable suspicion of the presence of illegal drugs that gave rise to a concern that guns were present; defendant conceded that probable cause existed to search the car in which he was a passenger since the officer smelled marijuana emanating from the car, which meant the officer was reasonably suspicious that other illegal drugs were present, as well as guns, and the officer thus had the right to pat-down defendant, at which time the cocaine was located. Commonwealth v. Webb, 62 Va. Cir. 110, 2003 Va. Cir. LEXIS 73 (Roanoke 2003).

Probable cause to search. — Public safety is a clear exigent circumstance justifying the police officers' entry into a defendant's residence in response to an alarm call; if the police have reason to believe that someone might be hurt or that an intruder is on the premises, they are permitted to enter the premises to check for such activity. Commonwealth v. Swartz, 66 Va. Cir. 513, 2003 Va. Cir. LEXIS 255 (Fairfax County 2003).

Consent to warrantless search was voluntary. — Defendant's motion to suppress evidence was denied because, based on the totality of the circumstances, defendant's waiver of his rights and consent to search his home was voluntarily made and, thus, lawfully obtained; the officer removed defendant's handcuffs, read him his rights, received permission to search the house, and asked defendant if anything illegal would be found, to which defendant responded affirmatively. Commonwealth v. Swartz, 66 Va. Cir. 513, 2003 Va. Cir. LEXIS 255 (Fairfax County 2003).

Consent to search not valid. — Where the police officers, after hearing a noise in defendant's apartment, asked defendant's boyfriend's consent to search the apartment, and the boyfriend granted consent, the consent to search exception to the warrant requirement under § 19.2-59 was not established; defendant's boyfriend, who was not a co-tenant in the apartment, lacked the apparent authority to consent to the search, as there was no effort made to ascertain whether the boyfriend was a co-tenant of the apartment; nor was the exigent circumstance exception established. Commonwealth v. Gordon, — Va. Cir. —, 2003 Va. Cir. LEXIS 170 (Roanoke Sept. 8, 2003).

Search held invalid. — Police officer's search of defendant without probable cause to believe a crime was being committed rendered the search of defendant, which showed defendant had crack cocaine on defendant's person, illegal; even if probable cause had existed, suppression would have still been required because the facts did not justify a warrantless search. Commonwealth v. Niblett, 61 Va. Cir. 736, 2002 Va. Cir. LEXIS 316 (Roanoke 2002).

Defendant's motion to suppress was granted, where the evidence showed that any alleged consent received by officers was the fruit of the poisonous tree that was not purged of an illegal taint, specifically, the illegal entry into a locked employee break room, especially where no intervening circumstances or significant passage of time between the illegal entry and the consent was present. Commonwealth v. Soy Hem, 62 Va. Cir. 480, 2003 Va. Cir. LEXIS 303 (Norfolk 2003).

Evidence obtained from a warrantless search of defendants' apartment was suppressed where no exigent circumstances existed, the evidence did not support a finding of hot pursuit, and consent obtained after the detective entered defendants' apartment could not retroactively validate a prior improper entry. Commonwealth v. Whitecotton, — Va. Cir. —, 2004 Va. Cir. LEXIS 228 (Roanoke Aug. 27, 2004).

§ 19.2-59.1. Strip searches prohibited; exceptions; how strip searches conducted.

A. No person in custodial arrest for a traffic infraction, Class 3 or Class 4 misdemeanor, or a violation of a city, county, or town ordinance, which is punishable by no more than thirty days in jail shall be strip searched unless there is reasonable cause to believe on the part of a law-enforcement officer authorizing the search that the individual is concealing a weapon. All strip searches conducted under this section shall be performed by persons of the same sex as the person arrested and on premises where the search cannot be observed by persons not physically conducting the search.

B. A regional jail superintendent or the chief of police or the sheriff of the county or city shall develop a written policy regarding strip searches.

C. A search of any body cavity must be performed under sanitary conditions and a search of any body cavity, other than the mouth, shall be conducted either by or under the supervision of medically trained personnel.

D. Strip searches authorized pursuant to the exceptions stated in subsection A of this section shall be conducted by a law-enforcement officer as defined in § 9.1-101.

E. The provisions of this section shall not apply when the person is taken into custody by or remanded to a law-enforcement officer pursuant to a circuit or district court order.

F. For purposes of this section, *"strip search"* shall mean having an arrested person remove or arrange some or all of his clothing so as to permit a visual inspection of the genitals, buttocks, anus, female breasts, or undergarments of such person.

G. Nothing in this section shall prohibit a sheriff or a regional jail superintendent from requiring that inmates take hot water and soap showers and be subjected to visual inspection upon assignment to the general population area of the jail or upon determination by the sheriff or regional jail superintendent that the inmate must be held at the jail by reason of his inability to post bond after reasonable opportunity to do so.

History.
1981, c. 608; 1995, c. 112.

Cross references.
As to punishment for Class 3 and Class 4 misdemeanors, see § 18.2-11.

CASE NOTES

Expansive definition of "strip search." — The definition of "strip search" contained in this section is much more expansive than the traditional definition of such a search, because the statute is restricted to non-jailable offenses and offenses punishable by no more than 30 days in jail. McCloud v. Commonwealth, 35 Va. App. 276, 544 S.E.2d 866, 2001 Va. App. LEXIS 213 (2001).

Prohibition inapplicable to arrests for felonies. — By its own terms, this section does not apply to felony offenses and, accordingly, was not implicated where a defendant was arrested for possession of a stolen vehicle, a felony under Virginia law. McCloud v. Commonwealth, 35 Va. App. 276, 544 S.E.2d 866, 2001 Va. App. LEXIS 213 (2001).

This section does not apply to felony detainees, and does not provide a statutory suppression remedy for alleged violations. Craddock v. Commonwealth, 40 Va. App. 539, 580 S.E.2d 454, 2003 Va. App. LEXIS 296 (2003).

Where appellant was subjected to a visual body cavity search while being processed for detention into a jail and appellant argued that there was no medically trained personnel present at the time of the search, appellant was not subject to the provisions of § 19.2-59.1, because appellant had been charged with a felony. Winston v. Commonwealth, 51 Va. App. 74, 654 S.E.2d 340, 2007 Va. App. LEXIS 485 (2007).

Exclusion of evidence not mandated. — The fact that a search violates a legislative mandate without violating the Constitution does not provide for the exclusion of such evidence. Taylor v. Commonwealth, 28 Va. App. 638, 507 S.E.2d 661 (1998).

Denial of defendant's motion to suppress drugs was proper because, even if there was a U.S. Const., Amend. IV violation, defendant almost certainly would have been denied bail and committed to jail. Once inside, the deputies would have had a reason to believe that defendant was hiding contraband, which would have justified a body cavity search. Bowe v. Commonwealth, 2010 Va. App. LEXIS 136 (Apr. 6, 2010).

Evidence should have been suppressed. — Trial court erred in denying defendant's motion to suppress evidence obtained as a result of the lawful arrest of defendant on an outstanding warrant, as the search of defendant at a lockup violated defendant's Fourth Amendment rights in a case where defendant was later convicted of possession of cocaine with intent to distribute; contrary to the Commonwealth's argument, the search of defendant was not a less intrusive strip search, but was a more intrusive visual body cavity search where police officers had defendant bend over and spread defendant's buttock cheeks, and the search was unreasonable because police did not have a "clear indication" that evidence was located within defendant's body and the police officers did not show that they faced exigent circumstances that required such an invasive search be performed. King v. Commonwealth, 49 Va. App. 717, 644 S.E.2d 391, 2007 Va. App. LEXIS 194 (2007).

§ 19.2-60. Motion for return of seized property and to suppress.

A person aggrieved by an allegedly unlawful search or seizure may move the court to return any seized property and to suppress it for use as evidence. The court shall receive evidence on any issue of fact necessary to the decision of the motion. If the motion is granted by a court of record, any seized property shall be restored as soon as practicable unless otherwise subject to lawful detention, and such property shall not be admissible in evidence at any hearing or trial. If the motion is granted by a court not of record, such property shall not be admissible in evidence at any hearing or trial before that court, but the ruling shall have no effect on any hearing or trial in a court of record.

History.
1975, c. 495.

Law Review.
For review of Fourth Circuit cases on habeas corpus and prisoners' rights, see 36 Wash. & Lee L. Rev. 603 (1979).

CASE NOTES

I. In General.
II. Motion to Suppress.
  A. Search and Seizure.
  B. Suppression of Statements, DNA, etc.

I. IN GENERAL.

This section is a procedural statute. Troncoso v. Commonwealth, 12 Va. App. 942, 407 S.E.2d 349 (1991).

Rules governing suppression. — A motion under this section must be decided according to the established rules governing the suppression of evidence. Accordingly, suppression is properly denied absent a showing that the evidence was seized pursuant to a constitutional violation or pursuant to the violation of a statute which expressly provides suppression as a remedy for its breach. Troncoso v. Commonwealth, 12 Va. App. 942, 407 S.E.2d 349 (1991).

Commonwealth's limited right of appeal. — The legislature has narrowly limited the Commonwealth's right to appeal suppression orders of the trial courts to orders which are based on constitutional violations; therefore, where the Commonwealth appealed an order suppressing certain evidence solely on the grounds that the evidence was obtained in violation of § 19.2-59 and this section, the court of appeals would not entertain the Commonwealth's appeal. Commonwealth v. Ragland, 7 Va. App. 452, 374 S.E.2d 183 (1988).

Commonwealth's interlocutory appeal not allowed based on former § 19.2-83. — Where the trial court's suppressing order was not based on a violation of a provision of the Virginia or federal Constitutions, but was based on former § 19.2-83, which limited the authority of a police officer to stop, question and search a suspicious person, the interlocutory appeal by the Commonwealth from the order suppressing evidence of cocaine found on the defendant when law-enforcement officers searched him was not one which the Commonwealth was permitted to appeal. Commonwealth v. Brown, 8 Va. App. 41, 378 S.E.2d 623 (1989).

Entry of a knowing and voluntary, but non-conditional plea waived appeal from denial of motion to suppress. — Because defendant did not enter a conditional guilty plea pursuant to § 19.2-254, to a charge of possession of Oxycodone, but he entered said plea voluntarily and intelligently, he waived his right to appeal from the judgment denying his motion to suppress the evidence seized against him. Hill v. Commonwealth, 47 Va. App. 667, 626 S.E.2d 459, 2006 Va. App. LEXIS 63 (2006).

Where entry reasonable pursuant to emergency doctrine. — Officers' entry of appellant's home was reasonable under the emergency doctrine and appellant's motion to suppress was properly denied because evidence of appellant brandishing and using guns in the home permitted a reasonable officer to conclude that appellant's young daughter might be threatened with serious injury and in need of immediate aid; any error regarding the warrant was harmless because the shotguns and ammunition found pursuant to the warrant were merely cumulative of the weapons found in plain view pursuant to the lawful entry. Stallings v. Commonwealth, 2007 Va. App. LEXIS 451 (Dec. 18, 2007).

II. MOTION TO SUPPRESS.

A. Search and Seizure.

Consent to search. — Although no warrant exception justified police entry into the mother's apartment where defendant lived, the consent obtained thereafter from the mother was sufficiently an act of free will to purge the primary taint and thus, the trial court properly denied defendant's motion to suppress inculpatory evidence found in defendant's bedroom. Kyer v. Commonwealth, 45 Va. App. 473, 612 S.E.2d 213, 2005 Va. App. LEXIS 193 (2005).

Trial court did not err in denying defendant's motion to suppress, as there was no evidence that the police coerced defendant into consenting to the search; defendant never testified he heard any threats, saw any brandished firearms, observed an overwhelming number of officers, experienced any overt or implicit coercion, or felt he had no choice but to consent. Elliott v. Commonwealth, 61 Va. App. 48, 733 S.E.2d 146, 2012 Va. App. LEXIS 335 (2012).

Since a police officer conducting a traffic stop of defendant's vehicle had already given defendant her documentation back and had informed her that he was only going to give her a warning for her speeding violation while advising her to slow down before he continued questioning her, the traffic stop had concluded, and the ensuing encounter between the officer and defendant needed to proceed on a consensual basis in order for it to be lawful. The continued encounter was not consensual as, when the officer questioned defendant about the possession of illegal drugs, he had not informed defendant that she was free to leave, nor would a reasonable person have felt free to leave since the circumstances did not change from when the officer originally had seized her based on probable cause for the traffic stop; thus, defendant's motion to suppress was properly granted. Commonwealth v. Crooks, 2012 Va. App. LEXIS 364 (Nov. 15, 2012).

Consensual encounter. — Trial court did not err in denying defendant's motion to suppress a firearm seized from defendant's person. Since defendant did not submit to the officer's assertion of authority when he instructed defendant to take his hands out of his pockets after officers approached him on the streets while investigating a report of drug activity, the encounter remained consensual. Blanchard v. Commonwealth, 2012 Va. App. LEXIS 110 (Apr. 10, 2012).

Trial court did not err in denying defendant's motion to suppress evidence a police officer obtained from his person after conducting a traffic stop because defendant was not illegally detained, and the search was consensual; when the officer sought permission to search defendant's vehicle the encounter was consensual, and defendant was not seized for purposes of the Fourth Amendment, and a reasonable person would have recognized that the traffic investigation was concluded and that he or she was free to leave and to refuse the officer's request to search. Mayo v. Commonwealth, 2013 Va. App. LEXIS 57 (Feb. 19, 2013).

Third party consent. — As the peremptory manner in which a homeowner gained access to defendant's rented bedroom, unannounced and without knocking despite knowing defendant was present, would lead a reasonable person to believe that the room was under the homeowner's control as well, an officer's presence in the room was lawful and did not violate defendant's Fourth Amendment rights. Thus, defendant's motion to suppress was properly denied. Sourdiff v. Commonwealth, 2008 Va. App. LEXIS 534 (Dec. 9, 2008).

Abandoned property admissible. — Trial court erred in granting defendant's motion to suppress, because defendant was unable to meet defendant's burden of proving that defendant retained a reasonable expectation of privacy in the item after defendant tossed it out the window of the moving vehicle, where the evidence did not establish that defendant was subject to a seizure of defendant's person when defendant discarded plastic bag out the window. Commonwealth v. Kennedy, 2009 Va. App. LEXIS 26 (Jan. 27, 2009).

No reasonable expectation of privacy. — Trial court properly denied defendant's suppression motion as defendant surrendered his expectation of privacy in a tissue and its contents by voluntarily and intentionally dropping them to the ground in a quasi-public place during a consensual encounter with the police; notwithstanding any subjective intention to step on the tissue and to retain or regain control of it, the officers' recovery of the tissue was not an unreasonable search or seizure. Mayfield v. Commonwealth, No. 2713-03-1, 2005 Va. App. LEXIS 14 (Ct. of Appeals Jan. 11, 2005).

Defendant's motion to suppress was properly denied as he failed to show a reasonable expectation of privacy in a motel room where no evidence beyond his presence in the room tended to show that he was in the room with the registered owner's consent. Sharpe v. Commonwealth, 44 Va. App. 448, 605 S.E.2d 346, 2004 Va. App. LEXIS 594 (2004).

Defendant was not entitled to have DNA evidence suppressed because the use of a buccal swab to obtain defendant's DNA profile for comparison with DNA evidence recovered from the victim did not violate defendant's rights under the Fourth Amendment; defendant's reasonable expectation of privacy in the DNA sample ended when defendant voluntarily provided it to police for DNA testing and comparison in another case, without limiting its subsequent use for the same purpose in other investigations. Pharr v. Commonwealth, 50 Va. App. 89, 646 S.E.2d 453, 2007 Va. App. LEXIS 246 (2007).

No privacy interest in garbage cans. — Discarded garbage placed on the side of the street for pickup did not fall within any recognized Fourth Amendment privacy interest, and defendant did not have a legitimate privacy interest in it merely because the trash, which defendant testified he placed about two to three feet from the street, could be within the curtilage. Commonwealth v. Bryant, — Va. App. —, — S.E.2d —, 2005 Va. App. LEXIS 179 (May 3, 2005).

Search of backpack. — Defendant was not entitled to suppression of evidence seized from a backpack in defendant's grandfather's house after the grandfather gave consent, because it was objectively reasonable for the police officer to conclude that the grandfather's consent to search included the authority to consent to a search of the backpack and defendant was present but failed to object to search. Glenn v. Commonwealth, 275 Va. 123, 654 S.E.2d 910, 2008 Va. LEXIS 16 (2008).

Denial of defendant's motion to suppress was proper, where the officer had the driver's unrestricted consent to search the car containing defendant's bookbag; defendant left the bookbag in the car, knowing the car was to be searched; and defendant failed to make any objection to the search of the bookbag, despite ample opportunity to do so. Vaughan v. Commonwealth, 53 Va. App. 435, 672 S.E.2d 909, 2009 Va. App. LEXIS 82 (2009).

Handgun seized following a warrantless search of defendant's backpack was not admissible based on abandonment, where the trial court made no factual finding that defendant left the backpack in the office to conceal it from police, or otherwise intended to discard it or its contents. Nor was the fact that defendant told the officer that the handgun was in the backpack an "independent source," as the information obtained by the officer during the warrantless search was clearly used to secure defendant's admission. Knight v. Commonwealth, 61 Va. App. 297, 734 S.E.2d 716, 2012 Va. App. LEXIS 406 (2012).

Search warrant not supported by probable cause. — Although a search warrant affidavit failed to provide a sufficient nexus between drugs and defendant's residence to support probable cause under the Fourth Amendment, it was not so lacking in probable cause as to render official belief in the warrant objectively unreasonable. The good faith exception prevented application of the exclusionary rule, and defendant's pre-trial motion to suppress evidence was properly denied. Sowers v. Commonwealth, 49 Va. App. 588, 643 S.E.2d 506, 2007 Va. App. LEXIS 172 (2007).

Good faith exception. — Where defendant was convicted of second-degree murder, items seized at defendant's residence pursuant to a search warrant were properly admitted because: (1) the totality of the circumstances could be considered when deciding the question of good faith; and (2) the Leon good-faith exception to the exclusionary rule applied since the warrant stated that the residence was located on the same street as the shooting and the criminal complaint listed defendant's address, which was the same address as the residence. Adams v. Commonwealth, 275 Va. 260, 657 S.E.2d 87, 2008 Va. LEXIS 40 (2008).

Exclusionary rule of U.S. Const. amend. IV did not mandate suppression of evidence found during a search of defendant as the searching officer relied on information provided by a dispatcher that there was outstanding warrant for defendant's arrest. Thus,

the officer was objectively reasonable in arresting and searching defendant incident to that arrest. Bellamy v. Commonwealth, 60 Va. App. 125, 724 S.E.2d 232, 2012 Va. App. LEXIS 130 (2012).

"Good faith" exception applied and motion to suppress should have been denied, because, while the officer mistakenly failed to indicate that the information in the affidavit came from an informant rather than from the officer's personal knowledge, there was no reason to believe that the magistrate would have been misled to conclude that the officer was the source of the information since the affidavit itself indicated that the informant was the source of the information. Commonwealth v. Becerra-Ochoa, 2013 Va. App. LEXIS 62 (Feb. 26, 2013).

Search incident to valid arrest. — Motion to suppress was improperly granted because defendant was not seized for purposes of the Fourth Amendment when the officer parked 20 to 30 feet from the car where defendant was sitting and asked for and received identification; once the officer learned of the outstanding warrant for defendant, the encounter became a lawful seizure and evidence found during the search incident to defendant's arrest was lawfully obtained. Commonwealth v. Belfield, — Va. App. —, — S.E.2d —, 2007 Va. App. LEXIS 256 (June 26, 2007).

Cocaine found on defendant during a search incident to defendant's arrest for public drunkenness was erroneously suppressed as a police officer had probable cause to arrest defendant for public drunkenness under § 18.2-388, since defendant was found drunk and sleeping in a car in a parking lot open to the public and routinely used by apartment residents and guests; it did not matter for Fourth Amendment purposes that defendant was charged under a City ordinance with a more narrow scope than the state public drunkenness statute. Commonwealth v. Carter, — Va. App. —, — S.E.2d —, 2007 Va. App. LEXIS 344 (Sept. 14, 2007).

Denial of defendant's motion to suppress was proper, because the officer had probable cause to believe that defendant had or was committing crime of possessing marijuana based on the strong odor emanating from defendant; thus, the officer had probable cause to arrest defendant and therefore, the officer was entitled to conduct a full search of defendant's person. Askew v. Commonwealth, 2009 Va. App. LEXIS 133 (Mar. 24, 2009).

Denial of defendant's motion to suppress evidence seized from defendant's person incident to a warrantless arrest was upheld, because the officers had probable cause for the warrantless arrest given verified information from a confidential informant regarding defendant's identity, automobile, and destination, and the officers' observations of defendant's suspicious behavior and interactions with a man at the subject location. Robinson v. Commonwealth, 53 Va. App. 732, 675 S.E.2d 206, 2009 Va. App. LEXIS 174 (2009).

There was no error in the denial of a motion to suppress evidence obtained in a search incident to arrest because the initial encounter between defendant and a police officer was consensual where the officer made no show of force or authority nor did she physically restrain defendant in any way during the encounter and the interaction prior to defendant's arrest lasted only five to seven minutes. Muhammad v. Commonwealth, 2010 Va. App. LEXIS 163 (Apr. 24, 2010).

Trial court did not err in refusing to suppress evidence because evidence obtained from independent sources provided probable cause for defendant's arrest and the accompanying search of his vehicle for a crime committed only hours earlier; the focus on defendant as a suspect did not begin with the placement of a global positioning system device on his vehicle. Hill v. Commonwealth, No. 1828-11-3, 2012 Va. App. LEXIS 318 (Oct. 9, 2012).

Inevitable discovery doctrine. — Trial court properly denied defendant's motion to suppress, because even assuming, without deciding, that the state trooper violated defendant's Fourth Amendment rights by searching a cigarette box without probable cause, the evidence was nonetheless admissible under the inevitable discovery doctrine, as there was a reasonable probability that the evidence would have been discovered during a search incident to a lawful arrest, made after the trooper searched defendant's vehicle pursuant to defendant's consent. Bell v. Commonwealth, 2009 Va. App. LEXIS 9 (Jan. 13, 2009).

Probable cause to arrest found. — Denial of motion to suppress was proper because the officers had probable cause to arrest defendant based on the officer's belief that defendant constructively possessed the cocaine found in the console of the vehicle; among other things, the vehicle's owner admitted possessing smoking devices found in the vehicle but denied any knowledge of the container where the drugs were found and the officers were armed with the additional knowledge that defendant had just engaged in suspicious behavior suggestive of a drug transaction with a person traveling in a rental vehicle, and they observed a large bulge in his pants pocket that defendant admitted was a roll of cash. Dodd v. Commonwealth, 50 Va. App. 301, 649 S.E.2d 222, 2007 Va. App. LEXIS 316 (2007).

Trial court erred in suppressing a firearm found at the scene because the officers had probable cause to arrest defendant based on information received from an informant that the officers spoke to face-to-face; when officers first encountered defendant the defendant was nervous and determined to convince the officers that the defendant did not have a gun, even though the officers never mentioned that officers suspected the defendant had one; and an officer then found a gun in a vehicle the exact place defendant had been standing when the officers first spotted defendant. Commonwealth v. Moody, 2008 Va. App. LEXIS 438 (Sept. 30, 2008).

Grant of motion to suppress was error, where an officer had probable cause to arrest defendant after noticing a car parked next to a closed salvage yard, seeing defendant flee from the salvage yard, finding the lock on the salvage yard gate broken, discovering a hacksaw inside a duffle bag underneath a truck in the salvage yard, and finding, during consensual search, used car parts in the trunk of defendant's car. Commonwealth v. Butler, 2009 Va. App. LEXIS 20 (Jan. 15, 2009).

Trial court did not err by denying defendant's motion to suppress because the totality of the circumstances provided police officers with probable cause to arrest defendant for a robbery; the police had received an anonymous tip linking defendant to the crimes, had observed him attempt to flee, located a cap matching a description of the cap the robber wore inside the residence where he was found, and had obtained an eyewitness identification of defendant as the robber. Smith v. Commonwealth, 2009 Va. App. LEXIS 269 (June 16, 2009).

Defendant's suppression motion was properly denied where the police possessed probable cause to arrest defendant when defendant arrived at a parking lot to sell marijuana because an informant identified defendant as a marijuana dealer, and the police overheard a phone call with a person identified as defendant arranging for a marijuana purchase at the parking lot. Gholston v. Commonwealth, 2010 Va. App. LEXIS 202 (2010).

Defendant's motion to suppress evidence was properly denied because recovery of a firearm and cocaine evidence stemmed from a search incident to a lawful arrest where officers stopped defendant's car for failing to stop at a stop sign and an officer smelled marijuana coming from the car, which gave the officers probable cause to not only search the car but to search the individuals within the car. Price v. Commonwealth, 2010 Va. App. LEXIS 194 (May 11, 2010).

Trial court did not err in denying defendant's motion to suppress cocaine the police discovered in defendant's vehicle incident to an arrest on a separate charge because the police did not rely on the passenger of the vehicle as an informant since the passenger was not an informant, and his reliability and basis of knowledge were not factors in determining whether the police had probable cause to arrest defendant; unlike an anonymous tipster, the passenger was known to the police and personally spoke with them, and by telling the police that defendant was the driver and possessed the cocaine, the passenger was subjecting himself to possible arrest if the information proved false under § 18.2-461, placed his credibility at risk, and he could not lie with impunity. Jones v. Commonwealth, 2011 Va. App. LEXIS 98 (Mar. 22, 2011).

Trial court did not err in denying defendant's motion to suppress cocaine the police discovered in defendant's vehicle incident to an arrest on a separate charge because the police had probable cause to arrest defendant since a reasonable officer could conclude that there was probable cause to believe that defendant committed the crime of possession of cocaine, either solely or jointly; it was an entirely reasonable inference from the facts that either defendant or a passenger had knowledge of, and exercised dominion and control over, the cocaine. Jones v. Commonwealth, 2011 Va. App. LEXIS 98 (Mar. 22, 2011).

Trial court did not err in denying defendant's motion to suppress, where it was clear that the trial court was referring to the probable cause standard when it denied the motion by stating that the officer "had reason to believe" that a crime was being committed and there

was abundant evidence that defendant was disregarding the officer's signal or attempting to escape or elude the officer. Proffitt v. Commonwealth, 2011 Va. App. LEXIS 339 (2011).

Trial court erred in granting defendant's motion to suppress his statement to an arresting officer that he had taken an item from a store because under the totality of the circumstances, there was probable cause to arrest defendant since he matched the description given by an eyewitness and was apprehended near the scene of the crime; when the arrest officer found defendant in a library he knew that a shoplifting had occurred at the store located across the street and that the suspect was a white male wearing a gray hooded sweatshirt who fled toward the library. Commonwealth v. Hicks, 2012 Va. App. LEXIS 33 (Feb. 7, 2012).

Trial court properly denied defendant's motion to suppress drug evidence found in a search incident to defendant's arrest. Assessing defendant's encounter with the officer objectively, the officer had probable cause to arrest defendant for misdemeanor littering under § 33.1-346 from the moment defendant removed his coat and dropped it in the street while running from the officer. Bynum v. Commonwealth, 2012 Va. App. LEXIS 408 (Dec. 18, 2012).

No probable cause to arrest. — Motion to suppress heroin was improperly denied because the informant's tip did not provide probable cause to arrest defendant. The informant provided no basis for the claim that defendant was in possession of drugs; the informant did not provide such detailed information that a court could infer that the informant had personal knowledge of the alleged illegal activity; and the informant's history of reliability was not so great that it could, standing alone, support a finding of probable cause. Byrd v. Commonwealth, 50 Va. App. 542, 651 S.E.2d 414, 2007 Va. App. LEXIS 394 (2007).

Defendant's motion to suppress evidence resulting from the search of his person was properly granted because detectives lacked probable cause to arrest defendant; the detectives had insufficient knowledge to provide them with probable cause to believe that defendant was a drug source, there was no evidence that the detectives observed anything other than innocent behavior when defendant approached the driver of a car, and the detectives overheard none of the conversation between defendant and the driver. Commonwealth v. Williams, — Va. App. —, — S.E.2d —, 2008 Va. App. LEXIS 229 (May 13, 2008).

Because an officer lacked probable cause to arrest defendant for possession of marijuana, reliance upon the officer's detection of an unidentified "faint odor" was insufficient to create probable cause, and defendant's suspicious behavior as an intoxicated person did not warrant any further investigation, denial of her suppression motion was reversed. Buhrman v. Commonwealth, 275 Va. 501, 659 S.E.2d 325, 2008 Va. App. LEXIS 43 (2008).

Defendant not in custody. — Where defendant voluntarily accompanied officers to the police station, the detectives told defendant he was not under arrest and was free to leave, and the behavior of the officers supported their statements, the evidence supported a finding that defendant was not in custody when he made his first confession. Olson v. Commonwealth, — Va. App. —, — S.E.2d —, 2008 Va. App. LEXIS 95 (Feb. 26, 2008).

Plain view doctrine. — Motion to suppress was properly denied because the police officer did not violate defendant's constitutional rights under the Fourth Amendment by using a flashlight to illuminate contraband in defendant's pocket during the night hours; the officers' use of a flashlight to illuminate the interior of defendant's jacket pocket, which illuminated what defendant had exposed in plain view, did not change the plain view nature of the discovery. Gibson v. Commonwealth, 50 Va. App. 744, 653 S.E.2d 626, 2007 Va. App. LEXIS 446 (2007).

Reasonable, articulable suspicion. — Firearm should have been suppressed because the seizure that led to its discovery was unreasonable under the Fourth Amendment; although the officer had reasonable suspicion to believe that defendant possessed a firearm, nothing in the record provided reasonable suspicion for the belief that defendant was carrying the firearm in a legally proscribed manner. The informant provided no explanation for the basis for the belief that defendant might have had an outstanding warrant, and knowledge that defendant possessed a handgun and was trying to sell it in a high-crime, high-drug area contributed nothing to the reasonable, articulable suspicion required for a *Terry* stop. Goodman v. Commonwealth, — Va. App. —, — S.E.2d —, 2007 Va. App. LEXIS 383 (Oct. 16, 2007).

Trial court erred in granting defendant's motion to suppress evidence a police officer obtained pursuant to a traffic stop of his vehicle because a broken brake light provided the officer with reasonable suspicion to conduct a traffic stop; because § 46.2-1014.1 required defendant's vehicle to be equipped with a supplemental center high mount stop light, and the officer observed that the light was defective, the officer had reasonable suspicion to believe defendant was in violation of § 46.2-1003. Commonwealth v. Gaskins, 2011 Va. App. LEXIS 180 (May 24, 2011).

Denial of defendant's motion to suppress was proper, because the information provided to the officers by the two unwitting informants gave the officers reasonable suspicion to justify the seizure, and the informants' reliability was based on the female informant's previously having provided information and completed two controlled buys, and the male informant's prediction of defendant's arrival in a green car. Johnson v. Commonwealth, 2009 Va. App. LEXIS 193 (Apr. 28, 2009).

Trial court did not err in denying defendant's motion to suppress evidence because police officers had a particularized and objective basis for suspecting that defendant was involved in criminal activity since defendant was loitering in a known open-air drug market and was talking to people whom a trained and experienced police officer knew to be drug dealers; defendant was observed waving at vehicles in the area of high drug activity, which the officer, who was an expert in street-level drug transactions, testified was behavior consistent with soliciting potential drug sales. Baker v. Commonwealth, 2010 Va. App. LEXIS 444 (Nov. 9, 2010).

Trial court did not err in denying defendant's motion to suppress drugs seized from his car because defendant's brief detention was based upon a reasonable suspicion of criminal activity, and because defendant's uncle ran to defendant's car, a police officer's suspicions of criminal activity were specifically and reasonably directed toward defendant; when the uncle exited defendant's vehicle at the officer's approach and dropped a baggie of cocaine the officer's original suspicions were confirmed with respect to the uncle, and with respect to defendant, the officer's original suspicions were not only unresolved but based upon his experience in narcotics transactions, were also heightened due to the uncle's proximity to him. Perry v. Commonwealth, 2010 Va. App. LEXIS 406 (Oct. 19, 2010).

Motion to suppress was properly denied where officer had reasonable, articulable suspicion to stop defendant's vehicle based on the officer's observation that the license plate decal referring to the month of registration on defendant's car appeared to be ripped in half. Based on that circumstance, a reasonable officer certainly would have suspected that the decal was cut up or altered radically and therefore, had been mutilated under § 46.2-607. Williams v. Commonwealth, 2011 Va. App. LEXIS 41 (Feb. 8, 2011).

Evidence found during an investigatory stop was admissible, because the circumstances justified reasonable suspicion that defendant might not have been using an unregistered truck consistent with the statutory exemptions for farm use vehicles; the truck displayed a store-bought farm use tag, three people were in the truck, and the truck was on the road late at night in the winter after a snowstorm. Shifflett v. Commonwealth, 58 Va. App. 732, 716 S.E.2d 132, 2011 Va. App. LEXIS 314 (2011).

Motion to suppress was properly denied, because, police had a reasonable, articulable suspicion that defendant was engaged in criminal activity, i.e., that he was in possession of contraband when they seized defendant, and defendant did not merely refuse to consent or cooperate, he initially agreed to both a pat down and a search of his outer clothing for drugs, weapons, and other illegal items and then lied about the existence of interior pockets. Hargrove v. Commonwealth, 2012 Va. App. LEXIS 25 (Jan. 31, 2012).

Trial court did not err in denying defendant's motion to suppress a firearm seized from defendant's person. The officer had reasonable suspicion under U.S. Const. amend. IV that defendant possessed a concealed weapon, justifying a pat down, as defendant kept placing his hands in his pockets despite instructions to remove them, he was sweating profusely on a cold night, and he was nervous. Blanchard v. Commonwealth, 2012 Va. App. LEXIS 110 (Apr. 10, 2012).

Defendant's motion to suppress was properly denied, where the officer's observations of defendant and another sitting in a vehicle in an area known for drug trafficking and making furtive gestures contributed to providing a reasonable officer with reasonable,

articulable suspicion that defendant was connected with criminal activity that was afoot. Beasley v. Commonwealth, 60 Va. App. 381, 728 S.E.2d 499, 2012 Va. App. LEXIS 232 (2012).

Police officer had reasonable suspicion to believe that criminal activity was foot and was duty bound to further investigate after the officer observed two individuals in a stairwell of an apartment complex known as a high crime area and, upon the officer's arrival, defendant's companion threw down an object, which the officer suspected was drugs. Ferguson v. Commonwealth, 2013 Va. App. LEXIS 33 (Jan. 29, 2013).

Reasonable suspicion that criminal activity was afoot. — Motion to suppress was properly denied because the officer had reasonable suspicion to believe that criminal activity was afoot, thereby supporting the stop and frisk under *Terry*. Defendant walked away from the car at a fast pace as the officer approached, despite the fact that defendant had only been at the car window a few seconds; as defendant walked away, defendant was digging in defendant's pocket, causing the officer to believe defendant was reaching for a weapon; and defendant failed to heed the officer's repeated demands to stop. Thomas v. Commonwealth, — Va. App. —, — S.E.2d —, 2007 Va. App. LEXIS 384 (Oct. 16, 2007).

Trial court's order suppressing a baggie containing cocaine was erroneous because the investigatory stop of defendant was supported by reasonable suspicion that criminal activity was afoot; the evidence showed that defendant waived the baggie at two complete strangers, kissed it, and exclaimed "Woo" before driving off, and that the off-duty officer witnessing the behavior recognized the baggie as the type used to package cocaine. Commonwealth v. Jenkins, — Va. App. —, — S.E.2d —, 2007 Va. App. LEXIS 377 (Oct. 9, 2007).

Motion to suppress should not have been granted where the totality of the circumstances supported an officer's reasonable suspicion to detain defendant; the officer observed a known drug user put his hands into a car in which defendant sat, the user withdrew his hands when he saw the officer approach, defendant moved his hands to the glove compartment and then to the floorboard, and the officer conducted a protective sweep. Commonwealth v. Granger, — Va. App. —, — S.E.2d —, 2008 Va. App. LEXIS 68 (Feb. 12, 2008).

Trial court did not err in denying defendant's motion to suppress evidence obtained as the result of an investigative detention because defendant's apparent attempt to move his hand-rolled cigarette to a place where police officers could not see it, together with his headlong flight when the officers approached him, met the standard of a reasonable suspicion of criminal activity; the trial judge did not err in considering defendant's flight from the officers in deciding his motion to suppress because defendant had not yet been seized at the time he ran away. Carter v. Commonwealth, — Va. App. —, — S.E.2d —, 2008 Va. App. LEXIS 177 (Apr. 15, 2008).

Motion to suppress a butterfly knife was properly denied where an officer had a reasonable articulable suspicion to detain defendant and determine whether he was involved in the use of narcotics. The totality of the circumstances were that: (1) the police spotted defendant, a habitual user of narcotics, loitering in an area known for drug distribution and use; (2) he entered a van, traveled to another location with two other men, and then huddled with them outside the van while one of the men was bent over and using a lighter in a manner consistent with inhaling crack cocaine; (3) defendant repeatedly looked over his shoulder, as if watching for the police or others; and (4) one of the men fled as the police officers converged, consistent with a diversionary tactic commonly used to divert officers' attention and permit the other members of the group to dispose of contraband. Thompson v. Commonwealth, 51 Va. App. 205, 656 S.E.2d 409, 2008 Va. App. LEXIS 59 (2008), rev'd, 277 Va. 280, 673 S.E.2d 469 (2009) (as to whether butterfly knife was weapon of like kind).

Trial court did not err by denying defendant's motion to suppress because the facts known to officers at the time of the traffic stop of defendant were sufficient to justify the stop and constituted reasonable articulable facts of criminal activity; the police had determined that defendant was a suspect in a series of commercial burglaries and tracked his vehicle to an office park when no business was being conducted, and the person who left the building carrying a concealed object matched defendant's description and got in a car known to be registered to him. Baker v. Commonwealth, 2011 Va. App. LEXIS 358 (Nov. 22, 2011).

Trial court did not err in denying defendant's motion to suppress cocaine that he spit from his mouth because the facts were sufficient to establish both reasonable suspicion for defendant's detention at the time he was removed from a car and probable cause to search him when an officer ordered him to open his mouth; the totality of the circumstances, viewed in light of the officer's experience, were sufficient to provide him with reasonable suspicion to believe criminal activity was afoot and that defendant was involved in it. King v. Commonwealth, 2012 Va. App. LEXIS 143 (May 8, 2012).

Lack of reasonable suspicion to initiate a pat down. — Denial of motion to suppress was error, because the officer lacked reasonable suspicion to pat down defendant based only on the fact that defendant was loitering in front of a store known to be the site of drug distribution and drug arrests and defendant appeared nervous; no other facts suggested that defendant was involved in the distribution of drugs, such as hand-to-hand transaction, contact with other, or maintenance of a stash. Thompson v. Commonwealth, 54 Va. App. 1, 675 S.E.2d 832, 2009 Va. App. LEXIS 212 (2009).

Trial court erred in denying defendant's motion to suppress a glass pipe a police officer recovered during a pat down because the officer failed to articulate any facts and circumstances that, when viewed objectively, would lead any reasonable police officer to conclude that defendant was armed or dangerous; although defendant seemed nervous at the prospect of being patted down, the record contained no factual evidence from which any reasonable police officer could infer that he was either violent or that he was in possession of a weapon. Baker v. Commonwealth, 57 Va. App. 181, 700 S.E.2d 160, 2010 Va. App. LEXIS 404 (2010).

Tip failed to support deputy's answer and resulting evidence inadmissible. — Evidence was properly suppressed because, even if the informant was known and met the highest indicia of reliability, the tip failed to support the deputy's seizure of defendant because the tip did not relay information describing possible illegal activity that was corroborated by the officer. Commonwealth v. Johnson, 2008 Va. App. LEXIS 394 (Aug. 11, 2008).

Legal basis to detain. — Denial of defendant's motion to suppress was proper where the police officer had a legal basis to detain defendant based on defendant's presence in a restaurant parking lot at 12:40 a.m., when the restaurant was closed, and the posted warning sign that reserved use of the parking lot for patrons only; the fact that the officer's suspicion of trespassing could have been wrong did not make it unreasonable. Raab v. Commonwealth, 50 Va. App. 577, 652 S.E.2d 144, 2007 Va. App. LEXIS 444 (2007).

Protective sweep. — Because defendant claimed to be "heavily armed," and the police believed that another person might be in the residence, a protective sweep that took place immediately after defendant was arrested outside the residence did not violate the Fourth Amendment, and the officers could seize a gun that was found in plain sight; therefore, the trial court properly denied defendant's § 19.2-60 motion to suppress. Williams v. Commonwealth, 49 Va. App. 439, 642 S.E.2d 295, 2007 Va. App. LEXIS 113 (2007).

Investigatory stop. — Given the circumstances, in which officers stopped defendant after a reported bank robbery, they had ample reason to restrain defendant by handcuffing defendant and placing defendant in a patrol car during an investigatory stop. The officers faced exactly the kind the situation the Fourth Amendment placed outside the reach of "unrealistic second-guessing" by courts. Archie v. Commonwealth, — Va. App. —, — S.E.2d —, 2007 Va. App. LEXIS 286 (July 31, 2007).

Denial of defendant's motion to suppress was proper because the investigatory stop was based on reasonable, articulable suspicion that defendant was trespassing on the subject property, owned by the housing authority; defendant's subsequent admission to trespassing led to his arrest and a valid search, which led to the discovery of the drugs. Watson v. Commonwealth, — Va. App. —, — S.E.2d —, 2007 Va. App. LEXIS 408 (Nov. 13, 2007).

Trial court properly admitted a firearm into evidence where defendant's actions, walking around to the passenger side of the parked car after being told to stop by the officers, sitting down in the car, and making furtive gestures underneath the passenger seat, provided reasonable suspicion criminal activity was afoot; in addition, the driver's consent to search the vehicle provided an independent basis for the search of the vehicle. Woodhouse v.

Commonwealth, — Va. App. —, — S.E.2d —, 2008 Va. App. LEXIS 1 (Jan. 8, 2008).

Because a dog's alert created probable cause to search defendant's car, defendant's motion to suppress the firearm found in the vehicle's trunk was properly denied. Jones v. Commonwealth, 2007 Va. App. LEXIS 499 (Oct. 30, 2007), aff'd, 277 Va. 171, 670 S.E.2d 727 (2009).

Evidence supported the denial of defendant's motion to suppress because the police developed, first, reasonable suspicion for the detention and, then, probable cause for defendant's arrest, and the evidence supported a finding that, at the time of the seizure, reasonable suspicion existed to believe defendant could have been involved in a crime; when the officer first approached defendant she knew that he fit the robber's general description, defendant admitted that he had just come from the shopping center in which the robbery had occurred, and once the seizure had occurred, officers worked to confirm or dispel the suspicions supporting the detention. Clark v. Commonwealth, 2011 Va. App. LEXIS 282 (Sept. 20, 2011).

Reasonable suspicion required to make investigatory stop. — Trial court erred in denying defendant's motion to suppress because the officer lacked the reasonable suspicion required to conduct an investigative traffic stop under the Fourth Amendment; the anonymous tip received by the officer failed to include predictions about defendant's future behavior and the officer observed defendant driving within the speed limit and did not see defendant's car swerve. Harris v. Commonwealth, 276 Va. 689, 668 S.E.2d 141, 2008 Va. LEXIS 108 (2008), cert. denied, 2009 U.S. LEXIS 7645 (U.S. 2009).

Evidence deemed admissible. — Trial court correctly refused to suppress either the weapon found on the defendant during a pat down search, following a tip from a concerned citizen that the defendant was brandishing a weapon, or the crack cocaine found on the defendant during a search incident to the defendant's arrest because the tip provided information permitting the officers to reasonably infer that it: (1) came from a concerned citizen making a contemporaneous, eyewitness report; (2) involved an open and obvious crime rather than mere concealed illegality; and (3) described criminality posing an imminent danger to the public, therefore, the officers correctly concluded the totality of the circumstances raised a reasonable suspicion to believe that criminal activity may be afoot. Jackson v. Commonwealth, 39 Va. App. 624, 576 S.E.2d 206, 2003 Va. App. LEXIS 37 (2003).

Defendant's broad and unfocused questions to law-enforcement officers, and continuous insistence on desiring to talk to them about his passenger's involvement in suspicious activity, despite numerous warnings given to him regarding his rights under Miranda, established that police did not violate his right to counsel and right to remain silent; thus, the trial court properly denied suppression of the evidence seized and his statements, and his convictions for possession with intent to distribute and transporting more than one ounce of cocaine into the Commonwealth with the intent to distribute were affirmed. Medley v. Commonwealth, 44 Va. App. 19, 602 S.E.2d 411, 2004 Va. App. LEXIS 453 (2004).

Trial court properly denied suppression of the evidence seized against defendant, where officers had reason to believe that defendant was involved in a drug transaction in a high-drug trafficking area, defendant had prior arrests for narcotics violations, intelligence supplied information that defendant possessed a firearm in that same location, and an officer knew that defendant had been previously convicted of a felony when he felt a gun on defendant's waistband. Spinner v. Commonwealth, No. 2548-03-3, 2004 Va. App. LEXIS 490 (Ct. of Appeals Oct. 12, 2004).

In the prosecution of possession of cocaine with intent to distribute, the trial court did not err in denying defendant's motion to suppress evidence seized from his person, because: (1) defendant's non-verbal response to an investigating officer intimated that defendant was inviting a pat-down frisk of his person, by automatically assuming the frisk position; and (2) defendant could not be heard to complain by his voluntary acts of submitting to a pat-down frisk, given that the encounter was brief and defendant was not boxed in; moreover, the record adequately reflected that it was immediately apparent to the officer from his initial pat-down that the flat oblong, odd shaped rock he felt in defendant's pant pocket was crack cocaine. Graham v. Commonwealth, — Va. App. —, — S.E.2d —, 2005 Va. App. LEXIS 287 (July 19, 2005).

Defendant's motion to suppress evidence was properly denied; although defendant's property was transferred to federal authorities, it never lost its status as evidence, and defendant failed to formally move for the return of his property as required by §§ 19.2-58 and 19.2-60, so defendant's prostitution-related convictions were appropriate. United States v. Jenkins, — F.3d —, 2005 U.S. App. LEXIS 18376 (4th Cir. Aug. 25, 2005), cert. denied, — U.S. —, 126 S. Ct. 1092, 163 L. Ed. 2d 907 (2006).

Based on a citizen informant's statement that defendant confessed the burglary to her, the victim's information, and the victim's sister's statement that defendant's DVD collection was bigger after the burglary, the officer had probable cause to obtain a search warrant and to freeze the scene by excluding people from the premises for a reasonable time while obtaining a warrant; that same information provided officers with at least reasonable suspicion to detain defendant for a reasonable period of time while obtaining and executing a search warrant. Because the evidence supported a finding that the actions of the police were reasonable under the circumstances, their decision to freeze the scene by requiring defendant to stay and preventing others from entering did not compel the conclusion that her consent to the search of her house was involuntary, and, furthermore, the officers' failure to clearly indicate to defendant that she had a legal right to delimit the scope of the search did not compel the conclusion that her consent to search the house was involuntary. Thomas v. Commonwealth, — Va. App. —, — S.E.2d —, 2005 Va. App. LEXIS 363 (Sept. 20, 2005).

Under the plain feel exception, the officer's belief that the substance was marijuana upon patting defendant's pocket and without further manipulating its contents, if found credible by the trial court, was sufficient to provide probable cause to seize the contents of the pocket; thus, where the events leading up to the same were consensual, the trial court properly denied defendant's motion to suppress the contraband seized. Taylor v. Commonwealth, — Va. App. —, — S.E.2d —, 2006 Va. App. LEXIS 78 (Mar. 7, 2006).

Motion to suppress was erroneously granted because the search of defendant's purse did not violate the Fourth Amendment where it was conducted incident to a valid arrest. The officer's had probable cause to stop defendant's vehicle for a traffic violation, the officers did not impermissibly extend scope of the stop by asking defendant questions about drug paraphernalia, and the officers had probable cause to arrest defendant based on her admission to possession of a crack cocaine stem. Commonwealth v. Briggs, — Va. App. —, — S.E.2d —, 2006 Va. App. LEXIS 125 (Apr. 4, 2006).

Defendant's motion to suppress a photograph was properly denied as two officers did not turn a consensual encounter into a seizure when they photographed defendant; the officers only had a conversation with defendant and asked for permission to photograph him. They did not coerce defendant into compliance as neither officer physically touched defendant, made any threats or demands, drew their weapons, or engaged in any other form of aggressive behavior. Clay v. Commonwealth, — Va. App. —, — S.E.2d —, 2006 Va. App. LEXIS 118 (Mar. 28, 2006).

Trial court did not err in denying defendant's motion to suppress the cocaine seized from his person after his valid arrest merely because the police conducted a warrantless strip and body cavity search, as an officer removed a protruding bag of suspected narcotics from defendant's anus without exposing his genitals or anal cavity upon being told by defendant's wife that such would be found therein; hence, the search was incidental to defendant's arrest, not an improper strip or body cavity search, and was not unreasonable under the Fourth Amendment. Nowlin v. Commonwealth, — Va. App. —, — S.E.2d —, 2006 Va. App. LEXIS 552 (Dec. 12, 2006).

Evidence obtained in a warrantless search was admissible because the officers were justified in searching for a weapon, seizing that weapon, and arresting defendant after defendant raised his arms in air and revealed a bulge in his clothing that the officer tapped with a flashlight causing a noise he believed indicated the presence of a "heavy metal object," which the officer then believed to be a weapon. Taylor v. Commonwealth, — Va. App. —, — S.E.2d —, 2007 Va. App. LEXIS 54 (Feb. 20, 2007).

Defendant's motion to suppress was properly denied, as evidence of wire transfers from defendant to Trinidad and Tobago, the last one being only three days before the first package of cocaine arrived at defendant's apartment, was admissible because it was not so remote in time as to be without probative value; nor was it speculative. Patton v. Commonwealth, — Va. App. —, — S.E.2d —, 2007 Va. App. LEXIS 295 (Aug. 7, 2007).

Because the facts and circumstances surrounding defendant's arrest outside of his home justified a warrantless search of that home, after officers broke through the barricaded door of the home after apprehending defendant, pursuant to either the exigent circumstances or protective sweep exceptions to the warrant requirement, the Court of Appeals did not err in reversing the circuit court's denial of defendant's motion to suppress the evidence seized as a result. Commonwealth v. Robertson, 275 Va. 559, 659 S.E.2d 321, 2008 Va. LEXIS 49 (2008).

Defendant's motion to suppress was properly denied since the officers had reasonable articulable suspicion that defendant possessed a concealed weapon, a "black object" in a bag in defendant's vehicle, and that such possession rendered defendant potentially armed and dangerous. The officer's search of the bag was reasonable, as the bag was within defendant's immediate control, was big enough to contain a weapon, and the officer felt a hard object inside before the officer opened the bag. Jones v. Commonwealth, 52 Va. App. 548, 665 S.E.2d 261, 2008 Va. App. LEXIS 410 (2008).

Denial of defendant's motion to suppress drugs discovered during a pat down was proper, because the officer's initial approach was consensual, the officer did not seize defendant until the officer discovered that defendant was trespassing, and the officer's frisk of defendant, to determine if defendant was armed, did not exceed its proper constitutional scope. Bandy v. Commonwealth, 52 Va. App. 510, 664 S.E.2d 519, 2008 Va. App. LEXIS 382 (2008).

Denial of defendant's motion to suppress was not erroneous since the facts omitted from the affidavit in support of the search warrant did not have a bearing on the existence of probable cause. In addition, the fact that the police initiated contact with the victim was not material to whether there was probable cause defendant obtained money from the victim by false pretenses. Milian v. Commonwealth, 2008 Va. App. LEXIS 435 (Sept. 23, 2008).

Trial court did not err in denying defendant's motion to suppress, because a reasonably prudent police officer, under the circumstances, would have conducted a pat-down search for the officer's safety and the protection of others after encountering defendant in a parking lot at 3:00 a.m. when responding to a "narcotics-in-progress" call and defendant admitted that defendant was not a registered guest at the motel. Miller v. Commonwealth, 2008 Va. App. LEXIS 495 (Nov. 4, 2008).

Denial of motion to suppress was proper where the officer handling the narcotics detection dog testified that the officer and the dog trained for eight hours every two weeks, the dog had been with the police for four and a half years, and the dog received training at Virginia Police Work Dog Association, the dog's training and experience was sufficient to establish the dog's reliability and supported a finding of probable cause for the officer's search of defendant's vehicle. Jones v. Commonwealth, 277 Va. 171, 670 S.E.2d 727, 2009 Va. LEXIS 10 (2009).

Trial court properly denied defendant's motion to suppress, because defendant's encounter with the officers could not be fairly characterized as a seizure; an officer did nothing more than initiate a conversation with defendant and ask if defendant would identify himself, defendant willingly produced ID card, and there was no threat, show of force, or intimidation. Venable v. Commonwealth, 2008 Va. App. LEXIS 570 (Dec. 30, 2008).

Because the trial court explicitly declined to credit the portion of defendant's mother's testimony that supported defendant's argument that her consent to a search of her residence was coerced, defendant's motion to suppress was properly denied. Waller v. Commonwealth, 2009 Va. App. LEXIS 103 (Mar. 4, 2009).

Police had probable cause to seize the firearm and reasonable suspicion to detain defendant where the firearm, which was under the armrest of defendant's car, was sufficiently hidden to give police officers probable cause to believe the object was evidence that defendant had committed the crime of concealing a weapon. The fact that defendant had been sitting alone in the car was sufficient to provide a reasonable officer with probable cause to believe that defendant had a firearm "about his person," in violation of § 18.2-308. White v. Commonwealth, 2009 Va. App. LEXIS 107 (Mar. 4, 2009).

Denial of defendant's motion to suppress was proper, where the police officer initiated a consensual encounter with defendant, which developed into reasonable suspicion of trespassing after the police officer observed defendant enter housing authority property posted with "no trespassing" signs and exit the property almost immediately, providing no credibility for defendant's story about coming from defendant's girlfriend's residence. Pettis v. Commonwealth, 2009 Va. App. LEXIS 135 (Mar. 24, 2009).

Trial court correctly denied defendant's motion to suppress evidence a police officer recovered from his person because the seizure of defendant was reasonable under the totality of the circumstances; the officer was justified in detaining defendant in order to conduct a pat-down search for weapons and to protect his personal safety because defendant persistently attempted to reach into his pants pocket. Pettaway v. Commonwealth, 2009 Va. App. LEXIS 178 (Apr. 21, 2009).

Denial of motion to suppress was proper where defendant voluntarily consented to a search of defendant's person; at the time that defendant told the officer "you can search me if you want," defendant's identification had been returned and defendant was told that defendant was free to leave, defendant remained at the scene to make sure defendant's friend, who had been arrested on an outstanding warrant, was okay. Samy v. Commonwealth, 2009 Va. App. LEXIS 194 (Apr. 28, 2009).

Trial court erred in granting defendant's motion to suppress, because the evidence, viewed in the light most favorable to defendant, compelled the conclusion that the search of defendant's vehicle was reasonable under the Fourth Amendment; the proper test was whether the van was apparently rather than actually mobile. Commonwealth v. Grimes, 2009 Va. App. LEXIS 248 (June 2, 2009).

Trial court erred in granting defendant's motion to suppress evidence, where the initial encounter between defendant and the officer was consensual, the officer had probable cause to arrest and detain defendant after learning that defendant's driver's license was suspended, and the police dog alert, occurring during the lawful detention, provided the officer with probable cause to search defendant's vehicle under the automobile exception. Commonwealth v. Boyd, 2010 Va. App. LEXIS 432 (Nov. 5, 2010).

Trial court properly denied defendant's motion to suppress, where the police had probable cause and exigent circumstances to enter defendant's home without a warrant; the police needed to gain control of the situation and arrest defendant once they believed that defendant had committed the charged crimes, in order to prevent defendant from washing away DNA evidence from defendant's person and clothing and to minimize any danger to the community. West v. Commonwealth, 54 Va. App. 345, 678 S.E.2d 836, 2009 Va. App. LEXIS 305 (2009).

Failure to suppress evidence was not erroneous, as defendant was not seized until the officer tackled defendant, by which point the officer had more than reasonable suspicion to stop defendant because defendant had committed a traffic violation by not obeying a stop sign while being pursued by officer, giving the officer sufficient justification to stop defendant. Rhoades v. Commonwealth, 2009 Va. App. LEXIS 322 (July 21, 2009).

Trial court did not err in denying defendant's motion to suppress a handgun that defendant accidentally dropped while fleeing from a police officer because suppression was not required under the exclusionary rule, and the recovery of the handgun by the officer was not fruit of the poisonous tree since the handgun was discovered by means sufficiently attenuated from the officer's initial seizure of defendant, which occurred prior to defendant's flight on foot; because defendant's accidental loss of the handgun during his flight was an independent source for the discovery and recovery of the handgun, separate and sufficiently distinguishable from the officer's seizure of defendant, the discovery of the handgun was not fruit of the poisonous tree since its discovery was not the foreseeable result of the earlier seizure of defendant by the police, and its admissibility was not an "exploitation" of any police action that was illegal. Fitchett v. Commonwealth, 56 Va. App. 741, 697 S.E.2d 28, 2010 Va. App. LEXIS 339 (2010).

Where the police received an anonymous tip of drug activity at defendant's residence involving a white male and a black male and an officer observed, through defendant's open doorway, a black male with a white substance run toward the back of the house, the circumstances provided probable cause for the warrantless search under the exigent circumstances exception to the warrant requirement and the evidence recovered was admissible. Smith v. Commonwealth, 56 Va. App. 592, 696 S.E.2d 211, 2010 Va. App. LEXIS 316 (2010).

Motion to suppress was properly denied, where defendant was still in custody for driving on a suspended license when an officer saw a marijuana stem in defendant's vehicle, and thus, the officers had probable cause to search the vehicle based on the observation of what they believed to be contraband based on prior narcotics experience and specialized training in drug recognition. Dorrough v. Commonwealth, 2010 Va. App. LEXIS 250 (June 22, 2010).

Trial court erred in granting defendant's motion to suppress, because the officer had a valid basis for the stop where the vehicle matched the description of a vehicle used to flee a shooting and was observed close to the scene within minutes of the shooting, and officers observed various traffic offenses, and the command to exit the vehicle at gunpoint was reasonable where the officer had reason to believe that the driver might be armed and dangerous. Commonwealth v. Hairston, 2010 Va. App. LEXIS 333 (Aug. 17, 2010).

Because the initial encounter between defendant and a police officer was consensual, and because a seizure did not take place until a drug dog alerted and provided probable cause to believe that defendant was involved in criminal activity, the trial court properly denied defendant's motion to suppress. Lewis v. Commonwealth, 2011 Va. App. LEXIS 354 (Nov. 15, 2011).

Trial court did not err in denying defendant's motion to suppress, because the officer had probable cause based on his detection of the odor of marijuana, and thus, an independent source existed for the search of defendant's residence and the evidence seized from his person would have been inevitably found during a search incident to arrest. Krebs v. Commonwealth, 2011 Va. App. LEXIS 400 (Dec. 13, 2011).

Evidence deemed inadmissible. — Where a police officer did not have specific and articulable facts upon which to conclude that defendant was armed and dangerous before frisking defendant for weapons during a traffic stop, the search was unreasonable under the Fourth Amendment; as a result, the trial judge erred in failing to suppress the evidence. Christian v. Commonwealth, No. 0303-03-1, 2004 Va. App. LEXIS 190 (Ct. of Appeals Mar. 2, 2004).

Circuit court properly granted defendant's motion to suppress evidence seized as a result of a traffic stop on grounds that said evidence failed to show a reasonable articulable suspicion that defendant was violating § 46.2-848 or attempting to avoid or evade the checkpoint, and the arresting officer never articulated a reasonable basis as to why he made a vehicle stop of defendant, did not testify that he believed defendant was evading a roadblock, and never stated that he believed that defendant violated, or was about to violate, the law. Commonwealth v. Wells, 2007 Va. App. LEXIS 9 (Jan. 9, 2007).

Motion to suppress evidence obtained pursuant to a traffic stop of defendant's antique vehicle was improperly denied as the evidence was obtained in violation of U.S. Const., Amend. IV. The trooper stopped the vehicle solely because it displayed no inspection sticker even though, as the trooper acknowledged, exceptions to this requirement were specifically provided in §§ 46.2-730, 46.2-1157, and 46.2-1163 for antique vehicles displaying antique tags, and the trooper did not articulate any reasons for suspecting that defendant was operating his vehicle in violation of the permitted uses. Campbell v. Commonwealth, 2007 Va. App. LEXIS 50 (Feb. 13, 2007).

Trial court erred in denying defendant's motion to suppress because the objective facts in the record did not support a lawful detention of defendant, in that, defendant's mere presence, asleep in the victim's residence after a New Year's party, did not create a reasonable suspicion that he was involved in the victim's domestic dispute with her boyfriend. Moreover, the victim specifically told the officer that defendant was not involved. Lantion v. Commonwealth, — Va. App. —, — S.E.2d —, 2007 Va. App. LEXIS 51 (Feb. 13, 2007).

Even if an officer's initial investigative detention of defendant were lawful, the officer's frisk of defendant for weapons was not supported by a reasonable belief that defendant was armed and presently dangerous, and thus, the evidence pursuant to the frisk should have been suppressed. The officer testified that when he awoke defendant, who had been asleep on a bed, defendant merely rolled over and looked at the officer, making no threatening gestures; thus, defendant's admission to the officer upon questioning that he possessed a pocketknife did not establish dangerousness. Lantion v. Commonwealth, — Va. App. —, — S.E.2d —, 2007 Va. App. LEXIS 51 (Feb. 13, 2007).

Methamphetamine discovered on spoon in defendant's pocket was the fruit of an unconstitutional search and should have been suppressed; the investigator articulated no reason for believing, before attempting to frisk defendant, that defendant was armed and dangerous but testified that she became concerned defendant might be armed and dangerous after defendant avoided the investigator's attempt to frisk him. Hamm v. Commonwealth, — Va. App. —, — S.E.2d —, 2007 Va. App. LEXIS 134 (Apr. 3, 2007).

Search of defendant following a traffic stop violated the Fourth Amendment, and the denial of defendant's motion to suppress was error. A deputy's act of directing defendant to the rear of the car near where another officer stood, followed by the deputy's persistence in seeking permission to search, conveyed to a reasonable person in defendant's position that there was not freedom to leave and converted the encounter into a seizure unsupported by reasonable suspicion or probable cause. Dorsey v. Commonwealth, — Va. App. —, — S.E.2d —, 2007 Va. App. LEXIS 176 (May 1, 2007).

Trial judge erred in denying defendant's motion to suppress evidence found in defendant's house pursuant to a search warrant, as the warrant was not supported by Fourth Amendment probable cause due to the affidavit's failure to provide a nexus between defendant's drug possession and his residence. The affidavit asserted that defendant had marijuana on defendant's person and that the officer merely "suspected cocaine residue." Cunningham v. Commonwealth, 49 Va. App. 605, 643 S.E.2d 514, 2007 Va. App. LEXIS 174 (2007).

Deputy did not have reasonable suspicion to make a traffic stop, and defendant's suppression motion was properly granted, as a belief based on a mistaken understanding of the law as to whether a broken passenger side mirror was a violation of law could not constitute the reasonable suspicion required for a constitutional traffic stop since the deputy did not make a mistake of fact about the scope of activities proscribed by the law, and the mistake of law was not objectively reasonable. Commonwealth v. Snyder, 2007 Va. App. LEXIS 307 (Aug. 14, 2007).

Trial court properly granted defendant's motion to suppress evidence where the game warden was not authorized to conduct a warrantless search of defendant's person and the fruits of that search were thus not admissible, and the Commonwealth was barred from arguing that the game warden affected a custodial arrest because that argument was not presented before the trial court. Commonwealth v. Wilkins, 2008 Va. App. LEXIS 302 (June 24, 2008).

Due to the officers' lack of a reasonable and articulable suspicion that defendant was engaged in criminal activity, defendant's seizure and the ensuing search of defendant's vehicle were invalid under the Fourth Amendment; thus, any evidence obtained by the officers during the search of defendant's vehicle should have been suppressed. Middlebrooks v. Commonwealth, 52 Va. App. 469, 664 S.E.2d 499, 2008 Va. App. LEXIS 376 (2008).

Although the police officers were authorized to stop defendant's vehicle based upon their reasonable belief that a traffic violation had occurred when defendant stopped in the middle of a travel lane, the trial court erred in denying the motion to suppress because the officers had no reasonable suspicion that defendant had engaged in criminal activity or was armed and dangerous and, thus, there was no justification for a pat down of defendant. Lightfoot v. Commonwealth, 2008 Va. App. LEXIS 459 (Oct. 14, 2008).

Trial court erred in denying defendant's motion to suppress, because defendant's activities, being in a "high crime area" in the middle of the morning and walking 15 feet to a townhouse upon seeing an officer, did not provide the officer with reasonable suspicion that criminal activity was afoot. Jones v. Commonwealth, 53 Va. App. 171, 670 S.E.2d 31, 2008 Va. App. LEXIS 561 (2008).

Evidence found after the officer stopped defendant's vehicle should have been suppressed, because the fact that defendant was parked at the rear customer entrance to a gas station, at night, in an area where there had been robberies and burglaries, and that defendant appeared to be looking or reaching for something inside the vehicle was insufficient to support an investigative stop. Rudolph v. Commonwealth, 277 Va. 209, 722 S.E.2d 527, 2009 Va. LEXIS 34, cert. denied, 130 S. Ct. 738, 175 L. Ed. 2d 514, 2009 U.S. LEXIS 8721 (U.S. 2009).

Trial court erred in denying defendant's motion to suppress,

because, at time of the officer searched defendant's pants, the officer did not have probable cause to believe that the pants, which were not on defendant, contained contraband or evidence of a crime; among other things, there was no evidence that defendant possessed or displayed a weapon during the argument with defendant's girlfriend. Garland v. Commonwealth, 2009 Va. App. LEXIS 222 (May 12, 2009).

Where defendant's grandmother had the apparent authority to consent to the search of a car parked in the grandmother's driveway, there was no evidence that the grandmother withdrew consent to search, and the police were not aware that defendant's father was the owner of the car and thus, the fact that the father did not want the car searched was not a basis for withdrawal of consent, the motion to suppress was erroneously granted. Commonwealth v. Ferrell, 2011 Va. App. LEXIS 47 (Feb. 10, 2011).

Defendant's consent to search, the search, and the evidence seized were the product of an illegal detention, occurring while the defendant was illegally detained and under circumstances in which she was not free to leave or disregard the officer's inquiries. At the time of the encounter, defendant was stopped in a rural area in the nighttime, the police emergency lights were activated the entire time, traffic was light, defendant was the only adult in her vehicle while there were two police officers present at the scene, defendant requested to search the vehicle after the purpose of the initial stop was completed, the officer was in his uniform and his weapon was displayed, and he made this request only after he had informed defendant of illegal drug trafficking in the area and had asked her if she had anything illegal in the vehicle; thus, defendant's motion to suppress was properly granted. Commonwealth v. Crooks, 2012 Va. App. LEXIS 364 (Nov. 15, 2012).

Trial court erred in denying defendant's motion to suppress on the ground that the community caretaker doctrine was applicable, because the evidence presented failed to implicate public safety concerns or a safeguarding of personal property where the officer testified that he searched defendant's backpack because he was "curious" about its weight, without testifying that he thought the weight was suspicious of activity that posed danger to the public. Knight v. Commonwealth, 61 Va. App. 297, 734 S.E.2d 716, 2012 Va. App. LEXIS 406 (2012).

B. Suppression of Statements, DNA, etc.

Statements knowingly and voluntarily made. — Police officers did not violate defendant's Fifth Amendment rights, and his waiver of those rights and his subsequent statements to the police were both voluntary and intelligently and knowingly made and should not have been suppressed. Timely *Miranda* warnings were given twice, defendant said that he understood them but wished to answer police questions, he was 20 years old and aware of what was happening, there was no indication of any coercion, and the police did not use a certain two-step procedure, which in another state had been used essentially to trick suspects into making incriminating statements and allegedly "waiving" their rights and which the United States Supreme Court had already declared was illegal and forbidden. Commonwealth v. Kadian, — Va. App. —, — S.E.2d —, 2006 Va. App. LEXIS 246 (May 30, 2006).

Admission of defendant's statements to police was proper where defendant was not threatened during the encounter with police, was advised of Miranda rights in writing and orally, indicated that defendant understood them, and voluntarily, knowingly, and intelligently waived those rights. Angel v. Commonwealth, 2009 Va. App. LEXIS 125 (Mar. 24, 2009).

Denial of defendant's motion to suppress inculpatory statements made to detectives was proper, as the finding that defendant voluntarily waived defendant's Miranda rights before talking to police was proper; contrary to defendant's claim, defendant's condition did not affect the voluntariness of the waiver, as defendant provided police with specific, accurate information about defendant's work and educational history, and defendant's description of the events surrounding the shooting was consistent with the physical evidence and the statements of witnesses. Oliver v. Commonwealth, 2009 Va. App. LEXIS 297 (June 30, 2009).

Although defendant invoked the right to counsel, the trial court erred in suppressing defendant's statement to police, because defendant later reinitiated communication with the police and waived defendant's Miranda rights; defendant's waiver was voluntarily, knowingly, and intelligently made and defendant was aware of nature of defendant's Fifth Amendment rights and the potential consequences of abandoning them. Commonwealth v. Edwards, 2009 Va. App. LEXIS 325 (July 21, 2009).

Defendant's motion to suppress statements made during police interrogation was properly denied, where defendant knowing and intelligently waived defendant's Fifth Amendment privilege against self-incrimination and the detectives' conduct was not coercive and did not overbear defendant's free will; thus, defendant's confession was freely and voluntarily given. Lewis v. Commonwealth, 2009 Va. App. LEXIS 357 (Aug. 11, 2009).

Defendant not in custody when statements made. — Trial court did not err in denying defendant's motion to suppress statements she made to detectives in the audio-visual room of a police station because defendant was not in custody at the time she made the incriminating statements when she was not under formal arrest, and her freedom of movement was not restricted, and, therefore, the detectives were not required to advise defendant of her Miranda rights; defendant voluntarily went to the police station, and a reasonable person would not think that they were in custody merely because they were moved to another location within the police station and would not have concluded from the duration and character of the interview that she was not free to leave. Durand v. Commonwealth, 2009 Va. App. LEXIS 419 (Sept. 22, 2009).

Suppression of DNA evidence. — Although defendant's counsel was not notified and thus was not present when a DNA sample was taken, there was no error and no violation of defendant's Sixth Amendment right to counsel, and a trial court properly denied defendant's motion to suppress the DNA evidence, which was derived from a DNA sample taken after defendant was indicted and had retained counsel. The Sixth Amendment right to have counsel present at the critical stages of a criminal proceeding did not extend to preparatory steps, which included the gathering of evidence, such as the taking of fingerprints or DNA evidence, because the risk that counsel's absence at such stages might derogate from a defendant's right to a fair trial was slight. Wilson v. Commonwealth, — Va. App. —, — S.E.2d —, 2006 Va. App. LEXIS 243 (May 30, 2006).

Waiver of Miranda rights. — Decision granting defendant's motion to suppress defendant's statements was reversed; an investigator's termination of interrogation for a period of approximately ten minutes did not, in itself, impact the presumption that defendant's waiver of *Miranda* rights continued. Police were not required to repeat *Miranda* warnings after the initial interrogation ended. Commonwealth v. Wimbish, — Va. App. —, — S.E.2d —, 2006 Va. App. LEXIS 435 (Oct. 3, 2006).

Statements admissible. — Denial of motion to suppress was proper, because defendant's statement made it unclear whether defendant had requested the presence of an attorney during custodial interrogation, or whether defendant had simply expressed a desire to have an attorney appointed to represent defendant at trial and thus, the police were permitted to ask defendant limited questions solely for the purpose of clarifying the statement. Stevens v. Commonwealth, 57 Va. App. 566, 704 S.E.2d 585, 2011 Va. App. LEXIS 31 (2011), aff'd, 2012 Va. App. LEXIS 15 (Va. 2012).

Statements admissible under public safety exception. — Admission of statements defendant made before police advised defendant of defendant's Miranda rights was not error, because the public safety exception to Miranda permitted the officer to ask defendant whether the weapon, five feet away from the officer, was loaded and an immediate danger. Since warnings were not required, there was no taint to statements made after defendant was advised of defendant's Miranda rights. Anderson v. Commonwealth, 2009 Va. App. LEXIS 114 (Mar. 17, 2009), aff'd, 279 Va. 85, 688 S.E.2d 605, 2010 Va. LEXIS 13 (2010).

Admissability of out-of-court identification. — Denial of motion to suppress a witness's out-of-court identification based on a single photograph was upheld because the officer, who was investigating an unrelated burglary, had no knowledge that a credit card forgery had previously occurred at the same location and thus, there was no possibility that the officer could have manipulated the witness or misled the witness into identifying defendant as the person who had used the stolen credit card. Logan v. Commonwealth, 51 Va. App. 111, 655 S.E.2d 30, 2008 Va. App. LEXIS 2 (2008).

Unequivocal request for counsel during interrogation. —

In a prosecution for first-degree murder, breaking and entering while armed with a deadly weapon, and two counts of using of a firearm in the commission of a felony, because the record evidence showed that defendant failed to make an unequivocal request for an attorney prior to confessing to his crimes, given the surrounding circumstances in which he made his statements concerning counsel, including the tone of the interview and defendant's demeanor, the trial court did not err by admitting his confession into evidence. West v. Commonwealth, 2008 Va. App. LEXIS 241 (May 20, 2008).

Erroneous denial of defendant's motion to suppress a confession necessitated a new trial, because defendant unambiguously invoked his Fifth Amendment right to counsel before the confession was made and the error was not harmless where the erroneously admitted confession was the only evidence actually placing defendant at the scene of the robbery homicides; the only other evidence linking defendant to the crimes was the testimony of an individual who said he acted as a middleman and who did not name defendant until over a year after the crimes, one day before he himself was scheduled to be tried for the robbery homicides and related crimes. Stevens v. Commonwealth, 2010 Va. App. LEXIS 244 (June 22, 2010).

Out of court statements deemed admissible. — Suppression of statement erroneous where defendant was not in custody at the time statement was made and thus, no Miranda violation occurred; defendant was not restrained and could have easily ended conversation at any time by disconnecting call. Commonwealth v. Carruitero, — Va. App. —, — S.E.2d —, 2007 Va. App. LEXIS 148 (Apr. 10, 2007).

Out of court identifications deemed admissible. — Trial court did not err in admitting out-of-court and in-court identifications by several witnesses based on the use of a single photograph because, while discrepancies existed in the witnesses' descriptions of defendant and three witnesses who made positive out-of-court identifications were unable to identify defendant at the suppression hearing, such issues went to weight of the evidence, not its admissibility. Rountree v. Commonwealth, — Va. App. —, — S.E.2d —, 2007 Va. App. LEXIS 279 (July 24, 2007).

Anonymous tip admissible. — Denial of defendant's motion to suppress was proper, because the anonymous tip described a progression of incidents that were corroborated by the officer as the officer approached the scene; among other things, defendant's physical characteristics matched those described, and defendant was running from the apartment complex and had cuts on defendant's face. Roberts v. Commonwealth, 2009 Va. App. LEXIS 67 (Feb. 10, 2009).

Evidence deemed inadmissible. — Defendant's motion to suppress was properly denied because although defendant was in custody when he identified shorts containing contraband as his, he was not subject to "interrogation" where an "objective observer" would not have perceived the words and actions related to defendant's clothes as being intended to elicit incriminating information from defendant, and thus, Miranda safeguards were not implicated. Emerson v. Commonwealth, 43 Va. App. 263, 597 S.E.2d 242, 2004 Va. App. LEXIS 274 (2004).

Motion to suppress was properly granted as to pre-Miranda warning inculpatory statements because the officers deliberately engaged in a two-stop interrogation strategy, after which no curative measures were taken, and because a reasonable officer would have realized that the questions asked were likely to elicit incriminating responses. Commonwealth v. Bowman, — Va. App. —, — S.E.2d —, 2007 Va. App. LEXIS 318 (Aug. 27, 2007).

Evidence of a drug transaction was properly suppressed because: (1) a hand-to-hand transaction occurred within the curtilage of a home in which defendant had a reasonable expectation of privacy; (2) a detective lacked probable cause to enter defendant's backyard prior to observing the drug transaction; (3) the detective could not have seen the transaction without intruding into the curtilage by climbing a fence; and (4) the detective was not in a place from which he could legitimately view that transaction for purposes of the Fourth Amendment. Commonwealth v. Hackett, — Va. App. —, — S.E.2d —, 2008 Va. App. LEXIS 120 (Mar. 11, 2008).

Defendant's statements to police should have been suppressed because the officers made it clear that defendant was not free to leave and was in custody, when one officer told another to handcuff defendant and the second officer restrained defendant before putting the handcuffs on, and thus, defendant should have been

Mirandized before being asked potentially incriminating questions. White v. Commonwealth, 2009 Va. App. LEXIS 107 (Mar. 4, 2009).

Harmless error. — In a case in which defendant was indicted for murdering his wife but was convicted of voluntary manslaughter, even if the trial court erred in denying defendant's motion to suppress the interrogation transcript, defendant's testimony at trial during his case-in-chief waived his right to object to the same evidence on appeal, rendering any error harmless. Abdul-Wasi v. Commonwealth, — Va. App. —, — S.E.2d —, 2005 Va. App. LEXIS 180 (May 3, 2005).

CIRCUIT COURT OPINIONS

Return of illegally seized property. — Exclusionary rule of the Fourth Amendment applied to the suppressed evidence of a criminal action in the quasi-criminal forfeiture action; defendant was entitled to the return of money illegally seized. Commonwealth v. Turner, 58 Va. Cir. 576, 2000 Va. Cir. LEXIS 627 (Charlottesville 2000).

Timely execution of search warrant. — Despite an eight-day delay in executing a search warrant, its underlying probable cause was not stale because it suggested a continuing enterprise of drug sales; because no constitutional violation existed and defendant was not prejudiced, defendant's motion to suppress was denied. Commonwealth v. Roy, 55 Va. Cir. 299, 2001 Va. Cir. LEXIS 522 (Richmond 2001).

Inaccurate description of location in warrant. — Where the description of the unit to be searched in a warrant directly conflicted with its actual location, there was insufficient evidence for the police to determine which unit to search; as a result, defendant was entitled to suppress the evidence found. Commonwealth v. Carr, 61 Va. Cir. 491, 2003 Va. Cir. LEXIS 224 (Charlottesville 2003).

Pat-down exceeded acceptable scope of frisk. — Defendant's motion to suppress marijuana a police officer seized from his person was granted because even though the stop and frisk for weapons was permissible under Terry, lifting up defendant's shirt and looking inside his clothing during the pat-down exceeded the acceptable scope of the frisk; the officer's testimony merely disclosed that he saw a bulge and assumed it was a weapon, but a soft bulge in a defendant's waistband was not enough information to justify a conclusion that the item was immediately apparent as contraband. Commonwealth v. Wichael, 84 Va. Cir. 83, 2011 Va. Cir. LEXIS 275 (Augusta County Dec. 20, 2011).

Consent to search. — Although a police officer's initial approach and demand that defendant produce some identification at the officer's instruction was not a consensual search. Commonwealth v. Forest, 62 Va. Cir. 340, 2003 Va. Cir. LEXIS 292 (Norfolk 2003).

Statements knowingly and voluntarily made. — Circuit court denied defendant's motion to suppress statements he made to the police during video-recorded questioning following his arrest because the recording on the whole indicated that defendant was not so impaired as to preclude a voluntary confession, and the conduct of the investigators who conducted the interview did not rise to the level of being coercive and defeating defendant's free will. Commonwealth v. Wilkins, 82 Va. Cir. 20, 2010 Va. Cir. LEXIS 318 (Augusta County Apr. 19, 2010).

Statements admissible. — Defendant's statements to police were admissible as they were unsolicited and not the result of interrogation or its functional equivalent. Commonwealth v. Adderley, 74 Va. Cir. 292, 2007 Va. Cir. LEXIS 186 (Virginia Beach 2007).

Defendant knowingly and intelligently waived his U.S. Const. amend. V right to remain silent as the evidence showed that defendant understood what he was doing when he executed the waiver form. He was advised of his rights in writing and orally in Vietnamese, his native language, and he showed that he was capable of asking appropriate questions when he did not understand something; thus, defendant's motion to suppress his statements was denied. Commonwealth v. Nguyen, 2012 Va. Cir. LEXIS 24 (Fairfax County Feb. 27, 2012).

Evidence deemed admissible. — Because police officers were dispatched to an apartment based on an informant's report of an "urgent" or "high priority" domestic disturbance and because the

officers believed that they heard someone scream after they encountered defendant, who was both drunk and bellicose, at the door, the officers' entry into the apartment did not violate defendant's Fourth Amendment rights. Commonwealth v. Soriano, 68 Va. Cir. 50, 2005 Va. Cir. LEXIS 25 (Fairfax County 2005).

Because a pat-down search of a defendant, after defendant had already told the searching officer that he had two knives on him, did not move out of the bounds of a reasonable Terry stop and could not be characterized as custody associated with a formal arrest, defendant was not entitled to Miranda warnings; hence, without any custody, defendant's statement that the hard tube-like mound in his pocket was marijuana, as well as the marijuana seized as a result, were both admissible. Commonwealth v. Herring, — Va. Cir. —, 2006 Va. Cir. LEXIS 8 (Charlottesville Feb. 13, 2006).

Motion to suppress evidence seized from defendant's residence was denied because the dog sniff was performed based on the consent of the homeowner's daughter, who the police reasonably believed had authority to grant such consent. Commonwealth v. Hoa Lam, — Va. Cir. —, 2006 Va. Cir. LEXIS 26 (Fairfax County Jan. 5, 2006).

Although the evidence of field sobriety tests conducted on defendant by a university police officer who was outside the university police department's patrol area may have been gathered in violation of the "color of office" doctrine, the officer's actions were in reliance on the authority of former § 19.2-17, which the officer reasonably and in good faith believed to be the established law. Therefore, defendant's motion to suppress the evidence of the field sobriety tests was denied. Commonwealth v. Thompson, 69 Va. Cir. 283, 2005 Va. Cir. LEXIS 321 (Charlottesville 2005).

Defendant's motion to suppress was denied, as officers testified that they witnessed an improper lane change made by defendant in heavy traffic. Because the officers witnessed defendant driving in a manner that suggested defendant was violating traffic ordinances, there was an objective basis for stopping defendant's car. Commonwealth v. Clark, — Va. Cir. —, 2006 Va. Cir. LEXIS 274 (Roanoke County Oct. 16, 2006).

Where officers responded to an apartment property manager's tip regarding trespassing and drug activity, detained two defendants, and seized a bag from defendants, suppression was not warranted, because the officers executed a proper Terry stop since the tip came from a known informant and the officers had a reasonable belief that criminal activity was afoot; the officers had a reasonable suspicion that there could be a weapon in the bag based on a reasonable suspicion of drug activity and the actions and words of both defendants. Commonwealth v. Cosentine, — Va. Cir. —, 2003 Va. Cir. LEXIS 384 (Loudoun County Mar. 24, 2003).

Evidence obtained during search of defendant's house and neighbor's attic was admissible because the affidavit supporting the search warrant for defendant's home met the test for probable cause and thus, search of defendant's home and derivative search of the neighbor's attic were permissible. Commonwealth v. Adderley, 74 Va. Cir. 292, 2007 Va. Cir. LEXIS 186 (Virginia Beach 2007).

Defendant's motion to suppress was partially denied because: (1) a traffic stop was proper since officers had probable cause to believe that the occupants committed a traffic infraction because the driver turned right through a red light; and (2) defendant's arrest was supported by probable cause since an officer saw in plain view a plastic bag filled with marijuana near defendant. Commonwealth v. Andrews, — Va. Cir. —, 2007 Va. Cir. LEXIS 260 (Prince William County June 1, 2007).

Defendant's motion to suppress drug paraphernalia that a police officer seized during a search of his person was denied because the search, which was not a pretext for investigation, would have inevitably yielded the contraband found on defendant; even if the officer lacked probable cause to arrest defendant, defendant was plainly intoxicated and seeking help from the police, and if the officer had not arrested defendant, he would have ultimately and inevitably discovered the drugs as incident to a search while transporting defendant in the police car because defendant would have been subject to a limited search pursuant to standard police procedure. Commonwealth v. Poole, 74 Va. Cir. 561, 2006 Va. Cir. LEXIS 328 (Charlottesville Dec. 12, 2006).

Defendant's statements to police were admissible, as defendant knowingly and intelligently waived defendant's Miranda rights; defendant testified that defendant knew that defendant had a right not to talk to police and that defendant did not ask for counsel. The items seized from a car defendant had been passenger in were admissible, as the search did not violate defendant's rights under the Fourth Amendment where vehicle owner gave police permission for the search and defendant had neither standing to object to the vehicle search nor an expectation of privacy in it. Commonwealth v. Porter, 74 Va. Cir. 343, 2007 Va. Cir. LEXIS 286 (Roanoke County 2007).

Evidence deemed inadmissible. — Motion to suppress evidence found in the trunk of a car after consent to search was given was granted because officers failed to return defendant's license after checking for outstanding warrants; the officers had no warrant, and there was no reasonable articulable suspicion that criminal activity was afoot where a car was stopped merely because officers suspected that the driver had a suspended license. Commonwealth v. Washington, 64 Va. Cir. 149, 2004 Va. Cir. LEXIS 185 (Norfolk 2004).

Court granted a defendant's motion to suppress since the officer directed her to get in his police van, and, with his badge and gun showing, threatened prosecution, and obtained statements and evidence in the custodial interrogation without giving Miranda warnings. It was not shown that defendant was free to leave the van. Commonwealth v. Meyers, 65 Va. Cir. 398, 2004 Va. Cir. LEXIS 285 (Fauquier County 2004).

As defendant's arrest for driving under the influence was made by an officer who did not have the statutory authority to make an arrest outside of a university's jurisdiction, the arrest was not a lawful arrest sufficient to implement the implied consent law, § 18.2-268.2. Defendant's motion to suppress a certificate of the breath test analysis therefore had to be granted. Commonwealth v. Thompson, 69 Va. Cir. 283, 2005 Va. Cir. LEXIS 321 (Charlottesville 2005).

Since the officer lacked reasonable, articulable suspicion of criminal activity that would have permitted a *Terry* stop and there was no reason to believe that defendant needed police assistance, defendant was entitled to suppression of drugs seized when the officer approached defendant's car parked on the side of the road during the early morning hours. In re Commonwealth, 2008 Va. Cir. LEXIS 114 (Roanoke County Sept. 4, 2008).

CHAPTER 6.

INTERCEPTION OF WIRE, ELECTRONIC OR ORAL COMMUNICATIONS.

§ 19.2-61. Definitions.

As used in this chapter:

"*Aggrieved person*" means a person who was a party to any intercepted wire, electronic or oral communication or a person against whom the interception was directed;

"*Aural transfer*" means a transfer containing the human voice at any point between and including the point of origin and the point of reception;

"*Communications common carrier*" means any person engaged as a common carrier for hire in communication by wire or radio or in radio transmission of energy;

"*Contents*" when used with respect to any wire, electronic or oral communication, includes any information concerning the substance, purport or meaning of that communication;

"*Electronic, mechanical or other device*" means any device or apparatus that can be used to intercept a wire, electronic or oral communication other than:

(a) Any telephone or telegraph instrument, equipment or facility, or any component thereof, (i) furnished to the subscriber or user by a provider of wire or electronic communication service in the ordinary course of its business and being used by the subscriber or user in the ordinary course of its business or furnished by the subscriber or user for connection to the facilities of such service and used in the ordinary course of the subscriber's or user's business; or (ii) being used by a communications common carrier in the ordinary course of its business, or by an investigative or law-enforcement officer in the ordinary course of his duties;

(b) A hearing aid or similar device being used to correct subnormal hearing to not better than normal;

"*Electronic communication*" means any transfer of signs, signals, writing, images, sounds, data, or intelligence of any nature transmitted in whole or in part by a wire, radio, electromagnetic, photoelectronic or photooptical system. The term does not include:

1. Any wire communication or oral communication as defined herein;

2. Any communication made through a tone-only paging device;

3. Any communication from an electronic or mechanical device which permits the tracking of the movement of a person or object; or

4. Any electronic funds transfer information stored by a financial institution in a communications system used for the electronic storage and transfer of funds;

"*Electronic communication service*" means any service which provides to users thereof the ability to send or receive wire or electronic communications;

"*Electronic communication system*" means any wire, radio, electromagnetic, photooptical or photoelectronic facilities for the transmission of wire or electronic communications, and any computer facilities or related electronic equipment for the electronic storage of such communications;

"*Electronic storage*" means any temporary, intermediate storage of a wire or electronic communication incidental to the electronic transmission thereof and any storage of such communication by an electronic communication service for purposes of backup protection of such communication;

"*Intercept*" means any aural or other means of acquisition of the contents of any wire, electronic or oral communication through the use of any electronic, mechanical or other device;

"*Investigative or law-enforcement officer*" means any officer of the United States or of a state or political subdivision thereof, who is empowered by law to conduct investigations of or to make arrests for offenses enumerated in this chapter, and any attorney authorized by law to prosecute or participate in the prosecution of such offenses;

"*Judge of competent jurisdiction*" means a judge of any circuit court of the Commonwealth with general criminal jurisdiction;

"*Monitor*" or "*monitoring*" means the actual auditory or visual acquisition of an intercepted communication by any means;

"*Oral communication*" means any oral communication uttered by a person exhibiting an expectation that such communication is not subject to interception under circumstances justifying such expectations but does not include any electronic communication;

"*Pen register*" means a device or process that records or decodes dialing, routing, addressing or signaling information transmitted by an instrument or facility from which a wire or electronic communication is transmitted; however, such information shall not include the contents of any communication. The term does not include any device or process used by a provider or customer of a wire or electronic communication service for billing, or recording as an incident to billing, for communications services provided by such provider or any device or process used by a provider or customer of a wire communication service for cost accounting or other like purposes in the ordinary course of the provider's or customer's business;

"*Person*" means any employee or agent of the Commonwealth or a political subdivision thereof, and any individual, partnership, association, joint stock company, trust or corporation;

"*Readily accessible to the general public*" means, with respect to a radio communication, that such communication is not (i) scrambled or encrypted; (ii) transmitted using modulation techniques whose essential parameters have been withheld from the public with the intention of preserving the privacy of such communication; (iii) carried on a subcarrier or other signal subsidiary to a radio transmission; (iv) transmitted over a communication system provided by a communications common carrier, unless the communication is a tone-only paging system communication; or (v) transmitted on frequencies allocated under Part 25, subpart D, E, or F of Part 74, or Part 94 of the Rules of the Federal Communications Commission, unless, in the case of a communication transmitted on a frequency allocated under Part 74 that is not exclusively allocated to broadcast auxiliary services, the communication is a two-way voice communication by radio;

"*Remote computing service*" means the provision to the public of computer storage or processing services by means of an electronic communications system;

"*Trap and trace device*" means a device or process that captures the incoming electronic or other impulses that identify the originating number or other dialing, routing, addressing and signaling information reasonably likely to identify the source of a wire or electronic communication; however, such information shall not include the contents of any communication;

"*User*" means any person or entity who uses an electronic communication service and is duly authorized by the provider of such service to engage in such use;

"*Wire communication*" means any aural transfer made in whole or in part through the use of facilities for the transmission of communications by the aid of wire, cable, or other like connection, including the use of such connection in a switching station, furnished or operated by any person engaged in providing or operating such facilities for the transmission of communications.

History.
Code 1950, § 19.1-89.1; 1973, c. 442; 1975, c. 495; 1988, c. 889; 2002, cc. 588, 623; 2005, c. 934.

Law Review.
For 2007 annual survey article, "Electronic Data: A Commentary on the Law in Virginia in 2007," see 42 U. Rich. L. Rev. 355 (2007).

Michie's Jurisprudence.
For related discussion, see 16 M.J. Right of Privacy, § 1; 18 M.J. Telegraph and Telephone Companies, § 2.

CASE NOTES

Definitions of "intercept" in this section and § 19.2-68 B 5 compared. — Prior to the 1980 amendment of § 19.2-68, adding subdivision B 5 thereof, "intercept" was defined in former subsection (3) of this section and meant an "aural acquisition." Under that definition, a wiretap order could only be entered by a judge sitting in the jurisdiction where the conversation would be heard. Thus, a wiretap order could be entered, for example, in Richmond, where the listening post would be located, while the actual conversation might occur in Franklin County. This would deprive the local authorities of knowledge of the investigation involving their jurisdiction. To avoid this result, the General Assembly enacted § 19.2-68 B 5, defining "intercept" as the physical act of acquiring the means to intercept the conversation. Smith v. Commonwealth, 3 Va. App. 650, 353 S.E.2d 159 (1987), appeal dismissed, 234 Va. 573, 363 S.E.2d 703 (1988).

"Oral communication." — Defendant's statements confiding incriminating information did not constitute an oral communication within the meaning of this section, and, thus, defendant's convictions for the rape and forcibly sodomy of defendant's teenage stepdaughter based in part on such evidence were upheld. Carpenter v. Commonwealth, 51 Va. App. 84, 654 S.E.2d 345, 2007 Va. App. LEXIS 463 (2007).

Applied in Newton v. Commonwealth, 29 Va. App. 433, 512 S.E.2d 846.

§ 19.2-62. Interception, disclosure, etc., of wire, electronic or oral communications unlawful; penalties; exceptions.

A. Except as otherwise specifically provided in this chapter any person who:

1. Intentionally intercepts, endeavors to intercept or procures any other person to intercept or endeavor to intercept, any wire, electronic or oral communication;

2. Intentionally uses, endeavors to use, or procures any other person to use or endeavor to use any electronic, mechanical or other device to intercept any oral communication;

3. Intentionally discloses, or endeavors to disclose, to any other person the contents of any wire, electronic or oral communication knowing or having reason to know that the information was obtained through the interception of a wire, electronic or oral communication; or

4. Intentionally uses, or endeavors to use, the contents of any wire, electronic or oral communication, knowing or having reason to know that the information was obtained through the interception of a wire, electronic or oral communication; shall be guilty of a Class 6 felony.

B. 1. It shall not be unlawful under this chapter for an operator of a switchboard, or an officer, employee or agent of a provider of wire or electronic communications service, whose facilities are used in the transmission of a wire communication, to intercept, disclose or use that communication in the normal course of his employment while engaged in any activity which is a necessary incident to the rendition of his service or to the protection of the rights or property of the provider of that service. However, a provider of wire communication service to the public shall not utilize service observing or random monitoring except for mechanical or service quality control checks. It shall not be a criminal offense under this chapter for providers of wire or electronic communications service, their officers, employees and agents, landlords, custodians, or other persons pursuant to a court order under this chapter, to provide information facilities or technical assistance to an investigative or law-enforcement officer, who, pursuant to this chapter, is authorized to intercept a wire, electronic or oral communication.

2. It shall not be a criminal offense under this chapter for a person to intercept a wire, electronic or oral communication, where such person is a party to the communication or one of the parties to the communication has given prior consent to such interception.

3. It shall not be a criminal offense under this chapter for any person:

(a) To intercept or access an electronic communication made through an electronic communication system that is configured so that such electronic communication is readily accessible to the general public;

(b) To intercept any radio communication which is transmitted (i) by any station for the use of the general public, or that relates to ships, aircraft, vehicles, or persons in distress, (ii) by any governmental, law-enforcement, civil defense, private land mobile, or public safety communications system, including police and fire, readily accessible to the general public, (iii) by a station operating on an authorized frequency within the bands allocated to the amateur, citizens band, or general mobile radio services; or (iv) by any marine or aeronautical communications system;

(c) To intercept any wire or electronic communication the transmission of which is causing harmful interference to any lawfully operating station or consumer electronic equipment, to the extent necessary to identify the source of such interference;

(d) Using the same frequency to intercept any radio communication made through a system that utilizes frequencies monitored by individuals engaged in the provision or the use of such system, if such communication is not scrambled or encrypted;

(e) To use a pen register or a trap and trace device pursuant to §§ 19.2-70.1 and 19.2-70.2; or

(f) Who is a provider of electronic communication service to record the fact that a wire or electronic communication was initiated or completed in order to protect such provider, another provider furnishing service toward the completion of the wire or electronic communication, or a user of that service, from fraudulent, unlawful or abusive use of such service.

C. A person or entity providing an electronic communication service to the public shall not intentionally divulge the contents of any communication, other than one to such person or entity or an agent thereof, while in transmission on that service to any person or entity other than an addressee or intended recipient of such communication or an agent of the addressee or intended recipient. However, a person or entity providing electronic communication service to the public may divulge the contents of any such communication:

1. As authorized in subdivision B 1 of this section or § 19.2-67;

2. With the lawful consent of the originator or any addressee or intended recipient of such communication;

3. To a person employed or authorized, or whose facilities are used, to forward such communication to its destination; or

4. Which were inadvertently obtained by the service provider and which appear to pertain to the commission of a crime, to a law-enforcement agency.

Conduct otherwise an offense under this subsection that consists of or relates to the interception of a satellite transmission that is not encrypted or scrambled and that is transmitted (i) to a broadcasting station for purposes of retransmission to the general public, or (ii) as an audio subcarrier intended for redistribution to facilities open to the public, but not including data transmissions or telephone calls, is not an offense under this section unless the conduct is for the purposes of direct or indirect commercial advantage or private financial gain. Further, private viewing of a satellite video communication that is not scrambled or encrypted and interception of a radio communication that is transmitted on frequencies allocated under subpart D of Part 74 of the Rules of the Federal Communications Commission that is not scrambled or encrypted when the viewing or interception is not done for a tortious or illegal purpose or for purposes of direct or indirect commercial advantage or private commercial gain, shall not be offenses under this chapter.

Violation of this subsection shall be punishable as a Class 1 misdemeanor.

History.
Code 1950, § 19.1-89.2; 1973, c. 442; 1975, c. 495; 1988, c. 889; 2004, c. 149.

Cross references.
As to punishment for Class 6 felonies, see § 18.2-10. As to punishment for Class 1 misdemeanors, see § 18.2-11.

Law Review.
For an article, "I Spy: The Newsgatherer Under Cover," see 33 U. Rich. L. Rev. 1185 (2000). For note, "Bartnicki v. Vopper: A Public Concern Exception for the Press and its Disclosure of unlawfully Obtained Information," see 11 Geo. Mason. L. Rev. 441 (2002).

CASE NOTES

Marital communications. — Defendant's statements confiding incriminating information did not constitute an oral communication within the meaning of § 19.2-61, the wiretap statute, and, thus, defendant's convictions for the rape and forcibly sodomy of defendant's teenage stepdaughter based in part on such evidence were upheld. Carpenter v. Commonwealth, 51 Va. App. 84, 654 S.E.2d 345, 2007 Va. App. LEXIS 463 (2007).

OPINIONS OF THE ATTORNEY GENERAL

Telephone company employees may disclose contents of intercepted telephone conversations both to law-enforcement officers and in testimony at a criminal trial for the offense of fraudulently obtaining or using telephone service. See opinion of Attorney General to The Honorable Harvey L. Bryant, Commonwealth's Attorney for the City of Virginia Beach, 04-021 (5/27/04).

§ 19.2-63. Manufacture, possession, sale or advertising of certain devices unlawful; penalties; exceptions.

A. Except as otherwise specifically provided in this chapter, any person who intentionally:

1. Manufactures, assembles, possesses, or sells any electronic, mechanical, or other device, knowing or having reason to know that the design of such device renders it primarily useful for the purpose of the surreptitious interception of wire, electronic or oral communications; or

2. Places in any newspaper, magazine, handbill, or other publication any advertisement of:

(a) Any electronic, mechanical, or other device knowing or having reason to know that the design of such device renders it primarily useful for the purpose of the surreptitious interception of wire, electronic or oral communications, or

(b) Any other electronic, mechanical, or other device where such advertisement promotes the use of such device for the purpose of the surreptitious interception of wire, electronic or oral communications; shall be guilty of a Class 6 felony.

B. It shall not be unlawful under this section for:

1. A provider of wire or electronic communication service or an officer, agent, or employee of, or a person under contract with, such provider in the normal course of the provider's business, or

2. An officer, agent, or employee of, or a person under contract with the United States, the Commonwealth or a political subdivision thereof, in the normal course of the activities of the United States, the Commonwealth, or a political subdivision thereof, to manufacture, assemble, possess, or sell any electronic, mechanical, or other device knowing or having reason to know that the design of such device renders it primarily useful for the purpose of the surreptitious interception of wire, electronic or oral communications.

History.
Code 1950, § 19.1-89.3; 1973, c. 442; 1975, c. 495; 1988, c. 889.

Cross references.
As to punishment for Class 6 felonies, see § 18.2-10.

§ 19.2-63.1. Supervision and control of devices; unauthorized possession.

Any electronic, mechanical or other device as defined in this chapter which is in the possession of any sheriff's office or police department of a county, city or town, or in the possession of any employee of such office, shall be under the direct control and supervision of the sheriff or chief of police of the office or department or his designee who is an employee of the office or department. Unauthorized possession of any such device under the provisions of this section by any such employee is unlawful, notwithstanding the provisions of subdivision B 2 of § 19.2-63, and a Class 1 misdemeanor.

History.
1978, c. 63; 1988, c. 889; 2011, c. 193.

Cross references.
As to punishment for Class 1 misdemeanors, see § 18.2-11.

The 2011 amendments.
The 2011 amendment by c. 193 added "or his designee who is an employee of the office or department" at the end of the first sentence.

CASE NOTES

Virginia wiretap statute is patterned on a federal statute covering the same subject. Morton v. Commonwealth, 227 Va. 216, 315 S.E.2d 224, cert. denied, 469 U.S. 862, 105 S. Ct. 198, 83 L. Ed. 2d 130 (1984). See 18 U.S.C.A. § 2517.

Void-for-vagueness doctrine inapplicable. — The portions of the "Virginia Wiretap Statute" which prescribe the procedure for obtaining and conducting a wiretap are not penal in nature, and thus, the void-for-vagueness doctrine is not applicable to them. Smith v. Commonwealth, 3 Va. App. 650, 353 S.E.2d 159 (1987), appeal dismissed, 234 Va. 573, 363 S.E.2d 703 (1988).

§ 19.2-64. Forfeiture of unlawful devices.

Any electronic, mechanical or other device used, manufactured, assembled, possessed, sold, or advertised in violation of § 19.2-62 or § 19.2-63 may be seized and forfeited to the Commonwealth, and turned over to the court of record in the city or county in which it was seized and such property shall be disposed of in such manner as the court may direct.

History.
Code 1950, § 19.1-89.4; 1973, c. 442; 1975, c. 495.

Law Review.
For survey of Virginia criminal law for the year 1972-1973, see 59 Va. L. Rev. 1458 (1973).

§ 19.2-65. When intercepted communications and evidence derived therefrom not to be received in evidence.

Whenever any wire or oral communication has been intercepted, no part of the contents of such communication and no evidence derived therefrom may be received in evidence in any trial, hearing or other proceeding in or before any court, grand jury, department, officer, commission, regulatory body, legislative committee or other agency of this Commonwealth or a political subdivision thereof if the disclosure of that information would be in violation of this chapter.

History.
Code 1950, § 19.1-89.5; 1973, c. 442; 1975, c. 495.

Law Review.
For survey of Virginia criminal law for the year 1972-1973, see 59 Va. L. Rev. 1458 (1973). For 2007 annual survey article, "Electronic Data: A Commentary on the Law in Virginia in 2007," see 42 U. Rich. L. Rev. 355 (2007).

CASE NOTES

Admissible communications. — A recording of a whispered conversation between defendant and his mother's boyfriend in a police interrogation room while only defendant, the boyfriend, and defendant's mother were present was admissible against defendant because he had no reasonable expectation of privacy under the circumstances. Belmer v. Commonwealth, 36 Va. App. 448, 553 S.E.2d 123, 2001 Va. App. LEXIS 531 (2001).

Applied in Morton v. Commonwealth, 227 Va. 216, 315 S.E.2d 224 (1984).

§ 19.2-66. When Attorney General or Chief Deputy Attorney General may apply for order authorizing interception of communications.

A. The Attorney General or Chief Deputy Attorney General, if the Attorney General so designates in writing, in any case where the Attorney General is authorized by law to prosecute or pursuant to a request in his official capacity of an attorney for the Commonwealth in any city or county, may apply to a judge of competent jurisdiction for an order authorizing the interception of wire, electronic or oral communications by the Department of State Police, when such interception may reasonably be expected to provide evidence of the commission of a felonious offense of extortion, bribery, kidnapping, murder, any felony violation of § 18.2-248 or 18.2-248.1, any felony violation of Chapter 29 (§ 59.1-364 et seq.) of Title 59.1, any felony violation of Article 2 (§ 18.2-38 et seq.), Article 2.1 (§ 18.2-46.1 et seq.), Article 2.2 (§ 18.2-46.4 et seq.), Article 5 (§ 18.2-58 et seq.), Article 6 (§ 18.2-59 et seq.) or any felonies that are not Class 6 felonies in Article 7 (§ 18.2-61 et seq.) of Chapter 4 of Title 18.2, or any conspiracy to commit any of the foregoing offenses. The Attorney General or Chief Deputy Attorney General may apply for authorization for the observation or monitoring of the interception by a police department of a county or city, by a sheriff's office, or by law-enforcement officers of the United States. Such application shall be made, and such order may be granted, in conformity with the provisions of § 19.2-68.

B. The application for an order under subsection B of § 19.2-68 shall be made as follows:

1. In the case of an application for a wire or electronic interception, a judge of competent jurisdiction shall have the authority to issue an order under subsection B of § 19.2-68 if there is probable cause to believe that an offense was committed, is being committed, or will be committed or the person or persons whose communications are to be intercepted live, work, subscribe to a wire or electronic communication system, maintain an address or a post office box, or are making the communication within the territorial jurisdiction of the court.

2. In the case of an application for an oral intercept, a judge of competent jurisdiction shall have the authority to issue an order under subsection B of § 19.2-68 if there is probable cause to believe that an offense was committed, is being committed, or will be committed or the physical location of the oral communication to be intercepted is within the territorial jurisdiction of the court.

C. For the purposes of an order entered pursuant to subsection B of § 19.2-68 for the interception of a wire or electronic communication, such communication shall be deemed to be intercepted in the jurisdiction where the order is entered, regardless of the physical location or the method by which the communication is captured or routed to the monitoring location.

History.
Code 1950, § 19.1-89.6; 1973, c. 442; 1975, c. 495; 1976, c. 271; 1979, c. 602; 1982, cc. 40, 274; 1988, cc. 855, 889; 2002, cc. 588, 623; 2004, c. 122; 2005, c. 934; 2011, cc. 403, 414; 2013, cc. 448, 664.

Cross references.
As to punishment for class 6 felonies, see § 18.2-10.

The 2011 amendments.
The 2011 amendments by cc. 403 and 414 are identical, and rewrote the first paragraph in subsection B, which read: "The application for an order under subsection B of § 19.2-68 for the interception of a wire, electronic or oral communication shall be made in the jurisdiction where there is probable cause to believe that an offense listed in subsection A of this section was committed, is being committed, or will be committed"; in subsections B 1 and B 2, inserted "there is probable cause to believe that an offense was committed, is being committed, or will be committed or"; and redesignated former subdivision B 3 as subsection C.

The 2013 amendments.
The 2013 amendments by cc. 448 and 664 are identical, and inserted "by a sheriff's office" in the next-to-last sentence in subsection A.

Law Review.
For 2003/2004 survey of criminal law and procedure, see 39 U. Rich. L. Rev. 133 (2004).

Michie's Jurisprudence.
For related discussion, see 18 M.J. Telegraph and Telephone Companies, § 2.

CASE NOTES

Void-for-vagueness doctrine inapplicable. — The portions of the "Virginia Wiretap Statute" which prescribe the procedure for obtaining and conducting a wiretap are not penal in nature, and thus, the void-for-vagueness doctrine is not applicable to them. Smith v. Commonwealth, 3 Va. App. 650, 353 S.E.2d 159 (1987), appeal dismissed, 234 Va. 573, 363 S.E.2d 703 (1988).

This section must be read with § 19.2-68. — This section, which delineates the parties who may initiate an application for a wiretap and the crimes for which a wiretap can be obtained, is subordinate to and must be read with § 19.2-68. Smith v. Commonwealth, 3 Va. App. 650, 353 S.E.2d 159 (1987), appeal dismissed, 234 Va. 573, 363 S.E.2d 703 (1988).

Section 19.2-68 qualifies this section. — Section 19.2-68 outlines the procedural requirements of a wiretap application and clearly qualifies this section. Smith v. Commonwealth, 3 Va. App. 650, 353 S.E.2d 159 (1987), appeal dismissed, 234 Va. 573, 363 S.E.2d 703 (1988).

Definition of "intercept" in § 19.2-68 B 5 applies to both this section and § 19.2-68. For purposes of these sections, "intercept" means the physical act (such as splicing) by which the interceptor gains the ability to exercise dominion and control over the communication. Smith v. Commonwealth, 3 Va. App. 650, 353 S.E.2d 159 (1987), appeal dismissed, Nationwide Mut. Ins. Co. v. Scott, 234 Va. 573, 363 S.E.2d 703 (1988).

Interception occurred when telephone line broken and splicing occurred. — Interception of telephone conversations occurred in Franklin County when telephone line was broken and splicing occurred, even though the intercepted conversations could not have been transcribed but for the listening post in Henry County where they were monitored. Thus, intercept order entered by a judge in Franklin County was valid. Smith v. Commonwealth, 3 Va. App. 650, 353 S.E.2d 159 (1987), appeal dismissed, 234 Va. 573, 363 S.E.2d 703 (1988).

Applied in Morton v. Commonwealth, 227 Va. 216, 315 S.E.2d 224 (1984).

§ 19.2-67. Disclosure of information obtained by authorized means.

A. Any investigative or law-enforcement officer, or police officer of a county or city, who, by any means authorized by this chapter, has obtained knowledge of the contents of any wire, electronic or oral communication, or evidence derived therefrom, may disclose such contents to another investigative or law-enforcement officer, or police officer of a county or city, to the extent that such disclosure is appropriate to the proper performance of the official duties of the officer making or receiving the disclosure.

B. Any investigative or law-enforcement officer or police officer of a county or city, who, by any means authorized by this chapter, has obtained knowledge of the contents of any wire, electronic or oral communication or evidence derived therefrom may use such contents to the extent such use is appropriate to the proper performance of his official duties.

C. Any person who has received, by any means authorized by this chapter, any information concerning a wire, electronic or oral communication, or evidence derived therefrom intercepted in accordance with the provisions of this chapter may disclose the contents of that communication or such derivative evidence while giving testimony under oath or affirmation in any criminal proceeding for an offense specified in § 19.2-66, or any conspiracy or attempt to commit the same, in any court of the United States or of any state or in any federal or state grand jury proceeding.

D. No wire, electronic or oral communication which is a privileged communication between the parties to the conversation which is intercepted in accordance with, or in violation of, the provisions of this chapter shall lose its privileged character, nor shall it be disclosed or used in any way.

E. When an investigative or law-enforcement officer, or police officer of a county or city, while engaged in intercepting wire, electronic or oral communications in the manner authorized herein, or observing or monitoring such interception intercepts, observes or monitors wire, electronic or oral communications relating to offenses other than those specified in the order of authorization, the contents thereof, and evidence derived therefrom, shall not be disclosed or used as provided in subsections A, B and C of this section, unless such communications or derivative evidence relates to a felony, in which case use or disclosure may be made as provided in subsections A, B and C of this section. Such use and disclosure pursuant to subsection C of this section shall be permitted only when approved by a judge of competent jurisdiction where such judge finds, on subsequent application, that such communications were otherwise intercepted in accordance with the provisions of this chapter. Violations of this subsection E shall be punishable as provided in § 19.2-62.

History.
Code 1950, § 19.1-89.7; 1973, c. 442; 1975, c. 495; 1976, c. 231; 1979, c. 602; 1983, c. 536; 1988, c. 889.

§ 19.2-68. Application for and issuance of order authorizing interception; contents of order; recording and retention of intercepted communications, applications and orders; notice to parties; introduction in evidence of information obtained.

A. Each application for an order authorizing the interception of a wire, electronic or oral communication shall be made in writing upon oath or affirmation to the appropriate judge of competent jurisdiction and shall state the applicant's authority to make such application. Each application shall be verified by the Attorney General to the best of his knowledge and belief and shall include the following information:

1. The identity of the attorney for the Commonwealth and law-enforcement officer who requested the Attorney General to apply for such order;

2. A full and complete statement of the facts and circumstances relied upon by the applicant to justify his belief that an order should be issued, including (i) details as to the particular offense that has been, is being or is about to be committed, (ii) except as provided in subsection I, a particular description of the nature and location of the facilities from which or the place where the communication is to be intercepted, (iii) a particular description of the type of communications sought to be intercepted, (iv) the identity of the person, if known, committing the offense and whose communications are to be intercepted;

3. A full and complete statement as to whether or not other investigative procedures have been tried and failed or why they reasonably appear to be unlikely to succeed if tried or to be too dangerous;

4. A statement of the period of time for which the interception is required to be maintained. If the nature of the investigation is such that the authorization for interception should not automatically terminate when the described type of communication has been first obtained, a particular description of facts establishing probable cause to believe that additional communications of the same type will occur thereafter;

5. A full and complete statement of the facts concerning all previous applications known to the individual authorizing and making the application, made to any judge for authorization to intercept wire, electronic or oral communications involving any of the same persons, facilities or places specified in the application, and the action taken by the judge on each such application;

6. Where the application is for the extension of an order, a statement setting forth the results thus far obtained from the interception, or a reasonable explanation of the failure to obtain such results; and

7. If authorization is requested for observation or monitoring by a police department of a county or city, by a sheriff's office, or by law-enforcement officers of the United States, a statement containing the name of the police department, sheriff's office, or United States agency and an explanation of the reasons such observation or monitoring is necessary.

The judge may require the applicant to furnish additional testimony or documentary evidence in support of the application.

B. Upon such application the judge may enter an ex parte order, as requested or as modified, authorizing interception of wire, electronic or oral communications if the judge determines on the basis of the facts submitted by the applicant that:

1. There is probable cause for belief that an individual is committing, has committed or is about to commit an offense enumerated in § 19.2-66 of this chapter;

2. There is probable cause for belief that particular communications concerning that offense will be obtained through such interception;

3. Normal investigative procedures have been tried and have failed, or reasonably appear to be unlikely to succeed if tried, or to be too dangerous; and interception under this chapter is the only alternative investigative procedure available;

4. Except as provided in subsection I, there is probable cause for belief that the facilities from which, or the place where, the wire, electronic or oral communications are to be intercepted are being used, or are about to be used, in connection with the commission of such offense, or are leased to, listed in the name of, or commonly used by such person;

5. A wire, electronic or oral communication authorized to be intercepted pursuant to this section may be monitored at any location within the Commonwealth of Virginia.

C. Each order authorizing the interception of any wire, electronic or oral communication shall specify:

1. The identity of the person, if known, whose communications are to be intercepted;

2. The nature and location of the communications facilities as to which, or the place where, authority to intercept is granted;

3. A particular description of the type of communication sought to be intercepted, and a statement of the particular offense enumerated in § 19.2-66 to which it relates;

4. That such interception is to be conducted only by the Department of State Police;

5. If observation or monitoring by the police department of a county or city, by a sheriff's office, or by law-enforcement officers of the United States is authorized, only that police department, sheriff's office, or agency or the officers from any police department of a town which originated the investigation leading to the application shall observe or monitor the interception; and

6. The period of time during which such interception is authorized, including a statement as to whether or not the interception shall automatically terminate when the described communication has been first obtained.

An order authorizing the interception of a wire, electronic or oral communication shall, upon request of the applicant, direct that a provider of wire or electronic communications service, landlord, custodian or other person shall furnish the Department of State Police forthwith all information, facilities and technical assistance necessary to accomplish the interception unobtrusively and with a minimum of interference with the services that such service provider, landlord, custodian or person is providing the person whose communications are to be intercepted. Any provider of wire or electronic communications service, landlord, custodian or other person furnishing such facilities or technical assistance shall be compensated therefor by the Commonwealth for reasonable and actual expenses incurred in providing such facilities or assistance, to be paid out of the criminal fund.

D. No order entered under this section may authorize the interception of any wire, electronic or oral communication for any period longer than is necessary to achieve the objective of the authorization, nor in any event longer than 30 days which period begins to run on the earlier of the day on which the investigative or law-enforcement officer begins to conduct an interception under the order or 10 days after the date of entry of the order. Extensions of an order may be granted, but only upon application for an extension made in accordance with subsection A of this section and the court's making the findings required by subsection B of this section. The period of extension shall be no longer than the authorizing judge deems necessary to achieve the purposes for which it was granted and in no event for longer than 30 days. Every order and extension thereof shall contain a provision that the authorization to intercept shall be executed as soon as practicable, shall be conducted in such a way as to minimize the interception of communications not otherwise subject to interception under this chapter, and must terminate upon attainment of the authorized objective, or in any event in 30 days. In the event the intercepted communication is in a code or foreign language, and an expert in that foreign language or code is not reasonably available during the interception period, minimization may be accomplished as soon as practicable after such interception.

E. Whenever an order authorizing interception is entered pursuant to this chapter, the order shall require reports to be made to the judge who issued the order showing what progress has been made toward achievement of the authorized objective and the need for continued interception. Such reports shall be made at such intervals as the judge shall require.

F. 1. The contents of any wire, electronic or oral communication intercepted by any means authorized by this chapter shall, if possible, be recorded on tape or wire or other comparable device. Should it not be possible to record the intercepted communi-cation, a detailed resume of such communication shall forthwith be reduced to writing and filed with the court. The recording of the contents of any wire, electronic or oral communication under this subsection shall be done in such way as will protect the recording from editing or other alterations and shall not be duplicated except upon order of the court as hereafter provided. Immediately upon the expiration of the period of the order, or extensions thereof, such recording or detailed resume shall be made available to the judge issuing such order and sealed under his directions. Custody of any recordings or detailed resumes shall be vested with the court and shall not be destroyed for a period of 10 years from the date of the order and then only by direction of the court; provided, however, should any interception fail to reveal any information related to the offense or offenses for which it was authorized, such recording or resume shall be destroyed after the expiration of 60 days after the notice required by subdivision 4 of this subsection is served. Duplicate recordings may be made for use or disclosure pursuant to the provisions of subsections A and B of § 19.2-67 for investigations. The presence of the seal provided for by this subsection, or a satisfactory explanation for the absence thereof, shall be a prerequisite for the use or disclosure of the contents of any wire, electronic or oral communication or evidence derived therefrom under subsection C of § 19.2-67.

2. Applications made and orders granted or denied under this chapter shall be sealed by the judge. Custody of the applications and orders shall be wherever the judge directs. Such applications and orders shall be disclosed only upon a showing of good cause before a judge of competent jurisdiction and shall not be destroyed except on order of the issuing or denying judge, and in any event shall be kept for 10 years.

3. Any violation of the provisions of this subsection may be punished as contempt of the issuing or denying court.

4. Within a reasonable time but not later than 90 days after the filing of an application for an order of authorization which is denied or the termination of the period of an order or extensions thereof, the issuing or denying judge shall cause to be served, on the persons named in the order or the application, and such other parties to intercepted communications as the judge may determine in his discretion that is in the interest of justice, an inventory which shall include notice of:

(a) The fact of the entry of the order or the application;

(b) The date of the entry and the period of authorized interception, or the denial of the application;

(c) The fact that during the period wire, electronic or oral communications were or were not intercepted; and

(d) The fact that unless he files a motion with the court within 60 days after the service of notice upon him, the recordation or resume may be destroyed in accordance with subdivision 1 of this subsection.

The judge, upon the filing of a motion, shall make available to such person or his counsel for inspection the intercepted communications, applications and orders. The serving of the inventory required by this subsection may be postponed for additional periods, not to exceed 30 days each, upon the ex parte showing of good cause to a judge of competent jurisdiction.

G. The contents of any intercepted wire, electronic or oral communication or evidence derived therefrom shall not be received in evidence or otherwise disclosed in any trial, hearing or other proceeding in a state court unless each party to the communication and to such proceeding, not less than 10 days before the trial, hearing or proceeding, has been furnished with a copy of the court order, accompanying application under which the interception was authorized and the contents of any intercepted wire, electronic or oral communication that is to be used in any trial, hearing or other proceeding in a state court. This 10-day period may be waived by the judge if he finds that it was not possible to furnish the party with the above information 10 days before the trial, hearing or proceeding and that the party will not be prejudiced by the delay in receiving such information; provided that such information in any event shall be given prior to the day of the trial, and the inability to comply with such 10-day period shall be grounds for the granting of a continuance to either party.

The judge who considers an application for an interception under this chapter, whether issuing or denying the order, shall be disqualified from presiding at any trial resulting from or in any manner connected with such interception, regardless of whether the evidence acquired thereby is used in such trial.

H. Any aggrieved person in any trial, hearing or proceeding in or before any court, department, officer, agency, regulatory body or other authority of the Commonwealth, or a political subdivision thereof, may move to suppress the contents of any intercepted wire, electronic or oral communication, or evidence derived therefrom, on the grounds that:

1. The communication was unlawfully intercepted, or was not intercepted in compliance with this chapter; or

2. The order of the authorization or approval under which it was intercepted is insufficient on its face; or

3. The interception was not made in conformity with the order of authorization or approval; or

4. The interception is not admissible into evidence in any trial, proceeding or hearing in a state court under the applicable rules of evidence.

Such motion shall be made before the trial, hearing or proceeding unless there was no opportunity to make such motion or the person was not aware of the grounds of the motion. If the motion is granted

pursuant to subdivision 1, 2 or 3 of this subsection, the contents of the intercepted wire, electronic or oral communication or evidence derived therefrom shall be treated as having been obtained in violation of this chapter. The judge, upon the filing of such motion by the aggrieved person, shall make available to the aggrieved person, or his counsel, for inspection the intercepted communication.

I. The requirements of subdivision 2 of subsection A and subdivision 4 of subsection B of this section relating to the specification of the facilities from which, or the place where, the communication is to be intercepted do not apply if:

1. In the case of an application with respect to the interception of an oral communication:

(a) The application contains a full and complete statement as to why such specification is not practical and identifies the person committing the offense and whose communications are to be intercepted; and

(b) The judge finds that such specification is not practical; or

2. In the case of an application with respect to a wire or electronic communication:

(a) the application identifies the person believed to be committing the offense and whose communications are to be intercepted and the applicant makes a showing of a purpose, on the part of that person, to thwart interception by changing facilities; and

(b) the judge finds that such purpose has been adequately shown.

The interception of a communication under an order issued pursuant to this subsection shall not begin until the facilities from which, or the place where, the communication is to be intercepted is ascertained by the person implementing the interception order. A provider of wire or electronic communications service that has received an order issued pursuant to this subdivision 2 may move the court to modify or quash the order on the ground that its assistance with respect to the interception cannot be performed in a timely or reasonable fashion. The court, upon notice to the Attorney General, shall decide the motion expeditiously.

History.

Code 1950, § 19.1-89.8; 1973, c. 442; 1975, c. 495; 1976, c. 163; 1977, c. 335; 1979, c. 602; 1980, c. 244; 1988, c. 889; 2002, c. 91; 2005, c. 934; 2013, cc. 448, 664.

The 2013 amendments.

The 2013 amendments by cc. 448 and 664 are nearly identical, and inserted "by a sheriff's office" and "sheriff's office" in subdivisions A 7 and C 5.

Michie's Jurisprudence.

For related discussion, see 18 M.J. Telegraph and Telephone Companies, § 2.

CASE NOTES

Void-for-vagueness doctrine inapplicable. — The portions of the "Virginia Wiretap Statute" which prescribe the procedure for obtaining and conducting a wiretap are not penal in nature, and thus, the void-for-vagueness doctrine is not applicable to them. Smith v. Commonwealth, 3 Va. App. 650, 353 S.E.2d 159 (1987), appeal dismissed, 234 Va. 573, 363 S.E.2d 703 (1988).

Section 19.2-66 must be read with this section. — Section 19.2-66, which delineates the parties who may initiate an application for a wiretap and the crimes for which a wiretap can be obtained, is subordinate to and must be read with this section. Smith v. Commonwealth, 3 Va. App. 650, 353 S.E.2d 159 (1987), appeal dismissed, 234 Va. 573, 363 S.E.2d 703 (1988).

This section qualifies § 19.2-66. — This section outlines the procedural requirements of a wiretap application and clearly qualifies § 19.2-66. Smith v. Commonwealth, 3 Va. App. 650, 353 S.E.2d 159 (1987), appeal dismissed, 234 Va. 573, 363 S.E.2d 703 (1988).

Definitions of "intercept" in this section and § 19.2-61 compared. — Prior to the 1980 amendment of this section, adding subdivision B 5, "intercept" was defined in § 19.2-61 and meant an "aural acquisition." Under that definition, a wiretap order could only be entered by a judge sitting in the jurisdiction where the conversation would be heard. Thus, a wiretap order could be entered, for example, in Richmond, where the listening post would be located, while the actual conversation might occur in Franklin County. This would deprive the local authorities of knowledge of the investigation involving their jurisdiction. To avoid this result, the General Assembly enacted subdivision B 5 of this section, defining "intercept" as the physical act of acquiring the means to intercept the conversation. Smith v. Commonwealth, 3 Va. App. 650, 353 S.E.2d 159 (1987), appeal dismissed, 234 Va. 573, 363 S.E.2d 703 (1988).

Definition of "intercept" in subdivision B 5 of this section applies to both § 19.2-66 and this section. For purposes of these sections, "intercept" means the physical act (such as splicing) by which the interceptor gains the ability to exercise dominion and control over the communication. Smith v. Commonwealth, 3 Va. App. 650, 353 S.E.2d 159 (1987), appeal dismissed, 234 Va. 573, 363 S.E.2d 703 (1988).

Legislature intended in subdivision B 5 to distinguish between "intercept" and "monitor." Smith v. Commonwealth, 3 Va. App. 650, 353 S.E.2d 159 (1987), appeal dismissed, 234 Va. 573, 363 S.E.2d 703 (1988).

Interception occurred when telephone line was broken and splicing occurred. — Interception of telephone conversations occurred in Franklin County when telephone line was broken and splicing occurred, even though the intercepted conversations could not have been transcribed but for the listening post in Henry County where they were monitored. Thus, intercept order entered by a judge in Franklin County was valid. Smith v. Commonwealth, 3 Va. App. 650, 353 S.E.2d 159 (1987), appeal dismissed, 234 Va. 573, 363 S.E.2d 703 (1988).

§ 19.2-69. Civil action for unlawful interception, disclosure or use.

Any person whose wire, electronic or oral communication is intercepted, disclosed or used in violation of this chapter shall (i) have a civil cause of action against any person who intercepts, discloses or uses, or procures any other person to intercept, disclose or use such communications, and (ii) be entitled to recover from any such person:

1. Actual damages but not less than liquidated damages computed at the rate of $400 a day for each day of violation or $4,000, whichever is higher;

2. Punitive damages; and

3. A reasonable attorney's fee and other litigation costs reasonably incurred.

A good faith reliance on a court order or legislative authorization shall constitute a complete defense to any civil or criminal action brought under this chapter or under any other law.

History.
Code 1950, § 19.1-89.9; 1973, c. 442; 1975, c. 495; 1988, c. 889; 2010, c. 343.

The 2010 amendments.
The 2010 amendment by c. 343 substituted "$400" for "$100" and "$4,000" for "$1,000."

§ 19.2-70. Reports to be filed by courts and Attorney General.

All courts of the Commonwealth and the Attorney General shall file all reports required by 18 U.S.C.A. § 2519. The Attorney General shall file a written report with the Clerks of the Senate and House of Delegates on or before December 31 of each year setting forth the number of applications made pursuant to this chapter, the number of interceptions authorized, the number of arrests resulting from each application, the number of convictions including a breakdown by offense, the cost of each application granted and the number of requests denied. Such information shall be made available by such Clerks to any member of the General Assembly upon request. However, notwithstanding the above requirements, no report shall be made concerning a granted application until after all inventories associated with such application are served pursuant to subdivision F 4 of § 19.2-68.

History.
Code 1950, § 19.1-89.10; 1973, c. 442; 1975, c. 495; 2011, cc. 403, 414.

The 2011 amendments.
The 2011 amendments by cc. 403 and 414 are identical, and added the last sentence.

Law Review.
For survey of Virginia criminal law for the year 1972-1973, see 59 Va. L. Rev. 1458 (1973).

§ 19.2-70.1. General prohibition on pen register and trap and trace device use; exceptions.

Except as provided in this section, no person may install or use a pen register or a trap and trace device without first obtaining a court order under § 19.2-70.2.

However, a court order shall not be required for use of a pen register or trap and trace device by a provider of electronic or wire communication service (i) relating to the operation, maintenance, and testing of a wire or electronic communication service or to the protection of the rights or property of the provider, or to the protection of users of that service from abuse of service or unlawful use of service; (ii) to record the fact that a wire or electronic communication was initiated or completed in order to protect such provider, another provider furnishing service toward the completion of the wire communication, or a user of that service, from fraudulent, unlawful or abusive use of service; or (iii) where the consent of the user of that service has been obtained.

Any person who knowingly violates this section shall be guilty of a Class 1 misdemeanor.

History.
1988, c. 889.

Cross references.
As to punishment for Class 1 misdemeanors, see § 18.2-11.

§ 19.2-70.2. Application for and issuance of order for a pen register or trap and trace device; assistance in installation and use.

A. An investigative or law-enforcement officer may make application for an order or an extension of an order authorizing or approving the installation and use of a pen register or a trap and trace device, in writing under oath or equivalent affirmation, to a court of competent jurisdiction. The application shall include:

1. The identity of the officer making the application and the identity of the law-enforcement agency conducting the investigation; and

2. A certification by the applicant that the information likely to be obtained is relevant to an ongoing criminal investigation being conducted by that agency.

The application may include a request that the order require information, facilities and technical assistance necessary to accomplish the installation be furnished.

B. An application for an ex parte order authorizing the installation and use of a pen register or trap and trace device may be filed in the jurisdiction where the person or persons who subscribe to the wire or electronic communication system live, work, or maintain an address or a post office box. For the purposes of an order entered pursuant to this section for the installation and use of a pen register or trap and trace device, such installation shall be deemed to occur in the jurisdiction where the order is entered, regardless of the physical location or the method by which the information is captured or routed to the law-enforcement officer that made the application. Upon application, the court shall enter an ex parte order authorizing the installation and use of a pen register or a trap and trace device if the court finds that the investigative or law-enforcement officer has certified to the court that the information likely to be obtained by such installation and use is relevant to an ongoing criminal investigation.

The order shall specify:

1. The identity, if known, of the person in whose name the telephone line or other facility to which the pen register or trap and trace device is to be attached or applied is listed or to whom the line or other facility is leased;

2. The identity, if known, of the person who is the subject of the criminal investigation;

3. The attributes of the communications to which the order applies, including the number or other identifier and, if known, the location of the telephone line or other facility to which the pen register or trap and trace device is to be attached or applied; and

4. A statement of the offense to which the information likely to be obtained by the pen register or trap and trace device relates.

C. Installation and use of a pen register or a trap and trace device shall be authorized for a period not to exceed 60 days. Extensions of the order may be granted, but only upon application made and order issued in accordance with this section. The period of an extension shall not exceed 60 days.

D. An order authorizing or approving the installation and use of a pen register or a trap and trace device shall direct that:

1. The order and application be sealed until otherwise ordered by the court;

2. Information, facilities and technical assistance necessary to accomplish the installation be furnished if requested in the application; and

3. The person owning or leasing the line or other facility to which the pen register or trap and trace device is attached or applied, or who is obligated by the order to provide assistance to the applicant, not disclose the existence of the pen register or trap and trace device or the existence of the investigation to the listed subscriber, or to any other person, unless or until otherwise ordered by the court.

E. Upon request of an investigative or a law-enforcement officer authorized by the court to install and use a pen register, a provider of wire or electronic communication service, a landlord, custodian or any other person so ordered by the court shall, as soon as practicable, furnish the officer with all information, facilities, and technical assistance necessary to accomplish the installation of the pen register unobtrusively and with a minimum of interference with the services that the person so ordered by the court accords the party with respect to whom the installation and use is to take place.

F. Upon request of an investigative or law-enforcement officer authorized by the court to receive the results of a trap and trace device under this section, a provider of wire or electronic communication service, a landlord, custodian or any other person so ordered by the court shall, as soon as practicable, install the device on the appropriate line and furnish the officer with all additional information, facilities and technical assistance, including installation and operation of the device, unobtrusively and with a minimum of interference with the services that the person so ordered by the court accords the party with respect to whom the installation and use is to take place. Unless otherwise ordered by the court, the results of the trap and trace device shall be furnished to the investigative or law-enforcement officer designated by the court at reasonable intervals during regular business hours for the duration of the order. Where the law-enforcement agency implementing an ex parte order under this subsection seeks to do so by installing and using its own pen register or trap and trace device on a packet-switched data network of a provider of electronic communication service to the public, the agency shall ensure that a record will be maintained that will identify (i) any officer or officers who installed the device and any officer or officers who accessed the device to obtain information from the network; (ii) the date and time the device was installed, the date and time the device was uninstalled, and the date, time, and duration of each time the device is accessed to obtain information; (iii) the configuration of the device at the time of its installation and any subsequent modification thereof; and (iv) any information that has been collected by the device. To the extent that the pen register or trap and trace device can be set automatically to record this information electronically, the record shall be maintained electronically throughout the installation and use of such device. The record maintained hereunder shall be provided ex parte and under seal of the court that entered the ex parte order authorizing the installation and use of the device within 30 days after termination of the order, including any extensions thereof.

G. A provider of a wire or electronic communication service, a landlord, custodian or other person who furnishes facilities or technical assistance pursuant to this section shall be reasonably compensated for reasonable and actual expenses incurred in providing such facilities and assistance. The expenses shall be paid out of the criminal fund.

H. No cause of action shall lie in any court against a provider of a wire or electronic communication service, its officers, employees, agents or other specified persons for providing information, facilities, or assistance in accordance with the terms of a court order issued pursuant to this section. Good faith reliance on a court order, a legislative authorization or a statutory authorization is a complete defense against any civil or criminal action based upon a violation of this chapter.

History.
1988, c. 889; 2002, cc. 588, 623; 2005, c. 934.

§ 19.2-70.3. Obtaining records concerning electronic communication service or remote computing service.

A. A provider of electronic communication service or remote computing service, which, for purposes of subdivisions A 2 through A 4, includes a foreign corporation that provides such services, shall disclose a record or other information pertaining to a subscriber to or customer of such service, excluding the contents of electronic communications, to an investigative or law-enforcement officer only pursuant to:

1. A subpoena issued by a grand jury of a court of this Commonwealth;

2. A search warrant issued by a magistrate, general district court or a circuit court;

3. A court order for such disclosure issued as provided in this section; or

4. The consent of the subscriber or customer to such disclosure.

B. A court shall issue an order for disclosure under this section only if the investigative or law-enforcement officer shows that there is reason to believe the records or other information sought are relevant and material to an ongoing criminal investigation, or the investigation of any missing child as defined in § 52-32, missing senior adult as defined in § 52-34.4, or an incapacitated person as defined in § 64.2-2000 who meets the definition of a missing senior adult except for the age requirement. Upon issuance of an order for disclosure under this section, the order and any written application or statement of facts may be sealed by the court for 90 days for good cause shown upon application of the attorney for the Commonwealth in an ex parte proceeding. The order and any written application or statement of facts may be sealed for additional 90-day periods for good cause shown upon subsequent application of the attorney for the Commonwealth in an ex parte proceeding. A court issuing an order pursuant to this section, on a motion made promptly by the service provider, may quash or modify the order, if the information or records requested are unusually voluminous in nature or compliance with such order would otherwise cause an undue burden on such provider.

C. A provider of electronic communication service or remote computing service, including a foreign corporation that provides such services, shall disclose the contents of electronic communications to an investigative or law-enforcement officer only pursuant to a search warrant issued by a magistrate, a juvenile and domestic relations district court, a general district court, or a circuit court, based upon complaint on oath supported by an affidavit as required in § 19.2-54, or judicial officer or court of any of the several states of the United States or its territories, or the District of Columbia when the warrant issued by such officer or such court complies with the provisions of subsection E. In the case of a search warrant directed to a foreign corporation the affidavit shall state that the complainant believes that the records requested are actually or constructively possessed by a foreign corporation that provides electronic communication service or remote computing service within the Commonwealth of Virginia. If satisfied that probable cause has been established for such belief and as required by Chapter 5 (§ 19.2-52 et seq.), the magistrate, the juvenile and domestic relations district court, the general district court, or the circuit court shall issue a warrant identifying those records to be searched for and commanding the person seeking such warrant to properly serve the warrant upon the foreign corporation.

D. In order to comply with the requirements of § 19.2-54, any search of the records of a foreign corporation shall be deemed to have been made in the same place wherein the search warrant was issued.

E. A Virginia corporation or other entity that provides electronic communication services or remote computing services to the general public, when properly served with a search warrant and affidavit in support of the warrant, issued by a judicial officer or court of any of the several states of the United States or its territories, or the District of Columbia with jurisdiction over the matter, to produce a record or other information pertaining to a subscriber to or customer of such service or the contents of electronic communications, or both, shall produce the record or other information or the contents of electronic communications as if that warrant had been issued by a Virginia court. The provisions of this subsection shall only apply to a record or other information or contents of electronic communications relating to the commission of a criminal offense that is substantially similar to (i) a violent felony as defined in § 17.1-805, (ii) an act of violence as defined in § 19.2-297.1, (iii) any offense for which registration is required pursuant to § 9.1-902, (iv) computer fraud pursuant to § 18.2-152.3, or (v) identity theft pursuant to § 18.2-186.3. The search warrant shall be enforced and executed in the Commonwealth as if it were a search warrant described in subsection C.

F. The provider of electronic communication service or remote computing service may verify the authenticity of the written reports or records that it discloses pursuant to this section, excluding the contents of electronic communications, by providing an affidavit from the custodian of those written reports or records or from a person to whom said custodian reports certifying that they are true and complete and that they are prepared in the regular course of business. When so authenticated, the written reports and records are admissible in evidence as a business records exception to the hearsay rule.

G. No cause of action shall lie in any court against a provider of a wire or electronic communication service, its officers, employees, agents, or other specified persons for providing information, facilities, or assistance in accordance with the terms of a court order, warrant or subpoena under this section.

H. For the purposes of this section:

"Foreign corporation" means any corporation or other entity, whose primary place of business is located outside of the boundaries of the Commonwealth, that makes a contract or engages in a terms of service agreement with a resident of the Commonwealth to be performed in whole or in part by either party in the Commonwealth, or a corporation that has been issued a certificate of authority pursuant to § 13.1-759 to transact business in the Commonwealth. The making of the contract or terms of service agreement or the issuance of a certificate of authority shall be considered to be the agreement of the foreign corporation or entity that a search warrant or subpoena, which has been properly served on it, has the same legal force and effect as if served personally within the Commonwealth.

"Properly served" means delivery of a search warrant or subpoena by hand, by United States mail, by commercial delivery service, by facsimile or by any other manner to any officer of a corporation or its general manager in the Commonwealth, to any natural person designated by it as agent for the service of process, or if such corporation has designated a corporate agent, to any person named in the latest annual report filed pursuant to § 13.1-775.

History.
1988, c. 889; 2009, c. 378; 2010, cc. 319, 473, 582, 720, 721; 2011, c. 392.

Editor's note.
At the direction of the Virginia Code Commission, the reference to "37.2-1000" was changed to "64.2-2000" to conform to the recodification of Title 64.1 by Acts 2012, c. 614, effective October 1, 2012.

At the direction of the Virginia Code Commission, subsection E as added by Acts 2010, c. 721, was redesignated as subsection F and the remaining subsections were redesignated accordingly.

The 2009 amendments.
The 2009 amendment by c. 378 substituted "relevant and material to an ongoing criminal investigation" for "relevant to a legitimate law enforcement inquiry" in the first sentence in subsection B; and added subsections C, D, and F; and redesignated former subsection C as subsection E.

The 2010 amendments.
The 2010 amendment by c. 319 inserted "for judicial officer or court of another any of the several states of the United States or its territories, or the District of Columbia when the warrant issued by such officer or such court complies with the provisions of subsection E" at the end of the first sentence of subsection C; added subsection E; and redesignated former subsections C through F as subsections D through G.

The 2010 amendment by c. 473 are nearly the same as c. 319 amendments, but, inserted "or judicial officer or court of any of the several states of the United States or its territories, or the District of Columbia when the warrant issued by such officer or such court complies with the provisions of subsection E" in the first sentence of subsection C; inserted subsection E; and redesignated former subsections E and F as subsections F and G.

Subsection C is set out in the form above at the direction of the Virginia Code Commission.

The 2010 amendment by c. 582 added the language beginning "or the investigation of any missing child" at the end of the first sentence in subsection B.

The 2010 amendment by c. 720 inserted "which, for purposes of subdivisions A 2 through A 4, includes a foreign corporation that provides such services" in the introductory language of subsection A.

The 2010 amendment by c. 721 deleted "The foreign corporation may verify the authenticity of records that it produces by providing an affidavit from the person in custody of those records certifying that they are true and complete." at the end of subsection C; inserted subsection F and redesignated former subsections E and F as subsections G and H.

The 2011 amendments.
The 2011 amendment by c. 392 added the second and third sentences in subsection B.

CASE NOTES

Applicability. — Defendant's motion to suppress was properly denied because, in part, even if a detective violated 18 U.S.C.S. § 2703 and § 19.2-70.3, those statutes did not provide suppression of the evidence in federal court as a remedy. United States v. Clenney, 631 F.3d 658, 2011 U.S. App. LEXIS 2117 (4th Cir. 2011).

CHAPTER 7.
ARREST.

Section
19.2-71. Who may issue process of arrest.

Section

§ 19.2-71. Who may issue process of arrest.

A. Process for the arrest of a person charged with a criminal offense may be issued by the judge, or clerk of any circuit court, any general district court, any juvenile and domestic relations district court, or any magistrate as provided for in Chapter 3 (§ 19.2-26 et seq.) of this title. However, no magistrate may issue an arrest warrant for a felony offense upon the basis of a complaint by a person other than a law-enforcement officer or an animal control officer without prior authorization by the attorney for the Commonwealth or by a law-enforcement agency having jurisdiction over the alleged offense.

B. No law-enforcement officer shall seek issuance of process by any judicial officer, for the arrest of a person for the offense of capital murder as defined in § 18.2-31, without prior authorization by the attorney for the Commonwealth. Failure to comply with the provisions of this subsection shall not be (i) a basis upon which a warrant may be quashed or deemed invalid, (ii) deemed error upon which a conviction or sentence may be reversed or vacated, or (iii) a basis upon which a court may prevent or delay execution of sentence.

History.
Code 1950, § 19.1-90; 1960, c. 366; 1975, c. 495; 1999, c. 266; 2002, c. 310; 2009, cc. 291, 344; 2010, c. 240; 2011, cc. 205, 223.

Editor's note.
Acts 1993, c. 930, cl. 3, as amended by Acts 1994, c. 564, cl. 2, and Acts 1996, c. 616, cl. 4, provides that the amendment to this section by Acts 1993, c. 930, cl. 1, shall become effective June 1, 1998, "if state funds are provided, including all local costs, to carry out the purposes of this bill by the General Assembly." The funding was not provided.

The 2009 amendments.
The 2009 amendments by cc. 291 and 344 are nearly identical, and added the last sentence of subsection A. In addition, c. 291 added "having jurisdiction over the alleged offense" at the end of subsection A. The section is set out in the form above at the direction of the Virginia Code Commission.

The 2010 amendments.
The 2010 amendment by c. 240 inserted "or an animal control officer" following "law-enforcement officer" in the second sentence of subsection A.

The 2011 amendments.
The 2011 amendments by cc. 205 and 223 are identical, and substituted "without prior authorization by the attorney for the Commonwealth or by a law-enforcement agency" for "without prior consultation by the magistrate with the attorney for the Commonwealth or, if no attorney for the Commonwealth is available, without prior consultation with a law-enforcement agency" in subsection A.

Law Review.
For note, "Criminal Procedure and Criminal Law: Virginia Supreme Court Decisions During the 70's," see 15 U. Rich. L. Rev. 585 (1981).

Michie's Jurisprudence.
For related discussion, see 5B M.J. Criminal Procedure, § 19.

CASE NOTES

Applied in Evans v. Sturgill, 430 F. Supp. 1209 (W.D. Va. 1977); Estate of Hackler v. Hackler, 44 Va. App. 51, 602 S.E.2d 426, 2004 Va. App. LEXIS 454 (2004).

OPINIONS OF THE ATTORNEY GENERAL

Show cause summons. — Service of a criminal show cause summons does not constitute an "arrest" or trigger the reporting requirements of § 19.2-390. See opinion of Attorney General to The Honorable Dennis S. Proffitt, Chesterfield County Sheriff, 09-070, 2009 Va. AG LEXIS 48 (10/26/09).

Prosecutorial discretion. — While a prosecutor is permitted to move to amend a misdemeanor charge alleging a violation of a municipal ordinance to the equivalent misdemeanor charge alleging a violation of state law when such an arrest or summons was made by an officer of a local police department or a deputy of a local sheriff's department, any such amendment is subject to judicial review and may be made only by an appropriate judicial officer. See opinion of Attorney General to The Honorable Richard K. Newman, Commonwealth Attorney for the City of Hopewell, 11-080, 2012 Va. AG LEXIS 8 (2/17/12).

§ 19.2-72. When it may issue; what to recite and require.

On complaint of a criminal offense to any officer authorized to issue criminal warrants he shall examine on oath the complainant and any other witnesses, or when such officer shall suspect that an offense punishable otherwise than by a fine has been committed he may, without formal complaint, issue a summons for witnesses and shall examine such witnesses. A written complaint shall be required if the complainant is not a law-enforcement officer. If upon such examination such officer finds that there is probable cause to believe the accused has committed an offense, such officer shall issue a warrant for his arrest, except that no magistrate may issue an arrest warrant for a felony offense upon the basis of a complaint by a person other than a law-enforcement officer or an animal control officer without prior authorization by the attorney for the Commonwealth or by a law-enforcement agency having jurisdiction over the alleged offense. The warrant shall (i) be directed to an appropriate officer or officers, (ii) name the accused or, if his name is unknown, set forth a description by which he can be identified with reasonable certainty, (iii) describe the offense charged with reasonable certainty, (iv) command that the accused be arrested and brought before a court of appropriate jurisdiction in the county, city or town in which the offense was allegedly committed, and (v) be signed by the issuing officer. The warrant shall require the officer to whom it is directed to summon such witnesses as shall be therein named to appear and give evidence on the examination. But in a city or town having a police force, the warrant shall be directed "To any policeman, sheriff or his deputy sheriff of such city (or town)," and shall be executed by the policeman, sheriff or his deputy sheriff into whose hands it shall come or be delivered. A sheriff or his deputy may execute an arrest warrant throughout the county in which he serves and in any city or town surrounded thereby and effect an arrest in any city or town surrounded thereby as a result of a criminal act committed during the execution of such warrant. A jail officer as defined in § 53.1-1 employed at a regional jail or jail farm is authorized to execute a warrant of arrest upon an accused in his jail. The venue for the prosecution of such criminal act shall be the jurisdiction in which the offense occurred.

History.
   Code 1950, § 19.1-91; 1960, c. 366; 1975, c. 495; 1991, c. 420; 2000, c. 170; 2007, c. 412; 2009, cc. 291, 344; 2010, c. 240; 2011, cc. 205, 223; 2013, c. 207.

Cross references.
   As to issuance of summons instead of warrant in certain cases, see § 19.2-73. For constitutional provision as to general warrants, see Va. Const., Art. I, § 10.

The 2007 amendments.
   The 2007 amendment by c. 412, in the next-to-last sentence, inserted "or town" following "and in any city" and "and effect an arrest in any city or town surrounded thereby as a result of a criminal act committed during the execution of such warrant" at the end; and added the last sentence.

The 2009 amendments.
   The 2009 amendments by cc. 291 and 344 are nearly identical, and added the second sentence; and in the third sentence, added

the exception at the end. In addition, c. 291 inserted "having jurisdiction over the alleged offense" at the end of the third sentence. The sentence has been set out in the form above at the direction of the Virginia Code Commission.

The 2010 amendments.
   The 2010 amendment by c. 240 inserted "or an animal control officer" following "a law-enforcement officer" in the third sentence of the paragraph.

The 2011 amendments.
   The 2011 amendments by cc. 205 and 223 are identical, and in the second sentence, deleted "whenever practicable" following "complaint shall be required," and in the third sentence, substituted "without prior authorization by the attorney for the Commonwealth or by a law-enforcement agency" for "without prior consultation by the magistrate with the attorney for the Commonwealth or, if no attorney for the Commonwealth is available, without prior consultation with a law-enforcement agency."

The 2013 amendments.
   The 2013 amendment by c. 207 inserted the next-to-last sentence.

Law Review.
   For note, "Using DNA Profiles to Obtain 'John Doe' Arrest Warrants and Indictments," see 58 Wash. & Lee L. Rev. 1585 (2001).

Michie's Jurisprudence.
   For related discussion, see 2A M.J. Arrest, § 4; 5B M.J. Criminal Procedure, §§ 12, 17; 19 M.J. Warrants, § 2.

CASE NOTES

   Section mandatory. — This section leaves an officer into whose hands a warrant is delivered no choice. The warrant shall be executed by the officer into whose hands it is delivered. Hearn v. Hudson, 549 F. Supp. 949 (W.D. Va. 1982).
   Sufficiency of recitation of offense in warrant. — Warrants of arrest are required to recite the offense charged, but the same particularity is not expected or required as in indictments. Lacey v. Palmer, 93 Va. 159, 24 S.E. 930 (1896). See also Satterfield v. Commonwealth, 105 Va. 867, 52 S.E. 979 (1906).
   Motion by defendants, company and debt collector, for sanctions, attorney's fees, and costs pursuant to Fed. R. Civ. P. 11 and § 1692k(a)(3) of the Fair Debt Collection Practices Act (FDCPA) was granted where plaintiff's contention that the debt collector lacked standing to seek a warrant for her arrest was meritless; Virginia law made clear that any person could lawfully seek to have a criminal warrant issued, and such warrant would issue if the officer investigating the complaint found that there was probable cause to believe that a criminal offense took place. Guidry v. Clare, 442 F. Supp. 2d 282, 2006 U.S. Dist. LEXIS 56447 (E.D. Va. 2006).
   Probation violation. — Fourth Amendment and § 19.2-72 do not require sworn statements for the seizure of a probationer whose sentence to confinement has been suspended based on his failure to comply with specified terms and conditions of his probation. Unsworn written statements under § 53.1-149, which showed that appellant had had only limited contact with probation authorities and that he still owed over $51,000 in restitution, and appellant's failure to comply with a show cause order were a sufficient basis for the trial court to issue a capias for appellant's arrest. Pierce v. Commonwealth, 48 Va. App. 660, 633 S.E.2d 755, 2006 Va. App. LEXIS 407 (2006).
   Applied in Evans v. Sturgill, 430 F. Supp. 1209 (W.D. Va. 1977); Zuniga v. Commonwealth, 7 Va. App. 523, 375 S.E.2d 381 (1988).

CIRCUIT COURT OPINIONS

   False arrest claim failed. — Students' false arrest and false imprisonment claims against a college president failed as there was no allegation implicating the president in any way in the students' arrests, and a magistrate issued warrants for the arrest of the students. Long v. Commonwealth, 2007 Va. Cir. LEXIS 78 (Norfolk Apr. 13, 2007).

OPINIONS OF THE ATTORNEY GENERAL

Withdrawal or dismissal of warrant or summons. — Neither a chief of police nor a Commonwealth's attorney has the authority to unilaterally withdraw or dismiss a lawfully issued arrest warrant or summons. See opinion of Attorney General to The Honorable Ralph B. Robertson, Judge, Richmond General District Court, Criminal Division, 03-025 (5/30/03).

"Unarrest" of lawfully arrested person not authorized. — There is no authority or process by which a police officer or a Commonwealth's attorney may "unarrest" a person who is lawfully arrested on a warrant or summons. See opinion of Attorney General to The Honorable Ralph B. Robertson, Judge, Richmond General District Court, Criminal Division, 03-025 (5/30/03).

§ 19.2-73. Issuance of summons instead of warrant in certain cases.

A. In any misdemeanor case or in any class of misdemeanor cases, or in any case involving complaints made by any state or local governmental official or employee having responsibility for the enforcement of any statute, ordinance or administrative regulation, the magistrate or other issuing authority having jurisdiction may issue a summons instead of a warrant when there is reason to believe that the person charged will appear in the courts having jurisdiction over the trial of the offense charged.

B. If any person under suspicion for driving while intoxicated has been taken to a medical facility for treatment or evaluation of his medical condition, the officer at the medical facility may issue, on the premises of the medical facility, a summons for a violation of § 18.2-266, 18.2-266.1, 18.2-272 or 46.2-341.24 and for refusal of tests in violation of subsection A of § 18.2-268.3 or subsection A of § 46.2-341.26:3, in lieu of securing a warrant and without having to detain that person, provided that the officer has probable cause to place him under arrest. The issuance of such summons shall be deemed an arrest for purposes of Article 2 (§ 18.2-266 et seq.) of Chapter 7 of Title 18.2.

C. Any person on whom such summons is served shall appear on the date set forth in same, and if such person fails to appear in such court at such time and on such date then he shall be treated in accordance with the provisions of § 19.2-128, regardless of the disposition of, and in addition to, the charge upon which he was originally arrested.

History.
Code 1950, § 19.1-146; 1972, c. 461; 1975, c. 495; 1978, c. 500; 1981, c. 382; 2005, c. 425; 2010, c. 840.

Editor's note.
Acts 2010, c. 840, cl. 2, provides: "That the provisions of this act may result in a net increase in periods of imprisonment or commitment. Pursuant to § 30-19.1:4, the estimated amount of the necessary appropriation cannot be determined for periods of imprisonment in state adult correctional facilities; therefore, Chapter 781 of the Acts of Assembly of 2009 requires the Virginia Criminal Sentencing Commission to assign a minimum fiscal impact of $50,000. Pursuant to § 30-19.1:4, the estimated amount of the necessary appropriation is $0 for periods of commitment to the custody of the Department of Juvenile Justice."

The 2010 amendments.
The 2010 amendment by c. 840, in subsection B, in the first sentence, deleted "arresting" preceding "officer" and added "and without having to detain that person, provided that the officer has probable cause to place him under arrest," and added the last sentence.

Law Review.
For annual survey article, "Criminal Law and Procedure," see 46 U. Rich. L. Rev. 59 (2011).

Michie's Jurisprudence.
For related discussion, see 5B M.J. Criminal Procedure, § 12; 11B M.J. Justices and Magistrates, § 33.

CASE NOTES

Constraint. — In a trial on the offense of driving under the influence, the circuit court properly admitted results of a blood test from a sample collected while defendant was in the hospital. Subsection B of § 19.2-73 authorized issuance of a summons, and an arrest followed by a release on a summons satisfied the requirement of "constraining" the arrestee's liberty under the implied consent statutes. Reading §§ 19.2-73 and 19.2-74 in pari materia with the implied consent statute, an arrest followed by a release on summons satisfies the requirement of "constraining" the arrestee's personal liberty, for purposes of implicating the statutory duty to provide a blood or breath sample. Young v. Commonwealth, 57 Va. App. 731, 706 S.E.2d 53, 2011 Va. App. LEXIS 77 (2011).

Applied in Commonwealth v. Rafferty, 241 Va. 319, 402 S.E.2d 17 (1991).

OPINIONS OF THE ATTORNEY GENERAL

Withdrawal or dismissal of warrant or summons. — Neither a chief of police nor a Commonwealth's attorney has the authority to unilaterally withdraw or dismiss a lawfully issued arrest warrant or summons. See opinion of Attorney General to The Honorable Ralph B. Robertson, Judge, Richmond General District Court, Criminal Division, 03-025 (5/30/03).

"Unarrest" of lawfully arrested person not authorized. — There is no authority or process by which a police officer or a Commonwealth's attorney may "unarrest" a person who is lawfully arrested on a warrant or summons. See opinion of Attorney General to The Honorable Ralph B. Robertson, Judge, Richmond General District Court, Criminal Division, 03-025 (5/30/03).

§ 19.2-73.1. Notice of issuance of warrant or summons; appearance; failure to appear.

In any misdemeanor case or in any class of misdemeanor cases and in a Class 5 or Class 6 felony case, the chief of police of the city or county or his designee, or the sheriff or deputy sheriff of the county, if the county has no police department, in which the case is pending may notify the accused of the issuance of the warrant or summons and direct the accused to appear at the time and place directed for the purpose of the execution of the summons or warrant. However, the issuing judicial officer may direct the execution of such process prior to any such notification. If the accused does not appear, then the warrant or summons shall be executed and returned as provided by § 19.2-76.

History.
1979, c. 335; 1991, c. 162; 1993, c. 350.

§ 19.2-73.2. Law-enforcement officers to issue subpoenas; penalty.

Law-enforcement officers as defined in § 9.1-101 and state police officers, in the course of their duties, in the investigation of any Class 3 or Class 4 misdemeanor or any traffic infraction, may, within seventy-two hours of the time of the offense, issue a subpoena to any witness to appear in court and testify with respect to any such criminal charge or traffic infraction brought against any person as a result of such investigation. The return of service thereof shall be made within seventy-two hours after service to the appropriate court clerk. A subpoena so issued shall have the same force and effect as if issued by the court.

Any person failing to appear in response to a subpoena issued as provided in this section shall be punished as provided by law.

History.
  1995, c. 335.

§ 19.2-74. Issuance and service of summons in place of warrant in misdemeanor case; issuance of summons by special policemen and conservators of the peace.

A. 1. Whenever any person is detained by or is in the custody of an arresting officer for any violation committed in such officer's presence which offense is a violation of any county, city or town ordinance or of any provision of this Code punishable as a Class 1 or Class 2 misdemeanor or any other misdemeanor for which he may receive a jail sentence, except as otherwise provided in Title 46.2, or for offenses listed in subsection D of § 19.2-81, or an arrest on a warrant charging an offense for which a summons may be issued, and when specifically authorized by the judicial officer issuing the warrant, the arresting officer shall take the name and address of such person and issue a summons or otherwise notify him in writing to appear at a time and place to be specified in such summons or notice. Upon the giving by such person of his written promise to appear at such time and place, the officer shall forthwith release him from custody. However, if any such person shall fail or refuse to discontinue the unlawful act, the officer may proceed according to the provisions of § 19.2-82.

Anything in this section to the contrary notwithstanding, if any person is believed by the arresting officer to be likely to disregard a summons issued under the provisions of this subsection, or if any person is reasonably believed by the arresting officer to be likely to cause harm to himself or to any other person, a magistrate or other issuing authority having jurisdiction shall proceed according to the provisions of § 19.2-82.

2. Whenever any person is detained by or is in the custody of an arresting officer for a violation of any county, city, or town ordinance or of any provision of this Code, punishable as a Class 3 or Class 4 misdemeanor or any other misdemeanor for which he cannot receive a jail sentence, except as otherwise provided in Title 46.2, or to the offense of public drunkenness as defined in § 18.2-388, the arresting officer shall take the name and address of such person and issue a summons or otherwise notify him in writing to appear at a time and place to be specified in such summons or notice. Upon the giving of such person of his written promise to appear at such time and place, the officer shall forthwith release him from custody. However, if any such person shall fail or refuse to discontinue the unlawful act, the officer may proceed according to the provisions of § 19.2-82.

3. Any person so summoned shall not be held in custody after the issuance of such summons for the purpose of complying with the requirements of Chapter 23 (§ 19.2-387 et seq.) of this title. Reports to the Central Criminal Records Exchange concerning such persons shall be made after a disposition of guilt is entered as provided for in § 19.2-390.

Any person refusing to give such written promise to appear under the provisions of this section shall be taken immediately by the arresting or other police officer before a magistrate or other issuing authority having jurisdiction, who shall proceed according to provisions of § 19.2-82.

Any person who willfully violates his written promise to appear, given in accordance with this section, shall be treated in accordance with the provisions of § 19.2-128, regardless of the disposition of, and in addition to, the charge upon which he was originally arrested.

Any person charged with committing any violation of § 18.2-407 may be arrested and immediately brought before a magistrate who shall proceed as provided in § 19.2-82.

B. Special policemen of the counties as provided in § 15.2-1737, special policemen or conservators of the peace appointed under Chapter 2 (§ 19.2-12 et seq.) of this title and special policemen appointed by authority of a city's charter may issue summonses pursuant to this section, if such officers are in uniform, or displaying a badge of office. On application, the chief law-enforcement officer of the county or city shall supply each officer with a supply of summons forms, for which such officer shall account pursuant to regulation of such chief law-enforcement officer.

C. The summons used by a law-enforcement officer pursuant to this section shall be in form the same as the uniform summons for motor vehicle law violations as prescribed pursuant to § 46.2-388.

History.
  Code 1950, § 19.1-92.1; 1973, c. 98; 1974, c. 481; 1975, c. 495; 1976, c. 753; 1978, c. 500; 1979, cc. 679, 680; 1980, c. 492; 1981, c. 382; 1982, cc. 485, 500; 1984, c. 24; 1988, c. 455; 1995, c. 471; 2010, c. 840.

Cross references.

As to limitation on powers of registered armed security officers, see § 9.1-146. As to punishment for Class 1, Class 2, Class 3, and Class 4 misdemeanors, see § 18.2-11.

Editor's note.

Acts 2010, c. 840, cl. 2, provides: "That the provisions of this act may result in a net increase in periods of imprisonment or commitment. Pursuant to § 30-19.1:4, the estimated amount of the necessary appropriation cannot be determined for periods of imprisonment in state adult correctional facilities; therefore, Chapter 781 of the Acts of Assembly of 2009 requires the Virginia Criminal Sentencing Commission to assign a minimum fiscal impact of $50,000. Pursuant to § 30-19.1:4, the estimated amount of the necessary appropriation is $0 for periods of commitment to the custody of the Department of Juvenile Justice."

The 2010 amendments.

The 2010 amendment by c. 840 substituted "as otherwise provided in Title 46.2, or for offenses listed in subsection D of § 19.2-81" for "as otherwise provided in Title 46.2, or § 18.2-266" in the first sentence in subdivision A 1.

Law Review.

For survey of Virginia criminal law for the year 1978-1979, see 66 Va. L. Rev. 241 (1980). For survey of Virginia criminal law and procedure for the year 2004-2005, see 40 U. Rich. L. Rev. 197 (2005). For 2006 survey article, "Criminal Law and Procedure," see 41 U. Rich. L. Rev. 83 (2006). For 2007 annual survey article, "Criminal Law and Procedure," see 42 U. Rich. L. Rev. 311 (2007).

Michie's Jurisprudence.

For related discussion, see 5B M.J. Criminal Procedure, § 12.

CASE NOTES

Section does not require arresting officers to issue plaintiff a summons instead of executing the warrant by arresting him. Hearn v. Hudson, 549 F. Supp. 949 (W.D. Va. 1982).

Objective standard applied to determine whether statutory circumstances obtain. — Although § 19.2-74 refers to a predictive estimation of the accused person's future conduct, the standard for determining satisfaction of the statute is objective, whether evidence supports a reasonable belief that the statutory circumstances obtain. Fox v. Commonwealth, 43 Va. App. 446, 598 S.E.2d 770, 2004 Va. App. LEXIS 306 (2004).

A police officer is entitled to detain briefly an individual who has committed an offense, in order to obtain information required for the issuance of a summons; the arresting officer had probable cause to charge defendant with violating a city ordinance, "pedestrian in the roadway," and after informing defendant that he intended to issue him a summons, the officer legally detained him. Beale v. Commonwealth, No. 1412-96-1 (Ct. of Appeals Apr. 1, 1997).

This statute does not contemplate a custodial situation equivalent to an actual custodial arrest, and under it, a suspect is detained, or in the custody of the police officer, only long enough for the officer to take down the name and address of the person and issue a summons. Lovelace v. Commonwealth, 258 Va. 588, 522 S.E.2d 856 (1999).

Custodial arrest authorized in certain cases. — Although this section provides that, in misdemeanor cases, an arresting officer shall issue the offender a summons and shall thereafter release the offender from custody, this section in conjunction with § 19.2-82 permits such an officer to effect a warrantless custodial arrest if the offender fails or refuses to discontinue the unlawful act or refuses to give a written promise to appear or if the officer reasonably believes the offender will likely disregard the summons or do harm to himself or others. Commonwealth v. Dickson, No. 2503-00-1, 2001 Va. App. LEXIS 221 (Ct. of Appeals Apr. 23, 2001).

Defendant's custodial arrest complied with § 19.2-74 and a search incident to defendant's arrest complied with the Fourth Amendment as the circumstances supported a belief that defendant was likely to disregard the summons for a Class 1 misdemeanor or that he was a danger to himself or others where defendant fled when the officer exited his vehicle and discarded a concealed handgun as he ran, from which the serial number had been obliterated; whether the arresting officer actually held that belief was immaterial. Fox v. Commonwealth, 43 Va. App. 446, 598 S.E.2d 770, 2004 Va. App. LEXIS 306 (2004).

Custodial arrest authorized where defendant failed to comply with prior court order. — Officer had ample reason to arrest defendant rather than issue summons and release him based on defendant's failure to comply with prior court order that he stay away from certain property; thus, defendant's motion to suppress was properly denied since the subject evidence was found during a search incident to a valid arrest. Ross v. Commonwealth, No. 0342-04-2, 2004 Va. App. LEXIS 637 (Ct. of Appeals Dec. 28, 2004).

Custodial arrest not authorized. — Evidence discovered during a search incident to an arrest should have been suppressed as fruit of the poisonous tree because a full custodial arrest, necessary to justify a search incident to arrest, was not permitted when police stopped defendant and determined he was driving on a suspended license. Moore v. Commonwealth, 45 Va. App. 146, 609 S.E.2d 74, 2005 Va. App. LEXIS 80 (2005), aff'd, — Va. App. —, 622 S.E.2d 253 (2005). But see Virginia v. Moore, — U.S. —, 128 S.Ct. 1598 (2008).

Constraint. — In a trial on the offense of driving under the influence, the circuit court properly admitted results of a blood test from a sample collected while defendant was in the hospital. Subsection B of § 19.2-73 authorized issuance of a summons, and an arrest followed by a release on a summons satisfied the requirement of "constraining" the arrestee's liberty under the implied consent statutes. Reading §§ 19.2-73 and 19.2-74 in pari materia with the implied consent statute, an arrest followed by a release on summons satisfies the requirement of "constraining" the arrestee's personal liberty, for purposes of implicating the statutory duty to provide a blood or breath sample. Young v. Commonwealth, 57 Va. App. 731, 706 S.E.2d 53, 2011 Va. App. LEXIS 77 (2011).

Search pursuant to issuance of citation or summons. — Class 3 and 4 misdemeanors are similar in nature and duration to a traffic stop and do not contemplate a custodial situation equivalent to an actual custodial arrest. Thus, an "arrest" that is effected by issuing a citation or summons rather than taking the suspect into custody does not, by itself, justify a full field-type search. However, such an encounter between police and an individual may involve some degree of danger to the officer or need to preserve or discover evidence sufficient to warrant an additional intrusion. Farrow v. Commonwealth, 31 Va. App. 517, 525 S.E.2d 11 (2000).

When an officer "arrested" defendant for trespass he did not use the correct procedure, under § 19.2-74, when he placed her in custody, rather than issuing her a summons, because trespass was a class 1 misdemeanor, but, if there was a statutory violation, it did not require that evidence seized from defendant in a search incident to her arrest be suppressed, because exclusion of evidence was not an available remedy for a statutory violation, where no constitutional violation occurred. Coppedge v. Commonwealth, No. 2920-03-1, 2005 Va. App. LEXIS 23 (Ct. of Appeals Jan. 18, 2005).

Search incident to an arrest. — Where officers had reason to believe that defendant was driving on a suspended license, they had probable cause to arrest defendant, and thus, even though the arrest violated § 19.2-74, the arrest, and the search incident to that arrest, did not violate the Fourth Amendment; since there was no Fourth Amendment violation, the exclusionary rule did not apply, and since § 19.2-74 did not provide for exclusion of evidence retrieved from a search subsequent to that arrest, the trial court did not err in refusing to suppress evidence recovered during a search incident to defendant's arrest. Moore v. Commonwealth, 47 Va. App. 55, 622 S.E.2d 253, 2005 Va. App. LEXIS 536 (2005). See also the following note.

Police officers were authorized to issue only a summons to defendant for driving with a suspended license, since none of the exceptions in § 19.2-74 were present. Therefore, the officers' full field-type search of defendant's person after improperly arresting him violated his rights, since the "search incident to arrest" exception to the Fourth Amendment did not include a "search incident to citation." Moore v. Commonwealth, 272 Va. 717, 636 S.E.2d 395, 2006 Va. LEXIS 99 (2006), rev'd, remanded, 553 U.S. 164, 128 S. Ct. 1598, 2008 U.S. LEXIS 3674, 170 L. Ed. 2d 559 (U.S. 2008) rev'd, Virginia v. Moore, — U.S. —, 128 S.Ct. 1598 (2008) (see the following note).

Warrantless arrest for driving with a suspended license was reasonable under the Fourth Amendment, even if it was not permitted under § 19.2-74. Therefore, the crack cocaine and cash that the arrestee was carrying and that was discovered in a search incidental to the arrest did not need to be suppressed. Virginia v. Moore, 553 U.S. 164, 128 S. Ct. 1598, 170 L. Ed. 2d 559, 2008 U.S. LEXIS 3674 (2008).

Denial of defendant's motion to suppress was proper as defendant was arrested for trespassing under § 18.2-119, and the Fourth Amendment's exclusionary rule did not require the exclusion of the evidence seized from defendant during a search incident to a valid seizure for a misdemeanor violation for which § 19.2-74 required release on a summons. Simmons v. Commonwealth, 2008 Va. App. LEXIS 360 (July 29, 2008).

Issuance of summons to appear. — Traffic summons was one type of public record as an officer took the name and address of a person who had committed a crime and issued a summons to appear at a time and place to be specified in such summons, under § 19.2-74 A. 1. and 2., and the person then gave his written promise to appear at such time and place before the officer released him from custody, and any person refusing to give such written promise to appear under the provisions of § 19.2-74 was to be taken immediately by the arresting or other police officer before a magistrate or other issuing authority having jurisdiction, under § 19.2-74 A. 3. Hines v. Commonwealth, 39 Va. App. 752, 576 S.E.2d 781, 2003 Va. App. LEXIS 92 (2003).

Failure to raise argument in the trial court. — Ends of justice exception to Va. Sup. Ct. R. 5A:18 did not excuse defendant's failure to raise in the trial court the argument that defendant could not be convicted of obstructing justice because defendant was authorized to resist an unlawful arrest as the claimed error was not clear, substantial, and material. The trial court made an express finding that defendant's attempt to flee gave officers reason to believe, for purposes of § 19.2-74, that defendant was a flight risk. Coleman v. Commonwealth, 2008 Va. App. LEXIS 463 (Oct. 14, 2008).

Applied in Fisher v. Washington Metro. Area Transit Auth., 690 F.2d 1133 (4th Cir. 1982); Addison v. Commonwealth, 224 Va. 713, 299 S.E.2d 521 (1983); Coston v. Commonwealth, 29 Va. App. 350, 512 S.E.2d 158 (1999); West v. Commonwealth, 36 Va. App. 237, 549 S.E.2d 605, 2001 Va. App. LEXIS 432 (2001).

CIRCUIT COURT OPINIONS

Custodial arrest authorized in certain cases. — Petitioner's custodial arrest for the misdemeanor offense of public drunkenness complied with this section and the Fourth Amendment because this section specifically excludes the offense of public drunkenness from its release from custody requirement and permits police to make custodial arrests of intoxicated persons and to search or question those persons incident to that arrest. Petitioner was taken into custody "for his safety" and officers could not release him where he was extremely intoxicated, his father had requested that he be removed from the father's home, and they had probable cause to arrest him for the murder of his wife. Hudson v. Dir. of the Dep't of Corr., 67 Va. Cir. 319, 2005 Va. Cir. LEXIS 147 (Clarke County May 16, 2005).

Where, after stopping defendant for speeding, an officer learned that defendant had committed his third driving under suspension violation, subdivision A 1 of this section applied; since defendant had repeatedly refused to cease his unlawful activity, the officer appropriately exercised his discretion in arresting defendant, and a subsequent search of the passenger compartment of the vehicle was constitutional. Commonwealth v. Williams, 68 Va. Cir. 265, 2005 Va. Cir. LEXIS 198 (Charlottesville July 19, 2005).

No probable cause for arrest. — As an officer did not and could not arrest defendant for the misdemeanor offense of possession of marijuana based on the marijuana found in defendant's car pursuant to a consent search, and as defendant withdrew his consent to a search of his person (including his wallet) before the officer found any incriminating evidence, the officer's search of defendant's wallet violated defendant's rights under U.S. Const., Amend. IV, and the methampetamine tablets found in the wallet were sup-

pressed. Commonwealth v. Johnson, 84 Va. Cir. 518, 2012 Va. Cir. LEXIS 108 (Augusta County June 15, 2012).

Suspended statements from illegal detention. — After a summons was issued, the defendant should have been free to leave a traffic stop and, where police lacked reasonable suspicion that he was acting illegally, his detention was an illegal seizure and any statements had to be suppressed. Commonwealth v. Hooks, 61 Va. Cir. 720, 2002 Va. Cir. LEXIS 312 (Fairfax County 2002).

§ 19.2-74.1. Repealed by Acts 1981, c. 382.

§ 19.2-75. Copy of process to be left with accused; exception.

Except as provided in § 46.2-936, any process issued against a person charged with a criminal offense shall be in duplicate and the officer serving such process shall leave a copy with the person charged.

History.
   Code 1950, § 19.1-92; 1960, c. 366; 1975, c. 495.

Michie's Jurisprudence.
   For related discussion, see 5B M.J. Criminal Procedure, § 23; 19 M.J. Warrants, § 4.

CASE NOTES

Purpose of section. — The purpose of requiring a copy of a criminal process to be left with a defendant is to inform him of the specific charge made against him so that he may intelligently prepare his defense. Dorchincoz v. Commonwealth, 191 Va. 33, 59 S.E.2d 863 (1950); Gooch v. City of Lynchburg, 201 Va. 172, 110 S.E.2d 236 (1959); Hammer v. Commonwealth, 207 Va. 135, 148 S.E.2d 878 (1966).

This section merely provides for the service of process against a person charged with a criminal offense once process is actually issued. It is not directed to or intended to be determinative of whether or not written notice or warrant must be issued before an accused may be tried for a misdemeanor. Gooch v. City of Lynchburg, 201 Va. 172, 110 S.E.2d 236 (1959).

This section does not apply to an indictment. Rose v. Commonwealth, 189 Va. 771, 55 S.E.2d 33 (1949).

Compliance with the section is not jurisdictional, and objection to noncompliance is waived if not taken advantage of at the trial. Rose v. Commonwealth, 189 Va. 771, 55 S.E.2d 33 (1949).

But is presumed. — Where there is no showing that the accused did not receive a copy of the original process under which he was apprehended, the presumption is that this section was complied with. Rose v. Commonwealth, 189 Va. 771, 55 S.E.2d 33 (1949).

Failure to comply is not necessarily reversible error. — While it is the duty of the arresting officer to comply with this section, his failure to do so does not constitute reversible error unless it affirmatively appears that defendant was prejudiced thereby. Dorchincoz v. Commonwealth, 191 Va. 33, 59 S.E.2d 863 (1950); Hammer v. Commonwealth, 207 Va. 135, 148 S.E.2d 878 (1966).

Failure to leave duplicate copy of process was not reversible under the facts of the case. Dorchincoz v. Commonwealth, 191 Va. 33, 59 S.E.2d 863 (1950).

Formal warrant unnecessary when summons is issued under former § 46.1-178 (now § 46.2-936). — The clear and necessary implication to be drawn from this section, when read along with former § 46.1-178 (now § 46.2-936), which provides for the issuance of a summons for misdemeanors under former Title 46.1 (now Title 46.2), is that when a summons is issued under former § 46.1-178 (now § 46.2-936) there is no need for the issuance or service of a formal warrant. Tate v. Lamb, 195 Va. 1005, 81 S.E.2d 743 (1954).

§ 19.2-76. Execution and return of warrant, capias or summons; arrest outside county or city where charge is to be tried.

A law-enforcement officer may execute within his jurisdiction a warrant, capias or summons issued anywhere in the Commonwealth. A jail officer as defined in § 53.1-1 employed at a regional jail or jail farm may execute upon a person being held in his jail a warrant, capias or summons issued anywhere in the Commonwealth. A warrant or capias shall be executed by the arrest of the accused, and a summons shall be executed by delivering a copy to the accused personally.

If the accused is a corporation, partnership, unincorporated association or legal entity other than an individual, a summons may be executed by service on the entity in the same manner as provided in Title 8.01 for service of process on that entity in a civil proceeding. However, if the summons is served on the entity by delivery to a registered agent or to any other agent who is not an officer, director, managing agent or employee of the entity, such agent shall not be personally subject to penalty for failure to appear as provided in § 19.2-128, nor shall the agent be subject to punishment for contempt for failure to appear under his summons as provided in § 19.2-129.

The law-enforcement officer or jail officer executing a warrant or capias shall endorse the date of execution thereon and make return thereof to a judicial officer. The law-enforcement officer executing a summons shall endorse the date of execution thereon and make return thereof to the court to which the summons is returnable.

Whenever a person is arrested upon a warrant or capias in a county or city other than that in which the charge is to be tried, the law-enforcement officer or jail officer making the arrest shall either (i) bring the accused forthwith before a judicial officer in the locality where the arrest was made or where the charge is to be tried or (ii) commit the accused to the custody of an officer from the county or city where the charge is to be tried who shall bring the accused forthwith before a judicial officer in the county or city in which the charge is to be tried. The judicial officer before whom the accused is brought shall immediately conduct a bail hearing and either admit the accused to bail or commit him to jail for transfer forthwith to the county or city where the charge is to be tried.

History.

Code 1950, §§ 19.1-98, 19.1-99; 1960, c. 366; 1975, c. 495; 1979, c. 661; 1993, c. 431; 1994, c. 933; 1997, c. 10; 1998, c. 615; 2013, c. 207.

Cross references.

As to summons for use of toll facility without payment of toll, see § 46.2-819.3.

The 2013 amendments.

The 2013 amendment by c. 207 inserted the second sentence in the first paragraph; and inserted "or jail officer" in the first sentence of the third and fourth paragraphs.

Michie's Jurisprudence.

For related discussion, see 5B M.J. Criminal Procedure, §§ 13, 17, 19; 19 M.J. Warrants, § 4.

CASE NOTES

Section is absolutely unambiguous on how the officer is to execute the warrant. Hearn v. Hudson, 549 F. Supp. 949 (W.D. Va. 1982).

An accused may waive irregularities in the warrant of his arrest, and where he has done so, and the justice has jurisdiction of his person and of the offense with which he is charged, and hears the charge on its merits, the judgment of the justice is final and conclusive, and the guilt or innocence of the accused of that charge can never again be called in question. Jones v. Morris, 97 Va. 43, 33 S.E. 377 (1899).

Arresting officer's failure to take defendant before a magistrate in the county or corporation in which the accused was arrested, as required by this section, was a mere procedural violation of this section which did not prejudice defendant and which did not involve an error of constitutional dimension giving rise to an application of the exclusionary rule. Tharp v. Commonwealth, 221 Va. 487, 270 S.E.2d 752 (1980).

Effect of delay in taking defendant before magistrate. — Where defendant was legally seized and constitutionally detained, delay in taking him before a magistrate did not mean that the probable cause to hold him for the crimes stated in the warrants somehow evaporated, so as to require exclusion of the evidence developed during his detention. Horne v. Commonwealth, 230 Va. 512, 339 S.E.2d 186 (1986).

In the Commonwealth, not every violation of the requirement that a suspect be taken before a magistrate without unnecessary delay results in the exclusion of evidence. Horne v. Commonwealth, 230 Va. 512, 339 S.E.2d 186 (1986).

Where defendant was unlawfully arrested in Berryville, subsequently held in custody on Fairfax County warrants and ultimately transported to Fairfax County where he was admitted to bail, the failure of Berryville or Fairfax County officers to take him before a magistrate in Clarke County violated the clear directive in this section. However, the failure to abide by the statute was a mere procedural violation which did not involve an error of constitutional dimension giving rise to an application of the exclusionary rule. The delay in taking defendant before a magistrate, although a patent violation of statute, did not abridge his Eighth Amendment rights. Terrell v. Commonwealth, No. 0230-85 (Ct. of Appeals Oct. 10, 1986).

The clear legislative mandate in this section was not followed, where from the time Berryville officers took defendant into custody, at some time after 1:00 p.m., until the Fairfax County officers arrived at approximately 5:15 p.m., defendant was not taken before a magistrate. Given the affirmative obligation on law-enforcement officers imposed by this section, the Commonwealth bore the burden of showing the unavailability of such official. Therefore, Berryville officers violated this section. The Fairfax County officers also violated this section when they took custody of defendant and transported him back to their jurisdiction without first taking him before a magistrate in Clarke County. Terrell v. Commonwealth, No. 0230-85 (Ct. of Appeals Oct. 10, 1986).

Applied in Rowe v. Grizzard, 591 F. Supp. 389 (E.D. Va. 1984).

CIRCUIT COURT OPINIONS

Procedural error. — Arresting officer's failure to take defendant before a magistrate in the county or corporation in which the accused was arrested as required by this section was a mere procedural error and suppression of evidence and statements was not warranted as a result. Commonwealth v. Arava, 56 Va. Cir. 240, 2001 Va. Cir. LEXIS 133 (Arlington County 2001).

OPINIONS OF THE ATTORNEY GENERAL

Absent consent of a dwelling owner, a law-enforcement officer must obtain a warrant before entering a dwelling for the purpose of serving a summons for a misdemeanor. See opinion of Attorney General to The Honorable Gary W. Waters, Sheriff for the City of Portsmouth, 03-064 (9/16/03).

Execution of criminal warrants. — Officers of a regional jail do not have the authority to execute criminal warrants in the jail. See opinion of Attorney General to The Honorable Roy F. Evans, Jr., Commonwealth's Attorney for Smyth County, 06-005 (3/22/06).

Show cause summons. — Service of a criminal show cause summons does not constitute an "arrest" or trigger the reporting requirements of § 19.2-390. See opinion of Attorney General to The Honorable Dennis S. Proffitt, Chesterfield County Sheriff, 09-070, 2009 Va. AG LEXIS 48 (10/26/09).

§ 19.2-76.1. Submission of quarterly reports concerning unexecuted felony and misdemeanor warrants and other criminal process; destruction; dismissal.

It shall be the duty of the chief law-enforcement officer of the police department or sheriff's office, whichever is responsible for such service, in each county, town or city of the Commonwealth to submit quarterly reports to the attorney for the Commonwealth for the county, town or city concerning unexecuted felony and misdemeanor arrest warrants, summonses, capiases or other unexecuted criminal processes as hereinafter provided. The reports shall list those existing felony arrest warrants in his possession that have not been executed within seven years of the date of issuance, those misdemeanor arrest warrants, summonses and capiases and other criminal processes in his possession that have not been executed within three years from the date of issuance, and those unexecuted misdemeanor arrest warrants, summonses and capiases in his possession that were issued for a now deceased person, based on mistaken identity or as a result of any other technical or legal error. The reports shall be submitted in writing no later than the tenth day of April, July, October, and January of each year, together with the unexecuted felony and misdemeanor warrants, or other unexecuted criminal processes listed therein. Upon receipt of the report and the warrants listed therein, the attorney for the Commonwealth shall petition the circuit court of the county or city for the destruction of such unexecuted felony and misdemeanor warrants, summonses, capiases or other unexecuted criminal processes. The attorney for the Commonwealth may petition that certain of the unexecuted warrants, summonses, capiases and other unexecuted criminal processes not be destroyed based upon justifiable continuing, active investigation of the cases. The circuit court shall order the destruction of each such unexecuted felony warrant and each unexecuted misdemeanor warrant, summons, capias and other criminal process except (i) any warrant which charges capital murder and (ii) any unexecuted criminal process whose preservation is deemed justifiable by the court. No arrest shall be made under the authority of any warrant or other process which has been ordered destroyed pursuant to this section. Nothing in this section shall be construed to relate to or affect the time within which a prosecution for a felony or a misdemeanor shall be commenced.

Notwithstanding the foregoing, an attorney for the Commonwealth may at any time move for the dismissal and destruction of any unexecuted warrant or summons issued by a magistrate upon presentation of such warrant or summons to the court in which the warrant or summons would otherwise be returnable. The court shall not order the dismissal and destruction of any warrant which charges capital murder and shall not order the dismissal and destruction of an unexecuted criminal process whose preservation is deemed justifiable by the court. Dismissal of such a warrant or summons shall be without prejudice.

As used herein, the term "chief law-enforcement officer" refers to the chiefs of police of cities, counties and towns and sheriffs of cities and counties, unless a political subdivision has otherwise designated its chief law-enforcement officer by appropriate resolution or ordinance, in which case the local designation shall be controlling.

History.
1976, c. 252; 1979, c. 34; 1982, c. 608; 1985, c. 199; 1990, c. 626; 1991, c. 542; 1993, c. 550; 2003, c. 147; 2010, c. 652; 2011, cc. 336, 347.

The 2010 amendments.
The 2010 amendment by c. 652 inserted the second paragraph.

The 2011 amendments.
The 2011 amendments by cc. 336 and 347 are identical, and in the second paragraph, inserted "and destruction" in the first sentence and added the second sentence.

CASE NOTES

Validity of capias. — Even if the capias at issue was subject to being destroyed under § 19.2-76.1 as more than three years old, because it had not in fact been ordered destroyed, it remained valid for purposes of providing the authority to arrest defendant for a probation violation. Boone v. Commonwealth, 60 Va. App. 419, 728 S.E.2d 517, 2012 Va. App. LEXIS 241 (2012).

OPINIONS OF THE ATTORNEY GENERAL

"Unarrest" of lawfully arrested person not authorized. — There is no authority or process by which a police officer or a Commonwealth's attorney may "unarrest" a person who is lawfully arrested on a warrant or summons. See opinion of Attorney General to The Honorable Ralph B. Robertson, Judge, Richmond General District Court, Criminal Division, 03-025 (5/30/03).

§ 19.2-76.2. Mailing of summons in certain cases.

Notwithstanding the provisions of § 19.2-76, whenever a summons for a violation of a county, city or town parking ordinance is served in any county, city or town it may be executed by mailing by first-class mail a copy thereof to the address of the owner of the vehicle as shown on the records of the Department of Motor Vehicles. In addition, whenever a summons for a violation of a county, city or town trash ordinance punishable as a misdemeanor under § 15.2-901 is served in any county, city or town, it may be executed by mailing a copy by first-class mail to the person who occupies the subject premises. If the person fail to appear on the date of return set out in the summons mailed pursuant to this section, the summons shall be executed in the manner set out in § 19.2-76.3 of this Code.

No proceedings for contempt or arrest of a person summoned by mailing shall be instituted for his failure to appear on the return date of the summons.

History.
1977, c. 233; 1978, c. 781; 1983, c. 254; 1984, c. 119.

OPINIONS OF THE ATTORNEY GENERAL

Withdrawal or dismissal of warrant or summons. — Neither a chief of police nor a Commonwealth's attorney has the authority to unilaterally withdraw or dismiss a lawfully issued arrest warrant or summons. See opinion of Attorney General to The Honorable Ralph B. Robertson, Judge, Richmond General District Court, Criminal Division, 03-025 (5/30/03).

§ 19.2-76.3. Failure to appear on return date for summons issued under § 19.2-76.2.

A. If any person fails to appear on the date of the return contained in the summons issued in accordance with § 19.2-76.2, then a summons shall be delivered to the sheriff of the county, city or town for service on that person as set out in § 8.01-296.

B. If such person then fails to appear on the date of return as contained in the summons so issued, a summons shall be executed in the manner set out in § 19.2-76.

C. No proceedings for contempt or arrest of any person summoned under the provisions of this section shall be instituted unless such person has been personally served with a summons and has failed to appear on the return date contained therein.

History.
1983, c. 254; 1994, c. 642.

§ 19.2-77. Escape, flight and pursuit; arrest anywhere in Commonwealth.

Whenever a person in the custody of an officer shall escape or whenever a person shall flee from an officer attempting to arrest him, such officer, with or without a warrant, may pursue such person anywhere in the Commonwealth and, when actually in close pursuit, may arrest him wherever he is found. If the arrest is made in a county or city adjoining that from which the accused fled, or in any area of the Commonwealth within one mile of the boundary of the county or city from which he fled, the officer may forthwith return the accused before the proper official of the county or city from which he fled. If the arrest is made beyond the foregoing limits, the officer shall proceed according to the provisions of § 19.2-76, and if such arrest is made without a

warrant, the officer shall procure a warrant from the magistrate serving the county or city wherein the arrest was made, charging the accused with the offense committed in the county or city from which he fled.

History.
Code 1950, § 19.1-94; 1960, c. 366; 1975, c. 495; 1992, c. 881; 2008, cc. 551, 691.

Cross references.
As to jurisdiction and authority of special police officers, see § 15.2-1744. As to warrants for escaped patients of state hospital, see §§ 37.2-834 and 37.2-835.

The 2008 amendments.
The 2008 amendments by cc. 551 and 691 are identical and substituted "magistrate serving the county" for "magistrate of the county" in the last sentence.

Law Review.
For survey of Virginia law on criminal procedure for the year 1972-1973, see 59 Va. L. Rev. 1478 (1973).

Michie's Jurisprudence.
For related discussion, see 2A M.J. Arrest, § 7; 16 M.J. Searches and Seizures, § 7.

CASE NOTES

"Close pursuit" is a relative term and has reference to time or distance, or both, depending on the facts of the case. Callands v. Commonwealth, 208 Va. 340, 157 S.E.2d 198 (1967); Reyes v. Slayton, 331 F. Supp. 325 (W.D. Va. 1971).

Close pursuit is pursuit instituted immediately and with intent to recapture or reclaim, as where a thief is fleeing with stolen goods. Reyes v. Slayton, 331 F. Supp. 325 (W.D. Va. 1971). Officer was in "close pursuit" where he was directly behind defendant the entire time he followed him, and he activated his lights as soon as it was safe to pull defendant over. Hamm v. City of Norton, No. 1607-98-3 (Ct. of Appeals Sept. 28, 1999).

Failure to heed officer's lights and siren constituted flight. — Under the facts, where defendant disregarded the officer's pursuit and his emergency lights and siren and attempted to find refuge beyond the officer's jurisdiction, his failure to heed the officer's lights and siren constituted flight from an attempt to arrest; the fact that defendant was not speeding or was not driving so as to elude officer did not mean that he was not fleeing from officer. Neiss v. Commonwealth, 16 Va. App. 807, 433 S.E.2d 262 (1993).

OPINIONS OF THE ATTORNEY GENERAL

Absent consent of a dwelling owner, a law-enforcement officer must obtain a warrant before entering a dwelling for the purpose of serving a summons for a misdemeanor. See opinion of Attorney General to The Honorable Gary W. Waters, Sheriff for the City of Portsmouth, 03-064 (9/16/03).

§ 19.2-78. Uniform of officer making arrest.

All officers whose duties are to make arrests acting under the authority of any law of this Commonwealth or any subdivision thereof, who shall make any arrest, search or seizure on any public road or highway of this Commonwealth shall be dressed at the time of making any such arrest, search or seizure in such uniform as he may customarily wear in the performance of his duties which will clearly show him to casual observation to be an officer.

Nothing in this section shall render unlawful any arrest, search or seizure by an officer who is not in such customary uniform.

History.
Code 1950, §§ 19.1-95, 19.1-96; 1960, c. 366; 1975, c. 495.

Cross references.
As to unlawful wearing of officer's uniform, see § 18.2-175. For provisions concerning adoption of uniforms for State Police, see §§ 52-9.1 and 52-9.2.

§ 19.2-79. Arrest by officers of other states of United States.

Any member of a duly organized state, county or municipal peace unit of another state of the United States who enters this Commonwealth in close pursuit, and continues within this Commonwealth in such close pursuit, of a person in order to arrest him on the ground that he has committed a felony in such other state shall have the same authority to arrest and hold in custody such person as members of a duly organized state, county or municipal peace unit of this Commonwealth have to arrest and hold in custody a person on the ground that he has committed a felony in this Commonwealth, if the state from which such person has fled extends similar privileges to any member of a duly organized state, county or municipal peace unit of this Commonwealth.

If an arrest is made in this Commonwealth by an officer of another state in accordance with the provisions of the first paragraph of this section, he shall without unnecessary delay take the person arrested before a judge of a general district court, or of the circuit court, of the county or city in which the arrest was made, who shall conduct a hearing for the purpose of determining the lawfulness of the arrest. If the judge determines that the arrest was lawful he shall commit the person arrested to await for a reasonable time the issuance of an extradition warrant by the Governor. If the judge determines that the arrest was unlawful he shall discharge the person arrested.

The first paragraph of this section shall not be construed so as to make unlawful any arrest in this Commonwealth which would otherwise be lawful.

For the purpose of this section the word "State" shall include the District of Columbia.

History.
Code 1950, § 19.1-97; 1960, c. 366; 1975, c. 495.

Law Review.
For essay, "In the Aftermath of Soering, Is Interstate Extradition to Virginia Illegal?", see 48 Wash. & Lee L. Rev. 1477 (1991).

Michie's Jurisprudence.
For related discussion, see 2A M.J. Arrest, § 7; 5B M.J. Criminal Procedure, §§ 13, 17.

§ 19.2-80. Duty of arresting officer; bail.

In any case in which an officer does not issue a summons pursuant to § 19.2-74 or § 46.2-936, a law-enforcement officer making an arrest under a warrant or capias shall bring the arrested person without unnecessary delay before a judicial officer. The judicial officer shall immediately conduct a bail hearing and either admit the accused to bail or commit him to jail. However, if (i) the accused is charged with a misdemeanor and is brought before a judge of the court having jurisdiction to try the case and (ii) both the accused and the Commonwealth consent, the judge may proceed to trial instead of conducting a bail hearing.

History.
Code 1950, § 19.1-98; 1960, c. 366; 1975, c. 495; 1979, c. 679; 1986, c. 327; 1997, c. 10.

Michie's Jurisprudence.
For related discussion, see 5B M.J. Criminal Procedure, §§ 13, 14, 17, 19.

CASE NOTES

Term "forthwith," as used in § 19.2-82, is synonymous with standard used in this section, and the same remedies for a violation of this section should apply to a violation of § 19.2-82. Slade v. Commonwealth, No. 0786-85 (Ct. of Appeals Feb. 4, 1987).

Officer cannot hold prisoner unreasonable time before making return. — Under this section there must be a reasonable time allowed for making return of the warrant of arrest, and some latitude must be given the officers in keeping a prisoner in custody after he has been arrested and before he is taken to the justice. But it is not permissible to trifle with him, and detain and interrogate him, for the ulterior purpose of extracting a confession as to his own guilt, or getting information from him as to the guilt of others, and it matters not at all that the process of arrest was in its inception regular and valid, and that it was obtained on probable cause. Sands & Co. v. Norvell, 126 Va. 384, 101 S.E. 569 (1919).

False imprisonment may result not only from the arrest of a person without any valid warrant, but also from the unlawful detention of a prisoner who has been lawfully arrested. Unreasonable delay in presenting a prisoner for examination or trial, and a fortiori mistreatment after arrest followed by release without any hearing before the magistrate, are instances in point. Sands & Co. v. Norvell, 126 Va. 384, 101 S.E. 569 (1919).

Statement admissible despite delay. — Failure promptly to present a defendant as required by this section is a mere procedural violation where it involves no constitutional error, thus, a statement obtained without infringing constitutional safeguards is admissible. Alatishe v. Commonwealth, 12 Va. App. 376, 404 S.E.2d 81 (1991).

Even where appeals court assumed without deciding that the delay in bringing a defendant before the magistrate violated § 19.2-80, such violation did not require exclusion of his statements. Lewis v. Commonwealth, No. 3064-01-1, 2002 Va. App. LEXIS 640 (Ct. of Appeals Oct. 22, 2002).

Where defendant was taken before a magistrate only 15 minutes after his arrest, evidence obtained pertaining to the case should not have been suppressed as the product of a violation of this section. Pearson v. Commonwealth, 221 Va. 936, 275 S.E.2d 893 (1981).

Appearance before magistrate did not constitute hearing contemplated by this section. — Where plaintiff who had served sentence was arrested under bench warrant mistakenly issued for failure to serve such sentence, appearance before night magistrate who did nothing beyond signing a form committing the plaintiff to jail, did not constitute the advertisement hearing contemplated by this section. McDonald v. Dunning, 760 F. Supp. 1156 (E.D. Va. 1991).

OPINIONS OF THE ATTORNEY GENERAL

Bringing arrestee to magistrate's office. — There is no requirement that law-enforcement officer bring arrestee to nearest magistrate's office. See opinion of Attorney General to The Honorable Danny R. Fox, Sheriff for Mecklenburg County, 04-015 (4/13/04).

§ 19.2-80.1. When arrested person operating motor vehicle; how vehicle removed from scene of arrest.

In any case in which a police officer arrests the operator of a motor vehicle and there is no legal cause for the retention of the motor vehicle by the officer, the officer shall allow the person arrested to designate another person who is present at the scene of the arrest and a licensed driver to drive the motor vehicle from the scene to a place designated by the person arrested. If such a designation is not made, the officer may cause the vehicle to be taken to the nearest appropriate place for safekeeping.

History.
  1981, c. 306.

CASE NOTES

Police had legitimate reason to impound and inventory vehicle where there was no other licensed driver present at the scene who could have been designated by the defendant to drive the vehicle. Butler v. Commonwealth, 31 Va. App. 614, 525 S.E.2d 58 (2000).

§ 19.2-80.2. Duty of arresting officer; providing magistrate or court with criminal history information.

In any case in which an officer proceeds under §§ 19.2-76, 19.2-80 and 19.2-82, such officer shall, to the extent possible, obtain and provide the magistrate or court with the arrested person's criminal history information prior to any proceeding under Article 1 (§ 19.2-119 et seq.) of Chapter 9 of this title. A pretrial services agency established pursuant to § 19.2-152.2 may, in lieu of the arresting officer, provide the criminal history to the magistrate or court.

History.
  1999, cc. 829, 846; 2007, c. 133.

The 2007 amendments.
  The 2007 amendment by c. 133, in the last sentence, substituted "pretrial services agency" for "pretrial services program" and "§ 19.2-152.2" for "§ 19.2-152.4."

§ 19.2-81. Arrest without warrant authorized in certain cases.

A. The following officers shall have the powers of arrest as provided in this section:
  1. Members of the State Police force of the Commonwealth;
  2. Sheriffs of the various counties and cities, and their deputies;
  3. Members of any county police force or any duly constituted police force of any city or town of the Commonwealth;

  4. The Commissioner, members and employees of the Marine Resources Commission granted the power of arrest pursuant to § 28.2-900;
  5. Regular conservation police officers appointed pursuant to § 29.1-200;
  6. United States Coast Guard and United States Coast Guard Reserve commissioned, warrant, and petty officers authorized under § 29.1-205 to make arrests;
  7. The special policemen of the counties as provided by § 15.2-1737, provided such officers are in uniform, or displaying a badge of office;
  8. Conservation officers appointed pursuant to § 10.1-115;
  9. Full-time sworn members of the enforcement division of the Department of Motor Vehicles appointed pursuant to § 46.2-217;
  10. Special agents of the Department of Alcoholic Beverage Control; and
  11. Campus police officers appointed under Chapter 17 (§ 23-232 et seq.) of Title 23.

B. Such officers may arrest without a warrant any person who commits any crime in the presence of the officer and any person whom he has reasonable grounds or probable cause to suspect of having committed a felony not in his presence.

Such officers may arrest without a warrant any person whom the officer has probable cause to suspect of operating any watercraft or motorboat while (i) intoxicated in violation of subsection B of § 29.1-738 or a substantially similar ordinance of any county, city, or town in the Commonwealth or (ii) in violation of an order issued pursuant to § 29.1-738.4 and may thereafter transfer custody of the person arrested to another officer, who may obtain a warrant based upon statements made to him by the arresting officer.

C. **(Effective until July 1, 2014)** Any such officer may, at the scene of any accident involving a motor vehicle, watercraft as defined in § 29.1-712 or motorboat, or at any hospital or medical facility to which any person involved in such accident has been transported, or in the apprehension of any person charged with the theft of any motor vehicle, on any of the highways or waters of the Commonwealth, upon reasonable grounds to believe, based upon personal investigation, including information obtained from eyewitnesses, that a crime has been committed by any person then and there present, apprehend such person without a warrant of arrest. For purposes of this section, "the scene of any accident" shall include a reasonable location where a vehicle or person involved in an accident has been moved at the direction of a law-enforcement officer to facilitate the clearing of the highway or to ensure the safety of the motoring public.

C. **(Effective July 1, 2014)** Any such officer may, at the scene of any accident involving a motor vehicle, watercraft as defined in § 29.1-733.2 or motorboat, or at any hospital or medical facility to which any person involved in such accident has been transported, or in the apprehension of any person charged with the theft of any motor vehicle, on any of the highways or waters of the Commonwealth, upon reasonable grounds to believe, based upon personal investigation, including information obtained from eyewitnesses, that a crime has been committed by any person then and there present, apprehend such person without a warrant of arrest. For purposes of this section, "the scene of any accident" shall include a reasonable location where a vehicle or person involved in an accident has been moved at the direction of a law-enforcement officer to facilitate the clearing of the highway or to ensure the safety of the motoring public.

D. Such officers may, within three hours of the alleged offense, arrest without a warrant at any location any person whom the officer has probable cause to suspect of driving or operating a motor vehicle, watercraft or motorboat while intoxicated in violation of § 18.2-266, 18.2-266.1, 46.2-341.24, or subsection B of § 29.1-738; or a substantially similar ordinance of any county, city, or town in the Commonwealth, whether or not the offense was committed in such officer's presence. Such officers may, within three hours of the alleged offense, arrest without a warrant at any location any person whom the officer has probable cause to suspect of operating a watercraft or motorboat in violation of an order issued pursuant to § 29.1-738.4, whether or not the offense was committed in such officer's presence.

E. Such officers may arrest, without a warrant or a capias, persons duly charged with a crime in another jurisdiction upon receipt of a photocopy of a warrant or a capias, telegram, computer printout, facsimile printout, a radio, telephone or teletype message, in which photocopy of a warrant, telegram, computer printout, facsimile printout, radio, telephone or teletype message shall be given the name or a reasonably accurate description of such person wanted and the crime alleged.

F. Such officers may arrest, without a warrant or a capias, for an alleged misdemeanor not committed in his presence when the officer receives a radio message from his department or other law-enforcement agency within the Commonwealth that a warrant or capias for such offense is on file.

G. Such officers may also arrest without a warrant for an alleged misdemeanor not committed in their presence involving (i) shoplifting in violation of § 18.2-96 or 18.2-103 or a similar local ordinance, (ii) carrying a weapon on school property in violation of § 18.2-308.1, (iii) assault and battery, (iv) brandishing a firearm in violation of § 18.2-282, or (v) destruction of property in violation of § 18.2-137, when such property is located on premises used for business or commercial purposes, or a similar local ordinance, when any such arrest is based on probable cause upon reasonable complaint of the person who observed the alleged offense. The arresting officer may issue a summons to any person arrested under this section for a misdemeanor violation involving shoplifting.

History.

Code 1950, § 19.1-100; 1960, c. 366; 1974, c. 241; 1975, c. 495; 1976, cc. 515, 570; 1977, c. 97; 1979, c. 268; 1982, c. 272; 1983, c. 206; 1984, c. 534; 1985, c. 507; 1988, cc. 353, 744, 752, 853; 1989, c. 726; 1990, cc. 635, 744, 784; 1995, c. 465; 1996, cc. 866, 929, 1015; 1998, c. 684; 2004, c. 949; 2005, cc. 88, 435; 2008, cc. 460, 737; 2010, c. 840; 2011, cc. 510, 643; 2012, c. 776; 2013, c. 787.

Subsection C set out twice. — The first version of subsection C above is effective until July 1, 2014. The second version of subsection C above is effective July 1, 2014.

Cross references.

For arrests without warrants in cases of flight and pursuit, see § 19.2-77. For statute authorizing arrests without warrants in connection with the extradition of criminals, see § 19.2-100.

Editor's note.

Acts 2008, c. 460, cl. 2, provides: "That the provisions of this act may result in a net increase in periods of imprisonment or commitment. Pursuant to § 30-19.1:4, the estimated amount of the necessary appropriation is $12,475 for periods of imprisonment in state adult correctional facilities and $0 for periods of commitment to the custody of the Department of Juvenile Justice."

Acts 2010, c. 840, cl. 2, provides: "That the provisions of this act may result in a net increase in periods of imprisonment or commitment. Pursuant to § 30-19.1:4, the estimated amount of the necessary appropriation cannot be determined for periods of imprisonment in state adult correctional facilities; therefore, Chapter 781 of the Acts of Assembly of 2009 requires the Virginia Criminal Sentencing Commission to assign a minimum fiscal impact of $50,000. Pursuant to § 30-19.1:4, the estimated amount of the necessary appropriation is $0 for periods of commitment to the custody of the Department of Juvenile Justice."

Acts 2012, c. 776, cl. 2, provides: "That the provisions of this act may result in a net increase in periods of imprisonment or commitment. Pursuant to § 30-19.1:4, the estimated amount of the necessary appropriation is $0 for periods of imprisonment in state adult correctional facilities and is $0 for periods of commitment to the custody of the Department of Juvenile Justice."

Acts 2013, c. 787, cl. 3 provides: "That the provisions of this act shall become effective on July 1, 2014."

The 2008 amendments.

The 2008 amendment by c. 460 added subdivision 9; and made related changes.

The 2008 amendment by c. 737 inserted the present second sentence in the third paragraph following subdivision 8 [now subdivision 9].

The 2010 amendments.

The 2010 amendment by c. 840 added the subsection designations; deleted the last paragraph in subsection B, which dealt with an officer's power to arrest without a warrant persons intoxicated while in violation of subsection B of § 29.1-738 or of an order issued pursuant to § 29.1-738.4; and rewrote subsection D, in part by adding the last sentence.

The 2011 amendments.

The 2011 amendment by c. 510 added the last paragraph in subsection B.

The 2011 amendment by c. 643 added subdivision A 10 and made a related change.

The 2012 amendments.

The 2012 amendment by c. 776 inserted subdivision A 11 and made a related change.

The 2013 amendments.

The 2013 amendment by c. 787, effective July 1, 2014, substituted "§ 29.1-733.2" for "§ 29.1-712" in subsection C.

Law Review.

For comment on the presence requirement and the "police-team" rule in arrest for misdemeanors, see 26 Wash. & Lee L. Rev. 119 (1969). For survey of recent legislation on criminal procedure — authority of police to question and search suspicious persons, see 5 U. Rich. L. Rev. 191 (1970). For survey of Virginia criminal law and procedure for the year 1969-1970, see 56 Va. L. Rev. 1572 (1970).

For note comparing Virginia law with a model implied consent statute for drunken drivers, see 12 Wm. & Mary L. Rev. 654 (1971). For survey of Virginia law on criminal procedure for the year 1973-1974, see 60 Va. L. Rev. 1505 (1974). For survey of Virginia law on criminal procedure for the year 1977-1978, see 64 Va. L. Rev. 1419 (1978). For survey of Virginia law on criminal procedure for the year 1978-1979, see 66 Va. L. Rev. 261 (1980). For note on the constitutionality of an identification requirement for lawfully stopped persons, see 37 Wash. & Lee L. Rev. 253 (1980). For note, "Criminal Procedure and Criminal Law: Virginia Supreme Court Decisions During the 70's," see 15 U. Rich. L. Rev. 585 (1981). For article, "State Court Activism and Searches Incident to Arrest," see 68 Va. L. Rev. 1085 (1982). For note on stop and frisk based upon anonymous telephone tips, see 39 Wash. & Lee L. Rev. 1437 (1982). For comment on spouse abuse in Virginia, see 17 U. Rich. L. Rev. 633 (1983). For 1985 survey of Virginia criminal procedure, see 19 U. Rich. L. Rev. 697 (1985). For comment on what standard governs investigative stops in Virginia, see 9 G.M.U. L. Rev. 313 (1987). For 2003/2004 survey of criminal law and procedure, see 39 U. Rich. L. Rev. 133 (2004). For note, "New Theories of Guilt on Appeal in Virginia Criminal Cases," see 50 Wm. and Mary L. Rev. 2177 (2009).

Michie's Jurisprudence.
For related discussion, see 2A M.J. Arrest, §§ 4, 6, 8, 9, 10, 12; 16 M.J. Right of Privacy, § 1.

CASE NOTES

I. In General.
II. Illustrative Cases.

I. IN GENERAL.

Editor's note.
Some of the cases annotated below were decided under former § 19.2-83.

The test of constitutional validity is whether at the moment of arrest the arresting officer had knowledge of sufficient facts and circumstances to warrant a reasonable man in believing that an offense has been committed. DePriest v. Commonwealth, 4 Va. App. 577, 359 S.E.2d 540 (1987), cert. denied, 488 U.S. 985, 109 S. Ct. 541, 102 L. Ed. 2d 571 (1988).

Section violation does not necessarily result in Fourth Amendment violation. — Violation of this section did not necessarily result in a Fourth Amendment violation or warrant application of the exclusionary rule, where a police officer had probable cause to arrest defendant on a "peeping tom" charge and anything seized as a result of that arrest was subject to being used against him. Lovelace v. Commonwealth, No. 0822-88-4 (Ct. of Appeals Apr. 24, 1990).

There is no Fourth Amendment violation for misdemeanor arrests committed outside the presence of the arresting state officer. Penn v. Commonwealth, 13 Va. App. 399, 412 S.E.2d 189 (1991), aff'd, 244 Va. 218, 420 S.E.2d 713 (1992).

There is no constitutional violation where state police officers make warrantless arrests for misdemeanors not committed in their presence. Penn v. Commonwealth, 13 Va. App. 399, 412 S.E.2d 189 (1991), aff'd, 244 Va. 218, 420 S.E.2d 713 (1992).

Purpose of provision for arrest at scene of accident. — The legislature intended for the provisions of this section, inter alia, to facilitate the timely arrest of persons in motor vehicle accidents involving alcohol or other intoxicants so that they may be tested under the implied consent law to determine their blood alcohol content. Smith v. Commonwealth, 32 Va. App. 228, 527 S.E.2d 456, 2000 Va. App. LEXIS 281 (2000).

The term "accident" means an event occurring by chance or from unknown causes or an unfortunate event; there is nothing inherent in the meaning of the word that suggests that it applies only when a vehicle strikes or collides with a person or property. Leveroni v. County of Arlington, 18 Va. App. 626, 445 S.E.2d 723 (1994).

Trial court did not err in ruling that an "accident" occurred sufficient to authorize warrantless arrest, where defendant's ve-

hicle went far enough off paved roadway to become mired in mud up to its axles. Ferrufino v. Commonwealth, No. 1930-98-4, 1999 Va. App. LEXIS 626 (Nov. 9, 1999).

Lineal and temporal criteria for arrest at scene of accident. — The time and place elements of the res gestae doctrine are applicable by analogy to a court's determination of whether a warrantless arrest occurred "at the scene of any accident," and whether an arrest occurred at the scene of an accident depends upon whether the relevant factors are linked by time and place or by any reasonable temporal and/or lineal criteria. Smith v. Commonwealth, 32 Va. App. 228, 527 S.E.2d 456, 2000 Va. App. LEXIS 281 (2000).

Arrest at scene of accident shown. — A defendant was arrested at the scene of an accident within the meaning of this section where the evidence established that the arresting officer arrived at the intersection at which the accident occurred within minutes of its occurrence, and that from that intersection he could see the tow truck and the house where defendant's vehicle was parked and that he then proceeded directly to that location, which was about 100 yards away, arriving twenty to thirty seconds later; under a res gestae analysis of time and place, the officer's arrest of the defendant, at this location and so close in time to the accident, met the lineal and temporal requirements necessary to constitute an arrest at the scene of the accident. Smith v. Commonwealth, 32 Va. App. 228, 527 S.E.2d 456, 2000 Va. App. LEXIS 281 (2000).

Surveillance and legitimate inquiry. — This section does not deny to the police the authority to discharge their proper and expected function of maintaining public order through surveillance and legitimate inquiry. Troncoso v. Commonwealth, 12 Va. App. 942, 407 S.E.2d 349 (1991).

Departure from misdemeanor presence rule contrary to legislative intent. — A careful reading of the statute indicates that any departure from the misdemeanor presence rule, except as specified by the statute, is contrary to the legislative intent. Penn v. Commonwealth, 13 Va. App. 399, 412 S.E.2d 189 (1991), aff'd, 244 Va. 218, 420 S.E.2d 713 (1992).

Protective search of area of suspect's immediate control. — Police officers may, whenever they possess an articulable and objectively reasonable belief that a suspect is presently or potentially dangerous, conduct a protective search of the area within the suspect's immediate control. If the suspect moves about, an officer is justified in staying with the individual during the course of the stop and conducting a protective search of the areas which come within the suspect's immediate control, even if this action necessitates entry into the suspect's home. Servis v. Commonwealth, 6 Va. App. 507, 371 S.E.2d 156 (1988).

It makes no difference that the object removed from subject's person is not a weapon. To justify removal, it is only necessary that the officer reasonably believes the object could be a weapon. Lansdown v. Commonwealth, 226 Va. 204, 308 S.E.2d 106 (1983), cert. denied, 465 U.S. 1104, 104 S. Ct. 1604, 80 L. Ed. 2d 134 (1984).

When pat-down search authorized. — The authority to conduct a pat-down search does not automatically accompany an investigative detention. Only where the officer can point to particular facts from which he reasonably inferred that the individual was armed and dangerous is he justified in searching for weapons. Williams v. Commonwealth, 4 Va. App. 53, 354 S.E.2d 79 (1987).

To justify removal of item from pocket of defendant during pat-down search, it was not necessary that the item actually be a weapon. Officer was entitled to remove the item if he reasonably believed that it could be a weapon. Williams v. Commonwealth, 4 Va. App. 53, 354 S.E.2d 79 (1987).

Pat-down search for weapons held reasonable. — Even though the officers who detained defendant had no information that he was armed or that he had a past history of violence, they acted reasonably when conducting a protective pat-down search for weapons in light of the fact that they had a reasonable suspicion that defendant was presently engaged in narcotics distribution. Williams v. Commonwealth, 4 Va. App. 53, 354 S.E.2d 79 (1987).

Search of passenger compartment subsequent to arrest authorized. — Once defendant was lawfully arrested for reckless driving, police officer was authorized to undertake a related search of the vehicle's passenger compartment. Joe v. Commonwealth, No. 1996-93-1, 1995 Va. App. LEXIS 33 (Jan. 10, 1995).

Good faith. — Under this section the good faith of the arresting officer is not a factor. Foote v. Commonwealth, 11 Va. App. 61, 396 S.E.2d 851 (1990).

Arrest upon knowledge of existence of unexecuted felony warrant. — An officer has probable cause, and indeed the legal duty, to arrest upon knowledge of the existence of an unexecuted felony warrant for the suspect. Crowder v. Commonwealth, 213 Va. 151, 191 S.E.2d 239 (1972).

Where the arresting officer was acting on personal knowledge of the existence of felony warrants commanding the arrest of defendant, it would be a strained construction of the law to vitiate an arrest made under such circumstances, notwithstanding a statute which permits the arrest had the required information and allegation come to him by radio, telegram or teletype. Crowder v. Commonwealth, 213 Va. 151, 191 S.E.2d 239 (1972).

Arrest resulting from mistake of law should be judged by same test as one stemming from mistake of fact, viz., whether the arresting officer acted "in good faith and with probable cause." This test "has been consistently read as meaning good faith and 'reasonable belief' in the validity of the arrest." DeChene v. Smallwood, 226 Va. 475, 311 S.E.2d 749, cert. denied, 469 U.S. 857, 105 S. Ct. 184, 83 L. Ed. 2d 118 (1984).

Where conduct which prompted arrest occurred in officer's presence, the legality of the arrest will turn on whether the officer acted in good faith and with reasonable belief in the validity of the arrest. DeChene v. Smallwood, 226 Va. 475, 311 S.E.2d 749, cert. denied, 469 U.S. 857, 105 S. Ct. 184, 83 L. Ed. 2d 118 (1984).

An offense is committed within the presence of an officer, within the meaning of the misdemeanor presence rule, when he has direct personal knowledge, through his sight, hearing, or other senses that it is then and there being committed. Penn v. Commonwealth, 13 Va. App. 399, 412 S.E.2d 189 (1991), aff'd, 244 Va. 218, 420 S.E.2d 713 (1992).

When an officer came upon defendant's vehicle with its hazard lights operating, while defendant went into a building to make a delivery, defendant had not terminated the operation of the vehicle and he committed the crime of operating the vehicle without a license in the officer's presence, authorizing the officer to arrest him without a warrant. Harris v. Commonwealth, No. 1615-01-2, 2002 Va. App. LEXIS 365 (Ct. of Appeals July 2, 2002).

Eyewitness testimony of sexual assault sufficiently independent of evidence obtained by GPS device. — Exclusionary rule under Va. Const., Art. I, § 10, did not bar the eyewitness testimony of the officers who saw defendant commit a sexual assault, which was a new and distinct offense, and sufficiently independent of any information obtained by them from the GPS that they had placed on a van driven by defendant without a warrant. Foltz v. Commonwealth, 58 Va. App. 107, 706 S.E.2d 914, 2011 Va. App. LEXIS 165 (2011).

Officer's personal knowledge of offense. — Unless the arrest is one within the various statutory exceptions to the general rule, a police officer may not arrest a misdemeanant without a warrant except when an officer has personal knowledge acquired by his personal senses that an offense was committed in his presence. Durant v. City of Suffolk, 4 Va. App. 445, 358 S.E.2d 732 (1987).

A legal warrantless arrest cannot be effectuated based upon the officer having information from others which leads him to believe an offense is being committed in his presence. Penn v. Commonwealth, 13 Va. App. 399, 412 S.E.2d 189 (1991), aff'd, 244 Va. 218, 420 S.E.2d 713 (1992).

Information received from a third party, even a fellow law-enforcement officer, is an inadequate substitute for the arresting officer's own observations and perceptions. Penn v. Commonwealth, 13 Va. App. 399, 412 S.E.2d 189 (1991), aff'd, 244 Va. 218, 420 S.E.2d 713 (1992).

Misdemeanor committed, but not in officer's presence. — If the officer has information that a misdemeanor has been committed, but not in his presence, he must obtain a warrant and make the arrest pursuant to that warrant. Penn v. Commonwealth, 13 Va. App. 399, 412 S.E.2d 189 (1991), aff'd, 244 Va. 218, 420 S.E.2d 713 (1992).

Suspicion of narcotics possession and distribution gives rise to inference of dangerousness. — Suspicion of narcotics possession and distribution is a circumstance which, standing alone, gives rise to an inference of dangerousness, so as to confer authority to conduct a pat-down search. Williams v. Commonwealth, 4 Va. App. 53, 354 S.E.2d 79 (1987).

Commonwealth's interlocutory appeal not allowed based on this section. — Where the trial court's suppressing order was not based on a violation of a provision of the Virginia or federal Constitutions, but was based on this section, which limits the authority of a police officer to stop, question and search a suspicious person, the interlocutory appeal by the Commonwealth from the order suppressing evidence of cocaine found on the defendant when law-enforcement officers searched him was not one which the Commonwealth is permitted to appeal. Commonwealth v. Brown, 8 Va. App. 41, 378 S.E.2d 623 (1989).

Third sentence of section applies to defendant charged with offense in another jurisdiction. — Where defendant is charged with an offense in another jurisdiction, it is the third sentence of this section, and not the first sentence, by which the lawfulness of defendant's arrest is to be judged. Grajales v. Commonwealth, No. 0508-85 (Ct. of Appeals Nov. 12, 1986).

Warrantless arrest of a person charged with a crime in another jurisdiction. — Three conditions are necessary to empower a police officer to effectuate a warrantless arrest of a person charged with a crime in another jurisdiction: an officer must be given the name or a description of the person wanted, a description of the crime, and an allegation that such person is likely to flee the Commonwealth. Foote v. Commonwealth, 11 Va. App. 61, 396 S.E.2d 851 (1990).

A reasonably accurate description should address gender, race, age, height, weight, hair color, and any unique characteristics. Foote v. Commonwealth, 11 Va. App. 61, 396 S.E.2d 851 (1990).

Where radio transmission informed a deputy sheriff that the driver of a suspicious truck was wanted, that the deputy should use caution, and that the driver was a "Rambo-type" suspect, this transmission did not meet the statutory requirements authorizing a warrantless arrest of a person charged with a crime in another jurisdiction. Foote v. Commonwealth, 11 Va. App. 61, 396 S.E.2d 851 (1990).

Applied in Lowe v. Commonwealth, 218 Va. 670, 239 S.E.2d 112 (1977); Thompson v. Commonwealth, 10 Va. App. 117, 390 S.E.2d 198 (1990); Poindexter v. Commonwealth, 16 Va. App. 730, 432 S.E.2d 527 (1993); Chambers v. City of Roanoke, — F. Supp. 2d —, 2003 U.S. Dist. LEXIS 377 (W.D. Va. Jan. 13, 2003); Harris v. Commonwealth, 39 Va. App. 670, 576 S.E.2d 228, 2003 Va. App. LEXIS 39 (2003); United States v. Day, 591 F.3d 679, 2010 U.S. App. LEXIS 429 (4th Cir. 2010).

II. ILLUSTRATIVE CASES.

Probable cause to make warrantless arrest. — The events witnessed by the police officer during his surveillance provided him with a suspicion of criminal activity, but not probable cause, where he did not observe suspected narcotics change hands, nor did he observe the exchange of any object which in his experience suggested narcotics, and there was no evidence that the area under surveillance was noted for heroin transactions or that the transactions observed were furtive in nature. DePriest v. Commonwealth, 4 Va. App. 577, 359 S.E.2d 540 (1987), cert. denied, 488 U.S. 985, 109 S. Ct. 541, 102 L. Ed. 2d 571 (1988).

Where the defendant and codefendant were stopped and patted down for weapons but not subjected to further investigation until another police officer arrived, the initial stop did not constitute an arrest; the defendant was not actually arrested until the other officer arrived on the scene and found a substance he suspected was heroin in the pocket of codefendant, and the discovery of this substance, along with the other officer's prior observations, provided probable cause to arrest defendant. DePriest v. Commonwealth, 4 Va. App. 577, 359 S.E.2d 540 (1987), cert. denied, 488 U.S. 985, 109 S. Ct. 541, 102 L. Ed. 2d 571 (1988).

Arrest was supported by probable cause. — Where police articulated facts supporting reasonable suspicion that appellant was the person they sought for leaving the scene of an accident without filing a report, and it was appellant's action that produced in plain view the cocaine that gave them probable cause to arrest him, notwithstanding that the police described their actions as an investigatory detention, not an arrest, arrest of the appellant which was supported by probable cause occurred when the cocaine was discovered as a result of Terry stop and appellant was placed in handcuffs, and police did not violate this section which prohibits warrantless arrest for a misdemeanor. Mazza v. Commonwealth, 16 Va. App. 907, 434 S.E.2d 339 (1993).

Officer had probable cause to arrest defendant for driving under the influence of alcohol, in violation of § 18.2-266, because a reasonable person could have properly inferred from the totality of the circumstances that defendant had drunk enough alcohol, at the time of the accident, to observably affect his manner, disposition, speech, muscular movement, general appearance, or behavior, since: (1) the officer knew that defendant had been in a bar until nearly closing time; (2) the officer knew that defendant struck the victim while driving his motorcycle; (3) the officer observed at the hospital that defendant had a quite strong odor of alcohol about his person; and (4) the officer saw that, although defendant's only apparent injuries were scrapes and bruises, defendant's speech was slurred. Bristol v. Commonwealth, 47 Va. App. 584, 625 S.E.2d 676, 2006 Va. App. LEXIS 53 (2006), reversed, remanded, 272 Va. 568, 636 S.E.2d 460 (2006), as to validity of arrest.

Because a police officer heard a judge orally order that a capias be issued for defendant's failure to appear, the officer had sufficient probable cause and authority to arrest defendant under § 19.2-81. Jones v. Commonwealth, — Va. App. —, — S.E.2d —, 2007 Va. App. LEXIS 29 (Jan. 30, 2007).

Because defendant's post-entry assaults on police officers were outside the scope of the exclusionary rule, and because police officers had probable cause under § 19.2-81 to make a warrantless arrest for public intoxication, the Fourth Amendment was irrelevant; since defendant had no right to resist the arrest, defendant's motion to suppress was properly denied and defendant was properly convicted of assault and battery on a police officer and obstruction of justice. Messier v. Commonwealth, 2007 Va. App. LEXIS 201 (May 15, 2007).

Trial court did not err in denying defendant's motion to suppress cocaine the police discovered in defendant's vehicle incident to an arrest on a separate charge because the police had probable cause to arrest defendant since a reasonable officer could conclude that there was probable cause to believe that defendant committed the crime of possession of cocaine, either solely or jointly; it was an entirely reasonable inference from the facts that either defendant or a passenger had knowledge of, and exercised dominion and control over, the cocaine. Jones v. Commonwealth, 2011 Va. App. LEXIS 98 (Mar. 22, 2011).

Where, at night, an officer observed a van operating in a grossly reckless manner under circumstances suggesting that its occupants were engaged in "possibly criminal behavior" or that they were fleeing from the scene of a crime; the situation appeared sufficiently aggravated that he felt it necessary to radio for assistance; after attempting unsuccessfully to elude arrest, the driver brought the van to a halt in an unlit area; with "no rear windows or side windows" in the van, the actions of the occupants were hidden from the officer; none of the occupants could produce any personal identification or any registration for the van; and the officer stated that he was concerned about the occupants possibly having weapons to make an assault on him regarding the traffic stop, the intrusion that occurred when the officer ordered the defendant from the van and detained him until he was frisked by another officer was reasonably warranted. Lansdown v. Commonwealth, 226 Va. 204, 308 S.E.2d 106 (1983), cert. denied, 465 U.S. 1104, 104 S. Ct. 1604, 80 L. Ed. 2d 134 (1984).

Arrest on reasonable belief is valid. — In United States v. Gearhart, 326 F.2d 412 (4th Cir. 1964), the court said that an arrest was in order, because, in the aggregate, the sheriff had "reasonable grounds to believe" that a crime had been committed by the defendant.

A police officer may arrest, without a warrant, one whom he has reasonable grounds or probable cause to suspect of having committed a felony even though the crime is not committed in his presence. Crowder v. Commonwealth, 213 Va. 151, 191 S.E.2d 239 (1972).

Protective search held reasonable. — Police officer had an articulable and objectively reasonable basis for suspecting that the defendant was potentially dangerous, where the hour was late and the area was rural, the police had been called to the scene to investigate a possible break-in to the motel room in which the defendant was found, the defendant appeared nervous, highly upset, and under the influence of some intoxicant, twice he gave false answers to the police about to whom the rooms were registered, chairs were piled against the door to block entry, and when asked for his identification, the defendant quickly retreated into the room without responding. Based on the totality of the circum-

stances, the officer could reasonably suspect that the defendant was the reported burglar who might be armed and potentially dangerous. Accordingly, he was justified in conducting a pat-down of the defendant's outer clothing and a protective search of the area within the defendant's immediate control, as well as monitoring the defendant's movements during the course of the stop. Therefore, his warrantless entry into the motel room was reasonable. Servis v. Commonwealth, 6 Va. App. 507, 371 S.E.2d 156 (1988).

Warrantless arrests at hospital of any person involved in accident. — This section authorizes law-enforcement officers to make warrantless arrests at a hospital of any person involved in a motor vehicle accident even though the crime was not committed in the officer's presence, provided the officer is in uniform or displaying a badge of office and has reasonable grounds to believe based upon personal investigation that a crime arising from the accident was committed by that person. Paige v. City of Lynchburg, 10 Va. App. 162, 390 S.E.2d 524 (1990).

Warrantless arrest of defendant in the hospital at 4:35 p.m. was invalid, where the motor vehicle accident occurred at 3:00 p.m. The officer had no authority without a warrant to arrest the accused except at the scene of the motor vehicle accident for driving under the influence and after his driver's license had been revoked, offenses which were committed not in his presence. Thomas v. Town of Marion, 226 Va. 251, 308 S.E.2d 120 (1983).

After-the-fact appraisal does not lessen cause to stop, question, and search. — An officer's concessions on the witness stand that he had no reason to stop the vehicle other than the actions of the vehicle itself and that the defendant individually did nothing to indicate he possessed a concealed weapon, posed any danger to the officer, or had committed any crime, obviously were the result of an after-the-fact appraisal of the situation. They neither lessen the fact that he did have ample cause to stop the vehicle nor take away from his on-the-scene concern for his safety and his fear that the vehicle's occupants might have weapons to make an assault on him. In determining whether to detain the defendant, the officer was entitled to rely upon the totality of the circumstances — the whole picture. Lansdown v. Commonwealth, 226 Va. 204, 308 S.E.2d 106 (1983), cert. denied, 465 U.S. 1104, 104 S. Ct. 1604, 80 L. Ed. 2d 134 (1984).

Defendant's identification. — Police officers were authorized to seek defendant's identification, where they saw him and others engaged in a drug transaction and stopped the vehicle he was driving. Smith v. Commonwealth, No. 0138-89-2 (Ct. of Appeals Oct. 16, 1990).

Suppression of evidence not appropriate for noncompliance with section. — Where officers who arrested defendant were wearing plain clothes at the time they placed defendant under arrest, and in addition, the trial court specifically found that the officers had no chance to display their badges prior to arresting defendant, suppression of evidence was not the appropriate remedy for the officers' failure to comply with this section. Graves v. Commonwealth, No. 1113-88-2 (Ct. of Appeals July 17, 1990).

Although defendant's warrantless arrest for littering violated this section because the misdemeanor offense was not committed in the presence of the arresting officer, such a violation of state law did not warrant application of the exclusionary rule to suppress the cocaine discovered in the search. Penn v. Commonwealth, 13 Va. App. 399, 412 S.E.2d 189 (1991), aff'd, 244 Va. 218, 420 S.E.2d 713 (1992).

Suppression of evidence. — Not every violation of this section necessarily results in the exclusion of evidence; where an illegal arrest under this section does not violate any constitutional rights, the defendant is not entitled to have evidence seized pursuant to that arrest excluded. Penn v. Commonwealth, 13 Va. App. 399, 412 S.E.2d 189 (1991), aff'd, 244 Va. 218, 420 S.E.2d 713 (1992).

The exclusionary rule adopted in Mapp v. Ohio, 367 U.S. 643, 81 S. Ct. 1684, 6 L. Ed. 2d 1081 (1961), does not operate to exclude evidence where the defendant claims that rights provided to him under state statute have been violated, but fails to allege a deprivation of constitutional rights. Penn v. Commonwealth, 13 Va. App. 399, 412 S.E.2d 189 (1991), aff'd, 244 Va. 218, 420 S.E.2d 713 (1992).

In the absence of any deprivation of constitutional rights, an arrest in violation of state statute does not require exclusion of any evidence obtained as a result of the arrest. Penn v. Commonwealth,

13 Va. App. 399, 412 S.E.2d 189 (1991), aff'd, 244 Va. 218, 420 S.E.2d 713 (1992).

Under Virginia law, no suppression of evidence is required when evidence is obtained in violation of state law but no constitutional violation has occurred. Penn v. Commonwealth, 13 Va. App. 399, 412 S.E.2d 189 (1991), aff'd, 244 Va. 218, 420 S.E.2d 713 (1992).

A violation of this section does not require the exclusion of evidence absent a constitutional violation. Hailey v. Commonwealth, No. 0627-99-3, 2000 Va. App. LEXIS 593 (Ct. of Appeals Aug. 15, 2000).

Cocaine found in defendant's vehicle was admissible because a police officer had probable cause under subsection B of § 19.2-81 to arrest defendant for public intoxication, in violation of § 18.2-388, as the officer testified that as the officer approached defendant's parked vehicle and spoke with defendant there was a very strong odor of alcohol coming from defendant's breath, defendant's speech was slurred, and defendant's eyes were very bloodshot. Furthermore, the officer's search of defendant's vehicle was a proper search incident to arrest under then existing law, as defendant was in custody and an occupant of the vehicle. McGhee v. Commonwealth, 280 Va. 620, 701 S.E.2d 58, 2010 Va. LEXIS 260 (2010).

Section 52-21, relating to procedure after arrest without warrant, held not applicable where the record showed that the accident occurred in Stafford County and defendant was taken directly from the scene to a Fredericksburg hospital and arrested at the hospital and upon his release, officer took the accused to a Stafford County magistrate and obtained a warrant since the warrantless arrest at the hospital following the accident was made pursuant to this section. Walter v. Commonwealth, 8 Va. App. 485, 382 S.E.2d 484 (1989).

The defendant's warrantless arrest for driving under the influence of alcohol was unlawful where the police officer had not observed the defendant driving, and the police officer's only source of knowledge that the defendant drove in that city was the radio call for assistance. Durant v. City of Suffolk, 4 Va. App. 445, 358 S.E.2d 732 (1987).

Warrantless arrest was lawful where defendant was asked whether he would accompany police officer in the police car to speak to another officer and he agreed and was arrested by the other officer after the other officer identified defendant as the person he had seen trespassing. James v. Commonwealth, 8 Va. App. 98, 379 S.E.2d 378 (1989).

Petit larceny is a continuing offense, and where two police officers observed the defendant and the radio in question in his car, a misdemeanor was being committed in their presence which permitted them to arrest the defendant without a warrant pursuant to this section. Ford v. Commonwealth, No. 0885-89-4 (Ct. of Appeals Nov. 6, 1990).

Warrantless arrest invalid. — Officer made an invalid warrantless arrest for a misdemeanor not committed in his presence as the single-vehicle accident occurred on or beside a private road in a gated, guarded residential complex; thus, the exceptions to the warrant requirement in § 19.2-81 did not apply. Therefore, the implied consent law did not apply to permit the certificate of analysis of defendant's breath test to be admitted into evidence. Roseborough v. Commonwealth, 281 Va. 233, 704 S.E.2d 414, 2011 Va. LEXIS 147 (2011).

"Accident" found. — Where defendant's car came in contact with sign 20 feet from the hard surface, which resulted from her admitted failure to pay attention, this event was an accident within the meaning of the statute. Leveroni v. County of Arlington, 18 Va. App. 626, 445 S.E.2d 723 (1994).

CIRCUIT COURT OPINIONS

Lack of signature on warrant. — Defendant was not entitled to have evidence seized during an arrest and statements made in course of and following the arrest suppressed because the lack of a magistrate's signature on an otherwise valid warrant did not render defendant's arrest unlawful under § 19.2-81, where the facts otherwise failed to set forth a violation of defendant's rights under the Fourth Amendment. Commonwealth v. Osborne, 72 Va. Cir. 601, 2005 Va. Cir. LEXIS 376 (Scott County 2005).

"In the presence" requirement. — Court rejected "police team" argument to satisfy the "in the presence" requirement for misdemeanor arrests under § 19.2-81. Commonwealth v. Coakley, 56 Va. Cir. 99, 2001 Va. Cir. LEXIS 446 (Norfolk 2001).

Trial court did not violate petitioner's Fourth Amendment rights by denying his motion to suppress, despite his claim that the police officers lacked probable cause to arrest him for being drunk in public where he was inside his parents' home when he was arrested, because there was evidence that petitioner was extremely intoxicated and had been in public when he left his home where his wife's dead body was found and went to his parents' home. The officers' failure to observe petitioner's intoxication "in public," prior to arresting him, may have constituted a violation of § 19.2-81, which authorized a warrantless arrest of any person who committed a crime in the presence of an officer, but it did not strip the officers of probable cause to arrest him and did not warrant exclusion of evidence or statements obtained as a result of the arrest. Hudson v. Dir. of the Dep't of Corr., 67 Va. Cir. 319, 2005 Va. Cir. LEXIS 147 (Clarke County May 16, 2005).

Park ranger's arrest of defendant not improper. — Park rangers were permitted to exercise the powers of a conservator of the peace when engaged in the performance of their official duties; as a conservator of the peace, a ranger was permitted to make an arrest for a misdemeanor committed in his presence. A ranger's arrest of defendant for driving under the influence based on the ranger's observations of defendant was proper. Commonwealth v. Stickle, 72 Va. Cir. 494, 2007 Va. Cir. LEXIS 154 (Loudoun County 2007).

Objective standard. — Correct inquiry is whether, based on an objective standard, a deputy had sufficient information to support probable cause for an arrest for a crime. Commonwealth v. May, 63 Va. Cir. 474, 2003 Va. Cir. LEXIS 339 (Loudoun County 2003).

While defendant argued that the arrest was illegal because a deputy did not have probable cause to arrest defendant for the felony of grand larceny for which defendant was subsequently charged, the deputy did have probable cause to believe that defendant committed the crime of petit larceny in the deputy's presence because: (1) the victim of the grand larceny told the deputy that the victim's purse had been stolen and described two individuals that the victim suspected of taking the purse; (2) because the deputy had no information that the purse had been recovered, the deputy had reason to believe that the asportation of the stolen purse continued; (3) the deputy had reason to believe that the purse the deputy saw near defendant was the one that the victim reported as being stolen; and (4) because the purse had some value, it was the subject of, at least, petit larceny. Commonwealth v. May, 63 Va. Cir. 474, 2003 Va. Cir. LEXIS 339 (Loudoun County 2003).

Court stated that §§ 18.2-266, 19.2-81, and 46.2-100, read together, require that an individual drive or operate, or be in actual physical control of a motor vehicle in the presence of the arresting officer for an arrest to be valid. Commonwealth v. Coakley, 56 Va. Cir. 99, 2001 Va. Cir. LEXIS 446 (Norfolk 2001).

Information obtained from National Criminal Information Center sufficient to support arrest under a warrant from a foreign jurisdiction. — Determination that there was an outstanding warrant for defendant through a check using the National Criminal Information Center enabled officers to arrest defendant despite the fact that the officers did not have an actual copy of the warrant. Commonwealth v. Makeen, 62 Va. Cir. 269, 2003 Va. Cir. LEXIS 293 (Norfolk 2003).

Defendant's refusal to submit not unlawful in absence of valid arrest. — Court found the driving under the influence (DUI) defendant was improperly charged under § 18.2-268 [see now § 18.2-268.1 et seq.] with refusing to submit to a breath or blood test since the defendant was not legally under arrest for DUI, as the defendant's arrest was in violation of former § 19.2-81; therefore, when the defendant was read his implied consent rights under former § 18.2-268 (requiring the defendant to have been lawfully arrested in order to be subject to former § 18.2-268's mandate to submit) the defendant's refusal to submit did not constitute a violation of former § 18.2-268, and his refusal to submit was not admissible since the test itself, even if he had consented to the test, was inadmissible. Commonwealth v. Coakley, 56 Va. Cir. 99, 2001 Va. Cir. LEXIS 446 (Norfolk 2001).

OPINIONS OF THE ATTORNEY GENERAL

Execution of misdemeanor capias not in officer's possession. — A law-enforcement officer has the authority to execute a misdemeanor capias, not in his possession, based upon an official dispatch from another county, provided the officer informs the accused of the existence of, and the charges contained in, the capias and delivers the capias to the accused as soon thereafter as is practicable. See opinion of Attorney General to Mr. George S. Webb, III, Commonwealth's Attorney for Madison County, 05-017 (4/26/05).

Law-enforcement officers may inquire into immigration status. — Virginia law-enforcement officers, including conservation officers, may inquire into the immigration status of persons stopped or arrested; however, persons tasked with enforcing zoning laws lack the authority to investigate criminal violations of the law, including criminal violations of the immigration laws of the United States. See opinion of Attorney General to The Honorable Robert G. Marshall, Member, Virginia House of Delegates, 10-047, 2010 Va. AG LEXIS 37 (7/30/10).

§ 19.2-81.1. Arrest without warrant by correctional officers in certain cases.

Any correctional officer, as defined in § 53.1-1, may arrest, in the same manner as provided in § 19.2-81, persons for crimes involving:

(a) The escape of an inmate from a correctional institution, as defined in § 53.1-1;

(b) Assisting an inmate to escape from a correctional institution, as defined in § 53.1-1;

(c) The delivery of contraband to an inmate in violation of § 18.2-474 or § 18.2-474.1; and

(d) Any other criminal offense which may contribute to the disruption of the safety, welfare, or security of the population of a correctional institution.

History.
1976, c. 752.

§ 19.2-81.2. Power of correctional officers and designated noncustodial employees to detain.

A. A correctional officer, as defined in § 53.1-1, who has completed the minimum training standards established by the Department of Criminal Justice Services, or other noncustodial employee of the Department of Corrections who has been designated to carry a weapon by the Director of the Department of Corrections pursuant to § 53.1-29 of the Code and who has completed the basic course in detention training as approved by the Department of Criminal Justice Services, may, while on duty in or on the grounds of a correctional institution, or with custody of prisoners without the confines of a correctional institution, detain any person whom he has reasonable suspicion to believe has committed a violation of §§ 18.2-473 through 18.2-475, or of aiding or abetting a prisoner in violating the provisions of § 53.1-203. Such detention shall be for the purpose of summoning a law-enforcement officer in order that the law-enforcement officer can arrest the person who is alleged to have violated any of the above sections.

B. Any employee of the Department of Corrections having the authority to detain any person pursuant to subsection A hereof shall not be held civilly liable for unlawful detention, slander, malicious prosecution, false imprisonment, false arrest, or assault and battery of the person so detained, whether such detention takes place within or without the grounds of a correctional institution, provided that, in causing the detention of such person, the employee had at the time of the detention reasonable suspicion to believe that the person committed a violation for which the detention was undertaken.

C. It is the purpose and intent of this section to ensure that the safety, stability, welfare and security of correctional institutions be preserved insofar as possible.

History.
1976, c. 740; 1979, c. 642; 1984, cc. 720, 779.

The number of this section was assigned by the Virginia Code Commission, the number in the 1976 act having been 19.2-81.1.

§ 19.2-81.3. Arrest without a warrant authorized in cases of assault and battery against a family or household member and stalking and for violations of protective orders; procedure, etc.

A. Any law-enforcement officer with the powers of arrest under subsection A of § 19.2-81 may arrest without a warrant for an alleged violation of § 18.2-57.2, 18.2-60.4, or 16.1-253.2 regardless of whether such violation was committed in his presence, if such arrest is based on probable cause or upon personal observations or the reasonable complaint of a person who observed the alleged offense or upon personal investigation.

B. A law-enforcement officer having probable cause to believe that a violation of § 18.2-57.2 or 16.1-253.2 has occurred shall arrest and take into custody the person he has probable cause to believe, based on the totality of the circumstances, was the predominant physical aggressor unless there are special circumstances which would dictate a course of action other than an arrest. The standards for determining who is the predominant physical aggressor shall be based on the following considerations: (i) who was the first aggressor, (ii) the protection of the health and safety of family and household members, (iii) prior complaints of family abuse by the allegedly abusing person involving the family or household members, (iv) the relative severity of the injuries inflicted on persons involved in the incident, (v) whether any injuries were inflicted in self-defense, (vi) witness statements, and (vii) other observations.

C. A law-enforcement officer having probable cause to believe that a violation of § 18.2-60.4 has occurred that involves physical aggression shall arrest and take into custody the person he has probable cause to believe, based on the totality of the circumstances, was the predominant physical aggressor unless there are special circumstances which would dictate a course of action other than an arrest. The standards for determining who is the predominant physical aggressor shall be based on the following considerations: (i) who was the first aggressor, (ii) the protection of the health and safety of the person to whom the protective order was issued and the person's family and household members, (iii) prior acts of violence, force, or threat, as defined in § 19.2-152.7:1, by the person against whom the protective order was issued against the person protected by the order or the protected person's family or household members, (iv) the relative severity of the injuries inflicted on persons involved in the incident, (v) whether any injuries were inflicted in self-defense, (vi) witness statements, and (vii) other observations.

D. Regardless of whether an arrest is made, the officer shall file a written report with his department, which shall state whether any arrests were made, and if so, the number of arrests, specifically including any incident in which he has probable cause to believe family abuse has occurred, and, where required, including a complete statement in writing that there are special circumstances that would dictate a course of action other than an arrest. The officer shall provide the allegedly abused person or the person protected by an order issued pursuant to § 19.2-152.8, 19.2-152.9, or 19.2-152.10, both orally and in writing, information regarding the legal and community resources available to the allegedly abused person or person protected by the order. Upon request of the allegedly abused person or person protected by the order, the department shall make a summary of the report available to the allegedly abused person or person protected by the order.

E. In every case in which a law-enforcement officer makes an arrest under this section for a violation of § 18.2-57.2, he shall petition for an emergency protective order as authorized in § 16.1-253.4 when the person arrested and taken into custody is brought before the magistrate, except if the person arrested is a minor, a petition for an emergency protective order shall not be required. Regardless of whether an arrest is made, if the officer has probable cause to believe that a danger of acts of family abuse exists, the law-enforcement officer shall seek an emergency protective order under § 16.1-253.4, except if the suspected abuser is a minor, a petition for an emergency protective order shall not be required.

F. A law-enforcement officer investigating any complaint of family abuse, including but not limited to assault and battery against a family or household member shall, upon request, transport, or arrange for the transportation of an abused person to a hospital or safe shelter, or to appear before a magistrate. Any local law-enforcement agency may adopt a policy requiring an officer to transport or arrange for transportation of an abused person as provided in this subsection.

G. The definition of "family or household member" in § 16.1-228 applies to this section.

H. As used in this section, a "law-enforcement officer" means (i) any full-time or part-time employee of a police department or sheriff's office which is part of or administered by the Commonwealth or any political subdivision thereof, and any campus police officer appointed under Chapter 17 (§ 23-232 et seq.) of Title 23, and who is responsible for the prevention and detection of crime and the enforcement of the penal, traffic or highway laws of this Commonwealth and (ii) any member of an auxiliary police force established pursuant to § 15.2-1731. Part-time employees are compensated officers who are not full-time employees as defined by the employing police department or sheriff's office.

History.
1991, c. 715; 1992, c. 886; 1995, cc. 413, 433; 1996, c. 866; 1997, c. 603; 1998, c. 569; 1999, cc. 697, 721, 807; 2002, cc. 810, 818; 2004, c. 1016; 2008, cc. 551, 691; 2011, cc. 445, 480; 2012, cc. 776, 827.

Cross references.
As to arrest policies and procedures in domestic violence and family abuse cases, see § 9.1-1300.

Editor's note.
Acts 2011, cc. 445 and 480, cl. 2 provides: "That the provisions of this act may result in a net increase in periods of imprisonment or commitment. Pursuant to § 30-19.1:4, the estimated amount of the necessary appropriation is $93,767 for periods of imprisonment in state adult correctional facilities and cannot be determined for periods of commitment to the custody of the Department of Juvenile Justice."

Acts 2012, c. 776, cl. 2, provides: "That the provisions of this act may result in a net increase in periods of imprisonment or commitment. Pursuant to § 30-19.1:4, the estimated amount of the necessary appropriation is $0 for periods of imprisonment in state adult correctional facilities and is $0 for periods of commitment to the custody of the Department of Juvenile Justice."

The 2008 amendments.
The 2008 amendments by cc. 551 and 691 are identical, and deleted one of the section symbols preceding "18.2-87.2" in subsection A; and substituted "a hospital or safe shelter, or to appear before a magistrate" for "a hospital, safe shelter, or magistrate" in subsection E.

The 2011 amendments.
The 2011 amendments by cc. 245 and 480 are identical, and added present subsection C and redesignated former subsections C through G as subsections D through H; in subsection D, inserted "or the person protected by an order issued pursuant to § 19.2-152.8, 19.2-152.9, or 19.2-152.10" and "or person protected by the order" in the second sentence, and inserted "or person protected by the order" two times in the last sentence; and inserted "for a violation of § 18.2-57.2," in the first sentence of subsection E.

The 2012 amendments.
The 2012 amendment by c. 776 substituted "with the powers of arrest under subsection A of § 19.2-81" for "as defined in § 19.2-81" and inserted "and any campus police officers appointed under Chapter 17 (§ 23-232 et seq.) of Title 23" in subsection H.

The 2012 amendment by c. 827, effective April 18, 2012, deleted "subsection B of" preceding "§ 15.2-1731" at the end of H (ii).

Law Review.
For 2003/2004 survey of family and juvenile law, see 39 U. Rich. L. Rev. 241 (2004).

Michie's Jurisprudence.
For related discussion, see 9B M.J. Husband and Wife, § 87.

CASE NOTES

Applicability. — Virginia statutory law provided support for officers' actions when they entered a bathroom in plaintiff's home because the officers' actions were justified by the exigent circumstances in responding to a domestic situation where there may have been a gun in the residence. Trull v. Smolka, 2011 U.S. App. LEXIS 3404 (4th Cir. Feb. 18, 2011), cert. denied, 2011 U.S. LEXIS 6760, 132 S. Ct. 106, 181 L. Ed. 2d 33 (U.S. 2011).

OPINIONS OF THE ATTORNEY GENERAL

Attorney General declined to render opinion on matter delegated to Department of Criminal Justice Services. — The Attorney General declined to render an opinion on what constitutes "special circumstances which would dictate a course of action other than an arrest" under subsection B as the Department of Criminal Justice Services was the appropriate agency to make such a determination. See opinion of Attorney General to The Honorable Matthew J. Britton, Commonwealth's Attorney for King George County, 01-001 (6/27/01).

§ 19.2-81.4. Repealed by Acts 2008, cc. 600 and 771, cl. 2.

Cross references.
For current provisions as to arrest policies and procedures in domestic violence and family abuse cases, see § 9.1-1300.

§ 19.2-81.5. Cooperation with a law-enforcement officer.

Upon receipt of a request and documentation of an indictment or issuance of a warrant from a law-enforcement agency, any public agency within the Commonwealth may disclose to the requesting law-enforcement agency from agency records, to the extent permitted by federal law, the address of an individual who has been indicted or for whom a warrant for arrest for a crime punishable by incarceration has been issued.

History.
1998, c. 436.

§ 19.2-81.6. Authority of law-enforcement officers to arrest illegal aliens.

All law-enforcement officers enumerated in § 19.2-81 shall have the authority to enforce immigration laws of the United States, pursuant to the provisions of this section. Any law-enforcement officer enumerated in § 19.2-81 may, in the course of acting upon reasonable suspicion that an individual has committed or is committing a crime, arrest the individual without a warrant upon receiving confirmation from the Bureau of Immigration and Customs Enforcement of the United States Department of Homeland Security that the individual (i) is an alien illegally present in the United States, and (ii) has previously been convicted of a felony in the United States and deported or left the United States after such conviction. Upon receiving such confirmation, the officer shall take the individual forthwith before a magistrate or other issuing authority and proceed pursuant to § 19.2-82.

History.
2004, cc. 360, 412.

OPINIONS OF THE ATTORNEY GENERAL

Virginia law-enforcement officers have authority to detain and arrest individuals who have committed violations of the laws of the United States and other states, and such authority extends to violations of federal criminal immigration law. It would not be advisable to enforce such violations outside of the scope of an agreement with federal authorities. See opinion of Attorney General to The Honorable Kenneth W. Stolle, Member, Senate of Virginia, and The Honorable David B. Albo, Member, House of Delegates, 07-086 (10/15/07).

Law-enforcement officers may inquire into immigration status. — Virginia law-enforcement officers, including conservation officers, may inquire into the immigration status of persons stopped or arrested; however, persons tasked with enforcing zoning laws lack the authority to investigate criminal violations of the law, including criminal violations of the immigration laws of the United States. See opinion of Attorney General to The Honorable Robert G. Marshall, Member, Virginia House of Delegates, 10-047, 2010 Va. AG LEXIS 37 (7/30/10).

§ 19.2-82. Procedure upon arrest without warrant.

A. A person arrested without a warrant shall be brought forthwith before a magistrate or other issuing authority having jurisdiction who shall proceed to examine the officer making the arrest under oath. If the magistrate or other issuing authority having jurisdiction has lawful probable cause upon which to believe that a criminal offense has been committed, and that the person arrested has committed such offense, he shall issue either a warrant under the provisions of § 19.2-72 or a summons under the provisions of § 19.2-73.

As used in this section the term "brought before a magistrate or other issuing authority having jurisdiction" shall include a personal appearance before such authority or any two-way electronic video and audio communication meeting the requirements of § 19.2-3.1, in order that the accused and the arresting officer may simultaneously see and speak to such magistrate or authority. If electronic means are used, any documents filed may be transmitted in accordance with § 19.2-3.1.

If a warrant is issued the case shall thereafter be disposed of under the provisions of §§ 19.2-183 through 19.2-190, if the issuing officer is a judge; under the provisions of §§ 19.2-119 through 19.2-134, if the issuing officer is a magistrate or other issuing officer having jurisdiction.

If such warrant or summons is not issued, the person so arrested shall be released.

B. A warrant may be issued pursuant to this section, where the person has been arrested in accordance with § 19.2-81.6, and the magistrate or other issuing authority examines the officer making the arrest under oath, and finds lawful probable cause to believe the arrested individual meets the conditions of clauses (i) and (ii) of § 19.2-81.6. If such warrant is issued, it shall recite § 19.2-81.6 and the applicable violation of federal criminal law previously confirmed with Immigration and Customs Enforcement. Upon the person being taken into federal custody, such state warrant shall be dismissed. Any warrant issued under this subsection shall expire within 72 hours, or when the person is taken into federal custody, whichever occurs first. Recurrent applications for a warrant under this subsection shall not be permitted within a six-month period except where confirmation has been received from Immigration and Customs Enforcement that the arrested person will be taken into federal custody.

History.

Code 1950, § 19.1-100.1; 1968, c. 639; 1975, c. 495; 1981, c. 382; 1983, c. 564; 1984, c. 766; 1991, c. 41; 2002, c. 310; 2004, cc. 360, 412; 2009, c. 669.

The 2009 amendments.

The 2009 amendment by c. 669, in subsection B, deleted "the Bureau" preceding "Immigration and Customs" in the second sentence and added "except where confirmation has been received from Immigration and Customs Enforcement that the arrested person will be taken into federal custody" in the last sentence.

Michie's Jurisprudence.

For related discussion, see 2A M.J. Arrest, §§ 8, 12; 5B M.J. Criminal Procedure, §§ 13, 17, 19, 21; 19 M.J. Warrants, § 2.

CASE NOTES

Term "forthwith," as used in this section, is synonymous with standard used in § 19.2-80, and the same remedies for a violation of § 19.2-80 should apply to a violation of this section. Slade v. Commonwealth, No. 0786-85 (Ct. of Appeals Feb. 4, 1987).

Failure promptly to present defendant as required by this section is a mere procedural violation where it involves no constitutional error. Frye v. Commonwealth, 231 Va. 370, 345 S.E.2d 267 (1986).

Delay in presentment violates constitution only if exculpatory evidence thereby lost. — While, under Virginia law, an arresting officer must take an accused before a judicial officer with reasonable promptness and without unreasonable delay, violation of this requirement reaches constitutional dimension only if it results in the defendant's loss of exculpatory evidence. Frye v. Commonwealth, 231 Va. 370, 345 S.E.2d 267 (1986).

And evidence need not be excluded unless loss of exculpatory evidence results. — A violation of the prompt presentment provision of this section does not require the exclusion of evidence unless the violation caused a loss of exculpatory evidence. Jumper v. Commonwealth, No. 0497-85 (Ct. of Appeals Oct. 10, 1986).

Failure to have accused appear before magistrate. — Where the officer who had arrested the defendant for driving while intoxicated had appeared before a magistrate and obtained a warrant for the defendant's arrest without the defendant being present, it was undeniable that the probable cause determination did not adhere to the procedure set forth in this section but this violation alone did not constitute reversible error where it did not infringe any constitutional right of the defendant. Jones v. Town of Marion, 28 Va. App. 791, 508 S.E.2d 921 (1999), aff'd, 259 Va. 7, 524 S.E.2d 866 (2000).

Effect of delay in taking defendant before magistrate. — Where defendant was legally seized and constitutionally detained, delay in taking him before a magistrate did not mean that the probable cause to hold him for the crimes stated in the warrants somehow evaporated, so as to require exclusion of the evidence developed during his detention. Horne v. Commonwealth, 230 Va. 512, 339 S.E.2d 186 (1986).

In the Commonwealth, not every violation of the requirement that a suspect be taken before a magistrate without unnecessary delay results in the exclusion of evidence. Horne v. Commonwealth, 230 Va. 512, 339 S.E.2d 186 (1986).

Confessions held not excludable despite unreasonable delay. — Assuming, without deciding, that the arresting officers failed to present defendant to the magistrate before an unreason-

able period of time had elapsed, thereby violating this section, this violation does not result in exclusion of the confession obtained from him in the interim interrogation. Frye v. Commonwealth, 231 Va. 370, 345 S.E.2d 267 (1986).

Warrant issued after arrest irrelevant in false arrest action. — In an action under 42 U.S.C. § 1983 alleging that defendant officer denied plaintiff due process by subjecting him to a false arrest for being drunk in public, the arrest warrant issued by the magistrate subsequent to the arrest did not establish as a matter of law that probable cause existed for the defendant to arrest the plaintiff. Robinson v. Goff, 517 F. Supp. 350 (W.D. Va. 1981).

When a defendant officer in a civil action relies upon probable cause as a defense to a charge of illegal arrest under 42 U.S.C. § 1983, he must establish that probable cause existed at the time the arrest was made. A warrant, subsequently issued by a magistrate, is irrelevant to the determination of whether the officer arresting an individual without a warrant had probable cause to arrest. Robinson v. Goff, 517 F. Supp. 350 (W.D. Va. 1981).

Search incident to illegal arrest. — Where officers had reason to believe that defendant was driving on a suspended license, they had probable cause to arrest defendant, and thus, even though the arrest violated § 19.2-74, the arrest, and the search incident to that arrest, did not violate the Fourth Amendment; since there was no Fourth Amendment violation, the exclusionary rule did not apply, and since § 19.2-74 did not provide for exclusion of evidence retrieved from a search subsequent to that arrest, the trial court did not err in refusing to suppress evidence recovered during a search incident to defendant's arrest. Moore v. Commonwealth, 47 Va. App. 55, 622 S.E.2d 253, 2005 Va. App. LEXIS 536 (2005). But see Virginia v. Moore, — U.S. —, 128 S.Ct. 1598 (2008).

Police officers were authorized to issue only a summons to defendant for driving with a suspended license, since none of the exceptions in § 19.2-74 were present. Therefore, the officers' full field-type search of defendant's person after improperly arresting him violated his rights, since the "search incident to arrest" exception to the Fourth Amendment did not include a "search incident to citation." Moore v. Commonwealth, 272 Va. 717, 636 S.E.2d 395, 2006 Va. LEXIS 99 (2006), rev'd, remanded, 553 U.S. 164, 128 S. Ct. 1598, 2008 U.S. LEXIS 3674, 170 L. Ed. 2d 559 (U.S. 2008) rev'd, Virginia v. Moore, — U.S. —, 128 S.Ct. 1598 (2008) (see the following note).

Warrantless arrest for driving with a suspended license was reasonable under the Fourth Amendment, even if it was not permitted under § 19.2-74. Therefore, the crack cocaine and cash that the arrestee was carrying and that was discovered in a search incidental to the arrest did not need to be suppressed. Virginia v. Moore, 553 U.S. 164, 128 S. Ct. 1598, 170 L. Ed. 2d 559, 2008 U.S. LEXIS 3674 (2008).

CIRCUIT COURT OPINIONS

Delay. — Even assuming that the delay in taking defendant to the magistrate was unnecessary, there was only a procedural violation that did not amount to a constitutional error and, suppression of evidence and statements was not warranted as a result. Commonwealth v. Arava, 56 Va. Cir. 240, 2001 Va. Cir. LEXIS 133 (Arlington County 2001).

OPINIONS OF THE ATTORNEY GENERAL

Virginia law-enforcement officers have authority to detain and arrest individuals who have committed violations of the laws of the United States and other states, and such authority extends to violations of federal criminal immigration law. It would not be advisable to enforce such violations outside of the scope of an agreement with federal authorities. See opinion of Attorney General to The Honorable Kenneth W. Stolle, Member, Senate of Virginia, and The Honorable David B. Albo, Member, House of Delegates, 07-086 (10/15/07).

§ 19.2-82.1. Giving false identity to law-enforcement officer; penalty.

Any person who falsely identifies himself to a law-enforcement officer with the intent to deceive the law-enforcement officer as to his real identity after having been lawfully detained and after being requested to identify himself by a law-enforcement officer, is guilty of a Class 1 misdemeanor.

History.
2006, c. 387.

Cross references.
As to punishment for Class 1 misdemeanor, see § 18.2-11.

Law Review.
For 2006 survey article, "Criminal Law and Procedure," see 41 U. Rich. L. Rev. 83 (2006).

§ 19.2-83. Repealed by Acts 1994, c. 273.

§ 19.2-83.1. Report of arrest of school employees and adult students for certain offenses.

A. Every state official or agency and every sheriff, police officer, or other local law-enforcement officer or conservator of the peace having the power to arrest for a felony, upon arresting a person who is known or discovered by the arresting official to be a full-time, part-time, permanent, or temporary teacher or other employee in any public school division in this Commonwealth for a felony or a Class 1 misdemeanor or an equivalent offense in another state shall file a report of such arrest with the division superintendent of the employing division as soon as practicable. The contents of the report required pursuant to this section shall be utilized by the local school division solely to implement the provisions of subsection B of § 22.1-296.2 and § 22.1-315.

B. Every state official or agency and every sheriff, police officer, or other local law-enforcement officer or conservator of the peace having the power to arrest for a felony, shall file a report, as soon as practicable, with the division superintendent of the school division in which the student is enrolled upon arresting a person who is known or discovered by the arresting official to be a student age 18 or older in any public school division in this Commonwealth for:

1. A firearm offense pursuant to Article 4 (§ 18.2-279 et seq.), 5 (§ 18.2-288 et seq.), 6 (§ 18.2-299 et seq.), 6.1 (§ 18.2-307.1 et seq.), or 7 (§ 18.2-308.1 et seq.) of Chapter 7 of Title 18.2;

2. Homicide, pursuant to Article 1 (§ 18.2-30 et seq.) of Chapter 4 of Title 18.2;

3. Felonious assault and bodily wounding, pursuant to Article 4 (§ 18.2-51 et seq.) of Chapter 4 of Title 18.2;

4. Criminal sexual assault, pursuant to Article 7 (§ 18.2-61 et seq.) of Chapter 4 of Title 18.2;

5. Manufacture, sale, gift, distribution or possession of Schedule I or II controlled substances, pursuant to Article 1 (§ 18.2-247 et seq.) of Chapter 7 of Title 18.2;

6. Manufacture, sale or distribution of marijuana or synthetic cannabinoids pursuant to Article 1 (§ 18.2-247 et seq.) of Chapter 7 of Title 18.2;

7. Arson and related crimes, pursuant to Article 1 (§ 18.2-77 et seq.) of Chapter 5 of Title 18.2;

8. Burglary and related offenses, pursuant to §§ 18.2-89 through 18.2-93;

9. Robbery pursuant to § 18.2-58;

10. Prohibited criminal street gang activity pursuant to § 18.2-46.2; or

11. Recruitment of juveniles for criminal street gang pursuant to § 18.2-46.3.

History.
1991, c. 2; 1996, cc. 958, 960; 1997, c. 721; 2001, c. 591; 2004, c. 517; 2011, cc. 384, 410; 2013, c. 746.

Editor's note.
Acts 2011, cc. 384 and 410, cl. 3 provides: "That the provisions of this act may result in a net increase in periods of imprisonment or commitment. Pursuant to § 30-19.1:4, the estimated amount of the necessary appropriation cannot be determined for periods of imprisonment in state adult correctional facilities; therefore, Chapter 874 of the Acts of Assembly of 2010 requires the Virginia Criminal Sentencing Commission to assign a minimum fiscal impact of $50,000. Pursuant to § 30-19.1:4, the estimated amount of the necessary appropriation cannot be determined for periods of commitment to the custody of the Department of Juvenile Justice."

Acts 2013, c. 746, cl. 2 provides: "That the provisions of this act are declaratory of existing law."

The 2011 amendments.
The 2011 amendments by cc. 384 and 410, effective March 23, 2011, are identical, and, inserted "or synthetic cannabinoids" in subdivision B 6.

The 2013 amendments.
The 2013 amendment by c. 746 inserted "6.1 (§ 18.2-307.1 et seq.)," and substituted "18.2-308.1" for "18.2-308" in subdivision B 1.

Michie's Jurisprudence.
For related discussion, see 16 M.J. Schools, § 14.

§ 19.2-83.2. Jail officer to ascertain citizenship of inmate.

Whenever any person is taken into custody at any jail, the sheriff or other officer in charge of such facility shall inquire as to whether the person (i) was born in a country other than the United States, and (ii) is a citizen of a country other than the United States. The sheriff or other officer in charge of such facility shall make an immigration alien query to the Law Enforcement Support Center of the United States Immigration and Customs Enforcement for any person who (i) was born in a country other than the United States, and (ii) is a citizen of a country other than the United States, or for whom the answer to (i) or (ii) is unknown. The sheriff or other officer in charge shall communicate the results of any immigration alien query to the Local Inmate Data System of the State Compensation Board. The State Compensation Board shall communicate, on a monthly basis, the results of any immigration alien query that results in a confirmation that the person is illegally present in the United States to the Central Criminal Records Exchange of the Department of State Police in a format approved by the Exchange. The information received by the Central Criminal Records Exchange concerning the person's immigration status shall be recorded in the person's criminal history record.

History.
2008, cc. 180, 415.

Editor's note.
Acts 2008, cc. 180 and 415, cl. 2 provides: "That the State Compensation Board shall maintain in the Local Inmate Data System, and the Department of Corrections shall maintain in its offender management system, a specific data field for the entry of the response received from the Law Enforcement Support Center of the United States Immigration and Customs Enforcement pursuant to the request made in accordance with § 19.2-83.2 or 53.1-218 of the Code of Virginia for information on an inmate's immigration status."
Acts 2008, cc. 180 and 415, cl. 3 provides: "That the Department of Corrections shall confirm the validity of the social security numbers given by inmates and omit from its database those social security numbers determined to be fictitious."

CHAPTER 8.

EXTRADITION OF CRIMINALS.

ARTICLE 1.

FUGITIVES FROM FOREIGN NATIONS.

§ 19.2-84. Governor to surrender on requisition of President.

The Governor shall whenever required by the executive authority of the United States, pursuant to the Constitution and laws thereof, deliver over to justice any person found within the Commonwealth, who is charged with having committed any crime without the jurisdiction of the United States.

History.
Code 1950, § 19.1-47; 1960, c. 366; 1975, c. 495.

Law Review.
For essay, "In the Aftermath of Soering, Is Interstate Extradition to Virginia Illegal?", see 48 Wash. & Lee L. Rev. 1477 (1991).

Michie's Jurisprudence.
For related discussion, see 8A M.J. Extradition, § 2.

ARTICLE 2.

UNIFORM CRIMINAL EXTRADITION ACT.

Michie's Jurisprudence.
For related discussion, see 8A M.J. Extradition, § 2.

§ 19.2-85. Definitions.

When appearing in this chapter:
(1) The term *"Governor"* includes any person performing the functions of Governor by authority of the law of this Commonwealth;
(2) The term *"executive authority"* includes the Governor, and any person performing the functions of Governor in a state other than this Commonwealth;
(3) The term *"State,"* referring to a state other than this Commonwealth, includes any other state or territory, organized or unorganized, of the United States of America, and the District of Columbia; and
(4) The term *"judge"* means a judge of a court of record having criminal jurisdiction.

History.
Code 1950, § 19.1-49; 1960, c. 366; 1975, c. 495.

Uniform law cross references.
For other signatory state provisions, see:
Alaska: Alaska Stat. §§ 12.70.010 to 12.70.290.
Arizona: A.R.S. §§ 13-3841 to 13-3870.01.
Arkansas: A.C.A. §§ 16-94-201 to 16-94-231.
California: Cal. Pen. Code, § 1548 et seq.
Colorado: C.R.S. §§ 16-19-101 through 16-19-134.
Connecticut: Conn. Gen. Stat. §§ 54-157 to 54-185.
Delaware: 11 Del. Ch. § 2501 et seq.
Florida: Fla. Stat. § 941.01 et seq.
Georgia: O.C.G.A. §§ 17-13-20 to 17-13-49.
Hawaii: H.R.S. §§ 832-1 to 832-27.

Idaho: Idaho Code § 19-4501 et seq.
Illinois: 725 I.L.C.S. 225/1 to 225/32.
Indiana: Burns Ind. Code Ann., IC 35-33-10-3.
Iowa: Iowa Code §§ 820.1 to 820.29.
Kansas: K.S.A. §§ 22-2701 to 22-2730.
Kentucky: K.R.S. §§ 440.150 to 440.420.
Maine: 15 M.R.S. §§ 201 to 229.
Maryland: Md. Criminal Procedure Code Ann. §§ 9-101 through 9-128.
Michigan: M.C.L.S. §§ 780.1 to 780.31.
Minnesota: Minn. Stat. §§ 629.01 to 629.29.
Missouri: §§ 548.011 through 548.300 R.S. Mo.
Montana: Mont. Code Anno. §§ 46-30-101 to 46-30-413.
Nebraska: R.R.S. Neb. §§ 29-729 to 29-758.
Nevada: N.R.S. §§ 179.177 to 179.235.
New Hampshire: R.S.A. §§ 612:1 to 612:30.
New Jersey: N.J. Stat. § 2A-160-1 et seq.
New Mexico: N.M. Stat. Ann. §§ 31-4-1 to 31-4-30.
New York: NY CLS CPL §§ 570.02 to 570.66.
North Carolina: N.C. Gen. Stat. §§ 15A-721 to 15A-751.
Ohio: ORC Ann. 2963.01 et seq.
Oklahoma: 22 Okl. St. §§ 1141.1 to 1141.30.
Oregon: O.R.S. §§ 133.743 to 133.857.
Pennsylvania: 42 Pa. C.S. § 9121 et seq.
Puerto Rico: 34 L.P.R.A. § 1881 et seq.
Rhode Island: R.I. Gen. Laws § 12-9-1 et seq.
South Dakota: S.D. Codified Laws §§ 23-24-1 through 23-24-39.
Tennessee: Tenn. Code Ann. § 40-9-101 et seq.
Texas: Tex. Code Crim. Proc., art. 51.13.
Utah: Utah Code Ann. § 77-30-1 et seq.
Vermont: 13 V.S.A. §§ 4941 to 4969.
Virgin Islands: 5 V.I.C. §§ 3801 through 3829.
Washington: Rev. Code Wash. §§ 10.88.200 to 10.88.930.
West Virginia: W. Va. Code § 5-1-7 et seq.
Wisconsin: Wis. Stat. § 976.03.
Wyoming: Wyo. Stat. §§ 7-3-201 through 7-3-227.

Law Review.
For essay, "In the Aftermath of Soering, Is Interstate Extradition to Virginia Illegal?", see 48 Wash. & Lee L. Rev. 1477 (1991).

CASE NOTES

Matters of extradition are constitutionally controlled by U.S. Const., Art. IV, § 2, cl. 2. They are statutorily controlled by the Uniform Criminal Extradition Act (this article) and the Interstate Agreement on Detainers (§ 53.1-210 et seq.). Arebaugh v. Dalton, 600 F. Supp. 1345 (E.D. Va. 1985).

Governor of asylum state must make findings and conclusions. — While the Constitution mandates that a fugitive in one state "shall" be returned to the demanding state, the Governor of the asylum state must make factual findings and legal conclusions following specific inquiries prior to granting extradition. First, he must determine whether the accused has been charged with a crime under the laws of the demanding state, and second, whether the accused was within the demanding state at the time of the offense. The former is generally a question of law but it may be a question of fact. The latter is generally a question of fact. The Governor's factual determination may not be set aside unless it appears conclusively that the accused could not be a fugitive. Arebaugh v. Dalton, 600 F. Supp. 1345 (E.D. Va. 1985).

Governor's determination of probable cause precludes further judicial inquiry in asylum state. — Once the Governor of the asylum state has acted on a requisition for extradition based on the demanding state's judicial determination that probable cause existed, no further judicial inquiry may be had on that issue in the asylum state. Arebaugh v. Dalton, 600 F. Supp. 1345 (E.D. Va. 1985).

Habeas court in asylum state cannot discharge person arrested on merely contradictory evidence. — A habeas court in an asylum state cannot discharge one who has been arrested under a governor's warrant where there is merely contradictory evidence on the subject of presence in or absence from the State, as habeas corpus is not the proper proceeding to try the question of alibi, or any question as to the guilt or innocence of the accused. Only when it is conclusively proved that no question can be made

that the person was not within the demanding state when the crime is said to have been committed is he to be released. Manning v. Commonwealth, 1 Va. App. 60, 334 S.E.2d 151 (1985).

Only function of an Attorney General, in extradition proceedings, is to assist the Governor in determining whether extradition ought to be granted. In this sense, he is entitled to absolute immunity because of the quasi-judicial function he is performing. If it be deemed that his duty in this connection be that of an advocate, he is entitled to the absolute immunity accorded public prosecutors. Arebaugh v. Dalton, 600 F. Supp. 1345 (E.D. Va. 1985).

Immunity of Governor and Attorney General where statutory duty breached. — If the Governor and Attorney General, in acting on an extradition request, breach some statutory duty or are derelict in their statutory duties, they are, nevertheless, entitled to absolute immunity from damages. Arebaugh v. Dalton, 600 F. Supp. 1345 (E.D. Va. 1985).

Governor immune since he acts in judicial capacity. — When the Governor of an asylum state acts on an extradition request he performs a judicial function. Accordingly, he would be entitled to absolute immunity in carrying out this function. Arebaugh v. Dalton, 600 F. Supp. 1345 (E.D. Va. 1985).

Judicial immunity of magistrate ordering temporary confinement of extradited prisoner. — Even if, as prison inmate contended, state magistrates have no authority under the Virginia Uniform Criminal Extradition Act (UCEA) (this article) to order temporary confinement of extradited prisoners, judicial immunity would still be appropriate. The very applicability of the UCEA with regard to the inmate's transfer represented an unsettled and disputed point of law. In contrast, the general authority of magistrates to commit persons accused of crimes to jail is well established in Virginia by statute. Pressly v. Gregory, 831 F.2d 514 (4th Cir. 1987).

§ 19.2-86. Fugitives from justice; duty of Governor.

Subject to the provisions of this chapter, the provisions of the Constitution of the United States controlling, and any and all acts of Congress enacted in pursuance thereof, the Governor shall have arrested and delivered up to the executive authority of any other of the United States any person charged in that state with treason, felony, or other crime, who has fled from justice and is found in this Commonwealth.

History.
Code 1950, § 19.1-50; 1960, c. 366; 1975, c. 495.

Law Review.
For essay, "In the Aftermath of Soering, Is Interstate Extradition to Virginia Illegal?", see 48 Wash. & Lee L. Rev. 1477 (1991).

CASE NOTES

A charge of crime is not merged in the conviction and sentence, for the purpose of extradition, but the criminal is still charged with the crime until completion of the sentence imposed upon him. United States ex rel. Faris v. McClain, 42 F. Supp. 429 (M.D. Pa. 1942).

Inapplicable to non-fleers. — Since this section addresses the extradition only of persons who have "fled from justice," and defendant was clearly not such a person, defendant's contentions with respect to the Uniform Criminal Extradition Act were without merit. Stewart v. Bailey, 7 F.3d 384 (4th Cir. 1993).

§ 19.2-87. Form of demand.

No demand for the extradition of a person charged with, or convicted of, crime in another state shall be recognized by the Governor unless in writing alleging, except in cases arising under § 19.2-91, that the accused was present in the demanding state at the time of the commission of the alleged crime and that thereafter he fled from such state, and accompanied: (1) by a copy of an indictment found, (2) by a copy or an information supported by an affidavit filed in the state having jurisdiction of the crime, (3) by a copy of an affidavit made before a magistrate in such state together with a copy of any warrant which was issued thereupon, or (4) by a copy of a judgment of conviction or of a sentence imposed in execution thereof together with a statement by the executive authority of the demanding state that the person claimed has escaped from confinement or has broken the terms of his bail, probation or parole. The indictment, information or affidavit made before the magistrate must substantially charge the person demanded with having committed a crime under the law of that state; and the copy of the indictment, information, affidavit, judgment of conviction or sentence must be authenticated by the executive authority making the demand.

History.
Code 1950, § 19.1-51; 1960, c. 366; 1975, c. 495.

CIRCUIT COURT OPINIONS

Request for extradition and affadavit incorrect. — Because the Florida extradition warrant signed by the Governor of Florida and its underlying request for extradition and probable cause affidavit were incorrect on their face, and because the office of the Secretary of the Commonwealth failed to provide a resident 10 days in which to respond to Florida's extradition warrant, the resident was entitled to have the petition for writ of habeas corpus be granted. Cole v. Commonwealth, 84 Va. Cir. 367, 2012 Va. Cir. LEXIS 38 (Fairfax County Mar. 14, 2012).

§ 19.2-88. Governor may investigate case.

When a demand shall be made upon the Governor by the executive authority of another state for the surrender of a person so charged with, or convicted of, crime, the Governor may call upon the Attorney General or any other officer of this Commonwealth to investigate or assist in investigating the demand and to report to him the situation and circumstances of the person so demanded and whether he ought to be surrendered.

History.
Code 1950, § 19.1-52; 1960, c. 366; 1975, c. 495.

CASE NOTES

Only function of an Attorney General, in extradition proceedings, is to assist the Governor in determining whether extradition ought to be granted. In this sense, he is entitled to absolute immunity because of the quasi-judicial function he is performing. If it be deemed that his duty in this connection be that of an advocate, he is entitled to the absolute immunity accorded public prosecutors. Arebaugh v. Dalton, 600 F. Supp. 1345 (E.D. Va. 1985).

Immunity of Governor and Attorney General where statutory duty breached. — If the Governor and Attorney General, in acting on an extradition request, breach some statutory duty or are

derelict in their statutory duties, they are, nevertheless, entitled to absolute immunity from damages. Arebaugh v. Dalton, 600 F. Supp. 1345 (E.D. Va. 1985).

§ 19.2-89. Extradition of persons imprisoned or awaiting trial in another state.

When it is desired to have returned to this Commonwealth a person charged in this Commonwealth with a crime and such person is imprisoned or is held under criminal proceedings then pending against him in another state, the Governor may agree with the executive authority of such other state for the extradition of such person before the conclusion of such proceedings or his term of sentence in such other state, upon condition that such person be returned to such other state at the expense of this Commonwealth as soon as the prosecution in this Commonwealth is terminated.

History.
Code 1950, § 19.1-53; 1960, c. 366; 1975, c. 495.

Law Review.
For essay, "In the Aftermath of Soering, Is Interstate Extradition to Virginia Illegal?," see 48 Wash. & Lee L. Rev. 1477 (1991).

§ 19.2-90. Extradition of persons who have left demanding state involuntarily.

The Governor may also surrender on demand of the executive authority of any other state any person in this Commonwealth who is charged in the manner provided in §§ 19.2-109 to 19.2-111, with having violated the laws of the state whose executive authority is making the demand, even though such person left the demanding state involuntarily.

History.
Code 1950, § 19.1-54; 1960, c. 366; 1975, c. 495.

§ 19.2-91. Extradition of persons not in demanding state at time of commission of crime.

The Governor may also surrender, on demand of the executive authority of any other state, any person in this Commonwealth charged in such other state in the manner provided in § 19.2-87 with committing an act in this Commonwealth, or in a third state, intentionally resulting in a crime in the state whose executive authority is making the demand. The provisions of this chapter not otherwise inconsistent shall apply to such cases, even though the accused was not in that state at the time of the commission of the crime, and has not fled therefrom.

History.
Code 1950, § 19.1-55; 1960, c. 366; 1975, c. 495.

CIRCUIT COURT OPINIONS

Request for extradition and affadavit incorrect. — Because the Florida extradition warrant signed by the Governor of Florida and its underlying request for extradition and probable cause affidavit were incorrect on their face, and because the office of the Secretary of the Commonwealth failed to provide a resident 10 days in which to respond to Florida's extradition warrant, the resident was entitled to have the petition for writ of habeas corpus be granted. Cole v. Commonwealth, 84 Va. Cir. 367, 2012 Va. Cir. LEXIS 38 (Fairfax County Mar. 14, 2012).

§ 19.2-92. Issuance of Governor's warrant of arrest; its recitals.

If the Governor decides that a demand for the extradition of a person, charged with, or convicted of, crime in another state should be complied with, he shall sign a warrant of arrest, which shall be sealed with the state seal, and be directed to the sheriff or sergeant of any county or city or to any peace officer or other person whom he may think fit to entrust with the execution thereof. The warrant must substantially recite the facts necessary to the validity of its issuance. Any electronically transmitted facsimile of a Governor's warrant shall be treated as an original document, provided the original is received within four working days of receipt of the facsimile.

History.
Code 1950, § 19.1-56; 1960, c. 366; 1975, c. 495; 2001, cc. 214, 226; 2011, c. 59.

The 2011 amendments.
The 2011 amendment by c. 59 inserted "working" in the last sentence.

§ 19.2-93. Manner and place of execution of warrant.

Such warrant shall authorize the officer or other person to whom it is directed to arrest the accused at any time and at any place where he may be found within the Commonwealth and to command the aid of all peace officers or other persons in the execution of the warrant and to deliver the accused, subject to the provisions of this chapter, to the duly authorized agent of the demanding state.

History.
Code 1950, § 19.1-57; 1960, c. 366; 1975, c. 495.

§ 19.2-94. Assistance to arresting officer.

Every officer or other person empowered to make the arrest, as provided in the preceding section, shall have the same authority, in arresting the accused, to command assistance therein as the sheriffs and sergeants of the several counties and cities of this Commonwealth have by law in the execution of any criminal process directed to them, with like penalties against those who refuse to render their assistance.

History.
Code 1950, § 19.1-58; 1960, c. 366; 1975, c. 495.

§ 19.2-95. Rights of accused persons; application for writ of habeas corpus.

No person arrested upon such warrant shall be delivered over to the agent whom the executive authority demanding him shall have appointed to receive him unless he shall first be taken forthwith before a judge of a circuit or general district court in the Commonwealth, who shall inform him of the demand made for his surrender and of the crime with which he is charged, and that he has the right to demand and procure legal counsel; and if the prisoner or his counsel shall state that he or they desire to test the legality of his arrest, the judge shall fix a reasonable time to be allowed him within which to apply for a writ of habeas corpus. When such writ is applied for, notice thereof and of the time and place of hearing thereon shall be given to the attorney for the Commonwealth of the county or city in which the arrest is made and in which the accused is in custody, and to the agent of the demanding state.

History.
Code 1950, § 19.1-59; 1960, c. 366; 1975, c. 495; 2005, c. 839.

Michie's Jurisprudence.
For related discussion, see 9A M.J. Habeas Corpus, § 16.

CASE NOTES

A petitioner is required to exhaust his state remedies as a prerequisite to seeking habeas corpus in a federal court to avoid extradition. Tickle v. Summers, 270 F.2d 848 (4th Cir. 1959).

§ 19.2-96. Penalty for noncompliance with preceding section.

Any officer who shall deliver to the agent for extradition of the demanding state a person in his custody under the Governor's warrant in willful disobedience to the last preceding section shall be guilty of a Class 1 misdemeanor.

History.
Code 1950, § 19.1-60; 1960, c. 366; 1975, c. 495.

Cross references.
As to punishment for Class 1 misdemeanors, see § 18.2-11.

§ 19.2-97. Confinement in jail when necessary.

The officer or persons executing the Governor's warrant of arrest, or the agent of the demanding state to whom the prisoner may have been delivered, may, when necessary, confine the prisoner in the jail of any county or city through which he may pass; and the keeper of such jail shall receive and safely keep the prisoner until the officer or person having charge of him is ready to proceed on his route, such officer or person being chargeable with the expense of keeping.

History.
Code 1950, § 19.1-61; 1960, c. 366; 1975, c. 495.

§ 19.2-98. Same; for prisoners being taken through Commonwealth.

The officer or agent of a demanding state to whom a prisoner may have been delivered following extradition proceedings in another state or to whom a prisoner may have been delivered after waiving extradition in such other state, and who is passing through this Commonwealth with such prisoner for the purpose of returning immediately such prisoner to the demanding state may, when necessary, confine the prisoner in the jail of any county or city through which he may pass; and the keeper of such jail shall receive and safely keep the prisoner until the officer or agent having charge of him is ready to proceed on his route, such officer or agent, however, being chargeable with the expense of keeping, provided, however, that such officer or agent shall deliver to the jailer the warrant or legal order authorizing custody of the prisoner. Such prisoner shall not be entitled to demand a new requisition while in this Commonwealth.

History.
Code 1950, § 19.1-62; 1960, c. 366; 1975, c. 495.

§ 19.2-99. Arrest prior to requisition.

Whenever: (1) any person within this Commonwealth shall be charged on the oath of any credible person before any judge, magistrate or other officer authorized to issue criminal warrants in this Commonwealth with the commission of any crime in any other state and, except in cases arising under § 19.2-91, (a) with having fled from justice, (b) with having been convicted of a crime in that state and of having escaped from confinement, or (c) of having broken the terms of his bail, probation, or parole, or (2) complaint shall have been made before any such judge, magistrate or other officer in this Commonwealth setting forth on the affidavit of any credible person in another state that a crime has been committed in such other state and that the accused has been charged in such state with the commission of the crime, and, except in cases arising under § 19.2-91, (a) has fled from justice, (b) having been convicted of a crime in that state has escaped from confinement, or (c) broken the terms of his bail, probation or parole, and that the accused is believed to be in this Commonwealth, such judge, magistrate or other officer shall issue a warrant directed to any sheriff or to any peace officer commanding him to apprehend the person named therein, wherever he may be found in this Commonwealth, and to bring him before any judge who may be available in or convenient of access to the place where the arrest may be made, to answer the charge of complaint and affidavit. A certified copy of the sworn charge or complaint and affidavit upon which the warrant is issued shall be attached to the warrant.

History.
Code 1950, § 19.1-63; 1960, c. 366; 1975, c. 495.

§ 19.2-100. Arrest without warrant.

The arrest of a person may be lawfully made also by any peace officer or private person without a warrant upon reasonable information that the accused stands charged in the courts of a state with a crime punishable by death or imprisonment for a term exceeding one year. But when so arrested the accused shall be taken before a judge, magistrate or other officer authorized to issue criminal warrants in this Commonwealth with all practicable speed and complaint made against him under oath setting forth the ground for the arrest as in the preceding section; and thereafter his answer shall be heard as if he had been arrested on a warrant.

History.
Code 1950, § 19.1-64; 1960, c. 366; 1975, c. 495.

Cross references.
For arrest without warrant in cases of flight and pursuit, see § 19.2-77. For other statutes authorizing arrests without warrants, see §§ 19.2-81 and 52-20.

Michie's Jurisprudence.
For related discussion, see 2A M.J. Arrest, §§ 5, 12.

CASE NOTES

Reasonable information that accused stands charged with crime. — Where a Kentucky warrant on its face charged accused with the commission of a felony, it constituted "reasonable information" to a deputy sheriff of Virginia that accused stood charged in the courts of another state with a crime, punishable by "imprisonment for a term exceeding one year," and justified the local officer in arresting him without a warrant within the meaning of this section. Mullins v. Sanders, 189 Va. 624, 54 S.E.2d 116 (1949).

The person arrested must be taken before a judicial officer within a reasonable time, or without unnecessary delay, in order that a charge may be formulated against him. Mullins v. Sanders, 189 Va. 624, 54 S.E.2d 116 (1949).

Unreasonable delay constitutes false imprisonment. — Unreasonable delay in failing to comply with such statutory mandate constitutes false imprisonment. Moreover, any person who causes, induces, aids, assists or encourages an officer to delay unreasonably in bringing the arrested person before the committing judicial officer is likewise liable for such unlawful imprisonment. Mullins v. Sanders, 189 Va. 624, 54 S.E.2d 116 (1949).

Question for jury. — Whether an arrested person has been brought before a magistrate "with all practicable speed," as is required by this section, or without unnecessary delay, depends upon the circumstances of the particular case. Ordinarily, this is a question for the jury unless the facts are undisputed. Mullins v. Sanders, 189 Va. 624, 54 S.E.2d 116 (1949).

§ 19.2-101. Confinement to await requisition; bail.

If from the examination before the judge it appears that the person held pursuant to either of the two preceding sections is the person charged with having committed the crime alleged and, except in cases arising under § 19.2-91, that he has fled from justice, the judge shall, by a warrant reciting the accusation, commit him to jail for such a time, not exceeding thirty days, specified in the warrant as will enable the arrest of the accused to be made under a warrant of the Governor on a requisition of the executive authority of the state having jurisdiction of the offense, unless the accused give bail as provided in the next section, or until he shall be legally discharged.

History.
Code 1950, § 19.1-65; 1960, c. 366; 1975, c. 495.

CASE NOTES

The impact of this section and § 19.2-103 is that an individual arrested in this State as a fugitive from justice in another state cannot be confined in jail upon the warrant of the judge or trial justice for longer than ninety days, sixty days of which must be on a recommitment order of a judge or trial justice. At the end of this time period, if no governor's warrant has been issued, it appears that the accused must be released. Speaks v. Pittsylvania County, 355 F. Supp. 1129 (W.D. Va. 1973).

The time period specified in this section begins to run from the date of execution of the warrant. Unless recommitted under § 19.2-103, the Commonwealth is required to release defendant on this warrant at the end of thirty days. Speaks v. Pittsylvania County, 355 F. Supp. 1129 (W.D. Va. 1973).

§ 19.2-102. In what cases bail allowed; conditions of bond.

Unless the offense with which the prisoner is charged is shown to be an offense punishable by death or life imprisonment under the laws of the state in which it was committed, any judge, magistrate or other person authorized by law to admit persons to bail in this Commonwealth may admit the person arrested to bail by bond, with sufficient sureties, and in such sum as he deems proper, conditioned upon his appearance before a judge at a time specified in such bond and upon his surrender for arrest upon the warrant of the Governor of this Commonwealth.

History.
Code 1950, § 19.1-66; 1960, c. 366; 1975, c. 495.

§ 19.2-103. Discharge, recommitment or renewal of bail.

If the accused is not arrested under warrant of the Governor by the expiration of the time specified in the warrant or bond, any judge in this Commonwealth may discharge him or may recommit him for a further period not to exceed sixty days, or such judge may again take bail for his appearance and surrender, as provided in the preceding section, but within a period not to exceed sixty days after the date of such new bond.

History.
Code 1950, § 19.1-67; 1960, c. 366; 1975, c. 495.

CASE NOTES

The impact of this section and § 19.2-101 is that an individual arrested in this State as a fugitive from justice in another state cannot be confined in jail upon the warrant of the judge, trial justice, or justice of the peace for longer than ninety days, sixty days of which must be on a recommitment order of a judge or trial

justice. At the end of this time period, if no governor's warrant has been issued, it appears that the accused must be released. Speaks v. Pittsylvania County, 355 F. Supp. 1129 (W.D. Va. 1973).

§ 19.2-104. Forfeiture of bail.

If the prisoner is admitted to bail and fails to appear and surrender himself according to the conditions of his bond, any judge of a circuit or general district court by proper order, shall declare the bond forfeited and order his immediate arrest without warrant if he be within this Commonwealth. Recovery may be had on such bond in the name of the Commonwealth as in the case of other bonds given by the accused in criminal proceedings within this Commonwealth.

History.
Code 1950, § 19.1-68; 1960, c. 366; 1975, c. 495.

§ 19.2-105. Persons under criminal prosecution in this Commonwealth at time of requisition.

If a criminal prosecution has been instituted against such person under the laws of this Commonwealth and is still pending, the Governor, in his discretion, either may surrender him on demand of the executive authority of another state or hold him until he has been tried and discharged or convicted and punished in this Commonwealth.

History.
Code 1950, § 19.1-69; 1960, c. 366; 1975, c. 495.

§ 19.2-106. When guilt or innocence of accused inquired into.

The guilt or innocence of the accused as to the crime of which he is charged may not be inquired into by the Governor or in any proceeding after the demand for extradition accompanied by a charge of crime in legal form as above provided shall have been presented to the Governor, except as it may be involved in identifying the person held as the person charged with the crime.

History.
Code 1950, § 19.1-70; 1960, c. 366; 1975, c. 495.

§ 19.2-107. Governor may recall warrant or issue alias.

The Governor may recall his warrant of arrest or may issue another warrant whenever he deems it proper.

History.
Code 1950, § 19.1-71; 1960, c. 366; 1975, c. 495.

§ 19.2-108. Fugitives from this Commonwealth; duty of Governor.

Whenever the Governor shall demand a person charged with crime or with escaping from confinement or breaking the terms of his bail, probation or parole in this Commonwealth, from the executive authority of any other state, or from the chief justice or an associate justice of the Supreme Court of the District of Columbia authorized to receive such demand under the laws of the United States, he shall issue a warrant under the seal of this Commonwealth to some agent commanding him to receive the person so charged if delivered to him and convey him to the proper officer of the county or city in this Commonwealth in which the offense was committed. Nothing herein shall prevent the sheriff or police chief of a county or city who has been directed to execute such warrant from authorizing a private prisoner transportation company meeting the minimum qualifications set by the Department of Criminal Justice Services to receive and return the person to the Commonwealth.

History.
Code 1950, § 19.1-72; 1960, c. 366; 1975, c. 495; 2009, c. 848.

The 2009 amendments.
The 2009 amendment by c. 848 added the last sentence.

Law Review.
For essay, "In the Aftermath of Soering, Is Interstate Extradition to Virginia Illegal?," see 48 Wash. & Lee L. Rev. 1477 (1991).

OPINIONS OF THE ATTORNEY GENERAL

Governor may appoint any agent he chooses to retrieve and return to court a fugitive located in another state. See opinion of Attorney General to The Honorable H. S. Caudill, Sheriff for Tazewell County, 02-096 (12/20/02).

§ 19.2-109. Application for requisition for return of person charged with crime.

When the return to this Commonwealth of a person charged with crime in this Commonwealth is required, the attorney for the Commonwealth shall present to the Governor his written application for a requisition for the return of the person charged, in which application shall be stated the name of the person so charged, the crime charged against him, the approximate time, place and circumstances of its commission, the state in which he is believed to be, including the location of the accused therein at the time the application is made, and certifying that, in the opinion of the attorney for the Commonwealth, the ends of justice require the arrest and return of the accused to this Commonwealth for trial and that the proceeding is not instituted to enforce a private claim.

History.
Code 1950, § 19.1-73; 1960, c. 366; 1975, c. 495.

§ 19.2-110. Application for requisition for return of escaped convict, etc.

When the return to this Commonwealth is required of a person who has been convicted of a crime in this Commonwealth and has escaped from confinement or broken the terms of his bail, probation or parole, the attorney for the Commonwealth, of the county or city in which the offense was committed, or the warden of the institution or sheriff of the county or city from which the escape was made, shall present to the Governor a written application for a requisition for the return of such person, in which application shall be stated the name of the person, the crime of which he was convicted, the circumstances of his escape from confinement or of the breach of the terms of his bail, probation or parole and the state in which he is believed to be, including the location of the person therein at the time application is made.

History.
Code 1950, § 19.1-74; 1960, c. 366; 1975, c. 495.

§ 19.2-111. Form of such applications; copies, etc.

The application shall be verified by affidavit, shall be executed in duplicate and shall be accompanied by two certified copies of the indictment returned, or information and affidavit filed, or of the complaint made to the judge of a circuit or general district court or other officer issuing the warrant stating the offense with which the accused is charged, or of the judgment of conviction or of the sentence. The attorney for the Commonwealth, warden or sheriff may also attach such further affidavits and other documents in duplicate as he shall deem proper to be submitted with such application. One copy of the application, with the action of the Governor indicated by endorsement thereon, and one of the certified copies of the indictment, complaint, information, and affidavits, or of the judgment of conviction or of the sentence shall be filed in the office of the Secretary of the Commonwealth, to remain of record in that office. The other copies of all papers shall be forwarded with the Governor's requisition.

History.
Code 1950, § 19.1-75; 1960, c. 366; 1975, c. 495.

§ 19.2-112. Costs and expenses of extradition.

A. The expenses incident to the extradition of any person under the four preceding sections may be paid out of the state treasury, on warrants of the Comptroller issued upon vouchers signed by the Governor, or such other person as may be designated by him for such purpose.

B. If the person extradited is found guilty, or if the person was extradited after illegally leaving the Commonwealth while on parole or on probation, the person extradited, and not the Commonwealth, shall be responsible for the costs and expenses of extradition. The state treasury shall continue to reimburse local jurisdictions for the costs and expenses of extradition. The fugitive shall pay the costs and expenses of his extradition into the state treasury.

History.

Code 1950, § 19.1-76; 1960, c. 366; 1975, c. 495; 1999, c. 322; 2002, c. 622.

§ 19.2-113. Immunity from service of process in certain civil actions.

A person brought into this Commonwealth by, or after waiver of, extradition based on a criminal charge shall not be subject to service of personal process in civil actions arising out of the same facts as the criminal proceeding to answer which he is being or has been returned, until he has been convicted in the criminal proceeding, or, if acquitted, until he has had reasonable opportunity to return to the state from which he was extradited.

History.

Code 1950, § 19.1-77; 1960, c. 366; 1975, c. 495.

§ 19.2-114. Written waiver of extradition proceedings.

Any person arrested in this Commonwealth charged with having committed any crime in another state or alleged to have escaped from confinement, or broken the terms of his bail, probation or parole may waive the issuance and service of the warrant provided for in §§ 19.2-92 and 19.2-93 and all other procedures incidental to extradition proceedings by executing or subscribing in the presence of a judge of a circuit or district court within this Commonwealth a writing which states that he consents to return to the demanding state. However, before the waiver is executed or subscribed by the person, it shall be the duty of the judge to inform the person of his rights to the issuance and service of a warrant of extradition and to obtain a writ of habeas corpus as provided for in § 19.2-95.

If and when such consent has been duly executed, it shall forthwith be forwarded to the office of the Governor and filed therein. The judge shall direct the officer having the person in custody to promptly deliver him to the duly accredited agent of the demanding state, and shall deliver or cause to be delivered to such agent a copy of the consent.

This section shall not be deemed to limit the rights of the accused person to return voluntarily and without formality to the demanding state, nor shall this waiver procedure be deemed to be an executive procedure or to limit the powers, rights or duties of the officers of the demanding state or of this Commonwealth.

History.

Code 1950, § 19.1-78; 1960, c. 366; 1975, c. 495; 1992, c. 306.

Law Review.

For essay, "In the Aftermath of Soering, Is Interstate Extradition to Virginia Illegal?," see 48 Wash. & Lee L. Rev. 1477 (1991).

Michie's Jurisprudence.

For related discussion, see 9A M.J. Habeas Corpus, § 16.

§ 19.2-115. Nonwaiver by this Commonwealth.

Nothing in this chapter contained shall be deemed to constitute a waiver by this Commonwealth of its right, power or privilege to try such demanded person for crime committed within this Commonwealth, or of its right, power or privilege to regain custody of such person by extradition proceedings or otherwise for the purpose of trial, sentence or punishment for any crime committed within this Commonwealth, nor shall any proceedings had under this chapter which result in, or fail to result in, extradition be deemed a waiver by this Commonwealth of any of its rights, privileges or jurisdiction in any way whatsoever.

History.

Code 1950, § 19.1-79; 1960, c. 366; 1975, c. 495.

Law Review.

For essay, "In the Aftermath of Soering, Is Interstate Extradition to Virginia Illegal?," see 48 Wash. & Lee L. Rev. 1477 (1991).

§ 19.2-116. No right of asylum; no immunity from other criminal prosecutions while in this Commonwealth.

After a person has been brought back to this Commonwealth by, or after waiver of, extradition proceedings he may be tried in this Commonwealth for other crimes which he may be charged with having committed here as well as that specified in the requisition for his extradition.

History.

Code 1950, § 19.1-80; 1960, c. 366; 1975, c. 495.

Law Review.

For essay, "In the Aftermath of Soering, Is Interstate Extradition to Virginia Illegal?," see 48 Wash. & Lee L. Rev. 1477 (1991).

§ 19.2-117. Interpretation of article.

The provisions of this article shall be so interpreted and construed as to effectuate its general purposes to make uniform the law of those states which enact statutes similar thereto.

History.

Code 1950, § 19.1-81; 1960, c. 366; 1975, c. 495.

§ 19.2-118. Short title.

This article may be cited as the Uniform Criminal Extradition Act.

History.

Code 1950, § 19.1-82; 1960, c. 366; 1975, c. 495.

CASE NOTES

Applied in Arebaugh v. Dalton, 600 F. Supp. 1345 (E.D. Va. 1985).

CHAPTER 9.

BAIL AND RECOGNIZANCES.

Article 1. Bail.

ARTICLE 1.

BAIL.

Michie's Jurisprudence.

For related discussion, see 2B M.J. Bail and Recognizance, §§ 2, 8, 16, 29; 5B M.J. Criminal Procedure, §§ 14, 19, 20.

§ 19.2-119. Definitions.

As used in this chapter:

"*Bail*" means the pretrial release of a person from custody upon those terms and conditions specified by order of an appropriate judicial officer.

"*Bond*" means the posting by a person or his surety of a written promise to pay a specific sum, secured or unsecured, ordered by an appropriate judicial officer as a condition of bail to assure performance of the terms and conditions contained in the recognizance.

"*Criminal history*" means records and data collected by criminal justice agencies or persons consisting of identifiable descriptions and notations of arrests, detentions, indictments, informations or other formal charges, and any deposition arising therefrom.

"*Judicial officer*" means, unless otherwise indicated, any magistrate serving the jurisdiction, any judge of a district court and the clerk or deputy clerk of any district court or circuit court within their respective cities and counties, any judge of a circuit court, any judge of the Court of Appeals and any justice of the Supreme Court of Virginia.

"*Person*" means any accused, or any juvenile taken into custody pursuant to § 16.1-246.

"*Recognizance*" means a signed commitment by a person to appear in court as directed and to adhere to any other terms ordered by an appropriate judicial officer as a condition of bail.

History.

Code 1950, § 19.1-109.1; 1973, c. 485; 1974, c. 114; 1975, c. 495; 1984, c. 703; 1991, c. 581; 1993, c. 636; 1999, cc. 829, 846; 2008, cc. 551, 691.

The 2008 amendments.

The 2008 amendments by cc. 551 and 691 are identical and substituted "magistrate serving the jurisdiction" for "magistrate within his jurisdiction" in the definition for "Judicial officer."

CASE NOTES

Immunity of magistrates for acts in judicial capacity. — As judicial officers, magistrates are entitled to absolute immunity for acts performed in their judicial capacity. That immunity is vitiated only when the judicial officer acts in the clear absence of all jurisdiction. Pressly v. Gregory, 831 F.2d 514 (4th Cir. 1987).

OPINIONS OF THE ATTORNEY GENERAL

Surety bail bondsman. — A surety bail bondsman who executes a secured bail bond as a disclosed agent-in-fact for the stated corporate surety is not personally liable to the Commonwealth when the criminal defendant absconds, and the bond is forfeited. See opinion of Attorney General to The Honorable James S. Mathews, Judge, Norfolk General District Court, 09-025, 2009 Va. AG LEXIS 28 (6/1/09).

§ 19.2-120. Admission to bail.

Prior to conducting any hearing on the issue of bail, release or detention, the judicial officer shall, to the extent feasible, obtain the person's criminal history.

A. A person who is held in custody pending trial or hearing for an offense, civil or criminal contempt, or otherwise shall be admitted to bail by a judicial officer, unless there is probable cause to believe that:

1. He will not appear for trial or hearing or at such other time and place as may be directed, or

2. His liberty will constitute an unreasonable danger to himself or the public.

B. The judicial officer shall presume, subject to rebuttal, that no condition or combination of conditions will reasonably assure the appearance of the person or the safety of the public if the person is currently charged with:

1. An act of violence as defined in § 19.2-297.1;

2. An offense for which the maximum sentence is life imprisonment or death;

3. A violation of § 18.2-248, 18.2-248.01, 18.2-255, or 18.2-255.2 involving a Schedule I or II controlled substance if (i) the maximum term of imprisonment is 10 years or more and the person was previously convicted of a like offense or (ii) the person was previously convicted as a "drug kingpin" as defined in § 18.2-248;

4. A violation of § 18.2-308.1, 18.2-308.2, or 18.2-308.4 and which relates to a firearm and provides for a mandatory minimum sentence;

5. Any felony, if the person has been convicted of two or more offenses described in subdivision 1 or 2, whether under the laws of the Commonwealth or substantially similar laws of the United States;

6. Any felony committed while the person is on release pending trial for a prior felony under federal or state law or on release pending imposition or execution of sentence or appeal of sentence or conviction;

7. An offense listed in subsection B of § 18.2-67.5:2 and the person had previously been convicted of an offense listed in § 18.2-67.5:2 or a substantially similar offense under the laws of any state or the United States and the judicial officer finds probable cause to believe that the person who is currently charged with one of these offenses committed the offense charged;

8. A violation of § 18.2-374.1 or 18.2-374.3 where the offender has reason to believe that the solicited person is under 15 years of age and the offender is at least five years older than the solicited person;

9. A violation of § 18.2-46.2, 18.2-46.3, 18.2-46.5, or 18.2-46.7;

10. A violation of § 18.2-36.1, 18.2-51.4, 18.2-266, or 46.2-341.24 and the person has, within the past five years of the instant offense, been convicted three times on different dates of a violation of any combination of these Code sections, or any ordinance of any county, city, or town or the laws of any other state or of the United States substantially similar thereto, and has been at liberty between each conviction;

11. A second or subsequent violation of § 16.1-253.2 or 18.2-60.4 or a substantially similar offense under the laws of any state or the United States;

12. A violation of subsection B of § 18.2-57.2; or

13. A violation of subsection C of § 18.2-460 charging the use of threats of bodily harm or force to knowingly attempt to intimidate or impede a witness.

C. The judicial officer shall presume, subject to rebuttal, that no condition or combination of conditions will reasonably assure the appearance of the person or the safety of the public if the person is being arrested pursuant to § 19.2-81.6.

D. A judicial officer who is a magistrate, clerk, or deputy clerk of a district court or circuit court may not admit to bail, that is not set by a judge, any person who is charged with an offense giving rise to a rebuttable presumption against bail as set out in subsection B or C without the concurrence of an attorney for the Commonwealth. For a person who is charged with an offense giving rise to a rebuttable presumption against bail, any judge may set or admit such person to bail in accordance with this section after notice and an opportunity to be heard has been provided to the attorney for the Commonwealth.

E. The court shall consider the following factors and such others as it deems appropriate in determining, for the purpose of rebuttal of the presumption against bail described in subsection B, whether there are conditions of release that will reasonably assure the appearance of the person as required and the safety of the public:

1. The nature and circumstances of the offense charged;

2. The history and characteristics of the person, including his character, physical and mental condition, family ties, employment, financial resources, length of residence in the community, community ties, past conduct, history relating to drug or alcohol abuse, criminal history, membership in a criminal street gang as defined in § 18.2-46.1, and record concerning appearance at court proceedings; and

3. The nature and seriousness of the danger to any person or the community that would be posed by the person's release.

F. The judicial officer shall inform the person of his right to appeal from the order denying bail or fixing terms of bond or recognizance consistent with § 19.2-124.

G. If the judicial officer sets a secured bond and the person engages the services of a licensed bail bondsman, the magistrate executing recognizance for the accused shall provide the bondsman, upon request, with a copy of the person's Virginia criminal history record, if readily available, to be used by the bondsman only to determine appropriate reporting requirements to impose upon the accused upon his release. The bondsman shall pay a $15 fee payable to the state treasury to be credited to the Literary Fund, upon requesting the defendant's Virginia criminal history record issued pursuant to § 19.2-389. The bondsman shall review the record on the premises and promptly return the record to the magistrate after reviewing it.

History.
1975, c. 495; 1978, c. 755; 1979, c. 649; 1987, c. 390; 1991, c. 581; 1993, c. 636; 1996, c. 973; 1997, cc. 6, 476; 1999, cc. 829, 846; 2000, c. 797; 2002, cc. 588, 623; 2004, cc. 308, 360, 406, 412, 461, 819, 954, 959; 2005, c. 132; 2006, c. 504; 2007, cc. 134, 386, 745, 923; 2008, c. 596; 2010, c. 862; 2011, cc. 445, 450, 480; 2012, c. 467.

Editor's note.
Acts 2006, c. 504, provided in cl. 2: "That the provisions of this act shall not become effective unless an appropriation of funds effectuating the purposes of this act is included in the general appropriation act for the period of July 1, 2006, through June 30, 2008, passed during the 2006 Session of the General Assembly and signed into law by the Governor." Such an appropriation was not made. Had an appropriation been made, Acts 2006, c. 504, would have amended subdivision B 7 by substituting "A violation of § 18.2-67.3 or conspiracy to commit an offense under that section; or any other offense" for "An offense" and "if the person" for "and the person."

Acts 2007, cc. 745 and 923, cl. 2, provides: "That the provisions of this act may result in a net increase in periods of imprisonment or commitment. Pursuant to § 30-19.1:4, the estimated amount of the necessary appropriation cannot be determined for periods of imprisonment in state adult correctional facilities and is $0 for periods of commitment to the custody of the Department of Juvenile Justice."

Acts 2011, cc. 445 and 480, cl. 2 provides: "That the provisions of this act may result in a net increase in periods of imprisonment or commitment. Pursuant to § 30-19.1:4, the estimated amount of the necessary appropriation is $93,767 for periods of imprisonment in state adult correctional facilities and cannot be determined for periods of commitment to the custody of the Department of Juvenile Justice."

The 2007 amendments.
The 2007 amendments by cc. 134 and 386 are identical, and in subsection B, inserted subdivision 8 and redesignated former subdivisions 8 and 9 as subdivisions 9 and 10.

The 2007 amendments by cc. 745 and 923 are identical, and added subdivision B 10 [now B 11] and made related changes.

The 2008 amendments.
The 2008 amendment by c. 596 deleted "or" at the end of subdivision B 10; substituted "; or" for a period at the end of subdivision B 11; and added subdivision B 12.

The 2010 amendments.
The 2010 amendment by c. 862 added subsection F.

The 2011 amendments.
The 2011 amendments by cc. 445 and 480 are identical, and inserted "or 18.2-60.4" in subdivision B 11.

The 2011 amendment by c. 450 added subdivision B 13 and made related changes.

The 2012 amendments.
The 2012 amendment by c. 467 added subsection D; and redesignated former subsections D through F as subsections E through G.

Law Review.
For 2003/2004 survey of criminal law and procedure, see 39 U. Rich. L. Rev. 133 (2004).

CASE NOTES

Pretrial detention regulatory rather than punitive. — This section allowing pretrial detention is not punishment in the usual sense; it serves a regulatory function by providing for pretrial detention only if the accused is a threat to abscond or poses a risk to the safety of the community rather than a punitive function. Dorsey v. Commonwealth, 32 Va. App. 154, 526 S.E.2d 787 (2000).

Bond not necessarily required. — Once an accused is admitted to bail, a bond may be, but is not necessarily required. Heacock v. Commonwealth, 228 Va. 235, 321 S.E.2d 645 (1984).

Pre-conviction bail granted. — Trial court did not abuse its discretion in allowing defendant, an accused murderer, to pre-conviction bail; pursuant to subsection B of § 19.2-120, the trial court found that defendant's history and characteristics, and the lack of danger he would pose to the community if released, outweighed the circumstances and nature of the offenses charged. Commonwealth v. Jawad, No. 1828-02-1, 2002 Va. App. LEXIS 703 (Ct. of Appeals Nov. 25, 2002).

Trial court's decision to grant defendant's motion for pre-conviction bail was sound judicial discretion, not arbitrary discretion, because the record fairly supported the trial court's action; the trial court considered the factors of subsection D of § 19.2-120 and found that defendant successfully rebutted the presumption that no conditions of bail would reasonably assure defendant's appearance at trial or the safety of the public. Commonwealth v. Lee, — Va. App. —, — S.E.2d —, 2008 Va. App. LEXIS 156 (Apr. 8, 2008).

Bail may be denied and revoked upon finding of probable cause. — If an application for bail, i.e., release from custody, can be denied upon a finding of probable cause to believe that the accused will not appear or will constitute an unreasonable danger while at liberty, bail can be revoked upon such a finding. Heacock v. Commonwealth, 228 Va. 235, 321 S.E.2d 645 (1984).

Revocation of bail did not violate defendant's substantive due process rights. — Where a trial court revoked the defendant's bail after finding, based on evidence presented at a joinder hearing, that the defendant posed a danger to the community, the defendant's pretrial detention did not violate his substantive or procedural due process rights. Dorsey v. Commonwealth, 32 Va. App. 154, 526 S.E.2d 787 (2000).

Denial of bail upheld. — Where the record demonstrated defendant's extensive criminal record, his general and specific threats against the lives of witnesses against him, and his lack of ties to the community of the forum, denial of bail was within the trial court's discretion and the trial court made the requisite findings under subdivisions A 1 and A 2 and both were supported by the record. Fisher v. Commonwealth, 236 Va. 403, 374 S.E.2d 46 (1988), cert. denied, 490 U.S. 1028, 109 S. Ct. 1766, 104 L. Ed. 2d 201 (1989).

CIRCUIT COURT OPINIONS

Bail during Commonwealth's pretrial appeal. — Presumption against bail for a murder charge applied in a bail determination under § 19.2-406; the burden on the Commonwealth to show good cause why bail should not have been reduced or defendant released on his own recognizance during the Commonwealth's pretrial appeal did not eliminate the presumption against bail for defendant's murder charge. Commonwealth v. Ludwig, 69 Va. Cir. 460, 2006 Va. Cir. LEXIS 87 (Loudoun County 2006).

Suppressed or excluded statements may be considered at a bail determination hearing. Commonwealth v. Ludwig, 69 Va. Cir. 460, 2006 Va. Cir. LEXIS 87 (Loudoun County 2006).

§ 19.2-120.1. Presumption of no bail for illegal aliens charged with certain crimes.

A. In addition to the presumption against the admission to bail under subsection B of § 19.2-120, the judicial officer shall presume, subject to rebuttal, that no condition or combination of conditions will reasonably assure the appearance of the person or the safety of the public if (i) the person is currently charged with an offense listed in subsection A of § 19.2-297.1, subsection C of § 17.1-805, any offense under Chapter 4 (§ 18.2-30 et seq.) of Title 18.2 except any offense under subsection A of § 18.2-57.2, any felony offense under Article 1 (§ 18.2-247 et seq.) of Chapter 7 of Title 18.2, or any offense under Article 2 (§ 18.2-266 et seq.), or any local ordinance substantially similar thereto, 4 (§ 18.2-279 et seq.), 5 (§ 18.2-288 et seq.), 6 (§ 18.2-299 et seq.), 6.1 (§ 18.2-307.1 et seq.), or 7 (§ 18.2-308.1 et seq.) of Chapter 7 of Title 18.2, and (ii) the person has been identified as being illegally present in the United States by United States Immigration and Customs Enforcement.

B. Notwithstanding subsection A, no presumption shall exist under this section as to any misdemeanor offense, or any felony offense under Article 1 (§ 18.2-247 et seq.) of Chapter 7 of Title 18.2, unless United States Immigration and Customs Enforcement has guaranteed that, in all such cases in the Commonwealth, it will issue a detainer for the initiation of removal proceedings and agree to reimburse for the cost of incarceration from the time of the issuance of the detainer.

History.
2008, cc. 469, 834; 2013, c. 746.

Editor's note.
Acts 2013, c. 746, cl. 2 provides: "That the provisions of this act are declaratory of existing law."

The 2013 amendments.
The 2013 amendment by c. 746 inserted "6.1 (§ 18.2-307.1 et seq.)," and substituted "18.2-308.1" for "18.2-308" in subsection A, and made minor stylistic changes.

§ 19.2-121. Fixing terms of bail.

If the person is admitted to bail, the terms thereof shall be such as, in the judgment of any official granting or reconsidering the same, will be reasonably fixed to assure the appearance of the accused and to assure his good behavior pending trial. The judicial officer shall take into account (i) the nature and circumstances of the offense; (ii) whether a firearm is alleged to have been used in the offense; (iii) the weight of the evidence; (iv) the financial resources of the accused or juvenile and his ability to pay bond; (v) the character of the accused or juvenile including his family ties, employment or involvement in education; (vi) his length of residence in the community; (vii) his record of convictions; (viii) his appearance at court proceedings or flight to avoid prosecution or failure to appear at court proceedings; (ix) whether the person is likely to obstruct or attempt to obstruct justice, or threaten, injure, or intimidate, or attempt to threaten, injure, or intimidate a prospective witness, juror, or victim; and (x) any other information available which the court considers relevant to the determination of whether the accused or juvenile is unlikely to appear for court proceedings.

In any case where the accused has appeared and otherwise met the conditions of bail, no bond therefor shall be used to satisfy fines and costs unless agreed to by the person who posted such bond.

History.
1975, c. 495; 1978, c. 755; 1980, c. 190; 1991, c. 581; 1992, c. 576; 1993, c. 636; 1999, cc. 829, 846.

§ 19.2-122. Repealed by Acts 1986, c. 327.

§ 19.2-123. Release of accused on secured or unsecured bond or promise to appear; conditions of release.

A. Any person arrested for a felony who has previously been convicted of a felony, or who is presently on bond for an unrelated arrest in any jurisdiction, or who is on probation or parole, may be released only upon a secure bond. This provision may be waived with the approval of the judicial officer and with the concurrence of the attorney for the Commonwealth or the attorney for the county, city or town. Subject to the foregoing, when a person is arrested for either a felony or a misdemeanor, any judicial officer may impose any one or any combination of the following conditions of release:

1. Place the person in the custody and supervision of a designated person, organization or pretrial services agency which, for the purposes of this section, shall not include a court services unit established pursuant to § 16.1-233;

2. Place restrictions on the travel, association or place of abode of the person during the period of release and restrict contacts with household members for a period not to exceed 72 hours;

2a. Require the execution of an unsecured bond;

3. Require the execution of a secure bond which at the option of the accused shall be satisfied with sufficient solvent sureties, or the deposit of cash in lieu thereof. Only the actual value of any interest in real estate or personal property owned by the proposed surety shall be considered in determining solvency and solvency shall be found if the value of the proposed surety's equity in the real estate or personal property equals or exceeds the amount of the bond;

3a. Require that the person do any or all of the following: (i) maintain employment or, if unemployed, actively seek employment; (ii) maintain or commence an educational program; (iii) avoid all contact with an alleged victim of the crime and with any potential witness who may testify concerning the offense; (iv) comply with a specified curfew; (v) refrain from possessing a firearm, destructive device, or other dangerous weapon; (vi) refrain from excessive use of alcohol, or use of any illegal drug or any controlled substance not prescribed by a health care provider; and (vii) submit to testing for drugs and alcohol until the final disposition of his case;

3b. Place a prohibition on a person who holds an elected constitutional office and who is accused of a felony arising from the performance of his duties from physically returning to his constitutional office;

3c. Require the accused to accompany the arresting officer to the jurisdiction's fingerprinting facility and submit to having his photograph and fingerprints taken prior to release; or

4. Impose any other condition deemed reasonably necessary to assure appearance as required, and to assure his good behavior pending trial, including a condition requiring that the person return to custody after specified hours or be placed on home electronic incarceration pursuant to § 53.1-131.2 or, when the person is required to execute a secured bond, be subject to monitoring by a GPS (Global Positioning System) tracking device, or other similar device. The defendant may be ordered by the court to pay the cost of the device.

Upon satisfaction of the terms of recognizance, the accused shall be released forthwith.

In addition, where the accused is an individual receiving services in a state training center for individuals with intellectual disability, the judicial officer may place the individual in the custody of the director of the training center, if the director agrees to accept custody. The director is hereby authorized to take custody of the individual and to maintain him at the training center prior to a trial or hearing under such circumstances as will reasonably assure the appearance of the accused for the trial or hearing.

B. In any jurisdiction served by a pretrial services agency which offers a drug or alcohol screening or testing program approved for the purposes of this subsection by the chief general district court judge, any such person charged with a crime may be requested by such agency to give voluntarily a urine sample, submit to a drug or alcohol screening, or take a breath test for presence of alcohol. A sample may be analyzed for the presence of phencyclidine (PCP), barbiturates, cocaine, opiates or such other drugs as the agency may deem appropriate prior to any hearing to establish bail. The judicial officer and agency shall inform the accused or juvenile being screened or tested that test results shall be used by a judicial officer only at a bail hearing and only to determine appropriate conditions of release or to reconsider the conditions of bail at a subsequent hearing. All screening or test results, and any pretrial investigation report containing the screening or test results, shall be confidential with access thereto limited to judicial officers, the attorney for the Commonwealth, defense counsel, other pretrial ser-

vice agencies, any criminal justice agency as defined in § 9.1-101 and, in cases where a juvenile is screened or tested, the parents or legal guardian or custodian of such juvenile. However, in no event shall the judicial officer have access to any screening or test result prior to making a bail release determination or to determining the amount of bond, if any. Following this determination, the judicial officer shall consider the screening or test results and the screening or testing agency's report and accompanying recommendations, if any, in setting appropriate conditions of release. In no event shall a decision regarding a release determination be subject to reversal on the sole basis of such screening or test results. Any accused or juvenile whose urine sample has tested positive for such drugs and who is admitted to bail may, as a condition of release, be ordered to refrain from use of alcohol or illegal drugs and may be required to be tested on a periodic basis until final disposition of his case to ensure his compliance with the order. Sanctions for a violation of any condition of release, which violations shall include subsequent positive drug or alcohol test results or failure to report as ordered for testing, may be imposed in the discretion of the judicial officer and may include imposition of more stringent conditions of release, contempt of court proceedings or revocation of release. Any test given under the provisions of this subsection which yields a positive drug or alcohol test result shall be reconfirmed by a second test if the person tested denies or contests the initial drug or alcohol test positive result. The results of any drug or alcohol test conducted pursuant to this subsection shall not be admissible in any judicial proceeding other than for the imposition of sanctions for a violation of a condition of release.

C. [Repealed.]

D. Nothing in this section shall be construed to prevent an officer taking a juvenile into custody from releasing that juvenile pursuant to § 16.1-247. If any condition of release imposed under the provisions of this section is violated, a judicial officer may issue a capias or order to show cause why the recognizance should not be revoked.

E. Nothing in this section shall be construed to prevent a court from imposing a recognizance or bond designed to secure a spousal or child support obligation pursuant to § 16.1-278.16, Chapter 5 (§ 20-61 et seq.) of Title 20, or § 20-114 in addition to any recognizance or bond imposed pursuant to this chapter.

History.
Code 1950, § 19.1-109.2; 1973, c. 485; 1975, c. 495; 1978, cc. 500, 755; 1979, c. 518; 1981, c. 528; 1984, c. 707; 1989, c. 369; 1991, cc. 483, 512, 581, 585; 1992, c. 576; 1993, c. 636; 1999, cc. 829, 846; 2000, cc. 885, 1020, 1041; 2001, c. 201; 2006, c. 296; 2008, cc. 129, 884; 2011, cc. 799, 837; 2012, cc. 476, 507; 2013, c. 614.

The 2008 amendments.
The 2008 amendment by c. 129 added subsection E.
The 2008 amendment by c. 884, inserted subdivision A 3b and made minor stylistic changes.

The 2011 amendments.

The 2011 amendments by cc. 799 and 837 are identical, and in the first paragraph in subdivision A 4, added "or, when the person is required to execute a secured bond, be subject to monitoring by a GPS (Global Positioning System) tracking device, or other similar device" in the first sentence, and added the last sentence.

The 2012 amendments.

The 2012 amendments by cc. 476 and 507 are identical, and in the third paragraph in subdivision A 4, substituted "is an individual receiving services in a state training center for individuals with intellectual disability" for "is a resident of a state training center for the mentally retarded," "individual" for "person" and "training center" for "state facility" in the first sentence and substituted "The director" for "Such director" and "the individual" for "such person" in the second sentence.

The 2013 amendments.

The 2013 amendments by c. 614 added subdivision A 3c.

Law Review.

For survey of Virginia law on criminal procedure for the year 1972-1973, see 59 Va. L. Rev. 1478 (1973). For survey on legal issues involving children in Virginia for 1989, see 23 U. Rich. L. Rev. 705 (1989).

CASE NOTES

Discriminatory or arbitrary administration of bail system. — Where a state engages in discriminatory or arbitrary administration of a bail system, this gives rise to a constitutional claim. Wilborn v. Peyton, 287 F. Supp. 787 (W.D. Va. 1968) (decided under former § 19.1-110).

Bond not necessarily required. — Once an accused is admitted to bail, a bond may be, but is not necessarily required. Heacock v. Commonwealth, 228 Va. 235, 321 S.E.2d 645 (1984).

Waiver of right to bail. — See Wilborn v. Peyton, 287 F. Supp. 787 (W.D. Va. 1968) (decided under former § 19.1-110).

§ 19.2-124. Appeal from bail, bond, or recognizance order.

A. If a judicial officer denies bail to a person, requires excessive bond, or fixes unreasonable terms of a recognizance under this article, the person may appeal the decision of the judicial officer.

If the initial bail decision on a charge brought by a warrant or district court capias is made by a magistrate, clerk, or deputy clerk, the person shall first appeal to the district court in which the case is pending.

If the initial bail decision on a charge brought by direct indictment or presentment or circuit court capias is made by a magistrate, clerk, or deputy clerk, the person shall first appeal to the circuit court in which the case is pending.

If the appeal of an initial bail decision is taken on any charge originally pending in a district court after that charge has been appealed, certified, or transferred to a circuit court, the person shall first appeal to the circuit court in which the case is pending.

Any bail decision made by a judge of a court may be appealed successively by the person to the next higher court, up to and including the Supreme Court of Virginia, where permitted by law.

B. The attorney for the Commonwealth may appeal a bail, bond, or recognizance decision to the same court to which the accused person is required to appeal under subsection A.

C. The court granting or denying such bail may, upon appeal thereof, and for good cause shown, stay execution of such order for so long as reasonably practicable for the party to obtain an expedited hearing before the next higher court. No such stay may be granted after any person who has been granted bail has been released from custody on such bail.

D. No filing or service fees shall be assessed or collected for any appeal taken pursuant to this section.

History.

Code 1950, §§ 19.1-109.3, 19.1-112; 1960, c. 366; 1973, cc. 130, 485; 1975, c. 495; 1978, c. 755; 1984, c. 703; 1991, c. 581; 1999, cc. 829, 846; 2007, cc. 462, 549; 2010, cc. 404, 592; 2013, cc. 408, 474.

The 2007 amendments.

The 2007 amendments by cc. 462 and 549 are identical, and added subsection C.

The 2010 amendments.

The 2010 amendments by cc. 404 and 592 are identical, and in subsection A, substituted "the decision of the judicial officer" for "therefrom successively to the next higher court or judge thereof, up to and including the Supreme Court of Virginia or any justice thereof where permitted by law" in the introductory paragraph and added the second to last paragraphs; and rewrote subsection B.

The 2013 amendments.

The 2013 amendments by cc. 408 and 474 are identical, and added subsection C and redesignated former subsection C as D.

Law Review.

For survey of Virginia criminal law for the year 1971-1972, see 58 Va. L. Rev. 1206 (1972). For survey of Virginia law on criminal procedure for the year 1972-1973, see 59 Va. L. Rev. 1478 (1973).

CASE NOTES

Federal habeas corpus. — A federal court may grant habeas corpus relief prior to the state trial if the setting of bail is arbitrary or discriminatory in violation of constitutional requirements. Bowring v. Cox, 334 F. Supp. 334 (W.D. Va. 1971).

When prisoner's continued confinement will endanger his life. — A prisoner indicted for a felony will be let out on bail, when his continued confinement will endanger his life. Commonwealth v. Seemes, 38 Va. (11 Leigh) 665 (1841); Archer's Case, 47 Va. (6 Gratt.) 705 (1849).

What evidence to be considered. — When a prisoner, who has been remanded for trial by the examining court to the higher court, on a charge of felony, and against whom a bill of indictment has been found by the grand jury, applies to the higher court to be let to bail, on the ground that there is only a slight suspicion of guilt against him, that judgment, and the finding of the bill, are not conclusive evidence against the application, but the court may examine other evidence. It is a question for the exercise of the sound discretion of the court, and if the court is satisfied that there is material evidence for the Commonwealth that is not before the court, was not before the examining court, or spread on the record, the court ought not to sustain the motion. Commonwealth v. Rutherford, 26 Va. (5 Rand.) 646 (1826).

Revocation of bail appealable. — The revocation of a defendant's bail has the same effect as a denial of bail and is appealable under this section. Dorsey v. Commonwealth, 32 Va. App. 154, 526 S.E.2d 787 (2000).

OPINIONS OF THE ATTORNEY GENERAL

Civil proceeding. — Appeal of a determination of bond from a general district court to a circuit court is civil in nature; therefore, the fees and costs for such appeal should be calculated, taxed, and collected as a civil proceeding. See opinion of Attorney General to The Honorable Michael D. Wolfe, Clerk of the Circuit Court of Alleghany County, 05-065 (10/4/05).

§ 19.2-125. Release pending appeal from conviction in court not of record.

A person who has been convicted of an offense in a district court and who has noted an appeal shall be given credit for any bond that he may have posted in the court from which he appeals and shall be treated in accordance with the provisions of this article.

History.
Code 1950, § 19.1-109.4; 1973, c. 485; 1975, c. 495; 1978, c. 755; 1999, cc. 829, 846.

Law Review.
For survey of Virginia law on criminal procedure for the year 1972-1973, see 59 Va. L. Rev. 1478 (1973).

§ 19.2-126. Repealed by Acts 1999, cc. 829 and 846.

§ 19.2-127. Conditions of release of material witness.

If it appears by affidavit that the testimony of a person is material in any criminal proceeding, and it reasonably appears that it will be impossible to secure his presence by a subpoena, a judge shall inquire into the conditions of his release pursuant to this article.

History.
Code 1950, § 19.1-109.6; 1973, c. 485; 1975, c. 495; 1999, cc. 829, 846.

Law Review.
For survey of Virginia law on criminal procedure for the year 1972-1973, see 59 Va. L. Rev. 1478 (1973).

§ 19.2-128. Penalties for failure to appear.

A. Whoever, having been released pursuant to this chapter or § 19.2-319 or on a summons pursuant to § 19.2-73 or § 19.2-74, willfully fails to appear before any court or judicial officer as required, shall, after notice to all interested parties, incur a forfeiture of any security which may have been given or pledged for his release, unless one of the parties can show good cause for excusing the absence, or unless the court, in its sound discretion, shall determine that neither the interests of justice nor the power of the court to conduct orderly proceedings will be served by such forfeiture.

B. Any person (i) charged with a felony offense or (ii) convicted of a felony offense and execution of sentence is suspended pursuant to § 19.2-319 who willfully fails to appear before any court as required shall be guilty of a Class 6 felony.

C. Any person (i) charged with a misdemeanor offense or (ii) convicted of a misdemeanor offense and execution of sentence is suspended pursuant to

§ 19.2-319 who willfully fails to appear before any court as required shall be guilty of a Class 1 misdemeanor.

History.
Code 1950, § 19.1-109.7; 1973, c. 485; 1975, c. 495; 1981, c. 382; 1982, c. 271; 1999, c. 821.

Cross references.
As to punishment for Class 6 felonies, see § 18.2-10. As to punishment for Class 1 misdemeanors, see § 18.2-11.

Law Review.
For survey of Virginia law on criminal procedure for the year 1972-1973, see 59 Va. L. Rev. 1478 (1973). For survey of Virginia law on criminal law and procedure for the year 2007-2008, see 43 U. Rich. L. Rev. 149 (2008).

CASE NOTES

"Willfully," as used in subsection A of this section, has the customary meaning that the act must have been done purposely, intentionally, or designedly. Hunter v. Commonwealth, 15 Va. App. 717, 427 S.E.2d 197 (1993).

Notice of continuances. — An accused who is given notice of the original trial date is charged with notice of those dates to which his or her case is expressly continued when such action is duly recorded in the order of the court; also if the attorney had actual notice of the client's trial date, the fact finder may infer from that evidence that the client also had actual notice of the trial date. Hunter v. Commonwealth, 15 Va. App. 717, 427 S.E.2d 197 (1993).

Continuance no relief from appearance requirement. — Pre-trial continuance of the jury trial scheduled for January 10, 1992, did not relieve the defendant, who had been declared a fugitive, from appearing on January 10, 1992, as required by his bond; the appellant was required to appear on this date under the terms of his bond as charged in the indictment. Sloan v. Commonwealth, No. 0934-93-3 (Ct. of Appeals Oct. 4, 1994).

Judicial notice. — Trial court did not err in taking notice of its judicial records and the facts regarding the date and time of defendant's scheduled hearings because the trial court reasonably concluded that (1) the Commonwealth requested it take judicial notice of the entire record regarding defendant's failure to appear, (2) the trial court took such notice, and (3) the statements of the trial court, more specifically the facts recited by the trial court in rendering its decision, and the evidence and arguments of the parties demonstrated clearly that the trial court was taking note of its entire record. Williams v. Commonwealth, 57 Va. App. 750, 706 S.E.2d 530, 2011 Va. App. LEXIS 96 (2011).

Applicable to defendant who has pled guilty and is awaiting sentencing. — Trial court did not err in holding that the failure to appear statute, subsection B of § 19.2-128, applied to a person such as defendant, who had pled guilty and was awaiting sentencing when defendant failed to appear. If the statute was not read to apply to those people who had pled guilty and were awaiting sentencing, no repercussions would attach to a defendant who pled guilty and did not show up at sentencing, which would require the absurd result that the trial court would have no alternative but to jail such people until sentencing. Bowling v. Commonwealth, 51 Va. App. 102, 654 S.E.2d 354, 2007 Va. App. LEXIS 461 (2007).

Evidence was sufficient to establish willful failure to appear where the defendant had notice of the original trial date, all continuances were duly recorded by order of the court, thereby charging the defendant with notice of the trial date, and defense counsel was aware of the trial date and, in fact, had asked for it. Poindexter v. Commonwealth, No. 0457-98-2 (Ct. of Appeals Apr. 27, 1999).

Evidence supported defendant's conviction for a subsection B of § 19.2-128 violation as defendant willfully failed to appear since: (1) a bail bond agreement was introduced, which provided that defendant could not leave the Commonwealth; (2) defendant understood that defendant could not leave the Commonwealth; (3) defendant went to New York twice; and (4) defendant failed to contact the clerk's office or defendant's appointed counsel after defendant was arrested in New York on both visits. Deslandes v.

Commonwealth, 2008 Va. App. LEXIS 352 (July 8, 2008).

Evidence sufficient to infer willful failure to appear. — Based on the evidence that defendant had notice of the date, time and place of his scheduled felony trial, that he failed to appear, that he purposefully engaged in conduct that prevented receipt of notice, and that he left the state in violation of the conditions of his bail bond, the jury could reasonably infer that defendant willfully failed to appear at his felony trial. Hunter v. Commonwealth, 15 Va. App. 717, 427 S.E.2d 197 (1993).

Where defendant contended that because he was incarcerated in Maine at the time of trial he did not have the intent to "willfully" fail to appear, the facts and circumstances of this case showed that the defendant escaped from jail, fled to Maine, was captured and held in jail, and did not inform his counsel or the Commonwealth of his whereabouts. Neither the Commonwealth nor defendant's counsel had any idea of his location until he was returned by Maine. Upon this evidence the jury was entitled to infer that his intent was not to appear for trial. Hooper v. Commonwealth, No. 2100-96-1 (Ct. of Appeals Sept. 23, 1997).

Traffic summons was a public record as it became the charging document on which a general district court tried an accused, under § 16.1-129, and if an accused willfully violated his written promise to appear in court, given when he signed the summons, he could be convicted for failure to appear under § 19.2-128, regardless of the disposition of, and in addition to, the charge upon which he was originally arrested, under subdivision A 3 of § 19.2-74, and, given this statutory scheme, each signed summons clearly could constitute a separate offense under § 18.2-168, regarding forgery of a public document. Hines v. Commonwealth, 39 Va. App. 752, 576 S.E.2d 781, 2003 Va. App. LEXIS 92 (2003).

Court records reflecting that defendant was recognized to appear in court on the specified date as part of his bond was prima facie evidence proving defendant's knowledge of the court date; thus, the evidence was sufficient to sustain defendant's conviction for felony failure to appear since defendant failed to show why his absence was not willful. Gillard v. Commonwealth, No. 0037-02-2, 2003 Va. App. LEXIS 437 (Ct. of Appeals Aug. 19, 2003).

Where the state showed that defendant's failure to appear was "willful," and she failed to rebut that showing, the evidence supported conviction; defendant had notice but did not appear so it was inferred her failure to appear was willful. James v. Commonwealth, No. 3005-02-3, 2003 Va. App. LEXIS 617 (Ct. of Appeals Dec. 2, 2003).

Evidence that defendant knew he had an upcoming review hearing, yet failed to maintain contact with his attorney and failed to keep his attorney or the court advised of his whereabouts, and that defendant knew maintaining contact with his probation officer was a condition imposed by the trial judge, yet failed to do so and specifically testified that he "absconded," was sufficient to support a conviction for failure to appear. Ferguson v. Commonwealth, — Va. App. —, — S.E.2d —, 2007 Va. App. LEXIS 72 (Feb. 27, 2007).

Conviction for felony failure to appear under § 19.2-128 was supported by evidence defendant's name and address was clearly and correctly present on the face of the subpoena, which clearly indicated the date and time defendant was expected to appear, included the name, address, and phone number of the court, and instructed defendant to "PLEASE NOTE CHANGE OF COURT DATE FROM 6/22/05." Koral v. Commonwealth, — Va. App. —, — S.E.2d —, 2007 Va. App. LEXIS 213 (May 22, 2007).

Although defendant was incarcerated in Maryland on the day of defendant's North Carolina trial, there was sufficient evidence that defendant violated subsection B of § 19.2-128 since: (1) defendant left Virginia in violation of the conditions of defendant's bond; (2) defendant did not contact or attempt to contact defendant's attorney or the trial court to notify them of defendant's whereabouts; (3) defendant's Maryland probation officer testified that defendant's real name and birth date were other than those given to the North Carolina authorities at the time of defendant's arrest; and (4) the jury could infer that defendant's failure to appear was willful, and that defendant presented a false identification card when defendant was arrested to evade prosecution. Nelson v. Commonwealth, 50 Va. App. 413, 650 S.E.2d 562, 2007 Va. App. LEXIS 343 (2007).

Evidence was sufficient to support defendant's conviction for failure to appear in violation of § 19.2-128 because defendant was charged with notice of the trial date since the documents that the trial court noticed proved that defendant was given notice of his original trial date by a recognizance bond, which he signed, and established that the trial court entered an order continuing defendant's case; those documents provided prima facie evidence that defendant's failure to appear was willful, and the trial court was entitled to infer that defendant's failure to appear was willful. Williams v. Commonwealth, 57 Va. App. 750, 706 S.E.2d 530, 2011 Va. App. LEXIS 96 (2011).

Evidence of willfulness insufficient. — "Willfulness" element of felony failure to appear, subsection B of § 19.2-128, was not proven because defendant, who did not have a driver's license, contacted three people to transport him to court on the required date and contacted the clerk of the circuit court to inform the circuit court of his lack of transportation. Abell v. Commonwealth, — Va. App. —, — S.E.2d —, 2007 Va. App. LEXIS 94 (Mar. 13, 2007).

Trial court erred in convicting defendant of failure to appear in violation of § 19.2-128 because the evidence was insufficient to show that defendant's failure to appear was willful; the evidence was insufficient to show that defendant had notice of the order to appear on a certain date, and although the trial court had made an oral ruling setting a new trial date, it did not enter the written order memorializing that action until the actual date on which defendant was required to appear. Williams v. Commonwealth, 57 Va. App. 750, 706 S.E.2d 530, 2011 Va. App. LEXIS 96 (2011).

Evidence insufficient to prove actual notice. — Evidence was insufficient to support defendant's conviction for felony failure to appear, as it did not show that she had notice of the date and time of the hearing she was supposed to attend, which was set out in the warrant allegedly served upon her, or that the trial court took judicial notice of the hearing date and time contained in the warrant; accordingly, it was not shown that she willfully failed to appear at that hearing, and, thus, her conviction for felony failure to appear had to be reversed. Edmonds v. Commonwealth, 43 Va. App. 197, 597 S.E.2d 210, 2004 Va. App. LEXIS 275 (2004).

Conviction for willfully failing to appear in violation of subsection B of § 19.2-128 was reversed because the trial court failed to instruct the jury on the standard procedure of trial court, which included notification to the accused of the date the accused must reappear after a continuance has been granted due to the accused's failure to have counsel, leaving the jury with insufficient evidence to prove actual notice. Thomas v. Commonwealth, 48 Va. App. 605, 633 S.E.2d 229, 2006 Va. App. LEXIS 379 (2006).

Evidence held insufficient. — The evidence was insufficient to support the defendant's conviction for willfully failing to appear, where the only evidence presented by the Commonwealth was that the defendant was not in court on a specific date, but the record did not indicate that the defendant was required to appear on that date and, instead, reflected that she was scheduled to appear on a later date. Wiglesworth v. Commonwealth, No. 1291-99-2, 2000 Va. App. LEXIS 276 (Ct. of Appeals Apr. 11, 2000).

The evidence was insufficient to convict defendant of the felony of willfully failing to appear in the trial court since the applicable statute required that in order to be convicted under that statute, § 19.2-128 B(i), a person had to be charged with a felony; where defendant had not been charged with a felony for purposes of appearing in front of the trial court, but instead was supposed to appear before the trial court at a show cause hearing on a probation violation defendant could not be convicted under it. Lawson v. Commonwealth, 38 Va. App. 93, 561 S.E.2d 775, 2002 Va. App. LEXIS 212 (2002).

Applied in Bottoms v. Commonwealth, 281 Va. 23, 704 S.E.2d 406, 2011 Va. LEXIS 22 (2011).

§ 19.2-129. Power of court to punish for contempt.

Nothing in this chapter shall interfere with or prevent the exercise by any court of the Commonwealth of its power to punish for contempt, except that a person shall not be sentenced for contempt and under the provisions of § 19.2-128 for the same absence.

History.

Code 1950, § 19.1-109.8; 1973, c. 485; 1975, c. 495.

Law Review.
For survey of Virginia law on criminal procedure for the year 1972-1973, see 59 Va. L. Rev. 1478 (1973).

§ 19.2-130. Bail in subsequent proceeding arising out of initial arrest.

Any person admitted to bail by a judge or clerk of a district court or by a magistrate shall not be required to be admitted to bail in any subsequent proceeding arising out of the initial arrest unless the court having jurisdiction of such subsequent proceeding deems the initial amount of bond or security taken inadequate. When the court having jurisdiction of the proceeding believes the amount of bond or security inadequate or excessive, it may change the amount of such bond or security, require new and additional sureties, or set other terms of bail as are appropriate to the case, including, but not limited to, drug and alcohol monitoring. The court may, after notice to the parties, initiate a proceeding to alter the terms and conditions of bail on its own motion.

History.
Code 1950, § 19.1-111.1; 1972, c. 366; 1975, c. 495; 1978, c. 755; 1991, c. 581; 2008, cc. 363, 812.

The 2008 amendments.
The 2008 amendments by cc. 363 and 812 are identical, and substituted "security inadequate or excessive, it may change the amount of such bond or security, require new and additional sureties, or set other terms of bail as are appropriate to the case, including, but not limited to, drug and alcohol monitoring" for "security inadequate, it may increase the amount of such bond or security or require new and additional sureties" in the second sentence and added the last sentence.

Law Review.
For survey of Virginia criminal law for the year 1971-1972, see 58 Va. L. Rev. 1206 (1972).

§ 19.2-130.1. Bail terms set by court on a capias to be honored by magistrate.

A magistrate who is to set the terms of bail of a person arrested and brought before him pursuant to § 19.2-234 shall, unless circumstances exist that require him to set more restrictive terms, set the terms of bail in accordance with the order of the court that issued the capias, if such an order is affixed to or made a part of the capias by the court.

History.
2010, cc. 312, 375; 2011, c. 112.

The 2011 amendments.
The 2011 amendment by c. 112 substituted "shall, unless circumstances exist that require him to set more restrictive terms, set the terms of bail" for "shall do so."

§ 19.2-131. Bail for person held in jurisdiction other than that of trial.

In any case in which a person charged with a misdemeanor or felony, or a juvenile taken into custody pursuant to § 16.1-246 is held in some county, city or town other than that in which he is to be tried upon such charge, he may be admitted to bail by any judicial officer of the county, city or town in which he is so held in accordance with the provisions of law concerning the granting of bail in cases in which persons are so admitted to bail, when held in the county, city or town in which they are to be tried.

In such case, such judicial officer before whom he is brought may, without trial or examination, let him to bail, upon taking a recognizance for his appearance before the court having cognizance of the case. The fact of taking such recognizance shall be certified by the court or officer taking it upon the warrant under which such person was arrested or taken into custody and the warrant and recognizance shall be returned forthwith to the clerk of the court before whom the accused or juvenile taken into custody pursuant to § 16.1-246 is to appear. And to such court, the judicial officer who issued such warrant shall recognize or cause to be summoned such witnesses as he may think proper.

History.
Code 1950, §§ 19.1-118, 19.1-119; 1960, c. 366; 1975, c. 495; 1978, c. 755; 1992, c. 576.

§ 19.2-132. Motion to increase amount of bond fixed by judicial officer; when bond may be increased.

If the amount of any bond fixed by a judicial officer is subsequently deemed insufficient, or the security taken inadequate, or if it appears that bail should have been denied or that the person has violated a term or condition of his release, or has been convicted of or arrested for a felony or misdemeanor, the attorney for the Commonwealth of the county or city in which the person is held for trial may, on reasonable notice to the person and, if such person has been admitted to bail, to any surety on the bond of such person, move the appropriate judicial officer to increase the amount of such bond or to revoke bail. The court may grant such motion and may require new or additional sureties therefor, or both or revoke bail. Any surety in a bond for the appearance of such person may take from his principal collateral or other security to indemnify such surety against liability. The failure to notify the surety will not prohibit the court from proceeding with the bond hearing.

The court ordering any increase in the amount of such bond, ordering new or additional sureties, or revoking such bail may, upon appeal, and for good cause shown, stay execution of such order for so long as reasonably practicable for such person to obtain an expedited hearing before the court to which such order has been appealed.

History.
Code 1950, § 19.1-120; 1960, c. 366; 1975, c. 495; 1978, c. 755; 1989, c. 519; 1991, c. 581; 1999, cc. 829, 846; 2010, cc. 404, 592; 2013, cc. 408, 474.

Cross references.

As to constitutional provision against excessive bail, see Va. Const., Art. I, § 9.

The 2010 amendments.

The 2010 amendments by cc. 404 and 592 are identical, and deleted the subsection A designation; in the first sentence, substituted "If the amount of any bond fixed by a judicial officer" for "Although a person has been admitted to bail, if the amount of any bond," inserted "or that the person has violated a term or condition of his release, or has been convicted of or arrested for a felony or misdemeanor" and "if such person has been admitted to bail" and deleted "court, or the" preceding "appropriate judicial officer," and deleted "in accordance with subsection B" following "court may" in the second sentence; and deleted subsection B.

The 2013 amendments.

The 2013 amendments by cc. 408 and 474 are identical, and added the second paragraph.

Michie's Jurisprudence.

For related discussion, see 9B M.J. Indemnity, § 3.

CASE NOTES

Revocation of bail. — Nothing in this section prohibits or limits a trial court in an appropriate case from revoking the defendant's bail sua sponte upon learning information that establishes probable cause to believe the defendant is a danger to society. Dorsey v. Commonwealth, 32 Va. App. 154, 526 S.E.2d 787 (2000).

§§ 19.2-132.1, 19.2-133. Repealed by Acts 1991, c. 581.

Cross references.

For current provision relating to when accused admitted to bail may be subject to a motion to increase his bond or revoke bail, see subsection B of § 19.2-132. For current provision relating to when bail may be increased or new sureties required and right of surety to take indemnity, see subsection A of § 19.2-132.

§ 19.2-134. When bail piece to be delivered to accused; form of bail piece.

In all cases in which recognizances, at the suit of the Commonwealth, may have been, or shall hereafter be entered into, it shall be the duty of the clerk of the court in which, or in the clerk's office of which, any recognizance is filed, to deliver to the accused and his sureties upon request, a bail piece, in substance, as follows: "A. B. of the county or city of ......, is delivered to bail, unto C. D. of the county or city of ......, at the suit of the Commonwealth. Given under my hand, this day of ...., in the year ...."

History.

Code 1950, § 19.1-123; 1960, c. 366; 1975, c. 495; 1991, c. 581; 1992, c. 576.

ARTICLE 2.

RECOGNIZANCES.

§ 19.2-135. Commitment for trial; recognizance; notice to attorney for Commonwealth; remand on violation of condition.

When a judicial officer considers that there is sufficient cause for charging the accused or juvenile

taken into custody pursuant to § 16.1-246 with a felony, unless it be a case wherein it is otherwise specially provided, the commitment shall be for trial or hearing. Any recognizance taken of the accused or juvenile shall be upon the following conditions: (1) that he appear to answer for the offense with which he is charged before the court or judge before whom the case will be tried at such time as may be stated in the recognizance and at any time or times to which the proceedings may be continued and before any court or judge thereafter in which proceedings on the charge are held; (2) that he shall not depart from the Commonwealth unless the judicial officer taking recognizance or a court in a subsequent proceeding specifically waives such requirement; and (3) that he shall keep the peace and be of good behavior until the case is finally disposed of. Every such recognizance shall also include a waiver such as is required by § 49-12 in relation to the bonds therein mentioned and though such waiver be not expressed in the recognizance it shall be deemed to be included therein in like manner and with the same effect as if it was so expressed. The judge shall return to the clerk of the court wherein the accused or juvenile is to be tried, or the case be heard as soon as may be, a certificate of the nature of the offense, showing whether the accused or juvenile was committed to jail or recognized for his appearance; and the clerk, as soon as may be, shall inform the attorney for the Commonwealth of such certificate.

The court may, in its discretion, in the event of a violation of any condition of a recognizance taken pursuant to this section, remand the principal to jail until the case is finally disposed of, and if the principal is remanded to jail, the surety is discharged from liability.

When a recognizance is taken of a witness in a case against an accused or juvenile, the condition thereof shall be that he appear to give evidence in such case and that he shall not depart from the Commonwealth without the leave of such court or judge.

History.

Code 1950, §§ 19.1-125, 19.1-128, 19.1-133; 1960, c. 366; 1968, c. 639; 1975, c. 495; 1977, c. 287; 1978, c. 755; 1979, c. 735; 1988, c. 688; 1992, c. 576.

Michie's Jurisprudence.

For related discussion, see 3A M.J. Bonds, § 22; 5B M.J. Criminal Procedure, § 64.

CASE NOTES

Standing of Commonwealth to challenge 1979 amendment. — The Commonwealth had no standing to assert the constitutional rights of those posting cash bonds where the Commonwealth argued that the classification created by the 1979 amendment to this section discriminated against those posting cash bonds in violation of the equal protection clause. Esper Bonding Co. v. Commonwealth, 222 Va. 595, 283 S.E.2d 185 (1981).

Form of condition. — A recognizance should show on its face that the condition it contains is to do some act, for the performance of which such an obligation may be properly taken, and that the court or officer before whom it is taken has authority to act in cases of that general character. Cannon v. Commonwealth, 96 Va. 573, 32 S.E. 33 (1899).

Both the principal and his surety were estopped to question the constitutionality of the good behavior condition in this section and in the bonds executed under it where they accepted the benefits conferred by the section. Bisping v. Commonwealth, 218 Va. 753, 240 S.E.2d 656, cert. denied, 435 U.S. 1007, 98 S. Ct. 1878, 56 L. Ed. 2d 389 (1978).

Judge need not find accused "guilty" of crime to revoke bail. — To revoke bail, the judge is not required to find that the accused was "guilty" of a crime or that a breach of the good behavior condition upon which he had been admitted to bail has been established by a preponderance of the evidence. Heacock v. Commonwealth, 228 Va. 235, 321 S.E.2d 645 (1984).

§ 19.2-136. How bonds in recognizances payable; penalty.

Bonds in recognizances in criminal or juvenile cases shall be payable to the county or city in which the case is prosecuted. The treasurer or director of finance of such locality may engage in collection activity regarding the judgment of default rendered pursuant to § 19.2-143. Any responses to the judgment of default rendered pursuant to § 19.2-143 shall be filed with the court, with notice given to such locality. Every bond under this title shall be in such sum as the court or officer requiring it may direct.

History.
Code 1950, § 19.1-127; 1960, c. 366; 1973, c. 485; 1975, c. 495; 1978, c. 755; 1991, c. 581; 2011, c. 802; 2012, c. 408.

Cross references.
As to increase in amount of bail, see § 19.2-132. As to recognizance containing waiver, see § 19.2-135. As to recognizance for mentally incapacitated persons, see § 19.2-141. As to effect of defects in form of recognizance, see § 19.2-146.

The 2011 amendments.
The 2011 amendment by c. 802 rewrote the first two sentences, which read: "Bonds in recognizances in criminal or juvenile cases, where the violation is committed against the Commonwealth or where the Commonwealth is a party, shall be payable to the Commonwealth of Virginia. Bonds in recognizances in criminal cases where the violation is a violation of a county, city or town ordinance, shall be payable to such county, city or town"; and added the third sentence.

The 2012 amendments.
The 2012 amendment by c. 408 substituted "to the county or city in which the case is prosecuted" for "to the county, city or town wherein the recognizance was taken" at the end of the first sentence, substituted "locality" for "county, city or town" in the second sentence, and substituted "notice given to such locality" for "notice given to the county, city or town wherein the recognizance was taken" at the end of the third sentence.

Law Review.
For note, "Grand Jury Reform: A Proposal for Change in Virginia," see 23 U. Rich. L. Rev. 279 (1989).

Michie's Jurisprudence.
For related discussion, see 2B M.J. Bail and Recognizance, §§ 12, 15; 5B M.J. Criminal Procedure, § 64.

CASE NOTES

The examining court must enter of record that the prisoner was bailable and fix the amount of bail. Saunders v. Commonwealth, 44 Va. (3 Gratt.) 214 (1846).

§ 19.2-137. Order of court on recognizance.

When such recognizance is taken by a court of a person to answer a charge or of a witness to give evidence it shall be sufficient for the order of the court taking the recognizance to state that the party or parties recognized were duly recognized upon a bond in such sum as the court may have directed with such surety as the court may have accepted for his or their appearance before such court at such time as may have been prescribed by the court to answer for the offense with which such person is charged or to give evidence, as the case may be.

History.
Code 1950, § 19.1-129; 1960, c. 366; 1975, c. 495; 1991, c. 581.

Michie's Jurisprudence.
For related discussion, see 2B M.J. Bail and Recognizance, § 3; 5B M.J. Criminal Procedure, § 64.

§§ 19.2-138 through 19.2-140. Repealed by Acts 1987, c. 670.

Cross references.
As to cash bonds, see § 19.2-143.

§ 19.2-141. How recognizance taken for incapacitated or insane person or one under disability.

A recognizance which would be taken of a person but for his being a minor, insane or otherwise mentally incapacitated, may be taken of another person and without further surety, if such other person is deemed sufficient, for the performance by such minor, insane or otherwise incapacitated person, of the conditions of the recognizance.

History.
Code 1950, § 19.1-134; 1960, c. 366; 1975, c. 495; 1997, c. 801.

Editor's note.
Acts 1997, c. 801, cl. 2, provides: "That the provisions of this act shall become effective on January 1, 1998. The powers granted and duties imposed pursuant to this act shall apply prospectively to guardians and conservators appointed by court order entered on or after that date, or modified on or after that date if the court so directs, without regard to when the petition was filed. The procedures specified in this act governing proceedings for appointment of a guardian or conservator or termination or other modification of a guardianship shall apply on and after that date without regard to when the petition therefor was filed or the guardianship or conservatorship created."

Michie's Jurisprudence.
For related discussion, see 2B M.J. Bail and Recognizance, § 12; 5B M.J. Criminal Procedure, § 64.

§ 19.2-142. Where recognizance taken out of court to be sent.

A person taking a recognizance out of court shall forthwith transmit it to the clerk of the court for appearance before which it is taken; or, if it be not for appearance before a court, to the clerk of the circuit court of the county or city in which it is taken; and it shall remain filed in the clerk's office.

History.
Code 1950, § 19.1-136; 1960, c. 366; 1975, c. 495.

Michie's Jurisprudence.
For related discussion, see 2B M.J. Bail and Recognizance, § 18.

§ 19.2-143. Where default recorded; process on recognizance; forfeiture on recognizance; when copy may be used; cash bond.

When a person, under recognizance in a case, either as party or witness, fails to perform the condition of appearance thereof, if it is to appear before a court of record, or a district court, a hearing shall be held upon reasonable notice to all parties affording them opportunity to show cause why the recognizance or any part thereof should not be forfeited. The show cause notice shall be issued within 45 days of the breach of the condition of appearance.

If the court finds the recognizance or any part thereof should be forfeited, the default shall be recorded therein, unless the defendant or juvenile is brought before the court within 150 days of the findings of default. After 150 days of the finding of default, his default shall be recorded therein, and if it is to appear before a district court, his default shall be entered by the judge of such court, on the case papers unless the defendant or juvenile has been delivered or appeared before the court. The process on any such forfeited recognizance shall be issued from the court before which the appearance was to be, and wherein such forfeiture was recorded or entered. Any such process issued by a judge shall be made returnable before, and tried by, such judge, who shall promptly transmit to the clerk of the circuit court of his county or city wherein deeds are recorded an abstract of such judgment as he may render thereon, which shall be forthwith docketed by the clerk of such court.

If the defendant or juvenile appears before or is delivered to the court within 24 months of the findings of default, the court shall remit any bond previously ordered forfeited by the courts, less such costs as the court may direct.

If it is brought to the attention of the court that the defendant or juvenile is incarcerated in another state or country within 48 months of the finding of default, thereby preventing his delivery or appearance within that period, the court shall remit any bond previously ordered forfeited. If the defendant or juvenile left the Commonwealth with the permission of the court, the bond shall be remitted without deduction of costs; otherwise, the cost of returning him to the Commonwealth shall be deducted from the bond.

Evidence that the defendant or juvenile is incarcerated or subject to court process in another jurisdiction on the day his appearance is required or a medical certificate from a duly licensed physician that the defendant was physically unable to so appear shall be considered evidence of good cause why the recognizance should not be forfeited.

If such recognizance so forfeited is not for such appearance, process thereon shall be issued from the court in which it was taken, or the court to which it was made returnable, and in a proceeding in one court on a recognizance entered in another a copy thereof shall be evidence in like manner as the original would be if it had been entered in the court wherein the proceeding is being had thereon.

However, when any defendant or juvenile who posted a cash bond and failed to appear is tried in his absence and is convicted, the court or judge trying the case shall first apply the cash bond, or so much thereof as may be necessary, to the payment of any fines or costs, or both, adjudged against the defendant or juvenile or imposed by law. Any remaining funds shall be forfeited without further notice. However, if a rehearing is granted, the court may remit part or all of such cash bond not applied ultimately to fines or costs, and order a refund of the same by the State Treasurer, or by the treasurer or director of finance of the locality, if the bond was collected by a locality pursuant to § 19.2-136, but only if good cause is shown.

If the defendant or juvenile posted a cash bond and failed to appear, but is not tried in his absence, the bond shall be forfeited promptly without further notice. However, if the defendant or juvenile appears in court within 60 days after the bond is forfeited, the judge may remit part or all of any bond previously forfeited and order a refund of the same by the State Treasurer, or by the treasurer or director of finance of the locality, if the bond was collected by a locality pursuant to § 19.2-136.

History.
Code 1950, § 19.1-137; 1960, c. 366; 1962, c. 499; 1970, c. 371; 1973, c. 409; 1975, c. 495; 1978, c. 755; 1979, c. 735; 1987, c. 670; 1988, c. 443; 1990, c. 624; 2000, c. 885; 2003, c. 840; 2005, c. 585; 2006, cc. 296, 316; 2011, c. 802; 2012, c. 408.

Cross references.
As to when penalty of recognizance remitted, see § 19.2-145. As to action on recognizance not being defeated by defect in form of recognizance, see § 19.2-146. As to limitation of action on recognizance, see § 8.01-246.

The 2011 amendments.
The 2011 amendment by c. 802, in the last two paragraphs, inserted "or by the treasurer or director of finance of the county, city or town, if the bond was collected by a county, city or town pursuant to § 19.2-136."

The 2012 amendments.
The 2012 amendment by c. 408 substituted "locality" for "county, city or town" in the last two paragraphs.

Michie's Jurisprudence.
For related discussion, see 2B M.J. Bail and Recognizance, §§ 3, 27, 28.

CASE NOTES

Bail revocation and bond forfeiture proceedings may be combined. — While nothing in the statutes requires that a bail revocation proceeding and a bond forfeiture proceeding be combined for hearing, nothing forbids such a procedure. Heacock v. Commonwealth, 228 Va. 235, 321 S.E.2d 645 (1984) (decided prior to the 1987 amendment).

Improper to use finding of probable cause to revoke bail as proof in bond forfeiture proceeding. — The surety was denied procedural due process in a bond forfeiture hearing by the treatment of the finding of probable cause in the bail revocation hearing as prima facie proof for purposes of the bond forfeiture proceeding. Heacock v. Commonwealth, 228 Va. 235, 321 S.E.2d 645 (1984) (decided prior to the 1987 amendment).

Judge need not find accused "guilty" of crime to revoke bail. — To revoke bail, the judge is not required to find that the accused was "guilty" of a crime or that a breach of the good behavior condition upon which he had been admitted to bail has been established by a preponderance of the evidence. Heacock v. Commonwealth, 228 Va. 235, 321 S.E.2d 645 (1984).

Standard of proof in bail revocation and bond forfeiture proceedings compared. — Probable cause is the standard of proof in a bail revocation proceeding. On the other hand, the effort of the Commonwealth to collect a debt due by reason of the forfeiture of the recognizance is a matter purely civil, and the Commonwealth must prove its case by a preponderance of the evidence. Heacock v. Commonwealth, 228 Va. 235, 321 S.E.2d 645 (1984) (decided prior to the 1987 amendment).

Burden of proof. — The movant in a show-cause proceeding has the burden of proving the premise of the show-cause order, and, if the movant makes a prima facie case, the burden shifts to the other party to go forward with the evidence. Heacock v. Commonwealth, 228 Va. 235, 321 S.E.2d 645 (1984).

Surety is essential party to bond forfeiture proceeding. — A surety on a cash recognizance has no viable due process complaint about the proceeding to revoke bail. He was not a party to that proceeding and, accordingly, had no standing to challenge lack of notice and no right to call or cross-examine witnesses. As surety on the cash recognizance, however, he is an essential party to the bond forfeiture proceeding and, under the provisions of § 19.2-135 and this section, is entitled to notice and hearing. Heacock v. Commonwealth, 228 Va. 235, 321 S.E.2d 645 (1984) (decided prior to the 1987 amendment).

Limitation of notice requirement. — The notice required by this section is limited to "a hearing ... to show cause" why a bail bond should not be forfeited. The statutory language cannot be stretched to include a requirement for notice to a surety of the nonappearance of a defendant. Commonwealth v. Allstate Bonding Co., 246 Va. 189, 435 S.E.2d 396 (1993).

Lack of standing. — Where sureties failed to satisfy dual burden assumed under the bond agreement of taking some action to secure the defendant's appearance and of ascertaining whether the action was successful, they were in no position to complain when the Commonwealth failed to notify them of the defendants' nonappearance until 13 months to more than three years after the fact. Commonwealth v. Allstate Bonding Co., 246 Va. 189, 435 S.E.2d 396 (1993).

Since a surety has no standing to challenge lack of notice of a defendant's bail revocation hearing, there is no reason why a surety would have standing to challenge lack of notice of a defendant's initial nonappearance. Commonwealth v. Allstate Bonding Co., 246 Va. 189, 435 S.E.2d 396 (1993).

§ 19.2-144. Forfeiture of recognizance while in military or naval service.

If in any motion, action, suit or other proceeding made or taken in any court of this Commonwealth on a forfeited bail bond or forfeited recognizance, or to enforce the payment of the bond in any manner or any judgment thereon, or to forfeit any bail bond or recognizance, it appears that the person for whose alleged default such bail bond or recognizance was forfeited or judgment rendered, or such motion is made or proceeding taken, was prevented from complying with the condition of such bail bond or recognizance by reason of his having enlisted or been

drafted in the army or navy of the United States, then judgment or decree on such motion, action, suit or other proceeding shall be given for the defendant.

History.
Code 1950, § 19.1-139; 1960, c. 366; 1975, c. 495; 1991, c. 581.

§ 19.2-145. How penalty remitted.

When in an action or on a motion to extend the period for enforcement of a judgment on a recognizance the penalty is adjudged to be forfeited the court may on an application of a defendant or juvenile remit the penalty or any part of it and render judgment on such terms and conditions as it deems reasonable.

History.
Code 1950, § 19.1-140; 1960, c. 366; 1975, c. 495; 1978, c. 755; 1982, c. 153.

Cross references.
As to discharge of recognizance in misdemeanor cases where injured party acknowledges satisfaction, etc., see §§ 19.2-151 and 19.2-152.

Michie's Jurisprudence.
For related discussion, see 2B M.J. Bail and Recognizance, § 20.

CASE NOTES

Court has discretion. — The statute invests the courts with discretionary powers to meet the exigencies of particular cases by remitting the penalty in whole or in part, and rendering judgment on such terms and conditions as it deems reasonable. Caldwell v. Commonwealth, 55 Va. (14 Gratt.) 698 (1858); Bolanz v. Commonwealth, 65 Va. (24 Gratt.) 31 (1873); Bowling v. Commonwealth, 123 Va. 340, 96 S.E. 739 (1918).

This section, which is an extension of the common-law rule, invests the courts with discretionary power to meet the exigencies of the particular case. Bisping v. Commonwealth, 218 Va. 753, 240 S.E.2d 656, cert. denied, 435 U.S. 1007, 98 S. Ct. 1878, 56 L. Ed. 2d 389 (1978).

Section does not apply when final judgment entered. — The discretion vested in the trial court by this section is limited to cases in which there is a pending action or scire facias on the recognizance which has been forfeited, and does not extend to cases in which final judgment has been entered in the action or scire facias. In the latter class of cases the recognizance, as such, no longer remains in court. Jordan v. Commonwealth, 135 Va. 560, 115 S.E. 569 (1923).

This is true where the trial court did not pass on the merits of the case, but denied relief solely on the ground that it had no control over the final judgment on the scire facias which had been entered at a former term. Jordan v. Commonwealth, 135 Va. 560, 115 S.E. 569 (1923).

Impossibility of performance as excuse for breach. — Bail will generally be exonerated from liability where the performance of the conditions of the recognizance are rendered impossible by the act of God, the act of the law, or the act of the obligee. Caldwell v. Commonwealth, 55 Va. (14 Gratt.) 698 (1858); Bowling v. Commonwealth, 123 Va. 340, 96 S.E. 739 (1918).

The prisoner's confinement in the state correctional facility for another felony having rendered it impossible for him to appear at the court at the time prescribed by the recognizance, it constitutes a good defense for the bail to the scire facias. Caldwell v. Commonwealth, 55 Va. (14 Gratt.) 698 (1858).

Where the bail was guilty of no negligence whatever, and, without fault on his part, the attorney for the Commonwealth, with full knowledge of the facts voluntarily suffered the principal to be taken out of the control of his bondsmen by federal authority, by which act the latter was rendered powerless to produce the principal at the time and place of trial the bail should be exonerated from liability upon recognizance. Bowling v. Commonwealth, 123 Va. 340, 96 S.E. 739 (1918).

It is not competent for the accused to absolve himself or his bail by accepting a federal office. Bolanz v. Commonwealth, 65 Va. (24 Gratt.) 31 (1873).

Discretion not abused. — Where the record conclusively showed that the principal, while on bail, violated the specific good behavior condition of the recognizances by committing additional crimes of the same nature and character as his earlier convictions, and no evidence was adduced at the scire facias (now motion to extend) hearing by either the principal or the surety in explanation, excuse, mitigation or palliation of the principal's flagrant violation of the condition, the trial court did not abuse its discretion in failing to remit the whole or any part of the forfeiture. Bisping v. Commonwealth, 218 Va. 753, 240 S.E.2d 656, cert. denied, 435 U.S. 1007, 98 S. Ct. 1878, 56 L. Ed. 2d 389 (1978).

§ 19.2-146. Defects in form of recognizance not to defeat action or judgment.

No action or judgment on a recognizance shall be defeated or arrested by reason of any defect in the form of the recognizance, if it appear to have been taken by a court or officer authorized to take it and be substantially sufficient.

History.
Code 1950, § 19.1-141; 1960, c. 366; 1975, c. 495.

Cross references.
As to form and sufficiency of recognizance, etc., see § 19.2-135.

Michie's Jurisprudence.
For related discussion, see 2B M.J. Bail and Recognizance, §§ 12, 13.

CASE NOTES

The words "action or judgment" as used in this section are broad enough to include a proceeding by scire facias. The award of execution on a recognizance is commonly spoken of as a judgment on a scire facias. Walker v. Commonwealth, 144 Va. 648, 131 S.E. 230 (1926).

"Substantially sufficient." — A recognizance is not invalid because it required defendant in a prosecution for violation of the prohibition law to appear not before the court or any court, but only before the judge of the court, and, it appearing that the recognizance was "taken by a court, or officer, authorized to take it," the recognizance was certainly "substantially sufficient" within this section. Alls v. Commonwealth, 131 Va. 640, 108 S.E. 645 (1921).

A substantially sufficient memorandum of the recognizance taken by a justice of the peace, is protected under this section. Walker v. Commonwealth, 144 Va. 648, 131 S.E. 230 (1926).

Recognizance held not substantially sufficient as required by this section. Commonwealth v. Fulks, 94 Va. 585, 27 S.E. 498 (1897).

Variance held immaterial. — Pursuant to this section and §§ 19.2-135 and 19.2-136, it was held that where the condition of the recognizance of one accused of a felony was for his personal appearance "to answer the charge against him," and the language of the scire facias of such recognizance was for his personal appearance "to answer as of a felony whereof he stands accused," the variance was immaterial, no form of language being prescribed for the recognizance. Allen v. Commonwealth, 90 Va. 356, 18 S.E. 437 (1893).

For other instances of variance between the scire facias and the recognizance, see Wood v. Commonwealth, 25 Va. (4 Rand.) 329 (1826); Bias v. Floyd, 34 Va. (7 Leigh) 640 (1836); Alls v. Commonwealth, 131 Va. 640, 108 S.E. 645 (1921).

§ 19.2-147. Docketing judgment on forfeited recognizance or bond.

Whenever a judgment is entered in any court of record in favor of the Commonwealth of Virginia upon a forfeited recognizance or bond, the clerk of the court in which the judgment is rendered shall certify an abstract of the same to the clerk of the circuit court of the county or city wherein the judgment debtor resides or of any city or county in which he may own real property, who shall thereupon enter the abstract of judgment upon his judgment docket.

History.
Code 1950, § 19.1-142; 1960, c. 366; 1975, c. 495; 1994, c. 432.

§ 19.2-148. Surety discharged on payment of amount, etc., into court.

A surety on a bond in a recognizance may, after default, pay into the court from which the process has issued, or may issue thereon, the amount for which he is bound, with such costs as the court may direct, and be thereupon discharged.

History.
Code 1950, § 19.1-143; 1960, c. 366; 1975, c. 495; 1991, c. 581.

Cross references.
As to procedure for discharge of surety by surrender of principal, see §§ 19.2-149 and 19.2-150.

Michie's Jurisprudence.
For related discussion, see 2B M.J. Bail and Recognizance, §§ 19, 25.

§ 19.2-149. How surety on a bond in recognizance may surrender principal and be discharged from liability.

A bail bondsman or his licensed bail enforcement agent on a bond in a recognizance may at any time arrest his principal and surrender him to the court before which the recognizance was taken or before which such principal's appearance is required, or to the sheriff, sergeant or jailer of the county or city wherein the court before which such principal's appearance is required is located; in addition to the above authority, upon the application of the surety, the court, or the clerk thereof, before which the recognizance was taken, or before which such principal's appearance is required, shall issue a capias for the arrest of such principal, and such capias may be executed by such bail bondsman or his licensed bail enforcement agent, or by any sheriff, sergeant or police officer, and the person executing such capias shall deliver such principal and such capias to the sheriff or jailer of the county or the sheriff, sergeant or jailer of the city in which the appearance of such principal is required, and thereupon the surety or the property bail bondsman shall be discharged from liability for any act of the principal subsequent thereto. Such sheriff, sergeant or jailer shall thereafter deliver such capias to the clerk of such court, with his endorsement thereon acknowledging delivery of such principal to his custody.

History.
Code 1950, § 19.1-144; 1960, c. 366; 1975, c. 495; 1991, c. 581; 2004, c. 460.

Cross references.
As to right of surety to take indemnity from bail, see § 19.2-132. As to how penalty remitted, see § 19.2-145. As to discharge of surety upon payment, see § 19.2-148.

Editor's note.
Acts 2004, c. 460, cl. 5 provides: "That the provisions of this act, except for § 16.1-77, shall become effective on July 1, 2005."

Law Review.
For note on liability of bail bondsmen under 42 U.S.C. § 1983, see 42 Wash. & Lee L. Rev. 215 (1985).

Michie's Jurisprudence.
For related discussion, see 2B M.J. Bail and Recognizance, §§ 19, 25.

CASE NOTES

Nothing in this section imparted legal justification to beat the victim and handcuff him for six hours to a door before surrendering him to jail. The fact finder could have found beyond a reasonable doubt that defendant detained the victim, by force, without legal justification, and with the intent to deprive him of his personal liberty. The evidence was sufficient to prove beyond a reasonable doubt that the bondsman committed abduction. Perry v. Commonwealth, No. 0237-95-2 (Ct. of Appeals July 9, 1996).

Fugitive recovery agent exceeded authority. — Evidence was sufficient to convict a fugitive recovery agent of violating § 18.2-174 in connection with his stop of a vehicle in which he thought a fugitive might be riding, as he exceeded the scope of the authority granted him under this section and by: (1) wearing a misleading badge representing that he was part of a "special investigations unit" of a law-enforcement body; (2) by stating that he was with a "violent crimes unit"; and (3) by interrogating the woman he stopped about her possible drunk driving after he realized that the fugitive was not in the car. English v. Commonwealth, 43 Va. App. 370, 598 S.E.2d 322, 2004 Va. App. LEXIS 294 (2004).

§ 19.2-150. Proceeding when surety surrenders principal.

If the surrender is to the court, the court shall make such order as it deems proper; if the surrender is to a sheriff or jailer, the officer to whom the accused has been surrendered shall give the surety a certificate of the fact. After such surrender the person shall be treated in accordance with the provisions of Article 1 (§ 19.2-119 et seq.) of Chapter 9 of this title unless the court or judge thereof has reason to believe that no one or more conditions of release will reasonably assure that the person will not flee or pose a danger to any other person or to the community.

History.
Code 1950, § 19.1-145; 1960, c. 366; 1973, c. 485; 1975, c. 495; 1978, c. 755; 1999, cc. 829, 846.

Michie's Jurisprudence.
For related discussion, see 2B M.J. Bail and Recognizance, §§ 19, 25; 5B M.J. Criminal Procedure, § 64.

ARTICLE 3.
SATISFACTION AND DISCHARGE.

Michie's Jurisprudence.
For related discussion, see 4A M.J. Compromise and Settlement, § 6; 5B M.J. Criminal Procedure, § 11.

§ 19.2-151. Satisfaction and discharge of assault and similar charges.

When a person is in jail or under a recognizance to answer a charge of assault and battery or other misdemeanor, or has been indicted for an assault and battery or other misdemeanor for which there is a remedy by civil action, unless the offense was committed (i) by or upon any law-enforcement officer, (ii) riotously in violation of §§ 18.2-404 to 18.2-407, (iii) against a family or household member in violation of § 18.2-57.2, or (iv) with intent to commit a felony, if the person injured appears before the court which made the commitment or took the recognizance, or before the court in which the indictment is pending, and acknowledges in writing that he has received satisfaction for the injury, the court may, in its discretion, by an order, supersede the commitment, discharge the recognizance, or dismiss the prosecution, upon payment by the defendant of costs accrued to the Commonwealth or any of its officers.

History.
Code 1950, § 19.1-18; 1960, c. 366; 1968, c. 639; 1975, c. 495; 1997, c. 532; 1999, c. 963.

CASE NOTES

Section accords with policy of the law. — Private adjustment of prosecutions for misdemeanors, provided for by this section, is in accord with the general policy of the law. Of course, compounding or concealing crimes, or stifling prosecutions to defeat the ends of justice, will not be permitted, but in prosecutions not involving any great offense against the public, the courts will encourage settlements between the parties as less injurious to the public than litigation. Glidewell v. Murray-Lacy & Co., 124 Va. 563, 98 S.E. 665 (1919).

It applies to misdemeanors involving civil wrongs. — This section applies to those classes of misdemeanors which also involve the infliction of a civil wrong. The course adopted for the disposal of a criminal charge is set out in the statute and is judicial in nature. It contemplates acknowledgment of satisfaction for the civil wrong, and the dismissal of the criminal charge then rests in the judicial discretion of the justice (now judge or court). Darnell v. Davis, 190 Va. 701, 58 S.E.2d 68 (1950).

It may apply though formalities not strictly followed. — The fact that the formalities of this section were not strictly followed will not prevent its application, where it appears that the aggrieved party received satisfaction, appeared before the justice (now judge or court) and the warrant was dismissed. Orndorff v. Bond, 185 Va. 497, 39 S.E.2d 352 (1946).

And there may be estoppel to allege irregularity. — In an action for abuse of process, where defendants claimed that the settlement with plaintiff was in accordance with this section, plaintiff cannot complaint of an alleged irregularity in the dismissal of the warrant against him, when what was done was upon his own proposition. Glidewell v. Murray-Lacy & Co., 124 Va. 563, 98 S.E. 665 (1919).

Dismissal of warrant is discretionary. — Under the explicit terms of this section, the written request for dismissal of the warrant is addressed to the discretion of the judicial officer empowered to take the action authorized and allowed by law, and his action terminates the prosecution. Darnell v. Davis, 190 Va. 701, 58 S.E.2d 68 (1950).

And warrant may be dismissed though costs not paid. — There is no merit in the contention that a justice of the peace (now judge or court) has no right or jurisdiction to dismiss a warrant under this section where the defendant fails to pay the costs accrued. Darnell v. Davis, 190 Va. 701, 58 S.E.2d 68 (1950).

The words "or other misdemeanor," following "assault and battery," are not limited to other misdemeanors of the same kind as assault and battery. Glidewell v. Murray-Lacy & Co., 124 Va. 563, 98 S.E. 665 (1919).

Settlement not a concealing or compounding of offense. — Defendants, who procured plaintiff's arrest for a misdemeanor, upon obtaining a settlement of their claim against plaintiff, had him released and the warrant dismissed. It was held that the transaction did not fall within the condemnation of § 18.2-462 against concealing or compounding offenses, but was within the spirit, if not within the terms, of this section. Glidewell v. Murray-Lacy & Co., 124 Va. 563, 98 S.E. 665 (1919).

Applied in Commonwealth v. Jackson, 255 Va. 552, 499 S.E.2d 276 (1998).

§ 19.2-152. Order discharging recognizance or superseding commitment; judgment for costs.

Every order discharging a recognizance shall be filed with the clerk before the session of the court at which the party was to appear. Where a person is held under a commitment, any order superseding a commitment shall be delivered to the jailer, who shall forthwith discharge the witnesses, if any, and the accused or juvenile, and judgment against the accused or juvenile shall be entered in the court for the costs of the prosecution.

History.
Code 1950, § 19.1-19; 1960, c. 366; 1975, c. 495; 1978, c. 755.

ARTICLE 4.

BAIL BONDSMEN.

§§ 19.2-152.1 through 19.2-152.1:7. Repealed by Acts 2004, c. 460, effective July 1, 2005.

ARTICLE 5.

PRETRIAL SERVICES ACT.

§ 19.2-152.2. Purpose; establishment of pretrial services and services agencies.

It is the purpose of this article to provide more effective protection of society by establishing pretrial services agencies that will assist judicial officers in discharging their duties pursuant to Article 1 (§ 19.2-119 et seq.) of Chapter 9 of this title. Such agencies are intended to provide better information and services for use by judicial officers in determining the risk to public safety and the assurance of appearance of persons age 18 or over or persons under the age of 18 who have been transferred for trial as adults held in custody and charged with an offense, other than an offense punishable by death, who are pending trial or hearing. Any city, county or combination thereof may establish a pretrial services agency and any city, county or combination thereof required to submit a community-based cor-

rections plan pursuant to § 53.1-82.1 shall establish a pretrial services agency.

History.
1994, 2nd Sp. Sess., cc. 1, 2; 1999, cc. 829, 846; 2004, c. 378; 2007, c. 133.

Cross references.
As to dissemination of juvenile record information, see § 19.2-389.1. As to limitations on the release of criminal incident information, see § 2.2-3706. As to the confidentiality of court records, see § 16.1-305.

The 2007 amendments.
The 2007 amendment by c. 133 substituted "pretrial services agencies" for "programs" in the first sentence, substituted "agencies" for "programs" in the second sentence and in the last sentence, substituted "pretrial services agency" for "pretrial services program" in two places.

§ 19.2-152.3. Department of Criminal Justice Services to prescribe standards; biennial plan.

The Department of Criminal Justice Services shall prescribe standards for the development, implementation, operation and evaluation of services authorized by this article. The Department of Criminal Justice Services shall develop risk assessment and other instruments to be used by pretrial services agencies in assisting judicial officers in discharging their duties pursuant to Article 1 (§ 19.2-119 et seq.) of Chapter 9 of this title. Any city, county or combination thereof which establishes pretrial services pursuant to this article shall submit a biennial plan to the Department of Criminal Justice Services for review and approval.

History.
1994, 2nd Sp. Sess., cc. 1, 2; 1999, cc. 829, 846; 2007, c. 133.

The 2007 amendments.
The 2007 amendment by c. 133 substituted "services" for "programs" in the first sentence, substituted "pretrial services agencies" for "pretrial services programs" in the second sentence and substituted "pretrial services" for "a pretrial services program" in the last sentence.

§ 19.2-152.4. Mandated services.

Any city, county or combination thereof which elects or is required to establish a pretrial services agency shall provide all information and services for use by judicial officers as set forth in Article 1 (§ 19.2-119 et seq.) of Chapter 9 of this title.

History.
1994, 2nd Sp. Sess., cc. 1, 2; 1999, cc. 829, 846; 2007, c. 133.

The 2007 amendments.
The 2007 amendment by c. 133 substituted "pretrial services agency" for "pretrial services program."

§ 19.2-152.4:1. Form of oath of office for local pretrial services officer; authorization to seek capias.

Every pretrial services officer who is an employee of a local pretrial services agency established by any city, county or combination thereof or operated pursuant to this article shall take an oath of office as prescribed in § 49-1 and to provide services pursuant to the requirements of this article before entering the duties of his office. The oath of office shall be taken before any general district or circuit court judge in any county or city which has established services for use by judicial officers pursuant to this article.

In addition, any officer of a pretrial services agency established or operated pursuant to this article may seek a capias from any judicial officer for the arrest of any person under the agency's custody and supervision for failure to comply with any conditions of release imposed by a judicial officer, for failure to comply with the conditions of pretrial supervision as established by a pretrial services agency, or when there is reason to believe that the person will fail to appear, will leave, or has left the jurisdiction to avoid prosecution.

History.
2000, c. 1040; 2007, c. 133.

The 2007 amendments.
The 2007 amendment by c. 133 deleted "warrant or" following "may seek a" in the second paragraph.

§ 19.2-152.4:2. Confidentiality of records of and reports on adult persons under investigation by or in the custody or supervision of a local pretrial services agency.

A. Any pretrial investigation report prepared by a local pretrial services officer is confidential and is exempt from the Virginia Freedom of Information Act (§ 2.2-3700 et seq.). Such reports shall be filed as a part of the case record. Such reports shall be sealed upon receipt by the court and made available only by court order; except that such reports shall be available upon request to (i) any criminal justice agency, as defined in § 9.1-101, of this or any other state or of the United States; (ii) any agency where the accused is referred for assessment or treatment; or (iii) counsel for the person who is the subject of the report.

B. Any report on the progress of an accused under the supervision or custody of a pretrial services agency and any information relative to the identity of or inferring personal characteristics of an accused, including demographic information, diagnostic summaries, records of office visits, medical, substance abuse, psychiatric or psychological records or information, substance abuse screening, assessment and testing information, and other sensitive information not explicitly classified as criminal history record information, is exempt from the Virginia Freedom of Information Act (§ 2.2-3700 et seq.). However, such information may be disseminated to criminal justice agencies as defined in § 9.1-101 in the discretion of the custodian of these records.

History.
2002, c. 769; 2007, c. 133.

The 2007 amendments.
The 2007 amendment by c. 133 deleted "no right of review or correction by subject of record or report" from the end in the section heading.

§ 19.2-152.4:3. Duties and responsibilities of local pretrial services officers.

A. Each local pretrial services officer, for the jurisdictions served, shall:

1. Investigate and interview defendants arrested on state and local warrants and who are detained in jails located in jurisdictions served by the agency while awaiting a hearing before any court that is considering or reconsidering bail, at initial appearance, advisement or arraignment, or at other subsequent hearings;

2. Present a pretrial investigation report with recommendations to assist courts in discharging their duties related to granting or reconsidering bail;

3. Supervise and assist all defendants residing within the jurisdictions served and placed on pretrial supervision by any judicial officer within the jurisdictions to ensure compliance with the terms and conditions of bail;

4. Conduct random drug and alcohol tests on any defendant under supervision for whom a judicial officer has ordered testing or who has been required to refrain from excessive use of alcohol or use of any illegal drug or controlled substance or other defendant-specific condition of bail related to alcohol or substance abuse;

5. Seek a capias from any judicial officer pursuant to § 19.2-152.4:1 for any defendant placed under supervision or the custody of the agency who fails to comply with the conditions of bail or supervision, when continued liberty or noncompliance presents a risk of flight, a risk to public safety or risk to the defendant;

6. Seek an order to show cause why the defendant should not be required to appear before the court in those cases requiring a subsequent hearing before the court;

7. Provide defendant-based information to assist any law-enforcement officer with the return to custody of defendants placed on supervision for which a capias has been sought; and

8. Keep such records and make such reports as required by the Commonwealth of Virginia Department of Criminal Justice Services.

B. Each local pretrial services officer, for the jurisdictions served, may provide the following optional services, as appropriate and when available resources permit:

1. Conduct, subject to court approval, drug and alcohol screenings, or tests at investigation pursuant to subsection B of § 19.2-123 or following release to supervision, and conduct or facilitate the

preparation of screenings or assessments or both pursuant to state approved protocols;

2. Facilitate placement of defendants in a substance abuse education or treatment program or services or other education or treatment service when ordered as a condition of bail;

3. Sign for the custody of any defendant investigated by a pretrial services officer, and released by a court to pretrial supervision as the sole term and condition of bail or when combined with an unsecured bond;

4. Provide defendant information and investigation services for those who are detained in jails located in jurisdictions served by the agency and are awaiting an initial bail hearing before a magistrate;

5. Supervise defendants placed by any judicial officer on home electronic monitoring as a condition of bail and supervision;

6. Prepare, for defendants investigated, the financial statement-eligibility determination form for indigent defense services; and

7. Subject to approved procedures and if so requested by the court, coordinate for defendants investigated, services for court-appointed counsel and for interpreters for foreign-language speaking and hearing-impaired defendants.

History.
2003, c. 603; 2007, c. 133; 2008, cc. 551, 691.

The 2007 amendments.
The 2007 amendment by c. 133 substituted "agency" for "program" in subdivisions A 1 and B 4; and inserted "or services" following "treatment program" in subdivision B 2.

The 2008 amendments.
The 2008 amendments by cc. 551 and 691 are identical and deleted "local" preceding "magistrate" at the end of subdivision B 4.

§ 19.2-152.5. Community criminal justice boards.

Each city, county or combination thereof establishing a pretrial services agency shall also establish a community criminal justice board pursuant to § 9.1-178.

History.
1994, 2nd Sp. Sess., cc. 1, 2; 2007, c. 133.

The 2007 amendments.
The 2007 amendment by c. 133 substituted "pretrial services agency" for "pretrial services program."

§ 19.2-152.6. Withdrawal from pretrial services.

Any participating city or county may, at the beginning of any calendar quarter, by ordinance or resolution of its governing authority, notify the Department of Criminal Justice Services of its intention to withdraw from participation in pretrial services. Such withdrawal shall be effective as of the last day of the quarter in which such notice is given.

History.
1994, 2nd Sp. Sess., cc. 1, 2; 2007, c. 133.

The 2007 amendments.
The 2007 amendment by c. 133 substituted "participation in pretrial services" for "the pretrial services program."

§ 19.2-152.7. Funding; failure to comply.

Counties and cities shall be required to establish a pretrial services agency only to the extent funded by the Commonwealth through the general appropriation act. The Department of Criminal Justice Services shall periodically review each agency established under this article to determine compliance with the submitted plan and operating standards. If the Department determines that any agency is not in substantial compliance with the submitted plan or standards, the Department may suspend all or any portion of financial aid made available to the locality for purposes of this article until there is compliance.

History.
1994, 2nd Sp. Sess., cc. 1, 2; 2007, c. 133.

The 2007 amendments.
The 2007 amendment by c. 133 substituted "agency" for "program" in the first and second sentences and substituted "any agency" for "a program" in the second sentence.

Michie's Jurisprudence.
For related discussion, see 2B M.J. Bail and Recognizance, § 2.

CHAPTER 9.1.

PROTECTIVE ORDERS.

§ 19.2-152.7:1. Definitions.

As used in this chapter:

"Act of violence, force, or threat" means any act involving violence, force, or threat that results in bodily injury or places one in reasonable apprehension of death, sexual assault, or bodily injury. Such act includes, but is not limited to, any forceful detention, stalking, criminal sexual assault in violation of Article 7 (§ 18.2-61 et seq.) of Chapter 4 of Title 18.2, or any criminal offense that results in bodily injury or places one in reasonable apprehension of death, sexual assault, or bodily injury.

History.
2011, cc. 445, 480.

Editor's note.
Acts 2011, cc. 445 and 480, cl. 2 provides: "That the provisions of this act may result in a net increase in periods of imprisonment or commitment. Pursuant to § 30-19.1:4, the estimated amount of the necessary appropriation is $93,767 for periods of imprisonment in state adult correctional facilities and cannot be determined for

periods of commitment to the custody of the Department of Juvenile Justice."

§ 19.2-152.8. Emergency protective orders authorized.

A. Any judge of a circuit court, general district court, juvenile and domestic relations district court or magistrate may issue a written or oral ex parte emergency protective order pursuant to this section in order to protect the health or safety of any person.

B. When a law-enforcement officer or an alleged victim asserts under oath to a judge or magistrate that such person is being or has been subjected to an act of violence, force, or threat and on that assertion or other evidence the judge or magistrate finds that (i) there is probable danger of a further such act being committed by the respondent against the alleged victim or (ii) a petition or warrant for the arrest of the respondent has been issued for any criminal offense resulting from the commission of an act of violence, force, or threat, the judge or magistrate shall issue an ex parte emergency protective order imposing one or more of the following conditions on the respondent:

1. Prohibiting acts of violence, force, or threat or criminal offenses resulting in injury to person or property;

2. Prohibiting such contacts by the respondent with the alleged victim or the alleged victim's family or household members as the judge or magistrate deems necessary to protect the safety of such persons; and

3. Such other conditions as the judge or magistrate deems necessary to prevent (i) acts of violence, force, or threat, (ii) criminal offenses resulting in injury to person or property, or (iii) communication or other contact of any kind by the respondent.

C. An emergency protective order issued pursuant to this section shall expire at 11:59 p.m. on the third day following issuance. If the expiration occurs on a day that the court is not in session, the emergency protective order shall be extended until 11:59 p.m. on the next day that the court which issued the order is in session. The respondent may at any time file a motion with the court requesting a hearing to dissolve or modify the order. The hearing on the motion shall be given precedence on the docket of the court.

D. A law-enforcement officer may request an emergency protective order pursuant to this section and, if the person in need of protection is physically or mentally incapable of filing a petition pursuant to § 19.2-152.9 or 19.2-152.10, may request the extension of an emergency protective order for an additional period of time not to exceed three days after expiration of the original order. The request for an emergency protective order or extension of an order may be made orally, in person or by electronic means, and the judge of a circuit court, general district court, or juvenile and domestic relations district court or a magistrate may issue an oral

emergency protective order. An oral emergency protective order issued pursuant to this section shall be reduced to writing, by the law-enforcement officer requesting the order or the magistrate, on a preprinted form approved and provided by the Supreme Court of Virginia. The completed form shall include a statement of the grounds for the order asserted by the officer or the alleged victim of such crime.

E. The court or magistrate shall forthwith, but in all cases no later than the end of the business day on which the order was issued, enter and transfer electronically to the Virginia Criminal Information Network the respondent's identifying information and the name, date of birth, sex, and race of each protected person provided to the court or magistrate. A copy of an emergency protective order issued pursuant to this section containing any such identifying information shall be forwarded forthwith to the primary law-enforcement agency responsible for service and entry of protective orders. Upon receipt of the order by the primary law-enforcement agency, the agency shall forthwith verify and enter any modification as necessary to the identifying information and other appropriate information required by the Department of State Police into the Virginia Criminal Information Network established and maintained by the Department pursuant to Chapter 2 (§ 52-12 et seq.) of Title 52 and the order shall be served forthwith upon the respondent and due return made to the court. However, if the order is issued by the circuit court, the clerk of the circuit court shall forthwith forward an attested copy of the order containing the respondent's identifying information and the name, date of birth, sex, and race of each protected person provided to the court to the primary law-enforcement agency providing service and entry of protective orders and upon receipt of the order, the primary law-enforcement agency shall enter the name of the person subject to the order and other appropriate information required by the Department of State Police into the Virginia Criminal Information Network established and maintained by the Department pursuant to Chapter 2 (§ 52-12 et seq.) of Title 52 and the order shall be served forthwith upon the respondent. Upon service, the agency making service shall enter the date and time of service and other appropriate information required into the Virginia Criminal Information Network and make due return to the court. One copy of the order shall be given to the alleged victim of such crime. The judge or magistrate who issues an oral order pursuant to an electronic request by a law-enforcement officer shall verify the written order to determine whether the officer who reduced it to writing accurately transcribed the contents of the oral order. The original copy shall be filed with the clerk of the appropriate district court within five business days of the issuance of the order. If the order is later dissolved or modified, a copy of the dissolution or modification order shall also be attested, forwarded forthwith to the primary law-enforcement agency responsible for service and entry of protective orders, and upon receipt of the order by the primary law-enforcement agency, the agency shall forthwith verify and enter any modification as necessary to the identifying information and other appropriate information required by the Department of State Police into the Virginia Criminal Information Network as described above and the order shall be served forthwith and due return made to the court. Upon request, the clerk shall provide the alleged victim of such crime with information regarding the date and time of service.

F. The issuance of an emergency protective order shall not be considered evidence of any wrongdoing by the respondent.

G. As used in this section, a "law-enforcement officer" means any (i) person who is a full-time or part-time employee of a police department or sheriff's office which is part of or administered by the Commonwealth or any political subdivision thereof and who is responsible for the prevention and detection of crime and the enforcement of the penal, traffic or highway laws of the Commonwealth and (ii) member of an auxiliary police force established pursuant to § 15.2-1731. Part-time employees are compensated officers who are not full-time employees as defined by the employing police department or sheriff's office.

H. Neither a law-enforcement agency, the attorney for the Commonwealth, a court nor the clerk's office, nor any employee of them, may disclose, except among themselves, the residential address, telephone number, or place of employment of the person protected by the order or that of the family of such person, except to the extent that disclosure is (i) required by law or the Rules of the Supreme Court, (ii) necessary for law-enforcement purposes, or (iii) permitted by the court for good cause.

I. As used in this section, "copy" includes a facsimile copy.

J. No fee shall be charged for filing or serving any petition pursuant to this section.

K. No emergency protective order shall be issued pursuant to this section against a law-enforcement officer for any action arising out of the lawful performance of his duties.

History.
1997, c. 831; 1998, cc. 569, 684; 1999, c. 371; 2001, c. 474; 2002, cc. 507, 706, 810, 818; 2003, c. 730; 2008, cc. 73, 246; 2009, cc. 341, 732; 2011, cc. 445, 480; 2012, cc. 146, 637, 827.

Cross references.
As to penalty for violation of stalking protective order, see § 18.2-60.4.

Editor's note.
Acts 2011, cc. 445 and 480, cl. 2 provides: "That the provisions of this act may result in a net increase in periods of imprisonment or commitment. Pursuant to § 30-19.1:4, the estimated amount of the necessary appropriation is $93,767 for periods of imprisonment in state adult correctional facilities and cannot be determined for periods of commitment to the custody of the Department of Juvenile Justice."

The 2008 amendments.
The 2008 amendments by cc. 73 and 246 are identical, and in subsection C, substituted "shall expire at the end of the third day following issuance" for "shall expire 72 hours after issuance" at the end of the first sentence, and in the second sentence, deleted "of the 72-hour period" following "If the expiration" and substituted "the end" for "5 p.m."; rewrote subsection E; and added subsection K.

The 2009 amendments.
The 2009 amendment by c. 341, in subsection B, inserted "sexual battery in violation of § 18.2-67.4, aggravated sexual battery in violation of § 18.2-67.3" twice and made a related change; and in subdivisions B 1 and B 3, inserted "acts of sexual battery."

The 2009 amendment by c. 732, in subsection C, in the first sentence, substituted "11:59 p.m. on" for "the end of," in the second sentence, substituted "on a day" for "at a time" and "11:59 p.m. on" for "the end of" and deleted "business" preceding "day that the"; in subsection E, in the first sentence, inserted "electronically to the Virginia Criminal Information Network the respondent's" and "and the name, date of birth, sex, and race of each protected person," and deleted "electronically to the Virginia Criminal Information Network" from the end, in the second sentence, deleted "and an addendum" preceding "containing any such," in the third sentence, deleted "and addendum" preceding "by the primary," in the fourth sentence, deleted "and an addendum" following "copy of the order," inserted "the respondent's" and "and the name, date of birth, sex, and race of each protected person provided to the court" and deleted "and addendum" following "receipt of the order"; and deleted subsection K, which read: "If any identifying information in the addendum is determined to be incorrect by the entering agency, the agency shall enter the corrected information into the Virginia Criminal Information Network."

The 2011 amendments.
The 2011 amendments by cc. 445 and 480 are identical, and rewrote the first paragraph in subsection B; in subdivision B 1, substituted "force, or threat or criminal offenses resulting in injury to person or property" for "acts of sexual battery, or acts of stalking in violation of § 18.2-60.3"; in subdivision B 2, deleted "of such crime" following "victim"; in subdivision B 3, added the clause (i) designation, and therein substituted "acts of violence, force, or threat" for "acts of stalking, acts of sexual battery, or" and added the clause (ii) and (iii) designations; and in subsection D, subdivided the former first sentence, adding the language beginning "and, if the person in need of protection" in the first sentence and "The request for an emergency protective order or extension of an order may be made" in the second sentence.

The 2012 amendments.
The 2012 amendment by c. 146 added subsection K.
The 2012 amendment by c. 637 substituted "or the alleged victim's family" for "or such person's family" in subdivision B 2.
The 2012 amendment by c. 827, effective April 18, 2012, deleted "subsection B of" preceding "§ 15.2-1731" in G (ii).

OPINIONS OF THE ATTORNEY GENERAL

Petition for protective orders by law enforcement on behalf of minors. — Law-enforcement officers may file petitions for emergency protective orders on behalf of minors who are victims of family abuse, stalking, sexual assault or other acts of criminal violence. See opinion of Attorney General to The Honorable Charniele L. Herring, Member, House of Delegates, 10-116, 2011 Va. AG LEXIS 2 (01/21/11).

Petition by unemancipated minors for protective orders. — A minor may seek an emergency protective order in certain situations, but a minor who has not been emancipated, however mature that individual may be, can seek a protective order only through a next friend. See opinion of Attorney General to The Honorable Charniele L. Herring, Member, House of Delegates, 10-116, 2011 Va. AG LEXIS 2 (01/21/11).

Petition by emancipated minors for protective orders. — Emancipated minor may file petitions for protective orders under applicable statutes. See opinion of Attorney General to The Honorable Charniele L. Herring, Member, House of Delegates, 10-116, 2011 Va. AG LEXIS 2 (01/21/11).

§ 19.2-152.9. Preliminary protective orders.

A. Upon the filing of a petition alleging that (i) the petitioner is or has been, within a reasonable period of time, subjected to an act of violence, force, or threat, or (ii) a petition or warrant has been issued for the arrest of the alleged perpetrator for any criminal offense resulting from the commission of an act of violence, force, or threat, the court may issue a preliminary protective order against the alleged perpetrator in order to protect the health and safety of the petitioner or any family or household member of the petitioner. The order may be issued in an ex parte proceeding upon good cause shown when the petition is supported by an affidavit or sworn testimony before the judge or intake officer. Immediate and present danger of any act of violence, force, or threat or evidence sufficient to establish probable cause that an act of violence, force, or threat has recently occurred shall constitute good cause.

A preliminary protective order may include any one or more of the following conditions to be imposed on the respondent:

1. Prohibiting acts of violence, force, or threat or criminal offenses that may result in injury to person or property;

2. Prohibiting such other contacts by the respondent with the petitioner or the petitioner's family or household members as the court deems necessary for the health and safety of such persons; and

3. Such other conditions as the court deems necessary to prevent (i) acts of violence, force, or threat, (ii) criminal offenses that may result in injury to person or property, or (iii) communication or other contact of any kind by the respondent.

B. The court shall forthwith, but in all cases no later than the end of the business day on which the order was issued, enter and transfer electronically to the Virginia Criminal Information Network the respondent's identifying information and the name, date of birth, sex, and race of each protected person provided to the court. A copy of a preliminary protective order containing any such identifying information shall be forwarded forthwith to the primary law-enforcement agency responsible for service and entry of protective orders. Upon receipt of the order by the primary law-enforcement agency, the agency shall forthwith verify and enter any modification as necessary to the identifying information and other appropriate information required by the Department of State Police into the Virginia Criminal Information Network established and maintained by the Department pursuant to Chapter 2 (§ 52-12 et seq.) of Title 52 and the order shall be served forthwith on the alleged perpetrator in person as provided in § 16.1-264, and due return made to the court. However, if the order is issued by the circuit court, the clerk of the circuit court shall forthwith forward an attested copy of the order containing the respondent's identifying information and the name, date of birth, sex, and race of each protected person provided to the court to the primary law-enforcement agency providing service and entry of protective orders and upon receipt of the order, the primary law-enforcement agency shall enter the name of the person subject to the order and other appropriate information required by the Department of State Police into the Virginia Criminal Information Network established and maintained by the Department pursuant to Chapter 2 (§ 52-12 et seq.) of Title 52 and the order shall be served forthwith on the alleged perpetrator in person as provided in § 16.1-264. Upon service, the agency making service shall enter the date and time of service and other appropriate information required by the Department of State Police into the Virginia Criminal Information Network and make due return to the court. The preliminary order shall specify a date for the full hearing. The hearing shall be held within 15 days of the issuance of the preliminary order. If the respondent fails to appear at this hearing because the respondent was not personally served, the court may extend the protective order for a period not to exceed six months. The extended protective order shall be served as soon as possible on the respondent. However, upon motion of the respondent and for good cause shown, the court may continue the hearing. The preliminary order shall remain in effect until the hearing. Upon request after the order is issued, the clerk shall provide the petitioner with a copy of the order and information regarding the date and time of service. The order shall further specify that either party may at any time file a motion with the court requesting a hearing to dissolve or modify the order. The hearing on the motion shall be given precedence on the docket of the court.

Upon receipt of the return of service or other proof of service pursuant to subsection C of § 16.1-264, the clerk shall forthwith forward an attested copy of the preliminary protective order to primary law-enforcement agency and the agency shall forthwith verify and enter any modification as necessary into the Virginia Criminal Information Network as described above. If the order is later dissolved or modified, a copy of the dissolution or modification order shall also be attested, forwarded forthwith to the primary law-enforcement agency responsible for service and entry of protective orders, and upon receipt of the order by the primary law-enforcement agency, the agency shall forthwith verify and enter any modification as necessary to the identifying information and other appropriate information required by the Department of State Police into the Virginia Criminal Information Network as described above and the order shall be served forthwith and due return made to the court.

C. The preliminary order is effective upon personal service on the alleged perpetrator. Except as otherwise provided, a violation of the order shall constitute contempt of court.

D. At a full hearing on the petition, the court may issue a protective order pursuant to § 19.2-152.10 if the court finds that the petitioner has proven the allegation that the petitioner is or has been, within a reasonable period of time, subjected to an act of violence, force, or threat by a preponderance of the evidence.

E. No fees shall be charged for filing or serving petitions pursuant to this section.

F. Neither a law-enforcement agency, the attorney for the Commonwealth, a court nor the clerk's office, nor any employee of them, may disclose, except among themselves, the residential address, telephone number, or place of employment of the person protected by the order or that of the family of such person, except to the extent that disclosure is (i) required by law or the Rules of the Supreme Court, (ii) necessary for law-enforcement purposes, or (iii) permitted by the court for good cause.

G. As used in this section, "copy" includes a facsimile copy.

History.

1997, c. 831; 1998, cc. 569, 684; 1999, c. 371; 2001, c. 101; 2002, cc. 507, 810, 818; 2003, c. 730; 2008, cc. 73, 128, 246; 2009, cc. 341, 732; 2011, cc. 445, 480.

Cross references.

As to penalty for violation of stalking protective order, see § 18.2-60.4.

Editor's note.

Acts 2011, cc. 445 and 480, cl. 2 provides: "That the provisions of this act may result in a net increase in periods of imprisonment or commitment. Pursuant to § 30-19.1:4, the estimated amount of the necessary appropriation is $93,767 for periods of imprisonment in state adult correctional facilities and cannot be determined for periods of commitment to the custody of the Department of Juvenile Justice."

The 2008 amendments.

The 2008 amendments by cc. 73 and 246 are identical and rewrote subsection B and added subsection H.

The 2008 amendment by c. 128 inserted the eighth and ninth sentences in the first paragraph of subsection B.

The 2009 amendments.

The 2009 amendment by c. 341, in subsection A, inserted "sexual battery in violation of § 18.2-67.4, aggravated sexual battery in violation of § 18.2-67.3" twice; in subdivisions A 1 and A 3, inserted "acts of sexual battery"; in subsection B, in the first paragraph, substituted "perpetrator" for "stalker" twice; and in subsection D, inserted "sexual battery in violation of § 18.2-67.4, aggravated sexual battery in violation of § 18.2-67.3."

The 2009 amendment by c. 732, in subsection B, in the first sentence, inserted "electronically to the Virginia Criminal Information Network the respondent's" and "and the name, date of birth, sex, and race of each protected person," and deleted "electronically to the Virginia Criminal Information Network" from the end; in the second sentence, deleted "and an addendum" preceding "containing any such," in the third sentence, deleted "and addendum'" preceding "by the primary," in the fourth sentence, deleted "and an addendum" following "copy of the order," inserted "the respondent's" and "and the name, date of birth, sex, and race of each protected person provided to the court" and deleted "and addendum" following "receipt of the order"; and deleted subsection H, which read: "If any identifying information in the addendum is determined to be incorrect by the entering agency, the agency shall enter the corrected information into the Virginia Criminal Information Network."

The 2011 amendments.

The 2011 amendments, by cc. 445 and 480, are identical, and in the first paragraph in subsection A, in the first sentence, rewrote

clause (i), which read "the petitioner is or has been, within a reasonable period of time subjected to stalking, sexual battery in violation of § 18.2-67.4, aggravated sexual battery in violation of § 18.2-67.3, or a criminal offense resulting in a serious bodily injury to the petitioner, and," in clause (ii), inserted "petition or" and substituted "for any criminal offense resulting from the commission of an act of violence, force, or threat" for "of such act or acts," and rewrote the last sentence; in subdivision A 1, inserted "acts of violence, force, or threat or" and deleted "acts of sexual battery, or acts of stalking in violation of § 18.2-60.3" from the end; in subdivision A 3, added the clause designations, and substituted "violence, force, or threat" for "stalking, acts of sexual battery"; in subsection C, deleted "in § 16.1-253.2" following "provided"; and in subsection D, substituted "allegation that the petitioner is or has been, within a reasonable period of time, subjected to an act of violence, force, or threat" for "allegation of a criminal offense resulting in a serious bodily injury to the petitioner, sexual battery in violation of § 18.2-67.4, aggravated sexual battery in violation of § 18.2-67.3, or stalking."

Law Review.

For article, "Family Law," see 35 U. Rich. L. Rev. 651 (2001).

CIRCUIT COURT OPINIONS

Expungement of preliminary protective order not authorized. — Absent a provision allowing expungement of a preliminary protective order, issued pursuant to § 19.2-152.9, the superior court judge declined to order the same. Petition for Expungement, 74 Va. Cir. 463, 2008 Va. Cir. LEXIS 2 (Newport News 2008).

OPINIONS OF THE ATTORNEY GENERAL

Petition by unemancipated minors for protective orders. — A minor may seek an emergency protective order in certain situations, but a minor who has not been emancipated, however mature that individual may be, can seek a protective order only through a next friend. See opinion of Attorney General to The Honorable Charniele L. Herring, Member, House of Delegates, 10-116, 2011 Va. AG LEXIS 2 (01/21/11).

Petition by emancipated minors for protective orders. — Emancipated minor may file petitions for protective orders under applicable statutes. See opinion of Attorney General to The Honorable Charniele L. Herring, Member, House of Delegates, 10-116, 2011 Va. AG LEXIS 2 (01/21/11).

§ 19.2-152.10. Protective order.

A. The court may issue a protective order pursuant to this chapter to protect the health and safety of the petitioner and family or household members of a petitioner upon (i) the issuance of a petition or warrant for, or a conviction of, any criminal offense resulting from the commission of an act of violence, force, or threat or (ii) a hearing held pursuant to subsection D of § 19.2-152.9. A protective order issued under this section may include any one or more of the following conditions to be imposed on the respondent:

1. Prohibiting acts of violence, force, or threat or criminal offenses that may result in injury to person or property;

2. Prohibiting such contacts by the respondent with the petitioner or family or household members of the petitioner as the court deems necessary for the health or safety of such persons; and

3. Any other relief necessary to prevent (i) acts of violence, force, or threat, (ii) criminal offenses that may result in injury to person or property, or (iii)

communication or other contact of any kind by the respondent.

B. The protective order may be issued for a specified period of time up to a maximum of two years. The protective order shall expire at 11:59 p.m. on the last day specified or at 11:59 p.m. on the last day of the two-year period if no date is specified. Prior to the expiration of the protective order, a petitioner may file a written motion requesting a hearing to extend the order. Proceedings to extend a protective order shall be given precedence on the docket of the court. The court may extend the protective order for a period not longer than two years to protect the health and safety of the petitioner or persons who are family or household members of the petitioner at the time the request for an extension is made. The extension of the protective order shall expire at 11:59 p.m. on the last day specified or at 11:59 p.m. on the last day of the two-year period if no date is specified. Nothing herein shall limit the number of extensions that may be requested or issued.

C. A copy of the protective order shall be served on the respondent and provided to the petitioner as soon as possible. The court, including a circuit court if the circuit court issued the order, shall forthwith, but in all cases no later than the end of the business day on which the order was issued, enter and transfer electronically to the Virginia Criminal Information Network the respondent's identifying information and the name, date of birth, sex, and race of each protected person provided to the court and shall forthwith forward the attested copy of the protective order and containing any such identifying information to the primary law-enforcement agency responsible for service and entry of protective orders. Upon receipt of the order by the primary law-enforcement agency, the agency shall forthwith verify and enter any modification as necessary to the identifying information and other appropriate information required by the Department of State Police into the Virginia Criminal Information Network established and maintained by the Department pursuant to Chapter 2 (§ 52-12 et seq.) of Title 52 and the order shall be served forthwith upon the respondent and due return made to the court. Upon service, the agency making service shall enter the date and time of service and other appropriate information required into the Virginia Criminal Information Network and make due return to the court. If the order is later dissolved or modified, a copy of the dissolution or modification order shall also be attested, forwarded forthwith to the primary law-enforcement agency responsible for service and entry of protective orders, and upon receipt of the order by the primary law-enforcement agency, the agency shall forthwith verify and enter any modification as necessary to the identifying information and other appropriate information required by the Department of State Police into the Virginia Criminal Information Network as described above and the order shall be served forthwith and due return made to the court.

D. Except as otherwise provided, a violation of a protective order issued under this section shall constitute contempt of court.

E. The court may assess costs and attorneys' fees against either party regardless of whether an order of protection has been issued as a result of a full hearing.

F. Any judgment, order or decree, whether permanent or temporary, issued by a court of appropriate jurisdiction in another state, the United States or any of its territories, possessions or Commonwealths, the District of Columbia or by any tribal court of appropriate jurisdiction for the purpose of preventing violent or threatening acts or harassment against or contact or communication with or physical proximity to another person, including any of the conditions specified in subsection A, shall be accorded full faith and credit and enforced in the Commonwealth as if it were an order of the Commonwealth, provided reasonable notice and opportunity to be heard were given by the issuing jurisdiction to the person against whom the order is sought to be enforced sufficient to protect such person's due process rights and consistent with federal law. A person entitled to protection under such a foreign order may file the order in any appropriate district court by filing with the court, an attested or exemplified copy of the order. Upon such a filing, the clerk shall forthwith forward an attested copy of the order to the primary law-enforcement agency responsible for service and entry of protective orders which shall, upon receipt, enter the name of the person subject to the order and other appropriate information required by the Department of State Police into the Virginia Criminal Information Network established and maintained by the Department pursuant to Chapter 2 (§ 52-12 et seq.) of Title 52. Where practical, the court may transfer information electronically to the Virginia Criminal Information Network.

Upon inquiry by any law-enforcement agency of the Commonwealth, the clerk shall make a copy available of any foreign order filed with that court. A law-enforcement officer may, in the performance of his duties, rely upon a copy of a foreign protective order or other suitable evidence which has been provided to him by any source and may also rely upon the statement of any person protected by the order that the order remains in effect.

G. Either party may at any time file a written motion with the court requesting a hearing to dissolve or modify the order. Proceedings to modify or dissolve a protective order shall be given precedence on the docket of the court.

H. Neither a law-enforcement agency, the attorney for the Commonwealth, a court nor the clerk's office, nor any employee of them, may disclose, except among themselves, the residential address, telephone number, or place of employment of the person protected by the order or that of the family of such person, except to the extent that disclosure is

(i) required by law or the Rules of the Supreme Court, (ii) necessary for law-enforcement purposes, or (iii) permitted by the court for good cause.

I. No fees shall be charged for filing or serving petitions pursuant to this section.

J. As used in this section:

"*Copy*" includes a facsimile copy; and

"*Protective order*" includes an initial, modified or extended protective order.

History.

1997, c. 831; 1998, cc. 569, 684; 1999, c. 371; 2002, cc. 507, 810, 818; 2003, c. 730; 2008, cc. 73, 246; 2009, cc. 341, 732; 2010, cc. 425, 468; 2011, cc. 445, 480; 2012, cc. 152, 261.

Cross references.

As to penalty for violation of stalking protective order, see § 18.2-60.4.

Editor's note.

Acts 2011, cc. 445 and 480, cl. 2 provides: "That the provisions of this act may result in a net increase in periods of imprisonment or commitment. Pursuant to § 30-19.1:4, the estimated amount of the necessary appropriation is $93,767 for periods of imprisonment in state adult correctional facilities and cannot be determined for periods of commitment to the custody of the Department of Juvenile Justice."

Acts 2012, cc. 152 and 261, cl. 2 provides: "That beginning July 1, 2013, any circuit court clerk who does not use the Statewide Case Management System operated and maintained by the Executive Secretary of the Supreme Court shall provide protective orders directly to the Virginia Criminal Information Network in an electronic format approved by the Department of State Police; and that until July 1, 2013, such clerks shall forthwith forward the protective order to the primary law-enforcement agency providing service and entry of protective orders for entry into the Virginia Criminal Information Network."

The 2008 amendments.

The 2008 amendments by cc. 73 and 246 are identical, and rewrote subsection B; in the first paragraph of subsection E, substituted "shall forthwith forward an attested copy of the order to the primary law-enforcement agency responsible for service and entry of protective orders" for "shall forward forthwith an attested copy of the order to the local police department or sheriff's office" in the third sentence, and added the fourth sentence; and added subsection J.

The 2009 amendments.

The 2009 amendment by c. 341, in subsection A, inserted "sexual battery in violation of § 18.2-67.4, aggravated sexual battery in violation of § 18.2-67.3" twice; and in subdivisions A 1 and A 3, inserted "acts of sexual battery."

The 2009 amendment by c. 732, in subsection B, in the second sentence, substituted "11:59 p.m. on" for "the end of," "specified or at 11:59 p.m. on the last day of the two-year period" for "identified for the two-year period and,'" and "specified" for "identified, it shall expire at the end of the two years following the date of issuance," in the fourth sentence, inserted "electronically to the Virginia Criminal Information Network the respondent's" and "and the name, date of birth, sex, and race of each protected person," and deleted "electronically to the Virginia Criminal Information Network" following "provided to the court" and "an addendum" preceding "containing any such," in the fifth sentence, deleted "and addendum" following "receipt of the order," in the sixth sentence, deleted "and an addendum" following "copy of the order," inserted "the respondent's" and "and the name, date of birth, sex, and race of each protected person provided to the court" and deleted "and addendum" following "receipt of the order"; and deleted subsection J, which read: "If any identifying information in the addendum is determined to be incorrect by the entering agency, the agency shall enter the corrected information into the Virginia Criminal Information Network."

The 2010 amendments.

The 2010 amendments by cc. 425 and 468 are identical, and divided former subsection B into subsections B and C by inserting

the C designation following the second sentence; redesignated former subsections C through I as subsections D through J; in subsection B, substituted "of time up to a maximum of" for "however, unless otherwise authorized by law, a protective order may not be issued under this section for a period longer than" near the end of the first sentence, and added the last five sentences; added the definition of "Protective order" in subsection J and made related changes.

The 2011 amendments.

The 2011 amendments by cc. 445 and 480 are identical, and in the first paragraph in subsection A, rewrote clause (i), which read: "the issuance of a petition or warrant for sexual battery in violation of § 18.2-67.4, aggravated sexual battery in violation of § 18.2-67.3, or a criminal offense resulting in a serious bodily injury to the petitioner, or a violation of § 18.2-60.3," and deleted clause (iii), which read: "a conviction for sexual battery in violation of § 18.2-67.4, aggravated sexual battery in violation of § 18.2-67.3, a criminal offense resulting in a serious bodily injury to the petitioner, or a violation of § 18.2-60.3"; in subdivision A 1, inserted "acts of violence, force, or threat or" and deleted "act of sexual battery, or acts of stalking in violation of § 18.2-60.3" from the end; and in subdivision A 3, added clause (i), added the clause (ii) designation, and therein deleted "acts of sexual battery, or acts of stalking" from the end, and inserted "or (iii)."

The 2012 amendments.

The 2012 amendments by cc. 152 and 261 are identical, and in subsection C, inserted "including a circuit court if the circuit court issued the order" in the second sentence, and deleted the former fourth sentence, which read: "However, if the order is issued by the circuit court, the clerk of the circuit court shall forthwith forward an attested copy of the order containing the respondent's identifying information and the name, date of birth, sex, and race of each protected person provided to the court to the primary law-enforcement agency providing service and entry of protective orders and upon receipt of the order, the primary law-enforcement agency shall enter the name of the person subject to the order and other appropriate information required by the Department of State Police into the Virginia Criminal Information Network established and maintained by the Department pursuant to Chapter 2 (§ 52-12 et seq.) of Title 52 and the order shall be served forthwith on the respondent."; and made minor stylistic changes.

OPINIONS OF THE ATTORNEY GENERAL

Petition for protective orders by law enforcement on behalf of minors. — Law-enforcement officers may file petitions for emergency protective orders on behalf of minors who are victims of family abuse, stalking, sexual assault or other acts of criminal violence. See opinion of Attorney General to The Honorable Charniele L. Herring, Member, House of Delegates, 10-116, 2011 Va. AG LEXIS 2 (01/21/11).

Petition by unemancipated minors for protective orders. — A minor may seek an emergency protective order in certain situations, but a minor who has not been emancipated, however mature that individual may be, can seek a protective order only through a next friend. See opinion of Attorney General to The Honorable Charniele L. Herring, Member, House of Delegates, 10-116, 2011 Va. AG LEXIS 2 (01/21/11).

Petition by emancipated minors for protective orders. — Emancipated minor may file petitions for protective orders under applicable statutes. See opinion of Attorney General to The Honorable Charniele L. Herring, Member, House of Delegates, 10-116, 2011 Va. AG LEXIS 2 (01/21/11).

§ 19.2-152.11. Venue for protective orders.

Proceedings in which a protective order is sought pursuant to this chapter shall be commenced where (i) either party has his principal residence; (ii) the act of violence, force, or threat by the respondent against the petitioner occurred; or (iii) a protective order was issued if, at the time the proceeding is commenced, the order is in effect to protect the petitioner or a family or household member of the petitioner.

History.
2012, c. 637.

CHAPTER 10.

DISABILITY OF JUDGE OR ATTORNEY FOR COMMONWEALTH; COURT-APPOINTED COUNSEL; INTERPRETERS; TRANSCRIPTS.

ARTICLE 1.

DISABILITY OF JUDGE.

§ 19.2-153. When judge cannot sit on trial; how another judge procured to try the case.

When the judge of a circuit court in which a prosecution is pending is connected with the accused or party injured, or is so situated in respect to the case as in his opinion to render it improper that he should preside at the trial, or if he has rejected a plea bargain agreement submitted by both parties and the parties do not agree that he may hear the case, he shall enter the fact of record and the clerk of the court shall at once certify this fact to the Chief Justice of the Supreme Court and thereupon another judge shall be appointed, in the manner prescribed by § 17.1-105, to preside at the trial.

History.
Code 1950, § 19.1-7; 1960, c. 366; 1975, c. 495; 1984, c. 585; 1985, c. 253.

Law Review.
For article, "Signaling and Plea Bargaining's Innocence Problem," see 66 Wash. & Lee L. Rev. 73 (2009).

Michie's Jurisprudence.
For related discussion, see 11A M.J. Judges, § 14.

CASE NOTES

Resentencing by another judge. — Prosecutor's references to defendant's refusal to accept plea offer during sentencing hearing were improper and trial judge erred in overruling defense counsel's objections to the statements; Court of Appeals could not conclude that the comments were harmless and remanded the case for resentencing by another judge. Craddock v. Commonwealth, 16 Va. App. 402, 429 S.E.2d 889 (1993).

CIRCUIT COURT OPINIONS

Circuit Court rejects the contention that it is solely the individual judge and not a court that is deemed to reject a plea agreement. — This section does not authorize a defendant to seek to present a proposed agreed disposition, one by one, to each individual judge in that circuit, and, if unsuccessful, to every other circuit court judge in the Commonwealth, hoping to eventually find a judge who was willing to accept the agreed disposition rejected by all of his or her colleagues. Commonwealth v. Stepek, 2007 Va. Cir. LEXIS 183 (Fairfax County Aug. 23, 2007).

§ 19.2-154. Death or disability of judge during trial; how another judge procured to continue with trial.

If by reason of death, sickness or other disability the judge who presided at a criminal jury trial is unable to proceed with and finish the trial, another judge of that court or a judge designated by the Chief Justice of the Supreme Court or by a justice designated by him for that purpose, may proceed with and finish the trial or, in his discretion, may grant and preside at a new trial. If by reason of such disability, the judge who presided at any trial is unable to perform the duties to be performed by the court after a finding of guilty by the jury or the court, another judge of that court, or a judge designated as provided in the preceding sentence, may perform those duties or, in his discretion, may grant and preside at a new trial. Before proceeding with the trial or performing such duties, such judge shall certify that he has familiarized himself with the record of the trial.

History.
1975, c. 495.

ARTICLE 2.

DISABILITY OF ATTORNEY FOR COMMONWEALTH.

§ 19.2-155. Disqualification or temporary disability of attorney for Commonwealth; appointment of substitute; powers, duties and compensation of such appointee.

If the attorney for the Commonwealth of any county or city is connected by blood or marriage with the accused, or is so situated with respect to such accused as to render it improper, in his opinion, concurred in by the judge, for him to act, or if such attorney for the Commonwealth of any county or city is unable to act, or to attend to his official duties as attorney for the Commonwealth, due to sickness, disability or other reason of a temporary nature, then upon notification by such attorney for the Commonwealth, or upon the certificate of his attending physician, or the clerk of the court, which fact shall be entered of record, the judge of the circuit court shall appoint from another jurisdiction an attorney for the Commonwealth or an assistant attorney for the Commonwealth, with the consent of such attorney for the Commonwealth or assistant, who is not authorized by law to engage in private practice for such case or cases, term or terms of court, or period or periods of time, as may be necessary or desirable, and the same to be forthwith entered of record. However, if the circuit court determines that the appointment of such attorney for the Commonwealth or such assistant attorney for the Commonwealth is not appropriate or that such

an attorney or assistant is unavailable, or for other good cause, then the circuit court may appoint an attorney-at-law who shall be compensated pursuant to § 19.2-332. Such appointee shall act in place of, and otherwise perform the duties and exercise the powers of, such disqualified or disabled attorney for the Commonwealth, in regard to such case or cases, for the term or terms of the court, or the period or periods of time, for which the appointment and designation is made, or until the disqualified or disabled attorney for the Commonwealth shall again be able to attend to his duties as such. Nothing herein shall prevent a court from appointing as a special assistant attorney for the Commonwealth, without additional compensation, an attorney employed by a state agency when such appointment is requested by the attorney for the Commonwealth and the court determines such appointment will aid in the prosecution of a particular case or cases.

An attorney for the Commonwealth or assistant attorney for the Commonwealth who is required by law to devote full time to his duties as such shall not receive additional compensation for services rendered on appointment pursuant to this section. However, such attorney for the Commonwealth or assistant may receive reimbursement for actual expenses incurred, as approved by the Compensation Board to be paid by the Compensation Board, provided such expenses are not otherwise reimbursed by the county or city which he is elected or appointed to serve or by the Compensation Board.

History.
Code 1950, §§ 19.1-9, 19.1-10; 1960, c. 366; 1975, c. 495; 1983, c. 362; 1985, c. 321; 1996, c. 968.

Michie's Jurisprudence.
For related discussion, see 4A M.J. Commonwealth's and State's Attorney, § 9; 11A M.J. Judges, § 14.

CASE NOTES

Appointment of substitute in disciplinary action against attorney. — Section 54.1-3935 as it stood prior to the 1980 amendment did not prohibit the appointment of a substitute attorney for the Commonwealth pursuant to this section or the designation of a substitute judge in accordance with § 17-7 [see now § 17.1-105] in a disciplinary proceeding brought against an attorney. Blue v. Virginia State Bar ex rel. First Dist. Comm., 222 Va. 357, 282 S.E.2d 6 (1981).

Appointment of prosecutor retained by victim's family to act as special prosecutor. — Trial judge violated defendant's due process rights by appointing private prosecutor retained by victim's family to act as special prosecutor after Commonwealth's attorney withdrew from the case. Adkins v. Commonwealth, 26 Va. App. 14, 492 S.E.2d 833 (1997).

The general statutory language, "or other reason of a temporary nature," must be restricted in its meaning to conditions analogous to "sickness" or "disability." In re Morrissey, 246 Va. 333, 433 S.E.2d 918 (1993).

CIRCUIT COURT OPINIONS

Failure to raise issue. — Because defendant's trial counsel never raised an issue at trial or on direct appeal that the appointment of a special prosecutor to retry defendant did not comport with § 19.2-155, the issue was not cognizable in defendant's habeas corpus proceeding. Pease v. Huffman, 72 Va. Cir. 610, 2005 Va. Cir. LEXIS 377 (Wise County 2005).

§ 19.2-156. Prolonged absence of attorney for Commonwealth.

If it shall be necessary for the attorney for the Commonwealth of any county or city to absent himself for a prolonged period of time from the performance of the duties of his office, then, upon notification by such attorney for the Commonwealth, or by the court on its own motion, and the facts being entered of record, the judge of the circuit court shall appoint an attorney-at-law as acting attorney for the Commonwealth to serve for such length of time as may be necessary. Such acting attorney for the Commonwealth shall act in place of and otherwise perform the duties and exercise the powers of such regular attorney for the Commonwealth, and while so acting shall receive the salary and allowance for expenses fixed by the State Compensation Board for such regular attorney for the Commonwealth, who during such length of time shall not receive any such salary or allowance.

History.
Code 1950, § 19.1-11; 1960, c. 366; 1975, c. 495.

Law Review.
For 2006 survey article, "Election Law," see 41 U. Rich. L. Rev. 121 (2006).

CASE NOTES

Trial court authority to appoint. — Trial court was authorized to appoint an attorney-at-law to fulfill the duties of the duly-elected Commonwealth's attorney while he was serving with his military unit in Iraq and, thus, petitioner's application for writ of mandamus and/or prohibition was denied; although § 2.2-2800 would prohibit petitioner from serving both the federal government and the state government at the same time, § 2.2-2802 contained an exception for Virginia office holders who were called into active military service and prevented from vacating or forfeiting their office. In re Hannett, 270 Va. 223, 619 S.E.2d 465, 2005 Va. LEXIS 82 (2005).

OPINIONS OF THE ATTORNEY GENERAL

Commonwealth's attorney involuntarily recalled to active military duty has the sole discretion to appoint an assistant Commonwealth's attorney to perform the duties of the office during his absence. See opinion of Attorney General to The Honorable Gordon E. Hannett, Floyd County Commonwealth's Attorney, 05-040 (5/5/05).

Person appointed pursuant to the provisions of this section upon the resignation of the regular Commonwealth's attorney may act in place of and otherwise perform the duties and exercise the powers of that office. See opinion of Attorney General to The Honorable Gordon E. Hannett, Floyd County Commonwealth's Attorney, 05-040 (5/5/05).

ARTICLE 3.
APPOINTMENT OF ATTORNEY FOR ACCUSED.

Michie's Jurisprudence.
For related discussion, see 5B M.J. Criminal Procedure, §§ 20, 24, 41, 77, 100; 9A M.J. Habeas Corpus, §§ 8, 15.

§ 19.2-157. Duty of court when accused appears without counsel.

Except as may otherwise be provided in §§ 16.1-266 through 16.1-268, whenever a person charged with a criminal offense the penalty for which may be death or confinement in the state correctional facility or jail, including charges for revocation of suspension of imposition or execution of sentence or probation, appears before any court without being represented by counsel, the court shall inform him of his right to counsel. The accused shall be allowed a reasonable opportunity to employ counsel or, if appropriate, the statement of indigence provided for in § 19.2-159 may be executed.

History.
Code 1950, §§ 19.1-241.1, 19.1-241.7; 1964, c. 657; 1966, c. 460; 1973, c. 316; 1975, c. 495; 1978, c. 362.

Cross references.
As to supplementing compensation of public defender by county or city, see § 19.2-163.01:1. As to Supreme Court of Virginia rules governing petitions for writ of actual innocence, see Rule 5:7B, Rules of the Virginia Supreme Court. As to Court of Appeals rules governing petitions for writ of actual innocence, see Rule 5A:5(b), Rules of the Virginia Supreme Court.

Law Review.
For note on the indigent in Virginia, see 51 Va. L. Rev. 163 (1965). For comment, "Right to Court-Appointed Counsel for Misdemeanants in Virginia," see 4 U. Rich. L. Rev. 306 (1970). For survey of Virginia law on criminal procedure for the year 1972-1973, see 59 Va. L. Rev. 1478 (1973). For article discussing the requirement of counsel in misdemeanor cases and its implementation in Virginia, see 30 Wash. & Lee L. Rev. 431 (1973). For note, "Criminal Procedure and Criminal Law: Virginia Supreme Court Decisions During the 70's," see 15 U. Rich. L. Rev. 585 (1981).

CASE NOTES

This section and §§ 19.2-159 and 19.2-160 provide procedural guidelines which are not jurisdictional requirements. Compliance with the provisions of § 19.2-160, for example, may establish a prima facie case of waiver; noncompliance may make more difficult the Commonwealth's burden of proving waiver. Van Sant v. Commonwealth, 224 Va. 269, 295 S.E.2d 883 (1982).

No person may be deprived of his liberty who has been denied assistance of counsel as guaranteed by the Sixth Amendment. This holding is applicable to all criminal prosecutions, including prosecutions for violations of municipal ordinances. The denial of the assistance of counsel will preclude the imposition of a jail sentence. Argersinger v. Hamlin, 407 U.S. 25, 92 S. Ct. 2006, 32 L. Ed. 2d 530 (1972).

No imprisonment may be imposed at the trial of a misdemeanor, even though local law permits it, unless the accused is represented by counsel. Argersinger v. Hamlin, 407 U.S. 25, 92 S. Ct. 2006, 32 L. Ed. 2d 530 (1972).

Absent a knowing and intelligent waiver, no person may be imprisoned for any offense, whether classified as petty, misdemeanor, or felony, unless he was represented by counsel at his trial. Argersinger v. Hamlin, 407 U.S. 25, 92 S. Ct. 2006, 32 L. Ed. 2d 530 (1972).

Noncompliance with section does not prove Commonwealth failed to establish waiver. — Although compliance with the requirements of this section and following sections may be sufficient to establish a prima facie case of waiver, and noncompliance may make it more difficult for the Commonwealth to meet its burden of establishing a waiver, noncompliance alone does not prove that the Commonwealth has failed to meet its burden of proving that the defendant waived his right to counsel. Bolden v. Commonwealth, 11 Va. App. 187, 397 S.E.2d 534 (1990), cert.

denied, 502 U.S. 943, 112 S. Ct. 382, 116 L. Ed. 2d 333 (1991).

This section does not grant new rights to an accused not already embodied in the Sixth Amendment to the Constitution and by the Fourteenth Amendment made applicable to the states. Timmons v. Peyton, 360 F.2d 327 (4th Cir.), cert. denied, 385 U.S. 960, 87 S. Ct. 396, 17 L. Ed. 2d 305 (1966).

Sections 19.2-157 through 19.2-161 deal with matters of procedure. Arey v. Peyton, 209 Va. 370, 164 S.E.2d 691 (1968).

No continuing obligation to represent. — Under the facts of the instant case, the defendant was not deprived of effective representation of counsel because appointed counsel did not recognize a continuing obligation of representation between stages of the proceedings. Jackson v. Cox, 435 F.2d 1089 (4th Cir. 1970).

Appointed counsel after defendant requested public defender. — Defendant's right to counsel was violated when the trial court proceeded to trial without defendant being represented by counsel despite the fact that defendant, who alleged defendant had retained counsel, requested a public defender and the record contained no facts supporting a conclusion that defendant was attempting to delay the proceedings or that defendant acted in bad faith. Fattaleh v. Commonwealth, — Va. App. —, — S.E.2d —, 2006 Va. App. LEXIS 391 (Aug. 22, 2006).

An indigent accused is entitled to have counsel appointed at a preliminary hearing. The purpose of this rule is to protect the indigent accused against an erroneous or improper prosecution. This rule should apply only to those preliminary hearings held after June 22, 1970. Noe v. Cox, 320 F. Supp. 849 (W.D. Va. 1970).

Preliminary hearing is critical stage of proceedings. — The preliminary hearing, even one whose sole purpose is merely to determine whether or not sufficient evidence exists to hold an accused, is a critical stage of the proceedings. Grey v. Slayton, 345 F. Supp. 1278 (W.D. Va. 1972).

But not retroactively. — The holding that a preliminary hearing, even one whose sole purpose is merely to determine whether or not sufficient evidence exists to hold an accused, is a critical stage is not retroactive. Grey v. Slayton, 345 F. Supp. 1278 (W.D. Va. 1972).

Since the preliminary hearing in Virginia was not critical at the time of the hearing, then nonobservance of this section did not violate petitioner's constitutional rights. Grey v. Slayton, 345 F. Supp. 1278 (W.D. Va. 1972).

Court-appointed investigator not constitutionally required. — An indigent defendant has no constitutional right to the appointment, at public expense, of an investigator to assist in his defense. When a trial court employs an investigator at public expense, it is an act of judicial grace not constitutionally required. Stockton v. Commonwealth, 227 Va. 124, 314 S.E.2d 371, cert. denied, 469 U.S. 873, 105 S. Ct. 229, 83 L. Ed. 2d 158 (1984).

Right to counsel at both appellate levels. — This section, when considered with § 19.2-326, provides an indigent with a statutory right to court-appointed counsel at both appellate levels. Dodson v. Director of Dep't of Cors., 233 Va. 303, 355 S.E.2d 573 (1987).

Court-appointed counsel on appeal. — This section, when considered with § 19.2-326, provides an indigent with a statutory right to court-appointed counsel at both appellate levels. Dodson v. Director of Dep't of Cors., 233 Va. 303, 355 S.E.2d 573 (1987).

Failure to appoint counsel to assist indigent defendant in making appeal from a conviction is a denial of equal protection and due process guaranteed to him under the federal Constitution and the Virginia Bill of Rights. Cabaniss v. Cunningham, 206 Va. 330, 143 S.E.2d 911 (1965); Via v. Peyton, 208 Va. 387, 158 S.E.2d 127 (1967).

Appellant may allege ineffective counsel on appeal to Virginia Supreme Court. — The General Assembly intended to provide an accused who is indigent a right to counsel in the Virginia Supreme Court. Therefore, appellant is not precluded from raising the allegation that his counsel rendered ineffective assistance in an appeal to the court. Dodson v. Director of Dep't of Cors., 233 Va. 303, 355 S.E.2d 573 (1987).

Burden of proving waiver. — The burden is on the Commonwealth to prove waiver of the right to counsel by clear, precise and unequivocal evidence. Sargent v. Commonwealth, 5 Va. App. 143, 360 S.E.2d 895 (1987).

Failure to appoint counsel was error. — Defendant did not voluntarily waive his right to counsel when he signed a waiver because there was no evidence that the trial court made defendant aware of the dangers and disadvantages of waiving his right to counsel. Nothing in § 19.2-159 or in the financial statement form required child care payments to be made pursuant to a court order; deducting defendant's child care payments, his income was below 125 percent of the poverty guidelines, and he was entitled to court-appointed counsel. Blue v. Commonwealth, 49 Va. App. 704, 644 S.E.2d 385, 2007 Va. App. LEXIS 195 (2007).

Applied in Lemke v. Commonwealth, 218 Va. 870, 241 S.E.2d 789 (1978).

CIRCUIT COURT OPINIONS

Section inapplicable. — A petitioner had no right to appointed counsel in trials of his parking citations because there was no threat of confinement for a parking ticket. In re Scott, 80 Va. Cir. 558, 2010 Va. Cir. LEXIS 89 (Norfolk July 13, 2010).

§ 19.2-158. When person not free on bail shall be informed of right to counsel and amount of bail.

Every person charged with an offense described in § 19.2-157, who is not free on bail or otherwise, shall be brought before the judge of a court not of record, unless the circuit court issues process commanding the presence of the person, in which case the person shall be brought before the circuit court, on the first day on which such court sits after the person is charged, at which time the judge shall inform the accused of the amount of his bail and his right to counsel. The court shall also hear and consider motions by the person or Commonwealth relating to bail or conditions of release pursuant to Article 1 (§ 19.2-119 et seq.) of Chapter 9 of this title. If the court not of record sits on a day prior to the scheduled sitting of the court which issued process, the person shall be brought before the court not of record.

No hearing on the charges against the accused shall be had until the foregoing conditions have been complied with, and the accused shall be allowed a reasonable opportunity to employ counsel of his own choice, or, if appropriate, the statement of indigence provided for in § 19.2-159 may be executed.

History.
Code 1950, §§ 19.1-241.2, 19.1-241.8; 1964, c. 657; 1966, c. 460; 1973, c. 316; 1975, c. 495; 1998, c. 773; 1999, cc. 829, 846.

Law Review.
For article discussing the requirement of counsel in misdemeanor cases and its implementation in Virginia, see 30 Wash. & Lee L. Rev. 431 (1973).

CASE NOTES

Compliance with this section is a matter of state law, and where the state trial court decided after a hearing that the section was not violated, a federal court will not, in a habeas corpus proceeding, disturb that finding, unless the state criminal process, taken as a whole, impugns the concept of fundamental fairness. Barksdale v. Robinson, 397 F. Supp. 267 (W.D. Va. 1975).

The constitutional right to counsel is satisfied if counsel is appointed in sufficient time to allow counsel to become familiar with the case, to confer with his client and to prepare for and participate in the trial. Even if a significant and unjustified delay in appointing counsel occurs, that delay does not rise to constitutional dimension if the record affirmatively shows that no prejudice resulted. Graves v. Commonwealth, 12 Va. App. 53, 402 S.E.2d 500 (1991).

Effect of failure to appoint counsel. — While there was a failure to appoint counsel for defendant charged with a felony on the first day a municipal court sat after petitioner's arrest, as provided by this section and Rule 3A:5 (b) (1) (now repealed) of the Supreme Court, such a violation of the statute and rule does not affect the jurisdiction of a court of record to subsequently try defendant for a felony. Ferguson v. Superintendent of Va. State Penitentiary, 215 Va. 269, 208 S.E.2d 749 (1974).

The failure of the trial court to appoint counsel for the appellant until 25 days after his arrest, in violation of the requirements of this section, was not a denial of his constitutional right to counsel warranting a reversal of his conviction for distribution of cocaine. Graves v. Commonwealth, 12 Va. App. 53, 402 S.E.2d 500 (1991).

Applied in Ferguson v. Boyd, 566 F.2d 873 (4th Cir. 1977).

§ 19.2-159. Determination of indigency; guidelines; statement of indigence; appointment of counsel.

A. If the accused shall claim that he is indigent, and the charge against him is a criminal offense which may be punishable by death or confinement in the state correctional facility or jail, subject to the provisions of § 19.2-160, the court shall determine from oral examination of the accused or other competent evidence whether or not the accused is indigent within the contemplation of law pursuant to the guidelines set forth in this section.

B. In making its finding, the court shall determine whether or not the accused is a current recipient of a state or federally funded public assistance program for the indigent. If the accused is a current recipient of such a program and does not waive his right to counsel or retain counsel on his own behalf, he shall be presumed eligible for the appointment of counsel. This presumption shall be rebuttable where the court finds that a more thorough examination of the financial resources of the defendant is necessary. If the accused shall claim to be indigent and is not presumptively eligible under the provisions of this section, then a thorough examination of the financial resources of the accused shall be made with consideration given to the following:

1. The net income of the accused, which shall include his total salary and wages minus deductions required by law. The court also shall take into account income and amenities from other sources including but not limited to social security funds, union funds, veteran's benefits, other regular support from an absent family member, public or private employee pensions, dividends, interests, rents, estates, trusts, or gifts.

2. All assets of the accused which are convertible into cash within a reasonable period of time without causing substantial hardship or jeopardizing the ability of the accused to maintain home and employment. Assets shall include all cash on hand as well as in checking and savings accounts, stocks, bonds, certificates of deposit, and tax refunds. All personal property owned by the accused which is readily convertible into cash shall be considered, except

property exempt from attachment. Any real estate owned by the accused shall be considered in terms of the amounts which could be raised by a loan on the property. For purposes of eligibility determination, the income, assets, and expenses of the spouse, if any, who is a member of the accused's household, shall be considered, unless the spouse was the victim of the offense or offenses allegedly committed by the accused.

3. Any exceptional expenses of the accused and his family which would, in all probability, prohibit him from being able to secure private counsel. Such items shall include but not be limited to costs for medical care, family support obligations, and child care payments.

The available funds of the accused shall be calculated as the sum of his total income and assets less the exceptional expenses as provided in paragraph 3 above. If the accused does not waive his right to counsel or retain counsel on his own behalf, counsel shall be appointed for the accused if his available funds are equal to or below 125 percent of the federal poverty income guidelines prescribed for the size of the household of the accused by the federal Department of Health and Human Services. The Supreme Court of Virginia shall be responsible for distributing to all courts the annual updates of the federal poverty income guidelines made by the Department.

If the available funds of the accused exceed 125 percent of the federal poverty income guidelines and the accused fails to employ counsel and does not waive his right to counsel, the court may, in exceptional circumstances, and where the ends of justice so require, appoint an attorney to represent the accused. However, in making such appointments, the court shall state in writing its reasons for so doing. The written statement by the court shall be included in the permanent record of the case.

C. If the court determines that the accused is indigent as contemplated by law pursuant to the guidelines set forth in this section, the court shall provide the accused with a statement which shall contain the following:

"I have been advised this ....day of ...., 20 .., by the (name of court) court of my right to representation by counsel in the trial of the charge pending against me; I certify that I am without means to employ counsel and I hereby request the court to appoint counsel for me."

.... (signature of accused)

The court shall also require the accused to complete a written financial statement to support the claim of indigency and to permit the court to determine whether or not the accused is indigent within the contemplation of law. The accused shall execute the said statements under oath, and the said court shall appoint competent counsel to represent the accused in the proceeding against him, including an appeal, if any, until relieved or replaced by other counsel.

The executed statements by the accused and the order of appointment of counsel shall be filed with and become a part of the record of such proceeding.

All other instances in which the appointment of counsel is required for an indigent shall be made in accordance with the guidelines prescribed in this section.

D. Except in jurisdictions having a public defender, or unless (i) the public defender is unable to represent the defendant by reason of conflict of interest or (ii) the court finds that appointment of other counsel is necessary to attain the ends of justice, counsel appointed by the court for representation of the accused shall be selected by a fair system of rotation among members of the bar practicing before the court whose names are on the list maintained by the Indigent Defense Commission pursuant to § 19.2-163.01. If no attorney who is on the list maintained by the Indigent Defense Commission is reasonably available, the court may appoint as counsel an attorney not on the list who has otherwise demonstrated to the court's satisfaction an appropriate level of training and experience. The court shall provide notice to the Commission of the appointment of the attorney.

History.
Code 1950, § 19.1-241.3; 1964, c. 657; 1966, c. 460; 1975, c. 495; 1976, c. 553; 1978, c. 720; 1984, c. 709; 2004, cc. 884, 921; 2006, cc. 680, 708; 2008, cc. 122, 154.

Cross references.
As to eligibility for public guardian or conservator, see § 64.2-2010.

Editor's note.
Acts 2008, cc. 122 and 154, cl. 2 repealed Acts 2006, cc. 680 and 708, cl. 2, which provided a July 1, 2008, expiration date for the 2006 amendments to this section. Therefore, the 2006 amendments will not expire.

The 2006 amendments.
The 2006 amendments by cc. 680 and 708 are nearly identical, and added the last two sentences of subsection D; chapter 708 also inserted the subsection designations.
This section has been set out in the form above at the direction of the Virginia Code Commission.

The 2008 amendments.
The 2008 amendments by cc. 122 and 154 are identical, and inserted "or unless (i) the public defender is unable to represent the defendant by reason of conflict of interest or (ii) the court finds that appointment of other counsel is necessary to attain the ends of justice," and made related changes, in subsection D.

Law Review.
For comment, "Right to Court-Appointed Counsel for Misdemeanants in Virginia," see 4 U. Rich. L. Rev. 306 (1970). For article discussing the requirement of counsel in misdemeanor cases and its implementation in Virginia, see 30 Wash. & Lee L. Rev. 431 (1973). For note, "Criminal Procedure and Criminal Law: Virginia Supreme Court Decisions During the 70's," see 15 U. Rich. L. Rev. 585 (1981).

CASE NOTES

This section and §§ 19.2-157 and 19.2-160 provide procedural guidelines which are not jurisdictional requirements. Compliance with the provisions of § 19.2-160, for example, may establish a prima facie case of waiver; noncompliance may make more difficult the Commonwealth's burden of proving waiver. Van Sant v. Commonwealth, 224 Va. 269, 295 S.E.2d 883 (1982).

Term "an appeal" is used in its generic sense and simply means that an indigent is entitled to counsel throughout the appellate process. Dodson v. Director of Dep't of Cors., 233 Va. 303, 355 S.E.2d 573 (1987).

Failure of Commonwealth to show asset was readily convertible to cash. — In conviction for perjury based upon appellant's statement of indigence for the appointment of counsel, the record failed to disclose that the motor vehicles upon which the Commonwealth relied to support the conviction were available to appellant so as to be readily convertible to cash; therefore, there was insufficient evidence to support the conviction. Smith v. Commonwealth, 12 Va. App. 606, 405 S.E.2d 626 (1991).

Failure to appoint counsel was error. — Defendant did not voluntarily waive his right to counsel when he signed a waiver because there was no evidence that the trial court made defendant aware of the dangers and disadvantages of waiving his right to counsel. Nothing in § 19.2-159 or in the financial statement form required child care payments to be made pursuant to a court order; deducting defendant's child care payments, his income was below 125 percent of the poverty guidelines, and he was entitled to court-appointed counsel. Blue v. Commonwealth, 49 Va. App. 704, 644 S.E.2d 385, 2007 Va. App. LEXIS 195 (2007).

Applied in Harris v. Commonwealth, 20 Va. App. 194, 455 S.E.2d 759 (1995).

CIRCUIT COURT OPINIONS

Defendant not eligible once husband's income and assets were considered. — Defendant did not meet the eligibility requirements for court-appointed counsel under § 19.2-159, where defendant's husband, with whom defendant resided, had an annual income of $42,000 and a home valued at approximately $300,000, and defendant had a job for $10 per hour, because 125% of the applicable federal poverty income guideline for such a household was $25,000. Commonwealth v. Thomas, — Va. Cir. —, 2006 Va. Cir. LEXIS 179 (Fairfax County Sept. 13, 2006).

§ 19.2-159.1. Interrogation by court; filing; change in circumstances; investigation by attorney for Commonwealth.

A. The court shall thoroughly interrogate any person making the statement of indigency required in § 19.2-159 and shall further advise such person of the penalty which might result from false swearing, as provided in § 19.2-161.

B. The statement and oath of the defendant shall be filed with the papers in the case, and shall follow and be in effect at all stages of the proceedings against him without further oath. In the event the defendant undergoes a change of circumstances so that he is no longer indigent, the defendant shall thereupon obtain private counsel and shall forthwith advise the court of the change of circumstances. The court shall grant reasonable continuance to allow counsel to be obtained and to prepare for trial. When private counsel has been retained, appointed counsel shall forthwith be relieved of further responsibility and compensated for his services, pro rata, pursuant to § 19.2-163.

C. Upon the request of the court, it shall be the duty of the attorney for the Commonwealth of the county or city in which such statement and oath was made to make an investigation as to the indigency of the defendant, or of any other person making such statement. The attorney for the Commonwealth is authorized to delegate the responsibility for such investigation to any subordinate in his office, or to any agency, state or local, which possesses the facilities to quickly make such investigation. Such investigation shall be reduced to writing and forwarded to the court in which the statement and oath was made within fourteen days after such request by the court is made. Such report shall be placed with the papers in the case.

History.
Code 1950, § 19.1-241.3:1; 1975, c. 580; 1977, c. 6; 1981, c. 289; 1984, c. 709.

The number of this section was assigned by the Virginia Code Commission, the number in the 1975 act having been 19.1-241.3:1.

CASE NOTES

Continuance motion was not one contemplated by section. — Although defendant's father had apparently undertaken to retain counsel for him immediately prior to trial, the defendant advised the court that he "didn't have anything to do with" this effort, had not spoken with such attorney, and remained unable to compensate counsel. Under such circumstances, defendant's continuance motion was clearly not one contemplated by this section. A trial court's decision to deny a continuance will not be reversed on appeal unless there was a clear abuse of discretion and prejudice to the defendant. The record demonstrated no prejudice to defendant from the ruling. Armstead v. Commonwealth, No. 2251-96-1 (Ct. of Appeals Sept. 23, 1997).

Abuse of discretion. — When a previously indigent accused obtains retained counsel, due to the hiring of counsel by the accused's parent, the trial court's failure to substitute retained counsel, and to grant a reasonable continuance to permit retained counsel an opportunity to prepare for trial, was inconsistent with the requirements of subsection B of § 19.2-159.1. London v. Commonwealth, 49 Va. App. 230, 638 S.E.2d 721, 2006 Va. App. LEXIS 578 (2006).

§ 19.2-160. Appointment of counsel or waiver of right.

If the charge against the accused is a crime the penalty for which may be incarceration, and the accused is not represented by counsel, the court shall ascertain by oral examination of the accused whether or not the accused desires to waive his right to counsel.

In the event the accused desires to waive his right to counsel, and the court ascertains that such waiver is voluntary and intelligently made, then the court shall provide the accused with a statement to be executed by the accused to document his waiver. The statement shall be in a form designed and provided by the Supreme Court. Any executed statement herein provided for shall be filed with and become a part of the record of such proceeding.

In the absence of a waiver of counsel by the accused, and if he shall claim that he is indigent, the court shall proceed in the same manner as is provided in § 19.2-159.

Should the defendant refuse or otherwise fail to sign either of the statements described in this section and § 19.2-159, the court shall note such re-

fusal on the record. Such refusal shall be deemed to be a waiver of the right to counsel, and the court, after so advising the accused and offering him the opportunity to rescind his refusal shall, if such refusal is not rescinded and the accused's signature given, proceed to hear and decide the case. However, if, prior to the commencement of the trial, the court states in writing, either upon the request of the attorney for the Commonwealth or, in the absence of the attorney for the Commonwealth, upon the court's own motion, that a sentence of incarceration will not be imposed if the defendant is convicted, the court may try the case without appointing counsel, and in such event no sentence of incarceration shall be imposed.

History.
Code 1950, § 19.1-241.9; 1973, c. 316; 1975, c. 495; 1978, c. 365; 1979, c. 468; 1983, c. 97; 1989, c. 385.

Law Review.
For survey of Virginia Law on criminal procedure for the year 1972-1973, see 59 Va. L. Rev. 1478 (1973). For article discussing the requirement of counsel in misdemeanor cases and its implementation in Virginia, see 30 Wash. & Lee L. Rev. 431 (1973). For survey of Virginia law on criminal procedure for the year 1978-1979, see 66 Va. L. Rev. 261 (1980). For note on competence to plead guilty and to stand trial when a criminal defendant waives counsel, see 68 Va. L. Rev. 1139 (1982).

CASE NOTES

This section and §§ 19.2-157 and 19.2-159 provide procedural guidelines which are not jurisdictional requirements. Compliance with the provisions of this section, for example, may establish a prima facie case of waiver; noncompliance may make more difficult the Commonwealth's burden of proving waiver. Van Sant v. Commonwealth, 224 Va. 269, 295 S.E.2d 883 (1982).

Burden of proof of waiver. — Absent a knowing and intelligent waiver, no person may be imprisoned for any offense unless he is represented by counsel at trial. The burden is on the Commonwealth to prove waiver of the right to counsel by clear, precise, and unequivocal evidence. Van Sant v. Commonwealth, 224 Va. 269, 295 S.E.2d 883 (1982).

The burden is on the Commonwealth to prove waiver of the right to counsel by clear, precise and unequivocal evidence. Sargent v. Commonwealth, 5 Va. App. 143, 360 S.E.2d 895 (1987).

Right to counsel did not attach where defendant only sentenced to pay a fine. — Trial court did not err by admitting evidence of an uncounseled misdemeanor conviction in order to elevate defendant's third offense of petit larceny to a felony, where despite defendant's contention to the contrary she did not have the right to counsel for a prior misdemeanor conviction, as she was only sentenced to pay a fine; moreover, any violation of the statutory right to counsel did not mandate exclusion of the conviction order. Kapoor v. Commonwealth, No. 2582-03-4, 2004 Va. App. LEXIS 557 (Ct. of Appeals Nov. 16, 2004).

Trial judge's failure to advise petitioner of the hazards of a pro se defense, or to inquire whether petitioner's choice to proceed pro se was an informed choice, or, indeed, even to acknowledge petitioner's desire to waive counsel, taken together with the judge's effort to force petitioner to proceed with counsel he did not want, deprived petitioner of his Sixth Amendment guarantees. Van Sant v. Gondles, 596 F. Supp. 484 (E.D. Va. 1983), aff'd, 742 F.2d 1450 (4th Cir. 1984).

Trial judge's failure to allow petitioner a continuance requested for purpose of preparing his own defense without even an inquiry into petitioner's level of preparedness, taken in light of petitioner's representations of unpreparedness, deprived petitioner of effective self-representation. Van Sant v. Gondles, 596 F. Supp. 484 (E.D. Va. 1983), aff'd, 742 F.2d 1450 (4th Cir. 1984).

The fact that a defendant had other retained counsel representing her at trial in the general district court did not necessarily prove that she was ineligible to receive the benefit of court-appointed counsel on appeal to the circuit court. Lemke v. Commonwealth, 218 Va. 870, 241 S.E.2d 789 (1978).

Applied in Harris v. Commonwealth, 20 Va. App. 194, 455 S.E.2d 759 (1995).

§ 19.2-161. Penalty for false swearing with regard to statement of indigence.

Any person charged with a felony who shall falsely swear or who shall execute the statement provided for in § 19.2-159 knowing such statement to be false, shall be guilty of perjury, punishable as a Class 5 felony.

Any person charged with a misdemeanor punishable by confinement in jail who shall falsely swear or who shall execute the statement provided for in § 19.2-159 knowing such statement to be false shall be guilty of a Class 1 misdemeanor.

History.
Code 1950, §§ 19.1-241.6, 19.1-241.12; 1964, c. 657; 1973, c. 316; 1975, c. 495.

Cross references.
As to punishment for Class 5 felonies, see § 18.2-10. As to punishment for Class 1 misdemeanors, see § 18.2-11.

Law Review.
For survey of Virginia law on criminal procedure for the year 1972-1973, see Va. L. Rev. 1478 (1973). For note, "Lying on the Stand Won't Cost You a Dime: Should Courts Recognize a Civil Action in Tort for Perjury," see 44 Wash. & Lee L. Rev. 1257 (1988).

CASE NOTES

Failure of Commonwealth to show asset was readily convertible to cash. — In conviction for perjury based upon appellant's statement of indigence for the appointment of counsel, the record failed to disclose that the motor vehicles upon which the Commonwealth relied to support the conviction were available to appellant so as to be readily convertible to cash; therefore, there was insufficient evidence to support the conviction. Smith v. Commonwealth, 12 Va. App. 606, 405 S.E.2d 626 (1991).

§ 19.2-162. Continuances to be granted if necessary.

Courts before which criminal proceedings are pending shall afford such continuances and take such other action as is necessary to comply with the provisions of this chapter.

History.
Code 1950, §§ 19.1-241.4, 19.1-241.10; 1964, c. 657; 1973, c. 316; 1975, c. 495.

Law Review.
For survey of Virginia law on criminal procedure for the year 1972-1973, see 59 Va. L. Rev. 1478 (1973).

CASE NOTES

In order to work a delay by the last minute change of counsel, exceptional circumstances must exist. Shifflett v. Commonwealth, 218 Va. 25, 235 S.E.2d 316 (1977).

No adequate cause to delay trial. — There were no circum-

stances suggesting adequate cause to delay a trial on a motion for a continuance to enable the defendant to retain counsel of his own choosing, where the only ground assigned was that the defendant needed more time in preparing his defense, and where the record showed that the defendant had adequate time to prepare his defense if he had cooperated with his court-appointed attorney. Shifflett v. Commonwealth, 218 Va. 25, 235 S.E.2d 316 (1977).

Surprise. — When a litigant is surprised in the midst of a trial, that is precisely the situation in which a continuance may be appropriate. Bennett v. Commonwealth, 236 Va. 448, 374 S.E.2d 303 (1988), cert. denied, 490 U.S. 1028, 109 S. Ct. 1765, 104 L. Ed. 2d 200 (1989).

Defendant could not successfully attack the trial court's decision to grant continuance on the ground that his right of surprise was undermined since there is no such right. Bennett v. Commonwealth, 236 Va. 448, 374 S.E.2d 303 (1988), cert. denied, 490 U.S. 1028, 109 S. Ct. 1765, 104 L. Ed. 2d 200 (1989).

Discretion of trial court. — A motion for a continuance in order to obtain the presence of a missing witness is addressed to the sound discretion of the trial court whose decision will not be reversed unless the record affirmatively shows an abuse of such discretion. Shifflett v. Commonwealth, 218 Va. 25, 235 S.E.2d 316 (1977); Van Sant v. Commonwealth, 224 Va. 269, 295 S.E.2d 883 (1982).

The same standard of appellate review applies to the denial of a request for a recess during the trial as to a request for a continuance; the decision whether to grant a continuance is a matter within the sound discretion of the trial court, and abuse of discretion and prejudice to the complaining party are essential to reversal. Lowery v. Commonwealth, 9 Va. App. 304, 387 S.E.2d 508 (1990).

There was no abuse of discretion in the trial court's granting the Commonwealth a continuance from 12:25 p.m. on October 20, to the start of trial on October 21, in order to allow the authentication of important papers. Bennett v. Commonwealth, 236 Va. 448, 374 S.E.2d 303 (1988), cert. denied, 490 U.S. 1028, 109 S. Ct. 1765, 104 L. Ed. 2d 200 (1989).

The court did not abuse its discretion in refusing a continuance to obtain the presence of a missing witness where it was not indicated that the person whose presence was sought was a material witness, and where there was a lack of due diligence in obtaining his presence. Shifflett v. Commonwealth, 218 Va. 25, 235 S.E.2d 316 (1977).

When the Commonwealth was obviously surprised by defendant's evidence, the trial court's grant of a four-day continuance was not an abuse of discretion, despite the fact that the jury had been empaneled. Bennett v. Commonwealth, 236 Va. 448, 374 S.E.2d 303 (1988), cert. denied, 490 U.S. 1028, 109 S. Ct. 1765, 104 L. Ed. 2d 200 (1989).

Continuance properly granted. — Continuance was necessary where motion was made in order to secure the testimony of a material witness and a subpoena had been requested and issued, but service was unobtainable due to the witness' absence from the state, and there was no evidence that the defense encouraged and/or participated in the witness' departure from the state. Cherricks v. Commonwealth, 11 Va. App. 96, 396 S.E.2d 397 (1990).

§ 19.2-163. Compensation of court-appointed counsel.

Upon submission to the court, for which appointed representation is provided, of a detailed accounting of the time expended for that representation, made within 30 days of the completion of all proceedings in that court, counsel appointed to represent an indigent accused in a criminal case shall be compensated for his services on an hourly basis at a rate set by the Supreme Court of Virginia in a total amount not to exceed the amounts specified in the following schedule:

1. In a district court, a sum not to exceed $120, provided that, notwithstanding the foregoing limitation, the court in its discretion, and subject to

guidelines issued by the Executive Secretary of the Supreme Court of Virginia, may waive the limitation of fees up to (i) an additional $120 when the effort expended, the time reasonably necessary for the particular representation, the novelty and difficulty of the issues, or other circumstances warrant such a waiver; or (ii) an amount up to $650 to defend, in the case of a juvenile, an offense that would be a felony if committed by an adult that may be punishable by confinement in the state correctional facility for a period of more than 20 years, or a charge of violation of probation for such offense, when the effort expended, the time reasonably necessary for the particular representation, the novelty and difficulty of the issues, or other circumstances warrant such a waiver; or (iii) such other amount as may be provided by law. Such amount shall be allowed in any case wherein counsel conducts the defense of a single charge against the indigent through to its conclusion or a charge of violation of probation at any hearing conducted under § 19.2-306; thereafter, compensation for additional charges against the same accused also conducted by the same counsel shall be allowed on the basis of additional time expended as to such additional charges;

2. In a circuit court (i) to defend a felony charge that may be punishable by death an amount deemed reasonable by the court; (ii) to defend a felony charge that may be punishable by confinement in the state correctional facility for a period of more than 20 years, or a charge of violation of probation for such offense, a sum not to exceed $1,235, provided that, notwithstanding the foregoing limitation, the court in its discretion, and subject to guidelines issued by the Executive Secretary of the Supreme Court of Virginia, may waive the limitation of fees up to an additional $850 when the effort expended, the time reasonably necessary for the particular representation, the novelty and difficulty of the issues, or other circumstances warrant such a waiver; (iii) to defend any other felony charge, or a charge of violation of probation for such offense, a sum not to exceed $445, provided that, notwithstanding the foregoing limitation, the court in its discretion, and subject to guidelines issued by the Executive Secretary of the Supreme Court of Virginia, may waive the limitation of fees up to an additional $155 when the effort expended, the time reasonably necessary for the particular representation, the novelty and difficulty of the issues, or other circumstances warrant such a waiver; and (iv) in the circuit court only, to defend any misdemeanor charge punishable by confinement in jail or a charge of violation of probation for such offense, a sum not to exceed $158. In the event any case is required to be retried due to a mistrial for any cause or reversed on appeal, the court may allow an additional fee for each case in an amount not to exceed the amounts allowable in the initial trial. In the event counsel is appointed to defend an indigent charged with a felony that may be punishable by death, such counsel shall continue to receive com-

pensation as provided in this paragraph for defending such a felony, regardless of whether the charge is reduced or amended to a felony that may not be punishable by death, prior to final disposition of the case. In the event counsel is appointed to defend an indigent charged with any other felony, such counsel shall receive compensation as provided in this paragraph for defending such a felony, regardless of whether the charge is reduced or amended to a misdemeanor or lesser felony prior to final disposition of the case in either the district court or circuit court.

Counsel appointed to represent an indigent accused in a criminal case, who are not public defenders, may request an additional waiver exceeding the amounts provided for in this section. The request for any additional amount shall be submitted to the presiding judge, in writing, with a detailed accounting of the time spent and the justification for the additional amount. The presiding judge shall determine, subject to guidelines issued by the Executive Secretary of the Supreme Court of Virginia, whether the request for an additional amount is justified in whole or in part, by considering the effort expended and the time reasonably necessary for the particular representation, and, if so, shall forward the request as approved to the chief judge of the circuit court or district court for approval.

If at any time the funds appropriated to pay for waivers under this section become insufficient, the Executive Secretary of the Supreme Court of Virginia shall so certify to the courts and no further waivers shall be approved.

The circuit or district court shall direct the payment of such reasonable expenses incurred by such court-appointed counsel as it deems appropriate under the circumstances of the case. Counsel appointed by the court to represent an indigent charged with repeated violations of the same section of the Code of Virginia, with each of such violations arising out of the same incident, occurrence, or transaction, shall be compensated in an amount not to exceed the fee prescribed for the defense of a single charge, if such offenses are tried as part of the same judicial proceeding. The trial judge shall consider any guidelines established by the Supreme Court but shall have the sole discretion to fix the amount of compensation to be paid counsel appointed by the court to defend a felony charge that may be punishable by death.

The circuit or district court shall direct that the foregoing payments shall be paid out by the Commonwealth, if the defendant is charged with a violation of a statute, or by the county, city or town, if the defendant is charged with a violation of a county, city or town ordinance, to the attorney so appointed to defend such person as compensation for such defense.

Counsel representing a defendant charged with a Class 1 felony, or counsel representing an indigent prisoner under sentence of death in a state habeas corpus proceeding, may submit to the court, on a monthly basis, a statement of all costs incurred and fees charged by him in the case during that month. Whenever the total charges as are deemed reasonable by the court for which payment has not previously been made or requested exceed $1,000, the court may direct that payment be made as otherwise provided in this section.

When such directive is entered upon the order book of the court, the Commonwealth, county, city or town, as the case may be, shall provide for the payment out of its treasury of the sum of money so specified. If the defendant is convicted, the amount allowed by the court to the attorney appointed to defend him shall be taxed against the defendant as a part of the costs of prosecution and, if collected, the same shall be paid to the Commonwealth, or the county, city or town, as the case may be. In the event that counsel for the defendant requests a waiver of the limitations on compensation, the court shall assess against the defendant an amount equal to the pre-waiver compensation limit specified in this section for each charge for which the defendant was convicted. An abstract of such costs shall be docketed in the judgment docket and execution lien book maintained by such court.

Any statement submitted by an attorney for payments due him for indigent representation or for representation of a child pursuant to § 16.1-266 shall, after the submission of the statement, be forwarded forthwith by the clerk to the Commonwealth, county, city or town, as the case may be, responsible for payment.

For the purposes of this section, the defense of a case may be considered conducted through to its conclusion and an appointed counsel entitled to compensation for his services in the event an indigent accused fails to appear in court subject to a capias for his arrest or a show cause summons for his failure to appear and remains a fugitive from justice for one year following the issuance of the capias or the summons to show cause, and appointed counsel has appeared at a hearing on behalf of the accused.

Effective July 1, 2007, the Executive Secretary of the Supreme Court of Virginia shall track and report the number and category of offenses charged involving adult and juvenile offenders in cases in which court-appointed counsel is assigned. The Executive Secretary shall also track and report the amounts paid by waiver above the initial cap to court-appointed counsel. The Executive Secretary shall provide these reports to the Governor, members of the House Appropriations Committee, and members of the Senate Finance Committee on a quarterly basis.

History.
Code 1950, §§ 14.1-184, 14.1-184.1, 19.1-241.5, 19.1-241.11; 1964, cc. 386, 651, 657; 1968, c. 481; 1973, c. 316; 1975, c. 495; 1976, c. 553; 1980, c. 626; 1981, cc. 472, 486; 1985, c. 525; 1986, c. 425; 1987, c. 638; 1988, cc. 465, 472; 1989, c. 565; 1994, c. 451; 1995, cc.

571, 713; 1997, c. 492; 1998, cc. 440, 451; 2000, cc. 436, 448; 2001, c. 509; 2006, c. 332; 2007, cc. 938, 946; 2008, c. 760; 2009, c. 284.

Cross references.
As to punishment for Class 1 felonies, see § 18.2-10.

Editor's note.
Acts 2000, cc. 436 and 448, cl. 2 provide: "That this act shall be effective if funds are appropriated by the 2000 Session of the General Assembly, subject to the restrictions of paragraphs a, b, c, and d.

"a. If the funds appropriated by the 2000 Session of the General Assembly are less than $8,173,204 for FY 2001 and $8,591,029 for FY 2002, the increases in fees authorized in this act for counsel appointed pursuant to § 19.2-163 shall be prorated by the Executive Secretary of the Supreme Court as provided for in paragraphs b, c, and d.

"b. A proration factor for each year shall be derived by dividing the actual amounts included in the appropriation act for an increase in fees pursuant to this act for each year by the amounts in paragraph a above for each fiscal year.

"c. The increase in fees for each year, derived by subtracting the fees authorized in § 19.2-163 as of January 1, 2000, from the fees included in this act, shall be multiplied by the proration factor derived in paragraph b above.

"d. The actual fees to be paid to counsel appointed pursuant to this act shall not exceed the sum of the existing fees authorized in § 19.2-163 as of January 1, 2000, plus the prorated increase derived in paragraph c above."

An appropriation of an additional $5.2 million was made to the general fund for FY 2002 to provide for additional expenses under HB 1312 (c. 436) and a related Senate Bill. No appropriation was made as an increase for FY 2001.

Acts 2012, Sp. Sess. I, c. 3, as amended by Acts 2013, c. 806, effective for the biennium ending June 30, 2014, Item 42 E 2 provides: "The Chief Justice of the Supreme Court of Virginia shall determine how the amounts appropriated to Other Courts Costs and Allowances (Criminal Fund) will be allocated, consistent with statutory provisions in the Code of Virginia. Funds within these appropriations are to be used to fund fully the statutory caps on compensation applicable to attorneys appointed by the court to defend criminal charges. Should this appropriation not be sufficient to fund fully all of the statutory caps on compensation as established by § 19.2-163, Code of Virginia, that this appropriation shall be applied first to fully fund the statutory caps for the most serious noncapital felonies and then, should funds still remain in this appropriation, to the other statutory caps, in declining order of the severity of the charges to which each cap is applicable."

Acts 2012, Sp. Sess. I, c. 3, as amended by Acts 2013, c. 806, effective for the biennium ending June 30, 2014, Item 42 E 4 provides: "Notwithstanding the provisions of § 19.2-163, Code of Virginia, the amount of compensation allowed to counsel appointed by the court to defend a felony charge that may be punishable by death shall be calculated on an hourly basis at a rate set by the Supreme Court of Virginia."

The 2007 amendments.
The 2007 amendments by cc. 938 and 946 are nearly identical, and rewrote the introductory paragraph; in subdivision 1, divided the former sentence into two sentences by substituting "Such" for "such," added the proviso in the first sentence and deleted "without a requirement for accounting of time devoted thereto" following "§ 19.2-306 in the last sentence; and in subdivision 2, in the first sentence, inserted the proviso in clauses (ii) and (iii) and inserted "in the circuit court only" in clause (iv), added the present second, third and last paragraphs and inserted the next-to-last sentence in the seventh paragraph.

The 2008 amendments.
The 2008 amendment by c. 760 inserted the clause (i) and (iii) designators and inserted clause (ii) in subdivision 1; and substituted "20 years" for "twenty years" in clause (ii) in subdivision 2.

The 2009 amendments.
The 2009 amendment by c. 284 inserted "or counsel representing an indigent prisoner under sentence of death in a state habeas corpus proceeding" in the seventh paragraph.

Law Review.

For note, "Judicial Problems in Administering Court-Appointment of Counsel for Indigents," see 28 Wash. & Lee L. Rev. 120 (1971). For survey of Virginia law on criminal procedure for the year 1972-1973, see 59 Va. L. Rev. 1478 (1973). For article discussing the requirement of counsel in misdemeanor cases and its implementation in Virginia, see 30 Wash. & Lee L. Rev. 431 (1973). For 1985 survey of Virginia criminal procedure, see 19 U. Rich. L. Rev. 697 (1985). For survey on legal issues involving children in Virginia for 1989, see 23 U. Rich. L. Rev. 705 (1989). For 2003/2004 survey of family and juvenile law, see 39 U. Rich. L. Rev. 241 (2004). For foreword to 2007 annual survey of Virginia law, "Has a New Day Dawned for Indigent Defense in Virginia?," see 42 U. Rich. L. Rev. 93 (2007). For 2007 annual survey article, "Criminal Law and Procedure," see 42 U. Rich. L. Rev. 311 (2007).

CASE NOTES

Constitutionality. — This section, which provides a scheme and guidelines for compensating court-appointed counsel, is narrowly tailored to serve a compelling state interest and, therefore, is constitutional; it can not be said that, by establishing a statutory cap on attorney's fees, the state has deprived indigent defendants of their constitutional right to effective assistance of counsel. Webb v. Commonwealth, 32 Va. App. 337, 528 S.E.2d 138, 2000 Va. App. LEXIS 325 (2000).

The compensation allowable under this section for attorneys defending felony cases is not inadequate and does not operate to deny a defendant his right to conflict-free and effective assistance of counsel on grounds that it creates a financial disincentive for a lawyer to effectively represent his client. Webb v. Commonwealth, 32 Va. App. 337, 528 S.E.2d 138, 2000 Va. App. LEXIS 325 (2000).

Possibility of repayment does not chill exercise of convicted criminal's right to counsel. — The possibility that at some future date a convicted criminal might be called upon to repay the State an attorney's fee incurred in his defense of the commission by him of a criminal act doesn't "chill" the exercise of his constitutional entitlement to legal representation. Wicks v. City of Charlottesville, 215 Va. 274, 208 S.E.2d 752 (1974), appeal dismissed, 421 U.S. 901, 95 S. Ct. 1548, 43 L. Ed. 2d 769 (1975).

Basis for judgment for court costs where there is conviction. — A judgment rendered against a defendant for court costs in a criminal case where there is a conviction is not rendered on any demand for a debt or liability contracted by him. Wicks v. City of Charlottesville, 215 Va. 274, 208 S.E.2d 752 (1974), appeal dismissed, 421 U.S. 901, 95 S. Ct. 1548, 43 L. Ed. 2d 769 (1975).

Appropriateness addresses whether the purpose of the expense is suitable for the particular case. An expense would not be justified, even if reasonable in amount, if it served little or no purpose in the particular case. Singleton v. Commonwealth, 16 Va. App. 841, 433 S.E.2d 507 (1993).

Compensation for investigative services for indigent defendants not mandated. — Denial of defendant's request for appointment of an investigator was affirmed because neither § 19.2-332 nor § 19.2-163 mandated the appointment of experts to assist indigent defendants and their counsel. Dowdy v. Commonwealth, 278 Va. 577, 686 S.E.2d 710, 2009 Va. LEXIS 108 (2009).

ARTICLE 3.1.

INDIGENT DEFENSE.

§ 19.2-163.01. Virginia Indigent Defense Commission established; powers and duties.

A. The Virginia Indigent Defense Commission (hereinafter Indigent Defense Commission or Commission) is established. The Commission shall be supervisory and shall have sole responsibility for the powers, duties, operations, and responsibilities set forth in this section.

The Commission shall have the following powers and duties:

1. To publicize and enforce the qualification standards for attorneys seeking eligibility to serve as court-appointed counsel for indigent defendants pursuant to § 19.2-159.

2. To develop initial training courses for attorneys who wish to begin serving as court-appointed counsel, and to review and certify legal education courses that satisfy the continuing requirements for attorneys to maintain their eligibility for receiving court appointments.

3. To maintain a list of attorneys admitted to practice law in Virginia who are qualified to serve as court-appointed counsel for indigent defendants based upon the official standards and to disseminate the list by July 1 of each year and updates throughout the year to the Office of the Executive Secretary of the Supreme Court for distribution to the courts. In establishing and updating the list, the Commission shall consider all relevant factors, including but not limited to, the attorney's background, experience, and training and the Commission's assessment of whether the attorney is competent to provide quality legal representation.

4. To establish official standards of practice for court-appointed counsel and public defenders to follow in representing their clients, and guidelines for the removal of an attorney from the official list of those qualified to receive court appointments and to notify the Office of the Executive Secretary of the Supreme Court of any attorney whose name has been removed from the list.

5. To develop initial training courses for public defenders and to review and certify legal education courses that satisfy the continuing requirements for public defenders to maintain their eligibility.

6. To periodically review and report to the Virginia State Crime Commission, the House and the Senate Committees for Courts of Justice, the House Committee on Appropriations, and the Senate Committee on Finance on the caseload handled by each public defender office.

7. To maintain all public defender and regional capital defender offices established by the General Assembly.

8. To hire and employ and, at its pleasure, remove an executive director, counsel, and such other persons as it deems necessary, and to authorize the executive director to appoint, after prior notice to the Commission, a deputy director, and for each of the above offices a public defender or capital defender, as the case may be, who shall devote his full time to his duties and not engage in the private practice of law.

9. To authorize the public defender or capital defender to employ such assistants as authorized by the Commission.

10. To authorize the public defender or capital defender to employ such staff, including secretarial and investigative personnel, as may be necessary to

carry out the duties imposed upon the public defender office.

11. To authorize the executive director of the Commission, in consultation with the public defender or capital defender to secure such office space as needed, to purchase or rent office equipment, to purchase supplies and to incur such expenses as are necessary to carry out the duties imposed upon him.

12. To approve requests for appropriations and receive and expend moneys appropriated by the General Assembly of Virginia, to receive other moneys as they become available to it and expend the same in order to carry out the duties imposed upon it.

13. To require and ensure that each public defender office collects and maintains caseload data and fields in a case management database on an annual basis.

14. To report annually on or before October 1 to the Virginia State Crime Commission, the House and Senate Committees for Courts of Justice, the House Committee on Appropriations, and the Senate Committee on Finance on the state of indigent criminal defense in the Commonwealth, including Virginia's ranking amongst the 50 states in terms of pay allowed for court-appointed counsel appointed pursuant to § 19.2-159 or subdivision C 2 of § 16.1-266.

B. The Commission shall adopt rules and procedures for the conduct of its business. The Commission may delegate to the executive director or, in the absence of the executive director, the deputy executive director, such powers and duties conferred upon the Commission as it deems appropriate, including powers and duties involving the exercise of discretion. The Commission shall ensure that the executive director complies with all Commission and statutory directives. Such rules and procedures may include the establishment of committees and the delegation of authority to the committees. The Commission shall review and confirm by a vote of the Commission its rules and procedures and any delegation of authority to the executive director at least every three years.

C. The executive director shall, with the approval of the Commission, fix the compensation of each public defender and all other personnel in each public defender office. The executive director shall also exercise and perform such other powers and duties as may be lawfully delegated to him and such powers and duties as may be conferred or imposed upon him by law.

History.
2004, cc. 884, 921; 2005, c. 230; 2006, cc. 429, 501; 2007, c. 371; 2008, cc. 536, 815; 2010, c. 314.

Editor's note.
Acts 2004, cc. 884 and 921, cl. 2, provide: "That the persons responsible for appointing members to the Virginia Indigent Defense Commission may, by agreement, make the initial appointments for such lengths of time as to allow the appointment terms to be staggered."

The 2007 amendments.
The 2007 amendment by c. 371 inserted "executive director of the Commission, in consultation with the" to subdivision A 11; and inserted "or, in the absence of the executive director, the deputy executive director" in the second sentence of subsection B.

The 2008 amendments.
The 2008 amendments by cc. 536 and 815 are identical, and in subdivision A 12, inserted "and to receive and distribute funds from a county or city as provided by § 19.2-163.01:1" at the end and made a related change; and inserted the second through the fourth sentences in subsection C.

The 2010 amendments.
The 2010 amendment by c. 314, in subdivision A 12, deleted "and to receive and distribute funds from a county or city as provided by § 19.2-163.01:1" from the end; and in subsection C, deleted the second through fourth sentences, which read: "When funds are received from a county or city as provided in § 19.2-163.01:1, the executive director, in accordance with policies adopted by the Commission, shall use the funds to adjust the compensation of the public defender and other personnel in the public defender's office in the county or city from which such funds are received. The adjustments to the compensation shall be effective only for the period for which such funds are provided by the county or city."

Law Review.
For 2003/2004 survey of family and juvenile law, see 39 U. Rich. L. Rev. 241 (2004). For foreword to 2007 annual survey of Virginia law, "Has a New Day Dawned for Indigent Defense in Virginia?," see 42 U. Rich. L. Rev. 93 (2007).

OPINIONS OF THE ATTORNEY GENERAL

Locality does not have authority to supplement the salaries of the public defender or his staff. See opinion of Attorney General to The Honorable Mitchell Van Yahres, Member, House of Delegates, 05-033 (12/2/05).

§ 19.2-163.01:1. Supplementing compensation of public defender.

A. The governing body of any county or city may supplement the compensation of the public defender or any of his deputies or employees above the compensation fixed by the executive director, in such amounts as it may deem expedient. Such additional compensation shall be wholly payable from the funds of any such county or city.

B. Due to the privileged and protected nature of the attorney-client relationship and the statutory scope of representation provided in §§ 19.2-157 and 19.2-163.3, no county or city providing a supplement to compensation under this section shall place any condition or requirement upon the receipt of such funds.

C. Funds provided by any county or city under this section shall be paid directly to the employees with notice to the Indigent Defense Commission of any amount so provided.

History.
2008, cc. 536, 815; 2010, c. 314.

The 2010 amendments.
The 2010 amendment by c. 314, in subsection C, inserted "directly to the employees with notice" and substituted "of any amount so provided" for "in accordance with any required state procedures and processes."

§ 19.2-163.02. Membership of Indigent Defense Commission; expenses.

The Virginia Indigent Defense Commission shall consist of 14 members as follows: the chairmen of the House and Senate Committees for Courts of Justice or their designees who shall be members of the Courts of Justice committees; the chairman of the Virginia State Crime Commission or his designee; the Executive Secretary of the Supreme Court or his designee; two attorneys officially designated by the Virginia State Bar; two persons appointed by the Governor; three persons appointed by the Speaker of the House of Delegates; and three persons appointed by the Senate Committee on Rules. At least one of the appointments made by the Governor, one of the appointments made by the Speaker, and one of the appointments made by the Senate Committee on Rules, shall be an attorney in private practice with a demonstrated interest in indigent defense issues. Persons who are appointed by virtue of their office shall hold terms coincident with their terms of office. If the chairman of the Virginia State Crime Commission is (i) the chairman of the House Committee for Courts of Justice, then the vice-chairman of the Committee shall serve in the position designated for the Committee chairman or (ii) the chairman of the Senate Committee for Courts of Justice, then the Senate Committee on Rules, upon the recommendation of the chairman of the Committee, shall appoint a member of the Committee to serve in the position designated for the Committee chairman. All other members shall be appointed for terms of three years and may be reappointed.

The Commission shall elect a chairman and a vice-chairman from among its membership annually. The chairman or his designee shall preside at all regular and called meetings of the Commission and shall have no additional duties or authority unless set by statute or by resolution of the Commission and annually confirmed by the Commission. A majority of the members shall constitute a quorum. The Commission shall meet at least four times each year. The meetings of the Commission shall be held at the call of the chairman or whenever three of the members so request.

Members shall be paid reasonable and necessary expenses incurred in the performance of their duties. Legislative members shall receive compensation as provided in § 30-19.12 and nonlegislative citizen members shall receive compensation for their services as provided in §§ 2.2-2813 and 2.2-2825.

History.

2004, cc. 884, 921; 2005, cc. 176, 758; 2006, cc. 429, 501; 2008, c. 115.

Editor's note.

Acts 2005, c. 758, cl. 2, provides: "That this act shall not be construed to affect existing appointments, made by the Senate Committee on Privileges and Elections, for which the terms have not expired. However, any new appointments made after July 1, 2005 shall be made in accordance with the provisions of this act."

The 2008 amendments.

The 2008 amendment by c. 115 inserted "who shall be members of the Courts of Justice committees" near the beginning of the first sentence of the first paragraph.

§ 19.2-163.03. Qualifications for court-appointed counsel.

A. Initial qualification requirements. An attorney seeking to represent an indigent accused in a criminal case, in addition to being a member in good standing of the Virginia State Bar, shall meet the specific criteria required for each type or level of case. The following criteria shall be met for qualification and subsequent court appointment:

1. Misdemeanor case. To initially qualify to serve as counsel appointed pursuant to § 19.2-159 for an indigent defendant charged with a misdemeanor, the attorney shall:

(i) if an active member of the Virginia State Bar for less than one year, have completed six hours of MCLE-approved continuing legal education developed by the Indigent Defense Commission, or

(ii) if an active member of the Virginia State Bar for one year or more, either complete the six hours of approved continuing legal education developed by the Commission, or certify to the Commission that he has represented, in a district court within the past year, four or more defendants charged with misdemeanors, or

(iii) be qualified pursuant to this section to serve as counsel for an indigent defendant charged with a felony.

2. Felony case.

a. To initially qualify to serve as counsel appointed pursuant to § 19.2-159 for an indigent defendant charged with a felony, the attorney shall (i) have completed the six hours of MCLE-approved continuing legal education developed by the Commission, and (ii) certify that he has participated as either lead counsel or co-counsel in four felony cases from their beginning through to their final resolution, including appeals, if any.

b. If the attorney has been an active member of the Virginia State Bar for more than one year and certifies that he has participated, within the past year, as lead counsel in four felony cases through to their final resolution, including appeals, if any, the requirement to complete six hours of continuing legal education and the requirement to participate as co-counsel shall be waived.

c. If the attorney has been an active member of the Virginia State Bar for more than one year and certifies that he has participated, within the past five years, as lead counsel in five felony cases through to their final resolution, including appeals, if any, the requirement to participate as either lead counsel or co-counsel in four felony cases within the past year shall be waived.

3. Juvenile and domestic relations case.

a. To initially qualify to serve as appointed counsel in a juvenile and domestic relations district court pursuant to subdivision C 2 of § 16.1-266, the attorney shall (i) have completed the six hours of MCLE-approved continuing legal education developed by the Commission, (ii) have completed four additional hours of MCLE-approved continuing legal education on representing juveniles developed by the Commission, and (iii) certify that he has participated as either lead counsel or co-counsel in four cases involving juveniles in a juvenile and domestic relations district court.

b. If the attorney has been an active member of the Virginia State Bar for more than one year and certifies that he has, within the past year, been lead counsel in four cases involving juveniles in juvenile and domestic relations district court, the requirement to complete the 10 hours of continuing legal education shall be waived.

c. If the attorney has been an active member of the Virginia State Bar for more than one year and certifies that he has participated, within the past five years, in five cases involving juveniles in a juvenile and domestic relations district court, the requirement to participate as either lead counsel or co-counsel in four juvenile cases shall be waived.

B. Requalification requirements. After initially qualifying as provided in subsection A, an attorney shall maintain his eligibility for certification biennially by notifying the Commission of completion of at least six hours of Commission and MCLE-approved continuing legal education. The Commission shall provide information on continuing legal education programs that have been approved.

In addition, to maintain eligibility to accept court appointments under subdivision C 2 of § 16.1-266, an attorney shall complete biennially thereafter four additional hours of MCLE-approved continuing legal education on representing juveniles, certified by the Commission.

C. Waiver and exceptions. The Commission or the court before which a matter is pending, may, in its discretion, waive the requirements set out in this section for individuals who otherwise demonstrate their level of training and experience. A waiver of such requirements pursuant to this subsection shall not form the basis for a claim of error at trial, on appeal, or in any habeas corpus proceeding.

History.
2004, cc. 884, 921; 2006, c. 708; 2007, c. 571.

Editor's note.
Acts 2004, c. 884, cl. 4, provides: "That the provisions of § 19.2-163.03 shall become effective July 1, 2005."

Acts 2004, c. 921, cl. 4, provides: "That § 19.2-163.03 shall become effective July 1, 2005, only if funds are appropriated by the General Assembly to carry out the purposes of that section." Funding was provided in Acts 2004, Sp. Sess. I, c. 4, Item 39.

The 2007 amendments.
The 2007 amendment by c. 571 rewrote the section.

§ 19.2-163.04. Public Defender offices.

Public defender offices are established in:
a. The City of Virginia Beach;

b. The City of Petersburg;

c. The Cities of Buena Vista, Lexington, Staunton and Waynesboro and the Counties of Augusta and Rockbridge;

d. The City of Roanoke;

e. The City of Portsmouth;

f. The City of Richmond;

g. The Counties of Clarke, Frederick, Page, Shenandoah and Warren, and the City of Winchester;

h. The City and County of Fairfax;

i. The City of Alexandria;

j. The City of Radford and the Counties of Bland, Pulaski and Wythe;

k. The Counties of Fauquier, Loudoun and Rappahannock;

l. The City of Suffolk;

m. The City of Franklin and the Counties of Isle of Wight and Southampton;

n. The City of Bedford and the County of Bedford;

o. The City of Danville;

p. The Counties of Halifax, Lunenburg and Mecklenburg;

q. The City of Fredericksburg and the Counties of King George, Stafford and Spotsylvania;

r. The City of Lynchburg;

s. The City of Martinsville and the Counties of Henry and Patrick;

t. The City of Charlottesville and the County of Albemarle;

u. The City of Norfolk;

v. The County of Arlington and the City of Falls Church;

w. The City of Newport News;

x. The City of Chesapeake; and

y. The City of Hampton.

History.
2004, cc. 884, 921; 2004, Sp. Sess. I, c. 4, cl. 2; 2005, c. 951; 2006, Sp. Sess. I, c. 2.

Editor's note.
Acts 2004, Special Session I, c. 4, cl. 2, as amended by Acts 2005, c. 951, and as amended by Acts 2006, Sp. Sess. I, c. 2, amended § 19.2-163.2, from which this section is derived. At the direction of the Virginia Code Commission, effect has been given in this section, as set out above, to Acts 2004, Special Session I, c. 4, cl. 2, as amended by Acts 2005, c. 951, and Acts 2006, Sp. Sess. I, c. 2, by adding subdivisions v, w, x and y.

ARTICLE 4.

PUBLIC DEFENDERS.

§§ 19.2-163.1, 19.2-163.2. Repealed by Acts 2004, cc. 884 and 921.

Cross references.
For current provisions relating to public defenders offices, see § 19.2-163.04.

Editor's note.
Repealed § 19.2-163.2 was amended by Acts 2004, Sp. Sess. I, c. 4. At the direction of the Virginia Code Commission the amendments have been incorporated into § 19.2-163.04.

§ 19.2-163.3. Duties of public defenders.

Public defenders shall carry out the following duties in accordance with the guidance, policies, and authorizations of the Indigent Defense Commission:

(a) To assist the executive director of the Commission in securing office space, to employ a staff, to fix salaries and to do such other things necessary to carry out the duties imposed upon them with the approval of the Commission.

(b) To represent or supervise assistants in representing within their respective jurisdictions as set out in § 19.2-163.04 indigent persons charged with a crime or offense when such persons are entitled to be represented by law by court-appointed counsel in a court of record or a court not of record.

(c) To represent or supervise assistants in representing indigent persons who are entitled to be represented by court-appointed counsel in an appeal of their conviction to the Court of Appeals or the Supreme Court of Virginia.

(d) To submit such reports as required by the Commission.

History.
Code 1950, § 19.1-32.4; 1972, c. 800; 1975, c. 495; 1978, c. 698; 1979, c. 194; 1990, c. 734; 1992, c. 80; 2007, c. 680.

Cross references.
As to supplementing compensation of public defender by county or city, see § 19.2-163.01:1.

The 2007 amendments.
The 2007 amendment by c. 680, in the introductory paragraph, deleted "and their assistants" preceding "shall carry," and added the language beginning "in accordance with" to the end; substituted "assist the executive director of the Commission in securing" for "secure" in subsection (a); inserted "or supervise assistants in representing" in subsections (b) and (c); and deleted subsection (d), which read: "To represent indigent prisoners when a habeas corpus proceeding is brought by such prisoners"; and redesignated subsection (e) as (d).

CASE NOTES

Applied in Mackall v. Murray, 109 F.3d 957 (4th Cir. 1997).

§ 19.2-163.4. Inapplicability of §§ 17.1-606 and 19.2-163 where public defender offices established; exception.

In counties and cities in which public defender offices are established pursuant to § 19.2-163.04, defense services for indigents charged with jailable offenses shall be provided by the public defenders unless (i) the public defender is unable to represent the defendant or petitioner by reason of conflict of interest or (ii) the court finds that appointment of other counsel is necessary to attain the ends of justice. Except for the provisions of § 19.2-163 relating to reasonable expenses, §§ 17.1-606 and 19.2-163 shall not apply when defense services are provided by the public defenders.

History.
Code 1950, § 19.1-32.5; 1972, c. 800; 1975, cc. 476, 495; 1992, c. 80; 1994, c. 415.

Cross references.
As to counsel in capital cases, see § 19.2-163.7.

§ 19.2-163.4:1. Repayment of representation costs by convicted persons.

In any case in which an attorney from a public defender or capital defender office represents an indigent person charged with an offense and such person is convicted, the sum that would have been allowed a court-appointed attorney as compensation and as reasonable expenses shall be taxed against the person defended as a part of the costs of the prosecution, and, if collected, shall be paid to the Commonwealth or, if payment was made to the Commonwealth by a locality for defense of a local ordinance violation, to the appropriate county, city or town. An abstract of such costs shall be docketed in the judgment lien docket and execution book of the court.

History.
2004, cc. 884, 921.

§ 19.2-163.5. Legal services to public defenders and/or assistant public defenders.

At the request of a public defender, the Attorney General shall provide legal services to such attorney, his assistants, or members of his staff in any proceeding brought against him, his assistants, or staff for money damages, when the cause of action allegedly arises out of the duties of his office.

Any costs chargeable against the defendant or defendants in any such case shall be paid by the Commonwealth from the appropriation for the payment of criminal charges.

History.
1978, c. 698.

§ 19.2-163.6. Repealed by Acts 2004, c. 884 and 921.

ARTICLE 4.1.

COUNSEL IN CAPITAL CASES.

Michie's Jurisprudence.
For related discussion, see 5B M.J. Criminal Procedure, § 24.

§ 19.2-163.7. Counsel in capital cases.

In any case in which an indigent defendant is charged with a capital offense, the judge of the circuit court, upon request for the appointment of counsel, shall appoint at least two attorneys from the list or lists established by the Supreme Court and the Indigent Defense Commission or as provided in subsection C of § 19.2-163.8 to represent the defendant at trial and, if the defendant is sentenced to death, on appeal. In all cases where counsel is appointed under this section after July 1, 2004, one of the attorneys appointed shall be from a capital defense unit maintained by the Indigent Defense Commission. This section shall be construed in conformity with the provisions of § 19.2-163.4. If prior to indictment the attorney for the Commonwealth declares in writing that the Commonwealth will not seek the death penalty, the capital defense unit attorney may upon motion before the circuit court seek to withdraw as counsel. The circuit court judge having heard the motion to withdraw shall permit the capital defense unit attorney to withdraw and shall appoint another attorney pursuant to the provisions of § 19.2-159. If the sentence of death is affirmed on appeal, the court shall, within 30 days after the decision of the Supreme Court of Virginia, appoint counsel from the same list, or such other list as the Supreme Court and the Commission may establish, to represent an indigent prisoner under sentence of death in a state habeas corpus proceeding. The Attorney General shall have no standing to object to the appointment of counsel for the petitioner.

History.
1991, c. 664; 1995, c. 503; 2001, c. 766; 2002, c. 614; 2004, cc. 329, 884, 921.

Effect of amendment.
The 2004 amendment by cc. 884 and 921 are identical, and substituted "Indigent Defense" for "Public Defender" twice, deleted "pursuant to § 19.2-163.8" preceding "to represent the defendant" in the first sentence, and substituted "30" for "thirty" in the present sixth sentence.

Law Review.
For article, "And Death Shall Have No Dominion: How to Achieve Categorical Exemption of Mentally Retarded Defendants from Execution," see 45 U. Rich. L. Rev. 961 (2011).

CASE NOTES

Defendant's right to counsel adequately safeguarded. — Virginia's statutory scheme for identifying and appointing qualified attorneys to represent indigent defendants in capital murder cases adequately safeguards those defendants' constitutionally guaranteed right to counsel. Bailey v. Commonwealth, 259 Va. 723, 529 S.E.2d 570, 2000 Va. LEXIS 59, cert. denied, 531 U.S. 995, 121 S. Ct. 488, 148 L. Ed. 2d 460 (2000).

State supreme court dismissed the petition filed by petitioner for a writ of habeas corpus in petitioner's capital murder case; petitioner did not show that petitioner's right to counsel was not adequately safeguarded, as the trial court was required to appoint only "one or more" attorneys to work on petitioner's case, one attorney was left on petitioner's case after the second attorney withdrew, petitioner agreed that it was not necessary to appoint a second counsel, and the record showed that the trial court was prepared to appoint co-counsel if the trial court felt that was necessary. Jackson v. Warden of the Sussex I State Prison, 2005 Va. LEXIS 107 (June 16, 2005).

No automatic appointment of counsel. — While Virginia law provided for appointment of an attorney to represent indigent capital petitioners in state post-conviction proceedings upon request, these sections did not provide for automatic appointment of counsel in all cases involving indigent capital defendants, which was required to satisfy the opt-in provisions of federal law. Satcher v. Netherland, 944 F. Supp. 1222 (E.D. Va. 1996), aff'd in part and rev'd in part on other grounds sub nom. Satcher v. Pruett, 126 F.3d 561 (4th Cir.), cert. denied, 522 U.S. 1010, 118 S. Ct. 595, 139 L. Ed. 2d 431 (1997).

Trial court has discretion to stay execution to allow time for counsel to prepare. — This section is not an empty mandate requiring appointment of counsel irrespective of whether there is sufficient time prior to the execution date for appointed counsel to prepare a petition for a writ of habeas corpus. In order for a prisoner to receive the intended protection of this section, he must be allowed a reasonable period of time during which to consult with counsel and to have counsel prepare his petition. Thus, this section implicitly provides the trial court with discretionary authority to stay execution of a death sentence in order to comply with the intent of the statute. Davidson v. Commonwealth, 246 Va. 168, 432 S.E.2d 178 (1993).

Undue defense. — Since July 1, 1992, Virginia has required appointment of competent counsel to represent indigent petitioners in its post-conviction proceedings. Although the parties dispute whether Virginia's system satisfies the requirements of § 107 of the Antiterrorism and Effective Death Penalty Act of 1996, the dispute was irrelevant because the system was not set up until after the defendant's Virginia habeas petition had been finally denied by the Virginia Supreme Court. Accordingly, Virginia's disposition of the defendant's petition should not have received the added deference afforded by the Act, because by the time it denied the petition, Virginia had not yet set up the appointment procedures the Act requires as the price of deference. Bennett v. Angelone, 92 F.3d 1336 (4th Cir.), cert. denied, 519 U.S. 1002, 117 S. Ct. 503, 136 L. Ed. 2d 395 (1996).

§ 19.2-163.8. List of qualified attorneys.

A. The Supreme Court and the Indigent Defense Commission, in conjunction with the Virginia State Bar, shall adopt standards for attorneys admitted to practice law in Virginia who are qualified to represent defendants charged with capital murder or sentenced to death, which take into consideration, to the extent practicable, the following criteria: (i) license or permission to practice law in Virginia; (ii) general background in criminal litigation; (iii) demonstrated experience in felony practice at trial and appeal; (iv) experience in death penalty litigation; (v) familiarity with the requisite court system; (vi) current training in death penalty litigation; (vii) current training in the analysis and introduction of forensic evidence, including deoxyribonucleic acid (DNA) testing and the evidence of a DNA profile comparison to prove or disprove the identity of any person; and (viii) demonstrated proficiency and commitment to quality representation.

B. The Supreme Court and the Indigent Defense Commission shall maintain a list of attorneys admitted to practice law in Virginia who are qualified to represent defendants charged with capital murder or sentenced to death. In establishing such a list, the Court and the Commission shall consider all relevant factors, including but not limited to, the attorney's background, experience, and training and the Court's and the Commission's assessment of whether the attorney is competent to provide quality legal representation.

C. Notwithstanding the requirements of § 19.2-163.7, the judge of the circuit court may appoint counsel who is not included on the list, but who otherwise qualifies under the standards established and maintained by the Court and the Commission.

D. Noncompliance with the requirements of this article shall not form the basis for a claim of error at trial, on appeal, or in any habeas corpus proceeding.

The performance of habeas corpus counsel appointed pursuant to this article shall not form a basis for relief in any subsequent habeas corpus proceeding.

E. The Supreme Court and the Indigent Defense Commission shall, in conjunction with the Virginia State Bar, promulgate and thereafter maintain standards for the qualifications of counsel who shall be considered eligible to be placed on the list of qualified attorneys.

History.

1991, c. 664; 2001, c. 766; 2004, cc. 884, 921.

CASE NOTES

No automatic appointment of counsel. — While Virginia law provided for appointment of an attorney to represent indigent capital petitioners in state post-conviction proceedings upon request, these sections did not provide for automatic appointment of counsel in all cases involving indigent capital defendants, which was required to satisfy the opt-in provisions of federal law. Satcher v. Netherland, 944 F. Supp. 1222 (E.D. Va. 1996), aff'd in part and rev'd in part on other grounds sub nom. Satcher v. Pruett, 126 F.3d 561 (4th Cir.), cert. denied, 522 U.S. 1010, 118 S. Ct. 595, 139 L. Ed. 2d 431 (1997).

Undue defense. — Since July 1, 1992, Virginia has required appointment of competent counsel to represent indigent petitioners in its post-conviction proceedings. Although the parties dispute whether Virginia's system satisfies the requirements of § 107 of the Antiterrorism and Effective Death Penalty Act of 1996, the dispute was irrelevant because the system was not set up until after the defendant's Virginia habeas petition had been finally denied by the Virginia Supreme Court. Accordingly, Virginia's disposition of the defendant's petition should not have received the added deference afforded by the Act, because by the time it denied the petition, Virginia had not yet set up the appointment procedures the Act requires as the price of deference. Bennett v. Angelone, 92 F.3d 1336 (4th Cir.), cert. denied, 519 U.S. 1002, 117 S. Ct. 503, 136 L. Ed. 2d 395 (1996).

ARTICLE 5.

INTERPRETERS.

Michie's Jurisprudence.
For related discussion, see 5B M.J. Criminal Procedure, § 38.

§ 19.2-164. Interpreters for non-English-speaking persons (Supreme Court Rule 2:507 derived in part from this section).

In any criminal case in which a non-English-speaking person is the accused, an interpreter for the non-English-speaking person shall be appointed. In any criminal case in which a non-English-speaking person is a victim or witness, an interpreter shall be appointed by the judge of the court in which the case is to be heard unless the court finds that the person does not require the services of a court-appointed interpreter. An English-speaking person fluent in the language of the country of the accused, a victim or a witness shall be appointed by the judge of the court in which the case is to be heard, unless such person obtains an interpreter of his own choos-

ing who is approved by the court as being competent. The compensation of an interpreter appointed by the court pursuant to this section shall be fixed by the court in accordance with guidelines set by the Judicial Council of Virginia and shall be paid from the general fund of the state treasury as part of the expense of trial. Such fee shall not be assessed as part of the costs unless (i) an interpreter has been appointed for the defendant, (ii) the defendant fails to appear, (iii) the interpreter appears in the case and no other case on that date, and (iv) the defendant is convicted of a failure to appear on that date the interpreter appeared in the case, then the court, in its discretion, may assess as costs the fee paid to the interpreter. Whenever a person communicates through an interpreter to any person under such circumstances that the communication would be privileged, and such person could not be compelled to testify as to the communications, this privilege shall also apply to the interpreter. The provisions of this section shall apply in both circuit courts and district courts.

History.

Code 1950, § 19.1-246.1; 1966, c. 240; 1974, c. 110; 1975, c. 495; 1978, c. 601; 1982, c. 444; 1985, c. 396; 1995, c. 546; 1996, c. 402; 2003, c. 1011; 2007, c. 383.

Cross references.

As to interpreters for the deaf in criminal cases, see now § 19.2-164.1. As to privileged communications by interpreters for the deaf in civil cases, see § 8.01-400.1. As to the visual electronic recording of the testimony of a deaf individual and the interpretation thereof for use in verification of the official transcript of civil proceedings, see § 8.01-406.

Editor's note.

At the direction of the Virginia Code Commission, the notation to the Virginia Rules of Evidence was added to the catchline of this section. Acts 2012, cc. 688 and 708, cl. 6 provides: "That pursuant to the authority set forth in §§ 30-146 and 30-147 of the Code of Virginia, the Virginia Code Commission shall direct any party with whom the Virginia Code Commission contracts to publish the Code of Virginia to include in the catchline of every section of the Code of Virginia from which any rule contained in the Rules of Evidence has been derived a notation specifying such rule."

The 2007 amendments.

The 2007 amendment by c. 383 inserted "unless" and clauses (i) through (iv) in the fifth sentence.

Law Review.

For survey of Virginia criminal law for the year 1973-1974, see 60 Va. L. Rev. 1499 (1974). For survey of Virginia law on evidence for the year 1977-1978, see 64 Va. L. Rev. 1451 (1978).

CASE NOTES

Transcribed testimony properly admitted. — Trial court did not abuse its discretion in admitting the transcribed testimony of the victim; although the interpreter had difficulty conveying a precise translation of some words and concepts, the interpreter performed her duties within reasonable limits of accuracy. Majette v. Commonwealth, No. 1400-01-1, 2002 Va. App. LEXIS 512 (Ct. of Appeals Aug. 20, 2002).

Adequate interpreter services provided. — Trial court did not err in denying defendant's motion to set aside the jury's verdict finding him guilty of involuntary manslaughter and reckless driving in a case where defendant, a Somalia native who had been in the United States for six years and who understood English, struck and fatally injured a pedestrian while defendant was driving a taxicab; defendant's due process rights were not violated because he was provided with adequate interpreter services and the evidence showed that he understood the trial process, which meant he was given a fair chance to defend himself against the State's accusations. Takow v. Commonwealth, 2006 Va. App. LEXIS 255 (June 6, 2006).

Interpreter not required. — Trial court's decision not to provide the victim with a translator during the victim's testimony did not violate § 19.2-164, because the witness clearly understood what was asked of him, and although the witness may have spoken with some minor imperfections, those imperfections did not establish that the victim was a non-English speaking person as set forth in § 19.2-164. Tharp v. Commonwealth, 2011 Va. App. LEXIS 308 (Oct. 11, 2011).

Challenges to interpreter waived. — Because defendant made no objection at a preliminary hearing to the victim's use of an interpreter pursuant to § 19.2-164, defendant's arguments challenging the interpreter were waived under Va. Sup. Ct. R. 5A:18. McDowell v. Commonwealth, 2009 Va. App. LEXIS 253 (June 9, 2009).

Applied in Saunders v. Commonwealth, 38 Va. App. 192, 562 S.E.2d 367, 2002 Va. App. LEXIS 238 (2002).

§ 19.2-164.1. Interpreters for the deaf (Supreme Court Rule 2:507 derived in part from this section).

In any criminal case in which a deaf person is the accused, an interpreter for the deaf person shall be appointed. In any criminal case in which a deaf person is the victim or a witness, an interpreter for the deaf person shall be appointed by the court in which the case is to be heard unless the court finds that the deaf person does not require the services of a court-appointed interpreter and the deaf person waives his rights. Such interpreter shall be procured by the judge of the court in which the case is to be heard through the Department for the Deaf and Hard-of-Hearing.

The compensation of an interpreter appointed by the court pursuant to this section shall be fixed by the court and paid from the general fund of the state treasury as part of the expense of trial. Such fee shall not be assessed as part of the costs.

Any person entitled to the services of an interpreter under this section may waive these services for all or a portion of the proceedings. Such a waiver shall be made by the person upon the record after an opportunity to consult with legal counsel. A judicial officer, utilizing an interpreter obtained in accordance with this section, shall explain to the deaf person the nature and effect of any waiver. Any waiver shall be approved in writing by the deaf person's legal counsel. If the person does not have legal counsel, approval shall be made in writing by a judicial officer. A person who waives his right to an interpreter may provide his own interpreter at his own expense without regard to whether the interpreter is qualified under this section.

The provisions of this section shall apply in both circuit courts and district courts.

Whenever a person communicates through an interpreter to any person under such circumstances that the communication would be privileged, and such person could not be compelled to testify as to the communications, this privilege shall also apply to the interpreter.

In any judicial proceeding, the judge on his own motion or on the motion of a party to the proceeding may order all of the testimony of a deaf person and the interpretation thereof to be visually electronically recorded for use in verification of the official transcript of the proceedings.

History.
1982, c. 444; 1985, c. 396; 1995, c. 546; 1996, c. 402.

Cross references.
As to interpreters for the deaf in civil proceedings, see § 8.01-384.1.

Editor's note.
At the direction of the Virginia Code Commission, the notation to the Virginia Rules of Evidence was added to the catchline of this section. Acts 2012, cc. 688 and 708, cl. 6 provides: "That pursuant to the authority set forth in §§ 30-146 and 30-147 of the Code of Virginia, the Virginia Code Commission shall direct any party with whom the Virginia Code Commission contracts to publish the Code of Virginia to include in the catchline of every section of the Code of Virginia from which any rule contained in the Rules of Evidence has been derived a notation specifying such rule."

ARTICLE 6.

RECORDING EVIDENCE AND INCIDENTS OF TRIAL.

Michie's Jurisprudence.
For related discussion, see 1B M.J. Appeal and Error, § 204; 5A M.J. Courts, §§ 26, 27; 5B M.J. Criminal Procedure, §§ 35, 40, 69; 9A M.J. Habeas Corpus, § 17.

§ 19.2-165. Recording evidence and incidents of trial in felony cases; cost of recording; cost of transcripts; certified transcript deemed prima facie correct; request for copy of transcript.

In all felony cases, the court or judge trying the case shall by order entered of record provide for the recording verbatim of the evidence and incidents of trial either by a court reporter or by mechanical or electronic devices approved by the court. The expense of reporting or recording the trial of criminal cases shall be paid by the Commonwealth out of the appropriation for criminal charges, upon approval of the trial judge. However, if the defendant is convicted, the Commonwealth shall be entitled to receive the amount allocated to the court reporter fund under the fixed felony fee. Localities that maintain mechanical or electronic devices for this purpose shall be entitled to retain their reasonable expenses attributable to the cost of operating and maintaining such equipment.

In all felony cases where it appears to the court from the affidavit of the defendant and other evidence that the defendant intends to seek an appeal and is financially unable to pay such costs or to bear the expense of a copy of the transcript of the evidence for an appeal, the trial court shall, upon the motion of counsel for the defendant, order the evidence transcribed for such appeal and all costs therefor paid by the Commonwealth out of the appropriation for criminal charges. If the conviction is not reversed, all costs paid by the Commonwealth, under the provisions hereof, shall be assessed against the defendant.

The reporter or other individual designated to report and record the trial shall file the original shorthand notes or other original records with the clerk of the circuit court who shall preserve them in the public records of the court for not less than five years if an appeal was taken and a transcript was prepared, or ten years if no appeal was taken. The transcript in any case certified by the reporter or other individual designated to report and record the trial shall be deemed prima facie a correct statement of the evidence and incidents of trial.

Upon the request of any counsel of record, or of any party not represented by counsel, and upon payment of the reasonable cost thereof, the court reporter covering any proceeding shall provide the requesting party with a copy of the transcript of such proceeding or any requested portion thereof.

The court shall not direct the court reporter to cease recording any portion of the proceeding without the consent of all parties or of their counsel of record.

The administration of this section shall be under the direction of the Supreme Court of Virginia.

History.
Code 1950, § 17-30.1; 1952, c. 642; 1956, c. 699; 1962, c. 419; 1964, c. 533; 1968, c. 358; 1975, cc. 495, 640; 1983, c. 505; 1984, c. 752; 1994, c. 497; 1999, c. 9.

Law Review.
For note on the indigent in Virginia, see 51 Va. L. Rev. 163 (1965). For survey of Virginia law on criminal law and procedure for the year 1969-1970, see 56 Va. L. Rev. 1572 (1970).

CASE NOTES

This section is plain. Hudgins v. Circuit Court, 294 F. Supp. 258 (E.D. Va. 1968).

Refusal to provide an indigent defendant with a free transcript constitutes a denial of constitutional rights. Cabaniss v. Cunningham, 206 Va. 330, 143 S.E.2d 911 (1965).

As does counsel's failure to advise of right to such transcript. — An indigent defendant is denied his constitutional right to a free transcript where his counsel fails to advise him of this right. Cabaniss v. Cunningham, 206 Va. 330, 143 S.E.2d 911 (1965).

And it makes no difference that court-appointed counsel may think there are no grounds for review. Cabaniss v. Cunningham, 206 Va. 330, 143 S.E.2d 911 (1965).

Nor does it matter whether the trial judge may think an appeal to be frivolous. Cabaniss v. Cunningham, 206 Va. 330, 143 S.E.2d 911 (1965).

In camera hearing. — The in camera hearing was a stage of the trial where something could be done to affect the defendant's interests, therefore, the defendant was entitled to have a court reporter present. The in camera hearing was not merely to determine a legal question. Testimony was heard to determine whether appellant was promised immunity from prosecution. Defense counsel was given the right to cross-examine the witness. The witness was taken to the judge's chambers for the purpose of asking him

substantive evidentiary questions. Brittingham v. Commonwealth, 10 Va. App. 530, 394 S.E.2d 336 (1990).

Section inapplicable in habeas corpus. — This section is not applicable to the initial request for a transcript if for the purpose of habeas corpus. McLaren v. Peyton, 262 F. Supp. 120 (W.D. Va. 1966).

No provision is made for a transcript of the evidence of the criminal trial for use in applying for habeas corpus. Hudgins v. Circuit Court, 294 F. Supp. 258 (E.D. Va. 1968); Hogan v. Aiken, 339 F. Supp. 1005 (W.D. Va. 1972).

The use of a narrative statement is recognized by Sup. Ct. Rule 5:9 as a proper method of furnishing a record of evidence and incidents of trial for appeal. Houghtaling v. Commonwealth, 209 Va. 309, 163 S.E.2d 560 (1968), cert. denied, 394 U.S. 1021, 89 S. Ct. 1642, 23 L. Ed. 2d 46 (1969).

Applied in Crumble v. Commonwealth, 2 Va. App. 231, 343 S.E.2d 359 (1986); Jones v. Commonwealth, 29 Va. App. 503, 513 S.E.2d 431 (1999); Dickerson v. Commonwealth, 36 Va. App. 8, 548 S.E.2d 230, 2001 Va. App. LEXIS 398 (2001).

OPINIONS OF THE ATTORNEY GENERAL

Court has discretion in choosing and contracting for private court reporting services. — It is within the discretion of the court to establish procedures for choosing and contracting for private court reporting services, and the court may exercise its discretion in choosing those people it determines to be trustworthy for the task. See opinion of Attorney General to The Honorable Clifford R. Weckstein, Judge, Twenty-Third Judicial Circuit, 02-004 (4/12/02).

§ 19.2-165.1. Payment of medical fees in certain criminal cases; reimbursement.

A. Except as provided in subsection B, all medical fees expended in the gathering of evidence for all criminal cases where medical evidence is necessary to establish a crime has occurred and for cases involving abuse of children under the age of 18 shall be paid by the Commonwealth out of the appropriation for criminal charges, provided that any medical evaluation, examination, or service rendered be performed by a physician or facility specifically designated by the attorney for the Commonwealth in the city or county having jurisdiction of such case for such a purpose. If no such physician or facility is reasonably available in such city or county, then the attorney for the Commonwealth may designate a physician or facility located outside and adjacent to such city or county.

Where there has been no prior designation of such a physician or facility, such medical fees shall be paid out of the appropriation for criminal charges upon authorization by the attorney for the Commonwealth of the city or county having jurisdiction over the case. Such authorization may be granted prior to or within 48 hours after the medical evaluation, examination, or service rendered.

B. All medical fees expended in the gathering of evidence through physical evidence recovery kit examinations conducted on victims complaining of sexual assault under Article 7 (§ 18.2-61 et seq.) of Chapter 4 of Title 18.2 shall be paid by the Commonwealth pursuant to subsection F of § 19.2-368.11:1. Victims complaining of sexual assault shall not be required to participate in the criminal justice system or cooperate with law-enforcement authorities in order to be provided with such forensic medical exams.

C. Upon conviction of the defendant in any case requiring the payment of medical fees authorized by this section, the court shall order that the defendant reimburse the Commonwealth for payment of such fees.

History.
1976, c. 292; 1982, c. 507; 1987, c. 330; 1997, c. 322; 1999, c. 853; 2000, c. 292; 2003, cc. 28, 772; 2008, cc. 203, 251.

The 2008 amendments.
The 2008 amendments by cc. 203 and 251 are identical, and in subsection A, inserted "Except as provided in subsection B" and substituted "expended" for "involved" in the first sentence and deleted the last sentence requiring reimbursement of medical fees; and added subsections B and C.

§ 19.2-166. Court reporters.

Each judge of a court of record having jurisdiction over criminal proceedings shall be authorized, in all felony cases and habeas corpus proceedings to appoint a court reporter to report proceedings or to operate mechanical or electrical devices for recording proceedings, to transcribe the report or record of such proceedings, to perform any stenographic work related to such report, record or transcript including work pertinent to the court's findings of fact and conclusions of law pertinent thereto. Such reporter shall be paid by the Commonwealth on a per diem or work basis as appropriate out of the appropriation for criminal charges.

History.
Code 1950, § 17-30.1:1; 1968, c. 486; 1975, c. 495; 2003, c. 140.

CHAPTER 11.

PROCEEDINGS ON QUESTION OF INSANITY.

§ 19.2-167. Accused not to be tried while insane or feebleminded.

No person shall, while he is insane or feebleminded, be tried for a criminal offense.

History.
Code 1950, § 19.1-227; 1960, c. 366; 1964, c. 231; 1968, c. 789; 1975, c. 495.

Law Review.
For note on partial responsibility as a mitigating factor, see 18 Wash. & Lee L. Rev. 118 (1961). For comment on the procedural methods for raising insanity in criminal actions in Virginia, see 18 Wash. & Lee L. Rev. 365 (1961). For an article, "An End to Insanity: Recasting the Role of Mental Disability in Criminal Cases," see 86 Va. L. Rev. 1199 (2000).

Michie's Jurisprudence.
For related discussion, see 5B M.J. Criminal Procedure, §§ 24, 41, 43; 10A M.J. Insane and Other Incompetent Persons, §§ 2, 3, 6, 43, 47, 50; 4A M.J. Continuances, § 47; 6A M.J. Discovery, § 38; 9A M.J. Habeas Corpus, § 8; 20 M.J. Witnesses, § 8.

CASE NOTES

Article sets forth procedure for commitment. — This article sets forth the procedure for the commitment to a state hospital for observation of a person charged with crime when there is reason to believe that his mental condition makes such confinement necessary. Barber v. Commonwealth, 206 Va. 241, 142 S.E.2d 484 (1965).

This section is merely declaratory of the common law. Delp v. Commonwealth, 172 Va. 564, 200 S.E. 594 (1939); Thomas v. Cunningham, 313 F.2d 934 (4th Cir. 1963).

Insanity and feeblemindedness are placed on the same plane with respect to criminal liability. Graham v. Gathright, 345 F. Supp. 1148 (W.D. Va. 1972).

Commitment proceedings as to persons accused of crime are for their protection. Timmons v. Peyton, 240 F. Supp. 749 (E.D. Va. 1965), rev'd on other grounds, 360 F.2d 327 (4th Cir.), cert. denied, 385 U.S. 960, 87 S. Ct. 396, 17 L. Ed. 2d 305 (1966).

What emerges from this humane legislation is the assurance by the Commonwealth that one whose mental capacity to cope with the exigencies of a trial is in doubt shall not be put in jeopardy without a preliminary inquiry into his present mental condition. Thomas v. Cunningham, 313 F.2d 934 (4th Cir. 1963); Kibert v. Peyton, 383 F.2d 566 (4th Cir. 1967).

An accused is presumed to be sane at trial unless his mental condition is called into question by proof to the contrary. Thomas v. Cunningham, 313 F.2d 934 (4th Cir. 1963); Poteat v. Peyton, 270 F. Supp. 220 (W.D. Va. 1967); Jefferson v. Commonwealth, 214 Va. 747, 204 S.E.2d 258 (1974).

But he must have opportunity to raise issue of insanity. — While efforts to overcome the presumption of sanity may be circumscribed by state prescriptions as to the quantum of proof and legal tests of insanity, procedural due process requires that a state shall afford an accused adequate opportunity to raise the issue. Thomas v. Cunningham, 313 F.2d 934 (4th Cir. 1963).

Or the protection is illusory. — The protection afforded the defendant by this section is illusory, however, if, when a reasonable doubt as to his sanity arises, neither court nor counsel seeks to utilize the procedures provided by the state for determining competency. Kibert v. Peyton, 383 F.2d 566 (4th Cir. 1967).

Separate hearing on issue of sanity was unjustified where the court, upon the concurrence of two qualified psychologists, considered defendant mentally competent to stand trial for murder, and the jury affirmed such a conclusion. Wilson v. Cox, 312 F. Supp. 209 (W.D. Va. 1970).

Availability of psychiatric testimony. — The right to a judicial determination of fitness to stand trial is not to be confused with the contention that a state is constitutionally obligated to provide at public expense the services of psychiatrists whose expert testimony may later prove useful in establishing the affirmative defense of lack of criminal responsibility. While the availability of such evidence at state expense may be invaluable to an indigent accused unable to employ his own psychiatrists, this would appear to be a merely incidental consequence of the primary statutory objective of preserving his right to a fair trial by first resolving his mental capacity to understand the charges and the nature of the proceedings against him. Thomas v. Cunningham, 313 F.2d 934 (4th Cir. 1963).

Ake v. Oklahoma to be applied prospectively. — The rule announced in *Ake v. Oklahoma*, 105 S. Ct. 1087 (1985) (that due process of law was denied where no psychiatrist was appointed to examine the defendant, to help him prepare his case, to serve as an expert witness for the defense, and to assist in the defense at trial) should be applied only to those cases tried subsequent to Feb. 26, 1985. Snurkowski v. Commonwealth, 2 Va. App. 532, 348 S.E.2d 1 (1986).

Refusal to appoint second psychiatrist not error. — The trial court did not err in refusing to appoint a second independent private psychiatrist, where soon after defendant was formally charged, his counsel moved for the appointment of a private psychiatrist to examine and evaluate the defendant and to aid in his defense and that motion was granted. *Ake v. Oklahoma*, 470 U.S. 68, 105 S. Ct. 1087, 84 L. Ed. 2d 53 (1985) does not require the appointment of a psychiatrist of the defendant's choice. The United States Supreme Court was careful not to prescribe the method for the selection of the independent psychiatrist. Beaver v. Commonwealth, 232 Va. 521, 352 S.E.2d 342, cert. denied, 483 U.S. 1033, 107 S. Ct. 3277, 97 L. Ed. 2d 781 (1987).

Plea of guilty by insane defendant. — A man whose mind is so crippled by psychosis that he cannot understand the proceedings or confer intelligently about the case is in no position to plead guilty or to consent to such a plea in his behalf. If a trial court accepts a plea of guilty from such a man, the resulting judgment is vulnerable to collateral attack. Thomas v. Cunningham, 313 F.2d 934 (4th Cir. 1963).

§ 19.2-168. Notice to Commonwealth of intention to present evidence of insanity; continuance if notice not given.

In any case in which a person charged with a crime intends (i) to put in issue his sanity at the time of the crime charged and (ii) to present testimony of an expert to support his claim on this issue at his trial, he, or his counsel, shall give notice in writing to the attorney for the Commonwealth, at least 60 days prior to his trial, of his intention to present such evidence. However, if the period between indictment and trial is less than 120 days, the person or his counsel shall give such notice no later than 60 days following indictment. In the event that such notice is not given, and the person proffers such evidence at his trial as a defense, then the court may

in its discretion, either allow the Commonwealth a continuance or, under appropriate circumstances, bar the defendant from presenting such evidence. The period of any such continuance shall not be counted for speedy trial purposes under § 19.2-243.

History.

Code 1950, § 19.1-227.1; 1970, c. 336; 1975, c. 495; 1986, c. 535; 2008, c. 372.

The 2008 amendments.

The 2008 amendment by c. 372 substituted "60 days prior" for "twenty one days prior" near the end of clause (ii) in the first sentence; and inserted the second sentence.

Law Review.

For survey of Virginia law on criminal law and procedure for the year 1969-1970, see 56 Va. L. Rev. 1572 (1970). For comment on the insanity defense in Virginia, see 17 U. Rich. L. Rev. 129 (1982). For article, "Virginia's Capital Murder Sentencing Proceeding: A Defense Perspective," see 18 U. Rich. L. Rev. 341 (1984).

CASE NOTES

Statute inapplicable in juvenile proceedings. — The reference in this section to "any person" who intends to raise an insanity defense does not include juveniles, and such a defense may not be raised in delinquency proceedings. Commonwealth v. Chatman, 260 Va. 562, 538 S.E.2d 304, 2000 Va. LEXIS 131 (2000).

Commonwealth entitled to other sanity evaluations. — Subsection E of § 19.2-169.5 clearly provides that the Commonwealth is entitled not only to the report ordered under § 19.2-169.5, but also to the results of any other evaluation of the defendant's sanity when notice is given by the defense pursuant to this section; subsection E of § 19.2-169.5 cannot be read as applying only to the report ordered. Blevins v. Commonwealth, 11 Va. App. 429, 399 S.E.2d 173 (1990).

Disclosure of mental health records to the Commonwealth. — Psychiatric, psychological, medical, and other records produced by the mental health experts in the course of fulfilling their court-ordered responsibilities under § 19.2-169.5 are protected under that statute from being disclosed to the Commonwealth until the defendant gives notice under this section. Schwartz v. Commonwealth, 45 Va. App. 407, 611 S.E.2d 631, 2005 Va. App. LEXIS 156 (2005).

Plea of "not guilty by reason of insanity" not required to preserve defense of insanity. Thus, trial judge erred when he ruled that the trial could not proceed in an orderly fashion on the defendant's insanity defense unless the defendant entered a formal plea of "not guilty by reason of insanity." Jones v. Commonwealth, 28 Va. App. 444, 506 S.E.2d 27 (1998).

Equal protection not denied. — Defendant juvenile was not denied his equal protection rights under U.S. Const. amend. XIV, § 1 because he had no right in juvenile court to assert an insanity defense to attempting to poison his mother's tea with intent to kill or injure her in violation of § 18.2-54.1 as defendant suffered no disparate treatment as he had the same ability as an adult to assert an insanity defense under § 19.2-168 in the trial court, but he did not exercise his right under § 16.1-270 to be tried as adult and to assert the insanity defense available to him under the adult system. D.L.G. v. Commonwealth, 60 Va. App. 77, 724 S.E.2d 208, 2012 Va. App. LEXIS 123 (2012).

Applied in Shifflett v. Commonwealth, 221 Va. 760, 274 S.E.2d 305 (1981).

§ 19.2-168.1. Evaluation on motion of the Commonwealth after notice.

A. If the attorney for the defendant gives notice pursuant to § 19.2-168, and the Commonwealth thereafter seeks an evaluation of the defendant's sanity at the time of the offense, the court shall appoint one or more qualified mental health experts to perform such an evaluation. The court shall order the defendant to submit to such an evaluation and advise the defendant on the record in court that a refusal to cooperate with the Commonwealth's expert could result in exclusion of the defendant's expert evidence. The qualification of the experts shall be governed by subsection A of § 19.2-169.5. The location of the evaluation shall be governed by subsection B of § 19.2-169.5. The attorney for the Commonwealth shall be responsible for providing the experts the information specified in subsection C of § 19.2-169.5. After performing their evaluation, the experts shall report their findings and opinions, and provide copies of psychiatric, psychological, medical or other records obtained during the course of the evaluation to the attorneys for the Commonwealth and the defense.

B. If the court finds, after hearing evidence presented by the parties, that the defendant has refused to cooperate with an evaluation requested by the Commonwealth, it may admit evidence of such refusal or, in the discretion of the court, bar the defendant from presenting expert psychiatric or psychological evidence at trial on the issue of his sanity at the time of the offense.

History.
1982, c. 653; 1986, c. 535.

Law Review.
For comment suggesting the need for reform of the insanity defense in Virginia, see 13 U. Rich. L. Rev. 397 (1979). For review of Fourth Circuit cases on criminal procedure, see 36 Wash. & Lee L. Rev. 485 (1979). For survey of Virginia law on criminal procedure for the year 1978-1979, see 66 Va. L. Rev. 261 (1980). For article, "The Role of Mental Health Professionals in the Criminal Process: The Case for Informed Speculation," see 66 Va. L. Rev. 427 (1980). For comment on the insanity defense in Virginia, see 17 U. Rich. L. Rev. 129 (1982).

CASE NOTES

There exists no constitutional right to the appointment of a private psychiatrist of the defendant's own choosing at public expense. Satterfield v. Zahradnick, 572 F.2d 443 (4th Cir.), cert. denied, 436 U.S. 920, 98 S. Ct. 2270, 56 L. Ed. 2d 762 (1978), decided under repealed § 19.2-169.

Liability for expenses where hospitalized under Title 37.2. — A person is liable for the expenses of his care, treatment, and maintenance when confined to a state hospital pursuant to former Title 37.1 [now Title 37.2], even though he previously had been confined to the facility pursuant to former § 19.2-169 as a person charged with crime. Commonwealth, Dep't of Mental Health & Mental Retardation v. Jenkins, 224 Va. 456, 297 S.E.2d 692 (1982).

Refusal to cooperate with Commonwealth's mental health expert. — Based on defendant's admissions to an inmate that defendant's only chance to get less than 20 years was to act strangely, and to the trial court that defendant understood that a refusal to cooperate with the Commonwealth's mental health expert could result in exclusion of defendant's own expert's opinion, the trial court did not err in finding that any mental illness asserted by defendant did not preclude defendant from cooperating with the Commonwealth's expert. Grattan v. Commonwealth, 2008 Va. App. LEXIS 516 (Nov. 25, 2008), aff'd, 278 Va. 602, 685 S.E.2d 634, 2009 Va. LEXIS 103 (2009).

Exclusion of expert's testimony under § 19.2-168.1 was affirmed because having found defendant competent to stand trial, it was reasonable for the court to conclude that defendant understood the

court's repeated instructions that he was required to cooperate with the Commonwealth's mental health evaluators and its constant warnings about the potential ramifications of his refusal to do so. Grattan v. Commonwealth, 278 Va. 602, 685 S.E.2d 634, 2009 Va. LEXIS 103 (2009).

§ 19.2-169. Repealed by Acts 1982, c. 653.

Cross references.
For present provisions covering the subject matter of the repealed section, see §§ 19.2-168.1 and 19.2-169.1.

§ 19.2-169.1. Raising question of competency to stand trial or plead; evaluation and determination of competency.

A. *Raising competency issue; appointment of evaluators.* — If, at any time after the attorney for the defendant has been retained or appointed and before the end of trial, the court finds, upon hearing evidence or representations of counsel for the defendant or the attorney for the Commonwealth, that there is probable cause to believe that the defendant, whether a juvenile transferred pursuant to § 16.1-269.1 or adult, lacks substantial capacity to understand the proceedings against him or to assist his attorney in his own defense, the court shall order that a competency evaluation be performed by at least one psychiatrist or clinical psychologist who is qualified by training and experience in forensic evaluation.

B. *Location of evaluation.* — The evaluation shall be performed on an outpatient basis at a mental health facility or in jail unless the court specifically finds that outpatient evaluation services are unavailable or unless the results of outpatient evaluation indicate that hospitalization of the defendant for evaluation on competency is necessary. If the court finds that hospitalization is necessary, the court, under authority of this subsection, may order the defendant sent to a hospital designated by the Commissioner of Behavioral Health and Developmental Services as appropriate for evaluations of persons under criminal charge. The defendant shall be hospitalized for such time as the director of the hospital deems necessary to perform an adequate evaluation of the defendant's competency, but not to exceed 30 days from the date of admission to the hospital.

C. *Provision of information to evaluators.* — The court shall require the attorney for the Commonwealth to provide to the evaluators appointed under subsection A any information relevant to the evaluation, including, but not limited to (i) a copy of the warrant or indictment; (ii) the names and addresses of the attorney for the Commonwealth, the attorney for the defendant, and the judge ordering the evaluation; (iii) information about the alleged crime; and (iv) a summary of the reasons for the evaluation request. The court shall require the attorney for the defendant to provide any available psychiatric records and other information that is deemed relevant. The court shall require that information be provided to the evaluator within 96 hours of the issuance of the court order pursuant to this section.

D. *The competency report.* — Upon completion of the evaluation, the evaluators shall promptly submit a report in writing to the court and the attorneys of record concerning (i) the defendant's capacity to understand the proceedings against him; (ii) his ability to assist his attorney; and (iii) his need for treatment in the event he is found incompetent but restorable, or incompetent for the foreseeable future. No statements of the defendant relating to the time period of the alleged offense shall be included in the report.

E. *The competency determination.* — After receiving the report described in subsection D, the court shall promptly determine whether the defendant is competent to stand trial. A hearing on the defendant's competency is not required unless one is requested by the attorney for the Commonwealth or the attorney for the defendant, or unless the court has reasonable cause to believe the defendant will be hospitalized under § 19.2-169.2. If a hearing is held, the party alleging that the defendant is incompetent shall bear the burden of proving by a preponderance of the evidence the defendant's incompetency. The defendant shall have the right to notice of the hearing, the right to counsel at the hearing and the right to personally participate in and introduce evidence at the hearing.

The fact that the defendant claims to be unable to remember the time period surrounding the alleged offense shall not, by itself, bar a finding of competency if the defendant otherwise understands the charges against him and can assist in his defense. Nor shall the fact that the defendant is under the influence of medication bar a finding of competency if the defendant is able to understand the charges against him and assist in his defense while medicated.

History.

1982, c. 653; 1983, c. 373; 1985, c. 307; 2003, c. 735; 2007, c. 781; 2009, cc. 813, 840.

Cross references.

As to representation by counsel in proceeding for commitment, see § 19.2-182.

The 2007 amendments.

The 2007 amendment by c. 781 deleted "or master's level psychologist" following "clinical psychologist" in subsection A and made related changes; substituted "the court finds that hospitalization is necessary" for "either finding is made" in the second sentence in subsection B; added the last sentence to subsection C; inserted "but restorable, or incompetent for the foreseeable future" to the end of the first sentence of subsection D; and made minor stylistic changes.

The 2009 amendments.

The 2009 amendments by cc. 813 and 840 are identical, and substituted "Behavioral Health and Developmental Services" for "Mental Health, Mental Retardation and Substance Abuse Services" in subsection B.

Law Review.

For note, "Law and Morality 'Unspeakable Justice': The Oswaldo Martinez Case and the Failure of the Legal System to Adequately Provide for Incompetent Defendants," see 48 Wm. & Mary L. Rev. 2075 (2007). For article, "Reconceptualizing Competence: An Appeal," see 66 Wash. & Lee L. Rev. 259 (2009). For annual survey article, "Criminal Law and Procedure," see 46 U. Rich. L. Rev. 59 (2011).

CASE NOTES

I. GENERAL CONSIDERATION.

Editor's note.

Many of the cases cited in the following annotations were decided under repealed § 19.2-169.

As to constitutionality of procedure under former § 19.2-169, see Payne v. Slayton, 329 F. Supp. 886 (W.D. Va. 1971).

Former § 19.2-169 was enacted in clear recognition of the State's constitutional obligation to provide a hearing on the question of whether a person to be tried is in such a mental condition that his confinement in a hospital for the insane or colony for the feebleminded for proper care and observation is necessary to attain the ends of justice. Thomas v. Cunningham, 313 F.2d 934 (4th Cir. 1963).

Due process requires state to provide means to raise issue. — Due process requires that the State must provide an adequate means by which an accused can raise the issue of insanity at the time of trial and at the commission of the alleged offense. Hodnett v. Slayton, 343 F. Supp. 1142 (W.D. Va. 1972), appeal dismissed, 471 F.2d 648 (4th Cir. 1973).

Trial court's refusal to suspend proceedings as denial of due process. — Where insanity at the time of the trial was established by reliable and uncontroverted sworn medical testimony, on the strength of this prima facie showing, the trial court's refusal to suspend the proceedings and its decision to hold trial the very next morning was so arbitrary as to constitute a denial of due process. Thomas v. Cunningham, 313 F.2d 934 (4th Cir. 1963).

Procedures must be set in motion whenever bona fide doubt as to competency exists. — State hearing procedures must be set in motion whenever it appears in the course of the proceedings that a bona fide doubt as to a defendant's competency exists. McLaughlin v. Royster, 346 F. Supp. 297 (E.D. Va. 1972).

Commitment proceedings as to persons accused of crime are for their protection. Timmons v. Peyton, 240 F. Supp. 749 (E.D. Va. 1965), rev'd on other grounds, 360 F.2d 327 (4th Cir.), cert. denied, 385 U.S. 960, 87 S. Ct. 396, 17 L. Ed. 2d 305 (1966).

Failure to raise question. — The protection afforded the defendant is illusory if, when a reasonable doubt as to his sanity arises, neither court nor counsel seeks to utilize the procedures provided by the State for determining competency. Kibert v. Peyton, 383 F.2d 566 (4th Cir. 1967).

There exists no constitutional right to the appointment of a private psychiatrist of the defendant's own choosing at public expense. Satterfield v. Zahradnick, 572 F.2d 443 (4th Cir.), cert. denied, 436 U.S. 920, 98 S. Ct. 2270, 56 L. Ed. 2d 762 (1978).

No constitutional guarantee of examination. — There is no constitutional guarantee that every person indicted for a felony is entitled to a mental examination. Kerns v. Peyton, 292 F. Supp. 182 (W.D. Va. 1968); Newman v. Peyton, 303 F. Supp. 462 (W.D. Va. 1969).

A state prisoner who alleges mental incapacity to stand trial is not entitled as a matter of right to pretrial commitment and examination at state expense. Morris v. Peyton, 283 F. Supp. 63 (W.D. Va. 1968).

No obligation on court where defendant's mental health not in doubt. — Former § 19.2-169 placed no obligation upon the court or the attorney for the Commonwealth in cases where there was no reason to doubt petitioner's mental health. Newman v. Peyton, 303 F. Supp. 462 (W.D. Va. 1969). See also Kerns v. Peyton, 292 F. Supp. 182 (W.D. Va. 1968).

Former § 19.2-169 placed no obligation upon the court to appoint a committee except where the court or attorney for the Commonwealth had reason to believe that the person to be tried was in such mental condition that his confinement in a hospital for the insane or colony for the feebleminded for proper care and observation was necessary to attain the ends of justice. Wood v. Commonwealth, 146 Va. 296, 135 S.E. 895 (1926); Delp v. Commonwealth, 172 Va. 564, 200 S.E. 594 (1939); Tilton v. Commonwealth, 196 Va. 774, 85 S.E.2d 368 (1955).

State must assure indigent defendant access to competent psychiatrist who will conduct an appropriate examination and assist in evaluation, preparation, and presentation of the defense when the defendant demonstrates to the trial judge that his sanity at the time of the offense is to be a significant factor at trial. Tuggle v. Commonwealth, 230 Va. 99, 334 S.E.2d 838 (1985), cert. denied, 478 U.S. 1010, 106 S. Ct. 3309, 92 L. Ed. 2d 722 (1986).

Indigent entitled to psychiatrist in capital case on issue of future dangerousness. — When the prosecution in a capital sentencing proceeding presents psychiatric evidence of an indigent defendant's future dangerousness, due process requires that a state provide the defendant the assistance of a psychiatrist on the issue. Where the Commonwealth presented psychiatric evidence that defendant showed a high probability of future dangerousness, even though defendant's trial and direct appeal predated the decision of the United States Supreme Court in *Ake v. Oklahoma*, 470 U.S. 68, 105 S. Ct. 1087, 84 L. Ed. 2d 53 (1985), in light of that decision the trial court erred in denying his motion for an independent psychiatrist to rebut the Commonwealth's psychiatric evidence of future dangerousness. Tuggle v. Commonwealth, 230 Va. 99, 334 S.E.2d 838 (1985), cert. denied, 478 U.S. 1010, 106 S. Ct. 3309, 92 L. Ed. 2d 722 (1986).

Ake v. Oklahoma **to be applied prospectively.** — The rule announced in *Ake v. Oklahoma*, 105 S. Ct. 1087 (1985) (that due process of law was denied where no psychiatrist was appointed to examine the defendant, to help him prepare his case, to serve as an expert witness for the defense, and to assist in the defense at trial) should be applied only to those cases tried subsequent to Feb. 26, 1985. Snurkowski v. Commonwealth, 2 Va. App. 532, 348 S.E.2d 1 (1986).

Commitment to a hospital or other means of inquisition is not granted ex mero motu; it is not a perfunctory order. Hawks v. Peyton, 370 F.2d 123 (4th Cir. 1966), cert. denied, 387 U.S. 925, 87 S. Ct. 2044, 18 L. Ed. 2d 982 (1967). See also Kerns v. Peyton, 292 F. Supp. 182 (W.D. Va. 1968).

Use of competency evaluation of a witness. — Trial court did not err in refusing to admit into evidence a competency evaluation of a co-conspirator who testified against defendant because nothing in the competency report about the co-conspirator suggested he was untruthful, given to making up facts, had impaired memory functions, had any cognitive impairments, and nothing suggested his mental conditions made him more likely to lie than anyone else. Waters v. Commonwealth, 43 Va. App. 636, 600 S.E.2d 918, 2004 Va. App. LEXIS 399 (2004).

Applied in Washington v. Commonwealth, 228 Va. 535, 323 S.E.2d 577 (1984).

II. ACTION BY THE COURT.

Action by court is discretionary. — Under former § 19.2-169 the lower court, after hearing the evidence, could in its discretion commit a person held for trial to the Commissioner of Mental Health, Mental Retardation and Substance Abuse Services [now the Commissioner of Behavioral Health and Developmental Services] at the proper hospital, pending determination of his mental condition. Delp v. Commonwealth, 172 Va. 564, 200 S.E. 594 (1939).

The language of former § 19.2-169 imported the exercise of discretion by the trial court in deciding whether the circumstances warranted further inquiry into defendant's mental condition, rather than the imposition of a mandate requiring such action regardless of the circumstances. Elkins v. Commonwealth, 208 Va. 336, 157 S.E.2d 243 (1967).

And will not be disturbed absent abuse. — The trial court's choice is discretionary and its denial of defendant's motion for a mental examination before trial will not be disturbed unless it is clearly shown that the trial court abused its discretion. Poteat v. Peyton, 270 F. Supp. 220 (W.D. Va. 1967).

The use of former § 19.2-169 was entirely discretionary with the trial court. The failure of the trial court to exercise such discretion

was reviewable only in the event of clear abuse of judicial discretion. Morris v. Peyton, 283 F. Supp. 63 (W.D. Va. 1968).

Denial of a motion for pretrial examination cannot be assailed except for abuse of discretion. Thomas v. Cunningham, 313 F.2d 934 (4th Cir. 1963); Poteat v. Peyton, 270 F. Supp. 220 (W.D. Va. 1967); Morris v. Peyton, 283 F. Supp. 63 (W.D. Va. 1968).

The denial of a motion for a pretrial examination or the denial of a motion for a continuance in order to effectuate a mental examination cannot be assailed except for a clear abuse of discretion. Ashby v. Cox, 344 F. Supp. 759 (W.D. Va. 1972).

While the Supreme Court has the power to review the action of the trial court in committing or refusing to commit persons to the Commissioner of Mental Health, Mental Retardation and Substance Abuse Services [now the Commissioner of Behavioral Health and Developmental Services], it will not disturb the trial court's ruling unless it plainly appears that the discretion of the trial court has been abused. Delp v. Commonwealth, 172 Va. 564, 200 S.E. 594 (1939); Tilton v. Commonwealth, 196 Va. 774, 85 S.E.2d 368 (1955).

Denial of motion held not an abuse. — Where there was no prima facie showing of insanity that would cause the court to doubt the defendant's sanity, there was no abuse of discretion by the trial court in denying defendant's motion. Poteat v. Peyton, 270 F. Supp. 220 (W.D. Va. 1967).

A trial judge did not abuse his discretion in denying a pretrial examination under former § 19.2-169 where testimony indicated that petitioner understood the nature of the charges against him and that he was aware that he was subject to punishment for them if found guilty, where the reason for an expert witness's lack of faith in the petitioner's ability to stand trial was not his present mental condition or competence but was caused by petitioner's memory lapse occasioned by heavy drinking, where the petitioner appeared normal while in court, and the petitioner's own testimony revealed nothing which indicated any mental defect or disease at the time of trial, and where there was no evidence that the petitioner had any prior history of mental instability. South v. Slayton, 336 F. Supp. 879 (W.D. Va. 1972).

The trial court has the inherent power to require defendant to be examined by a psychiatric committee in order that his examiners might report their opinion as to his sanity at the time of his alleged crimes and testify to such opinion if called by the Commonwealth as rebuttal witnesses. Shifflett v. Commonwealth, 221 Va. 760, 274 S.E.2d 305 (1981).

Second psychiatric opinion. — Trial court properly denied defendant's motion for a second psychiatric opinion, where defendant was cogent and responsive, her trial testimony was detailed, and there was no evidence that her mental condition had changed since her first psychiatric evaluation. Rothwell v. Commonwealth, No. 1342-98-1 (Ct. of Appeals Jan. 4, 2000).

Judge may invoke procedure sua sponte. — Since a defendant cannot always be expected to demand a sanity examination for himself, the judge may invoke the procedure sua sponte. Thomas v. Cunningham, 313 F.2d 934 (4th Cir. 1963).

No error in failing to order sua sponte evaluation. — Trial court did not err in failing to order sua sponte an evaluation of defendant's competency to stand trial under the terms of § 19.2-169.1 because there was no probable cause to believe that defendant lacked substantial capacity to understand the criminal proceedings against him or to assist his counsel in his defense; when entering his plea defendant stated his full name, gave his date of birth, and indicated that he fully understood the grand larceny charge for which he was being prosecuted, defendant pleaded not guilty to that charge and acknowledged that he was doing so knowingly and voluntarily, at the end of the colloquy, the trial court found that defendant had entered a free and voluntary plea of not guilty, and at no time did defense counsel raise with the trial court any issue regarding defendant's competency to stand trial. Anderson v. Commonwealth, 2011 Va. App. LEXIS 80 (Mar. 8, 2011).

And should do so when adequate showing has been made. — When an adequate showing has been made to raise the issue of the defendant's sanity, the trial court should order a hearing sua sponte. McLaughlin v. Royster, 346 F. Supp. 297 (E.D. Va. 1972).

III. PROOF.

An accused is presumed to be sane at the trial unless his mental condition is called into question by proof to the contrary. Payne v. Slayton, 329 F. Supp. 886 (W.D. Va. 1971).

An accused is presumed to be sane at the trial and during the commission of the offense, and it is his burden to prove the contrary. Graham v. Gathright, 345 F. Supp. 1148 (W.D. Va. 1972).

A simple suggestion of mental deficiency is not enough to require deferment of trial. Hawks v. Peyton, 370 F.2d 123 (4th Cir. 1966), cert. denied, 387 U.S. 925, 87 S. Ct. 2044, 18 L. Ed. 2d 982 (1967).

Fact that defendant had been in a mental institution on different occasions did not make out a prima facie case of insanity where that fact was not established before the trial court. Poteat v. Peyton, 270 F. Supp. 220 (W.D. Va. 1967).

Burden on accused upon motion for pretrial commitment. — In proceeding on a motion for pretrial commitment for observation and report, an accused was not required to prove actual insanity, as is necessary where lack of criminal responsibility is asserted as an affirmative defense. His sole burden was to adduce facts sufficient to create in the court's mind reasonable grounds to doubt his sanity. Thomas v. Cunningham, 313 F.2d 934 (4th Cir. 1963); Ashby v. Cox, 344 F. Supp. 759 (W.D. Va. 1972).

In proceeding on a motion for pretrial commitment, an accused met his burden of creating a reasonable doubt as to his sanity where two specialists testified without contradiction or reservation that accused was presently in the grip of a serious psychosis, disabling him from assisting his counsel. Thomas v. Cunningham, 313 F.2d 934 (4th Cir. 1963).

In Virginia, unlike the federal practice, the burden rests upon the accused to prove his mental incompetency. Timmons v. Peyton, 240 F. Supp. 749 (E.D. Va. 1965), rev'd on other grounds, 360 F.2d 327 (4th Cir.), cert. denied, 385 U.S. 960, 87 S. Ct. 396, 17 L. Ed. 2d 305 (1966).

The duty of carrying the burden of proving a defendant's insanity at the time of trial falls upon the petitioner's attorney to present the issue to the court when he has reasonable belief that his client's mental condition is of a nature which may render him incompetent to stand trial and which may also raise a question of his client's sanity at the time of the crime. Payne v. Slayton, 329 F. Supp. 886 (W.D. Va. 1971).

The burden of proof on the issue of insanity rests with the accused. Hodnett v. Slayton, 343 F. Supp. 1142 (W.D. Va. 1972), appeal dismissed, 471 F.2d 648 (4th Cir. 1973).

Petitioner need not prove actual insanity. — In proceeding on a motion for pretrial commitment for observation and report, the petitioner is not required to prove actual insanity, but only to adduce facts sufficient to create in the court's mind reasonable grounds to doubt his sanity. Morris v. Peyton, 283 F. Supp. 63 (W.D. Va. 1968).

The question of whether or not the defendant knows right from wrong is not relevant to the question of whether he should have been afforded a pretrial mental examination. Ashby v. Cox, 344 F. Supp. 759 (W.D. Va. 1972).

Efforts to overcome presumption of sanity may be circumscribed by state. — The Supreme Court of the United States has stated that a defendant's efforts to overcome the presumption of sanity may be circumscribed by state prescriptions as to the quantum of proof and legal tests of sanity. Payne v. Slayton, 329 F. Supp. 886 (W.D. Va. 1971).

But due process requires opportunity to raise issue. — Although efforts to overcome the presumption of sanity may be circumscribed by state rules as to the quantum of proof and legal tests of insanity, due process requires that a state shall afford the accused adequate opportunity to raise the issue. Graham v. Gathright, 345 F. Supp. 1148 (W.D. Va. 1972).

Before indigent defendant is entitled to psychiatric assistance, he must make a threshold showing to the trial court that his sanity is likely to be a significant factor in his defense. Tuggle v. Commonwealth, 230 Va. 99, 334 S.E.2d 838 (1985), cert. denied, 478 U.S. 1010, 106 S. Ct. 3309, 92 L. Ed. 2d 722 (1986).

Evidence supported the trial court's finding of competency. — Credible evidence supported the trial court's finding of competency, and the appeals court would not disturb it on appeal; a hospital treatment team submitted a report stating that defendant was competent to be sentenced, and two of the doctors involved in the report pointed out that the dissociative episodes defendant demonstrated were generally quite brief, lasting from just five to six minutes. Orndorff v. Commonwealth, 45 Va. App. 822, 613 S.E.2d 876, 2005 Va. App. LEXIS 288 (2005), aff'd in part, rev'd in

part, 2006 Va. LEXIS 43 (Va. 2006).

Finding that defendant was competent to stand trial was supported by evidence that defendant understood the nature of the proceedings against defendant, had substantial capacity to meaningfully participate in defendant's defense should defendant have chosen to do so, and was capable of understanding the consequences of defendant's failure to cooperate with the Commonwealth's mental health expert's efforts to evaluate defendant. Grattan v. Commonwealth, 2008 Va. App. LEXIS 516 (Nov. 25, 2008), aff'd, 278 Va. 602, 685 S.E.2d 634, 2009 Va. LEXIS 103 (2009).

IV. PRACTICE AND PROCEDURE.

Proof of reasonable ground for questioning mental capacity entitles a person to a preliminary inquiry upon his mental capability to understand the nature of the charge against him and to assist in his defense. Owsley v. Peyton, 368 F.2d 1002 (4th Cir. 1966).

Hearing contemplated. — Former § 19.2-169 contemplated that the court would rule on the suggestion "after hearing evidence." Hawks v. Peyton, 370 F.2d 123 (4th Cir. 1966), cert. denied, 387 U.S. 925, 87 S. Ct. 2044, 18 L. Ed. 2d 982 (1967).

Presence of accused at hearing. — If the personal presence of the party sought to be committed is required at any hearing prescribed, it will present grave difficulties with respect to many suspected mentally ill persons accused of crime, and will, in effect, prejudice the rights of an accused, as many such persons are not in condition to appear in court. Timmons v. Peyton, 240 F. Supp. 749 (E.D. Va. 1965), rev'd on other grounds, 360 F.2d 327 (4th Cir.), cert. denied, 385 U.S. 960, 87 S. Ct. 396, 17 L. Ed. 2d 305 (1966).

Precommitment hearing does not decide issue of competency. — The precommitment hearing does not decide the issue of competency, but rather the existence of reason to believe that the defendant may be incompetent. McLaughlin v. Royster, 346 F. Supp. 297 (E.D. Va. 1972).

Separate hearing on issue of sanity was unjustified where the court, upon the concurrence of two qualified psychologists, considered defendant mentally competent to stand trial for murder, and the jury affirmed such a conclusion. Wilson v. Cox, 312 F. Supp. 209 (W.D. Va. 1970).

The report from the hospital does not conclude the issue of competency. Counsel has a duty to explore the matter further and adduce evidence in court, when there is reason for doubt as to the mental condition of the accused. McLaughlin v. Royster, 346 F. Supp. 297 (E.D. Va. 1972).

Effective assistance of counsel. — If reasonable grounds exist for questioning the sanity or competency of a defendant and counsel fails to explore the matter, the defendant has been denied effective assistance of counsel. Wood v. Zahradnick, 430 F. Supp. 107 (E.D. Va. 1977), aff'd, 578 F.2d 980 (4th Cir. 1978).

Where the facts known or reasonably ascertainable by counsel prior to trial were sufficient to inject the issues of whether the defendant was incompetent to stand trial or whether he was not responsible for his acts in the case, counsel had an affirmative obligation to make suitable inquiry to determine whether these defenses could be advanced. Counsel's failure to do so rendered his assistance ineffective within the meaning of the sixth amendment. Wood v. Zahradnick, 430 F. Supp. 107 (E.D. Va. 1977), aff'd, 578 F.2d 980 (4th Cir. 1978).

The defense attorney's failure to explore the mental condition of his client deprived his client of his right to effective assistance of counsel where the trial was certain to result in his conviction unless an insanity defense prevailed and where the circumstances suggested such a defense. Wood v. Zahradnick, 578 F.2d 980 (4th Cir. 1978).

The failure of the defendant's lawyer to explore the matter and adduce evidence in court where there was reason for doubt as to the mental condition of the accused constituted a denial of his right to effective assistance of counsel. Kibert v. Peyton, 383 F.2d 566 (4th Cir. 1967).

Defense of incompetency cannot be waived. — The defense of incompetency to stand trial cannot be waived by the incompetent, and his counsel cannot waive it for him by failing to move for examination of his competency. Kibert v. Peyton, 383 F.2d 566 (4th Cir. 1967).

The due process right to face trial only while capable of understanding and assisting in the proceedings is not subject to waiver. McLaughlin v. Royster, 346 F. Supp. 297 (E.D. Va. 1972).

Effect of evaluation request on speedy trial right. — Where record clearly indicated that the substantial delay of trial was occasioned by defendant's motion for an evaluation pursuant to this section and his conduct in relation to the evaluation, i.e., waiting almost five months to supply information necessary for the examination to commence, no denial of speedy trial occurred. Jones v. Commonwealth, 13 Va. App. 566, 414 S.E.2d 193 (1992).

While defendant argued that the tolling of the statutory speedy trial period ended when the doctor who evaluated him issued her report opining that defendant was competent to stand trial, the court rejected this, concluding that, pursuant to subsection E of § 19.2-169.1, only the court, not the evaluator, could determine whether a criminal defendant was competent to stand trial. Although the trial court did not make a competency determination until eight months after the doctor issued her report, this did not violate the statutory mandate to promptly determine whether defendant was competent to stand trial as subsection E of § 19.2-169.1 required the trial court to promptly determine a defendant's competency only after receiving the evaluator's report concerning a defendant's competency, and the trial court made a competency decision two months after receiving the report, which had been sent to the wrong court initially. Brown v. Commonwealth, 57 Va. App. 381, 702 S.E.2d 582, 2010 Va. App. LEXIS 490 (2010).

Defendant may subsequently raise defense of insanity at time of offense. — Even if the trial court determines that the accused has the capacity to stand trial, he is not precluded from, and must be given the opportunity of, raising a defense of insanity at the time of the commission of the offense. Graham v. Gathright, 345 F. Supp. 1148 (W.D. Va. 1972).

On habeas corpus a federal court may, in its discretion, entertain and consider a review of the issue of insanity at the time of trial, even where the state court has previously determined the same issue after hearing. It is not, however, required to do so. Owsley v. Cunningham, 190 F. Supp. 608 (E.D. Va. 1961).

Where no hearing has ever been had in any state court proceeding on the issue of insanity at the time of trial, either at or immediately prior to the trial on the merits or by way of post-conviction remedies in the state court, it seems appropriate that a federal court should grant a plenary hearing. Owsley v. Cunningham, 190 F. Supp. 608 (E.D. Va. 1961).

While the provisions of former §§ 19.2-169 and 19.2-170 were discretionary, the failure of the trial court to exercise such discretion, while reviewable on direct appeal in the event of a clear abuse of judicial discretion, did not preclude the accused from proving his lack of mental capacity under his plea of not guilty, and the jury could find the accused not guilty by reason of insanity. The trial court, in exercising its discretion by denying the motion to commit, conducted a hearing on the reasonable necessity of such commitment for observation and report. Any error of the state court in evaluating the issue of mental competency would not go to jurisdiction; it is only the denial of the opportunity to tender the issue of insanity which affords the right to present the issue of insanity in habeas corpus proceedings. Owsley v. Cunningham, 190 F. Supp. 608 (E.D. Va. 1961).

Since due process entitled an accused to have the matter of sanity thoroughly canvassed and the Commonwealth provided the means for it, a federal court was obliged to scrutinize the procedures by which an accused's claim was rejected. Thomas v. Cunningham, 313 F.2d 934 (4th Cir. 1963).

Petition for habeas corpus on the grounds of alleged insanity at the time of trial was entertained by a federal court even though the petitioner never took a direct appeal from his convictions. Thomas v. Cunningham, 313 F.2d 934 (4th Cir. 1963).

When the opportunity to raise the issue of the defendant's sanity has been provided, a federal court in a habeas corpus proceeding need not inquire again into the mental fitness of the state prisoner. Hodnett v. Slayton, 343 F. Supp. 1142 (W.D. Va. 1972), appeal dismissed, 471 F.2d 648 (4th Cir. 1973).

Where the issue is insanity at the time of trial, a federal court is obliged to examine the procedures by which this claim was rejected, but it is not required to review the merits of the determination where the State has done so. Graham v. Gathright, 345 F. Supp. 1148 (W.D. Va. 1972).

Under the rule governing federal habeas corpus proceedings, a federal district court cannot rely upon the state court's findings as sufficient basis to decide a defendant's claim of incompetence to stand trial where no specific finding of fact was made by the state court as to petitioner's condition when he was tried, and where the ruling against petitioner was apparently based upon a restrictive rule of the relevance of evidence, which kept the state court from deciding the central issue of competency. McLaughlin v. Royster, 346 F. Supp. 297 (E.D. Va. 1972).

On the issue of the competency of a petitioner to stand trial, he has the right to a federal hearing. McLaughlin v. Royster, 346 F. Supp. 297 (E.D. Va. 1972).

Liability for expenses where hospitalized under Title 37.2. — A person is liable for the expenses of his care, treatment, and maintenance when confined to a state hospital pursuant to former Title 37.1 [now Title 37.2], even though he previously had been confined to the facility pursuant to former § 19.2-169 as a person charged with crime. Commonwealth, Dep't of Mental Health & Mental Retardation v. Jenkins, 224 Va. 456, 297 S.E.2d 692 (1982).

Appointment on prior occasions did not preclude status as "independent" psychiatrist. — Doctor was not precluded from being an "independent" psychiatrist simply because he had been appointed by the court on prior occasions. Hogan v. Commonwealth, 5 Va. App. 36, 360 S.E.2d 371 (1987).

Ordering of examination not a finding of probable cause. — Where the court ordered the psychiatric examination solely because "this is a capital murder case," the court did not, merely by ordering the psychiatric examination pursuant to §§ 19.2-169.1 and 19.2-169.5, as a matter of law, find probable cause. Tuggle v. Commonwealth, 230 Va. 99, 334 S.E.2d 838 (1985), cert. denied, 478 U.S. 1010, 106 S. Ct. 3309, 92 L. Ed. 2d 722 (1986).

Withdrawal of notice of intent did not moot issue of error in denying motion for psychiatric assistance. — The issue of whether the court erred in denying defendant's pre-trial motion for independent psychiatric assistance was not moot, where defendant withdrew his notice of intent to rely on an insanity defense because of his belief that he had not been given sufficient opportunity to develop evidence of his mental state at the time of the offense. Hogan v. Commonwealth, 5 Va. App. 36, 360 S.E.2d 371 (1987).

Issue of whether defendant met burden not addressed on appeal where psychiatrist provided. — It is not necessary to address the issue on appeal whether defendant carried the threshold burden required in Ake v. Oklahoma, 470 U.S. 68, 105 S. Ct. 1087, 84 L. Ed. 2d 53 (1985), where the trial court did, in fact, provide him with the services of an independent psychiatrist. Hogan v. Commonwealth, 5 Va. App. 36, 360 S.E.2d 371 (1987).

Erroneous burden shifting. — With regard to defendant's conviction for murder and the affirmation of the denial of defendant's motion for a new trial based on after-discovered evidence, the trial court erred by concluding that defendant failed to meet her burden of proving reasonable diligence as to the alleged new evidence that she suffered from dissociative identity disorder to support an insanity defense, which was not asserted by her at trial, as the trial court improperly shifted the focus of the reasonable diligence inquiry by effectively assigning to defendant's counsel the responsibility for reaching a different medical diagnosis. Error was also found by the trial court misapplying the materiality standard since it should have made its own determination of the materiality of the alleged new evidence instead of relying upon the jury's rejection of defendant's mitigation evidence presented during the sentencing phase of defendant's trial. Orndorff v. Commonwealth, 271 Va. 486, 628 S.E.2d 344, 2006 Va. LEXIS 43 (2006).

Rehearing not required. — The trial court properly denied the defendant's motion for a new preliminary hearing, as there was no probable cause to believe that he lacked substantial capacity to understand the proceedings against him or to assist his attorney in his own defense where he made numerous appearances before both the general district and circuit courts prior to the preliminary hearing, appropriately participated in such proceedings and failed to raise the issue of competency, either through counsel or otherwise. Stoneman v. Commonwealth, No. 3069-96-3 (Ct. of Appeals June 9, 1998).

CIRCUIT COURT OPINIONS

Effect of evaluation request on speedy trial right. — Defendant's motion to dismiss an indictment charging him with murder on the ground that his right to a speedy trial under § 19.2-243 had been violated was denied because the speedy trial clock could not have resumed running based solely upon the issuance of a competency report, and until the circuit court determined the issue of defendant's competency, no trial could take place; it is the circuit court, not the Commissioner of Mental Health, Mental Retardation and Substance Abuse Services, which determines a defendant's competency to stand trial. Commonwealth v. Brown, 2009 Va. Cir. LEXIS 56 (Fairfax Aug. 10, 2009).

OPINIONS OF THE ATTORNEY GENERAL

Competency evaluation report ordered by and submitted to a court as part of the court's record is open to inspection under § 17.1-208, provided such report is not sealed by court order. See opinion of Attorney General to The Honorable George E. Schaefer, Clerk of Norfolk Circuit Court, 08-099, 2009 Va. AG LEXIS 13 (2/25/09).

§ 19.2-169.2. Disposition when defendant found incompetent.

A. Upon finding pursuant to subsection E of § 19.2-169.1 that the defendant, including a juvenile transferred pursuant to § 16.1-269.1, is incompetent, the court shall order that the defendant receive treatment to restore his competency on an outpatient basis or, if the court specifically finds that the defendant requires inpatient hospital treatment, at a hospital designated by the Commissioner of Behavioral Health and Developmental Services as appropriate for treatment of persons under criminal charge. Any reports submitted pursuant to subsection D of § 19.2-169.1 shall be made available to the director of the community services board or behavioral health authority or his designee or to the director of the treating inpatient facility or his designee.

B. If, at any time after the defendant is ordered to undergo treatment under subsection A of this section, the director of the community services board or behavioral health authority or his designee or the director of the treating inpatient facility or his designee believes the defendant's competency is restored, the director or his designee shall immediately send a report to the court as prescribed in subsection D of § 19.2-169.1. The court shall make a ruling on the defendant's competency according to the procedures specified in subsection E of § 19.2-169.1.

C. The clerk of court shall certify and forward forthwith to the Central Criminal Records Exchange, on a form provided by the Exchange, a copy of an order for treatment issued pursuant to subsection A.

History.

1982, c. 653; 2003, c. 735; 2007, c. 781; 2008, cc. 751, 788; 2009, cc. 813, 840.

The 2007 amendments.

The 2007 amendment by c. 781, in subsection A, inserted "to the director of the community services board or behavioral health authority or his designee or" and "inpatient" following "of the treating," and added "or his designee" to the end in the last sentence; and, in subsection B, substituted "community services

board or behavioral health authority or his designee or the director of the treating inpatient facility or his designee" for "treatment facility."

The 2008 amendments.

The 2008 amendments by cc. 751 and 788 are identical and added subsection C.

The 2009 amendments.

The 2009 amendments by cc. 813 and 840 are identical, and substituted "Behavioral Health and Developmental Services" for "Mental Health, Mental Retardation and Substance Abuse Services" in subsection A.

Law Review.

For annual survey article on legal issues involving children, see 38 U. Rich. L. Rev. 161 (2003).

CASE NOTES

Applied in Burns v. Commonwealth, 279 Va. 243, 688 S.E.2d 263, 2010 Va. LEXIS 19 (2010).

CIRCUIT COURT OPINIONS

Effect of evaluation request on speedy trial right. — Defendant's motion to dismiss an indictment charging him with murder on the ground that his right to a speedy trial under § 19.2-243 had been violated was denied because the speedy trial clock could not have resumed running based solely upon the issuance of a competency report, and until the circuit court determined the issue of defendant's competency, no trial could take place; it is the circuit court, not the Commissioner of Mental Health, Mental Retardation and Substance Abuse Services, which determines a defendant's competency to stand trial. Commonwealth v. Brown, 2009 Va. Cir. LEXIS 56 (Fairfax Aug. 10, 2009).

OPINIONS OF THE ATTORNEY GENERAL

Involuntary treatment of individuals in jail. — A local court in limited circumstances may issue an order under subsection A of this section or § 19.2-169.3 authorizing the superintendent of a regional jail to force an individual in custody to take prescribed medication for treatment of mental illness. Further, the court having jurisdiction over such individual's trial may enter such an order to restore competency pursuant to those provisions. Additionally, when a court previously has entered an order to restore competency, any court with jurisdiction may enter the order pursuant to § 37.2-1101, as limited by § 37.2-1102(3). See opinion of Attorney General to The Honorable William J. Howell, Speaker, House of Delegates, 07-006 (9/20/07).

§ 19.2-169.3. Disposition of the unrestorably incompetent defendant; capital murder charge; sexually violent offense charge.

A. If, at any time after the defendant is ordered to undergo treatment pursuant to subsection A of § 19.2-169.2, the director of the community services board or behavioral health authority or his designee or the director of the treating inpatient facility or his designee concludes that the defendant is likely to remain incompetent for the foreseeable future, he shall send a report to the court so stating. The report shall also indicate whether, in the board, authority, or inpatient facility director's or his designee's opinion, the defendant should be released, committed pursuant to Article 5 (§ 37.2-814 et seq.) of Chapter

8 of Title 37.2, committed pursuant to Chapter 9 (§ 37.2-900 et seq.) of Title 37.2, or certified pursuant to § 37.2-806 in the event he is found to be unrestorably incompetent. Upon receipt of the report, the court shall make a competency determination according to the procedures specified in subsection E of § 19.2-169.1. If the court finds that the defendant is incompetent and is likely to remain so for the foreseeable future, it shall order that he be (i) released, (ii) committed pursuant to Article 5 (§ 37.2-814 et seq.) of Chapter 8 of Title 37.2, or (iii) certified pursuant to § 37.2-806. However, if the court finds that the defendant is incompetent and is likely to remain so for the foreseeable future and the defendant has been charged with a sexually violent offense, as defined in § 37.2-900, he shall be screened pursuant to the procedures set forth in §§ 37.2-903 and 37.2-904. If the court finds the defendant incompetent but restorable to competency in the foreseeable future, it may order treatment continued until six months have elapsed from the date of the defendant's initial admission under subsection A of § 19.2-169.2.

B. At the end of six months from the date of the defendant's initial admission under subsection A of § 19.2-169.2 if the defendant remains incompetent in the opinion of the board, authority, or inpatient facility director or his designee, the director or his designee shall so notify the court and make recommendations concerning disposition of the defendant as described in subsection A. The court shall hold a hearing according to the procedures specified in subsection E of § 19.2-169.1 and, if it finds the defendant unrestorably incompetent, shall order one of the dispositions described in subsection A. If the court finds the defendant incompetent but restorable to competency, it may order continued treatment under subsection A of § 19.2-169.2 for additional six-month periods, provided a hearing pursuant to subsection E of § 19.2-169.1 is held at the completion of each such period and the defendant continues to be incompetent but restorable to competency in the foreseeable future.

C. If any defendant has been charged with a misdemeanor in violation of Article 3 (§ 18.2-95 et seq.) of Chapter 5 of Title 18.2 or Article 5 (§ 18.2-119 et seq.) of Chapter 5 of Title 18.2, other than a misdemeanor charge pursuant to § 18.2-130 or Article 2 (§ 18.2-415 et seq.) of Chapter 9 of Title 18.2, and is being treated pursuant to subsection A of § 19.2-169.2, and after 45 days has not been restored to competency, the director of the community service board, behavioral health authority, or the director of the treating inpatient facility, or any of their designees, shall send a report indicating the defendant's status to the court. The report shall also indicate whether the defendant should be released or committed pursuant to § 37.2-817 or certified pursuant to § 37.2-806. Upon receipt of the report, if the court determines that the defendant is still incompetent, the court shall order that the defen-

dant be released, committed, or certified, and may dismiss the charges against the defendant.

D. Unless an incompetent defendant is charged with capital murder or the charges against an incompetent criminal defendant have been previously dismissed, charges against an unrestorably incompetent defendant shall be dismissed on the date upon which his sentence would have expired had he been convicted and received the maximum sentence for the crime charged, or on the date five years from the date of his arrest for such charges, whichever is sooner.

E. If the court orders an unrestorably incompetent defendant to be screened pursuant to the procedures set forth in §§ 37.2-903 and 37.2-904, it shall order the attorney for the Commonwealth in the jurisdiction wherein the defendant was charged and the Commissioner of Behavioral Health and Developmental Services to provide the Director of the Department of Corrections with any information relevant to the review, including, but not limited to: (i) a copy of the warrant or indictment, (ii) a copy of the defendant's criminal record, (iii) information about the alleged crime, (iv) a copy of the competency report completed pursuant to § 19.2-169.1, and (v) a copy of the report prepared by the director of the defendant's community services board, behavioral health authority, or treating inpatient facility or his designee pursuant to this section. The court shall further order that the defendant be held in the custody of the Department of Behavioral Health and Developmental Services for secure confinement and treatment until the Commitment Review Committee's and Attorney General's review and any subsequent hearing or trial are completed. If the court receives notice that the Attorney General has declined to file a petition for the commitment of an unrestorably incompetent defendant as a sexually violent predator after conducting a review pursuant to § 37.2-905, the court shall order that the defendant be released, committed pursuant to Article 5 (§ 37.2-814 et seq.) of Chapter 8 of Title 37.2, or certified pursuant to § 37.2-806.

F. In any case when an incompetent defendant is charged with capital murder, notwithstanding any other provision of this section, the charge shall not be dismissed and the court having jurisdiction over the capital murder case may order that the defendant receive continued treatment under subsection A of § 19.2-169.2 for additional six-month periods without limitation, provided that (i) a hearing pursuant to subsection E of § 19.2-169.1 is held at the completion of each such period, (ii) the defendant remains incompetent, (iii) the court finds continued treatment to be medically appropriate, and (iv) the defendant presents a danger to himself or others.

G. The attorney for the Commonwealth may bring charges that have been dismissed against the defendant when he is restored to competency.

History.
1982, c. 653; 1999, cc. 946, 985; 2003, cc. 915, 919, 989, cls. 4, 5,

1018, cls. 4, 5, 1042, cls. 10, 11; 2006, cc. 863, 914; 2007, cc. 781, 876; 2008, cc. 406, 796; 2009, cc. 813, 840; 2012, cc. 668, 800.

Editor's note.

Acts 1999, cc. 946 and 985, cl. 3, as amended by Acts 2000, c. 1024, and Acts 2001, c. 776, cl. 3, had provided that the amendments by Acts 1999, cc. 946 and 985 would be effective July 1, 2003.

Acts 2002, c. 899, Items 49 C and 331 C 1, prior to amendment by Acts 2003, c. 1042, had provided: "The effective date of Chapters 946 and 985 of the 1999 Acts of Assembly, which establishes the civil commitment and treatment of sexual predators, is postponed to January 1, 2004."

Acts 2002, c. 899, and Acts 2003, c. 1042, in Item 49 E, provide: "E. The Attorney General shall review the decision of the U.S. Supreme Court in the case of Kansas v. Crane, decided on January 22, 2002, and determine what effect this decision may have on the implementation of Chapters 946 and 985 of the Acts of Assembly of 1999. The Attorney General shall make a report of his review, including any recommended changes to this legislation, to the Governor and the General Assembly by September 1, 2002."

Acts 2003, cc. 989 and 1018, cl. 3, provide: "That an emergency exists and this act is in force from its passage [April 2, 2003], notwithstanding the provisions of Items 49 C and 331 C1 of Chapter 899 of the Acts of Assembly of 2002."

Acts 2003, cc. 989 and 1018, cl. 4, provide: "That, notwithstanding the provisions of Items 49 C and 331 C1 of Chapter 899 of the Acts of Assembly of 2002, the provisions of Chapters 946 and 985, as they may be amended, of the Acts of Assembly of 1999 shall become effective on the effective date of this act [April 2, 2003.]"

Acts 2003, cc. 989 and 1018, cl. 5, provide: "That the third enactments of Chapter 946 and Chapter 985, as amended, of the Acts of Assembly of 1999 are amended and reenacted as follows: "3. That the effective date of this act is the date of enactment of House Bill 1400, House Bill 2445 or Senate Bill 1149 of the 2003 General Assembly Session, whichever is the first to be enacted. "3. That the effective date of this act is the date of enactment of House Bill 1400, House Bill 2445 or Senate Bill 1149 of the 2003 General Assembly Session, whichever is the first to be enacted."

Acts 2003, c. 1042, cls. 10 and 11, also amended cl. 3 of Acts 1999, cc. 946 and 985, in an identical fashion.

Acts 2002, c. 899, as amended by Acts 2003, c. 1042, in Items 59 C 1 and 331 C 1, provide that the provisions of Title 37.1, Chapter 2, Article 1.1 "shall be effective upon passage of House Bill 2445 of the 2003 General Assembly Session, Senate Bill 1149 of the 2003 General Assembly Session, or this act, whichever is first to be enacted." See also Acts 2002, c. 899, Item 421 H, as added by Acts 2003, c. 1042.

House Bill 2445 (Chapter 989) and Senate Bill 1149 (Chapter 1018) of the 2003 General Assembly were enacted on April 2, 2003, the date they were approved by the Governor.

Acts 2012, cc. 668 and 800, cl. 2 provides: "That the Director, in coordination with the Department, shall develop protocols to assess whether the individual meets the definition of a sexually violent predator and shall report to the General Assembly on protocol objectives, design, methodology, statistical considerations, embedded assumptions, risk assessments, and organization of the full assessment process. All measures shall be consistent with evidenced-based best practices. The primary tool of the protocols shall be a risk assessment instrument and corresponding reference score designated by the Commissioner. The Director shall submit the report to the Governor and the General Assembly by January 1, 2013."

Acts 2012, cc. 668 and 800, cl. 3 provides: "That the provisions of this act shall become effective on January 1, 2013."

The 2007 amendments.

The 2007 amendment by c. 781 inserted "or his designee" throughout; in subsection A, inserted "the director of the community services board or behavioral health authority" and "inpatient" following "director of the treating"; inserted "board, authority, or inpatient facility" in subsections A and B; and substituted "community services board, behavioral health authority, or treating inpatient facility" for "treating facility" in subsection D.

The 2007 amendment by c. 876, in subsection A, deleted "reviewed for commitment pursuant to Chapter 9 (§ 37.2-900 et seq.) of Title 37.2, or (iv)" following "(iii)," and inserted the second to last sentence.

The 2008 amendments.

The 2008 amendments by cc. 406 and 796 are nearly identical, and inserted subsection C and redesignated former subsections C through F as subsections D through G.

The 2009 amendments.

The 2009 amendments by cc. 813 and 840 are identical, and substituted "Behavioral Health and Developmental Services" for "Mental Health, Mental Retardation and Substance Abuse Services" twice in subsection E.

The 2012 amendments.

The 2012 amendment by c. 668, effective January 1, 2013, substituted "he shall be screened pursuant to the procedures set forth in §§ 37.2-903 and 37.2-904" for "he shall be reviewed for commitment pursuant to Chapter 9 (§ 37.2-900 et seq.) of Title 37.2" at the end of the fifth sentence of subsection A, and substituted "provide the Director of the Department of Corrections with" for "provide the Commitment Review Committee established pursuant to § 37.2-902 with" in the first sentence of subsection E.

The 2012 amendment by c. 800, effective January 1, 2013, made the same amendments as c. 668 and in addition, substituted "screened pursuant to the procedures set forth in §§ 37.2-903 and 37.2-904" for "reviewed for commitment pursuant to § 37.2-904" in subsection E.

Law Review.

For note, "Law and Morality 'Unspeakable Justice': The Oswaldo Martinez Case and the Failure of the Legal System to Adequately Provide for Incompetent Defendants," see 48 Wm. & Mary L. Rev. 2075 (2007).

CASE NOTES

Liability for expenses when hospitalized under Title 37.2. — A person is liable for the expenses of his care, treatment, and maintenance when confined to a state hospital pursuant to Title 37.1 [now Title 37.2], even though he previously had been confined to the facility pursuant to former § 19.2-169 as a person charged with crime. Commonwealth, Dep't of Mental Health & Mental Retardation v. Jenkins, 224 Va. 456, 297 S.E.2d 692 (1982).

Sufficiency of the evidence. — Evidence was sufficient to support the civil commitment of an inmate as a sexually violent predator because the inmate was incarcerated upon a conviction for a sexually violent offense, the inmate was clearly diagnosed with the mental abnormality of pedophilia by experts, and there was clear and convincing evidence that because of his mental abnormality the inmate found it difficult to control his predatory behavior, which made it likely that he would engage in sexually violent acts. Shivaee v. Commonwealth, 270 Va. 112, 613 S.E.2d 570, 2005 Va. LEXIS 68, cert. denied, 546 U.S. 1005, 126 S. Ct. 626, 163 L. Ed. 2d 509 (2005).

CIRCUIT COURT OPINIONS

Second grand jury indictment following release from hospital permitted. — Defendant first indicted capital murder and robbery was found to be mentally incompetent and confined to a state hospital, accordingly the indictment was dismissed; however, later indictment for the same crimes obtained upon the defendant's release from the hospital could not be dismissed on the ground of the passage of time. Commonwealth v. Sink, 61 Va. Cir. 279, 2003 Va. Cir. LEXIS 18 (Portsmouth 2003).

OPINIONS OF THE ATTORNEY GENERAL

Involuntary treatment of individuals in jail. — A local court in limited circumstances may issue an order under subsection A of § 19.2-169.2 or this section authorizing the superintendent of a regional jail to force an individual in custody to take prescribed medication for treatment of mental illness. Further, the court having jurisdiction over such individual's trial may enter such an order to restore competency pursuant to those provisions. Additionally, when a court previously has entered an order to restore competency, any court with jurisdiction may enter the order pursuant to § 37.2-1101, as limited by § 37.2-1102(3). See opinion of Attorney General to The Honorable William J. Howell, Speaker, House of Delegates, 07-006 (9/20/07).

§ 19.2-169.4. Litigating certain issues when the defendant is incompetent.

A finding of incompetency does not preclude the adjudication, at any time before trial, of a motion objecting to the sufficiency of the indictment, nor does it preclude the adjudication of similar legal objections which, in the court's opinion, may be undertaken without the personal participation of the defendant.

History.
1982, c. 653.

§ 19.2-169.5. Evaluation of sanity at the time of the offense; disclosure of evaluation results.

A. Raising issue of sanity at the time of offense; appointment of evaluators. — If, at any time before trial, the court finds, upon hearing evidence or representations of counsel for the defendant, that there is probable cause to believe that the defendant's sanity will be a significant factor in his defense and that the defendant is financially unable to pay for expert assistance, the court shall appoint one or more qualified mental health experts to evaluate the defendant's sanity at the time of the offense and, where appropriate, to assist in the development of an insanity defense. Such mental health expert shall be (i) a psychiatrist, a clinical psychologist, or an individual with a doctorate degree in clinical psychology who has successfully completed forensic evaluation training as approved by the Commissioner of Behavioral Health and Developmental Services and (ii) qualified by specialized training and experience to perform forensic evaluations. The defendant shall not be entitled to a mental health expert of his own choosing or to funds to employ such expert.

B. Location of evaluation. — The evaluation shall be performed on an outpatient basis, at a mental health facility or in jail, unless the court specifically finds that outpatient services are unavailable, or unless the results of the outpatient evaluation indicate that hospitalization of the defendant for further evaluation of his sanity at the time of the offense is necessary. If either finding is made, the court, under authority of this subsection, may order that the defendant be sent to a hospital designated by the Commissioner of Behavioral Health and Developmental Services as appropriate for evaluation of the defendant under criminal charge. The defendant shall be hospitalized for such time as the director of the hospital deems necessary to perform an adequate evaluation of the defendant's sanity at the time of the offense, but not to exceed 30 days from the date of admission to the hospital.

C. Provision of information to evaluator. — The court shall require the party making the motion for the evaluation, and such other parties as the court deems appropriate, to provide to the evaluators appointed under subsection A any information relevant to the evaluation, including, but not limited to (i) copy of the warrant or indictment; (ii) the names and addresses of the attorney for the Commonwealth, the attorney for the defendant and the judge who appointed the expert; (iii) information pertaining to the alleged crime, including statements by the defendant made to the police and transcripts of preliminary hearings, if any; (iv) a summary of the reasons for the evaluation request; (v) any available psychiatric, psychological, medical or social records that are deemed relevant; and (vi) a copy of the defendant's criminal record, to the extent reasonably available.

D. The evaluators shall prepare a full report concerning the defendant's sanity at the time of the offense, including whether he may have had a significant mental disease or defect which rendered him insane at the time of the offense. The report shall be prepared within the time period designated by the court, said period to include the time necessary to obtain and evaluate the information specified in subsection C.

E. Disclosure of evaluation results. — The report described in subsection D shall be sent solely to the attorney for the defendant and shall be deemed to be protected by the lawyer-client privilege. However, the Commonwealth shall be given the report in all felony cases, the results of any other evaluation of the defendant's sanity at the time of the offense, and copies of psychiatric, psychological, medical, or other records obtained during the course of any such evaluation, after the attorney for the defendant gives notice of an intent to present psychiatric or psychological evidence pursuant to § 19.2-168.

F. In any case where the defendant obtains his own expert to evaluate the defendant's sanity at the time of the offense, the provisions of subsections D and E, relating to the disclosure of the evaluation results, shall apply.

History.
1982, c. 653; 1986, c. 535; 1987, c. 439; 1996, cc. 937, 980; 2005, c. 428; 2009, cc. 813, 840.

The 2009 amendments.
The 2009 amendments by cc. 813 and 840 are identical and substituted "Behavioral Health and Developmental Services" for "Mental Health, Mental Retardation and Substance Abuse Services" in subsections A and B.

Law Review.
For comment on the insanity defense in Virginia, see 17 U. Rich. L. Rev. 129 (1982). For survey of Virginia criminal law and procedure for the year 2004-2005, see 40 U. Rich. L. Rev. 197 (2005).

CASE NOTES

Editor's note.
Many of the cases cited in the following annotations were decided under repealed §§ 19.2-169 and 19.2-170.

Due process requires that State must provide adequate means by which accused can raise issue of insanity at the time of trial and at the commission of the alleged offense. Hodnett v. Slayton, 343 F. Supp. 1142 (W.D. Va. 1972), appeal dismissed, 471 F.2d 648 (4th Cir. 1973).

State must assure indigent defendant access to competent psychiatrist who will conduct an appropriate examination and assist in evaluation, preparation, and presentation of the defense when the defendant demonstrates to the trial judge that his sanity at the time of the offense is to be a significant factor at trial. Tuggle v. Commonwealth, 230 Va. 99, 334 S.E.2d 838 (1985), cert. denied, 478 U.S. 1010, 106 S. Ct. 3309, 92 L. Ed. 2d 722 (1986).

Indigent entitled to psychiatrist in capital case on issue of future dangerousness. — When the prosecution in a capital sentencing proceeding presents psychiatric evidence of an indigent defendant's future dangerousness, due process requires that a state provide the defendant the assistance of a psychiatrist on the issue. Where the Commonwealth presented psychiatric evidence that defendant showed high probability of future dangerousness, even though defendant's trial and direct appeal predated in light of the trial court erred in denying his motion for an independent psychiatrist to rebut the Commonwealth's psychiatric evidence of future dangerousness. Tuggle v. Commonwealth, 230 Va. 99, 334 S.E.2d 838 (1985), cert. denied, 478 U.S. 1010, 106 S. Ct. 3309, 92 L. Ed. 2d 722 (1986).

***Ake v. Oklahoma* to be applied prospectively.** — The rule announced in *Ake v. Oklahoma*, 470 U.S. 68, 105 S. Ct. 1087, 84 L. Ed. 2d 53 (1985) (that due process of law was denied where no psychiatrist was appointed to examine the defendant, to help him prepare his case, to serve as an expert witness for the defense, and to assist in the defense at trial) should be applied only to those cases tried subsequent to Feb. 26, 1985. Snurkowski v. Commonwealth, 2 Va. App. 532, 348 S.E.2d 1 (1986).

Examination by staff clinical psychologist and mental health professionals satisfied requirements. — The trial court correctly ruled that the examination and evaluation of defendant by a staff clinical psychologist and the mental health professionals at Central State Hospital satisfied the requirements of both subsection A and the due process requirements defined in *Ake v. Oklahoma*, 470 U.S. 68, 105 S. Ct. 1087, 84 L. Ed. 2d 53 (1985). Funk v. Commonwealth, 8 Va. App. 91, 379 S.E.2d 371 (1989).

Before indigent defendant is entitled to psychiatric assistance, he must make a threshold showing to the trial court that this sanity is likely to be a significant factor in his defense. Tuggle v. Commonwealth, 230 Va. 99, 334 S.E.2d 838 (1985), cert. denied, 478 U.S. 1010, 106 S. Ct. 3309, 92 L. Ed. 2d 722 (1986).

Right of defendant to raise defense of insanity at time of offense despite competency finding. — Even if the trial court determines that the accused has the capacity to stand trial, he is not precluded from, and must be given the opportunity of, raising a defense of insanity at the time of the commission of the offense. Graham v. Gathright, 345 F. Supp. 1148 (W.D. Va. 1972).

The trial court has the inherent power to require defendant to be examined by a psychiatric committee in order that his examiners might report their opinion as to his sanity at the time of his alleged crimes and testify to such opinion if called by the Commonwealth as rebuttal witnesses. Shifflett v. Commonwealth, 221 Va. 760, 274 S.E.2d 305 (1981).

Commonwealth entitled to other sanity evaluations. — Subsection E of this section clearly provides that the Commonwealth is entitled not only to the report ordered under this section, but also to the results of any other evaluation of the defendant's sanity when notice is given by the defense pursuant to § 19.2-168; subsection E of this section cannot be read as applying only to the report ordered. Blevins v. Commonwealth, 11 Va. App. 429, 399 S.E.2d 173 (1990).

Disclosure of mental health records to the Commonwealth. — Psychiatric, psychological, medical, and other records produced by the mental health experts in the course of fulfilling their court-ordered responsibilities under § 19.2-169.5 are protected under that statute from being disclosed to the Commonwealth until the defendant gives notice pursuant to § 19.2-168. Schwartz v. Commonwealth, 45 Va. App. 407, 611 S.E.2d 631, 2005 Va. App. LEXIS 156 (2005).

Trial court did not abuse its discretion in denying defendant access to a psychologist's testimony and notes and a county mental health center's notes regarding her father's alleged killer, a crime in which defendant was an alleged conspirator, as the Commonwealth would have had access to those documents if they were released to defendant. Schwartz v. Commonwealth, 45 Va. App. 407, 611 S.E.2d 631, 2005 Va. App. LEXIS 156 (2005).

Inquiry into competency to stand trial not limited. — Neither former § 19.2-169 nor former § 19.2-170, though preceded by § 19.2-168 requiring notice of an insanity defense, contained any language expressly or impliedly limiting the committee's (now evaluators') inquiry to competency to stand trial, or forbidding it to go into the question of insanity at the time of the alleged offense. Shifflett v. Commonwealth, 221 Va. 760, 274 S.E.2d 305 (1981).

Burden of proving insanity. — An accused is presumed to be sane at the trial and during the commission of the offense, and it is his burden to prove the contrary. Graham v. Gathright, 345 F. Supp. 1148 (W.D. Va. 1972).

The duty of carrying the burden of proving a defendant's insanity at the time of trial falls upon the petitioner's attorney to present the issue to the court when he has reasonable belief that his client's mental condition is of a nature which may render him incompetent to stand trial and which may also raise a question of his client's sanity at the time of the crime. Payne v. Slayton, 329 F. Supp. 886 (W.D. Va. 1971).

The burden of proof on the issue of insanity rests with the accused. Hodnett v. Slayton, 343 F. Supp. 1142 (W.D. Va. 1972), appeal dismissed, 471 F.2d 648 (4th Cir. 1973).

In Virginia, unlike the federal practice, the burden rests upon the accused to prove his mental incompetency. Timmons v. Peyton, 240 F. Supp. 749 (E.D. Va. 1965), rev'd on other grounds, 360 F.2d 327 (4th Cir.), cert. denied, 385 U.S. 960, 87 S. Ct. 396, 17 L. Ed. 2d 305 (1966).

Ordering of examination not a finding of probable cause. — Where the court ordered the psychiatric examination solely because "this is a capital murder case," the court did not, merely by ordering the psychiatric examination pursuant to § 19.2-169.1 and this section, as a matter of law, find probable cause. Tuggle v. Commonwealth, 230 Va. 99, 334 S.E.2d 838 (1985), cert. denied, 478 U.S. 1010, 106 S. Ct. 3309, 92 L. Ed. 2d 722 (1986).

Effective assistance of counsel. — If reasonable grounds exist for questioning the sanity or competency of a defendant and counsel fails to explore the matter, the defendant has been denied effective assistance of counsel. Wood v. Zahradnick, 430 F. Supp. 107 (E.D. Va. 1977), aff'd, 578 F.2d 980 (4th Cir. 1978).

Where the facts known or reasonably ascertainable by counsel prior to trial were sufficient to inject the issues of whether the defendant was incompetent to stand trial or whether he was not responsible for his acts in the case, counsel had an affirmative obligation to make suitable inquiry to determine whether these defenses could be advanced. Counsel's failure to do so rendered his assistance ineffective within the meaning of the sixth amendment. Wood v. Zahradnick, 430 F. Supp. 107 (E.D. Va. 1977), aff'd, 578 F.2d 980 (4th Cir. 1978).

The defense attorney's failure to explore the mental condition of his client deprived his client of his right to effective assistance of counsel where the trial was certain to result in his conviction unless an insanity defense prevailed and where the circumstances suggested such a defense. Wood v. Zahradnick, 578 F.2d 980 (4th Cir. 1978).

Consideration of insanity in federal habeas proceedings. — While the provisions of former §§ 19.2-169 and 19.2-170 were discretionary, the failure of the trial court to exercise such discretion, while reviewable on direct appeal in the event of a clear abuse of judicial discretion, did not preclude the accused from proving his lack of mental capacity under his plea of not guilty, and the jury could find the accused not guilty by reason of insanity. The trial court, in exercising its discretion by denying the motion to commit, conducted a hearing on the reasonable necessity of such commitment for observation and report. Any error of the state court in evaluating the issue of mental competency would not go to jurisdiction; it is only the denial of the opportunity to tender the issue of insanity which affords the right to present the issue of insanity in habeas corpus proceedings. Owsley v. Cunningham, 190 F. Supp. 608 (E.D. Va. 1961).

§ 19.2-169.6. (Effective until July 1, 2014) Inpatient psychiatric hospital admission from local correctional facility.

A. Any inmate of a local correctional facility who is not subject to the provisions of § 19.2-169.2 may be hospitalized for psychiatric treatment at a hospital designated by the Commissioner of Behavioral Health and Developmental Services as appropriate for treatment of persons under criminal charge if:

1. The court with jurisdiction over the inmate's case, if it is still pending, on the petition of the person having custody over an inmate or on its own motion, holds a hearing at which the inmate is represented by counsel and finds by clear and convincing evidence that (i) the inmate has a mental illness; (ii) there exists a substantial likelihood that, as a result of a mental illness, the inmate will, in the near future, (a) cause serious physical harm to himself or others as evidenced by recent behavior causing, attempting, or threatening harm and any other relevant information or (b) suffer serious harm due to his lack of capacity to protect himself from harm as evidenced by recent behavior and any other relevant information; and (iii) the inmate requires treatment in a hospital rather than the local correctional facility. Prior to making this determination, the court shall consider the examination conducted in accordance with § 37.2-815 and the preadmission screening report prepared in accordance with § 37.2-816 and conducted in-person or by means of a two-way electronic video and audio communication system as authorized in § 37.2-804.1 by an employee or designee of the local community services board or behavioral health authority who is skilled in the assessment and treatment of mental illness, who is not providing treatment to the inmate, and who has completed a certification program approved by the Department of Behavioral Health and Developmental Services as provided in § 37.2-809. The examiner appointed pursuant to § 37.2-815, if not physically present at the hearing, shall be available whenever possible for questioning during the hearing through a two-way electronic video and audio or telephonic communication system as authorized in § 37.2-804.1. Any employee or designee of the local community services board or behavioral health authority, as defined in § 37.2-809, representing the board or authority that prepared the preadmission screening report shall attend the hearing in person or, if physical attendance is not practicable, shall participate in the hearing through a two-way electronic video and audio communication system as authorized in § 37.2-804.1. When the hearing is held outside the service area of the community services board or behavioral health authority that prepared the preadmission screening report, and it is not practicable for a representative of the board or authority to attend or participate in the hearing, arrangements shall be made by the board or authority for an employee or designee of the board or

authority serving the area in which the hearing is held to attend or participate on behalf of the board or authority that prepared the preadmission screening report; or

2. Upon petition by the person having custody over an inmate, a magistrate finds probable cause to believe that (i) the inmate has a mental illness; (ii) there exists a substantial likelihood that, as a result of a mental illness, the inmate will, in the near future, (a) cause serious physical harm to himself or others as evidenced by recent behavior causing, attempting, or threatening harm and any other relevant information or (b) suffer serious harm due to his lack of capacity to protect himself from harm as evidenced by recent behavior and any other relevant information; and (iii) the inmate requires treatment in a hospital rather than a local correctional facility, and the magistrate issues a temporary detention order for the inmate. Prior to the filing of the petition, the person having custody shall arrange for an evaluation of the inmate conducted in-person or by means of a two-way electronic video and audio communication system as authorized in § 37.2-804.1 by an employee or designee of the local community services board or behavioral health authority who is skilled in the assessment and treatment of mental illness and who has completed a certification program approved by the Department as provided in § 37.2-809. After considering the evaluation of the employee or designee of the local community services board or behavioral health authority, and any other information presented, and finding that probable cause exists to meet the criteria, the magistrate may issue a temporary detention order in accordance with the applicable procedures specified in §§ 37.2-809 through 37.2-813. The person having custody over the inmate shall notify the court having jurisdiction over the inmate's case, if it is still pending, and the inmate's attorney prior to the detention pursuant to a temporary detention order or as soon thereafter as is reasonable.

Upon detention pursuant to this subdivision, a hearing shall be held either before the court having jurisdiction over the inmate's case or before a district court judge or a special justice, as defined in § 37.2-100, in accordance with the provisions of §§ 37.2-815 through 37.2-821, in which case the inmate shall be represented by counsel as specified in § 37.2-814. The hearing shall be held within 48 hours of execution of the temporary detention order issued pursuant to this subdivision. If the 48-hour period terminates on a Saturday, Sunday, legal holiday, or day on which the court is lawfully closed, the inmate may be detained until the close of business on the next day that is not a Saturday, Sunday, legal holiday, or day on which the court is lawfully closed. Any employee or designee of the local community services board or behavioral health authority, as defined in § 37.2-809, representing the board or authority that prepared the preadmission screening report shall attend the hearing in person or, if physical attendance is not practicable, shall participate in the hearing through a two-way electronic video and audio communication system as authorized in § 37.2-804.1. When the hearing is held outside the service area of the community services board or behavioral health authority that prepared the preadmission screening report, and it is not practicable for a representative of the board or authority to attend or participate in the hearing, arrangements shall be made by the board or authority for an employee or designee of the board or authority serving the area in which the hearing is held to attend or participate on behalf of the board or authority that prepared the preadmission screening report. The judge or special justice conducting the hearing may order the inmate hospitalized if, after considering the examination conducted in accordance with § 37.2-815, the preadmission screening report prepared in accordance with § 37.2-816, and any other available information as specified in subsection C of § 37.2-817, he finds by clear and convincing evidence that (1) the inmate has a mental illness; (2) there exists a substantial likelihood that, as a result of a mental illness, the inmate will, in the near future, (a) cause serious physical harm to himself or others as evidenced by recent behavior causing, attempting, or threatening harm and any other relevant information or (b) suffer serious harm due to his lack of capacity to protect himself from harm as evidenced by recent behavior and any other relevant information; and (3) the inmate requires treatment in a hospital rather than a local correctional facility. The examiner appointed pursuant to § 37.2-815, if not physically present at the hearing, shall be available whenever possible for questioning during the hearing through a two-way electronic video and audio or telephonic communication system as authorized in § 37.2-804.1. The examination and the preadmission screening report shall be admitted into evidence at the hearing.

B. In no event shall an inmate have the right to make application for voluntary admission as may be otherwise provided in § 37.2-805 or 37.2-814 or be subject to an order for mandatory outpatient treatment as provided in § 37.2-817.

C. If an inmate is hospitalized pursuant to this section and his criminal case is still pending, the court having jurisdiction over the inmate's case may order that the admitting hospital evaluate the inmate's competency to stand trial and his mental state at the time of the offense pursuant to §§ 19.2-169.1 and 19.2-169.5.

D. An inmate may not be hospitalized longer than 30 days under subsection A unless the court which has criminal jurisdiction over him or a district court judge or a special justice, as defined in § 37.2-100, holds a hearing and orders the inmate's continued hospitalization in accordance with the provisions of subdivision A 2. If the inmate's hospitalization is continued under this subsection by a court other than the court which has jurisdiction over his crimi-

nal case, the facility at which the inmate is hospitalized shall notify the court with jurisdiction over his criminal case and the inmate's attorney in the criminal case, if the case is still pending.

E. Hospitalization may be extended in accordance with subsection D for periods of 60 days for inmates awaiting trial, but in no event may such hospitalization be continued beyond trial, nor shall such hospitalization act to delay trial, as long as the inmate remains competent to stand trial. Hospitalization may be extended in accordance with subsection D for periods of 180 days for an inmate who has been convicted and not yet sentenced, or for an inmate who has been convicted of a crime and is in the custody of a local correctional facility after sentencing, but in no event may such hospitalization be continued beyond the date upon which his sentence would have expired had he received the maximum sentence for the crime charged. Any inmate who has not completed service of his sentence upon discharge from the hospital shall serve the remainder of his sentence.

F. For any inmate who has been convicted and not yet sentenced, or who has been convicted of a crime and is in the custody of a local correctional facility after sentencing, the time the inmate is confined in a hospital for psychiatric treatment shall be deducted from any term for which he may be sentenced to any penal institution, reformatory or elsewhere.

G. Any health care provider, as defined in § 32.1-127.1:03, or other provider rendering services to an inmate who is the subject of a proceeding under this section, upon request, shall disclose to a magistrate, the court, the inmate's attorney, the inmate's guardian ad litem, the examiner appointed pursuant to § 37.2-815, the community service board or behavioral health authority preparing the preadmission screening pursuant to § 37.2-816, or the sheriff or administrator of the local correctional facility any and all information that is necessary and appropriate to enable each of them to perform his duties under this section. These health care providers and other service providers shall disclose to one another health records and information where necessary to provide care and treatment to the inmate and to monitor that care and treatment. Health records disclosed to a sheriff or administrator of the local correctional facility shall be limited to information necessary to protect the sheriff or administrator of the local correctional facility and his employees, the inmate, or the public from physical injury or to address the health care needs of the inmate. Information disclosed to a law-enforcement officer shall not be used for any other purpose, disclosed to others, or retained.

Any health care provider disclosing records pursuant to this section shall be immune from civil liability for any harm resulting from the disclosure, including any liability under the federal Health Insurance Portability and Accountability Act (42 U.S.C. § 1320d et seq.), as amended, unless the person or provider disclosing such records intended the harm or acted in bad faith.

H. Any order entered where an inmate is the subject of proceedings under this section shall provide for the disclosure of medical records pursuant to subsection G. This subsection shall not preclude any other disclosures as required or permitted by law.

History.

1982, c. 653; 1986, c. 629; 1987, c. 96; 1990, c. 76; 1995, c. 844; 2005, c. 716; 2008, cc. 779, 782, 850, 870; 2010, cc. 340, 406; 2012, c. 801.

Editor's note.

Acts 2012, c. 801, cl. 2, provides: "That the provisions of this act shall expire on July 1, 2014."

The 2012 amendments.

The 2012 amendment by c. 801, expiring July 1, 2014, in the first sentence of subdivision A 1, inserted the A 1 (ii) (a) designation, substituted "or" for "if any" at the end of A 1 (ii) (a), and inserted A 1 (ii) (b); in the first sentence of subdivision A 2, inserted the A 2 (ii) (a) designation, substituted "or" for "if any" at the end of A 2 (ii) (a), and inserted A 2 (ii) (b); in the last paragraph of subsection A, in the first sentence, deleted the (a) designation following "held either", and deleted the (b) designation following "inmate's case or", and in the sixth sentence, inserted the (2) (a) designation, and substituted "any other relevant information or (b) suffer serious harm due to his lack of capacity to protect himself from harm as evidenced by recent behavior and any other relevant information" for "other relevant information, if any."

§ 19.2-169.6. (Effective July 1, 2014) Inpatient psychiatric hospital admission from local correctional facility.

A. Any inmate of a local correctional facility who is not subject to the provisions of § 19.2-169.2 may be hospitalized for psychiatric treatment at a hospital designated by the Commissioner of Behavioral Health and Developmental Services as appropriate for treatment of persons under criminal charge if:

1. The court with jurisdiction over the inmate's case, if it is still pending, on the petition of the person having custody over an inmate or on its own motion, holds a hearing at which the inmate is represented by counsel and finds by clear and convincing evidence that (i) the inmate has a mental illness; (ii) there exists a substantial likelihood that, as a result of a mental illness, the inmate will, in the near future, cause serious physical harm to himself or others as evidenced by recent behavior causing, attempting, or threatening harm and other relevant information, if any; and (iii) the inmate requires treatment in a hospital rather than the local correctional facility. Prior to making this determination, the court shall consider the examination conducted in accordance with § 37.2-815 and the preadmission screening report prepared in accordance with § 37.2-816 and conducted in-person or by means of a two-way electronic video and audio communication system as authorized in § 37.2-804.1 by an employee or designee of the local community services board or behavioral health authority who is skilled in the assessment and treatment of mental illness,

who is not providing treatment to the inmate, and who has completed a certification program approved by the Department of Behavioral Health and Developmental Services as provided in § 37.2-809. The examiner appointed pursuant to § 37.2-815, if not physically present at the hearing, shall be available whenever possible for questioning during the hearing through a two-way electronic video and audio or telephonic communication system as authorized in § 37.2-804.1. Any employee or designee of the local community services board or behavioral health authority, as defined in § 37.2-809, representing the board or authority that prepared the preadmission screening report shall attend the hearing in person or, if physical attendance is not practicable, shall participate in the hearing through a two-way electronic video and audio communication system as authorized in § 37.2-804.1. When the hearing is held outside the service area of the community services board or behavioral health authority that prepared the preadmission screening report, and it is not practicable for a representative of the board or authority to attend or participate in the hearing, arrangements shall be made by the board or authority for an employee or designee of the board or authority serving the area in which the hearing is held to attend or participate on behalf of the board or authority that prepared the preadmission screening report; or

2. Upon petition by the person having custody over an inmate, a magistrate finds probable cause to believe that (i) the inmate has a mental illness; (ii) there exists a substantial likelihood that, as a result of a mental illness, the inmate will, in the near future, cause serious physical harm to himself or others as evidenced by recent behavior causing, attempting, or threatening harm and other relevant information, if any; and (iii) the inmate requires treatment in a hospital rather than a local correctional facility, and the magistrate issues a temporary detention order for the inmate. Prior to the filing of the petition, the person having custody shall arrange for an evaluation of the inmate conducted in-person or by means of a two-way electronic video and audio communication system as authorized in § 37.2-804.1 by an employee or designee of the local community services board or behavioral health authority who is skilled in the assessment and treatment of mental illness and who has completed a certification program approved by the Department as provided in § 37.2-809. After considering the evaluation of the employee or designee of the local community services board or behavioral health authority, and any other information presented, and finding that probable cause exists to meet the criteria, the magistrate may issue a temporary detention order in accordance with the applicable procedures specified in §§ 37.2-809 through 37.2-813. The person having custody over the inmate shall notify the court having jurisdiction over the inmate's case, if it is still pending, and the inmate's attorney prior to

the detention pursuant to a temporary detention order or as soon thereafter as is reasonable.

Upon detention pursuant to this subdivision, a hearing shall be held either (a) before the court having jurisdiction over the inmate's case or (b) before a district court judge or a special justice, as defined in § 37.2-100, in accordance with the provisions of §§ 37.2-815 through 37.2-821, in which case the inmate shall be represented by counsel as specified in § 37.2-814. The hearing shall be held within 48 hours of execution of the temporary detention order issued pursuant to this subdivision. If the 48-hour period terminates on a Saturday, Sunday, legal holiday, or day on which the court is lawfully closed, the inmate may be detained until the close of business on the next day that is not a Saturday, Sunday, legal holiday, or day on which the court is lawfully closed. Any employee or designee of the local community services board or behavioral health authority, as defined in § 37.2-809, representing the board or authority that prepared the preadmission screening report shall attend the hearing in person or, if physical attendance is not practicable, shall participate in the hearing through a two-way electronic video and audio communication system as authorized in § 37.2-804.1. When the hearing is held outside the service area of the community services board or behavioral health authority that prepared the preadmission screening report, and it is not practicable for a representative of the board or authority to attend or participate in the hearing, arrangements shall be made by the board or authority for an employee or designee of the board or authority serving the area in which the hearing is held to attend or participate on behalf of the board or authority that prepared the preadmission screening report. The judge or special justice conducting the hearing may order the inmate hospitalized if, after considering the examination conducted in accordance with § 37.2-815, the preadmission screening report prepared in accordance with § 37.2-816, and any other available information as specified in subsection C of § 37.2-817, he finds by clear and convincing evidence that (1) the inmate has a mental illness; (2) there exists a substantial likelihood that, as a result of a mental illness, the inmate will, in the near future, cause serious physical harm to himself or others as evidenced by recent behavior causing, attempting, or threatening harm and other relevant information, if any; and (3) the inmate requires treatment in a hospital rather than a local correctional facility. The examiner appointed pursuant to § 37.2-815, if not physically present at the hearing, shall be available whenever possible for questioning during the hearing through a two-way electronic video and audio or telephonic communication system as authorized in § 37.2-804.1. The examination and the preadmission screening report shall be admitted into evidence at the hearing.

B. In no event shall an inmate have the right to make application for voluntary admission as may be otherwise provided in § 37.2-805 or 37.2-814 or be subject to an order for mandatory outpatient treatment as provided in § 37.2-817.

C. If an inmate is hospitalized pursuant to this section and his criminal case is still pending, the court having jurisdiction over the inmate's case may order that the admitting hospital evaluate the inmate's competency to stand trial and his mental state at the time of the offense pursuant to §§ 19.2-169.1 and 19.2-169.5.

D. An inmate may not be hospitalized longer than 30 days under subsection A unless the court which has criminal jurisdiction over him or a district court judge or a special justice, as defined in § 37.2-100, holds a hearing and orders the inmate's continued hospitalization in accordance with the provisions of subdivision A 2. If the inmate's hospitalization is continued under this subsection by a court other than the court which has jurisdiction over his criminal case, the facility at which the inmate is hospitalized shall notify the court with jurisdiction over his criminal case and the inmate's attorney in the criminal case, if the case is still pending.

E. Hospitalization may be extended in accordance with subsection D for periods of 60 days for inmates awaiting trial, but in no event may such hospitalization be continued beyond trial, nor shall such hospitalization act to delay trial, as long as the inmate remains competent to stand trial. Hospitalization may be extended in accordance with subsection D for periods of 180 days for an inmate who has been convicted and not yet sentenced, or for an inmate who has been convicted of a crime and is in the custody of a local correctional facility after sentencing, but in no event may such hospitalization be continued beyond the date upon which his sentence would have expired had he received the maximum sentence for the crime charged. Any inmate who has not completed service of his sentence upon discharge from the hospital shall serve the remainder of his sentence.

F. For any inmate who has been convicted and not yet sentenced, or who has been convicted of a crime and is in the custody of a local correctional facility after sentencing, the time the inmate is confined in a hospital for psychiatric treatment shall be deducted from any term for which he may be sentenced to any penal institution, reformatory or elsewhere.

G. Any health care provider, as defined in § 32.1-127.1:03, or other provider rendering services to an inmate who is the subject of a proceeding under this section, upon request, shall disclose to a magistrate, the court, the inmate's attorney, the inmate's guardian ad litem, the examiner appointed pursuant to § 37.2-815, the community service board or behavioral health authority preparing the preadmission screening pursuant to § 37.2-816, or the sheriff or administrator of the local correctional facility any and all information that is necessary and appropriate to enable each of them to perform his duties under this section. These health care providers and other service providers shall disclose to one another health records and information where necessary to provide care and treatment to the inmate and to monitor that care and treatment. Health records disclosed to a sheriff or administrator of the local correctional facility shall be limited to information necessary to protect the sheriff or administrator of the local correctional facility and his employees, the inmate, or the public from physical injury or to address the health care needs of the inmate. Information disclosed to a law-enforcement officer shall not be used for any other purpose, disclosed to others, or retained.

Any health care provider disclosing records pursuant to this section shall be immune from civil liability for any harm resulting from the disclosure, including any liability under the federal Health Insurance Portability and Accountability Act (42 U.S.C. § 1320d et seq.), as amended, unless the person or provider disclosing such records intended the harm or acted in bad faith.

H. Any order entered where an inmate is the subject of proceedings under this section shall provide for the disclosure of medical records pursuant to subsection G. This subsection shall not preclude any other disclosures as required or permitted by law.

History.
1982, c. 653; 1986, c. 629; 1987, c. 96; 1990, c. 76; 1995, c. 844; 2005, c. 716; 2008, cc. 779, 782, 850, 870; 2010, cc. 340, 406.

The 2008 amendments.
The 2008 amendment by c. 779 substituted "and that there exists a substantial likelihood that, as a result of mental illness, the defendant will, in the near future, cause serious physical harm to himself or others as evidenced by recent behavior causing, attempting, or threatening harm and other relevant information, if any" for "and is imminently dangerous to himself or others" in clause (ii) in subdivision A 1, in clause (i) in subdivision A 2 and in clause (i) in subsection C; moved the clause (i) designator to follow "the defendant" in subdivision A 2; substituted "and the continued substantial likelihood that, as a result of mental illness, the defendant will, in the near future, cause serious physical harm to himself or others as evidenced by recent behavior causing, attempting, or threatening such harm and other relevant information, if any, and" for "and being imminently dangerous" in subsection B; in subsection C, inserted "and that there continues to exist a substantial likelihood that, as a result of mental illness, the defendant will, in the near future, cause serious physical harm to himself or others as evidenced by recent behavior causing, attempting, or threatening harm and other relevant information, if any" at the end of clause (i); deleted former clause (ii), which read: "be immently dangerous to self or others"; redesignated former clause (iii) as clause (ii); and made a minor stylistic change.
The 2008 amendment by c. 782 added subsections D and E.
The 2008 amendments by cc. 850 and 870 are identical and rewrote the section.

The 2010 amendments.
The 2010 amendments by cc. 340 and 406 are nearly identical, and rewrote the section.

§ 19.2-169.7. Disclosure by defendant during evaluation or treatment; use at guilt phase of trial.

No statement or disclosure by the defendant concerning the alleged offense made during a compe-

tency evaluation ordered pursuant to § 19.2-169.1, a mental state at the time of the offense evaluation ordered pursuant to § 19.2-169.5, or treatment ordered pursuant to § 19.2-169.2 or § 19.2-169.6 may be used against the defendant at trial as evidence or as a basis for such evidence, except on the issue of his mental condition at the time of the offense after he raises the issue pursuant to § 19.2-168.

History.
1982, c. 653.

Law Review.
For an article relating to all published Virginia criminal law decisions between July 1, 1997, and July 1, 1998, see 32 U. Rich. L. Rev. 1091 (1998). For an article, "An End to Insanity: Recasting the Role of Mental Disability in Criminal Cases," see 86 Va. L. Rev. 1199 (2000).

CASE NOTES

Applicability. — This section explicitly refers to statements "concerning the alleged offense"; it does not bar irrelevant or highly prejudicial statements. Thus, in view of defendant's concession that the questions did not directly relate to the offense and in the absence of a record of the trial judge's ruling, which is presumed to be correct, the court had no basis to resolve this issue in her favor. Zelenak v. Commonwealth, 23 Va. App. 259, 475 S.E.2d 853 (1996), aff'd on reh'g en banc, 25 Va. App. 295, 487 S.E.2d 873 (1997).
Where defendant admitted that the cross-examination questions concerning her abuse by her family did not relate directly to the offense, they were properly admissible. Zelenak v. Commonwealth, 25 Va. App. 295, 487 S.E.2d 873 (1997).

§§ 19.2-170 through 19.2-174. Repealed by Acts 1982, c. 653.

Cross references.
For present provisions covering the subject matter of the repealed sections, see §§ 19.2-168.1 and 19.2-169.1 through 19.2-169.7.

§ 19.2-174.1. Information required prior to admission to a mental health facility.

Prior to any person being placed into the custody of the Commissioner for evaluation or treatment pursuant to §§ 19.2-169.2, 19.2-169.3, 19.2-169.6, 19.2-182.2, and 19.2-182.3, and Chapter 9 (§ 37.2-900 et seq.) of Title 37.2, the court or special justice shall provide the Commissioner with the following, if available: (i) the commitment order, (ii) the names and addresses for the attorney for the Commonwealth, the attorney for the person and the judge holding jurisdiction over the person, (iii) a copy of the warrant or indictment, and (iv) a copy of the criminal incident information as defined in § 2.2-3706 or a copy of the arrest report or a summary of the facts relating to the crime. The party requesting the placement into the Commissioner's custody or, in the case of admissions pursuant to §§ 19.2-169.3 and 19.2-169.6, and Chapter 9 (§ 37.2-900 et seq.) of Title 37.2, the person having custody over the defendant or inmate shall gather the above information for submission to the court at the hearing. If the information is not available at the hearing, it shall be provided by the party requesting placement or the person having custody directly to the Commissioner within 96 hours of the person being placed into the Commissioner's custody. If the 96-hour period expires on a Saturday, Sunday or legal holiday, the 96 hours shall be extended to the next day that is not a Saturday, Sunday or legal holiday.

History.
1995, c. 645; 1999, cc. 946, 985; 2001, c. 837; 2003, c. 989, cls. 4, 5, 1018, cls. 4, 5, 1042, cls. 10, 11; 2010, cc. 340, 406.

Editor's note.
Acts 1999, cc. 946 and 985, cl. 3, as amended by Acts 2000, c. 1024, and Acts 2001, c. 776, cl. 3, had provided that the amendments by Acts 1999, cc. 946 and 985 would be effective July 1, 2003.

Acts 2002, c. 899, Items 49 C and 331 C 1, prior to amendment by Acts 2002, c. 1042, had provided: "The effective date of Chapters 946 and 985 of the 1999 Acts of Assembly, which establishes the civil commitment and treatment of sexual predators, is postponed to January 1, 2004."

Acts 2002, c. 899, and Acts 2003, c. 1042, in Item 49 E, provides: "E. The Attorney General shall review the decision of the U.S. Supreme Court in the case of Kansas v. Crane, decided on January 22, 2002, and determine what effect this decision may have on the implementation of Chapters 946 and 985 of the Acts of Assembly of 1999. The Attorney General shall make a report of his review, including any recommended changes to this legislation, to the Governor and the General Assembly by September 1, 2002."

Acts 2003, cc. 989 and 1018, cl. 3, provide: "That an emergency exists and this act is in force from its passage [April 2, 2003], notwithstanding the provisions of Items 49 C and 331 C1 of Chapter 899 of the Acts of Assembly of 2002."

Acts 2003, cc. 989 and 1018, cl. 4, provide: "That, notwithstanding the provisions of Items 49 C and 331 C1 of Chapter 899 of the Acts of Assembly of 2002, the provisions of Chapters 946 and 985, as they may be amended, of the Acts of Assembly of 1999 shall become effective on the effective date of this act [April 2, 2003.]"

Acts 2003, cc. 989 and 1018, cl. 5, provide: "That the third enactments of Chapter 946 and Chapter 985, as amended, of the Acts of Assembly of 1999 are amended and reenacted as follows:

"3. That the effective date of this act is the date of enactment of House Bill 1400, House Bill 2445 or Senate Bill 1149 of the 2003 General Assembly Session, whichever is the first to be enacted.

"3. That the effective date of this act is the date of enactment of House Bill 1400, House Bill 2445 or Senate Bill 1149 of the 2003 General Assembly Session, whichever is the first to be enacted."

Acts 2003, c. 1042, cls. 10 and 11 also amended cls. 3 of Acts 1999, cc. 946 and 985, in an identical fashion.

Acts 2002, c. 899, as amended by Acts 2003, c. 1042, in Items 49 C 1 and 331 C 1, provide that the provisions of Title 37.1, Chapter 2, Article 1.1 "shall be effective upon passage of House Bill 2445 of the 2003 General Assembly Session, Senate Bill 1149 of the 2003 General Assembly Session, or this act, whichever is first to be enacted." See also Acts 2002, c. 899, Item 421 H, as added by Acts 2003, c. 1042.

House Bill 2445 (Chapter 989) and Senate Bill 1149 (Chapter 1018) of the 2003 General Assembly were enacted on April 2, 2003, the date they were approved by the Governor.

The 2010 amendments.
The 2010 amendments by cc. 340 and 406 are identical, and deleted "19.2-176, 19.2-177.1" following "19.2-169.6" in the first sentence; in the second sentence, deleted "19.2-176, and 19.2-177.1" following "19.2-169.6" and inserted "or inmate"; and made minor stylistic changes.

§ 19.2-175. Compensation of experts.

Each psychiatrist, clinical psychologist or other expert appointed by the court to render professional service pursuant to § 19.2-168.1, 19.2-169.1, 19.2-169.5, 19.2-182.8, 19.2-182.9, 19.2-264.3:1, 19.2-

264.3:3 or 19.2-301, who is not regularly employed by the Commonwealth of Virginia except by the University of Virginia School of Medicine and the Medical College of Virginia Commonwealth University, shall receive a reasonable fee for such service. For any psychiatrist, clinical psychologist, or other expert appointed by the court to render such professional services who is regularly employed by the Commonwealth of Virginia, except by the University of Virginia School of Medicine or the Medical College of Virginia Commonwealth University, the fee shall be paid only for professional services provided during nonstate hours that have been approved by his employing agency as being beyond the scope of his state employment duties. The fee shall be determined in each instance by the court that appointed the expert, in accordance with guidelines established by the Supreme Court after consultation with the Department of Behavioral Health and Developmental Services. Except in capital murder cases the fee shall not exceed $750, but in addition if any such expert is required to appear as a witness in any hearing held pursuant to such sections, he shall receive mileage and a fee of $100 for each day during which he is required so to serve. An itemized account of expense, duly sworn to, must be presented to the court, and when allowed shall be certified to the Supreme Court for payment out of the state treasury, and be charged against the appropriations made to pay criminal charges. Allowance for the fee and for the per diem authorized shall also be made by order of the court, duly certified to the Supreme Court for payment out of the appropriation to pay criminal charges.

History.
Code 1950, § 19.1-233; 1960, c. 366; 1968, c. 657; 1970, c. 640; 1975, c. 495; 1976, c. 140; 1978, cc. 195, 794; 1979, c. 516; 1982, c. 653; 1986, c. 535; 1990, c. 697; 1995, c. 645; 2003, cc. 1031, 1040; 2006, cc. 114, 170; 2007, c. 829; 2009, cc. 813, 840; 2010, cc. 340, 406.

Editor's note.
Acts 2001, c. 480, which would have amended this section by substituting "$800" for "$400" in the third sentence, provided in cl. 2, "That the provisions of this act shall not become effective unless an appropriation effectuating the purposes of this act is included in the 2001 Appropriation Act, passed during the 2001 Session of the General Assembly and signed into law by the Governor." Such an appropriation was not made.

The 2007 amendments.
The 2007 amendment by c. 829, substituted "$750" for "$400" in the fourth sentence.

The 2009 amendments.
The 2009 amendments by cc. 813 and 840 are identical, and substituted "Behavioral Health and Developmental Services" for "Mental Health, Mental Retardation and Substance Abuse Services" in the third sentence; and made a minor stylistic change in the first sentence.

The 2010 amendments.
The 2010 amendments by cc. 340 and 406 are identical, and in the first sentence, deleted "subsection A of § 19.2-176" following "19.2-169.5" and made a minor stylistic change.

Law Review.
For comment on the insanity defense in Virginia, see 17 U. Rich. L. Rev. 129 (1982). For 2006 survey article, "Criminal Law and Procedure," see 41 U. Rich. L. Rev. 83 (2006).

§ 19.2-176. Repealed by Acts 2010, cc. 340 and 406, cl. 2.

Editor's note.

Former § 19.2-176, authorizing evaluation for determination of insanity after conviction but before sentence, was derived from Code 1950, § 19.1-234; 1960, c. 366; 1964, c. 231; 1966, c. 715; 1972, c. 295; 1975, c. 495; 1982, c. 653; 1986, c. 629; 1990, c. 76; 2008, cc. 779, 850, 870.

§ 19.2-177. Repealed by Acts 1988, cc. 787, 873.

Cross references.

As to determination of mental illness after sentencing, see now § 19.2-177.1.

§ 19.2-177.1. Repealed by Acts 2010, cc. 340 and 406, cl. 2.

Editor's note.

Former § 19.2-177.1, relating to determination of mental illness after sentencing, was enacted by Acts 1988, c. 787, and amended by Acts 1995, c. 844; 2005, c. 716; 2008, cc. 779, 850, 870.

§ 19.2-178. Where prisoner kept when no vacancy in facility or hospital.

When a court shall have entered any of the orders provided for in § 19.2-168.1, 19.2-169.1, 19.2-169.5, or 19.2-169.6, the sheriff of the county or city or the proper officer of the penal institution shall immediately proceed to ascertain whether a vacancy exists at the proper facility or hospital and until it is ascertained that there is a vacancy such person shall be kept in the jail of such county or city or in such custody as the court may order, or in the penal institution in which he is confined, until there is room in such facility or hospital. Any person whose care and custody is herein provided for shall be taken to and from the facility or hospital to which he was committed by an officer of the penal institution having custody of him, or by the sheriff of the county or city whose court issued the order of commitment, and the expenses incurred in such removals shall be paid by such penal institution, county or city.

History.

Code 1950, § 19.1-236; 1960, c. 366; 1975, c. 495; 1995, c. 645; 2010, cc. 340, 406.

The 2010 amendments.

The 2010 amendments by cc. 340 and 406 are identical, and in the first sentence, deleted "19.2-176, or § 19.2-177.1," and made minor stylistic changes.

§ 19.2-179. Repealed by Acts 1981, c. 310.

§ 19.2-180. Sentence or trial of prisoner when restored to sanity.

When a prisoner whose trial or sentence was suspended by reason of his being found to be insane or feebleminded, has been found to be mentally competent and is brought from a hospital and committed to jail, if already convicted, he shall be sentenced, and if not, the court shall proceed to try him as if no delay had occurred on account of his insanity or feeblemindedness.

History.

Code 1950, § 19.1-238; 1960, c. 366; 1975, c. 495.

§ 19.2-181. Repealed by Acts 1991, c. 427.

Cross references.

For provisions pertaining to disposition of persons acquitted by reason of insanity, see § 19.2-182.2 et seq.

§ 19.2-182. Representation by counsel in proceeding for commitment.

A. In any proceeding for commitment under this title, the judge before whom or upon whose order the proceeding is being held, shall ascertain if the person whose commitment is sought is represented by counsel. If the person is not represented by counsel, the judge shall appoint an attorney at law to represent him in the proceeding. The attorney shall receive a fee of twenty-five dollars for his services, to be paid by the Commonwealth.

B. Any attorney representing any person in any proceeding for commitment under this title shall, prior to such proceeding, personally consult with such person.

History.

Code 1950, § 19.1-239.1; 1966, c. 715; 1975, c. 495; 1991, c. 427.

§ 19.2-182.1. Repealed by Acts 1982, c. 653.

CHAPTER 11.1.

DISPOSITION OF PERSONS ACQUITTED BY REASON OF INSANITY.

Michie's Jurisprudence.

For related discussion, see 10A M.J. Insane and Other Incompetent Persons, §§ 3, 5, 43, 47, 48.

---

§ 19.2-182.2. Verdict of acquittal by reason of insanity to state the fact; temporary custody and evaluation.

When the defense is insanity of the defendant at the time the offense was committed, the jurors shall be instructed, if they acquit him on that ground, to state the fact with their verdict. The court shall place the person so acquitted (the acquittee) in temporary custody of the Commissioner of Behavioral Health and Developmental Services (hereinafter referred to in this chapter as the Commissioner) for evaluation as to whether the acquittee may be released with or without conditions or requires commitment. The evaluation shall be conducted by (i) one psychiatrist and (ii) one clinical psychologist. The psychiatrist or clinical psychologist shall be skilled in the diagnosis of mental illness and intellectual disability and qualified by training and experience to perform such evaluations. The Commissioner shall appoint both evaluators, at least one of whom shall not be employed by the hospital in which the acquittee is primarily confined. The evaluators shall determine whether the acquittee currently has mental illness or intellectual disability and shall assess the acquittee and report on his condition and need for hospitalization with respect to the factors set forth in § 19.2-182.3. The evaluators shall conduct their examinations and report their findings separately within 45 days of the Commissioner's assumption of custody. Copies of the report shall be sent to the acquittee's attorney, the attorney for the Commonwealth for the jurisdiction where the person was acquitted and the community services board or behavioral health authority as designated by the Commissioner. If either evaluator recommends conditional release or release without conditions of the acquittee, the court shall extend the evaluation period to permit the hospital in which the acquittee is confined and the appropriate community services board or behavioral health authority to jointly prepare a conditional release or discharge plan, as applicable, prior to the hearing.

History.

1991, c. 427; 1993, c. 295; 1996, cc. 937, 980; 2007, cc. 485, 565; 2009, cc. 813, 840; 2012, cc. 476, 507.

The 2007 amendments.

The 2007 amendments by cc. 485 and 565 are identical, and substituted "or behavioral health authority as designated by the Commissioner" for "serving the locality where the acquittee was acquitted" at the end of the next-to-last sentence and inserted "or behavioral health authority" following "community services board" in the last sentence.

The 2009 amendments.

The 2009 amendments by cc. 813 and 840 are identical, and substituted "Commissioner of Behavioral Health and Developmental Services" for "Commissioner of Mental Health, Mental Retarda-

tion and Substance Abuse Services" in the second sentence and "currently has mental illness or mental retardation" for "is currently mentally ill or mentally retarded" in the sixth sentence; and made minor stylistic changes throughout the section.

The 2012 amendments.

The 2012 amendments by cc. 476 and 507 are identical, and substituted "intellectual disability" for "mental retardation" twice, and made a minor stylistic change.

Law Review.

For an article, "The Confusion of Cause and Reasons in Forensic Psychology: Deconstructing Mens Rea and Other Mental Events," see 33 U. Rich. L. Rev. 107 (1999).

CASE NOTES

Editor's note.

The cases annotated below were decided under prior law.

Court of appeals had no jurisdiction of appeal from commitment order. — The court of appeals had no jurisdiction of an appeal from a commitment order under subsection (1) of former § 19.2-181; an examination of former § 17-116.05 (see now § 17.1-405) revealed no proceeding remotely resembling the proceeding at issue. Antzes v. Commonwealth, 13 Va. App. 172, 409 S.E.2d 172 (1991) (decided under prior law).

Court of appeals had no jurisdiction of an appeal from a subsection (1) of former § 19.2-181 commitment order, as none has been conferred by the legislature; if the hearing held under subsection (1) of former § 19.2-181 was criminal in nature, the court of appeals had no jurisdiction, as there had been no final conviction of a crime from which to appeal (see § 17-116.05:1 (i) [see now § 17.1-406]); furthermore, conferral of jurisdiction on the court of appeals by subsection (5) of former § 19.2-181 did not apply to a commitment proceeding under subsection (1) of former § 19.2-181. Antzes v. Commonwealth, 13 Va. App. 172, 409 S.E.2d 172 (1991) (decided under prior law).

Administrative procedures under this section not proper as jury instructions. — The detailed administrative procedures to be followed by the court and the Commissioner of Mental Health, Mental Retardation and Substance Abuse Services [now the Commissioner of Behavioral Health and Developmental Services] under this section when a defendant is acquitted by reason of insanity are directed to the court and are not the concern of the jury and thus are not proper as jury instructions. Spruill v. Commonwealth, 221 Va. 475, 271 S.E.2d 419 (1980).

Trial court properly refused to instruct jury on the consequences of a verdict of not guilty by reason of insanity although defendant argued that the jury should have been told that, pursuant to a finding of not guilty by reason of insanity, defendant would not be set free but instead would be committed to the custody of state mental health authorities. As interpreted by the Virginia Supreme Court, the language in the statute that details these consequences specifically directs itself to the attention of the court. Furthermore, the court of appeals presumed that the jury conscientiously followed the explicit cautionary instruction. Miller v. Commonwealth, 15 Va. App. 301, 422 S.E.2d 795 (1992), aff'd, 246 Va. 336, 437 S.E.2d 411 (1993) (decided under former § 19.2-181).

Informing jury of consequences of acquittal by reason of insanity. — Due process under the United States and Virginia Constitutions did not require that the jury be informed during the guilt phase that an acquittal by reason of insanity would not entitle defendant to be released and could result in his commitment to a mental health facility. Such information would encourage an acquittal irrespective of the evidence. Holmes v. Commonwealth, 2008 Va. App. LEXIS 515 (Nov. 25, 2008).

Commitment procedures for insanity acquittees distinguished from that for other persons. — Virginia's scheme for the commitment of insanity acquittees is different in a number of respects from its scheme for the commitment of persons other than insanity acquittees. A person other than an insanity acquittee may be committed only if the factfinder determines that there is clear and convincing evidence that the person is insane and dangerous; he is given the right to a jury trial at the precommitment stage; he is automatically released after 180 days and if the State wishes to confine him for a longer period, it must initiate a fresh commitment proceeding every 180 days; and, finally, before the 180-day period has run, he has an unlimited right to seek release. Harris v. Ballone, 681 F.2d 225 (4th Cir. 1982).

Differences in standards for incarceration constitutional. — It is not a denial of due process for a person who has committed a criminal act to be incarcerated as long as he is considered dangerous. This aspect of Virginia's scheme does not deny equal protection because a different standard (i.e., insane and dangerous) is used for persons other than insanity acquittees. The fact that an insanity acquittee has already been shown beyond a reasonable doubt to have committed at least one dangerous act justifies the distinction Virginia has drawn. Harris v. Ballone, 681 F.2d 225 (4th Cir. 1982).

Person may not be incarcerated solely because he is insane (at least in the absence of any showing that an involuntary confinement is necessary to ensure his own survival or safety or to alleviate or cure his illness). Harris v. Ballone, 681 F.2d 225 (4th Cir. 1982).

Hearing rights of insanity acquittees generally. — While the Code of Virginia does not explicitly guarantee to insanity acquittees the right to receive advance notice of hearings, to present evidence, and to cross-examine experts, neither does it explicitly deny them. Harris v. Ballone, 681 F.2d 225 (4th Cir. 1982).

Denial of jury trial and automatic release constitutional. — The denial of a jury trial at the precommitment stage and the denial of automatic release after 180 days are clearly not unconstitutional as denying due process, nor equal protection of the laws. The fact that an insanity acquittee has already been shown beyond a reasonable doubt to have committed at least one dangerous act provides a rational basis for the distinctions drawn by the General Assembly. Harris v. Ballone, 681 F.2d 225 (4th Cir. 1982).

Standard of proof under former section held constitutional. — The requirement of subsection (3) of former section 19.2-181 that the judge be "satisfied" that the insanity acquittee qualified for commitment invoked at least the preponderance-of-the-evidence standard, and the use of that standard was constitutionally permissible. Harris v. Ballone, 681 F.2d 225 (4th Cir. 1982).

Although clear-and-convincing standard used for other committees. — The clear-and-convincing-evidence standard is required for the commitment of persons other than insanity acquittees, but the situation of an insanity acquittee is distinguishable because an insanity acquittee has already been shown beyond a reasonable doubt to have committed at least one dangerous act. Harris v. Ballone, 681 F.2d 225 (4th Cir. 1982).

One-per-year restriction does not deny equal protection. — That no similar restriction is imposed on committed persons other than insanity acquittees does not make the rule limiting applications for discharge to one-per-year unconstitutional under the equal protection clause. The obvious rationale for this restriction is to encourage the patient who has demonstrated dangerousness to cooperate with the treating physicians in curing his ills, and the General Assembly could rationally have distinguished between insanity acquittees and other committed persons in evaluating the wisdom of imposing such a restriction. Harris v. Ballone, 681 F.2d 225 (4th Cir. 1982).

Nor due process. — The force of the argument that the one-per-year restriction on applications for a release order denies due process because it creates the possibility that an insanity acquittee will remain committed for almost a year after the justification for his commitment has ceased to exist is substantially diluted by the fact that the hospital where the insanity acquittee is committed is free to apply for his release as often as it wishes. Harris v. Ballone, 681 F.2d 225 (4th Cir. 1982).

Burden of proof. — Both in habeas corpus proceedings and other statutory proceedings for the release of a person committed to a mental institution after his acquittal of a criminal offense on the ground of insanity, the burden of proving eligibility for release rests on the petitioner. Blalock v. Markley, 207 Va. 1003, 154 S.E.2d 158 (1967).

Where language of the statute improperly placed upon insanity acquittee the burden of proving, even if she was not insane, that she was not dangerous, it violated protections of the Due Process Clause. Williams v. Commonwealth, 18 Va. App. 384, 444 S.E.2d 16 (1994) (decided under former § 19.2-181).

Applied in Eastlack v. Commonwealth, 282 Va. 120, 710 S.E.2d 723, 2011 Va. LEXIS 126 (2011).

§ 19.2-182.3. Commitment; civil proceedings.

Upon receipt of the evaluation report and, if applicable, a conditional release or discharge plan, the court shall schedule the matter for hearing on an expedited basis, giving the matter priority over other civil matters before the court, to determine the appropriate disposition of the acquittee. Except as otherwise ordered by the court, the attorney who represented the defendant at the criminal proceedings shall represent the acquittee through the proceedings pursuant to this section. The matter may be continued on motion of either party for good cause shown. The acquittee shall be provided with adequate notice of the hearing, of the right to be present at the hearing, the right to the assistance of counsel in preparation for and during the hearing, and the right to introduce evidence and cross-examine witnesses at the hearing. The hearing is a civil proceeding.

At the conclusion of the hearing, the court shall commit the acquittee if it finds that he has mental illness or intellectual disability and is in need of inpatient hospitalization. For the purposes of this chapter, mental illness includes any mental illness, as defined in § 37.2-100, in a state of remission when the illness may, with reasonable probability, become active. The decision of the court shall be based upon consideration of the following factors:

1. To what extent the acquittee has mental illness or intellectual disability, as those terms are defined in § 37.2-100;

2. The likelihood that the acquittee will engage in conduct presenting a substantial risk of bodily harm to other persons or to himself in the foreseeable future;

3. The likelihood that the acquittee can be adequately controlled with supervision and treatment on an outpatient basis; and

4. Such other factors as the court deems relevant.

If the court determines that an acquittee does not need inpatient hospitalization solely because of treatment or habilitation he is currently receiving, but the court is not persuaded that the acquittee will continue to receive such treatment or habilitation, it may commit him for inpatient hospitalization. The court shall order the acquittee released with conditions pursuant to §§ 19.2-182.7, 19.2-182.8, and 19.2-182.9 if it finds that he is not in need of inpatient hospitalization but that he meets the criteria for conditional release set forth in § 19.2-182.7. If the court finds that the acquittee does not need inpatient hospitalization nor does he meet the criteria for conditional release, it shall release him without conditions, provided the court has approved a discharge plan prepared by the appropriate community services board or behavioral health authority in consultation with the appropriate hospital staff.

History.
  1991, c. 427; 1993, c. 295; 2005, c. 716; 2012, cc. 476, 507.

The 2012 amendments.
  The 2012 amendments by cc. 476 and 507 are identical, and substituted "intellectual disability" for "mental retardation" in the second paragraph and in subdivision 1; and in the last paragraph, substituted "§§ 19.2-182.7, 19.2-182.8, and 19.2-182.9" for "§§ 19.2-182.7 through 19.2-182.9" in the second sentence.

CASE NOTES

  Mental illness. — The term "mental illness" in this section is not limited solely to the definition of "mentally ill" in § 37.1-1 [see now § 37.2-100]. Mercer v. Commonwealth, 259 Va. 235, 523 S.E.2d 213 (2000).
  Continued commitment does not establish nature of an individual's particular condition. — It is simply not the case that a person committed to a mental hospital in Virginia must remain insane throughout the duration of his commitment. Given the specific provisions of § 19.2-182.3, the mere fact of continued commitment does not establish the nature or characteristics of the individual's particular condition, much less his ability to understand and appreciate the requirements of state and federal habeas litigation. Farabee v. Johnson, — F.3d —, 2005 U.S. App. LEXIS 7030 (4th Cir. Apr. 22, 2005).
  Applied in Eastlack v. Commonwealth, 282 Va. 120, 710 S.E.2d 723, 2011 Va. LEXIS 126 (2011).

§ 19.2-182.4. Confinement and treatment; interfacility transfers; out-of-hospital visits; notice of change in treatment.

  A. Upon commitment of an acquittee for inpatient hospitalization, the Commissioner shall determine the appropriate placement for him, based on his clinical needs and security requirements. The Commissioner may make interfacility transfers and treatment and management decisions regarding acquittees in his custody without obtaining prior approval of or review by the committing court. If the Commissioner is of the opinion that a temporary visit from the hospital would be therapeutic for the acquittee and that such visit would pose no substantial danger to others, the Commissioner may grant such visit not to exceed forty-eight hours.
  B. The Commissioner shall give notice of the granting of an unescorted community visit to any victim of a felony offense against the person punishable by more than five years in prison that resulted in the charges on which the acquittee was acquitted or the next-of-kin of the victim at the last known address, provided the person seeking notice submits a written request for such notice to the Commissioner.
  C. The Commissioner shall notify the attorney for the Commonwealth for the committing jurisdiction in writing of changes in an acquittee's course of treatment which will involve authorization for the acquittee to leave the grounds of the hospital in which he is confined.

History.
  1991, c. 427; 1993, c. 295; 2006, c. 358.

§ 19.2-182.5. Review of continuation of confinement hearing; procedure and reports; disposition.

  A. The committing court shall conduct a hearing twelve months after the date of commitment to assess the need for inpatient hospitalization of each acquittee who is acquitted of a felony by reason of insanity. A hearing for assessment shall be conducted at yearly intervals for five years and at biennial intervals thereafter. The court shall schedule the matter for hearing as soon as possible after it becomes due, giving the matter priority over all pending matters before the court.
  B. Prior to the hearing, the Commissioner shall provide to the court a report evaluating the acquittee's condition and recommending treatment, to be prepared by a psychiatrist or a psychologist. The psychologist who prepares the report shall be a clinical psychologist and any evaluating psychiatrist or clinical psychologist shall be skilled in the diagnosis of mental illness and qualified by training and experience to perform forensic evaluations. If the examiner recommends release or the acquittee requests release, the acquittee's condition and need for inpatient hospitalization shall be evaluated by a second person with such credentials who is not currently treating the acquittee. A copy of any report submitted pursuant to this subsection shall be sent to the attorney for the Commonwealth for the jurisdiction from which the acquittee was committed.
  C. The acquittee shall be provided with adequate notice of the hearing, of the right to be present at the hearing, the right to the assistance of counsel in preparation for and during the hearing, and the right to introduce evidence and cross-examine witnesses at the hearing. Written notice of the hearing shall be provided to the attorney for the Commonwealth for the committing jurisdiction. The hearing is a civil proceeding.
  According to the determination of the court following the hearing, and based upon the report and other evidence provided at the hearing, the court shall (i) release the acquittee from confinement if he does not need inpatient hospitalization and does not meet the criteria for conditional release set forth in § 19.2-182.7, provided the court has approved a discharge plan prepared jointly by the hospital staff and the appropriate community services board or behavioral health authority; (ii) place the acquittee on conditional release if he meets the criteria for conditional release, and the court has approved a conditional release plan prepared jointly by the hospital staff and the appropriate community services board or behavioral health authority; or (iii) order that he remain in the custody of the Commissioner if he continues to require inpatient hospitalization based on consideration of the factors set forth in § 19.2-182.3.
  D. An acquittee who is found not guilty of a misdemeanor by reason of insanity on or after July 1, 2002, shall remain in the custody of the Commis-

sioner pursuant to this chapter for a period not to exceed one year from the date of acquittal. If, prior to or at the conclusion of one year, the Commissioner determines that the acquittee meets the criteria for conditional release or release without conditions pursuant to § 19.2-182.7, emergency custody pursuant to § 37.2-808, temporary detention pursuant to §§ 37.2-809 to 37.2-813, or involuntary commitment pursuant to Article 5 (§ 37.2-814 et seq.) of Chapter 8 of Title 37.2, he shall petition the committing court. Written notice of an acquittee's scheduled release shall be provided by the Commissioner to the attorney for the Commonwealth for the committing jurisdiction not less than thirty days prior to the scheduled release. The Commissioner's duty to file a petition upon such determination shall not preclude the ability of any other person meeting the requirements of § 37.2-808 to file the petition.

History.
  1991, c. 427; 1993, c. 295; 1996, cc. 937, 980; 2002, c. 750; 2007, cc. 485, 565.

Editor's note.
  Acts 2002, c. 750, cl. 2, provides: "That, on or before October 1, 2002, the Commissioner shall implement the provisions of this act for misdemeanor acquittees who are in the custody of the Commissioner on the effective date of this act."

The 2007 amendments.
  The 2007 amendments by cc. 485 and 565 are identical, and inserted "or behavioral health authority" following "community services board" in clauses (i) and (ii) of the last paragraph in subsection C.

CASE NOTES

Confinement not limited in duration. — The provisions of the Code dealing with the disposition of persons acquitted by reason of insanity do not limit the length of time that an acquittee can be confined for inpatient treatment, and it is conceivable that an acquittee could be confined for inpatient treatment for many years or for the remainder of his life, if the acquittee continues to be mentally ill and in need of inpatient treatment. Commonwealth v. Chatman, 260 Va. 562, 538 S.E.2d 304, 2000 Va. LEXIS 131 (2000).
  Continued confinement after mental health review hearings. — Under § 19.2-182.5, a prisoner was not unlawfully confined for 11 years, after being found not guilty by reason of insanity, because at each of his mental health review hearings, the prisoner had been found to be mentally ill and unsuitable for release and his commitment had been renewed; thus, he was no longer confined on the original commitment, and instead, was confined under the most recent decision that his confinement should be continued. McKinney v. Kilgore, — F. Supp. 2d —, 2005 U.S. Dist. LEXIS 8384 (W.D. Va. Apr. 29, 2005).
  Applied in Eastlack v. Commonwealth, 282 Va. 120, 710 S.E.2d 723, 2011 Va. LEXIS 126 (2011).

§ 19.2-182.6. Petition for release; conditional release hearing; notice; disposition.

A. The Commissioner may petition the committing court for conditional or unconditional release of the acquittee at any time he believes the acquittee no longer needs hospitalization. The petition shall be accompanied by a report of clinical findings supporting the petition with respect to the factors set forth in § 19.2-182.3 and by a conditional release or discharge plan, as applicable, prepared jointly by the hospital and the appropriate community services board or behavioral health authority. The acquittee may petition the committing court for release only once in each year in which no annual judicial review is required pursuant to § 19.2-182.5. The party petitioning for release shall transmit a copy of the petition to the attorney for the Commonwealth for the committing jurisdiction.

B. 1. When a petition for release is made by the acquittee, the court shall order the Commissioner to appoint two persons in the same manner as set forth in § 19.2-182.2 to assess and report on the acquittee's need for inpatient hospitalization by reviewing his condition with respect to the factors set forth in § 19.2-182.3. The evaluators shall conduct their evaluations and report their finding in accordance with the provisions of § 19.2-182.2, except that the evaluations shall be completed and findings reported within 45 days of issuance of the court's order for evaluation.

2. When a petition for release is made by the Commissioner no further evaluations of the acquittee shall be required unless otherwise deemed necessary by the court. If the court determines that further evaluation is necessary, the court shall order the Commissioner to appoint two persons in the same manner as set forth in § 19.2-182.2 to assess and report on the acquittee's need for inpatient hospitalization by reviewing his condition with respect to the factors set forth in § 19.2-182.3. The evaluators shall conduct their evaluations and report their finding in accordance with the provisions of § 19.2-182.2, except that the evaluations shall be completed and findings reported within 45 days of issuance of the court's order for evaluation.

The Commissioner shall give notice of the hearing to any victim of the act resulting in the charges on which the acquittee was acquitted or the next of kin of the victim at the last known address, provided the person submits a written request for such notification to the Commissioner.

C. Upon receipt of the reports of evaluation, the court shall conduct a hearing on the petition. The hearing shall be scheduled on an expedited basis and given priority over other civil matters before the court. The acquittee shall be provided with adequate notice of the hearing, of the right to be present at the hearing, the right to the assistance of counsel in preparation for and during the hearing, and the right to introduce evidence and cross-examine witnesses. Written notice of the hearing shall be provided to the attorney for the Commonwealth for the committing jurisdiction. The hearing is a civil proceeding.

At the conclusion of the hearing, based upon the report and other evidence provided at the hearing, the court shall order the acquittee (i) released from confinement if he does not need inpatient hospitalization and does not meet the criteria for conditional release set forth in § 19.2-182.3, provided the court has approved a discharge plan prepared jointly by the hospital and the appropriate community services board or behavioral health authority; (ii) placed on conditional release if he meets the criteria for such release as set forth in § 19.2-182.7, and the court has approved a conditional release plan prepared jointly by the hospital and the appropriate community services board or behavioral health authority; or (iii) retained in the custody of the Commissioner if he continues to require inpatient hospitalization based on consideration of the factors set forth in § 19.2-182.3.

D. Persons committed pursuant to this chapter shall be released only in accordance with the procedures set forth governing release and conditional release.

History.
1991, c. 427; 1993, c. 295; 2007, cc. 485, 565, 785.

The 2007 amendments.
The 2007 amendments by cc. 485 and 565 are identical, and inserted "or behavioral health authority" following "community services board" at the end of the second sentence in subsection A and at the end of clauses (i) and (ii) in the last paragraph of subsection C.

The 2007 amendment by c. 785 inserted "with respect to the factors set forth in § 19.2-182.3" in subsection A; inserted the subdivision designators, substituted "When a petition for release is made by the acquittee" for "Upon receipt of a petition for release" in subdivision B 1; added subdivision B 2 and made related changes.

§ 19.2-182.7. Conditional release; criteria; conditions; reports.

At any time the court considers the acquittee's need for inpatient hospitalization pursuant to this chapter, it shall place the acquittee on conditional release if it finds that (i) based on consideration of the factors which the court must consider in its commitment decision, he does not need inpatient hospitalization but needs outpatient treatment or monitoring to prevent his condition from deteriorating to a degree that he would need inpatient hospitalization; (ii) appropriate outpatient supervision and treatment are reasonably available; (iii) there is significant reason to believe that the acquittee, if conditionally released, would comply with the conditions specified; and (iv) conditional release will not present an undue risk to public safety. The court shall subject a conditionally released acquittee to such orders and conditions it deems will best meet the acquittee's need for treatment and supervision and best serve the interests of justice and society.

The community services board or behavioral health authority as designated by the Commissioner shall implement the court's conditional release orders and shall submit written reports to the court on the acquittee's progress and adjustment in the community no less frequently than every six months. An aquittee's conditional release shall not be revoked solely because of his voluntary admission to a state hospital.

After a finding by the court that the acquittee has violated the conditions of his release but does not require inpatient hospitalization pursuant to § 19.2-182.8, the court may hold the acquittee in contempt of court for violation of the conditional release order.

History.
1991, c. 427; 1999, cc. 700, 746; 2007, cc. 485, 565; 2008, c. 810.

The 2007 amendments.
The 2007 amendments by cc. 485 and 565 are identical, and substituted "or behavioral health authority as designated by the Commissioner" for "serving the locality in which the acquittee will reside upon release" in the second paragraph.

The 2008 amendments.
The 2008 amendment by c. 810 added the last sentence to the second paragraph.

§ 19.2-182.8. Revocation of conditional release.

If at any time the court that released an acquittee pursuant to § 19.2-182.7 finds reasonable ground to believe that an acquittee on conditional release (i) has violated the conditions of his release or is no longer a proper subject for conditional release based on application of the criteria for conditional release and (ii) requires inpatient hospitalization, it may order an evaluation of the acquittee by a psychiatrist or clinical psychologist, provided the psychiatrist or clinical psychologist is qualified by training and experience to perform forensic evaluations. If the court, based on the evaluation and after hearing evidence on the issue, finds by a preponderance of the evidence that an acquittee on conditional release (a) has violated the conditions of his release or is no longer a proper subject for conditional release based on application of the criteria for conditional release and (b) has mental illness or intellectual disability and requires inpatient hospitalization, the court may revoke the acquittee's conditional release and order him returned to the custody of the Commissioner.

At any hearing pursuant to this section, the acquittee shall be provided with adequate notice of the hearing, of the right to be present at the hearing, the right to the assistance of counsel in preparation for and during the hearing, and the right to introduce evidence and cross-examine witnesses at the hearing. The hearing shall be scheduled on an expedited basis and shall be given priority over other civil matters before the court. Written notice of the hearing shall be provided to the attorney for the Commonwealth for the committing jurisdiction. The hearing is a civil proceeding.

History.
1991, c. 427; 1993, c. 295; 1996, cc. 937, 980; 2006, cc. 343, 369, 370; 2008, c. 810; 2012, cc. 476, 507.

The 2008 amendments.
The 2008 amendment by c. 810 deleted the last sentence of the first paragraph, which read: "An acquittee's conditional release

shall not be revoked solely because of his voluntary hospital admission."

The 2012 amendments.

The 2012 amendments by cc. 476 and 507 are identical, and substituted in the second sentence of the first paragraph, substituted the clause (a) designator for the former clause (i) designator and "(b) has mental illness or intellectual disability" for "(ii) is mentally ill or mentally retarded."

CASE NOTES

Applied in Eastlack v. Commonwealth, 282 Va. 120, 710 S.E.2d 723, 2011 Va. LEXIS 126 (2011).

§ 19.2-182.9. Emergency custody of conditionally released acquittee.

When exigent circumstances do not permit compliance with revocation procedures set forth in § 19.2-182.8, any district court judge or a special justice, as defined in § 37.2-100, or a magistrate may issue an emergency custody order, upon the sworn petition of any responsible person or upon his own motion based upon probable cause to believe that an acquittee on conditional release (i) has violated the conditions of his release or is no longer a proper subject for conditional release and (ii) requires inpatient hospitalization. The emergency custody order shall require the acquittee within his judicial district to be taken into custody and transported to a convenient location where a person designated by the community services board or behavioral health authority who is skilled in the diagnosis and treatment of mental illness shall evaluate such acquittee and assess his need for inpatient hospitalization. A law-enforcement officer who, based on his observation or the reliable reports of others, has probable cause to believe that any acquittee on conditional release has violated the conditions of his release and is no longer a proper subject for conditional release and requires emergency evaluation to assess the need for inpatient hospitalization, may take the acquittee into custody and transport him to an appropriate location to assess the need for hospitalization without prior judicial authorization. The evaluation shall be conducted immediately. The acquittee shall remain in custody until a temporary detention order is issued or until he is released, but in no event shall the period of custody exceed four hours. However, upon a finding by a district court judge, special justice as defined in § 37.2-100, or magistrate that good cause exists to grant an extension, the district court judge, special justice, or magistrate shall extend the emergency custody order, or shall issue an order extending the period of emergency custody, one time for an additional period not to exceed two hours. Good cause for an extension includes the need for additional time to allow (a) the community services board to identify a suitable facility in which the person can be temporarily detained pursuant to this section or (b) a medical evaluation of the person to be

completed if necessary. If it appears from all evidence readily available (i) that the acquittee has violated the conditions of his release or is no longer a proper subject for conditional release and (ii) that he requires emergency evaluation to assess the need for inpatient hospitalization, the district court judge or a special justice, as defined in § 37.2-100, or magistrate, upon the advice of such person skilled in the diagnosis and treatment of mental illness, may issue a temporary detention order authorizing the executing officer to place the acquittee in an appropriate institution for a period not to exceed 48 hours prior to a hearing. If the 48-hour period terminates on a Saturday, Sunday, legal holiday, or day on which the court is lawfully closed, the acquittee may be detained until the next day which is not a Saturday, Sunday, legal holiday, or day on which the court is lawfully closed.

The committing court or any district court judge or a special justice, as defined in § 37.2-100, shall have jurisdiction to hear the matter. Prior to the hearing, the acquittee shall be examined by a psychiatrist or licensed clinical psychologist, provided the psychiatrist or clinical psychologist is skilled in the diagnosis of mental illness, who shall certify whether the person is in need of hospitalization. At the hearing the acquittee shall be provided with adequate notice of the hearing, of the right to be present at the hearing, the right to the assistance of counsel in preparation for and during the hearing, and the right to introduce evidence and cross-examine witnesses at the hearing. Following the hearing, if the court determines, based on a preponderance of the evidence presented at the hearing, that the acquittee (i) has violated the conditions of his release or is no longer a proper subject for conditional release and (ii) has mental illness or intellectual disability and is in need of inpatient hospitalization, the court shall revoke the acquittee's conditional release and place him in the custody of the Commissioner.

When an acquittee on conditional release pursuant to this chapter is taken into emergency custody, detained, or hospitalized, such action shall be considered to have been taken pursuant to this section, notwithstanding the fact that his status as an insanity acquittee was not known at the time of custody, detention, or hospitalization. Detention or hospitalization of an acquittee pursuant to provisions of law other than those applicable to insanity acquittees pursuant to this chapter shall not render the detention or hospitalization invalid. If a person's status as an insanity acquittee on conditional release is not recognized at the time of emergency custody or detention, at the time his status as such is verified, the provisions applicable to such persons shall be applied and the court hearing the matter shall notify the committing court of the proceedings.

History.

1991, c. 427; 1993, c. 295; 1996, cc. 937, 980; 2001, c. 837; 2005, c. 716; 2006, cc. 343, 370; 2008, c. 810; 2009, cc. 21, 838; 2012, cc. 476, 507.

The 2008 amendments.

The 2008 amendment by c. 810 deleted the last sentence of the second paragraph, which read: "An acquittee's conditional release shall not be revoked solely because of his voluntary hospital admission."

The 2009 amendments.

The 2009 amendment by c. 21, effective February 23, 2009, inserted the sixth and seventh sentences in the first paragraph.

The 2009 amendments by c. 838, effective April 8, 2009, added nearly identical sentences as c. 21, but inserted "district court judge, special justice, or" preceding "magistrate shall extend" in the sixth sentence and made a minor stylistic change in the seventh sentence. The first paragraph has been set out in the form above at the direction of the Virginia Code Commission.

The 2012 amendments.

The 2012 amendments by cc. 476 and 507 are identical, and substituted "intellectual disability" for "mental retardation" in clause (ii) of the second paragraph.

Law Review.

For annual survey article, "Health Care Law," see 44 U. Rich. L. Rev. 473 (2009).

§ 19.2-182.10. Release of person whose conditional release was revoked.

If an acquittee is returned to the custody of the Commissioner for inpatient treatment pursuant to revocation proceedings, and his condition improves to the degree that, within 60 days of resumption of custody following the hearing, the acquittee, in the opinion of hospital staff treating the acquittee and the supervising community services board or behavioral health authority, is an appropriate candidate for conditional release, he may be, with the approval of the court, conditionally released as if revocation had not taken place. If treatment is required for longer than 60 days, the acquittee shall be returned to the custody of the Commissioner for a period of hospitalization and treatment which is governed by the provisions of this chapter applicable to committed acquittees.

History.

1991, c. 427; 1993, c. 295; 2006, cc. 199, 225; 2007, cc. 485, 565.

The 2007 amendments.

The 2007 amendments by cc. 485 and 565 are identical, and inserted "or behavioral health authority" following "community services board" in the first sentence.

§ 19.2-182.11. Modification or removal of conditions; notice; objections; review.

A. The committing court may modify conditions of release or remove conditions placed on release pursuant to § 19.2-182.7, upon petition of the supervising community services board or behavioral health authority, the attorney for the Commonwealth, or the acquittee or upon its own motion based on reports of the supervising community services board or behavioral health authority. However, the acquittee may petition only annually commencing six months after the conditional release order is issued. Upon petition, the court shall require the supervising community services board or behavioral

health authority to provide a report on the acquittee's progress while on conditional release.

B. As it deems appropriate based on the community services board's or behavioral health authority's report and any other evidence provided to it, the court may issue a proposed order for modification or removal of conditions. The court shall provide notice of the order, and their right to object to it within ten days of its issuance, to the acquittee, the supervising community services board or behavioral health authority and the attorney for the Commonwealth for the committing jurisdiction and for the jurisdiction where the acquittee is residing on conditional release. The proposed order shall become final if no objection is filed within ten days of its issuance. If an objection is so filed, the court shall conduct a hearing at which the acquittee, the attorney for the Commonwealth, and the supervising community services board or behavioral health authority have an opportunity to present evidence challenging the proposed order. At the conclusion of the hearing, the court shall issue an order specifying conditions of release or removing existing conditions of release.

History.

1991, c. 427; 2007, cc. 485, 565.

The 2007 amendments.

The 2007 amendments by cc. 485 and 565 are identical, and inserted "or behavioral health authority" following "community services board" three times in subsection A and twice in subsection B; and inserted "or behavioral health authority's" following "community services board's" in the first sentence of subsection B.

§ 19.2-182.12. Representation of Commonwealth and acquittee.

The attorney for the Commonwealth shall represent the Commonwealth in all proceedings held pursuant to this chapter. The court shall appoint counsel for the acquittee unless the acquittee waives his right to counsel. The court shall consider appointment of the person who represented the acquittee at the last proceeding.

History.

1991, c. 427; 1993, c. 295.

§ 19.2-182.13. Authority of Commissioner; delegation to board; liability.

The Commissioner may delegate any of the duties and powers imposed on or granted to him by this chapter to an administrative board composed of persons with demonstrated expertise in such matters. The Department of Behavioral Health and Developmental Services shall assist the board in its administrative and technical duties. Members of the board shall exercise their powers and duties without compensation and shall be immune from personal liability while acting within the scope of their duties except for intentional misconduct.

History.

1991, c. 427; 2009, cc. 813, 840.

The 2009 amendments.

The 2009 amendments by cc. 813 and 840 are identical, and substituted "Department of Behavioral Health and Developmental Services" for "Department of Mental Health, Mental Retardation and Substance Abuse Services."

§ 19.2-182.14. Escape of persons placed or committed; penalty.

Any person placed in the temporary custody of the Commissioner pursuant to § 19.2-182.2 or committed to the custody of the Commissioner pursuant to § 19.2-182.3 who escapes from such custody shall be guilty of a Class 6 felony.

History.

1993, c. 295.

Cross references.

As to punishment for Class 6 felonies, see § 18.2-10.

§ 19.2-182.15. Escape of persons placed on conditional release; penalty.

Any person placed on conditional release pursuant to § 19.2-182.7 who leaves the Commonwealth without permission from the court which conditionally released the person shall be guilty of a Class 6 felony.

History.

1993, c. 295.

Cross references.

As to punishment for Class 6 felonies, see § 18.2-10.

§ 19.2-182.16. Copies of orders to Commissioner.

Copies of all orders and notices issued pursuant to this chapter shall be sent to the Commissioner of the Department of Behavioral Health and Developmental Services.

History.

1993, c. 295; 2009, cc. 813, 840.

The 2009 amendments.

The 2009 amendments by cc. 813 and 840 are identical, and substituted "Department of Behavioral Health and Developmental Services" for "Department of Mental Health, Mental Retardation and Substance Abuse Services."

CHAPTER 12.

PRELIMINARY HEARING.

§ 19.2-183. Examination of witnesses; assistance of counsel; evidentiary matters and remedies; power to adjourn case.

A. The judge before whom any person is brought for an offense shall, as soon as may be practical, in the presence of such person, examine on oath the witnesses for and against him. Before conducting the hearing or accepting a waiver of the hearing, the judge shall advise the accused of his right to counsel and, if the accused is indigent and the offense charged be punishable by confinement in jail or the state correctional facility, the judge shall appoint counsel as provided by law.

B. At the hearing the judge shall, in the presence of the accused, hear testimony presented for and against the accused in accordance with the rules of evidence applicable to criminal trials in this Commonwealth. In felony cases, the accused shall not be called upon to plead, but he may cross-examine any witness who testifies on behalf of the Commonwealth or on behalf of any other defendant, introduce witnesses in his own behalf, and testify in his own behalf.

C. A judge may adjourn a trial, pending before him, not exceeding 10 days at one time, without the consent of the accused.

D. At any preliminary hearing under this section, certificates of analysis and reports prepared pursuant to §§ 19.2-187 and 19.2-188 shall be admissible without the testimony of the person preparing such certificate or report.

History.

Code 1950, §§ 19.1-101, 19.1-102; 1960, c. 366; 1968, c. 639; 1973, c. 485; 1975, c. 495; 1982, c. 513; 2010, c. 555.

The 2010 amendments.

The 2010 amendment by c. 555 substituted "any witness who testifies on behalf of the Commonwealth or on behalf of any other defendant" for "witnesses" in subsection B; added subsection D; and made a minor stylistic change.

Michie's Jurisprudence.
For related discussion, see 5B M.J. Criminal Procedure, §§ 17, 18, 20, 24.

CASE NOTES

Purpose. — This section's purpose is to provide for the orderly and expeditious handling of criminal charges to determine whether they should go forward; it authorizes continuances of up to ten days without the consent of the accused, but it does not forbid granting longer continuances for good cause. Ricks v. Commonwealth, No. 0882-89-1 (Ct. of Appeals, Feb. 12, 1991).

The preliminary hearing is essentially a screening process. Its primary purpose is to determine whether there is "sufficient cause" for charging the accused with the crime alleged, that is, whether there is reasonable ground to believe that the crime has been committed and whether the accused is the person who committed it. Moore v. Commonwealth, 218 Va. 388, 237 S.E.2d 187 (1977).

A preliminary hearing may not be used for the purpose of discovery. Foster v. Commonwealth, 209 Va. 297, 163 S.E.2d 565 (1968).

Neither this section nor any rule of court gives counsel for the accused the right to call witnesses at the preliminary hearing for the purpose of discovery. Williams v. Commonwealth, 208 Va. 724, 160 S.E.2d 781, cert. denied, 393 U.S. 1006, 89 S. Ct. 497, 21 L. Ed. 2d 470 (1968); Foster v. Commonwealth, 209 Va. 297, 163 S.E.2d 565 (1968).

Because a preliminary hearing is essentially a screening process, the Code of Virginia prescribed as early as 1849, and still prescribes, that the examining judge "shall examine on oath the witnesses for and against ... [the accused]." Defense counsel therefore had the right to present evidence for accused, that is, to show there was no reasonable ground for belief that he had committed murder. But counsel could not complain of the county judge's actions at the preliminary hearing on the ground that they were denied the right to discover evidence that might be used by the Commonwealth at a subsequent trial in the circuit court. Williams v. Commonwealth, 208 Va. 724, 160 S.E.2d 781, cert. denied, 393 U.S. 1006, 89 S. Ct. 497, 21 L. Ed. 2d 470 (1968).

Refusal to permit witnesses to testify. — Where counsel for defendant made no suggestion to the police court that the testimony of any of the witnesses not permitted to testify would tend to show either that the crime had not been committed or that any of the defendants had not committed the crime, and there was no showing that defendant was prejudiced by the court's action in refusing to permit the witnesses to testify, the trial court committed no error in overruling defendant's motion to quash the indictment because he was denied a proper preliminary hearing. Foster v. Commonwealth, 209 Va. 297, 163 S.E.2d 565 (1968).

§ 19.2-183.1. Joint preliminary hearings.

Upon motion of the attorney for the Commonwealth, preliminary hearings for persons alleged to have participated in contemporaneous and related acts or occurrences or in a series of such acts or occurrences constituting an offense or offenses may be heard jointly if jurisdiction over each person and offense lies in the same court, unless the court finds that such joint preliminary hearing would constitute prejudice to a defendant. Upon such a finding, the court shall order that the preliminary hearing for that defendant be held separately.

History.
1993, cc. 462, 489.

Michie's Jurisprudence.
For related discussion, see 5B M.J. Criminal Procedure, § 20.

§ 19.2-184. Witnesses may be separated (Subsection (a) of Supreme Court Rule 2:615 derived in part from this section).

While a witness is under such examination all other witnesses may by order of the judge be excluded from the place of examination and kept separate from each other.

History.
Code 1950, § 19.1-104; 1960, c. 366; 1968, c. 639; 1975, c. 495.

Editor's note.
At the direction of the Virginia Code Commission, the notation to the Virginia Rules of Evidence was added to the catchline of this section. Acts 2012, cc. 688 and 708, cl. 6 provides: "That pursuant to the authority set forth in §§ 30-146 and 30-147 of the Code of Virginia, the Virginia Code Commission shall direct any party with whom the Virginia Code Commission contracts to publish the Code of Virginia to include in the catchline of every section of the Code of Virginia from which any rule contained in the Rules of Evidence has been derived a notation specifying such rule."

Michie's Jurisprudence.
For related discussion, see 20 M.J. Witnesses, § 35.

§ 19.2-185. Testimony may be reduced to writing and subscribed.

When the judge deems it proper the testimony of the witnesses may be reduced to writing, and, if required by him, shall be signed by them respectively.

The judge of the court of record to which the case may be or has been certified may order the testimony of the witnesses at the preliminary hearing to be reduced to writing.

History.
Code 1950, § 19.1-105; 1960, c. 366; 1968, c. 639; 1975, c. 495.

CASE NOTES

Failure to record preliminary hearing as error of judgment by counsel. — In a prosecution under § 18.2-361, defense counsel's failure to record the preliminary hearing constitutes a serious error of judgment in a case where the credibility of the prosecutrix is at issue. Lankford v. Foster, 546 F. Supp. 241 (W.D. Va. 1982), aff'd, 716 F.2d 896 (4th Cir. 1983), cert. denied, 467 U.S. 1214, 104 S. Ct. 2655, 81 L. Ed. 2d 362 (1984).

Circuit court authorized defendant to employ court reporter because transcript of the preliminary hearing may be an effective tool for cross-examining and impeaching witnesses at trial. However, the responsibility for employing the court reporter and having her present rested with the defendant, and the court's denial of a motion for continuance based on the court reporter's absence, did not result in an abuse of discretion. Lebedun v. Commonwealth, 27 Va. App. 697, 501 S.E.2d 427 (1998).

§ 19.2-186. When accused to be discharged, tried, committed or bailed by judge.

The judge shall discharge the accused if he considers that there is not sufficient cause for charging him with the offense.

If a judge considers that there is sufficient cause only to charge the accused with an offense which the judge has jurisdiction to try, then he shall try the accused for such offense and convict him if he deems him guilty and pass judgment upon him in accordance with law just as if the accused had first been brought before him on a warrant charging him with such offense.

If a judge considers that there is sufficient cause to charge the accused with an offense that he does not have jurisdiction to try then he shall certify the case to the appropriate court having jurisdiction and shall commit the accused to jail or let him to bail pursuant to the provisions of Article 1 (§ 19.2-119 et seq.) of Chapter 9 of this title.

History.
Code 1950, § 19.1-106; 1960, c. 366; 1968, c. 639; 1973, c. 485; 1975, c. 495; 1999, cc. 829, 846.

Michie's Jurisprudence.
For related discussion, see 2B M.J. Bail and Recognizance, § 8; 5B M.J. Criminal Procedure, §§ 19, 21.

CASE NOTES

The word "shall" in the clause "then he shall try the accused for such an offense" means the court has the responsibility to proceed to try the accused on the misdemeanor, either at the time of the hearing (but subsequent to the finding of no probable cause on the felony) or at some later time. Moore v. Commonwealth, 218 Va. 388, 237 S.E.2d 187 (1977).

"Shall" is directory only. — It is manifest from the statutes that the General Assembly intended "shall," in the clause "then he shall try the accused for such offense," to be directory only, and not mandatory. Moore v. Commonwealth, 218 Va. 388, 237 S.E.2d 187 (1977).

And district court need not immediately try accused on merits of lesser misdemeanor offense. — The district court has the potential jurisdiction to proceed under certain circumstances to try the accused for a lesser misdemeanor offense included within the felony charge then before the court. But, the district court, when it makes a finding of no probable cause, is not required to proceed immediately to try the accused on the merits of such lesser offense, although the court may elect to do so. Moore v. Commonwealth, 218 Va. 388, 237 S.E.2d 187 (1977).

Under this section, the court, in order to try the defendant for the lesser offense, must find not only lack of probable cause on the felony charge but also sufficient cause to charge the accused with the misdemeanor. And even then, as we construe the statute, the court is not obligated as a part of that proceeding to try the defendant at that time on the merits of the misdemeanor. Moore v. Commonwealth, 218 Va. 388, 237 S.E.2d 187 (1977).

Where the defendant is not before the court on a felony, the only options open to the court are a finding of guilty or not guilty. Greenwalt v. Commonwealth, 224 Va. 498, 297 S.E.2d 709 (1982).

Municipal court had jurisdiction to convict defendants of lesser misdemeanor offenses included within felonies then before the circuit court. Rouzie v. Commonwealth, 215 Va. 174, 207 S.E.2d 854 (1974).

But such convictions placed defendants in double jeopardy. — Municipal court convictions for lesser misdemeanors placed defendants in danger, absent a double jeopardy bar, of prosecution for identical or greater included offenses. Rouzie v. Commonwealth, 215 Va. 174, 207 S.E.2d 854 (1974).

The county judge had only one issue to decide when he presided at a preliminary hearing: whether there was sufficient cause for charging accused with murder, or, in other words, whether there was reasonable ground to believe that a murder had been committed and accused was the person who had committed the murder. Williams v. Commonwealth, 208 Va. 724, 160 S.E.2d 781, cert. denied, 393 U.S. 1006, 89 S. Ct. 497, 21 L. Ed. 2d 470 (1968).

Dismissal of felony warrant is not acquittal or finding of not guilty. — A mere dismissal of a felony warrant at a preliminary hearing indicates only a finding of lack of probable cause. Since jeopardy has not attached, discharge cannot operate as an acquittal, or finding of not guilty, of any lesser included misdemeanor offense. Moore v. Commonwealth, 218 Va. 388, 237 S.E.2d 187 (1977).

Retrial precluded after swearing of witness and dismissal on refusal of Commonwealth to proceed. — Where the trial court ruled against prosecuting defendant on a felony charge, but found probable cause supporting a misdemeanor charge and accordingly swore in a witness, but the attorney for the Commonwealth refused to question the witness, stating that he wished to secure a grand jury for a felony charge, upon which the judge properly dismissed the case, the attorney for the Commonwealth could not prosecute the case anew on a felony charge, as double jeopardy had attached. The Commonwealth had the opportunity to question the sworn witness, defendant had risked a determination of guilt, and absent manifest necessity defendant could not be retried for the same offense. Goolsby v. Hutto, 529 F. Supp. 92 (E.D. Va. 1981), aff'd, 691 F.2d 199 (4th Cir. 1982).

CIRCUIT COURT OPINIONS

Double jeopardy. — Defendant's double jeopardy rights were not violated when a prosecutor had a felony charge reinstated after taking a dismissal of a lesser included misdemeanor charge on appeal; although jeopardy attached when a general district court tried defendant on a lesser offense, the judgment was annulled when defendant exercised the right to appeal and sought a trial de novo in a circuit court. Commonwealth v. Painter, 64 Va. Cir. 455, 2004 Va. Cir. LEXIS 161 (Rockingham County 2004), aff'd, 47 Va. App. 225, 623 S.E.2d 408 (2005).

§ 19.2-187. Admission into evidence of certain certificates of analysis.

In any hearing or trial of any criminal offense or in any proceeding brought pursuant to Chapter 22.1 (§ 19.2-386.1 et seq.), a certificate of analysis of a person performing an analysis or examination, duly attested by such person, shall be admissible in evidence as evidence of the facts therein stated and the results of the analysis or examination referred to therein, provided (i) the certificate of analysis is filed with the clerk of the court hearing the case at least seven days prior to the proceeding if the attorney for the Commonwealth intends to offer it into evidence in a preliminary hearing or the accused intends to offer it into evidence in any hearing or trial, or (ii) the requirements of subsection A of § 19.2-187.1 have been satisfied and the accused has not objected to the admission of the certificate pursuant to subsection B of § 19.2-187.1, when any such analysis or examination is performed in any laboratory operated by the Division of Consolidated Laboratory Services or the Department of Forensic Science or authorized by such Department to conduct such analysis or examination, or performed by a person licensed by the Department of Forensic Science pursuant to § 18.2-268.9 or 46.2-341.26:9 to conduct such analysis or examination, or performed by the Federal Bureau of Investigation, the federal Postal Inspection Service, the federal Bureau of Alcohol, Tobacco and Firearms, the Naval Criminal Investigative Service, the National Fish and Wildlife Forensics Laboratory, the federal Drug Enforcement Administration, the Forensic Document Laboratory of the U.S. Department of Homeland Security, or the U.S. Secret Service Laboratory.

In a hearing or trial in which the provisions of subsection A of § 19.2-187.1 do not apply, a copy of such certificate shall be mailed or delivered by the clerk or attorney for the Commonwealth to counsel of record for the accused at no charge at least seven days prior to the hearing or trial upon request made by such counsel to the clerk with notice of the request to the attorney for the Commonwealth. The request to the clerk shall be on a form prescribed by the Supreme Court and filed with the clerk at least 10 days prior to the hearing or trial. In the event that a request for a copy of a certificate is filed with the clerk with respect to a case that is not yet before the court, the clerk shall advise the requester that he must resubmit the request at such time as the case is properly before the court in order for such request to be effective. If, upon proper request made by counsel of record for the accused, a copy of such certificate is not mailed or delivered by the clerk or attorney for the Commonwealth to counsel of record for the accused in a timely manner in accordance with this section, the accused shall be entitled to continue the hearing or trial.

The certificate of analysis of any examination conducted by the Department of Forensic Science relating to a controlled substance, marijuana, or synthetic cannabinoids as defined in § 18.2-248.1:1 shall be mailed or forwarded by personnel of the Department of Forensic Science to the attorney for the Commonwealth of the jurisdiction where such offense may be heard. The attorney for the Commonwealth shall acknowledge receipt of the certificate on forms provided by the laboratory.

Any such certificate of analysis purporting to be signed by any such person shall be admissible as evidence in such hearing or trial without any proof of the seal or signature or of the official character of the person whose name is signed to it.

For the purposes of this section and §§ 19.2-187.01, 19.2-187.1, and 19.2-187.2, the term "certificate of analysis" includes reports of analysis and results of laboratory examination.

History.
Code 1950, § 19.1-106.1; 1974, c. 200; 1975, c. 495; 1976, c. 245; 1983, c. 178; 1984, c. 607; 1988, c. 494; 1990, cc. 737, 825; 1992, c. 56; 1994, cc. 41, 375; 1995, c. 437; 1999, c. 296; 2000, c. 336; 2002, c. 832; 2005, cc. 868, 881; 2006, c. 294; 2009, Sp. Sess. I, cc. 1, 4; 2010, c. 656; 2011, cc. 384, 410, 645.

Editor's note.
Acts 2011, cc. 384 and 410, cl. 3 provides: "That the provisions of this act may result in a net increase in periods of imprisonment or commitment. Pursuant to § 30-19.1:4, the estimated amount of the necessary appropriation cannot be determined for periods of imprisonment in state adult correctional facilities; therefore, Chapter 874 of the Acts of Assembly of 2010 requires the Virginia Criminal Sentencing Commission to assign a minimum fiscal impact of $50,000. Pursuant to § 30-19.1:4, the estimated amount of the necessary appropriation cannot be determined for periods of commitment to the custody of the Department of Juvenile Justice."

The 2009 amendments.
The 2009 amendments by Sp. Sess. I, c. 1, effective August 21, 2009, and Sp. Sess. I, c. 4, effective September 15, 2009, are

identical, and rewrote the first paragraph; and in the second paragraph, added "In a hearing or trial in which the provisions of subsection A of § 19.2-187.1 do not apply" at the beginning of the first sentence, inserted "the hearing or" preceding "trial" at the end of the second sentence, and substituted "accused" for "defendant" near the end of the last sentence.

The 2010 amendments.
The 2010 amendment by c. 656 inserted the last paragraph.

The 2011 amendments.
The 2011 amendments by cc. 384 and 410, effective March 23, 2011, are identical, and inserted "synthetic cannabinoids as defined in § 18.2-248.1:1" and made a related change in the first sentence of the third paragraph, and made a minor stylistic change.
The 2011 amendment by c. 645, in the first paragraph, inserted "the Forensic Document Laboratory of the U.S. Department of Homeland Security" and substituted "U.S. Secret Service Laboratory" for "United States Secret Service Laboratory."

Law Review.
For survey of Virginia criminal procedure for the year 1975-1976, see 62 Va. L. Rev. 1412 (1976). For 1995 survey of criminal law and procedure, see 29 U. Rich. L. Rev. 951 (1995). For an article on bifurcated sentencing in noncapital felony cases in Virginia, see 30 U. Rich. L. Rev. 465 (1996). For an article, "Criminal Law and Procedure," see 31 U. Rich. L. Rev. 1015 (1997). For 2006 survey article, "Criminal Law and Procedure," see 41 U. Rich. L. Rev. 83 (2006). For 2007 annual survey article, "Criminal Law and Procedure," see 42 U. Rich. L. Rev. 311 (2007).

Michie's Jurisprudence.
For related discussion, see 5B M.J. Criminal Procedure, §§ 23, 56; 6B M.J. Drugs and Druggists, § 5; 7B M.J. Evidence, §§ 86, 199.

CASE NOTES

I. In General.
II. Requirements of Certificate of Analysis.
III. Request for Copy of Certificate.

I. IN GENERAL.

Purpose of statute. — The purpose of § 19.2-187 is to ensure that a breath test certificate to be used in evidence is lodged timely in a secure and appropriate place, accessible to the accused, and available to the accused upon request; the statute sets forth a specific statement of admissibility of certificates and once its provisos are satisfied, the statement is complete, and a certificate thus qualified is properly received into evidence. Cephas v. Commonwealth, No. 3359-01-4, 2003 Va. App. LEXIS 114 (Ct. of Appeals Mar. 4, 2003).

Admission of a certificate of analysis prepared by a forensic scientist that detailed the results of tests he performed to determine that the two substances found on defendant's person were crack cocaine and marijuana was not error, and § 19.2-187 allowing for the admission of certain writings even though they would otherwise be considered inadmissible hearsay was not implicated, as the forensic scientist who prepared the certificate was present, he testified and authenticated the certificate, and he was available to be cross-examined. Bell v. Commonwealth, 49 Va. App. 570, 643 S.E.2d 497, 2007 Va. App. LEXIS 152 (2007).

Purpose of provisos and the second paragraph of this section. — The purpose of the provisos is to ensure that the certificate to be used in evidence is lodged timely in a secure and appropriate place, accessible to the accused, and available to him upon request. Stokes v. Commonwealth, 11 Va. App. 550, 399 S.E.2d 453 (1991).

The second paragraph of this section serves an entirely different purpose: it provides for the coordination of governmental agencies to facilitate the development of his case by the attorney for the Commonwealth. Stokes v. Commonwealth, 11 Va. App. 550, 399 S.E.2d 453 (1991).

Had the legislature intended the provisions of the second paragraph of this section to be a condition of admissibility, it would have incorporated those requirements as enumerated provisos into the first paragraph. Stokes v. Commonwealth, 11 Va. App. 550, 399 S.E.2d 453 (1991).

Exception to hearsay rule. — This section creates an exception to the hearsay rule and permits the written analysis to be admitted into evidence without requiring the in-court presence of the person who prepared the document. Allen v. Commonwealth, 3 Va. App. 657, 353 S.E.2d 162 (1987).

This section was enacted to allow into evidence a written report of an analysis or examination conducted by specified laboratories, without requiring that the technicians be present. Myrick v. Commonwealth, 13 Va. App. 333, 412 S.E.2d 176 (1991).

Court rejected petitioner's claim that he was denied the effective assistance of counsel at trial due to his counsel's failure to raise the issue that the Commonwealth violated his right to confront and cross-examine witnesses when it introduced certificates of analysis in an attempt to authenticate several letters allegedly written by petitioner. The record, including the certificates of analysis, showed that the Commonwealth complied with the requirements of § 19.2-187 as the certificates were attested to by the scientists who performed the handwriting analysis and, therefore, the scientists were not required to appear at trial; also petitioner admitted to the police that he wrote the letters. Powell v. Warden of the Sussex I State Prison, — Va. —, — S.E.2d —, 2005 Va. LEXIS 106 (Nov. 8, 2005).

This section imposes a condition for the exoneration of an otherwise hearsay document from the application of the hearsay rule, thus making that document admissible. Winston v. Commonwealth, 16 Va. App. 901, 434 S.E.2d 4 (1993).

No violation of Confrontation Clause. — Defendant waived her Sixth Amendment rights to confrontation by failing to avail herself of her statutory right under § 19.2-187.1 to subpoena the operator of a breath test in her driving under the influence trial under § 18.2-266. Thus, it was proper to admit the certificate of the blood alcohol analysis without live testimony of the operator pursuant to §§ 18.2-268.9 and 19.2-187. McKeel v. Commonwealth, — Va. App. —, — S.E.2d —, 2006 Va. App. LEXIS 575 (Dec. 19, 2006).

Defendant's failure to timely notify the Commonwealth of his desire to confront forensic analyst at trial on drug charges constituted a waiver of his right to confrontation in that the procedure of §§ 19.2-187 and 19.2-187.1 adequately protected defendant's Confrontation Clause rights. Brooks v. Commonwealth, 49 Va. App. 155, 638 S.E.2d 131, 2006 Va. App. LEXIS 574 (2006).

Because defendant did not timely notify the Commonwealth of defendant's desire to confront a forensic analyst at trial, the procedure in §§ 19.2-187 and 19.2-187.1 adequately protected defendant's Sixth Amendment Confrontation Clause rights; therefore, the trial court did not err in admitting a certificate of analysis when the forensic scientist did not testify. Morton v. Commonwealth, — Va. App. —, — S.E.2d —, 2007 Va. App. LEXIS 39 (Feb. 6, 2007).

Because defendant, charged with possession of cocaine with intent to distribute, in violation of § 18.2-248, neglected to inform the Commonwealth of his desire to have the scientist who prepared the certificate of analysis present until the day of trial, defendant waived his Confrontation Clause rights. Thus, no error resulted in admitting the certificate of analysis without the scientist's testimony. McCray v. Commonwealth, — Va. App. —, — S.E.2d —, 2008 Va. App. LEXIS 36 (Jan. 22, 2008).

Defendant was properly convicted of driving while intoxicated because the trial court did not violate defendant's constitutional right to confrontation when it admitted his blood alcohol breath analysis into evidence in accordance with the terms of § 19.2-187; because defendant did not subpoena the booking tech who administered the blood alcohol breath analysis, he waived his opportunity to cross-examine potential witnesses. Ki-Ho Min v. Commonwealth, — Va. App. —, — S.E.2d —, 2008 Va. App. LEXIS 144 (Mar. 25, 2008).

Defendant waived the constitutional right to confront the person who performed a certificate of analysis on the substance found under the car seat in which he was sitting because defendant did not follow the procedures provided by §§ 19.2-187 and 19.2-187.1; defendant never notified the Commonwealth or the trial court of his desire to confront the witness until the middle of trial. Cypress v.

Commonwealth, — Va. App. —, — S.E.2d —, 2007 Va. App. LEXIS 497 (Jan. 3, 2007).

Defendant waived the constitutional right to confront the person who prepared the certificates of analysis that were performed on the substances found in defendant's apartment and on his person because defendant did not follow the procedures of §§ 19.2-187 and 19.2-187.1; defendant did not notify the Commonwealth or the trial court of his desire to confront the witness until the middle of trial. Briscoe v. Commonwealth, — Va. App. —, — S.E.2d —, 2007 Va. App. LEXIS 498 (Jan. 18, 2007).

In defendants' prosecutions for drug-related offenses, the admission of analysts' certificates of analysis, without the analysts' live testimony, pursuant to §§ 19.2-187 and 19.2-187.1, violated defendants' rights to confrontation because the statutory procedure allowing defendants to call the analysts as adverse witnesses impermissibly relieved the prosecution of the duty to present witnesses and required defendants to call those witnesses, as defendants were not given a period of time, after notice, in which to object to the admission of the certificates absent the analysts' testimony. Cypress v. Commonwealth, 280 Va. 305, 699 S.E.2d 206, 2010 Va. LEXIS 225 (2010).

In defendants' prosecutions for drug-related offenses, the admission of analysts' certificates of analysis, without the analysts' live testimony, pursuant to §§ 19.2-187 and 19.2-187.1, violated defendants' rights to confrontation because neither defendant waived this objection by not using § 19.2-187.1's procedure for calling the analysts to testify, as this procedure impermissibly burdened and did not adequately protect defendants' confrontation rights. Cypress v. Commonwealth, 280 Va. 305, 699 S.E.2d 206, 2010 Va. LEXIS 225 (2010).

Violation of confrontation clause. — In defendants' prosecutions for drug-related offenses, the admission of analysts' certificates of analysis, without the analysts' live testimony, pursuant to §§ 19.2-187 and 19.2-187.1, violated defendants' rights to confrontation because the certificates were testimonial as: (1) each attested that an analyst performed an analysis and that the certificate accurately reflected the results of the analysis; and (2) each showed the substance analyzed was cocaine and the amount of cocaine, so the certificates were functionally identical to live testimony. Cypress v. Commonwealth, 280 Va. 305, 699 S.E.2d 206, 2010 Va. LEXIS 225 (2010).

Chain of custody. — Because the Commonwealth established that evidence submitted was the same as that tested and that it had not been altered, substituted or contaminated prior to testing, any lack of proof regarding identity of the "authorized agent" at testing laboratory who received the evidence was harmless. Harris v. Commonwealth, No. 0909-99-1 (Ct. of Appeals Mar. 7, 2000).

Transfer does not eliminate benefit of prima facie proof. — Because the Commonwealth presented a duly attested certificate of analysis, it established its prima facie evidence of chain of custody. The Commonwealth did not lose the benefit of its prima facie proof when the cocaine was transferred between regional laboratories within the Division of Forensic Science [now the Department of Forensic Science]. While the relevant statutory sections are construed strictly against the Commonwealth, no language in § 19.2-187.01 compels the conclusion that the General Assembly intended to eliminate the presumed, valid chain of custody when items are transferred between Division laboratories. Dunn v. Commonwealth, 20 Va. App. 217, 456 S.E.2d 135 (1995).

In-court appearance of certificate preparer to "certify" document. — Commonwealth incorrectly argued that in-court appearance of preparer of a certificate of analysis to "certify" the document was sufficient to render its out-of-court statements admissible for their truth. Assuming that trooper authenticated the certificate, its contents were inadmissible because they were offered to prove the truth of the matter asserted and did not fall within an exception to the hearsay rule. Hughes v. Commonwealth, No. 2802-96-4 (Ct. of Appeals Nov. 25, 1997).

Duplicate originals are made at the same time, by the same mechanical impression, and each is an exact counterpart of the other. A duplicate original is accorded the same dignity as an original and, if otherwise proper, is similarly admissible in evidence. Winston v. Commonwealth, 16 Va. App. 901, 434 S.E.2d 4 (1993).

Since the duplicate originals of certificates of fingerprint analysis were as reliable and trustworthy as the originals, and the prosecution properly filed them with the clerk, they were admissible under this section. Compliance with § 8.01-390 was unnecessary. Lovak v. Commonwealth, No. 2001-93-4 (Ct. of Appeals March 14, 1995).

Filing of copy raised "best evidence" question. — Defendant's objection on the ground that a copy rather than the original was filed raised a "best evidence" question, which was whether a copy of the certificate of analysis qualified as an original or could be filed in lieu of the original for the purposes of pretrial filing as required by this section. Myrick v. Commonwealth, 13 Va. App. 333, 412 S.E.2d 176 (1991).

While this section provides for pretrial filing of a certificate, rather than for its admissibility in evidence, the purpose of the filing requirement is solely to satisfy the statutory prerequisites in order for the certificate to be admissible at trial; thus, in considering whether a copy, rather than the original, can be filed under this section, the same requirements for admitting a copy into evidence must be satisfied. Myrick v. Commonwealth, 13 Va. App. 333, 412 S.E.2d 176 (1991).

Trial court did not err in ruling that a photocopy of a certificate of analysis could be filed in lieu of an original certificate under this section, provided the proof established that the photocopy was a replica of the original. Myrick v. Commonwealth, 13 Va. App. 333, 412 S.E.2d 176 (1991).

Error found in admitting test results. — Where the record before the appellate court contained no evidence that the field test used by detective had been approved by the division, the appellate court could not determine the reliability of the field test kit used to support detective's testimony that the substance tested positive as cocaine, therefore, the trial court erred when it permitted the detective to testify to the result produced by the test. Galbraith v. Commonwealth, 18 Va. App. 734, 446 S.E.2d 633 (1994).

In this instance, the court of appeals was "unable to say what effect the inadmissible evidence had on the fact finder's decision," despite "independent evidence of the nature of the controlled substance," thus defendant's conviction was reversed. Payne v. Commonwealth, No. 2870-95-4, 1997 Va. App. LEXIS 166 (Ct. of Appeals Mar. 25, 1997).

Opinion testimony. — This section does not allow opinions into evidence without expert testimony. Barber v. Commonwealth, 19 Va. App. 497, 452 S.E.2d 873 (1995).

Opportunity to cross-examine the chemist who performed the tests and who prepared the certificate eliminated the hearsay problem associated with the admission of the certificate when the Commonwealth failed to comply with the filing requirements of this section. Lewis v. Commonwealth, No. 0430-96-2 (Ct. of Appeals June 3, 1997).

Virginia's statutory scheme provides a mechanism for governmental and judicial economy by obviating the need for the prosecution to call the preparer and chain of custody witness. The statutes provide a defendant with adequate notice that the prosecution intends to rely on the certificate and affords a defendant the absolute right to call the preparer or chain of custody witness as an adverse witness should he so desire. Wingfield v. Commonwealth, No. 3000-95-2 (Ct. of Appeals Apr. 1, 1997).

Admission proper. — There was no abuse of discretion in the trial court's admission of certificates of analysis, because the senior analyst from the Division of Forensic Science who testified made her own conclusions from the data to determine the rarity of defendant's DNA profile. Pope v. Commonwealth, 60 Va. App. 486, 729 S.E.2d 751, 2012 Va. App. LEXIS 250 (2012).

II. REQUIREMENTS OF CERTIFICATE OF ANALYSIS.

This section is mandatory, not discretionary. Lewis v. Commonwealth, No. 2479-99-1, 2000 Va. App. LEXIS 560 (Ct. of Appeals Aug. 1, 2000).

Burden of proof. — When the Commonwealth seeks to admit a certificate of analysis containing hearsay evidence, it has the burden of proving that the certificate satisfies the requirements of this section. Taylor v. Commonwealth, 28 Va. App. 1, 502 S.E.2d 113 (1998).

Strict compliance. — This section demands strict compliance. Basfield v. Commonwealth, No. 0291-89-2 (Ct. of Appeals Oct. 2, 1990).

Strict compliance with the pretrial filing provisions of this section is required. Myrick v. Commonwealth, 13 Va. App. 333, 412 S.E.2d

176 (1991); Taylor v. Commonwealth, 28 Va. App. 1, 502 S.E.2d 113 (1998).

A certificate of analysis is not admissible if the Commonwealth fails strictly to comply with the provisions of this section. Bottoms v. Commonwealth, 20 Va. App. 466, 457 S.E.2d 796 (1995).

Where defense counsel sent the Commonwealth's Attorney's Office a copy of the letter it sent to the circuit court clerk requesting a certificate of analysis, that the letter did not include a "cc:" reference indicating the Commonwealth was to receive a copy did not render defendant's notice deficient because such a notation was not required by § 19.2-187. Dotson v. Commonwealth, No. 1416-02-2, 2003 Va. App. LEXIS 282 (Ct. of Appeals May 6, 2003).

Trial court erred in admitting a certificate of analysis establishing that the substances seized from defendant were marijuana and cocaine, because his attorney requested the certificate in the manner provided for in § 19.2-187 and the evidence failed to show a copy of such certificate was mailed or delivered to counsel of record for the accused at least seven days prior to the hearing or trial upon request made by such counsel; moreover, assuming without deciding that the evidence other than the certificate of analysis would have been sufficient to support a finding that the substances seized from defendant and admitted at trial were, in fact, cocaine and marijuana, the appeals court could not conclude, without usurping the trial court's fact-finding function, that the error did not influence the fact-finder. Bell v. Commonwealth, 47 Va. App. 126, 622 S.E.2d 751, 2005 Va. App. LEXIS 493 (2005).

Filing requirements and legislative intent. There is no indication that the legislature intended that the filing requirements of this section relate only to the seven consecutive days immediately preceding a hearing or trial. Mostyn v. Commonwealth, 14 Va. App. 920, 420 S.E.2d 519 (1992).

Timing of indictment, filing of certificate. — This section contains no requirement that the indictment precede the filing of the certificate. The provisos of the statute having been satisfied, the trial court did not err in admitting the certificate into evidence. Blackwell v. Commonwealth, No. 0124-94-3 (Ct. of Appeals July 25, 1995).

Commencement of bench trial. — For most purposes, a bench trial begins when the trial court starts to hear evidence because at that point, a bench trial commences for double jeopardy purposes and likewise triggers the timing of the speedy trial statute; there is no reason why the same principle should not also govern the commencement of bench trials for purposes of § 19.2-187's pretrial disclosure requirements. Bolden v. Commonwealth, 49 Va. App. 285, 640 S.E.2d 526, 2007 Va. App. LEXIS 52 (2007).

Authentication of date stamp. — The Commonwealth must authenticate a date stamp used as proof that a certificate was timely filed with the circuit court but the court may take judicial notice of the date stamp's authenticity where the identity of the official date stamp of the court clerk's office is easily ascertainable from a reliable source such that a reasonably informed person would not regard the identity of the trial court's official date stamp as reasonably subject to dispute. Taylor v. Commonwealth, 28 Va. App. 1, 502 S.E.2d 113 (1998).

Signature requirement. — In order to be admissible as an exception to the hearsay rule, a certificate introduced under this section must bear the examiner's signature as part of an attestation clause included on the certificate. Petit Frere v. Commonwealth, 19 Va. App. 460, 452 S.E.2d 682 (1995).

Signature need not be notarized. — This section does not require notarization of the preparer's signature. Petit Frere v. Commonwealth, 19 Va. App. 460, 452 S.E.2d 682 (1995).

This section should be construed strictly against the Commonwealth and in favor of the accused, particularly the filing requirements. Gray v. Commonwealth, 220 Va. 943, 265 S.E.2d 705 (1980).

Although the court must construe this section strictly against the Commonwealth and in favor of the accused, this section only requires that the certificate be filed. Mostyn v. Commonwealth, 14 Va. App. 920, 420 S.E.2d 519 (1992).

Because this statute deals with criminal matters, and it undertakes to make admissible evidence which otherwise might be objectionable, it should be construed strictly against the Commonwealth and in favor of the accused. Winston v. Commonwealth, 16 Va. App. 901, 434 S.E.2d 4 (1993).

This section should be construed strictly against the Commonwealth and in favor of the accused, because it undertakes to make admissible evidence which otherwise might be subject to a valid hearsay objection. Coleman v. Commonwealth, 27 Va. App. 768, 501 S.E.2d 461 (1998).

Statute sets forth specific safeguards with which Commonwealth must comply. — The statute sets forth specific safeguards with which the Commonwealth must comply when it seeks to have a certificate of drug analysis admitted into evidence without independently proving the test results or authenticity of the report. Myrick v. Commonwealth, 13 Va. App. 333, 412 S.E.2d 176 (1991); Taylor v. Commonwealth, 28 Va. App. 1, 502 S.E.2d 113 (1998).

This section provides a basis for admitting into evidence the results of an analysis performed by the Division of Forensic Science [now the Department of Forensic Science] or the Division of Consolidated Laboratory Services when the certificate showing the results is attested by the person who performed the test, without requiring that person to appear at trial. Galbraith v. Commonwealth, 18 Va. App. 734, 446 S.E.2d 633 (1994).

Statement of admissibility is complete when the provisos are satisfied. — The first paragraph of this section sets forth a specific statement of admissibility of certificates of laboratory analysis subject to provisos expressly stated: When those provisos are satisfied, the statement of admissibility is complete, and a certificate thus qualified is properly received into evidence. Stokes v. Commonwealth, 11 Va. App. 550, 399 S.E.2d 453 (1991).

Once the integrity of the chain is properly established and the remaining provisions of this section and § 19.2-187.01 are satisfied, a certificate of analysis shall be admissible as evidence of facts therein stated and the results of the analysis or examination referred to therein. Crews v. Commonwealth, 18 Va. App. 115, 442 S.E.2d 407 (1994).

The admissibility of a certificate of blood analysis prepared pursuant to former § 18.2-268 (now § 18.2-268.1 et seq.) is governed by the requirements of this section. Basfield v. Commonwealth, No. 0291-89-2 (Ct. of Appeals Oct. 2, 1990); Basfield v. Commonwealth, 11 Va. App. 122, 398 S.E.2d 80 (1990).

Failure to comply with filing provisions renders certificate inadmissible. — In the absence of the preparer of the certificate of analysis as a witness at trial, the failure of the Commonwealth fully to comply with the filing provisions of this section renders the certificate inadmissible. Gray v. Commonwealth, 220 Va. 943, 265 S.E.2d 705 (1980).

If the preparer of the certificate is not produced as a witness at trial, the failure of the Commonwealth fully to comply with the filing provisions of this section renders the certificate inadmissible. Nonnemacker v. Commonwealth, No. 0367-88-2 (Ct. of Appeals Sept. 11, 1990).

A certificate of analysis is not admissible if the commonwealth fails strictly to comply with the provisions of this section. Woodward v. Commonwealth, 16 Va. App. 672, 432 S.E.2d 510 (1993).

As defendant's request to the Commonwealth for copy of the analysis of his breath alcohol content was in proper form, but the certificate was not provided as required by § 19.2-187, his conviction of driving under the influence was reversed; and since the trial court expressly ruled that the remaining evidence was by itself insufficient to convict, the warrant was dismissed. Dotson v. Commonwealth, No. 1416-02-2, 2003 Va. App. LEXIS 282 (Ct. of Appeals May 6, 2003).

Manner in which certificates marked not prescribed. — Section 19.2-187 does not prescribe the manner in which a clerk's office must mark certificates of analysis; accordingly, if there is an objective basis in the record from which a fact finder can determine if and when the certificate was filed in the court, § 19.2-187 is satisfied. Cephas v. Commonwealth, No. 3359-01-4, 2003 Va. App. LEXIS 114 (Ct. of Appeals Mar. 4, 2003).

Prejudice to defendant need not be shown. — Prejudice to the defendant from a failure to comply with this section need not be shown in order to hold evidence inadmissible. Woodward v. Commonwealth, 16 Va. App. 672, 432 S.E.2d 510 (1993).

Defendant's conviction for possession of heroin was reversed and the case remanded for new trial because the admission of a certificate of analysis is always deemed prejudicial. Sheppard v. Commonwealth, No. 1270-03-1, 2004 Va. App. LEXIS 340 (Ct. of Appeals July 13, 2004).

Certificates admissible although improperly filed. —

Where certificates of analysis of the controlled substances found in the defendant's vehicle pertaining to each of the charges were filed with the clerk of the court more than seven days before the trial, but the certificates, although filed in the defendant's files, were not filed in the correct ones, and the record did not reflect that the defendant had been harmed in any manner by the way the certificates were filed, the trial court properly admitted the certificates into evidence. Burns v. Commonwealth, No. 1571-89-4 (Ct. of Appeals Dec. 11, 1990).

Certificate inadmissible absent strict compliance. — In the absence of strict compliance with filing requirement of this section, the certificates were inadmissible and prejudice to the defendant would be presumed. Allen v. Commonwealth, 3 Va. App. 657, 353 S.E.2d 162 (1987).

Although the legislature has excepted a certificate of analysis prepared in accordance with this section from the disability of hearsay, a certificate lacking the requisite attestation clause or otherwise not in "strict compliance" with the statute remains "subject to a valid hearsay objection." Payne v. Commonwealth, No. 2870-95-4, 1997 Va. App. LEXIS 166 (Ct. of Appeals Mar. 25, 1997).

Filing in general district court not authorized as substitute for filing in circuit court. — This section requires that the certificate shall be filed with the clerk of the court hearing the case at least seven days prior to hearing or trial. The statute does not authorize filing in the general district court as a substitute for the proviso that the certificate be filed in the circuit court at least seven days prior to the hearing in the circuit court. Allen v. Commonwealth, 3 Va. App. 657, 353 S.E.2d 162 (1987).

Trial court did not err in admitting certificate of analysis. — Defendant's claim that the trial court erred in admitting a breath test certificate because the Commonwealth did not prove the certificate was filed seven days prior to trial with the clerk of the trial court as required by § 19.2-187, was without merit, as the order of the general district court transferring the case to the trial court was stamped "filed"; when the order arrived in the trial court clerk's office and was stamped as "filed," it was accompanied by the other papers in the case, including the certificate, all of which were "filed" when the order was filed with the clerk. Cephas v. Commonwealth, No. 3359-01-4, 2003 Va. App. LEXIS 114 (Ct. of Appeals Mar. 4, 2003).

Because this section did not not require a preliminary finding of fact that no alcohol was consumed by a defendant between her act of driving and the blood alcohol test, the trial court properly admitted the certificate of analysis. Acheson v. Commonwealth, No. 1706-03-4, 2004 Va. App. LEXIS 566 (Ct. of Appeals Nov. 16, 2004).

On appeal from a conviction of possession of cocaine, pursuant to § 18.2-250, the appeals court found that no error resulted from the trial court's admission of a certificate of analysis, as such was turned over to defendant's first counsel, but lost as a result of transferring defendant's case file to his second counsel, and absent evidence to the contrary, such did not impute fault to the Commonwealth. Hobson v. Commonwealth, — Va. App. —, — S.E.2d —, 2007 Va. App. LEXIS 388 (Oct. 23, 2007).

Certificate of analysis confirming the substance defendant distributed was cocaine was lodged in the file for a related case charging distribution of cocaine. Thus, the certificate was accessible and available to defendant, satisfying both the letter and spirit of § 19.2-187. Stevens v. Commonwealth, 2008 Va. App. LEXIS 412 (Sept. 2, 2008).

Certificate properly admitted. — Certificate of analysis was properly admitted as it was filed in compliance with this section where it was filed in the general district court, a stapled packet of paperwork was received by the trial court from the general district court, and despite the trial court clerk's failure to mark the certificate as filed, it had identical holes to other district court documents the clerk had marked as filed; further, a second copy of the certificate was stapled to the Commonwealth's response to the trial court's discovery order. Holmes v. Commonwealth, No. 2929-03-1, 2004 Va. App. LEXIS 601 (Ct. of Appeals Dec. 7, 2004).

Evidence sufficient to support finding of compliance with this section. — Evidence consisting of the notation that the document was filed on a certain date with the initials of the deputy clerk on the face of the certificate was sufficient to support the finding of the trial court that it was filed in compliance with this section. Carter v. Commonwealth, No. 1930-89-2 (Ct. of Appeals March 26, 1991).

The notation that the document had been "filed" and date and initials of the deputy clerk who filed it were sufficient for the trial court to determine that the certificate had been filed in that court. Carter v. Commonwealth, 12 Va. App. 156, 403 S.E.2d 360 (1991).

Where the trial judge found the original was simply missing without explanation, and the record contained no evidence or testimony from the clerk's office that the certificate in fact had been filed but was misplaced, there was no evidence in the record to support a finding that the certificate was filed in accordance with the mandates of this section. The evidence that the police had in their possession a copy of a certificate stamped "filed on May 27, 1988," was insufficient to establish that the original certificate was properly filed. Johnson v. Commonwealth, No. 1573-89-3 (Ct. of Appeals April 9, 1991).

Where the record was clear that the challenged certificate of analysis was properly filed with the clerk "at least seven days prior" to trial in compliance with this section, and it was thereafter accessible and available to defendant because it was lodged with another certificate which related to simultaneously tried offenses, both the letter and spirit of this section were fully satisfied. Harshaw v. Commonwealth, 16 Va. App. 69, 427 S.E.2d 733 (1993).

Trial court reasonably inferred from partially legible information on copy of certificate of analysis from Bureau of Forensic Science in cocaine distribution case that certificate was filed in the proper court at least seven days prior to trial. Waller v. Commonwealth, 27 Va. App. 71, 497 S.E.2d 508 (1998).

This section does not require that the certificates must be filed according to any particular system, only in a way which is accessible to the accused and available to him on request; therefore there was no requirement for evidence showing that certificate filed in cocaine buyer's file also was filed in defendant's file. Waller v. Commonwealth, 27 Va. App. 71, 497 S.E.2d 508 (1998).

The Commonwealth complied with the statute and, therefore, the court properly admitted a certificate of blood alcohol analysis into evidence where the attorney for the Commonwealth timely mailed a copy of the certificate to defendant's counsel prior to trial in the circuit court, notwithstanding defendant's counsel's contention that he never received the document. Johnson v. Commonwealth, No. 2371-97-2 (Ct. of Appeals Oct. 27, 1998).

The presence of a certificate of analysis in the proper circuit court case file at least seven days before trial was sufficient to permit its admissibility under the statute even without proof of filing. Hopkins v. Commonwealth, No. 0644-98-2 (Ct. of Appeals Apr. 27, 1999).

III. REQUEST FOR COPY OF CERTIFICATE.

Failure to specifically request certificate. — Where the defendant chose to move the trial court to enter a discovery order, which was a request directed to the trial court and not a direct request to the clerk or the Commonwealth's Attorney, the fact that a copy of the request had to be mailed to the opposing counsel was not sufficient to alert either the clerk or the Commonwealth's Attorney that the motion was a request pursuant to this section, and because the defendant did not make a sufficient request, the trial court did not err in admitting the certificate of analysis even though the defendant had not been provided with a copy of it seven days before trial. Smith v. Commonwealth, No. 2077-99-2, 2000 Va. App. LEXIS 520 (Ct. of Appeals July 18, 2000).

Request for discovery rather than proceeding under this section. — Because a defendant, who was charged with misdemeanor possession of marijuana, chose to seek discovery of a certificate of analysis under Rule 3A:11, which is not applicable to misdemeanor cases, instead of directly proceeding under this section, his request for the certificate of analysis was not valid and the court did not err in admitting the certificate into evidence even though a copy of it had not been provided to the defendant seven days before trial. Lewis v. Commonwealth, No. 2479-99-1, 2000 Va. App. LEXIS 560 (Ct. of Appeals Aug. 1, 2000).

The trial court did not err in admitting into evidence a certificate of analysis because defendant failed to satisfy the requirement of § 19.2-187 where he chose discovery under Va. Sup. Ct. Rule 3A:11, which was a method not available to him as he was charged with a misdemeanor, not a felony. Lewis v. Commonwealth, No. 2479-99-1, 2001 Va. App. LEXIS 604 (Ct. of Appeals Mar. 20, 2001).

Appellant entitled to subpoena writings used by chemist. — In trial for possession of cocaine with the intent to distribute,

pursuant to Supreme Court Rule 3A:11, appellant was entitled to subpoena all writings used by chemist to conclude that the substance examined and tested by him was cocaine. Ellis v. Commonwealth, 14 Va. App. 18, 414 S.E.2d 615 (1992).

Failure to comply with mailing provisions. — Clerk failed to comply with appellant's request for a copy of certificate prior to his trial. Because the mailing requirement was not satisfied, trooper's hearsay statements contained in the certificate were not admissible as evidence of the facts and the results of the analysis referred to therein. Hughes v. Commonwealth, No. 2802-96-4 (Ct. of Appeals Nov. 25, 1997).

Defendant's claim that court erred in admitting certificate of analysis because Commonwealth failed to mail or deliver a copy of the certificate upon request of the defendant, as required by this section, was without merit. Defendant never made a direct request for the certificate as provided under this section, and instead endorsed the discovery order which directed that all discovery would take place in the Commonwealth Attorney's office, and failed to appear at the prosecutor's office for discovery of the certificate. By failing to conduct discovery as prescribed by the discovery order, defendant waived any objection concerning delivery of the certificate to him. Coleman v. Commonwealth, 27 Va. App. 768, 501 S.E.2d 461 (1998).

Untimely delivery. — Delivery of the certificate of analysis to defendant's counsel three days before trial was not timely. Copeland v. Commonwealth, 19 Va. App. 515, 452 S.E.2d 876 (1995).

Continuance not remedy for noncompliance. — Continuance for seven days after trial had begun would not allow the Commonwealth to comply with clause (ii) of this section [now the second paragraph]. Clause (ii) requires that the certificate be mailed or delivered to counsel "at least seven days prior to ... trial." A continuance of any length after the trial had begun would not have remedied the Commonwealth's noncompliance. Bottoms v. Commonwealth, 20 Va. App. 466, 457 S.E.2d 796 (1995).

Continuance properly granted. — Trial court did not abuse its discretion in granting the Commonwealth a continuance, even though it had not complied with this section, as the Commonwealth had complied with § 19.2-187 by the continued date, when the bench trial actually began and the trial court began to take evidence. Bolden v. Commonwealth, 49 Va. App. 285, 640 S.E.2d 526, 2007 Va. App. LEXIS 52 (2007).

CIRCUIT COURT OPINIONS

Applicability. — Although Virginia case law has required strict compliance with § 19.2-187, which requires the Commonwealth to file a certificate of analysis at least one week prior to trial in a DUI case, where § 19.2-187 is not implicated, denial of a continuance does not preclude the granting of a nolle prosequi under § 19.2-265.3, even where both motions are predicated on the same assertions. Commonwealth v. Van Luu, 79 Va. Cir. 43, 2009 Va. Cir. LEXIS 69 (Fairfax Apr. 14, 2009).

Exception to hearsay rule. — Trial court overruled defendant's objection to the admission of a laboratory certificate of analysis stating that the substance defendant possessed was cocaine, as statutory law allowed for the admission of such evidence, and gave the accused the right to summon the person performing the chemical analysis and examine him as an adverse witness; as a result, admission of that evidence was recognized as an exception to the hearsay rule and defendant's confrontation clause rights were not violated since the statute gave him a right to confront the person who authored the certificate. Commonwealth v. Williams, 69 Va. Cir. 277, 2005 Va. Cir. LEXIS 322 (Charlottesville 2005).

OPINIONS OF THE ATTORNEY GENERAL

Accused, or his counsel, need not be in possession of copy of certificate of analysis within seven days of hearing or trial. — Requirement that copy of certificate of analysis be "mailed or delivered" to counsel for accused at least seven days before hearing or trial does not impose condition that the accused, or his counsel, be in possession of such copy within seven days of hearing or trial. See opinion of Attorney General to The Honorable George W. Grayson, Member, House of Delegates, 00-099 (11/20/00).

§ 19.2-187.01. Certificate of analysis as evidence of chain of custody of material described therein.

A report of analysis duly attested by the person performing such analysis or examination in any laboratory operated by (i) the Division of Consolidated Laboratory Services, the Department of Forensic Science or any of its regional laboratories, or by any laboratory authorized by such Division or Department to conduct such analysis or examination; (ii) the Federal Bureau of Investigation; (iii) the federal Bureau of Alcohol, Tobacco and Firearms; (iv) the Naval Criminal Investigative Service; (v) the federal Drug Enforcement Administration; (vi) the Postal Inspection Service; (vii) the U.S. Secret Service; or (viii) the Forensic Document Laboratory of the U.S. Department of Homeland Security shall be prima facie evidence in a criminal or civil proceeding as to the custody of the material described therein from the time such material is received by an authorized agent of such laboratory until such material is released subsequent to such analysis or examination. Any such certificate of analysis purporting to be signed by any such person shall be admissible as evidence in such hearing or trial without any proof of the seal or signature or of the official character of the person whose name is signed to it. The signature of the person who received the material for the laboratory on the request for laboratory examination form shall be deemed prima facie evidence that the person receiving the material was an authorized agent and that such receipt constitutes proper receipt by the laboratory for purposes of this section.

History.

1979, c. 364; 1989, c. 458; 1990, cc. 548, 825; 1991, c. 687; 1993, c. 32; 1994, c. 375; 1995, c. 437; 2005, cc. 868, 881; 2011, c. 645.

The 2011 amendments.

The 2011 amendment by c. 645, in the first sentence, substituted "U.S. Secret Service" for "United States Secret Service" in clause (i), added clause (viii), and made a related change.

Law Review.

For survey of Virginia law on evidence for the year 1978-1979, see 66 Va. L. Rev. 293 (1980).

Michie's Jurisprudence.

For related discussion, see 5B M.J. Criminal Procedure, § 56.

CASE NOTES

The underlying rationale of this section was to relieve the Commonwealth of having to call into court every employee who handled tested material to prove its chain of custody. Dunn v. Commonwealth, 20 Va. App. 217, 456 S.E.2d 135 (1995).

This section relieves the Commonwealth of having to present testimony regarding the chain of custody of an analyzed or examined substance, provided certain safeguards are met. Harris v. Commonwealth, 261 Va. 185, 541 S.E.2d 547, 2001 Va. LEXIS 7 (2001).

Standard of proof. — The chain of custody rule requires a showing with reasonable certainty that the item has not been altered, substituted, or contaminated prior to analysis, in any way that would affect the results of the analysis. In proving the chain of custody, however, the Commonwealth is not required to exclude every conceivable possibility of substitution, alteration or tampering. Feltner v. Commonwealth, No. 2596-95-4 (Ct. of Appeals Oct. 1, 1996).

The statutory scheme for establishing proper receipt is not the only method of proof available to the Commonwealth. This section does not require the signature of the person who received the evidence to be on the certificate of analysis; rather, it specifies that a signature on the request for laboratory examination form is prima facie evidence that the individual is an authorized agent of the laboratory. This section does not specifically require the Commonwealth to identify the recipient of analyzed material evidence only through a request for laboratory examination form. The agency relationship may be established by other evidence. Feltner v. Commonwealth, No. 2596-95-4 (Ct. of Appeals Oct. 1, 1996).

"Laboratory." — A common-sense analysis of the 1991 amendment to this section belies appellant's argument and confirms that "laboratory" refers not to one specific testing site (for example, Building A of the Northern Laboratory of the Division of Forensic Science), but to the entire state-approved entity, such as the laboratories that comprise either of the Division systems or the other enumerated agencies. Dunn v. Commonwealth, 20 Va. App. 217, 456 S.E.2d 135 (1995).

Section has no filing requirement for certificates of analysis. — Where, in possession of cocaine case, certificate of analysis was not timely filed according to § 19.2-187 and where defendant contended that admission of certificate prejudiced him by establishing link in chain-of-custody of cocaine before trial, certificate was properly admitted for this limited purpose since this section provides that certificate of analysis from any laboratory operated by Division of Consolidated Laboratory Services is prima facie evidence of laboratory's custody of evidence and unlike § 19.2-187, this section does not make filing of certificate with court seven days prior to trial prerequisite to admission into evidence. Smith v. Commonwealth, No. 0783-87-2 (Ct. of Appeals Mar. 21, 1989).

The trial court did not err in allowing the Commonwealth to rely on certificates of analysis to establish prima facie evidence of the chain of custody of a sample, notwithstanding that the certificates were not timely filed according to § 19.2-187. Jackson v. Commonwealth, No. 0075-98-4 (Ct. of Appeals Feb. 23, 1999).

This section does not specifically require the Commonwealth to identify the recipient of analyzed material evidence only through a request for laboratory examination form; the agency relationship prescribed by this section may be established by other evidence. Harshaw v. Commonwealth, 16 Va. App. 69, 427 S.E.2d 733 (1993).

Once the integrity of the chain is properly established and the remaining provisions of § 19.2-187 and this section are satisfied, a certificate of analysis shall be admissible as evidence of facts therein stated and the results of the analysis or examination referred to therein. Crews v. Commonwealth, 18 Va. App. 115, 442 S.E.2d 407 (1994).

Forensic scientists need not physically receive mail for purposes of chain of custody. — Nothing in § 19.2-187.01 requires the forensic scientists in the Virginia Division of Forensic Science [now the Department of Forensic Science] to physically receive the mail from the postman or sign the postal receipts; postal receipts addressed to the Division give rise to a presumption of receipt by the Division. Martin v. Commonwealth, No. 1221-02-2, 2003 Va. App. LEXIS 341 (Ct. of Appeals June 17, 2003).

Presumption of regularity. — In cases where authorized personnel handle a tested material, a "presumption of regularity" attaches at the moment the material is received by an authorized agent of any of the listed entities until it is released after analysis. Dunn v. Commonwealth, 20 Va. App. 217, 456 S.E.2d 135 (1995).

Forensic scientist could properly testify regarding his analysis of gunshot residue test, notwithstanding Commonwealth's failure to introduce certificate of analysis, where Commonwealth did not rely upon certificate of analysis and its accompanying attestation to establish chain of custody, but upon testimony of scientist and investigating officer who administered test. Hill v. Commonwealth, No. 2336-98-1 (Ct. of Appeals Nov. 23, 1999).

Appellant entitled to subpoena writings used by chemist. — In trial for possession of cocaine with the intent to distribute, pursuant to Sup. Ct. R. 3A:11, appellant was entitled to subpoena all writings used by chemist to conclude that the substance examined and tested by him was cocaine. Ellis v. Commonwealth, 14 Va. App. 18, 414 S.E.2d 615 (1992).

Specific statute governs over general one. — When one statute speaks to a subject in a general way and another deals with a part of the same subject in a more specific manner, the two should be harmonized, if possible, and where they conflict, the latter prevails, and because § 18.2-268 (now repealed) is more specific than this code section statute and directly applies to blood alcohol test results, § 18.2-268 (now repealed) is applicable to the facts of this case. Hilberath v. Commonwealth, No. 0351-92-4 (Ct. of Appeals Mar. 8, 1994).

Transfer does not eliminate benefit of prima facie proof. — Because the Commonwealth presented a duly attested certificate of analysis, it established its prima facie evidence of chain of custody. The Commonwealth did not lose the benefit of its prima facie proof when the cocaine was transferred between regional laboratories within the Division of Forensic Science [now the Department of Forensic Science]. While the relevant statutory sections are construed strictly against the Commonwealth, no language in this section compels the conclusion that the General Assembly intended to eliminate the presumed, valid chain of custody when items are transferred between Division laboratories. Dunn v. Commonwealth, 20 Va. App. 217, 456 S.E.2d 135 (1995).

Receipt by authorized agent. — Because Commonwealth established that evidence submitted was the same as that tested and that it had not been altered, substituted or contaminated prior to testing, any lack of proof regarding identity of the "authorized agent" at testing laboratory who received the evidence was harmless. Harris v. Commonwealth, No. 0909-99-1 (Ct. of Appeals Mar. 7, 2000).

The record sufficiently established an unbroken chain in the custody of the subject cocaine where the informant gave the police officer the substance obtained from defendant within minutes of the transaction, and he subsequently sealed and mailed it to the forensic laboratory for analysis, together with a request for analysis which fully and correctly identified the instant offense and related evidence. Crews v. Commonwealth, 18 Va. App. 115, 442 S.E.2d 407 (1994).

Valid chain of custody established. — Appellate court rejected defendant's claim that the Commonwealth failed to establish a valid chain of custody for drugs that were admitted into evidence at trial, in part because defendant failed to challenge the fact that a state trooper who testified did not identify the drugs as the drugs he purchased from defendant when the Commonwealth offered the drugs as evidence. Smith v. Commonwealth, No. 2268-02-2, 2004 Va. App. LEXIS 66 (Ct. of Appeals Feb. 10, 2004).

Where the Commonwealth proved with reasonable certainty that there had been no substitution, contamination, or alteration of cigar butts and green plant material seized from defendant's car, the trial court properly found that the Commonwealth established the chain of custody and properly permitted the introduction of the certificate of analysis into evidence in defendant's prosecution for possession of marijuana. Tyler v. Commonwealth, No. 0096-04-2, 2005 Va. App. LEXIS 112 (Ct. of Appeals Mar. 22, 2005).

Circuit court did not abuse its discretion in admitting the certificate of analysis into evidence when the circuit court, which observed the evidence, made a factual finding that the discrepancies between the descriptions on the request for examination form and certificate of analysis were not contradictory, and the Commonwealth presented sufficient evidence to establish with reasonable certainty that there had been no alteration or substitution of the evidence. Herndon v. Commonwealth, 280 Va. 138, 694 S.E.2d 618, 2010 Va. LEXIS 70 (2010).

Certificates of analysis properly admitted. — Trial court properly admitted into evidence two certificates of analysis as evidence of the chain of custody of the drugs seized during the drug sales under § 19.2-187.01 where: (1) the initials on the postal receipts matched those on the Request for Laboratory Examination; (2) a police officer mailed the narcotics to the Virginia Division of Forensic Science [now the Department of Forensic Science], which verified its receipt by executing the Request for Laboratory Examination; (3) the receipt alone established prima facie evidence of the chain of custody; and (4) that the initials on the postal receipts were not consistent with the signatures on the two Requests for Laboratory Examination did not undermine the statutory inference under § 19.2-187.01. Martin v. Commonwealth, No.

1221-02-2, 2003 Va. App. LEXIS 341 (Ct. of Appeals June 17, 2003).

Trial court was authorized to admit authenticated certificates of analysis that permitted a prima facie inference that the Commonwealth's forensic science department maintained a proper chain of custody at all times while the relevant testing samples in defendant's case were in the laboratory; too, since the certificates were not testimonial in nature, the inference did not violate the Confrontation Clause and the chain-of-custody proof was sufficient to support defendant's convictions. Anderson v. Commonwealth, 48 Va. App. 704, 634 S.E.2d 372, 2006 Va. App. LEXIS 414 (2006), aff'd, 274 Va. 469, 650 S.E.2d 702, 2007 Va. LEXIS 115 (Va. 2007).

Court affirmed defendant's drug conviction under § 18.2-248 because defendant's objection to the chain of custody of evidence could not be sustained as the Commonwealth had established prima facie evidence that the Division of Forensic Science (DFS) properly had custody of the evidence under § 19.2-187.01; section 19.2-187.01 authorized the trial court to receive a certificate of analysis as evidence of the chain of custody of the material tested. When the Commonwealth presented a duly attested certificate of analysis, it established "prima facie evidence" that DFS had custody of the material described therein from the time such material was received by an authorized agent of such laboratory until such material was released. Mitchell v. Commonwealth, — Va. App. —, — S.E.2d —, 2006 Va. App. LEXIS 499 (Nov. 7, 2006).

Admission of the certificate of analysis relating to defendant's DNA sample did not violate the Confrontation Clause because the author of the certificate of analysis appeared at trial, testified as to its contents, and defendant had an opportunity to cross-examine the author. In addition, defendant suffered no Confrontation Clause violation regarding the presumption contained in § 19.2-187.01, because it was not testimonial in nature. Anderson v. Commonwealth, 274 Va. 469, 650 S.E.2d 702, 2007 Va. LEXIS 115 (2007), cert. denied, Anderson v. Virginia, 553 U.S. 1054, 128 S. Ct. 2473, 2008 U.S. LEXIS 4189 (U.S. 2008).

Applied in Alvarez v. Commonwealth, 24 Va. App. 768, 485 S.E.2d 646 (1997); Johnson v. Commonwealth, 259 Va. 654, 529 S.E.2d 769, 2000 Va. LEXIS 60; Wimbish v. Commonwealth, 51 Va. App. 474, 658 S.E.2d 715, 2008 Va. App. LEXIS 168 (2008); Hargrove v. Commonwealth, 53 Va. App. 545, 673 S.E.2d 896, 2009 Va. App. LEXIS 123 (2009).

§ 19.2-187.02. Admissibility of written reports or records of blood alcohol tests conducted in the regular course of providing emergency medical treatment.

A. Notwithstanding any other provision of law, the written reports or records of blood alcohol tests conducted upon persons receiving medical treatment in a hospital or emergency room are admissible in evidence as a business records exception to the hearsay rule in prosecutions for any violation of § 18.2-266 (driving while intoxicated) or a substantially similar local ordinance, § 18.2-36.1 (involuntary manslaughter resulting from driving while intoxicated), § 18.2-36.2 (involuntary manslaughter resulting from boating while intoxicated), § 18.2-51.4 (maiming resulting from driving while intoxicated), § 18.2-51.5 (maiming resulting from boating while intoxicated), § 29.1-738 (boating while intoxicated), or § 46.2-341.24 (driving a commercial vehicle while intoxicated).

B. The provisions of law pertaining to confidentiality of medical records and medical treatment shall not be applicable to reports or records of blood alcohol tests sought or admitted as evidence under the provisions of this section in prosecutions as specified in subsection A. Owners or custodians of such reports or records may disclose them, in accordance with regulations concerning patient privacy promulgated by the U.S. Department of Health and Human Services, without obtaining consent or authorization for such disclosure. No person who is involved in taking blood or conducting blood alcohol tests shall be liable for civil damages for breach of confidentiality or unauthorized release of medical records because of the evidentiary use of blood alcohol test results under this section, or as a result of that person's testimony given pursuant to this section.

History.
2002, c. 749; 2005, c. 801; 2007, cc. 379, 679.

Editor's note.
Acts 2007, cc. 379 and 679, cl. 2, provides: "That the provisions of this act may result in a net increase in periods of imprisonment or commitment. Pursuant to § 30-19.1:4, the estimated amount of the necessary appropriation cannot be determined for periods of imprisonment in state adult correctional facilities and cannot be determined for periods of commitment to the custody of the Department of Juvenile Justice."

The 2007 amendments.
The 2007 amendments by cc. 379 and 679 are nearly identical, and inserted "§ 18.2-36.2 (involuntary manslaughter resulting from boating while intoxicated)" and "§ 18.2-51.5 (maiming resulting from boating while intoxicated), § 29.1-738 (boating while intoxicated)" in subsection A.

Law Review.
For article reviewing recent developments and changes in legislation, case law, and Virginia Supreme Court Rules affecting civil litigation, "Civil Practice and Procedure," see 40 U. Rich. L. Rev. 95 (2005).

CASE NOTES

Admission of hospital toxicology report held proper. — Where blood tests were performed by medical personnel in a hospital emergency room, and the toxicology report was shown to be a business record, recorded in the regular course of hospital business, contemporaneously made, and authenticated by its authorized custodian, such acted as sufficient foundation for the admissibility of the hospital blood test as a business record; further, blood tests performed by medical personnel in a hospital emergency room are not subject to the requirements of § 18.2-268.5. Stevens v. Commonwealth, 44 Va. App. 122, 603 S.E.2d 642, 2004 Va. App. LEXIS 496 (2004).

Blood tests performed by medical personnel in a hospital emergency room are not subject to the requirements of § 18.2-268.5; further, that statute applies only to blood drawn under the implied consent law. Stevens v. Commonwealth, 46 Va. App. 234, 616 S.E.2d 754, 2005 Va. App. LEXIS 407 (2005), aff'd, — Va. —, 634 S.E.2d 305 (2006).

Blood alcohol tests properly admitted as business record. — In a prosecution for aggravated involuntary manslaughter, the trial court did not commit reversible error in allowing into evidence the results of a blood alcohol content test performed on a blood sample taken from a defendant in violation of his Fourth, Fifth, and Fourteenth Amendment rights, as: (1) a test conducted by hospital personnel had been independently performed and the written report thereof was admissible under subsection A of § 19.2-187.02; (2) defendant consented to a second blood test administered by a deputy sheriff under the implied consent law; (3) evidence of defendant's intoxication was overwhelming despite testing over three times the legal limit; and (4) it was unreasonable to believe that the jury would have rejected the hospital-administered test and accepted, instead, the implied consent law test. Stevens v. Commonwealth, 272 Va. 481, 634 S.E.2d 305, 2006 Va. LEXIS 87

(2006), cert. denied, 549 U.S. 1350, 127 S. Ct. 2053, 167 L. Ed. 2d 784, 2007 U.S. LEXIS 4119 (U.S. 2007).

OPINIONS OF THE ATTORNEY GENERAL

Because this section is procedural in nature, the Commonwealth may introduce into evidence the written results of a blood alcohol test, even though the accident giving rise to the charge of involuntary manslaughter as a result of driving while intoxicated occurred before the effective date of the statute. See opinion of Attorney General to The Honorable Michael J. Bush, Commonwealth's Attorney for Russell County, 02-128 (12/18/02).

§ 19.2-187.1. Procedures for notifying accused of certificate of analysis; waiver; continuances.

A. In any trial and in any hearing other than a preliminary hearing, in which the attorney for the Commonwealth intends to offer a certificate of analysis into evidence in lieu of testimony pursuant to § 19.2-187, the attorney for the Commonwealth shall:

1. Provide by mail, delivery, or otherwise, a copy of the certificate to counsel of record for the accused, or to the accused if he is proceeding pro se, at no charge, no later than 28 days prior to the hearing or trial;

2. Provide simultaneously with the copy of the certificate so provided under subdivision 1 a notice to the accused of his right to object to having the certificate admitted without the person who performed the analysis or examination being present and testifying;

2a. When the attorney for the Commonwealth intends to present such testimony through two-way video conferencing, attach to the copy of the certificate provided under subdivision 1 a notice on a page separate from the notice in subdivision 2 specifying that the person who performed the analysis or examination may testify by two-way video conferencing and that the accused has a right to object to such two-way video testimony; and

3. File a copy of the certificate and notice with the clerk of the court hearing the matter (i) on the day that the certificate and notice are provided to the accused or (ii) in the case of a breath test certificate for a violation of any offense listed in subsection E of § 18.2-270, no later than three business days following the day that the certificate and notice are provided to the accused.

B. The accused may object in writing to admission of the certificate of analysis, in lieu of testimony, as evidence of the facts stated therein and of the results of the analysis or examination. Such objection shall be filed with the court hearing the matter, with a copy to the attorney for the Commonwealth, no more than 14 days after the certificate and notice were filed with the clerk by the attorney for the Commonwealth or the objection shall be deemed waived. If timely objection is made, the certificate shall not be admissible into evidence unless (i) the testimony of the person who performed the analysis or examination is admitted into evidence describing the facts and results of the analysis or examination during the Commonwealth's case-in-chief at the hearing or trial and that person is present and subject to cross-examination by the accused, (ii) the objection is waived by the accused or his counsel in writing or before the court, or (iii) the parties stipulate before the court to the admissibility of the certificate. If the accused demands, at hearing or trial, the presence of the person who performed the analysis or examination and he is thereafter found guilty of the charge or charges for which he demanded the presence of such witness, $50 for expenses related to the witness's appearance at hearing or trial shall be charged to the accused as court costs.

B1. When the attorney for the Commonwealth gives notice to the accused of intent to present testimony by two-way video conferencing, the accused may object in writing to the admission of such testimony and may file an objection as provided in subsection B. The provisions of subsection B shall apply to such objection mutatis mutandis.

B2. The two-way video testimony permitted by this section shall comply with the provisions of subsection B of § 19.2-3.1. In addition, unless otherwise agreed by the parties and the court, (i) all orders pertaining to witnesses apply to witnesses testifying by video conferencing; (ii) upon request, all materials read or used by the witness during his testimony shall be identified on the video; and (iii) any witness testifying by video conferencing shall certify at the conclusion of his testimony, under penalty of perjury, that he did not engage in any off-camera communications with any person during his testimony.

C. Where the person who performed the analysis and examination is not available for hearing or trial and the attorney for the Commonwealth has used due diligence to secure the presence of the person, the court shall order a continuance. Any continuances ordered pursuant to this subsection shall total not more than 90 days if the accused has been held continuously in custody and not more than 180 days if the accused has not been held continuously in custody.

D. Any objection by counsel for the accused, or the accused if he is proceeding pro se, to timeliness of the receipt of notice required by subsection A shall be made before hearing or trial upon his receipt of actual notice unless the accused did not receive actual notice prior to hearing or trial. A showing by the Commonwealth that the notice was mailed, delivered, or otherwise provided in compliance with the time requirements of this section shall constitute prima facie evidence that the notice was timely received by the accused. If the court finds upon the accused's objection made pursuant to this subsection, that he did not receive timely notice pursuant to subsection A, the accused's objection shall not be deemed waived and if the objection is made prior to

hearing or trial, a continuance shall be ordered if requested by either party. Any continuance ordered pursuant to this subsection shall be subject to the time limitations set forth in subsection C.

E. Nothing in this section shall prohibit the admissibility of a certificate of analysis when the person who performed the analysis and examination testifies at trial or the hearing concerning the facts stated therein and of the results of the analysis or examination.

F. The accused in any hearing or trial in which a certificate of analysis is offered into evidence shall have the right to call the person performing such analysis or examination or involved in the chain of custody as a witness therein, and examine him in the same manner as if he had been called as an adverse witness. Such witness shall be summoned and appear at the cost of the Commonwealth; however, if the accused calls the person performing such analysis or examination as a witness and is found guilty of the charge or charges for which such witness is summoned, $50 for expenses related to that witness's appearance at hearing or trial shall be charged to the accused as court costs.

History.

1976, c. 245; 1979, c. 364; 2009, Sp. Sess. I, cc. 1, 4; 2010, cc. 555, 656, 800; 2011, c. 32.

The 2009 amendments.

The 2009 amendments by Sp. Sess. I, c. 1, effective August 21, 2009, and Sp. Sess. I, c. 4, effective September 15, 2009, are identical, and rewrote the section.

The 2010 amendments.

The 2010 amendment by c. 555 inserted the last sentence in subsection B; inserted subsection E; redesignated former subsection E as subsection F; and inserted "however, if the accused calls the person performing such analysis or examination as a witness and is found guilty of the charge or charges for which such witness is summoned, $50 for expenses related to that witness's appearance at hearing or trial shall be charged to the accused as court costs" at the end of subsection F.

The 2010 amendment by c. 656 inserted "in lieu of testimony" in the introductory language of subsection A; and substituted "Provide simultaneously with" for "Attach to" in subdivision A 2.

The 2010 amendment by c. 800 added subdivision A 2a and subsections B1 and B2.

The 2011 amendments.

The 2011 amendment by c. 32 added the subdivision A 3 (i) designation and subdivision A 3 (ii).

Law Review.

For survey of Virginia criminal procedure for the year 1975-1976, see 62 Va. L. Rev. 1412 (1976). For survey of Virginia law on criminal law and procedure for the year 2007-2008, see 43 U. Rich. L. Rev. 149 (2008). For Essay, "The Confrontation Clause and the High Stakes of the Court's Consideration of Briscoe v. Virginia," see 95 Va. L. Rev. In Brief 97 (2010).

Michie's Jurisprudence.

For related discussion, see 5B M.J. Criminal Procedure, § 56.

CASE NOTES

Virginia's statutory scheme provides a mechanism for governmental and judicial economy by obviating the need for the prosecution to call the preparer and chain of custody witness. The statutes provide a defendant with adequate notice that the prosecution intends to rely on the certificate and affords a defendant the absolute right to call the preparer or chain of custody witness as an adverse witness should he so desire. Wingfield v. Commonwealth, No. 3000-95-2 (Ct. of Appeals Apr. 1, 1997).

Failure to offer proof of who had possession at given time. — Where defendant's argument was that he rebutted the prima facie proof of the chain of custody when he proved that analyst could not account for the substance while it was in the possession of other persons at the forensic lab and he could not verify that those persons or someone else did not alter, contaminate, or substitute the substance during the time that analyst could not account for it, a defendant does not rebut the presumption of an unbroken chain of custody by failing to offer proof of who had possession of the substance at a given time or by failing to account for how the person handled the substance at that time. A defendant cannot rebut the presumption by offering evidence that tends to prove only a single link in the chain and by then claiming that the evidence failed to prove or account for other links. Waller v. Commonwealth, No. 1873-95-2 (Ct. of Appeals Aug. 12, 1997).

Varying descriptions of substances. — Where defendant argued that the description of the substance that was analyzed at the laboratory and returned to the court so differed from the description of the substance that was delivered to the lab that there could be no "reasonable assurance" that they were the same substance, and therefore, he argued that the varying descriptions between the two substances rebutted the prima facie case established by the attested certificate and that the trial court erred by admitting the substance and certificate of analysis into evidence, the argument failed because the descriptions were not so dissimilar that they proved that the substance analyzed was different from that submitted. Moreover, the identifying numbers and initials of those persons who delivered and analyzed the substance and their testimony that the substance appeared to be that which they delivered and analyzed was sufficient to prove with "reasonable assurance" that they were the same. Waller v. Commonwealth, No. 1873-95-2 (Ct. of Appeals Aug. 12, 1997).

Access to materials used in preparation of paper. — The truth-finding process may not require that work papers or memoranda that assisted in the preparation of scientific paper be revealed, but it does require that if the scientist used information contained in other authorities to reach his conclusion, the accused is entitled to know what they are so that the challenge anticipated by this section effectively can be made; Supreme Court Rule 3A:11 provides the vehicle to enable the accused to make an intelligent challenge. Ellis v. Commonwealth, 14 Va. App. 18, 414 S.E.2d 615 (1992).

Appellant entitled to subpoena writings used by chemist. — In trial for possession of cocaine with the intent to distribute, pursuant to Supreme Court Rule 3A:11, appellant was entitled to subpoena all writings used by chemist to conclude that the substance examined and tested by him was cocaine. Ellis v. Commonwealth, 14 Va. App. 18, 414 S.E.2d 615 (1992).

Admission of certificate violated Confrontation Clause. — Trial court erred in admitting into evidence a certificate of blood alcohol analysis because the attestation clause included in the certificate was testimonial in nature, and its admission, over the objection of defendant, constituted a violation of the Confrontation Clause when the facts establishing the validity and admissibility of the breath-test result had to be proved by live, in-court testimony; while there is no constitutional requirement that the factual predicates in § 18.2-268.9 be established prior to the admission of the results of the test, once the General Assembly conditions the validity and admissibility of the breath-test results on the proof of those facts, the Commonwealth must prove those facts through live, in-court testimony and not by affidavit. Grant v. Commonwealth, 54 Va. App. 714, 682 S.E.2d 84, 2009 Va. App. LEXIS 390 (2009).

In defendants' prosecutions for drug-related offenses, the admission of analysts' certificates of analysis, without the analysts' live testimony, pursuant to §§ 19.2-187 and 19.2-187.1, violated defendants' rights to confrontation because the statutory procedure allowing defendants to call the analysts as adverse witnesses impermissibly relieved the prosecution of the duty to present witnesses and required defendants to call those witnesses, as defendants were not given a period of time, after notice, in which to object to the admission of the certificates absent the analysts'

testimony. Cypress v. Commonwealth, 280 Va. 305, 699 S.E.2d 206, 2010 Va. LEXIS 225 (2010).

In defendants' prosecutions for drug-related offenses, the admission of analysts' certificates of analysis, without the analysts' live testimony, pursuant to §§ 19.2-187 and 19.2-187.1, violated defendants' rights to confrontation because neither defendant waived this objection by not using § 19.2-187.1's procedure for calling the analysts to testify, as this procedure impermissibly burdened and did not adequately protect defendants' confrontation rights. Cypress v. Commonwealth, 280 Va. 305, 699 S.E.2d 206, 2010 Va. LEXIS 225 (2010).

In defendants' prosecutions for drug-related offenses, the admissions of analysts' certificates of analysis, without the analysts' live testimony, pursuant to §§ 19.2-187 and 19.2-187.1, violated defendants' rights to confrontation because the certificates were testimonial as: (1) each attested that an analyst performed an analysis and that the certificate accurately reflected the results of the analysis; and (2) each showed the substance analyzed was cocaine and the amount of cocaine, so the certificates were functionally identical to live testimony. Cypress v. Commonwealth, 280 Va. 305, 699 S.E.2d 206, 2010 Va. LEXIS 225 (2010).

No violation of defendant's right of confrontation occurred, where defendant had the express statutory right pursuant to this section to subpoena the chemist performing the analysis on the seized cocaine or the person involved in the chain of custody to testify at trial and be available for his examination. Defendant's choice not to avail himself of that process does not constitute a denial of his confrontation right. Wingfield v. Commonwealth, No. 3000-95-2 (Ct. of Appeals Apr. 1, 1997).

Defendant waived her Sixth Amendment rights to confrontation by failing to avail herself of her statutory right under § 19.2-187.1 to subpoena the operator of a breath test in her driving under the influence trial under § 18.2-266. Thus, it was proper to admit the certificate of the blood alcohol analysis without live testimony of the operator pursuant to §§ 18.2-268.9 and 19.2-187. McKeel v. Commonwealth, — Va. App. —, — S.E.2d —, 2006 Va. App. LEXIS 575 (Dec. 19, 2006).

Defendant's failure to timely notify the Commonwealth of his desire to confront forensic analyst at trial on drug charges constituted a waiver of his right to confrontation in that the procedure of §§ 19.2-187 and 19.2-187.1 adequately protected defendant's Confrontation Clause rights. Brooks v. Commonwealth, 49 Va. App. 155, 638 S.E.2d 131, 2006 Va. App. LEXIS 574 (2006).

No violation of Confrontation Clause. — Because defendant did not timely notify the Commonwealth of defendant's desire to confront a forensic analyst at trial, the procedure in §§ 19.2-187 and 19.2-187.1 adequately protected defendant's Sixth Amendment Confrontation Clause rights; therefore, the trial court did not err in admitting a certificate of analysis when the forensic scientist did not testify. Morton v. Commonwealth, — Va. App. —, — S.E.2d —, 2007 Va. App. LEXIS 39 (Feb. 6, 2007).

Because defendant, charged with possession of cocaine with intent to distribute, in violation of § 18.2-248, neglected to inform the Commonwealth of his desire to have the scientist who prepared the certificate of analysis present until the day of trial, defendant waived his Confrontation Clause rights. Thus, no error resulted in admitting the certificate of analysis without the scientist's testimony. McCray v. Commonwealth, — Va. App. —, — S.E.2d —, 2008 Va. App. LEXIS 36 (Jan. 22, 2008).

Defendant was properly convicted of driving while intoxicated because the trial court did not violate defendant's constitutional right to confrontation when it admitted his blood alcohol breath analysis into evidence in accordance with the terms of § 19.2-187; because defendant did not subpoena the booking tech who administered the blood alcohol breath analysis, he waived his opportunity to cross-examine potential witnesses. Ki-Ho Min v. Commonwealth, — Va. App. —, — S.E.2d —, 2008 Va. App. LEXIS 144 (Mar. 25, 2008).

Defendant waived the constitutional right to confront the person who performed a certificate of analysis on the substance found under the car seat in which he was sitting because defendant did not follow the procedures provided by §§ 19.2-187 and 19.2-187.1; defendant never notified the Commonwealth or the trial court of his desire to confront the witness until the middle of trial. Cypress v. Commonwealth, — Va. App. —, — S.E.2d —, 2007 Va. App. LEXIS 497 (Jan. 3, 2007).

Defendant waived the constitutional right to confront the person who prepared the certificates of analysis that were performed on the substances found in defendant's apartment and on his person because defendant did not follow the procedures provided by §§ 19.2-187 and 19.2-187.1; defendant did not notify the Commonwealth or the trial court of his desire to confront the witness until the middle of trial. Briscoe v. Commonwealth, — Va. App. —, — S.E.2d —, 2007 Va. App. LEXIS 498 (Jan. 18, 2007).

Admission of a ballistics certificate did not violate defendant's Confrontation Clause rights because, although the ballistics certificate contained testimonial hearsay, defendant waived his right to confront the preparer of the certificate by failing to call the analyst as permitted by subsection E of § 19.2-187.1. Miller v. Commonwealth, 2009 Va. App. LEXIS 421 (Sept. 22, 2009).

There was no abuse of the circuit court's discretion in admitting the certificate of analysis in evidence because neither the sheriff's captain nor the postal workers were "vital links" in the chain of custody; no contention was made at trial that the captain ever had any contact with the evidence and he was not shown to be a link in the chain. Branham v. Commonwealth, 283 Va. 273, 720 S.E.2d 74, 2012 Va. LEXIS 18 (2012).

Admission of certificate not harmless error. — Trial court's error in admitting into evidence a certificate of blood alcohol analysis was not harmless beyond a reasonable doubt because in order to convict defendant of a per se violation under clause (i) of § 18.2-266 or invoke the presumption of intoxication afforded by subdivision A 3 of § 18.2-269 the trial court had to rely on the facts recited in the attestation clause in order to conclude that the test was conducted in accordance with the relevant statutes; the only evidence that the breath test was administered either as provided by Title 18.2, Chapter Seven, Article Two of the Virginia Code or in accordance with the provisions of §§ 18.2-268.1 through 18.2-268.12, as required by § 18.2-269, was in the attestation clause on the certificate of analysis, and because the use of the attestation clause in the case violated the Confrontation Clause, it could not be used to prove that the breath test was administered in accordance with the relevant statutes. Grant v. Commonwealth, 54 Va. App. 714, 682 S.E.2d 84, 2009 Va. App. LEXIS 390 (2009).

Reopening case to allow analyst to testify. — Where certificates of analysis pertaining to drugs and a firearm had been admissible at the time defendant was initially found guilty in a bench trial, since he had not availed himself of his right under § 19.2-187.1 to call the scientists who prepared the certificates as witnesses, the trial court did not err in reopening the case to allow the scientists to testify and defendant to cross-examine them, because Confrontation Clause law had changed in the interim, and this procedure protected defendant's constitutional rights to confrontation and a fair trial. Morgan v. Commonwealth, 61 Va. App. 58, 733 S.E.2d 151, 2012 Va. App. LEXIS 336 (2012).

Applied in Dunn v. Commonwealth, 20 Va. App. 217, 456 S.E.2d 135 (1995).

CIRCUIT COURT OPINIONS

Right to examine forensic scientist. — Trial court overruled defendant's objection to the admission of a laboratory certificate of analysis stating that the substance defendant possessed was cocaine, as statutory law allowed for the admission of such evidence, and gave the accused the right to summon the person performing the chemical analysis and examine him as an adverse witness; as a result, admission of that evidence was recognized as an exception to the hearsay rule and defendant's confrontation clause rights were not violated since the statute gave him a right to confront the person who authored the certificate. Commonwealth v. Williams, 69 Va. Cir. 277, 2005 Va. Cir. LEXIS 322 (Charlottesville 2005).

§ 19.2-187.2. Procedure for subpoena duces tecum of analysis evidence.

No subpoena duces tecum shall issue for the production of writings or documents used to reach the conclusion contained in a certificate of analysis prepared pursuant to § 19.2-187 except upon affida-

vit that the requested writings or documents are material. Upon a showing by the Commonwealth that the production of such writings and documents would place an undue burden on the Department of Forensic Science, the court may order that the subpoena duces tecum be satisfied by making the writings and documents available for inspection by the requesting party at the laboratory site where the analysis was performed or at the laboratory operated by the Department of Forensic Science which is closest to the court in which the case is pending.

History.
1993, c. 629; 2005, cc. 868, 881.

CIRCUIT COURT OPINIONS

Expert's documents material to defense. — Defendant was entitled to obtain the writing and notes that the Commonwealth's handwriting expert used to prepare his certificate of analysis regarding whether the writings on the business checks that defendant allegedly used to embezzle were in fact written entirely in her own hand, as without those documents, defense counsel could not effectively exercise the right to cross-examine the Commonwealth's handwriting expert; accordingly, the materials sought were material to the defense of defendant and the Commonwealth was required to provide them to defendant. Commonwealth v. Hayslett, 62 Va. Cir. 31, 2003 Va. Cir. LEXIS 70 (Roanoke 2003).

§ 19.2-188. Reports by Chief Medical Examiner received as evidence.

A. Reports of investigations made by the Chief Medical Examiner, his assistants or medical examiners, and the records and certified reports of autopsies made under the authority of Title 32.1, shall be received as evidence in any court or other proceeding, and copies of photographs, laboratory findings and reports in the office of the Chief Medical Examiner or any medical examiner, when duly attested by the Chief Medical Examiner or one of his Assistant Chief Medical Examiners, shall be received as evidence in any court or other proceeding for any purpose for which the original could be received without proof of the official character or the person whose name is signed thereto.

B. Any statement of fact or of opinion in such reports and records concerning the physical or medical cause of death and not alleging any conduct by the accused shall be admissible as competent evidence of the cause of death in any preliminary hearing.

History.
Code 1950, § 19.1-45; 1960, c. 366; 1975, c. 495; 2003, c. 459; 2009, c. 640.

The 2009 amendments.
The 2009 amendment by c. 640 inserted the A designation at the beginning of the first paragraph and added subsection B.

Law Review.
For survey of Virginia law on evidence for the year 1969-1970, see 56 Va. L. Rev. 1325 (1970). For comment on the admissibility of documentary evidence and the right to confrontation, see 12 Wm. & Mary L. Rev. 440 (1970). For survey of Virginia law on evidence for

the year 1971-1972, see 58 Va. L. Rev. 1268 (1972). For survey of Virginia law on evidence for the year 1973-1974, see 60 Va. L. Rev. 1543 (1974).

Michie's Jurisprudence.
For related discussion, see 5C M.J. Dead Bodies, § 5; 7B M.J. Evidence, §§ 84, 221; 9B M.J. Homicide, §§ 59, 76.

CASE NOTES

Constitutionality. — The constitutional right of confrontation is not violated when the report of a state chemist is admitted into evidence. Robertson v. Cox, 320 F. Supp. 900 (W.D. Va. 1970).

The admission of a laboratory report in evidence under this section violates no constitutional right of a defendant. The right to be confronted with one's accusers and witnesses does not operate to exclude proper documentary evidence. Robertson v. Commonwealth, 211 Va. 62, 175 S.E.2d 260 (1970).

Right to confront witness not denied. — Admission in a rape prosecution of reports of the Chief Medical Examiner's office indicating presence of seminal fluid in vaginal swabs does not violate the accused's right to confrontation of the witnesses against him. Robertson v. Cox, 320 F. Supp. 900 (W.D. Va. 1970).

The purpose of this section is primarily to obviate the necessity of summoning as witnesses those physicians or technicians who, in their official capacity, are required to make pathological, bacteriological and toxicological investigations, as well as postmortem examinations. Such a provision is not only expedient and convenient — it prevents the delay that would result if the limited number of physicians, chemists and technicians were forced to testify whenever a report made by them was offered in evidence. Robertson v. Commonwealth, 211 Va. 62, 175 S.E.2d 260 (1970).

The effect of this section is to make reports of investigations of the Chief Medical Examiner admissible as prima facie evidence of the facts stated therein, thus obviating the necessity of summoning as witnesses those persons performing the particular tests involved. Bass v. Commonwealth, 212 Va. 699, 187 S.E.2d 188 (1972).

Effect of statement in death certificate signed by attending physician concerning cause of death. — Although signed by the decedent's attending physician, a statement in a death certificate concerning the cause of death was but the expression of an opinion and was not, therefore, competent to show the cause of the decedent's death. Ward v. Commonwealth, 216 Va. 177, 217 S.E.2d 810 (1975).

This section merely constitutes a statutory exception to the hearsay rule and does not eliminate the necessity of identifying the substance tested with the person from whom obtained. Bass v. Commonwealth, 212 Va. 699, 187 S.E.2d 188 (1972).

This section provides a statutory exception to the hearsay rule by permitting investigation reports and autopsy reports of the Chief Medical Examiner or his assistants to be received in evidence without requiring the investigating official to testify. Fitzgerald v. Commonwealth, 223 Va. 615, 292 S.E.2d 798 (1982).

Only facts contained in certificate are accorded dignity of prima facie evidence. — Reports of investigations made by the Chief Medical Examiner or his assistants or by medical examiners, as well as the records and reports of autopsies, shall be prima facie evidence of the facts stated therein in any court or other proceeding; and copies of such reports of investigations, and copies of the records and reports of autopsies, duly attested, shall be received in evidence for any purpose for which the original could be received, without any proof of the official character of the person whose name is signed thereto. The language of this section means that only facts contained in the certificate are accorded the dignity of prima facie evidence. Robertson v. Commonwealth, 211 Va. 62, 175 S.E.2d 260 (1970).

Prima facie evidence of facts stated. — Reports of the medical examiner introduced pursuant to this section are prima facie evidence of the facts stated therein. Quintana v. Commonwealth, 224 Va. 127, 295 S.E.2d 643 (1982), cert. denied, 460 U.S. 1029, 103 S. Ct. 1280, 75 L. Ed. 2d 501 (1983).

Opinion in medical examiner's report. — Opinion in a medical examiner's report is not competent evidence. Quintana v. Commonwealth, 224 Va. 127, 295 S.E.2d 643 (1982), cert. denied, 460 U.S. 1029, 103 S. Ct. 1280, 75 L. Ed. 2d 501 (1983).

Where, in a prosecution for murder, the crucial issue was whether death was brought about by criminal agency, the ultimate question was whether the decedent jumped intentionally, fell accidentally, or was thrown to her death, and the facts and circumstances shown by the testimony of lay witnesses were sufficient to enable a jury to decide that question, the deputy chief medical examiner's opinion as to whether death was brought about by criminal agency, which opinion was based largely, if not entirely, upon the same facts and circumstances, was inadmissible. Bond v. Commonwealth, 226 Va. 534, 311 S.E.2d 769 (1984).

Autopsy report was properly admitted without redaction of the chief medical examiner's opinion as to the cause of a newborn baby's death where the opinion evidence was cumulative of other evidence as to the cause of death, which was admitted without objection. Corrales v. Commonwealth, No. 2797-01-2, 2002 Va. App. LEXIS 687 (Ct. of Appeals Nov. 19, 2002).

Expressions of opinion in medical examiner's report. — Expressions of opinion are not admissible merely because they are included in a medical examiner's report; only statements of fact are admissible under this statutory exception to the rule excluding hearsay evidence. Hopkins v. Commonwealth, 230 Va. 280, 337 S.E.2d 264 (1985), cert. denied, 475 U.S. 1098, 106 S. Ct. 1498, 89 L. Ed. 2d 898 (1986).

Introduction of report where investigating official testifies. — There is no preclusive language in this section barring introduction of the reports if the investigating official testifies; this section does not require an election by the Commonwealth to introduce the relevant evidence either by a qualified witness or by the written reports. Fitzgerald v. Commonwealth, 223 Va. 615, 292 S.E.2d 798 (1982), cert. denied, 459 U.S. 1228, 103 S. Ct. 1235, 75 L. Ed. 2d 469 (1983).

Admission of report harmless error. — Because of defendant's confession as to the cause of death of defendant's wife, as adduced at trial, any error in the admission of an autopsy report prepared by a then deceased medical examiner and the testimony of a later medical examiner based on the report was harmless beyond a reasonable doubt. Abney v. Commonwealth, 51 Va. App. 337, 657 S.E.2d 796, 2008 Va. App. LEXIS 103 (2008).

Admission of autopsy report not error although pathologist testified at trial. — Fact that the pathologist who performed the autopsy on the victim testified at trial did not render the admission of the autopsy report error. Gray v. Commonwealth, 233 Va. 313, 356 S.E.2d 157, cert. denied, 484 U.S. 873, 108 S. Ct. 207, 98 L. Ed. 2d 158 (1987).

Applied in Rife v. Blankenship, 721 F.2d 983 (4th Cir. 1983).

§ 19.2-188.1. Testimony regarding identification of controlled substances.

A. In any preliminary hearing on a violation of Article 1 (§ 18.2-247 et seq.) of Chapter 7 of Title 18.2 or a violation of subdivision 6 of § 53.1-203, any law-enforcement officer shall be permitted to testify as to the results of field tests that have been approved by the Department of Forensic Science pursuant to regulations adopted in accordance with the Administrative Process Act (§ 2.2-4000 et seq.), regarding whether or not any substance the identity of which is at issue in such hearing is a controlled substance, imitation controlled substance, or marijuana, as defined in § 18.2-247.

B. In any trial for a violation of § 18.2-250.1, any law-enforcement officer shall be permitted to testify as to the results of any marijuana field test approved as accurate and reliable by the Department of Forensic Science pursuant to regulations adopted in accordance with the Administrative Process Act (§ 2.2-4000 et seq.), regarding whether or not any plant material, the identity of which is at issue, is marijuana provided the defendant has been given written notice of his right to request a full chemical analysis. Such notice shall be on a form approved by the Supreme Court and shall be provided to the defendant prior to trial.

In any case in which the person accused of a violation of § 18.2-250.1, or the attorney of record for the accused, desires a full chemical analysis of the alleged plant material, he may, by motion prior to trial before the court in which the charge is pending, request such a chemical analysis. Upon such motion, the court shall order that the analysis be performed by the Department of Forensic Science and shall prescribe in its order the method of custody, transfer, and return of evidence submitted for chemical analysis.

History.
1991, c. 477; 1993, c. 33; 2005, cc. 868, 881; 2006, c. 447; 2013, c. 60.

Cross references.
As to the powers and duties of the Department of Criminal Justice Services and the Criminal Justice Services Board, see § 9.1-102.

Editor's note.
Acts 2006, c. 447, cl. 2, provides: "That the Board of Forensic Science shall promulgate regulations to implement the provisions of this act to be effective within 280 days of its enactment in accordance with § 2.2-4011 A [see now § 2.2-4011 B] of the Code of Virginia."

The 2013 amendments.
The 2013 amendment by c. 60, in subsection A, inserted "or a violation of subdivision 6 of § 53.1-203" near the beginning of the first sentence, and made a minor stylistic change.

Law Review.
For 2006 survey article, "Criminal Law and Procedure," see 41 U. Rich. L. Rev. 83 (2006).

CASE NOTES

This section permits any law-enforcement officer to testify at a preliminary hearing as to the results of field tests which have been approved by the Division of Forensic Science [now the Department of Forensic Science] pursuant to regulations adopted in accordance with the Administrative Process Act (former § 9-6.14:1 et seq. — see now § 2.2-4000 et seq.). Galbraith v. Commonwealth, 18 Va. App. 734, 446 S.E.2d 633 (1994).

Error found in admitting test results. — Where the record before the appellate court contained no evidence that the field test used by detective had been approved by the division, the appellate court could not determine the reliability of the field test kit used to support detective's testimony that the substance tested positive as cocaine, therefore, the trial court erred when it permitted the detective to testify to the result produced by the test. Galbraith v. Commonwealth, 18 Va. App. 734, 446 S.E.2d 633 (1994).

§ 19.2-188.2. Certificate of surgeon as evidence.

A. In any criminal proceeding, the certificate of a duly qualified surgeon stating that he has removed organs or other body parts from a decedent for transplant in accordance with Chapter 8 (§ 32.1-277 et seq.) of Title 32.1, shall be admissible in evidence as evidence of the facts stated therein. The certificate shall be competent evidence to show that such organs or body parts were functional at the time of

recovery and not affected by any injury or illness that caused the decedent's death.

B. A copy of the certificate shall be filed with the attorney for the Commonwealth in the jurisdiction in which the decedent's fatal injury occurred. The certificate shall not be admitted into evidence unless the attorney for the Commonwealth has provided a copy of the certificate to counsel for the defendant at least fourteen days prior to the proceeding in which it is to be offered into evidence.

C. Any such certificate, when properly notarized, purporting to be signed by the surgeon who removed the organs or other body parts shall be admissible in evidence without proof of seal or signature of the person whose name is signed to it. In any hearing or trial the accused shall have the right to call the person signing the certificate and the provisions of § 19.2-187.1 shall apply, mutatis mutandis.

History.
1997, c. 557.

§ 19.2-188.3. Admissibility of affidavits by government officials regarding a search of government records (Subdivision (10)(b) of Supreme Court Rule 2:803 derived from this section).

In any hearing or trial, an affidavit signed by a government official who is competent to testify, deemed to have custody of an official record, or signed by his designee, stating that after a diligent search, no record or entry of such record is found to exist among the records in his custody, is admissible as evidence that his office has no such record or entry, provided that, if the hearing or trial is a proceeding other than a preliminary hearing, the procedures set forth in subsection G of § 18.2-472.1 for admission of an affidavit have been satisfied, mutatis mutandis, and the accused has not objected to the admission of the affidavit pursuant to the procedures set forth in subsection H of § 18.2-472.1, mutatis mutandis. Nothing in this section shall be construed to affect the admissibility of affidavits in civil cases under § 8.01-390.

History.
2010, c. 464; 2011, c. 285.

Editor's note.
At the direction of the Virginia Code Commission, the notation to the Virginia Rules of Evidence was added to the catchline of this section. Acts 2012, cc. 688 and 708, cl. 6 provides: "That pursuant to the authority set forth in §§ 30-146 and 30-147 of the Code of Virginia, the Virginia Code Commission shall direct any party with whom the Virginia Code Commission contracts to publish the Code of Virginia to include in the catchline of every section of the Code of Virginia from which any rule contained in the Rules of Evidence has been derived a notation specifying such rule."

The 2011 amendments.
The 2011 amendment by c. 285 inserted "if the hearing or trial is a proceeding other than a preliminary hearing" following "provided that."

§ 19.2-189. Commitment of accused for further examination.

If the accused be committed, it shall be by an order of the judge stating that he is committed for further examination on a day specified in the order. And on that day he may be brought before such judge by his verbal order to the officer by whom he was committed, or by a written order to a different person.

History.

Code 1950, § 19.1-107; 1960, c. 366; 1968, c. 639; 1975, c. 495.

CASE NOTES

A warrant of commitment before indictment must describe the offense plainly and fully. Young v. Commonwealth, 40 Va. (1 Rob.) 744 (1842).

§ 19.2-190. To whom, and when, examination and recognizance to be certified.

Every examination and recognizance for a felony taken under this chapter, shall, by the person taking it, be certified to the clerk of the circuit court of the county or city in which the party charged is to be tried, or the witness is to appear, on or before the first day of its next term. If he fails he may be compelled to do so by attachment as for a contempt.

History.

Code 1950, § 19.1-108; 1960, c. 366; 1975, c. 495.

Michie's Jurisprudence.

For related discussion, see 5B M.J. Criminal Procedure, § 22.

CHAPTER 13.
GRAND JURIES.

Article 1. In General.

ARTICLE 1.
IN GENERAL.

Michie's Jurisprudence.

For related discussion, see 9A M.J. Grand Jury, §§ 2, 20.

§ 19.2-191. Functions of a grand jury.

The functions of a grand jury are twofold:

(1) To consider bills of indictment prepared by the attorney for the Commonwealth and to determine whether as to each such bill there is sufficient probable cause to return such indictment "a true bill."

(2) To investigate and report on any condition that involves or tends to promote criminal activity, either in the community or by any governmental authority, agency or official thereof. These functions may be exercised by either a special grand jury or a regular grand jury as hereinafter provided.

History.

1975, c. 495; 1980, c. 517; 2001, c. 4.

Law Review.

For survey of Virginia law on criminal procedure for the year 1974-1975, see 61 Va. L. Rev. 1713 (1975).

CASE NOTES

Applied in Powell v. Commonwealth, 261 Va. 512, 552 S.E.2d 344, 2001 Va. LEXIS 86 (2001).

§ 19.2-192. Secrecy in grand jury proceedings.

Except as otherwise provided in this chapter, every member of a regular or special grand jury shall keep secret all proceedings which occurred during sessions of the grand jury; provided, however, in a prosecution for perjury of a witness examined before a regular grand jury, a regular grand juror may be required by the court to testify as to the testimony given by such witness before the regular grand jury.

History.
1975, c. 495.

Law Review.
For note, "Disclosure of Grand Jury Materials to Foreign Authorities Under Federal Rule of Criminal Procedure 6(e)," see 70 Va. L. Rev. 1623 (1984).

Michie's Jurisprudence.
For related discussion, see 9A M.J. Grand Jury, §§ 21, 48.

CASE NOTES

Considerations in disclosure. — Plaintiff's request to depose a state court grand juror about statements he made as to grand jury deliberations of the charges lodged against plaintiff was denied, because it was clear that any such testimony ran afoul of the prohibition against disclosing grand jury proceedings, and plaintiff had offered no authority supporting the proposition that one may depose grand jurors at all, let alone that justice so required in his case. Plaster v. Brown, — F. Supp. 2d —, 2006 U.S. Dist. LEXIS 213 (W.D. Va. Jan. 4, 2006).

Plaintiff's request to depose a state court grand juror about statements he made as to grand jury deliberations of the charges lodged against plaintiff was denied because, given the cloak of secrecy that the law imposed on grand jury deliberations, it was difficult to see how deposition testimony concerning statements made by a grand juror regarding the grand jury's deliberations could reasonably be calculated to lead to the discovery of admissible evidence; as such, the testimony was outside the permissible scope of discovery. Plaster v. Brown, — F. Supp. 2d —, 2006 U.S. Dist. LEXIS 213 (W.D. Va. Jan. 4, 2006).

§ 19.2-192.1. Sealing of indictment.

Upon ex parte motion by the Commonwealth and for good cause shown, the circuit court may seal an indictment until such time as the defendant is arrested.

History.
2002, c. 130.

Editor's note.
Acts 2002, c. 130, cl. 2, provides: "That the provisions of this act are declaratory of existing law."

ARTICLE 2.

REGULAR GRAND JURIES.

Michie's Jurisprudence.
For related discussion, see 9A M.J. Grand Jury, §§ 3, 4, 9 — 15, 17, 30, 39, 47.

§ 19.2-193. Number of regular grand juries.

There shall be a regular grand jury at each term of the circuit court of each county and city, unless the court, on the motion of the attorney for the Commonwealth or with his concurrence, finds that it is unnecessary or impractical to impanel a grand jury for the particular term and enters an order to that effect.

Whenever the number of cases to be considered by the grand jury at a given term is so great as to hamper the intelligent consideration thereof by a single grand jury, the court may order two or more regular grand juries to be impanelled to sit separately at the same or a different time during the term.

Whenever a regular grand jury has been discharged, the court, during the term, may impanel another regular grand jury.

History.
Code 1950, § 19.1-147; 1960, c. 366; 1975, c. 495.

Law Review.
For comment on grand juries, see 22 Wash. & Lee L. Rev. 325 (1965).

CASE NOTES

Time of impaneling special grand juries. — Under the provisions of this section and § 19.2-206, special grand juries may be summoned and impaneled at any regular or special term of the court when so ordered by the judge. Wright v. Commonwealth, 114 Va. 872, 77 S.E. 503 (1913).

§ 19.2-194. When and how grand jurors to be selected and summoned; lists to be delivered to clerk.

The judge or judges regularly presiding in the circuit court of each county and city shall annually, in the month of June, July, or August, select from citizens of the county or city at least 60 persons and not more than 120 persons 18 years of age or over, of honesty, intelligence, impartiality, and good demeanor and suitable in all respects to serve as grand jurors, who, except as hereinafter provided, shall be the grand jurors for the county or city from which they are selected for the next 12 months. The judge or judges making the selection shall at once furnish to the clerk of the circuit court a list of those selected for that county or city.

The clerk, not more than 20 days before the commencement of each term of his court at which a regular grand jury is required, shall issue a venire facias to the sheriff of his county or city, commanding him to summon not less than five nor more than nine of the persons selected as aforesaid (the number to be designated by the judge of the court by an order entered of record) to be named in the writ to appear on the first day of the court to serve as grand jurors. Those persons who are to be summoned shall be randomly selected but no such person shall be required to appear more than once until all the others have been summoned once, nor more than twice until the others have been twice summoned, and so on. The Circuit Court of James City County, or the judge thereof in vacation, shall select the grand jurors for each court from such county and the City of Williamsburg in such proportion from each as he may think proper.

Any person who has legal custody of and is responsible for a child 16 years of age or younger or a person having a mental or physical impairment requiring continuous care during normal court hours shall be excused from jury service upon his request.

History.
Code 1950, § 19.1-148; 1960, c. 366; 1971, Ex. Sess., c. 262; 1973, cc. 401, 439; 1974, c. 618; 1975, c. 495; 1991, c. 226; 2003, c. 825; 2004, c. 306; 2008, c. 644.

The 2008 amendments.
The 2008 amendments by c. 644, in the first paragraph, inserted "impartiality"; and inserted "Those persons who are to be summoned shall be randomly selected but" at the beginning of the second sentence in the second paragraph.

Law Review.
For article summarizing published Virginia criminal law decisions between July 1, 2002 and July 1, 2003, see 38 U. Rich. L. Rev. 87 (2003).

CASE NOTES

There can be no arbitrary and systematic exclusion of persons from juries whether those excluded be of a particular race or of a particular class, or whether the exclusion results from legislative action or from arbitrary and capricious action of those charged with providing grand jury lists. Scales v. Commonwealth, 214 Va. 728, 204 S.E.2d 273 (1974), cert. denied, 419 U.S. 1123, 95 S. Ct. 808, 42 L. Ed. 2d 823 (1975).

The list mentioned in this section is for the regular grand jury. McDaniel v. Commonwealth, 165 Va. 709, 181 S.E. 534 (1935).

Objections to the mode of summoning a grand jury must be made a preliminary stage of the case before a plea to the merits, otherwise they are to be considered as waived. Early v. Commonwealth, 86 Va. 921, 11 S.E. 795 (1890); Curtis v. Commonwealth, 87 Va. 580, 13 S.E. 73 (1891); Taylor v. Commonwealth, 90 Va. 109, 17 S.E. 812 (1893); Bailey v. Commonwealth, 193 Va. 814, 71 S.E.2d 368, cert. denied, 344 U.S. 886, 73 S. Ct. 186, 97 L. Ed. 686 (1952).

Unless the proceeding be void ab initio. — Curtis v. Commonwealth, 87 Va. 589, 13 S.E. 73 (1891); Bailey v. Commonwealth, 193 Va. 814, 71 S.E.2d 368, cert. denied, 344 U.S. 886, 73 S. Ct. 186, 97 L. Ed. 686 (1952).

And cannot be raised for the first time on appeal. — Objection that the grand jury was not selected as required by law cannot be raised for the first time in the appellate court. Taylor v. Commonwealth, 90 Va. 109, 17 S.E. 812 (1893).

Applied in Muhammad v. Commonwealth, 269 Va. 451, 619 S.E.2d 16, 2005 Va. LEXIS 85 (2005).

§ 19.2-195. Number and qualifications of grand jurors.

A regular grand jury shall consist of not less than five nor more than seven persons. Each grand juror shall be a citizen of this Commonwealth, eighteen years of age or over, and shall have been a resident of this Commonwealth one year and of the county or corporation in which the court is to be held six months, and in other respects a qualified juror, and, when the grand juror is for a circuit court of a county, not an inhabitant of a city, except in those

cases in which the circuit court of the county has jurisdiction in the city.

History.
Code 1950, § 19.1-150; 1960, c. 366; 1973, c. 439; 1974, c. 617; 1975, c. 495; 1991, c. 226.

Michie's Jurisprudence.
For related discussion, see 11B M.J. Jury, § 15.

CASE NOTES

Constitutionality. — This section is not repugnant to Amendments Five and Fourteen of the United States Constitution. Hausenfluck v. Commonwealth, 85 Va. 702, 8 S.E. 683 (1889).

There is a constitutional right to a jury drawn from a group which represents a cross section of the community. — And a cross section of the community includes persons with varying degrees of training and intelligence and with varying economic and social positions. Under the United States Constitution, the jury is not to be made the representative of the most intelligent, the most wealthy, or the most successful, nor of the least intelligent, the least wealthy, or the least successful. It is a democratic institution, representative of all qualified classes of people. Witcher v. Peyton, 405 F.2d 725 (4th Cir. 1969).

A grand jury should be composed of persons qualified to serve in that capacity under the law, such qualifications being regulated by statute in Virginia. Commonwealth v. Burton, 31 Va. (4 Leigh) 645 (1832); Commonwealth v. St. Clair, 42 Va. (1 Gratt.) 556 (1844); Shinn v. Commonwealth, 73 Va. (32 Gratt.) 899 (1879).

The phrase, "in other respects a qualified juror," must be interpreted according to the common law, and statutory requirements of jurors. Booth v. Commonwealth, 57 Va. (16 Gratt.) 519 (1861); Waller v. Commonwealth, 178 Va. 294, 16 S.E.2d 808 (1941).

Residence in the county. — The court has heretofore decided that residence, within the county, is a necessary qualification of grand jurors. The peculiar functions and duties of grand juries, as well as the structure of the clause of the act under consideration, would warrant, if necessary, the reading of it with the words "of the county," at the end of each disqualification. Commonwealth v. Towles, 32 Va. (5 Leigh) 743 (1835); Moran v. Commonwealth, 36 Va. (9 Leigh) 651 (1839). See also Commonwealth v. Cherry, 4 Va. (2 Va. Cas.) 20 (1815); McCue v. Commonwealth, 103 Va. 870, 49 S.E. 623 (1905).

Residence in the State. — A naturalized citizen of the United States or a native citizen of any other state of the union, domiciled in Virginia, being entitled to all the privileges of a citizen of this State, is a citizen and qualified as such to serve on grand juries. Commonwealth v. Cherry, 4 Va. (2 Va. Cas.) 20 (1815); Commonwealth v. Towles, 32 Va. (5 Leigh) 743 (1835).

Common-law exceptions. — Therefore, it is a good exception at common law to one returned on a grand jury, that he is an alien, or villain, or minor, or that he is outlawed for a crime, or that he was not returned by the proper officer, or that he was returned at the instance of the prosecutor. Booth v. Commonwealth, 57 Va. (16 Gratt.) 519 (1861); Waller v. Commonwealth, 178 Va. 294, 16 S.E.2d 808 (1941).

Being a prohibition officer did not constitute any disqualification to serve as a grand juror. As a matter of public policy it may have been true that, when there were a large number of indictments for violation of the former Prohibition Act under consideration, the courts should have excluded persons who were then actually engaged in enforcing this statute from serving on the grand jury. This, however, was left to the sound discretion of the trial courts. Webb v. Commonwealth, 137 Va. 833, 120 S.E. 155 (1923).

Effect of former service as juror. — A plea in abatement will not lie to an indictment because two or more of the grand jurors which found the indictment had served on another grand jury at the same term. Richardson v. Commonwealth, 76 Va. 1007 (1882).

Selection of jurors must always accord with the fact that the proper functioning of the jury system, and indeed, of democracy itself, requires that the jury be a body truly representative of the community, and not the organ of any special group or class. If that requirement is observed, the officials charged with choosing federal jurors may exercise some discretion to the end that competent jurors may be called. But they must not allow the desire for competent jurors to lead them into selections which do not comport with the concept of the jury as a cross section of the community. Tendencies, no matter how slight, toward the selection of jurors by any method other than a process which will insure a trial by a representative group are undermining processes weakening the institution of jury trial, and should be sturdily resisted. That the motives influencing such tendencies may be of the best must not blind courts to the dangers of allowing any encroachment whatsoever on this essential right. Steps innocently taken may one by one lead to the irretrievable impairment of substantial liberties. Witcher v. Peyton, 405 F.2d 725 (4th Cir. 1969).

In the selection of juries recognition must be given to the fact that those eligible for jury service are to be found in every stratum of society. Jury competence is an individual rather than a group or class matter. That fact lies at the very heart of the jury system. To disregard it is to open the door to class distinctions and discriminations which are abhorrent to the democratic ideals of trial by jury. Witcher v. Peyton, 405 F.2d 725 (4th Cir. 1969).

Attacking jury selection procedure. — It is not necessary to a successful attack upon a jury selection procedure that petitioner obtain an admission from the judge and jury commissioners that they have discriminated. Witcher v. Peyton, 405 F.2d 725 (4th Cir. 1969).

Want of qualifications or other objections to a grand jury are to be made effective by a plea in abatement. Commonwealth v. Cherry, 4 Va. (2 Va. Cas.) 20 (1815); Commonwealth v. Long, 4 Va. (2 Va. Cas.) 318 (1822); Moore v. Commonwealth, 36 Va. (9 Leigh) 639 (1838). See also Lawrence v. Commonwealth, 86 Va. 573, 10 S.E. 840 (1890).

Motion to quash. — The incompetency of one grand juror is sufficient to render an indictment defective, when found by a grand jury of which he is a member. For such defect the indictment will be quashed. Commonwealth v. Burton, 31 Va. (4 Leigh) 645 (1832); Shinn v. Commonwealth, 73 Va. (32 Gratt.) 899 (1879).

When made. — In the case of a grand jury, a party indicted is not bound to object to a grand juror for any disqualification before he is sworn, for he is no party to the selection and constitution of the grand inquest of the county. But when he is indicted he becomes a party, and it is competent for him to avail himself of the disqualification. Commonwealth v. Cherry, 4 Va. (2 Va. Cas.) 20 (1815); Commonwealth v. Carter, 4 Va. (2 Va. Cas.) 319 (1822); Hunter v. Matthews, 39 Va. (12 Leigh) 228 (1841).

After indictment found. — Objection to the qualification of an individual grand juror can be taken after indictment found. Commonwealth v. Long, 4 Va. (2 Va. Cas.) 318 (1822); Commonwealth v. St. Clair, 42 Va. (1 Gratt.) 556 (1844); Day v. Commonwealth, 43 Va. (2 Gratt.) 562 (1845).

Must be before plea to merits. — Objections to the competency or qualifications of a particular grand juror must be made at a preliminary stage of the case, before a plea to the merits; otherwise, they are considered waived. Early v. Commonwealth, 86 Va. 921, 11 S.E. 795 (1890); Taylor v. Commonwealth, 90 Va. 109, 17 S.E. 812 (1893); Bailey v. Commonwealth, 193 Va. 814, 71 S.E.2d 368, cert. denied, 344 U.S. 886, 73 S. Ct. 186, 97 L. Ed. 686 (1952).

Unless the proceedings are void from the beginning. Curtis v. Commonwealth, 87 Va. 589, 13 S.E. 73 (1891); Bailey v. Commonwealth, 193 Va. 814, 71 S.E.2d 368, cert. denied, 344 U.S. 886, 73 S. Ct. 186, 97 L. Ed. 686 (1952).

Objections waived by pleading general issue. — A plea in abatement raising objections to the manner of organizing the jury, or to the qualification of grand jurors, is waived by pleading the general issue alone. Early v. Commonwealth, 86 Va. 921, 11 S.E. 795 (1890); Bailey v. Commonwealth, 193 Va. 814, 71 S.E.2d 368, cert. denied, 344 U.S. 886, 73 S. Ct. 186, 97 L. Ed. 686 (1952).

If a defendant may legally waive an indictment and be tried for a felony without any indictment at all, it seems clear that his constitutional rights are not violated by requiring that if he questions the validity of an indictment that is made he shall do so before he goes to trial on a plea of not guilty and is convicted. Bailey v. Commonwealth, 193 Va. 814, 71 S.E.2d 368, cert. denied, 344 U.S. 886, 73 S. Ct. 186, 97 L. Ed. 686 (1952).

By pleading the general issue alone, a defendant has always been understood to waive the right to interpose afterwards a plea in abatement. The settled doctrine, however, is that the judge may permit a pleading to be withdrawn, and another one to be substituted, whenever by so doing he does not violate any positive rule of law or of established practice. But such a discretion will rarely, if ever, be exercised in aid of an attempt to rely upon a merely dilatory or formal defense. Bailey v. Commonwealth, 193 Va. 814, 71 S.E.2d 368, cert. denied, 344 U.S. 886, 73 S. Ct. 186, 97 L. Ed. 686 (1952).

Cannot be raised for first time in appellate court. — Objection that the grand jury was not constituted, and foreman not selected and sworn as required by law, cannot be raised for the first time in the appellate court, but must be by plea in abatement. Taylor v. Commonwealth, 90 Va. 109, 17 S.E. 812 (1893).

§ 19.2-196. How deficiency of jurors supplied.

If a sufficient number of grand jurors do not appear, the court may order the deficiency to be supplied from the bystanders or from a list furnished by the judge to the sheriff or sergeant.

History.
Code 1950, § 19.1-151; 1960, c. 366; 1975, c. 495.

Cross references.
As to when new foreman or juror may be sworn in, see § 19.2-197.

CASE NOTES

Replacement procedure. — If one of the grand jurors summoned lacks the necessary legal qualifications, the court must discharge him and order another to be sworn in his place. Commonwealth v. Burton, 31 Va. (4 Leigh) 645 (1832); Richardson v. Commonwealth, 76 Va. 1007 (1882).

§ 19.2-197. Foreman of grand jury; oaths of jurors and witnesses.

From among the persons summoned who attend the court shall select a foreman who shall be sworn as follows: "You shall diligently inquire, and true presentment make, of all such matters as may be given you in charge, or come to your knowledge, touching the present service. You shall present no person through prejudice or ill-will, nor leave any unpresented through fear or favor, but in all your presentments you shall present the truth, the whole truth, and nothing but the truth. So help you God." The other grand jurors shall afterwards be sworn as follows: "The same oath that your foreman has taken on his part, you and each of you shall observe and keep on your part. So help you God." Any witness testifying before the grand jury may be sworn by the foreman.

History.
Code 1950, § 19.1-152; 1960, c. 366; 1975, c. 495.

Cross references.
As to effect of omission from indictment of statement concerning oaths, see § 19.2-226.

CASE NOTES

The fact that the oath was administered to the grand jury by a clerk de facto is not sufficient to avoid a prosecution for gaming. Hord v. Commonwealth, 31 Va. (4 Leigh) 674 (1833).

§ 19.2-198. When new foreman or juror may be sworn in.

If the foreman or any grand juror, at any time after being sworn, fail or be unable to attend another may be sworn in his stead.

History.
Code 1950, § 19.1-153; 1960, c. 366; 1975, c. 495.

Cross references.
As to how deficiency of jurors may be supplied, see § 19.2-196.

§ 19.2-199. Judge to charge grand jury.

The grand jury, after being sworn, shall be charged by the judge of the court and shall then be sent to their room. In the charge given by the court to a regular grand jury, the court shall instruct it to advise the court after their considerations of the bills of indictment whether it desires to be impanelled as a special grand jury to consider any matters provided for in subdivision (2) of § 19.2-191.

History.
Code 1950, § 19.1-154; 1960, cc. 366, 467; 1975, c. 495.

Law Review.
For survey of Virginia law on criminal procedure for the year 1974-1975, see 61 Va. L. Rev. 1713 (1975).

CASE NOTES

Section directory. — Failure to charge the grand jury, as provided by former § 3982, did not vitiate an indictment found by them. The provision was directory only. Porterfield v. Commonwealth, 91 Va. 801, 22 S.E. 352 (1895).

Charge not improper. — The court's statement in its charge that the attorney for the Commonwealth sends only enough witnesses before the grand jury to show probable cause was not improper or prejudicial to defendant. Britt v. Commonwealth, 202 Va. 906, 121 S.E.2d 495 (1961).

§ 19.2-200. Duties of grand jury.

The grand jury shall inquire of and present all felonies, misdemeanors and violations of penal laws committed within the jurisdiction of the respective courts wherein it is sworn; except that no presentment shall be made of a matter for which there is no corporal punishment, but only a fine, where the fine is limited to an amount not exceeding five dollars. After a regular grand jury has concluded its deliberation on bills of indictment and made its return thereon, the court shall inquire of it whether it recommends that a special grand jury be impanelled to perform any of the functions provided for in subdivision (2) of § 19.2-191. If a majority of the grand jurors responds in the affirmative, the court shall impanel so many of that jury as answer in the affirmative and are also willing to serve thereon, plus any additional members as may be necessary to complete the panel, as a special grand jury and if a minority of the grand jurors responds in the affirmative, the court may impanel a special grand jury in the same manner.

History.
Code 1950, § 19.1-155; 1960, c. 366; 1975, c. 495; 1978, c. 741; 1980, c. 134.

Law Review.
For survey of Virginia law on criminal procedure for the year 1974-1975, see 61 Va. L. Rev. 1713 (1975).

Michie's Jurisprudence.
For related discussion, see 9A M.J. Grand Jury, § 20.

§ 19.2-201. Officers to give information of violation of penal laws to attorney for Commonwealth.

Every commissioner of the revenue, sheriff, constable or other officer shall promptly give information of the violation of any penal law to the attorney for the Commonwealth, who shall forthwith institute and prosecute all necessary and proper proceedings in such case, whether in the name of the Commonwealth or of a county or corporation, and may in such case issue or cause to be issued a summons for any witnesses he may deem material to give evidence before the court or grand jury. Except as otherwise provided in this chapter, no attorney for the Commonwealth shall go before any grand jury except when duly sworn to testify as a witness, but he may advise the foreman of a regular grand jury or any member or members thereof in relation to the discharge of their duties.

History.
Code 1950, § 19.1-156; 1960, c. 366; 1975, c. 495.

Law Review.
For note, "Grand Jury Reform: A Proposal for Change in Virginia," see 23 U. Rich. L. Rev. 279 (1989).

Michie's Jurisprudence.
For related discussion, see 9A M.J. Grand Jury, § 24.

CASE NOTES

It is the purpose of this section to give the grand jury the benefit of the advice of the attorney for the Commonwealth relative to the discharge of their duties, without permitting him, by his presence, or otherwise, to influence them in reaching a conclusion during their deliberations. Hall v. Commonwealth, 143 Va. 554, 130 S.E. 416 (1925).

Duty of sheriff. — This section makes it the duty of the sheriff to give information of the violation of any penal law to the attorney for the Commonwealth, whose duty it is to institute a prosecution in such case. This duty imposed upon the sheriff necessarily carries with it the implied power to investigate, inquire into, and ascertain if an offense has been or is being committed. Carico v. Wilmore, 51 F. 196 (W.D. Va. 1892).

Permissible communications with grand jury. — A Commonwealth's attorney may advise the grand jury on a legal issue and the law in regard to the various indictments that they are considering, but he may not specifically refer to the indictment against the accused. Pease v. Commonwealth, 24 Va. App. 397, 482 S.E.2d 851 (1997).

A Commonwealth's attorney is not permitted by his presence or otherwise to influence a grand jury in reaching a conclusion during their deliberations. Pease v. Commonwealth, 24 Va. App. 397, 482 S.E.2d 851 (1997).

Consultation by the regular grand jury with the attorney for the Commonwealth during deliberations to obtain advice on a legal issue was not error, as such action is explicitly provided for in this section, and his advice to them was properly limited to this matter. Vihko v. Commonwealth, 10 Va. App. 498, 393 S.E.2d 413 (1990).

Appearance of attorney for the Commonwealth. — An indictment will not be quashed because the attorney for the Commonwealth appeared before the grand jury during their deliberation when not sworn as a witness, where it appears from the evidence that he did not advise them to find the indictment, did not know of their finding until the presentment was made, and was not in the room when they had under consideration or deliberation the indictment or the presentment upon which the indictment was found. Mullins v. Commonwealth, 115 Va. 945, 79 S.E. 324 (1913).

Presence does not invalidate indictment unless accused prejudiced. — Notwithstanding this section forbidding an attorney for the Commonwealth to go before a grand jury during their deliberations, the mere presence of the attorney for the Commonwealth in the grand jury room does not invalidate an indictment found at the time, if it satisfactorily appears that the accused was not prejudiced thereby. Draper v. Commonwealth, 132 Va. 648, 111 S.E. 471 (1922), overruled on other grounds, as stated in Cooper v. Commonwealth, 277 Va. 377, 673 S.E.2d 185 (2009.

Prejudicial conduct before grand jury found. — Where prosecutor initiated contact with grand jury regarding defendant's witness, about whom he told them that her testimony would not be truthful, and actually examined this witness for the grand jury, such conduct substantially influenced their decision to return murder indictment, to the prejudice of the defendant. Therefore, the indictment was quashed. Pease v. Commonwealth, 24 Va. App. 397, 482 S.E.2d 851 (1997).

CIRCUIT COURT OPINIONS

No private right of action. — Police officer, who claimed that other police officers conspired to conceal events surrounding the death of a suspect and compelled him to testify falsely about those events, did not have a private right of action against a city or its employees to recover damages he sustained when he was terminated from the city's police department. Young v. City of Norfolk, 62 Va. Cir. 307, 2003 Va. Cir. LEXIS 296 (Norfolk 2003).

Termination from employment. — To the extent that an employee alleged that the employee's termination resulted from complying with the employee's obligations under subsection C of § 63.2-526, and §§ 19.2-201 and 19.2-208, to report welfare fraud and to testify before a grand jury, the employee made out a claim under the Type 1 exception to the "employment-at-will" doctrine. McClosky v. Warren Co. Dep't of Soc. Servs., 81 Va. Cir. 35, 2010 Va. Cir. LEXIS 102 (Warren County July 15, 2010).

Deputies had a *Bowman* claim for complying with a duty to report sheriff's misconduct. — Sheriff's deputies had no right to bring a claim under *Bowman v. State Bank of Keysville*, 229 Va. 534, 331 S.E.2d 797 (1985), for wrongful termination against the sheriff based on either § 15.2-1722 or the Virginia Fraud Against Taxpayers Act, § 8.01-216.1 et seq.; however, they did state a *Bowman* claim based on their duty under § 19.2-201 to report wrongful conduct. Bowman v. Hunt, 2011 Va. Cir. LEXIS 116 (Franklin County Aug. 16, 2011).

§ 19.2-202. How indictments found and presentment made.

At least four of a regular grand jury must concur in finding or making an indictment or presentment. It may make a presentment or find an indictment upon the information of two or more of its own body, or on the testimony of witnesses called on by the grand jury, or sent to it by the court. If only one of their number can testify as to an offense, he shall be sworn as any other witness. When a presentment or indictment is so made or found, the names of the grand jurors giving the information, or of the witnesses, shall be written at the foot of the presentment or indictment.

History.
Code 1950, § 19.1-157; 1960, c. 366; 1975, c. 495.

Cross references.
As to indorsement of complaining witness' name, see § 19.2-228.

Michie's Jurisprudence.
For related discussion, see 9A M.J. Grand Jury, § 32.

CASE NOTES

Provision as to indorsement of names merely directory. — The requirement of this section that the names of witnesses shall be written at the foot of the indictment is merely directory, and noncompliance therewith does not invalidate the indictment. Shelton v. Commonwealth, 89 Va. 450, 16 S.E. 355 (1892); Porterfield v. Commonwealth, 91 Va. 801, 22 S.E. 352 (1895); Clopton v. Commonwealth, 109 Va. 813, 63 S.E. 1022 (1909). See also Hall v. Commonwealth, 143 Va. 554, 130 S.E. 416 (1925).

Although this section provides for the endorsement of names of witnesses who testify before a regular grand jury, the requirement is directory and an omission is not grounds to quash the indictment. Vihko v. Commonwealth, 10 Va. App. 498, 393 S.E.2d 413 (1990).

Omission does not exclude witnesses. — The omission of the names of witnesses in the indorsement of an indictment will not operate to exclude such witnesses from testifying at the trial. Lawrence v. Commonwealth, 71 Va. (30 Gratt.) 845 (1878), overruled on another point, Jones v. Commonwealth, 87 Va. 63, 12 S.E. 226 (1890).

The failure of the foreman of the grand jury to write the word "foreman" after his name is a matter of no moment. The entry on the order book showing the finding of the grand jury is sufficient evidence of that fact, and makes it immaterial whether the words "a true bill" were in fact indorsed on the indictment or not. Hall v. Commonwealth, 143 Va. 554, 130 S.E. 416 (1925).

§ 19.2-203. Indictments ignored may be sent to another grand jury; what irregularities not to vitiate indictment, etc.

Although a bill of indictment be returned not a true bill the same or another bill of indictment against the same person for the same offense may be sent to, and acted on, by the same or another grand jury. No irregularity in the time or manner of selecting the jurors, or in the writ of venire facias, or in the manner of executing the same, shall vitiate any presentment, indictment or finding of a grand jury.

History.
Code 1950, § 19.1-158; 1960, c. 366; 1975, c. 495.

Law Review.
For note, "Criminal Procedure and Criminal Law: Virginia Supreme Court Decisions During the 70's," see 15 U. Rich. L. Rev. 585 (1981).

Michie's Jurisprudence.
For related discussion, see 5B M.J. Criminal Procedure, § 21; 9A M.J. Grand Jury, § 19; 9B M.J. Indictments, Informations and Presentments, § 31.

CASE NOTES

Due process. — Imposition of a sentence against defendant after he violated the terms of an agreement that allowed him to withdraw a guilty plea to a felony in a circuit court did not violate the final disposition rule, speedy trial, or double jeopardy. Urbina v.

Commonwealth, No. 2467-02-4, 2003 Va. App. LEXIS 551 (Ct. of Appeals Nov. 4, 2003).

Effect of section. — This section allows the prosecutor, once having failed to establish probable cause, to seek, perhaps armed with more or newly discovered evidence, another indictment on the same charge. Moore v. Commonwealth, 218 Va. 388, 237 S.E.2d 187 (1977).

Bringing indictment after finding of no probable cause by district court. — Failure of the General Assembly to bar forever the bringing of an indictment after a finding of no probable cause by a district court was intentional. Such a provision would have been totally inconsistent with the provisions of former § 19.1-158 (now this section). Moore v. Commonwealth, 218 Va. 388, 237 S.E.2d 187 (1977).

§ 19.2-204. Penalties on officers and jurors for failure of duty.

A court whose officer fails without good cause, when it is his duty, to summon a grand jury and return a list of its names shall fine him twenty dollars. A person summoned and failing to attend a court as a grand juror shall be fined by the court not less than five dollars nor more than twenty dollars, unless, after being summoned to show cause against the fine, he gives a reasonable excuse for his failure.

History.
Code 1950, § 19.1-159; 1960, c. 366; 1975, c. 495.

Michie's Jurisprudence.
For related discussion, see 9A M.J. Grand Jury, § 16.

§ 19.2-205. Pay and mileage of grand jurors.

Every person who serves upon a grand jury, regular or special, shall receive the same compensation and mileage allowed jurors in civil cases by § 17.1-618 and the same shall be paid out of the county or corporation levy.

History.
Code 1950, § 19.1-160; 1960, c. 366; 1974, c. 207; 1975, c. 495.

Michie's Jurisprudence.
For related discussion, see 9A M.J. Grand Jury, § 13.

ARTICLE 3.

SPECIAL GRAND JURIES.

Michie's Jurisprudence.
For related discussion, see 9A M.J. Grand Jury, §§ 13, 20, 21, 24, 31, 39, 41, 42, 44.

§ 19.2-206. When impanelled.

A. Special grand juries may be impanelled by a circuit court (i) at any time upon its own motion, (ii) upon recommendation of a minority of the members of a regular grand jury that a special grand jury be impanelled, to perform the functions provided for in subdivision (2) of § 19.2-191, or (iii) upon request of the attorney for the Commonwealth to investigate and report on any condition that involves or tends to promote criminal activity and consider bills of indictment to determine whether there is sufficient probable cause to return each such indictment as a "true bill."

B. A special grand jury shall be impanelled by a circuit court upon the recommendation of a majority of the members of a regular grand jury if the court finds probable cause to believe that a crime has been committed which should be investigated by a special grand jury impanelled to perform the functions provided for in subdivision (2) of § 19.2-191.

History.
Code 1950, § 19.1-149; 1960, c. 366; 1975, c. 495; 1978, c. 741; 1980, c. 134; 1987, c. 136; 2001, c. 4.

Law Review.
For article, "Criminal Law and Procedure," see 35 U. Rich. L. Rev. 537 (2001).

CASE NOTES

Under this section a special grand jury may be summoned without a writ of venire facias. Robinson v. Commonwealth, 88 Va. 900, 14 S.E. 627 (1892). See also Combs v. Commonwealth, 90 Va. 88, 17 S.E. 881 (1893).

The statute does not require the order of the judge to be entered of record. Mesmer v. Commonwealth, 67 Va. (26 Gratt.) 976 (1875).

When court may summon a special grand jury. — Under the provisions of this section and § 19.2-193, special grand juries may be summoned and impaneled at any regular term of the court when so ordered by the judge. Wright v. Commonwealth, 114 Va. 872, 77 S.E. 503 (1913).

Where one of the grand jury finding an indictment was incompetent, and for that reason the grand jury is dismissed and the indictment quashed the court may direct a special grand jury to be summoned and impaneled at the same term. An indictment found by this grand jury is valid. Shinn v. Commonwealth, 73 Va. (32 Gratt.) 899 (1879).

Powers of special grand jury. — A special grand jury is qualified to perform any business that may properly come before it, and generally has the same powers as a regular grand jury. Lyles v. Commonwealth, 88 Va. 396, 13 S.E. 802 (1891). As to how indictments are found and presentments made, see § 19.2-202.

§ 19.2-207. Composition of a special grand jury.

Special grand juries shall consist of not less than seven and not more than 11 members, and shall be summoned from a list prepared by the court. Members of a special grand jury shall possess the same qualifications as those prescribed for members of a regular grand jury, including indifferent in the cause to be conducted by the special grand jury. In order to determine a potential juror's qualifications, the presiding judge shall examine each juror individually and under oath. He shall then certify in writing and not under seal that he has examined the members of the special grand jury and has found that they are qualified and are impartial and disinterested in the subject matter and outcome of the investigation. The examination shall be recorded by a court reporter and conducted pursuant to the requirements of secrecy provided for in this chapter. The court shall appoint one of the members as foreman.

History.
1975, c. 495; 2008, c. 644.

The 2008 amendments.

The 2008 amendment by c. 644 substituted "11 members" for "eleven members" in the first sentence, inserted "including indifferent in the cause to be conducted by the special grand jury" in the second sentence, and inserted the third, fourth, and fifth sentences.

§ 19.2-208. Subpoena power of special grand jury.

The special grand jury may subpoena persons to appear before it to testify and to produce specified records, papers, and documents or other tangible things, but before any witness testifies, he shall be warned by the foreman that he need not answer any questions or produce any evidence that would tend to incriminate him, and that the witness may have counsel of his own procurement present when he appears to testify, and at the same time the foreman also shall warn each witness that he may later be called upon to testify in any case that might grow out of the investigation and report of the special grand jury.

A witness who has been called to testify or produce specified records, papers and documents or other tangible things before a grand jury requested by the attorney for the Commonwealth, and who refuses to testify or produce specified records, papers and documents or other tangible things by expressly invoking his right not to incriminate himself, may be compelled to testify or produce specified records, papers and documents or other tangible things by the presiding judge. Such witness who refuses to testify or produce specified records, papers and documents or other tangible things after being ordered to do so by the presiding judge may be held in contempt and may be incarcerated until the contempt is purged by compliance with the order or the grand jury is discharged. When a witness is compelled to testify or produce specified records, papers and documents or other tangible things after expressly invoking his right not to incriminate himself, and the presiding judge has determined that the assertion of the right is bona fide, the compelled testimony, or any information directly or indirectly derived from such testimony or other information, shall not be used against the witness in any criminal proceeding except a prosecution for perjury.

Notwithstanding the provisions of this section, all provisions of this Code relative to immunity granted to witnesses who testify before a grand jury shall remain applicable.

The foreman shall administer the oath prescribed by law for witnesses, and any member of the special grand jury may examine a witness.

History.

1975, c. 495; 2001, c. 4; 2003, c. 565.

Law Review.

For 1991 survey on criminal law and procedure, see 25 U. Rich. L. Rev. 731 (1991). For article, "Criminal Law and Procedure," see 35 U. Rich. L. Rev. 537 (2001). For article summarizing published Virginia criminal law decisions between July 1, 2002 and July 1, 2003, see 38 U. Rich. L. Rev. 87 (2003).

CASE NOTES

A defendant found guilty of contempt for failing to produce documents subpoenaed by a special grand jury was denied due process of law where the notice to the defendant of the hearing at which he was convicted of indirect contempt was insufficient to show that there would be a hearing before the court to determine whether he should be adjudged in contempt. The trial court abused its discretion in not granting a continuance. Davis v. Commonwealth, 219 Va. 395, 247 S.E.2d 681 (1978).

CIRCUIT COURT OPINIONS

Termination from employment. — To the extent that an employee alleged that the employee's termination resulted from complying with the employee's obligations under subsection C of § 63.2-526, and §§ 19.2-201 and 19.2-208, to report welfare fraud and to testify before a grand jury, the employee made out a claim under the Type 1 exception to the "employment-at-will" doctrine. McClosky v. Warren Co. Dep't of Soc. Servs., 81 Va. Cir. 35, 2010 Va. Cir. LEXIS 102 (Warren County July 15, 2010).

OPINIONS OF THE ATTORNEY GENERAL

Immunity of witness. — A witness who testifies or produces evidence pursuant to a special grand jury subpoena is afforded use immunity and derivative use immunity; such a witness, however, is not granted transactional immunity, as he is not absolutely immune from future prosecution based on the mere fact of his prior testimony. See opinion of Attorney General to The Honorable David M. Hicks, Commonwealth's Attorney for the City of Richmond, 04-34 (7/6/04).

§ 19.2-209. Presence of counsel for a witness.

Any witness appearing before a special grand jury shall have the right to have counsel of his own procurement present when he testifies. Such counsel shall have the right to consult with and advise the witness during his examination, but shall not have the right to conduct an examination of his own of the witness.

History.

1975, c. 495.

§ 19.2-210. Presence of attorney for the Commonwealth.

The attorney for the Commonwealth shall not be present at any time while the special grand jury is in session except that during the investigatory stage of its proceedings he may be present. When the special grand jury is impanelled upon motion of the court or recommendation of a regular grand jury, he may be present during the investigatory stage only when his presence is requested by the special grand jury and may interrogate witnesses provided the special grand jury requests or consents to such interrogation. When the special grand jury was impanelled upon his request, he may examine any witness called to testify or produce evidence, but his examination of a witness shall in no way affect the right of any grand juror to examine the witness.

The attorney for the Commonwealth shall not be present during or after the investigative stage of the proceedings at any time while the special grand jury is discussing, evaluating or considering the testimony of a witness or is deliberating in order to reach decisions or prepare its report, except that he may be present when his legal advice is requested by the special grand jury.

History.
  1975, c. 495; 2001, c. 4.

Law Review.
  For article, "Criminal Law and Procedure," see 35 U. Rich. L. Rev. 537 (2001).

CASE NOTES

The role of special personnel is not limited to educating the grand jurors in the areas of expertise in order that they may successfully conduct their own investigation and examination, or simply to providing documentary evidence and reports. They may, and most often do, conduct the investigation. The limitation which the statute places on the appointed personnel is that they may not participate in the grand jury's deliberations. Vihko v. Commonwealth, 10 Va. App. 498, 393 S.E.2d 413 (1990).

Grand jury may direct special counsel to draft report. — So long as the grand jury arrived at its conclusions through untrammeled deliberations, it may then direct special counsel to draft its report. Vihko v. Commonwealth, 10 Va. App. 498, 393 S.E.2d 413 (1990).

§ 19.2-211. Provision for special counsel and other personnel.

At the request of the special grand jury, the court may designate special counsel to assist it in its work, and may also provide it with appropriate specialized personnel for investigative purposes.

History.
  1975, c. 495.

CASE NOTES

The role of special personnel is not limited to educating the grand jurors in the areas of expertise in order that they may successfully conduct their own investigation and examination, or simply to providing documentary evidence and reports. They may, and most often do, conduct the investigation. The limitation which the statute places on the appointed personnel is that they may not participate in the grand jury's deliberations. Vihko v. Commonwealth, 10 Va. App. 498, 393 S.E.2d 413 (1990).

§ 19.2-212. Provision for court reporter; use and disposition of notes, tapes and transcriptions.

A. A court reporter shall be provided for a special grand jury to record, manually or electronically, and transcribe all oral testimony taken before a special grand jury, but such reporter shall not be present during any stage of its deliberations. The notes, tapes and transcriptions of the reporter are for the sole use of the special grand jury, and the contents thereof shall not be divulged by anyone except as hereinafter provided. After the special grand jury has completed its use of the notes, tapes and transcriptions, the foreman shall cause them to be

sealed, the container dated, and delivered to the court.

The court shall cause the sealed container to be kept safely. If any witness testifying before the special grand jury is prosecuted subsequently for perjury, the court, on motion of either the attorney for the Commonwealth or the defendant, shall permit them both to have access to the testimony given by the defendant when a witness before the special grand jury, and the testimony shall be admissible in the perjury case.

If no prosecution for perjury is instituted within three years from the date of the report of the special grand jury, the court shall cause the sealed container to be destroyed; however, on motion of the attorney for the Commonwealth, the court may extend the time period for destruction if the grand jury was impanelled at the request of the attorney for the Commonwealth.

B. Upon motion to the presiding judge, the attorney for the Commonwealth shall be permitted to review any evidence that was presented to the special grand jury, and shall be permitted to make notes and to duplicate portions of the evidence as he deems necessary for use in a criminal investigation or proceeding. The attorney for the Commonwealth shall maintain the secrecy of all information obtained from a review or duplication of the evidence presented to the special grand jury. Upon motion to the presiding judge by a person indicted after a special grand jury investigation, similar permission to review, note or duplicate evidence shall be extended if it appears that the permission is consistent with the ends of justice and is necessary to reasonably inform such person of the nature of the evidence to be presented against him, or to adequately prepare his defense.

History.
  1975, c. 495; 2001, c. 4; 2003, c. 96; 2008, c. 644.

The 2008 amendments.
  The 2008 amendment by c. 644 substituted "after a special grand jury investigation" for "by a special grand jury" in the last sentence of subsection B.

CASE NOTES

Secrecy is to protect proceedings from public exposure. — The characteristic secrecy associated with grand jury proceedings is intended to protect proceedings from public exposure. Vihko v. Commonwealth, 10 Va. App. 498, 393 S.E.2d 413 (1990).

The rationale for nondisclosure of grand jury proceedings to the public is twofold: (1) to protect the reputation of suspected individuals from the stigma which investigation alone can bring; and (2) to promote public cooperation in investigations by providing some anonymity and reducing the risk of recrimination. Vihko v. Commonwealth, 10 Va. App. 498, 393 S.E.2d 413 (1990).

Primary function of recording proceedings. — While the better practice is to record all proceedings before the grand jury, other than their deliberations, the primary function of recording the proceedings is to maintain a record and transcript for the use, benefit, and convenience of the grand juries. The record is not maintained to provide those under investigation with a record to assure that all formalities attendant to the proceedings have been followed. Vihko v. Commonwealth, 10 Va. App. 498, 393 S.E.2d 413 (1990).

Trial judge only authorized official to monitor scope of disclosure. — The trial judge is the only official authorized by statute to allow access to and to monitor the scope of disclosure of the grand jury's notes, tapes, transcriptions, and report after sealing and filing with the court. Vihko v. Commonwealth, 10 Va. App. 498, 393 S.E.2d 413 (1990) (decided prior to 2001 amendments).

Evidence viewed by grand jury no bar to use at trial. — The fact that a grand jury previously viewed or considered evidence, standing alone, is no bar to its subsequent use at trial. Vihko v. Commonwealth, 10 Va. App. 498, 393 S.E.2d 413 (1990).

§ 19.2-213. Report by special grand jury; return of true bill.

At the conclusion of its investigation and deliberation, a special grand jury impanelled by the court on its own motion or on recommendation of a regular grand jury shall file a report of its findings with the court, including therein any recommendations that it may deem appropriate, after which it shall be discharged. Such report shall be sealed and not open to public inspection, other than by order of the court.

A majority, but not less than five, of the members of a special grand jury convened upon request of the attorney for the Commonwealth must concur in order to return a "true bill" of indictment. A "true bill" may be returned upon the testimony of, or evidence produced by, any witness who was called by the grand jury, upon evidence presented or sent to it.

History.
1975, c. 495; 1978, c. 638; 2001, c. 4.

Law Review.
For survey of Virginia criminal procedure for the year 1977-1978, see 64 Va. L. Rev. 1419 (1978).

CASE NOTES

Trial judge only authorized official to monitor scope of disclosure. — The trial judge is the only official authorized by statute to allow access to and to monitor the scope of disclosure of the grand jury's notes, tapes, transcriptions, and report after sealing and filing with the court. Vihko v. Commonwealth, 10 Va. App. 498, 393 S.E.2d 413 (1990).

CIRCUIT COURT OPINIONS

Need for grand jury materials. — As the circuit court presiding over a special grand jury could not determine from the record to what extent, if at all, a town had a particularized need for grand jury materials to defend against a suit, it sent the report of the special grand jury to the federal district court in which the suit was pending for that court's ruling on the issue. In re Special Grand Jury Report, 54 Va. Cir. 482, 2001 Va. Cir. LEXIS 208 (Roanoke County 2001).

§ 19.2-213.1. Discharge of special grand jury.

If a special grand jury has not filed a report pursuant to § 19.2-213 within six months of its impanelling, the circuit court appointing it shall discharge it; provided, however, if such court, in its discretion, determines that the special grand jury is making progress in its investigation, the court may direct that special grand jury to continue its investigation pursuant to this article.

History.
1978, c. 638.

Law Review.
For survey of Virginia criminal procedure for the year 1977-1978, see 64 Va. L. Rev. 1419 (1978).

§ 19.2-214. Prosecutions resulting from report.

Any bill of indictment for alleged criminal offenses, which may follow as a result of the report of the special grand jury, shall be prepared by the attorney for the Commonwealth for presentation to a regular grand jury.

History.
1975, c. 495.

§ 19.2-215. Costs of special grand jury.

All costs incurred for services provided by the court for a special grand jury shall be paid by the Commonwealth.

History.
1975, c. 495.

ARTICLE 4.

MULTI-JURISDICTION GRAND JURIES.

Michie's Jurisprudence.
For related discussion, see 9A M.J. Grand Jury, § 46 — 50.

§ 19.2-215.1. Functions of a multijurisdiction grand jury.

The functions of a multijurisdiction grand jury are:

1. To investigate any condition that involves or tends to promote criminal violations of:

a. Title 10.1 for which punishment as a felony is authorized;

b. § 13.1-520;

c. §§ 18.2-47 and 18.2-48;

d. §§ 18.2-111 and 18.2-112;

e. Article 6 (§ 18.2-59 et seq.) of Chapter 4 of Title 18.2;

f. Article 7.1 (§ 18.2-152.1 et seq.) of Chapter 5 of Title 18.2;

g. Article 1 (§ 18.2-247 et seq.) and Article 1.1 (§ 18.2-265.1 et seq.) of Chapter 7 of Title 18.2;

h. Article 1 (§ 18.2-325 et seq.) and Article 1.1:1 (§ 18.2-340.15 et seq.) of Chapter 8 of Title 18.2, Chapter 29 (§ 59.1-364 et seq.) of Title 59.1 or any other provision prohibiting, limiting, regulating, or otherwise affecting gaming or gambling activity;

i. § 18.2-434, when violations occur before a multijurisdiction grand jury;

j. Article 2 (§ 18.2-438 et seq.) and Article 3 (§ 18.2-446 et seq.) of Chapter 10 of Title 18.2;

k. § 18.2-460 for which punishment as a felony is authorized;

l. Article 1.1 (§ 18.2-498.1 et seq.) of Chapter 12 of Title 18.2;

m. Article 1 (§ 32.1-310 et seq.) of Chapter 9 of Title 32.1;

n. Chapter 4.2 (§ 59.1-68.6 et seq.) of Title 59.1;

o. Article 9 (§ 3.2-6570 et seq.) of Chapter 65 of Title 3.2;

p. Article 1 (§ 18.2-30 et seq.) of Chapter 4 of Title 18.2;

q. Article 2.1 (§ 18.2-46.1 et seq.) and Article 2.2 (§ 18.2-46.4 et seq.) of Chapter 4 of Title 18.2;

r. Article 5 (§ 18.2-186 et seq.) and Article 6 (§ 18.2-191 et seq.) of Chapter 6 of Title 18.2;

s. Chapter 6.1 (§ 59.1-92.1 et seq.) of Title 59.1;

t. § 18.2-178 where the violation involves insurance fraud;

u. § 18.2-356;

v. Article 9 (§ 18.2-246.1 et seq.) of Chapter 6 of Title 18.2;

w. Article 2 (§ 18.2-38 et seq.) of Chapter 4 of Title 18.2;

x. Malicious felonious assault and malicious bodily wounding under Article 4 (§ 18.2-51 et seq.) of Chapter 4 of Title 18.2;

y. Article 5 (§ 18.2-58 et seq.) of Chapter 4 of Title 18.2;

z. Felonious sexual assault under Article 7 (§ 18.2-61 et seq.) of Chapter 4 of Title 18.2;

aa. Arson in violation of § 18.2-77 when the structure burned was occupied or a Class 3 felony violation of § 18.2-79;

bb. Chapter 13 (§ 18.2-512 et seq.) of Title 18.2; and

cc. Any other provision of law when such condition is discovered in the course of an investigation that a multijurisdiction grand jury is otherwise authorized to undertake and to investigate any condition that involves or tends to promote any attempt, solicitation or conspiracy to violate the laws enumerated in this section.

2. To report evidence of any criminal offense enumerated in subdivision 1 and for which a court reporter has recorded all oral testimony as provided by § 19.2-215.9 to the attorney for the Commonwealth or United States attorney of any jurisdiction where such offense could be prosecuted or investigated and, when appropriate, to the Attorney General.

3. To consider bills of indictment prepared by a special counsel to determine whether there is sufficient probable cause to return each such indictment as a "true bill." Only bills of indictment which allege an offense enumerated in subdivision 1 may be submitted to a multijurisdiction grand jury.

4. The provisions of this section shall not abrogate the authority of an attorney for the Commonwealth in a particular jurisdiction to determine the course of a prosecution in that jurisdiction.

History.
1983, c. 543; 1991, c. 616; 1995, c. 552; 2000, c. 359; 2002, cc. 588, 623; 2004, cc. 396, 435; 2008, c. 704; 2009, c. 491; 2011, c. 504; 2013, cc. 83, 314, 459.

The 2008 amendments.
The 2008 amendment by c. 704 deleted "and" at the end of subdivision 1 q; redesignated former subdivision 1 r as subdivision 1 s; and inserted subdivision 1 r.

The 2009 amendments.
The 2009 amendment by c. 491 inserted subdivision 1 s and redesignated former subdivision 1 s as subdivision 1 t; and made a related change.

The 2011 amendments.
The 2011 amendment by c. 504 added subdivision 1 t and made a related change; and redesignated former subdivision 1 t as subdivision 1 u.

The 2013 amendments.
The 2013 amendment by c. 83 added subdivision 1 u and redesignated accordingly, and made a related change.
The 2013 amendment by c. 314 added subdivision 1 u, and made a related change. Subdivision 1 u as added by c. 314, was redesignated as 1 v at the direction of the Virginia Code Commission.
The 2013 amendment by c. 459 added subdivisions 1 u through 1 z and redesignated former subdivision 1 u as present 1 aa and made related changes; and inserted "and for which a court reporter has recorded all oral testimony as provided by § 19.2-215.9" in subdivision 2. Subdivisions 1 u through 1 z, as added by c. 459, were redesignated as 1 w through 1 bb at the direction of the Virginia Code Commission.

Law Review.
For article, "Criminal Law and Procedure," see 35 U. Rich. L. Rev. 537 (2001). For 2003/2004 survey of criminal law and procedure, see 39 U. Rich. L. Rev. 133 (2004).

CASE NOTES

Construction with § 18.2-262. — In order to give full force and effect both to this section, addressing the narrow, specific exemption for multi-jurisdictional grand juries, and to § 18.2-262, addressing grand juries generally, the later enacted statutory scheme (§ 19.2-215.1 et seq.) is construed to control testimony before multi-jurisdiction grand juries. Tharpe v. Commonwealth, 18 Va. App. 37, 441 S.E.2d 228 (1994).

§ 19.2-215.2. Application for such grand jury.

Provided the Attorney General has approved the application in writing prior to submission, application for a multi-jurisdiction grand jury may be made to the Supreme Court of Virginia by two or more attorneys for the Commonwealth from jurisdictions which would be within the original scope of the investigation. The application shall be in writing and shall state (i) which jurisdictions will be involved in the original scope of the investigation, (ii) in which jurisdiction it is requested that the multijurisdiction grand jury be convened, (iii) the name or names of the attorneys for the Commonwealth or their assistants who will serve as special counsel to the grand jury, (iv) the name of the attorney who shall direct the grand jury proceedings. The presiding judge may extend or limit the jurisdictional territory of the investigation, for good cause shown, upon the motion of a grand jury already convened. Notice of every such application shall be given to the attorneys for the Commonwealth in the jurisdictions named in the application and, if the original scope of the investigation is extended into other jurisdictions, notice of such extension shall be given to the attorneys for the Commonwealth in the jurisdictions into which the investigation is extended.

History.
1983, c. 543.

§ 19.2-215.3. When impaneled; impaneling order.

Upon application by two or more attorneys for the Commonwealth, the Chief Justice of the Supreme Court, or any justice designated by the Chief Justice, may within twenty days thereafter order the impaneling of a multi-jurisdiction grand jury for a term of twelve months. The term of such a grand jury may be extended for successive periods of not more than six months by the Chief Justice, or by any justice designated by the Chief Justice, upon the petition of a majority of the members of the grand jury.

The impaneling order shall designate the jurisdiction requested on the application as the jurisdiction where the multi-jurisdiction grand jury shall be convened and shall, unless all judges of that circuit have recused themselves, appoint a judge of the circuit court of that jurisdiction as the presiding judge. The impaneling order shall also designate special counsel and each special counsel who will assist the multi-jurisdiction grand jury as listed in the application. The presiding judge shall substitute or appoint additional special counsel upon motion of special counsel.

History.
1983, c. 543; 2010, c. 438.

The 2010 amendments.
The 2010 amendment by c. 438, in the second paragraph, deleted "shall appoint a judge of a circuit court from one of the jurisdictions named on the application as the presiding judge and" following "impaneling order," and inserted "the jurisdiction requested on the application as the jurisdiction" and "and shall, unless all judges of that circuit have recused themselves, appoint a judge of the circuit court of that jurisdiction as the presiding judge."

§ 19.2-215.4. Number and qualifications of jurors; grand jury list; when convened; compensation of jurors.

A. A multi-jurisdiction grand jury shall consist of not less than seven nor more than 11 members. Each member of a multi-jurisdiction grand jury shall be a citizen of this Commonwealth, 18 years of age or older, and a resident of this Commonwealth for one year and of one of the jurisdictions named in the application for six months.

B. The presiding judge shall determine the number of grand jurors to be drawn and shall draw them so that, to the extent practicable, each of the jurisdictions named in the application is represented by at least one juror residing in that jurisdiction, but in no event shall said panel have more than 11 members. The grand jurors shall be summoned from a list prepared by the presiding judge. In the preparation of this list, the presiding judge shall select only persons who have been selected as regular grand jurors pursuant to the provisions of § 19.2-194 in the jurisdiction named in the application. Members of a multi-jurisdiction grand jury shall possess the same qualifications as those prescribed for members of a regular grand jury, including indifference in the cause.

C. The provisions of § 19.2-192 dealing with secrecy in grand jury proceedings are incorporated herein by reference.

D. The presiding judge shall determine the time, date and place within the designated jurisdiction where the multi-jurisdiction grand jury is to be convened. The presiding judge shall also appoint one of the grand jurors to serve as foreman. Members of the multi-jurisdiction grand jury shall be compensated according to the provisions of § 19.2-205. The expense of a multi-jurisdiction grand jury shall be borne by the Commonwealth.

History.
1983, c. 543; 2008, c. 644.

The 2008 amendments.
The 2008 amendment by c. 644, in subsection A, substituted "11" for "eleven" and "18" for "eighteen"; in subsection B, substituted "11" for "eleven" and added the last sentence.

§ 19.2-215.5. Subpoena power; counsel for witness; oath.

A multi-jurisdiction grand jury has statewide subpoena power and may subpoena persons to appear before it to testify or to produce evidence in the form of specified records, papers, documents or other tangible things. Mileage and such other reasonable expenses as are approved by the presiding judge shall be paid such persons from funds appropriated for such purpose.

A witness before a multi-jurisdiction grand jury shall be entitled to the presence of counsel in the grand jury room, but he may not participate in the proceedings.

The foreman shall administer the oath required by law for witnesses.

History.
1983, c. 543.

§ 19.2-215.6. Role and presence of special counsel; examination of witnesses.

Special counsel may be present during the investigatory stage of a multi-jurisdiction grand jury proceeding and may examine any witness who is called to testify or produce evidence. The examination of a witness by special counsel shall in no way affect the right of any grand juror to examine the witness.

Special counsel, however, may not be present at any time during the deliberations of a multi-jurisdiction grand jury except when the grand jury requests the legal advice of special counsel as to specific questions of law.

History.
1983, c. 543.

§ 19.2-215.7. Warnings given to witnesses; when witness in contempt; use of testimony compelled after witness invokes right against self-incrimination.

A. Every witness testifying before a multi-jurisdiction grand jury shall be warned by special counsel or by the foreman of the grand jury that he need not answer any question that would tend to incriminate him, and that he may later be called upon to testify in any case that may result from the grand jury proceedings.

B. A witness who has been called to testify or produce evidence before a multi-jurisdiction grand jury, and who refuses to testify or produce evidence by expressly invoking his right not to incriminate himself, may be compelled to testify or produce evidence by the presiding judge. A witness who refuses to testify or produce evidence after being ordered to do so by the presiding judge may be held in contempt and may be incarcerated until the contempt is purged by compliance with the order.

C. When a witness is compelled to testify or produce evidence after expressly invoking his right not to incriminate himself, and the presiding judge has determined that the assertion of the right is bona fide, the compelled testimony, or any information directly or indirectly derived from such testimony or other information, shall not be used against the witness in any criminal proceeding except a prosecution for perjury.

History.
1983, c. 543.

CASE NOTES

Appellant never invoked her constitutional privilege against self-incrimination before a multi-jurisdiction grand jury where the record indicated that appellant was advised that she need not answer any incriminating questions but that if she refused to answer, she could be compelled to do so, and appellant indicated in writing that she understood this warning, but she testified about the drug crimes without affirmatively invoking her privilege. Tharpe v. Commonwealth, 18 Va. App. 37, 441 S.E.2d 228 (1994).

§ 19.2-215.8. Returning a "true bill" of indictment; jurisdiction to be set out.

In order to return a "true bill" of indictment, a majority, but in no instance less than five, of the multi-jurisdiction grand jurors must concur in that finding. A multi-jurisdiction grand jury may return a "true bill" of indictment upon the testimony of, or evidence produced by, any witness who was called by the grand jury, upon evidence presented to it by special counsel, or upon evidence sent to it by the presiding judge.

Every "true bill" of indictment returned by a multi-jurisdiction grand jury shall state in which jurisdiction or jurisdictions the offense is alleged to have occurred. Thereafter, when venue is proper in more than one jurisdiction, the presiding judge who directed the grand jury proceeding shall elect in which one of the jurisdictions named in the indictment the indictment is to be prosecuted.

History.
1983, c. 543.

§ 19.2-215.9. Court reporter provided; safekeeping of transcripts, notes, etc.; when disclosure permitted; access to record of testimony and evidence.

A. A court reporter shall be provided for a multi-jurisdiction grand jury to record, manually or electronically, and transcribe all oral testimony taken before a multi-jurisdiction grand jury, but such a reporter shall not be present during any stage of its deliberations. Such transcription shall include the original or copies of all documents, reports or other evidence presented to the multi-jurisdiction grand jury. The notes, tapes and transcriptions of the reporter are for the use of the multi-jurisdiction grand jury, and the contents thereof shall not be used or divulged by anyone except as provided in this article. After the multi-jurisdiction grand jury has completed its use of the notes, tapes and transcriptions, the foreman shall cause them to be delivered to the presiding judge.

B. The presiding judge shall cause the notes, tapes and transcriptions or other evidence to be kept safely. Upon motion to the presiding judge, special counsel shall be permitted to review any of the evidence which was presented to the multi-jurisdiction grand jury, and shall be permitted to make notes and to duplicate portions of the evidence as he deems necessary for use in a criminal investigation or proceeding. Special counsel shall maintain the secrecy of all information obtained from a review or duplication of the evidence presented to the multi-jurisdiction grand jury, except that this information may be disclosed pursuant to the provisions of subdivision 2 of § 19.2-215.1. Upon motion to the presiding judge by a person indicted by a multi-jurisdiction grand jury, similar permission to review, note or duplicate evidence shall be extended if it appears that the permission is consistent with the ends of justice and is necessary to reasonably inform such person of the nature of the evidence to be presented against him, or to adequately prepare his defense.

C. If any witness who voluntarily testified or produced evidence before the multi-jurisdiction grand jury is prosecuted on the basis of his testimony or the evidence he produced, or if any witness who was compelled to testify or to produce evidence is prosecuted for perjury on the basis of his testimony or the evidence he produced before the multi-jurisdiction grand jury, the presiding judge, on motion of either the Commonwealth or the defendant, shall permit both the Commonwealth and the defendant access to the testimony of or evidence produced by the defendant before the multi-jurisdiction grand jury. The testimony and the evidence produced by the defendant voluntarily before the multi-jurisdiction grand jury shall then be admissible in the trial of the criminal offense with which the defendant is charged, for the purpose of impeaching the defendant.

History.
1983, c. 543.

§ 19.2-215.10. Participation by Office of Attorney General; assistance of special counsel permitted in certain prosecutions.

Upon request by the applicants or upon motion to the presiding judge by special counsel, the Office of Attorney General may participate as special counsel in the multi-jurisdiction grand jury proceedings and any prosecutions arising therefrom. In any prosecution arising out of the multi-jurisdiction grand jury, the attorney for the Commonwealth may also obtain the assistance of the special counsel to the grand jury as a special assistant attorney for the Commonwealth.

History.
1983, c. 543.

§ 19.2-215.11. Discharge of grand jury.

At any time during the original or extended term of a multi-jurisdiction grand jury, the presiding judge may discharge the grand jury if, in the opinion of the presiding judge, the existence of the multi-jurisdiction grand jury is no longer necessary.

History.
1983, c. 543.

CHAPTER 14.

PRESENTMENTS, INDICTMENTS AND INFORMATIONS.

Article 1. Necessity for Indictment, etc.

ARTICLE 1.

NECESSITY FOR INDICTMENT, ETC.

§ 19.2-216. Definition of indictment, presentment and information.

An indictment is a written accusation of crime, prepared by the attorney for the Commonwealth and returned "a true bill" upon the oath or affirmation of a legally impanelled grand jury.

A presentment is a written accusation of crime prepared and returned by a grand jury from their own knowledge or observation, without any bill of indictment laid before them.

An information is a written accusation of crime or a complaint for forfeiture of property or money or for imposition of a penalty, prepared and presented by a competent public official upon his oath of office.

History.
1975, c. 495.

§ 19.2-217. When information filed; prosecution for felony to be by indictment or presentment; waiver; process to compel appearance of accused.

An information may be filed by the attorney for the Commonwealth based upon a complaint in writing verified by the oath of a competent witness; but no person shall be put upon trial for any felony, unless an indictment or presentment shall have first been found or made by a grand jury in a court of competent jurisdiction or unless such person, by writing signed by such person before the court having jurisdiction to try such felony or before the judge of such court shall have waived such indictment or presentment, in which event he may be tried on a warrant or information. If the accused be in custody, or has been recognized or summoned to answer such information, presentment or indictment, no other process shall be necessary; but the court may, in its discretion, issue process to compel the appearance of the accused.

History.

Code 1950, § 19.1-162; 1960, c. 366; 1975, c. 495.

Law Review.

For article, "Is the Grand Jury Necessary?," see 45 Va. L. Rev. 461 (1959). For comment on arraignment, pretrial motions, and pleas, see 22 Wash. & Lee L. Rev. 336 (1965). For survey of Virginia criminal law for the year 1971-1972, see 58 Va. L. Rev. 1206 (1972).

Michie's Jurisprudence.

For related discussion, see 5B M.J. Criminal Procedure, §§ 12, 20, 21; 8B M.J. Forgery, § 12; 9A M.J. Grand Jury, § 31; 9B M.J. Indictments, Informations and Presentments, §§ 7, 50.

CASE NOTES

This section is a criminal statute and applies only to a criminal proceeding. Lawrence v. Commonwealth, 206 Va. 51, 141 S.E.2d 735 (1965).

It is not applicable to a proceeding under former § 53-296, the recidivist statute. Lawrence v. Commonwealth, 206 Va. 51, 141 S.E.2d 735 (1965).

There is no constitutional requirement that prosecutions for felony be by indictment. The requirement is merely statutory and may be waived. Livingston v. Commonwealth, 184 Va. 830, 36 S.E.2d 561 (1946); Bailey v. Commonwealth, 193 Va. 814, 71 S.E.2d 368, cert. denied, 344 U.S. 886, 73 S. Ct. 186, 97 L. Ed. 686 (1952); Council v. Smyth, 201 Va. 135, 109 S.E.2d 116 (1959); Cunningham v. Hayes, 204 Va. 851, 134 S.E.2d 271, cert. denied, 376 U.S. 973, 84 S. Ct. 1140, 12 L. Ed. 2d 86 (1964); Henson v. Commonwealth, 208 Va. 120, 155 S.E.2d 346 (1967).

While this section prevents the trial of a person on a felony charge except upon a presentment or indictment found by a grand jury, this is purely a statutory requirement and is not predicated upon any constitutional guarantee. Benson v. Commonwealth, 190 Va. 744, 58 S.E.2d 312 (1950); Scales v. Commonwealth, 214 Va. 728, 204 S.E.2d 273 (1974), cert. denied, 419 U.S. 1123, 95 S. Ct. 808, 42 L. Ed. 2d 823 (1975).

Options open to Commonwealth. — When the Commonwealth seeks to prosecute an adult for a felony, it has several options how to proceed, including direct indictment, information, presentment, or arrest warrant followed by a preliminary hearing. Burfoot v. Commonwealth, 23 Va. App. 38, 473 S.E.2d 724 (1996).

Indictment for felony not jurisdictional. — This section is a clear expression of the legislative policy that the requirement of an indictment in the prosecution for a felony may be waived, and hence is not jurisdictional. Hanson v. Smyth, 183 Va. 384, 32 S.E.2d 142

(1944); Bailey v. Commonwealth, 193 Va. 814, 71 S.E.2d 368, cert. denied, 344 U.S. 886, 73 S. Ct. 186, 97 L. Ed. 686 (1952); Council v. Smyth, 201 Va. 135, 109 S.E.2d 116 (1959).

The requirement for indictment is not jurisdictional and constitutionally imposed but is only statutory and procedural. Triplett v. Commonwealth, 212 Va. 649, 186 S.E.2d 16 (1972).

Nor is preliminary hearing. — The requirement of a preliminary hearing (assuming waiver) of one arrested on a charge of a felony is not jurisdictional and its denial does not violate the "due process" and "equal protection" of the laws clause of the Fourteenth Amendment of the Constitution of the United States. Dunnivan v. Peyton, 292 F. Supp. 173 (W.D. Va. 1968).

But denial may be reversible error. — Where the defendant insists upon his statutory rights to a preliminary hearing and indictment, the failure of the trial court to adhere to those procedural requirements is reversible error. Triplett v. Commonwealth, 212 Va. 649, 186 S.E.2d 16 (1972).

Defects in form. — Failure of the grand jury foreman to sign the indictments was a defect in form only and accordingly, when the indictments were returned by the grand jury in open court, that defect in form was cured and the indictments became valid instruments under which to try defendant. Although the written charges did not contain the signature of the grand jury foreman, they had been "returned in open court" by the grand jury as true bills and, thus, became valid indictments. Reed v. Commonwealth, 281 Va. 471, 706 S.E.2d 854, 2011 Va. LEXIS 50 (2011).

The term "indictment" in this section means and includes an indictment which has been properly amended by the court. Farewell v. Commonwealth, 167 Va. 475, 189 S.E. 321 (1937).

Bringing indictment after finding of no probable cause by district court. — Failure of the General Assembly to bar forever the bringing of an indictment after a finding of no probable cause by a district court was intentional. Such a provision would have been totally inconsistent with the provisions of former § 19.1-158 (now § 19.2-203). Moore v. Commonwealth, 218 Va. 388, 237 S.E.2d 187 (1977), decided under former §§ 19.1-162 and 19.1-163.1.

Plea cannot be entered at preliminary hearing. — The procedure prescribed for waiving an indictment does not permit a plea to be entered at a preliminary hearing on a felony charge. Timmons v. Peyton, 240 F. Supp. 749 (E.D. Va. 1965), rev'd on other grounds, 360 F.2d 327 (4th Cir.), cert. denied, 385 U.S. 960, 87 S. Ct. 396, 17 L. Ed. 2d 305 (1966).

Virginia does not permit a plea to be entered at a preliminary hearing on a felony charge. Dunnivan v. Peyton, 292 F. Supp. 173 (W.D. Va. 1968).

Failure of record to show indictment returned will not vitiate conviction. — Where the requirement for an indictment is not jurisdictional, the failure of the record to show affirmatively that the indictment was returned into court by the grand jury is not such a defect as will render null and void the judgment of conviction based thereon. Hanson v. Smyth, 183 Va. 384, 32 S.E.2d 142 (1944).

Motion to quash information not available when defects not shown on record or by bill of exception. — A motion to quash an information on the ground that it is not founded upon a complaint in writing verified by the oath of a competent witness, as required by this section, is not available where the defect is not apparent upon the face of the information, and not incorporated in the record by proper bill of exceptions. Quillin v. Commonwealth, 105 Va. 874, 54 S.E. 333 (1906).

The question of the sufficiency of an indictment cannot be raised more than four years after a conviction in a collateral proceeding by habeas corpus. Council v. Smyth, 201 Va. 135, 109 S.E.2d 116 (1944).

A misdemeanor may be tried on a presentment or information as well as on indictment. Jones v. Commonwealth, 60 Va. (19 Gratt.) 478 (1868).

Conviction of robbery where indictment charged only attempted robbery. — See Henson v. Commonwealth, 208 Va. 120, 155 S.E.2d 346 (1967).

Inapplicable to juvenile conviction. — Defendant's sentence to a mandatory five-year term under § 18.2-308.2 for possession of a firearm by a convicted felon, was affirmed as he had been convicted of possessing a firearm after conviction of a felony in violation of § 18.2-308.2 when he was 14, which would have been classified as a violent felony under subsections B and C of § 17.1-805, if he had been tried as an adult; defendant's argument that his juvenile conviction could not serve as the necessary predicate act for § 18.2-308.2 because he was not convicted under an indictment was rejected, and § 19.2-217, relied upon by defendant, was inapplicable. Parks v. Commonwealth, No. 2780-02-1, 2003 Va. App. LEXIS 385 (Ct. of Appeals July 8, 2003).

Applied in Wilson v. Commonwealth, 31 Va. App. 495, 525 S.E.2d 1 (2000); Grier v. Commonwealth, 35 Va. App. 560, 546 S.E.2d 743, 2001 Va. App. LEXIS 297 (2001); Edwards v. Commonwealth, 41 Va. App. 752, 589 S.E.2d 444, 2003 Va. App. LEXIS 637 (2003).

§ 19.2-217.1. Central file of capital murder indictments.

Upon the return by a grand jury of an indictment for capital murder and the arrest of the defendant, the clerk of the circuit court in which such indictment is returned shall forthwith file a certified copy of the indictment with the clerk of the Supreme Court of Virginia. All such indictments shall be maintained in a single place by the clerk of the Supreme Court, and shall be available to members of the public upon request. Failure to comply with the provisions of this section shall not be (i) a basis upon which an indictment may be quashed or deemed invalid; (ii) deemed error upon which a conviction may be reversed or a sentence vacated; or (iii) a basis upon which a court may prevent or delay execution of a sentence.

History.
1993, c. 319.

§ 19.2-218. Preliminary hearing required for person arrested on charge of felony; waiver.

No person who is arrested on a charge of felony shall be denied a preliminary hearing upon the question of whether there is reasonable ground to believe that he committed the offense and no indictment shall be returned in a court of record against any such person prior to such hearing unless such hearing is waived in writing by the accused.

History.
Code 1950, § 19.1-163.1; 1960, c. 389; 1975, c. 495.

Law Review.
For survey of Virginia law on criminal law for the year 1971-1972, see 58 Va. L. Rev. 1206 (1972). For annual survey article, "Criminal Law and Procedure," see 44 U. Rich. L. Rev. 339 (2009).

Michie's Jurisprudence.
For related discussion, see 5B M.J. Criminal Procedure, §§ 17, 21; 9B M.J. Infants, § 13; 12B M.J. Mayhem, § 5.

CASE NOTES

Purpose of section. — It may reasonably be assumed from the language used in this section that it was enacted to change the effect of previous court decisions and to grant an accused the right to a preliminary hearing when he has been arrested on a warrant charging a felony before an indictment has been returned by a grand jury. Webb v. Commonwealth, 204 Va. 24, 129 S.E.2d 22 (1963).

This section does not require a preliminary hearing after indictment. Braxton v. Peyton, 365 F.2d 563 (4th Cir.), cert.

denied, 385 U.S. 939, 87 S. Ct. 306, 17 L. Ed. 2d 218 (1966); May v. Peyton, 268 F. Supp. 928 (W.D. Va. 1967), rev'd on other grounds, 398 F.2d 476 (4th Cir. 1968), cert. denied, 402 U.S. 948, 91 S. Ct. 1602, 29 L. Ed. 2d 117 (1971).

This section does not require a preliminary hearing after indictment. The federal courts have upheld the constitutionality of this interpretation of this section and have not required the state to provide a preliminary hearing when the accused has been previously indicted by a grand jury. Couser v. Cox, 324 F. Supp. 1140 (W.D. Va. 1971).

Requirement not jurisdictional. — The requirement of this section is procedural only, and not jurisdictional, and any defect in connection with the required hearing must be raised before trial, or forever lost as a ground of objection. Snyder v. Commonwealth, 202 Va. 1009, 121 S.E.2d 452 (1961); Gibson v. Peyton, 262 F. Supp. 574 (W.D. Va. 1966).

The preliminary hearing granted by this section is not jurisdictional. Ashby v. Cox, 344 F. Supp. 759 (W.D. Va. 1972).

In Virginia, a preliminary hearing in an adult criminal case is merely a procedural requirement, not jurisdictionally significant. Nottingham v. Zahradnick, 573 F.2d 193 (4th Cir.), cert. denied, 439 U.S. 970, 99 S. Ct. 464, 58 L. Ed. 2d 430 (1978).

Since a preliminary hearing in an adult case is a procedural and not a jurisdictional requirement, where an adult defendant whose victim was a juvenile was given a preliminary hearing in the criminal division of a general district court the declaration of a mistrial by the circuit court judge on the ground that the defendant had been denied a hearing in the juvenile court under subsection I of § 16.1-241 was not required under the doctrine of "manifest necessity," jeopardy attached, and the defendant could not be retried. Nottingham v. Zahradnick, 573 F.2d 193 (4th Cir.), cert. denied, 439 U.S. 970, 99 S. Ct. 464, 58 L. Ed. 2d 430 (1978).

Nor constitutionally mandated. — An accused has a statutory right in Virginia to a preliminary hearing before his indictment but he still does not have a constitutional right to a preliminary hearing. McCormick v. Peyton, 274 F. Supp. 797 (W.D. Va. 1967).

There is no constitutional right to a preliminary hearing. Ashby v. Cox, 344 F. Supp. 759 (W.D. Va. 1972).

The requirement of a preliminary hearing of one arrested on a charge of a felony is not jurisdictional, and its denial does not violate the "due process" and "equal protection" of the law clauses of § 1 of the Fourteenth Amendment to the Constitution of the United States and Va. Const., Art. I, § 8. Webb v. Commonwealth, 204 Va. 24, 129 S.E.2d 22 (1963).

The requirement for a preliminary hearing under this section is not jurisdictional and constitutionally imposed but is only statutory and procedural. Triplett v. Commonwealth, 212 Va. 649, 186 S.E.2d 16 (1972).

Defendant's conviction for assaulting a police officer in violation of subsection C of § 18.2-57 had to stand, as defendant was not denied the right to a preliminary hearing on that charge after the district court terminated the charge by entering a nolle prosequi officer and the Commonwealth then obtained a direct indictment for the same offense and proved its case in the trial court. Since the case had been terminated in the district court once the nolle prosequi order was entered, defendant was not under actual arrest for that charge as required by the preliminary hearing statute, § 19.2-218, and not holding the preliminary hearing was a statutory, not constitutional, matter, which meant that defendant's due process rights under Va. Const., Art. I, § 11 were not violated because a preliminary hearing was not held. Wright v. Commonwealth, 52 Va. App. 690, 667 S.E.2d 787, 2008 Va. App. LEXIS 509 (2008).

Options open to Commonwealth. — When the Commonwealth seeks to prosecute an adult for a felony, it has several options how to proceed, including direct indictment, information, presentment, or arrest warrant followed by a preliminary hearing. Burfoot v. Commonwealth, 23 Va. App. 38, 473 S.E.2d 724 (1996).

The preliminary hearing and proceedings attendant thereto are of a procedural nature in Virginia. Bird v. Peyton, 287 F. Supp. 860 (W.D. Va. 1968).

There is no guarantee provided for a preliminary hearing in either the Virginia or the United States Constitutions. Bird v. Peyton, 287 F. Supp. 860 (W.D. Va. 1968).

The right to a preliminary hearing is given only by statute. Bird v. Peyton, 287 F. Supp. 860 (W.D. Va. 1968).

In the absence of a statute providing otherwise a preliminary hearing is not a prerequisite or an indispensable step in the prosecution of a person accused of crime. Couser v. Cox, 324 F. Supp. 1140 (W.D. Va. 1971).

Insistence on right to preliminary hearing and indictment. — Where the defendant insists upon his statutory rights to a preliminary hearing and indictment, the failure of the trial court to adhere to those procedural requirements is reversible error. Triplett v. Commonwealth, 212 Va. 649, 186 S.E.2d 16 (1972).

Waiver valid despite defendant's mistaken belief he would be admitted into drug court program. — Although defendant waived the right to a preliminary hearing based on the expectation that he would be admitted into the drug court program, the later determination that he was not eligible for the program did not render his otherwise voluntary waiver invalid. Angelina v. Commonwealth, — Va. App. —, — S.E.2d —, 2005 Va. App. LEXIS 233 (June 14, 2005).

The Virginia preliminary hearing is a "critical stage" of the criminal process. Noe v. Cox, 320 F. Supp. 849 (W.D. Va. 1970).

And an indigent accused is entitled to have counsel appointed. The purpose of this rule is to protect the indigent accused against an erroneous or improper prosecution. This rule should apply only to those preliminary hearings held after June 22, 1970. Noe v. Cox, 320 F. Supp. 849 (W.D. Va. 1970).

The purposes and procedures of the preliminary hearing in Virginia are so similar to those in North Carolina that, in Virginia, as in North Carolina, the safeguards provided by the preliminary hearing may not be fully utilized unless the accused is assisted by counsel. Noe v. Cox, 320 F. Supp. 849 (W.D. Va. 1970).

The procedure in a state court in its preliminary hearing is a matter for state direction so long as the proceedings do not amount to such a gross unfairness as to violate the defendant's right to due process as guaranteed by the Fourteenth Amendment. Bird v. Peyton, 287 F. Supp. 860 (W.D. Va. 1968).

Failure to appoint a reporter for petitioner in the preliminary hearing does not violate any constitutional rights of petitioner. Bird v. Peyton, 287 F. Supp. 860 (W.D. Va. 1968).

Action of grand jury preempting right to preliminary hearing. — Where a grand jury finds that there is reasonable cause to believe that defendant has committed a felony before defendant is arrested, its action preempts defendant's right to a preliminary hearing. Webb v. Commonwealth, 204 Va. 24, 129 S.E.2d 22 (1963).

A suspect is not entitled to a preliminary hearing if he has not been arrested or charged with any offense prior to indictment by a grand jury. Land v. Commonwealth, 211 Va. 223, 176 S.E.2d 586 (1970).

Determination by a grand jury of probable cause to indict preempts an adult defendant's right to a preliminary hearing. Nottingham v. Zahradnick, 573 F.2d 193 (4th Cir.), cert. denied, 439 U.S. 970, 99 S. Ct. 464, 58 L. Ed. 2d 430 (1978).

Section deals only with person who is "arrested." — Former § 19.1-163.1 (now this section) dealt by its very language only with a person who was "arrested," meaning, within this context, a person who was detained in custody by authority of law or one who was under a legal restraint. Moore v. Commonwealth, 218 Va. 388, 237 S.E.2d 187 (1977).

Defendant was properly indicted without a preliminary hearing where the Commonwealth took a nolle prosequi of the offenses charged in the original warrants because the nolle prosequi terminated the charges as if they had never existed and the defendant was not under arrest as required by this statute. Armel v. Commonwealth, 28 Va. App. 407, 505 S.E.2d 378 (1998).

Direct indictment by grand jury following arrest and hearing on different charge. — Where the defendant was originally detained on a noncapital charge of first-degree murder, was granted a preliminary hearing on that charge, and was certified to the grand jury, and where the attorney for the Commonwealth then obtained indictments for both capital murder and first-degree murder and proceeded to trial on the capital but not the noncapital offense, the procedure employed in obtaining the indictment was not manipulative, and it did not work a denial of any statutory right to which the defendant was entitled, since defendant was not arrested on the charge of capital murder, but was indicted on that charge directly by the grand jury. Waye v. Commonwealth, 219 Va. 683, 251 S.E.2d 202, cert. denied, 442 U.S. 924, 99 S. Ct. 2850, 61 L. Ed. 2d 292 (1979).

A person who had been dismissed after a probable cause hearing, and whose freedom of movement and liberty was not subject to any legal restriction, was not a person who "is arrested on a charge of felony" within the meaning of former § 19.1-163.1 (now this section). Moore v. Commonwealth, 218 Va. 388, 237 S.E.2d 187 (1977).

Bringing indictment after finding of no probable cause by district court. — Failure of the General Assembly to bar forever the bringing of an indictment after a finding of no probable cause by a district court was intentional. Such a provision would have been totally inconsistent with the provisions of former § 19.1-158 (now § 19.2-203). Moore v. Commonwealth, 218 Va. 388, 237 S.E.2d 187 (1977) (decided under former §§ 19.1-162 and 19.1-163.1).

CIRCUIT COURT OPINIONS

Waiver based on plea agreement. — Because defendant specifically waived the right to a preliminary hearing under § 19.2-218 in reliance on a plea agreement, and because defendant complied with defendant's modified obligation to provide a "very specific" description of the driver of a stolen vehicle, defendant was entitled to have the agreement enforced. Commonwealth v. Brown, 79 Va. Cir. 659, 2007 Va. Cir. LEXIS 334 (Alexandria Nov. 2, 2007).

Nolle prossing case and obtaining straight indictment was not prohibited. — Prosecutor's action in nolle prossing a case and then obtaining a straight indictment was not manipulative and did not deprive defendant of his statutory right to have a preliminary hearing under § 19.2-218; defendant was not entitled to a dismissal of the case against him. Commonwealth v. Muth, 72 Va. Cir. 261, 2006 Va. Cir. LEXIS 222 (Fairfax County 2006).

§ 19.2-218.1. Preliminary hearings involving certain sexual crimes against spouses.

A. In any preliminary hearing of a charge for a violation under § 18.2-61, 18.2-67.1, or 18.2-67.2 where the complaining witness is the spouse of the accused, upon a finding of probable cause the court may request that its court services unit, in consultation with any appropriate social services organization, local community services board, or other community mental health services organization, prepare a report analyzing the feasibility of providing counseling or other forms of therapy for the accused and the probability such treatment will be successful. Based upon this report and any other relevant evidence, the court may, with the consent of the accused, the complaining witness and the attorney for the Commonwealth in any case involving a violation of § 18.2-61, 18.2-67.1, or 18.2-67.2, authorize the accused to submit to and complete a designated course of counseling or therapy. In such case, the hearing shall be adjourned until such time as counseling or therapy is completed or terminated. Upon the completion of counseling or therapy by the accused and after consideration of a final evaluation to be furnished to the court by the person responsible for conducting such counseling or therapy and such further report of the court services unit as the court may require, and after consideration of the views of the complaining witness, the court, in its discretion, may discharge the accused if the court finds such action will promote maintenance of the family unit and be in the best interest of the complaining witness.

B. No statement or disclosure by the accused concerning the alleged offense made during counseling or any other form of therapy ordered pursuant to this section or § 18.2-61, 18.2-67.1, 18.2-67.2, or 19.2-218.2 may be used against the accused in any trial as evidence, nor shall any evidence against the accused be admitted which was discovered through such statement or disclosure.

History.
1986, c. 516; 2005, c. 631; 2012, cc. 476, 507.

The 2012 amendments.
The 2012 amendments by cc. 476 and 507 are identical, and substituted "local community services board" for "local board of mental health and mental retardation" in the first sentence of subsection A.

Michie's Jurisprudence.
For related discussion, see 15 M.J. Rape, § 3.

CASE NOTES

Not applicable where defendant fails to request report at preliminary hearing. — After defendant had a preliminary hearing in juvenile and domestic relations court, and a grand jury indicted defendant on charges of forcible sodomy and animate object sexual penetration against his wife, violations of §§ 18.2-67.1 and 18.2-67.2, defendant was not entitled under § 19.2-218.2 to return the case to the juvenile and domestic relations court for a hearing to authorize the preparation of a report to address the feasibility of counseling or therapy pursuant to § 19.2-218.1 where defendant failed to make the request for such a report at the preliminary hearing. Wilson v. Commonwealth, 58 Va. App. 513, 711 S.E.2d 251, 2011 Va. App. LEXIS 230 (2011).

§ 19.2-218.2. Hearing before juvenile and domestic relations district court required for persons accused of certain violations against their spouses.

A. In any case involving a violation of § 18.2-61, 18.2-67.1, or 18.2-67.2 where the complaining witness is the spouse of the accused, where a preliminary hearing pursuant to § 19.2-218.1 has not been held prior to indictment or trial, the court shall refer the case to the appropriate juvenile and domestic relations district court for a hearing to determine whether counseling or therapy is appropriate prior to further disposition unless the hearing is waived in writing by the accused. The court conducting this hearing may order counseling or therapy for the accused in compliance with the guidelines set forth in § 19.2-218.1.

B. After such hearing pursuant to which the accused has completed counseling or therapy and upon the recommendation of the juvenile and domestic relations district court judge conducting the hearing, the judge of the circuit court may dismiss the charge with the consent of the attorney for the Commonwealth and if the court finds such action will promote maintenance of the family unit and be in the best interest of the complaining witness.

History.
1986, c. 516; 2005, c. 631.

Editor's note.
Acts 1993, c. 930, cl. 3, as amended by Acts 1994, c. 564, cl. 2, and Acts 1996, c. 616, cl. 4, provides that the amendment to this section by Acts 1993, c. 930, cl. 1, shall become effective June 1, 1998, "if state funds are provided, including all local costs, to carry out the purposes of this bill by the General Assembly." The funding was not provided.

Michie's Jurisprudence.
For related discussion, see 15 M.J. Rape, § 3.

CASE NOTES

Not applicable where defendant fails to request report at preliminary hearing. — After defendant had a preliminary hearing in juvenile and domestic relations court, and a grand jury indicted defendant on charges of forcible sodomy and animate object sexual penetration against his wife, violations of §§ 18.2-67.1 and 18.2-67.2, defendant was not entitled under § 19.2-218.2 to return the case to the juvenile and domestic relations court for a hearing to authorize the preparation of a report to address the feasibility of counseling or therapy pursuant to § 19.2-218.1 where defendant failed to make the request for such a report at the preliminary hearing. Wilson v. Commonwealth, 58 Va. App. 513, 711 S.E.2d 251, 2011 Va. App. LEXIS 230 (2011).

§ 19.2-219. When capias need not be issued; summons; judgment.

No capias need be issued on a presentment or indictment of an offense for which there is no punishment but a fine or forfeiture, limited to an amount not exceeding twenty dollars; but a summons to answer such presentment or indictment may be issued against the accused; and if it be served ten days before the return day thereof, and he does not appear, judgment may be rendered against him for the penalty. If he appear, the court may, unless he demand a jury, hear and determine the matter and give judgment thereon.

History.
Code 1950, § 19.1-164; 1960, c. 366; 1975, c. 495.

ARTICLE 2.

FORM AND REQUISITES.

§ 19.2-220. Contents of indictment in general.

The indictment or information shall be a plain, concise and definite written statement, (1) naming the accused, (2) describing the offense charged, (3) identifying the county, city or town in which the accused committed the offense, and (4) reciting that the accused committed the offense on or about a certain date. In describing the offense, the indictment or information may use the name given to the offense by the common law, or the indictment or information may state so much of the common law or statutory definition of the offense as is sufficient to advise what offense is charged.

History.
1975, c. 495.

Michie's Jurisprudence.

For related discussion, see 9B M.J. Indictments, Informations and Presentments, § 19; 12A M.J. Larceny, §§ 12, 19; 19 M.J. Venue, § 15.

CASE NOTES

I. In General.
II. Illustrative Cases.

I. IN GENERAL.

Purpose of an indictment is to give the accused notice of the nature and character of the offense charged. The requirements of an indictment are prescribed by this section, which provides that an indictment shall be a "plain, concise, and definite written statement ... describing the offense charged." Cantwell v. Commonwealth, 2 Va. App. 606, 347 S.E.2d 523 (1986).

The function of an indictment is to give an accused notice of the nature and character of the accusations against him or her in order that the accused can adequately prepare to defend against his or her accuser. Sims v. Commonwealth, 28 Va. App. 611, 507 S.E.2d 648 (1998).

The indictment fulfilled the purpose of informing defendant of the charge against him and was not deficient for failing to state that defendant had a prior conviction on a violent felony that could net defendant a five-year mandatory minimum sentence as the indictment sufficiently alleged the underlying offense and its elements, and the statute the Commonwealth incorporated by reference sufficiently informed defendant that he could receive a mandatory minimum sentence if the Commonwealth showed a prior conviction for a "violent felony." Thomas v. Commonwealth, 37 Va. App. 748, 561 S.E.2d 56, 2002 Va. App. LEXIS 176 (2002).

An indictment must give the accused notice of the nature and character of the offense charged so he can make his defense, although in charging a statutory offense it is not necessary to follow the identical words of the statute. Wilder v. Commonwealth, 217 Va. 145, 225 S.E.2d 411 (1976).

A criminal defendant enjoys the right to be advised of the cause and nature of the accusation lodged against him and this right is fully honored by this section and § 19.2-221. Simpson v. Commonwealth, 221 Va. 109, 267 S.E.2d 134 (1980).

The indictment should "cite the statute or ordinance that defines the offense or, if there is no defining statute or ordinance, prescribes the punishment for the offense." "Both the United States and Virginia Constitutions recognize that a criminal defendant enjoys the right to be advised of the cause and nature of the accusation lodged against him. The important concerns evident in these provisions are fully honored by this section and § 19.2-221." Rush v. Commonwealth, No. 2058-94-2 (Ct. of Appeals Mar. 26, 1996).

An indictment, in order to be sufficient, must give an accused notice of the nature and character of the offense charged so he can make his defense. Commonwealth v. Dalton, 259 Va. 249, 524 S.E.2d 860 (2000).

It is not necessary to include in the indictment an allegation of every fact in the chain of circumstances comprising the offense charged. Howard v. Commonwealth, 221 Va. 904, 275 S.E.2d 602 (1981).

Ordinarily, an indictment sufficiently charges a statutory offense if it follows the language of the statute but this rule does not apply when the statutory language does not in itself fully and clearly set forth all the material elements of the offense. Sims v. Commonwealth, 28 Va. App. 611, 507 S.E.2d 648 (1998).

References at the foot of the charge to particular criminal statutes fail to save an indictment otherwise defective. Such references support, but do not replace, the "definite written statement," required in the body of an indictment. Wilder v. Commonwealth, 217 Va. 145, 225 S.E.2d 411 (1976).

A defendant cannot be charged in one count with two or more independent offenses. The reason for the rule is to prevent confusion, multiplication of issues, and prejudice to the defendant. Walker v. Commonwealth, 12 Va. App. 438, 404 S.E.2d 394 (1991).

The indorsement is not a substantive part of an indictment and is not determinative of the legal sufficiency of the accusation to charge the crime for which it is sought to hold the accused to answer; it neither strengthens nor weakens the legal force of the averments in the charging portion of the indictment. Wilder v. Commonwealth, 217 Va. 145, 225 S.E.2d 411 (1976).

Indictment must contain an averment of facts essential to the punishment to be inflicted. McKinley v. Commonwealth, 217 Va. 1, 225 S.E.2d 352 (1976).

But punishment need not be affirmatively set forth. — Although it is fundamental that when a statute contains more than one grade of offense carrying different punishments, the indictment must contain an assertion of the facts essential to the punishment sought to be imposed, this section does not require an indictment to affirmatively set forth the punishment for the offense. Sloan v. Commonwealth, 35 Va. App. 240, 544 S.E.2d 375, 2001 Va. App. LEXIS 180 (2001).

Where an offense is punishable with a higher penalty because it is a second or subsequent offense of the same kind, the more severe punishment cannot be inflicted unless the indictment charges that it is a second or subsequent offense. McKinley v. Commonwealth, 217 Va. 1, 225 S.E.2d 352 (1976).

An indictment need not be drafted in the exact words of the applicable statute so long as the accused is given notice of the nature and character of the offense charged. Black v. Commonwealth, 223 Va. 277, 288 S.E.2d 449 (1982).

Indictment cannot be collaterally attacked unless defect jurisdictional. — As long as the indictment is not so defective as to deprive the court of jurisdiction to render the judgment of conviction, a petitioner may not collaterally attack the sufficiency of the indictment by a petition for a writ of habeas corpus. Abney v. Warden, Mecklenburg Correctional Center, 1 Va. App. 26, 332 S.E.2d 802 (1985).

Indictment not invalidated by surplusage. — Additional unnecessary language included in indictment which is surplusage does not invalidate the indictment. Black v. Commonwealth, 223 Va. 277, 288 S.E.2d 449 (1982).

When an allegation of variance is based on unnecessary words in an indictment, the unnecessary word or words in the indictment must be descriptive of that which is "legally essential" to the charge. Stated another way, the unnecessary language must have a material effect on the offense charged and on the proof required to convict under that charge. Hairston v. Commonwealth, 2 Va. App. 211, 343 S.E.2d 355 (1986).

If the unnecessary word or words inserted in the indictment describe, limit or qualify the words which it was necessary to insert therein, then they are descriptive of the offense charged in the indictment and cannot be rejected as surplusage. The offense as charged must be proved. Hairston v. Commonwealth, 2 Va. App. 211, 343 S.E.2d 355 (1986).

Signature of grand jury foreman on indictments. — Failure of the grand jury foreman to sign the indictments was a defect in form only and accordingly, when the indictments were returned by the grand jury in open court, that defect in form was cured and the indictments became valid instruments under which to try defendant. Although the written charges did not contain the signature of the grand jury foreman, they had been "returned in open court" by the grand jury as true bills and, thus, became valid indictments. Reed v. Commonwealth, 281 Va. 471, 706 S.E.2d 854, 2011 Va. LEXIS 50 (2011).

II. ILLUSTRATIVE CASES.

Use of term "on or about" in the indictment was consistent with the provisions of this section, where defendant requested no bill of particulars regarding the date or time of the crime charged, counsel for the accused during cross examination made a concerted effort to fix the date of February 17 with certainty before presenting an alibi defense, and the complaining witnesses were two young children, ages 9 and 10. Marlowe v. Commonwealth, 2 Va. App. 619, 347 S.E.2d 167 (1986).

Time was not an element of sexual offenses alleged, and both indictments and Commonwealth's response to bill of particulars sufficiently informed defendant of relevant offense dates. Booker v. Commonwealth, No. 1603-98-1 (Ct. of Appeals Aug. 3, 1999).

Evidence was not deficient in defendant's case where he was charged with and convicted of aggravated sexual battery; where the indictment stated that the charged events occurred "on or about" a certain date through a certain other date, the trial court had a basis for ruling that the dates contained in the indictment were sufficiently narrow to apprise defendant of the charges against him and allow him to prepare a defense. Clifford v. Commonwealth, 48 Va. App. 499, 633 S.E.2d 178, 2006 Va. App. LEXIS 364 (2006), rev'd, on other grounds, 274 Va. 23, 645 S.E.2d 295 (2007).

By citation of subdivision 2 of § 53.1-203 in the indictment, defendant was informed of essential elements of the case against him. He suffered no prejudice by the omission in the body of the indictment of the words "for the purpose of," and failure to use that phrase did not invalidate the indictment. Reed v. Commonwealth, 3 Va. App. 665, 353 S.E.2d 166 (1987).

Incorporation by reference to section under which defendant charged. — The inference to be drawn from the provisions of this section and Rule 3A:6 (a) is clearly that incorporation by reference to the section under which defendant is charged is contemplated by the rule. Reed v. Commonwealth, 3 Va. App. 665, 353 S.E.2d 166 (1987).

Incorporation by reference. — Pursuant to § 19.2-220 and Va. Sup. Ct. R. 3A:6(a), the citation to § 18.2-51.2 in the indictment incorporated by reference the complete definition of aggravated malicious wounding and supplemented the charging language of the indictment; therefore, the statutory citation, coupled with the facts alleged, was sufficient to set forth all relevant elements of the aggravated malicious wounding offense. Robinson v. Commonwealth, No. 1623-02-2, 2003 Va. App. LEXIS 327 (Ct. of Appeals June 3, 2003).

Indictment which cited the statute under which defendant was charged provided adequate notice to defendant of the charges against him. Walshaw v. Commonwealth, 44 Va. App. 103, 603 S.E.2d 633, 2004 Va. App. LEXIS 483 (2004).

Evidence was sufficient to convict defendant of breaking and entering under § 18.2-91 and there was not a fatal variance between the evidence offered at trial and the indictment, which charged defendant with breaking and entering with the intent to commit larceny, as: (1) § 18.2-91 was cited in the indictment in accordance with § 19.2-220 and Va. Sup. Ct. R. 3A:6(a); (2) the citation in the indictment to § 18.2-91 incorporated by reference the complete definition of the offense set forth in the statute and supplemented the charging language of the indictment; (3) as the statute's title reflected, the offense could be committed with the "intent to commit larceny, assault and battery or other felony"; (4) although the body of the charge omitted reference to the intent to commit assault and battery, that specific intent was alleged in the indictment; (5) in reciting an abbreviated title of the charged offense, the indictment specifically referenced the "intent to commit A and B," or assault and battery; and (6) the arrest warrant underlying the felony charge specifically accused defendant of breaking and entering in the nighttime the dwelling house of the victim with the intent to commit assault and battery. Barth v. Commonwealth, 2007 Va. App. LEXIS 56 (Feb. 20, 2007).

Proof of commission of crime on date other than that alleged. — To require that a child or any witness be able to recall the exact date an event occurred in his or her life in order to obtain a conviction would too often preclude prosecutions in this type of case where the victims are children and the crimes are not discovered until some time after their commission. The Commonwealth's case would too often fail because it could not specify the exact date of the offense against the child. It is this same reasoning which permits the Commonwealth to prove the commission of the crime charged on a date different than that alleged in the indictment. Marlowe v. Commonwealth, 2 Va. App. 619, 347 S.E.2d 167 (1986).

Need not prove ultimate ownership of property taken in robbery prosecution. — Because robbery is a crime against the person, the prosecution need not prove the ultimate ownership of the property taken but need only prove that the possessory rights of the victim were superior to those of the thief. As such, it is not "legally essential" to allege or identify the ultimate owner of the property taken. Hairston v. Commonwealth, 2 Va. App. 211, 343 S.E.2d 355 (1986).

Although the woman named in the indictment as the owner of the automobile did not have legal title to the property, conviction for destruction of property was sufficiently supported by the evidence. The evidence proved that the woman had possession of the automobile and that she was to receive title to it under an agreement with her former husband, who did have legal title to the property. Proof that the person alleged in the indictment

to be the owner of such property has actual or constructive possession of the property is sufficient in a prosecution for this offense. Tammaro v. Commonwealth, No. 0504-94-1 (Ct. of Appeals March 21, 1995).

No requirement of prior notice to defendant. — Even though the Commonwealth failed to inform defendant that he was being charged as a second offender, defendant was validly convicted of use of firearm as a second offense; Ansell v. Commonwealth, 219 Va. 759, 250 S.E.2d 760 (1979), makes clear that § 18.2-53.1 has no requirement of prior notice to the defendant. Stubblefield v. Commonwealth, 10 Va. App. 343, 392 S.E.2d 197 (1990).

Defendant implicitly acknowledged fair notice that indictment charged him with capital murder at the pre-trial hearings when he moved to quash the indictment, assigning only challenges to the facial constitutionality of the capital statutes. Boggs v. Commonwealth, 229 Va. 501, 331 S.E.2d 407 (1985), cert. denied, 475 U.S. 1031, 106 S. Ct. 1240, 89 L. Ed. 2d 347 (1986).

Indictment described the crime with sufficient specificity to provide notice. — Where a defendant fired a weapon from inside a building at a fleeing victim, the indictment charging him with shooting at or against an occupied building or dwelling house, putting the lives of the occupants in peril, in violation of § 18.2-279, sufficiently placed him on notice of the nature and character of the offense charged, and the proof at trial did not fatally vary from the allegations of the indictment, as defendant fired "at" a portion of the building, and the portion of the statute referenced in the indictment did not specify where the shooter had to be located in reference to the building. King v. Commonwealth, 40 Va. App. 193, 578 S.E.2d 803, 2003 Va. App. LEXIS 61 (2003).

Indictment was not void when it was amended because the original indictment did describe a crime under subsection A of § 18.2-67.1 with sufficient specificity to provide notice to defendant as it alleged that defendant "caused" the victim to commit sodomy in violation of § 18.2-67.1 and the indictment mentioned only two people, defendant and the victim; as the language of the indictment did not exclude the possibility that defendant was the person with whom the victim was "caused" to commit sodomy, the use of "caused," as opposed to "engaged in," in that context was not a fatal variance. Nelson v. Commonwealth, 41 Va. App. 716, 589 S.E.2d 23, 2003 Va. App. LEXIS 615 (2003), aff'd, 268 Va. 665, 604 S.E.2d 76 (2004).

Time as an element of the offense of credit card theft. — Defendant's convictions for credit card theft were proper because she provided no case law or authority to support her contention that time was an element of the offense of credit card theft. As time was not an element of the offense, the Commonwealth was not required to prove the exact date of the offenses, as long as the evidence established beyond a reasonable doubt that the crimes occurred and that defendant committed the crimes; there was sufficient evidence to show that defendant obtained the credit cards and received the credit cards and, therefore, the trial court did not err in finding the evidence sufficient to prove the offenses. Trang Chau v. Commonwealth, 2011 Va. App. LEXIS 30 (Feb. 1, 2011).

Necessity for bill of particulars at discretion of court. — Whether the Commonwealth is required to file a bill of particulars rests with the discretion of the trial court. A bill of particulars is not required where the indictments provide the defendant adequate notice of the nature and the character of the offense charged so he can make his defense. Curmak v. Commonwealth, No. 0037-94-2 (Ct. of Appeals March 14, 1995).

Defendant's argument that the Commonwealth was required to allege every fact that supported the charge against him was without merit. If appellant desired more information about which facts the Commonwealth intended to rely on, he had the right to ask for a bill of particulars, and the trial court did not err in failing to order a bill of particulars. Rush v. Commonwealth, No. 2060-94-2 (Ct. of Appeals April 2, 1996).

Although the child sexual assault victim could not recall the specific dates of the incidents, the trial court did not err when it denied defendant's motion for a bill of particulars as to the precise day, date, and time of each alleged offense; the indictments were sufficient to apprise defendant of the nature of the crimes with which he was charged. Christopher v. Commonwealth, — Va. App. —, — S.E.2d —, 2006 Va. App. LEXIS 590 (Dec. 28, 2006).

Fatal variance. — Trial court erred in convicting defendant on a charge of attempted breaking and entering, as the variance between the shop or business identified as the place that defendant attempted to break into and the evidence at trial which showed that he tried to break into a shop by another name was a fatal variance between the charge and the proof; the evidence did not prove the crime charged, and, thus, the judgment of conviction had to be reversed and the indictment had to be dismissed. Dotson v. Commonwealth, No. 1410-02-2, 2003 Va. App. LEXIS 531 (Ct. of Appeals Oct. 21, 2003).

Character of offense not changed by an amendment. — Trial court did not err in allowing an amendment to a statutory burglary indictment, as the addition of an assault and battery mens rea to the original indictment changed one of its specific elements, but not its general nature or character. Hicks v. Commonwealth, No. 1421-03-3, 2004 Va. App. LEXIS 172 (Ct. of Appeals Apr. 13, 2004).

Applied in Dowdy v. Commonwealth, 220 Va. 114, 255 S.E.2d 506 (1979); Wall Distribs., Inc. v. City of Newport News, 228 Va. 358, 323 S.E.2d 75 (1984); KMA, Inc. v. City of Newport News, 228 Va. 365, 323 S.E.2d 78 (1984); Willis v. Commonwealth, 10 Va. App. 430, 393 S.E.2d 405 (1990); Terry v. Cross, 112 F. Supp. 2d 543, 2000 U.S. Dist. LEXIS 13315 (E.D. Va. 2000); Powell v. Commonwealth, 261 Va. 512, 552 S.E.2d 344, 2001 Va. LEXIS 86 (2001).

CIRCUIT COURT OPINIONS

Indictment found to be sufficient. — In a case in which defendant was convicted of violating former § 3.1-796.124 [now § 3.2-6571] and he filed a motion to set aside based on alleged deficiencies in the indictment, since he did not raise the issue of the validity of the indictment until 16 months after trial, defendant had waived his right to be more fully advised of the cause and nature of his accusation. Additionally, it was obvious that defendant, the Commonwealth, and the court all were fully aware of the cause and nature of the offense for which he was being tried and of which he was convicted. Commonwealth v. Taylor, 77 Va. Cir. 102, 2008 Va. Cir. LEXIS 228 (Chesapeake 2008).

§ 19.2-221. Form of prosecutions generally; murder and manslaughter.

The prosecutions for offenses against the Commonwealth, unless otherwise provided, shall be by presentment, indictment or information. While any form of presentment, indictment or information which informs the accused of the nature and cause of the accusation against him shall be good the following shall be deemed sufficient for murder and manslaughter:

Commonwealth of Virginia .... county (or city) to-wit: The grand jurors of the Commonwealth of Virginia, in and for the body of the county (or city) of ...., upon their oaths present that A .... B ...., on the .... day of ...., 20 ...., in the county (or city) of .... feloniously did kill and murder one C .... D .... against the peace and dignity of the Commonwealth.

A grand jury may, in case of homicide, which in their opinion amounts to manslaughter only, and not to murder, find an indictment against the accused for manslaughter and in such case the indictment shall be sufficient if it be in form or effect as follows:

Commonwealth of Virginia .... county (or city) to-wit: The grand jurors of the Commonwealth of Virginia, in and for the body of the county (or city) of ...., upon their oaths present that A .... B ...., on the .... day of ...., 20 ...., in the county (or city) of

.... feloniously and unlawfully did kill and slay one C .... D ...., against the peace and dignity of the Commonwealth.

History.
Code 1950, § 19.1-166; 1960, c. 366; 1975, c. 495.

Law Review.
For survey of Virginia criminal procedure for the year 1975-1976, see 62 Va. L. Rev. 1412 (1976).

Michie's Jurisprudence.
For related discussion, see 9B M.J. Homicide, §§ 51, 54; 9B M.J. Indictments, Informations and Presentments, § 23; 19 M.J. Venue, § 15.

CASE NOTES

A criminal defendant enjoys the right to be advised of the cause and nature of the accusation lodged against him and this right is fully honored by § 19.2-220 and this section. Simpson v. Commonwealth, 221 Va. 109, 267 S.E.2d 134 (1980).

The indictment should also "cite the statute or ordinance that defines the offense or, if there is no defining statute or ordinance, prescribes the punishment for the offense." "Both the United States and Virginia Constitutions recognize that a criminal defendant enjoys the right to be advised of the cause and nature of the accusation lodged against him. The important concerns evident in these provisions are fully honored by § 19.2-220 and this section." Rush v. Commonwealth, No. 2058-94-2 (Ct. of Appeals Mar. 26, 1996).

This section merely prescribes short form indictments for murder and manslaughter. Warlitner v. Commonwealth, 217 Va. 348, 228 S.E.2d 698 (1976), cert. denied, 430 U.S. 957, 97 S. Ct. 1604, 51 L. Ed. 2d 807 (1977).

It does not mention, much less establish, any presumptions or burdens. Warlitner v. Commonwealth, 217 Va. 348, 228 S.E.2d 698 (1976), cert. denied, 430 U.S. 957, 97 S. Ct. 1604, 51 L. Ed. 2d 807 (1977).

And nothing in Mullaney v. Wilbur, 421 U.S. 684, 95 S. Ct. 1881, 44 L. Ed. 2d 508 (1975) casts any shadow upon the constitutionality of this section. Warlitner v. Commonwealth, 217 Va. 348, 228 S.E.2d 698 (1976), cert. denied, 430 U.S. 957, 97 S. Ct. 1604, 51 L. Ed. 2d 807 (1977).

The statutory short form of indictment for murder includes the charge of murder of the first degree. Kibert v. Commonwealth, 216 Va. 660, 222 S.E.2d 790 (1976).

When the accused pleads guilty to an indictment for murder, he confesses "to the highest degree of the offense which the indictment charges and of which he can be convicted under its averments." Kibert v. Commonwealth, 216 Va. 660, 222 S.E.2d 790 (1976).

The object of the forms of indictment for murder and manslaughter set out in this section was to eliminate the excessive verbiage used in the old common-law forms and to substitute therefor a short, simple statement of the offense charged. Hurd v. Commonwealth, 159 Va. 880, 165 S.E. 536 (1932).

Short form approved by state and federal courts. — The short form allowed by this section as a form for indictment has been approved by both the federal and the State courts. Davis v. Slayton, 353 F. Supp. 571 (W.D. Va. 1973).

Sufficiency of indictment challenged in federal habeas corpus proceedings. — If an accused is aware of the actual charge against him, and the indictment provides sufficient information upon which to prepare a defense, there has been no violation of any constitutional right cognizable in a federal habeas corpus proceeding. Claytor v. Slayton, 342 F. Supp. 767 (W.D. Va. 1972).

Inmate was denied habeas corpus relief on his claim that his counsel was ineffective for failing to object to the amendment of the murder indictment on the day of trial to add the words "willfully, deliberately, and with premeditation," because Virginia law permitted the use of short-form indictments in charging defendants with murder, and therefore the original indictment would have been sufficient to charge the inmate with first-degree murder; this charge implicitly included the "willful, deliberate, and premeditated" language of the amended indictment. Coleman v. Johnson, — F. Supp. 2d —, 2005 U.S. Dist. LEXIS 33709 (E.D. Va. Sept. 6, 2005).

The omission of the words "unlawful act" and "with malice aforethought" in an indictment for murder does not constitute a fatal defect. Coleman v. Smyth, 166 F. Supp. 934 (E.D. Va.), appeal dismissed, 260 F.2d 518 (4th Cir. 1958), cert. denied, 359 U.S. 946, 79 S. Ct. 726, 3 L. Ed. 2d 679 (1959).

Indictment for murder in first degree need not charge specially facts showing the offense. — Even before this section was enacted it had been held in Commonwealth v. Miller, 3 Va. (1 Va. Cas.) 310 (1812), that it was unnecessary for an indictment for murder in the first degree to charge specially facts that would show the offense to have been murder in the first degree, and there have been a number of subsequent cases to the same effect. McGrady v. Cunningham, 296 F.2d 600 (4th Cir. 1961), cert. denied, 369 U.S. 855, 82 S. Ct. 944, 8 L. Ed. 2d 14 (1962).

An indictment for murder in the first degree under this section need not charge specifically the facts showing the offense. Ward v. Commonwealth, 205 Va. 564, 138 S.E.2d 293 (1964); Simpson v. Commonwealth, 221 Va. 109, 267 S.E.2d 134 (1980).

An indictment need not designate the degree of the offense charged nor allege facts which would describe that degree. This "short form" indictment, therefore, is sufficient to charge murder either in the first or second degree. Hale v. Cox, 336 F. Supp. 1364 (W.D. Va. 1972).

It is not necessary that the indictment should charge murder in the first degree or use that description which, according to the statute, constitutes that degree of offense. Ward v. Commonwealth, 205 Va. 564, 138 S.E.2d 293 (1964); Simpson v. Commonwealth, 221 Va. 109, 267 S.E.2d 134 (1980).

An indictment which charged that the defendant "feloniously and unlawfully did kill and murder" one named person did not void a conviction of second-degree murder. Claytor v. Slayton, 342 F. Supp. 767 (W.D. Va. 1972).

Manner of killing. — Under an indictment for murder in the form prescribed either by this section or Rule 3A:7, Form 5 of the Supreme Court, the Commonwealth may prove a killing in any manner or in different manners. Thus, the Commonwealth was not required to elect whether it was proceeding against the defendant on the theory that the killing was willful, deliberate and premeditated or under the felony-murder doctrine that the killing occurred in the commission of abduction. Akers v. Commonwealth, 216 Va. 40, 216 S.E.2d 28 (1975).

Forms held sufficient. — In a prosecution for homicide, it was contended that the short form of indictment, drawn according to this section, did not give sufficient notice of the cause and nature of the accusation. It was held that there was no merit in this contention. Hurd v. Commonwealth, 159 Va. 880, 165 S.E. 536 (1932); Bausell v. Commonwealth, 165 Va. 669, 181 S.E. 453 (1935); Maxwell v. Commonwealth, 167 Va. 490, 187 S.E. 506 (1936).

The short form of indictment prescribed by this section is sufficient to support a conviction of murder in the first degree. Hobson v. Youell, 177 Va. 906, 15 S.E.2d 76 (1941).

An indictment which substantially follows the statutory short form as prescribed for homicide is sufficient. Coleman v. Smyth, 166 F. Supp. 934 (E.D. Va.), appeal dismissed, 260 F.2d 518 (4th Cir. 1958), cert. denied, 359 U.S. 946, 79 S. Ct. 726, 3 L. Ed. 2d 679 (1959).

Accused contended that a demurrer to the indictment should have been sustained because it was not alleged that he did some act towards the commission of the offense charged. It was held that under this section, the indictment was sufficient and the demurrer was properly overruled. Pamplin v. Commonwealth, 167 Va. 470, 188 S.E. 147 (1936).

The proposition that the short statutory form of indictment for murder includes the charge of murder in the first degree is now the established law in this Commonwealth. Barber v. Commonwealth, 206 Va. 241, 142 S.E.2d 484 (1965).

Under a short form murder indictment, defendant could be convicted of first or second-degree murder. Burton v. Cox, 312 F. Supp. 264 (W.D. Va. 1970).

The short form of indictment is by this section sufficient to convict on first as well as second-degree murder. Davis v. Slayton, 353 F. Supp. 571 (W.D. Va. 1973).

Defendant's first-degree murder conviction was affirmed, despite his allegation that the short-form indictment that was filed against him did not specifically state all the elements of first-degree murder and that the trial court erred in refusing to amend the charge, as Virginia law required proof of both malice or premeditation as elements of the offense for conviction, and such did not have to be stated in the indictment. Scott v. Commonwealth, No. 0831-04-1, 2005 Va. App. LEXIS 131 (Ct. of Appeals Mar. 29, 2005).

There is no requirement in Virginia that a warrant have the same particularity of an indictment. Ward v. Peyton, 349 F.2d 359 (4th Cir. 1965), cert. denied, 382 U.S. 995, 86 S. Ct. 578, 15 L. Ed. 2d 481 (1966).

Hence, no constitutional right of petitioner was denied by the difference between the language of the warrant upon which the preliminary hearing was held and the language of the indictment upon which he was convicted. Ward v. Peyton, 349 F.2d 359 (4th Cir. 1965), cert. denied, 382 U.S. 995, 86 S. Ct. 578, 15 L. Ed. 2d 481 (1966).

A plea of guilty to an indictment is a plea of guilty to the highest degree of the offense charged in the indictment. Hale v. Cox, 336 F. Supp. 1364 (W.D. Va. 1972).

When an individual pleads guilty, he pleads guilty to the highest offense charged in the indictment. Davis v. Slayton, 353 F. Supp. 571 (W.D. Va. 1973).

And plea valid despite lack of knowledge as to presumption. — Where it is clear that a petitioner knew and understood the offense charged in the indictment, and that the indictment provided him with sufficient information upon which to prepare a defense, even if the petitioner did not also understand the presumption of a charge of second-degree murder arising from an indictment for murder under this section, there nevertheless has been no violation of any constitutional right where the petitioner pleads guilty to first-degree murder. Hale v. Cox, 336 F. Supp. 1364 (W.D. Va. 1972).

Defendant pled guilty to first-degree murder. — Since the indictment was sufficient to convict on first as well as second-degree murder, the defendant's plea of guilty was a plea of guilty to first-degree murder. Davis v. Slayton, 353 F. Supp. 571 (W.D. Va. 1973).

Every unlawful homicide is presumed to be murder in the second degree. Hale v. Cox, 336 F. Supp. 1364 (W.D. Va. 1972).

With the burden on the Commonwealth to elevate the offense to murder in the first degree. — See Hale v. Cox, 336 F. Supp. 1364 (W.D. Va. 1972).

Where defendant was tried on an indictment charging manslaughter but was convicted of murder, it was held that the conviction was not void but only voidable, since all the parties and the court had considered the indictment to be one for murder and defendant had pleaded guilty under that assumption. Frye v. Cunningham, 205 Va. 671, 139 S.E.2d 107 (1964); Hayes v. Peyton, 364 F.2d 303 (4th Cir.), cert. denied, 385 U.S. 981, 87 S. Ct. 530, 17 L. Ed. 2d 442 (1966).

Applied in Spain v. Commonwealth, 7 Va. App. 385, 373 S.E.2d 728 (1988).

CIRCUIT COURT OPINIONS

Bill of particulars. — Where defendant was charged with second degree murder, as the indictment did not have to allege he acted with malice, he was not entitled to a bill of particulars under § 19.2-230 concerning evidence on the issue of whether he acted with malice. Commonwealth v. Kuhne, 80 Va. Cir. 299, 2010 Va. Cir. LEXIS 49 (Fairfax County Apr. 22, 2010).

§ 19.2-222. Repealed by Acts 1996, c. 676.

§ 19.2-223. Charging several acts of embezzlement; description of money.

In a prosecution against a person accused of embezzling or fraudulently converting to his own use bullion, money, bank notes or other security for money or items of personal property subject to larceny it shall be lawful in the same indictment or accusation to charge and thereon to proceed against the accused for any number of distinct acts of such embezzlements or fraudulent conversions which may have been committed by him within six months from the first to the last of the acts charged in the indictment; and it shall be sufficient to allege the embezzlement or fraudulent conversion to be of money without specifying any particular money, gold, silver, note or security. Such allegation, so far as it regards the description of the property, shall be sustained if the accused be proved to have embezzled any bullion, money, bank note or other security for money or items of personal property subject to larceny although the particular species be not proved.

And in a prosecution for the larceny of United States currency or for obtaining United States currency by a false pretense or token, or for receiving United States currency knowing the same to have been stolen, it shall be sufficient if the accused be proved guilty of the larceny of national bank notes or United States treasury notes, certificates for either gold or silver coin, fractional coin, currency, or any other form of money issued by the United States government, or of obtaining the same by false pretense or token, or of receiving the same knowing it to have been stolen although the particular species be not proved.

History.
Code 1950, § 19.1-168; 1960, c. 366; 1975, c. 495; 1989, c. 370.

Cross references.
As to what is deemed embezzlement, see §§ 18.2-111 and 18.2-112.

Michie's Jurisprudence.
For related discussion, see 2B M.J. Autrefois, Acquit and Convict, § 6; 6B M.J. Embezzlement, § 7; 9B M.J. Indictments, Informations and Presentments, § 23; 12A M.J. Larceny, § 15; 15 M.J. Receiving Stolen Goods, § 3.

CASE NOTES

Charge of larceny of United States currency sufficient. — Prior to the passage of this section in 1870, it had been decided that in an indictment for larceny, a description of the subject as "United States currency," was not sufficient. In consequence of that decision, this section was passed, by which, among other things, it was enacted that "in a prosecution for the larceny of United States currency," it shall be sufficient if the accused be proved guilty of the larceny of national bank notes, or "United States treasury notes." An indictment now charging the offense as a larceny of "United States currency," does charge an indictable offense under the section. Dull v. Commonwealth, 66 Va. (25 Gratt.) 965 (1875). See Holly v. Commonwealth, 113 Va. 769, 75 S.E. 88 (1912).

Possession and larceny need not be charged. — It is sufficient for an indictment under this section, for embezzlement, to conform to the language of the statute in its description of the offense. Possession need not be alleged, nor need larceny be charged. "Embezzle" has as fixed a meaning as "steal," and to charge that defendants "did feloniously ... embezzle and convert to their use," etc., is a sufficient allegation. Commonwealth v. Davis, 17 Va. L. Reg. 516 (1911).

No objection can be urged to an indictment for embezzlement because of the number of transactions contained in the indictment, as the statute allows this to be done. Commonwealth v. Davis, 17 Va. L. Reg. 516 (1911).

Distinct acts of embezzlement for six-month period may be joined. — This section allows the prosecutor to proceed against an accused for "any number of distinct acts of such embezzlements" as may have been committed within a six-month period. The thrust of this section, therefore, is to allow joinder under one charge of separate crimes committed within the specified period where said joinder, absent statutory authority, possibly might run afoul of the rule of duplicity of charges. Mechling v. Slayton, 361 F. Supp. 770 (E.D. Va. 1973).

Although the rule of duplicity prohibits the simultaneous charging of several unrelated crimes in one indictment, pursuant to this section, distinct acts of embezzlement for a six-month period are "related" such that they may be grouped together under one charge. Mechling v. Slayton, 361 F. Supp. 770 (E.D. Va. 1973).

Charge of continuous plan, etc., and single offense sufficient. — An indictment did not contravene this section because it charged "a continuous plan or scheme and a single offense of embezzlement." Challenor v. Commonwealth, 209 Va. 789, 167 S.E.2d 116 (1969).

Evidence relating to earlier embezzlement held inadmissible. — Where it was manifest from the evidence that the two crimes of embezzlement charged in the indictment were not part of a continuous scheme and occurred at times separated by several years the court erred in refusing to strike the evidence relating to the earlier embezzlement. Webb v. Commonwealth, 204 Va. 24, 129 S.E.2d 22 (1963).

§ 19.2-224. In prosecution for forgery, unnecessary to set forth copy of forged instrument.

In a prosecution for forging or altering any instrument or other thing, or attempting to employ as true any forged instrument or other thing, or for any of the offenses mentioned in Article 1 (§ 18.2-168 et seq.) of Chapter 6 of Title 18.2, it shall not be necessary to set forth any copy or facsimile of such instrument or other thing; but it shall be sufficient to describe the same in such manner as would sustain an indictment for stealing such instrument or other thing, supposing it to be the subject of larceny.

History.
Code 1950, § 19.1-169; 1960, c. 366; 1975, c. 495.

Michie's Jurisprudence.
For related discussion, see 5A M.J. Counterfeiting, § 4; 8B M.J. Forgery, § 14.

CASE NOTES

Description as would sustain larceny indictment sufficient. — In a prosecution for forging, or attempting to employ as true any forged instrument, it is sufficient to describe the same in the indictment in such manner as would sustain an indictment for the larceny of such instrument. Coleman v. Commonwealth, 66 Va. (25 Gratt.) 865 (1874).

No necessity for setting out endorsement. — On the trial when the note was offered in evidence, it was objected to on the ground of variance. It was not necessary to set out in the indictment the endorsements upon the note, or any other matter written upon the same paper, constituting no part of the note itself, and not entering into the essential description of the instrument. Perkins v. Commonwealth, 48 Va. (7 Gratt.) 650 (1850).

The description of the writing in the indictment, as the endorsement of a person whose name is forged, will not vitiate the indictment, though the simulated liability might not be that of a technical endorser, but of a different character. Powell v. Commonwealth, 52 Va. (11 Gratt.) 822 (1854).

Nor maker and place of payment. — An indictment charged

the forgery of an endorsement on a negotiable note, which was described as to the amount, date to whom payable and when due but did not state who was the maker of the note or where it was payable. It was a good indictment. Cocke v. Commonwealth, 54 Va. (13 Gratt.) 750 (1855).

Variance in indictment and forged order. — The difference between "account" as set out in the indictment and "acct" as written in a forged order, is not a material variance, which will exclude the order as evidence. Burress v. Commonwealth, 68 Va. (27 Gratt.) 934 (1876), overruled on other grounds, Keister's Ex'rs v. Philips' Ex'r, 124 Va. 591, 98 S.E. 676 (1919).

§ 19.2-225. Allegation of intent.

Where an intent to injure, defraud or cheat is required to constitute an offense, it shall be sufficient, in an indictment or accusation therefor, to allege generally an intent to injure, defraud or cheat without naming the person intended to be injured, defrauded or cheated; and it shall be sufficient, and not be deemed a variance, if there appear to be an intent to injure, defraud or cheat the United States, or any state, or any county, corporation, officer or person.

History.
Code 1950, § 19.1-170; 1960, c. 366; 1975, c. 495.

Michie's Jurisprudence.
For related discussion, see 5A M.J. Counterfeiting, § 4; 8B M.J. Forgery, § 12; 12A M.J. Larceny, § 16.

CASE NOTES

This section applies to an indictment for an attempt to poison. The word "injure" is more apposite to the offense of poisoning or attempting to poison than to forgery, cheating, and like offenses. Davis v. Commonwealth, 99 Va. 838, 38 S.E. 191 (1901).

§ 19.2-226. What defects in indictments not to vitiate them.

No indictment or other accusation shall be quashed or deemed invalid:

(1) For omitting to set forth that it is upon the oaths of the jurors or upon their oaths and affirmations;

(2) For the insertion of the words "upon their oath," instead of "upon their oaths";

(3) For not in terms alleging that the offense was committed "within the jurisdiction of the court" when the averments show that the case is one of which the court has jurisdiction;

(4) For the omission or misstatement of the title, occupation, estate, or degree of the accused or of the name or place of his residence;

(5) For omitting the words "with force and arms" or the statement of any particular kind of force and arms;

(6) For omitting to state, or stating imperfectly, the time at which the offense was committed when time is not the essence of the offense;

(7) For failing to allege the kind or value of an instrument which caused death or to allege that it was of no value;

(8) For omitting to charge the offense to be "against the form of the statute or statutes";

(9) For the omission or insertion of any other words of mere form or surplusage; or

(10) For omitting or stating incorrectly the Virginia crime code references for the particular offense or offenses covered.

Nor shall it be abated for any misnomer of the accused; but the court may, in case of a misnomer appearing before or in the course of a trial, forthwith cause the indictment or accusation to be amended according to the fact.

History.
Code 1950, § 19.1-172; 1960, c. 366; 1975, c. 495; 2003, c. 148.

Cross references.
For section prescribing oath of grand jury, see § 19.2-197. As to amendments of indictments generally, see § 19.2-231.

Editor's note.
Acts 2003, c. 148, cl. 2, provides: "That this act shall become effective on October 1, 2004."

Acts 2003, c. 148, cl. 3, effective October 1, 2004, provides: "That the charging and dispositional documents incorporating Virginia crime codes developed pursuant to this act shall indicate clearly that the crime codes are to be entered in a portion of such documents labeled 'for administrative use only' or words to that effect."

Michie's Jurisprudence.
For related discussion, see 3A M.J. Burglary and Housebreaking, § 9; 9B M.J. Indictments, Informations and Presentments, §§ 23, 31, 32, 34, 37; 14B M.J. Perjury, § 11; 15 M.J. Rape, § 13; 19 M.J. Venue, § 15.

CASE NOTES

I. General Consideration.
II. Jurisdiction and Venue.
III. Designation of Time.
IV. Instrument Causing Death.
V. Surplusage.
VI. Misnomer.

I. GENERAL CONSIDERATION.

For history and general consideration of statute, see Commonwealth v. Peas, 43 Va. (2 Gratt.) 629 (1834).

Constitutionality. — The constitutional guarantee that the accused in all criminal prosecutions has the right to be confronted with the witnesses against him, etc., is not violated by this section. Shiflett v. Commonwealth, 90 Va. 386, 18 S.E. 838 (1894).

Extends to most defects in form. — The provisions of this act dispense with the necessity of formal allegations in an indictment, and declare that "no indictment shall be quashed, or deemed invalid," for any of certain enumerated causes. So far as these provisions extend they secure an indictment against objections, however raised. They seem to extend to most if not all defects of form. Lazier v. Commonwealth, 51 Va. (10 Gratt.) 708 (1853).

Absence of the foreman's signature from an indictment, although not specified in § 19.2-226 as an insubstantial defect in form, is nonetheless a defect in form only and does not render the indictment so defective as to be in violation of the constitution under § 19.2-227. Reed v. Commonwealth, 281 Va. 471, 706 S.E.2d 854, 2011 Va. LEXIS 50 (2011).

Failure of grand jury foreman to sign indictments is defect in form only. — Failure of the grand jury foreman to sign the indictments was a defect in form only and accordingly, when the indictments were returned by the grand jury in open court, that defect in form was cured and the indictments became valid instruments under which to try defendant. The absence of the foreman's signature from an indictment, although not specified in § 19.2-226 as an insubstantial defect in form, was nonetheless a defect in form only and did not render the indictment so defective as to be in violation of the constitution under Va. Code Ann. § 19.2-227. Reed v. Commonwealth, 281 Va. 471, 706 S.E.2d 854, 2011 Va. LEXIS 50 (2011).

Power of trial courts to make amendments. — It clearly seems to be the legislative intent to empower the trial courts to make amendments to defective indictments when the defects are much greater, and might be more fatal than those listed as inconsequential and without need of amendment in this section. Farewell v. Commonwealth, 167 Va. 475, 189 S.E. 321 (1937).

Alteration of printed form not alteration of indictment. — Where indictment was drawn on paper containing a printed form originally designed for use as an information, and this form was merely altered to conform to a proper form of an indictment and the blanks filled in with typewritten matter which conclusively demonstrated the charge against the accused, a motion to quash, on the ground that the indictment was altered, was properly overruled. McCann v. Commonwealth, 174 Va. 429, 4 S.E.2d 768 (1939).

Need not prove ultimate ownership of property taken in robbery prosecution. — Because robbery is a crime against the person, the prosecution need not prove the ultimate ownership of the property taken but need only prove that the possessory rights of the victim were superior to those of the thief. As such, it is not "legally essential" to allege or identify the ultimate owner of the property taken. Hairston v. Commonwealth, 2 Va. App. 211, 343 S.E.2d 355 (1986).

II. JURISDICTION AND VENUE.

Jurisdiction must appear. — Notwithstanding this section, dispensing with the necessity for merely formal allegations in an information or indictment, it is still necessary that it be shown in terms or by proper averments that the case is one of which the court had jurisdiction. Commonwealth v. Guigon, 1 Va. Dec. 597 (1886). See Lazier v. Commonwealth, 51 Va. (10 Gratt.) 708 (1853); Anderson v. Commonwealth, 100 Va. 860, 42 S.E. 865 (1902), overruled on another point, Kelley v. Commonwealth, 140 Va. 522, 125 S.E. 437 (1924).

The naming of the county in the margin is not indispensable, if it be found in the body of the indictment. Tefft v. Commonwealth, 35 Va. (8 Leigh) 721 (1837).

Venue in caption applies to whole indictment and each count thereof. — An indictment contained two counts. The caption was "Virginia — Roanoke County, to wit." The petitioner demurred to the entire indictment alleging as to the second count that it had no caption and no venue was laid. The caption applies to the whole indictment and to each count in it. Wright v. Commonwealth, 82 Va. 183 (1886).

Averment as to precise place not necessary. — In a prosecution for stabbing with intent to kill, where the indictment which was made by the grand jury of the Hustings Court of the City of Richmond charged the assault to have been made at the said city and within the jurisdiction of the said Hustings Court of the City of Richmond, this was sufficient. It was not necessary to state the place in the city where the assault was made. Baccigalupo v. Commonwealth, 74 Va. (33 Gratt.) 807 (1880).

Except in case of local offense. — Where an offense is local in its nature, place is of its essence, and it is essential that the place should be set forth in the indictment, and the proof must correspond. Morgan v. Commonwealth, 90 Va. 80, 21 S.E. 826 (1893). See Farewell v. Commonwealth, 167 Va. 475, 189 S.E. 321 (1937).

Uncertainty as to where offense committed objectionable. — Where the indictment in the caption names one county and in the body of it speaks of the defendant as of another county, the charging the offense to have been committed in the county aforesaid, is error, it not being alleged with sufficient certainty that the offense was committed in the county in which the indictment was found. Bell v. Commonwealth, 49 Va. (8 Gratt.) 600 (1851).

Presentment for playing cards, "at or near" a place, is objectionable for uncertainty. Bishop v. Commonwealth, 54 Va. (13 Gratt.) 785 (1856).

Sufficient averment. — An indictment charging that the prisoner, "at the county and within the jurisdiction of the court, feloniously and maliciously did stab one P.T. with intention to maim, etc., and kill him," will not be quashed upon objection that it

does not allege that P.T. was within the county or jurisdiction. Commonwealth v. Woodson, 36 Va. (9 Leigh) 669 (1839).

Insufficient averment. — An indictment which charges that an offense was committed "within the jurisdiction of the court," but does not state where the offense was committed, is bad on demurrer. Early v. Commonwealth, 93 Va. 765, 24 S.E. 936 (1896).

III. DESIGNATION OF TIME.

Omission to state, or imperfect statement of time does not hurt indictment. Sledd v. Commonwealth, 60 Va. (19 Gratt.) 813 (1870); Rhodes v. Commonwealth, 78 Va. 692 (1884).

The Commonwealth may prove the commission of the crime charged on a date different from that alleged, and sustain a conviction thereof. Parish v. Commonwealth, 206 Va. 627, 145 S.E.2d 192 (1965), cert. denied, 384 U.S. 942, 86 S. Ct. 1463, 16 L. Ed. 2d 540 (1966); Pasanello v. Commonwealth, 206 Va. 640, 145 S.E.2d 200 (1965).

And it need not be alleged when not of the essence. Savage v. Commonwealth, 84 Va. 582, 5 S.E. 563 (1888); Arrington v. Commonwealth, 87 Va. 96, 12 S.E. 224 (1890).

Defendant to be given as precise a date as possible. — While time may not be of the essence in a particular case, it is, nonetheless, preferable and required that the defendant be given as precise a date of the alleged offense as possible. Clinebell v. Commonwealth, 3 Va. App. 362, 349 S.E.2d 676 (1986), aff'd in part, rev'd in part, 235 Va. 319, 368 S.E.2d 263 (1988).

In a felony case when time is not the essence of the offense, the Commonwealth may prove the commission of a crime charged on a date different from that alleged in the indictment. Harris v. Commonwealth, 185 Va. 26, 37 S.E.2d 868 (1946).

It becomes necessary, therefore, to inquire whether time is of the essence of the offense. Cool v. Commonwealth, 94 Va. 799, 26 S.E. 411 (1896).

For instance, when statute applicable depends on date of offense. — When there are two statutes, either of which may apply to the offense charged, and the one of subsequent date changes the nature of the offense or the punishment of the same, the indictment must by proper averment as to time refer to the statute under which it was found so that the court may see the exact character of the offense, and the nature and measure of the punishment to be imposed. Time is of the essence of the offense. Cool v. Commonwealth, 94 Va. 799, 26 S.E. 411 (1896).

When any time stated in an indictment is to be proved by a matter of record, a variance will be fatal, and in an indictment for perjury the day on which the perjury was committed must be truly laid. Rhodes v. Commonwealth, 78 Va. 692 (1884).

Reasonable doubt as to date permissible where time not element of offense. — When time is not an element of the crime charged, the jury verdict will stand if the evidence is sufficient to prove beyond a reasonable doubt that a crime occurred and that the defendant committed the crime, even though the evidence is such that there may be a reasonable doubt as to the day on which the offense occurred. Such a result does not constitute a denial of due process of law. Marlowe v. Commonwealth, 2 Va. App. 619, 347 S.E.2d 167 (1986).

Statutory rape. — In a statutory rape case, where the age of the victim is not in dispute, time is not of the essence of the offense charged. Clinebell v. Commonwealth, 3 Va. App. 362, 349 S.E.2d 676 (1986), aff'd in part, rev'd in part, 235 Va. 319, 368 S.E.2d 263 (1988).

Sexual offenses. — Time was not an element of sexual offenses alleged, and both indictments and Commonwealth's response to bill of particulars sufficiently informed defendant of relevant offense dates. Booker v. Commonwealth, No. 1603-98-1 (Ct. of Appeals Aug. 3, 1999).

Time is not an element of offense of rape, and Commonwealth is not required to prove exact date of an offense against a child as long as evidence establishes beyond a reasonable doubt that a crime occurred and that defendant committed the crime. Felder v. Commonwealth, No. 1617-98-2 (Ct. of Appeals Aug. 3, 1999).

Evidence was not deficient in defendant's case where he was charged with and convicted of aggravated sexual battery; where the indictment stated that the charged events occurred "on or about" a certain date through a certain other date, the trial court had a basis for ruling that the dates contained in the indictment were sufficiently narrow to apprise defendant of the charges against him and allow him to prepare a defense. Clifford v. Commonwealth, 48 Va. App. 499, 633 S.E.2d 178, 2006 Va. App. LEXIS 364 (2006), rev'd, on other grounds, 274 Va. 23, 645 S.E.2d 295 (2007).

Although the child sexual assault victim could not recall the specific dates of the incidents, the trial court did not err when it denied defendant's motion for a bill of particulars as to the precise day, date, and time of each alleged offense; the indictments were sufficient to apprise defendant of the nature of the crimes with which he was charged. Christopher v. Commonwealth, — Va. App. —, — S.E.2d —, 2006 Va. App. LEXIS 590 (Dec. 28, 2006).

Credit card theft. — Defendant's convictions for credit card theft were proper under subdivision 6 of § 19.2-226 because she provided no case law or authority to support her contention that time was an element of the offense of credit card theft. As time was not an element of the offense of credit card theft, the Commonwealth was not required to prove the exact date of the offenses, as long as the evidence established beyond a reasonable doubt that the crimes occurred and that defendant committed the crimes; there was sufficient evidence to show that defendant obtained the credit cards and received the credit cards and, therefore, the trial court did not err in finding the evidence sufficient to prove the offenses. Trang Chau v. Commonwealth, 2011 Va. App. LEXIS 30 (Feb. 1, 2011).

Unnecessary to aver precise time of sale of intoxicating liquor. — It is unnecessary to allege in an indictment for the unlawful sale of intoxicating liquors the precise time when the sale was made. Clopton v. Commonwealth, 109 Va. 813, 63 S.E. 1022 (1909). See also Savage v. Commonwealth, 84 Va. 582, 5 S.E. 563 (1888); Arrington v. Commonwealth, 87 Va. 96, 12 S.E. 224 (1890).

But it must be shown that offense not barred. — While it is unnecessary in a prosecution for the unlawful sale of ardent spirits for the indictment to state the precise time of the sale, it is necessary that such facts should be stated in the indictment as will show that the offense charged was committed within the period of limitation fixed by the statute. Shiflett v. Commonwealth, 114 Va. 876, 77 S.E. 606 (1913).

Using figures instead of words in setting out the dates of an indictment is not a fatal defect under this section. Lazier v. Commonwealth, 51 Va. (10 Gratt.) 708 (1853); Cady v. Commonwealth, 51 Va. (10 Gratt.) 776 (1854).

IV. INSTRUMENT CAUSING DEATH.

It is unnecessary to state the weapon with which the assault was made in an indictment for malicious assault with intent to kill. Jackson v. Commonwealth, 96 Va. 107, 30 S.E. 452 (1898).

An indictment sufficiently charges the means by which life was extinguished, when in one count it charges that the prisoner did strike, kick and beat deceased upon the belly, stomach and back, and, in another count, that he did strike, push or knock the deceased down upon the floor, and that while lying there, he, upon the stomach, belly, back, legs and hands of her did then and there strike, beat and kick, giving several mortal wounds, or one mortal wound. Johnson v. Commonwealth, 111 Va. 877, 69 S.E. 1104 (1911).

Averment that killing was done with loaded shotgun would have been quite sufficient, without specifying the kind of missiles employed. Green v. Commonwealth, 122 Va. 862, 94 S.E. 940 (1918).

V. SURPLUSAGE.

Unnecessary and irrelevant matter in an indictment may generally be treated as surplusage if, when stricken out, enough remains to sufficiently charge the offense. Commonwealth v. Moseley, 4 Va. (2 Va. Cas.) 154 (1819); Commonwealth v. Bennet, 4 Va. (2 Va. Cas.) 235 (1820); Pomeroy v. Commonwealth, 4 Va. (2 Va. Cas.) 342 (1823); Lazier v. Commonwealth, 51 Va. (10 Gratt.) 708 (1853); Thompson v. Commonwealth, 61 Va. (20 Gratt.) 724 (1870).

When an allegation of variance is based on unnecessary words in an indictment, the unnecessary word or words in the indictment must be descriptive of that which is "legally essential" to the charge. Stated another way, the unnecessary language must have a material effect on the offense charged and on the proof required to convict under that charge. Hairston v. Commonwealth,

2 Va. App. 211, 343 S.E.2d 355 (1986).

If the unnecessary word or words inserted in the indictment describe, limit or qualify the words which it was necessary to insert therein, then they are descriptive of the offense charged in the indictment and cannot be rejected as surplusage. The offense as charged must be proved. Hairston v. Commonwealth, 2 Va. App. 211, 343 S.E.2d 355 (1986).

When commencement or caption states name of court and term at which indictment was found, it is surplusage, and a mistake does not invalidate it. Bell v. Commonwealth, 49 Va. (8 Gratt.) 600 (1851).

Conclusions of law, summing up the offense unnecessarily, may be regarded as surplusage, as where an indictment for taking a voluntary false oath, not amounting to perjury, concludes, "And so the said A.B. did commit perjury, etc." Hawley v. Commonwealth, 75 Va. 847 (1880).

Anything more than proper endorsement is surplusage. — The only proper endorsement on an indictment is a "true bill" or, "not a true bill" with the name of the foreman. Anything more is not a part of the finding of the grand jury, but mere surplusage. Thompson v. Commonwealth, 61 Va. (20 Gratt.) 724 (1870).

Inclusion and omission of "feloniously." — The law in this State has been declared to be that the omission of the word "feloniously" in an indictment charging a statutory felony is not error if the acts constituting the crime are sufficiently set forth. It logically follows that the converse of the proposition is equally true, i.e., that the inclusion of the word "feloniously" in an indictment charging a statutory misdemeanor does not make the charge a felony; and this section provides that no indictment shall be quashed or deemed invalid for the omission or the insertion of any words of mere form or surplusage. Young v. Commonwealth, 155 Va. 1152, 156 S.E. 565 (1931).

Inconsistent averments as surplusage. — An indictment for murder which describes the wound in one place as above the nipple of the left breast, and subsequently, as below the nipple of the left breast, is not void for repugnancy and inconsistency, as the latter recitation is surplusage, and covered by this section. Robertson v. Commonwealth, 1 Va. Dec. 851, 20 S.E. 362 (1894).

The objection made to the first count of an indictment that it is insensible, or contradictory and repugnant, in speaking of the "aforesaid 14th day of December" when no other day than the 9th of December is before mentioned is not a fatal defect under this section. The word "aforesaid" before "the 14th of December" is mere surplusage. Lazier v. Commonwealth, 51 Va. (10 Gratt.) 708 (1853).

And allegation as to previous conviction. — An indictment for murder is not bad on demurrer because it contains a count charging that the accused had been twice before sentenced in the United States to confinement in the penitentiary. The count charging the previous convictions must be rejected as surplusage. But if the prisoner objects to the introduction of evidence of such former convictions, his objection should be sustained, as such evidence tends to unduly prejudice the prisoner before the jury. Wright v. Commonwealth, 109 Va. 847, 65 S.E. 19 (1909).

Also, alleging time in continuando. — A count of an indictment alleging an offense as committed upon a certain day, and going on to charge it in the continuando, is not defective. The continuando is mere surplusage. Burner v. Commonwealth, 54 Va. (13 Gratt.) 778 (1856).

"Jr." mere surplusage. — "Jr." is not part of a person's name, but is mere descriptio persona and may be rejected as surplusage for purposes of this section. Bassett v. Commonwealth, 222 Va. 844, 284 S.E.2d 844 (1981), cert. denied, 456 U.S. 938, 102 S. Ct. 1996, 72 L. Ed. 2d 458 (1982), cert. denied, 499 U.S. 983, 111 S. Ct. 1639, 113 L. Ed. 2d 734 (1991).

"Inc." mere surplusage. — Evidence that defendant's employer owned a truck and tools that were supplied to defendant but not returned by him was sufficient to sustain defendant's conviction for grand larceny, in violation of § 18.2-95, even though the indictment charged defendant with stealing the truck and tools from a corporation and the Commonwealth did not prove that defendant's employer was a corporation. Commonwealth v. Nuckles, 266 Va. 519, 587 S.E.2d 695, 2003 Va. LEXIS 107 (2003).

Reference to city code was mere surplusage. — Because a warrant provided defendant with notice of the nature and character of the offense with which defendant was charged, and because §§ 16.1-137 and 19.2-226 authorized the trial court to amend the warrant to delete reference to a city code, which was mere surplusage, the trial court properly denied defendant's motion to dismiss, and found defendant guilty of a second offense of driving under the influence under § 18.2-266. Dennis v. Commonwealth, 2008 Va. App. LEXIS 530 (Dec. 9, 2008).

VI. MISNOMER.

Misnomer not fatal if identity clear. — Misnomer of a victim will not render an indictment fatally defective when the victim's identity is made clear at trial. Bassett v. Commonwealth, 222 Va. 844, 284 S.E.2d 844 (1981), cert. denied, 456 U.S. 938, 102 S. Ct. 1996, 72 L. Ed. 2d 458 (1982), cert. denied, 499 U.S. 983, 111 S. Ct. 1639, 113 L. Ed. 2d 734 (1991).

When the identity of the accused was never at any time questioned or doubted, the action of the trial court in permitting the attorney for the Commonwealth to change the name in the indictment from R.A. Kitchen to Ira Kitchen, is fully authorized by this section and § 19.2-231. Kitchen v. Commonwealth, 132 Va. 700, 111 S.E. 111 (1922).

But when entire name wrong, correction not allowed. — By mistake a wrong name was inserted in an indictment for a misdemeanor, though the record of the court and the indorsement on the indictment shows the correct name. Under the statute allowing the correction of a "misnomer," then just passed, the indictment cannot be amended by striking out the wrong name and inserting the name of the person intended. Commonwealth v. Buzzard, 46 Va. (5 Gratt.) 694 (1848).

Section authorizes amendment. — Pursuant to this section, where defendants indicted jointly for a misdemeanor have been duly summoned, but failed to appear, the court may, in their absence, amend the indictment against "S.C.," and make it read "S.S. alias S.C." Shiflett v. Commonwealth, 90 Va. 386, 18 S.E. 838 (1894).

§ 19.2-227. When judgment not to be arrested or reversed.

Judgment in any criminal case shall not be arrested or reversed upon any exception or objection made after a verdict to the indictment or other accusation, unless it be so defective as to be in violation of the Constitution.

History.
Code 1950, § 19.1-165; 1960, c. 366; 1975, c. 495.

Law Review.
For annual survey article, "Criminal Law and Procedure," see 46 U. Rich. L. Rev. 59 (2011).

Michie's Jurisprudence.
For related discussion, see 1A M.J. Adultery, Fornication and Lewdness, § 4; 1B M.J. Appeal and Error, § 285; 5A M.J. Counterfeiting, § 6; 5B M.J. Criminal Procedure, § 69; 9B M.J. Indictments, Informations and Presentments, § 56; 11A M.J. Judgments and Decrees, § 136; 12B M.J. Mayhem, § 5; 14B M.J. Pleading, § 21.

CASE NOTES

The intent of the act is, that where a real felony or offense is charged in an indictment or information, though defectively charged, after plea and verdict such want of form shall not be availed of by the defendant. Commonwealth v. Richards, 3 Va. (1 Va. Cas.) 1 (1810); Taylor v. Commonwealth, 4 Va. (2 Va. Cas.) 94 (1817); Commonwealth v. Ervin, 4 Va. (2 Va. Cas.) 337 (1823); Burgess v. Commonwealth, 4 Va. (2 Va. Cas.) 483 (1825); Stephen v. Commonwealth, 29 Va. (2 Leigh) 759 (1830).

Legislative prerogative. — This section was intended to meet cases, and to require persons charged with crime to assert their rights and to make their defenses before verdict, and thereafter to cut off all defenses not made before verdict unless prohibited by the Constitution. The Constitution gives to the accused the right to demand the cause and nature of his accusation, and this right cannot be taken away from him, but there is no inhibition on the legislature to fix a stage of the procedure beyond which he cannot go in the assertion of his constitutional right. Flanary v. Commonwealth, 133 Va. 665, 112 S.E. 604 (1922).

Collateral attack barred unless defects in indictment jurisdictional. — As long as the indictments on which a defendant was convicted were not so defective so as to deprive the court of jurisdiction to render the judgments of conviction, a petitioner may not collaterally attack the sufficiency of the indictments. Kahaliqi v. Commonwealth, No. 1611-00-4, 2001 Va. App. LEXIS 185 (Ct. of Appeals Apr. 10, 2001).

If an alleged defect be matter of form or surplusage only it is cured by the criminal statute of jeofails. Lithgow v. Commonwealth, 4 Va. (2 Va. Cas.) 297 (1822).

Certainty in charge required. — The statute of jeofails was not intended to introduce a carelessness or laxity in pleading, but merely to cure those defects which the over nicety of the courts had introduced into the common law, and which did not put the rights of the Commonwealth or the accused into jeopardy. According to the very terms of the statute, the offense must be charged with sufficient certainty in the indictment or other accusation, for judgment to be given thereon according to the very right of the case. There must still be some certainty in the charge. Commonwealth v. Peas, 43 Va. (2 Gratt.) 629 (1834); Commonwealth v. Ailstock, 44 Va. (3 Gratt.) 650 (1846); Old v. Commonwealth, 59 Va. (18 Gratt.) 915 (1867).

Omission to state court where grand jury impanelled is cured. — The omission to state in what court of the county the grand jury was impanelled (the county itself being mentioned), if an error, is cured. Trimble v. Commonwealth, 4 Va. (2 Va. Cas.) 143 (1818).

And omission to state offense was "unlawfully" committed. — The omission to state in an indictment that the offense was committed unlawfully, is cured by the statute of jeofails. Commonwealth v. Bennett, 4 Va. (2 Va. Cas.) 235 (1820).

Defective spelling of date. — An indictment for grand larceny, charged the goods to have been stolen on the "21st of December, one thousand eight hundred and twenty-thee," leaving out the "r" in the last word. This is cured by the statute of jeofails. Aldridge v. Commonwealth, 4 Va. (2 Va. Cas.) 447 (1824).

A mistake in the name of the month in which the deceased died, where it is clear from the rest of the indictment that it was a mistake, and it is clear what month was intended, is one of form cured by the statute of jeofails. Commonwealth v. Ailstock, 44 Va. (3 Gratt.) 650 (1846).

Omission of time of offense. — An indictment for unlawfully transporting ardent spirits accurately charged accused with the offense in every particular except as to the date of the commission of the offense. There was no demurrer or other objection to the indictment until after a verdict of conviction, which was abundantly supported by the testimony. If objection had been raised because of the omission of the date of the offense, it could have been corrected at the bar by the prosecuting attorney on mere motion under § 19.2-231. It was held that under this section, accused could not raise the objection on appeal that the indictment was defective for failure to state the time of the commission of the offense. Flanary v. Commonwealth, 133 Va. 665, 112 S.E. 604 (1922). See also Honaker v. Commonwealth, 136 Va. 752, 118 S.E. 85 (1923).

Absence of the foreman's signature from an indictment, although not specified in § 19.2-226 as an insubstantial defect in form, is nonetheless a defect in form only and does not render the indictment so defective as to be in violation of the constitution under § 19.2-227. Reed v. Commonwealth, 281 Va. 471, 706 S.E.2d 854, 2011 Va. LEXIS 50 (2011).

Signature of grand jury foreman. — Failure of the grand jury foreman to sign the indictments was a defect in form only and accordingly, when the indictments were returned by the grand jury in open court, that defect in form was cured and the indictments became valid instruments under which to try defendant. The absence of the foreman's signature from an indictment, although not specified in § 19.2-226 as an insubstantial defect in form, was nonetheless a defect in form only and did not render the indictment so defective as to be in violation of the constitution under § 19.2-227. Reed v. Commonwealth, 281 Va. 471, 706 S.E.2d 854, 2011 Va. LEXIS 50 (2011).

Failure to allege incorporation of the owner of property stolen. — See Lithgow v. Commonwealth, 4 Va. (2 Va. Cas.) 297 (1822).

Former conviction alleged by recital only sustained. — A conviction for a second offense in violating the former prohibition law was sustained, notwithstanding the fact that a former conviction was alleged by way of recital only, where no objection to the indictment was made by demurrer or otherwise. Cooper v. Commonwealth, 134 Va. 545, 113 S.E. 863 (1922).

But omission to charge intent not cured. — In a prosecution for unlawful and malicious cutting, accused contended on appeal that the indictment was not in compliance with § 18.2-51, in that it failed to charge that the cutting was done with the intent to maim, disable, or kill, as required by the statute. It was held that where no felony is alleged in an indictment, it would be violative of constitutional rights to find one guilty of that grade of offense, and, therefore, this section did not cure the defect in the indictment. Tompkins v. Commonwealth, 177 Va. 858, 13 S.E.2d 409 (1941).

Applied in Evans v. Commonwealth, 226 Va. 292, 308 S.E.2d 126 (1983); Stamper v. Commonwealth, 228 Va. 707, 324 S.E.2d 682 (1985); Waters v. Commonwealth, 29 Va. App. 133, 510 S.E.2d 262 (1999).

CIRCUIT COURT OPINIONS

Indictment found to be sufficient. — In a case in which defendant was convicted of violating former § 3.1-796.124 [now § 3.2-6571] and he filed a motion to set aside based on alleged deficiencies in the indictment, since he did not raise the issue of the validity of the indictment until 16 months after trial, defendant had waived his right to be more fully advised of the cause and nature of his accusation. Additionally, it was obvious that defendant, the Commonwealth, and the court all were fully aware of the cause and nature of the offense for which he was being tried and of which he was convicted. Commonwealth v. Taylor, 77 Va. Cir. 102, 2008 Va. Cir. LEXIS 228 (Chesapeake 2008).

§ 19.2-228. Name and address of complaining witness to be written on indictment, etc., for misdemeanor.

In a prosecution for a misdemeanor the name and address of the complaining witness, if there be one, shall be written at the foot of the presentment, indictment or information when it is made, found or filed. In case the grand jury that brings in such presentment or indictment or the attorney for the Commonwealth who files such information fail to write the name of a complaining witness at the foot of the presentment, indictment or information, then the name of a complaining witness may be entered of record as such by the court on the motion of the defendant or the attorney for the Commonwealth at any time before the judgment.

History.
Code 1950, § 19.1-173; 1960, c. 366; 1975, c. 495.

Michie's Jurisprudence.
For related discussion, see 5B M.J. Criminal Procedure, § 100.

CASE NOTES

This is not a penal statute, and there is no reason why it should be construed strictly and not carry into effect the obvious intention of the legislature. Wortham v. Commonwealth, 26 Va. (5 Rand.) 669 (1827).

Requirement merely directory. — The requirement of the statutes is merely directory, not mandatory, and a failure to observe it will not invalidate an indictment. Porterfield v. Commonwealth,

91 Va. 801, 22 S.E. 352 (1895). See also Commonwealth v. Dever, 37 Va. (10 Leigh) 685 (1840); Commonwealth v. Williams, 40 Va. (5 Gratt.) 702 (1848); Shelton v. Commonwealth, 89 Va. 450, 16 S.E. 355 (1892).

It applies only to misdemeanors. — This section does not require name of prosecutor to be written at foot of an indictment for a felony, but only for a misdemeanor. Thompson v. Commonwealth, 88 Va. 45, 13 S.E. 304 (1891).

And then only to volunteer prosecutors. — A volunteer informer ought to be made a prosecutor, and liable for costs in case of failure. But one who is compelled to be an informer, cannot be considered a prosecutor. Wortham v. Commonwealth, 26 Va. (5 Rand.) 669 (1827).

A private person may be prosecutor, and liable to pay the costs of the defendant, notwithstanding he was not named at the foot of the information it appearing sufficiently by the presentment, and other proceedings in the cause, that he was the person who instituted the prosecution. After verdict rendered it was too late for the prosecutor to show, by parol testimony, that he was called on by the grand jury, and did not voluntarily go before them to give them information. Commonwealth v. Dove, 4 Va. (2 Va. Cas.) 29 (1815).

Costs to prosecutor when indictment quashed because of incapacity of juror. — When in a prosecution for a misdemeanor at the instance of a voluntary prosecutor, the defendant filed a plea in abatement, that one of the grand jurors who found the indictment was not a freeholder, and the issue made upon that plea was found for the defendant, and the indictment quashed, the court gave judgment for the costs against the prosecutor. Commonwealth v. St. Clair, 42 Va. (1 Gratt.) 556 (1844).

An indictment will not be dismissed, though the prosecutor be insolvent, if the court would ex officio have directed a prosecution to be instituted. Commonwealth v. Hill, 36 Va. (9 Leigh) 601 (1838).

Prosecutor a competent witness in support of indictment. — On an indictment for an assault and battery on the voluntary information of the person assaulted, the informer and prosecutor, being the only witness for the prosecution, is a competent witness, though liable for costs in case defendant is acquitted. Baker v. Commonwealth, 4 Va. (2 Va. Cas.) 353 (1823); Gilliam v. Commonwealth, 31 Va. (4 Leigh) 688 (1834).

§ 19.2-229. When complaining witness required to give security for costs.

For good cause the court may require a complaining witness to give security for the costs and if he fails to do so dismiss the prosecution at his costs.

History.
Code 1950, § 19.1-174; 1960, c. 366; 1975, c. 495.

Michie's Jurisprudence.
For related discussion, see 5B M.J. Criminal Procedure, § 101; 9B M.J. Indictments, Informations and Presentments, § 17.

§ 19.2-230. Bill of particulars.

A court of record may direct the filing of a bill of particulars at any time before trial. A motion for a bill of particulars shall be made before a plea is entered and at least seven days before the day fixed for trial and the bill of particulars shall be filed within such time as is fixed by the court.

History.
1975, c. 495.

Michie's Jurisprudence.
For related discussion, see 3A M.J. Bill of Particulars, § 7; 5B M.J. Criminal Procedure, § 31.

CASE NOTES

A defendant is not entitled to a bill of particulars as a matter of right; whether the Commonwealth is required to file a bill of particulars rests within the discretion of the trial court. Quesinberry v. Commonwealth, 241 Va. 364, 402 S.E.2d 218, cert. denied, 502 U.S. 834, 112 S. Ct. 113, 116 L. Ed. 2d 82 (1991), and overruled in part on other grounds by Jay v. Commonwealth, 275 Va. 510, 659 S.E.2d 311, 2008 Va. LEXIS 53 (2008).

Limitations on use. — As long as an indictment sufficiently recites the elements of the offense, the commonwealth is not required to include all evidence upon which it plans to rely to prove a particular offense, and an accused should not be permitted to use a bill of particulars to expand the scope of discovery in a criminal case. Sims v. Commonwealth, 28 Va. App. 611, 507 S.E.2d 648 (1998).

Purpose of bill of particulars is to state sufficient facts regarding the crime to inform an accused in advance of the offense for which he is to be tried; he is entitled to no more. Swisher v. Commonwealth, 256 Va. 471, 506 S.E.2d 763 (1998), cert. denied, 528 U.S. 812, 120 S. Ct. 46, 145 L. Ed. 2d 41 (1999).

Omission of judge's name from bill of particulars as testifying witness not error. — Despite defendant's arguments on appeal that: (1) by requesting a list of witnesses in his bill of particulars, the Commonwealth was required to provide him with the names of the witnesses it intended to call and that failure to do so should have prevented the non-disclosed witness from testifying; and (2) the Commonwealth deliberately misled him in its response to his bill of particulars and that such prosecutorial misconduct was also a basis for vacating his conviction, because defendant cited no authority in his opening brief to support either argument, and no discovery order requiring the production of witnesses had been entered, no error affecting the outcome of the trial resulted. Bennett v. Commonwealth, 2007 Va. App. LEXIS 155 (Apr. 17, 2007).

Bill of particulars and arrest warrant were sufficient. — Both the arrest warrant and the Commonwealth's response to a bill of particulars sufficiently informed defendant as to the general nature and character of the conduct for which he was to be tried, and Virginia jurisprudence required no more; the bill of particulars was relief available to an accused, at the discretion of the court, to supplement a charging instrument that failed to fully and clearly set forth all the material elements of the offense, but not to expand the scope of discovery in a criminal case. Raja v. Commonwealth, 40 Va. App. 710, 581 S.E.2d 237, 2003 Va. App. LEXIS 318 (2003).

Bill of particulars not required. — To be sufficient, an indictment must give the accused "notice of the nature and character of the offense charged so he can make his defense"; when an indictment meets that standard, a bill of particulars is not required. Strickler v. Commonwealth, 241 Va. 482, 404 S.E.2d 227, cert. denied, 502 U.S. 944, 112 S. Ct. 386, 116 L. Ed. 2d 337 (1991).

Whether the Commonwealth is required to file a bill of particulars rests with the discretion of the trial court. A bill of particulars is not required where the indictments provide the defendant adequate notice of the nature and the character of the offense charged so he can make his defense. Curmak v. Commonwealth, No. 0037-94-2 (Ct. of Appeals March 14, 1995).

A defendant is not entitled to a bill of particulars as a matter of right, but is provided in the discretion of the court. Roach v. Commonwealth, 251 Va. 324, 468 S.E.2d 98, cert. denied, 519 U.S. 951, 117 S. Ct. 365, 136 L. Ed. 2d 256 (1996), overruled in part on other grounds by Morrisette v. Warden of the Sussex I State Prison, 270 Va. 188, 613 S.E.2d 551 (2005).

A defendant is not entitled to a bill of particulars as a matter of right. Goins v. Commonwealth, 251 Va. 442, 470 S.E.2d 114, cert. denied, 519 U.S. 887, 117 S. Ct. 222, 136 L. Ed. 2d 154 (1996).

Whether to require the Commonwealth to file a bill of particulars is a matter that rests within the sound discretion of the trial court. Mickens v. Commonwealth, 252 Va. 315, 478 S.E.2d 302 (1996), cert. denied, 520 U.S. 1269, 117 S. Ct. 2442, 138 L. Ed. 2d 202 (1997).

Denial of bill of particulars harmless error. — The trial court acted within its discretion in denying a defendant's motion for a bill of particulars specifying what time the alleged burglary occurred, what crime the defendant intended to commit when he gained entry and what force the defendant allegedly used to seize the victim for purposes of a charge of abduction where the defendant was on notice from the preliminary hearing of the time the alleged burglary occurred, the indictments indicated the predicate offenses the commonwealth intended to prove and the commonwealth was not required to describe the nature of the force used when abducting the victim; to the extent the indictment for burglary may have been insufficient to apprise the defendant of the nature and character of the offense, the trial court's error in refusing to order a bill of particulars was harmless beyond a reasonable doubt where the defendant was aware of the predicate offenses the commonwealth intended to prove and was not surprised by or unprepared for the proof adduced at trial. Sims v. Commonwealth, 28 Va. App. 611, 507 S.E.2d 648 (1998).

Failure to order bill of particulars when Commonwealth amended indictment. — Trial judge did not abuse his discretion by failing to order a bill of particulars when the Commonwealth amended one of the three rape indictments to allege a new offense date. The indictment was sufficient to apprise the appellant of the nature and character of the offense, as he had already entered his plea prior to his bill of particulars request. In a statutory rape case, when the age of the victim is not in dispute, time is not of the essence of such an offense, and the Commonwealth is not required to specify the exact date. Yeager v. Commonwealth, 16 Va. App. 761, 433 S.E.2d 248 (1993).

CIRCUIT COURT OPINIONS

Reciprocal discovery. — Defendant, who filed a motion for a bill of particulars, was entitled to discover the place and time of the crime charged, and this provided reciprocal discovery sufficient to render the pre-trial alibi notice requirement of Supreme Court Rule 3A:11(c)(2) consistent with defendant's due process rights. Commonwealth v. Thasoonthorn, 55 Va. Cir. 28, 2001 Va. Cir. LEXIS 233 (Fairfax County 2001).

Bill of particulars not required. — Defendants who were charged with violations of § 18.2-152.3:1 were not entitled to a bill of particulars when the indictment sufficiently set forth where and when the offenses were allegedly committed. Routing information, names of electronic mail service providers and their subscribers, and the identity of the recepients did not need to be provided when the act of transmission was the act that was circumscribed by the statute. Commonwealth v. Jaynes, 64 Va. Cir. 443, 2004 Va. Cir. LEXIS 155 (Loudoun County 2004).

Where the Commonwealth intended to prove "vileness" as an aggravating factor in support of the death penalty, it was not required to identify the components of the vileness factor on which it intended to offer evidence because the indictment, the discovery responses, and defendant's opportunity to hear the evidence presented at the preliminary hearing adequately informed him of the charged offense. Commonwealth v. Waddler, 65 Va. Cir. 418, 2004 Va. Cir. LEXIS 296 (Portsmouth 2004).

Where defendant was charged with second degree murder, as the indictment did not have to allege he acted with malice, he was not entitled to a bill of particulars under § 19.2-230 concerning evidence on the issue of whether he acted with malice. Commonwealth v. Kuhne, 80 Va. Cir. 299, 2010 Va. Cir. LEXIS 49 (Fairfax County Apr. 22, 2010).

ARTICLE 3.

AMENDMENTS.

§ 19.2-231. Amendment of indictment, presentment or information.

If there be any defect in form in any indictment, presentment or information, or if there shall appear to be any variance between the allegations therein and the evidence offered in proof thereof, the court may permit amendment of such indictment, presentment or information, at any time before the jury returns a verdict or the court finds the accused guilty or not guilty, provided the amendment does not change the nature or character of the offense charged. After any such amendment the accused shall be arraigned on the indictment, presentment or information as amended, and shall be allowed to plead anew thereto, if he so desires, and the trial shall proceed as if no amendment had been made; but if the court finds that such amendment operates as a surprise to the accused, he shall be entitled, upon request, to a continuance of the case for a reasonable time.

History.

Code 1950, §§ 19.1-175 through 19.1-177; 1960, c. 366; 1975, c. 495.

Cross references.

As to amendment in case of misnomer, see § 19.2-226.

Law Review.

For an article, "Criminal Law and Procedure," see 31 U. Rich. L. Rev. 1015 (1997).

Michie's Jurisprudence.

For related discussion, see 4A M.J. Continuances, §§ 3, 17, 47; 9B M.J. Indictments, Informations and Presentments, §§ 36, 50; 12A M.J. Lotteries, § 5; 14B M.J. Perjury, § 5; 16 M.J. Seduction, § 12; 16 M.J. Sodomy, § 4.

CASE NOTES

I. In General.
II. Character or Nature of Offense.

I. IN GENERAL.

Policy. — The judicial and legislative policy is to have both civil and criminal cases tried on their merits and as far as possible to ignore mere formal defects. Collins v. City of Radford, 134 Va. 518, 113 S.E. 735 (1922); Jolly v. Commonwealth, 136 Va. 756, 118 S.E. 109 (1923). See also Guynn v. Commonwealth, 163 Va. 1042, 177 S.E. 227 (1934).

The policy of the legislature is to try criminal cases on their merits as far as possible, and to ignore mere formal defects. This is demonstrated by the liberal provisions for amendment provided by the statute. Martin v. Warden, Va. State Penitentiary, 2 Va. App. 6, 341 S.E.2d 202 (1986).

Purpose. — The purpose of this section is to permit the court to amend defective indictments, including such indictments as would be fatally defective if objected to at the proper time and an amendment not made. Farewell v. Commonwealth, 167 Va. 475, 189 S.E. 321 (1937).

The manifest purpose of this section is to allow amendments which avoid unnecessary delays and further the ends of justice, without prejudice to the substantial right of the accused to be informed of the accusation, and to one fair trial on the merits. Sullivan v. Commonwealth, 157 Va. 867, 161 S.E. 297 (1931); Farewell v. Commonwealth, 167 Va. 475, 189 S.E. 321 (1937).

This section permits the trial court to amend an indictment at any time before the verdict is returned or a finding of guilt is made, provided the amendment does not change the nature or character of the offense charged. Trusty v. Commonwealth, No. 0278-93-1 (Ct. of Appeals Dec. 20, 1994); Crawford v. Commonwealth, No. 1844-99-3, 2000 Va. App. LEXIS 367 (Ct. of Appeals May 16, 2000).

Liberally construed. — This section is remedial, and in accordance with the accepted rule should be construed liberally to correct the evil at which it is directed, and to promote the remedy thereby provided. The legislative intent is to simplify criminal procedure. A narrow construction of this section would defeat its wise purpose. Sullivan v. Commonwealth, 157 Va. 867, 161 S.E. 297 (1931); Livingston v. Commonwealth, 184 Va. 830, 36 S.E.2d 561 (1946).

This section is remedial in nature and is to be liberally construed in order to achieve the laudable purpose of avoiding further unnecessary delay in the criminal justice process by allowing amendment, rather than requiring reindictment by a grand jury. Willis v. Commonwealth, 10 Va. App. 430, 393 S.E.2d 405 (1990).

This section is to be construed liberally. Cantwell v. Commonwealth, 2 Va. App. 606, 347 S.E.2d 523 (1986).

Even indictments which are fatally defective may be amended under this provision if such amendment is made at the proper time. Martin v. Warden, Va. State Penitentiary, 2 Va. App. 6, 341 S.E.2d 202 (1986).

Although the evidence at trial showed that defendant attempted to break and enter at a shop or business different than the shop or business named in the indictment, the Commonwealth did not attempt to amend the indictment to correct the defect, especially since amendments to change the location of an offense were liberally allowed and such an amendment would not have changed the nature or character of the offense; since the Commonwealth did not amend the defect, the evidence did not prove the charge alleged in the indictment and, thus, defendant's conviction had to be reversed and the indictment had to be dismissed. Dotson v. Commonwealth, No. 1410-02-2, 2003 Va. App. LEXIS 531 (Ct. of Appeals Oct. 21, 2003).

Amendment satisfies constitutional provision. — An amendment under this section, setting out more definitely and specifically, either the cause and nature of the charge, or the date, or the place of the offense, satisfies the constitutional provision, giving to the accused in a criminal prosecution "the right to demand the cause and nature of his accusation." The amendment is but a stage in the procedure taking place before trial. Puckett v. Commonwealth, 134 Va. 574, 113 S.E. 853 (1922); Farewell v. Commonwealth, 167 Va. 475, 189 S.E. 321 (1937). See Woods v. Commonwealth, 140 Va. 491, 124 S.E. 458 (1924).

This section authorizes, before the general issue is pleaded, any amendment of the indictment which does not change the nature of the offense charged. Thus, the accused is given timely and ample opportunity to avail himself of his constitutional right to be informed of the nature and cause of the accusation against him. That satisfies such constitutional requirement. Forester v. Commonwealth, 210 Va. 764, 173 S.E.2d 851 (1970).

Substantial rights of accused protected. — An amendment, when allowed under this section, must provide that the substantial rights of the accused are protected by informing him of the nature and character of the accusations. Willis v. Commonwealth, 10 Va. App. 430, 393 S.E.2d 405 (1990).

Indictment merely defective and indictment fatally invalid distinguished. — There is a marked difference between an indictment which is merely defective so that it may be amended or the defendant may be given further information by a bill of particulars, and an indictment so fatally invalid that a prosecution cannot be based upon it. Snead v. Smyth, 273 F.2d 838 (4th Cir. 1959).

No amendment where indictment invalid. — Because the indictment found by the grand jury stated no offense and was invalid, it necessarily follows the trial court had no power to amend the indictment. Wilder v. Commonwealth, 217 Va. 145, 225 S.E.2d 411 (1976).

This section authorizes a trial court "to amend an indictment at any time before the verdict is returned or a finding of guilt is made, provided that the amendment does not change the nature or character of the offense charged." Davis v. Commonwealth, No. 2626-95-2 (Ct. of Appeals Apr. 1, 1997).

Amendment on day of trial. — The amendment of an indictment for robbery on the day of the trial has been declared proper. Owsley v. Cunningham, 190 F. Supp. 608 (E.D. Va. 1961).

Objection that indictment failed to negative exceptions waived. — Accused was indicted for the possession of a still and stilling material. To the indictment accused demurred on the ground that it did not negative the exceptions contained in the prohibition act. The demurrer was not interposed until after the jury had been impaneled and duly sworn to try the issue of fact. It was held that the point was waived by failure to interpose the demurrer in time. If there had been merit in the point, the indictment could and doubtless would have been amended under this section which authorizes amendments of indictments for misdemeanors which do not change the nature of the offense charged, at any time before judgment is entered. Gilreath v. Commonwealth, 136 Va. 709, 118 S.E. 100 (1923).

Opportunity to plead anew. — Court of Appeals would not consider defendant's argument that he was entitled to "plead anew" after Commonwealth's amendment of indictments, since defendant at trial never requested opportunity to plead anew to amended indictments. Majette v. Commonwealth, No. 2307-98-2 (Ct. of Appeals Jan. 27, 2000).

Objection because of variance between allegation and proof cannot be raised for the first time on appeal. — The reason for such holding is that if the attention of the trial court had been called to the alleged variance, it could have been cured by an amendment to the indictment under this section. Booth v. Commonwealth, 165 Va. 794, 183 S.E. 257 (1936).

If there shall appear to be any variance between the allegations therein and the evidence offered in proof thereof, the court may permit amendment of such indictment at any time before the jury returns a verdict or the court finds the accused guilty or not guilty, provided the amendment does not change the nature or character of the offense charged; any objection to deficiencies in arraignment on the amended indictment was not presented to the trial court and, therefore, is not before this court on appeal. Barnett v. Commonwealth, No. 2622-95-1 (Ct. of Appeals Sept. 24, 1996).

Where indictment was sufficient to sustain a conviction of abduction "with the intent to deprive such other person of his personal liberty," and Commonwealth introduced evidence to show that the abduction was with intent to defile and offered an instruction setting forth the punishment for that offense, failure of defendant to object to variance at time of offer of evidence and fact that only assignment of error was to the action of the trial court in failing to quash the indictment would preclude the Supreme Court from considering the question of variance on appeal. McKinley v. Commonwealth, 217 Va. 1, 225 S.E.2d 352 (1976) (decided under former §§ 18.1-36, 18.1-37 and 18.1-38).

Surprise at trial is prejudice. — By directly linking the finding of "surprise" to an entitlement to a continuance, the Legislature declared that a surprise caused by amending an indictment at trial per se prejudices the accused. To alleviate that prejudice, a trial judge must grant the accused a continuance for a reasonable period of time. Crawford v. Commonwealth, 23 Va. App. 661, 479 S.E.2d 84 (1996).

Trial court did not err in refusing to grant continuance. — Although this section mandates that when an amendment operates as a surprise to the accused he shall be entitled, upon request, to a continuance of the case for a reasonable time, where attorney for the Commonwealth made clear to the defense as early as two months before trial, and at a pretrial conference, the nature and character of the charges and the theory upon which the commonwealth was proceeding, the court did not err in refusing to grant the motion for a continuance. Willis v. Commonwealth, 10 Va. App. 430, 393 S.E.2d 405 (1990).

Trial court did not err in denying defendant a continuance after the Commonwealth was permitted to amend the indictment to cover an additional period of time, because defendant failed to prove that the amendment operated as a surprise or that defendant was prejudiced by the denial of the motion; defendant was aware of the evidence against defendant and made no showing of a specific need for time for additional investigation to prepare a defense. Ortiz v. Commonwealth, 276 Va. 705, 667 S.E.2d 751, 2008 Va. LEXIS 122 (2008).

Trial court did not err in denying defendant's motion for a continuance after the Commonwealth amended an indictment to change name of owner of dwelling defendant burglarized; the amendment did not change defendant's theory of defense, he knew the company named in amendment bought the dwelling in a foreclosure sale a month before the burglary so there was no surprise, and as defendant failed to present evidence of a need for further investigation after the amendment, he failed to establish any prejudice caused by the amendment. Basim Dauwd Jami v. Commonwealth, 2009 Va. App. LEXIS 102 (Mar. 10, 2009).

Trial court did not err in denying defendant's motion for a continuance because defendant failed to show that the amendment to the indictment operated as a surprise or that the denial of a continuance caused prejudice; all of the crimes charged, attempted rape, abduction with intent to defile, and misdemeanor assault and battery, took place at the same time and place, and involved related,

sexual conduct against the victim, and the evidence defendant needed to defend against the charges would not have changed because of the amendment to the abduction charge. Gay v. Commonwealth, 2011 Va. App. LEXIS 134 (Apr. 19, 2011).

Technical correction permitted after jury returns verdict. — There was no defect in form in the conspiracy indictments on which a defendant was tried nor was there any variance between the allegations listed and the evidence offered at trial where the indictments mistakenly classified the conspiracy charges as Class 6 felonies, rather than Class 5 felonies, and the fact that the indictments contained surplus language and were subject to a technical correction after the jury had returned its verdict did not render them defective and in need of a substantive amendment under this section to sustain their validity. Sloan v. Commonwealth, 35 Va. App. 240, 544 S.E.2d 375, 2001 Va. App. LEXIS 180 (2001).

Applied in Edwards v. Commonwealth, 218 Va. 994, 243 S.E.2d 834 (1978); Chiang v. Commonwealth, 6 Va. App. 13, 365 S.E.2d 778 (1988); Thomas v. Commonwealth, 256 Va. 38, 501 S.E.2d 391 (1998); Powell v. Commonwealth, 261 Va. 512, 552 S.E.2d 344, 2001 Va. LEXIS 86 (2001).

II. CHARACTER OR NATURE OF OFFENSE.

Amendment changing nature of charge prohibited. — Under this section, an amendment to an original summons charging failure to yield the right-of-way, so as to charge reckless driving, was not possible since it would have changed the nature of the offense charged. Miles v. Commonwealth, 205 Va. 462, 138 S.E.2d 22 (1964).

While, under this section, defective indictments may be amended, the trial court does not have the power to change by amendment the character of an offense as found by the grand jury. Puckett v. Commonwealth, 134 Va. 574, 113 S.E. 853 (1922); Evans v. Commonwealth, 183 Va. 775, 33 S.E. 636 (1945).

An indictment under former § 18.2-68 for seduction could not be amended by inserting the word "unmarried" before the word "female" as such would change the charge from misdemeanor to felony. Evans v. Commonwealth, 183 Va. 775, 33 S.E. 636 (1945).

Amendment to include alternative theory of capital murder not permitted. — The pre-trial amendment of an indictment charging one theory of capital murder to include an alternative and additional theory of capital murder does not constitute an amendment contemplated by the provisions of this section to correct a variance between the allegation of the original indictment and the proof the Commonwealth expects to adduce at the subsequent trial; despite the liberal construction afforded to promote the remedial purpose of this section, because such an amended indictment materially changes the nature of the offense originally charged, it should not be permitted. Powell v. Commonwealth, 261 Va. 512, 552 S.E.2d 344, 2001 Va. LEXIS 86 (2001).

Character of offense not changed. — Where an indictment erroneously charged that the accused was previously convicted for a violation of a certain section of the prohibition law, when, as a matter of fact, he was convicted for the violation of a different section, an amendment correcting the error does not change the character of the offense even though the effect of the amendment was to charge the accused with a second violation, the punishment for which was a felony. Kelley v. Commonwealth, 140 Va. 522, 125 S.E. 437 (1924).

Where an indictment charged that accused "did unlawfully and feloniously store for sale ardent spirits," and also charged that the accused had previously been convicted of a violation of the same law, the allowance of an amendment striking out the words "and feloniously" did not change the character of the offense within the meaning of this section. Kelley v. Commonwealth, 140 Va. 522, 125 S.E. 437 (1924).

Where accused was indicted for breaking and entering a motor sales company with intent to steal, etc., and the indictment was amended to charge breaking and entering the garage building belonging to the motor sales company, etc., the amendment did not change the offense charged but enlarged on the description and made the charge clearer. Robinson v. Commonwealth, 190 Va. 134, 56 S.E.2d 367 (1949).

Trial counsel's failure to object to any defect in the indictment resulted in no prejudice to petitioner, where the defective language, if any, was subject to a curative amendment under this section and such amendment would not have changed the nature or character of the offense. Martin v. Warden, Va. State Penitentiary, 2 Va. App. 6, 341 S.E.2d 202 (1986).

Where the time period charged in the indictment was narrowed, the word "feloniously" was struck from the indictment, and the amount in question was amended, the amendments did not change the nature of the offense; they merely had the effect of reducing the charge from a felony to a misdemeanor. Hall v. Commonwealth, 2 Va. App. 159, 342 S.E.2d 640 (1986).

The amendment to defendant's burglary indictment, which added the aggravated circumstance of committing the felony while armed with a deadly weapon, did not change the nature or character of the offense. Hawkins v. Commonwealth, No. 0188-87-1 (Ct. of Appeals Jan. 3, 1989).

Where both an arrest warrant and a summons charged defendant with violating a city ordinance and § 18.2-266, each of which is a misdemeanor, and the defendant was convicted on the summons and appealed, and on appeal, the circuit court granted the Commonwealth's motion to amend the summons to delete the reference to the city ordinance, this action was proper, as the amendment did not change the nature or character of the offense charged. Hill v. Commonwealth, No. 1240-91-4 (Ct. of Appeals Feb. 2, 1993).

In this case, defendant was charged with felony embezzlement both prior to and after the trial court amended the indictment by adding the phrase "such automobile having a value of $200.00 or more." Although the Commonwealth's amendment more clearly described the automobile allegedly embezzled by appellant, it did not change the nature or character of the offense charged. Davis v. Commonwealth, No. 2626-95-2 (Ct. of Appeals Apr. 1, 1997).

Where defendant could originally have been convicted of violating the statute in any of three ways, trial court's amendment which struck second clause of indictment as unconstitutional, did not change the nature or character of the offense. Wilson v. Commonwealth, 31 Va. App. 495, 525 S.E.2d 1 (2000).

Presentments issued by grand jury charging defendant with causing or creating a public nuisance or of permitting the continuation of a public nuisance were not fatally defective after the trial court amended the presentments to cover a one-year time period, which was the allotted time-period for prosecution of a misdemeanor, instead of the two-year time period that had been set forth; the trial court's amendment merely narrowed the time alleged in the presentments and did not change the nature of the offenses charged against defendant. Niazi v. Commonwealth, No. 2283-02-2, 2004 Va. App. LEXIS 102 (Ct. of Appeals Mar. 9, 2004).

Trial court did not err in allowing an amendment to a statutory burglary indictment, as the addition of an assault and battery mens rea to the original indictment changed one of its specific elements, but not its general nature or character. Hicks v. Commonwealth, No. 1421-03-3, 2004 Va. App. LEXIS 172 (Ct. of Appeals Apr. 13, 2004).

Indictments were properly amended to change the dates of the incidents under § 19.2-231 as the amendment did not change the nature or character of the offense charged; assuming that the amendments to an indictment were a surprise to defendant for purposes of Va. Const., Art. I, § 8, defendant was entitled to a continuance, which defendant refused. Haley v. Commonwealth, 2007 Va. App. LEXIS 402 (Nov. 6, 2007).

Original indictment did not charge a non-offense where: (1) by its reference to § 18.2-308.2, the indictment provided defendant with notice of the nature and character of the offense with which he was charged; (2) the amended indictment tracked the language of § 18.2-308.2 to charge that defendant carried in a concealed manner a dirk, bowie knife, switchblade knife, ballistic knife, machete, or razor or any weapon of like kind; (3) the nature of the charged offense was not changed; and (4) defendant did not claim surprise regarding the charged offense or request a continuance of the trial date. Thompson v. Commonwealth, 51 Va. App. 205, 656 S.E.2d 409, 2008 Va. App. LEXIS 59 (2008), rev'd, 277 Va. 280, 673 S.E.2d 469 (2009) (as to whether butterfly knife was weapon of like kind).

Trial court did not err in allowing the amendment of indictment under § 19.2-231, prior to arraignment, from charging indecent liberties with a child, to aggravated sexual battery, because the underlying conduct of both charges was essentially the same, and the purpose and subject matter of each charge were similar. Pulliam v. Commonwealth, 55 Va. App. 710, 688 S.E.2d 910, 2010 Va. App. LEXIS 73 (2010).

Amendment to an indictment was proper where the offense with which defendant was charged was plainly described in the body of the indictment as possession of cocaine while a prisoner and where the amendment of the statutory provision cited at the foot of the indictment did not change that description and, thus, did not affect the nature or character of the offense charged. Mosby v. Commonwealth, No. 2990-08-3, 2010 Va. App. LEXIS 120 (Ct. of Appeals Mar. 30, 2010).

Pursuant to § 19.2-231, the trial court properly allowed the prosecution, after trial began, to amend a charge of rape (§ 18.2-61) to object sexual penetration (§ 18.2-67.2), because the amendment did not change the nature or character of the underlying conduct, penetrating victim's vagina against her will by force, only the object used to accomplish the penetration. Jackson v. Commonwealth, 2012 Va. App. LEXIS 224 (July 10, 2012).

No error in amendment which substituted § 18.2-257 for § 18.2-26. — Where prior to trial, the trial court granted the Commonwealth's motion to amend second count of indictment, and where the nature of the amendment changed the attempt statute on which the Commonwealth was relying from § 18.2-26, the general attempt statute, to § 18.2-257, which covers attempts to violate the Drug Control Act, the trial court did not err in granting the Commonwealth's motion to amend the indictment against defendant. The amendment did not change the nature or character of the offense charged; it merely substituted reference to § 18.2-257, the specific provision covering attempts to commit drug offenses, for § 18.2-26, the general provision covering attempts to commit general, non-capital felonies. Robinson v. Commonwealth, No. 1840-90-1 (Ct. of Appeals July 21, 1992).

Amendment providing for greater punishment. — That an amendment to an indictment allowed under this section authorizes a greater punishment than that authorized for the offense charged in the original indictment does not of itself change the character of the offense charged. Sullivan v. Commonwealth, 157 Va. 867, 161 S.E. 297 (1931).

Amendment to an indictment, charging defendant with being the principal, or a principal administrator, organizer, or leader of a continuing criminal enterprise engaged, during a one-year period, in the distribution of at least five kilograms of a mixture containing cocaine base, which served only to change punishment by increasing amount of cocaine base possessed by defendant, and did not add a new charge or otherwise change the nature or character of the offense charged was permissible under § 19.2-231. Dunaway v. Commonwealth, 52 Va. App. 281, 663 S.E.2d 117, 2008 Va. App. LEXIS 326 (2008).

Section authorizes amendment of date of crime. — An indictment originally alleged that the perjury was committed on September 20th, while the proof tended to show that it was committed on September 19th. It was held that an amendment was clearly authorized by this section. Robinson v. Commonwealth, 165 Va. 876, 183 S.E. 254 (1936).

Date alleged in indictment. — Defendant made no showing that some grave injustice or the denial of essential rights occurred to justify application of the "good cause" and "ends of justice" exceptions to Va. Sup. Ct. R. 5A:18 where, had defendant challenged the sufficiency of the evidence of his possession of burglary tools on the date they were found, the Commonwealth could have sought an amendment of the indictment. Jarvis v. Commonwealth, — Va. App. —, — S.E.2d —, 2005 Va. App. LEXIS 415 (Oct. 18, 2005).

How omission of date of offense corrected. — There was no demurrer or other objection to the indictment until after a verdict of conviction, which was abundantly supported by the testimony. If objection had been raised because of the omission of the date of the offense, it could have been corrected at the bar by the prosecuting attorney on mere motion under this section, but such motion is barred after verdict by § 19.2-227. Flanary v. Commonwealth, 133 Va. 665, 112 S.E. 604 (1922). See Salyer v. Commonwealth, 165 Va. 744, 181 S.E. 435 (1935).

Failure to allege time of offense no ground for setting aside verdict. — Failure to allege in an indictment the time of the offense, even in a case in which time was essential, was not, in view of this section, a ground for setting aside the verdict where no objection was timely made to the indictment. Puckett v. Commonwealth, 134 Va. 574, 113 S.E. 853 (1922).

The accused waived his right to object to murder indictment for failure to allege any date on which the offense charged was committed, by not objecting before pleading, though such would not have been the case prior to this section providing for amendment of indictment before defendant pleads. Puckett v. Commonwealth, 134 Va. 574, 113 S.E. 853 (1922).

Nor is failure to allege that act was committed feloniously. — An indictment for receiving stolen goods omitted to allege that the accused "feloniously" committed the act. The demurrer to the indictment did not specify the grounds upon which it was based. If it had done so, and had pointed out this objection, the trial court could, and would, have directed an amendment of the indictment pursuant to the provisions of this section. Jolly v. Commonwealth, 136 Va. 756, 118 S.E. 109 (1923).

How indictment for felony and misdemeanor amended when only misdemeanor proved. — When under an indictment charging both a misdemeanor and a felony, it was clear that the proof only supported a charge of misdemeanor, aggravated by the fact of a prior conviction, the court should have amended that part of the indictment alleging prior conviction to conform to the proof, pursuant to this section, and proceeded with the trial upon the amended indictment as if it had charged a misdemeanor only in the beginning. Keeney v. Commonwealth, 147 Va. 678, 137 S.E. 478 (1927).

Amendment of indictment which includes various intents improperly drafted in the disjunctive is permitted under this section. Wilson v. Commonwealth, 31 Va. App. 495, 525 S.E.2d 1 (2000).

Therefore, the fact that the grand jury may have indicted the accused for having acted with one intent did not preclude his conviction for violating the statute with a different intent, also included in the indictment. Wilson v. Commonwealth, 31 Va. App. 495, 525 S.E.2d 1 (2000).

Amending the indictment to change the intent. — Trial court did not err by amending the indictment, which charged breaking and entering with the intent to commit destruction of property, by adding the phrase "or indecent exposure" where: (1) the amendment permitted the Commonwealth to satisfy its burden of proof with either of two specific alternatives; (2) the modification of the original indictment did not change the general nature or character of the crime charged; (3) only the intent changed, and as amended the indictment still charged a misdemeanor of the same general nature or class; (4) the amendment did not surprise defendant because the original indictment included a count that charged indecent exposure; (5) the amendment did not prejudice defendant because the trial court continued the case after making the amendment; and (6) the trial court convicted defendant of the charge as originally stated. Esquibele v. Commonwealth, No. 2500-03-4, 2004 Va. App. LEXIS 586 (Ct. of Appeals Nov. 30, 2004).

Amendment charging second offense not error. — Where the accused was indicted for transporting and having for sale ardent spirits, and the indictment charged that "the transportation" was the second offense, it was not error to allow an amendment by substituting the word "acts" for the word "transportation" and by inserting after the words "a second offense," the words "under this statute." The stricken words might be treated as surplusage. Staples v. Commonwealth, 140 Va. 583, 125 S.E. 319 (1924).

Variance of name between allegation and proof not reversible error. — Where there was a variance between the given name of the person killed in the indictment and the proof, but the case proceeded upon the idea that they were one and the same person under this section, the point is purely technical and not ground for reversal. Brown v. Commonwealth, 138 Va. 807, 122 S.E. 421 (1924).

Amendment of victim's name. — Change in the name of victim did not create a new offense nor did it change the nature or character of the offense for which appellant was indicted, therefore, trial court did not err when it permitted indictment to be amended to indicate the name of a victim who was present at the same time and place as the person originally named as the victim in the indictment. Phan v. Commonwealth, 18 Va. App. 360, 444 S.E.2d 9 (1994).

No error in permitting sexual offense amendment. — Amendment of the indictment, which occurred nearly three months before trial, did not change the nature or character of the offense with which appellant was charged. The amendment affected only the manner in which the aggravated sexual battery was committed — from defendant touching the child to forcing the child to touch him — and appellant remained charged with the same crime committed against the same victim during the same period of time. He had ample opportunity to prepare a defense to the amended charge. Thus, the trial judge did not err in permitting the amendment, and in denying appellant's motion to dismiss the indictment. Atorick v. Commonwealth, No. 2934-95-4 (Ct. of Appeals July 8, 1997).

CIRCUIT COURT OPINIONS

Enforcement of guilty plea after amendment of indictment. — Defendant's motion to enforce an oral plea agreement was denied because he subsequently voluntarily agreed to amend the indictment, from distribution of imitation cocaine to distribution of cocaine, thus creating a new charge and thus invalidating and waiving the original plea agreement to distribution of imitation cocaine. Commonwealth v. Carter, 64 Va. Cir. 224, 2004 Va. Cir. LEXIS 183 (Norfolk 2004).

ARTICLE 4.
PROCESS.

§ 19.2-232. What process to be awarded against accused on indictment, etc.

When an indictment or presentment is found or made, or information filed, the court, or the judge thereof, shall award process against the accused to answer the same, if he be not in custody. Such process, if the prosecution be for a felony, shall be a capias; if it be for a misdemeanor, for which imprisonment may be imposed, it may be a capias or summons, in the discretion of the court or judge; in all other cases, it shall be, in the first instance a summons, but if a summons be returned executed and the defendant does not appear, or be returned not found, the court or judge may award a capias. The officer serving the summons or capias shall also serve a copy of the indictment, presentment or information therewith.

History.
Code 1950, § 19.1-178; 1960, c. 366; 1975, c. 495; 1980, c. 349.

Cross references.
As to when capias need not be filed, but a summons issued, see § 19.2-219. As to where process of arrest issued during term may be executed, see § 19.2-236. As to process on indictment or presentment for misdemeanor, see § 19.2-237.

Law Review.
For comment, "Immunity from Service of Nonresident Criminal Defendants," see 20 Wash. & Lee L. Rev. 375 (1963).

Michie's Jurisprudence.
For related discussion, see 5B M.J. Criminal Procedure, §§ 12, 45; 19 M.J. Warrants, § 2.

CASE NOTES

For history of this section, see Jones v. Commonwealth, 86 Va. 661, 10 S.E. 1005 (1890).

Every state may control the remedies furnished in her courts, and may at any time change the forms of procedure therein, and the laws in force in that respect at time of trial must prevail. Jones v. Commonwealth, 86 Va. 661, 10 S.E. 1005 (1890);

Wilson v. Commonwealth, 86 Va. 666, 10 S.E. 1007 (1890).

Preliminary examination not required. — By this section an examination by a justice of the peace is not required, and the accused need not have such preliminary examination. Jones v. Commonwealth, 86 Va. 661, 10 S.E. 1005 (1890).

A warrant of arrest is unnecessary when the accused is in custody when the indictment is found. Waller v. Commonwealth, 84 Va. 492, 5 S.E. 364 (1888).

§ 19.2-233. How awarded, directed, returnable and executed.

Sections 8.01-292 and 8.01-295 shall apply to process in criminal, as well as in civil cases; and the court may, in the same case against the same person, award at the same time, or different times, several writs of summons or capias directed to officers of different counties or cities. An officer having a capias under which the accused is let to bail shall give a certificate of the fact, which shall protect him against any other capias which may have been issued for the same offense. A summons shall be served by delivering a copy thereof to the party in person and the clerk issuing such summons shall deliver or transmit therewith as many copies thereof as there are persons named therein on whom it is to be served.

History.
Code 1950, § 19.1-179; 1960, c. 366; 1975, c. 495.

§ 19.2-234. Procedure when person arrested under capias.

An officer who, under a capias from any court, arrests a person accused of an offense shall proceed in accordance with § 19.2-80 and Article 1 (§ 19.2-119 et seq.) of Chapter 9 of Title 19.2 regarding bail.

History.
Code 1950, § 19.1-183; 1960, c. 366; 1975, c. 495; 1986, c. 327.

Michie's Jurisprudence.
For related discussion, see 5B M.J. Criminal Procedure, § 12.

§ 19.2-235. Clerks to mail process to officers in other counties, etc.

The clerk of every court shall forward, by mail, all process issued for the Commonwealth, directed to the officer of any county or city other than his own.

History.
Code 1950, § 19.1-181; 1960, c. 366; 1975, c. 495.

Cross references.
As to effect on proceedings when corporation fails to appear in answer to process, see § 19.2-238.

CASE NOTES

Section is constitutional. — The constitutional guarantee that the accused in all criminal prosecutions has the right to be confronted with the witnesses against him, etc., is not violated by this section. Shiflett v. Commonwealth, 90 Va. 386, 18 S.E. 838 (1894).

It displaces the rule of the common law that judgment for

corporal punishment can be pronounced against a man only when he is personally present. Shiflett v. Commonwealth, 90 Va. 386, 18 S.E. 838 (1894).

Defendant has duty to appear in person. — Authority, conferred by this section, to try a misdemeanor charge in the absence of the accused is not a right given him; it is a privilege accorded only to the court. It does not relax the defendant's obligation to appear in obedience to the mandate of the summons. Nor does this section abridge the power of the court to require his submission in person to its jurisdiction — perhaps to answer its judgment. Souther v. Reid, 101 F. Supp. 806 (E.D. Va. 1951).

§ 19.2-236. Where process of arrest may be executed.

When process of arrest in a criminal prosecution is issued from a court, either against a party accused or a witness, the officer to whom it is directed or delivered may execute it in any part of the Commonwealth.

History.
Code 1950, § 19.1-182; 1960, c. 366; 1975, c. 495.

§ 19.2-237. Process on indictment or presentment for misdemeanor.

On any indictment or presentment for a misdemeanor process shall be issued immediately. If the accused appear and plead to the charge, the trial shall proceed without delay, unless good cause for continuance be shown. If, in any misdemeanor case the accused fails to appear and plead, when required the court may either award a capias or proceed to trial in the same manner as if the accused had appeared, plead not guilty and waived trial by jury, provided, that the court shall not in any such case enforce a jail sentence.

History.
Code 1950, §§ 19.1-180, 19.1-184; 1960, c. 366; 1975, c. 495; 1979, c. 468.

Cross references.
As to right of court to award at same time several writs of summons or capias directed to officers of different counties, see § 19.2-233. As to when felony cases shall be tried, see §§ 19.2-241, 19.2-243.

Law Review.
For an article relating to all published Virginia criminal law decisions between July 1, 1997, and July 1, 1998, see 32 U. Rich. L. Rev. 1091 (1998).

Michie's Jurisprudence.
For related discussion, see 5B M.J. Criminal Procedure, §§ 25, 29, 30, 34, 39, 45; 12A M.J. Lotteries, § 6; 19 M.J. Warrants, § 2.

CASE NOTES

Section is constitutional. — The constitutional guarantee that the accused in all criminal prosecutions has the right to be confronted with the witnesses against him, etc., is not violated by this section. Shiflett v. Commonwealth, 90 Va. 386, 18 S.E. 838 (1894).

The requirements of this section are met where an accused has voluntarily waived his right to be present at trial but was present at the hearing where sentence was imposed. Hohman v. Commonwealth, No. 0815-95-4 (Ct. of Appeals Dec. 31, 1996).

Under this section, no arraignment or plea of the accused

is necessary in a misdemeanor case. Bare v. Commonwealth, 122 Va. 783, 94 S.E. 168 (1917); Foy v. Commonwealth, 132 Va. 671, 111 S.E. 269 (1922).

If the accused in a prosecution for a misdemeanor, is absent, no arraignment can be made because of his absence, but nevertheless the court may proceed to trial just as if he had appeared and pleaded not guilty. If he is present when his case is called, he should plead, if he desires to make defense, and if he goes to trial without pleading, he thereby waives his right to do so. Bare v. Commonwealth, 122 Va. 783, 94 S.E. 168 (1917).

No plea is necessary in a misdemeanor case. However, in such a case an accused may plead as he has been advised, demur or move to quash, he may plead to the jurisdiction or he may plead guilty. He may plead former jeopardy and not guilty, or he may stand mute. If, upon his trial for a misdemeanor, he be present when his case is called, he should plead such defenses as he deems proper, and if he goes to trial without a specific plea, he thereby waives his right to make that plea thereafter, and cannot thereafter take advantage of his failure. Royals v. City of Hampton, 201 Va. 552, 111 S.E.2d 795 (1960).

Presence of accused not necessary. — A prisoner indicted under § 18.2-415 for a disturbance of religious worship, who was duly summoned but failed to appear, may be tried in his absence without the award of a capias for his arrest. Shiflett v. Commonwealth, 90 Va. 386, 18 S.E. 838 (1894).

Continuance. — Upon indictment for carrying on a lottery business, when accused "appears and pleads to the charge" and moves for a continuance, it is not error to deny the motion. Lawrence v. Commonwealth, 86 Va. 573, 10 S.E. 840 (1890).

Forfeiture of rights found. — Appellant, by his conduct of knowingly and voluntarily failing to appear for his trial, forfeited both his constitutional rights of confrontation and due process and his statutory rights under this section. Hohman v. Commonwealth, No. 0815-95-4 (Ct. of Appeals Dec. 31, 1996).

The proper method of raising the question of former jeopardy is by special plea of former acquittal or conviction. Royals v. City of Hampton, 201 Va. 552, 111 S.E.2d 795 (1960).

Applied in Head v. Commonwealth, 3 Va. App. 163, 348 S.E.2d 423 (1986).

§ 19.2-238. Summons against corporation; proceedings; expense of publication.

A summons against a corporation to answer an indictment, presentment or information may be served as provided in §§ 8.01-299 through 8.01-301; and if the defendant after being so served fail to appear, the court may proceed to trial and judgment, without further process, as if the defendant had appeared, plead not guilty and waived trial by jury. And when, in any such case, publication of a copy of the process is required according to such sections, the expense of such publication may be certified by the court to the Comptroller, and shall be paid out of the state treasury; but the same shall be taxed with other costs and collected from the defendant, if judgment be for the Commonwealth, and be paid into the state treasury by the officer collecting the same.

History.
Code 1950, § 19.1-186; 1960, c. 366; 1975, c. 495.

Michie's Jurisprudence.
For related discussion, see 9B M.J. Indictments, Informations and Presentments, § 5.

CHAPTER 15.
TRIAL AND ITS INCIDENTS.

Article 1. Jurisdiction.

ARTICLE 1.

JURISDICTION.

§ 19.2-239. Jurisdiction in criminal cases.

The circuit courts, except where otherwise provided, shall have exclusive original jurisdiction for the trial of all presentments, indictments and informations for offenses committed within their respective circuits.

History.
Code 1950, § 19.1-187; 1960, c. 366; 1975, c. 495.

Michie's Jurisprudence.
For related discussion, see 4A M.J. Continuances, § 19; 5A M.J. Courts, § 39.

CASE NOTES

Generally, charges may be tried only in the circuit courts having territorial jurisdiction over the locations where the crimes occurred and in which venue is laid. Foster-Zahid v. Commonwealth, 23 Va. App. 430, 477 S.E.2d 759 (1996).

Claim involved territorial jurisdiction rather than venue. — Where defendant claimed that the circuit court lacked jurisdiction to try defendant because the Commonwealth failed to prove that defendant's offense occurred within the territorial jurisdiction of the circuit court where defendant was tried, defendant's claim pertained to territorial jurisdiction, rather than venue. Gordon v. Commonwealth, 38 Va. App. 818, 568 S.E.2d 452, 2002 Va. App. LEXIS 521 (2002).

Claim of lack of territorial jurisdiction was waived. — Where defendant did not dispute that defendant's alleged drug offense occurred in Virginia, but merely claimed that the Commonwealth failed to prove that the offense occurred in the specific territorial jurisdiction where defendant had been tried and convicted, defendant's claim, like that based on improper venue, was waived because defendant's objection to the circuit court's territorial jurisdiction was untimely. Gordon v. Commonwealth, 38 Va. App. 818, 568 S.E.2d 452, 2002 Va. App. LEXIS 521 (2002).

Territorial jurisdiction distinguished from subject matter jurisdiction. — Unlike the subject matter jurisdiction described in § 17.1-513, which may not be waived, the jurisdiction described in § 19.2-239 refers to a circuit court's authority over persons, things, or occurrences located in a defined geographic area, which is properly categorized as "territorial jurisdiction" and may be waived by failing to timely raise the issue. Gordon v. Commonwealth, 38 Va. App. 818, 568 S.E.2d 452, 2002 Va. App. LEXIS 521 (2002).

Transfers between circuit courts implicated territorial jurisdiction but not subject matter jurisdiction. — Transfer of defendant's criminal trial from Norfolk (Virginia) (the place of the offense), to Arlington (Virginia) and the subsequent transfer back to Norfolk after the jury verdicts did not implicate subject matter jurisdiction since both the Arlington and Norfolk circuit courts had subject matter jurisdiction over defendant's charges under § 17.1-513. The only question was whether a violation of § 19.2-239 occurred when the Arlington circuit court conducted the trial; this issue went solely to the circuit court's lack of authority to exercise territorial jurisdiction and was waived by defendant's failure to timely object. Porter v. Commonwealth, 276 Va. 203, 661 S.E.2d 415, 2008 Va. LEXIS 78 (2008), cert. denied, 129 S. Ct. 1999, 173 L. Ed. 2d 1097, 2009 U.S. LEXIS 3047 (U.S. 2009).

Jurisdiction may exist where the immediate harm occurs, even if the criminal act does not physically occur there. Foster-Zahid v. Commonwealth, 23 Va. App. 430, 477 S.E.2d 759 (1996).

Nolo contendere plea. — By pleading nolo contendere, defendant, in essence, admitted as true each factual allegation set forth in the indictment, including the fact that the offense occurred in the Commonwealth. Jones v. Commonwealth, 42 Va. App. 142, 590 S.E.2d 572, 2004 Va. App. LEXIS 2 (2004).

Effect of plea agreement. — Acceptance of defendant's plea agreement, which provided that the trial court would impose sentence on two counts of aggravated sexual battery and would withhold decision on the other two counts, did not divest the trial court of its jurisdiction to adjudicate the charges. Holden v. Commonwealth, 26 Va. App. 403, 494 S.E.2d 892 (1998).

The trial court had jurisdiction over a prosecution for embezzlement where the defendant took a guitar amplifier belonging to the victim with him when he moved from Virginia to West Virginia and then used it as collateral for a loan he secured from a pawn shop in West Virginia, as the crime commenced when the defendant appropriated the amplifier to his own use and removed it, without authorization, to West Virginia. Bescher v. Commonwealth, No. 1489-97-4 (Ct. of Appeals April 14, 1998).

Jurisdiction proven. — In a murder case, the trial court had territorial jurisdiction under §§ 19.2-239 and 17.1-513 because the facts and circumstances proved that the killing occurred in Richmond, Virginia. The undisputed evidence showed that the stabbing occurred at a rooming house in Richmond, Virginia; diagrams of the residence indicated that it was in Richmond; Richmond police and a Richmond prosecutor investigated the case; physical evidence was analyzed in Richmond; and defendant's arrest warrant had a Richmond address. Dixon v. Commonwealth, 2006 Va. App. LEXIS 165 (May 2, 2006).

Trial court did not err in convicting defendant of attempted murder because the trial court was not deprived of subject matter jurisdiction when it failed to arraign defendant on the charge when defendant was fully aware of the attempted murder charge and was in no way prejudiced by the omission of a formal arraignment; defendant's continued silence in the face of repeated references to the attempted murder charge was tantamount to a waiver of his right to be arraigned and to enter a not guilty plea, and having failed to raise any objection, defendant waived any defect. Simmons v. Commonwealth, 54 Va. App. 594, 681 S.E.2d 56, 2009 Va. App. LEXIS 367 (2009).

Because defendant admitted that the events in question occurred at the apartment of the victim's grandmother, and because the grandmother and defendant's girlfriend testified that the apartment was in a locality in Virginia, the evidence was sufficient to establish the trial court's subject matter jurisdiction under §§ 19.2-239 and 17.1-513. Torres v. Commonwealth, 2010 Va. App. LEXIS 420 (Nov. 2, 2010).

Applied in Owusu v. Commonwealth, 11 Va. App. 671, 401 S.E.2d 431 (1991); Curtis v. Commonwealth, 13 Va. App. 622, 414 S.E.2d 421 (1992); Penn v. Commonwealth, 32 Va. App. 422, 528 S.E.2d 179, 2000 Va. App. LEXIS 329 (2000); Thomas v. Commonwealth, 36 Va. App. 326, 549 S.E.2d 648, 2001 Va. App. LEXIS 448 (2001); Morris v. Commonwealth, 51 Va. App. 459, 658 S.E.2d 708, 2008 Va. App. LEXIS 170 (2008).

§ 19.2-240. Clerks shall make out criminal docket.

Before every term of any court in which criminal cases are to be tried the clerk of the court shall make out a separate docket of criminal cases then pending, in the following order, numbering the same:

1. Felony cases;
2. Misdemeanor cases.

He shall docket all felony cases in the order in which the indictments are found and all misdemeanor cases in the order in which the presentments or indictments are found or informations are filed or appeals are allowed by magistrates and as soon as any presentments or indictments are made at a term of court he shall forthwith docket the same in the order required above.

Traffic infractions shall be docketed with misdemeanor cases.

Cases appealed from the juvenile and domestic relations district court shall not be placed on the criminal docket except for cases involving criminal offenses committed by adults as provided in § 16.1-302. Cases transferred to a circuit court from a juvenile and domestic relations district court pursuant to Article 7 (§ 16.1-269.1 et seq.) of Chapter 11 of Title 16.1 shall be docketed as provided in this section upon return of a true bill of indictment by the grand jury.

History.
Code 1950, § 19.1-189; 1960, c. 366; 1975, c. 495; 1977, c. 585; 1990, c. 258; 1994, cc. 859, 949.

Editor's note.
Acts 1993, c. 930, cl. 3, as amended by Acts 1994, c. 564, cl. 2, and Acts 1996, c. 616, cl. 4, provides that the amendment to this section by Acts 1993, c. 930, cl. 1, shall become effective June 1, 1998, "if state funds are provided, including all local costs, to carry out the purposes of this bill by the General Assembly." The funding was not provided.

Michie's Jurisprudence.
For related discussion, see 5A M.J. Courts, § 10; 5B M.J. Criminal Procedure, §§ 25, 39.

§ 19.2-241. Time within which court to set criminal cases for trial.

The judge of each circuit court shall fix a day of his court when the trial of criminal cases will commence, and may make such general or special order in reference thereto, and to the summoning of witnesses, as may seem proper, but all criminal cases shall be disposed of before civil cases, unless the court shall direct otherwise.

When an indictment is found against a person for felony or when an appeal has been perfected from the conviction of a misdemeanor or traffic infraction, the accused, if in custody, or if he appear according to his recognizance, may be tried at the same term and shall be tried within the time limits fixed in § 19.2-243; provided that no trial shall be held on the first day of the term unless it be with consent of the attorney for the Commonwealth and the accused and his attorney.

History.
Code 1950, §§ 19.1-188 through 19.1-190; 1960, c. 366; 1972, c. 705; 1975, c. 495; 1977, c. 585; 1978, c. 410.

Cross references.
As to continuance when indictment or presentment is amended, see § 19.2-231. As to time of trial for misdemeanors, see § 19.2-237. As to continuance when warrant for misdemeanor is amended or new warrant is issued, see § 16.1-137. As to continuance where member or officer of General Assembly in session is involved, see § 30-5.

Law Review.
For survey of Virginia criminal law for the year 1971-1972, see 58 Va. L. Rev. 1206 (1972).

Michie's Jurisprudence.
For related discussion, see 4A M.J. Continuances, § 19; 5B M.J. Criminal Procedure, §§ 25, 39.

CASE NOTES

The purpose of this section is to secure to the accused the speedy trial guaranteed by the Constitution, and to further the policy of the law to expedite the trial of criminal cases. Either the Commonwealth or the accused, moving for a continuance, must show good cause. Benton v. Commonwealth, 90 Va. 328, 18 S.E. 282 (1893); Thompson v. Commonwealth, 131 Va. 847, 109 S.E. 447 (1921).

While in the orderly administration of justice some delay is unavoidable and some is essential to due process, courts must inquire into the reasons for the delay. Stephens v. Commonwealth, 225 Va. 224, 301 S.E.2d 22 (1983).

The burden is on the prosecution to prove excusable delay. Stephens v. Commonwealth, 225 Va. 224, 301 S.E.2d 22 (1983).

The protections granted under this section and § 19.2-243 are not self-operative and may be claimed or waived. Stephens v. Commonwealth, 225 Va. 224, 301 S.E.2d 22 (1983).

This section is directory merely, it being not otherwise intended for the benefit of the accused than as a means of insuring a speedy trial. Wash v. Commonwealth, 57 Va. (16 Gratt.) 530 (1861); Hall v. Commonwealth, 89 Va. 171, 15 S.E. 517 (1893); Benton v. Commonwealth, 90 Va. 328, 18 S.E. 282 (1893).

Order in which cases tried is in discretion of court. — The order in which cases on the docket shall be tried rests in the sound discretion of the court, and this section specifically authorizes the court to make such special orders in reference thereto as may seem proper. Jones v. Commonwealth, 135 Va. 545, 115 S.E. 572 (1923).

And setting of trial date is under supervision of court. — This provision contemplates an orderly procedure for setting criminal cases and expressly places the control of that process under the supervision of the trial court, not a party litigant. Williams v. Commonwealth, 2 Va. App. 566, 347 S.E.2d 146 (1986).

What is "good cause" is in discretion of trial court. — Under this section, whether good cause is shown upon a motion for a continuance is a question which rests largely in the discretion of the trial court, and, while the exercise of such discretion is reviewable, the judgment of the trial court in that respect will not be reversed unless plainly erroneous. Lufty v. Commonwealth, 126 Va. 707, 100 S.E. 829 (1919).

But such discretion may not be arbitrarily exercised to grant the Commonwealth a continuance, without good cause, when the prisoner demands trial. Benton v. Commonwealth, 90 Va. 328, 18 S.E. 282 (1893).

Prejudice against accused is not good cause for continuance. — Affidavits of the prevalence of bitter and general prejudice against the accused do not of themselves constitute good ground for a continuance. Joyce v. Commonwealth, 78 Va. 287 (1884).

Where there was adequate inquiry into the possible prejudicial effect news coverage may have had on the jury at a defendant's trial, and where, in the second trial of the defendant, after he had been convicted in his previous trial, the jurors were examined thoroughly on voir dire to guard against the possibility of unfair publicity affecting their verdict, and where such safeguards were diligently undertaken, it cannot be said that the trial judge committed constitutional error or even abused his discretion in disallowing the defendant's motion for a continuance and proceeding with the trial as provided for in this section. A contrary rule would endanger the defendant's right to a speedy trial and such delays in criminal proceedings are not to be invoked lightly. Couser v. Cox, 324 F. Supp. 1140 (W.D. Va. 1971).

Nor is want of time for counsel to consult authorities. — Under this section, the indictment and trial of a prisoner for rape forty-eight hours after the alleged commission of the crime is left to the sound discretion of the trial judge. Want of time for counsel for the defendant to consult authorities on the law of the case is not sufficient ground to support a motion for a continuance. Wright v. Commonwealth, 114 Va. 872, 77 S.E. 503 (1913).

Nor is temporary incompetency of witness for Commonwealth. — See Benton v. Commonwealth, 90 Va. 328, 18 S.E. 282 (1893).

Motion for continuance may be made before arraignment. — It is competent for the prisoner to move for a continuance before his formal arraignment. Joyce v. Commonwealth, 78 Va. 287 (1884).

On indictment for capital felony it was held error not to entertain a motion for continuance before arraignment. Anderson v. Commonwealth, 84 Va. 77, 3 S.E. 803 (1887).

It is not error to pass over a term in granting a continuance, on the prisoner's motion. Bolanz v. Commonwealth, 65 Va. (24 Gratt.) 31 (1873).

Tolling of speedy trial period. — Statutory speedy trial period was tolled beginning February 8, 2008, under the exception in § 19.2-243 that provides for tolling in the event of a continuance requested by defendant, by joint motion, or by the Commonwealth without objection by defendant. Since defendant did not object to the continuances imposed, the continuances tolled the statutory speedy trial period, and this tolling lasted until July 10, 2009, the date on which the circuit court found defendant competent to stand trial, which was three days before trial. Brown v. Commonwealth, 57 Va. App. 381, 702 S.E.2d 582, 2010 Va. App. LEXIS 490 (2010).

Applied in Wolkind v. Selph, 473 F. Supp. 675 (E.D. Va. 1979); Powell v. Commonwealth, 29 Va. App. 745, 514 S.E.2d 785 (1999); Howard v. Commonwealth, 281 Va. 455, 706 S.E.2d 885, 2011 Va. LEXIS 47 (2011).

CIRCUIT COURT OPINIONS

Second grand jury indictment following incompetency finding permitted. — When the defendant first indicted by a grand jury for capital murder and robbery was found to be mentally incompetent and confined to a state hospital, the indictment against the defendant was dismissed; however, the trial court found that a later indictment for the same crimes obtained upon the defendant's release from the hospital could not be dismissed on the ground of the passage of time as the defendant alleged. Common-

wealth v. Sink, 61 Va. Cir. 279, 2003 Va. Cir. LEXIS 18 (Portsmouth 2003).

§ 19.2-242. Accused discharged from jail if not indicted in time.

A person in jail on a criminal charge shall be discharged from imprisonment if a presentment, indictment or information be not found or filed against him before the end of the second term of the court at which he is held to answer, unless it appear to the court that material witnesses for the Commonwealth have been enticed or kept away or are prevented from attendance by sickness or inevitable accident, and except, also, in the cases provided in §§ 19.2-168.1 and 19.2-169.1. A discharge under the provisions of this section shall not, however, prevent a reincarceration after a presentment or indictment has been found.

History.
Code 1950, § 19.1-163; 1960, c. 366; 1975, c. 495.

Cross references.
As to within what time an indictment for felony must be tried, see § 19.2-243.

Law Review.
For comment, "The Defendant's Dilemma: Valid Charge or Speedy Trial," see 27 Wash. & Lee L. Rev. 175 (1970). For comment, "Jury Trials for Juvenile Delinquents in Virginia," see 28 Wash. & Lee L. Rev. 135 (1971).

CASE NOTES

The simple requirement of the statute is that some indictment shall be found before the end of the second term, or else the accused shall be discharged from imprisonment, although liable to be again arrested and tried upon any indictment that may be subsequently found against him. Waller v. Commonwealth, 84 Va. 492, 5 S.E. 364 (1888).

The word "term," as used in this statute, ought to be construed to mean, not the stated time when a court should be held, but the actual session of the court. Ex parte Santee, 4 Va. (2 Va. Cas.) 363 (1823); Commonwealth v. Cawood, 4 Va. (2 Va. Cas.) 527 (1826); Commonwealth v. Adcock, 49 Va. (8 Gratt.) 661 (1851); Brown v. Hume, 57 Va. (16 Gratt.) 456 (1864).

Second term must be grand jury term. — The second term of the court, spoken of in the statute, is the second term at which a grand jury is directed to be summoned. Jones v. Commonwealth, 60 Va. (19 Gratt.) 478 (1868).

Term at which accused is sent on not counted. — Where during a term of the court accused is sent on for indictment, that term is not considered one of the two terms at which he must be indicted under this section. Bell's Case, 48 Va. (7 Gratt.) 646 (1850); Jones v. Commonwealth, 60 Va. (19 Gratt.) 478 (1868); Glover v. Commonwealth, 86 Va. 382, 10 S.E. 420 (1889).

Special session not counted. — A special session of court held for the trial of offenses is not the third (now second) term within the meaning of the statute, but is a substitute for it, and therefore, where there was a failure to hold two regular terms, and then a special session was held, at which the prisoner was not tried, but being indicted at the regular term succeeding the special session, he ought not to be discharged from the crime, but may be tried. Commonwealth v. Lovett, 4 Va. (2 Va. Cas.) 74 (1817).

Indictment must be recorded. — Although a prisoner has in fact been arraigned on, and has pleaded to, an indictment not appearing by the record to have been found by the grand jury, and if a third actual term has passed without such record of the findings, he is entitled under this section to be discharged from the crime. Commonwealth v. Cawood, 4 Va. (2 Va. Cas.) 527 (1826);

Commonwealth v. Adcock, 49 Va. (8 Gratt.) 661 (1851).

Indictment for different offenses sufficient. — A prisoner was arrested for housebreaking with intent to kill and rob. Subsequently he was indicted for burglary and grand larceny, and was held under this indictment until the grand jury, the third which had met since his arrest, indicted him for a felonious assault. Upon the last indictment he was tried and convicted. The prisoner contended that he was entitled to his discharge because the indictment on which he was tried was not found until the third term at which a grand jury was impaneled after his arrest. It was held, that the simple requirement of the statute is that some indictment shall be found before the end of the second term, or else the accused shall be discharged from imprisonment. Manifestly the present case does not come within the statute, for here the accused was indicted by the first grand jury that met after his arrest, and the Commonwealth has only done what she has a right to do, exercise her election as to the indictment upon which the prisoner should be tried. Waller v. Commonwealth, 84 Va. 492, 5 S.E. 364 (1888).

But information for felony insufficient. — The filing of the information being unauthorized in the case of a felony, is of no avail, and an indictment must be found within the time prescribed by the statute. Jones v. Commonwealth, 60 Va. (19 Gratt.) 478 (1868).

A misdemeanor may be tried on a presentment or information, as well as on an indictment, while a felony can be tried on an indictment only, and the kind of accusation must be made within the period limited by the statute, which the nature of the offense requires. The offense in this case being a felony, it was necessary that an indictment should be found against the prisoner "before the end of the second term of the court, in which he is held to answer, unless, etc." Jones v. Commonwealth, 60 Va. (19 Gratt.) 478 (1868).

A second indictment proper when verdict set aside. — Where a second indictment was for the same act of embezzling as the first, under which the prisoner had been indicted, tried and convicted in time and the verdict set aside for variance, the second indictment was proper and in time. The prisoner was not entitled to be discharged. Commonwealth v. Adcock, 49 Va. (8 Gratt.) 661 (1851).

Question must be raised in trial court. — After the indictment is found, the question whether two terms have elapsed since the prisoner has been held to answer, without any indictment against him, should be raised by plea or otherwise. If this is not done, the question cannot be brought before the appellate court. Glover v. Commonwealth, 86 Va. 382, 10 S.E. 420 (1889).

Writ of error only extends to matters after indictment. — This motion was made before any indictment was found. The point was not raised by plea or otherwise after the indictment was found, and consequently is not brought up for review by writ of error. The writ extends only to such matters as occurred after the indictment was found. Glover v. Commonwealth, 86 Va. 382, 10 S.E. 420 (1889).

Remedy by habeas corpus before indictment found. — Where before indictment found, there was a motion made and properly overruled to discharge prisoner on the ground that two terms had elapsed since he had been held to answer without any indictment against him, the remedy was not by writ of error, but by habeas corpus, which is too late after final judgment. Bell v. Commonwealth, 49 Va. (8 Gratt.) 600 (1851); Glover v. Commonwealth, 86 Va. 382, 10 S.E. 420 (1889).

§ 19.2-243. Limitation on prosecution of felony due to lapse of time after finding of probable cause; misdemeanors; exceptions.

Where a district court has found that there is probable cause to believe that an adult has committed a felony, the accused, if he is held continuously in custody thereafter, shall be forever discharged from prosecution for such offense if no trial is commenced in the circuit court within five months from the date such probable cause was found by the district court; and if the accused is not held in custody but has been recognized for his appearance in the circuit court to answer for such offense, he shall be forever dis-

charged from prosecution therefor if no trial is commenced in the circuit court within nine months from the date such probable cause was found.

If there was no preliminary hearing in the district court, or if such preliminary hearing was waived by the accused, the commencement of the running of the five and nine months periods, respectively, set forth in this section, shall be from the date an indictment or presentment is found against the accused.

If an indictment or presentment is found against the accused but he has not been arrested for the offense charged therein, the five and nine months periods, respectively, shall commence to run from the date of his arrest thereon.

Where a case is before a circuit court on appeal from a conviction of a misdemeanor or traffic infraction in a district court, the accused shall be forever discharged from prosecution for such offense if the trial de novo in the circuit court is not commenced (i) within five months from the date of the conviction if the accused has been held continuously in custody or (ii) within nine months of the date of the conviction if the accused has been recognized for his appearance in the circuit court to answer for such offense.

The provisions of this section shall not apply to such period of time as the failure to try the accused was caused:

1. By his insanity or by reason of his confinement in a hospital for care and observation;

2. By the witnesses for the Commonwealth being enticed or kept away, or prevented from attending by sickness or accident;

3. By the granting of a separate trial at the request of a person indicted jointly with others for a felony;

4. By continuance granted on the motion of the accused or his counsel, or by concurrence of the accused or his counsel in such a motion by the attorney for the Commonwealth, or by the failure of the accused or his counsel to make a timely objection to such a motion by the attorney for the Commonwealth, or by reason of his escaping from jail or failing to appear according to his recognizance;

5. By continuance ordered pursuant to subsection I or J of § 18.2-472.1 or subsection C or D of § 19.2-187.1;

6. By the inability of the jury to agree in their verdict; or

7. By a natural disaster, civil disorder, or act of God.

But the time during the pendency of any appeal in any appellate court shall not be included as applying to the provisions of this section.

For the purposes of this section, an arrest on an indictment or warrant or information or presentment is deemed to have occurred only when such indictment, warrant, information, or presentment or the summons or capias to answer such process is served or executed upon the accused and a trial is deemed commenced at the point when jeopardy would attach or when a plea of guilty or nolo contendere is tendered by the defendant. The lodging of a detainer or its equivalent shall not constitute an arrest under this section.

History.

Code 1950, § 19.1-191; 1960, c. 366; 1974, c. 391; 1975, c. 495; 1984, c. 618; 1988, c. 33; 1993, c. 425; 1995, cc. 37, 352; 2002, c. 743; 2005, c. 650; 2007, c. 944; 2009, Sp. Sess. I, cc. 1, 4.

Cross references.

As to time for trial of criminal cases generally, see §§ 19.2-237 and 19.2-241. As to discharge of accused when not indicted before end of second term, etc., see § 19.2-242. As to the right to speedy trial, see Va. Const., Art. I, § 8.

The 2007 amendments.

The 2007 amendment by c. 944, in the first paragraph, deleted "general" preceding "district court" and substituted "an adult" for "the accused" in the first sentence.

The 2009 amendments.

The 2009 amendments by Sp. Sess. I, c. 1, effective August 21, 2009, and Sp. Sess. I, c. 4, effective September 15, 2009, are identical, and added subdivision 5 and redesignated the following subdivisions accordingly.

Law Review.

For survey of Virginia criminal law and procedure for the year 1970-1971, see 57 Va. L. Rev. 1438 (1971). For survey of Virginia law on criminal procedure for the year 1972-1973, see 59 Va. L. Rev. 1478 (1973). For survey of Virginia law on criminal procedure for the year 1974-1975, see 61 Va. L. Rev. 1713 (1975). For note, "Criminal Procedure and Criminal Law: Virginia Supreme Court Decisions During the 70's," see 15 U. Rich. L. Rev. 585 (1981). For an article, "Criminal Law and Procedure," see 31 U. Rich. L. Rev. 1015 (1997). For an article relating to all published Virginia criminal law decisions between July 1, 1997, and July 1, 1998, see 32 U. Rich. L. Rev. 1091 (1998). For 2000 survey of Virginia criminal law and procedure, see 34 U. Rich. L. Rev. 749 (2000). For article, "Legal Issues Involving Children," see 35 U. Rich. L. Rev. 741 (2001). For article surveying developments in criminal law and procedure in Virginia from July 2001 to September 2002, see 37 U. Rich. L. Rev. 45 (2002). For survey of Virginia criminal law and procedure for the year 2004-2005, see 40 U. Rich. L. Rev. 197 (2005). For 2007 annual survey article, "Criminal Law and Procedure," see 42 U. Rich. L. Rev. 311 (2007). For annual survey essay, "A Vanishing Virginia Constitution?," see 46 U. Rich. L. Rev. 347 (2011).

Michie's Jurisprudence.

For related discussion, see 2B M.J. Autrefois, Acquit and Convict, §§ 2, 22, 26; 4A M.J. Continuances, § 3; 5B M.J. Criminal Procedure, §§ 25, 39; 10A M.J. Injunctions, § 28; 12A M.J. Limitation of Actions, § 21.

CASE NOTES

I. General Consideration.
II. Terms of Court.
III. Exceptions and Excuses for Failure to Try.

I. GENERAL CONSIDERATION.

This section is not itself unconstitutional. Nail v. Slayton, 353 F. Supp. 1013 (W.D. Va. 1972).

But its procedural application may result in the deprivation of an individual's Sixth Amendment rights. Nail v. Slayton, 353 F. Supp. 1013 (W.D. Va. 1972).

This section is subordinate to constitutional right to speedy trial guaranteed by both the federal and state Constitutions. Holliday v. Commonwealth, 3 Va. App. 612, 352 S.E.2d 362 (1987).

This section is the statutory embodiment of the constitu-tional right to a speedy trial. Sheard v. Commonwealth, 12 Va. App. 227, 403 S.E.2d 178 (1991).

Section requires trial of incarcerated defendant commence within five months after probable cause found. This statutory requirement, however, does not apply to delays caused by continuances granted on the incarcerated defendant's motion. O'Dell v. Commonwealth, 234 Va. 672, 364 S.E.2d 491, cert. denied, 488 U.S. 871, 109 S. Ct. 186, 102 L. Ed. 2d 154 (1988).

Five-month requirement translates to 152 and fraction days. — The five-month requirement of this section translates to 152 and a fraction days. The Commonwealth is required to commence trial within that time. Ballance v. Commonwealth, 21 Va. App. 1, 461 S.E.2d 401 (1995); Robinson v. Commonwealth, 28 Va. App. 148, 502 S.E.2d 704 (1998).

When five-month period commences. — Under § 1-13.3 [see now § 1-210], when a statute or rule of court requires a notice to be given or any other act to be done within a certain time after any event or judgment, that time shall be in addition to the day on which the event or judgment took place; thus here, the five month speedy trial time allowance under this section did not begin to run until the day after defendant's probable cause hearing. Randolph v. Commonwealth, 22 Va. App. 334, 470 S.E.2d 132 (1996).

The five-month period begins to run on the day after the preliminary hearing at which probable cause is found. Robinson v. Commonwealth, 28 Va. App. 148, 502 S.E.2d 704 (1998).

A trial starts with arraignment when applying the rights defined in the statute, regardless of whether an evidentiary proceeding followed the arraignment. Hutchins, Jr. v. Commonwealth, No. 1439-97-3 (Ct. of Appeals Jan. 19, 1999).

The time elapsing from the finding of probable cause to the initial trial date, even though the accused concurs in the trial date, is not a continuance within the contemplation of subdivision 4 of the statute, but counts against the Commonwealth in a calculation of compliance. Ballance v. Commonwealth, 21 Va. App. 1, 461 S.E.2d 401 (1995).

This section addresses the commencement of trial, not the conclusion of proceedings. The enumerated exceptions to the statute's applicability address this requirement. The final paragraph of the statute serves the same purpose. It relates to appeals addressing matters necessary to be resolved prior to the commencement of trial. Morgan v. Commonwealth, 19 Va. App. 637, 453 S.E.2d 914 (1995).

This section uses the word "commenced" repeatedly and purposefully to define compliance with the time periods prescribed as the statutory measure of the right of an accused to a speedy trial; nowhere does the statute, including the last unnumbered paragraph, require that the trial, once timely commenced, be concluded before the termination of the time period. Johnson v. Commonwealth, 252 Va. 425, 478 S.E.2d 539 (1996).

Trial commences for jury trial when first juror is sworn for voir dire, not when the jury is sworn to try the case, which is when jeopardy attaches. Hutchins v. Commonwealth, 30 Va. App. 574, 518 S.E.2d 838 (1999), rev'd on other grounds.

The sole object of this section is to secure a speedy trial to the accused, and to guard against a protracted imprisonment or harassment by a criminal prosecution. Commonwealth v. Adcock, 49 Va. (8 Gratt.) 661 (1851); Wadley v. Commonwealth, 98 Va. 803, 35 S.E. 452 (1900); Mealy v. Commonwealth, 193 Va. 216, 68 S.E.2d 507 (1952).

This section was designed to implement the constitutional guarantee of a speedy trial under the provisions of Va. Const., Art. I, § 8. Brooks v. Peyton, 210 Va. 318, 171 S.E.2d 243 (1969).

This section is intended to assure the defendant's right to a speedy trial and society's interest in swift and certain justice. Clark v. Commonwealth, 4 Va. App. 3, 353 S.E.2d 790 (1987).

Purpose. — The legislative purpose of this limitations statute was to clarify when the right to a speedy trial is infringed and to simplify the courts' application of it. Holliday v. Commonwealth, 3 Va. App. 612, 352 S.E.2d 362 (1987).

The speedy trial statute was enacted to clarify and augment the constitutional guarantees of the Sixth Amendment to the United States Constitution and Va. Const., Art. I, § 8. Bunton v. Commonwealth, 6 Va. App. 557, 370 S.E.2d 470 (1988).

This section is conceptually and functionally related to the constitutional guarantee of a speedy trial. Fowlkes v. Commonwealth, 218 Va. 763, 240 S.E.2d 662 (1978).

This section is the interpretation by the legislature of what constitutes a "speedy trial," as that term is used in the Bills of Rights. Flanary v. Commonwealth, 184 Va. 204, 35 S.E.2d 135 (1945); Delph v. Slayton, 343 F. Supp. 449 (W.D. Va. 1972), aff'd in part, vacated in part, 471 F.2d 648 (4th Cir. 1973).

This section is merely a codification of what the legislature deems to be a speedy trial under Va. Const., Art. I, § 8. Delph v. Slayton, 343 F. Supp. 449 (W.D. Va. 1972), aff'd in part, vacated in part, 471 F.2d 648 (4th Cir. 1973).

This section is the statutory embodiment of the constitutional right to a speedy trial. Clark v. Commonwealth, 4 Va. App. 3, 353 S.E.2d 790 (1987).

At the very least this section is indicative of the legislative efforts to preclude any undue delay giving rise to a deprivation of one's right to a speedy trial. Clark v. Oliver, 346 F. Supp. 1345 (E.D. Va. 1972).

Construction of section. — This section must be construed so as to assure both a defendant's constitutional right to a speedy trial and society's interest in swift and certain justice. Clark v. Commonwealth, 4 Va. App. 3, 353 S.E.2d 790 (1987).

Imposition of a sentence against defendant after he violated the terms of an agreement that allowed him to withdraw a guilty plea to a felony in a circuit court did not violate speedy trial. Urbina v. Commonwealth, No. 2467-02-4, 2003 Va. App. LEXIS 551 (Ct. of Appeals Nov. 4, 2003).

Trial court did not err in denying defendant's motions to dismiss the indictments issued against him, as the Commonwealth did not violate his statutory speedy trial rights; defendant's trial was commenced within five months from the date that probable cause was found by the district court, which is all that the speedy trial statute required, despite the fact that the trial in which he was actually convicted, held because two previous juries caused a mistrial because they were unable to reach a verdict, was commenced more than five months after the probable cause finding. Thomas v. Commonwealth, No. 0155-03-1, 2004 Va. App. LEXIS 271 (Ct. of Appeals June 8, 2004).

Literal language, reason, and spirit of section considered. — In applying the provisions of this section the court will look at its literal language and also to its reason and spirit. Clark v. Commonwealth, 4 Va. App. 3, 353 S.E.2d 790 (1987).

Time for retrial. — When the trial of an accused has been commenced within the applicable time period prescribed by statute and, on appeal, a conviction is reversed and the case remanded for retrial, the time for retrial rests within the discretion of the trial court, a discretion measured and controlled by the constitutional standards of reasonableness and fairness; upon retrial following reversal on appeal, the right of the accused to a speedy trial is governed exclusively by the constitutional mandate. Johnson v. Commonwealth, 252 Va. 425, 478 S.E.2d 539 (1996).

This section is not applicable to recidivist proceedings because they are not criminal prosecutions. Tyson v. Hening, 205 Va. 389, 136 S.E.2d 832, cert. denied, 379 U.S. 867, 85 S. Ct. 139, 13 L. Ed. 2d 71 (1964).

Delay prior to preliminary hearing and indictment. — Where the delay of which the defendant complains occurred prior to the preliminary hearing and the issuance of the indictment, the limitation periods of this section are not applicable. His claim, therefore, must be based on the constitutional guarantees of a speedy trial. Holliday v. Commonwealth, 3 Va. App. 612, 352 S.E.2d 362 (1987).

The protection granted an accused under this section is not self-operative. It may be claimed or it may be waived. Brooks v. Peyton, 210 Va. 318, 171 S.E.2d 243 (1969); Stephens v. Commonwealth, 225 Va. 224, 301 S.E.2d 22 (1983); Laidler v. Commonwealth, No. 0161-99-4, 2000 Va. App. LEXIS 227 (Ct. of Appeals Mar. 28, 2000).

Accused is not required to take any action to avail himself of his statutory right to speedy trial. The affirmative duty to act in bringing about a speedy trial rests with the Commonwealth, and the accused may stand mute without waiving his right so long as his actions do not constitute a concurrence in or necessitate the delay. Cantwell v. Commonwealth, 2 Va. App. 606, 347 S.E.2d 523 (1986).

An accused may remain silent, making no demands, without forfeiting the right to have the charges against him or her timely heard. Bunton v. Commonwealth, 6 Va. App. 557, 370 S.E.2d 470 (1988).

"The failure ... of ... [appellant] to insist at the docket call on [February 22, 1994], to set the trial within the prescribed period did not extend the period within which [appellant] must be brought to trial." Stinnie v. Commonwealth, 21 Va. App. 610, 466 S.E.2d 752 (1996).

"[A] defendant does not waive his right to a speedy trial merely because he remains silent or does not demand that a trial date be set within the prescribed period." Stinnie v. Commonwealth, 21 Va. App. 610, 466 S.E.2d 752 (1996).

This section is inapplicable to retrial following reversal on appeal. Morgan v. Commonwealth, 19 Va. App. 637, 453 S.E.2d 914 (1995).

Scope of review. — Proper assessment and determination of the merits of a claim pursuant to this section involve a review of the whole record and a consideration of the trial court orders in the context of the record that comes before the Court of Appeals. Baity v. Commonwealth, 16 Va. App. 497, 431 S.E.2d 891 (1993).

Waiver. — Failure to invoke the provisions of this section until after final judgment is a waiver of the protection afforded thereunder. Brooks v. Peyton, 210 Va. 318, 171 S.E.2d 243 (1969).

Although counsel and trial judge informally discussed speedy trial requirements, record failed to show that defendant alleged a speedy trial violation or moved to dismiss indictments based on § 19.2-243, and therefore Rule 5A:18 barred consideration of speedy trial issue on appeal. Laidler v. Commonwealth, No. 0161-99-4 (Ct. of Appeals Mar. 28, 2000).

The protection granted an accused under this section is not self-operative; it may be claimed or it may be waived. Laidler v. Commonwealth, No. 0161-99-4 (Ct. of Appeals Mar. 28, 2000).

Waiver by guilty plea. — A guilty plea waives any contention that the speedy trial provisions of this section were violated. Williams v. Commonwealth, 33 Va. App. 725, 536 S.E.2d 916, 2000 Va. App. LEXIS 734 (2000).

It is the duty of officers to obtain trial. — It is the duty of officers charged with the responsibility of enforcing the criminal laws of the Commonwealth to prepare for and obtain a trial of an accused within the three regular terms of court specified in this section. Flanary v. Commonwealth, 184 Va. 204, 35 S.E.2d 135 (1945).

Affirmative duty rests on Commonwealth to bring about speedy trial, and accused may stand mute without waiving his rights so long as his actions do not constitute concurrency in or necessitate delay of trial. Moten v. Commonwealth, 7 Va. App. 438, 374 S.E.2d 704 (1988).

The burden rests with the prosecuting authority to ensure that an accused is accorded his or her constitutional and statutory right. Bunton v. Commonwealth, 6 Va. App. 557, 370 S.E.2d 470 (1988).

Burden to explain delay. — If the accused is not tried within the time specified in this section, the burden is on the Commonwealth to explain the delay. Powell v. Commonwealth, 29 Va. App. 745, 514 S.E.2d 785 (1999).

When an accused asserts that he has been denied a speedy trial, the burden is on the Commonwealth to explain and excuse the delay. Heath v. Commonwealth, 32 Va. App. 176, 526 S.E.2d 798, 2000 Va. App. LEXIS 278 (2000), aff'd, 261 Va. 389, 541 S.E.2d 906 (2001).

It is the prosecution which has the responsibility of vindicating society's interests in swift and certain justice, and the burden of demonstrating that a delay in commencing trial is excused under this section lies upon the Commonwealth. Heath v. Commonwealth, 32 Va. App. 176, 526 S.E.2d 798, 2000 Va. App. LEXIS 278 (2000), aff'd, 261 Va. 389, 541 S.E.2d 906 (2001).

The section was enacted for the prisoner's protection. — The constitutional guarantee of a speedy trial carried into this section is for the prisoner's protection, and as against him is no warrant for undue haste. Smith v. Commonwealth, 155 Va. 1111, 156 S.E. 577 (1931).

Trial need not be complete. — Under this section the trial need not be a complete trial in which final judgment is entered not later than during the third term; if the accused is actually brought to trial within the time required, this section has been sufficiently complied with. Butts v. Commonwealth, 145 Va. 800, 133 S.E. 764 (1926).

This code section requires the timely commencement of trial, not that trial be concluded within the specified five month period. Riddick v. Commonwealth, 22 Va. App. 136, 468 S.E.2d 135 (1996).

Final judgment need not be entered during third term. — Where an accused is actually brought to trial within the time required by this section, but from some adventitious cause, without fault on the part of the Commonwealth, final judgment cannot be entered during such term, or where a further delay for a reasonable time is necessary to consider some motion or application of the accused, this section has been sufficiently complied with. Howell v. Commonwealth, 186 Va. 894, 45 S.E.2d 165 (1947).

Plea is analogous to autrefois acquit or convict. — Defendants were entitled to no more under their motion that they be forever discharged from prosecution for the offense charged in a second indictment, than under their plea of former discharge under the first indictment, and both are analogous to the plea of autrefois acquit or convict. Commonwealth v. Davis, 17 Va. L. Reg. 509 (1911).

Applicability of five month limitation. — In the instant case, the five month limitation would have applied only if defendant had been "continuously in custody," and he had not been in continuous custody, since his second arrest began a separate confinement. Robbs v. Commonwealth, 252 Va. 433, 478 S.E.2d 699 (1996).

Larceny and embezzlement are not the same offense for determining time limits under this section. Cera v. Commonwealth, No. 0432-94-4 (Ct. of Appeals May 2, 1995).

What law governs. — The question of a prisoner's right to be discharged because of failure to try him, arising after this section went into operation, must be governed by this section. Commonwealth v. Adcock, 49 Va. (8 Gratt.) 661 (1851).

Scope of review by federal court. — Unless this section is itself a violation of the Sixth Amendment because of its very terms, so that the requisite federal question under 28 U.S.C. § 2254 (a) is present, the federal courts cannot review the manner in which the state courts choose to apply or even misapply their own statutes as long as such application or misapplication does not violate an individual's federal rights. Delph v. Slayton, 343 F. Supp. 449 (W.D. Va. 1972), aff'd in part, vacated in part on other grounds, 471 F.2d 648 (4th Cir. 1973).

The federal court is not bound by the state's interpretation of what constitutes a speedy trial. If this section is itself a violation of the Sixth Amendment or if the time involved in a case in face deprives petitioner of a speedy trial, the federal court may invalidate the state statute or the state procedure. Nail v. Slayton, 353 F. Supp. 1013 (W.D. Va. 1972).

Habeas corpus. — Since the right to a discharge under a statute, which provides that if a person is not tried within a specified time he shall be discharged, is not absolute in the sense that a mere lapse of time ousts the court of jurisdiction, a judgment of conviction is not void so as to subject it to collateral attack by writ of habeas corpus. Brooks v. Peyton, 210 Va. 318, 171 S.E.2d 243 (1969).

Defendant deprived of right to speedy trial. — Where the continuance of the proceeding to the next term of court was not on the motion of either the accused or the Commonwealth, and the continuance was not the cause of failure to try the accused, the delay caused by the continuance could not be excluded from the provisions of this section. Nelms v. Commonwealth, 11 Va. App. 639, 400 S.E.2d 799 (1991).

Where the Commonwealth, without any hindrance or delay from the defendant, could have fixed the trial date at its convenience within the five-month period and instead voluntarily chose to set the trial date after the five-month period had expired, this section barred the prosecution of the defendant. Taylor v. Commonwealth, 12 Va. App. 425, 404 S.E.2d 86 (1991).

Defendant's right to speedy trial was violated where the defendant was held continuously in custody from September 8, 1988, the date probable cause was found by the district court, until his trial began on October 2, 1989; during such period the case was not continued as a result of continuances requested or concurred in by the defendant. May v. Commonwealth, No. 1090-92-3 (Ct. of Appeals July 27, 1993).

The Commonwealth has the burden of showing that defendant's suppression motion and the time taken by the trial court to rule thereon caused a delay which was attributable to him; where nothing in the record showed that the filing of the motion necessitated a slow-down of the judicial process, his subsequent trial was held in violation of the nine month limitation provision. Robbs v. Commonwealth, 252 Va. 433, 478 S.E.2d 699 (1996).

When the district court certified and transferred defendant for trial as an adult in the circuit court, the district court necessarily found the requisite probable cause contemplated by the speedy trial statute. Because the transfer order directed that defendant be "remanded to jail," the prescribed five month limitation of this section commenced on October 4, 1995. It was immaterial that such custody coincided with detention of defendant incidental to an unrelated commitment. Irrespective of the trial court's order to quash, the initial indictments of defendant were a nullity, obtained without the benefit of the enabling order required by subsection B of § 16.1-269.6, and the court simply remedied of record an error or oversight in the proceedings, without disturbing the legal efficacy of the pending transfer order or effecting a nolle prosequi. Accordingly, defendant was held continuously in custody from the finding of probable cause in the district court on October 4, 1995, until trial on July 11, 1996, in violation of this section, and the court had to reverse and dismiss the convictions. Price v. Commonwealth, 25 Va. App. 655, 492 S.E.2d 447 (1997), aff'd, 256 Va. 373, 506 S.E.2d 317 (1998).

Where not only was no order entered setting an initial trial date for defendant's jury trial, but no order was entered setting a continued trial date, the Commonwealth had not borne its burden by proving a delay countenanced by this section; therefore, defendant's convictions for second degree murder and use of a firearm in the commission of murder were reversed. Powell v. Commonwealth, 29 Va. App. 745, 514 S.E.2d 785 (1999).

The defendant was not prosecuted in a timely manner where, after the conclusion of appellate proceedings in a civil matter ancillary to the criminal proceeding, 12 months elapsed to the date of her trial and the record reflected no justifiable basis for the delay. Battle v. Commonwealth, No. 1757-97-1 (Ct. of Appeals Dec. 8, 1998).

Defendant's right to speedy trial was not violated because, although he objected to a continuance being counted against him, he agreed to the trial date, which fell outside of the speedy trial time frame in the § 19.2-243. Accordingly, the trial court did not err in finding that defendant was tried within the statutory speedy trial period. Hall v. Commonwealth, 2009 Va. App. LEXIS 467 (Oct. 20, 2009).

Defendant not deprived of right to speedy trial. — See Nail v. Slayton, 353 F. Supp. 1013 (W.D. Va. 1972).

Where an indictment was presented at the November term of the grand jury and was returned "not a true bill" on November 19, 1984, this action by the grand jury operated to discharge appellant on the charge. Presumably the grand jury determined that there was not sufficient cause to hold him. Had appellant not been incarcerated on an unrelated criminal conviction, he would have been entitled to be discharged from custody once the grand jury failed to return an indictment against him. Therefore, as of November 19, 1984, this section ceased to apply. A second grand jury returned a true bill of indictment on February 19, 1985, for the same offense, and appellant was brought to trial within two months of that indictment. There was no denial of a speedy trial within the contemplation of this section. Presley v. Commonwealth, 2 Va. App. 348, 344 S.E.2d 195 (1986); Rogers v. Commonwealth, 5 Va. App. 337, 362 S.E.2d 752 (1987).

The failure to try the defendant in accordance with this section resulted from his motion for time to prepare for trial pro se after dismissing counsel; unlike a continuance granted to an individual accused of a felony to initially obtain counsel, a continuance of a trial, previously set, requested by the accused to prepare for trial, benefits only him. Stinnie v. Commonwealth, 22 Va. App. 726, 473 S.E.2d 83 (1996).

Because the defendant never announced that he was ready for trial until the Commonwealth tried to set a trial date, and did in fact not even stand ready for trial on the first date set, and because the Commonwealth was ready to proceed well within the remaining time under this section, the defendant's statutory speedy trial rights were not violated. Jefferson v. Commonwealth, 23 Va. App. 652, 479 S.E.2d 80 (1996).

Defendant's right to speedy trial was not violated where the continuances that delayed his trial beyond the five-month period provided by this section were attributable to, or acquiesced in, by the defense. Watkins v. Commonwealth, 26 Va. App. 335, 494 S.E.2d 859 (1998).

A defendant was not denied his right to a speedy trial when the Commonwealth commenced trial 183 days after the general district court made its finding of probable cause and 92 of those days were chargeable to the defendant; the defendant was chargeable with the periods that elapsed due to his own motions for continuances and also with the period that elapsed when the defendant failed to object to a motion for continuance made by the Commonwealth. Robinson v. Commonwealth, 28 Va. App. 148, 502 S.E.2d 704 (1998).

Speedy trial requirement was not violated where defendant's trial was timely commenced but was disrupted by mistrial when prosecution unintentionally failed to comply with discovery order; retrial was merely an extension of the earlier proceeding and did not implicate a new speedy trial timeframe. Fisher v. Commonwealth, 26 Va. App. 788, 497 S.E.2d 162 (1988).

A defendant was not denied the right to a speedy trial although there was a 16-month interval between the preliminary hearing and the trial, where the defendant either requested or agreed to every continuance granted by the circuit court under the original indictments and where, when the time attributable to those continuances was subtracted from the total time the case was pending in the circuit court before trial, the record showed that the defendant was tried within the time restrictions imposed by this section. Johnson v. Commonwealth, 259 Va. 654, 529 S.E.2d 769, 2000 Va. LEXIS 60, cert. denied, 531 U.S. 981, 121 S. Ct. 432, 148 L. Ed. 2d 439 (2000).

Where defendant agreed, within the five-month period fixed by § 19.2-243, to an original trial date beyond the five-month period, because defendant's agreement to the trial date was confirmed by the trial court before he was indicted, defendant was not charged with the time pending before his indictment, but the time between his indictment and his trial was removed from the five-month period; when that time was subtracted from the total time defendant was held continuously in custody from the date of his preliminary hearing, defendant was tried well within the five-month limitation period of § 19.2-243, and there was no speedy trial violation. Hudson v. Commonwealth, 267 Va. 36, 591 S.E.2d 679, 2004 Va. LEXIS 14 (2004).

Because a delay for counsel's motion to withdraw and two later continuances were properly attributed to defendant, he was held in custody for 120 days from the finding of probable cause until his release to pre-trial services; consequently, defendant's right to a speedy trial under § 19.2-243 was not violated. Booker v. Commonwealth, — Va. App. —, — S.E.2d —, 2006 Va. App. LEXIS 591 (Dec. 28, 2006).

Process which resulted in a trial on the merits within the statutorily described time did not support a presumption of prejudice. Jones v. Commonwealth, 2008 Va. App. LEXIS 84 (Feb. 19, 2008).

Because defendant did not object to the continuance from January 26th to February 8th, the speedy trial statute by its own terms did not apply to that period. It necessarily followed that defendant could not preserve a right he never had by simply refusing to waive it. Sigsby v. Commonwealth, — Va. App. —, — S.E.2d —, 2008 Va. App. LEXIS 137 (Mar. 18, 2008).

Delay based on conduct of defendant. — Trial court properly denied defendant's motion to dismiss the two criminal charges filed against him on the allegation that his speedy trial rights under § 19.2-243 had been violated as defendant only could have been considered to have been held in continuous custody beyond the five-month time period allowed in the statute by virtue of his own conduct in refusing to sign a personal recognizance bond since he had been physically released before the speedy trail deadline date. White v. Commonwealth, 37 Va. App. 658, 561 S.E.2d 12, 2002 Va. App. LEXIS 162 (2002).

Detention as fugitive out-of-state. — Detention in North Carolina on accusation of being a fugitive is not the same as "arrest thereon" as used in this section with respect to Virginia indictment against defendant. His detention in North Carolina gave Virginia no rights with respect to him; thus, this section first came into play with defendant's arrest upon his delivery to Virginia authorities, not 11 months earlier when he was detained in North Carolina on the fugitive warrant. Williamson v. Commonwealth, 13 Va. App. 655, 414 S.E.2d 609 (1992).

Review confined to record in determining responsibility for delay. — In determining responsibility for the delay of a criminal trial, the court must confine its review to the record before it. Because of the fragility of memories, representations of counsel or even of the trial judge, if not supported by the record, are insufficient. Williams v. Commonwealth, 2 Va. App. 566, 347 S.E.2d 146 (1986).

Inadequate record. — Because the transcript that was provided did not include the hearing during which the issue of whether a witness was "kept away" under subdivision 2 of § 19.2-243, the transcript was insufficient to permit resolution of appellate issues under Va. Sup. Ct. R. 5A:8(b)(4)(ii). Gardner v. Commonwealth, No. 2367-09-1, 2010 Va. App. LEXIS 482 (Ct. of Appeals Dec. 14, 2010).

Delay held too great and without good cause. — Where a federal prisoner had been prejudiced by the delay in state prosecution of over a year, in spite of his repeated efforts to bring the case to trial, the delay was too great and without good cause. Taylor v. Virginia, 353 F. Supp. 1323 (W.D. Va. 1973).

A 55-day delay which occurred as a result of a continuance granted on motion of the Commonwealth was not chargeable against the Commonwealth since when the motion was made, the defendant was present in court with his attorney and the defense attorney did not simply remain passive, but expressly affirmed the attorney for the Commonwealth's assertion to the court that the motion was "by agreement," and twice affirmatively stated, "we have no objection." Corey v. Commonwealth, 8 Va. App. 281, 381 S.E.2d 19 (1989).

Defendant held for trial within meaning of section. — Since at all times subsequent to his indictment for an escape felony defendant was held by the Commonwealth in its penal institutions and was available for trial in the court in which the case was pending, he was being held for trial within the meaning of this section and was entitled to claim its protection. Knott v. Commonwealth, 215 Va. 531, 211 S.E.2d 86 (1975).

Applied in Foster v. Commonwealth, 8 Va. App. 167, 380 S.E.2d 12 (1989); Arnold v. Commonwealth, 18 Va. App. 218, 443 S.E.2d 183 (1994); Yiaadey v. Commonwealth, 29 Va. App. 535, 513 S.E.2d 446 (1999); Harris v. Commonwealth, 258 Va. 576, 520 S.E.2d 825 (1999); Bonds v. Beale, 145 F. Supp. 2d 708, 2001 U.S. Dist. LEXIS 5572 (E.D. Va. 2001); Ragsdale v. Commonwealth, 38 Va. App. 421, 565 S.E.2d 331, 2002 Va. App. LEXIS 366 (2002); Bailey v. Commonwealth, 38 Va. App. 794, 568 S.E.2d 440, 2002 Va. App. LEXIS 527 (2002).

II. TERMS OF COURT.

This section contemplates terms actually held, not terms merely provided for by law. Ex parte Santee, 4 Va. (2 Va. Cas.) 363 (1823); Commonwealth v. Cawood, 4 Va. (2 Va. Cas.) 527 (1826); Brown v. Hume, 57 Va. (16 Gratt.) 456 (1864).

The word "term" in this section ought to be construed to mean, not the stated time when a court should be held, but the actual session of the court, and this construction must be given to the word in all three of the clauses of this section. Therefore, where a prisoner was remanded for trial by the examining court in July, 1822, and at the October term the court did not sit, and at the May term, 1823, the cause was continued for the Commonwealth, and at the third term, in October, 1823, there was no court, the prisoner was not entitled to be forever discharged of the crime. Ex parte Santee, 4 Va. (2 Va. Cas.) 363 (1823).

And not partial ones. — This section contemplates complete terms, not partial ones. Bell v. Commonwealth, 49 Va. (8 Gratt.) 600 (1851); Sands v. Commonwealth, 61 Va. (20 Gratt.) 800 (1871).

All terms of court, criminal and civil, must be considered regular terms for purposes of the time limitation imposed by this section. Woodard v. Commonwealth, 214 Va. 495, 201 S.E.2d 785 (1974).

Special sessions are not included. — A special session was not one of the terms contemplated by this section. Commonwealth v. Lovett, 4 Va. (2 Va. Cas.) 74 (1817).

Term of indictment is not to be counted. — The term at which a prisoner is indicted for a felony is not to be counted as one of the terms contemplated by this section. The terms are those after the prisoner has been indicted and held for trial. Kibler v. Commonwealth, 94 Va. 804, 26 S.E. 858 (1897); Flanary v. Commonwealth, 184 Va. 204, 35 S.E.2d 135 (1945); Butts v. Commonwealth, 145 Va. 800, 133 S.E. 764 (1926).

Defendant was indicted and held for trial at the July term, which is therefore excluded from computation of three regular terms within the meaning of this section. Woodard v. Commonwealth, 214 Va. 495, 201 S.E.2d 785 (1974).

Nor term at which case is continued by agreement of counsel. Kibler v. Commonwealth, 94 Va. 804, 26 S.E. 858 (1897).

Nor is term at which prisoner is first held for trial. — The three terms spoken of in this section are three terms after that at which the prisoner is first held for trial. And though a prisoner has been arrested and committed to jail, or gives bail to appear and does appear, or is brought into court, on the first day of a term of a court, that term is not to be counted as one of the three terms aforesaid. Bell's Case, 48 Va. (7 Gratt.) 646 (1850); Bell v. Commonwealth, 49 Va. (8 Gratt.) 600 (1851); Sands v. Commonwealth, 61 Va. (20 Gratt.) 800 (1871).

When case continued without being set for trial, time period which follows is not tolled. — When an accused appears before a trial court for the appointment of counsel and the case is continued to the next docket call without being set for trial, the period of time which follows is not tolled under this section. Nelms v. Commonwealth, 11 Va. App. 639, 400 S.E.2d 799 (1991).

Original indictment supplanted by second indictment. — When an original indictment is supplanted by a second indictment, the terms contemplated by the statute are to be counted from the time of the second indictment. Brooks v. Peyton, 210 Va. 318, 171 S.E.2d 243 (1969); Miller v. Commonwealth, 217 Va. 929, 234 S.E.2d 269 (1977), cert. denied, 434 U.S. 1016, 98 S. Ct. 735, 54 L. Ed. 2d 762 (1978).

III. EXCEPTIONS AND EXCUSES FOR FAILURE TO TRY.

Failure to commence trial was caused by court. — Where failure to commence trial of accused within the statutorily mandated time limitations was caused solely by the trial court's failure, well within the statutory time limitation, to fix a timely trial date, the accused has been denied his statutory right to a speedy trial; thus the initial 15 days granted to the accused to obtain his own counsel was not a delay contemplated and accommodated by the time limitation of this section and could not toll the applicable nine month limitation. Baity v. Commonwealth, 16 Va. App. 497, 431 S.E.2d 891 (1993).

Enumeration does not exclude other excuses in pari ratione. — The exceptions or excuses for failure to try the prisoner enumerated in this section are not intended to exclude others of a similar nature, or in pari ratione. The prisoner is entitled to his discharge only if the Commonwealth has been in default for three terms without any of the excuses for the failure enumerated in this section, or any like excuses fairly implied by the courts from the reason and spirit of the law. Commonwealth v. Adcock, 49 Va. (8 Gratt.) 661 (1851).

The General Assembly has enumerated circumstances which excuse "the failure to try." This enumeration was not intended to exclude other circumstances in pari ratione. Knott v. Commonwealth, 215 Va. 531, 211 S.E.2d 86 (1975).

The granting of separate trials at the request of a defendant, when he has been indicted on different charges, is not in pari ratione with the statutory listed excuse. The case of a defendant indicted for two completely different felonies is in no way analogous to that of a defendant jointly indicted with others for the commission of a felony. The statute speaks to a situation where only one crime is involved, the witnesses against all defendants are most likely the same witnesses, and the exhibits are the same. For these and other reasons, the granting of separate trials to persons jointly indicted would necessarily bring about delay which should be charged to a defendant who seeks a severance. Walker v. Commonwealth, 225 Va. 5, 301 S.E.2d 28 (1983).

This section sets forth five circumstances that excuse the failure to try an accused within the prescribed time period, including those instances where the delay was caused by continuance granted on the motion of the accused, or by his concurrence in a motion by the Commonwealth. The enumerated exceptions are not all-inclusive; others of a similar nature may be implied. The exceptions, both express and implied, often look to the defendant's actions which tend to delay the trial. Cantwell v. Commonwealth, 2 Va. App. 606, 347 S.E.2d 523 (1986).

The Commonwealth must be at fault, to entitle prisoner to

his discharge under this section. Ex parte Santee, 4 Va. (2 Va. Cas.) 363 (1823).

Burden is on the Commonwealth to prove that the delay in trying appellant was excusable, based either on one of the reasons enumerated in the statute or on appellant's waiver of his right to be tried within the designated period. Shavin v. Commonwealth, 17 Va. App. 256, 437 S.E.2d 411 (1993).

Federal injunction against trial obtained by prisoner is an excuse. — A prisoner was not entitled to be discharged from prosecution on the ground that four regular terms of court elapsed after the indictment was found without a trial, where the trial was prevented by an injunction from a federal court obtained at the instance of the prisoner. Wadley v. Commonwealth, 98 Va. 803, 35 S.E. 452 (1900).

While an injunction from a federal court is not among the exceptions enumerated in this section, it is within its spirit and reason. The object of this section is to insure speedy trials, and, in enumerating certain exceptions, it was not intended to exclude others of like nature. Wadley v. Commonwealth, 98 Va. 803, 35 S.E. 452 (1900).

As is reversal of prior conviction. — Where a prisoner pleaded that he had been held for trial more than four terms after indictment, a replication that during that period the prisoner had been convicted and the conviction reversed, and that he had been held until reversal for punishment, not for trial, was held sufficient. Smith v. Commonwealth, 85 Va. 924, 9 S.E. 148 (1889). See also Commonwealth v. Adcock, 49 Va. (8 Gratt.) 661 (1851).

If a prisoner has been tried and convicted of a crime, and a new trial awarded to him, although he should not be tried again until after the third term, subsequent to his examination, he is not entitled to a discharge. Vance v. Commonwealth, 4 Va. (2 Va. Cas.) 162 (1819).

New prosecution after case nolle prossed started speedy trial clock anew. — By reconsidering its decision in a prior proceeding to grant the Commonwealth's nolle prosequi motion and not running the speedy trial deadline anew in the second proceeding, the trial court erred in concluding that the Virginia Speedy Trial Act, § 19.2-243, barred defendant's prosecution under a second set of indictments. Commonwealth v. Smith, 2012 Va. App. LEXIS 372 (Nov. 20, 2012).

Right to speedy trial exists even if defendant was detained in a different jurisdiction. — Defendant's right to a speedy trial under this section required that he be tried within five months after he was detained in Virginia following indictment even though he was detained in a different jurisdiction from that in which his charge was pending. Funk v. Commonwealth, 16 Va. App. 694, 432 S.E.2d 193 (1993).

The right to speedy trial or discharge may be waived. — Failure to invoke the constitutional provision until after verdict and final judgment is a waiver, and right to discharge may not be asserted for the first time in the Supreme Court on a record involving the merits of the case. Butts v. Commonwealth, 145 Va. 800, 133 S.E. 764 (1926); Rose v. Commonwealth, 189 Va. 771, 55 S.E.2d 33 (1949).

The right to a speedy trial may be waived if the defendant is aware of his rights. Delph v. Slayton, 343 F. Supp. 449 (W.D. Va. 1972), aff'd in part, vacated in part, 471 F.2d 648 (4th Cir. 1973).

A defendant may agree to a general waiver of his or her statutory speedy trial rights, in which instance the accused foregoes his or her rights granted by this section. Additionally, an accused may make a limited waiver of that right, in which instance the accused foregoes the statutory protection for a specified period of time. Mitchell v. Commonwealth, 30 Va. App. 520, 518 S.E.2d 330 (1999).

Where a defendant affirmatively agreed to a trial date beyond the statutory time period, he waived his right to be tried within the time periods set by statute. Hudson v. Commonwealth, 39 Va. App. 240, 572 S.E.2d 486, 2002 Va. App. LEXIS 697 (2002), aff'd, 267 Va. 36, 591 S.E.2d 679 (2004).

And consent by the prisoner to a continuance which would prevent the operation of this section is such a waiver, and may be given either in person or by counsel, at all events before arraignment. Kibler v. Commonwealth, 94 Va. 804, 26 S.E. 858 (1897); Butts v. Commonwealth, 145 Va. 800, 133 S.E. 764 (1926); Flanary v. Commonwealth, 184 Va. 204, 35 S.E.2d 135 (1945). On the question of the necessity for the presence of the accused when his counsel moves for a continuance after arraignment, see the cases above cited and Benton v. Commonwealth, 91 Va. 782, 21 S.E. 495 (1895).

Subdivision (4) of this section amounts to a provision for a waiver of the right to a speedy trial when defendant requests a continuance. Delph v. Slayton, 343 F. Supp. 449 (W.D. Va. 1972), aff'd in part, vacated in part on other grounds, 471 F.2d 648 (4th Cir. 1973).

Where a defendant moves for, or concurs in the continuance of a trial date, such action tolls the running of the speedy trial bar and that time is specifically excepted under subdivision 4. Mitchell v. Commonwealth, 30 Va. App. 520, 518 S.E.2d 330 (1999).

Defendant's actions in acquiescing with and agreeing to the order, signed by the defendant and his counsel, which was entered well within the five-month period, constituted a continuance of the trial date within the intendment of subdivision (4) of this section. The defendant made no objection to this continuance, and, in fact, affirmatively agreed to the trial date. Commonwealth v. Hutchins, 260 Va. 293, 533 S.E.2d 622, 2000 Va. LEXIS 122 (2000).

However, continuance moved for or concurred in by defendant, while not included in the timeframe within which the Commonwealth must commence trial, does not waive or bar a defendant's right to assert a speedy trial claim. Mitchell v. Commonwealth, 30 Va. App. 520, 518 S.E.2d 330 (1999).

Continuance requested by defendant. — When the defendant requests and is granted a continuance for an indefinite period of time, the speedy trial period will not recommence until the defendant announces to the Commonwealth that he stands ready for trial; where the accused affirmatively acts and invites the delay in the commencement of trial by such motion, there is no violation of his speedy trial right. Heath v. Commonwealth, 32 Va. App. 176, 526 S.E.2d 798, 2000 Va. App. LEXIS 278 (2000), aff'd, 261 Va. 389, 541 S.E.2d 906 (2001).

Defendant's § 19.2-243 right to a speedy trial was not violated because, after defendant's arrest, his counsel requested a continuance of slightly over two months, and, at a later docket call date, new defense counsel requested another continuance and agreed to set the trial on a date that was well outside the 152-day deadline; subdivision 4 of this section tolls the statutory speedy trial clock based on actions taken by the accused or his counsel. Although defendant argued that he did not consent to new defense counsel's representation, the transcript made clear that counsel appeared on defendant's behalf to serve as his advocate, and defendant introduced no evidence to nullify this attorney/client relationship. Wyant v. Commonwealth, 2008 Va. App. LEXIS 574 (Dec. 30, 2008).

Continuance not objected to by defendant. — Where defendant, who was charged with issuing bad checks, did not object to a continuance to allow for the completion of an expert handwriting analysis based in part upon a handwriting exemplar provided by defendant, any delay in prosecuting defendant did not count toward the nine-month statutory period for prosecuting defendant under the speedy trial statute. Hunt v. Commonwealth, — Va. App. —, — S.E.2d —, 2006 Va. App. LEXIS 22 (Jan. 24, 2006).

There was no violation of § 19.2-243, because defendant could not complain of continuances agreed to by defense counsel or a continuance due to the unavailability of a material witness for the Commonwealth for medical reasons. Withee v. Commonwealth, 2008 Va. App. LEXIS 488 (Nov. 4, 2008).

No violation of defendant's statutory speedy trial rights occurred because defendant's trial occurred within the five-month period specified by § 19.2-243; the five-month speedy trial period was tolled because defendant failed to object to the continuance effected on the trial court's motion. Howard v. Commonwealth, 55 Va. App. 417, 686 S.E.2d 537, 2009 Va. App. LEXIS 569 (2009), aff'd, 281 Va. 455, 706 S.E.2d 885, 2011 Va. LEXIS 47 (2011).

Trial court properly denied defendant's motion to dismiss on statutory speedy trial grounds where the speedy trial statute was tolled during a joint continuance period and, therefore, defendant's trial occurred 126 days after the finding of probable cause, well within the statutory limit. The trial court's entry of the joint continuance order, endorsed by defendant's counsel, combined with a transcript of defendant's statements from that date, and defendant's admission in a subsequent hearing that he did not say anything about the continuance, supported the trial court's determination. Wimbush v. Commonwealth, 2010 Va. App. LEXIS 185 (May 11, 2010).

Tolling provisions of § 19.2-243, the speedy trial statute, applied to a trial court order entered sua sponte continuing defendant's

trial date where defendant did not object to the continuance. Howard v. Commonwealth, 281 Va. 455, 706 S.E.2d 885, 2011 Va. LEXIS 47 (2011).

Expressing a desire for separate trials does not thereby instigate a proceeding which should have caused any undue delay. Walker v. Commonwealth, 225 Va. 5, 301 S.E.2d 28 (1983).

Defendant may request or concur in continuance and simultaneously waive his statutory speedy trial rights. However, the two are separate and distinct. Mitchell v. Commonwealth, 30 Va. App. 520, 518 S.E.2d 330 (1999).

A continuance has the effect of excluding the time for the delay from the period attributable to the Commonwealth. A waiver, however, foregoes the accused's right to assert the speedy trial statute as a bar to prosecution notwithstanding the effect of the statute. Mitchell v. Commonwealth, 30 Va. App. 520, 518 S.E.2d 330 (1999).

But silence or failure to demand trial is not a waiver. — Proof that the accused remained silent or that he did not demand a trial is not sufficient to overcome the prima facie case made by accused when he has established the fact that three regular terms of the circuit court have been held without trial of an indictment for a felony pending therein. Flanary v. Commonwealth, 184 Va. 204, 35 S.E.2d 135 (1945).

The mere silence of the accused or his failure to demand that his case be submitted to a jury within the time prescribed by this section does not estop him from claiming its benefits. Howell v. Commonwealth, 186 Va. 894, 45 S.E.2d 165 (1947).

The silence of the defendant except to request separate trials is not sufficient to preclude defendant from availing himself of the protections of this section or the constitutional guarantee of a speedy trial. Walker v. Commonwealth, 225 Va. 5, 301 S.E.2d 28 (1983).

A defendant does not waive his right to a speedy trial merely because he remains silent or does not demand that a trial date be set within the prescribed period. Godfrey v. Commonwealth, 227 Va. 460, 317 S.E.2d 781 (1984).

The defendant's attorney's failure to insist on a trial date within the statutory limit does not dispense with the requirements of this section. Nelms v. Commonwealth, 11 Va. App. 639, 400 S.E.2d 799 (1991).

Defendant's conviction was reversed where he was held continuously in custody and not tried within five months of preliminary hearing; no continuances were requested by or chargeable to him and his filing of motion for psychiatric examination did not necessitate a slow-down of the judicial process. Heath v. Commonwealth, No. 0203-98-2 (Ct. of Appeals July 6, 1999).

Nor is failure to object to continuance requested by Commonwealth. — See Flanary v. Commonwealth, 184 Va. 204, 35 S.E.2d 135 (1945).

The accused does not waive his right to a speedy trial simply by failing to oppose a motion for a continuance made by the Commonwealth. When the accused and his attorney do not object to a continuance, it is not the same as the accused being a proponent of the continuance. Pittman v. Commonwealth, 10 Va. App. 693, 395 S.E.2d 473 (1990).

Although silence itself does not constitute a waiver of rights pursuant to the speedy trial statute, silence in response to court's interpretation of a pre-existing written waiver may estop an accused from challenging the tolling of the statute until he or she registers an objection or revokes the waiver. Shavin v. Commonwealth, 17 Va. App. 256, 437 S.E.2d 411 (1993).

Defendant did not waive speedy trial right. — Where defense counsel made it clear in both words and by his specific objection to the order of continuance that he intended to rely upon the defendant's speedy trial right, even though he stated that his objection was "technical," and where defense counsel, both verbally and by written objection noted on the order, advised the trial court that the defense was not waiving its speedy trial rights, defendant did not waive his speedy trial right. Pittman v. Commonwealth, 10 Va. App. 693, 395 S.E.2d 473 (1990).

Waiver found. — By signing order which contained language that the defendant's motion for a continuance also constituted a waiver of his statutory speedy trial rights, defendant waived his right to a statutory speedy trial claim for delays preceding the waiver and until such time as the waiver ceased to be effective. Without such language, defendant's motion would have merely been a continuance and would have only tolled the clock prospectively. Mitchell v. Commonwealth, 30 Va. App. 520, 518 S.E.2d 330 (1999).

When defendant, who was charged with two sets of charges, was questioned by the trial court as to waiving his right to speedy trial, without distinguishing between the two sets of charges, and, with benefit of counsel, waived his speedy trial right, and did not object when trial dates on each set of charges were set beyond the speedy trial limit, he effectively waived his right to speedy trial as to both sets of charges. Commonwealth v. Gregory, 263 Va. 134, 557 S.E.2d 715, 2002 Va. LEXIS 5 (2002), cert. denied, 537 U.S. 838, 123 S. Ct. 156, 154 L. Ed. 2d 59 (2002).

Where the trial record unambiguously established that a continuance of defendant's trial date was ordered upon his motion, and by agreeing or requesting the same without objection, defendant waived his statutory right to a trial within five months of the date the indictment against him was filed. Tate v. Commonwealth, No. 2230-03-1, 2004 Va. App. LEXIS 484 (Ct. of Appeals Oct. 12, 2004).

Because defendant's failure to raise an objection to the trial date constituted an acquiescence to a continuance, defendant's statutory speedy trial rights under § 19.2-243 were not violated. Newsome v. Commonwealth, 2009 Va. App. LEXIS 59 (Feb. 10, 2009).

Waiver not found. — Defendant did not waive right to a speedy trial when his counsel, after objecting to a continuance granted on the Commonwealth's motion, provided an available trial date that he knew to be beyond the statutory five month speedy trial period. Baker v. Commonwealth, 25 Va. App. 19, 486 S.E.2d 111 (1997).

Appellant's request for seven separate jury trials did not constitute a waiver of his speedy trial rights under this section, thus, Commonwealth's failure to try appellant on the charges at issue within five months of his preliminary hearing resulted in a violation of this section. Norton v. Commonwealth, 19 Va. App. 97, 448 S.E.2d 892 (1994).

Filing of motions by a defendant will not in every case justify a delay beyond the time required by this section to bring him to trial. When the legislature prescribed the time period in which a defendant should be brought to trial, it necessarily envisioned that discovery and other pretrial motions would be made and decided within that time frame. The burden is always upon the Commonwealth to show that any delay was justified under one of the exceptions, express or implied, to this section. Cantwell v. Commonwealth, 2 Va. App. 606, 347 S.E.2d 523 (1986).

Where the delay from the date of the indictment to the trial was about six and one-half months, but excluding the time allowed for the continuance attributable to the defendant, the trial was held within the five-month period prescribed by this section, there was no violation of the defendant's statutory right to a speedy trial. Stewart v. Commonwealth, No. 0198-86-2 (Ct. of Appeals Sept. 16, 1987).

Time before appointment of counsel not chargeable to defendant. — The passage of time prior to the date counsel is appointed to represent a defendant is not chargeable to him. Jefferson v. Commonwealth, 33 Va. App. 230, 532 S.E.2d 899, 2000 Va. App. LEXIS 606 (2000).

Docketing hearing was not continuance chargeable to defendant. — When defendant first appeared on July 9, 2007, before the trial court, which after asking for the name of defendant's attorney set a trial date of October 31, 2007, within the five-month period prescribed by § 19.2-243, the July 9 proceeding was not a continuance, but a docketing hearing to set the initial trial date. Thus, the period between July 9 and October 31 was not chargeable to defendant. Plather v. Commonwealth, 2009 Va. App. LEXIS 144 (Mar. 24, 2009).

Delay chargeable to defendant. — Where delay of trial was from statutory limit of 152 days to 279 days due to time between filing of defendant's first motion for psychological evaluation and second psychological report delay was properly chargeable to defendant since need for second evaluation and consequent transfer order was defendant's frustration of initial evaluation. Moten v. Commonwealth, 7 Va. App. 438, 374 S.E.2d 704 (1988).

Absent satisfactory explanation by the Commonwealth for delay extending beyond the statutory period, the prosecution will be dismissed. However, delay which is attributable to the defendant "will not be counted in determining whether the Commonwealth complied" with the statutory mandate. Thomas v. Commonwealth, 16 Va. App. 851, 434 S.E.2d 319 (1993).

Where transcript from the hearing indicated that both defendant and the Commonwealth agreed to a specified court date to determine the status of defendant's competency evaluation, the number of days between the court's receipt of psychological evaluation of defendant's competency and the hearing to determine defendant's competency status were chargeable to defendant under this section. Blair v. Commonwealth, No. 2550-98-1, 2000 Va. App. LEXIS 405 (Ct. of Appeals May 30, 2000).

Commonwealth did not fail to bring defendant to trial within the time period required by § 19.2-243 where 55 days were excludable based on defendant's request for different court-appointed counsel. Angelina v. Commonwealth, — Va. App. —, — S.E.2d —, 2005 Va. App. LEXIS 233 (June 14, 2005).

Speedy trial right had not been violated, even though his trial did not take place until more than five months from a probable cause finding had passed; Two delays, one caused by a motion for substitution of counsel and one caused by a continuance requested by defendant's counsel, were attributable to defendant and once those delays were subtracted, defendant's right to a speedy trial was not violated because it was commenced within the statutory time period. Wallace v. Commonwealth, — Va. App. —, — S.E.2d —, 2005 Va. App. LEXIS 413 (Oct. 18, 2005).

Continuance for want of time to try case is no excuse. — Where a prisoner charged with felony was indicted at the first term of the circuit court after his examination, and the case was continued at that term for want of time to try it, and at the second term, the case was continued on the motion of the prisoner, upon the ground of the absence of a material witness for him, and at each of the three succeeding terms the case was again continued for want of time to try it, upon the expiration of the last of the five terms, the prisoner became entitled, under this section, to be forever discharged of the crime imputed to him. Green v. Commonwealth, 40 Va. (1 Rob.) 731 (1842).

Absence of accused when continuance requested. — No problem is presented because the accused was not present when the request for a continuance was made and granted under this section. Delph v. Slayton, 343 F. Supp. 449 (W.D. Va. 1972), aff'd in part, vacated in part on other grounds, 471 F.2d 648 (4th Cir. 1973).

Unexpected circumstances that may warrant a delay. — Time limitations for the commencement of criminal trials specified in this section contemplate that circumstances beyond the control of the trial judge and the parties, such as the sickness of a witness, or those caused, requested or concurred in by the accused, may warrant a delay in the trial to ensure a fair trial to both the accused and the Commonwealth. Baity v. Commonwealth, 16 Va. App. 497, 431 S.E.2d 891 (1993).

Commonwealth has the duty to explain the delay after the defendant raises the issue. Without anything in a court order or elsewhere in the record to show that a defendant agreed to or concurred in the delay of his trial, or instigated a proceeding which of necessity brought about a delay of his trial, the delay must be attributed to the Commonwealth. Bunton v. Commonwealth, 6 Va. App. 557, 370 S.E.2d 470 (1988).

Opportunity to explain reason for delay does not expire with statutory time period. — While most reasons for delay will be documented in records or orders of proceedings prior to the speedy trial hearing, other documentation and the explanation for the delay may become a part of the record for the first time at the speedy trial hearing. The opportunity to prove or document the reason for the delay does not expire with the running of the statutory time period during which the trial must be had. Bunton v. Commonwealth, 6 Va. App. 557, 370 S.E.2d 470 (1988).

Responsibility of trial judge. — Although in setting its docket the trial judge should consider counsel's available dates and whether the date selected is convenient for counsel, absent defendant's request for a continuance or concurrence in the Commonwealth's request or waiver of the right to a speedy trial, the trial judge has the responsibility to commence the trial within the statutorily specified time regardless of whether the date is convenient for counsel. Baker v. Commonwealth, 25 Va. App. 19, 486 S.E.2d 111 (1997).

The failure of the judge who had agreed to try defendant to appear on the trial date is not an excuse similar to those set out specifically in this section, since it would permit a judge, through inadvertence or dereliction, to circumvent the legislative determination of the requirements of a speedy trial. Woodard v.

Commonwealth, 214 Va. 495, 201 S.E.2d 785 (1974).

Ideally, the court's order should specify the reasons for continuances or failure to try within the statutory time limit and state the positions of the parties' with regard to that order. Without anything in a court order or elsewhere in the record to show that a defendant agreed to or concurred in the delay of his trial, or instigated a proceeding which of necessity brought about a delay of his trial, the delay must be attributed to the Commonwealth. Cantwell v. Commonwealth, 2 Va. App. 606, 347 S.E.2d 523 (1986).

An order granting a continuance speaks for itself, and the record must reflect the reason for any delay of defendant's trial. Godfrey v. Commonwealth, 227 Va. 460, 317 S.E.2d 781 (1984).

Defendant's failure to object to Commonwealth's motion for continuance. — Under the 1995 amendment to this section, a defendant is charged with any delay resulting from the Commonwealth's motion for a continuance if the defendant fails to make a timely objection to such motion. Robinson v. Commonwealth, 28 Va. App. 148, 502 S.E.2d 704 (1998).

The defendant's failure to make a timely objection to a continuance caused the delay resulting from this continuance to be charged to the defendant. Mitchell v. Commonwealth, No. 1738-00-2, 2001 Va. App. LEXIS 328 (Ct. of Appeals June 12, 2001).

Trial court did not err in denying defendant's motion to dismiss the charges against him based on an alleged speedy trial violation, as defendant did not object to the Commonwealth's motion for continuance of his trial; indeed, defendant suggested the new date, which was beyond the nine-month period for trying a case following a finding of probable cause, and defendant acquiesced in the selection of that date. Keene v. Commonwealth, No. 2200-02-2, 2003 Va. App. LEXIS 526 (Ct. of Appeals Oct. 21, 2003).

Statutory speedy trial period was tolled beginning February 8, 2008, under the exception in § 19.2-243 that provides for tolling in the event of a continuance requested by defendant, by joint motion, or by the Commonwealth without objection by defendant. Since defendant did not object to the continuances imposed, the continuances tolled the statutory speedy trial period, and this tolling lasted until July 10, 2009, the date on which the circuit court found defendant competent to stand trial, which was three days before trial. Brown v. Commonwealth, 57 Va. App. 381, 702 S.E.2d 582, 2010 Va. App. LEXIS 490 (2010).

Continuance extended period although trial date not set previously. — Continuance granted on motion of defendant extended the speedy trial period, despite defendant's argument that since no trial date had been set previously, no continuance cognizable under this section occurred. Townes v. Commonwealth, 234 Va. 307, 362 S.E.2d 650 (1987), cert. denied, 485 U.S. 971, 108 S. Ct. 1249, 99 L. Ed. 2d 447 (1988).

Tolling of statute of limitations. — Delays in the commencement of trial will toll the running of the time limitations; however, that delay which is inherent in the process of fixing a timely trial date and which is accommodated by the statutory time limitations is not a delay that extends these time limitations. Baity v. Commonwealth, 16 Va. App. 497, 431 S.E.2d 891 (1993).

Where a defendant was directly indicted, without prior arrest on the charges, the time prescribed by this section did not begin to run until the date of his arrest; and since he was not held in continuous custody from that time, but was released on bail, the nine month statutory period applied. Harris v. Commonwealth, 21 Va. App. 347, 464 S.E.2d 516 (1995).

Denial of defendant's motion to dismiss the case for an alleged violation of the statutory right to a speedy trial under § 19.2-243 was affirmed because counsel for defendant had agreed to a trial date that was outside of the limitations period and such agreement tolled the limitations period. Thompson v. Commonwealth, — Va. App. —, — S.E.2d —, 2006 Va. App. LEXIS 242 (May 30, 2006).

Defendant's convictions for possession of cocaine and forging a public document were reversed because the Commonwealth failed to bring defendant to trial within the five-month speedy trial provision; while defendant's non-availability pursuant to a federal writ ad prosequendum tolled the running of the statute, once the terms of the writ were fulfilled, defendant's unavailability ended and the statutory clock resumed. The Commonwealth presented no evidence that defendant was in custody for more than one day. Jiron-Garcia v. Commonwealth, 48 Va. App. 638, 633 S.E.2d 744, 2006 Va. App. LEXIS 401 (2006).

Defendant's right to a speedy trial was not violated because

excusable delay occurred, and defendant acquiesced in the setting of the trial date outside the parameters of § 19.2-243; because the trial court granted the Commonwealth's motion to continue the case with no objection from defendant's counsel, and the case was continued on joint motion two other times, the statutory time limit was tolled. Smith v. Commonwealth, 2009 Va. App. LEXIS 269 (June 16, 2009).

Defendant failed to preserve for appeal his claim of a violation of his constitutional speedy trial rights because defendant's brief reference to the constitutional issue in his written motion to dismiss due to a violation of § 19.2-243 was insufficient to preserve the claim for appeal; the ends-of-justice exception to Va. Sup. Ct. R. 5A:18 did not apply because defendant's trial did not violate the speedy trial statute since it was tolled for 42 days, and defendant made no allegation that he was prejudiced by the fact that assuming no tolling of § 19.2-243, his trial occurred twelve days beyond the five-month statutory limit. Howard v. Commonwealth, 55 Va. App. 417, 686 S.E.2d 537, 2009 Va. App. LEXIS 569 (2009), aff'd, 281 Va. 455, 706 S.E.2d 885, 2011 Va. LEXIS 47 (2011).

While defendant argued that the tolling of the statutory speedy trial period ended when the doctor who evaluated him issued her report opining that defendant was competent to stand trial, the court rejected this, concluding that pursuant to subsection E of § 19.2-169.1, only the court, not the evaluator, could determine whether a criminal defendant was competent to stand trial. Although the trial court did not make a competency determination until eight months after the doctor issued her report, this did not violate the statutory mandate to promptly determine whether defendant was competent to stand trial as subsection E of § 19.2-169.1 required the trial court to promptly determine a defendant's competency only after receiving the evaluator's report concerning a defendant's competency, and the trial court made a competency decision two months after receiving the report, which had been sent to the wrong court initially. Brown v. Commonwealth, 57 Va. App. 381, 702 S.E.2d 582, 2010 Va. App. LEXIS 490 (2010).

Effect of correction of inadvertent omission on tolling of section. — Where the record clearly established that trial was continued from August 11, 1997, upon defendant's motion, and the disputed nunc pro tunc order simply corrected the inadvertent omission of a contemporaneous order memorializing the event, as otherwise reflected in the record, then this section was tolled on August 11, 1997. Michael v. Commonwealth, No. 2451-98-1, 2000 Va. App. LEXIS 421 (Ct. of Appeals June 6, 2000).

Continuances requested by defendant when Commonwealth discovered that evidence was lost or missing and when the Commonwealth advised defendant of information which he wanted to investigate would be attributed to defendant, absent a showing of bad faith on the part of the Commonwealth. Taylor v. Commonwealth, 4 Va. App. 45, 354 S.E.2d 74 (1987).

Initial appearance without counsel. — When an accused first appears before a trial court in a felony case without counsel and the matter is continued to permit the accused to obtain private counsel, that delay does not toll the time limitations contained in this section for the commencement of the accused's trial; rather, that delay is inherent in the orderly process of fixing a trial date and is necessarily included within or factored into the time limitations of this section. Baity v. Commonwealth, 16 Va. App. 497, 431 S.E.2d 891 (1993).

Failure of counsel to appear chargeable to defendant. — Failure of defense counsel to appear at a docket call is not a delay inherent in the process of preparing the matter for trial, and such failure to appear requires a continuance as effectively as though defense counsel had moved for a continuance. Accordingly, any delay resulting from counsel's failure to appeal is chargeable to the defendant. Jefferson v. Commonwealth, 33 Va. App. 230, 532 S.E.2d 899, 2000 Va. App. LEXIS 606 (2000).

Defendant joined Commonwealth in request for continuance but later rescinded. — Where defendant joined with the Commonwealth in a request for a continuance of the case from April 18 to May 19, 1989, a period of 30 days, even though defendant rescinded his concurrence the following day by moving to dismiss the indictment, this period of time was excepted from application of the statute under subdivision (4). Braxton v. Commonwealth, No. 0800-89-3 (Ct. of Appeals July 24, 1990).

Defendant's responsibility to provide adequate record. — While the Commonwealth must prove that a given delay was excusable, the defendant has the responsibility of providing the court with an adequate record when he or she seeks to avoid being charged with the delay attributed to his or her own motion for continuance on the grounds that such motion was necessitated by prosecutorial efforts to hinder or impede the defendant's timely preparation for trial. Robinson v. Commonwealth, 28 Va. App. 148, 502 S.E.2d 704 (1998).

Nunc pro tunc order stating continuance granted was invalid. — Where neither defendant nor Commonwealth requested a continuance, and trial judge did not grant a continuance, rather the parties and trial judge agreed upon a date on which they would convene in order to schedule the case for trial, the trial judge's entry of an order nunc pro tunc stating that the appellant moved for and was granted a continuance did not establish that a continuance was granted. The trial court attempted, after the fact, to establish that it had granted a continuance, when, in fact, the parties and the court merely agreed to a date on which they would schedule trial. Thus, the trial court's order nunc pro tunc was invalid, and the Commonwealth failed to bring the appellant to trial within the period prescribed by this section. Blackburn v. Commonwealth, No. 2166-96-3 (Ct. of Appeals Oct. 14, 1997).

Where case had been continued by agreement but no court entry upon the record reflected such a continuance, because trial court never considered a motion for a continuance and never ordered a continuance, there was no defect or omission in the record. Therefore, the trial court lacked authority to issue an order nunc pro tunc reciting that a continuance had been granted when in fact the court had not granted a motion for a continuance on the motion of or with the concurrence of the defendant. The nunc pro tunc order was thus invalid and could not bar appellant's speedy trial claim. Blevins v. Commonwealth, No. 1264-96-3 (Ct. of Appeals Sept. 30, 1997).

Court's continuance order did not cause "failure to try." — Court's order continuing the case to the next term of court did not cause a "failure to try the accused." Where the accused had simply been brought before the court for the appointment of counsel, no trial date had been set and no attempt was made to set one, the effect of appointing counsel was to prepare the matter for trial, and did not cause a failure to try the defendant. Nelms v. Commonwealth, 11 Va. App. 639, 400 S.E.2d 799 (1991).

The burden is on the Commonwealth to prove excuse for the failure to try defendant before three regular terms had passed. Woodard v. Commonwealth, 214 Va. 495, 201 S.E.2d 785 (1974); Robinson v. Commonwealth, 28 Va. App. 148, 502 S.E.2d 704 (1998).

The burden is on the prosecution to prove excusable delay. Stephens v. Commonwealth, 225 Va. 224, 301 S.E.2d 22 (1983).

While in the orderly administration of justice some delay is unavoidable and some is essential to due process, courts must inquire into the reasons for the delay. Stephens v. Commonwealth, 225 Va. 224, 301 S.E.2d 22 (1983).

If a defendant is not tried within the time specified in this section, the burden is on the Commonwealth to explain the delay. Godfrey v. Commonwealth, 227 Va. 460, 317 S.E.2d 781 (1984).

In Virginia, when a defendant asserts that he has been denied a speedy trial, the burden is on the Commonwealth to explain the delay. Cantwell v. Commonwealth, 2 Va. App. 606, 347 S.E.2d 523 (1986); Moten v. Commonwealth, 7 Va. App. 438, 374 S.E.2d 704 (1988).

Argument that continuance was for defendant's benefit held untenable. — See Woodard v. Commonwealth, 214 Va. 495, 201 S.E.2d 785 (1974).

Delay attributed to defendant's actions. — Delay in bringing defendant to trial beyond the statutorily prescribed time was attributed to his actions, where defense counsel's request to withdraw was necessitated by defendant's uncooperative attitude and two subsequent continuances were attributable to him even though he was not informed and did not consent to either continuance. Shearer v. Commonwealth, 9 Va. App. 394, 388 S.E.2d 828 (1990).

Where record clearly indicated that the substantial delay of trial was occasioned by defendant's motion for an evaluation pursuant to § 19.2-169.1 and his conduct in relation to the evaluation; i.e., waiting almost five months to supply information necessary for the examination to commence, no denial of speedy trial occurred. Jones v. Commonwealth, 13 Va. App. 566, 414 S.E.2d 193 (1992).

Where the accused affirmatively acts and invites a delay in the commencement of trial by a motion for continuance, there is no violation of his speedy trial rights. Stinnie v. Commonwealth, 22 Va. App. 726, 473 S.E.2d 83 (1996).

Request for psychiatric evaluation. — Where the court had granted the defendant's motion requesting a psychiatric evaluation to determine his competency to stand trial, the period following the granting of such motion was for the defendant's benefit and, notwithstanding the absence of a formal motion to continue the matter to permit the examination to be conducted, the de facto continuance which resulted was caused by his action and was to be subtracted from time limit set by this section. Heath v. Commonwealth, 32 Va. App. 176, 526 S.E.2d 798, 2000 Va. App. LEXIS 278 (2000), aff'd, 261 Va. 389, 541 S.E.2d 906 (2001).

Exception for confinement in hospital. — A trial court's order continuing a defendant's case because the defendant was receiving medical treatment at a diagnostic center stated a reason for the continuance sufficiently similar to the medical treatment provision enumerated in the speedy trial statute to bring that continuance within the spirit of the statute and to toll the running of the speedy trial period until the end of the defendant's confinement for medical care. Mitchell v. Commonwealth, No. 1738-00-2, 2001 Va. App. LEXIS 328 (Ct. of Appeals June 12, 2001).

Hospitalization exception inapplicable. — Confinement exception is not applicable where the defendant was hospitalized and released before any trial dates were set. No delay in the trial was caused by the defendant's emergency hospitalization for treatment. Therefore, it could not be charged to the defendant. Taylor v. Commonwealth, 12 Va. App. 425, 404 S.E.2d 86 (1991).

Illness of witness for Commonwealth. — Delay from February 5 to May 14 was not chargeable to the Commonwealth in light of unavailability of Commonwealth's witness due to prostate surgery and relocation to North Carolina, notwithstanding fact that witness was able to return to work "in early March." Wiggins v. Commonwealth, No. 0187-99-1 (Ct. of Appeals Dec. 28, 1999).

Defendant not held continuously. — Where, less than five months after his arrest, defendant was released on bond, failed to appear for trial, and was re-arrested on a capias and incarcerated, he had not been held "continuously in custody" on the drug charges; therefore, when he was released on bond, the five-month limit of § 19.2-243 ceased to apply, and the nine-month limitation came into play. McCray v. Commonwealth, 44 Va. App. 334, 605 S.E.2d 291, 2004 Va. App. LEXIS 579 (2004).

Presumption of accuracy of order. — Where a defendant does not object to the accuracy of an order within 21 days after its entry, an appellate court may presume that the order, as the final pronouncement on the subject, rather than a transcript that may be flawed by omissions, accurately reflects what transpired. Thomas v. Commonwealth, 16 Va. App. 851, 434 S.E.2d 319 (1993).

Court must confine review to record. — In assessing responsibility for delay in trying a defendant, the court must confine its review to the record. Representations of counsel, or even of the trial judge, if not supported by the record, are insufficient. Thus, continuances must be documented to enable the court to review and evaluate them when they are challenged. Thomas v. Commonwealth, 16 Va. App. 851, 434 S.E.2d 319 (1993).

Appellate review of responsibility for delay. — In assessing responsibility for delay in trying a defendant, the Supreme Court will confine the review to the record that comes before it. Representations of counsel, or even of the trial judge, if not supported by the record, are insufficient. Godfrey v. Commonwealth, 227 Va. 460, 317 S.E.2d 781 (1984).

CIRCUIT COURT OPINIONS

Construction. — The speedy trial statute should be construed to assure both a defendant's constitutional right to a speedy trial and society's interest in swift and certain justice. Commonwealth v. Jordan, 54 Va. Cir. 312, 2000 Va. Cir. LEXIS 603 (Suffolk 2000).

Section is inapplicable. — Parking violations were not traffic infractions required to be tried in General District Court within nine months as provided in § 19.2-243. In re Scott, 80 Va. Cir. 558, 2010 Va. Cir. LEXIS 89 (Norfolk July 13, 2010).

Defendant not deprived of right to speedy trial. — Defendant's motion to dismiss an indictment charging him with murder on the ground that his right to a speedy trial under § 19.2-243 had been violated was denied because the speedy trial clock could not have resumed running based solely upon the issuance of a competency report, and until the circuit court determined the issue of defendant's competency, no trial could take place; it is the court, not the Commissioner of Mental Health, Mental Retardation and Substance Abuse Services, which determines a defendant's competency to stand trial. Commonwealth v. Brown, 2009 Va. Cir. LEXIS 56 (Fairfax Aug. 10, 2009).

Running of time period. — If an indictment or presentment is found against an accused but he has not been arrested for the offense charged therein, the five-month period within which he must be brought to trial runs from the date of his arrest, and, in the absence of a preliminary hearing, the five-month period runs from the date of indictment or the date of arrest, whichever comes later. Commonwealth v. Jordan, 54 Va. Cir. 312, 2000 Va. Cir. LEXIS 603 (Suffolk 2000).

When defendant must speak. — Arrest which begins the running of the time within which a defendant must be brought to trial involves the arrest for the offense described in the indictment for which defendant is tried. Commonwealth v. Jordan, 54 Va. Cir. 312, 2000 Va. Cir. LEXIS 603 (Suffolk 2000).

Under paragraph 4., an accused may stand mute when the court sets a trial date, without waiving his rights to speedy trial, but he must speak or risk waiving his speedy trial rights when the court continues the trial to a subsequent date. Commonwealth v. Jordan, 54 Va. Cir. 312, 2000 Va. Cir. LEXIS 603 (Suffolk 2000).

Defendant's failure to object to nolle prosequi of first indictment. — Defendant's right to a speedy trial was not violated by the issuance of a second indictment for use of a firearm in the commission of a felony after the first indictment was nolle prosequi because when the first indictment was nolle prosequi, without objection by defendant, the warrants were laid to rest and the speedy clock trial stopped running. Commonwealth v. Waddler, 66 Va. Cir. 257, 2004 Va. Cir. LEXIS 330 (Portsmouth Dec. 3, 2004).

Exception for confinement in hospital. — When the defendant first indicted by a grand jury for capital murder and robbery was found mentally incompetent and confined to a state hospital the indictment against the defendant was dismissed; however, the trial court found that a later indictment against the defendant for the same crimes obtained upon the defendant's release from the hospital could not be dismissed on the ground of the passage of time as the defendant alleged. Commonwealth v. Sink, 61 Va. Cir. 279, 2003 Va. Cir. LEXIS 18 (Portsmouth 2003).

Waiver. — Defendant's motion to dismiss an indictment charging him with murder on the ground that his right to a speedy trial under § 19.2-243 had been violated was denied because defendant failed to advise the circuit court of any objection to prolonging the effect of an indefinite continuance, and that period of time had to be excluded from the computation of the five-month speedy trial period; because a failure to object to a continuance is the functional equivalent of presenting a motion for a continuance or acquiescing in the granting of such a motion, a defendant can no longer stand mute, yet claim that the speedy trial clock had not been tolled. Commonwealth v. Brown, 2009 Va. Cir. LEXIS 56 (Fairfax Aug. 10, 2009).

ARTICLE 2.

VENUE.

§ 19.2-244. Venue in general.

Except as otherwise provided by law, the prosecution of a criminal case shall be had in the county or city in which the offense was committed. Except as to motions for a change of venue, all other questions of venue must be raised before verdict in cases tried by a jury and before the finding of guilty in cases tried by the court without a jury.

History.
1975, c. 495.

Cross references.
For prosecution of offenses relating to credit cards in any county or city in which any act of the crime was committed or any issuer sustained financial loss, see § 18.2-198.1.

Michie's Jurisprudence.
For related discussion, see 4A M.J. Conspiracy, § 9; 19 M.J. Venue, §§ 14, 15.

CASE NOTES

Venue not substantive element of crime and similar to jurisdiction. — Even though venue is an element which the prosecution must prove, it is not a substantive element of the crime and is similar in nature to jurisdiction. Venue is usually determined by the court as a matter of law where the facts established it or not in dispute and where it is established by a preponderance of the evidence. Harris v. Commonwealth, No. 0849-88-2 (Ct. of Appeals Aug. 21, 1990).

The Commonwealth may prove venue by either direct or circumstantial evidence. Davis v. Commonwealth, 14 Va. App. 709, 419 S.E.2d 285 (1992).

Burden of proof. — The burden in a criminal case is upon the Commonwealth to prove venue by evidence which is either direct or circumstantial. Pollard v. Commonwealth, 220 Va. 723, 261 S.E.2d 328 (1980).

Allegations of venue contained solely in an indictment cannot supply proof, since the mere fact that police of a certain jurisdiction investigate a crime cannot support an inference that the crime occurred within their jurisdiction. Sutherland v. Commonwealth, 6 Va. App. 378, 368 S.E.2d 295 (1988).

Standard of proof. — To prove venue, the Commonwealth must produce evidence sufficient to give rise to a strong presumption that the offense was committed within the jurisdiction of the court, and this may be accomplished either by direct or circumstantial evidence. Foster-Zahid v. Commonwealth, 23 Va. App. 430, 477 S.E.2d 759 (1996).

Motion to strike to challenge venue. — The Virginia Supreme Court has impliedly upheld the use of the motion to strike to challenge venue. Sutherland v. Commonwealth, 6 Va. App. 378, 368 S.E.2d 295 (1988).

When objection must be made. — An objection to venue must be raised before verdict. Day v. Commonwealth, 12 Va. App. 1078, 407 S.E.2d 52 (1991).

Evidence offered to prove venue must furnish the foundation for a "strong presumption" that the offense was committed within the jurisdiction of the court. Pollard v. Commonwealth, 220 Va. 723, 261 S.E.2d 328 (1980).

Ordinarily, a criminal case must be prosecuted in the county or city in which the offense was committed. To prove venue, the Commonwealth must produce evidence sufficient to give rise to a "strong presumption" that the offense was committed within the jurisdiction of the court, and this may be accomplished by either direct or circumstantial evidence. Cheng v. Commonwealth, 240 Va. 26, 393 S.E.2d 599 (1990).

The evidence to establish venue in a criminal case must be sufficient to present a "strong presumption" that the offense was committed within the jurisdiction of the court. Davis v. Commonwealth, 14 Va. App. 709, 419 S.E.2d 285 (1992).

Motion sufficient to put court on notice that venue in question. — At the close of the Commonwealth's evidence, defendant moved to strike the evidence for failure of the Commonwealth to prove that he did take, steal, and carry away automobile from Chesterfield County. In other words, the Commonwealth failed to establish that the crime occurred in Chesterfield County. While defendant could have stated his venue objection more clearly, the court finds that his objection was sufficient to put the trial court on notice that venue was in question. Sutherland v. Commonwealth, 6 Va. App. 378, 368 S.E.2d 295 (1988).

Issue of venue submitted to jury. — The exact physical location of a murdered body within the river constituted a factual question which the jury could appropriately decide. However, the exact location of the boundary between Virginia and Maryland involves an interpretation of § 7.1-7 [now § 1-308] and represents a legal question outside the jury's province. If it were impossible for the jurors to interpret the evidence concerning the body's exact placement so as to conclude under § 7.1-7 [now § 1-308] that the body lay in Virginia, then the trial court should not have submitted the issue of venue to the jury. Traverso v. Commonwealth, 6 Va. App. 172, 366 S.E.2d 719 (1988).

Evidence held sufficient to prove venue. — Evidence was sufficient to prove venue in Augusta County where investigating officer testified that offending firearms were found on property in Craigsville, and trial court, without objection, took judicial notice that Craigsville was located in Augusta County, expressly rejecting testimony of both defendant and his estranged wife to the contrary. Lawhorn v. Commonwealth, No. 2100-98-3 (Ct. of Appeals Oct. 26, 1999).

Ordinarily, a criminal case had to be prosecuted in the county or city in which the offense was committed, under this section; despite special venue provision of former subsection A of § 18.2-60.3, there was no error in the refusal to grant defendant's motion to strike a stalking charge based upon an allegation of improper venue, as the evidence gave rise to a strong presumption that at least one of the stalking events occurred within the jurisdiction of the court where defendant was tried. Raja v. Commonwealth, 40 Va. App. 710, 581 S.E.2d 237, 2003 Va. App. LEXIS 318 (2003).

Defendant's two grand larceny and two uttering a forged check convictions were reversed on appeal, as the trial court erred in finding the evidence insufficient to establish venue, no evidence was presented by the Commonwealth as to the location of the alleged crimes, and the Commonwealth failed to ask the court to take judicial notice of that location. Harris v. Commonwealth, — Va. App. —, — S.E.2d —, 2006 Va. App. LEXIS 493 (Oct. 31, 2006).

It was clearly established that the charged larceny was committed in Henrico County under circumstances in which the Commonwealth presented evidence from an employee of the Henrico County store from which inkjet cartridges were allegedly stolen, who verified that inkjet cartridges found among those in a box found in defendant's car were those missing from his store; moreover, witnesses identified defendant as the individual shown leaving the store carrying a box similar to the one found in his car on the store's security videotape. Based on these facts, the Commonwealth presented sufficient evidence to support the trial court's venue findings. Brown v. Commonwealth, — Va. App. —, — S.E.2d —, 2007 Va. App. LEXIS 223 (May 29, 2007).

Venue was established in the proper county in defendant's trial for possession of heroin and possession of cocaine because the evidence raised a strong presumption that the offense occurred in the county when defendant possessed cocaine and heroin there; knowing and intentional possession of a controlled substance is an ongoing and continuing offense, and self-induced intoxication or unconsciousness will not be considered a defense to possession of drugs. Morris v. Commonwealth, 51 Va. App. 459, 658 S.E.2d 708, 2008 Va. App. LEXIS 170 (2008).

After defendant's wallet containing cocaine was discovered in an airport, the evidence was sufficient to establish a strong presumption that defendant's crime occurred in Loudoun County, and venue for defendant's trial was proper. All portions of the airport in which a person would lose a wallet were in Loudoun County, and the only portions of the airport in Fairfax County were parts of a few runways, the green open areas surrounding those runways, and parts of a few access roads. Hockensmith v. Commonwealth, 2008 Va. App. LEXIS 500 (Nov. 12, 2008).

Conviction of assault in violation of Virginia Beach, Va., City Code § 23-11 was affirmed because, although defendant claimed that the alleged assault did not occur within the city boundaries, the trial court found that the assault and battery occurred forty yards from the shoreline within the territorial limits of the city. Bostic v. City of Virginia Beach, 2011 Va. App. LEXIS 35 (Feb. 8, 2011).

Venue was proper in Mecklenburg County, Virginia, for defendant's trial for forgery because the fact that the victim filed a civil lawsuit in Mecklenburg, while not dispositive, was competent circumstantial evidence to establish venue when taken together with the totality of the evidence in the record; defendant pointed to no authority that prohibited a subsequent trial court from looking to that civil judgment in addition to other evidence in the record to establish venue in a related criminal case, and the evidence only had to establish a strong presumption of venue. Duckworth v. Commonwealth, 2011 Va. App. LEXIS 60 (Feb. 22, 2011).

Trial court did not err in convicting defendant of forgery in violation of § 18.2-172 because venue was proper in Mecklenburg County, Virginia since the evidence established a strong presumption that defendant deposited or placed the forged instrument with another person or firm in Mecklenburg County pursuant to § 19.2-245.1, and the record did not suggest the involvement of an alternate jurisdiction from which defendant could reasonably have perpetrated the forgery; the victim's attorney sent an unsigned note to defendant's residence in Mecklenburg County, and although the record was silent as to who received the note, the only logical inference flowing from the evidence was that defendant passed the instrument back to either the victim, who resided in Mecklenburg, or the attorney, whose principal place of business was also in Mecklenburg. Duckworth v. Commonwealth, 2011 Va. App. LEXIS 60 (Feb. 22, 2011).

Venue over charges for three counts of causing a juvenile to assist in the distribution of marijuana to a third party, in violation of clause (ii) of subsection A of § 18.2-255, was proper in Hanover County where the nature of the crime was not that of a continuing crime, but one in which different elements of a single crime occur in different jurisdictions, and the record clearly showed that the juvenile distributed the marijuana he received from defendant to a third party in Hanover County. Kelso v. Commonwealth, 282 Va. 134, 710 S.E.2d 470, 2011 Va. LEXIS 128 (2011).

Trial court did not err in denying defendant's challenge to venue because pursuant to §§ 18.2-374.3 and 19.2-244, venue was proper in Louisa County since a detective, who was posing as 13-year-old girl, received defendant's personal electronic contacts there; defendant chose to communicate online with the undercover officer, and the victim actually received his communications, which was a critical portion of the offense proscribed by subsection A of § 18.2-374.3, while in Louisa County. Spiker v. Commonwealth, 58 Va. App. 466, 711 S.E.2d 228, 2011 Va. App. LEXIS 221 (2011).

Evidence held insufficient to prove venue in prosecution for grand larceny resulting in conviction for receiving stolen property. Pollard v. Commonwealth, 220 Va. 723, 261 S.E.2d 328 (1980).

Where the body of a murder victim was found six to seven and one-half feet from the Virginia shoreline, and the only evidence introduced concerning the low water mark showed that on the day the body was found, the river level was at the actual low water mark, therefore, unless a line could be drawn between two headlands in order to form a new low water mark, the body's placement would have been six to seven and one-half feet beyond the Virginia border. Since victim's body lay six to seven and one-half feet from the Commonwealth of Virginia, venue did not lie in Loudoun County and the appellant's conviction was reversed. Traverso v. Commonwealth, 6 Va. App. 172, 366 S.E.2d 719 (1988).

A forgery prosecution may take place "in any county or city where the writing was forged, or where the same was used or passed, or attempted to be used or passed, or deposited or placed with another person, firm, association, or corporation either for collection or credit;" "the burden is upon the Commonwealth to prove venue by evidence which is either direct or circumstantial. Such evidence must furnish the foundation for a "strong presumption" that the offense was committed within the jurisdiction of the court," which the court did not adequately establish. Long v. Commonwealth, No. 2031-95-4 (Ct. of Appeals Mar. 25, 1997).

Appellant was not indicted for stealing blank checks from doctor or for forgery. Rather, she was charged with larceny of U.S. currency from a bank. The record was devoid of any reference to the location of the bank -- the alleged situs of the crime. While sufficient evidence established that the appellant removed the bank checks in the county, the court of appeals could not infer upon that finding alone that a subsequent, separate and distinct offense of larceny of money from the bank likewise occurred in the county. Lacking such proof, the Commonwealth failed to prove that the larceny occurred within the trial court's jurisdiction. Turner v. Commonwealth, No. 2804-96-2 (Ct. of Appeals Oct. 14, 1997).

Offense of felony eluding a law-enforcement officer resulting in serious injury to another occurred in second county, not first county, and thus the trial court erred in denying defendant's challenge to venue in first county as the evidence showed that even though defendant was speeding in his vehicle and driving it recklessly in order to elude a police chase in the first county, the element of causing serious injury to another person only occurred in the second county. Thomas v. Commonwealth, 38 Va. App. 319, 563 S.E.2d 406, 2002 Va. App. LEXIS 303 (2002).

Where a Portsmouth officer activated his lights just after crossing into Chesapeake, but there was no evidence that he was within proximity of defendant at the time or that defendant was aware he was being followed by police, the trial court erred in determining that the Circuit Court of Portsmouth had venue to try defendant for eluding police. Ross v. Commonwealth, No. 0246-04-1, 2005 Va. App. LEXIS 61 (Ct. of Appeals Feb. 15, 2005).

Venue was improper for defendant's trial for unauthorized use of an automobile in violation of § 19.2-244 because although the trial court found that defendant unlawfully used the car, the only evidence of that use was in jurisdictions other than the city where defendant was tried, and even though defendant was charged with the larceny of the car in the city, the trial court specifically acquitted him of that offense; the Commonwealth may not rely on a greater offense to prove venue where the evidence fails to prove the defendant committed the greater offense and the lesser-included offense could not be properly charged in the jurisdiction. Taylor v. Commonwealth, 58 Va. App. 185, 708 S.E.2d 241, 2011 Va. App. LEXIS 140 (2011).

Defendant's conviction of altering the serial number of a firearm in violation of § 18.2-311.1 was reversed; as there was no evidence he removed the serial number in Brunswick County, the Commonwealth failed to meet its burden under § 19.2-244 to show that venue was proper in that county. Bonner v. Commonwealth, 61 Va. App. 247, 734 S.E.2d 692, 2012 Va. App. LEXIS 399 (2012).

Venue for transportation of controlled substance. — Venue properly exists in each jurisdiction through which the statutory minimum quantity of a controlled substance was transported, but not in those jurisdictions where less than the required amount was transported; venue was, accordingly, not appropriate in the city in which a package containing one gram of cocaine was delivered to the defendant, where the package in question contained a much larger quantity when it had been transported to another city but all but one gram had been removed prior to the controlled delivery to the defendant. Green v. Commonwealth, 32 Va. App. 438, 528 S.E.2d 187, 2000 Va. App. LEXIS 335 (2000).

Venue for conduct during high-speed chase. — Venue was proper in Greene County where the evidence was sufficient to raise a strong presumption that defendant's conduct in Greene County during a high-speed chase in several counties endangered the operation of a police vehicle and other persons as: (1) defendant was driving in excess of 90 miles per hour when the radar registered his speed in Greene County; (2) his speed increased beyond 100 miles per hour after the officer activated his lights and siren and joined the pursuit; (3) defendant was not fully in control of his vehicle and was passing other cars without signaling; (4) he also drove at the excessive speed through an intersection of two highways in Greene County that was controlled by a traffic signal; and (5) both the length of time during which the activity occurred in Greene County and the span of distance over which it took place supported venue in Greene County. Paytes v. Commonwealth, No. 2681-02-2, 2004 Va. App. LEXIS 80 (Ct. of Appeals Feb. 17, 2004).

Venue for causing a juvenile to assist in distributing marijuana. — Because causing a juvenile to assist in the distribution of marijuana in violation of subsection A of § 18.2-255 was a continuing offense, venue was proper in the county where the juvenile sold the marijuana pursuant to § 19.2-244. Kelso v. Commonwealth, 57 Va. App. 30, 698 S.E.2d 263, 2010 Va. App. LEXIS 350 (2010), aff'd, 282 Va. 134, 710 S.E.2d 470, 2011 Va. LEXIS 128 (2011).

Child abduction. — Where the evidence established that the father was a resident of Fairfax County at the time of the abduction by out-of-state mother and that the child was to be returned to Fairfax County pursuant to a valid and enforceable custody order, the harm contemplated by this section was clearly established as occurring in this locus for venue purposes. Foster-Zahid v. Commonwealth, 23 Va. App. 430, 477 S.E.2d 759 (1996).

Defendant's failure to relinquish custody of her minor child to the father in Virginia Beach constituted an offense committed within that circuit under § 19.2-244. Accordingly, venue was proper in that jurisdiction as that was the jurisdiction to which the defendant was ordered to relinquish temporary custody and from which the defendant withheld custody of their child from the father. Dunn v. Commonwealth, No. 1689-02-1, 2003 Va. App. LEXIS 219 (Ct. of Appeals Apr. 15, 2003).

Venue of crime of conspiracy. — Under this section, the crime of conspiracy is deemed to have been committed in any city or county in which an act in furtherance of the conspiracy took place, as well as in the place where the conspiracy was entered into. The fact that the agreement forming the basis of the conspiracy may have been entered into in Chesapeake, the place where defendant was incarcerated, does not restrict venue to Chesapeake only. Henry v. Commonwealth, 2 Va. App. 194, 342 S.E.2d 655 (1986).

Evidence supported the determination that venue in a prosecution for conspiracy to distribute marijuana lay in Hanover County, where a co-conspirator resided in Hanover County, an undercover officer telephoned the co-conspirator at her house there on several occasions, and where he spoke with both the defendant and the co-conspirator, who were then in Hanover County, concerning the purchase of marijuana. Williams v. Commonwealth, No. 2203-97-2 (Ct. of Appeals July 7, 1998).

Crimes committed on Roanoke County property located in City of Salem. — When former § 17-126.2 and this section are considered together, it is plain that the General Assembly intended that a crime committed on Roanoke County property located in the City of Salem not only should be treated for all intents and purposes as if it happened in Roanoke County, but also that Roanoke County should have full concurrent criminal jurisdiction over the area in question including search and seizure for criminal law enforcement. Garza v. Commonwealth, 228 Va. 559, 323 S.E.2d 127 (1984).

Venue for altering serial number of firearm. — As the offense of altering or removing a serial number of a firearm, § 18.2-311.1, constitutes a discrete act rather than a continuing offense, under § 19.2-244, venue is proper where the alteration or removal was done. Bonner v. Commonwealth, 61 Va. App. 247, 734 S.E.2d 692, 2012 Va. App. LEXIS 399 (2012).

Merit of exception based upon failure to prove venue. — It seldom happens that there is any real merit in an exception based upon a failure to prove venue, unless the question has been developed and made the subject of serious inquiry before verdict. Sutherland v. Commonwealth, 6 Va. App. 378, 368 S.E.2d 295 (1988).

Applied in Spitzer v. Commonwealth, 233 Va. 7, 353 S.E.2d 711 (1987); Thomas v. Commonwealth, 36 Va. App. 326, 549 S.E.2d 648, 2001 Va. App. LEXIS 448 (2001); Hedrick v. Warden of Sussex I State Prison, 264 Va. 486, 570 S.E.2d 840, 2002 Va. LEXIS 161 (2002).

§ 19.2-245. Offenses committed without and made punishable within Commonwealth; embezzlement or larceny committed within Commonwealth; where prosecuted.

Prosecution for offenses committed wholly or in part without and made punishable within this Commonwealth may be in any county or city in which the offender is found or to which he is sent by any judge or court; and if any person shall commit larceny or embezzlement beyond the jurisdiction of this Commonwealth and bring the stolen property into the same he shall be liable to prosecution and punishment for larceny or embezzlement in any county or city into which he shall have taken the property as if the same had been wholly committed therein; and if any person shall commit larceny or embezzlement within this Commonwealth and take the stolen property into any county or city other than the county or city within which the same was committed he shall be liable to prosecution and punishment for such larceny or embezzlement in any such county or city into which he shall have taken the property as if the same had been wholly committed therein; provided, that if any person shall commit embezzlement within this Commonwealth he shall be liable as aforesaid or to prosecution and punishment for his offense in the county or city in which he was legally obligated to deliver the embezzled funds or property.

History.
Code 1950, § 19.1-220; 1960, c. 366; 1975, c. 495; 1977, c. 216.

Cross references.
For rule of court requiring that questions of venue in criminal cases be raised in the trial court, see Rule 1:2.

Michie's Jurisprudence.
For related discussion, see 5B M.J. Criminal Procedure, §§ 1, 10; 12A M.J. Larceny, § 11.

CASE NOTES

History of section. — See Howell v. Commonwealth, 187 Va. 34, 46 S.E.2d 37 (1948).

The legislature has power to fix the venue of criminal prosecutions in a place other than that in which the crime was committed in the absence of a constitutional limitation. Lovelace v. Commonwealth, 205 Va. 541, 138 S.E.2d 253 (1964).

The constitutionality of this section, so far as it declares the crime of larceny, is clear. It makes statutory the principle that every act of removal or change of possession of stolen property is a new violation of the owner's right. Howell v. Commonwealth, 187 Va. 34, 46 S.E.2d 37 (1948).

The constitutionality of this section insofar as it describes the crime of larceny is clear. Lovelace v. Commonwealth, 205 Va. 541, 138 S.E.2d 253 (1964).

No double jeopardy violation. — There was no double jeopardy violation in prosecuting defendant for embezzlement from her employer's clinic in Tazewell County after she pled guilty to embezzlement from a different clinic in Russell County owned by the same employer, because, although § 19.2-245 allowed a prosecution wholly in Russell County for the embezzlement occurring in both Tazewell County and Russell County, defendant failed to prove that the Russell County conviction encompassed same embezzlement for which she was indicted in Tazewell County. Hatfield v. Commonwealth, 2008 Va. App. LEXIS 486 (Nov. 4, 2008).

Its true meaning is that venue is given in any county in which the defendant may be found to have committed the offense by bringing in the stolen goods, to the same extent as if the crime "had been wholly committed" in that county. Howell v. Commonwealth, 187 Va. 34, 46 S.E.2d 37 (1948); Lovelace v. Commonwealth, 205 Va. 541, 138 S.E.2d 253 (1964).

In a prosecution for bringing into Virginia property stolen in another state, an accused who, when arrested, was in jail in the county in which he had sold the property, having been brought there from out of the state on a different charge, was "found" in that county in the sense intended by this section as a prerequisite to the court's jurisdiction. Howell v. Commonwealth, 187 Va. 34, 46 S.E.2d 37 (1948).

To be applicable, this section requires proof that the accused participated in taking the stolen property into the county where the prosecution is brought. Nelson v. Commonwealth, 12 Va. App. 268, 403 S.E.2d 384 (1991).

This section clearly has in view more than one place of venue. Howell v. Commonwealth, 187 Va. 34, 46 S.E.2d 37 (1948); Lovelace v. Commonwealth, 205 Va. 541, 138 S.E.2d 253 (1964).

It is not an attempt to enforce the criminal laws of another state, but defines and punishes an offense committed in this state. Howell v. Commonwealth, 187 Va. 34, 46 S.E.2d 37 (1948); Lovelace v. Commonwealth, 205 Va. 541, 138 S.E.2d 253 (1964).

The crime continues and accompanies the defendant into every county into which he goes with stolen property. Lovelace v. Commonwealth, 205 Va. 541, 138 S.E.2d 253 (1964).

Fact that part of crime committed in another state does not affect venue. — In a prosecution for subornation of perjury the fact that the suborner and the perjurer discussed some details of the crime in another state does not affect the venue under this section. Mundy v. Commonwealth, 161 Va. 1049, 171 S.E. 691 (1933).

This section gives Virginia jurisdiction over embezzlement of-fenses, even though most or all of the illegal acts took place in another state. Keselica v. Commonwealth, 24 Va. App. 115, 480 S.E.2d 756 (1997).

Embezzlement of computer. — The fact that the consignment contract was silent as to where the computer was to be returned did not mean that there was no venue in which the appellant could be prosecuted for embezzlement. Jackson v. Commonwealth, No. 1552-95-2 (Ct. of Appeals Dec. 31, 1996).

Where appellant was legally obligated to return the computer to victim in Powhatan County, the fact that he would have been legally obligated to return the computer to her wherever she was does not defeat Powhatan County as a proper venue. Furthermore, the consignment contract was executed in Powhatan County. The contract was for a period of sixty days. At the end of sixty days, the appellant had the legal duty to either return the computer to her or pay Williams $850. Accordingly, Powhatan County was a proper venue in which to prosecute the charge. Jackson v. Commonwealth, No. 1552-95-2 (Ct. of Appeals Dec. 31, 1996).

Embezzlement of rented car. — A rental agreement provided that a car was to be returned to the owner in the City of Lynchburg at a specified time. The Corporation Court of the City of Lynchburg had venue to try defendant on a charge of embezzling the car. Stegall v. Commonwealth, 208 Va. 719, 160 S.E.2d 566 (1968).

§ 19.2-245.01. Offenses involving reports or statements concerning cigarette sales or stamping.

Any criminal violation of Chapter 42 (§ 3.2-4200 et seq.) of Title 3.2, Article 10 (§ 18.2-246.6 et seq.) of Chapter 6 of Title 18.2, or § 18.2-514 involving reports or statements concerning cigarette sales or stamping may be prosecuted in the City of Richmond.

History.
2009, c. 847; 2013, c. 625.

Editor's note.
Acts 2013, c. 625, cl. 2 provides: "That the provisions of this act may result in a net increase in periods of imprisonment or commitment. Pursuant to § 30-19.1:4, the estimated amount of the necessary appropriation cannot be determined for periods of imprisonment in state adult correctional facilities; therefore, Chapter 3 of the Acts of Assembly of 2012, Special Session I, requires the Virginia Criminal Sentencing Commission to assign a minimum fiscal impact of $50,000. Pursuant to § 30-19.1:4, the estimated amount of the necessary appropriation cannot be determined for periods of commitment to the custody of the Department of Juvenile Justice."

The 2013 amendments.
The 2013 amendment by c. 625 substituted "Article 10 (§ 18.2-246.6 et seq.) of Chapter 6 of Title 18.2, or § 18.2-514" for "or of § 18.2-246.13 or 18.2-514."

§ 19.2-245.1. Forgery; where prosecuted.

If any person commits forgery, that forgery may be prosecuted in any county or city (i) where the writing was forged, or where the same was used or passed, or attempted to be used or passed, or deposited or placed with another person, firm, association, or corporation either for collection or credit for the account of any person, firm, association, or corporation or (ii) where the writing is found in the possession of the defendant.

History.
1979, c. 30; 2000, c. 327.

CASE NOTES

A forgery prosecution may take place "in any county or city where the writing was forged, or where the same was used or passed, or attempted to be used or passed, or deposited or placed with another person, firm, association, or corporation either for collection or credit;" "the burden is upon the Commonwealth to prove venue by evidence which is either direct or circumstantial. Such evidence must furnish the foundation for a "strong presumption" that the offense was committed within the jurisdiction of the court," which the court did not adequately establish. Long v. Commonwealth, No. 2031-95-4 (Ct. of Appeals Mar. 25, 1997) (decided prior to the 2000 amendment, providing for prosecution where the writing is found).

Venue found improper. — Prosecution failed to establish requisite venue in Henrico County, where record established only that defendant possessed a forged check in Henrico County after having attempted to pass it at an unspecified store. Copeland v. Commonwealth, No. 1851-98-2 (Ct. of Appeals June 29, 1999).

Venue was proper in Mecklenburg County, Virginia, for defendant's trial for forgery because the fact that the victim filed a civil lawsuit in Mecklenburg, while not dispositive, was competent circumstantial evidence to establish venue when taken together with the totality of the evidence in the record; defendant pointed to no authority that prohibited a subsequent trial court from looking to that civil judgment in addition to other evidence in the record to establish venue in a related criminal case, and the evidence only had to establish a strong presumption of venue. Duckworth v. Commonwealth, 2011 Va. App. LEXIS 60 (Feb. 22, 2011).

Venue proper. — Trial court did not err in convicting defendant of forgery in violation of § 18.2-172 because venue was proper in Mecklenburg County, Virginia since the evidence established a strong presumption that defendant deposited or placed the forged instrument with another person or firm in Mecklenburg County pursuant to § 19.2-245.1, and the record did not suggest the involvement of an alternate jurisdiction from which defendant could reasonably have perpetrated the forgery; the victim's attorney sent an unsigned note to defendant's residence in Mecklenburg County, and although the record was silent as to who received the note, the only logical inference flowing from the evidence was that defendant passed the instrument back to either the victim, who resided in Mecklenburg, or the attorney, whose principal place of business was also in Mecklenburg. Duckworth v. Commonwealth, 2011 Va. App. LEXIS 60 (Feb. 22, 2011).

§ 19.2-245.2. Tax offenses; where prosecuted.

If an offense involving tax, as defined in Title 58.1, is committed, that offense may be prosecuted in either any county or city where a false or fraudulent tax return, document, or statement was filed, or the county or city where the offender resides. However, venue shall not be in the City of Richmond solely because a false or fraudulent tax return, document or statement was filed directly with the Department of Taxation.

History.
1990, c. 631.

§ 19.2-246. Injury inflicted by person within Commonwealth upon one outside Commonwealth.

If a mortal wound or other violence or injury be inflicted by a person within this Commonwealth upon one outside of the same, or upon one in this Commonwealth who afterwards dies from the effect thereof out of the Commonwealth, the offender shall be amenable to prosecution and punishment for the offense in the courts of the county or city in which he was at the time of the commission thereof as if the same had been committed in such county or city.

History.
Code 1950, § 19.1-221; 1960, c. 366; 1975, c. 495.

Michie's Jurisprudence.
For related discussion, see 19 M.J. Venue, § 14.

CASE NOTES

For the history of this section and related statutes, see Covington v. Commonwealth, 136 Va. 665, 116 S.E. 462 (1923).

The effect of this section and § 18.2-27 is merely to give the courts of the counties or corporations, in which the accused and the deceased may have been, respectively, at the time of the commission of the offense, concurrent jurisdiction, so that the offender may be prosecuted and punished in either county, where the offense is not wholly committed within one county. Covington v. Commonwealth, 136 Va. 665, 116 S.E. 462 (1923).

There is nothing incongruous or objectionable in the like result being accomplished by two separate statutes, as by this section and § 18.2-27, which is attained in the cases of §§ 19.2-248 and 19.2-249 by single statutes. Covington v. Commonwealth, 136 Va. 665, 116 S.E. 462 (1923).

§ 19.2-247. Venue in certain homicide cases.

Where evidence exists that a homicide has been committed either within or without this Commonwealth, under circumstances which make it unknown where such crime was committed, the offense shall be amenable to prosecution in the courts of the county or city where the body of the victim may be found or, if the victim was removed from the Commonwealth for medical treatment prior to death and died outside the Commonwealth, in the courts of the county or city from which the victim was removed for medical treatment prior to death, as if the offense has been committed in such county or city. In a prosecution for capital murder pursuant to subdivision 8 of § 18.2-31, the offense may be prosecuted in any jurisdiction in the Commonwealth in which any one of the killings may be prosecuted.

History.
Code 1950, § 19.1-221.1; 1973, c. 308; 1975, c. 495; 1996, c. 959; 2002, c. 503.

Michie's Jurisprudence.
For related discussion, see 19 M.J. Venue, § 14.

CASE NOTES

Prosecution did not violate the double jeopardy clause of the United States Constitution by indicting defendant on rape charge in Portsmouth, in addition to the murder charge tried in Norfolk for no evidence was presented that the rape occurred in Norfolk or that the victim was transported to Norfolk by the defendant prior to the commission of such offense, and the Norfolk court did not have jurisdiction to try appellant for rape. Vanegas v. Commonwealth, 17 Va. App. 451, 438 S.E.2d 289 (1993).

Court correctly refused to instruct jury on venue issue. — Trial court correctly refused to instruct the jury on the issue of venue, where the uncertainty of whether the fatal wound was inflicted in Richmond or Chesterfield County was determinative of venue as a matter of law. Harris v. Commonwealth, No. 0849-88-2 (Ct. of Appeals Aug. 21, 1990).

Applied in Hedrick v. Warden of Sussex I State Prison, 264 Va. 486, 570 S.E.2d 840, 2002 Va. LEXIS 161 (2002).

§ 19.2-248. Venue when mortal wound, etc., inflicted in one county and death ensues in another.

If a mortal wound, or other violence or injury, be inflicted, or poison administered in one county or city, and death ensues therefrom in another county or city, the offense may be prosecuted in either.

History.
Code 1950, § 19.1-223; 1960, c. 366; 1975, c. 495.

Cross references.
As to offenses committed without and made punishable within the state, see § 19.2-245. As to how and where homicide is prosecuted and punished if death occurs outside the state, see § 18.2-37.

Michie's Jurisprudence.
For related discussion, see 9B M.J. Homicide, § 50; 19 M.J. Venue, § 14.

§ 19.2-249. Offenses committed on boundary of two counties, two cities, or county and city, etc.; where prosecuted.

An offense committed on the boundary of two counties, or on the boundary of two cities, or on the boundary of a county and city, or within 300 yards thereof, may be alleged to have been committed, and may be prosecuted and punished, in either county, in either city, or the county or city, and any sheriff, deputy sheriff, or other police officer shall have jurisdiction to make arrests and preserve the peace for a like distance on either side of the boundary line between such counties, such cities, or such county and city.

History.
Code 1950, § 19.1-222; 1960, c. 366; 1975, c. 495; 1978, c. 354; 2003, c. 116.

Law Review.
For 2007 annual survey article, "Electronic Data: A Commentary on the Law in Virginia in 2007," see 42 U. Rich. L. Rev. 355 (2007).

Michie's Jurisprudence.
For related discussion, see 19 M.J. Venue, § 14.

CASE NOTES

Place of arrest. — Where a York County deputy made traffic stop in the City of Williamsburg, defendant was arrested for the DUI charge in Williamsburg, while the record did not reflect where defendant was arrested on the habitual offender charge, it was clear that she was not arrested for that offense at the stop. Johnson v. Commonwealth, No. 1005-04-1, 2005 Va. App. LEXIS 105 (Ct. of Appeals Mar. 15, 2005).

Because a campus police officer's concurrent jurisdiction under §§ 19.2-249, 19.2-250, and 23-234 extended up to one mile beyond the city's corporate limits, the officer was well within the statutorily prescribed jurisdiction when the officer stopped and arrested defendant for drunk driving 200 yards into the adjoining county.

Boatwright v. Commonwealth, 50 Va. App. 169, 647 S.E.2d 515, 2007 Va. App. LEXIS 281 (2007).

This section was held applicable to information proceedings for the forfeiture of an automobile while being used in the illegal transportation of intoxicating liquors. Commercial Credit Co. v. Commonwealth, 155 Va. 1033, 155 S.E. 689 (1930).

Suppression of evidence. — Assuming that an investigator's actions violated §§ 18.2-146 and 19.2-249, that violation did not entitle defendant to suppression of the evidence because the statutes did not provide for the remedy of exclusion. Hill v. Commonwealth, No. 1828-11-3, 2012 Va. App. LEXIS 318 (Oct. 9, 2012).

CIRCUIT COURT OPINIONS

Search and seizure. — Though officer who detained the defendant and his companions exceeded his statutory authority under § 19.2-249, he did not violate the Fourth Amendment, therefore the defendant was not entitled to have evidence seized pursuant to the arrest excluded. Commonwealth v. Dawson, 61 Va. Cir. 309, 2003 Va. Cir. LEXIS 35 (Roanoke 2003).

§ 19.2-249.1. Offenses committed within towns situated in two or more counties; where prosecuted.

An offense or traffic infraction committed within a town situated in two or more counties within the Commonwealth may be alleged to have been committed, and may be prosecuted and punished, in any one of such counties.

History.
1984, c. 278.

§ 19.2-249.2. Venue for prosecution of computer crimes.

For the purpose of venue under the Virginia Computer Crimes Act (§ 18.2-152.1 et seq.), any violation of the article shall be considered to have been committed in any county or city:

1. In which any act was performed in furtherance of any course of conduct that violated this article;

2. In which the owner has his principal place of business in the Commonwealth;

3. In which any offender had control or possession of any proceeds of the violation or of any books, records, documents, property, financial instrument, computer software, computer program, computer data, or other material or objects that were used in furtherance of the violation;

4. From which, to which, or through which any access to a computer or computer network was made whether by wires, electromagnetic waves, microwaves, optics or any other means of communication;

5. In which the offender resides; or

6. In which any computer that is an object or an instrument of the violation is located at the time of the alleged offense.

History.
2005, cc. 746, 761, 827.

CASE NOTES

Establishing venue. — Commonwealth established venue in Virginia Beach under subdivisions 4 and 6 of § 19.2-249.2 during defendant's trial for harassment by computer in violation of § 18.2-152.7:1 because the evidence was sufficient to prove a strong presumption that the victim received the e-mails defendant sent her while she resided in Virginia Beach, on a computer located within Virginia Beach; the victim lived in Virginia Beach, and she testified that all the offensive e-mails were sent to her e-mail account in the City of Virginia Beach. Barson v. Commonwealth, 2010 Va. App. LEXIS 427 (Nov. 2, 2010).

§ 19.2-250. How far jurisdiction of corporate authorities extends.

A. Notwithstanding any other provision of this article and except as provided in subsection B hereof, the jurisdiction of the corporate authorities of each town or city, in criminal cases involving offenses against the Commonwealth, shall extend within the Commonwealth one mile beyond the corporate limits of such town or city; except that such jurisdiction of the corporate authorities of towns situated in counties having a density of population in excess of 300 inhabitants per square mile, or in counties adjacent to cities having a population of 170,000 or more, shall extend for 300 yards beyond the corporate limits of such town or, in the case of the criminal jurisdiction of an adjacent county, for 300 yards within such town.

B. Notwithstanding any other provision of this article, the jurisdiction of the authorities of Chesterfield County and Henrico County, in criminal cases involving offenses against the Commonwealth, shall extend one mile beyond the limits of such county into the City of Richmond.

History.
Code 1950, § 15.1-141; 1962, c. 623; 1975, c. 495; 1978, c. 379; 1998, c. 428; 2007, c. 813.

Editor's note.
Acts 2007, c. 813, cl. 2, provides: "That the provisions of this act shall not affect the powers of any locality with respect to any ordinance, resolution or bylaw validly adopted and not repealed or rescinded prior to July 1, 2007."

The 2007 amendments.
The 2007 amendment by c. 813 substituted "Chesterfield County and Henrico County" for "a county adjoining the City of Richmond and having a population between 209,200 and 209,500 or a county adjoining the City of Richmond and having a population between 217,800 and 217,900, according to the 1990 census" in subsection B.

Michie's Jurisprudence.
For related discussion, see 2A M.J. Arrest, § 7; 5A M.J. Courts, § 43; 12A M.J. Licenses, § 10; 13B M.J. Municipal Corporations, § 25.

CASE NOTES

Purpose of section. — This section does not purport to extend the effect of municipal ordinances beyond the corporate limits of a city. It is a statute of enforcement of the effective law within the area specified. Its purpose is plain, that is, to prevent the territory contiguous to a city from becoming a refuge for criminals, and to confer on the corporation courts of cities power to enforce the police regulations and law of the area involved. Murray v. City of Roanoke, 192 Va. 321, 64 S.E.2d 804 (1951); Kelley v. County of Brunswick, 200 Va. 45, 104 S.E.2d 7 (1958).

This section does not extend the effect of city ordinances beyond city limits; rather, it confers on city police officers the authority to enforce the statutes of the Commonwealth or law of the jurisdiction

involved. Hoambrecker v. City of Lynchburg, 13 Va. App. 511, 412 S.E.2d 729 (1992).

"Jurisdiction" defined. — The word "jurisdiction" as used in this section broadly means the power, right, or authority in the courts to hear, determine, and enforce the law in cases, causes or controversies. It is the power to try and declare the law. It is the authority by which judicial officers take cognizance of, and apply and enforce, the law, as distinguished from the power to enact law. Murray v. City of Roanoke, 192 Va. 321, 64 S.E.2d 804 (1951).

Section 19.2-54 and this section must be read together and harmonized. Robertson v. Rogers, 2 Va. App. 503, 346 S.E.2d 41 (1986), aff'd, 360 S.E.2d 715 (1987).

Exclusionary rule did not apply. — Where appellant asserted that LSD was seized from him in a search pursuant to an unlawful arrest because investigator exceeded his jurisdictional authority under this section, that claim of illegality as to the arrest did not involve a claim that federal constitutional protections were violated which would implicate the exclusionary rule. Even if investigator violated this section or exceeded the common-law authority of a private citizen in arresting appellant for a misdemeanor, he nonetheless constitutionally detained appellant. The exclusionary rule did not apply. Accordingly, the trial court properly denied the appellant's motion to suppress the evidence. Wright v. Commonwealth, No 2528-96-3 (Ct. of Appeals Dec. 9, 1997).

Filing of affidavits required by § 19.2-54 in the City of Danville, rather than defendant's residence of Pittsylvania County, was appropriate where the Circuit Court of the City of Danville, pursuant to this section, had jurisdiction over the crime and the area where the search was made. Robertson v. Rogers, 2 Va. App. 503, 346 S.E.2d 41 (1986), aff'd, 360 S.E.2d 715 (1987).

Taxation beyond city limits. — This section is unconstitutional insofar as it authorizes the levy by a city of a license tax upon a circus exhibition beyond its corporate limits for the sole purpose of raising revenue to defray the general expenses of the city government. Robinson v. City of Norfolk, 108 Va. 14, 60 S.E. 762 (1908); City of Charlottesville v. Marks' Shows, Inc., 179 Va. 321, 18 S.E.2d 890 (1942).

Gambling ordinance purporting to be effective outside city limits invalid. — The City of Roanoke had no power under this section to enact a gambling ordinance effective outside the city limits. Murray v. City of Roanoke, 192 Va. 321, 64 S.E.2d 804 (1951).

A town ordinance prohibiting drunken driving had no effect beyond the corporate limits. Kelley v. County of Brunswick, 200 Va. 45, 104 S.E.2d 7 (1958).

Where offense occurred, not where officer was located, is determinative. — A police officer located outside the one-mile jurisdictional limit of a town had the authority to arrest a speeding driver where the officer employed radar to observe a violation within that limit. Where the arresting officer was located when he observed the speeding violation was irrelevant; the relevant question was whether the offense occurred within the town's jurisdiction as defined by this section. Breitbach v. Commonwealth, 35 Va. App. 604, 546 S.E.2d 764, 2001 Va. App. LEXIS 300 (2001).

City police officer had the authority to stop and arrest appellant within one mile of city limits as long as it was for an offense against the Commonwealth or the county in which the arrest was made. Hoambrecker v. City of Lynchburg, 13 Va. App. 511, 412 S.E.2d 729 (1992).

Although route defendant actually traveled extended more than one mile beyond city, officer had authority to arrest him where location was still physically within one mile of city limits. Hamm v. City of Norton, No. 1607-98-3 (Ct. of Appeals Sept. 28, 1999).

Status of policeman acting outside one-mile area. — If a policeman acts outside the one-mile area from the city limits, his status is that of any other private citizen. Moore v. Oliver, 347 F. Supp. 1313 (W.D. Va. 1972).

Although uniformed police officer was outside of jurisdictional boundary limits set out in subsection A of § 19.2-250, the officer had the same authority to arrest as did a private citizen and could make an extraterritorial arrest under those circumstances in which a private citizen would be authorized to make an arrest, including when a breach of the peace was committed in the officer's or citizen's presence; defendant's dangerous conduct, on a public highway, in and of itself was a breach of the peace under any definition of that concept, and the officer properly detained defendant after observing the dangerous conduct, and defendant's conviction for refusing to submit to a breath test, in violation of § 18.2-268.3, was affirmed. Hudson v. Commonwealth, 266 Va. 371, 585 S.E.2d 583, 2003 Va. LEXIS 84 (2003).

Defendant was properly convicted of assault and battery on a police officer under subsection C of § 18.2-57 because while defendant claimed that the officer's public duties were limited to one mile outside the geographic borders of Virginia Beach under § 19.2-250, a law-enforcement mutual aid agreement permitted by § 15.2-1726 gave the officer authority to perform his public duties in Chesapeake based on the immediate threat to public safety presented by defendant's erratic driving. Rowe v. Commonwealth, 2008 Va. App. LEXIS 242 (May 20, 2008), aff'd, 277 Va. 495, 675 S.E.2d 161, 2009 Va. LEXIS 59 (2009).

Arrest held valid. — Assuming arguendo that a detective arrested defendant for his criminal activity in the county where the arrest occurred — not for his activity in the officer's own county — the arrest, though it violated subsection A of § 19.2-250, was constitutional, because the officer had reasonable suspicion to arrest defendant for possessing cocaine in the county of the arrest, and defendant's subsequent confession furnished probable cause to arrest for possession in the officer's county. Commonwealth v. Coleman, No. 1672-03-2, 2004 Va. App. LEXIS 6 (Ct. of Appeals Jan. 6, 2004).

Because a campus police officer's concurrent jurisdiction under §§ 19.2-249, 19.2-250, and 23-234 extended up to one mile beyond the city's corporate limits, the officer was well within the statutorily prescribed jurisdiction when the officer stopped and arrested defendant for drunk driving 200 yards into the adjoining county. Boatwright v. Commonwealth, 50 Va. App. 169, 647 S.E.2d 515, 2007 Va. App. LEXIS 281 (2007).

OPINIONS OF THE ATTORNEY GENERAL

Town police department could not patrol and enforce laws one mile beyond corporate limits of town. — A town police department could not patrol and enforce the laws of the Commonwealth one mile beyond the corporate limits of the town where the density of population in the county within one mile of the town was less than 300 inhabitants per square mile, although the county density, particularly in the east end, exceeded 300 inhabitants per square mile. See opinion of Attorney General to The Honorable Joe T. May, Member, House of Delegates, 01-045 (6/19/01).

Jurisdiction of a town police department in cases involving offenses against the Commonwealth extends one mile beyond the corporate limits of the town, where the population density of the county in which the town is located, is 25.5 inhabitants per square mile, under the threshold of 300 inhabitants per square mile prescribed in subsection A of this section. See opinion of Attorney General to The Honorable E. Carter Nettles, Jr., Commonwealth's Attorney for Sussex County, 03-097 (12/2/03).

Jurisdiction of a town police department does not include the authority to enforce town ordinances outside the corporate limits of the town; therefore, the town is not entitled to any fines collected for violations of state law occurring outside its corporate limits. See opinion of Attorney General to The Honorable E. Carter Nettles, Jr., Commonwealth's Attorney for Sussex County, 03-097 (12/2/03).

Limit on law-enforcement authority. — This section does not confer law-enforcement authority to local police departments outside of the corporate limits of the localities that they serve. See opinion of Attorney General to The Honorable Thomas D. Jones, Sheriff, Charlotte County, 08-028 (7/28/08).

§ 19.2-251. When and how venue may be changed.

A circuit court may, on motion of the accused or of the Commonwealth, for good cause, order the venue for the trial of a criminal case in such court to be changed to some other circuit court. Such motion when made by the accused may be made in his absence upon a petition signed and sworn to by him.

Whenever the mayor of any city, or the sheriff of any county, shall call on the Governor for military force to protect the accused from violence, the judge of the circuit court of the city or county having jurisdiction of the offense shall, upon a petition signed and sworn to by the accused, whether he be present or not, at once order the venue to be changed to the circuit court of a city or county sufficiently remote from the place where the offense was committed to insure the safe and impartial trial of the accused.

History.
Code 1950, § 19.1-224; 1960, c. 366; 1975, c. 495.

Cross references.
As to custody of defendant when venue changed, see § 19.2-252. As to procedure upon and after change of venue, see § 19.2-253. As to constitutional provision prohibiting local, special or private laws for change of venue in civil and criminal cases, see Va. Const., Art. IV, § 14 (2).

Law Review.
For comment on change of venue in criminal cases, see 26 Wash. & Lee L. Rev. 89 (1969).

Michie's Jurisprudence.
For related discussion, see 11B M.J. Jury, § 4; 19 M.J. Venue, §§ 14, 17, 117.1, 20.

CASE NOTES

I. Right and Power to Change.
II. Grounds for Change.
III. Proceedings.

I. RIGHT AND POWER TO CHANGE.

This section is not in conflict with Va. Const., Art. I, § 8. Newberry v. Commonwealth, 192 Va. 819, 66 S.E.2d 841 (1951).

The purpose of a change of venue is to accord litigants, both the Commonwealth and the defendant, a fair and impartial trial. Newcomer v. Commonwealth, 220 Va. 64, 255 S.E.2d 485 (1979).

Under this section, the courts have power whenever necessary to allow a change of venue. Wormeley v. Commonwealth, 51 Va. (10 Gratt.) 658 (1853); Muscoe v. Commonwealth, 87 Va. 460, 12 S.E. 790 (1891); Bowles v. Commonwealth, 103 Va. 816, 48 S.E. 527 (1904), overruled on other grounds, Graham v. Commonwealth, 127 Va. 808, 103 S.E. 565 (1920).

Question of change of venue is within sound judicial discretion of the trial judge. Evans v. Commonwealth, 161 Va. 992, 170 S.E. 756 (1933); Poindexter v. Commonwealth, 218 Va. 314, 237 S.E.2d 139 (1977); Newcomer v. Commonwealth, 220 Va. 64, 255 S.E.2d 485 (1979); Watkins v. Commonwealth, 229 Va. 469, 331 S.E.2d 422 (1985), cert. denied, 475 U.S. 1099, 106 S. Ct. 1503, 89 L. Ed. 2d 903 (1986).

It is only where the record affirmatively shows an abuse of discretion that the trial court's ruling on a motion for a change of venue will be reversed. Poindexter v. Commonwealth, 218 Va. 314, 237 S.E.2d 139 (1977); Newcomer v. Commonwealth, 220 Va. 64, 255 S.E.2d 485 (1979); Watkins v. Commonwealth, 229 Va. 469, 331 S.E.2d 422 (1985), cert. denied, 475 U.S. 1099, 106 S. Ct. 1503, 89 L. Ed. 2d 903 (1986).

An application for a change of venue in a criminal case on the ground of local prejudice rendering impossible an impartial trial is a matter addressed to the sound discretion of the trial court and its ruling on this question will not be reversed on appeal unless the record clearly shows abuse of that discretion. Farrow v. Commonwealth, 197 Va. 353, 89 S.E.2d 312 (1955).

Change of venue is within the sound discretion of the trial court, and refusal to grant it will not constitute reversible error unless the record affirmatively shows an abuse of discretion. Stockton v.

Commonwealth, 227 Va. 124, 314 S.E.2d 371, cert. denied, 469 U.S. 873, 105 S. Ct. 229, 83 L. Ed. 2d 158 (1984).

The trial court must be allowed a wide discretion in deciding motions for change of venue. Looney v. Commonwealth, 115 Va. 921, 78 S.E. 625 (1913); Taylor v. Commonwealth, 122 Va. 886, 94 S.E. 795 (1918); Thompson v. Commonwealth, 131 Va. 847, 109 S.E. 447 (1921). See Wormeley v. Commonwealth, 51 Va. (10 Gratt.) 658 (1953); Poindexter v. Commonwealth, 218 Va. 314, 237 S.E.2d 139 (1977); Newcomer v. Commonwealth, 220 Va. 64, 255 S.E.2d 485 (1979).

Liberal construction. — Statutes conferring the right to a change of venue are enacted with the view of according litigants a fair and impartial trial, and being in furtherance of justice should be liberally construed so as not to defeat the right. Ramsay v. Harrison, 119 Va. 682, 89 S.E. 977 (1916).

Questions of venue not raised at the trial stage are waived. Loomis v. Peyton, 323 F. Supp. 246 (W.D. Va. 1971).

There is a presumption that a defendant can receive a fair trial from the citizens of the county or city in which the offense occurred. To overcome this presumption, the accused has the burden of clearly showing that there is such a widespread feeling of prejudice on the part of the citizenry as will be reasonably certain to prevent a fair and impartial trial. Stockton v. Commonwealth, 227 Va. 124, 314 S.E.2d 371, cert. denied, 469 U.S. 873, 105 S. Ct. 229, 83 L. Ed. 2d 158 (1984).

Trial court's discretion in ruling upon a motion for change of venue will not be disturbed in the absence of a clear showing of abuse. LeVasseur v. Commonwealth, 225 Va. 564, 304 S.E.2d 644 (1983), cert. denied, 464 U.S. 1063, 104 S. Ct. 744, 79 L. Ed. 2d 202 (1984).

Applied in Taylor v. Commonwealth, 58 Va. App. 185, 708 S.E.2d 241, 2011 Va. App. LEXIS 140 (2011).

II. GROUNDS FOR CHANGE.

Grounds must exist at time of trial. — Conditions which obtain when the trial was had and not those which existed at the time of the homicide are looked to under this section. Thompson v. Commonwealth, 131 Va. 847, 109 S.E. 447 (1921); Evans v. Commonwealth, 161 Va. 992, 170 S.E. 756 (1933).

On a change of venue motion courts must look to the conditions at the time of the trial, not to the conditions at the time of the crime. Newcomer v. Commonwealth, 220 Va. 64, 255 S.E.2d 485 (1979).

Mere belief or fears of defendant not sufficient. — The venue will not be changed for the mere belief of the party or his witnesses that he cannot have a fair trial in the county. Facts and circumstances must appear satisfying to the court. Wormeley v. Commonwealth, 51 Va. (10 Gratt.) 658 (1853); Muscoe v. Commonwealth, 87 Va. 460, 12 S.E. 790 (1891); Bowles v. Commonwealth, 103 Va. 816, 48 S.E. 527 (1904); Wright v. Commonwealth, 114 Va. 872, 77 S.E. 503 (1913).

Sheer volume of publicity is not alone sufficient to justify a change of venue. LeVasseur v. Commonwealth, 225 Va. 564, 304 S.E.2d 644 (1983), cert. denied, 464 U.S. 1063, 104 S. Ct. 744, 79 L. Ed. 2d 202 (1984).

Showing of either extensive publicity or widespread knowledge of the crime or the accused is insufficient by itself to justify a change of venue. Stockton v. Commonwealth, 227 Va. 124, 314 S.E.2d 371, cert. denied, 469 U.S. 873, 105 S. Ct. 229, 83 L. Ed. 2d 158 (1984).

Fair trial. — Under this section a change of venue should be ordered when necessary to secure a fair trial. Evans v. Commonwealth, 161 Va. 992, 170 S.E. 756 (1933).

Miscarriage of justice. — A criminal case ought not to be sent elsewhere for trial, unless it is made to appear to the court in which the case is pending that a trial in the vicinage is likely to result in a miscarriage of justice. Muscoe v. Commonwealth, 87 Va. 460, 12 S.E. 790 (1891).

Local prejudice of such a character as to prevent a fair and impartial trial in the county or district where the action is brought is a well recognized ground for a change of venue. Uzzle v. Commonwealth, 107 Va. 919, 60 S.E. 52 (1908); Burton v. Commonwealth, 107 Va. 931, 60 S.E. 55 (1908); Jones v. Commonwealth, 111 Va. 862, 69 S.E. 953 (1911); Ramsay v. Harrison, 119 Va. 682, 89 S.E. 977 (1916).

Race prejudice. — It was good cause for change of venue under this section that it appeared that the white people of the county

were so greatly aroused against the accused, who was a black man, that it was probable that he might not obtain a fair trial. Uzzle v. Commonwealth, 107 Va. 919, 60 S.E. 52 (1908); Burton v. Commonwealth, 107 Va. 931, 60 S.E. 55 (1908).

Prejudice not shown by brevity of jury's deliberations. — Defendant's contention that prejudice on the part of the jury was proved by the fact they deliberated only a relatively short time was without merit. Rees v. Commonwealth, 203 Va. 850, 127 S.E.2d 406 (1962), cert. denied, 372 U.S. 964, 83 S. Ct. 1088, 10 L. Ed. 2d 128, rehearing denied, 373 U.S. 947, 83 S. Ct. 1533, 10 L. Ed. 2d 702 (1963).

Pretrial publicity did not result in prejudice. — Pretrial publicity involving a single newspaper article, which was not read by any member of defendant's jury, was not enough to overcome the presumption that defendant would receive a fair trial in the jurisdiction where the offense occurred and, therefore, the trial court did not err in denying defendant's motion for a change of venue. Pritchett v. Commonwealth, 2008 Va. App. LEXIS 594 (Oct. 14, 2008).

Raising of fund to prosecute prisoner is not ground for a change of venue. Wormeley v. Commonwealth, 51 Va. (10 Gratt.) 658 (1853).

III. PROCEEDINGS.

When motion for jury from another county should precede. — Where an application for a change of venue is based simply on the ground of difficulty in obtaining jurors in the county free from exceptions, it must be preceded by an application to summon jurors from beyond such county. But this rule has no application where the motion for a change of venue is based upon the ground that there exists such prejudice and excitement against the accused as to endanger the fairness and impartiality of a trial conducted in the county. Wright v. Commonwealth, 74 Va. (33 Gratt.) 880 (1880); Joyce v. Commonwealth, 78 Va. 287 (1884); Waller v. Commonwealth, 84 Va. 492, 5 S.E. 364 (1888); Uzzle v. Commonwealth, 107 Va. 919, 60 S.E. 52 (1908); Burton v. Commonwealth, 107 Va. 931, 60 S.E. 55 (1908); Jones v. Commonwealth, 111 Va. 862, 69 S.E. 953 (1911); Looney v. Commonwealth, 115 Va. 921, 78 S.E. 625 (1913).

Renewal of motion for change. — Although a motion for a change of venue may have been properly overruled at one term of the court, it is renewable at a subsequent time whenever the exigencies of the situation may call it into requisition. Looney v. Commonwealth, 115 Va. 921, 78 S.E. 625 (1913).

The burden of proof is on the prisoner to show to the satisfaction of the trial court good cause to have the trial of the case removed to a county other than that in which the crime is committed. Slayton v. Commonwealth, 185 Va. 371, 38 S.E.2d 485 (1946); Rees v. Commonwealth, 203 Va. 850, 127 S.E.2d 406 (1962), cert. denied, 372 U.S. 964, 83 S. Ct. 1088, 10 L. Ed. 2d 128, rehearing denied, 373 U.S. 947, 83 S. Ct. 1533, 10 L. Ed. 2d 702 (1963).

The burden is upon the one requesting a change of venue to show clearly that there is such a widespread feeling of prejudice on the part of the citizens of the county as will be reasonably certain to prevent a fair and impartial trial. Farrow v. Commonwealth, 197 Va. 353, 89 S.E.2d 312 (1955).

Affidavits as to prejudice by disinterested persons required. — An application by defendant for a change of venue, on the ground of general prejudice existing against him in the town or county where the cause is to be tried, should be supported by the affidavits of disinterested individuals. Boswell v. Flockheart, 35 Va. (8 Leigh) 364 (1837); Wormeley v. Commonwealth, 51 Va. (10 Gratt.) 658 (1853); Muscoe v. Commonwealth, 87 Va. 460, 12 S.E. 790 (1891).

Statements of facts and circumstances in affidavits. — The affidavits in support of the motion for a change of venue, especially where opposed by counter affidavits of disinterested persons, should state the facts and circumstances tending to show that a fair and impartial trial cannot be had where the case is pending. King v. Commonwealth, 4 Va. (2 Va. Cas.) 78 (1817); Ramsay v. Harrison, 119 Va. 682, 89 S.E. 977 (1916).

Where the affidavits introduced by the Commonwealth stand unchallenged by counter affidavits or other evidence, the affidavits should be taken to prove what is within them. Poindexter v. Commonwealth, 218 Va. 314, 237 S.E.2d 139 (1977).

Effect of evidence opposing change. — A prisoner was

indicted for murder. Several witnesses testified that not greater than the usual prejudice existed, and in their opinion a fair trial could be had. It was held, that a change of venue was properly denied. Muscoe v. Commonwealth, 87 Va. 460, 12 S.E. 790 (1891).

Facts considered as established. — Upon an application for a change of venue in a criminal case, facts stated in the petition for removal which the Commonwealth does not attempt to controvert and which the accused is not permitted to sustain by proof, must be considered as established. Uzzle v. Commonwealth, 107 Va. 919, 60 S.E. 52 (1908); Burton v. Commonwealth, 107 Va. 931, 60 S.E. 55 (1908).

Evidence insufficient. — Defendant was not entitled to a change of venue of venire where there was no evidence of inflammatory newspaper or radio coverage of the case, no evidence of mass prejudice, hostility or threat of mob action, either before the jury was sworn or during the course of the trial, nor unusual difficulty in securing an impartial jury. Rees v. Commonwealth, 203 Va. 850, 127 S.E.2d 406 (1962), cert. denied, 372 U.S. 964, 83 S. Ct. 1088, 10 L. Ed. 2d 128, rehearing denied, 373 U.S. 947, 83 S. Ct. 1533, 10 L. Ed. 2d 702 (1963).

When jury subsequently secured after refusal of motion there is a presumption that motion unfounded. — Wright v. Commonwealth, 74 Va. (33 Gratt.) 880 (1880); Looney v. Commonwealth, 115 Va. 921, 78 S.E. 625 (1913); Taylor v. Commonwealth, 122 Va. 886, 94 S.E. 795 (1918). See also Joyce v. Commonwealth, 78 Va. 287 (1884); Waller v. Commonwealth, 84 Va. 492, 5 S.E. 364 (1888); Bowles v. Commonwealth, 103 Va. 816, 48 S.E. 527 (1904), overruled on another point, Graham v. Commonwealth, 127 Va. 808, 103 S.E. 565 (1920).

CIRCUIT COURT OPINIONS

Media coverage. — Defendant was not entitled to a change of venue pursuant to § 19.2-251, based on alleged heavy reporting by multiple news outlets, as defendant only alleged potential prejudice as a result of the sheer volume of media coverage, defendant did not allege or show that any media reports were inaccurate or intemperate. Commonwealth v. Boughton, 74 Va. Cir. 538, 2006 Va. Cir. LEXIS 323 (Chesapeake 2006).

§ 19.2-252. Court ordering change of venue may admit accused to bail and recognize witnesses; remand of accused not admitted to bail.

When the venue is so changed, the court making the order may admit the accused to bail and shall recognize the witnesses and the accused if admitted to bail and the bail be given, to appear on some certain day before the court to which the case is removed; if the accused be not admitted to bail or the bail required be not given, the court shall remand him to its own jail and order its officer to remove him thence to the jail of the court to which the case is removed, so that he shall be there before the day for the appearance of the witnesses.

History.
Code 1950, § 19.1-225; 1960, c. 366; 1975, c. 495.

Michie's Jurisprudence.
For related discussion, see 19 M.J. Venue, §§ 23, 25.

§ 19.2-253. Procedure upon and after change of venue.

The clerk of the court which orders a change of venue shall certify copies of the recognizances aforesaid and of the record of the case to the clerk of the

court to which the case is removed, who shall thereupon issue a venire facias, directed to the officer of such court; and such court shall proceed with the case as if the prosecution had been originally therein; and for that purpose the certified copies aforesaid shall be sufficient.

History.
Code 1950, § 19.1-226; 1960, c. 366; 1975, c. 495.

Michie's Jurisprudence.
For related discussion, see 19 M.J. Venue, §§ 17, 25.

ARTICLE 3.

ARRAIGNMENT; PLEAS; TRIAL WITHOUT JURY.

Michie's Jurisprudence.
For related discussion, see 1A M.J. Abatement, Survival and Revival, § 27; 4A M.J. Continuances, § 48; 5B M.J. Criminal Procedure, §§ 29, 30 - 34, 38, 43, 45, 49, 70, 78, 95; 9B M.J. Indictments, Informations and Presentments, § 52; 11B M.J. Jury, §§ 14, 63.

§ 19.2-254. Arraignment; pleas; when court may refuse to accept plea.

Arraignment shall be conducted in open court. It shall consist of reading to the accused the charge on which he will be tried and calling on him to plead thereto. In a felony case, arraignment is not necessary when waived by the accused. In a misdemeanor case, arraignment is not necessary when waived by the accused or his counsel, or when the accused fails to appear.

An accused may plead not guilty, guilty or nolo contendere. The court may refuse to accept a plea of guilty to any lesser offense included in the charge upon which the accused is arraigned; but, in misdemeanor and felony cases the court shall not refuse to accept a plea of nolo contendere.

With the approval of the court and the consent of the Commonwealth, a defendant may enter a conditional plea of guilty in a felony case, reserving the right, on appeal from the judgment, to a review of the adverse determination of any specified pretrial motion. If the defendant prevails on appeal, he shall be allowed to withdraw his plea.

History.
1975, c. 495; 1987, c. 357.

Law Review.
For 2006 survey article, "Criminal Law and Procedure," see 41 U. Rich. L. Rev. 83 (2006). For article, "Prosecutorial Power: A Transnational Symposium: The Worldwide Accountability Deficit for Prosecutors," see 67 Wash & Lee L. Rev. 1587 (2010).

CASE NOTES

Rejection of guilty plea. — Under the Virginia Constitution, the statutes and the Rules of the Supreme Court of Virginia, a trial court may reject a guilty plea to the whole of an indictment tendered without a plea agreement only when it determines that the plea is constitutionally invalid; further, this determination extends only to ensuring that a guilty plea is made voluntarily, intelligently and knowingly. Graham v. Commonwealth, 11 Va. App. 133, 397 S.E.2d 270 (1990).

Plea of nolo contendere. — See Jefferson v. Commonwealth, 27 Va. App. 477, 500 S.E.2d 219 (1998).

When an accused enters a voluntary and intelligent plea of nolo contendere to an offense, he waives all defenses except those jurisdictional. Therefore, by entering a plea of nolo contendere to a conspiracy charge, appellant foreclosed the opportunity to appeal the trial court's denial of his pretrial motion to dismiss. Clauson v. Commonwealth, 29 Va. App. 282, 511 S.E.2d 449 (1999).

By pleading nolo contendere, defendant, in essence, admitted as true each factual allegation set forth in the indictment, including the fact that the offense occurred in the Commonwealth. Jones v. Commonwealth, 42 Va. App. 142, 590 S.E.2d 572, 2004 Va. App. LEXIS 2 (2004).

Arraignment waived. — Trial court did not err in convicting defendant of attempted murder because defendant was fully aware of the attempted murder charge and was in no way prejudiced by the omission of a formal arraignment, defendant's continued silence in the face of repeated references to the attempted murder charge was tantamount to a waiver of his right to be arraigned and to enter a not guilty plea, and having failed to raise any objection, defendant waived any defect; neither § 19.2-254 nor § 19.2-259 expressly provides that formal arraignment and entry of a plea are jurisdictional requirements, but, to the contrary, § 19.2-254 expressly provides that a defendant can waive arraignment. Simmons v. Commonwealth, 54 Va. App. 594, 681 S.E.2d 56, 2009 Va. App. LEXIS 367 (2009).

Issues on appeal limited to those specifically reserved. — Defendant waived his right to challenge on appeal the legality of a traffic checkpoint where he entered into a conditional plea agreement that specifically preserved only the pretrial motions and argument made on a certain date, and where defendant raised no issue of the validity of the checkpoint in those motions or on that date. Wilkins v. Commonwealth, No. 2758-99-2, 2001 Va. App. LEXIS 211 (Ct. of Appeals Apr. 17, 2001).

Withdrawal permitted after prevail on appeal. — On appeal, the holding that defendant had not been in custody was reversed and therefore he had been entitled to Miranda warnings before police asked him about a weapon. Even if the Commonwealth was correct about the inevitable discovery of the weapon or the application of the public safety exception, defendant entered a conditional guilty plea pursuant to § 19.2-254 that allowed him to withdraw his plea if he prevailed on appeal. Hasan v. Commonwealth, 276 Va. 674, 667 S.E.2d 568, 2008 Va. LEXIS 120 (2008).

Because defendant entered a conditional guilty plea pursuant to § 19.2-254 and prevailed on appeal regarding the suppression of the evidence at issue, § 19.2-254 mandated that the case be remanded to permit the possible withdrawal of the plea. Baker v. Commonwealth, 57 Va. App. 181, 700 S.E.2d 160, 2010 Va. App. LEXIS 404 (2010).

Waiver by entering Alford plea. — Defendant by knowingly, intelligently, and voluntarily entering Alford pleas waived his right to appeal the denial of his motion to suppress a statement he made to police before he was Mirandized. Zimmer v. Commonwealth, No. 2623-00-2, 2001 Va. App. LEXIS 695 (Ct. of Appeals Dec. 27, 2001).

Alford plea. — Trial court did not err in finding that defendant violated his probation by refusing to admit that he committed the charged crime during court-ordered sex offender treatment because his Alford plea did not contain an implicit promise that he would never be required to admit his guilt; a defendant who enters an Alford plea is not an innocent person for the purposes of criminal sentencing and probation, and to mitigate the possibility that an innocent person would so plead, a factual basis is required supporting the finding of guilt before an Alford plea could be accepted. Carroll v. Commonwealth, 54 Va. App. 730, 682 S.E.2d 92, 2009 Va. App. LEXIS 392 (2009), aff'd, 280 Va. 641, 701 S.E.2d 414, 2010 Va. LEXIS 277 (2010).

Entry of a knowing and voluntary, but non-conditional plea waived appeal from denial of motion to suppress. — Because defendant did not enter a conditional guilty plea to a charge of possession of Oxycodone, in violation of § 18.2-250, but he entered said plea voluntarily and intelligently, he waived his right to appeal from the judgment denying his motion to suppress the evidence seized against him. Hill v. Commonwealth, 47 Va. App. 667, 626 S.E.2d 459, 2006 Va. App. LEXIS 63 (2006).

Lack of consent by Commonwealth. — Defendant's appeal based on his conditional guilty plea to a drug charge that reserved a challenge to the denial of his motion to suppress was properly dismissed because the mandatory language of § 19.2-254 required the Commonwealth's consent to a conditional plea, which it did not give. Witcher v. Commonwealth, 47 Va. App. 273, 623 S.E.2d 432, 2005 Va. App. LEXIS 526 (2005).

Conditional plea to misdemeanor vacated. — Although § 19.2-254 did not permit defendant to enter a conditional plea to a misdemeanor, defendant's guilty plea for obstruction of justice was vacated because it was not entered knowingly and intelligently; defendant informed the court that defendant wished to preserve right to appeal the denial of the motion to suppress and entered a guilty plea on understanding that an appeal was allowed. Cross v. Commonwealth, 49 Va. App. 484, 642 S.E.2d 763, 2007 Va. App. LEXIS 137 (2007).

Review on appeal not waived. — An accused, with the approval of the court and the consent of the Commonwealth, may enter a conditional plea of guilty in a felony case, reserving the right, on appeal from the judgment, to a review of the adverse determination of any specified pretrial motion; defendant did not waive his right to have the trial court's denial of his double jeopardy motion reviewed by entry of guilty plea. Johnson v. Commonwealth, 38 Va. App. 137, 562 S.E.2d 341, 2002 Va. App. LEXIS 228 (2002).

Attempt by defendant to have unwritten plea agreement accepted. — Trial court did not err by making a factual determination that the parties had not yet entered into a plea agreement with regard to defense counsel trying to stop a trial for defendant based on a purported oral plea agreement with the Commonwealth, which the Commonwealth confirmed was made because, although the parties may have reached an agreement, the agreement was not binding on the trial court because it had not been presented to the court in writing for the court to have either accepted or rejected it. Forcing the trial court to halt the trial in order to consider an orally proffered agreement undermined the clear purpose of Va. Sup. Ct. R. 3A:8(c), which was to ensure that plea agreements were fully disclosed to both the trial court and the defendant, and, considering the multiple continuances in the case, the trial court did not abuse its discretion when it refused to stop the trial for the purpose of entertaining defendant's last-minute motion for consideration of an unwritten plea agreement. Wilson v. Commonwealth, 46 Va. App. 408, 617 S.E.2d 431, 2005 Va. App. LEXIS 324 (2005), rev'd, remanded as to issue of recusal, 630 S.E.2d 326, 2006 Va. LEXIS 60 (2006).

Applied in Smith v. Commonwealth, 27 Va. App. 357, 499 S.E.2d 11 (1998); Jones v. Commonwealth, 28 Va. App. 444, 506 S.E.2d 27 (1998); White v. Commonwealth, 46 Va. App. 123, 616 S.E.2d 49, 2005 Va. App. LEXIS 325 (2005).

CIRCUIT COURT OPINIONS

Enforcement of plea. — Because defendant specifically waived the right to a preliminary hearing under § 19.2-218 in reliance on a plea agreement, and because defendant complied with defendant's modified obligation to provide a "very specific" description of the driver of a stolen vehicle, defendant was entitled to have the agreement enforced. Commonwealth v. Brown, 79 Va. Cir. 659, 2007 Va. Cir. LEXIS 334 (Alexandria Nov. 2, 2007).

§ 19.2-254.1. Procedure in traffic infraction cases.

In a traffic infraction case, as defined in § 46.2-100, involving an offense included in the uniform fine schedule established pursuant to § 16.1-69.40:1, a defendant may elect to enter a written appearance and waive court hearing, except in instances in which property damage or personal injury resulted. Arraignment is not necessary when waived by the accused or his counsel, when the accused fails to appear, or when such written appearance has been elected.

An accused may plead not guilty, guilty, or nolo contendere; and the court shall not refuse to accept a plea of nolo contendere. A plea of guilty may be entered in writing without court appearance.

When an accused tenders payment without executing a written waiver of court hearing and entry of guilty plea, such tender of payment shall itself be deemed a waiver of court hearing and entry of guilty plea.

In districts with traffic violations bureaus on July 1, 1977, the chief judge of the district may designate the traffic violations bureau for the receipt of a written appearance, waiver of court hearing and guilty plea.

History.
1977, c. 585; 1978, c. 605; 1992, c. 54.

§ 19.2-254.2. Procedure in nontraffic offenses for which prepayment is authorized.

In any prepayable nontraffic offense case as defined in § 16.1-69.40:2 a defendant may elect to enter a written appearance and waive court hearing. Arraignment is not necessary when waived by the accused or his counsel, when the accused fails to appear, or when such written appearance has been elected.

An accused may plead not guilty, guilty, or nolo contendere; and the court shall not refuse to accept a plea of nolo contendere. A plea of guilty may be entered in writing without court appearance.

When an accused tenders payment without executing a written waiver of court hearing and entry of guilty plea, such tender of payment shall itself be deemed a waiver of court hearing and entry of guilty plea. Likewise when a person charged with a prepayable nontraffic offense fails to enter a written or court appearance, he shall be deemed to have waived court hearing and the case may be heard in his absence. In all other respects prepayable traffic offenses shall be treated as all other misdemeanors.

History.
1978, c. 605; 1992, c. 54.

Cross references.
As to doubling of otherwise applicable fines set forth in Rule 3B:2 in the case of a waiver of appearance and plea of guilty under § 16.1-69.40:1 or § 19.2-254.2 for a violation of Chapter 8 (§ 46.2-800 et seq.) of Title 46.2 in a designated highway safety corridor, see § 46.2-947.

§ 19.2-255. Defendant allowed to plead several matters of law or fact.

The defendant in any criminal prosecution may plead as many several matters, whether of law or fact, as he shall think necessary, and he may file pleas in bar at the same time with pleas in abatement, or within a reasonable time thereafter; but

the issues on the pleas in abatement shall be first tried.

History.
Code 1950, § 19.1-242; 1960, c. 366; 1975, c. 495.

§ 19.2-256. Approvers.

Approvers shall not be admitted in any case.

History.
Code 1950, § 19.1-244; 1960, c. 366; 1975, c. 495.

CASE NOTES

The doctrine of "approvement" was never the law of this state. Oliver v. Commonwealth, 77 Va. 590 (1883).

An approver is one who being indicted for treason, or felony, and arraigned, confesses the fact before he pleads, and accuses others, his accomplices, in order to obtain his pardon. His approvement is equivalent to an indictment, and if he supports it in all respects, and the person accused by him is found guilty, the approver is entitled to his pardon, but if he is acquitted, the approver receives judgment to be hanged, upon his own confession of the indictment. Byrd v. Commonwealth, 4 Va. (2 Va. Cas.) 490 (1826).

The admissibility of an accomplice does not depend on the ancient, and exploded doctrine of approvement. Byrd v. Commonwealth, 4 Va. (2 Va. Cas.) 490 (1826).

§ 19.2-257. Trial without jury in felony cases.

Upon a plea of guilty in a felony case, tendered in person by the accused after being advised by counsel, the court shall hear and determine the case without the intervention of a jury; or if the accused plead not guilty, with his consent after being advised by counsel and the concurrence of the attorney for the Commonwealth and of the court entered of record, the court shall hear and determine the case without the intervention of a jury. In such cases the court shall have and exercise all the powers, privileges and duties given to juries by any statute relating to crimes and punishments.

History.
Code 1950, § 19.1-192; 1960, c. 366; 1975, c. 495.

Cross references.
As to right of defendant in criminal prosecution to plead several matters of law or fact, see § 19.2-255. For constitutional provision as to trial without jury in felony cases, see Va. Const., Art. I, § 8.

Law Review.
For survey of Virginia criminal law and procedure for the year 1970-1971, see 57 Va. L. Rev. 1438 (1971). For note, "Criminal Procedure and Criminal Law: Virginia Supreme Court Decisions During the 70's," see 15 U. Rich. L. Rev. 585 (1981).

CASE NOTES

The language of this section is both expansive and mandatory. Knight v. Johnson, 529 F. Supp. 1309 (E.D. Va. 1982), rev'd on other grounds, 699 F.2d 162 (4th Cir.), cert. denied, 464 U.S. 832, 104 S. Ct. 112, 78 L. Ed. 2d 113 (1983).

Consent required before defendant can waive right to jury trial not unconstitutional. — There is no violation of any constitutional right of a defendant in requiring consent of the prosecution and the court in order for the defendant to waive his right to a jury trial. Vines v. Muncy, 553 F.2d 342 (4th Cir.), cert. denied, 434 U.S. 851, 98 S. Ct. 163, 54 L. Ed. 2d 120 (1977).

A jury may be waived only with the consent of the defendant, the Commonwealth, and the court. The statutory requirement of consent by the Commonwealth and by the court does not violate any constitutional right of the defendant. Pope v. Commonwealth, 234 Va. 114, 360 S.E.2d 352 (1987), cert. denied, 485 U.S. 1015, 108 S. Ct. 1489, 99 L. Ed. 2d 716 (1988).

The Virginia Constitution and statutes are silent as to whether an accused will be permitted to withdraw a waiver of a trial by jury once that waiver has been exercised; and, if so, when such withdrawal of the waiver must be exercised. Thomas v. Commonwealth, 218 Va. 553, 238 S.E.2d 834 (1977).

A defendant has no right to a jury trial if he pleads guilty in person, voluntarily, and after having been advised by counsel. Hancock v. Slayton, 341 F. Supp. 436 (W.D. Va. 1972).

Necessity for renewal of waiver motion. — The defendant argued on appeal that since the case had to be recessed that the trial judge should have reconsidered the motion to withdraw the waiver of a jury trial because the reasons for denying the motion no longer existed. However, the defendant did not renew his motion to withdraw the waiver of a jury trial and did not request the trial judge to reconsider his ruling in any manner. Therefore, the trial judge had no opportunity to rule upon the question the defendant presented on appeal. Weis v. Commonwealth, No. 1986-95-2 (Ct. of Appeals Jan. 7, 1997).

Where guilty plea to whole of an indictment, error to submit issues to jury. — Where a guilty plea to the whole of an indictment has been tendered, it is reversible error for a trial court to submit the degree of guilt or the question of punishment to the jury. Graham v. Commonwealth, 11 Va. App. 133, 397 S.E.2d 270 (1990).

The requirement that a plea of guilty be entered in person is statutory. Gross v. Smyth, 182 Va. 724, 30 S.E.2d 570 (1944).

And may be waived. — The requirement that a plea of guilty be made in person, being only statutory, may be waived. Cottrell v. Commonwealth, 187 Va. 351, 46 S.E.2d 413 (1948).

Denial of right to withdraw waiver held abuse of discretion. — A motion to withdraw a waiver of a jury trial made 11 days before the defendant's cases were set for trial was seasonably made, and the trial judge abused his discretion in denying the defendant the right to withdraw his waiver where the motion was not for the purpose of delay and granting the motion would not have resulted in an unreasonable delay of the trial thereby impeding the cause of justice. Thomas v. Commonwealth, 218 Va. 553, 238 S.E.2d 834 (1977).

Jury trial cannot be waived unless the accused is represented by counsel. Mitchell v. Youell, 130 F.2d 880 (4th Cir. 1942).

But this requirement is likewise statutory. — The requirement of advice of counsel prior to waiver of a jury creates only a statutory right involving trial procedure, a violation of which would be subject only to direct attack and not by a collateral attack in a habeas corpus proceeding. Thornhill v. Smyth, 185 Va. 986, 41 S.E.2d 11 (1947).

Guilty plea tendered in mid-trial irrelevant to right to enter plea. — The fact that a plea is tendered mid-trial is irrelevant to the analysis regarding a defendant's right to enter a plea of guilty; no limitations either under the Virginia Constitution, statutes or Rules of Court exist which provide a time by which a defendant must enter his plea of guilty. Graham v. Commonwealth, 11 Va. App. 133, 397 S.E.2d 270 (1990).

Valid plea of guilty which is accepted by the trial court is equivalent to a conviction of the offense to which it is directed. The effect is to authorize imposition of the sentence prescribed by law for that offense. Knight v. Johnson, 529 F. Supp. 1309 (E.D. Va. 1982), rev'd on other grounds, 699 F.2d 162 (4th Cir.), cert. denied, 464 U.S. 832, 104 S. Ct. 112, 78 L. Ed. 2d 113 (1983).

Effect of plea. — A plea of guilty waives all but jurisdictional objections and the objection that no offense is charged. Hancock v. Slayton, 341 F. Supp. 436 (W.D. Va. 1972).

If a plea of guilty is made, the prosecution is entirely relieved of the burden of proving any facts. Hancock v. Slayton, 341 F. Supp. 436 (W.D. Va. 1972).

A guilty plea constitutes a waiver of all nonjurisdictional defenses. Knight v. Johnson, 529 F. Supp. 1309 (E.D. Va. 1982), rev'd on other grounds, 699 F.2d 162 (4th Cir.), cert. denied, 464 U.S. 832,

104 S. Ct. 112, 78 L. Ed. 2d 113 (1983).

Judge may hear evidence in accepting guilty plea. — In accepting a plea of guilty, any trial judge is free to hear the evidence he deems necessary to an understanding of the case and to the fixing of an appropriate sentence. Kibert v. Commonwealth, 216 Va. 660, 222 S.E.2d 790 (1976).

This does not mean that evidence must be heard upon a plea of guilty. Kibert v. Commonwealth, 216 Va. 660, 222 S.E.2d 790 (1976).

Not only is proof unnecessary to fix the degree of the crime upon a plea of guilty in a murder case, but the introduction of evidence to sustain a conviction upon a guilty plea is equally unnecessary in any criminal case. Kibert v. Commonwealth, 216 Va. 660, 222 S.E.2d 790 (1976).

Appeal. — Since a plea of guilty is itself a conviction by the defendant's own hand, it would seem senseless for a defendant to also want to claim the right to appeal his conviction, unless perhaps the guilty plea was coerced. Hancock v. Slayton, 341 F. Supp. 436 (W.D. Va. 1972).

A plea of guilty affords a defendant the right to appeal jurisdictional defects or questions concerning the length of his sentence only. Hancock v. Slayton, 341 F. Supp. 436 (W.D. Va. 1972).

Trial order recited that both the Commonwealth's attorney and the trial court concurred in defendant's jury trial waiver and a bench trial; this recitation satisfied the requirements of Va. Const., Art. 1, § 8, and of § 19.2-257 regarding waiver of a jury trial. Defendant made no objection to the trial court that the trial order did not accurately reflect the proceedings at his trial; thus, defendant's assertion that the order was inaccurate was waived and would not be considered on appeal. Lindsey v. Commonwealth, — Va. App. —, — S.E.2d —, 2006 Va. App. LEXIS 433 (Oct. 3, 2006).

Upon a plea of guilty in a felony case the court is required to try the case. Sentence cannot be imposed upon the plea alone. McGrady v. Cunningham, 296 F.2d 600 (4th Cir. 1961), cert. denied, 369 U.S. 855, 82 S. Ct. 944, 8 L. Ed. 2d 14 (1962).

Voluntary guilty plea stands unless induced by threats, misrepresentation or improper promises. — A plea of guilty entered by one fully aware of the direct consequences, including the actual value of any commitments made to him by the court, prosecutor, or his own counsel, must stand unless induced by threats (or promises to discontinue improper harassment), misrepresentation (including unfulfilled or unfulfillable promises), or perhaps by promises that are by their nature improper as having no proper relationship to the prosecutor's business (e.g., bribes). Brown v. Peyton, 435 F.2d 1352 (4th Cir. 1970), cert. denied, 406 U.S. 931, 92 S. Ct. 1785, 32 L. Ed. 2d 133 (1972).

Review of promises which might have induced guilty plea. — The United States Supreme Court's decision in *Brady v. United States*, 397 U.S. 742, 90 S. Ct. 1463, 25 L. Ed. 2d 747 (1970), provides the standard by which reviewing courts may now measure any promises which might have induced the defendant's guilty plea. Simply because the promise made by the judge induced the defendant to plead guilty does not make that plea involuntary. The promise must be of the prohibited type to affect the voluntariness of the defendant's plea. Brown v. Peyton, 435 F.2d 1352 (4th Cir. 1970), cert. denied, 406 U.S. 931, 92 S. Ct. 1785, 32 L. Ed. 2d 133 (1972).

The judge's participation in the plea discussion did not in itself render the plea involuntary. Brown v. Peyton, 435 F.2d 1352 (4th Cir. 1970), cert. denied, 406 U.S. 931, 92 S. Ct. 1785, 32 L. Ed. 2d 133 (1972).

This section vests the trial court with almost unfettered authority as to a post-guilty plea hearing. Knight v. Johnson, 529 F. Supp. 1309 (E.D. Va. 1982), rev'd on other grounds, 699 F.2d 162 (4th Cir.), cert. denied, 464 U.S. 832, 104 S. Ct. 112, 78 L. Ed. 2d 113 (1983).

The right to have the jury both try the issue of guilt and fix the penalty is a part of the right of trial by jury. Huggins v. Commonwealth, 213 Va. 327, 191 S.E.2d 734 (1972).

The established practice is one trial on guilt and punishment. Snider v. Cox, 212 Va. 13, 181 S.E.2d 617 (1971).

And change of that general practice is left to the legislature. Snider v. Cox, 212 Va. 13, 181 S.E.2d 617 (1971).

A trial to determine punishment alone is permitted where, under newly announced constitutional principles, a felon's sentence has been set aside, not because the jury that tried him could not constitutionally find him guilty, but because the jury as then constituted could not constitutionally impose the death sentence. Snider v. Cox, 212 Va. 13, 181 S.E.2d 617 (1971).

Although a felon's sentence was set aside because the jury as then constituted could not constitutionally impose the death sentence, the exclusion of jurors opposed to capital punishment did not result in an unrepresentative jury on the issue of guilt or substantially increase the risk of conviction, and there was no error in the action of the state courts in granting a new trial on the issue of punishment only. Snider v. Winstead, 339 F. Supp. 897 (W.D. Va. 1972).

No clearly established federal right to have death sentence decided by jury. — Because a federal habeas petitioner had pled guilty to two counts of capital murder for hire in the deaths of her husband and stepson, the inmate had no clearly established right under federal law to have her sentence decided by a jury. Thus, counsel's failure to question the constitutionality of § 19.2-257 did not amount to ineffectiveness. Lewis v. Wheeler, 609 F.3d 291, 2010 U.S. App. LEXIS 11377 (4th Cir. 2010), cert. denied, 131 S. Ct. 60, 177 L.Ed.2d 1148, 2010 U.S. LEXIS 5735 (U.S. 2010).

Effect of former law. — Former Va. Const., 1902, § 8, former § 19-166 (now this section) and former § 19-223 did no more than authorize and require a trial court, when a plea of guilty was entered in a criminal case, to dispose of the case without the intervention of the jury. The alternate provisions relating to a plea of guilty were intended only to make clear that the requirement of consent and concurrence entered of record did not apply when a guilty plea was entered and that it was mandatory for the court to dispose of the case without the intervention of a jury. Kibert v. Commonwealth, 216 Va. 660, 222 S.E.2d 790 (1976).

Guilty plea held not voluntary. — Where the defendant's guilty plea to a short form indictment of murder was based upon the advice of counsel who mistakenly understood that the Commonwealth would have the burden of raising the degree of the offense to first-degree murder through a showing of evidence of premeditation, when in fact the Virginia Supreme Court has determined that a guilty plea is always to the highest degree of the offense charged in the indictment and that the statutory short form of indictment for murder includes murder in the first degree, the plea could not be viewed as voluntary, intelligent or made with an awareness of the likely consequences. Harlow v. Murray, 443 F. Supp. 1327 (W.D. Va.), aff'd, 588 F.2d 1348 (4th Cir. 1978).

If the jury cannot agree on a punishment and if the defendant, the attorney for the Commonwealth, and the court agree, in the manner provided in this section, then the court shall fix punishment. Carcamo v. Commonwealth, No. 1554-95-4 (Ct. of Appeals Sept. 17, 1996).

Applied in Knight v. Johnson, 699 F.2d 162 (4th Cir. 1983); Smallwood v. Commonwealth, 14 Va. App. 527, 418 S.E.2d 567 (1992); Miller v. Commonwealth, 16 Va. App. 977, 434 S.E.2d 897 (1993).

§ 19.2-258. Trial of misdemeanors by court without jury; failure to appear deemed waiver of jury.

In all cases of a misdemeanor upon a plea of guilty, tendered in person by the accused or his counsel, the court shall hear and determine the case without the intervention of a jury. If the accused plead not guilty, in person or by his counsel, the court, in its discretion, with the concurrence of the accused and the attorney for the Commonwealth, may hear and determine the case without the intervention of a jury. In each instance the court shall have and exercise all the powers and duties vested in juries by any statute relating to crimes and punishments.

When a person charged with a misdemeanor has been admitted to bail or released upon his own recognizance for his appearance before a court of record having jurisdiction of the case, for a hearing thereon and fails to appear in accordance with the condition of his bail or recognizance, he shall be deemed to have waived trial by a jury and the case may be heard in his absence as upon a plea of not guilty.

History.
Code 1950, § 19.1-193; 1960, c. 366; 1975, c. 495.

Cross references.
For constitutional provisions as to trial by jury, see Va. Const., Art. I, § 8.

CASE NOTES

Failure to appear. — Defendant's failure to appear for trial in circuit court constituted a waiver of his right to trial by jury. Prezechowski v. Commonwealth, No. 0945-98-3 (Ct. of Appeals June 1, 1999).

The failure to include in the record the defendant's consent to waive his right to be tried by a jury or the concurrence by the attorney for the Commonwealth and the court required that the conviction be set aside. Wright v. Commonwealth, 4 Va. App. 303, 357 S.E.2d 547 (1987).

The Virginia Constitution and statutes are silent as to whether an accused will be permitted to withdraw a waiver of a trial by jury once that waiver has been exercised; and if so, when such withdrawal of the waiver must be exercised. Thomas v. Commonwealth, 218 Va. 553, 238 S.E.2d 834 (1977).

Necessity for renewal of waiver motion. — The defendant argued on appeal that since the case had to be recessed that the trial judge should have reconsidered the motion to withdraw the waiver of a jury trial because the reasons for denying the motion no longer existed. However, the defendant did not renew his motion to withdraw the waiver of a jury trial and did not request the trial judge to reconsider his ruling in any manner. Therefore, the trial judge had no opportunity to rule upon the question the defendant presented on appeal. Weis v. Commonwealth, No. 1986-95-2 (Ct. of Appeals Jan. 7, 1997).

Denial of right to withdraw waiver held abuse of discretion. — A motion to withdraw a waiver of a jury trial made 11 days before the defendant's case was set for trial was seasonably made, and the trial judge abused his discretion in denying the defendant the right to withdraw his waiver where the motion was not for the purpose of delay and granting the motion would not have resulted in an unreasonable delay of the trial thereby impeding the cause of justice. Thomas v. Commonwealth, 218 Va. 553, 238 S.E.2d 834 (1977).

Applied in Head v. Commonwealth, 3 Va. App. 163, 348 S.E.2d 423 (1986); Sisk v. Commonwealth, 3 Va. App. 459, 350 S.E.2d 676 (1986).

§ 19.2-258.1. Trial of traffic infractions; measure of proof; failure to appear.

For any traffic infraction cases tried in a district court, the court shall hear and determine the case without the intervention of a jury. For any traffic infraction case appealed to a circuit court, the defendant shall have the right to trial by jury. The defendant shall be presumed innocent until proven guilty beyond a reasonable doubt.

When a person charged with a traffic infraction fails to enter a written or court appearance, he shall be deemed to have waived court hearing and the case may be heard in his absence, after which he shall be notified of the court's finding. He shall be advised that if he fails to comply with any order of the court therein, the court may order suspension of his driver's license as provided in § 46.2-395 but the court shall not issue a warrant for his failure to appear pursuant to § 46.2-938.

History.

1977, c. 585; 1978, c. 605; 1989, c. 705; 2001, c. 414.

Law Review.

For article, "Appeal De Novo in Virginia: An Examination of Its Present Utility," see 42 Wash. & Lee L. Rev. 1149 (1985).

§ 19.2-259. On trial for felony, accused to be present; when court may enter plea for him, and trial go on.

A person tried for felony shall be personally present during the trial. If when arraigned he will not plead or answer and does not confess his guilt the court shall have the plea of not guilty entered and the trial shall proceed as if the accused had put in that plea. But for the purposes of this section a motion for a continuance, whether made before or after arraignment, shall not be deemed to be part of the trial.

History.

Code 1950, § 19.1-240; 1960, c. 366; 1975, c. 495.

Cross references.

As to presence of accused in prosecution of a misdemeanor, see § 19.2-237. As to trial without jury, see §§ 19.2-257 and 19.2-258.

Law Review.

For survey of Virginia law on criminal law for the year 1971-1972, see 58 Va. L. Rev. 1206 (1972).

CASE NOTES

I. Presence of Accused.
   A. In General.
   B. Waiver.
   C. When Essential.
   D. When Not Essential.
   E. Must Be Shown by Record.
II. Pleading.

I. PRESENCE OF ACCUSED.

A. In General.

Source of right. — A defendant's right to be present at trial arises from two sources, the Sixth Amendment and this section. Hunter v. Commonwealth, 13 Va. App. 187, 409 S.E.2d 483 (1991).

An accused's right to be present at trial arises from both the sixth amendment and this section. Cruz v. Commonwealth, 24 Va. App. 454, 482 S.E.2d 880 (1997).

Presence required when interests of prisoner affected. — It has been uniformly held that, in a trial for felony, it is absolutely necessary to a valid conviction that the prisoner shall be present in court whenever anything is done in his case in any way affecting his interest. Thus, it is the well-established practice that a prisoner accused of felony must be arraigned in person, and must plead in person; and, in all the subsequent proceedings, he must appear in person, not by attorney; and such appearance in person must be shown by the record. Boswell v. Commonwealth, 61 Va. (20 Gratt.) 860 (1871); Lawrence v. Commonwealth, 71 Va. (30 Gratt.) 845 (1878), overruled on another point, Jones v. Commonwealth, 87 Va. 63, 12 S.E. 226 (1890); Longley v. Commonwealth, 99 Va. 807, 37 S.E. 339 (1900); Gilligan v. Commonwealth, 99 Va. 816, 37 S.E. 962 (1901); O'Boyle v. Commonwealth, 100 Va. 785, 40 S.E. 121 (1901); Bowles v. Commonwealth, 103 Va. 816, 48 S.E. 527 (1904), over-

ruled on another point, Graham v. Commonwealth, 127 Va. 808, 103 S.E. 565 (1920).

The rule is that the accused must be present on his arraignment when any evidence is given or excluded, when the jury is charged, when the trial court wishes to communicate with the jury in answering questions by them, and when the jury receives further instructions. Lewis v. Commonwealth, 212 Va. 411, 184 S.E.2d 818 (1971).

Where the court without consulting or notifying either the Commonwealth or the defendant, responded to jury questions apparently through the bailiff, and the jury subsequently reached a guilty verdict without pursuing either request further, the trial court clearly erred in communicating with the jury in the defendant's absence and his conviction was reversed. Swilling v. Commonwealth, No. 1214-86-1 (Ct. of Appeals June 7, 1988).

The right of one charged with felony to be personally present throughout his trial was a basic principle of the common law, and the first sentence of this section is but a legislative declaration of that principle. Williams v. Commonwealth, 188 Va. 583, 50 S.E.2d 407 (1948).

This section is merely declaratory of the common-law principle. Near v. Cunningham, 313 F.2d 929 (4th Cir. 1963), commented on in 21 Wash. & Lee L. Rev. 346 (1964).

The common-law doctrine relating to the right of a person indicted for a felony to be present during his trial has been enacted into this section. Root v. Cunningham, 344 F.2d 1 (4th Cir.), cert. denied, 382 U.S. 866, 86 S. Ct. 135, 15 L. Ed. 2d 104 (1965). But see, United States v. Rhodes, 32 F.3d 867 (4th Cir. 1994), cert. denied, 513 U.S. 1164, 115 S. Ct. 1130, 130 L. Ed. 2d 1092 (1995).

This section requiring the presence of the accused at every stage of his trial is merely declaratory of a common-law right, and his absence at any critical stage is a violation of his constitutional right. Timmons v. Peyton, 360 F.2d 327 (4th Cir.), cert. denied, 385 U.S. 960, 87 S. Ct. 396, 17 L. Ed. 2d 305 (1966).

The provision that "a person tried for felony shall be personally present during the trial" is declaratory of a principle of the common law, and is an essential part of the process of law provided for the trial of persons charged with a felony. Conformity to the rule is essential to jurisdiction and the accused cannot waive it. Lewis v. Commonwealth, 212 Va. 411, 184 S.E.2d 818 (1971).

This provision is merely declaratory of a principle of the common law; it is an essential part of the process of law without which the courts have no jurisdiction to pronounce judgment; and it is a right which the accused cannot waive. Bilokur v. Commonwealth, 221 Va. 467, 270 S.E.2d 747 (1980).

The accused has an inalienable right to be present throughout his trial. Root v. Cunningham, 344 F.2d 1 (4th Cir.), cert. denied, 382 U.S. 866, 86 S. Ct. 135, 15 L. Ed. 2d 104 (1965). But see, United States v. Rhodes, 32 F.3d 867 (4th Cir. 1994), cert. denied, 513 U.S. 1164, 115 S. Ct. 1130, 130 L. Ed. 2d 1092 (1995).

And such right is to be carefully guarded. Root v. Cunningham, 344 F.2d 1 (4th Cir.), cert. denied, 382 U.S. 866, 86 S. Ct. 135, 15 L. Ed. 2d 104 (1965). But see, United States v. Rhodes, 32 F.3d 867 (4th Cir. 1994), cert. denied, 513 U.S. 1164, 115 S. Ct. 1130, 130 L. Ed. 2d 1092 (1995).

But it must not be so enlarged as to exceed its true scope and purpose. Root v. Cunningham, 344 F.2d 1 (4th Cir.), cert. denied, 382 U.S. 866, 86 S. Ct. 135, 15 L. Ed. 2d 104 (1965). But see, United States v. Rhodes, 32 F.3d 867 (4th Cir. 1994), cert. denied, 513 U.S. 1164, 115 S. Ct. 1130, 130 L. Ed. 2d 1092 (1995).

The statutory phrase "during the trial" has been defined as every stage of the trial from the accused's arraignment to his sentence, when anything is to be done which can affect his interest. Bilokur v. Commonwealth, 221 Va. 467, 270 S.E.2d 747 (1980); Jones v. Commonwealth, 227 Va. 425, 317 S.E.2d 482 (1984).

A person tried for a felony has the right to be personally present during the trial. This right has been read very broadly. The Supreme Court has defined the phrase "during the trial" to mean "every stage of the trial from [the accused's] arraignment to his sentence, when anything is to be done which can affect his interest." Brittingham v. Commonwealth, 10 Va. App. 530, 394 S.E.2d 336 (1990).

The in camera hearing was a stage of the trial where something could be done to affect the defendant's interests, therefore, the defendant was entitled to have a court reporter present. The in camera hearing was not merely to determine a legal question.

Testimony was heard to determine whether appellant was promised immunity from prosecution. Defense counsel was given the right to cross-examine the witness. The witness was taken to the judge's chambers for the purpose of asking him substantive evidentiary questions. Brittingham v. Commonwealth, 10 Va. App. 530, 394 S.E.2d 336 (1990).

The rule is well established that a person on trial for a felony cannot appear by attorney. Lawrence v. Commonwealth, 71 Va. (30 Gratt.) 845 (1878), overruled on another point, Jones v. Commonwealth, 87 Va. 63, 12 S.E. 226 (1890); Bond v. Commonwealth, 83 Va. 581, 3 S.E. 149 (1887); Shelton v. Commonwealth, 89 Va. 450, 16 S.E. 355 (1892); Snodgrass v. Commonwealth, 89 Va. 679, 17 S.E. 238 (1893); Coleman v. Commonwealth, 90 Va. 635, 19 S.E. 161 (1894).

The test for determining whether this section has been violated is whether or not the interest of the defendant has been affected by the action of the judge in defendant's absence. Rogers v. Commonwealth, 183 Va. 190, 31 S.E.2d 576 (1944); Thomas v. Commonwealth, 183 Va. 501, 32 S.E.2d 711 (1945); Carpenter v. Commonwealth, 193 Va. 851, 71 S.E.2d 377 (1952).

No violation found. — Where the trial court took the issue of its power to vacate a previously suspended sentence under advisement and, after ruling by letter opinion, held a further hearing where the decision was announced and final judgment was pronounced in defendant's presence, the trial court did not sentence defendant in his absence. Murphy v. Commonwealth, No. 0552-01-1, 2002 Va. App. LEXIS 216 (Ct. of Appeals Apr. 9, 2002).

Insufficient evidence of prejudice caused by continuance. — Where defendant fails to appear at trial and defense counsel requests a continuance, the Commonwealth cannot establish prejudice which the continuance causes only by showing that witnesses may be lost or not available for a second trial. Cruz v. Commonwealth, 23 Va. App. 113, 474 S.E.2d 835 (1996), aff'd on reh'g en banc, 24 Va. App. 454, 482 S.E.2d 880 (1997).

How irregularity cured. — If, in the absence of the accused, a motion for new trial is made and overruled, and afterwards during same term, in his presence, the overruling is rescinded, and he is invited to renew the motion, but refuses, the irregularity is thereby cured. Boswell v. Commonwealth, 61 Va. (20 Gratt.) 860 (1871); Bond v. Commonwealth, 83 Va. 581, 3 S.E. 149 (1887). See also Thomas v. Commonwealth, 183 Va. 501, 32 S.E.2d 711 (1945).

Due process. — Even if petitioner was entitled to be present at the time of presentation and argument of certain motions, and even if a ruling on the motions by the state court when petitioner was not present affected his interest, this does not bring into focus the due process clause of the Fourteenth Amendment of the United States Constitution. Owsley v. Cunningham, 190 F. Supp. 608 (E.D. Va. 1961).

Forfeiture of right. — While the accused cannot waive his right to be present during trial, the Supreme Court has never held that an accused cannot forfeit the right accorded by this section. Quintana v. Commonwealth, 224 Va. 127, 295 S.E.2d 643 (1982), cert. denied, 460 U.S. 1029, 103 S. Ct. 1280, 75 L. Ed. 2d 501 (1983).

An accused may forfeit both the constitutional right and statutory right to be present at trial. Cruz v. Commonwealth, 24 Va. App. 454, 482 S.E.2d 880 (1997).

Record supported the trial court's judgment that defendant was warned he could be tried in absentia if he did not appear for trial, and the trial court did not abuse its discretion when it allowed the Commonwealth to try defendant in absentia on a charge of conspiracy to commit grand larceny. Sullivan v. Commonwealth, No. 2300-02-4, 2004 Va. App. LEXIS 67 (Ct. of Appeals Feb. 10, 2004).

B. Waiver.

Defendant may waive his right to be present at beginning of his trial after presence at arraignment just as he may waive his right to be present at any later stage. Head v. Commonwealth, 3 Va. App. 163, 348 S.E.2d 423 (1986), overruled on other grounds, Cruz v. Commonwealth, 24 Va. App. 454, 482 S.E.2d 880 (1997).

An accused can waive his right to be present for the entire trial. Cruz v. Commonwealth, 24 Va. App. 454, 482 S.E.2d 880 (1997).

Requirements. — The waiver of the right to be present at a jury viewing of the crime scene must be given knowingly and intelligently and with sufficient awareness of its likely consequences. Hunter v. Commonwealth, 23 Va. App. 306, 477 S.E.2d 1 (1996).

No express statutory waiver of right to be present upon failure to appear. — There is no express statutory authorization for holding that a person not appearing at his felony trial will be deemed to have waived his right to be present. Sisk v. Commonwealth, 3 Va. App. 459, 350 S.E.2d 676 (1986).

Judge should inform defendant of possible waiver of right to be present. — It is recommended that the trial judge inform the defendant, upon accepting his plea, that failure to appear after arraignment may be deemed a waiver or forfeiture of his right to be present during the trial and that the trial will commence in his absence. The arraignment is a significant stage of the proceedings because it is generally considered the point at which a criminal trial begins. Sisk v. Commonwealth, 3 Va. App. 459, 350 S.E.2d 676 (1986).

Even without a prior warning that he could be tried in his absence if he failed to appear, the trial court properly found that the defendant voluntarily waived his right to be present at trial where, at the conclusion of the Commonwealth's evidence, the trial judge instructed the parties to coordinate a date to complete the trial, and the defendant failed to appear at the next three scheduled trial dates. Sykes v. Commonwealth, No. 2125-97-1 (Ct. of Appeals July 7, 1998).

Voluntary waiver found. — Defendant waived his right to be present at trial, where he and his attorney signed document entitled "Agreement Setting Case For Trial," which included both scheduled trial date and warning that failure to appear for trial could result in defendant being tried and convicted in his absence. Hutchings v. Commonwealth, No. 2935-98-2 (Ct. of Appeals Feb. 8, 2000).

Trial court did not err in convicting defendant of attempted murder because defendant was fully aware of the attempted murder charge and was in no way prejudiced by the omission of a formal arraignment, defendant's continued silence in the face of repeated references to the attempted murder charge was tantamount to a waiver of his right to be arraigned and to enter a not guilty plea, and having failed to raise any objection, defendant waived any defect; neither § 19.2-254 nor § 19.2-259 expressly provides that formal arraignment and entry of a plea are jurisdictional requirements, but, to the contrary, § 19.2-254 expressly provides that a defendant can waive arraignment. Simmons v. Commonwealth, 54 Va. App. 594, 681 S.E.2d 56, 2009 Va. App. LEXIS 367 (2009).

Defendant's unlawful wounding conviction was affirmed as defendant failed to object under Va, Sup. Ct. R. 5A:18 to the trial court's communication with the jury outside of defendant and counsel's presence allegedly in violation of the Sixth Amendment, U.S. Const. amend. VI, and §§ 19.2-259 and 19.2-263.1 until after the jury had been discharged, depriving the trial court of a chance to take corrective action or to declare a mistrial; defendant did not claim that the good cause or ends of justice exceptions to Rule 5A:18 applied, and the Rule 5A:18 exceptions were not considered sua sponte. Maxwell v. Commonwealth, 2013 Va. App. LEXIS 120 (Apr. 16, 2013).

Voluntary absence at trial, standing alone, does not constitute a knowing and intelligent waiver. Hunter v. Commonwealth, 13 Va. App. 187, 409 S.E.2d 483 (1991).

Defendant's voluntary absence alone does not constitute a knowing and intelligent waiver of his right to be present at trial; the "voluntariness" of such waiver is a fact specific question. Cruz v. Commonwealth, 24 Va. App. 454, 482 S.E.2d 880 (1997).

Bond warning that failure to appear could result in trial and conviction of defendant in his absence was not a sufficient basis upon which to find a knowing and intelligent waiver where the bond may have been too casually considered for the defendant to have known the consequences of his act, and there was no other evidence that the defendant knew or should have known or understood the consequences of his action. Sisk v. Commonwealth, 3 Va. App. 459, 350 S.E.2d 676 (1986).

As to waiver by defendant of right to be present at a view by the jury, overruling Noell v. Commonwealth, 135 Va. 600, 115 S.E. 679 (1932), to the extent that it elevated to jurisdictional stature the right of an accused to be present at a view and made the right not subject to waiver, see Jones v. Commonwealth, 227 Va. 425, 317 S.E.2d 482 (1984).

For cases holding that defendant cannot waive right to be present at all stages of his trial, see Jackson v. Commonwealth, 60

Va. (19 Gratt.) 656 (1870); Bond v. Commonwealth, 83 Va. 581, 3 S.E. 149 (1887); Jones v. Commonwealth, 87 Va. 63, 12 S.E. 226 (1890); Shelton v. Commonwealth, 89 Va. 450, 16 S.E. 355 (1892); Noell v. Commonwealth, 135 Va. 600, 115 S.E. 679 (1923); Near v. Cunningham, 313 F.2d 929 (4th Cir. 1963), commented on in 21 Wash. & Lee L. Rev. 346 (1964). But see Hagood v. Commonwealth, 157 Va. 918, 162 S.E. 10 (1932).

C. When Essential.

Imposition of sentence in defendant's absence held error. — None of the factors that underlie the decision to proceed with the trial of a defendant in absentia is present after the fact finder has determined guilt. Factors such as the loss or disappearance of witnesses, the difficulty of rescheduling the case, the burden of multiple trials where there are multiple defendants, denying an absent defendant the opportunity to obstruct the course of justice, and other prejudices to the Commonwealth cease to be compelling reasons for proceeding with the imposition of sentence. For these reasons, the trial court erred in imposing sentence on the defendant in absentia. Head v. Commonwealth, 3 Va. App. 163, 348 S.E.2d 423 (1986), overruled on other grounds, Cruz v. Commonwealth, 24 Va. App. 454, 482 S.E.2d 880 (1997).

Evidence read to jury. — Upon a trial for felony it is the right of the prisoner to be present from the arraignment to the verdict. And if the evidence of a witness on the trial, which has been reduced to writing, or any part of it, is read to the jury in the absence of the prisoner, it is error, for which the verdict will be set aside. Jackson v. Commonwealth, 60 Va. (19 Gratt.) 656 (1870).

Viewing of crime scene by jury. — An accused on trial for a felony has the right to be present in person during the trial; this includes every stage of the trial from arraignment to sentencing, when anything is to be done which can affect his interest. This definition encompasses a viewing of the crime scene by the jury. Hunter v. Commonwealth, 23 Va. App. 306, 477 S.E.2d 1 (1996).

D. When Not Essential.

Inquiry into and consideration of purely legal matters by trial judge. — The prisoner's right of personal presence in a felony case from arraignment to sentence must not be so enlarged as to exceed its true scope and thereby made to include all inquiry into and consideration of purely legal matters by the trial judge which are in fact and reality merely careful and prudent preparations for the resumption and conduct of the trial. Williams v. Commonwealth, 188 Va. 583, 50 S.E.2d 407 (1948); Carpenter v. Commonwealth, 193 Va. 851, 71 S.E.2d 377 (1952).

Pretrial conference on sanity of defendant. — A conference called pursuant to former § 19.2-169 (see now § 19.2-169.1) held in chambers on defendant's motion five days before the date set for trial, was not a "stage of the trial proper" within the intendment of this section. Quintana v. Commonwealth, 224 Va. 127, 295 S.E.2d 643 (1982), cert. denied, 460 U.S. 1029, 103 S. Ct. 1280, 75 L. Ed. 2d 501 (1983).

Pre-arraignment hearing concerning restraining of defendant. — A decision following a pretrial hearing, at which the defendant was not present, that the defendant should be shackled during subsequent proceedings was not a ruling that so affected the defendant's interests that his presence was mandated where the hearing was held six months before the trial finally commenced and nothing bearing on the merits of the case was discussed, considered or decided. Graham v. Commonwealth, 31 Va. App. 662, 525 S.E.2d 567 (2000).

The consideration of instruction in chambers in the absence of accused is unobjectionable. When the instructions are given or rejected by the court he must be present. Hagood v. Commonwealth, 157 Va. 918, 162 S.E. 10 (1932); Carpenter v. Commonwealth, 193 Va. 851, 71 S.E.2d 377 (1952).

The consideration of instructions by the trial court in chambers out of the presence of the defendant and the jury violates no right guaranteed by either the state or federal Constitutions. Root v. Cunningham, 344 F.2d 1 (4th Cir.), cert. denied, 382 U.S. 866, 86 S. Ct. 135, 15 L. Ed. 2d 104 (1965). But see, United States v. Rhodes, 32 F.3d 867 (4th Cir. 1994), cert. denied, 513 U.S. 1164, 115 S. Ct. 1130, 130 L. Ed. 2d 1092 (1995).

And consideration of sentence in chambers is unobjectionable. — Appellate court refused to review defendant's claim that the trial court violated his rights under the Sixth Amendment to the U.S. Constitution and § 19.2-259 when it did not permit him to attend a meeting it held in chambers to consider defendant's objections to the sentence the court imposed because the court considered all issues defendant raised during a hearing it held six weeks later, which defendant did attend. Baldwin v. Commonwealth, 43 Va. App. 415, 598 S.E.2d 754, 2004 Va. App. LEXIS 309 (2004).

As is statement to jury concerning securing sleeping clothes. — In prosecution for homicide, the jury was told by the judge in the absence of accused, that if any of them wanted pajamas, nightclothes or anything like that they should get the sergeant to telephone for them but they should not telephone themselves. It was held that this action of the judge was not a violation of this section, since it was inconceivable that his remarks could have affected in the slightest degree the interests of accused. Rogers v. Commonwealth, 183 Va. 190, 31 S.E.2d 576 (1944).

Direction as to delivery of transcript of evidence. — Where the presiding judge who heard the evidence and argument of counsel died, the direction by a temporarily presiding judge that a transcript of the evidence be taken to the appointed judge was no part of the trial and this section was inapplicable. Johnson v. Commonwealth, 184 Va. 466, 35 S.E.2d 770 (1945).

Precautionary remarks to jurors. — On the first day of a trial for murder, when only 14 of the necessary 20 prospective jurors had been selected, it was necessary to recess until the panel could be completed. The court, in the absence of accused, but in the presence of his counsel, instructed the prospective jurors not to discuss the case with anyone. When the court's attention was called to the fact that accused was absent from the courtroom, accused was brought in and the proceeding was repeated in his presence. It was held that it was inconceivable that the precautionary remarks of the judge could have affected in the slightest degree the interests of accused. Thomas v. Commonwealth, 183 Va. 501, 32 S.E.2d 711 (1945).

Suspensions of trial. — One of the defendants on trial for homicide was taken ill in jail, so that upon the advice of physicians the trial was suspended from time to time during two days because of his absence from the courthouse. This section provides that a person tried for a felony shall be personally present during the trial, but it also provides that a motion for a continuance, whether made before or after the arraignment, shall not be deemed a part of the trial. These suspensions were not part of the trial, and were not grounds for a reversal of the conviction of accused. The right of accused to be present was not thereby denied, but, on the contrary, accorded. Seymour v. Commonwealth, 133 Va. 775, 112 S.E. 806 (1922).

Abscondment during trial. — The general disruption to the proper administration of the criminal justice system is such that the Commonwealth should not have to prove any special prejudice when the defendant absconds after the trial has commenced. Barfield v. Commonwealth, 20 Va. App. 447, 457 S.E.2d 786 (1995).

When the trial court determines that a defendant has voluntarily and knowingly absconded from the jurisdiction after his trial has commenced, public policy dictates that a trial court, exercising its sound discretion, may proceed with the trial in the defendant's absence. Barfield v. Commonwealth, 20 Va. App. 447, 457 S.E.2d 786 (1995).

Denial of second motion to strike evidence made in judge's chambers. — In rape prosecution where first motion to strike evidence was made in defendant's presence, denial of second motion made in judge's chambers in defendant's absence while instructions were being discussed, was not prejudicial denial of accused's right to be present during trial. Carpenter v. Commonwealth, 193 Va. 851, 71 S.E.2d 377 (1952).

It is not necessary that a prisoner be present in a felony case when bills of exceptions are presented to and signed by the judge. Thurman v. Commonwealth, 107 Va. 912, 60 S.E. 99 (1908).

Accused has right to be present at view. — A view of the crime scene is part of the trial of a felony case at which an accused has a right to be present. Jones v. Commonwealth, 227 Va. 425, 317 S.E.2d 482 (1984).

This right may be waived. — The defendant in a felony case may waive his right to be present at a view of the scene of the crime. Jones v. Commonwealth, 227 Va. 425, 317 S.E.2d 482 (1984).

But view conducted in his absence must not prejudice

right to fair trial. — Even though an accused may waive his right to attend a view, the event must be conducted in a manner free from any prejudice to his right to a fair trial. In his absence, no evidence should be taken and no tests conducted. Neither should there be permitted any irregularity or misconduct which might tend to influence the trier of fact. Jones v. Commonwealth, 227 Va. 425, 317 S.E.2d 482 (1984).

Trial judge's conference with a juror whom the judge had observed dropping his head and closing his eyes during testimony of the State Chemist did not constitute a part of the defendant's trial, within the meaning of this section. Rather, the judge's action was merely administrative in nature and, accordingly, he was not obligated to notify the defendant and his counsel in advance of the conference or to advise them afterward what took place in chambers. This duty of notification and advice arises only when an ex parte communication relates to some aspect of the trial. Furthermore, the trial judge's remarks were innocuous. The trial judge merely sought to impress upon the juror the necessity to hear and consider every word of testimony before deciding whether to convict the defendant. And, in telling the juror that the case was a serious one carrying a heavy penalty, the judge only stated what was fact. Ellis v. Commonwealth, 227 Va. 419, 317 S.E.2d 479 (1984).

Appointment of new counsel. — This section does not require defendant's presence at the performance of the ministerial acts prior to trial of relieving previously-appointed counsel and appointing new counsel. Although defendant has the right to counsel, he is not guaranteed the services of a particular lawyer. For the purposes of this section, this means he does not have the right to insist that the court appoint his choice of counsel. Doxie v. Commonwealth, No. 0063-85 (Ct. of Appeals Aug. 26, 1986).

When trial may proceed in defendant's absence. — If the defendant is found to have voluntarily waived his right to be present, and it is further found that the burden of a continuance would be prejudicial to the Commonwealth's case, then the trial may, in the sound discretion of the court, properly proceed in the defendant's absence. Head v. Commonwealth, 3 Va. App. 163, 348 S.E.2d 423 (1986), overruled on other grounds, Cruz v. Commonwealth, 24 Va. App. 454, 482 S.E.2d 880 (1997).

Where the record in this case was totally devoid of any assurance, or even hint, that the defendant would be available in the future, and as far as the trial court was aware, the defendant could have fled the jurisdiction or the country for parts unknown, never to be heard from again, under such circumstances, there was no abuse of discretion in proceeding with the trial in the defendant's absence. Cruz v. Commonwealth, 23 Va. App. 113, 474 S.E.2d 835 (1996), aff'd on reh'g en banc, 24 Va. App. 454, 482 S.E.2d 880 (1997).

Where the record was devoid of any indication that defendant would be available for trial in the future and could have even fled the jurisdiction, trial court did not abuse its discretion to proceed to trial in the defendant's absence. Cruz v. Commonwealth, 24 Va. App. 454, 482 S.E.2d 880 (1997).

Voluntary absence found. — Where defendant's explanation that he missed trial because he drank too much and overslept clearly supported the trial court's finding that his absence was, indeed, voluntary, and where the "Appearance at Trial" form provided defendant both notice of his trial date and a warning that this failure to appear could result in a trial in his absence, the trial court properly found that defendant was voluntarily absent from trial and that he had notice both of the trial date and the possibility he would be tried in his absence if he failed to appear. Cruz v. Commonwealth, 23 Va. App. 113, 474 S.E.2d 835 (1996), aff'd on reh'g en banc, 24 Va. App. 454, 482 S.E.2d 880 (1997).

Factors considered in deciding to proceed with trial in defendant's absence. — It is not appropriate for every case to proceed to trial in the defendant's absence. In each instance, the decision must rest in the sound discretion of the trial judge who should consider, inter alia, the likelihood that the trial could soon take place with the defendant present, the difficulty of rescheduling, the burden on the Commonwealth in securing the attendance of witnesses on another date, and any other factors given to explain the defendant's absence. Head v. Commonwealth, 3 Va. App. 163, 348 S.E.2d 423 (1986), overruled on other grounds, Cruz v. Commonwealth, 24 Va. App. 454, 482 S.E.2d 880 (1997).

Jury deliberations. — Defendant does not have a right to be present in the courtroom while the jury is deliberating in another room. Remington v. Commonwealth, 262 Va. 333, 551 S.E.2d 620, 2001 Va. LEXIS 107 (2001), cert. denied, 535 U.S. 1062, 122 S. Ct. 1928, 152 L. Ed. 2d 834 (2002).

E. Must Be Shown by Record.

The record must show that a person indicted for felony was personally present during the trial therefor. It must show that he was arraigned in person, pleaded in person and was personally present whenever anything was done in his case in any way affecting his interests. The record can alone be looked to for the evidence to prove such presence at every stage of the trial. Jackson v. Commonwealth, 60 Va. (19 Gratt.) 656 (1870); Boswell v. Commonwealth, 61 Va. (20 Gratt.) 860 (1871); Cluverius v. Commonwealth, 81 Va. 787 (1886); Snodgrass v. Commonwealth, 89 Va. 679, 17 S.E. 238 (1893); Coleman v. Commonwealth, 90 Va. 635, 19 S.E. 161 (1894); Benton v. Commonwealth, 91 Va. 782, 21 S.E. 495 (1895); Gilligan v. Commonwealth, 99 Va. 816, 37 S.E. 962 (1901); Bowles v. Commonwealth, 103 Va. 816, 48 S.E. 527 (1904), overruled on another point, Graham v. Commonwealth, 127 Va. 808, 103 S.E. 565 (1920).

His presence must be shown by the record when motion for new trial is made and overruled. Bond v. Commonwealth, 83 Va. 581, 3 S.E. 149 (1887).

Presence inferred from record. — The whole record is to be looked to, and if anything appears in the record from which this presence must be necessarily inferred, it is all that the law requires. Lawrence v. Commonwealth, 71 Va. (30 Gratt.) 845 (1878), overruled on another point, Jones v. Commonwealth, 87 Va. 63, 12 S.E. 226 (1890); Cluverius v. Commonwealth, 81 Va. 787 (1886); Benton v. Commonwealth, 91 Va. 782, 21 S.E. 495 (1895).

Where at the end of the record of the proceedings of the court on the day of the conviction, it is stated, "And thereupon the accused was remanded to jail," this is conclusive that he had been personally present during all the proceedings had that day. Cluverius v. Commonwealth, 81 Va. 787 (1886).

The fact that a person charged with felony appears by attorney, does not show that he was not then personally present in court, and if it otherwise appears from the record that he was then personally present it will be sufficient. Lawrence v. Commonwealth, 71 Va. (30 Gratt.) 845 (1878), overruled on another point, Jones v. Commonwealth, 87 Va. 63, 12 S.E. 226 (1890); Benton v. Commonwealth, 91 Va. 782, 21 S.E. 495 (1895).

II. PLEADING.

The defendant must plead or the court plead for him before the trial may proceed. Crutchfield v. Commonwealth, 187 Va. 291, 46 S.E.2d 340 (1948).

Without a plea entered in person by the accused, or by the court, there can be no trial of a felony charge. Cassidy v. Peyton, 210 Va. 80, 168 S.E.2d 125 (1969).

A plea of nolo contendere is not such a confession of guilt under this section as is sufficient to sustain a conviction of felony. Cassidy v. Peyton, 210 Va. 80, 168 S.E.2d 125 (1969).

While a plea of nolo contendere is permissible in a misdemeanor case, such a plea cannot be accepted in a felony case. Cassidy v. Peyton, 210 Va. 80, 168 S.E.2d 125 (1969).

Effect when no plea properly made. — A plea of not guilty was withdrawn, a plea of guilty was rejected by the court, and the plea of nolo contendere was improperly received. Therefore, it follows that the case was tried without a joinder of issue upon any valid plea. Without a plea entered in person by the accused, or by the court, there can be no trial of a felony charge. This section concludes this question. Roach v. Commonwealth, 157 Va. 954, 162 S.E. 50 (1932).

ARTICLE 4.

TRIAL BY JURY.

Michie's Jurisprudence.
For related discussion, see 5B M.J. Criminal Procedure, §§ 23, 26, 38, 43, 48; 11B M.J. Jury, §§ 3, 20, 47, 54, 55; 13B M.J. New Trials, § 11.

§ 19.2-260. Provisions of Title 8.01 apply except as provided in this article.

Except as otherwise provided in this article, trial by jury in criminal cases shall be regulated as provided for in Chapter 11 (§ 8.01-336 et seq.) of Title 8.01.

History.
1975, c. 495; 1977, c. 624.

CASE NOTES

Prejudice not shown by mere fact that defendant was black and victim and jurors were white. — The allegation that defendant's sentence of death was racially motivated because he was black but the victim and all the jurors were white was insufficient to establish systematic exclusion of blacks from membership on juries, where he did not challenge the racial composition of the jury at trial, and nothing in the record suggests that his sentence resulted from racial prejudice. Watkins v. Commonwealth, 229 Va. 469, 331 S.E.2d 422 (1985), cert. denied, 475 U.S. 1099, 106 S. Ct. 1503, 89 L. Ed. 2d 903 (1986).

Denial of motion to withdraw waiver of jury trial was improper. — Denial of defendant's motion to withdraw his waiver of his right to a jury trial was improper because the record failed to show that the motion was made solely for the purpose of delay or whether defendant's request for a jury trial could have been accommodated at the time it was made. The record also failed to disclose the number of witnesses that would have been inconvenienced by the continuance, or the difficulty that rescheduling the trial would present to those witnesses. Cokes v. Commonwealth, 280 Va. 92, 694 S.E.2d 582, 2010 Va. LEXIS 60 (2010).

Voir dire permitted regarding gangs. — Defendant's convictions for second-degree murder, use of a firearm during the commission of a felony, and possession of a firearm by a convicted felon were proper because at least some of defendant's proffered gang evidence was erroneously excluded and that evidence was to be admissible on retrial. The evidence of the victim's friend and the victim's gang membership was going to be squarely before the jury and on remand, defendant was entitled to voir dire the venire panel regarding that issue. Cousins v. Commonwealth, 56 Va. App. 257, 693 S.E.2d 283, 2010 Va. App. LEXIS 214 (2010).

Applied in Brown v. Commonwealth, 29 Va. App. 199, 510 S.E.2d 751 (1999).

§ 19.2-261. Charging grand jury in presence of person selected as juror.

The court shall not charge the grand jury in the presence of any person selected as a juror to try any person indicted by the said grand jury. A violation of this provision shall constitute reversible error in any criminal case tried by a jury composed of one or more such veniremen.

History.
Code 1950, § 8-208.20; 1973, c. 439; 1975, c. 495.

§ 19.2-262. Waiver of jury trial; numbers of jurors in criminal cases; how jurors selected from panel.

A. In any criminal case in which trial by jury is dispensed with as provided by law, the whole matter of law and fact shall be heard and judgment given by the court. In appeals from juvenile and domestic relations district courts, the infant, through his guardian ad litem or counsel, may waive a jury.

B. Twelve persons from a panel of not less than 20 shall constitute a jury in a felony case. Seven persons from a panel of not less than 13 shall constitute a jury in a misdemeanor case.

C. The parties or their counsel, beginning with the attorney for the Commonwealth, shall alternately strike off one name from the panel until the number remaining shall be reduced to the number required for a jury.

D. In any case in which persons indicted for felony are tried jointly, if counsel or the accused are unable to agree on the full number to be stricken, or, if for any other reason counsel or the accused fail or refuse to strike off the full number of jurors allowed such party, the clerk shall place in a box ballots bearing the names of the jurors whose names have not been stricken and shall cause to be drawn from the box such number of ballots as may be necessary to complete the number of strikes allowed the party or parties failing or refusing to strike. Thereafter, if the opposing side is entitled to further strikes, they shall be made in the usual manner.

History.
Code 1950, § 8-208.21; 1973, c. 439; 1974, c. 611; 1975, cc. 495, 578; 1979, c. 230; 1997, cc. 516, 518; 2005, c. 356.

Editor's note.
Acts 1993, c. 930, cl. 3, as amended by Acts 1994, c. 564, cl. 2, and Acts 1996, c. 616, cl. 4, provides that the amendment to this section by Acts 1993, c. 930, cl. 1, shall become effective June 1, 1998, "if state funds are provided, including all local costs, to carry out the purposes of this bill by the General Assembly." The funding was not provided.

Law Review.
For article, "Trial by Jury and Speedy Justice," see 28 Wash. & Lee L. Rev. 309 (1971). For survey of Virginia law on pleading and practice for the year 1972-1973, see 59 Va. L. Rev. 1559 (1973). For survey of Virginia criminal procedure for the year 1977-1978, see 64 Va. L. Rev. 1419 (1978).

Research references.
Ward Wagner, Jr., Art of Advocacy: Jury Selection (Matthew Bender).

CASE NOTES

Waiver not ground for seating partial panel. — Under appropriate circumstances, a waiver of peremptory strikes by one or both parties is helpful and useful to the alleviation of an overcrowded docket. However, where a defendant has alerted the court to the existence of a potential problem and elects to stand on the statutory mandate of a panel of 20 jurors, he is entitled to a full panel of impartial jurors and may not be required to accept a lesser number simply because the Commonwealth agrees to waive one or more of its peremptory strikes. Fuller v. Commonwealth, 14 Va. App. 277, 416 S.E.2d 44 (1992).

Defendant may not be forced to use peremptory strikes to exclude certain veniremen. — It is prejudicial error for the trial court to force a defendant to use the peremptory strikes afforded him by this section to exclude a venireman who is not free from exception. Breeden v. Commonwealth, 217 Va. 297, 227 S.E.2d 734 (1976).

Refusal to remove partial juror not harmless error even if peremptory strike used. — A trial court's refusal to remove a juror who is not impartial does not constitute harmless error even if counsel uses a peremptory strike to exclude the juror. David v. Commonwealth, 26 Va. App. 77, 493 S.E.2d 379 (1997).

Effect of leading questions. — Answers to leading questions by the trial court or the attorney for the Commonwealth do not per se remove the taint resulting from expressed impression of guilt or bias. Proof that a prospective juror is impartial and fair should come from the juror and not be based on his or her mere assent to persuasive suggestions. Williams v. Commonwealth, 14 Va. App. 208, 415 S.E.2d 856 (1992).

Sufficient race-neutral explanation found. — Commonwealth's concerns with jurors who were not paying attention, one of whom was seen smiling at appellant, provided sufficient race-neutral explanations for the use of two of its peremptory strikes. Allred v. Commonwealth, No. 0223-94-2 (Ct. of Appeals March 14, 1995).

Peremptory strikes in capital murder trial. — There is no basis in Virginia law for additional peremptory strikes in a capital murder trial. Buchanan v. Commonwealth, 238 Va. 389, 384 S.E.2d 757 (1989), cert. denied, 493 U.S. 1063, 110 S. Ct. 880, 107 L. Ed. 2d 963 (1990).

Because peremptory challenges are a creature of statute and are not required by the Constitution, it is for the state to determine the number of peremptory challenges allowed; a defendant is only denied a "right" to peremptory challenges in a state capital proceeding when he does not receive that which state law provides. Goins v. Angelone, 52 F. Supp. 2d 638 (E.D. Va. 1999), appeal dismissed, 226 F.3d 312 (4th Cir. 2000).

Peremptory strikes may not be combined by co-defendants. — Defendant argued that he and the codefendant were each entitled to exercise four peremptory strikes pursuant to this section. However, the codefendants together were statutorily assured no more than four peremptory strikes. Because the trial court permitted a total of six peremptory challenges, there was no error. Banks v. Commonwealth, No. 2990-95-3 (Ct. of Appeals Feb. 4, 1997).

Number of peremptory strikes in case of joinder. — Defendants jointly tried are together entitled only to the four peremptory challenges provided by this section. Allowing each defendant three challenges, rather than four as requested, was within the discretion of the trial court. Adkins v. Commonwealth, 24 Va. App. 159, 480 S.E.2d 777 (1997).

Failure to select jury free from prejudice. — Where jurors in question were closely associated with either the accused or the victim and their respective families and the information to which they were exposed and/or conclusions they had formed, coupled with their associations, raised reasonable doubt that they could stand indifferent in the cause, the trial court failed in its duty to procure a jury free from prejudice when it declined to select other jurors. Williams v. Commonwealth, 14 Va. App. 208, 415 S.E.2d 856 (1992).

Refusal to strike for cause held proper. — Trial court's decision to deny defendant's motion to strike a prospective juror for cause was not manifestly erroneous and would not be reversed, as the trial court reasonably concluded that the prospective juror's apparent equivocation over whether she could be impartial was due to her nervousness about reaching a decision and wondering later whether it was the correct decision rather than any problem with being impartial. Weeks v. Commonwealth, No. 1939-02-3, 2003 Va. App. LEXIS 364 (Ct. of Appeals June 24, 2003).

The trial court erred in refusing to strike potential juror for cause, where although she stated that she would attempt not to base her judgment on information she had gained through the news media, she could not assure the court that she would render her verdict based solely on the evidence adduced at trial. Her answers raised a reasonable doubt as to her qualification to serve as a juror, a doubt that should have been resolved by granting defendant's motion to strike her for cause. DeHart v. Commonwealth, 19 Va. App. 139, 449 S.E.2d 59 (1994).

Restoration of juror removed for cause was reversible error. — A trial court's restoration to a jury panel of a venire member previously removed for cause, in order to have a full 20-member panel, was prejudicial, reversible error notwithstanding the fact that the Commonwealth had agreed to use its first peremptory strike to remove that member. Winston v. Commonwealth, 32 Va. App. 864, 531 S.E.2d 59, 2000 Va. App. LEXIS 529 (2000).

Decision of court to use procedure in subsection (4) (now subsection D) not reversible error. — Where Commonwealth refused to exercise right to strike three of four prospective jurors, decision of trial court to use procedure specified in subsection (4) (now subsection D) of this section was not reversible error. Reid v. Commonwealth, No. 0894-94-1 (Ct. of Appeals Oct. 10, 1995).

Too few jurors; mistrial mandatory. — Despite the accused's willingness to proceed with a jury of less than 12 members following the illness of a juror, where the Commonwealth insisted upon its co-equal right to a jury of 12 members, the trial court properly declared that a mistrial was mandatory; and a second trial for the same offenses did not violate double jeopardy principles. King v. Commonwealth, 40 Va. App. 364, 579 S.E.2d 634, 2003 Va. App. LEXIS 255 (2003).

Section not violated. — The trial court did not violate defendant's rights to strike a member of the jury pool chosen to sit on the jury, as provided by § 19.2-262, after another chosen juror was excused, as: (1) defendant was not forced to choose between two jurors that he had previously struck; (2) his prejudice argument based on his belief that the previous jury was a better jury for him than the jury that heard the case lacked merit; and (3) both sides knew which jurors the opposing party had struck the first time, and this foresight did not prejudice either party, as the reasons for those strikes were not disclosed by either party and none of the jurors knew who originally struck the excused juror. Moreover, the trial court was not faced with replacing a juror after the jury had been sworn, as provided by § 8.01-361, nor was the trial court faced with seating additional, alternate jurors, as provided by § 8.01-360. Waddler v. Commonwealth, 50 Va. App. 113, 646 S.E.2d 896, 2007 Va. App. LEXIS 248 (2007).

Applied in Strickler v. Commonwealth, 241 Va. 482, 404 S.E.2d 227 (1991); Atkins v. Commonwealth, 257 Va. 160, 510 S.E.2d 445 (1999).

§ 19.2-262.1. Joinder of defendants.

On motion of the Commonwealth, for good cause shown, the court shall order persons charged with participating in contemporaneous and related acts or occurrences or in a series of acts or occurrences constituting an offense or offenses, to be tried jointly unless such joint trial would constitute prejudice to a defendant. If the court finds that a joint trial would constitute prejudice to a defendant, the court shall order severance as to that defendant or provide such other relief justice requires.

History.
1993, cc. 462, 489; 1997, c. 518.

Law Review.
For 2000 survey of Virginia criminal law and procedure, see 34 U. Rich. L. Rev. 749 (2000).

CASE NOTES

Discretion of trial court generally. — The risk of prejudice will vary with the facts of each case and the decision to permit a joint trial is entrusted to the sound discretion of the trial court. Pitt v. Commonwealth, 28 Va. App. 730, 508 S.E.2d 891 (1999).

Discretion of trial court limited. — This section limits the discretion of the trial court as to joinder of defendants and requires a court to provide separate trials for individual defendants unless good cause exists for joinder and no prejudice would result from a joint trial; in determining whether a joint trial would prejudice a defendant, the court should require the party moving for severance to establish that actual prejudice would result from a joint trial. Goodson v. Commonwealth, 22 Va. App. 61, 467 S.E.2d 848 (1996).

Balancing tests. — In determining the propriety of ordering a joint trial of multiple defendants, the degree of prejudice may be balanced against the effectiveness of using other measures to cure any such risk, such as limiting instructions. Barnes v. Commonwealth, 22 Va. App. 406, 470 S.E.2d 579 (Va. App. 1996).

Actual prejudice must be demonstrated. — On appeal, a defendant must demonstrate that actual prejudice would result from a joint trial, and actual prejudice results only when there is a serious risk that a joint trial would compromise a specific trial right of the defendant or prevent the jury from making a reliable judgment about guilt or innocence. Strope v. Commonwealth, No. 1549-98-4, 2000 Va. App. LEXIS 310 (Ct. of Appeals Apr. 18, 2000).

Antagonistic defenses insufficient. — Actual prejudice does not exist merely because codefendants may have positions that are hostile to one another. Strope v. Commonwealth, No. 1549-98-4, 2000 Va. App. LEXIS 310 (Ct. of Appeals Apr. 18, 2000).

Good cause. — The need for numerous witnesses who would otherwise have had to appear at two separate trials constituted good cause for the joinder of the defendants' trials. Dearing v. Commonwealth, 259 Va. 117, 524 S.E.2d 121 (2000).

Prejudice does not exist merely because a co-defendant has a better chance of acquittal if tried separately. Barnes v. Commonwealth, 22 Va. App. 406, 470 S.E.2d 579 (Va. App. 1996).

Defendant was not prejudiced by a joint trial because he could not have compelled his codefendant to testify even if they had been tried separately. Dearing v. Commonwealth, 259 Va. 117, 524 S.E.2d 121 (2000).

Failure to show prejudice. — Despite the varying degrees of culpability that the defendant claimed, the defendant failed to show that the defendant suffered actual prejudice during the course of the trial as the record failed to show that the defendant's trial rights were affected or that the jury process was compromised. Accordingly, the trial court did not err by denying the defendant's motion to sever the trial. Turner v. Commonwealth, No. 1641-01-3, 2002 Va. App. LEXIS 707 (Ct. of Appeals Nov. 26, 2002).

Because defendant could point to no trial right that was compromised or any basis for concluding that the jury was prevented from making a reliable judgment about defendant's guilt or innocence, the trial court did not abuse its discretion by refusing defendant's request for a separate trial under § 19.2-262.1 and Va. Sup. Ct. R. 3A:10(a). Allen v. Commonwealth, 58 Va. App. 618, 712 S.E.2d 748, 2011 Va. App. LEXIS 258 (2011).

Right to confront witnesses was not violated by joint trial. — Where defendant in a joint criminal trial left the courtroom when a codefendant testified, and declined an offer to cross-examine the codefendant, defendant did not show actual prejudice from the joint trial, and was not deprived of any trial right, as defendant chose not to exercise his right to cross-examine, in favor of a different strategy. Duenas v. Commonwealth, No. 1429-01-3, 2002 Va. App. LEXIS 582 (Ct. of Appeals Oct. 1, 2002).

Prejudice requiring severance results only where there is a serious risk that a joint trial would compromise a specific trial right of one of the defendant's, or prevent the jury from making a reliable judgment about guilt or innocence; prejudice may be found where evidence, inadmissible against a defendant if tried alone, is admitted in a joint trial against a codefendant. Pitt v. Commonwealth, 28 Va. App. 730, 508 S.E.2d 891 (1999).

A defendant has no right to exclude relevant and competent evidence, such as the testimony of a former co-defendant. Barnes v. Commonwealth, 22 Va. App. 406, 470 S.E.2d 579 (Va. App. 1996).

Prejudice from admission of evidence. — Prejudice may result when evidence inadmissible against a defendant, if tried alone, is admitted against a codefendant in a joint trial. Strope v. Commonwealth, No. 1549-98-4, 2000 Va. App. LEXIS 310 (Ct. of Appeals Apr. 18, 2000).

Failure to show prejudice. — Defendant complained of prejudice in joinder with codefendant which would allow evidence admissible against codefendant but inadmissible against him, but failed to point out any trial right, as opposed to trial tactics, which was compromised or any basis for concluding that the jury was prejudiced by the joinder. Adkins v. Commonwealth, 24 Va. App. 159, 480 S.E.2d 777 (1997).

There was nothing in the record that suggested that joinder prejudiced defendant's defense by rendering him unable to call his codefendant as a witness. Even had the two men been tried separately, the codefendant, if called to testify, could have asserted his Fifth Amendment right against self-incrimination. Dickerson v. Commonwealth, 29 Va. App. 252, 511 S.E.2d 434 (1999).

Court did not err ordering defendant to be tried jointly with his codefendant where good cause for joinder was shown based on the number of witnesses, and defendant did not suffer prejudice from being unable to call his codefendant as a witness; even if the trial

court granted the codefendant immunity, however, it could not compel him to testify if he decided to assert his Fifth Amendment privilege. Byrd v. Commonwealth, No. 2550-02-1, 2003 Va. App. LEXIS 708 (Ct. of Appeals Dec. 30, 2003).

Applied in Davis v. Commonwealth, 36 Va. App. 291, 549 S.E.2d 631, 2001 Va. App. LEXIS 445 (2001).

CIRCUIT COURT OPINIONS

Antagonistic defenses insufficient. — Defendants' criminal cases, arising from an incident where they allegedly used violence to commit a robbery, were subject to joinder under § 19.2-262.1 because the Commonwealth showed good cause on the basis of judicial economy and defendants would not be prejudiced merely because they intended to implicate each other. Commonwealth v. Moeller, 72 Va. Cir. 402, 2007 Va. Cir. LEXIS 20 (Fairfax County 2007).

Failure to show prejudice. — Joinder of three defendants' trials on home invasion charges was proper under § 19.2-262.1 and Va. Sup. Ct. R. 3A:10 because all defendants were charged with the same offenses, which allegedly arose out of the same events. Moreover, the joinder of defendants' trials would promote efficiency and judicial economy, and defendants' argument that they would be prejudiced because they would be unable to compel each other to testify under U.S. Const., Amend. V, was without merit. Commonwealth v. Rice, 81 Va. Cir. 215, 2010 Va. Cir. LEXIS 301 (Hanover County Sept. 23, 2010).

§ 19.2-263. Repealed by Acts 1993, cc. 462 and 489.

Cross references.
As to present provisions relating to severance of a joint trial, see § 19.2-262.1.

§ 19.2-263.1. Contact between judge and juror prohibited.

No judge shall communicate in any way with a juror in a criminal proceeding concerning the juror's conduct or any aspect of the case during the course of the trial outside the presence of the parties or their counsel.

History.
1985, c. 176.

Law Review.
For 1985 survey of Virginia criminal procedure, see 19 U. Rich. L. Rev. 697 (1985).

CASE NOTES

Communication with jury. — Defendant's contention that the trial court erred in entering the jury room to answer a written question the jury posed about sentencing was waived and would not be considered the "ends-of-justice" exception to the requirement that objections to be reviewed on appeal had to be raised at trial; defendant and defense counsel's silence when the trial court asked whether the response should be phrased in open court with the jury or whether the trial court could step into the jury room and respond meant defendant on appeal was trying to take advantage of an error for which he was responsible since his failure to object at trial and his subsequent objection on appeal was inviting error and then trying to benefit from it, which the appellate court would not allow. Pope v. Commonwealth, 2006 Va. App. LEXIS 500 (Nov. 7, 2006).

Failure to object. — Defendant's unlawful wounding conviction was affirmed as defendant failed to object under Va, Sup. Ct. R. 5A:18 to the trial court's communication with the jury outside of defendant and counsel's presence allegedly in violation of the Sixth

Amendment, U.S. Const. amend. VI, and §§ 19.2-259 and 19.2-263.1 until after the jury had been discharged, depriving the trial court of a chance to take corrective action or to declare a mistrial; defendant did not claim that the good cause or ends of justice exceptions to Rule 5A:18 applied, and the Rule 5A:18 exceptions were not considered sua sponte. Maxwell v. Commonwealth, 2013 Va. App. LEXIS 120 (Apr. 16, 2013).

§ 19.2-263.2. Jury instructions.

A proposed jury instruction submitted by a party, which constitutes an accurate statement of the law applicable to the case, shall not be withheld from the jury solely for its nonconformance with model jury instructions.

History.
1992, c. 522.

Editor's note.
Acts 1992, c. 522, which enacted this section, in cl. 2 provides that the provisions of the 1992 act are declaratory of existing law.

Law Review.
For a case note, "The Extension of the Bruton Rule at the Expense of Judicial Efficiency in Gray v. Maryland," see 33 U. Rich. L. Rev. 227 (1999). For article surveying developments in criminal law and procedure in Virginia from July 2001 to September 2002, see 37 U. Rich. L. Rev. 45 (2002).

CASE NOTES

Trial court's issued instructions were not basis for reversal. — Because defendant's unwillingness to submit to a breath test without access to counsel amounted to an unreasonable refusal under subsection A of § 18.2-268.3, the trial court properly instructed the jury on said issue. Thus, defendant's conviction of unreasonably refusing to submit to a breath test, after having been convicted of two predicate offenses within ten years, in violation of § 18.2-268.3, was upheld on appeal. Brothers v. Commonwealth, 50 Va. App. 468, 650 S.E.2d 874, 2007 Va. App. LEXIS 370 (2007).

Refusal of instruction held error. — Trial court's refusal of a proffered instruction on the sole ground that it was not the model instruction was reversible error, as it violated the statutory dictate of this section, and because, had the trial court given defendant's proffered instruction, the jury would have been clearly informed that a manslaughter conviction was legally insufficient to sustain the charge of use of a firearm during the commission of a murder. Gaines v. Commonwealth, 38 Va. App. 326, 563 S.E.2d 410, 2002 Va. App. LEXIS 304 (2002), aff'd, 39 Va. App. 562, 574 S.E.2d 775 (2003).

Refusal of instruction held proper. — Defendant's proffered instruction was properly refused, as such was likely to be obvious to any rational juror applying his or her common sense, and was covered by other, more general jury instructions, which allowed defense counsel to argue these principles forcefully to the jury in closing argument. Hales v. Commonwealth, No. 2989-03-2, 2005 Va. App. LEXIS 109 (Ct. of Appeals Mar. 22, 2005).

§ 19.2-263.3. Juror information confidential.

A. The court may, upon motion of either party or its own motion, and for good cause shown, issue an order regulating the disclosure of the personal information of a juror who has been impaneled in a criminal trial to any person, other than to counsel for either party. Good cause shown includes, but is not limited to, a determination by the court that there is a likelihood of bribery, tampering, or physical injury to or harassment of a juror if his personal information is disclosed. An order regulating the disclosure of information may be modified, and the personal information of the jurors in a criminal case may be disseminated to a person having a legitimate interest or need for the information, with restrictions upon its use and further dissemination as may be deemed appropriate by the court.

B. In addition to the provisions of subsection A, the Supreme Court shall prescribe and publish rules that provide for the protection of the personal information of a juror in a criminal trial.

C. For purposes of this section, *"personal information"* means any information collected by the court, clerk, or jury commissioner at any time about a person who is selected to sit on a criminal jury and includes, but is not limited to, a juror's name, age, occupation, home and business addresses, telephone numbers, email addresses, and any other identifying information that would assist another in locating or contacting the juror.

History.
2008, c. 538.

§ 19.2-264. When jury need not be kept together in felony case; sufficient compliance with requirement that jury be kept together.

In any case of a felony the jury shall not be kept together unless the court otherwise directs. Whenever a jury is required to be kept together, it shall be deemed sufficient compliance although the court for good cause permits one or more of such jurors to be separated from the others; provided all such jurors, whether separated or not, be kept in charge of officers provided therefor.

History.
Code 1950, §§ 8-208.31, 8-208.32; 1973, c. 439; 1975, c. 495.

CASE NOTES

Whether to allow jury to separate is matter within trial judge's discretion. McFalls v. Peyton, 270 F. Supp. 577 (W.D. Va. 1967), aff'd, 401 F.2d 890 (4th Cir. 1968), cert. denied, 394 U.S. 951, 89 S. Ct. 1292, 22 L. Ed. 2d 486 (1969).

As to the exercise of the judge's discretion as to whether the jury should separate, it is to be remembered that the statutes or decisions of many states expressly allow the separation of the jury even in capital cases. Other states have provided the contrary. The practice has varied, with perhaps a slight present tendency in the more conservative direction. If the mere opportunity for prejudice or corruption is to raise a presumption that they exist, it will be hard to maintain jury trial under the conditions of the present day. Rich v. United States, 330 F. Supp. 949 (E.D. Va. 1967), appeal dismissed, 447 F.2d 990 (4th Cir. 1968), cert. denied, 394 U.S. 993, 89 S. Ct. 1473, 22 L. Ed. 2d 769, reh'g denied, 395 U.S. 931, 89 S. Ct. 1777, 23 L. Ed. 2d 252 (1969).

Exercise of trial judge's discretion in absence of accused. — While it is true that whether to allow the jury to separate is a matter within the trial judge's discretion, it is not to be presumed that the discretion is to be exercised in a vacuum; in other words, in the absence of the accused in contravention of § 19.2-259. Near v. Cunningham, 313 F.2d 929 (4th Cir. 1963), commented on in 21 Wash. & Lee L. Rev. 346 (1964).

Abuse of discretion. — In capital cases, where objection is interposed to the jury being permitted to separate after deliberations have been commenced, this may be an abuse of discretion, especially where no admonitions were given or where the inconvenience to the jurors is likely to touch upon their ability to give proper consideration to the case when they resume their deliberations. Rich v. United States, 330 F. Supp. 949 (E.D. Va. 1967), appeal dismissed, 447 F.2d 990 (4th Cir. 1968), cert. denied, 394 U.S. 993, 89 S. Ct. 1473, 22 L. Ed. 2d 769, reh'g denied, 395 U.S. 931, 89 S. Ct. 1777, 23 L. Ed. 2d 252 (1969).

Separation with consent of accused and Commonwealth. — Where the jury has been permitted to separate by the court upon the consent of the accused and the Commonwealth, prejudice will not be presumed in favor of the accused, and the burden will be upon him to show that the jury, during such separation, were guilty of misconduct to his prejudice. Powell v. Commonwealth, 182 Va. 327, 28 S.E.2d 687 (1944); Near v. Commonwealth, 202 Va. 20, 116 S.E.2d 85 (1960), cert. denied, 365 U.S. 873, 81 S. Ct. 907, 5 L. Ed. 2d 862 (1961), 369 U.S. 862, 82 S. Ct. 951, 8 L. Ed. 2d 19 (1962).

Refusal to sequester not error where jurors warned and questioned. — There was no error in denial of defendant's motion to sequester the jury during the three-day trial, where the trial judge, when he dismissed the jurors for the day, warned them to avoid news accounts of the trial and to refrain from discussing the case among themselves or with others, and when they reassembled, he questioned them on the subject and all replied that they had complied with his instructions. Boggs v. Commonwealth, 229 Va. 501, 331 S.E.2d 407 (1985), cert. denied, 475 U.S. 1031, 106 S. Ct. 1240, 89 L. Ed. 2d 347 (1986), 495 U.S. 940, 110 S. Ct. 2193, 109 L. Ed. 2d 521 (1990).

Media coverage does not mandate sequestration. — Sequestration is not mandated by the mere fact that the offense has received coverage in the news media. Pope v. Commonwealth, 234 Va. 114, 360 S.E.2d 352 (1987), cert. denied, 485 U.S. 1015, 108 S. Ct. 1489, 99 L. Ed. 2d 716 (1988).

If prejudice is shown, it is grounds for a new trial in any case where the jury is permitted to separate and the jurors have been subjected to outside influence. This is equally true both for a criminal case and with respect to a civil case involving a de minimis amount. Rich v. United States, 330 F. Supp. 949 (E.D. Va. 1967), appeal dismissed, 447 F.2d 990 (4th Cir. 1968), cert. denied, 394 U.S. 993, 89 S. Ct. 1473, 22 L. Ed. 2d 769, reh'g denied, 395 U.S. 931, 89 S. Ct. 1777, 23 L. Ed. 2d 2521 (1969).

Separation of jury as grounds for habeas corpus. — In a petition for habeas corpus, accused was entitled to a hearing where it was alleged that, in the absence of the accused, the trial judge had exercised his discretion to allow the jury to separate during the trial and that thereafter the jurors mingled with the spectators and heard prejudicial remarks. Near v. Cunningham, 313 F.2d 929 (4th Cir. 1963), commented on in 21 Wash. & Lee L Rev. 346 (1964).

Applied in George v. Angelone, 901 F. Supp. 1070 (E.D. Va. 1995).

§ 19.2-264.1. Views by juries.

The jury in any criminal case may, at the request of either the attorney for the Commonwealth or any defendant, be taken to view the premises or place in question, or any property, matter or thing relating to the case, when it shall appear to the court that such view is necessary to a just decision.

History.
Code 1950, § 8-216; 1977, c. 624.

CASE NOTES

Jury view of scene not abuse of discretion. — Trial court's decision to allow the jury to view the crime scene was not an abuse of discretion because it helped the jury understand the layout of the apartment complex, the location of the window and the parking lot, and how these factors related to the crimes. Smith v. Commonwealth, 48 Va. App. 521, 633 S.E.2d 188, 2006 Va. App. LEXIS 366 (2006).

View of prison facility. — With regard to defendant's convictions on two capital murder counts and the imposition of two death sentences against him, the trial court did not abuse its discretion in denying defendant's motion for a view of the prison facility since evidence on the general nature of prison life in a maximum-security facility was not even relevant to the determination of his future dangerousness. Prieto v. Commonwealth, 283 Va. 149, 721 S.E.2d 484, 2012 Va. LEXIS 20 (2012).

Applied in Tross v. Commonwealth, 21 Va. App. 362, 464 S.E.2d 523 (1995).

ARTICLE 4.1.

TRIAL OF CAPITAL CASES.

Michie's Jurisprudence.
For related discussion, see 5B M.J. Criminal Procedure, §§ 56, 59, 65, 70, 80; 9B M.J. Homicide, § 132.1.

§ 19.2-264.2. Conditions for imposition of death sentence.

In assessing the penalty of any person convicted of an offense for which the death penalty may be imposed, a sentence of death shall not be imposed unless the court or jury shall (1) after consideration of the past criminal record of convictions of the defendant, find that there is a probability that the defendant would commit criminal acts of violence that would constitute a continuing serious threat to society or that his conduct in committing the offense for which he stands charged was outrageously or wantonly vile, horrible or inhuman in that it involved torture, depravity of mind or an aggravated battery to the victim; and (2) recommend that the penalty of death be imposed.

History.
1977, c. 492.

The numbers of §§ 19.2-264.2 through 19.2-264.5 were assigned by the Virginia Code Commission, the numbers in the 1977 act having been 19.2-264.1 through 19.2-264.4.

Cross references.
As to review of death sentences by Supreme Court, see § 17.1-313.

Law Review.
For survey of Virginia criminal procedure for the year 1976-1977, see 63 Va. L. Rev. 1408 (1977). For article, "Psychiatry and the Death Penalty: Emerging Problems in Virginia," see 66 Va. L. Rev. 167 (1980). For survey of Virginia law on criminal procedure for the year 1978-1979, see 66 Va. L. Rev. 261 (1980). For comment discussing possible effects on Virginia's death penalty law in the light of recent United States Supreme Court decisions, see 15 U. Rich. L. Rev. 951 (1981). For comment on Virginia's death penalty, see 17 U. Rich. L. Rev. 603 (1983). For article, "Virginia's Capital Murder Sentencing Proceeding: A Defense Perspective," see 18 U. Rich. L. Rev. 341 (1984). For article, "Virginia's Capital Jurors," 44 Wm. & Mary L. Rev. 2063 (2003). For case note, "Atkins v. Virginia: Nothing Left of the Independent Legislative Power to Punish and Define Crime," 11 Geo. Mason L. Rev. 805 (2003).

CASE NOTES

I. General Consideration.
II. Aggravating Criteria.
   A. Vileness.
   B. Future Dangerousness.

III. Practice and Procedure.

I. GENERAL CONSIDERATION.

Constitutionality of article. — This article is not facially unconstitutional under the Eighth and Fourteenth Amendments. Smith v. Commonwealth, 219 Va. 455, 248 S.E.2d 135 (1978), cert. denied, 441 U.S. 967, 99 S. Ct. 2419, 60 L. Ed. 2d 1074 (1979); Evans v. Commonwealth, 222 Va. 766, 284 S.E.2d 816 (1981), cert. denied, 455 U.S. 1038, 102 S. Ct. 1741, 72 L. Ed. 2d 155 (1982), 498 U.S. 927, 111 S. Ct. 309, 112 L. Ed. 2d 295 (1990); Stamper v. Baskerville, 531 F. Supp. 1122 (E.D. Va. 1982), cert. denied, 459 U.S. 1225, 103 S. Ct. 123, 75 L. Ed. 2d 466 (1993).

Virginia's capital murder statutes are not unconstitutional. Clark v. Commonwealth, 220 Va. 201, 257 S.E.2d 784 (1979), cert. denied, 444 U.S. 1049, 100 S. Ct. 741, 62 L. Ed. 2d 736 (1980); Pope v. Commonwealth, 234 Va. 114, 360 S.E.2d 352 (1987), cert. denied, 485 U.S. 1015, 108 S. Ct. 1489, 99 L. Ed. 2d 716 (1988).

The death penalty under Virginia capital murder statute does not constitute cruel and unusual punishment nor deny a defendant due process or equal protection. Stamper v. Commonwealth, 220 Va. 260, 257 S.E.2d 808 (1979), cert. denied, 445 U.S. 972, 100 S. Ct. 1666, 64 L. Ed. 2d 249 (1980).

The statutory definitions of the two aggravating circumstances are not so vague as to vest the sentencing authority with standard-less sentencing power. Smith v. Commonwealth, 219 Va. 455, 248 S.E.2d 135 (1978), cert. denied, 441 U.S. 967, 99 S. Ct. 2419, 60 L. Ed. 2d 1074 (1979); Martin v. Commonwealth, 221 Va. 436, 271 S.E.2d 123 (1980).

The fact that the statutory alternative to the capital penalty is one which permits parole does not mean that the sentencing authority is constitutionally overbroad. Mercy by parole is not unconstitutional. Smith v. Commonwealth, 219 Va. 455, 248 S.E.2d 135 (1978), cert. denied, 441 U.S. 967, 99 S. Ct. 2419, 60 L. Ed. 2d 1074 (1979).

This section is not unconstitutionally vague. Briley v. Commonwealth, 221 Va. 563, 273 S.E.2d 57 (1980).

The dichotomy between "past criminal record of convictions" in this section and "prior history" in subsection C of § 19.2-264.4 does not render the statutory scheme unconstitutionally vague. LeVasseur v. Commonwealth, 225 Va. 564, 304 S.E.2d 644 (1983), cert. denied, 464 U.S. 1063, 104 S. Ct. 744, 79 L. Ed. 2d 202 (1984).

This section and § 19.2-264.4 C are not unconstitutional as being overly broad and impermissibly vague. Hoke v. Commonwealth, 237 Va. 303, 377 S.E.2d 595, cert. denied, 491 U.S. 910, 109 S. Ct. 3201, 105 L. Ed. 2d 709 (1989).

The statutory scheme violates neither the Eighth nor the Fourteenth Amendment to the federal Constitution. Watkins v. Commonwealth, 238 Va. 341, 385 S.E.2d 50 (1989), cert. denied, 494 U.S. 1074, 110 S. Ct. 1797, 108 L. Ed. 2d 798 (1990).

Defendant was not denied meaningful appellate review because the Virginia statutory death sentencing scheme adequately requires the trial judge or jury to specify the findings that justified imposition of a death sentence. Stockton v. Commonwealth, 241 Va. 192, 402 S.E.2d 196, cert. denied, 502 U.S. 280, 112 S. Ct. 280, 116 L. Ed. 2d 231 (1991).

The individualized sentencing required by the Constitution is satisfied when, having established the statutory predicate, the sentencing body then proceeds to consider whether the death penalty should be imposed in each specific case. Royal v. Commonwealth, 250 Va. 110, 458 S.E.2d 575 (1995), cert. denied, 516 U.S. 1097, 116 S. Ct. 823, 133 L. Ed. 2d 766 (1996).

Constitutionality claim was functional equivalent of "successive petition." — Where the substance of petitioner's claim—the constitutionality of Virginia's capital sentencing scheme—had been litigated, evaluated, and affirmed in several different forums, the claim raised no new or colorable issues; as such, it was the functional equivalent of a "successive petition" for habeas corpus within the meaning of Rule 9(b) of the Rules governing 2254 Cases. Jones v. Murray, 802 F. Supp. 1412 (E.D. Va.), aff'd, 976 F.2d 169 (4th Cir. 1992).

Aggravating factors not vague and overbroad. — The aggravating factors which a jury must find in order to impose the death penalty are not unconstitutionally vague and overbroad. Gray v. Commonwealth, 233 Va. 313, 356 S.E.2d 157, cert. denied, 484 U.S. 873, 108 S. Ct. 207, 98 L. Ed. 2d 158 (1987).

Aggravating circumstances part of means to narrow class of persons. — Future dangerousness and the other aggravating circumstances provided in the Virginia death penalty statutes are only a part of the means by which Virginia attempts to narrow the class of persons who receive the death penalty. Giarratano v. Procunier, 891 F.2d 483 (4th Cir. 1989), cert. denied, 498 U.S. 881, 111 S. Ct. 222, 112 L. Ed. 2d 178 (1990).

Difference in language of this section and subsection C of § 19.2-264.4 not unconstitutional. — Virginia's sentencing scheme is not overbroad, vague and facially unconstitutional merely because this section allows a jury to examine an accused's past criminal record while subsection C of § 19.2-264.4 provides for examination of his prior history. Gray v. Commonwealth, 233 Va. 313, 356 S.E.2d 157, cert. denied, 484 U.S. 873, 108 S. Ct. 207, 98 L. Ed. 2d 158 (1987).

Former statutes not presumptively unconstitutional. — The former death penalty statutes, enacted in 1975, were not rendered presumptively unconstitutional by decisions of the United States Supreme Court invalidating the death penalty statutes of other states. Smith v. Commonwealth, 219 Va. 455, 248 S.E.2d 135 (1978), cert. denied, 441 U.S. 967, 99 S. Ct. 2419, 60 L. Ed. 2d 1074 (1979).

Retroactive application not unconstitutional. — The application of the 1977 death penalty law to a defendant who committed his crime while the 1975 death penalty law was in effect was not a violation of the ex post facto clauses of the state and federal Constitutions, since the 1975 law was presumptively valid, in spite of decisions of the United States Supreme Court invalidating the death penalty statutes of other states, and since the changes incorporated in the 1977 law are both ameliorative and procedural. Smith v. Commonwealth, 219 Va. 455, 248 S.E.2d 135 (1978), cert. denied, 441 U.S. 967, 99 S. Ct. 2419, 60 L. Ed. 2d 1074 (1979).

Where two or more persons take direct part in inflicting fatal injuries, each joint participant is an "immediate perpetrator" for the purposes of the capital murder statutes. Thomas v. Taylor, 170 F.3d 466 (4th. Cir. 1999).

Prosecutorial discretion does not invalidate statute. — Existence of discretion in prosecutors to decide whether to charge capital murder or to accept a plea to a lesser offense does not lead to arbitrary imposition of the death penalty and does not invalidate Virginia's capital-murder statutes. Correll v. Commonwealth, 232 Va. 454, 352 S.E.2d 352, cert. denied, 482 U.S. 931, 107 S. Ct. 3219, 96 L. Ed. 2d 705 (1987).

Potential dangerousness or outrageous vileness must be found. — A jury may find either that the defendant is potentially dangerous or that the crime was outrageously vile and on the basis of these findings, it may recommend the death penalty. The jury may find these aggravating criteria and still not recommend death; what the statute does do, however, is prohibit the jury from recommending death unless it finds the presence of one or the other or both of these aggravating criteria. Briley v. Bass, 584 F. Supp. 807 (E.D. Va.), aff'd, 742 F.2d 155 (4th Cir.), cert. denied, 469 U.S. 893, 105 S. Ct. 270, 83 L. Ed. 2d 206 (1984).

Under this section, the death penalty may not be imposed unless the court or jury shall find one or both of two aggravating factors termed "future dangerousness" and "vileness." Yeatts v. Commonwealth, 242 Va. 121, 410 S.E.2d 254 (1991), cert. denied, 503 U.S. 946, 112 S. Ct. 1500, 117 L. Ed. 2d 639 (1992).

Petitioner's challenge to allegedly perjured testimony of a prosecution witness that petitioner had stated he could "do it again" in reference to a vile rape-murder to justify imposition of the death penalty for potential dangerousness failed, because either future dangerousness or vileness was sufficient to support imposition of the death penalty. Swisher v. True, 325 F.3d 225, 2003 U.S. App. LEXIS 5939 (4th Cir. 2003), cert. denied, 539 U.S. 971, 123 S. Ct. 2668, 156 L. Ed. 2d 679 (2003).

And this section not unconstitutional in not requiring both. — This section is not unconstitutional in not requiring a finding of both "future dangerousness" and "vileness" before imposition of the death penalty. A jury must find either future dangerousness or depravity before it may impose the death sentence, but it need not find both. Briley v. Bass, 584 F. Supp. 807 (E.D. Va.), aff'd, 742 F.2d 155 (4th Cir.), cert. denied, 469 U.S. 893, 105 S. Ct. 270, 83 L. Ed. 2d 206 (1984).

Where jury chose "or" without indicating factor and judge ordered jury to elect between circumstances. — Where confusion was created because the jury had not struck out the "and/or" provision pertaining to the aggravating circumstances on the jury form, where after the jury redeliberated, it again chose "or" without indicating a factor, and where defendant contended that the judge's statement to the jury that it must elect between the aggravating circumstances ruled out the possibility that the jury would select life imprisonment if it could not reach a unanimous decision on which aggravating factor was present, and in effect, the judge directed a verdict, even if the claim were not defaulted, it would have little merit because the jury obviously chose death as the penalty and it simply needed some guidance on expressing which factor it found to justify the penalty. Fitzgerald v. Thompson, 943 F.2d 463 (4th Cir. 1991), cert. denied, 502 U.S. 1112, 112 S. Ct. 1219, 117 L. Ed. 2d 456 (1992).

By refusing to question prospective jurors on racial prejudice, trial judge failed to adequately protect petitioner's constitutional right to an impartial jury. Turner v. Murray, 476 U.S. 28, 106 S. Ct. 1683, 90 L. Ed. 2d 27 (1986).

A capital defendant accused of an interracial crime is entitled to have prospective jurors informed of the race of the victim and questioned on the issue of racial bias. Turner v. Murray, 476 U.S. 28, 106 S. Ct. 1683, 90 L. Ed. 2d 27 (1986).

Applied in Coppola v. Commonwealth, 220 Va. 243, 257 S.E.2d 797 (1979); Clanton v. Commonwealth, 223 Va. 41, 286 S.E.2d 172 (1982); Fitzgerald v. Commonwealth, 223 Va. 615, 292 S.E.2d 798 (1982); Coleman v. Commonwealth, 226 Va. 31, 307 S.E.2d 864 (1983); Jones v. Commonwealth, 228 Va. 427, 323 S.E.2d 554 (1984); Briley v. Bass, 750 F.2d 1238 (4th Cir. 1984); Tuggle v. Commonwealth, 230 Va. 99, 334 S.E.2d 838 (1985); Wise v. Commonwealth, 230 Va. 322, 337 S.E.2d 715 (1985); Beaver v. Commonwealth, 232 Va. 521, 352 S.E.2d 342 (1987); Townes v. Commonwealth, 234 Va. 307, 362 S.E.2d 650 (1987); Smith v. Commonwealth, 239 Va. 243, 389 S.E.2d 871 (1990); George v. Commonwealth, 242 Va. 264, 411 S.E.2d 12 (1991); Jones v. Murray, 947 F.2d 1106 (4th Cir. 1991); Wise v. Williams, 982 F.2d 142 (4th Cir. 1992); Spencer v. Murray, 5 F.3d 758 (4th Cir. 1993); Goins v. Commonwealth, 251 Va. 442, 470 S.E.2d 114 (1996); Beaver v. Thompson, 93 F.3d 1186 (4th Cir. 1996); Mickens v. Commonwealth, 252 Va. 315, 478 S.E.2d 302 (1996); Royal v. Netherland, 4 F. Supp. 2d 540 (E.D. Va. 1998); Roach v. Angelone, 176 F.3d 210 (4th Cir. 1999); Lenz v. Warden of the Sussex I State Prison, 267 Va. 318, 593 S.E.2d 292, 2004 Va. LEXIS 46 (2004); Jackson v. Warden of the Sussex I State Prison, 271 Va. 434, 627 S.E.2d 776, 2006 Va. LEXIS 32 (2006); Elliott v. Warden of the Sussex I State Prison, 274 Va. 598, 652 S.E.2d 465, 2007 Va. LEXIS 137 (2007).

II. AGGRAVATING CRITERIA.

A. Vileness.

The second clause of this section provides specific criteria which must be met before the death penalty can be imposed on the basis of this clause. The conduct in committing the offense must be deemed to be outrageously or wantonly vile, horrible or inhuman, and second, the jury must conclude that the conduct establishes one of the following: torture of the victim, an aggravated battery of the victim, or the perpetrator's depravity of mind. Turner v. Commonwealth, 221 Va. 513, 273 S.E.2d 36 (1980), cert. denied, 451 U.S. 1011, 101 S. Ct. 2347, 68 L. Ed. 2d 863 (1981).

In capital sentencing, finding of vileness must be based on vile, horrible, or inhuman conduct involving torture or aggravated battery to victim, yet proof of any one component will support a finding of vileness. Beck v. Commonwealth, 253 Va. 373, 484 S.E.2d 898, cert. denied, 522 U.S. 1018, 118 S. Ct. 608, 139 L. Ed. 2d 495 (1997).

The words "depravity of mind" as used in this article mean a degree of moral turpitude and psychical debasement surpassing that inherent in the definition of ordinary legal malice and premeditation. Smith v. Commonwealth, 219 Va. 455, 248 S.E.2d 135 (1978), cert. denied, 441 U.S. 967, 99 S. Ct. 2419, 60 L. Ed. 2d 1074 (1979); Briley v. Commonwealth, 221 Va. 563, 273 S.E.2d 57 (1980); Bunch v. Commonwealth, 225 Va. 423, 304 S.E.2d 271, cert. denied, 464 U.S. 977, 104 S. Ct. 414, 78 L. Ed. 2d 352 (1983); Turner v. Commonwealth, 234 Va. 543, 364 S.E.2d 483, cert. denied, 486 U.S. 1017, 108 S. Ct. 1756, 100 L. Ed. 2d 218 (1988).

Depravity of mind established. — The defendant's actions established depravity of mind, that is, a degree of moral turpitude

and physical debasement surpassing that inherent in the definition of ordinary legal malice and premeditation, where the defendant shot the victims in front of their loved ones and family members after having forcibly invaded the sanctity of their homes, the killings were unprovoked, premeditated and methodical, and the defendant showed no mercy towards his victims. Walker v. Commonwealth, 258 Va. 54, 515 S.E.2d 565 (1999), cert. denied, 528 U.S. 1125, 120 S. Ct. 955, 145 L.Ed. 2d 829 (2000).

Sufficient evidence of defendant's "depravity of mind" existed in a case where defendant recruited two people to kill her husband and stepson so she could take control of her husband's assets and obtain the proceeds of her stepson's life insurance policies; the husband and the stepson would not have been killed but for the fact that defendant was the mastermind behind their murders, defendant initiated a new plan to kill the two men after the first plan failed, and defendant did not report the murders for at least 45 minutes after the two murderers shot the husband and stepson, accordingly, imposing a death sentence on defendant was proper. Lewis v. Commonwealth, 267 Va. 302, 593 S.E.2d 220, 2004 Va. LEXIS 47, cert. denied, 543 U.S. 904, 125 S. Ct. 201, 160 L. Ed. 2d 177 (2004).

Fact that defendant was the mastermind of a murder for hire plot and that defendant gave specific directions for the manner in which the victim was to be murdered supported a finding of depravity of mind and thus satisfied the statutory predicate of vileness. Teleguz v. Commonwealth, 273 Va. 458, 643 S.E.2d 708, 2007 Va. LEXIS 64 (2007), cert. denied, Teleguz v. Virginia, 522 U.S. 1191, 2008 U.S. LEXIS 1412, 128 S.Ct. 1228 (2008).

Evidence was sufficient to support a finding that defendant's conduct involved depravity of mind in that he acted with a degree of moral turpitude and surpassing that inherent in the definition of ordinary legal malice and premeditation, and a finding of depravity of mind was sufficient by itself to support a finding of vileness under § 19.2-264.2. Morva v. Commonwealth, 278 Va. 329, 683 S.E.2d 553, 2009 Va. LEXIS 84 (2009), cert. denied, 131 S. Ct. 97, 178 L. Ed. 2d 61, 2010 U.S. LEXIS 5806 (U.S. 2010).

Vileness factor does not include requirement that defendant's mental state embrace the intent to commit an outrageously or wantonly vile murder. Reid v. Commonwealth, 256 Va. 561, 506 S.E.2d 787 (1998), cert. denied, 528 U.S. 833, 120 S. Ct. 91, 145 L. Ed. 2d 77 (1999).

Psychological torture as proof of depravity. — Depravity of mind, an aspect of the vileness predicate, can be established by proof of psychological torture. Poyner v. Commonwealth, 229 Va. 401, 329 S.E.2d 815, cert. denied, 474 U.S. 865, 106 S. Ct. 189, 88 L. Ed. 2d 158, 474 U.S. 888, 106 S. Ct. 208, 88 L. Ed. 2d 178 (1985). See also Mueller v. Murray, 252 Va. 356, 478 S.E.2d 542 (1996).

Depravity of mind can be established by proof of psychological torture of the victim. Mueller v. Commonwealth, 244 Va. 386, 422 S.E.2d 380 (1992), cert. denied, 507 U.S. 1043, 113 S. Ct. 1880, 123 L. Ed. 2d 498 (1993), overruled in part on other grounds by Morrisette v. Warden of the Sussex I State Prison, 270 Va. 188, 613 S.E.2d 551 (2005).. See also Mueller v. Murray, 252 Va. 356, 478 S.E.2d 542 (1996).

Evidence of sexual mutilation, whether occurring before or after death, evinces a depravity of mind within the meaning of this section. Mueller v. Commonwealth, 244 Va. 386, 422 S.E.2d 380 (1992), cert. denied, 507 U.S. 1043, 113 S. Ct. 1880, 123 L. Ed. 2d 498 (1993), overruled in part on other grounds by Morrisette v. Warden of the Sussex I State Prison, 270 Va. 188, 613 S.E.2d 551 (2005).. See also Mueller v. Murray, 252 Va. 356, 478 S.E.2d 542 (1996).

The words "aggravated battery" as used in this article mean a battery which, qualitatively and quantitatively, is more culpable than the minimum necessary to accomplish an act of murder. Smith v. Commonwealth, 219 Va. 455, 248 S.E.2d 135 (1978), cert. denied, 441 U.S. 967, 99 S. Ct. 2419, 60 L. Ed. 2d 1074 (1979); Briley v. Commonwealth, 221 Va. 563, 273 S.E.2d 57 (1980); Whitley v. Commonwealth, 223 Va. 66, 286 S.E.2d 162, cert. denied, 459 U.S. 882, 74 L. Ed. 2d 148, 103 S. Ct. 181 (1982); Turner v. Commonwealth, 234 Va. 543, 364 S.E.2d 483, cert. denied, 486 U.S. 1017, 108 S. Ct. 1756, 100 L. Ed. 2d 218 (1988); Mueller v. Commonwealth, 244 Va. 386, 422 S.E.2d 380 (1992), cert. denied, 507 U.S. 1043, 113 S. Ct. 1880, 123 L. Ed. 2d 498 (1993). See also Mueller v. Murray, 252 Va. 356, 478 S.E.2d 542 (1996).

"Aggravated battery" means a battery which, qualitatively and quantitatively, is more culpable than the minimum necessary to accomplish an act of murder. Edmonds v. Commonwealth, 229 Va. 303, 329 S.E.2d 807, cert. denied, 474 U.S. 975, 106 S. Ct. 339, 88 L. Ed. 2d 324 (1985).

Aggravated battery committed where defendant robbed, raped, and forced victim to await execution. Hedrick v. Commonwealth, 257 Va. 328, 513 S.E.2d 634, cert. denied, 528 U.S. 952, 120 S. Ct. 376, 145 L. Ed. 2d 294 (1999).

The terms "depravity of mind" and "aggravated battery" are used in this section in the disjunctive, therefore, it was not necessary to discuss depravity of mind in a hearing where both aggravated battery and depravity of mind were found. Turner v. Commonwealth, 234 Va. 543, 364 S.E.2d 483, cert. denied, 486 U.S. 1017, 108 S. Ct. 1756, 100 L. Ed. 2d 218 (1988).

Depravity of mind may exist alone to support vileness finding. — This section and subsection C of § 19.2-264.4 define vileness as conduct that involves torture, depravity of mind, or aggravated battery to the victim; the use of the disjunctive word "or," rather than the conjunctive "and," signifies the availability of alternative choices. Hence, depravity of mind can exist independently of the presence of torture or aggravated battery and may alone support a finding of vileness as a basis for a sentence of death. Bunch v. Commonwealth, 225 Va. 423, 304 S.E.2d 271, cert. denied, 464 U.S. 977, 104 S. Ct. 414, 78 L. Ed. 2d 352 (1983), 505 U.S. 1230, 112 S. Ct. 3056, 120 L. Ed. 2d 922 (1992).

Number or nature of batteries inflicted upon victim is the essence of the test whether the defendant's conduct was outrageously or wantonly vile, horrible or inhuman in that it involved an aggravated battery. Boggs v. Commonwealth, 229 Va. 501, 331 S.E.2d 407 (1985), cert. denied, 475 U.S. 1031, 106 S. Ct. 1240, 89 L. Ed. 2d 347 (1986), 495 U.S. 940, 110 S. Ct. 2193, 109 L. Ed. 2d 521 (1990).

The number or nature of the batteries inflicted upon the victim is a proper test as to whether the defendant's conduct was outrageous or wantonly vile, horrible, or inhuman in that it involved an aggravated battery. Boggs v. Bair, 892 F.2d 1193 (4th Cir. 1989), cert. denied, 495 U.S. 940, 110 S. Ct. 2193, 109 L. Ed. 2d 521 (1990).

A killing inflicted by multiple gunshot wounds may constitute an "aggravated battery" within the meaning of this section where there is an appreciable lapse of time between the first shot and the last, and where death does not result instantaneously from the first. Barnes v. Commonwealth, 234 Va. 130, 360 S.E.2d 196 (1987), cert. denied, 484 U.S. 1036, 108 S. Ct. 763, 98 L. Ed. 2d 779 (1988).

Where the evidence established that the defendant shot one victim three times and the other victim seven times, such multiple gunshots established aggravated battery which would support a finding of vileness. Walker v. Commonwealth, 258 Va. 54, 515 S.E.2d 565 (1999), cert. denied, 528 U.S. 1125, 120 S. Ct. 955, 145 L.Ed. 2d 829 (2000).

If the killing of any victim in a multiple homicide meets the test of this section, the death penalty may be imposed; the tests required by this section contain no requirement that, in the case of multiple homicides, all killings must meet the test of vileness before the ultimate penalty may be imposed, and there is no legislative intent within the statutory framework to impose such a requirement. Barnes v. Commonwealth, 234 Va. 130, 360 S.E.2d 196 (1987), cert. denied, 484 U.S. 1036, 108 S. Ct. 763, 98 L. Ed. 2d 779 (1988).

Order or gunshot wounds not required to be proved. — The statutory scheme contains no requirement that the Commonwealth prove the order in which multiple gunshot wounds were inflicted in order to establish which caused death, or indeed, whether death might not have resulted if any wound had been avoided. The "more culpable than the minimum" standard articulated in Smith v. Commonwealth, 219 Va. 455, 248 S.E.2d 135 (1978), cert. denied, 441 U.S. 967, 99 S. Ct. 2419, 60 L. Ed. 2d 1074 (1979) contains no such requirement, and the Supreme Court declines to impose such a requirement now. Barnes v. Commonwealth, 234 Va. 130, 360 S.E.2d 196 (1987), cert. denied, 484 U.S. 1036, 108 S. Ct. 763, 98 L. Ed. 2d 779 (1988).

"Outrageously or wantonly vile," etc., have accepted meanings. — The terms "outrageously or wantonly vile," "horrible or inhuman," and "depravity of mind or aggravated battery to the victim" used in this section are commonly used and each has an accepted meaning. Clark v. Commonwealth, 220 Va. 201, 257

S.E.2d 784 (1979), cert. denied, 444 U.S. 1049, 100 S. Ct. 741, 62 L. Ed. 2d 736 (1980).

It is not required that the three statutory terms of torture, depravity of mind, and aggravated battery be considered together in determining vileness, with the result that depravity of mind does not exist in the situation where there is no torture and where there is no aggravated battery to the victim. A mere inspection of the statutory language in question demonstrates clearly that the term "vileness" includes three separate and distinct factors, with the proof of any one factor being sufficient to support a finding of vileness and hence a sentence of death. Bunch v. Commonwealth, 225 Va. 423, 304 S.E.2d 271, cert. denied, 464 U.S. 977, 104 S. Ct. 414, 78 L. Ed. 2d 352 (1983), 505 U.S. 1230, 112 S. Ct. 3056, 120 L. Ed. 2d 922 (1992).

Where the statute provides that the death penalty shall not be imposed unless the fact finder determines either that the defendant, based on his criminal record, would be "a continuing serious threat to society," the future dangerousness predicate, or that the defendant's "conduct in committing the offense ... was outrageously or wantonly vile, horrible or inhuman in that it involved depravity of mind or an aggravated battery to the victim," the vileness predicate, executing two persons in their home and then stripping their bodies of jewelry and stealing their personal property, manifestly demonstrated a depravity of mind. Sheppard v. Commonwealth, 250 Va. 379, 464 S.E.2d 131 (1995), cert. denied, 517 U.S. 1110, 116 S. Ct. 1332, 134 L. Ed. 2d 483 (1996).

Thus, failure to give definitional instruction not error. — While the terms "outrageously or wantonly vile," "horrible or inhuman," and "depravity of mind or aggravated battery to the victim" may have been defined in an instruction to the jury in a manner satisfactory to the Supreme Court, the fact that the trial court did not choose to give such a definitional instruction did not constitute reversible error. Clark v. Commonwealth, 220 Va. 201, 257 S.E.2d 784 (1979), cert. denied, 444 U.S. 1049, 100 S. Ct. 741, 62 L. Ed. 2d 736 (1980); Briley v. Commonwealth, 221 Va. 563, 273 S.E.2d 57 (1980).

Whether decedent remained conscious is immaterial. — For purposes of the "vileness" determination, it is immaterial whether the decedent remained conscious during the course of several assaults. Boggs v. Commonwealth, 229 Va. 501, 331 S.E.2d 407 (1985), cert. denied, 475 U.S. 1031, 106 S. Ct. 1240, 89 L. Ed. 2d 347 (1986).

Conduct held to be vile and to constitute psychological torture. — Conduct of defendant in pointing a gun at victim and forcing her to get inside car while on a public street in broad daylight, in making victim disrobe, in raping her, in shooting her in the head, and in pushing her nude body out of a car onto a parking lot behind a church, and then in driving around in victim's car selling and giving away candy he found in the back seat, was vile and constituted psychological torture of the victim. Poyner v. Commonwealth, 229 Va. 401, 329 S.E.2d 815, cert. denied, 474 U.S. 865, 106 S. Ct. 189, 88 L. Ed. 2d 158, 474 U.S. 888, 106 S. Ct. 208, 88 L. Ed. 2d 178 (1985), 506 U.S. 958, 113 S. Ct. 419, 121 L. Ed. 2d 342 (1992).

Defendant's conduct in shooting a defenseless woman in the back of the head, a woman begging for her life after she had complied with all his demands, showed a degree of moral turpitude and psychical debasement surpassing that inherent in the definition of ordinary legal malice and premeditation, and amounted to psychological torture of his victim. Poyner v. Commonwealth, 229 Va. 401, 329 S.E.2d 815, cert. denied, 474 U.S. 865, 106 S. Ct. 189, 88 L. Ed. 2d 158, 474 U.S. 888, 106 S. Ct. 208, 88 L. Ed. 2d 178 (1985), 506 U.S. 958, 113 S. Ct. 419, 121 L. Ed. 2d 342 (1992).

Aggravated battery committed where victim was choked, kicked, and stabbed. — The murder of the victim was clearly an aggravated battery, one which, qualitatively and quantitatively, is more culpable than the minimum necessary to accomplish an act of murder, where the defendant choked his victim, kicked him repeatedly, and finally inflicted two knife wounds, either of which could ultimately have resulted in death. These acts exceeded the minimum necessary to accomplish the victim's murder. Correll v. Commonwealth, 232 Va. 454, 352 S.E.2d 352, cert. denied, 482 U.S. 931, 107 S. Ct. 3219, 96 L. Ed. 2d 705 (1987).

Use of victim's body as target for knife-throwing. — Defendant's conduct revealed his horrifying depravity of mind, a degree of moral turpitude and psychical debasement surpassing that inherent in the definition of ordinary legal malice and premeditation, since only an evil, distorted imagination could have conceived the villainous plan to kill the victim by using his prostrate body as a target for knife-throwing. Correll v. Commonwealth, 232 Va. 454, 352 S.E.2d 352, cert. denied, 482 U.S. 931, 107 S. Ct. 3219, 96 L. Ed. 2d 705 (1987).

Wounds held to satisfy "vileness" test. — Proof of the multiple wounds sustained by victim, particularly a neck wound, which, even considered alone, constituted an aggravated battery in light of the savage, methodical manner in which it was inflicted, leaving the victim to suffer an interval of agony awaiting death, was held to satisfy the test for the "vileness" predicate under this section. Edmonds v. Commonwealth, 229 Va. 303, 329 S.E.2d 807, cert. denied, 474 U.S. 975, 106 S. Ct. 339, 88 L. Ed. 2d 324 (1985).

Where defendant could have taken money bags and purse and fled without harming victim but instead, he followed victim to rear of store, grabbed her from behind by hair, and cut her throat, where cut was five inches long, beginning near her left ear and extending downward and into larynx, where wound was two inches deep and where victim stumbled out of building into street, clutching her neck with both hands in effort to stop bleeding, evidence supported trial court's finding of "vileness" predicate. Stout v. Commonwealth, 237 Va. 126, 376 S.E.2d 288, cert. denied, 492 U.S. 925, 109 S. Ct. 3263, 106 L. Ed. 2d 609 (1989).

Evidence that victim was raped and sodomized and was bound at her wrists and ankles so snugly that she could not have freed herself, that a gag was placed tightly over her mouth and that defendant plunged a knife into her back, muffled her screams with a pillow, then stabbed her in her stomach to a depth of 6 ½ inches and, as she continued to scream, held the pillow over her face for four to five minutes until she died, was sufficient evidence of "vileness." Hoke v. Commonwealth, 237 Va. 303, 377 S.E.2d 595, cert. denied, 491 U.S. 910, 109 S. Ct. 3201, 105 L. Ed. 2d 709 (1989).

Although victim would have died "shortly" from the gunshot wound to his head, his death was not instantaneous, and the jury could have found that he was still alive but unconscious when his hands were severed; accordingly, the evidence was sufficient to support the jury's finding of vileness based upon aggravated battery. Stockton v. Commonwealth, 241 Va. 192, 402 S.E.2d 196, cert. denied, 502 U.S. 280, 112 S. Ct. 280, 116 L. Ed. 2d 231 (1991).

State supreme court found that the death penalty was not an excessive or disproportionate punishment for defendant who was convicted of killing a 79-year-old woman who was stabbed five times in the neck and face, anally sodomized with her cane, and had the cane driven into her mouth. Jackson v. Commonwealth, 266 Va. 423, 587 S.E.2d 532, 2003 Va. LEXIS 101 (2003), cert. denied, 543 U.S. 842, 125 S. Ct. 281, 160 L. Ed. 2d 68 (2004).

Motion to strike properly overruled. — In a capital murder case, the circuit court properly overruled defendant's motion to strike evidence regarding the "vileness" aggravator, as the evidence showed: (1) that defendant committed an aggravated battery on the murder victim, as the killing was inflicted by multiple gunshot wounds, and there was a lapse of time between the first shot and the last, and death did not result instantaneously from the first; and (2) the depravity of defendant's mind, as he repeatedly shot the victim in front of her husband and left them both to die merely so he could rob them. Green v. Commonwealth, 266 Va. 81, 580 S.E.2d 834, 2003 Va. LEXIS 55 (2003), cert. denied, 540 U.S. 1194, 124 S. Ct. 1448, 158 L. Ed. 2d 107 (2004).

Jury justified in vileness verdict. — Where defendant apparently held his gun to the heads of his wife and five-month-old child, killed them in deliberate execution-type murders, carefully arranged their bodies, secured the house, and then fled, his murders were "more depraved" than ordinary murders, the jury justifiably found these murders to be "outrageously or wantonly vile, horrible or inhuman." Stewart v. Commonwealth, 245 Va. 222, 427 S.E.2d 394, cert. denied, 510 U.S. 848, 114 S. Ct. 143, 126 L. Ed. 2d 105 (1993).

The jury could have found that the defendant's killing of his wife and two-year old son were characterized by "vileness" where the evidence established that, several months before the killings, the defendant began to make elaborate efforts to divert suspicion away from himself, that the defendant obtained the murder weapon several weeks in advance of the killings, that the defendant shot his wife three times in the head while she was sleeping and that he shot his child twice in the head as the child was climbing out of bed.

Bailey v. Commonwealth, 259 Va. 723, 529 S.E.2d 570, 2000 Va. LEXIS 59, cert. denied, 531 U.S. 995, 121 S. Ct. 488, 148 L. Ed. 2d 460 (2000).

A rational sentencer could have found that the murder of victim involved either depravity of mind or an aggravated battery where despite defendant's emphasis that the murder could not possibly be considered an aggravated battery because he rapidly fired two successive shots into victim's chest, either one of which may have been fatal, defendant shot victim in the head before he fired the two shots into victim's chest, and, between the shot to the head and the shots to the chest, enough time elapsed for officer to talk to defendant and for two customers to escape from the store. Turner v. Williams, 35 F.3d 872 (4th Cir. 1994), cert. denied, 514 U.S. 1017, 115 S. Ct. 1359, 131 L. Ed. 2d 216 (1995), overruled in part by O'Dell v. Netherland, 95 F.3d 1214 (4th Cir. 1996).

Any error in the jury instruction on the vileness predicate did not provide a basis for granting a writ of habeas corpus because defendant's death sentence still rested on firm ground relative to his future dangerousness. George v. Angelone, 100 F.3d 353 (4th Cir. 1996), cert. denied, 519 U.S. 1103, 117 S. Ct. 854, 136 L. Ed. 2d 829 (1997).

Death sentence based on jury's finding of "vileness" in capital murder case in which evidence showed that defendant stabbed victim 10 times and used knife blade as a saw, was not disproportionate to sentences for similar offenses and would be upheld. Yarbrough v. Commonwealth, 262 Va. 388, 551 S.E.2d 306, 2001 Va. LEXIS 112 (2001), cert. denied, 535 U.S. 1060, 122 S. Ct. 1925, 152 L. Ed. 2d 832 (2002).

Ineffective assistance of counsel claim. — State inmate who pled guilty to capital murder for hire in the deaths of her husband and stepson was properly denied relief under 28 U.S.C.S. § 2254. Counsel were not ineffective for not presenting evidence of her prescription drug addiction to rebut the vileness aggravator in § 19.2-264.2, as it would have undermined their trial strategy by supporting a future-dangerousness aggravator and undercutting their portrayal of the inmate as a remorseful, previously nonviolent defendant who assisted police in arresting her coconspirators. Lewis v. Wheeler, 609 F.3d 291, 2010 U.S. App. LEXIS 11377 (4th Cir. 2010), cert. denied, 131 S. Ct. 60, 177 L.Ed.2d 1148, 2010 U.S. LEXIS 5735 (U.S. 2010).

B. Future Dangerousness.

"Future dangerousness" predicate constitutional. — The aggravating predicate of "future dangerousness" contained in Virginia's capital punishment scheme is constitutional. Giarratano v. Procunier, 891 F.2d 483 (4th Cir. 1989), cert. denied, 498 U.S. 881, 111 S. Ct. 222, 112 L. Ed. 2d 178 (1990).

Since the supreme court had previously determined that § 19.2-264.2 was not unconstitutionally vague, no additional instructions regarding the definition of "probability" were needed in order for the jury to properly understand and determine defendant's future dangerousness under the other instructions given to the jury in his case. Porter v. Commonwealth, 276 Va. 203, 661 S.E.2d 415, 2008 Va. LEXIS 78 (2008), cert. denied, 129 S. Ct. 1999, 173 L. Ed. 2d 1097, 2009 U.S. LEXIS 3047 (U.S. 2009).

Motion to strike properly overruled. — In a capital murder case, the circuit court properly overruled defendant's motion to strike evidence regarding the "future dangerousness" aggravator, based on defendant's killing a robbery victim with multiple gunshots in front of her husband and leaving them both to die, and his other bad acts, including an assault on a friend and his disruptive behavior and threats to correctional officers. Green v. Commonwealth, 266 Va. 81, 580 S.E.2d 834, 2003 Va. LEXIS 55 (2003), cert. denied, 540 U.S. 1194, 124 S. Ct. 1448, 158 L. Ed. 2d 107 (2004).

Circumstances of crime may be sufficient alone. — The facts and circumstances surrounding a capital murder may be sufficient, standing alone, to support a finding of future dangerousness. Schmitt v. Commonwealth, 262 Va. 127, 547 S.E.2d 186, 2001 Va. LEXIS 85 (2001).

Where finding of vileness absent, finding of future dangerousness supported death penalty. — Where trial court found that "future dangerousness" predicate, had been proved beyond reasonable doubt, and where if finding of vileness were absent trial court's finding of future dangerousness was sufficient to support imposition of death penalty. Stout v. Commonwealth, 237 Va. 126,

376 S.E.2d 288, cert. denied, 492 U.S. 925, 109 S. Ct. 3263, 106 L. Ed. 2d 609 (1989).

Verdict based solely upon "future dangerousness" renders moot on appeal all issues related to the "vileness" predicate. Fisher v. Commonwealth, 236 Va. 403, 374 S.E.2d 46 (1988), cert. denied, 490 U.S. 1028, 109 S. Ct. 1766, 104 L. Ed. 2d 201 (1989).

Where jury made no finding of "vileness" but based its verdict upon the "future dangerousness" predicate alone, and defendant, on appeal, assigned error to court's finding of sufficient evidence of a "depraved mind" and "aggravated battery" to warrant instructing jury on "vileness," and refusal to submit case to the jury on "future dangerousness" alone, a verdict based solely upon "future dangerousness" rendered moot on appeal all issues related to the "vileness" predicate. Fisher v. Commonwealth, 236 Va. 403, 374 S.E.2d 46 (1988), cert. denied, 490 U.S. 1028, 109 S. Ct. 1766, 104 L. Ed. 2d 201 (1989).

Evidence sufficient to support "future dangerousness" predicate. — Where defendant had prior convictions of assault, attempted arson, carrying a concealed weapon, resisting arrest, and burglary, and in addition, his prior history, by his own admission, suggested a life of increasingly violent crime and, moreover, the brutality of the crime itself could not, and should not, be ignored in assessing defendant's future dangerousness, the evidence was sufficient to support the "future dangerousness" predicate. Hoke v. Commonwealth, 237 Va. 303, 377 S.E.2d 595, cert. denied, 491 U.S. 910, 109 S. Ct. 3201, 105 L. Ed. 2d 709 (1989).

Facts and circumstances may be sufficient to support a finding of "future dangerousness," as here where the defendant killed a defenseless 70-year-old neighbor who had been his friend because he wanted her money. Roach v. Commonwealth, 251 Va. 324, 468 S.E.2d 98, cert. denied, 519 U.S. 951, 117 S. Ct. 365, 136 L. Ed. 2d 256 (1996), overruled in part on other grounds by Morrisette v. Warden of the Sussex I State Prison, 270 Va. 188, 613 S.E.2d 551 (2005).

Where the Commonwealth presented evidence that the defendant had previously been convicted of carnal knowledge, forgery, assault and unauthorized use of a motor vehicle, that he regularly stole from friends and acquaintances, and that he had punched a pregnant woman in the stomach in a rage, and where the defendant had committed two brutal, unprovoked murders within a six month period, the Commonwealth proved beyond a reasonable doubt that the defendant would be a continuing serious threat to society. Walker v. Commonwealth, 258 Va. 54, 515 S.E.2d 565 (1999), cert. denied, 528 U.S. 1125, 120 S. Ct. 955, 145 L.Ed. 2d 829 (2000).

Where the defendant murdered the victim, an innocent employee of a pool hall, to facilitate a robbery and to avoid being identified as its perpetrator, the jury was entitled to find that this violent, calculated action was strong evidence that the defendant was a dangerous person who would commit future criminal acts of violence. Lovitt v. Commonwealth, 260 Va. 497, 537 S.E.2d 866, 2000 Va. LEXIS 149 (2000), cert. denied, 534 U.S. 815, 122 S. Ct. 41, 151 L. Ed. 2d 14 (2001).

The evidence was sufficient to support the jury's finding of future dangerousness where the defendant murdered an innocent security guard to facilitate a robbery and to avoid being apprehended at the robbery scene; the jury was entitled to find that this violent, premeditated action was strong evidence that the defendant was a dangerous person who would commit future criminal acts of violence, and the jury could also consider the defendant's criminal record and the fact that the defendant had committed another armed robbery one month before the robbery in which the guard was killed. Schmitt v. Commonwealth, 262 Va. 127, 547 S.E.2d 186, 2001 Va. LEXIS 85 (2001).

Despite defendant's lack of a serious criminal record, the evidence that he had been a drug dealer for many years and had talked, planned, and attempted to set in motion many plans for killing and robbing drug suppliers (and that he celebrated after the murder in question) provided a sufficient basis for the jury to have found that a death sentence was warranted under the future dangerousness criterion. Wolfe v. Commonwealth, 265 Va. 193, 576 S.E.2d 471, 2003 Va. LEXIS 32, cert. denied, 540 U.S. 1019, 124 S. Ct. 566, 157 L. Ed. 2d 434 (2003).

Factors considered in determining whether continuing serious threat to society exists. — In making a determination that there is a probability that defendant would commit criminal acts of violence that would constitute a continuing serious threat to society, the factfinder is entitled to consider not only the defendant's past criminal record of convictions, but also any matter which the court deems relevant to sentence, the prior history of the defendant or the circumstances surrounding the commission of the offense, and the heinousness of the crime. Edmonds v. Commonwealth, 229 Va. 303, 329 S.E.2d 807, cert. denied, 474 U.S. 975, 106 S. Ct. 339, 88 L. Ed. 2d 324 (1985).

In considering the defendant's future dangerousness, a jury was entitled to consider his extensive criminal record, which included an attempted robbery conviction and three burglary convictions, and that the defendant had committed several criminal offenses while released in the community on supervised probation or parole, since this evidence demonstrated that the defendant did not refrain from further serious criminal activity, even when the consequences of such criminal behavior would be especially severe. Lovitt v. Commonwealth, 260 Va. 497, 537 S.E.2d 866, 2000 Va. LEXIS 149 (2000), cert. denied, 534 U.S. 815, 122 S. Ct. 41, 151 L. Ed. 2d 14 (2001).

Future dangerousness consideration not limited to defendant's prior criminal record. — The statutory provisions governing the imposition of the death penalty do not limit consideration of whether a defendant will be a future danger to the defendant's prior criminal record. Royal v. Commonwealth, 250 Va. 110, 458 S.E.2d 575 (1995), cert. denied, 516 U.S. 1097, 116 S. Ct. 823, 133 L. Ed. 2d 766 (1996).

The circumstances of the crime appropriately may be considered when determining whether the statutory predicate of future dangerousness exists. Royal v. Commonwealth, 250 Va. 110, 458 S.E.2d 575 (1995), cert. denied, 516 U.S. 1097, 116 S. Ct. 823, 133 L. Ed. 2d 766 (1996).

Circumstances of crime and defendant's lack of remorse are proper factors to be considered on the issue of the probability that he will constitute a continuing serious threat to society. Frye v. Commonwealth, 231 Va. 370, 345 S.E.2d 267 (1986).

Defendant's statement as to large number of crimes he committed was relevant to future dangerousness. — Defendant's assertion to investigator in sheriff's department that he had perpetrated about 3,000 acts of breaking and entering was relevant to the question of his future dangerousness. Frye v. Commonwealth, 231 Va. 370, 345 S.E.2d 267 (1986).

Escape plan relevant to future dangerousness. — Evidence of a defendant's plan to escape is relevant and admissible to show his future dangerousness. Frye v. Commonwealth, 231 Va. 370, 345 S.E.2d 267 (1986).

Motion for appointment of prison risk assessment expert properly denied. — Defendant's motion requesting the appointment of a prison risk assessment expert failed to address the statutory factors regarding future dangerousness under § 19.2-264.2 and subsection C of § 19.2-264.4 as being individualized and particularized as to defendant's prior history, conviction record, and the circumstances of his crime; as Virginia Supreme Court precedent rendered inadmissible the statistical speculation defendant offered, defendant failed to show the required particularized need for the expert's assistance. In light of the inadmissibility of the evidence defendant sought to introduce through the expert, he also failed to establish how he was prejudiced by the lack of the expert's assistance; accordingly, the circuit court did not abuse its discretion in denying the prison expert motion. Porter v. Commonwealth, 276 Va. 203, 661 S.E.2d 415, 2008 Va. LEXIS 78 (2008), cert. denied, 129 S. Ct. 1999, 173 L. Ed. 2d 1097, 2009 U.S. LEXIS 3047 (U.S. 2009).

Conduct held to constitute continuing serious threat to society. — Actions of defendant who killed five women in an 11-day-period, striking boldly in broad daylight because he knew he would kill his victim and there would be no witness to identify him, selecting his victims on impulse, ignoring pleas for mercy and cries of fear and anguish, and later showing no remorse, graphically illustrated the probability that he would commit criminal acts of violence that would constitute a continuing serious threat to society. Poyner v. Commonwealth, 229 Va. 401, 329 S.E.2d 815, cert. denied, 474 U.S. 865, 106 S. Ct. 189, 88 L. Ed. 2d 158, 474 U.S. 888, 106 S. Ct. 208, 88 L. Ed. 2d 178 (1985), 506 U.S. 958, 113 S. Ct. 419, 121 L. Ed. 2d 342 (1992).

Where defendant conceded at trial that he had previously been convicted of at least 25 separate felonies, and when arrested for the crime at issue was engaged in a "fencing" operation for stolen goods in Charlotte, the record supported a finding of "future dangerousness." Fisher v. Commonwealth, 236 Va. 403, 374 S.E.2d 46 (1988), cert. denied, 490 U.S. 1028, 109 S. Ct. 1766, 104 L. Ed. 2d 201 (1989).

Expert testimony regarding prison life. — Although defendant claimed that the circuit court erred in denying his motion for appointment of an expert on prison risk assessment and that in doing so the court violated his due process rights and his rights against cruel and unusual punishment under the United States Constitution because the testimony that the expert would have provided was relevant and mitigating and any relevant mitigating evidence had to be admitted, the circuit court did not abuse its discretion when it found that defendant failed to demonstrate the particularized need necessary for appointment of the expert since the expert's anticipated testimony was not in rebuttal to any specific evidence concerning prison life. Moreover, under § 19.2-264.2 and subsection C of § 19.2-264.4, the relevant evidence surrounding a determination of future dangerousness consisted of the defendant's history and the circumstances of the defendant's offense, and thus, to be admissible, evidence related to a prison environment had to connect the specific characteristics of the particular defendant to his future adaptability in the prison environment; therefore, because the expert's proposed testimony concerning prison life was inadmissible, the lack of that expert assistance did not result in a fundamentally unfair trial. Morva v. Commonwealth, 278 Va. 329, 683 S.E.2d 553, 2009 Va. LEXIS 84 (2009), cert. denied, 131 S. Ct. 97, 178 L. Ed. 2d 61, 2010 U.S. LEXIS 5806 (U.S. 2010).

III. PRACTICE AND PROCEDURE.

Part Three A of the Rules of the Supreme Court applicable to guilty plea in capital case. — There is no provision in this article concerning the entry by an accused of a plea of guilty in a capital murder case. There is no conflict, therefore, between this article and Rule 3A:13 (a) of the Rules of the Supreme Court, and, hence, pursuant to Rule 3A:18, the provisions of Part Three A shall be applicable to the entry of a plea of guilty in a capital case. Pruett v. Commonwealth, 232 Va. 266, 351 S.E.2d 1 (1986), cert. denied, 482 U.S. 931, 107 S. Ct. 3220, 96 L. Ed. 2d 706 (1987).

Submission only of punishment question to jury upon plea of guilty properly denied. — In a prosecution for capital murder, after the trial court denied defendant's motion for two juries, the trial court correctly denied defendant's motion to permit him to plead guilty and submit to the jury the question of punishment alone. Rule 3A:13 (a) of the Rules of the Supreme Court provides that "[t]he accused is entitled to a trial by jury only in a circuit court on a plea of not guilty." Pruett v. Commonwealth, 232 Va. 266, 351 S.E.2d 1 (1986), cert. denied, 482 U.S. 931, 107 S. Ct. 3220, 96 L. Ed. 2d 706 (1987).

Burden of proving aggravating circumstances. — In the sentencing stage of a capital murder trial, the prosecution has the burden of proving aggravating circumstances beyond a reasonable doubt. Waye v. Commonwealth, 219 Va. 683, 251 S.E.2d 202, cert. denied, 442 U.S. 924, 99 S. Ct. 2850, 61 L. Ed. 2d 292 (1979).

Jury at liberty to recommend life term. — It is clear from the statutory context that, even when the Commonwealth establishes either or both aggravating circumstances, the jury is at liberty, in consideration of circumstances in mitigation, to recommend a sentence of imprisonment for life. Smith v. Commonwealth, 219 Va. 455, 248 S.E.2d 135 (1978), cert. denied, 441 U.S. 967, 99 S. Ct. 2419, 60 L. Ed. 2d 1074 (1979).

Denial of motion to preclude imposition of the death penalty was not error, where the motion was based on a statistical study published in a law review article suggesting that racial factors may have influenced the imposition of the death penalty in the 1970's. This precise issue was resolved by the United States Supreme Count in McCleskey v. Kemp, 481 U.S. 279, 107 S. Ct. 1756, 95 L. Ed. 2d 262 (1987). Barnes v. Commonwealth, 234 Va. 130, 360 S.E.2d 196 (1987), cert. denied, 484 U.S. 1036, 108 S. Ct. 763, 98 L. Ed. 2d 779 (1988).

Jury must consider all evidence relevant to sentencing. — The jury in a capital murder case has the duty to consider all the evidence relevant to sentencing, both favorable and unfavorable, before determining whether the defendant has such a propensity to violence as to make him a menace to society, or whether the crime of which he has been convicted is so atrocious that he should be executed. Stamper v. Commonwealth, 220 Va. 260, 257 S.E.2d 808

(1979), cert. denied, 445 U.S. 972, 100 S. Ct. 1666, 64 L. Ed. 2d 249 (1980).

Use in evidence of record of previous convictions. — In a capital murder case, in determining defendant's proclivity for violence, the jury may obtain from the mere record of previous convictions an inaccurate or incomplete impression of the defendant's temperament and disposition. Stamper v. Commonwealth, 220 Va. 260, 257 S.E.2d 808 (1979), cert. denied, 445 U.S. 972, 100 S. Ct. 1666, 64 L. Ed. 2d 249 (1980).

The fact that at the sentencing phase of defendant's capital murder trial, the jury was advised that the defendant had been convicted in Maryland of conspiracy to distribute controlled drugs, a felony, and had been sentenced to serve three years in the state correctional facility was not erroneous. Clark v. Commonwealth, 220 Va. 201, 257 S.E.2d 784 (1979), cert. denied, 444 U.S. 1049, 100 S. Ct. 741, 62 L. Ed. 2d 736 (1980).

Use of defendant's juvenile record in capital sentencing. — Virginia law does not prohibit the use of a defendant's juvenile record in capital sentencing. Peterson v. Murray, 904 F.2d 882 (4th Cir.), cert. denied, 498 U.S. 992, 111 S. Ct. 537, 112 L. Ed. 2d 547 (1990).

Testimony of victim of prior crime. — In the sentencing phase of a capital murder trial, the probative value of testimony by the victim of a previous armed robbery by the defendant was sufficient to outweigh its prejudicial effect for the reason that such testimony was relevant to a consideration of the defendant's history and background and to a determination by the jury whether there was a probability that he would "constitute a continuing serious threat to society." Stamper v. Commonwealth, 220 Va. 260, 257 S.E.2d 808 (1979), cert. denied, 445 U.S. 972, 100 S. Ct. 1666, 64 L. Ed. 2d 249 (1980).

Evidence admissible on question of propensity or violence. — Testimony that a defendant who committed murder deliberately and for hire, referred to his victim as "a beast," and then expressed no regret or remorse for the act he committed, is obviously proper testimony for a jury to consider in determining whether such person would in all probability commit criminal acts of violence in the future. Had the defendant manifested remorse, sorrow, or grief for the murder that he had committed, this would have been a circumstance in mitigation admissible in evidence at the sentencing phase. Clark v. Commonwealth, 220 Va. 201, 257 S.E.2d 784 (1979), cert. denied, 444 U.S. 1049, 100 S. Ct. 741, 62 L. Ed. 2d 736 (1980).

A defendant's propensity for future criminal acts of violence is an acceptable consideration in determining whether to impose the death penalty. Turner v. Commonwealth, 221 Va. 513, 273 S.E.2d 36 (1980), cert. denied, 451 U.S. 1011, 101 S. Ct. 2347, 68 L. Ed. 2d 863 (1981).

The presence or absence of a criminal record is pertinent to the dangerousness standard. Bunch v. Commonwealth, 225 Va. 423, 304 S.E.2d 271, cert. denied, 464 U.S. 977, 104 S. Ct. 414, 78 L. Ed. 2d 352 (1983), 505 U.S. 1230, 112 S. Ct. 3056, 120 L. Ed. 2d 922 (1992).

It is fallacious to argue that a defendant without a criminal record but who commits a murder satisfying the vileness standard cannot be sentenced to death and, conversely, that a defendant as to whom the dangerousness standard is satisfied but whose crime does not meet the vileness test cannot be sentenced to death either. This section and subsection C of § 19.2-264.4 state the dangerousness and vileness standards in the disjunctive; only one, not both, need be present to support a valid sentence of death. Bunch v. Commonwealth, 225 Va. 423, 304 S.E.2d 271, cert. denied, 464 U.S. 977, 104 S. Ct. 414, 78 L. Ed. 2d 352 (1983), 505 U.S. 1230, 112 S. Ct. 3056, 120 L. Ed. 2d 922 (1992).

Evidence inadmissible on question of propensity or violence. — Trial court correctly barred defendant's mental health expert's generalized testimony and did not abuse its discretion in doing so because the proffer of the expert's testimony on future dangerousness in a prison setting failed to meet the test of relevance. Neither the actual proffer, counsel's argument, nor the expert's explanations on voir dire tied his proposed opinion testimony on future dangerousness in a prison environment to defendant's history and background, and the circumstances of his offense, to defendant's character, history, and background or was specific to defendant, relevant to his future adaptability. Juniper v.

Commonwealth, 271 Va. 362, 626 S.E.2d 383, 2006 Va. LEXIS 29 (2006).

Evidence of prior act of violence is certainly probative of the probability that the accused would commit other criminal acts of violence. When offered for that purpose, the evidence should be considered relevant and admissible. Pruett v. Commonwealth, 232 Va. 266, 351 S.E.2d 1 (1986), cert. denied, 482 U.S. 931, 107 S. Ct. 3220, 96 L. Ed. 2d 706 (1987).

Evidence of prior unadjudicated criminal conduct, while generally not admissible in the guilt phase of capital-murder trial, may be used in the penalty phase to prove the defendant's propensity to commit criminal acts of violence in the future. Watkins v. Commonwealth, 229 Va. 469, 331 S.E.2d 422 (1985), cert. denied, 475 U.S. 1099, 106 S. Ct. 1503, 89 L. Ed. 2d 903 (1986).

Trial court may properly refuse to define statutory terms included in aggravating circumstances upon which a sentence of death may be based. Bunch v. Commonwealth, 225 Va. 423, 304 S.E.2d 271, cert. denied, 464 U.S. 977, 104 S. Ct. 414, 78 L. Ed. 2d 352 (1983), 505 U.S. 1230, 112 S. Ct. 3056, 120 L. Ed. 2d 922 (1992).

Aggravating circumstances on vileness are unconstitutionally vague unless limitations instructions. — Aggravating circumstances based on vileness are unconstitutionally vague unless the jury is given some limiting instruction that guides their discretion. More specific guidelines enable the courts to review rationally the sentence imposed. The instruction given by the trial court was that the jury could impose a sentence of death if they found the murder "wantonly vile, horrible or inhuman" in that it involved an aggravated battery "beyond the minimum necessary to accomplish the act of murder." This was, to some extent, self-limiting, for it did not include any statutory vileness factors except that of aggravated battery. Boggs v. Bair, 892 F.2d 1193 (4th Cir. 1989), cert. denied, 495 U.S. 940, 110 S. Ct. 2193, 109 L. Ed. 2d 521 (1990).

Instruction on culpability upheld. — An instruction to the jury that they could impose death if they found the murder wantonly vile, horrible or inhuman in that it involved an aggravated battery beyond the minimum necessary to accomplish the act of murder, sufficiently instructed the jury that it should not apply a cold, factual analysis about the cause of death, but instead should reach a moral judgment about whether the wounds were excessive in a way that was more culpable than murder generally, and it satisfied the constitutional requirements set by the Supreme Court. Boggs v. Bair, 695 F. Supp. 864 (E.D. Va. 1988), aff'd in part and rev'd in part, 892 F.2d 1193 (4th Cir. 1989), cert. denied, 495 U.S. 940, 110 S. Ct. 2193, 109 L. Ed. 2d 521 (1990).

Jury entitled to hear of parole ineligibility. — Where defendant represented to the trial court that he would not have been eligible for parole if he were convicted of capital murder, "future dangerousness" was an issue in the sentencing phase of the capital murder trial; therefore, the jury was entitled to be informed of defendant's parole ineligibility. Mickens v. Commonwealth, 249 Va. 423, 457 S.E.2d 9 (1995).

Refusal to instruct on eligibility for parole if life sentence imposed. — In sentencing phase of capital murder trial, trial court did not err in refusing to instruct jury with respect to defendant's eligibility for parole if life imprisonment were imposed, and in permitting the question of the death penalty to go to jury. Stamper v. Commonwealth, 220 Va. 260, 257 S.E.2d 808 (1979), cert. denied, 445 U.S. 972, 100 S. Ct. 1666, 64 L. Ed. 2d 249 (1980).

The court did not err in refusing to grant proffered instructions defining the terms "vile" and "wantonly," where the language of this section defining these terms was recited in an instruction which was given the jury. Justus v. Commonwealth, 220 Va. 971, 266 S.E.2d 87 (1980), cert. denied, 455 U.S. 983, 102 S. Ct. 1491, 71 L. Ed. 2d 693 (1982).

The court properly refused an instruction offered by the defendant which would have told the jury that if it could not reach agreement as to the appropriate punishment, the court would dismiss it and impose a life sentence. Justus v. Commonwealth, 220 Va. 971, 266 S.E.2d 87 (1980), cert. denied, 455 U.S. 983, 102 S. Ct. 1491, 71 L. Ed. 2d 693 (1982).

Commonwealth could rebut defendant's closing argument. — Since in the sentencing stage of a capital murder trial, the prosecution has the burden of proving aggravating circumstances beyond a reasonable doubt, it was not improper to permit the attorney for the Commonwealth to rebut the defendant's closing argument in the sentencing stage of the trial. Waye v. Commonwealth, 219 Va. 683, 251 S.E.2d 202, cert. denied, 442 U.S. 924, 99 S. Ct. 2850, 61 L. Ed. 2d 292 (1979).

Raising claims on habeas allowed. — Where Slayton v. Parrigan, 215 Va. 27, 205 S.E.2d 680 (1974) generally says that claims that could have been raised on direct appeal, but were not, cannot be raised on state collateral review, and where Hawks v. Cox, 211 Va. 91, 175 S.E.2d 271 (1970) has been read to say that claims raised and decided against petitioner on direct review cannot be raised on state habeas, defendant's various challenges to the application of the vileness factor were raised on direct appeal and therefore the Supreme Court of Virginia on collateral review must have dismissed these claims under Hawks, not Slayton. Accordingly, because Hawks did not bar federal appellate court from reviewing the merits of federal constitutional claims properly raised on direct appeal, the court in the instant case rejected the Commonwealth's argument that defendant was procedurally barred from raising these claims on federal habeas. Turner v. Williams, 35 F.3d 872 (4th Cir. 1994), cert. denied, 514 U.S. 1017, 115 S. Ct. 1359, 131 L. Ed. 2d 216 (1995), overruled in part by O'Dell v. Netherland, 95 F.3d 1214 (4th Cir. 1996).

Additional claims carried no weight. — Where defendant claimed that the Supreme Court of Virginia's appellate review of his sentence was inadequate and further argued that the Virginia system did not provide capital defendants meaningful appellate review, even in cases in which the results appear arbitrary, since the Virginia courts applied a constitutionally sufficient limiting construction for the vileness factor in defendant's case, it was clear from the United States Supreme Court's cases that these additional claims carried no constitutional weight. Turner v. Williams, 35 F.3d 872 (4th Cir. 1994), cert. denied, 514 U.S. 1017, 115 S. Ct. 1359, 131 L. Ed. 2d 216 (1995), overruled in part by O'Dell v. Netherland, 95 F.3d 1214 (4th Cir. 1996).

Reaching merits of claim not barred. — Where defendant sought the benefit of a rule that a vague aggravating factor must be supplemented with constitutionally sufficient limiting instructions or appellate review, and where the Commonwealth responded that defendants' claim was barred under Teague v. Lane, 489 U.S. 288, 109 S. Ct. 1060, 103 L. Ed. 2d 334 (1989) because it would require the court to announce new constitutional rules of criminal procedure on collateral review, in challenging the Commonwealth's application of its vileness factor in his case, defendant did not seek the benefit of a new rule, for purposes of Teague. Accordingly, Teague did not bar the court from reaching the merits. Turner v. Williams, 35 F.3d 872 (4th Cir. 1994), cert. denied, 514 U.S. 1017, 115 S. Ct. 1359, 131 L. Ed. 2d 216 (1995), overruled in part by O'Dell v. Netherland, 95 F.3d 1214 (4th Cir. 1996).

§ 19.2-264.3. Procedure for trial by jury.

A. In any case in which the offense may be punishable by death which is tried before a jury the court shall first submit to the jury the issue of guilt or innocence of the defendant of the offense charged in the indictment, or any other offense supported by the evidence for which a lesser punishment is provided by law and the penalties therefor.

B. If the jury finds the defendant guilty of an offense for which the death penalty may not be imposed, it shall fix the punishment as provided in § 19.2-295.1.

C. If the jury finds the defendant guilty of an offense which may be punishable by death, then a separate proceeding before the same jury shall be held as soon as is practicable on the issue of the penalty, which shall be fixed as is provided in § 19.2-264.4.

If the sentence of death is subsequently set aside or found invalid, and the defendant or the Commonwealth requests a jury for purposes of resentencing, the court shall impanel a different jury on the issue of penalty.

History.
1977, c. 492; 1983, c. 519; 1994, cc. 828, 860, 862, 881.

Law Review.
For survey of Virginia criminal procedure for the year 1976-1977, see 63 Va. L. Rev. 1408 (1977). For article, "Psychiatry and the Death Penalty: Emerging Problems in Virginia," see 66 Va. L. Rev. 167 (1980). For comment discussing possible effects on Virginia's death penalty law in the light of recent United States Supreme Court decisions, see 15 U. Rich. L. Rev. 951 (1981). For article, "Virginia's Capital Murder Sentencing Proceeding: A Defense Perspective," see 18 U. Rich. L. Rev. 341 (1984).

CASE NOTES

Constitutionality. — As to the constitutionality of this article, see note under § 19.2-264.2.

This section requires that the same jury determine both guilt and punishment. This statutory procedure is constitutional. Pope v. Commonwealth, 234 Va. 114, 360 S.E.2d 352 (1987), cert. denied, 485 U.S. 1015, 108 S. Ct. 1489, 99 L. Ed. 2d 716 (1988).

Subsection B of § 19.2-264.4 does not contain a relaxed evidentiary standard or produce unreliable determinations of aggravating factors, but rather evidence relevant to sentencing in the penalty phase of a capital murder trial is admissible, subject to the rules of evidence governing admissibility, and the Supreme Court of Virginia has held that subsection B of § 19.2-264.4 does not permit admission of irrelevant evidence, in particular presentence reports from probation officers and hearsay evidence; thus, a circuit court properly refused to dismiss the indictments where defendant's complaints about the constitutionality of subsection B of § 19.2-264.4 were merely hypothetical in nature. Jackson v. Commonwealth, 267 Va. 178, 590 S.E.2d 520, 2004 Va. LEXIS 8 (2004), cert. denied, 543 U.S. 891, 125 S. Ct. 168, 160 L. Ed. 2d 155 (2004).

Death penalty is not unconstitutional, per se. It does not violate the proscription against cruel and unusual punishment as stated in the Eighth Amendment to the federal Constitution. Stockton v. Commonwealth, 227 Va. 124, 314 S.E.2d 371, cert. denied, 469 U.S. 873, 105 S. Ct. 229, 83 L. Ed. 2d 158 (1984).

The purpose of the 1983 amendment to this section is straightforward: to establish new procedures for resentencing in capital cases where a prior death sentence is vacated and to apply the amendment only to those defendants whose sentences were vacated following the amendment's enactment is entirely rational, therefore, resentencing defendant to death after his first death sentence was vacated did not violate his equal protection rights, even though others were not so resentenced prior to the 1983 amendment. Evans v. Thompson, 881 F.2d 117 (4th Cir. 1989), cert. denied, 497 U.S. 1010, 110 S. Ct. 3255, 111 L. Ed. 2d 764 (1990).

The 1983 amendment to subsection C did not constitute a violation of the ex post facto clause. Turner v. Commonwealth, 234 Va. 543, 364 S.E.2d 483, cert. denied, 486 U.S. 1017, 108 S. Ct. 1756, 100 L. Ed. 2d 218 (1988).

Following the *Patterson v. Commonwealth*, 222 Va. 653, 283 S.E.2d 212 (1981) decision, the General Assembly in 1983 amended subsection C to permit resentencing of a capital defendant by a different jury where a prior sentence of death has been set aside or declared invalid. The Supreme Court of Virginia upheld the 1983 amendment against the contention that it constituted an ex post facto law. Turner v. Commonwealth, 234 Va. 543, 364 S.E.2d 483, cert. denied, 486 U.S. 1017, 108 S. Ct. 1756, 100 L. Ed. 2d 218 (1988).

Where defendant murdered a deputy sheriff, was convicted and sentenced to death, but had his death sentence overturned, all prior to the March, 1983, amendment to this section, then was resentenced to death after the amendment to this section, the defendant did not have his rights violated under the ex post facto clause since the change in this section was merely an adjustment in the method of administering defendant's punishment that was collateral to the penalty itself and defendant was on notice when he murdered the deputy sheriff that the imposition of death was a possible penalty. Evans v. Thompson, 881 F.2d 117 (4th Cir. 1989), cert. denied, 497

U.S. 1010, 110 S. Ct. 3255, 111 L. Ed. 2d 764 (1990).

Death penalty availability. — State supreme court granted the petition for writ of mandamus filed by the Commonwealth Attorney, as the trial court did not have the discretion to prohibit the Commonwealth Attorney from seeking the death penalty; the Commonwealth Attorney was entitled to seek the death penalty pursuant to statutory law, his limited right of appeal did not include allowing him to appeal the trial court's prohibition, and the trial court erred by exercising an executive function in determining that the Commonwealth Attorney was prohibited from seeking it in defendant's case where defendant was charged with capital murder pursuant to § 18.2-31. In re Horan, 271 Va. 258, 634 S.E.2d 675, 2006 Va. LEXIS 23 (2006).

Failure to question jury as to bias in favor of death penalty. — In a prosecution for robbery and capital murder, the refusal by the trial judge to ask the jury whether, if the jury should happen to convict the defendant of capital murder, each juror would be able to consider voting for a sentence less than death, or to ask an equivalent question, was prejudicial error invalidating the sentence to death. Patterson v. Commonwealth, 222 Va. 653, 283 S.E.2d 212 (1981).

Correctness of "vileness" instruction unimportant where instruction and proof as to "dangerousness" sufficient. — Where it is clear that there was evidence sufficient to sustain the "dangerousness" finding and that the instruction on such ground was not open to attack, it is unimportant whether the instructions on "vileness" were strictly correct or not. Briley v. Bass, 742 F.2d 155 (4th Cir.), cert. denied, 469 U.S. 893, 105 S. Ct. 270, 83 L. Ed. 2d 206 (1984).

Where the attack of the petitioner is on the trial instruction on the "vileness" ground, but the petitioner does not question the correctness of the court's instruction on the adequacy of the evidence to support a finding on the ground of "dangerousness," and, the jury has returned a verdict finding the death sentence warranted under both the "vileness" and the "dangerousness" standard, it is of no importance whether the instruction on "vileness" was correct so long as the instruction on "dangerousness" was correct, provided the verdict of the jury was unanimous on the "dangerousness" ground. Briley v. Bass, 742 F.2d 155 (4th Cir.), cert. denied, 469 U.S. 893, 105 S. Ct. 270, 83 L. Ed. 2d 206 (1984).

Instruction as to effect of nonunanimous verdict properly denied. — Defense counsel request to ask prospective jurors whether they understood "that should their verdict not be unanimous, then the court would impose a proper sentence" was properly denied. While this was a correct statement of law it concerned a procedural matter and was not one which should have been the subject of an instruction because it would have been an open invitation for the jury to avoid its responsibility and to disagree. This view is not changed by the fact that the attorney for the Commonwealth was permitted to ask the jurors if they knew a death verdict must be unanimous. Pruett v. Commonwealth, 232 Va. 266, 351 S.E.2d 1 (1986), cert. denied, 482 U.S. 931, 107 S. Ct. 3220, 96 L. Ed. 2d 706 (1987).

Instruction held erroneous. — Harmful, reversible error occurred in a capital murder prosecution when the trial court instructed the jury in such a manner that the jury could have believed that it could convict the defendant of capital murder though it was unable to determine who fired the fatal shots or if it determined that the defendant's brother fired the fatal shots; the error was compounded when the Commonwealth was permitted to argue to the jury that it could convict the defendant regardless of who pulled the trigger. Johnson v. Commonwealth, 220 Va. 146, 255 S.E.2d 525 (1979), cert. denied, 454 U.S. 920, 102 S. Ct. 422, 70 L. Ed. 2d 231 (1981).

Comment by prosecution that defendant had conceded guilt not reversible. — Comment made by the attorney for the Commonwealth during his closing argument that "[t]he defense conceded [guilt] in their voir dire of you and in their opening statement" was not reversible error, where in view of the well-nigh-conclusive nature of the evidence of defendant's guilt, the defense adopted the tactic of conceding culpability in the early stages of the trial in aid of a later effort in the penalty phase to save defendant from the electric chair and defense counsel admitted that he conceded guilt to some of the prospective jurors during voir dire and, although he did not use precise language of concession, he effectively conceded guilt to all the actual jurors in his opening statement. Pruett v. Commonwealth, 232 Va. 266, 351 S.E.2d 1 (1986), cert. denied, 482 U.S. 931, 107 S. Ct. 3220, 96 L. Ed. 2d 706 (1987).

When prevalence of crime in community may be raised. — A Commonwealth's attorney may properly argue on the question of punishment the prevalence of crime in the community, the personal safety of its inhabitants and the jury's duty to uphold the law, so long as the thrust of the argument is to deter the defendant as well as others from committing similar crimes in the community. Hill v. Commonwealth, No. 1898-93-2 (Ct. of Appeals July 5, 1995).

A juvenile who is convicted by a jury of capital murder should be sentenced by the jury pursuant to this section and § 19.2-264.4. Thomas v. Commonwealth, 244 Va. 1, 419 S.E.2d 606, cert. denied, 506 U.S. 958, 113 S. Ct. 421, 121 L. Ed. 2d 343 (1992).

Applied in Waye v. Commonwealth, 219 Va. 683, 251 S.E.2d 202 (1979); Justus v. Commonwealth, 220 Va. 971, 266 S.E.2d 87 (1980); Turner v. Commonwealth, 221 Va. 513, 273 S.E.2d 36 (1980); Briley v. Commonwealth, 221 Va. 563, 273 S.E.2d 57 (1980); Ball v. Commonwealth, 221 Va. 754, 273 S.E.2d 790 (1981); Quintana v. Commonwealth, 224 Va. 127, 295 S.E.2d 643 (1982); Evans v. Commonwealth, 228 Va. 468, 323 S.E.2d 114 (1984); Briley v. Bass, 750 F.2d 1238 (4th Cir. 1984); Edmonds v. Commonwealth, 229 Va. 303, 329 S.E.2d 807 (1985); Watkins v. Commonwealth, 229 Va. 469, 331 S.E.2d 422 (1985); Boggs v. Commonwealth, 229 Va. 501, 331 S.E.2d 407 (1985); Yeatts v. Commonwealth, 242 Va. 121, 410 S.E.2d 254 (1991); George v. Commonwealth, 242 Va. 264, 411 S.E.2d 12 (1991); Wolfe v. Commonwealth, 265 Va. 193, 576 S.E.2d 471, 2003 Va. LEXIS 32; Johnson v. Commonwealth, 267 Va. 53, 591 S.E.2d 47, 2004 Va. LEXIS 7 (2004); Juniper v. Commonwealth, 271 Va. 362, 626 S.E.2d 383, 2006 Va. LEXIS 29 (2006).

§ 19.2-264.3:1. Expert assistance when defendant's mental condition relevant to capital sentencing.

A. Upon (i) motion of the attorney for a defendant charged with or convicted of capital murder and (ii) a finding by the court that the defendant is financially unable to pay for expert assistance, the court shall appoint one or more qualified mental health experts to evaluate the defendant and to assist the defense in the preparation and presentation of information concerning the defendant's history, character, or mental condition, including (i) whether the defendant acted under extreme mental or emotional disturbance at the time of the offense; (ii) whether the capacity of the defendant to appreciate the criminality of his conduct or to conform his conduct to the requirements of the law was significantly impaired at the time of the offense; and (iii) whether there are any other factors in mitigation relating to the history or character of the defendant or the defendant's mental condition at the time of the offense. The mental health expert appointed pursuant to this section shall be (i) a psychiatrist, a clinical psychologist, or an individual with a doctorate degree in clinical psychology who has successfully completed forensic evaluation training as approved by the Commissioner of Behavioral Health and Developmental Services and (ii) qualified by specialized training and experience to perform forensic evaluations. The defendant shall not be entitled to a mental health expert of the defendant's own choosing or to funds to employ such expert.

B. Evaluations performed pursuant to subsection A may be combined with evaluations performed pursuant to § 19.2-169.5 and shall be governed by subsections B and C of § 19.2-169.5.

C. The expert appointed pursuant to subsection A shall submit to the attorney for the defendant a report concerning the history and character of the defendant and the defendant's mental condition at the time of the offense. The report shall include the expert's opinion as to (i) whether the defendant acted under extreme mental or emotional disturbance at the time of the offense, (ii) whether the capacity of the defendant to appreciate the criminality of his conduct or to conform his conduct to the requirements of the law was significantly impaired, and (iii) whether there are any other factors in mitigation relating to the history or character of the defendant or the defendant's mental condition at the time of the offense.

D. The report described in subsection C shall be sent solely to the attorney for the defendant and shall be protected by the attorney-client privilege. However, the Commonwealth shall be given the report and the results of any other evaluation of the defendant's mental condition conducted relative to the sentencing proceeding and copies of psychiatric, psychological, medical or other records obtained during the course of such evaluation, after the attorney for the defendant gives notice of an intent to present psychiatric or psychological evidence in mitigation pursuant to subsection E.

E. In any case in which a defendant charged with capital murder intends, in the event of conviction, to present testimony of an expert witness to support a claim in mitigation relating to the defendant's history, character or mental condition, he or his attorney shall give notice in writing to the attorney for the Commonwealth, at least 60 days before trial, of his intention to present such testimony. In the event that such notice is not given and the defendant tenders testimony by an expert witness at the sentencing phase of the trial, then the court may, in its discretion, upon objection of the Commonwealth, either allow the Commonwealth a continuance or, under appropriate circumstances, bar the defendant from presenting such evidence.

F. 1. If the attorney for the defendant gives notice pursuant to subsection E and the Commonwealth thereafter seeks an evaluation concerning the existence or absence of mitigating circumstances relating to the defendant's mental condition at the time of the offense, the court shall appoint one or more qualified experts to perform such an evaluation. The court shall order the defendant to submit to such an evaluation, and advise the defendant on the record in court that a refusal to cooperate with the Commonwealth's expert could result in exclusion of the defendant's expert evidence. The qualification of the experts shall be governed by subsection A. The location of the evaluation shall be governed by subsection B of § 19.2-169.5. The attorney for the Commonwealth shall be responsible for providing the experts the information specified in subsection C of § 19.2-169.5. After performing their evaluation, the experts shall report their findings and opinions and provide copies of psychiatric, psychological, medical or other records obtained during the course of the evaluation to the attorneys for the Commonwealth and the defense.

2. If the court finds, after hearing evidence presented by the parties, out of the presence of the jury, that the defendant has refused to cooperate with an evaluation requested by the Commonwealth, the court may admit evidence of such refusal or, in the discretion of the court, bar the defendant from presenting his expert evidence.

G. [Repealed.]

History.
1986, c. 535; 1987, c. 439; 1996, cc. 937, 980; 2003, cc. 1031, 1040; 2009, cc. 813, 840; 2010, c. 559.

The 2009 amendments.
The 2009 amendments by cc. 813 and 840 are identical, and substituted "Commissioner of Behavioral Health and Developmental Services" for "Commissioner of Mental Health, Mental Retardation and Substance Abuse Services" near the end of subsection A.

The 2010 amendments.
The 2010 amendment by c. 559 substituted "60 days" for "21 days" in subsection E.

Law Review.
For article summarizing published Virginia criminal law decisions between July 1, 2002 and July 1, 2003, see 38 U. Rich. L. Rev. 87 (2003).

CASE NOTES

Clause (ii) of subsection A does not require experience in capital murder cases as a qualification for an appointed expert. The relevant part of this section simply requires specialized training and experience to perform forensic evaluations. Cherrix v. Commonwealth, 257 Va. 292, 513 S.E.2d 642, cert. denied, 528 U.S. 873, 120 S. Ct. 177, 145 L. Ed. 2d 149 (1999).

Waiver of Fifth Amendment privilege. — When a defendant has given notice that he intends to present evidence of his mental condition in the penalty phase of the trial, he waives his Fifth Amendment privilege against the introduction of psychiatric testimony by the prosecution. Savino v. Commonwealth, 239 Va. 534, 391 S.E.2d 276, cert. denied, 498 U.S. 882, 111 S. Ct. 229, 112 L. Ed. 2d 184 (1990).

The defendant waived his Fifth Amendment rights by requesting a psychiatric evaluation pursuant to this section. This section, both on its face and by operation, provided the defense with adequate notice of the waiver. Savino v. Murray, 82 F.3d 593 (4th Cir.), cert. denied, 518 U.S. 1036, 117 S. Ct. 1, 135 L. Ed. 2d 1098 (1996).

Defendant's Sixth Amendment right to counsel was not violated, where he was on notice that, by virtue of this section, an examination would be conducted by the Commonwealth's expert in an effort to produce evidence against his interests. Savino v. Commonwealth, 239 Va. 534, 391 S.E.2d 276, cert. denied, 498 U.S. 882, 111 S. Ct. 229, 112 L. Ed. 2d 184 (1990).

Fact that defendant may not have received from appointed expert the opinion he wanted is completely immaterial. Defendant does not have a constitutional right to choose a psychiatrist of his personal liking or to receive funds to hire his own. Put another way, defendant has no right to "shop around" at state expense until he finds a doctor who will give him the opinion he wants. Pruett v. Commonwealth, 232 Va. 266, 351 S.E.2d 1 (1986), cert. denied, 482 U.S. 931, 107 S. Ct. 3220, 96 L. Ed. 2d 706 (1987).

Assuming that the expert witness's diagnosis was flawed, petitioner did not show that trial counsel was unreasonable in relying upon it or in failing to conduct a more thorough investigation of his own; it followed, then, that the state supreme court was reasonable and correct in dismissing petitioner's related ineffective assistance claim under the performance prong of *Strickland.* Orbe v. True, 233

F. Supp. 2d 749, 2002 U.S. Dist. LEXIS 22958 (E.D. Va. 2002).

Defendant's refusal to cooperate. — Trial court did not abuse its discretion by excluding defendant's expert witness testimony concerning mitigation factors at sentencing where defendant knowingly and intelligently refused to cooperate. Muhammad v. Commonwealth, 269 Va. 451, 619 S.E.2d 16, 2005 Va. LEXIS 85 (2005), cert. denied, — U.S. —, 126 S. Ct. 2035, 164 L. Ed. 2d 794 (2006) and overruled in part on other grounds by Jay v. Commonwealth, 275 Va. 510, 659 S.E.2d 311, 2008 Va. LEXIS 53 (2008).

Trial court did not abuse its discretion in denying defendant's motion to appoint a substitute expert for the Commonwealth of Virginia based on the trial court's finding that defendant, after the trial court granted defendant's motion for the appointment of a mental health expert, refused to cooperate with the mental health expert for the Commonwealth of Virginia. Further, the trial court did not err by imposing the sanction of allowing defendant to present testimony from his mental health expert as long as the jury was informed of defendant's refusal to cooperate with the Commonwealth's mental health expert. Juniper v. Commonwealth, 271 Va. 362, 626 S.E.2d 383, 2006 Va. LEXIS 29 (2006).

Trial court informed the inmate, pursuant to § 19.2-264.3:1, that if he did not submit to a psychiatric evaluation by the government's experts, he would not be able to present expert testimony of his own and the inmate indicated that he understood; after the inmate refused to be examined by the government's psychiatrist, the trial court once again questioned him about the consequences of his doing so, and he once again indicated that he understood. Thus, the state court's determination that the inmate waived the presentation of expert mitigation evidence was neither inconsistent with the facts in the record nor contrary to clearly established law. Muhammad v. Kelly, 575 F.3d 359, 2009 U.S. App. LEXIS 17645 (4th Cir. 2009).

Failure to present the testimony of a habeas inmate's mental health expert at sentencing was not ineffective assistance where the inmate refused to cooperate with the Commonwealth's expert even after the trial court explained to him the ramifications. Teleguz v. Warden of the Sussex I State Prison, 279 Va. 1, 688 S.E.2d 865, 2010 Va. LEXIS 7 (2010).

Counsel was not ineffective in failing to present a mental health evaluation and testimony of an expert hired by the defense to evaluate petitioner and assist in the preparation and presentation of information regarding his mental health because petitioner failed to submit to the evaluation of the state's expert. In the face of the trial court's evident disinclination to admit the expert's testimony absent compliance, petitioner could not demonstrate that more vigorous argument from counsel would have likely affected the trial court's decision. Teleguz v. Kelly, 2011 U.S. Dist. LEXIS 83884 (Aug. 1, 2011).

Opinion on future dangerousness permitted. — This section differentiates between a defendant's statements made during psychiatric evaluation and an expert's opinion based upon such statements. Because this section does not preclude use of the opinion of the state's examiner for establishing an aggravating circumstance, an expert's opinion on future dangerousness is also permitted. Savino v. Murray, 82 F.3d 593 (4th Cir.), cert. denied, 518 U.S. 1036, 117 S. Ct. 1, 135 L. Ed. 2d 1098 (1996).

Indigent defendant was not entitled to select his examining psychiatrist if the state was paying for the examination. Mackall v. Commonwealth, 236 Va. 240, 372 S.E.2d 759 (1988), cert. denied, 492 U.S. 925, 109 S. Ct. 3261, 106 L. Ed. 2d 607 (1989).

Indigent defendant was not entitled to a second psychiatric examination at state expense where the Commonwealth already had paid for his first examination. Mackall v. Commonwealth, 236 Va. 240, 372 S.E.2d 759 (1988), cert. denied, 492 U.S. 925, 109 S. Ct. 3261, 106 L. Ed. 2d 607 (1989).

Scope of expert's testimony. — Subsection F of § 19.2-264.3:1 does not limit the scope of the expert's examination to matters of mitigation and, therefore, the Commonwealth's mental health expert may evaluate a defendant's future dangerousness. Prieto v. Commonwealth, 283 Va. 149, 721 S.E.2d 484, 2012 Va. LEXIS 20 (2012).

Expert qualified. — With regard to defendant's convictions on two capital murder counts and the imposition of two death sentences against him, the trial court did not abuse its discretion by allowing a particular doctor as the Commonwealth's mental health expert under subsection F of § 19.2-264.3:1 because he satisfied the professional requirements for appointment and defendant presented no evidence that would have supported disqualifying the doctor as the mental health expert. Prieto v. Commonwealth, 283 Va. 149, 721 S.E.2d 484, 2012 Va. LEXIS 20 (2012).

Applied in Mu'Min v. Commonwealth, 239 Va. 433, 389 S.E.2d 886 (1990); Cardwell v. Netherland, 971 F. Supp. 997 (E.D. Va. 1997); Jackson v. Commonwealth, 255 Va. 625, 499 S.E.2d 538 (1998); Ramdass v. Angelone, 28 F. Supp. 2d 343 (E.D. Va. 1998); Joseph v. Angelone, 184 F.3d 320 (4th Cir. 1999); Burns v. Warden of the Sussex I State Prison, 268 Va. 1, 597 S.E.2d 195, 2004 Va. LEXIS 78 (2004).

§ 19.2-264.3:1.1. Capital cases; determination of mental retardation.

A. As used in this section and § 19.2-264.3:1.2, the following definition applies:

"Mentally retarded" means a disability, originating before the age of 18 years, characterized concurrently by (i) significantly subaverage intellectual functioning as demonstrated by performance on a standardized measure of intellectual functioning administered in conformity with accepted professional practice, that is at least two standard deviations below the mean and (ii) significant limitations in adaptive behavior as expressed in conceptual, social and practical adaptive skills.

B. Assessments of mental retardation under this section and § 19.2-264.3:1.2 shall conform to the following requirements:

1. Assessment of intellectual functioning shall include administration of at least one standardized measure generally accepted by the field of psychological testing and appropriate for administration to the particular defendant being assessed, taking into account cultural, linguistic, sensory, motor, behavioral and other individual factors. Testing of intellectual functioning shall be carried out in conformity with accepted professional practice, and whenever indicated, the assessment shall include information from multiple sources. The Commissioner of Behavioral Health and Developmental Services shall maintain an exclusive list of standardized measures of intellectual functioning generally accepted by the field of psychological testing.

2. Assessment of adaptive behavior shall be based on multiple sources of information, including clinical interview, psychological testing and educational, correctional and vocational records. The assessment shall include at least one standardized measure generally accepted by the field of psychological testing for assessing adaptive behavior and appropriate for administration to the particular defendant being assessed, unless not feasible. In reaching a clinical judgment regarding whether the defendant exhibits significant limitations in adaptive behavior, the examiner shall give performance on standardized measures whatever weight is clinically appropriate in light of the defendant's history and characteristics and the context of the assessment.

3. Assessment of developmental origin shall be based on multiple sources of information generally accepted by the field of psychological testing and appropriate for the particular defendant being as-

sessed, including, whenever available, educational, social service, medical records, prior disability assessments, parental or caregiver reports, and other collateral data, recognizing that valid clinical assessment conducted during the defendant's childhood may not have conformed to current practice standards.

C. In any case in which the offense may be punishable by death and is tried before a jury, the issue of mental retardation, if raised by the defendant in accordance with the notice provisions of subsection E of § 19.2-264.3:1.2, shall be determined by the jury as part of the sentencing proceeding required by § 19.2-264.4.

In any case in which the offense may be punishable by death and is tried before a judge, the issue of mental retardation, if raised by the defendant in accordance with the notice provisions of subsection E of § 19.2-264.3:1.2, shall be determined by the judge as part of the sentencing proceeding required by § 19.2-264.4.

The defendant shall bear the burden of proving that he is mentally retarded by a preponderance of the evidence.

D. The verdict of the jury, if the issue of mental retardation is raised, shall be in writing, and, in addition to the forms specified in § 19.2-264.4, shall include one of the following forms:

(1) "We the jury, on the issue joined, having found the defendant guilty of (here set out the statutory language of the offense charged), and that the defendant has proven by a preponderance of the evidence that he is mentally retarded, fix his punishment at (i) imprisonment for life or (ii) imprisonment for life and a fine of $_____.

Signed

_____ fore-
man"

or

(2) "We the jury, on the issue joined, having found the defendant guilty of (here set out the statutory language of the offense charged) find that the defendant has not proven by a preponderance of the evidence that he is mentally retarded.

Signed

_____ fore-
man"

History.
2003, cc. 1031, 1040; 2009, cc. 813, 840.

Editor's note.
Acts 2003, cc. 1031 and 1040, cls. 2, provide: "That an emergency exists and this act is in force from its passage."

Acts 2003, c. 1031 was approved April 29, 2003, and Acts 2003, c. 1040 was approved May 1, 2003.

The 2009 amendments.
The 2009 amendments by cc. 813 and 840 are identical, and substituted "Commissioner of Behavioral Health and Developmental Services" for "Commissioner of Mental Health, Mental Retardation and Substance Abuse Services" in the last sentence of subdivision B 1.

Law Review.

For article, "The Challenge of Implementing Atkins v. Virginia: How Legislatures and Courts Can Promote Accurate Assessments and Adjudications of Mental Retardation if Death Penalty Cases," see 41 U. Rich. L. Rev. 811 (2007). For article, "And Death Shall Have No Dominion: How to Achieve Categorical Exemption of Mentally Retarded Defendants from Execution," see 45 U. Rich. L. Rev. 961 (2011).

CASE NOTES

Resentencing defendant after determination of mental retardation claim. — Although § 8.01-654.2 is silent regarding the procedure to be followed once a death row inmate's mental retardation issue was resolved on remand, the Supreme Court of Virginia concluded that, upon a finding that he was not mentally retarded, the sentence of death entered remained in full force and effect, but upon a finding that he was mentally retarded, the trial court shall enter an order vacating the sentence of death and re-sentence defendant in accordance with subsection D of this section. Burns v. Warden of the Sussex I State Prison, 269 Va. 351, 609 S.E.2d 608, 2005 Va. LEXIS 33 (2005).

Determination of mental retardation claim by judge or jury. — Because defendant, who was sentenced to death, was originally tried by a jury, § 8.01-654.2 requires that, on remand, he be entitled to have his claim of mental retardation determined by a jury in accordance with subsection C of this section. Burns v. Warden of the Sussex I State Prison, 269 Va. 351, 609 S.E.2d 608, 2005 Va. LEXIS 33 (2005).

In a capital case, defendant unsuccessfully argued that the circuit court erred in not requiring that the issue of mental retardation be determined separately from the other sentencing issues. The language in subsection C of § 19.2-264.3:1.1 directing that the issue of mental retardation shall be determined by the jury as part of the sentencing proceeding required by § 19.2-264.4 clearly mandated that the issue of mental retardation be determined by the jury as part of the sentencing phase. Prieto v. Commonwealth, 278 Va. 366, 682 S.E.2d 910, 2009 Va. LEXIS 94 (2009), cert. denied, 177 L. Ed. 2d 332, 2010 U.S. LEXIS 4926 (U.S. 2010).

Because, pursuant to § 8.01-654.2, the jury provisions of § 19.2-264.3:1.1 applied to Atkins claims brought in state court, the inmate, who was sentenced to death, was not entitled to a jury to decide his Atkins claim because he was in federal court; thus, the federal district court did not err by refusing to empanel a jury to determine the inmate's mental retardation claim. Walker v. Kelly, 593 F.3d 319, 2010 U.S. App. LEXIS 1844 (4th Cir. 2010), cert. denied, 130 S. Ct..3318, 176 L. Ed. 2d 1215, 2010 U.S. LEXIS 4160 (U.S. 2010).

Evidence generally. — Section 8.01-654.2 directs that, if the court concludes that a capital murder defendant's claim of mental retardation is not frivolous, whether on direct appeal or in a habeas corpus proceeding, the court must remand the matter "to the circuit court" for a determination regarding mental retardation consistent with §§ 19.2-264.3:1.1 and 19.2-264.3:1.2. Nothing in that directive precludes the use of a jury to determine the issue of mental retardation if the issue arose in the context of a habeas corpus proceeding. Burns v. Warden of the Sussex I State Prison, 268 Va. 1, 597 S.E.2d 195, 2004 Va. LEXIS 78 (2004).

Case was remanded to the district court to make a determination regarding the habeas corpus petitioner's mental retardation, considering all evidence pertaining to the developmental origin, intellectual functioning, and adaptive behavior aspects. Walker v. True, 399 F.3d 315, 2005 U.S. App. LEXIS 2775 (4th Cir. 2005).

Prisoner sought habeas relief from his death sentence, asserting that his death sentence violated Atkins because of his mental retardation. In denying the petition, the district court relied on two IQ tests administered to the prisoner around his eighteenth birthday; yet, the court failed to consider: (1) the prisoner's claim that the first IQ test was inadequate; (2) the impact of the standard margin of error on the second test; and (3) that state law required the consideration of other factors, rather than just IQ tests, in making an intelligence assessment as to mental capacity. Walton v. Johnson, 407 F.3d 285, 2005 U.S. App. LEXIS 7336 (4th Cir. 2005).

If an expert, skilled in administering, scoring and interpreting

standardized measures of adaptive behavior, determines in his or her opinion that such a test is not appropriate for a particular defendant or that administering a standardized measure of adaptive behavior is not feasible, the expert can still testify as to the defendant's mental retardation and explain why a measure of adaptive behavior was not administered to the defendant. The decision about which tests to administer to a defendant and the manner in which they are given goes to the weight to be accorded an expert's opinion regarding mental retardation, not to the admissibility of the opinion. Atkins v. Commonwealth, 272 Va. 144, 631 S.E.2d 93, 2006 Va. LEXIS 67 (2006), overruled on other grounds, Jay v. Commonwealth, 275 Va. 510, 659 S.E.2d 311, 2008 Va. LEXIS 53 (2008).

Mental retardation claim not supported by evidence. — Supreme court was not required to remand defendant's case for consideration of his mental retardation claim since, inter alia, his expert witness testified that he was not mentally retarded and the scores he received on two IQ tests were not below the threshold for being classified as mentally retarded. Johnson v. Commonwealth, 267 Va. 53, 591 S.E.2d 47, 2004 Va. LEXIS 7 (2004), vacated and remanded, 125 S.Ct. 1589, 161 L.Ed.2d 270, 2005 U.S. LEXIS 2208, for further consideration in light of Roper v. Simmons, 544 U.S. 551, 161 L.Ed.2d 1, 125 S.Ct. 1183 (2005).

State inmate was denied federal habeas relief on a claim that he could not be executed because of mental retardation where the state court determined that the inmate had failed to produce evidence that he had a qualifying IQ under a statutorily accepted test, failed to present sufficient evidence showing the required limitations in adaptive behavior, and as a result, failed to show that he was mentally retarded as defined in § 19.2-264.3:1.1. Bell v. True, 413 F. Supp. 2d 657, 2006 U.S. Dist. LEXIS 4608 (W.D. Va. 2006).

Denial of federal habeas corpus relief was affirmed holding that petitioner was not mentally retarded where the petitioner failed to satisfy the statutory definition of mental retardation under Virginia law, § 19.2-264.3:1.1(A)(i), because the petitioner failed to allege sufficient facts demonstrating that his IQ score (intellectual functioning) was 70 or less before he turned 18 as the petitioner only offered speculation that a "standard measurement error" (so-called "Flynn effect") actually lowered his given score of 77 enough to meet Virginia's mental retardation standard. Walton v. Johnson, 440 F.3d 160, 2006 U.S. App. LEXIS 5898 (4th Cir. 2006), cert. denied, — U.S. —, 126 S. Ct. 2377, 165 L. Ed. 2d 298 (2006).

Inmate was properly denied habeas corpus relief on his claim that he could not be executed because he was mentally retarded because he failed to show that he was mentally retarded under Virginia law, as he received a score of 76 on an IQ test, and only speculation on the court's part would lower the inmate's score to 70 or less. Hedrick v. True, 443 F.3d 342, 2006 U.S. App. LEXIS 7904 (4th Cir. 2006), cert. denied, 548 U.S. 928, 127 S. Ct. 10, 165 L. Ed. 2d 992 (2006).

Since the petitioner provided no documentation that he was diagnosed as being mentally retarded before the age of 18 in accordance with the legal definition of mental retardation established by the legislature, the petitioner failed to demonstrate that his counsel's performance was deficient or that there is a reasonable probability that, but for counsel's alleged error, the result of his conviction on three counts of capital murder and the imposition of the death sentence, would have been different. Winston v. Warden of the Sussex I State Prison, 2007 Va. LEXIS 43 (Mar. 7, 2007).

Where defendant sought habeas corpus relief from his state court convictions that included capital murder during the commission of a robbery, and where a federal habeas court conducted an evidentiary hearing regarding defendant's claim that his death sentence constituted cruel and unusual punishment, the evidence was sufficient to conclude that defendant did not qualify as "mentally retarded" under subsection A of § 19.2-264.3:1.1, because although defendant presented sufficient evidence demonstrating "significantly sub average intellectual functioning," the test scores were not adjusted based on the standard error of measurement of the WAIS-II score, since such adjustments were speculative and not fully supported by expert evidence; but the "Flynn effect" was properly accounted for in analyzing defendant's intellectual functioning, however defendant did not meet his burden in proving that he had significant limitations in adaptive behavior based on evidence of his employment history, use of language, understanding of money concepts, self-direction, and relationships with others. Green v. Johnson, — F. Supp. 2d —, 2007 U.S. Dist. LEXIS 21711 (E.D. Va. Mar. 26, 2007), aff'd, 515 F.3d 290, 2008 U.S. App. LEXIS 2967 (4th Cir. Va. 2008).

State supreme court dismissed the petition for writ of habeas corpus filed by petitioner, who was convicted of two counts of capital murder for hire and who was sentenced to death following petitioner's guilty plea to seven felonies; while petitioner's primary claim was that petitioner received ineffective assistance of counsel because counsel allegedly failed to conduct an adequate investigation of mitigation evidence and counsel failed to present such mitigation evidence, petitioner could not show that petitioner was prejudiced by the alleged failures, including the failure to present evidence of mental retardation when there was no evidence that petitioner was mentally retarded. Lewis v. Warden of the Fluvanna Corr. Ctr., 274 Va. 93, 645 S.E.2d 492, 2007 Va. LEXIS 95 (2007), supplemental op., 2007 Va. LEXIS 68 (Va. June 8, 2007).

Where a state inmate claimed that he was mentally retarded and, therefore, that his sentence violated the Eighth Amendment, the inmate was not entitled to federal habeas corpus relief because (1) the state court's conclusion that the inmate failed to prove that his mental retardation claim was not frivolous for purposes of § 8.01-654.2 was entitled to deference given that it was not objectively unreasonable to conclude that the test in clause (i) of subsection A of § 19.2-264.3:1.1 could not be satisfied where three of the inmate's four intelligence quotient scores exceeded 70, the maximum score for a mental retardation classification; and (2) the inmate failed to prove that he had significant limitations in adaptive behavior. Green v. Johnson, 515 F.3d 290, 2008 U.S. App. LEXIS 2967 (4th Cir. 2008), cert. denied, stay denied, 128 S. Ct. 2527, 2008 U.S. LEXIS 4519 (U.S. 2008).

Evidence in the record supported the federal district court's finding that the state inmate, who was sentenced to death, failed to prove that he was mentally retarded under subsection A of § 19.2-264.3:1.1, and thus was not eligible for the death penalty under the United States Supreme Court's holding in Atkins (interpreting U.S. Const., Amend. VIII); the record on appeal showed that the district court was presented with conflicting evidence concerning the inmate's adaptive skills, but it was not persuaded by the inmate's evidentiary presentation and concluded that he failed to meet his burden of proving, by a preponderance of the evidence, the necessary fact that he suffered from significant limitations in adaptive behavior. While the district court's finding was not necessarily compelled by the evidence in the record, there was sufficient evidence in the record to support it; thus, based on the record, the district court did not clearly err. Walker v. Kelly, 593 F.3d 319, 2010 U.S. App. LEXIS 1844 (4th Cir. 2010), cert. denied, 130 S. Ct..3318, 176 L. Ed. 2d 1215, 2010 U.S. LEXIS 4160 (U.S. 2010).

Evidence of petitioner state death row inmate's retardation, believed to have been destroyed but found just before the federal district court's evidentiary hearing, should not have been excluded on the grounds that rendered an Atkins-related ineffective assistance of counsel claim unexhausted under 28 U.S.C.S. § 2254(b)(1), (d), as it did not fundamentally alter the claim as it had been considered by the state courts; § 2254(d) and deference did not apply to the Atkins-related ineffective assistance of counsel claim since the state supreme court had denied an evidentiary hearing and had thus precluded discovery, but deference under § 2254(e)(1) would apply to relevant factual findings. Winston v. Kelly, 592 F.3d 535, 2010 U.S. App. LEXIS 1845 (4th Cir. 2010), cert. denied, 131 S. Ct. 136, 2010 U.S. LEXIS 5952, 178 L. Ed. 2d 83 (U.S. 2010).

Death penalty. — The authorized punishment for conviction of class 1 felonies is death, if the person so convicted was 16 years of age or older at the time of the offense and is not determined to be mentally retarded, but the finding of mental retardation does not increase the penalty for the crime beyond the statutory maximum, rather, a defendant facing the death penalty may avoid that penalty if defendant successfully raises and proves by a preponderance of the evidence that defendant is mentally retarded; the state does not have a corollary duty to prove that a defendant is not retarded in order to be entitled to the death penalty, and accordingly, an increase in a defendant's sentence is not predicated on the outcome of the mental retardation determination, only a decrease. Walker v. True, 399 F.3d 315, 2005 U.S. App. LEXIS 2775 (4th Cir. 2005).

Inmate diligently pursued his habeas corpus claims that Atkins barred his execution and that he received ineffective assistance of counsel through the failure to investigate this claim; and it was not wholly implausible that he could establish his claims even in light of the deferential standards of the Anti-Terrorism and Effective Death Penalty Act of 1996, 110 Stat. 1214. In reaching that conclusion, however, the court did not decide that the inmate was entitled to an evidentiary hearing, but rather exercised its discretion to grant that hearing; the court granted the inmate a hearing on his counsel's ineffective assistance both as cause and prejudice to excuse the procedural default of his Atkins claim and as a free standing constitutional claim. Winston v. Kelly, 624 F. Supp. 2d 478, 2008 U.S. Dist. LEXIS 42565 (W.D. Va. 2008).

Petitioner state death row inmate established counsel's ineffectiveness by showing counsel failed to review the inmate's school records and interview school officials, which would have revealed an IQ score of below 70 to show retardation under subsection A of § 19.2-264.3:1.1, and, in turn, that would have prompted them to press their expert to explore further the merits of mental retardation as a sentencing defense. Winston v. Pearson, 683 F.3d 489, 2012 U.S. App. LEXIS 12937 (4th Cir. 2012).

Applied in Atkins v. Commonwealth, 266 Va. 73, 581 S.E.2d 514, 2003 Va. LEXIS 71 (2003); Burns v. Commonwealth, 279 Va. 243, 688 S.E.2d 263, 2010 Va. LEXIS 19 (2010).

CIRCUIT COURT OPINIONS

Age of origination, not of diagnosis, relevant. — Department of Medical Assistance Services' interpretation of definition of Mental Retardation/Intellectual Disability so as to require the diagnosis prior to age eighteen, rather than the origination of the disability before age eighteen, was unreasonable, arbitrary, and capricious; the department could not interpret the definition of Mental Retardation/Intellectual Disability in such a way so as to conflict with the plain language of that definition. Pape v. Pane, 2011 Va. Cir. LEXIS 79 (Fairfax County May 13, 2011).

§ 19.2-264.3:1.2. Expert assistance when issue of defendant's mental retardation relevant to capital sentencing.

A. Upon (i) motion of the attorney for a defendant charged with or convicted of capital murder and (ii) a finding by the court that the defendant is financially unable to pay for expert assistance, the court shall appoint one or more qualified mental health experts to assess whether or not the defendant is mentally retarded and to assist the defense in the preparation and presentation of information concerning the defendant's mental retardation. The mental health expert appointed pursuant to this section shall be (a) a psychiatrist, a clinical psychologist or an individual with a doctorate degree in clinical psychology, (b) skilled in the administration, scoring and interpretation of intelligence tests and measures of adaptive behavior and (c) qualified by experience and by specialized training, approved by the Commissioner of Behavioral Health and Developmental Services, to perform forensic evaluations. The defendant shall not be entitled to a mental health expert of the defendant's own choosing or to funds to employ such expert.

B. Evaluations performed pursuant to subsection A may be combined with evaluations performed pursuant to § 19.2-169.1, 19.2-169.5, or 19.2-264.3:1.

C. The expert appointed pursuant to subsection A shall submit to the attorney for the defendant a report assessing whether the defendant is mentally retarded. The report shall include the expert's opinion as to whether the defendant is mentally retarded.

D. The report described in subsection C shall be sent solely to the attorney for the defendant and shall be protected by the attorney-client privilege. However, the Commonwealth shall be given a copy of the report, the results of any other evaluation of the defendant's mental retardation and copies of psychiatric, psychological, medical or other records obtained during the course of the evaluation, after the attorney for the defendant gives notice of an intent to present evidence of mental retardation pursuant to subsection E.

E. In any case in which a defendant charged with capital murder intends, in the event of conviction, to present testimony of an expert witness to support a claim that he is mentally retarded, he or his attorney shall give notice in writing to the attorney for the Commonwealth, at least 21 days before trial, of his intention to present such testimony. In the event that such notice is not given and the defendant tenders testimony by an expert witness at the sentencing phase of the trial, then the court may, in its discretion, upon objection of the Commonwealth, either allow the Commonwealth a continuance or, under appropriate circumstances, bar the defendant from presenting such evidence.

F. 1. If the attorney for the defendant gives notice pursuant to subsection E and the Commonwealth thereafter seeks an evaluation concerning the existence or absence of the defendant's mental retardation, the court shall appoint one or more qualified experts to perform such an evaluation. The court shall order the defendant to submit to such an evaluation, and advise the defendant on the record in court that a refusal to cooperate with the Commonwealth's experts could result in exclusion of the defendant's expert evidence. The qualification of the experts shall be governed by subsection A. The attorney for the Commonwealth shall be responsible for providing the experts the information specified in subsection C of § 19.2-169.5. After performing their evaluation, the experts shall report their findings and opinions and provide copies of psychiatric, psychological, medical or other records obtained during the course of the evaluation to the attorneys for the Commonwealth and the defense.

2. If the court finds, after hearing evidence presented by the parties, out of the presence of the jury, that the defendant has refused to cooperate with an evaluation requested by the Commonwealth, the court may admit evidence of such refusal or, in the discretion of the court, bar the defendant from presenting his expert evidence.

History.
2003, cc. 1031, 1040; 2009, cc. 813, 840.

Editor's note.
Acts 2003, cc. 1031 and 1040, cls. 2, provide: "That an emergency exists and this act is in force from its passage."

Acts 2003, c. 1031 was approved April 29, 2003, and Acts 2003, c. 1040 was approved May 1, 2003.

The 2009 amendments.
The 2009 amendments by cc. 813 and 840 are identical, and substituted "Commissioner of Behavioral Health and Developmental Services" for "Commissioner of Mental Health, Mental Retardation and Substance Abuse Services" in subsection A; and made minor stylistic changes.

CASE NOTES

Use of jury to determine mental retardation. — Section 8.01-654.2 directs that, if the court concludes that a capital murder defendant's claim of mental retardation is not frivolous, whether on direct appeal or in a habeas corpus proceeding, the court must remand the matter "to the circuit court" for a determination regarding mental retardation consistent with §§ 19.2-264.3:1.1 and 19.2-264.3:1.2. Nothing in that directive precludes the use of a jury to determine the issue of mental retardation if the issue arose in the context of a habeas corpus proceeding. Burns v. Warden of the Sussex I State Prison, 268 Va. 1, 597 S.E.2d 195, 2004 Va. LEXIS 78 (2004).

Qualifications of witness not established. — Clinical psychologist appointed by the court was erroneously allowed to testify and express an opinion about whether defendant, in capital murder case, was mentally retarded because the Commonwealth failed to establish that the psychologist possessed the qualifications required by subsection A of this section. Atkins v. Commonwealth, 272 Va. 144, 631 S.E.2d 93, 2006 Va. LEXIS 67 (2006), overruled on other grounds, Jay v. Commonwealth, 275 Va. 510, 659 S.E.2d 311, 2008 Va. LEXIS 53 (2008).

Death penalty. — The authorized punishment for conviction of class 1 felonies is death, if the person so convicted was 16 years of age or older at the time of the offense and is not determined to be mentally retarded, but the finding of mental retardation does not increase the penalty for the crime beyond the statutory maximum death, rather, a defendant facing the death penalty may avoid that penalty if defendant successfully raises and proves by a preponderance of the evidence that defendant is mentally retarded; the state does not have a corollary duty to prove that a defendant is not retarded in order to be entitled to the death penalty, and accordingly, an increase in a defendant's sentence is not predicated on the outcome of the mental retardation determination, only a decrease. Walker v. True, 399 F.3d 315, 2005 U.S. App. LEXIS 2775 (4th Cir. 2005).

Applied in Burns v. Commonwealth, 279 Va. 243, 688 S.E.2d 263, 2010 Va. LEXIS 19 (2010).

§ 19.2-264.3:1.3. Expert assistance for indigent defendants in capital cases.

A. In any case in which an indigent defendant (i) is charged with a capital offense and (ii) is found by the court to be financially unable to pay for expert assistance, the defendant or his attorney may, upon notice to the Commonwealth, move in circuit court for the court to designate another judge in the same circuit to hear an ex parte request for the appointment of a qualified expert to assist in the preparation of the defendant's defense. No ex parte proceeding, communication, or request may be considered pursuant to this section unless a proper showing is made in an adversarial proceeding before the trial judge demonstrating a particularized need for confidentiality. Any such proceeding, communication, or request shall be transcribed and made part of the record available for appellate review or any other post conviction review.

B. The motion for the appointment of a qualified expert shall be in writing, filed under seal, and shall be heard ex parte as soon as practicable by the designated judge. Upon hearing the ex parte request, the designated judge shall find, by clear and convincing evidence, a particularized need for confidentiality has been demonstrated before considering the request for expert services. After a hearing upon the motion, the court may order the appointment of a qualified expert upon a showing that the provision of the requested expert services would materially assist the defendant in preparing his defense and the lack of such confidential assistance would result in a fundamentally unfair trial. Any expert appointed pursuant to this subsection shall be compensated in accordance with § 19.2-332. The designated judge shall direct requests for scientific investigations to the Department of Forensic Science or Division of Consolidated Laboratory Services whenever practicable.

C. All ex parte hearings conducted under this section shall be on the record, and the record of the hearings, together with all papers filed and orders entered in connection with ex parte requests for expert assistance, shall be kept under seal as part of the record of the case. Following decision on the motion, whether it is granted or denied, the motion shall remain under seal. On motion of any party, and for good cause shown, the court may unseal the record after the trial is concluded. Following final judgment and after all appeals have been exhausted, the court shall unseal all records and other material sealed pursuant to this section. No ex parte ruling by a designated judge pursuant to this section in a proceeding where the Commonwealth is excluded shall be the subject of a claim of error on appeal, or form the basis for relief in any postconviction litigation on behalf of the defendant.

D. This section does not apply to the appointment of a mental health expert pursuant to § 19.2-264.3:1 or 19.2-264.3:1.2.

History.
  2010, c. 789.

§ 19.2-264.3:2. Notice to the defendant of intention to present evidence of unadjudicated criminal conduct.

Upon motion of the defendant, in any case in which the offense for which the defendant is to be tried may be punishable by death, if the attorney for the Commonwealth intends to introduce during a sentencing proceeding held pursuant to § 19.2-264.4 evidence of defendant's unadjudicated criminal conduct, the attorney for the Commonwealth shall give notice in writing to the attorney for the defendant of such intention. The notice shall include a description of the alleged unadjudicated criminal conduct and, to the extent such information is available, the time and place such conduct will be alleged to have occurred.

The court shall specify the time by which such notice shall be given.

History.
  1993, c. 377.

CASE NOTES

Sufficiency of notice of unadjudicated conduct. — Because the Commonwealth of Virginia's notice of unadjudicated conduct incidents advised defendant of two separate assaults at the victim's place of work, the trial court properly concluded that defendant had fair notice of the Commonwealth's intent to prove assault. Furthermore, even if the notice was not sufficient to advise defendant of the alleged incidents to which a witness testified, such error was harmless as the witness's testimony was merely cumulative of other incidents of assault by defendant. Juniper v. Commonwealth, 271 Va. 362, 626 S.E.2d 383, 2006 Va. LEXIS 29 (2006).

Applied in Swisher v. Commonwealth, 256 Va. 471, 506 S.E.2d 763 (1998).

§ 19.2-264.3:3. Limitations on use of statements or disclosure by defendant during evaluations.

No statement or disclosure by the defendant made during a competency evaluation performed pursuant to § 19.2-169.1, an evaluation performed pursuant to § 19.2-169.5 to determine sanity at the time of the offense, treatment provided pursuant to § 19.2-169.2 or § 19.2-169.6, a mental condition evaluation performed pursuant to § 19.2-264.3:1 or a mental retardation evaluation performed pursuant to § 19.2-264.3:1.2, and no evidence derived from any such statements or disclosures may be introduced against the defendant at the sentencing phase of a capital murder trial for the purpose of proving the aggravating circumstances specified in § 19.2-264.4. Such statements or disclosures shall be admissible in rebuttal only when relevant to issues in mitigation raised by the defense.

History.
  2003, cc. 1031, 1040.

Editor's note.
  Acts 2003, cc. 1031 and 1040, cls. 2, provide: "That an emergency exists and this act is in force from its passage."
  Acts 2003, c. 1031 was approved April 29, 2003, and Acts 2003, c. 1040 was approved May 1, 2003.

§ 19.2-264.3:4. Notice of expert testimony in capital case.

Whenever the defendant, the defendant's attorney, or the attorney for the Commonwealth in a capital case intends to introduce expert opinion testimony at trial, the defendant, defendant's attorney, or attorney for the Commonwealth shall notify the opposing party in writing of such party's intention to present such testimony at least 60 days before the trial. The written notice shall include copies of any written reports of the witness, a summary of the proposed expert testimony that describes the witness's opinions and the basis and reasons for those opinions, and the witness's qualifications and contact information.

History.
  2010, c. 789.

§ 19.2-264.4. Sentence proceeding.

A. Upon a finding that the defendant is guilty of an offense which may be punishable by death, a proceeding shall be held which shall be limited to a determination as to whether the defendant shall be sentenced to death or life imprisonment. Upon request of the defendant, a jury shall be instructed that for all Class 1 felony offenses committed after January 1, 1995, a defendant shall not be eligible for parole if sentenced to imprisonment for life. In case of trial by jury, where a sentence of death is not recommended, the defendant shall be sentenced to imprisonment for life.

A1. In any proceeding conducted pursuant to this section, the court shall permit the victim, as defined in § 19.2-11.01, upon the motion of the attorney for the Commonwealth, and with the consent of the victim, to testify in the presence of the accused regarding the impact of the offense upon the victim. The court shall limit the victim's testimony to the factors set forth in clauses (i) through (vi) of subsection A of § 19.2-299.1.

B. In cases of trial by jury, evidence may be presented as to any matter which the court deems relevant to sentence, except that reports under the provisions of § 19.2-299, or under any rule of court, shall not be admitted into evidence.

Evidence which may be admissible, subject to the rules of evidence governing admissibility, may include the circumstances surrounding the offense, the history and background of the defendant, and any other facts in mitigation of the offense. Facts in mitigation may include, but shall not be limited to, the following: (i) the defendant has no significant history of prior criminal activity, (ii) the capital felony was committed while the defendant was under the influence of extreme mental or emotional disturbance, (iii) the victim was a participant in the defendant's conduct or consented to the act, (iv) at the time of the commission of the capital felony, the capacity of the defendant to appreciate the criminality of his conduct or to conform his conduct to the requirements of law was significantly impaired, (v) the age of the defendant at the time of the commission of the capital offense, or (vi) even if § 19.2-264.3:1.1 is inapplicable as a bar to the death penalty, the subaverage intellectual functioning of the defendant.

C. The penalty of death shall not be imposed unless the Commonwealth shall prove beyond a reasonable doubt that there is a probability based upon evidence of the prior history of the defendant or of the circumstances surrounding the commission of the offense of which he is accused that he would commit criminal acts of violence that would constitute a continuing serious threat to society, or that his conduct in committing the offense was outrageously or wantonly vile, horrible or inhuman, in that it involved torture, depravity of mind or aggravated battery to the victim.

D. In the event the jury cannot agree as to the penalty, the court shall dismiss the jury, and impose a sentence of imprisonment for life.

History.
1977, c. 492; 1980, c. 160; 1990, cc. 316, 754; 1998, c. 485; 2000, c. 838; 2003, cc. 1031, 1040; 2010, c. 658.

Cross references.
As to punishment for Class I felonies, see § 18.2-10.

The 2010 amendments.
The 2010 amendment by c. 658 deleted former subsection D concerning the written form of the jury's verdict; and redesignated former subsection E as subsection D.

Law Review.
For survey of Virginia criminal procedure for the year 1976-1977, see 63 Va. L. Rev. 1408 (1977). For article, "Psychiatry and the Death Penalty: Emerging Problems in Virginia," see 66 Va. L. Rev. 167 (1980). For survey of Virginia law on criminal procedure for the year 1978-1979, see 66 Va. L. Rev. 261 (1980). For article, "The Role of Mental Health Professionals in the Criminal Process: The Case for Informed Speculation," see 66 Va. L. Rev. 427 (1980). For a comment discussing possible effects on Virginia's death penalty law in the light of recent United States Supreme Court decisions, see 15 U. Rich. L. Rev. 951 (1981). For comment on Virginia's death penalty, see 17 U. Rich. L. Rev. 603 (1983). For article, "Virginia's Capital Murder Sentencing Proceeding: A Defense Perspective," see 18 U. Rich. L. Rev. 341 (1984). For note, "The Meaning of 'Life' for Virginia Jurors and Its Effect on Reliability in Capital Sentencing," see 75 Va. L. Rev. 1605 (1989). For 1991 survey on criminal law and procedure, see 25 U. Rich. L. Rev. 731 (1991). For a note, "Due Process on the Uncharted Seas of Irrelevance: Limiting the Presence of Victim Impact Evidence at Capital Sentencing After *Payne v. Tennessee*," see 55 Wash. & Lee L. Rev. 295 (1998). For 2000 survey of Virginia criminal law and procedure, see 34 U. Rich. L. Rev. 749 (2000). For article, "Virginia's Capital Jurors," 44 Wm. & Mary L. Rev. 2063 (2003). For case note, "Atkins v. Virginia: Nothing Left of the Independent Legislative Power to Punish and Define Crime," 11 Geo. Mason L. Rev. 805 (2003). For article, "And Death Shall Have No Dominion: How to Achieve Categorical Exemption of Mentally Retarded Defendants from Execution," see 45 U. Rich. L. Rev. 961 (2011).

CASE NOTES

I. GENERAL CONSIDERATION.

Constitutionality. — As to constitutionality of this article, see note under § 19.2-264.2.

The statutory definitions of the two aggravating circumstances are not so vague as to vest the sentencing authority with standardless sentencing power. Smith v. Commonwealth, 219 Va. 455, 248 S.E.2d 135 (1978), cert. denied, 441 U.S. 967, 99 S. Ct. 2419, 60 L. Ed. 2d 1074 (1979).

The fact that the statutory alternative to the capital penalty is one which permits parole does not mean that the sentencing authority is constitutionally overbroad. Mercy by parole is not unconstitutional. Smith v. Commonwealth, 219 Va. 455, 248 S.E.2d 135 (1978), cert. denied, 441 U.S. 967, 99 S. Ct. 2419, 60 L. Ed. 2d 1074 (1979).

The Supreme Court rejected defendant's contention that Virginia's capital sentencing statute is unconstitutional as being overbroad and vague, and because of its racially discriminatory application. Jenkins v. Commonwealth, 244 Va. 445, 423 S.E.2d 360 (1992), cert. denied, 507 U.S. 1036, 113 S. Ct. 1862, 123 L. Ed. 2d

483 (1993), overruled in part on other grounds by Jay v. Commonwealth, 275 Va. 510, 659 S.E.2d 311, 2008 Va. LEXIS 53 (2008).

The dichotomy between "past criminal record of convictions" in § 19.2-264.2 and "prior history" in subsection C of this section does not render the statutory scheme unconstitutionally vague. LeVasseur v. Commonwealth, 225 Va. 564, 304 S.E.2d 644 (1983), cert. denied, 464 U.S. 1063, 104 S. Ct. 744, 79 L. Ed. 2d 202 (1984).

Subsection C of this section and § 19.2-264.2 are not unconstitutional as being overly broad and impermissibly vague. Hoke v. Commonwealth, 237 Va. 303, 377 S.E.2d 595, cert. denied, 491 U.S. 910, 109 S. Ct. 3201, 105 L. Ed. 2d 709 (1989).

Subsection C is not unconstitutionally vague and overbroad in violation of the accused's rights under the Eighth and Fourteenth Amendments to the United States Constitution. Evans v. Commonwealth, 222 Va. 766, 284 S.E.2d 816 (1981), cert. denied, 498 U.S. 927, 111 S. Ct. 309, 112 L. Ed. 2d 295 (1990), cert. denied, 455 U.S. 1038, 102 S. Ct. 1741, 72 L. Ed. 2d 155 (1982); Hoke v. Commonwealth, 237 Va. 303, 377 S.E.2d 595, cert. denied, 491 U.S. 910, 109 S. Ct. 3201, 105 L. Ed. 2d 709 (1989).

Due process does not require that the Commonwealth limit itself to a pretrial construction of the character of defendant's conduct. Furthermore, defendant has no constitutional right to a bill of particulars if the indictments are sufficient to give him notice of the nature and character of the offenses charged so that he can make his defense. Williams v. Commonwealth, 248 Va. 528, 450 S.E.2d 365 (1994), cert. denied, 515 U.S. 1161, 115 S. Ct. 2616, 132 L. Ed. 2d 858 (1995).

Death penalty is not unconstitutional, per se. It does not violate the proscription against cruel and unusual punishment as stated in the Eighth Amendment to the federal Constitution. Stockton v. Commonwealth, 227 Va. 124, 314 S.E.2d 371, cert. denied, 469 U.S. 873, 105 S. Ct. 229, 83 L. Ed. 2d 158 (1984).

Death penalty statutes are not facially unconstitutional. Stockton v. Commonwealth, 227 Va. 124, 314 S.E.2d 371, cert. denied, 469 U.S. 873, 105 S. Ct. 229, 83 L. Ed. 2d 158 (1984).

Language of this section is not vague and overbroad. Stockton v. Commonwealth, 227 Va. 124, 314 S.E.2d 371, cert. denied, 469 U.S. 873, 105 S. Ct. 229, 83 L. Ed. 2d 158 (1984).

Failure to list mitigating factors not unconstitutional. — A verdict form used in a capital murder case which lists the aggravating factors but does not list any mitigating factors is not unconstitutional. Clark v. Commonwealth, 220 Va. 201, 257 S.E.2d 784 (1979), cert. denied, 444 U.S. 1049, 100 S. Ct. 741, 62 L. Ed. 2d 736 (1980).

Virginia's death penalty scheme is not invalid for failure to instruct the jury on statutory mitigating factors mentioned in this section. Clozza v. Murray, 913 F.2d 1092 (4th Cir. 1990), cert. denied, 499 U.S. 913, 111 S. Ct. 1123, 113 L. Ed. 2d 231 (1991).

Authority of Commonwealth Attorney to seek death penalty. — State Supreme Court granted the petition for writ of mandamus filed by the Commonwealth Attorney, as the trial court did not have the discretion to prohibit the Commonwealth Attorney from seeking the death penalty; the Commonwealth Attorney was entitled to seek that penalty pursuant to statutory law and the trial court erred by exercising an executive function in determining that the Commonwealth Attorney was prohibited from seeking it in defendant's case where defendant was charged with capital murder pursuant to § 18.2-31. In re Horan, 271 Va. 258, 634 S.E.2d 675, 2006 Va. LEXIS 23 (2006).

Subsection C standard sufficient. — Subsection C has a common sense meaning which a jury can understand and thus supplies a sufficient standard for a jury to predict future criminal conduct. Bassett v. Commonwealth, 222 Va. 844, 284 S.E.2d 844 (1981), cert. denied, 456 U.S. 938, 102 S. Ct. 1996, 72 L. Ed. 2d 458 (1982).

"Vileness" predicate constitutional. — The "vileness" predicate is constitutionally valid. Watkins v. Commonwealth, 238 Va. 341, 385 S.E.2d 50 (1989), cert. denied, 494 U.S. 1074, 110 S. Ct. 1797, 108 L. Ed. 2d 798 (1990).

"Future dangerousness" predicate constitutional. — The aggravating predicate of "future dangerousness" contained in Virginia's capital punishment scheme is constitutional. Giarratano v. Procunier, 891 F.2d 483 (4th Cir. 1989), cert. denied, 498 U.S. 881, 111 S. Ct. 222, 112 L. Ed. 2d 178 (1990).

State inmate was denied habeas relief on a claim that the aggravating factor of future dangerousness violated the Eighth

Amendment where the inmate presented no compelling reason why the court should have departed from judicial precedent finding that the statute was constitutional. Bell v. True, 413 F. Supp. 2d 657, 2006 U.S. Dist. LEXIS 4608 (W.D. Va. 2006).

The language "evidence of the prior history of the defendant" of this section is not unconstitutionally vague. LeVasseur v. Commonwealth, 225 Va. 564, 304 S.E.2d 644 (1983), cert. denied, 464 U.S. 1063, 104 S. Ct. 744, 79 L. Ed. 2d 202 (1984).

Dichotomy between "past criminal record of convictions" in § 19.2-264.2 and "prior history" in subsection C of this section does not render the statutory scheme unconstitutionally vague. LeVasseur v. Commonwealth, 225 Va. 564, 304 S.E.2d 644 (1983), cert. denied, 464 U.S. 1063, 104 S. Ct. 744, 79 L. Ed. 2d 202 (1984).

Difference in language of § 19.2-264.2 and subsection C of this section not unconstitutional. — Virginia's sentencing scheme is not overbroad, vague and facially unconstitutional merely because § 19.2-264.2 allows a jury to examine an accused's past criminal record while subsection C of this section provides for examination of his prior history. Gray v. Commonwealth, 233 Va. 313, 356 S.E.2d 157, cert. denied, 484 U.S. 873, 108 S. Ct. 207, 98 L. Ed. 2d 158 (1987).

Aggravating circumstances part of means to narrow class of persons. — Future dangerousness and the other aggravating circumstances provided in the Virginia death penalty statutes are only a part of the means by which Virginia attempts to narrow the class of persons who receive the death penalty. Giarratano v. Procunier, 891 F.2d 483 (4th Cir. 1989), cert. denied, 498 U.S. 881, 111 S. Ct. 222, 112 L. Ed. 2d 178 (1990).

The individualized sentencing required by the Constitution is satisfied when, having established the statutory predicate, the sentencing body then proceeds to consider whether the death penalty should be imposed in each specific case. Royal v. Commonwealth, 250 Va. 110, 458 S.E.2d 575 (1995), cert. denied, 516 U.S. 1097, 116 S. Ct. 823, 133 L. Ed. 2d 766 (1996).

Victim impact evidence not limited by statute. — No language in subsection A1 of § 19.2-264.4 supported the theory that persons not referred to in that statutory provision were automatically barred from providing victim impact statements, especially since the determination of who had relevant victim impact testimony depended on the circumstances of the individual case; thus, the trial court did not err in allowing a cousin and the victim's fiance from providing such testimony even though they were not family members. Thomas v. Commonwealth, 263 Va. 216, 559 S.E.2d 652, 2002 Va. LEXIS 27 (2002).

It is the jury's duty to consider all the evidence, both favorable and unfavorable, before fixing punishment. Watkins v. Commonwealth, 229 Va. 469, 331 S.E.2d 422 (1985), cert. denied, 475 U.S. 1099, 106 S. Ct. 1503, 89 L. Ed. 2d 903 (1986).

Separate jury for sentencing phase not constitutionally mandated. — Even if the sentence was imposed by a jury other than the one which decided the question of guilt, the sentencing jury would necessarily have access to the evidence presented in the guilt phase of the trial. Such a system would give no greater assurance of impartiality than the system now used but it would needlessly require two separate trials in which the same evidence would be presented. This kind of cumbersome procedure is not mandated by the United States or Virginia Constitutions. Watkins v. Commonwealth, 229 Va. 469, 331 S.E.2d 422 (1985), cert. denied, 475 U.S. 1099, 106 S. Ct. 1503, 89 L. Ed. 2d 503 (1986).

Where the jury's verdict, employing the statutory language, found both the "future dangerousness" and the "vileness" predicates in fixing the death sentence and the trial court polled the jury, and each juror affirmed that this was his or her verdict, the jury based the sentence of death upon both predicates, i.e., findings that there was a probability that the defendant would commit criminal acts of violence that would constitute a continuing serious threat to society and defendant's conduct in committing the offense was outrageously or wantonly vile, horrible or inhuman. Hoke v. Commonwealth, 237 Va. 303, 377 S.E.2d 595, cert. denied, 491 U.S. 910, 109 S. Ct. 3201, 105 L. Ed. 2d 709 (1989).

A juvenile who is convicted by a jury of capital murder should be sentenced by the jury pursuant to § 19.2-264.3 and this section. Thomas v. Commonwealth, 244 Va. 1, 419 S.E.2d 606, cert. denied, 506 U.S. 958, 113 S. Ct. 421, 121 L. Ed. 2d 343 (1992).

Guilty plea with regard to first victim no bar to prosecu-

tion for second victim's death. — Defendant's guilty plea to first-degree murder with regard to death of one victim did not bar, on double jeopardy grounds, capital murder prosecution with regard to death of second victim. Same conduct is used to support more than one conviction in a single proceeding. Defendant can be prosecuted in single proceeding for both murder charges involving victims. Thomas v. Commonwealth, 244 Va. 1, 419 S.E.2d 606, cert. denied, 506 U.S. 958, 113 S. Ct. 421, 121 L. Ed. 2d 343 (1992).

Applied in Mason v. Commonwealth, 219 Va. 1091, 254 S.E.2d 116 (1979); Johnson v. Commonwealth, 220 Va. 146, 255 S.E.2d 525 (1979); Giarratano v. Commonwealth, 220 Va. 1064, 266 S.E.2d 94 (1980); Turner v. Commonwealth, 221 Va. 513, 273 S.E.2d 36 (1980); Briley v. Commonwealth, 221 Va. 532, 273 S.E.2d 48 (1980); Briley v. Commonwealth, 221 Va. 563, 273 S.E.2d 57 (1980); Ball v. Commonwealth, 221 Va. 754, 273 S.E.2d 790 (1981); Fitzgerald v. Commonwealth, 223 Va. 615, 292 S.E.2d 798 (1982); Quintana v. Commonwealth, 224 Va. 127, 295 S.E.2d 643 (1982); Stamper v. Baskerville, 531 F. Supp. 1122 (E.D. Va. 1982); Coleman v. Commonwealth, 226 Va. 31, 307 S.E.2d 864 (1983); Evans v. Commonwealth, 228 Va. 468, 323 S.E.2d 114 (1984); Boggs v. Commonwealth, 229 Va. 501, 331 S.E.2d 407 (1985); Townes v. Commonwealth, 234 Va. 307, 362 S.E.2d 650 (1987); DeLong v. Commonwealth, 234 Va. 357, 362 S.E.2d 669 (1987); Spencer v. Commonwealth, 238 Va. 563, 385 S.E.2d 850 (1989); Mu'Min v. Commonwealth, 239 Va. 433, 389 S.E.2d 886 (1990); Yeatts v. Commonwealth, 242 Va. 121, 410 S.E.2d 254 (1991); George v. Commonwealth, 242 Va. 264, 411 S.E.2d 12 (1991); Fitzgerald v. Thompson, 943 F.2d 463 (4th Cir. 1991); DeLong v. Thompson, 790 F. Supp. 594 (E.D. Va. 1991); King v. Commonwealth, 243 Va. 353, 416 S.E.2d 669 (1992); Dubois v. Commonwealth, 246 Va. 260, 435 S.E.2d 636 (1993); Breard v. Commonwealth, 248 Va. 68, 445 S.E.2d 670 (1994); Satcher v. Netherland, 944 F. Supp. 1222 (E.D. Va. 1996); Beaver v. Thompson, 93 F.3d 1186 (4th Cir. 1996); Cardwell v. Netherland, 971 F. Supp. 997 (E.D. Va. 1997); Weeks v. Angelone, 4 F. Supp. 2d 497 (E.D. Va. 1998); Payne v. Commonwealth, 257 Va. 216, 509 S.E.2d 293 (1999); Commonwealth v. Shifflett, 257 Va. 34, 510 S.E.2d 232 (1999); Atkins v. Commonwealth, 257 Va. 160, 510 S.E.2d 445 (1999); Bramblett v. Commonwealth, 257 Va. 263, 513 S.E.2d 400 (1999); Hedrick v. Commonwealth, 257 Va. 328, 513 S.E.2d 634; Cherrix v. Commonwealth, 257 Va. 292, 513 S.E.2d 642; Runyon v. Commonwealth, 29 Va. App. 573, 513 S.E.2d 872 (1999); Wolfe v. Commonwealth, 265 Va. 193, 576 S.E.2d 471, 2003 Va. LEXIS 32; Atkins v. Commonwealth, 266 Va. 73, 581 S.E.2d 514, 2003 Va. LEXIS 71 (2003); Emmett v. Warden of the Sussex I State Prison, 269 Va. 164, 609 S.E.2d 602, 2005 Va. LEXIS 18 (2005); Jackson v. Warden of the Sussex I State Prison, 271 Va. 434, 627 S.E.2d 776, 2006 Va. LEXIS 32 (2006); Wilson v. Commonwealth, 54 Va. App. 631, 681 S.E.2d 74, 2009 Va. App. LEXIS 363 (2009).

II. MITIGATING FACTORS.

List of mitigating circumstances not exclusive. — The list of mitigating circumstances which the factfinder is required to consider in pari materia with aggravating circumstances is illustrative and not exclusive. Smith v. Commonwealth, 219 Va. 455, 248 S.E.2d 135 (1978), cert. denied, 441 U.S. 967, 99 S. Ct. 2419, 60 L. Ed. 2d 1074 (1979).

A list of five nonexclusive mitigating circumstances appears in this section, but the defense is permitted to introduce any evidence relevant to the penalty decision, including the circumstances surrounding the offense, the history and background of the defendant, and any other facts in mitigation of the offense. Briley v. Bass, 750 F.2d 1238 (4th Cir. 1984), cert. denied, 470 U.S. 1088, 105 S. Ct. 1885, 85 L. Ed. 2d 152 (1985).

The effect of a defendant's incarceration upon relatives is not a mitigating circumstance for the jury to consider. Coppola v. Commonwealth, 220 Va. 243, 257 S.E.2d 797 (1979), cert. denied, 444 U.S. 1103, 100 S. Ct. 1069, 62 L. Ed. 2d 788 (1980).

Prison conditions not a mitigating factor. — Evidence regarding the conditions of prison life, specifically life without parole in a maximum security prison, is not proper mitigating evidence. Walker v. Commonwealth, 258 Va. 54, 515 S.E.2d 565 (1999), cert. denied, 528 U.S. 1125, 120 S. Ct. 955, 145 L.Ed. 2d 829 (2000).

Expert testimony regarding prison life. — Although defendant claimed that the circuit court erred in denying his motion for appointment of an expert on prison risk assessment and that in

doing so the court violated his due process rights and his rights against cruel and unusual punishment under the United States Constitution because the testimony that the expert would have provided was relevant and mitigating and any relevant mitigating evidence had to be admitted, the circuit court did not abuse its discretion when it found that defendant failed to demonstrate the particularized need necessary for appointment of the expert since the expert's anticipated testimony was not in rebuttal to any specific evidence concerning prison life. Moreover, under § 19.2-264.2 and subsection C of § 19.2-264.4, the relevant evidence surrounding a determination of future dangerousness consisted of the defendant's history and the circumstances of the defendant's offense, and thus, to be admissible, evidence related to a prison environment had to connect the specific characteristics of the particular defendant to his future adaptability in the prison environment; therefore, because the expert's proposed testimony concerning prison life was inadmissible, the lack of that expert assistance did not result in a fundamentally unfair trial. Morva v. Commonwealth, 278 Va. 329, 683 S.E.2d 553, 2009 Va. LEXIS 84 (2009), cert. denied, 131 S. Ct. 97, 178 L. Ed. 2d 61, 2010 U.S. LEXIS 5806 (U.S. 2010).

Sub-average intellectual functioning. — Inmate contended that trial counsel unreasonably failed to present evidence about his sub-average intellectual functioning; this claim implicated the weighing process and the prejudice inquiry distilled to whether there was a reasonable probability that, but for counsel's deficient performance, at least one jury member would have found the mitigating circumstances to outweigh the aggravating circumstances. The inmate's claim focused on the manner in which counsel chose to present evidence of the inmate's intellectual functioning rather than on counsel's failure to present that evidence; however, the jury had the evidence and the court could not presume that the jury did not conscientiously review them or understand from them that the inmate had, for example, a borderline intellect and severe verbal processing problems or that he was at risk of being easily manipulated. Winston v. Kelly, 624 F. Supp. 2d 478, 2008 U.S. Dist. LEXIS 42565 (W.D. Va. 2008).

In a capital case, defendant unsuccessfully argued that the circuit court erred in not requiring that the issue of mental retardation be determined separately from the other sentencing issues. The language in subsection C of § 19.2-264.3:1.1 directing that the issue of mental retardation shall be determined by the jury as part of the sentencing proceeding required by § 19.2-264.4 clearly mandated that the issue of mental retardation be determined by the jury as part of the sentencing phase. Prieto v. Commonwealth, 278 Va. 366, 682 S.E.2d 910, 2009 Va. LEXIS 94 (2009), cert. denied, 177 L. Ed. 2d 332, 2010 U.S. LEXIS 4926 (U.S. 2010).

Imposition of the death sentence is not per se precluded where defendant is 21 years of age. Age is merely a fact to be weighed by the jury. Peterson v. Commonwealth, 225 Va. 289, 302 S.E.2d 520, cert. denied, 464 U.S. 865, 104 S. Ct. 202, 78 L. Ed. 2d 176 (1983).

Refusal to permit testimony as to parole eligibility was proper. — Refusal of the court, during the penalty phase, to permit the Chairman of the Virginia Parole Board to testify concerning defendant's parole eligibility was not error, as during the penalty phase it was the jury's duty to assess the penalty, irrespective of considerations of parole. Poyner v. Commonwealth, 229 Va. 401, 329 S.E.2d 815, cert. denied, 474 U.S. 865, 106 S. Ct. 189, 88 L. Ed. 2d 158, 474 U.S. 888, 106 S. Ct. 208, 88 L. Ed. 2d 178 (1985), 506 U.S. 958, 113 S. Ct. 419, 121 L. Ed. 2d 342 (1992).

Constitutional right to have jury consider all mitigating factors before deciding punishment was not impaired by the trial court's refusal to give some instruction especially drawing the jury's attention to evidence in mitigation, where defendant was given a full opportunity to adduce evidence in mitigation, the jury was instructed to consider "all the evidence," and the burden of proof was properly allocated. An instruction is improper which singles out one portion of the evidence for special emphasis. LeVasseur v. Commonwealth, 225 Va. 564, 304 S.E.2d 644 (1983), cert. denied, 464 U.S. 1063, 104 S. Ct. 744, 79 L. Ed. 2d 202 (1984).

Evidence of petitioner state death row inmate's retardation, believed to have been destroyed but found just before the federal district court's evidentiary hearing, should not have been excluded on the grounds that rendered an Atkins-related ineffective assistance of counsel claim unexhausted under 28 U.S.C.S. § 2254(b)(1), (d), as it did not fundamentally alter the claim as it had been considered by the state courts, but while the new evidence that classified the inmate as mentally retarded and the I.Q. score were material to the Atkins-related claims, there was no reason to believe they would have persuaded the jury as mitigating evidence, and thus, a claim that counsel was ineffective in the penalty phase of the trial due to inadequate evidence in mitigation failed since the inmate had not shown that there was a reasonable probability that, but for his counsel's failures, a single juror would have voted against death. Winston v. Kelly, 592 F.3d 535, 2010 U.S. App. LEXIS 1845 (4th Cir. 2010), cert. denied, 131 S. Ct. 136, 2010 U.S. LEXIS 5952, 178 L. Ed. 2d 83 (U.S. 2010).

Failure to instruct as to certain mitigating factors. — Trial counsel and the trial court knew from the voir dire that two jurors felt that neither age nor troubled background were mitigating factors; although each juror's promise that they would consider these mitigating factors if so instructed was enough to satisfy the requirements of Morgan, the failure of the trial court to then instruct the jury as to these mitigating factors tread on the guarantees of the Eighth Amendment. The trial court notably failed to include Virginia's statutory language on mitigation, which listed the age of the defendant at the time of the commission of the capital offense as one example of mitigation; given the two jurors' responses and the inmate's youth (he was 20 years old at the time of the offense) and counsel's strategic decision to offer the abusive background as a mitigating factor, failure to instruct the jury to consider the mitigating factors of age and troubled background was a defect of constitutional proportion. Jackson v. Kelly, 2010 U.S. Dist. LEXIS 29710 (E.D. Va. 2010), rev'd, 9 Fed. Appx. 110, 2011 U.S. App. LEXIS 8438 (4th Cir. Va. 2011).

Failure to instruct that unanimity as to mitigating factors unnecessary. — Trial court's instruction that any decision the jury made regarding punishment was to be unanimous, created a reasonable probability that the inmate's jurors believed, as a result, that any finding of mitigation had to be unanimous; the instructions did not comply with the law clearly established in Mills and McKoy, and the Virginia Supreme Court's conclusions as to the adequacy of how counsel and the trial court handled the jury instructions revealed a fundamental misunderstanding of clearly established federal law. In holding that the trial court's unanimity instruction did not preclude the jury from considering mitigating evidence, and that counsel was not unreasonable for failing to request an instruction that was not necessary or required, the Virginia Supreme Court ignored the significant constitutional requirement that jurors be permitted not only to consider mitigation, but also to give it meaningful effect in their sentencing decision. Jackson v. Kelly, 2010 U.S. Dist. LEXIS 29710 (E.D. Va. 2010), rev'd, 9 Fed. Appx. 110, 2011 U.S. App. LEXIS 8438 (4th Cir. Va. 2011).

Evidence admissible on issue of mitigation. — Evidence of a good previous record, and extenuating circumstances tending to explain, but not excuse, his commission of the crime, is admissible mitigating evidence for the jury to consider in determining whether the defendant will probably be a continuing serious threat to society, or whether his conduct in committing the murder was outrageously or wantonly vile, horrible or inhuman. Coppola v. Commonwealth, 220 Va. 243, 257 S.E.2d 797 (1979), cert. denied, 444 U.S. 1103, 100 S. Ct. 1069, 62 L. Ed. 2d 788 (1980).

Evidence irrelevant to issue of mitigation. — Evidence that the children of defendant were embarrassed and humiliated by the prosecution of their father for the heinous crime of capital murder is irrelevant on the issue of mitigation. Coppola v. Commonwealth, 220 Va. 243, 257 S.E.2d 797 (1979), cert. denied, 444 U.S. 1103, 100 S. Ct. 1069, 62 L. Ed. 2d 788 (1980).

Age of defendant as a mitigating factor. — The Constitution does not require juvenile transfer hearings nor does it require additional procedural safeguards for juveniles tried for capital crimes. Besides, Virginia's death penalty statutes provide for individualized consideration of all those tried on capital charges, with "the age of the defendant at the time of ... the capital offense," a statutorily prescribed mitigating factor the jury may consider in determining whether to fix punishment at death or life imprisonment. Thomas v. Commonwealth, 244 Va. 1, 419 S.E.2d 606, cert. denied, 506 U.S. 958, 113 S. Ct. 421, 121 L. Ed. 2d 343 (1992).

Mental illness as a mitigating factor. — In a prosecution for capital murder and robbery, even if a jury finds that defendant was mentally ill, it may conclude that the alleged mental illness does not mitigate the offenses. Swann v. Commonwealth, 247 Va. 222, 441 S.E.2d 195, cert. denied, 513 U.S. 889, 115 S. Ct. 234, 130 L. Ed. 2d 158 (1994).

Trial court's failure to find merit in defendant's allegation that his history of mental health problems and failure to receive adequate treatment when in state custody as a juvenile were mitigating factors was not in error since, inter alia, the expert called by defendant did not testify that defendant lacked the ability to appreciate the criminality of his conduct or that his condition significantly impairs his ability to conform his conduct to the requirements of the law. Powell v. Commonwealth, 267 Va. 107, 590 S.E.2d 537, 2004 Va. LEXIS 6, cert. denied, — U.S. —, 125 S. Ct. 86, 160 L. Ed. 2d 157 (2004).

Mitigating circumstances held properly considered. — Trial court gave proper consideration to mitigating circumstance, although the trial judge's oral articulation of his reasons for sustaining the death sentence did not specifically mention the mitigating circumstance of defendant's being the first person to arouse suspicion that the victim's death was not from natural causes, where the trial judge did say he considered the post sentence report that described that mitigating circumstance. Any doubt about the matter was laid to rest in the court's sentencing order, which expressly stated that the court had considered all of the evidence in this case, the report of the probation officer, the matters brought out on cross-examination of the probation officer and such additional facts as were presented by the defendant. Williams v. Commonwealth, 234 Va. 168, 360 S.E.2d 361 (1987), cert. denied, 484 U.S. 1020, 108 S. Ct. 733, 98 L. Ed. 2d 681 (1988).

III. AGGRAVATING FACTORS.

A. Vileness.

The words "depravity of mind" as used in the death penalty statute mean a degree of moral turpitude and psychical debasement surpassing that inherent in the definition of ordinary legal malice and premeditation. Smith v. Commonwealth, 219 Va. 455, 248 S.E.2d 135 (1978), cert. denied, 441 U.S. 967, 99 S. Ct. 2419, 60 L. Ed. 2d 1074 (1979); Bunch v. Commonwealth, 225 Va. 423, 304 S.E.2d 271, cert. denied, 464 U.S. 977, 104 S. Ct. 414, 78 L. Ed. 2d 352 (1983), 505 U.S. 1230, 112 S. Ct. 3056, 120 L. Ed. 2d 922 (1992).

Vileness factor does not include requirement that defendant's mental state embrace the intent to commit an outrageously or wantonly vile murder. Reid v. Commonwealth, 256 Va. 561, 506 S.E.2d 787 (1998), cert. denied, 528 U.S. 833, 120 S. Ct. 91, 145 L. Ed. 2d 77 (1999).

The words "aggravated battery" as used in the death penalty statute mean a battery which, qualitatively and quantitatively, is more culpable than the minimum necessary to accomplish an act of murder. Smith v. Commonwealth, 219 Va. 455, 248 S.E.2d 135 (1978), cert. denied, 441 U.S. 967, 99 S. Ct. 2419, 60 L. Ed. 2d 1074 (1979).

Terms "depravity of mind," "vileness," and "aggravated battery" do not vest unbridled discretion in the sentencing body. Stockton v. Commonwealth, 227 Va. 124, 314 S.E.2d 371, cert. denied, 469 U.S. 873, 105 S. Ct. 229, 83 L. Ed. 2d 158 (1984).

Depravity of mind may exist alone to support vileness finding. — Section 19.2-264.2 and subsection C of this section define vileness as conduct that involves torture, depravity of mind, or aggravated battery to the victim; the use of the disjunctive word "or," rather than the conjunctive "and," signifies the availability of alternative choices. Hence, depravity of mind can exist independently of the presence of torture or aggravated battery and may alone support a finding of vileness as a basis for a sentence of death. Bunch v. Commonwealth, 225 Va. 423, 304 S.E.2d 271, cert. denied, 464 U.S. 977, 104 S. Ct. 414, 78 L. Ed. 2d 352 (1983), 505 U.S. 1230, 112 S. Ct. 3056, 120 L. Ed. 2d 922 (1992).

Aggravated battery proven. — Medical evidence showed that both victims were shot in the face from close range and that both shots would have been fatal. Victim, however, was able to get out of her bed and walk to bedroom, where she was again struck in the face by a blast from defendant's shotgun, this one killing her instantaneously. Hence, it was clear beyond any doubt that there was an appreciable lapse of time between the first shot that struck victim and the last and that death did not result instantaneously from the first. It was just as clear that the battery to victim was more culpable than the minimum necessary to accomplish her murder, and therefore, that the battery was aggravated. Thomas v. Commonwealth, 244 Va. 1, 419 S.E.2d 606, cert. denied, 506 U.S. 958, 113 S. Ct. 421, 121 L. Ed. 2d 343 (1992).

Aggravated battery is not proven where evidence shows that the victim died almost instantaneously from a single gunshot wound. However, proof of infliction of multiple wounds may meet the test for an aggravated battery. Watkins v. Commonwealth, 229 Va. 469, 331 S.E.2d 422 (1985), cert. denied, 475 U.S. 1099, 106 S. Ct. 1503, 89 L. Ed. 2d 903 (1986).

A death sentence based upon vileness is not supported by the evidence where the victim died almost instantaneously from a single gunshot wound. Peterson v. Commonwealth, 225 Va. 289, 302 S.E.2d 520, cert. denied, 464 U.S. 865, 104 S. Ct. 202, 78 L. Ed. 2d 176 (1983).

The fact that the defendant conceded he had committed an aggravated battery did not relieve the Commonwealth of the duty of showing the defendant's conduct to be outrageously or wantonly vile, horrible or inhuman. Justus v. Commonwealth, 220 Va. 971, 266 S.E.2d 87 (1980), cert. denied, 455 U.S. 983, 102 S. Ct. 1491, 71 L. Ed. 2d 693 (1982).

Photographs of pregnant victim of rape-murder are admissible where the evidence was admitted to show that the defendant's conduct was outrageously and wantonly vile, horrible and inhuman, and that it involved torture, depravity of mind, or aggravated battery to the victim. Justus v. Commonwealth, 220 Va. 971, 266 S.E.2d 87 (1980), cert. denied, 455 U.S. 983, 102 S. Ct. 1491, 71 L. Ed. 2d 693 (1982).

Motion to strike properly overruled. — In a capital murder case, the circuit court properly overruled defendant's motion to strike evidence regarding the "vileness" aggravator, as the evidence showed: (1) that defendant committed an aggravated battery on the murder victim, as the killing was inflicted by multiple gunshot wounds, and there was a lapse of time between the first shot and the last, and death did not result instantaneously from the first; and (2) the depravity of defendant's mind as he repeatedly shot the victim in front of her husband and left them both to die merely so he could rob them. Green v. Commonwealth, 266 Va. 81, 580 S.E.2d 834, 2003 Va. LEXIS 55 (2003), cert. denied, 540 U.S. 1194, 124 S. Ct. 1448, 158 L. Ed. 2d 107 (2004).

Evidence sufficient to establish "vileness" predicate. — Conduct of defendant, who violently raped and sodomized his 15-year old victim, severely injuring her before strangling her to death, and subjected her to both physical and psychological torture before strangling her so tightly that the rope left a "deep dent" in her neck, surpassed the degree of "depravity of mind" which has been held sufficient to establish the "vileness" predicate. Spencer v. Commonwealth, 240 Va. 78, 393 S.E.2d 609, cert. denied, 498 U.S. 908, 111 S. Ct. 281, 112 L. Ed. 2d 235 (1990).

Where the evidence established that the defendant shot one victim three times and the other victim seven times, such multiple gunshots established aggravated battery which would support a finding of vileness. Walker v. Commonwealth, 258 Va. 54, 515 S.E.2d 565 (1999), cert. denied, 528 U.S. 1125, 120 S. Ct. 955, 145 L.Ed. 2d 829 (2000).

With regard to proof of vileness, the defendant's actions established depravity of mind, that is, a degree of moral turpitude and physical debasement surpassing that inherent in the definition of ordinary legal malice and premeditation where the defendant shot the victims in front of their loved ones and family members after having forcibly invaded the sanctity of their homes, the killings were unprovoked, premeditated and methodical and the defendant showed no mercy towards his victims. Walker v. Commonwealth, 258 Va. 54, 515 S.E.2d 565 (1999), cert. denied, 528 U.S. 1125, 120 S. Ct. 955, 145 L.Ed. 2d 829 (2000).

Vileness predicate established where defendant, in an attempt to avoid arrest, shot the trooper at least six times from close range with high-powered revolver, two of the shots being independently fatal. The officer posed no threat to defendant in connection with this routine traffic stop; the trooper died with his service revolver still enclosed in its holster. Then, the defendant left and returned to the scene, falsely claiming that he attempted to render assistance to the victim when his real purpose was to retrieve incriminating evidence. Weeks v. Commonwealth, 248 Va. 460, 450

S.E.2d 379 (1994), cert. denied, 516 U.S. 829, 116 S. Ct. 100, 133 L. Ed. 2d 55 (1995).

Ample evidence of vileness and future dangerousness. — Where defendant was the sole participant in prior murders and arson and suggested the robberies, the rapes, and the execution-type killings of victims in the instant case, and the arson of their house, evidence amply justified the jury's finding of vileness and future dangerousness. Williams v. Commonwealth, 248 Va. 528, 450 S.E.2d 365 (1994), cert. denied, 515 U.S. 1161, 115 S. Ct. 2616, 132 L. Ed. 2d 858 (1995).

B. Future Dangerousness.

"Future dangerousness" supplies a sufficient standard for the sentencing body to predict future criminal conduct. Stockton v. Commonwealth, 227 Va. 124, 314 S.E.2d 371, cert. denied, 469 U.S. 873, 105 S. Ct. 229, 83 L. Ed. 2d 158 (1984).

Motion to strike properly overruled. — In a capital murder case, the circuit court properly overruled defendant's motion to strike evidence regarding the "future dangerousness" aggravator, based on defendant's killing a robbery victim with multiple gunshots in front of her husband and leaving them both to die, and his other bad acts, including an assault on a friend and his disruptive behavior and threats to correctional officers. Green v. Commonwealth, 266 Va. 81, 580 S.E.2d 834, 2003 Va. LEXIS 55 (2003), cert. denied, 540 U.S. 1194, 124 S. Ct. 1448, 158 L. Ed. 2d 107 (2004).

Verdict based solely upon "future dangerousness" renders moot on appeal all issues related to the "vileness" predicate. Fisher v. Commonwealth, 236 Va. 403, 374 S.E.2d 46 (1988), cert. denied, 490 U.S. 1028, 109 S. Ct. 1766, 104 L. Ed. 2d 201 (1989).

Where jury made no finding of "vileness" but based its verdict upon the "future dangerousness" predicate alone, and defendant, on appeal, assigned error to court's finding of sufficient evidence of a "depraved mind" and "aggravated battery" to warrant instructing jury on "vileness," and refusal to submit case to the jury on "future dangerousness" alone, a verdict based solely upon "future dangerousness" rendered moot on appeal all issues related to the "vileness" predicate. Fisher v. Commonwealth, 236 Va. 403, 374 S.E.2d 46 (1988), cert. denied, 490 U.S. 1028, 109 S. Ct. 1766, 104 L. Ed. 2d 201 (1989).

Factors considered in determining whether continuing serious threat to society exists. — In making a determination that there is a probability that defendant would commit criminal acts of violence that would constitute a continuing serious threat to society, the factfinder is entitled to consider not only the defendant's past criminal record of convictions, but also any matter which the court deems relevant to sentence, the prior history of the defendant or the circumstances surrounding the commission of the offense, and the heinousness of the crime. Edmonds v. Commonwealth, 229 Va. 303, 329 S.E.2d 807, cert. denied, 475 U.S. 975, 106 S. Ct. 339, 88 L. Ed. 2d 324 (1985).

Where court stated orally defendant's conduct involved depravity of mind, but the court's sentencing order stated only that there was a probability that the defendant would commit criminal acts of violence that would constitute a continuing serious threat to society, the court's sentence of death was not predicated upon statutory aggravator of vileness. Walton v. Commonwealth, 256 Va. 85, 501 S.E.2d 134, cert. denied, 525 U.S. 1046, 119 S. Ct. 602, 142 L. Ed. 2d 544 (1998).

Future dangerousness consideration not limited to defendant's prior criminal record. — The statutory provisions governing the imposition of the death penalty do not limit consideration of whether a defendant will be a future danger to the defendant's prior criminal record. Royal v. Commonwealth, 250 Va. 110, 458 S.E.2d 575 (1995), cert. denied, 516 U.S. 1097, 116 S. Ct. 823, 133 L. Ed. 2d 766 (1996).

Where defendant with a criminal history killed an 80-year-old man and an 81-year-old woman by shooting both victims in the head, later shot another victim in the head simply because he wanted to drive his car, and while he was incarcerated, described the murders to several inmates, including details of how the defendant had laughed at the victims while carrying out the murders, there was sufficient evidence to support a finding of future dangerousness. Walton v. Commonwealth, 256 Va. 85, 501 S.E.2d 134, cert. denied, 525 U.S. 1046, 119 S. Ct. 602, 142 L. Ed. 2d 544 (1998).

It is not necessary that a defendant have a prior criminal

record before the Commonwealth presents evidence of "future dangerousness" to the trier of fact. Goins v. Commonwealth, 251 Va. 442, 470 S.E.2d 114, cert. denied, 519 U.S. 887, 117 S. Ct. 222, 136 L. Ed. 2d 154 (1996).

The circumstances of the crime appropriately may be considered when determining whether the statutory predicate of future dangerousness exists. Royal v. Commonwealth, 250 Va. 110, 458 S.E.2d 575 (1995), cert. denied, 516 U.S. 1097, 116 S. Ct. 823, 133 L. Ed. 2d 766 (1996).

Circumstances of crime and defendant's lack of remorse are proper factors to be considered on the issue of the probability that he will constitute a continuing serious threat to society. Frye v. Commonwealth, 231 Va. 370, 345 S.E.2d 267 (1986).

Escape plan relevant to future dangerousness. — Evidence of a defendant's plan to escape is relevant and admissible to show his future dangerousness. Frye v. Commonwealth, 231 Va. 370, 345 S.E.2d 267 (1986).

Defendant's statement as to large number of crimes he committed was relevant to future dangerousness. — Defendant's assertion to investigator in sheriff's department that he had perpetrated about 3,000 acts of breaking and entering was relevant to the question of his future dangerousness. Frye v. Commonwealth, 231 Va. 370, 345 S.E.2d 267 (1986).

Where defendant conceded at trial that he had previously been convicted of at least 25 separate felonies, and when arrested for the crime at issue was engaged in a "fencing" operation for stolen goods in Charlotte, the record supported a finding of "future dangerousness." Fisher v. Commonwealth, 236 Va. 403, 374 S.E.2d 46 (1988), cert. denied, 490 U.S. 1028, 109 S. Ct. 1766, 104 L. Ed. 2d 201 (1989).

Admission as to other similar murder was relevant to future violent acts. — Defendant's admission regarding a different murder and information about the particulars thereof, which were strikingly similar to the execution style of the murder at issue, were relevant evidence of defendant's propensity to commit violent acts in the future, and the trial court did not err in admitting this evidence. Gray v. Commonwealth, 233 Va. 313, 356 S.E.2d 157, cert. denied, 484 U.S. 873, 108 S. Ct. 207, 98 L. Ed. 2d 158 (1987).

Admission of videotaped confession during penalty phase. — Where defendant's videotaped confession to five murders was highly reliable and wholly relevant to the issue of future dangerousness, there was no error in admitting the full videotape into evidence during penalty phase of trial for two of the murders. Poyner v. Commonwealth, 229 Va. 401, 329 S.E.2d 815, cert. denied, 474 U.S. 865, 106 S. Ct. 189, 88 L. Ed. 2d 158, 474 U.S. 888, 106 S. Ct. 208, 88 L. Ed. 2d 178 (1985), 506 U.S. 958, 113 S. Ct. 419, 121 L. Ed. 2d 342 (1992).

Evidence that defendant was on parole on date of offense. — Defendant's objection to evidence offered during penalty phase to show that he was, on the date of the offense, free on parole from a sentence imposed for a prior crime was without merit. This section requires the jury, as a prerequisite to imposition of the death penalty based on the "future dangerousness" predicate, to consider the "prior history" of the defendant. Pope v. Commonwealth, 234 Va. 114, 360 S.E.2d 352 (1987), cert. denied, 485 U.S. 1015, 108 S. Ct. 1489, 99 L. Ed. 2d 716 (1988).

Ineligibility for parole. — Although due process entitles a defendant in a capital case to inform the jury that he will be ineligible for parole where the prosecution asserts future dangerousness as a basis for imposition of the death penalty, this rule has not been extended to cases where parole ineligibility has not been established as a matter of state law at the time of the jury's future dangerousness deliberations. Ramdass v. Angelone, 530 U.S. 156, 120 S. Ct. 2113, 147 L. Ed. 2d 125, 2000 U.S. LEXIS 3965 (2000).

Evidence of prior unadjudicated criminal conduct, while generally not admissible in the guilt phase of capital-murder trial, may be used in the penalty phase to prove the defendant's propensity to commit criminal acts of violence in the future. Watkins v. Commonwealth, 229 Va. 469, 331 S.E.2d 422 (1985), cert. denied, 475 U.S. 1099, 106 S. Ct. 1503, 89 L. Ed. 2d 903 (1986).

Evidence of unadjudicated criminal activity may be used in the sentencing phase of a capital murder case. Beaver v. Commonwealth, 232 Va. 521, 352 S.E.2d 342, cert. denied, 483 U.S. 1033, 107 S. Ct. 3277, 97 L. Ed. 2d 781 (1987).

The use of prior criminal convictions and prior unadjudicated criminal conduct as evidence of "future dangerousness" has been consistently approved. Watkins v. Commonwealth, 238 Va. 341, 385 S.E.2d 50 (1989), cert. denied, 494 U.S. 1074, 110 S. Ct. 1797, 108 L. Ed. 2d 798 (1990).

Evidence of a prior act of violence is certainly probative of the probability that the accused would commit other criminal acts of violence. When offered for that purpose, the evidence should be considered relevant and admissible. Pruett v. Commonwealth, 232 Va. 266, 351 S.E.2d 1 (1986), cert. denied, 482 U.S. 931, 107 S. Ct. 3220, 96 L. Ed. 2d 706 (1987).

Testimony of victim of prior crime. — In the sentencing phase of a capital murder trial, the probative value of testimony by the victim of a previous armed robbery by the defendant was sufficient to outweigh its prejudicial effect for the reason that such testimony was relevant to a consideration of defendant's history and background and to a determination by the jury whether there was a probability that he would "constitute a continuing serious threat to society." Stamper v. Commonwealth, 220 Va. 260, 257 S.E.2d 808 (1979), cert. denied, 445 U.S. 972, 100 S. Ct. 1666, 64 L. Ed. 2d 249 (1980).

Evidence of defendant's juvenile record in Georgia which listed four separate charges of theft and commitment to Georgia juvenile institutions on three occasions was admissible in the sentence phase of defendant's capital murder trial. Beaver v. Commonwealth, 232 Va. 521, 352 S.E.2d 342, cert. denied, 483 U.S. 1033, 107 S. Ct. 3277, 97 L. Ed. 2d 781 (1987).

Evidence of prior convictions and sentences. — Evidence of prior convictions is admissible under this section as well as evidence of the sentences imposed. The sentence reflects the gravity of the offense and the offender's propensity for violence. Bassett v. Commonwealth, 222 Va. 844, 284 S.E.2d 844 (1981), cert. denied, 456 U.S. 938, 102 S. Ct. 1996, 72 L. Ed. 2d 458 (1982); 499 U.S. 983, 111 S. Ct. 1639, 113 L. Ed. 2d 734 (1991).

Evidence of prior convictions is admissible in the penalty trial, even where defendant has pleaded not guilty to the charges and has appealed the convictions. Peterson v. Commonwealth, 225 Va. 289, 302 S.E.2d 520, cert. denied, 464 U.S. 865, 104 S. Ct. 202, 78 L. Ed. 2d 176 (1983).

The statute does not restrict the admissible evidence to the record of convictions. In fairness to the defendant, however, the preferred practice is to make known to him before trial the evidence that is to be adduced at the penalty stage if he is found guilty. Peterson v. Commonwealth, 225 Va. 289, 302 S.E.2d 520, cert. denied, 464 U.S. 865, 104 S. Ct. 202, 78 L. Ed. 2d 176 (1983).

The presence or absence of a criminal record is pertinent to the dangerousness standard. Bunch v. Commonwealth, 225 Va. 423, 304 S.E.2d 271, cert. denied, 464 U.S. 977, 104 S. Ct. 414, 78 L. Ed. 2d 352 (1983), 505 U.S. 1230, 112 S. Ct. 3056, 120 L. Ed. 2d 922 (1992).

It is fallacious to argue that a defendant without a criminal record but who commits a murder satisfying the vileness standard cannot be sentenced to death and, conversely, that a defendant as to whom the dangerousness standard is satisfied but whose crime does not meet the vileness test cannot be sentenced to death either. Section 19.2-264.2 and subsection C of this section state the dangerousness and vileness standards in the disjunctive; only one, not both, need be present to support a valid sentence of death. Bunch v. Commonwealth, 225 Va. 423, 304 S.E.2d 271, cert. denied, 464 U.S. 977, 104 S. Ct. 414, 78 L. Ed. 2d 352 (1983), 505 U.S. 1230, 112 S. Ct. 3056, 120 L. Ed. 2d 922 (1992).

Although the trial court ruled the jury could consider the aggravating circumstance of vileness but not dangerousness, it was not error for the court to permit the attorney for the Commonwealth in his closing argument to comment upon evidence which pertained to dangerousness. The trial court's ruling on dangerousness did not foreclose the attorney for the Commonwealth from commenting on evidence that tended to establish both dangerousness and vileness. It was not improper for the attorney for the Commonwealth to comment upon this evidence in an effort, as he told the jury, to show that defendant's stated desire "to kill somebody" indicated "a depraved person." Bunch v. Commonwealth, 225 Va. 423, 304 S.E.2d 271, cert. denied, 464 U.S. 977, 104 S. Ct. 414, 78 L. Ed. 2d 352 (1983), 505 U.S. 1230, 112 S. Ct. 3056, 120 L. Ed. 2d 922 (1992).

The trial court did not err in admitting, in the sentencing phase, evidence of defendant's confession to and sentence in a previous capital murder, as evidence of prior crimes committed by the defendant was relevant on the issue of defendant's propensity to commit violent acts in the future. Payne v. Commonwealth, 233 Va. 460, 357 S.E.2d 500, cert. denied, 484 U.S. 933, 108 S. Ct. 308, 98 L. Ed. 2d 267 (1987).

Admissibility of crimes committed after alleged crimes at bar. — The court did not err in admitting evidence of his convictions for abduction and attempted robbery which occurred a week after the present robbery and murder. Joseph v. Commonwealth, 249 Va. 78, 452 S.E.2d 862, cert. denied, 516 U.S. 876, 116 S. Ct. 204, 133 L. Ed. 2d 137 (1995).

Evidence sufficient to support "future dangerousness" predicate. — Where defendant had prior convictions of assault, attempted arson, carrying a concealed weapon, resisting arrest, and burglary, and in addition, his prior history, by his own admission, suggested a life of increasingly violent crime and, moreover, the brutality of the crime itself could not, and should not, be ignored in assessing defendant's future dangerousness, the evidence was sufficient to support the "future dangerousness" predicate. Hoke v. Commonwealth, 237 Va. 303, 377 S.E.2d 595, cert. denied, 491 U.S. 910, 109 S. Ct. 3201, 105 L. Ed. 2d 709 (1989).

Evidence, that defendant had six prior convictions for burglary, three as a juvenile and three as an adult, that two weeks after he was released from the penitentiary to enter a "halfway house," he committed the first of a series of brutal rape-murders of women and that within 90 days, he had committed three similar murders, employing the same modus operandi, was overwhelming proof of "future dangerousness." Spencer v. Commonwealth, 240 Va. 78, 393 S.E.2d 609, cert. denied, 498 U.S. 908, 111 S. Ct. 281, 112 L. Ed. 2d 235 (1990).

The defendant's "future dangerousness" was clearly shown by his planning and executing the murders of five innocent persons, three of whom were children, and where four of the five murder victims received multiple gunshot wounds. Goins v. Commonwealth, 251 Va. 442, 470 S.E.2d 114, cert. denied, 519 U.S. 887, 117 S. Ct. 222, 136 L. Ed. 2d 154 (1996).

Future dangerousness finding was properly supported by defendant's own admission that he planned and executed the killing of former employee, killed two others, his statement that he "loved to kill," and his violence in jail while awaiting trial. Beck v. Commonwealth, 253 Va. 373, 484 S.E.2d 898, cert. denied, 522 U.S. 1018, 118 S. Ct. 608, 139 L. Ed. 2d 495 (1997).

Where the Commonwealth presented evidence that the defendant had previously been convicted of carnal knowledge, forgery, assault and unauthorized use of a motor vehicle, that he regularly stole from friends and acquaintances and that he had punched a pregnant woman in the stomach in a rage and where the defendant had committed two brutal, unprovoked murders within a six-month period, the Commonwealth proved beyond a reasonable doubt that the defendant would be a continuing serious threat to society. Walker v. Commonwealth, 258 Va. 54, 515 S.E.2d 565 (1999), cert. denied, 528 U.S. 1125, 120 S. Ct. 955, 145 L.Ed. 2d 829 (2000).

Testimony by an expert witness that the defendant showed a probability for committing criminal acts of violence which would constitute a continuing serious threat to society was not testimony upon the ultimate fact in issue, where the expert witness did not express an opinion upon what sentence defendant should receive. Payne v. Commonwealth, 233 Va. 460, 357 S.E.2d 500, cert. denied, 484 U.S. 933, 108 S. Ct. 308, 98 L. Ed. 2d 267 (1987).

Motion for appointment of prison risk assessment expert properly denied. — Defendant's motion requesting the appointment of a prison risk assessment expert failed to address the statutory factors regarding future dangerousness under § 19.2-264.2 and subsection C of § 19.2-264.4 as being individualized and particularized as to defendant's prior history, conviction record, and the circumstances of his crime; as Virginia Supreme Court precedent rendered inadmissible the statistical speculation defendant offered, defendant failed to show the required particularized need for the expert's assistance. In light of the inadmissibility of the evidence defendant sought to introduce through the expert, he also failed to establish how he was prejudiced by the lack of the expert's assistance; accordingly, the circuit court did not abuse its discretion in denying the prison expert motion. Porter v. Commonwealth, 276 Va. 203, 661 S.E.2d 415, 2008 Va. LEXIS 78 (2008), cert. denied, 129 S. Ct. 1999, 173 L. Ed. 2d 1097, 2009 U.S. LEXIS 3047 (U.S. 2009).

Failure to further investigate possible defense where evidence might support "dangerousness" finding. — Even if

defendant's attorneys should have made further investigation into defendant's mental and emotional condition, their failure to do so, under the circumstances of the case, did not result in any prejudice to defendant, where the testimony of two doctors as to his mental and emotional condition would have presented evidence supporting the potential "dangerousness" circumstance for imposing the death penalty — a condition which, according to the judgment of the attorney for the Commonwealth and the jury's verdict, had not been established at trial. Virginia Dep't of Cors. v. Clark, 227 Va. 525, 318 S.E.2d 399 (1984).

On review, even if the future dangerousness aggravating circumstance was taken out of this case, including all evidence improperly admitted or excluded and any improper comments by the prosecution on that invalid aggravating circumstance, the sentence would have been the same. Tuggle v. Netherland, 79 F.3d 1386 (4th Cir.), cert. denied, 519 U.S. 894, 117 S. Ct. 237, 136 L. Ed. 2d 166 (1996).

Jury instructions regarding future dangerousness. — In a capital murder case, a habeas petitioner failed to demonstrate that counsel's performance was deficient or that there was a reasonable probability that, but for counsel's alleged errors, the result of the proceeding would have been different where counsel failed to object to the trial court's future dangerousness instruction because the jury instruction followed the future dangerousness language of § 19.2-264.4 and, therefore, was not unconstitutionally vague. Juniper v. Warden of the Sussex I State Prison, 281 Va. 277, 707 S.E.2d 290, 2011 Va. LEXIS 61, cert. denied, 2011 U.S. LEXIS 8795, 181 L. Ed. 2d 532 (U.S. 2011).

IV. PRACTICE AND PROCEDURE.

Evidence admissible at penalty phase. — In the penalty trial, the evidence presented may include the circumstances surrounding the offense, the history and background of the defendant, and facts in mitigation. Stockton v. Commonwealth, 227 Va. 124, 314 S.E.2d 371, cert. denied, 469 U.S. 873, 105 S. Ct. 229, 83 L. Ed. 2d 158 (1984).

Petitioner's claim of ineffective assistance of counsel asserted in his petition for a writ of habeas corpus was found meritless with regard to petitioner alleging he was denied the effective assistance of counsel during the penalty phase because counsel failed to object during closing argument to the Commonwealth's mention of him having sex with a woman involved in the case while she was unconscious as the claim satisfied neither the performance nor the prejudice prong of the two-part test enunciated in *Strickland*. The record, including the trial transcript, demonstrated that the prosecutor's argument was a proper comment based upon the evidence and was concerning a sexual encounter he allegedly had with the woman while she was sedated and was admissible to prove his motive to kill the victim, which was a circumstance surrounding the offense. Elliott v. Warden of the Sussex I State Prison, 274 Va. 598, 652 S.E.2d 465, 2007 Va. LEXIS 137 (2007).

In a capital case in which defendant was sentenced to death, defendant unsuccessfully argued that the admission of his previous death sentence was irrelevant to his future dangerousness and undermined the jury's obligation to consider the mitigating evidence. Pursuant to subsection B of § 19.2-264.4, the history and background of defendant could be admitted, and § 19.2-295.1 provided that upon his conviction for a felony, the Commonwealth shall present his prior criminal history, including prior convictions and the punishments imposed, by certified, attested or exemplified copies of the final order, including adult convictions. Prieto v. Commonwealth, 278 Va. 366, 682 S.E.2d 910, 2009 Va. LEXIS 94 (2009), cert. denied, 177 L. Ed. 2d 332, 2010 U.S. LEXIS 4926 (U.S. 2010).

Evidence inadmissible at penalty phase. — Virginia does not permit the admission of hearsay evidence contained in affidavits by a defendant's family members during penalty phase proceedings. Lovitt v. Warden, 266 Va. 216, 585 S.E.2d 801, 2003 Va. LEXIS 81 (2003), cert. denied, 541 U.S. 1006, 124 S. Ct. 2018, 158 L. Ed. 2d 523 (2004); habeas corpus dismissed, stay vacated sub nom. Lovitt v. True, 330 F. Supp. 2d 603 (E.D. Va. 2004).

Subsection B of § 19.2-264.4 does not contain a relaxed evidentiary standard or produce unreliable determinations of aggravating factors, but rather evidence relevant to sentencing in the penalty phase of a capital murder trial is admissible, subject to the rules of evidence governing admissibility, and the Supreme Court of Virginia has held that subsection B of § 19.2-264.4 does not permit admission of irrelevant evidence, in particular presentence reports from probation officers and hearsay evidence; thus, a circuit court properly refused to dismiss the indictments where defendant's complaints about the constitutionally of subsection B of § 19.2-264.4 were merely hypothetical in nature. Jackson v. Commonwealth, 267 Va. 178, 590 S.E.2d 520, 2004 Va. LEXIS 8 (2004), cert. denied, 543 U.S. 891, 125 S. Ct. 168, 160 L. Ed. 2d 155 (2004).

Trial court correctly barred defendant's mental health expert's generalized testimony and did not abuse its discretion in doing so because the proffer of the expert's testimony on future dangerousness in a prison setting failed to meet the test of relevance. Neither the actual proffer, counsel's argument, nor the expert's explanations on voir dire tied his proposed opinion testimony on future dangerousness in a prison environment to defendant's history and background, and the circumstances of his offense, to defendant's character, history, and background or was specific to defendant, relevant to his future adaptability. Juniper v. Commonwealth, 271 Va. 362, 626 S.E.2d 383, 2006 Va. LEXIS 29 (2006).

Trial court did not err in refusing to allow defendant to testify during sentencing phase that he was incarcerated on earlier charges arising from same incident before those charges were nolle prosequied because the jury's consideration of defendant's prior incarceration addressed none of the purposes of sentencing; in applying the factors of subsection B of § 19.2-264.4 as they related to § 19.2-295.1, defendant's pretrial incarceration was not relevant to circumstances surrounding the offense, the history and background of defendant, circumstances that tended to explain the offense, defendant's criminal record, mental condition and intellectual functioning of defendant, the age of defendant, or any other factor in mitigation of the offense. Jones v. Commonwealth, 54 Va. App. 414, 679 S.E.2d 568, 2009 Va. App. LEXIS 338 (2009).

Circuit court erred in admitting a witness's victim impact testimony, as neither the witness nor the witness's parent was a victim of the capital murders for which defendant had been found guilty; the witness's testimony, by the Commonwealth's own admission at trial, was solely presented as victim impact testimony of unrelated and unadjudicated criminal conduct. Andrews v. Commonwealth, 280 Va. 231, 699 S.E.2d 237, 2010 Va. LEXIS 239 (2010), cert. denied, 131 S. Ct. 2999, 2011 U.S. LEXIS 4469, 180 L. Ed. 2d 827 (U.S. 2011).

Two-stage procedure. — Virginia's capital punishment statute involves a two-stage determination; the jury first decides whether the prosecutor has established one or both of the statutory aggravating factors, including "vileness" and "future dangerousness"; if the jury finds neither aggravator satisfied, it must impose a sentence of life imprisonment; if the jury finds one or both of the aggravators established, however, it has full discretion to impose either a death sentence or a sentence of life imprisonment. Tuggle v. Netherland, 516 U.S. 10, 116 S. Ct. 283, 133 L. Ed. 2d 251 (1995), cert. denied, 519 U.S. 894, 117 S. Ct. 237, 136 L. Ed. 2d 166 (1996).

Defendant, convicted of two counts of capital murder, was not entitled to a bifurcated penalty phase where in one proceeding the jury had to find one or more of the aggravating factors making defendant eligible for a sentence of death, followed by a second proceeding in which the jurors considered the mitigating evidence to determine whether to impose a sentence of death or life imprisonment without paroled. Lawlor v. Commonwealth, 285 Va. 187, 738 S.E.2d 847, 2013 Va. LEXIS 13 (2013).

Relevance of victim impact testimony in capital case. — Victim impact testimony is relevant to punishment in a capital murder prosecution in Virginia. The trial court did not err in admitting the testimony in the instant case. Weeks v. Commonwealth, 248 Va. 460, 450 S.E.2d 379 (1994), cert. denied, 516 U.S. 829, 116 S. Ct. 100, 133 L. Ed. 2d 55 (1995).

Under Virginia's modern, bifurcated capital procedure, victim impact evidence is probative, for example, of the depravity of mind component of the vileness predicate, which the jury in the instant case found as a basis for imposing the death penalty. Weeks v. Commonwealth, 248 Va. 460, 450 S.E.2d 379 (1994), cert. denied, 516 U.S. 829, 116 S. Ct. 100, 133 L. Ed. 2d 55 (1995).

Trial court did not err in refusing to allow defendant to call the father of one of the decedents as a witness to testify about remarks attributed to him by the news media to the effect that as a Christian he could not hope that jurors imposed the death penalty because the testimony did not fall within the scope of victim impact

testimony authorized under § 19.2-299.1 and witness opinion on what the jury should decide as the appropriate sentence in a given case was not admissible. Juniper v. Commonwealth, 271 Va. 362, 626 S.E.2d 383, 2006 Va. LEXIS 29 (2006).

With regard to defendant's convictions on two capital murder counts and the imposition of two death sentences against him, the trial court did not abuse its discretion in refusing to grant a mistrial or bar subsequent testimony from the sister of one of the murder/rape victims because no reasonable juror could conclude from the sister's testimony that she was attempting to implicate defendant in her own rape that occurred years prior and the trial judge promptly, explicitly and carefully instructed the jury to disregard the inappropriate testimony that the sister made that her rapist "got away with it." Prieto v. Commonwealth, 283 Va. 149, 721 S.E.2d 484, 2012 Va. LEXIS 20 (2012).

Evidence of victim's convictions not required. — In the penalty phase of a capital murder trial, this section did not require the circuit court to admit into evidence the victim's prior convictions; those convictions had no relevance to the issue of whether the defendant's acts were vile, inhuman or showed depravity of mind or to the issue of whether the defendant would constitute a serious continuing threat to society. Lenz v. Commonwealth, 261 Va. 451, 544 S.E.2d 299, 2001 Va. LEXIS 58 (2001), cert. denied, 534 U.S. 1003, 122 S. Ct. 481, 151 L. Ed. 2d 395 (2001).

Submission of both vileness and future dangerousness to jury. — Where the evidence was sufficient to submit the issues of both vileness and future dangerousness to the jury, the defendant could not assert that the evidence of both should have been stricken because the prosecutor's argument on the issue of future dangerousness, which the jury did not find, may have made it easier for the jury to find vileness. Kasi v. Commonwealth, 256 Va. 407, 508 S.E.2d 57 (1998), cert. denied, 527 U.S. 1038, 119 S. Ct. 2399, 144 L. Ed. 2d 798 (1999) overruled in part on other grounds by Jay v. Commonwealth, 275 Va. 510, 659 S.E.2d 311, 2008 Va. LEXIS 53 (2008).

Exclusion of references to victim's murder conviction. — In a capital murder case in which defendant, a prison inmate, was convicted of killing another inmate, the trial court did not err in excluding references during the penalty phase to the victim's murder conviction and life sentence, as the victim's conviction had no relevance to defendant's sentencing. Remington v. Commonwealth, 262 Va. 333, 551 S.E.2d 620, 2001 Va. LEXIS 107 (2001), cert. denied, 535 U.S. 1062, 122 S. Ct. 1928, 152 L. Ed. 2d 834 (2002).

Photographs admissible. — Introduction of photographs of each victim's head showing that each had been shot in the head and that parts of the head were partially burned were relevant not only to establish defendant's future dangerousness by indicating the atrociousness of the murders, but also to corroborate the testimony of confession. The fact that the autopsy reports reflect the same facts as the photographs did not make the photographs inadmissible. Williams v. Commonwealth, 248 Va. 528, 450 S.E.2d 365 (1994), cert. denied, 515 U.S. 1161, 115 S. Ct. 2616, 132 L. Ed. 2d 858 (1995).

Autopsy photographs introduced at the penalty phase which showed the close range at which the defendant shot the victim were relevant on the issue of whether the defendant's conduct was outrageously vile. Walker v. Commonwealth, 258 Va. 54, 515 S.E.2d 565 (1999), cert. denied, 528 U.S. 1125, 120 S. Ct. 955, 145 L.Ed. 2d 829 (2000).

Subsection C permits admission into evidence of unadjudicated misconduct. — Under subsection C, a sentencing jury shall consider evidence of a defendant's "prior history" in determining whether he "would commit criminal acts of violence that would constitute a continuing serious threat to society"; this provision permits the admission into evidence of unadjudicated misconduct. Stockton v. Commonwealth, 241 Va. 192, 402 S.E.2d 196, cert. denied, 502 U.S. 280, 112 S. Ct. 280, 116 L. Ed. 2d 231 (1991).

Where defendant argued that Virginia's capital sentencing scheme was unconstitutional because it failed to require proof beyond a reasonable doubt of the commission of unadjudicated crimes and thus permitted the jury to consider unreliable and prejudicial evidence, contention that evidence of unadjudicated criminal activity is "not reliable" was rejected and argument that such evidence was "highly inflammatory and inherently prejudicial" was also rejected. Stockton v. Commonwealth, 241 Va. 192, 402 S.E.2d 196, cert. denied, 502 U.S. 280, 112 S. Ct. 280, 116 L. Ed. 2d 231 (1991).

Aggravating circumstances to be proven beyond reasonable doubt. — The Commonwealth is charged in a capital murder case with the burden of not only proving guilt beyond a reasonable doubt but of proving aggravating circumstances beyond a reasonable doubt. Justus v. Commonwealth, 220 Va. 971, 266 S.E.2d 87 (1980), cert. denied, 455 U.S. 983, 102 S. Ct. 1491, 71 L. Ed. 2d 693 (1982).

Each piece of evidence need not be proved beyond reasonable doubt. — Where the ultimate issue of fact is the defendant's future dangerousness, the Commonwealth is required to prove this beyond a reasonable doubt, but each piece of evidence offered to prove the ultimate issue of fact need not also be tested by some standard of proof; that evidence is tested by the credibility or weight the fact finder chooses to give it. Walker v. Commonwealth, 258 Va. 54, 515 S.E.2d 565 (1999), cert. denied, 528 U.S. 1125, 120 S. Ct. 955, 145 L.Ed. 2d 829 (2000).

Failure to instruct that unanimity as to mitigating factors unnecessary. — It was not error to fail to instruct the jury in a capital murder case that its finding of mitigating factors need not be unanimous. Clark v. Commonwealth, 220 Va. 201, 257 S.E.2d 784 (1979), cert. denied, 444 U.S. 1049, 100 S. Ct. 741, 62 L. Ed. 2d 736 (1980).

Instruction failing to advise death penalty not mandatory. — In the penalty trial phase of a prosecution for capital murder following rape, an instruction which failed explicitly to advise the jury that, even though it might find aggravating circumstances, the death penalty is not mandatory, while not artfully drawn, was not error, since, read as a whole, the instruction fairly expounded the thrust of the statute. Smith v. Commonwealth, 219 Va. 455, 248 S.E.2d 135 (1978), cert. denied, 441 U.S. 967, 99 S. Ct. 2419, 60 L. Ed. 2d 1074 (1979).

Jury must consider all evidence relevant to sentencing. — The jury in a capital murder case has the duty to consider all the evidence relevant to sentencing, both favorable and unfavorable, before determining whether the defendant has such a propensity to violence as to make him a menace to society, or whether the crime of which he has been convicted is so atrocious that he should be executed. Stamper v. Commonwealth, 220 Va. 260, 257 S.E.2d 808 (1979), cert. denied, 445 U.S. 972, 100 S. Ct. 1666, 64 L. Ed. 2d 249 (1980).

Jury at liberty to recommend life term. — It is clear from the statutory context that, even when the Commonwealth establishes either or both aggravating circumstances, the jury is at liberty, in consideration of circumstances in mitigation, to recommend a sentence of imprisonment for life. Smith v. Commonwealth, 219 Va. 455, 248 S.E.2d 135 (1978), cert. denied, 441 U.S. 967, 99 S. Ct. 2419, 60 L. Ed. 2d 1074 (1979).

Subsection C provides that the death penalty shall not be imposed unless the Commonwealth proves one of the two aggravating circumstances beyond a reasonable doubt. The statute does not require that, upon such proof, the jury must impose the extreme penalty but only that, absent such proof, it shall not do so. By requiring the jury to consider circumstances both in aggravation of and in mitigation of the offense, the statute clearly contemplates that, notwithstanding a showing of the former, the jury is at liberty in consideration of the latter to recommend the lesser penalty. Such discretion in the sentencing authority is not constitutionally infirm. Smith v. Commonwealth, 219 Va. 455, 248 S.E.2d 135 (1978), cert. denied, 441 U.S. 967, 99 S. Ct. 2419, 60 L. Ed. 2d 1074 (1979).

Use of "and/or" on jury form. — On habeas petition, federal court would defer to state court on defendant's contention that the use of the conjunction "and/or" on jury form permitted the jury to sentence defendant to death without unanimity on either one of the two aggravating factors, and that his counsel was prejudicially ineffective for failing to object to the wording of the "and/or" verdict form. Moreover, even if the court were permitted to consider the question de novo, Virginia precedent does not appear to support this claim. Barnabei v. Angelone, 214 F.3d 463, 2000 U.S. App. LEXIS 12183 (4th Cir.), cert. denied, 530 U.S. 1300, 121 S. Ct. 24, 147 L. Ed. 2d 1047 (2000).

Unanimity as to aggravating factors unnecessary. — In imposing the death penalty following a capital murder conviction, the jury's verdict was not required to be unanimous as to the aggravating factors relied upon. Clark v. Commonwealth, 220 Va. 201, 257 S.E.2d 784 (1979), cert. denied, 444 U.S. 1049, 100 S. Ct. 741, 62 L. Ed. 2d 736 (1980); Briley v. Bass, 584 F. Supp. 807 (E.D. Va.), aff'd, 742 F.2d 155 (4th Cir.), cert. denied, 469 U.S. 893, 105 S. Ct. 270, 83 L. Ed. 2d 206 (1984).

Unanimity as to finding one or both aggravating factors is necessary. — In a capital case in which defendant had been sentenced to death, the verdict form in defendant's second trial was defective in failing to explicitly set out the unanimity required in the jury finding of one or both of the aggravating factors beyond a reasonable doubt. Additionally, Article I, § 8 of the Constitution of Virginia provided that a jury's verdict in a criminal case had to be unanimous. Prieto v. Commonwealth, 278 Va. 366, 682 S.E.2d 910, 2009 Va. LEXIS 94 (2009), cert. denied, 177 L. Ed. 2d 332, 2010 U.S. LEXIS 4926 (U.S. 2010).

Remaining aggravating factors will support sentence even if one invalidated. — When a jury makes separate findings of specific statutory aggravating circumstances, any of which could support a sentence of death, and one of the circumstances subsequently is invalidated, the remaining valid circumstance, or circumstances will support the sentence. Tuggle v. Commonwealth, 230 Va. 99, 334 S.E.2d 838 (1985), cert. denied, 478 U.S. 1010, 106 S. Ct. 3309, 92 L. Ed. 2d 722 (1986) (granting habeas relief in part because of disagreement with this holding).

The mere fact that the jury deliberated no more than 25 minutes before returning death verdict in sentencing stage of capital murder prosecution provides no indication that it did not maturely, carefully, and calmly deliberate the full range of issues or that it did not make an individualized decision on the defendant's sentence. All the period of deliberation indicates is that the jury labored under no uncertainty concerning the punishment it should fix. Waye v. Commonwealth, 219 Va. 683, 251 S.E.2d 202, cert. denied, 442 U.S. 924, 99 S. Ct. 2850, 61 L. Ed. 2d 292 (1979).

Court would not notice objection to jury verdict. — Where defense counsel responded to the trial judge's inquiry at trial by stating affirmatively that he had no objection to an instruction on vileness, and the Commonwealth did not argue vileness, and the jury based its verdict fixing punishment at death solely upon the finding that defendant posed "a continuing serious threat" to society, the Supreme Court would not notice an objection to it on appeal. Peterson v. Commonwealth, 225 Va. 289, 302 S.E.2d 520, cert. denied, 464 U.S. 865, 104 S. Ct. 202, 78 L. Ed. 2d 176 (1983).

Capital murder verdict form must allow for life sentence and fine. — Section 18.2-10(g) and subdivision D 1 of this section are in conflict; § 18.2-10, the statute that prescribes the punishment for capital murder, is the more specific of the two and, accordingly, it must prevail; thus, at a minimum, a jury must receive a verdict form that, in addition to addressing the imposition of a sentence of death and the imposition of a sentence of life imprisonment, also allows the jury to impose a sentence of life imprisonment and a fine of up to $100,000. Powell v. Commonwealth, 261 Va. 512, 552 S.E.2d 344, 2001 Va. LEXIS 86 (2001).

In a capital case in which defendant was sentenced to death, the sentencing phase verdict forms provided to the jury in the second trial were defective in that they did not include a life without parole sentence option, the Commonwealth unsuccessfully argued that the General Assembly's amendment of § 19.2-264.4 after the *Powell* decision was a rejection of the holding in that decision. Section 19.2-264.4 established the sentencing procedure in a capital murder case and recognized that a jury must be instructed upon request of the defendant that a life sentence means life without parole, but nothing in § 19.2-264.4 dictated required jury instructions. Prieto v. Commonwealth, 278 Va. 366, 682 S.E.2d 910, 2009 Va. LEXIS 94 (2009), cert. denied, 177 L. Ed. 2d 332, 2010 U.S. LEXIS 4926 (U.S. 2010).

In a capital case, the sentencing phase verdict forms provided to the jury in the second trial were defective in that they did not include a life without parole sentence option, and the Commonwealth's argument that any error in the verdict form was cured by the jury instructions was without merit. Pursuant to the *Powell* and *Morrisette* decisions, a verdict form had to provide the jury with the explicit option of imposing a life sentence even if the jury finds one or both aggravating factors. Prieto v. Commonwealth, 278 Va. 366, 682 S.E.2d 910, 2009 Va. LEXIS 94 (2009), cert. denied, 177 L. Ed. 2d 332, 2010 U.S. LEXIS 4926 (U.S. 2010).

Form verdict which follows statute is constitutional. —

Listing of aggravating factors in the form verdict without comparable listing of mitigating factors benefits rather than prejudices the accused. Aggravating factors are expressly limited to those specified by statute, while any circumstances in mitigation may be considered. Hence, the form verdict, which follows the language of the statute, is constitutional. Watkins v. Commonwealth, 229 Va. 469, 331 S.E.2d 422 (1985), cert. denied, 475 U.S. 1099, 106 S. Ct. 1503, 89 L. Ed. 2d 903 (1986).

Verdict form must include option of life imprisonment and fine. — In 1991, the General Assembly amended § 18.2-10 to include the additional option of imposing a fine of not more than $100,000 in addition to a sentence of life imprisonment, but failed to amend this section to reflect this change in the range of sentences available for capital murder, and the two statutes have since remained in conflict; because § 18.2-10, the statute that prescribes the punishment for capital murder, is the more specific of the two, it must prevail and, thus, at a minimum, a jury in a capital case must receive a verdict form that, in addition to addressing the imposition of a sentence of death and the imposition of a sentence of life imprisonment, also allows the jury to impose a sentence of life imprisonment and a fine of up to $100,000. Accordingly, in a capital murder trial, the trial court must give the jury verdict forms providing expressly for the imposition of a sentence of imprisonment for life and a fine of not more than $100,000 when the jury finds that one or both of the aggravating factors have been proven beyond a reasonable doubt. Powell v. Commonwealth, 261 Va. 512, 552 S.E.2d 344, 2001 Va. LEXIS 86 (2001).

Questioning of jurors held to resolve possible ambiguity in form of verdict. — Where in the form of verdict furnished the jury, the two grounds of vileness and dangerousness were stated both conjunctively and in the alternative ("and/or") and in answer, the jury, in its finding pursuant to the form of verdict submitted to it, struck out "or," leaving "and" and the trial judge took note of this action by the jury and specifically inquired of the foreman of the jury whether the striking of "or" meant that the jury was not only "unanimous in the final verdict" but also "unanimous in finding the two lawful provisions that you must find in order to impose a death sentence," to which the foreman responded affirmatively and the court then addressed the same inquiry to all members of the jury and the record stated, "[t]he members of the jury answered affirmatively," the jury thus unanimously found both "vileness" and "dangerousness" as a warrant for the death sentence. Briley v. Bass, 742 F.2d 155 (4th Cir.), cert. denied, 469 U.S. 893, 105 S. Ct. 270, 83 L. Ed. 2d 206 (1984).

Jury instructions and form verdict ensure consideration of factors for and against death penalty. — The jury is instructed to consider mitigating circumstances, and the form verdict reflects that a jury may sentence a defendant to death only after having considered the evidence in mitigation of the offense. These safeguards sufficiently satisfy the constitutional requirement that the jury's discretion be guided and channeled by requiring examination of specific factors that argue in favor of or against imposition of the death penalty, thus eliminating total arbitrariness and capriciousness in its imposition. Watkins v. Commonwealth, 229 Va. 469, 331 S.E.2d 422 (1985), cert. denied, 475 U.S. 1099, 106 S. Ct. 1503, 89 L. Ed. 2d 903 (1986).

Defendant may not argue that lesser sentence is for life until defendant dies. — The defendant does not have the right to argue to a jury that the lesser sentence is a sentence for life imprisonment, until the defendant dies and that any lesser definition would have to deal with parole, pardon, and probation. If the jury is not to be concerned with what may later happen to a defendant sentenced to the state correctional facility, no inference can be drawn or argued one way or the other as to whether he will serve his full term. Williams v. Commonwealth, 234 Va. 168, 360 S.E.2d 361 (1987), cert. denied, 484 U.S. 1020, 108 S. Ct. 733, 98 L. Ed. 2d 681 (1988), questioned, Yarbrough v. Commonwealth, 258 Va. 347, 519 S.E.2d 602 (1999).

Improper to tell jury that judge shares responsibility for death sentence. — It is improper for the jury to be told that the trial judge shares a responsibility for the death sentence. Such a comment is misleading, because it fails to place before the jury accurate information explaining the limits on the court's power to set aside the jury's verdict, as while it is true that the trial court in a proper case may set aside a sentence of death, the court does not have unlimited discretion to do so in any case. Frye v. Common-

wealth, 231 Va. 370, 345 S.E.2d 267 (1986).

Death sentence and life sentence for codefendants respectively. — A death sentence against one defendant will be upheld when a sentence of life imprisonment, or less, has been imposed upon a codefendant, provided the death sentence is in accord with the general statewide standard. Coppola v. Commonwealth, 220 Va. 243, 257 S.E.2d 797 (1979), cert. denied, 444 U.S. 1103, 100 S. Ct. 1069, 62 L. Ed. 2d 788 (1980).

A codefendant is not necessarily entitled to commutation of a death sentence because an equally culpable confederate, on substantially the same evidence, has been sentenced to life imprisonment. Coppola v. Commonwealth, 220 Va. 243, 257 S.E.2d 797 (1979), cert. denied, 444 U.S. 1103, 100 S. Ct. 1069, 62 L. Ed. 2d 788 (1980).

Result of codefendant's trial irrelevant. — Evidence as to the result of another defendant's trial for the same crime is irrelevant to the determination by the jury of the appropriate punishment for the defendant whose sentence is being weighed. Coppola v. Commonwealth, 220 Va. 243, 257 S.E.2d 797 (1979), cert. denied, 444 U.S. 1103, 100 S. Ct. 1069, 62 L. Ed. 2d 788 (1980).

Elimination for bias in favor of death penalty permitted. — The process of selection of an impartial jury permits elimination for cause of those veniremen who are biased in favor of the death penalty under all circumstances as well as those who are biased against its imposition under all circumstances. Patterson v. Commonwealth, 222 Va. 653, 283 S.E.2d 212 (1981).

And refusal to question jury as to bias invalidates sentence. — In a prosecution for robbery and capital murder, the refusal by the trial judge to ask the jury whether, if the jury should happen to convict the defendant of capital murder, each juror would be able to consider voting for a sentence less than death, or to ask an equivalent question, was prejudicial error invalidating the sentence to death. Patterson v. Commonwealth, 222 Va. 653, 283 S.E.2d 212 (1981).

The use of a transcript from a previous trial of the accused is unobjectionable. Bassett v. Commonwealth, 222 Va. 844, 284 S.E.2d 844 (1981), cert. denied, 456 U.S. 938, 102 S. Ct. 1996, 72 L. Ed. 2d 458 (1982); 499 U.S. 983, 111 S. Ct. 1639, 113 L. Ed. 2d 734 (1991).

Use in evidence of mere record of previous convictions. — In a capital murder case, in determining the defendant's proclivity for violence, the jury may obtain from the mere record of previous convictions an inaccurate or incomplete impression of the defendant's temperament and disposition. Stamper v. Commonwealth, 220 Va. 260, 257 S.E.2d 808 (1979), cert. denied, 445 U.S. 972, 100 S. Ct. 1666, 64 L. Ed. 2d 249 (1980).

Use of defendant's juvenile record. — Virginia law does not prohibit the use of a defendant's juvenile record in capital sentencing. Peterson v. Murray, 904 F.2d 882 (4th Cir.), cert. denied, 498 U.S. 992, 111 S. Ct. 537, 112 L. Ed. 2d 547 (1990).

Cross-examination of psychologist's testimony as to defendant's mental capacity. — Where the issue of the defendant's mental capacity at the time of the crime was relevant and was placed in issue by the defendant, through opinion testimony of psychologists as matter in mitigation, the Commonwealth, on cross-examination, was entitled to explore the scope and limits of the doctor's opinion on this subject. Washington v. Commonwealth, 228 Va. 535, 323 S.E.2d 577 (1984), cert. denied, 471 U.S. 1111, 105 S. Ct. 2347, 85 L. Ed. 2d 863 (1985).

Instruction on specific mitigating factors not required. — In defendant's case, the trial court's instruction was consistent with the sentencing statute; the statute establishes a capital defendant's right to present mitigating evidence during the sentencing hearing. It neither imposes nor implies an obligation to instruct the jury about specific mitigating factors. Buchanan v. Angelone, 103 F.3d 344 (4th Cir. 1996), aff'd, 522 U.S. 269, 118 S. Ct. 757, 139 L. Ed. 2d 702 (1998).

Trial tactics may require that certain evidence in mitigation not be presented. — Although a defendant in a capital case has the constitutional right to present virtually unlimited evidence in mitigation, trial counsel has a tactical responsibility to determine the extent of such evidence to be presented. Consequently, the posture of a given case may well justify, if not require, an effective attorney to refrain from presenting such evidence. Virginia Dep't of Cors. v. Clark, 227 Va. 525, 318 S.E.2d 399 (1984).

Attorney for the Commonwealth may not argue possibility

of executive clemency, nor may the court make any comment to the jury about what might happen after the sentence is imposed. This principle applies in capital murder cases as well. Williams v. Commonwealth, 234 Va. 168, 360 S.E.2d 361 (1987), cert. denied, 484 U.S. 1020, 108 S. Ct. 733, 98 L. Ed. 2d 681, cert. denied, 484 U.S. 1020, 108 S. Ct. 733, 98 L. Ed. 2d 681 (1988).

Right of Commonwealth to make closing rebuttal. — Since this section places upon the Commonwealth the burden of proving aggravating circumstances beyond a reasonable doubt, the Commonwealth has·the right to make a closing rebuttal during the penalty trial. Smith v. Commonwealth, 219 Va. 455, 248 S.E.2d 135 (1978), cert. denied, 441 U.S. 967, 99 S. Ct. 2419, 60 L. Ed. 2d 1074 (1979), aff'd, 477 U.S. 527, 106 S. Ct. 2661, 91 L. Ed. 2d 434 (1986).

Court to impose life sentence when further deliberations would be fruitless. — Subsection E of this section becomes applicable only after it has become apparent to the trial judge, following a reasonable period of deliberation, that further deliberations would be fruitless and that the jury's deadlock is final. Eaton v. Commonwealth, 240 Va. 236, 397 S.E.2d 385 (1990), cert. denied, 502 U.S. 824, 112 S. Ct. 88, 116 L. Ed. 2d 60 (1991).

In a capital case in which defendant argued that the circuit court erred in denying his motion to bar a retrial and impose a life sentence as set forth in subsection E of § 19.2-264.4 [now subsection D], the circuit court did not abuse its discretion in denying defendant's motion to declare a mistrial on the grounds that the jury was hung because it could not agree on a verdict since: (1) the trial had been in progress for approximately four weeks; (2) the jury had successfully arrived at a verdict of guilty in the guilt or innocence phase; (3) the jury had been deliberating the determination of mental retardation for approximately a day and a half; and (4) the jury foreman's note did not state that the jury was unable to reach a unanimous decision, only that it appeared to be unable to do so. Prieto v. Commonwealth, 278 Va. 366, 682 S.E.2d 910, 2009 Va. LEXIS 94 (2009), cert. denied, 177 L. Ed. 2d 332, 2010 U.S. LEXIS 4926 (U.S. 2010).

Federal district court properly denied an inmate's request for a writ of habeas corpus. under 28 U.S.C.S. § 2254 following his conviction for capital murder, § 18.2-31.4, and the imposition of the death penalty based on future dangerousness under § 19.2-264.4 where counsel was not ineffective under U.S. Const., amend. VI, in failing to object to the prosecutor's alleged consideration of race in seeking the death penalty; the prosecutor's mere mention of race did not amount to clear evidence that she decided to indict petitioner for capital murder and reject his plea offer because of his Caucasian race. The prosecutor's statements evidenced her intent to be evenhanded regardless of the fact that petitioner was Caucasian. Orbe v. True, — F.3d —, 2003 U.S. App. LEXIS 24896 (4th Cir. Dec. 11, 2003), cert. denied, 541 U.S. 970, 124 S. Ct. 1740, 158 L. Ed. 2d 419 (2004); Burns v. Commonwealth, 279 Va. 243, 688 S.E.2d 263, 2010 Va. LEXIS 19 (2010).

CIRCUIT COURT OPINIONS

Commonwealth not required to identify components of vileness factor. — Where the Commonwealth intended to prove "vileness" as an aggravating factor in support of the death penalty, it was not required to identify the components of the vileness factor on which it intended to offer evidence because the indictment, the discovery responses, and defendant's opportunity to hear the evidence presented at the preliminary hearing adequately informed him of the charged offense. Commonwealth v. Waddler, 65 Va. Cir. 418, 2004 Va. Cir. LEXIS 296 (Portsmouth 2004).

§ 19.2-264.5. Post-sentence reports.

When the punishment of any person has been fixed at death, the court shall, before imposing sentence, direct a probation officer of the court to thoroughly investigate the history of the defendant and any and all other relevant facts, to the end that the court may be fully advised as to whether the sentence of death is appropriate and just. Reports shall be made, presented and filed as provided in

§ 19.2-299 except that, notwithstanding any other provision of law, such reports shall in all cases contain a Victim Impact Statement. Such statement shall contain the same information and be prepared in the same manner as Victim Impact Statements prepared pursuant to § 19.2-299.1. After consideration of the report, and upon good cause shown, the court may set aside the sentence of death and impose a sentence of imprisonment for life. Notwithstanding any other provision of law, if the court sets aside the sentence of death and imposes a sentence of imprisonment for life, it shall include in the sentencing order an explanation for the reduction in sentence.

History.
1977, c. 492; 1993, c. 978; 2004, c. 298.

Law Review.
For survey of Virginia criminal procedure for the year 1976-1977, see 63 Va. L. Rev. 1408 (1977). For article, "Psychiatry and the Death Penalty: Emerging Problems in Virginia," see 66 Va. L. Rev. 167 (1980). For article, "Virginia's Capital Murder Sentencing Proceeding: A Defense Perspective," see 18 U. Rich. L. Rev. 341 (1984). For a note, "Due Process on the Uncharted Seas of Irrelevance: Limiting the Presence of Victim Impact Evidence at Capital Sentencing After *Payne v. Tennessee*," see 55 Wash. & Lee L. Rev. 295 (1998).

CASE NOTES

Constitutionality. — As to constitutionality of this article, see note under § 19.2-264.2.

Virginia's capital sentencing procedure statutes are not facially invalid on grounds that the death penalty is cruel and unusual punishment under the Eighth and Fourteenth Amendments. Mason v. Commonwealth, 219 Va. 1091, 254 S.E.2d 116, cert. denied, 444 U.S. 919, 100 S. Ct. 239, 62 L. Ed. 2d 176 (1979).

This section does not unconstitutionally discriminate against a capital defendant because its "good cause" provision imposes upon him a heavier burden in reducing a capital verdict than in reducing a noncapital verdict. Bassett v. Commonwealth, 222 Va. 844, 284 S.E.2d 844 (1981), cert. denied, 456 U.S. 938, 102 S. Ct. 1996, 72 L. Ed. 2d 458 (1982); 499 U.S. 983, 111 S. Ct. 1639, 113 L. Ed. 2d 734 (1991).

The provisions of this section are clear and provide a meaningful review by a trial court of a death sentence, thus, this section is facially constitutional. Breard v. Commonwealth, 248 Va. 68, 445 S.E.2d 670, cert. denied, 513 U.S. 971, 115 S. Ct. 442, 130 L. Ed. 2d 353 (1994).

Court found no reason to depart from its prior precedent and it had already rejected defendant's arguments that the death penalty on its face and as applied violated the Sixth Amendment, the Eighth Amendment, and the Fourteenth Amendment to the United States Constitution, as well as Va. Const., Art. I, §§ 8, 9, and 11, where defendant contended that: (1) the aggravating factor of future dangerousness was unconstitutionally vague because it did not provide meaningful guidance to the sentencing jury so as to avoid an arbitrary and capricious infliction of the death penalty; (2) Virginia's capital murder statutes did not require instructions to the jury regarding the duty to consider mitigating evidence, the meaning of mitigating evidence, the absence of any burden of proof on a defendant with regard to the mitigation evidence presented, and the liberty that each juror had to consider and give effect to mitigating evidence; (3) the use of unadjudicated conduct to prove the aggravating factor of future dangerousness failed to comport with the constitutional requirement of reliability for capital sentencing; (4) a sentence of death under § 19.2-264.5 was unconstitutional because a trial court could consider hearsay evidence contained in a post-sentence report; (5) a sentence of death under § 19.2-264.5 was unconstitutional because a trial court was not required to set aside a death penalty upon a showing of good cause;

(6) Virginia's death penalty statutes did not provide for meaningful appellate review, including the proportionality review; and (7) the expedited review of death penalty cases was unconstitutional. Jackson v. Commonwealth, 267 Va. 178, 590 S.E.2d 520, 2004 Va. LEXIS 8 (2004), cert. denied, 543 U.S. 891, 125 S. Ct. 168, 160 L. Ed. 2d 155 (2004).

Defendant's claim that § 19.2-264.5 was unconstitutional as applied, failed, as the record indicated that the trial court considered defendant's lack of remorse; the statutory sentencing report; the evidence adduced at trial, including defendant's mitigating evidence in the penalty phase; the duration of voir dire and the resulting impartiality of the jury; the seriousness with which jurors undertook and completed their deliberations; the jury's finding of both aggravating factors; and the egregiousness of the offense in denying defendant's motion to set aside the jury's recommendation. Lawlor v. Commonwealth, 285 Va. 187, 738 S.E.2d 847, 2013 Va. LEXIS 13 (2013).

Trial court not required to review records from other cases. — A trial court is not required to obtain from the Supreme Court and review the records of prior capital murder cases maintained pursuant to § 17.1-313 E before determining whether a death sentence was appropriate or setting it aside for "good cause shown" pursuant to this section. Bailey v. Commonwealth, 259 Va. 723, 529 S.E.2d 570, 2000 Va. LEXIS 59, cert. denied, 531 U.S. 995, 121 S. Ct. 488, 148 L. Ed. 2d 460 (2000).

Proportionality review not required. — There is a distinction between the appropriateness review conducted by the trial court pursuant to this section and the proportionality review conducted by the Supreme Court pursuant to subdivision C 2 of § 17.1-313; the proportionality review conducted by the Supreme Court in all death sentence cases suffices to secure the constitutional right of the defendant to such a review and such a review need not be conducted by the trial court. Bailey v. Commonwealth, 259 Va. 723, 529 S.E.2d 570, 2000 Va. LEXIS 59, cert. denied, 531 U.S. 995, 121 S. Ct. 488, 148 L. Ed. 2d 460 (2000).

The death penalty statutes do not require a proportionality review by the trial court. Lovitt v. Commonwealth, 260 Va. 497, 537 S.E.2d 866, 2000 Va. LEXIS 149 (2000), cert. denied, 534 U.S. 815, 122 S. Ct. 41, 151 L. Ed. 2d 14 (2001).

Role of trial court when death penalty is sought. — State supreme court granted the petition for writ of mandamus filed by the Commonwealth Attorney, as the trial court did not have the discretion to prohibit the Commonwealth Attorney from seeking the death penalty; the Commonwealth Attorney was entitled to seek that penalty pursuant to statutory law and the trial court erred by exercising an executive function in determining that the Commonwealth Attorney was prohibited from seeking it in defendant's case where defendant was charged with capital murder pursuant to § 18.2-31. In re Horan, 271 Va. 258, 634 S.E.2d 675, 2006 Va. LEXIS 23 (2006).

Jurisdiction of trial court to impose life sentence after remand. — Defendant had been sentenced to death, but the case was remanded to determine whether he was mentally retarded. That the mandate related solely to the issue of mental retardation did not divest the trial court of jurisdiction to consider other legal issues the parties raised on remand, including defendant's motion under § 19.2-264.5 requesting the imposition of a life sentence. In re Commonwealth, 278 Va. 1, 677 S.E.2d 236, 2009 Va. LEXIS 78 (2009).

The statutes do not limit evidence of victim impact to that received from the victim's family members; rather, the circumstances of the individual case will dictate what evidence will be necessary and relevant, and from what sources it may be drawn. Beck v. Commonwealth, 253 Va. 373, 484 S.E.2d 898, cert. denied, 522 U.S. 1018, 118 S. Ct. 608, 139 L. Ed. 2d 495 (1997).

Post-sentence report requirement restricted to jury cases. — While this section does not expressly restrict its post sentence report requirement to jury cases, such a restriction is implicit in its language. The provision clearly contemplates a situation in which a fact finder first fixes punishment, then the trial court imposes sentence. Such a sequence generally does not occur in bench trials, in which the fact finder and the sentencer are the same entity, the trial judge. Correll v. Commonwealth, 232 Va. 454, 352 S.E.2d 352, cert. denied, 482 U.S. 931, 107 S. Ct. 3219, 96 L. Ed. 2d 705 (1987).

Hearsay evidence may be considered in sentencing phase. — During the sentencing phase of a capital murder case, the court may consider hearsay evidence, favorable or unfavorable to the defendant, contained in a postsentence report. This is implicit from the language of this section and § 19.2-299, which permit a probation officer "to thoroughly investigate and report upon the history of the accused and any other and all other relevant facts." O'Dell v. Commonwealth, 234 Va. 672, 364 S.E.2d 491, cert. denied, 488 U.S. 871, 109 S. Ct. 186, 102 L. Ed. 2d 154 (1988).

The phrase "upon good cause shown" contained in this section merely reiterates the rule applicable in all cases, misdemeanor, felony, or capital, when the court must consider altering a jury verdict. The same criterion applies in capital as well as noncapital cases. Bassett v. Commonwealth, 222 Va. 844, 284 S.E.2d 844 (1981), cert. denied, 456 U.S. 938, 102 S. Ct. 1996, 72 L. Ed. 2d 458 (1982); 499 U.S. 983, 111 S. Ct. 1639, 113 L. Ed. 2d 734 (1991).

Consideration of presentence report together with evidence from sentencing hearing. — Where no presentence report is received in a bench trial, this section requires the court to consider a post sentence report before imposing the death penalty. However, the tenor of this section is complied with and no prejudice results to the defendant where the trial judge considers a presentence report in conjunction with the evidence adduced in the sentencing hearing and, in a single step, fixes and imposes a sentence of death. Correll v. Commonwealth, 232 Va. 454, 352 S.E.2d 352, cert. denied, 482 U.S. 931, 107 S. Ct. 3219, 96 L. Ed. 2d 705 (1987).

Counsel's failure to object to court's plan to consider presentence report was not prejudicial in the sentencing phase on grounds that it allowed the court to consider damaging evidence about his criminal past in fixing sentence, rather than giving him one opportunity to convince the court, before it saw the report, to sentence him to life imprisonment. Nothing contained in the report was inadmissible in the sentencing phase; indeed, much of the information in the report was revealed by the testimony. As the presentence report was admissible, counsel were under no duty to object to its admission. Correll v. Commonwealth, 232 Va. 454, 352 S.E.2d 352, cert. denied, 482 U.S. 931, 107 S. Ct. 3219, 96 L. Ed. 2d 705 (1987).

Failure to object to court's departure from sentencing scheme of this section did not prejudice defendant's rights on appeal, since counsel's failure to object was irrelevant in view of the ruling that consideration of a presentence report satisfies the statutory requirements in a bench trial. Correll v. Commonwealth, 232 Va. 454, 352 S.E.2d 352, cert. denied, 482 U.S. 931, 107 S. Ct. 3219, 96 L. Ed. 2d 705 (1987).

Failure to interview parents or wife. — The defendant was not denied any statutory rights in the sentencing phase of his capital murder trial as the result of the probation officer's failure to interview the defendant's parents or wife. Stamper v. Commonwealth, 220 Va. 260, 257 S.E.2d 808 (1979), cert. denied, 445 U.S. 972, 100 S. Ct. 1666, 64 L. Ed. 2d 249 (1980).

A probation report which used information from a prior presentence report was not erroneously admitted at the sentencing phase of a capital murder trial where the probation officer did not use information from the presentence report until after the accuracy of this information was confirmed in an interview with the defendant, who was given opportunity to cross-examine the probation officer thoroughly on the report and to introduce relevant evidence on his own behalf to supplement or contradict the report. Stamper v. Commonwealth, 220 Va. 260, 257 S.E.2d 808 (1979), cert. denied, 445 U.S. 972, 100 S. Ct. 1666, 64 L. Ed. 2d 249 (1980).

Inclusion of recommendation of sentence in probation report. — Where an objection was raised to the report of a probation officer, which included a recommendation of what sentence should be imposed, but where the trial judge indicated that the probation officer's recommendation was not relevant and would not influence the court in its decision, it must be assumed that the recommendation did not influence the court. Accordingly, inclusion of the recommendation, if error, was harmless. Waye v. Commonwealth, 219 Va. 683, 251 S.E.2d 202, cert. denied, 442 U.S. 924, 99 S. Ct. 2850, 61 L. Ed. 2d 292 (1979).

Although original sentencing order was entered in error for failure of the trial court to consider the probation report required by this section, where the trial judge recognized the omission, vacated the order, directed the probation officer to prepare a report, authorized a private psychiatric examination, and afforded defendant a second opportunity to show good cause why the death penalty should not be imposed, the error was cured, and absent anything to support defendant's claim that the final sentencing order was the product of passion or prejudice, such assignment of error would be rejected. Edmonds v. Commonwealth, 229 Va. 303, 329 S.E.2d 807, cert. denied, 474 U.S. 975, 106 S. Ct. 339, 88 L. Ed. 2d 324 (1985).

Victim impact statement contained in a post-sentence report did not create an impermissible risk that the capital sentencing decision would be made in an arbitrary manner, where the statement was not read to the jury nor was the jury ever made aware of its existence. Smith v. Commonwealth, 239 Va. 243, 389 S.E.2d 871 (1990), cert. denied, 498 U.S. 881, 111 S. Ct. 221, 112 L. Ed. 2d 177 (1990).

Defendant not entitled to victim impact statement. — Defendant was not entitled to a new sentencing hearing on grounds that the post-sentence report did not contain a victim impact statement; the victim impact statement requirement did not confer any rights on defendant. Remington v. Commonwealth, 262 Va. 333, 551 S.E.2d 620, 2001 Va. LEXIS 107 (2001), cert. denied, 535 U.S. 1062, 122 S. Ct. 1928, 152 L. Ed. 2d 834 (2002).

Applied in Johnson v. Commonwealth, 220 Va. 146, 255 S.E.2d 525 (1979); Justus v. Commonwealth, 220 Va. 971, 266 S.E.2d 87 (1980); Turner v. Commonwealth, 221 Va. 513, 273 S.E.2d 36 (1980); Briley v. Commonwealth, 221 Va. 532, 273 S.E.2d 48 (1980); Briley v. Commonwealth, 221 Va. 563, 273 S.E.2d 57 (1980); Patterson v. Commonwealth, 222 Va. 653, 283 S.E.2d 212 (1981); Quintana v. Commonwealth, 224 Va. 127, 295 S.E.2d 643 (1982); Peterson v. Commonwealth, 225 Va. 289, 302 S.E.2d 520 (1983); Bunch v. Commonwealth, 225 Va. 423, 304 S.E.2d 271 (1983); Coleman v. Commonwealth, 226 Va. 31, 307 S.E.2d 864 (1983); Stockton v. Commonwealth, 227 Va. 124, 314 S.E.2d 371 (1984); Boggs v. Commonwealth, 229 Va. 501, 331 S.E.2d 407 (1985); Tuggle v. Commonwealth, 230 Va. 99, 334 S.E.2d 838 (1985); Clanton v. Blair, 619 F. Supp. 1491 (E.D. Va. 1985); Williams v. Commonwealth, 234 Va. 168, 360 S.E.2d 361 (1987); DeLong v. Commonwealth, 234 Va. 357, 362 S.E.2d 669 (1987); Yeatts v. Commonwealth, 242 Va. 121, 410 S.E.2d 254 (1991); George v. Commonwealth, 242 Va. 264, 411 S.E.2d 12 (1991); Chandler v. Commonwealth, 249 Va. 270, 455 S.E.2d 219 (1995); Hedrick v. Commonwealth, 257 Va. 328, 513 S.E.2d 634; Juniper v. Commonwealth, 271 Va. 362, 626 S.E.2d 383, 2006 Va. LEXIS 29 (2006); Jackson v. Warden of the Sussex I State Prison, 271 Va. 434, 627 S.E.2d 776, 2006 Va. LEXIS 32 (2006).

CIRCUIT COURT OPINIONS

Defendant not entitled to counsel at probation officer's presentence interview. — Defendant was not entitled to have counsel present at the probation officer's presentence interview that would provide a presentence report as recognized in § 19.2-264.5. The Sixth Amendment right to counsel only applied to critical stages of a criminal proceeding and the interview was not a critical stage because the probation officer did not have an adversarial role in interviewing a defendant. Commonwealth v. Prieto, 75 Va. Cir. 212, 2008 Va. Cir. LEXIS 53 (Fairfax County 2008).

ARTICLE 5.

MISCELLANEOUS PROVISIONS.

§ 19.2-265. Opening statement of counsel.

On the trial of any case of felony or misdemeanor and before any evidence is submitted on either side, the attorney for the Commonwealth and counsel for the accused, respectively, shall have the right to make an opening statement of their case.

History.
Code 1950, § 19.1-245; 1960, c. 366; 1975, c. 495.

Michie's Jurisprudence.
For related discussion, see 5B M.J. Criminal Procedure, § 65; 19 M.J. Trial, § 11.

CASE NOTES

This section confers the right to make an opening statement, but does not make it obligatory on either party. Johnson v. Commonwealth, 111 Va. 877, 69 S.E. 1104 (1911).

Counsel cannot put his client's character into evidence through his opening statement, particularly when the jury has already been instructed that counsels' statements are not to be viewed as evidence. Fields v. Commonwealth, 2 Va. App. 300, 343 S.E.2d 379 (1986).

Counsel cannot argue during opening statement. — The trial court did not abuse its discretion in ruling that defendant's counsel could not use the opening statement for argument. Spencer v. Commonwealth, 238 Va. 295, 384 S.E.2d 785 (1989), cert. denied, 493 U.S. 1093, 110 S. Ct. 1171, 107 L. Ed. 2d 1073 (1990).

§ 19.2-265.01. Victims, certain members of the family and support persons not to be excluded.

During the trial of every criminal case and in all court proceedings attendant to trial, whether before, during or after trial, including any proceedings occurring after an appeal by the defendant or the Commonwealth, at which attendance by the defendant is permitted, whether in a circuit or district court, any victim as defined in § 19.2-11.01 may remain in the courtroom and shall not be excluded unless the court determines, in its discretion, the presence of the victim would impair the conduct of a fair trial. In any case involving a minor victim, the court may permit an adult chosen by the minor to be present in the courtroom during any proceedings in addition to or in lieu of the minor's parent or guardian.

The attorney for the Commonwealth shall give prior notice when practicable of such trial and attendant proceedings and changes in the scheduling thereof to any known victim and to any known adult chosen in accordance with this section by a minor victim, at the address or telephone number, or both, provided in writing by such person.

History.
1993, cc. 447, 452; 1994, cc. 361, 598; 1995, c. 687; 1996, c. 546; 1999, c. 844; 2000, c. 339.

Editor's note.
At the direction of the Code Commission, Acts 1994, c. 361, which amended this section, was not given effect due to a conflict. The amendment would have added the second sentence dealing with the same subject matter but using different language.

Michie's Jurisprudence.
For related discussion, see 5B M.J. Criminal Procedure, § 38; 20 M.J. Witnesses, § 35.

CASE NOTES

No abuse of discretion in allowing victim witness to stay in courtroom. — Circuit court did not abuse its discretion under § 19.2-265.01 by allowing a murder victim's son, who was a victim within the meaning of subsection B of § 19.2-11.01, to remain in the courtroom after he testified during the guilt phase of the trial because the circuit court correctly concluded that the victim's son did not learn anything while he was present in the court that would have changed or affected his victim impact testimony during the penalty phase, and, thus, defendant was not prejudiced by the fact that the son testified during the penalty phase after having heard much of the testimony during the guilt phase. Jackson v. Commonwealth, 267 Va. 178, 590 S.E.2d 520, 2004 Va. LEXIS 8 (2004), cert. denied, 543 U.S. 891, 125 S. Ct. 168, 160 L. Ed. 2d 155 (2004).

Because defendant provided no specific reason for finding that a victim witness's presence in the courtroom during the testimony of other witnesses would impair the fairness of the trial, the trial court did not abuse its discretion by allowing the victim witness to remain in the courtroom. Hernandez-Guerrero v. Commonwealth, 46 Va. App. 366, 617 S.E.2d 410, 2005 Va. App. LEXIS 311 (2005).

Circuit court properly found a probationer in violation of his probation, as testimony from a victim-witness in a city prosecution, which was underlying basis for the issuance of a capias in the revocation matter, was relevant; further, that witness was exempt from sequestration, as she could not have shaped her testimony to correspond to the contents of the probationer's letter to the judge or the testimony of the probation officer. Osborne v. Commonwealth, — Va. App. —, — S.E.2d —, 2005 Va. App. LEXIS 376 (Oct. 4, 2005).

No exception exists to allow defendant's family to remain in court at guilt phase and also testify at penalty phase. — Defendant was not denied the effective assistance of counsel where his counsel did not object to the exclusion of defendant's family from the courtroom during the guilt phase of his trial because those family members were expected to testify during the penalty phase; the court rejected defendant's argument that counsel's failure to object sent a false message that his family did not care enough to be with him during his trial. Defendant could not show that an objection would be successful; so he failed to establish the performance prong of the *Strickland* test; there was no exception under § 19.2-265.01 that would allow defendant's family to remain in the courtroom during trial and still be able to testify at the penalty phase. Jackson v. Warden of the Sussex I State Prison, 271 Va. 434, 627 S.E.2d 776, 2006 Va. LEXIS 32 (2006).

§ 19.2-265.1. Exclusion of witnesses (Subsection (a) of Supreme Court Rule 2:615 derived in part from this section and subsection (c) of Supreme Court Rule 2:615 derived from this section).

In the trial of every criminal case, the court, whether a court of record or a court not of record, may upon its own motion and shall upon the motion of either the attorney for the Commonwealth or any defendant, require the exclusion of every witness to be called, including, but not limited to, police officers or other investigators; however, each defendant who is an individual and one officer or agent of each defendant which is a corporation or association shall be exempt from the rule of this section as a matter of right. Additionally, any victim as defined in § 19.2-11.01 who is to be called as a witness shall be exempt from the rule of this section as a matter of law unless, in accordance with the provisions of § 19.2-265.01, his exclusion is otherwise required.

History.
Code 1950, § 8-211.1; 1966, c. 268; 1975, c. 652; 1977, c. 624; 1990, c. 572; 2004, c. 311.

Editor's note.
At the direction of the Virginia Code Commission, the notation to the Virginia Rules of Evidence was added to the catchline of this section. Acts 2012, cc. 688 and 708, cl. 6 provides: "That pursuant to the authority set forth in §§ 30-146 and 30-147 of the Code of Virginia, the Virginia Code Commission shall direct any party with whom the Virginia Code Commission contracts to publish the Code of Virginia to include in the catchline of every section of the Code of Virginia from which any rule contained in the Rules of Evidence has been derived a notation specifying such rule."

Law Review.
For survey on evidence in Virginia for 1989, see 23 U. Rich. L. Rev. 647 (1989).

Michie's Jurisprudence.
For related discussion, see 20 M.J. Witnesses, § 35.

CASE NOTES

Statute held mandatory. — Former § 8-211.1 permitted of no rational construction but that "upon the motion of any party" a trial court "shall" exclude "every witness" during the trial of "every case …." Johnson v. Commonwealth, 217 Va. 682, 232 S.E.2d 741 (1977).

Absolute right to exclude witnesses. — A defendant's right to exclusion of witnesses at trial is absolute. Cuozzo v. Commonwealth, No. 1843-98-2, 2000 Va. App. LEXIS 603 (Ct. of Appeals Aug. 15, 2000).

Testimony of witness violating order directing his exclusion. — The presence of a witness in the courtroom, in disobedience of the order of exclusion, does not disqualify such witness from testifying. On the contrary, it is generally held that it is within the sound discretion of the trial court to permit the testimony of a witness who has violated an order directing his exclusion from the courtroom. Brickhouse v. Commonwealth, 208 Va. 533, 159 S.E.2d 611 (1968), decided under former § 8-211.1.

Where information was communicated to a witness in violation of an exclusion order pertaining only to documentary evidence regarding her marital status, and the witness did not in any way change her testimony upon learning of its existence, the trial court did not abuse its discretion in allowing this witness to testify later at trial. Bennett v. Commonwealth, 236 Va. 448, 374 S.E.2d 303 (1988), cert. denied, 490 U.S. 1028, 109 S. Ct. 1765, 104 L. Ed. 2d 200 (1989).

The trial court erred in refusing to admit into evidence the testimony of a defense witness who had remained in the courtroom in violation of an order excluding witnesses where the excluded testimony addressed the credibility of the only witness against the defendant and the weight to be given to his testimony, and where violation of the exclusion order was unintentional, both on his part and on the part of defense counsel, and there was no showing that his presence in the courtroom influenced his testimony. Jury v. Commonwealth, 10 Va. App. 718, 395 S.E.2d 213 (1990).

Trial court has discretion whether witness prevented from testifying. — A trial court has discretion to decide whether a witness who violates an exclusion order should be prevented from testifying. Jury v. Commonwealth, 10 Va. App. 718, 395 S.E.2d 213 (1990).

Factors considered in determining whether witness should be prevented from testifying. — Factors to be considered in determining whether a witness who violates an exclusion order should be prevented from testifying include whether prejudice will result to the defendant and whether the violation of the rule resulted from intentional impropriety. Jury v. Commonwealth, 10 Va. App. 718, 395 S.E.2d 213 (1990).

Mistrial was not mandated by the trial court's decision not to exclude the testimony of a witness who discussed court proceedings with another potential witness, where there was no showing that either participant in the conversation was aware of the order excluding them from the courtroom or that defendant was prejudiced by their conversation. Wolfe v. Commonwealth, 265 Va. 193, 576 S.E.2d 471, 2003 Va. LEXIS 32, cert. denied, 540 U.S. 1019, 124 S. Ct. 566, 157 L. Ed. 2d 434 (2003).

Circuit court properly found a probationer in violation of his probation, as testimony from a victim-witness in a city prosecution, which was underlying basis for the issuance of a capias in the revocation matter, was relevant; and further, that witness was exempt from sequestration, as she could not have shaped her testimony to correspond to the contents of the probationer's letter to the judge or the testimony of the probation officer. Osborne v. Commonwealth, — Va. App. —, — S.E.2d —, 2005 Va. App. LEXIS 376 (Oct. 4, 2005).

Where record demonstrates defendant requested wit-

nesses be excluded from courtroom, and the Commonwealth assured the trial court that it was not going to call investigator for State Corporation Commission as a witness but needed him present as a consultant during trial, defendant then told trial court that he was going to call investigator for two matters. The trial court did not force defendant to call investigator as his own witness. Rather, defendant, after requesting that the witnesses be excluded, determined that he might want to call investigator as his own witness. Pursuant to this section, the trial court then was required to exclude investigator, as well as all other potential witnesses, from the courtroom during the trial. Chiang v. Commonwealth, 6 Va. App. 13, 365 S.E.2d 778 (1988).

Constitutionality of former statute. — So much of former § 8-211.1 as required the exclusion of each witness "whose presence is not necessary to the proceedings" was void for indefiniteness. Jefferson v. Commonwealth, 212 Va. 255, 183 S.E.2d 734 (1971).

Applied in Church v. Commonwealth, 230 Va. 208, 335 S.E.2d 823 (1985); Wolfe v. Commonwealth, 265 Va. 193, 576 S.E.2d 471, 2003 Va. LEXIS 32.

§ 19.2-265.2. Judicial notice of laws (Supreme Court Rule 2:202 derived in part from this section).

A. Whenever, in any criminal case it becomes necessary to ascertain what the law, statutory or otherwise, of this Commonwealth, of another state, of the United States, of another country, or of any political subdivision or agency of the same is, or was, at any time, the court shall take judicial notice thereof whether specially pleaded or not.

B. The court, in taking such notice, shall consult any book, record, register, journal, or other official document or publication purporting to contain, state, or explain such law, and may consider any evidence or other information or argument that is offered on the subject.

History.
1978, c. 328.

Editor's note.
At the direction of the Virginia Code Commission, the notation to the Virginia Rules of Evidence was added to the catchline of this section. Acts 2012, cc. 688 and 708, cl. 6 provides: "That pursuant to the authority set forth in §§ 30-146 and 30-147 of the Code of Virginia, the Virginia Code Commission shall direct any party with whom the Virginia Code Commission contracts to publish the Code of Virginia to include in the catchline of every section of the Code of Virginia from which any rule contained in the Rules of Evidence has been derived a notation specifying such rule."

Law Review.
For survey of Virginia law on evidence for year 1977-1978, see 64 Va. L. Rev. 1451 (1978).

CASE NOTES

Effect where notice not shown in record on appeal. — Where the record on appeal for a case in which the defendant was convicted under § 18.2-270 for a second and subsequent offense of driving under the influence of intoxicants did not show that the trial court took judicial notice of North Carolina's laws and, further, even assuming the court took judicial notice of those laws, it failed to enter of record the provisions of the laws it noticed, the Commonwealth was not relieved from proving the provisions of those laws and their similarity to Virginia's. Rufty v. Commonwealth, 221 Va. 836, 275 S.E.2d 584 (1981).

Trial court is not required to formally admit ordinances of jurisdiction where it sits, because it is required to take judicial notice of those laws. Oulds v. Commonwealth, No. 2062-98-3 (Ct. of Appeals Sept. 28, 1999).

Judicial notice of city ordinances. — This statute eliminates the requirement of introducing an authenticated copy of a city ordinance into evidence and that the ordinance be "specially pleaded" in those cases where proof of the terms of such an ordinance is necessary to establish the elements of the offense. Oulds v. Commonwealth, 260 Va. 210, 532 S.E.2d 33 (2000).

Prosecutor was not required to introduce a city ordinance that defendant violated into evidence before the trial court, pursuant to § 19.2-265.2, could take judicial notice of the city ordinance. Cubitt v. Commonwealth, No. 3462-01-1, 2002 Va. App. LEXIS 747 (Ct. of Appeals Dec. 17, 2002).

Notice of prior conviction as evidence of ordinance. — In convicting defendant of driving under the influence (DUI), the trial court did not err in admitting evidence of prior DUI conviction, as the arrest warrant constituted an official document, and the trial court properly consulted the warrant as evidence of the ordinance under which defendant was previously convicted in taking judicial notice of its provisions. Webb v. Commonwealth, No. 2749-01-2, 2003 Va. App. LEXIS 138 (Ct. of Appeals Mar. 18, 2003).

CIRCUIT COURT OPINIONS

Compact incorporated into Virginia Code. — Circuit court need not take judicial notice of the Washington Metropolitan Area Transit Authority Compact, because the Compact was, itself, the law of the Commonwealth of Virginia as the Compact was entered into by the Commonwealth of Virginia, and was incorporated in the Code of Virginia at §§ 56-529 and 56-530. Commonwealth v. Fox, 78 Va. Cir. 40, 2008 Va. Cir. LEXIS 177 (Fairfax County 2008).

§ 19.2-265.3. Nolle prosequi; discretion of court upon good cause shown.

Nolle prosequi shall be entered only in the discretion of the court, upon motion of the Commonwealth with good cause therefor shown.

History.
1979, c. 641.

Law Review.
For annual survey article, "Criminal Law and Procedure," see 44 U. Rich. L. Rev. 339 (2009).

Michie's Jurisprudence.
For related discussion, see 4A M.J. Commonwealth's and State's Attorney, §§ 4, 7; 5B M.J. Criminal Procedure, § 27; 6A M.J. Dismissal, Discontinuance and Nonsuit, §§ 38, 39.

CASE NOTES

"Good cause" for a nolle prosequi was demonstrated where: (1) the Commonwealth had not obtained documents indispensable to prosecution of defendant on the scheduled trial date; (2) the Commonwealth's dilemma was fully disclosed to the court in support of a related continuance motion; (3) when the motion was denied, the Commonwealth quickly sought to nolle prosequi the charges, clearly prompted by those evidentiary concerns presented to the court moments earlier; and (4) acting in this context, the court granted the motion, implicitly finding that the circumstances constituted sufficient "good cause" to justify the requested relief. Harris v. Commonwealth, No. 2087-97-4 (Ct. of Appeals Oct. 20, 1998).

Retrial precluded after swearing of witness and dismissal on refusal of Commonwealth to proceed. — Where the trial court ruled against prosecuting defendant on a felony charge, but found probable cause supporting a misdemeanor charge and accordingly swore in a witness, but the attorney for the Commonwealth refused to question the witness, stating that he wished to secure a grand jury for a felony charge, upon which the judge properly dismissed the case, the attorney for the Commonwealth could not prosecute the case anew on a felony charge, as double jeopardy attached. The Commonwealth had the opportunity to question the sworn witness, defendant had risked a determination of guilt, and absent manifest necessity defendant could not be retried for the same offense. Goolsby v. Hutto, 529 F. Supp. 92 (E.D. Va. 1981), aff'd, 691 F.2d 199 (4th Cir. 1982).

Jeopardy attaches upon denial of motion and swearing of first witness. — When the general district court denied the motion for nolle prosequi, set the case for trial, and called and swore the first witness, the defendant was then subjected either to conviction or acquittal. The fact that the witness gave no evidence because the attorney for the Commonwealth refused to examine him, required the acquittal of the defendant by the general district court, just as his conviction would have been required had the witness given evidence sufficient to sustain his guilt. Goolsby v. Hutto, 691 F.2d 199 (4th Cir. 1982).

Entry of nolle prosequi prior to jury being empaneled or sworn. — Jeopardy had not yet attached in a prosecution for murder because the jury had not been empaneled or sworn, and thus, the entry of a nolle prosequi did not bar reindictment and reprosecution. Cantrell v. Commonwealth, 7 Va. App. 269, 373 S.E.2d 328 (1988), cert. denied, 496 U.S. 911, 110 S. Ct. 2600, 110 L. Ed. 2d 280 (1990).

Where the jury had not been empaneled and sworn in defendant's case, and no mistrial was declared, the attorney for the Commonwealth was not required to prove "manifest necessity" in support of his motion to nolle prosequi; rather, the attorney for the Commonwealth was merely required to show good cause, and the trial court, in its discretion, could grant the motion. Cantrell v. Commonwealth, 7 Va. App. 269, 373 S.E.2d 328 (1988), cert. denied, 496 U.S. 911, 110 S. Ct. 2600, 110 L. Ed. 2d 280 (1990).

Dismissal of charges against defendant did not constitute nolle prosequi. — Trial court erred in denying defendant's motion to dismiss criminal charges, as the prosecution's dismissal of an earlier indictment for the same charges did not act as a nolle prosequi under § 19.2-265.3, as the trial court denied the prosecution's motion for a continuance because the prosecution failed to work with federal authorities to obtain defendant's presence at trial, and was not prepared to proceed without defendant's presence, so the dismissal was with prejudice. Roe v. Commonwealth, 271 Va. 453, 628 S.E.2d 526, 2006 Va. LEXIS 46 (2006).

Defendant not prejudiced by nolle prosequi on first degree murder count in capital trial. — Defendant was not prejudiced by the granting of a motion to enter a nolle prosequi on the first-degree murder count, despite his claim that the jury was not cognizant of its option to consider the evidence within the framework of a first-degree murder alternative, since the "framework" in which the evidence was adduced was constructed at the time the robbery and capital murder counts of the indictment were read to the jury and the defendant entered his pleas of not guilty. The framework in which the evidence was considered by the jury was that fashioned by the instructions. Those instructions defined first-degree and second-degree murder as well as capital murder. Boggs v. Commonwealth, 229 Va. 501, 331 S.E.2d 407 (1985), cert. denied, 475 U.S. 1031, 106 S. Ct. 1240, 89 L. Ed. 2d 347 (1986), 495 U.S. 940, 110 S. Ct. 2193, 109 L. Ed. 2d 521 (1990).

No constructive nolle prosequi by withholding finding on guilty pleas. — The trial court could not constructively enter a nolle prosequi on the three first-degree murder indictments by withholding a finding on the guilty pleas. Rea v. Commonwealth, 14 Va. App. 940, 421 S.E.2d 464 (1992).

Subsequent indictments of enhanced offenses. — Trial judge erred in refusing to dismiss indictments of enhanced offenses that were obtained after the trial judge granted the Commonwealth's motion to nolle prosequi, as the bringing of more serious charges under the facts of this case represented prosecutorial vindictiveness. Battle v. Commonwealth, 12 Va. App. 624, 406 S.E.2d 195 (1991).

Nolle prosequi was properly granted based on the unexpected absence of a witness for the Commonwealth. Rogers v. Commonwealth, No. 1086-97-1 (Ct. of Appeals April 14, 1998).

Trial court did not err by granting the Commonwealth's motion to nolle prosequi the issuing multiple worthless checks indictment and prosecute defendant under three separate indictments of § 18.2-181, because the prosecutor was exercising the Commonwealth's right to elect which two statutes to proceed under. Moore

v. Commonwealth, 59 Va. App. 795, 722 S.E.2d 668, 2012 Va. App. LEXIS 81 (2012).

Court declined to speculate whether good cause existed. — Defendant's conviction for petit larceny was proper because, in view of defendant's tactical decision to withdraw her appeal, the appellate court declined to speculate whether good cause existed to support the nolle prosequi entry or whether the Commonwealth moved to enter the nolle prosequi in violation of defendant's due process rights. Gordon v. Commonwealth, 2011 Va. App. LEXIS 330 (Nov. 1, 2011).

Defendant not entitled to dismissal in later proceeding. — Defendant was not entitled to dismissal based on the prosecutor's nolle prosequi of prior charges, which were identical to charges in the later proceeding, because under § 19.2-265.3, absent vindictive intent resulting in oppressive and unfair trial tactics, or other prosecutorial misconduct, courts deferred to the prosecutor in these circumstances; the presence or absence of good cause in the prior proceeding could not have been collaterally reviewed by the trial court in the later proceeding. It changed nothing that, in the earlier proceeding, an unsuccessful continuance motion preceded the motion for nolle prosequi. Duggins v. Commonwealth, 59 Va. App. 785, 722 S.E.2d 663, 2012 Va. App. LEXIS 80 (2012).

CIRCUIT COURT OPINIONS

"Good cause" for a nolle prosequi was demonstrated. — Pursuant to the court's discretion, the Commonwealth was entitled to nolle prosequi defendant's case pursuant to § 19.2-265.3 because its failure to subpoena a doctor as a necessary witness for trial amounted to a mere oversight, or a lack of adequate foresight and preparation. It did not constitute bad faith or prosecutorial misconduct. Commonwealth v. Van Luu, 79 Va. Cir. 43, 2009 Va. Cir. LEXIS 69 (Fairfax Apr. 14, 2009).

Nolle prosequi granted where defendant failed to show existence of cooperation agreement. — Commonwealth's motion for nolle prosequi was granted where defendant failed to show that the government made a firm promise of commitment supporting the existence of cooperation agreement and, even if there had been agreement as to the terms asserted by defendant or the Commonwealth, such terms simply did not contain the terms essential to such an agreement since the agreement suggested by both sides contained no discussion of what level of cooperation would be required of defendant in order for her to satisfy the purported cooperation agreement nor who would determine whether defendant had fulfilled her part of the cooperation agreement. In addition, defendant's own evidence was that she failed to comply with the cooperation requirement. Commonwealth v. Stewart, 66 Va. Cir. 135, 2004 Va. Cir. LEXIS 325 (Portsmouth Oct. 22, 2004).

Nolle prosequi may be granted. — Although Virginia case law has required strict compliance with § 19.2-187, which requires the Commonwealth to file a certificate of analysis at least one week prior to trial in a DUI case, where § 19.2-187 is not implicated, denial of a continuance does not preclude the granting of a nolle prosequi under § 19.2-265.3, even where both motions are predicated on the same assertions. Commonwealth v. Van Luu, 79 Va. Cir. 43, 2009 Va. Cir. LEXIS 69 (Fairfax Apr. 14, 2009).

OPINIONS OF THE ATTORNEY GENERAL

Commonwealth's attorney has no authority to dismiss any misdemeanor or felony charge that led to the lawful arrest of an accused, without a showing of good cause to the court. See opinion of Attorney General to The Honorable Ralph B. Robertson, Judge, Richmond General District Court, Criminal Division, 03-025 (5/30/03).

§ 19.2-265.4. Failure to provide discovery.

A. In any criminal prosecution for a felony in a circuit court or for a misdemeanor brought on direct indictment, the attorney for the Commonwealth shall have a duty to adequately and fully provide discovery as provided under Rule 3A:11 of the Rules of the Supreme Court. Rule 3A:11 shall be construed to apply to such felony and misdemeanor prosecutions. This duty to disclose shall be continuing and shall apply to any additional evidence or material discovered by the Commonwealth prior to or during trial which is subject to discovery or inspection and has been previously requested by the accused. In any criminal prosecution for a misdemeanor by trial de novo in circuit court, the attorney for the Commonwealth shall have a duty to adequately and fully provide discovery as provided under Rule 7C:5 of the Rules of the Supreme Court.

B. If at any time during the course of the proceedings it is brought to the attention of the court that the attorney for the Commonwealth has failed to comply with this section, the court may order the Commonwealth to permit the discovery or inspection, grant a continuance, or prohibit the Commonwealth from introducing evidence not disclosed, or the court may enter such other order as it deems just under the circumstances.

History.
1985, c. 538; 1995, c. 504; 2004, c. 348.

Law Review.
For 2003/2004 survey of criminal law and procedure, see 39 U. Rich. L. Rev. 133 (2004).

Michie's Jurisprudence.
For related discussion, see 5B M.J. Criminal Procedure, § 23; 6A M.J. Discovery, § 8.

CASE NOTES

Duty of court to impose sanctions upon deliberate attempt to use improper evidence. — When it appears to a trial court that a party has deliberately attempted to introduce evidence which it knows is improper or inadmissible, either because it was not disclosed during discovery or because it otherwise is inadmissible under rules of evidence, it is the duty and responsibility of the court to deter such inappropriate tactics by taking such action, imposing such sanctions, or granting such relief as it deems appropriate. Stotler v. Commonwealth, 2 Va. App. 481, 346 S.E.2d 39 (1986).

No duty to impose sanctions unless failure to comply intentional. — There is no duty upon the court to impose sanctions or grant other relief unless the failure to comply was intentional and the party violating the discovery order deliberately attempted to introduce improper evidence. Synder v. Commonwealth, 10 Va. App. 67, 389 S.E.2d 727 (1990).

Sanctions where Commonwealth deliberately fails to comply with discovery order. — When it is brought to the attention of a court that the Commonwealth has failed to comply with a discovery order, the court may prohibit the Commonwealth from introducing the evidence or enter such other order as it deems just under the circumstances. Certain circumstances may dictate a citation for contempt and/or require referral of the matter to the appropriate ethics committee of the bar. Stotler v. Commonwealth, 2 Va. App. 481, 346 S.E.2d 39 (1986).

Prejudice required to show grounds for reversal or other remedy. — When an accused alleging a discovery violation shows no prejudice, he can claim no reversible error; thus, a defendant who alleges the remedy fashioned for any discovery violation is insufficient also must show prejudice in order to claim entitlement to relief. Miles v. Commonwealth, No. 0692-00-4, 2001 Va. App. LEXIS 183 (Ct. of Appeals Apr. 10, 2001).

Where the Commonwealth failed to provide an inculpatory recorded telephone conversation between defendant and his mother

prior to seeking its admission at trial, as required by a discovery order, admission of the evidence was upheld because defendant failed to show prejudice by demonstrating how timely disclosure would have changed his trial strategy or affected the outcome of the trial. Romero-Diaz v. Commonwealth, No. 0489-09-4, 2010 Va. App. LEXIS 180 (Ct. of Appeals May 4, 2010).

Failure to comply with discovery not reversible absent prejudice. — A trial court's admission of relevant and material evidence at trial which was not disclosed as required by a discovery order is not reversible error in the absence of a showing of prejudice. Stotler v. Commonwealth, 2 Va. App. 481, 346 S.E.2d 39 (1986).

Defendant's convictions for carjacking, robbery, abduction, and use of a firearm in the commission of those felonies were proper because, as a sanction for non-disclosure, the trial court did not allow the introduction of a photo spread, nor did it consider the derivative identification as substantive evidence of the identity of the perpetrator. The trial court did not abuse its discretion in formulating the relief granted. Thompson v. Commonwealth, 2010 Va. App. LEXIS 415 (Oct. 26, 2010).

No abuse of discretion where court refused to exclude challenged evidence. — In the absence of evidence that late disclosure prejudiced the defense, or absent an objection and a trial court finding that the prosecutor deliberately violated his discovery duties, it is not an abuse of discretion for the trial court to refuse to exclude the challenged evidence. Moreno v. Commonwealth, 10 Va. App. 408, 392 S.E.2d 836 (1990).

Court did not err in failing to review statements where no motion made. — Where appellant contended that trial court erred in failing to review the alibi witness statements in camera, appellant did not move the trial court to review the witness statements, nor did he move that the documents be placed under seal for the record on appeal. The court of appeals did not need to rule upon the non-exercise of a judicial power that was not invoked. While the trial court could have reviewed the statements in camera sua sponte, it was not required to do so. Allen v. Commonwealth, No. 2737-96-2 (Ct. of Appeals Feb. 10, 1998).

The remedial relief to be granted by the trial court following a discovery violation or upon the late disclosure of evidence is within the trial court's discretion and will not be disturbed on appeal unless plainly wrong. Where no prejudice has been shown by permitting the witness to testify after the late disclosure of the discoverable evidence, the trial court does not err by admitting the evidence after granting a continuance. Moreno v. Commonwealth, 10 Va. App. 408, 392 S.E.2d 836 (1990).

There was no violation of discovery order where the Commonwealth disclosed information as soon as it was received, and no prejudice where the information was disclosed in time to be put to use. Bennett v. Commonwealth, 236 Va. 448, 374 S.E.2d 303 (1988), cert. denied, 490 U.S. 1028, 109 S. Ct. 1765, 104 L. Ed. 2d 200 (1989).

No violation of discovery where disclosure was timely. — There was no error when a trial court found that the prosecution had timely provided defendant with certain discovery materials, even though the prosecution did not give the materials, including the prior inconsistent statement and the criminal record of his co-conspirator, to defendant before trial; defendant received the materials in enough time, because the trial court granted defendant a 10-minute recess to prepare to cross-examine the co-conspirator. Additionally, there was no evidence that defendant was prejudiced by the alleged *Brady* violation, and absent such proof of prejudice, any violation did not take on constitutional proportions or deprive defendant of his due process right to a fair trial. Wilson v. Commonwealth, — Va. App. —, — S.E.2d —, 2006 Va. App. LEXIS 243 (May 30, 2006).

Applied in Smith v. Commonwealth, 239 Va. 243, 389 S.E.2d 871 (1990); Conway v. Commonwealth, 11 Va. App. 103, 397 S.E.2d 263 (1990); Conway v. Commonwealth, 12 Va. App. 711, 407 S.E.2d 310 (1991).

CIRCUIT COURT OPINIONS

Disclosure of confidential informant required. — Commonwealth was required to disclose identity of confidential informant who arranged a drug purchase at which defendant was arrested since the informant was with officers when the purchase was set up and since the informant could possibly testify on issues of entrapment or accommodation, which was information that could be essential to preparation of the defense. Commonwealth v. Cashwell, 66 Va. Cir. 63, 2004 Va. Cir. LEXIS 262 (Nelson County 2004).

Brady violation not found. — Discovery of a weapon over a month after the shooting for which defendant was convicted of murder, miles away from the scene of the shooting, and determined not to be the murder weapon, was not exculpatory or material evidence; therefore, no *Brady* violation occurred. Bonhom v. Angelone, 58 Va. Cir. 358, 2002 Va. Cir. LEXIS 44 (Fairfax County 2002).

Motion to dismiss denied. — Defendant's motion to dismiss based on the Commonwealth's alleged discovery violation was denied. He had the opportunity to inspect evidence pursuant to the court's discovery order; he elicited testimony about certain evidence at issue; certain evidence discovered post-trial was inculpatory and not exculpatory, and the late discovery of inculpatory evidence neither changed the defense strategy nor denied him a fair trial. Commonwealth v. Javier-Paz, 2012 Va. Cir. LEXIS 19 (Fairfax County Feb. 9, 2012).

§ 19.2-265.5. Prosecuting misdemeanor cases without attorney.

Notwithstanding any of the provisions of § 19.2-265.1, whenever in a misdemeanor case neither an attorney for the Commonwealth nor any other attorney for the prosecution is present, the complaining witness may be allowed to remain in court throughout the entire trial if necessary for the orderly presentation of witnesses for the prosecution.

History.
1987, c. 659.

§ 19.2-265.6. Effect of dismissal of criminal charges.

No dismissal of any criminal charge by a court shall bar subsequent prosecution of the charge unless jeopardy attached at the earlier proceeding or unless the dismissal order explicitly states that the dismissal is with prejudice.

History.
2007, c. 419.

Law Review.
For 2007 annual survey article, "Criminal Law and Procedure," see 42 U. Rich. L. Rev. 311 (2007).

§ 19.2-266. Exclusion of persons from trial; photographs and broadcasting permitted under designated guidelines; exceptions.

In the trial of all criminal cases, whether the same be felony or misdemeanor cases, the court may, in its discretion, exclude from the trial any persons whose presence would impair the conduct of a fair trial, provided that the right of the accused to a public trial shall not be violated.

A court may solely in its discretion permit the taking of photographs in the courtroom during the progress of judicial proceedings and the broadcasting of judicial proceedings by radio or television and the use of electronic or photographic means for the perpetuation of the record or parts thereof in criminal and in civil cases, but only in accordance with the rules set forth hereunder. In addition to such rules, the Supreme Court and the Court of Appeals shall have the authority to promulgate any other rules they deem necessary to govern electronic media and still photography coverage in their respective courts. The following rules shall serve as guidelines, and a violation of these rules may be punishable as contempt:

Coverage Allowed.

1. The presiding judge shall at all times have authority to prohibit, interrupt or terminate electronic media and still photography coverage of public judicial proceedings. The presiding judge shall advise the parties of such coverage in advance of the proceedings and shall allow the parties to object thereto. For good cause shown, the presiding judge may prohibit coverage in any case and may restrict coverage as he deems appropriate to meet the ends of justice.

2. Coverage of the following types of judicial proceedings shall be prohibited: adoption proceedings, juvenile proceedings, child custody proceedings, divorce proceedings, temporary and permanent spousal support proceedings, proceedings concerning sexual offenses, proceedings for the hearing of motions to suppress evidence, proceedings involving trade secrets, and in camera proceedings.

3. Coverage of the following categories of witnesses shall be prohibited: police informants, minors, undercover agents and victims and families of victims of sexual offenses.

4. Coverage of jurors shall be prohibited expressly at any stage of a judicial proceeding, including that portion of a proceeding during which a jury is selected. The judge shall inform all potential jurors at the beginning of the jury selection process of this prohibition.

5. To protect the attorney-client privilege and the right to counsel, there shall be no recording or broadcast of sound from such conferences which occur in a court facility between attorneys and their clients, between co-counsel of a client, between adverse counsel, or between counsel and the presiding judge held at the bench or in chambers.

Location of Equipment and Personnel.

1. The location of recording and camera equipment shall be strictly regulated so as not to be intrusive.

2. Media personnel shall not enter or leave the courtroom once the proceedings are in session except during a court recess or adjournment.

3. Electronic media equipment and still photography equipment shall not be taken into the courtroom or removed from the designated media area except at the following times:

a. Prior to the convening of proceedings;

b. During any luncheon recess;

c. During any court recess with the permission of the trial judge; and

d. After adjournment for the day of the proceedings.

Official Representatives of the Media.

The Virginia Association of Broadcasters and the Virginia Press Association may designate one person to represent the television media, one person to represent the radio broadcasters, and one person to represent still photographers in each jurisdiction in which electronic media and still photographic coverage is desired. The names of the persons so designated shall be forwarded to the chief judge of the court in the county or city in which coverage is desired so that arrangements can be made for the "pooling" of equipment and personnel. Such persons shall also be the only persons authorized to speak for the media to the presiding judge concerning the coverage of any judicial proceedings.

Equipment and Personnel.

1. No distracting lights or sounds shall be permitted.

2. Not more than two television cameras shall be permitted in any proceeding.

3. Not more than one still photographer, utilizing not more than two still cameras with not more than two lenses for each camera and related equipment for print purposes, shall be permitted in any proceeding.

4. Not more than one audio system for broadcast purposes shall be permitted in any proceeding. Audio pickup for all media purposes shall be accomplished with existing audio systems present in the court facility. If no technically suitable audio system exists in the court facility, microphones and related wiring essential for media purposes may be installed and maintained at media expense. The microphones and wiring must be unobtrusive and shall be located in places designated in advance of any proceeding by the chief judge of the court in which coverage is desired.

5. Any "pooling" arrangements among the media required by these limitations on equipment and personnel shall be the sole responsibility of the media without calling upon the presiding judge to mediate any dispute as to the appropriate media representative or equipment authorized to cover a particular proceeding. In the absence of advance media agreement on disputed equipment or personnel issues, the presiding judge may exclude all contesting media personnel from a proceeding.

6. In no event shall the number of personnel in the designated area exceed the number necessary to operate the designated equipment.

7. Only television photographic and audio equipment which does not produce distracting sound or light shall be employed to cover judicial proceedings. No artificial lighting device of any kind shall be employed in connection with the television camera.

8. Only still camera equipment which does not produce distracting sound or light shall be employed to cover judicial proceedings. No artificial lighting device of any kind shall be employed in connection with a still camera.

9. With the concurrence of the chief judge of the court in which coverage is desired, modifications and additions may be made in light sources existing in the facility, provided such modifications or additions are installed and maintained without public expense.

Impermissible Use of Media Material.

None of the film, video tape, still photographs or audio reproductions developed during or by virtue of coverage of a judicial proceeding shall be admissible as evidence (i) in the proceeding out of which it arose, (ii) in any proceeding subsequent and collateral thereto, or (iii) upon any retrial or appeal of such proceedings.

All electronic media and still photography coverage of public judicial proceedings authorized by this section, with the exception of electronic or photographic means authorized for the perpetuation of the record or parts thereof shall be conducted at no cost to the Commonwealth.

History.
Code 1950, § 19.1-246; 1960, c. 366; 1971, Ex. Sess., c. 28; 1975, c. 495; 1978, c. 477; 1987, c. 580; 1989, c. 582; 1990, c. 243; 1992, c. 557.

Cross references.
As to exclusion of witnesses in civil cases, see § 8.01-375.

Law Review.
For survey of Virginia statutory changes in substantive criminal law for the year 1970-1971, see 57 Va. L. Rev. 1467 (1971). For survey of Virginia law on criminal law for the year 1971-1972, see 58 Va. L. Rev. 1206 (1972). For comment on the fair trial-free press controversy, see 11 U. Rich. L. Rev. 177 (1976). For survey of Virginia law on evidence for the year 1977-1978, see 64 Va. L. Rev. 1451 (1978). For note on public access to criminal trials, see 15 U. Rich. L. Rev. 741 (1981). For comment on the prejudicial effects of cameras in the courtroom, see 16 U. Rich. L. Rev. 867 (1982). For 1987 survey of Virginia criminal procedure, see 21 U. Rich. L. Rev. 727 (1987). For article, "Cameras in Virginia Courtrooms," see 26 U. Rich. L. Rev. 921 (1992). For article, "Dancing in the Courthouse": The First Amendment Right of Access Opens a New Round, see 29 U. Rich. L. Rev. 237 (1995).

Michie's Jurisprudence.
For related discussion, see 5B M.J. Criminal Procedure, § 38; 19 M.J. Trial, §§ 1, 3; 20 M.J. Witnesses, § 35.

CASE NOTES

Constitutionality. — This section, permitting the closure by the court of a criminal trial to the public and press, upon the unobjected-to request of the defendant, without requiring the court to make specific findings as to whether alternative solutions would have met the need to ensure fairness and without the specific finding of an overriding interest, violates the right of the public and press to attend criminal trials implicit in the guarantees of the

First Amendment. Richmond Newspapers, Inc. v. Virginia, 448 U.S. 555, 100 S. Ct. 2814, 65 L. Ed. 2d 973 (1980).

This section, if properly applied in the context of a pretrial suppression hearing, is constitutional. Richmond Newspapers, Inc. v. Commonwealth, 222 Va. 574, 281 S.E.2d 915 (1981).

Neither this section nor Rule 1:14 violates the equal protection clause of the Constitution of the United States. Diehl v. Commonwealth, 9 Va. App. 191, 385 S.E.2d 228 (1989).

This section merely restates certain inherent powers of a trial court. A court must have the power and authority to remove persons from the courtroom who are causing a disturbance or are otherwise disrupting the orderly conduct of a trial, and a judge is vested with such discretion absent the provisions of this section. Richmond Newspapers, Inc. v. Commonwealth, 222 Va. 574, 281 S.E.2d 915 (1981).

Section applies primarily to spectators. — Although the word "persons" may include witnesses, the court has read this section to apply primarily to spectators. Johnson v. Commonwealth, 217 Va. 682, 232 S.E.2d 741 (1977), decided under this section and former § 8-211.1 before the enactment of Title 8.01. See § 8.01-375 and the note thereto.

A **"public trial"** is a trial which is not limited or restricted to any particular class of the community, but is open to the observation of all. Cumbee v. Commonwealth, 219 Va. 1132, 254 S.E.2d 112 (1979).

Classes of excludable persons not particularized. — The Supreme Court has not particularized those classes of persons who may properly be excluded without impairing the nature of a public trial either from a constitutional standpoint or under this section. Cumbee v. Commonwealth, 219 Va. 1132, 254 S.E.2d 112 (1979).

Much must be left to the discretion of the court in excluding from the courtroom extraneous influences on the trial of a criminal case. Doyle v. Commonwealth, 100 Va. 808, 40 S.E. 925 (1902).

Limits of judge's discretion. — In exercising his discretion under this section, the trial judge must not act arbitrarily nor violate or abridge guaranteed constitutional rights. Richmond Newspapers, Inc. v. Commonwealth, 222 Va. 574, 281 S.E.2d 915 (1981).

The separation of witnesses in the trial of a case is not grantable as a matter of right. It is a matter which lies within the sound discretion of the court, subject to review and reversal upon a showing of abuse of discretion or prejudice resulting therefrom. The particular facts in each case must be considered in determining whether the court abused its authority in that case. Huffman v. Commonwealth, 185 Va. 524, 39 S.E.2d 291 (1946); Near v. Commonwealth, 202 Va. 20, 116 S.E.2d 85 (1960), cert. denied, 365 U.S. 873, 81 S. Ct. 907, 5 L. Ed. 2d 862 (1961), 369 U.S. 862, 82 S. Ct. 951, 8 L. Ed. 2d 19 (1962).

Neither the accused nor the Commonwealth, as a matter of right, is entitled to have the witnesses separated, as this is a matter within the sound discretion of the court, subject to review and reversal upon a showing of abuse of discretion or prejudice resulting therefrom. Yorke v. Commonwealth, 212 Va. 776, 188 S.E.2d 77 (1972).

The better practice is to grant a motion for exclusion when it is seasonably made in good faith in the absence of some showing of a good reason for its denial. Yorke v. Commonwealth, 212 Va. 776, 188 S.E.2d 77 (1972).

No reversal unless record discloses abuse of discretion. — As both the common law and this section give the trial court discretion in the matter, the Supreme Court will not reverse its ruling unless the record discloses an abuse of that discretion. Burford v. Commonwealth, 179 Va. 752, 20 S.E.2d 509 (1942); Hampton v. Commonwealth, 190 Va. 531, 58 S.E.2d 288, cert. denied, 339 U.S. 989, 70 S. Ct. 1013, 94 L. Ed. 1390 (1950), 340 U.S. 914, 71 S. Ct. 286, 95 L. Ed. 660 (1951); Campbell v. Commonwealth, 194 Va. 825, 75 S.E.2d 468 (1953).

No reversal where record failed to show actual prejudice. — Defendant's four capital murder convictions, and conviction for use of a firearm in the commission of murder, were not reversed, despite his contention that he was deprived of a fair trial when the trial court allowed spectators in the courtroom to wear badges displaying photographs of the victims, where the court took active steps to ensure that the jurors were not negatively influenced by the spectators, including segregating the jurors from persons in the hallways and elevators, and by excluding the victim's family

members, many of whom were wearing the badges, from the front row of the gallery, and there were always some people seated in the front row between the spectators wearing the badges and the jury. Cooper v. Commonwealth, No. 0819-03-4, 2004 Va. App. LEXIS 403 (Ct. of Appeals Aug. 24, 2004).

Failure to exclude certain witnesses held not error. — Failure of the court upon motion by defendant to exclude the sheriff and one of his deputies as well as another witness was not error where the Commonwealth's case would have been complete even if the sheriff and deputy had not testified, and where the testimony of the other witness was harmless. Near v. Commonwealth, 202 Va. 20, 116 S.E.2d 85 (1960), cert. denied, 365 U.S. 873, 81 S. Ct. 907, 5 L. Ed. 2d 862 (1961), 369 U.S. 862, 82 S. Ct. 951, 8 L. Ed. 2d 19 (1962).

Pretrial suppression hearings should be open absent overriding interest. — Absent an overriding interest articulated in findings, pretrial suppression hearings should be open to the public. This holding is mandated by Va. Const., Art. I, § 12. Richmond Newspapers, Inc. v. Commonwealth, 222 Va. 574, 281 S.E.2d 915 (1981).

Closure of hearing justified when fair trial jeopardized. — An "overriding interest" exists to justify closure of a pretrial suppression hearing when a fair trial for the defendant is likely to be jeopardized by an open pretrial hearing. Richmond Newspapers, Inc. v. Commonwealth, 222 Va. 574, 281 S.E.2d 915 (1981).

Alternatives must be considered before closure employed. — Before closing a pretrial suppression hearing to the public, the trial court should consider whether there are alternatives available which would eliminate the likelihood of prejudice to the accused. While there are fewer alternatives available at pretrial than at trial, they should be explored before closure is employed. Richmond Newspapers, Inc. v. Commonwealth, 222 Va. 574, 281 S.E.2d 915 (1981).

Only part of hearing should be closed where possible. — When it is not possible to hold the entire pretrial suppression hearing in public, only that portion that would be prejudicial should be closed. Richmond Newspapers, Inc. v. Commonwealth, 222 Va. 574, 281 S.E.2d 915 (1981).

Right of public to be heard on closure issue. — Before a pretrial suppression hearing is closed, interested members of the public should have the right to be heard, with the assistance of counsel if desired. Richmond Newspapers, Inc. v. Commonwealth, 222 Va. 574, 281 S.E.2d 915 (1981).

Notice to public of closure motion. — For intervention to take place, the public must have notice of the closure motion. For this reason, motions to close a pretrial suppression hearing should be made in writing and filed with the court before the day of the hearing involved, and the public must be given reasonable notice that a closure hearing will be conducted. Richmond Newspapers, Inc. v. Commonwealth, 222 Va. 574, 281 S.E.2d 915 (1981).

Receipt of information in camera at closure hearing. — There is the danger that the information sought be kept from the public will be disclosed in the hearing on closure, thereby negating the purpose of closure. To protect against this, the trial court may hear or observe this information in camera in order to establish to what extent its release would be prejudicial to the defendant. Richmond Newspapers, Inc. v. Commonwealth, 222 Va. 574, 281 S.E.2d 915 (1981).

Burden at closure hearing. — At the hearing on closure of a pretrial suppression hearing, the burden will be on the moving party to show that an open hearing would jeopardize the defendant's right to a fair trial. The intervenors, however, shall have the burden of showing that reasonable alternatives to closure are available. Richmond Newspapers, Inc. v. Commonwealth, 222 Va. 574, 281 S.E.2d 915 (1981).

Cameras were allowed in the courtroom since the record failed to demonstrate good cause; the only evidence presented by defendant was the testimony of one experienced trial attorney who opined that permitting cameras in court to document the proceedings may have an adverse effect upon the interest of a defendant, and he offered no proof to support his opinion. Diehl v. Commonwealth, 9 Va. App. 191, 385 S.E.2d 228 (1989).

Defendant's constitutional right to a public trial was abridged where at the beginning of his incest case and before the first witness, the prosecutor moved to remove spectators at least while the victim was testifying, and in granting the motion, the trial court stated that the courtroom was to be cleared in view of the type of case, and thereafter and for the remainder of the trial, all persons except the actual participants in the proceedings were barred from the courtroom. Cumbee v. Commonwealth, 219 Va. 1132, 254 S.E.2d 112 (1979).

For a case involving former D.R. 7-107, Trial Publicity (see now Rule 3.6 of the Rules of Professional Conduct), see Hirschkop v. Virginia State Bar, 421 F. Supp. 1137 (E.D. Va. 1976), aff'd in part and rev'd in part, 594 F.2d 356 (4th Cir. 1979).

Applied in Brown v. City of Danville, 44 Va. App. 586, 606 S.E.2d 523, 2004 Va. App. LEXIS 627 (2004).

§ 19.2-266.1. Conviction of lesser offense on indictment for homicide.

In any trial upon an indictment charging homicide, the jury or the court may find the accused not guilty of the specific offense charged in the indictment, but guilty of any degree of homicide supported by the evidence for which a lesser punishment is provided by law.

History.
1975, c. 495.

Michie's Jurisprudence.
For related discussion, see 5B M.J. Criminal Procedure, §§ 11, 62, 70.

CASE NOTES

Either party may request lesser-included offense instruction. — This section does not limit the offering of lesser-included instructions to the accused; the Commonwealth may request an instruction on a lesser-included offense, and the trial court may grant such instruction, over the objection of the defense, as long as the evidence supports such an instruction. Craig v. Commonwealth, 34 Va. App. 155, 538 S.E.2d 355, 2000 Va. App. LEXIS 837 (2000).

§ 19.2-266.2. Defense objections to be raised before trial; hearing; bill of particulars.

A. Defense motions or objections seeking (i) suppression of evidence on the grounds such evidence was obtained in violation of the provisions of the Fourth, Fifth or Sixth Amendments to the Constitution of the United States or Article I, Section 8, 10 or 11 of the Constitution of Virginia proscribing illegal searches and seizures and protecting rights against self-incrimination; (ii) dismissal of a warrant, information, or indictment or any count or charge thereof on the ground that: (a) the defendant would be deprived of a speedy trial in violation of the provisions of the Sixth Amendment to the Constitution of the United States, Article I, Section 8 of the Constitution of Virginia, or § 19.2-243; or (b) the defendant would be twice placed in jeopardy in violation of the provisions of the Fifth Amendment to the Constitution of the United States or Article I, Section 8 of the Constitution of Virginia; or (iii) dismissal of a warrant, information, or indictment or any count or charge thereof on the ground that a statute upon which it was based is unconstitutional shall be raised by motion or objection.

B. Such a motion or objection in a proceeding in circuit court shall be raised in writing, before trial. The motions or objections shall be filed and notice given to opposing counsel not later than seven days before trial in circuit court or, if made under clause (ii) of subsection A, at such time prior to trial in circuit court as the grounds for the motion or objection shall arise, whichever occurs last. A hearing on all such motions or objections shall be held not later than three days prior to trial in circuit court, unless such period is waived by the accused, as set by the trial judge. The circuit court may, however, for good cause shown and in the interest of justice, permit the motions or objections to be raised at a later time.

C. To assist the defense in filing such motions or objections in a timely manner, the circuit court shall, upon motion of the defendant, direct the Commonwealth to file a bill of particulars pursuant to § 19.2-230. The circuit court shall fix the time within which such bill of particulars is to be filed. Upon further motion of the defendant, the circuit court may, upon a showing of good cause, direct the Commonwealth to supplement its bill of particulars. The attorney for the Commonwealth shall certify that the matters stated in the bill of particulars are true and accurate to the best of his knowledge and belief.

D. In a criminal proceeding in district court, any motion or objection as described in subsection A may be raised prior to or at such proceeding. In the event such a motion or objection is raised, the district court shall, upon motion of the Commonwealth grant a continuance for good cause shown.

History.
1987, c. 710; 2005, cc. 622, 694; 2006, cc. 578, 862.

Editor's note.
The section above was recodified at the direction of the Virginia Code Commission. It was formerly codified at § 19.2-399.

Law Review.
For 2006 survey article, "Criminal Law and Procedure," see 41 U. Rich. L. Rev. 83 (2006).

Michie's Jurisprudence.
For related discussion, see 7B M.J. Evidence, § 56.

CASE NOTES

This statute operates to require a court to order a bill of particulars only where the defendant seeks: (1) suppression of evidence as violative of search and seizure or self-incrimination protections, or (2) dismissal of an indictment on the ground that the statute on which it was based is unconstitutional; where a defendant does not allege any grounds to bring this section into play and makes constitutional claims that relate only to the non-specificity of the indictment, this section does not require the court to order a bill of particulars. Sims v. Commonwealth, 28 Va. App. 611, 507 S.E.2d 648 (1998).

Waiver of written motion requirement found. — Trial judge's decision to rule on the substantive merits of defendant's objection at trial to admission of hospital bed statement effectively waived the requirement that a written motion be made in advance. Accordingly, defendant's objection to admission of his statement may be considered on appeal. Wheaton v. Commonwealth, No. 1409-95-2 (Ct. of Appeals Apr. 22, 1997).

Failure to raise objections before trial. — Trial court did not err in refusing to consider defendant's untimely motion to suppress, because defendant neither complied with pretrial filing requirements of this section, nor made any showing as to what "good cause" existed for his not having motion timely heard pretrial, or why "in the interest of justice" it was necessary to hear his motion at trial. Graves v. Commonwealth, No. 1316-98-3 (Ct. of Appeals June 29, 1999).

Defendant's argument that the statute he was prosecuted under was unconstitutional was not properly presented to the trial court in the manner prescribed by statute, and, as a result, the argument was not preserved for appeal. Johnson v. Commonwealth, 37 Va. App. 634, 561 S.E.2d 1, 2002 Va. App. LEXIS 160 (2002).

In defendant's possession of a firearm conviction, the trial court did not err in admitting defendant's statements to police that he picked up the firearm in an alley, as defendant's failure to file a motion to suppress did not meet the notice requirements of § 19.2-266.2 and therefore, defendant waived the argument on appeal. Greene v. Commonwealth, No. 3343-01-2, 2002 Va. App. LEXIS 717 (Ct. of Appeals Dec. 3, 2002).

Inmate was not entitled to habeas corpus relief on his claim that his rights under the Fifth and Sixth Amendments were violated when the Commonwealth was permitted to introduce during sentencing a tape recording between the inmate and an informant during which the inmate confessed to the bank robbery and murder because the inmate waived any such objection by failing to file a timely pretrial suppression motion. Schmitt v. True, 387 F. Supp. 2d 622, 2005 U.S. Dist. LEXIS 20335 (E.D. Va. 2005).

Appellate court declined to address the merits of defendant's claim that the trial court erred in refusing to suppress the cocaine discovered on defendant's person during a search, because § 19.2-266.2 provided the trial court with "a freestanding basis" for denying defendant's motion and defendant did not argue that defendant was misled by the Commonwealth or its witnesses or otherwise prevented by the Commonwealth from discovering relevant facts. Womack v. Commonwealth, 2009 Va. App. LEXIS 257 (June 9, 2009).

Objection must be raised in writing before trial. — Because the plain language of § 19.2-266.2 requires without exception that defense motions or objections seeking dismissal of an indictment on the ground that the defendant would be twice placed in jeopardy in violation of the provisions of the Fifth Amendment to the Constitution of the United States or Va. Const., Art. I, § 8, be raised in writing before trial, a defendant must raise such an objection in writing before trial to preserve his or her objection, even if the trial court may be incapable of ruling on the motion until after the defendant is convicted and sentenced. Williams v. Commonwealth, 57 Va. App. 750, 706 S.E.2d 530, 2011 Va. App. LEXIS 96 (2011).

Defendant waived his objection that double jeopardy barred his multiple convictions for violations of § 20-61 because defendant failed to raise his double jeopardy objection in writing before trial, as required by § 19.2-266.2; defendant did not argue that the good cause or ends of justice exception to § 19.2-266.2 had to be invoked. Williams v. Commonwealth, 57 Va. App. 750, 706 S.E.2d 530, 2011 Va. App. LEXIS 96 (2011).

Failure to file motion to suppress waived constitutional challenge. — Defendant waived his claim that evidence introduced in his trial was unconstitutionally seized because he failed to file a pretrial motion to suppress the evidence; further, defendant failed to object to the admissibility of the evidence at trial, and thus his claim was unpreserved for appeal pursuant to Va. Sup. Ct. R. 5A:18. Arrington v. Commonwealth, 53 Va. App. 635, 674 S.E.2d 554, 2009 Va. App. LEXIS 146 (2009).

Failure to give prior notice of constitutional challenge. — In a charge of DUI as a second offense, the trial court properly refused to consider defendant's constitutional challenge to the local code section relating to the prior DUI, Newport News, Va., City Code § 26-72, because defendant failed to give notice of his intent to challenge the local code section's constitutionality as required by § 19.2-266.2, and failed to show good cause for that failure. Artis v. Commonwealth, 2008 Va. App. LEXIS 502 (Nov. 12, 2008).

Failure to raise argument until closing argument. — Defendant's failure to comply with the statutory requirements of § 19.2-266.2 barred his raising an issue as to his consent to a search of his car and motel room on appeal; defendant filed no pretrial motions contesting the validity of his consent, made no objection during the Commonwealth's case to the admissibility of the drugs or the search of the car or the motel room, made a motion

to strike only based on the sufficiency of the evidence on a conspiracy charge, and did not raise the consent issue until closing argument. Wilson v. Commonwealth, No. 0433-02-2, 2002 Va. App. LEXIS 735 (Ct. of Appeals Dec. 10, 2002).

Reliability of informant. — Any lack of detail in the informant's stated basis of knowledge as to defendant's predicted criminal activity was compensated for by the informant's history of reliability, where the informant had a record of providing reliable information to the police for almost two years and leading to the arrest of more than 50 people and informed the police that he was watching defendant bring heroin to the subject of a search warrant; thus, defendant was not entitled to have the evidence suppressed. Beuns v. Commonwealth, — Va. App. —, — S.E.2d —, 2008 Va. App. LEXIS 206 (Apr. 29, 2008).

Although a search warrant was facially valid, given the informant's motive to lie and the absence of evidence corroborating his allegations or establishing his reliability in some other way, probable cause was lacking; therefore, defendant's motion to suppress was properly granted. Commonwealth v. Thomas, 2011 Va. App. LEXIS 267 (Aug. 16, 2011).

Motions to suppress evidence. — Trial court did not err in denying defendant's motions to suppress evidence regarding the detention of defendant or the single-photograph identification of defendant, as the detention of defendant in a nearby park a short time after a woman was attacked was justified and the identification of defendant after the woman was attacked and a witness observed defendant at the scene of the attack was not unduly suggestive. Blevins v. Commonwealth, 40 Va. App. 412, 579 S.E.2d 658, 2003 Va. App. LEXIS 254 (2003).

Where defendant was charged with possession of heroin and cocaine with intent to distribute, both seized from his person during a warrantless arrest, the trial court refused to hear his untimely motion to suppress pursuant to § 19.2-266.2; because defendant failed to request a pretrial hearing on his motion to suppress as required by § 19.2-266.2, he waived his right to challenge his arrest on appeal. Moody v. Commonwealth, No. 3183-02-1, 2003 Va. App. LEXIS 624 (Ct. of Appeals Dec. 9, 2003).

Where defendant wishes to file a motion to suppression evidence after the statutory deadline, if the argument is not presented to the trial court in the manner set forth in § 19.2-266.2, then defendant has not preserved it for appeal. Moody v. Commonwealth, No. 3183-02-1, 2003 Va. App. LEXIS 624 (Ct. of Appeals Dec. 9, 2003).

Denial of defendant's motion to suppress was upheld since defendant, a juvenile, was not in custody when the associate principal questioned him because the associate principal was not a law-enforcement officer or state officer acting in that capacity, thus, Miranda warning was not required; in addition, the associate principal did not threaten defendant with disciplinary action if he remained silent or refused to cooperate indicating the statement was voluntarily made. J.D. v. Commonwealth, 42 Va. App. 329, 591 S.E.2d 721, 2004 Va. App. LEXIS 31 (2004).

Trial court erred in granting defendant's motion to suppress evidence seized in an investigatory stop and consent to search, as the police officer who stopped defendant's car had observed an air freshener hanging from the rear view mirror and determined that it was so big as to constitute a possible obstruction to the driver's view, which was a violation of § 46.2-1054; pursuant to a review of the officer's investigatory stop, the trial court should have merely determined whether the officer, under the totality of the circumstances, had a reasonable and articulable belief that the freshener could have constituted a violation of § 46.2-1054, not whether it in fact was such an obstruction, as that was an inquiry for the trial court or jury. Commonwealth v. Bryant, No. 0076-04-1, 2004 Va. App. LEXIS 283 (Ct. of Appeals June 15, 2004).

Trial court erred in denying defendant's motion to suppress evidence, as the police did not have probable cause to arrest defendant and, thus, their search of him that revealed a toy gun in his pocket also was not supported by the necessary probable cause; accordingly, his subsequent confessions at the police station to two burglaries should have been suppressed. Hardin v. Commonwealth, No. 0690-03-1, 2004 Va. App. LEXIS 319 (Ct. of Appeals July 6, 2004).

Although a state trooper told defendant that defendant was not under arrest, defendant's hands were in handcuffs and defendant was placed in a locked patrol car; therefore, because the trooper was required to give Miranda warnings before questioning defendant, the trial court erred in denying defendant's motion to suppress. Dixon v. Commonwealth, 270 Va. 34, 613 S.E.2d 398, 2005 Va. LEXIS 54 (2005).

Because an informant's identification, coupled with the police officers' corroboration, provided probable cause to approach a vehicle, and because cocaine was in plain view on defendant's lap in the passenger seat, there was probable cause to arrest defendant for possession of cocaine; therefore, the trial court properly denied defendant's motion to suppress. Turner v. Commonwealth, — Va. App. —, — S.E.2d —, 2006 Va. App. LEXIS 314 (July 18, 2006).

Because defendant's foot was partially outside of defendant's right shoe, the shoelaces were untied, and there was a bulge under defendant's foot that prevented the foot from completely fitting the shoe, a police officer's belief that defendant possessed a weapon in the shoe was reasonable and did not violate the Fourth Amendment; therefore, the trial court properly denied defendant's motion to suppress. Ford v. Commonwealth, — Va. App. —, — S.E.2d —, 2006 Va. App. LEXIS 316 (July 18, 2006).

Because defendant's post-entry assaults on police officers were outside the scope of the exclusionary rule, and because police officers had probable cause under § 19.2-81 to make a warrantless arrest for public intoxication, the Fourth Amendment was irrelevant; since defendant had no right to resist the arrest, defendant's motion to suppress was properly denied and defendant was properly convicted of assault and battery on a police officer and obstruction of justice. Messier v. Commonwealth, 2007 Va. App. LEXIS 201 (May 15, 2007).

Although a police officer lawfully stopped a truck in which defendant was a passenger, the police officer had no reasonable belief that defendant was involved in criminal activity; therefore, because there was conflicting evidence as to whether defendant consented to a search of defendant's person, the trial court properly granted defendant's suppression motion. Commonwealth v. Swift, 2008 Va. App. LEXIS 457 (Oct. 14, 2008).

Because a police officer, responding to a "shots-fired" call, had reasonable cause to stop a vehicle in which defendant was a passenger that made a wide turn, and based on the officer's knowledge of defendant's history with guns and defendant's bending movements as the vehicle passed the officer, the trial court erred in granting defendant's motion to suppress. Commonwealth v. Calloway, 2009 Va. App. LEXIS 343 (Aug. 4, 2009).

Because the police possessed reasonable suspicion to suspect that defendant was wanted by the police when they detained defendant, they were justified in stopping defendant's vehicle and detaining defendant to confirm defendant's identity; consequently, the trial court did not err in denying defendant's motion to suppress evidence found during a subsequent search. Sidney v. Commonwealth, 2009 Va. App. LEXIS 600 (Aug. 19, 2009).

While the trial court properly found that the information possessed by a police officer was sufficient for probable cause to arrest, it erred in holding that a formal arrest had to precede the search of defendant's person; accordingly, the trial court erred in granting defendant's motion to suppress. Commonwealth v. Turner, 2011 Va. App. LEXIS 87 (Mar. 8, 2011).

Because the stop of defendant's vehicle was based on suspicion that defendant possessed drugs, a 15-minute detention to check defendant's license and registration and obtain a dog to sniff the vehicle did not violate the Fourth Amendment; therefore, defendant's motion to suppress was properly denied. Mitchell v. Commonwealth, 2011 Va. App. LEXIS 287 (Sept. 27, 2011).

Defendant's due process rights were not violated and the trial court did not err by denying defendant's motion to suppress the victim's identification of defendant from a photo array because a police officer's statement that the suspect was in the array did not make it impermissibly suggestive, and defendant's elongated photo did not create a very substantial likelihood of irreparable misidentification. Smith v. Commonwealth, 61 Va. App. 112, 733 S.E.2d 683, 2012 Va. App. LEXIS 348 (2012).

Trial court correctly denied defendant's motion to suppress because a deputy's stop of defendant's vehicle was based on a reasonable, articulable suspicion that the vehicle had defective brake lights, in violation of §§ 46.2-1002 and 46.2-1003. Otey v. Commonwealth, 61 Va. App. 346, 735 S.E.2d 255, 2012 Va. App. LEXIS 421 (2012).

Motion not timely. — In failing to comply with § 19.2-266.2, defendant waived the opportunity to pursue defendant's constitu-

tional claim. Accordingly, there was no abuse of discretion in the denial of defendant's motion to suppress on the ground that the motion was not timely filed. Cooke v. Commonwealth, — Va. App. —, — S.E.2d —, 2008 Va. App. LEXIS 208 (Apr. 29, 2008).

"Good cause" for failure to raise issue prior to trial not found. — Defendant failed to establish that defendant had "good cause" for the failure to argue, before trial, a motion to suppress based on failure to be informed of defendant's Miranda rights, where defendant, as the person to whom the rights were read and of whom questions were asked, was in the best position to know whether to raise such an issue in a motion to suppress. Naar v. Commonwealth, 2009 Va. App. LEXIS 166 (Apr. 14, 2009).

Motion to suppress defendant's statement properly denied. — Because defendant's statement was given in a noncustodial setting, Miranda warnings were administered to him out of an abundance of caution, and law enforcement did not apply any coercive tactics or take advantage of defendant's disability in order to obtain a statement, said statement was properly admitted. Smith v. Commonwealth, — Va. App. —, — S.E.2d —, 2008 Va. App. LEXIS 27 (Jan. 15, 2008).

Trial court's judgment denying motion to suppress affirmed on other grounds. — Police had probable cause to arrest defendant after a person told them defendant tried to sell property that was reported stolen, and although the appellate court found that the trial court's reason for denying defendant's motion to suppress evidence was erroneous, it affirmed the trial court's judgment because police could have arrested defendant and conducted a search incident to arrest. Williams v. Commonwealth, No. 2854-01-1, 2003 Va. App. LEXIS 294 (Ct. of Appeals May 13, 2003).

Trial court erred in denying defendant's motion to suppress since the pat-down search of defendant exceeded the reasonable measures needed to assure officer safety; none of the four police officers who responded to a report that a group of black males were smoking marijuana at a street corner had a reasonable belief that defendant, a member of the group, was armed and dangerous, and, thus, the resulting pat-down search of him after an officer found a gun on another member of the group was not justified. El-Amin v. Commonwealth, No. 1472-02-2, 2003 Va. App. LEXIS 315 (Ct. of Appeals May 27, 2003).

Commonwealth's right to appeal from the suppression of evidence. — Procedure set forth in § 19.2-266.2 for suppression motions is directly related to the provisions of § 19.2-398, the Commonwealth's right to appeal evidence excluded as a result of a suppression hearing; the Commonwealth would be prejudiced by allowing a defendant to disregard, without good cause, the dictates of § 19.2-266.2. Wilson v. Commonwealth, No. 0433-02-2, 2002 Va. App. LEXIS 735 (Ct. of Appeals Dec. 10, 2002).

Counsel's strategic decision not ineffective although cause of habeas procedural default. — Federal district court properly denied a state death row inmate's habeas corpus petition because defense counsel were not ineffective under the Sixth Amendment for failing to move to suppress a taped conversation between the inmate and a Commonwealth witness, which contained both incriminating statements and statements that supported the inmate's claim that he fatally shot a security guard unintentionally, at least seven days before trial as required by § 19.2-266.2; although the claim was procedurally defaulted under state law because defense counsel did not comply with § 19.2-266.2 and could not, therefore, be reviewed by the federal habeas court, the default was the result of counsels' strategic, albeit unsuccessful, gamble that the Commonwealth would move to admit the tape during the guilt phase of trial, rather than wait until the penalty phase, which is what occurred. Schmitt v. Kelly, — F.3d —, 2006 U.S. App. LEXIS 17658 (4th Cir. July 13, 2006).

Failure to raise double jeopardy issue. — Court of appeals declined to address defendant's claim that § 19.2-266.2 did not bar his double jeopardy argument due to the Commonwealth's failure to raise the lack of compliance with § 19.2-266.2 before the trial court because defendant provided no principles of law or authority to support his argument that the Commonwealth's failure barred it from relying on § 19.2-266.2 on appeal. Williams v. Commonwealth, 57 Va. App. 750, 706 S.E.2d 530, 2011 Va. App. LEXIS 96 (2011).

Applied in Upchurch v. Commonwealth, 31 Va. App. 48, 521 S.E.2d 290 (1999); Schmitt v. Commonwealth, 262 Va. 127, 547 S.E.2d 186, 2001 Va. LEXIS 85 (2001); Morrison v. Commonwealth,

37 Va. App. 273, 557 S.E.2d 724, 2002 Va. App. LEXIS 1 (2002); Brooks v. Commonwealth, 49 Va. App. 155, 638 S.E.2d 131, 2006 Va. App. LEXIS 574 (2006); McGhee v. Commonwealth, 280 Va. 620, 701 S.E.2d 58, 2010 Va. LEXIS 260 (2010).

CIRCUIT COURT OPINIONS

Commonwealth not required to identify components of aggravating factor. — Where the Commonwealth intended to prove "vileness" as an aggravating factor in support of the death penalty, it was not required to identify the components of the vileness factor on which it intended to offer evidence because the indictment, the discovery responses, and defendant's opportunity to hear the evidence presented at the preliminary hearing adequately informed him of the charged offense. Commonwealth v. Waddler, 65 Va. Cir. 418, 2004 Va. Cir. LEXIS 296 (Portsmouth 2004).

Inevitable discovery. — Because a police officer's initial confrontation with defendant was a proper Fourth Amendment *Terry* stop and the contraband in defendant's pocket would have inevitably been discovered as the result of a search incident to arrest, defendant's motion to suppress was denied. Commonwealth v. Webster, 68 Va. Cir. 430, 2005 Va. Cir. LEXIS 249 (Roanoke County Aug. 25, 2005).

Miranda warnings not given. — Because defendants were handcuffed for over an hour and not free to leave in spite of a statement by the police to the contrary, they were entitled to Miranda warnings about their right to remain silent and the right to counsel; because the warnings were not given, defendants' motions to suppress were granted. Commonwealth v. Hughes, 69 Va. Cir. 482, 2006 Va. Cir. LEXIS 85 (Martinsville 2006).

Motion for bill of particulars granted. — Defendant filed a motion for a bill of particulars under subsection C of § 19.2-266.2, seeking information about searches or seizures that might have affected his rights under U.S. Const., Amend. IV; and statements he allegedly made that might affect his rights under U.S. Const., Amends. V and VI. He was entitled to this information because it related to his rights against self-incrimination and illegal searches and seizures, which were specifically referred to in subsection A of § 19.2-266.2. Commonwealth v. Kuhne, 80 Va. Cir. 299, 2010 Va. Cir. LEXIS 49 (Fairfax County Apr. 22, 2010).

Motion for bill of particulars denied. — Defendant filed a motion for a bill of particulars under subsection C of § 19.2-266.2, seeking information regarding hearsay statements the prosecution might seek to introduce that might implicate his right of confrontation, and statements allegedly made at any identification procedure that might affect his rights under U.S. Const., Amends. V and VI. As the right to confrontation was not listed in subsection A of § 19.2-266.2, and as his U.S. Const., Amend V rights were not implicated by the indentification procedure, he was not entitled to the requested information. Commonwealth v. Kuhne, 80 Va. Cir. 299, 2010 Va. Cir. LEXIS 49 (Fairfax County Apr. 22, 2010).

OPINIONS OF THE ATTORNEY GENERAL

Applicability in district courts. — This section applies only to proceedings in circuit courts and not to proceedings in district courts. See opinion of Attorney General to Delegate Robert Hurt, 05-016 (5/17/05).

§ 19.2-266.3. Continuances; appearances of parties.

When the court grants a continuance in advance of the date of a scheduled trial or hearing, if the defendant acknowledges in writing, on a form provided by the Office of the Executive Secretary of the Supreme Court, that he promises to appear in court on the date and time of the newly scheduled trial or hearing, the court shall not require counsel or the defendant to appear on the date when the trial or hearing was originally scheduled. However, if the defendant is in violation of the terms of his pretrial release or has failed to appear at any court proceeding, the court may require the defendant to appear on the date when the trial or hearing was originally scheduled as a condition of any continuance granted.

History.
2013, c. 154.

CHAPTER 16.

EVIDENCE AND WITNESSES.

Article 1. In General.

ARTICLE 1.

IN GENERAL.

§ 19.2-267. Provisions applicable to witnesses in criminal as well as civil cases; obligation to attend; summons.

Sections 8.01-396.1, 8.01-402, 8.01-405, 8.01-407, and 8.01-408 to 8.01-410, inclusive, shall apply to a criminal as well as a civil case in all respects, except that a witness in a criminal case shall be obliged to attend, and may be proceeded against for failing to do so, although there may not previously have been any payment, or tender to him of anything for attendance, mileage, or tolls. In a criminal case a summons for a witness may be issued by the attorney for the Commonwealth or other attorney charged with the responsibility for the prosecution of a violation of any ordinance or by the attorney for the defendant; however, any attorney who issues such a summons shall, at the time of the issuance, file with the clerk of the court the names and addresses of such witnesses.

History.
Code 1950, § 19.1-262; 1960, c. 366; 1962, c. 374; 1975, c. 495; 1977, c. 624; 1991, c. 38; 1994, c. 543; 2007, c. 552; 2008, c. 124.

Cross references.
As to summons for witnesses in criminal cases, see also §§ 19.2-72 and 19.2-131. As to exclusion of witnesses in civil cases, see § 8.01-375.

The 2007 amendments.
The 2007 amendment by c. 552 inserted "or by the attorney for the defendant" following "ordinance" in the last sentence.

The 2008 amendments.
The 2008 amendment by c. 124 substituted "8.01-405, 8.01-407, and 8.01-408 to 8.01-410" for "8.01-405, and 8.01-407 to 8.01-410."

Law Review.
For annual survey of Virginia labor and employment law, see 40 U. Rich. L. Rev. 241 (2005). For 2007 annual survey article, "Criminal Law and Procedure," see 42 U. Rich. L. Rev. 311 (2007).

Michie's Jurisprudence.
For related discussion, see 5B M.J. Criminal Procedure, § 64.

CASE NOTES

Because such filing is a directory rather than a mandatory requirement, failure to file the names and addresses of such witnesses under this section with the clerk does not prevent the witnesses from being called to testify. Caccioppo v. Commonwealth, 20 Va. App. 534, 458 S.E.2d 592 (1995).

Where a defendant's substantive rights were not affected by the Commonwealth's failure to file the names and addresses of witnesses being summoned at the time of the issuance of the summonses, the trial court did not abuse its discretion in permitting the witnesses to testify. Abraham v. Commonwealth, 32 Va. App. 22, 526 S.E.2d 277 (2000).

Nothing in this section prohibits the witnesses summoned by the Commonwealth from testifying due to the Commonwealth's failure to file their names or addresses with the clerk; nor is there any suggestion in the statute that such a remedy was intended by the legislature. Abraham v. Commonwealth, 32 Va. App. 22, 526 S.E.2d 277 (2000).

In response to defendant's pretrial motion, the prosecutor proffered that her office had filed the returns of service for its witnesses and, thus, the names of its witnesses were available to defendant, despite defendant's suggestion that no evidence in the record supports the Commonwealth's assertion; the rule is well settled that a unilateral avowal of counsel, if unchallenged, constitutes a proper proffer. Maldonado v. Commonwealth, — Va. App. —, — S.E.2d —, 2006 Va. App. LEXIS 589 (Dec. 28, 2006).

Expert testimony admissible in criminal case. — Where a firearms expert's testimony was within her area of expertise, was not within the range of the jury's common experience, was relevant, and assisted the trier of fact in understanding the evidence, the trial court did not abuse its discretion in admitting this expert testimony under § 8.01-401.1. McCormick v. Commonwealth, No. 3058-01-2, 2003 Va. App. LEXIS 311 (Ct. of Appeals May 20, 2003).

§ 19.2-267.1. Authority of law-enforcement officer to issue summons to witness; failure to appear.

A summons may be issued by a law-enforcement officer during the course of his immediate investigation of an alleged misdemeanor for which an arrest warrant is not required pursuant to § 19.2-81 to any person he reasonably believes was a witness to the offense. The summons shall command the person to appear and testify at the trial of any criminal charge brought against any person as the result of the offense.

A summons issued pursuant to this section shall have the same force as if issued by the court. The failure of any person so summoned to appear after receiving written notice of the date, time and place of the trial at least five days prior to the trial shall be punishable as contempt of the court in accordance with § 18.2-456 (5).

History.
1983, c. 224.

§ 19.2-267.2. Response to subpoena for information stored in electronic format.

When a subpoena has been served pursuant to Rule 3A:12 of the Rules of the Supreme Court on a person who is not a party to the action requiring the production of information that is stored in an electronic format, the person shall produce a tangible copy of the information. If a tangible copy cannot be produced, the person shall permit the parties to review the information on a computer or by electronic means during normal business hours, provided that the information can be accessed and isolated. If a tangible copy cannot reasonably be produced and the information is commingled with information other than that requested in the subpoena and cannot reasonably be isolated, the person may file a motion for a protective order or motion to quash.

History.
2002, c. 764.

§ 19.2-268. Right of accused to testify.

In any case of felony or misdemeanor, the accused may be sworn and examined in his own behalf, and if so sworn and examined, he shall be deemed to have waived his privilege of not giving evidence against himself, and shall be subject to cross-examination as any other witness; but his failure to testify shall create no presumption against him, nor be the subject of any comment before the court or jury by the prosecuting attorney.

History.
Code 1950, § 19.1-264; 1960, c. 366; 1975, c. 495.

Cross references.
As to when statement by accused as a witness is not received in evidence, see § 19.2-270. As to testimony of husband and wife, see § 8.01-398 and §§ 19.1-271.1 and 19.2-271.2. As to right to refuse to testify, see Va. Const., Art. I, § 8. As to competency of interested party, see § 8.01-396.

Law Review.
For survey of Virginia criminal law for the year 1971-1972, see 58 Va. L. Rev. 1206 (1972). For note on the problem of partially silent defendants, see 69 Va. L. Rev. 155 (1983).

Michie's Jurisprudence.
For related discussion, see 2A M.J. Argument and Conduct of Counsel, §§ 9, 15; 4A M.J. Commonwealth's and State's Attorney, § 3; 5B M.J. Criminal Procedure, §§ 55, 59, 61; 7B M.J. Evidence, § 231; 20 M.J. Witnesses, §§ 5, 39, 81, 82.

CASE NOTES

I. In General.
II. Failure to Testify.

I. IN GENERAL.

History of section. — See Enoch v. Commonwealth, 141 Va. 411, 126 S.E. 222 (1925).

The object of this section was to afford the accused opportunity to testify or not, as his interest might dictate, and not to deprive him of his right to deny his guilt by plea and rest upon the legal presumption of innocence. Price v. Commonwealth, 77 Va. 393 (1883). See Blair v. Commonwealth, 166 Va. 715, 185 S.E. 900 (1936); Elliott v. Commonwealth, 172 Va. 595, 1 S.E.2d 273 (1939).

This section must be given a reasonable construction. Enoch v. Commonwealth, 141 Va. 411, 126 S.E. 222 (1925).

And should be liberally construed in favor of the accused, so as to give him the fullest right to testify in his own behalf, and that this right should not be any further impaired than the language of the statute necessarily requires. Enoch v. Commonwealth, 141 Va. 411, 126 S.E. 222 (1925).

When accused testifies he subjects himself to all the terms of this section. — This section permits the accused himself to testify, but to do so he must accept all of the terms of the section, and (1) "be deemed to have waived his privilege of not giving evidence against himself," and (2) "be subject to cross-examination as any other witness." The right to cross-examine him "as any other witness" implied the right to impeach his credibility by the same rules as those applicable to other witnesses. To discredit the witness, if there be reason to doubt his truthfulness, is one of the legitimate and leading objects of cross-examination. Smith v. Commonwealth, 136 Va. 773, 118 S.E. 107 (1923). See Watson v. Commonwealth, 87 Va. 608, 13 S.E. 22 (1891); Thaniel v. Commonwealth, 132 Va. 795, 111 S.E. 259 (1922); Smith v. Commonwealth, 182 Va. 585, 30 S.E.2d 26 (1944).

This section permits an accused to testify in his own behalf in any criminal proceeding, subject to cross-examination as any other witness. Powell v. Commonwealth, 13 Va. App. 17, 409 S.E.2d 622 (1991).

Once defendant in robbery trial testified on direct examination about his adversarial relationship with witness in an effort to discredit her testimony, Commonwealth could explore on cross examination additional matters relating to the case, even those that were beyond the scope of matters raised on direct examination. Drumgoole v. Commonwealth, 26 Va. App. 783, 497 S.E.2d 159 (1998).

And waives his rights under § 19.2-270. — Under § 19.2-270 no statement made by a witness upon a legal examination, unless made when examined as a witness in his own behalf, can be used as evidence against him. But where, under this section, a prisoner subsequently goes on the stand as a witness in his own behalf, he thereby waives the right afforded him by § 19.2-270, and may be cross-examined as to his statement at such examination, and the Commonwealth may contradict his testimony thus adduced. Thaniel v. Commonwealth, 132 Va. 795, 111 S.E. 259 (1922); Smith v. Commonwealth, 136 Va. 773, 118 S.E. 107 (1923).

But waiver must always be made understandingly and willingly. — The waiver of the privilege of the accused not to give evidence against himself must always be made understandingly and willingly, and generally after being fully warned by the court. Powell v. Commonwealth, 167 Va. 558, 189 S.E. 433 (1937).

Whenever the accused, because of some incident in the trial and through no fault of his, is forced to testify for fear that adverse inferences might be drawn from his failure, then he has not volunteered as a witness and has not waived his rights. Such waiver only follows where liberty of choice has been fully accorded. Powell v. Commonwealth, 167 Va. 558, 189 S.E. 433 (1937).

If it cannot be said that the accused voluntarily took the stand and testified, then it cannot be said that he intended to waive his statutory right. Blair v. Commonwealth, 166 Va. 715, 185 S.E. 900 (1936).

As to the matter testified about by accused he waives his privilege and becomes subject to cross-examination as any other witness. Enoch v. Commonwealth, 141 Va. 411, 126 S.E. 222 (1925).

Manifestly, an accused who takes the stand waives his right against self-incrimination in its entirety, not just selectively, and may be cross-examined on any subject related to the offenses for which he is on trial. Wells v. Commonwealth, 32 Va. App. 775, 531 S.E.2d 16, 2000 Va. App. LEXIS 498 (2000).

Testimony stricken where defendant refused to submit to cross-examination. — The trial court properly struck the defendant's testimony where, during a recess following his direct examination, he made it clear to the court that he would not resume the witness stand and submit to cross-examination, and the trial court was not required to go through a fruitless charade to demonstrate the situation. Tate, Jr. v. Commonwealth, No. 3017-97-2 (Ct. of Appeals Mar. 30, 1998).

Inferences permitted by waiver. — The waiver of the privilege against self-incrimination goes so far as to permit inferences to be drawn from prior omissions or failures or refusals to testify at a time when the privilege existed and the inference would have been prohibited. Sims v. Slayton, 333 F. Supp. 246 (W.D. Va. 1971).

Inferences from silence as to certain matters. — Where the accused takes the stand in his own behalf and voluntarily testifies for himself, he may not stop short in his testimony by omitting and failing to explain incriminating circumstances and events already in evidence, in which he participated and concerning which he is fully informed, without subjecting his silence to the inferences naturally to be drawn from it. Wells v. Commonwealth, 32 Va. App. 775, 531 S.E.2d 16, 2000 Va. App. LEXIS 498 (2000).

A court does not err in instructing a jury that it may draw inferences from the selective silence of a testifying accused and any inferences that a jury may draw are also appropriate subjects for argument by the Commonwealth. Wells v. Commonwealth, 32 Va.

App. 775, 531 S.E.2d 16, 2000 Va. App. LEXIS 498 (2000).

Right of Commonwealth to comment on silence. — An accused, by taking the stand, waives not only his right against self-incrimination but also his right not to have the Commonwealth comment on his failure to testify on a particular issue or subject. Wells v. Commonwealth, 32 Va. App. 775, 531 S.E.2d 16, 2000 Va. App. LEXIS 498 (2000).

Construction of "subject to cross-examination as any other witness." — There was some doubt as to the meaning of the phrase, "subject to cross-examination as any other witness." This doubt was as to whether the accused waives his privilege of not testifying against himself and may stop any stage when a question is asked which would tend to incriminate him. This was settled by expressly declaring that if the accused be "so sworn and examined, he shall be deemed to have waived his privilege of not giving evidence against himself." Thaniel v. Commonwealth, 132 Va. 795, 111 S.E. 259 (1922).

This section does not extend the class of cases in which the right of cross-examination was given, but simply defines the extent of the right where it already existed. If the right to cross-examination did not exist before, it has not been conferred now. Enoch v. Commonwealth, 141 Va. 411, 126 S.E. 222 (1925).

Extent of right to cross-examine. — To guard against false testimony, the right of cross-examination was conferred. It would seem that this safeguard did not extend any further than the benefit conferred, and that if the benefit was limited the safeguard should be also. Enoch v. Commonwealth, 141 Va. 411, 126 S.E. 222 (1925).

The statute did not attempt to confer upon the Commonwealth the right to examine the accused, but only to cross-examine him under given conditions. This right to cross-examine, however, could only exist where there had been a prior examination in chief. Enoch v. Commonwealth, 141 Va. 411, 126 S.E. 222 (1925).

When the accused voluntarily takes the stand he loses his character as a party, becomes a mere witness, and may be examined as fully as any other witness; he may be examined and must answer concerning all matters that are relevant to the case, whether testified to on the direct examination or not. Bourne v. Commonwealth, No. 0309-02-4, 2003 Va. App. LEXIS 111 (Ct. of Appeals Mar. 4, 2003).

By taking the stand, defendant subjected himself to cross-examination about any relevant matter, including whether he was driving at the time of the accident and with whom he discussed the issue; the challenged cross-examination also affected defendant's credibility, as it was closely related to defendant's direct examination, in which defendant denied telling the victim's former girlfriend or any member of the victim's family that he had been driving. Bourne v. Commonwealth, No. 0309-02-4, 2003 Va. App. LEXIS 111 (Ct. of Appeals Mar. 4, 2003).

Cross-examination as to prior felony convictions. — The Commonwealth may ask a defendant who testifies in a criminal proceeding the number of times he has been convicted of a felony, but not the names of the felonies, other than perjury, and not the nature or details thereof. Thus, a defendant in a criminal trial who has been convicted of one or more felonies is not subject to as comprehensive cross-examination as nondefendant witnesses, notwithstanding the provisions of this section. Sadoski v. Commonwealth, 219 Va. 1069, 254 S.E.2d 100 (1979).

Impeachment. — This right to cross-examination implies the right to impeach the credibility of the accused under the same rules applicable to any other witness. Carson v. Commonwealth, 188 Va. 398, 49 S.E.2d 704 (1948).

Impeachment with previously suppressed statement. — A statement made by defendant which was not a confession of guilt but a statement inconsistent with the statements made by him at the trial, was admissible to impeach his credibility. Carson v. Commonwealth, 188 Va. 398, 49 S.E.2d 704 (1948).

Statement of a witness that he fails to recollect or does not recall his former statement constitutes an adequate foundation for his impeachment, even where the statement with which the impeachment will be accomplished has been suppressed as a result of a Miranda violation. Bourne v. Commonwealth, No. 0309-02-4, 2003 Va. App. LEXIS 111 (Ct. of Appeals Mar. 4, 2003).

Statement obtained in violation of Miranda may be used to impeach a defendant's trial testimony if that testimony is inconsistent with the suppressed statement; the shield provided by Miranda is not to be perverted to a license to testify inconsistently, or even perjuriously, free from the risk of confrontation with prior inconsistent utterances. Bourne v. Commonwealth, No. 0309-02-4, 2003 Va. App. LEXIS 111 (Ct. of Appeals Mar. 4, 2003).

Effect of accused's testimony as to collateral matter. — It could never have been intended that the accused should be deemed to have waived his constitutional right of silence before the jury because he had testified to such collateral matters as the qualification of jurors, change of venue, etc., before the judge in the absence of the jury. So far as the merits of the case are concerned, the guilt or innocence of the accused had not been sworn and examined in his own behalf "in any case of felony." Enoch v. Commonwealth, 141 Va. 411, 126 S.E. 222 (1925).

An accused does not waive his privilege against self-incrimination by testifying before trial or, in a jury trial, outside the presence of the jury as to collateral matters, such as venue or the admissibility of a confession. Wells v. Commonwealth, 32 Va. App. 775, 531 S.E.2d 16, 2000 Va. App. LEXIS 498 (2000).

Selective suppression of incriminating facts prohibited. — The defendant may not testify freely as to events and circumstances which tend to support his defense, and selectively suppress other relevant facts and matters that tend to incriminate him. Sims v. Slayton, 333 F. Supp. 246 (W.D. Va. 1971).

Claimed error as to the judge's impartiality was not preserved for appellate review. — Defendant's claim of error as to the court's comments to her outside of the presence of the jury to compose herself, were not preserved for appellate review as she failed to object to such and failed to show how they could have had a negative impact on the jury's perception of her credibility. Cary v. Commonwealth, No. 2031-03-1, 2004 Va. App. LEXIS 623 (Ct. of Appeals Dec. 21, 2004), aff'd, — Va. —, 623 S.E.2d 906 (2006).

Applied in Powell v. Commonwealth, 261 Va. 512, 552 S.E.2d 344, 2001 Va. LEXIS 86 (2001).

II. FAILURE TO TESTIFY.

No comment by prosecuting attorney on failure of accused to testify. — The statutes expressly provide that the failure of the accused to testify shall create no presumption against him, nor be the subject of comment by the prosecuting attorney. Price v. Commonwealth, 77 Va. 393 (1883).

The inhibition against comment upon the failure of the accused to testify contained in this section is so positive, so clear and so direct, that it is unnecessary to enter the realm of speculation to discover the intention of the lawmakers. In unambiguous language they have said it shall not be done. Elliott v. Commonwealth, 172 Va. 595, 1 S.E.2d 273 (1939).

Provision prohibiting comment must be strictly observed. — The requirement of this section, that failure of a defendant to testify shall not be subject of comment before the court or jury must be strictly observed. Banovitch v. Commonwealth, 196 Va. 210, 83 S.E.2d 369 (1954); Dunn v. Commonwealth, 222 Va. 750, 284 S.E.2d 807 (1981).

When failure to testify instruction given. — A failure to testify instruction should always be given if requested by a defendant. Hines v. Commonwealth, 217 Va. 905, 234 S.E.2d 262 (1977).

While the better practice is that a failure to testify instruction not be given over defendant's objection, there will be cases in which a cautionary instruction may be given by a court in the exercise of its sound discretion and where no prejudice will result. Hines v. Commonwealth, 217 Va. 905, 234 S.E.2d 262 (1977).

Prosecutor's comment not prejudice per se. — While a comment by a prosecutor on the failure of the accused to testify is improper, there is no rigid rule that such a statement constitutes prejudice per se. Dunn v. Commonwealth, 222 Va. 750, 284 S.E.2d 807 (1981).

Test as to whether prosecutor's remark prohibited. — In determining whether a remark falls within the boundary of the prohibition that a prosecutor shall not make an adverse comment before the jury on a defendant's failure to testify, the test is whether, in the circumstances of the particular case, the language used was manifestly intended or was of such character that the jury would naturally and necessarily take it to be a comment on the failure of the accused to testify. Hines v. Commonwealth, 217 Va. 905, 234 S.E.2d 262 (1977).

The test is whether, in the circumstances of the particular case, the language used was manifestly intended or was of such character that the jury would naturally and necessarily take it to be a comment on the failure of the accused to testify. Quintana v. Commonwealth, 224 Va. 127, 295 S.E.2d 643 (1982), cert. denied, 460 U.S. 1029, 103 S. Ct. 1280, 75 L. Ed. 2d 501 (1983).

When prosecutor's comment harmless. — A comment by a prosecutor on the failure of the accused to testify is harmless only where the court is able to declare a belief that it was harmless beyond a reasonable doubt. Dunn v. Commonwealth, 222 Va. 750, 284 S.E.2d 807 (1981).

As a general rule, any comment that the attorney for the Commonwealth makes referring to defendant's election not to testify is a violation of his rights against self-incrimination as guaranteed by U.S. Const., Amend. V and Va. Const., Art. I, § 8, and as explicated in this section. Johnson v. Commonwealth, 236 Va. 48, 372 S.E.2d 134 (1988).

Prosecutorial comment may become proper under invited error doctrine. — It is generally error for the prosecutor to comment on the defendant's failure to testify. Such comment, however, may become proper under the invited error doctrine when the area has been opened to fair comment by the argument and comment of defense counsel or of a pro se defendant. Lincoln v. Commonwealth, 217 Va. 370, 228 S.E.2d 688 (1976).

Even though a defendant does not testify, demonstrative conduct on his part in some circumstances may open the door to fair comment on his failure to testify. Lincoln v. Commonwealth, 217 Va. 370, 228 S.E.2d 688 (1976); Johnson v. Commonwealth, 236 Va. 48, 372 S.E.2d 134 (1988).

Prosecution's response held justified. — Defendant's counsel, in his summation, represented to the jury that the defendant did not testify because "we don't feel . . . the jury are going to convict . . . on the evidence of two convicted felons" and because "we didn't think it was necessary." By so doing, the defense invited the prosecution's response, which did not go beyond meeting the argument advanced by the defendant. In these circumstances, the response was fully justified and did not constitute error. Lincoln v. Commonwealth, 217 Va. 370, 228 S.E.2d 688 (1976).

The prosecutor can no more comment now than he could before the statute on the failure of the accused to testify. Before the statute the accused could not testify. It is now his privilege to testify, but it is his right to stand mute. His liberty of choice must be fully accorded him, and cannot be made the subject of comment. But the restraint of the statute cannot be extended so as to prevent proper comment and emphasis upon the testimony of other witnesses simply because it could only be contradicted by the accused and he stands mute. Miller v. Commonwealth, 153 Va. 890, 149 S.E. 459 (1929). See Blair v. Commonwealth, 166 Va. 715, 185 S.E. 900 (1936); Powell v. Commonwealth, 167 Va. 558, 189 S.E. 433 (1937).

But prosecutor may comment on testimony of other witnesses. — Assuming the validity of this section and construing it, certainly it does not mean that because a prosecutor may not comment upon the failure of the accused to testify, therefore he cannot allude to, rely upon and comment upon the evidence of the witnesses who have actually testified. Miller v. Commonwealth, 153 Va. 890, 149 S.E. 459 (1929).

Section does not apply to extrajudicial statement. — The provision in this section that the failure of an accused to testify shall create no presumption against him applies to testimony in court and not to an extrajudicial statement. Thus, it does not prohibit admission of testimony that an accused remained silent in the face of an accusation. Owens v. Commonwealth, 186 Va. 689, 43 S.E.2d 895 (1947).

Objectionable comment. — Where accused did not testify and the attorney for the Commonwealth, in his closing argument, said that accused had not denied what a witness for the Commonwealth had stated, the trial court should have declared a mistrial. Elliott v. Commonwealth, 172 Va. 595, 1 S.E.2d 273 (1939).

Where the prosecution in a burglary trial continuously asserted that the defendant was required to explain his possession of the stolen goods, and the prosecution similarly in closing argument placed the burden on the defendant personally to deny that he had stolen the goods, the prosecution made improper reference to the defendant's failure to testify. Shipwash v. Collins, 475 F. Supp. 1000 (W.D. Va. 1979).

Unobjectionable comment. — Remark of prosecuting attorney to the jury that prisoner had not accounted for his whereabouts at time of homicide nor his flight from the State, without allusion to his failure to testify, comes not within this section. Sutton v. Commonwealth, 85 Va. 128, 7 S.E. 323 (1888).

Likewise, in a prosecution for seduction, prosecuting attorney's remark that no witness has gone upon the stand to deny statements of two witnesses that defendant had had intercourse with the prosecutrix, was unobjectionable. Miller v. Commonwealth, 153 Va. 890, 149 S.E. 459 (1929).

Remarks of prosecuting attorney that "though he had no right to swear any man accused of crime, he had the right to prove his statements," is not a violation of this section. Sawyers v. Commonwealth, 88 Va. 356, 13 S.E. 708 (1891).

In a burglary prosecution, where defendant chose not to testify, and the prosecutor asked the jurors if they had "heard from that witness stand any evidence" that the defendant had denied his guilt, any witness who had spoken with the defendant could have supplied such evidence if, in fact, the defendant had uttered such a denial. Hence, the prosecutor's reference to the lack of such evidence, like a comment that incriminating evidence had not been contradicted, could not be characterized fairly as a remark that the jury naturally and necessarily would interpret as a comment on the fact that defendant had exercised his right not to testify. Johnson v. Commonwealth, 236 Va. 48, 372 S.E.2d 134 (1988).

Time for exception to comment. — If the exception to such comment is not taken until after verdict it is too late, if, under all the circumstances, the court can see that a proper verdict has been rendered and the accused not injured by the comment. Price v. Commonwealth, 77 Va. 393 (1883); Norfolk & W.R.R. v. Shott, 92 Va. 34, 22 S.E. 811 (1895).

Defendant held not improperly compelled to testify. — Where the Commonwealth disclosed the incriminating statement well before the investigator testified and in ample time for defendant's counsel to advise him whether or not to take the witness stand, admission of the statement did not improperly compel defendant to testify. Bennett v. Commonwealth, 236 Va. 448, 374 S.E.2d 303 (1988), cert. denied, 490 U.S. 1028, 109 S. Ct. 1765, 104 L. Ed. 2d 200 (1989).

Burden is on Commonwealth to show objectionable comment was harmless. Joyner v. Commonwealth, 192 Va. 471, 65 S.E.2d 555 (1951).

§ 19.2-268.1. Contradiction by prior inconsistent writing (Subdivision (b)(i) of Supreme Court Rule 2:613 derived in part from this section).

A witness in a criminal case may be cross-examined as to previous statements made by him in writing or reduced into writing, relative to the subject matter of the proceeding, without such writing being shown to him; but if it is intended to contradict such witness by the writing, his attention must, before such contradictory proof can be given, be called to the particular occasion on which the writing is supposed to have been made, and he may be asked if he did not make a writing of the purport of the one to be offered to contradict him, and if he denies making it, or does not admit its execution, it shall then be shown to him, and if he admits its genuineness, he shall be allowed to make his own explanation of it; but it shall be competent for the court at any time during the trial to require the production of the writing for its inspection, and the court may thereupon make such use of it for the purpose of the trial as it may think best.

History.
Code 1950, § 8-293; 1958, c. 380; 1960, c. 114; 1964, c. 356; 1977, c. 624.

Cross references.
As to contradiction of witnesses by prior inconsistent writings in civil cases, see § 8.01-404.

Editor's note.

At the direction of the Virginia Code Commission, the notation to the Virginia Rules of Evidence was added to the catchline of this section. Acts 2012, cc. 688 and 708, cl. 6 provides: "That pursuant to the authority set forth in §§ 30-146 and 30-147 of the Code of Virginia, the Virginia Code Commission shall direct any party with whom the Virginia Code Commission contracts to publish the Code of Virginia to include in the catchline of every section of the Code of Virginia from which any rule contained in the Rules of Evidence has been derived a notation specifying such rule."

Law Review.

For note on the problem of partially silent defendants, see 69 Va. L. Rev. 155 (1983).

Michie's Jurisprudence.

For related discussion, see 20 M.J. Witnesses, § 57.

CASE NOTES

This section does not provide authority for trial court to order the disclosure of otherwise non-discoverable material. Rather, the section was intended to be used as an evidentiary rule by the trial court to order the production, inspection and use of a written statement once a witness has been cross-examined about the existence or contents of a prior statement. Newton v. Commonwealth, 29 Va. App. 433, 512 S.E.2d 846, cert. denied, 528 U.S. 1025, 120 S. Ct. 540, 145 L. Ed. 2d 419 (1999).

Presupposition of writing's existence. — If the prior inconsistent statement was in writing or reduced to writing, such as in the form of a transcript, the court may require the party to produce the writing. However, this section presupposes the existence of a writing. Edwards v. Commonwealth, 19 Va. App. 568, 454 S.E.2d 1 (1995).

Necessity of laying of foundation. — A witness may be impeached by showing that he has formerly made statements inconsistent with his present testimony. An attorney may impeach a witness in this manner, provided a foundation is first laid by calling his attention to the statement and then questioning him about it. Edwards v. Commonwealth, 19 Va. App. 568, 454 S.E.2d 1 (1995).

Impeachment evidence which may be used. — After the foundation is laid, the witness may then usually be impeached by the introduction of evidence to prove that the prior inconsistent statement was in fact made. Such evidence includes the testimony of another witness who heard the prior inconsistent statement, or the transcript of a prior hearing. Edwards v. Commonwealth, 19 Va. App. 568, 454 S.E.2d 1 (1995).

Courts can require a direct reading from an available transcript instead of paraphrased questions, and it was well within the court's discretion to control the conduct of cross-examination. Edwards v. Commonwealth, 19 Va. App. 568, 454 S.E.2d 1 (1995).

If a witness denies or is unable to recall a prior statement, a party may impeach him by introducing other evidence, such as another witness who heard the inconsistent statement. If a transcript is available, the court may require its production pursuant to the mandate of this section even if there are other means of impeachment. Edwards v. Commonwealth, 19 Va. App. 568, 454 S.E.2d 1 (1995).

This section does not determine the outcome of the instant case because there was no evidence that a transcript was available or that the disputed testimony had been reduced to writing. If a transcript is available, an attorney may read from the transcript to impeach a witness by prior inconsistent statements. Edwards v. Commonwealth, 19 Va. App. 568, 454 S.E.2d 1 (1995).

Use of transcribed questions. — Where Commonwealth's witnesses in a murder trial had given statements to investigating officers which were inconsistent with their trial testimony, the court did not commit reversible error by requiring defense counsel to read the transcribed questions and answers contained in those statements during cross-examination in an attempt to attack the credibility of the witnesses' prior inconsistent statements. Scott v. Commonwealth, 7 Va. App. 552, 372 S.E.2d 771 (1988), cert. denied, 490 U.S. 1095, 109 S. Ct. 2441, 104 L. Ed. 2d 997 (1989).

Court did not abuse its discretion in refusing to admit transcript. — Where trial court refused to admit into evidence the transcription of witness' prior statement to police, made at the time of his arrest, which directly contradicted witness' trial testimony, where defendant's attorney cross-examined witness as to a portion of the testimony, and where defendant asserted that the entire statement was inconsistent with witness' trial testimony and, therefore, should have been admitted in its entirety, because the trial court determined that admission of the written statement would have added nothing not already in the record, the trial court did not abuse its discretion in refusing to admit the transcript. Smith v. Commonwealth, 15 Va. App. 507, 425 S.E.2d 95 (1992).

The court erred in requiring a transcript as the only means of impeaching a witness based on inconsistent statements made at an earlier hearing. Although laying a foundation prior to the introduction of impeachment evidence is a separate and necessary step in the impeachment process, it is not contingent on the existence of a transcript. While using a transcript, if available, is the preferable means of laying an impeachment foundation, it is not the only means. This rule also applies once the initial foundation has been laid. Edwards v. Commonwealth, 19 Va. App. 568, 454 S.E.2d 1 (1995).

Objection to use of such writing must be made at trial. — Although defendant argued that the trial court erred in not requiring the Commonwealth to produce the inconsistent writing used to impeach defense witness, defendant failed to properly raise the issue at trial and also failed to raise the issue on appeal, causing the matter to be barred. Wilson v. Commonwealth, 25 Va. App. 263, 487 S.E.2d 857 (1997).

Applied in Smith v. Commonwealth, 19 Va. App. 594, 453 S.E.2d 572 (1995).

§ 19.2-268.2. Recent complaint hearsay exception (Subdivision (23) of Supreme Court Rule 2:803 derived from this section).

Notwithstanding any other provision of law, in any prosecution for criminal sexual assault under Article 7 (§ 18.2-61 et seq.) of Chapter 4 of Title 18.2, a violation of §§ 18.2-361, 18.2-366, 18.2-370 or § 18.2-370.1, the fact that the person injured made complaint of the offense recently after commission of the offense is admissible, not as independent evidence of the offense, but for the purpose of corroborating the testimony of the complaining witness.

History.
1993, c. 592.

Editor's note.

At the direction of the Virginia Code Commission, the notation to the Virginia Rules of Evidence was added to the catchline of this section. Acts 2012, cc. 688 and 708, cl. 6 provides: "That pursuant to the authority set forth in §§ 30-146 and 30-147 of the Code of Virginia, the Virginia Code Commission shall direct any party with whom the Virginia Code Commission contracts to publish the Code of Virginia to include in the catchline of every section of the Code of Virginia from which any rule contained in the Rules of Evidence has been derived a notation specifying such rule."

Law Review.

For an article, "Criminal Law and Procedure," see 31 U. Rich. L. Rev. 1015 (1997). For annual survey article on legal issues involving children, see 38 U. Rich. L. Rev. 161 (2003). For 2006 survey article, "Criminal Law and Procedure," see 41 U. Rich. L. Rev. 83 (2006).

CASE NOTES

Only the fact of the complaint, not the details given therein may be admitted, and the scope of admission rests with the sound discretion of the trial court. Woodard v. Commonwealth, 19 Va. App. 24, 448 S.E.2d 328 (1994).

The initial determination of timeliness under the recent complaint rule is committed to the sound discretion of the trial court, and thereafter, timeliness is a matter for the trier of fact to consider in weighing the evidence. Woodard v. Commonwealth, 19 Va. App. 24, 448 S.E.2d 328 (1994).

Timeliness. — Under this section, timeliness, in relation to the reasons for the delay of the rape complaint, must initially be decided by the trial judge in order to determine whether evidence of the complaint can be admitted. Terry v. Commonwealth, 24 Va. App. 627, 484 S.E.2d 614 (1997).

Delayed complaints of sexual assault are admissible for purpose of corroborating testimony of a complaining witness, where delay is credibly explained or consistent with circumstances. Bartz v. Commonwealth, No. 1374-98-2 (Ct. of Appeals June 29, 1999).

Trial court was not required under § 19.2-268.2 to make an express factual finding prior to the admittance into evidence of the child's stepmother's testimony, and there was sufficient evidence of the child's fear that she would not have been believed and of her fear of reprisals by defendant, to explain the delay in the child's complaint to her stepmother. Almond v. Commonwealth, No. 3071-01-2, 2002 Va. App. LEXIS 746 (Ct. of Appeals Dec. 17, 2002).

A rape victim's complaint corroborates more than his or her testimony; it also corroborates the occurrence of the rape itself. No reason justifies limiting the recent complaint rule to corroboration of a victim's testimony. The rule is also applicable to corroborate other independent evidence of the offense; however, the complaint alone does not constitute sufficient evidence of the offense. Woodard v. Commonwealth, 19 Va. App. 24, 448 S.E.2d 328 (1994).

This statute was inapplicable in this case. Child's statement that he had been sexed was uniquely probative of the charge of sexual abuse; as such, it was "independent evidence of the offense." Moreover, that statement was not made "for the purpose of corroborating the testimony of the complaining witness"; the child never testified in court. Jenkins v. Commonwealth, 254 Va. 333, 492 S.E.2d 131 (1997).

Trial court did not abuse its discretion in admitting evidence of the victim's hearsay complaint of the rape, which occurred in July, where the school-age victim testified that she told no one about the offense until school commenced after the summer recess, over defendant's objection on the ground that these reports were not recent complaints and, thus, not admissible. Woodard v. Commonwealth, 19 Va. App. 24, 448 S.E.2d 328 (1994).

Error in admitting complaint. — In the absence of an explanation for the extraordinary 16-month delay between alleged molestation and child's statements about the alleged incident to her stepmother, the evidence failed to provide a foundation from which the trial judge could have found that the complaint met the statutory requirement under this section that it was made "recently after commission of the offense." Castelow v. Commonwealth, 29 Va. App. 305, 512 S.E.2d 137 (1999).

No error in admitting victim's complaint. — The plain language of § 19.2-268.2 does not limit the number of recent complaints of sexual assault that the Commonwealth may introduce into evidence to corroborate a victim's testimony, and there is also no case law barring the Commonwealth from presenting more than two corroborating witnesses. Longfield v. Commonwealth, No. 0303-01-2, 2002 Va. App. LEXIS 33 (Ct. of Appeals Jan. 29, 2002).

While victim did not tell her father or mother about the rape until ten months later, she explained the reasons for the delay: (1) victim was afraid mother would not believe her because defendant was her mother's good friend; (2) she did not tell her father for fear that he would hurt the defendant and end up in jail; and (3) she felt responsible for rape because she insisted on staying home instead of going with her mother. Thus, the trial court did not err by holding the complaint sufficiently recent to be admissible. Terry v. Commonwealth, 24 Va. App. 627, 484 S.E.2d 614 (1997).

The trial court did not abuse its discretion in admitting a statement made by the victim to a school counselor regarding multiple rapes by the defendant, who was her uncle, though it was made long after the event, where the rapes occurred when she was between 11 and 14 years old, the complaint was made when she was 15 years old, and the defendant threatened her with regard to telling anyone about the incidents. Hutchison v. Commonwealth, No. 0131-97-3 (Ct. of Appeals April 28, 1998).

Minor victim's statements regarding sexual assaults were prop-

erly admitted, since her delay in reporting assaults to her mother was explained by threat of harm from defendant if she were to tell anyone. Booker v. Commonwealth, No. 1603-98-1 (Ct. of Appeals Aug. 3, 1999).

Trial court did not abuse its discretion in admitting a complaining witness' recent complaints of rape where it was impossible to separate the admissible portions from the inadmissible and the trial court judge specifically said he would not consider the inadmissible portions. The fact of the complaint of rape laid in the details of the complaining witness' statement and the complaint would have been incomplete without those details. Breeden v. Commonwealth, 43 Va. App. 169, 596 S.E.2d 563, 2004 Va. App. LEXIS 257 (2004).

Sexual assault victim's letter to her grandmother complaining of defendant's conduct fell within the "recent complaint" hearsay exception and was admissible, not as independent evidence, but to corroborate the victim's testimony. Wilson v. Commonwealth, 46 Va. App. 73, 615 S.E.2d 500, 2005 Va. App. LEXIS 268 (2005).

In an action charging defendant with various sexually based crimes, admission of a letter that the victim wrote to a school counselor as a recent complaint under § 19.2-268.2 was proper where, inter alia, the delay in reporting was adequately explained by the victim, who stated that the victim did not think anyone would believe the victim and the victim was concerned about the victim's niece's father going to jail; defendant's other challenges to the letter were waived by a failure to object or raise the issue in the trial court and a failure to proffer a curative instruction. Williams v. Commonwealth, 2008 Va. App. LEXIS 460 (Oct. 14, 2008).

Social worker's testimony regarding a statement by the victim was admissible as a recent complaint, under § 19.2-268.2, because neither § 19.2-268.2, nor the common law conditioned admissibility of the victim's complaint on whether the complaint was the victim's first outcry; instead, all that was required was that the complaint was made recently after commission of the offense. Anderson v. Commonwealth, 2011 Va. App. LEXIS 214 (June 28, 2011).

Error in using victim's out-of-court statement to convict defendant. — Although the trial court properly admitted an out-of-court statement, which defendant's stepdaughter gave to a detective as a recent complaint of criminal sexual assault, pursuant to § 19.2-268.2, the court erred by using the stepdaughter's statement to convict defendant of forcible sodomy because testimony which the stepdaughter gave at defendant's trial did not corroborate her out-of-court statement and there was no other evidence that established the elements of the offense. However, the stepdaughter's testimony and defendant's admission that he rubbed his stepdaughter's genitalia were sufficient to prove that he committed animate object sexual penetration and aggravated sexual battery, and the appellate court affirmed the trial court's judgment convicting defendant of those crimes. Fincham v. Commonwealth, No. 3361-02-2, 2004 Va. App. LEXIS 259 (Ct. of Appeals June 8, 2004).

Applied in Brown v. Commonwealth, 37 Va. App. 169, 554 S.E.2d 711, 2001 Va. App. LEXIS 635 (2001); Anderson v. Commonwealth, 282 Va. 457, 717 S.E.2d 623, 2011 Va. LEXIS 226 (2011).

§ 19.2-269. Convicts as witnesses (Supreme Court Rule 2:609 derived from this section).

A person convicted of a felony or perjury shall not be incompetent to testify, but the fact of conviction may be shown in evidence to affect his credit.

History.

Code 1950, § 19.1-265; 1960, c. 366; 1975, c. 495.

Cross references.

As to what constitutes a felony, see § 18.2-8. As to penalties for conviction of perjury, see § 18.2-434.

Editor's note.

At the direction of the Virginia Code Commission, the notation to the Virginia Rules of Evidence was added to the catchline of this section. Acts 2012, cc. 688 and 708, cl. 6 provides: "That pursuant to the authority set forth in §§ 30-146 and 30-147 of the Code of

Virginia, the Virginia Code Commission shall direct any party with whom the Virginia Code Commission contracts to publish the Code of Virginia to include in the catchline of every section of the Code of Virginia from which any rule contained in the Rules of Evidence has been derived a notation specifying such rule."

Law Review.

For article on evidence of other crimes in criminal cases, see 3 U. Rich. L. Rev. 62 (1968). For survey of Virginia criminal law for the year 1971-1972, see 58 Va. L. Rev. 1206 (1972). For review of Fourth Circuit cases on evidence, see 36 Wash. & Lee L. Rev. 562 (1979). For survey of Virginia law on evidence for the year 1978-1979, see 66 Va. L. Rev. 293 (1980). For 1987 survey of Virginia evidence law, see 21 U. Rich. L. Rev. 775 (1987). For survey on evidence in Virginia for 1989, see 23 U. Rich. L. Rev. 647 (1989).

Michie's Jurisprudence.

For related discussion, see 1A M.J. Accomplices and Accessories, § 6; 5B M.J. Criminal Procedure, § 59; 20 M.J. Witnesses, §§ 6, 39, 66.

CASE NOTES

Law prior to adoption of section. — Prior to the adoption of this section as § 4779 of the Code of 1919, convicted felons, as a rule, could not testify unless pardoned or punished, and a person convicted of perjury could not testify although pardoned or punished. Lincoln v. Commonwealth, 217 Va. 370, 228 S.E.2d 688 (1976).

Purpose of section. — This section makes material changes in the law governing the competency of witness to testify, so as to remove practically all disqualifications, and permit the courts to hear all evidence bearing on the question at issue just as is usual in the business affairs of life. In pursuance of this policy the law with reference to the testimony of those convicted of felony or perjury was changed. Epes' Adm'r v. Hardaway, 135 Va. 80, 115 S.E. 712 (1923).

Impeachment. — It is not proper to ask a witness if he has been indicted, and it is not proper to show that he has been convicted of an ordinary misdemeanor, but it may, for purposes of impeachment, be shown by the witness himself that he has been convicted of felony or of perjury. Smith v. Commonwealth, 155 Va. 1111, 156 S.E. 577 (1931).

A defendant/witness may be impeached by showing that he has been previously convicted of a felony. Powell v. Commonwealth, 13 Va. App. 17, 409 S.E.2d 622 (1991).

Effect of impeachment. — If a witness is impeached, it only goes to his credit, not to his competency. He is a competent witness even if he has convicted of perjury. Patterson v. Commonwealth, 139 Va. 589, 123 S.E. 657 (1924), appeal dismissed, 270 U.S. 632, 46 S. Ct. 349, 70 L. Ed. 771 (1926).

Entitlement to discount testimony. — At defendant's trial for grand larceny involving a stolen vehicle, the trial court was entitled to discount the defense testimony of defendant's girlfriend, who was a convicted felon. Randolph v. Commonwealth, No. 2162-02-1, 2003 Va. App. LEXIS 511 (Ct. of Appeals Oct. 14, 2003).

In defendant's prosecution for drug possession, although defendant denied knowledge of the drugs found in a car he was borrowing, the trial court was entitled to consider defendant's prior felony conviction in assessing his credibility under § 19.2-269. Etheridge v. Commonwealth, 2009 Va. App. LEXIS 134 (Mar. 24, 2009).

Defendant's conviction for grand larceny of a string trimmer was appropriate because the evidence was sufficient and the trial judge was entitled to consider defendant's prior felony conviction in assessing his credibility. Swiggett v. Commonwealth, 2010 Va. App. LEXIS 53 (Feb. 9, 2010).

Proof of prior conviction. — It has long been well settled in this state that the character of a witness for veracity cannot be impeached by proof of a prior conviction of crime, unless the crime be a felony or one which involved moral turpitude or the character of the witness for veracity. McLane v. Commonwealth, 202 Va. 197, 116 S.E.2d 274 (1960); Lincoln v. Commonwealth, 217 Va. 370, 228 S.E.2d 688 (1976).

By Commonwealth. — This section means that the fact of conviction of a felony may be shown by the Commonwealth. Harmon v. Commonwealth, 212 Va. 442, 185 S.E.2d 48 (1971).

"Conviction" includes guilty plea. — For the limited purposes of this section, the word "conviction" includes a guilty plea accepted by the court but for which no order has been entered stating a finding of guilt or imposing sentence; proof of such a guilty plea may be shown to impeach a witness. Jewel v. Commonwealth, 260 Va. 430, 536 S.E.2d 905, 2000 Va. LEXIS 145 (2000).

Felony, other than perjury, and the details thereof may not be shown. Harmon v. Commonwealth, 212 Va. 442, 185 S.E.2d 48 (1971).

So long as the defendant answers truthfully the inquiry as to a prior felony conviction, the name of the crime cannot be shown. Harmon v. Commonwealth, 212 Va. 442, 185 S.E.2d 48 (1971).

When the Commonwealth attempts to impeach the credibility of the accused by showing prior felony convictions, in order to avoid undue prejudice to the accused, neither the nature of the felony, other than perjury, nor the details of the crime are admissible; only the fact of a conviction can be shown. Powell v. Commonwealth, 13 Va. App. 17, 409 S.E.2d 622 (1991).

For purposes of impeachment, the fact of a prior conviction of a felony may be shown against a party-witness in a civil case, but the name of the felony, other than perjury, and the details thereof may not be shown. Payne v. Carroll, 250 Va. 336, 461 S.E.2d 837 (1995).

Witnesses other than defendant may be asked names of felonies for which they have been convicted. This rule is not limited to witnesses for the Commonwealth. Dammerau v. Commonwealth, 3 Va. App. 285, 349 S.E.2d 409 (1986), overruled on other grounds, Vescuso v. Commonwealth, 5 Va. App. 59, 360 S.E.2d 547 (1987).

Prior conviction must involve moral turpitude. — It must be clearly shown that the prior conviction was for an offense involving moral turpitude; otherwise the inquiry should not be permitted. Chrisman v. Commonwealth, 3 Va. App. 89, 348 S.E.2d 399 (1986).

And character of witness for veracity. — The character of a witness' veracity cannot be impeached by proof of a prior conviction of crime, unless the crime be one which involved the character of the witness for veracity. Chrisman v. Commonwealth, 3 Va. App. 89, 348 S.E.2d 399 (1986).

Misdemeanor must involve moral turpitude. — If the crime be a misdemeanor, the right to inquire is limited to those that involve moral turpitude. Chrisman v. Commonwealth, 3 Va. App. 89, 348 S.E.2d 399 (1986).

Indecent exposure conviction not admissible. — It was error to admit into evidence the fact of the defendant's prior conviction of indecent exposure. Chrisman v. Commonwealth, 3 Va. App. 89, 348 S.E.2d 399 (1986).

Since it is not determinative of veracity. — The crime of indecent exposure is neither a crime of treason nor a felony, nor is it a crime of the sort known as crimen falsi at the Roman or common law. It does not involve deception, trickery, forgery, lying, cheating or stealing. It is not an infamous crime. It does not involve moral turpitude as that phrase has been applied at common law relating to incompetency or impeachment. It is not determinative of the character of a person for veracity. Chrisman v. Commonwealth, 3 Va. App. 89, 348 S.E.2d 399 (1986).

Effect of voluntarily taking stand in own defense. — When a defendant voluntarily takes the stand in his own defense and opens up matters by his own testimony, he subjects himself to cross-examination on the matters relevantly raised by that testimony. Harmon v. Commonwealth, 212 Va. 442, 185 S.E.2d 48 (1971).

Where defendant takes the witness stand in his own defense and testifies on direct examination that he has been convicted previously of a certain number of felonies, he may be cross-examined only with respect to the correctness of the number stated and, if his answers are truthful, without regard to the names or the nature of the offenses. McAmis v. Commonwealth, 225 Va. 419, 304 S.E.2d 2 (1983).

Where defendant on direct examination goes beyond merely testifying he has been convicted previously of a certain number of felonies and discloses additional information concerning his convictions, he may be held to have opened the door to inquiry concerning the names of the offenses. McAmis v. Commonwealth, 225 Va. 419, 304 S.E.2d 2 (1983).

When an accused testifies on his own behalf he may determine that it is in his best interests as a trial tactic to reveal the fact of his prior felony convictions in terms of bolstering his credibility with the trier of fact. If this is done truthfully and not in a manner calculated to mislead, it does not open the door for the Commonwealth on cross-examination to establish the names and nature of the prior felony convictions. Joyner v. Commonwealth, 10 Va. App. 290, 392 S.E.2d 822 (1990).

This section permits the examination of a defendant as to any prior felony convictions should he become a witness in his own behalf. The sole purpose of such inquiry is to attack the defendant's credibility as a witness. His answer is not to be considered as evidence of his guilt or innocence of the crime charged. Harmon v. Commonwealth, 212 Va. 442, 185 S.E.2d 48 (1971).

Right of cross-examination not unlimited. — Where the Commonwealth attempts to impeach the accused under this section by establishing the number of prior convictions, the Commonwealth's right to cross-examine him about the name and nature of the prior convictions is not unlimited. Powell v. Commonwealth, 13 Va. App. 17, 409 S.E.2d 622 (1991).

Cross-examination of defendant as to prior felony convictions. — The Commonwealth may ask a defendant who testifies in a criminal proceeding the number of times he has been convicted of a felony, but not the names of the felonies, other than perjury, and not the nature or details thereof. Thus, a defendant in a criminal trial who has been convicted of one or more felonies is not subject to as comprehensive cross-examination as nondefendant witnesses, notwithstanding the provisions of § 19.2-268. Sadoski v. Commonwealth, 219 Va. 1069, 254 S.E.2d 100 (1979).

Effect of defendant's disclosure of felony on direct examination. — Where the accused has disclosed on direct examination the nature of the felony conviction, he does not open the door for the Commonwealth to introduce evidence concerning the nature or character of another felony conviction he may have either purposefully or mistakenly misrepresented without first exploring the other alternatives to prove that the accused had more than one felony conviction and testified untruthfully. Able v. Commonwealth, 16 Va. App. 542, 431 S.E.2d 337 (1993).

Reversible error in permitting evidence of names rather than number. — The trial court committed reversible error in permitting the Commonwealth to introduce evidence of the names rather than only the number of a defendant's prior felony convictions. Joyner v. Commonwealth, 10 Va. App. 290, 392 S.E.2d 822 (1990).

Error not harmless. — In a cocaine possession conviction based on a bench trial, admission of the nature of defendant's prior conviction was not harmless error because it was impossible to determine if this evidence, which potentially prejudiced the trial court's decision, was limited to credibility. Lawrence v. Commonwealth, 2009 Va. App. LEXIS 426 (Sept. 29, 2009).

Erroneous admission of questions about prior convictions held harmless. — Although robbery defendant opened the door to questioning about one prior conviction for grand larceny, trial court abused its discretion in allowing the Commonwealth to question defendant as to the identity and nature of a second felony conviction and a misdemeanor conviction; the abuse was harmless error since defendant failed to show that admission of this testimony prejudiced his ability to receive a fair trial. Cole v. Commonwealth, 16 Va. App. 113, 428 S.E.2d 303 (1993).

Details of prior convictions. — Unless the defendant answers untruthfully any questions concerning the number of his felony convictions or voluntarily puts into issue the details of his prior convictions, the Commonwealth may not inquire as to the details of a prior offense. If a defendant answers falsely, however, he opens the door to the Commonwealth's impeachment of his response, and the Commonwealth may be permitted to inquire into the nature or character of the prior convictions. Farrow v. Commonwealth, No. 0861-89-3 (Ct. of Appeals Oct. 23, 1990).

Commonwealth's evidence was competent, not inherently incredible, and sufficient to prove beyond a reasonable doubt attempted rape and abduction with intent to defile, because jury believed the victim's version of what happened and the Commonwealth's evidence and rejected defendant's version of those events, and the jury was permitted to consider defendant's prior felony convictions in assessing his credibility; the victim testified that defendant held her down, partially removed her pants, exposed his penis, pulled out a knife, and repeatedly threatened to kill the victim. Gay v.

Commonwealth, 2011 Va. App. LEXIS 134 (Apr. 19, 2011).

Defendant, who misstated the number of his convictions and qualified his answer by stating that the convictions were received "when I was younger," opened the door to further inquiry by the Commonwealth in order to identify which of the felonies he was admitting to in attempting to account for his prior convictions. Farrow v. Commonwealth, No. 0861-89-3 (Ct. of Appeals Oct. 23, 1990).

Jury is entitled to know both the number and the nature of a witness' felony convictions, but not the details thereof, in order to evaluate his testimony and determine what credit it should be given. Johnson v. Commonwealth, 224 Va. 525, 298 S.E.2d 99 (1982).

The triers of fact were entitled to know the number and nature, but not the details, of the felony convictions of a witness for the Commonwealth who had been granted immunity from prosecutions, so that they could evaluate his testimony and determine what credit it should be given. Hummel v. Commonwealth, 217 Va. 548, 231 S.E.2d 216 (1977), cert. denied, 440 U.S. 935, 99 S. Ct. 1278, 59 L. Ed. 2d 492 (1979).

While naming a prior felony conviction similar in nature to the offense for which a defendant is on trial during cross-examination of the defendant would be highly prejudicial to him, the naming of the prior convictions of a witness for the Commonwealth who has been granted immunity from prosecution in order to attack his credibility does not present the same risk of undue prejudice. Hummel v. Commonwealth, 217 Va. 548, 231 S.E.2d 216 (1977), cert. denied, 440 U.S. 935, 99 S. Ct. 1278, 59 L. Ed. 2d 492 (1979).

Probative value of prior conviction outweighs prejudicial effect. — Some prejudice rises against a defendant when it is disclosed that he has been convicted of a felony, but its probative value as to his credit outweighs the prejudicial effect. Harmon v. Commonwealth, 212 Va. 442, 185 S.E.2d 48 (1971).

Exclusion of nature of prior convictions deemed harmless error. — Although a trial court erred in excluding defense counsel's attempts to question a malicious wounding victim as to the nature of his prior convictions, it was deemed harmless error because the jury knew that the victim was a convicted felon, as were the four defendants involved in the jailhouse attack, the jury was informed as to the number of prior convictions, and the nature of those felonies was not of particular importance, nor was it likely that they would have added to the impeachment potential. Justus v. Commonwealth, Nos. 1220-03-3, 1234-03-3, 1291-03-3, 2004 Va. App. LEXIS 256 (Ct. of Appeals June 1, 2004).

Indictment inadmissible where accused was convicted of lower offense. — It was error not to forbid the introduction before the jury of the record of the indictment of accused for housebreaking, upon which he was convicted of a mere assault and battery. Boggs v. Commonwealth, 199 Va. 478, 100 S.E.2d 766 (1957).

It was improper for the attorney for the Commonwealth to ask defendant whether he had been convicted of malicious wounding (a felony) when in fact he had been indicted for malicious wounding but convicted only of assault and battery (a misdemeanor). But defendant was not manifestly prejudiced by the question where no testimony was given in response to the question and where the trial court took prompt, direct and positive action in instructing the jury to disregard the question and all its effects. McLane v. Commonwealth, 202 Va. 197, 116 S.E.2d 274 (1960).

Effect of felony under federal statute declared misdemeanor by state statute. — The conviction of a crime in a federal court, which is a felony under the federal statutes but which is declared to be a misdemeanor by the Virginia statutes, is not admissible in evidence under this section. Burford v. Commonwealth, 179 Va. 752, 20 S.E.2d 509 (1942).

Adjudication as juvenile delinquent may not be shown. — In view of the provisions of the juvenile statutes no error was committed in refusing to allow defendant's counsel to ask a witness for the prosecution whether he had ever been adjudged a juvenile delinquent in a proceeding in a juvenile court involving a felonious offense or larceny, the purpose of the question being to affect the credibility of the witness. Questions which refer to the disposition of the child in a juvenile court are not permitted. Kiracofe v. Commonwealth, 198 Va. 833, 97 S.E.2d 14 (1957).

Question about felony conviction asked in conjunction with prejudicial questions about prior conduct. — That a question about a felony conviction may be improper when asked of an accused in conjunction with prejudicial questions about prior conduct, see Williams v. Commonwealth, 203 Va. 837, 127 S.E.2d 423 (1962).

Only a conviction, not a revocation of probation, may be used to impeach the credibility of a witness. Willis v. Commonwealth, No. 1195-95-3 (Ct. of Appeals April 23, 1996).

Witness not incompetent to testify. — Under § 19.2-269, a witness is not incompetent to testify simply because he has a criminal record. Lester v. Commonwealth, No. 1719-03-3, 2004 Va. App. LEXIS 198 (Ct. of Appeals Apr. 27, 2004).

Impeachment by juvenile adjudication. — Defendant's convictions for first-degree murder and use of a firearm in the commission of a felony were proper because, although she sought pretrial disclosure by the Commonwealth of the criminal records of several witnesses for the Commonwealth, including both adult and juvenile records, review of defendant's several motions in limine relating to juvenile records demonstrated that she sought juvenile records as part of general impeachment preparations. Bias or motivation was never identified as a justification; consequently, juvenile adjudications were not permitted to be used for the impeachment of a witness on the subject of general credibility. Thomas v. Commonwealth, 279 Va. 131, 688 S.E.2d 220, 2010 Va. LEXIS 11, cert. denied, 131 S. Ct. 143, 178 L. Ed. 2d 8, 2010 U.S. LEXIS 6109 (U.S. 2010).

Applied in Epps v. Commonwealth, 59 Va. App. 71, 717 S.E.2d 151, 2011 Va. App. LEXIS 351 (2011).

CIRCUIT COURT OPINIONS

Impeachment following removal of political disabilities of witness. — Motion in limine by an accident victim in a negligence action was denied to the extent that the motion requested that a motorist was to be barred from impeaching the victim with the victim's felony convictions because, under § 19.2-269, the fact of the convictions could be used as evidence to affect the victim's credibility, even though the victim's political disabilities had been removed by the Governor of Virginia. Sulton v. FedEx Ground Package Sys., 80 Va. Cir. 385, 2010 Va. Cir. LEXIS 62 (Fairfax County June 1, 2010).

§ 19.2-269.1. Inmates as witnesses in criminal cases.

Whenever the Commonwealth or a defendant in a criminal prosecution in any circuit court in this Commonwealth requires as a witness in his behalf, an inmate in a state or local correctional facility as defined in § 53.1-1, the court, on the application of such defendant or his attorney, or the attorney for the Commonwealth, shall issue an order to the Director of the Department of Corrections to deliver such witness to the sheriff of the jurisdiction of the court issuing the order. If authorized by the court, the clerk of the circuit court or a deputy clerk may issue these orders on behalf of the court. The sheriff shall go where such witness may then be and carry him to the court to testify as such witness, and after he has testified and been released as such witness, carry him back to the place whence he came, for all of which service the sheriff shall be paid out of the criminal expense funds in the state treasury such compensation as the court in which the case is pending may certify to be reasonable.

History.
Code 1950, § 8-300; 1966, c. 227; 1974, cc. 44, 45; 1977, c. 624; 2002, cc. 515, 544.

§ 19.2-269.2. Nondisclosure of addresses or telephone numbers of crime victims and witnesses.

During any criminal proceeding, upon motion of the defendant or the attorney for the Commonwealth, a judge may prohibit testimony as to the current residential or business address or telephone number of a victim or witness if the judge determines that this information is not material under the circumstances of the case.

History.
1989, c. 170; 1994, cc. 845, 931.

§ 19.2-270. When statement by accused as witness not received as evidence.

In a criminal prosecution, other than for perjury, or in an action on a penal statute, evidence shall not be given against the accused of any statement made by him as a witness upon a legal examination, in a criminal or civil action, unless such statement was made when examined as a witness in his own behalf.

History.
Code 1950, § 19.1-267; 1960, c. 366; 1975, c. 495; 1988, c. 366.

Cross references.
As to right of accused to testify, see § 19.2-268.

Law Review.
For survey on evidence in Virginia for 1989, see 23 U. Rich. L. Rev. 647 (1989). For survey of Virginia criminal law and procedure for the year 2004-2005, see 40 U. Rich. L. Rev. 197 (2005).

Michie's Jurisprudence.
For related discussion, see 5B M.J. Criminal Procedure, § 60; 7B M.J. Evidence, §§ 231, 234; 8B M.J. Forgery, § 17; 20 M.J. Witnesses, §§ 39, 80, 81.

CASE NOTES

Constitutionality. — The effect of this section is to conform the procedure in this state with the general rule that a defendant's testimony at a former trial is admissible in evidence against him in later proceedings and does not violate his constitutional privilege against compulsory self-incrimination. Consequently, the statute is not in derogation of the federal and state constitutional provisions. Harbaugh v. Commonwealth, 209 Va. 695, 167 S.E.2d 329 (1969).

This section benefits both the witness-in-jeopardy and the accused by immunizing the witness. Benefit to the witness from use of immunity is manifest. The benefit to the accused lies in taking away the obstacle to confrontation posed by the witness' continued assertion of the Fifth Amendment privilege. A third, and equally important, benefit accrues to the truthfinding process. As the trial judge stated: "The reason behind this statute . . . is obvious. There is a search for justice and we must have the truth." Cunningham v. Commonwealth, 2 Va. App. 358, 344 S.E.2d 389 (1986).

Protection provided witness limited. — This section by its terms confers only use immunity, i.e., it protects the witness only from the use of the specific testimony compelled from him under the grant of immunity, but not from evidence obtained as a result of such testimony. Such limited protection is obviously not coextensive with the constitutional privilege against self-incrimination and cannot overcome the privilege, once validly asserted. Gosling v. Commonwealth, 14 Va. App. 158, 415 S.E.2d 870 (1992).

Witness testimony should only be compelled if incrimination clearly impossible. — When a witness declares his belief that an answer to a question would incriminate, or tend to incriminate him, the court cannot compel him to answer, unless it is perfectly clear, from a careful consideration of all the circumstances in the case, that the witness is mistaken and that the answer cannot possibly have such tendency. Gosling v. Commonwealth, 14 Va. App. 158, 415 S.E.2d 870 (1992).

Immunization cures any possible prejudice. — Although no Virginia cases on point can be found, immunization has been held in other jurisdictions to cure any possible prejudice, because the defendant is enabled to cross-examine. Cunningham v. Commonwealth, 2 Va. App. 358, 344 S.E.2d 389 (1986).

No statement made by witness upon legal examination, unless made when examined as a witness in his own behalf, can be used as evidence against him. Smith v. Commonwealth, 136 Va. 773, 118 S.E. 107 (1923).

Where defendant formerly a witness in his own behalf. — Where the defendant's testimony at his brother's trial constituted statements that he made when examined as a witness on his own behalf, he was not entitled to any protection under this section when the prosecutor sought to use that testimony against him. Thornton v. Commonwealth, 22 Va. App. 2, 467 S.E.2d 820 (1996).

Testimony from a prior trial that ends in a mistrial is admissible under the statute. Moore v. Commonwealth, No. 0063-98-4 (Ct. of Appeals Feb. 23, 1999).

Waiver. — A defendant who chooses to testify waives his privilege against compulsory self-incrimination with respect to the testimony he gives, and that waiver is no less effective or complete because the defendant may have been motivated to take the witness stand in the first place only by reason of the strength of the lawful evidence adduced against him. Harbaugh v. Commonwealth, 209 Va. 695, 167 S.E.2d 329 (1969).

A defendant in a criminal case who takes the stand in his own behalf and testifies without asserting his privilege against self-incrimination thereby waives the privilege as to the testimony given so that it may be used against him in a subsequent trial of the same case. The fact that the defendant does not take the stand at the second trial does not prevent the use of his testimony given at the former trial if it would otherwise be admissible. Harbaugh v. Commonwealth, 209 Va. 695, 167 S.E.2d 329 (1969).

Statements at coroner's inquest are inadmissible. — On a trial for murder, statements made by the accused on his examination at the inquest before the coroner's jury cannot be given in evidence against him, under the express provisions of this section. Mullins v. Commonwealth, 113 Va. 787, 75 S.E. 193 (1912).

But cross-examination as to statements made before coroner is permissible. Thaniel v. Commonwealth, 132 Va. 795, 111 S.E. 259 (1922).

The fact that defendant took the stand at his second trial only after the State threatened to introduce his prior testimony does not have the effect of compelling his testimony at the second trial since the State could constitutionally introduce that evidence. Smith v. Slayton, 369 F. Supp. 1213 (W.D. Va. 1973).

The decision of the defendant to take the stand at his second trial, apparently to avoid the effect that his prior testimony might have upon the jury, does not rise to the level of an unconstitutional coercion or compulsion on the part of the Commonwealth. Smith v. Slayton, 369 F. Supp. 1213 (W.D. Va. 1973).

The use of prior testimony from defendant's first trial for purposes of rebuttal or impeachment is certainly a natural consequence of taking the stand in one's own defense. Smith v. Slayton, 369 F. Supp. 1213 (W.D. Va. 1973).

Statement of witness for accused in conflict with his former testimony. — Evidence shall not be given against the accused of any statement made by him as a witness upon a legal examination. Therefore, evidence that the statements of witnesses for the accused conflict with the testimony of the accused as delivered on his examination as a witness at a former trial is inadmissible. Kirby v. Commonwealth, 77 Va. 681 (1883), superseded by statute as stated in Frazier v. Commonwealth, 40 Va. App. 350, 579 S.E.2d 628 (2003).

But statements of joint interest when witness is subsequently indicted are admissible. — Statements made by a person as a witness upon a legal examination touching a matter in which he is jointly interested with another are not excluded under this section when he is subsequently indicted for crime. Hansel v. Commonwealth, 118 Va. 803, 88 S.E. 166 (1916).

Statement inadmissible. — In a prosecution for violation of the

Prohibition Act, a witness testified as to a statement of accused that he had given away some of the beverages found on his premises. Accused denied having made such statements, and the purpose of the testimony was to impeach his credibility. The statement was not shown to have been made by the accused "when examined as a witness in his own behalf," and, therefore, was not admissible. Neal v. Commonwealth, 124 Va. 842, 98 S.E. 629 (1919).

Denial of due process where defense witness arrested in violation of section. — See Bray v. Peyton, 429 F.2d 500 (4th Cir. 1970).

Witness' silence correctly honored where trial court properly heard and considered several questions that defendant proposed to ask witness, recognized an incriminating dimension to the inquiries, and thereby declined to compel witness' testimony. Gosling v. Commonwealth, 14 Va. App. 158, 415 S.E.2d 870 (1992).

Defendant's testimony from prior trial admissible. — Trial court properly admitted defendant's prior testimony from her boyfriend's trial for failure to appear because, as an exception to the statute, regarding the personal and familial aspect of the defendant and her boyfriend's relationship, defendant testified at her own trial that she encouraged her boyfriend to flee during his drug/weapons trial because she was concerned about her boyfriend and the father of her child going to prison. Frazier v. Commonwealth, 268 Va. 412, 601 S.E.2d 624, 2004 Va. LEXIS 126 (2004).

Applied in Johnson v. Riddle, 222 Va. 428, 281 S.E.2d 843 (1981).

§ 19.2-270.1. Use of photographs as evidence in certain larceny and burglary prosecutions.

In any prosecution for larceny under the provisions of §§ 18.2-95, 18.2-96 or § 18.2-98, or for shoplifting under the provisions of § 18.2-103, or for burglary under the provisions of §§ 18.2-89, 18.2-90, 18.2-91 or § 18.2-92, photographs of the goods, merchandise, money or securities alleged to have been taken or converted shall be deemed competent evidence of such goods, merchandise, money or securities and shall be admissible in any proceeding, hearing or trial of the case to the same extent as if such goods, merchandise, money or securities had been introduced as evidence. Such photographs shall bear a written description of the goods, merchandise, money or securities alleged to have been taken or converted, the name of the owner of such goods, merchandise, money or securities and the manner of the identification of same by such owner, or the name of the place wherein the alleged offense occurred, the name of the accused, the name of the arresting or investigating police officer or conservator of the peace, the date of the photograph and the name of the photographer. Such writing shall be made under oath by the arresting or investigating police officer or conservator of the peace, and the photographs identified by the signature of the photographer. Upon the filing of such photograph and writing with the police authority or court holding such goods and merchandise as evidence, such goods or merchandise shall be returned to their owner, or the proprietor or manager of the store or establishment wherein the alleged offense occurred.

History.
1976, c. 577; 1985, c. 184; 1987, c. 493; 1995, c. 447.

Law Review.
For survey of Virginia tort law for the year 1975-1976, see 62 Va. L. Rev. 1489 (1976).

Michie's Jurisprudence.
For related discussion, see 5B M.J. Criminal Procedure, § 56; 14B M.J. Photographs and Photographers, § 5.

CASE NOTES

This section provides an alternative means of establishing an adequate foundation to authenticate a photograph which is offered under the independent silent witness theory in prosecutions under §§ 18.2-95 and 18.2-96. Saunders v. Commonwealth, 1 Va. App. 396, 339 S.E.2d 550 (1986).

Photograph as silent witness. — A photograph of the goods or merchandise alleged to have been taken or converted, which bears the sworn writing of the arresting officer and the photographer's signature, shall be deemed competent evidence of such goods or merchandise and shall be admissible to the same extent as if such goods and merchandise had been introduced as evidence. When a photograph is so authenticated and admitted it becomes not just an illustration of the testimony of a witness but an independent silent witness constituting substantive evidence. Saunders v. Commonwealth, 1 Va. App. 396, 339 S.E.2d 550 (1986).

The trial court did not err in admitting photographs of recovered, stolen property in a larceny prosecution where the Commonwealth failed to comply with this section because they were received as illustrative, rather than substantive, evidence, and, thus, were not subject to the requirements of this section. Saunders v. Commonwealth, 1 Va. App. 396, 339 S.E.2d 550 (1986).

§ 19.2-270.1:1. Computer and electronic data in obscenity, etc. cases; access to defendant.

When computer data or electronic data, stored in any form, the possession of which is otherwise unlawful, are seized as evidence in a criminal prosecution of any offense involving obscenity or child pornography, neither the original data nor a copy thereof shall be released to the defendant or his counsel, nor shall a court order the release of such evidence to the defendant or his counsel except as provided herein. The defendant and his counsel shall be allowed the reasonable opportunity to review such evidence in accordance with the rules of discovery. Upon a finding that the production of the original data or a copy thereof to counsel or his designee is necessary and material to the defense of the accused, the court may order such production only under terms that restrict access to specifically identified recipients, prohibit any duplication of the data beyond what is reasonably necessary for the purpose of the production, and require the return of the data to the law-enforcement agency maintaining custody or control of the seized data for appropriate disposition.

History.
2006, c. 601.

§ 19.2-270.2. Disposition of money, securities or documents seized upon arrest, etc., and pertinent as evidence.

A. When in the course of investigation or arrest, the investigating or arresting officer shall seize or come into the possession of moneys, cash, or negotiable or nonnegotiable instruments or securities, hereinafter called "moneys or securities," taken or retained unlawfully from a financial institution or other person, and such moneys or securities, or a portion thereof, shall be pertinent evidence in a pending prosecution or appeal therefrom, the officer or agency having possession thereof, may retain, pending such prosecution or appeal thereof, sufficient of such moneys or securities as shall be necessary to prove the crime of grand larceny or other crimes requiring a specific amount in value. The court upon motion of the attorney for the Commonwealth and for good cause shown may order the release of all moneys or securities, subject to the provisions of this section. The remaining excess moneys or securities, if any, may be released to the owner thereof, upon proper receipt therefor, which release shall be with the consent of the attorney for the Commonwealth. The officer or agency authorizing such release shall make an appropriate record of such moneys or securities released, including designation or copying of serial numbers, and such record or receipt shall be admissible into evidence in any proceeding, hearing or trial of the case to the same extent as if such moneys or securities had been introduced. Such record or receipt shall contain the name of the financial institution or person from whom such moneys or securities were taken, the place from which taken, the name of the accused, and the name of the arresting officer or officers coming into initial possession of such moneys or securities. Pictures shall be taken of any instruments or securities and such pictures shall be attached to the receipt or record above and shall contain further, in the case of such copying, the date of the photograph and the name of the photographer.

B. When in the course of investigation or arrest, the investigating or arresting officer seizes or comes into the possession of moneys or securities under the provisions of this section, and such moneys or securities, or a portion thereof, are introduced as an exhibit in a prosecution or appeal therefrom, the court may, with the consent of the attorney for the Commonwealth, authorize the clerk of the circuit court, upon all appeal rights being exhausted, to deposit such moneys or cash in an interest-bearing account.

History.
1980, c. 423; 1991, c. 680; 1995, c. 447.

Michie's Jurisprudence.
For related discussion, see 16 M.J. Searches and Seizures, § 11.

CASE NOTES

Inapplicable as to introduction of seized items. — This section permits police authorities to retain monies and securities pending trial or appeal, or to release the items when good cause is shown and does not involve the admissibility of the items as evidence; this statute has no application to the introduction into evidence of the money and checks or copies thereof against this defendant. Nestle v. Commonwealth, 22 Va. App. 336, 470 S.E.2d 133 (1996).

§ 19.2-270.3. Admissible evidence as to identity of party presenting bad check, draft or order.

In any prosecution under § 18.2-181 or § 18.2-182 for the presentation of a bad check, draft or order, the following shall be admissible in any proceeding, hearing or trial of the case:

1. The unpaid or dishonored check, draft or order, bearing a notation thereon of the full name, residence address, home telephone number, and either the driver's license, social security or other governmentally issued identification number of the person who delivered such check, draft or order to the payee, the cashing party or its representative, and bearing the initials of the representative of the payee or cashing party to whom the check, draft or order was delivered, as evidence that such information was transcribed on such check, draft or order at the time of such delivery; or

2. A composite photograph of the check, draft or order, and of the person delivering such check, draft or order, and of other documentation identifying such person, such as a driver's license, social security card, or other governmentally issued identification card, taken together at the time the check, draft or order was delivered by such person to the payee, the cashing party or its representative.

If such evidence is introduced, it may invoke an inference sufficient for the trier of fact to find that the person whose identifying information appears on the check, draft or order was the person who delivered the check, draft or order in question to the payee, cashing party or its representative.

History.
1981, c. 292; 1991, c. 633.

Michie's Jurisprudence.
For related discussion, see 3A M.J. Banks and Banking, § 89.

CASE NOTES

This section does not create a rebuttable presumption that a bad check was presented by the person whose name, address, telephone number, and social security or other identifying number are noted thereon. If the legislative purpose was to create such a rebuttable presumption, the statutory language fell short of accomplishing that end. Such a presumption might have been specifically created, but, significantly, was not. Edwards v. Commonwealth, 227 Va. 349, 315 S.E.2d 239 (1984).

Statutory words "may be deemed competent evidence with respect to the identity of the person who delivered the check," are not equivalent to the words "shall be sufficient evidence to show, prima facie, that the person whose identifying data is written on the face of a bad check, is the person who presented it." Edwards v. Commonwealth, 227 Va. 349, 315 S.E.2d 239 (1984).

Identifying data must be shown to pertain to presenter. — The opening paragraph of this section makes admissible and competent, as to the identity of the presenter, only that evidence specified in the following numbered subdivisions. Thus when subdivision 1, which refers only to identifying data of the person who delivered such check, is relied on, the identifying data must still be shown somehow to pertain to the presenter of a bad check, and the presenter's identity must still be shown by some other means. Edwards v. Commonwealth, 227 Va. 349, 315 S.E.2d 239 (1984).

§ 19.2-270.4. When donation, destruction, or return of exhibits received in evidence authorized.

A. Except as provided in § 19.2-270.4:1 and unless objection with sufficient cause is made, the trial court in any criminal case may order the donation or destruction of any or all exhibits received in evidence during the course of the trial (i) in any misdemeanor case, at any time after the expiration of the time for filing an appeal from the final judgment of the court if no appeal is taken or if an appeal is taken, at any time after exhaustion of all appellate remedies and (ii) in any felony case, upon notice in the sentencing order or otherwise to the attorney for the Commonwealth, the defendant at his last known address, and attorney of record for the defendant in the case, after more than one year has expired from exhaustion of all appellate remedies, or, if no appeal is taken, after more than one year from the time for seeking appellate remedies has expired; and in the event the defendant is found not guilty by a court of law, the court may, upon entry of the final order, order the destruction, donation, or return of the exhibits; provided, however, if a petition for writ of habeas corpus is filed within such one-year period, then such order shall not be entered until exhaustion of such habeas corpus proceedings. Notwithstanding the foregoing, in all cases concluded prior to July 1, 2005, the notice requirement in this section shall not apply. The order of donation or destruction may require that photographs be made of all exhibits ordered to be donated or destroyed and that such photographs be appropriately labeled for future identification. In addition, the order shall state the nature of the exhibit subject to donation or destruction, identify the case in which such exhibit was received and from whom such exhibit was received, if known, and the manner by which the exhibit is to be destroyed or to whom donated. However, any money introduced into evidence, unless it is stolen from a third party, shall be subject to forfeiture by law-enforcement officials as otherwise provided by law, and if no forfeiture action is taken or if funds remain after any such forfeiture, the clerk shall escheat such funds as otherwise provided by law. No notice to the defendant shall be required in the case of exhibits the disposal or destruction of which is controlled by § 19.2-386.23 or 19.2-386.24, in any case in which such exhibits may be seized and forfeited to the Commonwealth under Chapter 22.1 (§ 19.2-386.1 et seq.) or Chapter 22.2 (§ 19.2-386.15 et seq.), or any other forfeiture provisions, or in any case where such exhibits are deemed contraband.

B. Except as provided in § 19.2-270.4:1, a circuit court for good cause shown, on notice to the attorney for the Commonwealth and any attorney for a defendant in the case, may order the return of any or all exhibits to the owners thereof, notwithstanding the pendency of any appeal or petition for a writ of habeas corpus. The order may be upon such conditions as the court deems appropriate for future identification and inclusion in the record of a case subject to retrial. In addition, the owner shall acknowledge in a sworn affidavit to be filed with the record of the case, that he has retaken possession of such exhibit or exhibits.

C. Any photographs taken pursuant to an order of donation or destruction or an order returning exhibits to the owners shall be retained with the record in the case and, if necessary, shall be admissible in any subsequent trial of the same cause, subject to all other rules of evidence.

D. Upon petition of any organization which is exempt from taxation under § 501 (c) (3) of the Internal Revenue Code, the court in its sound discretion may order the donation of an exhibit to such charitable organization.

History.

1984, c. 621; 1989, c. 481; 1994, c. 536; 2001, cc. 873, 874, 875; 2008, c. 805; 2010, cc. 352, 366, 454.

Cross references.

As to the contents of the record on appeal before the Virginia Supreme Court, see Rule 5:10, Rules of the Virginia Supreme Court.

Editor's note.

Acts 2001, cc. 873 and 874, cl. 3, provide: "That an emergency exists and the provisions of this act, except for the provisions of Chapter 19.2, consisting of sections 19.2-327.2 through 19.2-327.6, are in force from its passage [May 2, 2001]."

The 2008 amendments.

The 2008 amendment by c. 805, in subsection A, inserted "in any misdemeanor case" at the beginning of clause (i), redesignated the former clause (ii) as a continuation of clause (i), inserted present clause (ii); and in subsection B, inserted "or petition for a writ of habeas corpus" at the end of the first sentence.

The 2010 amendments.

The 2010 amendment by c. 352 in subsection A, inserted "in the sentencing order or otherwise" and "and in the event the defendant is found not guilty by a court of law, the court may, upon entry of the final order, order the destruction, donation, or return of the exhibits" in the first sentence, and inserted the second and fifth sentences.

The 2010 amendments by cc. 366 and 454 are nearly identical, and inserted the last sentence in subsection A.

CASE NOTES

Habeas petition denied. — Petition for a writ of habeas corpus was dismissed because the chief court clerk, who obtained an order to destroy the trial exhibits in the defendant's case after the defendant's conviction was affirmed by the Supreme Court of Virginia in order to create storage space, did not act in bad faith in destroying the evidence, was not aware that the new statute had gone into effect, and was not aware that potentially exculpatory DNA evidence was destroyed in the destruction of the exhibits. Lovitt v. Warden, 266 Va. 216, 585 S.E.2d 801, 2003 Va. LEXIS 81 (2003), cert. denied, 541 U.S. 1006, 124 S. Ct. 2018, 158 L. Ed. 2d 523 (2004); habeas corpus dismissed, stay vacated sub nom. Lovitt v. True, 330 F. Supp. 2d 603 (E.D. Va. 2004).

OPINIONS OF THE ATTORNEY GENERAL

Requirement for motion to preserve evidence. — Unless a court imposes a death sentence or a defendant files a motion to store, retain, and preserve human biological evidence, the trial court, in a criminal case that has not been appealed, may order the donation or destruction of such evidence after the time period for appeal of the final judgment has expired. See opinion of Attorney General to The Honorable Yvonne G. Smith, Clerk, Circuit Court of Henrico County, 03-094 (10/31/03).

§ 19.2-270.4:1. Storage, preservation and retention of human biological evidence in felony cases.

A. Notwithstanding any provision of law or rule of court, upon motion of a person convicted of a felony but not sentenced to death or his attorney of record to the circuit court that entered the judgment for the offense, the court shall order the storage, preservation, and retention of specifically identified human biological evidence or representative samples collected or obtained in the case for a period of up to 15 years from the time of conviction, unless the court determines, in its discretion, that the evidence should be retained for a longer period of time. Upon the filing of such a motion, the defendant may request a hearing for the limited purpose of identifying the human biological evidence or representative samples that are to be stored in accordance with the provisions of this section. Upon the granting of the motion, the court shall order the clerk of the circuit court to transfer all such evidence to the Department of Forensic Science. The Department of Forensic Science shall store, preserve, and retain such evidence. If the evidence is not within the custody of the clerk at the time the order is entered, the court shall order the governmental entity having custody of the evidence to transfer such evidence to the Department of Forensic Science. Upon the entry of an order under this subsection, the court may upon motion or upon good cause shown, with notice to the convicted person, his attorney of record and the attorney for the Commonwealth, modify the original storage order, as it relates to time of storage of the evidence or samples, for a period of time greater than or less than that specified in the original order.

B. In the case of a person sentenced to death, the court that entered the judgment shall, in all cases, order any human biological evidence or representative samples to be transferred by the governmental entity having custody to the Department of Forensic Science. The Department of Forensic Science shall store, preserve, and retain such evidence until the judgment is executed. If the person sentenced to death has his sentence reduced, then such evidence shall be transferred from the Department to the original investigating law-enforcement agency for storage as provided in this section.

C. Pursuant to standards and guidelines established by the Department of Forensic Science, the order shall state the method of custody, transfer and return of any evidence to insure and protect the Commonwealth's interest in the integrity of the evidence. Pursuant to standards and guidelines established by the Department of Forensic Science, the Department of Forensic Science, local law-enforcement agency or other custodian of the evidence shall take all necessary steps to preserve, store, and retain the evidence and its chain of custody for the period of time specified.

D. In any proceeding under this section, the court, upon a finding that the physical evidence is of such a nature, size or quantity that storage, preservation or retention of all of the evidence is impractical, may order the storage of only representative samples of the evidence. The Department of Forensic Science shall take representative samples, cuttings or swabbings and retain them. The remaining evidence shall be handled according to § 19.2-270.4 or as otherwise provided for in the Code.

E. An action under this section or the performance of any attorney representing the petitioner under this section shall not form the basis for relief in any habeas corpus or appellate proceeding. Nothing in this section shall create any cause of action for damages against the Commonwealth, or any of its political subdivisions or officers, employees or agents of the Commonwealth or its political subdivisions.

History.
2001, cc. 873, 874, 875; 2002, c. 832; 2005, cc. 868, 881.

Editor's note.
Acts 2001, cc. 873, 874, cl. 3, provides: "That an emergency exists and the provisions of this act, except for the provisions of Chapter 19.2, consisting of sections 19.2-327.2 through 19.2-327.6, are in force from its passage [May 2, 2001]."

Law Review.
For article, "Criminal Law and Procedure," see 35 U. Rich. L. Rev. 537 (2001).

CASE NOTES

No bad faith in destruction of trial exhibits. — Petition for a writ of habeas corpus was dismissed because the chief court clerk, who obtained an order to destroy the trial exhibits in the defendant's case after the defendant's conviction was affirmed by the Supreme Court of Virginia in order to create storage space, did not act in bad faith in destroying the evidence, was not aware that the new statute had gone into effect, and was not aware that potentially exculpatory DNA evidence was destroyed in the destruction of the exhibits. Lovitt v. Warden, 266 Va. 216, 585 S.E.2d 801, 2003 Va. LEXIS 81 (2003), cert. denied, 541 U.S. 1006, 124 S. Ct. 2018, 158 L. Ed. 2d 523 (2004); habeas corpus dismissed, stay vacated sub nom. Lovitt v. True, 330 F. Supp. 2d 603 (E.D. Va. 2004).

CIRCUIT COURT OPINIONS

Request limited to specifically identified human biological evidence. — Trial court denied the defendant's motion to preserve biological evidence as the defendant made a blanket request for all evidence; however, pursuant to subsection A of § 19.2-270.4:1, the defendant could only request the court to preserve specifically identified human biological evidence. Commonwealth v. Stevens, 60 Va. Cir. 432, 2002 Va. Cir. LEXIS 415 (Richmond 2002).

Request for storage of hair samples granted. — Defendant's request, after his conviction for statutory burglary and attempted grand larceny, for new scientific testing of hair samples found at the scene of the crime, pursuant to § 19.2-327.1, was denied where the results thereof would not have resulted in a changed outcome

because the trial court had given no weight to the prior analysis of such hair fragments and there was sufficient other evidence to support the conviction; however, the court granted defendant's motion to store, preserve, and retain his human biological evidence for a period of 15 years pursuant to § 19.2-270.4:1. Neal v. Commonwealth's Att'y, 60 Va. Cir. 440, 2002 Va. Cir. LEXIS 305 (Roanoke 2002).

OPINIONS OF THE ATTORNEY GENERAL

Requirement for motion to preserve evidence. — Unless a court imposes a death sentence or a defendant files a motion to store, retain, and preserve human biological evidence, the trial court, in a criminal case that has not been appealed, may order the donation or destruction of such evidence after the time period for appeal of the final judgment has expired. See opinion of Attorney General to The Honorable Yvonne G. Smith, Clerk, Circuit Court of Henrico County, 03-094 (10/31/03).

§ 19.2-270.5. DNA profile admissible in criminal proceeding.

In any criminal proceeding, DNA (deoxyribonucleic acid) testing shall be deemed to be a reliable scientific technique and the evidence of a DNA profile comparison may be admitted to prove or disprove the identity of any person. This section shall not otherwise limit the introduction of any relevant evidence bearing upon any question at issue before the court, including the accuracy and reliability of the procedures employed in the collection and analysis of a particular DNA sample. The court shall, regardless of the results of the DNA analysis, if any, consider such other relevant evidence of the identity of the accused as shall be admissible in evidence.

At least twenty-one days prior to commencement of the proceeding in which the results of a DNA analysis will be offered as evidence, the party intending to offer the evidence shall notify the opposing party, in writing, of the intent to offer the analysis and shall provide or make available copies of the profiles and the report or statement to be introduced. In the event that such notice is not given, and the person proffers such evidence, then the court may in its discretion either allow the opposing party a continuance or, under appropriate circumstances, bar the person from presenting such evidence. The period of any such continuance shall not be counted for speedy trial purposes under § 19.2-243. If the opposing party intends to object to the admissibility of such evidence he shall give written notice of that fact and the basis for his objections at least ten days prior to commencement of the proceedings.

History.
1990, c. 669; 1997, c. 315; 2002, cc. 627, 885.

Law Review.
For note, "DNA Fingerprinting: The Virginia Approach," see 35 Wm. & Mary L. Rev. 767 (1994). For an article relating to all published Virginia criminal law decisions between July 1, 1997, and July 1, 1998, see 32 U. Rich. L. Rev. 1091 (1998).

CASE NOTES

Virginia's statute governing admission of DNA evidence was simply a rule of evidence, merely stating that such evidence is to be treated as scientifically reliable, and did not shift the burden of proof to the defendant or determine his guilt. Satcher v. Netherland, 944 F. Supp. 1222 (E.D. Va. 1996), aff'd in part and rev'd in part on other grounds sub nom. Satcher v. Pruett, 126 F.3d 561 (4th Cir.), cert. denied, 522 U.S. 1010, 118 S. Ct. 595, 139 L. Ed. 2d 431 (1997).

Profiles, reports or statements. — A probability calculation or probability report indicating statistical probability of a DNA match constitutes a "profile," "report" or "statement" within meaning of this section. Beverly v. Commonwealth, No. 0852-98-2 (Ct. of Appeals June 29, 1999).

This section does not require that copies of profiles, statements or reports to be introduced be attached to the notice; it requires only that they be "provided or made available." Beverly v. Commonwealth, No. 0852-98-2 (Ct. of Appeals June 29, 1999).

Prosecution's filing of third DNA notice less than 21 days before trial was irrelevant to the report's admissibility, where report had previously been timely attached to both first and second DNA notices. Beverly v. Commonwealth, No. 0852-98-2 (Ct. of Appeals June 29, 1999).

The supplemental report prepared by the expert merely completed the summary of the analysis contained in expert's earlier report, and it thus constituted additional analysis of the DNA evidence in question, not an analysis of new evidence requiring additional notice to defendant. Hills v. Commonwealth, 32 Va. App. 479, 528 S.E.2d 730, 2000 Va. App. LEXIS 388 (2000).

Where notice not given, options of court. — The statute provides that, in the event timely notice is not given, "then the court may in its discretion either allow ... a continuance or ... bar... such evidence." That language expressly limits the court's discretion by the disjunctive "or" to a choice of "either" of two defined options. Stated differently, if a trial court determines that the evidence is admissible, the statute requires the court to grant a motion to interrupt and postpone the progress of the trial to afford the defense a period of time for consultation with other experts and preparation of an appropriate response to the new evidence. Caprio v. Commonwealth, 254 Va. 507, 493 S.E.2d 371 (1997).

Extrapolation of blood profile frequency was within contemplation of statute. — Extrapolation of blood profile frequency based upon expert's analysis of a series of DNA profiles and reports was a matter within the contemplation of the statute. Caprio v. Commonwealth, 254 Va. 507, 493 S.E.2d 371 (1997).

Exclusion of hypothesis. — While defendant's hypothesis that the DNA evidence did not consider the existence of an identical twin or close relative to defendant—a circumstance which would diminish the probability that he was the perpetrator—was conceivable, it had no basis in the record. The Commonwealth must only exclude hypotheses of innocence that reasonably flow from the evidence, not from defendant's imagination, therefore, the evidence provided ample support for the convictions. Taylor v. Commonwealth, No. 1767-93-1 (Ct. of Appeals Feb. 28, 1995).

Harmless error. — Even assuming that the Commonwealth did not comply with § 19.2-270.5 regarding a DNA certificate, any error was harmless under § 8.01-678 because the forensic scientist who prepared the DNA certificate testified at trial, explaining the testing conducted, and, thus, the certificate was duplicative of her testimony; even without the certificate, the evidence against defendant was overwhelming as he was seen in the vicinity of the bank shortly after the robbery wearing the same clothes as the perpetrator. Whitted v. Commonwealth, 2008 Va. App. LEXIS 248 (May 20, 2008).

CIRCUIT COURT OPINIONS

Where court offers a continuance. — Petitioner was not denied his right to due process warranting habeas relief by the trial court's refusal to bar DNA evidence that the Commonwealth untimely disclosed because, although § 19.2-270.5 required the trial court to provide petitioner with an opportunity for the defense to consult with other experts and prepare an appropriate response to the new evidence, the trial court asked petitioner if he wanted a continuance in the event it did not find appropriate circumstances to bar admission of the evidence but petitioner declined. Hudson v. Dir. of the Dep't of Corr., 67 Va. Cir. 319, 2005 Va. Cir. LEXIS 147 (Clarke County May 16, 2005).

§ 19.2-270.6. Evidence of abuse admissible in certain criminal trials (Supreme Court Rule 2:409 derived from this section).

In any criminal prosecution alleging personal injury or death, or the attempt to cause personal injury or death, relevant evidence of repeated physical and psychological abuse of the accused by the victim shall be admissible, subject to the general rules of evidence.

History.
1993, c. 5.

Editor's note.
At the direction of the Virginia Code Commission, the notation to the Virginia Rules of Evidence was added to the catchline of this section. Acts 2012, cc. 688 and 708, cl. 6 provides: "That pursuant to the authority set forth in §§ 30-146 and 30-147 of the Code of Virginia, the Virginia Code Commission shall direct any party with whom the Virginia Code Commission contracts to publish the Code of Virginia to include in the catchline of every section of the Code of Virginia from which any rule contained in the Rules of Evidence has been derived a notation specifying such rule."

Michie's Jurisprudence.
For related discussion, see 7B M.J. Evidence, § 47.

§ 19.2-270.7. Determining decibel level of sound with proper equipment; certificate as to accuracy of equipment.

A law-enforcement officer may use equipment deemed proper pursuant to subsection C of § 2.2-1112 to determine the decibel level of any sound, including noise. The results of such determinations shall be accepted as prima facie evidence of the decibel level of the sound in any court or legal proceeding where the decibel level of the sound is at issue.

In any court or legal proceeding in which any question arises about the calibration or accuracy of such equipment used to determine the decibel level of sound, a certificate, or a true copy thereof, showing the calibration or testing for accuracy of the equipment, and when and by whom the calibration or test was made, shall be admissible as evidence of the facts therein stated. No calibration or testing of such equipment shall be valid for longer than 12 months.

History.
2010, c. 558.

§ 19.2-271. Certain judicial officers incompetent to testify under certain circumstances (Supreme Court Rule 2:605 derived from this section).

No judge shall be competent to testify in any criminal or civil proceeding as to any matter which came before him in the course of his official duties.

No clerk of any court, magistrate, or other person having the power to issue warrants, shall be competent to testify in any criminal or civil proceeding, except proceedings wherein the defendant is charged with perjury, as to any matter which came before him in the course of his official duties. Such person shall be competent to testify in any criminal proceeding wherein the defendant is charged pursuant to the provisions of § 18.2-460 or in any proceeding authorized pursuant to § 19.2-353.3. Notwithstanding any other provision of this section, any judge, clerk of any court, magistrate, or other person having the power to issue warrants, who is the victim of a crime, shall not be incompetent solely because of his office to testify in any criminal or civil proceeding arising out of the crime.

History.
Code 1950, §§ 19.1-267, 19.1-268; 1960, c. 366; 1975, c. 495; 1976, c. 269; 1989, c. 738; 1990, c. 602.

Editor's note.
At the direction of the Virginia Code Commission, the notation to the Virginia Rules of Evidence was added to the catchline of this section. Acts 2012, cc. 688 and 708, cl. 6 provides: "That pursuant to the authority set forth in §§ 30-146 and 30-147 of the Code of Virginia, the Virginia Code Commission shall direct any party with whom the Virginia Code Commission contracts to publish the Code of Virginia to include in the catchline of every section of the Code of Virginia from which any rule contained in the Rules of Evidence has been derived a notation specifying such rule."

Law Review.
For note, "Lying on the Stand Won't Cost You a Dime: Should Courts Recognize a Civil Action in Tort for Perjury?," see 44 Wash. & Lee L. Rev. 1257 (1988).

Michie's Jurisprudence.
For related discussion, see 8B M.J. Forgery, § 17; 9A M.J. Habeas Corpus, § 23; 20 M.J. Witnesses, §§ 80, 111.1.

CASE NOTES

This section is not a blanket prohibition against clerks testifying; it prohibits, instead, clerks testifying regarding factual matters which have come before them in the course of their official duties. This section does not prevent a clerk from testifying how and whether he has performed a ministerial function. Carter v. Commonwealth, No. 1930-89-2 (Ct. of Appeals March 26, 1991); Carter v. Commonwealth, 12 Va. App. 156, 403 S.E.2d 360 (1991).

This section is intended to protect an accused against the testimony of certain judicial officers before whom he has appeared as to admissions or confessions made by him. Baylor v. Commonwealth, 190 Va. 116, 56 S.E.2d 77 (1949).

But it has no application to an extrajudicial statement. Owens v. Commonwealth, 186 Va. 689, 43 S.E.2d 895 (1947).

Therefore, statement of accused to judge after judgment is admissible. — Where the testimony of the mayor in whose court case was first tried did not embrace any statements made by the accused on his trial, but embraced a statement made by the accused after judgment had been pronounced against him, it was held that the court did not err in admitting this evidence as it did not violate this section. Pflaster v. Town of Berryville, 157 Va. 859, 161 S.E. 58 (1931).

Error to allow judge's testimony. — Trial court erred in allowing the sitting circuit judge to testify in defendant's civil and criminal contempt case where he defied the trial court's order to have a deputy at the courthouse entrance during weekly business hours, and he took down signs ordered to be posted by the trial court about when the courthouse would be closed absent a deputy at the front entrance despite at least one request by the trial court that a sign and corresponding order be returned; the court itself, and not the trial judge, was the victim of defendant's contemptuous conduct and other statutory authority, such as § 18.2-459, did not permit a judicial officer who simply witnesses contemptuous behavior to testify. Epps v. Commonwealth, 47 Va. App. 687, 626 S.E.2d 912, 2006 Va. App. LEXIS 102 (2006).

Because it was the court as an institution which was harmed by contemptuous behavior, a judge was not a "victim" under § 19.2-271 for purposes of a contempt proceeding; a trial court erred in finding that a judge was a victim of alleged contempt, and in permitting the judge to testify. Commonwealth v. Epps, 273 Va. 410, 641 S.E.2d 77, 2007 Va. LEXIS 35 (2007).

No error to allow judge's testimony. — Because a judge passively witnessed defendant's conduct, and did not preside over any of the proceedings, he was properly allowed to testify, despite defendant's claim that the judge was not listed as a witness on the bill of particulars and no discovery order requiring the production of witnesses had been entered; moreover, defendant's claim that the judge's testimony was cumulative was not addressed, as such was raised for the first time on appeal. Bennett v. Commonwealth, 2007 Va. App. LEXIS 155 (Apr. 17, 2007).

Defendant's constitutional right of confrontation was not violated by admission into evidence in criminal proceeding of certificate prepared by general district court judge, which detailed circumstances of offense. Baugh v. Commonwealth, 14 Va. App. 368, 417 S.E.2d 891 (1992), overruled in part by Gilman v. Commonwealth, 275 Va. 222, 657 S.E.2d 474, 2008 Va. LEXIS 23 (2008).

Virginia legislature does not intend to give birth to a constitutional right to cross-examine a juvenile and domestic relations district court (JDR court) judge at an appeal of a petty direct summary contempt proceeding, a right that a defendant does not otherwise have in the JDR court or the circuit court, as: (1) a JDR court proceeding is not a criminal prosecution within the scope of the Sixth Amendment; (2) there is no constitutional right to trial at the JDR court and no constitutional right of appeal; (3) there is a statutory prohibition against calling a judge as a witness; and (4) the Virginia general assembly provides a statutory right of appeal with the caveat that a certificate from the JDR court can be used in such an appeal. Gilman v. Commonwealth, 48 Va. App. 16, 628 S.E.2d 54, 2006 Va. App. LEXIS 130 (2006), rehearing granted, 48 Va. App. 236, 629 S.E.2d 720 (2006), opinion withdrawn, vacated by 2006 Va. App. LEXIS 456 (Oct. 10, 2006).

Defendant must articulate basis for challenge. — It may be inappropriate to deny a challenge to a magistrate's neutrality in every instance, but where the defendant has not articulated a basis for his challenge, the trial court is justified in disallowing the defense to interrogate magistrate. Singleton v. Commonwealth, No. 1481-85 (Ct. of Appeals Aug. 31, 1987).

Applied in Bartlett v. Bank of Carroll, 218 Va. 240, 237 S.E.2d 115 (1977).

CIRCUIT COURT OPINIONS

Magistrate's testimony not allowed. — In a malicious prosecution action, a magistrate's testimony was not permitted, as it was irrelevant; neither defendant police officer nor the jury was entitled to place more reliance on arrest warrants issued by one magistrate over another because of one magistrate's additional education or job experience. Archer v. Fink, 56 Va. Cir. 253, 2001 Va. Cir. LEXIS 455 (Charlottesville 2001).

§ 19.2-271.1. Competency of husband and wife to testify.

Husband and wife shall be competent witnesses to testify for or against each other in criminal cases, except as otherwise provided.

History.
Code 1950, § 8-287; 1977, c. 624.

Cross references.
As to competency of husband and wife to testify for or against each other in civil cases, see § 8.01-398.

Michie's Jurisprudence.

For related discussion, see 9B M.J. Husband and Wife, § 87; 20 M.J. Witnesses, § 7.

CASE NOTES

Determination to be made at time of trial. — "The privilege of an accused to prevent his spouse from testifying against him is determined at the time of trial and depends upon the couple being validly married at that time." Livingston v. Commonwealth, 21 Va. App. 621, 466 S.E.2d 757 (1996).

The Commonwealth's attorney had the burden of first obtaining the consent of the accused husband before it could call the wife as a witness against him. Livingston v. Commonwealth, 21 Va. App. 621, 466 S.E.2d 757 (1996).

A person is not incompetent to testify against his spouse under Virginia law. Shiflett v. Virginia, 447 F.2d 50 (4th Cir. 1971), cert. denied, 405 U.S. 994, 92 S. Ct. 1267, 31 L. Ed. 2d 462 (1972), decided under former § 8-287.

And he can testify freely unless the spouse objects. Shiflett v. Virginia, 447 F.2d 50 (4th Cir. 1971), cert. denied, 405 U.S. 994, 92 S. Ct. 1267, 31 L. Ed. 2d 462 (1972), decided under former § 8-287.

In which event the spouse is privileged to prevent any testimony. — See Shiflett v. Virginia, 447 F.2d 50 (4th Cir. 1971), cert. denied, 405 U.S. 994, 92 S. Ct. 1267, 31 L. Ed. 2d 462 (1972), decided under former § 8-287.

§ 19.2-271.2. Testimony of husband and wife in criminal cases (Subsection (b) of Supreme Court Rule 2:504 derived from this section).

In criminal cases husband and wife shall be allowed, and, subject to the rules of evidence governing other witnesses, may be compelled to testify in behalf of each other, but neither shall be compelled to be called as a witness against the other, except (i) in the case of a prosecution for an offense committed by one against the other, against a minor child of either, or against the property of either; (ii) in any case where either is charged with forgery of the name of the other or uttering or attempting to utter a writing bearing the allegedly forged signature of the other; or (iii) in any proceeding relating to a violation of the laws pertaining to criminal sexual assault (§§ 18.2-61 through 18.2-67.10), crimes against nature (§ 18.2-361) involving a minor as a victim and provided the defendant and the victim are not married to each other, incest (§ 18.2-366), or abuse of children (§§ 18.2-370 through 18.2-371). The failure of either husband or wife to testify, however, shall create no presumption against the accused, nor be the subject of any comment before the court or jury by any attorney.

Except in the prosecution for a criminal offense as set forth in (i), (ii) or (iii) above, in any criminal proceeding, a person has a privilege to refuse to disclose, and to prevent anyone else from disclosing, any confidential communication between his spouse and him during their marriage, regardless of whether he is married to that spouse at the time he objects to disclosure. For the purposes of this section, *"confidential communication"* means a communication made privately by a person to his spouse that is not intended for disclosure to any other person.

History.

Code 1950, § 8-288; 1950, p. 664; 1958, c. 231; 1960, c. 469; 1977, c. 624; 1988, c. 482; 1993, c. 637; 1996, c. 423; 2005, c. 809.

Editor's note.

At the direction of the Virginia Code Commission, the notation to the Virginia Rules of Evidence was added to the catchline of this section. Acts 2012, cc. 688 and 708, cl. 6 provides: "That pursuant to the authority set forth in §§ 30-146 and 30-147 of the Code of Virginia, the Virginia Code Commission shall direct any party with whom the Virginia Code Commission contracts to publish the Code of Virginia to include in the catchline of every section of the Code of Virginia from which any rule contained in the Rules of Evidence has been derived a notation specifying such rule."

Law Review.

For survey of Virginia law on evidence for the year 1977-1978, see 64 Va. L. Rev. 1451 (1978). For comment on confidential communication privileges under federal and Virginia law, see 13 U. Rich. L. Rev. 593 (1979).

Michie's Jurisprudence.

For related discussion, see 6A M.J. Divorce and Alimony, § 33; 9B M.J. Husband and Wife, § 87; 20 M.J. Witnesses, § 7.

CASE NOTES

Editor's note.

Many of the cases cited in the following annotations were decided under former § 8-288, which was comparable to this section, and under this section as it read prior to the 1996 amendment eliminating defendant spouse's privilege to ban witness spouse from testifying against him.

Consent of defendant spouse no longer required. — In 1996, the legislature amended this statute to eliminate the defendant spouse's privilege to bar the witness spouse from testifying against the defendant, while preserving in the witness spouse the privilege to avoid compelled testimony, subject to certain statutory exceptions. Turner v. Commonwealth, 33 Va. App. 88, 531 S.E.2d 619, 2000 Va. App. LEXIS 566 (2000).

The language of this section is mandatory. Jones v. Commonwealth, 218 Va. 732, 240 S.E.2d 526 (1978).

The context of the phrase "criminal cases" indicates that the legislature intended for the marital privilege of this section to apply in an adversarial trial proceeding. Livingston v. Commonwealth, 21 Va. App. 621, 466 S.E.2d 757 (1996).

"Subject to the exception stated in § 8.01-398" is construed as a cross-reference which embodies the proviso in § 8.01-398 concerning confidential communications. This has the effect of retaining, as a part of the law of criminal procedure, the historic interspousal confidential communication privilege which was formerly contained in § 8-289, notwithstanding the apparent confinement of its successor statute, the present § 8.01-398, to "civil actions." In the absence of an express enactment to that effect, the supreme court will not assume that the General Assembly intended to abrogate this long-standing rule. Church v. Commonwealth, 230 Va. 208, 335 S.E.2d 823 (1985).

This section does not prohibit testimony at pretrial hearing to determine marital status. — Although husband faced trial for criminal charges, this section would not apply to prohibit his wife from testifying at a pretrial hearing to determine the marital status of the parties. Bennett v. Commonwealth, 236 Va. 448, 374 S.E.2d 303 (1988), cert. denied, 490 U.S. 1028, 109 S. Ct. 1765, 104 L. Ed. 2d 200 (1989).

A person is not incompetent to testify against his spouse under Virginia law. Shiflett v. Virginia, 447 F.2d 50 (4th Cir. 1971), cert. denied, 405 U.S. 994, 92 S. Ct. 1267, 31 L. Ed. 2d 462 (1972).

And he can testify freely unless the spouse objects. Shiflett v. Virginia, 447 F.2d 50 (4th Cir. 1971), cert. denied, 405 U.S. 994, 92 S. Ct. 1267, 31 L. Ed. 2d 462 (1972).

In which event the spouse is privileged to prevent any

testimony. — See Shiflett v. Virginia, 447 F.2d 50 (4th Cir. 1971), cert. denied, 405 U.S. 994, 92 S. Ct. 1267, 31 L. Ed. 2d 462 (1972).

And this is only circumstance in which section does not apply. — This section does not apply only if the Commonwealth attempts to call the wife as a witness against her husband and the husband objects. Jones v. Commonwealth, 218 Va. 732, 240 S.E.2d 526 (1978).

Exercise of privilege rested with testifying spouse. — Trial court erred in limiting defendant's cross-examination of the alleged shooting victim's wife, as neither the Commonwealth nor the victim had the right to invoke spousal immunity if the victim's wife was willing to testify, as the spousal immunity privilege rested with the testifying spouse, not defendant spouse, under § 19.2-271.2; in addition, even if there had been a privileged marital communication, the privilege was waived when the victim testified, without objection, concerning what the victim had told the victim's wife. Holt v. Commonwealth, No. 2542-01-3, 2003 Va. App. LEXIS 215 (Ct. of Appeals Apr. 8, 2003).

Privilege determined at time of trial. — The privilege of an accused to prevent his spouse from testifying against him is determined at the time of trial and depends upon the couple being validly married at that time. Stewart v. Commonwealth, 219 Va. 887, 252 S.E.2d 329 (1979).

"The privilege of an accused to prevent his spouse from testifying against him is determined at the time of trial and depends upon the couple being validly married at that time." Livingston v. Commonwealth, 21 Va. App. 621, 466 S.E.2d 757 (1996).

Thus, divorce decree after commission of offense terminated privilege. — A decree which granted a defendant's wife a divorce from bed and board after the charged offense of grand larceny of the wife's personal property was allegedly committed by defendant terminated defendant's privilege of preventing his wife from testifying against him, and, thus, she could testify against him in grand larceny prosecution. Stewart v. Commonwealth, 219 Va. 887, 252 S.E.2d 329 (1979).

Interspousal confidential communication privilege survived dissolution of marriage. — The confidential communications made by the defendant to his wife during their marriage must be treated as privileged if the case is tried again. Church v. Commonwealth, 230 Va. 208, 335 S.E.2d 823 (1985).

Offense committed prior to marriage. — Neither spouse may testify for or against the other in the prosecution of either for an offense committed before marriage. Stevens v. Commonwealth, 207 Va. 371, 150 S.E.2d 229 (1966).

Marriage must be valid. — This rule operates only where there is a valid marriage. United States v. Neeley, 475 F.2d 1136 (4th Cir. 1973).

When the defendant has never legally divorced his third wife, he cannot rely on any exclusionary rules based on the existence of subsequent valid marriages. United States v. Neeley, 475 F.2d 1136 (4th Cir. 1973).

Prior marriage in effect. — At defendant's request, a California court entered a final order of divorce nunc pro tunc, dissolving wife's first marriage and validating her subsequent marriage to defendant; but upon subsequent proceedings on behalf of wife and the former husband, that court set aside the nunc pro tunc judgment; therefore, wife's first marriage was still in effect, precluding husband from objecting to her testimony under this section, and the giving of effect to the California court's most recent order was proper under subsection B of § 8.01-389. Bennett v. Commonwealth, 236 Va. 448, 374 S.E.2d 303 (1988), cert. denied, 490 U.S. 1028, 109 S. Ct. 1765, 104 L. Ed. 2d 200 (1989).

This section provides no exception where an alibi defense is asserted. Jones v. Commonwealth, 218 Va. 732, 240 S.E.2d 526 (1978).

When extrajudicial statements admissible. — Where the wife's extrajudicial statements are made with the actual or constructive knowledge and with the express or tacit consent of the husband, they are admissible in evidence against him. Coppola v. Commonwealth, 220 Va. 243, 257 S.E.2d 797 (1979), cert. denied, 444 U.S. 1103, 100 S. Ct. 1069, 62 L. Ed. 2d 788 (1980).

Statute pertained specifically to testimony in criminal cases, and did not apply to a report of earlier extrajudicial statements. Wolfe v. Commonwealth, 37 Va. App. 136, 554 S.E.2d 695, 2001 Va. App. LEXIS 629 (2001).

Once the defendant's wife invoked the marital privilege, she could not be compelled to testify; she was, therefore, unavailable for the purpose of admitting her hearsay statement to the police made following her arrest. Therefore, the trial court did not error in admitting into evidence the confession the defendant's wife made to the police, after she invoked the spousal privilege at trial and refused to testify, because the confession was admissible as a declaration against the wife's interest. Nowlin v. Commonwealth, 40 Va. App. 327, 579 S.E.2d 367, 2003 Va. App. LEXIS 218 (2003), . But see Crawford v. Washington, 541 U.S. 36, 124 S. Ct. 1354, 158 L. Ed. 2d 177 (2004).

Because defendant's communication to his estranged wife over a cell phone concerned acts for which the wife had a right of action against defendant, neither § 8.01-398 nor the exception in § 19.2-271.2 forbade her testimony as to his statement. Braxton v. Commonwealth, — Va. App. —, — S.E.2d —, 2006 Va. App. LEXIS 313 (July 18, 2006).

Defendant's convictions for rape and forcible sodomy of defendant's teenage stepdaughter were not obtained in violation of defendant's ex post facto clause rights; admission was proper of the testimony of the victim's mother, defendant's wife, of statements that defendant made to her and a tape recording the mother made containing defendant's incriminating statements under amendments to §§ 8.01-398 and 19.2-271.2 since the evidence did not change the quantum of proof necessary to obtain the convictions but only changed the admissibility of evidence that could be offered to obtain the convictions. Carpenter v. Commonwealth, 51 Va. App. 84, 654 S.E.2d 345, 2007 Va. App. LEXIS 463 (2007).

Inapplicable in criminal investigations. — This section lists several exceptions to the general rule that an accused's spouse may not be called as a witness against him without his consent. These exceptions use the terms "prosecution," "case," and "proceeding" to describe situations in which an accused's spouse may testify against him. By using these terms interchangeably, the legislature thus defined "criminal cases" as "prosecutions" and "proceedings" and did not intend to include criminal investigation. Livingston v. Commonwealth, 21 Va. App. 621, 466 S.E.2d 757 (1996).

The language of this section clearly contemplates an adversarial proceeding such as a preliminary hearing or trial, not pretrial criminal investigation by the police. Furthermore, case law interpreting the marital privilege of this section has dealt only with a trial. Livingston v. Commonwealth, 21 Va. App. 621, 466 S.E.2d 757 (1996).

The "criminal case" contemplated by this section would encompass only potential testimony of wife at the trial on the misdemeanor marijuana possession charge and at the preliminary hearing and trial on the felony cocaine charge. Thus, the trial court did not err in denying appellant's motion to suppress the drugs seized from his home. Livingston v. Commonwealth, 21 Va. App. 621, 466 S.E.2d 757 (1996).

The rationale of the co-conspirator exception to the hearsay rule nullifies the application of the spousal privilege to extrajudicial statements made by one spouse when acting in concert with the other spouse and the fact that the accused is not charged with conspiring with his spouse is of no consequence since admissions of one spouse that are expressly adopted by the other spouse are clearly admissible. Stumpf v. Commonwealth, 8 Va. App. 200, 379 S.E.2d 480 (1989).

Argument prohibited by section. — The argument that if the wife had been called to testify for the defendant, her testimony would have been unfavorable is the kind of argument which this section was intended to prohibit. Jones v. Commonwealth, 218 Va. 732, 240 S.E.2d 526 (1978).

Exception inapplicable. — In the absence of a prosecution for an offense committed by one spouse against the other, the statutory exception to spousal privilege contained in this section is inapplicable. Creech v. Commonwealth, 242 Va. 385, 410 S.E.2d 650 (1991).

Where defendant's wife's property was destroyed along with defendant's house in a fire; defendant was indicted and tried solely for arson of his house; and defendant was neither charged with, nor tried for, any offense against his wife; it was error to allow defendant's wife to testify at his arson trial without his consent. Creech v. Commonwealth, 242 Va. 385, 410 S.E.2d 650 (1991).

Section 19.2-271.2(i) did not apply because the husband was not the victim of the offense; the husband did not rely on defendant's deceit, as he testified that he had no knowledge that defendant had written the check, he was not defrauded, and he parted with nothing of value because the bank had earlier closed the account from which defendant wrote the check. Lindsey v. Commonwealth, 2007 Va. App. LEXIS 480 (Dec. 27, 2007).

Section 19.2-271.2(ii) did not apply because defendant was indicted for uttering a check with insufficient funds, she was not charged with "forgery or uttering." Lindsey v. Commonwealth, 2007 Va. App. LEXIS 480 (Dec. 27, 2007).

Statutory requirements of § 19.2-271.2(ii) are met only when the Commonwealth specifically charges forgery, or uttering, or attempting to utter a document bearing the alleged forged name of the spouse. Lindsey v. Commonwealth, 2007 Va. App. LEXIS 480 (Dec. 27, 2007).

Burden of obtaining consent of accused upon Commonwealth. — The language employed shows the plain intent of the legislature to place upon the Commonwealth the burden of first obtaining the consent of the accused husband before it will be allowed to call the wife as a witness against him. Wilson v. Commonwealth, 157 Va. 962, 162 S.E. 15 (1932); Brown v. Commonwealth, 208 Va. 512, 158 S.E.2d 663 (1968).

The evil which the legislature sought to correct was exemplified in the case at bar, viz.: the intentional effort of the attorney for the Commonwealth was to force the accused to object to the introduction of his wife as a witness against him, and thus, perhaps, have the jury place upon him the odium of seeking to prevent a fair investigation of the transaction. An accused should not, by willful act, be placed in such an attitude before the jury by the representative of the Commonwealth. Wilson v. Commonwealth, 157 Va. 962, 162 S.E. 15 (1932); Brown v. Commonwealth, 208 Va. 512, 158 S.E.2d 663 (1968). See also Roller v. Commonwealth, 161 Va. 1104, 172 S.E. 242 (1932).

The Commonwealth's attorney has " 'the burden of first obtaining the consent of the accused husband before it will be allowed to call the wife as a witness against him.' " Livingston v. Commonwealth, 21 Va. App. 621, 466 S.E.2d 757 (1996).

Adoption of wife's words by accused made them his own. — Where a defendant in a confession agreed with his wife's statement concerning what happened in the incident in which the defendant was involved, it was necessary to give content to his indication of acquiescence. His adoption of her words made them his own, and did not constitute testimony by the wife over the defendant's objection. Shiflett v. Virginia, 447 F.2d 50 (4th Cir. 1971), cert. denied, 405 U.S. 994, 92 S. Ct. 1267, 31 L. Ed. 2d 462 (1972).

Effect of dismissal of charge of offense committed against spouse. — Where the defendant was originally charged with the attempted murder of his wife, but the Commonwealth elected not to prosecute that offense and that charge was dismissed prior to trial, and the defendant was brought to trial under indictments charging him with the murder of another and using a firearm in the commission of that felony, neither of the indictments charged that defendant committed an offense against his wife, so neither was a prosecution for an offense committed against the wife. Therefore, the wife was incompetent to testify against her husband. Jenkins v. Commonwealth, 219 Va. 764, 250 S.E.2d 763 (1979).

Comment by attorney for the Commonwealth in violation of section was not harmless error. — A comment by the attorney for the Commonwealth in violation of this section concerning the failure of the defendant's wife to testify concerning his alibi was not harmless error where it may have contributed to the quantum of punishment. Jones v. Commonwealth, 218 Va. 732, 240 S.E.2d 526 (1978).

Mother not barred from testifying against father in incest case. — A minor daughter's participation in an incestuous relationship did not mean that the offense was not committed "against" her so as to bring her mother's testimony within the exception to the statutory bar. The daughter's participation resulted from the father's intimidation and coercion and offense was as much "against" her as if the father had assaulted or maimed her. Cumbee v. Commonwealth, 219 Va. 1132, 254 S.E.2d 112 (1979).

This section should be given a reasonable construction; it is not a penal statute that must be construed strictly against the Commonwealth. Brown v. Commonwealth, 223 Va. 601, 292 S.E.2d 319 (1982).

Spouse may testify in prosecution for offenses against self and third party. — Where one spouse has testified in a criminal

prosecution against the other, whatever marital harmony once existed has been dissipated, and the spousal privilege no longer serves a useful purpose. Accordingly, where one spouse is indicted for an offense against the other and an offense against a third party, and both offenses arose from a common criminal enterprise, the witness-spouse can testify against the defendant-spouse in the prosecution of both charges. Brown v. Commonwealth, 223 Va. 601, 292 S.E.2d 319 (1982).

Attire observations not per se admissible. — There is no per se rule allowing the admission of spouse's observations of other's attire. Some acts, such as cross-dressing, or wearing bloody clothing, might be considered confidential communications. Edwards v. Commonwealth, 20 Va. App. 470, 457 S.E.2d 797 (1995).

Testimony in prosecution for property offense permitted. — This section permits spousal testimony in prosecutions for offenses committed by one spouse against the property as well as the person of the other, and accordingly a wife is a competent witness against her husband in his prosecution for larceny of her property. Hudson v. Commonwealth, 223 Va. 596, 292 S.E.2d 317 (1982).

Testimony properly admitted. — Wife's description of the defendant's clothing, which he displayed in public when he left the home, was not a confidential communication. Further, it is reasonable to infer that clothing worn in public was not intended to be kept private or confidential. Therefore, the wife's testimony about the defendant's attire on the evening of the offense was properly admitted. Edwards v. Commonwealth, 20 Va. App. 470, 457 S.E.2d 797 (1995).

The wife's testimony about the defendant's interest in purchasing a car and his intent to test-drive a car with an older couple was also not the sort of communication a spouse would reasonably consider of a secret nature between husband and wife. The information was not conveyed with an expression of confidentiality, nor did its content imply that it should be kept confidential. In fact, the defendant not only expressed his intent to the victim and his wife, but also arranged to meet them in a public place, further supporting a finding that this communication was not a marital secret. Edwards v. Commonwealth, 20 Va. App. 470, 457 S.E.2d 797 (1995).

Defendant's wife's testimony that the defendant instructed her over the phone to meet him at his relative's house was not disclosure of a secret communication because it lacked any objective indicia of confidential intent. If anything, the defendant's actions indicate the opposite, since he instructed her to meet him at a place where other people would be present to witness the meeting. Edwards v. Commonwealth, 20 Va. App. 470, 457 S.E.2d 797 (1995).

When the wife testified that she looked through the defendant's belongings, which he had deposited in their bedroom outside of her presence, and found a wallet containing the victim's driver's license and credit card, she was not describing a communication. While a spouse's conduct may convey information to the other spouse and would, therefore, be privileged, a spouse's conduct which does not convey information to the other spouse is not privileged. The former wife's discovery of the contents of the wallet conveyed information to her, as did the fact that she discovered it among the defendant's belongings. However, the defendant's conduct — leaving the wallet among his belongings — was not observed by the former wife and did not convey information to her. Edwards v. Commonwealth, 20 Va. App. 470, 457 S.E.2d 797 (1995).

Where defendant was violently assaulting wife when her father, the victim of the instant offense, came to her aid, and ignoring victim's command to stop, defendant continued "beating" and "banging" wife, and "grabbed" the knife from victim's hand, wounding victim with it as he retreated, defendant's assault on victim clearly attended defendant's attack on wife and, therefore, "arose from a common criminal enterprise." Accordingly, wife's testimony was properly admitted into evidence. Bowe v. Commonwealth, No. 2285-94-3 (Ct. of Appeals March 5, 1996).

In light of the 1996 amendment to this section eliminating the defendant spouse's privilege to bar the witness spouse from testifying against the defendant, a defendant's argument that the trial court erred in admitting his wife's testimony over his objection was without merit where the wife testified willingly. Turner v. Commonwealth, 33 Va. App. 88, 531 S.E.2d 619, 2000 Va. App. LEXIS 566 (2000).

Spouse's testimony of defendant's possession and use of a firearm the spouse owned was properly admitted in convicting defendant on possession and reckless handling of a firearm charges as the narrow statutory exception applied to the rule against admitting the testimony of one spouse against another since the evidence showed the prosecutions against defendant were for offenses committed by one spouse against another, in this case, by defendant against the spouse. Kirby v. Commonwealth, 264 Va. 440, 570 S.E.2d 832, 2002 Va. LEXIS 164 (2002).

Defendant's wife's testimony at defendant's preliminary hearing was properly admitted at defendant's trial where: (1) the wife voluntarily testified at the preliminary hearing, although she could have invoked the marital privilege; (2) she chose not to testify at the trial; and (3) in neither instance was she compelled to testify against defendant; after the wife accused defendant of premeditated murder in open court, any marital harmony they might have previously enjoyed was overtaken by events and applying the privilege could not be justified either by § 19.2-271.2 or its underlying public policy. Pryor v. Commonwealth, 48 Va. App. 1, 628 S.E.2d 47, 2006 Va. App. LEXIS 131 (2006).

Applied in Gazette, Inc. v. Harris, 229 Va. 1, 325 S.E.2d 713 (1985).

§ 19.2-271.3. Communications between ministers of religion and persons they counsel or advise (Supreme Court Rule 2:503 derived in part from this section).

No regular minister, priest, rabbi or accredited practitioner over the age of eighteen years, of any religious organization or denomination usually referred to as a church, shall be required in giving testimony as a witness in any criminal action to disclose any information communicated to him by the accused in a confidential manner, properly entrusted to him in his professional capacity and necessary to enable him to discharge the functions of his office according to the usual course of his practice or discipline, where such person so communicating such information about himself or another is seeking spiritual counsel and advice relative to and growing out of the information so imparted.

History.
1985, c. 570.

Editor's note.
At the direction of the Virginia Code Commission, the notation to the Virginia Rules of Evidence was added to the catchline of this section. Acts 2012, cc. 688 and 708, cl. 6 provides: "That pursuant to the authority set forth in §§ 30-146 and 30-147 of the Code of Virginia, the Virginia Code Commission shall direct any party with whom the Virginia Code Commission contracts to publish the Code of Virginia to include in the catchline of every section of the Code of Virginia from which any rule contained in the Rules of Evidence has been derived a notation specifying such rule."

Law Review.
For a survey on evidence in Virginia for 1989, see 23 U. Rich. L. Rev. 647 (1989).

Michie's Jurisprudence.
For related discussion, see 20 M.J. Witnesses, § 28.

CASE NOTES

Privilege limited to accused, not witness. — Defendant erroneously claimed a "priest-penitent" privilege justified his failure to present the testimony of the minister who allegedly heard potential witness's confession of the murder since this section creates a "priest-penitent" privilege in criminal cases, but limits the privilege to "information communicated to the minister by the

accused." Defendant, not witness is the accused in this case. O'Dell v. Commonwealth, 234 Va. 672, 364 S.E.2d 491, cert. denied, 488 U.S. 871, 109 S. Ct. 186, 102 L. Ed. 2d 154 (1988).

The pastoral privilege belongs to the clergyman, not to the layman, leaving it to his conscience to decide when disclosure is appropriate. Nestle v. Commonwealth, 22 Va. App. 336, 470 S.E.2d 133 (1996).

§ 19.2-271.4. Privileged communications by certain public safety personnel.

A. A person who is a member of a critical incident stress management team, established pursuant to subdivision A 13 of § 32.1-111.3, shall not disclose nor be compelled to testify regarding any information communicated to him by emergency medical services or public safety personnel who are the subjects of peer support services regarding a critical incident. Such information shall also be exempt from the Virginia Freedom of Information Act (§ 2.2-3700 et seq.).

B. A person whose communications are privileged under subsection A may waive the privilege.

C. The provisions of this section shall not apply when:

1. Criminal activity is revealed;

2. A member of a critical incident stress management team is a witness or a party to a critical incident that prompted the peer support services;

3. A member of a critical incident stress management team reveals the content of privileged information to prevent a crime against any other person or a threat to public safety;

4. The privileged information reveals intent to defraud or deceive the investigation into the critical incident; or

5. A member of a critical incident stress management team reveals the content of privileged information to the employer of the emergency medical services or public safety personnel regarding criminal acts committed or information that would indicate that the emergency medical services or public safety personnel pose a threat to themselves or others.

History.
2012, cc. 148, 320.

ARTICLE 2.

WITNESSES FROM OR FOR ANOTHER STATE.

§ 19.2-272. Definitions.

"*Witness*" as used in this article shall include a person whose testimony is desired in any proceeding or investigation by a grand jury or in a criminal action, prosecution or proceeding.

The word "*state*" shall include any territory of the United States and the District of Columbia.

The word "*summons*" shall include a subpoena (both subpoena ad testificandum and subpoena duces tecum), order or other notice requiring the appearance of a witness or production of documents.

History.
Code 1950, § 19.1-269; 1960, c. 366; 1975, c. 495; 1988, c. 34.

Uniform law cross references.
For other signatory state provisions, see:
Alabama: Code of Ala. §§ 12-21-280 to 12-21-285.
Alaska: Alaska Stat. §§ 12.50.010 to 12.50.080.
Arizona: A.R.S. §§ 13-4091 to 13-4096.
Arkansas: A.C.A. §§ 16-43-402 to 16-43-409.
California: California Pen. Code §§ 1334 to 1334.6.
Colorado: C.R.S. §§ 16-9-201 to 16-9-205.
Delaware: 11 Del. C. §§ 3521 to 3526.
Florida: Fla. Stat. §§ 942.01 to 942.06.
Georgia: O.C.G.A. §§ 24-10-90 to 24-10-97.
Hawaii: H.R.S. §§ 836-1 to 836-6.
Idaho: Idaho Code §§ 19-3005 to 19-3013.
Illinois: 725 I.L.C.S. 220/1 to 220/6.
Indiana: Burns Ind. Code Ann. §§ 35-37-5-1 to 35-37-5-9.
Iowa: Iowa Code §§ 819.1 through 819.5.
Kansas: K.S.A. §§ 22-4201 through 22-4206.
Kentucky: K.R.S. §§ 421.230 to 421.270.
Maine: 15 M.R.S. §§ 1411 to 1415.
Maryland: Md. Courts and Judicial Proceedings Code Ann. §§ 9-301 to 9-307.
Massachusetts: Mass. Ann. Laws ch. 233 §§ 10 to 13D.
Michigan: M.C.L.S. §§ 767.91 to 767.95.
Mississippi: Miss. Code Ann. §§ 99-9-27 to 99-9-35.
Missouri: §§ 491.400 to 491.450 R.S.Mo.
Nebraska: R.R.S. Neb. §§ 29-1906 to 29-1911.
Nevada: Nev. Rev. Stat. §§ 174.395 to 174.445.
New Hampshire: New Hampshire 59 R.S.A. §§ 613:1 to 613:3.
New Jersey: N.J. Stat. §§ 2A:81-18 to 2A:81-23.
New Mexico: N.M. Stat. Ann. §§ 38-8-1 to 31-8-6.
New York: NY CLS CPL §§ 640.10 to 640.20.
North Carolina: N.C. Gen. Stat. §§ 15A-811 to 15A-816.
Ohio: O.R.C. Ann. §§ 2939.25 to 2939.29.
Oklahoma: 22 Okl. St. §§ 721 to 727.
Oregon: O.R.S. §§ 136.623 to 136.637.
Pennsylvania: 42 Pa.C.S. §§ 5961 through 5965.
Puerto Rico: 34 L.P.R.A. § 1471.
Rhode Island: R.I. Gen. Laws 12-16-1 to 12-16-7.
South Carolina: S.C. Code Ann. §§ 19-9-10 to 19-9-120.
Tennessee: Tenn. Code Ann. §§ 40-17-201 to 40-17-212.
Texas: Tex. Code Crim. Proc. art. 24.28.
Utah: Utah Code Ann. §§ 77-21-1 to 77-21-5.
Vermont: 13 V.S.A. §§ 6641 through 6649.
Virgin Islands: 5 V.I.C. § 3861 to 3865.
Washington: Rev. Code Wash. §§ 10.55.010 to 10.55.130.
West Virginia: W. Va. Code §§ 62-6A-1 to 62-6A-6.

Michie's Jurisprudence.
For related discussion, see 5B M.J. Criminal Procedure, § 64; 14B M.J. Process, § 4.

CASE NOTES

Purpose. — The uniform act relative to out-of-state witnesses was passed in furtherance of the common-law rule and did not supplant it. Its purpose was to compel the attendance of nonresident witnesses in criminal proceedings, granting them immunity from the service of process while in attendance upon the court. Davis v. Hackney, 196 Va. 651, 85 S.E.2d 245 (1955).

Uniform act did not supplant the common law but was enacted in furtherance of the common law. Lester v. Bennett, 1 Va. App. 47, 333 S.E.2d 366 (1985).

Applied in Coleman v. Commonwealth, 226 Va. 31, 307 S.E.2d 864 (1983).

§ 19.2-273. Certificate that witness is needed in another state; hearing.

If a judge of a court of record in any state which by its laws has made provisions for commanding per-sons within that state to attend and testify in this Commonwealth certifies under the seal of such court (1) that there is a criminal prosecution pending in such court or that a grand jury investigation has commenced or is about to commence, (2) that a person being within this Commonwealth is a material witness in such prosecution or grand jury investigation and (3) that his presence will be required for a specified number of days, upon presentation of such certificate to any judge of a court of record in the county or city in which such person is, such judge shall fix a time and place for hearing and shall make an order directing the witness to appear at a time and place certain for the hearing.

History.
Code 1950, § 19.1-270; 1960, c. 366; 1975, c. 495.

§ 19.2-274. When court to order witness to attend.

If at such hearing the judge determines that the witness is material and necessary, that it will not cause undue hardship to the witness to be compelled to attend and testify in the prosecution or grand jury investigation in the other state and that the laws of the state in which the prosecution is pending, or grand jury investigation has commenced or is about to commence (and of any other state through which the witness may be required to pass by ordinary course of travel) will give to him protection from arrest and the service of civil and criminal process, the judge shall issue a summons, with a copy of the certificate attached, directing the witness to attend and testify in the court where the prosecution is pending, or where a grand jury investigation has commenced or is about to commence at a time and place specified in the summons. In any such hearing the certificate shall be prima facie evidence of all the facts stated therein.

History.
Code 1950, § 19.1-271; 1960, c. 366; 1975, c. 495.

§ 19.2-275. Arrest of witness.

If the certificate recommends that the witness be taken into immediate custody and delivered to an officer of the requesting state to assure his attendance in the requesting state, such judge may, in lieu of notification of the hearing, direct that such witness be forthwith brought before him for the hearing; and the judge at the hearing being satisfied of the desirability of such custody and delivery, for which determination the certificate shall be prima facie proof of such desirability, may, in lieu of issuing subpoena or summons, order that the witness be forthwith taken into custody and delivered to an officer of the requesting state.

History.
Code 1950, § 19.1-272; 1960, c. 366; 1975, c. 495.

§ 19.2-276. Penalty for failure to attend and testify.

If the witness who is summoned as above provided, after being paid or tendered by some properly authorized person reimbursement for reasonable travel and lodging expenses as provided in § 2.2-2823 for each day he is required to travel and attend as a witness, fails without good cause to attend and testify as directed in the summons, he shall be punished in the manner provided for the punishment of any witness who disobeys a Virginia circuit court summons.

History.
Code 1950, § 19.1-273; 1960, c. 366; 1975, c. 495; 1987, c. 125.

§ 19.2-277. Summoning witnesses in another state to testify in this Commonwealth.

If a person in any state which by its laws has made provision for commanding persons within its borders to attend and testify in criminal prosecutions or grand jury investigations commenced or about to commence in this Commonwealth is a material witness in a prosecution pending in a court of record in this Commonwealth, or in a grand jury investigation which has commenced or is about to commence, a judge of such court may issue a certificate under the seal of the court stating these facts and specifying the number of days the witness will be required. The certificate may include a recommendation that the witness be taken into immediate custody and delivered to an officer of this Commonwealth to assure his attendance in this Commonwealth. This certificate shall be presented to a judge of a court of record in the county in which the witness is found.

History.
Code 1950, § 19.1-274; 1960, c. 366; 1975, c. 495.

CASE NOTES

Recommendation that a witness be taken into custody to assure attendance not required. — Permissive language of this section in allowing that a certificate from a Virginia court may include a recommendation that the witness be taken into immediate custody and delivered to an officer of this Commonwealth to assure his attendance in this Commonwealth, does not require that a party always request a recommendation to take the witness into custody, especially where the witnesses have assured numerous officials that they would be present. Gray v. Commonwealth, 16 Va. App. 513, 431 S.E.2d 86 (1993).

§ 19.2-278. Reimbursement for daily mileage to such witnesses; issuance of warrant necessary to make tender.

If the witness is summoned to attend and testify in this Commonwealth he shall receive such reimbursement for his daily mileage as prescribed in § 2.2-2823 for each day that he is required to travel

and attend as a witness. A witness who has appeared in accordance with the provisions of the summons shall not be required to remain within this Commonwealth a longer period of time than the period mentioned in the certificate, unless otherwise ordered by the court.

The judge issuing the certificate prescribed in § 19.2-277 may, by order, direct the clerk of the court involved to issue such warrant or warrants payable out of the state treasury, as may be necessary to make the tender hereinabove prescribed; and after the entry of such order, such clerk, upon application of the attorney for the Commonwealth of the county or city involved, or of the accused, if certificate for the attendance of witness has been issued by such judge on his behalf as authorized by § 19.2-330, shall issue such warrant or warrants and deliver them to the said attorney for the Commonwealth, who shall, forthwith, cause such tender to be made. Upon issuance of any such warrant or warrants said clerk shall deliver a certified copy of the court's order to the Supreme Court, and the said warrant or warrants shall be paid out of the state treasury upon presentation.

Unless and until appropriate forms shall be obtained, such warrants may be issued on the regular forms provided for the payment of witness fees and allowances, but in such event the clerk issuing the same shall make a notation thereon that they were issued pursuant to the provisions of this section.

History.
Code 1950, § 19.1-275; 1960, c. 366; 1972, c. 719; 1975, c. 495; 1976, c. 308; 1977, c. 483; 1978, c. 195.

§ 19.2-279. Penalty for failure of such witnesses to testify.

If such witness, after coming into this Commonwealth, fails without good cause to attend and testify as directed in the summons, he shall be punished in the manner provided for the punishment of any witness who disobeys a summons issued from a court of record in this Commonwealth.

History.
Code 1950, § 19.1-276; 1960, c. 366; 1975, c. 495.

§ 19.2-280. Exemption of such witnesses from arrest or service of process.

If a person comes into this Commonwealth in obedience to a summons directing him to attend and testify in this Commonwealth he shall not while in this Commonwealth pursuant to such summons be subject to arrest or the service of process, civil or criminal, in connection with matters which arose before his entrance into this Commonwealth under the summons.

If a person passes through this Commonwealth while going to another state in obedience to a summons to attend and testify in that state or while returning therefrom, he shall not while so passing through this Commonwealth be subject to arrest or the service of process, civil or criminal, in connection with matters which arose before his entrance into this Commonwealth under the summons.

History.

Code 1950, § 19.1-277; 1960, c. 366; 1975, c. 495.

Michie's Jurisprudence.

For related discussion, see 2A M.J. Arrest, § 2; 14B M.J. Process, § 4.

CASE NOTES

Persons not in state in obedience to summons. — This section provides no basis upon which a person may claim immunity from arrest or service of process, where he is not in this State in obedience to a summons to attend and testify in a criminal proceeding. Lester v. Bennett, 1 Va. App. 47, 333 S.E.2d 366 (1985).

Out-of-state witness immune from process though not summoned under this article. — The enactment of this article did not supplant, but rather supplemented, the common-law rules on the subject. Hence a resident of Tennessee who voluntarily accepted service and appeared to testify in a criminal proceeding in Virginia, was privileged against service of civil process in Virginia, though he had not been summoned according to the procedure provided in the Uniform Act. Davis v. Hackney, 196 Va. 651, 85 S.E.2d 245 (1955).

The privilege from process extends to the property of the witness reasonably necessary to his attendance as well as to his person; and is based on considerations too important to yield to the personal advantage or disadvantage of individual suitors. Davis v. Hackney, 196 Va. 651, 85 S.E.2d 245 (1955).

The automobile in which a witness came to Virginia to testify was immune from attachment, even though it had been bought from the party against whom the witness came to testify and had not been paid for. Davis v. Hackney, 196 Va. 651, 85 S.E.2d 245 (1955).

§ 19.2-281. Construction of article.

This article shall be so interpreted and construed as to effectuate its general purpose to make uniform the law of the states which enact it.

History.

Code 1950, § 19.1-278; 1960, c. 366; 1975, c. 495.

§ 19.2-282. How article cited.

This article may be cited as the "Uniform Act to Secure the Attendance of Witnesses from without a State in Criminal Proceedings."

History.

Code 1950, § 19.1-279; 1960, c. 366; 1975, c. 495.

Michie's Jurisprudence.

For related discussion, see 5B M.J. Criminal Procedure, § 64; 14B M.J. Process, § 4.

CHAPTER 17.

CONVICTIONS; EFFECT THEREOF.

Article 1. Proof and Verdicts.

ARTICLE 1.

PROOF AND VERDICTS.

§ 19.2-283. How accused may be convicted of felony.

No person shall be convicted of felony, unless by his confession of guilt in court, or by his plea, or by the verdict of a jury, accepted and recorded by the court, or by judgment of the court trying the case without a jury according to law.

History.

Code 1950, § 19.1-248; 1960, c. 366; 1975, c. 495.

Cross references.

As to trial without jury, see §§ 19.2-257 and 19.2-258. As to constitutional provision for criminal trials, see Va. Const., Art. I, § 8.

Michie's Jurisprudence.

For related discussion, see 5B M.J. Criminal Procedure, §§ 50, 78.

CASE NOTES

What constitutes a "conviction" for purposes of impeachment. — A conviction occurs when an accused enters a plea of guilty that is voluntarily and intelligently made; it is not necessary for the final judgment or sentencing order to have been entered for the prior conviction to be used for impeachment purposes when the accused testifies in another case. Jewel v. Commonwealth, 30 Va. App. 416, 517 S.E.2d 264 (1999), aff'd, 260 Va. 430, 536 S.E.2d 905 (2000).

Verdict never accepted or recorded by court. — Where a pool of the jury revealed that they had agreed to a two-thirds majority verdict, and after questioning the jurors and determining that all of them did not agree the trial court declared a mistrial and discharged them, defendant was not convicted at that trial, because the court never accepted or recorded the jury's verdict, and the fact that a harsher sentence was given at a second trial did not violate defendant's constitutional rights. Price v. Slayton, 347 F. Supp. 1269 (W.D. Va. 1972).

§ 19.2-284. Proof of ownership in offense relating to property.

In a prosecution for an offense committed upon, relating to or affecting real estate, or for stealing, embezzling, destroying, injuring or fraudulently receiving or concealing any personal estate it shall be sufficient to prove that when the offense was committed the actual or constructive possession, or a general or special property, in the whole or any part of such estate was in the person or entity alleged in the indictment or other accusation to be the owner thereof.

History.
Code 1950, § 19.1-247; 1960, c. 366; 1975, c. 495.

Law Review.
For a note, "Pleading for Theft Consolidation in Virginia: Larceny, Embezzlement, False Pretenses and § 19.2-284," see 55 Wash. & Lee L. Rev. 249 (1998).

Michie's Jurisprudence.
For related discussion, see 12A M.J. Larceny, § 14.

CASE NOTES

Object of section. — This section does not dispense with the necessity of stating in an indictment for larceny the name of the owner of the stolen property, nor enable any person to be such owner who was not capable of being so at common law. Its only object was to get rid of the difficulties often existing at common law in regard to the proper person to be stated as the owner of property in an indictment for larceny or other offenses against property. Hughes v. Commonwealth, 58 Va. (17 Gratt.) 565 (1867).

This section has no application to proving a violation of § 18.2-81; § 18.2-81 is silent on the issue of ownership. Section 18.2-81 proscribes not only burning another person's property, but the broader offense of burning any property with malice or the intent to defraud an insurance company or another person; thus, § 18.2-81 requires proof only of malice or intent to defraud. Proof of ownership, or of an insurable interest, is not an element of malicious burning under § 18.2-81, and this section does not make it such. Hamm v. Commonwealth, 16 Va. App. 150, 428 S.E.2d 517 (1993).

Allegation as to owner must be proved. — On a trial for larceny, to convict the prisoner, there must be satisfactory proof that the property stolen was the property of the person stated in the indictment. Jones v. Commonwealth, 58 Va. (17 Gratt.) 563 (1866); Robinson v. Commonwealth, 73 Va. (32 Gratt.) 866 (1879); Prather v. Commonwealth, 85 Va. 122, 7 S.E. 178 (1888).

But it is only necessary to prove absolute or special ownership. — To sustain an indictment for larceny it is only necessary to prove that the goods alleged to have been stolen are either the absolute or the special property of the alleged owner. Latham v. Commonwealth, 184 Va. 934, 37 S.E.2d 36 (1946).

Carrier has special ownership in property transported. — Since the initial carrier is liable for loss, damage or injury to property in interstate commerce, it follows as a corollary that the initial carrier has a legal or special ownership in the property transported. Latham v. Commonwealth, 184 Va. 934, 37 S.E.2d 36 (1946).

Variance between indictment and proof at trial as to ownership. — When the Commonwealth alleged in an indictment that the money obtained by the defendant was the property of a named individual, her grandfather, but the evidence showed the money was the property of the bank in which the grandfather

maintained a savings account, it proved a different offense, resulting in a fatal variance and requiring that the defendant's conviction be reversed. Gardner v. Commonwealth, 262 Va. 18, 546 S.E.2d 686, 2001 Va. LEXIS 80 (2001).

Where the indictment omitted the word "Inc.," the significance of the term related solely to the legal status of the victim and not to the identity of the victim or the manner in which the crime was committed. Nuckles v. Commonwealth, 266 Va. 519, 587 S.E.2d 695, 2002 Va. App. LEXIS 665 (2003), reversing Nuckles v. Commonwealth, 2002 Va. App. LEXIS 665 (Va. Ct. App. Nov. 5, 2002).

Constructive possession. — Conviction for destruction of property was sufficiently supported by the evidence although the woman named in the indictment as the owner of the automobile which the defendant damaged did not have legal title to the property. The evidence proved that the woman had possession of the automobile and that she was to receive title to it under an agreement with her former husband, who did have legal title to the property. Proof that the person alleged in the indictment to be the owner of such property has actual or constructive possession of the property is sufficient in a prosecution for this offense. Tammaro v. Commonwealth, No. 0504-94-1 (Ct. of Appeals March 21, 1995).

§ 19.2-285. Accused guilty of part of offense charged; sentence; on new trial what tried.

If a person indicted of a felony be by the jury acquitted of part of the offense charged, he shall be sentenced for such part as he is so convicted of, if the same be substantially charged in the indictment, whether it be felony or misdemeanor. If the verdict be set aside and a new trial granted the accused, he shall not be tried for any higher offense than that of which he was convicted on the last trial.

History.
Code 1950, § 19.1-249; 1960, c. 366; 1975, c. 495.

Cross references.
As to conviction for attempt on indictment for felony and as to general verdict of not guilty, see § 19.2-286.

Michie's Jurisprudence.
For related discussion, see 2B M.J. Autrefois, Acquit and Convict, §§ 2, 11, 17, 21; 5B M.J. Criminal Procedure, §§ 11, 62, 70; 9B M.J. Homicide, § 100; 13B M.J. New Trials, § 67; 16 M.J. Robbery, § 8.

CASE NOTES

History of legislation resulting in this section. — See Cates v. Commonwealth, 111 Va. 837, 69 S.E. 520 (1910).

Sections 18.2-31 and 18.2-32 and this section are in pari materia and should be read together. Tucker v. Commonwealth, 159 Va. 1038, 167 S.E. 253 (1933); Puckett v. Commonwealth, 182 Va. 237, 28 S.E.2d 619 (1944).

"Higher offense" within the meaning of this section is to be determined by the maximum of the penalty affixed to the offense. Benton v. Commonwealth, 91 Va. 782, 21 S.E. 495 (1895).

For section to apply, crime must be substantially charged in the indictment. — One indicted for felony may be convicted of part of an offense charged but the statute does not apply unless the particular crime of which one was convicted was substantially charged in the indictment. Myers v. Commonwealth, 148 Va. 725, 138 S.E. 483 (1927).

Crime convicted of not different in nature from that in indictment. — Defendant was not convicted of a crime different in nature from that charged in the indictment where the original indictment charged the crime of breaking and entering a dwelling house with the intent to maim, and was amended to charge breaking and entering with the intent to commit murder, nor did the trial court err in permitting the amendment. Smith v. Commonwealth, 10 Va. App. 592, 394 S.E.2d 30 (1990).

Circuit courts do not lose jurisdiction because conviction for lesser included offense. — Former § 17-123 (see now § 17.1-513) provides that the circuit court has jurisdiction of all indictments for felonies. Since the defendant was indicted for a felony, the case had to be tried in the circuit court. Circuit courts do not lose jurisdiction to convict and sentence a defendant merely because the conviction turns out to be for a lesser included misdemeanor offense. Jimenez v. Commonwealth, 10 Va. App. 277, 392 S.E.2d 827 (1990), reversed on other grounds, 241 Va. 244, 402 S.E.2d 678 (1991).

On indictment for felony, defendant may be convicted of lower offense. — On an indictment for malicious cutting and wounding with intent to maim, disfigure, disable and kill, the defendant may be convicted of unlawful cutting and wounding with like intent, or of assault and battery. Montgomery v. Commonwealth, 98 Va. 840, 36 S.E. 371 (1900).

Jury verdict finding accused guilty of a lesser degree of homicide will not be disturbed even though the evidence adduced tends to prove murder in the first degree and none other. Blankenship v. Commonwealth, 193 Va. 587, 70 S.E.2d 335 (1952).

Evidence sufficient to sustain a conviction of a felony charged in an indictment is alike sufficient to sustain a conviction of a lesser offense substantially charged in the indictment. Fleming v. Commonwealth, 170 Va. 636, 196 S.E. 696 (1938).

Of what offenses accused may be convicted under indictment charging murder in first degree. — Under this section upon an indictment charging murder in the first degree, accused might be convicted not only of murder in the first degree but of murder in the second degree or manslaughter, and accused might be found guilty of an attempt to commit murder, first or second degree, or manslaughter, and where an indictment specifically charges an attempt to commit murder, the jury can find the accused guilty of an attempt to commit murder in the second degree, and impose the penalty of one year in jail. Lee v. Commonwealth, 144 Va. 594, 131 S.E. 212 (1926).

Conviction of lower offense is acquittal of higher offense. — A person indicted for murder and convicted of murder in the second degree is not again liable to conviction for murder in the first degree. Benton v. Commonwealth, 91 Va. 782, 21 S.E. 495 (1895). See also, Bateman v. Commonwealth, 183 Va. 253, 32 S.E.2d 134 (1944).

A conviction of the defendant of murder in the second degree acquits him of murder in the first degree. Carson v. Commonwealth, 188 Va. 398, 49 S.E.2d 704 (1948).

The conviction of the accused of the lower offense of voluntary manslaughter is an acquittal of the higher offenses of first and second-degree murder. Kuckenbecker v. Commonwealth, 199 Va. 619, 101 S.E.2d 523 (1958).

Where the indictment charged the accused with murder, the effect of a verdict finding him guilty of involuntary manslaughter, under the provisions of this section, was to acquit him of murder in either degree and voluntary manslaughter. Taylor v. Commonwealth, 186 Va. 587, 43 S.E.2d 906 (1947).

On new trial accused cannot be tried for any higher offense than that of which he was convicted on the last trial. Lane v. Commonwealth, 190 Va. 58, 55 S.E.2d 450 (1949).

If an accused is fairly acquitted of a higher offense included in the indictment, and, upon conviction of a lesser offense, applies for and obtains a new trial, he does not thereby waive the advantage of the acquittal of the higher offense thus obtained. He is not, however, acquitted of the offense in respect to which he asks for a new trial. He may be tried again for that offense with all its incidents and consequences. Lane v. Commonwealth, 190 Va. 58, 55 S.E.2d 450 (1949).

Where defendant was indicted for armed robbery, but was tried as an accessory to armed robbery and convicted for receiving stolen property, and the conviction was affirmed by the Supreme Court, he could not be retried for any crime of greater gravity than the receipt of stolen goods. Dove v. Peyton, 343 F.2d 210 (4th Cir. 1965).

And the same rule applies to a trial upon an indictment with one count that governs in a trial upon an indictment with several counts. Lane v. Commonwealth, 190 Va. 58, 55 S.E.2d 450 (1949).

Effect of conviction as to crimes of equal degree. — Housebreaking in the nighttime with intent to commit larceny, and grand larceny, are of equal degree. A conviction of either, when set aside at the instance of the accused, as a waiver of his jeopardy as to both, and upon a new trial he may be put upon trial upon the whole indictment in which both are charged. Benton v. Commonwealth, 91 Va. 782, 21 S.E. 495 (1895).

Effect of conviction of felony punishable as misdemeanor. — Conviction of unlawful shooting is a conviction of a felony, though punished by imprisonment in jail and a fine, and after reversal of the sentence a second trial may be had for the felony, and not merely for a misdemeanor, notwithstanding this section. Forbes v. Commonwealth, 90 Va. 550, 19 S.E. 164 (1894).

Under this section, one indicted for felony, may be convicted of an attempt to commit such felony; and one prosecuted for grand larceny, may be found guilty of petit larceny. Commonwealth v. Worrell, 5 Va. L. Reg. (n.s.) 836 (1920).

And conviction of attempt is acquittal of felony. — A person indicted for rape may be found not guilty of rape, but of an attempt to commit rape, but a verdict of guilty of an attempt to commit rape is an acquittal of the offense of rape, and if such verdict be set aside, the accused cannot on a second trial, be convicted of rape, as this is a higher offense. Cates v. Commonwealth, 111 Va. 837, 69 S.E. 520 (1910).

No conviction for assault in prosecution for sodomy where no charge of force. — Where in an indictment for sodomy no charge of assault was involved, because no force against, or lack of consent on the part of, the prosecutrix is averred, there can be no conviction of assault. Nor is the case in any way within this section authorizing a conviction for a part only of the larger offense charged. Wise v. Commonwealth, 135 Va. 757, 115 S.E. 508 (1923).

Section applies to robbery. — It was argued by counsel for defendant that this section applies to cases of homicide, malicious wounding, etc., but that it is not applicable to a case of robbery. The argument was more specious than sound, and if permitted to prevail, the defendant would go hence without punishment, although his guilt were firmly established by the evidence. Maxwell v. Commonwealth, 165 Va. 860, 183 S.E. 452 (1936).

Indecent exposure not lesser offense of sodomy. — Indecent exposure, though it may occur in almost all cases of sodomy where two persons are involved, is not a fact that must be charged or proved to sustain a conviction of sodomy in any case. Therefore, indecent exposure is not a lesser offense included in the offense of sodomy. Ashby v. Commonwealth, 208 Va. 443, 158 S.E.2d 657 (1968), cert. denied, 393 U.S. 1111, 89 S. Ct. 884, 21 L. Ed. 2d 808 (1969).

Instructions as to lesser offenses. — In murder prosecution where facts were sufficient to establish the killing of the deceased by the defendant and defendant was convicted of involuntary manslaughter the court did not err in instructing the jury as to voluntary manslaughter, involuntary manslaughter, or assault and battery, because there was no evidence which tended to prove the commission of any of these lesser offenses. Blankenship v. Commonwealth, 193 Va. 587, 70 S.E.2d 335 (1952).

Instruction as to higher offense in new trial for lower offense is immaterial. — Where the accused was tried upon an indictment containing only one count and was found guilty, not of murder but of voluntary manslaughter, action of the court in defining the degrees of murder becomes immaterial upon a new trial in view of this section. Bevley v. Commonwealth, 185 Va. 210, 38 S.E.2d 331 (1946).

Applied in Jones v. Commonwealth, 217 Va. 226, 228 S.E.2d 124 (1976); Edenton v. Commonwealth, 227 Va. 413, 316 S.E.2d 736 (1984).

§ 19.2-286. Conviction of attempt or as accessory on indictment for felony; effect of general verdict of not guilty.

On an indictment for felony the jury may find the accused not guilty of the felony but guilty of an attempt to commit such felony, or of being an accessory thereto; and a general verdict of not guilty, upon such indictment, shall be a bar to a subsequent prosecution for an attempt to commit such felony, or of being an accessory thereto.

History.

Code 1950, § 19.1-254; 1960, c. 366; 1975, c. 495.

Michie's Jurisprudence.

For related discussion, see 1A M.J. Accomplices and Accessories, § 8; 2A M.J. Attempts and Solicitations, § 6; 2B M.J. Autrefois, Acquit and Convict, §§ 2, 3, 21; 5B M.J. Criminal Procedure, § 11.

CASE NOTES

Upon conviction of lessor offense, higher offense no longer available. — Under this section a person indicted for rape may be found not guilty of rape, but of an attempt to commit rape, but a verdict of guilty of an attempt to commit rape is an acquittal of the offense of rape, and if such verdict be set aside, the accused cannot on a second trial, be convicted of rape, as this is a higher offense barred by § 19.2-285. Cates v. Commonwealth, 111 Va. 837, 69 S.E. 520 (1910).

Conviction of attempt is acquittal of main offense. — The result of a verdict which finds the accused guilty of an attempt to produce an abortion is to acquit him of the principal offense of abortion or miscarriage under § 18.2-71. Anderson v. Commonwealth, 190 Va. 665, 58 S.E.2d 72 (1950).

Accessory after the fact. — Before a defendant can be tried and convicted of being an accessory after the fact, he must be charged with that offense. Therefore, unless such a charge is specifically made, neither the state nor an accused is entitled to an accessory-after-the-fact instruction. Commonwealth v. Dalton, 259 Va. 249, 524 S.E.2d 860 (2000).

In deleting the modifier, "after the fact," the General Assembly indicated its intention to eliminate accessories after the fact from the application of this section. Commonwealth v. Dalton, 259 Va. 249, 524 S.E.2d 860 (2000).

Accessory before the fact instruction. — Trial court did not err in submitting a murder charge to the jury based on the theory that defendant was "an accessory before the fact or co-conspirator" in the commission of the charged murder; the Commonwealth is entitled to an accessory before the fact instruction on a felony indictment even when the defendant is not charged in the indictment with being an accessory before the fact to the felony. Schwartz v. Commonwealth, 45 Va. App. 407, 611 S.E.2d 631, 2005 Va. App. LEXIS 156 (2005).

Indictment charging crime also embraces attempt. — Indictment charging that petitioner "feloniously did enter the storehouse," etc., although charging the consummated crime of storebreaking, also embraced the lesser offense of attempting to enter without breaking or attempting to break and enter. Willoughby v. Smyth, 194 Va. 267, 72 S.E.2d 636 (1952).

Refusal of accessory after the fact instruction appropriate. — Defendant's convictions for first-degree murder and use of a firearm in the commission of a felony were appropriate because her argument that the trial court erred in refusing to allow her to proceed on the theory that she was an accessory after the fact and refusing an instruction that would have permitted the jury to make that finding was without merit under § 19.2-286 and Va. Sup. Ct. R. 3A:17(c). Before a defendant could be tried and convicted of being an accessory after the fact, she must have been charged with that offense; unless such a charge was specifically made, neither the Commonwealth nor an accused was entitled to an accessory-after-the-fact instruction and accessory after the fact was not a lesser included offense of murder. Thomas v. Commonwealth, 279 Va. 131, 688 S.E.2d 220, 2010 Va. LEXIS 11, cert. denied, 131 S. Ct. 143, 178 L. Ed. 2d 8, 2010 U.S. LEXIS 6109 (U.S. 2010).

§ 19.2-287. Verdict and judgment, when jury agree as to some and disagree as to others.

When two or more persons are charged and tried jointly, the jury may render a verdict as to any of them as to whom they agree. Thereupon judgment shall be entered according to the verdict; and as to the others the case shall be tried by another jury.

History.

Code 1950, § 19.1-256; 1960, c. 366; 1975, c. 495.

Michie's Jurisprudence.

For related discussion, see 5B M.J. Criminal Procedure, § 26.

CASE NOTES

New trial as to some. — Where several prisoners were tried together for the same felony and found guilty, the court may grant a new trial to one of them, and render a judgment against the others. Kemp v. Commonwealth, 59 Va. (18 Gratt.) 969 (1868).

Reversal as to some. — Two persons were indicted jointly and both the defendants were found guilty. One of them applied for a new trial, which was overruled, and he obtained a writ of error. The other did not apply for a new trial and there was a judgment against him. The judgment may be reversed as to the one who appealed, without reversing the judgment against the other who did not apply for a new trial. Jones v. Commonwealth, 72 Va. (31 Gratt.) 830 (1878).

§ 19.2-288. Verdict when accused found guilty of punishable homicide.

If a person indicted for murder be found by the jury guilty of any punishable homicide, they shall in their verdict fix the degree thereof and ascertain the extent of the punishment to be inflicted within the bounds prescribed by §§ 18.2-30 to 18.2-36.

History.

Code 1950, § 19.1-250; 1960, c. 366; 1975, c. 495.

Cross references.

As to trial without jury in felony case or plea of guilty, see § 19.2-257. As to definition of capital murder, see § 18.2-31. As to definition of first and second degree murder, see § 18.2-32. As to how murder in first degree and in the second degree are punished, see § 18.2-32. As to how lesser degrees of homicide are punished, see §§ 18.2-35 and 18.2-36.

Michie's Jurisprudence.

For related discussion, see 5B M.J. Criminal Procedure, § 78; 9B M.J. Homicide, § 121.

CASE NOTES

Effect of former law. — See Kibert v. Commonwealth, 216 Va. 660, 222 S.E.2d 790 (1976).

Failure of verdict to specify degree of crime erroneous. — Where a person is tried upon an indictment for murder the verdict should specify the degree of the crime of which he is convicted. If it does not so specify, it is erroneous. Commonwealth v. Williamson, 4 Va. (2 Va. Cas.) 211 (1820); Briggs v. Commonwealth, 82 Va. 554 (1886).

But verdict valid if punishment indicates degree. — A verdict which does not expressly find the degree may nevertheless be valid if the assessment of punishment clearly indicates such degree. Hobson v. Youell, 177 Va. 906, 15 S.E.2d 76 (1941).

Upon a plea of guilty, the court cannot submit the degree of guilt and the question of punishment to a jury for its determination. Upon a plea of guilty to the whole indictment, the court has no authority to submit the degree of guilt and the question of the punishment to be inflicted upon the accused to a jury for its determination. The accused and the public are both entitled to the independent judgment of the court upon the degree of his guilt and the punishment to be inflicted uninfluenced by the judgment or advice of the "jury" or other bystanders. Dixon v. Commonwealth, 161 Va. 1098, 172 S.E. 277 (1934); Hobson v. Youell, 177 Va. 906, 15 S.E.2d 76 (1941).

Fixing punishment by agreement permissible. — The practice, developed in a number of trial courts, whereby upon the arraignment of the accused and his plea of guilty, one of the attorneys, in the presence of the other, states to the court the essential facts constituting the crime charged and the punishment agreed upon, whereupon the court accepts such recommendation and, without examining the witnesses, fixes the punishment accordingly, is permissible under this section but such practice may be abused and should not be extended. Hobson v. Youell, 177 Va. 906, 15 S.E.2d 76 (1941).

§ 19.2-289. Conviction of petit larceny.

In a prosecution for grand larceny, if it be found that the thing stolen is of less value than $200, the jury may find the accused guilty of petit larceny.

History.
Code 1950, § 19.1-252; 1960, c. 366; 1966, c. 247; 1975, c. 495; 1981, c. 197.

Michie's Jurisprudence.
For related discussion, see 12A M.J. Larceny, §§ 12, 32.

§ 19.2-290. Conviction of petit larceny though thing stolen worth more than $200.

In a prosecution for petit larceny, though the thing stolen be of the value of $200 or more, the jury may find the accused guilty; and upon a conviction under this section or § 19.2-289 the accused shall be sentenced for petit larceny.

History.
Code 1950, § 19.1-253; 1960, c. 366; 1966, c. 247; 1975, c. 495; 1981, c. 197.

Michie's Jurisprudence.
For related discussion, see 12A M.J. Larceny, §§ 12, 32.

CASE NOTES

Discrepancies between indictment and evidence as to value of property stolen are contemplated by this section. Holly v. Commonwealth, 113 Va. 769, 75 S.E. 88 (1912).

§ 19.2-291. Faulty counts; motion to strike; general verdict of guilty.

When there are several counts in the indictment one or more of which are faulty, the accused may move to strike the faulty count or counts or move the court to instruct the jury to disregard them. If he does neither and a general verdict of guilty is found, judgment shall be entered against the accused, if any count be good, though others be faulty, unless the court can plainly see that the verdict could not have been found on the good count. If the accused demurs to the faulty count or moves the court to instruct the jury to disregard it and his demurrer or motion is overruled and there is a general verdict of guilty and it cannot be seen on which count the verdict was founded, if the jury has been discharged, it shall be set aside; but if it is manifest that it could not have been found on the bad count, the verdict shall be allowed to stand.

History.
Code 1950, § 19.1-255; 1960, c. 366; 1975, c. 495.

Michie's Jurisprudence.
For related discussion, see 6A M.J. Demurrers, § 5; 9B M.J. Indictments, Informations and Presentments, § 55; 19 M.J. Verdict, § 13.

CASE NOTES

When judgment not affected by bad count. — In a prosecution for violation of a city ordinance no demurrer to the warrant, which contained two counts, was interposed and no motion was made to instruct the jury to disregard the first count. There was a general verdict of guilty, which might well have been found under the second count. Under this section, even if the first count was bad, the regularity of the judgment was not affected thereby. Collins v. City of Radford, 134 Va. 518, 113 S.E. 735 (1922).

Since each of the four judgments of conviction against defendant were supported by sufficient evidence to prove him guilty beyond a reasonable doubt, the trial court did not err in denying defendant's motion to strike the charges against him on which he was convicted. Payne v. Commonwealth, No. 3339-02-3, 2003 Va. App. LEXIS 616 (Ct. of Appeals Dec. 2, 2003).

A motion to exclude evidence which could only be applicable to the faulty count, is in effect a motion to disregard that count. Rand v. Commonwealth, 50 Va. (9 Gratt.) 738 (1852).

§ 19.2-291.1. Report of conviction of school employees for certain offenses.

The clerk of any circuit court or any district court in the Commonwealth shall report to the Superintendent of Public Instruction and the division superintendent of any employing school division the conviction of any person, known by such clerk to hold a license issued by the Board of Education, for any felony involving the sexual molestation, physical or sexual abuse, or rape of a child or involving drugs pursuant to Article 1 (§ 18.2-247 et seq.) of Chapter 7 of Title 18.2.

History.
2008, cc. 474, 827.

ARTICLE 2.

FORMER JEOPARDY.

§ 19.2-292. Acquittal by jury on merits bar to further prosecution for same offense.

A person acquitted upon the facts and merits on a former trial, may plead such acquittal in bar of a second prosecution for the same offense, notwithstanding any defect in the form or substance of the indictment or accusation on which he was acquitted, unless the case be for a violation of the law relating to the state revenue and the acquittal be reversed on a writ of error on behalf of the Commonwealth.

History.
Code 1950, § 19.1-257; 1960, c. 366; 1975, c. 495.

Cross references.
As to other provisions providing for appeal in prosecutions for violation of state revenue laws, see § 19.2-317.

Michie's Jurisprudence.
For related discussion, see 2B M.J. Autrefois, Acquit and Convict, §§ 2, 6, 7, 9, 10, 12; 5B M.J. Criminal Procedure, § 8.

CASE NOTES

Section does not apply when warrants were quashed because void. — This section, providing immunity against a second trial for the same offense, speaks only of cases in which there has first been an acquittal "by the jury upon the facts and merits." It does not in terms at least, apply to a case, where no jury was sworn, but the warrant of a justice of the peace was quashed and dismissed on the ground that the statute under which it was issued was unconstitutional and void. Commonwealth v. Perrow, 124 Va. 805, 97 S.E. 820 (1919).

Nor when indictment was dismissed for variance. — When defendant was acquitted on the first trial because of a variance between the indictment and the proof, this acquittal could not be pleaded in bar to a second trial on the same crime. Burress v. Commonwealth, 68 Va. (27 Gratt.) 934 (1876), overruled on another point, Keister's Ex'rs v. Philips' Ex'x, 124 Va. 585, 98 S.E. 674 (1919).

Nor when quashed for racial discrimination in selection of grand jury. — Where former indictments against defendant were quashed on his motion because of racial discrimination in the selection of the grand jury, and a jury verdict on one of them was set aside and annulled, and subsequently another grand jury returned indictments against defendant substantially identical with the former ones, pleas of autrefois acquit would not lie to the new indictments, for defendant was not in jeopardy under the invalid indictments. Mealy v. Commonwealth, 193 Va. 216, 68 S.E.2d 507 (1952).

Acquittal on defective indictment. — This section was intended to apply when a person had been brought to trial under a defective indictment upon the facts and merits, and acquitted. He may then plead such acquittal in bar of a second prosecution for the same offense, notwithstanding the defective indictment. Burress v. Commonwealth, 68 Va. (27 Gratt.) 934 (1876), overruled on another point, Keister's Ex'rs v. Philips' Ex'x, 124 Va. 585, 98 S.E. 674 (1919); Rosser v. Commonwealth, 159 Va. 1028, 167 S.E. 257 (1933).

Voluntary de novo appeal did not constitute new trial. — Appellate court did not reach defendant's issue of whether two charges constituted the "same offense," under § 19.2-292, because the charges at issue were brought as a part of a single prosecution, and it was well settled that an appeal de novo from a general district court to a circuit court annulled the former judgment as completely as if no trial had ever occurred; thus, defendant's argument that her voluntary appeal, after her conviction for a misbranding charge in district court, constituted a new trial, was without merit. McClellan v. Commonwealth, 39 Va. App. 759, 576 S.E.2d 785, 2003 Va. App. LEXIS 95 (2003).

Former trial by court or jury may constitute jeopardy. — The spirit and purpose of the immunity intended to be secured by the doctrine of double jeopardy is violated whenever a defendant in any criminal case has been formerly tried by competent authority — whether court or jury — and discharged upon a defense constituting a bar to the proceeding, whether that defense is rested upon the law or the facts. Adkins v. Commonwealth, 175 Va. 590, 9 S.E.2d 349 (1940).

§ 19.2-293. When acquittal not a bar to further prosecution for same offense.

A person acquitted of an offense on the ground of a variance between the allegations and the proof of the indictment or other accusation, or upon an exception to the form or substance thereof, may be arraigned again on a new indictment or other proper accusation, and tried and convicted for the same offense, notwithstanding such former acquittal.

History.
Code 1950, § 19.1-258; 1960, c. 366; 1975, c. 495.

Cross references.
As to discharge of accused for failure to try within time prescribed, see § 19.2-243. As to effect of verdict of not guilty of felony

on subsequent prosecution for attempt, see § 19.2-286. For constitutional provisions as to former jeopardy, see Va. Const., Art. I, § 8.

Michie's Jurisprudence.
For related discussion, see 2B M.J. Autrefois, Acquit and Convict, § 6; 10A M.J. Instructions, § 35.

CASE NOTES

Discharge of jury after excluding state's evidence does not bar subsequent prosecution. — The court discharged the jury after sustaining motion of the defendant to exclude the Commonwealth's evidence on the ground of variance. The discharge of the jury on such ground did not bar a subsequent prosecution. Robinson v. Commonwealth, 73 Va. (32 Gratt.) 866 (1879).

Nor does verdict set aside for variance. — A second indictment being for the same act of embezzling as the first, and the prisoner having been indicted, tried and convicted in time, and the verdict set aside for variance between allegation and proof as to ownership of the property, the second indictment was proper and in time, and the prisoner is not entitled to be discharged. Commonwealth v. Adcock, 49 Va. (8 Gratt.) 661 (1851). See also, Robinson v. Commonwealth, 73 Va. (32 Gratt.) 866 (1879).

Section 19.2-243 is to be read as a proviso to this section, so as to authorize the trial and conviction of a party upon a new indictment or proper accusation who has been acquitted on the ground of variance, or upon an exception to the form or substance of the indictment, only if this new indictment is found and the trial had within three terms after the prisoner was first held for trial. Commonwealth v. Adcock, 49 Va. (8 Gratt.) 661 (1851).

When discharge upon demurrer bars further prosecution. — Where defendant was indicted and charged with the commission of the crime of bigamy and with counselling, aiding and abetting and assisting in the commission of the crime of bigamy, and a demurrer to that indictment was sustained on the ground that as a matter of law an unmarried man was not included within the language of the statute defining bigamy and could not be an accessory to the crime, and it was ordered that "the defendant be discharged from said indictment and may go thereof without day," the order discharging defendant "without day" was an ultimate decision upon a question of law, and when defendant was arraigned upon a second indictment charging him with aiding and abetting in the commission of the crime of bigamy the trial court erred in sustaining a demurrer to a plea of autrefois acquit to the second indictment. Adkins v. Commonwealth, 175 Va. 590, 9 S.E.2d 349 (1940).

Sufficiency of evidence argument considered. — Court of appeals addressed defendant's argument that the evidence was insufficient to support his convictions even though his convictions were reversed due to a fatal variance between the indictments and the proof offered at trial because if successful, it could impose a double jeopardy bar to reprosecution under properly worded indictments. Purvy v. Commonwealth, 59 Va. App. 260, 717 S.E.2d 847, 2011 Va. App. LEXIS 389 (2011).

CIRCUIT COURT OPINIONS

Prior dismissal did not bar retrial. — Where a dismissal in a prior case in a circuit court was entered before a jury was empaneled and before an arraignment, and was not intended to have been with prejudice or amounting to an acquittal, double jeopardy did not bar retrial of the same charges in a city court. Commonwealth v. Hagwood, 63 Va. Cir. 212, 2003 Va. Cir. LEXIS 356 (Charlottesville 2003).

§ 19.2-294. Offense against two or more statutes or ordinances.

If the same act be a violation of two or more statutes, or of two or more ordinances, or of one or more statutes and also one or more ordinances, conviction under one of such statutes or ordinances shall be a bar to a prosecution or proceeding under the other or others. Furthermore, if the same act be a violation of both a state and a federal statute, a prosecution under the federal statute shall be a bar to a prosecution under the state statute. The provisions of this section shall not apply to any offense involving an act of terrorism as defined in § 18.2-46.4.

For purposes of this section, a prosecution under a federal statute shall be deemed to be commenced once jeopardy has attached.

History.
Code 1950, § 19.1-259; 1960, c. 366; 1975, c. 495; 1987, c. 241; 2002, cc. 588, 623; 2003, c. 736.

Law Review.
For note, "Commonwealth Right of Appeal in Criminal Proceedings," see 43 Wash. & Lee L. Rev. 295 (1986). For comment on multiple murder, multiple punishment and double jeopardy in Virginia, see 9 G.M.U. L. Rev. 107 (1986). For an article, "Criminal Law and Procedure," see 31 U. Rich. L. Rev. 1015 (1997). For article summarizing published Virginia criminal law decisions between July 1, 2002 and July 1, 2003, see 38 U. Rich. L. Rev. 87 (2003).

Michie's Jurisprudence.
For related discussion, see 2B M.J. Autrefois, Acquit and Convict, §§ 18, 20, 28; 3A M.J. Burglary and Housebreaking, §§ 11, 21; 5A M.J. Courts, § 62; 5B M.J. Criminal Procedure, § 87; 9A M.J. Habeas Corpus, § 18.

CASE NOTES

I. In General.
II. Illustrative Cases.

I. IN GENERAL.

Applicability. — This section is implicated only when both convictions are for violations of a statute or a local ordinance or a combination of such; as such, the statute does not apply if one of the charges is a common-law offense. Morris v. Commonwealth, 45 Va. App. 181, 609 S.E.2d 92, 2005 Va. App. LEXIS 79 (2005).

For a case discussing the history of this section and § 19.2-294.1 and the cases interpreting those sections, see Lash v. County of Henrico, 13 Va. App. 251, 410 S.E.2d 689 (1991), overruled on other grounds, Hall v. Commonwealth, 14 Va. App. 892, 421 S.E.2d 455 (1992).

The purpose of this section is to remove the hardship manifest in Arrington v. Commonwealth, 87 Va. 96, 12 S.E. 224 (1890), in which a prisoner had "committed" but a single act, but inasmuch as it violated two statutes, he was convicted under both. Owens v. Commonwealth, 129 Va. 757, 105 S.E. 531 (1921).

Preventive effect. — Although the language of this section does not state that it provides a defense of former jeopardy, it amounts to such a defense in purpose and desired effect. Like the Fifth Amendment bar of former jeopardy, this section prevents the Commonwealth from subjecting an accused to the hazards of vexatious, multiple prosecutions. Phillips v. Commonwealth, 257 Va. 548, 514 S.E.2d 340 (1999).

This section is applicable only to criminal proceedings. It does not apply to a proceeding under § 18.2-336 [see now § 19.2-386.30] to forfeit property used in connection with a lottery, for that is a civil case. Quidley v. Commonwealth, 190 Va. 1029, 59 S.E.2d 52 (1950).

This section applies only to multiple or successive prosecutions. — The plain language of this statute bespeaks a legislative intent that it applies only to multiple or successive prosecutions. Hall v. Commonwealth, 14 Va. App. 892, 421 S.E.2d 455 (1992).

When defendant was charged with multiple arson counts, § 19.2-294 did not bar his convictions of those counts, because that statute only barred multiple or successive prosecutions, and defendant was

tried in a single, simultaneous, prosecution for all the offenses alleged. Schwartz v. Commonwealth, 41 Va. App. 61, 581 S.E.2d 891, 2003 Va. App. LEXIS 339 (2003), aff'd, 267 Va. 751, 594 S.E.2d 925 (2004).

This section does not apply to simultaneous prosecutions. Slater v. Commonwealth, 15 Va. App. 593, 425 S.E.2d 816 (1993).

Simultaneous prosecutions not barred. — This section does not bar multiple convictions arising out of the same act if they are prosecuted simultaneously. Thus where warrants for involuntary manslaughter and driving while under the influence of alcohol were issued at the same time, although the charges were heard at different times in different courts, because the charges were initiated simultaneously, the proceedings were concurrent, not successive, and thus, both convictions were permitted under this section. Doss v. Commonwealth, No. 2003-93-3, 1995 Va. App. LEXIS 425 (May 9, 1995).

Defendant's convictions in the circuit court for cruelty to animals in violation of § 3.1-796.122, after defendant had already been convicted in district court for failure to provide care for the same animals under § 3.1-796.68, did not violate § 19.2-294 because the cruelty convictions occurred as part of the same prosecution as her convictions for failure to provide care, and § 19.2-294 did not apply to simultaneous prosecutions. Hillman v. Commonwealth, No. 1211-01-3, 2002 Va. App. LEXIS 195 (Ct. of Appeals Apr. 2, 2002).

Evidence that defendant used his finger to rub his 12-year-old stepdaughter's genitalia and also touched his stepdaughter's breasts was sufficient to sustain his convictions for animate object sexual penetration and aggravated sexual battery, and nothing in § 19.2-294 barred defendant's convictions for both crimes in a single, simultaneous prosecution. Fincham v. Commonwealth, No. 3361-02-2, 2004 Va. App. LEXIS 259 (Ct. of Appeals June 8, 2004).

Trial court did not err in failing to dismiss indictments for robbery and possession of a firearm after a felony conviction on double jeopardy grounds, as the prosecutions against defendant were simultaneous, not successive, because they were joined in a single evidentiary hearing in the general district court; thus, upon an adjudication on misdemeanor charges, the later events in the circuit court on the felony charges were merely a continuation of the same prosecution. Morris v. Commonwealth, 45 Va. App. 181, 609 S.E.2d 92, 2005 Va. App. LEXIS 79 (2005).

Simultaneous initiation of charges is not exclusive measure of whether convictions arise from a single prosecution; rather, the more significant and compelling factor is whether the offenses were prosecuted in a single, concurrent evidentiary hearing. Phillips v. Commonwealth, 27 Va. App. 674, 500 S.E.2d 848 (1998).

Multiple convictions arising from same act not necessarily precluded. — This section does not preclude multiple convictions arising from the same act, provided the related offenses are prosecuted simultaneously. Hairston v. Commonwealth, No. 2777-95-3, 1996 Va. App. LEXIS 814 (Dec. 31, 1996).

Where felony and misdemeanor charges are instituted at separate times, but are heard simultaneously in a single proceeding, they are part of a single prosecution, even though jurisdictional limitations necessitate that they be concluded in different courts. Phillips v. Commonwealth, 27 Va. App. 674, 500 S.E.2d 848 (1998).

Conspiracy test. — The court has adopted the "totality of the circumstances" test established by the Fourth Circuit in United States v. MacDougall, 790 F.2d 1135 (4th Cir. 1986), to determine whether the evidence proves a single conspiracy or multiple conspiracies. Bolton v. Commonwealth, 19 Va. App. 376, 451 S.E.2d 687 (1994).

The MacDougall test examines five criteria: (1) the time periods of the alleged conspiracy(ies); (2) the places where the alleged activities occurred; (3) the people involved; (4) the overt acts alleged; and (5) the substantive statutes involved. Bolton v. Commonwealth, 19 Va. App. 376, 451 S.E.2d 687 (1994).

Multiple convictions for "same act" in same trial. — This section does not bar multiple convictions for the "same act" when those convictions are obtained in a single trial; however, multiple convictions and punishments for the "same act" may be precluded by the double jeopardy clause, even though obtained in a single trial. Hall v. Commonwealth, 14 Va. App. 892, 421 S.E.2d 455 (1992).

This section does not bar multiple convictions for separate crimes arising out of the same act when those convictions are obtained in a single trial. Thus, even if the challenged convictions arose out of the "same act," this section would not impose a bar if the convictions were obtained in a single proceeding. Because convictions were obtained in a single trial, defendant's contention that this section precluded his convictions for abduction, robbery and use of a firearm in the commission of a felony was without merit. Phoung v. Commonwealth, 15 Va. App. 457, 424 S.E.2d 712 (1992).

Capital murder convictions following defendant's guilty pleas to the lesser included first-degree murder offenses were not precluded because this section applies only to successive proceedings or prosecutions, and does not bar multiple convictions for the same act when those convictions are obtained in a single trial. Rea v. Commonwealth, 14 Va. App. 940, 421 S.E.2d 464 (1992).

Amenability of one charge to early conclusion. — Where charges are brought simultaneously, the amenability of one to early conclusion, while the other requires further proceedings, does not alter the fact that the proceedings are concurrent, not successive, prosecutions. Slater v. Commonwealth, 15 Va. App. 593, 425 S.E.2d 816 (1993).

Multiple convictions for "same act" through successive prosecutions. — This section bars the Commonwealth from securing multiple convictions for the "same act" through successive prosecutions or proceedings after having previously obtained a conviction. Hall v. Commonwealth, 14 Va. App. 892, 421 S.E.2d 455 (1992).

Two prosecutions involving single element insufficient to invoke double jeopardy protection. — Defendant was properly convicted of operating a motor vehicle after been declared an habitual offender, as the same evidence was not required to sustain both charges for DUI and for driving after having been declared a habitual offender; thus, the fact that the two prosecutions involved the single, overlapping element was not enough to invoke the protection of § 19.2-294. Belvin v. Commonwealth, No. 2568-01-1, 2002 Va. App. LEXIS 620 (Ct. of Appeals Oct. 15, 2002).

Pleading did not transform single prosecution into separate prosecutions. — By electing to plead guilty to three charges and not guilty to the remainder, defendant neither transformed the single prosecution into two separate prosecutions nor captured for himself any special protections against successive prosecutions under the double jeopardy clause. The convictions were thus obtained in a single trial and not barred by this section. Rea v. Commonwealth, 14 Va. App. 940, 421 S.E.2d 464 (1992).

Simultaneous prosecutions found. — Prosecutions were simultaneous, not successive, because they were joined in a single evidentiary hearing in the general district court. Thus, the later events in the circuit court on the felony charges were merely a continuation of the same prosecution. Phillips v. Commonwealth, 257 Va. 548, 514 S.E.2d 340 (1999).

Under § 19.2-294, defendant's guilty plea to reckless driving did not bar his prosecution for felony eluding arising from the same incident; as arrest warrants for the two offenses were issued on the same date, the misdemeanor and felony charges were brought in a "single proceeding," even though, due to jurisdictional constraints, they were resolved by two different courts. Hall v. Commonwealth, No. 1731-11-2, 2012 Va. App. LEXIS 306 (Oct. 2, 2012).

Section applies only to statutory offenses. — This section does not bar a defendant's conviction and punishment for both voluntary manslaughter and unlawful wounding, since it applies only where two or more statutory offenses are involved, and manslaughter is a common-law offense. Blythe v. Commonwealth, 222 Va. 722, 284 S.E.2d 796 (1981).

This section is not applicable when one crime is a common-law offense. Darnell v. Commonwealth, 12 Va. App. 948, 408 S.E.2d 540 (1991).

Statutory protection afforded by this section did not apply where one of defendant's criminal violations was for attempted murder, a common-law offense. Coleman v. Commonwealth, No. 2871-97-2, 1999 Va. App. LEXIS 445 (July 20, 1999).

Conviction is necessary under first sentence. — Under the first sentence of this section a mere proceeding or prosecution which does not result in a conviction does not bar another prosecution in a state court. Owens v. Commonwealth, 129 Va. 757, 105 S.E. 531 (1921), overruled on other grounds, Watkins v. Commonwealth, 238 Va. 341, 385 S.E.2d 50 (1989); Wheeler v. Commonwealth, 192 Va. 665, 66 S.E.2d 605 (1951); Dykeman v. Commonwealth, 201 Va. 807, 113 S.E.2d 867 (1960).

This section contemplates a conviction of an act or offense prohibited by two or more statutes or ordinances. Hundley v. Commonwealth, 193 Va. 449, 69 S.E.2d 336 (1952); Kelley v. County of Brunswick, 200 Va. 45, 104 S.E.2d 7 (1958).

The statute only bars prosecutions or proceedings after there has been a conviction. Hall v. Commonwealth, 14 Va. App. 892, 421 S.E.2d 455 (1992).

But first sentence applies only to state statutes and municipal ordinances. — The first sentence of this section applies only where state statutes and municipal ordinances are involved. Sigmon v. Commonwealth, 200 Va. 258, 105 S.E.2d 171 (1958).

The second sentence of this section does not create an absolute bar, which may be invoked by persons prosecuted in the state court at any time before conviction, without any reference to the time when either prosecution was commenced; it only refers to prosecutions in the federal court which have been commenced before the state court takes jurisdiction of the case. Owens v. Commonwealth, 129 Va. 757, 105 S.E. 531 (1921).

By the second sentence of this section, the legislature only intended to provide that if, when a prosecution under a state law was commenced, the accused could show that before that time there had been a prosecution against him under a federal statute for the same act, then the prosecution in the state court should be barred. Owens v. Commonwealth, 129 Va. 757, 105 S.E. 531 (1921); Sigmon v. Commonwealth, 200 Va. 258, 105 S.E.2d 171 (1958).

Charges arising from joint federal and state investigation does not necessarily bar state prosecution. — Under this section, a prosecution under state law for an offense arising out of a joint federal and state investigation is barred where a defendant has been charged in a federal warrant for the same acts. However, the mere fact that charges may be the result of a joint federal and state investigation does not necessarily bar a state prosecution. Billington v. Commonwealth, 13 Va. App. 341, 412 S.E.2d 461 (1991).

Even if some of the events of state prosecutions are recited in an affidavit for a federal search warrant, a later state prosecution is not barred where the search warrant is based on other information developed during the investigation. Billington v. Commonwealth, 13 Va. App. 341, 412 S.E.2d 461 (1991).

State prosecution not barred where it commenced prior to federal prosecution. — Section 19.2-294 did not bar state prosecution of defendant because the state action commenced before the federal prosecution; the state court proceedings at issue commenced upon issuance of the arrest warrants whereas the federal proceedings did not commence until the federal indictment was returned. Green v. Commonwealth, No. 2508-02-2, 2003 Va. App. LEXIS 516 (Ct. of Appeals Oct. 14, 2003).

Court first taking jurisdiction has priority. — See Owens v. Commonwealth, 129 Va. 757, 105 S.E. 531 (1921).

Conduct constituting "same act." — Although this section does not afford a blanket bar to multiple convictions where one such occurrence of driving a motor vehicle is involved, where one occurrence of driving cannot be separated factually into separate and distinct acts of driving and constitutes one distinct, continuous and unaltered course of driving bounded closely in terms of place and time, such conduct is the "same act" of driving for purposes of this section claim. Lash v. County of Henrico, 13 Va. App. 251, 410 S.E.2d 689 (1991), overruled on other grounds, Hall v. Commonwealth, 14 Va. App. 892, 421 S.E.2d 455 (1992).

This section applies to violation of any two or more statutes, not just driving while intoxicated and reckless driving, and it is applicable only if "the same act" is a violation of two or more statutes, not to offenses growing out of the same act or acts, and § 19.2-294 does not contemplate a continuous, uninterrupted course of operation of a motor vehicle. Brown v. Commonwealth, No. 2028-03-2, 2004 Va. App. LEXIS 363 (Ct. of Appeals July 27, 2004).

Convictions of malicious wounding and stabbing arose from same act. — Defendant's act of stabbing the victim clearly was the identical act that was used to convict him of malicious wounding and of stabbing in the commission of a felony; therefore, multiple convictions arising out of the "same act" were obtained. Hall v. Commonwealth, 14 Va. App. 892, 421 S.E.2d 455 (1992).

The inclusion of the words "same act or acts" in § 19.2-294.1 broadens the scope of that section over that of this section, which is limited to multiple prosecutions for the "same act." Lash v. County of Henrico, 13 Va. App. 251, 410 S.E.2d 689 (1991), overruled on other grounds, Hall v. Commonwealth, 14 Va. App. 892, 421 S.E.2d 455 (1992).

Test of identity of acts or offenses is whether the same evidence is required to sustain them; if not, then the fact that several charges relate to and grow out of one transaction or occurrence does not make a single act or offense where two separate acts or offenses are defined by statute. Hundley v. Commonwealth, 193 Va. 449, 69 S.E.2d 336 (1952); Owsley v. Cunningham, 190 F. Supp. 608 (E.D. Va. 1961).

A conviction of one statutory offense does not bar conviction under another statutory offense if each offense could have been proved without the necessity of proving the other. Fitzgerald v. Commonwealth, 11 Va. App. 625, 401 S.E.2d 208 (1991).

In determining whether the conduct underlying the convictions is based upon the same act, the particular criminal transaction must be examined to determine whether the acts are the same in terms of time, situs, victim, and the nature of the act itself. Hall v. Commonwealth, 14 Va. App. 892, 421 S.E.2d 455 (1992).

The test of whether there are separate acts sustaining several offenses is whether the same evidence is required to sustain them. Slade v. Commonwealth, No. 2664-98-3, 2000 Va. App. LEXIS 514 (Ct. of Appeals July 18, 2000).

To establish the applicability of this section, a defendant is required to do no more than to show that the "act" which served as the basis for the one conviction was "the same act" which was used to convict him of the other charge. Slade v. Commonwealth, No. 2664-98-3, 2000 Va. App. LEXIS 514 (Ct. of Appeals July 18, 2000).

Introduction of evidence of federal crimes to prove intent not bar to state prosecution. — The mere fact that the prosecution introduced and relied upon evidence of federal crimes to prove a defendant's intent with respect to the different acts for which he was being prosecuted under state law did not bar his prosecution. Billington v. Commonwealth, 13 Va. App. 341, 412 S.E.2d 461 (1991).

No double jeopardy where state and federal offenses involve different acts. — Defendant's motion to dismiss the heroin transport charges against him in the Commonwealth court was denied because the previous dismissal of the heroin distribution charges against the defendant in the federal court did not warrant a finding of double jeopardy as the defendant was charged with different acts, that is the transportation of heroin across the Commonwealth's border in the Commonwealth court and the distribution of heroin in the federal court. Londono v. Commonwealth, 40 Va. App. 377, 579 S.E.2d 641, 2003 Va. App. LEXIS 257 (2003).

Determination of simultaneous or successive charges. — It is the time of their institution which determines whether multiple charges are simultaneous or successive. Hairston v. Commonwealth, No. 2777-95-3, 1996 Va. App. LEXIS 814 (Dec. 31, 1996).

Collection of evidence is not step in prosecution of crime. — A step in the process of prosecution, under a federal statute, must first be begun against a defendant for the "same act" before this section is a bar to a later state prosecution; the collection of evidence by a federal grand jury which coincidentally, inadvertently or unavoidably includes evidence of a state crime is not "a step in the prosecution, under federal statute," of that crime and does not bar prosecution by the state for that crime. Billington v. Commonwealth, 13 Va. App. 341, 412 S.E.2d 461 (1991).

The mere fact that evidence of a state crime may be captured in the broad sweep of an inquiry before a federal grand jury does not bar prosecution by the state for that crime. Billington v. Commonwealth, 13 Va. App. 341, 412 S.E.2d 461 (1991).

The mere fact that evidence of a state crime may be captured in the broad sweep of an inquiry before a federal grand jury does not bar prosecution by the state for that crime. There must be a step in the process of prosecution, under a federal statute for the "same act" before this section is a bar to a later state prosecution. The mere collection of evidence by a federal grand jury which coincidentally, inadvertently or unavoidably includes evidence of a state crime is not such a step and does not bar prosecution by the state for that crime. Phau v. Commonwealth, No. 0539-90-3 (Ct. of Appeals Sept. 29, 1992).

Where an indictment for murder followed statutory short form and did not allege that the murder was committed while the accused was in the act of committing or attempting to commit robbery, the proof required to sustain the conviction was entirely different from that required to sustain conviction under a previous indictment for robbery only. Owsley v. Cunningham, 190 F. Supp. 608 (E.D. Va. 1961).

One occasion of driving an automobile may give rise to several acts and offenses, and the test of whether there are separate acts sustaining several offenses is whether the same evidence is required to sustain them. Estes v. Commonwealth, 212 Va. 23, 181 S.E.2d 622 (1971).

Manner of raising defense. — A defense under the provisions of this section is not exactly one of former jeopardy, yet it amounts to such a defense in purpose and desired effect. A mere motion to dismiss or quash is not sufficient to constitute a plea of former jeopardy. Such a defense must be raised by a formal plea in writing, duly sworn to, and setting forth all the facts and circumstances necessary to identify the accused and the offense. Sigmon v. Commonwealth, 200 Va. 258, 105 S.E.2d 171 (1958), holding that defendant's motion to quash, would, in this instance, be considered sufficient as a plea of former jeopardy under this section.

This section is not exactly a defense of former jeopardy. Yet, it amounts to such a defense in purpose and desired effect. Epps v. Commonwealth, 216 Va. 150, 216 S.E.2d 64 (1975).

Time for raising defense. — To argue a violation of this section, a defendant must present his plea in writing seven days prior to the trial date and, if the rule establishing this time limit is not followed, a defendant is deemed to have waived these concerns although, for good cause shown, a circuit court can allow an oral motion prior to trial. Clay v. Commonwealth, No. 0619-99-2, 2000 Va. App. LEXIS 644 (Ct. of Appeals Sept. 5, 2000).

Question cannot be raised for first time on appeal. — On appeal from a conviction for driving an automobile while under the influence of intoxicants, the accused contended that, because he had been tried upon a charge of being intoxicated and had been acquitted, this was an adjudication of driving an automobile while under the influence of intoxicants and, under this section, barred the second prosecution. However, it was held that the accused could not raise this question for the first time on appeal. Owens v. Commonwealth, 147 Va. 624, 136 S.E. 765 (1927).

A defense under this section was not made in the lower court and it cannot be raised for the first time on appeal. This is so because the defense is akin to that of former jeopardy which is an affirmative defense and if not raised in proper time is deemed to have been waived. Hubbard v. Commonwealth, 207 Va. 673, 152 S.E.2d 250 (1967).

Where defendant was convicted of both murder and malicious discharge of a firearm, in a case where there was testimony that another person was about three to four feet from the murder victim at the time of the killing, and the other person was knocked back and could not hear, defendant did not preserve defendant's argument that § 19.2-294 required the Commonwealth to elect which charge the Commonwealth would present to the jury, as the argument was not presented to the trial court; the Virginia Court of Appeals would not consider an argument on appeal that was not presented to the trial court, under Va. Sup. Ct. R. 5A:18. Proctor v. Commonwealth, 40 Va. App. 233, 578 S.E.2d 822, 2003 Va. App. LEXIS 182 (2003).

Applied in Mason v. Commonwealth, 217 Va. 321, 228 S.E.2d 683 (1976); Wade v. Commonwealth, 9 Va. App. 359, 388 S.E.2d 277 (1990); Ali v. Commonwealth, 280 Va. 665, 701 S.E.2d 64, 2010 Va. LEXIS 273 (2010).

II. ILLUSTRATIVE CASES.

Acts occurred at separate times and places. — Because the felony obstruction of justice prosecution was not based on the same act as the misdemeanor obstruction of justice conviction, § 19.2-294 did not bar his prosecution for felony obstruction of justice. Roach v. Commonwealth, 51 Va. App. 741, 660 S.E.2d 348, 2008 Va. App. LEXIS 212 (2008).

Prosecutions not based on same evidence as earlier convictions. — State prosecutions on ten charges of embezzlement, violations of § 18.2-111, convictions were not barred under § 19.2-294, although defendant had previously pled guilty on federal charges of mail fraud, in violation of 18 U.S.C.S. § 1341, and money laundering, in violation of 18 U.S.C.S. § 1956, because the evidence necessary to prove the federal offenses was different from that required to prove the state offenses where the acts involved in embezzling the funds were not the same as the acts of laundering the money and engaging in mail fraud. Rodis v. Commonwealth, 2010 Va. App. LEXIS 195 (May 11, 2010).

Multiple violations under a single statute not barred. — Conviction for committing three acts of aggravated sexual battery did not violate § 19.2-294, as defendant was convicted in a simultaneous prosecution for multiple violations of a single statute and § 19.2-294 only barred successive convictions under two or more statutes. De'Armond v. Commonwealth, 51 Va. App. 26, 654 S.E.2d 317, 2007 Va. App. LEXIS 460 (2007).

Prosecution for attempted murder after conviction of obstructing justice. — This section is not a bar to prosecution for attempted murder after a conviction of obstructing justice; while obstructing justice may be a statutory offense, attempted murder is a common-law offense. Martin v. Commonwealth, 242 Va. 1, 406 S.E.2d 15, cert. denied, 502 U.S. 945, 112 S. Ct. 388, 116 L. Ed. 2d 339 (1991).

Conviction of being a felon in possession of a handgun not based on the same evidence as earlier conviction for carrying a concealed weapon. — Defendant's conviction of possession of a firearm by a felon, § 18.2-308.2, was affirmed; the possession by a felon conviction was based on different evidence than the conviction for carrying a concealed weapon, § 18.2-308, which was based on the same incident, and therefore § 19.2-294 did not bar the possession by a felon conviction. Jefferson v. Commonwealth, 43 Va. App. 361, 597 S.E.2d 290, 2004 Va. App. LEXIS 277 (2004).

Reckless driving and driving under the influence. — In apparent response to Hundley v. Commonwealth, 193 Va. 449, 69 S.E.2d 336 (1952), the legislature changed the focus from "the same act" in cases involving concurrent charges of reckless driving and driving under the influence arising from one occurrence to whether the offenses arose from one continuous, uninterrupted course of operation of a motor vehicle. Lash v. County of Henrico, 13 Va. App. 251, 410 S.E.2d 689 (1991), overruled on other grounds, Hall v. Commonwealth, 14 Va. App. 892, 421 S.E.2d 455 (1992).

Reckless driving and speeding are separate and distinct offenses; nothing in the language of § 19.2-294.1 precludes the Commonwealth or a locality from convicting a person for both DUI and speeding. White v. Commonwealth, 26 Va. App. 410, 494 S.E.2d 896 (1998).

Prosecution for eluding a police officer after DUI conviction. — Although defendant had already been convicted of driving under the influence under § 18.2-266 from the same incident, his conviction for eluding a police officer under subsection B of § 46.2-817 was not barred by § 19.2-294 because the specific acts serving as a basis for prosecution of the offenses were separate and distinct in that the same evidence would not produce a conviction for both offenses. Wolford v. Commonwealth, 2006 Va. App. LEXIS 513 (Nov. 14, 2006).

Conviction of driving under influence and of driving on suspended license. — The defendant's conviction of driving under the influence was not barred, under this section, by his contemporaneous conviction of driving on a suspended license, or vice versa, because the defendant could have been convicted of driving under the influence without evidence of the suspension of his driver's license, and he could have been convicted of driving on a suspended license without evidence of his intoxication. Estes v. Commonwealth, 212 Va. 23, 181 S.E.2d 622 (1971).

Operating vehicle while under influence and driving after adjudged habitual offender. — Operating a motor vehicle while under the influence of alcohol and driving a motor vehicle upon a highway after having been adjudged an habitual offender are separate acts. Slater v. Commonwealth, 15 Va. App. 593, 425 S.E.2d 816 (1993).

Speeding and being adjudged an habitual offender. — Habitual offender charge was not barred by a prior speeding conviction because while the defendant's method of operating a motor vehicle was at issue in both charges, the nature of the specific act peculiar to each prosecution was different, the nature of each specific act was separate and distinct, and the speeding charge and habitual offender charge required different evidence. Terry v. Commonwealth, No. 0959-02-3, 2003 Va. App. LEXIS 220 (Ct. of Appeals Apr. 15, 2003).

Driving on suspended license and driving after being adjudged an habitual offender. — Charges of driving on a suspended license and driving after being adjudged an habitual offender did not constitute double jeopardy even though they arose

from the same act of driving. While driving was conduct common and necessary to each charge, the legal disability on defendant relating to each was different, and thus the evidence would not produce a conviction for both offenses. Johnson v. Commonwealth, 38 Va. App. 137, 562 S.E.2d 341, 2002 Va. App. LEXIS 228 (2002).

Aggravated involuntary manslaughter and driving while intoxicated. — Vehicular aggravated involuntary manslaughter conviction did not violate § 19.2-294, because defendant's conduct supported both defendant's conviction for manslaughter and the previous conviction for driving while intoxicated, where each act had a distinct victim and the nature of the act specific to each prosecution was distinct. Davis v. Commonwealth, 57 Va. App. 446, 703 S.E.2d 259, 2011 Va. App. LEXIS 3 (2011).

A prior administrative suspension of the defendant's driver's license did not bar a subsequent criminal trial for driving under the influence of alcohol. Kenison v. Commonwealth, No. 1688-97-4, 1999 Va. App. LEXIS 131 (Feb. 23, 1999).

Prosecution for hit and run after conviction for fleeing police. — The defendant's conviction of fleeing a police officer in Fairfax County did not bar his subsequent hit and run conviction in Arlington County. Even though the hit and run was the culmination of the same flight from police that gave rise to the Fairfax County conviction, the Arlington conviction was not based on the "same act" that served as the basis for the Fairfax conviction. Treu v. Commonwealth, 12 Va. App. 996, 406 S.E.2d 676 (1991).

Theft of several articles at same time. — The rule that the theft of several articles at one and the same time constitutes an indivisible offense, and a conviction or acquittal of any one or more of them is a bar to a subsequent prosecution for the larceny of the others, applies only to a case involving multiple larceny prosecutions predicated upon the theft of multiple articles stolen contemporaneously. Jones v. Commonwealth, 218 Va. 757, 240 S.E.2d 658, cert. denied, 435 U.S. 909, 98 S. Ct. 1459, 55 L. Ed. 2d 500, 439 U.S. 892, 99 S. Ct. 249, 58 L. Ed. 2d 238 (1978), overruled in part by Hudgins v. Commonwealth, 269 Va. 607, 611 S.Ed.2d 362 (2005).

Conviction of aggravated sexual battery and rape. — Defendant was not prosecuted under two statutes for a single act as proscribed by this section; instead, he was prosecuted for two separate acts, each constituting a distinct offense; when defendant moistened his finger and inserted it into his step-daughter's vagina (this act completed the offense of aggravated sexual battery) and then immediately thereafter, penetrated her vagina with his penis, (this act completed the offense of rape), defendant could have been convicted of each offense without evidence of the other, and this section did not bar his prosecution for both crimes because each offense was based on a different act arising from the same incident and each required different evidence to sustain a conviction. Thomas v. Commonwealth, No. 1743-88-3 (Ct. of Appeals Feb. 27, 1990).

This section does not prohibit defendant's prosecution in a single trial for aggravated malicious wounding and use of a firearm in the commission of the aggravated malicious wounding. Powell v. Commonwealth, No. 0554-89-1 (Ct. of Appeals Oct. 6, 1992).

Conviction of robbery and larceny. — In terms of time and situs, the robbery of a motel clerk and the larceny of the motel's courtesy car by the defendant involved two separate and distinct acts of caption and two different acts of asportation. Therefore, the acts which constituted the two offenses of which defendant was convicted were not "the same act" within the meaning of this section. Jones v. Commonwealth, 218 Va. 757, 240 S.E.2d 658, cert. denied, 435 U.S. 909, 99 S. Ct. 249, 55 L. Ed. 2d 500, 439 U.S. 892, 99 S. Ct. 249, 58 L. Ed. 2d 238 (1978), overruled in part by Hudgins v. Commonwealth, 269 Va. 607, 611 S.Ed.2d 362 (2005).

Conviction for burglary and grand larceny. — The double jeopardy clause does not bar conviction and sentence at one trial for burglary under § 18.2-91 and grand larceny under § 18.2-95 arising from a unitary criminal transaction, since each offense rests on different necessary elements. The clause is infringed only if all the components of a crime defined under one statute must also be proved to convict under another. The test to be applied is whether each provision requires proof of an additional fact which the other does not. Downey v. Peyton, 451 F.2d 236 (4th Cir. 1971).

Conviction of breaking and entering and destroying private property. — This section is inapplicable where the "same act" involved was the breaking of the doors of the places broken into.

This act, although common to both the convictions of breaking and entering and the convictions for destroying private property, was a violation of § 18.2-137, destroying private property, but was not a violation of § 18.2-91, statutory burglary. Thus, the same act was a violation of only one of the two statutes, not both. Fitzgerald v. Commonwealth, 11 Va. App. 625, 401 S.E.2d 208 (1991).

Prosecution for both breaking and entering and destroying private property was not barred because the breaking of a door may have been one continuous act, but the act of entering the property with intent to commit larceny, although immediately following the breaking, was a separate act from the breaking. Fitzgerald v. Commonwealth, 11 Va. App. 625, 401 S.E.2d 208 (1991).

Cruelty to animals and discharging firearm based on same act. — The Commonwealth was barred from prosecuting a defendant for cruelty to an animal after the defendant had already been convicted of discharging a firearm within the city limits, where the Commonwealth could successfully prosecute the defendant for cruelty to an animal only by proving, as charged in the indictment, that he shot the animal, and this same act of shooting was the basis for the earlier discharging a firearm conviction. Slade v. Commonwealth, No. 2664-98-3, 2000 Va. App. LEXIS 514 (Ct. of Appeals July 18, 2000).

Felony charges of distributing marijuana on school property not barred under the provisions of this section due to two prior misdemeanor convictions based on the same acts as the felony charges. Phillips v. Commonwealth, 27 Va. App. 674, 500 S.E.2d 848 (1998).

Conviction for five capital murders. — Although defendant was convicted of five charges of capital murder, each based separately upon proof beyond a reasonable doubt, the jury fixed only one death sentence for each victim. Under these circumstances, he was not subjected to multiple punishments for what he claimed was the same act or offense. Williams v. Commonwealth, 248 Va. 528, 450 S.E.2d 365 (1994), cert. denied, 515 U.S. 1161, 115 S. Ct. 2616, 132 L. Ed. 2d 858 (1995).

Prior conviction of illegal manufacture of liquor. — Under this section a misdemeanor indictment charging illegal possession of a still in violation of former § 4-77 (see now § 4.1-314) would fall only upon conviction of a charge of the greater and inclusive offense of illegal manufacture of liquor in violation of former § 4-57 (see now § 4.1-300) by the use of the identical still. Wheeler v. Commonwealth, 192 Va. 665, 66 S.E.2d 605 (1951), overruled on other grounds, Watkins v. Commonwealth, 238 Va. 341, 385 S.E.2d 50 (1989).

Prior conviction of illegal sale of liquor. — Under this section, a prior conviction in a trial justice court for the illegal sale of liquor is a bar to a prosecution for illegal possession of the identical liquor. Wheeler v. Commonwealth, 192 Va. 665, 66 S.E.2d 605 (1951), overruled on other grounds, Watkins v. Commonwealth, 238 Va. 341, 385 S.E.2d 50 (1989).

Uttering a forged note is not the "same act" as obtaining money by means thereof. Bullock v. Commonwealth, 205 Va. 867, 140 S.E.2d 821, cert. denied, 382 U.S. 927, 86 S. Ct. 310, 15 L. Ed. 2d 341 (1965), rehearing denied, 382 U.S. 1000, 86 S. Ct. 530, 15 L. Ed. 2d 489 (1966).

Indecent exposure not included in offense of sodomy. — The misdemeanor of indecent exposure is not included within the offense of sodomy because the elements of indecent exposure are not included within the elements of sodomy. Similarly, the elements of indecent exposure with lascivious intent are not included within the offense of sodomy, nor are the elements of sodomy included within the offense of indecent exposure with lascivious intent. So even if a prior conviction of indecent exposure with lascivious intent was based on the same evidence as a later prosecution for sodomy, this section is not applicable. Ashby v. Commonwealth, 208 Va. 443, 158 S.E.2d 657 (1968), cert. denied, 393 U.S. 1111, 89 S. Ct. 884, 21 L. Ed. 2d 808 (1969).

Severance not found. — Omission from the indictment of the language in the warrant, "or concealed weapon," simply removed surplusage, without affecting the substantive allegation. Therefore, the felony prosecution continued, uninterrupted, through a procedurally regular course from its genesis in the criminal complaint to conviction in the trial court. Hairston v. Commonwealth, No. 2777-95-3, 1996 Va. App. LEXIS 814 (Dec. 31, 1996).

The procurement of arrest warrants on different dates does not automatically trigger the successive prosecution bar under this section. Since the bar is intended to protect an accused from the "hazards of vexatious, multiple prosecutions," the bar does not preclude the prosecution of charges in a single, evidentiary hearing, even though the arrest warrants were obtained on different dates. Phillips v. Commonwealth, 257 Va. 548, 514 S.E.2d 340 (1999).

Subsequent prosecution under valid warrant. — Where a city ordinance was invalid and the city warrant issued under that ordinance was disposed of by a nolle prosequi — which barred prosecution under that particular warrant — this did not prevent later prosecution of the defendant under a valid warrant for the offense for which he was arrested. Lowery v. Commonwealth, 205 Va. 575, 138 S.E.2d 300 (1964).

For a case indicating that courts will decide, case by case, whether particular acts in violation of §§ 46.2-817 and 46.2-852 can produce multiple convictions without violating this section or § 19.2-294.1, see Lash v. County of Henrico, 13 Va. App. 251, 410 S.E.2d 689 (1991), overruled on other grounds, Hall v. Commonwealth, 14 Va. App. 892, 421 S.E.2d 455 (1992).

CIRCUIT COURT OPINIONS

Only applies to convictions. — Trial court found that § 19.2-294, which provided statutory double jeopardy protection to defendants, did not apply in defendant's case to prohibit a prosecution in the trial court against him for carnal knowledge in a case where the county juvenile court had already dismissed a charge of contributing to the delinquency of a minor against him; this section applies only to convictions and the dismissal of the charge in the county juvenile court did not involve a conviction against defendant. Commonwealth v. Hopkinson, 67 Va. Cir. 520, 2004 Va. Cir. LEXIS 362 (Loudoun County July 19, 2004).

Simultaneous prosecutions not barred. — Requirements for proving a concealed weapons misdemeanor under § 18.2-308 were distinct from the requirements of § 18.2-308.2, although the two charges were commenced at the same or concurrent time, and the prosecutions were not sequential in nature simply because the misdemeanor was more amenable to an expeditious resolution than the felony; thus, no violation of § 19.2-294 resulted. Commonwealth v. Turner, 62 Va. Cir. 209, 2003 Va. Cir. LEXIS 312 (Charlottesville 2003).

The fact that misdemeanor charges were brought to an early conclusion under the jurisdiction of the General District Court, did not make the subsequent prosecution of the felony cases in the Circuit Court a successive prosecution that violated the provisions of § 19.2-294; the prosecutions were simultaneous. Commonwealth v. Johnson, 68 Va. Cir. 482, 2001 Va. Cir. LEXIS 539 (Nelson County 2001).

State prosecution was not barred by § 19.2-294 on the basis of a federal prosecution because there was no showing that the acts for which defendant was charged, producing child pornography, also constituted a violation of a federal statute, which prohibited possession of child pornography transported in interstate commerce; defendant was charged federally with possessing child pornography that was transported in interstate commerce, but in the state case, defendant was charged with producing or creating child pornography images on a different date. Although he may have victimized the same child on more than one of these various occasions, the specific acts on which each prosecution was based were different in terms of when they occurred, as well as in the nature of the acts themselves. Commonwealth v. Allen, — Va. Cir. —, 2007 Va. Cir. LEXIS 100 (Fairfax County May 3, 2007).

A prior administrative suspension of driver's license. — Sixty-day administrative license suspension requirement in § 46.2-391.2 is civil, and not criminal, like its seven-day counterpart, and a subsequent driving under the influence (DUI) prosecution thus does not violate double jeopardy or § 19.2-294. Accordingly, such a suspension did not bar a DUI prosecution under § 18.2-266. Commonwealth v. Stump, 69 Va. Cir. 433, 2006 Va. Cir. LEXIS 95 (Roanoke 2006).

Simultaneous prosecutions not barred. — Double jeopardy pursuant to Va. Const. art. I, § 8, U.S. Const. amend. V, or § 19.2-294 did not bar defendant's felony prosecution for charges stemming from the making and storing of hazardous materials for the purpose of manufacturing fireworks, violations of §§ 18.2-85,

10.1-1455, after he pleaded guilty to violations of Norfolk, Va. City Code §§ 17.1-43, 17.1-44(25), because each of the four statutes required different elements of proof. Commonwealth v. Saunders, 78 Va. Cir. 345, 2009 Va. Cir. LEXIS 173 (Norfolk May 27, 2009).

Acts occurred at separate times and places. — Defendant failed to show that trial counsel's arguments to support a motion to dismiss under § 19.2-294 fell below an objective standard of reasonableness state charges for producing child pornography under § 18.2-374.1 and federal charges for possession of images of child pornography under 18 U.S.C.S. 2252A(a)(5)(B) involved two distinct acts and required different evidence to sustain them; the federal possession charge required only a showing that the pornographic images defendant possessed in 2004 were produced by someone using materials that had entered interstate commerce, and the state charge of production required the Commonwealth to show that defendant created the pornographic images in 2003. Allen v. Johnson, 2012 Va. Cir. LEXIS 72 (Fairfax County July 20, 2012).

Motion to dismiss. — Defendant failed to show that trial counsel's arguments to support a motion to dismiss under § 19.2-294 fell below an objective standard of reasonableness state charges for producing child pornography under § 18.2-374.1 and federal charges for possession of images of child pornography under 18 U.S.C.S. 2252A(a)(5)(B) involved two distinct acts and required different evidence to sustain them; the federal possession charge required only a showing that the pornographic images defendant possessed in 2004 were produced by someone using materials that had entered interstate commerce, and the state charge of production required the Commonwealth to show that defendant created the pornographic images in 2003. Allen v. Johnson, 2012 Va. Cir. LEXIS 72 (Fairfax County July 20, 2012).

§ 19.2-294.1. Dismissal of one of dual charges for driving while intoxicated and reckless driving upon conviction of other charge.

Whenever any person is charged with a violation of § 18.2-266 or any similar ordinances of any county, city, or town and with reckless driving in violation of § 46.2-852 or any ordinance of any county, city or town incorporating § 46.2-852, growing out of the same act or acts and is convicted of one of these charges, the court shall dismiss the remaining charge.

History.
Code 1950, § 19.1-259.1; 1960, c. 493; 1975, c. 495; 1997, c. 691; 2004, c. 937.

Editor's note.
Acts 2004, c. 937, cl. 2, provides: "That the Department of Motor Vehicles shall determine the impact on its recordkeeping system if the penalties currently applicable to a third conviction of § 18.2-266 were applicable without regard to the time period in which the offenses were committed."

Law Review.
For survey of Virginia criminal law and procedure for the year 1970-1971, see 57 Va. L. Rev. 1438 (1971). For 2003/2004 survey of criminal law and procedure, see 39 U. Rich. L. Rev. 133 (2004).

Michie's Jurisprudence.
For related discussion, see 2B M.J. Automobiles, §§ 118, 123; 2B M.J. Autrefois, Acquit and Convict, § 2; 20 M.J. Witnesses, § 111.1.

CASE NOTES

For a case discussing the history of § 19.2-294 and this section and the cases interpreting those sections, see Lash v. County of Henrico, 13 Va. App. 251, 410 S.E.2d 689 (1991),

overruled on other grounds, Hall v. Commonwealth, 14 Va. App. 892, 421 S.E.2d 455 (1992).

Construction. — Because this section relates to matters of a penal nature and is remedial in character, it must be construed strictly against the Commonwealth and favorably to the accused. Padgett v. Commonwealth, 220 Va. 758, 263 S.E.2d 388 (1980).

It is the commonality of the underlying offending conduct, the continuous, uninterrupted operation of a motor vehicle, that invokes the preclusive effect of this section. Harris v. City of Va. Beach, 19 Va. App. 214, 450 S.E.2d 401 (1994).

Although DUI and reckless driving are "separate and distinct" violations, a "conviction of one offense ... preclude[s] conviction of the other, whenever both 'gr[o]w' from the same 'continuous, uninterrupted course of operation of a motor vehicle.'" "It is the commonality of the underlying offending conduct, the continuous, uninterrupted operation of a motor vehicle, that invokes the preclusive effect of the statute." Lankford v. Commonwealth, No. 0581-95-2 (Ct. of Appeals Mar. 26, 1996).

Reckless driving and speeding are separate and distinct offenses; nothing in the language of this section precludes the Commonwealth or a locality from convicting a person for both DUI and speeding. White v. Commonwealth, 26 Va. App. 410, 494 S.E.2d 896 (1998).

The language, "the same act or acts," means "the same act or acts" of driving and contemplates a continuous, uninterrupted course of operation of a motor vehicle, without regard to the crossing of the boundary line between two localities. Padgett v. Commonwealth, 220 Va. 758, 263 S.E.2d 388 (1980).

The inclusion of the words "same act or acts" in this section broadens the scope of this section over that of § 19.2-294, which is limited to multiple prosecutions for the "same act." Lash v. County of Henrico, 13 Va. App. 251, 410 S.E.2d 689 (1991), overruled on other grounds, Hall v. Commonwealth, 14 Va. App. 892, 421 S.E.2d 455 (1992).

Where a DUI conviction is for a purely federal offense, the prohibition on dual convictions under this section is not triggered. United States v. Koonge, No. 99-4350, 2000 U.S. App. LEXIS 11438 (4th Cir. May 19, 2000).

Assimilation of section into federal law. — This provision controls the penalties when a person is charged with both reckless driving and driving while intoxicated and therefore is assimilated into federal law. United States v. Jones, No. 99-4879, 2000 U.S. App. LEXIS 23291 (4th Cir. Sept. 14, 2000).

This section merely requires a court to dismiss the charge of driving while intoxicated if the defendant is convicted of reckless driving. The term "charge" connotes a criminal action. By its terms, this section does not preclude civil action for compensatory relief or a suit to render nondischargeable a claim for compensatory relief. Hildebrand v. Kugler, 170 Bankr. 291 (Bankr. E.D. Va. 1994).

Reckless driving and driving under the influence. — In apparent response to Hundley v. Commonwealth, 193 Va. 449, 69 S.E.2d 336 (1952), the legislature changed the focus from "the same act" in cases involving concurrent charges of reckless driving and driving under the influence arising from one occurrence to whether the offenses arose from one continuous, uninterrupted course of operation of a motor vehicle. Lash v. County of Henrico, 13 Va. App. 251, 410 S.E.2d 689 (1991), overruled on other grounds, Hall v. Commonwealth, 14 Va. App. 892, 421 S.E.2d 455 (1992).

Two offenses subject to this section, driving under the influence and reckless driving, are "separate and distinct" violations, but the legislature intended that a conviction of one offense precludes conviction of the other, whenever both grow from the same continuous, uninterrupted course of operation of a motor vehicle so the statute is applicable where the two offenses grow out of the same act or acts of driving, and it is the commonality of the underlying offending conduct, the continuous, uninterrupted operation of a motor vehicle, that invokes the preclusive effect of the statute. Brown v. Commonwealth, No. 2028-03-2, 2004 Va. App. LEXIS 363 (Ct. of Appeals July 27, 2004).

Section 19.2-294.1 required the dismissal of defendant's indictment for felony driving under the influence, fourth offense, in violation of §§ 18.2-266 and 18.2-270 because defendant had been previously convicted of reckless driving in the general district court arising out of the same act or acts that were the basis of the felony indictment for driving under the influence. Lawson v. Commonwealth, 61 Va. App. 292, 734 S.E.2d 714, 2012 Va. App. LEXIS 402 (2012).

Dismissal mandatory. — Hence, when a person is convicted of driving under the influence of intoxicants, it is mandatory for the court to dismiss the reckless driving charge. Crawley v. Wilkerson, 283 F. Supp. 447 (W.D. Va. 1968).

Reversal of subsequent conviction necessitated. — Where defendant was charged and convicted of both this section's offenses, driving while intoxicated (DWI) and reckless driving, and the evidence was undisputed that the alleged misconduct was intimately related in time and distance, arising from and connected by one continuous, uninterrupted operation of defendant's motor vehicle, under such circumstances, the legislature clearly intended that a conviction of one offense result in a dismissal of the other. Accordingly, defendant's subsequent conviction for DWI should be reversed. Harris v. City of Va. Beach, 19 Va. App. 214, 450 S.E.2d 401 (1994).

Annulment of bar to conviction on appeal. — A person's conviction for driving under the influence of intoxicants constituted a bar to convicting such person of reckless driving, but when that person's conviction is annulled by an appeal, the bar to a conviction for reckless driving is also annulled. Crawley v. Wilkerson, 283 F. Supp. 447 (W.D. Va. 1968).

This section is irrelevant to prosecutions under federal regulations. — See United States v. Eubanks, 435 F.2d 1261 (4th Cir. 1971).

Commonwealth was not barred from prosecuting DUI charge. — The Commonwealth was not barred from prosecuting the defendant on his DUI charge by the provisions of this section; the language, "the same act or acts" used in this section means "the same act or acts" of driving and contemplates a continuous, uninterrupted course of operation of a motor vehicle; when appellant stopped his vehicle to use the bathroom, his course of operation of his vehicle was interrupted. When he started again on his course, that act of driving under the influence of alcohol constituted a separate offense subject to prosecution under the code section prohibiting driving under the influence of alcohol. Munden v. Commonwealth, No. 0105-90-2 (Ct. of Appeals June 4, 1991).

For a case indicating that courts will decide, case by case, whether particular acts in violation of §§ 46.2-817 and 46.2-852 can produce multiple convictions without violating § 19.2-294 or this section, see Lash v. County of Henrico, 13 Va. App. 251, 410 S.E.2d 689 (1991), overruled on other grounds, Hall v. Commonwealth, 14 Va. App. 892, 421 S.E.2d 455 (1992).

ARTICLE 3.

CONVICTION OF ALIENS.

§ 19.2-294.2. Procedure when aliens convicted of certain felonies; duties of probation and parole officer.

A. Whenever a person is (i) convicted in a circuit court of any felony and (ii) referred to a probation or parole officer for a report pursuant to § 19.2-299, or for probation supervision, the probation or parole officer shall inquire as to the citizenship of such person. If upon inquiry it is determined that the person may be an alien based upon his failure to produce evidence of United States citizenship, the probation or parole officer shall report this determination to the Central Criminal Records Exchange of the Department of State Police on forms provided by the Exchange.

B. The inquiry required by this section need not be made if it is apparent that a report on alien status has previously been made to the Central Criminal Records Exchange pursuant to this section.

C. It shall be the responsibility of the Central Criminal Records Exchange of the Department of State Police to review arrest reports submitted by law-enforcement agencies and reports of suspected alien-status inquiries made by probation or parole officers, and to report within sixty days of final disposition to the Law Enforcement Support Center of the United States Immigration and Customs Enforcement the identity of all convicted offenders suspected of being an alien.

History.
1985, c. 247; 1994, c. 579; 2008, cc. 180, 415.

The number of this section was assigned by the Code Commission, the number in the 1985 act having been 19.2-249.2.

Editor's note.
Acts 2004, c. 82, cl. 1, provides: "The State Compensation Board shall (i) maintain in the Local Inmate Data System (LIDS) specific data fields for an inmate's country of birth and country of citizenship, (ii) require all jail facilities that are subject to LIDS reporting to complete the additional fields for all inmates housed at such facilities, (iii) annually encourage all jail facilities subject to LIDS reporting to request compensation from the United States Department of Justice State Criminal Alien Assistance Program (SCAAP) for costs associated with incarcerating undocumented aliens; (iv) provide information to all jail facilities on the eligibility requirements to obtain such funds; and (v) monitor local jail participation in the SCAAP program."

Acts 2008, cc. 180 and 415, cl. 3 provides: "That the Department of Corrections shall confirm the validity of the social security numbers given by inmates and omit from its database those social security numbers determined to be fictitious."

The 2008 amendments.
The 2008 amendments by cc. 180 and 415 are identical and substituted "Law Enforcement Support Center of the United States Immigration and Customs Enforcement" for "Immigration and Naturalization Service" in subsection C.

Michie's Jurisprudence.
For related discussion, see 1B M.J. Aliens, § 4.

CHAPTER 18.

SENTENCE; JUDGMENT; EXECUTION OF SENTENCE.

Article 1. General Provisions.

ARTICLE 1.

GENERAL PROVISIONS.

§ 19.2-295. Ascertainment of punishment.

A. Within the limits prescribed by law, the term of confinement in the state correctional facility or in jail and the amount of fine, if any, of a person convicted of a criminal offense, shall be ascertained by the jury, or by the court in cases tried without a jury.

B. In any case in which a jury has fixed a sentence as provided in this chapter and the sentence is modified by the court pursuant to the authority contained within this chapter, the court shall file with the record of the case a written explanation of such modification including the cause therefor.

History.
Code 1950, §§ 19.1-291, 19.1-292; 1960, c. 366; 1975, c. 495; 2007, c. 259.

The 2007 amendments.
The 2007 amendment by c. 259 designated the provisions of the section as subsection A and added subsection B.

Law Review.
For discussion of jury sentencing, see 53 Va. L. Rev. 968 (1967). For survey of Virginia criminal law and procedure for the year 1970-1971, see 57 Va. L. Rev. 1438 (1971). For survey of Virginia law on criminal procedure for the year 1974-1975, see 61 Va. L. Rev. 1713 (1975). For article, "The Constitutionality of Harsher Sentences on Retrial in Virginia," see 62 Va. L. Rev. 1337 (1976). For survey of Virginia criminal procedure for the year 1975-1976, see 62 Va. L. Rev. 1412 (1976). For comment on sentencing in criminal cases, see 13 U. Rich. L. Rev. 899 (1979). For note, "Criminal Procedure and Criminal Law: Virginia Supreme Court Decisions During the 70's," see 15 U. Rich. L. Rev. 585 (1981). For an article on bifurcated sentencing in noncapital felony cases in Virginia, see 30 U. Rich. L. Rev. 465 (1996). For a note, "The Supreme Court's Backwards Proportionality Jurisprudence: Comparing Judicial Review of Excessive Criminal Punishments and Excessive Punitive Damages Awards," see 86 Va. L. Rev. 1249 (2000). For survey of Virginia law on criminal law and procedure for the year 2007-2008, see 43 U. Rich. L. Rev. 149 (2008).

Michie's Jurisprudence.
For related discussion, see 5B M.J. Criminal Procedure, §§ 38, 49, 50, 70, 72, 78, 79, 81, 95; 11B M.J. Jury, § 11.

CASE NOTES

Constitutionality. — Virginia's method of sentencing in a jury trial under this section and former § 53-272 (now §§ 53.1-151 and

53.1-186) does not violate due process. Roman v. Parrish, 328 F. Supp. 882 (E.D. Va. 1971).

Defendant's Sixth Amendment rights were not violated in a case where defendant was convicted of voluntary manslaughter, a jury recommended a three-year prison sentence pursuant to § 19.2-295, and the trial court imposed a three-year period of postrelease supervision; the postrelease supervision portion of defendant's sentence was imposed pursuant to statutory law, was within that statute's permissible range, and did not require the trial court to find any additional facts that were not implicit in the jury's finding of guilt. Alston v. Commonwealth, 274 Va. 759, 652 S.E.2d 456, 2007 Va. LEXIS 133 (2007).

The right to have the jury both try the issue of guilt and fix the penalty is a part of the right of trial by jury. Huggins v. Commonwealth, 213 Va. 327, 191 S.E.2d 734 (1972).

Due process clause not contrary to conclusion that jury sentencing preferable. Nothing in the due process clause of the Fourteenth Amendment intrudes upon the conclusion of this state that jury sentencing is preferable, whether in a unitary or bifurcated trial. Vines v. Muncy, 553 F.2d 342 (4th Cir.), cert. denied, 434 U.S. 851, 98 S. Ct. 163, 54 L. Ed. 2d 120 (1977).

No due process right to be sentenced by jury. — Nothing in the United States or Virginia Constitution gives a defendant the right to be sentenced by a jury or solely by a jury and the imposition of postrelease periods of suspended incarceration and supervision pursuant to § 19.2-295.2 does not violate any due process right of a defendant to be sentenced by a jury under this section. Boyd v. Commonwealth, 28 Va. App. 537, 507 S.E.2d 107 (1998).

The choice of sentencing procedures is a matter of legislative determination. Duncan v. Commonwealth, 2 Va. App. 342, 343 S.E.2d 392 (1986).

Right granted adults to have their sentences fixed by juries is purely statutory in both origin and nature. Ballard v. Commonwealth, 228 Va. 213, 321 S.E.2d 284 (1984), cert. denied, 470 U.S. 1085, 105 S. Ct. 1848, 85 L. Ed. 2d 146 (1985).

Juveniles not denied equal protection by different sentencing procedure. — Juveniles are not deprived of equal protection by the Virginia procedure in criminal cases, whereby an adult tried by jury has his sentence fixed by the jury under this section, while a juvenile transferred to circuit court and tried by jury has his sentence fixed by the judge under § 16.1-272. Ballard v. Commonwealth, 228 Va. 213, 321 S.E.2d 284 (1984), cert. denied, 470 U.S. 1085, 105 S. Ct. 1848, 85 L. Ed. 2d 146 (1985).

Rational basis exists for different sentencing procedure for juveniles. — A rational basis does exist for the classification under which sentences of adults are fixed by juries but sentences of juveniles transferred to the circuit court are fixed by the judge. While, for the purpose of determining guilt or innocence, a transferred juvenile is treated as an adult, and although he may be subject to adult penalties in the sentencing phase of his case, § 16.1-272 permits a circuit court to treat him in all respects as a juvenile, with the full panoply of beneficent alternatives available in juvenile court, including the use of a juvenile probation officer. Ballard v. Commonwealth, 228 Va. 213, 321 S.E.2d 284 (1984), cert. denied, 470 U.S. 1085, 105 S. Ct. 1848, 85 L. Ed. 2d 146 (1985).

Criminal defendant entitled to decision on sentence by jury and by trial judge. — Under the practice in this state, the convicted criminal defendant is entitled to "two decisions" on the sentence, one by the jury and the other by the trial judge in the exercise of his statutory right to suspend. Vines v. Muncy, 553 F.2d 342 (4th Cir.), cert. denied, 434 U.S. 851, 98 S. Ct. 163, 54 L. Ed. 2d 120 (1977).

His ultimate sentence does not therefore rest with the jury alone but is always subject to the control of the trial judge. Vines v. Muncy, 553 F.2d 342 (4th Cir.), cert. denied, 434 U.S. 851, 98 S. Ct. 163, 54 L. Ed. 2d 120 (1977).

Under the practice in this state, the punishment as fixed by the jury is not final or absolute, since its finding on the proper punishment is subject to suspension by the trial judge, in whole or in part, on the basis of any mitigating facts that the convicted defendant can marshal. Vines v. Muncy, 553 F.2d 342 (4th Cir.), cert. denied, 434 U.S. 851, 98 S. Ct. 163, 54 L. Ed. 2d 120 (1977).

Any criticism of jury sentencing because it lacks the objectivity and principled decision of a judge is overcome by the existence of the power in the trial judge to bring his so-called superior judgment to bear upon the issue of proper punishment in reaching his

decision whether to suspend the sentence or not. Vines v. Muncy, 553 F.2d 342 (4th Cir.), cert. denied, 434 U.S. 851, 98 S. Ct. 163, 54 L. Ed. 2d 120 (1977).

The power to impose sentences in all misdemeanor and felony cases resides in the jury. Witcher v. Peyton, 382 F.2d 707 (4th Cir. 1967).

Consideration of mitigating circumstances is for the court. — By vesting the trial court with discretionary authority to suspend or modify the sentence imposed by the jury, the legislature intended to leave the consideration of mitigating circumstances to the court. Reese v. Commonwealth, No. 1279-03-4, 2004 Va. App. LEXIS 316 (Ct. of Appeals July 6, 2004).

Policies behind right to jury trial not impaired. — The choice a defendant must make is whether or not to be tried by a jury, and since both the prosecutor and trial judge must concur in a waiver, it is not always his or her choice at that. But, a defendant, as a matter of law, suffers no prohibited burden of waiving the opportunity for a suspended sentence by being tried by a jury, because former § 53-272 (now §§ 53.1-151 and 53.1-186) specifically provides for suspension or probation by the judge after the jury's verdict of guilty and sentence under this section. Thus, this section and former § 53-272 (now §§ 53.1-151 and 53.1-186) on their faces do not appreciably impair the policies behind the right to a jury trial. Roman v. Parrish, 328 F. Supp. 882 (E.D. Va. 1971).

And fundamentally fair. — The federal district court cannot concern itself with what would be the most desirable method of sentencing under this state's law so long as the method employed is not fundamentally unfair, which that court has found it is not as far as this section and former § 53-272 (now §§ 53.1-151 and 53.1-186) are concerned. Roman v. Parrish, 328 F. Supp. 882 (E.D. Va. 1971).

The established practice is one trial on guilt and punishment. Snider v. Cox, 212 Va. 13, 181 S.E.2d 617 (1971).

And change of that general practice is left to the legislature. Snider v. Cox, 212 Va. 13, 181 S.E.2d 617 (1971).

A trial to determine punishment alone is permitted where, under newly announced constitutional principles, a felon's sentence has been set aside, not because the jury that tried him could not constitutionally find him guilty, but because the jury as then constituted could not constitutionally impose the death sentence. Snider v. Cox, 212 Va. 13, 181 S.E.2d 617 (1971).

Although a felon's sentence was set aside because the jury as then constituted could not constitutionally impose the death sentence, the exclusion of jurors opposed to capital punishment did not result in an unrepresentative jury on the issue of guilt or substantially increase the risk of conviction, and there was no error in the action of the state courts in granting a new trial on the issue of punishment only. Snider v. Winstead, 339 F. Supp. 897 (W.D. Va. 1972).

The verdict of the jury is the fixing of maximum punishment which may be served. Vines v. Muncy, 553 F.2d 342 (4th Cir.), cert. denied, 434 U.S. 851, 98 S. Ct. 163, 54 L. Ed. 2d 120 (1977).

Under such practice, the convicted defendant is entitled to "two decisions" on the sentence, one by the jury and the other by the trial judge in the exercise of his statutory right to suspend, rendering the jury's finding little more than an advisory opinion or first step decision. Reese v. Commonwealth, No. 1279-03-4, 2004 Va. App. LEXIS 316 (Ct. of Appeals July 6, 2004).

When harsher sentence upon retrial permissible. — A jury's imposition upon retrial of a harsher sentence than that given at an earlier trial does not offend due process so long as the jury is not informed of the prior sentence and the second sentence is not otherwise shown to be a product of vindictiveness. Cooper v. Mitchell, 647 F.2d 437 (4th Cir.), cert. denied, 454 U.S. 849, 102 S. Ct. 171, 70 L. Ed. 2d 139 (1981).

A defendant cannot receive a harsher sentence at a second trial where the sentence was imposed by a jury at the first trial. Levine v. Peyton, 444 F.2d 525 (4th Cir.), cert. denied, 404 U.S. 995, 92 S. Ct. 536, 30 L. Ed. 2d 547 (1971).

Harsher sentence improper. — Judgment was reversed and the case was remanded for a new sentencing hearing on defendant's robbery, conspiracy, and wearing a mask in public convictions as the ends of justice exception in Va. Sup. Ct. R. 5A:18 applied because defendant was sentenced to a maximum total sentence of 33 years in violation of § 19.2-295, when the jury imposed a maximum total sentence of 15 years of imprisonment. Gibbs v.

Commonwealth, No. 1726-11-1, 2012 Va. App. LEXIS 324 (Oct. 16, 2012).

The jury's use of the word "recommend" instead of the more commonly used word, "fix" was a mere irregularity which would have been amendable before the jury was discharged, and the judgment entered on such a verdict was not void and could not be successfully attacked by means of habeas corpus. Smyth v. Bunch, 202 Va. 126, 116 S.E.2d 33 (1960), cert. denied, 364 U.S. 935, 81 S. Ct. 382, 5 L. Ed. 2d 366 (1961).

Suspension of sentence or probation. — Even though this section provides for imposition of sentence by the jury, former § 53-272 (now §§ 53.1-151 and 53.1-186) allows the trial judge to suspend that sentence or place the defendant on probation. Roman v. Parrish, 328 F. Supp. 882 (E.D. Va. 1971).

Only excessive part of sentence is void. — Where the sentence imposed is in excess of that prescribed by law, that part of the sentence which is excessive is invalid. Deagle v. Commonwealth, 214 Va. 304, 199 S.E.2d 509 (1973).

A sentence in excess of one prescribed by law is not void ab initio because of the excess, but is good insofar as the power of the court extends, and is invalid only as to the excess. Deagle v. Commonwealth, 214 Va. 304, 199 S.E.2d 509 (1973).

Response to inquiry by jury as to time defendant would actually serve. — Where the jury wanted to know whether if they gave defendant life imprisonment or any long term of years they would have any assurance that he would not "get out," the proper response to such inquiries was stated in Coward v. Commonwealth, 164 Va. 639, 178 S.E. 797 (1935), to be, that it is the duty of the jury if they find the accused guilty to impose such punishment as they consider to be just under the evidence and within the limits stated in the court's instructions; and that they must not concern themselves with what may afterwards happen. Jones v. Commonwealth, 194 Va. 273, 72 S.E.2d 693 (1952), commented on in 39 Va. L. Rev. 273, 10 Wash. & Lee L. Rev. 219 (1953).

Response to inquiry by jury as to whether sentences would be served consecutively. — Since the trial judge did not know whether he would modify the jury's recommended sentences by running the sentences concurrently or otherwise suspending the sentences, he properly refused to instruct the jury on the presumption that sentences were to run consecutively; to advise the jury about the trial court's discretion would have been confusing. May v. Commonwealth, No. 0140-01-2, 2002 Va. App. LEXIS 398 (Ct. of Appeals July 23, 2002).

Punishment for robbery. — The import of this section is that the jury, upon determining a petitioner's guilt of robbery, has to set the sentence between the statutory limits for robbery as set forth in § 18.2-58. Roman v. Parrish, 328 F. Supp. 882 (E.D. Va. 1971).

If a jury returns with less than a five-year punishment for robbery, it will be sent back to set punishment within the limits of § 18.2-58. Roman v. Parrish, 328 F. Supp. 882 (E.D. Va. 1971).

Procedure where death sentence set aside. — Where the portion of the judgment order sentencing the defendant to death in accordance with the jury verdict must be set aside because the death penalty has been ruled invalid, the case should be remanded for a new trial on the issue of punishment since it would be sheer speculation to conclude that, if death had not then been a permissible punishment, the jury would have fixed the punishment at life imprisonment. Hodges v. Commonwealth, 213 Va. 316, 191 S.E.2d 794 (1972).

Applied in George v. Angelone, 901 F. Supp. 1070 (E.D. Va. 1995); Runyon v. Commonwealth, 29 Va. App. 573, 513 S.E.2d 872 (1999).

OPINIONS OF THE ATTORNEY GENERAL

Trial court may not order a person convicted of a felony to serve any confinement in jail on weekends or nonconsecutive days. — The plain language of § 53.1-131.1, limits the court's authority to convictions for misdemeanors, traffic offenses and violations of Chapter 5 (§ 20-61 et seq.) Title 20. See opinion of Attorney General to The Honorable Harvey L. Bryant, Commonwealth's Attorney, City of Virginia Beach, 12-062, 2012 Va. AG LEXIS 30 (7/20/2012).

§ 19.2-295.1. Sentencing proceeding by the jury after conviction.

In cases of trial by jury, upon a finding that the defendant is guilty of a felony or a Class 1 misdemeanor, or upon a finding in the trial de novo of an appealed misdemeanor conviction that the defendant is guilty of a Class 1 misdemeanor, a separate proceeding limited to the ascertainment of punishment shall be held as soon as practicable before the same jury. At such proceeding, the Commonwealth may present any victim impact testimony pursuant to § 19.2-295.3 and shall present the defendant's prior criminal history, including prior convictions and the punishments imposed, by certified, attested or exemplified copies of the final order, including adult convictions and juvenile convictions and adjudications of delinquency. Prior convictions shall include convictions and adjudications of delinquency under the laws of any state, the District of Columbia, the United States or its territories. The Commonwealth shall provide to the defendant 14 days prior to trial notice of its intention to introduce copies of final orders evidencing the defendant's prior criminal history, including prior convictions and punishments imposed. Such notice shall include (i) the date of each prior conviction, (ii) the name and jurisdiction of the court where each prior conviction was had, (iii) each offense of which he was convicted, and (iv) the punishment imposed. Prior to commencement of the trial, the Commonwealth shall provide to the defendant photocopies of certified copies of the final orders which it intends to introduce at sentencing. After the Commonwealth has introduced in its case-in-chief of the sentencing phase such evidence of prior convictions or victim impact testimony, or both, or if no such evidence is introduced, the defendant may introduce relevant, admissible evidence related to punishment. Nothing in this section shall prevent the Commonwealth or the defendant from introducing relevant, admissible evidence in rebuttal.

If the jury cannot agree on a punishment, the court shall impanel a different jury to ascertain punishment, unless the defendant, the attorney for the Commonwealth, and the court agree, in the manner provided in § 19.2-257, that the court shall fix punishment.

If the sentence imposed pursuant to this section is subsequently set aside or found invalid solely due to an error in the sentencing proceeding, the court shall impanel a different jury to ascertain punishment, unless the defendant, the attorney for the Commonwealth and the court agree, in the manner provided in § 19.2-257, that the court shall fix punishment.

History.

1994, cc. 828, 860, 862, 881; 1995, c. 567; 1996, c. 664; 2001, c. 389; 2007, cc. 388, 478; 2012, c. 134.

Cross references.

As to punishment for Class 1 misdemeanors, see § 18.2-11.

The 2007 amendments.

The 2007 amendments by cc. 388 and 478 are identical and rewrote the first paragraph.

The 2012 amendments.

The 2012 amendment by c. 134, in the second paragraph, substituted "the court shall impanel a different jury to ascertain punishment, unless" for "and if" and "that" for "then."

Law Review.

For an article relating to all published Virginia criminal law decisions between July 1, 1997, and July 1, 1998, see 32 U. Rich. L. Rev. 1091 (1998). For a review of criminal law in Virginia for year 1999, see 33 U. Rich. L. Rev. 857 (1999). For 2003/2004 survey of criminal law and procedure, see 39 U. Rich. L. Rev. 133 (2004). For 2006 survey article, "Criminal Law and Procedure," see 41 U. Rich. L. Rev. 83 (2006). For 2007 annual survey article, "Criminal Law and Procedure," see 42 U. Rich. L. Rev. 311 (2007).

Michie's Jurisprudence.

For related discussion, see 5B M.J. Criminal Procedure, §§ 70, 78.

CASE NOTES

I. Sentencing Proceedings Generally.
II. Introduction of evidence.
    A. Evidence of Prior Convictions.
    B. Other Relevant Evidence.

I. SENTENCING PROCEEDINGS GENERALLY.

Purpose of bifurcated proceeding. — This section establishes the procedure for bifurcating felony trials by jury; the purpose of such bifurcated trials is to allow the trier of fact to consider the prior record of the accused for sentencing purposes while avoiding the risk of prejudice to the accused when determining guilt or innocence. Byrd v. Commonwealth, 30 Va. App. 371, 517 S.E.2d 243 (1999).

No ex post facto violation. — The court rejects the defendant's contention that the construction of the statute violates constitutional protections against ex post facto laws. The enactment of this section and its application in this case do not violate ex post facto protections. Bunn v. Commonwealth, 21 Va. App. 593, 466 S.E.2d 744 (1996).

Section 19.2-295.1 was procedural in nature, and the trial court did not violate defendant's rights under U.S. Const., Art. 1, § 10, or Va. Const., Art. 1, § 9, to be free from ex post facto laws by applying it during defendant's trial on charges that he violated former § 18.1-191 by committing fornication with his daughter in 1969 and 1970, even though § 19.2-295.1 was not enacted into law at the time defendant committed the offenses. Pilcher v. Commonwealth, No. 2483-01-3, 2003 Va. App. LEXIS 402 (Ct. of Appeals July 15, 2003).

This section does not convey a substantive right; procedural in nature, it permits bifurcating the trial and sentencing proceedings. Riley v. Commonwealth, 21 Va. App. 330, 464 S.E.2d 508 (1995).

This section requires a bifurcated proceeding in all felony trials and a jury verdict of guilty emanating from the guilt phase of the bifurcated trial, approved by the trial court, resolves that issue, leaving sentence as the sole question remaining to be decided by an additional verdict incidental to a "separate proceeding." Gray v. Commonwealth, 28 Va. App. 227, 503 S.E.2d 252 (1998).

Limitations on jury's ascertainment of punishment. — The Legislature intended the procedures outlined in this section for the jury's ascertainment of punishment to be subject to: (1) the provisions of § 19.2-295, which require the jury's sentence to be within the limits prescribed by law; (2) the provisions of § 19.2-295.2, which permit the trial court to impose a suspended term of incarceration and postrelease supervision when the jury's sentence includes an active term of incarceration; and (3) the provisions of § 19.2-303, which permit the trial court to suspend some or all of a

sentence and impose probation. Boyd v. Commonwealth, 28 Va. App. 537, 507 S.E.2d 107 (1998).

Jurors in Virginia are neither required nor entitled to consider parole eligibility in non-capital felony cases, either by the federal constitution or the law extant in the Commonwealth. The recent abolishment of parole for all felonies committed after January 1, 1995, does not require departure from the rule. Walker v. Commonwealth, 25 Va. App. 50, 486 S.E.2d 126 (1997).

This section contains no provision requiring that the jury be told of defendant's parole ineligibility and the appellate court is not at liberty to create such a requirement for noncapital cases where it does not exist. Mosby v. Commonwealth, 24 Va. App. 284, 482 S.E.2d 72 (1997).

Because this section is directory and procedural, the Commonwealth's failure to precisely comply with its provisions does not result in the de facto inadmissibility of evidence of defendant's prior convictions. Lee v. Commonwealth, No. 0139-95-3 (Ct. of Appeals March 4, 1997).

This section is procedural in nature and does not convey a substantive right. As such, the statute's notice provisions are merely directory, and precise compliance was not essential to the validity of the proceedings. Lebedun v. Commonwealth, 27 Va. App. 697, 501 S.E.2d 427 (1998).

No due process right to be sentenced by jury. — Nothing in the United States or Virginia Constitution gives a defendant the right to be sentenced by a jury or solely by a jury and the imposition of postrelease periods of suspended incarceration and supervision pursuant to § 19.2-295.2 does not violate any due process right of a defendant under this section, which provides for bifurcated jury sentencing. Boyd v. Commonwealth, 28 Va. App. 537, 507 S.E.2d 107 (1998).

In determining what evidence should be considered by sentencing jury, a trial court should be guided by the cases decided under § 19.2-264.4, the corresponding statute for capital murder cases. Runyon v. Commonwealth, 29 Va. App. 573, 513 S.E.2d 872 (1999).

Remedy for error in jury instruction. — Although the trial court erred by denying defendant's request for a jury instruction regarding his ineligibility for parole during the penalty phase of his trial, § 19.2-295.1 only entitled him to a resentencing hearing, not a new trial. Hills v. Commonwealth, 262 Va. 807, 553 S.E.2d 722, 2001 Va. LEXIS 127 (2001).

On Allen charge regarding sentencing unanimity court properly did not instruct jury on statutory procedure. — Trial court's Allen charge to the jury on a question of whether sentencing reverted to the court if the jury was unable to reach unanimity on sentencing was justified since that question justified an Allen charge. The charge properly did not instruct the jury regarding the procedure because the jury never indicated it could not reach agreement on a sentence and the delivery of such an instruction would improperly encourage the jury to quickly pass the matter of sentencing to the court if it had difficulty reaching unanimity. Workman v. Commonwealth, — Va. App. —, — S.E.2d —, 2005 Va. App. LEXIS 303 (Aug. 2, 2005), rev'd, remanded, 272 Va. 633, 636 S.E.2d 368 (2006).

Purpose of notice provisions. — The purpose of the notice provisions in this section is to provide defense counsel with the opportunity to know in advance what convictions the Commonwealth intends to introduce and to investigate their validity. Lebedun v. Commonwealth, 27 Va. App. 697, 501 S.E.2d 427 (1998).

Where notice of prior convictions included erroneous dates. — The Commonwealth was properly permitted to introduce evidence of prior convictions of the defendant, notwithstanding that the notice of intention to produce such evidence erroneously stated the dates of the prior convictions, since the conviction order and documentation delivered to the defendant sufficiently apprised him of the correct conviction dates. Lebedun v. Commonwealth, No. 0233-97-4 (Ct. of Appeals July 7, 1998).

Notice to the defendant of the Commonwealth's intention to introduce a prior conviction into evidence was sufficient, notwithstanding that the notice stated an incorrect date for the conviction, where the defendant also received copies of the conviction order listing the correct date and he admitted that the conviction actually occurred. Bender v. Commonwealth, No. 0176-98-1 (Ct. of Appeals Feb. 23, 1999).

Where the defendant received a photocopy of the front

side of the "warrant for arrest" relating to the conviction in issue. While this portion of the warrant did not reflect the conviction, defendant was clearly notified of the Commonwealth's intention to introduce such evidence during the sentencing phase of the trial. Thus, the Commonwealth's failure to precisely comply with the procedural requirements of this section violated no substantive right and resulted in no prejudice to the defendant. Evans v. Commonwealth, No. 0870-95-2 (Ct. of Appeals April 2, 1996).

Not rule of exclusion. — This section creates a category of evidentiary admissibility; it is not a rule of evidentiary exclusion. Evidence that is otherwise admissible is not dependent upon the statute for admissibility. Gilley v. Commonwealth, 21 Va. App. 740, 467 S.E.2d 312 (1996).

Introduction of punishment imposed for prior convictions improper. — Proof of the punishment imposed for prior convictions is not relevant to the issue whether the accused is guilty of the offense, and therefore, the trial judge erred in refusing to redact references to defendant's jail sentence from the conviction order when it was entered as evidence during the guilt determination phase of the trial. Burke v. Commonwealth, 27 Va. App. 489, 500 S.E.2d 225 (1998).

However, error in allowing evidence of prior punishment to be entered during guilt determination phase of jury trial was clearly harmless, where jury's knowledge of prior punishment could have only affected the sentence they imposed, and they eventually would have been exposed to defendant's punishment for the prior offense before deciding his punishment. Burke v. Commonwealth, 27 Va. App. 489, 500 S.E.2d 225 (1998).

In the prosecution's case in chief at the penalty phase of the trial of a non-capital felony or a Class 1 misdemeanor, it may introduce records showing only the fact of a conviction of a criminal offense, including the name of the crime, the date of the conviction, and the court in which the conviction occurred. Information in the record concerning proceedings subsequent to conviction, such as sentence, suspension, probation, or other rehabilitative efforts, must be redacted before the record is received in evidence. Gillespie v. Commonwealth, 272 Va. 753, 636 S.E.2d 430, 2006 Va. LEXIS 94 (2006) (decided prior to 2007 amendments).

Defendant's sentence for burglary was reversed because, during its case in chief at the sentencing phase, the prosecution introduced evidence of the sentence he received for a grand larceny conviction, as well as his drug treatment. Under § 19.2-295.1, the prosecution could introduce only evidence of defendant's convictions, but not sentencing information, unless necessary for rebuttal. Gillespie v. Commonwealth, 272 Va. 753, 636 S.E.2d 430, 2006 Va. LEXIS 94 (2006) (decided prior to 2007 amendments).

Introduction of prior convictions during guilt phase improper. — Trial judge erred in admitting defendant's two prior robbery convictions during the guilt phase of the trial because the felony convictions, which had to be proved to invoke § 19.2-297.1, were not elements of the malicious wounding offense proscribed by § 18.2-51; § 19.2-297.1 unambiguously related to the punishment to be imposed upon conviction. Washington v. Commonwealth, 44 Va. App. 157, 604 S.E.2d 92, 2004 Va. App. LEXIS 503 (2004).

New trial required where improper evidence admitted during guilt phase. — Because the improper evidence of other crimes was presented during the guilt phase of defendant's criminal trial, not in the sentencing proceeding, the remedy of a new sentencing proceeding afforded by § 19.2-295.1, was inapplicable and a new trial should have been ordered. Young v. Commonwealth, 273 Va. 528, 643 S.E.2d 491, 2007 Va. LEXIS 55 (2007).

Guilty plea following verdict untimely. — A defendant may plead guilty at any time prior to the return of the jury's verdict concluding the guilt phase of a bifurcated trial; however, following publication of a guilty verdict and its acceptance by the trial court, a plea of guilty is untimely and may not upset the procedural course of a bifurcated trial. Daye v. Commonwealth, 21 Va. App. 688, 467 S.E.2d 287 (1996).

Failure to preserve issue for appellate review. — Defendant did not argue in the trial court, as he did on appeal, that the testimony of two officers at the penalty phase of his trial was barred under the bifurcated sentencing statute, and thus this argument was barred on appeal. Macklin v. Commonwealth, 2007 Va. App. LEXIS 269 (June 26, 2007).

Applied in Livingston v. Commonwealth, 21 Va. App. 621, 466 S.E.2d 757 (1996); Dingus v. Commonwealth, 23 Va. App. 382, 477

S.E.2d 303 (1996); Booker v. Commonwealth, 276 Va. 37, 661 S.E.2d 461, 2008 Va. LEXIS 84 (2008); Nelson v. Commonwealth, 2010 Va. App. LEXIS 42 (2010).

II. INTRODUCTION OF EVIDENCE.

A. Evidence of Prior Convictions.

"Record of conviction" under this section includes the indictment for a prior conviction as well as the final order. Brooks v. Commonwealth, 24 Va. App. 523, 484 S.E.2d 127 (1997).

But evidence of non-final prior convictions cannot be introduced. — Remand was required for resentencing of defendant convicted of grand larceny as the trial court erred in considering one of defendant's prior convictions that was not final and the appellate court could not say the error was harmless, especially since the trial court imposed a sentence at the high end of the permissible range. Smith v. Commonwealth, No. 2320-02-1, 2004 Va. App. LEXIS 117 (Ct. of Appeals Mar. 23, 2004).

Prior convictions under local laws. — Because the word "include" is susceptible to more than one meaning and because it is not immediately clear from the word's context which meaning is meant to apply, the statute's provision that prior convictions shall include convictions under the laws of any state, the District of Columbia, the United States or its territories is ambiguous; however, consistent with the manifest purpose of the statute, which is to allow the jury to consider defendant's current record of criminal convictions, § 19.2-295.1 does not provide an exclusive definition of the term "prior convictions" and, thus, does not prohibit the presentation at sentencing of convictions under local laws. Rather, the statute's provision that prior convictions shall include convictions under the laws of any state, the District of Columbia, the United States or its territories indicates that the prior convictions the Commonwealth may present at sentencing are not limited to convictions under the statutes contained in the Code of Virginia; accordingly, the trial court did not err in allowing the Commonwealth to present evidence of defendant's misdemeanor driving under the influence of alcohol conviction for violating a city code. Auer v. Commonwealth, 46 Va. App. 637, 621 S.E.2d 140, 2005 Va. App. LEXIS 416 (Oct. 25, 2005).

Nolle prossed charges not admissible. — The language of this section is clear and its intent plain in that it limits the introduction of evidence by the Commonwealth to charges for which the defendant has been convicted; there is no basis upon which to enlarge the legislature's manifest intent in adopting this statute by permitting the introduction of evidence of charges that were nolle prossed. Byrd v. Commonwealth, 30 Va. App. 371, 517 S.E.2d 243 (1999).

Proof requirements. — The Commonwealth was not required to prove the contents of a written order reflecting the fact of defendant's conviction; rather, it was required to prove the fact of the conviction itself. Folson v. Commonwealth, 23 Va. App. 521, 478 S.E.2d 316 (1996).

The trial court did not err by allowing indictments to be read to the jury. Palmer v. Commonwealth, No. 2507-95-2 (Ct. of Appeals Aug. 5, 1997).

Convictions from special courts-martial. — Trial court did not violate § 19.2-295.1 by admitting, during the sentencing phase of defendant's bifurcated jury trial, criminal convictions he received from special courts-martial under the Uniform Code of Military Justice (UCMJ), as the provisions of the UCMJ constituted laws of the United States and defendant did not raise on appeal any constitutional objections in contest of his UCMJ convictions. Oliver v. Commonwealth, 46 Va. App. 613, 620 S.E.2d 567, 2005 Va. App. LEXIS 411 (Oct. 18, 2005).

Admission of prior traffic record. — Because the General Assembly does not expressly refer to § 46.2-943, a statute related to sentencing proceedings in bifurcated trials for traffic offenses, when it enacted § 19.2-295.1, it did not intend to impose the § 19.2-295.1 notice requirements as a prerequisite for the admissibility of a defendant's prior traffic record into evidence pursuant to § 46.2-943; § 46.2-943 is the more specific statute, and § 19.2-295.1 notice requirements do not apply to the admission of a defendant's prior traffic record into evidence pursuant to § 46.2-943. Ngomondjami v. Commonwealth, 54 Va. App. 310, 678 S.E.2d 281, 2009 Va. App. LEXIS 296 (2009).

Introduction of prior convictions proper. — The bifurcated procedure established in this section clearly manifests a legislative intent to provide juries with information specific only to sentencing, apart from considerations of guilt or innocence, thereby similarly situating juries in felony cases with their counterparts in bifurcated capital cases; thus the trial court properly allowed the Commonwealth to disclose to the jury defendant's prior convictions, together with the attendant sentences, during the sentencing phase of his trial. Gilliam v. Commonwealth, 21 Va. App. 519, 465 S.E.2d 592 (1996).

The obvious purpose of this section is to allow the jury, which will be recommending sentence, to consider the defendant's most current record of criminal convictions. Nothing in the language or logic of the statute suggests that the legislature intended to limit the jury's consideration to anything other than the defendant's complete criminal record. Bunn v. Commonwealth, 21 Va. App. 593, 466 S.E.2d 744 (1996).

The clear and obvious reading of the statute is that "prior convictions" refers to convictions obtained prior "to the [bifurcated sentencing] proceeding." Bunn v. Commonwealth, 21 Va. App. 593, 466 S.E.2d 744 (1996).

When the Legislature enacted the bifurcated trial statute, they incorporated the term "record of conviction" aware that its meaning includes both convictions and punishment, thereby intending to assist the jury in fashioning a sentence suitable both to defendant and the offense. Burke v. Commonwealth, 27 Va. App. 489, 500 S.E.2d 225 (1998).

Nothing in this section required the Commonwealth to introduce a document that was signed by the judge who convicted defendant of rape to have that document considered by the trial court that convicted defendant of robbery, and the court that convicted defendant of robbery did not err when it considered documents that were not signed by the judge but were properly authenticated by his clerk. Seaton v. Commonwealth, 42 Va. App. 739, 595 S.E.2d 9, 2004 Va. App. LEXIS 165 (2004).

Proof of a defendant's prior predicate convictions is admissible during the guilt phase of the trial. This reading comports with the plain language of § 19.2-295.1 and gives full meaning, force and effect to §§ 19.2-295.1 and 19.2-297.1. Washington v. Commonwealth, 272 Va. 449, 634 S.E.2d 310, 2006 Va. LEXIS 73 (2006).

Trial court did not err in permitting the prosecutor to cross-examine defendant about his prior conviction for possession of cocaine because defendant introduced evidence concerning his history and background, and the prosecutor was entitled to cross-examine him about specific acts in order to rebut his testimony; during the sentencing hearing, defendant stated that he was "deeply sorry" for his actions, and he testified that he had a chemical addiction to cocaine and that his criminal record was a reflection of that addiction. Ali v. Commonwealth, 2009 Va. App. LEXIS 500 (Nov. 10, 2009), aff'd in part, rev'd in part, 280 Va. 665, 701 S.E.2d 64 (2010).

In a capital case in which defendant was sentenced to death, defendant unsuccessfully argued that the admission of his previous death sentence was irrelevant to his future dangerousness and undermined the jury's obligation to consider the mitigating evidence. Pursuant to subsection B of § 19.2-264.4, the history and background of defendant could be admitted, and § 19.2-295.1 provided that upon his conviction for a felony, the Commonwealth shall present his prior criminal history, including prior convictions and the punishments imposed, by certified, attested or exemplified copies of the final order, including adult convictions. Prieto v. Commonwealth, 278 Va. 366, 682 S.E.2d 910, 2009 Va. LEXIS 94 (2009), cert. denied, 177 L. Ed. 2d 332, 2010 U.S. LEXIS 4926 (U.S. 2010).

Introduction of prior convictions proper in recidivist crimes. — Defendant moved to bifurcate the guilt phase of the trial so that the jury would not be aware of his prior larceny convictions until it determined whether he was guilty of petit larceny in violation of §§ 18.2-96 and 18.2-104, but the trial court stated that there was no authority for such a procedure and that it was for the legislature to change the manner of proof in recidivist crimes. When the legislature enacted and amended § 19.2-295.1, it chose not to create a separate bifurcated procedure of the guilt phase for these offenses, thus, the trial court did not err. Elem v. Commonwealth, 55 Va. App. 55, 683 S.E.2d 830, 2009 Va. App. LEXIS 462 (2009).

Introduction of prior convictions improper. — The trial court erroneously permitted the jury to consider as convictions for purposes of fixing punishment three offenses for which the defendant had previously been found guilty but not sentenced that were thus incomplete records of conviction not contemplated by this statute. Webb v. Commonwealth, 31 Va. App. 466, 524 S.E.2d 164 (2000).

Probation violation inadmissible. — Trial court erroneously considered evidence of a defendant's prior probation revocation in the penalty determination phase of a bifurcated criminal jury trial as part of the record of conviction, as such was not a continuation and part of the sentencing process imposed for a criminal conviction; to the extent that *Merritt v. Commonwealth,* 32 Va. App. 506, 528 S.E. 2d 743 (2000) conflicted with this holding, it was expressly overruled. Jaccard v. Commonwealth, 268 Va. 56, 597 S.E.2d 30, 2004 Va. LEXIS 87 (2004).

Prior sentencing evidence. — Defendant's contention that it was error for the trial court to allow the admission of prior sentencing evidence had to be rejected. Such evidence was admissible under the explicit provisions of § 19.2-295.1. Pcelinski v. Commonwealth, — Va. App. —, — S.E.2d —, 2008 Va. App. LEXIS 81 (Feb. 19, 2008).

Prior sentencing order properly admitted. — Where this section requires the Commonwealth to present evidence of a defendant's past criminal convictions by introduction of his record of conviction, the record of conviction is the trial court's sentencing order; thus the entire order, including the sentence imposed, which is the record of conviction, was properly submitted to the jury. Davis v. Commonwealth, No. 0126-95-4 (Ct. of Appeals Jan. 23, 1996).

When evidence of prior sentences may lead the jury to speculate that parole is still available to the defendant, a trial judge is required to instruct the jury that defendant, if convicted, will be ineligible for parole. Hartigan v. Commonwealth, 31 Va. App. 243, 522 S.E.2d 406 (1999).

Sufficient evidence of prior convictions. — Where the certifications by the clerk and judge verified not only the accuracy of the photocopies, but also reflected the state of Maryland's determination that "the originals together, constitute the record of the proceedings," in the case, the evidence contained in these properly admitted documents, viewed in the aggregate, was sufficient to establish defendant's prior convictions. Folson v. Commonwealth, 23 Va. App. 521, 478 S.E.2d 316 (1996).

Admission of evidence of nolle prossed charges harmless error. — The admission of evidence of charges that had been nolle prossed was harmless error because, even if the jury had treated these charges as convictions, this evidence was merely cumulative of overwhelming evidence that the appellant had been convicted of numerous similar offenses and, although the jury was free to impose a maximum sentence of 10 years imprisonment, it only imposed a mid-range sentence of five years. Byrd v. Commonwealth, 30 Va. App. 371, 517 S.E.2d 243 (1999).

B. Other Relevant Evidence.

Construction with § 19.2-264.4. — The factors a jury may consider in mitigation of a capital offense under subsection B of § 19.2-264.4 may also be considered by the trial court in determining what evidence is relevant to punishment under this section, except that evidence of unadjudicated criminal activity is admissible in capital cases, whereas this section only permits the introduction of the record of convictions. Byrd v. Commonwealth, 30 Va. App. 371, 517 S.E.2d 243 (1999).

In determining what evidence is relevant to punishment, the trial court may be guided in the exercise of its discretion, subject to the rules of evidence governing admissibility, by the factors set forth in § 19.2-264.4(B) as interpreted in Coppola v. Commonwealth, 220 Va. 243, 257 S.E.2d 797 (1979). Commonwealth v. Shifflett, 257 Va. 34, 510 S.E.2d 232 (1999).

Unsworn or out-of-court evidence may be considered. — The court must be allowed to consider all relevant evidence in the exercise of its discretion in sentencing; such evidence includes any responsible unsworn or out-of-court information relative to the circumstances of the crime, subject to the requirement that the information bear some indicia of reliability. Payan v. Commonwealth, No. 2373-99-4, 2000 Va. App. LEXIS 379 (Ct. of Appeals May 16, 2000).

Admission of evidence at resentencing hearing. — Trial court erred under § 19.2-295.1 in admitting at a resentencing hearing, over defendant's objection, a summary of facts created by the trial court that had not been presented to the original jury. Booker v. Commonwealth, 60 Va. App. 35, 723 S.E.2d 621, 2012 Va. App. LEXIS 108 (2012).

Evidence of codefendant's sentence. — Trial court properly precluded the jury from hearing testimony regarding codefendant's sentence during the penalty phase, although the trial judge was permitted to consider such evidence in determining whether to impose the jury's recommended sentence. Howell v. Commonwealth, 2012 Va. App. LEXIS 205 (June 19, 2012).

Admissible mitigating evidence. — The kind of evidence contemplated bears upon the record of the defendant and the nature of his crime. Evidence of a good previous record, and extenuating circumstances tending to explain, but not excuse, the commission of a noncapital crime is admissible mitigating evidence. Commonwealth v. Shifflett, 257 Va. 34, 510 S.E.2d 232 (1999).

Recidivism evidence. — Section 19.2-297.1 did not forbid recidivism evidence from being presented in the guilt phase of a jury trial, and neither the jury bifurcation statute, § 19.2-295.1, nor Va. Sup. Ct. R. 3A:17.1 were inconsistent with this interpretation; recidivism evidence was properly admitted in a prosecution for malicious wounding "after having been twice convicted of a violent felony." Washington v. Commonwealth, 46 Va. App. 276, 616 S.E.2d 774, 2005 Va. App. LEXIS 320 (2005), aff'd, 272 Va. 449, 634 S.E.2d 310 (2006).

Defendant may testify as to involvement in planning or participation in crime. — A defendant is entitled during the sentencing phase of the trial to account for or explain his participation or degree of culpability in the offense for which he has been found guilty, because those facts are relevant to and have a bearing upon the appropriate punishment to be imposed for the defendant's criminal conduct. Kearney v. Commonwealth, 32 Va. App. 790, 531 S.E.2d 23, 2000 Va. App. LEXIS 534 (2000).

Evidence of defendant's problems with drug use. — Because defendant did not object to admission of defendant's extensive prior convictions or other exhibits that also informed the jury of defendant's problems with drug use, the same information defendant argued should have been redacted from a specific exhibit pursuant to former § 19.2-295.1, any error in admitting that exhibit without redaction was harmless. Adams v. Commonwealth, 2009 Va. App. LEXIS 112 (Mar. 17, 2009).

Evidence of defendant's pretrial incarceration irrelevant. — Trial court did not err in refusing to allow defendant to testify during sentencing phase that he was incarcerated on earlier charges arising from same incident before those charges were nolle prosequied because the jury's consideration of defendant's prior incarceration addressed none of the purposes of sentencing; in applying the factors of subsection B of § 19.2-264.4 as they related to § 19.2-295.1, defendant's pretrial incarceration was not relevant to circumstances surrounding the offense, the history and background of defendant, circumstances that tended to explain the offense, defendant's criminal record, mental condition and intellectual functioning of defendant, the age of defendant, or any other factor in mitigation of the offense. Jones v. Commonwealth, 54 Va. App. 414, 679 S.E.2d 568, 2009 Va. App. LEXIS 338 (2009).

Discretion is vested in trial court to determine, subject to rules of evidence governing admissibility, the evidence which may be adduced in mitigation of the offense. Runyon v. Commonwealth, 29 Va. App. 573, 513 S.E.2d 872 (1999).

Impact of defendant's incarceration. — The trial court did not abuse its discretion by refusing to allow evidence concerning the impact of defendant's incarceration upon his family and his employment. Commonwealth v. Shifflett, 257 Va. 34, 510 S.E.2d 232 (1999).

In the punishment phase of a bifurcated trial, the trial judge can allow the jury to consider conviction orders that include recital of the punishment imposed. Burke v. Commonwealth, 27 Va. App. 489, 500 S.E.2d 225 (1998).

Minimum sentence rendered error involving defendant's evidence harmless. — Assuming that the trial court erred in limiting appellant's evidence of employment history and family during the sentencing phase, this error was harmless and did not affect appellant's sentence, as he received the minimum sentence allowed for the offense committed. Carcamo v. Commonwealth, No. 1554-95-4 (Ct. of Appeals Sept. 17, 1996).

Defendant may produce relevant admissible evidence. — The statutory language simply sets forth the order of proof at the sentencing proceeding. However, the language does not prohibit the defendant from introducing relevant, admissible evidence related to punishment if the Commonwealth chooses not to produce evidence of the defendant's prior convictions, or if the defendant has no criminal record that the Commonwealth can introduce. Pierce v. Commonwealth, 21 Va. App. 581, 466 S.E.2d 130 (1996).

Rebuttal evidence permitted. — This section permits the Commonwealth to introduce relevant, admissible evidence to rebut any evidence introduced by the defendant on the issue of sentencing, but the admissibility of rebuttal evidence is generally restricted in scope to refuting matters brought out by its proponent's adversary. Byrd v. Commonwealth, 30 Va. App. 371, 517 S.E.2d 243 (1999).

This section prohibits the Commonwealth from offering into evidence more than certified copies of criminal convictions, and permits the defendant to introduce any evidence relevant to the issue of punishment, but in the event the defendant offers evidence on the issue of punishment, the Commonwealth may offer relevant, admissible evidence in rebuttal. Jones v. Commonwealth, No. 0406-99-2, 2000 Va. App. LEXIS 578 (Ct. of Appeals Aug. 1, 2000).

If defendant offers sentencing information in rebuttal at the penalty phase, as allowed by § 19.2-295.1, the prosecution may introduce evidence of sentencing and prior efforts to rehabilitate if the trial court deems it relevant and admissible to rebut defendant's evidence. Gillespie v. Commonwealth, 272 Va. 753, 636 S.E.2d 430, 2006 Va. LEXIS 94 (2006).

Rebuttal of defendant's good character. — This section goes beyond the common-law rule of evidence, which disallows proof of a defendant's specific bad acts to rebut the defendant's character evidence, and where a defendant puts on evidence that he has been of good character or has a history and background of being a good, law-abiding, caring or remorseful person, the Commonwealth may, subject to the trial court's sound discretion, introduce evidence of specific acts in the defendant's history and background that rebuts the defendant's contention or proves that the defendant has a history or background of criminal or bad acts or is not of good character. Pughsley v. Commonwealth, 33 Va. App. 640, 536 S.E.2d 447, 2000 Va. App. LEXIS 700 (2000).

When a defendant convicted of unlawful wounding offered evidence in mitigation through his testimony that he did not intend to cut the victim or anyone else, he put his intent or lack thereof in issue as it might bear on the determination of an appropriate sentence for his crime, and a photograph of another person cut by the defendant in the same incident then became relevant evidence to rebut this evidence by depicting both the number of wounds and their severity. Jones v. Commonwealth, No. 0406-99-2, 2000 Va. App. LEXIS 578 (Ct. of Appeals Aug. 1, 2000).

Error for court to exclude appellant's background and family information. — Where after sentencing hearing, trial court allowed appellant to proffer excluded evidence, and appellant testified that his father had been killed when he was nine, that he had no male role models, that his mother abused drugs and alcohol, that his half-brother had been shot, and that he had no fixed home before he came to Virginia at the age of 22, the excluded evidence in this case clearly was relevant to appellant's background and family situation at the time of the earlier conviction and was also probative of his current situation. It was error for the trial court to exclude this information from the jury's purview. Taylor v. Commonwealth, No. 1776-96-4 (Ct. of Appeals Dec. 30, 1997).

Any error from exclusion of additional mitigating evidence was harmless, where defense proved extensive facts concerning defendant's mental deficiencies and "hard life," and evidence was clearly presented to jury that defendant's problems flowed from extenuating circumstances. Hostetter v. Commonwealth, No. 2378-98-3 (Ct. of Appeals Feb. 15, 2000).

Evidence of adverse effect on wife's medical condition properly excluded. — In malicious wounding case, defendant's proffered evidence that his incarceration would adversely affect his wife, who had a medical condition, was not a mitigating circumstance that the jury could properly consider. Caudill v. Commonwealth, 27 Va. App. 81, 497 S.E.2d 513 (1998).

Harmless error in refusing to admit mitigating evidence. — A defendant's suicidal mindset on the evening when he was charged with operating a vehicle after having been declared an habitual offender offered an insubstantial explanation for his behavior, and the trial court's refusal to admit evidence regarding his medical condition and mental state at the time of the offense, if error, was harmless, as such evidence would clearly have had no effect on the jury's determination of sentence. Thomas v. Commonwealth, No. 1883-99-4, 2000 Va. App. LEXIS 641 (Ct. of Appeals Sept. 5, 2000).

CIRCUIT COURT OPINIONS

Introduction of prior conviction did not impede impartial jury. — Commonwealth could introduce evidence of defendant's prior larceny convictions in the guilt phase of a concealment trial under §§ 18.2-103 and 18.2-104, and upon request, a limiting instruction would be given that the evidence could be considered only as proof of defendant's prior predicate convictions, and not as proof that defendant committed the concealment; defendant's request for a separate proceeding after a preliminary finding of culpability, but before defendant was convicted, was rejected as under § 19.2-295.1, a separate proceeding to determine punishment occurred only after a defendant was convicted of a felony. Commonwealth v. Dickens, 77 Va. Cir. 57, 2008 Va. Cir. LEXIS 124 (Fairfax County 2008).

§ 19.2-295.2. Postrelease supervision of felons sentenced for offenses committed on and after January 1, 1995, and on and after July 1, 2000.

A. At the time the court imposes sentence upon a conviction for any felony offense committed (i) on or after January 1, 1995, the court may, and (ii) on or after July 1, 2000, shall, in addition to any other punishment imposed if such other punishment includes an active term of incarceration in a state or local correctional facility, except in cases in which the court orders a suspended term of confinement of at least six months, impose a term of postrelease supervision of not less than six months nor more than three years, as the court may determine. Such additional term shall be suspended and the defendant placed under postrelease supervision upon release from the active term of incarceration. The period of supervision shall be established by the court; however, such period shall not be less than six months nor more than three years. Periods of postrelease supervision imposed pursuant to this section upon more than one felony conviction may be ordered to run concurrently. Periods of postrelease supervision imposed pursuant to this section may be ordered to run concurrently with any period of probation the defendant may also be subject to serve.

B. The period of postrelease supervision shall be under the supervision and review of the Virginia Parole Board. The Board shall review each felon prior to release and establish conditions of postrelease supervision. Failure to successfully abide by such terms and conditions shall be grounds to terminate the period of postrelease supervision and recommit the defendant to the Department of Corrections or to the local correctional facility from which he was previously released. Procedures for any such termination and recommitment shall be conducted in the same manner as procedures for the revocation of parole.

C. Postrelease supervision programs shall be operated through the probation and parole districts established pursuant to § 53.1-141.

D. Nothing in this section shall be construed to prohibit the court from exercising any authority otherwise granted by law.

History.
1994, 2nd Sp. Sess., cc. 1, 2; 1995, cc. 502, 574; 2000, c. 767.

Law Review.
For an article, "Criminal Law and Procedure," see 31 U. Rich. L. Rev. 1015 (1997). For article summarizing published Virginia criminal law decisions between July 1, 2002 and July 1, 2003, see 38 U. Rich. L. Rev. 87 (2003). For survey of Virginia law on criminal law and procedure for the year 2007-2008, see 43 U. Rich. L. Rev. 149 (2008).

Michie's Jurisprudence.
For related discussion, see 5B M.J. Criminal Procedure, § 70; 14A M.J. Pardon, Probation and Parole, § 5.

CASE NOTES

Statute to be interpreted liberally. — Section 19.2-295.2 is more similar to probation than to traditional penal codes and, therefore, should be interpreted liberally. Alston v. Commonwealth, 49 Va. App. 115, 637 S.E.2d 344, 2006 Va. App. LEXIS 544 (2006).

Application of statute does not require additional fact-finding by court. — Section does not require that a trial court find proof of particular facts independent of the jury's finding of guilt. Alston v. Commonwealth, 49 Va. App. 115, 637 S.E.2d 344, 2006 Va. App. LEXIS 544 (2006).

This statute clearly provides the court independent authority to control the imposition of sentence, giving it discretion to suspend or increase a jury's recommendation; while defendant's codefendants received lighter sentences, they did not have defendant's extensive criminal record. Accordingly, there was no abuse of discretion in imposing the jury sentence and the additional one year suspended term under this section. Allard v. Commonwealth, 24 Va. App. 57, 480 S.E.2d 139 (1997).

No due process right to be sentenced by jury. — Nothing in the United States or Virginia Constitution gives a defendant the right to be sentenced by a jury or solely by a jury and the imposition of postrelease periods of suspended incarceration and supervision pursuant to this section does not violate any due process right of a defendant to be sentenced by a jury. Boyd v. Commonwealth, 28 Va. App. 537, 507 S.E.2d 107 (1998).

Statute does not violate separation of powers doctrine. — Imposition of a term of post-release supervision pursuant to § 19.2-295.2 did not violate the separation of powers doctrine under Va. Const., Art. III, § 1, because the Virginia Parole Board only provided conduct standards for defendant upon release, but defendant remained subject to the length of punishment imposed by the judiciary. Akbar v. Commonwealth, 2010 Va. App. LEXIS 154 (Apr. 27, 2010).

Postrelease supervision upon revocation of probation. — Contention that the trial court abused its discretion by sentencing defendant to one-year of postrelease supervision upon defendant's service of two years in prison after revocation of defendant's probation because this exceeded the original sentence the trial court imposed and suspended, two years in prison for cocaine possession, could not be considered by the appellate court because defendant did not object during the trial proceedings, and no other circumstance existed that would warrant considering the contention. McCoy v. Commonwealth, No. 1475-01-1, 2002 Va. App. LEXIS 436 (Ct. of Appeals July 30, 2002).

Subsection A of 19.2-295.2 unambiguously required that a court impose a sentence of postrelease supervision at the time of conviction, and thus, the trial court erred in imposing an additional term of postrelease supervision after defendant's probation was revoked. Lamb v. Commonwealth, 40 Va. App. 52, 577 S.E.2d 530, 2003 Va. App. LEXIS 120 (2003).

Where defendant violated his probation conditions, the trial court only had the authority to revoke suspension of the original three years to which it sentenced defendant; it did not have the authority to impose a period of postrelease supervision. Roundtree v. Commonwealth, No. 0298-03-1, 2003 Va. App. LEXIS 599 (Ct. of Appeals Nov. 18, 2003).

Suspended sentence and postrelease supervision properly imposed. — Defendant's sentence to three years of incarceration plus an additional six months, suspended upon a condition of six months of postrelease supervision, for unlawfully throwing a missile at or against an occupied building pursuant to § 18.2-279, was not in error on the ground that it exceeded the jury's recommendation of three years; this section permits a trial court to impose a suspended term of incarceration and postrelease supervision when a jury's sentence includes an active term of incarceration, and the trial court did not make additional fact findings in imposing the sentence beyond those found by the jury. Perry v. Commonwealth, 2006 Va. App. LEXIS 270 (June 20, 2006).

Imposition of postrelease terms of suspended incarceration and supervision. — Trial court did not err in imposing an additional sentence of three years supervision on to defendant's life sentence after defendant pled guilty to first degree murder in exchange for the life sentence; although the plea agreement was a contract, contract law included the law in force on the date the contract was formed, which included the suspended sentence and postrelease supervision provisions of subdivision (g) of § 18.2-10 and § 19.2-295.2. Wright v. Commonwealth, 49 Va. App. 58, 636 S.E.2d 489, 2006 Va. App. LEXIS 503 (2006).

Imposition of terms of suspended incarceration and supervision proper though not mentioned in plea agreement. — Defendant entered into a plea agreement with the Commonwealth pursuant to Va. Sup. Ct. R. 3A:8(c)(1)(C). As contract principles applied to plea agreements, and the law in effect when the contract was made became part of the contract, the trial court, after accepting the plea agreement, properly imposed terms of suspended incarceration and postrelease supervision under §§ 18.2-10 (g) and 19.2-295.2 A, even though such terms were not mentioned in the plea agreement. Wright v. Commonwealth, 275 Va. 77, 655 S.E.2d 7, 2008 Va. LEXIS 12 (2008).

Postrelease supervision properly imposed. — Where a trial court did not make factual determinations beyond those implicit in the jury's conviction, it did not violate *Blakely* by adding three years of postrelease supervision to defendant's sentence pursuant to § 19.2-295.2, as a statute could provide for such sentencing components without violating the right to a jury trial. Alston v. Commonwealth, 49 Va. App. 115, 637 S.E.2d 344, 2006 Va. App. LEXIS 544 (2006).

As defendant's sentence, which included three years of imprisonment fixed by the jury and a three-year term of postrelease supervision imposed by the trial court under § 19.2-295.2, was within the 10-year range set by the legislature for voluntary manslaughter, it was not illegal. Alston v. Commonwealth, 49 Va. App. 115, 637 S.E.2d 344, 2006 Va. App. LEXIS 544 (2006).

Defendant's Sixth Amendment rights were not violated in a case where defendant was convicted of voluntary manslaughter, a jury recommended a three-year prison sentence pursuant to § 19.2-295, and the trial court imposed a three-year period of postrelease supervision; the postrelease supervision portion of defendant's sentence was imposed pursuant to statutory law, was within that statute's permissible range, and did not require the trial court to find any additional facts that were not implicit in the jury's finding of guilt. Alston v. Commonwealth, 274 Va. 759, 652 S.E.2d 456, 2007 Va. LEXIS 133 (2007).

Determination of sentence. — Because the three-year term of postrelease supervision was to be added to the 10-year term that could have been imposed for the offenses for which defendant was convicted, the sentences totaling 10.5 years imposed by the trial court were within the statutory ranges for the offenses and, therefore, were not illegal. Williams v. Commonwealth, 270 Va. 580, 621 S.E.2d 98, 2005 Va. LEXIS 96 (2005).

Section 19.2-295.2 does not direct the trial court to suspend a part of the traditional sentence under § 18.2-10, but instead to add a period of postrelease supervision when less than six months of the traditional sentence is suspended. The legislature did not create a conflict with the prior sentencing structure, but instead changed it. Alston v. Commonwealth, 49 Va. App. 115, 637 S.E.2d 344, 2006 Va. App. LEXIS 544 (2006).

Because it was unclear as to whether a trial court, which sentenced defendant following his convictions for second-degree murder and use of a firearm during a felony, intended to sentence defendant to the maximum term of postrelease supervision under § 19.2-295.2, the cause was remanded for entry of a specific term. Alston v. Commonwealth, — Va. App. —, — S.E.2d —, 2008 Va. App. LEXIS 4 (Jan. 8, 2008).

Claim that the imposition of a two-year term of postrelease supervision under § 19.2-295.2 violated the separation of powers doctrine was barred by Va. Sup Ct. R. 5A:18 where defendant failed to make his argument before the trial court; the ends of justice exception to Rule 5A:18 did not apply where defendant did not show that a miscarriage of justice actually occurred. Fitzpatrick v. Commonwealth, 2008 Va. App. LEXIS 52 (Feb. 5, 2008).

§ 19.2-295.2:1. Postrelease supervision of felons sentenced for certain offenses committed on or after July 1, 2006.

A. For offenses committed on or after July 1, 2006:

1. At the time the court imposes a sentence upon a conviction for a first violation of subsection A of § 18.2-472.1 the court shall impose an added term of postrelease supervision of six months.

2. For a second or subsequent violation of subsection A of § 18.2-472.1 when both violations occurred after July 1, 2006, or a first violation of subsection B of § 18.2-472.1, the court shall impose an added term of postrelease supervision by the Department of Corrections of two years.

3. For a second or subsequent violation of subsection B of § 18.2-472.1 when both violations occurred after July 1, 2006, the court shall impose an added term of postrelease supervision by the Department of Corrections of five years.

Any terms of postrelease supervision imposed pursuant to this section shall be in addition to any other punishment imposed, including any periods of active incarceration or suspended periods of incarceration, if any.

B. The court shall order that any term of postrelease supervision imposed pursuant to this section be suspended, and the defendant be placed on active supervision under a postrelease supervision program operated by the Department of Corrections. The court shall order that the defendant be subject to electronic monitoring by means of a GPS (Global Positioning System) tracking device, or other similar device during this period of postrelease supervision. Failure to successfully abide by the terms and conditions of the postrelease supervision program shall be grounds to terminate the period of postrelease supervision and recommit the defendant to the Department of Corrections or to a local correctional facility. Procedures for any such termination shall be conducted after a hearing in the court which originally sentenced the defendant, conducted in a manner consistent with a revocation hearing under § 19.2-306, mutatis mutandis.

C. Nothing in this section shall be construed to prohibit the court from exercising any authority otherwise granted by law.

History.
2006, cc. 857, 914.

§ 19.2-295.3. Admission of victim impact testimony.

Whether by trial or upon a plea of guilty, upon a finding that the defendant is guilty of a felony, the court shall permit the victim, as defined in § 19.2-11.01, upon motion of the attorney for the Commonwealth, to testify in the presence of the accused regarding the impact of the offense upon the victim. The court shall limit the victim's testimony to the factors set forth in clauses (i) through (vi) of subsection A of § 19.2-299.1. In the case of trial by jury, the court shall permit the victim to testify at the sentencing hearing conducted pursuant to § 19.2-295.1 or in the case of trial by the court or a guilty plea, the court shall permit the victim to testify before the court prior to the imposition of a sentence. Victim impact testimony in all capital murder cases shall be admitted in accordance with § 19.2-264.4.

History.
1998, c. 485; 2004, c. 310.

CASE NOTES

Family member statements were properly admitted since the murder was determined to be a direct consequence of the conspiracy to commit robbery. — Since it could not be said that the trial court was plainly wrong when it determined that a murder was a direct consequence of a conspiracy to commit a robbery, the victim impact testimony was properly admitted under subsection B of § 19.2-11.01 even though defendant was acquitted of the murder. Furthermore, the admissibility of the victim impact testimony was relevant and within the sound discretion of the trial court even if the witnesses were not deemed "victims" under subsection B of § 19.2-11.01. Rock v. Commonwealth, 45 Va. App. 254, 610 S.E.2d 314, 2005 Va. App. LEXIS 107 (2005).

Relevant evidence not limited by statute. — There is no sound reason why relevant victim impact testimony that may be considered by a jury in a capital case should not likewise be considered in a non-capital case. Rock v. Commonwealth, 45 Va. App. 254, 610 S.E.2d 314, 2005 Va. App. LEXIS 107 (2005).

Evidence admissible during Commonwealth's case-in-chief. — Pursuant to § 19.2-295.3, the victim was properly permitted to testify during the Commonwealth's case-in-chief of the sentencing phase of defendant's rape trial; the victim had a qualified, statutorily protected right to be heard at sentencing, and it was within the trial judge's ultimate discretion to decide when the victim would be heard. Washington v. Commonwealth, 48 Va. App. 486, 632 S.E.2d 625, 2006 Va. App. LEXIS 349 (2006).

CIRCUIT COURT OPINIONS

Nolle prosequi. — When defendant agreed to a plea bargain which involved a charge being nolle prosequied, and pled guilty pursuant to the plea bargain, the prosecutor could not have a victim impact statement related to the nolle prosequied charge included in the presentence investigation report, because that would violate the spirit of § 19.2-295.3, regarding the admission of victim impact testimony, which was only admitted after a defendant was found guilty, and the "bargained for exchange" of the plea bargain. Commonwealth v. Summit, 62 Va. Cir. 477, 2003 Va. Cir. LEXIS 157 (Roanoke 2003).

§ 19.2-296. Withdrawal of plea of guilty.

A motion to withdraw a plea of guilty or nolo contendere may be made only before sentence is imposed or imposition of a sentence is suspended; but to correct manifest injustice, the court within twenty-one days after entry of a final order may set aside the judgment of conviction and permit the defendant to withdraw his plea.

History.
1975, c. 495.

Law Review.
For survey of Virginia criminal procedure for the year 1975-1976, see 62 Va. L. Rev. 1412 (1976).

Michie's Jurisprudence.
For related discussion, see 5B M.J. Criminal Procedure, § 75.

CASE NOTES

Standard codified in this section. — In a post-sentence situation concerning withdrawal of a guilty plea entered after a plea agreement, judicial discretion is involved, and the applicable standard for exercising this discretion was enunciated in former Rule 3A:25(d) and is codified in this section. Lilly v. Commonwealth, 218 Va. 960, 243 S.E.2d 208 (1978).

Whether or not accused should be allowed to withdraw plea of guilty for the purpose of submitting a not guilty plea is a matter that rests within the sound discretion of the trial court and is to be determined by the facts and circumstances of each case. Jones v. Commonwealth, 29 Va. App. 503, 513 S.E.2d 431 (1999).

Motion to withdraw plea should be granted if it appears from the surrounding circumstances that the plea of guilty was submitted in good faith under an honest mistake of material fact or facts, or if it was induced by fraud, coercion or undue influence and would not otherwise have been made. Jones v. Commonwealth, 29 Va. App. 503, 513 S.E.2d 431 (1999).

A defendant has no absolute right to withdraw a plea of guilty or nolo contendere; rather, such privilege is permissive. Moreno v. Commonwealth, No. 1126-98-4 (Ct. of Appeals May 4, 1999).

Least surprise or influence causing plea sufficient for withdrawal. — Generally, the withdrawal of a plea of guilty should not be denied in any case where it is in the least evident that the ends of justice will be subserved by permitting not guilty to be pleaded in its place; the least surprise or influence causing a defendant to plead guilty when he has any defense at all should be sufficient grounds for permitting a change of plea from guilty to not guilty. Lynch v. Commonwealth, No. 0512-00-2, 2001 Va. App. LEXIS 275 (Ct. of Appeals May 22, 2001).

Manifest injustice. — Trial court properly denied her motion to withdraw her guilty plea because defendant's arrest warrant was for a felony, defendant was familiar with the system due to defendant's prior convictions, and defendant understood the maximum punishment; therefore, pursuant to § 19.2-296, a "manifest injustice" did not occur. Milton v. Commonwealth, 2012 Va. App. LEXIS 316 (Oct. 9, 2012).

Defense to charges not enought to set aside guilty plea. — Defense to the charges is not by itself sufficient to require a trial court to set aside a guilty plea because the guilty plea must also be entered inadvisedly; any number of circumstances might render a plea inadvised, including the fact that an attorney overlooked a viable defense or the defendant did not understand the nature of the charges. Pritchett v. Commonwealth, 2013 Va. App. LEXIS 117 (Apr. 16, 2013).

Defendant is allowed to withdraw his or her guilty plea in situations where the defendant would not have pled guilty but for some external circumstance such as coercion, or poor or erroneous advice from counsel; a defendant who wishes to withdraw his or her guilty plea must do more than tender a defense. Pritchett v. Commonwealth, 2013 Va. App. LEXIS 117 (Apr. 16, 2013).

In resolving the question of whether the trial court abused its discretion in denying a motion for withdrawal of a guilty plea after sentencing to correct some manifest injustice resulting from a plea agreement, not only what the trial court may have told, or failed to tell, the defendant before accepting his plea but also the events that occurred after acceptance of the plea and before sentencing must be considered. If, upon the whole record, it appears that the defendant, at any time before sentencing, was fairly warned or otherwise made aware that the court was not bound to follow the recommendation of the attorney for the Commonwealth, then the defendant is in no position to claim that his plea was rendered "unknowing and involuntary," resulting in manifest injustice. Lilly v. Commonwealth, 218 Va. 960, 243 S.E.2d 208 (1978).

In determining whether a trial court abused its discretion in denying a motion to withdraw a plea of guilty, an appellate court should consider not only what the trial court may have told, or failed to tell, the defendant before accepting his plea but also the events that occurred after acceptance of the plea and before sentencing. Underwood v. Commonwealth, No. 0872-98-3, 2000 Va. App. LEXIS 224 (Ct. of Appeals Mar. 28, 2000).

Determining whether court erred in declining to allow withdrawal of a guilty plea requires an examination of the circumstances confronting the accused immediately prior to and at the time he or she pleaded to the charge. Jones v. Commonwealth, 29 Va. App. 503, 513 S.E.2d 431 (1999).

Habeas case law was inapplicable. — Habeas case law was inapplicable in considering defendant's motion to withdraw a guilty plea prior to sentencing under § 19.2-296 as: (1) when a case remained within the jurisdiction of the trial court to permit the withdrawal of a guilty plea, the presumptions that favored the Commonwealth in a habeas proceeding did not apply; (2) when defendant filed the § 19.2-296 motion, defendant was necessarily seeking to repudiate the admission of guilt and some, if not all, of the admissions made in the guilty plea colloquy; and (3) the proper granting of a motion to withdraw a guilty plea under § 19.2-296 was not dependent upon a determination that defendant failed to receive adequate legal representation from counsel. Justus v. Commonwealth, 274 Va. 143, 645 S.E.2d 284, 2007 Va. LEXIS 74 (2007).

Defendant entitled to withdraw guilty plea. — Ends of justice would be served in permitting defendant to withdraw defendant's guilty pleas and plead not guilty to the charges against defendant under § 19.2-296 as defendant's motion to withdraw the guilty pleas was made in good faith and premised upon a reasonable basis for substantive, and not "merely dilatory or formal," defenses to the charges since: (1) during the plea hearing, the trial court clearly was made aware by defense counsel that defendant was living with the victim in the home defendant was accused of having burglarized and damaged; (2) defendant provided an affidavit that evidenced that defendant had resided in this home at the time of the alleged burglary; (3) neither counsel's representation nor the affidavit were inherently incredible and they supported absolute defenses to the charges because a person could not unlawfully break and enter a home that person had the right to occupy, or damage that person's own property; and (4) an affidavit provided an evidentiary basis for defendant's claim of self-defense, and was not inherently incredible. Justus v. Commonwealth, 274 Va. 143, 645 S.E.2d 284, 2007 Va. LEXIS 74 (2007).

Trial court erred in not permitting defendant to withdraw defendant's guilty plea because the motion to withdraw was made in good faith, as defendant contended that defendant was not provided by jail officials with bipolar medication before the plea hearing to treat defendant's depression. Furthermore, the motion to withdraw was premised upon a reasonable basis that defendant was able to present substantive, and not merely dilatory or formal, defenses to the charges of construction fraud, as defendant contended that the proffer of evidence by the Commonwealth of Virginia showed that defendant lacked the requisite intent to defraud when defendant entered into two renovation contracts and received advance payment for the purchase of supplies and labor. Bottoms v. Commonwealth, 281 Va. 23, 704 S.E.2d 406, 2011 Va. LEXIS 22 (2011).

Trial court erred in denying motion to withdraw guilty pleas, where the trial court rejected defendant's argument that a reasonable defense was sufficient grounds for granting the motion to withdraw, although it was clear from case law that such grounds were sufficient cause to grant the motion, and the proffered defense was a substantive defense recognized by law and not merely dilatory or formal in nature. Terry v. Commonwealth, 2012 Va. App. LEXIS 193 (June 12, 2012).

Defendant not entitled to withdraw guilty plea. — Trial court did not err in denying defendant's motion to withdraw his plea of guilty for manifest injustice, where court had advised

defendant that his guilty plea was a waiver of all his rights incident to trial and that only issue before court was defendant's sentence; moreover, defendant did not avail himself of opportunity to make a statement before he was sentenced, or ask any questions of trial court. Underwood v. Commonwealth, No. 0872-98-3 (Ct. of Appeals Mar. 28, 2000).

Where defendant failed to demonstrate an actual conflict of interest with counsel, the trial court did not abuse its discretion or infringe upon defendant's Sixth Amendment guarantees when it denied counsel's motion to withdraw under Alford. Dillard v. Commonwealth, No. 0679-02-1, 2003 Va. App. LEXIS 207 (Ct. of Appeals Apr. 8, 2003).

Trial court properly denied defendant's motion pursuant to § 19.2-296 to withdraw his guilty plea to second degree murder, as defendant did not file the motion until his conviction had been reversed based on an illegal sentence, and defendant failed to show that he entered the plea based on an official misrepresentation concerning his sentence or a mistake of fact. Leneave v. Commonwealth, No. 2197-03-2, 2004 Va. App. LEXIS 480 (Ct. of Appeals Oct. 5, 2004).

Defendant was not entitled to withdraw his guilty pleas where, among other things, the evidence showed that the trial judge questioned defendant extensively to ensure that he was entering the pleas voluntarily, knowingly, and with a clear understanding of their effect, defendant acknowledged that the charges and the plea agreement had been read verbatim to him and that he understood them, and defendant told the trial judge that he was entering his pleas freely and voluntarily and that no one, including his attorney, had threatened or forced him to plead guilty or made any promises concerning his pleas of guilty. Stevenson v. Commonwealth, No. 2350-02-1, 2004 Va. App. LEXIS 89 (Ct. of Appeals Feb. 24, 2004).

Defendant's motion to withdraw his guilty plea to malicious wounding was properly denied as he did not establish he pled guilty due to a mistake of fact. Moreover, withdrawal of the plea would not promote the ends of justice; as the motion to withdraw the plea was not heard until nine months after he pled guilty and 21 months after the crime, a new trial would cause chaos. Johnson v. Commonwealth, No. 3206-03-2, 2005 Va. App. LEXIS 67 (Ct. of Appeals Feb. 15, 2005).

Where defendant testified he pled guilty to malicious wounding because his counsel misinformed him that he faced a life sentence, and counsel denied this, defendant's motion to withdraw his guilty plea on grounds of mistake of fact was properly denied because the trial court was entitled to believe counsel. Johnson v. Commonwealth, No. 3206-03-2, 2005 Va. App. LEXIS 67 (Ct. of Appeals Feb. 15, 2005).

Where defendant did not offer any real substantive defense to charges against defendant, which included the robbery of a store where five former coworkers recognized defendant as the assailant, defendant was not entitled to withdraw defendant's guilty plea filed pursuant to § 19.2-296. The trial court could have concluded that defendant's claim of mistaken identity offered no real substantive defense and that defendant's claim that defendant was not thinking properly when defendant pled guilty did not mean defendant was not competent to plead guilty. Coleman v. Commonwealth, 51 Va. App. 284, 657 S.E.2d 164, 2008 Va. App. LEXIS 92 (2008).

Trial court properly denied defendant's motion to withdraw his guilty pleas to malicious wounding, using a firearm in the commission of malicious wounding, conspiracy to commit robbery, and wearing body armor because defendant's justifications for withdrawing his guilty pleas did not constitute evidence of reasonable grounds for trying the matter; defendant claimed no mistake of fact and did not assert that he entered his pleas with surprise or influence or out of fear, fraud, or official misrepresentation. Chaney v. Commonwealth, — Va. App. —, — S.E.2d —, 2008 Va. App. LEXIS 153 (Apr. 1, 2008).

Denial of defendant's motion to withdraw his guilty plea pursuant to § 19.2-296 was proper because defendant's only basis to withdraw his plea was that the sentencing guidelines came out higher than he expected, which, since the trial court informed him that his juvenile record would be used to compute his recommended sentence, was not a good faith basis; the reason that the guidelines required a higher sentence than defendant expected was that he failed to tell his attorney that he had a criminal record as a juvenile. Thompson v. Commonwealth, 2009 Va. App. LEXIS 314 (July 14, 2009).

As the evidence clearly showed the victim was not capable of giving consent, defendant's assertions regarding possible defenses and his ignorance of the law regarding consent and mental retardation did not rise to the "more severe standard" applicable under § 19.2-296 after sentencing, which required defendant to show denial of his motion would create a manifest injustice. Sene v. Commonwealth, 2009 Va. App. LEXIS 333 (July 28, 2009).

In a case in which defendant pled guilty to violating §§ 18.2-90, 18.2-47, 18.2-67.1 and 18.2-53.1, he argued unsuccessfully that the circuit court abused its discretion in denying his motion to withdraw his guilty pleas prior to sentencing; defendant failed to show a good faith basis for seeking to withdraw his guilty pleas. He was clearly aware of the potential range of punishments available to the court at the time he pled guilty; as such, the fact that the sentencing guidelines recommended a higher sentence than he had hoped did not constitute a good faith basis for rescinding his pleas. Mack v. Commonwealth, 2009 Va. App. LEXIS 417 (Sept. 22, 2009).

Trial court did not err in refusing defendant's motion to withdraw his guilty plea because defendant failed to establish a good faith basis for seeking to withdraw his plea and to proffer evidence of a reasonable basis for contesting guilt, and defendant knew, prior to entering his plea, exactly what his sentence was going to be and that it would run concurrent to his sentence in an earlier case; a reasonable defense is a defense that reasonably supports the defendant's proffer, it is not a defense that is based solely upon a challenge to the credibility of a victim's testimony, especially when a defendant has admitted to the substance of such testimony. Williams v. Commonwealth, 59 Va. App. 238, 717 S.E.2d 837, 2011 Va. App. LEXIS 392 (2011).

In a case in which defendant appealed his conviction for grand larceny, in violation § 18.2-95, the trial court did not abuse its discretion in denying his motion to withdraw his guilty plea prior to sentencing. He had 14 prior felony convictions, several for grand larceny, and he also had numerous misdemeanor convictions for petit larceny; for him to argue that he was confused or subjected to undue influence by his attorney was nothing more than a dilatory attempt to postpone his trial. Terrell v. Commonwealth, 2012 Va. App. LEXIS 243 (July 24, 2012).

Denial of defendant's motion to withdraw his guilty plea was upheld, because defendant failed to show guilty plea was entered by mistake or misconception of nature of charges, or through fear, and evidence supported the trial court's finding that defendant took a look at what the consequences might be after he pled guilty and had buyer's remorse. Branch v. Commonwealth, 60 Va. App. 540, 729 S.E.2d 777, 2012 Va. App. LEXIS 256 (2012).

Trial court did not err in denying defendant's motion to withdraw his guilty plea under § 19.2-296 as there was no good faith basis for the withdrawal of the plea. While defendant sought to withdraw his plea on the basis that his new attorney, retained since the guilty plea hearing, concluded that his plea was entered inadvisably, defendant had not been able on the day he entered his guilty plea to articulate any valid reason why he was unsatisfied with his attorney and wished to hire a new one. Vasquez v. Commonwealth, 2013 Va. App. LEXIS 22 (Jan. 22, 2013).

Trial court did not err in denying defendant's motion to withdraw his guilty pleas because it followed the requirements of Va. Sup. Ct. R. 3A:8(c)(2); the trial court properly could consider the statements defendant made during the colloquy in assessing whether defendant's guilty pleas were entered into inadvisedly or based on a mistake concerning the trial court's ability to reject the recommendation of the prosecution. Pritchett v. Commonwealth, 2013 Va. App. LEXIS 117 (Apr. 16, 2013).

Defendant was not entitled to withdraw his Alford pleas on grounds that he misunderstood their nature and effect, or that he mistakenly entered into plea agreement because he feared his co-defendant would testify untruthfully. Moreno v. Commonwealth, No. 1126-98-4 (Ct. of Appeals May 4, 1999).

Trial court properly exercised its discretion when it denied defendant's motion to withdraw his Alford guilty pleas because defendant's request was not made in good faith; defendant did not have a viable or reasonable defense and never provided any proof to support his allegations that counsel told defendant that he could receive only the midpoint or below of the sentencing guidelines, failed to investigate and present mitigating evidence, and failed to adequately prepare for trial. Gallimore v. Commonwealth, — Va. App. —, — S.E.2d —, 2008 Va. App. LEXIS 174 (Apr. 15, 2008).

Where defendant entered Alford pleas to rape, conspiracy to commit a felony, and unlawful videotaping of a minor, defendant's motion to withdraw the pleas based on undue influence was properly denied because: (1) nothing "undue" was found regarding defendant feeling pressured and fearful as defendant faced the prospect of fighting the charges alone and the possibility of multiple life sentences being imposed; and (2) defendant failed to proffer a "reasonable defense" to the charges. Rice v. Commonwealth, 2008 Va. App. LEXIS 287 (June 17, 2008).

As defendant had not shown there was a manifest injustice to be corrected, the trial court did not abuse its discretion in denying defendant's motion to withdraw defendant's Alford guilty plea; defendant's claim that defendant was not mentally stable fell short of satisfying the manifest injustice standard, as defendant demonstrated that defendant was competent to enter the guilty plea and that defendant was entering it knowingly, freely, and voluntarily. Howell v. Commonwealth, 60 Va. App. 737, 732 S.E.2d 722, 2012 Va. App. LEXIS 322 (2012).

Failure to file motion to withdraw plea. — Defendant's plea was valid because the trial court conducted an extensive colloquy with him to ensure his plea of guilty was made knowingly, intelligently, and voluntarily and defendant, at no time, raised any issues regarding the voluntary nature of his plea. During the 15 months following his plea, defendant never challenged the trial court's acceptance of his plea; there was also no merit to his contention that he had little or no opportunity to challenge the voluntary nature of his plea in the trial court. Swilling v. Commonwealth, 2009 Va. App. LEXIS 24 (Jan. 27, 2009).

Withdrawal of guilty plea not permitted. — The trial court did not abuse his discretion in refusing to allow the defendant to withdraw his guilty plea, notwithstanding the assertion that the guilty plea was not made knowingly, where there was an extensive colloquy prior to the acceptance of the plea, the defendant signed a stipulation admitting the crime, and both the defendant and his counsel acknowledged that the entire matter had been explained to the defendant prior to the hearing and that he understood the charge against him and the consequences of pleading guilty. Johnson v. Commonwealth, No. 1587-97-2 (Ct. of Appeals Dec. 15, 1998).

Trial judge did not abuse his discretion by denying defendant's post-sentence motion to withdraw his guilty pleas where the evidence showed that the pleas were made voluntarily and that the motion was prompted by defendant's disappointment in the sentence he received. Bowman v. Commonwealth, No. 0952-00-2, 2001 Va. App. LEXIS 479 (Ct. of Appeals Aug. 14, 2001).

Trial court did not err in finding that defendant was prohibited from possessing a firearm on the porch of his home and therefore, the trial court did not abuse its discretion in denying defendant's motion to withdraw his guilty plea. Plumley v. Commonwealth, No. 1799-02-3, 2003 Va. App. LEXIS 501 (Ct. of Appeals Oct. 7, 2003).

Denial of motion to withdraw guilty plea was upheld where the evidence indicated that defendant fully and completely understood the plea agreement he entered into; the plea agreement defendant signed made no mention of eight-year cap and the guilty plea form that defendant signed before trial did not indicate that defendant had a particular expectation regarding what his sentence would be. Harris v. Commonwealth, No. 2917-02-1, 2003 Va. App. LEXIS 514 (Ct. of Appeals Oct. 14, 2003).

Since there was no question that the trial court imposed sentence and/or imposed suspension of sentence for all charges well before defendant sought to withdraw his guilty pleas, the trial court, pursuant to § 19.2-296, lacked any authority to consider defendant's motion and, thus did not err in refusing to do so. Staten v. Commonwealth, No. 2165-02-2, 2004 Va. App. LEXIS 45 (Ct. of Appeals Feb. 3, 2004).

Defendant was not entitled to withdraw his guilty pleas where, among other things, the evidence showed that the trial judge questioned defendant extensively to ensure that he was entering the pleas voluntarily, knowingly, and with a clear understanding of their effect, defendant acknowledged that the charges and the plea agreement had been read verbatim to him and that he understood them, and defendant told the trial judge that he was entering his pleas freely and voluntarily and that no one, including his attorney, had threatened or forced him to plead guilty or made any promises concerning his pleas of guilty. Stevenson v. Commonwealth, No. 2350-02-1, 2004 Va. App. LEXIS 89 (Ct. of Appeals Feb. 24, 2004).

Trial court did not have jurisdiction to consider defendant's motion to withdraw his guilty plea under this section, as defendant's original sentencing order remained valid as to all portions that were not in excess of the sentencing court's statutory authority. McKenney v. Commonwealth, Nos. 3330-02-2, 0473-03-2, 2004 Va. App. LEXIS 157 (Ct. of Appeals Apr. 6, 2004).

Defendant's motion to withdraw his Alford plea was properly denied; he had been fully advised of the consequences of his plea and understood them, and trial court did not credit his claim that he felt pressured into accepting the plea bargain. Wilson v. Commonwealth, No. 2175-03-2, 2004 Va. App. LEXIS 248 (Ct. of Appeals June 1, 2004).

Trial court did not abuse its discretion in denying defendant's motion for leave to withdraw defendant's guilty pleas. The evidence did not support defendant's allegation that the police fraudulently induced defendant to plead guilty to drug charges, as defendant was asked twice whether defendant was promised anything and defendant answered no, and defendant gave the same answer on defendant's guilty plea form. Jones v. Commonwealth, — Va. App. —, — S.E.2d —, 2006 Va. App. LEXIS 568 (Dec. 19, 2006).

Trial court did not err in denying defendant's motion to withdraw his guilty pleas to robbery and use of a firearm in the commission of a robbery because the trial court was not required to grant the motion based on defendant's alleged defense, which simply claim that he was in the wrong place at the wrong time; defendant presented no affidavits and submitted no evidence in support of his motion, and the record did not support defendant's allegation that he was pressured into accepting the plea agreement. Booker v. Commonwealth, 2008 Va. App. LEXIS 171 (Apr. 8, 2008).

Circuit court did not err in denying defendant's motion to withdraw his guilty pleas because defendant did not offer any affidavits to support his motion, and he offered conflicting explanations as to why he decided to plead guilty, which suggested an attempt to avoid the consequences of his actions; defendant's motion appeared to have represented simply an attempt to avoid jail, and he did not offer a reasonable foundation for a defense. Hughes v. Commonwealth, — Va. App. —, — S.E.2d —, 2008 Va. App. LEXIS 236 (May 13, 2008).

Withdrawal of plea of nolo contendere. — Defendant was entitled to withdraw the disputed plea of nolo contendere if the record established any defense at all to the indictments, and it was reasonably probable that nondisclosure of the exculpatory impeachment evidence had the least influence on such plea. Jefferson v. Commonwealth, 27 Va. App. 477, 500 S.E.2d 219 (1998).

Defendant was not permitted to withdraw his plea of nolo contendere where record failed to show that defendant's plea was involuntary, induced by fraud, coercion, or undue influence, or based upon any surprise or honest mistake of material fact; to the contrary, the record contained evidence that defendant fully understood the nature and effect of his plea and that defendant's nolo contendere plea was freely and voluntarily given. Horn v. Commonwealth, No. 1317-02-3, 2003 Va. App. LEXIS 702 (Ct. of Appeals Dec. 30, 2003).

Because defendant neither argued why defendant's § 19.2-296 motion to withdraw a plea of nolo contendere should be granted, nor proffered the evidence defendant intended to elicit or the argument defendant made on appeal, defendant's argument was waived pursuant to Va. Sup. Ct. R. 5A:18. Stone v. Commonwealth, 2011 Va. App. LEXIS 288 (Sept. 27, 2011).

Improper standard applied. — Trial court erred in denying defendant's motion to withdraw his guilty plea, because it did not follow the correct standard in denying the motion; the trial court did not consider whether defendant's proffered defense was reasonable, and not merely dilatory or formal, but found that defendant was advised by two experienced attorneys and relied on his answers during the colloquy. Hubbard v. Commonwealth, 60 Va. App. 200, 725 S.E.2d 163, 2012 Va. App. LEXIS 168 (2012).

Order granting a writ of habeas corpus was error because, after sentencing, the rule of § 19.2-296 applied to motions to withdraw guilty pleas, and there was no evidence that the inmate was denied effective assistance of counsel relating to his motion to withdraw his Alford plea to grand larceny or that manifest injustice occurred; if the case had gone to trial, the inmate's sole defense would have been his own self-serving and uncorroborated testimony that he had been given permission to remove air conditioning units he was charged with stealing. He would have been subject to cross-examination with regard to his changing accounts of the person who had allegedly given him permission, his precipitate flight from the scene when confronted by the owner, and his two prior larceny convictions. Johnson v. Anis, 284 Va. 462, 731 S.E.2d 914, 2012 Va. LEXIS 164 (2012).

Defendant's purported misunderstanding of procedural matters was belied by record, and even if his misunderstanding was genuine, his reluctance to submit to normal legal procedure could not be deemed manifest injustice under this section. Atabaki v. Commonwealth, No. 1411-98-4 (Ct. of Appeals Feb. 8, 2000).

Jurisdiction on appeal. — Because a motion to withdraw a guilty plea under § 19.2-296 is designed by statute to be filed and disposed of while the circuit court retains jurisdiction over the case, the motion is criminal in nature; such motion does not challenge the jurisdiction of the circuit court. Thus, defendant's appeal was subject to the criminal appellate jurisdiction of the Court of Appeals under subsection A of § 17.1-406. Williams v. Commonwealth, 263 Va. 189, 557 S.E.2d 233, 2002 Va. LEXIS 22 (2002).

Preservation of issue on appeal. — Defendant's appellate argument that his guilty pleas were involuntary because the trial court did not specifically advise him of the appellate consequences of the pleas was defaulted because defendant never questioned the voluntariness of pleas before the trial court, did not object to the trial court's acceptance of his pleas either during trial or post-trial, and did not move to withdraw his pleas. Cook v. Commonwealth, — Va. App. —, — S.E.2d —, 2005 Va. App. LEXIS 429 (Nov. 1, 2005).

Applied in Manning v. Commonwealth, 22 Va. App. 252, 468 S.E.2d 705 (1996); Williams v. Commonwealth, 263 Va. 189, 557 S.E.2d 233, 2002 Va. LEXIS 22 (2002); Epps v. Commonwealth, 59 Va. App. 71, 717 S.E.2d 151, 2011 Va. App. LEXIS 351 (2011); Booker v. Commonwealth, 61 Va. App. 323, 734 S.E.2d 729, 2012 Va. App. LEXIS 407 (2012).

CIRCUIT COURT OPINIONS

Withdrawal of plea allowed where defendant's attorney misinformed defendant of the immigration consequences of the plea. — Defendant's motion to withdraw his guilty plea to charges of distribution of marijuana was granted, because defendant's attorney incorrectly advised defendant that the guilty plea would not render him deportable pursuant to 8 U.S.C.S. § 1227(a)(2)(B)(i), so defendant received ineffective assistance of counsel, and the guilty plea was not voluntary and knowing. Commonwealth v. Tahmas, — Va. Cir. —, 2005 Va. Cir. LEXIS 132 (Fairfax County July 26, 2005).

§ 19.2-297. Repealed by Acts 1994, c. 706.

§ 19.2-297.1. Sentence of person twice previously convicted of certain violent felonies.

A. Any person convicted of two or more separate acts of violence when such offenses were not part of a common act, transaction or scheme, and who has been at liberty as defined in § 53.1-151 between each conviction, shall, upon conviction of a third or subsequent act of violence, be sentenced to life imprisonment and shall not have all or any portion of the sentence suspended, provided it is admitted, or found by the jury or judge before whom he is tried, that he has been previously convicted of two or more such acts of violence. For the purposes of this section, *"act of violence"* means (i) any one of the following violations of Chapter 4 (§ 18.2-30 et seq.) of Title 18.2:

a. First and second degree murder and voluntary manslaughter under Article 1 (§ 18.2-30 et seq.);

b. Mob-related felonies under Article 2 (§ 18.2-38 et seq.);

c. Any kidnapping or abduction felony under Article 3 (§ 18.2-47 et seq.);

d. Any malicious felonious assault or malicious bodily wounding under Article 4 (§ 18.2-51 et seq.);

e. Robbery under § 18.2-58 and carjacking under § 18.2-58.1;

f. Except as otherwise provided in § 18.2-67.5:2 or § 18.2-67.5:3, criminal sexual assault punishable as a felony under Article 7 (§ 18.2-61 et seq.); or

g. Arson in violation of § 18.2-77 when the structure burned was occupied or a Class 3 felony violation of § 18.2-79.

(ii) conspiracy to commit any of the violations enumerated in clause (i) of this section; and (iii) violations as a principal in the second degree or accessory before the fact of the provisions enumerated in clause (i) of this section.

B. Prior convictions shall include convictions under the laws of any state or of the United States for any offense substantially similar to those listed under "act of violence" if such offense would be a felony if committed in the Commonwealth.

The Commonwealth shall notify the defendant in writing, at least thirty days prior to trial, of its intention to seek punishment pursuant to this section.

C. Any person sentenced to life imprisonment pursuant to this section shall not be eligible for parole and shall not be eligible for any good conduct allowance or any earned sentence credits under Chapter 6 (§ 53.1-186 et seq.) of Title 53.1. However, any person subject to the provisions of this section, other than a person who was sentenced under subsection A of § 18.2-67.5:3 for criminal sexual assault convictions specified in subdivision f, (i) who has reached the age of sixty-five or older and who has served at least five years of the sentence imposed or (ii) who has reached the age of sixty or older and who has served at least ten years of the sentence imposed may petition the Parole Board for conditional release. The Parole Board shall promulgate regulations to implement the provisions of this subsection.

History.
1994, cc. 828, 860, 862, 881; 1994, 2nd Sp. Sess., cc. 1, 2; 1995, c. 834; 1996, c. 539.

Cross references.
As to presumption of no bail for illegal aliens charged with certain crimes, see § 19.2-120.1. As to requirement of saliva or tissue sample for DNA analysis after arrest for a violent felony, see § 19.2-310.2:1. As to punishment for Class 3 felonies, see § 18.2-10.

Law Review.
For 2007 annual survey article, "Criminal Law and Procedure," see 42 U. Rich. L. Rev. 311 (2007).

Michie's Jurisprudence.
For related discussion, see 2B M.J. Bail and Recognizance, § 9.

CASE NOTES

Introduction of recidivism evidence. — This section did not forbid recidivism evidence from being presented in the guilt phase of a jury trial, and neither the jury bifurcation statute, § 19.2-295.1, nor Va. Sup. Ct. R. 3A:17.1 were inconsistent with this interpretation; recidivism evidence was properly admitted in a prosecution for malicious wounding "after having been twice convicted of a violent felony." Washington v. Commonwealth, 46 Va. App. 276, 616 S.E.2d 774, 2005 Va. App. LEXIS 320 (2005), aff'd, 272 Va. 449, 634 S.E.2d 310 (2006).

Introduction of prior convictions during guilt phase. — Trial judge erred in admitting defendant's two prior robbery convictions during the guilt phase of the trial because the felony convictions, which had to be proved to invoke § 19.2-297.1, were not elements of the malicious wounding offense proscribed by § 18.2-51; this section unambiguously related to the punishment to be imposed upon conviction. Washington v. Commonwealth, 44 Va. App. 157, 604 S.E.2d 92, 2004 Va. App. LEXIS 503 (2004).

Proof of a defendant's prior predicate convictions is admissible during the guilt phase of the trial. This reading comports with the plain language of § 19.2-295.1 and gives full meaning, force and effect to §§ 19.2-295.1 and 19.2-297.1. Washington v. Commonwealth, 272 Va. 449, 634 S.E.2d 310, 2006 Va. LEXIS 73 (2006).

To meet its burden of proof, the Commonwealth needed to show that defendant had been "before sentenced in the United States;" accordingly, the trial court correctly admitted into evidence copies of orders showing defendant's prior sentences so that the Commonwealth could prove its case in chief. Person v. Commonwealth, No. 1989-92-2 (Ct. of Appeals Apr. 12, 1994) (decided under former § 19.2-297).

Robbery offenses not substantially similar. — Based on a comparison of the elements of the crimes of robbery in Maryland and Virginia, an appellant may be convicted in Maryland of behavior that would not have been a crime in Virginia, which compels the conclusion that the offenses are not substantially similar for purposes of § 19.2-297.1 as in Maryland, in cases not involving capital or felony murder, a defendant can be convicted of an afterthought robbery, but Virginia's appellate courts have expressly rejected the notion of robbery as an afterthought crime in the non-capital murder context. Dean v. Commonwealth, 61 Va. App. 209, 734 S.E.2d 673, 2012 Va. App. LEXIS 394 (2012).

CIRCUIT COURT OPINIONS

The presumption against bail for a murder charge applied in a bail determination under § 19.2-406. — The burden on the Commonwealth to show good cause why bail should not have been reduced or defendant released on his own recognizance during the Commonwealth's pretrial appeal did not eliminate the presumption against bail for defendant's murder charge. Commonwealth v. Ludwig, 69 Va. Cir. 460, 2006 Va. Cir. LEXIS 87 (Loudoun County 2006).

§ 19.2-298. Pronouncement of sentence.

After a finding of guilty, sentence shall be pronounced, or decision to suspend the imposition of sentence shall be announced, without unreasonable delay. Pending pronouncement, the court may commit the accused to jail or may continue or alter the bail except that in those cases where the accused is convicted of a murder in the first degree, the court shall commit him to jail and he shall not be allowed bail pending the pronouncement of sentence. Before pronouncing the sentence, the court shall inquire of the accused if he desires to make a statement and if he desires to advance any reason why judgment should not be pronounced against him.

Whenever any person willfully and knowingly fails to surrender or submit to the custody of a sheriff as ordered by a court, any law-enforcement officer, with or without a warrant, may arrest such person anywhere in the Commonwealth. If the arrest is made in the county or city in which the person was ordered to surrender, or in an adjoining county or city, the officer may forthwith return the accused before the proper court. If the arrest is made beyond the foregoing limits, the officer shall proceed according to the provisions of § 19.2-76, and if such arrest is made without a warrant, the officer shall procure a warrant from the magistrate serving the county or city wherein the arrest was made, charging the accused with contempt of court.

History.

1975, c. 495; 1976, c. 285; 2009, c. 192.

The 2009 amendments.

The 2009 amendment by c. 192 added the last paragraph.

Law Review.

For article, "The Constitutionality of Harsher Sentences on Retrial in Virginia," see 62 Va. L. Rev. 1337 (1976). For survey of Virginia criminal procedure for the year 1975-1976, see 62 Va. L. Rev. 1412 (1976). For an article on bifurcated sentencing in noncapital felony cases in Virginia, see 30 U. Rich. L. Rev. 465 (1996). For an article relating to all published Virginia criminal law decisions between July 1, 1997, and July 1, 1998, see 32 U. Rich. L. Rev. 1091 (1998). For annual survey article, "Criminal Law and Procedure," see 46 U. Rich. L. Rev. 59 (2011).

Michie's Jurisprudence.

For related discussion, see 5B M.J. Criminal Procedure, §§ 27, 70, 72.

CASE NOTES

Allocution and closing argument distinguished. — Allocution is the defendant's right to speak on his own behalf after the fact finder determines guilt but before the judge pronounces sentence. The defendant's closing argument is not allocution, but is his opportunity to present arguments in mitigation before the fact finder deliberates. Bassett v. Commonwealth, 222 Va. 844, 284 S.E.2d 844 (1981), cert. denied, 456 U.S. 938, 102 S. Ct. 1996, 72 L. Ed. 2d 458 (1982); 499 U.S. 983, 111 S. Ct. 1639, 113 L. Ed. 2d 734 (1991).

The right of allocution is not constitutionally required. Stamper v. Baskerville, 531 F. Supp. 1122 (E.D. Va. 1982), cert. denied, 459 U.S. 1225, 103 S. Ct. 123, 75 L. Ed. 2d 466 (1993).

Court rejected petitioner's claim that he was denied the effective assistance of counsel at trial due to his counsel's failure to raise the issue that the trial court violated his rights under the Fifth and Fourteenth Amendments as well as under § 19.2-298 when it failed to allow petitioner to allocute before he was sentenced because there is no constitutional "right" to an allocution before sentencing. The record demonstrated that petitioner was prone to making statements detrimental to his case and he did not allege what he would have said if he had been given the opportunity to address the court or how such a statement would have impacted the sentence he received. Powell v. Warden of the Sussex I State Prison, — Va. —, — S.E.2d —, 2005 Va. LEXIS 106 (Nov. 8, 2005).

Denial of due process to refuse defendant's request to speak. — When a defendant effectively communicates his desire to the trial judge to speak prior to the imposition of sentence, it is a denial of due process for the court not to grant defendant's request. Stamper v. Baskerville, 531 F. Supp. 1122 (E.D. Va. 1982), cert. denied, 459 U.S. 1225, 103 S. Ct. 123, 75 L. Ed. 2d 466 (1993).

Sentence in absentia. — Trial court erred in imposing a jail sentence in absentia. Robinson v. Commonwealth, No. 2901-01-1, 2003 Va. App. LEXIS 183 (Ct. of Appeals Apr. 1, 2003).

Effect of acceptance of plea agreement. — Acceptance of defendant's plea agreement, which provided that the trial court would impose sentence on two counts of aggravated sexual battery and would withhold decision on the other two counts, did not divest the trial court of its jurisdiction to adjudicate the charges. Holden v. Commonwealth, 26 Va. App. 403, 494 S.E.2d 892 (1998).

No clear error shown. — At habeas corpus hearing, where the record showed that the defendant, who was represented at trial by experienced criminal lawyers, did not inform the trial judge of his desire to address the court before sentencing and the judge failed to inform him of his right to speak under this section, but counsel was well aware of the omission at trial and chose to forbear objecting for tactical reasons, there was no "clear error." Stamper v. Baskerville, 531 F. Supp. 1122 (E.D. Va. 1982), cert. denied, 459 U.S. 1225, 103 S. Ct. 123, 75 L. Ed. 2d 466 (1993).

Harmless error. — Trial court's failure to afford defendant a right of allocution under § 19.2-298 was harmless error as defendant's refusal to proffer an allocution statement deprived the trial court of an opportunity to correct its mistake, and precluded the appellate court from determining whether defendant received a fair trial and substantial justice. Montgomery v. Commonwealth, 56 Va. App. 695, 696 S.E.2d 261, 2010 Va. App. LEXIS 324 (2010).

Applied in Stamper v. Commonwealth, 220 Va. 260, 257 S.E.2d 808 (1979); Lamb v. Commonwealth, 40 Va. App. 52, 577 S.E.2d 530, 2003 Va. App. LEXIS 120 (2003).

§ 19.2-298.01. Use of discretionary sentencing guidelines.

A. In all felony cases, other than Class 1 felonies, the court shall (i) have presented to it the appropriate discretionary sentencing guidelines worksheets and (ii) review and consider the suitability of the applicable discretionary sentencing guidelines established pursuant to Chapter 8 (§ 17.1-800 et seq.) of Title 17.1. Before imposing sentence, the court shall state for the record that such review and consideration have been accomplished and shall make the completed worksheets a part of the record of the case and open for inspection. In cases tried by a jury, the jury shall not be presented any information regarding sentencing guidelines.

B. In any felony case, other than Class 1 felonies, in which the court imposes a sentence which is either greater or less than that indicated by the discretionary sentencing guidelines, the court shall file with the record of the case a written explanation of such departure.

C. In felony cases, other than Class 1 felonies, tried by a jury and in felony cases tried by the court without a jury upon a plea of not guilty, the court shall direct a probation officer of such court to prepare the discretionary sentencing guidelines worksheets. In felony cases tried upon a plea of guilty, including cases which are the subject of a plea agreement, the court shall direct a probation officer of such court to prepare the discretionary sentencing guidelines worksheets, or, with the concurrence of the accused, the court and the attorney for the Commonwealth, the worksheets shall be prepared by the attorney for the Commonwealth.

D. Except as provided in subsection E, discretionary sentencing guidelines worksheets prepared pursuant to this section shall be subject to the same distribution as presentence investigation reports prepared pursuant to subsection A of § 19.2-299.

E. Following the entry of a final order of conviction and sentence in a felony case, the clerk of the circuit court in which the case was tried shall cause a copy of such order or orders, the original of the discretionary sentencing guidelines worksheets prepared in the case, and a copy of any departure explanation prepared pursuant to subsection B to be forwarded to the Virginia Criminal Sentencing Commission within five days. Similarly, the statement required by §§ 19.2-295 and 19.2-303 and regarding departure from or modification of a sentence fixed by a jury shall be forwarded to the Virginia Criminal Sentencing Commission.

F. The failure to follow any or all of the provisions of this section or the failure to follow any or all of the provisions of this section in the prescribed manner shall not be reviewable on appeal or the basis of any other post-conviction relief.

G. The provisions of this section shall apply only to felony cases in which the offense is committed on or after January 1, 1995, and for which there are discretionary sentencing guidelines. For purposes of the discretionary sentencing guidelines only, a person sentenced to a boot camp incarceration program pursuant to § 19.2-316.1, a detention center incarceration program pursuant to § 19.2-316.2 or a diversion center incarceration program pursuant to § 19.2-316.3 shall be deemed to be sentenced to a term of incarceration.

History.
1994, 2nd Sp. Sess., cc. 1, 2; 1996, c. 552; 1997, c. 345; 1998, cc. 200, 353; 1999, c. 286; 2007, c. 259.

Cross references.
As to inspection of confidential Department of Juvenile Justice records for the purpose of preparing discretionary sentencing guidelines worksheets, see § 16.1-300. As to punishment for Class 1 felonies, see § 18.2-10.

The 2007 amendments.
The 2007 amendment by c. 259 added the second sentence in subsection E.

CASE NOTES

Constitutionality. — The legislature acted within its authority when it created the sentencing guidelines and provided that those guidelines would be discretionary and not mandatory; it confirmed the discretionary aspect of the guidelines by leaving their implementation solely within the discretion of the trial courts and by excluding decisions relating to the application of the guidelines from appellate review. This structural determination denies a defendant no substantive or procedural right that he is entitled under the law to enjoy. Jett v. Commonwealth, 34 Va. App. 252, 540 S.E.2d 511, 2001 Va. App. LEXIS 46 (2001).

If a sentence is within the range set by the legislature for the crime with which the defendant was convicted, an appellate court will not interfere with the judgment; thus defendant's life sentence would not be disturbed. Hunt v. Commonwealth, 25 Va. App. 395, 488 S.E.2d 672 (1997).

Trial court did not abuse its discretion in imposing a 43-year sentence against defendant, as said sentence was within the ranges set by the legislature and well below the total statutory maximum for the various felony offenses for which he was convicted. Clark v. Commonwealth, — Va. App. —, — S.E.2d —, 2008 Va. App. LEXIS 234 (May 13, 2008).

References in a victim impact statement and a pre-sentence report relating to defendant's conduct towards a former girlfriend did not violate Apprendi v. New Jersey, 530 U.S. 466 (2000), as defendant entered a no contest plea, which allowed the trial court to consider defendant guilty for sentencing purposes; although the trial court departed from the sentencing guidelines, the guidelines were discretionary under § 19.2-298.01, and the sentences imposed

were within the authorized ranges. Myers v. Commonwealth, 2008 Va. App. LEXIS 385 (Aug. 12, 2008).

Defendant's 10-year sentence for felony embezzlement under § 18.2-111 was proper as the failure to follow any or all of the sentencing guidelines under § 19.2-298.01 was not reviewable on appeal. Greene v. Commonwealth, 2008 Va. App. LEXIS 319 (July 15, 2008).

The sentencing guidelines are not binding on trial judges, rather, the guidelines are merely a tool to assist trial judges in fixing an appropriate punishment; Virginia trial courts have discretion to fix an appropriate sentence, and failure to follow the guidelines does not deny equal protection of the law. Brooks v. Commonwealth, No. 2540-02-3, 2004 Va. App. LEXIS 29 (Ct. of Appeals Jan. 28, 2004).

Although defendant was granted habeas corpus relief, defendant's claim that he suffered prejudice under *Strickland* because defendant's conviction of common-law involuntary manslaughter and aggravated involuntary manslaughter subjected defendant to an increased range of punishment under the sentencing guidelines was rejected because the guidelines provided by § 19.2-298.01 were discretionary, rather than mandatory; the trial court was required only to consider the sentencing guidelines before sentencing defendant and to file with the record of the case a written explanation of any departure from the indicated range of punishment. West v. Dir. of the Dep't of Corr., 273 Va. 56, 639 S.E.2d 190, 2007 Va. LEXIS 17 (2007).

Scientific evidence in presentence report. — In order to admit scientific evidence in the risk assessment portion of the presentence report the Commonwealth had the burden of proving that a penile plethysmograph examination was a reliable scientific method of determining a convicted sex offender's risk to reoffend. Billips v. Commonwealth, 274 Va. 805, 652 S.E.2d 99, 2007 Va. LEXIS 122 (2007).

Scope of review. — Review of trial court's imposition on three related counts of sentence of 75 years and $800,000.00 fine was limited to whether the sentence fell within the permissible statutory range. Smith v. Commonwealth, 26 Va. App. 620, 496 S.E.2d 117 (1998).

Sentencing court's use of voluntary sentencing guidelines in effect at the time of defendant's sentencing, as opposed to those in effect at the time of his crime, was not an ex post facto violation because the guidelines were mere tools to assist the sentencing court in pronouncing sentence, their application did not rise to the level of an ex post facto violation, and the scope of the appellate court's review was whether the sentence imposed fell within the range prescribed by the legislature. Luttrell v. Commonwealth, 42 Va. App. 461, 592 S.E.2d 752, 2004 Va. App. LEXIS 83 (2004).

When defendant said the sex offender risk assessment instrument incorporated into the sentence imposed on him was unreliable in predicting recidivism, this issue was not reviewable on appeal under subsection F of § 19.2-298.01, so the trial court's consideration of the instrument as a factor in applying discretionary sentencing guidelines was no basis for review of defendant's sentence. Luttrell v. Commonwealth, 42 Va. App. 461, 592 S.E.2d 752, 2004 Va. App. LEXIS 83 (2004).

Defendant's sentence, which departed from the sentencing guidelines, was affirmed as: (1) subsection F of § 19.2-298.01 prohibited appellate review of application of the sentencing guidelines; (2) the sentences were not beyond the statutory maximum on either charge; (3) defendant waived his claims that the trial court violated his constitutional right to a fair trial and deprived him of his right to liberty without due process under the Fifth, Sixth, and Fourteenth Amendments as he objected only to the trial court's failure to impose the discretionary sentencing guidelines; and (4) there were no grounds to invoke the good cause or ends of justice exceptions to Rule 5A:18. Burpo v. Commonwealth, No. 2831-02-2, 2004 Va. App. LEXIS 123 (Ct. of Appeals Mar. 23, 2004).

Because defendant's sentence of 27 months imprisonment for drunk driving and for driving with a suspended license fell below the midpoint of the range prescribed by § 18.2-266 and subdivision C 1 of § 18.2-270, it was consonant with the Assimilative Crimes Act's "like punishment" requirement, and even if the district court should have more adequately considered Virginia'a sentencing guidelines, those guidelines were entirely discretionary, and deviations from them were not reviewable on appeal. United States v. Finley, 531 F.3d 288, 2008 U.S. App. LEXIS 13762 (4th Cir. 2008).

Defendant's sentence for possession of cocaine with intent to distribute was not subject to appellate review because it was within the applicable sentencing range of 5 to 40 years, and § 19.2-298.01 provided that a failure to sentence consistent with the discretionary sentencing guideline recommendation was not reviewable on appeal. Tunstall v. Commonwealth, 2009 Va. App. LEXIS 65 (Feb. 10, 2009).

Defendant was unable to object to sentences imposed on certain felony convictions because pursuant to subsection F of § 19.2-298.01, the failure to follow certain sentencing provisions in the prescribed manner did not provide any basis for relief. Melendez v. Commonwealth, 2010 Va. App. LEXIS 171 (May 4, 2010).

No abuse of discretion. — Defendant did not show an abuse of discretion in sentencing for his felony convictions because the sentences were within the statutory maximum. Melendez v. Commonwealth, 2010 Va. App. LEXIS 171 (May 4, 2010).

Sentence was proper. — Defendant, who was convicted of possession of heroin and cocaine with intent to distribute and possession with intent to distribute a controlled substance within 1,000 feet of a school, was properly sentenced because the sentences were within the statutory sentencing range. Murphy v. Commonwealth, 2010 Va. App. LEXIS 103 (Mar. 23, 2010).

Sentence for taking indecent liberties with a minor was affirmed where, before passing sentence, the trial court emphasized the seriousness of the offense committed, addressed two of the arguments made by the defense in mitigation of the offense, explained that it did not feel either of those claims undermined the seriousness of the criminal acts committed against the victim, and gave reasons for exceeding the sentencing guidelines: "gravity of the offense" and "failure to truly accept responsibility"; contrary to defendant's contention, the record did not reflect that the trial court refused to consider any of the mitigating facts or circumstances presented on his behalf. The sentence imposed by the trial court was within the range set by the legislature. Harmon v. Commonwealth, 2012 Va. App. LEXIS 107 (Apr. 10, 2012).

Applied in Runyon v. Commonwealth, 29 Va. App. 573, 513 S.E.2d 872 (1999).

CIRCUIT COURT OPINIONS

Sentencing guidelines not binding on trial judges. — A trial court properly departed from the discretionary sentencing guidelines by filing a written explanation for its departure, citing the violent nature of the crime committed, coupled with defendant's extensive criminal record, and defendant was sentenced within the statutory range for grand larceny from the person, and below the mandatory minimum sentence imposed for a conviction of robbery. Scott v. Warden, Coffeewood Corr. Ctr., — Va. Cir. —, 2004 Va. Cir. LEXIS 27 (Fairfax County Mar. 1, 2004).

Effective for felony offenses committed after January 1, 1995, sentencing guidelines are to be prepared and must be considered by the judge at sentencing. These "guidelines" are precisely that and impose no mandatory sentencing duty on the court. Commonwealth v. Boone, 73 Va. Cir. 277, 2007 Va. Cir. LEXIS 232 (Portsmouth Apr. 26, 2007).

Post-trial relief. — Failure of a court to follow sentencing guidelines was not a basis for post-trial relief; a petition for a writ of habeas corpus that alleged, inter alia, that the petitioner's counsel did not know the sentencing guidelines, was denied. Beddard v. Mahon, 58 Va. Cir. 111, 2001 Va. Cir. LEXIS 398 (Fauquier County 2001).

§§ 19.2-298.1 through 19.2-298.4. Repealed by Acts 2003, c. 584.

Cross references.
For current registration provisions, see the Sex Offender and Crimes Against Minors Registry Act, §§ 9.1-900 et seq.

§ 19.2-299. Investigations and reports by probation officers in certain cases.

A. When a person is tried in a circuit court (i) upon a charge of assault and battery in violation of § 18.2-57 or 18.2-57.2, stalking in violation of § 18.2-60.3, sexual battery in violation of § 18.2-67.4, attempted sexual battery in violation of § 18.2-67.5, or driving while intoxicated in violation of § 18.2-266, and is adjudged guilty of such charge, unless waived by the court and the defendant and the attorney for the Commonwealth, the court may, or on motion of the defendant shall; or (ii) upon a felony charge not set forth in subdivision (iii) below, the court may when there is a plea agreement between the defendant and the Commonwealth and shall when the defendant pleads guilty without a plea agreement or is found guilty by the court after a plea of not guilty; or (iii) the court shall when a person is charged and adjudged guilty of a felony violation, or conspiracy to commit or attempt to commit a felony violation, of § 18.2-46.2, 18.2-46.3, 18.2-48, clause (2) or (3) of § 18.2-49, § 18.2-61, 18.2-63, 18.2-64.1, 18.2-64.2, 18.2-67.1, 18.2-67.2, 18.2-67.3, 18.2-67.4:1, 18.2-67.5, 18.2-67.5:1, 18.2-355, 18.2-356, 18.2-357, 18.2-361, 18.2-362, 18.2-366, 18.2-368, 18.2-370, 18.2-370.1, or 18.2-370.2, or any attempt to commit or conspiracy to commit any felony violation of § 18.2-67.5, 18.2-67.5:2, or 18.2-67.5:3, direct a probation officer of such court to thoroughly investigate and report upon the history of the accused, including a report of the accused's criminal record as an adult and available juvenile court records, any information regarding the accused's participation or membership in a criminal street gang as defined in § 18.2-46.1, and all other relevant facts, to fully advise the court so the court may determine the appropriate sentence to be imposed. Unless the defendant or the attorney for the Commonwealth objects, the court may order that the report contain no more than the defendant's criminal history, any history of substance abuse, any physical or health-related problems as may be pertinent, and any applicable sentencing guideline worksheets. This expedited report shall be subject to all the same procedures as all other sentencing reports and sentencing guidelines worksheets. The probation officer, after having furnished a copy of this report at least five days prior to sentencing to counsel for the accused and the attorney for the Commonwealth for their permanent use, shall submit his report in advance of the sentencing hearing to the judge in chambers, who shall keep such report confidential. Counsel for the accused may provide the accused with a copy of the presentence report. The probation officer shall be available to testify from this report in open court in the presence of the accused, who shall have been provided with a copy of the presentence report by his counsel or advised of its contents and be given the right to cross-examine the investigating officer as to any matter contained therein and to present any additional facts bearing upon the matter. The report of the investigating officer shall at all times be kept confidential by each recipient, and shall be filed as a part of the record in the case. Any report so filed shall be made available only by court order and shall be sealed upon final order by the court, except that such reports or copies thereof shall be available at any time to any criminal justice agency, as defined in § 9.1-101, of this or any other state or of the United States; to any agency where the accused is referred for treatment by the court or by probation and parole services; and to counsel for any person who has been indicted jointly for the same felony as the person subject to the report. Subject to the limitations set forth in § 37.2-901, any report prepared pursuant to the provisions hereof shall without court order be made available to counsel for the person who is the subject of the report if that person (i) is charged with a felony subsequent to the time of the preparation of the report or (ii) has been convicted of the crime or crimes for which the report was prepared and is pursuing a post-conviction remedy. The presentence report shall be in a form prescribed by the Department of Corrections. In all cases where such report is not ordered, a simplified report shall be prepared on a form prescribed by the Department of Corrections. For the purposes of this subsection, information regarding the accused's participation or membership in a criminal street gang may include the characteristics, specific rivalries, common practices, social customs and behavior, terminology, and types of crimes that are likely to be committed by that criminal street gang.

B. As a part of any presentence investigation conducted pursuant to subsection A when the offense for which the defendant was convicted was a felony, the court probation officer shall advise any victim of such offense in writing that he may submit to the Virginia Parole Board a written request (i) to be given the opportunity to submit to the Board a written statement in advance of any parole hearing describing the impact of the offense upon him and his opinion regarding the defendant's release and (ii) to receive copies of such other notifications pertaining to the defendant as the Board may provide pursuant to subsection B of § 53.1-155.

C. As part of any presentence investigation conducted pursuant to subsection A when the offense for which the defendant was convicted was a felony drug offense set forth in Article 1 (§ 18.2-247 et seq.) of Chapter 7 of Title 18.2, the presentence report shall include any known association of the defendant with illicit drug operations or markets.

D. As a part of any presentence investigation conducted pursuant to subsection A, when the offense for which the defendant was convicted was a felony, not a capital offense, committed on or after January 1, 2000, the defendant shall be required to undergo a substance abuse screening pursuant to § 18.2-251.01.

History.
Code 1950, § 53-278.1; 1952, c. 233; 1972, c. 516; 1974, c. 121; 1975, cc. 371, 495; 1979, c. 286; 1980, c. 733; 1981, c. 263; 1983, c. 541; 1987, c. 676; 1989, c. 169; 1991, cc. 43, 229; 1992, c. 77; 1993, cc. 466, 492; 1994, 2nd Sp. Sess., cc. 1, 2; 1995, cc. 687, 778; 1997,

c. 691; 1998, cc. 783, 840; 1999, cc. 891, 903, 913; 2001, c. 647; 2003, cc. 146, 613; 2004, cc. 308, 459, 819; 2005, cc. 188, 219, 631; 2006, cc. 99, 863, 914, 916; 2010, c. 223.

Cross references.
As to inspection of confidential Department of Juvenile Justice records for the purpose of preparing presentence reports, see § 16.1-300.

Editor's note.
The above section is former § 53-278.1 as amended by Acts 1975, c. 371. Pursuant to Acts 1975, c. 593, cl. 2, it has been substituted for § 19.2-299 as enacted by Acts 1975, c. 495.
Acts 1998, cc. 783 and 840, cl. 2, provide: "That the provisions of this act amending or adding §§ 16.1-273, 18.2-251.01, 18.2-252, 19.2-299 and 19.2-299.2, except for subsection A (ii) of § 19.2-299.2, shall become effective July 1, 1999."

The 2010 amendments.
The 2010 amendment by c. 223, in the tenth sentence in subsection A, substituted "Subject to the limitations set forth in § 37.2-901, any report" for "Any report," added the clause (i) designator, added clause (ii) and made a related change.

Law Review.
For survey of Virginia law on criminal law for the year 1971-1972, see 58 Va. L. Rev. 1206 (1972). For survey of Virginia law on criminal procedure for the year 1974-1975, see 61 Va. L. Rev. 1713 (1975). For article, "The Constitutionality of Harsher Sentences on Retrial in Virginia," see 62 Va. L. Rev. 1337 (1976). For survey of Virginia criminal procedure for the year 1975-1976, see 62 Va. L. Rev. 1412 (1976). For comment on sentencing in criminal cases, see 13 U. Rich. L. Rev. 899 (1979). For survey of Virginia criminal law and procedure for the year 2004-2005, see 40 U. Rich. L. Rev. 197 (2005).

Michie's Jurisprudence.
For related discussion, see 5B M.J. Criminal Procedure, §§ 70, 78.

CASE NOTES

Section is procedural statute and does not violate constitutional prohibition against ex post facto laws. McClain v. Commonwealth, 189 Va. 847, 55 S.E.2d 49 (1949).
This section is a procedural statute. Smyth v. White, 195 Va. 169, 77 S.E.2d 454 (1953).
Its provisions may be waived with the consent of the accused, the attorney for the Commonwealth, and the court. Smyth v. White, 195 Va. 169, 77 S.E.2d 454 (1953).
This section sets forth a permissible practice only, which is not required unless requested by the defendant. Hawks v. Peyton, 288 F. Supp. 94 (W.D. Va. 1968).
And noncompliance cannot be reached by habeas corpus. — The failure to comply with the statute cannot be reached by writ of habeas corpus. Smyth v. White, 195 Va. 169, 77 S.E.2d 454 (1953); Hawks v. Peyton, 288 F. Supp. 94 (W.D. Va. 1968).
Allegation that no presentence report was made is not grounds for the grant of a writ of habeas corpus. Hawks v. Peyton, 288 F. Supp. 94 (W.D. Va. 1968).
"History of the accused" includes, but is not restricted to, the defendant's history of criminal convictions. Thomas v. Commonwealth, 18 Va. App. 656, 446 S.E.2d 469 (1994).
Criminal history in presentence report. — Although defendant's prior perjury conviction was improperly admitted since defendant did not testify and defendant's credibility was not at issue, the error was harmless under § 8.01-678 since defendant's criminal history was properly before the trial court during sentencing as part of a presentence report under § 19.2-299. Pierce v. Commonwealth, 50 Va. App. 609, 652 S.E.2d 785, 2007 Va. App. LEXIS 419 (2007).
Pre-sentence report properly recounted the history of defendant's relationship to a former girlfriend under subsection A of § 19.2-299, even though the report included unadjudicated criminal acts committed against the girlfriend as the goal of defendant's intrusion into the home of the girlfriend's sibling was to force the girlfriend to come to that home and bring their child so that defendant could

"blow her head off" with a shotgun defendant possessed. Myers v. Commonwealth, 2008 Va. App. LEXIS 385 (Aug. 12, 2008).

Review of presentence report of co-defendant in related case. — Defendant was not entitled to have defendant's sentence set aside because the trial court's sua sponte review of the presentence report of the defendant in a related case was not improper pursuant to § 19.2-299, which governed presentence reports, in that the statute provided that presentence reports were available to courts and did not limit courts to a review of presentence reports in particular cases. Stewart v. Commonwealth, No. 2453-11-4, 2012 Va. App. LEXIS 327 (Oct. 16, 2012).

Judge retains discretionary sentencing authority. — This section does not affect a transfer of discretionary authority from the judge of the trial court to a probation officer of the court. Judges are not bound to the conclusions presented in probation officers' reports. Bassett v. Commonwealth, 13 Va. App. 580, 414 S.E.2d 419 (1992).

A defendant convicted of a felony has an absolute right to have a presentence investigation and report prepared upon his request and submitted to the court prior to the pronouncement of sentence. Duncan v. Commonwealth, 2 Va. App. 342, 343 S.E.2d 392 (1986).

Defendant waives right against self-incrimination by pleading guilty. — By pleading guilty, a defendant waives his Fifth Amendment right against self-incrimination as to matters germane to the offense for which he has pled guilty and is to be sentenced. Edmundson v. Commonwealth, 13 Va. App. 476, 412 S.E.2d 727 (1992).

The waiver of the right against compulsory self-incrimination is not unlimited; it does not allow the law-enforcement authorities to inquire about unrelated matters which have no bearing upon the disposition of the case before the trial court. Edmundson v. Commonwealth, 13 Va. App. 476, 412 S.E.2d 727 (1992).

Inquiry held within scope of waiver of right against self-incrimination. — Where the trial court was considering a presentence report in order to determine an appropriate sentence and disposition, and the defendant had given conflicting reports about the extent of his drug use or habit, the inquiry into the conflicting reports was relevant to the case for which he had pled guilty and within the scope of the waiver of his right against compulsory self-incrimination. Edmundson v. Commonwealth, 13 Va. App. 476, 412 S.E.2d 727 (1992).

The effect of the 1975 amendment to former § 53-278.1 (transferred hereto) was such that, when an accused is found guilty of any felony by either the court or a jury, the court may, and upon defendant's motion shall, direct an investigation by a probation officer and consider his report before imposing sentence. Upon defendant's motion, he is entitled to this presentence procedure as a matter of right. Smith v. Commonwealth, 217 Va. 329, 228 S.E.2d 557 (1976).

Impact statement may be source for restitution amount. — The legislature intended that the victim impact statement be used by trial judge to determine the amount of restitution. Alger v. Commonwealth, 19 Va. App. 252, 450 S.E.2d 765 (1994).

Time of reference to probation officer. — The time before sentence when the case is referred to the probation officer for investigation and report is not important. What is important is that the accused shall be adjudged guilty only on evidence admissible on that issue, and before the court hears the probation officer's report. McClain v. Commonwealth, 189 Va. 847, 55 S.E.2d 49 (1949).

This section does not contemplate that the probation officer recommend what sentence should be imposed. Linton v. Commonwealth, 192 Va. 437, 65 S.E.2d 534 (1951).

Use of voluntary sentencing guidelines as "tool" does not violate section. — When the sentence imposed by the trial court is within the statutory range established by the legislature, use of judicially implemented voluntary sentencing guidelines as a "tool" to assist the court in determining the appropriate sentence does not violate this section. Hudson v. Commonwealth, 10 Va. App. 158, 390 S.E.2d 509 (1990).

Failure to afford opportunity of cross-examining officer where his appointment not required. — Where a report of a probation officer was not required but the court appointed such officer at defendants' counsel's request failure to afford defendant's counsel opportunity to cross-examine the probation officer and,

after scrutiny of the report, to present any additional facts bearing on the matter was reversible error. Having availed itself of the provisions of the statute, the court should have been governed by its terms. Linton v. Commonwealth, 192 Va. 437, 65 S.E.2d 534 (1951).

Hearsay evidence may be considered in sentencing phase. — During the sentencing phase of a capital murder case, the court may consider hearsay evidence, favorable or unfavorable to the defendant, contained in a postsentence report. This is implicit from the language of § 19.2-264.5 and this section, which permit a probation officer "to thoroughly investigate and report upon the history of the accused and any other and all other relevant facts." O'Dell v. Commonwealth, 234 Va. 672, 364 S.E.2d 491, cert. denied, 488 U.S. 871, 109 S. Ct. 186, 102 L. Ed. 2d 154 (1988).

Testimony regarding drug associations at sentencing. — Defendant was not deprived of due process at sentencing where Commonwealth elicited testimony regarding charges that were nolle prosequied, because there was no evidence that the Commonwealth agreed not to elicit testimony regarding defendant's drug associations at sentencing, and the testimony regarding such "associations" was admissible under subsection C of § 19.2-299. Sizer v. Commonwealth, 2010 Va. App. LEXIS 337 (Aug. 17, 2010).

Error in denying motion for presentencing report not cured. — The proceedings conducted in reliance upon the second paragraph of former § 53-272 prior to the 1976 amendment did not cure the original error in denying defendant's motion for a presentencing probation report pursuant to former § 53-278.1, predecessor to this section. Smith v. Commonwealth, 217 Va. 329, 228 S.E.2d 557 (1976).

Construction with appellate rules. — Narrative portion of presentence report was not a proper substitute for properly designated portions of transcript or statement of facts, or copies of orders, as required by appellate rule. Jones v. Commonwealth, No. 1128-98-4 (Ct. of Appeals Mar. 21, 2000).

Sentencing judge's right to read report. — Concomitant with the defendant's right to the presentence report is the right to have the sentencing judge read the report before passing sentence. Harley v. Commonwealth, No. 1717-95-2 (Ct. of Appeals July 23, 1996).

Scientific evidence in presentence report. — In order to admit scientific evidence in the risk assessment portion of the presentence report the Commonwealth had the burden of proving that a penile plethysmograph examination was a reliable scientific method of determining a convicted sex offender's risk to reoffend. Billips v. Commonwealth, 274 Va. 805, 652 S.E.2d 99, 2007 Va. LEXIS 122 (2007).

Use of information from confidential informants permitted. — Inclusion of information under this section from confidential informants does not violate the Fifth, Sixth, and Fourteenth Amendments. Furthermore, this section is not void for vagueness and does not require the disclosure of the identities of the informants used to prepare a defendant's presentence report. Moses v. Commonwealth, 27 Va. App. 293, 498 S.E.2d 451 (1998).

Applied in Knight v. Johnson, 699 F.2d 162 (4th Cir. 1983); Crank v. Rogers, 1 Va. App. 491, 339 S.E.2d 909 (1986); Wheeler v. Gilmore, 998 F. Supp. 666 (E.D. Va. 1998).

OPINIONS OF THE ATTORNEY GENERAL

Provision of report to defendant not authorized. — It is a violation of this section for a defense attorney to copy a defendant's presentence report or to provide the original or a copy of such report to the defendant. See opinion of Attorney General to The Honorable Thomas B. Hoover, Judge, Ninth Judicial Circuit, 03-009 (3/31/03)(But see 2005 amendments to this section).

§ 19.2-299.1. When Victim Impact Statement required; contents; uses.

The presentence report prepared pursuant to § 19.2-299 shall, with the consent of the victim, as defined in § 19.2-11.01, in all cases involving offenses other than capital murder, include a Victim Impact Statement. Victim Impact Statements in all cases involving capital murder shall be prepared and submitted in accordance with the provisions of § 19.2-264.5.

A Victim Impact Statement shall be kept confidential and shall be sealed upon entry of the sentencing order. If prepared by someone other than the victim, it shall (i) identify the victim, (ii) itemize any economic loss suffered by the victim as a result of the offense, (iii) identify the nature and extent of any physical or psychological injury suffered by the victim as a result of the offense, (iv) detail any change in the victim's personal welfare, lifestyle or familial relationships as a result of the offense, (v) identify any request for psychological or medical services initiated by the victim or the victim's family as a result of the offense, and (vi) provide such other information as the court may require related to the impact of the offense upon the victim.

If the court does not order a presentence investigation and report, the attorney for the Commonwealth shall, at the request of the victim, submit a Victim Impact Statement. In any event, a victim shall be advised by the local crime victim and witness assistance program that he may submit in his own words a written Victim Impact Statement prepared by the victim or someone the victim designates in writing.

The Victim Impact Statement may be considered by the court in determining the appropriate sentence. A copy of the statement prepared pursuant to this section shall be made available to the defendant or counsel for the defendant without court order at least five days prior to the sentencing hearing. The statement shall not be admissible in any civil proceeding for damages arising out of the acts upon which the conviction was based. The statement, however, may be utilized by the Virginia Workers' Compensation Commission in its determinations on claims by victims of crimes pursuant to Chapter 21.1 (§ 19.2-368.1 et seq.) of this title.

History.
1983, c. 541; 1984, c. 282; 1987, c. 676; 1989, c. 374; 1993, cc. 436, 569; 1995, cc. 687, 720; 1996, c. 398.

Cross references.
As to use of victim impact statements for Commitment Review Committee assessments of prisoners eligible for commitment as sexually violent predators, see § 37.2-904.

Law Review.
For a note, "Due Process on the Uncharted Seas of Irrelevance: Limiting the Presence of Victim Impact Evidence at Capital Sentencing After *Payne v. Tennessee*," see 55 Wash. & Lee L. Rev. 295 (1998).

Michie's Jurisprudence.
For related discussion, see 5B M.J. Criminal Procedure, §§ 70, 80.

CASE NOTES

Relevance of victim impact testimony in capital case. — Victim impact testimony is relevant to punishment in a capital murder prosecution in Virginia. The trial court did not err in admitting the testimony in the instant case. Weeks v. Common-wealth, 248 Va. 460, 450 S.E.2d 379 (1994), cert. denied, 516 U.S. 829, 116 S. Ct. 100, 133 L. Ed. 2d 55 (1995).

Under Virginia's modern, bifurcated capital procedure, victim impact evidence is probative, for example, of the depravity of mind component of the vileness predicate, which the jury in the instant case found as a basis for imposing the death penalty. Weeks v. Commonwealth, 248 Va. 460, 450 S.E.2d 379 (1994), cert. denied, 516 U.S. 829, 116 S. Ct. 100, 133 L. Ed. 2d 55 (1995).

Trial court did not err in refusing to allow defendant to call the father of one of the decedents as a witness to testify about remarks attributed to him by the news media to the effect that as a Christian he could not hope that jurors imposed the death penalty because the testimony did not fall within the scope of victim impact testimony authorized under § 19.2-299.1 and witness' opinion on what the jury should decide as the appropriate sentence in a given case was not admissible. Juniper v. Commonwealth, 271 Va. 362, 626 S.E.2d 383, 2006 Va. LEXIS 29 (2006).

The statutes do not limit evidence of victim impact to that received from the victim's family members; rather, the circumstances of the individual case will dictate what evidence will be necessary and relevant, and from what sources it may be drawn. Beck v. Commonwealth, 253 Va. 373, 484 S.E.2d 898, cert. denied, 522 U.S. 1018, 118 S. Ct. 608, 139 L. Ed. 2d 495 (1997).

Former girlfriend's psychological harm was the "direct result" of the felonies committed by defendant during a home intrusion, and the victim impact statement of the girlfriend was properly included in the pre-sentence report under subsection B of § 19.2-11.01 and § 19.2-299.1 as the goal of the home intrusion of the girlfriend's sibling was to force the girlfriend to come to that home and bring their child so that defendant could "blow her head off" with a shotgun defendant possessed; the girlfriend clearly suffered "psychological" harm as she "was scared to death" and "was waiting in horror to hear what happened" to her sibling and the sibling's family. Myers v. Commonwealth, 2008 Va. App. LEXIS 385 (Aug. 12, 2008).

Restitution may be ordered for insurer. — The statutes declare a legislative intent to provide restitution for the victims of crimes, including corporations. One cannot conclude that the legislature intended by the most recent legislation to limit the power of the courts to order restitution. Therefore, it was proper for the court in the instant case to order defendant burglar to pay restitution to insurance carrier of victims. Alger v. Commonwealth, 19 Va. App. 252, 450 S.E.2d 765 (1994).

Objection failed to preserve appellate issue. — Defendant objected to officers' testimony at the penalty phase of his trial based on relevance and prejudice, but the trial court was not presented with the issue of whether the officers were "victims" under the victim impact statute, § 19.2-299.1, and, thus, defendant's objection lacked the requisite specificity to preserve his appellate argument that the officers' testimony was inadmissible under that statute. Macklin v. Commonwealth, 2007 Va. App. LEXIS 269 (June 26, 2007).

§ 19.2-299.2. Alcohol and substance abuse screening and assessment for designated Class 1 misdemeanor convictions.

A. When a person is convicted of any offense committed on or after January 1, 2000, under Article 1 (§ 18.2-247 et seq.) or Article 1.1 (§ 18.2-265.1 et seq.) of Chapter 7 of Title 18.2, and such offense is punishable as a Class 1 misdemeanor, or when a person is convicted for a second offense of petit larceny, the court shall order the person to undergo a substance abuse screening as part of the sentence if the defendant's sentence includes probation supervision by a local community-based probation services agency established pursuant to Article 9 (§ 9.1-173 et seq.) of Chapter 1 of Title 9.1 or participation in a local alcohol safety action program. Whenever a court requires a person to enter into and successfully complete an alcohol safety action program pursuant to § 18.2-271.1 for a second offense of the type described therein, or orders an evaluation of a person to be conducted by an alcohol safety action program pursuant to any provision of § 46.2-391, the alcohol safety action program shall assess such person's degree of alcohol abuse before determining the appropriate level of treatment to be provided or to be recommended for such person being evaluated pursuant to § 46.2-391.

The court may order such screening upon conviction as part of the sentence of any other Class 1 misdemeanor if the defendant's sentence includes probation supervision by a local community-based probation services agency established pursuant to Article 9 (§ 9.1-173 et seq.) of Chapter 1 of Title 9.1, participation in a local alcohol safety action program or any other sanction and the court has reason to believe the defendant has a substance abuse or dependence problem.

B. A substance abuse screening ordered pursuant to this section shall be conducted by the local alcohol safety action program. When an offender is ordered to enter local community-based probation services established pursuant to Article 9 (§ 9.1-173 et seq.) of Chapter 1 of Title 9.1, rather than the local alcohol safety action program, the local community-based probation services agency shall be responsible for the screening. However, if a local community-based probation services agency has not been established for the locality, the local alcohol safety action program shall conduct the screening as part of the sentence.

C. If the screening indicates that the person has a substance abuse or dependence problem, an assessment shall be completed and if the assessment confirms that the person has a substance abuse or dependence problem, as a condition of a suspended sentence and probation, the court shall order the person to complete the substance abuse education and intervention component, or both as appropriate, of the local alcohol safety action program or such other agency providing treatment programs or services, if available, such as in the opinion of the court would be best suited to the needs of the person. If the referral is to the local alcohol safety action program, the program may charge a fee for the education and intervention component, or both, not to exceed $300, based upon the defendant's ability to pay.

History.
1998, cc. 783, 840; 1999, cc. 891, 913; 2000, cc. 958, 980, 1040; 2007, c. 133; 2008, c. 762.

Cross references.
As to punishment for Class 1 misdemeanors, see § 18.2-11.

Editor's note.
Acts 1998, cc. 783 and 840, cl. 2, provide: "That the provisions of this act amending or adding §§ 16.1-273, 18.2-251.01, 18.2-252, 19.2-299 and 19.2-299.2, except for subsection A(ii) of § 19.2-299.2, shall become effective July 1, 1999."

Acts 2000, cc. 958 and 980, cl. 3, provide: "That the provisions of this act shall be effective October 1, 2000."

The 2007 amendments.
The 2007 amendment by c. 133 substituted "community-based probation services agency" for "community-based probation program" in two places in subsections A and B; substituted "local community-based probation services" for "programming under the local community-based probation program" in the second sentence of subsection B; and in subsection C, in the first sentence, inserted "agency providing" following "such other" and "or services" following "treatment programs."

The 2008 amendments.
The 2008 amendment by c. 762 inserted "or when a person is convicted for a second offense of petit larceny" following "Class 1 Misdemeanor" in the first sentence in subsection A.

§ 19.2-300. Deferring for mental examination sentence of person convicted of offense indicating sexual abnormality.

In the case of the conviction in any circuit court of any person for any criminal offense which indicates sexual abnormality, the trial judge may on his own initiative, or shall upon application of the attorney for the Commonwealth, the defendant, or counsel for defendant or other person acting for the defendant, defer sentence until the report of a mental examination conducted as provided in § 19.2-301 of the defendant can be secured to guide the judge in determining what disposition shall be made of the defendant.

History.
Code 1950, § 53-278.2; 1950, p. 897; 1970, c. 62; 1975, c. 495; 1990, c. 697.

Law Review.
For a review of criminal law in Virginia for year 1999, see 33 U. Rich. L. Rev. 857 (1999).

Michie's Jurisprudence.
For related discussion, see 5B M.J. Criminal Procedure, § 70; 9B M.J. Incest, § 2; 10A M.J. Insane and Other Incompetent Persons, § 43; 15 M.J. Rape, § 27; 16 M.J. Sodomy, § 4.

CASE NOTES

"Sexual abnormality." — When dealing with sexually abnormal behavior, the Virginia legislature does not make a distinction between "force" and "violence." Simerly v. Commonwealth, 29 Va. App. 710, 514 S.E.2d 387 (1999).

If the question to be answered is whether the defendant's conduct indicates "sexual abnormality," the answer should never rest upon the victim's conduct. The victim's decision to avoid violence does not make the defendant's conduct any less "abnormal." Simerly v. Commonwealth, 29 Va. App. 710, 514 S.E.2d 387 (1999).

Defendant was convicted of an offense that "indicates sexual abnormality" where the record was replete with evidence that defendant used force to commit rape. Because the defendant's counsel requested that the court defer sentencing until he could be given a mental examination but the trial court refused, the case was reversed and remanded for resentencing after the receipt of the report of mental examination. Simerly v. Commonwealth, 29 Va. App. 710, 514 S.E.2d 387 (1999).

Mental evaluation not mandatory when imposing sentence for violation of probation. — Decision to order a mental examination under § 19.2-300 is not discretionary when a defendant who has been convicted of an offense indicating sexual abnormality requests such an evaluation prior to sentencing for that conviction; however, it is not mandatory before revoking a suspended sentence due to a probation violation, as the previously imposed sentence is merely being modified. Alsberry v. Commonwealth, 39 Va. App. 314, 572 S.E.2d 522, 2002 Va. App. LEXIS 721 (2002).

Trial court did not abuse its discretion in refusing to order a mental evaluation before imposing a sentence for defendant's probation violation; defendant could have requested an evaluation when he was first sentenced, but he did not do so, and this request was made during the hearing on his fourth probation violation, more than six years after defendant's abnormal behavior first came to light. Alsberry v. Commonwealth, 39 Va. App. 314, 572 S.E.2d 522, 2002 Va. App. LEXIS 721 (2002).

Scientific evidence in presentence report. — In order to admit scientific evidence in the risk assessment portion of the presentence report the Commonwealth had the burden of proving that a penile plethysmograph examination was a reliable scientific method of determining a convicted sex offender's risk to reoffend. Billips v. Commonwealth, 274 Va. 805, 652 S.E.2d 99, 2007 Va. LEXIS 122 (2007).

Applied in Justus v. Commonwealth, 220 Va. 471, 266 S.E.2d 87 (1980).

§ 19.2-301. Judge shall require examination under § 19.2-300; by whom made; report; expenses of psychiatrist.

The judge shall order the defendant examined by at least one psychiatrist or clinical psychologist who is qualified by specialized training and experience to perform such evaluations. Upon a finding by the court that a psychiatrist or clinical psychologist is not reasonably available for the instant case, the court may appoint a state licensed clinical social worker who has been certified by the Commonwealth as a sex offender treatment provider as defined in § 54.1-3600 and qualified by experience and by specialized training approved by the Commissioner of Behavioral Health and Developmental Services to perform such evaluations. The examination shall be performed on an outpatient basis at a mental health facility or in jail. However, if the court specifically finds that outpatient examination services are unavailable or if the results of outpatient examination indicate that hospitalization of the defendant for further examination is necessary, the court may order the defendant sent to a hospital designated by the Commissioner of Behavioral Health and Developmental Services as appropriate for examination of persons convicted of crimes. The defendant shall then be hospitalized for such time as the director of the hospital deems necessary to perform an adequate examination, but not to exceed 30 days from the date of admission to the hospital. Upon completion of the examination, the examiners shall prepare a written report of their findings and conclusions and shall furnish copies of such report to the defendant, counsel for the defendant, and the attorney for the Commonwealth at least five days prior to sentencing and shall furnish a copy of the report to the judge in advance of the sentencing hearing. The report of the examiners shall at all times be kept confidential by each recipient, except to the extent necessary for the prosecution or defense of any offense, and shall be filed as part of the record in the case and the defendant's copy shall be returned to the court at the conclusion of sentencing. Any report so filed shall be sealed upon the entry of the sentencing order by the court and made available only by court order, except that such report or copies thereof shall be available at any time to the office of the Attorney General for assessment for civil commitment as provided in Chapter 9 (§ 37.2-900 et seq.) of Title 37.2; any criminal justice agency, as defined in § 9.1-101, of this or any other state or of the United States; to any agency where the accused is referred for treatment by the court or by probation and parole services; and to counsel for any person who has been indicted jointly for the same felony as the person who is the subject of the report. Any such report shall without court order be made available to counsel for the person who is the subject of the report if that person is charged with a felony subsequent to the time of the preparation of the report.

History.
Code 1950, § 53-278.3; 1950, p. 898; 1970, c. 62; 1975, cc. 286, 495; 1990, c. 697; 2002, c. 662; 2003, c. 886; 2007, c. 440; 2009, cc. 813, 840.

Editor's note.
The above section is former § 53-278.3 as amended by Acts 1975, c. 286. Pursuant to Acts 1975, c. 593, cl. 2, it has been substituted for § 19.2-301 as enacted by Acts 1975, c. 495.

The 2007 amendments.
The 2007 amendment by c. 440 inserted the second sentence.

The 2009 amendments.
The 2009 amendments by cc. 813 and 840 are identical, and substituted "Commissioner of Behavioral Health and Developmental Services" for "Commissioner of Mental Health, Mental Retardation and Substance Abuse Services" in the second and fourth sentences.

Michie's Jurisprudence.
For related discussion, see 10A M.J. Insane and Other Incompetent Persons, § 43.

CASE NOTES

Applied in Justus v. Commonwealth, 220 Va. 471, 266 S.E.2d 87 (1980).

§ 19.2-302. Construction and administration of §§ 19.2-300 and 19.2-301.

Nothing contained in § 19.2-300 or 19.2-301 shall be construed to conflict with or repeal any statute in regard to the Department of Behavioral Health and Developmental Services, and such sections shall be administered with due regard to the authority of, and in cooperation with, the Commissioner of Behavioral Health and Developmental Services.

History.
Code 1950, § 53-278.4; 1950, p. 898; 1975, c. 495; 2009, cc. 813, 840.

The 2009 amendments.
The 2009 amendments by cc. 813 and 840 are identical, and substituted "Behavioral Health and Developmental Services" for "Mental Health, Mental Retardation and Substance Abuse Services" twice; and made a minor stylistic change.

Michie's Jurisprudence.

For related discussion, see 5B M.J. Criminal Procedure, § 70; 9B M.J. Incest, § 2.

§ 19.2-303. Suspension or modification of sentence; probation; taking of fingerprints and blood, saliva, or tissue sample as condition of probation.

After conviction, whether with or without jury, the court may suspend imposition of sentence or suspend the sentence in whole or part and in addition may place the defendant on probation under such conditions as the court shall determine, including monitoring by a GPS (Global Positioning System) tracking device, or other similar device, or may, as a condition of a suspended sentence, require the defendant to make at least partial restitution to the aggrieved party or parties for damages or loss caused by the offense for which convicted, or to perform community service, or both, under terms and conditions which shall be entered in writing by the court. The defendant may be ordered by the court to pay the cost of the GPS tracking device or other similar device. If, however, the court suspends or modifies any sentence fixed by a jury pursuant to § 19.2-295, the court shall file a statement of the reasons for the suspension or modification in the same manner as the statement required pursuant to subsection B of § 19.2-298.01. The judge, after convicting the defendant of a felony, shall determine whether a copy of the defendant's fingerprints are on file at the Central Criminal Records Exchange. In any case where fingerprints are not on file, the judge shall require that fingerprints be taken as a condition of probation. Such fingerprints shall be submitted to the Central Criminal Records Exchange under the provisions of subsection D of § 19.2-390.

In those courts having electronic access to the Local Inmate Data System (LIDS) within the courtroom, prior to or upon sentencing, the clerk of court shall also determine by reviewing LIDS whether a blood, saliva, or tissue sample has been taken for DNA analysis and submitted to the DNA data bank maintained by the Department of Forensic Science pursuant to Article 1.1 (§ 19.2-310.2 et seq.) of Chapter 18 of this title. In any case in which the clerk has determined that a DNA sample or analysis is not stored in the DNA data bank, or in any case in which electronic access to LIDS is not available in the courtroom, the court shall order that the defendant appear within 30 days before the sheriff or probation officer and allow the sheriff or probation officer to take the required sample. The order shall also require that, if the defendant has not appeared and allowed the sheriff or probation officer to take the required sample by the date stated in the order, then the sheriff or probation officer shall report to the court the defendant's failure to appear and provide the required sample.

After conviction and upon sentencing of an active participant or member of a criminal street gang, the court may, as a condition for suspending the imposition of the sentence in whole or in part or for placing the accused on probation, place reasonable restrictions on those persons with whom the accused may have contact. Such restrictions may include prohibiting the accused from having contact with anyone whom he knows to be a member of a criminal street gang, except that contact with a family or household member, as defined in § 16.1-228, shall be permitted unless expressly prohibited by the court.

In any case where a defendant is convicted of a violation of § 18.2-48, 18.2-61, 18.2-63, 18.2-67.1, 18.2-67.2, 18.2-67.3, 18.2-370, or 18.2-370.1, committed on or after July 1, 2006, and some portion of the sentence is suspended, the judge shall order that the period of suspension shall be for a length of time at least equal to the statutory maximum period for which the defendant might originally have been sentenced to be imprisoned, and the defendant shall be placed on probation for that period of suspension subject to revocation by the court. The conditions of probation may include such conditions as the court shall determine, including active supervision. Where the conviction is for a violation of clause (iii) of subsection A of § 18.2-61, subdivision A 1 of § 18.2-67.1, or subdivision A 1 of § 18.2-67.2, the court shall order that at least three years of the probation include active supervision of the defendant under a postrelease supervision program operated by the Department of Corrections, and for at least three years of such active supervision, the defendant shall be subject to electronic monitoring by means of a GPS (Global Positioning System) tracking device, or other similar device.

If a person is sentenced to jail upon conviction of a misdemeanor or a felony, the court may, at any time before the sentence has been completely served, suspend the unserved portion of any such sentence, place the person on probation for such time as the court shall determine, or otherwise modify the sentence imposed.

If a person has been sentenced for a felony to the Department of Corrections but has not actually been transferred to a receiving unit of the Department, the court which heard the case, if it appears compatible with the public interest and there are circumstances in mitigation of the offense, may, at any time before the person is transferred to the Department, suspend or otherwise modify the unserved portion of such a sentence. The court may place the person on probation for such time as the court shall determine.

History.

1975, c. 495; 1982, cc. 458, 636; 1983, c. 431; 1984, c. 32; 1992, c. 391; 1993, c. 448; 2006, cc. 436, 483, 853, 914; 2007, cc. 259, 528; 2011, cc. 799, 837.

The 2007 amendments.

The 2007 amendment by c. 259 added the second sentence in the first paragraph.

The 2007 amendment by c. 528 inserted "and blood, saliva, or tissue sample" in the section heading; and added the second paragraph.

The 2011 amendments.
The 2011 amendments by cc. 799 and 837 are identical, and in the first paragraph, inserted "including monitoring by a GPS (Global Positioning System) tracking device, or other similar device" in the first sentence, and added the second sentence.

Law Review.
For survey of Virginia law on criminal procedure for the year 1974-1975, see 61 Va. L. Rev. 1713 (1975). For article, "The Constitutionality of Harsher Sentences on Retrial in Virginia," see 62 Va. L. Rev. 1337 (1976). For survey of Virginia criminal procedure for the year 1975-1976, see 62 Va. L. Rev. 1412 (1976). For an article relating to all published Virginia criminal law decisions between July 1, 1997, and July 1, 1998, see 32 U. Rich. L. Rev. 1091 (1998). For 2006 survey article, "Criminal Law and Procedure," see 41 U. Rich. L. Rev. 83 (2006). For annual survey of Virginia law article, "Criminal Law and Procedure," see 47 U. Rich. L. Rev. 143 (2012).

Michie's Jurisprudence.
For related discussion, see 5B M.J. Criminal Procedure, §§ 70, 75, 76.

CASE NOTES

Editor's note.
Many of the cases cited in the following annotations were decided under former § 53-272.

I. In General.
II. Modification or Suspension of Sentence.
III. Conditions on Suspension or Probation.

I. IN GENERAL.

Constitutionality. — Statutes such as former § 53-272, which confer upon the trial court power to suspend sentences, are constitutional. Richardson v. Commonwealth, 131 Va. 802, 109 S.E. 460 (1921).

No infringement of pardoning power. — Former § 53-272, relating to suspension of sentence and placing on probation by the court, did not contravene the constitutional provisions vesting the pardoning power in the executive. Richardson v. Commonwealth, 131 Va. 802, 109 S.E. 460 (1921). See Wilborn v. Saunders, 170 Va. 153, 195 S.E. 723 (1938).

Legislative intent. — This section reflects the legislature's intent to provide for the review and suspension of sentences imposed for all felony convictions provided the defendant has not been sent to the Department of Corrections. Esparza v. Commonwealth, 29 Va. App. 600, 513 S.E.2d 885 (1999).

The legislature did not intend to limit the application of this section to cases of convictions obtained upon a plea of not guilty or an open plea entered without agreement. Esparza v. Commonwealth, 29 Va. App. 600, 513 S.E.2d 885 (1999).

Defendant did not show that an exception existed to the state supreme court rule that the trial court lacked jurisdiction to modify a sentence where the request was made more than 21 days after the sentencing order was entered; although § 19.2-303 provided for an exception to the state supreme court rule, the exception did not apply to defendant's case as it gave the trial court the power to "suspend or otherwise modify" a sentence before a defendant was sent to the Department of Corrections and the legislature did not intend that the trial court could "suspend" defendant's already suspended sentence. Patterson v. Commonwealth, 39 Va. App. 610, 575 S.E.2d 583, 2003 Va. App. LEXIS 34 (2003).

Purpose. — The purpose of former § 53-272 was to restore to a useful place in society an offender who is a good social risk. Slayton v. Commonwealth, 185 Va. 357, 38 S.E.2d 479 (1946).

Former § 53-272 was enacted to the end that the criminal might be reformed, so that he might be restored to a useful place in society and be self-sustaining thereafter. Wilborn v. Saunders, 170 Va. 153, 195 S.E. 723 (1938).

Both this section and § 19.2-306 serve the same rehabilitative purpose. Esparza v. Commonwealth, 29 Va. App. 600, 513 S.E.2d 885 (1999).

Liberal construction. — Former § 53-272 was highly remedial and should be liberally construed. Richardson v. Commonwealth, 131 Va. 802, 109 S.E. 460 (1921); Dyke v. Commonwealth, 193 Va. 478, 69 S.E.2d 483 (1952).

The statutes obviously confer upon trial courts wide latitude and much discretion in matters of suspension and probation to provide a remedial tool in the rehabilitation of criminals and, to that end, should be liberally construed. Wright v. Commonwealth, 32 Va. App. 148, 526 S.E.2d 784, appeal dismissed, 261 Va. 1, 539 S.E.2d 432 (2000).

Due process. — The imposition of postrelease periods of suspended incarceration and supervision pursuant to this section and § 19.2-295.2 does not violate any due process right of a defendant to be sentenced by a jury. Boyd v. Commonwealth, 28 Va. App. 537, 507 S.E.2d 107 (1998).

Applicable to plea agreements. — There is nothing in the statutory scheme as articulated by the legislature to suggest the post-sentencing rehabilitative purposes and goals of this section are inapplicable to felons convicted pursuant to a plea agreement. Esparza v. Commonwealth, 29 Va. App. 600, 513 S.E.2d 885 (1999).

Alternative dispositions. — Former § 53-272 provided two alternatives: (1) that the convicted person may be placed on probation conditioned upon his good behavior for a definite period until the further order of the court; and (2) that his sentence may be suspended without any express limitation as to the duration of the suspension. White v. Commonwealth, 170 Va. 641, 196 S.E. 610 (1938).

This section did not authorize a trial court to vacate a previous conviction if defendant complied with conditions that may have been imposed upon defendant for the suspension of the imposition of defendant's sentence. Epps v. Commonwealth, 59 Va. App. 71, 717 S.E.2d 151, 2011 Va. App. LEXIS 351 (2011).

Not applicable to request for new trial. — This section applies to a request for sentence modification when a prisoner has not been transferred to the department of corrections rather than a request for a new trial. Hillman v. Commonwealth, No. 2194-93-4 (Ct. of Appeals May 16, 1995).

Jurisdiction. — Commonwealth was incorrect that the court lacked jurisdiction because § 19.2-303 gave the trial court jurisdiction over all felony convictions provided that defendant had not been sent to the Department of Corrections. To the extent that the Commonwealth challenged the merits of the motion to reconsider on the basis that a purely legal argument could not constitute circumstances in mitigation of the offense, that argument did not need to be reached because the trial court denied the motion to reconsider without reaching its merits, reiterating that the evidence that defendant wanted to present had no bearing on the sentences that it imposed. Pagan v. Commonwealth, 2011 Va. App. LEXIS 7 (Jan. 11, 2011).

Final judgment subject to review. — After the trial court has adjudged the defendant guilty and has suspended either the imposition or the execution of sentence, or commitment of the defendant, and has fixed the terms of his probation, it has made a complete disposition of the case within the purview of the statute. Its action is then final and subject to review. The happening of an event, which brings into operation the right of revocation, does not alter the finality of the judgment previously entered. Fuller v. Commonwealth, 189 Va. 327, 53 S.E.2d 26 (1949).

A final judgment is not obtained when the judge overrules a motion for a new trial, and adjudges the defendant guilty but suspends imposition of sentence pending a report from the probation officer and in order to permit the defendant to perfect his appeal. Fuller v. Commonwealth, 189 Va. 327, 53 S.E.2d 26 (1949).

Final disposition not found. — Initial order finding that the evidence supported a determination of guilt against defendant for violating § 58.1-1815 regarding the failure to pay withholding tax was not a conviction and did not impose a sentence. Instead that order continued the case and deferred final disposition for nearly a year, which meant that defendant could not claim that the trial court in its initial order entered a suspended sentence regarding defendant pursuant to § 19.2-303 because that statute applied only after a conviction and the initial order did not enter a conviction or sentence. Gibson v. Commonwealth, 276 Va. 176, 662 S.E.2d 54, 2008 Va. LEXIS 86 (2008).

Appeal from order where sentence is suspended. — A sentencing order entered by a trial court is a complete disposition of the case, even if the order suspends the imposition of sentence, and is, thus, a final, appealable order. Oliver v. Commonwealth, 35 Va. App. 286, 544 S.E.2d 870, 2001 Va. App. LEXIS 196 (2001).

Orders of suspension and probation with regard to sentences on several convictions of grand larceny spoke as of the day they were entered, and the defendant's probation ran from that date. There was no merit in the Commonwealth's contention that by virtue of former § 19.1-294 (now § 19.2-308) the defendant was placed on probation for successive periods. Vick v. Commonwealth, 201 Va. 474, 111 S.E.2d 824 (1960).

Applied in Stamper v. Commonwealth, 228 Va. 707, 324 S.E.2d 682 (1985); Anderson v. Commonwealth, 25 Va. App. 565, 490 S.E.2d 274 (1997); Rogers v. Commonwealth, 29 Va. App. 580, 513 S.E.2d 876 (1999); Reinke v. Commonwealth, 51 Va. App. 357, 657 S.E.2d 805, 2008 Va. App. LEXIS 111 (2008).

II. MODIFICATION OR SUSPENSION OF SENTENCE.

This section invests courts with discretionary authority to modify a sentence post-conviction in all felony cases, including those in which the defendant has been sentenced pursuant to a plea agreement so long as the defendant is in the local jail and has not been delivered to the Department of Corrections. Esparza v. Commonwealth, 29 Va. App. 600, 513 S.E.2d 885 (1999).

Trial court did not err in modifying defendant's sentence to impose the same sentence on defendant's first habitual petit larceny conviction as it did on defendant's other habitual petit larceny conviction, as the trial court had the statutory authority to modify the sentence, defendant's sentence could be modified because defendant was in jail and not in the Department of Correction, modification conformed defendant's sentence to defendant's plea bargain and the trial court's sentencing intent, and the modification was not entered more than 21 days after entry of a final sentencing order. Hilleary v. Commonwealth, No. 0423-02-4, 2003 Va. App. LEXIS 144 (Ct. of Appeals Mar. 18, 2003).

Circuit court retained jurisdiction under § 19.2-303 to modify defendant's sentences even though an appeal was pending because the requirements of § 19.2-303 were met at the time the circuit court addressed the motion. Harris v. Commonwealth, 57 Va. App. 205, 700 S.E.2d 475, 2010 Va. App. LEXIS 422 (2010).

This section operated as a statutory exception to Va. Sup. Ct. R. 1:1, and where the requirements of § 19.2-303 were satisfied, the trial court retained jurisdiction to modify defendant's sentences even after twenty-one days from entry of the final order because defendant had not yet been transferred to the Department of Corrections. Harris v. Commonwealth, 57 Va. App. 205, 700 S.E.2d 475, 2010 Va. App. LEXIS 422 (2010).

Convicted criminal entitled to decision on sentence by jury and by judge. — Under the practice in this State, the convicted criminal defendant is entitled to "two decisions" on the sentence, one by the jury and the other by the trial judge in the exercise of his statutory right to suspend. Vines v. Muncy, 553 F.2d 342 (4th Cir.), cert. denied, 434 U.S. 851, 98 S. Ct. 163, 54 L. Ed. 2d 120 (1977).

His ultimate sentence does not therefore rest with the jury alone, but is always subject to the control of the trial judge. Vines v. Muncy, 553 F.2d 342 (4th Cir.), cert. denied, 434 U.S. 851, 98 S. Ct. 163, 54 L. Ed. 2d 120 (1977).

Under the practice in this State, the punishment as fixed by the jury is not final or absolute, since its finding on the proper punishment is subject to suspension by the trial judge, in whole or in part, on the basis of any mitigating facts that the convicted defendant can marshal. Vines v. Muncy, 553 F.2d 342 (4th Cir.), cert. denied, 434 U.S. 851, 98 S. Ct. 163, 54 L. Ed. 2d 120 (1977).

Any criticism of jury sentencing on the ground that it lacks the objectivity and principled decision of a judge is overcome by the existence of the power in the trial judge to bring his so-called superior judgment to bear upon the issue of proper punishment in reaching his decision whether to suspend the sentence or not. Vines v. Muncy, 553 F.2d 342 (4th Cir.), cert. denied, 434 U.S. 851, 98 S. Ct. 163, 54 L. Ed. 2d 120 (1977).

The verdict of the jury is the fixing of maximum punishment which may be served. Vines v. Muncy, 553 F.2d 342 (4th Cir.),

cert. denied, 434 U.S. 851, 98 S. Ct. 163, 54 L. Ed. 2d 120 (1977).

While a trial judge may have the authority under this section to reduce a jury's recommended sentence, he or she does not have the authority to impose a sentence greater than the one recommended by the jury. Batts v. Commonwealth, 30 Va. App. 1, 515 S.E.2d 307 (1999).

There is no right to have the jury determine whether a sentence should be suspended. Virginia ex rel. Shifflett v. Cook, 333 F. Supp. 718 (W.D. Va. 1971).

Suspension conditioned on waiver of Fourth Amendment rights. — The sole statutory limitation placed upon a trial court's discretion in its determination of conditions for suspending sentence is one of reasonableness and the court acted reasonably and within its discretion when it conditioned the suspension of the defendant's sentence on his waiver of his Fourth Amendment right against unreasonable searches and seizures for one year. Anderson v. Commonwealth, 256 Va. 580, 507 S.E.2d 339 (1998).

Consideration of mitigation left to court. — By vesting the trial court with discretionary authority to suspend or modify the sentence imposed by the jury, the legislature intended to leave the consideration of mitigating circumstances to the court. Duncan v. Commonwealth, 2 Va. App. 342, 343 S.E.2d 392 (1986).

Circumstances in mitigation of offense. — Defendant failed to present evidence that would have justified a modification or suspension of her sentence under § 19.2-303 because the new evidence that she presented to the trial court was not evidence in mitigation of the offense within the meaning of § 19.2-303 since the evidence was only relevant to defendant's guilt or innocence; "circumstances in mitigation of the offense" under § 19.2-303, does not include evidence that bears solely on the question of guilt or innocence because § 19.2-303 clearly provides that the only remedy that may be utilized in light of the mitigating circumstances is modification or suspension of the defendant's sentence. Wilson v. Commonwealth, 54 Va. App. 631, 681 S.E.2d 74, 2009 Va. App. LEXIS 363 (2009).

As to distinction between suspension of sentence and probation, see Dyke v. Commonwealth, 193 Va. 478, 69 S.E.2d 483 (1952).

Suspension and probation distinguished. — This section, § 19.2-304 and former § 53-272 distinguish between a suspension, either of imposition of sentence or of execution of sentence, on the one hand, and probation, on the other. Grant v. Commonwealth, 223 Va. 680, 292 S.E.2d 348 (1982).

"Suspension of sentence" means either delay in its imposition or the staying of its execution. It is not a pardon, excuse, immunity, or relief from the punishment, but a mere suspension, or postponement, of its execution. Richardson v. Commonwealth, 131 Va. 802, 109 S.E. 460 (1921).

When defendant pled guilty to an offense and the trial court withheld a finding of guilt, and defendant was subsequently convicted of another offense, the trial court could enter an order nunc pro tunc to the prior proceedings finding defendant guilty of the offense to which he pled guilty, sentencing him to a suspended sentence, and revoking that suspension as to part of the sentence. Jefferson v. Commonwealth, No. 2301-02-2, 2004 Va. App. LEXIS 18 (Ct. of Appeals Jan. 13, 2004), aff'd, — Va. —, 607 S.E.2d 107 (2005).

And lies in the court's discretion. — The suspension of a sentence is left to the discretion of the trial court. Slayton v. Commonwealth, 185 Va. 357, 38 S.E.2d 479 (1946). See also Abdo v. Commonwealth, 218 Va. 473, 237 S.E.2d 900 (1977).

Suspension of a sentence is a matter of the trial court's discretion rather than the jury's. Virginia ex rel. Shifflett v. Cook, 333 F. Supp. 718 (W.D. Va. 1971).

The attorney for the Commonwealth may agree to recommend suspension. — An attorney for the Commonwealth may properly confer with the accused and his attorney, and in appropriate cases agree to recommend to the judge the exercise of his power to suspend a sentence. But the attorney for the Commonwealth can make no agreement which will bind the judge, and the appropriate action must be at last determined by the judge himself, though he will generally adopt such recommendation. Richardson v. Commonwealth, 131 Va. 802, 109 S.E. 460 (1921).

But the trial judge cannot enter into a binding agreement with the prisoner to excuse him forever from the penalties of his crime. When a trial judge suspends a sentence he does not make a contract with the accused, but only extends to him the opportunity which the State affords to repent and reform. Richardson v. Commonwealth, 131 Va. 802, 109 S.E. 460 (1921).

The rule that a court cannot amend a final judgment or order, after the adjournment of the term, has no application to an order suspending a sentence upon accused and discharging him from custody until the further order of the court. When the execution of a sentence was thus suspended, under former § 53-272, the case remained pending and the court did not thereby lose its control over the accused or his case. Richardson v. Commonwealth, 131 Va. 802, 109 S.E. 460 (1921).

No modification of sentencing order after felon released on parole. — Trial judge may not modify a sentencing order after a convicted felon has been released by the Department of Corrections on parole and impose for the first time a requirement of probation. Russnak v. Commonwealth, 10 Va. App. 317, 392 S.E.2d 491 (1990).

Modification allowed where defendant was never in custody of the Virginia Department of Corrections. — Trial court retained jurisdiction to modify defendant's sentence under the § 19.2-303 exception to Va. Sup. Ct. R. 1:1 while he was in the custody of the Federal Bureau of Prisons as defendant had never actually been in the custody of the Virginia Department of Corrections. Neely v. Commonwealth, 44 Va. App. 239, 604 S.E.2d 733, 2004 Va. App. LEXIS 530 (2004), aff'd, 271 Va. 1, 624 S.E.2d 657 (2006).

Circuit court did not lose jurisdiction to consider defendant's motion to modify his sentence under § 19.2-303 because time limitations imposed by Va. Sup. Ct. R. 1:1 did not impact jurisdiction where defendant had not been transferred to the Virginia Department of Corrections but had been in a federal correctional institution for crimes committed while he was on supervised probation relating to a suspended two-year state sentence for possession of cocaine. Commonwealth v. Neely, 271 Va. 1, 624 S.E.2d 657, 2006 Va. LEXIS 8 (2006).

Trial court erred in denying defendant's motion to suspend or modify sentence under § 19.2-303 on the ground that it did not have jurisdiction to entertain the motion because the trial court had jurisdiction to entertain the motion when defendant had been convicted of a felony and not yet transferred to the Department of Corrections; however, the error was harmless because defendant failed to present evidence that would have justified a modification or suspension of her sentence under § 19.2-303. Wilson v. Commonwealth, 54 Va. App. 631, 681 S.E.2d 74, 2009 Va. App. LEXIS 363 (2009).

Trial judge did not have authority to modify defendant's sentence pursuant to this section since the record did not disclose whether defendant had been transferred to the Department of Corrections when the trial judge overruled her motion on March 5, 1991; since the burden of proving appellate jurisdiction rested upon the defendant, defendant failed to prove on the record that the trial judge had authority to act and that her appeal was timely. D'Alessandro v. Commonwealth, 15 Va. App. 163, 423 S.E.2d 199 (1992).

In absence of proof that defendant had not yet been transferred to department of corrections, and in light of proof to the contrary, trial judge had no authority to modify defendant's sentences to run concurrently. Johnson v. Commonwealth, No. 0348-98-4 (Ct. of Appeals June 22, 1999).

Once a defendant has been transferred to the Department of Corrections and 21 days have passed since the court's last order, the court can no longer use § 19.2-303 to modify a sentence. A trial court improperly entered an amended sentencing order more than 21 days after entry of a sentencing order on revocation of a defendant's probation because the evidence showed defendant was in custody of the Department of Corrections. Ziats v. Commonwealth, 42 Va. App. 133, 590 S.E.2d 117, 2003 Va. App. LEXIS 701 (2003).

Because defendant received a fully suspended sentence and was not going to be transferred to the Department of Corrections at any time after his sentencing, the trial court did not have jurisdiction to modify defendant's suspended sentence under § 19.2-303. Smith v. Commonwealth, — Va. App. —, — S.E.2d —, 2008 Va. App. LEXIS 238 (May 20, 2008).

Trial court properly found that it had no authority under § 19.2-303 to modify defendant's sentence where he had already been transferred to the Virginia Department of Corrections because the legislature in § 19.2-303 had created an absolute event when a trial court could no longer modify a sentence and clearly limited the authority of the trial court to do so. The statute contained no exceptions. Stokes v. Commonwealth, 61 Va. App. 388, 736 S.E.2d 330, 2013 Va. App. LEXIS 17 (2013).

When read in conjunction with Va. Sup. Ct. R. 1:1, Va. Code Ann. § 19.2-303 establishes an absolute event, i.e., a transfer to the Virginia Department of Corrections, when a trial court can no longer modify a sentence. Because § 19.2-303 clearly allows a court to modify an unserved portion of a sentence any time before a person is transferred to the Department of Corrections, the operative date in question is when the court makes its ruling, not when the motion is filed, and not when the matter initially comes before the court. Stokes v. Commonwealth, 61 Va. App. 388, 736 S.E.2d 330, 2013 Va. App. LEXIS 17 (2013).

Court lacked authority to lengthen incarceration. — It was true that both the first and third orders fixed the grand larceny and burglary sentences to run consecutively. However, the second order providing that those sentences run concurrently became final under Rule 1:1 more than a year before the third order was entered. While the trial court still retained power under this section to modify the sentences in consideration of "circumstances in mitigation of the offense", the court had no authority to lengthen the period of incarceration. Robertson v. Superintendent of Wise Correctional Unit, 248 Va. 232, 445 S.E.2d 116 (1994).

Suspension must be ordered within 21 days of sentencing order. — Reading Rule 1:1 and former § 53-272 together, after the expiration of 21 days from the sentencing order if a defendant convicted of a felony has been committed and delivered to the state correctional facility and no order has been entered within 21 days after final judgment suspending the sentence, the trial court has no further authority to suspend the sentence. In re Commonwealth, Dep't of Cors., 222 Va. 454, 281 S.E.2d 857 (1981).

And taking motion under advisement is insufficient. — In view of Rule 1:1 and former § 53-272, where the trial court took under advisement motions to set aside the verdicts and judgments and to suspend or modify all or part of the sentences of defendants convicted of drug-related offenses within 21 days of the entry of sentencing orders, the court did not "modify, vacate, or suspend" the judgments, and, therefore, the motions and the orders entered thereon did not affect the finality of the sentencing orders and the court lost jurisdiction to act on the motions to suspend at the end of the 21-day period and delivery of the defendants to the state correctional facility. In re Commonwealth, Dep't of Cors., 222 Va. 454, 281 S.E.2d 857 (1981).

Order to suspend a sentence entered more than 21 days after sentencing. — Trial court acted properly when it suspended a sentence it imposed on defendant to hear defendant's motion to modify the sentence, even though the order suspending defendant's sentence was entered more than 21 days after defendant was sentenced to incarceration in the Virginia Department of Corrections, because defendant was still incarcerated in a county jail. Baldwin v. Commonwealth, 43 Va. App. 415, 598 S.E.2d 754, 2004 Va. App. LEXIS 309 (2004).

Use of writ of prohibition to bar suspension. — The Department of Corrections had standing to seek a writ of prohibition barring the trial court from ordering the release from custody and suspension of sentences of prisoners convicted of drug-related offenses, and still held in custody, where the trial court had taken under advisement the motions of the prisoners within 21 days of the entry of sentencing orders, but had not ordered the judgments modified, vacated or suspended within the 21-day period. In re Commonwealth, Dep't of Cors., 222 Va. 454, 281 S.E.2d 857 (1981).

A writ of prohibition could not be used to revoke the releases of prisoners from custody and the suspension of their sentences, even if the orders of the trial court were improperly entered for failure of the court to act within 21 days of entry of sentencing orders and before delivery to the state correctional facility, since the writ of prohibition is not available to correct errors already committed. In re Commonwealth, Dep't of Cors., 222 Va. 454, 281 S.E.2d 857 (1981).

Extended probation modified. — Defendant's extended probation imposed upon him as a condition of the suspension of his sentence was modified as the trial court had specified no period of probation. Hartless v. Commonwealth, 29 Va. App. 172, 510 S.E.2d 738 (1999).

Trial judge did not have authority to modify defendant's sentence. — Although a trial court normally retained jurisdiction for a certain time period over certain judgments, orders, and decrees, it did not have jurisdiction over defendant's motion to reduce his sentence as defendant's earlier concession that he had already been transferred to a Virginia Department of Corrections facility meant that the trial court was divested, at the time of the transfer, of its authority, pursuant to § 19.2-303, to retain jurisdiction over his case. Chilton v. Commonwealth, No. 0789-02-2, 2004 Va. App. LEXIS 38 (Ct. of Appeals Jan. 28, 2004).

Sentencing court lacked jurisdiction under this section to modify defendant's amended sentence or to reconsider the court's denial of defendant's motion to withdraw his guilty plea where: (1) the sentencing court properly vacated the portion of its original sentencing order that was in excess of the statutory maximum in § 18.2-181 and sentenced defendant to the statutory maximum, (2) the sentencing court properly vacated that portion of the original sentencing order that ordered a probation officer to set restitution and set a restitution amount as was required by subsection C of § 19.2-305.1, (3) otherwise, the original sentencing order remained a valid final order, and (4) defendant had been transferred to the Virginia Department of Corrections and his motions were filed more than 21 days after entry of the original sentencing order. McKenney v. Commonwealth, Nos. 3330-02-2, 0473-03-2, 2004 Va. App. LEXIS 157 (Ct. of Appeals Apr. 6, 2004).

Trial court properly held that it did not have jurisdiction to modify defendant's sentence under Rule 1:1 and § 19.2-303, as more than 21 days had passed since the sentence was imposed, and defendant had been transferred to the custody of the Virginia Department of Corrections (DOC); there was no exception that would allow the trial court to retain jurisdiction even though defendant's transfer to the DOC occurred in violation of the trial court's order retaining custody of defendant in the local jail for some indefinite period of time. Coe v. Commonwealth, No. 3293-02-2, 2004 Va. App. LEXIS 181 (Ct. of Appeals Mar. 2, 2004).

Sentencing order void ab initio. — Sentencing order was a final order under Va. Sup. Ct. R. 1:1 as it adjudicated guilt, imposed a sentence, remanded defendant to the sheriff's custody, and required that defendant register as a sex offender on his release; the sentencing order was void ab initio because § 19.2-303 did not authorize the trial court to reduce defendant's conviction from a felony to a misdemeanor after he had served the active portion of the sentence. The doctrine of invited error did not bar defendant's motion to vacate the sentencing order. Burrell v. Commonwealth, 283 Va. 474, 722 S.E.2d 272, 2012 Va. LEXIS 50 (2012).

Defendant did not prove jurisdiction. — Defendant had not shown that the trial court had jurisdiction to modify his sentence under § 19.2-303. His motion had been filed over 21 days from the entry of the final order, and neither the motion nor the record indicated that defendant had not yet been transferred to the Department of Corrections at the time the motion was filed. Monk v. Commonwealth, — Va. App. —, — S.E.2d —, 2007 Va. App. LEXIS 378 (Oct. 9, 2007).

No abuse of discretion in refusing to modify sentence imposed. — Because defendant never voiced any objection to the sentences imposed against him after entering guilty pleas to two indictments charging distribution of cocaine pursuant to a plea agreement, the trial court's denial of defendant's motion to modify the sentences was upheld on appeal. The appellate court found no abuse of discretion on the part of the trial court in failing to modify defendant's sentences since defendant responded to the trial court's questions regarding the plea agreement, found that it was voluntarily entered into, that defendant never voiced any objections, and because the sentences did not exceed the maximum allowable. Russell v. Commonwealth, — Va. App. —, — S.E.2d —, 2005 Va. App. LEXIS 263 (July 5, 2005).

III. CONDITIONS ON SUSPENSION OR PROBATION.

Power to place conditions on suspension. — Inherent in the power granted under this section and former § 53-272 to support imposition or execution is the power to place conditions on such suspension. Grant v. Commonwealth, 223 Va. 680, 292 S.E.2d 348 (1982).

Trial court was authorized to place conditions on that part of

defendant's sentence that was suspended, including lifetime probation under certain conditions, and, thus, the trial court did not err in placing conditions on defendant's suspended sentence that included lifetime probation in a case where defendant pled guilty to seven felonies arising out of the accidental shooting of a friend, as defendant could have received up to 105 years in prison and only received 65 years with 35 years of those suspended based on certain conditions, including the lifetime probation. Lathram v. Commonwealth, — Va. App. —, — S.E.2d —, 2006 Va. App. LEXIS 168 (May 2, 2006).

Good behavior is a condition of every suspension, with or without probation, whether expressly so stated or not. Coffey v. Commonwealth, 209 Va. 760, 167 S.E.2d 343 (1969).

Even though the language of the suspension does not in terms include a condition of good behavior, that condition is implicit in every such suspension whether with or without probation and whether or not expressly so stated and constitutes the origin and purpose of the suspension and probation statutes. Marshall v. Commonwealth, 202 Va. 217, 116 S.E.2d 270 (1960).

While the language of the suspensions did not in terms include a condition of good behavior, that condition is implicit in every such suspension and constitutes the origin and purpose of the suspension and probation statutes. When a trial court suspends a sentence it does not make a contract with the accused, but only extends to him the opportunity which the State affords him to repent and reform. Coffey v. Commonwealth, 209 Va. 760, 167 S.E.2d 343 (1969); Brown v. Slayton, 342 F. Supp. 61 (W.D. Va. 1972).

When defendant received a suspended sentence after pleading guilty, an implicit condition of that suspension was that he maintain good behavior, so, when he was subsequently convicted of another offense, his suspended sentence could be revoked. Jefferson v. Commonwealth, No. 2301-02-2, 2004 Va. App. LEXIS 18 (Ct. of Appeals Jan. 13, 2004), aff'd, — Va. —, 607 S.E.2d 107 (2005).

The first clause of this section gives broad power to the trial court to determine the conditions of a suspended sentence. Waiters v. Commonwealth, 33 Va. App. 739, 536 S.E.2d 923, 2000 Va. App. LEXIS 735 (2000).

The only limitation placed upon the discretion of the trial court in its determination of what conditions are to be imposed is that a condition be "reasonable." Jackson v. Commonwealth, 29 Va. App. 418, 512 S.E.2d 838 (1999).

The only limitation placed upon the discretion of the trial court is that the conditions of suspension must be reasonable in relation to the nature of the offense, the background of the offender and the surrounding circumstances. Waiters v. Commonwealth, 33 Va. App. 739, 536 S.E.2d 923, 2000 Va. App. LEXIS 735 (2000).

Restitution. — Trial court erred in requiring defendant to pay, as a condition of his suspended sentence, restitution that included the cost of the installation of a security system installed by the burglary victims after the burglary because, while related to defendant's burglary, the installation of a security system was not caused by the offense, and the attenuation was too great. Howell v. Commonwealth, 274 Va. 737, 652 S.E.2d 107, 2007 Va. LEXIS 121 (2007).

Restitution. — Under § 19.2-303 restitution was limited to damages caused by the offense; therefore, the trial court abused its discretion when it ordered defendant to pay restitution related to an "indirect" financial loss that occurred when a pipe burst inside a victim's home while the victim was convalescing elsewhere. Maye v. Commonwealth, 2011 Va. App. LEXIS 40 (Feb. 8, 2011).

Trial court did not abuse its discretion, pursuant to § 19.2-303, subsection B of § 19.2-305, and subsection A of § 19.2-305.1, by the amount of a restitution ordered because the finding by the trial court that the Commonwealth of Virginia Department of Medical Assistance Services received no value from the services rendered to Medicaid-eligible clients by defendant's employee, who actually had no training to be a personal care aide, was not plainly wrong or unsupported by the evidence. Burriesci v. Commonwealth, 59 Va. App. 50, 717 S.E.2d 140, 2011 Va. App. LEXIS 344 (2011).

Impact statement may be source for restitution amount. — The legislature intended that the victim impact statement be used by trial judge to determine the amount of restitution. Alger v. Commonwealth, 19 Va. App. 252, 450 S.E.2d 765 (1994).

Restitution may be ordered for insurer. — The statutes declare a legislative intent to provide restitution for the victims of crimes, including corporations. One cannot conclude that the legislature intended by the most recent legislation to limit the power of the courts to order restitution. Therefore, it was proper for the court in the instant case to order burglar to pay restitution to insurance carrier of victims. Alger v. Commonwealth, 19 Va. App. 252, 450 S.E.2d 765 (1994).

Return of sum paid by undercover agent as appropriate restitution. — A trial court's order that a defendant convicted of distribution of marijuana return the exact sum an undercover agent had paid the defendant for the illegal drugs was a reasonable and appropriate exercise of the court's discretion; at a minimum, the requirement prevented the defendant from profiting from the crime he committed. Waiters v. Commonwealth, 33 Va. App. 739, 536 S.E.2d 923, 2000 Va. App. LEXIS 735 (2000).

Supervised probation on resuspension of sentence. — The trial court had implicit statutory authority under § 19.2-306 to place defendant on supervised probation as a condition of resuspending the 1989 sentence, and it did not impermissibly modify or extend the 1989 sentencing order in violation of Va. Sup. Ct. R. 1:1, or its exceptions in § 19.2-303. Harrison v. Commonwealth, No. 0556-04-2, 2005 Va. App. LEXIS 115 (Ct. of Appeals Mar. 22, 2005).

Incarceration as condition of suspension. — Trial court had the authority to impose a period of incarceration as a condition of suspending the execution of a five-year penitentiary sentence. Nuckoles v. Commonwealth, 12 Va. App. 1083, 407 S.E.2d 355 (1991).

Submission to court-ordered child support upheld as condition. — That part of defendant's sentence, conditioning the suspension of part of said sentence on his submission to court-ordered child support, was upheld on appeal, and found not to be an abuse of the trial court's wide latitude afforded under § 19.2-303, as such was an important aspect of his rehabilitation and reintegration into his community. Martin v. Commonwealth, — Va. App. —, — S.E.2d —, 2006 Va. App. LEXIS 602 (Dec. 19, 2006).

Enforcement of probationary requirement. — A court's ability to revoke the suspension of a sentence and to impose that sentence permits it to enforce a probationary requirement as a condition of suspension. Hartless v. Commonwealth, 29 Va. App. 172, 510 S.E.2d 738 (1999).

Altering conditions of suspended sentence. — Court could remove a good behavior requirement as a probation condition but lacked jurisdiction to alter good behavior and related provisions imposed as conditions of the suspension of a sentence more than 21 days after entry of a sentencing order. McFarland v. Commonwealth, 39 Va. App. 511, 574 S.E.2d 311, 2002 Va. App. LEXIS 770 (2002).

When a trial court had subject matter jurisdiction over defendant's 1998 hearing to revoke his suspended sentence and extended defendant's period of suspension, the trial court did not err in revoking defendant's suspended sentence in 2010, pursuant to subsection A of § 19.2-306, because the suspension took place within the fourteen-year period established in the 1998 sentencing order; defendant was not entitled to collaterally attack the 1998 sentencing order because the order was not void. Dunham v. Commonwealth, 59 Va. App. 634, 721 S.E.2d 824, 2012 Va. App. LEXIS 49 (2012).

To be effective, probation must be concurrent with coordinate term of suspension of sentence. Hartless v. Commonwealth, 29 Va. App. 172, 510 S.E.2d 738 (1999).

Probation period. — Probation depends for enforceability upon the existence of a term of sentence suspension; therefore, the duration of probation cannot extend beyond the specified period of suspension. Hartless v. Commonwealth, 29 Va. App. 172, 510 S.E.2d 738 (1999).

Probation can be directed only under supervision of probation officers. — The probation of defendants in criminal cases can be directed and exercised only under the supervision of probation officers, duly appointed and qualified. Bryant v. Commonwealth, 198 Va. 148, 93 S.E.2d 130 (1956).

And a verbal order directing a husband to assist in the probation of his wife is wholly void and of no legal or binding force or effect. Bryant v. Commonwealth, 198 Va. 148, 93 S.E.2d 130 (1956).

Effect of acceptance of plea agreement. — Acceptance of defendant's plea agreement, which provided that the trial court would impose sentence on two counts of aggravated sexual battery and would withhold decision on the other two counts, did not divest

the trial court of its jurisdiction to adjudicate the charges. Holden v. Commonwealth, 26 Va. App. 403, 494 S.E.2d 892 (1998).

Effect of compliance by accused. — When the accused has complied with conditions specified, he has a right to rely upon them, and the suspension will stand. Griffin v. Cunningham, 205 Va. 349, 136 S.E.2d 840 (1964); Hamilton v. Commonwealth, 217 Va. 325, 228 S.E.2d 555 (1976).

Failure to comply. — A court which has ordered a suspension of sentence undoubtedly has the power to revoke it when the defendant has failed to comply with the conditions of the suspension. Griffin v. Cunningham, 205 Va. 349, 136 S.E.2d 840 (1964).

Where the trial court imposed a condition upon a probation to enter and successfully complete a Detention Center Incarceration Program, and while such might have been a condition of probation, merely entering the program was a prerequisite to and one of the conditions upon which the probationer's sentence was suspended; when he could no longer satisfy this condition, the court was authorized to reconsider the suspended sentences and determine what portion of the same or other alternatives were appropriate. Word v. Commonwealth, 41 Va. App. 496, 586 S.E.2d 282, 2003 Va. App. LEXIS 485 (2003).

Trial court did not abuse its discretion by imposing the entire original sentences that had been suspended against a defendant upon revocation of the suspended sentences, because § 19.2-306 did not provide a trial court with any discretion as to imposing the entire original sentence or a portion of the same upon revocation. As such, the trial court's imposition of the entire 26 years of imprisonment against the defendant was proper, because his suspended sentences were revoked due to his failure to report to his probation officer, his failure to make restitution, and his subsequent conviction for larceny. Commonwealth v. Payne, — Va. —, — S.E.2d —, 2003 Va. LEXIS 117 (July 11, 2003).

Showing performance of condition of suspension. — Where sentence is suspended upon the condition that the defendant keep the peace and not violate the law for one year, the better, though not essential, practice is for the defendant to show to the court that he has performed the condition of the suspension and obtain an order of complete discharge. Dyke v. Commonwealth, 193 Va. 478, 69 S.E.2d 483 (1952).

Evidence that the defendant continued to be employed by the victim after commission of the burglary and larceny, and evidence that he made restitution for the damage to the window and money stolen, was irrelevant to the issue of defendant's guilt. The evidence, at best, was relevant only to the issue of punishment. The trial court properly refused to admit the evidence before the jury in mitigation of punishment. Duncan v. Commonwealth, 2 Va. App. 342, 343 S.E.2d 392 (1986).

Decision to seek reincarceration after release not violation. — The Virginia Attorney General's decision to seek reincarceration of persons who had been sentenced for serious narcotics violations and then released by procedures which the Supreme Court of Virginia held to be void under Rule 1:1 and this section did not violate the Fourteenth Amendment, where there was nothing in the record to indicate that he undertook to have them reincarcerated for any reason other than the seriousness of the crimes involved and the public outcry against their release. Crowley v. Landon, 780 F.2d 440 (4th Cir. 1985).

Suspension of probation upon event enhancing purpose of probation. — The trial court is given broad discretion to suspend sentences and fix terms of probation. With this broad authority to fix the terms and conditions of probation, to increase or decrease the probation period, and to revoke or modify any condition of the probation, there is no reason or restriction that would preclude the trial court from suspending the probation upon the occurrence of events that enhance the purpose of probation. Sami v. Commonwealth, No. 0367-86-4 (Ct. of Appeals July 27, 1987).

Punishment not excessive. — Sentence for violation of § 18.2-248 to a term of nine years in the penitentiary, of which four-and-one-half years were suspended conditioned on appellant's good behavior for 40 years did not constitute excessive and unreasonable punishment. Worsham v. Commonwealth, No. 1944-93-2 (Ct. of Appeals March 14, 1995).

Revocation of suspended sentence justified. — Where the trial court's order suspending defendant's sentence was in writing and plainly stated that defendant was required to pay restitution for his victim's medical expenses not to exceed $10,000, and he had paid only a total of $865.00 during nearly three years on probation despite constant reminders from his probation officer to adhere to his payment schedule, revocation of defendant's probation was justified. Keeling v. Commonwealth, 25 Va. App. 312, 487 S.E.2d 881 (1997).

CIRCUIT COURT OPINIONS

Bond pending appeal. — Circuit court had authority to grant defendant's petition for bond pending an appeal by the Commonwealth, after the appellate court had reversed defendant's conviction, where defendant's original sentence had been suspended, in part, by the trial court pursuant to this section. Commonwealth v. Smith, 54 Va. Cir. 629, 1999 Va. Cir. LEXIS 727 (Richmond 1999).

Time limitations. — Because more than 21 days had lapsed since the entry of a final sentencing order, and because none of the exceptions in § 19.2-303 applied, the circuit court lacked jurisdiction to alter defendant's sentence under Va. Sup. Ct. R. 1:1. Commonwealth v. Flinchum, 79 Va. Cir. 549, 2009 Va. Cir. LEXIS 224 (Salem Nov. 30, 2009).

Postrelease periods contemplated by §§ 18.2-10 and 19.2-295.2 did not conflict with the trial court's sentencing powers under the statute. Commonwealth v. Washington, 55 Va. Cir. 358, 2001 Va. Cir. LEXIS 299 (Rockingham County 2001).

Polygraph testing of sex offenders constitutes a reasonable condition of probation pursuant to this section absent evidence that the procedures employed by the probation officer or polygraph examiner unduly burden the probationer's Fifth Amendment right against self-incrimination. Commonwealth v. Hill, 55 Va. Cir. 155, 2001 Va. Cir. LEXIS 259 (Fairfax County 2001).

Trial judge without authority to modify former sentence. — On motion brought by a legal permanent resident seeking reduction of a 12 months suspended sentence and inactive probation, already served, so as to avoid possible sanctions by the Immigration and Naturalization Service, the trial court did not have authority to grant complainant's application for writ of audita querela in order to modify her sentence, since it was entered pursuant to a guilty plea and had already been served. Commonwealth v. Sharma, 58 Va. Cir. 460, 2002 Va. Cir. LEXIS 70 (Fairfax County 2002).

Suspension of finding of guilt or innocence inappropriate. — Even if a trial court could suspend a finding of guilt or innocence, it was inappropriate to do so in defendant's case after she was found guilty of grand larceny; defendant's bona fide claim of right, based upon her belief that she owned the bracelet in question, was contradicted by credible and overwhelming evidence. Commonwealth v. Bryant, 57 Va. Cir. 162, 2001 Va. Cir. LEXIS 514 (Danville 2001).

Not applicable to improper driving violation. — Juvenile who was found guilty of improper driving could not be ordered to pay restitution because improper driving was a traffic infraction under § 46.2-869, not an offense under § 19.2-303, and was not a crime to which §§ 19.2-305.1 B or 19.2-305 B was applicable. Commonwealth v. Warwick, 78 Va. Cir. 336, 2009 Va. Cir. LEXIS 145 (Brunswick County May 18, 2009).

§ 19.2-303.1. Fixing period of suspension of sentence.

In any case where a court suspends the imposition or execution of a sentence, it may fix the period of suspension for a reasonable time, having due regard to the gravity of the offense, without regard to the maximum period for which the defendant might have been sentenced.

History.
1982, c. 636.

Michie's Jurisprudence.
For related discussion, see 5B M.J. Criminal Procedure, § 76.

CASE NOTES

Liberal construction. — The statutes obviously confer upon trial courts wide latitude and much discretion in matters of suspension and probation to provide a remedial tool in the rehabilitation of criminals and, to that end, should be liberally construed. Wright v. Commonwealth, 32 Va. App. 148, 526 S.E.2d 784, appeal dismissed, 261 Va. 1, 539 S.E.2d 432 (2000).

The court's authority to suspend execution is not absolute; the legislature has authorized suspension "for a reasonable time, having due regard to the gravity of the offense." Simmers v. Commonwealth, 11 Va. App. 375, 398 S.E.2d 693 (1990).

Facts may authorize or require longer suspension. — Under this section the court must consider that the facts surrounding a particular offense may well authorize, even require, a longer suspension than would be reasonable under less egregious circumstances. Simmers v. Commonwealth, 11 Va. App. 375, 398 S.E.2d 693 (1990).

Although defendant had no criminal history at the time defendant pled guilty to possession of illegal mushrooms, defendant's suspended sentence of 20 years was not unreasonable in light of the information produced at the sentencing hearing that defendant had an extensive history of illegal drug usage prior to defendant's conviction and sentencing for possession of illegal mushrooms; in light of that information, the lengthy suspended sentence was not unreasonable. Patterson v. Commonwealth, 39 Va. App. 610, 575 S.E.2d 583, 2003 Va. App. LEXIS 34 (2003).

When a trial court had subject matter jurisdiction over defendant's 1998 hearing to revoke his suspended sentence and extended defendant's period of suspension, the trial court did not err in revoking defendant's suspended sentence in 2010, pursuant to subsection A of § 19.2-306, because the suspension took place within the fourteen-year period established in the 1998 sentencing order; defendant was not entitled to collaterally attack the 1998 sentencing order because the order was not void. Dunham v. Commonwealth, 59 Va. App. 634, 721 S.E.2d 824, 2012 Va. App. LEXIS 49 (2012).

Authority to suspend sentence extends to revocation proceedings. — This section which expressly provides that a trial court may suspend a sentence for a reasonable time "in any case," pertains not only to a defendant's initial sentencing but also to sentencing in revocation proceedings and a court could, therefore, reimpose a five year suspension period in a revocation proceeding, even though that period would extend beyond the end of the five-year period originally imposed. Wright v. Commonwealth, 32 Va. App. 148, 526 S.E.2d 784, appeal dismissed, 261 Va. 1, 539 S.E.2d 432 (2000).

Section 19.2-303.1, which expressly provides that a trial court may suspend a sentence for a reasonable time, applies not only to a defendant's initial sentencing but also to a sentence imposed in a subsequent revocation proceeding. Keene v. Commonwealth, No. 0043-03-1, 2003 Va. App. LEXIS 679 (Ct. of Appeals Dec. 23, 2003).

Indefinite suspension and probation. — Where a defendant was convicted of robbery, for which the maximum sentence permitted is life in prison, the trial court did not impose a period of suspension or probation that exceeded the maximum when it ordered an indefinite period of suspension and an indefinite period of probation; such sentence was reasonable given the gravity of the offense. Cherry v. Commonwealth, No. 0468-00-1, 2001 Va. App. LEXIS 198 (Ct. of Appeals Apr. 17, 2001).

Lifetime probation. — Trial court was authorized to place conditions on that part of defendant's sentence that was suspended, including lifetime probation under certain conditions, and, thus, the trial court did not err in placing conditions on defendant's suspended sentence that included lifetime probation in a case where defendant pled guilty to seven felonies arising out of the accidental shooting of a friend, as defendant could have received up to 105 years in prison and only received 65 years with 35 years of those suspended based on certain conditions, including the lifetime probation. Lathram v. Commonwealth, — Va. App. —, — S.E.2d —, 2006 Va. App. LEXIS 168 (May 2, 2006).

Applied in Briggs v. Commonwealth, 21 Va. App. 338, 464 S.E.2d 512 (1995).

§ 19.2-303.2. Persons charged with first offense may be placed on probation.

Whenever any person who has not previously been convicted of any felony pleads guilty to or enters a plea of not guilty to any crime against property constituting a misdemeanor, under Articles 5, 6, 7 and 8 of Chapter 5 (§ 18.2-119 et seq.) of Title 18.2, the court, upon such plea if the facts found by the court would justify a finding of guilt, without entering a judgment of guilt and with the consent of the accused, may defer further proceedings and place him on probation subject to terms and conditions, which may include restitution for losses caused, set by the court. Upon violation of a term or condition, the court may enter an adjudication of guilt and proceed as otherwise provided. Upon fulfillment of the terms and conditions, the court shall discharge the person and dismiss the proceedings against him. Discharge and dismissal under this section shall be without adjudication of guilt and is a conviction only for the purpose of applying this section in subsequent proceedings.

History.
1985, c. 617.

Michie's Jurisprudence.
For related discussion, see 14A M.J. Pardon, Probation and Parole, § 5.

CASE NOTES

Applied in Epps v. Commonwealth, 59 Va. App. 71, 717 S.E.2d 151, 2011 Va. App. LEXIS 351 (2011).

§ 19.2-303.3. Sentence to local community-based probation services; services agency; requirements for participation; sentencing; and removal from probation; payment of costs towards supervision and services.

A. Any offender who is (i) convicted on or after July 1, 1995, of a misdemeanor or a felony that is not a felony act of violence as defined in § 19.2-297.1, and for which the court imposes a total sentence of 12 months or less, and (ii) no younger than 18 years of age or is considered an adult at the time of conviction may be sentenced to a local community-based probation services agency established pursuant to § 9.1-174 by the local governing bodies within that judicial district or circuit.

B. In those courts having electronic access to the Local Inmate Data System (LIDS) within the courtroom, at the time of sentencing, the clerk of court shall determine by reviewing LIDS, in any case where there is a felony conviction, whether a sample of the offender's blood, saliva, or tissue or an analysis of the sample is stored in the DNA data bank maintained by the Department of Forensic Science pursuant to Article 1.1 (§ 19.2-310.2 et seq.) of Chapter 18 of this title. If the clerk has determined that a DNA sample or analysis is not stored in the DNA data bank, or in any case in which electronic access to LIDS is not available in the courtroom, the court shall order that the offender appear within 30 days before the sheriff or community-based probation officer and allow the sheriff or community-based probation officer to take the required sample. The order shall also require that, if the offender has not appeared and allowed the sheriff or community-based probation officer to take the required sample by the date stated in the order, then the sheriff or community-based probation officer shall report to the court the offender's failure to appear and provide the required sample. The court may order the offender placed under local community-based probation services pursuant to § 9.1-174 upon a determination by the court that the offender may benefit from these services and is capable of returning to society as a productive citizen with a reasonable amount of supervision and intervention including services set forth in § 9.1-176. All or part of any sentence imposed that has been suspended, shall be conditioned upon the offender's successful completion of local community-based probation services established pursuant to § 9.1-174.

The court may impose terms and conditions of supervision as it deems appropriate, including that the offender abide by any additional requirements of supervision imposed or established by the local community-based probation services agency during the period of probation supervision.

C. Any sworn officer of a local community-based probation services agency established or operated pursuant to the Comprehensive Community Corrections Act for Local-Responsible Offenders (§ 9.1-173 et seq.) may seek a capias from any judicial officer for the arrest of any person on local community-based probation and under its supervision for (i) intractable behavior; (ii) refusal to comply with the terms and conditions imposed by the court; (iii) refusal to comply with the requirements of local community-based probation supervision established by the agency; or (iv) the commission of a new offense while on local community-based probation and under agency supervision. Upon arrest, the offender shall be brought for a hearing before the court of appropriate jurisdiction. After finding that the offender (a) exhibited intractable behavior as defined herein; (b) refused to comply with terms and conditions imposed by the court; (c) refused to comply with the requirements of local community-based probation supervision established by the agency; or (d) committed a new offense while on local community-based probation and under agency supervision, the court may revoke all or part of the suspended sentence and supervision, and commit the offender to serve whatever sentence was originally imposed or impose such other terms and conditions of probation as it deems appropriate or, in a case where the proceeding has been deferred, enter an adjudication of guilt and proceed as otherwise provided by law.

"Intractable behavior" is that behavior that, in the determination of the court, indicates an offender's unwillingness or inability to conform his behavior to that which is necessary for successful completion of local community-based probation or that the offender's behavior is so disruptive as to threaten the successful completion of the program by other participants.

D. An offender sentenced to or provided a deferred proceeding and placed on community-based probation pursuant to this section may be required to pay an amount towards the costs of his supervision and services received in accordance with subsection D of § 9.1-182.

History.
1994, 2nd Sp. Sess., cc. 1, 2; 1995, cc. 502, 574; 1999, c. 372; 2000, c. 1040; 2006, c. 883; 2007, cc. 133, 528.

The 2007 amendments.
The 2007 amendment by c. 133, in subsection B, in the first sentence of the first paragraph, substituted "under local community-based probation services" for "in a local community-based probation program" and "these services" for "the program" and deleted "programs and" following "including," and substituted "local community-based probation services" for "any program" in the last sentence; and substituted "local community-based probation services agency" for "program" in the last paragraph; inserted "community-based" preceding "board" in five places in subsection C and once in subsection D and "local community-based" preceding "probation" in two places in subsection C; and in subsection C, inserted "services" preceding "agency" in the first sentence and substituted "probation" for "supervision" in clause (d) of the last sentence.
The 2007 amendment by c. 528 inserted the first three sentences and deleted "Prior to or at the time of sentencing" at the beginning of the fourth sentence in subsection B.

CASE NOTES

Applied in Carroll v. Commonwealth, 54 Va. App. 730, 682 S.E.2d 92, 2009 Va. App. LEXIS 392 (2009).

§ 19.2-303.4. Payment of costs when proceedings deferred and defendant placed on probation.

A circuit or district court, which has deferred further proceedings, without entering a judgment of guilt, and placed a defendant on probation subject to terms and conditions pursuant to § 4.1-305, 16.1-278.8, 16.1-278.9, 18.2-57.3, 18.2-61, 18.2-67.1, 18.2-67.2, 18.2-251 or 19.2-303.2, shall impose upon the defendant costs.

History.
1995, c. 485; 2000, c. 186; 2002, c. 831; 2005, c. 631.

§ 19.2-303.5. (For expiration date, see Editor's notes) Immediate sanction probation programs.

There may be established in the Commonwealth up to two immediate sanction probation programs in accordance with the following provisions:
1. As a condition of a sentence suspended pursuant to § 19.2-303, a court may order a defendant convicted of a crime, other than a violent crime as defined in subsection C of § 17.1-805, to participate in an immediate sanction probation program.
2. If a participating offender fails to comply with any term or condition of his probation and the alleged probation violation is not that the offender committed a new crime or infraction, (i) his probation officer shall immediately issue a noncompliance letter pursuant to § 53.1-149 authorizing his arrest at any location in the Commonwealth and (ii) his probation violation hearing shall take priority on the court's docket. The probation officer may, in any event, exercise any other lawful authority he may have with respect to the offender.
3. When a participating offender is arrested pursuant to subdivision 2, the court shall conduct an immediate sanction hearing unless (i) the alleged probation violation is that the offender committed a new crime or infraction; (ii) the alleged probation violation is that the offender absconded for more than seven days; or (iii) the offender, attorney for the Commonwealth, or the court objects to such immediate sanction hearing. If the court conducts an immediate sanction hearing, it shall proceed pursuant to subdivision 4. Otherwise, the court shall proceed pursuant to § 19.2-306.
4. At the immediate sanction hearing, the court shall receive the noncompliance letter, which shall be admissible as evidence, and may receive other evidence. If the court finds good cause to believe that the offender has violated the terms or conditions of his probation, it may (i) revoke no more than 30 days of the previously suspended sentence and (ii) continue or modify any existing terms and conditions of probation. If the court does not modify the terms and conditions of probation or remove the defendant from the program, the previously ordered terms and conditions of probation shall continue to apply. The court may remove the offender from the immediate sanction probation program at any time.
5. The provisions of this section shall expire on July 1, 2012.

History.
2010, c. 845.

Editor's note.
Although subdivision 5 provides a July 1, 2012, expiration date for this section, Acts 2012, Sp. Sess. I, c. 3, Item 50 B purports to extend the date to July 1, 2014.
Acts 2010, c. 845, cls. 1 and 4, were codified as this section at the direction of the Virginia Code Commission.
Acts 2010, c. 845, cl. 2, provides: "That the Virginia Criminal Sentencing Commission shall report to the Chairmen of the House and Senate Courts of Justice Committees on or before January 12, 2012, on the operation and costs of any established immediate sanction probation program, including statistics on the characteristics of the participants and the outcomes of their participation."
Acts 2010, c. 845, cl. 3, provides: "That the Virginia Criminal Sentencing Commission may calculate the impact of a revocation of a suspended sentence for a participant in an immediate sanction probation program differently than the revocation of a sentence pursuant to § 19.2-306 of the Code of Virginia."
Acts 2012, Sp. Sess. I, c. 3, as amended by Acts 2013, c. 806, effective for the biennium ending June 30, 2014, Item 50 B provides: "B.1. Notwithstanding the provisions of § 19.2-303.5,

Code of Virginia, the provisions of that section shall not expire on July 1, 2012, but shall continue in effect until July 1, 2014, and may be implemented in up to four sites.

"2. The Virginia Criminal Sentencing Commission, with the concurrence of the chief judge of the circuit court and the Commonwealth's attorney of the locality, shall designate each immediate sanction probation program site. The Virginia Criminal Sentencing Commission shall develop guidelines and procedures for implementing the program, administer the program, and evaluate the results of the program. As part of its administration of the program, the commission shall designate a standard, validated substance abuse assessment instrument to be used by probation and parole districts to assess probationers subject to the immediate sanction probation program. The commission shall also determine outcome measures and collect data for evaluation of the results of the program at the designated sites. The commission shall present a report on the implementation of the immediate sanction probation program, including preliminary recidivism results to the Chief Justice, Governor, and the Chairmen of the House and Senate Courts of Justice Committees, the House Appropriations Committee, and the Senate Finance Committee by October 1, 2013."

§ 19.2-304. Increasing or decreasing probation period and modification of conditions.

The court may subsequently increase or decrease the probation period and may revoke or modify any condition of probation, but only upon a hearing after reasonable notice to both the defendant and the attorney for the Commonwealth.

History.
Code 1950, § 53-273; 1974, c. 205; 1975, c. 495.

Law Review.
For survey of Virginia criminal law and procedure for the year 1970-1971, see 57 Va. L. Rev. 1438 (1971). Cook v. Commonwealth, 211 Va. 290, 176 S.E.2d 815 (1970) was commented on in 6 U. Rich. L. Rev. 167 (1971). For article summarizing published Virginia criminal law decisions between July 1, 2002 and July 1, 2003, see 38 U. Rich. L. Rev. 87 (2003).

Michie's Jurisprudence.
For related discussion, see 5B M.J. Criminal Procedure, §§ 76, 77.

CASE NOTES

Suspension and probation distinguished. — This section, § 19.2-303 and former § 53-272 distinguish between a suspension, either of imposition of sentence or of execution of sentence, on the one hand, and probation, on the other. Grant v. Commonwealth, 223 Va. 680, 292 S.E.2d 348 (1982).

Effect of extending probation period. — An extension of the period of probation under this section has the effect of extending the time period during which revocation may occur under § 19.2-306. Cook v. Commonwealth, 211 Va. 290, 176 S.E.2d 815 (1970).

Where defendant's probation period had been extended under § 19.2-304, the trial court was entitled to revoke his suspended sentence, although the original period of suspension had expired, because, pursuant to subsection A of § 19.2-306, the trial court could revoke the suspension anytime during the probation period. Mohamed v. Commonwealth, 56 Va. App. 95, 691 S.E.2d 513, 2010 Va. App. LEXIS 145 (2010).

Fundamental fairness requires a judicial hearing of a summary nature for the probation period to be extended, since increasing the period of probation has the effect of extending the restraints on the probationer's liberty which are normally incident to his probation and extends the time period during which revocation may occur. Cook v. Commonwealth, 211 Va. 290, 176 S.E.2d 815 (1970).

Hearing required to extend probation. — Trial court erred in revoking defendant's suspended sentence, because defendant had no notice of the request to extend probation and was not given opportunity to be heard on whether probation should have been extended. Thus, the extension was invalid and the cause of revocation occurred beyond the one-year probation period and beyond the two-year period of suspension. Dudash v. Commonwealth, 2012 Va. App. LEXIS 415 (Dec. 18, 2012).

Suspension of probation upon event enhancing purpose of probation. — The trial court is given broad discretion to suspend sentences and fix the terms of probation. With this broad authority to fix the terms and conditions of probation, to increase or decrease the probation period, and to revoke or modify any condition of the probation, there is no reason or restriction that would preclude the trial court from suspending the probation upon the occurrence of events that enhance the purpose of probation. Sami v. Commonwealth, No. 0367-86-4 (Ct. of Appeals July 27, 1987).

Invalid order. — Where defendant was not present when the order was entered extending his period of probation, and no notice was given to him of the action proposed to be taken by the court, and he was afforded no opportunity to be heard on whether his period of probation should be extended, the order was not a valid order. Cook v. Commonwealth, 211 Va. 290, 176 S.E.2d 815 (1970).

Authority of court to modify condition of suspension. — Evidence supported the trial court's conclusion that a payment allotted to defendant's wife from defendant's military retirement benefit was a condition of defendant's suspended sentences rather than a condition of probation, and, thus, that the trial court correctly concluded it lacked authority under Va. Sup. Ct. R. 1:1 to modify the condition pursuant to § 19.2-304. Reinke v. Commonwealth, 51 Va. App. 357, 657 S.E.2d 805, 2008 Va. App. LEXIS 111 (2008).

Altering conditions of suspended sentence. — Court could remove a good behavior requirement as a probation condition but lacked jurisdiction to alter good behavior and related provisions imposed as conditions of the suspension of a sentence more than 21 days after entry of a sentencing order. McFarland v. Commonwealth, 39 Va. App. 511, 574 S.E.2d 311, 2002 Va. App. LEXIS 770 (2002).

Applied in Anderson v. Commonwealth, 25 Va. App. 565, 490 S.E.2d 274 (1997).

§ 19.2-305. Requiring fines, costs, restitution for damages, support or community services from probationer.

A. While on probation the defendant may be required to pay in one or several sums a fine or costs, or both such fine and costs, imposed at the time of being placed on probation as a condition of such probation, and the failure of the defendant to pay such fine or costs, or both such fine and costs, at the prescribed time or times may be deemed a breach of such probation. The provisions of this subsection shall also apply to any person ordered to pay costs pursuant to § 19.2-303.3.

B. A defendant placed on probation following conviction may be required to make at least partial restitution or reparation to the aggrieved party or parties for damages or loss caused by the offense for which conviction was had, or may be required to provide for the support of his wife or others for whose support he may be legally responsible, or may be required to perform community services. The defendant may submit a proposal to the court for making restitution, for providing for support or for performing community services.

C. No defendant shall be kept under supervised probation solely because of his failure to make full payment of fines, fees, or costs, provided that, following notice by the probation and parole officer to each court and attorney for the Commonwealth in whose jurisdiction any fines, fees, or costs are owed by the defendant, no such court or attorney for the Commonwealth objects to his removal from supervised probation.

History.
Code 1950, § 53-274; 1962, c. 143; 1975, c. 495; 1977, c. 682; 1978, c. 716; 1984, c. 32; 1995, c. 485; 2009, c. 240.

The 2009 amendments.
The 2009 amendment by c. 240 added subsection C.

Law Review.
For article on criminal restitution, a survey of its past history and an analysis of its present usefulness, see 5 U. Rich. L. Rev. 71 (1970). For survey of Virginia law on criminal law and procedure for the year 2007-2008, see 43 U. Rich. L. Rev. 149 (2008).

Michie's Jurisprudence.
For related discussion, see 5B M.J. Criminal Procedure, §§ 78, 90, 92.

CASE NOTES

Restitution provisions applicable to probationer. — By its terms, the restitution portion of this statute comes into play when the defendant is on probation. This is the import of the words "Such defendant." They refer to the first sentence where the defendant is described as one on probation. Baker v. Commonwealth, 230 Va. 252, 335 S.E.2d 276 (1985).

Payment of restitution. — Trial court erred in requiring defendant to pay, as a condition of his suspended sentence, restitution that included the cost of the installation of a security system installed by the burglary victims after the burglary because, while related to defendant's burglary, the installation of a security system was not caused by the offense, and the attenuation was too great. Howell v. Commonwealth, 274 Va. 737, 652 S.E.2d 107, 2007 Va. LEXIS 121 (2007).

Because defendant's plea agreement to receiving or concealing stolen property in violation of § 18.2-108 specifically waived any right of appeal from the decision of the trial court, not merely the conviction itself, the trial court did not err in ordering defendant to pay restitution pursuant to subsection B of § 19.2-305. Craig v. Commonwealth, 2011 Va. App. LEXIS 329 (Nov. 1, 2011).

Restitution was limited to damages caused by the offense. — Under § 19.2-305(B) restitution was limited to damages caused by the offense; therefore, the trial court abused its discretion when it ordered defendant to pay restitution related to an "indirect" financial loss that occurred when a pipe burst inside a victim's home while the victim was convalescing elsewhere. Maye v. Commonwealth, 2011 Va. App. LEXIS 40 (Feb. 8, 2011).

Trial court did not abuse its discretion, pursuant to § 19.2-303, subsection B of § 19.2-305, and subsection A of § 19.2-305.1, by the amount of a restitution ordered because the finding by the trial court that the Commonwealth of Virginia Department of Medical Assistance Services received no value from the services rendered to Medicaid-eligible clients by defendant's employee, who actually had no training to be a personal care aide, was not plainly wrong or unsupported by the evidence. Burriesci v. Commonwealth, 59 Va. App. 50, 717 S.E.2d 140, 2011 Va. App. LEXIS 344 (2011).

Payment of court costs. — Because defendant did not pay court costs during the original term of probation as required by a 1995 standing order that was incorporated into the sentencing order, defendant was still under the trial court's jurisdiction when it entered an order extending defendant's probation and thereafter found defendant in violation of probation. Heiderscheidt v. Commonwealth, 2009 Va. App. LEXIS 256 (June 9, 2009).

Court-ordered child support as condition of probation. — Probation condition that defendant report to the Division of Child Support Enforcement and submit to an order of support for any child that was not in his custody was not improper in defendant's conviction for driving after having been declared an habitual

offender because subsection B of § 19.2-305 authorized such a condition. Martin v. Commonwealth, 274 Va. 733, 652 S.E.2d 109, 2007 Va. LEXIS 124 (2007).

CIRCUIT COURT OPINIONS

Entry of judgment. — Where judgment was not entered and the restitution order was not docketed under the statute by order of the court or written request of the victim, criminal restitution could not be ordered. Commonwealth v. Mehryar, 57 Va. Cir. 496, 2000 Va. Cir. LEXIS 521 (Fairfax County Nov. 15, 2000).

Restitution provisions. — Court was granted statutory authority to require a defendant who was placed on probation to pay restitution pursuant to § 19.2-303 and this section. Commonwealth v. Washington, 55 Va. Cir. 358, 2001 Va. Cir. LEXIS 299 (Rockingham County 2001).

Postrelease supervision did equate to probation for purposes of ordering restitution. Commonwealth v. Washington, 55 Va. Cir. 358, 2001 Va. Cir. LEXIS 299 (Rockingham County 2001).

Not applicable to improper driving violation. — Juvenile who was found guilty of improper driving could not be ordered to pay restitution because improper driving was a traffic infraction under § 46.2-869, not an offense under § 19.2-303, and was not a crime to which §§ 19.2-305.1 B or 19.2-305 B was applicable. Commonwealth v. Warwick, 78 Va. Cir. 336, 2009 Va. Cir. LEXIS 145 (Brunswick County May 18, 2009).

OPINIONS OF THE ATTORNEY GENERAL

Payment of restitution. — A circuit court has the authority to order that payment of restitution be made prior to payment of court costs. See opinion of Attorney General to The Honorable Dollie M. Compton, Clerk, Circuit Court of Russell County, 00-097 (12/27/01).

§ 19.2-305.1. Restitution for property damage or loss; community service.

A. Notwithstanding any other provision of law, no person convicted of a crime in violation of any provision in Title 18.2, which resulted in property damage or loss, shall be placed on probation or have his sentence suspended unless such person shall make at least partial restitution for such property damage or loss, or shall be compelled to perform community services, or both, or shall submit a plan for doing that which appears to the court to be feasible under the circumstances.

B. Notwithstanding any other provision of law, any person who, on or after July 1, 1995, commits, and is convicted of, a crime in violation of any provision in Title 18.2 shall make at least partial restitution for any property damage or loss caused by the crime or for any medical expenses or expenses directly related to funeral or burial incurred by the victim or his estate as a result of the crime, may be compelled to perform community services and, if the court so orders, shall submit a plan for doing that which appears to be feasible to the court under the circumstances.

B1. Notwithstanding any other provision of law, any person, who on or after July 1, 2005 commits and is convicted of a crime in violation of § 18.2-248 involving the manufacture of any controlled substance, may be ordered, upon presentation of suitable evidence of such costs, by the court to reimburse the Commonwealth or the locality for the costs incurred by the jurisdiction, as the case may be, for the removal and remediation associated with the illegal manufacture of any controlled substance by the defendant.

C. At or before the time of sentencing, the court shall receive and consider any plan for making restitution submitted by the defendant. The plan shall include the defendant's home address, place of employment and address, social security number and bank information. If the court finds such plan to be reasonable and practical under the circumstances, it may consider probation or suspension of whatever portion of the sentence that it deems appropriate. By order of the court incorporating the defendant's plan or a reasonable and practical plan devised by the court, the defendant shall make restitution while he is free on probation or work release or following his release from confinement. Additionally, the court may order that the defendant make restitution during his confinement, if feasible, based upon both his earning capacity and net worth as determined by the court at sentencing.

D. At the time of sentencing, the court shall determine the amount to be repaid by the defendant and the terms and conditions thereof. If community service work is ordered, the court shall determine the terms and conditions upon which such work shall be performed. The court shall include such findings in the judgment order. The order shall specify that sums paid under such order shall be paid to the clerk, who shall disburse such sums as the court may, by order, direct. Any court desiring to participate in the Setoff Debt Collection Act (§§ 58.1-520 through 58.1-535) for the purpose of collecting fines or costs or providing restitution shall, at the time of sentencing, obtain the social security number of each defendant.

E. Unreasonable failure to execute the plan by the defendant shall result in revocation of the probation or imposition of the suspended sentence. A hearing shall be held in accordance with the provisions of this Code relating to revocation of probation or imposition of a suspended sentence before either such action is taken.

E1. A defendant convicted of an offense under § 18.2-374.1, 18.2-374.1:1, or 18.2-374.3 shall be ordered to pay mandatory restitution to the victim of the offense in an amount as determined by the court. For purposes of this subsection, "victim" means a person who is depicted in a still or videographic image involved in an offense under § 18.2-374.1, 18.2-374.1:1, or 18.2-374.3.

The Commonwealth shall make reasonable efforts to notify victims of offenses under § 18.2-374.1, 18.2-374.1:1, or 18.2-374.3.

F. If restitution is ordered to be paid by the defendant to the victim of a crime and the victim can no longer be located or identified, the clerk shall deposit any such restitution collected to the Criminal Injuries Compensation Fund for the benefit of crime victims. The administrator shall reserve a

sum sufficient in the Fund from which he shall make prompt payment to the victim for any proper claims. Before making the deposit he shall record the name, last known address and amount of restitution due each victim appearing from the clerk's report to be entitled to restitution.

G. If restitution pursuant to § 19.2-305 or this section is ordered to be paid by the defendant to the victim of a crime or other entity, and the Criminal Injuries Compensation Fund has made any payments to or on behalf of the victim for any loss, damage, or expenses included in the restitution order, then upon presentation by the Fund of a written request that sets forth the amount of payments made by the Fund to the victim or on the victim's behalf, the entity collecting restitution shall pay to the Fund as much of the restitution collected as will reimburse the Fund for its payments made to the victim or on the victim's behalf.

History.
1977, c. 682; 1978, c. 131; 1981, c. 224; 1984, cc. 32, 269; 1994, c. 197; 1995, cc. 434, 687; 2000, c. 775; 2002, cc. 810, 818; 2003, c. 982; 2005, c. 591; 2011, cc. 575, 588; 2013, c. 273.

Cross references.
For the Criminal Inquiries Compensation Fund, see § 19.2-368.18.

The 2011 amendments.
The 2011 amendments by cc. 575 and 588 are identical, and added subsection E1.

The 2013 amendments.
The 2013 amendment by c. 273 added subsection G.

Law Review.
For survey of Virginia criminal law for the year 1976-77, see 63 Va. L. Rev. 1396 (1977). For article, "Explaining Restitution," see 71 Va. L. Rev. 65 (1985).

Michie's Jurisprudence.
For related discussion, see 5B M.J. Criminal Procedure, § 90.

CASE NOTES

Intent that restitution be expressly ordered. — The legislature intended that the restitution requirement be expressly ordered. Russnak v. Commonwealth, 10 Va. App. 317, 392 S.E.2d 491 (1990).

Ability to pay is a necessary consideration in the trial court's determination of cause for the failure to pay restitution ordered as a condition of a suspended sentence, thus, where the evidence established that the failure resulted solely from an inability to pay and not a willful refusal, it was an abuse of discretion to automatically revoke the prior suspended sentence without considering reasonable alternatives to imprisonment. Duff v. Commonwealth, 16 Va. App. 293, 429 S.E.2d 465 (1993).

The phrase "such property damage or loss" in subsection A refers back to that which "resulted" from the crime in question; therefore, restitution may be ordered only for damage or loss resulting from or caused by the crime for which the person is convicted. Thompson v. Commonwealth, No. 0686-89-2 (Ct. of Appeals June 11, 1991).

Amount of restitution. — Trial court did not abuse its discretion, pursuant to § 19.2-303, subsection B of § 19.2-305, and subsection A of § 19.2-305.1, by the amount of a restitution ordered because the finding by the trial court that the Commonwealth of Virginia Department of Medical Assistance Services received no value from the services rendered to Medicaid-eligible clients by defendant's employee, who actually had no training to be a personal care aide, was not plainly wrong or unsupported by the evidence. Burriesci v. Commonwealth, 59 Va. App. 50, 717 S.E.2d 140, 2011 Va. App. LEXIS 344 (2011).

Restitution evidence was supported by a preponderance of the evidence; the victim prepared a list of stolen items with values and the list clearly bore some indicia of reliability, as the victim assessed the value of the stolen items not returned and gave that information to her insurance carrier and the police. Sigler v. Commonwealth, 61 Va. App. 674, 739 S.E.2d 272, 2013 Va. App. LEXIS 108 (Apr. 2, 2013).

Impact statement may be source for restitution amount. — The legislature intended that the victim impact statement be used by trial judge to determine the amount of restitution. Alger v. Commonwealth, 19 Va. App. 252, 450 S.E.2d 765 (1994).

Trial court required to set restitution amount. — Sentencing court properly vacated that portion of the original sentencing order that ordered a probation officer to set restitution and set a restitution amount as was required by subsection C. McKenney v. Commonwealth, Nos. 3330-02-2, 0473-03-2, 2004 Va. App. LEXIS 157 (Ct. of Appeals Apr. 6, 2004).

Cost of security system improper as part of restitution. — Trial court erred in requiring defendant to pay, as a condition of his suspended sentence, restitution that included the cost of the installation of a security system installed by the burglary victims after the burglary because, while related to defendant's burglary, the installation of a security system was not caused by the offense, and the attenuation was too great. Howell v. Commonwealth, 274 Va. 737, 652 S.E.2d 107, 2007 Va. LEXIS 121 (2007).

The sentencing court is given broad discretion as to whether it will order restitution in lieu of a suspended sentence. Therefore, there is an inherent uncertainty as to whether restitution will be ordered in the first instance, and if so, under what terms and conditions. Starr v. Virginia, 147 Bankr. 380 (Bankr. E.D. Va. 1991).

No implicit restitution arises from order silent on issue. — Because the statute requires the trial judge to include the terms of restitution in the sentencing order, no "implicit" requirement of "some form of restitution" arises from an order that is otherwise silent as to that issue. Russnak v. Commonwealth, 10 Va. App. 317, 392 S.E.2d 491 (1990).

When this section and § 19.2-306 are applied in conjunction, the requirement of subsection D of this section, that only "unreasonable" failure to pay restitution shall result in revocation of a suspended sentence, restricts the scope of the court's authority under § 19.2-306 to revoke a suspension for "any cause" deemed by it sufficient. Duff v. Commonwealth, 16 Va. App. 293, 429 S.E.2d 465 (1993).

A reasonable failure to pay restitution negates a reasonable cause to revoke a suspended sentence. Duff v. Commonwealth, 16 Va. App. 293, 429 S.E.2d 465 (1993).

Revocation justified. — Where the trial court's order suspending defendant's sentence was in writing and plainly stated that defendant was required to pay restitution for his victim's medical expenses not to exceed $10,000, and he had paid only a total of $865.00 during nearly three years on probation despite constant reminders from his probation officer to adhere to his payment schedule, revocation of defendant's probation was justified. Keeling v. Commonwealth, 25 Va. App. 312, 487 S.E.2d 881 (1997).

Court's alternative where failure to pay restitution not willful. — A court may modify restitution plan consistent with the defendant's ability to pay or employ some other means to permit the victim to recover the loss where the failure to follow the plan resulted solely from an inability to pay and was not a willful refusal. Duff v. Commonwealth, 16 Va. App. 293, 429 S.E.2d 465 (1993).

Joint and several liability proper. — Although defendant was acting in concert with others, he was guilty of all crimes committed and was fully responsible for the total loss which the victim sustained. Where the trial court determined that defendant would be jointly and severally liable for victim-company's total loss, it acted within its sentencing authority in ordering restitution in the amount of $42,804.46. Bazemore v. Commonwealth, 25 Va. App. 466, 489 S.E.2d 254 (1997).

Fraudulent conversion of property. — Trial court did not abuse its discretion by ordering defendant who was convicted of fraudulently converting a piece of farm equipment, in violation of

§ 18.2-115, to pay the unpaid secured balance which defendant owed on the equipment, rather than its diminished value as damaged or destroyed property. Landes v. Commonwealth, 37 Va. App. 710, 561 S.E.2d 37, 2002 Va. App. LEXIS 180 (2002).

Collateral source rule inapplicable. — Trial court erred in determining that collateral source rule precluded defendant's relief from restitution order following assault victim's settlement with insurer. Diedrich v. Commonwealth, No. 0962-98-1 (Ct. of Appeals June 29, 1999).

CIRCUIT COURT OPINIONS

Not applicable to improper driving violation. — Juvenile who was found guilty of improper driving could not be ordered to pay restitution because improper driving was a traffic infraction under § 46.2-869, not an offense under § 19.2-303, and was not a crime to which §§ 19.2-305.1 B or 19.2-305 B was applicable. Commonwealth v. Warwick, 78 Va. Cir. 336, 2009 Va. Cir. LEXIS 145 (Brunswick County May 18, 2009).

OPINIONS OF THE ATTORNEY GENERAL

Payment of restitution. — A circuit court has the authority to order that payment of restitution be made prior to payment of court costs. See opinion of Attorney General to The Honorable Dollie M. Compton, Clerk, Circuit Court of Russell County, 00-097 (12/27/01).

§ 19.2-305.2. Amount of restitution; enforcement.

A. The court, when ordering restitution pursuant to § 19.2-305.1, may require that such defendant, in the case of an offense resulting in damage to or loss or destruction of property of a victim of the offense (i) return the property to the owner or (ii) if return of the property is impractical or impossible, pay an amount equal to the greater of the value of the property at the time of the offense or the value of the property at the time of sentencing.

B. An order of restitution may be docketed as provided in § 8.01-446 when so ordered by the court or upon written request of the victim and may be enforced by a victim named in the order to receive the restitution in the same manner as a judgment in a civil action.

History.
1988, c. 679; 1989, c. 386.

Michie's Jurisprudence.
For related discussion, see 16 M.J. Restitution, § 1.

CASE NOTES

Docketing of restitution order as judgment against person does not improperly modify sentence by enhancing punishment, and requirement that restitution order be docketed "without delay" does not relate to entry of docketing order by circuit court. Frazier v. Commonwealth, 20 Va. App. 719, 460 S.E.2d 608 (1995).

Remedy for fraudulent conversion of property. — Trial court did not abuse its discretion by ordering defendant who was convicted of fraudulently converting a piece of farm equipment, in violation of § 18.2-115, to pay the unpaid secured balance which defendant owed on the equipment, rather than its diminished value as damaged or destroyed property. Landes v. Commonwealth, 37 Va. App. 710, 561 S.E.2d 37, 2002 Va. App. LEXIS 180 (2002).

Hearsay evidence allowed to determine value of stolen property. — Sentencing court properly considered hearsay statements from burglary victims regarding value of property stolen from them in setting defendant's restitution requirement as the evidence bore minimal indicia of reliability and defendant knew of the evidence far enough in advance that he could have refuted the evidence. Smith v. Commonwealth, 52 Va. App. 26, 660 S.E.2d 691, 2008 Va. App. LEXIS 247 (2008).

§ 19.2-305.3. Repealed by Acts 1997, c. 140.

§ 19.2-305.4. When interest to be paid on award of restitution.

The court, when ordering restitution pursuant to § 19.2-305 or 19.2-305.1, may provide in the order for interest on the restitution. If the court orders the payment of interest, it shall accrue from the date of the loss or damage unless the court specifies a different date in the order, at the rate specified in § 6.2-302.

History.
1996, c. 544; 2001, c. 122; 2005, cc. 14, 79.

Editor's note.
Effective October 1, 2010, "6.2-302" was substituted for "6.1-330.54" to conform to the recodification of Title 6.1 by Acts 2010, c. 794.

§ 19.2-306. Revocation of suspension of sentence and probation.

A. In any case in which the court has suspended the execution or imposition of sentence, the court may revoke the suspension of sentence for any cause the court deems sufficient that occurred at any time within the probation period, or within the period of suspension fixed by the court. If neither a probation period nor a period of suspension was fixed by the court, then the court may revoke the suspension for any cause the court deems sufficient that occurred within the maximum period for which the defendant might originally have been sentenced to be imprisoned.

B. The court may not conduct a hearing to revoke the suspension of sentence unless the court, within one year after the expiration of the period of probation or the period of suspension, issues process to notify the accused or to compel his appearance before the court. If neither a probation period nor a period of suspension was fixed by the court, then the court shall issue process within one year after the expiration of the maximum period for which the defendant might originally have been sentenced to be incarcerated. Such notice and service of process may be waived by the defendant, in which case the court may proceed to determine whether the defendant has violated the conditions of suspension.

C. If the court, after hearing, finds good cause to believe that the defendant has violated the terms of suspension, then: (i) if the court originally suspended the imposition of sentence, the court shall revoke the suspension, and the court may pronounce whatever sentence might have been originally imposed or (ii) if the court originally suspended the

execution of the sentence, the court shall revoke the suspension and the original sentence shall be in full force and effect. The court may again suspend all or any part of this sentence and may place the defendant upon terms and conditions or probation.

D. If any court has, after hearing, found no cause to impose a sentence that might have been originally imposed, or to revoke a suspended sentence or probation, then any further hearing to impose a sentence or revoke a suspended sentence or probation, based solely on the alleged violation for which the hearing was held, shall be barred.

E. Nothing contained herein shall be construed to deprive any person of his right to appeal in the manner provided by law to the circuit court having criminal jurisdiction from a judgment or order revoking any suspended sentence.

History.
Code 1950, § 53-275; 1958, c. 468; 1970, c. 275; 1975, c. 495; 1978, c. 687; 2002, c. 628.

Cross references.
As to eligibility for parole, see § 53.1-151. As to commencement of term of confinement, see § 53.1-186.

Law Review.
For survey of Virginia criminal law and procedure for the year 1970-1971, see 57 Va. L. Rev. 1438 (1971). For survey of Virginia law on criminal procedure for the year 1974-1975, see 61 Va. L. Rev. 1713 (1975). For 1995 survey of criminal law and procedure, see 29 U. Rich. L. Rev. 951 (1995).

Michie's Jurisprudence.
For related discussion, see 1B M.J. Appeal and Error, § 120.1; 5B M.J. Criminal Procedure, §§ 76, 77; 14A M.J. Pardon, Probation and Parole, § 5.

CASE NOTES

I. In General.
II. Limitation Period.
III. Revocation Hearing.
    A. Generally.
    B. Basis for Revocation.
    C. Terms and Conditions.

I. IN GENERAL.

Purpose. — Both this section and § 19.2-303 serve the same rehabilitative purpose. Esparza v. Commonwealth, 29 Va. App. 600, 513 S.E.2d 885 (1999).

Probation, suspension, distinct concepts. — In drafting conviction orders, sentencing judges must be cognizant that probation and suspension of sentence are separate and distinct concepts and that they may be fixed at different intervals to accomplish different goals. Sentencing orders frequently fail to clarify whether a period of suspension of sentence and a period of probation are fixed for the same or different periods of time, particularly where sentencing orders denominate probation as "unsupervised." Sentencing judges who intend that a sentence shall be suspended for a fixed period, even where the period of suspension is to expire at the same time as the period of probation, should clearly state the respective period of suspension and period of probation in the sentencing order. Carbaugh v. Commonwealth, 19 Va. App. 119, 449 S.E.2d 264 (1994).

The concepts are distinct but overlapping, in the sense that a sentence of confinement may be suspended without admitting the defendant to probation while a prerequisite to probation is that any sentence of confinement be first suspended. Collins v. Commonwealth, 269 Va. 141, 607 S.E.2d 719, 2005 Va. LEXIS 13 (2005).

Suspension of execution of sentence includes release under appeal bond. — Appeal of a criminal conviction does not affect the finality of judgment, but only suspends the execution of the sentence. Therefore, the execution of defendant's sentence was suspended when he was released under his appeal bond and he was subject to the implicit condition of good behavior. Collins v. Commonwealth, 269 Va. 141, 607 S.E.2d 719, 2005 Va. LEXIS 13 (2005).

When § 19.2-305.1 and this section are applied in conjunction, the requirement of § 19.2-305.1 D (now § 19.2-305.1 E) that only "unreasonable" failure to pay restitution shall result in revocation of a suspended sentence, restricts the scope of the court's authority under this section to revoke a suspension for "any cause" deemed by it sufficient. Duff v. Commonwealth, 16 Va. App. 293, 429 S.E.2d 465 (1993).

"If none" construed. — In order to give effect to the legislative purpose, the words "if none" in this section cannot sensibly refer solely to "period of probation." The words, "if none," may, however, reasonably be read to refer to the clause, "for any cause deemed by the judge sufficient which occurred at any time within the period of probation." This interpretation is grammatically sound and consistent with the legislative intent to grant judges broad powers to revoke suspended sentences. Carbaugh v. Commonwealth, 19 Va. App. 119, 449 S.E.2d 264 (1994).

The probation statutes are highly remedial and should be liberally construed to provide trial courts a valuable tool for rehabilitation of criminals. Grant v. Commonwealth, 223 Va. 680, 292 S.E.2d 348 (1982).

The statutes obviously confer upon trial courts wide latitude and much discretion in matters of suspension and probation to provide a remedial tool in the rehabilitation of criminals and, to that end, should be liberally construed. Wright v. Commonwealth, 32 Va. App. 148, 526 S.E.2d 784, appeal dismissed, 261 Va. 1, 539 S.E.2d 432 (2000).

Language "shall leave the jurisdiction of the court without the consent of the judge" manifestly applies primarily to a fugitive or to one who absconds. It does not apply to a person who departs the Commonwealth because he is in the custody of federal authorities. Rease v. Commonwealth, 227 Va. 289, 316 S.E.2d 148 (1984).

Power of courts to revoke suspensions and probation for breach of conditions must not be restricted beyond statutory limitations. Grant v. Commonwealth, 223 Va. 680, 292 S.E.2d 348 (1982).

Jurisdiction on appeal of probation revocation. — As a trial court's jurisdiction to revoke a convict's probation and suspension of sentence is part of a purely criminal process, and as under this section the trial court retained jurisdiction over the suspended portion of defendant's sentence during the two-year period of his probation and for one year thereafter, the trial court had jurisdiction over the suspended portion of defendant's sentence at the time it revoked defendant's probation. Accordingly, because defendant's appeal of the revocation order was an appeal from an action taken while the trial court retained jurisdiction over his sentence, his appeal was within the appellate court's jurisdiction under subsection A of § 17.1-406. Green v. Commonwealth, 263 Va. 191, 557 S.E.2d 230, 2002 Va. LEXIS 23 (2002).

Appeal of revocation proceeding based upon underlying conviction. — As a consequence, the fate of the underlying conviction will determine the outcome of an appeal of the revocation proceeding. Resio v. Commonwealth, 29 Va. App. 616, 513 S.E.2d 892 (1999).

Validity of district court's jurisdiction following appeal to circuit court. — Where defendant withdrew an appeal of a district court judgment more than 10 days after the date of the judgment, and a de novo hearing was not held, the judgment was stayed but remained valid; a circuit court's appellate order did not annul or abrogate the district court judgment. Commonwealth v. Diaz, 266 Va. 260, 585 S.E.2d 552, 2003 Va. LEXIS 90 (2003), reversing 38 VA. App. 713, 568 S.E.2d 401 (2002).

Trial court's authority. — Defendant's suspended sentence could not be modified as no jurisdiction existed under § 19.2-306 as the trial court's authority had to be predicated on revocation of the suspended sentence, which had not occurred in the instant case; no power was given to the trial court to enlarge or modify an original sentence. Smith v. Commonwealth, — Va. App. —, — S.E.2d —, 2008 Va. App. LEXIS 238 (May 20, 2008).

Appeal of conviction does not bar revocation of suspension. — Evidence that the trier of fact in a criminal proceeding found beyond a reasonable doubt that a defendant violated a state law is sufficient to support revocation of a suspended sentence, notwithstanding the pendency of such conviction on appeal. Simmonds v. Commonwealth, No. 2710-99-3, 2000 Va. App. LEXIS 662 (Ct. of Appeals Sept. 26, 2000).

Failure to preserve issue for review. — Where a defendant made no objection when the Commonwealth reminded the trial court at a revocation hearing that a term of defendant's probation was to remain drug and alcohol free, or when the trial court noted that defendant had been under the influence of alcohol contrary to the terms of his probation, and made no argument at the hearing that the trial court's consideration of his consumption of alcohol was a violation of his due process rights or otherwise improper, he was barred under Va. Sup. Ct. R. 5A:18 from raising this issue for the first time on appeal. Cappell v. Commonwealth, No. 0807-02-3, 2003 Va. App. LEXIS 313 (Ct. of Appeals May 27, 2003).

In a probation revocation hearing, where defendant failed to renew his motion to strike after he presented his evidence, his closing argument did not challenge the sufficiency of the evidence, and he made no motion to set aside the court's judgment, any claim on appeal that the order of revocation was not supported by sufficient evidence was not preserved for appeal; further, the appeals court refused to apply Va. Sup. Ct. R. 5A:18 because defendant did not affirmatively show that a miscarriage of justice occurred. Ramsey v. Commonwealth, No. 1732-03-2, 2004 Va. App. LEXIS 297 (Ct. of Appeals June 29, 2004). See also, Goode v. Commonwealth, 2007 Va. App. LEXIS 118 (Mar. 27, 2007).

Miscarriage of justice found. — There was a miscarriage of justice for Va. Sup. Ct. R. 5A:18 purposes in the revocation of defendant's 1999 sentences as the maximum sentence for the 1999 convictions was five years and 30 days under §§ 18.2-308.2, 18.2-10, and 18.2-250.1, and the revocation of defendant's 1999 suspended sentences occurred two years after the maximum period for which defendant might originally have been sentenced to imprisonment under subsection A of § 19.2-306. Keen v. Commonwealth, 2010 Va. App. LEXIS 268 (July 6, 2010).

Written statement of fact not provided. — Although defendant was not provided with a written statement issued by the court, the record clearly demonstrated that defendant received written notice from the Commonwealth and knew what probation violations were being lodged against defendant, as the Commonwealth provided defendant's attorney with a copy of the letter to trial court requesting that defendant's probation be revoked because of a violation of good behavior. Logan v. Commonwealth, 50 Va. App. 518, 651 S.E.2d 403, 2007 Va. App. LEXIS 393 (2007), rev'd on other grounds, remanded, 2008 Va. App. LEXIS 96 (2008).

Miscarriage of justice not found. — Order revoking defendant's suspended sentences for three distributing marijuana convictions was proper as defendant failed to object and did not show a miscarriage of justice under Va. Sup. Ct. R. 5A:18 since the trial court had jurisdiction to revoke defendant's suspended sentences under subsection A of § 19.2-306 since such revocation was allowed during the maximum period for which defendant might originally have been sentenced to imprisonment, or 30 years, under § 18.2-10. Keen v. Commonwealth, 2010 Va. App. LEXIS 268 (July 6, 2010).

Applied in Smith v. Commonwealth, 222 Va. 700, 284 S.E.2d 590 (1981); Wise v. Ritter, 25 Bankr. 440 (Bankr. E.D. Va. 1982); Vaughn v. Commonwealth, 12 Va. App. 924, 406 S.E.2d 419 (1991); Epps v. Commonwealth, 59 Va. App. 71, 717 S.E.2d 151, 2011 Va. App. LEXIS 351 (2011); Smith v. Commonwealth, 59 Va. App. 710, 722 S.E.2d 310, 2012 Va. App. LEXIS 56 (2012).

II. LIMITATION PERIOD.

When arrest allowed after expiration of probation and suspension. — To effect the legislative intent, the first sentence of this section must be read consistently so as to allow the arrest of a defendant within one year after the period of suspension fixed by the court in those cases where both a period of probation and a period of suspension have been prescribed and where the period of probation has expired. Carbaugh v. Commonwealth, 19 Va. App. 119, 449 S.E.2d 264 (1994).

Indefinite probation period. — Probation depends for enforceability upon the existence of a term of sentence suspension;

therefore, the duration of probation cannot extend beyond the specified period of suspension. Hartless v. Commonwealth, 29 Va. App. 172, 510 S.E.2d 738 (1999).

Defendant's extended probation imposed upon him as a condition of the suspension of his sentence was modified as the trial court had specified no period of probation. Hartless v. Commonwealth, 29 Va. App. 172, 510 S.E.2d 738 (1999).

Limitation upon period within which suspension revocable. — If the court fails to prescribe the period of probation in the suspending order, the statute limits the jurisdiction of the court to revoke the suspension to the maximum period for which the accused could originally have been imprisoned. Richardson v. Commonwealth, 131 Va. 802, 109 S.E. 460 (1921). This holding was made statutory by the 1938 amendment.

Where there was no express limitation as to the duration of the suspension, the jurisdiction of the court to revoke the suspension continued for the maximum period for which the defendant might originally have been imprisoned. Dyke v. Commonwealth, 193 Va. 478, 69 S.E.2d 483 (1952).

Former § 53-272 [now §§ 53.1-151 and 53.1-186] authorizes the suspension of imposition or execution of sentence during good behavior. Inherent in that optional authority is the power of the court to attach such reasonable terms and conditions to the suspension as it may deem proper. Such terms and conditions are probation only in the sense that they require the defendant to observe a specified course of conduct; but they are not the supervised probation referred to in the statute. If no period of supervised probation is added to the suspension of the sentence, then under the terms of this section the only limitation upon the time for revocation of the suspension is the maximum period for which the defendant might originally have been sentenced. Dyke v. Commonwealth, 193 Va. 478, 69 S.E.2d 483 (1952).

When a court in its order prescribes the period of suspension and supervised probation it may, under this section, revoke the suspension and probation only within the probation period. Vick v. Commonwealth, 201 Va. 474, 111 S.E.2d 824 (1960).

While petitioner was released from supervised probation by the judge, it is clear under Virginia law that a sentencing court retains the authority to activate petitioner's sentence at any time during the maximum period for which petitioner might have originally been sentenced. There is, therefore, no question that petitioner is "in custody" for purposes of the federal habeas corpus statutes. Hamilton v. Lumpkin, 389 F. Supp. 1069 (E.D. Va. 1975).

If a probation period or a period of suspension was "prescribed," within the meaning of this section, then running of the shorter time within which the court could revoke would be triggered; if such period was not "prescribed," then the time for revocation would extend through the maximum period for which defendant could originally have been sentenced. Grant v. Commonwealth, 223 Va. 680, 292 S.E.2d 348 (1982).

Where no time was set or "prescribed" for the suspension of imposition of defendant's sentence, the sentencing authority of the trial court under this section was still viable and extended through the maximum period for which defendant might originally have been sentenced to imprisonment, and thus the trial court had the power to revoke the suspension and to pronounce the sentence that might have been originally imposed. Grant v. Commonwealth, 223 Va. 680, 292 S.E.2d 348 (1982).

Where on November 10, 1983 (21 months after the original sentencing order), the trial court revoked appellant's suspended imposition of sentence and ordered him to serve 10 years in prison, but suspended five years for an unspecified time period, then the remaining suspension period ended, by operation of this section, on November 10, 1993; thus when on July 11, 1994, the trial court heard evidence that appellant committed a petit larceny on May 26, 1993, along with other parole violations starting in October 1993, both of these offenses occurred before November 10, 1993, and imposition of the five year previously suspended portion was proper. Briggs v. Commonwealth, 21 Va. App. 338, 464 S.E.2d 512 (1995).

Where a sentencing order imposes no term of suspension, the term of suspension is "the maximum period for which the defendant might originally have been sentenced to be imprisoned;" where the maximum period that the defendant could have been imprisoned was 12 months, and 12 months from the date of the sentencing order was July 28, 1993, and the conduct which was the cause of the

suspension proceeding occurred, on May 24, 1994, since the term of suspension of defendant's sentence had expired, this conduct could not support the revocation of the suspension. Klokow v. Commonwealth, No. 2659-94-3 (Ct. of Appeals Feb. 13, 1996).

When defendant received a suspended sentence that did not specify the period of suspension, the suspension could be revoked at any time within the maximum prison term that could have been imposed, which was five years, and, when the suspension was revoked and resuspended, upon defendant's violation of the conditions of suspension, a new five-year period within which the new suspension could be revoked started running, so the trial court had jurisdiction to, again, revoke the suspension within that time period, upon defendant's further violations of the conditions of the suspension. Keene v. Commonwealth, No. 0043-03-1, 2003 Va. App. LEXIS 679 (Ct. of Appeals Dec. 23, 2003).

Where defendant was arrested on a four-year-old bench warrant for violating probation, the trial court properly exercised its jurisdiction pursuant to § 19.2-306. The procedural law governing defendant's probation was governed by the version of § 19.2-306 in effect at the time defendant was placed on probation after serving a portion of an imposed sentence and the trial court issued the bench warrant well within the time period prescribed by the amendment to § 19.2-306 in effect at that time. Hunter v. Commonwealth, 56 Va. App. 582, 695 S.E.2d 567, 2010 Va. App. LEXIS 301 (2010).

Limitation on time of revocation. — In the absence of a specified period of probation or a specified period of suspension, a trial court may revoke a suspension of sentence for a probation violation only when the violation occurs within the maximum period for which the defendant might originally have been sentenced to be imprisoned. Hartless v. Commonwealth, 29 Va. App. 172, 510 S.E.2d 738 (1999).

Where issues raised by a bench warrant were extensions of defendant's underlying criminal case, a matter already and properly before a trial court, the trial court had constitutional and statutory authority, subject matter jurisdiction, to entertain the issues raised by the bench warrant; however, its exercise of that jurisdiction was constrained by the time requirement of § 19.2-306. Farmer v. Commonwealth, — Va. App. —, — S.E.2d —, 2008 Va. App. LEXIS 47 (Jan. 29, 2008).

Bench warrant issued was untimely. — A bench warrant issued more than one year after the conclusion of defendant's probation was untimely. Reinemer v. Commonwealth, 16 Va. App. 462, 431 S.E.2d 68 (1993).

One-year limit suspended when probationer arrested by another jurisdiction. — The legislature did not intend the statutory one-year limitation to restrict the power of the court to revoke probation circumstances when the probationer commits another crime within the probation period and is arrested by another jurisdiction, thereby placing himself beyond the jurisdiction and control of the sentencing court. In such cases, the one-year time constraint of this section is suspended. The time limit remains suspended, when the probation period expires during incarceration in the other jurisdiction, until the probationer is released by such other jurisdiction, provided the original court as soon as practicable has issued a warrant charging violation of probation and a detainer. Rease v. Commonwealth, 227 Va. 289, 316 S.E.2d 148 (1984).

Statute tolled for time period that probationer absconded from jurisdiction. — Had this section not been tolled, trial court could have revoked probationer's suspended sentence up until January 8, 1991 — four years plus one year following his conviction on January 8, 1986. However, by including in the calculations the fact that he absconded from the jurisdiction for two years less nine days, thereby tolling the statute of limitations for that period of time, the trial court's jurisdiction continued until December 31, 1992. Therefore, the trial court had jurisdiction when it revoked probationer's suspended sentence on September 11, 1991. Withrow v. Commonwealth, No. 2087-91-1 (Ct. of Appeals Feb. 16, 1993).

Trial court did not abuse its discretion when it revoked defendant's probation at a time beyond the time the trial court normally would have retained jurisdiction over defendant's probation and suspended sentence, as defendant's acts in absconding when defendant's probation officer no longer knew where defendant was located and defendant's arrest on a criminal charge in another state, were sufficient to trigger the tolling provisions of the statute permitting revocations of probation and suspended sentences, and permitted the trial court to revoke defendant's probation and suspended sentence at a time that normally would have been beyond the time the trial court retained jurisdiction over defendant's probation and suspended sentence. Allison v. Commonwealth, 40 Va. App. 407, 579 S.E.2d 655, 2003 Va. App. LEXIS 256 (2003).

Limitation period tolled by out-of-state incarceration. — Probation revocation hearing was not outside the one-year limitation of § 19.2-306. Appellant's probation had been tolled when he was incarcerated in California, during which he was beyond the jurisdiction and control of the Virginia trial court. Pierce v. Commonwealth, 48 Va. App. 660, 633 S.E.2d 755, 2006 Va. App. LEXIS 407 (2006).

Issuance of capias does not toll period for revocation of suspended sentence. — The time period during which a suspended sentence may be revoked for a violation of probation is not tolled by the mere issuance of a capias for a probationer's arrest. Smith v. Commonwealth, No. 0809-86-1 (Ct. of Appeals July 13, 1987).

Statute not tolled when defendant within reach of trial court's writ. — Even though defendant never reported to his probation officer, the tolling provision of this section did not apply where a trial court and the Commonwealth's agents knew his location, which was in reach of the trial court's writ, and the trial court had the power to retrieve defendant from any penal institution in the Commonwealth and have him produced for a revocation hearing. The trial court was constrained from exercising its subject matter jurisdiction to conduct a revocation hearing. Farmer v. Commonwealth, — Va. App. —, — S.E.2d —, 2008 Va. App. LEXIS 47 (Jan. 29, 2008).

When a state probation violation warrant merely has been issued but not served and a detainer has been lodged, a defendant has no constitutional or statutory right to force the trial court to decide the revocation issue. This is true even though the defendant was, for a brief time, held in federal custody in jail in an adjoining county. Accordingly, it is entirely proper for the trial court to defer decision on the probation violation until completion of defendant's federal incarceration. Rease v. Commonwealth, 227 Va. 289, 316 S.E.2d 148 (1984).

Effect of extending probation period. — An extension of the period of probation under § 19.2-304 has the effect of extending the time during which revocation may occur under this section. Cook v. Commonwealth, 211 Va. 290, 176 S.E.2d 815 (1970).

Meaning of "maximum period," etc. — The language of this section, "the maximum period for which the defendant might originally have been sentenced" and "the court may pronounce whatever sentence might have been originally imposed," does not mean the maximum punishment for the greatest or most serious offense charged in the indictment. If upon an indictment for murder one is found guilty of involuntary manslaughter and given a suspended jail sentence and fine, the statute does not contemplate that the suspension of sentence could be revoked at any time during the life of accused because he was simply indicted for murder which carries a punishment of death or life imprisonment. The test is not what is the maximum punishment which might be imposed under the indictment alone, but the maximum punishment which might be imposed under the indictment and the evidence. White v. Commonwealth, 170 Va. 641, 196 S.E. 610 (1938).

Hearing continued beyond period of probation on defendant's motion. — The appeal on an order revoking suspension of sentence came before the circuit court for hearing within the one-year period of probation during which defendant's sentence was suspended. On his motion the hearing was continued and not had until after the one-year period. Since the delay was on defendant's motion, he would not be heard to say the revocation was not timely made. Berry v. Commonwealth, 200 Va. 495, 106 S.E.2d 590 (1959).

Suspension revocation exhausted court's sentencing authority. — When the trial court revoked the suspension of the execution of defendant's original sentence and imposed the entirety of the remainder of the unserved portion of that sentence, the court exhausted the sentencing authority invested in it by § 19.2-306 and lost its jurisdiction to impose any additional terms, conditions, or supervision upon him; because the trial court was without jurisdiction to order him placed on probation upon his release from incarceration after serving his sentence in full, his subsequent

contempt conviction for violating that order was error. Grooms v. Commonwealth, No. 1439-02-3, 2003 Va. App. LEXIS 575 (Ct. of Appeals Nov. 12, 2003).

III. REVOCATION HEARING.

A. Generally.

Fundamental fairness requires a judicial hearing of a summary nature before the court can revoke a suspended sentence and thereby deprive the probationer of his liberty. The requirement of such a hearing is implicit in the statute. Cook v. Commonwealth, 211 Va. 290, 176 S.E.2d 815 (1970).

Since the revocation of a suspension of sentence deprives the probationer of his liberty, he is entitled to a judicial hearing thereon, but a summary hearing is sufficient. Slayton v. Commonwealth, 185 Va. 357, 38 S.E.2d 479 (1946).

Since the revocation of a suspension deprives the probationer of his liberty, he is entitled to a judicial hearing thereon. Griffin v. Cunningham, 205 Va. 349, 136 S.E.2d 840 (1964).

In a proceeding to revoke probation, an accused is entitled to a judicial hearing at which he has the right to appear and testify, and to be represented by counsel. Brown v. Slayton, 337 F. Supp. 10 (W.D. Va. 1971).

Judicial hearing defined. — A judicial hearing means a hearing in accordance with familiar principles governing the exercise of judicial discretion. Griffin v. Cunningham, 205 Va. 349, 136 S.E.2d 840 (1964).

Hearsay evidence. — A trial judge's action in taking cognizance of testimony that he heard in an earlier prosecution to which the defendant was a party is equivalent to admitting hearsay evidence in the revocation proceeding. Hess v. Commonwealth, 17 Va. App. 738, 441 S.E.2d 29 (1994).

Limited applicability of exclusionary rule. — Although a probation, parole, or suspended sentence revocation proceeding is not criminal in nature, the outcome of such a proceeding may result in the loss of one's liberty. Nevertheless, unless the evidence shows that the police officers who illegally seized the evidence also acted in bad faith, the exclusionary rule should not be used to prevent the evidence from being admitted into evidence in a secondary proceeding, such as a probation revocation hearing. Anderson v. Commonwealth, 20 Va. App. 361, 457 S.E.2d 396 (1995), aff'd, 251 Va. 437, 470 S.E.2d 862 (1996).

Arrest is not necessary where defendant is already in custody of court. — The purpose of the provision in this section that the court may "cause the defendant to be arrested," is that he may be brought before the court. There was no occasion for causing the defendant to be arrested when he was already in the custody of the court on a felony charge of malicious shooting at the time of the revocation. Berry v. Commonwealth, 200 Va. 495, 106 S.E.2d 590 (1959).

Failure to conduct preliminary hearing. — Even if there exists a requirement of a preliminary hearing in probation-revocation cases, the failure to conduct such a hearing is not a denial of a constitutional right. Brown v. Slayton, 337 F. Supp. 10 (W.D. Va. 1971).

Where an outstanding warrant to show cause why the suspended portion of his sentence should not be revoked remained unexecuted for a time during which the defendant was otherwise incarcerated, defendant lost no protected liberty interest as a result of the warrant. Defendant was not deprived of any due process rights since there was no duty to provide him a hearing until he was taken into custody as a parole violator by execution of the capias and show cause order upon him. Atkins v. Commonwealth, 2 Va. App. 329, 343 S.E.2d 385 (1986).

Absence of counsel at revocation proceeding. — A probation revocation proceeding at which petitioner alleges that he did not have the benefit of counsel may be a valid ground for the granting of the writ of habeas corpus. Cave v. Slayton, 353 F. Supp. 513 (W.D. Va. 1972).

Burden on defendant to place in record evidence. — Burden was on defendant, appealing the revocation of a suspended sentence, to place in the record all of the evidence that would prove a statutory bar to revocation. Of necessity, that would include evidence and a copy of any orders from the first hearing. Mann v. Commonwealth, No. 0308-89-1 (Ct. of Appeals Aug. 21, 1990).

A jury need not be impanelled to try the issue of the

sufficiency of the cause of revocation of the suspension. Slayton v. Commonwealth, 185 Va. 357, 38 S.E.2d 479 (1946); Berry v. Commonwealth, 200 Va. 495, 106 S.E.2d 590 (1959).

Proof beyond reasonable doubt. — The court of appeals held that although revocation of probation must be upon reasonable cause, an assessment of the sufficiency of the evidence to sustain an order is vested in the trial court and proof beyond a reasonable doubt is not required. The Supreme Court reversed Pannell v. Commonwealth, 34 Va. App. 287, 540 S.E.2d 527, 2001 Va. App. LEXIS 47 (2001) rev'd 263 Va. 497 (2002).

Judgment reversible only on clear showing of abuse of discretion. — The trial court's finding of fact and judgment as to an order of revocation are reversible only upon a clear showing of abuse of such discretion. Hamilton v. Commonwealth, 217 Va. 325, 228 S.E.2d 555 (1976).

Discretion of court. — The revocation of the suspension of a sentence is left to the discretion of the trial court. And there is no indication as to how the sufficiency of the cause of revocation is to be determined. Slayton v. Commonwealth, 185 Va. 357, 38 S.E.2d 479 (1946) wherein the court's discretion was held not abused.

A revocation of a suspended sentence lies in the discretion of the trial court and that discretion is quite broad. Hamilton v. Commonwealth, 217 Va. 325, 228 S.E.2d 555 (1976).

The question of whether to revoke the suspension of a sentence lies within the sound discretion of the trial court. Singleton v. Commonwealth, 11 Va. App. 575, 400 S.E.2d 205 (1991). See also, Preston v. Commonwealth, 14 Va. App. 731, 419 S.E.2d 288 (1992).

A trial court has broad discretion to revoke a suspended sentence and probation. Hill v. Commonwealth, No. 1835-92-3 (Ct. of Appeals Jan. 18, 1994).

Where the trial court imposed a condition upon a probation to enter and successfully complete a Detention Center Incarceration Program, and while such might have been a condition of probation, merely entering the program was a prerequisite to and one of the conditions upon which the probationer's sentence was suspended; when he could no longer satisfy this condition, the court was authorized to reconsider the suspended sentences and determine what portion of the same or other alternatives were appropriate. Word v. Commonwealth, 41 Va. App. 496, 586 S.E.2d 282, 2003 Va. App. LEXIS 485 (2003).

Trial court did not abuse its discretion in denying defendant's motion to continue his probation revocation proceedings on grounds that defense counsel had not yet had the opportunity to review the Commonwealth's sentencing guidelines report or to obtain evidence that defendant was eligible for a particular drug treatment program, because: (1) defendant failed to include the sentencing guidelines report as a part of the record on appeal, preventing the appeals court from concluding that defendant's inability to review the report before the revocation hearing resulted in any prejudice; and (2) defendant was not eligible for the particular drug treatment he sought, and thus, he could not demonstrate any prejudice resulting from his inability to present evidence that he was eligible for that program. Mock v. Commonwealth, — Va. App. —, — S.E.2d —, 2005 Va. App. LEXIS 243 (June 21, 2005).

Trial court did not abuse its discretion by imposing the entire original sentences that had been suspended against a defendant upon revocation of the suspended sentences, because this section did not provide a trial court with any discretion as to imposing the entire original sentence or a portion of the same upon revocation. As such, the trial court's imposition of the entire 26 years of imprisonment against the defendant was proper, because his suspended sentences were revoked due to his failure to report to his probation officer, his failure to make restitution, and his subsequent conviction for larceny. Commonwealth v. Payne, — Va. —, — S.E.2d —, 2003 Va. LEXIS 117 (July 11, 2003).

Because defendant's instant messaging took place sometime after a revocation hearing, the trial court properly exercised its discretion under subsection D of § 19.2-306 in revoking defendant's suspended sentence. Castle v. Commonwealth, 2011 Va. App. LEXIS 266 (Aug. 9, 2011).

If the presiding judge at the probation revocation hearing also presided at the probationer's criminal prosecution and the judge deems it necessary or desirable to consider evidence or aspects of the earlier criminal proceeding as a basis for revoking probation, the judge may in the exercise of sound discretion consider such evidence, provided that the judge delineates during the evidentiary portion of the revocation proceeding precisely the evidence that is being considered. Hess v. Commonwealth, 17 Va. App. 738, 441 S.E.2d 29 (1994).

Evidence of pre-suspension criminal record admissible. — Defendant's pre-suspension criminal record was admissible in revocation proceedings, as it was relevant to the trial court's determination of how much of the suspension to revoke. Pearson v. Commonwealth, 37 Va. App. 583, 560 S.E.2d 459, 2002 Va. App. LEXIS 141 (2002).

Imposition of new period of suspension in revocation proceeding. — Section 19.2-303.1, which expressly provides that a trial court may suspend a sentence for a reasonable time "in any case," pertains not only to a defendant's initial sentencing but also to sentencing in revocation proceedings and a court could, therefore, impose a five year suspension period in a revocation proceeding, even though that period would extend beyond the end of the five-year period originally imposed. Wright v. Commonwealth, 32 Va. App. 148, 526 S.E.2d 784, appeal dismissed, 261 Va. 1, 539 S.E.2d 432 (2000).

As defendant's first resentencing constituted a new sentencing event only in the imposition of previously suspended time and of reasonable conditions, which were within the statutorily limited powers of the circuit court, the period of suspension under § 19.2-306 included defendant's subsequent possession of heroin. Canty v. Commonwealth, 2011 Va. LEXIS 253 (Oct. 7, 2011).

The right to notice and hearing involves no constitutional question but is to be determined by reference to the probation statute. Berry v. Commonwealth, 200 Va. 495, 106 S.E.2d 590 (1959).

Proceedings held not to violate rights of defendant. — While under suspended sentence for a misdemeanor defendant was arrested on a charge of malicious shooting. When he pleaded not guilty to this charge in the county court, it being suggested in his presence by the prosecutor that he had nevertheless been involved in a violent breach of the peace, the court revoked the suspension. He appealed to the circuit court under this section. After his conviction of the felony, hearing was held in the circuit court, also without any warrant, summons, or rule charging violation of the terms of the suspension, and the revocation was affirmed. These actions violated no right of defendant. Berry v. Commonwealth, 200 Va. 495, 106 S.E.2d 590 (1959).

Use of polygraph results. — Trial court erred when it considered the results of a polygraph exam defendant took while enrolled in a counseling program for sex offenders and determined that defendant had violated the conditions of probation because he gave deceptive answers when asked if he had tried to meet with children or had sexual contacts with children. White v. Commonwealth, 41 Va. App. 191, 583 S.E.2d 771, 2003 Va. App. LEXIS 417 (2003).

B. Basis for Revocation.

The revocation of the suspended sentence must be based on reasonable cause, and must be based upon cause that occurred within the suspension of probation period. Bailey v. Commonwealth, 19 Va. App. 355, 451 S.E.2d 686 (1994).

Adequacy of grounds for revocation. — Whether or not a court has adequate grounds on which to revoke a petitioner's probation is more properly a question of the sufficiency of the evidence; as such, only in the case where the judgment is totally devoid of evidentiary support is there raised a federal question cognizable in the federal district court. Brown v. Slayton, 337 F. Supp. 10 (W.D. Va. 1971).

Trial court did not abuse its discretion in revoking suspended sentence for aggravated sexual battery involving children, where defendant took photographs of children in public places without having physical contact with the children on the advice of a psychiatrist for use as a masturbation tool to help defendant overcome his pedophila and conditions of the suspended sentence included that defendant was not to possess pornography or have contact with children. Levesque v. Commonwealth, No. 0312-00-3, 2001 Va. App. LEXIS 371 (Ct. of Appeals June 26, 2001).

Trial court did not abuse its discretion in revoking a portion of defendant's suspended sentence, where defendant committed institutional infractions by threatening correctional officers and threatening to commit arson and by committing two acts of indecent exposure. Artis v. Commonwealth, — Va. App. —, — S.E.2d —, 2006 Va. App. LEXIS 84 (Mar. 7, 2006).

After defendant was convicted of attempted robbery, the trial court properly revoked two previously suspended sentences. Since being put on probation and having the sentences suspended, defendant had tested positive for cocaine use, failed to report to his probation officer, failed to submit to urine screens, failed to report to drug court, and absconded from his probation supervision, in addition to his conviction. Brown v. Commonwealth, — Va. App. —, — S.E.2d —, 2006 Va. App. LEXIS 233 (Apr. 18, 2006).

Revocation of defendant's suspended sentence was upheld because the act upon which the revocation was based violated the good behavior condition of suspension, which was in effect even during the period of defendant's incarceration, and the court's written order prevailed over any apparently contradictory provisions contained in the transcript of the proceedings. Palmer v. Commonwealth, — Va. App. —, — S.E.2d —, 2006 Va. App. LEXIS 434 (Oct. 3, 2006).

Since the record indicated that a trial court placed significant weight upon defendant's new convictions in the revocation of the suspension of her prior sentences, defendant was entitled to a new hearing in light of the court's reversal of defendant's new convictions. Whitehead v. Commonwealth, 278 Va. 105, 677 S.E.2d 265, 2009 Va. LEXIS 62 (2009).

Trial court did not err in finding that defendant violated his probation by refusing to admit that he committed the charged crime during court-ordered sex offender treatment because his Alford plea did not contain an implicit promise that he would never be required to admit his guilt, and the record did not show that the trial court abused its discretion in ordering sex offender treatment as a condition of defendant's probation; a defendant who enters an Alford plea is not an innocent person for the purposes of criminal sentencing and probation, and to mitigate the possibility that an innocent person would so plead, a factual basis is required supporting the finding of guilt before an Alford plea could be accepted. Carroll v. Commonwealth, 54 Va. App. 730, 682 S.E.2d 92, 2009 Va. App. LEXIS 392 (2009), aff'd, 280 Va. 641, 701 S.E.2d 414, 2010 Va. LEXIS 277 (2010).

Trial court did not err in revoking defendant's previously suspended sentence under subsection A of § 19.2-306 because defendant had been found guilty of robbery, abduction, carjacking, and use of a firearm during each of those felonies. Thompson v. Commonwealth, 2010 Va. App. LEXIS 415 (Oct. 26, 2010).

Trial court had authority under § 19.2-306 to revoke defendant's suspended sentence for misconduct that occurred while defendant was serving time on work release because the sentencing summary did not state that the suspended sentence was conditioned "upon release" and the condition of good behavior was implicit in every order suspending sentence; that implicit condition attached from the moment following the pronouncement of a suspended sentence. Hodgins v. Commonwealth, 61 Va. App. 102, 733 S.E.2d 678, 2012 Va. App. LEXIS 346 (Nov. 6, 2012).

Trial court, because it committed no legal error in denying defendant's motion to withdraw defendant's guilty plea, properly considered defendant's new conviction in determining whether to revoke defendant's suspended sentence from a prior conviction. Further, in light of the evidence presented, the court did not abuse its discretion in revoking the entirety of defendant's suspended sentence in light of defendant's new conviction. Booker v. Commonwealth, 61 Va. App. 323, 734 S.E.2d 729, 2012 Va. App. LEXIS 407 (2012).

Section provides authority to revoke. — The authority of the trial court to revoke suspension of the execution of a sentence for any cause deemed by it sufficient which occurs within the period of suspension fixed by the court is provided by this section. Hamilton v. Commonwealth, 217 Va. 325, 228 S.E.2d 555 (1976).

This section provides the court with authority to revoke suspended sentences for violation occurring during the period of probation. Blankenship v. Commonwealth, No. 1490-88-1 (Ct. of Appeals Aug. 14, 1990).

This section authorizes a trial judge to revoke a suspended sentence based on criminal misconduct violating the conditions of suspension, even though committed while the convict is incarcerated and before his active probation begins. Haynes v. Commonwealth, No. 1593-92-2 (Ct. of Appeals Mar. 22, 1994).

Under this section, a court retains the authority to revoke a suspended sentence despite the proscriptions of the rule specifying that all final judgments, orders, and decrees shall remain under the control of the trial court and subject to be modified, vacated, or suspended for 21 days after the date of entry and no longer. Wright v. Commonwealth, 32 Va. App. 148, 526 S.E.2d 784, appeal dismissed, 261 Va. 1, 539 S.E.2d 432 (2000).

Revocation of suspended sentence did not exceed judge's authority. — Trial court had authority to revoke defendant's suspended sentence upon his violations of conditions of suspended sentence and probation, since § 19.2-306 provided that the court could revoke defendant's unspecified suspended sentence during the maximum prescribed sentence plus one year, and the court's action occurred well within the prescribed period. Derrick v. Commonwealth, No. 2722-00-3, 2002 Va. App. LEXIS 283 (Ct. of Appeals May 7, 2002).

Since defendant was arrested and brought before the trial court within one year from the end of defendant's initial period of suspension, as required by § 19.2-306, the trial court had the authority to revoke defendant's sentence and extend his probation. Vitkow v. Commonwealth, No. 0531-01-4, 2002 Va. App. LEXIS 310 (Ct. of Appeals May 14, 2002).

Where defendant's probation period had been extended under § 19.2-304, the trial court was entitled to revoke his suspended sentence, although the original period of suspension had expired, because, pursuant to subsection A of § 19.2-306, the trial court could revoke the suspension anytime during the probation period. Mohamed v. Commonwealth, 56 Va. App. 95, 691 S.E.2d 513, 2010 Va. App. LEXIS 145 (2010).

When defendant was convicted of taking indecent liberties with a child while in a custodial or supervisory relationship, it was not an abuse of discretion to revoke defendant's previously suspended sentence or to run the sentence consecutively to defendant's new sentence because, (1) by committing a new offense, defendant "forfeited" the "conditional freedom" inherent in the court's earlier decision to suspend part of defendant's sentence, (2) defendant did not claim the trial court based defendant's sentence or revocation on facially unlawful considerations or that either sentence exceeded applicable statutory limits, and (3) consecutive sentences were presumed, under § 19.2-308. Nicholson v. Commonwealth, 2011 Va. App. LEXIS 405 (Dec. 20, 2011).

Revocation should not be arbitrary. — The action of the court in revoking a suspension should not, under any circumstances, be arbitrary. Griffin v. Cunningham, 205 Va. 349, 136 S.E.2d 840 (1964); Hamilton v. Commonwealth, 217 Va. 325, 228 S.E.2d 555 (1976).

Cause for revoking must be reasonable. — The cause deemed by the court to be sufficient for revoking a suspension must be a reasonable cause. Hamilton v. Commonwealth, 217 Va. 325, 228 S.E.2d 555 (1976).

Because trial judge erred in imposing prison sentences in excess of maximum allowed by statute, he had no authority to later revoke suspended sentences on those convictions and incarcerate defendant on those revocations. McCray v. Commonwealth, No. 1276-99-2 (Ct. of Appeals Mar. 21, 2000).

Trial court did not abuse its discretion in revoking defendant's suspended sentence for defendant's failure to pay restitution for eight months as the evidence did not support defendant's argument that defendant had an inability to pay restitution as defendant paid for car insurance, gasoline, medical prescriptions, and even a second restitution in another county at a time when defendant's sentencing order stated defendant was required to pay "all income" towards defendant's restitution and she did not pay any restitution at all. Johnson v. Commonwealth, No. 0760-01-4 CHIEF, 2002 Va. App. LEXIS 628 (Ct. of Appeals Oct. 15, 2002).

Defendant's own statement sufficient to prove violation of conditions of probation. — Circuit court did not abuse its discretion in revoking defendant's previously suspended sentences and re-suspending them on the ground that defendant violated the terms of probation because the Commonwealth proved by defendant's own statement that she used alcohol on numerous occasions during the probationary period, and if credited by the trial court, defendant's statement was sufficient, standing alone, to prove that she was making a poor adjustment to supervision; the corpus delicti rule is not applicable to the probation revocation process, which deals solely with the possible modification of a judgment already rendered. Downey v. Commonwealth, 59 Va. App. 13, 716 S.E.2d 472, 2011 Va. App. LEXIS 323 (2011).

Conduct occurred before sentence was imposed. — Revocation was not proper when all of the conduct complained of in the revocation proceeding occurred before the suspended sentence at issue was imposed. Joyce v. Commonwealth, — Va. App. —, — S.E.2d —, 2006 Va. App. LEXIS 498 (Nov. 7, 2006).

Because the trial court expressly stated that it did not consider the charges pending against defendant in another jurisdiction at a prior revocation hearing, it did not abuse its discretion under § 19.2-306 in revoking defendant's suspended sentence on that basis at a subsequent revocation hearing. Clarke v. Commonwealth, 60 Va. App. 190, 725 S.E.2d 158, 2012 Va. App. LEXIS 166 (2012).

Continuance of revocation proceeding not required. — A conviction for petit larceny which occurred during the period of probation is sufficient cause to support revocation of the petitioner's suspended sentence even if evidence of the facts underlying the conviction is not presented. In addition, a continuance of the revocation proceeding is not required while an appeal of the underlying conviction is pending. Patterson v. Commonwealth, 12 Va. App. 1046, 407 S.E.2d 43 (1991).

The conviction of a subsequent criminal offense is not essential to warrant the revocation of a suspension of sentence. Slayton v. Commonwealth, 185 Va. 357, 38 S.E.2d 479 (1946); Berry v. Commonwealth, 200 Va. 495, 106 S.E.2d 590 (1959).

Even though defendant had been acquitted of alleged crimes, the conduct connected with the alleged crimes could properly be the basis for revocation of suspension. In a revocation proceeding proof beyond a reasonable doubt is not required. Marshall v. Commonwealth, 202 Va. 217, 116 S.E.2d 270 (1960).

Trial court did not abuse its discretion in revoking a defendant's suspended sentence where three witnesses placed him at the scene of a murder and one identified him as the shooter; the trial court — notwithstanding the fact that a jury had acquitted defendant of the murder — was entitled to find from this evidence that defendant was illicitly involved in the homicide and made deceitful statements to an officer to conceal his involvement, and on the basis of either of those findings, could have properly concluded that defendant failed to be of good behavior, amounting to substantial misconduct, during the period of the suspension of his sentence. Cappell v. Commonwealth, No. 0807-02-3, 2003 Va. App. LEXIS 313 (Ct. of Appeals May 27, 2003).

Defendant consented to procedure. — Revocation of defendant's probation was affirmed as defendant agreed to the procedure followed, in which federal drug charges that were pending at the time of a first revocation hearing were not to be considered, unless they resulted in convictions; defendant was convicted, and the drug offenses properly formed the basis of a second revocation hearing. Subsection D of § 19.2-306 did not bar later consideration of that not previously considered. Ford v. Commonwealth, — Va. App. —, — S.E.2d —, 2007 Va. App. LEXIS 106 (Mar. 20, 2007).

Failure to complete alternative sentencing program. — Revocation of defendant's suspended sentence based on his failure to complete an alternative sentencing program was erroneous because his failure to complete the program was not willful but based on an unforeseen medical condition. Peyton v. Commonwealth, 268 Va. 503, 604 S.E.2d 17, 2004 Va. LEXIS 147 (2004).

Bench warrant as support of revocation. — Trial court did not violate defendant's due process rights when it revoked defendant's probation, as the bench warrant expressly stated that defendant was removed from the shelter for inappropriate conduct, which provided a sufficient basis for revocation. Lawrence v. Commonwealth, No. 0716-01-4, 2002 Va. App. LEXIS 719 (Ct. of Appeals Dec. 3, 2002).

Proof of violation beyond reasonable doubt not required. — An alleged violation upon which revocation is based need not be proven beyond a reasonable doubt. Simmonds v. Commonwealth, No. 2710-99-3, 2000 Va. App. LEXIS 662 (Ct. of Appeals Sept. 26, 2000).

Judge's power of revocation. — If no cause arose during the probation period, the judge may also revoke the suspended sentence and probation for any "cause . . . which occurred . . . within the period of suspension fixed by the court." The words, "if neither," must then be read to refer both to "cause . . . which occurred . . . within the probation period" and "cause . . . which occurred . . . within the period of suspension fixed by the court." Carbaugh v. Commonwealth, 19 Va. App. 119, 449 S.E.2d 264 (1994).

Although the express wording of this section does not explicitly address a judge's power to revoke suspension and probation when no period of suspension was fixed, that power is implicit because, if the cause arose during a time that was neither within the probation period nor within a period of suspension, i.e., no period of suspension was expressly prescribed, the judge could revoke the suspended sentence and probation within the maximum period for which the defendant might originally have been sentenced to be imprisoned. Carbaugh v. Commonwealth, 19 Va. App. 119, 449 S.E.2d 264 (1994).

Evidence supported decision to revoke defendant's probation and suspended sentence. — Revocation of suspended sentence was upheld as defendant's termination from the detention center violated a condition of his probation and suspended sentences and the trial court considered the totality of the evidence before finding sufficient cause to revoke defendant's suspended sentences. Owens v. Commonwealth, No. 0146-03-4, 2004 Va. App. LEXIS 60 (Ct. of Appeals Feb. 10, 2004).

Circuit court properly found a probationer in violation of his probation, as: (1) testimony from a victim-witness in a city prosecution, which was underlying basis for the issuance of a capias in the revocation matter, was relevant; (2) that witness was exempt from sequestration, as she could not have shaped her testimony to correspond to the contents of the probationer's letter to the judge or the testimony of the probation officer; and (3) a denial of a continuance was not error, as the probationer's counsel stated that despite his unfamiliarity with the city action, he was prepared to try the issue of whether or not his client violated the terms of his probation. Osborne v. Commonwealth, — Va. App. —, — S.E.2d —, 2005 Va. App. LEXIS 376 (Oct. 4, 2005).

Revocation of defendant's suspended sentence was affirmed when defendant was convicted after the suspended sentence was imposed of additional crimes. Imposition of the unserved portions of the original sentences was not an abuse of discretion. Joyce v. Commonwealth, — Va. App. —, — S.E.2d —, 2006 Va. App. LEXIS 498 (Nov. 7, 2006).

Revocation of defendant's probation and suspension of sentence was affirmed because the fact that defendant threatened the trial judge, standing alone, was legally sufficient to support the revocation and did not reflect an abuse of discretion. Spencer v. Commonwealth, — Va. App. —, — S.E.2d —, 2007 Va. App. LEXIS 469 (Dec. 27, 2007).

Circuit court did not abuse its discretion in revoking a portion of an inmate's remaining suspended sentence for one conviction, imposing an active period of incarceration, and revoking and resuspending in full the sentence on a second conviction because the inmate violated the conditions of his probation by testing positive for cocaine use within days of leaving jail and by failing to report for a required meeting with his probation officer. Price v. Commonwealth, 51 Va. App. 443, 658 S.E.2d 700, 2008 Va. App. LEXIS 166 (2008).

During defendant's revocation hearing, evidence was admitted into the record without objection that defendant had violated the conditions of his probation by failing to abide by the law and by failing to report to his probation officer as instructed, and defendant pleaded "no contest" to felony petit larceny third or subsequent offense, which he committed the day after his initial meeting with his probation officer. Because the evidence clearly established that defendant was convicted of petit larceny third offense during his probation period, the appellate court concluded that the evidence was sufficient to establish that he violated the conditions of his probation. Myers v. Commonwealth, 2009 Va. App. LEXIS 558 (Dec. 15, 2009).

Evidence supported sentence after probation revocation. — One-year and six-month sentence for underlying robbery and attempted robbery offenses was properly imposed after probation revocation under circumstances in which, inter alia, defendant had problems with both alcohol and drugs, tested positive for marijuana three times in five months, and refused to enter substance abuse counseling. Parkins v. Commonwealth, — Va. App. —, — S.E.2d —, 2006 Va. App. LEXIS 489 (Oct. 31, 2006).

C. Terms and Conditions.

Good behavior is a condition of every suspension. — While the language of the suspensions did not in terms include a condition of good behavior, that condition is implicit in every such suspension and constitutes the origin and purpose of the suspension and probation statutes. When a trial court suspends a sentence it does not make a contract with the accused, but only extends to him the opportunity which the State affords him to repent and reform. Coffey v. Commonwealth, 209 Va. 760, 167 S.E.2d 343 (1969); Brown v. Slayton, 342 F. Supp. 61 (W.D. Va. 1972).

Good behavior is a condition of every suspension, with or without probation, whether expressly so stated or not. Rutherford v. Blankenship, 468 F. Supp. 1357 (W.D. Va. 1979).

Revocation of a defendant's suspended sentence was proper, since: (1) good behavior was an implicit condition of every suspended sentence, even though probation had not yet started; and (2) he violated that condition while his sentence was suspended when he was released under his appeal bond. Collins v. Commonwealth, 269 Va. 141, 607 S.E.2d 719, 2005 Va. LEXIS 13 (2005).

Trial court did not err in revoking defendant's suspended sentences and resuspending six months under § 19.2-306 without first finding that defendant signed the probation terms and conditions form because defendant violated her implied duty of good behavior during the term of her suspended sentences by continuing to use illegal drugs. Jennings v. Commonwealth, 2010 Va. App. LEXIS 112 (Mar. 23, 2010).

Incarceration as condition of suspension. — Trial court had the authority to impose a period of incarceration as a condition of suspending the execution of a five-year penitentiary sentence. Nuckoles v. Commonwealth, 12 Va. App. 1083, 407 S.E.2d 355 (1991).

Order not prescribing probation or probation period. — Order suspending jail sentence and placing defendant "upon his good behavior for a period of one year" upon condition that "he keep the peace and dignity and not violate any of the laws" for a period of one year, did not prescribe a probation or a probation period within the meaning of former § 53-272 and this section. Dyke v. Commonwealth, 193 Va. 478, 69 S.E.2d 483 (1952).

Probation as condition of suspension. — A court's ability to revoke the suspension of a sentence and to impose that sentence permits it to enforce a probationary requirement as a condition of suspension. Hartless v. Commonwealth, 29 Va. App. 172, 510 S.E.2d 738 (1999).

Implicit in the trial court's sentencing authority was its power to impose the entire suspended sentence, and then to resuspend all or a portion of the reimposed sentence under such terms and conditions it deemed appropriate, including placing defendant on supervised probation as a condition of resuspending the 1989 sentence, and it did not impermissibly modify or extend the 1989 sentencing order in violation of Va. Sup. Ct. R. 1:1. Harrison v. Commonwealth, No. 0556-04-2, 2005 Va. App. LEXIS 115 (Ct. of Appeals Mar. 22, 2005).

To be effective, probation must be concurrent with coordinate term of suspension of sentence. Hartless v. Commonwealth, 29 Va. App. 172, 510 S.E.2d 738 (1999).

Proportionality of sentence imposed after revocation. — Although § 19.2-306 gave the trial court broad discretion to revoke suspended sentences and impose whatever sentence might have been originally imposed, imposing the entire 26 years of defendant's suspended sentences for forgery based on a new larceny conviction, two missed probation meetings in 7 years, and a failure to pay complete restitution, was disproportionate to defendant's violations where, inter alia, defendant was a non-violent offender who had done well on probation and was being "monitored" only for restitution purposes. Payne v. Commonwealth, No. 1759-01-1, 2002 Va. App. LEXIS 515 (Ct. of Appeals Aug. 20, 2002).

A reasonable failure to pay restitution negates a reasonable cause to revoke a suspended sentence. Duff v. Commonwealth, 16 Va. App. 293, 429 S.E.2d 465 (1993).

Ability to pay is a necessary consideration in the trial court's determination of cause for the failure to pay restitution ordered as a condition of a suspended sentence thus, where the evidence established that the failure resulted solely from an inability to pay and not a willful refusal, it was an abuse of discretion to automatically revoke the prior suspended sentence without considering reasonable alternatives to imprisonment. Duff v. Commonwealth, 16 Va. App. 293, 429 S.E.2d 465 (1993).

Court's alternative where failure to pay restitution not willful. — A court may modify restitution plan consistent with the defendant's ability to pay or employ some other means to permit the victim to recover the loss where the failure to follow the plan

resulted solely from an inability to pay and was not a willful refusal. Duff v. Commonwealth, 16 Va. App. 293, 429 S.E.2d 465 (1993).

Revocation of suspended sentence did not exceed judge's authority. — When appellant was arrested in 1992 for driving under the influence of alcohol, he was still within the maximum period for which he might have been sentenced on the grand larceny charge. Thus, the trial judge did not exceed his authority when, in 1993, he revoked an additional nine months of the suspended sentence. Carbaugh v. Commonwealth, 19 Va. App. 119, 449 S.E.2d 264 (1994).

Trial court did not abuse its discretion in revoking defendant's suspended sentences where he lied to court, failed to make timely restitution, and continued to fraudulently obtain money from other individuals, in violation of condition that he obey laws of Commonwealth. Mitchell v. Commonwealth, No. 2313-98-1 (Ct. of Appeals Nov. 16, 1999).

Where a defendant was in possession of a sharp instrument, made threats to children and made improper use of the mail, the trial court did not abuse its discretion in revoking suspended sentences. Kibler v. Commonwealth, No. 0165-02-4, 2002 Va. App. LEXIS 718 (Ct. of Appeals Dec. 3, 2002).

Because the trial court had the statutory authority to enter an order revoking a probationer's suspended sentences, and resuspend them for a fixed period on certain conditions, a collateral attack against the content of that order raising a question of trial court error was prohibited, as: (1) the order's lack of a specific finding that the probationer violated the terms of his suspended sentences, and its arguable lack of clarity, did not divest the court of jurisdiction; and (2) at most, such errors or irregularities rendered the order merely voidable rather than void ab initio. Moreover, the probationer could have challenged the court's entry of the order upon a timely motion to the trial court or a timely direct appeal, but failed to do so. Crawley v. Commonwealth, — Va. App. —, — S.E.2d —, 2007 Va. App. LEXIS 217 (May 22, 2007).

Because the record showed that a probationer failed to comply with the terms of his suspended sentences within the period of suspension fixed by the court, the trial court had jurisdiction to revoke the probationer's suspended sentences and resuspend those sentences for a fixed period on certain conditions. Crawley v. Commonwealth, — Va. App. —, — S.E.2d —, 2007 Va. App. LEXIS 217 (May 22, 2007).

When a trial court had subject matter jurisdiction over defendant's 1998 hearing to revoke his suspended sentence and extended defendant's period of suspension, the trial court did not err in revoking defendant's suspended sentence in 2010, pursuant to subsection A of § 19.2-306, because the suspension took place within the fourteen-year period established in the 1998 sentencing order; defendant was not entitled to collaterally attack the 1998 sentencing order because the order was not void. Dunham v. Commonwealth, 59 Va. App. 634, 721 S.E.2d 824, 2012 Va. App. LEXIS 49 (2012).

Absence of explicit recitation re-suspending balance of original sentence. — Under subsection C of § 19.2-306, a first revocation order implicitly re-suspended the unserved balance of defendant's original sentence and did not implicitly discharge the remaining sentence, despite the absence of an explicit recitation re-suspending the balance of the original sentence; the trial court could not shorten a final sentence even if it wanted to, and certainly could not shorten defendant's sentence by accident or because his bad behavior required a revocation proceeding. Jacobs v. Commonwealth, 61 Va. App. 529, 738 S.E.2d 519, 2013 Va. App. LEXIS 77 (2013).

Appeal of condition barred by probationer's consent. — Because a probation condition that the probationer take his antipsychotic medication was imposed with his full and voluntary consent, any claim on appeal that the trial court erred in imposing sentence due to a violation of said condition was barred. Spencer v. Commonwealth, — Va. App. —, — S.E.2d —, 2007 Va. App. LEXIS 292 (Aug. 7, 2007).

Escape violated good behavior condition. — Appellant's contention that the sentencing order required only that he maintain good behavior for three years after release from confinement was without merit. This condition merely established the required period of good behavior after release. It had no effect on the implicit condition of suspension that appellant was to remain on good behavior from the time the sentencing order was entered. Therefore, when appellant escaped, he violated the condition of good behavior. Crowder v. Commonwealth, No. 2348-93-1 (Ct. of Appeals April 25, 1995).

Probation revocation based solely on failure to maintain good behavior upheld. — Trial court was justified in exercising its discretion to revoke appellant's suspended sentence and probation based solely on the fact that he failed to maintain good behavior when he did not report to his parole and probation officer upon being released from the penitentiary. Davis v. Commonwealth, 12 Va. App. 81, 402 S.E.2d 684 (1991).

Probation revocation upheld and sentence imposed. — Defendant's use of illegal drugs during the probationary period was inconsistent with the terms and conditions of the probation and evidenced her unwillingness to avail herself of the opportunity afforded by the court. Under such circumstances, the judgment of the trial court to convict defendant of possession of controlled substance and impose sentence clearly constituted no abuse of discretion. Connelly v. Commonwealth, 14 Va. App. 888, 420 S.E.2d 244 (1992).

Trial court did not abuse its discretion under § 19.2-306 in imposing all of defendant's previously suspended sentence where: (1) the evidence was uncontroverted that defendant violated the conditions of his probation by committing the misdemeanor destruction of private property and "Peeping Tom" offenses; (2) it was defendant's fourth violation of probation in less than four years; (3) defendant's other violations included failure to maintain his registration as a sex offender and hiding in the nurses' locker room at a hospital; (4) there was no question that the original sentence was warranted; and (5) defendant's probation officer testified that he was dangerous. Alsberry v. Commonwealth, 39 Va. App. 314, 572 S.E.2d 522, 2002 Va. App. LEXIS 721 (2002).

Condition to be of good behavior not violated. — Where the only changed circumstance that occurred between the date defendant was sentenced by the trial court and the date of the revocation hearing in the trial court was that the indictment against him, of which the court was aware at time of sentencing, has been tried and had resulted in a conviction in a federal court, this did not constitute a violation by defendant of the condition of his suspended sentence to be of good behavior. Hamilton v. Commonwealth, 217 Va. 325, 228 S.E.2d 555 (1976).

Presumption where ground of revocation not stated. — Where the ground upon which a suspension of sentence was revoked is not shown, the presumption is that it was upon a valid finding that the accused had in some manner violated the conditions of the suspension. Slayton v. Commonwealth, 185 Va. 357, 38 S.E.2d 479 (1946); Marshall v. Commonwealth, 202 Va. 217, 116 S.E.2d 270 (1960).

Basis for revocation order. — However, should Commonwealth elect to rely solely upon criminal conviction, without evidence of the related conduct, to establish the reasonable cause necessary to revocation, the "bare fact" of such conviction clearly becomes the basis for the revocation order. Resio v. Commonwealth, 29 Va. App. 616, 513 S.E.2d 892 (1999).

Trial court erred in revoking defendant's suspended sentence and probation imposed in defendant's distribution of imitation of cocaine case, as revocation was based on conduct that occurred before defendant's sentence in that case was imposed, and not after as was required by statute. Oliver v. Commonwealth, 38 Va. App. 845, 568 S.E.2d 465, 2002 Va. App. LEXIS 522 (2002).

Imposition of different conditions of resuspension of sentence. — Trial court, pursuant to § 19.2-306, in revoking defendant's sentences and resuspending them, had the discretion to impose different conditions on the resuspension of those sentences. Reinke v. Commonwealth, 51 Va. App. 357, 657 S.E.2d 805, 2008 Va. App. LEXIS 111 (2008).

Reinstatement of portion of original sentence. — Because defendant pleaded no contest to violating the terms of a suspended sentence, the trial court did not abuse its discretion under subsection A of § 19.2-306 by reinstating a total of six years of the original nine-year-and-six-month sentence. Vaughn v. Commonwealth, 2009 Va. App. LEXIS 71 (Feb. 17, 2009).

Effect of compliance by accused with conditions of suspension. — When the accused has complied with conditions specified, he has a right to rely upon them, and the suspension will

stand. Griffin v. Cunningham, 205 Va. 349, 136 S.E.2d 840 (1964).

Failure to comply. — A court which has ordered a suspension of sentence undoubtedly has the power to revoke it when the defendant has failed to comply with the conditions of the suspension. Griffin v. Cunningham, 205 Va. 349, 136 S.E.2d 840 (1964); Hamilton v. Commonwealth, 217 Va. 325, 228 S.E.2d 555 (1976).

Trial court acted within its discretion in revoking a defendant's probation where the defendant had violated two of the conditions of his probation by failing to make restitution payments to the elderly couple he had defrauded and by lying to his probation officer. Keselica v. Commonwealth, 34 Va. App. 31, 537 S.E.2d 611, 2000 Va. App. LEXIS 768 (2000).

Where defendant did not comply with a polygraph examination, which was a reasonable, additional probation requirement under the circumstances, the trial court properly revoked defendant's probation. Jones v. Commonwealth, No. 2637-02-1, 2003 Va. App. LEXIS 533 (Ct. of Appeals Oct. 28, 2003).

Substantial misconduct grounds for revocation of suspension. — The failure of a defendant to be of good behavior, amounting to substantial misconduct, during the period of the suspension would provide reasonable cause for revocation of the suspension whether or not good behavior was expressly stated to be a condition of the suspension. Marshall v. Commonwealth, 202 Va. 217, 116 S.E.2d 270 (1960); Brown v. Slayton, 342 F. Supp. 61 (W.D. Va. 1972); Hamilton v. Commonwealth, 217 Va. 325, 228 S.E.2d 555 (1976).

Proof of violation of conditions. — Inasmuch as a proceeding to revoke a suspension of a sentence for cause is not a trial for the commission of a new criminal offense, the alleged violation by the probationer of the conditions of the suspension of sentence need not be proven beyond a reasonable doubt. Slayton v. Commonwealth, 185 Va. 357, 38 S.E.2d 479 (1946); Marshall v. Commonwealth, 202 Va. 217, 116 S.E.2d 270 (1960).

Because sufficient evidence supported the other charged probation violations against the probationer, and because he requested the exact relief he sought to contest on appeal, the order finding that he was in violation of said probation by refusing to take antipsychotic drugs was upheld without reaching the merits of his claim. Spencer v. Commonwealth, — Va. App. —, — S.E.2d —, 2007 Va. App. LEXIS 292 (Aug. 7, 2007).

Evidence supported decision to revoke defendant's probation and suspended sentence. — Revocation of suspended sentence was upheld as defendant's termination from the detention center violated a condition of his probation and suspended sentences and the trial court considered the totality of the evidence before finding sufficient cause to revoke defendant's suspended sentences. Owens v. Commonwealth, No. 0146-03-4, 2004 Va. App. LEXIS 60 (Ct. of Appeals Feb. 10, 2004).

Suspended sentence revocable for substantial misconduct short of violation of law. — Defendant's suspended sentence for aggravated sexual battery on an 11-year-old, conditioned on good behavior, could be revoked for substantial misconduct not involving violation of law; therefore trial court did not abuse its discretion in revoking suspended sentence even absent proof that defendant violated law by writing letters in which he graphically described his desire to have sex with children. Holden v. Commonwealth, 27 Va. App. 38, 497 S.E.2d 492 (1998).

The trial judge erred by basing his decision to revoke probation and suspension of imposition of sentence upon testimony that he recalled from the misdemeanor prosecution, without his stating for or making part of the record the specific evidence upon which he relied to find that defendant had violated the conditions of probation and suspension of sentence. Hess v. Commonwealth, 17 Va. App. 738, 441 S.E.2d 29 (1994).

Failure to preserve issue for review. — Where a defendant made no objection when the Commonwealth reminded the trial court at a revocation hearing that a term of defendant's probation was to remain drug and alcohol free, or when the trial court noted that defendant had been under the influence of alcohol contrary to the terms of his probation, and made no argument at the hearing that the trial court's consideration of his consumption of alcohol was a violation of his due process rights or otherwise improper, he was barred under Va. Sup. Ct. R. 5A:18 from raising this issue for the first time on appeal. Cappell v. Commonwealth, No. 0807-02-3, 2003 Va. App. LEXIS 313 (Ct. of Appeals May 27, 2003).

CIRCUIT COURT OPINIONS

Constitutionality. — Affidavit from a custodian of state police records of sex offender registrations that stated that defendant failed to register as a sex offender was properly admitted into evidence at a probation revocation hearing where admission of the affidavit did not violate defendant's due process right to confront witnesses in a criminal trial. Commonwealth v. Dickens, 73 Va. Cir. 437, 2007 Va. Cir. LEXIS 229 (Norfolk July 18, 2007), aff'd, 52 Va. App. 412, 663 S.E.2d 548, 2008 Va. App. LEXIS 356 (2008).

The Sixth Amendment and Crawford did not apply in a probation revocation hearing because the full panoply of rights due a defendant in a criminal prosecution does not extend to parole revocation proceedings, neither does that panoply of rights apply in a probation revocation hearing. Commonwealth v. Dickens, 73 Va. Cir. 437, 2007 Va. Cir. LEXIS 229 (Norfolk July 18, 2007), aff'd, 52 Va. App. 412, 663 S.E.2d 548, 2008 Va. App. LEXIS 356 (2008).

The admission into evidence of an affidavit in a probation violation proceeding does not violate the due process guarantee of confrontation in a parole revocation proceeding. Commonwealth v. Dickens, 73 Va. Cir. 437, 2007 Va. Cir. LEXIS 229 (Norfolk July 18, 2007), aff'd, 52 Va. App. 412, 663 S.E.2d 548, 2008 Va. App. LEXIS 356 (2008).

One-year limit suspended when probationer arrested by another jurisdiction. — Trial court was not required to dispose of inmate's probation violation that resulted in a detainer on his record until the inmate had completed his federal prison sentence, and, thus, his speedy trial rights were not violated because the inmate was not within the trial court's jurisdiction. Offer v. Commonwealth, 63 Va. Cir. 380, 2003 Va. Cir. LEXIS 213 (Fairfax County 2003).

Right to counsel during plea. — Where a sentence imposed on a defendant qualified defendant for court appointed counsel, defendant's appearance without counsel when defendant pleaded guilty did not show that an intelligent waiver of defendant's right to counsel had occurred; therefore, defendant's suspended sentence could not subsequently be revoked. Commonwealth v. Walker, 60 Va. Cir. 149, 2002 Va. Cir. LEXIS 302 (Alexandria 2002).

Conviction in circuit court did not divest juvenile court of jurisdiction. — Despite the fact that defendant had already been tried and convicted on unrelated charges as an adult in the circuit court, the juvenile court retained jurisdiction to enforce its previous order revoking his probation and sentencing him to jail time, and the juvenile proceedings subsequent to his conviction were simply an exercise of the court's inherent authority to enforce its orders. Commonwealth v. Stewart, 71 Va. Cir. 313, 2006 Va. Cir. LEXIS 224 (Page County 2006).

OPINIONS OF THE ATTORNEY GENERAL

Constitutionality. — Although this section does not specify when a probation revocation hearing must be conducted, the lack of a specific time period in the statute does not violate the due process rights of a defendant. See opinion of Attorney General to The Honorable James F. Almand, Member, House of Delegates, 02-112 (12/12/02).

Timely issuance of process invokes the jurisdiction of the circuit court under this section to conduct a probation revocation hearing. See opinion of Attorney General to The Honorable James F. Almand, Member, House of Delegates, 02-112 (12/12/02).

§ 19.2-307. Contents of judgment order.

The judgment order shall set forth the plea, the verdict or findings and the adjudication and sentence, whether or not the case was tried by jury, and if not, whether the consent of the accused was concurred in by the court and the attorney for the Commonwealth. If the accused is found not guilty, or for any other reason is entitled to be discharged, judgment shall be entered accordingly. If an accused is tried at one time for two or more offenses, the court may enter one judgment order respecting all such offenses. The final judgment order shall be entered on a form promulgated by the Supreme Court.

History.
1975, c. 495; 1996, c. 60.

Michie's Jurisprudence.
For related discussion, see 5B M.J. Criminal Procedure, §§ 70, 73.

CASE NOTES

Authentication of orders. — Nothing in this section required the Commonwealth to introduce a document that was signed by a judge who convicted defendant of rape to have that document considered by the trial court that convicted defendant of robbery, and the court that convicted defendant of robbery did not err when it considered documents that were not signed by the judge but were properly authenticated by his clerk. Seaton v. Commonwealth, 42 Va. App. 739, 595 S.E.2d 9, 2004 Va. App. LEXIS 165 (2004).

Judge's notes complied with section. — Judge's notes clearly complied with the substance of § 19.2-307 as they listed defendant's guilty plea, the judge's finding of guilt, the sentence, and conditional suspension of the sentence. It was immaterial that the judge did not list whether the case was tried by a judge or jury, as all cases of that type in juvenile and domestic relations district court were tried by a judge. Sanders v. Commonwealth, 2008 Va. App. LEXIS 320 (July 15, 2008).

Requirements satisfied. — Defendant's prior conviction, in the general district court, of driving a motor vehicle after having been found to be an habitual offender was adequately proved by a record of his plea of guilty to the offense and his sentence, which comported with the prescribed punishment for the offense, notwithstanding a failure of the record to show a judicial finding of defendant's guilt. Wilson v. Commonwealth, 40 Va. App. 250, 578 S.E.2d 831, 2003 Va. App. LEXIS 193 (2003).

In light of the presumption of regularity, the absence of a mark on a prior juvenile adjudication indicating that a Boykin-type colloquy had been given, especially when there was no requirement in § 19.2-307 that the information be on the adjudication, defendant was properly convicted of violating § 18.2-308.2. Isaac v. Commonwealth, 2010 Va. App. LEXIS 423 (Nov. 2, 2010).

Requirements not satisfied. — At the sentencing phase of defendant's trial, the trial court erroneously admitted into evidence three documents which the Commonwealth contended were prior orders of conviction; these documents, as orders of conviction, failed in every respect to satisfy the requirements of this section. Bellinger v. Commonwealth, 23 Va. App. 471, 477 S.E.2d 779 (1996).

Trial court's judgment of conviction finding defendant guilty of possessing a firearm while under the age of 29, after having been convicted of a delinquent act that would have been a felony if committed by an adult, had to be reversed, as the juvenile court order that the trial court relied on did not make clear to which offense, or both, it was referring to when it stated "found guilty" in regard to charges against him when he was 15-years-old of grand larceny and petit larceny; accordingly, the juvenile court's judgment order was not sufficiently clear, and the Commonwealth could not definitively show that defendant had been adjudicated guilty of a delinquent act that would have been a felony had he been an adult. Johnson v. Commonwealth, — Va. App. —, — S.E.2d —, 2006 Va. App. LEXIS 91 (Mar. 14, 2006).

Conviction of felony domestic assault and battery was not supported by sufficient evidence because the warrant at issue, which alleged that defendant assaulted a family or household member "on or about 06/11/2004 to 06/13/2004," failed to indicate any finding of guilt and thus, was insufficient to prove a prior conviction on any date; nonetheless, the lesser-included misdemeanor was proven beyond a reasonable doubt. Sensabaugh v. Commonwealth, — Va. App. —, — S.E.2d —, 2007 Va. App. LEXIS 199 (May 15, 2007).

§ 19.2-308. When two or more sentences run concurrently.

When any person is convicted of two or more offenses, and sentenced to confinement, such sentences shall not run concurrently, unless expressly ordered by the court.

History.
Code 1950, § 19.1-294; 1960, c. 366; 1975, c. 495.

Michie's Jurisprudence.
For related discussion, see 5B M.J. Criminal Procedure, §§ 77, 78, 81.

CASE NOTES

Sentences run consecutively. — The general rule in Virginia, both before there was a statute on the subject and since, is that sentences run consecutively and not concurrently. The first statute appears in the Acts of 1877-78, p. 315. See Commonwealth v. Leath, 3 Va. (1 Va. Cas.) 151 (1805), where the rule was applied before any statute had been enacted on the subject, and Parsons v. Commonwealth, 154 Va. 832, 152 S.E. 547 (1930), where the rule was applied after the statute had been enacted. Hudson v. Youell, 179 Va. 442, 19 S.E.2d 705, cert. denied, 317 U.S. 630, 63 S. Ct. 47, 87 L. Ed. 508 (1942).

Trial court's refusal to run defendant's sentence with the time he was already serving on a different offense was a decision within the trial court's sound discretion. There was no abuse in the exercise of that discretion. Swilling v. Commonwealth, 2009 Va. App. LEXIS 24 (Jan. 27, 2009).

Circuit court did not err in dismissing an inmate's petition seeking an order requiring the Virginia Department of Corrections to comply with a judgment giving him credit for time spent incarcerated because the inmate was not entitled credit toward his Virginia sentence for the time he was incarcerated while he was in Virginia custody serving time for his West Virginia sentence; while in Virginia, the inmate remained in the custody of and subject to the jurisdiction of West Virginia under the Interstate Agreement on Detainers, Article V(g) of § 53.1-210 and W. Va. Code § 62-14-1, and the sentences imposed were to be served consecutively to and not concurrently with each other under § 19.2-308. Dorr v. Clarke, 284 Va. 514, 733 S.E.2d 235, 2012 Va. LEXIS 192 (2012).

Unless ordered to run concurrently. — The court is given express power to order sentences to run concurrently, but in the absence of express direction, they still run consecutively. Hudson v. Youell, 179 Va. 442, 19 S.E.2d 705, cert. denied, 317 U.S. 630, 63 S. Ct. 47, 87 L. Ed. 508 (1942).

Where the court said that each of four sentences was "to be computed from the date of this judgment," it was meant thereby that the sentences should run concurrently and not consecutively. Conner v. Commonwealth, 207 Va. 455, 150 S.E.2d 478 (1966).

Concurrent service is "expressly ordered," within the meaning of this section, whenever the order contains a direction compliance with which will produce that result. Perkins v. Peyton, 369 F.2d 590 (4th Cir. 1966).

Absent an express direction by the trial court that they are to run concurrently, multiple sentences are to run consecutively. Edmond v. Commonwealth, No. 2272-03-1, 2004 Va. App. LEXIS 610 (Ct. of Appeals Dec. 14, 2004).

Multiple sentences to confinement shall not run concurrently, unless expressly ordered by the court, and in the absence of express direction, they will run consecutively. Robertson v. Superintendent of Wise Correctional Unit, 248 Va. 232, 445 S.E.2d 116 (1994).

As this section is self-executing. — The legislative intent seems manifest that this section was intended to be self-executing. Hudson v. Youell, 179 Va. 442, 19 S.E.2d 705, cert. denied, 317 U.S. 630, 63 S. Ct. 47, 87 L. Ed. 508 (1942).

Sequence in which sentences must be served not specified by statute. — Nothing in former § 53-207 nor any other provision specifies the sequence in which sentences must be served. Shockley v. Slayton, 333 F. Supp. 868 (W.D. Va. 1971).

There is no constitutional or statutory requirement that sentences must be served in the order in which they are imposed by judgment. Shockley v. Slayton, 333 F. Supp. 868 (W.D. Va. 1971).

And it does not require the court to state sequence in its orders sentencing to imprisonment upon two or more convictions. Hudson v. Youell, 179 Va. 442, 19 S.E.2d 705, cert. denied, 317 U.S. 630, 63 S. Ct. 47, 87 L. Ed. 508 (1942).

Both the nature and sequence of service of multiple sentences are determined by the court or courts rendering judgment. Shockley v. Slayton, 333 F. Supp. 868 (W.D. Va. 1971).

Kind, amount, and sequence of punishment must be clearly specified. — So long as the kind, amount, and sequence of punishment were clearly specified before petitioner began to serve any of the sentences, none of his constitutional rights were violated. Shockley v. Slayton, 333 F. Supp. 868 (W.D. Va. 1971).

It prevails over former § 53-207. — Former § 53-207 (now § 53.1-186), stating that confinement shall commence from the date of the final judgment, must be read in conjunction with this section, and being general in its terms must give way to this section whenever they conflict, the latter being specific in its terms. Wilkinson v. Youell, 180 Va. 321, 23 S.E.2d 356 (1942); Conner v. Commonwealth, 207 Va. 455, 150 S.E.2d 478 (1966).

The provisions of former § 53-207 (now § 53.1-186) must be read with this section and does not control the sequence of sentence service. Perkins v. Peyton, 369 F.2d 590 (4th Cir. 1966).

Former section 53-207 (now § 53.1-186) is not mandatory and it must be read in conjunction with, and when in conflict must give way to, this section, which provides that multiple sentences shall run consecutively and not concurrently, unless otherwise directed by the court. Shockley v. Slayton, 333 F. Supp. 868 (W.D. Va. 1971).

Concurrent sentences cannot later be made consecutive. — Original sentences expressly ordering concurrent service within the meaning of this section are beyond the power of the trial judge later to make them consecutive. Perkins v. Peyton, 369 F.2d 590 (4th Cir. 1966).

Order that revoked sentences run consecutively was not an abuse of discretion. — Defendant's revoked sentences of six months, to be served consecutively, were affirmed as when defendant was originally sentenced, § 19.2-308 required that multiple sentences be served consecutively, unless expressly ordered otherwise; the trial court did not abuse its discretion in finding that the original conviction orders evinced an intent to impose consecutive terms for the suspended sentences. James v. Commonwealth, — Va. App. —, — S.E.2d —, 2006 Va. App. LEXIS 276 (June 27, 2006).

When defendant was convicted of taking indecent liberties with a child while in a custodial or supervisory relationship, it was not an abuse of discretion to revoke defendant's previously suspended sentence or to run the sentence consecutively to defendant's new sentence because, (1) by committing a new offense, defendant "forfeited" the "conditional freedom" inherent in the court's earlier decision to suspend part of defendant's sentence, (2) defendant did not claim the trial court based defendant's sentence or revocation on facially unlawful considerations or that either sentence exceeded applicable statutory limits, and (3) consecutive sentences were presumed, under § 19.2-308. Nicholson v. Commonwealth, 2011 Va. App. LEXIS 405 (Dec. 20, 2011).

This section does not apply to orders of suspension and probation. — It applies only to the serving of sentences to confinement in prison. An order granting probation is not a sentence to confinement. Vick v. Commonwealth, 201 Va. 474, 111 S.E.2d 824 (1960).

The suspended portions of a defendant's sentence would not run concurrently unless expressly so ordered by the court pursuant to this section. Malinowski v. Commonwealth, No. 1511-88-4 (Ct. of Appeals Aug. 14, 1990).

Reduction of time to be served on concurrent sentence in another state. — Where defendant received a 30-year sentence in Virginia to run concurrently with his Texas sentence, the fact that Texas reduced the time to be served on its 30-year sentence did not reduce the Virginia sentence. Murray v. Martinez, 234 Va. 270, 361 S.E.2d 136 (1987).

Definition of "concurrently." — Where the Attorney General, counsel for the respondent, contended that the purpose of the second order was to clarify the trial judge's intention that the prior 12-month sentence was to have run concurrently with the other unrelated convictions he had received and served locally and that use of the term "concurrent" in the second order was never intended to apply to the original two suspended sentences, the Supreme Court disagreed with that construction of the second order. Read together, the words "all sentences," "these sentences," and "concurrently," constituted an express directive that embraced the grand larceny and burglary sentences — the only sentences the trial court had jurisdiction to suspend — as well as the sentences imposed by other Virginia courts. Robertson v. Superintendent of Wise Correctional Unit, 248 Va. 232, 445 S.E.2d 116 (1994).

Response to inquiry by jury as to whether sentences would be served concurrently. — Since the trial judge did not know whether he would modify the jury's recommended sentences by running the sentences concurrently or otherwise suspending the sentences, he properly refused to instruct the jury on the presumption that sentences were to run consecutively; to advise the jury about the trial court's discretion would have been confusing. May v. Commonwealth, No. 0140-01-2, 2002 Va. App. LEXIS 398 (Ct. of Appeals July 23, 2002).

Trial court did not err in refusing to answer a jury question as to whether a defendant's sentences would run concurrently or consecutively where the decision was up to the trial court on some of the charges, because the jury would then speculate as to what the trial court was going to do. Reese v. Commonwealth, No. 1279-03-4, 2004 Va. App. LEXIS 316 (Ct. of Appeals July 6, 2004).

Concurrent sentences proper. — Subdivision C1 of § 18.2-374.1 does not prohibit mandatory minimum sentences imposed under that section from running concurrently as: (1) § 18.2-12.1, defining mandatory minimum, does not require that mandatory minimum sentences run consecutively; (2) § 19.2-308 provides that when any person is convicted of two or more offenses, and sentenced to confinement, such sentences shall not run concurrently, unless expressly ordered by the court; and (3) if subdivision C1 of § 18.2-374.1 were interpreted to require the mandatory minimum sentences to run consecutively, it would render superfluous the words the Virginia general assembly used in at least 11 other criminal statutes explicitly requiring that mandatory minimum sentences run consecutively. Commonwealth v. Jefferson, 60 Va. App. 749, 732 S.E.2d 728, 2012 Va. App. LEXIS 323 (2012).

Trial court did not abuse its discretion in ordering defendant's six § 18.2-374.1 sentences to run concurrently with each other as: (1) § 18.2-12.1, defining mandatory minimum, did not require that mandatory minimum sentences run consecutively; (2) § 19.2-308 provided that when any person was convicted of two or more offenses, and sentenced to confinement, such sentences were not to run concurrently, unless expressly ordered by the court; and (3) if subdivision C1 of § 18.2-374.1 were interpreted to require the mandatory minimum sentences to run consecutively, it would render superfluous the words the Virginia general assembly used in at least 11 other criminal statutes explicitly requiring that mandatory minimum sentences run consecutively. Commonwealth v. Jefferson, 60 Va. App. 749, 732 S.E.2d 728, 2012 Va. App. LEXIS 323 (2012).

Neither § 18.2-12.1, the mandatory minimum sentencing statute, nor § 18.2-53.1, the use or display of a firearm while commiting a felony, prohibit a trial court from running multiple sentences imposed for convictions of § 18.2-53.1 concurrently with each other. To the extent that the holding in *Bullock v. Commonwealth,* 631 S.E.2d 334 (2006), is inconsistent, it is overruled. Brown v. Commonwealth, 284 Va. 538, 733 S.E.2d 638, 2012 Va. LEXIS 190 (2012).

Applied in Wood v. Commonwealth, 12 Va. App. 1257, 408 S.E.2d 568 (1991); Pierce v. Commonwealth, 48 Va. App. 660, 633 S.E.2d 755, 2006 Va. App. LEXIS 407 (2006).

§ 19.2-308.1. When sentence may run concurrently with sentence in another jurisdiction.

Notwithstanding any other provision of law, in the event that a person is convicted of a criminal offense in any court of this Commonwealth and such person has also been sentenced to imprisonment for a term of one year or more by a court of the United States, or any other state or territory, and, at the time of sentencing in this Commonwealth, is incarcerated in a federal or state penal institution, the court may order the sentence to run concurrently with the sentence imposed by such other court.

History.
1977, c. 344.

Michie's Jurisprudence.
For related discussion, see 5B M.J. Criminal Procedure, § 78.

CASE NOTES

No right for time served in another state while on parole. — Although a Virginia court has authority to allow a sentence imposed in Virginia to run concurrently with a sentence from another jurisdiction, a criminal defendant is only entitled to credit as a matter of right for time spent in confinement while awaiting trial. Therefore, the petitioner was not entitled to credit for the time served on a sentence imposed in South Dakota while he was on parole on his Virginia sentence. Larson v. Beck, No. 0880-85 (Ct. of Appeals Dec. 13, 1985).

Reduction of time to be served on concurrent sentence in another state. — Where defendant received a 30-year sentence in Virginia to run concurrently with his Texas sentence, the fact that Texas reduced the time to be served on its 30-year sentence did not reduce the Virginia sentence. Murray v. Martinez, 234 Va. 270, 361 S.E.2d 136 (1987).

No error in denying concurrent sentence. — Given that the record on appeal adequately demonstrated that the sentencing judge correctly understood his discretion and sentenced defendant within the lawful scope of that discretion, the Court of Appeals of Virginia declined to apply the ends of justice exception to Va. Sup. Ct. R. 5A:18. As a result, no error resulted in the denial of defendant's request for a concurrent sentence. Scalf v. Commonwealth, 2008 Va. App. LEXIS 230 (May 13, 2008).

§ 19.2-309. Sentence of confinement for conviction of a combination of felony and misdemeanor offenses.

When any person is convicted of a combination of felony and misdemeanor offenses and sentenced to confinement therefor, in determining the sequence of confinement, the felony sentence and commitment shall take precedence and such person shall first be committed to serve the felony sentence.

History.
Code 1950, § 19.1-295; 1960, c. 366; 1975, c. 495.

CIRCUIT COURT OPINIONS

Applicability. — Prisoner was convicted of felony and misdemeanor offenses spanning the course of several years and each charge constituted its own separate case; therefore, § 19.2-309 did not apply and sentences were served in order of judgment with the remaining active time from the prisoner's first period of incarceration to be served first, and the time not physically served on each sentence to be served second. Commonwealth v. Demille, 78 Va. Cir. 137, 2009 Va. Cir. LEXIS 9 (Fairfax County 2009).

§ 19.2-309.1. Not set out.

History.
1988, cc. 764, 785.

Editor's note.
This section, relating to confinement to jail farms maintained by the Cities of Danville, Martinsville, and Newport News, was

enacted by Acts 1988, cc. 764 and 785. In furtherance of the general policy of the Virginia Code Commission to include in the Code only provisions having general and permanent application, this section, which is limited in its purpose and scope, is not set out here, but attention is called to it by this reference.

§ 19.2-310. Transfer of prisoners to custody of Director of Department of Corrections.

Every person sentenced by a court to the Department of Corrections upon conviction of a felony shall be conveyed to an appropriate receiving unit operated by the Department in the manner hereinafter provided. The clerk of the court in which the person is sentenced shall forthwith transmit to the Central Criminal Records Exchange the report of dispositions required by § 19.2-390. The clerk of the court within 30 days from the date of the judgment shall forthwith transmit to the Director of the Department a certified copy or copies of the order of trial and a certified copy of the complete final order, and if he fails to do so shall forfeit $50. The clerk of the court may transmit or make available a copy or copies of such orders electronically. Such copy or copies shall contain, as nearly as ascertainable, the birth date of the person sentenced. The sheriff shall certify to the Director of the Department any jail credits to which the person to be confined is entitled at such time as that person is transferred to the custody of the Director of the Department.

Following receipt of the order of trial and a certified copy of the complete final order, the Director or his designee shall dispatch a correctional officer to the county or city with a warrant directed to the sheriff authorizing him to deliver the prisoner to the correctional officer whose duty it shall be to take charge of the person and convey him to an appropriate receiving unit designated by the Director or his designee. The Director or his designee shall allocate space available in the receiving unit or units by giving first priority to the transportation, as the transportation facilities of the Department may permit, of those persons held in jails who in the opinion of the Director or his designee except as required by § 53.1-20 require immediate transportation to a receiving unit. In making such a determination of priority, the Director shall give due regard to the capacity of local as well as state correctional facilities and, to the extent feasible, shall seek to balance between local and state correctional facilities the excess of prisoners requiring detention.

History.
Code 1950, § 19.1-296; 1960, c. 366; 1966, c. 522; 1970, c. 67; 1972, c. 358; 1974, cc. 44, 45; 1975, c. 495; 1981, c. 529; 1982, cc. 476, 636; 1986, c. 606; 1990, cc. 676, 768; 2010, c. 352; 2011, c. 470.

The 2010 amendments.
The 2010 amendment by c. 352 substituted "so shall forfeit $50" for "so he shall forfeit $100" at the end of the third sentence of the first paragraph.

The 2011 amendments.
The 2011 amendment by c. 470, in the first paragraph, made a minor stylistic change in the third sentence and added the fourth sentence.

CASE NOTES

Right of transfer to state system not constitutionally protected. — Under this section and the priority system established pursuant to it, Virginia has not provided those inmates who are awaiting transfer from jail to the state system with an interest that is protected by the Constitution. The transfer is within the discretion of the Director of the Department of Corrections, taking into consideration the space available in the units, the transportation required, and the categories within the priority system. Miller v. Landon, 545 F. Supp. 81 (W.D. Va. 1982).

Applied in In re Commonwealth, Dep't of Cors., 222 Va. 454, 281 S.E.2d 857 (1981); Hill v. Hutto, 559 F. Supp. 390 (E.D. Va. 1983).

§ 19.2-310.01. Transmission of sentencing documents.

Within thirty days of the receipt of a request from the Department of Corrections for certified copies of sentencing documents for any misdemeanor conviction, the clerk of the court receiving such request shall transmit the requested documents to the Director of the Department. In accordance with the provisions of § 17.1-267, the requested documents shall be provided to the Director without the payment of any fee.

History.
1992, c. 498.

§ 19.2-310.1. Repealed by Acts 1982, c. 636.

Cross references.
For present provisions covering the subject matter of the repealed section, see § 53.1-21, subdivision B 4.

Editor's note.
The repealed section was enacted by Acts 1976, c. 287.

ARTICLE 1.1.

DNA ANALYSIS AND DATA BANK.

§ 19.2-310.2. Blood, saliva, or tissue sample required for DNA analysis upon conviction of certain crimes; fee.

A. Every person convicted of a felony on or after July 1, 1990, every person convicted of a felony offense under Article 7 (§ 18.2-61 et seq.) of Chapter 4 of Title 18.2 who was incarcerated on July 1, 1989, and every person convicted of a violation of (i) § 18.2-67.4, (ii) § 18.2-67.4:2, (iii) subsection C of § 18.2-67.5, (iv) § 18.2-130 or (v) § 18.2-370.6 shall have a sample of his blood, saliva or tissue taken for DNA (deoxyribonucleic acid) analysis to determine identification characteristics specific to the person. If a sample has been previously taken from the person as indicated by the Local Inmate Data System (LIDS), no additional sample shall be taken. The Department of Forensic Science shall provide to LIDS the most current information submitted to the DNA data bank on a weekly basis and shall remove from LIDS and the data bank persons no longer eligible to be in the data bank. A fee of $25 shall be charged for the withdrawal of this sample. The fee shall be taxed as part of the costs of the criminal case resulting in the conviction and one-half of the fee shall be paid into the general fund of the locality where the sample was taken and one-half of the fee shall be paid into the general fund of the state treasury. This fee shall only be taxed one time regardless of the number of samples taken. The assessment provided for herein shall be in addition to any other fees prescribed by law. The analysis shall be performed by the Department of Forensic Science or other entity designated by the Department. The identification characteristics of the profile resulting from the DNA analysis shall be stored and maintained by the Department in a DNA data bank and shall be made available only as provided in § 19.2-310.5.

B. After July 1, 1990, the blood, saliva or tissue sample shall be taken prior to release from custody. Notwithstanding the provisions of § 53.1-159, any person convicted of a felony who is in custody after July 1, 1990, shall provide a blood, saliva or tissue sample prior to his release. Every person so convicted after July 1, 1990, who is not sentenced to a term of confinement shall provide a blood, saliva or tissue sample as a condition of such sentence. A person required under this section to submit a sample for DNA analysis is not relieved from this requirement regardless of whether no blood, saliva, or tissue sample has been taken from the person or, if a sample has been taken, whether the sample or the results from the analysis of a sample cannot be found in the DNA data bank maintained by the Department of Forensic Science.

C. Nothing in this section shall prevent the Department of Forensic Science from including the identification characteristics of an individual's DNA profile in the DNA data bank as ordered by a circuit court pursuant to a lawful plea agreement.

D. A collection or placement of a sample for DNA analysis that was taken or retained in good faith does not invalidate the sample's use in the data bank pursuant to the provisions of this article. The detention, arrest, or conviction of a person based upon a data bank match or data bank information is not invalidated if it is determined that the sample was obtained, placed, or retained in the data bank in good faith, or if the conviction or juvenile adjudication that resulted in the collection of the DNA sample was subsequently vacated or otherwise altered in any future proceeding, including but not limited to post-trial or post-fact-finding motions, appeals, or collateral attacks.

E. The Virginia Department of Corrections and the Department of Forensic Science shall, on a quarterly basis, compare databases of offenders under the custody or supervision of the Department of Corrections with the DNA data bank of the Department of Forensic Science. The Virginia Department of Corrections shall require a DNA sample of those offenders under its custody or supervision if they are not identified in the DNA data bank.

F. Each community-based probation services agency established pursuant to § 9.1-174 shall determine by reviewing the Local Inmate Data System upon intake and again prior to discharge whether a blood, saliva, or tissue sample has been taken for DNA analysis for each offender required to submit a sample pursuant to this section and, if no sample has been taken, require an offender to submit a sample for DNA analysis.

G. The sheriff or regional jailer shall determine by reviewing the Local Inmate Data System upon intake and again prior to release whether a blood, saliva, or tissue sample has been taken for DNA analysis for each offender required to submit a sample pursuant to this section and, if no sample has been taken, require an offender to submit a sample for DNA analysis.

History.
1990, c. 669; 1993, c. 33; 1996, cc. 154, 952; 1998, c. 280; 2002, cc. 54, 753, 773; 2005, cc. 868, 881; 2007, c. 528; 2011, c. 247.

Editor's note.
Acts 2002, cc. 753 and 773, cl. 3, provide: "That the provisions of this act shall become effective on January 1, 2003."

Acts 2004, c. 82, cl. 1, provides: "The State Compensation Board shall (i) maintain in the Local Inmate Data System (LIDS) specific data fields for an inmate's country of birth and country of citizenship, (ii) require all jail facilities that are subject to LIDS reporting to complete the additional fields for all inmates housed at such facilities, (iii) annually encourage all jail facilities subject to LIDS reporting to request compensation from the United States Department of Justice State Criminal Alien Assistance Program (SCAAP) for costs associated with incarcerating undocumented aliens; (iv) provide information to all jail facilities on the eligibility requirements to obtain such funds; and (v) monitor local jail participation in the SCAAP program."

Acts 2007, c. 528, cl. 2, provides: "That the Secretary of Public Safety shall conduct a review of the procedures for collection of DNA samples pursuant to § 16.1-299.1 of the Code of Virginia and Article 1.1 (§ 19.2-310.2 et seq.) of Chapter 18 of Title 19.2 of the Code of Virginia. This review shall include a comparison of the data collected and maintained by the Virginia Department of Corrections, the Department of State Police, and any entity supervising parole or probation. The Secretary of Public Safety shall submit a status report by November 1, 2007, including any necessary recommendation regarding corrective actions to the Chairmen of the House Appropriations Committee, the Senate Finance Committee, the House Committee for Courts of Justice, and the Senate Committee for Courts of Justice."

The 2007 amendments.
The 2007 amendment by c. 528 inserted the A and B designations; inserted the third and sixth sentences in subsection A; added the last sentence in subsection B; and added subsections C through F.

The 2011 amendments.
The 2011 amendment by c. 247, in subsection A, in the first sentence, inserted "and every person convicted of a violation of (i) § 18.2-67.4, (ii) § 18.2-67.4:2, (iii) subsection C of § 18.2-67.5, (iv) § 18.2-130 or (v) § 18.2-370.6" and made a related change, and in the fifth sentence, deleted "felony" preceding "conviction"; and added subsection C and redesignated the remaining subsections accordingly.

Law Review.
For note, "DNA Fingerprinting: The Virginia Approach", see 35 Wm. & Mary L. Rev. 767 (1994). For 2000 survey of Virginia criminal law and procedure, see 34 U. Rich. L. Rev. 749 (2000). For article surveying developments in criminal law and procedure in Virginia from July 2001 to September 2002, see 37 U. Rich. L. Rev. 45 (2002).

CASE NOTES

Constitutionality of article. — Because prisoners' limited interest in not providing a blood sample required by this article is outweighed by the very important interest of the state in deterring and detecting recidivist acts, and because the DNA data bank bears a close and substantial relation to the State's interest, this article does not violate prisoners' Fourth Amendment rights. Jones v. Murray, 763 F. Supp. 842 (W.D. Va. 1991).

This article's blood sample providing requirement does not violate the ex post facto clause of the state Constitution since the requirement that prisoners provide blood samples is not punitive in nature; they are not being punished for a prior wrong and no additional time is added to their sentence, the blood sample is taken and analyzed for the sole purpose of establishing a data bank which will aid future law enforcement. Jones v. Murray, 763 F. Supp. 842 (W.D. Va. 1991).

The Commonwealth does not violate prisoners' right to privacy when it analyzes the blood samples of convicted felons and stores the profiles in a data bank under this article. Jones v. Murray, 763 F. Supp. 842 (W.D. Va. 1991).

The procurement of a blood sample for DNA analysis from a convicted felon under this section does not violate the Fourth Amendment guarantee against unreasonable searches and seizures or the Virginia Constitution; in the case of convicted felons who are in the custody of the Commonwealth, the minor intrusion caused by the taking of a blood sample is outweighed by the state's interest in determining inmates' identification characteristics specific to the person for improved law enforcement. Johnson v. Commonwealth, 259 Va. 654, 529 S.E.2d 769, 2000 Va. LEXIS 60, cert. denied, 531 U.S. 981, 121 S. Ct. 432, 148 L. Ed. 2d 439 (2000).

The Fifth Amendment right against self-incrimination, and the parallel right afforded by the Virginia Constitution, are not violated by the DNA statutes; the taking of a blood sample does not implicate any rights against self-incrimination, because such an act is not testimonial or communicative in nature. Johnson v. Commonwealth, 259 Va. 654, 529 S.E.2d 769, 2000 Va. LEXIS 60, cert. denied, 531 U.S. 981, 121 S. Ct. 432, 148 L. Ed. 2d 439 (2000).

Portion of DNA testing statute authorizing mandatory parole modification unconstitutional. — To the extent that the first five words of the third paragraph of this section: "Notwithstanding the provisions of § 53.1-159" authorize a modification of mandatory parole, this section violates the ex post facto clause. Therefore, those five words are unconstitutional and may not be enforced to modify the mandatory parole period. Otherwise, though, the mandatory DNA testing imposed on all incarcerated felons withstands Constitutional scrutiny. Jones v. Murray, 962 F.2d 302 (4th Cir.), cert. denied, 506 U.S. 977, 113 S. Ct. 472, 121 L. Ed. 2d 378 (1992).

Section constituted a reasonable regulation which was not penal in nature, and that the punishment of inmates for failure to comply with directives to provide a blood sample was contemplated as part of the sentence of every prisoner. Ewell v. Murray, 11 F.3d 482 (4th Cir. 1993), cert. denied, 511 U.S. 1111, 114 S. Ct. 2112, 128 L. Ed. 2d 671 (1994).

Requirement does not constitute an ex post facto law. — Reasonable prison regulations are not frozen at the time of each inmate's conduct, but rather, they may be subject to reasonable amendments as necessary for good prison administration, safety and efficiency, without implicating ex post facto concerns thus, Virginia's enactment of a requirement that inmates provide blood samples or suffer punishment for their refusal did not constitute an ex post facto law. Ewell v. Murray, 11 F.3d 482 (4th Cir. 1993), cert. denied, 511 U.S. 1111, 114 S. Ct. 2112, 128 L. Ed. 2d 671 (1994).

Prisoner must be given process before being held beyond parole release date. — While a prisoner who refuses to provide a blood sample prior to his release may be detained because they have not complied with the DNA statute, the prisoner must be given some process before he is held beyond his established parole release date; such procedures would provide that the state-created right to mandatory parole is not abrogated arbitrarily and that prisoners' liberty interests are not offended. Jones v. Murray, 763 F. Supp. 842 (W.D. Va. 1991), aff'd in part and rev'd in part, 962 F.2d 302 (4th Cir.), cert. denied, 506 U.S. 977, 113 S. Ct. 472, 121 L. Ed. 2d 378 (1992).

CIRCUIT COURT OPINIONS

No violation of Interstate Agreement on Detainers. — Where defendant had already been tried prior to detention in federal prison and the taking of blood samples under §§ 19.2-310.2 and 19.2-310.3 was not a penalty for being convicted, defendant's rights under § 53.1-210, art. III(d), of the Interstate Agreement on Detainers were not violated. Commonwealth v. Velasquez, 63 Va. Cir. 477, 2003 Va. Cir. LEXIS 259 (Fairfax County 2003).

OPINIONS OF THE ATTORNEY GENERAL

The term "tissue" as used in §§ 19.2-310.2 through 19.2-310.7 includes epidermal cells taken from a person's body. See opinion of Attorney General to The Honorable David A. Nutter, Member, House of Delegates, 02-150 (1/8/03).

§ 19.2-310.2:1. Saliva or tissue sample required for DNA analysis after arrest for a violent felony.

Every person arrested for the commission or attempted commission of a violent felony as defined in § 19.2-297.1 or a violation or attempt to commit a violation of § 18.2-31, 18.2-89, 18.2-90, 18.2-91, or 18.2-92, shall have a sample of his saliva or tissue taken for DNA (deoxyribonucleic acid) analysis to determine identification characteristics specific to the person. After a determination by a magistrate or a grand jury that probable cause exists for the arrest, a sample shall be taken prior to the person's release from custody. The analysis shall be performed by the Department of Forensic Science or other entity designated by the Department. The identification characteristics of the profile resulting from the DNA analysis shall be stored and maintained by the Department in a DNA data bank and shall be made available as provided in § 19.2-310.5.

The clerk of the court shall notify the Department of final disposition of the criminal proceedings. If the charge for which the sample was taken is dismissed or the defendant is acquitted at trial, the Department shall destroy the sample and all records thereof, provided there is no other pending qualifying warrant or capias for an arrest or felony conviction that would otherwise require that the sample remain in the data bank.

History.
2002, cc. 753, 773; 2003, c. 150; 2004, c. 445; 2005, cc. 868, 881; 2006, c. 182.

Editor's note.
Acts 2002, cc. 753 and 773, cl. 3, provide: "That the provisions of this act shall become effective on January 1, 2003."

Law Review.
For survey of Virginia law on criminal law and procedure for the year 2007-2008, see 43 U. Rich. L. Rev. 149 (2008).

CASE NOTES

Constitutionality. — Taking of defendant's DNA pursuant § 19.2-310.2:1, upon arrest for an unrelated felony, and as part of the routing booking process, did not violate the Fourth Amendment. Anderson v. Commonwealth, 274 Va. 469, 650 S.E.2d 702,

2007 Va. LEXIS 115 (2007), cert. denied, Anderson v. Virginia, 553 U.S. 1054, 128 S. Ct. 2473, 2008 U.S. LEXIS 4189 (U.S. 2008).

Obtaining DNA sample. — DNA testing statute, § 19.2-310.2:1, did not violate defendant's Fourth Amendment rights by authorizing police to obtain a sample of "saliva or tissue" for DNA testing from anyone arrested for certain violent felonies; a search of an arrestee, such as defendant for rape, robbery, and forcible sodomy, did not violate defendant's Fourth Amendment rights since no independent legal justification was required except for an arrest pursuant to probable cause, which occurred in defendant's case. Anderson v. Commonwealth, 48 Va. App. 704, 634 S.E.2d 372, 2006 Va. App. LEXIS 414 (2006), aff'd, 274 Va. 469, 650 S.E.2d 702, 2007 Va. LEXIS 115 (Va. 2007).

OPINIONS OF THE ATTORNEY GENERAL

Reasonable force used to obtain DNA sample. — This section requires a person lawfully arrested for a violent felony to provide a saliva or tissue sample for DNA analysis; therefore, reasonable force may be used, if necessary, to obtain a DNA sample from such an arrestee who refuses to comply with the applicable DNA statutes. See opinion of Attorney General to The Honorable William R. Janis, Member, House of Delegates, 02-138 (5/13/03).

§ 19.2-310.3. Procedures for withdrawal of blood, saliva or tissue sample for DNA analysis.

Each sample required pursuant to § 19.2-310.2 from persons who are to be incarcerated shall be withdrawn at the receiving unit or at such other place as is designated by the Department of Corrections or, in the case of a juvenile, the Department of Juvenile Justice. The required samples from persons who are not sentenced to a term of confinement shall be withdrawn at a time and place specified by the sentencing court. Only a correctional health nurse technician or a physician, registered nurse, licensed practical nurse, graduate laboratory technician, or phlebotomist shall withdraw any blood sample to be submitted for analysis. No civil liability shall attach to any person authorized to withdraw blood, saliva or tissue as provided herein as a result of the act of withdrawing blood, saliva or tissue from any person submitting thereto, provided the blood, saliva or tissue was withdrawn according to recognized medical procedures. However, no person shall be relieved from liability for negligence in the withdrawing of any blood, saliva or tissue sample.

Chemically clean sterile disposable needles and vacuum draw tubes or swabs shall be used for all samples. The tube or envelope containing the sample shall be sealed and labeled with the subject's name, social security number, date of birth, race and gender; the name of the person collecting the sample; and the date and place of collection. The tubes or envelopes containing the samples shall be secured to prevent tampering with the contents. The steps herein set forth relating to the taking, handling, identification, and disposition of blood, saliva or tissue samples are procedural and not substantive. Substantial compliance therewith shall be deemed to be sufficient. The samples shall be transported to the Department of Forensic Science not more than 15 days following withdrawal and shall

be analyzed and stored in the DNA data bank in accordance with §§ 19.2-310.4 and 19.2-310.5.

History.
1990, c. 669; 1997, c. 862; 1998, c. 280; 2003, c. 150; 2004, c. 440; 2005, cc. 868, 881.

Law Review.
For note, "DNA Fingerprinting: The Virginia Approach", see 35 Wm. & Mary L. Rev. 767 (1994).

CIRCUIT COURT OPINIONS

No violation of Interstate Agreement on Detainers. — Where defendant had already been tried prior to detention in federal prison and the taking of blood samples under §§ 19.2-310.2 and 19.2-310.3 was not a penalty for being convicted, defendant's rights under § 53.1-210, art. III(d), of the Interstate Agreement on Detainers were not violated. Commonwealth v. Velasquez, 63 Va. Cir. 477, 2003 Va. Cir. LEXIS 259 (Fairfax County 2003).

§ 19.2-310.3:1. Procedures for taking saliva or tissue sample for DNA analysis.

A. Each sample required pursuant to § 19.2-310.2:1 from persons arrested shall be taken before release from custody at such place as is designated by the law-enforcement agency responsible for arrest booking in the jurisdiction. Samples shall be taken in accordance with procedures adopted by the Department of Forensic Science. The sample shall be sealed and labeled with the subject's name, social security number, date of birth, race and gender; the name of the person collecting the sample; the date and place of collection; information identifying the arresting or accompanying officer; and the offense for which the person was arrested. The sample shall be secured to prevent tampering with the contents and be accompanied by a copy of the arrest warrant or capias. The steps herein set forth relating to the taking, handling, identification, and disposition of saliva or tissue samples are procedural and not substantive. The sample shall be transported to the Department of Forensic Science not more than 15 days following withdrawal and shall be analyzed and stored in the DNA data bank in accordance with §§ 19.2-310.4 and 19.2-310.5.

B. Substantial compliance therewith shall be deemed to be sufficient. If a sample has been previously taken from the individual as indicated by the Local Inmate Data System (LIDS), no additional sample shall be taken. No civil liability shall attach to any person authorized to take saliva or tissue as provided herein as a result of the act of taking saliva or tissue from any person submitting thereto, provided the saliva or tissue was taken according to recognized medical procedures. However, no person shall be relieved from liability for negligence in the taking of any saliva or tissue sample.

History.
2002, cc. 753, 773; 2003, c. 150; 2005, cc. 868, 881.

Editor's note.
Acts 2002, cc. 753 and 773, cl. 3, provide: "That the provisions of this act shall become effective on January 1, 2003."

CASE NOTES

Obtaining DNA sample. — DNA testing statute, § 19.2-310.2:1, did not violate defendant's Fourth Amendment rights by authorizing police to obtain a sample of "saliva or tissue" for DNA testing from anyone arrested for certain violent felonies; a search of an arrestee, such as defendant for rape, robbery, and forcible sodomy, did not violate defendant's Fourth Amendment rights since no independent legal justification was required except for an arrest pursuant to probable cause, which occurred in defendant's case. Anderson v. Commonwealth, 48 Va. App. 704, 634 S.E.2d 372, 2006 Va. App. LEXIS 414 (2006), aff'd, 274 Va. 469, 650 S.E.2d 702, 2007 Va. LEXIS 115 (Va. 2007).

§ 19.2-310.4. Procedures for conducting DNA analysis of blood, saliva or tissue sample.

Whether or not the results of an analysis are to be included in the data bank, the Department shall conduct the DNA analysis in accordance with procedures adopted by the Department to determine identification characteristics specific to the individual whose sample is being analyzed. The Director or his designated representative shall complete and maintain on file a form indicating the name of the person whose sample is to be analyzed, the date and by whom the blood, saliva or tissue sample was received and examined, and a statement that the seal on the tube or envelope containing the sample had not been broken or otherwise tampered with. The remainder of a blood, saliva or tissue sample submitted for analysis and inclusion in the data bank pursuant to § 19.2-310.2 or 19.2-310.2:1 may be divided, labeled as provided for the original sample, and securely stored by the Department in accordance with specific procedures adopted by regulation of the Department to ensure the integrity and confidentiality of the samples. All or part of the remainder of that sample may be used only (i) to create a statistical data base provided no identifying information on the individual whose sample is being analyzed is included or (ii) for retesting by the Department to validate or update the original analysis.

A report of the results of a DNA analysis conducted by the Department as authorized, including the profile and identifying information, shall be made and maintained at the Department. A certificate and the results of the analysis shall be admissible in any court as evidence of the facts therein stated. Except as specifically provided in this section and § 19.2-310.5, the results of the analysis shall be securely stored and shall remain confidential.

History.
1990, c. 669; 1998, c. 280; 2002, cc. 753, 773; 2003, c. 150; 2005, cc. 868, 881.

Editor's note.
Acts 2002, cc. 753 and 773, cl. 3, provide: "That the provisions of this act shall become effective on January 1, 2003."

Law Review.
For note, "DNA Fingerprinting: The Virginia Approach", see 35 Wm. & Mary L. Rev. 767 (1994).

§ 19.2-310.5. DNA data bank.

A. It shall be the duty of the Department to receive samples of human biological evidence and to analyze, classify, and file the results of DNA identification characteristics profiles of samples of human biological evidence submitted pursuant to § 19.2-310.2 or 19.2-310.2:1 and to make such information available as provided in this section. The results of an analysis and comparison of evidence submitted to the Department pursuant to § 9.1-1101 to the identification characteristics of human biological evidence so analyzed, classified, and filed shall be made available directly to duly authorized members of federal, state, and local law-enforcement agencies or private police departments that have been designated as criminal justice agencies by the Department of Criminal Justice Services as defined by § 9.1-101, attorneys for the Commonwealth or attorneys for the United States Department of Justice, or the Office of the Chief Medical Examiner upon request made in furtherance of an official investigation or prosecution of any criminal offense, or to an accused or his attorney pursuant to § 9.1-1104. The Department shall confirm whether or not there is a DNA profile on file for a specific individual if a federal, state or local law-enforcement officer requests that information in furtherance of an official investigation of any criminal offense. The name of the requestor and the purpose for which the information is requested shall be maintained on file with the Department.

B. The Department shall adopt regulations governing (i) the methods of obtaining information from the data bank in accordance with this section and (ii) procedures for verification of the identity and authority of the requestor. The Department shall specify the positions in that agency which require regular access to the data bank and samples submitted as a necessary function of the job.

C. The Department shall create a separate statistical data base comprised of DNA profiles of samples of human biological evidence of persons whose identity is unknown. Nothing in this section or § 19.2-310.6 shall prohibit the Department from sharing or otherwise disseminating the information in the statistical data base with law-enforcement or criminal justice agencies within or without the Commonwealth.

D. The Department may charge a reasonable fee to search and provide a comparative analysis of DNA profiles in the data bank to any authorized law-enforcement agency outside of the Commonwealth.

History.
1990, c. 669; 1998, c. 280; 2000, c. 284; 2002, cc. 753, 773; 2005, cc. 868, 881; 2010, c. 502; 2011, cc. 66, 171, 638.

Editor's note.
Acts 2002, cc. 753 and 773, cl. 3, provide: "That the provisions of this act shall become effective on January 1, 2003."

The 2010 amendments.

The 2010 amendment by c. 502 added the subsection A through D designations; substituted "samples of human biological evidence" for "blood, saliva or tissue samples" throughout the section; in subsection A, inserted "or to an accused or his attorney pursuant to § 9.1-1104" in the second sentence, deleted the former fourth sentence, which read: "A request may be made by personal contact, mail, or electronic means.", and deleted the last sentence, which read: "Upon his request, a copy of the request for search shall be furnished to any person identified and charged with an offense as the result of a search of information in the data bank."

The 2011 amendments.

The 2011 amendments by cc. 66 and 171 are identical, and rewrote the second sentence in subsection A, which read: "The results of an analysis and comparison of the identification characteristics from two or more samples of human biological evidence shall be made available directly to federal, state and local law-enforcement officers upon request made in furtherance of an official investigation of any criminal offense, or to an accused or his attorney pursuant to § 9.1-1104."

The 2011 amendment by c. 638 substituted "state and local law-enforcement agencies or private police departments that have been designated as criminal justice agencies by the Department of Criminal Justice Services as defined by § 9.1-101" for "state and local law-enforcement officers" in the second sentence in subsection A.

Law Review.

For note, "DNA Fingerprinting: The Virginia Approach", see 35 Wm. & Mary L. Rev. 767 (1994). For 2000 survey of Virginia criminal law and procedure, see 34 U. Rich. L. Rev. 749 (2000).

§ 19.2-310.6. Unauthorized uses of DNA data bank; forensic samples; penalties.

Any person who, without authority, disseminates information contained in the data bank shall be guilty of a Class 3 misdemeanor. Any person who disseminates, receives, or otherwise uses or attempts to so use information in the data bank, knowing that such dissemination, receipt, or use is for a purpose other than as authorized by law, shall be guilty of a Class 1 misdemeanor.

Except as authorized by law, any person who, for purposes of having DNA analysis performed, obtains or attempts to obtain any sample submitted to the Department of Forensic Science for analysis shall be guilty of a Class 5 felony.

History.

1990, c. 669; 2005, cc. 868, 881.

Cross references.

As to punishment for Class 5 felonies, see § 18.2-10. As to punishment for Class 1 and Class 3 misdemeanors, see § 18.2-11.

§ 19.2-310.7. Expungement when DNA taken for a felony conviction.

A person whose DNA profile has been included in the data bank pursuant to § 19.2-310.2 may request expungement on the grounds that the felony conviction on which the authority for including his DNA profile was based has been reversed and the case dismissed. The Department of Forensic Science shall purge all records and identifiable information in the data bank pertaining to the person and destroy all samples from the person upon receipt of (i) a written request for expungement pursuant to

this section and (ii) a certified copy of the court order reversing and dismissing the conviction.

History.

1990, c. 669; 2002, cc. 753, 773; 2005, cc. 868, 881.

Editor's note.

Acts 2002, cc. 753 and 773, cl. 3, provide: "That the provisions of this act shall become effective on January 1, 2003."

ARTICLE 2.

INDETERMINATE COMMITMENT.

§ 19.2-311. Indeterminate commitment to Department of Corrections in certain cases; duration and character of commitment; concurrence by Department.

A. The judge, after a finding of guilt, when fixing punishment in those cases specifically enumerated in subsection B of this section, may, in his discretion, in lieu of imposing any other penalty provided by law and, with consent of the person convicted, commit such person for a period of four years, which commitment shall be indeterminate in character. In addition, the court shall impose a period of confinement which shall be suspended. Subject to the provisions of subsection C hereof, such persons shall be committed to the Department of Corrections for confinement in a state facility for youthful offenders established pursuant to § 53.1-63. Such confinement shall be followed by at least one and one-half years of supervisory parole, conditioned on good behavior. The sentence of indeterminate commitment and eligibility for continuous evaluation and parole under § 19.2-313 shall remain in effect but eligibility for use of programs and facilities established pursuant to § 53.1-63 shall lapse if such person (i) exhibits intractable behavior as defined in § 53.1-66 or (ii) is convicted of a second criminal offense which is a felony. A sentence imposed for any second criminal offense shall run consecutively with the indeterminate sentence.

B. The provisions of subsection A of this section shall be applicable to first convictions in which the person convicted:

1. Committed the offense of which convicted before becoming twenty-one years of age;

2. Was convicted of a felony offense other than any of the following: capital murder, murder in the first degree or murder in the second degree or a violation of §§ 18.2-61, 18.2-67.1, 18.2-67.2 or subdivision A 1 of § 18.2-67.3; and

3. Is considered by the judge to be capable of returning to society as a productive citizen following a reasonable amount of rehabilitation.

C. Subsequent to a finding of guilt and prior to fixing punishment, the Department of Corrections shall, concurrently with the evaluation required by § 19.2-316, review all aspects of the case to determine whether (i) such defendant is physically and emotionally suitable for the program, (ii) such indeterminate sentence of commitment is in the best interest of the Commonwealth and of the person convicted, and (iii) facilities are available for the confinement of such person. After the review such person shall be again brought before the court, which shall review the findings of the Department. The court may impose a sentence as authorized in subsection A, or any other penalty provided by law.

D. Upon the defendant's failure to complete the program established pursuant to § 53.1-63 or to comply with the terms and conditions through no fault of his own, the defendant shall be brought before the court for hearing. Notwithstanding the provisions for pronouncement of sentence as set forth in § 19.2-306, the court, after hearing, may pronounce whatever sentence was originally imposed, pronounce a reduced sentence, or impose such other terms and conditions of probation as it deems appropriate.

History.
   Code 1950, § 19.1-295.1; 1966, c. 579; 1974, cc. 44, 45; 1975, c. 495; 1976, c. 498; 1980, c. 531; 1988, c. 38; 1990, c. 701; 1994, cc. 859, 949; 1996, cc. 755, 914; 1997, c. 387; 2000, cc. 668, 690.

Cross references.
   As to facilities for confinement of persons committed to the Department of Corrections under § 19.2-311 et seq., see §§ 53.1-63 through 53.1-67.

Editor's note.
   Acts 2000, c. 668, cl. 2 and Acts 2000, c. 690, cl. 3, provide: "That the Department of Corrections shall report annually to the General Assembly on or before December 1 on the utilization of the Youthful Offender Program by the Judiciary."

Law Review.
   For survey of Virginia criminal procedure for the year 1975-1976, see 62 Va. L. Rev. 1412 (1976).

Michie's Jurisprudence.
   For related discussion, see 9B M.J. Infants, § 13.

CASE NOTES

No language in this section directs the court to make any findings before it can deny alternative sentencing under this section. Rather, the language of this section gives the judge complete discretion whether to impose this sentencing alternative on defendants who qualify under its provisions. Crank v. Rogers, 1 Va. App. 491, 339 S.E.2d 909 (1986).

   The language of this section, unlike former 18 U.S.C. § 5010 (d) of the Federal Youth Corrections Act, does not require the trial court to find that the youthful offender would not benefit from treatment under the statute before imposing any other sentence. Crank v. Rogers, 1 Va. App. 491, 339 S.E.2d 909 (1986).

Nor does due process require considering alternatives. — Due process does not require the trial judge to indicate, before imposing sentence, that he has considered sentencing alternatives available under this section. Crank v. Rogers, 1 Va. App. 491, 339 S.E.2d 909 (1986).

In order to prevail on claim that defense counsel was ineffective for not requesting court to sentence defendant under provisions of this section, defendant must establish both that counsel's assistance was deficient and that this deficiency prejudiced this defense. Crank v. Rogers, 1 Va. App. 491, 339 S.E.2d 909 (1986).

Sentencing alternatives under this section differ from those required by § 18.2-53.1. Thus, a commitment under this section is contrary to the mandatory provision of § 18.2-53.1.

LaFleur v. Commonwealth, 6 Va. App. 190, 366 S.E.2d 712 (1988).

   Purpose of § 18.2-53.1 would be eroded by committing offender under this section in lieu of sentencing him under § 18.2-53.1. This would substitute a discretionary penalty for an inflexible one. The General Assembly has directed a contrary policy which courts must follow. LaFleur v. Commonwealth, 6 Va. App. 190, 366 S.E.2d 712 (1988).

   Conviction for use of firearm. — The mandatory sentence required upon a conviction for the use of a firearm during the commission of a felony prevents a trial court from sentencing a person to an indeterminate commitment to the Department of Corrections. LaFleur v. Commonwealth, 6 Va. App. 190, 366 S.E.2d 712 (1988).

   Sentence was voidable. — Although the trial court arguably erred in imposing a sentence for malicious wounding below the statutory minimum and in failing to impose a suspended sentence under subsection A of § 19.2-311, the errors only rendered the sentence voidable; however, because more than 21 days had passed since the entry of defendant's original sentencing order, the trial court no longer had jurisdiction to enter an amended order under Va. Sup. Ct. R. 1:1, and could not reacquire jurisdiction, even by entry of a nunc pro tunc order. Because a probation violation order attempted to revoke a sentence imposed by the amended sentencing order, it too was invalid. Gautier v. Commonwealth, 2007 Va. App. LEXIS 35 (Feb. 6, 2007).

§ 19.2-312. Repealed by Acts 1990, c. 701.

§ 19.2-313. Eligibility for release.

Any person committed under the provisions of § 19.2-311 shall be eligible for release at the discretion of the Parole Board upon certification by the Director of the Department of Corrections that the person has successfully completed the program established pursuant to § 53.1-63 and a determination that he has demonstrated that such release is compatible with the interests of society and of such person and his successful rehabilitation to that extent. The Department and Parole Board shall make continuous evaluation of his progress to determine his readiness for release. All such persons, in any event, shall be released after four years' confinement. Any person committed under § 19.2-311 who was convicted of a misdemeanor and is determined to be unsuitable for the program established pursuant to § 53.1-63 shall be released after one year of confinement or the maximum confinement for the misdemeanor whichever is less.

History.
   Code 1950, § 19.1-295.3; 1966, c. 579; 1975, cc. 495, 571; 2000, cc. 668, 690.

Editor's note.
   The above section is former § 19.1-295.3 as amended by Acts 1975, c. 571. Pursuant to § 1-13.39 (see now § 30-152), it has been substituted for § 19.2-313 as enacted by Acts 1975, c. 495.

   Acts 2000, c. 668, cl. 2 and Acts 2000, c. 690, cl. 3 provide: "That the Department of Corrections shall report annually to the General Assembly on or before December 1 on the utilization of the Youthful Offender Program by the Judiciary."

Law Review.
   For comment, "Obstacles to Holding a Parole Official in Virginia Liable for the Negligent Release or Supervision of a Parolee," see 22 U. Rich. L. Rev. 83 (1987).

§ 19.2-314. Supervision of persons released.

Every person released under § 19.2-313 shall receive intensive parole supervision for a period of at least one and one-half years and may have parole supervision continued for a longer period, if the Parole Board deems it advisable.

History.

Code 1950, § 19.1-295.4; 1966, c. 579; 1975, c. 495; 2000, cc. 668, 690.

Editor's note.

Acts 2000, c. 668, cl. 2 and Acts 2000, c. 690, cl. 3, provide: "That the Department of Corrections shall report annually to the General Assembly on or before December 1 on the utilization of the Youthful Offender Program by the Judiciary."

§ 19.2-315. Compliance with terms and conditions of parole; time on parole not counted as part of commitment period.

Every person on parole under § 19.2-314 shall comply with such terms and conditions as may be prescribed by the Board according to § 53.1-157 and shall be subject to the penalties imposed by law for a violation of such terms and conditions. Notwithstanding any other provision of the Code, if parole is revoked as a result of any such violation, such person may be returned to the institution established pursuant to § 53.1-63 upon the direction of the Parole Board with the concurrence of the Department of Corrections, provided such person has not been convicted since his release on parole of an offense constituting a felony under the laws of the Commonwealth. Time on parole shall not be counted as part of the four-year period of commitment under this section. In addition, such person may be brought before the sentencing court for imposition of all or part of the suspended sentence.

History.

Code 1950, § 19.1-295.5; 1966, c. 579; 1975, c. 495; 1984, c. 33; 2000, cc. 668, 690.

Editor's note.

Acts 2000, c. 668, cl. 2 and Acts 2000, c. 690, cl. 3, provide: "That the Department of Corrections shall report annually to the General Assembly on or before December 1 on the utilization of the Youthful Offender Program by the Judiciary."

§ 19.2-316. Evaluation and report prior to determining punishment.

Following conviction and prior to sentencing, the court shall order such defendant committed to the Department of Corrections for a period not to exceed 60 days from the date of referral for evaluation and diagnosis by the Department to determine the person's potential for rehabilitation through confinement and treatment in the facilities and programs established pursuant to § 53.1-63. The evaluation and diagnosis shall include a complete physical and mental examination of the defendant and may be conducted by the Department of Corrections at any state or local facility, probation and parole office, or other location deemed appropriate by the Department. The Department of Corrections shall conduct

the evaluation and diagnosis and shall review all aspects of the case within 60 days from the date of conviction or revocation of ordinary probation and shall recommend that the defendant be committed to the facility established pursuant to § 53.1-63 upon finding that (i) such defendant is physically and emotionally suitable for the program, (ii) such commitment is in the best interest of the Commonwealth and the defendant, and (iii) facilities are available for confinement of the defendant.

If the Director of the Department of Corrections determines such person should be confined in a facility other than one established pursuant to § 53.1-63, a written report giving the reasons for such decision shall be submitted to the sentencing court. The court shall not be bound by such written report in the matter of determining punishment. Additionally, the person may be committed or transferred to a state hospital operated by the Department of Behavioral Health and Developmental Services or other mental health hospital, as provided by law, during such 60-day period.

History.

Code 1950, § 19.1-295.6; 1966, c. 579; 1974, cc. 44, 1975, c. 495; 1990, c. 701; 2000, cc. 668, 690; 2012, cc. 476, 507.

Editor's note.

Acts 2000, c. 668, cl. 2 and Acts 2000, c. 690, cl. 3, provide: "That the Department of Corrections shall report annually to the General Assembly on or before December 1 on the utilization of the Youthful Offender Program by the Judiciary."

The 2012 amendments.

The 2012 amendments by cc. 476 and 507 are identical, and substituted "state hospital operated by the Department of Behavioral Health and Developmental Services or other mental health hospital" for "mental hospital or like institution" in the third sentence of the second paragraph; and made minor stylistic changes throughout.

ARTICLE 3.

BOOT CAMP INCARCERATION PROGRAM.

§ 19.2-316.1. Eligibility for participation; evaluation; sentencing; withdrawal or removal from program.

An individual may be eligible to be sentenced as provided herein if he (i) is convicted on or after January 1, 1991, of a nonviolent felony, or is deemed by the court to be nonviolent in character, (ii) is no older than twenty-four at the time of conviction for the offense, (iii) has never before been incarcerated upon a felony conviction in a correctional facility of any state, the District of Columbia, the United States or its territories, and (iv) has not been confined for more than twelve months nor for more than one term of confinement in a local correctional facility of any such jurisdiction; however, confinement for misdemeanor traffic convictions shall not be considered in determining eligibility.

Following conviction and prior to sentencing, upon motion of the defendant, the court may order such defendant committed to the Department of Corrections for a period not to exceed sixty days from the date of referral or the date of revocation of ordinary probation, as the case may be, for evaluation and diagnosis by the Department to determine suitability for participation in the Boot Camp Incarceration Program established pursuant to § 53.1-67.1. The evaluation and diagnosis shall include a complete physical and mental examination of the defendant and may be conducted by the Department of Corrections at any state or local facility, probation and parole office, or other location deemed appropriate by the Department.

The Department of Corrections shall conduct the evaluation and diagnosis and shall review all aspects of the case within sixty days from the date of conviction or revocation of ordinary probation and shall recommend that the defendant be committed to the Boot Camp Incarceration Program upon finding that (i) such defendant is physically and emotionally suitable for the program, (ii) such commitment is in the best interest of the Commonwealth and the defendant, and (iii) facilities are available for confinement of the defendant.

Upon receipt of such a recommendation and written consent of the defendant to participate in the program, and a determination by the court that the defendant will benefit from the program and is capable of returning to society as a productive citizen following a reasonable amount of intensive supervision and rehabilitation including program components set forth in § 53.1-67.1, and the defendant would otherwise be committed to the Department of Corrections for a period of confinement, the court shall impose such sentence of confinement as authorized by law and suspend the sentence and place the defendant on probation. Such probation shall be conditioned upon the defendant's entry into and successful completion of a Boot Camp Incarceration Program established by the Department of Corrections pursuant to § 53.1-67.1. The court may impose such other terms and conditions of probation as it deems appropriate.

Upon the defendant's (i) voluntary withdrawal from the program, (ii) removal from the program by the Department of Corrections for intractable behavior, or (iii) refusal to comply with the terms and conditions of probation imposed by the court, the defendant shall be brought before the court for hearing. Upon a finding that the defendant voluntarily chooses to withdraw from the program, exhibited intractable behavior as defined herein, or refused to comply with terms and conditions of probation, the court may revoke all or part of the suspended sentence and probation. Upon revocation of the suspension and probation, the provisions of §§ 53.1-191, 53.1-196 and 53.1-198 through 53.1-201 shall apply retroactively to the date of sentencing.

Upon the defendant's failure to complete the program or to comply with the terms and conditions of probation imposed by the court through no fault of his own, the defendant shall be brought before the court for hearing. Notwithstanding the provisions for pronouncement of sentence as set forth in § 19.2-306, the court, after hearing, may pronounce whatever sentence was originally imposed, pronounce a reduced sentence, or impose such other terms and conditions of probation as it deems appropriate.

"Intractable behavior" means that behavior which, in the determination of the Department of Corrections, (i) indicates an inmate's unwillingness or inability to conform his behavior to that necessary to his successful completion of the program or (ii) is so disruptive as to threaten the successful completion of the program by other participants.

"Nonviolent felony" means any felony except those considered an "act of violence" pursuant to § 19.2-297.1 or any attempt to commit any of those crimes.

History.
1990, c. 474; 1992, c. 861; 1994, c. 926; 1995, c. 117; 1996, cc. 809, 938; 2000, c. 769.

Cross references.
As to the Comprehensive Community Corrections Act for Local-Responsible Offenders, see § 9.1-173.

Editor's note.
Acts 1990, c. 474, cl. 2, and Acts 1992, c. 861, cl. 2, which provided for the expiration of the 1990 enactment of and the 1992 amendment to this section on December 31, 1995, was repealed by Acts 1995, c. 117, cl. 2.

Michie's Jurisprudence.
For related discussion, see 5B M.J. Criminal Procedure, § 70.

CASE NOTES

Intermediate scrutiny test must be applied to pilot boot camp incarceration program where the program only admitted male applicants. West v. Virginia Dep't of Cors., 847 F. Supp. 402 (W.D. Va. 1994).

Equal protection afforded to Christian and muslim inmates. — Inmate's 42 U.S.C. § 1983 action, alleging that defendants abridged his constitutional right to the free exercise of his Muslim religion and violated his rights under the Equal Protection Clause by treating Muslims less favorably than Christians, would fail, where evidence showed that Christian and Muslim inmates were afforded essentially equal opportunities for religious services in separate locations at the same times and both groups of inmates were subject to the same daily boot camp regimen and schedule; where prison officials addressed allegations of inferior space for holding religious services and authorizing Muslim inmates to hold their religious services in quieter and less crowded spaces; and where an exception to the SDC schedule was made permitting weekly Islamic study sessions for two hours on Friday afternoons with an Imam, a congregation leader, which plaintiff attended. In these circumstances, plaintiff's equal protection claim failed, for the record reflected that defendants afforded plaintiff reasonable opportunities for pursuing his faith which were comparable to those afforded to Christian inmates. Nor did equal protection require prisons to ensure that their libraries adhered to numerical parity in books congenial to various religions. Finally, claim of disparate treatment in holiday observances also failed because any differences in treatment were not the result of purposeful discrimination, but instead were justified as reasonably related to the legitimate penological objectives of the facility. Blagman v. White, 112 F. Supp. 2d 534, 2000 U.S. Dist. LEXIS 13799 (E.D. Va. 2000).

Equal protection violated. — Even if there were differences which justified treating male and female inmates differently, there was no compelling interest in providing male and female offenders with such unequal sentencing options where male offenders were allowed to be in a boot camp incarceration program; department of corrections did not even attempt to address what "acknowledged differences" would justify the provision of a boot camp program and favorable sentencing alternatives only to men, defendants were acting on the basis of archaic and stereotypic notions of the roles of men and women, and there was an inherent contradiction in the defendant's argument where on the one hand, defendants argue that the "acknowledged differences" between men and women justify the provision of a trial boot camp program for male inmates and on the other hand, defendants purport to want to use the results of the all-male boot camp incarceration program to determine whether the program should be extended to women. West v. Virginia Dep't of Cors., 847 F. Supp. 402 (W.D. Va. 1994).

Discretion of the court to modify suspended sentence. — Where the trial court imposed a condition upon a probation to enter and successfully complete a Detention Center Incarceration Program, and while such might have been a condition of probation, merely entering the program was a prerequisite to and one of the conditions upon which the probationer's sentence was suspended; when he could no longer satisfy this condition, the court was authorized to reconsider the suspended sentences and determine what portion of the same or other alternatives were appropriate. Word v. Commonwealth, 41 Va. App. 496, 586 S.E.2d 282, 2003 Va. App. LEXIS 485 (2003).

ARTICLE 4.

DETENTION CENTER INCARCERATION PROGRAM.

§ 19.2-316.2. Eligibility for participation in detention center incarceration program; evaluation; sentencing; withdrawal or removal from program.

A. A defendant who otherwise would have been sentenced to incarceration for a nonviolent felony as defined in § 19.2-316.1 or who has been previously incarcerated for a nonviolent felony as defined in § 19.2-316.1 but otherwise meets the following criteria and (i) who is determined by the court to need more security or supervision than provided by the diversion center incarceration program under § 53.1-67.7, (ii) whose age or physical condition disqualifies him from the Boot Camp Incarceration Program under § 53.1-67.1, and (iii) who can benefit from a regimented environment and structured program, may be considered for commitment to a detention center established under § 53.1-67.8 as follows:

1. Following conviction and prior to imposition of sentence or following a finding that the defendant's probation should be revoked, upon motion of the defendant or the attorney for the Commonwealth or upon the court's own motion, the court may order such defendant committed to the Department of Corrections for a period not to exceed 60 days from the date of commitment for evaluation and diagnosis by the Department to determine suitability for participation in the Detention Center Incarceration Program. The evaluation and diagnosis shall include a complete physical and mental examination of the defendant and may be conducted by the Department

at any state or local correctional facility, probation and parole office, or other location deemed appropriate by the Department. When a defendant who has not been charged with a new criminal offense and who may be subject to a revocation of probation, scores incarceration on the probation violation guidelines and agrees to participate, the probation and parole officer, with the approval of the court, may commit the defendant to the Department for such evaluation, for a period not to exceed 60 days.

2. Upon determination that (i) such defendant is physically and emotionally suited for the program, (ii) such commitment is in the best interest of the Commonwealth and the defendant, and (iii) facilities are available for the confinement of the defendant, the Department shall recommend to the court in writing that the defendant be committed to the Detention Center Incarceration Program.

3. Upon receipt of such a recommendation and a determination by the court that the defendant will benefit from the program and is capable of returning to society as a productive citizen following successful completion of the program, and if the defendant would otherwise be committed to the Department, the court (i) shall impose sentence, suspend the sentence, and place the defendant on probation or (ii) following a finding that the defendant has violated the terms and conditions of his probation previously ordered, shall place the defendant on probation pursuant to this section. Such probation shall be conditioned upon the defendant's entry into and successful completion of the Detention Center Incarceration Program. The court shall order that, upon successful completion of the program, the defendant shall be released from confinement and be under intensive probation supervision for a period to be specified by the court followed by an additional period of regular probation of not less than one year. The court shall further order that the defendant, following release from confinement, shall (a) make reasonable efforts to secure and maintain employment, (b) comply with a plan of restitution or community service, (c) comply with a plan for payment of fines, if any, and costs of court, and (d) undergo appropriate substance abuse treatment, if necessary. The court may impose such other terms and conditions of probation as it deems appropriate. A sentence to the Detention Center Incarceration Program shall not be imposed as an addition to an active sentence to a state correctional facility.

4. Upon the defendant's (i) voluntary withdrawal from the program, (ii) removal from the program by the Department for intractable behavior as defined in § 19.2-316.1, or (iii) failure to comply with the terms and conditions of probation, the court shall cause the defendant to show cause why his probation and suspension of sentence should not be revoked. Upon a finding that the defendant voluntarily withdrew from the program, was removed from the program by the Department for intractable behavior, or failed to comply with the terms and

conditions of probation, the court may revoke all or part of the probation and suspended sentence and commit the defendant as otherwise provided in this chapter.

B. Any offender as described in § 19.2-316.1 paroled under § 53.1-155 or mandatorily released under § 53.1-159 and for whom probable cause that a violation of parole or of the terms and conditions of mandatory release, other than for the occurrence of a new felony or Class 1 or Class 2 misdemeanor, has been determined under § 53.1-165, may be considered by the Parole Board for commitment to a detention center as established under § 53.1-67.8 as follows:

1. The Parole Board or its authorized hearing officer, with the violator's consent, may order the violator to be evaluated and diagnosed by the Department of Corrections to determine suitability for participation in the Detention Center Incarceration Program. The evaluation and diagnosis may be conducted by the Department at any state or local correctional facility, probation or parole office, or other location deemed appropriate by the Department.

2. Upon determination that (i) such commitment is in the best interest of the Commonwealth and the violator and (ii) facilities are available for the confinement of the violator, or upon receipt of a defendant's voluntary participation form from the probation and parole officer and a determination that (i) and (ii) have been met, the Department shall recommend to the Parole Board in writing that the violator be committed to the Detention Center Incarceration Program. The Department shall have the final authority to determine an individual's suitability for the program.

3. Upon receipt of such a recommendation and a determination by the Parole Board that the violator will benefit from the program and is capable of returning to society as a productive citizen following successful completion of the program, the violator shall be placed under parole supervision for a period of not less than one year. The Parole Board may impose such other terms and conditions of parole or mandatory release as it deems appropriate.

4. Upon the violator's (i) voluntary withdrawal from the program, (ii) removal from the program for intractable behavior as defined in § 19.2-316.1, or (iii) failure to comply with the terms and conditions of parole or mandatory release, the Department shall conduct a preliminary parole violation hearing to determine if probable cause exists to revoke his parole or mandatory release. Upon a finding that the violator voluntarily withdrew from the program, was removed from the program by the Department for intractable behavior, or failed to comply with the

terms and conditions of parole or mandatory release, the Parole Board shall revoke parole or mandatory release and recommit the violator as provided in § 53.1-165.

History.
1994, 2nd Sp. Sess., cc. 1, 2; 1995, cc. 502, 574; 2000, c. 338; 2002, c. 604; 2005, cc. 512, 580; 2008, cc. 362, 761.

Cross references.
As to punishment for misdemeanors, see § 18.2-11.

The 2008 amendments.
The 2008 amendments by cc. 362 and 761 are identical, and added the last sentence in subdivision A 1; inserted "or upon receipt of a defendant's voluntary participation form from the probation and parole officer and a determination that (i) and (ii) have been met" in clause (ii) of subdivision B 2; and deleted the former last sentence in subdivision B 3, which read: "The time spent in the program shall not be counted as service of any part of a term of imprisonment for which he was sentenced upon his conviction."

Law Review.
For survey of Virginia criminal law and procedure for the year 2004-2005, see 40 U. Rich. L. Rev. 197 (2005).

Michie's Jurisprudence.
For related discussion, see 5B M.J. Criminal Procedure, § 77.

CASE NOTES

Failure to complete alternative program must be willful. — Revocation of defendant's suspended sentence based on his failure to complete an alternative sentencing program was erroneous because his failure to complete the program was not willful but based on an unforeseen medical condition. Peyton v. Commonwealth, 268 Va. 503, 604 S.E.2d 17, 2004 Va. LEXIS 147 (2004).

Finding of ineligibility upheld. — Considering schizophrenic defendant's previous probation violations and her unsuitability for alternative programs, revocation of probation and imposition of remaining sentence upon the Department of Corrections' determination that defendant was ineligible for detention center program did not constitute an abuse of discretion, despite defendant's contention that by doing so the trial court violated the Americans with Disabilities Act, 42 U.S.C. § 12101 et seq. Wilson v. Commonwealth, 31 Va. App. 200, 522 S.E.2d 385 (1999).

Credit for time served in detention program. — Because defendant's participation in the § 19.2-316.2 Detention Center Incarceration Program was incarceration, even though served as a condition of probation, it could not be used upon revocation of probation to enlarge a sentencing order that had become final under Va. Sup. Ct. R. 1:1. Charles v. Commonwealth, 270 Va. 14, 613 S.E.2d 432, 2005 Va. LEXIS 56 (2005).

Applied in Word v. Commonwealth, 41 Va. App. 496, 586 S.E.2d 282, 2003 Va. App. LEXIS 485 (2003).

OPINIONS OF THE ATTORNEY GENERAL

Eligibility. — General Assembly intended that a court should not sentence the same defendant to active incarceration with the Department of Corrections and to the Detention Center Incarceration Program or the Diversion Center Incarceration Program. Further, in a situation where one court imposes a Detention or Diversion Center sentence that would be countermanded by another court's sentence for incarceration with the Department, the Department must give effect to the sentences imposed by both courts. See opinion of Attorney General to The Honorable G. Carter

Greer, Judge, City of Martinsville Circuit Court, 08-108, 2009 Va. AG LEXIS 17 (2/25/09).

ARTICLE 5.

DIVERSION CENTER INCARCERATION PROGRAM.

§ 19.2-316.3. Eligibility for participation in diversion center incarceration program; evaluation; sentencing; withdrawal or removal from program; payment for costs.

A. A defendant (i) who otherwise would have been sentenced to incarceration for a nonviolent felony as defined in § 19.2-316.1 and who the court determines requires more security or supervision than provided by intensive probation supervision or (ii) whose suspension of sentence would otherwise be revoked after a finding that the defendant has violated the terms and conditions of probation for a nonviolent felony as defined in § 19.2-316.1, may be considered for commitment to a diversion center established under § 53.1-67.7 as follows:

1. Following conviction and prior to imposition of sentence or following a finding that the defendant's probation should be revoked, upon motion of the defendant or the attorney for the Commonwealth or upon the court's own motion, the court may order such defendant committed to the Department of Corrections for a period not to exceed 45 days from the date of commitment for evaluation and diagnosis by the Department to determine suitability for participation in the Diversion Center Incarceration Program. The evaluation and diagnosis may be conducted by the Department at any state or local correctional facility, probation and parole office, or other location deemed appropriate by the Department. When a defendant who has not been charged with a new criminal offense and who may be subject to a revocation of probation, scores incarceration on the probation violation guidelines and agrees to participate, the probation and parole officer, with the approval of the court, may commit the defendant to the Department for such evaluation, for a period not to exceed 45 days.

2. Upon determination that (i) such commitment is in the best interest of the Commonwealth and the defendant and (ii) facilities are available for the confinement of the defendant, the Department shall recommend to the court in writing that the defendant be committed to the Diversion Center Incarceration Program.

3. Upon receipt of such a recommendation and a determination by the court that the defendant will benefit from the program and is capable of returning to society as a productive citizen following successful completion of the program, and if the defendant would otherwise be committed to the Department, the court (i) shall impose sentence, suspend the sentence, and place the defendant on probation pursuant to this section or (ii) following a finding that the defendant has violated the terms and conditions of his probation previously ordered, shall place the defendant on probation pursuant to this section. Such probation shall be conditioned upon the defendant's entry into and successful completion of the Diversion Center Incarceration Program. The court shall order that, upon successful completion of the program, the defendant shall be released from confinement and be under intensive probation supervision for a period to be specified by the court followed by an additional period of regular probation of not less than one year. The court shall further order that the defendant, prior to release from confinement, shall (a) make reasonable efforts to secure and maintain employment, (b) comply with a plan of restitution or community service, (c) comply with a plan for payment of fines, if any, and costs of court, and (d) undergo substance abuse treatment, if necessary. The court may impose such other terms and conditions of probation as it deems appropriate. A sentence to the Diversion Center Incarceration Program shall not be imposed in addition to an active sentence to a state correctional facility.

4. Upon the defendant's (i) voluntary withdrawal from the program, (ii) removal from the program by the Department for intractable behavior as defined in § 19.2-316.1, or (iii) failure to comply with the terms and conditions of probation, the court shall cause the defendant to show cause why his probation and suspension of sentence should not be revoked. Upon a finding that the defendant voluntarily withdrew from the program, was removed from the program by the Department for intractable behavior, or failed to comply with the terms and conditions of probation, the court may revoke all or part of the probation and suspended sentence, and commit the defendant as otherwise provided in this chapter.

B. Any offender as described in § 19.2-316.1 paroled under § 53.1-155 or mandatorily released under § 53.1-159 and for whom probable cause that a violation of parole or of the terms and conditions of mandatory release, other than the occurrence of a new felony or Class 1 or Class 2 misdemeanor, has been determined under § 53.1-165, may be considered by the Parole Board for commitment to a diversion center as established under § 53.1-67.7 as follows:

1. The Parole Board or its authorized hearing officer, with the violator's consent or upon receipt of a defendant's written voluntary agreement to participate form from the probation and parole officer, may order the violator to be evaluated and diagnosed by the Department of Corrections to determine suitability for participation in the Diversion Center Incarceration Program. The evaluation and diagnosis may be conducted by the Department at any state or local correctional facility, probation or parole office, or other location deemed appropriate by the Department.

2. Upon determination that (i) such commitment is in the best interest of the Commonwealth and the violator and (ii) facilities are available for the confinement of the violator, the Department shall recommend to the Parole Board in writing that the violator be committed to the Diversion Center Incarceration Program. The Department shall have the final authority to determine an individual's suitability for the program.

3. Upon receipt of such a recommendation and a determination by the Parole Board that the violator will benefit from the program and is capable of returning to society as a productive citizen following successful completion of the program and if the violator would otherwise be committed to the Department, the Parole Board shall restore the violator to parole supervision conditioned upon entry into and successful completion of the Diversion Center Incarceration Program. The Parole Board shall order that, upon successful completion of the program, the violator shall be placed under parole supervision for a period of not less than one year. The Parole Board may impose such other terms and conditions of parole or mandatory release as it deems appropriate. The time spent in the program shall not be counted as service of any part of a term of imprisonment for which he was sentenced upon his conviction.

4. Upon the violator's (i) voluntary withdrawal from the program, (ii) removal from the program by the Department for intractable behavior as defined in § 19.2-316.1, or (iii) failure to comply with the terms and conditions of parole or mandatory release, the Parole Board may revoke parole or mandatory release and recommit the violator as provided in § 53.1-165.

C. A person sentenced pursuant to this article shall be required to pay an amount to be determined by the Board of Corrections pursuant to regulation to defray the cost of his keep.

History.
1994, 2nd Sp. Sess., cc. 1, 2; 1995, cc. 502, 574; 2000, c. 338; 2002, c. 604; 2005, c. 604; 2008, cc. 384, 757.

Cross references.
As to punishment for Class 1 or Class 2 misdemeanors, see § 18.2-11.

The 2008 amendments.
The 2008 amendments by cc. 384 and 757 are identical, and added the last sentence to subdivision A 1; and inserted "or upon receipt of a defendant's written voluntary agreement to participate form from the probation and parole officer" in the first sentence in subdivision B 1.

CASE NOTES

Judge substantially followed statutory requirements despite statement that temporary detention of defendant, imposed pending determination of suitability for diversion program, would also be punishment for his violation of the terms and conditions of the previously suspended sentence. Rogers v. Commonwealth, 29 Va. App. 580, 513 S.E.2d 876 (1999).
Finding of ineligibility upheld. — Considering schizophrenic

defendant's previous probation violations and her unsuitability for alternative programs, revocation of probation and imposition of remaining sentence upon the Department of Corrections' determination that defendant was ineligible for detention center program did not constitute an abuse of discretion, despite defendant's contention that by doing so the trial court violated the Americans with Disabilities Act, 42 U.S.C. § 12101 et seq. Wilson v. Commonwealth, 31 Va. App. 200, 522 S.E.2d 385 (1999).

OPINIONS OF THE ATTORNEY GENERAL

Eligibility. — General Assembly intended that a court should not sentence the same defendant to active incarceration with the Department of Corrections and to the Detention Center Incarceration Program or the Diversion Center Incarceration Program. Further, in a situation where one court imposes a Detention or Diversion Center sentence that would be countermanded by another court's sentence for incarceration with the Department, the Department must give effect to the sentences imposed by both courts. See opinion of Attorney General to The Honorable G. Carter Greer, Judge, City of Martinsville Circuit Court, 08-108, 2009 Va. AG LEXIS 17 (2/25/09).

CHAPTER 19.
EXCEPTIONS AND WRITS OF ERROR.

Michie's Jurisprudence.
For related discussion, see 1B M.J. Appeal and Error, §§ 47, 56, 57, 85, 125, 204, 207, 208, 313, 328; 2B M.J. Autrefois, Acquit and Convict, § 10; 4A M.J. Contempt, § 35; 2B M.J. Bail and Recognizance, §§ 9, 12, 13, 15; 2B M.J. Bail and Recognizance, §§ 9, 12, 13, 15; 5B M.J. Criminal Procedure, §§ 41, 53, 69, 76, 85, 99.

§ 19.2-317. When writ of error lies in criminal case for accused; when for Commonwealth; when for county, city or town.

A. A writ of error shall lie in a criminal case to the judgment of a circuit court or the judge thereof, from the Court of Appeals as provided in § 17.1-406. It shall lie in any such case for the accused and if the case is for the violation of any law relating to the state revenue, it shall lie also for the Commonwealth.

B. A writ of error shall also lie for any county, city or town from the Supreme Court to the judgment of any circuit court declaring an ordinance of such county, city or town to be unconstitutional or otherwise invalid, except when the violation of any such ordinance is made a misdemeanor by state statute.

C. A writ of error shall also lie for the Commonwealth from the Supreme Court to a judgment of the Court of Appeals in a criminal case, except where the decision of the Court of Appeals is made final under § 17.1-410 or § 19.2-408.

History.

Code 1950, § 19.1-282; 1960, c. 366; 1975, c. 495; 1984, c. 703; 1997, c. 358.

Cross references.

As to appeals by the Commonwealth, see § 19.2-398 et seq.

Law Review.

For survey of Virginia criminal law and procedure for the year 1969-1970, see 56 Va. L. Rev. 1572 (1970). For note discussing the Virginia Judicial Council's intermediate appellate court proposal, see 16 U. Rich. L. Rev. 209 (1982).

CASE NOTES

This section grants only the right to seek to invoke appellate jurisdiction and does not mean that the jurisdiction may be invoked in every case. Saunders v. Reynolds, 214 Va. 697, 204 S.E.2d 421 (1974).

The right to appellate review is not a necessary element of due process. Saunders v. Reynolds, 214 Va. 697, 204 S.E.2d 421 (1974).

The due process clause of the Fourteenth Amendment to the Constitution of the United States does not require that petitioner be granted a writ of error as a matter of right. Saunders v. Reynolds, 214 Va. 697, 204 S.E.2d 421 (1974).

Decision to grant or refuse petition is based on merits of case. — A decision to grant or refuse a petition for writ of error is based upon one equally-applied criterion — the merits of the case. Saunders v. Reynolds, 214 Va. 697, 204 S.E.2d 421 (1974).

Thus, equal protection not denied where meritless petition refused. — So long as the court adheres to a merits review of each petition for writ of error, there is no denial of equal protection to the felon whose petition is refused because it is without merit. Saunders v. Reynolds, 214 Va. 697, 204 S.E.2d 421 (1974).

Writ of error lies only to final judgment. — The judgment to which a writ of error will lie under this section is a final judgment pronounced at the end of a trial, and not an intermediate ruling of the trial court made as an incident of the trial of the case against a defendant. Sturgill v. Commonwealth, 175 Va. 584, 7 S.E.2d 141 (1940); Fuller v. Commonwealth, 189 Va. 327, 53 S.E.2d 26 (1949).

And to rejection of plea. — While it is permissible for the defendant in a criminal trial to file a plea seeking a dismissal of the prosecution under the provisions of § 19.2-243, the rejection of the plea is but an antecedent incident to the trial of the indictment against the defendant, and is in no sense the pronouncement of a final judgment to which a writ of error will lie under this section. Sturgill v. Commonwealth, 175 Va. 584, 7 S.E.2d 141 (1940).

Judgment under statute authorizing probation. — After a trial court has adjudged a defendant "guilty" and has suspended either the imposition or the execution of sentence, or commitment of the defendant, and has fixed the terms of his probation under former § 53-272 (now §§ 53.1-151 and 53.1-186), its action is final and subject to review. And the revocation of the probation does not alter the finality of the judgment. Fuller v. Commonwealth, 189 Va. 327, 53 S.E.2d 26 (1949).

Judgment not final where trial court fails to impose sentence or fix terms of probation. — The trial court entered an order that defendant was guilty as charged, which recited that mitigating circumstances justified suspension of sentence, that before taking action the court desired to have a report of the probation officer, and that the court suspended imposition of any sentence temporarily for the purpose of allowing defendant time for presentation of a writ of error to the Supreme Court. It was held that the order was not a final judgment of the trial court as contemplated by the statute. Fuller v. Commonwealth, 189 Va. 327, 53 S.E.2d 26 (1949).

As to the State's inability to appeal in criminal cases prior to the 1986 amendment of Va. Const., Art. VI, § 1, see Commonwealth v. Willcox, 111 Va. 849, 69 S.E. 1027 (1911); Commonwealth v. Perrow, 124 Va. 805, 97 S.E. 820 (1919); City of Roanoke v. Donckers, 187 Va. 491, 47 S.E.2d 440 (1948); Peyton v. King, 210 Va. 194, 169 S.E.2d 569 (1969).

The State may appeal in criminal case involving revenue laws. — Under Va. Const., Art. I, § 8 and Art. VI, § 1, the legislature may allow the Commonwealth an appeal in any criminal case involving the revenue laws, regardless of the degree of punishment. Commonwealth v. Willcox, 111 Va. 849, 69 S.E. 1027 (1911); Commonwealth v. Perrow, 124 Va. 805, 97 S.E. 820 (1919).

Reading the second sentence of former § 17-116.08 (see now § 17.1-411) with the second sentence of this section, the Commonwealth is "also" assured, consistent with Va. Const., Art. VI, § 1, of the right to appeal to the Supreme Court adverse judgments in prosecutions for the violation of any law relating to the state revenue, even though in criminal prosecutions generally, according to this section, "the accused" only may appeal to the Supreme Court. Commonwealth v. Smith, 230 Va. 354, 337 S.E.2d 278 (1985).

State revenue case. — Where the defense to a prosecution for the unlawful sale of malt liquor was that the defendant had the right to sell it at the place where sold, under the revenue laws of the State, the case involved a violation of a law "relating to the state revenue" within the provisions of this section. Commonwealth v. Goodwin, 109 Va. 828, 64 S.E. 54 (1909).

Two felons who are not similarly situated need not be treated alike to the extent that each must be granted a writ regardless of the merits of his claims. Saunders v. Reynolds, 214 Va. 697, 204 S.E.2d 421 (1974).

Procedure of granting a writ of error to one felon and refusing it to another is not violative of the equal protection clause. Saunders v. Reynolds, 214 Va. 697, 204 S.E.2d 421 (1974).

Distinctions between felonies and misdemeanors do not violate equal protection. — With respect to appellate procedure, the distinctions between felonies and misdemeanors either do not exist or, where they do, they are based upon well-reasoned objectives which serve a legitimate state interest and protect the constitutional rights of defendants convicted of crime and thus do not violate equal protection. Saunders v. Reynolds, 214 Va. 697, 204 S.E.2d 421 (1974).

The equal protection clause of the Fourteenth Amendment to the United States Constitution is not violated by the procedure in which a person convicted of a misdemeanor in a court not of record is given an automatic appeal to a higher court while a person originally convicted in a court of record has no such automatic right of appeal to a higher court. Saunders v. Reynolds, 214 Va. 697, 204 S.E.2d 421 (1974).

For cases construing former § 19.2-317.1 relative to the ineffective assistance of counsel, see Frye v. Commonwealth, 231 Va. 370, 345 S.E.2d 267 (1986); Dowell v. Commonwealth, 3 Va. App. 555, 351 S.E.2d 915 (1987); Beaver v. Commonwealth, 232 Va. 521, 352 S.E.2d 342, cert. denied, 483 U.S. 1033, 107 S. Ct. 3277, 97 L. Ed. 2d 781 (1987); Payne v. Commonwealth, 233 Va. 460, 357 S.E.2d 500, cert. denied, 484 U.S. 933, 108 S. Ct. 308, 98 L. Ed. 2d 267 (1987); Payne v. Commonwealth, 5 Va. App. 498, 364 S.E.2d 765 (1988); Hill v. Commonwealth, 8 Va. App. 60, 379 S.E.2d 134 (1989).

Applied in Wolkind v. Selph, 473 F. Supp. 675 (E.D. Va. 1979); City of Va. Beach v. Murphy, 239 Va. 353, 389 S.E.2d 462 (1990).

§ 19.2-317.1. Repealed by Acts 1990, c. 74.

§ 19.2-318. Appeal on writ of error to judgment for contempt.

From a judgment for any civil contempt of court an appeal may be taken to the Court of Appeals. A writ of error shall lie from the Court of Appeals to a judgment for criminal contempt of court. This section shall also be construed to authorize an appeal from or writ of error to a judgment of a circuit court rendered on appeal from a judgment of a district court for civil or criminal contempt.

History.
Code 1950, § 19.1-283; 1960, c. 366; 1968, c. 639; 1975, c. 495; 1979, c. 649; 1984, c. 703.

CASE NOTES

This section does not allow a writ of error to an interlocutory judgment or order adjudicating one guilty of contempt. An order which reserves the imposition of penalty or punishment for a period to allow the contemnor to purge himself is such an order. E.I. Du Pont de Nemours & Co. v. Universal Moulded Prods. Corp., 189 Va. 523, 53 S.E.2d 835 (1949).

An order adjudging a defendant guilty of contempt is a final judgment to which a writ of error lies under this section. Weston v. Commonwealth, 195 Va. 175, 77 S.E.2d 405 (1953).

Decree not interlocutory where appellant was sentenced to 15 days in jail and execution of the sentence was suspended until a date certain. The fact that the court suspended execution of the sentence and continued the case until a date certain so that the appellant could purge himself of the civil contempt did not make the decree interlocutory. The contempt decree imposed a sentence and fully adjudicated all issues; it was final, and jurisdiction of the appeal was therefore proper. Peet v. Peet, 16 Va. App. 323, 429 S.E.2d 487 (1993).

Jurisdiction in appeal of proper divorce decree debt liability determination. — Where matter clearly arose out of the enforcement of a provision in a divorce decree requiring husband to hold wife harmless for their joint debt to bank, Court of Appeals had jurisdiction to consider the trial court's determination that husband failed to comply with the terms of the decree. Douglas v. Douglas, 17 Va. App. 380, 437 S.E.2d 244 (1993).

Civil contempt. — Section 19.2-318 did not provide appellate jurisdiction for either the Supreme Court of Virginia or the Court of Appeals of Virginia to review the judgment of the circuit court dismissing the rule to show cause and refusing to hold the property owner in civil contempt of court; therefore, finding no abrogation of the common-law rule in the current or former versions of § 19.2-318 that would give the court jurisdiction of the instant appeal, the court turned to subdivision A 3 of § 8.01-670. The General Assembly abrogated the common-law rule that appellate review of contempt proceedings was not available only with regard to judgments "for" contempt; consequently, the court did not have jurisdiction under subdivision A 3 of § 8.01-670 to review the judgment dismissing the rule to show cause and refusing to hold the property owner in civil contempt of court. Jenkins v. Mehra, 281 Va. 37, 704 S.E.2d 577, 2011 Va. LEXIS 18 (2011).

Applied in Nusbaum v. Berlin, 273 Va. 385, 641 S.E.2d 494, 2007 Va. LEXIS 26 (2007).

§ 19.2-319. When execution of sentence to be suspended; bail; appeal from denial.

If a person sentenced by a circuit court to death or confinement in the state correctional facility indicates an intention to apply for a writ of error, the circuit court shall postpone the execution of such sentence for such time as it may deem proper.

In any other criminal case wherein judgment is given by any court to which a writ of error lies, and in any case of judgment for any civil or criminal contempt, from which an appeal may be taken or to which a writ of error lies, the court giving such judgment may postpone the execution thereof for such time and on such terms as it deems proper.

In any case after conviction if the sentence, or the execution thereof, is suspended in accordance with this section, or for any other cause, the court, or the judge thereof, may, and in any case of a misdemeanor shall, set bail in such penalty and for appearance at such time as the nature of the case may require; provided that, if the conviction was for a violent felony as defined in § 19.2-297.1 and the defendant was sentenced to serve a period of incarceration not subject to suspension, then the court shall presume, subject to rebuttal, that no condition or combination of conditions of bail will reasonably assure the appearance of the convicted person or the safety of the public.

In any case in which the court denies bail, the reason for such denial shall be stated on the record of the case. A writ of error from the Court of Appeals shall lie to any such judgment refusing bail or requiring excessive bail, except that in any case where a person has been sentenced to death, a writ of error shall lie from the Supreme Court. Upon review by the Court of Appeals or the Supreme Court, if the decision by the trial court to deny bail is overruled, the appellate court shall either set bail or remand the matter to circuit court for such further action regarding bail as the appellate court directs.

History.
Code 1950, § 19.1-281; 1960, c. 366; 1975, c. 495; 1979, c. 649; 1984, c. 703; 1987, c. 175; 1988, c. 524; 1999, c. 821; 2008, cc. 126, 146.

Cross references.
As to increase or decrease in probation period and modification of conditions, see § 19.2-304. As to requiring restitution, etc., see §§ 19.2-305 to 19.2-305.4. As to revocation of suspension of sentence and probation, see § 19.2-306. As to eligibility for parole, see § 53.1-151. As to commencement of term of confinement, see § 53.1-186.

The 2008 amendments.
The 2008 amendments by cc. 126 and 146 are identical, and in the last sentence of the final paragraph, inserted "either" and "or remand the matter ... court directs."

Law Review.
For 2007 annual survey article, "Criminal Law and Procedure," see 42 U. Rich. L. Rev. 311 (2007).

CASE NOTES

Applicability. — Where a trial court required a driving under the influence defendant to turn in his license to the court clerk upon his conviction, § 19.2-319 did not provide him with any relief on appeal because the revocation of a driver's license was not a punishment that could be postponed pending appeal, rather it was an act of the State under its police power to protect the public.

Corbin v. Commonwealth, 44 Va. App. 196, 604 S.E.2d 111, 2004 Va. App. LEXIS 516 (2004).

Scope of section. — The statute does not purport to make the decision of the Court of Appeals final in a bail proceeding. It merely delineates the court to which an appeal is to be taken in a noncapital case as well as in a case where a death sentence has been imposed. In addition, the statute addresses only cases where bail has been refused or excessive bail required. It does not speak to the question whether the Commonwealth may appeal to the Supreme Court when the prisoner successfully has appealed to the Court of Appeals. Commonwealth v. Smith, 230 Va. 354, 337 S.E.2d 278 (1985).

This section grants discretionary authority to the trial court to set bail pending appeal. Strohecker v. Commonwealth, 23 Va. App. 242, 475 S.E.2d 844 (1996).

Scope of relief. — This section provides for the postponement of the execution of a sentence in order to give a defendant a fair opportunity to apply for a writ of error. Here, appellant made no assertion to the trial court that he needed additional time to prepare his petition for appeal; rather, from appellant's motion it appeared that he misconstrued the statute, requesting that execution of his sentence be postponed "pending action by the Court of Appeals ..." This section provides for no such relief. Thus, there was no prejudice to appellant by the trial court's refusal to suspend execution of this sentence. Strohecker v. Commonwealth, 23 Va. App. 242, 475 S.E.2d 844 (1996).

Trial court erred in denying defendant's motion for bail pending appeal after the trial court concluded that it lacked jurisdiction to consider the motion because defendant had already filed his notice of appeal in defendant's criminal case prior to filing the motion for bail; the trial court was either required to suspend execution of defendant's sentence upon defendant's indication that defendant would be filing a writ of error, at which point the trial court could consider whether to grant bail pursuant to § 19.2-319, or the trial court could otherwise suspend execution of the sentence at any time during the pendency of appeal and then consider a bail request pursuant to § 19.2-322.1. Askew v. Commonwealth, 49 Va. App. 127, 638 S.E.2d 118, 2006 Va. App. LEXIS 558 (2006).

Unlike § 19.2-120, this section contains no general standards by which exercise of discretion to grant or deny post-conviction bail may be measured. Although post-conviction bail is generally less liberally accorded than in the pretrial stage, the statute requires the trial judge to exercise not an arbitrary discretion, but a sound judicial discretion. Dowell v. Commonwealth, 6 Va. App. 225, 367 S.E.2d 742 (1988).

Section 19.2-319 gives the court broad discretion in determining whether and under what circumstances to grant bail pending appeal; thus, the trial court erred in concluding it lacked authority to condition defendant's release on bail pending an appeal of his felony convictions on his participation in an electronic home monitoring program. Staton v. Commonwealth, No. 2055-01-4, 2001 Va. App. LEXIS 673 (Ct. of Appeals Dec. 11, 2001).

Order postponing execution of judgment of conviction only suspends execution of judgment. — The circuit judge's order postponing execution of the judgment of conviction only acts to suspend execution of the judgment; it does not vacate the judgment or affect finality of the judgement. Preston v. Commonwealth, 14 Va. App. 731, 419 S.E.2d 288 (1992).

Trial court cannot refuse to suspend judgment. — To refuse to suspend a judgment of imprisonment is a denial of the right to a writ of error conferred by statute. This the trial court has no right to do. Ramey v. Commonwealth, 145 Va. 848, 133 S.E. 755 (1926).

But the period of suspension is within its discretion. — Under this section, the period of suspension of sentence in order to give accused time to apply for a writ of error is within the sound judicial discretion of the trial court. But this discretion cannot be exercised in such manner as to deprive one convicted of crime of a fair opportunity to apply for a writ of error. Ramey v. Commonwealth, 145 Va. 848, 133 S.E. 755 (1926); Dodson v. Commonwealth, 185 Va. 57, 37 S.E.2d 744 (1946).

This section grants the power of bail to the judge or the trial court to be exercised under a reasonable discretion, and unless it appear to the Supreme Court that such discretion has been abused, that court will not disturb the action of the trial court. Robinson v. Commonwealth, 190 Va. 134, 56 S.E.2d 367 (1949).

Test for determining post-conviction bail. — The primary test for determining whether the defendant should be released following a felony conviction still requires the trial court to consider questions essential to all bail decisions — whether the defendant will appear for hearing or at such other time and place as may be directed and whether the defendant's liberty will constitute an unreasonable danger to himself and the public. Dowell v. Commonwealth, 6 Va. App. 225, 367 S.E.2d 742 (1988).

The decision to grant or deny bail should be made by the trial judge upon consideration of the evidence and the total record, including factors such as the nature and circumstance of the offense, the fact of conviction, the quantum of punishment assessed, defendant's employment status, defendant's record of escape, if any, and defendant's propensity for violence, if any. Dowell v. Commonwealth, 6 Va. App. 225, 367 S.E.2d 742 (1988).

The trial judge may find relevant the age of the defendant, his health, his ties to the community, the pendency of other charges against the defendant, and other factors relevant to whether the defendant will appear when required to do so and whether the defendant's liberty represents an unreasonable danger to himself and the public. Because each case has its own unique factors, precise rules cannot be formulated. However, whatever factors are used and considered determinative must bear upon the essential questions whether the defendant will appear at further proceedings when required to do so and whether defendant represents an unreasonable danger to himself and the public. Dowell v. Commonwealth, 6 Va. App. 225, 367 S.E.2d 742 (1988).

And need not be for any specific length of time. — The trial court need not suspend the judgment for any specific length of time, but it should, upon request, suspend it for such length of time as, under all the circumstances, will enable the accused to obtain a copy of the record and present his petition for a writ of error to one of the judges of the Supreme Court. Ramey v. Commonwealth, 145 Va. 848, 133 S.E. 755 (1926).

Bail after conviction of felony. — While the trial court, by this section, is vested with discretion as to granting bail after conviction of a felony, it is not an arbitrary discretion but a sound judicial discretion. Judd, No. 2 v. Commonwealth, 146 Va. 276, 135 S.E. 713 (1926).

Discretion as to bail pending appeal. — This section grants the trial court discretion in felony cases whether to admit a convicted defendant to bail pending appeal. This power to grant bail contemplates that it will be exercised with a reasonable discretion, and unless it appears to an appellate court that such discretion has been abused, the appellate court should not disturb the action of the trial court. Commonwealth v. Smith, 230 Va. 354, 337 S.E.2d 278 (1985).

Appeal suspends execution of sentence. — Appeal of a criminal conviction does not affect the finality of the judgment, it only suspends execution of the sentence. Peterson v. Commonwealth, 225 Va. 289, 302 S.E.2d 520, cert. denied, 464 U.S. 865, 104 S. Ct. 202, 78 L. Ed. 2d 176 (1983).

Review based on trial court record. — As in any appellate proceeding, review of the trial court's decision whether to admit the defendant to bail pending appeal must be based on the record made in the trial court. The appellate court must not conduct a de novo hearing or substitute its judgment for that of the trial court. Commonwealth v. Smith, 230 Va. 354, 337 S.E.2d 278 (1985).

Postconviction bail held properly refused. — The trial court did not abuse its discretion in refusing postconviction bail, considering the nature and circumstances of the offense, the fact of conviction, the quantum of punishment assessed, defendant's lack of employment, defendant's record of escape, and defendant's apparent propensity for violence. Commonwealth v. Smith, 230 Va. 354, 337 S.E.2d 278 (1985).

Given the seriousness of the offense of rape and the punishment imposed, defendant, who wanted to return to Senegal, posed a danger to the community and of absconding if he remained at liberty while he appealed; thus, defendant was not entitled to a bail pending appeal. Sene v. Commonwealth, 2009 Va. App. LEXIS 333 (July 28, 2009).

Denial of bail not based upon exercise of sound judicial discretion. — Denial of bail based upon a conclusion that, although the defendant was not such a threat, his well-being and the peace of mind of the victim were reasons not based upon an exercise of sound judicial discretion and the trial judge erred in using these criteria as bases for his consideration of this matter. Dowell v.

Commonwealth, 6 Va. App. 225, 367 S.E.2d 742 (1988).

Requisites of recognizance. — A recognizance under this section must comply with §§ 19.2-135 and 19.2-136. Cannon v. Commonwealth, 96 Va. 573, 32 S.E. 33 (1899).

Trial court lacked jurisdiction to consider motion for bond pending appeal. — Trial court lacked jurisdiction to consider defendant's motion for bond pending appeal where: (1) there was no order suspending or vacating the May 4, 2005, sentencing order within 21 days of its entry, so the trial court retained jurisdiction over defendant's sentence only until May 25, 2005; (2) defendant filed his notice of appeal on May 20, 2005, which divested the trial court of jurisdiction to postpone or suspend the execution of defendant's sentence for purposes of the bond motion; (3) this section required the sentence or the execution of the sentence to be suspended before the trial court could set bail; and (4) no exception to Va. Sup. Ct. R. 1:1 applied. Bowen v. Commonwealth, 2006 Va. App. LEXIS 119 (Mar. 28, 2006).

Applied in Grant v. Commonwealth, 223 Va. 680, 292 S.E.2d 348 (1982).

CIRCUIT COURT OPINIONS

Discretion as to bail pending appeal. — As defendant had been sentenced to confinement in an adult detention center, not a state correctional facility the trial court had the discretion, but was not mandated, to postpone execution of her sentence pending appeal. Commonwealth v. Wright, 72 Va. Cir. 215, 2006 Va. Cir. LEXIS 220 (Fairfax County 2006).

Bond pending appeal. — Defendant's petition for bond pending an appeal by the Commonwealth of Virginia, after the appellate court had reversed defendant's conviction, was granted where defendant's original sentence had been suspended, in part, for any other cause pursuant to this section. Commonwealth v. Smith, 54 Va. Cir. 629, 1999 Va. Cir. LEXIS 727 (Richmond 1999).

§ 19.2-320. Petitioner for writ of error to comply with Rules of Court.

Any party for whom a writ of error lies may apply therefor by complying with the provisions of the Rules of the Supreme Court of Virginia relative to the appeal of criminal cases to the Court of Appeals, or where an appeal is taken to the Supreme Court, with the Rules of the Supreme Court relative to appeal of criminal cases to the Supreme Court.

History.
Code 1950, § 19.1-284; 1960, c. 366; 1975, c. 495; 1984, c. 703.

Cross references.
As to appeal to the Supreme Court, see Rule 5:1 et seq. As to appeal to the Court of Appeals, see Rule 5A:1 et seq.

CASE NOTES

The record must affirmatively show that all essential formalities in procedure have been complied with, and a failure to do so constitutes error on the face of the record of which advantage may be taken on a writ of error, even though objection was not made by the accused in the trial court. Spurgeon v. Commonwealth, 86 Va. 652, 10 S.E. 979 (1890).

A writ of error will not lie where the record does not show the judgment of the trial court, but merely recites that judgment was entered. Read v. Commonwealth, 90 Va. 168, 17 S.E. 855 (1893).

Omitted parts of record. — This section and § 8.01-673 authorize the court in any case to award certiorari by which the clerk of the court below is directed to send to the appeals court any and all parts of the record which have been omitted from the record transmitted. Washington v. Commonwealth, 216 Va. 185, 217 S.E.2d 815 (1975).

For the requirements of a sufficient assignment of error the court must look to decisions construing and implying the statutes. Harlow v. Commonwealth, 195 Va. 269, 77 S.E.2d 851 (1953).

§ 19.2-321. With whom petition for writ of error filed.

A. The petition to the Court of Appeals shall be filed with the Clerk of the Court in the manner and within the time provided by law.

B. The petition in a case wherein a writ of error lies from the Supreme Court shall be filed with the Clerk of that Court in the manner and within the time provided by law.

History.
Code 1950, § 19.1-285; 1960, c. 366; 1975, c. 495; 1976, c. 615; 1984, c. 703.

Cross references.
As to manner and time of filing petitions for appeal, see § 8.01-674.

Law Review.
For survey of Virginia practice and pleading for the year 1975-1976, see 62 Va. L. Rev. 1460 (1976).

§ 19.2-321.1. Motion in the Court of Appeals for delayed appeal in criminal cases.

A. *Filing and content of motion.* — When, due to the error, neglect, or fault of counsel representing the appellant, or of the court reporter, or of the circuit court or an officer or employee thereof, an appeal in a criminal case has (i) never been initiated; (ii) been dismissed for failure to adhere to proper form, procedures, or time limits in the perfection of the appeal; or (iii) been denied or the conviction has been affirmed, for failure to file or timely file the indispensible transcript or written statement of facts as required by law or by the Rules of the Supreme Court; then a motion for leave to pursue a delayed appeal may be filed in the Court of Appeals within six months after the appeal has been dismissed or denied, the conviction has been affirmed, or the circuit court judgment sought to be appealed has become final, whichever is later. Such motion shall identify the circuit court and the style, date, and circuit court record number of the judgment sought to be appealed, and, if one was assigned in a prior attempt to appeal the judgment, shall give the Court of Appeals record number in that proceeding, and shall set forth the specific facts establishing the said error, neglect, or fault. If the error, neglect, or fault is alleged to be that of an attorney representing the appellant, the motion shall be accompanied by the affidavit of the attorney whose error, neglect, or fault is alleged, verifying the specific facts alleged in the motion, and certifying that the appellant is not personally responsible, in whole or in part, for the error, neglect, or fault causing loss of the original opportunity for appeal.

B. *Service, response, and disposition.* — Such motion shall be served on the attorney for the Commonwealth or, if a petition for appeal was granted in the original attempt to appeal, upon the Attorney General, in accordance with the Rules of the Supreme Court. If the Commonwealth disputes the facts alleged in the motion, or contends that those facts do not entitle the appellant to a delayed appeal under this section, the motion shall be denied without prejudice to the appellant's right to seek a delayed appeal by means of petition for a writ of habeas corpus. Otherwise, the Court of Appeals shall, if the motion meets the requirements of this section, grant appellant leave to initiate or re-initiate pursuit of the appeal.

C. *Time limits when motion granted.* — If the motion is granted, all computations of time under the Rules of the Supreme Court shall run from the date of the order of the Court of Appeals granting the motion, or if the appellant has been determined to be indigent, from the date of the order by the circuit court appointing counsel to represent the appellant in the delayed appeal, whichever is later.

D. *Applicability.* — The provisions of this section shall not apply to cases in which the appellant is responsible, in whole or in part, for the error, neglect, or fault causing loss of the original opportunity for appeal, nor shall it apply in cases where the claim of error, neglect, or fault has already been alleged and rejected in a prior judicial proceeding.

History.
2005, c. 836; 2011, c. 278.

The 2011 amendments.
The 2011 amendment by c. 278, in the first sentence of subsection A, added clause (iii) and made related changes, and inserted "or denied, the conviction has been affirmed," following "after the appeal has been dismissed."

Law Review.
For article, "Professional Responsibility," see 43 U. Rich. L. Rev. 255 (2008).

CASE NOTES

Relationship with Rule 5A:8. — In a case in which defendant appealed his convictions for abduction with intent to defile, rape and use of a firearm in the commission of rape, arguing that the Commonwealth's use of its peremptory strikes to strike three African-American jurors violated the Equal Protection Clause of the Fourteenth Amendment, defendant failed to comply with both Va. Sup. Ct. R. 5A:8 and § 19.2-321.1. Defendant, who had been granted a delayed appeal, was required to file the transcripts by June 24, 2008, which was 60 days after counsel had been appointed, and he did not file the transcript of the voir dire until August 27, 2008, which was 124 days after counsel was appointed. Gilliam v. Commonwealth, 2009 Va. App. LEXIS 450 (Oct. 6, 2009).

Applied in Whitt v. Commonwealth, No. 0885-11-3, 61 Va. App. 637, 739 S.E.2d 254, 2013 Va. App. LEXIS 100 (Mar. 26, 2013).

§ 19.2-321.2. Motion in the Supreme Court for delayed appeal in criminal cases.

A. *Filing and content of motion.* — When, due to the error, neglect, or fault of counsel representing the appellant, or of the court reporter, or of the Court of Appeals or the circuit court or an officer or employee of either, an appeal from the Court of Appeals to the Supreme Court in a criminal case has (i) never been initiated; (ii) been dismissed for failure to adhere to proper form, procedures, or time limits in the perfection of the appeal; or (iii) been denied or the conviction has been affirmed, for failure to file or timely file the indispensible transcript or written statement of facts as required by law or by the Rules of the Supreme Court; then a motion for leave to pursue a delayed appeal may be filed in the Supreme Court within six months after the appeal has been dismissed or denied, the conviction has been affirmed, or the Court of Appeals judgment sought to be appealed has become final, whichever is later. Such motion shall identify by the style, date, and Court of Appeals record number of the judgment sought to be appealed, and, if one was assigned in a prior attempt to appeal the judgment to the Supreme Court, shall give the record number assigned in the Supreme Court in that proceeding, and shall set forth the specific facts establishing the said error, neglect, or fault. If the error, neglect, or fault is alleged to be that of an attorney representing the appellant, the motion shall be accompanied by the affidavit of the attorney whose error, neglect, or fault is alleged, verifying the specific facts alleged in the motion, and certifying that the appellant is not personally responsible, in whole or in part, for the error, neglect, or fault causing loss of the original opportunity for appeal.

B. *Service, response, and disposition.* — Such motion shall be served on the attorney for the Commonwealth or, if a petition for appeal was granted in the Court of Appeals or in the Supreme Court in the original attempt to appeal, upon the Attorney General, in accordance with Rule 5:4 of the Supreme Court. If the Commonwealth disputes the facts alleged in the motion, or contends that those facts do not entitle the appellant to a delayed appeal under this section, the motion shall be denied without prejudice to the appellant's right to seek a delayed appeal by means of petition for a writ of habeas corpus. Otherwise, the Supreme Court shall, if the motion meets the requirements of this section, grant appellant leave to initiate or re-initiate pursuit of the appeal from the Court of Appeals to the Supreme Court.

C. *Time limits when motion granted.* — If the motion is granted, all computations of time under the Rules of the Supreme Court shall run from the date of the order of the Supreme Court granting the motion, or if the appellant has been determined to be indigent, from the date of the order by the circuit court appointing counsel to represent the appellant in the delayed appeal, whichever is later.

D. *Applicability.* — The provisions of this section shall not apply to cases in which the appellant is responsible, in whole or in part, for the error, neglect, or fault causing loss of the original opportunity for appeal, nor shall it apply in cases where the claim of error, neglect, or fault has already been alleged and rejected in a prior judicial proceeding, nor shall it apply in cases in which a sentence of death has been imposed.

History.
2005, c. 836; 2011, c. 278.

The 2011 amendments.
The 2011 amendment by c. 278, in the first sentence of subsection A, added clause (iii) and made related changes, and inserted "or denied, the conviction has been affirmed," following "after the appeal has been dismissed."

§ 19.2-322. Repealed by Acts 1984, c. 703.

Cross references.
As to suspension of execution of judgment on appeal, see now § 19.2-322.1.

§ 19.2-322.1. Suspension of execution of judgment on appeal.

Execution of a judgment from which an appeal to the Court of Appeals or the Supreme Court is sought may be suspended during an appeal provided the appeal is timely prosecuted and an appeal bond is filed as provided in § 8.01-676.1.

History.
1984, c. 703.

Law Review.
For 2007 annual survey article, "Criminal Law and Procedure," see 42 U. Rich. L. Rev. 311 (2007).

CASE NOTES

Scope of relief. — Trial court erred in denying defendant's motion for bail pending appeal after the trial court concluded that it lacked jurisdiction to consider the motion because defendant had already filed his notice of appeal in defendant's criminal case prior to filing the motion for bail; the trial court was either required to suspend execution of defendant's sentence upon defendant's indication that defendant would be filing a writ of error, at which point the trial court could consider whether to grant bail pursuant to § 19.2-319, or the trial court could otherwise suspend execution of the sentence at any time during the pendency of appeal and then consider a bail request pursuant to § 19.2-322.1. Askew v. Commonwealth, 49 Va. App. 127, 638 S.E.2d 118, 2006 Va. App. LEXIS 558 (2006).

§ 19.2-323. Denial by judge or justice no bar to allowance by Court.

The denial of a writ of error by a judge or justice of an appellate court, in the vacation of that court, shall not prevent the allowance of the writ by the Court, if by it deemed proper, on presentation of the petition to that Court at its next term.

History.
Code 1950, § 19.1-287; 1960, c. 366; 1975, c. 495; 1976, c. 615; 1984, c. 703.

§ 19.2-324. Decision of appellate court.

The court from which a writ of error lies shall affirm the judgment, if there be no error therein, and reverse the same in whole or in part, if erroneous, and enter such judgment as the court whose error is sought to be corrected ought to have entered; or remand the cause and direct a new trial; affirming in those cases where the voices on both sides are equal.

History.
Code 1950, § 19.1-288; 1960, c. 366; 1975, c. 495.

CASE NOTES

Practice controlled by this section. — Section 8-352 (now § 8.01-430), with reference to the order to be entered by a trial court upon setting aside a verdict, and § 8-493 (now § 8.01-681), in reference to the order of reversal to be entered in the Supreme Court, do not apply to criminal cases. As to such cases the practice remains unchanged and is controlled by this section. Henderson v. Commonwealth, 130 Va. 761, 107 S.E. 700 (1921).

Reversal of judgment. — Where the presentment does not charge the offense, the appellate court will reverse the judgment against the accused, though no motion in arrest of judgment was made in the court below. Old v. Commonwealth, 59 Va. (18 Gratt.) 915 (1867).

Where act charged not criminal. — Where in a criminal case the Supreme Court reverses a judgment overruling a demurrer to the indictment on the ground that the act charged in the indictment did not constitute a crime, it may enter the order which the lower court ought to have entered, sustaining the demurrer and discharging the prisoner from further detention or prosecution under the indictment. Wise v. Commonwealth, 135 Va. 757, 115 S.E. 508 (1923).

Affirmance where no error in judgment. — A case was submitted to the Supreme Court upon a verdict of guilty of a violation of the Sunday law, accompanied by a certificate of facts. From these facts reasonably fair-minded men might draw different conclusions as to whether the work done was one of necessity. The court was not able to say that the verdict, approved by the trial court, was erroneous, and affirmed the judgment. Pirkey Bros. v. Commonwealth, 134 Va. 713, 114 S.E. 764 (1922).

Or court equally divided. — A point in a cause, in which the judges of the Supreme Court are equally divided, stands affirmed by virtue of this section, as well where it is a ruling of the court below in the progress of the cause, as where it is the final judgment of the court in the case. This decision is final and irreversible, and cannot be changed upon a second appeal in the cause. Chahoon v. Commonwealth, 62 Va. (21 Gratt.) 822 (1871).

Remand for variance between verdict and judgment. — On a trial for a felony, for which the shortest term of imprisonment was five years, the jury found the prisoner guilty, and fixed the term of his imprisonment in the state correctional facility at three years. Upon a writ of error, on the application of the prisoner, the judgment was reversed and the prisoner remanded for another trial. Jones v. Commonwealth, 61 Va. (20 Gratt.) 848 (1871). For other cases where there was a variance between verdict and judgment, see Brooks v. Commonwealth, 31 Va. (4 Leigh) 669 (1833); Sykes v. Moran, 31 O.I.C. 224 (1949); Mason v. Fairfax County Fire & Rescue Services, 60 O.I.C. 298 (1981); Smith v. Imperial Woven Label Co., 51 O.I.C. 255 (1969).

§ 19.2-324.1. Erroneously admitted evidence; appeal.

In appeals to the Court of Appeals or the Supreme Court, when a challenge to a conviction rests on a claim that the evidence was insufficient because the trial court improperly admitted evidence, the reviewing court shall consider all evidence admitted at trial to determine whether there is sufficient evidence to sustain the conviction. If the reviewing court determines that evidence was erroneously admitted and that such error was not harmless, the case shall be remanded for a new trial if the Commonwealth elects to have a new trial.

History.
2013, c. 675.

§ 19.2-325. Provisions which apply to criminal as well as civil cases; when plaintiff in error unable to pay printing costs.

Sections 8.01-675.1, 8.01-675.2, 8.01-675.3, 8.01-684 and 17.1-328 shall apply as well to criminal cases as to civil cases. In a felony case in the Court of Appeals or the Supreme Court, if the plaintiff in error files with the Clerk of the Court an affidavit that he is unable to pay or secure to be paid the costs of printing the record in the case, together with a certificate of the judge of the trial court to the effect that he has investigated the matter and is of opinion that the plaintiff in error is unable to pay, or secure to be paid, such costs, the printing shall be done as if the costs had been paid and the clerk shall not be required to account for and pay the same into the state treasury. However, if the costs are not paid or secured to be paid and upon the hearing of the case the judgment of the court below is wholly affirmed by the Court of Appeals and no appeal granted by the Supreme Court, or wholly affirmed by the Supreme Court where appeal is granted, the Court in affirming the judgment shall also give judgment in behalf of the Commonwealth against the plaintiff in error for the amount of the costs to be taxed by its clerk.

History.
Code 1950, § 19.1-289; 1960, c. 366; 1975, c. 495; 1984, c. 703.

Cross references.
For rule of decision in Supreme Court, see § 8.01-680 and note. As to fees charged by clerk of Supreme Court, see § 17.1-328.

CASE NOTES

Statutory construction. — Once defendant indicated defendant's intention to apply for a writ of error, which he was required to do within 30 days of defendant's conviction becoming final pursuant to § 19.2-325 and Va. Sup. Ct. R. 5A:6(a), defendant's sentence could be suspended pursuant to § 19.2-319 and, thus, the trial court erred in concluding that it was divested of jurisdiction to consider defendant's motion for bail because defendant had already filed defendant's notice of appeal in defendant's criminal case. Askew v. Commonwealth, 49 Va. App. 127, 638 S.E.2d 118, 2006 Va. App. LEXIS 558 (2006).

§ 19.2-326. Payment of expenses of appeals of indigent defendants.

In any felony or misdemeanor case wherein the judge of the circuit court, from the affidavit of the defendant or any other evidence certifies that the

defendant is financially unable to pay his attorneys' fees, costs and expenses incident to an appeal, the court to which an appeal is taken shall order the payment of such attorneys' fees in an amount not less than $300, costs or necessary expenses of such attorneys in an amount deemed reasonable by the court, by the Commonwealth out of the appropriation for criminal charges. If the conviction is upheld on appeal, the attorney's fees, costs and necessary expenses of such attorney paid by the Commonwealth under the provisions hereof shall be assessed against the defendant.

History.
Code 1950, § 17-30.2; 1962, c. 419; 1964, c. 651; 1975, c. 495; 1980, c. 626; 1984, c. 703.

Editor's note.
Acts 2012, Sp. Sess. I, c. 3, as amended by Acts 2013, c. 806, effective for the biennium ending June 30, 2014, Item 40 B provides: "Notwithstanding the provisions of § 19.2-326, Code of Virginia, the amount of attorney's fees allowed counsel for indigent defendants in appeals to the Supreme Court shall be in the discretion of the Supreme Court."

Law Review.
For note on the indigent in Virginia, see 51 Va. L. Rev. 163 (1965).

CASE NOTES

Right to counsel at both appellate levels. — Section 19.2-157, when considered with this section, provides an indigent with a statutory right to court-appointed counsel at both appellate levels. Dodson v. Director of Dep't of Cors., 233 Va. 303, 355 S.E.2d 573 (1987).

§ 19.2-327. How judgment of appellate court certified and entered.

The judgment of the Court of Appeals or of the Supreme Court shall be certified to the court to whose judgment the writ of error was allowed. The court or the clerk thereof shall cause the same to be entered on its order book as its own judgment.

History.
Code 1950, § 19.1-290; 1960, c. 366; 1975, c. 495; 1984, c. 703.

CASE NOTES

This section is substantially complied with by simply transcribing the judgment of the Supreme Court on the order book of the trial court. Reed v. Commonwealth, 98 Va. 817, 36 S.E. 399 (1900).

CHAPTER 19.1.

SCIENTIFIC ANALYSIS OF NEWLY DISCOVERED OR UNTESTED SCIENTIFIC EVIDENCE.

Section
19.2-327.01. [Repealed.]
19.2-327.1. Motion by a convicted felon or person adjudicated

delinquent for scientific analysis of newly discovered or previously untested scientific evidence; procedure.

§ 19.2-327.01. Repealed by Acts 2004, c. 337.

Editor's note.

Acts 2003, c. 1017, which enacted this section provided: "That the provisions of this act shall become effective on July 1, 2004." Acts 2004, c. 337, repealed Acts 2003, c. 1017, effective July 1, 2004. Thus, this section never became effective.

§ 19.2-327.1. Motion by a convicted felon or person adjudicated delinquent for scientific analysis of newly discovered or previously untested scientific evidence; procedure.

A. Notwithstanding any other provision of law or rule of court, any person convicted of a felony or any person who was adjudicated delinquent by a circuit court of an offense that would be a felony if committed by an adult may, by motion to the circuit court that entered the original conviction or the adjudication of delinquency, apply for a new scientific investigation of any human biological evidence related to the case that resulted in the felony conviction or adjudication of delinquency if: (i) the evidence was not known or available at the time the conviction or adjudication of delinquency became final in the circuit court or the evidence was not previously subjected to testing because the testing procedure was not available at the Department of Forensic Science at the time the conviction or adjudication of delinquency became final in the circuit court; (ii) the evidence is subject to a chain of custody sufficient to establish that the evidence has not been altered, tampered with, or substituted in any way; (iii) the testing is materially relevant, noncumulative, and necessary and may prove the actual innocence of the convicted person or the person adjudicated delinquent; (iv) the testing requested involves a scientific method employed by the Department of Forensic Science; and (v) the person convicted or adjudicated delinquent has not unreasonably delayed the filing of the petition after the evidence or the test for the evidence became available at the Department of Forensic Science.

B. The petitioner shall assert categorically and with specificity, under oath, the facts to support the items enumerated in subsection A and (i) the crime for which the person was convicted or adjudicated delinquent, (ii) the reason or reasons the evidence was not known or tested by the time the conviction or adjudication of delinquency became final in the circuit court, and (iii) the reason or reasons that the newly discovered or untested evidence may prove the actual innocence of the person convicted or adjudicated delinquent. Such motion shall contain all relevant allegations and facts that are known to the petitioner at the time of filing and shall enumerate and include all previous records, applications, petitions, and appeals and their dispositions.

C. The petitioner shall serve a copy of such motion upon the attorney for the Commonwealth. The Commonwealth shall file its response to the motion within 30 days of the receipt of service. The court shall, no sooner than 30 and no later than 90 days after such motion is filed, hear the motion. Motions made by a petitioner under a sentence of death shall be given priority on the docket.

D. The court shall, after a hearing on the motion, set forth its findings specifically as to each of the items enumerated in subsections A and B and either (i) dismiss the motion for failure to comply with the requirements of this section or (ii) dismiss the motion for failure to state a claim upon which relief can be granted or (iii) order that the testing be done by the Department of Forensic Science based on a finding of clear and convincing evidence that the requirements of subsection A have been met.

E. The court shall order the tests to be performed by the Department of Forensic Science and prescribe in its order, pursuant to standards and guidelines established by the Department, the method of custody, transfer, and return of evidence submitted for scientific investigation sufficient to insure and protect the Commonwealth's interest in the integrity of the evidence. The results of any such testing shall be furnished simultaneously to the court, the petitioner and his attorney of record and the attorney for the Commonwealth. The Department of Forensic Science shall give testing priority to cases in which a sentence of death has been imposed. The results of any tests performed and any hearings held pursuant to this section shall become a part of the record.

F. Nothing in this section shall constitute grounds to delay setting an execution date pursuant to § 53.1-232.1 or to grant a stay of execution that has been set pursuant to clause (iii) or (iv) of § 53.1-232.1.

G. An action under this section or the performance of any attorney representing the petitioner under this section shall not form the basis for relief in any habeas corpus proceeding or any other appeal. Nothing in this section shall create any cause of action for damages against the Commonwealth or any of its political subdivisions or any officers, employees or agents of the Commonwealth or its political subdivisions.

H. In any petition filed pursuant to this chapter, the petitioner is entitled to representation by counsel subject to the provisions of Article 3 (§ 19.2-157 et seq.) of Chapter 10.

History.

2001, cc. 873, 874; 2005, cc. 868, 881; 2013, c. 170.

Cross references.

As to Supreme Court of Virginia rules governing petitions for writ of actual innocence, see Rule 5:7B, Rules of the Virginia Supreme Court.

Editor's note.

Acts 2001, cc. 873 and 874, cl. 3, provide: "That an emergency exists and the provisions of this act, except for the provisions of

Chapter 19.2, consisting of sections 19.2-327.2 through 19.2-327.6, are in force from its passage [May 2, 2001]."

The 2013 amendments.

The 2013 amendment by c. 170, in subsection A, inserted "or any person who was adjudicated delinquent by a circuit court of an offense that would be a felony if committed by an adult," "or the adjudication of delinquency," and "or adjudication of delinquency" in three places, and substituted "actual innocence of the convicted person or the person adjudicated delinquent" for "convicted person's actual innocence," and "person convicted or adjudicated delinquent" for "convicted person"; in the first sentence of subsection B, inserted "or adjudicated delinquent" in clauses (i) and (iii), and "or adjudication of delinquency" in clause (ii), and inserted "and" following "petitions" in the last sentence; substituted "clause (iii) or (iv) of § 53.1-232.1" for "§ 53.1-232.1 (iii) or (iv)" in subsection F; and in subsection H, substituted "petitioner" for "defendant" and deleted "of this title" at the end.

Law Review.

For article, "Legal Issues Involving Children," see 35 U. Rich. L. Rev. 741 (2001). For 2003/2004 survey of criminal law and procedure, see 39 U. Rich. L. Rev. 133 (2004). For note, "How Wide Should the Actual Innocence Gateway Be? An Attempt to Clarify the Miscarriage of Justice Exception for Federal Habeas Corpus Proceedings," see 50 Wm. and Mary L. Rev. 669 (2008).

Michie's Jurisprudence.

For related discussion, see 9A M.J. Habeas Corpus, § 15.

CASE NOTES

Jurisdiction to hear appeals. — State supreme court held that it did not have jurisdiction to hear appeals from proceedings that were conducted in the circuit courts, pursuant to § 19.2-327.1, either on direct appeal or when the person seeking review filed a petition for a writ of habeas corpus, and it dismissed an inmate's petition for a writ of habeas corpus challenging a certificate of analysis and related test results that the Virginia Division of Forensic Science [now the Department of Forensic Science] filed in the circuit court. Harvey v. Warden of the Coffeewood Corr. Ctr., 268 Va. 5, 597 S.E.2d 58, 2004 Va. LEXIS 82 (2004).

Proving actual innocence. — Because an inmate's discovery that no Physical Evidence Recovery Kit was performed upon a victim by a forensic nurse and that vaginal swabs had been destroyed did not constitute evidence proving his innocence, a court summarily dismissed defendant's petition for a writ of actual innocence under § 19.2-327.1. In re Pierce, 44 Va. App. 611, 606 S.E.2d 536, 2004 Va. App. LEXIS 633 (2004).

In a capital murder case, a habeas petitioner's assertions of actual innocence were governed by §§ 19.2-327.1 to 19.2-327.6, 19.2-327.10 to 19.2-327.14, and were outside the scope of habeas corpus review. Juniper v. Warden of the Sussex I State Prison, 281 Va. 277, 707 S.E.2d 290, 2011 Va. LEXIS 61, cert. denied, 2011 U.S. LEXIS 8795, 181 L. Ed. 2d 532 (U.S. 2011).

No bad faith in destruction of trial exhibits. — Petition for a writ of habeas corpus was dismissed because the chief court clerk, who obtained an order to destroy the trial exhibits in the defendant's case after the defendant's conviction was affirmed by the Supreme Court of Virginia in order to create storage space, did not act in bad faith in destroying the evidence, was not aware that the new statute had gone into effect, and was not aware that potentially exculpatory DNA evidence was destroyed in the destruction of the exhibits. Lovitt v. Warden, 266 Va. 216, 585 S.E.2d 801, 2003 Va. LEXIS 81 (2003), cert. denied, 541 U.S. 1006, 124 S. Ct. 2018, 158 L. Ed. 2d 523 (2004); habeas corpus dismissed, stay vacated sub nom. Lovitt v. True, 330 F. Supp. 2d 603 (E.D. Va. 2004).

CIRCUIT COURT OPINIONS

Denial of motion. — Defendant's motion was denied because it was not properly before the court as it was not filed by his counsel; furthermore, the defendant was unable to produce any facts to even suggest that any evidence was still extant, and the Commonwealth represented that the evidence sought by the defendant was no longer in its custody or control. Commonwealth v. McClelland, 60 Va. Cir. 436, 2003 Va. Cir. LEXIS 64 (Richmond 2003).

Request denied where results of new testing would not change outcome. — Defendant's request, after his conviction for statutory burglary and attempted grand larceny, for new scientific testing of hair samples found at the scene of the crime, pursuant to § 19.2-327.1, was denied where the results thereof would not have resulted in a changed outcome because the trial court had given no weight to the prior analysis of such hair fragments and there was sufficient other evidence to support the conviction; however, the court granted defendant's motion to store, preserve, and retain his human biological evidence for a period of 15 years pursuant to § 19.2-270.4:1. Neal v. Commonwealth's Att'y, 60 Va. Cir. 440, 2002 Va. Cir. LEXIS 305 (Roanoke 2002).

CHAPTER 19.2.

ISSUANCE OF WRIT OF ACTUAL INNOCENCE.

Section
19.2-327.2. Issuance of writ of actual innocence based on biological evidence.
19.2-327.3. Contents and form of the petition based on previously unknown or untested human biological evidence of actual innocence.
19.2-327.4. Determination by the Supreme Court for findings of fact by the circuit court.
19.2-327.5. Relief under writ.
19.2-327.6. Claims of relief.

Michie's Jurisprudence.

For related discussion, see 1B M.J. Appeal and Error, §§ 129, 511.5.

---

§ 19.2-327.2. Issuance of writ of actual innocence based on biological evidence.

Notwithstanding any other provision of law or rule of court, upon a petition of a person who was convicted of a felony upon a plea of not guilty or who was adjudicated delinquent upon a plea of not guilty by a circuit court of an offense that would be a felony if committed by an adult, or for any person, regardless of the plea, sentenced to death, or convicted or adjudicated delinquent of (i) a Class 1 felony, (ii) a Class 2 felony, or (iii) any felony for which the maximum penalty is imprisonment for life, the Supreme Court shall have the authority to issue writs of actual innocence under this chapter. The writ shall lie to the circuit court that entered the felony conviction or adjudication of delinquency and that court shall have the authority to conduct hearings, as provided for in § 19.2-327.5, on such a petition as directed by order from the Supreme Court.

History.

2001, cc. 873, 874; 2009, cc. 139, 320; 2013, c. 170.

Cross references.

As to punishment for felonies, see § 18.2-10. As to Supreme Court of Virginia rules governing petitions for writ of actual innocence, see Rule 5:7B, Rules of the Virginia Supreme Court. As to Court of Appeals rules governing petitions for writ of actual innocence, see Rule 5A:5(b), Rules of the Virginia Supreme Court.

Editor's note.

Acts 2001, cc. 873 and 874, cl. 2, provide: "That the provisions of Chapter 19.2 of Title 19.2, consisting of sections 19.2-327.2 through 19.2-327.6, of this act shall become effective on November 15, 2002."

The 2009 amendments.

The 2009 amendments by cc. 139 and 320 are identical, and deleted "incarcerated" following "petition of a person."

The 2013 amendments.

The 2013 amendment by c. 170, in the first sentence, inserted "who was adjudicated delinquent upon a plea of not guilty by a circuit court of an offense that would be a felony if committed by an adult" and "or adjudicated delinquent"; and inserted "or adjudication of delinquency" in the last sentence.

Law Review.

For article, "Criminal Law and Procedure," see 35 U. Rich. L. Rev. 537 (2001).

CASE NOTES

Applied in Lovitt v. Warden, 266 Va. 216, 585 S.E.2d 801, 2003 Va. LEXIS 81 (2003).

§ 19.2-327.3. Contents and form of the petition based on previously unknown or untested human biological evidence of actual innocence.

A. The petitioner shall allege categorically and with specificity, under oath, the following: (i) the crime for which the petitioner was convicted or the offense for which the petitioner was adjudicated delinquent, and that such conviction or adjudication of delinquency was upon a plea of not guilty or that the person is under a sentence of death or convicted of (a) a Class 1 felony, (b) a Class 2 felony, or (c) any felony for which the maximum penalty is imprisonment for life; (ii) that the petitioner is actually innocent of the crime for which he was convicted or adjudicated delinquent; (iii) an exact description of the human biological evidence and the scientific testing supporting the allegation of innocence; (iv) that the evidence was not previously known or available to the petitioner or his trial attorney of record at the time the conviction or adjudication of delinquency became final in the circuit court, or if known, the reason that the evidence was not subject to the scientific testing set forth in the petition; (v) the date the test results under § 19.2-327.1 became known to the petitioner or any attorney of record; (vi) that the petitioner or his attorney of record has filed the petition within 60 days of obtaining the test results under § 19.2-327.1; (vii) the reason or reasons the evidence will prove that no rational trier of fact would have found proof of guilt or delinquency beyond a reasonable doubt; and (viii) for any conviction or adjudication of delinquency that became final in the circuit court after June 30, 1996, that the evidence was not available for testing under § 9.1-1104. The Supreme Court may issue a stay of execution pending proceedings under the petition. Nothing in this chapter shall constitute grounds to delay setting an execution date pursuant to § 53.1-232.1 or to grant a stay of execution that has been set pursuant to clause (iii) or (iv) of § 53.1-232.1.

B. Such petition shall contain all relevant allegations of facts that are known to the petitioner at the time of filing and shall enumerate and include all previous records, applications, petitions, and appeals and their dispositions. A copy of any test results shall be filed with the petition. The petition shall be filed on a form provided by the Supreme Court. If the petitioner fails to submit a completed form, the Court may dismiss the petition or return the petition to the prisoner pending the completion of such form. The petitioner shall be responsible for all statements contained in the petition. Any false statement in the petition, if such statement is knowingly or willfully made, shall be a ground for prosecution and conviction of perjury as provided for in § 18.2-434.

C. The Supreme Court shall not accept the petition unless it is accompanied by a duly executed return of service in the form of a verification that a copy of the petition and all attachments has been served on the attorney for the Commonwealth of the jurisdiction where the conviction or adjudication of delinquency occurred and the Attorney General or an acceptance of service signed by these officials, or any combination thereof. The Attorney General shall have 30 days after receipt of the record by the clerk of the Supreme Court in which to file a response to the petition. The response may contain a proffer of any evidence pertaining to the guilt or delinquency or innocence of the petitioner that is not included in the record of the case, including evidence that was suppressed at trial.

D. The Supreme Court may, when the case has been before a trial or appellate court, inspect the record of any trial or appellate court action, and the Court may, in any case, award a writ of certiorari to the clerk of the respective court below, and have brought before the Court the whole record or any part of any record.

E. In any petition filed pursuant to this chapter, the petitioner is entitled to representation by counsel subject to the provisions of Article 3 (§ 19.2-157 et seq.) of Chapter 10.

History.

2001, cc. 873, 874; 2003, c. 131; 2005, cc. 868, 881; 2009, cc. 139, 320; 2013, cc. 170, 180.

Cross references.

As to punishment for felonies, see § 18.2-10. As to Supreme Court of Virginia rules governing petitions for writ of actual innocence, see Rule 5:7B, Rules of the Virginia Supreme Court.

Editor's note.

Acts 2001, cc. 873 and 874, cl. 2, provide: "That the provisions of Chapter 19.2 of Title 19.2, consisting of sections 19.2-327.2 through 19.2-327.6, of this act shall become effective on November 15, 2002."

The 2009 amendments.

The 2009 amendments by cc. 139 and 320 are identical, and in the first sentence of subsection A, deleted former clause (vii), which read: "that the petitioner is currently incarcerated" and redesignated former clauses (viii) and (vix) as clauses (vii) and (viii).

The 2013 amendments.

The 2013 amendment by c. 170, in clause (i) of the first sentence in subsection A, inserted "or the offense for which the petitioner was adjudicated delinquent" and "or adjudication of delinquency," redesignated subclauses (1) through (3) as subclauses (a) through (c), inserted "or adjudicated delinquent" at the end of clause (ii), "or adjudication of delinquency" in clauses (iv) and (viii), and "or delinquency" in clause (vii), and substituted "clause (iii) or (iv) of § 53.1-232.1" for "§ 53.1-232.1 (iii) or (iv)" at the end in the last sentence; inserted "and" following "petition" in the first sentence of subsection B; in subsection C, inserted "or adjudication of delinquency" in the first sentence and substituted "guilt or delinquency of the petitioner" for "guilt of the defendant" in the last sentence; and in subsection E, substituted "petitioner" for "defendant" and deleted "of this title" at the end.

The 2013 amendment by c. 180, in the first sentence of subsection A, redesignated subclauses (1) through (3) as subclauses (a) through (c) in clause (i) and substituted "would have found proof" for "could have found proof" in clause (vii) and "clause (iii) or (iv) of § 53.1-232.1" for "§ 53.1-232.1 (iii) or (iv)" in the last sentence; inserted "or innocence" following "guilt" in the last sentence of subsection C; deleted "of this title" at the end of subsection E; and made a minor stylistic change.

Law Review.

For article, "Criminal Law and Procedure," see 35 U. Rich. L. Rev. 537 (2001).

§ 19.2-327.4. Determination by the Supreme Court for findings of fact by the circuit court.

If the Supreme Court determines from the petition, from any hearing on the petition, from a review of the records of the case, including the record of any hearing on a motion to test evidence pursuant to § 9.1-1104, or from any response from the Attorney General that a resolution of the case requires further development of the facts under this chapter, the court may order the circuit court to conduct a hearing within 90 days after the order has been issued to certify findings of fact with respect to such issues as the Supreme Court shall direct. The record and certified findings of fact of the circuit court shall be filed in the Supreme Court within 30 days after the hearing is concluded. The petitioner or his attorney of record, the attorney for the Commonwealth and the Attorney General shall be served a copy of the order stating the specific purpose and evidence for which the hearing has been ordered.

History.

2001, cc. 873, 874; 2005, cc. 868, 881.

Editor's note.

Acts 2001, cc. 873 and 874, cl. 2, provide: "That the provisions of Chapter 19.2 of Title 19.2, consisting of sections 19.2-327.2 through 19.2-327.6, of this act shall become effective on November 15, 2002."

Law Review.

For article, "Criminal Law and Procedure," see 35 U. Rich. L. Rev. 537 (2001).

§ 19.2-327.5. Relief under writ.

Upon consideration of the petition, the response by the Commonwealth, previous records of the case, the record of any hearing held under this chapter and the record of any hearings held pursuant to § 19.2-327.1, and if applicable, any findings certified from the circuit court pursuant to § 19.2-327.4, the Supreme Court shall either dismiss the petition for failure to state a claim or assert grounds upon which relief shall be granted; or upon a hearing the Court shall (i) dismiss the petition for failure to establish allegations sufficient to justify the issuance of the writ or (ii) only upon a finding of clear and convincing evidence that the petitioner has proven all of the allegations contained in clauses (iv) through (viii) of subsection A of § 19.2-327.3, and upon a finding that no rational trier of fact would have found proof of guilt or delinquency beyond a reasonable doubt, grant the writ, and vacate the conviction or adjudication of delinquency, or in the event that the Court finds that no rational trier of fact would have found sufficient evidence beyond a reasonable doubt as to one or more elements of the offense for which the petitioner was convicted or adjudicated delinquent, but the Court finds that there remains in the original trial record evidence sufficient to find the petitioner guilty or delinquent beyond a reasonable doubt of a lesser included offense, the Court shall modify the conviction or adjudication of delinquency accordingly and remand the case to the circuit court for resentencing. The burden of proof in a proceeding brought pursuant to this chapter shall be upon the convicted or delinquent person seeking relief. If a writ vacating a conviction or adjudication of delinquency is granted, the Court shall forward a copy of the writ to the circuit court, where an order of expungement shall be immediately granted.

History.

2001, cc. 873, 874; 2007, cc. 465, 824, 883, 905; 2009, cc. 139, 320; 2013, cc. 170, 180.

Editor's note.

Acts 2001, cc. 873 and 874, cl. 2, provide: "That the provisions of Chapter 19.2 of Title 19.2, consisting of sections 19.2-327.2 through 19.2-327.6, of this act shall become effective on November 15, 2002."

The 2009 amendments.

The 2009 amendments by cc. 139 and 320 are identical, and substituted "clauses (iv) through (viii)" for "clauses (iv) through (ix)" in clause (ii) of the first sentence.

The 2013 amendments.

The 2013 amendment by c. 170 inserted "or delinquency," "or adjudication of delinquency" in three places, "or adjudicated delinquent," and "or delinquent" in two places.

The 2013 amendment by c. 180, in the first sentence, inserted "Supreme" preceding "Court" near the beginning, substituted "would have found proof" for "could have found proof" and "would have found sufficient evidence" for "could have found sufficient evidence" and made minor stylistic changes.

Law Review.

For article, "Criminal Law and Procedure," see 35 U. Rich. L. Rev. 537 (2001).

§ 19.2-327.6. Claims of relief.

An action under this chapter or the performance of any attorney representing the petitioner under this chapter shall not form the basis for relief in any habeas corpus or appellate proceeding. Nothing in this chapter shall create any cause of action for damages against the Commonwealth or any of its political subdivisions or any officers, employees or agents of the Commonwealth or its political subdivisions.

History.
2001, cc. 873, 874.

Editor's note.
Acts 2001, cc. 873 and 874, cl. 2, provide: "That the provisions of Chapter 19.2 of Title 19.2, consisting of sections 19.2-327.2 through 19.2-327.6, of this act shall become effective on November 15, 2002."

CHAPTER 19.3.

ISSUANCE OF WRIT OF ACTUAL INNOCENCE BASED ON NONBIOLOGICAL EVIDENCE.

§ 19.2-327.10. Issuance of writ of actual innocence based on nonbiological evidence.

Notwithstanding any other provision of law or rule of court, upon a petition of a person who was convicted of a felony upon a plea of not guilty, or the petition of a person who was adjudicated delinquent, upon a plea of not guilty, by a circuit court of an offense that would be a felony if committed by an adult, the Court of Appeals shall have the authority to issue writs of actual innocence under this chapter. Only one such writ based upon such conviction or adjudication of delinquency may be filed by a petitioner. The writ shall lie to the circuit court that entered the conviction or the adjudication of delinquency and that court shall have the authority to conduct hearings, as provided for in this chapter, on such a petition as directed by order from the Court of Appeals. In accordance with §§ 17.1-411 and 19.2-317, either party may appeal a final decision of the Court of Appeals to the Supreme Court of Virginia. Upon an appeal from the Court of Appeals, the Supreme Court of Virginia shall have the authority to issue writs in accordance with the provisions of this chapter.

History.
2004, c. 1024; 2013, c. 170.

Cross references.
As to Court of Appeals rules governing petitions for writ of actual innocence, see Rule 5A:5(b), Rules of the Virginia Supreme Court.

Editor's note.
Acts 2004, c. 1024, cl. 2, provides: "That the Office of the Executive Secretary of the Supreme Court of Virginia shall report to the Chairmen of the Senate and House Courts of Justice Committees on January 1 of each year the number of petitions filed for writs of actual innocence pursuant to Chapter 19.3 of Title 19.2 and the dispositions thereof."

The 2013 amendments.
The 2013 amendment by c. 170 inserted "or the petition of a person who was adjudicated delinquent, upon a plea of not guilty, by a circuit court of an offense that would be a felony if committed by an adult" in the first sentence, "or adjudication of delinquency" in the second sentence, and "or the adjudication of delinquency" in the third sentence.

Law Review.
For 2003/2004 survey of criminal law and procedure, see 39 U. Rich. L. Rev. 133 (2004).

CASE NOTES

Standards of review. — State's highest court is bound by the factual findings of the trial court with regard to a petition for a writ of actual innocence based on nonbiological evidence, as approved by the appellate court, unless they are plainly wrong or without evidence to support them; the conclusions of law and conclusions based on mixed questions of law and fact of the appellate court disposing of a petition for a writ of actual innocence based on nonbiological evidence, in accordance with general principles of appellate review, are subject to de novo review. Carpitcher v. Commonwealth, 273 Va. 335, 641 S.E.2d 486, 2007 Va. LEXIS 36 (2007).

Petition denied. — Under the provisions of § 19.2-327.12, the Court of Appeals of Virginia did not abuse its discretion in certifying issues of fact to the circuit court regarding the credibility of a codefendant's recantation testimony that had to be resolved before it could determine the merits of an inmate's petition for a writ of actual innocence based on non-biological evidence, and after reviewing the same, properly denied said petition, as: (1) this kind of inquiry fell squarely within the scope of § 19.2-327.12; and (2) such did not erroneously add a credibility requirement to the statutes governing writs of actual innocence based on non-biological evidence. Moreover, because the inmate failed to meet his statutory burden of proof by showing the elements of subsection A of § 19.2-327.11, his petition for said writ was properly denied. Johnson v. Commonwealth, 273 Va. 315, 641 S.E.2d 480, 2007 Va. LEXIS 33 (2007).

Petition for a writ of actual innocence based on non-biological evidence was properly dismissed because the inmate failed to carry his burden of proof that the recantations from the victims, the inmate's sons, were true. The testimony of the boys at trial regarding the sodomy by their father was graphic and explicit and abundantly corroborated by physician testimony, photographs, and the inmate's admission that he sometimes slept with the boys. Haas v. Commonwealth, 283 Va. 284, 721 S.E.2d 479, 2012 Va. LEXIS 16 (2012).

Petition granted. — Because a certificate of analysis excluding the item tested from the statutory definition of "firearm" under subsection A of § 18.2-308.2 was issued after defendant's conviction became final, defendant's petition for a writ of actual innocence under § 19.2-327.10 et seq., was granted, and the conviction was ordered expunged pursuant to § 19.2-327.13. Copeland v. Commonwealth, 52 Va. App. 529, 664 S.E.2d 528, 2008 Va. App. LEXIS 381 (2008).

Applied in In re Lima, 44 Va. App. 571, 605 S.E.2d 794, 2004 Va.

App. LEXIS 614 (2004); Bell v. True, 413 F. Supp. 2d 657, 2006 U.S. Dist. LEXIS 4608 (W.D. Va. 2006).

§ 19.2-327.11. Contents and form of the petition based on previously unknown or unavailable evidence of actual innocence.

A. The petitioner shall allege categorically and with specificity, under oath, all of the following: (i) the crime for which the petitioner was convicted or the offense for which the petitioner was adjudicated delinquent, and that such conviction or adjudication of delinquency was upon a plea of not guilty; (ii) that the petitioner is actually innocent of the crime for which he was convicted or the offense for which he was adjudicated delinquent; (iii) an exact description of the previously unknown or unavailable evidence supporting the allegation of innocence; (iv) that such evidence was previously unknown or unavailable to the petitioner or his trial attorney of record at the time the conviction or adjudication of delinquency became final in the circuit court; (v) the date the previously unknown or unavailable evidence became known or available to the petitioner, and the circumstances under which it was discovered; (vi) that the previously unknown or unavailable evidence is such as could not, by the exercise of diligence, have been discovered or obtained before the expiration of 21 days following entry of the final order of conviction or adjudication of delinquency by the circuit court; (vii) the previously unknown or unavailable evidence is material and, when considered with all of the other evidence in the current record, will prove that no rational trier of fact would have found proof of guilt or delinquency beyond a reasonable doubt; and (viii) the previously unknown or unavailable evidence is not merely cumulative, corroborative or collateral. Nothing in this chapter shall constitute grounds to delay setting an execution date pursuant to § 53.1-232.1 or to grant a stay of execution that has been set pursuant to clause (iii) or (iv) of § 53.1-232.1 or to delay or stay any other appeals following conviction or adjudication of delinquency, or petitions to any court. Human biological evidence may not be used as the sole basis for seeking relief under this writ but may be used in conjunction with other evidence.

B. Such petition shall contain all relevant allegations of facts that are known to the petitioner at the time of filing, shall be accompanied by all relevant documents, affidavits and test results, and shall enumerate and include all relevant previous records, applications, petitions, and appeals and their dispositions. The petition shall be filed on a form provided by the Supreme Court. If the petitioner fails to submit a completed form, the Court of Appeals may dismiss the petition or return the petition to the petitioner pending the completion of such form. Any false statement in the petition, if such statement is knowingly or willfully made, shall be a ground for prosecution of perjury as provided for in § 18.2-434.

C. In cases brought by counsel for the petitioner, the Court of Appeals shall not accept the petition unless it is accompanied by a duly executed return of service in the form of a verification that a copy of the petition and all attachments have been served on the attorney for the Commonwealth of the jurisdiction where the conviction or adjudication of delinquency occurred and the Attorney General, or an acceptance of service signed by these officials, or any combination thereof. In cases brought by petitioners pro se, the Court of Appeals shall not accept the petition unless it is accompanied by a certificate that a copy of the petition and all attachments have been sent, by certified mail, to the attorney for the Commonwealth of the jurisdiction where the conviction or adjudication of delinquency occurred and the Attorney General. If the Court of Appeals does not summarily dismiss the petition, it shall so notify in writing the Attorney General, the attorney for the Commonwealth, and the petitioner. The Attorney General shall have 60 days after receipt of such notice in which to file a response to the petition that may be extended for good cause shown; however, nothing shall prevent the Attorney General from filing an earlier response. The response may contain a proffer of any evidence pertaining to the guilt or delinquency or innocence of the petitioner that is not included in the record of the case, including evidence that was suppressed at trial.

D. The Court of Appeals may inspect the record of any trial or appellate court action, and the Court may, in any case, award a writ of certiorari to the clerk of the respective court below, and have brought before the Court the whole record or any part of any record. If, in the judgment of the Court, the petition fails to state a claim, or if the assertions of previously unknown or unavailable evidence, even if true, would fail to qualify for the granting of relief under this chapter, the Court may dismiss the petition summarily, without any hearing or a response from the Attorney General.

E. In any petition filed pursuant to this chapter that is not summarily dismissed, the petitioner is entitled to representation by counsel subject to the provisions of Article 3 (§ 19.2-157 et seq.) and Article 4 (§ 19.2-163.3 et seq.) of Chapter 10. The Court of Appeals may, in its discretion, appoint counsel prior to deciding whether a petition should be summarily dismissed.

History.
    2004, c. 1024; 2013, cc. 170, 180.

Cross references.
    As to Court of Appeals rules governing petitions for writ of actual innocence, see Rule 5A:5(b), Rules of the Virginia Supreme Court.

The 2013 amendments.
    The 2013 amendment by c. 170, in subsection A, inserted "or the offense for which the petitioner was adjudicated delinquent" in clause (i), "or adjudication of delinquency" in clauses (i) and (iv), "or the offense for which he was adjudicated delinquent" in clause (ii),

substituted "or adjudication of delinquency by the circuit court" for "by the court" in clause (vi), and inserted "or delinquency" near the end in clause (vii), substituted "clause (iii) or (iv) of § 53.1-232.1 or to delay or stay any other appeals following conviction or adjudication of delinquency" for "clause (iii) or clause (iv) of § 53.1-232.1 or to delay or stay any other post-conviction appeals" in the next-to-last sentence; inserted "and" following "petitions" in the first sentence of subsection B; in subsection C, inserted "or adjudication of delinquency" following "conviction" in the first and second sentences and "or delinquency" following "guilt" in the last sentence; and in the first sentence of subsection E, substituted "petitioner" for "defendant" and deleted "of this title" at the end.

The 2013 amendment by c. 180 substituted "would have found proof" for "could have found proof" in clause (vii) of the first sentence in subsection A; inserted "or innocence" following "guilt" in the last sentence of subsection C; and substituted "Article 4 (§ 19.2-163.3 et seq.) of Chapter 10" for "Article 4 (§ 19.2-163.1 et seq.) of Chapter 10 of this title" in the first sentence of subsection E.

CASE NOTES

Previously unknown or unavailable evidence. — To obtain relief under § 19.2-327.11, the evidence supporting the allegation of innocence must have been previously unknown or unavailable to the petitioner or his trial attorney of record at the time the conviction became final in the circuit court; defendant's arguments, which could have been raised on direct appeal and a certificate of analysis which predated defendant's convictions and was introduced into evidence at trial, did not provide a basis for a Writ of Actual Innocence, and defendant's petition was dismissed. In re Neal, 44 Va. App. 89, 603 S.E.2d 170, 2004 Va. App. LEXIS 482 (2004).

Perjury analysis improper. — Appellate court erred by conducting an additional perjury analysis with regard to an inmate's petition for a writ of actual innocence based on non-biological evidence; a perjury analysis is not part of the "materiality" inquiry under subdivision A (vii) of § 19.2-327.11, which focuses on the truth of the evidence presented in support of a petition for a writ of actual innocence based on non-biological evidence. Carpitcher v. Commonwealth, 273 Va. 335, 641 S.E.2d 486, 2007 Va. LEXIS 36 (2007).

Must demonstrate that no rational trier of fact could have found him guilty. — Where a defendant's writ of actual innocence was construed to challenge the amendment of the warrant and the sufficiency of the evidence presented at trial, such claims provided him no valid basis for relief; further, the petition failed to explain how the existence of a police document indicating a different date of the offense would have affected the evidence proving his guilt. In re Bui, 44 Va. App. 91, 603 S.E.2d 171, 2004 Va. App. LEXIS 481 (2004).

Inmate failed to satisfy burden of proof. — Inmate's claim that because it could not be determined which, if any, version of a victim's testimony was true, the inmate met the burden of proving that the inmate was entitled to relief because "no rational trier of fact could have found proof of guilt beyond a reasonable doubt" was rejected as the requirements of subdivision A (vii) of § 19.2-327.11 were stated in the conjunctive; to meet the inmate's statutory burden, the inmate was required to prove both that the recantation evidence was true and that, when considered with all the other evidence in the current record, no rational trier of fact could have found the inmate guilty of the crimes. As the inmate failed to meet the inmate's burden of establishing the first component of the two-part statutory burden, the inmate failed to satisfy the inmate's burden of proof. Carpitcher v. Commonwealth, 273 Va. 335, 641 S.E.2d 486, 2007 Va. LEXIS 36 (2007).

Petition for a writ of actual innocence based on non-biological evidence was properly dismissed because the inmate failed to carry his burden of proof that the recantations from the victims, the inmate's sons, were true. The testimony of the boys at trial regarding the sodomy by their father was graphic and explicit and abundantly corroborated by physician testimony, photographs, and the inmate's admission that he sometimes slept with the boys. Haas v. Commonwealth, 283 Va. 284, 721 S.E.2d 479, 2012 Va. LEXIS 16 (2012).

Material evidence has to be true. — To be "material," within

the meaning of § 19.2-327.11, evidence supporting a petition for a writ of actual innocence based on non-biological evidence has to be true; evidence that is false cannot be "material." Carpitcher v. Commonwealth, 273 Va. 335, 641 S.E.2d 486, 2007 Va. LEXIS 36 (2007).

Increased understanding of English does not prove actual innocence. — Where defendant did not proffer new evidence in support of his actual innocence, but merely alleged that his better understanding of the English language and the judicial system since his conviction warranted a remedy, such progress was not evidence proving or disproving any fact in issue as to whether he committed the crimes for which he was convicted. In re Lima, 44 Va. App. 571, 605 S.E.2d 794, 2004 Va. App. LEXIS 614 (2004).

Recantation of testimony by witness. — Petition for writ of actual innocence was denied because the inmate did not prove which, if any, of the victim's three versions of her testimony was truthful; other than the recantation, there was no additional evidence tending to establish that the victim perjured herself during trial. Considering that the victim was threatened, intimidated and coerced to comply with the various demands that she change her trial testimony, a reasonable fact finder could disregard the recantation and conclude that the victim, during her trial testimony, was telling the truth; accordingly, the recantation, standing alone, was insufficient to prove that the victim's trial testimony was perjured. In re Carpitcher, 47 Va. App. 513, 624 S.E.2d 700, 2006 Va. App. LEXIS 33 (2006).

Under the provisions of § 19.2-327.12, the Court of Appeals of Virginia did not abuse its discretion in certifying issues of fact to the circuit court regarding the credibility of a co-defendant's recantation testimony that had to be resolved before it could determine the merits of an inmate's petition for a writ of actual innocence based on nonbiological evidence, and after reviewing the same, properly denied said petition, as: (1) this kind of inquiry fell squarely within the scope of § 19.2-327.12; and (2) such did not erroneously add a credibility requirement to the statutes governing writs of actual innocence based on nonbiological evidence. Moreover, because the inmate failed to meet his statutory burden of proof by showing the elements of subsection A of 19.2-327.11, his petition for said writ was properly denied. Johnson v. Commonwealth, 273 Va. 315, 641 S.E.2d 480, 2007 Va. LEXIS 33 (2007).

Victim's recantation testimony was not material under subdivision A (vii) of § 19.2-327.11 as the trial court was unable to determine whether the victim's recantation was true, and concluded that the victim was "threatened, intimidated, and coerced" to change the victim's trial testimony; the appellate court did not err in holding that an inmate was required, and failed, to prove that the victim's recantation was true since the victim's recantation testimony did no more than establish that the victim spoke falsely on one or more occasions. Carpitcher v. Commonwealth, 273 Va. 335, 641 S.E.2d 486, 2007 Va. LEXIS 36 (2007).

Defendant's petition for a writ of actual innocence based on newly-discovered, non-biological evidence was denied, although the codefendant's confession that he acted alone in killing the victim was credible, because the recantation did not provide the court with clear and convincing evidence that no rational fact finder could have found that defendant used deception to abduct the victim with the intent to have sexual intercourse with her against her will. Turner v. Commonwealth, 56 Va. App. 391, 694 S.E.2d 251, 2010 Va. App. LEXIS 263 (2010).

Recantation of testimony by victim. — In light of the strong corroborating evidence of the inmate's guilt in the current record, aside from the victim's testimony, and the trial court's consideration of the victim's recantations in 1992, the inmate did not meet his burden of showing that the victim's 2004 recantation, made almost 12 years after the inmate's trial, was true and not merely cumulative. The victim's trial testimony was found credible not based solely on its contents and the victim's demeanor, but rather in light of the strong corroborating evidence, which included the inmate's admission to the victim's mother that he had sex with her son and direct eyewitness testimony of sexual activity between the inmate and the victim. Moore v. Commonwealth, 53 Va. App. 334, 671 S.E.2d 429, 2009 Va. App. LEXIS 34 (2009).

Merely corroborative evidence insufficient. — Petitioner's request for a writ of actual innocence was dismissed with regard to his burglary conviction where the alleged newly discovered evidence found by petitioner merely corroborated testimony given at his trial and did not establish an alibi for him. In re Barron, 44 Va. App. 536, 605 S.E.2d 777, 2004 Va. App. LEXIS 607 (2004).

Writ of actual innocence denied. — Where a petitioning inmate failed to claim to have discovered any new evidence that demonstrated he was actually innocent of the crimes for which he was convicted and given suspended sentences, and proffered no evidence that was previously unknown or unavailable to him, his request for a writ of actual innocence was summarily denied. In re Adams, 44 Va. App. 266, 604 S.E.2d 746, 2004 Va. App. LEXIS 553 (2004).

Petition for a writ of actual innocence was dismissed because petitioner did not meet his burden to establish previously unavailable evidence sufficient to justify issuance of the writ. His witness did not establish an alibi for him, and through diligence petitioner could have produced this witness at trial. In re Bowling, 46 Va. App. 50, 615 S.E.2d 489, 2005 Va. App. LEXIS 269 (2005).

Petition for a writ of actual innocence was denied because the coconspirator's contention that he lied about the inmate's wanting to kill the victim was not credible; the coconspirator was unable to provide logical explanations for why he and another acted as he alleged after trial, and other evidence corroborated details of trial testimony that inmate orchestrated murder, including evidence of his proximity to the victim's house at the time of the murder. In re Johnson, 47 Va. App. 503, 624 S.E.2d 696, 2006 Va. App. LEXIS 31 (2006).

State inmate was not entitled to a writ of actual innocence on his claims that the prosecution withheld Brady material with respect to four witnesses where the inmate had access to the witnesses and could have interviewed them at any time, but failed to do so. Bell v. True, 413 F. Supp. 2d 657, 2006 U.S. Dist. LEXIS 4608 (W.D. Va. 2006).

Appeals court did not improperly dismiss defendant's petition for a writ of actual innocence and deny defendant's request to vacate defendant's convictions for murder and abduction with intent to defile, as nothing in a co-defendant's recantation or a circuit court's finding had any bearing on the question in defendant's petition; the evidentiary record on the issue, with and without the recantation, was essentially the same. Turner v. Commonwealth, 282 Va. 227, 717 S.E.2d 111, 2011 Va. LEXIS 192 (2011).

§ 19.2-327.12. Determination by Court of Appeals for findings of fact by the circuit court.

If the Court of Appeals determines from the petition, from any hearing on the petition, from a review of the records of the case, or from any response from the Attorney General that a resolution of the case requires further development of the facts, the court may order the circuit court in which the order of conviction or the adjudication of delinquency was originally entered to conduct a hearing within 90 days after the order has been issued to certify findings of fact with respect to such issues as the Court of Appeals shall direct. The record and certified findings of fact of the circuit court shall be filed in the Court of Appeals within 30 days after the hearing is concluded. The petitioner or his attorney of record, the attorney for the Commonwealth and the Attorney General shall be served a copy of the order stating the specific purpose and evidence for which the hearing has been ordered.

History.
2004, c. 1024; 2013, c. 170.

Cross references.
As to Court of Appeals rules governing petitions for writ of actual innocence, see Rule 5A:5(b), Rules of the Virginia Supreme Court.

The 2013 amendments.
The 2013 amendment by c. 170 inserted "or the adjudication of delinquency" following "conviction" in the first sentence.

CASE NOTES

Inmate's procedural due process rights not violated. — Appellate court did not deny an inmate procedural due process in refusing to permit the inmate to file an additional brief challenging the trial court's certified findings of fact as the trial court's findings were evaluative in nature, addressing the victim's veracity and whether the victim's recantation testimony was the product of duress; any briefing challenging these evaluations would have been unlikely to have provided analysis of substantive benefit to the appellate court. Carpitcher v. Commonwealth, 273 Va. 335, 641 S.E.2d 486, 2007 Va. LEXIS 36 (2007).

Applicability. — Under the provisions of § 19.2-327.12, the Court of Appeals of Virginia did not abuse its discretion in certifying issues of fact to the circuit court regarding the credibility of a codefendant's recantation testimony that had to be resolved before it could determine the merits of an inmate's petition for a writ of actual innocence based on nonbiological evidence, and after reviewing the same, properly denied said petition, as: (1) this kind of inquiry fell squarely within the scope of § 19.2-327.12; and (2) such did not erroneously add a credibility requirement to the statutes governing writs of actual innocence based on nonbiological evidence. Moreover, because the inmate failed to meet his statutory burden of proof by showing the elements of subsection A of § 19.2-327.11, his petition for said writ was properly denied. Johnson v. Commonwealth, 273 Va. 315, 641 S.E.2d 480, 2007 Va. LEXIS 33 (2007).

Applied in Haas v. Commonwealth, 283 Va. 284, 721 S.E.2d 479, 2012 Va. LEXIS 16 (2012).

§ 19.2-327.13. Relief under writ.

Upon consideration of the petition, the response by the Commonwealth, previous records of the case, the record of any hearing held under this chapter and, if applicable, any findings certified from the circuit court pursuant to an order issued under this chapter, the Court of Appeals, if it has not already summarily dismissed the petition, shall either dismiss the petition for failure to state a claim or assert grounds upon which relief shall be granted; or the Court shall (i) dismiss the petition for failure to establish previously unknown or unavailable evidence sufficient to justify the issuance of the writ, or (ii) only upon a finding that the petitioner has proven by clear and convincing evidence all of the allegations contained in clauses (iv) through (viii) of subsection A of § 19.2-327.11, and upon a finding that no rational trier of fact would have found proof of guilt or delinquency beyond a reasonable doubt, grant the writ, and vacate the conviction or finding of delinquency, or in the event that the Court finds that no rational trier of fact would have found sufficient evidence beyond a reasonable doubt as to one or more elements of the offense for which the petitioner was convicted or adjudicated delinquent, but the Court finds that there remains in the original trial record evidence sufficient to find the petitioner guilty or delinquent beyond a reasonable doubt of a lesser included offense, the Court shall modify the order of conviction or delinquency accordingly and remand the case to the circuit court that entered the conviction or adjudication of delinquency for resentencing. The burden of proof in a proceeding brought pursuant to this chapter shall be upon the convicted or delinquent person seeking relief. If a writ vacating a conviction or adjudication of delinquency is granted, and no appeal is made to the Supreme Court, or the Supreme Court denies the Commonwealth's petition for appeal or upholds the decision of the Court of Appeals to grant the writ, the Court of Appeals shall forward a copy of the writ to the circuit court, where an order of expungement shall be immediately granted.

History.
2004, c. 1024; 2007, cc. 465, 824, 883, 905; 2013, cc. 170, 180.

Cross references.
As to Court of Appeals rules governing petitions for writ of actual innocence, see Rule 5A:5(b), Rules of the Virginia Supreme Court.

The 2007 amendments.
The 2007 amendments by cc. 465, 824, 883, and 905 are identical, and added the last sentence.

The 2013 amendments.
The 2013 amendment by c. 170, in clause (ii) of the first sentence, inserted "or delinquency" in two places, "or finding of delinquency" following "conviction," "or adjudicated delinquent" following "convicted," "or delinquent" in two places, and "that entered the conviction or adjudication of delinquency," and "or adjudication of delinquency" near the beginning of the last sentence.
The 2013 amendment by c. 180, in the first sentence, substituted "would have found proof" for "could have found proof" and "would have found sufficient evidence" for "could have found sufficient evidence" and made a minor stylistic change.

CASE NOTES

Petition denied. — Petition for writ of actual innocence, based on an allegation that the detective's interview with a suspect in an unrelated crime implicated codefendant, was denied because the interrogation did not affect the sufficiency of evidence to support defendant's convictions or establish his innocence; there was a reasonable inference of concertive action by all three men there. In re Dicks, 46 Va. App. 44, 614 S.E.2d 677, 2005 Va. App. LEXIS 247 (2005).

Under the provisions of § 19.2-327.12, the Court of Appeals of Virginia did not abuse its discretion in certifying issues of fact to the circuit court regarding the credibility of a codefendant's recantation testimony that had to be resolved before it could determine the merits of an inmate's petition for a writ of actual innocence based on nonbiological evidence, and after reviewing the same, properly denied said petition, as: (1) this kind of inquiry fell squarely within the scope of § 19.2-327.12; and (2) such did not erroneously add a credibility requirement to the statutes governing writs of actual innocence based on nonbiological evidence. Moreover, because the inmate failed to meet his statutory burden of proof by showing the elements of subsection A of § 19.2-327.11, his petition for said writ was properly denied. Johnson v. Commonwealth, 273 Va. 315, 641 S.E.2d 480, 2007 Va. LEXIS 33 (2007).

Expungement appropriate. — Because a certificate of analysis excluding the item tested from the statutory definition of "firearm" under subsection A of § 18.2-308.2 was issued after defendant's conviction became final, defendant's petition for a writ of actual innocence under § 19.2-327.10 et seq., was granted, and the conviction was ordered expunged pursuant to § 19.2-327.13. Copeland v. Commonwealth, 52 Va. App. 529, 664 S.E.2d 528, 2008 Va. App. LEXIS 381 (2008).

Evidence insufficient. — Petition for a writ of actual innocence was dismissed because petitioner did not meet his burden under § 19.2-327.11 to establish previously unavailable evidence sufficient to justify issuance of the writ. His witness did not establish an alibi for him, and through diligence petitioner could have produced this witness at trial. In re Bowling, 46 Va. App. 50, 615 S.E.2d 489, 2005 Va. App. LEXIS 269 (2005).

In light of the strong corroborating evidence of the inmate's guilt in the current record, aside from the victim's testimony, and the trial court's consideration of the victim's recantations in 1992, the inmate did not meet his burden of showing that the victim's 2004 recantation, made almost 12 years after the inmate's trial, was true and not merely cumulative. The victim's trial testimony was found credible not based solely on its contents and the victim's demeanor, but rather in light of the strong corroborating evidence, which included the inmate's admission to the victim's mother that he had sex with her son and direct eyewitness testimony of sexual activity between the inmate and the victim. Moore v. Commonwealth, 53 Va. App. 334, 671 S.E.2d 429, 2009 Va. App. LEXIS 34 (2009).

Petition for a writ of actual innocence based on non-biological evidence was properly dismissed because the inmate failed to carry his burden of proof that the recantations from the victims, the inmate's sons, were true. The testimony of the boys at trial regarding the sodomy by their father was graphic and explicit and abundantly corroborated by physician testimony, photographs, and the inmate's admission that he sometimes slept with the boys. Haas v. Commonwealth, 283 Va. 284, 721 S.E.2d 479, 2012 Va. LEXIS 16 (2012).

Applied in In re Bui, 44 Va. App. 91, 603 S.E.2d 171, 2004 Va. App. LEXIS 481 (2004); In re Barron, 44 Va. App. 536, 605 S.E.2d 777, 2004 Va. App. LEXIS 607 (2004).

§ 19.2-327.14. Claims of relief.

An action under this chapter or the actions of any attorney representing the petitioner under this chapter shall not form the basis for relief in any habeas corpus proceeding. Nothing in this chapter shall create any cause of action for damages against the Commonwealth or any of its political subdivisions.

History.
2004, c. 1024.

CASE NOTES

Applied in Johnson v. Commonwealth, 273 Va. 315, 641 S.E.2d 480, 2007 Va. LEXIS 33 (2007).

CHAPTER 20.

TAXATION AND ALLOWANCE OF COSTS.

Michie's Jurisprudence.
For related discussion, see 5B M.J. Criminal Procedure, §§ 100, 102, 104.

§ 19.2-328. When jailers and sheriffs to summon or employ guards and other persons; allowances therefor.

Whenever in the discretion of the court it is necessary for the safekeeping of a prisoner under charge of, or sentence for, crime, whether the prisoner be in jail, hospital, court or elsewhere, the court may order the jailer to summon a sufficient guard, and whenever ordered by the court to do so, the sheriff of any county or city shall summon or employ temporarily such person or persons as may be needed to preserve proper order or otherwise to aid the court in its proper operation and functioning, and for such guard or other service the court may allow therefor so much as it deems proper, not exceeding the hourly equivalent of the minimum annual salary paid a full-time deputy sheriff who performs like services in the same county or city; in addition, mileage and other expenses for rendering the services shall be paid for each person, the same to be paid out of the budget allotted to the sheriff as approved by the Compensation Board, except when payment for such guard is otherwise provided under the provisions of § 53.1-94 of the Code of Virginia.

History.
Code 1950, § 19.1-308; 1960, c. 366; 1972, c. 225; 1973, c. 401; 1975, c. 495; 1981, c. 386; 1985, c. 321.

§ 19.2-329. Allowance to witnesses.

Sections 17.1-612 to 17.1-616, inclusive, shall apply to a person attending as a witness, under a recognizance or summons in a criminal case, as well as to a person attending under a summons in a civil case, except that a person residing out of this Commonwealth, who attends a court therein as a witness, shall be allowed by the court a proper compensation for attendance and travel to and from the place of his abode, the amount of the same to be fixed by the court.

History.
Code 1950, § 19.1-312; 1960, c. 366; 1975, c. 495; 1977, c. 483.

§ 19.2-330. Compensation to witnesses from out of Commonwealth.

Any witness from without the Commonwealth whose attendance is compelled under the provisions of Chapter 16, Article 2 (§ 19.2-272 et seq.) of this title shall be deemed to render a service within the meaning of § 19.2-332 and the compensation and expenses of such witness, whether on behalf of the Commonwealth or the accused, may be paid out of the state treasury in accordance with the provisions of such section. But the compensation and expenses of any witness summoned on behalf of an accused shall not be certified to the state treasury as a compensation under such section except in cases when the court or judge thereof is satisfied that the defendant is without means to pay same and is unable to provide the costs incident thereto.

History.
Code 1950, § 19.1-313; 1960, c. 366; 1975, c. 495.

§ 19.2-331. When Commonwealth pays witnesses in case of misdemeanor.

Payment shall not be made out of the state treasury to a witness attending for the Commonwealth in any prosecution for a misdemeanor unless it appears that the sum to which the witness is entitled cannot be obtained:

(1) If it be a case wherein there is a prosecutor and the defendant is convicted, by reason of the insolvency of the defendant, or

(2) If it be a case in which there is no prosecutor, by reason of the acquittal or insolvency of the defendant or other cause.

History.
Code 1950, § 19.1-314; 1960, c. 366; 1975, c. 495.

§ 19.2-332. Compensation to officer or other person for services not otherwise compensable.

Whenever in a criminal case an officer or other person renders any service required by law for which no specific compensation is provided, or whenever any other service has been rendered pursuant to the request or prior approval of the court, the court shall allow therefor such sum as it deems reasonable, including mileage at a rate provided by law, and such allowance shall be paid out of the state treasury from the appropriation for criminal charges on the certificate of the court stating the nature of the service. This section shall not prevent any payment under § 2.2-816, which could have been made if this section had not been enacted.

This section shall not be construed to authorize the payment of any additional compensation to an officer or other employee of the Commonwealth who is compensated for his services exclusively by salary unless it be otherwise expressly provided by law.

History.
Code 1950, § 19.1-315; 1960, c. 366; 1972, c. 719; 1975, c. 495.

CASE NOTES

Compensation for investigative services for indigent defendants not mandated. — Denial of defendant's request for appointment of an investigator was affirmed because neither § 19.2-332 nor § 19.2-163 mandated the appointment of experts to assist indigent defendants and their counsel. Dowdy v. Commonwealth, 278 Va. 577, 686 S.E.2d 710, 2009 Va. LEXIS 108 (2009).

§ 19.2-333. No state fees to attorney for the Commonwealth.

No fee to an attorney for the Commonwealth shall be payable out of the state treasury, unless it be expressly so provided.

History.
  Code 1950, § 19.1-316; 1960, c. 366; 1975, c. 495.

§ 19.2-334. By whom certificate of allowance to be made; vouchers to accompany it; proof of correctness; what entry to state.

Any other expense incident to a proceeding in a criminal case which is payable out of the state treasury otherwise than under §§ 2.2-816, 19.2-330 or § 19.2-332 shall be certified by the court. If it be a judge of a district court exercising jurisdiction, it shall be certified by such judge to the Supreme Court. With the certificate of allowance there shall be transmitted to the Supreme Court the vouchers on which it is made. The court, in passing upon any account for fees or expenses required to be certified by it under this section, before certifying the account, may, in its discretion, require proof of the correctness of any item thereof.

The entry of such certificate of allowance shall state how much thereof is on account of each person prosecuted.

History.
  Code 1950, §§ 19.1-317, 19.1-318; 1960, c. 366; 1975, c. 495; 1978, c. 195; 1979, c. 465.

§ 19.2-335. Judge of district court to certify to clerk of circuit court costs of proceedings in criminal cases before him.

A judge of a district court before whom there is any proceeding in a criminal case, including any proceeding which has been deferred upon probation of the defendant pursuant to § 16.1-278.8, 16.1-278.9, 18.2-61, 18.2-67.1, 18.2-67.2, 18.2-251 or 19.2-303.2, shall certify to the clerk of the circuit court of his county or city, and a judge or court before whom there is, in a criminal case, any proceeding preliminary to conviction in another court, upon receiving information of the conviction from the clerk of the court wherein it is, shall certify to such clerk, all the expenses incident to such proceedings which are payable out of the state treasury.

History.
  Code 1950, § 19.1-319; 1960, c. 366; 1968, c. 639; 1975, c. 495; 1995, c. 485; 2005, c. 631.

§ 19.2-336. Clerk to make up statement of whole cost, and issue execution therefor.

In every criminal case the clerk of the circuit court in which the accused is found guilty or is placed on probation during deferral of the proceedings pursuant to § 16.1-278.8, 16.1-278.9, 18.2-61, 18.2-67.1, 18.2-67.2, 18.2-251 or 19.2-303.2, or, if the conviction is in a district court, the clerk to which the judge thereof certifies as aforesaid, shall, as soon as may

be, make up a statement of all the expenses incident to the prosecution, including such as are certified under § 19.2-335, and execution for the amount of such expenses shall be issued and proceeded with. Chapter 21 (§ 19.2-339 et seq.) shall apply thereto in like manner as if, on the day of completing the statement, there was a judgment in such court in favor of the Commonwealth against the accused for such amount as a fine. However, in any case in which an accused waives trial by jury, at least 10 days before trial, but the Commonwealth or the court trying the case refuses to so waive, then the cost of the jury shall not be included in such statement or judgment recorded pursuant to § 17.1-275.5.

History.
  Code 1950, § 19.1-320; 1960, c. 366; 1970, c. 429; 1975, c. 495; 1978, c. 716; 1995, c. 485; 2005, c. 631; 2012, c. 714.

Cross references.
  As to costs on order discharging recognizance, see § 19.2-152. As to expense of publication of process against corporation being taxed as costs, see § 19.2-238.

The 2012 amendments.
  The 2012 amendment by c. 714 deleted "of this title" following "(§ 19.2-339 et seq.)" in the second sentence, and added "recorded pursuant to § 17.1-275.5" at the end of the third sentence.

CASE NOTES

Constitutionality. — Virginia's recoupment statutes, §§ 19.2-336 and 19.2-358, did not violate defendant's right to due process even though they placed the burden of proof on him to show that he was unable to pay court costs, or violate his right to equal protection even though they did not require that the trial court project his future ability to pay court costs before imposing the duty. Roads v. Commonwealth, 2013 Va. App. LEXIS 92 (Mar. 26, 2013).

Virginia's recoupment statutes, §§ 19.2-336 and 19.2-358, did not violate defendant's due process or equal protection rights as defendant would not be subject to enhanced punishment for a failure to pay court costs solely due to his future indigence, should it occur, since the penalties defendant feared would be imposed if he did not pay the costs could not be imposed absent an intentional refusal to obey the sentence or a failure to make a good faith effort to obtain the necessary funds under subsection B of § 19.2-358; if the default was excusable, the court could allow defendant additional time for payment, reduce the amount due or of each installment, or remit the unpaid portion in whole or in part under subsection C of § 19.2-358. Roads v. Commonwealth, 2013 Va. App. LEXIS 92 (Mar. 26, 2013).

Under this section the accused is liable for the costs of his conviction, without any formal entry of judgment therefor. Commonwealth v. McCue's Ex'rs, 109 Va. 302, 63 S.E. 1066 (1909).

Section does not invade right of trial by jury. — The taxing of the costs of the jury to a defendant in a criminal case is not an invasion of the constitutional right of the accused to a trial by jury. Kincaid v. Commonwealth, 200 Va. 341, 105 S.E.2d 846 (1958).

Defendant's understanding of the cost of a jury trial and her desire to avoid this expense did not constitute coercion rendering her waiver of a jury involuntary. Ohree v. Commonwealth, 26 Va. App. 299, 494 S.E.2d 484 (1998).

Costs are no part of the punishment of the accused. Anglea v. Commonwealth, 51 Va. (10 Gratt.) 696 (1853); Commonwealth v. McCue's Ex'rs, 109 Va. 302, 63 S.E. 1066 (1909).

But they are exacted simply to reimburse the State for necessary expenditures in the enforcement of its violated laws. Anglea v. Commonwealth, 51 Va. (10 Gratt.) 696 (1853); Commonwealth v. McCue's Ex'rs, 109 Va. 302, 63 S.E. 1066 (1909); Kincaid v. Commonwealth, 200 Va. 341, 105 S.E.2d 846 (1958).

This statute only subjects the accused to such costs as the

Commonwealth is bound to pay. Anglea v. Commonwealth, 51 Va. (10 Gratt.) 696 (1853). See Finch v. Commonwealth, 55 Va. (14 Gratt.) 643 (1858).

Authorized fees. — Court was authorized to assess a fee against defendant for the Commonwealth's attorney fee, the clerks fee, and the recording fee under this section. Ohree v. Commonwealth, 26 Va. App. 299, 494 S.E.2d 484 (1998).

Court was authorized to assess a fee for the Criminal Injuries Compensation Fund against a defendant convicted of welfare fraud; the Commonwealth and its citizens were injured by the defendant's commission of the crime. Ohree v. Commonwealth, 26 Va. App. 299, 494 S.E.2d 484 (1998).

An individual convicted of a crime against the Commonwealth can be said to have caused the Commonwealth to incur the expense of the prosecution of that individual; therefore the imposition of a courthouse maintenance fee upon a defendant convicted of welfare fraud furthered the legislature's goal of reimbursement and was valid. Ohree v. Commonwealth, 26 Va. App. 299, 494 S.E.2d 484 (1998).

Costs are not affected by a pardon. — A pardon releasing a prisoner from all pains, penalties and forfeitures incurred by his conviction and sentence was held not to release him from the costs incurred in his prosecution by the Commonwealth. Anglea v. Commonwealth, 51 Va. (10 Gratt.) 696 (1853).

The only officer empowered to institute proceedings for the collection of costs due the State in a criminal prosecution is the Comptroller. See § 8-758 (now § 8.01-196). If the claim for such costs be asserted in a chancery suit by the local attorney for the Commonwealth, without the consent and approval of the Comptroller, it is a proceeding without authority, the State does not thereby become a party, and is not bound by any decree affecting her rights. Commonwealth v. McCue's Ex'rs, 109 Va. 302, 63 S.E. 1066 (1909).

Applied in In re Thompson, 145 Bankr. 848 (Bankr. E.D. Va. 1992).

CIRCUIT COURT OPINIONS

Responsibility for costs. — Defendant's appeal of a district court conviction for unreasonably failing to permit his blood or breath to be tested when charged with driving while intoxicated was a criminal matter to which the same procedures applied as appeals from misdemeanor convictions, and defendant was therefore responsible for the jury expense incurred in the circuit court when defendant withdrew his appeal on the day of trial when a jury had been assembled and resolved his case via plea bargain; to avoid the charge, defendant would have had to have withdrawn his jury demand at least 10 days prior to trial. Commonwealth v. Franklin, 54 Va. Cir. 214, 2000 Va. Cir. LEXIS 579 (Northampton County 2000).

§ 19.2-337. Claims not presented in time to be disallowed.

If by reason of the failure of a person to present his claim in due time a sum be not included in such execution which would have been included if so presented, such claim, unless there be good cause for the failure, shall be disallowed.

History.
Code 1950, § 19.1-321; 1960, c. 366; 1975, c. 495.

§ 19.2-338. Collection by town of cost of transporting prisoners.

(1) Notwithstanding any provision of any charter or any law to the contrary, any town may provide that any person convicted of violating any ordinance of the town may be charged, in addition to all other costs, fines, fees and charges, the costs of transporting such person so convicted to and from a jail or other penal institution outside the corporate limits of such town designated by the town as a place of confinement for persons arrested for violating the ordinances of the town and required to be held in jail pending trial upon such charge. The cost of such transportation shall be taxed as a part of the costs payable by persons convicted of violating such ordinances.

(2) No officer transporting any person convicted of violating any ordinance of the town, as provided in subsection (1) hereof, shall charge or be paid, nor shall such town receive directly or indirectly, more than the cost of transporting such person when more than one person is transported.

History.
Code 1950, § 19.1-322; 1960, c. 366; 1975, c. 495; 1995, c. 51.

CHAPTER 21.

RECOVERY OF FINES AND PENALTIES.

ARTICLE 1.

PROCEEDINGS TO RECOVER.

§ 19.2-339. Word "fine" construed.

Whenever the word *"fine"* is used in this chapter, it shall be construed to refer solely to the pecuniary penalty imposed by a court or jury upon a defendant who has been found guilty of a crime. The word "fine" shall not include other forfeitures, penalties, costs, amercements or the like, even though they follow as a consequence of conviction of crime.

History.
Code 1950, § 19.1-323; 1960, c. 366; 1975, c. 495.

Cross references.
As to prohibition of excessive fines, see Va. Const., Art. I, § 9. As to power of Governor to remit fines, see Va. Const., Art. V, § 12, and § 19.2-363.

Law Review.
For a note, "The Supreme Court's Backwards Proportionality Jurisprudence: Comparing Judicial Review of Excessive Criminal Punishments and Excessive Punitive Damages Awards," see 86 Va. L. Rev. 1249 (2000).

Michie's Jurisprudence.
For related discussion, see 5B M.J. Criminal Procedure, § 90.

CASE NOTES

This section has no application to an action to recover statutory penalty for failure of telegraph company to promptly deliver a telegram. Western Union Tel. Co. v. Tyler, 90 Va. 297, 18 S.E. 280 (1893), appeal dismissed, 17 S. Ct. 1002, 41 L. Ed. 1180 (1896). See § 56-469.

Nor does this section apply to an action to recover statutory penalty for failure to construct cattle guards. Russell v. Louisville & N.R.R., 93 Va. 322, 25 S.E. 99 (1896).

Scope of authority of Workers' Compensation Commission. — Workers' Compensation Commission has the same authority as a court to punish for noncompliance with its discovery orders and it has the inherent authority to strike a party's defenses for failure to comply with a discovery order. Jeff Coal, Inc. v. Phillips, 16 Va. App. 271, 430 S.E.2d 712 (1993).

§ 19.2-340. Fines; how recovered; in what name.

When any statute or ordinance prescribes a fine, unless it is otherwise expressly provided or would be inconsistent with the manifest intention of the General Assembly, it shall be paid to the Commonwealth if prescribed by a statute and recoverable by presentment, indictment, information or warrant and paid to the locality if prescribed by an ordinance and recoverable by warrant. Fines imposed and costs taxed in a criminal or traffic prosecution, including a prosecution for a violation of an ordinance adopted pursuant to § 46.2-1220, for committing an offense shall constitute a judgment and, if not paid at the time they are imposed, execution may issue thereon in the same manner as upon any other monetary judgment, subject to the period of limitations provided by § 19.2-341.

History.
Code 1950, § 19.1-324; 1960, c. 366; 1975, c. 495; 1995, c. 438.

Michie's Jurisprudence.
For related discussion, see 5B M.J. Criminal Procedure, §§ 92, 95 - 97, 100, 104; 18 M.J. Trespass, § 1.

CASE NOTES

Applied in Holt v. Virginia, 567 F. Supp. 210 (W.D. Va. 1983).

§ 19.2-340.1. Disposition of fines in criminal cases.

When a law-enforcement officer of (i) the Department of State Police or (ii) any other division of the state government makes an arrest or issues a summons for a violation of a provision of the Code of Virginia, the person arrested or summoned shall be charged with a violation of that Code provision and shall not be charged with a substantially similar local ordinance. All fines collected upon conviction of any person so arrested or summoned shall be credited to the Literary Fund.

History.
2012, c. 749.

§ 19.2-341. Penalties other than fines; how recovered; in what name; limitation of actions.

When any statute or ordinance prescribes a monetary penalty other than a fine, unless it is otherwise expressly provided or would be inconsistent with the manifest intention of the General Assembly, it shall be paid to the Commonwealth if prescribed by a statute and paid to the locality if prescribed by an ordinance and recoverable by warrant, presentment, indictment, or information. Penalties imposed and costs taxed in any such proceeding shall constitute a judgment and, if not paid at the time they are imposed, execution may issue thereon in the same manner as upon any other monetary judgment. No such proceeding of any nature, however, shall be brought or had for the recovery of such a penalty or costs due the Commonwealth or any political subdivision thereof, unless within twenty years from the date of the offense or delinquency giving rise to imposition of such penalty if imposed by a circuit court, or within ten years if imposed by a general district court.

History.
Code 1950, § 19.1-324; 1960, c. 366; 1975, c. 495; 1983, c. 499; 1995, c. 438.

§ 19.2-342. Where and in what court proceeding to be.

In a proceeding under § 19.2-341, such warrant, presentment, indictment or information shall be in the county or city wherein the offense was committed or the delinquency occurred.

History.
Code 1950, § 19.1-325; 1960, c. 366; 1975, c. 495.

Michie's Jurisprudence.
For related discussion, see 18 M.J. Trespass, § 1.

§§ 19.2-343, 19.2-344. Reserved.

ARTICLE 2.

REPORTS, ETC., OF FINES AND COSTS.

§§ 19.2-345, 19.2-346. Repealed by Acts 1988, c. 509.

§ 19.2-347. Repealed by Acts 1983, c. 499.

ARTICLE 3.

COLLECTION AND DISPOSITION OF FINES.

Michie's Jurisprudence.
For related discussion, see 5B M.J. Criminal Procedure, §§ 91 - 93, 95, 96, 100, 104.

§ 19.2-348. Attorneys for Commonwealth or clerks to superintend issue of executions, etc.

The attorney for the Commonwealth or the clerk of the circuit court shall superintend the issuing of all executions or judgments for fines and penalties going wholly or in part to the Commonwealth or a county, city or town, in the circuit court or appropriate district court of his county or city.

History.
Code 1950, § 19.1-341.1; 1960, c. 366; 1975, c. 495; 1983, c. 499; 1992, c. 623; 1994, c. 811.

CASE NOTES

Exclusive authority transferred to attorneys for the Commonwealth. — This section and § 19.2-349 transferred exclusive authority from the Comptroller to attorneys for the Commonwealth to institute proceedings to collect fines, costs and forfeitures which have been imposed by the courts. Commonwealth v. Holland, 211 Va. 530, 178 S.E.2d 506 (1971).

§ 19.2-349. Responsibility for collections; clerks to report unsatisfied fines, etc.; duty of attorneys for Commonwealth; duties of Department of Taxation.

A. The clerk of the circuit court and district court of every county and city shall submit to the judge of his court, the Department of Taxation, the State Compensation Board and the attorney for the Commonwealth of his county or city a monthly report of all fines, costs, forfeitures and penalties which are delinquent more than 30 days, including court-ordered restitution of a sum certain, imposed in his court for a violation of state law or a local ordinance which remain unsatisfied, including those which are delinquent in installment payments. The monthly report shall include the social security number or driver's license number of the defendant, if known, and such other information as the Department of Taxation and the Compensation Board deem appropriate. The Executive Secretary shall make the report required by this subsection on behalf of those clerks who participate in the Supreme Court's automated information system.

B. It shall be the duty of the attorney for the Commonwealth to cause proper proceedings to be instituted for the collection and satisfaction of all fines, costs, forfeitures, penalties and restitution. The attorney for the Commonwealth shall determine whether it would be impractical or uneconomical for such service to be rendered by the office of the attorney for the Commonwealth. If the defendant does not enter into an installment payment agreement under § 19.2-354, the attorney for the Commonwealth and the clerk may agree to a process by which collection activity may be commenced 30 days after judgment.

If the attorney for the Commonwealth does not undertake collection, he shall contract with (i) private attorneys or private collection agencies, (ii) enter into an agreement with a local governing body, (iii) enter into an agreement with the county or city treasurer, or (iv) use the services of the Department of Taxation, upon such terms and conditions as may be established by guidelines promulgated by the Office of the Attorney General, the Executive Secretary of the Supreme Court with the Department of Taxation and the Compensation Board. If the attorney for the Commonwealth undertakes collection, he shall follow the procedures established by the Department of Taxation and the Compensation Board. Such guidelines shall not supersede contracts between attorneys for the Commonwealth and private attorneys and collection agencies when active collection efforts are being undertaken. As part of such contract, private attorneys or collection agencies shall be given access to the social security number of the defendant in order to assist in the collection effort. Any such private attorney shall be subject to the penalties and provisions of § 18.2-186.3.

The fees of any private attorneys or collection agencies shall be paid on a contingency fee basis out of the proceeds of the amounts collected. However, in no event shall such attorney or collection agency receive a fee for amounts collected by the Department of Taxation under the Setoff Debt Collection Act (§ 58.1-520 et seq.). A local treasurer undertaking collection pursuant to an agreement with the attorney for the Commonwealth may collect the administrative fee authorized by § 58.1-3958.

C. The Department of Taxation and the State Compensation Board shall be responsible for the collection of any judgment which remains unsatisfied or does not meet the conditions of § 19.2-354. Persons owing such unsatisfied judgments or failing to comply with installment payment agreements under § 19.2-354 shall be subject to the delinquent tax collection provisions of Title 58.1. The Department of Taxation and the State Compensation Board shall establish procedures to be followed by clerks of courts, attorneys for the Commonwealth, other state agencies and any private attorneys or collection agents and may employ private attorneys or collection agencies, or engage other state agencies to collect the judgment. The Department of Taxation and the Commonwealth shall be entitled to deduct a fee for services from amounts collected for violations of local ordinances.

The Department of Taxation and the State Compensation Board shall annually report to the Governor and the General Assembly the total of fines, costs, forfeitures and penalties assessed, collected, and unpaid and those which remain unsatisfied or do not meet the conditions of § 19.2-354 by each circuit and district court. The report shall include the procedures established by the Department of Taxation and the State Compensation Board pursuant to this section and a plan for increasing the collection of unpaid fines, costs, forfeitures and penalties. The Auditor of Public Accounts shall annually report to the Governor, the Executive Secretary of the Supreme Court and the General Assembly as to the adherence of clerks of courts, attorneys for the Commonwealth and other state agencies to the procedures established by the Department of Taxation and the State Compensation Board.

History.
Code 1950, § 19.1-341.2; 1960, c. 366; 1975, c. 495; 1979, c. 469; 1983, cc. 415, 499; 1988, cc. 742, 750, 770, 852; 1991, c. 202; 1992, c. 623; 1993, c. 269; 1994, cc. 841, 945; 2001, c. 414; 2003, c. 262; 2006, c. 359; 2007, c. 551; 2012, c. 615.

The 2007 amendments.
The 2007 amendment by c. 551 added the last two sentences in the second paragraph of subsection B.

The 2012 amendments.
The 2012 amendment by c. 615 substituted "30 days" for "15 days" in the first paragraph of subsection B.

§ 19.2-350. When sheriff not to receive fines.

No sheriff or other law-enforcement officer shall receive any fine, penalty or costs imposed by a court not of record, except under process duly issued.

History.
Code 1950, § 19.1-342; 1960, c. 366; 1975, c. 495.

Cross references.
As to payment of fine by person committed to jail until he pays a fine, see § 53.1-116.

§ 19.2-351. How fines disposed of; informer.

Although a law may allow an informer or person prosecuting to have part of a fine or penalty, the whole thereof shall go to the Commonwealth, unless the name of such informer or prosecutor be endorsed on, or written at the foot of, the presentment at the time it is made, or of the indictment before it is presented to the grand jury, or of the information before it is filed, or of the writ issued in the action, or the process on the warrant, or the notice of the motion before service of such writ, process, or notice.

History.
Code 1950, § 19.1-344; 1960, c. 366; 1975, c. 495.

Michie's Jurisprudence.
For related discussion, see 9B M.J. Informers, § 2.

§ 19.2-352. Officers to pay fines to clerks; default; forfeiture, etc.

Every sheriff or other officer receiving money under a writ of fieri facias or capias pro fine shall pay the same to the clerk of the court from which such process issued, on or before the return day of such process; and if such sheriff or other officer fail to pay the money, or fail to return such writ of fieri facias or capias pro fine, he shall, for every such failure, unless good cause be shown therefor, forfeit twenty dollars; and the clerk shall, within ten days from the return day of such process, report the failure to pay such money, or to return such process, to the attorney for the Commonwealth, who shall proceed at once against such officer in default to recover such money and the forfeiture aforesaid.

History.
Code 1950, § 19.1-345; 1960, c. 366; 1975, c. 495.

§ 19.2-353. Certain fines paid into Literary Fund.

The proceeds of all fines and penalties collected for offenses committed against the Commonwealth, and directed by Article VIII, Section 8 of the Constitution of Virginia to be set apart as a part of a perpetual and permanent literary fund, shall be paid and collected only in lawful money of the United States, and shall be paid into the state treasury to the credit of the Literary Fund, and shall be used for no other purpose whatsoever.

History.
Code 1950, § 19.1-346; 1960, c. 366; 1971, Ex. Sess., c. 1; 1975, c. 495.

Cross references.
As to monetary penalties for violation of Private Security Services Advisory Board regulations credited under this section, see § 9.1-150.

§ 19.2-353.1. Fieri facias and proceedings thereon.

Any writ of fieri facias issued under this chapter and the proceedings on the same shall conform to the writ of fieri facias and proceedings thereon under Article 19 (§ 8.01-196 et seq.) of Chapter 3 of Title 8.01.

History.
Code 1950, § 19.1-347; 1960, c. 366; 1975, c. 495.

§ 19.2-353.2. Repealed by Acts 1988, cc. 770, 852.

§ 19.2-353.3. Acceptance of checks and credit or debit cards in lieu of money; additional fee.

Notwithstanding the provisions of § 19.2-353, personal checks and credit or debit cards shall be accepted in lieu of money to collect and secure all fees, fines, restitution, forfeiture, penalties and costs collected for offenses tried in a district court, including motor vehicle violations, committed against the Commonwealth or against any county, city or town. Notwithstanding the provisions of § 19.2-353, personal checks shall be accepted in lieu of money to collect and secure all fees, fines, restitution, forfeiture, penalties and costs collected for offenses tried in a circuit court, including motor vehicle violations, committed against the Commonwealth or against any county, city or town. The clerk of any circuit court shall not be required to but may, in his discretion, accept credit or debit card payment in lieu of money to collect and secure all fees, including filing fees, fines, restitution, forfeitures, penalties, and costs collected. The Committee on District Courts shall devise a procedure for approving and accepting checks and credit or debit cards that shall be accepted by the district courts. Court personnel shall not be held to be guarantors of the payment made in such manner and shall not be personally liable for any sums uncollected. The clerk of the court, in addition to any fees, fines, restitution, forfeiture, penalties or costs, may add to such payment a sum not to exceed four percent of the amount paid for the transaction, or a flat fee not to exceed $2 per transaction, as a reasonable convenience fee for the acceptance of a credit or debit card.

If a check is returned unpaid by the financial institution on which it is drawn or notice is received from the credit or debit card issuer that payment will not be made, for any reason, the fees, fine, restitution, forfeiture, penalty or costs shall be treated as unpaid, and the court may pursue all available remedies to obtain payment. The clerk of the court to whom the dishonored check or credit or debit card was tendered may impose a fee of $50 or 10 percent of the value of the payment, whichever is greater, in addition to the fine and costs already imposed.

The clerk of court may refuse acceptance of checks or credit or debit cards of an individual if (i) he has been convicted of a violation of Chapter 6 (§ 18.2-168 et seq.) of Title 18.2 in which a check, credit or debit card, or credit or debit card information was used to commit the offense, (ii) he has previously tendered to the court a check which was not ultimately honored or a credit or debit card or credit or debit card information which did not ultimately result in payment by the credit or debit card issuer, (iii) authorization of payment is not given by the bank or credit or debit card issuer, (iv) the validity of the check or credit or debit card cannot be verified, or (v) the payee of the check is other than the court.

History.
1979, c. 525; 1988, cc. 770, 852; 1990, c. 899; 1994, cc. 432, 841, 945; 1997, c. 819; 1998, cc. 720, 731; 2001, cc. 481, 501; 2009, c. 594; 2012, cc. 420, 714.

Cross references.
As to authority of public body responsible for revenue collection to accept revenue by commercially acceptable means, see § 2.2-614.1.

Editor's note.
Acts 1993, c. 930, cl. 3, as amended by Acts 1994, c. 564, cl. 2, and Acts 1996, c. 616, cl. 4, provides that the amendment to this section by Acts 1993, c. 930, cl. 1, shall become effective June 1, 1998, "if state funds are provided to carry out the purposes of this bill by the General Assembly." The funding was not provided.

The 2009 amendments.
The 2009 amendment by c. 594 substituted "reasonable convenience fee" for "service charge" in the last sentence of the first paragraph.

The 2012 amendments.
The 2012 amendment by c. 420 substituted "impose a fee of $50 or 10 percent of the value of the payment" for "impose a fee of twenty dollars or ten percent of the value of the payment" near the end of the second paragraph.
The 2012 amendment by c. 714 substituted "credit or debit cards" for "credit cards" and "credit or debit card" for "credit or debit card" throughout the section; and inserted "for the transaction, or a flat fee not to exceed $2 per transaction," near the end of the first paragraph.

CASE NOTES

Applied in West v. Costen, 558 F. Supp. 564 (W.D. Va. 1983).

OPINIONS OF THE ATTORNEY GENERAL

Returned check fee. — The clerk of a circuit court cannot collect a returned check fee in a civil case. See opinion of Attorney

General to The Honorable Eugene C. Wingfield, Clerk of Court, Lynchburg Circuit Court, 12-028, 2012 Va. AG LEXIS 24 (6/8/2012).

§ 19.2-353.4. Repealed by Acts 1988, cc. 770, 852.

Editor's note.

The repealed section was enacted by Acts 1985, c. 200, and amended by Acts 1988, c. 757.

§ 19.2-353.5. Interest on fines and costs.

No interest shall accrue on any fine or costs imposed in a criminal case or in a case involving a traffic infraction for a period of forty days from the date of the final judgment imposing such fine or costs or during any period the defendant is incarcerated as a result of that case. In no event shall interest accrue in such cases during any period in which a fine, costs, or both a fine and costs are being paid in deferred or installment payments pursuant to an order of the court. Whenever interest on any unpaid fine or costs accrues, it shall accrue at the judgment rate of interest set forth in § 6.2-302.

History.

1987, c. 648; 1988, cc. 106, 508; 1995, cc. 375, 566; 1996, c. 226.

Editor's note.

Effective October 1, 2010, "6.2-302" was substituted for "6.1-330.54" to conform to the recodification of Title 6.1 by Acts 2010, c. 794.

Michie's Jurisprudence.

For related discussion, see 5A M.J. Costs, § 17.

ARTICLE 4.

PAYMENT OF FINES AND COSTS ON INSTALLMENT BASIS, ETC.

Michie's Jurisprudence.

For related discussion, see 5B M.J. Criminal Procedure, §§ 92, 98, 99.

§ 19.2-354. Authority of court to order payment of fine, costs, forfeitures, penalties or restitution in installments or upon other terms and conditions; community work in lieu of payment.

A. Whenever (i) a defendant, convicted of a traffic infraction or a violation of any criminal law of the Commonwealth or of any political subdivision thereof, or found not innocent in the case of a juvenile, is sentenced to pay a fine, restitution, forfeiture or penalty and (ii) the defendant is unable to make payment of the fine, restitution, forfeiture, or penalty and costs within 30 days of sentencing, the court shall order the defendant to pay such fine, restitution, forfeiture or penalty and any costs which the defendant may be required to pay in deferred payments or installments. The court may authorize the clerk to establish and approve the conditions of all deferred or installment payment agreements, pursuant to guidelines established by the court. As a condition of every such agreement, a defendant who enters into an installment or deferred payment agreement shall promptly inform the court of any change of mailing address during the term of the agreement. If the defendant is unable to make payment within 30 days of sentencing, the court may assess a one-time fee not to exceed $10 to cover the costs of management of the defendant's account until such account is paid in full. This one-time fee shall not apply to cases in which costs are assessed pursuant to § 17.1-275.1, 17.1-275.2, 17.1-275.3, 17.1-275.4, 17.1-275.7, 17.1-275.8, or 17.1-275.9. Installment or deferred payment agreements shall include terms for payment if the defendant participates in a program as provided in subsection B or C. The court, if such sum or sums are not paid in full by the date ordered, shall proceed in accordance with § 19.2-358.

B. When a person sentenced to the Department of Corrections or a local correctional facility owes any fines, costs, forfeitures, restitution or penalties, he shall be required as a condition of participating in any work release, home/electronic incarceration or nonconsecutive days program as set forth in § 53.1-60, 53.1-131, 53.1-131.1, or 53.1-131.2 to either make full payment or make payments in accordance with his installment or deferred payment agreement while participating in such program. If, after the person has an installment or deferred payment agreement, the person fails to pay as ordered, his participation in the program may be terminated until all fines, costs, forfeitures, restitution and penalties are satisfied. The Director of the Department of Corrections and any sheriff or other administrative head of any local correctional facility shall withhold such ordered payments from any amounts due to such person. Distribution of the money collected shall be made in the following order of priority to:

1. Meet the obligation of any judicial or administrative order to provide support and such funds shall be disbursed according to the terms of such order;

2. Pay any fines, restitution or costs as ordered by the court;

3. Pay travel and other such expenses made necessary by his work release employment or participation in an education or rehabilitative program, including the sums specified in § 53.1-150; and

4. Defray the offender's keep.

The balance shall be credited to the offender's account or sent to his family in an amount the offender so chooses.

The Board of Corrections shall promulgate regulations governing the receipt of wages paid to persons participating in such programs, the withholding of payments and the disbursement of appropriate funds.

C. The court shall establish a program and may provide an option to any person upon whom a fine and costs have been imposed to discharge all or part of the fine or costs by earning credits for the performance of community service work before or after imprisonment. The program shall specify the rate at which credits are earned and provide for the manner of applying earned credits against the fine or costs. The court shall have such other authority as is reasonably necessary for or incidental to carrying out this program.

D. When the court has authorized deferred payment or installment payments, the clerk shall give notice to the defendant that upon his failure to pay as ordered he may be fined or imprisoned pursuant to § 19.2-358 and his privilege to operate a motor vehicle will be suspended pursuant to § 46.2-395.

E. The failure of the defendant to enter into a deferred payment or installment payment agreement with the court or the failure of the defendant to make payments as ordered by the agreement shall allow the Tax Commissioner to act in accordance with § 19.2-349 to collect all fines, costs, forfeitures and penalties.

History.
Code 1950, § 19.1-347.1; 1971 Ex. Sess., c. 250; 1975, c. 495; 1977, c. 585; 1982, c. 244; 1984, c. 32; 1986, c. 230; 1988, cc. 770, 852; 1994, cc. 841, 945; 1995, cc. 380, 441; 1996, c. 273; 1998, c. 831; 1999, c. 9; 2001, c. 414; 2002, c. 831; 2009, c. 741; 2012, c. 615.

The 2009 amendments.
The 2009 amendment by c. 741 substituted "and may provide" for "to provide" in subsection C and made minor stylistic changes.

The 2012 amendments.
The 2012 amendment by c. 615, in subsection A, substituted "30 days" for "fifteen days" in the first and fourth sentences, and made a minor stylistic change.

Law Review.
For article, "Explaining Restitution," see 71 Va. L. Rev. 65 (1985).

OPINIONS OF THE ATTORNEY GENERAL

Establishment of time frame within which defendant may make deferred or installment payments of unpaid fines or costs. — The statute permits the court to establish a time frame within which a defendant may make deferred or installment payments of unpaid fines or costs. See opinion of Attorney General to The Honorable George W. Harris Jr., Judge, Twenty-Third Judicial District, 00-063 (11/28/00).

Authority of clerk to grant or deny request. — A clerk may grant or deny a request for time to pay when the guidelines established by the court authorize such a practice, and such decisions are final and are not appealable. See opinion of Attorney General to The Honorable George W. Harris Jr., Judge, Twenty-Third Judicial District, 00-063 (11/28/00).

No appeal of court decision regarding deferred or installment payments. — There is no authority for appeal of a court decision regarding deferred or installment payments. See opinion of Attorney General to The Honorable George W. Harris Jr., Judge, Twenty-Third Judicial District, 00-063 (11/28/00).

Restoration of driver's license after payment of reinstatement fee and entry into agreement for deferred or installment payments. — The court must restore the driver's license of a defendant after the defendant has paid the reinstatement fee to the Department of Motor Vehicles and an agreement has been entered to make deferred or installment payments of unpaid fines or costs ordered by the court. See opinion of Attorney General to The Honorable George W. Harris Jr., Judge, Twenty-Third Judicial District, 00-063 (11/28/00).

§ 19.2-355. Petition of defendant.

(a) In determining whether the defendant is unable to pay such fine forthwith, the court may require such defendant to file a petition, under oath, with the court, upon a form provided by the court, setting forth the financial condition of the defendant.

(b) Such form shall be a questionnaire, and shall include, but shall not be limited to: the name and residence of the defendant; his occupation, if any; his family status and the number of persons dependent upon him; his monthly income; whether or not his dependents are employed and, if so, their approximate monthly income; his banking accounts, if any; real estate owned by the defendant, or any interest he may have in real estate; income produced therefrom; any independent income accruing to the defendant; tangible and intangible personal property owned by the defendant, or in which he may have an interest; and a statement listing the approximate indebtedness of the defendant to other persons. Such form shall also include a payment plan of the defendant, if the court should exercise its discretion in permitting the payment of such fine and costs in installments or other conditions to be fixed by the court. At the end of such form there shall be printed in bold face type, in a distinctive color the following: THIS STATEMENT IS MADE UNDER OATH, ANY FALSE STATEMENT OF A MATERIAL FACT TO ANY QUESTION CONTAINED HEREIN SHALL CONSTITUTE PERJURY UNDER THE PROVISIONS OF § 18.2-434 OF THE CODE OF VIRGINIA. THE MAXIMUM PENALTY FOR PERJURY IS CONFINEMENT IN THE PENITENTIARY FOR A PERIOD OF TEN YEARS. A copy of the petition shall be retained by the defendant.

(c) If the defendant is unable to read or write, the court, or the clerk, may assist the defendant in completing the petition and require him to affix his mark thereto. The consequences of the making of a false statement shall be explained to such defendant.

History.
Code 1950, § 19.1-347.2; 1971, Ex. Sess., c. 250; 1975, c. 495.

OPINIONS OF THE ATTORNEY GENERAL

Petitions under statute are traffic matters, rather than civil cases. — Petitions filed by defendants under § 19.2-355, as permitted by the amended language in subsection B of § 46.2-395, are considered to be traffic matters, and are not to be considered civil cases. See opinion of Attorney General to The Honorable George W. Harris Jr., Judge, Twenty-Third Judicial District, 00-063 (11/28/00).

§ 19.2-356. Payment of fine or costs as condition of probation or suspension of sentence.

If a defendant is placed on probation, or imposition or execution of sentence is suspended, or both, the court may make payment of any fine, or costs, or fine and costs, either on a certain date or on an installment basis, a condition of probation or suspension of sentence.

History.
Code 1950, § 19.1-347.3; 1971, Ex. Sess., c. 250; 1975, c. 495; 1987, c. 238.

CASE NOTES

Court costs nondischargeable in bankruptcy. — The fact that in some instances punishment will be contingent on court costs is sufficient, for definitional purposes, to lift Virginia's requirement that convicted defendants pay court costs into the nondischargeability provisions of 11 U.S.C. § 523(a)(7). Thompson v. Virginia, 16 F.3d 576 (4th Cir.), cert. denied, 512 U.S. 1221 114 S. Ct. 2709, 129 L. Ed. 2d 836 (1994).

§ 19.2-357. Requiring that defendant be of peace and good behavior until fine and costs are paid.

If a defendant is permitted to pay a fine or fine and costs on an installment basis, or under such other conditions as the court shall fix under the provisions of § 19.2-354, the court may require as a condition that the defendant be of peace and good behavior until the fine and costs are paid.

History.
Code 1950, § 19.1-347.4; 1971, Ex. Sess., c. 250; 1975, c. 495.

§ 19.2-358. Procedure on default in deferred payment or installment payment of fine, costs, forfeiture, restitution or penalty.

A. When an individual obligated to pay a fine, costs, forfeiture, restitution or penalty defaults in the payment or any installment payment, the court upon the motion of the Commonwealth in the case of a conviction of a violation of a state law, or attorney for a locality or for the Commonwealth in the event of a conviction of a violation of a local law or ordinance, or upon its own motion, may require him to show cause why he should not be confined in jail or fined for nonpayment. A show cause proceeding shall not be required prior to issuance of a capias if an order to appear on a date certain in the event of nonpayment was issued pursuant to subsection A of § 19.2-354 and the defendant failed to appear.

B. Following the order to show cause or following a capias issued for a defendant's failure to comply with a court order to appear issued pursuant to subsection A of § 19.2-354, unless the defendant shows that his default was not attributable to an intentional refusal to obey the sentence of the court, or not attributable to a failure on his part to make a good faith effort to obtain the necessary funds for payment, or unless the defendant shows that any failure to appear was not attributable to an intentional refusal to obey the order of the court, the court

may order the defendant confined as for a contempt for a term not to exceed sixty days or impose a fine not to exceed $500. The court may provide in its order that payment or satisfaction of the amounts in default at any time will entitle the defendant to his release from such confinement or, after entering the order, may at any time reduce the sentence for good cause shown, including payment or satisfaction of such amounts.

C. If it appears that the default is excusable under the standards set forth in subsection B hereof, the court may enter an order allowing the defendant additional time for payment, reducing the amount due or of each installment, or remitting the unpaid portion in whole or in part.

D. Nothing in this section shall be deemed to alter or interfere with the collection of fines by any means authorized for the enforcement of money judgments rendered in favor of the Commonwealth or any locality within the Commonwealth.

History.
Code 1950, § 19.1-347.6; 1973, c. 342; 1975, c. 495; 1977, c. 223; 1987, c. 238; 1988, cc. 770, 852; 1992, c. 485; 1994, c. 546.

CASE NOTES

Constitutionality. — Virginia's recoupment statutes, §§ 19.2-336 and 19.2-358, did not violate defendant's due process or equal protection rights as defendant would not be subject to enhanced punishment for a failure to pay court costs solely due to his future indigence, should it occur, since the penalties defendant feared would be imposed if he did not pay the costs could not be imposed absent an intentional refusal to obey the sentence or a failure to make a good faith effort to obtain the necessary funds under subsection B of § 19.2-358; if the default was excusable, the court could allow defendant additional time for payment, reduce the amount due or of each installment, or remit the unpaid portion in whole or in part under subsection C of § 19.2-358. Roads v. Commonwealth, 2013 Va. App. LEXIS 92 (Mar. 26, 2013).

Virginia's recoupment statutes, §§ 19.2-336 and 19.2-358, did not violate defendant's right to due process even though they placed the burden of proof on him to show that he was unable to pay court costs, or violate his right to equal protection even though they did not require that the trial court project his future ability to pay court costs before imposing the duty. Roads v. Commonwealth, 2013 Va. App. LEXIS 92 (Mar. 26, 2013).

Confinement constituted involuntary servitude and was proscribed by Thirteenth Amendment. — Where the state's sole ground for detaining defendant at a state farm was his failure to pay costs of the criminal prosecution, defendant's confinement constituted involuntary servitude and his imprisonment for nonpayment of costs contravened the Thirteenth Amendment. Wright v. Matthews, 209 Va. 246, 163 S.E.2d 158 (1968) (Case construed former § 53-221 which was repealed by Acts 1982, c. 638. Former § 53-221 applied specifically to persons held to labor for the nonpayment of fines and costs).

Imposition of fine. — Because defendant failed to provide a record that sufficiently established that defendant was convicted of traffic infractions and not crimes, pursuant to Va. Sup. Ct. R. 5A:8(b)(4)(ii), defendant waived the argument on appeal that the trial court erred in imposing a fine under § 19.2-358. Turnbull v. County of Spotsylvania, 2012 Va. App. LEXIS 24 (Jan. 31, 2012).

ARTICLE 5.

RECEIPTS FOR FINES.

Michie's Jurisprudence.
For related discussion, see 5B M.J. Criminal Procedure, § 92; 11B M.J. Justices and Magistrates, § 33.

§ 19.2-359. Official receipts to be given for fines.

Every officer collecting a fine, fine and costs or costs when no fine is imposed shall give an official receipt therefor to the person making the payment, and the clerk of the court shall use the official receipt in receipting to a court not of record for payments made to the clerk; and when the fine, fine and costs or costs are collected by execution, the clerk shall receipt to the officer making payment to him upon the official receipts.

History.
Code 1950, § 19.1-348; 1960, c. 366; 1975, c. 495.

§ 19.2-360. Forms of receipts; distribution; record of disposition.

The Executive Secretary of the Supreme Court shall prescribe and prepare forms of official receipts for fines and distribute them to the clerks of the circuit courts and to the clerks of the district courts for their use. A record of the disposition of each receipt form shall be maintained as prescribed by the Executive Secretary.

History.
Code 1950, § 19.1-349; 1960, c. 366; 1972, c. 97; 1975, c. 495; 1977, c. 465.

§ 19.2-361. Misuse, misappropriation or willful failure to account for fines is embezzlement.

If any officer misuse, misappropriate, or willfully fail to return or account for, a fine collected by him he shall be deemed guilty of embezzlement and shall be punished as for the embezzlement of public funds and the failure, without good cause, to produce or account for any receipt form received by him shall be prima facie evidence of his embezzlement of the amount represented thereby.

History.
Code 1950, § 19.1-350; 1960, c. 366; 1975, c. 495.

ARTICLE 6.

RELIEF FROM FINES AND PENALTIES.

Michie's Jurisprudence.
For related discussion, see 4A M.J. Contempt, § 5; 5B M.J. Criminal Procedure, § 92.

§ 19.2-362. Court not to remit fine or penalty, other than fine for contempt, except as provided in § 19.2-358.

No court shall remit any fine or penalty, except for a contempt, which the court during the same term may remit either wholly or in part, and except as provided in § 19.2-358. This section shall not impair the judicial power of the court to set aside a verdict or judgment, or to grant a new trial.

History.
Code 1950, § 19.1-351; 1960, c. 366; 1971, Ex. Sess., c. 250; 1975, c. 495.

§ 19.2-363. Authority of Governor to grant relief from fines and penalties.

The Governor shall have power, in his discretion, to remit, in whole or in part, fines and penalties, in all cases of felony or misdemeanor, after conviction, whether paid into the state treasury or not, except when judgment shall have been rendered against any person for contempt of court, for nonperformance of or disobedience to some order, decree or judgment of such court, or when the fine or penalty has been imposed by the State Corporation Commission, or when the prosecution has been carried on by the House of Delegates. The Governor may, in his discretion, remit, refund or release, in whole or in part, any forfeited recognizance or any judgment rendered thereon, provided, in the opinion of the Governor, the evidence accompanying such application warrants the granting of the relief asked for. But the provisions of the three following sections and § 19.2-368 shall be complied with as a condition precedent to such action by the Governor; provided, that when the party against whom the fine or penalty has been imposed and judgment rendered therefor has departed this life leaving a spouse or children surviving, the Governor may remit such fine or penalty upon the certificate of the judge of the circuit court of the county or city wherein such fine or penalty was imposed and judgment rendered, that to enforce the same against the estate, real or personal, of the decedent, would impose hardship upon the spouse or children. In any case when the Governor remits, in whole or in part, a fine or penalty, if the same has been paid into the state treasury, on the order of the Governor such fine or penalty or so much thereof as is remitted shall be paid by the State Treasurer, on the warrant of the Comptroller, out of the fund into which the fine or penalty was paid.

History.
Code 1950, § 19.1-352; 1960, c. 366; 1975, c. 495.

Cross references.
For constitutional authority, see Va. Const., Art. V, § 12.

CASE NOTES

The revocation of a driver's license under former § 46.1-417 (now § 46.2-389) is not a part of the penalty inflicted within the meaning of this section which empowers the Governor to "remit fines and penalties," and a pardon granted to a driver under this section does not restore to him the right to operate an automobile free of the conditions which were imposed upon him when his license was renewed. Prichard v. Battle, 178 Va. 455, 17 S.E.2d 393 (1941).

§ 19.2-364. Petition for relief; in what court filed; notice to attorney for Commonwealth.

Such person or his personal representative, as the case may be, shall file a petition in the clerk's office of the circuit court of the county or city wherein such fine or penalty was imposed, or such liability established, at least fifteen days before the term of the court at which the same is to be heard, and shall set forth the grounds upon which relief is asked. Ten days' notice thereof in writing shall be given to the attorney for the Commonwealth of the county or city.

History.
  Code 1950, § 19.1-353; 1960, c. 366; 1975, c. 495.

§ 19.2-365. Duties of attorney for Commonwealth upon filing of such petition.

The attorney for the Commonwealth, at or before the hearing of such petition, shall file an answer to the same. He shall cause to be summoned such witnesses and shall introduce all such testimony as may be necessary and proper to protect the interest of the Commonwealth; and the petitioner may cause to be summoned such witnesses and shall introduce all such testimony as may be necessary and proper to protect his interest.

History.
  Code 1950, § 19.1-354; 1960, c. 366; 1975, c. 495.

§ 19.2-366. Duty of court in which petition filed; certificate and opinion.

The court wherein such petition is filed shall hear all such testimony as may be offered, either by the petitioner or attorney for the Commonwealth, and after the evidence has been heard shall cause to be made out by the clerk of the court a certificate of the facts proved, and file with the same an opinion, in writing, as to the propriety of granting the relief prayed for.

History.
  Code 1950, § 19.1-355; 1960, c. 366; 1975, c. 495.

§ 19.2-367. Proceedings to be according to common law.

All proceedings had before the court under the provisions of the three preceding sections shall be according to the course of the common-law practice, except that no formal pleadings shall be necessary.

History.
  Code 1950, § 19.1-356; 1960, c. 366; 1975, c. 495.

§ 19.2-368. Course of proceeding when relief asked of the Governor.

Whenever application shall be made to the Governor by or on behalf of any person desiring to be relieved, in whole or in part, of any such fine or penalty, the petition, answer, certificate of facts, and opinion of the court provided for in §§ 19.2-364, 19.2-365 and 19.2-366, duly authenticated by the clerk of the court, shall accompany the application, which shall be in writing. In all cases in which the Governor shall remit a fine or penalty he shall issue his order to the clerk of the court by which such fine or penalty was imposed; or if such fine or penalty was imposed by a court not of record, to the clerk of the circuit court of the county or city in which the judge of such court not of record holds office, and such court shall, at its next term, or immediately, if then in session, cause such order to be spread upon the law order book of its court; and the clerk of such court shall immediately, upon the receipt of such order, mark the judgment for such fine or penalty, and costs, or so much thereof as the person may have been relieved of, "remitted by the Governor," upon the Judgment Lien Docket of the court of the county or city in which it may have been recorded. The Governor shall communicate to the General Assembly at each session the particulars of every case of fine or penalty remitted, with his reason for remitting the same.

History.
  Code 1950, § 19.1-357; 1960, c. 366; 1975, c. 495.

CHAPTER 21.1.

COMPENSATING VICTIMS OF CRIME.

§ 19.2-368.1. Findings; legislative intent.

The General Assembly finds that many innocent persons suffer personal physical injury or death as a result of criminal acts or in their efforts to prevent crime or apprehend persons committing or attempting to commit crimes. Such persons or their dependents may thereby suffer disability, incur financial hardships or become dependent upon public assistance. The General Assembly finds and determines that there is a need for governmental financial assistance for such victims of crime. Therefore, it is the intent of the General Assembly that aid, care and support be provided by the Commonwealth as a matter of moral responsibility for such victims of crime.

History.
1976, c. 605.

Law Review.
For survey of Virginia criminal law for the year 1975-1976, see 62 Va. L. Rev. 1400 (1976). For article discussing victims' rights litigation, see 11 U. Rich. L. Rev. 447 (1977). For discussion of the elements of compensation and restitution in this chapter, see 11 U. Rich. L. Rev. 679 (1977). For survey of Virginia criminal law for the year 1977-1978, see 64 Va. L. Rev. 1407 (1978). For article, "Victimology and Mental Health Law: An Agenda," see 66 Va. L. Rev. 681 (1980).

Michie's Jurisprudence.
For related discussion, see 5B M.J. Criminal Procedure, §§ 11, 78, 90.

CASE NOTES

Order of statute follows a scheme which is significant and carries out the stated intentions of the legislature. Jennings v. Division of Crime Victims' Comp., 5 Va. App. 536, 365 S.E.2d 241 (1988).

Analysis in determining claims. — The analysis the director and the commission should have applied in determining claims was as follows: (1) determine eligibility; (2) determine whether the award is allowed; (3) determine the amount of the award; (4) apportion the award, if necessary; and (5) reduce the award to each claimant by the amount of payments received or to be received by that claimant from any collateral source as a result of the injury. Jennings v. Division of Crime Victims' Comp., 5 Va. App. 536, 365 S.E.2d 241 (1988).

Applied in Marchand v. Division of Crime Victims' Comp., 230 Va. 460, 339 S.E.2d 175 (1986).

NOTES FROM THE WORKERS' COMPENSATION COMMISSION

The Virginia Victims of Crime Act is remedial in nature. It provides a system of redress for specified individuals who have suffered loss due to the commission of a crime. Prior to its enactment, no such remedy existed, and the addition of this form of compensation was calculated to fill what was perceived to be agap in available remedies. This being the case, it is axiomatic that the statute be liberally construed to promote its beneficent purpose, and its provisions should be read so as to promote the ability of the enactment to remedy the mischief at which it is directed. Bailey v. Criminal Injuries Compensation Fund, 77 O.W.C. 150 (1998).

The Criminal Injuries Compensation Fund is remedial in nature. provides a system of redress for specified individuals who have suffered loss due to the commission of a crime. Prior to its enactment, no such remedy existed, and the addition of this form of compensation was calculated to fill what was perceived to be agap in available remedies. This being the case, it is axiomatic that the statute be liberally construed to promote its beneficent purpose. Its provisions should be read so as to promote the ability of the enactment to remedy the mischief at which it is directed. Morrison v. Victims of Crimes Compensation Act, 77 O.W.C. 239 (1998).

In evaluating a claim under the Virginia Victims of Crime Act, the Commission is to apply the following analysis: (1) determine eligibility; (2) determine whether the award is allowed; (3) determine the amount of the award; (4) apportion the award if necessary; and (5) reduce the award to each claimant as may be required under the Act. Bailey v. Criminal Injuries Compensation Fund, 77 O.W.C. 150 (1998).

Under the Compensation Victims of Crime Act, benefits are awarded to innocent persons who suffer personal physical injury or death because of criminal acts. Benefits may be reduced or rejected if the victim contributes to the infliction of the injuries. Creed v. Criminal Injuries Comp. Fund, 76 O.W.C. 173 (1997).

Where the police report of the crime does not indicate that the victim was engaged in any criminal conduct, or that he was armed, or that he contributed in any way to the infliction of his own injury, but at most suggests that he was present in someone's home where marijuana may have been sold, there is no basis for denying or reducing the claim. Bailey v. Criminal Injuries Compensation Fund, 77 O.W.C. 150 (1998).

The Commission adopted a policy on November 4, 1998, which provided that "[t]he Fund may pay up to one thousand dollars for crime scene clean-up when a crime resulting in physical injury occurs in a residence . . .. Requests for Awards for Crime Scene Clean-Up involving automobiles will be decided by the Commission judicially on a case-by-case basis." Montgomery v. Criminal Injuries Compensation Fund, 78 O.W.C. 276 (1999).

The Commission interprets its crime scene clean-up policy to cover replacement and clean-up of items damaged by stains resulting from the police use of graphite at the crime scene. However, it does not cover payment for items taken by the police as evidence. Montgomery v. Criminal Injuries Compensation Fund, 78 O.W.C. 276 (1999).

§ 19.2-368.2. Definitions.

For the purpose of this chapter:

"Claimant" means the person filing a claim pursuant to this chapter.

"Commission" means the Virginia Workers' Compensation Commission.

"Crime" means an act committed by any person in the Commonwealth of Virginia which would constitute a crime as defined by the Code of Virginia or at common law. However, no act involving the operation of a motor vehicle which results in injury shall constitute a crime for the purpose of this chapter unless the injuries (i) were intentionally inflicted through the use of such vehicle or (ii) resulted from a violation of § 18.2-51.4 or 18.2-266 or from a felony violation of § 46.2-894.

"Family," when used with reference to a person, means (i) any person related to such person within the third degree of consanguinity or affinity, (ii) any person residing in the same household with such person, or (iii) a spouse.

"Sexual abuse" means sexual abuse as defined in subdivision 6 of § 18.2-67.10 and acts constituting rape, sodomy, object sexual penetration or sexual battery as defined in Article 7 (§ 18.2-61 et seq.) of Chapter 4 of Title 18.2.

"Victim" means a person who suffers personal physical injury or death as a direct result of a crime including a person who is injured or killed as a result of foreign terrorism or who suffers personal emotional injury as a direct result of being the subject of a violent felony offense as defined in subsection C of § 17.1-805, or stalking as described in § 18.2-60.3, or attempted robbery or abduction.

History.

1976, c. 605; 1984, c. 619; 1988, c. 748; 1990, c. 620; 1997, cc. 528, 691; 1998, c. 484; 1999, c. 286; 2001, c. 855; 2008, c. 590; 2012, c. 38.

The 2008 amendments.

The 2008 amendment by c. 590 deleted the section symbol preceding "18.2-266" at the end of the definition of "Crime" and inserted "or stalking as described in § 18.2-60.3" near the end of the definition of "Victim."

The 2012 amendments.

The 2012 amendment by c. 38 added "or from a felony violation of § 46.2-894" at the end of the paragraph defining "Crime."

CASE NOTES

Analysis in determining claims. — The analysis the director and the commission should have applied in determining claims was as follows: (1) determine eligibility; (2) determine whether the award is allowed; (3) determine the amount of the award; (4) apportion the award, if necessary; and (5) reduce the award to each claimant by the amount of payments received or to be received by that claimant from any collateral source as a result of the injury. Jennings v. Division of Crime Victims' Comp., 5 Va. App. 536, 365 S.E.2d 241 (1988).

§ 19.2-368.3. Powers and duties of Commission.

The Commission shall have the following powers and duties in the administration of the provisions of this chapter:

1. To adopt, promulgate, amend and rescind suitable rules and regulations to carry out the provisions and purposes of this chapter, to include a distinct policy (i) for the payment of physical evidence recovery kit examinations and (ii) to require each health care provider as defined in § 8.01-581.1 that provides services under this chapter to negotiate with the Commission or its designee to establish prospective agreements relating to rates for payment of claims for such services allowed under § 19.2-368.11:1, such rates to discharge the obligation to the provider in full except where the provider is an agency of the Commonwealth and the claimant receives a third party recovery in addition to the payment from the Fund.

2. Notwithstanding the provisions of § 2.2-3706, to acquire from the attorneys for the Commonwealth, State Police, local police departments, sheriffs' departments, and the Chief Medical Examiner such investigative results, information and data as will enable the Commission to determine if, in fact, a crime was committed or attempted, and the extent, if any, to which the victim or claimant was responsible for his own injury. These data shall include prior adult arrest records and juvenile court disposition records of the offender. For such purposes and in accordance with § 16.1-305, the Commission may also acquire from the juvenile and domestic relations district courts a copy of the order of disposition relating to the crime. The use of any information received by the Commission pursuant to this subdivision shall be limited to carrying out the purposes set forth in this section, and this information shall be confidential and shall not be dissemi-

nated further. The agency from which the information is requested may submit original reports, portions thereof, summaries, or such other configurations of information as will comply with the requirements of this section.

3. To hear and determine all claims for awards filed with the Commission pursuant to this chapter, and to reinvestigate or reopen cases as the Commission deems necessary.

4. To require and direct medical examination of victims.

5. To hold hearings, administer oaths or affirmations, examine any person under oath or affirmation and to issue summonses requiring the attendance and giving of testimony of witnesses and require the production of any books, papers, documentary or other evidence. The powers provided in this subsection may be delegated by the Commission to any member or employee thereof.

6. To take or cause to be taken affidavits or depositions within or without the Commonwealth.

7. To render each year to the Governor and to the General Assembly a written report of its activities.

8. To accept from the government of the United States grants of federal moneys for disbursement under the provisions of this chapter.

History.

1976, c. 605; 1984, c. 619; 1986, c. 422; 1990, c. 551; 1992, c. 547; 1998, c. 484; 1999, cc. 703, 726; 2008, cc. 203, 251; 2010, c. 780.

Editor's note.

Acts 1993, c. 930, cl. 3, as amended by Acts 1994, c. 564, cl. 2, and Acts 1996, c. 616, cl. 4, provides that the amendment to this section by Acts 1993, c. 930, cl. 1, shall become effective June 1, 1998, "if state funds are provided, including all local costs, to carry out the purposes of this bill by the General Assembly." The funding was not provided.

The 2008 amendments.

The 2008 amendments by cc. 203 and 251 are identical and added "and to include a distinct policy for the payment of physical evidence recovery kit examinations" at the end of subdivision 1.

The 2010 amendments.

The 2010 amendment by c. 780, in subdivision 1, added the clause (i) designator and added clause (ii) and made a related change; and deleted subsection B, which read: "For the purpose of this section, 'debt collection activities' means repeatedly calling or writing to the claimant and threatening either to turn the matter over to a debt collection agency or to an attorney for collection, enforcement or filing of other process. The term shall not include routine billing or inquiries about the status of the claim."

Law Review.

For survey of Virginia criminal law for the year 1975-1976, see 62 Va. L. Rev. 1400 (1976).

Michie's Jurisprudence.

For related discussion, see 16 M.J. Right of Privacy, § 1.

CASE NOTES

Analysis in determining claims. — The analysis the director and the commission should have applied in determining claims was as follows: (1) determine eligibility; (2) determine whether the award is allowed; (3) determine the amount of the award; (4) apportion the award, if necessary; and (5) reduce the award to each claimant by the amount of payments received or to be received by that claimant from any collateral source as a result of the injury.

Jennings v. Division of Crime Victims' Comp., 5 Va. App. 536, 365 S.E.2d 241 (1988).

Applied in Marchand v. Division of Crime Victims' Comp., 230 Va. 460, 339 S.E.2d 175 (1986).

NOTES FROM THE WORKERS' COMPENSATION COMMISSION

The Commission has broad latitude in the information and data obtained through various police agencies that shall be used to decide whether a victim is responsible for his or her own injury. Creed v. Criminal Injuries Comp. Fund, 76 O.W.C 173 (1997).

Code § 19.2-368.3 authorizes the Commission to reinvestigate or reopen cases as it deems necessary, and it is appropriate to reopen this case where the accuracy of statements made to police investigators is questioned. Creed v. Criminal Injuries Comp. Fund, 76 O.W.C 173 (1997).

The Commission must determine whether the claimant has established by a preponderance of the evidence that he was the victim of a "crime." The fact that charges against the alleged perpetrator were dropped by the Commonwealth does not conclusively establish that the claimant was not a victim of a "crime." The evidence before the Deputy Commissioner clearly established that the claimant suffered injuries after an altercation meeting the legal definition of criminal battery. The Commission observed that the prosecution's apparent inability to secure a conviction was evidence that the acts were something other than criminal, but found the claimant's testimony about the altercation more compelling. In Re: Claim of John Doxey, CV File No. 02-0296 (October 28, 2002).

§ 19.2-368.3:1. Crime victims' ombudsman.

A. The Commission shall employ a crime victims' ombudsman and adequate staff to facilitate the prompt review and resolution of crime victim compensation claims and to assure that crime victims' rights are safeguarded and protected during the claims process. The ombudsman shall report directly to the Commission.

B. The ombudsman shall ensure that all parties, including service providers and Criminal Injuries Compensation Fund personnel, are acting in the best interests of the crime victim. The ombudsman shall also provide assistance to crime victims in filling out the necessary forms for compensation and obtaining necessary documentation.

History.
1998, c. 484.

§ 19.2-368.4. Persons eligible for awards.

A. The following persons shall be eligible for awards pursuant to this chapter unless the award would directly and unjustly benefit the person who is criminally responsible:

1. A victim of a crime or the parent or guardian of a minor who is the victim of a crime.

2. A surviving spouse, parent, grandparent, sibling or child, including posthumous children, of a victim of a crime who died as a direct result of such crime.

3. Any person, except a law-enforcement officer engaged in the performance of his duties, who is injured or killed while trying to prevent a crime or an attempted crime from occurring in his presence, or trying to apprehend a person who had committed a crime in his presence or had, in fact, committed a felony.

4. A surviving spouse, parent, grandparent, sibling or child, including posthumous children, of any person who dies as a direct result of trying to prevent a crime or attempted crime from occurring in his presence, or trying to apprehend a person who had committed a crime in his presence or had, in fact, committed a felony.

5. Any other person legally dependent for his principal support upon a victim of crime who dies as a result of such crime, or legally dependent for his principal support upon any person who dies as a direct result of trying to prevent a crime or an attempted crime from occurring in his presence or trying to apprehend a person who had committed a crime in his presence or had, in fact, committed a felony.

B. A person who is criminally responsible for the crime upon which a claim is based, or an accomplice or accessory of such person, shall not be eligible to receive an award with respect to such claim.

C. A resident of Virginia who is the victim of a crime occurring outside Virginia and any other person as defined in subsection A who is injured as a result of a crime occurring outside Virginia shall be eligible for an award pursuant to this chapter if (i) the person would be eligible for benefits had the crime occurred in Virginia and (ii) the state, country or territory in which the crime occurred does not have a crime victims' compensation program deemed eligible pursuant to the provisions of the federal Victims of Crime Act and does not compensate nonresidents.

History.
1976, c. 605; 1977, c. 215; 1978, c. 210; 1981, c. 592; 1984, c. 747; 1985, c. 446; 1986, c. 422; 1988, c. 406; 1990, c. 550; 1996, c. 86; 2002, c. 665.

Law Review.
For survey of Virginia criminal law for the year 1975-1976, see 62 Va. L. Rev. 1400 (1976). For article discussing victims' rights litigation, see 11 U. Rich. L. Rev. 447 (1977). For survey of Virginia criminal law for the year 1977-1978, see 64 Va. L. Rev. 1407 (1978).

CASE NOTES

Analysis in determining claims. — The analysis the director and the commission should have applied in determining claims was as follows: (1) determine eligibility; (2) determine whether the award is allowed; (3) determine the amount of the award; (4) apportion the award, if necessary; and (5) reduce the award to each claimant by the amount of payments received or to be received by that claimant from any collateral source as a result of the injury. Jennings v. Division of Crime Victims' Comp., 5 Va. App. 536, 365 S.E.2d 241 (1988).

NOTES FROM THE WORKERS' COMPENSATION COMMISSION

Persons who fail to fully cooperate with law-enforcement authorities, or who are criminally responsible for the crime upon which the claim is based, are not eligible for an award. Bailey v. Criminal Injuries Compensation Fund, 77 O.W.C 150 (1998).

The Commission must determine whether the claimant has established by a preponderance of the evidence that he was the victim of a "crime." The fact that charges against the alleged perpetrator were dropped by the Commonwealth does not conclusively establish that the claimant was not a victim of a "crime." The evidence before the Deputy Commissioner clearly established that the claimant suffered injuries after an altercation meeting the legal definition of criminal battery. The Commission observed that the prosecution's apparent inability to secure a conviction was evidence that the acts were something other than criminal, but found the claimant's testimony about the altercation more compelling. In Re: Claim of John Doxey, CV File No. 02-0296 (October 28, 2002).

§ 19.2-368.5. Filing of claims; deferral of proceedings; restitution.

A. A claim may be filed by a person eligible to receive an award, as provided in § 19.2-368.4, or if such person is a minor, by his parent or guardian. In any case in which the person entitled to make a claim is incapacitated, the claim may be filed on his behalf by his guardian, conservator or such other individual authorized to administer his estate.

B. A claim shall be filed by the claimant not later than one year after the occurrence of the crime upon which such claim is based, or not later than one year after the death of the victim. However, (i) in cases involving claims made on behalf of a minor or a person who is incapacitated, the provisions of subsection A of § 8.01-229 shall apply to toll the one-year period; (ii) in cases involving claims made by a victim against profits of crime held in escrow pursuant to Chapter 21.2 (§ 19.2-368.19 et seq.) of this title, the claim shall be filed within five years of the date of the special order of escrow; and (iii) in cases involving claims of sexual abuse of a minor, the claim shall be filed within 10 years after the minor's eighteenth birthday. For good cause shown, the Commission may extend the time for filing.

C. Claims shall be filed in the office of the Commission in person, by mail, or by electronic means in accordance with standards approved by the Commission. The Commission shall accept for filing all claims submitted by persons eligible under subsection A of this section and alleging the jurisdictional requirements set forth in this chapter and meeting the requirements as to form in the rules and regulations of the Commission.

D. Upon filing of a claim pursuant to this chapter, the Commission shall promptly notify the attorney for the Commonwealth of the jurisdiction wherein the crime is alleged to have occurred. If, within 10 days after such notification, the attorney for the Commonwealth so notified advises the Commission that a criminal prosecution is pending upon the same alleged crime, the Commission shall defer all proceedings under this chapter until such time as such criminal prosecution has been concluded in the circuit court unless notification is received from the attorney for the Commonwealth that no objection is made to a continuation of the investigation and determination of the claim. When such criminal prosecution has been concluded in the circuit court the attorney for the Commonwealth shall promptly

so notify the Commission. Nothing in this section shall be construed to mean that the Commission is to defer proceedings upon the filing of an appeal, nor shall this section be construed to limit the authority of the Commission to grant emergency awards as hereinafter provided. Upon awarding a claim pursuant to this chapter, the Commission shall promptly notify the attorney for the Commonwealth of the jurisdiction wherein the crime is alleged to have occurred. If a criminal prosecution occurs regarding the same alleged crime, the attorney for the Commonwealth shall request the court to order restitution. However, neither the lack of a restitution order, nor the failure of the attorney for the Commonwealth to request such an order, shall preclude the Fund from exercising its subrogation rights pursuant to § 19.2-368.15. Any such restitution shall be paid over to the Comptroller for deposit into the Criminal Injuries Compensation Fund to the extent of the amount of the award paid from the Fund.

History.
1976, c. 605; 1977, c. 215; 1978, c. 122; 1986, c. 457; 1992, c. 681; 1997, c. 801; 1998, c. 484; 2001, cc. 363, 855; 2002, c. 665; 2005, c. 683; 2006, c. 414; 2009, c. 381.

Editor's note.
Acts 1997, c. 801, cl. 2, provides: "That the provisions of this act shall become effective on January 1, 1998. The powers granted and duties imposed pursuant to this act shall apply prospectively to guardians and conservators appointed by court order entered on or after that date, or modified on or after that date if the court so directs, without regard to when the petition was filed. The procedures specified in this act governing proceedings for appointment of a guardian or conservator or termination or other modification of a guardianship shall apply on and after that date without regard to when the petition therefor was filed or the guardianship or conservatorship created."

The 2009 amendments.
The 2009 amendment by c. 381, in subsection C, in the first sentence, deleted "or" following "Commission in person" and inserted "or by electronic means in accordance with standards approved by the Commission."

Law Review.
For article, "Legal Issues Involving Children," see 35 U. Rich. L. Rev. 741 (2001).

NOTES FROM THE WORKERS' COMPENSATION COMMISSION

Victim whose claim initially denied in April 2002 because value of claim less than $100 allowed to petition for review of denial in June 2003, although crime occurred in December 2000 and Act prevented claims from being filed more than two years after crime; Fund continued to solicit medical information after denial and thus victim reasonably believed timely claim was being processed. In Re: Thomas, CV File No. 01-0420 (Nov. 17, 2003).

Victim assaulted on April 27, 2000, and filed claim on April 30, 2003; at time of crime, Act precluded claims filed more than two years after date of crime, but was amended in 2001 to enlarge period of filing 'for good cause shown'; Commission found that amendment was not retroactive and that claim thus was time-barred. In Re: Fell, CV File No. 00-1501 (Nov. 12, 2003).

In 2001, the General Assembly amended Code § 19.2-368.5, granting the Commission discretion to extend indefinitely, when good cause is shown, the date for filing a claim under the Act. The legislation did not include language declaring the General Assembly's intent that the new provision apply to claims arising before the statute was amended. Because retroactive effect will be given only where such intent is stated in clear, explicit and unequivocal terms, the Commission found that the amendment is to be applied prospectively only. The claimant's claim was governed by the statute effective on the date of her injury, and found to be untimely. May v. Criminal Injuries Compensation Fund, CV File No. 90-1399 (October 28, 2002).

§ 19.2-368.5:1. Failure to perfect claim; denial.

Notwithstanding the provisions of § 19.2-368.5, if, following the initial filing of a claim, a claimant fails to take such further steps to support or perfect the claim as may be required by the Commission within 180 days after written notice of such requirement is sent by the Commission to the claimant, the claimant shall be deemed in default. If the claimant is in default, the Commission shall notify the claimant that the claim is denied and the claimant shall be forever barred from reasserting it; however, the Commission may reopen the proceeding upon a showing by claimant that the failure to do the acts required by the Commission was beyond the control of the claimant.

History.
1981, c. 302; 1998, c. 484.

§ 19.2-368.5:2. Effect of filing a claim; stay of debt collection activities by health care providers.

A. Whenever a person files a claim under this chapter, all health care providers, as defined in § 8.01-581.1 that have been given notice of a pending claim, shall refrain from all debt collection activities relating to medical treatment received by the person in connection with such claim until an award is made on the claim or until a claim is determined to be noncompensable pursuant to § 19.2-368.11:1. The statute of limitations for collection of such debt shall be tolled during the period in which the applicable health care provider is required to refrain from debt collection activities hereunder.

B. For the purpose of this section, *"debt collection activities"* means repeatedly calling or writing to the claimant and threatening either to turn the matter over to a debt collection agency or to an attorney for collection, enforcement or filing of other process. The term shall not include routine billing or inquiries about the status of the claim.

History.
2005, c. 683.

§ 19.2-368.6. Assignment of claims; investigation; hearing; confidentiality of records; decisions.

A. A claim, when accepted for filing, shall be properly investigated, and, if necessary, assigned by the chairman to a commissioner, deputy commissioner or other proper party for disposition. All claims arising from the death of an individual shall be considered together by the same person.

B. The person to whom such claim is assigned shall examine the papers filed in support of the claim and shall thereupon cause an investigation to be conducted into the validity of the claim. The investigation shall include, but not be limited to, an examination of police, court and official records and reports concerning the crime, and an examination of medical and hospital reports relating to the injury upon which the claim is based. Health care providers, as defined in § 8.01-581.1, shall provide medical and hospital reports relating to the diagnosis and treatment of the injury upon which the claim is based to the Commission, upon request.

C. Claims shall be investigated and determined, regardless of whether the alleged criminal has been apprehended or prosecuted for, or convicted of, any crime based upon the same incident, or has been acquitted, or found not guilty of the crime in question owing to a lack of criminal responsibility or other legal exemption.

D. There shall be a rebuttable presumption that the claimant did not contribute to and was not responsible for the infliction of his injury.

E. The person to whom a claim is assigned may decide the claim in favor of a claimant on the basis of the papers filed in support thereof and the report of the investigation of the claim. If he is unable to decide the claim, upon the basis of the said papers and report, he shall order a hearing. At the hearing any relevant evidence, not legally privileged, shall be admissible. The hearing of any claim involving a claimant or victim who is a juvenile shall be closed. All records, papers, and reports involving such claim shall be confidential except as to the amount of the award and nonidentifying information concerning the claimant or victim.

F. For purposes of this chapter, confidentiality provided for by law applicable to a claimant's or victim's juvenile court records shall not be applicable to the extent that the Commission shall have access to those records only for the purposes set forth in this chapter.

G. After examining the papers filed in support of the claim, and the report of investigation, and after a hearing, if any, a decision shall be made either granting an award pursuant to § 19.2-368.11:1 of this chapter or denying the claim.

H. The person making a decision shall issue a written report setting forth such decision and his reasons therefor, and shall notify the claimant and furnish him a copy of such report.

History.
1976, c. 605; 1977, c. 215; 1994, c. 834; 1997, c. 528; 1998, c. 484.

Editor's note.
Acts 1993, c. 930, cl. 3, as amended by Acts 1994, c. 564, cl. 2, and Acts 1996, c. 616, cl. 4, provides that the amendment to this section by Acts 1993, c. 930, cl. 1, shall become effective June 1, 1998, "if state funds are provided, including all local costs, to carry out the

purposes of this bill by the General Assembly." The funding was not provided.

NOTES FROM THE WORKERS' COMPENSATION COMMISSION

The Commission has broad latitude to consider information and data obtained through various police agencies, and the director properly considered such statements in denying the claim. However, a factual dispute arises when the claimant challenges the accuracy of such statements, and that the Commission found it was necessary to refer the case to the evidentiary docket for findings of fact and credibility determinations. Migliorini v. Criminal Injuries Compensation Fund, 78 O.W.C. 218 (1999).

To qualify as a crime while operating a motor vehicle, the injury must have been intentionally inflicted through the vehicle's use or resulted from a violation of § 18.2-51.4 or § 18.2-266. These criminal code sections pertain to operating a motor vehicle while intoxicated by alcohol or drugs. Knoff v. Criminal Injuries Compensation Fund, 78 O.W.C. 106 (1999).

Where the record confirmed that the motor vehicle driver suffered a diabetic seizure and blacked out, and the driver's blood and alcohol tests revealed that he was not under the influence of drugs or alcohol, the record contains no evidence that the accident was intentional, and the Commission held that the accident was not within the definition of a crime for the purpose of compensating the victim of a crime. Knoff v. Criminal Injuries Compensation Fund, 78 O.W.C. 106 (1999).

The Commission must determine whether the claimant has established by a preponderance of the evidence that he was the victim of a "crime." The fact that charges against the alleged perpetrator were dropped by the Commonwealth does not conclusively establish that the claimant was not a victim of a "crime." The evidence before the Deputy Commissioner clearly established that the claimant suffered injuries after an altercation meeting the legal definition of criminal battery. The Commission observed that the prosecution's apparent inability to secure a conviction was evidence that the acts were something other than criminal, but found the claimant's testimony about the altercation more compelling. In Re: Claim of John Doxey, CV File No. 02-0296 (October 28, 2002).

§ 19.2-368.7. Review by Commission.

A. The claimant may, within forty-five days from the date of the report, apply in writing to the Commission for review of the decision by the full Commission. The Commission may extend the time for filing under this section for good cause shown.

B. Upon receipt of an application pursuant to subsection A of this section, or upon its own motion, the Commission shall review the record and affirm or modify the decision of the person to whom the claim was assigned. The action of the Commission in affirming or modifying such decision shall be final. If the Commission receives no application pursuant to subsection A of this section, or takes no action upon its own motion, the decision of the person to whom the claim was assigned shall become the final decision of the Commission.

C. The Commission shall promptly notify the claimant and the Comptroller of the final decision of the Commission and furnish each with a copy of the report setting forth the decision.

History.
1976, c. 605; 1977, c. 215; 1986, c. 457; 1989, c. 335; 2000, c. 455; 2001, c. 363.

NOTES FROM THE WORKERS' COMPENSATION COMMISSION

The statutory provisions relating to requests for review from decisions of the Crime Victims Director are not as rigid as those contained in other statutes and rules relating to appellate procedure. Code § 19.2-368.7 (A) states that, "The Commission may extend the time for filing under this section, upon good cause shown, for a period not to exceed two years from the date of the occurrence." Also, Code § 19.2-368.8(A) allows the Commission to reinvestigate or reopen a decision making or denying an award, except that the Commission shall not reopen or reinvestigate a case after the expiration of two years from the date of occurrence of the crime upon which the claim is based. Migliorini v. Criminal Injuries Compensation Fund, 78 O.W.C. 218 (1999).

Where the claimant had filed a timely request for reconsideration of the decision of the Crime Victims Director, and thereafter filed her request for review within twenty days of the date that request was denied, the Commission held that there was good cause to consider the claimant's review request. Migliorini v. Criminal Injuries Compensation Fund, 78 O.W.C. 218 (1999).

§ 19.2-368.8. Reinvestigation of decision; reconsideration of award; judicial review.

A. The Commission, on its own motion, or upon request of the claimant, may reinvestigate or reopen a decision making or denying an award. Except for claims of sexual abuse that occurred while the victim was a minor, the Commission shall not reopen or reinvestigate a case after the expiration of two years from the date of submission of the original claim. Any claim involving the sexual abuse of a minor that has been denied before July 1, 2001, because it was not timely filed may, upon application filed with the Commission, be reconsidered provided the application for reconsideration is filed within ten years after the minor's eighteenth birthday.

B. The Commission shall reconsider, at least annually, every award upon which periodic payments are being made. An order or reconsideration of an award shall not require refund of amounts previously paid unless the award was obtained by fraud. The right of reconsideration does not affect the finality of a Commission decision for the purposes of judicial review.

C. Within thirty days of the date of the report containing the final decision of the Commission, the claimant may, if in his judgment the award is improper, appeal such decision to the Court of Appeals, as provided in § 65.2-706. The Attorney General may appear in such proceedings as counsel for the Commission.

History.
1976, c. 605; 1977, c. 215; 1984, c. 703; 2001, c. 855; 2002, c. 665.

Law Review.
For article, "Legal Issues Involving Children," see 35 U. Rich. L. Rev. 741 (2001).

CASE NOTES

Commission should have flexibility in implementing decisions. — The provision for reconsideration indicates that once the decision is made, the commission should have flexibility in implementing it. Therefore, if an award is reduced because payments are to be received in the future but those payments are never received or not received in full, the commission need not reopen or reinvestigate the case pursuant to subsection A to order that payments be made. It need only consider that the collateral source funds were never paid or not paid in full and that the award already entered, or the balance after reduction by collateral payments, should be paid from the Crime Victims' Compensation Fund. Jennings v. Division of Crime Victims' Comp., 5 Va. App. 536, 365 S.E.2d 241 (1988).

Social security payments are funds to be received as a result of the injury from any other public source; as provided by subsection C of § 19.2-368.12, however, if the social security payments were to cease before the limit of the award is reached, the claimant would be entitled to the balance of an award from the Crime Victims' Compensation Fund. Jennings v. Division of Crime Victims' Comp., 5 Va. App. 536, 365 S.E.2d 241 (1988).

NOTES FROM THE WORKERS' COMPENSATION COMMISSION

The statutory provisions relating to requests for review from decisions of the Crime Victims Director are not as rigid as those contained in other statutes and rules relating to appellate procedure. Code § 19.2-368.7(A) states that, "The Commission may extend the time for filing under this section, upon good cause shown, for a period not to exceed two years from the date of the occurrence." Also, Code § 19.2-368.8(A) allows the Commission to reinvestigate or reopen a decision making or denying an award, except that the Commission shall not reopen or reinvestigate a case after the expiration of two years from the date of occurrence of the crime upon which the claim is based. Migliorini v. Criminal Injuries Compensation Fund, 78 O.W.C. 218 (1999).

Where the claimant had filed a timely request for reconsideration of the decision of the Crime Victims Director, and thereafter filed her request for review within twenty days of the date that request was denied, the Commission held that there was good cause to consider the claimant's review request. Migliorini v. Criminal Injuries Compensation Fund, 78 O.W.C. 218 (1999).

§ 19.2-368.9. Emergency awards.

Notwithstanding any other provisions of this chapter, if it appears to the Commission, that (1) such claim is one with respect to which an award probably will be made, and (2) undue hardship will result to the claimant if immediate payment is not made, the Commission may make an emergency award to the claimant, pending a final decision in the case, provided that (i) the amount of such emergency award shall not exceed $2,000, (ii) the amount of such emergency award shall be deducted from any final award made to the claimant, and (iii) the excess of the amount of such emergency award over the final award, or the full amount of the emergency award if no final award is made, shall be repaid by the claimant to the Commission.

History.
1976, c. 605; 1977, c. 215; 1985, c. 446.

Law Review.
For article, "Criminal Law and Procedure," see 35 U. Rich. L. Rev. 537 (2001).

§ 19.2-368.10. When awards to be made; reporting crime and cooperation with law enforcement.

No award shall be made unless the Commission finds that:

1. A crime was committed;
2. Such crime directly resulted in an individual becoming a victim as defined in § 19.2-368.2, on whose behalf a claim is filed; and
3. Police records show that such crime was promptly reported to the proper authorities. In no case may an award be made where the police records show that such report was made more than 120 hours after the occurrence of such crime, unless the Commission, for good cause shown, finds the delay to have been justified. The provisions of this subdivision shall not apply to claims of sexual abuse that occurred while the victim was a minor.

The Commission, upon finding that any claimant or award recipient has not fully cooperated with all law-enforcement agencies, may deny, reduce or withdraw any award, as the case may be.

History.
1976, c. 605; 1977, c. 215; 1985, c. 446; 2001, c. 855; 2005, c. 683.

Law Review.
For survey of Virginia criminal law for the year 1975-1976, see 62 Va. L. Rev. 1400 (1976).

CASE NOTES

Analysis in determining claims. — The analysis the director and the commission should have applied in determining claims was as follows: (1) determine eligibility; (2) determine whether the award is allowed; (3) determine the amount of the award; (4) apportion the award, if necessary; and (5) reduce the award to each claimant by the amount of payments received or to be received by that claimant from any collateral source as a result of the injury. Jennings v. Division of Crime Victims' Comp., 5 Va. App. 536, 365 S.E.2d 241 (1988).

NOTES FROM THE WORKERS' COMPENSATION COMMISSION

Persons who fail to fully cooperate with law-enforcement authorities, or who are criminally responsible for the crime upon which the claim is based, are not eligible for an award. Bailey v. Criminal Injuries Compensation Fund, 77 O.W.C 150 (1998).

The Commission may reduce the award or reject a crime victim's claim altogether, if the victim's conduct "contributed to the infliction of the injury." This latter criterion established the substantive basis for the Commission's inquiry, rather than the merely precatory reference to "innocence" found in the preamble at Section 19.2-368.1, since a provision specifically addressing the circumstances in question controls as opposed to a provision with an oblique reference. Bailey v. Criminal Injuries Compensation Fund, 77 O.W.C. 150 (1998).

Where the police report of the crime does not indicate that the victim was engaged in any criminal conduct, or that he was armed, or that he contributed in any way to the infliction of his own injury, but at most suggests that he was present in someone's home where marijuana may have been sold, there is no basis for denying or reducing the claim. Bailey v. Criminal Injuries Compensation Fund, 77 O.W.C. 150 (1998).

§ 19.2-368.11. Repealed by Acts 1986, c. 457.

§ 19.2-368.11:1. Amount of award.

A. Compensation for Total Loss of Earnings: An award made pursuant to this chapter for total loss of earnings which results directly from incapacity incurred by a crime victim shall be payable during total incapacity to the victim or to such other eligible person, at a weekly compensation rate equal to 66 ⅔ percent of the victim's average weekly wages. The total amount of weekly compensation shall not exceed $600. The victim's average weekly wages shall be determined as provided in § 65.2-101.

B. Compensation for Partial Loss of Earnings: An award made pursuant to this chapter for partial loss of earnings which results directly from incapacity incurred by a crime victim shall be payable during incapacity at a weekly rate equal to 66 ⅔ percent of the difference between the victim's average weekly wages before the injury and the weekly wages which the victim is able to earn thereafter. The combined total of actual weekly earnings and compensation for partial loss of earnings shall not exceed $600 per week.

C. Compensation for Loss of Earnings of Parent of Minor Victim: The parent or guardian of a minor crime victim may receive compensation for loss of earnings, calculated as specified in subsections A and B, for time spent obtaining medical treatment for the child and for accompanying the child to, attending or participating in investigative, prosecutorial, judicial, adjudicatory and post-conviction proceedings.

D. Compensation for Dependents of a Victim Who Is Killed: If death results to a victim of crime entitled to benefits, dependents of the victim shall be entitled to compensation in accordance with the provisions of §§ 65.2-512 and 65.2-515 in an amount not to exceed the maximum aggregate payment or the maximum weekly compensation which would have been payable to the deceased victim under this section.

E. Compensation for Unreimbursed Medical Costs, Funeral Expenses, Services, etc.: Awards may also be made on claims or portions of claims based upon the claimant's actual expenses incurred as are determined by the Commission to be appropriate, for (i) unreimbursed medical expenses or indebtedness reasonably incurred for medical expenses; (ii) expenses reasonably incurred in obtaining ordinary and necessary services in lieu of those the victim would have performed, for the benefit of himself and his family, if he had not been a victim of crime; (iii) expenses directly related to funeral or burial, not to exceed $5,000; (iv) expenses attributable to pregnancy resulting from forcible rape; (v) mental health counseling for survivors as defined under subdivisions A 2 and A 4 of § 19.2-368.4, not to exceed $2,500 per claim; (vi) reasonable and necessary moving expenses, not to exceed $1,000, incurred by a victim or survivors as defined under subdivisions A 2 and A 4 of § 19.2-368.4; and (vii) any other reasonable and necessary expenses and indebtedness incurred as a direct result of the injury or death upon which such claim is based, not otherwise specifically provided for. Notwithstanding any other provision of law, a person who is not eligible for an award under subsection A of § 19.2-368.4 who pays expenses directly related to funeral or burial is eligible for reimbursement subject to the limitations of this section.

F. Notwithstanding the provisions of subdivision 3 of § 19.2-368.10, §§ 19.2-368.5, 19.2-368.5:1, 19.2-368.6, 19.2-368.7, 19.2-368.8, subsection G of this section, and § 19.2-368.16, the Criminal Injuries Compensation Fund shall pay for physical evidence recovery kit examinations conducted on victims of sexual assault. Any individual that submits to and completes a physical evidence recovery kit examination shall be considered to have met the reporting and cooperation requirements of this chapter. Funds paid for physical evidence recovery kit collection shall not be offset against the Fund's maximum allowable award as provided in subsection H. Payments may be subject to negotiated agreements with the provider. Healthcare providers that complete physical evidence recovery kit examinations may bill the Fund directly subject to the provisions of § 19.2-368.5:2. The Commission shall develop policies for a distinct payment process for physical evidence recovery kit examination expenses as required under subdivision 1 of § 19.2-368.3.

In order for the Fund to consider additional crime-related expenses, victims shall file with the Fund following the provisions of this chapter and Criminal Injuries Compensation Fund policy.

G. Any claim made pursuant to this chapter shall be reduced by the amount of any payments received or to be received as a result of the injury from or on behalf of the person who committed the crime or from any other public or private source, including an emergency award by the Commission pursuant to § 19.2-368.9.

H. To qualify for an award under this chapter, a claim must have a minimum value of $100, and payments for injury or death to a victim of crime, to the victim's dependents or to others entitled to payment for covered expenses, after being reduced as provided in subsection G, shall not exceed $25,000 in the aggregate.

History.
1986, c. 457; 1988, c. 748; 1989, c. 335; 1990, c. 552; 1992, c. 687; 1996, c. 86; 1998, c. 484; 2000, c. 847; 2002, c. 665; 2005, c. 683; 2007, c. 381; 2008, cc. 203, 251.

The 2007 amendments.
The 2007 amendment by c. 381 substituted "$25,000" for "$15,000" in subsection G.

The 2008 amendments.
The 2008 amendments by cc. 203 and 251 are identical, and inserted subsection F; redesignated former subsections F and G as subsections G and H; and substituted "subsection G" for "subsection F" in subsection H.

Michie's Jurisprudence.
For related discussion, see 5B M.J. Criminal Procedure, § 2.

CASE NOTES

The language of former § 19.2-368.11 was mandatory rather than discretionary. It required compensation for loss of earnings in accordance with the Workers' Compensation Act schedule. Marchand v. Division of Crime Victims' Comp., 230 Va. 460, 339 S.E.2d 175 (1986).

Under the mandatory provision of former § 19.2-368.11, victim was entitled to receive the compensation for lost earnings prescribed in former § 65.1-56 (now § 65.2-503) for the loss of sight in his eye, subject of course to the statutory limitation of $12,500 in the aggregate. Marchand v. Division of Crime Victims' Comp., 230 Va. 460, 339 S.E.2d 175 (1986).

Limited purpose to provide some assistance to victims with no other source of aid. — The provision for reducing the award indicates that the statute has a limited purpose to provide some assistance for those victims or dependents who have no other source of aid. The statute plainly does not intend that payment from a collateral source to a claimant who may have no legal obligation to provide assistance to other dependents of the crime victim will preclude an award to other claimants. Jennings v. Division of Crime Victims' Comp., 5 Va. App. 536, 365 S.E.2d 241 (1988) (decided under § 19.2-368.12 (c) before the version of that subsection was deleted by Acts 1989, c. 335).

Amounts received from collateral sources more than maximum allowable amounts. — When one claimant receives from collateral sources more than the maximum allowable amount under subsection C it does not preclude an award to other claimants regardless of whether any other claimants receive collateral funds or not. Jennings v. Division of Crime Victims' Comp., 5 Va. App. 536, 365 S.E.2d 241 (1988) (decided under § 19.2-368.12 (c) before the version of that subsection was deleted by Acts 1989, c. 335).

Social security payments are funds to be received as a result of the injury from any other public source; as provided by subsection C of § 19.2-368.12, however, if the social security payments were to cease before the limit of the award is reached, the claimant would be entitled to the balance of an award from the Crime Victims' Compensation Fund. Jennings v. Division of Crime Victims' Comp., 5 Va. App. 536, 365 S.E.2d 241 (1988) (decided under § 19.2-368.12 (c) before the version of that subsection was deleted by Acts 1989, c. 335).

Analysis in determining claims. — The analysis the director and the commission should have applied in determining claims was as follows: (1) determine eligibility; (2) determine whether the award is allowed; (3) determine the amount of the award; (4) apportion the award, if necessary; and (5) reduce the award to each claimant by the amount of payments received or to be received by that claimant from any collateral source as a result of the injury. Jennings v. Division of Crime Victims' Comp., 5 Va. App. 536, 365 S.E.2d 241 (1988).

NOTES FROM THE WORKERS' COMPENSATION COMMISSION

The Act governing the Criminal Injuries Compensation Fund is remedial in nature. It provides a system of redress for specified individuals who have suffered loss due to the commission of a crime. The addition of this form of compensation was calculated to fill what was perceived to be a gap in available remedies. This being the case, it is axiomatic that the statute ... be liberally construed to promote its beneficent purpose," and its provisions "should be read so as to promote the ability of the enactment to remedy the mischief at which it is directed." Albrecht v. Criminal Injuries Compensation Fund, 78 O.W.C. 42 (1999).

Wage-loss benefits not appropriate where victim presented no medical evidence showing that a medical condition caused by the crime limited the amount of work the victim could perform. In Re: Mooring, CV File No. 01-0365 (Aug. 20, 2003).

A crime victim may be entitled to an award of compensation for partial loss of earnings equal to two-thirds of the difference between the victim's average weekly wage before the injury, and what the victim "is able to earn thereafter." The Commission observed that the quoted language is identical to that used by the legislature in Code § 65.2-502, and construed it accordingly. Before the Commission will award benefits for partial loss of earnings, the victim must prove that he has reasonably marketed his residual capacity, thereby affirmatively establishing the extent of his economic disability. Mooring v. Criminal Injuries Compensation Fund, CV File

No. 01-0365 (September 19, 2002).

Eligibility for a Crime Victim's award is decided in the following fashion: (1) is the claimant eligible for an award; (2) is an award allowed; (3) what is the amount of the award; and (4) must the award amount be reduced or rescinded. Albrecht v. Criminal Injuries Compensation Fund, 78 O.W.C. 42 (1999).

Subsections (A) and (B) of § 19.2-368.11:1 provide that awards for total or partial loss of earnings must result directly from "incapacity incurred by a crime victim." Subsections (A) and (B) of § 19.2-368.11:1 apply only to loss of earnings incurred by victims who survive a crime but are incapacitated by the crime. These subsections are inapplicable to loss of earnings for the victim of a homicide. Cincotta v. Criminal Injuries Compensation Fund, 78 O.W.C. 132 (1999).

Subsection (C) of § 19.2-368.11:1 provides compensation for loss of support for surviving dependents of a victim who is killed as a result of the crime. However, where the claimant is a 25-year-old adult and was not dependent upon his mother, the homicide victim, he does not qualify for this benefit. Cincotta v. Criminal Injuries Compensation Fund, 78 O.W.C. 132 (1999).

The statutes governing the Criminal Injuries Compensation Fund do not specifically address the issue of pre-authorization of medical services. Virginia Code § 19.2-368.11:1(D), which specifies that awards may be made on claims or portions of claims based upon the claimant's actual expenses incurred as are determined by the Commission to be appropriate, does not prohibit pre-authorization of payment prior to the receipt of medical treatment. Pre-authorization is simply a representation to the health care provider that the Fund will pay reasonable and necessary costs of treatment related to the assault at the usual and customary rate. Morrison v. Victims of Crimes Compensation Act, 77 O.W.C. 239 (1998).

Claims for psychological services for survivors of a homicide victim are limited to a maximum amount of $1,000, but that amount must be reduced for any payments [collateral resources] received or to be received as a result of the injury from or on behalf of the person who committed the crime or from any other public or private source. Albrecht v. Criminal Injuries Compensation Fund, 78 O.W.C. 42 (1999).

Where the crime victim is otherwise precluded from receiving necessary reconstructive dental work, and it is likely that an award will be issued, it is appropriate for the Criminal Injuries Compensation Fund to issue a statement of pre-authorization. Morrison v. Victims of Crimes Compensation Act, 77 O.W.C. 239 (1998).

The Commission adopted a policy on November 4, 1998, which provided that "[t]he Fund may pay up to one thousand dollars for crime scene clean-up when a crime resulting in physical injury occurs in a residence.... Requests for Awards for Crime Scene Clean-Up involving automobiles will be decided by the Commission judicially on a case-by-case basis." Montgomery v. Criminal Injuries Compensation Fund, 78 O.W.C. 276 (1999).

The Commission interprets its crime scene clean-up policy to cover replacement and clean-up of items damaged by stains resulting from the police use of graphite at the crime scene. However, it does not cover payment for items taken by the police as evidence. Montgomery v. Criminal Injuries Compensation Fund, 78 O.W.C. 276 (1999).

Expenses for damages to a stolen automobile and loss of use of the victim's dwelling during the police department's investigation are not compensable under the Crime Victim's Compensation Act. The Act makes no provision for reimbursement for property loss. Cincotta v. Criminal Injuries Compensation Fund, 78 O.W.C. 132 (1999).

The Commission has made several policy determinations regarding collateral payments. Aid to Families with Dependent Children (AFDC) benefits and food stamps will no longer be deducted from a criminal injuries award as a collateral resource. Similarly, annual leave or paid vacation time will not be deducted from a claimant's criminal injuries award for lost wages, although sick leave will be considered a collateral resource. Finally, when the Criminal Injuries Compensation Fund suspects that a claim may be compensable under the Virginia Workers' Compensation Act, the claim will no longer be denied on that basis. Rather, the claim will be deferred until a decision under the Virginia Workers' Compensation Act is made. At that point, the issue of collateral payments will be addressed by the Criminal Injuries Compensation Fund. Albrecht v. Criminal Injuries Compensation Fund, 78 O.W.C. 42 (1999).

In this case, the claimants request that they be reimbursed for their out-of-pocket expenses incurred for psychological counseling necessitated by the death of their son, who was a homicide victim. These expenses are in the nature of medical expenses, and the claimants established that their health insurance company will not pay for the first $1,000.00 of psychological counseling. While each has received proceeds of life insurance policies on the death of their son, the Commission noted that life insurance is generally designed to compensate for loss of companionship and financial support, not medical expenses. The Commission held, therefore, that the life insurance proceeds should not be deducted as a collateral resource from the awards for psychological counseling. Albrecht v. Criminal Injuries Compensation Fund, 78 O.W.C. 42 (1999).

Subsection (E) of § 19.2-368.11:1, informally referred to as the "collateral resource" rule, provides that any claim for crime victim's benefits shall be reduced by the amount of any payments received or to be received as a result of the injury from or on behalf of the person who committed the crime or from any other public or private source, including an emergency award by the Commission. The Commission has held that life insurance proceeds should not be considered a collateral resource to be deducted from the costs of survivor's psychological counseling. Cincotta v. Criminal Injuries Compensation Fund, 78 O.W.C. 132 (1999).

With respect to victims' estates, the Commission has held that only that amount of a deceased victim's estate that both (i) exceeds $10,000 and (ii) is actually received by the claimant may be deducted from an award for lost wages under the Act. Neither life insurance proceeds nor the value of a deceased victim's estate will be deducted from awards for funeral expenses. Cincotta v. Criminal Injuries Compensation Fund, 78 O.W.C. 132 (1999).

The Commission policy of awarding no more than $1,000.00 towards crime-scene clean-up costs described in *In Re: Montgomery,* 78 OWC 276 (1999), may be overcome. If the costs associated with crime-scene clean up exceed $1,000.00, and the clean-up costs directly flowed from the crime itself, not from police investigative methods, the Commission may award more than $1,000.00 as "other reasonable and necessary expenses and indebtedness incurred as a direct result of the injury or death upon which such claim is based." In Re: Constance D. Yount, CV File No. 01-0330 (October 16, 2001).

The collateral source rule did not prevent the claimant from recovering medical expenses in this matter. Recovery of those amounts paid by a private health insurer, over and above the victim's co-payment, would be barred by the rule. However, amounts received by the claimant pursuant to a policy of life insurance or inheritance of the victim's estate, are not considered collateral sources. In Re: Constance D. Yount, CV File No. 01-0330 (October 16, 2001).

§ 19.2-368.12. Awards not subject to execution or attachment; apportionment; reductions.

A. No award made pursuant to this chapter shall be subject to execution or attachment other than for expenses resulting from the injury which is the basis for the claim.

B. If there are two or more persons entitled to an award as a result of the death of a person which is the direct result of a crime, the award shall be apportioned among the claimants.

C. In determining the amount of an award, the Commission shall determine whether, because of his conduct, the victim of such crime contributed to the infliction of his injury, and the Commission shall reduce the amount of the award or reject the claim altogether, in accordance with such determination; provided, however, that the Commission may disregard for this purpose the responsibility of the victim for his own injury where the record shows that such responsibility was attributable to efforts by the victim to prevent a crime or an attempted crime from occurring in his presence, or to apprehend a person who had committed a crime in his presence or had, in fact, committed a felony.

History.
1976, c. 605; 1977, c. 215; 1989, c. 335.

Law Review.
For article on the need for reform of and a proposed revision of Virginia's Exemption Statutes, see 37 Wash. & Lee L. Rev. 127 (1980).

CASE NOTES

Analysis in determining claims. — The analysis the director and the commission should have applied in determining claims was as follows: (1) determine eligibility; (2) determine whether the award is allowed; (3) determine the amount of the award; (4) apportion the award, if necessary; and (5) reduce the award to each claimant by the amount of payments received or to be received by that claimant from any collateral source as a result of the injury. Jennings v. Division of Crime Victims' Comp., 5 Va. App. 536, 365 S.E.2d 241 (1988).

Illustrative cases. — Where record disclosed that although bad blood existed between victim and assailant, victim confronted assailant under circumstances involving the consumption of alcohol and intoxication, engaged in an argument with assailant, smacked assailant in the face, and later approached assailant outside and laid his hand upon assailant's shoulder, and it was then that assailant stabbed victim, these circumstances sufficiently demonstrated a contributory chain of causation flowing from the initial confrontation to the ultimate stabbing of victim by assailant, and thus supported the commission's determination that victim contributed to the infliction of his injuries. Hoban v. Virginia Workers' Comp. Comm'n, No. 2236-94-1 (Ct. of Appeals Nov. 7, 1995).

NOTES FROM THE WORKERS' COMPENSATION COMMISSION

§ 19.2-368.6(D) creates a rebuttable presumption that the victim did not contribute to her injury. Garwacke v. Criminal Injuries Compensation Fund, 78 O.W.C. 253 (1999).

The Commission may reduce the award or reject a crim victim's claim altogether, if the victim's conduct "contributed to the infliction of the injury . . ." This latter criterion establishes the substantive basis for the Commission's inquiry, rather than the merely precatory reference to "innocence" found in the preamble at Section 19.2-368.1, since a provision specifically addressing the circumstances in question controls as opposed to a provision with an oblique reference. Bailey v. Criminal Injuries Compensation Fund, 77 O.W.C. 150 (1998).

Where the police report of the crime does not indicate that the victim was engaged in any criminal conduct, or that he was armed, or that he contributed in any way to the infliction of his own injury, but at most suggests that he was present in someone's home where marijuana may have been sold, there is no basis for denying or reducing the claim. Bailey v. Criminal Injuries Compensation Fund, 77 O.W.C. 150 (1998).

The claimant, a minor, attended a party and drank some beer. Without her knowledge, the beer was spiked with a hallucinogen. Because of a reaction to that drug, the claimant required medical treatment. The Commission found that there was no evidence that her actions proximately contributed to her injury. She was not intoxicated, she did not consent to ingesting the drug, nor was she aware of, or able to reasonably foresee, that another person at the party would illegally and secretly place drugs into her drink. The Commission concluded that being at the party and drinking beer were not such acts as would alert the claimant that she was placing herself in imminent danger, and concluded that her actions did not proximately contribute to her injury. Garwacke v. Criminal Injuries Compensation Fund, 78 O.W.C. 253 (1999).

In determining the amount of an award, the Commission must

determine whether the crime victim contributed to the infliction of his injury. If it determines that the victim contributed to the infliction of his injury to some degree, the Commission is required to reduce the amount of the award, or reject the claim altogether. In this case, the Commission reduced the claimant's award by 50%, noting that the victim was apparently aware of the possibility of a fight with his assailant, and had been threatened with physical violence. Nevertheless, the victim decided to confront the assailant, was beaten during the confrontation, and died later from massive head trauma. In Re: Claim of Tiffany D. Compton, CV File No. 01-0211 (June 12, 2001).

The Commission reduced the victim's award by 25%, pursuant to Code § 19.2-368.12(C), for actions taken that contributed to the injury for which benefits are sought. The victim was drinking and wagering on a game of pool. When the assailant refused to pay on his wagering losses, the victim removed his jacket and challenged the assailant to a fight. Because the victim was engaged in illegal betting, and the evidence showed he provoked the attack that resulted, the Commission agreed that reducing the award by 25% was appropriate. In Re: Claim of Randy E. Grimstead, CV File No. 01-0460 (July 24, 2001).

§ 19.2-368.13. Repealed by Acts 1984, c. 619.

§ 19.2-368.14. Public record; exception.

Except as provided in § 19.2-368.6 concerning juvenile claimants or victims, the record of any proceedings under this chapter shall be a public record; provided, however, that any record or report obtained by the Commission, the confidentiality of which is protected by any other law or regulation, shall remain confidential, subject to such law or regulation.

History.
1976, c. 605; 1994, c. 834.

§ 19.2-368.15. Subrogation of Commonwealth to claimant's right of action; lien in favor of the Commonwealth; disposition of funds collected.

Acceptance of an award made pursuant to this chapter shall subrogate the Commonwealth, to the extent of such award, to any right or right of action accruing to the claimant or the victim to recover payments on account of losses resulting from the crime with respect to which the award is made. However, except as otherwise provided in subsection G of § 19.2-305.1, the Commonwealth shall not institute any proceedings in connection with its right of subrogation under this section within one year from the date of commission of the crime, unless any claimant or victim's right or action shall have been previously terminated. All funds collected by the Commonwealth in a proceeding instituted pursuant to this section shall be paid over to the Comptroller for deposit into the Criminal Injuries Compensation Fund.

Whenever any person receives an award from the Criminal Injuries Compensation Fund, the Commonwealth shall have a lien for the total amount paid by the Fund, or any portion thereof compromised pursuant to the authority granted under § 2.2-514, on the claim of such injured person or his

personal representative against the person, firm, or corporation who is alleged to have caused such injuries. The Fund's lien shall be inferior to any lien for payment of reasonable attorney fees and costs, but shall be superior to all other liens created by § 8.01-66.2. The injured person may file a petition or motion to reduce the lien and apportion the recovery pursuant to § 8.01-66.9. The Fund's lien shall become effective when notice is provided pursuant to § 8.01-66.5 and liability shall attach pursuant to § 8.01-66.6.

History.
1976, c. 605; 1983, c. 227; 2013, c. 273.

The 2013 amendments.
The 2013 amendment by c. 273 inserted "except as otherwise provided in subsection G of § 19.2-305.1" in the second sentence of the first paragraph, and added the second paragraph.

NOTES FROM THE WORKERS' COMPENSATION COMMISSION

Fund's right of subrogation extends to victim's personal representative; Act establishes right of subrogation to rights accruing to claimant or victim, but not explicitly victim's personal representative; Act defines "victim" as person injured or killed by crime, and thus subrogation rights found to extend to both living victim and deceased victim, through personal representative. In Re: Debt Set-Off Matter of Fitzgerald, CV File No. 00-705 (Apr. 30, 2003).

Fund's subrogation right based on rights accruing to victim, and because victim's receipt of homeowner's insurance benefits from tortfeasor's policy would not diminish tortfeasor's liability in civil claim by victim by action of collateral-source rule, Fund's subrogation right similarly not diminished. In Re: Debt Set-Off Matter of Bradsher, CV File No. 00-545 (Jan. 24, 2003).

A person, against whom subrogation recovery is sought by setting-off the subrogation amount against the person's tax refund, is entitled to a hearing before the Commission to determine if the underlying debt is valid. The mere fact that the person was convicted of the underlying crime, from which the debt to the state arose, does not eliminate the need for a hearing as to the validity of the debt for which a tax refund set-off is claimed. The alleged debtor was not a party to the proceeding before the Criminal Injuries Compensation Fund ("C.I.C.F."), and did not have notice of it. Accepting the debt determination of the C.I.C.F., without allowing the putative debtor a hearing on its validity, would result in an unlawful taking of property, and would deprive him of his due process rights. In Re: Debt Set-Off Matter of Christopher R. Kowalski, CV File No. 99-1056 (December 29, 2000).

The Commission is charged in subrogation cases involving tax refund forfeitures, pursuant to Virginia Code §§ 58.1-520 et seq., to determine whether the claim against the debtor is "valid." A conviction of the underlying crime does not preclude the defendant from challenging the underlying facts in a subsequent action for civil damages. A conviction or acquittal in the criminal action does not establish in a subsequent civil action the truth of the facts upon which such conviction was based. The conviction is inadmissible evidence for this purpose. Therefore, when the underlying debt is challenged by the defendant, the Commission must give him an opportunity to be heard, and the evidence presented should be considered before rendering a final decision. In Re: Claim of Michael D. McFarland, CV File No. 97-970 (February 22, 2001).

The Commission rejected the debtor's argument that any set-off against his tax return should be limited to the amount of restitution he was ordered to pay as a part of his conviction. The victim's right to seek civil redress under Code § 8.01-243(B) is not affected by any sentence imposed by the court resulting from a criminal conviction. The Fund's rights following entry of an award are coextensive with the victim's, and the fund is subrogated to the victim's right to redress. Accordingly, the Circuit Court's restitution order does not preclude the Fund from seeking to setoff any amounts paid by the

Fund exceeding the restitution order. McFarland v. Criminal Injuries Compensation Fund, CV File No. 97-970 (August 29, 2002).

§ 19.2-368.16. Claims to be made under oath.

All claims shall be made under oath. Any person who asserts a false claim under the provisions of this chapter shall be guilty of perjury and, in addition, shall be subject to prosecution under the provisions of Article 3 (§ 18.2-95 et seq.) of Chapter 5 of Title 18.2, and shall further forfeit any benefit received and shall reimburse and repay the Commonwealth for payments received or paid on his behalf pursuant to any of the provisions hereunder.

History.
1976, c. 605.

§ 19.2-368.17. Public information program.

The Commission shall establish and conduct a public information program to assure extensive and continuing publicity and public awareness of the provisions of this chapter. The public information program shall include brochures, posters and public service advertisements for television, radio and print media for dissemination to the public of information regarding the right to compensation for innocent victims of crime, including information on the right to file a claim, the scope of coverage, and the procedures to be utilized incident thereto.

Whenever a crime which directly resulted in personal physical injury to, or death of, an individual is reported within the time required by § 19.2-368.10, the law-enforcement agency to which the report is made shall make reasonable efforts, where practicable, to notify the victim or other potential claimant in writing on forms prepared by the Commission of his or her possible right to file a claim under this chapter. In any event, no liability or cause of action shall arise from the failure to so notify a victim of crime or other potential claimant.

History.
1976, c. 605; 1986, cc. 457, 472.

§ 19.2-368.18. Criminal Injuries Compensation Fund.

A. There is hereby created a special fund to be administered by the Comptroller, known as the Criminal Injuries Compensation Fund.

B. Whenever the costs provided for in §§ 17.1-275.1, 17.1-275.2, 17.1-275.3, 17.1-275.4, 17.1-275.7, 17.1-275.8, or § 17.1-275.9 or subsections B or C of § 16.1-69.48:1 are assessed, a portion of the costs, as specified in those sections, shall be paid over to the Comptroller to be deposited into the Criminal Injuries Compensation Fund. Under no condition shall a political subdivision be held liable for the payment of this sum.

C. No claim shall be accepted under the provisions of this chapter when the crime that gave rise to such claim occurred prior to July 1, 1977.

D. Sums available in the Criminal Injuries Compensation Fund shall be used for the purpose of payment of the costs and expenses necessary for the administration of this chapter and for the payment of claims pursuant to this chapter.

E. All revenues deposited into the Criminal Injuries Compensation Fund, and appropriated for the purposes of this chapter, shall be immediately available for the payment of claims.

History.
1976, c. 605; 1978, c. 413; 1980, c. 521; 1985, c. 230; 1988, c. 748; 1993, c. 434; 1996, cc. 760, 976; 2002, c. 831.

Cross references.
As to the authority to deposit unclaimed court ordered restitution payments into the Criminal Injuries Compensation Fund, see § 19.2-305.1. For provision that commissions shall not be allowed to a clerk of court on costs collected pursuant to this section, see § 58.1-3176.

Law Review.
For survey of Virginia criminal law for the year 1975-1976, see 62 Va. L. Rev. 1400 (1976). For survey of Virginia criminal law for the year 1977-1978, see 64 Va. L. Rev. 1407 (1978).

Michie's Jurisprudence.
For related discussion, see 5B M.J. Criminal Procedure, §§ 90, 99.

CASE NOTES

Purpose of 1985 amendment to subsection E. — Subsection E of this section was rewritten in 1985, apparently to remove any limitations on the receipt of federal funds, federal assistance having become available with the passage of the Comprehensive Crime Control Act of 1984. Another reason for the 1985 amendment to subsection E of this section may simply have been that the limitation of using funds from prior years could have proved burdensome. United States v. Robertson, 638 F. Supp. 1202 (E.D. Va. 1986).

"Additional costs" are form of punishment. — The "additional costs" mandated by the Virginia victim compensation statute are a form of punishment. United States v. Robertson, 638 F. Supp. 1202 (E.D. Va. 1986).

Special assessment inapplicable to drunk-driving offense committed on federal enclave. — As drunken driving offenses are excepted from Virginia's "additional cost" provision in this section, no punishment exists in state law similar to the federal assessments in the Assimilative Crimes Act, 18 U.S.C. § 13, and for that reason the special assessment cannot apply to drunken driving offenses committed in Virginia on a federal enclave. United States v. Robertson, 638 F. Supp. 1202 (E.D. Va. 1986).

CHAPTER 21.2.

PROFITS FROM CRIME.

§ 19.2-368.19. Definitions.

For purposes of this chapter, the following terms shall have the following meanings unless the context requires otherwise:

"*Defendant*" means any person who pleads guilty to, is convicted of, or is found not guilty by reason of insanity with respect to a felony resulting in physical injury to or death of another person.

"*Division*" means the Division of Crime Victims' Compensation.

"*Interested party*" means the victim, the defendant, and any transferee of proceeds due the defendant under a contract, the person with whom the defendant has contracted, the prosecuting attorney for the Commonwealth, and the Division of Crime Victims' Compensation.

"*Victim*" means a person who suffers personal, physical, mental, emotional, or pecuniary loss as a direct result of a crime and includes the spouse, parent, child, or sibling of the victim.

History.
1990, c. 549; 1992, c. 681.

Research references.
David B. Smith, Prosecution and Defense of Forfeiture Cases (Matthew Bender).

Michie's Jurisprudence.
For related discussion, see 14B M.J. Penalties and Forfeitures, § 4.

§ 19.2-368.20. Special order of escrow.

A. Any proceeds or profits received or to be received directly or indirectly, except property that may be forfeited to the Commonwealth pursuant to §§ 19.2-386.15 through 19.2-386.31, by a defendant or a transferee of that defendant from any source, as a direct or indirect result of his crime or sentence, or the notoriety which such crime or sentence has conferred upon him, shall be subject to a special order of escrow.

B. Income from the defendant's employment in a position unrelated to his crime or the notoriety which such crime has conferred upon him but obtained through the assistance of or rehabilitative training by correctional or mental health programs or personnel shall not be subject to a special order of escrow under this section, and nothing in this section shall be construed to prohibit or hinder the return of property belonging to victims of crime to its rightful owners. Any proceeds from a contract relating to a depiction or discussion of the defendant's crime in a movie, book, newspaper, magazine, radio or television production, or live entertainment or publication of any kind shall not be subject to a special order of escrow unless an integral part of the work is a depiction or discussion of the defendant's crime or an impression of the defendant's thoughts, opinions, or emotions regarding such crime.

C. Upon petition of the attorney for the Commonwealth filed at any time after conviction of such defendant or his acquittal by reason of insanity and after notice to the interested parties, a hearing upon the motion and a finding for the Commonwealth, for good cause shown, any circuit court in which the petition is filed shall order that such proceeds be subject to a special order of escrow.

1. The petition shall be filed in the circuit court of the jurisdiction where the defendant was convicted or acquitted by reason of insanity.

2. The petition shall set forth in general terms the causes for entry of the special order of escrow, and be signed by the attorney for the Commonwealth.

3. Upon the filing of the petition, the clerk shall forthwith issue a warrant directed to the sheriff or other law-enforcement officer of the county or city, commanding him to take the property into his possession and hold the same subject to further proceedings in the cause. If for any cause the warrant was not executed, other like warrants may be successively issued until one is executed. The officer serving the warrant shall take the property into his possession and forthwith return the warrant and report to the clerk in writing.

4. Any person concerned in interest may appear and make defense to the petition, which may be done by answer on oath.

5. When the case is ready for trial, such issues of fact as are made by the pleadings, or as the court may direct, the court shall determine the whole matter of law and fact.

6. Expenses and costs incurred in the proceedings shall be paid as the court, in its discretion, shall determine; except that no costs shall be adjudged against the Commonwealth.

An order issued under this section shall require that the defendant and the person with whom the defendant contracts pay to the Division any proceeds due the defendant under the contract and the proceeds shall be placed in a special escrow account for the victims of the defendant's crime.

History.
1990, c. 549; 1992, c. 681; 2006, c. 414.

Law Review.
For note, "Son of Sam Laws: A Victim of the First Amendment?," see 49 Wash. & Lee L. Rev. 629 (1992).

§ 19.2-368.21. Distribution.

A. Proceeds paid to the Division under § 19.2-368.20 shall be retained in escrow in the Criminal Injuries Compensation Fund for five years after the date of the order, but during that five-year period may be levied upon to satisfy a money judgment rendered by a court or award of the Workers' Compensation Commission in favor of a victim of an offense for which the defendant has been convicted or acquitted by reason of insanity, or a legal representative of the victim.

B. If ordered by a circuit court in the interest of justice, after motion, notice to all interested parties, and opportunity for hearing, such escrow fund shall be used to:

1. First, satisfy court ordered restitution against a defendant and in favor of a victim;

2. Satisfy a money judgment rendered in the court hearing the matter, in favor of a victim of any offense for which the defendant has been convicted;

3. Pay for legal representation of the defendant in criminal proceedings, including the appeals process, to the extent the defendant's representation was paid for by the Commonwealth or an agency thereof. No more than 25% of the total proceeds in escrow may be used for legal representation; and

4. Pay any fines or costs assessed against the defendant by a court of the Commonwealth.

C. At the end of the five-year period, the remaining proceeds shall be paid into the Literary Fund. However, (i) if a civil action under this section is pending against the defendant, the proceeds shall be held in escrow until completion of the action or (ii) if the defendant has appealed his conviction and the appeals process is not final, the proceeds shall be held in escrow until the appeals process is final, and upon disposition of the charges favorable to the defendant, the Division shall immediately pay any money in the escrow account to the defendant.

History.
1990, c. 549; 1992, c. 681; 2006, c. 414.

§ 19.2-368.22. Actions to defeat chapter void.

Any action taken by any person convicted of a felony, whether by way of execution of a power of attorney, creation of corporate entities, or otherwise, to defeat the purpose of this chapter shall be void.

History.
1990, c. 549; 1992, c. 59.

CHAPTER 22.

ENFORCEMENT OF FORFEITURES.

Section
19.2-369 through 19.2-386. [Repealed.]

§§ 19.2-369 through 19.2-386. Repealed by Acts 2012, cc. 283 and 756, cl. 2.

Cross references.
For current provisions as to enforcement of forfeitures, see Chapter 22 (§ 19.2-386.1 et seq.).

Editor's note.
Former §§ 19.2-369 through 19.2-386, pertaining to enforcement of forfeitures, derived from: **19.2-369: Code 1950, §§ 19.1-17, 19.1-358; Acts 1960, c. 366; 1975, c. 495. 19.2-370:** Code 1950, § 19.1-359; Acts 1960, c. 366; 1975, c. 495. **19.2-371:** Code 1950, § 19.1-360; Acts 1960, c. 366; 1975, c. 495. **19.2-372:** Code 1950, § 19.1-361; Acts 1960, c. 366; 1975, c. 495. **19.2-373:** Code 1950, § 19.1-362; Acts 1960, c. 366; 1975, c. 495. **19.2-374:** Code 1950, § 19.1-363; Acts 1960, c. 366; 1975, c. 495. **19.2-375:** Code 1950, § 19.1-363.1; Acts 1960, c. 366; 1975, c. 495. **19.2-376:** Code 1950, § 19.1-363.2; Acts 1960, c. 366; 1975, c. 495. **19.2-377:** Code 1950, § 19.1-364; Acts 1960, c. 366; 1975, c. 495. **19.2-378:** Code 1950, § 19.1-365; Acts 1960, c. 366; 1975, c. 495. **19.2-379:** Code 1950, § 19.1-366; Acts 1960, c. 366; 1975, c. 495. **19.2-380:** Code 1950, §

19.1-367; Acts 1960, c. 366; 1975, c. 495. **19.2-381:** Code 1950, § 19.1-368; Acts 1960, c. 366; 1975, c. 495. **19.2-382:** Code 1950, § 19.1-369; Acts 1960, c. 366; 1975, c. 495. **19.2-383:** Code 1950, § 19.1-370; Acts 1960, c. 366; 1975, c. 495. **19.2-384:** Code 1950, § 19.1-371; Acts 1960, c. 366; 1975, c. 495. **19.2-385:** Code 1950, § 19.1-372; Acts 1960, c. 366; 1975, c. 495; 2005, c. 681. **19.2-386:** Code 1950, § 19.1-373; Acts 1960, c. 366; 1975, c. 495.

CHAPTER 22.1.

ENFORCEMENT OF FORFEITURES.

Section
19.2-386.1.   Commencing an action of forfeiture.
19.2-386.2.   Seizure of named property.
19.2-386.2:1. Notice to Commissioner of Department of Motor Vehicles; duties of Commissioner.
19.2-386.3.   Notice of seizure for forfeiture and notice of motion for judgment.
19.2-386.4.   Records and handling of seized property.
19.2-386.5.   Release of seized property.
19.2-386.6.   Bond to secure possession.
19.2-386.7.   Sale of property liable to deterioration.
19.2-386.8.   Exemptions.
19.2-386.9.   Appearance by owner or lien holder.
19.2-386.10.   Trial.
19.2-386.11.   Judgment of condemnation; destruction.
19.2-386.12.   Sale of forfeited property.
19.2-386.13.   Writ of error and supersedeas.
19.2-386.14.   Sharing of forfeited assets.

§ 19.2-386.1. Commencing an action of forfeiture.

Except as otherwise specifically provided by law, whenever any property is forfeited to the Commonwealth by reason of the violation of any law, or if any statute provides for the forfeiture of any property or money, or if any property or money be seized as forfeited for a violation of any of the provisions of this Code, the Commonwealth shall follow the procedures set forth in this chapter.

An action against any property subject to seizure under the provisions of Chapter 22.2 (§ 19.2-386.15 et seq.) shall be commenced by the filing of an information in the clerk's office of the circuit court. Any information shall be filed in the name of the Commonwealth by the attorney for the Commonwealth or may be filed by the Attorney General if so requested by the attorney for the Commonwealth. Venue for an action of forfeiture shall lie in the county or city where (i) the property is located, (ii) the property is seized, or (iii) an owner of the property could be prosecuted for the illegal conduct alleged to give rise to the forfeiture. Such information shall (a) name as parties defendant all owners and lienholders then known or of record and the trustees named in any deed of trust securing such lienholder, (b) specifically describe the property, (c) set forth in general terms the grounds for forfeiture of the named property, (d) pray that the same be condemned and sold or otherwise be disposed of according to law, and (e) ask that all persons concerned or interested be notified to appear and show cause why such property should not be forfeited. In all cases, an information shall be filed within three years of the date of actual discovery by the Commonwealth of the last act giving rise to the forfeiture or the action for forfeiture will be barred.

History.
1989, c. 690; 1991, c. 560; 2002, cc. 588, 623; 2004, c. 995; 2012, cc. 283, 756.

Cross references.
As to seizure of property used in connection with or derived from terrorism, see §§ 19.2-386.15, 57-59. As to forfeiture for violation of the Virginia Computer Crimes Act, §§ 18.2-152.1 et seq., see § 19.2-386.17.

The 2012 amendments.
The 2012 amendments by c. 283 and 756 are identical, and substituted "Enforcement of Forfeitures" for "Forfeitures in Drug Cases" in the chapter heading; added the first paragraph hereof; and in the present second paragraph, substituted "Chapter 22.2 (§ 19.2-386.15 et seq.)" for "§ 19.2-386.15 or § 19.2-386.22" in the first sentence, and substituted the clause (a) through (e) designators for the former (i) through (v) designators in the fourth sentence.

Law Review.
For note, "Applying the Eighth Amendment to Civil Forfeiture After Austin v. United States: Excessiveness and Proportionality," see 36 Wm. & Mary L. Rev. 235 (1994).

Research references.
David B. Smith, Prosecution and Defense of Forfeiture Cases (Matthew Bender).

Michie's Jurisprudence.
For related discussion, see 6B M.J. Drugs and Druggists, § 5; 14B M.J. Penalties and Forfeitures, § 4.

CASE NOTES

Language of section is mandatory. — The language of §§ 18.2-249 [now 19.2-386.22] and 19.2-386.1 through 19.2-386.14 is plain, unambiguous, and mandatory. Jenkins v. Commonwealth, 13 Va. App. 420, 411 S.E.2d 841 (1991).

Court's authority dependent upon adherence to provisions of section. — The subject matter jurisdiction necessary to forfeiture is conferred upon the trial court only through these several statutes (§§ 18.2-249 [now 19.2-386.22] and 19.2-386.1 through 19.2-386.14) and the court's authority is dependent upon scrupulous adherence to their provisions. Jenkins v. Commonwealth, 13 Va. App. 420, 411 S.E.2d 841 (1991).

Jurisdiction contingent on filing of information. — If the Commonwealth wishes to obtain title to property through the forfeiture provisions of §§ 19.2-386.1 through 19.2-386.14, it must file an information for forfeiture within 90 days of the date it physically takes the property into its possession. Failure to do so deprives a trial court of jurisdiction to consider the information for forfeiture. Commonwealth v. Brunson, 248 Va. 347, 448 S.E.2d 393 (1994).

CIRCUIT COURT OPINIONS

Invocation of right against self-incrimination. — In a civil forfeiture action, where defendant had previously pleaded guilty to gambling activities, defendant was not entitled to subsequently invoke his Fifth Amendment rights to avoid self-incrimination in the subsequent civil action because the records sought by the State were germane to defendant's illegal gambling activities and, in particular, the issue of whether the items seized from his residence were used in connection with, or derived from, those activities; the State's motion to compel production was granted. Commonwealth v. $71,919.00 United States Currency, 65 Va. Cir. 118, 2004 Va. Cir. LEXIS 151 (Fairfax County 2004).

§ 19.2-386.2. Seizure of named property.

A. When any property subject to seizure under Chapter 22.2 (§ 19.2-386.15 et seq.) or other provision under the Code has not been seized at the time an information naming that property is filed, the clerk of the circuit court or a judge of the circuit court, upon motion of the attorney for the Commonwealth wherein the information is filed, shall issue a warrant to the sheriff or other state or local law-enforcement officer authorized to serve criminal process in the jurisdiction where the property is located, describing the property named in the complaint and authorizing its immediate seizure.

B. In all cases of seizure of real property, a notice of lis pendens shall be filed with the clerk of the circuit court of the county or city wherein the property is located and shall be indexed in the land records in the name or names of those persons whose interests appear to be affected thereby.

History.
1989, c. 690; 2002, cc. 588, 623; 2004, c. 995; 2006, c. 766; 2012, cc. 283, 756.

The 2012 amendments.
The 2012 amendments by cc. 283 and 756 are identical, and substituted "Chapter 22.2 (§ 19.2-386.15 et seq.) or other provision under the Code" for "§ 19.2-386.15 or § 19.2-386.22" near the beginning of subsection A.

CASE NOTES

Language of section is mandatory. — The language of §§ 18.2-249 [now 19.2-386.22] and 19.2-386.1 through 19.2-386.14 is plain, unambiguous, and mandatory. Jenkins v. Commonwealth, 13 Va. App. 420, 411 S.E.2d 841 (1991).

Court's authority dependent upon adherence to provisions of section. — The subject matter jurisdiction necessary to forfeiture is conferred upon the trial court only through these several statutes (§§ 18.2-249 [now 19.2-386.22] and 19.2-386.1 through 19.2-386.14) and the court's authority is dependent upon scrupulous adherence to their provisions. Jenkins v. Commonwealth, 13 Va. App. 420, 411 S.E.2d 841 (1991).

§ 19.2-386.2:1. Notice to Commissioner of Department of Motor Vehicles; duties of Commissioner.

If the property seized is a motor vehicle required by the motor vehicle laws of Virginia to be registered, the attorney for the Commonwealth shall forthwith notify the Commissioner of the Department of Motor Vehicles, by certified mail, of such seizure and the motor number of the vehicle so seized, and the Commissioner shall promptly certify to such attorney for the Commonwealth the name and address of the person in whose name such vehicle is registered, together with the name and address of any person holding a lien thereon, and the amount thereof. The Commissioner shall also forthwith notify such registered owner and lienor, in writing, of the reported seizure and the county or city wherein such seizure was made.

The certificate of the Commissioner, concerning such registration and lien, shall be received in evidence in any proceeding, either civil or criminal, under any provision of this chapter, in which such facts may be material to the issue involved.

History.
2012, cc. 283, 756.

CASE NOTES

Editor's note.
The annotations below were decided under prior law.

Nature of proceeding. — A proceeding under former § 4-56 to have an automobile condemned and sold because of a violation of the Alcoholic Beverage Control Act was a proceeding in rem rather than in personam, and was a civil action against an automobile and not a criminal action against a person. Ives v. Commonwealth, 182 Va. 17, 27 S.E.2d 906 (1943).

Former § 4-56 did not contemplate that there shall be two informations filed at the same time. It made no provision for an untimely information filed by the attorney for the Commonwealth. Such information being a nullity, the situation was the same as if there had been no information filed. Cason v. Commonwealth, 181 Va. 297, 24 S.E.2d 435 (1943).

An information filed by the Attorney General does not take the place of any other information. It is filed because of the lack of a previous information. Cason v. Commonwealth, 181 Va. 297, 24 S.E.2d 435 (1943).

Information need not designate time of appearance. — Subsection (d) of former § 4-56 did not contemplate that the information to be filed by the attorney for the Commonwealth should designate the day or time when the persons cited therein should appear. Ives v. Commonwealth, 182 Va. 17, 27 S.E.2d 906 (1943).

Variance between information and notice not fatal. — In a proceeding under former § 4-56 to have an automobile condemned and sold, there was no fatal variance because the time set for the confiscation as set out in the information and the time set out in the published notice are not the same, since the time for the hearing is fixed by the notice, which is the process. Ives v. Commonwealth, 182 Va. 17, 27 S.E.2d 906 (1943).

Commonwealth's failure to file its information within the statutory 60-day period was fatal to the forfeiture proceeding of an automobile suspected to have been used in illegal drug business. Haina v. Commonwealth, 235 Va. 571, 369 S.E.2d 401 (1988).

Notice to owner by registered mail not necessary. — In a proceeding under former § 4-56, there was no merit in a contention that a registered letter should have been mailed to the owner of the automobile at his last known address, where the automobile bore a New York license and the attorney for the Commonwealth had no means of knowing and did not know who was the owner of the vehicle or the last known address of such owner. Ives v. Commonwealth, 182 Va. 17, 27 S.E.2d 906 (1943).

No affidavit is required as a basis for publication, it being entirely different from the order of publication which is required under § 8.01-316. Ives v. Commonwealth, 182 Va. 17, 27 S.E.2d 906 (1943).

Two weeks' requirement met. — Where there were two publications of the notice required by subsection (d) of former § 4-56, one on March 25th and one on April 1st and the return day of the latter was on April 24th, the two weeks' requirement of the section was met. Ives v. Commonwealth, 182 Va. 17, 27 S.E.2d 906 (1943).

§ 19.2-386.3. Notice of seizure for forfeiture and notice of motion for judgment.

A. If an information has not been filed, then upon seizure of any property under Chapter 22.2 (§ 19.2-386.15 et seq.) or other provision under the Code, the agency seizing the property shall forthwith notify in writing the attorney for the Commonwealth

in the county or city in which the seizure occurred, who shall, within 21 days of receipt of such notice, file a notice of seizure for forfeiture with the clerk of the circuit court. Such notice of seizure for forfeiture shall specifically describe the property seized, set forth in general terms the grounds for seizure, identify the date on which the seizure occurred, and identify all owners and lien holders then known or of record, including the treasurer of the locality in which the seized property is located. The clerk shall forthwith mail by first-class mail notice of seizure for forfeiture to the last known address of all identified owners and lien holders. When property has been seized under Chapter 22.2 (§ 19.2-386.15 et seq.) or other provision under the Code prior to filing an information, then an information against that property shall be filed within 90 days of the date of seizure or the property shall be released to the owner or lien holder.

B. Except as to corporations, all parties defendant shall be served, in accordance with § 8.01-296, with a copy of the information and a notice to appear prior to any motion for default judgment on the information. The notice shall contain a statement warning the party defendant that his interest in the property shall be subject to forfeiture to the Commonwealth unless within 30 days after service on him of the notice, or before the date set forth in the order of publication with respect to the notice, an answer under oath is filed in the proceeding setting forth (i) the nature of the defendant's claim, (ii) the exact right, title or character of the ownership or interest in the property and the evidence thereof, and (iii) the reason, cause, exemption or defense he may have against the forfeiture of his interest in the property, including but not limited to the exemptions set forth in § 19.2-386.8. Service upon corporations shall be made in accordance with § 8.01-299 or subdivision 1 or 2 of § 8.01-301; however, if such service cannot be thus made, it shall be made by publication in accordance with § 8.01-317.

History.
1989, c. 690; 1991, c. 560; 1996, c. 673; 2002, cc. 588, 623; 2004, c. 995; 2011, c. 83; 2012, cc. 283, 756.

The 2011 amendments.
The 2011 amendment by c. 83 added "including the treasurer of the locality in which the seized property is located" in the second sentence in subsection A.

The 2012 amendments.
The 2012 amendments by cc. 283 and 756 are identical, and substituted "Chapter 22.2 (§ 19.2-386.15 et seq.) or other provision under the Code" for "§ 19.2-386.15 or § 19.2-386.22" twice in subsection A.

CASE NOTES

Notice and hearing required before forfeiture. — Forfeitures of rights and property cannot be adjudged by legislative act, and confiscation without a judicial hearing after due notice would be void as not being by due process of law. Boggs v. Commonwealth, 76 Va. 989 (1882).

Language of section is mandatory. — The language of

§§ 18.2-249 [now 19.2-386.22] and 19.2-386.1 through 19.2-386.14 is plain, unambiguous, and mandatory. Jenkins v. Commonwealth, 13 Va. App. 420, 411 S.E.2d 841 (1991).

Court's authority dependent upon adherence to provisions of section. — The subject matter jurisdiction necessary to forfeiture is conferred upon the trial court only through these several statutes (§§ 18.2-249 [now 19.2-386.22] and 19.2-386.1 through 19.2-386.14 and the court's authority is dependent upon scrupulous adherence to their provisions. Jenkins v. Commonwealth, 13 Va. App. 420, 411 S.E.2d 841 (1991).

Jurisdiction contingent upon filing of information. — If the Commonwealth wishes to obtain title to property through the forfeiture provisions of §§ 19.2-386.1 through 19.2-386.14, it must file an information for forfeiture within 90 days of the date it physically takes the property into its possession. Failure to do so deprives a trial court of jurisdiction to consider the information for forfeiture. Commonwealth v. Brunson, 248 Va. 347, 448 S.E.2d 393 (1994).

Jurisdiction not contingent on filing timely notice with clerk. — The provision in this statute which states that the Commonwealth's attorney "shall" file a notice of seizure for forfeiture with the clerk of the circuit court within 21 days from the date the Commonwealth's attorney receives notice of the seizure is directory, not mandatory, and the failure to file such notice within the time provided does not deprive the circuit court of jurisdiction. Commonwealth v. Wilks, 260 Va. 194, 530 S.E.2d 665, 2000 Va. LEXIS 89 (2000), distinguishing Commonwealth v. Brunson, 248 Va. 347, 448 S.E. 2d 393 (1994), which dealt with the time limitation for filing the information when property had already been seized.

CIRCUIT COURT OPINIONS

Police officer was not immune from liability for failure to file information. — City police officer was not immune from liability in a car owner's action for damages and injunctive relief arising out of his seizure of her car in alleged violation of the notification requirements of § 19.2-386.3 because the cloak of sovereign governmental immunity does not extend to intentional torts. Mallory v. City of Richmond, 69 Va. Cir. 100, 2005 Va. Cir. LEXIS 340 (Richmond 2005).

City is immune from respondeat superior liability for failure to file information. — City was immune from respondeat superior liability in a car owner's action for damages and injunctive relief arising out of the seizure of her car by a city police officer in alleged violation of the notification requirements of § 19.2-386.3 because municipalities were immune from liability for intentional torts committed by employees during the performance of a governmental function. Mallory v. City of Richmond, 69 Va. Cir. 100, 2005 Va. Cir. LEXIS 340 (Richmond 2005).

Claims in conversion and trespass arose from failure to file information. — Vehicle owner stated a claim against a city police officer in conversion and trespass to chattels by alleging that the officer's seizure of her vehicle without complying with the notice requirements of § 19.2-386.3 or notifying her before turning the vehicle over to the lienholder damaged her by depriving her of the opportunity to secure her property by establishing one of the exemptions outlined in § 19.2-386.8; the officer's demurrer and plea of sovereign immunity were therefore overruled. Mallory v. City of Richmond, 69 Va. Cir. 100, 2005 Va. Cir. LEXIS 340 (Richmond 2005).

§ 19.2-386.4. Records and handling of seized property.

Any agency seizing property under § 19.2-386.2, Chapter 22.2 (§ 19.2-386.15 et seq.), or other provision under the Code, pending forfeiture and final disposition, may do any of the following:

1. Place the property under constructive seizure by posting notice of seizure for forfeiture on the property or by filing notice of seizure for forfeiture in any appropriate public record relating to property;

2. Remove the property to a storage area for safekeeping or, if the property is a negotiable instrument or money, deposit it in an interest-bearing account;

3. Remove the property to a place designated by the circuit court in the county or city wherein the property was seized; or

4. Provide for another custodian or agency to take custody of the property and remove it to an appropriate location within or without the jurisdiction of the circuit court in the county or city wherein the property was seized or in which the complaint was filed.

A report regarding the type of property subject to forfeiture and its handling pursuant to this section and § 19.2-386.5, and the final disposition of the property shall be filed by the seizing agency with the Department of Criminal Justice Services in accordance with regulations promulgated by the Board.

History.
1989, c. 690; 1991, c. 560; 2002, cc. 588, 623; 2004, c. 995; 2012, cc. 283, 756.

The 2012 amendments.
The 2012 amendments by cc. 283 and 756 are identical, and substituted "under § 19.2-386.2, Chapter 22.2 (§ 19.2-386.15 et seq.), or other provision under the Code" for "§§ § 19.2-386.2, 19.2-386.15 or § 19.2-386.22" in the introductory paragraph.

CASE NOTES

Language of section is mandatory. — The language of §§ 18.2-249 [now § 19.2-386.22] and 19.2-386.1 through 19.2-386.14 is plain, unambiguous, and mandatory. Jenkins v. Commonwealth, 13 Va. App. 420, 411 S.E.2d 841 (1991).

Court's authority dependent upon adherence to provisions of section. — The subject matter jurisdiction necessary to forfeiture is conferred upon the trial court only through these several statutes (§§ 18.2-249 [now § 19.2-386.22] and 19.2-386.1 through 19.2-386.14) and the court's authority is dependent upon scrupulous adherence to their provisions. Jenkins v. Commonwealth, 13 Va. App. 420, 411 S.E.2d 841 (1991).

§ 19.2-386.5. Release of seized property.

At any time prior to the filing of an information, the attorney for the Commonwealth in the county or city in which the property has been seized pursuant to Chapter 22.2 (§ 19.2-386.15 et seq.) or other provision under the Code may, in his discretion, upon the payment of costs incident to the custody of the seized property, return the seized property to an owner or lien holder, without requiring that the owner or lien holder post bond as provided in § 19.2-386.6, if he believes the property is properly exempt from forfeiture pursuant to § 19.2-386.8.

History.
1989, c. 690; 2002, cc. 588, 623; 2004, c. 995; 2012, cc. 283, 756.

The 2012 amendments.
The 2012 amendments by cc. 283 and 756 are identical, and substituted "Chapter 22.2 (§ 19.2-386.15 et seq.) or other provision under the Code" for "§ 19.2-386.15 or § 19.2-386.22."

CASE NOTES

Language of section is mandatory. — The language of §§ 18.2-249 [now § 19.2-386.22] and 19.2-386.1 through 19.2-386.14 is plain, unambiguous, and mandatory. Jenkins v. Commonwealth, 13 Va. App. 420, 411 S.E.2d 841 (1991).

Court's authority dependent upon adherence to provisions of section. — The subject matter jurisdiction necessary to forfeiture is conferred upon the trial court only through these several statutes (§§ 18.2-249 [now § 19.2-386.22] and 19.2-386.1 through 19.2-386.14) and the court's authority is dependent upon scrupulous adherence to their provisions. Jenkins v. Commonwealth, 13 Va. App. 420, 411 S.E.2d 841 (1991).

§ 19.2-386.6. Bond to secure possession.

If the owner or lien holder of the named property desires to obtain possession thereof before the hearing on the information filed against the same, such property shall be appraised by the clerk of the court where such information is filed. The clerk shall promptly cause the property to be appraised at its fair cash value, and forthwith make return thereof in writing to the court. Any appraisal fee shall be taxed as costs as provided in § 19.2-386.12. Upon the return of the appraisal, the owner or lien holder may give a bond payable to the Commonwealth, in a penalty of the amount equal to the appraised value of the property plus the court costs which may accrue, with security to be approved by the clerk and conditioned for the performance of the final judgment of the court, on the trial of the information. A further condition shall be that, if upon the hearing on the information, the judgment of the court is that such property, or any part thereof, or such interest and equity as the owner or lien holder may have therein, is forfeited, judgment may thereupon be entered against the obligors on such bond for the penalty thereof, without further or other proceedings against them thereon, to be discharged by the payment of the appraised value of the property so seized and forfeited, and costs. Upon such judgment, execution may issue, on which the clerk shall endorse, "No security to be taken." Upon giving of the bond, the property shall be delivered to the owner or lien holder.

History.
1989, c. 690.

CASE NOTES

Language of section is mandatory. — The language of §§ 18.2-249 [now § 19.2-386.22] and 19.2-386.1 through 19.2-386.14 is plain, unambiguous, and mandatory. Jenkins v. Commonwealth, 13 Va. App. 420, 411 S.E.2d 841 (1991).

Court's authority dependent upon adherence to provisions of section. — The subject matter jurisdiction necessary to forfeiture is conferred upon the trial court only through these several statutes (§§ 18.2-249 [now § 19.2-386.22] and 19.2-386.1 through 19.2-386.14) and the court's authority is dependent upon scrupulous adherence to their provisions. Jenkins v. Commonwealth, 13 Va. App. 420, 411 S.E.2d 841 (1991).

Discharge of bond. — An automobile belonging to defendant was seized, while being used by persons other than defendant in the illegal transportation of whiskey. Upon request of defendant and in compliance with former § 4-56, an appraisal was made, defendant was required to execute a bond, and the automobile was returned to him. But before the hearing he made an attempt to surrender the vehicle to the authorities in an effort to escape liability on the bond, whereupon the court properly held that the bond was conditioned upon the parties' abiding by the order of the court, and was to be discharged under the authority of former § 4-56 by the payment of the appraised value of the vehicle. Wray v. Commonwealth, 191 Va. 738, 62 S.E.2d 889 (1951) (decided under former § 4-56).

§ 19.2-386.7. Sale of property liable to deterioration.

If the property seized is perishable or liable to deterioration, decay, or injury by being detained in custody pending the proceedings, the circuit court for the county or city in which the information is filed or in which the property is located, may order the same to be sold upon such notice as the court, in its discretion, may deem proper and hold the proceeds of sale pending the final disposition of such proceedings.

History.
1989, c. 690.

CASE NOTES

Language of section is mandatory. — The language of §§ 18.2-249 [now § 19.2-386.22] and 19.2-386.1 through 19.2-386.14 is plain, unambiguous, and mandatory. Jenkins v. Commonwealth, 13 Va. App. 420, 411 S.E.2d 841 (1991).

Court's authority dependent upon adherence to provisions of section. — The subject matter jurisdiction necessary to forfeiture is conferred upon the trial court only through these several statutes (§§ 18.2-249 [now § 19.2-386.22] and 19.2-386.1 through 19.2-386.14) and the court's authority is dependent upon scrupulous adherence to their provisions. Jenkins v. Commonwealth, 13 Va. App. 420, 411 S.E.2d 841 (1991).

§ 19.2-386.8. Exemptions.

The following exemptions shall apply to property otherwise subject to forfeiture:

1. No conveyance used by any person as a lawfully certified common carrier in the transaction of business as a common carrier may be forfeited under the provisions of this section unless the owner of the conveyance was a consenting party or privy to the conduct giving rise to forfeiture or knew or had reason to know of it.

2. No conveyance may be forfeited under the provisions of this section for any conduct committed by a person other than the owner while the conveyance was unlawfully in the possession of a person other than the owner in violation of the criminal laws of this Commonwealth, or any other state, the District of Columbia, the United States or any territory thereof.

3. No owner's interest may be forfeited under this chapter if the court finds that:

a. He did not know and had no reason to know of the conduct giving rise to forfeiture;

b. He was a bona fide purchaser for value without notice;

c. The conduct giving rise to forfeiture occurred without his connivance or consent, express or implied; or

d. The conduct giving rise to forfeiture was committed by a tenant of a residential or commercial property owned by a landlord, and the landlord did not know or have reason to know of the tenant's conduct.

4. No lien holder's interest may be forfeited under this chapter if the court finds that:

a. The lien holder did not know of the conduct giving rise to forfeiture at the time the lien was granted;

b. The lien holder held a bona fide lien on the property subject to forfeiture and had perfected the same in the manner prescribed by law prior to seizure of the property; and

c. The conduct giving rise to forfeiture occurred without his connivance or consent, express or implied.

In the event the interest has been sold to a bona fide purchaser for value in order to avoid the provisions of this chapter, the Commonwealth shall have a right of action against the seller of the property for the proceeds of the sale.

History.
1989, c. 690; 2005, c. 883.

CASE NOTES

Editor's note.
The cases noted below were decided under former § 4-56, now repealed, which covered the same subject matter as this section.

He must show he was ignorant of illegal use. — Under subsection (i) of former § 4-56 it was not required that it be shown that the lienor knew of the use to be made of the vehicle at the time the lien was created. Before a lien can be established against the interest of the Commonwealth, in the seized vehicle, the lien claimant must show that he was ignorant of its illegal use when it was so seized. Bandy v. Commonwealth, 185 Va. 1044, 41 S.E.2d 71 (1947).

Evidence necessary for conviction of bad faith. — A conviction of bad faith on the part of the automobile owner should be based upon some evidence of his criminal knowledge, connivance or consent to the unlawful use of his vehicle, or upon circumstances from which there may be fairly inferred such knowledge or consent. Patterson v. Commonwealth, 187 Va. 913, 48 S.E.2d 357 (1948), holding claimant had fully sustained the burden of proof (decided under former § 4-56).

Recording the lien of a North Carolina motor company on the face of a North Carolina title was insufficient where the alleged lien had not been perfected by registration of the chattel mortgage under the laws of North Carolina and there was no statutory provision in that state similar to subsection (i) of former § 4-56. Williams v. Commonwealth, 190 Va. 280, 56 S.E.2d 537 (1949).

Instance of innocent lienor. — Finance company, assignee of conditional sales contract under which a car had been sold to a reputed bootlegger, held an innocent lienor within the definition of subsection (i) of former § 4-56. Universal C.I.T. Credit Corp. v. Commonwealth, 196 Va. 72, 82 S.E.2d 593 (1954).

CIRCUIT COURT OPINIONS

Vehicle owner was deprived of opportunity to establish exemption. — Vehicle owner stated a claim against a city police

officer in conversion and trespass to chattels by alleging that the officer's seizure of her vehicle without complying with the notice requirements of § 19.2-386.3 or notifying her before turning the vehicle over to the lienholder damaged her by depriving her of the opportunity to secure her property by establishing one of the exemptions outlined in this section; the officer's demurrer and plea of sovereign immunity were therefore overruled. Mallory v. City of Richmond, 69 Va. Cir. 100, 2005 Va. Cir. LEXIS 340 (Richmond 2005).

§ 19.2-386.9. Appearance by owner or lien holder.

Any person claiming to be an owner or lien holder of the named property may appear at any time within thirty days after service on him of notice to appear or on or before the date certain set forth in any order of publication under § 8.01-317 or such longer time as the court in its discretion may allow to prevent a miscarriage of justice. Any person without actual or constructive notice of the forfeiture proceedings claiming to be an owner or lienholder may appear at any time before final judgment of the trial court and be made a party to the action. Such appearance shall be by answer, under oath, which shall clearly set forth (i) the nature of the defendant's claim; (ii) the exact right, title or character of the ownership or interest in the property and the evidence thereof; and (iii) the reason, cause, exemption or defense he may have against the forfeiture of the property.

History.
1989, c. 690; 1991, c. 560.

CASE NOTES

Priority of federal tax lien perfected at time of seizure. — Where the United States had no knowledge of the illegal use being made of property forfeited because of being used in a lottery and had properly perfected a tax lien thereon at the time of the seizure, said lien had priority over the forfeiture to the extent of the balance due thereon. Tri-Pharmacy, Inc. v. United States, 203 Va. 723, 127 S.E.2d 89 (1962) cert. denied, 371 U.S. 962, 83 S. Ct. 542, 9 L. Ed. 2d 509 (1963) (decided under prior law).

Ignorance of owner or lienor formerly no defense. — See Boggs v. Commonwealth, 76 Va. 989 (1882) (decided under prior law).; Quidley v. Commonwealth, 190 Va. 1029, 59 S.E.2d 52 (1950) (decided under prior law).

§ 19.2-386.10. Trial.

A. A party defendant who fails to appear as provided in § 19.2-386.9 shall be in default. The forfeiture shall be deemed established as to the interest of any party in default upon entry of judgment as provided in § 19.2-386.11. Within twenty-one days after entry of judgment, any party defendant against whom judgment has been so entered may petition the Department of Criminal Justice Services for remission of his interest in the forfeited property. For good cause shown and upon proof that the party defendant's interest in the property is exempt under subdivision 2, 3 or 4 of § 19.2-386.8, the Department of Criminal Justice Services shall grant the petition and direct the state treasury to either (i) remit to the party defendant an amount not exceeding the party defendant's interest in the proceeds of sale of the forfeited property after deducting expenses incurred and payable pursuant to subsection B of § 19.2-386.12 or (ii) convey clear and absolute title to the forfeited property in extinguishment of such interest.

If any party defendant appears in accordance with § 19.2-386.9, the court shall proceed to trial of the case, unless trial by jury is demanded by the Commonwealth or any party defendant. At trial, the Commonwealth has the burden of proving that the property is subject to forfeiture under this chapter. Upon such a showing by the Commonwealth, the claimant has the burden of proving that the claimant's interest in the property is exempt under subdivision 2, 3 or 4 of § 19.2-386.8. The proof of all issues shall be by a preponderance of the evidence.

B. The information and trial thereon shall be independent of any criminal proceeding against any party or other person for violation of law. However, upon motion and for good cause shown, the court may stay a forfeiture proceeding that is related to any indictment or information.

History.
  1989, c. 690; 1991, c. 560.

Law Review.
  For note, "Substantial Connection and The Illusive Facilitation Element for Civil Forfeiture of Narcoband in Drug Felony Cases," see 25 U. Rich. L. Rev. 171 (1991).

CASE NOTES

For case in which the order of the trial court confiscating and appropriating defendant's funds as an incidence of his criminal prosecution did not comply with statutory procedure and most significantly, the court did not act pursuant to an "information," with attendant rights, including notice right of trial "independent of any criminal proceeding," see Jenkins v. Commonwealth, 13 Va. App. 420, 411 S.E.2d 841 (1991).

§ 19.2-386.11. Judgment of condemnation; destruction.

A. If the forfeiture is established, the judgment shall be that the property be condemned as forfeited to the Commonwealth subject to any remission granted under subsection A of § 19.2-386.10 and further that the same be sold, unless (i) a sale thereof has been already made under § 19.2-386.7, (ii) the court determines that the property forfeited is of such minimal value that the sale would not be in the best interest of the Commonwealth or (iii) the court finds that the property may be subject to return to a participating agency. If the court finds that the property may be subject to return to an agency participating in the seizure in accordance with subsection C of § 19.2-386.14, the order shall provide for storage of the property until the determination to return it is made or, if return is not made, for sale of the property as provided in this section and § 19.2-386.12. If sale has been made,

the judgment shall be against the proceeds of sale, subject to the rights of any lien holder whose interest is not forfeited. If the property condemned has been delivered to the claimant under § 19.2-386.6, further judgment shall be against the obligors in the bond for the penalty thereof, to be discharged by the payment of the appraised value of the property, upon which judgment, process of execution shall be awarded and the clerk shall endorse thereon, "No security is to be taken."

B. Forfeited cash and negotiable instruments shall be disposed of pursuant to the provisions of § 19.2-386.12.

C. Contraband, the sale or possession of which is unlawful, weapons and property not sold because of the minimal value thereof, may be ordered destroyed by the court.

History.
  1989, c. 690; 1991, c. 560; 1993, c. 484.

CASE NOTES

Language of section is mandatory. — The language of §§ 18.2-249 [now § 19.2-386.22] and 19.2-386.1 through 19.2-386.14 is plain, unambiguous, and mandatory. Jenkins v. Commonwealth, 13 Va. App. 420, 411 S.E.2d 841 (1991).

Court's authority dependent upon adherence to provisions of section. — The subject matter jurisdiction necessary to forfeiture is conferred upon the trial court only through these several statutes (§§ 18.2-249 [now § 19.2-386.22] and 19.2-386.1 through 19.2-386.14) and the court's authority is dependent upon scrupulous adherence to their provisions. Jenkins v. Commonwealth, 13 Va. App. 420, 411 S.E.2d 841 (1991).

§ 19.2-386.12. Sale of forfeited property.

A. Any sale of forfeited property shall be made for cash, after due advertisement. The sale shall be by public sale or other commercially feasible means authorized by the court in the order of forfeiture and shall vest in the purchaser a clear and absolute title to the property sold subject to the rights of any lien holder whose interest is not forfeited. The proceeds of sale, and whatever may be realized on any bond given under § 19.2-386.6, and any money forfeited shall be paid over to the state treasury into a special fund of the Department of Criminal Justice Services in accordance with § 19.2-386.14.

B. In all cases of forfeiture under this section, the actual expenses incident to the custody, preservation, and management of the seized property prior to forfeiture, the actual expenses incident to normal legal proceedings to perfect the Commonwealth's interest in the seized property through forfeiture, and the actual expenses incident to the sale thereof, including commissions, shall be taxed as costs and shall be paid to the person or persons who incurred these costs out of the net proceeds from the sale of such property. If there are no proceeds, the actual expenses shall be paid by the Commonwealth from the Criminal Fund. Actual expenses in excess of the available net proceeds shall be paid by the Commonwealth from the Criminal Fund. The party or parties in interest to any forfeiture proceeding commenced under this section shall be entitled to reasonable attorney's fees and costs if the forfeiture proceeding is terminated in favor of such party or parties. Such fees and costs shall be paid by the Commonwealth from the Criminal Fund.

The residue, if any, shall be paid and disbursed as provided in subsection A of § 19.2-386.10 and § 19.2-386.14 and regulations promulgated by the Criminal Justice Services Board.

History.
1989, c. 690; 1991, c. 560.

CASE NOTES

Language of section is mandatory. — The language of §§ 18.2-249 [now § 19.2-386.22] and 19.2-386.1 through 19.2-386.14 is plain, unambiguous, and mandatory. Jenkins v. Commonwealth, 13 Va. App. 420, 411 S.E.2d 841 (1991).

Court's authority dependent upon adherence to provisions of section. — The subject matter jurisdiction necessary to forfeiture is conferred upon the trial court only through these several statutes (§§ 18.2-249 [now § 19.2-386.22] and 19.2-386.1 through 19.2-386.14) and the court's authority is dependent upon scrupulous adherence to their provisions. Jenkins v. Commonwealth, 13 Va. App. 420, 411 S.E.2d 841 (1991).

CIRCUIT COURT OPINIONS

Generally. — Both the "fruits" and "instrumentalities" of illegal drug transactions were to be subject to the same procedure for sale and compensation should the forfeiture proceeding be terminated in favor of one party; where defendant was entitled to return of illegally seized money, he was awarded attorney's fees. Commonwealth v. Turner, 58 Va. Cir. 576, 2000 Va. Cir. LEXIS 627 (Charlottesville 2000).

Editor's note.
The cases noted below were decided under former § 4-56, now repealed, which covered the same subject matter as this section.

Right of interested persons to contest forfeiture. — It is unquestioned that the legislature has the power to provide for the forfeiture of property used in the violation of a penal statute. In former § 4-56 the legislature exercised its power in that respect. However, before such forfeiture can be had, all persons interested in the seized property, whether owner or lienor, are made parties defendant to the information filed by the Commonwealth, and afforded an opportunity to contest the right of forfeiture. McNelis v. Commonwealth, 171 Va. 471, 198 S.E. 493 (1938).

But such proof need not be perfect or complete. — Former § 4-56 put upon the claimant the burden of satisfying the court that he was ignorant of the illegal use of his car, and that such use was without his connivance or consent, express or implied. But this does not mean that perfect or complete proof of innocence is required. The degree to which the proof ought to satisfy the court need be reasonable only. Patterson v. Commonwealth, 187 Va. 913, 48 S.E.2d 357 (1948); Cleek v. Commonwealth, 189 Va. 14, 52 S.E.2d 89 (1949); Universal C.I.T. Credit Corp. v. Commonwealth, 196 Va. 72, 82 S.E.2d 593 (1954).

Setting aside finding of trial court. — A finding of the trial court that a lien claimant has not successfully carried the required burden of proof cannot be set aside unless it appears from the evidence that such judgment is plainly wrong or without evidence to support it. Bandy v. Commonwealth, 185 Va. 1044, 41 S.E.2d 71 (1947).

§ 19.2-386.13. Writ of error and supersedeas.

For the purpose of review on a writ of error or supersedeas, a final judgment or order in the cause shall be deemed a final judgment or order within the meaning of subsection A of § 8.01-670.

History.
1989, c. 690; 2005, c. 681.

§ 19.2-386.14. Sharing of forfeited assets.

A. All cash, negotiable instruments, and proceeds from a sale conducted pursuant to § 19.2-386.7 or 19.2-386.12, after deduction of expenses, fees, and costs as provided in § 19.2-386.12, shall, as soon after entry of the forfeiture as is practicable, be distributed in a manner consistent with this chapter and Article VIII, Section 8 of the Constitution of Virginia.

A1. All cash, negotiable instruments and proceeds from a sale conducted pursuant to § 19.2-386.7 or 19.2-386.12, after deduction of expenses, fees and costs as provided in § 19.2-386.12, shall, as soon after entry of the forfeiture as is practicable, be paid over to the state treasury into a special fund of the Department of Criminal Justice Services for distribution in accordance with this section. The forfeited property and proceeds, less 10 percent, shall be made available to federal, state and local agencies to promote law enforcement in accordance with this section and regulations adopted by the Criminal Justice Services Board to implement the asset-sharing program.

The 10 percent retained by the Department shall be held in a nonreverting fund, known as the Asset Sharing Administrative Fund. Administrative costs incurred by the Department to manage and operate the asset-sharing program shall be paid from the Fund. Any amounts remaining in the Fund after payment of these costs shall be used to promote state or local law-enforcement activities. Distributions from the Fund for these activities shall be based upon need and shall be made from time to time in accordance with regulations promulgated by the Board.

B. Any federal, state or local agency or office that directly participated in the investigation or other law-enforcement activity which led, directly or indirectly, to the seizure and forfeiture shall be eligible for, and may petition the Department for, return of the forfeited asset or an equitable share of the net proceeds, based upon the degree of participation in the law-enforcement effort resulting in the forfeiture, taking into account the total value of all property forfeited and the total law-enforcement effort with respect to the violation of law on which the forfeiture is based. Upon finding that the petitioning agency is eligible for distribution and that all participating agencies agree on the equitable share of each, the Department shall distribute each share directly to the appropriate treasury of the participating agency.

If all eligible participating agencies cannot agree on the equitable shares of the net proceeds, the shares shall be determined by the Criminal Justice

Services Board in accordance with regulations which shall specify the criteria to be used by the Board in assessing the degree of participation in the law-enforcement effort resulting in the forfeiture.

C. After the order of forfeiture is entered concerning any motor vehicle, boat, aircraft, or other tangible personal property, any seizing agency may (i) petition the Department for return of the property that is not subject to a grant or pending petition for remission or (ii) request the circuit court to order the property destroyed. Where all the participating agencies agree upon the equitable distribution of the tangible personal property, the Department shall return the property to those agencies upon finding that (a) the agency meets the criteria for distribution as set forth in subsection B and (b) the agency has a clear and reasonable law-enforcement need for the forfeited property.

If all eligible participating agencies cannot agree on the distribution of the property, distribution shall be determined by the Criminal Justice Services Board as in subsection B, taking into consideration the clear and reasonable law-enforcement needs for the property which the agencies may have. In order to equitably distribute tangible personal property, the Criminal Justice Services Board may require the agency receiving the property to reimburse the Department in cash for the difference between the fair market value of the forfeited property and the agency's equitable share as determined by the Criminal Justice Services Board.

If a seizing agency has received property for its use pursuant to this section, when the agency disposes of the property (1) by sale, the proceeds shall be distributed as set forth in this section; or (2) by destruction pursuant to a court order, the agency shall do so in a manner consistent with this section.

D. All forfeited property, including its proceeds or cash equivalent, received by a participating state or local agency pursuant to this section shall be used to promote law enforcement but shall not be used to supplant existing programs or funds. The Board shall promulgate regulations establishing an audit procedure to ensure compliance with this section.

E. On or after July 1, 2012, but before July 1, 2014, local seizing agencies may contribute cash funds and proceeds from forfeited property to the Virginia Public Safety Foundation to support the construction of the Commonwealth Public Safety Memorial. Any funds contributed by seizing agencies shall be contributed only after an internal analysis to determine that such contributions will not negatively impact law-enforcement training or operations.

History.
1991, c. 560; 2012, cc. 126, 283, 373, 756.

Editor's note.
Acts 2012, Sp. Sess. I, c. 3, as amended by Acts 2013, c. 806, effective for the biennium ending June 30, 2014, Item 416 E provides: "Notwithstanding the provisions of §§ 19.2-386.14, 38.2-415, 46.2-1167 and 52-4.3, Code of Virginia, the Department of

State Police may use revenue from the State Asset Forfeiture Fund, the Insurance Fraud Fund, the Drug Investigation Trust Account - State, and the Safety Fund to modify, enhance or procure automated systems that focus on the Commonwealth's law enforcement activities and information gathering processes."

The 2012 amendments.
The 2012 amendments by cc. 126 and 373 are identical, and added subsection E and made minor stylistic changes.
The 2012 amendments by cc. 283 and 756 are identical, and added present subsection A and redesignated former subsection A as subsection A1; in subsection C, rewrote the first paragraph and added the third paragraph; and made minor stylistic changes.

CASE NOTES

Language of section is mandatory. — The language of §§ 18.2-249 [now § 19.2-386.22] and 19.2-386.1 through 19.2-386.14 is plain, unambiguous, and mandatory. Jenkins v. Commonwealth, 13 Va. App. 420, 411 S.E.2d 841 (1991).

Court's authority dependent upon adherence to provisions of section. — The subject matter jurisdiction necessary to forfeiture is conferred upon the trial court only through these several statutes (§§ 18.2-249 [now § 19.2-386.22] and 19.2-386.1 through 19.2-386.14) and the court's authority is dependent upon scrupulous adherence to their provisions. Jenkins v. Commonwealth, 13 Va. App. 420, 411 S.E.2d 841 (1991).

OPINIONS OF THE ATTORNEY GENERAL

The county treasurer is responsible for receiving any asset forfeiture funds, which must be held and used only for law-enforcement purposes; a sheriff may not establish a separate account or "treasury" for such funds separate and apart from the locality he serves. See opinion of Attorney General to The Honorable H. Roger Zurn, Jr., Treasurer, County of Loundon, 08-040 (8/26/08).

Guidelines of the Department of Criminal Justice Services do not require that asset forfeiture funds be paid only to law-enforcement agencies, but such funds only may be used for law-enforcement purposes. See opinion of Attorney General to The Honorable H. Roger Zurn, Jr., Treasurer, County of Loundon, 08-040 (8/26/08).

CHAPTER 22.2.

MISCELLANEOUS FORFEITURE PROVISIONS.

§ 19.2-386.15. Seizure of property used in connection with or derived from terrorism.

A. The following property shall be subject to lawful seizure by any law-enforcement officer charged with enforcing the provisions of Article 2.2 (§ 18.2-46.4 et seq.) of Chapter 4 of Title 18.2: all moneys or other property, real or personal, together with any interest or profits derived from the investment of such money and used in substantial connection with an act of terrorism as defined in § 18.2-46.4.

B. All seizures and forfeitures under this section shall be governed by the procedures contained in Chapter 22.1 (§ 19.2-386.1 et seq.) of this title.

History.
2002, cc. 588, 623, § 18.2-46.9; 2004, c. 995.

Effective date.
This chapter became effective April 21, 2004.

§ 19.2-386.16. Forfeiture of motor vehicles used in commission of certain crimes.

A. Any vehicle knowingly used by the owner thereof or used by another with his knowledge of and during the commission of, or in an attempt to commit, a second or subsequent offense of § 18.2-346, 18.2-347, 18.2-348, 18.2-349, 18.2-355, 18.2-356 or 18.2-357 or of a similar ordinance of any county, city or town or knowingly used for the transportation of any stolen goods, chattels or other property, when the value of such stolen goods, chattels or other property is $200 or more, or any stolen property obtained as a result of a robbery, without regard to the value of the property, shall be forfeited to the Commonwealth. The vehicle shall be seized by any law-enforcement officer arresting the operator of such vehicle for the criminal offense, and delivered to the sheriff of the county or city in which the offense occurred. The officer shall take a receipt therefor.

B. Any vehicle knowingly used by the owner thereof or used by another with his knowledge of and during the commission of, or in an attempt to commit, a misdemeanor violation of subsection D of § 18.2-47 or a felony violation of (i) Article 3 (§ 18.2-47 et seq.) of Chapter 4 of Title 18.2 or (ii) § 18.2-357 where the prostitute is a minor, shall be forfeited to the Commonwealth. The vehicle shall be seized by any law-enforcement officer arresting the operator of such vehicle for the criminal offense, and delivered to the sheriff of the county or city in which the offense occurred. The officer shall take a receipt therefor.

C. Forfeiture of such vehicle shall be enforced as is provided in Chapter 22.1 (§ 19.2-386.1 et seq.).

History.
Code 1950, §§ 18.1-103, 18.1-107.1; 1960, c. 358; 1966, c. 247; 1970, c. 353; 1975, cc. 14, 15, § 18.2-110; 1981, c. 188; 1982, c. 509; 1992, cc. 310, 725; 1993, cc. 609, 866; 2004, c. 995; 2010, c. 710; 2011, cc. 818, 852; 2012, cc. 283, 756.

The 2010 amendments.
The 2010 amendment by c. 710 inserted the subsection A, C, and D designations; and inserted subsection B.

The 2011 amendments.
The 2011 amendments, by cc. 818 and 852 are nearly identical, and in subsection B, inserted "a misdemeanor violation of subsection D of § 18.2-47 or" and substituted "Article 3 (§ 18.2-47 et seq.) of Chapter 4 of Title 18.2" for "Article 3, Chapter 4 of Title 18.2 (§§ 18.2-47 et seq.)."

The 2012 amendments.
The 2012 amendments by cc. 283 and 756 are identical, and rewrote subsection C and deleted former subsection D pertaining to use and operation of the vehicle after forfeiture.

§ 19.2-386.17. Forfeitures for computer crimes.

All moneys and other income, including all proceeds earned but not yet received by a defendant from a third party as a result of the defendant's violations of Article 7.1 (§ 18.2-152.1 et seq.) of Chapter 5 of Title 18.2, and all computer equipment, all computer software, and all personal property used in connection with any violation of such article known by the owner thereof to have been used in violation of such article, shall be subject to lawful seizure by a law-enforcement officer and forfeiture by the Commonwealth in accordance with the procedures set forth in Chapter 22.1 (§ 19.2-386.1 et seq.) of this title, applied mutatis mutandis.

History.
2003, cc. 987, 1016, § 18.2-152.16; 2004, c. 995.

Law Review.
For 2007 annual survey article, "Electronic Data: A Commentary on the Law in Virginia in 2007," see 42 U. Rich. L. Rev. 355 (2007).

§ 19.2-386.18. Forfeiture of unlawful electronic communication devices.

Any unlawful electronic communication device possessed, manufactured or sold in violation of §§ 18.2-190.2, 18.2-190.3 or § 18.2-190.4 may be seized and forfeited to the Commonwealth, and turned over to the circuit court in the city or county in which it was seized and such property shall be disposed of as provided by law.

History.
2002, c. 671, § 18.2-190.7; 2003, c. 354; 2004, c. 995.

§ 19.2-386.19. Seizure of property used in connection with money laundering.

The following property shall be subject to lawful seizure by any officer charged with enforcing the provisions of Article 9 (§ 18.2-246.1 et seq.) of Chapter 6 of Title 18.2: (i) all money, equipment, motor vehicles, and all other personal and real property of any kind or character used in substantial connection with the laundering of proceeds of some form of activity punishable as a felony under the laws of the Commonwealth, another state or territory of the United States, the District of Columbia, or the United States; (ii) all money or other property, real or personal, traceable to the proceeds of some form of activity punishable as a felony under the laws of the Commonwealth, another state or territory of the United States, the District of Columbia, or the United States, together with any interest or profits derived from the investment of such proceeds or other property; and (iii) all money, equipment, motor vehicles, and all other personal and real property of any kind or character used to or intended to be used to promote money laundering. Real property shall not be subject to seizure unless the minimum prescribed punishment for the violation is a term of imprisonment of not less than five years. All seizures and forfeitures under this section shall be governed by Chapter 22.1 (§ 19.2-386.1 et seq.), and the procedures specified therein shall apply, mutatis mutandis, to all forfeitures under Article 9 (§ 18.2-246.1 et seq.) of Chapter 6 of Title 18.2.

History.
1999, c. 348, § 18.2-246.4; 2003, cc. 541, 549; 2004, c. 995; 2012, cc. 283, 756.

The 2012 amendments.
The 2012 amendments by cc. 283 and 756 are identical, and inserted clause (iii) of the first sentence, and made related changes.

§ 19.2-386.20. Forfeiture of cigarettes sold or attempted to be sold in an unlawful delivery sale.

Any cigarettes sold or attempted to be sold in a delivery sale in violation of Article 10 (§ 18.2-246.6 et seq.) of Chapter 6 of Title 18.2 shall be forfeited to the Commonwealth and destroyed. All fixtures, equipment, materials and personal property used in substantial connection with a delivery sale or attempted delivery sale in a knowing and intentional violation of such article shall be subject to seizure and forfeiture according to the procedures contained in Chapter 22.1 (§ 19.2-386.1 et seq.) of this title, applied mutatis mutandis.

History.
2004, c. 995.

§ 19.2-386.21. Forfeiture of counterfeit and contraband cigarettes.

Counterfeit cigarettes possessed in violation of § 18.2-246.14 and cigarettes possessed in violation of § 58.1-1017 or 58.1-1017.1 shall be subject to seizure, forfeiture, and destruction by the Virginia Alcoholic Beverage Control Board or any law-enforcement officer of the Commonwealth. All fixtures, equipment, materials, and personal property used in substantial connection with (i) the sale or possession of counterfeit cigarettes in a knowing and intentional violation of Article 10 (§ 18.2-246.6 et seq.) of Chapter 6 of Title 18.2 or (ii) the sale or possession of cigarettes in a knowing and intentional violation of § 58.1-1017 or 58.1-1017.1 shall be subject to seizure and forfeiture according to the procedures contained in Chapter 22.1 (§ 19.2-386.1 et seq.), applied mutatis mutandis.

History.
2004, c. 995; 2013, c. 627.

The 2013 amendments.
The 2013 amendment by c. 627 inserted "and cigarettes possessed in violation of § 58.1-1017 or 58.1-1017.1" in the first sentence; and in the second sentence inserted "(i) the" and "or (ii) the sale or possession of cigarettes in a knowing and intentional violation of § 58.1-1017 or 58.1-1017.1," and made a stylistic change.

§ 19.2-386.22. Seizure of property used in connection with or derived from illegal drug transactions.

A. The following property shall be subject to lawful seizure by any officer charged with enforcing the provisions of Article 1 (§ 18.2-247 et seq.) of Chapter 7 of Title 18.2: (i) all money, medical equipment, office equipment, laboratory equipment, motor vehicles, and all other personal and real property of any kind or character, used in substantial connection with (a) the illegal manufacture, sale or distribution of controlled substances or possession with intent to sell or distribute controlled substances in violation of § 18.2-248, (b) the sale or distribution of marijuana or possession with intent to distribute marijuana in violation of subdivisions (a) (2), (a) (3) and (c) of § 18.2-248.1, (c) the sale or distribution of synthetic cannabinoids or possession with intent to distribute or manufacture synthetic cannabinoids in violation of subsections C and E of § 18.2-248.1:1, or (d) a drug-related offense in violation of § 18.2-474.1; (ii) everything of value furnished, or intended to be furnished, in exchange for a controlled substance in violation of § 18.2-248 or for marijuana in violation of § 18.2-248.1 or for synthetic cannabinoids in violation of § 18.2-248.1:1 or for a controlled substance, marijuana, or synthetic cannabinoids in violation of § 18.2-474.1; and (iii) all moneys or other property, real or personal, traceable to such an exchange, together with any interest or profits derived from the investment of such money or other property. Under the provisions of clause (i), real property shall not be subject to lawful seizure unless the minimum prescribed punishment for the violation is a term of not less than five years.

B. All seizures and forfeitures under this section shall be governed by the procedures contained in Chapter 22.1 (§ 19.2-386.1 et seq.) of this title.

History.
Code 1950, § 18.1-346; 1960, c. 358; 1970, c. 650; 1972, c. 799; 1973, c. 171; 1975, cc. 14, 15, § 18.2-249; 1976, c. 132; 1979, c. 435; 1982, c. 462; 1985, c. 569; 1986, cc. 449, 485; 1988, cc. 575, 753; 1989, cc. 638, 690; 1993, c. 825; 1999, c. 269; 2004, c. 995; 2011, cc. 384, 410.

Editor's note.
Acts 2011, cc. 384 and 410, cl. 3 provides: "That the provisions of this act may result in a net increase in periods of imprisonment or commitment. Pursuant to § 30-19.1:4, the estimated amount of the necessary appropriation cannot be determined for periods of imprisonment in state adult correctional facilities; therefore, Chapter 874 of the Acts of Assembly of 2010 requires the Virginia Criminal Sentencing Commission to assign a minimum fiscal impact of $50,000. Pursuant to § 30-19.1:4, the estimated amount of the necessary appropriation cannot be determined for periods of commitment to the custody of the Department of Juvenile Justice."

The 2011 amendments.
The 2011 amendments by cc. 384 and 410, effective March 23, 2011, are identical, and in subsection A, inserted clause (i) (c), redesignated former (i) (c) as (i) (d), and in (ii), inserted "or for synthetic cannabinoids in violation of § 18.2-248.1:1" and "synthetic cannabinoids," and made related changes.

CASE NOTES

The language of this section is plain, unambiguous, and mandatory. — The language of this section and §§ 19.2-386.1 through 19.2-386.14 is plain, unambiguous, and mandatory. Jenkins v. Commonwealth, 13 Va. App. 420, 411 S.E.2d 841 (1991).

The subject matter jurisdiction necessary to forfeiture is conferred upon the trial court only through these several statutes (this section and §§ 19.2-386.1 through 19.2-386.14) and the court's authority is dependent upon scrupulous adherence to their provisions. Jenkins v. Commonwealth, 13 Va. App. 420, 411 S.E.2d 841 (1991).

Forfeiture is appropriate. — It is well established that forfeiture is appropriate to afford the Commonwealth relief against property employed in defiance of the laws of the State. Jenkins v. Commonwealth, 13 Va. App. 420, 411 S.E.2d 841 (1991).

Forfeiture is not a criminal proceeding. — Forfeiture is, however, not a criminal proceeding but a "civil" action against "res" unlawfully employed by its owner or other person. Jenkins v. Commonwealth, 13 Va. App. 420, 411 S.E.2d 841 (1991).

Forfeiture is neither penalty nor punishment. — Although related to criminal activity, forfeiture is neither "penalty" nor "punishment" for an offense and remains entirely separate and distinct from a prosecution of its owner or other individual. Jenkins v. Commonwealth, 13 Va. App. 420, 411 S.E.2d 841 (1991).

Commonwealth's failure to file information within the statutory 60-day period was fatal to the forfeiture proceeding of an automobile suspected used in illegal drug business. Haina v. Commonwealth, 235 Va. 571, 369 S.E.2d 401 (1988).

"Substantial connection" existed between defendant's activity as a drug dealer and automobile used by him, even though it was registered to his sister, where he considered himself to be the owner of the vehicle and admitted to undercover officer that he regularly sold cocaine and in doing so used the vehicle; forfeiture was thus justified. Lee v. Commonwealth, 253 Va. 222, 482 S.E.2d 802 (1997).

"Substantial connection" existed between cash confis-

cated from defendant's apartment and defendant's illegal drug trafficking where defendant admitted the money was his and that he sold "eight to nine ounces" of cocaine per week, justifying forfeiture. Lee v. Commonwealth, 253 Va. 222, 482 S.E.2d 802 (1997).

For case in which the order of the trial court confiscating and appropriating defendant's funds as an incidence of his criminal prosecution did not comply with statutory procedure and most significantly, the court did not act pursuant to an "information," with attendant rights, including notice right of trial "independent of any criminal proceeding," see Jenkins v. Commonwealth, 13 Va. App. 420, 411 S.E.2d 841 (1991).

CIRCUIT COURT OPINIONS

Illegally seized property. — Exclusionary rule of the Fourth Amendment applied to the suppressed evidence of a criminal action in the quasi-criminal forfeiture action; defendant was entitled to the return of money illegally seized. Commonwealth v. Turner, 58 Va. Cir. 576, 2000 Va. Cir. LEXIS 627 (Charlottesville 2000).

Vehicle owner lacked standing to seek injunctive relief. — In an action against a city and a city police officer for the allegedly improper seizure of an owner's vehicle when the owner's son was arrested for possession of illegal drugs, the owner could not obtain a temporary and permanent injunction barring the city from handling vehicles seized pursuant to the authority granted by § 19.2-386.22 in any manner other than that set forth in the Virginia Code; she lacked standing to seek such relief. Mallory v. City of Richmond, 69 Va. Cir. 100, 2005 Va. Cir. LEXIS 340 (Richmond 2005).

§ 19.2-386.23. Disposal of seized controlled substances, marijuana, synthetic cannabinoids, and paraphernalia.

A. All controlled substances, imitation controlled substances, marijuana, synthetic cannabinoids as defined in § 18.2-248.1:1, or paraphernalia, the lawful possession of which is not established or the title to which cannot be ascertained, which have come into the custody of a peace officer or have been seized in connection with violations of Chapter 7 (§ 18.2-247 et seq.) of Title 18.2, shall be forfeited and disposed of as follows:

1. Upon written application by the Department of Forensic Science the court may order the forfeiture of any such substance or paraphernalia to the Department for research and training purposes and for destruction pursuant to regulations of the United States Department of Justice Drug Enforcement Administration and of the Board of Pharmacy once these purposes have been fulfilled.

2. In the event no application is made under subdivision 1 of this subsection, the court shall order the destruction of all such substances or paraphernalia, which order shall state the existence and nature of the substance or paraphernalia, the quantity thereof, the location where seized, the person or persons from whom the substance or paraphernalia was seized, if known, and the manner whereby such item shall be destroyed. However, the court may order that paraphernalia identified in subdivision 5 of § 18.2-265.1 not be destroyed and that it be given to a person or entity that makes a showing to the court of sufficient need for the property and an ability to put the property to a lawful and publicly

beneficial use. A return under oath, reporting the time, place and manner of destruction shall be made to the court and to the Board of Pharmacy by the officer to whom the order is directed. A copy of the order and affidavit shall be made a part of the record of any criminal prosecution in which the substance or paraphernalia was used as evidence and shall, thereafter, be prima facie evidence of its contents. In the event a law-enforcement agency recovers, seizes, finds, is given or otherwise comes into possession of any such substances or paraphernalia that are not evidence in a trial in the Commonwealth, the chief law-enforcement officer of the agency or his designee may, with the written consent of the appropriate attorney for the Commonwealth, order destruction of same; provided that, a statement under oath, reporting a description of the substances and paraphernalia destroyed, and the time, place and manner of destruction is made to the chief law-enforcement officer and to the Board of Pharmacy by the officer to whom the order is directed.

B. No such substance or paraphernalia used or to be used in a criminal prosecution under Chapter 7 (§ 18.2-247 et seq.) of Title 18.2 shall be disposed of as provided by this section until all rights of appeal have been exhausted, except as provided in § 19.2-386.24.

History.
Code 1950, § 54-524.101:5; 1973, c. 470; 1974, c. 113; 1975, cc. 14, 15, 607, § 18.2-253; 1979, cc. 435, 646; 1982, c. 462; 1990, c. 825; 1995, c. 578; 2001, c. 195; 2004, c. 995; 2005, cc. 868, 881; 2006, c. 107; 2011, cc. 384, 410.

Editor's note.
Acts 2011, cc. 384 and 410, cl. 3 provides: "That the provisions of this act may result in a net increase in periods of imprisonment or commitment. Pursuant to § 30-19.1:4, the estimated amount of the necessary appropriation cannot be determined for periods of imprisonment in state adult correctional facilities; therefore, Chapter 874 of the Acts of Assembly of 2010 requires the Virginia Criminal Sentencing Commission to assign a minimum fiscal impact of $50,000. Pursuant to § 30-19.1:4, the estimated amount of the necessary appropriation cannot be determined for periods of commitment to the custody of the Department of Juvenile Justice."

The 2011 amendments.
The 2011 amendments by cc. 384 and 410, effective March 23, 2011, are identical, and inserted "synthetic cannabinoids as defined in § 18.2-248.1:1" in the introductory language of subsection A.

CASE NOTES

Violation under section did not violate due process. — Where sheriff loaded marijuana on his private truck after police harvested it from fields, and where notice, as required by this section, was given to defendant, and no hearing was held as to propriety of destruction, due process clause was not violated since record contained no evidence that Commonwealth attempted to conceal from defendant fact of destruction of marijuana, since representative sample of 10 pounds was preserved and made available to him, and since reason for destruction was reasonable. Slayton v. Commonwealth, No. 0817-87-2 (Ct. of Appeals Mar. 7, 1989) (decided under prior law).

§ 19.2-386.24. Destruction of seized controlled substances, marijuana, or synthetic cannabinoids prior to trial.

Where seizures of controlled substances, marijuana, or synthetic cannabinoids are made in excess of 10 pounds in connection with any prosecution or investigation under Chapter 7 (§ 18.2-247 et seq.) of Title 18.2, the appropriate law-enforcement agency may retain 10 pounds of the substance randomly selected from the seized substance for representative purposes as evidence and destroy the remainder of the seized substance.

Before any destruction is carried out under this section, the law-enforcement agency shall cause the material seized to be photographed with identification case numbers or other means of identification and shall prepare a report identifying the seized material. It shall also notify the accused, or other interested party, if known, or his attorney, at least five days in advance that the photography will take place and that they may be present. Prior to any destruction under this section, the law-enforcement agency shall also notify the accused or other interested party, if known, and his attorney at least seven days prior to the destruction of the time and place the destruction will occur. Any notice required under the provisions of this section shall be by first-class mail to the last known address of the person required to be notified. In addition to the substance retained for representative purposes as evidence, all photographs and records made under this section and properly identified shall be admissible in any court proceeding for any purposes for which the seized substance itself would have been admissible.

History.
1979, c. 646, § 18.2-253.1; 1980, c. 179; 2004, c. 995; 2011, cc. 384, 410.

Editor's note.
Acts 2011, cc. 384 and 410, cl. 3 provides: "That the provisions of this act may result in a net increase in periods of imprisonment or commitment. Pursuant to § 30-19.1:4, the estimated amount of the necessary appropriation cannot be determined for periods of imprisonment in state adult correctional facilities; therefore, Chapter 874 of the Acts of Assembly of 2010 requires the Virginia Criminal Sentencing Commission to assign a minimum fiscal impact of $50,000. Pursuant to § 30-19.1:4, the estimated amount of the necessary appropriation cannot be determined for periods of commitment to the custody of the Department of Juvenile Justice."

The 2011 amendments.
The 2011 amendments by cc. 384 and 410, effective March 23, 2011, are identical, and inserted "synthetic cannabinoids" and made a related change in the first paragraph.

§ 19.2-386.25. Judge may order law-enforcement agency to maintain custody of controlled substances, etc.

Upon request of the clerk of any court, a judge of the court may order a law-enforcement agency to take into its custody or to maintain custody of substantial quantities of any controlled substances, imitation controlled substances, chemicals, marijuana, synthetic cannabinoids or paraphernalia used or to be used in a criminal prosecution under Chapter 7 (§ 18.2-247 et seq.) of Title 18.2. The court in its order may make provision for ensuring integrity of these items until further order of the court.

History.

1985, c. 377, § 18.2-253.2; 2004, c. 995; 2011, cc. 384, 410.

Editor's note.

Acts 2011, cc. 384 and 410, cl. 3 provides: "That the provisions of this act may result in a net increase in periods of imprisonment or commitment. Pursuant to § 30-19.1:4, the estimated amount of the necessary appropriation cannot be determined for periods of imprisonment in state adult correctional facilities; therefore, Chapter 874 of the Acts of Assembly of 2010 requires the Virginia Criminal Sentencing Commission to assign a minimum fiscal impact of $50,000. Pursuant to § 30-19.1:4, the estimated amount of the necessary appropriation cannot be determined for periods of commitment to the custody of the Department of Juvenile Justice."

The 2011 amendments.

The 2011 amendments by cc. 384 and 410, effective March 23, 2011, are identical, and inserted "synthetic cannabinoids."

§ 19.2-386.26. Seizure and forfeiture of drug paraphernalia.

All drug paraphernalia as defined in Article 1.1 (§ 18.2-247 et seq.) of Chapter 7 of Title 18.2 shall be forfeited to the Commonwealth and may be seized and disposed of in the same manner as provided in § 19.2-386.23, subject to the rights of an innocent lienor, to be recognized as under § 19.2-386.8.

History.

1981, c. 598, § 18.2-265.4; 1993, c. 866; 2004, c. 995; 2012, cc. 283, 756.

The 2012 amendments.

The 2012 amendments by cc. 283 and 756 are identical, and substituted "§ 19.2-386.8" for "§ 4.1-343."

§ 19.2-386.27. Forfeiture of firearms carried in violation of Article 6.1 (§ 18.2-307.1 et seq.).

Any weapon used in the commission of a violation of Article 6.1 (§ 18.2-307.1 et seq.) of Chapter 7 of Title 18.2 shall be forfeited to the Commonwealth and may be seized by an officer as forfeited, and such as may be needed for police officers, conservators of the peace, and the Department of Forensic Science shall be devoted to that purpose, subject to any registration requirements of federal law, and the remainder shall be disposed of as provided in § 19.2-386.29.

History.

2004, c. 995; 2005, cc. 868, 881; 2013, c. 746.

Editor's note.

Acts 2013, c. 746, cl. 2 provides: "That the provisions of this act are declaratory of existing law."

The 2013 amendments.

The 2013 amendment by c. 746 substituted "Article 6.1 (§ 18.2-307.1 et seq.) of Chapter 7 of Title 18.2" for "§ 18.2-308."

§ 19.2-386.28. Forfeiture of weapons that are concealed, possessed, transported or carried in violation of law.

Any firearm, stun weapon as defined by § 18.2-308.1, or any weapon concealed, possessed, transported or carried in violation of § 18.2-283.1, 18.2-287.01, 18.2-287.4, 18.2-308.1:2, 18.2-308.1:3, 18.2-308.1:4, 18.2-308.2, 18.2-308.2:01, 18.2-308.2:1, 18.2-308.4, 18.2-308.5, 18.2-308.7, or 18.2-308.8 shall be forfeited to the Commonwealth and disposed of as provided in § 19.2-386.29.

History.

2004, c. 995; 2007, c. 519; 2013, c. 746.

Editor's note.

Acts 2013, c. 746, cl. 2 provides: "That the provisions of this act are declaratory of existing law."

The 2007 amendments.

The 2007 amendment by c. 519 deleted "or taser" following "stun weapon."

The 2013 amendments.

The 2013 amendment by c. 746 inserted "18.2-287.01" and made minor stylistic changes.

§ 19.2-386.29. Forfeiture of certain weapons used in commission of criminal offense.

All pistols, shotguns, rifles, dirks, bowie knives, switchblade knives, ballistic knives, razors, slingshots, brass or metal knucks, blackjacks, stun weapons, and other weapons used by any person in the commission of a criminal offense, shall, upon conviction of such person, be forfeited to the Commonwealth by order of the court trying the case. The court shall dispose of such weapons as it deems proper by entry of an order of record. Such disposition may include the destruction of the weapons or, subject to any registration requirements of federal law, sale of the firearms to a licensed dealer in such firearms in accordance with the provisions of Chapter 22.1 (§ 19.2-386.1 et seq.) regarding sale of property forfeited to the Commonwealth.

The court may authorize the seizing law-enforcement agency to use the weapon for a period of time as specified in the order. When the seizing agency ceases to so use the weapon, it shall be disposed of as otherwise provided in this section.

However, upon petition to the court and notice to the attorney for the Commonwealth, the court, upon good cause shown, shall return any such weapon to its lawful owner after conclusion of all relevant proceedings if such owner (i) did not know and had no reason to know of the conduct giving rise to the forfeiture and (ii) is not otherwise prohibited by law from possessing the weapon. The owner shall acknowledge in a sworn affidavit to be filed with the record in the case or cases that he has retaken possession of the weapon involved.

History.
Code 1950, § 18.1-270; 1960, c. 358; 1975, cc. 14, 15, § 18.2-310; 1986, cc. 445, 641; 1988, c. 359; 1990, cc. 556, 944; 2004, c. 995; 2007, c. 519; 2012, cc. 283, 756.

Cross references.
As to disposal of unclaimed firearms in possession of Division of Capitol Police, see § 30-34.2:2.

The 2007 amendments.
The 2007 amendment by c. 519 deleted "and tasers" following "stun weapons" in the first sentence of the first paragraph.

The 2012 amendments.
The 2012 amendments by cc. 283 and 756 are identical, and substituted "Chapter 22.1 (§ 19.2-386.1 et seq.)" for "Chapter 22 (§ 19.2-369 et seq.) of this title" near the end of the first paragraph; and in the second paragraph, deleted the former first sentence, which read: "The proceeds of any sale of such weapon shall be paid in accordance with the provisions of Article VIII, Section 8 of the Constitution of Virginia." and deleted "In addition," from the beginning of the first sentence.

OPINIONS OF THE ATTORNEY GENERAL

Applicable statute in forfeiture of firearm used by person convicted under § 18.2-286. — Subsection A of § 29.1-521.2, with very rare possible exceptions, establishes the procedure to be used in forfeiting a firearm used by a person convicted of violating § 18.2-286, rather than § 19.2-386.29, which applies generally to criminal offenses. See opinion of Attorney General to The Honorable Phillip C. Steele, Commonwealth's Attorney for Giles County, 05-047 (8/19/05).

§ 19.2-386.30. Forfeiture of money, gambling devices, etc., seized from illegal gambling enterprise; innocent owners or lienors.

All money, gambling devices, office equipment and other personal property used in connection with an illegal gambling enterprise or activity, and all money, stakes and things of value received or proposed to be received by a winner in any illegal gambling transaction, which are lawfully seized by any law-enforcement officer or which shall lawfully come into his custody, shall be forfeited to the Commonwealth in accordance with the procedures contained in Chapter 22.1 (§ 19.2-386.1 et seq.).

History.
Code 1950, §§ 18.1-321, 18.1-323, 18.1-333, 18.1-341; 1960, c. 358; 1975, cc. 14, 15, 576, § 18.2-336; 2004, c. 995; 2012, cc. 283, 756.

The 2012 amendments.
The 2012 amendments by cc. 283 and 756 are identical, and rewrote the section.

Michie's Jurisprudence.
For related discussion, see 18 M.J. Taxation, § 86.

CASE NOTES

Nature of proceeding. — The proceeding to forfeit property under this section is against the property and not against the owner of the property or any other person. It is in rem wholly and not in personam. It is not a criminal proceeding. It is a civil case. Quidley v. Commonwealth, 190 Va. 1029, 59 S.E.2d 52 (1950) (decided under prior law).

For a forfeiture of money to be sustained, the Commonwealth must show a connection between the lottery operation and the money. Plummer v. Commonwealth, 215 Va. 185, 207 S.E.2d 861 (1974) (decided under prior law).

Mere possession of money and its availability and accessibility are not sufficient to sustain its forfeiture. Plummer v. Commonwealth, 215 Va. 185, 207 S.E.2d 861 (1974) (decided under prior law).

Forfeiture of property to the Commonwealth under this section occurred when it was seized. The subsequent forfeiture proceeding was required, not to complete the forfeiture, but to prove the illegal use for which the forfeiture was suffered. Therefore, a federal tax lien perfected after seizure was subordinate to the Commonwealth's interest. Tri-Pharmacy, Inc. v. United States, 203 Va. 723, 127 S.E.2d 89 (1962), cert. denied, 371 U.S. 962, 83 S. Ct. 542, 9 L. Ed. 2d 509 (1963) (decided under prior law).

Section 19.2-294 does not apply. — Section 19.2-294, providing that where the same act is a violation of two or more statute or ordinances, conviction under one statute or ordinance shall be a bar to prosecution under the other or others, does not apply to a proceeding under this section. Quidley v. Commonwealth, 190 Va. 1029, 59 S.E.2d 52 (1950) (decided under prior law).

Priority of federal tax lien perfected at time of seizure. — Where the United States had no knowledge of the illegal use being made of forfeited property and had properly perfected a tax lien thereon at the time of the seizure, said lien had priority over the forfeiture to the extent of the balance due thereon. Tri-Pharmacy, Inc. v. United States, 203 Va. 723, 127 S.E.2d 89 (1962), cert. denied, 371 U.S. 962, 83 S. Ct. 542, 9 L. Ed. 2d 509 (1963) (decided under prior law).

Evidence sufficient to prove property used in operation of lottery. — Evidence of the Commonwealth was sufficient to prove that certain forfeited property was used in the operation of a lottery. Tri-Pharmacy, Inc. v. United States, 203 Va. 723, 127 S.E.2d 89 (1962), cert. denied, 371 U.S. 962, 83 S. Ct. 542, 9 L. Ed. 2d 509 (1963) (decided under prior law).

§ 19.2-386.31. Seizure and forfeiture of property used in connection with the exploitation and solicitation of children.

All audio and visual equipment, electronic equipment, devices and other personal property used in connection with the possession, production, distribution, publication, sale, possession with intent to distribute or making of child pornography that constitutes a violation of § 18.2-374.1 or 18.2-374.1:1, or in connection with the solicitation of a person less than 18 years of age that constitutes a violation of § 18.2-374.3 shall be subject to lawful seizure by a law-enforcement officer and shall be subject to forfeiture to the Commonwealth pursuant to Chapter 22.1 (§ 19.2-386.1 et seq.). The Commonwealth shall file an information and notice of seizure in accordance with the procedures in Chapter 22.1 (§ 19.2-386.1 et seq.); however, any forfeiture action shall be stayed until conviction of the person whose property is subject to forfeiture. Upon his conviction, the court may dispose of the issue of forfeiture or may continue the civil case allowing the defendant time to answer, at the court's discretion.

History.
1986, c. 596, § 18.2-374.2; 1999, c. 659; 2004, c. 995; 2007, cc. 134, 386; 2012, cc. 283, 756.

The 2007 amendments.

The 2007 amendments by cc. 134 and 386 are identical, and in the first paragraph, inserted "possession," substituted "making of child pornography that constitutes a violation of § 18.2-374.1 or 18.2-374.1:1, or in connection with the solicitation of a person less than 18 years of age that constitutes a violation of § 18.2-374.3 shall be subject" for "making of sexually explicit visual material having a person less than 18 years of age as a subject shall be subject," and inserted "18.2-374.1:1, or 18.2-374.3" in the first sentence, and inserted "to the agency seizing such property" in the second sentence.

The 2012 amendments.

The 2012 amendments by cc. 283 and 756 are identical, and rewrote the section.

§ 19.2-386.32. Seizure and forfeiture of property used in connection with the abduction of children.

All moneys and other property, real and personal, owned by a person and used to further the abduction of a child in violation of § 18.2-47, 18.2-48, or 18.2-48.1 are subject to lawful seizure by a law-enforcement officer and are subject to forfeiture to the Commonwealth pursuant to Chapter 22.1 (§ 19.2-386.1 et seq.) by order of the court in which a conviction under § 18.2-47, 18.2-48, or 18.2-48.1 is obtained.

History.

2011, cc. 818, 852; 2012, cc. 283, 756.

The 2012 amendments.

The 2012 amendments by cc. 283 and 756 are identical, and substituted "Chapter 22.1 (§ 19.2-386.1 et seq.)" for "Chapter 22 (§ 19.2-369 et seq.)."

§ 19.2-386.33. Forfeiture of money, etc., derived from violation of §§ 2.2-3103 through 2.2-3112.

In addition to any other fine or penalty provided by law, any money or other thing of value derived by an officer or employee from a violation of §§ 2.2-3103 through 2.2-3112 shall be forfeited, in accordance with the procedures contained in Chapter 22.1 (§ 19.2-386.1 et seq.). If the thing of value received by the officer or employee in violation of §§ 2.2-3103 through 2.2-3112 increases in value between the time of the violation and the time of discovery of the violation, the greater value shall determine the amount of forfeiture.

History.

2012, cc. 283, 756.

§ 19.2-386.34. Forfeiture of vehicle used in a felony violation of § 18.2-266.

The vehicle solely owned and operated by the accused during the commission of a felony violation of § 18.2-266 shall be subject to seizure and forfeiture. After an arrest upon a felony violation of § 18.2-266, the vehicle may be forfeited to the Commonwealth pursuant to the procedures set forth in Chapter 22.1 (§ 19.2-386.1 et seq.). Any seizure shall be stayed until conviction and the exhaustion of all appeals at which time, if the information has been filed, the Commonwealth shall give notice of seizure to all appropriate parties pursuant to § 19.2-386.3.

An immediate family member of the owner of any motor vehicle for which an information has been filed under this section who was not the driver at the time of the violation may petition the court in which such information was filed for the release of the motor vehicle. If the immediate family member proves by a preponderance of the evidence that his immediate family has only one motor vehicle and will suffer a substantial hardship if that motor vehicle is seized and forfeited, the court, in its discretion, may release the vehicle.

In the event the vehicle was sold to a bona fide purchaser subsequent to the arrest but prior to seizure in order to avoid seizure and forfeiture, the Commonwealth shall have a right of action against the seller for the proceeds of the sale.

History.

2012, cc. 283, 756.

Editor's note.

Acts 2012, cc. 283 and 756, which enacted this section are nearly identical. The section has been set out in the form above at the direction of the Virginia Code Commission.

CHAPTER 23.

CENTRAL CRIMINAL RECORDS EXCHANGE.

§ 19.2-387. Exchange to operate as a division of Department of State Police; authority of Superintendent of State Police.

A. The Central Criminal Records Exchange shall operate as a separate division within the Department of State Police and shall be the sole criminal record-keeping agency of the Commonwealth, except for (i) the Department of Juvenile Justice pursuant to Chapter 10 (§ 16.1-222 et seq.) of Title 16.1, (ii) the Department of Motor Vehicles, (iii) for purposes of the DNA data bank, the Department of Forensic Science and (iv) for the purpose of making parole determinations pursuant to subdivisions 1, 2, 3 and 5 of § 53.1-136, the Virginia Parole Board.

B. The Superintendent of State Police is hereby authorized to employ such personnel, establish such offices, and acquire such equipment as shall be necessary to carry out the purposes of this chapter and is also authorized to enter into agreements with other state agencies for services to be performed for it by employees of such other agencies.

History.
  Code 1950, § 19.1-19.1:1; 1970, c. 101; 1975, c. 495; 1988, c. 541; 1990, c. 669; 1993, c. 313; 2001, cc. 203, 215; 2003, c. 431; 2005, cc. 868, 881.

Cross references.
  As to definitions relating to this chapter, see § 9.1-101. As to civil remedies for violation of this chapter, see § 9.1-135. As to criminal penalty for violation of this chapter, see § 9.1-136.

Michie's Jurisprudence.
  For related discussion, see 5B M.J. Criminal Procedure, § 2.

OPINIONS OF THE ATTORNEY GENERAL

  State Police may provide mental health information to FBI to determine a person's eligibility to possess, purchase, or transfer a firearm. — The Department of State Police has the authority to provide certain mental health information maintained in the Central Criminal Records Exchange to the Federal Bureau of Investigation, so long as it is (i) kept confidential; and (ii) used only to determine a person's eligibility to possess, purchase or transfer a firearm. See opinion of Attorney General to Colonel W. Gerald Massengill, Superintendent, Department of State Police, 01-062 (4/4/02).
  Duty of clerk of court when issuing concealed weapon permit. — When issuing a concealed weapon permit, the clerk of court has no duty to verify with the general district or the juvenile and domestic relations district court whether the applicant has any criminal charges or protective orders pending against him in those courts. The failure of a clerk to detect any existing protective orders or criminal charges does not constitute gross negligence, provided the clerk has followed the statutory requirements governing the issuance of a concealed weapon permit. See opinion of Attorney General to The Honorable Jack Kennedy, Clerk of the Circuit Court, Wise County and City of Norton, 11-018, 2011 Va. AG LEXIS 26 (5/13/11).

§ 19.2-387.1. Protective Order Registry; maintenance; access.

A. The Department of State Police shall keep and maintain a computerized Protective Order Registry. The purpose of the Registry shall be to assist the efforts of law-enforcement agencies to protect their communities and their citizens. The Department of State Police shall make Registry information available, upon request, to criminal justice agencies, including local law-enforcement agencies, through the Virginia Criminal Information Network (VCIN). Registry information provided under this section shall be used only for the purposes of the administration of criminal justice.

B. No liability shall be imposed upon any law-enforcement official who disseminates information or fails to disseminate information in good faith compliance with the requirements of this section, but this provision shall not be construed to grant immunity for gross negligence or willful misconduct.

History.
  2002, cc. 810, 818.

OPINIONS OF THE ATTORNEY GENERAL

  Duty of clerk of court when issuing concealed weapon permit. — When issuing a concealed weapon permit, the clerk of court has no duty to verify with the general district or the juvenile and domestic relations district court whether the applicant has any criminal charges or protective orders pending against him in those courts. The failure of a clerk to detect any existing protective orders or criminal charges does not constitute gross negligence, provided the clerk has followed the statutory requirements governing the issuance of a concealed weapon permit. See opinion of Attorney General to The Honorable Jack Kennedy, Clerk of the Circuit Court, Wise County and City of Norton, 11-018, 2011 Va. AG LEXIS 26 (5/13/11).

§ 19.2-388. Duties and authority of Exchange.

A. It shall be the duty of the Central Criminal Records Exchange to receive, classify and file criminal history record information as defined in § 9.1-101 and other records required to be reported to it by §§ 16.1-299 and 19.2-390. The Exchange is authorized to prepare and furnish to all state and local law-enforcement officials and agencies; to clerks of circuit courts, general district courts, and juvenile and domestic relations district courts; and to corrections and penal officials, forms which shall be used for the making of such reports.

B. Juvenile records received pursuant to § 16.1-299 shall be maintained separately from adult records.

History.
  Code 1950, § 19.1-19.2; 1966, c. 669; 1968, c. 537; 1970, c. 118; 1975, c. 495; 1976, c. 771; 1982, c. 33; 1993, cc. 468, 926; 1996, cc. 755, 914.

Editor's note.
  Acts 1996, cc. 755 and 914, cl. 7, provide: "[t]hat the provisions of this act shall apply to offenses committed and to records created and proceedings held with respect to those offenses on or after July 1, 1996."

§ 19.2-389. Dissemination of criminal history record information.

A. Criminal history record information shall be disseminated, whether directly or through an intermediary, only to:

1. Authorized officers or employees of criminal justice agencies, as defined by § 9.1-101, for purposes of the administration of criminal justice and the screening of an employment application or review of employment by a criminal justice agency with respect to its own employees or applicants, and dissemination to the Virginia Parole Board, pursuant to this subdivision, of such information on all state-responsible inmates for the purpose of making parole determinations pursuant to subdivisions 1, 2, 3, and 5 of § 53.1-136 shall include collective dissemination by electronic means every 30 days;

2. Such other individuals and agencies that require criminal history record information to implement a state or federal statute or executive order of the President of the United States or Governor that expressly refers to criminal conduct and contains requirements or exclusions expressly based upon such conduct, except that information concerning the arrest of an individual may not be disseminated to a noncriminal justice agency or individual if an interval of one year has elapsed from the date of the arrest and no disposition of the charge has been recorded and no active prosecution of the charge is pending;

3. Individuals and agencies pursuant to a specific agreement with a criminal justice agency to provide services required for the administration of criminal justice pursuant to that agreement which shall specifically authorize access to data, limit the use of data to purposes for which given, and ensure the security and confidentiality of the data;

4. Individuals and agencies for the express purpose of research, evaluative, or statistical activities pursuant to an agreement with a criminal justice agency that shall specifically authorize access to data, limit the use of data to research, evaluative, or statistical purposes, and ensure the confidentiality and security of the data;

5. Agencies of state or federal government that are authorized by state or federal statute or executive order of the President of the United States or Governor to conduct investigations determining employment suitability or eligibility for security clearances allowing access to classified information;

6. Individuals and agencies where authorized by court order or court rule;

7. Agencies of any political subdivision of the Commonwealth, public transportation companies owned, operated or controlled by any political subdivision, and any public service corporation that operates a public transit system owned by a local government for the conduct of investigations of applicants for employment, permit, or license whenever, in the interest of public welfare or safety, it is necessary to determine under a duly enacted ordinance if the past criminal conduct of a person with a conviction record would be compatible with the nature of the employment, permit, or license under consideration;

7a. Commissions created pursuant to the Transportation District Act of 1964 (§ 15.2-4500 et seq.) and their contractors, for the conduct of investigations of individuals who have been offered a position of employment whenever, in the interest of public welfare or safety and as authorized in the Transportation District Act of 1964, it is necessary to determine if the past criminal conduct of a person with a conviction record would be compatible with the nature of the employment under consideration;

8. Public or private agencies when authorized or required by federal or state law or interstate compact to investigate (i) applicants for foster or adoptive parenthood or (ii) any individual, and the adult members of that individual's household, with whom the agency is considering placing a child or from whom the agency is considering removing a child due to abuse or neglect, on an emergency, temporary, or permanent basis pursuant to §§ 63.2-901.1 and 63.2-1505, subject to the restriction that the data shall not be further disseminated to any party other than a federal or state authority or court as may be required to comply with an express requirement of law;

9. To the extent permitted by federal law or regulation, public service companies as defined in § 56-1, for the conduct of investigations of applicants for employment when such employment involves personal contact with the public or when past criminal conduct of an applicant would be incompatible with the nature of the employment under consideration;

10. The appropriate authority for purposes of granting citizenship and for purposes of international travel, including, but not limited to, issuing visas and passports;

11. A person requesting a copy of his own criminal history record information as defined in § 9.1-101 at his cost, except that criminal history record information shall be supplied at no charge to a person who has applied to be a volunteer with (i) a Virginia affiliate of Big Brothers/Big Sisters of America; (ii) a volunteer fire company; (iii) the Volunteer Emergency Families for Children; (iv) any affiliate of Prevent Child Abuse, Virginia; (v) any Virginia affiliate of Compeer; or (vi) any board member or any individual who has been offered membership on the board of a Crime Stoppers, Crime Solvers or Crime Line program as defined in § 15.2-1713.1;

12. Administrators and board presidents of and applicants for licensure or registration as a child welfare agency as defined in § 63.2-100 for dissemination to the Commissioner of Social Services' representative pursuant to § 63.2-1702 for the conduct of investigations with respect to employees of and volunteers at such facilities, caretakers, and other adults living in family day care homes or homes approved by family day care systems, and foster and adoptive parent applicants of private child-placing agencies, pursuant to §§ 63.2-1719, 63.2-1720, and 63.2-1721, subject to the restriction that the data shall not be further disseminated by the facility or agency to any party other than the data subject, the

Commissioner of Social Services' representative or a federal or state authority or court as may be required to comply with an express requirement of law for such further dissemination;

13. The school boards of the Commonwealth for the purpose of screening individuals who are offered or who accept public school employment and those current school board employees for whom a report of arrest has been made pursuant to § 19.2-83.1;

14. The State Lottery Department for the conduct of investigations as set forth in the State Lottery Law (§ 58.1-4000 et seq.), and the Department of Agriculture and Consumer Services for the conduct of investigations as set forth in Article 1.1:1 (§ 18.2-340.15 et seq.) of Chapter 8 of Title 18.2;

15. Licensed nursing homes, hospitals and home care organizations for the conduct of investigations of applicants for compensated employment in licensed nursing homes pursuant to § 32.1-126.01, hospital pharmacies pursuant to § 32.1-126.02, and home care organizations pursuant to § 32.1-162.9:1, subject to the limitations set out in subsection E;

16. Licensed homes for adults, licensed district homes for adults, and licensed adult day care centers for the conduct of investigations of applicants for compensated employment in licensed homes for adults pursuant to § 63.2-1720, in licensed district homes for adults pursuant to § 63.1-189.1, and in licensed adult day care centers pursuant to § 63.2-1720, subject to the limitations set out in subsection F;

17. The Alcoholic Beverage Control Board for the conduct of investigations as set forth in § 4.1-103.1;

18. The State Board of Elections and authorized officers and employees thereof and general registrars appointed pursuant to § 24.2-110 in the course of conducting necessary investigations with respect to voter registration, limited to any record of felony convictions;

19. The Commissioner of Behavioral Health and Developmental Services for those individuals who are committed to the custody of the Commissioner pursuant to §§ 19.2-169.2, 19.2-169.6, 19.2-182.2, 19.2-182.3, 19.2-182.8, and 19.2-182.9 for the purpose of placement, evaluation, and treatment planning;

20. Any alcohol safety action program certified by the Commission on the Virginia Alcohol Safety Action Program for (i) assessments of habitual offenders under § 46.2-360, (ii) interventions with first offenders under § 18.2-251, or (iii) services to offenders under § 18.2-51.4, 18.2-266, or 18.2-266.1;

21. Residential facilities for juveniles regulated or operated by the Department of Social Services, the Department of Education, or the Department of Behavioral Health and Developmental Services for the purpose of determining applicants' fitness for employment or for providing volunteer or contractual services;

22. The Department of Behavioral Health and Developmental Services and facilities operated by the Department for the purpose of determining an individual's fitness for employment pursuant to departmental instructions;

23. Pursuant to § 22.1-296.3, the governing boards or administrators of private or religious elementary or secondary schools which are accredited by a statewide accrediting organization recognized, prior to January 1, 1996, by the State Board of Education or a private organization coordinating such records information on behalf of such governing boards or administrators pursuant to a written agreement with the Department of State Police;

24. Public and nonprofit private colleges and universities for the purpose of screening individuals who are offered or accept employment;

25. Members of a threat assessment team established by a public institution of higher education pursuant to § 23-9.2:10 or by a private nonprofit institution of higher education, for the purpose of assessing or intervening with an individual whose behavior may present a threat to safety; however, no member of a threat assessment team shall redisclose any criminal history record information obtained pursuant to this section or otherwise use any record of an individual beyond the purpose that such disclosure was made to the threat assessment team;

26. Executive directors of community services boards or the personnel director serving the community services board for the purpose of determining an individual's fitness for employment pursuant to §§ 37.2-506 and 37.2-607;

27. Executive directors of behavioral health authorities as defined in § 37.2-600 for the purpose of determining an individual's fitness for employment pursuant to §§ 37.2-506 and 37.2-607;

28. The Commissioner of Social Services for the purpose of locating persons who owe child support or who are alleged in a pending paternity proceeding to be a putative father, provided that only the name, address, demographics and social security number of the data subject shall be released;

29. Authorized officers or directors of agencies licensed pursuant to Article 2 (§ 37.2-403 et seq.) of Chapter 4 of Title 37.2 by the Department of Behavioral Health and Developmental Services for the purpose of determining if any applicant who accepts employment in any direct care position has been convicted of a crime that affects his fitness to have responsibility for the safety and well-being of individuals with mental illness, intellectual disability, or substance abuse pursuant to §§ 37.2-416, 37.2-506, and 37.2-607;

30. The Commissioner of the Department of Motor Vehicles, for the purpose of evaluating applicants for and holders of a motor carrier certificate or license subject to the provisions of Chapters 20 (§ 46.2-2000 et seq.) and 21 (§ 46.2-2100 et seq.) of Title 46.2;

31. The chairmen of the Committees for Courts of Justice of the Senate or the House of Delegates for the purpose of determining if any person being

considered for election to any judgeship has been convicted of a crime;

32. Heads of state agencies in which positions have been identified as sensitive for the purpose of determining an individual's fitness for employment in positions designated as sensitive under Department of Human Resource Management policies developed pursuant to § 2.2-1201.1. Dissemination of criminal history record information to the agencies shall be limited to those positions generally described as directly responsible for the health, safety and welfare of the general populace or protection of critical infrastructures;

33. The Office of the Attorney General, for all criminal justice activities otherwise permitted under subdivision A 1 and for purposes of performing duties required by the Civil Commitment of Sexually Violent Predators Act (§ 37.2-900 et seq.);

34. Shipyards, to the extent permitted by federal law or regulation, engaged in the design, construction, overhaul, or repair of nuclear vessels for the United States Navy, including their subsidiary companies, for the conduct of investigations of applications for employment or for access to facilities, by contractors, leased laborers, and other visitors;

35. Any employer of individuals whose employment requires that they enter the homes of others, for the purpose of screening individuals who apply for, are offered, or have accepted such employment;

36. Public agencies when and as required by federal or state law to investigate (i) applicants as providers of adult foster care and home-based services or (ii) any individual with whom the agency is considering placing an adult on an emergency, temporary, or permanent basis pursuant to § 63.2-1601.1, subject to the restriction that the data shall not be further disseminated by the agency to any party other than a federal or state authority or court as may be required to comply with an express requirement of law for such further dissemination, subject to limitations set out in subsection G;

37. The Department of Medical Assistance Services, or its designee, for the purpose of screening individuals who, through contracts, subcontracts, or direct employment, volunteer, apply for, are offered, or have accepted a position related to the provision of transportation services to enrollees in the Medicaid Program or the Family Access to Medical Insurance Security (FAMIS) Program, or any other program administered by the Department of Medical Assistance Services;

38. The State Corporation Commission for the purpose of investigating individuals who are current or proposed members, senior officers, directors, and principals of an applicant or person licensed under Chapter 16 (§ 6.2-1600 et seq.) of Title 6.2. Notwithstanding any other provision of law, if an application is denied based in whole or in part on information obtained from the Central Criminal Records Exchange pursuant to § 6.2-1605, the Commissioner of Financial Institutions or his designee may disclose such information to the applicant or its designee;

39. The Department of Professional and Occupational Regulation for the purpose of investigating individuals for initial licensure pursuant to § 54.1-2106.1;

40. The Department for Aging and Rehabilitative Services and the Department for the Blind and Vision Impaired for the purpose of evaluating an individual's fitness for various types of employment and for the purpose of delivering comprehensive vocational rehabilitation services pursuant to Article 11 (§ 51.5-170 et seq.) of Chapter 14 of Title 51.5 that will assist the individual in obtaining employment;

41. Bail bondsmen, in accordance with the provisions of § 19.2-120;

42. The State Treasurer for the purpose of determining whether a person receiving compensation for wrongful incarceration meets the conditions for continued compensation under § 8.01-195.12;

43. The Department of Social Services and directors of local departments of social services for the purpose of screening individuals seeking to enter into a contract with the Department of Social Services or a local department of social services for the provision of child care services for which child care subsidy payments may be provided; and

44. Other entities as otherwise provided by law.

Upon an ex parte motion of a defendant in a felony case and upon the showing that the records requested may be relevant to such case, the court shall enter an order requiring the Central Criminal Records Exchange to furnish the defendant, as soon as practicable, copies of any records of persons designated in the order on whom a report has been made under the provisions of this chapter.

Notwithstanding any other provision of this chapter to the contrary, upon a written request sworn to before an officer authorized to take acknowledgments, the Central Criminal Records Exchange, or the criminal justice agency in cases of offenses not required to be reported to the Exchange, shall furnish a copy of conviction data covering the person named in the request to the person making the request; however, such person on whom the data is being obtained shall consent in writing, under oath, to the making of such request. A person receiving a copy of his own conviction data may utilize or further disseminate that data as he deems appropriate. In the event no conviction data is maintained on the data subject, the person making the request shall be furnished at his cost a certification to that effect.

B. Use of criminal history record information disseminated to noncriminal justice agencies under this section shall be limited to the purposes for which it was given and may not be disseminated further.

C. No criminal justice agency or person shall confirm the existence or nonexistence of criminal history record information for employment or licensing inquiries except as provided by law.

D. Criminal justice agencies shall establish procedures to query the Central Criminal Records Exchange prior to dissemination of any criminal history record information on offenses required to be reported to the Central Criminal Records Exchange to ensure that the most up-to-date disposition data is being used. Inquiries of the Exchange shall be made prior to any dissemination except in those cases where time is of the essence and the normal response time of the Exchange would exceed the necessary time period. A criminal justice agency to whom a request has been made for the dissemination of criminal history record information that is required to be reported to the Central Criminal Records Exchange may direct the inquirer to the Central Criminal Records Exchange for such dissemination. Dissemination of information regarding offenses not required to be reported to the Exchange shall be made by the criminal justice agency maintaining the record as required by § 15.2-1722.

E. Criminal history information provided to licensed nursing homes, hospitals and to home care organizations pursuant to subdivision A 15 shall be limited to the convictions on file with the Exchange for any offense specified in §§ 32.1-126.01, 32.1-126.02, and 32.1-162.9:1.

F. Criminal history information provided to licensed assisted living facilities, licensed district homes for adults, and licensed adult day care centers pursuant to subdivision A 16 shall be limited to the convictions on file with the Exchange for any offense specified in § 63.1-189.1 or 63.2-1720.

G. Criminal history information provided to public agencies pursuant to subdivision A 36 shall be limited to the convictions on file with the Exchange for any offense specified in § 63.2-1719.

H. Upon receipt of a written request from an employer or prospective employer, the Central Criminal Records Exchange, or the criminal justice agency in cases of offenses not required to be reported to the Exchange, shall furnish at the employer's cost a copy of conviction data covering the person named in the request to the employer or prospective employer making the request, provided that the person on whom the data is being obtained has consented in writing to the making of such request and has presented a photo-identification to the employer or prospective employer. In the event no conviction data is maintained on the person named in the request, the requesting employer or prospective employer shall be furnished at his cost a certification to that effect. The criminal history record search shall be conducted on forms provided by the Exchange.

History.
Code 1950, § 19.1-19.2; 1966, c. 669; 1968, c. 537; 1970, c. 118; 1975, c. 495; 1976, c. 771; 1977, c. 626; 1978, c. 350; 1979, c. 480; 1981, c. 207; 1985, c. 360; 1987, cc. 130, 131; 1988, c. 851; 1989, c. 544; 1990, c. 766; 1991, c. 342; 1992, cc. 422, 641, 718, 746, 791, 844; 1993, cc. 48, 313, 348; 1994, cc. 34, 670, 700, 830; 1995, cc. 409, 645, 731, 781, 809; 1996, cc. 428, 432, 747, 881, 927, 944; 1997, cc. 169, 177, 606, 691, 721, 743, 796, 895; 1998, cc. 113, 405, 445, 882; 1999, cc. 383, 685; 2001, cc. 552, 582; 2002, cc. 370, 587, 606; 2003, c. 731; 2005, cc. 149, 914, 928; 2006, cc. 257, 277, 644; 2007, cc. 12, 361, 495, 572; 2008, cc. 387, 689, 863; 2009, cc. 667, 813, 840; 2010, cc. 189, 340, 406, 456, 524, 563, 862; 2011, cc. 432, 449; 2012, cc. 40, 189, 386, 476, 507, 803, 835; 2013, cc. 165, 176, 261, 407, 491, 582.

Cross references.
As to Criminal Justice Services Board regulations and procedures for the interstate dissemination of criminal history record information, see § 9.1-128. As to Department of Criminal Justice Services licensing, certification, and registration requirements for Private Security Services Businesses, see § 9.1-139. As to background checks required for certain employees of localities, see § 15.2-1503.1. As to applicant preemployment information in localities, see § 15.2-1505.1. For requirement that a preschool or nursery school program operated by a private accredited school furnish documentary evidence that employees obtain criminal record checks as provided in subdivision A 11 of § 19.2-389, see § 63.2-1717 E 7. As to background checks, including a criminal history record check pursuant to § 19.2-389, and a search of the central registry maintained pursuant to § 63.2-1515, for compensated employment of persons in assisted living facilities, adult day care centers, and child welfare agencies, see § 63.2-1720. As to requirement of a search of the central registry maintained pursuant to § 63.2-1515 and a criminal records check as provided in subdivision A 11 of § 19.2-389 for employees or volunteers of a child day center that is exempt from licensure pursuant to § 63.2-1716, see § 63.2-1724.

Editor's note.
At the direction of the Virginia Code Commission, subdivision A 39 as added by Acts 2010, c. 862 was renumbered as subdivision A 40. In addition, Title 6.2 references in subdivision A 38 were substituted for Title 6.1 references to conform to Acts 2010, c. 794, effective October 1, 2010.

Acts 1990, c. 766, cl. 2 repeals cl. 2, c. 851 of Acts 1988, which provided for the expiration of the 1988 act.

At the direction of the Code Commission, Acts 1994, c. 700, which amended this section, was not given effect due to a conflict. The amendment would have conflicted with the amendment to this section in Acts 1994, c. 830.

Section 63.1-189.1, referred to in subdivision A 16 and subsection F of this section, contained in former Article 2 (§ 63.1-183 et seq.) of Chapter 9 of former Title 63.1, was repealed effective October 1, 2002, by Acts 2002, c. 747.

Acts 2005, c. 175, amended subdivision A 11 by adding clauses (vi) and (vii) as follows: "(vi) a council of Girl Scouts of the USA that serves Girl Scout troops in Virginia; or (vii) a council of Boy Scouts of America that serves Boy Scout troops in Virginia." The amendments were contingent on funding pursuant to Acts 2005, c. 175, cl. 2. The funding was not provided, so subdivision A 11 is set out above without the amendments by c. 175 at the direction of the Virginia Code Commission.

Acts 2009, c. 667, cl. 2, provides: "That the Department of Professional and Occupational Regulation shall obtain criminal history record information regarding individuals for initial licensure as a real estate licensee pursuant to § 54.1-2106.1."

Acts 2009, c. 667, cl. 3, provides: "That the Department of Professional and Occupational Regulation shall amend the renewal license application form to require applicants for a renewal real estate sales or brokerage license to state that they have no criminal convictions that have not been previously disclosed. Penalties for misrepresentation shall be established by the Real Estate Board."

Acts 2009, c. 667, cl. 4, provides: "That the State Police shall invoice the Department of Professional and Occupational Regulation for any costs and expenses of implementing the provisions of this act."

The 2007 amendments.
The 2007 amendment by c. 12 deleted "and" at the end of subdivision A 34; added subdivision A 35 [now A 36]; and redesignated the remaining subsection accordingly.

The 2007 amendment by c. 361 added subsection G [now H] and made minor stylistic changes.

The 2007 amendment by c. 495, in subdivision A 8, substituted "authorized or" for "and as," inserted "and the adult members of that individual's household," "or from whom the agency is considering removing a child due to abuse or neglect" and "and 63.2-1505" and deleted "by the agency" following "disseminated" and "for such further dissemination" from the end.

The 2007 amendment by c. 572, in subsection A, added subdivision A 35 and redesignated former subdivision A 35 as present subdivision A 36 [now A 37]; and added subsection G.

The 2008 amendments.

The 2008 amendments by cc. 387 and 689 are identical, and substituted "Agriculture and Consumer Services" for "Charitable Gaming" in subdivision A 14.

The 2008 amendment by c. 863 deleted "and" at the end of subdivision A 36; inserted subdivision A 37 and redesignated former subdivision A 37 as subdivision A 38.

The 2009 amendments.

The 2009 amendment by c. 667 inserted subdivision A 38 and redesignated former subdivision A 38 as subdivision A 39 and made a related change.

The 2009 amendments by cc. 813 and 840 are identical, and substituted "Commissioner of Behavioral Health and Developmental Services" for "Commissioner of the Department of Mental Health, Mental Retardation and Substance Abuse Services" in subdivision A 19 and "Behavioral Health and Developmental Services" for "Mental Health, Mental Retardation and Substance Abuse Services" in subdivisions A 21, A 22, and A 28.

The 2010 amendments.

The 2010 amendments by cc. 189 and 563 are nearly identical, and in subdivision A 7, inserted "public transportation companies owned, operated or controlled by any political subdivision, and any public transit system that operates a public transit system owned by a local government" and deleted "public" following "applicants for"; and added subdivision A 7a.

The 2010 amendments by cc. 340 and 406 are identical, and deleted "19.2-176, 19.2-177.1," following "19.2-169.6" in subdivision A 19.

The 2010 amendments by cc. 456 and 524 are identical, and redesignated former subdivisions A 25 through A 39 as subdivisions A 26 through A 40, respectively; added subdivision A 25; in subsection E, substituted "subdivision A 15" for "subdivision 15 of subsection A"; in subsection F, substituted "subdivision A 16" for "subdivision 16 of subsection A"; and in subsection G, substituted "subdivision A 36" for "subdivision 35 of subsection A."

The 2010 amendment by c. 862 added subdivision A 39, made a related change, and redesignated former subdivision A 39 as subdivision A 40.

The 2011 amendments.

The 2011 amendments by cc. 432 and 449 are nearly identical, and added subdivision A 40 and redesignated the remaining subdivisions accordingly.

The 2012 amendments.

The 2012 amendment by c. 40 added subdivision A 42, redesignated former subdivision A 42 as A 43, and made a related change.

The 2012 amendment by c. 189 substituted "§§ 63.2-1719, 63.2-1720, and 63.2-1721" for "§§ 63.2-1719 through 63.2-1721" in subdivision A 12, and rewrote subdivision A 38.

The 2012 amendment by c. 386 substituted "pursuant to §§ 63.2-1719, 63.2-1720, and 63.2-1721" for "pursuant to §§ 63.2-1719 through 63.2-1721" in subdivision A 12; and in subdivision A 25, inserted "or by a private nonprofit institution of higher education" and added the language beginning "however, no member of a threat assessment team" at the end.

The 2012 amendments by cc. 476 and 507 are identical, and substituted "§§ 63.2-1719, 63.2-1720, and 63.2-1721," for "§§ 63.2-1719 through 63.2-1721," in subdivision A 12; and in subdivision A 29, substituted "direct care position" for "direct consumer care position," "his fitness" for "their fitness," and "individuals with mental illness, intellectual disability, or substance abuse" for "persons with mental illness, mental retardation and substance abuse."

The 2012 amendments by cc. 803 and 835, cl. 59, are identical, and in subdivision A 28, deleted "of the Department" following "Commissioner"; and in subdivision A 40, substituted "Department for Aging and Rehabilitative Services" for "Department of Rehabili-

tative Services" and "Article 11 (§ 51.5-170 et seq.) of Chapter 14 of Title 51.5" for "Chapter 5 (§ 51.5-15 et seq.) of Title 51.5."

The 2013 amendments.

The 2013 amendments by cc. 165 and 582 are identical, and inserted "and holders of" preceding "a motor carrier certificate" in subdivision A 30.

The 2013 amendments by cc. 176 and 407 are identical, and deleted "or volunteer rescue squad" from the end of clause (ii) in subdivision A 11; and substituted "day care" for "day-care" in two places in subdivisions A 12 and A 16 and in subsection F.

The 2013 amendment by c. 261 added subdivision A 43, redesignated former subdivision A 43 as A 44, and made a related change.

The 2013 amendment by c. 491, in subdivision A 18, inserted "and general registrars appointed pursuant to § 24.2-110" and substituted "voter registration" for "registered voters."

Law Review.

For 2007 annual survey article, "Labor and Employment Law," see 42 U. Rich. L. Rev. 489 (2007).

CASE NOTES

Commonwealth's attorney authorized to review criminal background records of prospective jurors. — Because the Office of the Commonwealth's attorney is a criminal justice agency, and because the "administration of justice" includes the prosecution of criminal cases, subdivision A 1 of this section authorizes the Commonwealth's attorney to review the criminal background records of prospective jurors. Salmon v. Commonwealth, 32 Va. App. 586, 529 S.E.2d 815, 2000 Va. App. LEXIS 428 (2000).

Harmless error in refusal to require production of records. — Defendant's convictions for first-degree murder and use of a firearm in the commission of a felony were proper because, although defendant contended that she should have been provided the adult records of several of the Commonwealth's witnesses pursuant to subdivision A 38 of § 19.2-389, she failed to identify in the trial court or on appeal any prejudice allegedly flowing from the trial court's refusal to require production of those records; consequently, any error in such ruling was harmless as a matter of law. Thomas v. Commonwealth, 279 Va. 131, 688 S.E.2d 220, 2010 Va. LEXIS 11, cert. denied, 131 S. Ct. 143, 178 L. Ed. 2d 8, 2010 U.S. LEXIS 6109 (U.S. 2010).

Applied in Wheeler v. Gilmore, 998 F. Supp. 666 (E.D. Va. 1998).

OPINIONS OF THE ATTORNEY GENERAL

A commissioner of accounts is not permitted access to criminal history records of delinquent fiduciaries through the Virginia Criminal Information Network, unless such records are released pursuant to a circuit court order or rule. See opinion of Attorney General to The Honorable Thomas D. Horne, Judge, Twentieth Judicial Circuit, 00-011 (4/8/02).

State Police may provide mental health information to FBI to determine a person's eligibility to possess, purchase, or transfer a firearm. — The Department of State Police has the authority to provide certain mental health information maintained in the Central Criminal Records Exchange to the Federal Bureau of Investigation, so long as it is: (i) kept confidential; and (ii) used only to determine a person's eligibility to possess, purchase or transfer a firearm. See opinion of Attorney General to Colonel W. Gerald Massengill, Superintendent, Department of State Police, 01-062 (4/4/02).

Access to criminal justice information by nonlaw-enforcement personnel. — Nonlaw-enforcement personnel, such as E-911 dispatchers, may access criminal justice information generated from VCIN/NCIC terminals, provided the county E-911 office and the proposed agreement between the county sheriff's office, the county board of supervisors, and the local E-911 office satisfy the requirements of this section, and, further, that such access is authorized by the State Police. See opinion of Attorney General to The Honorable Clarence E. Phillips, Member, House of Delegates, 02-065 (8/20/02).

Private, nonprofit institutions of higher education may require criminal background searches as a condition of employment and may request that candidates for admission consent to a criminal background check as a condition of matriculation. See opinion of Attorney General to The Honorable Phillip P. Puckett, Member, Senate of Virginia, 06-046 (8/8/06).

Duty of clerk of court when issuing concealed weapon permit. — When issuing a concealed weapon permit, the clerk of court has no duty to verify with the general district or the juvenile and domestic relations district court whether the applicant has any criminal charges or protective orders pending against him in those courts. The failure of a clerk to detect any existing protective orders or criminal charges does not constitute gross negligence, provided the clerk has followed the statutory requirements governing the issuance of a concealed weapon permit. See opinion of Attorney General to The Honorable Jack Kennedy, Clerk of the Circuit Court, Wise County and City of Norton, 11-018, 2011 Va. AG LEXIS 26 (5/13/11).

§ 19.2-389.1. Dissemination of juvenile record information.

Record information maintained in the Central Criminal Records Exchange pursuant to the provisions of § 16.1-299 shall be disseminated only (i) to make the determination as provided in §§ 18.2-308.2 and 18.2-308.2:2 of eligibility to possess or purchase a firearm; (ii) to aid in the preparation of a pretrial investigation report prepared by a local pretrial services agency established pursuant to Article 5 (§ 19.2-152.2 et seq.) of Chapter 9, a presentence or post-sentence investigation report pursuant to § 19.2-264.5 or 19.2-299 or in the preparation of the discretionary sentencing guidelines worksheets pursuant to subsection C of § 19.2-298.01; (iii) to aid local community-based probation services agencies established pursuant to the Comprehensive Community Corrections Act for Local-Responsible Offenders (§ 9.1-173 et seq.) with investigating or serving adult local-responsible offenders and all court service units serving juvenile delinquent offenders; (iv) for fingerprint comparison utilizing the fingerprints maintained in the Automated Fingerprint Information System (AFIS) computer; (v) to attorneys for the Commonwealth to secure information incidental to sentencing and to attorneys for the Commonwealth and probation officers to prepare the discretionary sentencing guidelines worksheets pursuant to subsection C of § 19.2-298.01; (vi) to any full-time or part-time employee of the State Police, a police department or sheriff's office that is a part of or administered by the Commonwealth or any political subdivision thereof, and who is responsible for the prevention and detection of crime and the enforcement of the penal, traffic or highway laws of the Commonwealth, for purposes of the administration of criminal justice as defined in § 9.1-101; (vii) to the Department of Forensic Science to verify its authority to maintain the juvenile's sample in the DNA data bank pursuant to § 16.1-299.1; (viii) to the Office of the Attorney General, for all criminal justice activities otherwise permitted and for purposes of performing duties required by the Civil Commitment of Sexually Violent Predators Act (§ 37.2-900 et seq.); (ix) to the Virginia Criminal Sentencing Commission for research purposes; (x) to members of a threat assessment team established by a public institution of higher education pursuant to § 23-9.2:10 or by a private nonprofit institution of higher education, to aid in the assessment or intervention with individuals whose behavior may present a threat to safety; however, no member of a threat assessment team shall redisclose any juvenile record information obtained pursuant to this section or otherwise use any record of an individual beyond the purpose that such disclosure was made to the threat assessment team; and (xi) to any full-time or part-time employee of the State Police or a police department or sheriff's office that is a part of or administered by the Commonwealth or any political subdivision thereof for the purpose of screening any person for full-time or part-time employment with the State Police or a police department or sheriff's office that is a part of or administered by the Commonwealth or any political subdivision thereof.

History.
1993, cc. 468, 926; 1996, cc. 755, 870, 914; 2002, c. 701; 2003, cc. 107, 432; 2005, cc. 868, 881, 914; 2006, c. 502; 2007, c. 133; 2010, cc. 456, 524; 2011, c. 622; 2012, c. 386.

Editor's note.
Acts 1996, cc. 755 and 914, cl. 7, provide: "[t]hat the provisions of this act shall apply to offenses committed and to records created and proceedings held with respect to those offenses on or after July 1, 1996."

The 2007 amendments.
The 2007 amendment by c. 133 substituted "community-based probation services agencies" for "community-based probation programs" in clause (iii).

The 2010 amendments.
The 2010 amendment by c. 456 deleted "of this title" following "of Chapter 9," added clause (x), and made a related change.
The 2010 amendment by c. 524 added "(x) to members of a threat assessment team established by a public institution of higher education pursuant to § 23-9.2:10, to aid in the assessment or intervention with individuals whose behavior may present a threat to safety" and made a related change.

The 2011 amendments.
The 2011 amendment by c. 622 added clause (xi) and made a related change.

The 2012 amendments.
The 2012 amendment by c. 386, in clause (x), inserted "or by a private nonprofit institution of higher education" and "however, no member of a threat assessment team shall redisclose any juvenile record information obtained pursuant to this section or otherwise use any record of an individual beyond the purpose that such disclosure was made to the threat assessment team."

Law Review.
For annual survey article on legal issues involving children, see 38 U. Rich. L. Rev. 161 (2003).

§ 19.2-390. Reports to be made by local law-enforcement officers, conservators of the peace, clerks of court, Secretary of the Commonwealth and Corrections officials to State Police; material submitted by other agencies.

A. 1. Every state official or agency having the power to arrest, the sheriffs of counties, the police officials of cities and towns, and any other local law-enforcement officer or conservator of the peace having the power to arrest for a felony shall make a report to the Central Criminal Records Exchange, on forms provided by it, of any arrest, including those arrests involving the taking into custody of, or service of process upon, any person on charges resulting from an indictment, presentment or information, the arrest on capias or warrant for failure to appear, and the service of a warrant for another jurisdiction, on any of the following charges:

   a. Treason;

   b. Any felony;

   c. Any offense punishable as a misdemeanor under Title 54.1; or

   d. Any misdemeanor punishable by confinement in jail (i) under Title 18.2 or 19.2, except an arrest for a violation of § 18.2-119, Article 2 (§ 18.2-415 et seq.) of Chapter 9 of Title 18.2, or any similar ordinance of any county, city or town, (ii) under § 20-61, or (iii) under § 16.1-253.2.

The reports shall contain such information as is required by the Exchange and shall be accompanied by fingerprints of the individual arrested. Effective January 1, 2006, the corresponding photograph of the individual arrested shall accompany the report. Fingerprint cards prepared by a law-enforcement agency for inclusion in a national criminal justice file shall be forwarded to the Exchange for transmittal to the appropriate bureau. Nothing in this section shall preclude each local law-enforcement agency from maintaining its own separate photographic database. Fingerprints and photographs required to be taken pursuant to this subsection or subdivision A 3c of § 19.2-123 may be taken at the facility where the magistrate is located, including a regional jail, even if the accused is not committed to jail.

   2. For persons arrested and released on summonses in accordance with § 19.2-74, such report shall not be required until (i) a conviction is entered and no appeal is noted or if an appeal is noted, the conviction is upheld upon appeal or the person convicted withdraws his appeal; (ii) the court dismisses the proceeding pursuant to § 18.2-251; or (iii) an acquittal by reason of insanity pursuant to § 19.2-182.2 is entered. Upon such conviction or acquittal, the court shall remand the individual to the custody of the office of the chief law-enforcement officer of the county or city. It shall be the duty of the chief law-enforcement officer, or his designee who may be the arresting officer, to ensure that such report is completed after a determination of guilt or acquittal by reason of insanity. The court shall require the officer to complete the report immediately following the person's conviction or acquittal, and the individual shall be discharged from custody forthwith, unless the court has imposed a jail sentence to be served by him or ordered him committed to the custody of the Commissioner of Behavioral Health and Developmental Services.

B. Within 72 hours following the receipt of (i) a warrant or capias for the arrest of any person on a charge of a felony or (ii) a Governor's warrant of arrest of a person issued pursuant to § 19.2-92, the law-enforcement agency which received the warrant shall enter the person's name and other appropriate information required by the Department of State Police into the "information systems" known as the Virginia Criminal Information Network (VCIN), established and maintained by the Department pursuant to Chapter 2 (§ 52-12 et seq.) of Title 52 and the National Crime Information Center (NCIC), maintained by the Federal Bureau of Investigation. The report shall include the person's name, date of birth, social security number and such other known information which the State Police or Federal Bureau of Investigation may require. Where feasible and practical, the magistrate or court issuing the warrant or capias may transfer information electronically into VCIN. When the information is electronically transferred to VCIN, the court or magistrate shall forthwith forward the warrant or capias to the local police department or sheriff's office. When criminal process has been ordered destroyed pursuant to § 19.2-76.1, the law-enforcement agency destroying such process shall ensure the removal of any information relating to the destroyed criminal process from the VCIN and NCIC.

B1. Within 72 hours following the receipt of a written statement issued by a parole officer pursuant to § 53.1-149 or 53.1-162 authorizing the arrest of a person who has violated the provisions of his post-release supervision or probation, the law-enforcement agency that received the written statement shall enter, or cause to be entered, the person's name and other appropriate information required by the Department of State Police into the "information systems" known as the Virginia Criminal Information Network (VCIN), established and maintained by the Department pursuant to Chapter 2 (§ 52-12 et seq.) of Title 52.

C. The clerk of each circuit court and district court shall make an electronic report to the Central Criminal Records Exchange of (i) any dismissal, indefinite postponement or continuance, charge still pending due to mental incompetency or incapacity, nolle prosequi, acquittal, or conviction of, including any sentence imposed, or failure of a grand jury to return a true bill as to, any person charged with an offense listed in subsection A, including any action which may have resulted from an indictment, presentment or information, and (ii) any adjudication of delinquency based upon an act which, if committed by an adult, would require fingerprints to be filed pursuant to subsection A. In the case of offenses not required to be reported to the Exchange by subsection A, the reports of any of the foregoing dispositions shall be filed by the law-enforcement agency making the arrest with the arrest record required to be maintained by § 15.2-1722. Upon conviction of any person, including juveniles tried and convicted in the circuit courts pursuant to § 16.1-269.1, whether sentenced as adults or juveniles, for an offense for which registration is required as defined in § 9.1-902, the clerk shall within seven days of sentencing submit a report to the Sex Offender and Crimes Against Minors Registry. The report to the Registry shall include the name of the person convicted and all aliases which he is known to have used, the date and locality of the conviction for which registration is required, his date of birth, social security number, last known address, and specific reference to the offense for which he was convicted. No report of conviction or adjudication in a district court shall be filed unless the period allowed for an appeal has elapsed and no appeal has been perfected. In the event that the records in the office of any clerk show that any conviction or adjudication has been nullified in any manner, he shall also make a report of that fact to the Exchange and, if appropriate, to the Registry. In addition, each clerk of a circuit court, upon receipt of certification thereof from the Supreme Court, shall report to the Exchange or the Registry, or to the law-enforcement agency making the arrest in the case of offenses not required to be reported to the Exchange, on forms provided by the Exchange or Registry, as the case may be, any reversal or other amendment to a prior sentence or disposition previously reported. When criminal process is ordered destroyed pursuant to § 19.2-76.1, the clerk shall report such action to the law-enforcement agency that entered the warrant or capias into the VCIN.

D. In addition to those offenses enumerated in subsection A of this section, the Central Criminal Records Exchange may receive, classify and file any other fingerprints, photographs, and records of arrest or confinement submitted to it by any law-enforcement agency or any correctional institution.

E. Corrections officials, sheriffs, and jail superintendents of regional jails, responsible for maintaining correctional status information, as required by the regulations of the Department of Criminal Justice Services, with respect to individuals about whom reports have been made under the provisions of this chapter shall make reports of changes in correctional status information to the Central Criminal Records Exchange. The reports to the Exchange shall include any commitment to or release or escape from a state or local correctional facility, including commitment to or release from a parole or probation agency.

F. Any pardon, reprieve or executive commutation of sentence by the Governor shall be reported to the Exchange by the office of the Secretary of the Commonwealth.

G. Officials responsible for reporting disposition of charges, and correctional changes of status of individuals under this section, including those reports made to the Registry, shall adopt procedures reasonably designed at a minimum (i) to ensure that such reports are accurately made as soon as feasible by the most expeditious means and in no instance later than 30 days after occurrence of the disposition or correctional change of status and (ii) to report promptly any correction, deletion, or revision of the information.

H. Upon receiving a correction, deletion, or revision of information, the Central Criminal Records Exchange shall notify all criminal justice agencies known to have previously received the information.

As used in this section:

"Chief law-enforcement officer" means the chief of police of cities and towns and sheriffs of counties, unless a political subdivision has otherwise designated its chief law-enforcement officer by appropriate resolution or ordinance, in which case the local designation shall be controlling.

"Electronic report" means a report transmitted to, or otherwise forwarded to, the Central Criminal Records Exchange in an electronic format approved by the Exchange. The report shall contain the name of the person convicted and all aliases which he is known to have used, the date and locality of the conviction, his date of birth, social security number, last known address, and specific reference to the offense including the Virginia Code section and any subsection, the Virginia crime code for the offense, and the offense tracking number for the offense for which he was convicted.

History.

Code 1950, § 19.1-19.3; 1966, c. 669; 1968, c. 724; 1970, c. 191; 1971, Ex. Sess., c. 107; 1974, c. 575; 1975, cc. 495, 584; 1976, cc. 336, 572, 771; 1978, cc. 467, 825; 1979, c. 378; 1981, c. 529; 1982, cc. 33, 535; 1990, cc. 100, 692; 1992, c. 391; 1993, cc. 448, 468, 926; 1994, cc. 362, 428, 432; 1996, cc. 429, 755, 806, 914; 1997, cc. 27, 509, 747, 801; 2001, cc. 516, 536, 565; 2003, cc. 27, 584, 727; 2004, cc. 284, 406; 2005, cc. 187, 229; 2008, cc. 73, 246; 2009, cc. 249, 813, 840; 2010, c. 273; 2013, c. 614.

Editor's note.

The above section combines former § 19.1-19.3 as amended by Acts 1975, c. 584, and § 19.2-390 as enacted by Acts 1975, c. 495. The first sentence of subsection (a) is set out as amended by c. 584, and the last sentence of subsection (a) has been added pursuant to c. 495. See § 30-152.

Acts 1996, cc. 755 and 914, cl. 7, provide: "[t]hat the provisions of this act shall apply to offenses committed and to records created and proceedings held with respect to those offenses on or after July 1, 1996."

Acts 1997, c. 801, cl. 2, provides: "That the provisions of this act shall become effective on January 1, 1998. The powers granted and duties imposed pursuant to this act shall apply prospectively to guardians and conservators appointed by court order entered on or after that date, or modified on or after that date if the court so directs, without regard to when the petition was filed. The procedures specified in this act governing proceedings for appointment of a guardian or conservator or termination or other modification of a guardianship shall apply on and after that date without regard to when the petition therefor was filed or the guardianship or conservatorship created."

Acts 2008, cc. 73 and 246, cl. 2 provides: "That the amendments to § 19.2-390 of the Code of Virginia of this act that require an electronic report to be made to the Central Criminal Records Exchange shall not become effective as to any circuit court clerks not currently using the case management system of the Supreme Court of Virginia until July 1, 2009. Until July 1, 2009, the circuit court clerks shall forthwith forward the report to the Central Criminal Records Exchange, using such methods as may be established jointly with the Virginia State Police. All circuit court clerks who are using the case management system of the Supreme Court of Virginia shall provide the reports in electronic format pursuant to § 19.2-390."

The 2008 amendments.

The 2008 amendments by cc. 73 and 246 are identical, and deleted "systems" following "VCIN and NCIC" at the end of subsection B; in subsection C, substituted "shall make an electronic report" for "shall make a report" in the first sentence and deleted "system" following "VCIN" at the end of the subsection; and in subsection H, made a stylistic change and added the paragraph defining "Electronic report." For effective date and applicability, see Editor's note.

The 2009 amendments.

The 2009 amendment by c. 249 added clause (iii) and made related changes in the first paragraph of subdivision A 1 d.

The 2009 amendments by cc. 813 and 840 are identical, and substituted "Commissioner of Behavioral Health and Developmental Services" for "Commissioner of the Department of Mental Health, Mental Retardation and Substance Abuse Services" at the end of subdivision A 2.

The 2010 amendments.

The 2010 amendment by c. 273 added subsection B1 and made a minor stylistic change in subsection G.

The 2013 amendments.

The 2013 amendments by c. 614 added the last sentence in the last paragraph of subdivision A 1 d.

Law Review.

For survey of Virginia law on evidence for the year 1972-1973, see 59 Va. L. Rev. 1526 (1973).

CASE NOTES

National Criminal Information Center report as record of prior convictions. — Defendant's claim that a National Criminal Information Center report disclosing his prior convictions was not properly authenticated was rejected. Subsection C has extensive reporting requirements that attest to the regularity of the creation and preparation of the records; moreover, an officer testified that the report was consistent with his own search of defendant's criminal records. Hawes v. Commonwealth, No. 1094-03-4, 2004 Va. App. LEXIS 395 (Ct. of Appeals Aug. 17, 2004).

Copy of arrest report as evidence. — The fact that former § 8-266 provided that a copy of an arrest report filed with the Central Criminal Records Exchange could be admitted in evidence did not mean that all items in the report could be admitted for any purpose. The mere fact that a record or report qualifies as a public document does not automatically overcome the hearsay objection unless the document relates facts or events within the personal knowledge and observation of the recording official to which he could testify should he be called as a witness. Williams v. Commonwealth, 213 Va. 45, 189 S.E.2d 378 (1972).

Record of prior convictions properly admitted. — As defendant did not claim his two prior convictions listed in a copy of arrest report as evidence. were invalid, and the report's alleged incompleteness went to the weight to be given it, not its admissibility, the trial court properly admitted the report under the public records exception to the hearsay rule. Hawes v. Commonwealth, No. 1094-03-4, 2004 Va. App. LEXIS 395 (Ct. of Appeals Aug. 17, 2004).

OPINIONS OF THE ATTORNEY GENERAL

Information contained in indictments and capiases ordered sealed by a court prior to the arrest of the individual named in such indictments and capiases need not be entered in Network. — Subsection B does not require law-enforcement agencies to enter into the Virginia Criminal Information Network information contained in indictments and capiases ordered sealed by a court prior to the arrest of the individual named in such indictments and capiases. See opinion of Attorney General to The Honorable William W. Davenport, Commonwealth's Attor-

ney for Chesterfield County, 01-119 (4/4/02).

Show cause summons. — Service of a criminal show cause summons does not constitute an "arrest" or trigger the reporting requirements of § 19.2-390. See opinion of Attorney General to The Honorable Dennis S. Proffitt, Chesterfield County Sheriff, 09-070, 2009 Va. AG LEXIS 48 (10/26/09).

§ 19.2-390.01. Use of Virginia crime code references required.

If any criminal warrant, indictment, information, presentment, petition, summons, charging document issued by a magistrate, or dispositional document from a criminal trial, involves a jailable offense, it shall include the Virginia crime code references for the particular offense or offenses covered. When Virginia crime codes are provided on charging and dispositional documents, the Virginia crime codes shall be recorded and stored for adult offenders in: criminal history computer systems maintained by the State Police; court case management computer systems maintained by the Supreme Court of Virginia; probation and parole case management computer systems maintained by the Department of Corrections and the Virginia Parole Board; pretrial and community-based probation case management computer systems maintained by the Department of Criminal Justice Services; and jail management computer systems maintained by the State Compensation Board. The Department of Juvenile Justice shall record and store Virginia crime codes for particular offenses related to juveniles in case management computer systems.

Virginia crime codes shall only be used to facilitate administration and research, and shall not have any legal standing as they relate to a particular offense or offenses.

History.

2003, c. 148; 2007, c. 133.

Editor's note.

Acts 2003, c. 148, cl. 2, provides: "That this act shall become effective on October 1, 2004."

Acts 2003, c. 148, cl. 3, provides: "That the charging and dispositional documents incorporating Virginia crime codes developed pursuant to this act shall indicate clearly that the crime codes are to be entered in a portion of such documents labeled 'for administrative use only' or words to that effect."

The 2007 amendments.

The 2007 amendment by c. 133 substituted "pretrial and community-based probation" for "pretrial and community corrections" near the end of the second sentence.

§ 19.2-390.02. Policies and procedures for law enforcement to conduct in-person and photo lineups.

The Department of State Police and each local police department and sheriff's office shall establish a written policy and procedure for conducting in-person and photographic lineups.

History.

2005, cc. 187, 229.

§ 19.2-390.1. Sex Offender and Crimes Against Minors Registry; maintenance; access.

The Department of State Police shall keep and maintain a Sex Offender and Crimes Against Minors Registry, separate and apart from all other records maintained by it.

The Superintendent of State Police shall organize, equip, and staff, within the Department of State Police, the Sex Offender and Crimes Against Minors Registry. The Superintendent shall appoint and designate personnel as he deems necessary to carry out all duties and assignments related to the Sex Offender and Crimes Against Minors Registry as required by Chapter 9 (§ 9.1-900 et seq.) of Title 9.1.

History.
1994, c. 362; 1996, cc. 418, 542, 880; 1997, cc. 670, 672, 747; 1998, cc. 785, 834; 2000, c. 250; 2003, c. 584; 2006, cc. 857, 914.

Cross references.
As to Sex Offenders and Crimes Against Minors Registry, see § 9.1-900 et seq.

Editor's note.
At the direction of the Virginia Code Commission, the new subsection E added to § 19.2-390.1 by Acts 2003, c. 391 has been numbered § 9.1-916 and the new subsection H added to § 19.2-390.1 by Acts 2003, c. 391 has been numbered § 9.1-919. The new subsection G added to § 19.2-390.1 by Acts 2003, c. 391 is the same as § 9.1-917 added by Acts 2003, c. 584 (renumbered as § 9.1-918 at the direction of the Code Commission.)

Michie's Jurisprudence.
For related discussion, see 15 M.J. Rape, § 27.

CASE NOTES

Evidence from custodian of records of state police sex registry properly admitted. — Defendant's due process guarantees to confrontation under the Fourteenth Amendment were not violated by the admission of an affidavit of the custodian of records of a state police sex registry in defendant's probation revocation proceeding as: (1) the affidavit was a document establishing the absence of an objective fact; (2) it was prepared in a non-adversarial setting, was not accusatory, and was not prepared in anticipation of litigation; (3) the sex offender registry was a neutral repository that reflected the objective results of a search of public records; (4) the affidavit summarized the official registry, which was mandated by § 19.2-390.1; and (5) the affidavit fell within the official records exception to the hearsay rule under subsection B of § 8.01-390. Dickens v. Commonwealth, 52 Va. App. 412, 663 S.E.2d 548, 2008 Va. App. LEXIS 356 (2008).

§ 19.2-390.2. Repealed by Acts 2003, c. 584, cl. 2.

Cross references.
For current provisions relating to automatic notification of registration to certain entities, see § 9.1-914.

§ 19.2-390.3. Child Pornography Images Registry; maintenance; access.

A. The Office of the Attorney General, in cooperation with the Department of State Police, shall keep and maintain a Child Pornography Registry to be located within the State Police, separate and apart from all other records maintained by either department. The purpose of the Registry shall be to assist the efforts of law-enforcement agencies statewide to protect their communities from repeat child pornographers and to protect children from becoming victims of criminal offenders by aiding in identifying victims and perpetrators. Criminal justice agencies, including law-enforcement agencies, may request of the State Police a search and comparison of child pornography images contained within the Registry with those images obtained by criminal justice agencies during the course of official investigations.

B. The Registry shall include images of sexually explicit visual material in any form including any picture, photograph, drawing, sculpture, motion picture film, digital image or similar visual representation, presented as evidence and used in any conviction for any offense enumerated in §§ 18.2-374.1 and 18.2-374.1:1.

C. Registry information provided under this section shall be used for the purposes of the administration of criminal justice or for the protection of the public in general and children in particular. Use of the information or the images contained therein for purposes not authorized by this section is prohibited and a willful violation of this section with the intent to harass or intimidate another shall be punished as a Class 6 felony.

D. The Virginia Criminal Information Network and any form or document used by the Department of State Police to disseminate information from the Registry shall provide notice that any unauthorized possession, use or dissemination of the information or images is a crime punishable as a Class 6 felony.

History.
2003, cc. 935, 938.

Cross references.
As to penalty for Class 6 felony, see § 18.2-10.

Editor's note.
Acts 2003, cc. 935 and 938, cl. 3, provide: "The Superintendent of State Police, in consultation with the Office of the Attorney General, shall promulgate regulations governing the operation and maintenance of the Registry."

Acts 2003, cc. 935 and 938, cl. 4, provide: "On or before January 1, 2004, the Office of the Attorney General and the State Police shall develop and maintain a system for making certain a registry of information and images of child pornography is established, protected, and, where applicable, encrypted. The system shall be secure and not capable of being altered except by the State Police. The State Police shall remove all information that it knows to be inaccurate from the Registry."

Law Review.
For annual survey article on legal issues involving children, see 38 U. Rich. L. Rev. 161 (2003).

§ 19.2-391. Records to be made available to Exchange by state officials and agencies; duplication of records.

Each state official and agency shall make available to the Central Criminal Records Exchange such of their records as are pertinent to its functions and shall cooperate with the Exchange in the development and use of equipment and facilities on a joint basis, where feasible. No state official or agency shall maintain records which are a duplication of the records on deposit in the Central Criminal Records Exchange, except to the extent necessary for efficient internal administration of such agency. Furthermore, the Virginia Parole Board may receive and use electronically disseminated criminal history record information from the Central Criminal Records Exchange as required to make parole determinations pursuant to subdivisions 1, 2, 3, and 5 of § 53.1-136, provided the data is (i) temporarily stored with the Board solely for operational purposes, (ii) purged within thirty days of receipt of updated data by the Board, and (iii) accessed and viewed solely by Parole Board members and authorized staff pursuant to § 9.1-101 and § 9.1-130.

History.
Code 1950, § 19.1-19.4; 1966, c. 669; 1975, c. 495; 1993, c. 313.

§ 19.2-392. Fingerprints and photographs by police authorities.

A. All duly constituted police authorities having the power of arrest may take the fingerprints and photographs of: (i) any person arrested by them and charged with a felony or a misdemeanor an arrest for which is to be reported by them to the Central Criminal Records Exchange, or (ii) any person who pleads guilty or is found guilty after being summoned in accordance with § 19.2-74. Such authorities shall make such records available to the Central Criminal Records Exchange. Such authorities are authorized to provide, on the request of duly appointed law-enforcement officers, copies of any fingerprint records they may have, and to furnish services and technical advice in connection with the taking, classifying and preserving of fingerprints and fingerprint records.

B. Such police authorities may establish and collect a reasonable fee not to exceed $10 for the first card and $5 for each successive card for the taking of fingerprints when voluntarily requested by any person for purposes other than criminal violations.

History.
Code 1950, § 19.1-19.6; 1968, c. 722; 1975, c. 495; 1978, c. 825; 1985, c. 306; 2005, c. 347.

Cross references.
As to fingerprints and photographs of juveniles, see § 16.1-299.

§ 19.2-392.01. Judges may require taking of fingerprints and photographs in certain misdemeanor cases.

The judge of a district court may, in his discretion, on motion of the attorney for the Commonwealth, require the duly constituted police officers of the county, city or town within the territorial jurisdiction of the court to take the fingerprints and photograph of any person who has been arrested and charged with a misdemeanor other than a misdemeanor which is a violation of any provision of Title 46.2.

History.
1995, c. 407; 1996, cc. 755, 914.

Editor's note.
Acts 1996, cc. 755 and 914, cl. 7, provide: "[t]hat the provisions of this act shall apply to offenses committed and to records created and proceedings held with respect to those offenses on or after July 1, 1996."

§ 19.2-392.02. National criminal background checks by businesses and organizations regarding employees or volunteers providing care to children, the elderly and disabled.

A. For purposes of this section:

"*Barrier crime*" means any offense set forth in § 63.2-1719 or 63.2-1726.

"*Barrier crime information*" means the following facts concerning a person who has been arrested for, or has been convicted of, a barrier crime, regardless of whether the person was a juvenile or adult at the time of the arrest or conviction: full name, race, sex, date of birth, height, weight, fingerprints, a brief description of the barrier crime or offenses for which the person has been arrested or has been convicted, the disposition of the charge, and any other information that may be useful in identifying persons arrested for or convicted of a barrier crime.

"*Care*" means the provision of care, treatment, education, training, instruction, supervision, or recreation to children, the elderly or disabled.

"*Department*" means the Department of State Police.

"*Employed by*" means any person who is employed by, volunteers for, seeks to be employed by, or seeks to volunteer for a qualified entity.

"*Identification document*" means a document made or issued by or under the authority of the United States government, a state, a political subdivision of a state, a foreign government, political subdivision of a foreign government, an international governmental or an international quasi-governmental organization that, when completed with information concerning a particular individual, is of a type intended or commonly accepted for the purpose of identification of individuals.

"*Provider*" means a person who (i) is employed by a qualified entity, and has, seeks to have, or may have unsupervised access to a child or to an elderly or disabled person to whom the qualified entity provides care or (ii) owns, operates or seeks to own or operate a qualified entity.

"*Qualified entity*" means a business or organization that provides care to children, the elderly or disabled, whether governmental, private, for profit, nonprofit or voluntary, except organizations exempt pursuant to subdivision A 10 of § 63.2-1715.

B. Notwithstanding §§ 63.2-1719 to 63.2-1721 and 63.2-1724, a qualified entity may request the Department of State Police to conduct a national criminal background check on any provider who is employed by such entity. No qualified entity may request a national criminal background check on a provider until such provider has:

1. Been fingerprinted at any local or state law-enforcement agency and provided the fingerprints to the qualified entity; and

2. Completed and signed a statement, furnished by the entity, that includes (i) his name, address, and date of birth as it appears on a valid identification document, (ii) a disclosure of whether or not the provider has ever been convicted of or is the subject of pending charges for a criminal offense within or outside the Commonwealth, and if the provider has been convicted of a crime, a description of the crime and the particulars of the conviction, (iii) a notice to the provider that the entity may request a background check, (iv) a notice to the provider that he is entitled to obtain a copy of any background check report, to challenge the accuracy and completeness of any information contained in any such report, and to obtain a prompt determination as to the validity of such challenge before a final determination is made by the Department, and (v) a notice to the provider that prior to the completion of the background check the qualified entity may choose to deny the provider unsupervised access to children, the elderly or disabled for whom the qualified entity provides care.

C. Upon receipt of (i) a qualified entity's written request to conduct a background check on a provider, (ii) the provider's fingerprints, and (iii) a completed, signed statement as described in subsection B, the Department shall make a determination whether the provider has been convicted of or is the subject of charges of a barrier crime. To conduct its determination regarding the provider's barrier crime information, the Department shall access the national criminal history background check system, which is maintained by the Federal Bureau of Investigation and is based on fingerprints and other methods of identification, and shall access the Central Criminal Records Exchange maintained by the Department. If the Department receives a background report lacking disposition data, the Department shall conduct research in whatever state and local record-keeping systems are available in order to obtain complete data. The Department shall make reasonable efforts to respond to a qualified entity's inquiry within 15 business days.

D. Any background check conducted pursuant to this section for a provider employed by a private entity shall be screened by the Department of State Police. If the provider has been convicted of or is under indictment for a barrier crime, the qualified entity shall be notified that the provider is not qualified to work or volunteer in a position that involves unsupervised access to children, the elderly or disabled.

E. Any background check conducted pursuant to this section for a provider employed by a governmental entity shall be provided to that entity.

F. In the case of a provider who desires to volunteer at a qualified entity and who is subject to a national criminal background check, the Department and the Federal Bureau of Investigation may each charge the provider the lesser of $18 or the actual cost to the entity of the background check conducted with the fingerprints.

G. The failure to request a criminal background check pursuant to subsection B shall not be considered negligence per se in any civil action.

History.
2000, c. 860; 2005, c. 217.

CHAPTER 23.1.

EXPUNGEMENT OF CRIMINAL RECORDS.

§ 19.2-392.1. Statement of policy.

The General Assembly finds that arrest records can be a hindrance to an innocent citizen's ability to obtain employment, an education and to obtain credit. It further finds that the police and court records of those of its citizens who have been absolutely pardoned for crimes for which they have been unjustly convicted can also be a hindrance. This chapter is intended to protect such persons from the unwarranted damage which may occur as a result of being arrested and convicted.

History.
1977, c. 675; 1984, c. 642.

Law Review.
For survey of Virginia criminal procedure for the year 1976-1977, see 63 Va. L. Rev. 1408 (1977).

Michie's Jurisprudence.
For related discussion, see 5B M.J. Criminal Procedure, § 2.

CASE NOTES

Applied in Gregg v. Commonwealth, 227 Va. 504, 316 S.E.2d 741 (1984).

§ 19.2-392.2. Expungement of police and court records.

A. If a person is charged with the commission of a crime or any offense defined in Title 18.2, and

1. Is acquitted, or

2. A nolle prosequi is taken or the charge is otherwise dismissed, including dismissal by accord and satisfaction pursuant to § 19.2-151, he may file a petition setting forth the relevant facts and requesting expungement of the police records and the court records relating to the charge.

B. If any person whose name or other identification has been used without his consent or authorization by another person who has been charged or arrested using such name or identification, he may file a petition with the court disposing of the charge for relief pursuant to this section. Such person shall not be required to pay any fees for the filing of a petition under this subsection. A petition filed under this subsection shall include one complete set of the petitioner's fingerprints obtained from a law-enforcement agency.

C. The petition with a copy of the warrant or indictment if reasonably available shall be filed in the circuit court of the county or city in which the case was disposed of by acquittal or being otherwise dismissed and shall contain, except where not reasonably available, the date of arrest and the name of the arresting agency. Where this information is not reasonably available, the petition shall state the reason for such unavailability. The petition shall further state the specific criminal charge to be expunged, the date of final disposition of the charge as set forth in the petition, the petitioner's date of birth, and the full name used by the petitioner at the time of arrest.

D. A copy of the petition shall be served on the attorney for the Commonwealth of the city or county in which the petition is filed. The attorney for the Commonwealth may file an objection or answer to the petition within 21 days after it is served on him.

E. The petitioner shall obtain from a law-enforcement agency one complete set of the petitioner's fingerprints and shall provide that agency with a copy of the petition for expungement. The law-enforcement agency shall submit the set of fingerprints to the Central Criminal Records Exchange (CCRE) with a copy of the petition for expungement attached. The CCRE shall forward under seal to the court a copy of the petitioner's criminal history, a copy of the source documents that resulted in the CCRE entry that the petitioner wishes to expunge, and the set of fingerprints. Upon completion of the hearing, the court shall return the fingerprint card to the petitioner.

F. After receiving the criminal history record information from the CCRE, the court shall conduct a hearing on the petition. If the court finds that the continued existence and possible dissemination of information relating to the arrest of the petitioner causes or may cause circumstances which constitute a manifest injustice to the petitioner, it shall enter an order requiring the expungement of the police and court records, including electronic records, relating to the charge. Otherwise, it shall deny the petition. However, if the petitioner has no prior criminal record and the arrest was for a misdemeanor violation, the petitioner shall be entitled, in the absence of good cause shown to the contrary by the Commonwealth, to expungement of the police and court records relating to the charge, and the court shall enter an order of expungement.

G. The Commonwealth shall be made party defendant to the proceeding. Any party aggrieved by the decision of the court may appeal, as provided by law in civil cases.

H. Notwithstanding any other provision of this section, when the charge is dismissed because the court finds that the person arrested or charged is not the person named in the summons, warrant, indictment or presentment, the court dismissing the charge shall, upon motion of the person improperly arrested or charged, enter an order requiring expungement of the police and court records relating to the charge. Such order shall contain a statement that the dismissal and expungement are ordered pursuant to this subsection and shall be accompanied by the complete set of the petitioner's fingerprints filed with his petition. Upon the entry of such order, it shall be treated as provided in subsection K hereof.

I. Notwithstanding any other provision of this section, when a person has been granted an absolute pardon for the commission of a crime that he did not commit, he may file in the circuit court of the county or city in which the conviction occurred a petition setting forth the relevant facts and requesting expungement of the police records and the court records relating to the charge and conviction, and the court shall enter an order requiring expungement of the police and court records relating to the charge and conviction. Such order shall contain a statement that the expungement is ordered pursuant to this subsection. Upon the entry of such order, it shall be treated as provided in subsection K hereof.

J. Upon receiving a copy of a writ vacating a conviction pursuant to § 19.2-327.5 or 19.2-327.13, the court shall enter an order requiring expungement of the police and court records relating to the charge and conviction. Such order shall contain a statement that the expungement is ordered pursuant to this subsection. Upon the entry of the order, it shall be treated as provided in subsection K hereof.

K. Upon the entry of an order of expungement, the clerk of the court shall cause a copy of such order to be forwarded to the Department of State Police, which shall, pursuant to rules and regulations adopted pursuant to § 9.1-134, direct the manner by which the appropriate expungement or removal of such records shall be effected.

L. Costs shall be as provided by § 17.1-275, but shall not be recoverable against the Commonwealth.

M. Any order entered where (i) the court or parties failed to strictly comply with the procedures set forth in this section or (ii) the court enters an order of expungement contrary to law, shall be voidable upon motion and notice made within three years of the entry of such order.

History.

1977, c. 675; 1983, c. 394; 1984, c. 642; 1990, c. 603; 1992, c. 697; 2001, cc. 40, 345; 2007, cc. 465, 824, 883, 905; 2009, c. 618; 2011, c. 362.

Cross references.

As to petition for relief from identity fraud, see § 18.2-186.5.

The 2007 amendments.

The 2007 amendments by cc. 465, 824, 883, and 905, inserted "including electronic records" near the end of the second sentence in subsection F; and added subsection J.

In addition, the 2007 amendment by c. 824 added subsections K and L.

In addition, the 2007 amendment by c. 883 deleted "3. Is granted an absolute pardon for the commission of a crime for which he has been unjustly convicted" in subsection A; inserted subsection I and redesignated the remaining subsections accordingly; and made a related change in subsection H.

In addition, the 2007 amendment by c. 905 substituted "or any offense defined in Title 18.2, and" for "and" in subsection A.

The section is set out in the form above at the direction of the Virginia Code Commission.

The 2009 amendments.

The 2009 amendment by c. 618 added the last sentence in subsection B.

The 2011 amendments.

The 2011 amendment by c. 362, added the last sentence of subsection B, and added "and shall be accompanied by the complete set of the petitioner's fingerprints filed with his petition" at the end of the second sentence in subsection H.

Law Review.

For survey of Virginia criminal procedure for the year 1976-1977, see 63 Va. L. Rev. 1408 (1977). For an article relating to all published Virginia criminal law decisions between July 1, 1997, and July 1, 1998, see 32 U. Rich. L. Rev. 1091 (1998).

CASE NOTES

Proceedings appropriate for challenging outstanding judgments. — Expungement order proceedings involve a judicial determination and are therefore quite clearly appropriate vehicles for challenging the validity of outstanding criminal judgments. Snyder v. City of Alexandria, 870 F. Supp. 672 (E.D. Va. 1994).

Charge dismissed under first offender statute not "otherwise dismissed" for purposes of this section. — This section applies to innocent persons, not to those who are guilty. Under § 18.2-251, probation and ultimate dismissal is conditioned on a plea of guilty or a finding of guilt. One who is "guilty" cannot occupy the status of "innocent" so as to qualify under the expungement statute as a person whose charge has been "otherwise dismissed." Gregg v. Commonwealth, 227 Va. 504, 316 S.E.2d 741 (1984).

Because defendant's possession charge was not "otherwise dismissed" within the meaning of the expungement statute under subsection A, as the trial court had to find defendant guilty before disposing of her case pursuant to the first offender statute, § 18.2-251, defendant was not entitled to have the charge expunged from her record. Commonwealth v. Dotson, 276 Va. 278, 661 S.E.2d 473, 2008 Va. LEXIS 80 (2008).

Deferral of judgment and subsequent dismissal without determination of guilt. — A person deferred from judgment following a determination that the evidence is sufficient to support a conviction is not "innocent" of the offense regardless of the plea originally entered. Nor does a dismissal following satisfaction of the terms of that deferral render the case "otherwise dismissed" for purposes of expungement. Commonwealth v. Jackson, 255 Va. 552, 499 S.E.2d 276 (1998).

Repeal of the ordinance under which a person was ar-

rested does not render moot his request for expungement. Hearn v. Hudson, 549 F. Supp. 949 (W.D. Va. 1982).

Expungement order from federal court. — The administration of records related to law enforcement is a function close to the core of state government. An expungement order from a federal court would be a significant intrusion — and, in light of the availability of the state court procedure, an unnecessary intrusion — into the State's administration of its record-keeping. Hearn v. Hudson, 549 F. Supp. 949 (W.D. Va. 1982).

No fraud upon court in failing to tell of pending collateral action. — Defendant who was acquitted of charges of aggravated sexual battery of minor daughter did not commit a fraud on the court in his request for expungement of police and court records of the charge by failing to disclose that persons who made the sexual battery allegations were defendants in his civil action then pending for malicious prosecution, conspiracy, and intentional infliction of emotional distress. Ein v. Commonwealth, 246 Va. 396, 436 S.E.2d 610 (1993).

Charge "otherwise dismissed" for purposes of this section. — Neither petitioner entered a plea; each trial court took the charge under advisement while the petitioner performed agreed upon tasks with the understanding that, on doing so, the charge would be dismissed. As dismissals of the charges took place without a determination of guilt, without a finding of evidence sufficient to establish guilt, and without penalties or conditions imposed by judicial authority, petitioners were "innocent" so as to qualify for expungement of their criminal records under subdivision A 2 of § 19.2-392.2 as persons whose charges were "otherwise dismissed." Brown v. Commonwealth, 278 Va. 92, 677 S.E.2d 220, 2009 Va. LEXIS 70 (2009).

Trial court erred by finding that defendant could not, under subsection A of § 19.2-392.2, seek expungement of records pertaining to a possession of marijuana charge as the charge was amended to the completely separate and unrelated charge of reckless driving; since reckless driving was not a lesser-included offense of possession of marijuana, the elements of the offense of which defendant was convicted were not subsumed within the possession of marijuana charge and did not form the sole basis for the conviction. Thus, the possession of marijuana charge was necessarily "otherwise dismissed" within the intendment of subdivision A 2 of § 19.2-392.2. Dressner v. Commonwealth, 285 Va. 1, 736 S.E.2d 735, 2013 Va. LEXIS 9 (2013).

Not guilty by reason of insanity. — Circuit court properly denied appellant's petition for expungement of police and court records following finding that he was not guilty by reason of insanity because, while subdivision A 1 of § 19.2-392.2 permitted a person charged with commission of a crime to seek expungement if he had been acquitted of the crime, the term "acquitted" does not include acquittals by reason of insanity. Eastlack v. Commonwealth, 282 Va. 120, 710 S.E.2d 723, 2011 Va. LEXIS 126 (2011).

Expungement granted. — Trial court erred by finding that defendant could not, under subsection A of § 19.2-392.2, seek expungement of records pertaining to a possession of marijuana charge as the charge was necessarily "otherwise dismissed" within the intendment of subdivision A 2 of § 19.2-392.2, and defendant demonstrated the existence of manifest injustice through her loss of employment as a result of a background check that revealed the possession of marijuana charge; therefore, she had satisfied the requirements of the expungement statute and was entitled to have the records relating to the possession of marijuana charge expunged. Dressner v. Commonwealth, 285 Va. 1, 736 S.E.2d 735, 2013 Va. LEXIS 9 (2013).

Applied in Commonwealth v. Hill, 264 Va. 541, 570 S.E.2d 805, 2002 Va. LEXIS 170 (2002).

CIRCUIT COURT OPINIONS

Expungement granted. — Petitioner was entitled to expungement of a sexual battery charge under § 19.2-392.2 because he did not plead guilty to sexual battery and that charge was ultimately dropped; further, petitioner showed that the dissemination of information relating to that charge could cause him manifest injustice by prejudicing his opportunities for employment or housing. D.W. v. Commonwealth, 72 Va. Cir. 132, 2006 Va. Cir. LEXIS 300 (Charlottesville 2006).

Granting of petitioner's motion to expunge police and court records was proper because he neither pled guilty to reckless driving nor was there a finding of guilt as to the reckless driving charge; because improper driving was not a lesser-included offense of reckless driving, the reckless driving charge was "otherwise dismissed" within the meaning of the expungement statute, § 19.2-392.2. MacDonald v. Commonwealth, 83 Va. Cir. 485, 2011 Va. Cir. LEXIS 192 (Fairfax County Nov. 30, 2011).

Expungement denied. — Inmate's expungement petition, pursuant to this section, was denied where the inmate had a prior criminal record, the unrelated charge sought to be expunged was a felony, and he failed to establish by the greater weight of the evidence that the possible dissemination of such arrest record created a manifest injustice. Miller v. Commonwealth, 55 Va. Cir. 110, 2001 Va. Cir. LEXIS 246 (Fairfax County 2001).

Misdemeanor convictions could not be expunged from an individual's record where the individual pleaded guilty to and was found guilty of the crimes as the individual was not innocent of the crimes. Sanderlin v. Commonwealth, 58 Va. Cir. 375, 2002 Va. Cir. LEXIS 154 (Norfolk 2002).

Where an inmate was charged and convicted of criminal contempt for failing to appear, he was not innocent of the contempt charge for which he sought expungement; therefore, he was not entitled to relief. Brown v. Commonwealth, 60 Va. Cir. 214, 2002 Va. Cir. LEXIS 278 (Fairfax County 2002).

Because defendant pleaded guilty to two counts of burglary, defendant could not occupy the status of "innocent" so as to qualify for expungement under any applicable provision; defendant could not challenge the validity of the guilty pleas through an expungement proceeding. Woodward v. Commonwealth, 68 Va. Cir. 66, 2005 Va. Cir. LEXIS 58 (Fairfax County 2005). But see ; D.W. v. Commonwealth, 72 Va. Cir. 132, 2006 Va. Cir. LEXIS 300 (Charlottesville 2006).

Defendant failed to establish a right to expunge her record pursuant to § 19.2-392.2 under circumstances in which a court found that the evidence was sufficient to find guilt of a petit larceny charge, deferred judgment, and after defendant completed the terms imposed by the court, dismissed the charges. Newton v. Commonwealth, 71 Va. Cir. 160, 2006 Va. Cir. LEXIS 115 (Fairfax County 2006).

Petition to expunge petitioner's criminal record of petitioner's arrest for petit larceny under § 19.2-392.2 was denied because petitioner was not acquitted of the charge, the charge was not the subject of a nolle prosequi, nor was petitioner given an absolute pardon; the charge was dismissed because petitioner complied with terms of probation. Allman v. Commonwealth, 74 Va. Cir. 170, 2007 Va. Cir. LEXIS 277 (Roanoke County 2007).

§ 19.2-392.3. Disclosure of expunged records.

A. It shall be unlawful for any person having or acquiring access to an expunged court or police record to open or review it or to disclose to another person any information from it without an order from the court which ordered the record expunged.

B. Upon a verified petition filed by the attorney for the Commonwealth alleging that the record is needed by a law-enforcement agency for purposes of employment application as an employee of a law-enforcement agency or for a pending criminal investigation and that the investigation will be jeopardized or that life or property will be endangered without immediate access to the record, the court may enter an ex parte order, without notice to the person, permitting such access. An ex parte order may permit a review of the record, but may not permit a copy to be made of it.

C. Any person who willfully violates this section is guilty of a Class 1 misdemeanor.

History.
1977, c. 675; 1978, c. 713.

Cross references.
As to punishment for Class 1 misdemeanors, see § 18.2-11.

Law Review.
For survey of Virginia criminal procedure for the year 1976-77, see 63 Va. L. Rev. 1408 (1977).

CIRCUIT COURT OPINIONS

Violation not shown. — Detective did not violate the statute by testifying about a naval officer's alleged sexual abuse of a minor because the detective testified from her own notes and memory, not from expunged police or court records relating to the naval officer's arrest and trial. Morris v. Massingill, 61 Va. Cir. 532, 2003 Va. Cir. LEXIS 232 (Norfolk 2003).

§ 19.2-392.4. Prohibited practices by employers, educational institutions, agencies, etc., of state and local governments.

A. An employer or educational institution shall not, in any application, interview, or otherwise, require an applicant for employment or admission to disclose information concerning any arrest or criminal charge against him that has been expunged. An applicant need not, in answer to any question concerning any arrest or criminal charge that has not resulted in a conviction, include a reference to or information concerning arrests or charges that have been expunged.

B. Agencies, officials, and employees of the state and local governments shall not, in any application, interview, or otherwise, require an applicant for a license, permit, registration, or governmental service to disclose information concerning any arrest or criminal charge against him that has been expunged. An applicant need not, in answer to any question concerning any arrest or criminal charge that has not resulted in a conviction, include a reference to or information concerning charges that have been expunged. Such an application may not be denied solely because of the applicant's refusal to disclose information concerning any arrest or criminal charge against him that has been expunged.

C. A person who willfully violates this section is guilty of a Class 1 misdemeanor for each violation.

History.
1977, c. 675.

Cross references.
As to punishment for Class 1 misdemeanors, see § 18.2-11.

Law Review.
For survey of Virginia criminal procedure for the year 1976-77, see 63 Va. L. Rev. 1408 (1977).

CHAPTER 24.

INSPECTION WARRANTS.

Section
19.2-393. Definitions.
19.2-394. Issuance of warrant.

§ 19.2-393. Definitions.

An *"inspection warrant"* is an order in writing, made in the name of the Commonwealth, signed by any judge of the circuit court whose territorial jurisdiction encompasses the property or premises to be inspected or entered, and directed to a state or local official, commanding him to enter and to conduct any inspection, testing or collection of samples for testing required or authorized by state or local law or regulation in connection with the manufacturing, emitting or presence of a toxic substance, and which describes, either directly or by reference to any accompanying or attached supporting affidavit, the property or premises where the inspection, testing or collection of samples for testing is to occur. Such warrant shall be sufficiently accurate in description so that the official executing the warrant and the owner or custodian of the property or premises can reasonably determine from the warrant the activity, condition, circumstance, object or property of which inspection, testing or collection of samples for testing is authorized.

For the purposes of this chapter, *"manufacturing"* means producing, formulating, packaging, or diluting any substance for commercial sale or resale; *"emitting"* means the release of any substance, whether or not intentional or avoidable, into the work environment, into the air, into the water, or otherwise into the human environment; and *"toxic substance"* means any substance, including (i) any raw material, intermediate product, catalyst, final product and by-product of any operation conducted in a commercial establishment and (ii) any biological organism, that has the capacity, through its physical, chemical, or biological properties, to pose a substantial risk to humans, aquatic organisms or any other animal of illness, death or impairment of normal functions, either immediately or over a period of time.

History.
    1976, c. 625; 1979, c. 122.

Law Review.
    For survey of Virginia criminal procedure for the year 1975-1976, see 62 Va. L. Rev. 1412 (1976). For survey of Virginia law on administrative law and utility regulation for the year 1978-1979, see 66 Va. L. Rev. 193 (1980). For article, "Warrantless Searches and Seizures in Virginia," see 17 U. Rich. L. Rev. 721 (1983).

§ 19.2-394. Issuance of warrant.

An inspection warrant may be issued for any inspection, testing or collection of samples for testing or for any administrative search authorized by state or local law or regulation in connection with the presence, manufacturing or emitting of toxic substances, whether or not such warrant be constitutionally required. Nothing in this chapter shall be construed to require issuance of an inspection warrant where a warrant is not constitutionally required or to exclude any other lawful means of search, inspection, testing or collection of samples for testing, whether without warrant or pursuant to a search warrant issued under any other provision of the Code of Virginia. No inspection warrant shall be issued pursuant to this chapter except upon probable cause, supported by affidavit, particularly describing the place, things or persons to be inspected or tested and the purpose for which the inspection, testing or collection of samples for testing is to be made. Probable cause shall be deemed to exist if either reasonable legislative or administrative standards for conducting such inspection, testing or collection of samples for testing are satisfied with respect to the particular place, things or persons or there exists probable cause to believe that there is a condition, object, activity or circumstance which legally justifies such inspection, testing or collection of samples for testing. The supporting affidavit shall contain either a statement that consent to inspect, test or collect samples for testing has been sought and refused or facts or circumstances reasonably justifying the failure to seek such consent in order to enforce effectively the state or local law or regulation which authorizes such inspection, testing or collection of samples for testing. The issuing judge may examine the affiant under oath or affirmation to verify the accuracy of any matter indicated by the statement in the affidavit.

History.
    1976, c. 625; 1979, c. 122.

Law Review.
    For survey of Virginia law on governmental services and social welfare for the year 1978-1979, see 66 Va. L. Rev. 301 (1980).

CASE NOTES

Applied in Mosher Steel-Virginia v. Teig, 229 Va. 95, 327 S.E.2d 87 (1985).

§ 19.2-395. Duration of warrant.

An inspection warrant shall be effective for the time specified therein, for a period of not more than ten days, unless extended or renewed by the judicial officer who signed and issued the original warrant, upon satisfying himself that such extension or renewal is in the public interest. Such warrant shall be executed and returned to the judicial officer by whom it was issued within the time specified in the warrant or within the extended or renewed time. After the expiration of such time, the warrant, unless executed shall be void.

History.
    1976, c. 625.

Law Review.

For article, "Warrantless Searches and Seizures in Virginia," see 17 U. Rich. L. Rev. 721 (1983).

§ 19.2-396. Conduct of inspection, testing or collection of samples for testing; special procedure for dwelling.

An inspection, testing or collection of samples for testing pursuant to such warrant may not be made in the absence of the owner, custodian or possessor of the particular place, things or persons unless specifically authorized by the issuing judge upon a showing that such authority is reasonably necessary to effectuate the purpose of the law or regulation being enforced. An entry pursuant to this warrant shall not be made forcibly, except that the issuing judge may expressly authorize a forcible entry where facts are shown sufficient to create a reasonable suspicion of an immediate threat to public health or safety, or where facts are shown establishing that reasonable attempts to serve a previous warrant have been unsuccessful. In the case of entry into a dwelling, prior consent must be sought and refused and notice that a warrant has been issued must be given at least twenty-four hours before the warrant is executed, unless the issuing judge finds that failure to seek consent is justified and that there is a reasonable suspicion of an immediate threat to public health or safety.

History.

1976, c. 625; 1979, c. 122.

Law Review.

For survey of Virginia criminal procedure for the year 1975-1976, see 62 Va. L. Rev. 1412 (1976). For article, "Warrantless Searches and Seizures in Virginia," see 17 U. Rich. L. Rev. 721 (1983).

§ 19.2-397. Refusal to permit authorized inspection; penalty.

Any person who willfully refuses to permit an inspection, testing or collection of samples for testing lawfully authorized by warrant issued pursuant to this chapter shall be guilty of a Class 3 misdemeanor.

History.

1976, c. 625; 1979, c. 122.

Cross references.

As to punishment for Class 3 misdemeanors, see § 18.2-11.

CHAPTER 25.

APPEALS BY THE COMMONWEALTH.

§ 19.2-398. When appeal by the Commonwealth allowed.

A. In a felony case a pretrial appeal from a circuit court may be taken by the Commonwealth from:

1. An order of a circuit court dismissing a warrant, information or indictment, or any count or charge thereof on the ground that (i) the defendant was deprived of a speedy trial in violation of the provisions of the Sixth Amendment to the Constitution of the United States, Article I, Section 8 of the Constitution of Virginia, or § 19.2-243; or (ii) the defendant would be twice placed in jeopardy in violation of the provisions of the Fifth Amendment to the Constitution of the United States or Article I, Section 8 of the Constitution of Virginia; or

2. An order of a circuit court prohibiting the use of certain evidence at trial on the grounds such evidence was obtained in violation of the provisions of the Fourth, Fifth or Sixth Amendments to the Constitution of the United States or Article I, Section 8, 10 or 11 of the Constitution of Virginia prohibiting illegal searches and seizures and protecting rights against self-incrimination, provided the Commonwealth certifies that the appeal is not taken for purpose of delay and that the evidence is substantial proof of a fact material in the proceeding.

B. A petition for appeal may be taken by the Commonwealth in a felony case from any order of release on conditions pursuant to Article 1 (§ 19.2-119 et seq.) of Chapter 9 of this title.

C. A petition for appeal may be taken by the Commonwealth in a felony case after conviction where the sentence imposed by the circuit court is contrary to mandatory sentencing or restitution terms required by statute.

D. Nothing in this chapter shall affect the Commonwealth's right to appeal in civil matters or cases involving a violation of law relating to the state revenue or appeals pursuant to § 17.1-411 or subsection C of § 19.2-317.

E. A pretrial appeal may be taken in any criminal case from an order of a circuit court dismissing a warrant, information, summons, delinquency petition, or indictment, or any count or charge thereof, on the ground that a statute or local ordinance on which the order is based is unconstitutional.

History.

1985, c. 510; 1987, c. 710; 1998, c. 251; 1999, cc. 829, 846; 2002, cc. 611, 692; 2003, c. 109; 2005, cc. 622, 694; 2006, cc. 571, 876.

Editor's note.

Acts 1985, c. 510, cl. 2 provided that this chapter would take effect December 1, 1986, provided that a majority of those voting in a referendum in November 1986 voted in favor of an amendment to Va. Const., Art. VI, § 1, relating to the provisions of this chapter. Such an amendment to Va. Const., Art. VI, § 1, was ratified at the election held Nov. 4, 1986.

Law Review.

For note, "Double Jeopardy and the Commonwealth's Right to Writs of Error in Criminal Cases," see 20 U. Rich. L. Rev. 629 (1986). For note, "Commonwealth Right of Appeal in Criminal Proceedings," see 43 Wash. & Lee L. Rev. 295 (1986). For 1987 survey of Virginia criminal procedure, see 21 U. Rich L. Rev. 727 (1987). For an article relating to all published Virginia criminal law decisions between July 1, 1997, and July 1, 1998, see 32 U. Rich. L. Rev. 1091 (1998). For an article, "Final and Interlocutory Appeals in Virginia," see 8 Geo. Mason L. Rev. 337 (1999). For article surveying developments in criminal law and procedure in Virginia from July 2001 to September 2002, see 37 U. Rich. L. Rev. 45 (2002).

Michie's Jurisprudence.

For related discussion, see 1B M.J. Appeal and Error, §§ 57, 73, 85; 2B M.J. Autrefois, Acquit and Convict, § 10; 5B M.J. Criminal Procedure, § 69.

CASE NOTES

Constitutionality. — This section, which provides the Commonwealth a limited right to appeal interlocutory orders, does not violate the United States constitutional guarantee of equal protection. Commonwealth v. Ramey, 19 Va. App. 300, 450 S.E.2d 775 (1994).

The constitutional and statutory authority for Commonwealth appeals is narrowly circumscribed. It was not enacted to allow Commonwealth appeals from all allegedly erroneous pre-trial rulings by the trial court. Even if the trial court's ruling was erroneous, nonresponsive and exceeded the bounds of the relief requested, and even if it was intended to frustrate the Commonwealth's right of appeal, these facts do not provide a basis for the exercise of appellate jurisdiction. Commonwealth v. Brown, 8 Va. App. 41, 378 S.E.2d 623 (1989).

The purpose of Chapter 25 of Title 19.2, § 19.2-398 et. seq., is to afford the Commonwealth a limited right of appeal under certain carefully specified circumstances. Those appeals are pretrial, and the statutory scheme plainly contemplates that rulings on such appeals are interlocutory and reversible, as are the reviewed trial court rulings. Satchell v. Commonwealth, 20 Va. App. 641, 460 S.E.2d 253 (1995).

Section must be strictly construed against Commonwealth. — This section is in derogation of the general constitutional prohibition against appeals by the Commonwealth. It must be strictly construed against the state and limited in application to cases falling clearly within the language of the statute. Commonwealth v. Hawkins, 10 Va. App. 41, 390 S.E.2d 3 (1990).

This section does not permit appeal of a trial judge's evidentiary rulings at a hearing on a motion to suppress. Commonwealth v. Thornton, 24 Va. App. 478, 483 S.E.2d 487 (1997).

Right to appeal unconstitutional statute whether "facial" or "as applied" challenge. — The plain language of this section gives the Commonwealth the right to appeal whenever a statute is found unconstitutional, whether the finding is based on a "facial" or an "as applied" challenge. Commonwealth v. Johnson, No. 0629-90-4 (Ct. of Appeals Oct. 16, 1990).

Use of "shall" is directory only. — Language in § 19.2-400 stating what a notice of appeal "shall" contain, along with almost identical language in § 19.2-398, is directory only. Thus, the Commonwealth's failure to timely file the certification described in §§ 19.2-398 and 19.2-400 was not jurisdictional. Commonwealth v. Hackett, — Va. App. —, — S.E.2d —, 2008 Va. App. LEXIS 120 (Mar. 11, 2008).

Commonwealth's limited right of appeal. — The legislature has narrowly limited the Commonwealth's right to appeal suppression orders of the trial courts to orders which are based on constitutional violations; therefore, where the Commonwealth ap-pealed an order suppressing certain evidence solely on the grounds that the evidence was obtained in violation of §§ 19.2-59 and 19.2-60, the court of appeals would not entertain the Commonwealth's appeal. Commonwealth v. Ragland, 7 Va. App. 452, 374 S.E.2d 183 (1988).

Under this section the Commonwealth's right to appeal is limited to suppression orders granted on the basis of violation of specific provisions of the United States and the Virginia Constitutions. Commonwealth v. Rodgers, 21 Va. App. 745, 467 S.E.2d 813 (1996).

Commonwealth had a limited right to appeal the trial court's granting of defendant's motion to suppress, but the trial court's judgment had to be affirmed, as the Commonwealth's argument that the motion to suppress should not have been denied because the evidence showed that there was probable cause to make an arrest and to search incident to that arrest had to be rejected because that argument had not been raised in the trial court and, therefore, could not be considered for the first time on appeal. Commonwealth v. Flythe, No. 0759-03-1, 2003 Va. App. LEXIS 410 (Ct. of Appeals July 18, 2003).

Commonwealth's appeal of the trial court's dismissal of indictments filed against defendant charging him with possession of cocaine with intent to distribute and possession of a firearm while possessing cocaine with intent to distribute was dismissed; the record showed that the Commonwealth had submitted evidence, including sworn testimony, immediately prior to the trial court's ruling on defendant's motion to dismiss and the statute under which the Commonwealth appealed, clause (ii) of subdivision A 1 of § 19.2-398 expressly applied only to "pretrial appeals," which was not involved in the present case. Commonwealth v. Green, — Va. App. —, — S.E.2d —, 2006 Va. App. LEXIS 347 (Aug. 1, 2006).

Holding by appellate court in pre-trial suppression dispute is not stare decisis as to the admissibility issue raised in the post-trial appeal, and that issue is fully reviewable. Satchell v. Commonwealth, 20 Va. App. 641, 460 S.E.2d 253 (1995).

Grant of a motion to suppress evidence by defendant. — Commonwealth's appeal pursuant to § 19.2-398 of the trial court's grant of defendant's motion to suppress evidence was granted and the suppression was reversed, because the search that uncovered the evidence was a search incident to defendant's lawful arrest for bring drunk in public. Commonwealth v. Hamlet, No. 0256-03-2, 2003 Va. App. LEXIS 334 (Ct. of Appeals June 10, 2003).

Commonwealth's pretrial appeal of a suppression order was properly filed under this section where the record satisfactorily established that the court's decision was based upon constitutional grounds. Commonwealth v. Wilburn, No. 0884-91-4 (Ct. of Appeals Oct. 29, 1991).

Virginia Sup. Ct. R. 5A:18 did not preclude the court of appeals from considering a certain argument that the Commonwealth made in its appeal from a suppression order, pursuant to § 19.2-398, even though the Commonwealth admitted that there was merit to defendant's claim that the rule barred the Commonwealth from arguing on appeal, for lack of a proper preservation of the issue, that he had implicitly waived his Miranda rights. The court of appeals was not bound by concessions of law by the parties to a case, the issue of whether an officer had given defendant his Miranda warnings and defendant had chosen not to heed them was laid before the trial court as a factual predicate to the determination of the issue of whether the police had used illegal tactics in the interrogation, and, therefore, the rule did not bar the Commonwealth from advancing its argument of the implied waiver on appeal. Commonwealth v. Kadian, — Va. App. —, — S.E.2d —, 2006 Va. App. LEXIS 246 (May 30, 2006).

Suppression motion requirements must be followed. — Procedure set forth in § 19.2-266.2 for suppression motions is directly related to the provisions of § 19.2-398, the Commonwealth's right to appeal evidence excluded as a result of a suppression hearing; the Commonwealth would be prejudiced by allowing a defendant to disregard, without good cause, the dictates of § 19.2-266.2. Wilson v. Commonwealth, No. 0433-02-2, 2002 Va. App. LEXIS 735 (Ct. of Appeals Dec. 10, 2002).

Interlocutory appeal of suppression determination. — Following an interlocutory appeal by the Commonwealth pursuant to § 19.2-398 A 2, the appellate court determined that the trial court erred in granting defendant's motion to suppress drugs found in a vehicle recently occupied by defendant in relation to charges of possession of cocaine and heroin with intent to distribute, § 18.2-

248, because the automobile exception had no separate exigency requirement, and the search of the vehicle did not violate Virginia constitutional law prohibiting illegal searches and seizures. Commonwealth v. Rogers, — Va. App. —, — S.E.2d —, 2003 Va. App. LEXIS 85 (Feb. 25, 2003).

Although Va. Sup. Ct. R. 5A:3(c) allowed the Commonwealth to mail its petition appealing the trial court's judgment granting defendant's motion to suppress evidence to the court of appeals, it required the Commonwealth to obtain an official receipt showing that the petition was mailed on time and to produce that receipt on demand, and the appellate court held that because the Commonwealth could not produce a receipt showing that it mailed its petition on or before the date it was due, and could not otherwise show that its petition was filed on time, the court lacked jurisdiction to hear the Commonwealth's appeal. Commonwealth v. Green, No. 1845-03-2, 2004 Va. App. LEXIS 16 (Ct. of Appeals Jan. 13, 2004).

Commonwealth's interlocutory appeal of the pretrial suppression of defendant's statements, pursuant to § 19.2-398, was unsuccessful because the factual record supported the trial court's determination that defendant did not knowingly, intelligently, and voluntarily waive his previously invoked right to counsel with comments made after six hours in a windowless interrogation room. Once defendant requested counsel, the detectives should have scrupulously honored that request. Commonwealth v. Tucker, 2009 Va. App. LEXIS 489 (Nov. 3, 2009).

Scope of review. — The prosecutor's certification that "the evidence is essential to the prosecution" was not reviewable on appeal. Commonwealth v. Thomas, 23 Va. App. 598, 478 S.E.2d 715 (1996).

Trial court lacked authority to dismiss indictment after granting motion to suppress. Commonwealth v. Lane, No. 0318-99-2 (Ct. of Appeals Aug. 3, 1999).

Case was remanded to determine whether defendant, who had been sentenced to death, was mentally retarded. The Commonwealth could not use mandamus in the guise of an appeal to challenge the trial court's final judgment setting aside the death sentence based on a Brady violation, as the Commonwealth's appellate rights were strictly prescribed by Va. Const., Art. VI, § 1 and § 19.2-398. In re Commonwealth, 278 Va. 1, 677 S.E.2d 236, 2009 Va. LEXIS 78 (2009).

Appeal was outside scope of subdivision 2. — Commonwealth's appeal from an order granting a motion to suppress evidence, based on a finding that defendant's due process rights had been violated by a police identification procedure, was outside the scope of subdivision 2 and could not be maintained, where there was no finding that the evidence suppressed resulted from an illegal search or seizure or from an infringement of defendant's right against self-incrimination. Commonwealth v. Hawkins, 10 Va. App. 41, 390 S.E.2d 3 (1990).

Writ of mandamus filed by Commonwealth Attorney. — State supreme court granted the petition for writ of mandamus filed by the Commonwealth Attorney, as the trial court did not have the discretion to prohibit the Commonwealth Attorney from seeking the death penalty; the Commonwealth Attorney was entitled to seek the death penalty pursuant to statutory law, his limited right of appeal did not include allowing him to appeal the trial court's prohibition, and the trial court erred by exercising an executive function in determining that the Commonwealth Attorney was prohibited from seeking it in defendant's case where defendant was charged with capital murder pursuant to § 18.2-31. In re Horan, 271 Va. 258, 634 S.E.2d 675, 2006 Va. LEXIS 23 (2006).

Applied in Commonwealth v. Spencer, 21 Va. App. 156, 462 S.E.2d 899 (1995); Commonwealth v. Thornton, 24 Va. App. 478, 483 S.E.2d 487 (1997); Commonwealth v. Benjamin, 28 Va. App. 548, 507 S.E.2d 113 (1998); Franklin v. Commonwealth, — Va. App. —, — S.E.2d —, 2008 Va. App. LEXIS 175 (Apr. 15, 2008).

§ 19.2-399. Defense objections to be raised before trial; hearing; bill of particulars.

Editor's note.
This section is now codified at § 19.2-266.2.

§ 19.2-400. Appeal lies to the Court of Appeals; time for filing notice.

An appeal taken pursuant to § 19.2-398, including such an appeal in a capital murder case, shall lie to the Court of Appeals of Virginia.

No appeal shall be allowed the Commonwealth pursuant to subsection A of § 19.2-398 unless within seven days after entry of the order of the circuit court from which the appeal is taken, and before a jury is impaneled and sworn if there is to be trial by jury or, in cases to be tried without a jury, before the court begins to hear or receive evidence or the first witness is sworn, whichever occurs first, the Commonwealth files a notice of appeal with the clerk of the trial court. If the appeal relates to suppressed evidence, the attorney for the Commonwealth shall certify in the notice of appeal that the appeal is not taken for the purpose of delay and that the evidence is substantial proof of a fact material to the proceeding. All other requirements related to the notice of appeal shall be governed by Part Five A of the Rules of the Supreme Court. Upon the filing of a timely notice of appeal, the order from which the pretrial appeal is taken and further trial proceedings in the circuit court, except for a bail hearing, shall thereby be suspended pending disposition of the appeal.

An appeal by the Commonwealth pursuant to subsection C of § 19.2-398 shall be governed by Part Five A of the Rules of the Supreme Court.

History.
1987, c. 710; 2003, c. 109.

CASE NOTES

Purpose. — Purpose of this section is to prevent a circuit court from defeating the ability of the Commonwealth to pursue its appeal once the appeal is properly noted. West v. Commonwealth, 16 Va. App. 679, 432 S.E.2d 730 (1993).

Use of "shall" is directory only. — Language in § 19.2-400 stating what a notice of appeal "shall" contain, along with almost identical language in § 19.2-398, is directory only. Thus, the Commonwealth's failure to timely file the certification described in §§ 19.2-398 and 19.2-400 was not jurisdictional. Commonwealth v. Hackett, — Va. App. —, — S.E.2d —, 2008 Va. App. LEXIS 120 (Mar. 11, 2008).

Circuit court may reconsider its order. — This section did not bar circuit court from reconsidering its order granting motion to suppress after the Commonwealth had filed a notice of appeal from that order where trial court granted defendant's motion to suppress evidence in the circuit court. West v. Commonwealth, 16 Va. App. 679, 432 S.E.2d 730 (1993).

Commonwealth's limited right of appeal. — Commonwealth's appeal of the trial court's dismissal of indictments filed against defendant charging him with possession of cocaine with intent to distribute and possession of a firearm while possessing cocaine with intent to distribute was dismissed; the record showed that the Commonwealth had submitted evidence, including sworn testimony, immediately prior to the trial court's ruling on defendant's motion to dismiss and the statute under which the Commonwealth appealed, clause (ii) of subdivision A 1 of § 19.2-398 expressly applied only to "pretrial appeals," which was not involved in the present case. Commonwealth v. Green, — Va. App. —, — S.E.2d —, 2006 Va. App. LEXIS 347 (Aug. 1, 2006).

Tolling of dismissal order. — Appellate court, after finding that the trial court should not have entered its judgment suppressing evidence against defendant, found that it did not need to address the trial court's subsequent dismissal of the three indictments against defendant. Pursuant to § 19.2-400 and Va. Sup. Ct. R. 1:1, the Commonwealth's appeal of the trial court's ruling on the suppression order suspended the dismissal of the indictments pending the Commonwealth's appeal and since the Commonwealth prevailed, the indictments were treated as not having been dismissed at all. Commonwealth v. DeBusk, 2008 Va. App. LEXIS 268 (June 3, 2008).

Applied in Brown v. City of Danville, 44 Va. App. 586, 606 S.E.2d 523, 2004 Va. App. LEXIS 627 (2004).

§ 19.2-401. Cross appeal; when allowed; time for filing.

The defendant shall have no independent right of appeal pursuant to § 19.2-398. If the Commonwealth appeals, the defendant may cross appeal from any orders from which the Commonwealth may appeal, pursuant to § 19.2-398. The defendant shall be under no obligation to defend an appeal filed by the Commonwealth. However, when an appeal is taken by the Commonwealth, and the defendant wishes to defend or cross appeal, the circuit court shall, where the defendant is indigent, appoint counsel to represent the defendant on appeal. The remuneration to be awarded appointed counsel shall be governed by § 19.2-326.

In pretrial appeals, the defendant shall file a notice of cross appeal with the clerk of the circuit court within seven days following the notice of appeal filed by the Commonwealth.

Any brief on cross appeal shall be consolidated with the defendant's brief as appellee, if any.

History.
1987, c. 710; 2003, c. 109.

CASE NOTES

Applied in Commonwealth v. Thornton, 24 Va. App. 478, 483 S.E.2d 487 (1997).

§ 19.2-402. Petition for appeal; brief in opposition; time for filing.

A. When a notice of appeal has been filed pursuant to § 19.2-400, the Commonwealth may petition the Court of Appeals for an appeal pursuant to § 19.2-398. The Commonwealth shall be represented by the attorney for the Commonwealth prosecuting the case.

B. The provisions of this subsection apply only to pretrial appeals. The petition for a pretrial appeal shall be filed with the clerk of the Court of Appeals not more than 14 days after the date that the transcript or written statement of facts is filed, or if there are objections thereto, within 14 days after the judge signs the transcript or written statement. The accused may file a brief in opposition with the clerk of the Court of Appeals within 14 days after the filing of the petition for pretrial appeal. If the accused has filed a notice of cross appeal, he shall file a petition for cross appeal to be consolidated with, and filed within the same time period as, his

brief in opposition. The Commonwealth may file a brief in opposition to any petition for cross appeal within 10 days after the petition for cross appeal is filed. Except as specifically provided in this section, all other requirements for the petition for pretrial appeal and brief in opposition shall conform as nearly as practicable to Part Five A of the Rules of the Supreme Court of Virginia.

History.
1987, c. 710; 2003, c. 109.

CASE NOTES

Time requirement for filing interlocutory appeal by Commonwealth in criminal cases. — In reading §§ 17.1-408 and 19.2-402 and Va. Sup. Ct. R. 5A:12 together and giving effect to as much of their respective provisions as possible, in any interlocutory appeal by the Commonwealth in a criminal case, a petition for appeal that is compliant with the provisions of Va. Sup. Ct. R. 5A:12(c)(1) must be filed within fourteen days of the receipt by the clerk of the trial court of the transcript or written statement of facts or, if there are objections thereto, within fourteen days after the judge signs the transcript or written statement of facts, and, in such cases, the Virginia Court of Appeals has no authority to grant an extension of time for any reason, and any grant of such authority to that Court must come from the general assembly. Commonwealth v. Square, No. 2526-11-2, 2012 Va. App. LEXIS 202 (June 12, 2012).

Fourteen-day time limit in the more specific and more recent expression of legislative intent of § 19.2-402 applies to interlocutory appeals by the Commonwealth in criminal cases, rather than the forty-day time limit of § 17.1-408. Commonwealth v. Square, No. 2526-11-2, 2012 Va. App. LEXIS 202 (June 12, 2012).

Court of appeals lacked authority to grant extension. — When the Commonwealth's petition for an interlocutory appeal appealing an order granting a motion to suppress did not contain assignments of error, the appellate court erroneously granted an extension of time within which to file a proper petition and had no jurisdiction to consider the petition because (1) the requirement of assignments of error was jurisdictional, (2) the legislature intended in §§ 19.2-402 and 17.1-408 to expeditiously dispose of such appeals, (3) § 19.2-402 did not let the appellate court grant an extension in such cases, (4) § 19.2-402, reducing the time to file an interlocutory petition for appeal to fourteen days, governed, as the statute was a more specific and more recent expression of legislative intent, and (5) § 19.2-402's incorporation of Va. Sup. Ct. R. 5A:12 did not include authority to grant extensions of time, so (6) the general assembly did not intend to grant extensions to file a petition for appeal in these cases. Commonwealth v. Square, No. 2526-11-2, 2012 Va. App. LEXIS 202 (June 12, 2012).

Petition mailed by certified mail, return receipt requested, held untimely. — Although Va. Sup. Ct. R. 5A:3(c) allowed the Commonwealth to mail its petition appealing the trial court's judgment granting defendant's motion to suppress evidence to the court of appeals, it required the Commonwealth to obtain an official receipt showing that the petition was mailed on time and to produce that receipt on demand, and the appellate court held that because the Commonwealth could not produce a receipt showing that it mailed its petition on or before the date it was due, and could not otherwise show that its petition was filed on time, the court lacked jurisdiction to hear the Commonwealth's appeal. Commonwealth v. Green, No. 1845-03-2, 2004 Va. App. LEXIS 16 (Ct. of Appeals Jan. 13, 2004).

Incorporation of Va. Sup. Ct. R. 5A:12(a) does not apply to interlocutory appeals by the Commonwealth. — While § 19.2-402 incorporates by reference the requirements of the Rules of the Supreme Court Virginia applicable to the Virginia Court of Appeals, the authority to grant an extension of time as found in Va. Sup. Ct. R. 5A:12(a) does not apply to interlocutory appeals by the Commonwealth because the statute's plain language incorporates by reference only the substantive requirements for the petition as found in other subsections of Va. Sup. Ct. R. 5A:12. Commonwealth v. Square, No. 2526-11-2, 2012 Va. App. LEXIS 202 (June 12, 2012).

§ 19.2-403. Procedures on petition for pretrial appeal.

The procedures on a pretrial appeal to the Court of Appeals by the Commonwealth pursuant to § 19.2-398, and on a cross appeal of a pretrial appeal by the accused pursuant to § 19.2-401, shall be governed by the provisions of subsections C and D of § 17.1-407. The Court of Appeals, however, shall grant or deny the petition for a pretrial appeal, and the petition for cross appeal, if any, not later than 30 days after the brief in opposition is timely filed or the time for such filing has expired.

No petition for rehearing may be filed in any pretrial appeal pursuant to this chapter. If the petition for a pretrial appeal pursuant to this chapter is denied, the Court's mandate shall immediately issue and the clerk of the Court of Appeals shall return the record forthwith to the clerk of the trial court.

History.
1987, c. 710; 2003, c. 109.

§ 19.2-404. Procedures on awarded pretrial appeal.

This section applies only to pretrial appeals. If the Court of Appeals grants the Commonwealth's petition for a pretrial appeal, the Attorney General shall thereafter represent the Commonwealth during that appeal.

The Commonwealth shall file its opening brief in the office of the clerk of the Court of Appeals within 25 days after the date of the certificate awarding the appeal. The brief of the appellee shall be filed in the office of the clerk of the Court of Appeals within 25 days after the filing of the Commonwealth's opening brief. The Commonwealth may then file a reply brief, including its response to any cross appeal, in the office of the clerk of the Court of Appeals within 15 days after the filing of the brief of the accused. With the permission of a judge of the Court of Appeals, the time for filing any brief may be extended for good cause shown. Four copies of each brief shall be filed and three copies shall be mailed or delivered to opposing counsel on or before the date of filing. Except as specifically provided in this section, all other requirements of the brief shall conform as nearly as practicable to Part Five A of the Rules of the Supreme Court of Virginia. The Court of Appeals shall accelerate the appeal on its docket and render its decision not later than 60 days after the filing of the appellee's brief or after the time for filing such brief has expired.

When the opinion is rendered by the Court of Appeals, the mandate shall immediately issue and the clerk of the Court of Appeals shall return the record forthwith to the clerk of the trial court. No petition for rehearing may be filed.

History.
1987, c. 710; 2003, c. 109.

CASE NOTES

Holding by appellate court in pre-trial suppression dispute is not stare decisis as to the admissibility issue raised in the post-trial appeal, and that issue is fully reviewable. Satchell v. Commonwealth, 20 Va. App. 641, 460 S.E.2d 253 (1995).

§ 19.2-405. Pretrial appeals; record on appeal; transcript; written statement; time for filing.

This section applies only to pretrial appeals. The record on appeal shall conform, as nearly as practicable, to the requirements of Part Five A of the Rules of the Supreme Court for the record on appeal, except as hereinafter provided. The transcript or written statement of facts shall be filed by the Commonwealth with the clerk of the circuit court from which the appeal is being taken, within 25 days following entry of the order of the circuit court. Upon motion of the Commonwealth, the Court of Appeals may grant an extension of up to 45 days for filing the transcript or written statement for good cause shown. If the Commonwealth files a transcript or written statement, it shall also file with the clerk of the circuit court a notice, signed by the attorney for the Commonwealth, who is counsel for the appellant, identifying the transcript or written statement and reciting its delivery to the clerk. There shall be appended to the notice a certificate by the attorney for the Commonwealth that a copy of the notice has been mailed or delivered to opposing counsel.

Any party may object to the transcript or written statement on the ground that it is erroneous or incomplete. Notice of the objection specifying the errors alleged or deficiencies asserted shall be tendered to the trial judge within 10 days after the transcript or written statement is filed in the office of the clerk. The trial judge shall, within three days after the filing of such objection, either overrule the objection, or take steps deemed necessary to make the record complete or certify the respect in which the record is incomplete, and sign the transcript or written statement to verify its accuracy. The clerk of the trial court shall forthwith transmit the record to the clerk of the Court of Appeals.

History.
1987, c. 710; 2003, c. 109.

CIRCUIT COURT OPINIONS

Request denied where defendant could not file appeal. — Defendant's request for a transcript was denied because, as the defendant could not appeal the decision of the court, the defendant could not show a particularized need for a transcript. Commonwealth v. McClelland, 60 Va. Cir. 436, 2003 Va. Cir. LEXIS 64 (Richmond 2003).

§ 19.2-406. Bail pending pretrial appeal.

This section applies only to pretrial appeals. Upon a pretrial appeal being taken by the Commonwealth pursuant to § 19.2-398, if the defendant moves the trial court for release on bail, that court shall promptly, but in no event later than three days after the Commonwealth's notice of appeal is filed, hold a hearing to determine the issue of bail. The burden shall be upon the Commonwealth to show good cause why the bail should not be reduced or the accused released on his own recognizance. If it is determined that the accused shall be released on bail, bail shall be set and determined in accordance with Article 1 (§ 19.2-119 et seq.) of Chapter 9 of this title.

History.
1987, c. 710; 1999, cc. 829, 846; 2003, c. 109.

CIRCUIT COURT OPINIONS

Bail for murder charge. — Section 19.2-120 presumption against bail for a murder charge applied in a bail determination under § 19.2-406; the burden on the Commonwealth to show good cause why bail should not have been reduced or defendant released on his own recognizance during the Commonwealth's pretrial appeal did not eliminate the presumption against bail for defendant's murder charge. Commonwealth v. Ludwig, 69 Va. Cir. 460, 2006 Va. Cir. LEXIS 87 (Loudoun County 2006).

§ 19.2-407. Review by the Supreme Court.

Pursuant to § 17.1-409, the Supreme Court in its discretion may certify an appeal taken pursuant to § 19.2-398, or a cross appeal taken pursuant to § 19.2-401, for expedited review by the Supreme Court before it has been determined by the Court of Appeals. Such certification may be made only when the Supreme Court determines that at least one of the conditions set forth in subsection B of § 17.1-409 exists.

History.
1987, c. 710.

§ 19.2-408. Finality of decision of the Court of Appeals in pretrial appeals.

The decision of the Court of Appeals shall be final for purposes of a pretrial appeal pursuant to § 19.2-398, or a cross appeal of a pretrial appeal taken pursuant to § 19.2-401, and no further pretrial appeal shall lie to the Supreme Court.

History.
1987, c. 710; 2003, c. 109.

Law Review.
For an article, 'Final and Interlocutory Appeals in Virginia,' see 8 Geo. Mason L. Rev. 337 (1999).

Michie's Jurisprudence.
For related discussion, see 1B M.J. Appeal and Error, § 85.

CASE NOTES

Holding by appellate court in pre-trial suppression dispute is not stare decisis as to the admissibility issue raised in the

post-trial appeal, and that issue is fully reviewable. Satchell v. Commonwealth, 20 Va. App. 641, 460 S.E.2d 253 (1995).

§ 19.2-409. Exclusion of pretrial appeal period from time within which accused must be tried; reconsideration of issues after conviction.

This section applies only to pretrial appeals. The provisions of § 19.2-243 shall not apply to the period of time commencing when the Commonwealth's notice of pretrial appeal is filed pursuant to this chapter and ending 60 days after the Court of Appeals or Supreme Court issues its mandate disposing of the pretrial appeal. Such finality of the Court of Appeals' decision shall not preclude a defendant, if he is convicted, from requesting the Court of Appeals or Supreme Court on direct appeal to reconsider an issue which was the subject of the pretrial appeal.

History.
1987, c. 710; 2003, c. 109; 2007, c. 414.

The 2007 amendments.
The 2007 amendment by c. 414 substituted "60 days after" for "when" following "this chapter and ending" in the second sentence.

Law Review.
For an article, 'Final and Interlocutory Appeals in Virginia,' see 8 Geo. Mason L. Rev. 337 (1999). For 2007 annual survey article, "Criminal Law and Procedure," see 42 U. Rich. L. Rev. 311 (2007).

Michie's Jurisprudence.
For related discussion, see 1B M.J. Appeal and Error, § 73.

TITLE 22.1.

EDUCATION.

CHAPTER 12.

PUPIL TRANSPORTATION.

ARTICLE 1.

GENERAL PROVISIONS.

§ 22.1-176. Transportation of pupils authorized; when fee may be charged; contributions; regulations of Board of Education.

A. School boards may provide for the transportation of pupils, but nothing herein contained shall be construed as requiring such transportation except as provided in § 22.1-221.

B. When a school board provides transportation to pupils for extracurricular activities, other than those covered by an activity fund, which are sponsored by the pupils' school apart from the regular instructional program and which the pupils are not required to attend or participate in, the school board may accept contributions for such transportation or charge each pupil utilizing such transportation a reasonable fee not to exceed his pro rata share of the cost of providing such transportation. A school board may waive such fees for any pupil whose parent or guardian is financially unable to pay them.

C. When a school board provides transportation to pupils for field trips which are a part of the program of the pupils' school or are sponsored by such school, the school board may accept contributions for such transportation.

D. The Board of Education shall promulgate such regulations as shall be in the public interest to effect the intent of this section.

History.
Code 1950, §§ 22-72.1, 22-97.1; 1954, c. 291; 1956, Ex. Sess., c. 60; 1959, Ex. Sess., c. 79, § 1; 1968, c. 501; 1970, c. 156; 1971, Ex. Sess., c. 161; 1972, c. 86; 1975, cc. 308, 328; 1976, c. 99; 1978, cc. 430, 527; 1980, c. 559.

Cross references.
For section requiring the routing of school buses so as to avoid the necessity of pupils' crossing divided highways, see § 46.2-918.

OPINIONS OF THE ATTORNEY GENERAL

Local school boards may not charge for the transportation of students to and from school. See opinion of Attorney General to The Honorable John S. Reid, Member, House of Delegates, 07-053 (8/29/07).

Transportation to special program. — A local school board may not charge a fee for the transportation of a student enrolled in a specialty program located outside the boundaries of the student's base school. See opinion of Attorney General to The Honorable Jackson H. Miller, Member, House of Delegates, 10-016, 2010 Va. AG LEXIS 24 (3/18/10).

§ 22.1-176.1. Agreements to provide transportation for nonpublic school pupils.

Local school boards may enter into agreements with nonpublic schools within the school division to provide student transportation to and from such schools under such terms and conditions as the local school boards deem appropriate and responsible. Such terms may include, but are not limited to, arrangements relating to cost-sharing, fees, insurance, and liability.

History.
2007, c. 476.

§ 22.1-177. Regulations.

The Board may make regulations relating to the construction, design, operation, equipment, and color of public school buses and shall have the authority to issue an order prohibiting the operation on public streets and highways of any public school bus that does not comply with such regulations. Any such order shall be enforced by the Department of State Police.

Local school boards may, notwithstanding any regulation to the contrary, display decals depicting the flag of the United States on the sides and rear of school buses as long as any such decal does not obstruct the name of the school division or the number of the school bus and is no larger than 100 square inches. In addition, local school boards may, notwithstanding any regulation to the contrary, display decals relating to school bus safety. Local school divisions shall be responsible for the cost of the decals. Such decal shall not obstruct the name of the school division or the number of the school bus.

No regulation of the Board shall unreasonably limit the authority of any local school division to purchase and use school buses using compressed natural gas or other alternative fuels or convert its school buses to use compressed natural gas or other alternative fuels.

History.
Code 1950, § 22-276; 1958, c. 274; 1980, c. 559; 1991, c. 191; 2003, c. 162; 2007, c. 104; 2013, c. 778.

The 2013 amendments.
The 2013 amendment by c. 778, in the second paragraph, substituted "relating to school bus safety" for "relating to local

school division bus safety hotlines" at the end of the second sentence, and deleted "bearing the number of such safety hotline" at the end of the third sentence; and made a minor stylistic change.

§ 22.1-178. Requirements for persons employed to drive school buses.

A. No school board shall hire, employ, or enter into any agreement with any person for the purposes of operating a school bus transporting pupils unless the person proposed to so operate such school bus shall:

1. Have a physical examination of a scope prescribed by the Board of Education with the advice of the Medical Society of Virginia and furnish a form prescribed by the Board of Education showing the results of such examination.

2. Furnish a statement or copy of records from the Department of Motor Vehicles showing that the records of such Department do not disclose that the person, within the preceding five years, has been convicted upon a charge of driving under the influence of alcohol or drugs, convicted of a felony or assigned to any alcohol safety action program or driver alcohol rehabilitation program pursuant to § 18.2-271.1 or, within the preceding 12 months, has been convicted of two or more moving traffic violations or required to attend a driver improvement clinic by the Commissioner of the Department of Motor Vehicles pursuant to § 46.2-498.

3. Furnish a statement signed by two reputable persons who reside in the school division or in the applicant's community that the person is of good moral character.

4. Exhibit a license showing the person has successfully undertaken the examination prescribed by § 46.2-339.

5. Have reached the age of 18 on the first day of the school year.

B. Any school board may require proof of current certification or training in emergency first aid, cardiopulmonary resuscitation, and the use of an automated external defibrillator as a condition to employment to operate a school bus transporting pupils.

C. School boards may require persons accepting employment after July 1, 1994, as a driver of a school bus transporting pupils to agree, as a condition of employment, to submit to alcohol and controlled substance testing. Any such tests shall be conducted in compliance with Board of Education regulations.

D. The documents required pursuant to subdivisions A 1 and A 2 shall be furnished annually prior to the anniversary date of the employment agreement as a condition to continuing employment to operate a school bus.

E. The documents required pursuant to this section shall be filed with, and made a part of, the records of the school board employing such person as a school bus operator.

F. The State Department of Education shall furnish to the several division superintendents the necessary forms to be used by applicants in furnishing the information required by this section. Insofar as practicable, such forms shall be designed to limit paperwork, avoid the possibility of mistake, and furnish all parties involved with a complete and accurate record of the information required.

G. The physical examination required by subsection A may be performed and the report of the results signed by a licensed nurse practitioner or physician assistant.

History.
Code 1950, § 22-276.1; 1962, c. 544; 1966, c. 604; 1970, c. 696; 1972, c. 359; 1973, c. 170; 1976, cc. 116, 123; 1977, c. 393; 1978, c. 322; 1979, c. 126; 1980, c. 559; 1992, c. 130; 1993, c. 285; 1994, c. 104; 1998, c. 287; 2001, c. 445; 2006, c. 396; 2013, cc. 498, 530.

Editor's note.
Acts 2013, cc. 498 and 530, cl. 2 provides: "That the Board of Education, in conjunction with the Department of Health, shall adopt regulations and establish guidelines to implement the provisions of this act."

The 2013 amendments.
The 2013 amendments by cc. 498 and 530 are identical, and substituted "proof of current certification or training in emergency first aid, cardiopulmonary resuscitation, and the use of an automated external defibrillator" for "successful completion of the American National Red Cross first-aid course or its equivalent" in subsection B, and made minor stylistic changes.

Law Review.
For 2006 survey article, "Health Care Law," see 41 U. Rich. L. Rev. 179 (2006).

§ 22.1-179. Repealed by Acts 1992, c. 130, effective March 3, 1992.

Editor's note.
Former § 22.1-179, relating to completion of contract upon reaching age seventy, was derived from Code 1950, § 22-276.1; 1962, c. 544; 1966, c. 604; 1970, c. 696; 1972, c. 359; 1973, c. 170; 1976, cc. 116, 123; 1977, c. 393; 1978, c. 322; 1979, c. 126; 1980, c. 559.

§ 22.1-180. Requirements for persons employed to transport pupils attending religious or private schools.

No person, partnership, association or corporation operating any religious or private school shall hire, employ or enter into any agreement with any person for the purpose of transporting pupils by motor vehicle unless such person shall present the documents and meet the qualifications required of operators of public school buses by subsection A of § 22.1-178. The State Department of Education shall furnish the forms prescribed for the purposes of § 22.1-178 to any person, partnership, association or corporation who shall request such forms for the purpose of compliance with this section.

History.
Code 1950, § 22-276.2; 1968, c. 432; 1980, c. 559; 2005, c. 928.

§ 22.1-181. Training program for school bus operators.

The Board of Education shall develop a training program for persons applying for employment, and employed, to operate school buses and shall promote its implementation.

History.

Code 1950, § 22-276.3; 1977, c. 393; 1980, c. 559.

Cross references.

As to regulation of driver training schools, see § 46.2-1700, et seq.

§ 22.1-182. Use of school buses for public purposes.

The school board of any school division may enter into agreements with the governing body of any county, city or town in the school division, any state agency or any agency established or identified pursuant to United States Public Law 89-73 or any law amendatory or supplemental thereto providing for the use of the school buses of such school division by such agency or by departments, boards, commissions or officers of such county, city or town for public purposes, including transportation for the elderly. Each such agreement shall provide for reimbursing the school board in full for the proportionate share of any and all costs, both fixed and variable, of such buses incurred by such school board attributable to the use of such buses pursuant to such agreement. The governing body, state agency or agency established or identified pursuant to United States Public Law 89-73 or any law amendatory or supplemental thereto shall indemnify and hold harmless the school board from any and all liability of the school board by virtue of use of such buses pursuant to an agreement authorized herein.

History.

Code 1950, § 22-151.2; 1973, c. 368; 1975, c. 633; 1980, c. 559.

§ 22.1-183. When warning lights and identification to be covered.

It shall be unlawful for a school bus licensed in this Commonwealth to be operated on the public highways of this Commonwealth for the purpose of transporting persons or commodities other than school personnel, school children or elderly or mentally or physically handicapped persons unless the lettered identification and school bus traffic warning lights on the front and rear of such bus are covered with some opaque detachable material. This section shall not apply to any such bus when operated by a salesman or demonstrator in connection with a prospective sale or delivery of a bus.

History.

Code 1950, §§ 22-151.2, 22-280.1; 1973, c. 368; 1975, c. 633; 1980, c. 559.

§ 22.1-184. School bus emergency drills.

At every public school having public school buses there shall be held, at least once during the first ninety calendar days of each school session and oftener if necessary, a drill in leaving school buses under emergency circumstances.

History.

Code 1950, § 22-280.2; 1964, c. 174; 1980, c. 559.

§ 22.1-185. Shelters on bus routes.

The governing body of any county, city or town may expend funds for the construction and maintenance at points on school bus routes of such shelters, platforms or other structures as it may deem necessary or convenient for the protection and comfort of children of school age who go to such points to meet school buses.

History.

Code 1950, § 22-282; 1980, c. 559.

§ 22.1-186. Payments for transportation of pupils.

The regulations of the Board of Education governing state payments for pupil transportation shall provide for payments to school divisions for pupil transportation provided by the school divisions both through systems operated by the school divisions and through contracts with public transportation facilities.

History.

Code 1950, § 22-283.1; 1972, c. 699; 1980, c. 559.

§ 22.1-187. Exemption from payment of tolls by certain students, etc.

It shall be unlawful to collect any toll for the use of any road, highway, bridge or ferry in this Commonwealth, except those financed under the State Revenue Bond Act (§ 33.1-267 et seq.) or other act authorizing the construction by the State or a political subdivision thereof of projects financed by the issuance of bonds payable solely from tolls and other revenues of the project, (i) by any student or other person using the road, highway, bridge or ferry daily for going to or from immediate attendance upon any school, college, or other educational institution in this Commonwealth, or classes in water safety training conducted under the auspices of the American Red Cross or (ii) by the vehicle carrying the student or other person.

Any such student or other person or the parent or guardian of any such student may apply for and receive from the principal of any school, college, or other educational institution in this Commonwealth a card certifying that the student or other person uses such road, highway, bridge or ferry daily for regularly attending such school, college, educational institution or classes. Such card exhibited to the person in charge of any tollgate on any road, highway, bridge or ferry in this Commonwealth shall be accepted in lieu of all charges for the passage through such tollgate of any such student, person or the vehicle carrying him when using the road, highway, bridge or ferry daily for going to or from immediate attendance upon any such school, college, other educational institution, or classes.

Any person using any such card, except for the purpose herein specified, shall be guilty of a Class 4 misdemeanor.

History.
Code 1950, § 22-277; 1956, c. 237; 1958, c. 465; 1980, c. 559.

Cross references.
As to punishment for Class 4 misdemeanors, see § 18.2-11. As to inapplicability of certain laws to high-occupancy toll lanes, see § 33.1-56.5.

ARTICLE 2.
INSURANCE PROVISIONS.

Michie's Jurisprudence.
For related discussion, see 2B M.J. Automobiles, § 38; 16 M.J. Schools, § 111.1.

§ 22.1-188. Definitions.

As used in this article:

1. *"Vehicle"* means any vehicle owned or operated by, or owned or operated by any person under contract with, a county, city, town or school board in which any school pupils or personnel are transported at public expense to or from any public school.

2. *"School pupils and personnel"* includes school bus patrolmen when performing duties either in or outside a vehicle as prescribed by the Board of Education.

History.
1980, c. 559.

§ 22.1-189. Compliance with article prerequisite to receiving state school funds.

No school division in which any school pupils or personnel are transported at public expense to or from any public school in any vehicle shall receive any state school funds unless it complies with all applicable requirements of this article and submits satisfactory evidence to the Superintendent of Public Instruction of the effectuation of all requisite insurance.

History.
Code 1950, § 22-284; 1980, c. 559.

CASE NOTES

Vehicles covered. — This section and §§ 22.1-190 and 22.1-194 are designed for and limited to the operation of vehicles used for the transportation of school pupils and personnel. Crabbe v. County School Bd., 209 Va. 356, 164 S.E.2d 639 (1968) (decided under prior law).

§ 22.1-190. When insurance required and amount thereof.

A. Every vehicle shall be covered in a policy of liability and property damage insurance issued by an insurance carrier authorized to transact business in this Commonwealth, in the amounts of at least $50,000 for injury, including death, to one person; $500,000 for injury, including death, to all persons injured in any one accident; and $50,000 for damage, including destruction, to the property of any person, other than the insured. In addition, the policy of insurance shall provide coverage for loss or damage caused by an uninsured motorist in accordance with the provisions of § 38.2-2204 and in the amounts required by this section. The policy shall also provide for medical expense payment coverage in the minimum amount of $5,000 for each person injured. Taxicabs providing transportation of students under contract with a school division shall be covered by policies providing coverage of at least $50,000 for injury, including death, to one person; $200,000 for injury, including death, to all persons injured in any one accident; $10,000 for damage, including destruction, to the property of any person other than the insured; and medical expense payment coverage in the minimum amount of $1,000 for each person injured, or in such higher amounts as the contract with the school division or a local ordinance may prescribe.

B. The insurance so effected shall be subject to all laws of this Commonwealth regulating insurance.

C. This insurance shall not be required in cases when pupils are transported on a common carrier if such carrier is covered by a policy of insurance affording substantially the protection required by this article.

D. This insurance shall not be required in cases where pupils are transported in vehicles which are owned or operated by a county, city, town or school board which has qualified for and received a certificate of self-insurance from the Commissioner of the Department of Motor Vehicles, following a certification of financial responsibility equal to that required under subsection A of this section. The Commissioner of the Department of Motor Vehicles may require posting of a bond by a locality or school board as a condition to issuance of a certificate of financial responsibility pursuant to this subsection.

History.
Code 1950, § 22-285; 1958, c. 301; 1970, c. 681; 1976, c. 224; 1980, c. 559; 2012, c. 593.

The 2012 amendments.
The 2012 amendment by c. 593, in subsection A, substituted "to one person; $500,000 for injury, including death, to all persons injured in any one accident; and $50,000 for damage" for "to 1 person; $2500,000 for injury, including death, to all persons injured in any 1 accident; and $10,000 for damage" in the first sentence,

substituted "of $5,000 for each person injured" for "of $1,000" at the end of the third sentence, and added the fourth sentence.

Research references.

Virginia Forms (Matthew Bender). No. 1-204 Complaint — Personal Injury against Unknown Driver under Uninsured Motorist Statute; No. 1-217 Answer — Unknown Driver under Uninsured Motorist Statute.

CASE NOTES

Vehicles covered. — This section and §§ 22.1-189 and 22.1-194 are designed for and limited to the operation of vehicles used for the transportation of school pupils and personnel. Crabbe v. County School Bd., 209 Va. 356, 164 S.E.2d 639 (1968) (decided under prior law).

Failure to obtain certificate of self-insurance. — This section abrogated a school board's sovereign immunity up to the limits of its coverage under a self-insurance pool operated by the Virginia School Board Association, and the trial court properly held that a minor who was injured in a school bus accident and the minor's mother were not barred from suing the school board for negligence, and that the school board's liability for damages was not limited to $50,000 under subsection A of § 22.1-190 because the school board had not obtained a certificate of self-insurance from the Commissioner of the Virginia Department of Motor Vehicles, pursuant to subsection D of § 22.1-190. Frederick County Sch. Bd. v. Hannah, 267 Va. 231, 590 S.E.2d 567, 2004 Va. LEXIS 20 (2004).

§ 22.1-191. When Superintendent of Public Instruction to obtain insurance.

In every case in which a locality or its school board fails to obtain, or to require vehicles operated under contract with it to be covered by, the requisite insurance by the twentieth of July of any year or fails to notify the Superintendent of Public Instruction of the effectuation of requisite insurance on or before the first of August, it shall be the duty of the Superintendent of Public Instruction, on or before the first of September, to obtain insurance complying with the requirements of this article on all vehicles, as far as known to or reasonably ascertainable by him, to be used in the school division for school pupil and personnel transportation in the ensuing session and to expend for this purpose the requisite amount out of any state school funds otherwise distributable, or becoming distributable, to the school division so in default.

History.

Code 1950, § 22-287; 1980, c. 559.

§ 22.1-192. Injury and damage covered by policy.

Every policy of insurance issued in pursuance of the provisions of this article, in addition to compliance with other requirements of this article and with the requirements of other applicable laws, shall cover:

1. Injury, including death, to school pupils and personnel, except the driver when not a pupil, riding as passengers on any of the vehicles so insured when used to transport such persons at public expense;

2. Injury, including death, to any persons not passengers on any such vehicle;

3. Damage, including destruction, to property of any person other than the insured.

History.

Code 1950, § 22-288; 1962, c. 181; 1980, c. 559.

§ 22.1-193. Sufficiency of proof in action on policy; guest doctrine not applicable.

In case any school pupil or personnel, except the driver when not a pupil, whether riding in a vehicle or not, or any other person suffers injury, including death, or property damage, including destruction, through the ownership, maintenance, use or operation of a vehicle, it shall be sufficient, in an action for recovery upon the policy, to prove such facts and circumstances as are required to be shown in order to recover damages for death or injury to person or property caused by the negligent operation of privately owned motor vehicles in Virginia; provided that such pupils and personnel shall not be considered as guests, and § 8.01-63 shall not apply to them.

History.

Code 1950, § 22-289; 1980, c. 559.

§ 22.1-194. Liability of locality or school board owning or operating vehicle.

In case the locality or the school board is the owner, or operator through medium of a driver, of, or otherwise is the insured under the policy upon, a vehicle involved in an accident, the locality or school board shall be subject to action up to, but not beyond, the limits of valid and collectible insurance in force to cover the injury complained of or, in cases set forth in subsection D of § 22.1-190, up to but not beyond the amounts of insurance required under subsection A of § 22.1-190 and the defense of governmental immunity shall not be a bar to action or recovery. In case of several claims for damages arising out of a single accident involving a vehicle, the claims of pupils and school personnel, excluding driver when not a pupil, shall be first satisfied. In no event, except where approved self-insurance has been provided pursuant to subsection D of § 22.1-190, shall school funds be used to pay any claim or judgment or any person for any injury arising out of the operation of any such vehicle. The locality or school board may be sued alone or jointly with the driver, provided that in no case shall any member of a school board be liable personally in the capacity of school board member solely.

History.

Code 1950, § 22-290; 1976, c. 224; 1980, c. 559.

Editor's note.

At the direction of the Virginia Code Commission, "subsection D of § 22.1-190" was substituted for "22.1-190 D."

Law Review.

For a re-examination of sovereign tort immunity in Virginia, see 15 U. Rich. L. Rev. 247 (1981).

Research references.

Friend's Virginia Pleading and Practice (Matthew Bender). Chapter 35 Limitation of Actions: Statutes of Limitations; Immunities; Res Judicata and Collateral Estoppel. § 35.02 Immunities. Charles E. Friend.

Michie's Jurisprudence.

For related discussion, see 2B M.J. Automobiles, § 38.

CASE NOTES

This statute abrogates the immunity of a school board for acts of simple negligence to a limited degree and when the conditions of the statute are met, the defense of sovereign immunity will not bar an action for recovery of damages in an amount up to the limits of the insurance policy. Linhart v. Lawson, 261 Va. 30, 540 S.E.2d 875, 2001 Va. LEXIS 23 (2001).

This section abrogated a school board's sovereign immunity up to the limits of its coverage under a self-insurance pool operated by the Virginia School Board Association, and the trial court properly held that a minor who was injured in a school bus accident and the minor's mother were not barred from suing the school board for negligence, and that the school board's liability for damages was not limited to $50,000 under subsection A of § 22.1-190 because the school board had not obtained a certificate of self-insurance from the Commissioner of the Virginia Department of Motor Vehicles, pursuant to subsection D of § 22.1-190. Frederick County Sch. Bd. v. Hannah, 267 Va. 231, 590 S.E.2d 567, 2004 Va. LEXIS 20 (2004).

School boards liable for simple negligence. — In enacting this section, the general assembly created an exception to the common law principle that the liabilities of principals and agents are coterminous and imposed liability on a school board for simple negligence, even if its employee is liable only for acts of gross negligence. Linhart v. Lawson, 261 Va. 30, 540 S.E.2d 875, 2001 Va. LEXIS 23 (2001).

Immunity of individual employees preserved. — Governmental employees have always been subject to suit for gross negligence and the language in the statute authorizing a suit against an employee and school board jointly does no more than recognize that such an employee is amenable to suit; without more, the language of the statute is insufficient to convey a plainly manifest intent to abrogate a governmental employee's immunity for acts of simple negligence. Linhart v. Lawson, 261 Va. 30, 540 S.E.2d 875, 2001 Va. LEXIS 23 (2001).

Vehicles covered. — This section and §§ 22.1-189 and 22.1-190 are designed for and limited to the operation of vehicles used for the transportation of school pupils and personnel. Crabbe v. County School Bd., 209 Va. 356, 164 S.E.2d 639 (1968) (decided under prior law).

CIRCUIT COURT OPINIONS

No insurance coverage. — Even if the court were to accept the student's argument that the accident occurred during the unloading process, based on the facts, the Powell test, and other cases, the accident did not result from the ownership, maintenance, or use of the bus; the accident occurred after the bus driver removed the student from the bus, when he was on the sidewalk. The bus, at best, was merely the situs of the accident; therefore, there was no valid and collectible insurance in force to cover the injury complained of under § 22.1-194 and the county school board retained its immunity. Griffin v. Brunswick County Pub. Sch. Bd., 77 Va. Cir. 275, 2008 Va. Cir. LEXIS 267 (Brunswick County 2008).

§ 22.1-195. Recovery where vehicle operated under contract.

In case a vehicle involved in an accident is not owned by the county, city, town or school board but is operated under contract with the locality or school board, recovery may be had as provided for in § 22.1-193.

History.

Code 1950, § 22-291; 1980, c. 559.

Research references.

Friend's Virginia Pleading and Practice (Matthew Bender). Chapter 35 Limitation of Actions: Statutes of Limitations; Immunities; Res Judicata and Collateral Estoppel. § 35.02 Immunities. Charles E. Friend.

§ 22.1-196. Lapsed insurance.

If insurance is obtained but lapses while a vehicle is still being used or is proposed to be used to transport school pupils or personnel, no school funds remaining to be distributed to the school board so in default shall be distributed to it until the terms of this article in this regard have been fully complied with.

History.

Code 1950, § 22-292; 1980, c. 559.

§ 22.1-197. Distribution of funds when Superintendent effects insurance.

When the Superintendent of Public Instruction effects insurance as required by this article, he shall nevertheless not make any distribution of state school aid funds to the school board so in default until he has been furnished with satisfactory assurances that all vehicles required by this article to be covered by insurance have been duly insured.

History.

Code 1950, § 22-293; 1980, c. 559.

§ 22.1-198. Applicability of article not dependent upon approval of vehicles or allocability of state aid.

The provisions of this article apply to all vehicles whether or not the regulations of the Board of Education established pursuant to § 22.1-177 have been complied with and irrespective of whether or not any state aid for transporting school pupils and personnel in the particular vehicle has been, is, or will be allocable.

History.

Code 1950, § 22-294; 1980, c. 559.

TITLE 23.

EDUCATIONAL INSTITUTIONS.

CHAPTER 1.

GENERAL PROVISIONS.

§ 23-9.2:4. Payments to institutions of higher education for certain courses taken by law-enforcement officers.

The State Department of Criminal Justice Services is hereby authorized and directed to enter into contracts to make payments to accredited institutions of higher education within this Commonwealth for tuition, books and mandatory fees for law-enforcement officers of the Commonwealth, or its political subdivisions, departments or authorities, or of any county, city or town thereof enrolled on a full-time or part-time basis in courses included in an undergraduate or graduate program which leads to a degree or certificate in an area related to law enforcement or an area suitable for law-enforcement officers. No payments shall be made pursuant to this section to any institution of higher education operating within this Commonwealth whose primary campus is outside this Commonwealth. Assistance under this section may be granted only on behalf of an applicant who enters into an agreement to continue to serve as a law-enforcement officer in Virginia upon completion of his course of study for a period at least as long as the length of the course of study undertaken and paid for under the provisions of this section, and in the event such service is not completed, to repay the full amount of such payments on the terms and in the manner the State Department of Criminal Justice Services may prescribe.

Any person receiving the benefit of funds expended pursuant to this section shall be required to make reimbursement of such funds if he fails to satisfactorily complete the course or courses for which the funds were expended.

Any reimbursement of money advanced under the provisions of this section shall be returned to the State Department of Criminal Justice Services and used in accordance with the purposes of this section.

History.
1972, c. 697; 1974, c. 162; 1977, c. 162; 1982, c. 18; 1986, c. 236.

TITLE 27.

FIRE PROTECTION.

CHAPTER 1.

GENERAL PROVISIONS.

§ 27-1. Fire fighters, emergency medical technicians, and equipment may in emergencies go or be sent beyond territorial limits.

Whenever the necessity arises during any actual or potential emergency resulting from fire, personal injury, or other public disaster, the fire fighters or emergency medical technicians of any county, city or town may, together with all necessary equipment, lawfully go or be sent beyond the territorial limits of such county, city or town to any point within or without the Commonwealth, to assist in meeting such emergency.

In such event the acts performed for such purpose by such fire fighters or emergency medical technicians, and the expenditures made for such purpose by such county, city or town, shall be deemed conclusively to be for a public and governmental purpose and all of the immunities from liability enjoyed by a county, city or town when acting through its fire fighters or emergency medical technicians for a public or governmental purpose within its territorial limits shall be enjoyed by it to the same extent when such county, city or town is so acting, under this section or under other lawful authority, beyond its territorial limits.

The fire fighters or emergency medical technicians of any county, city or town, when acting hereunder, or under other lawful authority, beyond the territorial limits of such county, city or town, shall have all the immunities from liability and exemptions from laws, ordinances and regulations, and shall have all of the pension, relief, disability, workers' compensation and other benefits, enjoyed by them while performing their respective duties.

History.

1942, p. 376; Michie Code 1942, § 3032c; 1966, c. 134; 1977, c. 326; 1995, c. 461.

§ 27-2. Contracts of cities or towns to furnish fire protection; emergency medical services.

The governing body of any city or town may, in its discretion, authorize or require the fire department or emergency medical services department or division thereof to render aid in cases of actual or potential fire or medical emergency occurring beyond their limits, and may prescribe the conditions on which such aid may be rendered, and may enter into a contract, or contracts, with nearby, adjacent or adjoining counties and cities, within or without the Commonwealth, including the District of Columbia, for rendering aid in fire protection or in emergency medical response in such counties, cities, or any district, or sanitary district thereof or in the District of Columbia, on such terms as may be agreed upon by such governing body and the governing body of the District of Columbia or of such counties or cities and/or district, including sanitary districts; provided, that each of the parties to such agreement may contract as follows: (1) waive any and all claims against all the other parties thereto which may arise out of their activities outside their respective jurisdictions under such agreement; (2) indemnify and save harmless the other parties to such agreement from all claims by third parties for property damage or personal injury which may arise out of the activities of the other parties to such agreement outside their respective jurisdictions under such agreement. When the fire department or emergency medical services department or division of any city or town is operating under such permission or contract, or contracts, on any call beyond the corporate limits of the city or town, it shall be deemed to be operating in a governmental capacity, and subject only to such liability for injuries as it would be if it were operating within the corporate limits of such city or town.

History.

Code 1919, § 3033; 1938, p. 576; 1966, c. 134; 1968, c. 801; 1995, c. 461.

§ 27-2.1. Contracts for fire protection or emergency medical services for federal and state property.

Any county, city or town may contract with the federal or state governments to provide fire or emergency medical service to federal or state property

located within or without the boundaries of the county, city or town.

In the absence of a written contract, any acts performed and all expenditures made by a county, city or town in providing fire protection or emergency medical services to property owned by the federal government shall be deemed conclusively to be for a public and governmental purpose and all of the immunities from liability enjoyed by a county, city or town when acting through its fire fighters or emergency medical technicians for a public or governmental purpose within or without its territorial limits shall be enjoyed by it to the same extent when such county, city or town is so acting, under the provisions of this section, or under other lawful authority.

The fire fighters or emergency medical technicians of any county, city or town when acting hereunder, or under other lawful authority, shall have all of the immunities from liability and exemptions from laws, ordinances and regulations, and shall have all of the pension, relief, disability, workers' compensation and other benefits enjoyed by them while performing their respective duties.

The amount of compensation to the county, city or town pursuant to the contract shall be a matter within the sole discretion of the governing body of the county, city or town.

History.

1980, c. 729; 1995, c. 461.

§ 27-3. Contract of county with city or another county for fire protection; emergency medical services.

The governing body of any county adjoining or near any city, town, or county, within or without the Commonwealth, including the District of Columbia, having and maintaining fire-fighting or emergency medical services equipment may contract with any such city, town, or county, upon such terms as such governing body may deem proper, for fighting fires or responding to medical emergencies in such county, town, or city and may prescribe the terms and conditions upon which such services may be provided on privately owned property in the county, town, or city and may raise funds with which to pay for such services, by levying and collecting annually, at such rates as such governing body may deem sufficient, a special tax upon the property in such county, or in any magisterial district thereof, subject to local taxation.

History.

Code 1919, § 2743; 1942, p. 118; 1966, c. 134; 1995, c. 461.

§ 27-3.1. Public liability insurance to cover claims arising out of mutual aid agreements.

The governing body of any city, county or town in the Commonwealth is authorized to procure or extend the necessary public liability insurance to cover claims arising out of mutual aid agreements executed with other cities, counties, or towns outside the Commonwealth, including the District of Columbia.

History.
1968, c. 801; 1995, c. 461.

§ 27-4. Contract of county, city or town to furnish fire protection; emergency medical services.

Any county, city or town which operates firefighting equipment as provided for in § 27-15.2 and any county, city or town mentioned in § 27-23.6 may contract with counties, cities or towns in, adjacent to, or near such county, city or town, including the District of Columbia, for fire protection or emergency medical services in the manner provided for in § 27-2.

History.
1946, p. 609; Michie Suppl. 1946, § 2743m; 1948, p. 160; 1970, c. 187; 1991, c. 54; 1995, c. 461.

Editor's note.
Acts 1970, c. 187, cl. 3, provides that this section shall be liberally construed and is severable.

§ 27-5. Contracts as to installation of automatic sprinklers with incidental insurance clauses.

Nothing contained in Title 38.2 shall be construed as prohibiting the performance of any contract made for the introduction of automatic sprinklers for reducing the risk by fire on any property located in this Commonwealth and containing provisions for obtaining or guaranteeing insurance against loss or damage by fire or water for a specified time at a fixed rate; provided, that all insurance contracts issued as a result of such contracts shall be in the form required by law in this Commonwealth; provided, further, that the contract rate be less than the published rate on risks covered thereby or the rate used by insurance companies writing such risks.

History.
1930, p. 23; Michie Code 1942, § 4246c.

§ 27-5.1. Repealed by Acts 1986, c. 429.

Cross references.
As to the Statewide Fire Prevention Code, see now §§ 27-94 through 27-101.

§ 27-5.2. Repealed by Acts 1988, c. 891.

Cross references.
As to forest wardens and fires, see § 10.1-1135 et seq. As to fire hazards and closing of hunting and fishing seasons in forestlands, see § 10.1-1158 et seq.

§ 27-5.3. Certain counties authorized to accept grants and other federal assistance.

Any county having a population of more than 2,000 persons per square mile may apply for, accept and utilize grants and other assistance from the federal government pursuant to § 117 of the United States Housing Act of 1949 (79 Stat. 451, 477), as amended, for the purpose of carrying out programs of concentrated code enforcement and related activities.

History.
1966, c. 435.

§ 27-5.4. Repealed by Acts 1988, c. 891.

Cross references.
As to forest wardens and fires, see § 10.1-1135 et seq. As to fire hazards and closing of hunting and fishing seasons in forestlands, see § 10.1-1158 et seq.

§ 27-5.5. Plans of certain state structures to be submitted to local governing bodies; access of local fire officials to state structures; corrective actions.

A. Any agency, commission or institution of the Commonwealth engaging in the construction or renovation of a structure, the cost of which exceeds $25,000, shall submit, prior to the initiation of such construction or renovation, preliminary and working plans and specifications to the governing body, or its designee, of the political subdivision in which the structure is or will be located, provided that such governing body has submitted a written request for such plans and specifications to the Director of the Department of General Services and to such agency, commission or institution.

B. Every agency, commission or institution of the Commonwealth shall permit, at all reasonable hours, a local fire official reasonable access to existing structures or a structure under construction or renovation, for the purposes of performing an informational and advisory fire safety inspection. The local fire official may submit, subsequent to performing such inspection, his findings and recommendations including a list of corrective actions necessary to ensure that such structure is reasonably safe from the hazards of fire to the appropriate official of such agency, commission or institution, the Director of the Department of General Services, and the State Fire Marshal. Such agency, commission or institution shall notify, within sixty days of receipt of such findings and recommendations, the Director of the Department of General Services, the State Fire Marshal, and the local fire official of the corrective measures taken to eliminate the hazards reported by the local fire official. The State Fire Marshal shall have the same power in the enforcement of this section as is provided for the enforcement of the Statewide Fire Prevention Code (§ 27-94 et seq.).

History.
    1978, c. 197; 1989, c. 258.

CHAPTER 2.

FIRE/EMS DEPARTMENTS AND FIRE/EMS COMPANIES.

ARTICLE 1.

PROVISIONS APPLICABLE TO COUNTIES, CITIES AND TOWNS.

§ 27-6. Repealed by Acts 1970, c. 187.

§ 27-6.1. Establishment of fire/EMS department; chief, officers and employees.

The governing body of any city, town or county may establish as a department of government a fire/EMS department and may designate it by any name consistent with the names of its other governmental units. The head of such fire department shall be known as "the chief" or "the director." As many other officers and employees may be employed in such fire/EMS department as the governing body may approve.

History.
    1970, c. 187; 2001, c. 142; 2008, c. 410.

Editor's note.
    Acts 1970, c. 187, which added or amended many of the sections in this article, provides, in cl. 3, that the act shall be liberally construed and is severable.

OPINIONS OF THE ATTORNEY GENERAL

County may require reimbursement of costs for emergency services. — As the provision of emergency services by a county is discretionary, requiring reimbursement from a user of such services for the reasonable costs associated with the use of emergency equipment owned and maintained by the county is appropriate. See opinion of Attorney General to Ms. Deanis L. Simmons, County Attorney for Tazewell County, 00-068 (11/29/00).

§ 27-6.2. Applicant preemployment information with Arlington County Fire Department.

Applicants for employment with the Arlington County Fire Department, having a local ordinance adopted in accordance with § 19.2-389, shall be required to submit to fingerprinting and to provide personal descriptive information to be forwarded along with the applicant's fingerprints through the Central Criminal Records Exchange and the Federal Bureau of Investigation for the purpose of obtaining criminal history record information regarding such applicant; however, such applicants shall, if required by local ordinance, pay the cost of the fingerprinting or criminal records check or both.

The Central Criminal Records Exchange, upon receipt of an applicant's record or notification that no record exists, shall make a report to the fire chief or his designee, who must belong to a governmental entity. In determining whether a criminal conviction directly relates to a position, the locality shall consider the following criteria: (i) the nature and seriousness of the crime; (ii) the relationship of the crime to the work to be performed in the position applied for; (iii) the extent to which the position applied for might offer an opportunity to engage in further criminal activity of the same type as that in which the person had been involved; (iv) the relationship of the crime to the ability, capacity or fitness required to perform the duties and discharge the responsibilities of the position being sought; (v) the extent and nature of the person's past criminal activity; (vi) the age of the person at the time of the commission of the crime; (vii) the amount of time that has elapsed since the person's last involvement in the commission of a crime; (viii) the conduct and work activity of the person prior to and following the criminal activity; and (ix) evidence of the person's rehabilitation or rehabilitative effort while incarcerated or following release.

If an applicant is denied employment because of information appearing in his criminal history record, the locality shall provide a copy of the information obtained from the Central Criminal Records Exchange to the applicant. The information shall not be disseminated except as provided for in this section.

History.
2001, cc. 353, 373; 2003, c. 739.

§ 27-7. Bylaws of fire/EMS department; compensation of officers and employees; information on check stubs, time cards, etc.

The governing body of any city, town or county may empower the fire/EMS department therein to make bylaws to promote its objects consistent with the laws of this Commonwealth and ordinances of the city, town or county, and may provide for the compensation of the officers and employees of such department.

All check stubs or time cards purporting to be a record of time spent on the job by a fire fighter or emergency medical services personnel shall record all hours of employment, regardless of how spent. All check stubs or pay records purporting to show the hourly compensation of a fire fighter or emergency medical services personnel shall show the actual hourly wage to be paid. Nothing in this section shall require the showing of such information on check stubs, time cards or pay records; however, if such information shall be shown, the information shall be in compliance with this section.

History.
Code 1919, § 3126; 1970, c. 187; 1984, c. 595; 2001, c. 142.

§ 27-8. Who may form a fire/EMS company; limit on number of persons in combined companies.

Any number of persons, not less than twenty, may form themselves into a company for extinguishing fires or for performing emergency medical services,

or both. In any county in which two or more companies for extinguishing fires or for performing emergency medical services shall join together and singly use one fire/EMS station, the number of persons in the combined companies shall be not less than twenty. The minimum number of persons required by this section shall only apply to the formation of a fire company.

History.
Code 1919, § 3121; 1946, p. 110; 1970, c. 187; 2001, c. 142.

CIRCUIT COURT OPINIONS

Section not applicable. — County did not have the express statutory authority or the authority by implication to issue billings for a corporation's emergency medical services or to collect the proceeds from such billings because § 27-8 was not applicable to the corporation when the earliest definition of an Emergency Medical Services company existed in 1970, and the corporate charter for the corporation was issued in 1952; even if the corporation met the definition of an EMS company under § 27-8.1, the rules of statutory construction required that § 32.1-111.14 controlled because it addressed the powers of governing bodies over emergency services agencies in a specific manner. County of Campbell v. Altavista Lifesaving & First Aid Crew, Inc., 75 Va. Cir. 491, 2007 Va. Cir. LEXIS 304 (Campbell County 2007).

§ 27-8.1. Definitions.

"Emergency medical services personnel" means persons responsible for the direct provision of emergency medical or rescue services in a given medical emergency or emergency rescue including all persons who could be described as attendants, attendants-in-charge, or operators.

"Emergency medical services vehicle" means any vehicle, vessel, aircraft, or ambulance that holds a valid emergency medical services permit issue by the Office of Emergency Medical Services that is equipped, maintained or operated to provide emergency medical care or transportation of patients who are sick, injured, wounded, or otherwise incapacitated or helpless.

"Fire/EMS company" or *"Fire/EMS department"* means a volunteer fire-fighting or emergency medical services (EMS) organization organized pursuant to § 27-8 in any town, city or county of the Commonwealth, with the approval of the governing body thereof consisting of fire fighters or emergency medical services personnel, or both.

History.
1970, c. 187; 2001, c. 142.

CIRCUIT COURT OPINIONS

Corporation did not meet definition of emergency medical services. — County did not have the express statutory authority or the authority by implication to issue billings for a corporation's emergency medical services or to collect the proceeds from such billings because § 27-8 was not applicable to the corporation when the earliest definition of an Emergency Medical Services company existed in 1970, and the corporate charter for the corporation was issued in 1952; even if the corporation met the definition of an EMS company under § 27-8.1, the rules of statutory construction required that § 32.1-111.14 controlled because the statute addressed the powers of governing bodies over emergency services agencies in a specific manner. County of Campbell v. Altavista Lifesaving & First Aid Crew, Inc., 75 Va. Cir. 491, 2007 Va. Cir. LEXIS 304 (Campbell County 2007).

§ 27-9. Organization of company.

A writing stating the formation of such company, with the names of the members thereof thereto subscribed, shall be recorded in the court of the city or the court of the county wherein such fire company is. After which, the members of the company may make regulations for effecting its objects consistent with the laws of the Commonwealth, the ordinances of the city, town or county, and the bylaws of the fire/EMS department thereof. The principal officer of such fire company shall be known as "the chief."

History.
Code 1919, § 3122; 1970, c. 187; 2001, c. 142.

Cross references.
As to organization of fire company being prerequisite to appointment of officers, see § 27-13.

CASE NOTES

Organization of fire company prerequisite to appointment. — As a prerequisite to the authority of a town council to appoint a principal engineer or fire warden (now chief and other officers), there must have been organized a fire company under this article, because the language of § 27-13 limits the authority to appoint to such a case. Page v. Town of Warrenton, 210 F. 431 (4th Cir. 1913).

§ 27-10. Dissolution of company.

Whenever the fire/EMS department of the city, town, or county to which any fire/EMS company belongs shall ascertain that such company has failed, for three months successively, to consist of twenty effective members in the case of a fire company, or ascertain that it has failed for the like period to have or keep in good and serviceable condition, an engine, hose, emergency medical services vehicle and equipment and other proper implements, or the governing body of the county, city or town for any reason deems it advisable, such governing body may dissolve the company.

History.
Code 1919, § 3136; 1970, c. 187; 2001, c. 142.

CIRCUIT COURT OPINIONS

Authority to dissolve. — Fire Services Agreement entered into between the county and volunteer fire company could not be used to prevent the county from dissolving the volunteer fire company for the volunteer fire company's conduct in requesting that the county approve the purchase of a piece of fire-fighting equipment despite the volunteer fire company not using the proper procedure that would have allowed the county to first issue a recommendation regarding the purchase; while the county's alleged threat to revoke the volunteer fire company's funding and in effect dissolve it would not have been unlawful because the county had the authority to

dissolve pursuant to § 27-10, the county did not dissolve the volunteer fire company, but, instead restructured the volunteer fire company's operations. Am. Fire Equip., Inc. v. Widewater Volunteer Fire & Rescue Servs., 74 Va. Cir. 101, 2007 Va. Cir. LEXIS 138 (Spotsylvania County 2007).

§ 27-11. Duty of members on alarm of fire or call of a medical emergency.

Every member of the company shall, upon any alarm of fire or call of a medical emergency, attend according to the ordinances of the city, town or county or the bylaws, rules or regulations of the fire/EMS department or the company's regulations, and endeavor to extinguish such fire or assist in the medical emergency.

History.
Code 1919, § 3123; 1970, c. 187; 2001, c. 142.

§ 27-12. Repealed by Acts 1970, c. 187.

§ 27-13. Appointment of chief or director and other officers.

In every city, town or county in which there is any such company, there shall be appointed, at such time and in such manner as the governing body of such city, town or county may prescribe, a chief or director and as many other officers as such governing body may direct.

History.
Code 1919, § 3125; 1970, c. 187; 2008, c. 410.

CASE NOTES

Organization of fire company prerequisite to appointment. — As a prerequisite to the authority of a town council to appoint a principal engineer or fire warden (now chief and other officers), there must have been organized a fire company under this article, because the language of this section limits the authority to appoint to such a case. Page v. Town of Warrenton, 210 F. 431 (4th Cir. 1913).

§ 27-14. Ordinances as to fire/EMS departments, etc.

A. Such governing body may make such ordinances in relation to the powers and duties of fire/EMS departments, companies, chiefs or directors and other officers as it may deem proper, including billing property owners on behalf of volunteer fire departments as provided in § 38.2-2130.

B. The ordinances shall not require a minor who achieved certification under National Fire Protection Association 1001, level one, firefighter standards, as administered by the Department of Fire Programs, on or before January 1, 2006, between the ages of 15 and 16, to repeat the certification after his sixteenth birthday.

History.
Code 1919, § 3127; 1970, c. 187; 2001, c. 142; 2006, c. 462; 2008, c. 410; 2013, cc. 356, 616.

The 2013 amendments.

The 2013 amendments by cc. 356 and 616 are identical, and added "including billing property owners on behalf of volunteer fire departments as provided in § 38.2-2130" at the end of subsection A.

CIRCUIT COURT OPINIONS

County has authority to adopt code regarding emergency medical services permits. — Article III, Chapter 10 of the Campbell County, Va., Code complied with subdivision A 2 of § 32.1-111.14 because the statute granted permits to various fire and rescue organizations in the county in order to allow them to furnish emergency medical services in accordance with § 32.1-111.14; the other provisions of Article III were well within the authority of the county to enact ordinances and regulations regulating Emergency Medical Service companies and departments granted by subdivision A 8 of § 32.1-111.14 and § 27-14. County of Campbell v. Altavista Lifesaving & First Aid Crew, Inc., 75 Va. Cir. 491, 2007 Va. Cir. LEXIS 304 (Campbell County 2007).

OPINIONS OF THE ATTORNEY GENERAL

Billing for emergency services. — This section does not permit a locality to adopt an ordinance authorizing a volunteer fire department to assess and charge a fee to an individual's homeowners' or automobile insurance policy for responding to a fire emergency. See opinion of Attorney General to The Honorable Clarence E. "Bud" Phillips, Member, Virginia House of Delegates, 11-082, 2011 Va. AG LEXIS 55 (7/22/11).

§ 27-15. Repealed by Acts 1970, c. 187.

§ 27-15.1. Authority of chief, director or other officer in charge when answering alarm or operating at an emergency incident; penalty for refusal to obey orders.

While any fire/EMS department or fire/EMS company is in the process of answering an alarm or operating at an emergency incident where there is imminent danger or the actual occurrence of fire or explosion or the uncontrolled release of hazardous materials which threaten life or property and returning to the station, the chief, director, or other officer in charge of such fire/EMS department or company at that time shall have the authority to: (i) maintain order at such emergency incident or its vicinity, (ii) direct the actions of the fire fighters or emergency medical services personnel at the incident, (iii) notwithstanding the provisions of §§ 46.2-888 through 46.2-891, keep bystanders or other persons at a safe distance from the incident and emergency equipment, (iv) facilitate the speedy movement and operation of emergency equipment and fire fighters or emergency medical services personnel, (v) cause an investigation to be made into the origin and cause of the incident, and (vi) until the arrival of a police officer, direct and control traffic in person or by deputy and facilitate the movement of traffic. The fire chief, director, or other officer in charge shall display his fire fighter's or emergency medical services personnel's badge, or other proper means of identification. Notwithstanding any other provision of law, this authority shall extend to the activation of traffic control signals designed to facilitate the safe egress and ingress of emergency equipment at a fire/EMS station. Any person or persons refusing to obey the orders of the chief, director, or his deputies or other officer in charge at that time shall be guilty of a Class 4 misdemeanor. The chief, director, or other officer in charge shall have the power to make arrests for violation of the provisions of this section. The authority granted under the provisions of this section may not be exercised to inhibit or obstruct members of law-enforcement agencies or rescue squads from performing their normal duties when operating at such emergency incident, nor to conflict with or diminish the lawful authority, duties and responsibilities of forest wardens, including but not limited to the provisions of Chapter 11 of Title 10.1. Personnel from the news media, such as the press, radio and television, when gathering the news may enter at their own risk into the incident area only when the officer in charge has deemed the area safe and only into those areas of the incident that do not, in the opinion of the officer in charge, interfere with the fire/EMS department or fire fighters or emergency medical services personnel dealing with such emergencies, in which case the chief or other officer in charge may order such person from the scene of the emergency incident.

History.

1970, c. 187; 1977, c. 326; 1984, c. 644; 2001, c. 142; 2008, c. 410.

Cross references.

As to power of a fire chief to take property found at the scene of a fire or explosion, see § 27-34.1. As to punishment for Class 4 misdemeanors, see § 18.2-11.

§ 27-15.2. Purchase, maintenance, etc., of equipment; donated equipment.

A. The governing body of every city, town or county shall have power to provide for the purchase, operation, manning and maintenance of suitable equipment for fighting fires or performing emergency medical services in or upon the property of the city, town or county and of its inhabitants, and to prescribe the terms and conditions upon which the same will be used for fighting fires or performing emergency medical services in or upon privately owned property. All equipment purchased after October 1, 1970, shall be equipped with threads of USA Standard B2.3, B2.4 of the American Standards Association.

B. Any fire/EMS department of a city, town, or county, or any fire/EMS company donating equipment for fighting fires or performing emergency medical services to any fire/EMS department or any fire/EMS company, which equipment met existing engineering and safety standards at the time of its purchase by the donating entity, shall be immune from civil liability unless the donating entity acted with gross negligence or willful misconduct.

C. A safety inspection must be completed by a certified emergency vehicle service center and a report designating any deficiencies shall be provided prior to the change in ownership of the donated emergency vehicle.

History.
1970, c. 187; 2001, c. 142; 2010, c. 545.

The 2010 amendments.
The 2010 amendment by c. 545 inserted the subsection A designation, and added subsections B and C.

Research references.
Virginia Forms (Matthew Bender). No. 8A-1302 Consumer Lease/Option to Purchase under Uniform Commercial Code (Public Entity).

CIRCUIT COURT OPINIONS

Statutory authority not restricted. — County did not breach the Fire Services Agreement that it entered into with the volunteer fire company when it declined to approve the volunteer fire company's request to approve the purchase of a piece of fire-fighting equipment, despite the volunteer fire company's claim that the agreement was violated because the agreement provided that the county would not interfere with the volunteer fire company's operational control; the county's authority to purchase fire-fighting equipment, pursuant to § 27-15.2, could not be restricted by the Fire Services Agreement. Am. Fire Equip., Inc. v. Widewater Volunteer Fire & Rescue Servs., 74 Va. Cir. 101, 2007 Va. Cir. LEXIS 138 (Spotsylvania County 2007).

§ 27-15.3. Purchase of service-issued boots or helmet by certain firefighters.

A. Notwithstanding any other provision of law to the contrary, the governing body of any county, city, or town may allow any paid or volunteer firefighter for such jurisdiction with 10 or more years of service, but fewer than 20, to purchase the helmet or boots issued to the firefighter at fair market value.

B. Notwithstanding any other provision of law to the contrary, the governing body of any county, city, or town may allow any paid or volunteer firefighter for such jurisdiction with over 20 years of service to be given the helmet or boots issued to the firefighters or to purchase the helmet or boots issued to the firefighter at a price of $1.

History.
2011, c. 22.

§ 27-16. Repealed by Acts 1970, c. 187.

§ 27-17. Entry of buildings on fire and premises adjoining.

The chief of any fire/EMS department, or company or other authorized officer in command at a fire or medical emergency, and his subordinates, upon his order or direction, shall have the right at any time of the day or night to enter any building or upon any premises where a fire or medical emergency is in progress, or any building or premises adjacent thereto for the purpose of extinguishing the fire or performing emergency medical services.

History.
Code 1919, § 3130; 1970, c. 187; 2001, c. 142.

§ 27-17.1. Remaining on premises after fire extinguished.

The chief or other authorized officer of any fire/EMS department or fire/EMS company in command at a fire or medical emergency, and his subordinates upon his order or direction, shall have the right to remain at the scene of fire or medical emergency, including remaining in any building or house, for purposes of protecting the property and preventing the public from entry into the premises, until such reasonable time as the owner may resume responsibility for the protection of the property.

History.
1978, c. 149; 2001, c. 142.

§ 27-18. Repealed by Acts 1970, c. 187.

§ 27-19. Penalty for disobeying chief or other officer in command.

If any person at a fire or medical emergency refuses or neglects to obey any order duly given by the chief or other officer in command, he shall, upon conviction of such offense, be fined not to exceed $100.

History.
Code 1919, § 3132; 1970, c. 187; 2001, c. 142.

§ 27-20. Destruction of property to prevent spread of fire.

The chief, director, or other officer commanding in his absence, may direct the pulling down or destroying of any fence, house, or other thing which he may judge necessary to be pulled down or destroyed, to prevent the further spreading of a fire, and for this purpose may require such assistance from all present as he shall judge necessary.

History.
Code 1919, § 3133; 1970, c. 187; 2001, c. 142; 2008, c. 410.

CASE NOTES

Inapplicable where not acting in emergency. — This section and §§ 27-21 and 27-22 are not applicable to a case where the agents and officers of the city were engaged in pulling down the brick walls of a burned building several days after the fire in order to make the streets safe for passersby and were not acting in an emergency of a fire in progress. Burson v. City of Bristol, 176 Va. 53, 10 S.E.2d 541 (1940).

Evidence. — See Fardis & Boudouris v. E.I. DuPont de Nemours & Co., 123 Va. 88, 96 S.E. 164 (1918).

Applied in Page v. Town of Warrenton, 210 F. 431 (4th Cir. 1913).

§ 27-21. Owner may recover amount of actual damage.

The owner of such property shall be entitled to recover from the city, town or county the amount of the actual damage which he may have sustained by reason of the same having been pulled down or destroyed under such direction.

History.
Code 1919, § 3134; 1970, c. 187.

CASE NOTES

Where no fire company has been organized under the provisions of this article, the common-law rule, that no recovery can be had for private property destroyed to prevent the spread of fire, remains in force. Page v. Town of Warrenton, 210 F. 431 (4th Cir. 1913).

Sufficiency of declaration. — See Page v. Town of Warrenton, 210 F. 431 (4th Cir. 1913).

Inapplicable where not acting in emergency. — This section and §§ 27-20 and 27-22 are not applicable to a case where the agents and officers of the city were engaged in pulling down the brick walls of a burned building several days after the fire in order to make the streets safe for passersby and were not acting in an emergency of a fire in progress. Burson v. City of Bristol, 176 Va. 53, 10 S.E.2d 541 (1940).

§ 27-22. But not for property which would have been destroyed by the fire.

Section 27-21 shall not enable anyone to recover compensation for property which would have been destroyed by the fire, if the same had not been pulled down or destroyed under such direction, but only for what could have been saved with ordinary care and diligence, had no such direction been given.

History.
Code 1919, § 3135.

CASE NOTES

Inapplicable where not acting in emergency. — This section and §§ 27-20 and 27-21 are not applicable to a case where the agents and officers of the city were engaged in pulling down the brick walls of a burned building several days after the fire in order to make the streets safe for passersby and were not acting in an emergency of a fire in progress. Burson v. City of Bristol, 176 Va. 53, 10 S.E.2d 541 (1940).

§ 27-23. Repealed by Acts 1970, c. 187.

§ 27-23.1. Establishment of fire/EMS zones or districts; tax levies.

The governing bodies of the several cities or counties of this Commonwealth may create and establish, by designation on a map of the city or county showing current, official parcel boundaries, or by any other description which is legally sufficient for the conveyance of property or the creation of parcels, fire/EMS zones or districts in such cities or counties, within which may be located and established one or more fire/EMS departments, to be equipped with apparatus for fighting fires and protecting property and human life within such zones or districts from loss or damage by fire, illness or injury.

In the event of the creation of such zones or districts in any city or county, the city or county governing body may acquire, in the name of the city or county, real or personal property to be devoted to the uses aforesaid, and shall prescribe rules and regulations for the proper management, control and conduct thereof. Such governing body shall also have authority to contract with, or secure the services of, any individual corporation, organization or municipal corporation, or any volunteer fire fighters or emergency medical services personnel for such fire or emergency medical services protection as may be required.

To raise funds for the purposes aforesaid, the governing body of any city or county in which such zones or districts are established may levy annually a tax on the assessed value of all property real and personal within such zones or districts, subject to local taxation, which tax shall be extended and collected as other city or county taxes are extended and collected. However, any property located in Augusta County that has qualified for an agricultural or forestal use-value assessment pursuant to Article 4 (§ 58.1-3229 et seq.) of Chapter 32 of Title 58.1 may not be included within such a zone or district and may not be subject to such tax. In any city or county having a population between 25,000 and 25,500, the maximum rate of tax under this section shall be $0.30 on $100 of assessed value.

The amount realized from such levy shall be kept separate from all other moneys of the city or county and shall be applied to no other purpose than the maintenance and operation of the fire/EMS departments and companies established under the provisions of this section.

History.
1970, c. 187; 1972, c. 252; 1977, c. 326; 1978, c. 682; 1985, c. 343; 1993, c. 915; 2001, cc. 111, 142; 2007, c. 813.

Cross references.
As to the 1980, 1990 and 2000 United States Census figures for counties and cities of the Commonwealth of Virginia, see the Appendix to Title 15.2.

Editor's note.
Acts 2007, c. 813, cl. 2, provides: "That the provisions of this act shall not affect the powers of any locality with respect to any ordinance, resolution or bylaw validly adopted and not repealed or rescinded prior to July 1, 2007."

§ 27-23.2. Advances by city or county to fire/EMS district.

The governing body of any city or county in this Commonwealth may advance funds, not otherwise specifically allocated or obligated, from the general fund to a fire/EMS district to assist the fire district to exercise the powers set forth in § 27-23.1.

History.
1970, c. 187; 1985, c. 343; 2001, c. 142.

§ 27-23.3. Reimbursement for advances.

Notwithstanding the provisions of any other law, the governing body shall direct the treasurer to reimburse the general fund of the city or county from the proceeds of any funds to the credit of the fire/EMS district, not otherwise specifically allocated or obligated to the extent that the city or county has made advances to the fire/EMS district from such general fund to assist the district to exercise the powers set forth in § 27-23.1.

History.
1970, c. 187; 1985, c. 343; 2001, c. 142.

§ 27-23.4. Validation of prior advances.

The advancement of any funds heretofore advanced from the general fund by the governing body of any city or county in this Commonwealth for the benefit of a fire/EMS district in exercising the lawful powers of such fire/EMS district is hereby validated and confirmed.

History.
1970, c. 187; 1985, c. 343; 2001, c. 142.

§ 27-23.5. Exclusion of certain areas from fire/EMS districts and exemption of such areas from certain levies.

The governing body of any city or county having a fire/EMS district created under the provisions of § 27-23.1, prior to June 1 of any calendar year, may alter the boundaries of such fire/EMS district for the purpose of excluding an area of any such fire/EMS district which is also within the boundaries of a sanitary district providing fire protection or emergency medical services or under contract to a sanitary district providing fire protection or emergency medical services.

Any area excluded from a fire/EMS district as provided by this section shall not be subject to the levy set forth in § 27-23.1 for the year such area is excluded.

History.
1970, c. 187; 1985, c. 343; 2001, c. 142.

§ 27-23.6. Provision of fire-fighting or emergency medical services.

A. Any county, city or town may contract with or provide for any volunteer fire-fighting or emergency medical services companies or associations in the county, city or town for the fighting of fire or provision of emergency medical services in any county, city or town. If such provisions are made by the county, city or town, the fire-fighting or emergency medical services company shall be deemed to be an instrumentality of the county, city or town and as such exempt from suit for damages done incident to fighting fires or providing emergency medical services therein. The county, city or town may elect to provide for the matters authorized in §§ 27-4 and 27-39.

B. Any county, city or town may provide fire-fighting and emergency medical services to its citizens by using both government-employed and volunteer company or association firefighters and emergency medical services personnel. If such a system is utilized, the volunteer fire-fighting and emergency medical services companies and associations shall be deemed an instrumentality of the county, city or town, and as such exempt from suit for damages done incident to providing fire-fighting and emergency medical services to the county, city or town. The county, city or town may also elect to provide for matters authorized in §§ 27-4 and 27-39.

"Providing fire-fighting or emergency medical services" includes travel while performing fire, rescue or other emergency operations in fire-fighting apparatus or other emergency vehicles as described in §§ 46.2-1023 and 46.2-920, respectively.

History.
1970, c. 187; 1982, c. 239; 1991, c. 54; 2001, c. 142; 2002, c. 286.

Research references.
Friend's Virginia Pleading and Practice (Matthew Bender). Chapter 35 Limitation of Actions: Statute of Limitations; Immunities; Res Judicata and Collateral Estoppel. § 35.02 Immunities. Charles E. Friend.

Michie's Jurisprudence.
For related discussion, see 5A M.J. Counties, § 84.

CASE NOTES

Statute exemption is not different from immunity by general law. — Exemption provided by the statute is not different from the immunity provided by general law; there is no legal difference between the terms exemption and immunity; therefore, that the exemption provided owner of fire truck as an "instrumentality" of county was the equivalent of sovereign immunity to the extent of damages done incident to fighting fires. National R.R. Passenger Corp. v. Catlett Volunteer Fire Co., 241 Va. 402, 404 S.E.2d 216 (1991).

Exemption from suit is provided to fire-fighting companies and individual members. — Although this section does not in specific terms extend its exemption from suit to individual members of fire-fighting companies, if a contract exists between a fire-fighting company and a county, this section makes the fire-fighting company "an instrumentality of the contracting county and as such exempt from suit for damages done incident to fighting fires"; to this extent, the company would be entitled to the cloak of the county's sovereign immunity, and in turn, the cloak may be available to the company's members. National R.R. Passenger Corp. v. Catlett Volunteer Fire Co., 241 Va. 402, 404 S.E.2d 216 (1991).

Damages resulting from operation of truck en route to fire. — The exemption from suit for "damages done incident to fighting fires" encompasses damages resulting from the operation of a fire truck en route to a fire. National R.R. Passenger Corp. v. Catlett Volunteer Fire Co., 241 Va. 402, 404 S.E.2d 216 (1991).

Implied contract existed between owner of fire truck and county. — Where there was no express contract between owner of fire truck and county, the district court correctly imposed an implied-in-fact contract between them; the district judge surveyed the Virginia statutes concerning volunteer fire companies, reviewed the evidence supplied by owner of the fire truck concerning the ongoing close working relationship between owner of fire truck and county, and noted the requirement in Acts 1970, ch. 187, of which this section is a part, that the Act shall be liberally construed. National R.R. Passenger Corp. v. Catlett Volunteer Fire Co., 241 Va. 402, 404 S.E.2d 216 (1991).

Volunteer fireman's crossing railroad tracks without first

stopping was a discretionary act to which sovereign immunity attached; therefore, volunteer fireman was entitled to invoke the defense of sovereign immunity and was liable only for gross negligence. National R.R. Passenger Corp. v. Catlett Volunteer Fire Co., 241 Va. 402, 404 S.E.2d 216 (1991).

OPINIONS OF THE ATTORNEY GENERAL

Billing for emergency services. — Volunteer fire departments and rescue squads lack authority, either statutory or contractual, to bill home or automobile owners, or their insurance companies, for responding to a fire emergency. See opinion of Attorney General to The Honorable Clarence E. "Bud" Phillips, Member, Virginia House of Delegates, 11-052, 2011 Va. AG LEXIS 29 (5/13/11).

§ 27-23.7. Special levy for fire protection in certain counties.

Chapter 207 of the Acts of 1930, approved March 22, 1930 (codified as § 3144k of Michie Code of 1942), as amended, by Chapter 297 of the Acts of 1938, approved March 28, 1938, Chapter 392 of the Acts of 1940, approved April 1, 1940, Chapter 40 of the Acts of 1945, approved April 5, 1945, and Chapter 41 of the Acts of 1956, approved February 16, 1956, relating to special levy for fire protection in counties adjacent to a county containing more than 500 inhabitants a square mile, is continued in effect.

History.
1970, c. 187.

§ 27-23.8. Trial board for members of fire departments in certain counties.

Chapter 8 of the Acts of 1950, approved February 9, 1950, as amended, by Chapter 409 of the Acts of 1954, approved April 3, 1954, relating to trial board for members of fire departments in any county having a population of more than 2,000 per square mile is incorporated in this Code by this reference.

History.
1970, c. 187.

§ 27-23.9. Supervision and control of joint services of fire/EMS companies or departments.

Whenever two or more fire/EMS companies or departments are called to provide joint services in any district or political subdivision, the commander of the first company to arrive shall have general supervision and control of all such participating companies and departments until an officer of such district or political subdivision who is otherwise authorized by law to do so shall assume such general supervision and control.

History.
1970, c. 187; 2001, c. 142.

§ 27-23.10. Ordinances to effectuate purposes of § 27-23.9.

Every county, city and town is authorized to enact and enforce appropriate ordinances to effectuate the purposes of § 27-23.9.

History.
1970, c. 187.

ARTICLE 2.

IN COUNTIES GENERALLY.

§§ 27-24 through 27-29.1. Repealed by Acts 1970, c. 187.

CHAPTER 3.

LOCAL FIRE MARSHALS.

Section
27-30.   Appointment of fire marshal.
27-31.   Investigation of fires and explosions.
27-32.   Summoning witnesses and taking evidence.
27-32.1. Right of entry to investigate cause of fire or explosion.
27-32.2. Issuance of fire investigation warrant.
27-33.   Report of investigation.
27-34.   Duties and powers at fires.
27-34.1. Power of fire marshal or fire chief to take property found at scene of fire or explosion; restitution of such property.
27-34.2. Power to arrest, to procure and serve warrants and to issue summons; limitation on authority.
27-34.2:1. Police powers of fire marshals.
27-34.3. Power to order immediate compliance with law, etc., or prohibit use of building or equipment.
27-34.4. Inspection and review of plans of buildings under construction.
27-35.   Penalty for failure to discharge duty.
27-36.   Appointment, powers and duties of assistant fire marshals.
27-37.   Oath of fire marshal and assistants.
27-37.1. Right of entry to investigate releases of hazardous material, hazardous waste, or regulated substances.

§ 27-30. Appointment of fire marshal.

An officer, who shall be called a "fire marshal," may be appointed for each county, city or town, by the governing body thereof, whenever, in the opinion of such body, the appointment shall be deemed expedient. The term "fire marshal" as used in this chapter may include the local fire official and local arson investigator when appointed pursuant to this section.

History.
Code 1919, § 3137; 1970, c. 187; 1977, c. 334; 1984, c. 644.

Editor's note.
Acts 1970, c. 187, which added or amended many of the sections in this chapter, provides, in cl. 3, that the act shall be liberally construed and is severable.

§ 27-31. Investigation of fires and explosions.

Such fire marshal shall make an investigation into the origin and cause of every fire and explosion occurring within the limits for which he was appointed, and for any such service he shall receive such compensation as the governing body may allow.

History.
Code 1919, § 3138; 1997, c. 436.

§ 27-32. Summoning witnesses and taking evidence.

In making investigations pursuant to § 27-31, the fire marshal may issue a summons directed to a sheriff or sergeant of any county, city or town commanding the officer to summon witnesses to attend before him at such time and place as he may direct. Any such officer to whom the summons is delivered, shall forthwith execute it, and make return thereof to the fire marshal at the time and place named therein.

Witnesses, on whom the summons before mentioned is served, may be compelled by the fire marshal to attend and give evidence, and shall be liable in like manner as if the summons had been issued by a magistrate in a criminal case. They shall be sworn by the fire marshal before giving evidence, and their evidence shall be reduced to writing by him, or under his direction, and subscribed by them respectively.

History.
Code 1919, §§ 3138, 4808, 4810; 1970, c. 187; 1997, c. 436; 2008, cc. 551, 691.

§ 27-32.1. Right of entry to investigate cause of fire or explosion.

If in making such an investigation, the fire marshal shall make complaint under oath that there is good cause of suspicion or belief that the burning of or explosion on any land, building or vessel or of any object was caused by any act constituting a crime as defined in Article 1 (§ 18.2-77 et seq.) of Chapter 5 of Title 18.2 and that he has been refused admittance to the land, building or vessel or to examine the object in or on which any fire or explosion occurred within fifteen days after the extinguishment of such, any magistrate serving the city or county where the land, building, vessel or object is located may issue a warrant to the sheriff of the county or the sergeant of the city requiring him to enter such land, building or vessel or the premises upon which the object is located in the company of the fire marshal for the purposes of conducting a search for evidence showing that such fire or explosion was caused by any act defined in Article 1 of Chapter 5, of Title 18.2.

History.
1970, c. 187; 2008, cc. 551, 691.

Law Review.
For note, "Arson Investigations and the Fourth Amendment," see 30 Wash. & Lee L. Rev. 133 (1973).

§ 27-32.2. Issuance of fire investigation warrant.

If, in undertaking such an investigation, the fire marshal or investigator appointed pursuant to § 27-56 makes an affidavit under oath that the origin or cause of any fire or explosion on any land, building, or vessel, or of any object is undetermined and that he has been refused admittance thereto, or is unable to gain permission to enter such land, building, or vessel, or to examine such object, within 15 days after the extinguishing of such, any magistrate serving the city or county where the land, building, vessel, or object is located may issue a fire investigation warrant to the fire marshal or investigator appointed pursuant to § 27-56 authorizing him to enter such land, building, vessel, or the premises upon which the object is located for the purpose of determining the origin and source of such fire or explosion. If the fire marshal or investigator appointed pursuant to § 27-56, after gaining access to any land, building, vessel, or other premises pursuant to such a fire investigation warrant, has probable cause to believe that the burning or explosion was caused by any act constituting a criminal offense, he shall discontinue the investigation until a search warrant has been obtained pursuant to § 27-32.1, or consent to conduct the search has otherwise been given.

History.
1987, c. 701; 2008, cc. 551, 691; 2012, cc. 279, 330.

The 2012 amendments.
The 2012 amendments by cc. 279 and 330, are identical, and inserted "or investigator appointed pursuant to § 27-56" three times and made a minor stylistic change.

Michie's Jurisprudence.
For related discussion, see 2A M.J. Arson, § 2.

§ 27-33. Report of investigation.

The fire marshal shall make report to the governing body by whom he was appointed of any investigation made by him as soon thereafter as practicable, returning therewith the evidence taken by him and submitting such recommendations therein as he may think the public interest demands.

History.
Code 1919, § 3138.

§ 27-34. Duties and powers at fires.

Whenever any fire occurs, it shall be the duty of such fire marshal or his designated representative to be present at the same and advise and act in concert with such officers of police as may be present; and, for preserving order at and during the existence of such fire, and for the protection of property, he shall have concurrent powers with the officers of police, and the chief, director, or other officer in charge, but shall not exercise any authority which will conflict with the powers of any chief, director, or other officer in command of any fire department in the discharge of his special duties as such.

History.
Code 1919, § 3139; 1970, c. 187; 2008, c. 410.

§ 27-34.1. Power of fire marshal or fire chief to take property found at scene of fire or explosion; restitution of such property.

The fire chief, fire marshal or his designated representative is authorized to take and preserve any property found at the scene of a fire or explosion during his presence there while in the act of extinguishing such or found later with the consent of the owner or pursuant to § 27-32.1, which property indicates the fire or explosion was intentionally caused. Any person whose property is so taken and held may petition the circuit court of the county or city in which the property was taken or judge in vacation, for return of the property, and the court may order restitution upon such conditions as are appropriate for preservation of evidence, including the posting of bond.

History.
1970, c. 187; 1979, c. 189.

§ 27-34.2. Power to arrest, to procure and serve warrants and to issue summons; limitation on authority.

In addition to such other duties as may be prescribed by law, the local fire marshal and his assistants appointed pursuant to § 27-36 shall, if authorized by the governing body of the county, city or town appointing the local fire marshal, have the authority to arrest, to procure and serve warrants of arrest and to issue summons in the manner authorized by general law for violation of fire prevention and fire safety laws and related ordinances. The authority granted in this section shall not be exercised by any local fire marshal or assistant until such person has satisfactorily completed a training course designed specifically for local fire marshals and their assistants, which course shall be approved by the Virginia Fire Services Board.

The Department of Fire Programs in cooperation with the Department of Criminal Justice Services shall have the authority to design, establish and maintain the required courses of instruction through such agencies and institutions as the Departments jointly may deem appropriate and to approve such other courses as such Departments determine appropriate.

The authority granted in this section shall not be construed to authorize a fire marshal or his assistants to wear or carry firearms.

History.
1974, c. 334; 1975, c. 173; 1979, c. 402; 1984, c. 779; 1986, c. 60; 1988, c. 65; 1997, c. 436.

Law Review.
For survey of Virginia law on criminal procedure for the year 1973-74, see 60 Va. L. Rev. 1505 (1974).

§ 27-34.2:1. Police powers of fire marshals.

In addition to such other duties as may be prescribed by law, the local fire marshal and those assistants appointed pursuant to § 27-36 designated by the fire marshal shall, if authorized by the governing body of the county, city or town appointing the local fire marshal, have the same police powers as a sheriff, police officer or law-enforcement officer. The investigation and prosecution of all offenses involving hazardous materials, fires, fire bombings, bombings, attempts or threats to commit such offenses, false alarms relating to such offenses, possession and manufacture of explosive devices, substances and fire bombs shall be the responsibility of the fire marshal or his designee, if authorized by the governing body of the county, city or town appointing the local fire marshal. The police powers granted in this section shall not be exercised by any local fire marshal or assistant until such person has satisfactorily completed a course for fire marshals with police powers, designed by the Department of Fire Programs in cooperation with the Department of Criminal Justice Services, which course shall be approved by the Virginia Fire Services Board.

In addition, fire marshals with police powers shall continue to exercise those powers only upon satisfactory participation in in-service and advanced courses and programs designed by the Department of Fire Programs in cooperation with the Department of Criminal Justice Services, which courses shall be approved by the Virginia Fire Services Board.

History.
1977, c. 209; 1979, c. 446; 1984, c. 779; 1986, c. 60; 1988, c. 65; 2000, cc. 39, 390.

Law Review.
For survey of Virginia law on criminal procedure for the year 1978-1979, see 66 Va. L. Rev. 261 (1980).

§ 27-34.3. Power to order immediate compliance with law, etc., or prohibit use of building or equipment.

The local fire marshal shall, if authorized by the governing body of the county, city or town appointing him, have the authority to exercise the powers authorized by the Fire Prevention Code. However, an order prohibiting the use of a building or equipment issued pursuant to this section shall not be effective beyond the date of a determination made by the authorities identified in and pursuant to § 27-97, regardless of whether or not said determination overrules, modifies or affirms the order of the local fire marshal. If an order of the local fire marshal issued pursuant to this section conflicts to any degree with an order previously issued by an authority identified in and pursuant to § 27-97, the latter order shall prevail. The local fire marshal shall immediately report to the authorities identified in § 27-97 on the issuance and content of any order issued pursuant to this section.

History.
1975, c. 216; 1988, c. 199.

§ 27-34.4. Inspection and review of plans of buildings under construction.

Inspection of buildings other than state-owned buildings under construction and the review and approval of building plans for these structures for enforcement of the Uniform Statewide Building Code shall be the sole responsibility of the appropriate local building inspectors. Upon completion of such structures, responsibility for fire safety protection shall pass to the local fire marshal or official designated by the locality to enforce the Statewide Fire Prevention Code (§ 27-94 et seq.) in those localities which enforce the Statewide Fire Prevention Code.

History.
1980, c. 498; 1989, c. 258.

Law Review.
For comment on local liability for negligent inspection of buildings and equipment, see 18 U. Rich. L. Rev. 809 (1984).

§ 27-35. Penalty for failure to discharge duty.

For his failure to discharge any duty required of him by law the fire marshal shall be liable for each offense to a fine not exceeding $100, to be imposed by the governing body and to be collected as other fines are collected.

History.
Code 1919, § 3138.

§ 27-36. Appointment, powers and duties of assistant fire marshals.

The governing body of any county, city or town, or its designee may appoint one or more assistants, who, in the absence of the fire marshal, shall have the powers and perform the duties of the fire marshal.

History.
Code 1919, § 3140; 1970, c. 187; 1984, c. 644; 1998, c. 236.

§ 27-37. Oath of fire marshal and assistants.

The fire marshal and his assistants, before entering upon their duties, shall respectively take an oath, before any officer authorized to administer oaths, faithfully to discharge the duties of such office; the certificate of the oath shall be returned to and preserved by such governing body.

History.
Code 1919, § 3140.

§ 27-37.1. Right of entry to investigate releases of hazardous material, hazardous waste, or regulated substances.

The fire marshal shall have the right, if authorized by the governing body of the county, city, or town appointing the fire marshal, to enter upon any property from which a release of any hazardous material, hazardous waste, or regulated substance, as defined in § 10.1-1400 or 62.1-44.34:8, has occurred or is reasonably suspected to have occurred and which has entered into the ground water, surface water or soils of the county, city or town in order to investigate the extent and cause of any such release. If, in undertaking such an investigation, the fire marshal makes an affidavit under oath that the origin or cause of any such release is undetermined and that he has been refused admittance to the property, or is unable to gain permission to enter the property, any magistrate serving the city or county where the property is located may issue an investigation warrant to the fire marshal authorizing him to enter such property for the purpose of determining the origin and source of the release. If the fire marshal, after gaining access to any property pursuant to such investigation warrant, has probable cause to believe that the release was caused by any act constituting a criminal offense, he shall discontinue the investigation until a search warrant has been obtained or consent to conduct the search has otherwise been given.

History.
1992, c. 712; 2008, cc. 551, 691.

Research references.
Virginia Forms (Matthew Bender). No. 9-111 Affidavit for Investigative Search Warrant — Hazardous Materials; No. 9-112 Investigative Search Warrant — Hazardous Materials.

CHAPTER 4.

RELIEF FOR FIRE FIGHTERS AND DEPENDENTS.

Article 1. General Provisions.

ARTICLE 1.

GENERAL PROVISIONS.

§ 27-38. Repealed by Acts 1950, p. 316.

Cross references.
For present statute on the same subject as the repealed section, see § 15.2-1511.

§ 27-39. Counties, cities and towns authorized to provide relief.

Any county, city or town which operates fire-fighting equipment may provide for the relief of (1) any children and surviving spouse of any fire fighter who dies (2) and on or before July 1, 1977, shall provide for the relief of any fire fighter who is disabled by injury or illness as the direct or proximate result of the performance of his duty, including the presumption under § 27-40.1, in the service of the county, city or town or any political subdivision with which it contracts or has contracted for fire protection, whether such fire fighter be a member of a fire company of the county in which the injury occurred or of a political subdivision with which it contracts for fire protection. Such total disability retirement benefits shall be not less than those provided under the in-line-of-duty disability retirement provisions of § 51.1-157. Such relief of any children and surviving spouse of any fire fighter who dies shall be exclusive of, and not dependent upon, any payment under the Line of Duty Act (§ 9.1-400 et seq.).

History.
1946, p. 609; Michie Suppl. 1946, § 2743m; 1948, p. 161; 1970, c. 187; 1973, c. 543; 1976, c. 772; 1977, c. 326.

Editor's note.
Acts 1970, c. 187, cl. 3, provides that this section shall be liberally construed and is severable.

CASE NOTES

Applied in Pearson v. Canada Contracting Co., 232 Va. 177, 349 S.E.2d 106 (1986).

§ 27-40. Support of dependent children of firemen.

The governing bodies of cities of the first class may, by ordinance adopted by a recorded vote of a majority of the members elected to each branch, if there be more than one branch, appropriate money out of the public funds to aid in the support of dependent children of members of the fire departments of such cities who may have lost their lives through injuries received or illness incurred while in the performance of their duties as members of such fire departments; such aid to continue in the case of each such child until he or she shall have attained the age of sixteen years, and the payment of same to be made monthly to the lawful guardian of such dependent children and in such amounts as the governing body of such city may deem wise and just.

History.
1918, p. 224; Michie Code 1942, § 3035a.

§ 27-40.1. Presumption as to death or disability from respiratory diseases, hypertension or heart disease.

The death of, or any condition or impairment of health of salaried or volunteer fire fighters caused by respiratory diseases, hypertension or heart disease resulting in total or partial disability shall be presumed to have been suffered in the line of duty unless the contrary be shown by a preponderance of competent evidence; provided that prior to making any claim based upon such presumption for retirement, sickness or other benefits on account of such death or total or partial disability, such salaried or volunteer fire fighters shall have been found free from respiratory diseases, hypertension or heart disease, as the case may be, by a physical examination which shall include such appropriate laboratory and other diagnostic studies as such governing body shall prescribe and which shall have been conducted by physicians whose qualifications shall have been prescribed by such governing body; and provided, further, that any such fire fighter or, in the case of his death, any person entitled to make a claim for such benefits, claiming that his death or disability was suffered in the line of duty shall, if requested by such governing body or its authorized representative, submit himself, in the case of claim for disability benefits, to physical examination by any physician designated by such governing body, which examination may include such tests or studies as may reasonably be prescribed by the physician so designated or, in the case of a claim for death benefits, submit the body of the deceased fire fighter to a postmortem examination to be performed by the medical examiner for the county, city or town appointed under § 32.1-282. Such fire fighter or claimant shall have the right to have present at such examination, at his own expense, any qualified physician he may designate.

History.
1964, c. 216; 1972, c. 607; 1973, c. 543; 1976, c. 772; 1977, c. 326; 1978, c. 768.

The numbers of this section and § 27-40.2 were assigned by the Virginia Code Commission, the 1964 act having assigned no numbers.

Cross references.
As to the purchase of continued health insurance coverage by the surviving spouse and any dependents of an active or retired local law-enforcement officer, firefighter, etc., through the Department of Human Resource Management, see § 2.2-1205. As to the use of tobacco products by state employees, see § 2.2-2902. As to the Line of Duty Act, see § 9.1-400 et seq. As to payments to beneficiaries of certain deceased law-enforcement officers, firefighters and retirees, see § 9.1-402. As to use of tobacco products by government employees, see § 15.2-1504.

CASE NOTES

Former § 65.1-47.1 (now § 65.2-402) compared. — The language of this section mirrors and, in fact, formed the basis for former § 65.1-47.1. City of Waynesboro v. Harter, 222 Va. 564, 281 S.E.2d 911 (1981).

If this section makes an examination mandatory on the part of a city, former § 65.1-47.1 (now § 65.2-402), which contains the same language, must contain the same mandate. City of Waynesboro v. Harter, 222 Va. 564, 281 S.E.2d 911 (1981).

Applied in Berry v. County of Henrico, 219 Va. 259, 247 S.E.2d 389 (1978).

§ 27-40.1:1. Performance of physical examinations required by § 27-40.1.

Any county, city or town providing death, retirement, sickness or other benefits pursuant to the authority granted by § 27-39, or pursuant to any other provision of law or the charter of any city or town, or otherwise, shall do so exclusive of, and without regard to, any such benefits paid or payable out of the general fund of the state treasury pursuant to § 9.1-400 et seq. and shall by ordinance make provision for the employment of physicians and the performance of the physical examination required by § 27-40.1 and shall cause such examination to be made within ninety days after June 1, 1973, of every fire fighter in its service or the service of a political subdivision with which it has contracted for fire protection and of every fire fighter entering upon such service thereafter at the time of such entry, provided however, that any fire fighter employed by any such county, city or town which failed to cause such physical examination to be made on or before January 1, 1976, for any fire fighter employed prior to January 1, 1976, in its service or the service of a political subdivision with which it has contracted for fire protection shall be presumed to have been found free from respiratory disease, hypertension or heart disease as if such fire fighter had been examined pursuant to § 27-40.1. Such presumption shall also apply to the benefit of any fire fighter entering upon such service on or after January 1, 1976, unless said county, city or town shall cause such examination to be made of such fire fighter within ninety days after July 1, 1976. Every fire fighter entering upon such service on or after October 1, 1976, and thereafter,

shall be entitled to the benefit of such presumption unless such county, city or town shall cause such examination to be made of such fire fighter at the time of such entry.

History.
1973, c. 543; 1976, c. 772; 1977, c. 326.

§ 27-40.2. Employing such presumption in determining eligibility for benefits.

Such presumption, subject to the provisions of § 27-40.1, shall be employed in determining eligibility for death, retirement, sickness and other benefits provided pursuant to the authority granted by §§ 27-39, 27-40, or pursuant to any other provision of law or the charter of any city or town, or otherwise for persons who die or become totally or partially disabled; provided, however, that such presumption shall be used to determine eligibility for death benefits for all fire fighters employed by the City of Portsmouth when death occurs subsequent to July 1, 1972.

History.
1964, c. 216; 1972, c. 607; 1973, c. 543; 1974, c. 579; 1977, c. 326.

Cross references.
As to the purchase of continued health insurance coverage by the surviving spouse and any dependents of an active or retired local law-enforcement officer, firefighter, etc., through the Department of Human Resource Management, see § 2.2-1205. As to the Line of Duty Act, see § 9.1-400. As to continued health insurance coverage for disabled persons, their spouses and dependents, and for the surviving spouse and dependents of certain deceased law-enforcement officers, firefighters, see § 9.1-401. As to payments to beneficiaries of certain deceased law-enforcement officers, firefighters and retirees, see § 9.1-402.

§ 27-40.3. Definition.

For the purposes of this article the term "volunteer fire fighters" shall be defined as in § 27-42.

History.
1972, c. 607; 1977, c. 326.

§ 27-40.4. Income earned during disability retirement; reduction in benefits.

If any person is entitled to and receives pensions and benefits under this article and subsequently becomes employed, whether full-time or part-time, the pensions and benefits received shall be reduced by the amount of income received which exceeds the difference between the benefits received under this article and the amount of pay to which he would have been entitled had his employment progressed in the same rank and grade with credit for the level of seniority he would have attained had he not been disabled. Such a reduction in benefits shall continue until the time he becomes eligible for normal retirement, had he remained uninjured and continued his employment. For the purposes of this section, "income" means gross income received less deductions for social security taxes only.

Any person receiving pensions or benefits under the provisions of this article shall upon request, on or before May 1 of each year, provide a true and correct copy of all W-2 forms showing income received, or a statement under oath as to whether he has received compensation for work performed in the previous calendar year, to the governing body of the jurisdiction which is the source of the pension, or to that body's designee. Refusal to provide such documents shall be grounds for termination of benefits under this section, until such documents are produced. Production of the documents shall be required only until such time as the person shall be eligible for normal retirement, had he remained uninjured and continued his employment.

Nothing contained herein shall limit or restrict the right of any person to receive workers' compensation benefits under Title 65.2, as amended.

History.
  1983, c. 351.

ARTICLE 2.

RELIEF FOR VOLUNTEER FIRE FIGHTERS.

§ 27-41. Relief provided for.

Financial relief shall be extended by the counties, cities and towns of Virginia to volunteer fire fighters who are killed or injured while engaged in fighting fire or while responding to an alarm or returning from the scene of a fire, such relief to be paid in amounts and manner as hereinafter set forth.

History.
  1928, p. 1002; Michie Code 1942, § 3144a; 1970, c. 187; 1977, c. 326.

Editor's note.
  Acts 1970, c. 187, which amended this section and §§ 27-43 and 27-46, provides, in cl. 3, that the act shall be liberally construed and is severable.

§ 27-42. Definition of term "volunteer fire fighters."

For the purposes of this article the term *"volunteer fire fighters"* shall include only members of any organized fire-fighting company which has in its possession and operates fire-fighting apparatus and equipment, whose members serve without pay and whose names are maintained on a list kept by the secretary of such company. It shall be the responsibility of the secretary of such company to (i) file the list with the office of the clerk of the circuit court where such company is located, (ii) keep the list of such members up to date, and (iii) file the updated list with the clerk in a timely manner. The clerk shall not be responsible to obtain the list or an updated list from the secretary of the fire-fighting company if the list is not filed with the clerk.

History.
  1928, p. 1002; Michie Code 1942, § 3144b; 1977, c. 326; 2012, c. 802.

The 2012 amendments.
  The 2012 amendment by c. 802, substituted "are maintained on a list kept by the secretary of such company" for "have been duly certified by the secretary of such company as active members thereof to the clerk of the circuit court of the county or city as the case may be. The respective clerks shall keep a complete and accurate record of all names so certified in a book provided by the governing body of such county or city. Names shall be added to or stricken from such record upon the certificate of the secretary of any such company that such action has been decided by his organization in due form" and added the last two sentences.

§ 27-43. Payment on death.

Should any volunteer fire fighter be killed while actually engaged in fighting fire, or while going to a fire in answer to an alarm or returning therefrom, the governing body of the county, city or town in which his company is located shall pay to his personal representative, for the benefit of his estate, the sum of $1,000.

History.
  1928, p. 1002; Michie Code 1942, § 3144c; 1970, c. 187; 1977, c. 326.

§ 27-44. Payments for total and permanent disability.

Should any volunteer fire fighter be injured under circumstances set forth in § 27-43, so as to be totally and permanently disabled from making a livelihood, he shall be paid in like manner the sum of twenty-five dollars per week for forty weeks.

History.
  1928, p. 1002; Michie Code 1942, § 3144d; 1977, c. 326.

§ 27-45. Payments for partial disability.

Should a volunteer fire fighter be injured under circumstances set forth in § 27-43, so as to be prevented from attending to his usual occupation for a period greater than two weeks, but not permanently and totally disabled, he shall be paid in like manner the sum of twenty-five dollars per week until able to return to his usual occupation, provided, that the payments shall not continue in any event for a period greater than ten weeks.

History.
  1928, p. 1002; Michie Code 1942, § 3144e; 1977, c. 326.

§ 27-46. Payment for hospital and medical services.

In addition to the relief set forth in §§ 27-43 through 27-45, all necessary hospital charges and all necessary and proper medical, surgical, laboratory and operating room charges for any volunteer fire fighter arising out of any injury set forth in such sections shall be paid by such county, city or town.

History.
   1928, p. 1003; Michie Code 1942, § 3144f; 1970, c. 187; 1977, c. 326.

§ 27-47. Levy for funds.

All funds necessary to carry out the provisions of this article shall be raised in the case of a city by a general levy on all property therein subject to taxation for local purposes; and in the case of a county one-half thereof shall be raised by a general levy throughout the county and one-half by the levy within the town or magisterial district in which the fire company is located on all property therein subject to taxation for local purpose.

History.
   1928, p. 1003; Michie Code 1942, § 3144g.

OPINIONS OF THE ATTORNEY GENERAL

Billing for emergency services. — Section 27-14 does not permit a locality to adopt an ordinance authorizing a volunteer fire department to assess and charge a fee to an individual's homeowners' or automobile insurance policy for responding to a fire emergency. See opinion of Attorney General to The Honorable Clarence E. "Bud" Phillips, Member, Virginia House of Delegates, 11-082, 2011 Va. AG LEXIS 55 (7/22/11).

Volunteer fire departments and rescue squads lack authority, either statutory or contractual, to bill home or automobile owners, or their insurance companies, for responding to a fire emergency. See opinion of Attorney General to The Honorable Clarence E. "Bud" Phillips, Member, Virginia House of Delegates, 11-052, 2011 Va. AG LEXIS 29 (5/13/11).

§ 27-48. Disputed questions of fact.

Any disputed question of fact arising under the operation of this article shall be triable before the governing body of such county or city having jurisdiction of the company involved, and from the decision of such governing body the petitioner and the county or city, as the case may be, shall have an appeal of right to the circuit court of the county or the corporation court of the city. Such appeal on behalf of the county or city shall be taken by the attorney for the Commonwealth or the corporation counsel who shall prosecute the same in the trial court.

History.
   1928, p. 1003; Michie Code 1942, § 3144h.

§ 27-49. Special laws not affected.

This article shall not be construed to repeal any special act now in force in any county or city for the relief of volunteer fire fighters or to limit the enactment of further special and local laws for such purpose.

History.
   1928, p. 1003; Michie Code 1942, § 3144i; 1977, c. 326.

§ 27-50. Adoption of article by counties, cities and towns.

This article shall not become effective in any county, city or town until the governing body thereof shall adopt and approve the same by resolution duly passed and spread on its minutes.

History.
   1928, p. 1003; Michie Code 1942, § 3144j.

CHAPTER 5.

SAFETY PROVISIONS GENERALLY.

Article 1. Generally.

ARTICLE 1.

GENERALLY.

§ 27-51. Exits from public halls, theaters and opera houses.

All owners or lessees of public halls, theaters or opera houses situated in any city or town, or in any county which has elected to come under the provisions of Article 1 (§ 27-6.1 et seq.) of Chapter 2 of this title, shall provide suitable and sufficient exits from such buildings. The doors to the exits shall remain unlocked during all performances or public gatherings in the buildings, and shall in all cases open outwardly, and not inwardly.

History.
   Code 1919, § 3142; R. P. 1948, § 27-36.

§ 27-52. Inspection of buildings designated in preceding section.

In cities and towns having police and fire departments or having a fire inspector employed by such city or town, the respective heads of such departments and the mayor of such city or town shall, as a committee of three, or the fire inspector of such city or town, inspect at least semiannually, all buildings mentioned in § 27-51 which are located in their city or town, and see that the provisions thereof are complied with.

In cities and towns which do not possess police and fire departments or a fire inspector, the mayor and two members of the council to be selected by the mayor shall, as a committee of three, inspect all such buildings located in their city or town semiannually, and see that the provisions of § 27-51 are complied with. Any such building as to which such provisions have not been complied with, may be closed by order of the mayor of the city or town until the provisions are complied with.

History.
Code 1919, § 3143; R. P. 1948, § 27-37; 1974, c. 41.

§ 27-53. Penalty for violating § 27-51; separate offenses.

Any owner or lessee of any such building, who shall violate any of the provisions of § 27-51, shall be punishable by a fine of not less than $100 nor more than $500, or by confinement in jail not less than 6 nor more than 12 months, or by both. The continuation of any failure to comply with the provisions of such section for each week after notice has been given the owner or lessee of the buildings that the exits are unsafe or insufficient shall be deemed a separate offense.

History.
Code 1919, § 3144; R. P. 1948, § 27-38.

§ 27-54. Governing body to make additional safety provisions.

The governing body of any city or town, or of any such county, shall make such further provisions insuring the safety of the public using such buildings as is mentioned in § 27-51 as such governing body may see proper to make, not in conflict with such section.

History.
Code 1919, § 3145; R. P. 1948, § 27-39.

ARTICLE 2.

IN AREAS MADE HAZARDOUS BY DROUGHT.

§§ 27-54.1 through 27-54.4. Repealed by Acts 1988, c. 891.

Cross references.
As to forest wardens and fires, see § 10.1-1135 et seq. As to fire hazards and closing of hunting and fishing seasons in forestlands, see § 10.1-1158 et seq.

ARTICLE 3.

OPEN BURNING.

§ 27-54.5. Repealed by Acts 1988, c. 891.

Cross references.
As to forest wardens and fires, see § 10.1-1135 et seq. As to fire hazards and closing of hunting and fishing seasons in forestlands, see § 10.1-1158 et seq.

CHAPTER 6.

DEPARTMENT OF STATE POLICE; PUBLIC BUILDING SAFETY LAW; ARSON REPORTING IMMUNITY ACT.

Article 1. General Provisions.

ARTICLE 1.

GENERAL PROVISIONS.

§ 27-55. Department of State Police or successor agency to keep record of fires and explosions; when open to public inspection.

The Department of State Police or its successor agency shall keep in its office a record of all fires occurring in the Commonwealth, investigation of which is provided for in this article, together with all facts, statistics and circumstances concerning the same, including the origin of the fires. Such records shall not be open to public inspection, except insofar as the Department shall permit otherwise. Whenever the word "Department" appears in this article it shall be deemed to mean the Department of State Police or its successor agency in the Office of Public Safety.

History.
Code 1919, § 4148; 1918, p. 123; 1936, p. 259; 1948, p. 487; 1977, c. 613.

§ 27-56. Department to examine into origin of fires; appointment of arson investigators.

The Department shall examine, or cause examination to be made, into the origin and circumstances of all fires occurring in this Commonwealth, which may be brought to its attention by official report, or otherwise, and for that purpose shall have authority to call for and demand of the chief or other head officer of the fire department, and the chief or other head officer of the police department, of any city or town, and the sheriff of any county, for any information or assistance it may require in making or furthering such examination.

The Department shall appoint a chief arson investigator and assistant arson investigators, who shall have the same police powers as a sheriff in the investigation and prosecution of all offenses involving fires, fire bombings, bombings, attempts, threats to commit such offense, false alarms relating to any such offense, possession and manufacture of explosive devices, substances and firebombs.

History.
Code 1919, § 4186; 1977, c. 613.

Cross references.
As to the transfer of the office of the Chief Arson Investigator as a division to the Department of State Police, see Editor's note to § 36-131.

Law Review.
For note, "Arson Investigations and the Fourth Amendment," see 30 Wash. & Lee L. Rev. 133 (1973).

Michie's Jurisprudence.
For related discussion, see 8B M.J. Fires, § 2; 16 M.J. Searches and Seizures, § 8.

CASE NOTES

Applied in Bennett v. Commonwealth, 212 Va. 863, 188 S.E.2d 215 (1972).

§ 27-57. When insurance company to pay expenses of examination.

When such examination is made on the application of any fire insurance company, the necessary expenses attending the same shall be paid by such company.

History.
Code 1919, § 4186.

§ 27-58. Right to examine buildings or premises.

The Department, and such person or persons as it may appoint, shall have authority at all times of the day, in the performance of the duties imposed by the provisions of § 27-56, to enter upon and examine any building or premises where any fire has occurred, and any other buildings or premises immediately adjoining the same; provided, that such adjoining building is not at the time occupied and used as a dwelling house.

History.
Code 1919, § 4187; 1977, c. 613.

Law Review.
For survey of Virginia law on criminal law for the year 1971-72, see 58 Va. L. Rev. 1206 (1972). For note, "Arson Investigations and the Fourth Amendment," see 30 Wash. & Lee L. Rev. 133 (1973). For note, "Criminal Procedure and Criminal Law: Virginia Supreme Court Decisions During the 70's," see 15 U. Rich. L. Rev. 585 (1981).

CASE NOTES

Daytime entry, without warrant and without force. — A fire investigator's daytime entry, without a warrant and without force, under the authority of this section was a permissible inspection and does not violate the Fourth Amendment rights of the defendant. Bennett v. Commonwealth, 212 Va. 863, 188 S.E.2d 215 (1972).

§ 27-59. Criminal prosecutions.

If the Department shall be of opinion, after investigation as to the cause or origin of any fire, that there is sufficient evidence to charge any person with the crime of arson, or with incendiary burning of property, it shall furnish to the attorney for the Commonwealth of the city or county all such evidence, together with the names of witnesses, and all information obtained by it, including a copy of all pertinent and material testimony taken by it touching such offense.

History.
Code 1919, § 4188; 1918, p. 123; 1977, c. 613.

Law Review.
For note, "Arson Investigations and the Fourth Amendment," see 30 Wash. & Lee L. Rev. 133 (1973).

§ 27-60. Department to conduct investigations in certain cases; investigations may be private.

The Department may petition an appropriate judicial officer to summons and compel the attendance of witnesses to testify in relation to any matter which is, by the provisions of this chapter, a subject of inquiry and investigation. It may also administer oaths and affirmations to such witnesses, and false swearing in any such matter shall be deemed perjury, and shall be punished as such. It may in its discretion take or cause to be taken the testimony on oath of all persons supposed to be cognizant of any facts or to have means of knowledge in relation to the matters as to which any examination is, in this chapter, required to be made, and shall cause the same to be reduced to writing. Investigations in relation to such matters may, in the discretion of the Department, be private, and persons other than those required to be present by the provisions of this chapter may be excluded from that place where such examination is held, and witnesses may be kept separate and apart from each other, and not allowed to communicate with each other until they have been examined.

History.
Code 1919, § 4189; 1977, c. 613.

§ 27-61. When Department or fire chief may remedy inflammable or unsafe conditions.

The Department of Fire Programs, by its representative, or the chief or other head of the fire department of any county, city or town or district thereof, shall have the right, at all reasonable hours, for the purpose of examination, to enter into and upon any public school building or any other building or premises not at the time occupied and used as a dwelling house, within their respective jurisdictions, for examination as to combustible materials or inflammable or unsafe conditions in any such building or upon any such premises. Upon complaint of any person having an interest in any building or premises or property adjacent thereto, in his jurisdiction, an officer shall make an immediate investigation as to the presence of any combustible materials or the existence of inflammable or unsafe conditions in such buildings or upon such premises. Whenever any officer finds in any building or upon any premises combustible, inflammable or unsafe conditions, dangerous to the safety of the building or premises, or other property, he shall order the same to be removed or remedied, and the order shall, within a reasonable time to be fixed in the order, be complied with by the owner or occupant of the building or premises.

Any owner or occupant aggrieved by such order may within five days after notice of such order, appeal to the Department of Fire Programs, and the cause of his complaint shall be at once investigated by the Executive Director of the Department of Fire Programs, and unless by its authority such order is revoked, the order shall remain in force and the owner or occupant shall comply with the order.

Any owner or occupant of any building or premises failing to comply with any final order made or given under the authority of this section, shall be deemed guilty of a misdemeanor, and punished by a fine of not less than $5 nor more than $100 for each offense.

History.
Code 1919, § 4190; 1936, p. 776; 1977, c. 613; 1988, c. 199; 2007, cc. 647, 741.

§ 27-62. Penalty on local officers for violating law.

Any city, town or county officer referred to in this article who willfully neglects or refuses to comply with any of the requirements of this article shall be deemed guilty of a misdemeanor, and upon conviction thereof, be punished by a fine of not less than $5, nor more than $100.

History.
Code 1919, § 4192.

ARTICLE 2.

PUBLIC BUILDING SAFETY LAW.

§§ 27-63, 27-64. Repealed by Acts 1988, c. 199.

§ 27-65. Repealed by Acts 1981, c. 499.

§ 27-66. Repealed by Acts 1977, c. 613.

§ 27-66.1. Repealed by Acts 1989, c. 258.

Cross references.
As to qualifications of State Fire Marshal, see now § 36-139.2.

§ 27-67. Repealed by Acts 1981, c. 499.

Cross references.
For present provision relating to the qualifications, powers, and duties of the State Fire Marshal, see § 9.1-206.

§ 27-68. Repealed by Acts 1977, c. 613.

§ 27-69. Repealed by Acts 1981, c. 499.

Cross references.
For present provision relating to qualifications of the State Fire Marshal, see § 9.1-206.

§ 27-70. Repealed by Acts 1981, c. 499.

Cross references.
For present provision relating to qualifications of the State Fire Marshal, see § 9.1-206.

§ 27-70.1. Repealed by Acts 1988, c. 199.

§ 27-70.2. Repealed by Acts 1981, c. 499.

§ 27-71. Repealed by Acts 1977, c. 613.

§ 27-72. Repealed by Acts 1988, c. 199.

§ 27-73. Repealed by Acts 1989, c. 258.

§ 27-73.1. Repealed by Acts 1988, c. 199.

§§ 27-74 through 27-77. Repealed by Acts 1977, c. 613.

§§ 27-78, 27-78.1. Repealed by Acts 1989, c. 258.

Cross references.
As to inspection of certain state-owned and state-operated facilities, including, residential care facilities, and enforcement of safety standards, see § 9.1-207.

§ 27-79. Repealed by Acts 1988, c. 199.

§§ 27-79.1 through 27-79.8. Repealed by Acts 1981, c. 499.

§ 27-79.9. Repealed by Acts 1989, c. 258.

Cross references.
As to inspection of state-owned and state-operated facilities, including residential care facilities, and enforcement of safety standards, see § 9.1-207.

§§ 27-80 through 27-84. Repealed by Acts 1988, c. 199.

Editor's note.
Section 27-83.1 was previously repealed by Acts 1981, c. 499.

§§ 27-85, 27-85.1. Repealed by Acts 1981, c. 499.

§ 27-85.2. Repealed by Acts 1989, c. 258.

Cross references.
As to agreements between the Department of Fire Safety and other agencies for services related fire safety in public buildings, see § 9.1-208.

ARTICLE 3.
ARSON REPORTING IMMUNITY ACT.

§ 27-85.3. Short title.

This article shall be known as the Arson Reporting Immunity Act.

History.
1979, c. 279.

CASE NOTES

For discussion of failure to report suspected arson as partial basis for finding that insurance company acted in bad faith in handling claims, see A & E Supply Co. v. Nationwide Mut. Fire Ins. Co., 612 F. Supp. 760 (W.D. Va. 1985), rev'd on other grounds, 798 F.2d 669 (4th Cir. 1986), cert. denied, 479 U.S. 1091, 107 S. Ct. 1302, 94 L. Ed. 2d 158 (1987).

§ 27-85.4. Definitions.

For the purposes of this article:
"Action" includes nonaction or the failure to take action.
"Authorized agencies" means:
i. The chief or director of any municipal or county fire or police department or the sheriff of any county;
ii. The arson investigator of the State Police Department; the Alcohol, Tobacco and Firearms Division of the United States Department of the Treasury; or
iii. The attorney for the Commonwealth or other person responsible for prosecutions in the jurisdiction where the fire occurred.

"Insurance company" includes the Virginia Property Insurance Association.

History.
1979, c. 279; 1985, c. 58; 2008, c. 410.

§ 27-85.5. Disclosure of information.

A. Any authorized agency may, in writing, require an insurance company to release to the requesting agency any or all relevant information or evidence deemed material by the requesting agency in the insurance company's possession relating to the fire loss in question. Relevant information may include, but shall not be limited to:
1. Pertinent insurance policy information relevant to a fire loss under investigation and any application for such a policy;
2. Policy premium payment records;
3. History of previous claims made by the insured;
4. Material relating to the investigation of the loss, including statements of any person, proof of loss, and any other evidence relevant to the investigation.
B. 1. When an insurance company has reason to believe that a fire loss in which it has an interest may be of other than accidental cause, then, for the purpose of notification and for having such fire loss investigated, the company shall, in writing, notify an authorized agency and provide it with any or all material developed from the company's inquiry into the fire loss.
2. When an insurance company provides any one of the authorized agencies with notice of a fire loss, it shall be sufficient notice for the purpose of this article.
C. The authorized agency provided with information pursuant to subsections A or B of this section and in furtherance of its own purposes, may release or provide such information to any of the other authorized agencies.
D. Any insurance company providing information to an authorized agency or agencies pursuant to subsections A or B of this section shall have the right to request relevant information and receive, within a reasonable time, not to exceed thirty days, the information requested.
E. Any insurance company, or person acting in its behalf or authorized agency who releases information, whether oral or written, pursuant to subsections A or B of this section shall be immune from any liability arising out of a civil action, or penalty resulting from a criminal prosecution unless actual malice on the part of the insurance company or authorized agency is present.

History.
1979, c. 279.

Law Review.
For survey of Virginia law on criminal procedure for the year 1978-1979, see 66 Va. L. Rev. 261 (1980).

CASE NOTES

No immunity if report made in bad faith. — Insurer was incorrect that the Arson Reporting Immunity Act (ARIA), § 27-85.5, immunized it from liability without exception as the insured was alleging that the insurer's interaction with fire officials was without merit and in bad faith. In essence, the complaint was alleging that the insurer knew it did not have reason to report that the insured committed arson when it did so to arson investigators, in order to avoid its obligations under the insurance by having the insured criminally prosecuted — such conduct supported a claim of actual malice — the insured's allegations taken as true and in the light most favorable to him, stated a claim. Styles v. Liberty Mut. Fire Ins. Co., 2006 U.S. Dist. LEXIS 49294 (W.D. Va. July 7, 2006).

§ 27-85.6. Evidence.

Any authorized agency and insurance company described in § 27-85.4 or § 27-85.5 who receives any information furnished pursuant to this article, shall hold the information in confidence until such time as its release is required pursuant to a criminal or civil proceeding, except release in accordance with subsection C of § 27-85.5.

History.
1979, c. 279.

CASE NOTES

This section does not require a party to obtain a court order before it may produce documents which it has received pursuant to the Arson Reporting Immunity Act in response to discovery requests issued in a pending civil action. Front Royal Ins. Co. v. Gold Players, Inc., 187 F.R.D. 252 (W.D. Va. 1999).

CHAPTER 7.

LIQUEFIED PETROLEUM GASES.

§§ 27-86 through 27-90. Repealed by Acts 1995, c. 44.

Editor's note.
Former §§ 27-86 through 27-90, which defined liquefied petroleum gas, authorized promulgation of regulations regarding use, installation, etc. of liquefied petroleum gas, and provided penalties, were derived from Acts 1950, pp. 152. 153; 1964, c. 41; 1980, c. 670.

CHAPTER 8.

FIRE SERVICES TRAINING.

§§ 27-91 through 27-93. Repealed by Acts 1981, c. 154.

Cross references.
For provisions concerning the Department of Fire Programs, see § 9.1-200 et seq.

CHAPTER 9.

STATEWIDE FIRE PREVENTION CODE ACT.

§ 27-94. Short title.

This chapter may be cited as the "Virginia Statewide Fire Prevention Code Act."

History.
1986, c. 429.

Cross references.
As to exclusions for records relating to public safety under the Freedom of Information Act, see § 2.2-3705.2. As to exclusions for records relating to administrative investigations safety under the Freedom of Information Act, see § 2.2-3705.3. As to the requirements of this act applying to the siting of biotechnology research activities, see § 2.2-5509. For provision authorizing localities to provide for the issuance of permits for the display of fireworks, see § 15.2-974. As to the security of certain records submitted for the purpose of complying with the Uniform Statewide Building Code, § 36-97 et seq., or the Statewide Fire Prevention Code, § 27-94 et seq., see § 36-105.3. As to reduced cigarette ignition propensity standards, see § 59.1-293.1 et seq.

Editor's note.
Acts 2006, c. 164, effective March 23, 2006, provides: "§ 1. School fire drills during Standards of Learning assessments.
"Notwithstanding any Statewide Fire Prevention Code regulation promulgated pursuant to Chapter 9 (§ 27-94 et seq.) of Title 27 of the Code of Virginia to the contrary, the Board of Housing and Community Development shall promulgate regulations in accordance with the Administrative Process Act (§ 2.2-4000 et seq. of the Code of Virginia) to prohibit fire and evacuation drills from being conducted in schools during periods of mandatory testing required by the Board of Education. In the development of the regulations, the Board of Housing and Community Development shall seek input from the Virginia Department of Education and local school divisions."

§ 27-95. Definitions.

As used in this chapter, unless the context or subject matter requires otherwise, the following words or terms shall have the meaning herein ascribed to them:

"Board" means the Board of Housing and Community Development.

"Code provisions" means the provisions of the Fire Prevention Code as adopted and promulgated by the Board, and the amendments thereof as adopted and promulgated from time to time by such Board.

"Enforcement agency" means the agency or agencies of any local governing body or the State Fire Marshal charged with the administration or enforcement of the Fire Prevention Code.

"Fire Prevention Code" or *"Code"* means the Statewide Fire Prevention Code.

"Fire prevention regulation" means any law, rule, resolution, regulation, ordinance or code, general or special, or compilation thereof to safeguard life and property from the hazards of fire or explosion arising from the improper maintenance of life safety and fire prevention and protection materials, devices, systems and structures, and the unsafe storage, handling and use of substances, materials and devices, including explosives and blasting agents, wherever located, heretofore or hereafter enacted or adopted by the Commonwealth or any county or municipality, including departments, boards, bureaus, commissions or other agencies.

"Fire Services Board" means the Virginia Fire Services Board as provided for in § 9.1-202.

"Fireworks" means any firecracker, torpedo, sky-rocket, or other substance or object, of whatever form or construction, that contains any explosive or inflammable compound or substance, and is intended, or commonly known as fireworks, and which explodes, rises into the air or travels laterally, or fires projectiles into the air.

"Fireworks operator" or *"pyrotechnician"* means any person engaged in the design, setup, and firing of any fireworks other than permissible fireworks either inside a building or structure or outdoors.

"Inspection warrant" means an order in writing, made in the name of the Commonwealth, signed by any judge or magistrate whose territorial jurisdiction encompasses the building, structure or premises to be inspected or entered, and directed to a state or local official, commanding him to enter and to conduct any inspection, examination, testing or collection of samples for testing required or authorized by the Virginia Statewide Fire Prevention Code.

"Local government" means the governing body of any city, county or town in this Commonwealth.

"Permissible fireworks" means any sparklers, fountains, Pharaoh's serpents, caps for pistols, or pinwheels commonly known as whirligigs or spinning jennies.

"State Fire Marshal" means the State Fire Marshal as provided for by § 9.1-206.

History.
1986, c. 429; 1988, cc. 340, 549; 1989, c. 258; 2002, c. 856; 2010, cc. 587, 643.

The 2010 amendments.
The 2010 amendments by cc. 587 and 643 are identical, and

added the paragraph defining "Fireworks operator" or "pyrotechnician."

CASE NOTES

Applied in Saunders v. Commonwealth, No. 1195-10-1, 2011 Va. App. LEXIS 384 (Dec. 6, 2011).

§ 27-96. Statewide standards.

The purposes of this chapter are to provide for statewide standards for optional local enforcement to safeguard life and property from the hazards of fire or explosion arising from the improper maintenance of life safety and fire prevention and protection materials, devices, systems and structures, and the unsafe storage, handling, and use of substances, materials and devices, including fireworks, explosives and blasting agents, wherever located.

History.
1986, c. 429; 1988, c. 340; 2002, c. 856.

§ 27-96.1. Chapter inapplicable to certain uses of fireworks.

Unless prohibited by a local ordinance, the provisions of this chapter pertaining to fireworks shall not apply to the sale of or to any person using, igniting or exploding permissible fireworks on private property with the consent of the owner of such property.

History.
2002, c. 856.

§ 27-96.2. Exemptions generally.

The provisions of this chapter concerning fireworks shall have no application to any officer or member of the armed forces of this Commonwealth, or of the United States, while acting within the scope of his authority and duties as such, nor to any offer of sale or sale of fireworks to any authorized agent of such armed forces; nor shall it be applicable to the sale or use of materials or equipment, otherwise prohibited by this chapter, when such materials or equipment is used or to be used by any person for signaling or other emergency use in the operation of any boat, railroad train or other vehicle for the transportation of persons or property.

History.
2002, c. 856.

§ 27-97. Adoption of Fire Prevention Code.

The Board of Housing and Community Development is hereby empowered to adopt and promulgate a Statewide Fire Prevention Code which shall be cooperatively developed with the Fire Services Board pursuant to procedures agreed to by the two Boards. The Fire Prevention Code shall prescribe regulations to be complied with for the protection of life and property from the hazards of fire or explosion and for the handling, storage, sale and use of fireworks, explosives or blasting agents, and shall provide for the administration and enforcement of such regulations. The Fire Prevention Code shall require manufacturers of fireworks or explosives, as defined in the Code, to register and report information concerning their manufacturing facilities and methods of operation within the Commonwealth in accordance with regulations adopted by the Board. In addition to conducting criminal background checks pursuant to § 27-97.2, the Board shall also establish regulations for obtaining permits for the manufacturing, storage, handling, use, or sales of fireworks or explosives. In the enforcement of such regulations, the enforcing agency may issue annual permits for such activities to any state regulated public utility. Such permits shall not apply to the storage, handling, or use of explosives or blasting agents pursuant to the provisions of Title 45.1.

The Fire Prevention Code shall prohibit any person, firm, or corporation from transporting, manufacturing, storing, selling, offering for sale, exposing for sale, or buying, using, igniting, or exploding any fireworks except for those persons, firms, or corporations that manufacture, store, market and distribute fireworks for the sole purpose of fireworks displays permitted by an enforcement agency or by any locality.

The Fire Prevention Code shall supersede fire prevention regulations heretofore adopted by local governments or other political subdivisions. Local governments are hereby empowered to adopt fire prevention regulations that are more restrictive or more extensive in scope than the Fire Prevention Code provided such regulations do not affect the manner of construction, or materials to be used in the erection, alteration, repair, or use of a building or structure, including the voluntary installation of smoke alarms and regulation and inspections thereof in commercial buildings where such smoke alarms are not required under the provisions of the Code. The Fire Prevention Code shall prohibit any person not certified by the State Fire Marshal's Office as a fireworks operator or pyrotechnician to design, set up, or conduct or supervise the design, setup, or conducting of any fireworks display, either inside a building or structure or outdoors and shall require that at least one person holding a valid certification is present at the site where the fireworks display is being conducted. Certification shall not be required for the design, storage, sale, use, conduct, transportation, and set up of permissible fireworks or the supervision thereof or in connection with any fireworks display conducted by a volunteer fire department provided one member of the volunteer fire department holds a valid certification.

In formulating the Fire Prevention Code, the Board shall have due regard for generally accepted standards as recommended by nationally recognized organizations including, but not limited to, standards of the International Code Council, the National Fire Protection Association, and recognized organizations issuing standards for the protection of the public from the hazards of explosives and blasting agents. Such standards shall be based on the companion document to the model building code referenced by the Uniform Statewide Building Code.

The Fire Prevention Code shall require that buildings constructed prior to 1973 be maintained in accordance with state fire and public building regulations in effect prior to March 31, 1986, and that any building which is (i) more than 75 feet or more than six stories high and (ii) used, in whole or in part, as a dormitory to house students by any public or private institution of higher education shall be required to comply with the provisions of § 36-99.3. The Fire Prevention Code shall also require annual fire drills in all buildings having floors used for human occupancy located more than 75 feet above the lowest level of fire department vehicle access. The drills shall be conducted by building staff personnel or the owner of the building in accordance with a plan approved by the appropriate fire official and shall not affect other current occupants. The Board may modify, amend or repeal any Code provisions as the public interest requires. Any such Code changes shall be developed in cooperation with the Fire Services Board pursuant to procedures agreed to by the two Boards.

History.
1986, c. 429; 1988, cc. 199, 340; 1989, cc. 90, 420; 1990, c. 69; 1991, c. 53; 1994, c. 275; 1997, c. 584; 2000, cc. 951, 1065; 2002, c. 856; 2007, cc. 647, 741; 2010, cc. 587, 643.

Editor's note.
Acts 2007, cc. 647 and 741, cl. 3, provide: "That the provisions of this act shall become effective on July 1, 2008."

The 2010 amendments.
The 2010 amendments by cc. 587 and 643 are identical, and added the last two sentences of the third paragraph.

CASE NOTES

Illegal storage of fireworks. — Under former § 59.1-142, proof of illegal storage of fireworks could not support a verdict in which the jury found defendant "guilty of storing and offering for sale" illegal fireworks. Burnette v. Commonwealth, 203 Va. 455, 125 S.E.2d 171 (1962).

Sale of illegal fireworks. — Under former § 59.1-142, proof that illegal fireworks were stored in defendant's place of business in boxes marked with the names of other merchandise was not proof beyond a reasonable doubt that they were displayed for sale where there was nothing to indicate to a prospective customer that the boxes contained illegal fireworks which were being offered for sale. Burnette v. Commonwealth, 203 Va. 455, 125 S.E.2d 171 (1962).

OPINIONS OF THE ATTORNEY GENERAL

Locality may not selectively enforce open burning regulations on geographic basis. — A locality that chooses to enforce the Fire Prevention Code may not selectively enforce open burning regulations on a geographic basis. See opinion of Attorney General to The Honorable Emily Couric, Member, Senate of Virginia, 00-091 (11/18/00).

Storage of sparklers, fountains, and similar items. — The storage of items such as sparklers, fountains, and similar types of displays on private property is not prohibited by the Statewide Fire Prevention Code Act or the Fire Prevention Code, unless a locality adopts more restrictive provisions, as authorized by §§ 27-97 and former 59.1-148. See opinion of Attorney General to The Honorable Paul Clinton Harris Sr., Member, House of Delegates, 01-014 (2/16/01).

§ 27-97.1. Reports of stolen explosives.

Any person holding a permit for the manufacture, storage, handling, use or sale of explosives issued in accordance with the provisions of the Code shall report to the office of the chief arson investigator for the Commonwealth as well as the chief local law-enforcement official any theft or other unauthorized taking or disappearance of any explosives or blasting devices from their inventory. An initial verbal report shall be made within three days of the discovery of the taking or disappearance. A subsequent written report shall be filed within such time, and in such form, as is specified by the chief arson investigator.

Failure to comply with the provisions of this section shall constitute a Class 1 misdemeanor punishable by the same penalties applicable to violations of the Fire Prevention Code.

History.
1988, c. 340.

Cross references.
As to punishment for Class 1 misdemeanors, see § 18.2-11.

§ 27-97.2. Issuance of permit; background investigations.

A. The State Fire Marshal or other issuing authority shall consider all permit applications for manufacturing, storage, handling, use or sales of explosives and applications for certification as a blaster or as a fireworks operator or pyrotechnician, and may grant a valid permit or certification to applicants who meet the criteria established in the Statewide Fire Prevention Code. The State Fire Marshal shall require a background investigation, to include a national criminal history record information check, of all individual applicants and all designated persons representing an applicant that is not an individual, for a permit to manufacture, store, handle, use or sell explosives, and for any applicant for certification as a blaster or as a fireworks operator or pyrotechnician. Each such applicant shall submit his fingerprints to the State Fire Marshal on a form provided by the State Fire Marshal and provide personal descriptive information to be forwarded along with the applicant's fingerprints through the Central Criminal Records Exchange to the Federal Bureau of Investigation for the purpose of obtaining a national criminal history record check regarding such applicant. Any firm or company manufacturing, storing, using, or selling explosives shall provide to the enforcement agency, the State Fire Marshal or other issuing authority the name of a representative responsible for (i) ensuring compliance with state law and regulations relating to blasting agents and explosives and (ii) applying for permits. The State Fire Marshal or other issuing authority shall deny any application for a permit or for certification as a blaster or as a fireworks operator or pyrotechnician if the applicant or designated person representing an applicant has been convicted of any felony, whether such conviction occurred under the laws of the Commonwealth, or any other state, the District of Columbia, the United States or any territory thereof, unless his civil rights have been restored by the Governor or other appropriate authority. The provisions of this section shall not apply to the manufacturing, storage, handling, use or sales of permissible fireworks or in connection with any fireworks display conducted by a volunteer fire department provided one member of the volunteer fire department holds a valid certification.

B. No permit under this section shall be required of any person holding a certification or permit issued pursuant to the provisions of Title 45.1.

History.
2000, cc. 951, 1065; 2007, cc. 647, 741; 2010, cc. 587, 643.

The 2010 amendments.
The 2010 amendments by cc. 587 and 643 are identical, and in subsection A, inserted "or as a fireworks operator or pyrotechnician" three times and added the last sentence.

§ 27-98. Enforcement of Fire Prevention Code; appeals from decisions of local enforcing agencies; inspection of buildings.

Any local government may enforce the Fire Prevention Code in its entirety or with respect only to those provisions of the Fire Prevention Code relating to open burning, fire lanes, fireworks, and hazardous materials. If a local governing body elects to enforce only those provisions of the Fire Prevention Code relating to open burning, it may do so in all or in any designated geographic areas of its jurisdiction. The State Fire Marshal shall also have the authority, in cooperation with any local governing body, to enforce the Code. The State Fire Marshal shall also have authority to enforce the Code in those jurisdictions in which the local governments do not enforce the Code and may establish such procedures or requirements as may be necessary for the administration and enforcement of the Code in such jurisdictions. In addition, subject to the approval of the Board of Housing and Community Development, the State Fire Marshal may charge a fee to recover the actual cost of administering and enforcing the Code in jurisdictions for which he serves as the enforcement authority. No fee may be charged for the inspection of any school. The local governing body of any jurisdiction that enforces the Code may establish such procedures or requirements as may be necessary for the administration and enforcement of the Code. Appeals concerning the application of the Code by the local enforcing agency shall first lie to a local board of appeals and then to the State Building Code Technical Review Board. Appeals from the application of the Code by the State Fire Marshal shall be made directly to the State Building Code Technical Review Board as provided in Article 2 (§ 36-108 et seq.) of Chapter 6 of Title 36. Fees may be levied by the local governing body in order to defray the cost of such enforcement and appeals; however, for the City of Chesapeake no fee charged for the inspection of any place of religious worship designated as Assembly Group A-3 under the Fire Prevention Code shall exceed $50. For purposes of this section, "defray the cost" may include the fair and reasonable costs incurred for such enforcement during normal business hours, but shall not include overtime costs, unless conducted outside of the normal working hours established by the locality. A schedule of such costs shall be adopted by the local governing body in a local ordinance. A locality shall not charge an overtime rate for inspections conducted during the normal business hours established by the locality. Nothing herein shall be construed to prohibit a private entity from conducting such inspections, provided the private entity has been approved to perform such inspections in accordance with the written policy of the fire official for the locality. Any local fire code may provide for an appeal to a local board of appeals. If no local board of appeals exists, the State Building Code Technical Review Board shall hear appeals of any local fire code violation.

History.
  1986, c. 429; 1994, c. 275; 2000, cc. 941, 1001; 2001, c. 570; 2004, c. 787; 2008, c. 499; 2010, c. 102; 2012, cc. 607, 635.

The 2010 amendments.
  The 2010 amendment by c. 102 substituted "Article 2 (§ 36-108 et seq.) of Chapter 6 of Title 36" for "§ 36-108 et seq." in the ninth sentence and added the last two sentences.

The 2012 amendments.
  The 2012 amendment by c. 607 added the eleventh through fourteenth sentences.
  The 2012 amendment by c. 635 added "; however, for the City of Chesapeake no fee charged for the inspection of any place of religious worship designated as Assembly Group A-3 under the Fire Prevention Code shall exceed $50" at the end of the tenth sentence.

OPINIONS OF THE ATTORNEY GENERAL

Locality may not selectively enforce open burning regulations on geographic basis. — A locality that chooses to enforce the Fire Prevention Code may not selectively enforce open burning regulations on a geographic basis. See opinion of Attorney General to The Honorable Emily Couric, Member, Senate of Virginia, 00-091 (11/18/00).

§ 27-98.1. Inspections of buildings, structures, properties and premises.

In order to carry out the purposes of the Code and any regulations or standards adopted in pursuance

thereof, the local fire official, upon presenting appropriate credentials to the owner, operator, or agent in charge, is authorized, with the consent of the owner, operator, or agent in charge to enter a building, structure, property or premises for the purpose of conducting an inspection, examination, testing, collection of samples for testing, during regular working hours and at other reasonable times, and in a reasonable manner, to determine if the building, structures, systems, machines, apparatus, devices, equipment, and materials stored, used or handled, and all pertinent conditions therein, are in compliance with the requirements, regulations or standards set forth in the Code.

History.
  1988, c. 549.

§ 27-98.2. Issuance of warrant.

Search warrants for inspections or reinspections of buildings, structures, property, or premises subject to inspections pursuant to the Code, to determine compliance with regulations or standards set forth in the Code, shall be based upon a demonstration of probable cause and supported by affidavit. Such inspection warrants may be issued by any judge or magistrate having authority to issue criminal warrants whose territorial jurisdiction encompasses the building, structure, property or premises to be inspected or entered, if he is satisfied from the affidavit that there is probable cause for the issuance of an inspection warrant. No inspection warrant shall be issued pursuant to this chapter except upon probable cause, supported by affidavit, particularly describing the place, thing or property to be inspected, examined or tested and the purpose for which the inspection, examination, testing or collection of samples for testing is to be made. Probable cause shall be deemed to exist if such inspection, examination, testing or collection of samples are necessary to ensure compliance with the Fire Prevention Code for the protection of property from the hazards of fire or explosion. A supporting affidavit shall contain either a statement that consent to inspect, examine, test or collect samples for testing has been sought and refused, or facts or circumstances reasonably justifying the failure to seek such consent in order to enforce effectively the fire safety laws, regulations or standards of the Commonwealth which authorize such inspection, examination, testing or collection of samples for testing. In the case of an inspection program based upon legislative or administrative standards for selecting buildings, structures, or premises for inspections, the affidavit shall contain factual allegations sufficient to justify an independent determination by the judge or magistrate that the inspection program is based upon reasonable standards and that the standards are being applied to a particular place in a neutral and fair manner. The issuing judge or magistrate

r oath or affirmation to verify the accuracy of
matter in the affidavit.

. 549.

references.
Forms (Matthew Bender). No. 9-108 Affidavit for Fire
Warrant; No. 9-109 Fire Inspection Warrant; No. 9-110
ion Warrant Inventory.

Duration of warrant.

ction warrant shall be effective for the
d therein, for a period of not more than
unless extended or renewed by the
r who signed and issued the original
judicial officer may extend or renew
warrant upon application for exten-
setting forth the results which have
or a reasonable explanation of the
n such results. The extension or
the warrant shall not exceed seven
t shall be executed and returned to
t by whom it was issued within the
e warrant or within the extended
the return shall list any samples
the warrant. After the expiration
rrant, unless executed, shall be

History.

Res
Vi
Insp
Fire nder). No. 9-108 Affidavit for Fire
Fire Inspection Warrant; No. 9-110
ry.

§ 2

inspections, examina-
g, or collection of

No
owne
build ed in the absence of the
specif harge of the particular
upon or premises unless
neces suing judicial officer
regula ority is reasonably
warra es of a statute or
issuing try pursuant to this
entry ly, except that the
reason thorize a forcible
occupa fficient to create a
erty, o iate threat to an
welfare structure, prop-
structur ral safety and
are sho cent buildings,
serve a (ii) where facts
forcible le attempts to
issued j successful. If
enforcem ant shall be
official du to a law-
ny the fire

History.
1988, c. 549.

Research references.
Virginia Forms (Matthew Bender). No. 9-109 Fire Inspection
Warrant; No. 9-110 Fire Inspection Warrant Inventory.

§ 27-98.5. Review by courts.

A. No court of the Commonwealth shall have
jurisdiction to hear a challenge to the warrant prior
to its return to the issuing judge or magistrate
except as a defense in a contempt proceeding, unless
the owner or custodian of the building, structure,
property or premises to be inspected makes by
affidavit a substantial preliminary showing accompanied by an offer of proof that (i) a false statement,
knowingly and intentionally, or with reckless disregard for the truth, was included by the affiant in his
affidavit for the inspection warrant and (ii) the false
statement was necessary to the finding of probable
cause. The court shall conduct such expeditious in
camera view as the court may deem appropriate.

B. After the warrant has been executed and returned to the issuing judge, the validity of the
warrant may be reviewed either as a defense to any
citation issued by the fire official or otherwise by
declaratory judgment action brought in a circuit
court. In any such action, the review shall be confined to the face of the warrant and affidavits and
supporting materials presented to the issuing judge
unless the owner, operator, or agent in charge of
whose building, structure, property or premises has
been inspected makes a substantial showing by
affidavit accompanied by an offer of proof that (i) a
false statement, knowingly and intentionally, or
with reckless disregard for the truth, was made in
support of the warrant and (ii) the false statement
was necessary to the finding of probable cause. The
review shall only determine whether there is substantial evidence in the record supporting the decision to issue the warrant.

History.
1988, c. 549.

§ 27-99. State buildings.

The Fire Prevention Code shall be applicable to all
state-owned buildings and structures. Every agency,
commission or institution, including all institutions
of higher education, of the Commonwealth shall
permit, at all reasonable hours, a local fire official
reasonable access to existing structures or a structure under construction or renovation, for the purposes of performing an informational and advisory
fire safety inspection. The local fire official may
submit, subsequent to performing such inspection,
his findings and recommendations including a list of
corrective actions necessary to ensure that such
structure is reasonably safe from the hazards of fire
to the appropriate official of such agency, commission, or institution and the State Fire Marshal. Such

§ 27-101

agency, commission or institution shall notify, within 60 days of receipt of such findings and recommendations, the State Fire Marshal and the local fire official of the corrective measures taken to eliminate the hazards reported by the local fire official. The State Fire Marshal shall have the same power in the enforcement of this section as is provided for in § 27-98.

The State Fire Marshal may enter into an agreement as is provided for in § 9.1-207 with any local enforcement agency that enforces the Fire Prevention Code to enforce this section and to take immediate enforcement action upon verification of a complaint of an imminent hazard such as a chained or blocked exit door, improper storage of flammable liquids, use of decorative materials and overcrowding.

History.
1986, c. 429; 1989, c. 258; 1994, c. 275; 1997, c. 584; 2007, cc. 647, 741.

OPINIONS OF THE ATTORNEY GENERAL

Enforcement by municipality of Fire Prevention Code on state property. — A municipality has no authority to enforce the Statewide Fire Prevention Code on state property, including buildings, structures, and premises, if an agreement has not been entered into with the State Fire Marshall pursuant to § 27-99 or the Director of the Department of Housing and Community Development pursuant to former § 36-139.4, for the enforcement of the Code. See opinion of Attorney General to Mr. William C. Shelton, Director, Department of Housing and Community Development, 01-096 (3/26/02).

State-owned vehicular tunnels and other transportation-related structures, regardless of their age, are subject to the provisions of the Statewide Fire Prevention Code applicable to structures. See opinion of Attorney General to Mr. William C. Shelton, Department of Housing and Community Development, 03-115 (2/18/04).

§ 27-100. Violation a misdemeanor.

It shall be unlawful for any owner or any other person, firm, or corporation, on or after the effective date of any Code provisions, to violate any provisions of the Fire Prevention Code. Any such violation shall be deemed a Class 1 misdemeanor, and any owner, or any other person, firm, or corporation convicted of such violation shall be punished in accordance with the provisions of § 18.2-11.

History.
1986, c. 429.

Cross references.
As to punishment for Class 1 misdemeanors, see § 18.2-11.

§ 27-100.1. Seizure and destruction of certain fireworks.

Any law-enforcement officer arresting any person for a violation of this chapter related to fireworks shall seize any articles of fireworks in the possession or under the control of the person so arrested and shall hold the same until final disposition of any criminal proceeding instituted against such person. If a judgment of conviction is entered against such person, the court shall order destruction of such articles, upon expiration of the time allowed for appeal of such judgment of conviction.

History.
2002, c. 856.

§ 27-101. Injunction application.

Every court having jurisdiction under existing or any future law is and shall, upon the application of the enforcing agency or State Fire Marshal, issue a mandatory or restraining injunction in the enforcement of, or in prevention of the breach of, any of the provisions of this law or any rule or regulation made in pursuance thereof, the procedure for obtaining any such injunction in accordance with the laws then current governing actions generally except that the enforcing shall not be required to give bond as precedent to obtaining an injunction.

History.
1986, c. 429.